Merriam-Webster's Collegiate® Dictionary

ELEVENTH EDITION

Merriam-Webster's Collegiate® Dictionary

ELEVENTH EDITION

Merriam-Webster, Incorporated
Springfield, Massachusetts, U.S.A.

A GENUINE MERRIAM-WEBSTER

The name *Webster* alone is no guarantee of excellence. It is used by a number of publishers and may serve mainly to mislead an unwary buyer.

Merriam-Webster™ is the name you should look for when you consider the purchase of dictionaries or other fine reference books. It carries the reputation of a company that has been publishing since 1831 and is your assurance of quality and authority.

Copyright © 2014 by Merriam-Webster, Incorporated

Library of Congress Cataloging in Publication Data

Merriam-Webster's collegiate dictionary. — Eleventh ed.
     p.   cm.
   Includes index.
   ISBN 978-0-87779-807-1 (Laminated unindexed : alk. paper)
   ISBN 978-0-87779-808-8 (Jacketed hardcover unindexed : alk. paper)
   ISBN 978-0-87779-809-5 (Jacketed hardcover with digital download : alk. paper)
   ISBN 978-0-87779-810-1 (Leatherlook with digital download : alk. paper)
   ISBN 978-0-87779-811-8 (Luxury Leather)
   ISBN 978-0-87779-813-2 (Canadian)
   ISBN 978-0-87779-814-9 (International)
   1. English language—Dictionaries. I. Title: Collegiate dictionary. II. Merriam-Webster, Inc.
PE1628.M36   2003
423—dc21   2003003674
                                           CIP

Merriam-Webster's Collegiate® Dictionary, Eleventh Edition, principal copyright 2003

COLLEGIATE is a registered trademark of Merriam-Webster, Incorporated

Made in the United States of America

19th Printing Quad Graphics Versailles KY December 2014

Contents

Preface

When Webster's Collegiate Dictionary was first published, the year was 1898, and Americans were being exhorted to "remember the Maine." As the eleventh consecutive edition of this standard reference book appears, we have crossed the nearly inconceivable divide between the second and third millennia of the modern era, but since daily lives can scarcely be led in constant awareness of a span of time that vast, we now situate ourselves, for the most part, in the first decade of the twenty-first century. Over the time between these editions, the world has made its way through two global wars and many others of a more limited kind; wide-ranging social, political, and economic change (not to say, revolution); and successive waves of technological change that have transformed communication, transportation, information storage and retrieval, and great numbers of other human activities. At every turn these events and developments have had a major effect on the stock of words that English speakers use, and it has been the job of a good general dictionary to record these changes. The present book is the latest effort by the editorial team of Merriam-Webster to meet that responsibility.

Merriam-Webster's Collegiate Dictionary, Eleventh Edition, like all earlier editions is meant to serve the general public as its chief source of information about the words of our language. Its title may suggest a special appropriateness for the older student, but those who work in offices and those who read, think, and write at home will equally find it a trustworthy guide to the English of our day.

The ever-expanding vocabulary of our language exerts inexorable pressure on the contents of any dictionary. Words and senses are born at a far greater rate than that at which they die out. The 1664 pages of this Collegiate make it the most comprehensive ever published. And its treatment of words is as nearly exhaustive as the compass of an abridged work permits. As in all Merriam-Webster dictionaries, the information given is based on the collection of 15,700,000 citations maintained in the offices of this company. These citations show words used in a wide range of printed sources, and the collection is constantly being augmented through the efforts of the editorial staff. Thus, the user of the dictionary may be confident that entries in the Collegiate are based on current as well as older material. The citation files hold 5,700,000 more examples than were available to the editors of Webster's Third New International Dictionary, published in 1961, and 1,200,000 more than the editors of the Tenth Edition had at their disposal. The editors of this edition also had available to them a machine-readable corpus of over 76,000,000 words of text drawn from the wide and constantly changing range of publications that supply the paper slips in the citation files. It is now nearly four times the size of the corpus used by the editors of the Tenth Edition.

Those entries known to be trademarks or service marks are so labeled and are treated in accordance with a formula approved by the United States Trademark Association. No entry in this dictionary, however, should be regarded as affecting the validity of any trademark or service mark.

The best features of the vocabulary section in the last edition have been retained, reviewed, and improved for this one. Additional pictorial illustrations are present, and many of them were drawn especially for this book in order to supplement and clarify definitions. Synonym paragraphs and usage paragraphs are both here again, augmented in number. The dates of first use provided at most main entries have proved to be very popular with users of the Collegiate. For the Eleventh Edition, thousands of these dates have been pushed back in time, anywhere from a single year to several centuries from published materials (both print and electronic) not available ten years ago, from the continuing investigations of our own editors, and from the contributions of hundreds of interested readers. Two important changes in the treatment of the vocabulary have been made for this edition, one to provide additional information and the other to make information easier to find. All standard variants are now shown at the relevant main entry so that the reader may see at a glance whether they are equal variants with the main entry or are distinctly less frequent. And entries for abbreviations as well as for the symbols for chemical elements are now quickly found in the vocabulary section and need not be sought in a separate section tucked away in the back matter, as in the previous edition.

The front matter of this book establishes a context for understanding what this dictionary is and how it came to be, as well as how it may be used most effectively. The Explanatory Notes address themselves to the latter topic. They answer the user's questions about the conventions, devices, and techniques by which the editors have been able to compress mountains of information about English words into so few pages. All users of the dictionary are urged to read this section through and then consult it for special information as they need to. The brief essay on our language as it is recorded in Merriam-Webster dictionaries, and this Collegiate in particular, is meant to satisfy an interest in lexicography often expressed in the correspondence which our editors receive. The Guide to Pronunciation serves both to show how the pronunciations in this book are arrived at and to explain the mechanics of the respelling system in which they are set down.

The back matter retains five sections from the last edition of the Collegiate. These are Foreign Words and Phrases that occur frequently in English texts but have not become part of the English vocabulary; thousands of proper names brought together under the separate headings Biographical Names and Geographical Names; a gathering of important Signs and Symbols that cannot readily be alphabetized; and a Handbook of Style in which various stylistic conventions (as of punctuation and capitalization) are summarized and exemplified. All the sections have been carefully updated for this edition.

Looking at a copy of that long-ago first Collegiate Dictionary, one is struck by how different it is, as a physical book and as a work of reference, from the present edition. The board covers are heavy, the margins of the page are wide, and the type is relatively large; at the same time it holds only about 1100 pages and less than half the number of vocabulary entries of this Eleventh Edition. At that time the Merriam-Webster citation file was no more than in its infancy. Yet the editors of that book created it with the same careful, serious attention that the present editors have brought to their work.

We believe that this work sustains and advances the tradition of excellence in lexicography that is the heritage of Merriam-Webster, Incorporated. The editorial staff who produced it include a number of people who have made contributions to three or four successive editions of the Collegiate Dictionary. That experience and that continuity form an important part of what the Eleventh Edition is, as do the energy and care of those who have joined the staff just within the last few years. Some of the latter group will very likely contribute in major ways to the twelfth, the thirteenth, perhaps even the fourteenth edition of the Collegiate. In the meantime, the entire staff, whose names are given on the facing page, offer their work to people everywhere who need information about the vocabulary of English, in the assurance that it will prove a reliable companion.

Frederick C. Mish
Editor in Chief

Editorial Staff

²**pet** *adj* (1584) **1 :** kept or treated as a pet **2 :** expressing fondness or endearment ⟨a ~ name⟩ **3 :** FAVORITE ⟨a ~ project⟩

pharaoh ant *n* (ca. 1924) **:** a small red ant (*Monomorium pharaonis*) that is a common household pest

phar·ma·cy \'fär-mə-sē\ *n, pl* **-cies** [LL *pharmacia* administration of drugs, fr. Gk *pharmakeia*, fr. *pharmakeuein* to administer drugs, fr. *pharmakon* magic charm, poison, drug] (1651) **1 :** the art, practice, or profession of preparing, preserving, compounding, and dispensing medical drugs **2 a :** a place where medicines are compounded or dispensed **b :** DRUGSTORE **3 :** PHARMACOPOEIA 2

phase–contrast microscope *n* (1947) **:** a microscope that translates differences in phase of the light transmitted through or reflected by the object into differences of intensity in the image — called also *phase microscope*

Phi·lis·tine \'fi-lə-ˌstēn; fə-'lis-tən, -ˌtēn; 'fi-lə-stən\ *n* (14c) **1 :** a native or inhabitant of ancient Philistia — *often not cap* **2 a :** a person who is guided by materialism and is usu. disdainful of intellectual or artistic values **b :** one uninformed in a special area of knowledge — **philistine** *adj, often cap* — **phi·lis·tin·ism** \-lə-ˌstē-ˌni-zəm; -'lis-tə-, -ˌtē-, -lə-stə\ *n often cap*

pic·tur·esque \ˌpik-chə-'resk\ *adj* [F & It; F *pittoresque*, fr. It *pittoresco*, fr. *pittore* painter, fr. L *pictor*, fr. *pingere*] (1703) **1 a :** resembling a picture **:** suggesting a painted scene **b :** charming or quaint in appearance **2 :** evoking mental images **:** VIVID **syn** see GRAPHIC — **pic·tur·esque·ly** *adv* — **pic·tur·esque·ness** *n*

³**pig** *var of* PI

³**pilgrim·age** \'-aged; -ag·ing** (14c) **:** to go on a pilgrimage

³**pill** *vb* (1736) **1 :** to dose with pills **2 :** BLACKBALL ~ *vi* **:** to become rough with or mat into little balls ⟨brushed woolens often ~⟩

pil·lar \'pi-lər\ *n* [ME *piler*, fr. AF, fr. ML *pilare*, fr. L *pila*] (13c) **1 a :** a firm upright support for a superstructure **:** POST **b :** a usu. ornamental column or shaft; *esp* **:** one standing alone for a monument **2 a :** a supporting, integral, or upstanding member or part ⟨a ~ of society⟩ **b :** a fundamental precept ⟨the five ~s of Islam⟩ **3 :** a solid mass of coal, rock, or ore left standing to support a mine roof **4 :** a body part that resembles a column — **pil·lar·less** *adj* — **from pillar to post :** from one place or one predicament to another

pima cotton \'pē-mə\ *n* [*Pima* County, Arizona] (1925) **:** a cotton that produces fiber of exceptional strength and firmness and that was developed in the southwestern U.S. by selection and breeding of Egyptian cottons

pin·bone \'pin-ˌbōn\ *n* (1640) **:** the hipbone esp. of a quadruped — see COW illustration

pine nut *n* (bef. 12c) **:** the edible seed of any of several pines — compare PIÑON

pi·rosh·ki *or* **pi·rozh·ki** \pi-'rōsh-kē, ˌpir-əsh-'kē\ *n pl* [Russ *pirozhki*, pl. of *pirozhok*, dim. of *pirog* pastry] (1912) **:** small pastries with meat, cheese, or vegetable filling

plead \'plēd\ *vb* **plead·ed** \'plē-dəd\ *or* **pled** *also* **plead** \'pled\; **plead·ing** [ME *pleden, plaiden*, fr. AF *plaider, pleder*, fr. *plai* plea] *vi* (13c) **1 :** to argue a case or cause in a court of law **2 a :** to make an allegation in an action or other legal proceeding; *esp* **:** to answer the previous pleading of the other party by denying facts therein stated or by alleging new facts **b :** to conduct pleadings **3 :** to make a plea of a specified nature ⟨~ not guilty⟩ **4 a :** to argue for or against a claim **b :** to entreat or appeal earnestly ~ *vt* **1 :** to maintain (as a case or cause) in a court of law or other tribunal **2 :** to allege in or by way of a legal plea **3 :** to offer as a plea usu. in defense, apology, or excuse — **plead·able** \'plē-də-bəl\ *adj* — **plead·er** *n* — **plead·ing·ly** \'plē-diŋ-lē\ *adv*

plo·ver \'plə-vər, 'plō-\ *n, pl* **plover** *or* **plovers** [ME, fr. AF *plover, pluvier*, fr. VL **pluviarius*, fr. L *pluvia* rain — more at PLUVIAL] (14c) **1 :** any of a family (Charadriidae) of shorebirds that differ from the sandpipers in having a short hard-tipped bill and usu. a stouter more compact build **2 :** any of various birds (as a turnstone or sandpiper) related to the plovers

¹**plu·vi·al** \'plü-vē-əl\ *adj* [L *pluvialis*, fr. *pluvia* rain, fr. fem. of *pluvius* rainy, fr. *pluere* to rain — more at FLOW] (ca. 1656) **1 a :** of or relating to rain **b :** characterized by abundant rain **2 :** of a geologic change **:** resulting from the action of rain

¹**point·ed** \'pȯin-təd\ *adj* (14c) **1 a :** having a point **b :** being an arch with a pointed crown; *also* **:** marked by the use of a pointed arch ⟨~ architecture⟩ **2 a :** being to the point **:** PERTINENT **b :** aimed at a particular person or group **3 :** CONSPICUOUS, MARKED ⟨~ indifference⟩ **4 :** having points that contrast in color with the basic coat color ⟨a ~ cat⟩ — **point·ed·ly** *adv* — **point·ed·ness** *n*

²**pointed** *adj* [short for *appointed*] (1523) *obs* **:** SET, FIXED

¹**poise** \'pȯiz\ *vb* **poised; pois·ing** [ME, to weigh, ponder, fr. AF *peiser, poiser*, fr. L *pensare* — more at PENSIVE] *vt* (1598) **1 a :** BALANCE; *esp* **:** to hold or carry in equilibrium ⟨carried a water jar *poised* on her head⟩ **b :** to hold supported or suspended without motion in a steady position ⟨*poised* her fork and gave her guest a knowing look —Louis Bromfield⟩ **2 :** to hold or carry (the head) in a particular way **3 :** to put into readiness **:** BRACE ~ *vi* **1 :** to become drawn up into readiness **2 :** HOVER

²**pole** *vb* **poled; pol·ing** *vt* (1573) **1 :** to act upon with a pole **2 :** to impel or push with a pole ~ *vi* **1 :** to propel a boat with a pole **2 :** to use ski poles to gain speed

poleis *pl of* POLIS

post- *prefix* [ME, fr. L, fr. *post*; akin to Lith *pas* at, Gk *apo* away from — more at OF] **1 a :** after **:** subsequent **:** later ⟨*post*date⟩ **b :** behind **:** posterior **:** following after ⟨*post*lude⟩ ⟨*post*consonantal⟩ **2 a :** subsequent to **:** later than ⟨*post*operative⟩ **b :** posterior to ⟨*post*orbital⟩

post-abor·tion	post-di·vorce	post-mas·tec·to·my
post-ac·ci·dent	post-drug	post-mat·ing
post-ad·o·les·cent	post-ed·it·ing	post-me·di·e·val
post-am·pu·ta·tion	post–Ein·stein·ian	post-mid·night

po·sy \'pō-zē\ *n, pl* **posies** [alter. of *poesy*] (1533) **1 :** a brief sentiment, motto, or legend **2 a :** BOUQUET, NOSEGAY **b :** FLOWER

po·tas·si·um \pə-'ta-sē-əm\ *n often attrib* [NL, fr. *potassa* potash, fr. E *potash*] (ca. 1807) **:** a silver-white soft light low-melting monovalent metallic element of the alkali metal group that occurs abundantly in nature esp. combined in minerals — see ELEMENT table

Explanatory Chart

po·ten·tate \'pō-t'n-ˌtāt\ n (15c) : RULER, SOVEREIGN; broadly : one who wields great power or sway

pot·herb \'pät-ˌərb, -ˌhərb\ n (1538) : a usu. leafy herb that is cooked for use as greens; also : one (as mint) used to season food

pot lik·ker \-'li-kər\ Southern & Midland var of POT LIQUOR

pot·sherd \'pät-ˌshərd\ n [ME pot-sherd, fr. pot + shard shard] (14c) : a pottery fragment usu. unearthed as an archaeological relic

pouf also pouffe \'püf\ n [F pouf, something inflated, of imit. origin] (1817) 1 : PUFF 3b(3) 2 : a bouffant or fluffy part of a garment or accessory 3 : OTTOMAN — poufed or pouffed \'püft\ adj

poult \'pōlt\ n [ME polet, pulte young fowl — more at PULLET] (15c) : a young fowl; esp : a young turkey

pow·dery \'pau̇-də-rē\ adj (15c) 1 a : resembling or consisting of powder ⟨∼ snow⟩ b : easily reduced to powder : CRUMBLING 2 : covered with or as if with powder

prexy \'prek-sē\ also prex \'preks\ n, pl prex·ies also prex·es [prexy fr. prex, by shortening & alter. fr. president] (1828) slang : PRESIDENT — used chiefly of a college president

proph·et \'prä-fət\ n [ME prophete, fr. AF, fr. L propheta, fr. Gk prophētēs, fr. pro for + phanai to speak — more at FOR, BAN] (12c) 1 : one who utters divinely inspired revelations: as a often cap : the writer of one of the prophetic books of the Bible b cap : one regarded by a group of followers as the final authoritative revealer of God's will ⟨Muhammad, the Prophet of Allah⟩ 2 : one gifted with more than ordinary spiritual and moral insight; esp : an inspired poet 3 : one who foretells future events : PREDICTOR 4 : an effective or leading spokesman for a cause, doctrine, or group 5 Christian Science a : a spiritual seer b : disappearance of material sense before the conscious facts of spiritual Truth — proph·et·hood \-ˌhu̇d\ n

pro·pose \prə-'pōz\ vb pro·posed; pro·pos·ing [ME, fr. AF purposer, proposer, fr. L proponere (perf. indic. proposui) — more at PROPOUND] vi (14c) 1 : to form or put forward a plan or intention ⟨man ∼s, but God disposes⟩ 2 obs : to engage in talk or discussion 3 : to make an offer of marriage ∼ vt 1 a : to set before the mind (as for discussion, imitation, or action) ⟨∼ a plan for settling the dispute⟩ b : to set before someone and esp. oneself as an aim or intent ⟨proposed to spend the summer in Italy⟩ 2 a : to set forth for acceptance or rejection ⟨∼ terms for peace⟩ ⟨∼ a topic for debate⟩ b : to recommend to fill a place or vacancy : NOMINATE ⟨∼ them for membership⟩ c : to offer as a toast ⟨∼ the happiness of the couple⟩ — pro·pos·er n

¹pros·pect \'prä-ˌspekt\ n [ME, fr. L prospectus view, prospect, fr. prospicere to look forward, exercise foresight, fr. pro- forward + specere to look — more at PRO-, SPY] (15c) 1 : EXPOSURE 3b 2 a (1) : an extensive view (2) : a mental consideration : SURVEY b : a place that commands an extensive view : LOOKOUT c : something extended to the view : SCENE d archaic : a sketch or picture of a scene 3 obs : ASPECT 4 a : the act of looking forward : ANTICIPATION b : a mental picture of something to come : VISION c : something that is awaited or expected : POSSIBILITY d pl (1) : financial expectations (2) : CHANCES 5 : a place showing signs of containing a mineral deposit 6 a : a potential buyer or customer b : a likely candidate for a job or position — in prospect : possible or likely for the future

syn PROSPECT, OUTLOOK, ANTICIPATION, FORETASTE mean an advance realization of something to come. PROSPECT implies expectation of a particular event, condition, or development of definite interest or concern ⟨the prospect of a quiet weekend⟩. OUTLOOK suggests a forecasting of the future ⟨a favorable outlook for the economy⟩. ANTICIPATION implies a prospect or outlook that involves advance suffering or enjoyment of what is foreseen ⟨the anticipation of her arrival⟩. FORETASTE implies an actual though brief or partial experience of something forthcoming ⟨the frost was a foretaste of winter⟩.

¹pros·trate \'prä-ˌstrāt\ adj [ME prostrat, fr. AF, fr. L prostratus, pp. of prosternere, fr. pro- before + sternere to spread out, throw down — more at STREW] (14c) 1 : stretched out with face on the ground in adoration or submission; also : lying flat 2 : completely overcome and lacking vitality, will, or power to rise ⟨was ∼ from the heat⟩ 3 : trailing on the ground : PROCUMBENT ⟨∼ shrubs⟩

syn see PRONE

pro·ten·sive \-'ten(t)-siv\ adj [L protensus, pp. of protendere] (1671) 1 archaic : having continuance in time 2 archaic : having lengthwise extent or extensiveness — pro·ten·sive·ly adv

Protestant ethic n (1926) : an ethic that stresses the virtue of hard work, thrift, and self-discipline

prove \'prüv\ vb proved; proved or prov·en \'prü-vən, Brit also 'prō-\; prov·ing \'prü-viŋ\ [ME, fr. AF prover, pruver, fr. L probare to test, prove, fr. probus good, honest, fr. pro- for, in favor + -bus (akin to OE bēon to be) — more at PRO-, BE] vt (13c) 1 archaic : to learn or find out by experience 2 a : to test the truth, validity, or genuineness of ⟨the exception ∼s the rule⟩ ⟨∼ a will at probate⟩ b : to test the worth or quality of; specif : to compare against a standard — sometimes used with up or out c : to check the correctness of (as an arithmetic result) 3 a : to establish the existence, truth, or validity of (as by evidence or logic) ⟨∼ a theorem⟩ ⟨the charges were never proved in court⟩ b : to demonstrate as having a particular quality or worth ⟨the vaccine has been proven effective after years of tests⟩ ⟨proved herself a great actress⟩ 4 : to show (oneself) to be worthy or capable ⟨eager to ∼ myself in the new job⟩ ∼ vi : to turn out esp. after trial or test ⟨the new drug proved effective⟩ — prov·able \'prü-və-bəl\ adj — prov·able·ness n — prov·ably \-blē\ adv — prov·er \'prü-vər\ n

usage The past participle proven, orig. the past participle of preve, a Middle English variant of prove that survived in Scotland, has gradually worked its way into standard English over the past three and a half centuries. It seems to have first become established in legal use and to have come only slowly into literary use. Tennyson was one of its earliest frequent users, prob. for metrical reasons. It was disapproved by 19th century grammarians, one of whom included it in a list of "words that are not words." Surveys made some 50 or 60 years ago indicated that proved was about four times as frequent as proven. But our evidence from the last 30 or 35 years shows this no longer to be the case. As a past participle proven is now about as frequent as proved in all contexts. As an attributive adjective ⟨proved or proven gas reserves⟩ proven is much more common than proved.

provided conj [fr. pp. of provide] (15c) : on condition that : with the understanding : IF usage see PROVIDING

put–up \'pu̇t-ˌəp\ adj (1810) : arranged secretly beforehand ⟨a ∼ job⟩

---

primary stress
PAGE 12a

pronunciation
PAGES 12a, 13a

regional label
PAGE 18a

secondary stress
PAGE 12a

secondary variant
PAGE 11a

sense divider
PAGE 20a

sense letter
PAGE 20a

sense number
PAGE 20a

stylistic label
PAGES 18a, 19a

subject label
PAGE 19a

swung dash (boldface)
PAGE 13a

swung dash (lightface)
PAGE 19a

synonymous cross-reference
PAGE 23a

synonym paragraph
PAGES 23a, 24a

syn see
PAGES 23a, 24a

temporal label
PAGE 18a

undefined run-on entry
PAGES 11a, 12a

uppercase
PAGE 15a

usage note
PAGE 19a

usage paragraph
PAGES 19a, 20a

usage see
PAGE 20a

verbal illustration
PAGE 19a

Explanatory Notes

Entries

MAIN ENTRIES

A boldface letter or a combination of such letters, including punctuation marks and diacritics where needed, that is set flush with the left-hand margin of each column of type is a main entry or entry word. The main entry may consist of letters set solid, of letters joined by a hyphen or a slash, or of letters separated by one or more spaces:

> [1]**alone** . . . *adj*
>
> **au·to–da–fé** . . . *n*
>
> **and/or** . . . *conj*
>
> **automatic pilot** *n*

The material in lightface type that follows each main entry on the same line and on succeeding indented lines explains and justifies its inclusion in the dictionary.

Variation in the styling of compound words in English is frequent and widespread. It is often completely acceptable to choose freely among open, hyphenated, and closed alternatives (as *life style, life-style,* or *lifestyle*). However, to show all the stylings that are found for English compounds would require space that can be better used for other information. So this dictionary limits itself to a single styling for a compound:

> **peace·mak·er**
>
> **pell–mell**
>
> **boom box**

When a compound is widely used and one styling predominates, that styling is shown. When a compound is uncommon or when the evidence indicates that two or three stylings are approximately equal in frequency, the styling shown is based on the analogy of similar compounds.

ABBREVIATIONS AND SYMBOLS

Abbreviations and symbols for chemical elements are included as main entries in the vocabulary:

> **ca** *abbr* circa
>
> **Ca** *symbol* calcium

Abbreviations have been normalized to one form. In practice, however, there is considerable variation in the use of periods and in capitalization (as *mph, m.p.h., Mph,* and *MPH*), and stylings other than those given in this dictionary are often acceptable.

For a list of abbreviations regularly used in this dictionary, see the section Abbreviations in This Work elsewhere in the front matter. Many of these are also in general use, but as a rule an abbreviation is entered either in the vocabulary or in that list, not both.

ORDER OF MAIN ENTRIES

The main entries follow one another in alphabetical order letter by letter without regard to intervening spaces or hyphens: *battle royal* follows *battlement* and *earth-shattering* follows *earthshaking*. Those containing an Arabic numeral are alphabetized as if the numeral were

spelled out: *3-D* comes between *three-color* and *three-decker*. Those that often begin with the abbreviation *St.* in common usage have the abbreviation spelled out: *Saint Anthony's fire*.

Full words come before parts of words made up of the same letters. Solid compounds come first and are followed by hyphenated compounds and then open compounds. Lowercase entries come before entries that begin with a capital letter:

> [3]**semi** . . . *n*
>
> **semi-** . . . *prefix*
>
> **take·out** . . . *n*
>
> **take–out** . . . *adj*
>
> **take out** *vt*
>
> **tim·o·thy** . . . *n*
>
> **Tim·o·thy** . . . *n*

HOMOGRAPHS

When one main entry has exactly the same written form as another, the two are distinguished by superscript numerals preceding each word:

> [1]**melt** . . . *vb*   [1]**pine** . . . *n*
>
> [2]**melt** *n*   [2]**pine** *vi*

Sometimes such homographs are related: the two entries *melt* are derived from the same root. Sometimes there is no relationship: the two entries *pine* are unrelated beyond the accident of spelling. The order of homographs is usually historical: the one first used in English is entered first. A homograph derived from an earlier homograph by functional shift, however, follows its parent immediately, with the result that occasionally one homograph appears ahead of another that is older in usage. For example, of the three entries *kennel* the second (a verb) is derived from the first (a noun). Even though the unrelated third entry *kennel* was used in English many years before the second, it follows the two related entries.

Abbreviations and symbols that are homographs of other entries are listed last:

> [1]**bus** . . . *n*
>
> [2]**bus** *vb*
>
> [3]**bus** *abbr*

GUIDE WORDS

A pair of guide words is printed at the top of each page. The entries that fall alphabetically between the guide words are found on that page.

It is important to remember that alphabetical order rather than position of an entry on the page determines the selection of guide words. The first guide word is the alphabetically first entry on the page. The second guide word is usually the alphabetically last entry on the page:

> **glee • globular cluster**

The entry need not be a main entry. Another boldface word—a variant, an inflected form, or a defined or undefined run-on—may be selected as a guide word. For this reason the last printed main entry on a page is not always the last entry alphabetically:

IQ ● ironness

On the page where these guide words are used, *ironmongery* is the last printed entry, but *ironness,* a derivative word run on at ²*iron,* is the last entry alphabetically and so has been chosen as the second guide word.

All guide words must themselves be in alphabetical order from page to page throughout the dictionary; thus, the alphabetically last entry on a page is not used if it follows alphabetically the first guide word on the next page:

joint ● Jotun

On the page where these guide words are found, *Jotunn,* a variant at the entry *Jotun,* is the last entry alphabetically, but it is not used as the second guide word because it follows alphabetically the entry *Jotunheim,* which is the first guide word on the next page. To use *Jotunn* would violate the alphabetical order of guide words from page to page, and so the entry *Jotun* is the second guide word instead.

END-OF-LINE DIVISION

The centered dots within entry words indicate division points at which a hyphen may be put at the end of a line of print or writing. Thus the noun *pos·si·bil·i·ty* may be ended on one line with:

pos-

possi-

possibil-

possibili-

and continued on the next with:

sibility

bility

ity

ty

Centered dots are not shown after a single initial letter or before a single terminal letter because printers seldom cut off a single letter:

aswirl . . . *adj*

mouthy . . . *adj*

idea . . . *n*

Nor are they shown at second and succeeding homographs unless these differ among themselves:

¹**re·form** . . . *vb*   ¹**min·ute** . . . *n*

²**reform** *n*   ²**minute** *vt*

³**reform** *adj*   ³**mi·nute** . . . *adj*

There are acceptable alternative end-of-line divisions just as there are acceptable variant spellings and pronunciations. It is, for example, all but impossible to produce a convincing argument that either of the divisions *aus·ter·i·ty, au·ster·i·ty* is better than the other. But space cannot be taken for entries like *aus·ter·i·ty or au·ster·i·ty,* and *au·s·ter·i·ty* would likely be confusing to many. No more than one division is, therefore, shown for an entry in this dictionary.

Many words have two or more common pronunciation variants, and the same end-of-line division is not always appropriate for each of them. The division *fla·gel·lar,* for example, best fits the variant \flə-ˈje-lər\ whereas the division *flag·el·lar* best fits the variant \ˈfla-jə-lər\. In instances

like this, the division falling farther to the left is used, regardless of the order of the pronunciations:

fla·gel·lar \flə-ˈje-lər, ˈfla-jə-lər\

For more information on centered dots within entry words see the paragraph on hyphens in the Guide to Pronunciation.

A double hyphen at the end of a line in this dictionary stands for a hyphen that belongs at that point in a hyphenated word and that is retained when the word is written as a unit on one line.

lemon thyme *n* (1629) : a thyme (*Thymus citriodorus*) having lemon‑scented leaves used as a seasoning; *also* : its leaves

VARIANTS

When a main entry is followed by the word *or* and another spelling, the two spellings occur with equal or nearly equal frequency and can be considered equal variants. Both are standard, and either one may be used according to personal inclination:

ocher *or* **ochre**

If two variants joined by *or* are out of alphabetical order, they remain equal variants. The one printed first is, however, slightly more common than the second:

pol·ly·wog *or* **pol·li·wog**

When another spelling is joined to the main entry by the word *also,* the spelling after *also* occurs appreciably less often and thus is considered a secondary variant:

can·cel·la·tion *also* **can·cel·ation**

Secondary variants belong to standard usage and may be used according to personal inclination. If there are two secondary variants, the second is joined to the first by *or.* Once the word *also* is used to signal a secondary variant, all following variants are joined by *or*:

¹**Shake·spear·ean** *or* **Shake·spear·ian** *also* **Shak·sper·ean** *or* **Shak·sper·ian**

The use of *or* to indicate equal variants and *also* to indicate secondary variants applies not only to main entries, but to all boldface entry words, including inflected forms and run-on entries.

Variants of main entries whose spelling places them alphabetically more than a column away from the main entry are entered at their own alphabetical places as well as at the main entry:

gibe *or* **jibe** . . . *vb*

¹**jibe** *var of* GIBE

¹**rhyme** *also* **rime** . . . *n*

rhyme·ster *also* **rime·ster** . . . *n*

³**rime, rimester** *var of* RHYME, RHYMESTER

Variants having a usage label appear only at their own alphabetical places:

metre . . . *chiefly Brit var of* METER

agin . . . *dial var of* AGAINST

RUN-ON ENTRIES

The defined senses of a main entry may be followed by one or more derivatives or by a homograph with a different functional label. These are run-on entries. Each is introduced by a lightface dash and each has a functional label. They are not defined, however, since their meanings are readily derivable from the meaning of the root word:

> **slay** . . . *vb* . . . — **slay·er** *n*
>
> **spir·it·ed** . . . *adj* . . . — **spir·it·ed·ly** *adv* — **spir·it·ed·ness** *n*
>
> **stac·ca·to** . . . *adj* . . . — **staccato** *adv* — **staccato** *n*

The defined senses of a main entry may be followed by one or more phrases containing the entry word or an inflected form of it. These are also run-on entries. Each is introduced by a lightface dash but there is no functional label. They are, however, defined since their meanings are more than the sum of the meanings of their elements:

> **¹hole** . . . *n* . . . — **in the hole 1** : . . .
>
> **¹live** . . . *vb* . . . — **live it up** : . . .

Defined phrases of this sort are run on at the entry constituting the first major element in the phrase. The first major element is ordinarily a verb or a noun, but when these are absent another part of speech may serve instead:

> **¹but** . . . *conj* . . . — **but what** : . . .

When there are variants, however, the run-on appears at the entry constituting the first major invariable element in the phrase:

> **¹clock** . . . *n* . . . — **kill the clock** *or* **run out the clock** : . . .
>
> **¹hand** . . . *n* . . . — **on all hands** *or* **on every hand** : . . .

A run-on entry is an independent entry with respect to function and status. Labels at the main entry do not apply unless they are repeated.

Attention is called to the definition of *vocabulary entry* in this book. The term *dictionary entry* includes all vocabulary entries as well as all boldface entries in the separate sections of the back matter headed "Foreign Words and Phrases," "Biographical Names," and "Geographical Names."

Pronunciation

Pronunciation is indicated between a pair of reversed virgules \ \ following the entry word. The symbols used are listed in the chart printed inside the back cover of this dictionary and on the page facing the first page of the dictionary proper. An abbreviated list appears at the bottom of the second column on each right-hand page of the vocabulary. Explanations of the symbols are given in the Guide to Pronunciation.

SYLLABLES

A hyphen is used in the pronunciation to show syllabic division. These hyphens sometimes coincide with the centered dots in the entry word that indicate end-of-line division; sometimes they do not:

> **ab·sen·tee** \ˌab-sən-ˈtē\
>
> **¹met·ric** \ˈme-trik\

STRESS

A high-set mark \ˈ\ indicates primary (strongest) stress or accent; a low-set mark \ˌ\ indicates secondary (medium) stress or accent:

> **heart·beat** \ˈhärt-ˌbēt\

The stress mark stands at the beginning of the syllable that receives the stress.

Stress marks are an indication of the relative prominence of the syllables in a word. In running speech the primary stress can vary in English words for several contextual and semantic reasons. Because the variation is so great, this book shows the primary stress of a word in its pronunciation as a single word out of context.

VARIANT PRONUNCIATIONS

The presence of variant pronunciations indicates that not all educated speakers pronounce words the same way. A second-place variant is not to be regarded as less acceptable than the pronunciation that is given first. It may, in fact, be used by as many educated speakers as the first variant, but the requirements of the printed page make one precede the other:

> **apri·cot** \ˈa-prə-ˌkät, ˈā-\
>
> **for·eign** \ˈfȯr-ən, ˈfär-\

A variant that is appreciably less common than the preceding variant is preceded by the word *also*:

> **¹al·loy** \ˈa-ˌlȯi *also* ə-ˈlȯi\

A variant preceded by *sometimes* is even less common, though it does occur in educated speech:

> **in·vei·gle** \in-ˈvā-gəl *sometimes* -ˈvē-\

Sometimes a regional label precedes a variant:

> **¹great** \ˈgrāt, *Southern also* ˈgre(ə)t\

The label *dial* precedes a variant that is noteworthy or common in a dialect or dialects of American English, but that is not considered to be a standard pronunciation:

> **ask** \ˈask, ˈäsk; *dial* ˈaks\

The symbol \÷\ is placed before a pronunciation variant that occurs in educated speech but that is considered by some to be unacceptable:

> **nu·cle·ar** \ˈnü-klē-ər, ˈnyü-, ÷-kyə-lər\

This symbol refers only to the immediately following variant and not to subsequent variants separated from it by a comma or a semicolon.

PARENTHESES IN PRONUNCIATIONS

Symbols enclosed by parentheses represent elements that are present in the pronunciation of some speakers but are absent from the pronunciation of other speakers, or elements that are present in some but absent from other utterances of the same speaker:

> **¹twin·kle** \ˈtwiŋ-kəl\ *vb* . . . **twin·kling** \-k(ə-)liŋ\
>
> **sat·is·fac·to·ry** \ˌsa-təs-ˈfak-t(ə-)rē\
>
> **re·sponse** \ri-ˈspän(t)s\

Thus, the parentheses at *twinkling* mean that there are some who pronounce the \ə\ between \k\ and \l\ and others who do not pronounce it.

PARTIAL AND ABSENT PRONUNCIATIONS

When a main entry has less than a full pronunciation, the missing part is to be supplied from a pronunciation in a preceding entry or within the same pair of reversed virgules:

> **cham·pi·on·ship** \-ˌship\

Ma·dei·ra \mə-'dir-ə, -'der-\

The pronunciation of the first three syllables of *championship* is found at the main entry *champion*:

¹cham·pi·on \'cham-pē-ən\

The hyphens before and after \'der\ in the pronunciation of *Madeira* indicate that both the first and the last parts of the pronunciation are to be taken from the immediately preceding pronunciation.

Partial pronunciations are usually shown when two or more variants have a part in common. When a variation of stress is involved, a partial pronunciation may be terminated at the stress mark which stands at the beginning of a syllable not shown:

di·verse \dī-'vərs, də-', 'dī-ˌ\

an·cho·vy \'an-ˌchō-vē, an-'\

In general, no pronunciation is indicated for open compounds consisting of two or more English words that have own-place entry:

witch doctor *n*

A pronunciation is shown, however, for any element of an open compound that does not have entry at its own alphabetical place:

di·phos·pho·gly·cer·ic acid \(ˌ)dī-ˌfäs-fō-gli-ˌser-ik-\

sieve of Er·a·tos·the·nes \-ˌer-ə-'täs-thə-ˌnēz\

Only the first entry in a sequence of numbered homographs is given a pronunciation if their pronunciations are the same:

¹re·ward \ri-'wȯrd\

²reward

Pronunciations are shown for obsolete words only if they occur in Shakespeare:

clois·tress \'klȯi-strəs\ *n . . . obs*

The pronunciation of unpronounced derivatives and compounds run on at a main entry is a combination of the pronunciation at the main entry and the pronunciation of the suffix or final element as given at its alphabetical place in the vocabulary:

— oval·ness *n*

— shot in the dark

Thus, the pronunciation of *ovalness* is the sum of the pronunciations of *oval* and *-ness;* that of *shot in the dark,* the sum of the pronunciation of the four elements that make up the phrase.

The notation *sic* is used at a few pronunciation respellings which are correct but are at variance with the spelling of the word.

Ki·ri·bati \'kir-ə-ˌbas—*sic*\

Functional Labels

An italic label indicating a part of speech or some other functional classification follows the pronunciation or, if no pronunciation is given, the main entry. The main traditional parts of speech are indicated as follows:

¹bold . . . *adj*

hand·i·ly . . . *adv*

¹but . . . *conj*

oops . . . *interj*

bo·le·ro . . . *n*

²under *prep*

some·one . . . *pron*

¹shrink . . . *vb*

If a verb is both transitive and intransitive, the labels *vt* and *vi* introduce the subdivisions:

flat·ten . . . *vb* . . . *vt* . . . ~ *vi*

A boldface swung dash ~ is used to stand for the main entry (as *flatten*) and separate the subdivisions of the verb. If there is no subdivision, *vt* or *vi* takes the place of *vb*:

²fleece *vt*

ap·per·tain . . . *vi*

Labeling a verb as transitive, however, does not preclude occasional intransitive use (as in absolute constructions).

Other italicized labels used to indicate functional classifications that are not traditional parts of speech are:

geog *abbr*	**-itis** *n suffix*
poly- *comb form*	**-ize** *vb suffix*
-logy *n comb form*	**Ly·cra** . . . *trademark*
-iferous *adj comb form*	**-nd** *symbol*
super- *prefix*	**¹may** . . . *verbal auxiliary*
Gram·my . . . *service mark*	**gid·dy·ap** . . . *vb imper*
¹-ic *adj suffix*	**me·thinks** . . . *vb impersonal*
²-ward *or* **-wards** *adv suffix*	**NC–17** . . . *certification mark*

Two functional labels are sometimes combined:

zilch . . . *adj or n*

afloat . . . *adj or adv*

Functional labels are not shown for main entries that are noun phrases having a preposition in the middle:

ball of fire (ca. 1900) : a person of unusual energy . . .

Functional labels are also not shown for phrases that are defined run-on entries.

Inflected Forms

In comparison with some other languages, English does not have many inflected forms. Of those which it has, several are inflected forms of words belonging to small, closed groups (as the personal pronouns or the demonstratives). These forms can readily be found at their own alphabetical places with a full entry (as *whom,* the objective case form of *who*) or with a cross-reference in small capital letters to another entry (as *those,* the plural form of *that*).

Most other inflected forms, however, are covered explicitly or by implication at the main entry for the base form. These are the plurals of nouns, the principal parts of verbs (the past tense, the past participle when it differs from the past tense, and the present participle), and the comparative and superlative forms of adjectives and adverbs. In general, it may be said that when these inflected forms are created in a manner considered regular in English (as by adding *-s* or *-es* to nouns, *-ed* and *-ing* to verbs, and *-er* and *-est* to adjectives and adverbs) and when it seems that there is nothing about the formation likely to give the dictionary user doubts, the inflected form is not shown in order to save space for information more likely to be sought. Inflected forms are also not shown at undefined run-ons or at some entries bearing a limiting label:

gour·mand . . . *n* . . . **— gour·man·dize** . . . *vi*

¹fem·i·nine . . . *adj* . . . **— fem·i·nine·ness** . . . *n*

²**lake** *n* . . . — **laky** . . . *adj*

²**cote** . . . *vt* . . . *obs* : to pass by

crouse . . . *adj* . . . *chiefly Scot* : BRISK, LIVELY

On the other hand, if the inflected form is created in an irregular way or if the dictionary user is likely to have doubts about it (even though it is formed regularly), the inflected form is shown in boldface, either in full or cut back to a convenient and easily recognizable point. Full details about the kinds of entries at which inflected forms are shown and the kinds at which they are not shown are given in the three following sections.

NOUNS

The plurals of nouns are shown in this dictionary when suffixation brings about a change of final -*y* to -*i*-, when the noun ends in a consonant plus -*o*, when the noun ends in -*oo* or -*ey*, when the noun has an irregular plural or a zero plural or a foreign plural, when the noun is a compound that pluralizes any element but the last, when a final consonant is doubled, when the noun has variant plurals, and when it is believed that the dictionary user might have reasonable doubts about the spelling of the plural or when the plural is spelled in a way contrary to expectations:

²**spy** *n, pl* **spies**

si·lo . . . *n, pl* **silos**

²**shampoo** *n, pl* **shampoos**

gal·ley . . . *n, pl* **galleys**

¹**mouse** . . . *n, pl* **mice**

moose . . . *n, pl* **moose**

cri·te·ri·on . . . *n, pl* -**ria**

son–in–law . . . *n, pl* **sons–in–law**

¹**quiz** . . . *n, pl* **quiz·zes**

¹**fish** . . . *n, pl* **fish** *or* **fish·es**

cor·gi . . . *n, pl* **corgis**

³**dry** *n, pl* **drys**

Cutback inflected forms are used when the noun has three or more syllables:

ame·ni·ty . . . *n, pl* -**ties**

The plurals of nouns are usually not shown when the base word is unchanged by suffixation, when the noun is a compound whose second element is readily recognizable as a regular free form entered at its own place, or when the noun is unlikely to occur in the plural:

¹**night** . . . *n*

²**crunch** *n*

fore·foot . . . *n*

mo·nog·a·my . . . *n*

Nouns that are plural in form and that regularly occur in plural construction are labeled *n pl*:

munch·ies . . . *n pl*

Nouns that are plural in form but that are not always construed as plurals are appropriately labeled:

ro·bot·ics . . . *n pl but sing in constr*

two bits *n pl but sing or pl in constr*

A noun that is singular in construction takes a singular verb when it is used as a subject; a noun that is plural in construction takes a plural verb when it is used as a subject.

VERBS

The principal parts of verbs are shown in this dictionary when suffixation brings about a doubling of a final consonant or an elision of a final -*e* or a change of final -*y* to -*i*-, when final -*c* changes to -*ck* in suffixation, when the verb ends in -*ey*, when the inflection is irregular, when there are variant inflected forms, and when it is believed that the dictionary user might have reasonable doubts about the spelling of an inflected form or when the inflected form is spelled in a way contrary to expectations:

²**snag** *vt* **snagged; snag·ging**

¹**move** . . . *vb* **moved; mov·ing**

¹**cry** . . . *vb* **cried; cry·ing**

²**frolic** *vi* **frol·icked; frol·ick·ing**

¹**sur·vey** . . . *vb* **sur·veyed; sur·vey·ing**

¹**drive** . . . *vb* **drove** . . . ; **driv·en** . . . ; **driv·ing**

²**bus** *vb* **bused** *also* **bussed; bus·ing** *also* **bus·sing**

²**visa** *vt* **vi·saed** . . . ; **vi·sa·ing**

²**chagrin** *vt* **cha·grined** . . . ; **cha·grin·ing**

The principal parts of a regularly inflected verb are shown when it is desirable to indicate the pronunciation of one of the inflected forms:

learn . . . *vb* **learned** \'lərnd, 'lərnt\; **learn·ing**

rip·en . . . *vb* **rip·ened; rip·en·ing** \'rī-pə-niŋ, 'rīp-niŋ\

Cutback inflected forms are often used when the verb has three or more syllables, when it is a disyllable that ends in -*l* and has variant spellings, and when it is a compound whose second element is readily recognized as an irregular verb:

elim·i·nate . . . *vb* -**nat·ed; -nat·ing**

³**quarrel** *vi* -**reled** *or* -**relled; -rel·ing** *or* -**rel·ling**

¹**re·take** . . . *vt* -**took** . . . ; -**tak·en** . . . ; -**tak·ing**

The principal parts of verbs are usually not shown when the base word is unchanged by suffixation or when the verb is a compound whose second element is readily recognizable as a regular free form entered at its own place:

¹**jump** . . . *vb*

pre·judge . . . *vt*

Another inflected form of English verbs is the third person singular of the present tense, which is regularly formed by the addition of -*s* or -*es* to the base form of the verb. This inflected form is not shown except at a handful of entries (as *have* and *do*) for which it is in some way anomalous.

ADJECTIVES & ADVERBS

The comparative and superlative forms of adjectives and adverbs are shown in this dictionary when suffixation brings about a doubling of a final consonant or an elision of a final -*e* or a change of final -*y* to -*i*-, when the word ends in -*ey*, when the inflection is irregular, and when there are variant inflected forms:

¹**red** . . . *adj* **red·der; red·dest**

¹**tame** . . . *adj* **tam·er; tam·est**

¹**kind·ly** . . . *adj* **kind·li·er; -est**

¹**ear·ly** . . . *adv* **ear·li·er; -est**

dic·ey . . . *adj* **dic·i·er; -est**

¹**good** . . . *adj* **bet·ter** . . . ; **best**

¹**bad** . . . *adj* **worse** . . . ; **worst**

¹**far** . . . *adv* **far·ther** . . . *or* **fur·ther** . . . ; **far·thest** *or* **fur·thest**

The superlative forms of adjectives and adverbs of two or more syllables are usually cut back:

³**fancy** *adj* **fan·ci·er; -est**

¹**ear·ly** . . . *adv* **ear·li·er; -est**

The comparative and superlative forms of regularly inflected adjectives and adverbs are shown when it is desirable to indicate the pronunciation of the inflected forms:

¹**young** . . . *adj* **youn·ger** \'yəŋ-gər\; **youn·gest** \'yəŋ-gəst\

The inclusion of inflected forms in *-er* and *-est* at adjective and adverb entries means nothing more about the use of *more* and *most* with these adjectives and adverbs than that their comparative and superlative degrees may be expressed in either way; *lazier* or *more lazy; laziest* or *most lazy.*

At a few adjective entries only the superlative form is shown:

³**mere** *adj, superlative* **mer·est**

The absence of the comparative form indicates that there is no evidence of its use.

The comparative and superlative forms of adjectives and adverbs are not shown when the base word is unchanged by suffixation or when the word is a compound whose second element is readily recognizable as a regular free form entered at its own place:

¹**near** . . . *adv*

un·wary . . . *adj*

The comparative and superlative forms of adverbs are not shown when they are identical with the inflected forms of a preceding adjective homograph:

¹**hot** . . . *adj* **hot·ter; hot·test**

²**hot** *adv*

Capitalization

Most entries in this dictionary begin with a lowercase letter. A few of these have an italicized label *often cap*, which indicates that the word is as likely to be capitalized as not, that it is as acceptable with an uppercase initial as it is with one in lowercase. Some entries begin with an uppercase letter, which indicates that the word is usually capitalized. The absence of an initial capital or of an *often cap* label indicates that the word is not ordinarily capitalized:

lunk·head . . . *n*

gar·gan·tuan . . . *adj, often cap*

Mo·hawk . . . *n*

The capitalization of entries that are open or hyphenated compounds is similarly indicated by the form of the entry or by an italicized label:

obstacle course *n*

neo–Ex·pres·sion·ism . . . *n, often cap N*

off–off–Broadway *n, often cap both Os*

un–Amer·i·can . . . *adj*

Dutch oven *n*

Old Glory *n*

A word that is capitalized in some senses and lowercase in others shows variations from the form of the main entry by the use of italicized labels at the appropriate senses:

re·nais·sance . . . *n* . . . **1** *cap* . . . **2** *often cap*

Shet·land . . . *n* . . . **2** *often not cap*

Trin·i·ty . . . *n* . . . **2** *not cap*

Attributive Nouns

The italicized label *often attrib* placed after the functional label *n* indicates that the noun is often used as an adjective equivalent in attributive position before another noun:

¹**bot·tle** . . . *n, often attrib*

busi·ness . . . *n, often attrib*

Examples of the attributive use of these nouns are *bottle opener* and *business ethics.*

While any noun may occasionally be used attributively, the label *often attrib* is limited to those having broad attributive use. This label is not used when an adjective homograph (as *iron* or *paper*) is entered. And it is not used at open compounds (as *health food*) that may be used attributively with an inserted hyphen (as in *health-food store*).

Etymology

The matter in boldface square brackets preceding the definition is the etymology. Meanings given in roman type within these brackets are not definitions of the entry, but are meanings of the Middle English, Old English, or non-English words within the brackets.

The etymology traces a vocabulary entry as far back as possible in English (as to Old English), tells from what language and in what form it came into English, and (except in the case of such words outside the general vocabulary of English as *bascule* and *zloty*) traces the pre-English source as far back as possible if the source is an Indo-European language. These etyma are printed in italics.

OLD, MIDDLE, AND MODERN ENGLISH

The etymology usually gives the Middle English and the Old English forms of words in the following style:

¹**nap** . . . *vi* . . . [ME *nappen,* fr. OE *hnappian* . . .]

¹**old** . . . *adj* [ME, fr. OE *eald* . . .]

An etymology in which a word is traced back to Middle English but not to Old English indicates that the word is found in Middle English but not in those texts that have survived from the Old English period:

¹**slab** . . . *n* [ME *slabbe*]

¹**nag** . . . *n* . . . [ME *nagge;* akin to D *negge* small horse]

An etymology in which a word is traced back directly to Old English with no intervening mention of Middle English indicates that the word has not survived continuously from Old English times to the present. Rather, it died out after the Old English period and has been revived in modern times:

ge·mot . . . *n* [OE *gemōt* . . .]

thegn . . . *n* [OE . . .]

An etymology is not usually given for a word created in English by the combination of existing constituents or by functional shift. This indicates that the identity of the constituents is expected to be self-evident to the user.

book·shelf . . . *n* . . . : an open shelf for holding books

¹fire·proof . . . *adj* . . . : proof against or resistant to fire

off–put·ting . . . *adj* . . . : that puts one off : REPELLENT, DISCONCERTING

penal code *n* . . . : a code of laws concerning crimes and offenses and their punishment

³stalk *n* . . . 1 : the act of stalking

In the case of a family of words obviously related to a common English word but differing from it by containing various easily recognizable suffixes, an etymology is usually given only at the base word, even though some of the derivatives may have been formed in a language other than English:

¹equal . . . *adj* [ME, fr. L *aequalis*, fr. *aequus* level, equal] . . . **1 a** (1) : of the same measure, quantity, amount, or number as another

equal·i·ty . . . *n* . . . 1 : the quality or state of being equal

equal·ize . . . *vt* . . . 1 : to make equal

While *equalize* was formed in Modern English, *equality* was actually borrowed into Middle English (via Anglo‑French) from Latin *aequalitas*.

Incorporating material from major scholarly reference works completed in recent years, the etymologies of late Old and Middle English words borrowed from French now apply the label "Anglo-French" (abbreviated AF) to all medieval French words known to have been used in French documents written in Britain before about 1400. This treatment acknowledges that literate English speakers then were typically bilingual or trilingual readers and writers who cultivated distinctive varieties of Latin and French as well as of English, and that words moved easily from one to another of these three languages. The label "Anglo-French" should not be taken to mean that the etymon is attested exclusively in Anglo-French, for in the great majority of cases the word has a cognate form in the continental northern French of Picardy and Normandy or the French of Paris and its surroundings. Because Anglo‑French is one dialect of medieval French, it falls within the domain of wider labels "Old French" and "Middle French," which cover all dialects of French in their respective time frames. A similar caution applies to derivative words:

¹jour·ney . . . *n* . . . [ME, fr. AF *jurnee* day, day's journey, fr. *jur* day, fr. LL *diurnum* . . .]

This etymology does not mean that the derivation of *journey* from *jur* took place only in Anglo-French. Forms corresponding to Anglo-French *jurnee* exist in other dialects of Old and Middle French, as well as in Old Occitan, and the word survives in Modern French as *journée*, "day."

LANGUAGES OTHER THAN ENGLISH

The etymology gives the language from which words borrowed into English have come. It also gives the form or a transliteration of the word in that language if the form differs from that in English:

¹mar·ble . . . *n* [ME, fr. AF *marbre*, fr. L *marmor*, fr. Gk *marmaros*]

how·it·zer . . . *n* [D *houwitser*, ultim. fr. Czech *houfnice* ballista]

souk . . . *n* [Ar *sūq* market]

In a few cases the expression "ultim. fr." replaces the more usual "fr." This expression indicates that one or more intermediate steps have been omitted in tracing the derivation of the form preceding the expression from the form following it:

tri·lo·bite . . . *n* [ultim. fr. Gk *trilobos* three-lobed, fr. *tri-* + *lobos* lobe]

When a language name that is not itself an entry in the dictionary is used in an etymology, a short parenthetical definition will immediately follow the name:

kook·a·bur·ra . . . *n* [Wiradhuri (Australian aboriginal language of central New South Wales) *gugabarra*]

However, subfamily, language, or dialect names modified by qualifiers that simply add geographical orientation—as "Interior Salish," "MF (Picard dial.)," or "Southern Paiute"—will not be further defined as long as both the qualifier and the word being qualified are both entries in the dictionary.

Words cited from certain American Indian languages and from some other languages that are infrequently printed have been rendered with the phonetic symbols used by scholars of those languages. These symbols include the following: a raised dot to the right of a vowel letter to mark vowel length; a hook below a vowel letter to mark nasality; an apostrophe over a consonant letter to mark glottal release; a superscript *w* to the right of a consonant letter to mark labialization; the symbol ɔ to render \ȯ\; the symbol *i* to render a high central vowel; the Greek letters β, δ, and γ to render voiced labial, dental, and velar fricatives; the symbol θ to render \th\; the symbol *x* to render \k\; the symbol ʔ to render a glottal stop; and the symbol ƛ ("crossed lambda") for a voiceless lateral affricate. Examples of these symbols can be found at etymologies for the words *Athabascan*, *babassu*, *coho*, *fist*, *Lhasa apso*, *potlatch*, and *sego lily*.

ASSUMED OR RECONSTRUCTED FORMS

An asterisk placed before a word means that it is assumed to have existed or has been reconstructed by means of comparative evidence. In some cases, the assumption may be due to lack of evidence:

⁴bore *n* [ME **bore* wave, fr. ON *bāra*] (1601)

The word is unattested before Modern English, though the likelihood is strong that it was borrowed from Scandinavian much earlier. The case of the word *battlement* is somewhat different:

bat·tle·ment . . . *n* [ME *batelment*, fr. AF **bataillement*, fr. *batailler* to fortify with battlements — more at BATTLE]

It is highly probable that *bataillement* existed in Anglo‑French, given that both the underlying verb *batailler* and the Middle English derivative *batelment* are attested.

The asterisk is invariably used before words labeled VL, which stands for "Vulgar Latin," the traditional name for the unrecorded spoken Latin of both the uneducated and educated, especially in the final centuries of the Roman Empire. Vulgar Latin forms can be reconstructed on the basis of their later outcome in the Romance languages and of their relationship with known Latin words:

¹can·vas . . . *n* [ME *canevas*, fr. AF *canevas*, *chanevaz*, fr. VL **cannabaceus* hempen, fr. L *cannabis* hemp . . .]

WORDS OF UNKNOWN ORIGIN

When the source of a word appearing as a main entry is unknown, the expression "origin unknown" is usually used. Only in exceptional circumstances (as with some ethnic names) does the absence of an etymology mean that it has not been possible to furnish an informative etymology. More often, it means that no etymology is believed to be necessary. This is the case, for instance, with most of the entries identified as variants and with many derivatives.

ETYMOLOGIES OF TECHNICAL WORDS

Much of the technical vocabulary of the sciences and other specialized studies consists of words or word elements that are current in two or more languages, with only such slight modifications as are necessary to adapt them to the structure of the individual language in each case. Many words and word elements of this kind have become sufficiently a part of the general vocabulary of English as to require entry in an abridged dictionary. Because of the vast extent of the relevant published material in many languages and in many scientific and other specialized fields, it is impracticable to ascertain the language of origin of every such term. Yet it would not be accurate to formulate a statement about the origin of any such term in a way that could be interpreted as implying that it was coined in English. Accordingly, whenever a term that is entered in this dictionary belongs recognizably to this class of internationally current terms and whenever no positive evidence is at hand to show that it was coined in English, the etymology recognizes its international status and the possibility that it originated elsewhere than in English by use of the label ISV (for International Scientific Vocabulary):

meg·a·watt . . . *n* [ISV]

phy·lo·ge·net·ic . . . *adj* [ISV, fr. NL *phylogenesis* . . .]

¹**-ol** *n suffix* [ISV, fr. *alcohol*]

COMPRESSION OF INFORMATION

An etymology giving the name of a language (including ME or OE) and not giving the foreign (or Middle English or Old English) form indicates that this form is the same as that of the entry word:

ka·pok . . . *n* [Malay]

¹**po·grom** . . . *n* [Yiddish, fr. Russ . . .]

¹**dumb** . . . *adj* [ME, fr. OE . . .]

An etymology giving the name of a language (including ME or OE) and the form in that language but not giving the foreign (or Middle English or Old English) meaning indicates that this meaning is the same as that expressed in the first definition in the entry:

¹**wea·ry** . . . *adj* . . . [ME *wery*, fr. OE *wērig* . . .] . . . **1 :** exhausted in strength . . .

When a word from a foreign language (or Middle English or Old English) is a key element in the etymologies of several related entries that are found close together, the meaning of the word is usually given at only one of the entries:

ve·lo·ce . . . *adv or adj* [It, fr. L *veloc-, velox*]

ve·loc·i·pede . . . *n* [F *vélocipède*, fr. L *veloc-, velox + ped-, pes* foot — more at FOOT]

ve·loc·i·ty . . . *n* . . . [MF *velocité*, fr. L *velocitat-, velocitas*, fr. *veloc-, velox* quick; prob. akin to L *vegēre* to enliven — more at WAKE]

When an etymology includes the expression "by alter." and the altered form is not cited, the form is the term given in small capital letters as the definition:

ole . . . *adj* [by alter.] . . . **:** OLD

When the origin of a word is traced to the name of a person or place not further identified, additional information may be found in the Biographical Names or Geographical Names section in the back matter:

far·ad . . . *n* [Michael *Faraday*]

jodh·pur . . . *n* [*Jodhpur*, India]

RELATED WORDS

When a word of Indo-European origin has been traced back to the earliest language in which it is attested, words descended from the same Indo-European base in other languages (especially Old High German, Latin, Greek, and Sanskrit) are usually given:

na·vel . . . *n* [ME, fr. OE *nafela*; akin to OHG *nabalo* navel, L *umbilicus*, Gk *omphalos*]

¹**wind** . . . *n* . . . [ME, fr. OE; akin to OHG *wint* wind, L *ventus*, Gk *aēnai* to blow, Skt *vāti* it blows]

Sometimes, however, to avoid space-consuming repetition, the expression "more at" directs the user to another entry where the cognates are given:

ho·ly . . . *adj* . . . [ME, fr. OE *hālig*; akin to OE *hāl* whole — more at WHOLE]

Besides the use of "akin to" to denote relatedness, some etymologies make special use of "akin to" as part of a longer formula "of . . . origin; akin to. . . ." This formula indicates that a word was borrowed from some language belonging to a group of languages whose name is inserted in the blank before the word *origin*, that it is impossible to say that the word in question is a borrowing of a particular attested word in a particular language of the source group, and that the form cited in the blank after the expression *akin to* is related to the word in question as attested within the source group:

ba·nana . . . *n* . . . [Sp or Pg; Sp, fr. Pg, of African origin; akin to Wolof *banaana* banana]

²**briar** *n* [. . . F *bruyère* heath, fr. MF *bruiere*, fr. VL *brucaria*, fr. LL *brucus* heather, of Celt origin; akin to OIr *froech* heather; akin to Gk *ereikē* heather]

This last example shows the two contrasting uses of "akin to." The word cited immediately after "of Celt origin; akin to" is an attested Celtic word descended from the same etymon as the unattested Celtic source of the Latin word. The word cited after the second "akin to" is evidence that the Celtic etymon has deeper relations within Indo-European.

Dates

At most main entries a date will be found enclosed in parentheses immediately preceding the boldface colon or the number that introduces the first sense:

ex·po·sé *also* **ex·po·se** . . . *n* [F *exposé*, fr. pp. of *exposer*] (1803) **1 :** a formal statement of facts **2 :** an exposure of something discreditable

This is the date of the earliest recorded use in English, as far as it could be determined, of the sense which the date precedes. Several caveats are appropriate at this point. First, a few classes of main entries that are not complete words (as prefixes, suffixes, and combining forms) or are not generic words (as trademarks) are not given dates. Second, the date given applies only to the first sense of the word entered in this dictionary and not necessarily to the word's very earliest meaning in English. Many words, especially those with long histories, have obsolete, archaic, or uncommon senses that are not entered in this dictionary, and such senses have been excluded from consideration in determining the date:

green·horn . . . *n* [obs. *greenhorn* animal with green or young horns] (1682) **1 :** an inexperienced or naive person

The 1682 date is for sense 1, not for the word as a whole. *Greenhorn* also has an obsolete sense, "animal with green or young horns," that was recorded as early as 1460, but since this sense is not entered, it is ignored for purposes of dating. Third, the printed date should not be taken to mark the very first time that the word—or even the sense—was used in English. Many words were certainly in spoken use for decades or even longer before they passed into the written language. The date is for the earliest written or printed use that the editors have been able to discover. This fact means further that any date is subject to change as evidence of still earlier use may emerge, and many dates given now can confidently be expected to yield to others in future printings and editions.

A date will appear in one of three different styles:

nuclear family *n* (1947) **:** a family group that consists only of father, mother, and children

¹moon·light . . . *n* (14c) **:** the light of the moon

¹sheet . . . *n* [ME *shete,* fr. OE *scēte, scīete;* . . .] (bef. 12c) **1 a :** a broad piece of cloth; *esp* **:** BEDSHEET

The style that names a year (as 1947) is the one used for the period from the sixteenth century to the present. The style that names only a century (as 14c) is the one used for the period from the twelfth century through the fifteenth century, a span that roughly approximates the period of Middle English. The style (bef. 12c) is used for the period before the twelfth century back to the earliest records of English, a span that approximates the period of Old English. Words first attested after 1500 can usually be dated to a single year because the precise dates of publication of modern printed texts are known. If a word must be dated from a modern text of uncertain chronology, it will be assigned the latest possible date of the text's publication prefixed by the abbreviation *ca.* (for *circa*). For words from the Old and Middle English periods the examples of use on which the dates depend very often occur in manuscripts which are themselves of uncertain date and which may record a text whose date of composition is highly conjectural. To date words from these periods by year would frequently give a quite misleading impression of the state of our knowledge, and so the broader formulas involving centuries are used instead.

Each date reflects a particular instance of the use of a word, most often within a continuous text. In cases where the earliest appearance of a word dated by year is not from continuous text but from a source (as a dictionary or glossary) that defines or explains the word instead of simply using it, the year is preceded by *ca.*:

magnesium hydroxide *n* (ca. 1909) **:** a slightly alkaline crystalline compound $Mg(OH)_2$ . . .

In such instances, *ca.* indicates that while the source providing the date attests that the word was in use in the relevant sense at that time, it does not offer an example of the normal use of the word and thus gives no better than an approximate date for such use. For the example above no use has so far been found that is earlier than its appearance as an entry in Webster's New International Dictionary, published in 1909, so the date is given with the qualifying abbreviation.

Usage

USAGE LABELS

Three types of status labels are used in this dictionary —temporal, regional, and stylistic—to signal that a word or a sense of a word is not part of the standard vocabulary of English.

The temporal label *obs* for "obsolete" means that there is no evidence of use since 1755:

¹per·du . . . *n* . . . *obs*

gov·ern·ment . . . *n* . . . **2** *obs*

The label *obs* is a comment on the word being defined. When a thing, as distinguished from the word used to designate it, is obsolete, appropriate orientation is usually given in the definition:

¹cat·a·pult . . . *n* . . . **1 :** an ancient military device for hurling missiles

far·thin·gale . . . *n* . . . **:** a support (as of hoops) worn esp. in the 16th century beneath a skirt to expand it at the hipline

The temporal label *archaic* means that a word or sense once in common use is found today only sporadically or in special contexts:

¹goody . . . *n* . . . *archaic*

lon·gi·tude . . . *n* . . . **2** *archaic*

A word or sense limited in use to a specific region of the U.S. has a regional label. Some regional labels correspond loosely to areas defined in Hans Kurath's *Word Geography of the Eastern United States.* The adverb *chiefly* precedes a label when the word has some currency outside the specified region, and a double label is used to indicate considerable currency in each of two specific regions:

pung . . . *n* . . . *NewEng*

ban·quette . . . *n* . . . **1** . . . **b** *Southern*

³pas·tor . . . *n* . . . *chiefly Southwest*

do·gie . . . *n* . . . *chiefly West*

gal·lery . . . *n* . . . **2** . . . **b** *Southern & Midland*

¹pot·latch . . . *n* . . . **2** *Northwest*

smear·case . . . *n* . . . *chiefly Midland*

crul·ler . . . *n* . . . **2** *Northern & Midland*

Words current in all regions of the U.S. have no label.

A word or sense limited in use to one of the other countries of the English-speaking world has an appropriate regional label:

cut·ty sark . . . *n* . . . *chiefly Scot*

lar·ri·kin . . . *n* . . . *chiefly Austral*

in·da·ba . . . *n* . . . *chiefly SoAfr*

spal·peen . . . *n* . . . *chiefly Irish*

¹bon·net . . . *n* . . . **2 a** *Brit*

book off *vi* . . . *chiefly Canad*

¹din·kum . . . *adj* . . . *Austral & NewZeal*

gar·ron . . . *n* . . . *Scot & Irish*

The label *Brit* indicates that a word or sense is current in the United Kingdom or in more than one nation of the Commonwealth (as the United Kingdom, Australia, and Canada).

The label *dial* for "dialect" indicates that the pattern of use of a word or sense is too complex for summary labeling: it usually includes several regional varieties of American English or of American and British English:

least·ways . . . *adv* . . . *dial*

The label *dial Brit* indicates currency in several dialects of the Commonwealth; *dial Eng* indicates currency in one or more provincial dialects of England:

bo·gle . . . *n* . . . *dial Brit*

¹hob . . . *n* . . . **1** *dial Eng*

The stylistic label *slang* is used with words or senses that are especially appropriate in contexts of extreme informality, that are usually not limited to a particular region or area of interest, and that are composed typically of short-ened or altered forms or extravagant or facetious figures of speech:

> **⁴barb** *n* . . . *slang* : BARBITURATE
>
> **²skinny** *n* . . . *slang* : inside information : DOPE
>
> **bread·bas·ket** . . . *n* . . . **1** *slang* : STOMACH

There is no satisfactory objective test for slang, especially with reference to a word out of context. No word, in fact, is invariably slang, and many standard words can be given slang applications.

The stylistic label *nonstand* for "nonstandard" is used for a few words or senses that are disapproved by many but that have some currency in reputable contexts:

> **learn** . . . *vb* . . . **2 a** *nonstand*
>
> **ir·re·gard·less** . . . *adv* . . . *nonstand*

The stylistic labels *disparaging, offensive, obscene,* and *vulgar* are used for those words or senses that in common use are intended to hurt or shock or that are likely to give offense even when they are used without such an intent:

> **grin·go** . . . *n* . . . *often disparaging*
>
> **piss away** *vt* . . . *sometimes vulgar*

A subject label or guide phrase is sometimes used to indicate the specific application of a word or sense:

> **²break** *n* . . . **5** . . . **d** *mining*
>
> **an·ti·mag·net·ic** . . . *adj* . . . *of a watch*
>
> **¹hu·mor** . . . *n* . . . **2 a** *in medieval physiology*

In general, however, subject orientation lies in the definition:

> **Di·do** . . . *n* . . . : a legendary queen of Carthage in Virgil's *Aeneid* who kills herself when Aeneas leaves her
>
> **je·té** . . . *n* . . . : a springing jump in ballet made from one foot to the other in any direction

ILLUSTRATIONS OF USAGE

Definitions are sometimes followed by verbal illustrations that show a typical use of the word in context. These illustrations are enclosed in angle brackets, and the word being illustrated is usually replaced by a lightface swung dash. The swung dash stands for the boldface entry word, and it may be followed by an italicized suffix:

> **¹key** . . . *n* . . . **3 a** . . . ⟨the ∼ to a riddle⟩
>
> **com·mit** . . . *vt* . . . **1** . . . **c** . . . ⟨∼ it to memory⟩
>
> **²plummet** *vi* . . . **2** . . . ⟨prices ∼*ed*⟩
>
> **weak** . . . *adj* . . . **4** . . . **b** . . . (2) . . . ⟨history was my ∼*est* subject⟩

The swung dash is not used when the form of the boldface entry word is changed in suffixation, and it is not used for open compounds:

> **¹true** . . . *adj* . . . **8** . . . ⟨in the *truest* sense⟩
>
> **turn off** *vt* . . . **4** . . . ⟨*turn* the water *off*⟩

Illustrative quotations are also used to show words in typical contexts:

> **con·flict·ed** . . . *adj* . . . ⟨this unhappy and ∼ modern woman —John Updike⟩

Omissions in quotations are indicated by ellipses:

> **alien·ation** . . . *n* . . . **1** . . . ⟨∼ . . . from the values of one's society and family —S. L. Halleck⟩

USAGE NOTES

Definitions are sometimes followed by usage notes that give supplementary information about such matters as idiom, syntax, semantic relationship, and status. A usage note is introduced by a lightface dash:

> **¹inch** . . . *n* . . . **5** : . . . — usu. used in the phrase *give an inch*
>
> **²drum** . . . *vt* . . . **2** : . . . — usu. used with *out*
>
> **¹so** . . . *adv* . . . **1 a** : . . . — often used as a substitute for a preceding clause
>
> **¹sfor·zan·do** . . . *adj or adv* . . . : . . . — used as a direction in music
>
> **hajji** . . . *n* . . . : . . . — often used as a title

Two or more usage notes are separated by a semicolon:

> **²thine** *pron* . . . : that which belongs to thee — used without a following noun as a pronoun equivalent in meaning to the adjective *thy;* used esp. in ecclesiastical or literary language and still surviving in the speech of Friends esp. among themselves

Sometimes a usage note calls attention to one or more terms with the same denotation as the main entry:

> **water moccasin** *n* . . . **1** : a venomous semiaquatic pit viper (*Agkistrodon piscivorus*) chiefly of the southeastern U.S. that is closely related to the copperhead — called also *cottonmouth, cottonmouth moccasin*

The called-also terms are shown in italic type. If such a term falls alphabetically more than a column away from the main entry, it is entered at its own place with the sole definition being a synonymous cross-reference to the entry where it appears in the usage note:

> **cot·ton·mouth** . . . *n* . . . : WATER MOCCASIN
>
> **cottonmouth moccasin** *n* . . . : WATER MOCCASIN

Sometimes a usage note is used in place of a definition. Some function words (as conjunctions and prepositions) have little or no semantic content; most interjections express feelings but are otherwise untranslatable into meaning; and some other words (as oaths and honorific titles) are more amenable to comment than to definition:

> **¹of** . . . *prep* . . . **1** — used as a function word to indicate a point of reckoning
>
> **¹oyez** . . . *vb imper* . . . — used by a court or public crier to gain attention before a proclamation
>
> **¹or** . . . *conj* . . . **1** — used as a function word to indicate an alternative
>
> **gosh** . . . *interj* . . . — used as a mild oath to express surprise
>
> **sir** . . . *n* . . . **2 a** — used as a usu. respectful form of address

USAGE PARAGRAPHS

Brief usage paragraphs have been placed at a number of entries for terms that are considered to present problems of confused or disputed usage. A usage paragraph typically summarizes the historical background of the item and its associated body of opinion, compares these with available evidence of current usage, and often adds a few words of suitable advice for the dictionary user.

Each paragraph is signaled by an indented boldface italic *usage.* Where appropriate, discussion is keyed by sense number to the definition of the meaning in question. Most paragraphs incorporate appropriate verbal illustrations and illustrative quotations to clarify and exemplify the points being made:

> **ag·gra·vate** . . . *vt* . . . **1** *obs* **a** : to make heavy : BURDEN **b** : INCREASE **2** : to make worse, more serious, or more severe : intensify unpleasantly ⟨problems have been *aggravated* by neglect⟩ **3 a** : to rouse to displeasure or anger by usu. persistent and often petty goading **b** : to produce inflammation in
> *usage* Although *aggravate* has been used in sense 3a since the 17th century, it has been the object of disapproval only since about 1870. It is used in expository prose ⟨when his silly conceit . . . about his not-very-good early work has begun to *aggravate* us —William Styron⟩

but seems to be more common in speech and casual writing ⟨a good profession for him, because bus drivers get *aggravated* —Jackie Gleason (interview, 1986)⟩ ⟨& now this letter comes to *aggravate* me a thousand times worse —Mark Twain (letter, 1864)⟩. Sense 2 is far more common than sense 3a in published prose. Such is not the case, however, with *aggravation* and *aggravating. Aggravation* is used in sense 3 somewhat more than in its earlier senses; *aggravating* has practically no use other than to express annoyance.

When a second word is also discussed in a paragraph, the main entry for that word is followed by a run-on **usage** see . . . , which refers to the entry where the paragraph may be found:

²**af·fect** . . . *vb* . . . **usage** see EFFECT

Definitions

DIVISION OF SENSES

A boldface colon is used in this dictionary to introduce a definition:

¹**coo·per** . . . *n* . . . : one that makes or repairs wooden casks or tubs

It is also used to separate two or more definitions of a single sense:

un·cage . . . *vt* . . . : to release from or as if from a cage : free from restraint

Boldface Arabic numerals separate the senses of a word that has more than one sense:

¹**gloom** . . . *vb* . . . *vi* . . . **1** : to look, feel, or act sullen or despondent **2** : to be or become overcast **3** : to loom up dimly

Boldface lowercase letters separate the subsenses of a word:

¹**grand** . . . *adj* . . . **5 a** : LAVISH, SUMPTUOUS . . . **b** : marked by a regal form and dignity **c** : fine or imposing in appearance or impression **d** : LOFTY, SUBLIME

Lightface numerals in parentheses indicate a further division of subsenses:

take out *vt* **1 a** (1) : DEDUCT, SEPARATE (2) : EXCLUDE, OMIT (3) : WITHDRAW, WITHHOLD

A lightface colon following a definition and immediately preceding two or more subsenses indicates that the subsenses are subsumed by the preceding definition:

²**crunch** *n* . . . **3** : a tight or critical situation: as **a** : a critical point in the buildup of pressure between opposing elements . . . **b** : a severe economic squeeze . . . **c** : SHORTAGE

se·quoia . . . *n* . . . : either of two huge coniferous California trees of the bald cypress family that may reach a height of over 300 feet (90 meters): **a** : GIANT SEQUOIA **b** : REDWOOD 3a

The word *as* may or may not follow the lightface colon. Its presence (as at ²*crunch*) indicates that the following subsenses are typical or significant examples. Its absence (as at *sequoia*) indicates that the subsenses which follow are exhaustive.

The system of separating the various senses of a word by numerals and letters is a lexical convenience. It reflects something of their semantic relationship, but it does not evaluate senses or set up a hierarchy of importance among them.

Sometimes a particular semantic relationship between senses is suggested by the use of one of four italic sense dividers: *esp, specif, also,* or *broadly.*

The sense divider *esp* (for *especially*) is used to introduce the most common meaning subsumed in the more general preceding definition:

²**slick** *adj* . . . **3 a** : characterized by subtlety or nimble wit : CLEVER; *esp* : WILY

The sense divider *specif* (for *specifically*) is used to introduce a common but highly restricted meaning subsumed in the more general preceding definition:

pon·tiff . . . *n* . . . **2** : BISHOP; *specif, often cap* : POPE 1

The sense divider *also* is used to introduce a meaning that is closely related to but may be considered less important than the preceding sense:

chi·na . . . *n* . . . **1** : PORCELAIN; *also* : vitreous porcelain wares (as dishes, vases, or ornaments) for domestic use

The sense divider *broadly* is used to introduce an extended or wider meaning of the preceding definition:

flot·sam . . . *n* . . . **1** : floating wreckage of a ship or its cargo; *broadly* : floating debris

ORDER OF SENSES

The order of senses within an entry is historical: the sense known to have been first used in English is entered first. This is not to be taken to mean, however, that each sense of a multisense word developed from the immediately preceding sense. It is altogether possible that sense 1 of a word has given rise to sense 2 and sense 2 to sense 3, but frequently sense 2 and sense 3 may have arisen independently of one another from sense 1.

When a numbered sense is further subdivided into lettered subsenses, the inclusion of particular subsenses within a sense is based upon their semantic relationship to one another, but their order is likewise historical: subsense 1a is earlier than 1b, 1b is earlier than 1c, and so forth. Divisions of subsenses indicated by lightface numerals in parentheses are also in historical order with respect to one another. Subsenses may be out of historical order, however, with respect to the broader numbered senses:

¹**job** . . . *n* . . . (ca. 1627) **1 a** : a piece of work; *esp* : a small miscellaneous piece of work undertaken on order at a stated rate **b** : the object or material on which work is being done **c** : something produced by or as if by work ⟨do a better ∼ next time⟩ **d** : an example of a usu. specified type : ITEM ⟨a 14,000-square-foot ∼ with . . . seven bedrooms —Rick Telander⟩ **2 a** : something done for private advantage ⟨suspected the whole incident was a put-up ∼⟩ **b** : a criminal enterprise; *specif* : ROBBERY **c** : a damaging or destructive bit of work ⟨did a ∼ on him⟩ **3 a** (1) : something that has to be done : TASK (2) : an undertaking requiring unusual exertion ⟨it was a real ∼ to talk over that noise⟩ **b** : a specific duty, role, or function **c** : a regular remunerative position **d** *chiefly Brit* : state of affairs — usu. used with *bad* or *good* ⟨it was a good ∼ you didn't hit the old man —E. L. Thomas⟩ **4** : plastic surgery for cosmetic purposes ⟨a nose ∼⟩

At *job* the date indicates that the earliest unit of meaning, sense 1a, was born in the seventeenth century, and it is readily apparent how the following subsenses are linked to it and to each other by the idea of work. Even subsense 1d is so linked, because while it does not apply exclusively to manufactured items, it often does so, as the illustrative quotation suggests. Yet 1d did not exist before the 1920s, while 2a and 3a (1) both belong to the seventeenth century, although they are later than 1a. Even subsense 3d is earlier than 1d, as it is found in the works of Dickens.

Historical order also determines whether transitive or intransitive senses are given first at verbs which have both kinds. If the earliest sense is transitive, all the transitive senses precede all the intransitive senses.

OMISSION OF A SENSE

Occasionally the dictionary user, having turned to an entry, may not find a particular sense that was expected or hoped for. This usually means no more than that the editors judged the sense insufficiently common or otherwise important to include in a dictionary of this scope. Such a sense will frequently be found at the appropriate entry in a dictionary (as Webster's Third New International Dictionary) that has room for less common words and meanings. One special case is worth noting, however.

At times it would be possible to include the definition of a meaning for more than one entry (as at a simple verb and a verb-adverb collocation or at a verb and an adjective derived from a participle of that verb). To save space for other information such double coverage is avoided, and the meaning is generally defined only at the base form. For the derivative term the meaning is then considered to be essentially self-explanatory and is not defined. For example *cast off* has a sense "to get rid of" in such typical contexts as "cast off all restraint," and so has the simple verb *cast* in contexts like "cast all restraint to the winds." This meaning is defined as sense 1e(2) of *cast* and is omitted from the entry *cast off*, where the dictionary user will find a number of senses that cannot be considered self-explanatory in relation to the entries for *cast* and *off*. Likewise, the entry for the adjective *picked* gives only one sense —"CHOICE, PRIME"—which is not the meaning of *picked* in such a context as "the picked fruit lay stacked in boxes awaiting shipment." A definition suitable for this use is not given at *picked* because one is given at the first homograph *pick*, the verb from which the adjective *picked* is derived, as sense 3a—"to gather by plucking."

INFORMATION AT INDIVIDUAL SENSES

Information coming between the entry word and the first definition of a multisense word applies to all senses and subsenses. Information applicable only to some senses or subsenses is given between the appropriate boldface numeral or letter and the symbolic colon. A variety of kinds of information is offered in this way:

²**palm** *n* . . . 3 [L *palmus,* fr. *palma*]

²**rally** *n* . . . 4 *also* **ral·lye**

¹**disk** *or* **disc** . . . *n* . . . 4 . . . a *usu disc*

cru·ci·fix·ion . . . *n* . . . 1 a *cap*

¹**tile** . . . *n* . . . 1 *pl* **tiles** *or* **tile** a . . .

del·i·ca·tes·sen . . . *n pl* . . . 1 . . . 2 *sing, pl* **delicatessens**

fix·ing . . . *n* . . . 2 *pl*

²**die** . . . *n, pl* **dice** . . . *or* **dies** . . . 1 *pl* **dice** . . . 2 *pl* **dies** . . . 3 *pl* **dies**

¹**folk** . . . *n, pl* **folk** *or* **folks** . . . 5 **folks** *pl*

At *palm* the subetymology indicates that the third sense, while ultimately derived from the same source (Latin *palma*) as the other senses of the word, has a different immediate etymon (Latin *palmus*), from which it receives its meaning. At *rally* one is told that in the fourth sense the word has a variant spelling not used for other senses and that this variant is a secondary or less common one. At *disk* the italic abbreviation of sense 4a indicates that, while the spelling *disk* is overall somewhat the more common (since it precedes *disc* out of alphabetical order at the beginning of the entry), *disc* is the usual spelling for this particular sense. At *crucifixion* the label *cap* points out the one meaning of the word in which it is capitalized. At the first homograph *tile* no plural is shown at the beginning of the entry because the usual plural, *tiles,* is regular. The subsenses of sense 1, however, have a zero plural as well as the usual one, and so both plurals appear in boldface at sense 1. At *delicatessen* the situation is different: the entry as a whole is labeled a plural noun, but sense 2 is used as a singular. In this sense *delicatessen* can take the plural ending *-s* when needed, a fact that is indicated by the appearance of the plural in boldface at the sense. At *fixing* the italic abbreviation simply means that when used in this sense the word is always written in its plural form, *fixings*. At the second homograph *die* the actual distribution of the variant plurals can be given sense by sense in italic type because both variants are shown in boldface earlier in the entry. At the first homograph *folk* a singular noun is

shown with variant plurals of nearly equal frequency, when all senses are taken into account. The fifth sense, however, is unique in being always plural in form and construction. The form of the plural for this sense is *folks,* as shown, and the placement of the form before the label instead of after it (as at the senses of *die*) means that this sense is always plural.

When an italicized label or guide phrase follows a boldface numeral, the label or phrase applies only to that specific numbered sense and its subsenses. It does not apply to any other boldface numbered senses:

¹**boot** . . . *n* . . . 1 *archaic* . . . 2 *chiefly dial* . . . 3 *obs*

¹**fa·vor** . . . *n* . . . 2 *archaic* **a** . . . **b** (1) . . . (2) . . . 3

At *boot* the *archaic* label applies only to sense 1, the *chiefly dial* label only to sense 2, and the *obs* label only to sense 3. At *favor* the *archaic* label applies to all the subsenses of sense 2 but not to sense 3.

When an italicized label or guide phrase follows a boldface letter, the label or phrase applies only to that specific lettered sense and its subsenses. It does not apply to any other boldface lettered senses:

²**stour** *n* . . . 1 **a** *archaic* . . . **b** *dial Brit*

The *archaic* label applies to sense 1a but not to sense 1b. The *dial Brit* label applies to sense 1b but not to sense 1a.

When an italicized label or guide phrase follows a parenthesized numeral, the label or phrase applies only to that specific numbered sense:

in·car·na·tion . . . *n* . . . 1 **a** (1) . . . (2) *cap*

The *cap* label applies to sense 1a(2) and to no other subsenses of the word.

EXPANSIONS OF ABBREVIATIONS

Entries for abbreviations lack definitions. Instead such an entry is given an expansion, which is simply the full word or phrase from which the abbreviation was originally created. Because an expansion is not a definition, it is not introduced by a boldface colon. When more than one expansion is given for an abbreviation, the expansions are listed in alphabetical order and are separated by boldface numerals, except that closely related expansions are grouped together:

cir *abbr* **1** circle; circular **2** circuit **3** circumference

For an abbreviation that originated in another language, the foreign expansion is given in an etymology, followed by an idiomatic English equivalent. When such an expansion is listed along with other expansions in a single entry, alphabetical order within the entry is based on the foreign expansion rather than its English equivalent.

pp *abbr* **1** pages **2** per person **3** [L *per procurationem*] by proxy **4** pianissimo

Names of Plants, Animals & Microorganisms

The most familiar names of living and formerly living things are the common, or vernacular, names determined by popular usage, in which one organism may have several names (as *mountain lion, cougar,* and *painter*), different organisms may have the same name (as *dolphin*), and there may be variation in meaning or overlapping of the categories denoted by the names (as *whale, dolphin,* and *porpoise*).

In contrast, the scientific names of biological classification are governed by four highly prescriptive, internationally recognized codes of nomenclature for botany, zoology, bacteriology, and virology. The vocabularies of these nomenclatures have been developed and used by scientists for the purpose of identifying and indicating the relationships of plants, animals, and microorganisms. These systems of names classify each kind of organism into a hierarchy of groups—taxa—with each kind of organism having one—and only one—correct name and belonging to one—and only one—taxon at each level of classification in the hierarchy.

The taxonomic names of biological classification are used in this dictionary at entries that define common names of plants, animals, and microorganisms, as well as diseases of or products relating to plants, animals, or microorganisms that do not themselves have common names that qualify for entry here. Names from several different codes of nomenclature may appear in the same definition. Each is enclosed in parentheses, usually following an orienting noun:

Rocky Mountain spotted fever *n* . . . : an acute disease . . . that is caused by a rickettsia (*Rickettsia rickettsii*) usu. transmitted by an ixodid tick and esp. either the American dog tick or a wood tick (*Dermacentor andersoni*)

sand·fly fever . . . *n* . . . : a disease . . . caused by any of several single-stranded RNA viruses (genus *Phlebovirus* of the family *Bunyaviridae*) transmitted by the bite of a sand fly (esp. *Phlebotomus papatasii*) . . .

Within the parentheses the prescriptive principles of the relevant nomenclature hold, but as soon as the reader steps outside the parentheses the rules of general usage hold. For example, the genus name *Apatosaurus* for a group of large herbivorous dinosaurs is now the valid name in biological classification for the formerly accepted *Brontosaurus*. While *apatosaurus* is available as a common name, it has been slow in displacing *brontosaurus* in popular usage. So the main definition of the dinosaur is placed at the vocabulary entry for *brontosaurus*, while only a cross-reference in small capitals appears at *apatosaurus*. However, within the parenthetical identification, the genus name *Apatosaurus* appears first, with *Brontosaurus* listed second as a synonym:

apato·sau·rus . . . *n* . . . : BRONTOSAURUS

bron·to·sau·rus . . . *also* **bron·to·saur** . . . *n* . . . : any of a genus (*Apatosaurus* syn. *Brontosaurus*) of large sauropod dinosaurs of the Jurassic — called also *apatosaurus*

Taxonomic names are used in definitions in this dictionary to provide precise identifications through which defined terms may be pursued in technical writings. Because of their specialized nature, taxonomic names as such are not included as dictionary entries. However, many common names entered in this dictionary have been derived directly from genus names and other taxonomic names, often with little or no modification. In written text it is particularly important to distinguish between a common name and the taxonomic name from which it is derived. In contrast to the styling rules for taxonomic names (discussed below), common names (as "clostridium," "drosophila," and "enterovirus") are not usually capitalized or italicized, and common names derived from genus names can have a plural form even though genus names themselves are never pluralized.

The entries defining plants, animals, and microorganisms are usually oriented to higher taxa by common, vernacular terms within the definitions (as "alga" at *seaweed*, "thrush" at *robin*, and "picornaviruses" at *enterovirus*) or by technical adjectives (as "composite" at *daisy* and "oscine" at *warbler*.)

When the vernacular name of a plant or animal is used to identify the vernacular name of the taxonomic family to which the plant or animal belongs, that information will be given in parentheses in the definition of the plant or animal, and definitions for other organisms within that family will refer to the vernacular family name:

²rose . . . *n* . . . 1 a : any of a genus (*Rosa* of the family Rosaceae, the rose family) of usu. prickly shrubs . . .

ap·ple . . . *n, often attrib* . . . 1 : the fleshy usu. rounded red, yellow, or green edible pome of a usu. cultivated tree (genus *Malus*) of the rose family; *also* : an apple tree

¹squir·rel . . . *n* . . . 1 : any of various small or medium-sized rodents (family Sciuridae, the squirrel family): as . . .

chip·munk . . . *n* . . . : any of a genus (*Tamias*) of small striped No. American and Asian rodents of the squirrel family

LINNAEAN NOMENCLATURE OF PLANTS, ANIMALS & BACTERIA

The nomenclatural codes for botany, zoology, and bacteriology follow the binomial nomenclature of Carolus Linnaeus, who employed a New Latin vocabulary for the names of organisms and the names of ranks in the hierarchy of classification.

The fundamental taxon is the genus. It includes a group of closely related kinds of plants (as *Prunus,* which includes the wild and cultivated cherries, apricots, peaches, and almonds), a group of closely related kinds of animals (as *Canis,* which includes domestic dogs, coyotes, jackals, and wolves), or a group of closely related kinds of bacteria (as *Streptococcus,* which includes numerous pathogens of humans and domestic animals). The genus name is an italicized and capitalized singular noun.

The unique name of each kind of organism or species in the Linnaean systems is the binomial or species name, which consists of two parts: a genus name and an italicized lowercase word—the specific epithet—denoting the species. A trinomial is used to name a variety or a subspecies and consists of a binomial plus an italicized lowercase word denoting the variety or subspecies. For example, the cultivated cabbage (*Brassica oleracea capita*), the cauliflower (*Brassica oleracea botrytis*), and brussels sprouts (*Brassica oleracea gemmifera*) belong to the same species (*Brassica oleracea*) of cole.

The genus name in a binomial or trinomial may be abbreviated to its initial letter if it has previously been spelled out in full within the same text. In this dictionary, a genus name is abbreviated only when it is used more than once in senses not separated by a boldface sense number.

nas·tur·tium . . . *n* . . . : any of a genus (*Tropaeolum* of the family Tropaeolaceae, the nasturtium family) . . . ; *esp* : either of two widely cultivated ornamentals (*T. majus* and *T. minus*)

Names of taxa higher than the genus (as family, order, and class) are capitalized plural nouns that are often used with singular verbs and that are not abbreviated in normal use. They are not italicized.

¹bee·tle . . . *n* . . . 1 : any of an order (Coleoptera) of insects . . .

A genus name in good standing cannot be the name of two different groups of animals, groups of plants, or groups of bacteria. At least one of the applications must be invalid. However, since the nomenclatural codes are independent, an animal genus and a plant genus, for example, may validly receive the same name. Thus, a number of cabbage butterflies (as *Pieris rapae*) are placed in a genus of animals that has the same name as the plant genus to which the Japanese andromeda (*Pieris japonica*) belongs. Although no two higher taxa of plants or of bacteria are permitted to have the same name, the rules of zoological nomenclature do not apply to taxa above the family, and so, for example, it is possible for widely separated groups of animals to be placed in families or orders with identical taxonomic names.

Sometimes two or more different New Latin names can be found used in current literature for the same organism or group. This happens when old monographs and field guides are kept in print after name changes occur, when there are legitimate differences of opinion about the validity of the names, and when the rules of priority are not applied. To help the reader in recognizing an organism or group, some entries in this dictionary give two taxonomic names connected by "syn." (for "synonym"):

wa·ter·mel·on . . . *n* . . . **1 :** a large oblong or roundish fruit with a hard green or white rind . . . **2 :** a widely cultivated African vine (*Citrullus lunatus* syn. *C. vulgaris*) of the gourd family that bears watermelons

VIRUS NOMENCLATURE

The system of naming viruses evolved in a series of reports by the International Committee on Taxonomy of Viruses (ICTV) of the International Union of Microbiological Societies.

The report published in 2005 with the title *Virus Taxonomy: Eighth Report of the International Committee on Taxonomy of Viruses (8th Rept. of the ICTV)* is followed in this dictionary. In this landmark monograph, which contains the combined efforts of approximately 500 virus experts of the ICTV from around the world, the entire corpus of viruses is divided into 73 families, 298 genera, and about 1,950 species. The code of nomenclature presented there is independent of the three Linnaean systems governing the taxonomy of plants, animals, and bacteria and differs in the way names are constructed and written. However, the hierarchy of taxa, although presently incomplete, follows that of the Linnaean systems and includes the species, genus, subfamily, family, and order.

The higher taxa are based primarily on the characteristics of the nucleic acid of the included viruses. In this dictionary, when the common name for members of a family of viruses is defined, the definition will always mention whether the nucleic acid is DNA or RNA and whether it is single-stranded or double-stranded.

pox·vi·rus . . . *n* . . . **:** any of a family (*Poxviridae*) of brick-shaped or ovoid double-stranded DNA viruses that have . . .

ret·ro·vi·rus . . . *n* . . . **:** any of a family (*Retroviridae*) of single-stranded RNA viruses that produce reverse transcriptase . . .

Only the technical names for species, genera, and families of viruses are used in this dictionary and only those that are recognized or were formerly recognized as valid by the ICTV. In formal usage such names appear in italics and are preceded by the name of the taxon ("species," "genus," or "family") in roman before the italicized name.

As with the formal taxonomic names of Linnaean nomenclature, the formal names of virus taxonomy are used in definitions in this dictionary only in parentheses where the strict rules of the ICTV are applied rigorously.

The name of a species consists of an italicized phrase in which the first word is capitalized, other words are lowercase unless derived from a proper name (as in species *West Nile virus*, the causative agent of West Nile fever), and the last word is *virus* or *phage* or ends in *-virus*, sometimes followed by a number or letter or combination of both (as in species *Human immunodeficiency virus 1*, the most prevalent retrovirus causing AIDS).

The name of a genus is a single capitalized noun ending in *-virus*, sometimes followed by a capital letter (as in genus *Influenzavirus A*, which contains species *Influenza A virus*, the causative agent of the numerous forms of influenza collectively known as influenza A including the notorious variants of bird flu).

The name of a family is a single capitalized word ending in *-viridae* (as in family *Herpesviridae* or family *Poxviridae*).

In formal virus taxonomy, the valid technical name of every individual taxon is unique. In Linnaean taxonomy it is possible to have species in different genera or different families with the same name. A species of virus could be referenced without ambiguity by the species name alone provided the name itself is written in italics and preceded by the word "species" in roman. In this dictionary, definitions will contain some reference to both the genus and the family if the species has been classified to a genus and family, although it may be necessary to look up a common

name used in the definition in place of the technical genus or family name.

An added argument for making reference to the genus of the virus as well as the species is that in viral taxonomy a numbered series of species may be spread over several genera.

For example, in the herpesviruses (family *Herpesviridae*), the two forms of herpes simplex are caused by two viruses (species *Human herpesvirus 1* and species *Human herpesvirus 2*) assigned to the same genus (*Simplexvirus*) while the herpesvirus widely known as the Epstein-Barr virus (species *Human herpesvirus 4*) is placed in another genus (*Lymphocryptovirus*).

Just as with common names derived from the technical names of Linnaean taxonomy, widely used common names of diseases caused by viruses may imply that a virus of the wrong family causes the illness. Thus, chicken pox is not caused by a poxvirus, but by yet another herpesvirus (species *Human herpesvirus 3* of the genus *Varicellovirus*).

If there is no common name for the species, genus, or family to which a virus is assigned, the definition will characterize the nucleic acid of the virus and give the rest of the taxonomic information in parentheses:

hepatitis B *n* . . . **:** a sometimes fatal hepatitis caused by a double-stranded DNA virus (species *Hepatitis B virus* of the genus *Orthohepadnavirus*, family *Hepadnaviridae*) . . .

If there is a common name for members of a family (as picornavirus for the family *Picornaviridae*) entered and defined in this dictionary, it is available for use in defining:

hepatitis A *n* . . . **:** an acute usu. benign hepatitis caused by a picornavirus (species *Hepatitis A virus* of the genus *Hepatovirus*) . . .

Similarly, if a common name (as morbillivirus) is available for members of a genus, it is used in defining unless the name (as flavivirus) is used generally for members of the family, in which case to avoid ambiguity the technical genus name is given in parentheses along with the species name:

mea·sles . . . *n pl but sing or pl in constr* . . . **1 a :** an acute contagious disease that is caused by a morbillivirus (species *Measles virus*) and is marked . . .

West Nile virus *n* . . . **:** a flavivirus (species *West Nile virus* of the genus *Flavivirus*) that causes . . .

The *8th Rept. of the ICTV* adopts the convention of using roman type in writing subspecific taxa (as strains, subtypes, serotypes, and genotypes) and technical synonyms. This convention has been followed in this dictionary in those few cases where a subspecific taxon (as subtype H5N1) needed to be mentioned in a definition or a former but now invalid technical name (as Papovaviridae) was used in the definition of a common name for members of the defunct taxon.

bird flu *n* . . . **:** AVIAN INFLUENZA; *specif* **:** severe often fatal influenza A caused by strains of a subtype (H5N1) of the causative orthomyxovirus . . .

pa·po·va·vi·rus . . . *n* . . . **:** any of a former family (Papovaviridae) of double-stranded DNA viruses that included the papillomaviruses and polyomaviruses

The technical names of the two families to which the papovaviruses are now assigned can be found at the definitions of *papillomavirus* and *polyomavirus*.

Cross-Reference

Four different kinds of cross-references are used in this dictionary: directional, synonymous, cognate, and inflectional. In each instance the cross-reference is readily recognized by the lightface small capitals in which it is printed.

A cross-reference following a lightface dash and beginning with *see* or *compare* is a directional cross-reference. It directs the dictionary user to look elsewhere for further information. A *compare* cross-reference is regularly appended to a definition; a *see* cross-reference may stand alone:

wel·ter·weight . . . *n* . . . — compare LIGHTWEIGHT, MIDDLEWEIGHT

¹ri·al . . . *n* . . . — see MONEY table

A cross-reference immediately following a boldface colon is a synonymous cross-reference. It may stand alone as the only definitional matter for an entry or for a sense or subsense of an entry; it may follow an analytical definition; it may be one of two synonymous cross-references separated by a comma:

gar·ban·zo . . . *n* . . . : CHICKPEA

¹ne·glect . . . *vt* . . . **1** : to give little attention or respect to : DISREGARD

²main *adj* . . . **1** : CHIEF, PRINCIPAL

A synonymous cross-reference indicates that a definition at the entry cross-referred to can be substituted as a definition for the entry or the sense or subsense in which the cross-reference appears.

A cross-reference following an italic *var of* is a cognate cross-reference:

kaftan *var of* CAFTAN

Sometimes a cognate cross-reference has a limiting label preceding *var of* as a specific indication that the variant is not standard English:

haul·ier . . . *Brit var of* HAULER

²hist . . . *dial var of* HOIST

sher·ris . . . *archaic var of* SHERRY

A cross-reference following an italic label that identifies an entry as an inflected form of a noun, of an adjective or adverb, or of a verb is an inflectional cross-reference. Inflectional cross-references appear only when the inflected form falls at least a column away from the entry cross-referred to:

calves *pl of* CALF

³wound . . . *past and past part of* WIND

When guidance seems needed as to which one of several homographs or which sense of a multisense word is being referred to, a superscript numeral may precede the cross-reference or a sense number may follow it or both:

¹toss . . . *vt* . . . **3** . . . **c** : MATCH 5a

Synonyms

Brief paragraphs discriminating words of closely associated meaning from one another have been placed at a number of entries. They are signaled by an indented boldface italic *syn*. Each paragraph begins with a list of the words to be discussed in it, followed by a concise statement of the element of meaning that the words have in common. The discriminations themselves are amplified with verbal illustrations:

cautious . . . *adj* . . .
syn CAUTIOUS, CIRCUMSPECT, WARY, CHARY mean prudently watchful and discreet in the face of danger or risk. CAUTIOUS implies the exercise of forethought usu. prompted by fear of danger ⟨a *cautious* driver⟩. CIRCUMSPECT suggests less fear and stresses the surveying of all possible consequences before acting or deciding ⟨*circumspect* in his business dealings⟩. WARY emphasizes suspiciousness and alertness in watching for danger and cunning in escaping it ⟨keeps a *wary* eye on the competition⟩. CHARY implies a cautious reluctance to give, act, or speak freely ⟨*chary* of signing papers without having read them first⟩.

When a word is included in a synonym paragraph, the main entry for that word is followed by a run-on *syn* see . . . , which refers to the entry where the synonym paragraph appears:

cir·cum·spect . . . *adj* . . . *syn* see CAUTIOUS

When a word is a main entry at which there is a synonym paragraph and is also included in another paragraph elsewhere, the paragraph at the main entry is followed by a run-on *syn* see in addition . . . , which refers to the entry where the other paragraph may be found:

¹nat·u·ral . . . *adj* . . .
syn NATURAL, INGENUOUS, NAIVE, UNSOPHISTICATED, ARTLESS mean free from pretension or calculation . . . *syn* see in addition REGULAR

¹reg·u·lar . . . *adj* . . .
syn REGULAR, NORMAL, TYPICAL, NATURAL mean being of the sort or kind that is expected as usual, ordinary, or average . . .

Combining Forms, Prefixes & Suffixes

An entry that begins or ends with a hyphen is a word element that forms part of an English compound:

mega- *or* **meg-** *comb form* . . . **1** . . . **b** . . . ⟨*mega*hit⟩

-logy *n comb form* . . . **1** . . . ⟨phrase*ology*⟩

-lyze *vb comb form* . . . ⟨electro*lyze*⟩

-like *adj comb form* . . . ⟨bell-*like*⟩ ⟨lady*like*⟩

pre- *prefix* . . . **1 a** (1) . . . ⟨*pre*historic⟩

¹-ory *n suffix* . . . **1** . . . ⟨observat*ory*⟩

¹-ic *adj suffix* . . . **2 a** . . . ⟨alderman*ic*⟩

²-ly *adv suffix* . . . **1 a** . . . ⟨slow*ly*⟩

-ize *vb suffix* . . . **2 a** . . . ⟨crystall*ize*⟩

Combining forms, prefixes, and suffixes are entered in this dictionary for three reasons: to make easier the writing of etymologies of words in which these word elements occur over and over again; to make understandable the meaning of many undefined run-ons which for reasons of space would be omitted if they had to be given etymologies and definitions; and to make recognizable the meaningful elements of new words that are not well enough established in the language to warrant dictionary entry.

Lists of Undefined Words

Lists of undefined words occur after the entries of these prefixes and combining forms:

anti-	multi-	re-
co-	non-	self-
counter-	out-	sub-
hyper-	over-	super-
inter-	post-	ultra-
mis-	pre-	un-

These words are not defined because they are self-explanatory; their meanings are simply the sum of a meaning of the prefix or combining form and a meaning of the root word. Centered dots are shown to save the dictionary user the trouble of consulting another entry. The lists are not exhaustive of all the words that might be, or actually have been, formed with these prefixes and combining forms. The dictionary has room for only the most common or important examples.

The English Language in the Dictionary

In the offices where Merriam-Webster's Collegiate Dictionary, Eleventh Edition, was edited, several thousand letters and e-mails are received each year. The topics they articulate are enormously varied. Some merely ask for a particular bit of information about the English language that has been sought but not found in the dictionary. A few others are in hot pursuit of a special interest. Still others, their writers having come to think of the dictionary as an all-purpose reference book, ask questions about many other subjects besides words. A surprising number of correspondents, however, express considerable curiosity about how their dictionary—that formidably long and closely printed work with its many special abbreviations, symbols, and devices and its multitude of uses—came to be just the book it is.

They may ask quite directly such questions as how words make it into the dictionary or what it is that lexicographers do when they are editing or reediting a dictionary. But even questions of a very different sort on the surface may unwittingly reveal much the same interest. "Why did you fail to include word *x* in your book?" and "Why don't you still use the system of transcribing pronunciations with which I grew up instead of the present one with its 'upside-down *e*'?" may be in part expressions of annoyance at what is seen (not always accurately) as the dictionary's failure to do its job, but they are just as truly demands to know how dictionary editors make the decision to exclude some words from a given dictionary or to revise a long-standing feature of earlier editions. What follows is an effort to present a brief overview of the English language and its history and to provide brief and necessarily somewhat general answers to a few of the questions that users of this dictionary probably have about it, the processes that went into its making, and its relation to that fascinating and sometimes maddening marvel which we call the English language.

Language is the object of study of the academic discipline known as linguistics. Although the roots of linguistic science are found in earlier centuries, it is in most respects a modern creation, and the understanding of language that it offers us differs in a number of fundamental ways from the conceptions of language held by thinkers of the ancient and medieval worlds, the Renaissance, or the Enlightenment. This understanding does not differ, however, in every way. The use of language is still seen by linguists as a peculiarly human activity. We often use the word *language* to refer to the limited stock of movements or utterances by which some animals communicate a limited number of messages, but in doing so we recognize that we are speaking of something different in kind from our own language. Moreover, modern definitions of language are just as likely as earlier definitions to emphasize its functional aspect: language enables human beings, at least those who share a particular language, to communicate with each other by stating ideas, expressing feelings, and exchanging information.

Modern definitions of language, though, are more likely than older ones to stress some other aspects. One is the arbitrary nature of the relationship between the conventional sounds or other signs which serve as the vehicle of language and the meaning being conveyed by them. A few naive souls may believe that domestic swine are called pigs because their habits are so dirty, but it is clear to most that no inherent or necessary connection exists between the sequence of sounds \p\ plus \i\ plus \g\ and "any of various stout-bodied short-legged omnivorous artiodactyl mammals (family Suidae) with a thick bristly skin and a long mobile snout." A similarly naive Frenchman or German could insist with neither more nor less reason that *cochon* or *Schwein* is the word that naturally expresses the essential piggishness of the animal.

A linguistically oriented definition would also be likely to emphasize the systematic nature of language. Were it not for highly organized systems operating within any natural language, it could hardly be the subtle and effective tool of communication that it is. These systems are enormously complex both in themselves and in their mutual interaction, so complex indeed that no language has yet had its workings fully described; yet, paradoxically, and fortunately for the human race, any child with a normal ability to learn can, within a very few years, master at least the essentials of these systems for any one language with which it is in daily contact (or even two languages if the child's environment is bilingual). It is uncertain whether this is so because, as some linguists believe, at a profound level of structure the details that make English so different from other languages are unimportant and the systems of all languages are largely the same, but the fact that we learn our native language almost effortlessly up to a certain basic level of control is hardly to be denied.

The Systems of Language

The major systems that make up the broad comprehensive system of language itself are four in number: lexicon, grammar, semantics, and phonology. The one that dictionary editors and dictionary users are most directly concerned with is the vocabulary or *lexicon*, the collection of words and word elements which we put together in various ways to form larger units of discourse: phrases, clauses, sentences, paragraphs, and so forth. All languages have a lexicon, and all lexicons are governed by rules that permit some kinds of word formation, make others dubious, and render still others clearly impossible. In English we might say *versatileness* without hesitation if we needed such a word and could not for the moment think of *versatility*, even though the former is not normally part of our everyday working vocabulary; but *versatilize* might give us pause, and *nessversatile* we would simply never utter. The size of the lexicon varies considerably from language to language. The language of an isolated people, for example, may be perfectly adequate with a relatively small and fixed vocabulary, since it has no need of the coinages attendant upon modern technology, while English and other major languages have enormous stocks of words, to which they add year by year at a great rate. Since the dictionary is concentrated upon the lexicon, our discussion of the other systems of language, as it proceeds, will be largely concerned with how they are related to the lexicon and thus are important within the dictionary.

The grammatical system of language governs the way in which words are put together to form the larger units of discourse mentioned earlier. Grammar, of course, varies a great deal from language to language just as the lexicon does: in English, word order is a dominant factor in determining meaning, while the use of inflectional endings to mark the grammatical function of individual words within a sentence plays a clearly subordinate role, though important in some ways (as in indicating the number of a noun, the case of a personal pronoun, or the tense of a verb). Other languages show markedly different patterns, such as Latin with its elaborate set of paradigms for nouns, verbs, adjectives, and pronouns and its highly flexible word order. The semantic system of a language has to do with meanings and thus with the relation between the conventionalized symbols that constitute language and the external reality about which we need to communicate through language. The phonological system of a language is what allows a speaker of that language to transform a grammatical unit embodying a meaning into a flow of uttered sounds that can be heard and interpreted (accurately, if all goes well) by another speaker of the language. This system is always very tightly organized. The inventory of basic meaningful units of sound within a language (called *phonemes* by linguists) is never very large compared with the number of words and word elements in the lexicon; most speakers of English get by with about 40. Phonemes are identified by the fact that in some pairs of words they create a contrast that signals a difference in meaning: we consider the vowel sounds of *trip* and *trap* to be different phonemes because the difference in vowel sounds is the sole determinant of their being distinct words. Their consonant sounds are identical. Similarly, the initial consonant sounds of *pull* and *bull, tie* and *die,* and *come* and *gum* are contrasting phonemes. On the other hand, the sound at the beginning of *pit* and at the end of *tip* are phonetically quite different, but as they do not contrast meaningfully we do not perceive them as distinct phonemes. The combinations of these phonemes permitted in a given language are severely restricted, as are the ways in which speech sounds occur in conjunction with other significant elements of the phonological system such as stress (force or intensity) and intonation (the rise and fall in pitch of the voice as it moves through an utterance). In English, for example, it is possible for the consonants \str\ to occur in succession, but only at the beginning of a word (as in *strict*) or in the middle (as in *monstrous*), not at the end, and the sequence \pgr\ cannot occur at either the beginning or the end of a word but may occur in the middle (as in *upgrade*).

Variation and Change in Language

All of the systems of language are constantly in operation, and in a given language at a given time they may seem almost to be monolithic or at least to have sufficient identity that it makes sense, for example, to talk of *the* grammar of English. And, indeed, how could it be otherwise? Language would be a far more imperfect tool of communication than it is if the speakers of a language were not functioning within a system sufficiently unified to permit almost constant mutual intelligibility. Yet the impression of unity which we receive when we take a broad descriptive look at a single language at a particular time (taking a *synchronic* point of view, as linguists say) is more than a little misleading because it has failed to take account of the enormous variation that exists within the language.

Each of us speaks a distinctive form of English that is not identical in every particular with the form spoken by anyone else; linguists call this individual variety of a language an *idiolect.* Those whose idiolects share certain features of vocabulary, grammar, and phonology that are distinctively different from corresponding features shared by others who live in a different geographical area or belong to a different social group or who differ in some other way that affects their language are said to speak a *dialect* of the language. Researchers have identified a number of different geographical dialect areas within the United States, rather clearly marked on the Eastern seaboard but progressively less well defined as one moves west; yet, the dialects of American English do not differ overall very greatly from one another; some dialects of Great Britain are more strikingly divergent in phonology, for example, than are any two dialects within this country, and some dialects of other languages approach the condition of mutual unintel-

ligibility that is often taken to divide separate dialects from separate languages.

Nor is variation in language by any means confined to matters of idiolect or dialect. Variation may also be related to the several functional varieties of a language that people take up and discard as their roles and relationships change from moment to moment throughout the day. Such variation can involve vocabulary, pronunciation, and even grammar. A worker who queries one colleague concerning the whereabouts of another with "Seen John?" from which both the auxiliary verb *have* and the subject *you* have been deleted may not put the question in the same casual way to a superior.

If variation is one of the most prominent aspects of language as one considers it today, the inescapable fact that emerges from considering language historically (taking a *diachronic* point of view, as linguists say) is change. No living language stands still, however much we might wish at times that it would. Change over the short run is most readily noticed in the lexicon, as a comparison of successive editions of any modern dictionary will show; in grammar and phonology the forces of change typically operate much more slowly. Still, the cumulative effect of changes that are imperceptible as they occur can be impressive when measured across the centuries. The English of one's great-great-grandfather might not sound so very different from one's own. Perhaps it might seem a bit stiff and formal, a bit old-fashioned in its vocabulary, but the differences would not be dramatic. If we could somehow listen to an English-speaker of King Alfred's time, however, we would hear what all but a few scholars of historical English would take to be a foreign tongue.

The History of English

The history of English is conventionally, if perhaps too neatly, divided into three periods usually called Old English (or Anglo-Saxon), Middle English, and Modern English. The earliest period begins with the migration of certain Germanic tribes from the Continent to Britain in the fifth century A.D., though no records of their language survive from before the seventh century, and it continues until the end of the eleventh century or a bit later. By that time Latin, Old Norse (the language of the Viking invaders), and especially the Anglo-French of the dominant class after the Norman Conquest in 1066 had begun to have a substantial impact on the lexicon, and the well-developed inflectional system that typifies the grammar of Old English had begun to break down. The following brief sample of Old English prose illustrates several of the significant ways in which change has so transformed English that we must look carefully to find points of resemblance between the language of the tenth century and our own. It is taken from Aelfric's "Homily on St. Gregory the Great" and concerns the famous story of how that pope came to send missionaries to convert the Anglo-Saxons to Christianity after seeing Anglo-Saxon boys for sale as slaves in Rome:

> Eft he axode, hu ðære ðeode nama wære þe hi of comon. Him wæs geandwyrd, þæt hi Angle genemnode wæron. þa cwæð he, "Rihtlice hi sind Angle gehatene, for ðan ðe hi engla wlite habbað, and swilcum gedafenað þæt hi on heofonum engla geferan beon."

A few of these words will be recognized as identical in spelling with their modern equivalents—*he, of, him, for, and, on*—and the resemblance of a few others to familiar words may be guessed—*nama* to *name, comon* to *come, wære* to *were, wæs* to *was*—but only those who have made a special study of Old English will be able to read the passage with understanding. The sense of it is as follows: "Again he [St. Gregory] asked what might be the name of the people from which they came. It was answered to him that they were named Angles. Then he said, 'Rightly are they called Angles because they have the beauty of angels, and it is fitting that such as they should be angels' companions in heaven.' " Some of the words in the original have survived in altered form, including *axode (asked), hu (how), rihtlice (rightly), engla (angels), habbað (have), swilcum (such), heofonum (heaven)*, and *beon (be)*. Others, however, have vanished from our lexicon, mostly without leaving a trace, including several that were quite common words in Old English: *eft* "again," *ðeode* "people, nation," *cwæð* "said, spoke," *gehatene* "called, named," *wlite* "appearance, beauty," and *geferan* "companions." Recognition of some words is naturally hindered by the presence of two special characters, þ, called "thorn," and ð, called "edh," which served in Old English to represent the sounds now spelled with *th*.

Other points worth noting include the fact that the pronoun system did not yet, in the late tenth century, include the third person plural forms beginning with *th-*: *hi* appears where we would use *they*. Several aspects of word order will also strike the reader as oddly unlike ours. Subject and verb are inverted after an adverb—*þa cwæð he* "Then said he"—a phenomenon not unknown in Modern English but now restricted to a few adverbs such as *never* and requiring the presence of an auxiliary verb like *do* or *have*. In subordinate clauses the main verb must be last, and so an object or a preposition may precede it in a way no longer natural: *þe hi of comon* "which they from came," *for ðan ðe hi engla wlite habbað* "because they angels' beauty have."

Perhaps the most distinctive difference between Old and Modern English reflected in Aelfric's sentences is the elaborate system of inflections, of which we now have only remnants. Nouns, adjectives, and even the definite article are inflected for gender, case, and number: *ðære ðeode* "(of) the people" is feminine, genitive, and singular, *Angle* "Angles" is masculine, accusative, and plural, and *swilcum* "such" is masculine, dative, and plural. The system of inflections for verbs was also more elaborate than ours; for example, *habbað* "have" ends with the *-að* suffix characteristic of plural present indicative verbs. In addition, there were two imperative forms, four subjunctive forms (two for the present tense and two for the preterit, or past, tense), and several others which we no longer have. Even where Modern English retains a particular category of inflection, the form has often changed. Old English present participles ended in *-ende* not *-ing*, and past participles bore a prefix *ge-* (as *geandwyrd* "answered" above).

The period of Middle English extends roughly from the twelfth century through the fifteenth. The influence of French (and Latin, often by way of French) upon the lexicon continued throughout this period, the loss of some inflections and the reduction of others (often to a final unstressed vowel spelled *-e*) accelerated, and many changes took place within the phonological and grammatical systems of the language. A typical prose passage, especially one from the later part of the period, will not have such a foreign look to us as Aelfric's prose has; but it will not be mistaken for contemporary writing either. The following brief passage is drawn from a work of the late fourteenth century called *Mandeville's Travels*. It is fiction in the guise of travel literature, and, though it purports to be from the pen of an English knight, it was originally written in French and later translated into Latin and English. In this extract Mandeville describes the land of Bactria, apparently not an altogether inviting place, as it is inhabited by "full yuele [evil] folk and full cruell."

In þat lond ben trees þat beren wolle, as þogh it were of scheep; whereof men maken clothes, and all þing þat may ben made of wolle. In þat contree ben many ipotaynes, þat dwellen som tyme in the water, and somtyme on the lond: and þei ben half man and half hors, as I haue seyd before; and þei eten men, whan þei may take hem. And þere ben ryueres and watres þat ben fulle byttere, þree sithes more þan is the water of the see. In þat contré ben many griffounes, more plentee þan in ony other contree. Sum men seyn þat þei han the body vpward as an egle, and benethe as a lyoun: and treuly þei seyn soth þat þei ben of þat schappe. But o griffoun hath the body more gret, and is more strong, þanne eight lyouns, of suche lyouns as ben o this half; and more gret and strongere þan an hundred egles, suche as we han amonges vs. For o griffoun þere wil bere fleynge to his nest a gret hors, ʒif he may fynde him at the poynt, or two oxen ʒoked togidere, as þei gon at the plowgh.

The spelling is often peculiar by modern standards and even inconsistent within these few sentences (*contré* and *contree, o [griffoun]* and *a [gret hors], þanne* and þan, for example). Moreover, there is in addition to thorn another old character ʒ, "yogh," to make difficulty. It can represent several sounds but here may be thought of as equivalent to *y*. Even the older spellings (including those where *u* stands for *v* or vice versa) are recognizable, however, and there are only a few words like *ipotaynes* "hippopotamuses" and *sithes* "times" that have dropped out of the language altogether. We may notice a few words and phrases that have meanings no longer common such as *byttere* "salty," *o this half* "on this side of the world," and *at the poynt* "to hand," and the effect of the centuries-long dominance of French on the vocabulary is evident in many familiar words which could not have occurred in Aelfric's writing even if his subject had allowed them, words like *contree, ryueres, plentee, egle,* and *lyoun*.

In general word order is now very close to that of our time, though we notice constructions like *hath the body more gret* and *three sithes more þan is the water of the see*. We also notice that present tense verbs still receive a plural inflection as in *beren, dwellen, han,* and *ben* and that while nominative *þei* has replaced Aelfric's *hi* in the third person plural, the form for objects is still *hem*. All the same, the number of inflections for nouns, adjectives, and verbs has been greatly reduced, and in most respects Mandeville is closer to Modern than to Old English.

The period of Modern English extends from the sixteenth century to our own day. The early part of this period saw the completion of a revolution in the phonology of English that had begun in late Middle English and that effectively redistributed the occurrence of the vowel phonemes to something approximating their present pattern. (Mandeville's English would have sounded even less familiar to us than it looks.) Other important early developments include the stabilizing effect on spelling of the printing press and the beginning of the direct influence of Latin and, to a lesser extent, Greek on the lexicon. Later, as English came into contact with other cultures around the world and distinctive dialects of English developed in the many areas which Britain had colonized, numerous other languages made small but interesting contributions to our word-stock.

The historical aspect of English really encompasses more than the three stages of development just under consideration. English has what might be called a prehistory as well. As we have seen, our language did not simply spring into existence; it was brought from the Continent by Germanic tribes who had no form of writing and hence left no records. Philologists know that they must have spoken a dialect of a language that can be called West Germanic and that other dialects of this unknown language must have included the ancestors of such languages as German, Dutch, Low German, and Frisian. They know this because of certain systematic similarities which these languages share with each other but do not share with, say, Danish. However, they have had somehow to reconstruct what that language was like in its lexicon, phonology, grammar, and semantics as best they can through sophisticated techniques of comparison developed chiefly during the nineteenth century. Similarly, because ancient and modern languages like Old Norse and Gothic or Icelandic and Norwegian have points in common with Old English and Old High German or Dutch and English that they do not share with French or Russian, it is clear that there was an earlier unrecorded language that can be called simply Germanic and that must be reconstructed in the same way. Still earlier, Germanic was just a dialect (the ancestors of Greek, Latin, and Sanskrit were three other such dialects) of a language conventionally designated Indo-European, and thus English is just one relatively young member of an ancient family of languages whose descendants cover a fair portion of the globe. (For more detail on the Indo-European languages and their relationships, see the table having that title in the dictionary.)

The Dictionary and the Systems of English

By far the largest part of this volume is called "A Dictionary of the English Language" and so is naturally concerned with the systems of English that we have cursorily surveyed in their synchronic and diachronic aspects. In fact, information related to all four systems is given at most entries in the dictionary, as well as information related to what could reasonably be considered a fifth system of English and many other (though not all) languages —writing. The writing system provides an alternative to speech that permits long-distance transmission and visual reception of a communication and also enables a record to be kept for much longer than human memory can keep it. The writing system of Modern English allows for considerable variation, as is shown by the persistence of variant spellings like *veranda* and *verandah* or *judgment* and *judgement* and by the fact that many compound words have open, hyphenated, and solid stylings all in common use concurrently (as *decision maker, decision-maker,* and *decisionmaker*). At the same time, however, it tends to be a force for standardization and unification because recorded language creates a precedent for future language use and provides a basis on which language use can be taught to the younger members of a community. This conservative effect is one reason why spelling reformers have so far met with only modest success in their efforts.

We may now begin to look at the ways in which the specific systems of our language are treated in the dictionary and at the processes of lexicography which produce the information about these systems that the dictionary user encounters. A dictionary is necessarily and obviously concerned with the lexicon above all, and the information it can convey about the language systems is confined to the level of the word or short phrase. The result is that no dictionary of English, however good it may be, can provide all of the information about the English language that one might wish to have at one time or another. Thus, for example, details about such important aspects of phonology as the patterns of sentence stress and sentence intonation cannot be accommodated in a work of reference organized in terms of words, nor can grammatical topics such as word order in subordinate clauses or the structural relation of interrogative to declarative sentences.

The History of English in the Dictionary

A similar limitation applies to the treatment of the historical aspect of English; yet, Merriam-Webster's Collegiate Dictionary, Eleventh Edition, is able to offer a good deal of historical information about words. What we earlier called the prehistory of English is encountered in the etymologies that appear in square brackets ahead of the definitional material at many entries. An etymology tells us what is known of an English word before it became the word we enter in the dictionary; that is, if the word was created in English the etymology shows, to whatever extent is not already obvious from the shape of the word, what materials were used to form it, and if the word was borrowed into English the etymology traces the steps of the borrowing process backward from the point at which the word entered English to the earliest recorded ancestral language. Where it is most relevant, note is made of one or several words from other languages that are related ("akin") to the entry word but are not in the direct line of borrowing. Thus, a word like Aelfric's *heofon* (ignoring for the moment the dative plural inflection *-um* that it bears in the passage we looked at earlier) appears as part of this dictionary's etymology for the modern word *heaven:* [ME *heven,* fr. OE *heofon;* akin to OHG *himil* heaven]. Since *heaven* is a native English word, it has only two recorded

ancestors, Middle English *heven* and Old English *heofon.* Beyond those forms lie only the hypothetical, reconstructed forms of West Germanic, Germanic, and Indo-European. In this case one related West Germanic word is shown, Old High German *himil,* which is the parent of Modern German *Himmel* but only a second cousin of our English word. Similarly Mandeville's *contree* appears as the first element in the etymology of its modern descendant *country:* [ME *contree,* fr. AF *cuntree, contré,* fr. ML *contrata,* fr. L *contra* against, on the opposite side]. Here we see that our word can be traced back through three nouns of Middle English, Anglo-French, and Medieval Latin (all of which had the same basic meaning as the Modern English noun and so are not glossed) to a Latin preposition (which has a different meaning and so is glossed). The two etymological patterns are, as we would expect from what we know of the history of the English vocabulary, among the most common and are repeated with differing details at entry after entry throughout the book. Of course, borrowings that have occurred within the Modern English period are more various, and we find such exotic language names as Nahuatl (at *chocolate*), Taino (at ²*barbecue*), Tagalog (at *boondocks*), Malay (at ¹*amok*), and Kimbundu (at *banjo*) as well as the more familiar Russian (at *troika*), Italian (at ¹*ballot*), Arabic (at *mullah*), Spanish (at ¹*macho*), and Japanese (at *tycoon*).

An etymologist must know a good deal about the history of English and also about the relationships of sound and meaning and their changes over time that underlie the reconstruction of the Indo-European family, but even that considerable learning is not enough to do all that must be done to provide etymologies of English words in a dictionary such as this. A knowledge is also needed of the various processes by which words are created within Modern English: among the most important processes are shortening, or clipping (see ¹*prom*), functional shift (as the noun *commute* from the verb *commute*), back-formation (see *grid*), combination of initial letters (see *radar*), transfer of personal or place names (see *silhouette* and *denim*), imitation of sounds (see ¹*whiz*), folk etymology (see *Jerusalem artichoke*), and blending of two words (see *motel*). Also available to one who feels the need for a new word to name a new thing or express a new idea is the very considerable store of prefixes, suffixes, and combining forms that already exist in English. Some of these are native and others are borrowed from French, but the largest number have been taken directly from Latin or Greek, and they have been combined in many different ways often without any special regard for matching two elements from the same original language. The combination of these word elements has produced many scientific and technical terms of Modern English. Once in a while a word is created spontaneously out of the creative play of sheer imagination. (For examples of the latter sort of creation see the etymologies of *boondoggle* and *googol* in the dictionary. Such invention is common, as Merriam-Webster editors know from their mail, which frequently includes requests from coiners that their brand-new words be entered in the dictionary. Very few coinages of this kind ever come into common enough use to justify dictionary entry, however.)

An etymologist working on a new edition of the Collegiate Dictionary must review the etymologies at existing main entries and prepare such etymologies as are required for the main entries being added to the new edition. In the course of the former activity adjustments must sometimes be made either to incorporate a useful piece of information that has previously been overlooked or to revise the account of the word's origin in the light of new evidence. Such evidence may be unearthed by the etymologist or may be the product of published research by scholars of historical linguistics and others. In writing new etymologies this editor must, of course, be alive to the possible languages from which a new term may have been borrowed and to the possible ways in which one may have been created. New scientific and technical terms sometimes pose special difficulties. While they are most often formed from familiar word elements, occasionally a case like *methotrex-*

ate presents itself in which one part (here *-trexate*) resists identification.

When all attempts to provide a satisfactory etymology have failed, the editor has recourse to the formula "origin unknown." This formula seldom means that the editor is unaware of various speculations about the origin of the term but instead usually means that no single theory conceived by the etymologist or proposed by others is well enough backed by evidence to include in a serious work of reference, even when qualified by "probably" or "perhaps." Thus, our editors frequently have to explain to correspondents that the dictionary fails to state that the origin of *posh* is in the initial letters of the phrase "port out, starboard home"—supposedly a shipping term for the cooler accommodations on steamships plying between Britain and India from the mid-nineteenth century on—not because the story is unknown to us but because no evidence to support it has yet been produced. Some evidence exists that casts strong doubt on it; the word is not known earlier than 1918 (in a source unrelated to shipping), and the acronymic explanation does not appear until 1935. It therefore seems reasonable to consider the acronymic explanation a modern invention and assign *posh* the etymology [origin unknown]. The etymologist must sift such theories, often several conflicting theories of greater or lesser likelihood, and try to evaluate the evidence conservatively but fairly in arriving at the soundest possible etymology that the available information permits. Occasionally time will prove the result to be somewhat (or even quite) mistaken, and the etymology will need to be replaced by something better. This can happen even when the etymologist felt quite certain of the original etymology, and it is just one reason why dictionaries must be reedited from time to time if they are to remain reliable.

Historical information about words is also provided by the date appearing in parentheses just before the first or only definition at most main entries. The date given is for the earliest recorded use known to our editors of the first entered sense of that entry. In most cases the date is also, in effect, for the earliest use of the word itself that we know of. Some words, however, had early senses that later passed from common use without gaining special literary importance, and these senses are omitted from this dictionary. Because it would be misleading to give a date for a sense that the dictionary does not show, the date is always for the first sense actually defined at the entry. Because the senses of any word having more than one are always presented in historical order, with the one known to have been used first given first, the date serves as a link between the prehistory of the word shown in the etymology and its later recorded history of semantic development within the language as reflected in the order of definitions.

Evidence for the dates has come from a number of sources. Especially for words that have been a part of the language since before the twentieth century, the most important sources have been the major historical dictionaries of English. These works include for each sense dated examples of use from one or several authors including the earliest one available to the editors. Chief among these dictionaries is the majestic twenty-volume Oxford English Dictionary, Second Edition, now also available as OED Online in a form that permits electronic searches of the full text and that includes draft entries toward a Third Edition. Also of great importance have been the Middle English Dictionary, A Dictionary of American English, A Dictionary of Americanisms, The Scottish National Dictionary, and A Dictionary of the Older Scottish Tongue. Other dictionaries and studies that include dated quotations and have proved helpful in particular cases include Hobson-Jobson (a glossary of Anglo-Indian terms), The Stanford Dictionary of Anglicised Words and Phrases, Bailey's Early Modern English, Schäfer's Early Modern English Lexicography, Wright's English Dialect Dictionary, Cassidy and Le Page's Dictionary of Jamaican English, Branford's Dictionary of South African English, Avis's Dictionary of Canadianisms on Historical Principles, Cassidy and Hall's Dictionary of American Regional English, Wentworth's American Dialect Dictionary, Light-

er's Random House Historical Dictionary of American Slang, and the several editions of The Barnhart Dictionary of New English. The Century Dictionary and Cyclopedia and the successive editions of Merriam-Webster's unabridged dictionaries and their supplements of new words have also provided much assistance, for while these dictionaries do not incorporate dated quotations, an entry in one or another of them is sometimes earlier than any example of the word from running text that we have been able to find.

In recent years large, searchable text databases have come into use. Their primary purposes generally have nothing to do with the earliest occurrence of particular words. Nonetheless, several of them have been of great assistance to the editors of this work in the dating of entries. Earlier we mentioned OED Online, which frequently permits the finding of an earlier use lying so far undiscovered among the quotations at some entry other than the one for the word being dated. In addition, we have made important use of NEXIS, an immense collection of journalistic materials from 1975 forward; Literature Online, containing hundreds of thousands of poems, plays, and prose works in English; Accessible Archives, which features eighteenth- and nineteenth-century American periodicals; and Making of America, covering nineteenth- and early twentieth-century general-interest and technical periodicals and books.

The other major source of dates, especially for the period from 1890 to the present, is the Merriam-Webster file of examples of words used in context, which are called citations. More will be said of this collection later. Here it need only be noted that among the more than 15,700,000 slips which the file contains frequently appear one or more examples of a given word that are earlier than any quoted in other sources. And, of course, our citations have been essential to the dating of a considerable number of entries not included in any of the dictionaries mentioned above. The date of 1949 at *classical conditioning* is a case of the first sort, the earliest example in a reference source being from 1964, while the date of 1928 at *working papers* is of the second sort. Some of the older books in our editorial library and in other libraries to which our editors have access have occasionally supplemented the resources of the citation file in supplying dates.

Almost from the appearance of the first volume of The Oxford English Dictionary, scholars have been discovering earlier dates for particular words and senses by examining works not searched for examples by the dictionary's readers or by reading some works a second time and publishing the results of their findings in various journals. Many hundreds of entries in this dictionary include a date derived from one of these articles, and while far too many scholars and other interested students have participated in this work for a listing here to be practical, some collective acknowledgment of our debt to them is necessary. The date of 1676 at *menagerie* may be cited as an example of one derived from a source of this kind; the quotation discovered by this scholar is 36 years older than the earliest example that had previously been found.

The style of the date is determined by the period of English to which the sense being dated belongs: for entries from Old English we indicate simply that the example is from the period before the twelfth century (bef. 12c); for those from Middle English we indicate their century, as (14c); for those from Modern English we give a single year, as (1742).

Some caution needs to be exercised in interpreting the significance of a date. It is never meant to indicate the exact point at which a word entered the language. For one thing, words have often been in spoken use for many years before they come to be written down. For another, many texts from the earlier periods in which they might have been written down have not survived. Then, too, not all surviving texts, even for the earlier periods, have been read to collect examples for any historical dictionary, and obviously for the modern era only a very small sample of all published material has been examined in that way. One can perhaps with some justification think of the date as indicating a time by which one can be sure that the word was in use, but it will be safest simply to remember that the date actually belongs to the earliest occurrence known to the editors of this dictionary of the first entered sense of the word.

Leaving the historical aspect of English aside now, we may consider how information about the systems of English as they presently exist is recorded in this dictionary. The phonological system needs little more than a mention here. Its role in this dictionary is discussed in some detail in the "Guide to Pronunciation," which immediately follows this section, as is the way in which the pronunciations shown in the dictionary have been determined.

Semantics in the Dictionary

In turning to consider the coverage of the semantic system in the dictionary, we face several difficult problems. If one function of a dictionary is more important than its many others, surely that function is to define the meaning of words. But while definition is central to the dictionary and quite obviously is involved with semantics, for the most part it deals with individual words in isolation from other words and thus ignores, to a considerable extent, the systematic, relational side of English semantics. Another problem is that although we know quite a lot about the system of English phonology and a good deal (though less) about the grammatical system, our understanding of the semantic system is very imperfect, and much of what we do know about it does not come very obviously into play in a dictionary. Still, we will have a glimpse of this system when we consider the dictionary treatment of synonyms, and in the meantime there is much to be said about the defining of words. Perhaps the first thing that we need to remind ourselves of is that when we speak of the meaning of a word we are employing an artificial, if highly useful, convention. Meaning does not truly reside within the word but in the minds of those who hear or read it. This fact alone guarantees that meaning will be to a great degree amorphous; no two people have had exactly the same experience with what a word refers to and so the meaning of the word will be slightly or greatly different for each of us. It is obvious, then, that a dictionary which set itself the task of defining the meanings of words in their entirety would be a foolhardy enterprise. So dictionary editors invoke the traditional distinction between *denotation*—the direct and specific part of meaning which is sometimes indicated as the total of all the referents of a word and is shared by all or most people who use the word—and *connotation*—the more personal associations and shades of meaning that gather about a word as a result of individual experience and which may not be widely shared. The dictionary concerns itself essentially with the denotations of words.

For the editors of this dictionary the defining process began long before they actually sat down to examine critically the definitions of the last edition and to formulate trial definitions. It began with an activity that is called in our offices "reading and marking." Ordinarily each editor spends a portion of the working day reading a variety of newspapers, magazines, and books, looking for anything that might be useful to a definer of English words. Because both time and staff are limited and the scope of English seems nearly unlimited, changes in subject matter, geographical area covered, and individual publications must be made from time to time in a way carefully calculated to ensure the breadth and depth as well as the continuity of our coverage of the vocabulary of English. An editor who is reading and marking will, of course, be looking for examples of new words and for unusual applications of familiar words that suggest the possible emergence of a new meaning but will also be concerned to provide evidence of the current status of variant spellings, inflected forms, and the stylings of compound words, to collect examples that may be quotable as illustrations of typical use in the dictionary, and to record many other useful kinds of information. In each instance the reader will underline the word or

phrase that is of interest and mark off as much context as is considered helpful in clarifying the meaning. This example of a word used in context is called a *citation* of the word. Ideally the editor would like all citations to illuminate the meaning of the word, but some passages will remain obscure no matter how far they extend, and sometimes one must mark a citation simply for the occurrence of the word or meaning (especially when it is new), trusting that the reading-and-marking process will yield more helpful examples in the long run. In the case of ephemeral words, of course, this may never happen, but truly ephemeral words will not need to be defined for a dictionary. At this early stage of the dictionary-making process, editors do not make judgments about the likelihood of a word's establishing itself in the language. If a possible citation has even the barest potential to be useful at a later time, it is marked.

These samples of words in bracketed context are put onto 3 × 5 slips of paper, and the citation slips are placed in alphabetical order in rows of filing cabinets. (In recent years new citations have also been preserved in machine-readable form.) The slips will be used, as needed, by the editors in their roles as writers of definitions and certain other parts of dictionary entries. The editors engaged in this eleventh edition of the Collegiate reviewed every one of the more than a million citations that had been gathered since the tenth edition was prepared in the early 1990s. When necessary, they also drew upon the additional resources of what are called the "consolidated" files, those that contain all the citations (over fourteen million) that had been accumulated in our offices since the late nineteenth century and had been used in the editing of the many dictionaries this company published before the present one.

The actual defining process often begins with a number of special assignments called "group defining projects," which may range from a small set of words like those for the days of the week or the letters of the English alphabet (for which parallel, formulaic definitions are required) to the vocabulary of a large subject area such as music or anthropology. When these assignments have been completed, defining proceeds alphabetically, with the editors responsible for the terminology of the life sciences or the physical sciences and related technologies working independently of the editors responsible for defining the general vocabulary.

If you were a definer, you would typically be working at a given moment with a group of citations covering a relatively short segment of the alphabet, *gri-* to *gro-*, for example, and with the entries of the dictionary being reedited that fall within the same segment. Your job would be to determine, under the guidance of the citations, which existing entries could remain in the new edition essentially unchanged because their usage showed no significant alteration, which entries needed to be revised either by modification of existing definitions or by the addition of new ones, which old entries were expendable for the new edition, and what new entries should be added to keep coverage of the lexicon up-to-date. You would begin by reading and sorting out the citation slips, first by grammatical function, in the case of a word like *groom* that is both noun and verb, and then by meaning within each part of speech. For each group of citations that was covered by an adequate existing definition, you would need only to indicate that you had examined them and would do nothing to the definition. For definitions needing adjustment, you would indicate the change to be made. In many cases, you would have some citations left over that were not covered by an existing definition, and it would then be your job to determine whether that segment of meaning was perhaps relatively uncommon and not backed by a sufficient range and number of citations and so not needed for the dictionary or whether in fact it was a sense that dictionary users are entitled to find suitably defined when they come looking for it. In the former case you would reject the citations, and eventually they would find their way back to the files to await review for another dictionary (by which time perhaps the citational backing would be stronger and a definition needed). In the latter case the responsibility to frame the kind of definition that will adequately convey that particular segment of meaning to the dictionary user would be yours.

In writing that definition, you could follow any of a number of paths marked out by the instructions given to each definer. These include both the general policies and practices that govern all Merriam-Webster dictionaries and the more specific directions and prohibitions contained in the "style file," as it is called, for this particular dictionary.

The kind of definition that you would write in most cases is called an analytical definition. It consists in its purest form of the statement of a class to which the term being defined is assigned and a number of characteristics which differentiate the individual from other members of the class. For example, the first sense of *grove* is defined in this Collegiate as "a small wood without underbrush," assigning a grove to the more general class of woods and using "small" and "without underbrush" to indicate in what ways a grove is unlike other kinds of woods. Another possibility would be for you to define a synonym, as is done at the sixth sense of the noun *grip*, where the definition is "STAGEHAND." Defining by synonym tends to be inexact because even true synonyms do not have exactly the same meaning and is perhaps most useful in cases like the one just mentioned where one kind of referent has two or more names, a situation that occurs frequently with the common names of plants and animals. For this reason we link any synonym definition to an analytical definition by making the synonym a cross-reference (in small capital letters) to another entry where an analytical definition suitable for both words is given: at *stagehand* is the definition "a stage worker who handles scenery, properties, or lights," which is also a good definition of the sixth sense of *grip*.

Within these basic defining patterns many variations are permitted. Some analytical definitions may justifiably be truncated by the use of a related word within the definition in order to save precious space for more entries. For example, *gross domestic product* can be defined as "the gross national product excluding the value of net income earned abroad" because the meaning of *gross national product* is given as "the total value of the goods and services produced by the residents of a nation during a specified period (as a year)," and so the definition of *gross domestic product* need not give that information a second time.

It is also possible to add a synonymous cross-reference to an analytical definition and thereby incorporate at little cost of space a second version of the meaning that looks at it from a slightly different aspect. It is possible to add a parenthetical element that specifies one or several of the typical referents of the word or that indicates the sole or a typical object of a transitive verb. One may begin an adjective definition with one of a wide variety of formulas but others are forbidden. It is clear already that definers' instructions are elaborately detailed, and it would be tedious to rehearse them here. Their purpose is to assist in developing the definer's native talent so that the definitions that he or she writes are consistently good ones. What is a good definition? Many qualities could be mentioned, and probably different definers would rank the relative importance of those on any list differently; but all definers want their definitions to be objective in reflecting what the word means as it is actually used rather than what the definer or someone else thinks it ought to mean, and they want their definitions to be accurate, clear, informative, and concise. In short, they want their definitions to have the qualities that users have in mind when they call a dictionary they admire "authoritative."

In the course of your defining, you would have an opportunity fairly often to make another kind of decision: whether to include or omit a new candidate for main entry. Let us take as an example the word *bioterrorism*, which is one of many entries new to this edition of the Collegiate Dictionary. If you had been the definer who handled that word, you would have been faced with a group of about three dozen citations to read covering a span of twelve years, with the greatest concentration in the years from 1996 to the present. They would include extracts from such publications as *The Nation, Business Week, USA Today, Newsweek, The Ottawa Citizen, The Atlantic Monthly, The New York Times, The New Republic, The Journal of the American Medical Association, Commonweal,* and *Publishers Weekly*. In reading the citations, you would notice that while they varied in many details of context, they seem to be describing a straightforward and simple (not to say chilling) concept represented by the two elements that make up the word: *bio-* and *terrorism*. You might then have produced the following definition or one like it: "terrorism involving the use of biological weapons." (*Terrorism* is, of course, entered and defined at its own alphabetical place in the dictionary.)

The number and time span of the citations and the variety of the sources would already have told you that this was a very strong, and perhaps even an essential, candidate for entry in the new edition. There is no magic number of citations that guarantees entry and no particular span of years that must be reached. To a great extent the judgment made here must rest on your insight and experience as a definer who has seen the citational backing for many words, who has most likely defined words for other Merriam-Webster dictionaries in the past, and who thus has some sense of the relative importance and degree of establishment of new entries within the lexicon and of their likely staying power.

You would have noticed that in addition to the evidence for the noun *bioterrorism*, there were also fourteen citations for a word *bioterrorist*, some showing it used as a noun in the usual ways but several others showing it modifying another noun (as in "a bioterrorist plot"). Seeing both that these uses were less important than *bioterrorism* (though also well backed by citations) and that their meanings were easily inferred from the meaning of the main entry word, you would add them to your new main entry as an undefined run-on with a double functional label (*adj or n*). You would also notice ten citations for a noun *bioterror* with exactly the same meaning as *bioterrorism*. Our rules do not allow this word to be run on since its meaning is not easily inferred from the meaning of the main entry, but you might well make a separate main entry for it, defining it by synonymous cross-reference to *bioterrorism*.

To take one further example of a somewhat different kind, if you had been the life-sciences definer responsible for handling the term *genomics*, you would have read over 40 citations. Many of these would have been from sources such as *Science, Nature,* and *BioWorld Today,* likely to be seen chiefly by people with specialized interests; but you would also have seen examples from *The Wall Street Journal, Time, Wired,* and *The New Yorker*. In other words, the term is likely to be encountered by people with general interests and, given its nature, will probably be looked up in a dictionary fairly often. Such considerations would have led you to propose entry for the term and with a much higher priority than if the citational backing had been nearly all technical.

It is worth noting briefly that in the course of your work as a definer you would have been concerned with what the citations reveal about a word in addition to its meaning. The definer is initially responsible for most of the framework of the entry including not only spelling variants and run-ons but also inflected forms, usage notes, verbal illustrations, and temporal, regional, stylistic, and subject labels.

The other important part of these entries that is concerned with English semantics is the synonym paragraph. These paragraphs are not written by each individual definer as particular entries are encountered but are rather the special assignment of usually one editor, who decides which words will be included in a single paragraph and at which entry the paragraph will be placed. The synonym editor has a number of responsibilities in addition to the actual writing or revising of the synonym paragraph. Each entry for a term discussed in a paragraph must be checked to ensure that the definition of a given sense is fully consonant with its treatment in the paragraph, and the editor has the authority to make small adjustments of definitions so that no discrepancies which might puzzle a user remain.

Like the definer, this editor must read citations very carefully to see that the opening statement of the core meaning shared by the synonyms includes neither too much nor too little, that each discrimination of one word from the others is accurate, and that typical examples are chosen as a basis on which to frame verbal illustrations. It is particularly in these paragraphs that the dictionary user comes into contact with the systematic side of English semantics because here the concern is with the relationship of meanings instead of the meanings themselves as discrete entities. For example, the synonym paragraph at *splendid* in this dictionary states that *splendid, resplendent, gorgeous, glorious, sublime*, and *superb* mean "extraordinarily or transcendently impressive." This statement of meaning is at once too broad and too narrow to be a good definition for any of the words; it trims away the particular elements of meaning that make each word distinctive (the most important of which are stated in the following discussion). It does, however, give us an accurate notion of the point at which these words come into a precise semantic relationship with each other.

Grammar and Usage in the Dictionary

The last of the four systems of English whose reflection we may see, at least briefly and occasionally, in the dictionary is the grammatical system. As we saw earlier, this system involves chiefly the relationship between words as they form more complex units rather than individual words themselves. A descriptive grammar of English is a very different kind of book from a dictionary. Nevertheless, virtually every entry in this dictionary contains at least one piece of information about its grammatical nature and the kinds of relationships it can enter into, namely, the functional label which typically indicates the part of speech of the entry or, in the case of terminal word elements, the part of speech of the words that they form. If an entry is labeled *adv*, we know that it can describe the action of a verb but cannot itself be the main verb of a sentence, while an entry labeled *n* cannot link the subject of a sentence with a predicate adjective but can be the subject. Other parts of the entry also give us information that is grammatical in nature. One sort of information is offered by the boldface inflected forms that are shown at every entry for which they are irregular exceptions to the ordinary patterns of English inflection or may present some other sort of problem to the dictionary user. Another is offered by the undefined run-on entries. They illustrate the complex patterns by which one word or a number of words can be derived from a single base by means of affixation or functional shift. Certain kinds of usage notes following or standing in place of definitions also present grammatical information. Typical of the former kind of usage note is the one given at sense 2 of ¹*yoke*, "often used in negative constructions," and the one given at sense 2b of the verb ⁴*conk*, "usu. used with *off* or *out*." Typical of the latter are the several usage notes at the entry for the preposition *for*, "used as a function word to indicate duration of time or extent of space" at sense 9, for example, and the note given at sense 3c of *boy*, "used interjectionally to express intensity of feeling."

Usage is a concept that embraces many aspects of and attitudes toward language. Grammar is certainly only a small part of what goes to make up usage, though some people use one term for the other, as when they label what is really a controversial point of usage a grammatical error. Usage guidance is offered in this dictionary in many ways; it would be little exaggeration to say that any information a user seeks and finds in this book can offer some guidance as to usage. But usage information is chiefly conveyed through three devices: usage notes; temporal, regional, and stylistic labels; and usage paragraphs. The first two are developed by definers from their examination of citations, including sometimes (and particularly in the case of the labels) citations found in historical, dialect, and slang dictionaries as well as those in Merriam-Webster's citation file. The usage paragraphs like the synonym paragraphs are the result of a special project chiefly in the hands of one editor with assistance from several others. The editors attempted to select particular problems of confused or disputed usage that would be of broad general interest and could be treated at individual entries in the dictionary. The great majority of them involve words that have traditionally been points of dispute (a few of these are now probably more traditional than truly the subjects of heated dispute), but some are relatively new items for this kind of consideration. Several paragraphs deal with pronunciation, a subject rarely treated in books about usage.

The editors who wrote the paragraphs used several kinds of material: books describing one or another aspect of the history of usage as a problem in English; books and articles ruling on particular points of usage, whether the product of one person or a group; historical and other dictionaries; and above all citations of usage itself from our file. In digesting this mass of information and presenting it in a very brief compass, the editors have typically combined information on the history of the controversy, the current state of expressed opinion, illustrations of both old and modern use (often quoted), and practical advice. These paragraphs have profited greatly from the extensive research in the same materials that was carried out in the course of work on Merriam-Webster's Dictionary of English Usage.

It has been close to 250 years since Dr. Johnson published his great dictionary and 175 years since Noah Webster's American Dictionary of the English Language appeared. Even the more modest Collegiate series has passed its hundredth birthday. It seems clear that the long tradition of English dictionaries is not likely to wither and die. Indeed, dictionaries are likely to become, if anything, even more important to the general public in the future, at least as long as the vocabulary of English continues the rapid growth which began early in the twentieth century and which seems now to intensify year by year. As long as they are edited with a proper regard for the right of the dictionary user to have accurate information about what English words actually mean and how they are actually used, those dictionaries will continue to serve a useful purpose and to be needed. Though they are incomplete as descriptions of the systems of English and are edited by fallible humans whose best intentions sometimes fall short of the mark, such dictionaries will continue to form, as the best dictionaries have always done, a helpful bridge between what we know about language and how we use it. Movement across such a bridge is, of course, in both directions: our use of language furnishes the basis for our knowledge of it, but our knowledge of it also helps us to use it more effectively.

Guide to Pronunciation

Pronunciation is not an intrinsic component of the dictionary. For some languages, such as Spanish, Swahili, and Finnish, the correspondence between orthography and pronunciation is so close that a dictionary need only spell a word correctly to indicate its pronunciation. Modern English, however, displays no such consistency in sound and spelling, and so a dictionary of English must devote considerable attention to the pronunciation of the language. The English lexicon contains numerous eye rhymes such as *love, move,* and *rove,* words which do not sound alike despite their similar spellings. On the other hand, it also contains rhyming words such as *breeze, cheese, ease, frieze,* and *sleaze* whose rhymes are all spelled differently.

This grand mismatch between words that look alike and words that sound alike does at least serve to record something of the history of the English-speaking peoples and their language. Spelling often indicates whether a word comes down from the native Anglo-Saxon word stock or was adopted in successive ages from the speech of a missionary monk chanting Latin, a seafaring Viking dickering in Old Norse, a Norman nobleman giving orders in French, or a young immigrant to turn-of-the-century America. For example, the sound \sh\ is spelled as *sh* in native English *shore,* as *ch* in the French loan *champagne,* as *sk* in one pronunciation of the Norwegian loan *ski,* as *si* in the Renaissance Latin loan *emulsion,* and as *sch* in the recent Yiddish loan *schlep.* English vowels present different complexities of sound and spelling, due in large part to the fact that William Caxton introduced printing to England in A.D. 1476, many decades before the sound change known as the Great Vowel Shift had run its course. With the rise of printing came an increasingly fixed set of spelling conventions, but the conventionalized spellings soon lost their connection to pronunciation as the vowel shift continued. The stressed vowels of *sane* and *sanity* are therefore identical in spelling though now quite different in quality. For the trained observer the vagaries of English orthography contain a wealth of linguistic history; for most others, however, this disparity between sound and spelling is just a continual nuisance at school or work.

Readers often turn to the dictionary wanting to learn the exact pronunciation of a word, only to discover that the word may have several pronunciations, as is the case for *deity, economic, envelope,* and *greasy,* among many others. The inclusion of variant pronunciations disappoints those who want their dictionary to list one "correct" pronunciation. In truth, though, there can be no objective standard for correct pronunciation other than the usage of thoughtful and, in particular, educated speakers of English. Among such speakers one hears much variation in pronunciation.

Dictionaries of English before the modern era usually ignored pronunciation variants, instead indicating a single pronunciation by marking the entry word with diacritics to indicate stress and letter values. These systems were cumbersome, however, and reflected the dialectal biases of the editors more than the facts about how a word was actually spoken. Lexicographers came eventually to recognize the need for separate respellings which could record the entire range of accepted variants along with appropriate notes about dialectal distribution or usage.

This dictionary records many types of variation in pronunciation. Distinctions between British and American speech are frequently noted, as are differences among the three major dialect areas of the U.S.—Northern, Southern, and Midland. Words that have distinctive pronunciations in Canada, such as *decal* and *khaki,* have those pronunciations duly noted. Pronunciations peculiar to certain spheres of activity are also represented, as for example the variants of *athwart* and *tackle* heard in nautical use. Finally, a wide range of unpredictable variations are included, such as the pronunciation of *economic* with either \e\ or \ē\. Unpredictable variations frequently cut across the boundaries of geographical dialects, sometimes running along the lines of social class, ethnicity, or gender instead. In fine, this dictionary attempts to include—either explicitly or by implication—all pronunciation variants of a word that are used by educated speakers of the English language.

The pronunciations in this dictionary are informed chiefly by the Merriam-Webster pronunciation file. This file contains citations that are transcriptions of words used by native speakers of English in the course of utterances heard in speeches, interviews, and conversations. In this extensive collection of 3 × 5 slips of paper, one finds the pronunciations of a host of people: politicians, professors, curators, artists, musicians, doctors, engineers, preachers, activists, journalists, and many others. The Merriam-Webster pronunciation editors have been collecting these citations from live speech and from radio, television, and shortwave broadcasts since the 1930s. It is primarily on the basis of this large and growing file that questions of usage and acceptability in pronunciation are answered. All of the pronunciations recorded in this book can be documented as falling within the range of generally acceptable variation, unless they are accompanied by a restricting usage note or symbol or a regional label.

No system of indicating pronunciation is self-explanatory. The following discussion sets out the signification and use of the pronunciation symbols in this book, with special attention to those areas where experience has shown that dictionary users may have questions. More detailed information can be found in the Guide to Pronunciation in Webster's Third New International Dictionary. The order of symbols discussed below is the same as the order on the page of Pronunciation Symbols, with the exception that the symbols which are not letter characters are here listed first. Those characters which have corresponding symbols in the International Phonetic Alphabet (IPA) are shown with their IPA equivalents.

\ \ All pronunciation information is printed between reversed virgules. Pronunciation symbols are printed in roman type and all other information, such as labels and notes, is printed in italics.

\ ' \ A high-set stress mark precedes a syllable with primary (strongest) stress; a low-set mark precedes a syllable with secondary (medium) stress; a third level of weak stress requires no mark at all: \'pen-mən-ˌship\.

Since the nineteenth century the International Phonetics Association has recommended that stress marks precede the stressed syllable, and linguists worldwide have adopted this practice on the basic principle that before a syllable can be uttered the speaker must know what degree of stress to give it.

\ - \ Hyphens are used to separate syllables in pronunciation transcriptions. In actual speech, of course, there is no pause between the syllables of a word.

The placement of hyphens is based on phonetic principles, such as vowel length, nasalization, variation due to the position of a consonant in a syllable, and other nuances of the spoken word. The syllable breaks shown in this book reflect the careful pronunciation of a single word out of context. Syllabication tends to change in rapid or running speech: a consonant at the end of a syllable may shift into a following syllable, and unstressed vowels may be elided. The numerous variations in pronunciation that a word may have in running speech are of interest to phoneticians but are well outside the scope of a dictionary of general English.

The centered dots in boldface entry words indicate potential end-of-line division points and not syllabication. These division points are determined by considerations of both morphology and pronunciation, among others. Further discussion of end-of-line division is contained in the section of that name within the Explanatory Notes. In this book a consistent approach has been pursued, both toward word division based on traditional formulas and toward syllabication based on phonetic principles. As a result, the hyphens indicating syllable breaks and the centered dots indicating end-of-line division often do not fall in the same places.

\\( )\\ Parentheses are used in pronunciations to indicate that whatever is symbolized between them is present in some utterances but not in others; thus *factory* \\'fak-t(ə-)rē\\ is pronounced both \\'fak-tə-rē\\ and \\'fak-trē\\, *industry* \\'in-(ˌ)dəs-trē\\ is pronounced both \\'in-dəs-trē\\ and \\'in-ˌdəs-trē\\. In some phonetic environments, as in *fence* \\'fen(t)s\\ and *boil* \\'bȯi(-ə)l\\, it may be difficult to determine whether the sound shown in parentheses is or is not present in a given utterance; even the usage of a single speaker may vary considerably.

\\ , ; \\ Variant pronunciations are separated by commas; groups of variants are separated by semicolons. The order of variants does not mean that the first is in any way preferable to or more acceptable than the others. All of the variants in this book, except those restricted by a regional or usage label, are widely used in acceptable educated speech. If evidence reveals that a particular variant is used more frequently than another, the former will be given first. This should not, however, prejudice anyone against the second or subsequent variants. In many cases the numerical distribution of variants is equal, but one of them, of course, must be printed first.

\\ ÷ \\ The obelus, or division sign, is placed before a pronunciation variant that occurs in educated speech but that is considered by some to be questionable or unacceptable. This symbol is used sparingly and primarily for variants that have been objected to over a period of time in print by commentators on usage, in schools by teachers, or in correspondence that has come to the Merriam-Webster editorial department. In most cases the objection is based on orthographic or etymological arguments. For instance, the second variant of *cupola* \\'kyü-pə-lə, ÷-ˌlō\\, though used frequently in speech, is objected to because *a* is very rarely pronounced \\ō\\ in English. The pronunciation \\'lī-ˌber-ē\\ is similarly marked at the entry for *library* because some people insist that both *r*'s should be pronounced.

\\ ə \\ in unstressed syllables as in b**a**nana, c**o**llide, **a**but (IPA [ə]). This neutral vowel, called *schwa,* may be represented orthographically by any of the letters *a, e, i, o, u, y,* and by many combinations of letters. In running speech unstressed vowels are regularly pronounced as \\ə\\ in American and British speech.

Speakers of r-dropping dialects will often insert an \\r\\ after \\ə\\ when \\ə\\ precedes another vowel. (See the section on \\r\\.)

\\'ə, ˌə\\ in stressed syllables as in h**u**mdr**u**m, ab**u**t. (IPA [ʌ]).

Some speakers pronounce \\'ə\\ and \\ō\\ identically before \\l\\, with the result that word pairs like *gull* and *goal* are homophones. The sound produced in such cases is usually the same sound that other speakers use for \\ō\\.

\\ ᵊ \\ immediately preceding \\l\\, \\n\\, \\m\\, \\ŋ\\, as in b**a**t**tle,** c**o**t**ton,** and one pronunciation of op**e**n \\'ō-pᵊm\\ and of **and** \\ᵊŋ\\ as in one pronunciation of the phrase *lock and key* \\ˌläk-ᵊŋ-'kē\\. The symbol \\ᵊ\\ preceding these consonants does not itself represent a sound. It signifies instead that the following consonant is syllabic; that is, the consonant itself forms the nucleus of a syllable that does not contain a vowel.

In the pronunciation of some French or French-derived words \\ᵊ\\ is placed immediately after \\l\\, \\m\\, \\r\\ to indicate one nonsyllabic pronunciation of these consonants, as in the French words ta**ble** "table," pris**me** "prism," and ti**tre** "title," each of which in isolation and in some contexts is a one-syllable word.

\\ ər \\ as in f**ur**ther, m**er**ger, b**ir**d (IPA [ɝ, ɚ]). (See the section on \\r\\.) Actually, this is usually a single sound, not a sequence of \\ə\\ followed by \\r\\. Speakers of r-dropping dialects will pronounce \\ər\\ without r-color (IPA [ɜː, əː] when stressed, [ə] when unstressed) when it precedes a consonant or pause, but will insert a following \\r\\ when \\ər\\ precedes another vowel.

\\'ər-, 'ə-r\\ as in two different pronunciations of *hurry.* Most U.S. speakers pronounce \\'hər-ē\\ with the \\ər\\ representing the same sounds as in *bird* \\'bərd\\. Usually in metropolitan New York and southern England and frequently in New England and the southeastern U.S. the vowel is much the same as the vowel of *hum* followed by a syllable-initial variety of \\r\\. This pronunciation of *hurry* is represented as \\'hə-rē\\ in this book. Both types of pronunciation are shown for words composed of a single meaningful unit (or *morpheme*) as in *current, hurry,* and *worry.* In words such as *furry, stirring,* and *purring* in which a vowel or vowel-initial suffix is added to a word ending in *r* or *rr* (as *fur, stir,* and *purr*), the second type of pronunciation outlined above is heard only occasionally and is not shown in this dictionary.

\\ a \\ as in m**a**t, m**a**p, m**a**d, g**a**g, sn**a**p, p**a**tch (IPA [æ]). Some variation in this vowel is occasioned by the consonant that follows it; thus, for some speakers *map, mad,* and *gag* have noticeably different vowel sounds. There is a very small number of words otherwise identical in pronunciation that these speakers may distinguish solely by variation of this vowel, as in the two words *can* (put into cans; be able) in the sentence "Let's can what we can." However, this distinction is sufficiently infrequent that the traditional practice of using a single symbol is followed in this book.

Many varieties of English do not allow \\a\\ to be followed by an \\r\\ which begins the following syllable. In such a case, the sequence of \\a-r\\ is replaced by \\er\\, and word pairs like *arrow* and *aero* are homophones. This is not always indicated in transcription. The reader should assume that any sequences of \\a-r\\ will be \\er\\ for such speakers.

When it precedes \\ŋ\\, \\a\\ is often followed by a \\y\\ sound. The resulting vowel sounds much like \\ā\\ for many speakers.

\\ ā \\ as in d**ay**, f**a**de, d**a**te, **a**orta, dr**a**pe, c**a**pe (IPA [e, eɪ, eı]). In most English speech this is actually a diphthong. In lowland South Carolina, in coastal Georgia and Florida, and occasionally elsewhere \\ā\\ is pronounced as a monophthong. As a diphthong \\ā\\ has a first element \\e\\ or monophthongal \\ā\\ and a second element \\i\\.

Before \\l\\, speakers may lose the second element \\i\\ and insert \\ə\\. Thus, a word like *ale* would be IPA [eəl]. Alternately, many speakers will keep the second element \i\ and add a following \ə\ which creates a new syllable. Thus, the word *trail* will be \'trā-əl\, rhyming with *betrayal*.

\ **ä** \ as in b**o**ther, c**o**t (IPA [ɑ]). The symbol \ä\ represents the vowel of *cot, cod,* and the stressed vowel of *collar* in the speech of those who pronounce this vowel differently from the vowel in *caught, cawed,* and *caller,* represented by \ȯ\. In U.S. speech \ä\ is pronounced with little or no rounding of the lips, and it is fairly long in duration, especially before voiced consonants. In southern England \ä\ is usually accompanied by some lip rounding and is relatively short in duration. The vowel \ȯ\ generally has appreciable lip rounding. Many U.S. speakers do not distinguish between *cot—caught, cod—cawed,* and *collar—caller,* usually because they lack or have less lip rounding in the words transcribed with \ȯ\. Though the symbols \ä\ and \ȯ\ are used throughout this book to distinguish the members of the above pairs and similar words, the speakers who rhyme these pairs will automatically reproduce a sound that is consistent with their own speech.

In transcription of foreign words, the symbol \ä\ is also used to represent IPA [a], a vowel which is generally pronounced farther forward in the mouth than \ä\ but not as far forward as \a\. Some speakers may also have such a vowel in words like *balm* which contrasts with the vowel in words like *bomb.* Such a contrast is rare, however, and it is not represented in this dictionary.

Speakers of r-dropping dialects will usually insert an \r\ after \ä\ when \ä\ precedes another vowel. (See the section on \r\.)

\ **är** \ as in c**ar**, h**ear**t, **aar**dv**ar**k, baz**aar**, biz**ar**re (IPA [ɑɚ, aɚ, ɒɚ]). The initial element of this diphthong may vary from \ä\ to a vowel pronounced farther forward in the mouth than \ä\, or it may be a vowel with some lip rounding resembling \ȯ\. Speakers of r-dropping dialects will pronounce \är\ as a long vowel (IPA [ɑː, aː]) when it precedes a consonant or pause, and may distinguish \är\ in *cart* from \ä\ in *cot* by the length and quality of the vowel, not by the presence of \r\. However, speakers of r-dropping dialects will usually insert an \r\ after \är\ when it precedes a vowel. (See the section on \r\.)

\ **au̇** \ as in n**ow**, l**ou**d, **ou**t (IPA [aʊ, au]). The initial element of this diphthong may vary from \a\ to \ä\, the first being more common in Southern and south Midland speech than elsewhere. In coastal areas of the southern U.S. and in parts of Canada this diphthong is often realized as \əu̇\ when immediately preceding a voiceless consonant, as in the noun *house* and in *out.*

Many varieties of English do not allow \au̇\ to be followed by \l\ in the same syllable. Speakers of such varieties will insert a following \ə\ which creates a new syllable. This is indicated by the transcription \au̇(-ə)l\. For such speakers, *owl* will rhyme with *avowal.* Also, many varieties of English do not allow \au̇\ to be followed by \r\ in the same syllable. Speakers of such varieties will transform the following \r\ into \ər\, thus creating a new syllable. This is indicated by the transcription \au̇(-ə)r\. For such speakers, *scour* will rhyme with *plower.*

\ **b** \ as in **b**a**b**y, ri**b** (IPA [b]).

\ **ch** \ as in **ch**in, na**t**ure \'nā-chər\ (IPA [tʃ]). Actually, this sound is \t\ + \sh\. The distinction between the phrases *why choose* and *white shoes* is maintained by a difference in the syllabication of the \t\ and the \sh\ in each case and the consequent use of different varieties (or *allophones*) of \t\.

\ **d** \ as in **d**i**d**, a**dd**er (IPA [d]). (See the section on \t\ below for a discussion of the flap allophone of

\d\.) Many speakers pronounce \d\ like \j\ when it occurs before \r\ in the same syllable.

\ **e** \ as in b**e**t, b**e**d, p**e**ck (IPA [ɛ]). In Southern and Midland dialects this vowel before nasal consonants often has a raised articulation that approximates \i\, so that *pen* has nearly the pronunciation \'pin\.

Many varieties of English do not allow \e\ to be followed by an \r\ which begins the following syllable. In such a case, the sequence of \e-r\ is replaced by \er\, and word pairs like *very* and *vary* are homophones. This is not always indicated in transcription. The reader should assume that any sequences of \e-r\ will be \er\ for such speakers.

\ **er** \ as in b**are**, f**air**, w**ear**, derri**ere**, million**aire** (IPA [eɚ, ɛɚ]). The initial element of this diphthong may vary from \e\ to \ā\. Speakers of r-dropping dialects will pronounce \er\ without any r-color on the second element (IPA [eə, ɛə]) when it precedes a consonant or pause, but will usually insert an \r\ after \er\ when it precedes a vowel. (See the section on \r\.)

\ **'ē, ˌē** \ in stressed syllables as in b**ea**t, nose-bl**ee**d, even**ly**, eas**y** (IPA [i]). Many speakers will insert \ə\ after \ē\ when it precedes \l\. Additionally, some speakers pronounce \ē\ and \i\ identically before \l\, with the result that word pairs like *heel* and *hill* are homophones. The sound pronounced in such cases may be either \ē\ or \i\ as pronounced by those who distinguish the two.

\ **ē** \ in unstressed syllables, as in eas**y**, meal**y** (IPA [i, ɪ, ɪ]). Though the fact is not shown in this book, some dialects such as southern British and southern U.S. often, if not usually, pronounce \i\ instead of unstressed \ē\.

\ **f** \ as in **f**i**f**ty, cu**ff** (IPA [f]).

\ **g** \ as in **g**o, bi**g**, **g**ift (IPA [g]).

\ **h** \ as in **h**at, a**h**ead (IPA [h]).

\ **hw** \ as in **wh**ale as pronounced by those who do not have the same pronunciation for both *whale* and *wail.* Some U.S. speakers distinguish these two words as \'hwāl\ and \'wāl\ respectively, though frequently in the U.S. and usually in southern England \'wāl\ is used for both. Some linguists consider \hw\ to be a single sound, a voiceless \w\ (IPA [ʍ]).

\ **i** \ as in t**i**p, ban**i**sh, act**i**ve (IPA [ɪ]). Some speakers pronounce \ē\ and \i\ identically before \l\, with the result that word pairs like *heel* and *hill* are homophones. The sound pronounced in such cases may be either \ē\ or \i\ as pronounced by those who distinguish the two.

When it precedes \ŋ\, \i\ is often followed by a \y\ sound. The resulting sound often greatly resembles \ē\.

\ **ir** \ as in n**ear**, d**eer**, m**ere**, p**ier**, souven**ir** (IPA [iɚ, ɪɚ]). The initial element of this diphthong may vary from \ē\ to \i\. Speakers of r-dropping dialects will pronounce \ir\ without any r-color on the second element (IPA [iə, ɪə]) when it precedes a consonant or pause, but will usually insert an \r\ after \ir\ when it precedes a vowel. (See the section on \r\.)

\ **ī** \ as in s**i**te, s**i**de, b**uy**, tr**i**pe (IPA [aɪ, ai, ɑɪ, ɑi]). Actually, this sound is a diphthong, usually composed of \ä\ + \i\. In Southern speech, especially before a pause or voiced consonant, as in *shy* and *five,* the second element \i\ may not be pronounced (IPA [aːɪ]). Chiefly in eastern Virginia, coastal South Carolina, and parts of Canada the diphthong is approximately \'ə\ + \i\ before voiceless consonants, as in *nice* and *write* (IPA [ʌɪ]).

Many varieties of English do not allow \ī\ to be followed by \l\ in the same syllable. Speakers of such varieties will insert a following \ə\ which creates a new syllable. This is indicated by the transcription \ī(-ə)l\. For such speakers, *file* will rhyme with *denial.* Also, many varieties of English do not allow \ī\ to be followed by \r\ in the same syllable. Speakers of such varieties will transform the following \r\ into \ər\, thus creating a new syllable. This is indicated by the transcription \ī(-ə)r\. For such speakers, *fire* will rhyme with *higher.*

\ **j** \ as in **j**ob, **g**em, e**dg**e, **j**oin, **judg**e. Actually, this sound is \d\ + \zh\ (IPA [dʒ]). Assuming the anglicization of *Jeanne d'Arc* as \zhän-'därk\, the distinction between the sentences *They betray John Dark* and *They betrayed Jeanne d'Arc* is maintained by a difference in the syllabication of the \d\ and the \zh\ in each case and the consequent use of different varieties (or *allophones*) of \d\.

\ **k** \ as in **k**in, **c**oo**k**, a**ch**e (IPA [k]).

\ **k̲** \ as in German i**ch** "I," Bu**ch** "book," and one pronunciation of English lo**ch**. Actually, there are two distinct sounds in German; the \k̲\ in *ich* (IPA [ç]) is pronounced toward the front of the mouth and the \k̲\ in *Buch* is pronounced toward the back (IPA [x]). In English, however, no two words otherwise identical are distinguished by these two varieties of \k̲\, and therefore only a single symbol is necessary.

\ **l** \ as in **l**i**l**y, poo**l** (IPA [l, ɫ]). In words such as *battle* and *fiddle* the \l\ is a syllabic consonant (IPA [l̩]). (See the section on \ᵊ\ above.)

\ **m** \ as in **m**ur**m**ur, di**m**, ny**m**ph (IPA [m]). In pronunciation variants of some words, such as *open* and *happen,* \m\ is a syllabic consonant (IPA [m̩]). (See the section on \ᵊ\ above.)

\ **n** \ as in **n**o, ow**n** (IPA [n]). In words such as *cotton* and *sudden,* the \n\ is a syllabic consonant (IPA [n̩]). (See the section on \ᵊ\ above.)

\ **ⁿ** \ indicates that a preceding vowel or diphthong is pronounced with the nasal passages open, as in French *un bon vin blanc* \œⁿ-bōⁿ-vaⁿ-bläⁿ\ "a good white wine."

\ **ŋ** \ as in si**ng** \'siŋ\, si**ng**er \'siŋ-ər\, fi**ng**er \'fiŋ-gər\, i**nk** \'iŋk\ (IPA [ŋ]). In some rare contexts \ŋ\ may be a syllabic consonant (IPA [ŋ̍]). (See the section on \ᵊ\ above.)

\ **ō** \ as in b**o**ne, kn**ow**, b**eau** (IPA [o, oʊ, ou]). Especially in positions of emphasis, such as when it occurs at the end of a word or has primary stress, \ō\ tends to become diphthongal, moving from \ō\ toward a second element \u̇\. In southern England and in some U.S. speech, particularly in the Philadelphia area and in the Pennsylvania-Ohio-West Virginia border area, the first element is often approximately \ə\. In coastal South Carolina, Georgia, and Florida stressed \ō\ is often monophthongal when final, but when a consonant follows it is often a diphthong moving from \ō\ to \ə\. In this book the symbol \ō\ represents all of the above variants. As an unstressed vowel before another vowel, \ō\ is often pronounced as a schwa with slight lip rounding that is separated from the following vowel by the glide \w\, as in *following* \fä-lə-

win\. This reduced variant is not usually shown at individual entries.

\ **ȯ** \ as in s**aw**, **a**ll, gn**aw**, c**au**ght (IPA [ɔ]). (See the section on \ä\.)
Speakers of r-dropping dialects will usually insert an \r\ after \ȯ\ when \ȯ\ precedes another vowel. (See the section on \r\.)

\ **œ** \ as in French b**oeu**f "beef," German H**ö**lle "hell" (IPA [œ]). This vowel, which occurs only in foreign-derived terms and names, can be approximated by attempting to pronounce the vowel \e\ with the lips moderately rounded as for the vowel \u̇\. This vowel is often anglicized as the \ər\ of *bird* by those who do not "drop their r's" or as the corresponding vowel of *bird* used by those who do (see the section on \r\).
This symbol is also used to represent the vowel in French f**eu** "fire," German H**ö**hle "hole" (IPA [ø]). This vowel, which occurs primarily in foreign-derived terms and names, can be approximated by attempting to pronounce a monophthongal vowel \ā\ with the lips fully rounded as for the vowel \ü\. This vowel also occurs in Scots and thus is used in the pronunciation of *guidwillie,* mainly restricted to Scotland.

\ **ȯi** \ as in c**oi**n, destr**oy** (IPA [ɔɪ, ɔi, oɪ, oi]). In some Southern speech, especially before a consonant in the same word, the second element may disappear or be replaced by \ə\. Some utterances of *drawing* and *sawing* have a sequence of vowel sounds identical to that in *coin,* but because *drawing* and *sawing* are analyzed by many as two-syllable words they are transcribed with a parenthesized hyphen: \'drȯ(-)iŋ\, \'sȯ(-)iŋ\.
Many varieties of English do not allow \ȯi\ to be followed by \l\ in the same syllable. Speakers of such varieties will insert a following \ə\ which creates a new syllable. This is indicated by the transcription \ȯi(-ə)l\. For such speakers, *oil* will rhyme with *loyal.*

\ **ȯr** \ as in b**oar**, p**or**t, d**oor**, sh**ore** (IPA [oɚ, ɔɚ]). The initial element of this diphthong may vary from \ō\ to \ȯ\. Speakers of r-dropping dialects will usually pronounce \ȯr\ the same as \ȯ\. (See the section on \r\.) Historically, there has been a contrast between the vowel in words like *ore, bore, porch, sport,* and *hoarse* on one hand and the vowel in words like *or, for, torch, short,* and *horse* on the other hand. The vowel in the former set of words has been much like \ō\, and the vowel in the latter set like \ȯ\. However, the number of speakers that make such a distinction is currently very small, and we have not represented the distinction in this dictionary.

\ **p** \ as in **p**e**pp**er, li**p** (IPA [p]).

\ **r** \ as in **r**ed, **r**a**r**ity. What is transcribed here as \r\ in reality represents several distinct sounds. Before a stressed vowel \r\ denotes a continuant produced with the tongue tip slightly behind the teethridge (IPA [ɹ]). This sound is usually voiceless when it follows a voiceless stop, as in *pray, tree,* and *cram.*
In Received Pronunciation \r\ is sometimes pronounced as a flap (IPA [ɾ]) in the same contexts in which \t\ and \d\ occur as flaps in American English. (See the section on \t\ below.) Occasionally the flap may be heard after consonants, as in *bright* and *grow.* In other dialects of British English, particularly Scots, \r\ may be pronounced as an alveolar trill (IPA [r]) or as a uvular trill (IPA [ʀ]).
In some dialects, especially those of the southeastern U.S., eastern New England, New York City, and southern England, \r\ is not pronounced or is pronounced as \ə\ after a vowel in the same syllable. Such dialects are often referred to as r-dropping dialects. This term is somewhat misleading, since speakers of such dialects will often pronounce an \r\ in certain situations where speakers of non-

r-dropping dialects will not have an \r\. This matter is discussed in some of the other sections of this Guide.

\ s \ as in source, less (IPA [s]).

\ sh \ as in shy, mission, machine, special (IPA [ʃ]). Actually, this is a single sound, not two. When the two sounds \s\ and \h\ occur in sequence, they are separated by a hyphen in this book, as in *grasshopper* \'gras-ˌhä-pər\.

\ t \ as in tie, attack, late, later, latter (IPA [t]). In some contexts, as when a stressed or unstressed vowel precedes and an unstressed vowel or \ᵊl\ follows, the sound represented by t or tt is pronounced in most American speech as a voiced flap produced by the tongue tip tapping the teethridge (IPA [ɾ]). In similar contexts the sound represented by d or dd has the same pronunciation. Thus, the pairs *ladder* and *latter, leader* and *liter, parody* and *parity* are often homophones. At the end of a syllable \t\ often has an incomplete articulation with no release, or it is accompanied or replaced by a glottal closure. When \t\ occurs before the syllabic consonant \ᵊn\ as in *button* \'bə-tᵊn\, the glottal allophone is often heard. This may reflect a syllabication of \t\ with the preceding stressed syllable (i.e., \'bət-ᵊn\).

Many speakers pronounce \t\ like \ch\ when it occurs before \r\ in the same syllable.

\ th \ as in thin, ether (IPA [θ]). Actually, this is a single sound, not two. When the two sounds \t\ and \h\ occur in sequence they are separated by a hyphen in this book, as in *knighthood* \'nīt-ˌhud\. In some dialects of American English, \th\ is regularly replaced by \f\.

\ t͟h \ as in then, either, this (IPA [ð]). Actually, this is a single sound, not two. The difference between \th\ and \t͟h\ is that the former is pronounced without and the latter with vibration of the vocal cords.

\ ü \ as in rule, youth, union \'yün-yən\, few \'fyü\ (IPA [u]). As an unstressed vowel before another vowel, \ü\ is often pronounced as a schwa with slight lip rounding that is separated from the following vowel by the glide \w\, as in *valuing* \'val-yə-wiŋ\. This reduced variant is not usually shown at individual entries. Younger speakers of American English often use a more centralized and less rounded pronunciation of \ü\ in certain words (as *news* and *musician*), both in stressed and especially in unstressed syllables.

Some speakers pronounce \ü\ and \ù\ identically before \l\, with the result that word pairs like *pool* and *pull* are homophones. The sound pronounced in such cases may be either \ü\ or \ù\ as pronounced by those who distinguish the two.

\ ù \ as in pull, wood, book (IPA [ʊ]). Some speakers pronounce \ü\ and \ù\ identically before \l\, with the result that word pairs like *pool* and *pull* are homophones. The sound pronounced in such cases may be either \ü\ or \ù\ as pronounced by those who distinguish the two.

\ ue \ as in German füllen "to fill," hübsch "handsome" (IPA [y]). This vowel, which occurs only in foreign-derived terms and names, can be approximated by attempting to pronounce the vowel \i\ with the lips moderately rounded as for the vowel \ù\.

This symbol is also used to represent the vowel in French rue "street," German fühlen "to feel" (IPA [y]). This vowel, which occurs only in foreign-derived terms and names, can be approximated by attempting to pronounce the vowel \ē\ with the lips fully rounded as for the vowel \ü\.

\ ùr \ as in poor, tour, insure (IPA [uɚ, ʊɚ]). The initial element of this diphthong may vary from \ù\ to \ü\. Speakers of r-dropping dialects will pronounce \ùr\ without any r-color on the second element (IPA [uə, ʊə]) when it precedes a consonant or pause, but will usually insert an \r\ after \ùr\ when it precedes a vowel. (See the section on \r\.) Many speakers do not have the dipththong \ùr\ and have merged it with either \ər\ (when it follows palatal consonants such as \sh\, \ch\, or \y\ in words like *sure, mature,* or *obscure*) or \òr\ (in other environments). Similarly, many speakers of r-dropping dialects have merged \ùr\ with \ər\ and \ò\ in the same respective environments.

\ v \ as in vivid, invite (IPA [v]).

\ w \ as in we, away (IPA [w]).

\ y \ as in yard, young, cue \'kyü\, curable \'kyúr-ə-bəl\, few \'fyü\, fury \'fyúr-ē\, union \'yün-yən\ (IPA [j]). The sequences \lyü\, \syü\, and \zyü\ in the same syllable, as in *lewd, suit,* and *presume,* are common in southern British speech but are rare in American speech and only \lü\, \sü\, and \zü\ are shown in this dictionary. A sequence of \h\ and \y\ as in *hue* and *huge* is pronounced by some speakers as a \k\ articulated toward the front of the mouth (IPA [ç]).

\ ʸ \ indicates that during the articulation of the preceding consonant the tongue has substantially the position it has for the articulation of the \y\ of *yard*, as in French *digne* \dēnʸ\ "worthy." Thus \ʸ\ does not itself represent a sound but rather modifies the preceding symbol.

\ z \ as in zone, raise (IPA [z]).

\ zh \ as in vision, azure \'a-zhər\ (IPA [ʒ]). Actually, this is a single sound, not two. When the two sounds \z\ and \h\ occur in sequence, they are separated by a hyphen in this book, as in *hogshead* \'hògz-ˌhed, 'hägz-\.

Abbreviations in This Work

Additional abbreviations are entered in the main vocabulary of this dictionary.

A.&M. Agricultural and Mechanical
ab about
abbr abbreviation
abl ablative
Acad Academy
acc accusative
act active
A.D. anno Domini
adj adjective
adv adverb
AF Anglo-French
AFB Air Force Base
Afr African
Afrik Afrikaans
Agric Agriculture
Alb Albanian
alter alteration
Am America, American
Amer American
AmerF American French
AmerInd American Indian
AmerSp American Spanish
anc ancient, anciently
ant antonym
anthropol anthropologist, anthropology
aor aorist
Ar Arabic
Arab Arabian
Aram Aramaic
archaeol archaeologist
Arm Armenian
art article
astron astronomer, astronomy
attrib attributive, attributively
atty attorney
aug augmentative
Austral Australian
Av Avestan
AV Authorized Version
b born
bacteriol bacteriologist
B.C. before Christ, British Columbia
bef before
Belg Belgian
Beng Bengali
bet between
bib biblical
biochem biochemist
biol biologist
Braz Brazilian
BrazPg Brazilian Portuguese
Bret Breton
Brit Britain, British
bro brother
Bulg Bulgarian
c century
C centigrade, College
ca circa
Canad Canadian
CanF Canadian French
cap capital, capitalized
Catal Catalan
caus causative
Celt Celtic
cen central

cent century
chem chemist
Chin Chinese
comb combining
Comm Community
compar comparative
Confed Confederate
conj conjugation, conjunction
constr construction
contr contraction
Copt Coptic
Corn Cornish
criminol criminologist
d died
D Dutch
Dan Daniel, Danish
dat dative
dau daughter
def definite
dial dialect
dim diminutive
disc discovered
Dor Doric
dram dramatist
Du Dutch
DV Douay Version
e eastern
E east, eastern, English
econ economist
Ed Education
educ educator
EGmc East Germanic
Egypt Egyptian
emp emperor
Eng England, English
equiv equivalent
esp especially
est estimated
ethnol ethnologist
exc except
F Fahrenheit, French
fem feminine
Finn Finnish
fl flourished
Flem Flemish
fr from
Fr France, French
freq frequentative
Fris Frisian
ft feet
fut future
G German
Gael Gaelic
gen general, genitive
Ger German
Gk Greek
Gmc Germanic
Goth Gothic
gov governor
govt government
Gr Brit Great Britain
Heb Hebrew
hist historian
Hitt Hittite
Hung Hungarian
Icel Icelandic
IE Indo-European
imit imitative

imper imperative
incho inchoative
indef indefinite
indic indicative
infin infinitive
Inst Institute
instr instrumental
intens intensive
interj interjection
interrog interrogative
Ir Irish
irreg irregular
Is island
ISV International Scientific Vocabulary
It, Ital Italian
ital italic
Jav Javanese
Jp Japanese
L Latin
LaF Louisiana French
lat latitude
Lat Latin
LG Low German
LGk Late Greek
LHeb Late Hebrew
lit literally, literary
Lith Lithuanian
LL Late Latin
long longitude
m meters
manuf manufacturer
masc masculine
math mathematician
MBret Middle Breton
MD Middle Dutch
ME Middle English
Mech Mechanical
Med Medical
Mex Mexican, Mexico
MexSp Mexican Spanish
MF Middle French
MGk Middle Greek
MHG Middle High German
mi miles
mil military
min minister
MIr Middle Irish
ML Medieval Latin
MLG Middle Low German
ModE Modern English
ModGk Modern Greek
ModHeb Modern Hebrew
modif modification
MPers Middle Persian
MS manuscript
mt mountain
Mt Mount
MW Middle Welsh
n northern, noun
N north, northern
naut nautical
NE northeast
neut neuter
NewEng New England
NewZeal New Zealand
Nfld.&Lab. Newfoundland and Labrador

NL New Latin
No North
nom nominative
nonstand nonstandard
Norw Norwegian
nov novelist
n pl noun plural
NZ New Zealand
obs obsolete
occas occasionally
OCS Old Church Slavic
ODan Old Danish
OE Old English
OF Old French
OFris Old Frisian
OHG Old High German
OIr Old Irish
OIt Old Italian
OL Old Latin
ON Old Norse
OPers Old Persian
OPg Old Portuguese
OProv Old Provençal
OPruss Old Prussian
orig original, originally
ORuss Old Russian
OS Old Saxon
OSp Old Spanish
OSw Old Swedish
OW Old Welsh
PaG Pennsylvania German
part participle
pass passive
Pers Persian
perf perfect
perh perhaps
pers person
Pg Portuguese
philos philosopher

PhilSp Philippine Spanish
physiol physiologist
pl plural
Pol Polish
polit political, politician
pop population
Port Portuguese
pp past participle
prec preceding
prep preposition
pres present, president
prob probably
pron pronoun, pronunciation
pronunc pronunciation
prp present participle
Pruss Prussian
pseud pseudonym
psychol psychologist
R.C. Roman Catholic
REB Revised English Bible
redupl reduplication
refl reflexive
rel relative
resp respectively
rev revolution
Rom Roman, Romanian
RSV Revised Standard Version
Russ Russian
S south, southern
Sc Scottish, Scots
Scand Scandinavian
ScGael Scottish Gaelic
Sch School
Scot Scotland, Scottish
secy secretary
Sem Seminary, Semitic
Shak Shakespeare
sing singular

Skt Sanskrit
Slav Slavic
So South
SoAfr South Africa, South African
sociol sociologist
Sp, Span Spanish
specif specifically
spp species
St Saint
Ste Sainte
subj subjunctive
subsp subspecies
substand substandard
superl superlative
Sw, Swed Swedish
syn synonym, synonymy
Syr Syriac
Tag Tagalog
Tech Technology
theol theologian
Theol Theological
Toch Tocharian
trans translation
treas treasury
Turk Turkish
U University
ultim ultimately
usu usually
var variant, variety
v, vb verb
vi verb intransitive
VL Vulgar Latin
voc vocative
vt verb transitive
W Welsh, west, western
WGmc West Germanic
zool zoologist

Pronunciation Symbols

For more information see the Guide to Pronunciation.

ə	....	banana, collide, abut
ˈə, ˌə	....	humdrum, abut
ə	....	immediately preceding \l\, \n\, \m\, \ŋ\, as in battle, mitten, eaten, and sometimes open \ˈō-pᵊm\, lock and key \-ᵊŋ-\; immediately following \l\, \m\, \r\, as often in French table, prisme, titre
ər	....	further, merger, bird
ˈər- ˈə-r	....	as in two different pronunciations of hurry \ˈhər-ē, ˈhə-rē\
a	....	mat, map, mad, gag, snap, patch
ā	....	day, fade, date, aorta, drape, cape
ä	....	bother, cot
är	....	car, heart, bazaar, bizarre
au̇	....	now, loud, out
b	....	baby, rib
ch	....	chin, nature \ˈnā-chər\
d	....	did, adder
e	....	bet, bed, peck
er	....	bare, fair, wear, millionaire
ˈē, ˌē	....	beat, nosebleed, evenly, easy
ē	....	easy, mealy
f	....	fifty, cuff
g	....	go, big, gift
h	....	hat, ahead
hw	....	whale as pronounced by those who do not have the same pronunciation for both *whale* and *wail*
i	....	tip, banish, active
ir	....	near, deer, mere, pier
ī	....	site, side, buy, tripe
j	....	job, gem, edge, join, judge
k	....	kin, cook, ache
k̲	....	German ich, Buch; one pronunciation of loch
l	....	lily, pool
m	....	murmur, dim, nymph
n	....	no, own
ⁿ	....	indicates that a preceding vowel or diphthong is pronounced with the nasal passages open, as in French un bon vin blanc \œⁿ-bōⁿ-vaⁿ-bläⁿ\
ŋ	....	sing \ˈsiŋ\, singer \ˈsiŋ-ər\, finger \ˈfiŋ-gər\, ink \ˈiŋk\

ō	....	bone, know, beau
ȯ	....	saw, all, gnaw, caught
œ	....	French boeuf, feu, German Hölle, Höhle
ȯi	....	coin, destroy
ȯr	....	boar, port, door, shore
p	....	pepper, lip
r	....	red, rarity
s	....	source, less
sh	....	as in shy, mission, machine, special (actually, this is a single sound, not two); with a hyphen between, two sounds as in *grasshopper* \ˈgras-ˌhä-pər\
t	....	tie, attack, late, later, latter
th	....	as in thin, ether (actually, this is a single sound, not two); with a hyphen between, two sounds as in *knighthood* \ˈnīt-ˌhu̇d\
t̲h̲	....	then, either, this (actually, this is a single sound, not two)
ü	....	rule, youth, union \ˈyün-yən\, few \ˈfyü\
u̇	....	pull, wood, book
ue	....	German füllen, hübsch, fühlen, French rue
u̇r	....	boor, tour, insure
v	....	vivid, give
w	....	we, away
y	....	yard, young, cue \ˈkyü\, mute \ˈmyüt\, union \ˈyün-yən\
ʸ	....	indicates that during the articulation of the sound represented by the preceding character, the front of the tongue has substantially the position it has for the articulation of the first sound of *yard*, as in French digne \dēnʸ\
z	....	zone, raise
zh	....	as in vision, azure \ˈa-zhər\ (actually, this is a single sound, not two); with hyphen between, two sounds as in *hogshead* \ˈhȯgz-ˌhed, ˈhägz-\
\	....	reversed virgule used in pairs to mark the beginning and end of a transcription: \ˈpen\
ˈ	....	mark preceding a syllable with primary (strongest) stress: \ˈpen-mən-ˌship\
ˌ	....	mark preceding a syllable with secondary (medium) stress: \ˈpen-mən-ˌship\
-	....	mark of syllable division
( )	....	indicate that what is symbolized between is present in some utterances but not in others: *factory* \ˈfak-t(ə-)rē\
÷	....	indicates that many regard as unacceptable the pronunciation variant immediately following: *nuclear* \ˈnü-klē-ər, ˈnyü-, ÷-kyə-lər\

A Dictionary of the English Language

A

¹a \'ā\ *n, pl* **a's** *or* **as** \'āz\ *often cap, often attrib* (bef. 12c) **1 a** : the 1st letter of the English alphabet **b** : a graphic representation of this letter **c** : a speech counterpart of orthographic *a* **2** : the sixth tone of a C-major scale **3** : a graphic device for reproducing the letter *a* **4** : one designated *a* esp. as the first in order or class **5 a** : a grade rating a student's work as superior in quality **b** : one graded or rated with an A **6** : something shaped like the letter A **7** *cap* : the one of the four ABO blood groups characterized by the presence of antigens designated by the letter A and by the presence of antibodies against the antigens present in the B blood group

²a \ə, (')ā, *Canad* 'a\ *indefinite article* [ME, fr. OE *ān* one — more at ONE] (bef. 12c) **1** — used as a function word before singular nouns when the referent is unspecified ⟨*a* man overboard⟩ and before number collectives and some numbers ⟨*a* dozen⟩ **2** : the same ⟨birds of *a* feather⟩ ⟨swords all of *a* length⟩ **3 a** — used as a function word before a singular noun followed by a restrictive modifier ⟨*a* man who was here yesterday⟩ **b** : ANY ⟨*a* man who is sick can't work⟩ **c** — used as a function word before a mass noun to denote a particular type or instance ⟨*a* bronze made in ancient times⟩ **d** — used as a function word before a proper noun representing an example or type ⟨the attractions of *a* Boston or *a* Cleveland⟩ **e** — used as a function word before a proper noun to indicate limited knowledge about the referent ⟨*a* Mr. Smith called to inquire about the job⟩ **f** — used as a function word before a proper noun to distinguish the condition of the referent from a usual, former, or hypothetical condition ⟨*a* triumphant Ms. Jones greeted her supporters⟩ **4** — used as a function word before nouns to form adverbial phrases of quantity, amount, or degree ⟨felt *a* bit tired⟩ *usage* In speech and writing *a* is used before a consonant sound ⟨*a* door⟩ ⟨*a* human⟩. Before a vowel sound *an* is usual ⟨*an* icicle⟩ ⟨*an* honor⟩ but esp. in speech *a* is used occasionally, more often in some dialects than in others ⟨*a* apple⟩ ⟨*a* hour⟩ ⟨*a* obligation⟩. Before a consonant sound represented by a vowel letter *a* is usual ⟨*a* one⟩ ⟨*a* union⟩ but *an* also occurs though less frequently now than formerly ⟨*an* unique⟩ ⟨such *an* one⟩. Before unstressed or weakly stressed syllables with initial *h* both *a* and *an* are used in writing ⟨*a* historic⟩ ⟨*an* historic⟩. In the King James Version of the Old Testament and occasionally in writing and speech *an* is used before *h* in a stressed syllable ⟨*an* huntress⟩ ⟨*an* hundred⟩ ⟨children are *an* heritage of the Lord —Ps 127:3(AV)⟩.

³a \ə\ *prep* [ME, fr. OE *a-, an, on*] (bef. 12c) **1** *chiefly dial* : ON, IN, AT **2** : in, to, or for each ⟨twice *a* week⟩ *usage* see ²A

⁴a \ə\ *vb* [ME, contr. of *have*] (14c) *archaic* : HAVE ⟨I might *a* had husbands afore now —John Bunyan⟩

⁵a \ə\ *prep* [ME, by contr.] (15c) : OF — often attached to the preceding word ⟨kind*a*⟩ ⟨lott*a*⟩

⁶a *abbr* **1** absent **2** acceleration **3** acre **4** adult **5** alto **6** anode **7** answer **8** ante **9** anterior **10** are **11** area **12** atto- **13** author

¹a- \ə\ *prefix* [ME, fr. OE] **1** : on : in : at ⟨*a*bed⟩ **2** : in (such) a state or condition ⟨*a*fire⟩ **3** : in (such) a manner ⟨*a*loud⟩ **4** : in the act or process of ⟨gone *a*-hunting⟩ ⟨*a*tingle⟩

²a- \(')ā *also* (')a *or* (')ä\ *or* **an-** \(')an\ *prefix* [L & Gk; L, fr. Gk — more at UN-] : not : without ⟨*a*sexual⟩ — *a-* before consonants other than *h* and sometimes even before *h, an-* before vowels and usu. before *h* ⟨*a*chromatic⟩ ⟨*a*historical⟩ ⟨*an*astigmatic⟩ ⟨*an*hydrous⟩

-a- *comb form* [ISV] : replacing carbon esp. in a ring ⟨*a*za-⟩

-a \ə\ *n suffix* [NL, fr. *-a* (as in *magnesia*)] : OXIDE ⟨silic*a*⟩

A *abbr* **1** ace **2** adenine **3** ampere

A *symbol* argon

Å *abbr* angstrom unit

aa *abbr* ana

AA *abbr* **1** administrative assistant **2** Alcoholics Anonymous **3** antiaircraft **4** associate in arts **5** author's alterations

AAA *abbr* **1** Agricultural Adjustment Administration **2** American Automobile Association

AAAL *abbr* American Academy of Arts and Letters

AAAS *abbr* American Association for the Advancement of Science

AAC \,ā-,ā-'sē\ *n* [*A*dvanced *A*udio *C*oding] (1997) : a high-quality standardized computer file format for lossy compression and storage of digital audio data

AAFP *abbr* American Academy of Family Physicians

aah *also* **ah** \'ä, *often prolonged and/or followed by* ə\ *vi* (1843) : to exclaim in amazement, joy, or surprise ⟨oohing and ∼ing at the fireworks⟩ — **aah** *also* **ah** *n*

AAMC *abbr* Association of American Medical Colleges

A and M *abbr* **1** agricultural and mechanical **2** ancient and modern

A and R *abbr* artists and repertory; artists and repertoire

AAR *abbr* against all risks

aard·vark \'ärd-,värk\ *n* [obs. Afrik (now *erdvark*), fr. Afrik *aard* earth + *vark* pig] (1822) : a large burrowing nocturnal mammal (*Orycteropus afer*) of sub-Saharan Africa that has a long snout, extensible tongue, powerful claws, large ears, and heavy tail and feeds esp. on termites and ants

aard·wolf \-,wu̇lf\ *n, pl* **aard·wolves** \-,wu̇lvz\ [Afrik, fr. *aard* + *wolf*] (1833) : a maned striped nocturnal mammal (*Proteles cristatus*) of southern and eastern Africa that resembles the related hyenas and feeds chiefly on insects and esp. termites

aardwolf

Aar·on \'a-rən, 'er-ən\ *n* [LL, fr. Gk *Aarōn*, fr. Heb *Ahărōn*] (bef. 12c) : a brother of Moses and high priest of the Hebrews

Aa·ron·ic \a-'rä-nik, er-'ä-\ *adj* (1821) **1** : of or stemming from Aaron **2** : of or relating to the lower order of the Mormon priesthood

AARP *abbr* American Association of Retired Persons

AAS *abbr* associate in applied science

AASCU *abbr* American Association of State Colleges and Universities

AAU *abbr* Amateur Athletic Union

AAUP *abbr* American Association of University Professors

AAUW *abbr* American Association of University Women

AAVE *abbr* African-American Vernacular English

¹ab \'ab\ *n* (1956) : an abdominal muscle — usu. used in pl.

²ab *abbr* about

Ab \'äb, 'av, 'o̅v\ *n* [Heb *Ābh*] (ca. 1771) : the 11th month of the civil year or the 5th month of the ecclesiastical year in the Jewish calendar — see MONTH table

¹AB \'ā-'bē\ *n* (1927) : the one of the four ABO blood groups characterized by the presence of antigens designated by the letters A and B and by the absence of antibodies against these antigens

²AB *abbr* **1** able seaman; able-bodied seaman **2** airborne **3** airman basic **4** Alberta **5** [NL *artium baccalaureus*] bachelor of arts

ab- *prefix* [ME, fr. AF & L; AF, fr. L *ab-, abs-, a-*, fr. *ab, a* — more at OF] : from : away : off ⟨*ab*axial⟩

aba \ə-'bä, a-, 'ä-bə\ *n* [Ar *'abā'*] (1811) **1** : a loose sleeveless outer garment worn as traditional dress by men in the Middle East **2** : a fabric woven from the hair of camels or goats

ABA *abbr* **1** Amateur Boxing Association **2** American Bankers Association **3** American Bar Association **4** American Booksellers Association

ab·a·ca \,a-bə-'kä, ,ä-bə-\ *n* [Sp *abacá*, fr. Tag *abaká*] (ca. 1805) **1** : a strong fiber obtained from the leafstalk of a banana (*Musa textilis*) native to the Philippines — called also *Manila hemp* **2** : the plant that yields abaca

aback \ə-'bak\ *adv* (bef. 12c) **1** *archaic* : BACKWARD, BACK **2** : in a position to catch the wind upon the forward surface (as of a sail) **3** : by surprise : UNAWARES ⟨was taken ∼ by her sharp retort⟩

abac·te·ri·al \,ā-(,)bak-'tir-ē-əl\ *adj* (1888) : not caused by or characterized by the presence of bacteria ⟨∼ prostatitis⟩

aba·cus \'a-bə-kəs, ə-'ba-\ *n, pl* **aba·ci** \'a-bə-,sī, -,kē; ə-'ba-,kī\ *or* **aba·cus·es** [L, fr. Gk *abak-, abax*, lit., slab] (14c) **1** : an instrument for performing calculations by sliding counters along rods or in grooves **2** : a slab that forms the uppermost member or division of the capital of a column

¹abaft *adv* [ME, fr. *a-* + *baft* in the rear, fr. OE *bæftan*, fr. *be-* + *æftan* behind — more at AFT] (15c) : toward or at the stern : AFT

²abaft \ə-'baft\ *prep* (1594) : to the rear of; *specif* : toward the stern from

ab·a·lo·ne \,a-bə-'lō-nē, 'a-bə-,\ *n* [AmerSp *abulón*, fr. Rumsen (American Indian language of Monterey Bay, Calif.) *aulon*] (1850) : any of a genus (*Haliotis*) of edible rock-clinging gastropod mollusks that have a flattened shell slightly spiral in form, lined with mother-of-pearl, and with a row of apertures along its outer edge

¹aban·don \ə-'ban-dən\ *vt* [ME *abandounen*, fr. AF *abanduner* (*mettre*) *a bandun* to hand over, put in someone's control] (14c) **1 a** : to give up to the control or influence of another person or agent **b** : to give up with the intent of never again claiming a right or interest in ⟨∼ property⟩ **2** : to withdraw from often in the face of danger or encroachment ⟨∼ ship⟩ **3** : to withdraw protection, support, or help from ⟨he ∼ed his family⟩ **4** : to give (oneself) over unrestrainedly **5 a** : to cease from maintaining, practicing, or using ⟨∼ed their native

---

\ə\ **abut**	\ᵊ\ **kitten**, F **table** \ər\ **further** \a\ **ash** \ā\ **ace** \ä\ **mop**, **mar**
\au̇\ **out**	\ch\ **chin** \e\ **bet** \ē\ **easy** \g\ **go** \i\ **hit** \ī\ **ice** \j\ **job**
\ŋ\ **sing**	\ō\ **go** \ȯ\ **law** \ȯi\ **boy** \th\ **thin** \th̲\ **the** \ü\ **loot** \u̇\ **foot**
\y\ **yet**	\zh\ **vision**, **beige** \k, ⁿ, œ, ɶ, ʸ\ *see* Guide to Pronunciation

language⟩ **b :** to cease intending or attempting to perform ⟨~*ed* the escape⟩ — **aban·don·er** *n* — **aban·don·ment** \-dən-mənt\ *n*

syn ABANDON, DESERT, FORSAKE mean to leave without intending to return. ABANDON suggests that the thing or person left may be helpless without protection ⟨*abandoned* children⟩. DESERT implies that the object left may be weakened but not destroyed by one's absence ⟨a *deserted* town⟩. FORSAKE suggests an action more likely to bring impoverishment or bereavement to that which is forsaken than its exposure to physical dangers ⟨a *forsaken* lover⟩. ***syn*** see in addition RELINQUISH

[2]**abandon** *n* (1822) **:** a thorough yielding to natural impulses; *esp* **:** ENTHUSIASM, EXUBERANCE ⟨with reckless ~⟩

aban·doned \ə-ˈban-dənd\ *adj* (14c) **1 :** wholly free from restraint **2 :** given up **:** FORSAKEN

à bas \ä-ˈbä\ [F] (ca. 1897) **:** down with ⟨*à bas* the profiteers⟩

abase \ə-ˈbās\ *vt* **abased; abas·ing** [ME *abassen,* fr. AF *abesser, abaisser,* fr. *a-* (fr. L *ad-*) + *-besser,* fr. VL **bassiare* to lower] (15c) **1** *archaic* **:** to lower physically **2 :** to lower in rank, office, prestige, or esteem — **abase·ment** \-ˈbās-mənt\ *n*

abash \ə-ˈbash\ *vt* [ME *abaishen,* fr. AF *abaiss-, abair* to astonish, alter. of *esbair,* fr. *ex-* + *baer* to open wide, gape — more at ABEYANCE] (14c) **:** to destroy the self-possession or self-confidence of **:** DISCONCERT ***syn*** see EMBARRASS — **abash·ment** \-mənt\ *n*

abate \ə-ˈbāt\ *vb* **abat·ed; abat·ing** [ME, fr. AF *abatre* to strike down — more at REBATE] *vt* (13c) **1 a :** to put an end to ⟨~ a nuisance⟩ **b :** NULLIFY 1 ⟨~ a writ⟩ **2 a :** to reduce in degree or intensity **:** MODERATE ⟨may ~ their rancor to win peace⟩ **b :** to reduce in value or amount **:** make less esp. by way of relief ⟨~ a tax⟩ **3 :** DEDUCT, OMIT ⟨~ part of the price⟩ **4 a :** to beat down or cut away so as to leave a figure in relief **b** *obs* **:** BLUNT **5 :** DEPRIVE 2 ~ *vi* **1 :** to decrease in force or intensity **2 a :** to become defeated or become null or void **b :** to decrease in amount or value — **abat·er** *n*

syn ABATE, SUBSIDE, WANE, EBB mean to die down in force or intensity. ABATE stresses the idea of progressive diminishing ⟨the storm *abated*⟩. SUBSIDE implies the ceasing of turbulence or agitation ⟨the protests *subsided* after a few days⟩. WANE suggests the fading or weakening of something good or impressive ⟨*waning* enthusiasm⟩. EBB suggests the receding of something (as the tide) that commonly comes and goes ⟨the *ebbing* of daylight⟩. ***syn*** see in addition DECREASE

abate·ment \ə-ˈbāt-mənt\ *n* (14c) **1 :** the act or process of abating **:** the state of being abated **2 :** an amount abated; *esp* **:** a deduction from the full amount of a tax

ab·a·tis \ˈa-bə-ˌtē, ˈa-bə-təs\ *n, pl* **ab·a·tis** \ˈa-bə-ˌtēz\ *or* **ab·a·tis·es** \ˈa-bə-tə-səz\ [F, fr. *abattre* to strike down, slaughter, fr. OF *abatre*] (1766) **:** a defensive obstacle formed by felled trees with sharpened branches facing the enemy

ab·at·toir \ˈa-bə-ˌtwär, -ˌtwȯr, -ˌtȯr\ *n* [F, fr. *abattre*] (1820) **:** SLAUGHTERHOUSE

ab·ax·i·al \(ˌ)a-ˈbak-sē-əl\ *adj* (1857) **:** situated out of or directed away from the axis ⟨the ~ or lower surface of a leaf⟩

aba·ya \ə-ˈbī-ə\ *n* [Ar *ʿabāya*] (1836) **:** a loose-fitting full-length robe worn by some Muslim women

ab·ba·cy \ˈa-bə-sē\ *n, pl* **-cies** [ME *abbatie,* fr. LL *abbatia*] (15c) **:** the office, dignity, jurisdiction, or tenure of an abbot

Ab·bas·id \ə-ˈba-səd, ˈa-bə-səd\ *n* (1788) **:** a member of a dynasty of caliphs (750–1258) ruling the Islamic empire esp. from their capital Baghdad and claiming descent from Abbas the uncle of Muhammad

ab·ba·tial \ə-ˈbā-shəl, a-\ *adj* (ca. 1642) **:** of or relating to an abbot, abbess, or abbey

ab·bé \a-ˈbā, ˈa-ˌbā\ *n* [F, fr. LL *abbat-, abbas*] (1530) **:** a member of the French secular clergy in major or minor orders — used as a title

ab·bess \ˈa-bəs\ *n* [ME *abbesse,* fr. AF, fr. LL *abbatissa,* fem. of *abbat-, abbas*] (13c) **:** a woman who is the superior of a convent of nuns

Abbe·vil·li·an \ˌab-ˈvi-lē-ən, ˌa-bə-\ *adj* [*Abbeville,* France] (ca. 1934) **:** of or relating to an early Lower Paleolithic culture of Europe characterized by bifacial stone hand axes

ab·bey \ˈa-bē\ *n, pl* **abbeys** [ME, fr. AF *abbaie, abbeie,* fr. LL *abbatia* abbey, fr. *abbat-, abbas*] (13c) **1 a :** a monastery ruled by an abbot **b :** a convent ruled by an abbess **2 :** an abbey church

ab·bot \ˈa-bət\ *n* [ME *abbod,* fr. OE, fr. LL *abbat-, abbas,* fr. LGk *abbas,* fr. Aram *abbā* father] (bef. 12c) **:** the superior of a monastery for men

abbr *abbr* abbreviation

ab·bre·vi·ate \ə-ˈbrē-vē-ˌāt\ *vt* **-at·ed; -at·ing** [ME, fr. LL *abbreviatus,* pp. of *abbreviare* — more at ABRIDGE] (15c) **:** to make briefer; *esp* **:** to reduce to a shorter form intended to stand for the whole ***syn*** see SHORTEN — **ab·bre·vi·a·tor** \-ˌā-tər\ *n*

ab·bre·vi·a·tion \ə-ˌbrē-vē-ˈā-shən\ *n* (15c) **1 :** the act or result of abbreviating **:** ABRIDGMENT **2 :** a shortened form of a written word or phrase used in place of the whole ⟨*amt* is an ~ for *amount*⟩

[1]**ABC** \ˌā-(ˌ)bē-ˈsē\ *n, pl* **ABC's** *or* **ABCs** \-ˈsēz\ (13c) **1 :** ALPHABET — usu. used in pl. **2 a :** the rudiments of reading, writing, and spelling — usu. used in pl. **b :** the rudiments of a subject — usu. used in pl.

[2]**ABC** *abbr* **1** American Bowling Congress **2** American Broadcasting Companies **3** Australian Broadcasting Corporation

ABCD *abbr* accelerated business collection and delivery

abd *or* **abdom** *abbr* abdomen; abdominal

ABD \ˌā-(ˌ)bē-ˈdē\ *n, pl* **ABDs** *also* **ABD's** [*a*ll *b*ut *d*issertation] (1965) **:** a doctoral candidate who has completed required courses and examinations but not a dissertation

Ab·di·as \ab-ˈdī-əs\ *n* [LL, fr. Gk] (14c) **:** OBADIAH

ab·di·cate \ˈab-di-ˌkāt\ *vb* **-cat·ed; -cat·ing** [L *abdicatus,* pp. of *abdicare,* fr. *ab-* + *dicare* to proclaim — more at DICTION] *vt* (1541) **1 :** to cast off **:** DISCARD **2 :** to relinquish (as sovereign power) formally ~ *vi* **:** to renounce a throne, high office, dignity, or function — **ab·di·ca·ble** \-kə-bəl\ *adj* — **ab·di·ca·tion** \ˌab-di-ˈkā-shən\ *n* — **ab·di·ca·tor** \ˈab-di-ˌkā-tər\ *n*

syn ABDICATE, RENOUNCE, RESIGN mean to give up a position with no possibility of resuming it. ABDICATE implies a giving up of sovereign power or sometimes an evading of responsibility such as that of a parent ⟨*abdicated* the throne⟩. RENOUNCE may replace it but often implies additionally a sacrifice for a greater end ⟨*renounced* her inheritance by marrying a commoner⟩. RESIGN applies to the giving up of an unexpired office or trust ⟨*resigned* from the board⟩.

ab·do·men \ˈab-də-mən, -ˌdō-; əb-ˈdō-mən, ab-\ *n* [MF & L; MF, fr. L] (1543) **1 :** the part of the body between the thorax and the pelvis; *also* **:** the cavity of this part of the trunk containing the chief viscera **2 :** the posterior section of the body behind the thorax in an arthropod — see INSECT illustration — **ab·dom·i·nal** \ab-ˈdä-mə-nᵊl, əb-, -ˈdäm-nᵊl\ *adj* — **ab·dom·i·nal·ly** \-ē\ *adv*

ab·du·cens nerve \ab-ˈdü-ˌsenz-, -ˈdyü-\ *n* [NL *abducent-, abducens,* fr. L, prp. of *abducere*] (1947) **:** either of the sixth pair of cranial nerves that are motor nerves supplying the rectus on the outer and lateral side of each eye — called also *abducens*

ab·du·cent nerve \ab-ˈdü-sᵊnt-, -ˈdyü-\ *n* (1875) **:** ABDUCENS NERVE

ab·duct \ab-ˈdəkt, əb-; *2 also* ˈab-ˌ\ *vt* [L *abductus,* pp. of *abducere,* lit., to lead away, fr. *ab-* + *ducere* to lead — more at TOW] (1825) **1 :** to seize and take away (as a person) by force **2 :** to draw or spread away (as a limb or the fingers) from a position near or parallel to the median axis of the body or from the axis of a limb — **ab·duc·tor** \-ˈdək-tər\ *n*

ab·duct·ee \ˌab-ˌdək-ˈtē\ *n* (1975) **:** a person who has been abducted

ab·duc·tion \ab-ˈdək-shən, əb-\ *n* (1666) **1 :** the action of abducting **:** the condition of being abducted **2 :** the unlawful carrying away of a woman for marriage or intercourse

abeam \ə-ˈbēm\ *adv or adj* (ca. 1836) **:** off to the side of a ship or plane esp. at a right angle to the middle of the ship or plane's length

[1]**abe·ce·dar·i·an** \ˌā-bē-(ˌ)sē-ˈder-ē-ən\ *n* [ME *abecedary,* fr. ML *abecedarium* alphabet, fr. LL, neut. of *abecedarius* of the alphabet, fr. the letters *a* + *b* + *c* + *d*] (1603) **:** one learning the rudiments of something (as the alphabet)

[2]**abecedarian** *adj* (1665) **1 a :** of or relating to the alphabet **b :** alphabetically arranged **2 :** RUDIMENTARY

abed \ə-ˈbed\ *adv or adj* (13c) **:** in bed

Abel \ˈā-bəl\ *n* [LL, fr. Gk, fr. Heb *Hebhel*] (bef. 12c) **:** a son of Adam and Eve killed by his brother Cain

abe·lia \ə-ˈbēl-yə\ *n* [NL, fr. Clarke *Abel* †1826 Eng. botanist] (ca. 1899) **:** any of a genus (*Abelia*) of Asian or Mexican shrubs of the honeysuckle family having opposite leaves and white, red, or pink flowers

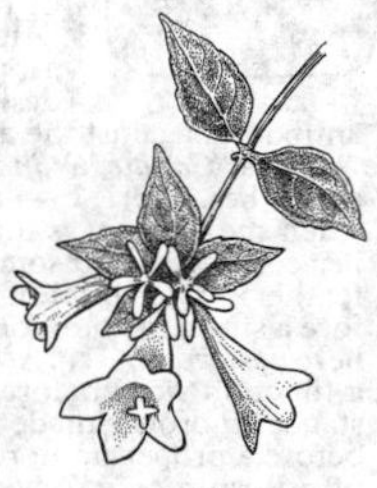
abelia

abe·li·an \ə-ˈbē-lē-ən\ *adj, often cap* [Niels *Abel* †1829 Norw. mathematician] (1847) **:** COMMUTATIVE 2 ⟨~ group⟩ ⟨~ ring⟩

Abe·na·ki \ˌa-bə-ˈnä-kē\ *also* **Ab·na·ki** \ab-ˈnä-kē\ *n, pl* **Abenaki** *or* **Abenakis** *also* **Abnaki** *or* **Abnakis** [Eastern Abenaki *wọpánahki,* Western Abenaki *wọbanakii,* lit., dawn land people, easterners] (1721) **1 :** a member of a group of American Indian peoples of northern New England and adjoining parts of Quebec **2 :** either of the two Algonquian languages spoken by the Abenaki peoples

Ab·er·deen An·gus \ˈa-bər-ˌdēn-ˈaŋ-gəs\ *n* [*Aberdeen & Angus,* counties in Scotland] (1862) **:** ANGUS

[1]**ab·er·rant** \ˈa-bər-ənt, ə-, -ˈbe-rənt; ˈa-bə-rənt, -ˌber-ənt, -ˌbe-rənt\ *adj* [L *aberrant-, aberrans,* prp. of *aberrare* to go astray, fr. *ab-* + *errare* to wander, err] (ca. 1780) **1 :** straying from the right or normal way **2 :** deviating from the usual or natural type **:** ATYPICAL — **ab·er·rance** \-ən(t)s\ *n* — **ab·er·ran·cy** \-ən(t)-sē\ *n* — **ab·er·rant·ly** *adv*

[2]**aberrant** *n* (1938) **1 :** an aberrant group, individual, or structure **2 :** a person whose behavior departs substantially from the standard

ab·er·rat·ed \ˈa-bə-ˌrā-təd\ *adj* [L *aberratus,* pp. of *aberrare*] (1893) **:** ABERRANT

ab·er·ra·tion \ˌa-bə-ˈrā-shən\ *n* [L *aberrare*] (1594) **1 :** the fact or an instance of being aberrant esp. from a moral standard or normal state **2 :** failure of a mirror, refracting surface, or lens to produce exact point-to-point correspondence between an object and its image **3 :** unsoundness or disorder of the mind **4 :** a small periodic change of apparent position in celestial bodies due to the combined effect of the motion of light and the motion of the observer **5 :** an aberrant individual — **ab·er·ra·tion·al** \-shnəl, -shə-nᵊl\ *adj*

abet \ə-ˈbet\ *vt* **abet·ted; abet·ting** [ME *abetten,* fr. AF *abeter,* fr. *a-* (fr. L *ad-*) + *beter* to bait, of Gmc origin; akin to OE *bǣtan* to bait] (14c) **1 :** to actively second and encourage (as an activity or plan) **2 :** to assist or support in the achievement of a purpose ***syn*** see INCITE — **abet·ment** \-mənt\ *n* — **abet·tor** *also* **abet·ter** \ə-ˈbe-tər\ *n*

abey·ance \ə-ˈbā-ən(t)s\ *n* [AF, fr. OF *abaer* to expect, await, lit., to gape, fr. *a-* + *baer* to gape, yawn — more at BAY] (1640) **1 :** a lapse in succession during which there is no person in whom a title is vested **2 :** temporary inactivity **:** SUSPENSION — **abey·ant** \-ənt\ *adj*

ab·hor \əb-ˈhȯr, ab-\ *vt* **ab·horred; ab·hor·ring** [ME *abhorren,* fr. L *abhorrēre,* fr. *ab-* + *horrēre* to shudder — more at HORROR] (15c) **:** to regard with extreme repugnance **:** LOATHE ***syn*** see HATE — **ab·hor·rer** \-ˈhȯr-ər\ *n*

ab·hor·rence \əb-ˈhȯr-ən(t)s, -ˈhär-\ *n* (1660) **1 a :** the act or state of abhorring **b :** the feeling of one who abhors **2 :** one that is abhorred

ab·hor·rent \-ənt\ *adj* [L *abhorrent-, abhorrens,* prp. of *abhorrēre*] (1599) **1 a** *archaic* **:** strongly opposed **b :** feeling or showing abhorrence **2 :** not agreeable **:** CONTRARY ⟨a notion ~ to their philosophy⟩ **3 :** being so repugnant as to stir up positive antagonism ⟨acts ~ to every right-minded person⟩ — **ab·hor·rent·ly** *adv*

Abib \ä-ˈvēv\ *n* [Heb *Ābhībh,* lit., ear of grain] (1530) **:** the first month of the ancient Hebrew calendar corresponding to Nisan — see MONTH table

abid·ance \ə-ˈbī-dᵊn(t)s\ *n* (1647) **1 :** an act or state of abiding **:** CONTINUANCE **2 :** COMPLIANCE ⟨~ by the rules⟩

abide \ə-ˈbīd\ *vb* **abode** \-ˈbōd\ *or* **abid·ed; abid·ing** [ME, fr. OE *ābīdan,* fr. *ā-,* perfective prefix + *bīdan* to bide; akin to OHG *ir-,* perfective prefix — more at BIDE] *vt* (bef. 12c) **1 :** to wait for **:** AWAIT **2 a :** to endure without yielding **:** WITHSTAND **b :** to bear patiently **:** TOLERATE ⟨cannot ~ such bigots⟩ **3 :** to accept without objection ⟨will ~ your decision⟩ ~ *vi* **1 :** to remain stable or fixed in a state **2 :** to continue in a place **:** SOJOURN ***syn*** see BEAR, CONTINUE — **abid·er** *n* — **abide by 1 :** to conform to ⟨*abide by* the rules⟩ **2 :** to acquiesce in ⟨will *abide by* your decision⟩

abid·ing \ə-ˈbī-diŋ\ *adj* (14c) **:** ENDURING, CONTINUING ⟨an ~ interest in nature⟩ — **abid·ing·ly** *adv*

ab·i·gail \ˈa-bə-ˌgāl\ *n* [*Abigail,* servant in *The Scornful Lady,* a play by Francis Beaumont & John Fletcher] (1671) : a lady's personal maid

abil·i·ty \ə-ˈbi-lə-tē\ *n, pl* **-ties** [ME *abilite,* fr. AF, fr. L *habilitat-, habilitas,* fr. *habilis* apt, skillful — more at ABLE] (14c) **1 a :** the quality or state of being able ⟨~ of soil to hold water⟩; *esp* : physical, mental, or legal power to perform **b :** competence in doing : SKILL **2 :** natural aptitude or acquired proficiency ⟨students with different *abilities*⟩

-ability *also* **-ibility** *n suffix* [ME *-abilite, -ibilite,* fr. AF *-abilité, -ibilité,* fr. L *-abilitas, -ibilitas,* fr. *-abilis, -ibilis* -able + *-tas* -ty] : capacity, fitness, or tendency to act or be acted on in a (specified) way ⟨agglutin*ability*⟩

ab in·i·tio \ˌab-ə-ˈni-shē-ˌō\ *adv* [L] (1599) : from the beginning

abio·gen·e·sis \ˌā-ˌbī-ō-ˈje-nə-səs\ *n* [NL, fr. ²*a-* + *bio-* + L *genesis*] (1870) : the origin of life from nonliving matter: as **a :** SPONTANEOUS GENERATION **b :** a theory in the evolution of early life on earth: organic molecules and subsequent simple life forms first originated from inorganic substances — **abi·og·e·nist** \ˌā-(ˌ)bī-ˈä-jə-nist\ *n*

abio·gen·ic \ˌā-ˌbī-ō-ˈje-nik\ *adj* (1874) : not produced by the action of living organisms — **abio·gen·i·cal·ly** \-ni-k(ə-)lē\ *adv*

abi·o·log·i·cal \ˌā-ˌbī-ə-ˈlä-ji-kəl\ *adj* (1868) : not biological; *esp* : not involving or produced by organisms ⟨~ synthesis of amino acids⟩

abi·ot·ic \ˌā-(ˌ)bī-ˈä-tik\ *adj* (1870) : not biotic : ABIOLOGICAL ⟨the ~ environment⟩ — **abi·ot·i·cal·ly** \-ti-k(ə-)lē\ *adv*

ab·ject \ˈab-ˌjekt\ *adj* [ME, fr. L *abjectus,* fr. pp. of *abicere* to cast off, fr. *ab-* + *jacere* to throw — more at JET] (15c) **1 :** sunk to or existing in a low state or condition ⟨to lowest pitch of ~ fortune thou art fallen —John Milton⟩ **2 a :** cast down in spirit : SERVILE, SPIRITLESS ⟨a man made ~ by suffering⟩ **b :** showing hopelessness or resignation ⟨~ surrender⟩ **3 :** expressing or offered in a humble and often ingratiating spirit ⟨~ flattery⟩ ⟨an ~ apology⟩ ***syn*** see MEAN — **ab·ject·ly** \ˈab-ˌjek(t)-lē, ab-ˈ\ *adv* — **ab·ject·ness** \-ˌjek(t)-nəs, -ˈjek(t)-\ *n*

ab·jec·tion \ab-ˈjek-shən\ *n* (15c) **1 :** a low or downcast state : DEGRADATION **2 :** the act of making abject : HUMBLING, REJECTION ⟨I protest . . . this vile ~ of youth to age —G. B. Shaw⟩

ab·ju·ra·tion \ˌab-jə-ˈrā-shən\ *n* (15c) **1 :** the act or process of abjuring **2 :** an oath of abjuring

ab·jure \ab-ˈju̇r\ *vt* **ab·jured; ab·jur·ing** [ME, fr. AF or L; AF *abjurer,* fr. L *abjurare,* fr. *ab-* + *jurare* to swear — more at JURY] (15c) **1 a :** to renounce upon oath **b :** to reject solemnly **2 :** to abstain from : AVOID ⟨~ extravagance⟩ — **ab·jur·er** *n*

syn ABJURE, RENOUNCE, FORSWEAR, RECANT, RETRACT mean to withdraw one's word or professed belief. ABJURE implies a firm rejecting or abandoning often made under oath ⟨*abjured* the errors of his former faith⟩. RENOUNCE may carry the meaning of disclaim or disown ⟨*renounced* abstract art and turned to portrait painting⟩. FORSWEAR may add an implication of perjury or betrayal ⟨I cannot *forswear* my principles⟩. RECANT stresses the withdrawing or denying of something professed or taught ⟨if they *recant* they will be spared⟩. RETRACT applies to the withdrawing of a promise, an offer, or an accusation ⟨the newspaper had to *retract* the story⟩.

abl *abbr* ablative

ab·late \a-ˈblāt\ *vb* **ab·lat·ed; ab·lat·ing** [L *ablatus* (pp. of *auferre* to remove), fr. *ab-* + *latus,* pp. of *ferre* — more at UKASE, BEAR, TOLERATE] *vt* (1542) : to remove or destroy esp. by cutting, abrading, or evaporating ~ *vi* : to become ablated; *esp* : VAPORIZE 1

ab·la·tion \a-ˈblā-shən\ *n* (15c) : the process of ablating: as **a :** surgical removal **b :** loss of a part (as ice from a glacier or the outside of a nose cone) by melting or vaporization

[1]**ab·la·tive** \ˈa-blə-tiv\ *adj* (ca. 1500) : of, relating to, or constituting a grammatical case expressing typically the relations of separation and source and also frequently such relations as cause or instrument — **ablative** *n*

[2]**ab·la·tive** \a-ˈblā-tiv\ *adj* (ca. 1569) **1 :** of or relating to ablation **2 :** tending to ablate ⟨~ material on a nose cone⟩ — **ab·la·tive·ly** *adv*

ablative absolute *n* (1631) : a construction in Latin in which a noun or pronoun and its adjunct both in the ablative case form together an adverbial phrase expressing generally the time, cause, or an attendant circumstance of an action

ab·laut \ˈä-ˌblau̇t, ˈa-; ˈäp-ˌlau̇t\ *n* [G, fr. *ab* away from + *Laut* sound] (1838) : a systematic variation of vowels in the same root or affix or in related roots or affixes esp. in the Indo-European languages that is usu. paralleled by differences in use or meaning (as in *sing, sang, sung, song*)

ablaze \ə-ˈblāz\ *adj or adv* (ca. 1676) **1 :** being on fire **2 :** radiant with light or emotion ⟨his face all ~ with excitement —Bram Stoker⟩

able \ˈā-bəl\ *adj* **abler** \-b(ə-)lər\; **ablest** \-b(ə-)ləst\ [ME, fr. AF, fr. L *habilis* apt, fr. *habēre* to have — more at HABIT] (14c) **1 a :** having sufficient power, skill, or resources to accomplish an object **b :** susceptible to action or treatment **2 :** marked by intelligence, knowledge, skill, or competence — **ably** \ˈā-b(ə-)lē\ *adv*

-able *also* **-ible** *adj suffix* [ME, fr. AF, fr. L *-abilis, -ibilis,* fr. *-a-, -i-,* verb stem vowels + *-bilis* capable or worthy of] **1 :** capable of, fit for, or worthy of (being so acted upon or toward) — chiefly in adjectives derived from verbs ⟨break*able*⟩ ⟨collect*ible*⟩ **2 :** tending, given, or liable to ⟨agree*able*⟩ ⟨perish*able*⟩ — **-ably** *also* **-ibly** *adv suffix*

able–bod·ied \ˌā-bəl-ˈbä-dēd\ *adj* (1600) : having a sound strong body

able–bodied seaman *n* (1708) : ABLE SEAMAN

abled \ˈā-bəld\ *adj* (1946) : capable of unimpaired function ⟨designed to be helpful to the less ~⟩ — compare DIFFERENTLY ABLED

able·ism \ˈā-bə-ˌli-zəm\ *n* (1981) : discrimination or prejudice against individuals with disabilities — **able·ist** \-ˌlist\ *adj*

able seaman *n* (1657) : an experienced deck-department seaman qualified to perform routine duties at sea

abloom \ə-ˈblüm\ *adj* (1729) : abounding with blooms : BLOOMING

ab·lut·ed \ə-ˈblü-təd, a-\ *adj* [back-formation fr. *ablution*] (1650) : washed clean

ab·lu·tion \ə-ˈblü-shən, a-\ *n* [ME, fr. MF or LL; MF, fr. LL *ablution-, ablutio,* fr. L *abluere* to wash away, fr. *ab-* + *lavere* to wash — more at LYE] (1533) **1 a :** the washing of one's body or part of it (as in a religious rite) **b** *pl* **:** the act or action of bathing **2** *pl, Brit* **:** a building housing bathing and toilet facilities on a military base — **ab·lu·tion·ary** \-shə-ˌner-ē, -ˌne-rē\ *adj*

ABM \ˌā-(ˌ)bē-ˈem\ *n, pl* **ABM's** *or* **ABMs** \-ˈemz\ (1963) : ANTIBALLISTIC MISSILE

abn *abbr* airborne

Abnaki *var of* ABENAKI

ab·ne·gate \ˈab-ni-ˌgāt\ *vt* **-gat·ed; -gat·ing** [back-formation fr. *abnegation*] (1543) **1 :** DENY, RENOUNCE ⟨*abnegated* their God⟩ **2 :** SURRENDER, RELINQUISH ⟨*abnegated* her powers⟩ — **ab·ne·ga·tor** \-ˌgā-tər\ *n*

ab·ne·ga·tion \ˌab-ni-ˈgā-shən\ *n* [LL *abnegation-, abnegatio,* fr. L *abnegare* to refute, fr. *ab-* + *negare* to deny — more at NEGATE] (14c) : DENIAL; *esp* : SELF-DENIAL

[1]**ab·nor·mal** \(ˌ)ab-ˈnȯr-məl, əb-\ *adj* [alter. of F *anormal,* fr. ML *anormalis,* fr. L *a-* + LL *normalis* normal] (1817) : deviating from the normal or average : UNUSUAL, EXCEPTIONAL ⟨~ behavior⟩ — **ab·nor·mal·ly** \-mə-lē\ *adv*

[2]**abnormal** *n* (1857) : an abnormal person

ab·nor·mal·i·ty \ˌab-nər-ˈma-lə-tē, -(ˌ)nȯr-\ *n, pl* **-ties** (1847) **1 :** something abnormal **2 :** the quality or state of being abnormal

abnormal psychology *n* (1888) : a branch of psychology concerned with mental and emotional disorders (as neuroses, psychoses, and mental retardation) and with certain incompletely understood normal phenomena (as dreams and hypnosis)

abo \ˈa-(ˌ)bō\ *n, pl* **ab·os** (1908) *Austral, often disparaging* : ABORIGINE

[1]**aboard** \ə-ˈbȯrd\ *adv or adj* (14c) **1 :** ALONGSIDE **2 a :** on, onto, or within a vehicle (as a car or ship) **b :** in or into a group, association, or organization ⟨her second promotion since coming ~⟩ **3** *baseball* **:** on base

[2]**aboard** *prep* (15c) : ON, ONTO, WITHIN ⟨go ~ ship⟩ ⟨~ a plane⟩

ABO blood group \ˌā-(ˌ)bē-ˈō-\ *n* (1949) : any of the four blood groups A, B, AB, and O comprising the ABO system

abode \ə-ˈbōd\ *n* [ME *abod,* fr. *abiden* to abide] (13c) **1** *obs* **:** WAIT, DELAY **2 :** a temporary stay : SOJOURN **3 :** the place where one abides : HOME

aboil \ə-ˈbȯi(-ə)l\ *adj or adv* (1810) **1 :** being at the boiling point : BOILING **2 :** intensely excited or stirred up ⟨the meeting was ~ with controversy⟩

abol·ish \ə-ˈbä-lish\ *vt* [ME *abolisshen,* fr. MF *aboliss-,* stem of *abolir,* fr. L *abolēre;* prob. akin to *adolescere* to grow up — more at ADULT] (15c) **1 :** to end the observance or effect of : ANNUL ⟨~ a law⟩ ⟨~ slavery⟩ **2 :** DESTROY — **abol·ish·able** \-li-shə-bəl\ *adj* — **abol·ish·er** *n* — **abol·ish·ment** \-mənt\ *n*

ab·o·li·tion \ˌa-bə-ˈli-shən\ *n* [MF, fr. L *abolition-, abolitio,* fr. *abolēre*] (1529) **1 :** the act of abolishing : the state of being abolished **2 :** the abolishing of slavery — **ab·o·li·tion·ary** \-ˈli-shə-ˌner-ē, -ˌne-rē\ *adj*

ab·o·li·tion·ism \-ˈli-shə-ˌni-zəm\ *n* (1807) : principles or measures fostering abolition esp. of slavery — **ab·o·li·tion·ist** \-ist\ *n or adj*

ab·oma·sum \ˌa-bō-ˈmā-səm\ *n, pl* **-sa** \-sə\ [NL, fr. L *ab-* + *omasum* ox's tripe] (1678) : the fourth compartment of the ruminant stomach that follows the omasum and has a true digestive function — compare RUMEN, RETICULUM — **ab·oma·sal** \-səl\ *adj*

A–bomb \ˈā-ˌbäm\ *n* (1945) : ATOMIC BOMB 1

abom·i·na·ble \ə-ˈbäm-nə-bəl, -ˈbä-mə-\ *adj* (14c) **1 :** worthy of or causing disgust or hatred : DETESTABLE ⟨the ~ treatment of the poor⟩ **2 :** quite disagreeable or unpleasant ⟨~ weather⟩ — **abom·i·na·bly** \-blē\ *adv*

abominable snow·man \-ˈsnō-mən, -ˌman\ *n, often cap A&S* (1921) : a mysterious creature with human or apelike characteristics reported to exist in the high Himalayas — called also *yeti*

abom·i·nate \ə-ˈbä-mə-ˌnāt\ *vt* **-nat·ed; -nat·ing** [L *abominatus,* pp. of *abominari,* lit., to deprecate as an ill omen, fr. *ab-* + *omin-, omen* omen] (1597) : to hate or loathe intensely : ABHOR ***syn*** see HATE — **abom·i·na·tor** \-ˌnā-tər\ *n*

abom·i·na·tion \ə-ˌbä-mə-ˈnā-shən\ *n* (14c) **1 :** something abominable **2 :** extreme disgust and hatred : LOATHING

ab·oral \(ˌ)a-ˈbȯr-əl\ *adj* (1857) : situated opposite to or away from the mouth ⟨a sea urchin's ~ surface⟩ — **ab·oral·ly** \-ə-lē\ *adv*

[1]**ab·orig·i·nal** \ˌa-bə-ˈrij-nəl, -ˈri-jə-nᵊl\ *adj* (1650) **1 :** being the first or earliest known of its kind present in a region ⟨~ forests⟩ ⟨~ rocks⟩ **2 a :** of or relating to aborigines **b** *often cap* **:** of or relating to the indigenous peoples of Australia ***syn*** see NATIVE — **ab·orig·i·nal·ly** *adv*

[2]**aboriginal** *n* (1749) **1 :** ABORIGINE 1 **2** *often cap* **:** ABORIGINE 2

ab·orig·i·ne \ˌa-bə-ˈrij-(ˌ)nē, -ˈri-jə-\ *n* [L *aborigines,* pl., fr. *ab origine* from the beginning] (1593) **1 :** an aboriginal inhabitant esp. as contrasted with an invading or colonizing people **2** *often cap* **:** a member of any of the indigenous peoples of Australia

[1]**aborn·ing** \ə-ˈbȯr-niŋ\ *adv* [¹*a-* + E dial. *borning* (birth)] (1837) : while being born or produced ⟨a resolution that died ~⟩

[2]**aborning** *adj* (1943) : being born or produced ⟨the ~ fiasco⟩

[1]**abort** \ə-ˈbȯrt\ *vb* [L *abortus,* pp. of *aboriri* to miscarry, fr. *ab-* + *oriri* to rise, be born — more at ORIENT] *vi* (1540) **1 :** to bring forth stillborn, nonviable, or premature offspring **2 :** to become checked in development so as to degenerate or remain rudimentary **3 :** to terminate a procedure prematurely ⟨the pilot decided to ~ due to mechanical difficulties⟩ ~ *vt* **1 a :** to induce the abortion of or give birth to prematurely **b :** to terminate the pregnancy of before term **2 a :** to terminate prematurely : CANCEL ⟨~ a project⟩ ⟨~ a spaceflight⟩ **b :** to stop in the early stages ⟨~ a disease⟩ — **abort·er** *n*

[2]**abort** *n* (1944) : the premature termination of a flight (as of an aircraft or spacecraft), a mission, or an action or procedure relating to a flight ⟨a launch ~⟩

abor·ti·fa·cient \ə-ˌbȯr-tə-ˈfā-shənt\ *n* (1857) : an agent (as a drug) that induces abortion — **abortifacient** *adj*

abor·tion \ə-ˈbȯr-shən\ *n* (ca. 1537) **1 :** the termination of a pregnancy after, accompanied by, resulting in, or closely followed by the death of the embryo or fetus: as **a :** spontaneous expulsion of a human fetus during the first 12 weeks of gestation — compare MISCARRIAGE **b :** induced expulsion of a human fetus **c :** expulsion of a fetus by a do-

mestic animal often due to infection at any time before completion of pregnancy — compare CONTAGIOUS ABORTION **2** : MONSTROSITY **3** : arrest of development (as of a part or process) resulting in imperfection; *also* : a result of such arrest
abor·tion·ist \-sh(ə-)nist\ *n* (1861) : one who induces abortions
abortion pill *n* (1871) : a drug taken orally to induce abortion esp. early in pregnancy; *esp* : RU-486
abor·tive \ə-ˈbȯr-tiv\ *adj* (14c) **1** *obs* : prematurely born **2** : FRUITLESS, UNSUCCESSFUL **3** : imperfectly formed or developed **4** : tending to cut short — **abor·tive·ly** *adv* — **abor·tive·ness** *n*
ABO system \ˌā-(ˌ)bē-ˈō-\ *n* (1944) : the basic system of antigens of human blood behaving in heredity as an allelic unit to produce any of the ABO blood groups
abound \ə-ˈbau̇nd\ *vi* [ME, fr. AF *abunder,* fr. L *abundare,* fr. *ab-* + *unda* wave — more at WATER] (14c) **1** : to be present in large numbers or in great quantity : be prevalent **2** : to be copiously supplied — used with *in* or *with* ⟨life ~*ed* in mysteries —Norman Mailer⟩ ⟨institutions ~ with evidence of his success —*Johns Hopkins Mag.*⟩
[1]**about** \ə-ˈbau̇t\ *adv* [ME, fr. OE *abūtan,* fr. [1]*a-* + *būtan* outside — more at BUT] (bef. 12c) **1 a** : reasonably close to ⟨~ a year ago⟩ **b** : ALMOST ⟨~ starved⟩ **c** : on the verge of — usu. used with *be* and a following infinitive ⟨is ~ to join the army⟩; used with a negative to express intention or determination ⟨not ~ to quit⟩ **2** : on all sides : AROUND **3 a** : in rotation **b** : around the outside **4** : HERE AND THERE **5** : in the vicinity : NEAR **6** : in the opposite direction ⟨face ~⟩ ⟨the other way ~⟩
[2]**about** *prep* (bef. 12c) **1** : in a circle around : on every side of : AROUND **2 a** : in the immediate neighborhood of : NEAR **b** : on or near the person of **c** : in the makeup of ⟨a mature wisdom ~ him⟩ **d** : at the command of ⟨has his wits ~ him⟩ **3** : engaged in ⟨act as if they know what they're ~ —T. S. Matthews⟩ **4 a** : with regard to : CONCERNING ⟨spoke ~ his past⟩ **b** : concerned with **c** : fundamentally concerned with or directed toward ⟨poker is ~ money —David Mamet⟩ **5** : over or in different parts of
[3]**about** *adj* (1815) **1** : moving from place to place; *specif* : being out of bed **2** : AROUND 2
about–face \ə-ˈbau̇t-ˈfās\ *n* [fr. the imper. phrase *about face*] (1861) **1** : a 180° turn to the right from the position of attention **2** : a reversal of direction **3** : a reversal of attitude, behavior, or point of view — **about–face** *vi*
about–turn \-ˈtərn\ *n* (1893) *Brit* : ABOUT-FACE
[1]**above** \ə-ˈbəv\ *adv* [ME, fr. OE *abufan,* fr. *a-* + *bufan* above, fr. *be-* + *ufan* above; akin to OE *ofer* over] (bef. 12c) **1 a** : in the sky : OVERHEAD ⟨the clouds ~⟩ **b** : in or to heaven **2 a** : in or to a higher place **b** : higher on the same page or on a preceding page **c** : UPSTAIRS **d** : above zero ⟨10 degrees ~⟩ **3** : in or to a higher rank or number ⟨30 and ~⟩ **4** *archaic* : in addition : BESIDES **5** : UPSTAGE
[2]**above** *prep* (bef. 12c) **1 a** : in or to a higher place than : OVER **b** : upriver of **2 a** : superior to (as in rank, quality, or degree) **b** : out of reach of ⟨~ suspicion⟩ **c** : in preference to **d** : too proud or honorable to stoop to ⟨not ~ taking undue credit⟩ **3** : exceeding in number, quantity, or size : more than ⟨men ~ 50 years old⟩ **4** : as distinct from and in addition to ⟨heard the whistle ~ the roar of the crowd⟩
[3]**above** *n, pl* **above** (13c) **1 a** : something that is above **b** : a person whose name is written above **2 a** : a higher authority **b** : HEAVEN
usage Although still objected to by some, the use of *above* as a noun in sense 1a ⟨none of the *above*⟩ ⟨the *above* is Theseus's opinion —William Blake⟩ and as an adjective ⟨without the *above* reserve —O. W. Holmes †1935⟩ ⟨I was brought up on the *above* words —Viscount Montgomery⟩ has been long established as standard.
[4]**above** *adj* (1604) : written or discussed higher on the same page or on a preceding page ***usage*** see [3]ABOVE
above all *adv* (14c) : before every other consideration : ESPECIALLY
[1]**above·board** \ə-ˈbəv-ˌbȯrd\ *adv* [fr. the difficulty of cheating at cards when the hands are above the table] (1594) : in a straightforward manner : OPENLY
[2]**aboveboard** *adj* (1648) : free from all traces of deceit or duplicity
above·ground \ə-ˈbəv-ˌgrau̇nd\ *adj* (1878) **1** : located or occurring on or above the surface of the ground **2** : existing, produced, or published by or within the establishment ⟨~ movies⟩ — **aboveground** *adv*
ab ovo \ab-ˈō-(ˌ)vō\ *adv* [L, lit., from the egg] (ca. 1586) : from the beginning
abp *abbr* archbishop
abr *abbr* abridged; abridgment
ab·ra·ca·dab·ra \ˌa-brə-kə-ˈda-brə\ *n* [LL] (1565) **1** : a magical charm or incantation **2** : unintelligible language
abrade \ə-ˈbrād\ *vb* **abrad·ed; abrad·ing** [L *abradere* to scrape off, fr. *ab-* + *radere* to scrape — more at RODENT] *vt* (1677) **1 a** : to rub or wear away esp. by friction : ERODE **b** : to irritate or roughen by rubbing **2** : to wear down in spirit : IRRITATE, WEARY ~ *vi* : to undergo abrasion — **abrad·able** \-ˈbrā-də-bəl\ *adj* — **abrad·er** *n*
Abra·ham \ˈā-brə-ˌham\ *n* [LL, fr. Gk *Abraam,* fr. Heb *'Abhrāhām*] (14c) : an Old Testament patriarch regarded by Jews as the founder of the Hebrew people through his son Isaac and by Muslims as the founder of the Arab peoples through his son Ishmael
abra·sion \ə-ˈbrā-zhən\ *n* [ML *abrasion-, abrasio,* fr. L *abradere*] (1554) **1 a** : a wearing, grinding, or rubbing away by friction **b** : IRRITATION **2** : an abraded area of the skin or mucous membrane
[1]**abra·sive** \ə-ˈbrā-siv, -ziv\ *adj* (1849) **1** : tending to abrade **2** : causing irritation ⟨~ manners⟩ — **abra·sive·ly** *adv* — **abra·sive·ness** *n*
[2]**abrasive** *n* (1853) : a substance (as emery or pumice) used for abrading, smoothing, or polishing
ab·re·ac·tion \ˌa-brē-ˈak-shən\ *n* [part trans. of G *Abreagierung* catharsis, fr. *ab* off, away + *Reagierung* reaction] (1912) : the expression and emotional discharge of unconscious material (as a repressed idea or emotion) by verbalization esp. in the presence of a therapist — **ab·re·act** \-ˈakt\ *vb*
abreast \ə-ˈbrest\ *adv or adj* (15c) **1** : beside one another with bodies in line ⟨columns of men five ~⟩ **2** : up to a particular standard or level esp. of knowledge of recent developments ⟨keeps ~ of the news⟩
abridge \ə-ˈbrij\ *vt* **abridged; abridg·ing** [ME *abregen,* fr. AF *abreger,* fr. LL *abbreviare,* fr. L *ad-* + *brevis* short — more at BRIEF] (14c) **1 a** *archaic* : DEPRIVE **b** : to reduce in scope : DIMINISH ⟨attempts to ~ the right of free speech⟩ **2** : to shorten in duration or extent ⟨modern transportation that ~*s* distance⟩ **3** : to shorten by omission of words without sacrifice of sense : CONDENSE ***syn*** see SHORTEN — **abridg·er** *n*
abridg·ment *or* **abridge·ment** \ə-ˈbrij-mənt\ *n* (15c) **1** : the action of abridging : the state of being abridged **2** : a shortened form of a work retaining the general sense and unity of the original
abroach \ə-ˈbrōch\ *adv or adj* (14c) **1** *archaic* : in a condition for letting out a liquid (as wine) **2** *archaic* : in action or agitation : ASTIR ⟨mischiefs that I set ~ —Shak.⟩
abroad \ə-ˈbrȯd\ *adv or adj* (13c) **1** : over a wide area : WIDELY **2** : away from one's home **3** : beyond the boundaries of one's country **4** : in wide circulation : ABOUT **5** : wide of the mark : ASTRAY
ab·ro·gate \ˈa-brə-ˌgāt\ *vt* **-gat·ed; -gat·ing** [L *abrogatus,* pp. of *abrogare,* fr. *ab-* + *rogare* to ask, propose a law — more at RIGHT] (1526) **1** : to abolish by authoritative action : ANNUL **2** : to treat as nonexistent ⟨*abrogating* their responsibilities⟩ ***syn*** see NULLIFY — **ab·ro·ga·tion** \ˌa-brə-ˈgā-shən\ *n*
abrupt \ə-ˈbrəpt\ *adj* [L *abruptus,* fr. pp. of *abrumpere* to break off, fr. *ab-* + *rumpere* to break — more at REAVE] (1530) **1 a** : characterized by or involving action or change without preparation or warning : UNEXPECTED ⟨came to an ~ stop⟩ ⟨an ~ turn⟩ ⟨an ~ decision to retire⟩ **b** : unceremoniously curt ⟨an ~ manner⟩ **c** : lacking smoothness or continuity ⟨an ~ transition⟩ **2** : giving the impression of being cut or broken off; *esp* : involving a sudden steep rise or drop ⟨~ hills⟩ ⟨a high ~ bank bounded the stream⟩ ***syn*** see PRECIPITATE, STEEP — **abrupt·ly** \ə-ˈbrəp(t)-lē\ *adv* — **abrupt·ness** \ə-ˈbrəp(t)-nəs\ *n*
abrup·tion \ə-ˈbrəp-shən\ *n* (1606) : a sudden breaking off or away
abs *abbr* **1** absolute **2** abstract
[1]**ABS** \ˌā-(ˌ)bē-ˈes\ *n* [*a*crylonitrile-*b*utadiene-*s*tyrene] (1964) : a tough rigid plastic used esp. for automobile parts and building materials
[2]**ABS** *abbr* **1** American Bible Society **2** antilock braking system
ab·scess \ˈab-ˌses\ *n, pl* **ab·scess·es** \ˈab-ˌse-səz, -ˌsēz; -sə-səz\ [L *abscessus,* lit., act of going away, fr. *abscedere* to go away, fr. *abs-, ab-* + *cedere* to go] (1615) : a localized collection of pus surrounded by inflamed tissue — **ab·scessed** \-ˌsest\ *adj*
ab·scise \ab-ˈsīz\ *vb* **ab·scised; ab·scis·ing** [L *abscisus,* pp. of *abscidere,* fr. *abs-* + *caedere* to cut] *vt* (1612) : to separate (as a flower from a stem) by abscission ~ *vi* : to separate by abscission
ab·scis·ic acid \ˌab-ˈsi-zik-, -sik-\ *n* [*absci*sion (var. of *abscission*) + *-ic*] (1968) : a plant hormone $C_{15}H_{20}O_4$ that is a sesquiterpene widespread in nature and that typically promotes leaf abscission and dormancy and has an inhibitory effect on cell elongation
ab·sci·sin \ˈab-sə-sən, ab-ˈsi-sᵊn\ *n* [*absci*sion + *-in*] (1961) : ABSCISIC ACID
ab·scis·sa \ab-ˈsi-sə\ *n, pl* **abscissas** *also* **ab·scis·sae** \-ˈsi-(ˌ)sē\ [NL, fr. L, fem. of *abscissus,* pp. of *abscindere* to cut off, fr. *ab-* + *scindere* to cut — more at SHED] (1694) : the horizontal coordinate of a point in a plane Cartesian coordinate system obtained by measuring parallel to the x-axis — compare ORDINATE

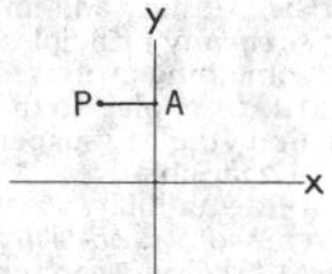

AP abscissa of point *P*

ab·scis·sion \ab-ˈsi-zhən\ *n* [ME *abscisioun,* fr. AF *abscission,* L *abscission-, abscissio,* fr. *abscindere*] (15c) **1** : the act or process of cutting off : REMOVAL **2** : the natural separation of flowers, fruit, or leaves from plants at a special separation layer
ab·scond \ab-ˈskänd, əb-\ *vi* [L *abscondere* to hide away, fr. *abs-* + *condere* to store up, conceal — more at CONDIMENT] (ca. 1578) : to depart secretly and hide oneself — **ab·scond·er** *n*
ab·seil \ˈab-ˌsāl, -ˌsī(-ə)l\ *vi* [G *abseilen,* fr. *ab* down, off + *Seil* rope] (1941) *chiefly Brit* : RAPPEL — **abseil** *n*
ab·sence \ˈab-sən(t)s\ *n* (14c) **1** : the state of being absent **2** : the period of time that one is absent **3** : WANT, LACK ⟨an ~ of detail⟩ **4** : inattention to present surroundings or occurrences ⟨~ of mind⟩
[1]**ab·sent** \ˈab-sənt\ *adj* [ME, fr. AF, fr. L *absent-, absens,* prp. of *abesse* to be absent, fr. *ab-* + *esse* to be — more at IS] (14c) **1** : not present or attending : MISSING **2** : not existing : LACKING ⟨danger in a situation where power is ~ —M. H. Trytten⟩ **3** : lost in thought : not attentive ***syn*** see ABSTRACTED — **ab·sent·ly** *adv*
[2]**ab·sent** \ab-ˈsent, ˈab-ˌ\ *vt* (15c) : to keep (oneself) away
[3]**ab·sent** \ˈab-sənt\ *prep* (1944) : in the absence of : WITHOUT
ab·sen·tee \ˌab-sən-ˈtē\ *n* (1605) : one that is absent: as **a** : a proprietor that lives away from his or her estate or business **b** : one missing from work or school — **absentee** *adj*
absentee ballot *n* (1889) : a ballot submitted (as by mail) in advance of an election by a voter who is unable to be present at the polls
ab·sen·tee·ism \ˌab-sən-ˈtē-ˌi-zəm\ *n* (1829) **1** : prolonged absence of an owner from his or her property **2** : chronic absence (as from work or school); *also* : the rate of such absence
ab·sent·mind·ed \ˌab-sənt-ˈmīn-dəd\ *adj* (1829) **1** : lost in thought and unaware of one's surroundings or actions : PREOCCUPIED; *also* : given to absence of mind **2** : indicative of or resulting from preoccupation or absence of mind ***syn*** see ABSTRACTED — **ab·sent·mind·ed·ly** *adv* — **ab·sent·mind·ed·ness** *n*
absent without leave *adj* (1793) : absent without authority from one's place of duty in the armed forces
ab·sinthe *also* **ab·sinth** \ˈab-(ˌ)sin(t)th\ *n* [F *absinthe,* fr. L *absinthium,* fr. Gk *apsinthion*] (1612) **1** : WORMWOOD 1 **2** : a green liqueur which is flavored with wormwood, anise, and other aromatic herbs and commercial production of which is banned in many countries for health concerns; *also* : a liqueur resembling absinthe
ab·so·lute \ˈab-sə-ˌlüt, ˌab-sə-ˈ\ *adj* [ME *absolut,* fr. AF, fr. L *absolutus,* fr. pp. of *absolvere* to set free, absolve] (14c) **1 a** : free from imperfection : PERFECT ⟨it is a most ~ and excellent horse —Shak.⟩ **b** : free or relatively free from mixture : PURE ⟨~ alcohol⟩ **c** : OUTRIGHT, UNMITIGATED ⟨an ~ lie⟩ **2** : being, governed by, or characteristic of a ruler or authority completely free from constitutional or other restraint ⟨~ power⟩ **3 a** : standing apart from a normal or usual syntactical relation with other words or sentence elements ⟨the ~ construction *this being the case* in the sentence "this being the case, let us

go"⟩ **b** *of an adjective or possessive pronoun* : standing alone without a modified substantive ⟨*blind* in "help the blind" and *ours* in "your work and ours" are ~⟩ **c** *of a verb* : having no object in the particular construction under consideration though normally transitive ⟨*kill* in "if looks could kill" is an ~ verb⟩ **4 :** having no restriction, exception, or qualification ⟨an ~ requirement⟩ ⟨~ freedom⟩ **5 :** POSITIVE, UNQUESTIONABLE ⟨~ proof⟩ **6 a :** independent of arbitrary standards of measurement **b :** relating to or derived in the simplest manner from the fundamental units of length, mass, and time ⟨~ electric units⟩ **c :** relating to, measured on, or being a temperature scale based on absolute zero ⟨~ temperature⟩; *specif* : KELVIN ⟨10° ~⟩ **7 :** FUNDAMENTAL, ULTIMATE ⟨~ knowledge⟩ **8 :** perfectly embodying the nature of a thing ⟨~ justice⟩ **9 :** being self-sufficient and free of external references or relationships ⟨an ~ term in logic⟩ ⟨~ music⟩ **10 :** being the true distance from an aircraft to the earth's surface ⟨~ altitude⟩ — **absolute** *n* — **ab·so·lute·ness** *n*

absolute ceiling *n* (ca. 1920) : the maximum height above sea level at which a particular airplane can maintain horizontal flight under standard air conditions — called also *ceiling*

absolute convergence *n* (1893) : convergence of a mathematical series when the absolute values of the terms are taken

absolute humidity *n* (1867) : the amount of water vapor present in a unit volume of air — compare RELATIVE HUMIDITY

ab·so·lute·ly \ˈab-sə-ˌlüt-lē, ˌab-sə-ˈ\ *adv* (14c) **1 :** in an absolute manner or condition — often used as an intensive ⟨~ brilliant⟩ **2 :** with respect to absolute values ⟨an ~ convergent series⟩

absolute magnitude *n* (1902) : a measure of the intrinsic luminosity of a celestial body (as a star) expressed as the apparent magnitude the body would have if viewed from a distance of 10 parsecs

absolute pitch *n* (1864) **1 :** the position of a tone in a standard scale independently determined by its rate of vibration **2 :** the ability to recognize or sing a given isolated note — called also *perfect pitch*

absolute space *n* (1710) : SPACE 4b

absolute value *n* (1889) **1 :** a nonnegative number equal in numerical value to a given real number **2 :** the positive square root of the sum of the squares of the real and imaginary parts of a complex number

absolute zero *n* (1808) : a theoretical temperature characterized by complete absence of heat and motion and equivalent to exactly −273.15°C or −459.67°F

ab·so·lu·tion \ˌab-sə-ˈlü-shən\ *n* (13c) : the act of absolving; *specif* : a remission of sins pronounced by a priest (as in the sacrament of reconciliation)

ab·so·lut·ism \ˈab-sə-ˌlü-ˌti-zəm\ *n* (1830) **1 a :** a political theory that absolute power should be vested in one or more rulers **b :** government by an absolute ruler or authority : DESPOTISM **2 :** advocacy of a rule by absolute standards or principles **3 :** an absolute standard or principle — **ab·so·lut·ist** \-ˌlü-tist\ *n or adj* — **ab·so·lu·tis·tic** \ˌab-sə-(ˌ)lü-ˈtis-tik\ *adj*

ab·so·lu·tive \ˌab-sə-ˈlü-tiv\ *adj* (1948) : of, relating to, or being an inflectional morpheme that typically marks the subject of an intransitive verb or the direct object of a transitive verb in an ergative language

ab·so·lut·ize \ˈab-sə-ˌlü-ˌtīz\ *vt* **-ized; -iz·ing** (1919) : to make absolute : convert into an absolute

ab·solve \əb-ˈzälv, -ˈsälv, -ˈzȯlv, -ˈsȯlv *also without* l\ *vt* **ab·solved; ab·solv·ing** [ME, fr. L *absolvere,* fr. *ab-* + *solvere* to loosen — more at SOLVE] (15c) **1 :** to set free from an obligation or the consequences of guilt **2 :** to remit (a sin) by absolution ***syn*** see EXCULPATE — **ab·solv·er** *n*

ab·sorb \əb-ˈsȯrb, -ˈzȯrb\ *vt* [AF *asorbir* to swallow up, fr. L *absorbēre,* fr. *ab-* + *sorbēre* to suck up; akin to Lith *surbti* to sip, Gk *rophein* to gulp down] (15c) **1 :** to take in and make part of an existent whole ⟨the capacity of China to ~ invaders⟩ **2 a :** to suck up or take up ⟨a sponge ~*s* water⟩ ⟨charcoal ~*s* gas⟩ ⟨plant roots ~ water⟩ **b :** to take in : ACQUIRE, LEARN ⟨convictions ~*ed* in youth —M. R. Cohen⟩ **c :** USE UP, CONSUME ⟨the fever ~*ed* her strength⟩ **3 :** to engage or engross wholly ⟨~*ed* in thought⟩ **4 a (1) :** to receive without recoil or echo ⟨provided with a sound-*absorbing* surface⟩ **(2) :** ENDURE, SUSTAIN ⟨~*ing* hardships⟩ **(3) :** ASSUME, BEAR ⟨the expenses were ~*ed* by the company⟩ **b :** to transform (radiant energy) into a different form esp. with a resulting rise in temperature ⟨the earth ~*s* the sun's rays⟩ — **ab·sorb·abil·i·ty** \əb-ˌsȯr-bə-ˈbi-lə-tē, -ˌzȯr-\ *n* — **ab·sorb·able** \əb-ˈsȯr-bə-bəl, -ˈzȯr-\ *adj* — **ab·sorb·er** *n*

ab·sor·bance \əb-ˈsȯr-bən(t)s, -ˈzȯr-\ *n* (1947) : the ability of a layer of a substance to absorb radiation expressed mathematically as the negative common logarithm of transmittance

ab·sor·ben·cy \əb-ˈsȯr-bən(t)-sē, -ˈzȯr-\ *n, pl* **-cies** (1859) **1 :** the quality or state of being absorbent **2** *or* **ab·sor·ban·cy :** ABSORBANCE

ab·sor·bent *also* **ab·sor·bant** \-bənt\ *adj* [L *absorbent-, absorbens,* prp. of *absorbēre*] (1718) : able to absorb ⟨as ~ as a sponge⟩ — **absorbent** *also* **absorbant** *n*

ab·sorb·ing *adj* (1876) : fully taking one's attention : ENGROSSING ⟨an ~ novel⟩ — **ab·sorb·ing·ly** \-biŋ-lē\ *adv*

ab·sorp·tance \əb-ˈsȯrp-tən(t)s, -ˈzȯrp-\ *n* [*absorp*tion + *-ance*] (ca. 1931) : the ratio of the radiant energy absorbed by a body to that incident upon it

ab·sorp·ti·om·e·try \əb-ˌsȯrp-shē-ˈä-mə-trē, -ˌzȯrp-\ *n* [*absorption* + *-metry*] (1951) : measurement of the amount of radiation absorbed (as by living tissue) esp. to determine density — compare DUAL-ENERGY X-RAY ABSORPTIOMETRY

ab·sorp·tion \əb-ˈsȯrp-shən, -ˈzȯrp-\ *n* [F & L; F, fr. L *absorption-, absorptio,* fr. *absorbēre*] (1741) **1 a :** the process of absorbing or of being absorbed — compare ADSORPTION **b :** interception of radiant energy or sound waves **2 :** entire occupation of the mind ⟨~ in his work⟩ — **ab·sorp·tive** \-tiv\ *adj*

absorption band *n* (1865) : a dark band in an absorption spectrum; *also* : ABSORPTION LINE

absorption line *n* (ca. 1889) : a dark line in an absorption spectrum

absorption spectrum *n* (1869) : an electromagnetic spectrum in which a decrease in intensity of radiation at specific wavelengths or ranges of wavelengths characteristic of an absorbing substance is manifested esp. as a pattern of dark lines or bands

ab·sorp·tiv·i·ty \əb-ˌsȯrp-ˈti-və-tē, -ˌzȯrp-\ *n, pl* **-ties** (ca. 1859) : the property of a body that determines the fraction of incident radiation absorbed by the body

ab·stain \əb-ˈstān, ab-\ *vi* [ME *absteinen,* fr. AF *asteign-, absteign-,* stem of *astenir, abstenir,* fr. L *abstinēre,* fr. *abs-, ab-* + *tenēre* to hold — more at THIN] (14c) : to refrain deliberately and often with an effort of self-denial from an action or practice ⟨~ from drinking⟩ — **ab·stain·er** *n*

ab·ste·mi·ous \ab-ˈstē-mē-əs\ *adj* [L *abstemius,* fr. *abs-* + *-temius;* akin to L *temetum* intoxicating drink] (1609) : marked by restraint esp. in the consumption of food or alcohol; *also* : reflecting such restraint ⟨an ~ diet⟩ — **ab·ste·mi·ous·ly** *adv* — **ab·ste·mious·ness** *n*

ab·sten·tion \əb-ˈsten(t)-shən, ab-\ *n* [LL *abstention-, abstentio,* fr. L *abstinēre*] (1521) : the act or practice of abstaining — **ab·sten·tious** \-shəs\ *adj*

ab·sti·nence \ˈab-stə-nən(t)s\ *n* [ME, fr. AF, fr. L *abstinentia,* fr. *abstinent-, abstinens,* prp. of *abstinēre*] (14c) **1 :** voluntary forbearance esp. from indulgence of an appetite or craving or from eating some foods **2 a :** habitual abstaining from intoxicating beverages **b :** abstention from sexual intercourse — **ab·sti·nent** \-nənt\ *adj* — **ab·sti·nent·ly** *adv*

abstr *abbr* abstract

[1]**ab·stract** \ab-ˈstrakt, ˈab-ˌ\ *adj* [ML *abstractus,* fr. L, pp. of *abstrahere* to drag away, fr. *abs-, ab-* + *trahere* to pull, draw] (14c) **1 a :** disassociated from any specific instance ⟨an ~ entity⟩ **b :** difficult to understand : ABSTRUSE ⟨~ problems⟩ **c :** insufficiently factual : FORMAL ⟨possessed only an ~ right⟩ **2 :** expressing a quality apart from an object ⟨the word *poem* is concrete, *poetry* is ~⟩ **3 a :** dealing with a subject in its abstract aspects : THEORETICAL ⟨~ science⟩ **b :** IMPERSONAL, DETACHED ⟨the ~ compassion of a surgeon —*Time*⟩ **4 :** having only intrinsic form with little or no attempt at pictorial representation or narrative content ⟨~ painting⟩ — **ab·stract·ly** \ab-ˈstrak(t)-lē, ˈab-ˌ\ *adv* — **ab·stract·ness** \ab-ˈstrak(t)-nəs, ˈab-ˌ\ *n*

[2]**ab·stract** \ˈab-ˌstrakt, *in sense 2 also* ab-ˈ\ *n* [ME, fr. L *abstractus*] (15c) **1 :** a summary of points (as of a writing) usu. presented in skeletal form; *also* : something that summarizes or concentrates the essentials of a larger thing or several things **2 :** an abstract thing or state **3 :** ABSTRACTION 4a

[3]**ab·stract** \ab-ˈstrakt, ˈab-ˌ, *in sense 3 usu* ˈab-ˌ\ *vt* (1542) **1 :** REMOVE, SEPARATE **2 :** to consider apart from application to or association with a particular instance **3 :** to make an abstract of : SUMMARIZE **4 :** to draw away the attention of **5 :** STEAL, PURLOIN ~ *vi* : to make an abstraction — **ab·stract·able** \-ˈstrak-tə-bəl, -ˌstrak-\ *adj* — **ab·strac·tor** *or* **ab·stract·er** \-tər\ *n*

ab·stract·ed \ab-ˈstrak-təd, ˈab-ˌ\ *adj* (1643) **1 :** withdrawn in mind : inattentive to one's surroundings ⟨said hello but seemed ~⟩ **2 :** ABSTRACT 4 ⟨~ geometric shapes⟩ — **ab·stract·ed·ly** *adv* — **ab·stract·ed·ness** *n*

syn ABSTRACTED, PREOCCUPIED, ABSENT, ABSENTMINDED, DISTRACTED mean inattentive to what claims or demands consideration. ABSTRACTED implies absorption of the mind in something other than one's surroundings, and often suggests reflection on weighty matters ⟨walking about with an *abstracted* air⟩. PREOCCUPIED often implies having one's attention so taken up by thoughts as to neglect others ⟨too *preoccupied* with her debts to enjoy the meal⟩. ABSENT stresses inability to fix the mind on present concerns due more to mental wandering than to concentration on other matters ⟨an *absent* stare⟩. ABSENTMINDED implies that the mind is fixed elsewhere and often refers to a habit of abstractedness ⟨so *absentminded,* he's been known to wear mismatched shoes⟩. DISTRACTED may suggest an inability to concentrate caused by worry, sorrow, or anxiety ⟨was too *distracted* by grief to continue working⟩.

abstract expressionism *n, often cap A&E* (1951) : an artistic movement of the mid-20th century comprising diverse styles and techniques and emphasizing esp. an artist's liberty to convey attitudes and emotions through nontraditional and usu. nonrepresentational means — **abstract expressionist** *n or adj, often cap A&E*

ab·strac·tion \ab-ˈstrak-shən, əb-\ *n* (1549) **1 a :** the act or process of abstracting : the state of being abstracted **b :** an abstract idea or term **2 :** absence of mind or preoccupation **3 :** abstract quality or character **4 a :** an abstract composition or creation in art **b :** ABSTRACTIONISM — **ab·strac·tion·al** \-shnəl, -shə-nᵊl\ *adj* — **ab·strac·tive** \ab-ˈstrak-tiv, ˈab-ˌ\ *adj*

ab·strac·tion·ism \ab-ˈstrak-shə-ˌni-zəm, əb-\ *n* (1926) : the principles or practice of creating abstract art — **ab·strac·tion·ist** \-sh(ə-)nist\ *adj or n*

abstract of title (1858) : a summary statement of the successive conveyances and other facts on which a title to a piece of land rests

ab·struse \əb-ˈstrüs, ab-\ *adj* [L *abstrusus,* fr. pp. of *abstrudere* to conceal, fr. *abs-, ab-* + *trudere* to push — more at THREAT] (1599) : difficult to comprehend : RECONDITE ⟨the ~ calculations of mathematicians⟩ — **ab·struse·ly** *adv* — **ab·struse·ness** *n*

ab·stru·si·ty \-ˈstrü-sə-tē\ *n, pl* **-ties** (1646) **1 :** the quality or state of being abstruse : ABSTRUSENESS **2 :** something that is abstruse

[1]**ab·surd** \əb-ˈsərd, -ˈzərd\ *adj* [MF *absurde,* fr. L *absurdus,* fr. *ab-* + *surdus* deaf, stupid] (1557) **1 :** ridiculously unreasonable, unsound, or incongruous ⟨an ~ argument⟩ **2 :** having no rational or orderly relationship to human life : MEANINGLESS ⟨an ~ universe⟩; *also* : lacking order or value ⟨an ~ existence⟩ **3 :** dealing with the absurd or with absurdism ⟨~ theater⟩ — **ab·surd·ly** *adv* — **ab·surd·ness** *n*

[2]**absurd** *n* (1946) : the state or condition in which human beings exist in an irrational and meaningless universe and in which human life has no ultimate meaning — usu. used with *the*

ab·surd·ism \əb-ˈsər-ˌdi-zəm, -ˈzər-\ *n* (1946) : a philosophy based on the belief that the universe is irrational and meaningless and that the search for order brings the individual into conflict with the universe — compare EXISTENTIALISM

\ə\ **abut** \ᵊ\ kitten, F table \ər\ **further** \a\ **ash** \ā\ **ace** \ä\ mop, **mar** \au̇\ **out** \ch\ **chin** \e\ **bet** \ē\ **easy** \g\ **go** \i\ **hit** \ī\ **ice** \j\ **job** \ŋ\ **sing** \ō\ **go** \ȯ\ **law** \ȯi\ **boy** \th\ **thin** \t͟h\ **the** \ü\ **loot** \u̇\ **foot** \y\ **yet** \zh\ **vision, beige** \k̲, ⁿ, œ, ue, ʸ\ *see* Guide to Pronunciation

ab·surd·ist \-dist\ *adj* (1946) : of, relating to, or characterized by the absurd or by absurdism : ABSURD ⟨~ literature⟩ ⟨an ~ sense of humor⟩ — **absurdist** *n*

ab·sur·di·ty \əb-ˈsər-də-tē, -ˈzər-\ *n, pl* **-ties** (1528) **1** : the quality or state of being absurd : ABSURDNESS **2** : something that is absurd

abub·ble \ə-ˈbə-bəl\ *adj* (ca. 1869) **1** : being in the process of bubbling **2** : being in a state of agitated activity or motion : ASTIR

abuild·ing \ə-ˈbil-diŋ\ *adj* (1535) : being in the process of building or of being built

abu·lia \ā-ˈbü-lē-ə, -ˈbyü-, ə-\ *n* [NL, fr. [2]*a-* + Gk *boulē* will] (ca. 1864) : abnormal lack of ability to act or to make decisions — **abu·lic** \-lik\ *adj*

abun·dance \ə-ˈbən-dən(t)s\ *n* (14c) **1** : an ample quantity : PROFUSION **2** : AFFLUENCE, WEALTH **3** : relative degree of plentifulness ⟨low ~*s* of uranium and thorium —H. C. Urey⟩

abun·dant \-dənt\ *adj* [ME, fr. AF, fr. L *abundant-, abundans,* prp. of *abundare* to abound] (14c) **1 a** : marked by great plenty (as of resources) ⟨a fair and ~ land⟩ **b** : amply supplied : ABOUNDING ⟨an area ~ with bird life⟩ **2** : occurring in abundance : AMPLE ⟨~ rainfall⟩ ***syn*** see PLENTIFUL — **abun·dant·ly** *adv*

[1]**abuse** \ə-ˈbyüs\ *n* [ME, fr. MF *abus,* fr. L *abusus,* fr. *abuti* to consume, fr. *ab-* + *uti* to use] (15c) **1** : a corrupt practice or custom **2** : improper or excessive use or treatment : MISUSE ⟨drug ~⟩ **3** *obs* : a deceitful act : DECEPTION **4** : language that condemns or vilifies usu. unjustly, intemperately, and angrily **5** : physical maltreatment

syn ABUSE, VITUPERATION, INVECTIVE, OBLOQUY, BILLINGSGATE mean vehemently expressed condemnation or disapproval. ABUSE, the most general term, usu. implies the anger of the speaker and stresses the harshness of the language ⟨scathing verbal *abuse*⟩. VITUPERATION implies fluent and sustained abuse ⟨a torrent of *vituperation*⟩. INVECTIVE implies a comparable vehemence but suggests greater verbal and rhetorical skill and may apply to a public denunciation ⟨blistering political *invective*⟩. OBLOQUY suggests defamation and consequent shame and disgrace ⟨subjected to *obloquy* and derision⟩. BILLINGSGATE implies practiced fluency and variety of profane or obscene abuse ⟨directed a stream of *billingsgate* at the cabdriver⟩.

[2]**abuse** \ə-ˈbyüz\ *vt* **abused; abus·ing** (15c) **1 a** : to put to a wrong or improper use ⟨~ a privilege⟩ **b** : to use excessively ⟨~ alcohol⟩; *also* : to use without medical justification ⟨~*ing* painkillers⟩ **2** *obs* : DECEIVE **3** : to use so as to injure or damage : MALTREAT **4** : to attack in words : REVILE — **abus·able** \-ˈbyü-zə-bəl\ *adj* — **abus·er** *n*

abu·sive \ə-ˈbyü-siv *also* -ziv\ *adj* (1583) **1** : characterized by wrong or improper use or action; *esp* : CORRUPT ⟨~ financial practices⟩ **2 a** : using harsh insulting language ⟨an angry and ~ crowd⟩ **b** : characterized by or serving for abuse ⟨~ language⟩ **c** : physically injurious ⟨~ behavior⟩ — **abu·sive·ly** *adv* — **abu·sive·ness** *n*

abut \ə-ˈbət\ *vb* **abut·ted; abut·ting** [ME *abutten,* fr. AF *aboter, abuter,* partly fr. OF *aboter* to border on, fr. *a-* (fr. L *ad-*) + *bout* blow, end, fr. *boter* to strike; partly fr. OF *abuter* to come to an end, fr. *a-* + *but* end, aim — more at [1]BUTT, [4]BUTT] *vi* (15c) **1** : to touch along a border or with a projecting part ⟨land ~*s* on the road⟩ **2 a** : to terminate at a point of contact **b** : to lean for support ~ *vt* **1** : to border on ⟨their property ~*s* our land⟩ **2** : to cause to abut

abu·ti·lon \ə-ˈbyü-tᵊl-ˌän, -tᵊl-ən\ *n* [NL, genus name, fr. Ar *awbūtīlūn* abutilon] (ca. 1578) : any of a genus (*Abutilon*) of plants of the mallow family often having lobed leaves and solitary bell-shaped flowers

abut·ment \ə-ˈbət-mənt\ *n* (1644) **1** : the place at which abutting occurs **2** : the part of a structure (as an arch or a bridge) that directly receives thrust or pressure

abut·tals \ə-ˈbə-tᵊlz\ *n pl* (1630) : the boundaries of lands with respect to adjacent lands

abut·ter \ə-ˈbə-tər\ *n* (1673) : one that abuts; *specif* : the owner of a contiguous property

abutting *adj* (1599) : that abuts or serves as an abutment : ADJOINING, BORDERING

abuzz \ə-ˈbəz\ *adj* (1859) : filled or resounding with or as if with a buzzing sound ⟨a lake ~ with outboards⟩; *esp* : filled with talk or excitement ⟨an office ~ with rumors⟩ ⟨a town ~ with anticipation of the big game⟩

aby *or* **abye** \ə-ˈbī\ *vt* [ME *abien,* fr. OE *ābycgan,* fr. *ā-* + *bycgan* to buy — more at ABIDE, BUY] (bef. 12c) *archaic* : to suffer a penalty for

abysm \ə-ˈbi-zəm\ *n* [ME *abime,* fr. AF *abisme,* modif. of LL *abyssus*] (14c) : ABYSS ⟨the dark backward and ~ of time —Shak.⟩

abys·mal \ə-ˈbiz-məl, a-\ *adj* (ca. 1656) **1 a** : having immense or fathomless extension downward, backward, or inward ⟨an ~ cliff⟩ **b** : immeasurably great : PROFOUND ⟨~ ignorance⟩ **c** : immeasurably low or wretched ⟨~ living conditions of the poor⟩ **2** : ABYSSAL 2 — **abys·mal·ly** \-mə-lē\ *adv*

abyss \ə-ˈbis, a- *also* ˈa-(ˌ)bis\ *n* [ME *abissus,* fr. LL *abyssus,* fr. Gk *abyssos,* fr. *abyssos,* adj., bottomless, fr. *a-* + *byssos* depth; perh. akin to Gk *bathys* deep] (14c) **1** : the bottomless gulf, pit, or chaos of the old cosmogonies **2 a** : an immeasurably deep gulf or great space **b** : intellectual or moral depths

abys·sal \ə-ˈbi-səl\ *adj* (1661) **1** : UNFATHOMABLE b **2** : of or relating to the bottom waters of the ocean depths

abyssal plain *n* (1954) : any of the great flat sediment-covered areas of ocean floor — see CONTINENTAL SHELF illustration

Ab·ys·sin·i·an \ˌa-bə-ˈsi-nē-ən, -ˈsin-yən\ *n* [*Abyssinia,* kingdom in Africa] (1876) : any of a breed of medium-sized slender domestic cats of African origin with short usu. brownish hair ticked with bands of darker color

ac *abbr* **1** account **2** acre **3** [L *ante cibum*] before meals

ac- — see AD-

-ac *n suffix* [NL *-acus,* fr. Gk *-akos,* var. of *-ikos* -ic after stems ending in *-i-*] : one affected with ⟨hemophili*ac*⟩

[1]**Ac** *abbr* altocumulus

[2]**Ac** *symbol* actinium

AC *abbr* **1** air-conditioning **2** alternating current **3** [ML *ante Christum*] before Christ **4** area code **5** athletic club

aca·cia \ə-ˈkā-shə\ *n* [NL, genus name, fr. L, acacia tree, fr. Gk *akakia*] (14c) **1** : GUM ARABIC **2** : any of a large genus (*Acacia*) of leguminous shrubs and trees of warm regions with leaves pinnate or reduced to phyllodes and white or yellow flower clusters

acad *abbr* academic; academy

ac·a·deme \ˈa-kə-ˌdēm, ˌa-kə-ˈ\ *n* [L *Academus* (in the phrase *inter silvas Academi* among the groves of Academus), fr. Gk *Akadēmos* — more at ACADEMY] (1588) **1 a** : a place of instruction **b** : the academic life, community, or world ⟨in the halls of ~⟩ **2** : ACADEMIC; *esp* : PEDANT

ac·a·de·mia \ˌa-kə-ˈdē-mē-ə\ *n* [NL, fr. L, academy] (1946) : ACADEME 1b

[1]**ac·a·dem·ic** \ˌa-kə-ˈde-mik\ *n* (1587) **1** : a member of an institution of learning **2** : a person who is academic in background, outlook, or methods **3** *pl* : academic subjects ⟨has no interest in ~*s*⟩

[2]**academic** *also* **ac·a·dem·i·cal** \-mi-kəl\ *adj* (1588) **1 a** : of, relating to, or associated with an academy or school esp. of higher learning **b** : of or relating to performance in academic courses ⟨~ excellence⟩ **c** : very learned but inexperienced in practical matters ⟨~ thinkers⟩ **d** : based on formal study esp. at an institution of higher learning **2** : of or relating to literary or artistic rather than technical or professional studies **3 a** : THEORETICAL, SPECULATIVE ⟨an ~ question⟩ **b** : having no practical or useful significance **4** : conforming to the traditions or rules of a school (as of literature or art) or an official academy : CONVENTIONAL ⟨~ painting⟩ — **ac·a·dem·i·cal·ly** \-mi-k(ə-)lē\ *adv*

academic freedom *n* (1863) : freedom to teach or to learn without interference (as by government officials)

ac·a·de·mi·cian \ˌa-kə-də-ˈmi-shən, ə-ˌka-də-\ *n* (1748) **1 a** : a member of an academy for promoting science, art, or literature **b** : a follower of an artistic or philosophical tradition or a promoter of its ideas **2** : ACADEMIC

ac·a·dem·i·cism \ˌa-kə-ˈde-mə-ˌsi-zəm\ *also* **acad·e·mism** \ə-ˈka-də-ˌmi-zəm\ *n* (1610) **1** : the doctrines of Plato's Academy; *specif* : the skeptical doctrines of the later Academy holding that nothing can be known — compare PYRRHONISM **2** : a formal academic quality (as in art or music) **3** : purely speculative thoughts and attitudes

academic year *n* (1828) : the annual period of sessions of an educational institution usu. beginning in September and ending in June

acad·e·my \ə-ˈka-də-mē\ *n, pl* **-mies** [L *academia,* fr. Gk *Akadēmeia,* fr. *Akadēmeia,* gymnasium where Plato taught, fr. *Akadēmos* Attic mythological hero] (1549) **1 a** : a school usu. above the elementary level; *esp* : a private high school **b** : a high school or college in which special subjects or skills are taught **c** : higher education — used with *the* ⟨the functions of the ~ in modern society⟩ **2** *cap* **a** : the school for advanced education founded by Plato **b** : the philosophical doctrines associated with Plato's Academy **3** : a society of learned persons organized to advance art, science, or literature **4** : a body of established opinion widely accepted as authoritative in a particular field

Aca·di·an \ə-ˈkā-dē-ən, a-\ *n* (1705) **1** : a native or inhabitant of Acadia **2** : a descendant of the French-speaking inhabitants of Acadia expelled after the French loss of the colony in 1755; *esp* : CAJUN — **Acadian** *adj*

acai *also* **açai** \ˌä-ˌsä-ˈē, -sī-ˈē\ *n* [BrazPg *açaí, fr. Tupi *iBasaí*] (1868) : a small dark purple fleshy berrylike fruit of a tall slender palm (*Euterpe oleracea*) of tropical Central and South America that is often used in beverages; *also* : the palm

acan·tho·ceph·a·lan \ə-ˌkan(t)-thə-ˈse-fə-lən\ *n* [ultim. fr. Gk *akantha* thorn, spine + *kephalē* head — more at CEPHALIC] (ca. 1889) : SPINY-HEADED WORM — **acanthocephalan** *adj*

acan·thus \ə-ˈkan(t)-thəs\ *n, pl* **acanthus** [NL, genus name, fr. Gk *akanthos,* an acanthus, fr. *akantha* thorn] (1551) **1** : any of a genus (*Acanthus* of the family Acanthaceae, the acanthus family) of prickly perennial herbs chiefly of the Mediterranean region **2** : an ornamentation (as in a Corinthian capital) representing or suggesting the leaves of the acanthus

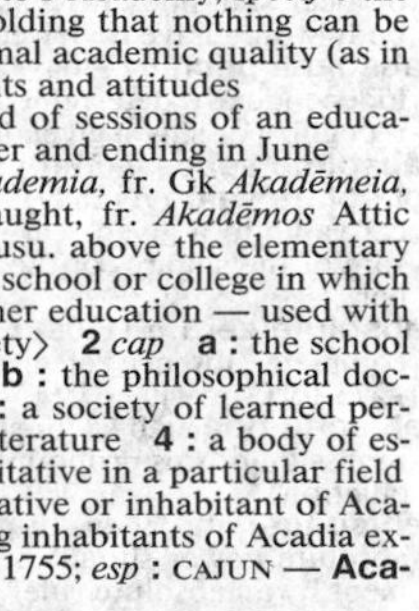

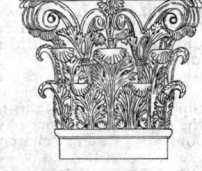

acanthus 2

a cap·pel·la *also* **a ca·pel·la** \ˌä-kə-ˈpe-lə\ *adv or adj* [It *a cappella* in chapel style] (ca. 1864) : without instrumental accompaniment

ac·a·ri·a·sis \ˌa-kə-ˈrī-ə-səs\ *n* (1828) : infestation with or disease caused by mites

acar·i·cide \ə-ˈker-ə-ˌsīd, -ˈka-rə-\ *n* [*acarus* + *-i-* + *-cide*] (ca. 1879) : a pesticide that kills mites and ticks — **acar·i·cid·al** \ə-ˌker-ə-ˈsī-dᵊl, -ˌka-rə-\ *adj*

ac·a·rid \ˈa-kə-rəd\ *n* (1881) : any of an order (Acari syn. Acarina) of arachnids including the mites and ticks — **acarid** *adj*

ac·a·rus \ˈa-kə-rəs\ *n, pl* **-ri** \-ˌrī\ [NL, genus name, fr. Gk *akari,* a mite] (1658) : MITE; *esp* : one of a formerly extensive genus (*Acarus*)

acat·a·lec·tic \(ˌ)ā-ˌka-tə-ˈlek-tik\ *adj* [LL *acatalecticus,* fr. *acatalectus,* fr. Gk *akatalēktos,* fr. *a-* + *katalēgein* to leave off — more at CATALECTIC] (1589) : not catalectic ⟨~ verse⟩ — **acatalectic** *n*

acau·les·cent \ˌā-kȯ-ˈle-sᵊnt\ *adj* [*a-* + L *caulis* stem — more at HOLE] (1854) : having no stem or appearing to have none

acc *abbr* accusative

ac·cede \ak-ˈsēd, ik-\ *vi* **ac·ced·ed; ac·ced·ing** [ME, fr. L *accedere* to go to, be added, fr. *ad-* + *cedere* to go] (15c) **1 a** : to become a party (as to an agreement) **b** : to express approval or give consent : give in to a request or demand **2** *archaic* : APPROACH **3** : to enter upon an office or position ***syn*** see ASSENT

accel *abbr* accelerando

[1]**ac·ce·le·ran·do** \(ˌ)ä-ˌche-lə-ˈrän-(ˌ)dō; ik-ˌse-, (ˌ)ak-\ *adv or adj* [It, lit., accelerating, fr. L *accelerandum,* gerund of *accelerare*] (ca. 1842) : gradually faster — used as a direction in music

[2]**accelerando** *n, pl* **-dos** (1889) : a gradual increase in tempo

ac·cel·er·ant \ik-ˈse-lə-rənt, ak-\ *n* (ca. 1909) : a substance used to accelerate a process (as the spreading of a fire)

ac·cel·er·ate \-lə-ˌrāt\ *vb* **-at·ed; -at·ing** [L *acceleratus,* pp. of *accelerare,* fr. *ad-* + *celer* swift — more at HOLD] *vt* (ca. 1530) **1** : to bring about at an earlier time ⟨~ their departure⟩ **2** : to cause to move faster ⟨*accelerated* his steps⟩; *also* : to cause to undergo acceleration **3 a** : to hasten the progress or development of ⟨~ our efforts⟩ **b** : INCREASE ⟨~ food production⟩ **4 a** : to enable (a student) to complete a course in less than usual time **b** : to speed up (as a course of study) ~ *vi* **1 a** : to move faster : gain speed ⟨the car slowly *accelerated*⟩ **b** : GROW, INCREASE ⟨inflation was *accelerating*⟩ **2** : to follow an accelerated educational program — **ac·cel·er·at·ing·ly** \-ˌrā-tiŋ-lē\ *adv*

ac·cel·er·a·tion \ik-ˌse-lə-ˈrā-shən, (ˌ)ak-\ *n* (1531) **1 :** the act or process of accelerating : the state of being accelerated **2 :** the rate of change of velocity with respect to time; *broadly* : change of velocity

acceleration of gravity (ca. 1889) : the acceleration of a body in free fall under the influence of earth's gravity expressed as the rate of increase of velocity per unit of time and assigned the standard value of 980.665 centimeters per second per second — called also *g*

acceleration principle *n* (ca. 1941) : a theory in economics: an increase or decrease in income induces a corresponding but magnified change in investment

ac·cel·er·a·tive \ik-ˈse-lə-ˌrā-tiv, ak-\ *adj* (ca. 1666) : of, relating to, or tending to cause acceleration : ACCELERATING

ac·cel·er·a·tor \ik-ˈse-lə-ˌrā-tər, ak-\ *n* (1552) : one that accelerates: as **a :** a muscle or nerve that speeds the performance of an action **b :** a device (as a pedal) for controlling the speed of a motor vehicle engine **c :** a substance that speeds a chemical reaction **d :** an apparatus for imparting high velocities to charged particles (as electrons) **e :** an item of computer hardware that increases the speed at which a program or function operates ⟨a graphics ~⟩

ac·cel·er·om·e·ter \ik-ˌse-lə-ˈrä-mə-tər, ak-\ *n* [ISV *accelera*tion + *-o-* + *-meter*] (ca. 1890) : an instrument for measuring acceleration or for detecting and measuring vibrations

[1]**ac·cent** \ˈak-ˌsent, ak-ˈ\ *vt* [MF *accenter,* fr. *accent* intonation, fr. L *accentus,* fr. *ad-* + *cantus* song — more at CHANT] (1530) **1 a :** to pronounce with accent : STRESS **b :** to mark with a written or printed accent **2 :** to give prominence to : make more prominent

[2]**ac·cent** \ˈak-ˌsent, *chiefly Brit* -sənt\ *n* (1530) **1 :** an articulative effort giving prominence to one syllable over adjacent syllables; *also* : the prominence thus given a syllable **2 :** a distinctive manner of expression: as **a :** an individual's distinctive or characteristic inflection, tone, or choice of words — usu. used in pl. **b :** a way of speaking typical of a particular group of people and esp. of the natives or residents of a region **3 :** rhythmically significant stress on the syllables of a verse usu. at regular intervals **4** *archaic* : UTTERANCE **5 a :** a mark (as ´, `, ˆ) used in writing or printing to indicate a specific sound value, stress, or pitch, to distinguish words otherwise identically spelled, or to indicate that an ordinarily mute vowel should be pronounced **b :** an accented letter **6 a :** greater stress given to one musical tone than to its neighbors **b :** ACCENT MARK 2 **7 a :** emphasis laid on a part of an artistic design or composition **b :** an emphasized detail or area; *esp* : a small detail in sharp contrast with its surroundings **c :** a substance or object used for emphasis **8 :** a mark placed to the right of a letter or number and usu. slightly above it: as **a :** a double prime **b :** PRIME **9 :** special concern or attention : EMPHASIS ⟨an ~ on youth⟩ — **ac·cent·less** \-ləs\ *adj*

accent mark *n* (1884) **1 a :** ACCENT 5a **b :** ACCENT 8 **2 a :** a symbol used to indicate musical stress **b :** a mark placed after a letter designating a note of music to indicate in which octave the note occurs

ac·cen·tu·al \ak-ˈsen(t)-sh(ə-)wəl, ik-\ *adj* [L *accentus*] (1610) : of, relating to, or characterized by accent; *specif* : based on accent rather than on quantity or syllabic recurrence ⟨~ poetry⟩ — **ac·cen·tu·al·ly** *adv*

ac·cen·tu·ate \ik-ˈsen(t)-shə-ˌwāt, ak-\ *vt* **-at·ed; -at·ing** [ML *accentuatus,* pp. of *accentuare,* fr. L *accentus*] (ca. 1731) : ACCENT, EMPHASIZE; *also* : INTENSIFY ⟨~*s* the feeling of despair⟩ — **ac·cen·tu·a·tion** \ik-ˌsen(t)-shə-ˈwā-shən, (ˌ)ak-\ *n*

ac·cept \ik-ˈsept, ak- *also* ek-\ *vb* [ME, fr. AF *accepter,* fr. L *acceptare,* freq. of *accipere* to receive, fr. *ad-* + *capere* to take — more at HEAVE] *vt* (14c) **1 a :** to receive willingly ⟨~ a gift⟩ **b :** to be able or designed to take or hold (something applied or added) ⟨a surface that will not ~ ink⟩ **2 :** to give admittance or approval to ⟨~ her as one of the group⟩ **3 a :** to endure without protest or reaction ⟨~ poor living conditions⟩ **b :** to regard as proper, normal, or inevitable ⟨the idea is widely ~*ed*⟩ **c :** to recognize as true : BELIEVE ⟨refused to ~ the explanation⟩ **4 a :** to make a favorable response to ⟨~ an offer⟩ **b :** to agree to undertake (a responsibility) ⟨~ a job⟩ **5 :** to assume an obligation to pay; *also* : to take in payment ⟨we don't ~ personal checks⟩ **6 :** to receive (a legislative report) officially ~ *vi* : to receive favorably something offered — usu. used with *of* ⟨a heart more disposed to ~ of his —Jane Austen⟩ — **ac·cept·ing·ly** \-ˈsep-tiŋ-lē\ *adv* — **ac·cept·ing·ness** \-tiŋ-nəs\ *n*

ac·cept·able \ik-ˈsep-tə-bəl, ak- *also* ek-\ *adj* (14c) **1 :** capable or worthy of being accepted ⟨no compromise would be ~⟩ **2 a :** WELCOME, PLEASING ⟨compliments are always ~⟩ **b :** barely satisfactory or adequate ⟨performances varied from excellent to ~⟩ — **ac·cept·abil·i·ty** \ik-ˌsep-tə-ˈbi-lə-tē, (ˌ)ak-, ek-\ *n* — **ac·cept·able·ness** \ik-ˈsep-tə-bəl-nəs, ak-\ *n* — **ac·cept·ably** \-blē\ *adv*

ac·cep·tance \ik-ˈsep-tən(t)s, ak-\ *n* (1574) **1 :** an agreeing either expressly or by conduct to the act or offer of another so that a contract is concluded and the parties become legally bound **2 :** the quality or state of being accepted or acceptable **3 :** the act of accepting : the fact of being accepted : APPROVAL **4 a :** the act of accepting a time draft or bill of exchange for payment when due according to the specified terms **b :** an accepted draft or bill of exchange **5 :** ACCEPTATION 2

ac·cep·tant \-tənt\ *adj* (1851) : willing to accept : RECEPTIVE

ac·cep·ta·tion \ˌak-ˌsep-ˈtā-shən\ *n* (15c) **1 :** ACCEPTANCE; *esp* : favorable reception or approval **2 :** a generally accepted meaning of a word or understanding of a concept

ac·cept·ed *adj* (15c) : generally approved or used ⟨an ~ convention⟩ — **ac·cept·ed·ly** *adv*

ac·cept·er \ik-ˈsep-tər, ak-\ *n* (1585) **1 :** one that accepts **2 :** ACCEPTOR 2

ac·cep·tive \ak-ˈsep-tiv\ *adj* (1596) **1 :** ACCEPTABLE **2 :** RECEPTIVE

ac·cep·tor \ik-ˈsep-tər, ak-\ *n* (14c) **1 :** ACCEPTER 1 **2 :** one that accepts an order or a bill of exchange **3 :** an atom, molecule, or subatomic particle capable of receiving another entity (as an electron) esp. to form a compound — compare DONOR 3a

[1]**ac·cess** \ˈak-ˌses *also* ik-ˈses\ *n* [ME, fr. AF & L; AF *acces,* fr. L *accessus* approach, fr. *accedere* to approach — more at ACCEDE] (14c) **1 a :** ONSET 2 **b :** a fit of intense feeling : OUTBURST **2 a :** permission, liberty, or ability to enter, approach, or pass to and from a place or to approach or communicate with a person or thing **b :** freedom or ability to obtain or make use of something **c :** a way or means of access **d :** the act or an instance of accessing **3 :** an increase by addition ⟨a sudden ~ of wealth⟩

[2]**access** *vt* (1962) : to get at : gain access to ⟨~*ed* the computer by phone⟩

ac·ces·si·ble \ik-ˈse-sə-bəl, ak-, ek-\ *adj* (15c) **1 :** providing access **2 a :** capable of being reached ⟨~ by rail⟩; *also* : being within reach ⟨fashions at ~ prices⟩ **b :** easy to communicate or deal with ⟨~ people⟩ **3 :** capable of being influenced : OPEN ⟨~ to new ideas⟩ **4 :** capable of being used or seen : AVAILABLE ⟨the collection is not currently ~⟩ **5 :** capable of being understood or appreciated ⟨the author's most ~ stories⟩ ⟨an ~ film⟩ — **ac·ces·si·bil·i·ty** \-ˌse-sə-ˈbi-lə-tē\ *n* — **ac·ces·si·ble·ness** \-ˈse-sə-bəl-nəs\ *n* — **ac·ces·si·bly** \-blē\ *adv*

[1]**ac·ces·sion** \ik-ˈse-shən, ak-\ *n* (1588) **1 a :** increase by something added **b :** acquisition of additional property (as by growth or increase of existing property) **2 :** something added : ACQUISITION **3 :** the act of assenting or agreeing **4 a :** the act of becoming joined : ADHERENCE **b :** the act by which one nation becomes party to an agreement already in force between other powers **5 a :** an act of coming near or to : APPROACH, ADMITTANCE **b :** the act of coming to high office or a position of honor or power ⟨her ~ to power⟩ **6 :** a sudden fit or outburst : ACCESS — **ac·ces·sion·al** \-ˈsesh-nəl, -ˈse-shə-nᵊl\ *adj*

[2]**accession** *vt* (1892) : to record in order of acquisition

ac·ces·so·ri·al \ˌak-sə-ˈsȯr-ē-əl\ *adj* (1726) **1 :** of or relating to an accessory ⟨~ liability⟩ **2 :** of, relating to, or constituting an accession : SUPPLEMENTARY ⟨~ services⟩

ac·ces·so·rise *Brit var of* ACCESSORIZE

ac·ces·so·rize \ik-ˈse-sə-ˌrīz, ak-\ *vb* **-rized; -riz·ing** *vt* (1939) : to furnish with accessories ~ *vi* : to wear clothing accessories

[1]**ac·ces·so·ry** *also* **ac·ces·sa·ry** \ik-ˈse-sə-rē, ak-, ek-, -ˈses-rē, *also* ə-ˈse-\ *n, pl* **-ries** (15c) **1 a :** a person not actually or constructively present but contributing as an assistant or instigator to the commission of an offense — called also *accessory before the fact* **b :** a person who knowing that a crime has been committed aids or shelters the offender with intent to defeat justice — called also *accessory after the fact* **2 a :** a thing of secondary or subordinate importance : ADJUNCT **b :** an object or device not essential in itself but adding to the beauty, convenience, or effectiveness of something else ⟨auto *accessories*⟩ ⟨clothing *accessories*⟩

[2]**accessory** *adj* (1607) **1 :** assisting as a subordinate; *esp* : contributing to a crime but not as the chief agent **2 :** aiding or contributing in a secondary way : SUPPLEMENTARY **3 :** present in a minor amount and not essential as a constituent ⟨an ~ mineral in a rock⟩

accessory fruit *n* (ca. 1900) : a fruit (as the apple) of which a conspicuous part consists of tissue other than that of the ripened ovary

accessory nerve *n* (ca. 1842) : either of a pair of motor nerves that are the 11th cranial nerves of higher vertebrates, arise from the medulla and the upper part of the spinal cord, and supply chiefly the pharynx and muscles of the upper chest, back, and shoulders

access time *n* (1950) : the time lag between the time stored information (as in a computer) is requested and the time it is delivered

ac·ciac·ca·tu·ra \(ˌ)ä-ˌchä-kə-ˈtu̇r-ə\ *n* [It, lit., crushing] (ca. 1819) : a discordant note sounded with a principal note or chord and immediately released

ac·ci·dence \ˈak-sə-dən(t)s, -ˌden(t)s\ *n* [ME, fr. MF, fr. L *accidentia* inflections of words, nonessential qualities, pl. of *accident-, accidens,* n.] (15c) : a part of grammar that deals with inflections

ac·ci·dent \ˈak-sə-dənt, -ˌdent; ˈaks-dənt\ *n* [ME, fr. MF, fr. L *accident-, accidens* nonessential quality, chance, fr. prp. of *accidere* to happen, fr. *ad-* + *cadere* to fall — more at CHANCE] (14c) **1 a :** an unforeseen and unplanned event or circumstance **b :** lack of intention or necessity : CHANCE ⟨met by ~ rather than by design⟩ **2 a :** an unfortunate event resulting esp. from carelessness or ignorance **b :** an unexpected and medically important bodily event esp. when injurious ⟨a cerebrovascular ~⟩ **c :** an unexpected happening causing loss or injury which is not due to any fault or misconduct on the part of the person injured but for which legal relief may be sought **d —** used euphemistically to refer to an involuntary act or instance of urination or defecation **3 :** a nonessential property or quality of an entity or circumstance ⟨the ~ of nationality⟩

[1]**ac·ci·den·tal** \ˌak-sə-ˈden-tᵊl\ *adj* (14c) **1 :** arising from extrinsic causes : INCIDENTAL, NONESSENTIAL **2 a :** occurring unexpectedly or by chance **b :** happening without intent or through carelessness and often with unfortunate results — **ac·ci·den·tal·ly** \-ˈdent-lē, -ˈden-tᵊl-ē\ *also* **ac·ci·dent·ly** \-ˈdent-lē\ *adv* — **ac·ci·den·tal·ness** \-ˈden-tᵊl-nəs\ *n*

syn ACCIDENTAL, FORTUITOUS, CASUAL, CONTINGENT mean not amenable to planning or prediction. ACCIDENTAL stresses chance ⟨any resemblance to actual persons is entirely *accidental*⟩. FORTUITOUS so strongly suggests chance that it often connotes entire absence of cause ⟨a series of *fortuitous* events⟩. CASUAL stresses lack of real or apparent premeditation or intent ⟨a *casual* encounter with a stranger⟩. CONTINGENT suggests possibility of happening but stresses uncertainty and dependence on other future events for existence or occurrence ⟨the *contingent* effects of the proposed law⟩.

[2]**accidental** *n* (1651) **1 :** a nonessential property **2 a :** a note foreign to a key indicated by a signature **b :** a prefixed sign indicating an accidental

accident insurance *n* (1851) : insurance against loss through accidental bodily injury to the insured

accident–prone *adj* (1926) **1 :** having a greater than average number of accidents **2 :** having personality traits that predispose to accidents

ac·cid·ie \ˈak-sə-dē\ *n* (13c) : ACEDIA

ac·cip·i·ter \ak-ˈsi-pə-tər, ik-\ *n* [NL, genus name, fr. L, hawk] (ca. 1828) : any of a genus (*Accipiter*) of medium-sized forest-inhabiting hawks that have short broad wings and a long tail and a characteristic flight pattern of several quick flaps and a glide — **ac·cip·i·trine** \-ˈsi-pə-ˌtrīn\ *adj or n*

\ə\ **abut** \ᵊ\ **kitten, F table** \ər\ **further** \a\ **ash** \ā\ **ace** \ä\ **mop, mar**
\au̇\ **out** \ch\ **chin** \e\ **bet** \ē\ **easy** \g\ **go** \i\ **hit** \ī\ **ice** \j\ **job**
\ŋ\ **sing** \ō\ **go** \ȯ\ **law** \ȯi\ **boy** \th\ **thin** \t͟h\ **the** \ü\ **loot** \u̇\ **foot**
\y\ **yet** \zh\ **vision, beige** \ḵ, ⁿ, œ, ue, ʸ\ *see* Guide to Pronunciation

[1]**ac·claim** \ə-ˈklām\ *vb* [L *acclamare,* lit., to shout at, fr. *ad-* + *clamare* to shout — more at CLAIM] *vt* (1606) **1 :** APPLAUD, PRAISE **2 :** to declare by acclamation ~ *vi* **:** to shout praise or applause — **ac·claim·er** *n*

[2]**acclaim** *n* (1667) **1 :** the act of acclaiming **2 :** PRAISE, APPLAUSE

ac·cla·ma·tion \ˌa-klə-ˈmā-shən\ *n* [L *acclamation-, acclamatio,* fr. *acclamare*] (1567) **1 :** a loud eager expression of approval, praise, or assent **2 :** an overwhelming affirmative vote by cheers, shouts, or applause rather than by ballot

ac·cli·mate \ˈa-klə-ˌmāt; ə-ˈklī-mət, -ˌmāt\ *vb* **-mat·ed; -mat·ing** [F *acclimater,* fr. *a-* (fr. L *ad-*) + *climat* climate] *vt* (1792) **:** to adapt to a new temperature, altitude, climate, environment, or situation ~ *vi* **:** to become acclimated

ac·cli·ma·tion \ˌa-klə-ˈmā-shən, -ˌklī-\ *n* (1801) **:** the process or result of acclimating; *esp* **:** physiological adjustment by an organism to environmental change

ac·cli·ma·tise *Brit var of* ACCLIMATIZE

ac·cli·ma·tize \ə-ˈklī-mə-ˌtīz\ *vb* **-tized; -tiz·ing** (1815) **:** ACCLIMATE — **ac·cli·ma·ti·za·tion** \ə-ˌklī-mə-tə-ˈzā-shən\ *n* — **ac·cli·ma·tiz·er** *n*

ac·cliv·i·ty \ə-ˈkli-və-tē, a-\ *n, pl* **-ties** [L *acclivitas,* fr. *acclivis* ascending, fr. *ad-* + *clivus* slope — more at DECLIVITY] (1614) **:** an ascending slope (as of a hill)

ac·co·lade \ˈa-kə-ˌlād, -ˌläd\ *n* [F, fr. *accoler* to embrace, fr. VL **accollare,* fr. L *ad-* + *collum* neck — more at COLLAR] (1623) **1 a :** a ceremonial embrace **b :** a ceremony or salute conferring knighthood **2 a :** a mark of acknowledgment **:** AWARD **b :** an expression of praise **3 :** a brace or a line used in music to join two or more staffs carrying simultaneous parts

ac·com·mo·date \ə-ˈkä-mə-ˌdāt\ *vb* **-dat·ed; -dat·ing** [L *accommodatus,* pp. of *accommodare,* fr. *ad-* + *commodare* to make fit, fr. *commodus* suitable — more at COMMODE] *vt* (1550) **1 :** to make fit, suitable, or congruous **2 :** to bring into agreement or concord **:** RECONCILE **3 :** to provide with something desired, needed, or suited **4 a :** to make room for **b :** to hold without crowding or inconvenience **5 :** to give consideration to **:** allow for ⟨~ the special interests of various groups⟩ ~ *vi* **:** to adapt oneself; *also* **:** to undergo visual accommodation ***syn*** see ADAPT, CONTAIN — **ac·com·mo·da·tive** \-ˌdā-tiv\ *adj* — **ac·com·mo·da·tive·ness** *n* — **ac·com·mo·da·tor** \-ˌdā-tər\ *n*

ac·com·mo·dat·ing *adj* (1775) **:** willing to please **:** HELPFUL, OBLIGING — **ac·com·mo·dat·ing·ly** \-ˌdā-tiŋ-lē\ *adv*

ac·com·mo·da·tion \ə-ˌkä-mə-ˈdā-shən\ *n* (1603) **1 :** something supplied for convenience or to satisfy a need: as **a :** lodging, food, and services or traveling space and related services — usu. used in pl. ⟨tourist ~*s* on the boat⟩ ⟨overnight ~*s*⟩ **b :** a public conveyance (as a train) that stops at all or nearly all points **c :** LOAN **2 :** the act of accommodating **:** the state of being accommodated: as **a :** the providing of what is needed or desired for convenience **b :** ADAPTATION, ADJUSTMENT **c :** a reconciliation of differences **:** SETTLEMENT **d :** the automatic adjustment of the eye for seeing at different distances effected chiefly by changes in the convexity of the crystalline lens; *also* **:** the range over which such adjustment is possible — **ac·com·mo·da·tion·al** \-shnəl, -shə-nᵊl\ *adj*

[1]**ac·com·mo·da·tion·ist** \-ˈdā-sh(ə-)nist\ *adj* (1919) **:** favoring or practicing accommodation or compromise

[2]**accommodationist** *n* (1964) **:** one who adapts to or compromises with an opposing view; *esp* **:** a black who adapts to the ideals or attitudes of whites — **ac·com·mo·da·tion·ism** \-ni-zəm\ *n*

accommodation ladder *n* (1754) **:** a light ladder or stairway hung over the side of a ship for ascending from or descending to small boats

ac·com·pa·ni·ment \ə-ˈkəm-pə-nē-mənt, -ˈkəmp-nē-\ *n* (1697) **1 :** an instrumental or vocal part designed to support or complement a melody **2 a :** an addition (as an ornament) intended to give completeness or symmetry **:** COMPLEMENT **b :** an accompanying situation or occurrence **:** CONCOMITANT — **ac·com·pa·ni·ment·al** \-ˌkəm-pə-nē-ˈmen-tᵊl, -ˌkəmp-nē-\ *adj*

ac·com·pa·nist \ə-ˈkəmp-nist, -ˈkəm-pə-\ *n* (ca. 1811) **:** one (as a pianist) who plays an accompaniment

ac·com·pa·ny \ə-ˈkəmp-nē, -ˈkämp-; -ˈkəm-pə-, -ˈkäm-\ *vb* **-nied; -ny·ing** [ME *accompanien* to make an associate, fr. AF *accompaigner,* fr. *a-* (fr. L *ad-*) + *cumpaing* companion — more at COMPANION] *vt* (15c) **1 :** to go with as an associate or companion **2 :** to perform an accompaniment to or for **3 a :** to cause to be in association ⟨*accompanied* their advice with a warning⟩ **b :** to be in association with ⟨the pictures that ~ the text⟩ ~ *vi* **:** to perform an accompaniment

ac·com·plice \ə-ˈkäm-pləs, -ˈkəm-\ *n* [alter. (fr. incorrect division of *a complice*) of *complice*] (1584) **:** one associated with another esp. in wrongdoing

ac·com·plish \ə-ˈkäm-plish, -ˈkəm-\ *vt* [ME *accomplisshen,* fr. AF *accompliss-,* stem of *accomplir,* fr. VL **accomplēre,* fr. L *ad-* + *complēre* to fill up — more at COMPLETE] (14c) **1 :** to bring about (a result) by effort ⟨have much to ~ today⟩ **2 :** to bring to completion **:** FULFILL ⟨~ a job⟩ **3 :** to succeed in reaching (a stage in a progression) ⟨would starve before ~*ing* half the distance —W. H. Hudson †1922⟩ **4** *archaic* **a :** to equip thoroughly **b :** PERFECT ***syn*** see PERFORM — **ac·com·plish·able** \-pli-shə-bəl\ *adj* — **ac·com·plish·er** *n*

ac·com·plished *adj* (15c) **1 a :** proficient as the result of practice or training ⟨an ~ dancer⟩; *also* **:** skillfully done or produced ⟨an ~ film⟩ **b :** having many social accomplishments **2 :** established beyond doubt or dispute ⟨an ~ fact⟩

ac·com·plish·ment \ə-ˈkäm-plish-mənt, -ˈkəm-\ *n* (15c) **1 :** the act of accomplishing **:** COMPLETION **2 :** something that has been accomplished **:** ACHIEVEMENT **3 a :** a quality or ability equipping one for society **b :** a special skill or ability acquired by training or practice

[1]**ac·cord** \ə-ˈkȯrd\ *vb* [ME, fr. AF *acorder,* fr. VL **accordare,* fr. L *ad-* + *cord-, cor* heart — more at HEART] *vt* (12c) **1 :** to bring into agreement **:** RECONCILE **2 :** to grant or give esp. as appropriate, due, or earned ~ *vi* **1** *archaic* **:** to arrive at an agreement **2** *obs* **:** to give consent **3 :** to be consistent or in harmony **:** AGREE — usu. used with *with* ⟨a theory that ~*s* with the known facts⟩ ***syn*** see GRANT

[2]**accord** *n* [ME, fr. AF *acord,* fr. *acorder*] (13c) **1 a :** AGREEMENT, CONFORMITY ⟨acted in ~ with the company's policy⟩ **b :** a formal reaching of agreement **:** COMPACT, TREATY **2 :** balanced interrelationship **:** HARMONY **3** *obs* **:** ASSENT **4 :** voluntary or spontaneous impulse to act ⟨gave generously of their own ~⟩

ac·cor·dance \ə-ˈkȯr-dᵊn(t)s\ *n* (14c) **1 :** AGREEMENT, CONFORMITY ⟨in ~ with a rule⟩ **2 :** the act of granting

ac·cor·dant \-dᵊnt\ *adj* (14c) **1 :** CONSONANT, AGREEING **2 :** HARMONIOUS, CORRESPONDENT — **ac·cor·dant·ly** *adv*

according as *conj* (15c) **1 :** in accord with the way in which **2 a :** depending on how **b :** depending on whether **:** IF

ac·cord·ing·ly \ə-ˈkȯr-diŋ-lē\ *adv* (14c) **1 :** in accordance **:** CORRESPONDINGLY **2 :** CONSEQUENTLY, SO

according to *prep* (14c) **1 :** in conformity with **2 :** as stated or attested by **3 :** depending on

[1]**ac·cor·di·on** \ə-ˈkȯr-dē-ən\ *n* [G *Akkordion,* fr. *Akkord* chord, fr. F *accord,* fr. OF *acord*] (1830) **:** a portable keyboard wind instrument in which the wind is forced past free reeds by means of a hand-operated bellows — **ac·cor·di·on·ist** \-dē-ə-nist\ *n*

[2]**accordion** *adj* (1852) **:** folding or creased or hinged to fold like an accordion ⟨an ~ pleat⟩ ⟨an ~ door⟩

ac·cost \ə-ˈkȯst, -ˈkäst\ *vt* [MF *accoster,* ultim. fr. L *ad-* + *costa* rib, side — more at COAST] (1597) **:** to approach and speak to often in a challenging or aggressive way

ac·couche·ment \ˌa-ˌküsh-ˈmä^{n}, ə-ˈküsh-ˌ\ *n* [F] (1744) **:** the time or act of giving birth

ac·cou·cheur \ˌa-ˌkü-ˈshər\ *n* [F] (1737) **:** one that assists at a birth; *esp* **:** OBSTETRICIAN

[1]**ac·count** \ə-ˈkau̇nt\ *n* [ME *acounte, accompte,* fr. AF *acunte,* fr. *acunter*] (14c) **1** *archaic* **:** RECKONING, COMPUTATION **2 a :** a record of debit and credit entries to cover transactions involving a particular item or a particular person or concern **b :** a statement of transactions during a fiscal period and the resulting balance **3 a :** a statement explaining one's conduct **b :** a statement or exposition of reasons, causes, or motives ⟨no satisfactory ~ of these phenomena⟩ **c :** a reason for an action **:** BASIS ⟨on that ~ I must refuse⟩ **4 a** (1) **:** a formal business arrangement providing for regular dealings or services (as banking, advertising, or store credit) and involving the establishment and maintenance of an account; *also* **:** CLIENT, CUSTOMER (2) **:** money deposited in a bank account and subject to withdrawal by the depositor **b :** an arrangement in which a person uses the Internet or e-mail services of a particular company **5 a :** VALUE, IMPORTANCE ⟨it's of no ~ to me⟩ **b :** ESTEEM ⟨stood high in their ~⟩ **6 :** ADVANTAGE ⟨turned her wit to good ~⟩ **7 a :** careful thought **:** CONSIDERATION ⟨have to take many things into ~⟩ **b :** a usu. mental record **:** TRACK ⟨keep ~ of all you do⟩ **8 :** a description of facts, conditions, or events **:** REPORT, NARRATIVE ⟨the newspaper ~ of the fire⟩ ⟨by all ~*s* they're well-off⟩; *also* **:** PERFORMANCE ⟨a straightforward ~ of the sonata⟩ — **on account :** with the price charged to one's account — **on account of :** for the sake of **:** by reason of — **on no account :** under no circumstances — **on one's own account 1 :** on one's own behalf **2 :** at one's own risk **3 :** by oneself **:** on one's own

[2]**account** *vb* [ME, fr. AF *acunter,* fr. *a-* (fr. L *ad-*) + *cunter* to count] *vt* (14c) **1 :** to think of as **:** CONSIDER ⟨~*s* himself lucky⟩ **2 :** to probe into **:** ANALYZE ~ *vi* **1 :** to furnish a justifying analysis or explanation — used with *for* ⟨couldn't ~ for the loss⟩ **2 a :** to be the sole or primary factor — used with *for* ⟨the pitcher ~*ed* for all three putouts⟩ **b :** to bring about the capture, death, or destruction of something — used with *for* ⟨~*ed* for two rabbits⟩

ac·count·abil·i·ty \ə-ˌkau̇n-tə-ˈbi-lə-tē\ *n* (1770) **:** the quality or state of being accountable; *esp* **:** an obligation or willingness to accept responsibility or to account for one's actions ⟨public officials lacking ~⟩

ac·count·able \ə-ˈkau̇n-tə-bəl\ *adj* (14c) **1 :** subject to giving an account **:** ANSWERABLE ⟨held her ~ for the damage⟩ **2 :** capable of being accounted for **:** EXPLAINABLE ***syn*** see RESPONSIBLE — **ac·count·able·ness** \-ˈkau̇n-tə-bəl-nəs\ *n* — **ac·count·ably** \-blē\ *adv*

ac·coun·tan·cy \ə-ˈkau̇n-tᵊn(t)-sē\ *n* (1836) **:** the profession or practice of accounting

[1]**ac·coun·tant** \ə-ˈkau̇n-tᵊnt\ *n* (15c) **1 :** one that gives an account or is accountable **2 :** one who is skilled in the practice of accounting or who is in charge of public or private accounts — **ac·coun·tant·ship** \-tᵊn(t)-ˌship\ *n*

[2]**accountant** *adj* (15c) *obs* **:** ACCOUNTABLE, ANSWERABLE ⟨I stand ~ for as great a sin —Shak.⟩

account executive *n* (1931) **:** a business executive (as in an advertising agency) responsible for dealing with a client's account

ac·count·ing \ə-ˈkau̇n-tiŋ\ *n* (1713) **1 :** the system of recording and summarizing business and financial transactions and analyzing, verifying, and reporting the results; *also* **:** the principles and procedures of accounting **2 a :** work done in accounting or by accountants **b :** an instance of applied accounting or of the settling or presenting of accounts **3 :** ACCOUNT 3

account payable *n, pl* **accounts payable** (1812) **:** the balance due to a creditor on a current account

account receivable *n, pl* **accounts receivable** (1812) **:** a balance due from a debtor on a current account

ac·cou·tre *or* **ac·cou·ter** \ə-ˈkü-tər\ *vt* **-cou·tred** *or* **-cou·tered; -cou·tring** *or* **-cou·ter·ing** \-ˈkü-tə-riŋ, -ˈkü-triŋ\ [F *accoutrer,* fr. MF *acoustrer,* fr. *a-* + *costure* seam, fr. VL **consutura* — more at COUTURE] (1596) **:** to provide with equipment or furnishings **:** OUTFIT ***syn*** see FURNISH

ac·cou·tre·ment *or* **ac·cou·ter·ment** \ə-ˈkü-trə-mənt, -ˈkü-tər-mənt\ *n* (1549) **1 a :** EQUIPMENT, TRAPPINGS; *specif* **:** a soldier's outfit usu. not including clothes and weapons — usu. used in pl. **b :** an accessory item of clothing or equipment — usu. used in pl. **2** *archaic* **:** the act of accoutring **3 :** an identifying and often superficial characteristic or device — usu. used in pl. ⟨~*s* of power that define our diplomacy —Elizabeth Drew⟩

ac·cred·it \ə-ˈkre-dət\ *vt* [L *accreditus,* pp. of *accredere* to give credence to, fr. *ad-* + *credere* to believe — more at CREED] (1535) **1 :** to give official authorization to or approval of: **a :** to provide with credentials; *esp* **:** to send (an envoy) with letters of authorization **b :** to recognize or vouch for as conforming with a standard **c :** to recognize (an educational institution) as maintaining standards that qualify the graduates for admission to higher or more specialized institutions or for professional practice **2 :** to consider or recognize as outstanding **3 :** ATTRIBUTE, CREDIT ***syn*** see APPROVE — **ac·cred·i·table** \-də-tə-bəl\ *adj* — **ac·cred·i·ta·tion** \ə-ˌkre-də-ˈtā-shən, -ˈdā-\ *n*

ac·crete \ə-ˈkrēt\ *vb* **ac·cret·ed; ac·cret·ing** [back-formation fr. *accretion*] *vi* (1784) **:** to grow or become attached by accretion ∼ *vt* **:** to cause to adhere or become attached; *also* **:** ACCUMULATE

ac·cre·tion \ə-ˈkrē-shən\ *n* [L *accretion-, accretio,* fr. *accrescere* — more at ACCRUE] (1615) **1 :** the process of growth or enlargement by a gradual buildup: as **a :** increase by external addition or accumulation (as by adhesion of external parts or particles) **b :** the increase of land by the action of natural forces **2 :** a product of accretion; *esp* **:** an extraneous addition ⟨∼*s* of grime⟩ — **ac·cre·tion·ary** \-shə-ˌner-ē, -ˌne-rē\ *adj* — **ac·cre·tive** \ə-ˈkrē-tiv\ *adj*

accretion disk *n* (1972) **:** a disk of usu. gaseous matter surrounding a massive celestial object (as a black hole) in which the matter gradually spirals in toward and accretes onto the object as a result of gravitational attraction

[1]**ac·cru·al** \ə-ˈkrü-əl\ *n* (1880) **1 :** the action or process of accruing **2 :** something that accrues or has accrued

[2]**accrual** *adj* (1917) **:** relating to or being a method of accounting that recognizes income when earned and expenses when incurred regardless of when cash is received or disbursed — compare CASH

ac·crue \ə-ˈkrü\ *vb* **ac·crued; ac·cru·ing** [ME *acreuen,* prob. fr. AF **acrue* increase, fr. *acreistre* to increase, fr. L *accrescere,* fr. *ad-* + *crescere* to grow — more at CRESCENT] *vi* (15c) **1 :** to come into existence as a legally enforceable claim **2 a :** to come about as a natural growth, increase, or advantage ⟨the wisdom that ∼*s* with age⟩ **b :** to come as a direct result of some state or action ⟨rewards due to the feminine will ∼ to me —Germaine Greer⟩ **3 :** to accumulate or be added periodically ⟨interest ∼*s* on a daily basis⟩ ∼ *vt* **:** to accumulate or have due after a period of time ⟨∼ vacation time⟩ — **ac·cru·able** \-ˈkrü-ə-bəl\ *adj* — **ac·crue·ment** \-ˈkrü-mənt\ *n*

acct *abbr* account; accountant

ac·cul·tur·ate \ə-ˈkəl-chə-ˌrāt, a-\ *vt* **-at·ed; -at·ing** [back-formation fr. *acculturation*] (1930) **:** to change through acculturation

ac·cul·tur·a·tion \ə-ˌkəl-chə-ˈrā-shən, a-\ *n* (1880) **1 :** cultural modification of an individual, group, or people by adapting to or borrowing traits from another culture; *also* **:** a merging of cultures as a result of prolonged contact **2 :** the process by which a human being acquires the culture of a particular society from infancy — **ac·cul·tur·a·tion·al** \-shnəl, -shə-nᵊl\ *adj* — **ac·cul·tur·a·tive** \ə-ˈkəl-chə-ˌrā-tiv, a-\ *adj*

ac·cu·mu·late \ə-ˈkyü-m(y)ə-ˌlāt\ *vb* **-lat·ed; -lat·ing** [L *accumulatus,* pp. of *accumulare,* fr. *ad-* + *cumulare* to heap up — more at CUMULATE] *vt* (15c) **:** to gather or pile up esp. little by little **:** AMASS ⟨∼ a fortune⟩ ∼ *vi* **:** to increase gradually in quantity or number

ac·cu·mu·la·tion \ə-ˌkyü-m(y)ə-ˈlā-shən\ *n* (15c) **1 :** something that has accumulated or has been accumulated **2 :** the action or process of accumulating **:** the state of being or having accumulated **3 :** increase or growth by addition esp. when continuous or repeated ⟨∼ of interest⟩

ac·cu·mu·la·tive \ə-ˈkyü-m(y)ə-ˌlā-tiv, -lə-\ *adj* (1647) **1 :** CUMULATIVE ⟨an age of rapid and ∼ change⟩ **2 :** tending or given to accumulation — **ac·cu·mu·la·tive·ly** *adv* — **ac·cu·mu·la·tive·ness** *n*

ac·cu·mu·la·tor \ə-ˈkyü-m(y)ə-ˌlā-tər\ *n* (1748) **:** one that accumulates: as **a :** a device (as in a hydraulic system) in which a fluid is collected and esp. in which it is kept under pressure as a means of storing energy **b** *Brit* **:** STORAGE BATTERY **c :** a part (as in a computer) where numbers are totaled or stored

ac·cu·ra·cy \ˈa-kyə-rə-sē, ˈa-k(ə-)rə-\ *n, pl* **-cies** (1662) **1 :** freedom from mistake or error **:** CORRECTNESS **2 a :** conformity to truth or to a standard or model **:** EXACTNESS **b :** degree of conformity of a measure to a standard or a true value — compare PRECISION 2a

ac·cu·rate \ˈa-kyə-rət, ˈa-k(ə-)rət\ *adj* [L *accuratus,* fr. pp. of *accurare* to take care of, fr. *ad-* + *cura* care] (1596) **1 :** free from error esp. as the result of care ⟨an ∼ diagnosis⟩ **2 :** conforming exactly to truth or to a standard **:** EXACT ⟨providing ∼ color⟩ **3 :** able to give an accurate result ⟨an ∼ gauge⟩ ***syn*** see CORRECT — **ac·cu·rate·ly** \ˈa-kyə-rət-lē, ˈa-k(ə-)rət-, ˈa-k(y)ərt-\ *adv* — **ac·cu·rate·ness** \-kyə-rət-nəs, -k(ə-)rət-nəs\ *n*

ac·cursed \ə-ˈkərst, -ˈkər-səd\ *or* **ac·curst** \ə-ˈkərst\ *adj* [ME *acursed,* fr. pp. of *acursen* to consign to destruction with a curse, fr. *a-* (fr. OE *ā,* perfective prefix) + *cursen* to curse — more at ABIDE] (13c) **1 :** being under or as if under a curse ⟨an ∼ people⟩ **2 :** DAMNABLE — **ac·curs·ed·ly** \-ˈkər-səd-lē\ *adv* — **ac·curs·ed·ness** \-ˈkər-səd-nəs\ *n*

accus *abbr* accusative

ac·cus·al \ə-ˈkyü-zəl\ *n* (1594) **:** ACCUSATION

ac·cu·sa·tion \ˌa-kyə-ˈzā-shən, -(ˌ)kyü-\ *n* (14c) **1 :** the act of accusing **:** the state or fact of being accused **2 :** a charge of wrongdoing

[1]**ac·cu·sa·tive** \ə-ˈkyü-zə-tiv\ *adj* [ME, fr. AF or L; AF *acusatif,* fr. L *accusativus,* fr. *accusatus,* pp. of *accusare*] (15c) **1 :** of, relating to, or being the grammatical case that marks the direct object of a verb or the object of any of several prepositions **2 :** ACCUSATORY ⟨an ∼ tone⟩

[2]**accusative** *n* (ca. 1620) **:** the accusative case of a language **:** a form in the accusative case

ac·cu·sa·to·ry \ə-ˈkyü-zə-ˌtȯr-ē\ *adj* (14c) **:** containing or expressing accusation **:** ACCUSING ⟨an ∼ look⟩

ac·cuse \ə-ˈkyüz\ *vb* **ac·cused; ac·cus·ing** [ME, fr. AF *accuser,* fr. L *accusare* to call to account, fr. *ad-* + *causa* lawsuit] *vt* (14c) **1 :** to charge with a fault or offense **:** BLAME **2 :** to charge with an offense judicially or by a public process ∼ *vi* **:** to bring an accusation — **ac·cus·er** \ə-ˈkyü-zər\ *n* — **ac·cus·ing·ly** \-ˈkyü-ziŋ-lē\ *adv*

ac·cused *n, pl* **accused** (1567) **:** one charged with an offense; *esp* **:** the defendant in a criminal case

ac·cus·tom \ə-ˈkəs-təm\ *vt* [ME, fr. AF *acostomer,* fr. *a-* (fr. L *ad-*) + *custume* custom] (15c) **:** to make familiar with something through use or experience — **ac·cus·tom·ation** \-ˌkəs-tə-ˈmā-shən\ *n*

ac·cus·tomed \ə-ˈkəs-təmd\ *adj* (15c) **1 :** often used or practiced **:** CUSTOMARY ⟨her ∼ cheerfulness⟩ **2 :** adapted to existing conditions ⟨eyes ∼ to the dark⟩ **3 :** being in the habit or custom ⟨∼ to winning⟩ ***syn*** see USUAL — **ac·cus·tomed·ness** \-təm(d)-nəs\ *n*

AC/DC \ˈā-(ˌ)sē-ˈdē-(ˌ)sē\ *adj* [fr. the likening of a bisexual person to an electrical appliance which can operate on either alternating or direct current] (ca. 1960) **:** BISEXUAL 1b

[1]**ace** \ˈās\ *n* [ME *as,* fr. AF, fr. L, unit, a copper coin] (14c) **1 a :** a die face marked with one spot **b :** a playing card marked in its center with one pip **c :** a domino end marked with one spot **2 :** a very small amount or degree **:** PARTICLE **3 :** a point scored esp. on a service (as in tennis or handball) that an opponent fails to touch **4 :** a golf score of one stroke on a hole; *also* **:** a hole made in one stroke **5 :** a combat pilot who has brought down at least five enemy airplanes **6 a :** a person who excels at something ⟨a computer ∼⟩ **b :** the best pitcher on a baseball team ⟨the ∼ of the staff⟩ — **ace in the hole 1 :** an ace dealt face down to a player (as in stud poker) and not exposed until the showdown **2 :** an effective and decisive argument or resource held in reserve — **within an ace of :** on the point of **:** very near to ⟨came *within an ace of* winning⟩

[2]**ace** *vt* **aced; ac·ing** (1923) **1 :** to score an ace against (an opponent) **2 :** to make (a hole in golf) in one stroke **3 :** to gain a decisive advantage over **:** DEFEAT — usu. used with *out* **4 a :** to earn a high grade on (as an examination); *esp* **:** to get an A on **b :** to perform extremely well in ⟨he *aced* every subject⟩

[3]**ace** *adj* (1926) **:** of first or high rank or quality ⟨an ∼ mechanic⟩

ACE *abbr* American Council on Education

-aceae *n pl suffix* [NL, fr. L, fem. pl. of *-aceus* -aceous] **:** plants of the nature of ⟨Ros*aceae*⟩ — in names of families of plants

ace·dia \ə-ˈsē-dē-ə\ *n* [LL, fr. Gk *akēdeia,* fr. *a-* + *kēdos* care, grief — more at HATE] (1607) **:** APATHY, BOREDOM

ACE inhibitor \ˌā-(ˌ)sē-ˈē-; ˈās-\ *n* [*a*ngiotensin *c*onverting *e*nzyme] (1982) **:** any of a group of antihypertensive drugs (as captopril) that relax arteries and promote renal excretion of salt and water by inhibiting the activity of angiotensin converting enzyme

Acel·da·ma \ə-ˈsel-də-mə\ *n* [Gk *Akeldama,* fr. Aram *ḥăqēl dĕmā,* lit., field of blood] (14c) **:** the potter's field bought with the money Judas had been paid for betraying Christ

acel·lu·lar \(ˌ)ā-ˈsel-yə-lər\ *adj* (1940) **1 :** containing no cells ⟨∼ vaccines⟩ **2 :** not divided into cells **:** consisting of a single complex cell — used esp. of protozoa and ciliates

acen·tric \(ˌ)ā-ˈsen-trik\ *adj* (1937) **:** lacking a centromere ⟨∼ chromosomes⟩

-aceous *adj suffix* [L *-aceus*] **1 a :** characterized by **:** full of ⟨set*aceous*⟩ **b :** consisting of ⟨diatom*aceous*⟩ **:** having the nature or form of ⟨tuff*aceous*⟩ **2 a :** of or relating to a group of animals typified by (such) a form ⟨cet*aceous*⟩ or characterized by (such) a feature ⟨crust*aceous*⟩ **b :** of or relating to a plant family ⟨solan*aceous*⟩

aceph·a·lous \(ˌ)ā-ˈse-fə-ləs, ə-ˈse-\ *adj* [Gk *akephalos,* fr. *a-* + *kephalē* head — more at CEPHALIC] (ca. 1731) **1 :** lacking a head or having the head reduced **2 :** lacking a governing head or chief

ace·quia \ə-ˈsā-kē-ə, ä-\ *n* [Sp, fr. Ar *al-sāqiya* the irrigation ditch] (1844) *Southwest* **:** an irrigation ditch or canal

acerb \ə-ˈsərb, a-\ *adj* [F or L; F *acerbe,* fr. L *acerbus;* akin to L *acer* sharp — more at EDGE] (1853) **:** ACERBIC ⟨∼ humor⟩

ac·er·bate \ˈa-sər-ˌbāt\ *vt* **-bat·ed; -bat·ing** (ca. 1731) **:** IRRITATE, EXASPERATE

acer·bic \ə-ˈsər-bik, a-\ *adj* (1865) **:** acid in temper, mood, or tone ⟨∼ commentary⟩ ⟨an ∼ reviewer⟩ — **acer·bi·cal·ly** \-bi-k(ə-)lē\ *adv*

acer·bi·ty \-bə-tē\ *n, pl* **-ties** (1572) **:** the quality of being acerbic

ac·er·o·la \ˌa-sə-ˈrō-lə\ *n* [AmerSp, fr. Sp, fruit of a shrub (*Crataegus azarolus*), fr. Ar *a(-zu'rūr)*] (1945) **:** any of various West Indian shrubs (genus *Malpighia* of the family Malpighiaceae) with mildly acid cherrylike fruits very rich in vitamin C

ace·sul·fame–K \ˈā-sē-ˌsəl-ˌfām-ˈkā\ *n* [*acet-* + *sulf-* + *-ame* (as in *aspartame*)] (1982) **:** a white crystalline powder $C_4H_4KNO_4S$ that is a cyclic organic potassium salt, has a sweetness much more intense than sucrose, and is used as a noncaloric sweetener in foods and beverages — called also *acesulfame potassium*

acet- *or* **aceto-** *comb form* [F & L; F *acét-,* fr. L *acet-,* fr. *acetum* vinegar; akin to L *acēre* to be sour, *acer* sharp — more at EDGE] **:** acetic acid **:** acetic ⟨*acet*yl⟩

ac·e·tab·u·lum \-ˈta-byə-ləm\ *n, pl* **-lums** *or* **-la** \-lə\ [L, lit., vinegar cup, fr. *acetum* vinegar] (1661) **1 :** a ventral sucker of a trematode **2 :** the cup-shaped socket in the hipbone — **ac·e·tab·u·lar** \-lər\ *adj*

ac·e·tal \ˈa-sə-ˌtal\ *n* [G *Azetal,* fr. *azet-* acet- + *Al*kohol alcohol] (1853) **:** any of various compounds characterized by the grouping $C(OR)_2$ and obtained esp. by heating aldehydes or ketones with alcohols

ac·et·al·de·hyde \ˌa-sə-ˈtal-də-ˌhīd\ *n* [ISV] (1877) **:** a colorless volatile water-soluble liquid aldehyde C_2H_4O used chiefly in organic synthesis

acet·amide \ə-ˈse-tə-ˌmīd, ˌa-sə-ˈta-ˌmīd\ *n* [ISV] (1869) **:** a white crystalline amide C_2H_5NO of acetic acid used esp. as a solvent and in organic synthesis

acet·amin·o·phen \ə-ˌsē-tə-ˈmi-nə-fən, ˌa-sə-tə-\ *n* [*acet-* + *amino* + *phen*ol] (1958) **:** a crystalline compound $C_8H_9NO_2$ that is a hydroxy derivative of acetanilide and is used in chemical synthesis and in medicine to relieve pain and fever

ac·et·an·i·lide *or* **ac·et·an·i·lid** \ˌa-sə-ˈta-nə-ˌlīd, -ləd\ *n* [ISV] (ca. 1864) **:** a white crystalline compound C_8H_9NO that is derived from aniline and acetic acid and is used esp. to relieve pain or fever

ac·e·tate \ˈa-sə-ˌtāt\ *n* (1788) **1 :** a salt or ester of acetic acid **2 :** CELLULOSE ACETATE; *also* **:** something (as a textile fiber) made from cellulose acetate **3 :** a phonograph recording disk made of an acetate or coated with cellulose acetate

ac·et·azol·amide \ˌa-sə-tə-ˈzō-lə-ˌmīd, -ˈzä-, -məd\ *n* [*acet-* + *azole* + *amide*] (1954) **:** a diuretic drug $C_4H_6N_4O_3S_2$ used esp. in the treatment of edema associated with congestive heart failure and of glaucoma and in the prevention and treatment of altitude sickness

ace·tic acid \ə-ˈsē-tik-\ *n* [prob. fr. F *acétique,* fr. L *acetum* vinegar] (1788) **:** a colorless pungent liquid acid $C_2H_4O_2$ that is the chief acid of vinegar and that is used esp. in synthesis (as of plastics)

acetic anhydride *n* (1866) **:** a colorless liquid $C_4H_6O_3$ with a pungent odor used in organic synthesis (as of cellulose acetate and aspirin)

ace·ti·fy \ə-ˈsē-tə-ˌfī, -ˈse-\ *vt* **-fied; -fy·ing** (ca. 1828) **:** to turn into acetic acid or vinegar — **ace·ti·fi·ca·tion** \-ˌsē-tə-fə-ˈkā-shən, -ˌse-\ *n*

ace·to·ace·tic acid \ˌa-sə-(ˌ)tō-ə-ˈsē-tik-, ə-ˌsē-tō-\ *n* [part trans. of G *Azetessigsäure,* fr. *azet-* acet- + *Essigsäure* acetic acid] (ca. 1900) **:** an unstable acid $C_4H_6O_3$ that is a ketone body found in abnormal quantities in the blood and urine in some conditions (as diabetes)

ac·e·tone \ˈa-sə-ˌtōn\ *n* [G *Azeton,* fr. L *acetum*] (1837) **:** a volatile fragrant flammable liquid ketone C_3H_6O used chiefly as a solvent and in organic synthesis and found in abnormal quantities in diabetic urine — **ac·e·ton·ic** \ˌa-sə-ˈtä-nik\ *adj*

ace·to·ni·trile \ə-ˌsē-tō-ˈnī-trəl, ˌa-sə-tō-, -ˌtrī(-ə)l\ *n* (1848) **:** the colorless liquid nitrile CH_3CN of acetic acid used chiefly in organic synthesis and as a solvent

ace·to·phe·net·i·din \ˌa-sə-(ˌ)tō-fə-ˈne-tə-dən, ə-ˌsē-tō-\ *n* [ISV] (1887) **:** PHENACETIN

ace·tous \ə-ˈsē-təs, ˈa-sə-təs\ *adj* (14c) **:** relating to or producing vinegar ⟨~ fermentation⟩; *also* **:** SOUR, VINEGARY

ace·tyl \ə-ˈsē-tᵊl, ˈa-sə-; ˈa-sə-ˌtēl\ *n* (ca. 1864) **:** the radical CH_3CO– of acetic acid — often used in combination

acet·y·late \ə-ˈse-tᵊl-ˌāt\ *vt* **-lat·ed; -lat·ing** (1864) **:** to introduce the acetyl radical into (a compound) — **acet·y·la·tion** \-ˌse-tᵊl-ˈā-shən\ *n* — **acet·y·la·tive** \-ˈset-ᵊl-ˌā-tiv\ *adj*

ace·tyl·cho·line \ə-ˌse-tᵊl-ˈkō-ˌlēn, -ˌsē-; ˈa-sə-ˌtēl-\ *n* [ISV] (1906) **:** a neurotransmitter $[C_7H_{16}NO_2]^+$ released at autonomic synapses and neuromuscular junctions and formed enzymatically in the tissues from choline

ace·tyl·cho·lin·es·ter·ase \-ˌkō-lə-ˈnes-tə-ˌrās, -ˌrāz\ *n* (1937) **:** an enzyme that occurs esp. in some nerve endings and in the blood and promotes the hydrolysis of acetylcholine

acetyl CoA \-ˌkō-ˈā\ *n* (1951) **:** ACETYL COENZYME A

acetyl coenzyme A *n* (1952) **:** a compound $C_{25}H_{38}N_7O_{17}P_3S$ formed as an intermediate in metabolism and active as a coenzyme in biological acetylations

acet·y·lene \ə-ˈse-tᵊl-ən, -tᵊl-ˌēn\ *n* (1851) **:** a colorless gaseous hydrocarbon HC≡CH used chiefly in organic synthesis and as a fuel (as in welding and soldering) — **acet·y·le·nic** \ə-ˌse-tᵊl-ˈē-nik, -ˈe-nik\ *adj*

ace·tyl·sa·lic·y·late \ə-ˌsē-tᵊl-sə-ˈli-sə-ˌlāt\ *n* (1893) **:** a salt or ester of acetylsalicylic acid

ace·tyl·sal·i·cyl·ic acid \ə-ˈsē-tᵊl-ˌsa-lə-ˌsi-lik-\ *n* [ISV] (1864) **:** ASPIRIN 1

ac·ey–deuc·ey *also* **ac·ey–deu·cy** \ˌā-sē-ˈdü-sē, -ˈdyü-\ *n* (1925) **:** a variation of backgammon in which a throw of a 1-2 wins extra turns

¹**Achae·an** \ə-ˈkē-ən\ *or* **Achai·an** \-ˈkī-ən, -ˈkā-ən\ *adj* (1567) **:** of, relating to, or characteristic of Achaea; *broadly* **:** of or relating to Greece

²**Achaean** *or* **Achaian** *n* (1607) **:** a native or inhabitant of Achaea; *broadly* **:** GREEK

Ach·ae·me·ni·an \ˌa-kə-ˈmē-nē-ən\ *adj* (1717) **:** of or relating to the Achaemenids

Ach·ae·me·nid \ə-ˈkē-mə-nəd\ *n, pl* **-menids** *also* **-men·i·dae** \ˌa-kə-ˈme-nə-ˌdē\ [Gk *Achaimenides,* fr. *Achaimenes,* 7th cent. B.C. king of Persia, founder of the dynasty + *-ides* (patronymic suffix)] (1889) **:** a member of the ruling house of ancient Persia generally considered historically important from the assumption of power by Cyrus the Great (559 B.C.) to the overthrow of Darius III (330 B.C.)

acha·la·sia \ˌā-kə-ˈlā-zh(ē-)ə\ *n* [NL, fr. *a-* + Gk *chalasis* slackening + NL *-ia*] (1914) **:** failure of a ring of muscle (as the anal sphincter or one of the esophagus) to relax

Acha·tes \ə-ˈkā-tēz\ *n* [L] (14c) **:** a faithful companion of Aeneas in Virgil's *Aeneid*

¹**ache** \ˈāk\ *vi* **ached; ach·ing** [ME *aken,* fr. OE *acan*] (bef. 12c) **1 a :** to suffer a usu. dull persistent pain ⟨an *aching* back⟩ **b :** to become distressed or disturbed (as with anxiety or regret) ⟨*aching* with sadness⟩ **c :** to feel compassion ⟨my heart ~*s* for those poor people⟩ **2 :** to experience a painful eagerness or yearning ⟨he is *aching* to go⟩

²**ache** *n* (bef. 12c) **1 :** a usu. dull persistent pain **2 :** a condition marked by aching

achene \ə-ˈkēn\ *n* [NL *achaenium,* fr. *a-* + Gk *chainein* to gape, yawn — more at YAWN] (1855) **:** a small dry indehiscent one-seeded fruit (as of a sunflower) developing from a simple ovary and usu. having a thin pericarp attached to the seed at only one point

Ach·er·on \ˈa-kə-ˌrän, -rən\ *n* [Gk *Acherōn*] (14c) **:** a river in Hades

Acheu·le·an *or* **Acheu·li·an** \ə-ˈshü-lē-ən\ *adj* [F *acheuléen,* fr. St. *Acheul,* near Amiens, France] (1877) **:** of or relating to a Lower Paleolithic culture originating in Africa and typified by bifacial tools with round cutting edges

à che·val \ˌä-shə-ˈväl\ *adv* [F, lit., on horseback] (1832) **1 :** with a leg on each side **:** ASTRIDE **2 :** in such a way as to be played or chanced simultaneously on two numbers or events (as in roulette)

achieve \ə-ˈchēv\ *vb* **achieved; achiev·ing** [ME *acheven,* fr. AF *achever* to finish, fr. *a-* (fr. L *ad-*) + *chef* end, head — more at CHIEF] *vt* (14c) **1 :** to carry out successfully **:** ACCOMPLISH ⟨~ a gradual increase in production⟩ **2 :** to get or attain as the result of exertion **:** REACH ⟨*achieved* a high degree of skill⟩ ⟨*achieved* greatness⟩ ~ *vi* **:** to attain a desired end or aim **:** become successful ***syn*** see PERFORM — **achiev·able** \-ˈchē-və-bəl\ *adj* — **achiev·er** *n*

achieved *adj* (15c) **:** brought to or marked by a high degree of development or refinement **:** FINISHED ⟨fully ~ poems⟩

achieve·ment \ə-ˈchēv-mənt\ *n* (15c) **1 :** the act of achieving **:** ACCOMPLISHMENT **2 a :** a result gained by effort **b :** a great or heroic deed **3 :** the quality and quantity of a student's work ***syn*** see FEAT

Achil·les \ə-ˈki-lēz\ *n* [L, fr. Gk *Achilleus*] (bef. 12c) **:** the greatest warrior among the Greeks at Troy and slayer of Hector

Achilles' heel *n* [fr. the story that Achilles was vulnerable only in the heel] (1840) **:** a vulnerable point

Achilles tendon *n* (1739) **:** the strong tendon joining the muscles in the calf of the leg to the bone of the heel — called also *Achilles*

ach·ing \ˈā-kiŋ\ *adj* (13c) **1 :** that aches ⟨an ~ back⟩ **2 :** causing or reflecting distress, deep emotion, or longing ⟨~ country ballads⟩

ach·ing·ly \-lē\ *adv* (1765) **1 :** in an aching manner ⟨~ sad songs⟩ **2 :** EXTREMELY, EXCEEDINGLY ⟨~ complicated⟩

achi·o·te \ˌä-chē-ˈō-tē\ *n* [AmerSp, fr. Nahuatl *āchiotl* the annatto tree] (1648) **:** a spice made from the red seed of the annatto tree; *also* **:** the seed from which the spice is made

achi·ral \ˌā-ˈkī-rəl\ *adj* (1921) **:** of, relating to, or being a molecule that is superimposable on its mirror image **:** not chiral

achlor·hy·dria \ˌā-ˌklȯr-ˈhī-drē-ə\ *n* [NL, fr. *a-* + ISV *chlor-* + *hydr-* + NL *-ia*] (1892) **:** absence of hydrochloric acid from the gastric juice — **achlor·hy·dric** \-ˈhī-drik\ *adj*

achon·drite \(ˌ)ā-ˈkän-ˌdrīt\ *n* (ca. 1904) **:** a stony meteorite without rounded grains — **achon·drit·ic** \ˌā-ˌkän-ˈdri-tik\ *adj*

achon·dro·pla·sia \ˌā-ˌkän-drə-ˈplā-zh(ē-)ə\ *n* [NL, fr. *a-* + *chondr-* + *-plasia*] (1881) **:** a genetic disorder disturbing normal growth of cartilage, resulting in a form of dwarfism characterized by a usu. normal torso and shortened limbs, and usu. inherited as an autosomal dominant trait — **achon·dro·plas·tic** \-ˈplas-tik\ *adj*

achoo *also* **ah·choo** \ä-ˈchü\ *interj* (1882) — used to represent the sound of a sneeze

ach·ro·mat \ˈa-krə-ˌmat\ *n* (1900) **:** ACHROMATIC LENS

ach·ro·mat·ic \ˌa-krə-ˈma-tik, (ˌ)ā-\ *adj* (1754) **1 :** refracting light without dispersing it into its constituent colors **:** giving images practically free from extraneous colors ⟨an ~ telescope⟩ **2 :** not readily colored by the usual staining agents **3 :** possessing no hue **:** being or involving black, gray, or white **:** NEUTRAL ⟨~ visual sensations⟩ **4 :** being without accidentals or modulation **:** DIATONIC — **ach·ro·mat·i·cal·ly** \-ti-k(ə-)lē\ *adv* — **achro·ma·tism** \(ˌ)ā-ˈkrō-mə-ˌti-zəm, a-\ *n* — **achro·ma·tize** \(ˌ)ā-ˈkrō-mə-ˌtīz, a-\ *vt*

achromatic lens *n* (1796) **:** a lens made by combining lenses of different glasses having different focal powers so that the light emerging from the lens forms an image practically free of chromatic aberration

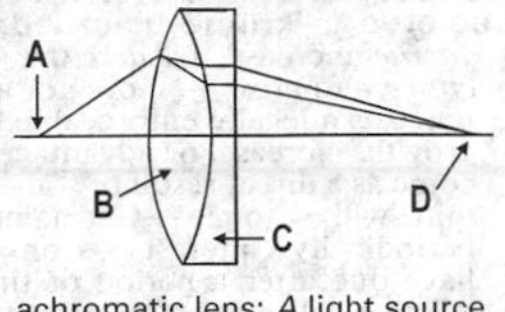

achromatic lens: *A* light source, *B* crown glass, *C* flint glass, *D* corrected wavelength focal point

achy \ˈā-kē\ *adj* **ach·i·er; ach·i·est** (1864) **:** afflicted with aches ⟨feeling tired and ~⟩ — **ach·i·ness** *n*

acic·u·lar \ə-ˈsi-kyə-lər\ *adj* [LL *acicula* (dim. of L *acus* needle) + E *-ar* — more at ACUTE] (1709) **:** shaped like a needle ⟨~ leaves⟩ ⟨~ crystals⟩

¹**ac·id** \ˈa-səd\ *adj* [F or L; F *acide,* fr. L *acidus,* fr. *acēre* to be sour — more at ACET-] (1626) **1 a :** sour, sharp, or biting to the taste ⟨an ~ flavor⟩ **b :** sharp, biting, or sour in manner, disposition, or nature ⟨an ~ individual⟩ ⟨an ~ personality⟩ **c :** sharply clear, discerning, or pointed ⟨an ~ wit⟩ ⟨~ criticism⟩ **d :** piercingly intense and often jarring ⟨~ yellow⟩ **2 a :** of, relating to, or being an acid; *also* **:** having the reactions or characteristics of an acid ⟨~ soil⟩ ⟨an ~ solution⟩ **b** *of salts and esters* **:** derived by partial exchange of replaceable hydrogen ⟨~ sodium carbonate $NaHCO_3$⟩ **c :** containing or involving the use of an acid (as in manufacture) ⟨an ~ bath⟩ **d :** marked by or resulting from an abnormally high concentration of acid ⟨~ indigestion⟩ **3 :** relating to or made by a process (as in making steel) in which the furnace is lined with acidic material and an acidic slag is used **4 :** rich in silica ⟨~ rocks⟩ — **ac·id·ly** *adv* — **ac·id·ness** *n*

²**acid** *n* (1650) **1 :** a sour substance; *specif* **:** any of various typically water-soluble and sour compounds that in solution are capable of reacting with a base to form a salt, redden litmus, and have a pH less than 7, that are hydrogen-containing molecules or ions able to give up a proton to a base, or that are substances able to accept an unshared pair of electrons from a base **2 :** something incisive, biting, or sarcastic ⟨a social satire dripping with ~⟩ **3 :** LSD — **ac·idy** \ˈa-sə-dē\ *adj*

ac·id–fast \ˈa-səd-ˌfast\ *adj* (1903) **:** not easily decolorized by acids

ac·id·head \-ˌhed\ *n* (1966) **:** an individual who uses LSD

acid·ic \ə-ˈsi-dik, a-\ *adj* (1866) **1 :** acid-forming **2 :** ACID

acid·i·fi·er \ə-ˈsi-də-ˌfī(-ə)r, a-\ *n* (1796) **:** one that acidifies; *esp* **:** a substance used to increase soil acidity

acid·i·fy \-ˌfī\ *vt* **-fied; -fy·ing** (1782) **1 :** to make acid **2 :** to convert into an acid — **acid·i·fi·ca·tion** \-ˌsi-də-fə-ˈkā-shən\ *n*

ac·i·dim·e·ter \ˌa-sə-ˈdi-mə-tər\ *n* (ca. 1828) **:** PH METER

acid·i·ty \ə-ˈsi-də-tē, a-\ *n, pl* **-ties** (1615) **1 :** the quality, state, or degree of being acid **2 :** the state of being excessively acid

acid·o·phil \ə-ˈsi-də-ˌfil, a-\ *also* **acid·o·phile** \-ˌfī(-ə)l\ *n* (1897) **:** a substance, tissue, or organism that stains readily with acid stains — **acidophil** *also* **acidophile** *adj*

ac·i·do·phil·ic \ˌa-sə-dō-ˈfi-lik\ *adj* (1895) **1 :** staining readily with acid stains **:** ACIDOPHIL **2 :** preferring or thriving in a relatively acid environment

ac·i·doph·i·lus \ˌa-sə-ˈdä-f(ə-)ləs\ *n* [NL, acidophilic] (1901) **:** a lactobacillus (*Lactobacillus acidophilus*) that is added esp. to dairy products (as yogurt and milk) or prepared as a dietary supplement, is part of the normal intestinal and vaginal flora, and is used therapeutically esp. to promote intestinal health; *also* **:** a preparation containing such bacteria

ac·i·do·sis \ˌa-sə-ˈdō-səs\ *n* [NL] (1900) **:** an abnormal condition characterized by reduced alkalinity of the blood and of the body tissues — **ac·i·dot·ic** \-ˈdä-tik\ *adj*

acid phosphatase *n* (1949) **:** a phosphatase (as the phosphomonoesterase from the prostate gland) optimally active in acid medium

acid precipitation *n* (1955) **:** precipitation (as rain or snow) having increased acidity caused by environmental factors (as atmospheric pollutants)

acid rain *n* (1845) **:** acid precipitation in the form of rain

acid rock *n* (1966) **:** rock music with lyrics and sound relating to or suggestive of drug-induced experiences

acid snow *n* (1981) **:** acid precipitation in the form of snow

acid test *n* (1854) **:** a severe or crucial test

acid·u·late \ə-ˈsi-jə-ˌlāt\ *vt* **-lat·ed; -lat·ing** [L *acidulus*] (1684) **:** to make acid or slightly acid — **acid·u·la·tion** \-ˌsi-jə-ˈlā-shən\ *n*

acid·u·lent \ə-ˈsi-jə-lənt\ *adj* [F *acidulant,* fr. prp. of *aciduler* to acidulate, fr. L *acidulus*] (1830) **:** ACIDULOUS

acid·u·lous \ə-ˈsi-jə-ləs\ *adj* [L *acidulus,* fr. *acidus*] (1769) **:** somewhat acid or harsh in taste or manner

acid–washed \ˈa-səd-ˌwȯsht, -ˌwäsht\ *also* **acid–wash** \-ˌwȯsh, -ˌwäsh\ *adj* (1987) **:** of, relating to, or being a fabric or a garment that has been treated with a bleach solution to produce a streaked or discolored appearance

ac·i·nar \ˈa-sə-nər, -ˌnär\ *adj* (1870) **:** of, relating to, or comprising an acinus ⟨pancreatic ~ cells⟩

ac·i·nus \ˈa-sə-nəs\ *n, pl* **-ni** \-ˌnī\ [NL, fr. L, berry, berry seed] (ca. 1751) **:** any of the small sacs terminating the ducts of some exocrine glands and lined with secretory cells — **ac·i·nous** \-nəs\ *adj*

ack *abbr* acknowledge; acknowledgment

ack–ack \ˈak-ˌak\ *n* [Brit. signalmen's former telephone pron. of *AA,* abbr. of *antiaircraft*] (1926) : an antiaircraft gun; *also* : antiaircraft fire

ackee *also* **akee** \ˈa-ˌkē, a-ˈkē\ *n* [origin unknown] (1794) : the fruit of an African tree (*Blighia sapida*) of the soapberry family grown in the Caribbean area, Florida, and Hawaii for its white or yellowish fleshy aril that is edible when ripe but is poisonous when immature or overripe and that has a toxic pink raphe attaching the aril to the seed; *also* : the tree

ac·knowl·edge \ik-ˈnä-lij, ak-\ *vt* **-edged; -edg·ing** [*ac-* (as in *accord*) + *knowledge*] (15c) **1** : to recognize the rights, authority, or status of **2** : to disclose knowledge of or agreement with **3 a** : to express gratitude or obligation for ⟨~ a gift⟩ **b** : to take notice of ⟨failed to ~ my greeting⟩ **c** : to make known the receipt of ⟨~ a letter⟩ **4** : to recognize as genuine or valid ⟨~ a debt⟩

syn ACKNOWLEDGE, ADMIT, OWN, AVOW, CONFESS mean to disclose against one's will or inclination. ACKNOWLEDGE implies the disclosing of something that has been or might be concealed ⟨*acknowledged* an earlier peccadillo⟩. ADMIT implies reluctance to disclose, grant, or concede and refers usu. to facts rather than their implications ⟨*admitted* the project was over budget⟩. OWN implies acknowledging something in close relation to oneself ⟨must *own* I know little about computers⟩. AVOW implies boldly declaring, often in the face of hostility, what one might be expected to be silent about ⟨*avowed* that he was a revolutionary⟩. CONFESS may apply to an admission of a weakness, failure, omission, or guilt ⟨*confessed* a weakness for sweets⟩.

ac·knowl·edged \-lijd\ *adj* (1598) : generally recognized, accepted, or admitted ⟨an ~ expert⟩ — **ac·knowl·edged·ly** \-lijd-lē, -li-jəd-\ *adv*

ac·knowl·edg·ment *or* **ac·knowl·edge·ment** \ik-ˈnä-lij-mənt, ak-\ *n* (1594) **1 a** : the act of acknowledging **b** : recognition or favorable notice of an act or achievement **2** : a thing done or given in recognition of something received **3** : a declaration or avowal of one's act or of a fact to give it legal validity

ACL \ˌā-(ˌ)sē-ˈel\ *n* (1981) : ANTERIOR CRUCIATE LIGAMENT

ACLS *abbr* advanced cardiac life support

ACLU *abbr* American Civil Liberties Union

ac·me \ˈak-mē\ *n* [Gk *akmē* point, highest point — more at EDGE] (1620) : the highest point or stage; *also* : one that represents perfection of the thing expressed ***syn*** see SUMMIT

ac·ne \ˈak-nē\ *n* [Gk *aknē* eruption of the face, MS var. of *akmē,* lit., point] (ca. 1828) : a disorder of the skin caused by inflammation of the skin glands and hair follicles; *specif* : a form found chiefly in adolescents and marked by pimples esp. on the face — **ac·ned** \-nēd\ *adj*

acne rosacea *n* [NL, rose-colored acne] (1833) : ROSACEA

acock \ə-ˈkäk\ *adj or adv* (1846) : being in a cocked position

acoe·lo·mate \(ˌ)ā-ˈsē-lə-ˌmāt\ *n* (ca. 1889) : an invertebrate lacking a coelom; *esp* : one belonging to the group comprising the flatworms and nemerteans and characterized by bilateral symmetry and a digestive cavity that is the only internal cavity — **acoelomate** *adj*

acold \ə-ˈkōld\ *adj* (14c) *archaic* : COLD, CHILLED ⟨the owl, for all his feathers, was ~ —John Keats⟩

ac·o·lyte \ˈa-kə-ˌlīt, -kō-\ *n* [ME, fr. AF & ML; AF, *acolit,* fr. ML *acoluthus,* fr. MGk *akolouthos,* fr. Gk, adj., following, fr. *a-, ha-* together (akin to Gk *homos* same) + *keleuthos* path] (14c) **1** : one who assists a member of the clergy in a liturgical service by performing minor duties **2** : one who attends or assists : FOLLOWER

ac·o·nite \ˈa-kə-ˌnīt\ *n* [MF or L; MF, fr. L *aconitum,* fr. Gk *akoniton*] (1548) **1** : MONKSHOOD **2** : the dried poisonous tuberous root of a common monkshood (*Aconitum napellus*) used esp. formerly for its medicinal properties (as in relieving pain)

acorn \ˈā-ˌkȯrn, -kərn\ *n* [ME *akern,* fr. OE *æcern;* akin to MHG *ackeran* acorns collectively, OIr *áirne* sloe, Lith *uoga* berry] (bef. 12c) : the nut of the oak usu. seated in or surrounded by a hard woody cupule of indurated bracts

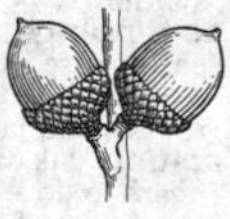
acorn

acorn squash *n* (1937) : an acorn-shaped dark green winter squash (*Cucurbita pepo*) with a ridged surface and mildly sweet yellow to orange flesh

acorn woodpecker *n* (1981) : a woodpecker (*Melanerpes formicivorus*) found from the U.S. Pacific coast south to Colombia that stores acorns in small holes which it digs esp. in the bark of trees

acorn worm *n* (ca. 1889) : any of a class (Enteropneusta) of burrowing wormlike marine animals having an acorn-shaped proboscis and classified with the hemichordates

acous·tic \ə-ˈküs-tik\ *or* **acous·ti·cal** \-ti-kəl\ *adj* [Gk *akoustikos* of hearing, fr. *akouein* to hear — more at HEAR] (1605) **1** : of or relating to the sense or organs of hearing, to sound, or to the science of sounds ⟨~ apparatus of the ear⟩ ⟨~ energy⟩: as **a** : deadening or absorbing sound ⟨~ tile⟩ **b** : operated by or utilizing sound waves **2** : of, relating to, or being a musical instrument whose sound is not electronically modified — **acous·ti·cal·ly** \-k(ə-)lē\ *adv*

ac·ous·ti·cian \ˌa-ˌkü-ˈsti-shən, ə-ˌkü-\ *n* (1859) : a specialist in acoustics

acous·tics \ə-ˈküs-tiks\ *n pl* (1683) **1** *sing in constr* : a science that deals with the production, control, transmission, reception, and effects of sound **2** *also* **acoustic** : the qualities that determine the ability of an enclosure (as an auditorium) to reflect sound waves in such a way as to produce distinct hearing

ACP *abbr* **1** African, Caribbean and Pacific (states) **2** American College of Physicians

acpt *abbr* acceptance

ac·quaint \ə-ˈkwānt\ *vt* [ME, fr. AF *acuinter, aquaynter,* fr. OF *acoins* familiar, fr. L *accognitus,* pp. of *accognoscere* to recognize, fr. *ad-* + *cognoscere* to know — more at COGNITION] (14c) **1** : to cause to know personally ⟨was ~*ed* with the mayor⟩ **2** : to make familiar : cause to know firsthand ***syn*** see INFORM

ac·quain·tance \ə-ˈkwān-tᵊn(t)s\ *n* (14c) **1 a** : the state of being acquainted **b** : personal knowledge : FAMILIARITY **2 a** : the persons with whom one is acquainted ⟨should auld ~ be forgot —Robert Burns⟩ **b** : a person whom one knows but who is not a particularly close friend ⟨a casual ~⟩ — **ac·quain·tance·ship** \-ˌship\ *n*

acquaintance rape *n* (1979) : rape committed by someone known to the victim

ac·qui·esce \ˌa-kwē-ˈes\ *vi* **-esced; -esc·ing** [F *acquiescer,* fr. L *acquiescere,* fr. *ad-* + *quiescere* to be quiet — more at QUIESCENT] (1651) : to accept, comply, or submit tacitly or passively — often used with *in* and sometimes with *to* ***syn*** see ASSENT

ac·qui·es·cence \-ˈe-sᵊn(t)s\ *n* (1646) **1** : the act of acquiescing : the state of being acquiescent **2** : an instance of acquiescing

ac·qui·es·cent \-ˈe-sᵊnt\ *adj* [L *acquiescent-, acquiescens,* prp. of *acquiescere*] (1753) : inclined to acquiesce — **ac·qui·es·cent·ly** *adv*

ac·quir·able \ə-ˈkwī-rə-bəl\ *adj* (1646) : capable of being acquired

ac·quire \ə-ˈkwī(-ə)r\ *vt* **ac·quired; ac·quir·ing** [ME *aqueren,* fr. AF *acquerre,* fr. L *acquirere,* fr. *ad-* + *quaerere* to seek, obtain] (15c) **1** : to get as one's own: **a** : to come into possession or control of often by unspecified means **b** : to come to have as a new or added characteristic, trait, or ability (as by sustained effort or natural selection) ⟨~ fluency in French⟩ ⟨bacteria that ~ tolerance to antibiotics⟩ **2** : to locate and hold (a desired object) in a detector ⟨~ a target by radar⟩

acquired immune deficiency syndrome *n* (1982) : AIDS

acquired immunodeficiency syndrome *n* (1982) : AIDS

acquired taste *n* (1840) : something or someone that is not easily or immediately liked or appreciated

ac·quir·ee \ə-ˌkwī(-ə)-ˈrē\ *n* (1969) : one (as a company) that is acquired : ACQUISITION

ac·quire·ment \ə-ˈkwī(-ə)r-mənt\ *n* (1630) **1** : a skill of mind or body usu. resulting from continued endeavor **2** : the act of acquiring

ac·quir·er \ə-ˈkwī(-ə)r-ər\ *n* (1768) : one that acquires; *esp* : a company that acquires another company

ac·qui·si·tion \ˌa-kwə-ˈzi-shən\ *n* [ME *acquisicioun,* fr. MF or L; MF *acquisition,* fr. L *acquisition-, acquisitio,* fr. *acquirere*] (14c) **1** : the act of acquiring **2** : something or someone acquired or gained ⟨the team announced two new ~*s*⟩ — **ac·qui·si·tion·al** \-shnəl, -shə-nᵊl\ *adj* — **ac·quis·i·tor** \ə-ˈkwi-zə-tər\ *n*

ac·quis·i·tive \ə-ˈkwi-zə-tiv\ *adj* (1835) : strongly desirous of acquiring and possessing ***syn*** see COVETOUS — **ac·quis·i·tive·ly** *adv* — **ac·quis·i·tive·ness** *n*

ac·quit \ə-ˈkwit\ *vt* **ac·quit·ted; ac·quit·ting** [ME *aquiten,* fr. AF *aquiter,* fr. *a-* (fr. L *ad-*) + *quite* free of — more at QUIT] (13c) **1 a** *archaic* : to pay off (as a claim or debt) **b** *obs* : REPAY, REQUITE **2** : to discharge completely (as from an obligation or accusation) ⟨the court *acquitted* the prisoner⟩ **3** : to conduct (oneself) usu. satisfactorily esp. under stress ⟨the recruits *acquitted* themselves like veterans⟩ ***syn*** see BEHAVE, EXCULPATE — **ac·quit·ter** *n*

ac·quit·tal \ə-ˈkwi-tᵊl\ *n* (15c) : a setting free from the charge of an offense by verdict, sentence, or other legal process

ac·quit·tance \ə-ˈkwi-tᵊn(t)s\ *n* (14c) : a document evidencing a discharge from an obligation; *esp* : a receipt in full

acr- *or* **acro-** *comb form* [MF or Gk; MF *acro-,* fr. Gk *akr-, akro-,* fr. *akros* topmost, extreme; akin to Gk *akmē* point — more at EDGE] **1** : beginning : end : tip ⟨*acro*nym⟩ **2 a** : top : peak : summit ⟨*acro*petal⟩ **b** : height ⟨*acro*phobia⟩

acre \ˈā-kər\ *n* [ME, fr. OE *æcer;* akin to OHG *ackar* field, L *ager,* Gk *agros,* and perh. to L *agere* to drive — more at AGENT] (bef. 12c) **1 a** *archaic* : a field esp. of arable land or pastureland **b** *pl* : LANDS, ESTATE **2** : any of various units of area; *specif* : a unit in the U.S. and England equal to 43,560 square feet (4047 square meters) — see WEIGHT table **3** : a broad expanse or great quantity ⟨~*s* of free publicity⟩

acre·age \ˈā-k(ə-)rij\ *n* (1859) : area in acres : ACRES

acre–foot \ˈā-kər-ˈfu̇t\ *n* (1900) : the volume (as of irrigation water) that would cover one acre to a depth of one foot

acre–inch \ˈā-kər-ˈinch\ *n* (ca. 1909) : one twelfth of an acre-foot

ac·rid \ˈa-krəd\ *adj* [modif. of L *acr-, acer* sharp — more at EDGE] (1712) **1** : sharp and harsh or unpleasantly pungent in taste or odor : IRRITATING **2** : deeply or violently bitter : ACRIMONIOUS ⟨an ~ denunciation⟩ ***syn*** see CAUSTIC — **acrid·i·ty** \a-ˈkri-də-tē, ə-\ *n* — **ac·rid·ly** \ˈa-krəd-lē\ *adv* — **ac·rid·ness** *n*

ac·ri·dine \ˈa-krə-ˌdēn\ *n* (ca. 1877) : a colorless crystalline compound $C_{13}H_9N$ occurring in coal tar and important as the parent compound of dyes and pharmaceuticals

acridine orange *n* (ca. 1909) : a basic orange dye structurally related to acridine and used esp. to stain nucleic acids

ac·ri·fla·vine \ˌa-krə-ˈflā-ˌvēn, -vən\ *n* [*acridine* + *flavine*] (1917) : a yellow dye $C_{14}H_{14}N_3Cl$ used as an antiseptic esp. for wounds

ac·ri·mo·ni·ous \ˌa-krə-ˈmō-nē-əs\ *adj* (1659) : caustic, biting, or rancorous esp. in feeling, language, or manner ⟨an ~ dispute⟩ — **ac·ri·mo·ni·ous·ly** *adv* — **ac·ri·mo·ni·ous·ness** *n*

ac·ri·mo·ny \ˈa-krə-ˌmō-nē\ *n, pl* **-nies** [MF or L; MF *acrimonie,* fr. L *acrimonia,* fr. *acr-, acer*] (1542) : harsh or biting sharpness esp. of words, manner, or disposition

ac·ri·tarch \ˈa-kri-ˌtärk\ *n* [Gk *akritos* uncertain (fr. *a-* + *kritos,* verbal of *krinein* to decide) + *archē* beginning — more at CERTAIN, ARCH-] (1963) : any of a group of fossil one-celled marine planktonic organisms of uncertain and possibly various taxonomic affinities held to represent the earliest known eukaryotes

ac·ro·bat \ˈa-krə-ˌbat\ *n* [F & Gk; F *acrobate,* fr. Gk *akrobatēs,* fr. *akr-* acr- + *bainein* to go — more at COME] (1825) **1** : one that performs gymnastic feats requiring skillful control of the body **2 a** : one skillful at exercises of intellectual or artistic dexterity **b** : one adept at swiftly changing or adapting a position or viewpoint ⟨a political ~⟩ — **ac·ro·bat·ic** \ˌa-krə-ˈba-tik\ *adj* — **ac·ro·bat·i·cal·ly** \-ti-k(ə-)lē\ *adv*

ac·ro·bat·ics \ˌa-krə-ˈba-tiks\ *n pl but sing or pl in constr* (1882) **1** : the art, performance, or activity of an acrobat **2** : a spectacular, showy, or startling performance or demonstration involving great agility or complexity

ac·ro·cen·tric \ˌa-krō-ˈsen-trik\ *adj* (1945) : having the centromere situated so that one chromosomal arm is much shorter than the other — **acrocentric** *n*

\ə\ **a**but \ᵊ\ kitten, F table \ər\ **fur**ther \a\ **a**sh \ā\ **a**ce \ä\ m**o**p, m**ar** \au̇\ **ou**t \ch\ **ch**in \e\ b**e**t \ē\ **ea**sy \g\ **g**o \i\ h**i**t \ī\ **i**ce \j\ **j**ob \ŋ\ si**ng** \ō\ g**o** \ȯ\ l**aw** \ȯi\ b**oy** \th\ **th**in \t͟h\ **th**e \ü\ l**oo**t \u̇\ f**oo**t \y\ **y**et \zh\ vi**s**ion, bei**ge** \k, ⁿ, œ, ue, ʸ\ *see* Guide to Pronunciation

ac·ro·lect \'a-krə-ˌlekt\ *n* [*acr-* + *-lect* (as in *dialect*)] (1964) : the language variety of a speech community closest to the standard or prestige form of a language

acro·le·in \ə-'krō-lē-ən\ *n* [ISV *acr-* (fr. L *acr-*, *acer*) + L *olēre* to smell — more at ODOR] (ca. 1857) : a colorless irritant pungent liquid aldehyde C_3H_4O used chiefly in organic synthesis

ac·ro·meg·a·ly \ˌa-krō-'me-gə-lē\ *n* [ISV] (1889) : a disorder caused by excessive production of growth hormone by the pituitary gland and marked esp. by progressive enlargement of hands, feet, and face — **ac·ro·me·gal·ic** \-mə-'ga-lik\ *adj or n*

ac·ro·nym \'a-krə-ˌnim\ *n* [*acr-* + *-onym*] (1943) : a word (as *NATO, radar,* or *laser*) formed from the initial letter or letters of each of the successive parts or major parts of a compound term; *also* : an abbreviation (as *FBI*) formed from initial letters : INITIALISM — **ac·ro·nym·ic** \ˌa-krə-'ni-mik\ *adj* — **ac·ro·nym·i·cal·ly** \-mi-k(ə-)lē\ *adv*

acrop·e·tal \ə-'krä-pə-tᵊl, a-\ *adj* [*acr-* + *-petal* (as in *centripetal*)] (1875) : proceeding from the base toward the apex or from below upward ⟨~ development of floral buds⟩ — **acrop·e·tal·ly** \-tᵊl-ē\ *adv*

ac·ro·pho·bia \ˌa-krə-'fō-bē-ə\ *n* [NL] (ca. 1888) : abnormal dread of being in a high place : fear of heights — **ac·ro·phobe** \'a-krə-ˌfōb\ *n* — **ac·ro·pho·bic** \-bik\ *adj*

acrop·o·lis \ə-'krä-pə-ləs\ *n* [Gk *akropolis,* fr. *akr-* acr- + *polis* city — more at POLICE] (1662) : the upper fortified part of an ancient Greek city (as Athens); *also* : a usu. fortified height of a city or district elsewhere (as in Central America)

ac·ro·some \'a-krə-ˌsōm\ *n* [ISV] (1899) : an anterior prolongation of a spermatozoon that releases egg-penetrating enzymes — **ac·ro·so·mal** \ˌa-krə-'sō-məl\ *adj*

[1]**across** \ə-'krȯs, *chiefly dial* -'krȯst\ *adv* [ME *acros,* fr. AF *an crois,* fr. *an* (fr. L *in*) + *crois* cross, fr. L *crux*] (14c) **1** : in a position reaching from one side to the other : CROSSWISE **2** : to or on the opposite side **3** : so as to be understandable, acceptable, or successful ⟨get an argument ~⟩

[2]**across** *adj* (ca. 1576) : being in a crossed position

[3]**across** *prep* (1591) **1 a** : from one side to the opposite side of : OVER, THROUGH ⟨swam ~ the river⟩ **b** : on the opposite side of ⟨lives ~ the street from us⟩ **2** : so as to intersect or pass through at an angle ⟨sawed ~ the grain of the wood⟩ **3** : so as to find or meet ⟨came ~ your football in the hall closet⟩ **4 a** : THROUGHOUT ⟨obvious interest ~ the nation —Robert Goralski⟩ **b** : so as to include or take into consideration all classes or categories ⟨~ differences, they insist, there can be no rational dialogue —Huston Smith⟩

across–the–board *adj* (1945) **1** : placed to win if a competitor wins, places, or shows ⟨an ~ racing bet⟩ **2** : embracing or affecting all classes or categories : BLANKET ⟨an ~ price increase⟩

acros·tic \ə-'krȯs-tik, -'kräs-\ *n* [MF & Gk; MF *acrostiche,* fr. Gk *akrostichis,* fr. *akr-* acr- + *stichos* line; akin to *steichein* to go — more at STAIR] (1530) **1** : a composition usu. in verse in which sets of letters (as the initial or final letters of the lines) taken in order form a word or phrase or a regular sequence of letters of the alphabet **2** : ACRONYM — **acrostic** *also* **acros·ti·cal** \-ti-kəl\ *adj* — **acros·ti·cal·ly** \-ti-k(ə-)lē\ *adv*

ac·ryl·am·ide \ˌa-krəl-'a-ˌmīd, ə-'kri-lə-\ *n* [*acrylic* + *amide*] (1893) : an amide C_3H_5NO that is derived from acrylic acid, that polymerizes readily, and that is used in the manufacture of synthetic textile fibers

ac·ry·late \'a-krə-ˌlāt\ *n* (1873) **1** : a salt or ester of acrylic acid **2** : ACRYLIC RESIN

[1]**acryl·ic** \ə-'kri-lik\ *adj* [ISV *acrolein* + *-yl* + [1]*-ic*] (1845) **1** : of or relating to acrylic acid or its derivatives ⟨~ polymers⟩ **2** : made or consisting of an acrylic ⟨an ~ window⟩

[2]**acrylic** *n* (1942) **1 a** : ACRYLIC RESIN **b** : a paint in which the vehicle is an acrylic resin **c** : a painting done in an acrylic resin **2** : ACRYLIC FIBER

acrylic acid *n* (1845) : an unsaturated liquid acid $C_3H_4O_2$ that polymerizes readily to form useful products (as constituents for varnishes and lacquers)

acrylic fiber *n* (1951) : a quick-drying synthetic textile fiber made by polymerization of acrylonitrile usu. with other monomers

acrylic resin *n* (1936) : a glassy thermoplastic made by polymerizing acrylic acid or methacrylic acid or a derivative of either and used for cast and molded parts or as coatings and adhesives

ac·ry·lo·ni·trile \ˌa-krə-lō-'nī-trəl, -ˌtrēl\ *n* [*acrylic* + *-o-* + *nitrile*] (1893) : a colorless volatile flammable liquid nitrile C_3H_3N used chiefly in organic synthesis and for polymerization

ACS *abbr* **1** American Chemical Society **2** American College of Surgeons

[1]**act** \'akt\ *n* [ME, partly fr. L *actus* doing, act, fr. *agere* to drive, do; partly fr. L *actum* thing done, record, fr. neut. of *actus,* pp. of *agere* — more at AGENT] (14c) **1 a** : the doing of a thing : DEED **b** : something done voluntarily **2** : a state of real existence rather than possibility **3** : the formal product of a legislative body : STATUTE; *also* : a decision or determination of a sovereign, a legislative council, or a court of justice **4** : the process of doing : ACTION ⟨caught in the ~⟩ **5** *often cap* : a formal record of something done or transacted **6** : one of the principal divisions of a theatrical work (as a play or opera) **7 a** : one of successive parts or performances (as in a variety show or circus) **b** : the performer or performers in such an act **c** : a performance or presentation identified with a particular individual or group **d** : the sum of a person's actions or effects that serve to create an impression or set an example ⟨a hard ~ to follow⟩ **8** : a display of affected behavior : PRETENSE — **into the act** *or* **in on the act** : into an undertaking or situation as an active participant

[2]**act** *vt* (1590) **1** *obs* : ACTUATE, ANIMATE **2 a** : to represent or perform by action esp. on the stage **b** : FEIGN, SIMULATE **c** : IMPERSONATE **3** : to play the part of as if in a play ⟨~ the man of the world⟩ **4** : to behave in a manner suitable to ⟨~ your age⟩ ~ *vi* **1 a** : to perform on the stage **b** : to behave as if performing on the stage : PRETEND **2** : to take action : MOVE ⟨think before ~*ing*⟩ ⟨~*ed* favorably on the recommendation⟩ **3** : to conduct oneself : BEHAVE ⟨~ like a fool⟩ **4** : to perform a specified function : SERVE ⟨trees ~*ing* as a windbreak⟩ **5** : to produce an effect : WORK ⟨wait for a medicine to ~⟩ **6** *of a play* : to be capable of being performed ⟨the play ~*s* well⟩ **7** : to give a decision or award ⟨adjourned without ~*ing* on the bill⟩ — **act·abil·i·ty** \ˌak-tə-'bi-lə-tē\ *n* — **act·able** \'ak-tə-bəl\ *adj*

[3]**act** *abbr* **1** active **2** actor **3** actual

[1]**ACT** *abbr* **1** Action for Children's Television **2** Association of Classroom Teachers **3** Australian Capital Territory

[2]**ACT** \ˌā-ˌsē-'tē\ *trademark* — used for a standardized achievement test to evaluate suitability for college admission

Ac·tae·on \ak-'tē-ən\ *n* [L, fr. Gk *Aktaiōn*] (14c) : a hunter turned into a stag and killed by his own hounds for having seen Artemis bathing

actg *abbr* acting

ACTH \ˌā-(ˌ)sē-(ˌ)tē-'āch\ *n* [*a*dreno*c*orticotropic *h*ormone] (1944) : a protein hormone of the anterior lobe of the pituitary gland that stimulates the adrenal cortex — called also *adrenocorticotropic hormone*

ac·tin \'ak-tən\ *n* [ISV, fr. L *actus*] (1942) : a cellular protein found esp. in microfilaments (as those comprising myofibrils) and active in muscular contraction, cellular movement, and maintenance of cell shape

actin- *or* **actini-** *or* **actino-** *comb form* [NL, ray, fr. Gk *aktin-, aktino-,* fr. *aktin-, aktis;* perh. akin to OE *ūhte* morning twilight, L *noct-, nox* night — more at NIGHT] **1** : having a radiate form ⟨*actino*lite⟩ **2** : actinic radiation (as X rays) ⟨*actino*meter⟩

[1]**act·ing** \'ak-tiŋ\ *n* (1598) : the art or practice of representing a character on a stage or before cameras

[2]**acting** *adj* (1797) **1** : holding a temporary rank or position : performing services temporarily ⟨~ president⟩ **2 a** : suitable for stage performance ⟨an ~ play⟩ **b** : prepared with directions for actors ⟨an ~ text of a play⟩

ac·tin·i·an \ak-'ti-nē-ən\ *n* [NL *actinia,* fr. Gk *aktin-, aktis*] (1869) : SEA ANEMONE

ac·tin·ic \ak-'ti-nik\ *adj* (1844) : of, relating to, resulting from, or exhibiting chemical changes produced by radiant energy esp. in the visible and ultraviolet parts of the spectrum ⟨~ light⟩ ⟨~ keratosis⟩ — **ac·tin·i·cal·ly** \-ni-k(ə-)lē\ *adv*

ac·ti·nide \'ak-tə-ˌnīd\ *n* [ISV] (1945) : any of the series of elements with increasing atomic numbers that begins with actinium or thorium and ends with lawrencium — see PERIODIC TABLE table

ac·tin·i·um \ak-'ti-nē-əm\ *n* [NL] (1900) : a radioactive trivalent metallic element that resembles lanthanum in chemical properties and that is found esp. in pitchblende — see ELEMENT table

ac·tin·o·lite \ak-'ti-nə-ˌlīt\ *n* (1794) : a bright green or grayish-green mineral of the amphibole group that is a silicate of calcium, magnesium, and iron occurring in fibrous, radiate, or columnar forms

ac·ti·nom·e·ter \ˌak-tə-'nä-mə-tər\ *n* (1833) : any of various instruments for measuring the intensity of incident radiation; *esp* : one in which the intensity of radiation is measured by the speed of a photochemical reaction — **ac·ti·no·me·tric** \-nō-'me-trik\ *adj* — **ac·ti·nom·e·try** \-'nä-mə-trē\ *n*

ac·ti·no·mor·phic \ˌak-(ˌ)ti-nō-'mȯr-fik, -tə-nō-; ak-ˌti-nō-\ *adj* [ISV] (1881) : being radially symmetrical and capable of division by any longitudinal plane into essentially symmetrical halves ⟨an ~ tulip flower⟩ — **ac·ti·no·mor·phy** \'ak-tə-nō-ˌmȯr-fē, ak-'ti-nō-\ *n*

ac·ti·no·my·ces \ˌak-(ˌ)ti-nō-'mī-ˌsēz, -tə-nō-; ak-ˌti-nō-\ *n, pl* **actinomyces** [NL, genus name, fr. *actin-* + Gk *mykēt-, mykēs* fungus; akin to Gk *myxa* mucus — more at MUCUS] (1882) : any of a genus (*Actinomyces*) of filamentous or rod-shaped bacteria that includes usu. commensal and sometimes pathogenic forms inhabiting mucosal surfaces esp. of the oral cavity of warm-blooded vertebrates

ac·ti·no·my·cete \-'mī-ˌsēt, -mī-'sēt\ *n* [ultim. fr. Gk *aktin-, aktis* + *mykēt-, mykēs*] (1883) : any of an order (Actinomycetales) of filamentous or rod-shaped bacteria (as the actinomyces and streptomyces)

ac·ti·no·my·cin \-'mī-sᵊn\ *n* (1940) : any of various red or yellow-red mostly toxic polypeptide antibiotics isolated from soil bacteria (esp. *Streptomyces antibioticus*); *specif* : one used to inhibit DNA or RNA synthesis

ac·ti·no·my·co·sis \-mī-'kō-səs\ *n* [NL] (1881) : infection with or disease caused by actinomyces; *esp* : a chronic disease of cattle, swine, and humans characterized by hard granulomatous masses usu. in the mouth and jaw — **ac·ti·no·my·cot·ic** \-'kä-tik\ *adj*

ac·tion \'ak-shən\ *n* [ME *accioun,* fr. AF *accion,* fr. L *action-, actio,* fr. *agere* to do — more at AGENT] (14c) **1** : the initiating of a proceeding in a court of justice by which one demands or enforces one's right; *also* : the proceeding itself **2** : the bringing about of an alteration by force or through a natural agency **3** : the manner or method of performing: **a** : an actor's or speaker's deportment or expression by means of attitude, voice, and gesture **b** : the style of movement of the feet and legs (as of a horse) **c** : a function of the body or one of its parts **4** : an act of will **5 a** : a thing done : DEED **b** : the accomplishment of a thing usu. over a period of time, in stages, or with the possibility of repetition **c** *pl* : BEHAVIOR, CONDUCT ⟨unscrupulous ~*s*⟩ **d** : INITIATIVE, ENTERPRISE ⟨a man of ~⟩ **6 a** (1) : an engagement between troops or ships (2) : combat in war ⟨gallantry in ~⟩ **b** (1) : an event or series of events forming a literary composition (2) : the unfolding of the events of a drama or work of fiction : PLOT (3) : the movement of incidents in a plot **c** : the combination of circumstances that constitute the subject matter of a painting or sculpture **7 a** : an operating mechanism **b** : the manner in which a mechanism or instrument operates **8 a** : the price movement and trading volume of a commodity, security, or market **b** : the process of betting including the offering and acceptance of a bet and determination of a winner **c** : financial gain or an opportunity for financial gain ⟨a piece of the ~⟩ **9** : sexual activity **10** : the most vigorous, productive, or exciting activity in a particular field, area, or group ⟨wants to be where the ~ is⟩

ac·tion·able \'ak-sh(ə-)nə-bəl\ *adj* (1591) **1** : subject to or affording ground for an action or suit at law **2** : capable of being acted on ⟨~ information⟩ — **ac·tion·ably** \-blē\ *adv*

ac·tion·er \'ak-sh(ə-)nər\ *n* (1973) : a film dominated by a high degree of exciting action

action figure *n* (1987) : a small-scale figure (as of a superhero) used esp. as a toy

ac·tion·less \'ak-shən-ləs\ *adj* (ca. 1817) : marked by inaction : IMMOBILE

action painting *n* (1952) : abstract expressionism marked esp. by the use of spontaneous techniques (as dribbling, splattering, or smearing) — **action painter** *n*

action potential *n* (1926) : a momentary reversal in electrical potential across a plasma membrane (as of a neuron or muscle fiber) that occurs when a cell has been activated by a stimulus

ac·ti·vate \ˈak-tə-ˌvāt\ *vb* **-vat·ed; -vat·ing** *vt* (1626) **:** to make active or more active: as **a** (1) **:** to make (as molecules) reactive or more reactive (2) **:** to convert (as a provitamin) into a biologically active derivative **b :** to make (a substance) radioactive **c :** to treat (as carbon or alumina) so as to improve adsorptive properties **d** (1) **:** to set up or formally institute (as a military unit) with the necessary personnel and equipment (2) **:** to put (an individual or unit) on active duty ~ *vi* **:** to become active — **ac·ti·va·tion** \ˌak-tə-ˈvā-shən\ *n* — **ac·ti·va·tor** \ˈak-tə-ˌvā-tər\ *n*

activated carbon *n* (1921) **:** a highly adsorbent powdered or granular carbon made usu. by carbonization and chemical activation and used chiefly for purifying by adsorption — called also *activated charcoal*

activation analysis *n* (1949) **:** NEUTRON ACTIVATION ANALYSIS

activation energy *n* (1924) **:** the minimum amount of energy required to convert a normal stable molecule into a reactive molecule

ac·tive \ˈak-tiv\ *adj* [ME, fr. AF or L; AF *actif,* fr. L *activus,* fr. *actus,* pp. of *agere* to drive, do — more at AGENT] (14c) **1 :** characterized by action rather than by contemplation or speculation ⟨an ~ life⟩ **2 :** producing or involving action or movement **3 a** *of a verb form or voice* **:** asserting that the person or thing represented by the grammatical subject performs the action represented by the verb ⟨*hits* in "he hits the ball" is ~⟩ **b :** expressing action as distinct from mere existence or state **4 :** quick in physical movement **:** LIVELY **5 :** marked by vigorous activity **:** BUSY ⟨the stock market was ~⟩ **6 :** requiring vigorous action or exertion ⟨~ sports⟩ **7 :** having practical operation or results **:** EFFECTIVE ⟨an ~ law⟩ **8 a :** disposed to action **:** ENERGETIC ⟨took an ~ interest⟩ **b :** engaged in an action or activity ⟨an ~ club member⟩ **c** *of a volcano* **:** currently erupting or likely to erupt — compare DORMANT 2a, EXTINCT 1b **d :** characterized by emission of large amounts of electromagnetic energy ⟨an ~ galactic nucleus⟩ **9 :** engaged in full-time service esp. in the armed forces ⟨~ duty⟩ **10 :** marked by present operation, transaction, movement, or use ⟨an ~ account⟩ **11 a :** capable of acting or reacting **:** reacting readily ⟨~ nitrogen⟩ ⟨~ ingredients⟩ **b :** tending to progress or to cause degeneration ⟨~ tuberculosis⟩ **c** *of an electronic circuit element* **:** capable of controlling voltages or currents **d** (1) **:** requiring the expenditure of energy ⟨~ calcium ion uptake⟩ (2) **:** functioning by the emission of radiant energy or sound ⟨radar is an ~ sensor⟩ **12 :** still eligible to win the pot in poker **13 :** moving down the line **:** visiting in the set — used of couples in contredanses or square dances — **active** *n* — **ac·tive·ly** *adv* — **ac·tive·ness** *n*

active immunity *n* (1895) **:** usu. long-lasting immunity that is acquired through production of antibodies within the organism in response to the presence of antigens — compare PASSIVE IMMUNITY

ac·tive–ma·trix \ˈak-tiv-ˌmā-triks\ *adj* (1980) **:** of, relating to, or being an LCD in which each pixel is individually controlled

active site *n* (1957) **:** a region on the surface of an enzyme whose shape permits binding only of a specific molecular substrate that then undergoes catalysis

active transport *n* (1922) **:** the movement of a chemical substance by the expenditure of energy against a gradient in concentration or in electrical potential across a plasma membrane

ac·tive·wear \ˈak-tiv-ˌwer\ *n* (1924) **:** SPORTSWEAR

ac·tiv·ism \ˈak-ti-ˌvi-zəm\ *n* (1915) **:** a doctrine or practice that emphasizes direct vigorous action esp. in support of or opposition to one side of a controversial issue — **ac·tiv·ist** \-vist\ *n or adj* — **ac·tiv·is·tic** \ˌak-ti-ˈvis-tik\ *adj*

ac·tiv·i·ty \ak-ˈti-və-tē\ *n, pl* **-ties** (1530) **1 :** the quality or state of being active **2 :** vigorous or energetic action **:** LIVELINESS **3 :** natural or normal function: as **a :** a process (as digestion) that an organism carries on or participates in by virtue of being alive **b :** a similar process actually or potentially involving mental function; *specif* **:** an educational procedure designed to stimulate learning by firsthand experience **4 :** an active force **5 a :** a pursuit in which a person is active **b :** a form of organized, supervised, often extracurricular recreation **6 :** an organizational unit for performing a specific function; *also* **:** its function or duties

act of God (1635) **:** an extraordinary interruption by a natural cause (as a flood or earthquake) of the usual course of events that experience, prescience, or care cannot reasonably foresee or prevent

ac·to·my·o·sin \ˌak-tə-ˈmī-ə-sən\ *n* [ISV *actin* + *-o-* + *myosin*] (1942) **:** a contractile complex of actin and myosin that together with ATP is active during muscular contraction

ac·tor \ˈak-tər *also* -ˌtȯr\ *n* (15c) **1 :** one that acts **:** DOER **2 a :** one who represents a character in a dramatic production **b :** a theatrical performer **c :** one who behaves as if acting a part **3 :** one that takes part in any affair — **ac·tor·ish** \-tə-rish\ *adj* — **ac·tor·ly** \-tər-lē\ *adj*

act out *vt* (1611) **1 a :** to represent in action ⟨children *act out* what they read⟩ **b :** to translate into action ⟨unwilling to *act out* their beliefs⟩ **2 :** to express (as an impulse or a fantasy) directly in overt behavior without modification to comply with social norms ~ *vi* **:** to behave badly or in a socially unacceptable often self-defeating manner esp. as a means of venting painful emotions (as fear or frustration)

ac·tress \ˈak-trəs\ *n* (1608) **:** a woman who is an actor — **ac·tressy** \-trə-sē\ *adj*

Acts \ˈakts\ *n pl but sing in constr* (1539) **:** a book in the New Testament narrating the beginnings of the Christian church — called also *Acts of the Apostles*; see BIBLE table

ac·tu·al \ˈak-ch(ə-w)əl, -sh(ə-w)əl; -chü-əl, -shü-\ *adj* [ME *actuel,* fr. LL *actualis,* fr. L *actus* act] (14c) **1** *obs* **:** ACTIVE **2 a :** existing in act and not merely potentially **b :** existing in fact or reality ⟨~ and imagined conditions⟩ **c :** not false or apparent ⟨~ costs⟩ **3 :** existing or occurring at the time ⟨caught in the ~ commission of a crime⟩

actual cash value *n* (ca. 1946) **:** money equal to the cost of replacing lost, stolen, or damaged property after depreciation

ac·tu·al·i·ty \ˌak-chə-ˈwa-lə-tē, ˌak-shə-\ *n, pl* **-ties** (1618) **1 :** the quality or state of being actual **2 :** something that is actual **:** FACT, REALITY ⟨possible risks which have been seized upon as *actualities* —T. S. Eliot⟩ — **in actuality :** in actual fact

ac·tu·al·ize \ˈak-ch(ə-w)ə-ˌlīz, -sh(ə-w)ə-ˌlīz\ *vb* **-ized; -iz·ing** *vt* (1701) **:** to make actual **:** REALIZE ~ *vi* **:** to become actual — **ac·tu·al·i·za·tion** \ˌak-ch(ə-w)ə-lə-ˈzā-shən, -sh(ə-w)ə-lə-\ *n*

ac·tu·al·ly \ˈak-ch(ə-w)ə-lē, -sh(ə-w)ə-lē; ˈaksh-lē, ˈaks-\ *adv* (15c) **1 :** in act or in fact **:** REALLY ⟨nominally but not ~ independent —Karl Loewenstein⟩ ⟨won't ~ arrive for an hour⟩ **2 :** in point of fact — used to suggest something unexpected ⟨he could ~ read the Greek⟩

ac·tu·ar·i·al \ˌak-chə-ˈwer-ē-əl, -shə-\ *adj* (1869) **1 :** of or relating to actuaries **2 :** relating to statistical calculation esp. of life expectancy — **ac·tu·ar·i·al·ly** \-ē-ə-lē\ *adv*

ac·tu·ary \ˈak-chə-ˌwer-ē, -shə-, -ˌwe-rē-\ *n, pl* **-ar·ies** [L *actuarius* shorthand writer, alter. of *actarius,* fr. *actum* record — more at ACT] (1553) **1** *obs* **:** CLERK, REGISTRAR **2 :** a person who calculates insurance and annuity premiums, reserves, and dividends

ac·tu·ate \ˈak-chə-ˌwāt, -shə-\ *vt* **-at·ed; -at·ing** [ML *actuatus,* pp. of *actuare* to execute, fr. L *actus* act] (1645) **1 :** to put into mechanical action or motion **2 :** to move to action ***syn*** see MOVE — **ac·tu·a·tion** \ˌak-chə-ˈwā-shən, -shə-\ *n*

ac·tu·a·tor \ˈak-chə-ˌwā-tər, -shə-\ *n* (1808) **:** one that actuates; *specif* **:** a mechanical device for moving or controlling something

act up *vi* (1903) **1 :** to act in a way different from that which is normal or expected: as **a :** to behave in an unruly, recalcitrant, or capricious manner ⟨the children were *acting up*⟩ **b :** SHOW OFF **c :** to function improperly ⟨this typewriter is *acting up* again⟩ **2 :** to become active or acute after being quiescent ⟨her rheumatism started to *act up*⟩

ACT UP *abbr* AIDS Coalition to Unleash Power

acu·ity \ə-ˈkyü-ə-tē, a-\ *n, pl* **-ities** [ME *acuite* acridity, fr. MF *acuité,* fr. ML *acuitat-, acuitas,* fr. L *acuere*] (1543) **:** keenness of perception

acu·le·ate \ə-ˈkyü-lē-ət\ *adj* [L *aculeatus* having stings, fr. *aculeus* sting, fr. *acus*] (1875) **:** relating to or being hymenopterans (as bees, ants, and many wasps) of a division (Aculeata) typically having the ovipositor modified into a stinger

acu·men \ə-ˈkyü-mən, ˈa-kyə-mən\ *n* [L *acumin-, acumen,* lit., point, fr. *acuere*] (ca. 1579) **:** keenness and depth of perception, discernment, or discrimination esp. in practical matters ***syn*** see DISCERNMENT

acu·mi·nate \ə-ˈkyü-mə-nət\ *adj* (1646) **:** tapering to a slender point

acu·pres·sure \ˈa-kyə-ˌpre-shər, ˈa-kə-\ *n* (1958) **:** the application of pressure (as with the thumbs or fingertips) to the same discrete points on the body stimulated in acupuncture that is used for its therapeutic effects (as the relief of tension or pain) — compare SHIATSU

acu·punc·ture \-ˌpəŋ(k)-chər\ *n* [L *acus* + E *puncture*] (1684) **:** an orig. Chinese practice of inserting fine needles through the skin at specific points esp. to cure disease or relieve pain (as in surgery) — **acupuncture** *vt* — **acu·punc·tur·ist** \-ˌpəŋ(k)-chə-rist\ *n*

acute \ə-ˈkyüt\ *adj* **acut·er; acut·est** [ME, fr. L *acutus,* pp. of *acuere* to sharpen, fr. *acus* needle; akin to L *acer* sharp — more at EDGE] (14c) **1 a** (1) **:** characterized by sharpness or severity ⟨~ pain⟩ (2) **:** having a sudden onset, sharp rise, and short course ⟨~ disease⟩ (3) **:** being, providing, or requiring short-term medical care (as for serious illness or traumatic injury) ⟨~ hospitals⟩ ⟨an ~ patient⟩ **b :** lasting a short time ⟨~ experiments⟩ **2 :** ending in a sharp point: as **a :** being or forming an angle measuring less than 90 degrees ⟨an ~ angle⟩ **b :** composed of acute angles ⟨an ~ triangle⟩ **3 a** *of an accent mark* **:** having the form ˊ **b :** marked with an acute accent **c :** of the variety indicated by an acute accent **4 a :** marked by keen discernment or intellectual perception esp. of subtle distinctions ⟨an ~ thinker⟩ **b :** responsive to slight impressions or stimuli ⟨~ hearing⟩ **5 :** felt, perceived, or experienced intensely ⟨~ distress⟩ **6 :** demanding urgent attention ⟨an ~ emergency⟩ — **acute·ly** *adv* — **acute·ness** *n*

syn ACUTE, CRITICAL, CRUCIAL mean of uncertain outcome. ACUTE stresses intensification of conditions leading to a culmination or breaking point ⟨an *acute* housing shortage⟩. CRITICAL adds to ACUTE implications of imminent change, of attendant suspense, and of decisiveness in the outcome ⟨the war has entered a *critical* phase⟩. CRUCIAL suggests a dividing of the ways and often a test or trial involving the determination of a future course or direction ⟨a *crucial* vote⟩. ***syn*** see in addition SHARP

ACV *abbr* **1** actual cash value **2** air-cushion vehicle

acy·clic \(ˌ)ā-ˈsī-klik, -ˈsi-\ *adj* (1853) **:** not cyclic: as **a :** not disposed in whorls or cycles **b :** having an open-chain structure **:** ALIPHATIC ⟨an ~ compound⟩

acy·clo·vir \(ˌ)ā-ˈsī-klō-ˌvir\ *n* [2*a-* + *cycl-* + *virus*] (1979) **:** a cyclic synthetic nucleoside $C_8H_{11}N_5O_3$ used esp. to treat the symptoms of chicken pox, shingles, and the genital form of herpes simplex

ac·yl \ˈa-səl\ *n, often attrib* [ISV, fr. *acid*] (1899) **:** a radical RCO– derived usu. from an organic acid by removal of the hydroxyl from all acid groups — often used in combination

ac·yl·ate \ˈa-sə-ˌlāt\ *vt* **-at·ed; -at·ing** (1903) **:** to introduce an acyl radical into — **ac·yl·a·tion** \ˌa-sə-ˈlā-shən\ *n*

1**ad** \ˈad\ *n, often attrib* (1841) **1 :** ADVERTISEMENT 2 **2 :** ADVERTISING

2**ad** *n* (ca. 1928) **:** ADVANTAGE 4

AD *abbr* **1** active duty **2** after date **3** Alzheimer's disease **4** anno Domini — often printed in small capitals and often punctuated **5** assembly district **6** assistant director **7** athletic director

A/D *abbr* analog/digital

ad- *or* **ac-** *or* **af-** *or* **ag-** *or* **al-** *or* **ap-** *or* **as-** *or* **at-** *prefix* [ME, fr. AF & L; AF, fr. L, fr. *ad* — more at AT] **1 :** to **:** toward — usu. *ac-* before *c, k,* or *q* ⟨*ac*culturation⟩ and *af-* before *f* ⟨*af*fluent⟩ and *ag-* before *g* ⟨*ag*gradation⟩ and *al-* before *l* ⟨*al*literation⟩ and *ap-* before *p* ⟨*ap*portion⟩ and *as-* before *s* ⟨*as*suasive⟩ and *at-* before *t* ⟨*at*tune⟩ and *ad-* before other sounds but sometimes *ad-* even before one of the listed consonants ⟨*ad*sorb⟩ **2 :** near **:** adjacent to — in this sense always in the form *ad-* ⟨*ad*renal⟩

1**-ad** *adv suffix* [L *ad*] **:** in the direction of **:** toward ⟨cephal*ad*⟩

2**-ad** *n suffix* [prob. fr. NL *-ad-, -as,* fr. Gk, suffix denoting descent from or connection with] **:** member of a botanical group ⟨bromeli*ad*⟩

Ada \ˈā-də\ *n* [fr. *Ada,* a trademark, fr. Augusta *Ada* Byron, Lady Lovelace †1852 Eng. mathematician] (1979) **:** a structured computer programming language

ADA *abbr* **1** American Dental Association **2** Americans for Democratic Action **3** average daily attendance **4** Americans with Disabilities Act **5** assistant district attorney

\ə\ **abut** \ᵊ\ kitten, F table \ər\ **further** \a\ **ash** \ā\ **ace** \ä\ **mop, mar** \au̇\ **out** \ch\ **chin** \e\ **bet** \ē\ **easy** \g\ **go** \i\ **hit** \ī\ **ice** \j\ **job** \ŋ\ **sing** \ō\ **go** \ȯ\ **law** \ȯi\ **boy** \th\ **thin** \t͟h\ **the** \ü\ **loot** \u̇\ **foot** \y\ **yet** \zh\ **vision, beige** \k̲, ⁿ, œ, ue, ʸ\ *see* Guide to Pronunciation

ad·age \ˈa-dij\ *n* [MF, fr. L *adagium*, fr. *ad-* + *-agium* (akin to *aio* I say); akin to Gk *ē* he said] (1513) **:** a saying often in metaphorical form that embodies a common observation

[1]**ada·gio** \ə-ˈdä-j(ē-ˌ)ō, ä-, -zh(ē-ˌ)ō\ *adv or adj* [It, fr. *ad* to + *agio* ease] (1683) **:** at a slow tempo — used chiefly as a direction in music

[2]**adagio** *n, pl* **-gios** (1699) **1 :** a musical composition or movement in adagio tempo **2 :** a ballet duet by a man and woman or a mixed trio displaying difficult feats of balance, lifting, or spinning

[1]**Ad·am** \ˈa-dəm\ *n* [ME, fr. LL, fr. Gk, fr. Heb *Ādhām*] (bef. 12c) **1 :** the first man and father by Eve of Cain and Abel **2 :** the unregenerate nature of man — used esp. in the phrase *the old Adam* — **Adam·ic** \ə-ˈda-mik\ *or* **Adam·i·cal** \-mi-kəl\ *adj*

[2]**Adam** *adj* [Robert *Adam* & James *Adam*] (1872) **:** of, relating to, or being an 18th century decorative style (as of furniture) characterized by straight lines, surface decoration, and conventional designs (as festooned garlands and medallions)

ad·a·mance \ˈa-də-mən(t)s\ *n* (1954) **:** ADAMANCY

ad·a·man·cy \-mən(t)-sē\ *n* [[2]*adamant* + *-cy*] (1937) **:** the quality or state of being adamant **:** OBSTINACY

adam–and–eve \ˌa-də-mən(d)-ˈēv\ *n* (1807) **:** PUTTYROOT

[1]**ad·a·mant** \ˈa-də-mənt, -ˌmant\ *n* [ME, fr. AF, fr. L *adamant-, adamas* hardest metal, diamond, fr. Gk] (14c) **1 :** a stone (as a diamond) formerly believed to be of impenetrable hardness **2 :** an unbreakable or extremely hard substance

[2]**adamant** *adj* (1897) **:** unshakable or insistent esp. in maintaining a position or opinion ***syn*** see INFLEXIBLE — **ad·a·mant·ly** *adv*

ad·a·man·tine \ˌa-də-ˈman-ˌtēn, -ˌtīn, -ˈman-tᵊn\ *adj* [ME, fr. L *adamantinus*, fr. Gk *adamantinos*, fr. *adamant-, adamas*] (13c) **1 :** made of or having the quality of adamant **2 :** rigidly firm **:** UNYIELDING ⟨~ discipline⟩ **3 :** resembling the diamond in hardness or luster

Adam's apple *n* (ca. 1755) **:** the projection in the front of the neck formed by the largest cartilage of the larynx

Adam's needle *n* (ca. 1760) **:** an often cultivated yucca (*Yucca filamentosa*) of coastal pine barrens of the eastern U.S. with a basal rosette of sharp-tipped leaves having loose threads along the margins

adapt \ə-ˈdapt\ *vb* [F or L; F *adapter*, fr. L *adaptare*, fr. *ad-* + *aptare* to fit, fr. *aptus* apt, fit] *vt* (15c) **:** to make fit (as for a new use) often by modification ~ *vi* **:** to become adapted — **adapt·ed·ness** *n*

syn ADAPT, ADJUST, ACCOMMODATE, CONFORM, RECONCILE mean to bring one thing into correspondence with another. ADAPT implies a modification according to changing circumstances ⟨*adapted* themselves to the warmer climate⟩. ADJUST suggests bringing into a close and exact correspondence or harmony such as exists between parts of a mechanism ⟨*adjusted* the budget to allow for inflation⟩. ACCOMMODATE may suggest yielding or compromising to effect a correspondence ⟨*accommodated* his political beliefs in order to win⟩. CONFORM applies to bringing into accordance with a pattern, example, or principle ⟨refused to *conform* to society's values⟩. RECONCILE implies the demonstration of the underlying compatibility of things that seem to be incompatible ⟨tried to *reconcile* what he said with what I knew⟩.

adapt·able \ə-ˈdap-tə-bəl, a-\ *adj* (1800) **:** capable of being or becoming adapted ***syn*** see PLASTIC — **adapt·abil·i·ty** \-ˌdap-tə-ˈbi-lə-tē\ *n*

ad·ap·ta·tion \ˌa-ˌdap-ˈtā-shən, -dəp-\ *n* (1610) **1 :** the act or process of adapting **:** the state of being adapted **2 :** adjustment to environmental conditions: as **a :** adjustment of a sense organ to the intensity or quality of stimulation **b :** modification of an organism or its parts that makes it more fit for existence under the conditions of its environment **3 :** something that is adapted; *specif* **:** a composition rewritten into a new form — **ad·ap·ta·tion·al** \-shnəl, -shə-nᵊl\ *adj* — **ad·ap·ta·tion·al·ly** *adv*

ad·ap·ta·tion·ist \ˌa-ˌdap-ˈtā-sh(ə-)nist, -dəp-\ *adj* (1978) **:** explaining or seeking to explain the evolution of traits in terms of their adaptive function or survival value — **adaptationist** *n*

adapt·er *also* **adap·tor** \ə-ˈdap-tər, a-\ *n* (1801) **1 :** one that adapts **2 a :** a device for connecting two parts (as of different diameters) of an apparatus **b :** an attachment for adapting apparatus for uses not orig. intended

adap·tion \ə-ˈdap-shən, a-\ *n* (1704) **:** ADAPTATION

adap·tive \ə-ˈdap-tiv, a-\ *adj* (1760) **1 :** showing or having a capacity for or tendency toward adaptation **2 a :** designed or intended to assist disabled persons **:** ASSISTIVE ⟨~ devices⟩ **b :** engaged in by disabled persons with the aid of equipment or techniques adapted for a disability ⟨~ skiing⟩ — **adap·tive·ly** *adv* — **adap·tive·ness** *n* — **ad·ap·tiv·i·ty** \ˌa-ˌdap-ˈti-və-tē\ *n*

adaptive optics *n pl but sing or pl in constr* (1975) **:** a telescopic system that improves image resolution by compensating for distortions caused by atmospheric turbulence

adaptive radiation *n* (ca. 1901) **:** evolutionary diversification of a generalized ancestral form with production of a number of adaptively specialized forms

adap·to·gen \ə-ˈdap-tə-jən\ *n* [ISV *adapt* + *-o-* + *-gen*] (1969) **:** a nontoxic substance and esp. a plant extract that is held to increase the body's ability to resist the damaging effects of stress and promote or restore normal physiological functioning — **adap·to·gen·ic** \ə-ˌdap-tə-ˈje-nik\ *adj*

Adar \ä-ˈdär, ˈä-\ *n* [ME, fr. Heb *Ădhār*] (14c) **:** the 6th month of the civil year or the 12th month of the ecclesiastical year in the Jewish calendar — see MONTH table

Adar Ri·shon \ä-ˌdär-rē-ˈshōn\ *n* [Heb *Ădhār Ri'shon* first Adar] (1905) **:** the intercalary month of the Jewish calendar that precedes Adar Sheni in leap years — see MONTH table

Adar She·ni \ä-ˌdär-shā-ˈnē\ *n* [Heb *Ădhār Shēnī* second Adar] (1891) **:** the month of the Jewish calendar that takes the place of Adar in leap years — see MONTH table

ad·ax·i·al \(ˌ)a-ˈdak-sē-əl\ *adj* (ca. 1900) **:** situated on the same side as or facing the axis (as of an organ) ⟨the ~ or upper surface of a leaf⟩

ADC *abbr* **1** aide-de-camp **2** Aid to Dependent Children **3** Air Defense Command **4** assistant division commander

add \ˈad\ *vb* [ME, fr. L *addere*, fr. *ad-* + *-dere* to put — more at DO] *vt* (14c) **1 :** to join or unite so as to bring about an increase or improvement ⟨~*s* 60 acres to his land⟩ ⟨wine ~*s* a creative touch to cooking⟩ **2 :** to say further **:** APPEND **3 :** to combine (numbers) into an equivalent simple quantity or number **4 :** to include as a member of a group ⟨don't forget to ~ me in⟩ ~ *vi* **1 a :** to perform addition **b :** to come together or unite by addition **2 a :** to serve as an addition ⟨the movie will ~ to his fame⟩ **b :** to make an addition ⟨~*ed* to her savings⟩ — **add·able** *or* **add·ible** \ˈa-də-bəl\ *adj*

ADD *abbr* **1** American Dialect Dictionary **2** attention deficit disorder

ad·dax \ˈa-ˌdaks\ *n, pl* **ad·dax·es** [L] (1693) **:** a large light-colored Saharan antelope (*Addax nasomaculatus*) that has long spiralling horns

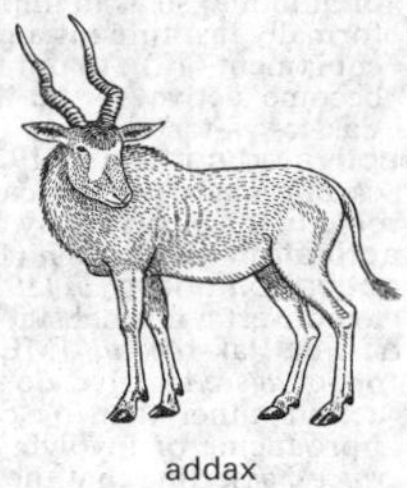

addax

ad·dend \ˈa-ˌdend, ə-ˈdend\ *n* [short for *addendum*] (1674) **:** a number to be added to another

ad·den·dum \ə-ˈden-dəm\ *n, pl* **-den·da** \-ˈden-də\ *also* **-den·dums** [L, neut. of *addendus*, gerundive of *addere*] (1684) **1 :** a thing added **:** ADDITION **2 :** a supplement to a book — often used in pl. but sing. in constr.

[1]**ad·der** \ˈa-dər\ *n* [ME, alter. (by false division of *a naddre*) of *naddre*, fr. OE *nǣdre*; akin to OHG *nātara* adder, L *natrix* water snake] (14c) **1 :** the common venomous viper (*Vipera berus*) of Europe; *broadly* **:** any of various snakes of the viper family — compare PUFF ADDER **2 :** any of several No. American snakes (as the hognose snakes) that are harmless but are popularly believed to be venomous

[2]**add·er** \ˈa-dər\ *n* (1580) **:** one that adds; *esp* **:** a device (as in a computer) that performs addition

ad·der's–tongue \ˈa-dərz-ˌtəŋ\ *n* (1578) **1 :** any of a genus (*Ophioglossum*, family Ophioglossaceae) of small ferns having a spore-bearing stalk resembling a serpent's tongue **2 :** DOGTOOTH VIOLET

[1]**ad·dict** \ə-ˈdikt\ *vt* [L *addictus*, pp. of *addicere* to favor, fr. *ad-* + *dicere* to say — more at DICTION] (1534) **1 :** to devote or surrender (oneself) to something habitually or obsessively ⟨~*ed* to gambling⟩ **2 :** to cause addiction to a substance in (a person or animal)

[2]**ad·dict** \ˈa-(ˌ)dikt\ *n* (1909) **1 :** one who is addicted esp. to a substance **2 :** DEVOTEE ⟨a detective novel ~⟩

ad·dic·tion \ə-ˈdik-shən, a-\ *n* (1599) **1 :** the quality or state of being addicted ⟨~ to reading⟩ **2 :** compulsive need for and use of a habit-forming substance (as heroin, nicotine, or alcohol) characterized by tolerance and by well-defined physiological symptoms upon withdrawal; *broadly* **:** persistent compulsive use of a substance known by the user to be harmful

ad·dic·tive \-ˈdik-tiv\ *adj* (1939) **:** causing or characterized by addiction ⟨an ~ drug⟩ ⟨an ~ personality⟩

add–in \ˈad-ˌin\ *adj* (1980) **:** being or able to be added to and enclosed within an existing system (as a computer) ⟨~ hardware⟩ — **add–in** *n*

Ad·di·son's disease \ˈa-də-sənz-\ *n* [Thomas *Addison* †1860 Eng. physician] (ca. 1856) **:** a destructive disease marked by deficient adrenocortical secretion and characterized by extreme weakness, loss of weight, low blood pressure, gastrointestinal disturbances, and brownish pigmentation of the skin and mucous membranes

ad·di·tion \ə-ˈdi-shən, a-\ *n* [*addicion* AF, fr. L *addition-, additio*, fr. *addere*] (14c) **1 :** a part added (as to a building or residential section) **2 :** the result of adding **:** INCREASE **3 :** the act or process of adding; *esp* **:** the operation of combining numbers so as to obtain an equivalent simple quantity **4 :** direct chemical combination of substances into a single product — **in addition :** [2]BESIDES, ALSO — **in addition to :** combined or associated with **:** [1]BESIDES 2

ad·di·tion·al \-ˈdish-nəl, -ˈdi-shə-nᵊl\ *adj* (ca. 1644) **:** existing by way of addition **:** ADDED ⟨~ information⟩

ad·di·tion·al·ly \-ˈdish-nə-lē, -ˈdi-shən-lē, ˈdi-shə-nᵊl-ē\ *adv* (1659) **:** in or by way of addition **:** FURTHERMORE

[1]**ad·di·tive** \ˈa-də-tiv\ *adj* (1699) **1 :** of, relating to, or characterized by addition ⟨an ~ process⟩ **2 :** produced by addition **3 :** characterized by, being, or producing effects (as drug responses or gene products) that when the causative factors act together are the sum of their individual effects — **ad·di·tive·ly** *adv* — **ad·di·tiv·i·ty** \ˌa-də-ˈti-və-tē\ *n*

[2]**additive** *n* (1945) **:** a substance added to another in relatively small amounts to effect a desired change in properties ⟨food ~*s*⟩

additive identity *n* (1953) **:** an identity element (as 0 in the group of whole numbers under the operation of addition) that in a given mathematical system leaves unchanged any element to which it is added

additive inverse *n* (1953) **:** a number that when added to a given number gives zero ⟨the *additive inverse* of 4 is –4⟩ — compare OPPOSITE 3

[1]**ad·dle** \ˈa-dᵊl\ *adj* [ME *adel* filth, fr. OE *adela*; akin to MLG *adele* liquid manure] (1682) **1** *of an egg* **:** ROTTEN **2 :** CONFUSED

[2]**addle** *vb* **ad·dled; ad·dling** \ˈad-liŋ, ˈa-dᵊl-iŋ\ *vt* (1682) **:** to throw into confusion **:** CONFOUND ~ *vi* **1 :** to become rotten **:** SPOIL **2 :** to become confused

ad·dle·pat·ed \ˈa-dᵊl-ˌpā-təd\ *adj* (1630) **1 :** being mixed up **:** CONFUSED **2 :** ECCENTRIC

addn *abbr* addition

addnl *abbr* additional

[1]**add–on** \ˈad-ˌän, -ˌȯn\ *n* (1941) **:** something added on: as **a :** a sum or amount added on **b :** something (as an accessory or added feature) that enhances the thing it is added to ⟨computer hardware ~*s*⟩

[2]**add–on** *adj* (1955) **1 :** being or able to be added on ⟨an ~ device⟩ **2 :** able to be added to ⟨~ certificates of deposit⟩

[1]**ad·dress** \ə-ˈdres, a- *also* ˈa-ˌdres\ *vb* [ME *adressen*, fr. AF *adrescer*, fr. *a-* (fr. L *ad-*) + *drescer* to direct, put right — more at DRESS] *vt* (14c) **1** *archaic* **a :** DIRECT, AIM **b :** to direct to go **:** SEND **2 a :** to direct the efforts or attention of (oneself) ⟨will ~ himself to the problem⟩ **b :** to deal with **:** TREAT ⟨intrigued by the chance to ~ important issues —I. L. Horowitz⟩ **3** *archaic* **:** to make ready; *esp* **:** DRESS **4 a :** to communicate directly ⟨~*es* his thanks to his host⟩ **b :** to speak or write directly to; *esp* **:** to deliver a formal speech to **5 a :** to mark directions for delivery on ⟨~ a letter⟩ **b :** to consign to the care of another (as an agent or factor) **6 :** to greet by a prescribed form **7 :** to adjust the club preparatory to hitting (a golf ball) **8 :** to identify (as a computer peripheral or memory location) by an address or a name for information transfer ~ *vi, obs* **:** to direct one's speech or attentions — **ad·dress·er** *n*

[2]**ad·dress** \ə-ˈdres, *for 4 & 5 & 7 also* ˈa-ˌdres\ *n* (1539) **1 :** dutiful and courteous attention esp. in courtship — usu. used in pl. **2 a :** readi-

ness and capability for dealing (as with a person or problem) skillfully and smoothly : ADROITNESS **b** *obs* : a making ready; *also* : a state of preparedness **3 a** : manner of bearing oneself ⟨a man of rude ~⟩ **b** : manner of speaking or singing : DELIVERY **4** : a formal communication; *esp* : a prepared speech delivered to a special audience or on a special occasion **5 a** : a place where a person or organization may be communicated with **b** : directions for delivery on the outside of an object (as a letter or package) **c** : the designation of place of delivery placed between the heading and salutation on a business letter **d** : the designation of a computer account from which one can send or receive e-mail **6** : a preparatory position of the player and club in golf **7 a** : a location (as in the memory of a computer) where particular information is stored **b** : a series of usu. alphanumeric characters that specifies the storage location (as on a network or in a computer's memory) of particular information ⟨an Internet ~⟩ ***syn*** see TACT

ad·dress·able \ə-ˈdre-sə-bəl\ *adj* (1953) **1** : able to be addressed : directly accessible ⟨~ registers in a computer⟩ **2** : of or relating to a subscription television system that uses decoders addressable by the system operator — **ad·dress·abil·i·ty** \ə-ˌdre-sə-ˈbi-lə-tē\ *n*

ad·dress·ee \ˌa-ˌdre-ˈsē, ə-\ *n* (1810) : one to whom something is addressed

ad·duce \ə-ˈdüs *also* -ˈdyüs\ *vt* **ad·duced; ad·duc·ing** [ME, fr. L *adducere,* lit., to lead to, fr. *ad-* + *ducere* to lead — more at TOW] (15c) : to offer as example, reason, or proof in discussion or analysis — **ad·duc·er** *n*

1**ad·duct** \ə-ˈdəkt, a-\ *vt* [L *adductus,* pp. of *adducere*] (ca. 1839) : to draw (as a limb) toward or past the median axis of the body; *also* : to bring together (similar parts) ⟨~ the fingers⟩

2**ad·duct** \ˈa-ˌdəkt\ *n* [G *Addukt,* fr. L *adductus*] (1941) : a chemical addition product ⟨~*s* form as carcinogenic metabolites bind to DNA⟩

ad·duc·tion \ə-ˈdək-shən, a-\ *n* (14c) **1** : the action of adducting : the state of being adducted **2** : the act or action of adducing

ad·duc·tor \-ˈdək-tər\ *n* [NL, fr. L, one that draws to, fr. *adducere*] (1615) **1** : a muscle that draws a part toward the median line of the body or toward the axis of an extremity **2** : a muscle that closes the valves of a bivalve mollusk

add up *vi* (1850) **1 a** : to come to the expected total ⟨the bill doesn't *add up*⟩ **b** : to form an intelligible pattern : make sense ⟨her story just doesn't *add up*⟩ **2 a** : AMOUNT 1b — used with *to* ⟨the play *adds up* to a lot of laughs⟩ **b** : to amount to a lot ⟨just a little each time, but it all *adds up*⟩ ~ *vt* : to form an opinion of ⟨*added* him *up* at a glance⟩

-ade *n suffix* [F, fr. MF, fr. Old Occitan *-ada,* fr. LL *-ata,* fr. L, fem. of *-atus* -ate] **1** : act : action ⟨block*ade*⟩ **2** : product; *esp* : sweet drink ⟨lime*ade*⟩

Adé·lie penguin \ə-ˈdā-lē-\ *n* [*Adélie* Coast, Antarctica] (1907) : a small antarctic penguin (*Pygoscelis adeliae*) — called also *Adélie*

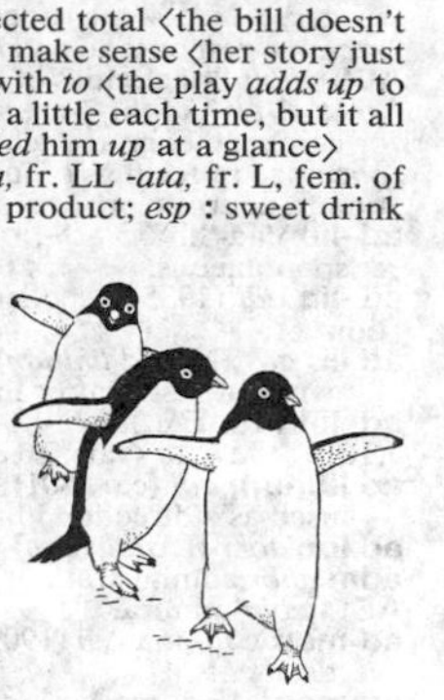

Adélie penguin

-adelphous *adj comb form* [prob. fr. NL *-adelphus,* fr. Gk *adelphos* brother, fr. *ha-, a-* together (akin to *homos* same) + *delphys* womb — more at SAME, DOLPHIN] : having (such or so many) stamen fascicles ⟨mon*adelphous*⟩

aden- *or* **adeno-** *comb form* [NL, fr. Gk, fr. *aden-, adēn;* akin to L *inguen* groin] : gland ⟨*aden*ine⟩ : adenoid ⟨*adeno*virus⟩

ad·e·nine \ˈa-də-ˌnēn\ *n* [ISV; fr. its presence in glandular tissue] (1885) : a purine base $C_5H_5N_5$ that codes hereditary information in the genetic code in DNA and RNA — compare CYTOSINE, GUANINE, THYMINE, URACIL

ad·e·ni·tis \ˌa-də-ˈnī-təs\ *n* [NL] (ca. 1848) : inflammation of a gland; *esp* : LYMPHADENITIS

ad·e·no·car·ci·no·ma \ˌa-dᵊn-(ˌ)ō-ˌkär-sə-ˈnō-mə\ *n* [NL] (ca. 1889) : a malignant tumor originating in glandular epithelium — **ad·e·no·car·ci·no·ma·tous** \-mə-təs\ *adj*

ad·e·no·hy·poph·y·sis \-hī-ˈpä-fə-səs\ *n, pl* **-y·ses** \-fə-ˌsēz\ [NL] (1935) : the anterior glandular lobe of the pituitary gland — **ad·e·no·hy·poph·y·se·al** \-(ˌ)hī-ˌpä-fə-ˈsē-əl\ *or* **ad·e·no·hy·po·phys·i·al** \-ˌhī-pə-ˈfi-zē-əl\ *adj*

1**ad·e·noid** \ˈa-də-ˌnȯid, ˈad-ˌnȯid\ *n* [Gk *adenoeidēs* glandular, fr. *adēn*] (ca. 1890) : either of two abnormally enlarged masses of lymphoid tissue at the back of the pharynx that usu. obstruct the nasal and ear passages; *also* : such a mass when not abnormally enlarged — usu. used in pl.

2**adenoid** *adj* (ca. 1947) **1** : of or relating to the adenoids **2** : relating to, affected with, or associated with abnormally enlarged adenoids ⟨a severe ~ condition⟩ ⟨~ facies⟩

ad·e·noi·dal \ˌa-də-ˈnȯi-dᵊl\ *adj* (1919) : exhibiting the characteristics (as snoring, mouth breathing, and voice nasality) of one affected with abnormally enlarged adenoids : ADENOID ⟨an ~ tenor⟩ — not usu. used technically

ad·e·no·ma \ˌa-də-ˈnō-mə\ *n, pl* **-mas** *also* **-ma·ta** \-mə-tə\ [NL *adenomat-, adenoma*] (1870) : a benign tumor of a glandular structure or of glandular origin — **ad·e·no·ma·tous** \-mə-təs\ *adj*

aden·o·sine \ə-ˈde-nə-ˌsēn, -sən\ *n* [ISV, blend of *adenine* and *ribose*] (ca. 1909) : a nucleoside $C_{10}H_{13}N_5O_4$ that is a constituent of RNA and yields adenine and ribose on hydrolysis

adenosine diphosphate *n* (1938) : ADP

adenosine mo·no·phos·phate \-ˌmä-nə-ˈfäs-ˌfāt, -ˌmō-\ *n* (1950) : AMP

adenosine 3′,5′–monophosphate \-ˌthrē-ˌfīv-\ *n* (1970) : CYCLIC AMP

adenosine tri·phos·pha·tase \-trī-ˈfäs-fə-ˌtās, -ˌtāz\ *n* (1943) : ATPASE

adenosine tri·phos·phate \-trī-ˈfäs-ˌfāt\ *n* (1938) : ATP

ad·e·no·vi·rus \ˌa-dᵊn-ō-ˈvī-rəs\ *n* (1956) : any of a family (*Adenoviridae*) of DNA viruses orig. identified in human adenoid tissue, causing infections of the respiratory system, conjunctiva, and gastrointestinal tract, and including some capable of inducing malignant tumors in experimental animals — **ad·e·no·vi·ral** \-rəl\ *adj*

ad·e·nyl·ate cy·clase \ə-ˌde-nᵊl-ət-ˈsī-ˌklās, -ˌāt-, -ˌklāz; ˌa-də-ˌnil-ət-, -ə-ˌlāt-\ *n* (1968) : an enzyme that catalyzes the formation of cyclic AMP from ATP

ad·e·nyl cyclase \ˈa-də-ˌnil-\ *n* [*aden*ine + *-yl*] (1968) : ADENYLATE CYCLASE

ad·e·nyl·ic acid \ˈa-də-ˌni-lik-\ *n* (1894) : AMP

1**ad·ept** \ˈa-ˌdept, ə-ˈdept, a-ˈ\ *n* [NL *adeptus* alchemist who has attained the knowledge of how to change base metals into gold, fr. L, pp. of *adipisci* to attain, fr. *ad-* + *apisci* to reach — more at APT] (1709) : a highly skilled or well-trained individual : EXPERT ⟨an ~ at chess⟩

2**adept** \ə-ˈdept *also* ˈa-ˌdept\ *adj* (ca. 1691) : thoroughly proficient : EXPERT ⟨~ at fixing cars⟩ ***syn*** see PROFICIENT — **adept·ly** \ə-ˈdep-(t)lē, a-\ *adv* — **adept·ness** \-ˈdep(t)-nəs\ *n*

ad·e·qua·cy \ˈa-di-kwə-sē\ *n, pl* **-cies** (1808) : the quality or state of being adequate

ad·e·quate \-kwət\ *adj* [L *adaequatus,* pp. of *adaequare* to make equal, fr. *ad-* + *aequare* to equal — more at EQUABLE] (ca. 1617) **1** : sufficient for a specific requirement ⟨~ taxation of goods⟩; *also* : barely sufficient or satisfactory ⟨her first performance was merely ~⟩ **2** : lawfully and reasonably sufficient ⟨~ grounds for a lawsuit⟩ ***syn*** see SUFFICIENT — **ad·e·quate·ly** *adv* — **ad·e·quate·ness** *n*

ad eun·dem \ˌad-ē-ˈən-dəm\ *or* **ad eundem gra·dum** \-ˈgrā-dəm\ *adv or adj* [NL *ad eundem gradum*] (1711) : to, in, or of the same rank — used esp. of the honorary granting of academic standing or a degree by a university to one whose actual work was done elsewhere

1**à deux** \(ˌ)ä-ˈdə(r), -ˈdœ\ *adv* [F] (1702) : privately or intimately with only two present ⟨dined *à deux*⟩

2**à deux** *adj* (1869) : involving two people esp. in private ⟨a cozy evening *à deux*⟩

ADF *abbr* automatic direction finder

ad fe·mi·nam \(ˈ)ad-ˈfe-mə-nəm, -ˌäm\ *adj* [NL, lit., to the woman] (1963) : marked by or being an attack on a woman's character rather than an answer to the contentions made — compare AD HOMINEM

ADH *abbr* antidiuretic hormone

ADHD *abbr* attention deficit/hyperactivity disorder

ad·here \ad-ˈhir, əd-\ *vb* **ad·hered; ad·her·ing** [MF or L; MF *adhérer,* fr. L *adhaerēre,* fr. *ad-* + *haerēre* to stick] *vi* (15c) **1** : to give support or maintain loyalty **2** *obs* : ACCORD 3 **3** : to hold fast or stick by or as if by gluing, suction, grasping, or fusing **4** : to bind oneself to observance ⟨~ to the rules⟩ ~ *vt* : to cause to stick fast ***syn*** see STICK

ad·her·ence \-ˈhir-ən(t)s\ *n* (1531) **1** : the act, action, or quality of adhering **2** : steady or faithful attachment : FIDELITY

1**ad·her·ent** \ad-ˈhir-ənt, əd-\ *adj* [ME, fr. AF or L; AF *adheirdant, adherent,* fr. L *adhaerent-, adhaerens,* prp. of *adhaerēre*] (15c) **1** : able or tending to adhere **2** : connected or associated with esp. by contract **3** : ADNATE — **ad·her·ent·ly** *adv*

2**adherent** *n* (15c) : one that adheres: as **a** : a follower of a leader, party, or profession **b** : a believer in or advocate esp. of a particular idea or church ***syn*** see FOLLOWER

ad·he·sion \ad-ˈhē-zhən, əd-\ *n* [F or L; F *adhésion,* fr. L *adhaesion-, adhaesio,* fr. *adhaerēre*] (1624) **1** : steady or firm attachment : ADHERENCE **2** : the action or state of adhering **3** : the abnormal union of separate tissue surfaces by new fibrous tissue resulting from an inflammatory process; *also* : the newly formed uniting tissue **4** : agreement to join ⟨~ of all nations to a copyright convention⟩ **5** : the molecular attraction exerted between the surfaces of bodies in contact — **ad·he·sion·al** \-ˈhēzh-nəl, -ˈhē-zhə-nᵊl\ *adj*

1**ad·he·sive** \-ˈhē-siv, -ziv\ *adj* (1670) **1** : tending to remain in association or memory **2** : tending to adhere or cause adherence **3** : prepared for adhering — **ad·he·sive·ly** *adv* — **ad·he·sive·ness** *n*

2**adhesive** *n* (1912) **1** : an adhesive substance (as glue or cement) **2** : a postage stamp with a gummed back

adhesive binding *n* (1955) : PERFECT BINDING — **ad·he·sive–bound** \-ˌbau̇nd\ *adj*

adhesive tape *n* (1918) : tape coated on one side with an adhesive mixture; *esp* : one used for covering wounds

1**ad hoc** \ˈad-ˈhäk, -ˈhōk; ˈäd-ˈhōk\ *adv* [L, for this] (1659) : for the particular end or case at hand without consideration of wider application

2**ad hoc** *adj* (1879) **1 a** : concerned with a particular end or purpose ⟨an *ad hoc* investigating committee⟩ **b** : formed or used for specific or immediate problems or needs ⟨*ad hoc* solutions⟩ **2** : fashioned from whatever is immediately available : IMPROVISED ⟨large *ad hoc* parades and demonstrations —Nat Hentoff⟩

1**ad ho·mi·nem** \(ˈ)ad-ˈhä-mə-ˌnem, -nəm\ *adj* [NL, lit., to the person] (1598) **1** : appealing to feelings or prejudices rather than intellect **2** : marked by or being an attack on an opponent's character rather than by an answer to the contentions made

2**ad hominem** *adv* (1962) : in an ad hominem manner ⟨was arguing *ad hominem*⟩

adi·a·bat·ic \ˌa-dē-ə-ˈba-tik, ˌā-ˌdī-ə-\ *adj* [Gk *adiabatos* impassable, fr. *a-* + *diabatos* passable, fr. *diabainein* to go across, fr. *dia-* + *bainein* to go — more at COME] (1859) : occurring without loss or gain of heat ⟨~ expansion of a gas⟩ — **adi·a·bat·i·cal·ly** \-ti-k(ə-)lē\ *adv*

adieu \ə-ˈdü, a-, -ˈdyü\ *n, pl* **adieus** *or* **adieux** \-ˈdüz, -ˈdyüz\ [ME, fr. AF *a deu, a dieu,* lit., to God] (14c) : FAREWELL — often used interjectionally

ad in·fi·ni·tum \ˌad-ˌin-fə-ˈnī-təm *also* ˌäd-\ *adv or adj* [L] (1581) : without end or limit

ad int *abbr* ad interim

1**ad in·ter·im** \ˈad-ˈin-tə-rəm, -ˌrim *also* ˈäd-\ *adv* [L] (1787) : for the intervening time : TEMPORARILY

2**ad interim** *adj* (1818) : made or serving ad interim

adi·os \ˌä-dē-ˈōs, ˌa-\ *interj* [Sp *adiós,* fr. *a Dios,* lit., to God] (1823) — used to express farewell

adip- *or* **adipo-** *comb form* [L *adip-, adeps,* prob. fr. Gk *aleipha* fat, oil, fr. *aleiphein* to rub with oil — more at ALIPHATIC] : fat ⟨*adipo*cyte⟩

adip·ic acid \ə-ˈdi-pik-\ *n* [ISV] (1877) : a white crystalline dicarboxylic acid $C_6H_{10}O_4$ formed by oxidation of various fats and also made synthetically for use esp. in the manufacture of nylon

---

\ə\ **abut** \ᵊ\ **kitten**, F table \ər\ **further** \a\ **ash** \ā\ **ace** \ä\ **mop, mar**
\au̇\ **out** \ch\ **chin** \e\ **bet** \ē\ **easy** \g\ **go** \i\ **hit** \ī\ **ice** \j\ **job**
\ŋ\ **sing** \ō\ **go** \ȯ\ **law** \ȯi\ **boy** \th\ **thin** \t͟h\ **the** \ü\ **loot** \u̇\ **foot**
\y\ **yet** \zh\ **vision, beige** \k̲, ⁿ, œ, ue, ʸ\ *see* Guide to Pronunciation

ad·i·po·cere \ˈa-də-pə-ˌsir\ *n* [modif. of F *adipocire*, fr. *adip-* + *cire* wax, fr. L *cera* — more at CERUMEN] (1803) : a waxy substance consisting chiefly of fatty acids and calcium soaps that is formed during decomposition of dead body fat in moist or wet anaerobic conditions

ad·i·po·cyte \ˈa-di-pō-ˌsīt\ *n* (1959) : FAT CELL

ad·i·pose \ˈa-də-ˌpōs\ *adj* [NL *adiposus*, fr. L *adip-*, *adeps*] (1743) : of or relating to animal fat; *broadly* : FAT — **ad·i·pos·i·ty** \ˌa-də-ˈpä-sə-tē\ *n*

adipose tissue *n* (1854) : connective tissue in which fat is stored and which has the cells distended by droplets of fat

Ad·i·ron·dack chair \ˌa-də-ˈrän-ˌdak-\ *n* [*Adirondack* Mountains, N.Y.] (1945) : a wooden lawn chair with a high slatted back, broad arms, and a seat that is lower in the back than the front

ad·it \ˈa-dət\ *n* [L *aditus* approach, fr. *adire* to go to, fr. *ad-* + *ire* to go — more at ISSUE] (1602) : a nearly horizontal passage from the surface in a mine

ADIZ *abbr* air defense identification zone

adj *abbr* **1** adjective **2** adjunct **3** adjustment **4** adjutant

ad·ja·cen·cy \ə-ˈjā-sᵊn(t)-sē\ *n, pl* **-cies** (1646) **1** : something that is adjacent **2** : the quality or state of being adjacent : CONTIGUITY

ad·ja·cent \ə-ˈjā-sᵊnt\ *adj* [ME, fr. AF or L; AF, *ajesaunt*, fr. L *adjacent-*, *adjacens*, prp. of *adjacēre* to lie near, fr. *ad-* + *jacēre* to lie; akin to L *jacere* to throw — more at JET] (15c) **1 a** : not distant : NEARBY ⟨the city and ~ suburbs⟩ **b** : having a common endpoint or border ⟨~ lots⟩ ⟨~ sides of a triangle⟩ **c** : immediately preceding or following **2** *of two angles* : having the vertex and one side in common — **ad·ja·cent·ly** *adv*

syn ADJACENT, ADJOINING, CONTIGUOUS, JUXTAPOSED mean being in close proximity. ADJACENT may or may not imply contact but always implies absence of anything of the same kind in between ⟨a house with an *adjacent* garage⟩. ADJOINING definitely implies meeting and touching at some point or line ⟨had *adjoining* rooms at the hotel⟩. CONTIGUOUS implies having contact on all or most of one side ⟨offices in all 48 *contiguous* states⟩. JUXTAPOSED means placed side by side esp. so as to permit comparison and contrast ⟨a skyscraper *juxtaposed* to a church⟩.

ad·jec·ti·val \ˌa-jik-ˈtī-vəl\ *adj* (1797) **1** : ADJECTIVE **2** : characterized by the use of adjectives — **ad·jec·ti·val·ly** \-və-lē\ *adv*

1**ad·jec·tive** \ˈa-jik-tiv *also* ˈa-jə-tiv\ *adj* [ME, fr. AF or LL; AF *adjectif*, fr. LL *adjectivus*, fr. L *adjectus*, pp. of *adjicere* to throw to, fr. *ad-* + *jacere* to throw — more at JET] (14c) **1** : of, relating to, or functioning as an adjective ⟨an ~ clause⟩ **2** : not standing by itself : DEPENDENT **3** : requiring or employing a mordant ⟨~ dyes⟩ **4** : PROCEDURAL ⟨~ law⟩ — **ad·jec·tive·ly** *adv*

2**adjective** *n* (14c) : a word belonging to one of the major form classes in any of numerous languages and typically serving as a modifier of a noun to denote a quality of the thing named, to indicate its quantity or extent, or to specify a thing as distinct from something else

ad·join \ə-ˈjȯin, a-\ *vb* [ME, fr. AF *ajoindre*, fr. L *adjungere*, fr. *ad-* + *jungere* to join — more at YOKE] *vt* (14c) **1** : to add or attach by joining **2** : to lie next to or in contact with ~ *vi* : to be close to or in contact with one another

ad·join·ing *adj* (15c) : touching or bounding at a point or line ***syn*** see ADJACENT

ad·joint \ˈa-ˌjȯint\ *n* [F, fr. pp. of *adjoindre* to adjoin] (1889) : the transpose of a matrix in which each element is replaced by its cofactor

ad·journ \ə-ˈjərn\ *vb* [ME *ajournen*, fr. OF *ajorner* to order to appear in court on a certain day, fr. *a-* (fr. L *ad-*) + *jour* day — more at JOURNEY] *vt* (15c) : to suspend indefinitely or until a later stated time ~ *vi* **1** : to suspend a session indefinitely or to another time or place **2** : to move to another place

ad·journ·ment \-mənt\ *n* (1607) **1** : the act of adjourning **2** : the state or interval of being adjourned

ad·judge \ə-ˈjəj\ *vt* **ad·judged; ad·judg·ing** [ME *ajugen*, fr. AF *ajuger*, fr. L *adjudicare*, fr. *ad-* + *judicare* to judge — more at JUDGE] (14c) **1 a** : to decide or rule upon as a judge : ADJUDICATE **b** : to pronounce judicially : RULE **2** *archaic* : SENTENCE, CONDEMN **3** : to hold or pronounce to be : DEEM ⟨~ the book a success⟩ **4** : to award or grant judicially in a case of controversy

ad·ju·di·cate \ə-ˈjü-di-ˌkāt\ *vb* **-cat·ed; -cat·ing** *vt* (1775) : to settle judicially ~ *vi* : to act as judge — **ad·ju·di·ca·tive** \-ˌkā-tiv, -kə-\ *adj* — **ad·ju·di·ca·tor** \-ˌkā-tər\ *n* — **ad·ju·di·ca·to·ry** \-ˈjü-di-kə-ˌtȯr-ē\ *adj*

ad·ju·di·ca·tion \ə-ˌjü-di-ˈkā-shən\ *n* [F or LL; F, fr. LL *adjudicatio*, fr. L *adjudicare*] (1691) **1** : the act or process of adjudicating **2 a** : a judicial decision or sentence **b** : a decree in bankruptcy

1**ad·junct** \ˈa-ˌjəŋ(k)t\ *n* [L *adjunctum*, fr. neut. of *adjunctus*, pp. of *adjungere*] (1588) **1** : something joined or added to another thing but not essentially a part of it **2 a** : a word or word group that qualifies or completes the meaning of another word or other words and is not itself a main structural element in its sentence **b** : an adverb or adverbial (as *heartily* in "They ate heartily" or *at noon* in "We left at noon") attached to the verb of a clause esp. to express a relation of time, place, frequency, degree, or manner — compare DISJUNCT 2 **3 a** : an associate or assistant of another **b** : an adjunct faculty member at a college or university **4** : ADJUVANT b — **ad·junc·tive** \a-ˈjəŋ(k)-tiv, ə-\ *adj*

2**adjunct** *adj* (1594) **1** : added or joined as an accompanying object or circumstance **2** : attached in a subordinate or temporary capacity to a staff ⟨an ~ professor⟩ — **ad·junct·ly** \ˈa-ˌjəŋ(k)-tlē, -ˌjəŋk-lē\ *adv*

ad·junc·tion \a-ˈjəŋ(k)-shən\ *n* (1618) : the act or process of adjoining

ad·ju·ra·tion \ˌa-jə-ˈrā-shən\ *n* (1611) **1** : a solemn oath **2** : an earnest urging or advising — **ad·jur·a·to·ry** \ə-ˈjür-ə-ˌtȯr-ē\ *adj*

ad·jure \ə-ˈju̇r\ *vt* **ad·jured; ad·jur·ing** [ME, fr. L *adjurare*, fr. *ad-* + *jurare* to swear — more at JURY] (14c) **1** : to command solemnly under or as if under oath or penalty of a curse **2** : to urge or advise earnestly ***syn*** see BEG

ad·just \ə-ˈjəst\ *vb* [ME *ajusten*, fr. OF *ajuster* to make conform, fr. *a-* (fr. L *ad-*) + *juste* right, exact — more at JUST] *vt* (14c) **1 a** : to bring to a more satisfactory state: (1) : SETTLE, RESOLVE (2) : RECTIFY **b** : to make correspondent or conformable : ADAPT **c** : to bring the parts of to a true or more effective relative position ⟨~ a carburetor⟩ **2** : to reduce to a system : REGULATE **3** : to determine the amount to be paid under an insurance policy in settlement of (a loss) ~ *vi* **1** : to adapt or conform oneself (as to new conditions) **2** : to achieve mental and behavioral balance between one's own needs and the demands of others ***syn*** see ADAPT — **ad·just·abil·i·ty** \-ˌjəs-tə-ˈbi-lə-tē\ *n* — **ad·just·able** \-ˈjəs-tə-bəl\ *adj* — **ad·jus·tive** \-ˈjəs-tiv\ *adj*

adjustable rate mortgage *n* (1981) : a mortgage having an interest rate which is usu. initially lower than that of a mortgage with a fixed rate but is adjusted periodically according to the cost of funds to the lender

ad·just·ed *adj* (1662) **1** : accommodated to suit a particular set of circumstances or requirements **2** : having achieved an often specified and usu. harmonious relationship with the environment or with other individuals ⟨a well-*adjusted* schoolchild⟩

ad·just·er *also* **ad·jus·tor** \ə-ˈjəs-tər\ *n* (1673) : one that adjusts; *esp* : an insurance agent who investigates personal or property damage and makes estimates for effecting settlements

ad·just·ment \ə-ˈjəs(t)-mənt\ *n* (1644) **1** : the act or process of adjusting **2** : a settlement of a claim or debt in a case in which the amount involved is uncertain or full payment is not made **3** : the state of being adjusted **4** : a means (as a mechanism) by which things are adjusted one to another **5** : a correction or modification to reflect actual conditions — **ad·just·men·tal** \ə-ˌjəs(t)-ˈmen-tᵊl, ˌa-ˌjəs(t)-\ *adj*

ad·ju·tan·cy \ˈa-jə-tən(t)-sē\ *n* (1775) : the office or rank of an adjutant

ad·ju·tant \ˈa-jə-tənt\ *n* [L *adjutant-*, *adjutans*, prp. of *adjutare* to help — more at AID] (1539) **1** : a staff officer in the army, air force, or marine corps who assists the commanding officer and is responsible esp. for correspondence **2** : one who helps : ASSISTANT

adjutant general *n, pl* **adjutants general** (1645) **1** : the chief administrative officer of an army who is responsible esp. for the administration and preservation of personnel records **2** : the chief administrative officer of a major military unit (as a division or corps)

1**ad·ju·vant** \ˈa-jə-vənt\ *adj* [F or L; F, fr. L *adjuvant-*, *adjuvans*, prp. of *adjuvare* to aid — more at AID] (1574) **1** : serving to aid or contribute : AUXILIARY **2** : assisting in the prevention, amelioration, or cure of disease ⟨~ chemotherapy following surgery⟩

2**adjuvant** *n* (1609) : one that helps or facilitates: as **a** : an ingredient (as in a prescription or a solution) that modifies the action of the principal ingredient **b** : something (as a drug or method) that enhances the effectiveness of medical treatment ⟨used chemotherapy as an ~ to surgery⟩ **c** : a substance (as one added to a vaccine) enhancing the immune response to an antigen

ADL *abbr* **1** activities of daily living **2** Anti-Defamation League

Ad·le·ri·an \äd-ˈlir-ē-ən, ad-\ *adj* [Alfred *Adler*] (1924) : of, relating to, or being a theory and technique of psychotherapy emphasizing the importance of feelings of inferiority, a will to power, and overcompensation in neurotic processes

1**ad–lib** \ˈad-ˈlib\ *vb* **ad–libbed; ad–lib·bing** [*ad lib*] *vt* (1919) : to deliver spontaneously ~ *vi* : to improvise esp. lines or a speech — **ad–lib** *n*

2**ad–lib** *adj* (1935) : spoken, composed, or performed without preparation

ad lib *adv* [NL *ad libitum*] (1794) **1** : in accordance with one's wishes **2** : without restraint or limit

1**ad li·bi·tum** \(ˌ)ad-ˈli-bə-təm\ *adv* [NL, in accordance with desire] (1610) : AD LIB ⟨rats fed *ad libitum*⟩

2**ad libitum** *adj* (ca. 1801) : omissible according to a performer's wishes — used as a direction in music; compare OBBLIGATO

ad loc *abbr* [L *ad locum*] to or at the place

adm *abbr* administration; administrative

ADM *abbr* admiral

ad·man \ˈad-ˌman\ *n* (1909) : a person who writes, solicits, or places advertisements

ad·mass \ˈad-ˌmas\ *n, often attrib* [*ad*vertising + *mass*] (1955) *chiefly Brit* : mass-media advertising; *also* : the society influenced by it

ad·mea·sure \ad-ˈme-zhər, -ˈmā-\ *vt* **-sured; -sur·ing** [ME *amesuren*, fr. AF *amesurer*, fr. *a-* (fr. L *ad-*) + *mesurer* to measure] (1641) : to determine the proper share of : APPORTION

ad·mea·sure·ment \-ˈme-zhər-mənt, -ˈmā-\ *n* (1523) **1** : determination and apportionment of shares **2** : determination or comparison of dimensions **3** : DIMENSIONS, SIZE

Ad·me·tus \ad-ˈmē-təs\ *n* [L, fr. Gk *Admētos*] (1567) : a king of Pherae who is saved by Apollo from his fated death when his wife Alcestis offers to die in his place

admin *abbr* administration; administrative

ad·min·is·ter \əd-ˈmi-nə-stər\ *vb* **-is·tered; -is·ter·ing** \-st(ə-)riŋ\ [ME *administren*, fr. AF *administrer*, fr. L *administrare*, fr. *ad-* + *ministrare* to serve, fr. *minister* servant — more at MINISTER] *vt* (14c) **1** : to manage or supervise the execution, use, or conduct of ⟨~ a trust fund⟩ **2 a** : to mete out : DISPENSE ⟨~ punishment⟩ **b** : to give ritually ⟨~ the last rites⟩ **c** : to give remedially ⟨~ a dose of medicine⟩ ~ *vi* **1** : to perform the office of administrator **2** : to furnish a benefit : MINISTER ⟨~ to an ailing friend⟩ **3** : to manage affairs — **ad·min·is·tra·ble** \-strə-bəl\ *adj* — **ad·min·is·trant** \-strənt\ *n*

ad·min·is·trate \-ˌstrāt\ *vb* **-trat·ed; -trat·ing** [L *administratus*, pp. of *administrare*] (1550) : ADMINISTER

ad·min·is·tra·tion \əd-ˌmi-nə-ˈstrā-shən, (ˌ)ad-\ *n* (14c) **1** : performance of executive duties : MANAGEMENT **2** : the act or process of administering **3** : the execution of public affairs as distinguished from policy-making **4 a** : a body of persons who administer **b** *often cap* : a group constituting the political executive in a presidential government **c** : a governmental agency or board **5** : the term of office of an administrative officer or body

ad·min·is·tra·tive \əd-ˈmi-nə-ˌstrā-tiv, -strə-\ *adj* (ca. 1731) : of or relating to administration or an administration : EXECUTIVE — **ad·min·is·tra·tive·ly** *adv*

administrative county *n* (1949) : a British local administrative unit often not coincident with an older county

administrative law *n* (1851) : law dealing with the establishment, duties, and powers of and available remedies against authorized agencies in the executive branch of the government

ad·min·is·tra·tor \əd-ˈmi-nə-ˌstrā-tər, -ˌstrā-ˌtȯr\ *n* (15c) **1** : a person legally vested with the right of administration of an estate **2 a** : one who administers esp. business, school, or governmental affairs **b** : a priest appointed to administer a diocese or parish temporarily

ad·min·is·tra·trix \-ˌmi-nə-ˈstrā-triks\ *n, pl* **-tra·tri·ces** \-ˈstrā-trə-ˌsēz\ [NL] (ca. 1623) : a woman who is an administrator esp. of an estate

ad·mi·ra·ble \ˈad-m(ə-)rə-bəl\ *adj* (15c) **1** : deserving the highest esteem : EXCELLENT **2** *obs* : exciting wonder : SURPRISING — **ad·mi-**

ra·bil·i·ty \ˌad-m(ə-)rə-ˈbi-lə-tē\ *n* — **ad·mi·ra·ble·ness** \ˈad-m(ə-)rə-bəl-nəs\ *n* — **ad·mi·ra·bly** \-blē\ *adv*

ad·mi·ral \ˈad-m(ə-)rəl\ *n* [ME, fr. AF *amiral* commander & ML *admiralis* emir, *admirallus* admiral, fr. Ar *amīr-al-* commander of the (as in *amīr-al-baḥr* commander of the sea)] (15c) **1** *archaic* **:** the commander in chief of a navy **2 a :** FLAG OFFICER **b :** a commissioned officer in the navy or coast guard who ranks above a vice admiral and whose insignia is four stars — compare GENERAL **3** *archaic* **:** FLAGSHIP **4 :** any of several brightly colored nymphalid butterflies — compare RED ADMIRAL

admiral of the fleet (1652) **:** the highest-ranking officer of the British navy

ad·mi·ral·ty \ˈad-m(ə-)rəl-tē\ *n* (15c) **1** *cap* **:** the executive department or officers formerly having general authority over British naval affairs **2 :** the court having jurisdiction over questions of maritime law; *also* **:** the system of law administered by admiralty courts

ad·mi·ra·tion \ˌad-mə-ˈrā-shən\ *n* (15c) **1** *archaic* **:** WONDER **2 :** an object of esteem **3 :** delighted or astonished approbation

ad·mire \əd-ˈmī(-ə)r\ *vb* **ad·mired; ad·mir·ing** [MF *admirer,* to marvel at, fr. L *admirari,* fr. *ad-* + *mirari* to wonder, fr. *mirus* astonishing] *vt* (1566) **1 :** to regard with admiration **2** *archaic* **:** to marvel at ~ *vi, dial* **:** to like very much ⟨I would ~ to know why not —A. H. Lewis⟩ ***syn*** see REGARD — **ad·mir·er** *n* — **ad·mir·ing·ly** \-ˈmī-riŋ-lē\ *adv*

ad·mis·si·ble \əd-ˈmi-sə-bəl, ad-\ *adj* [F, fr. ML *admissibilis,* fr. L *admissus,* pp. of *admittere*] (1611) **1 :** capable of being allowed or conceded **:** PERMISSIBLE ⟨evidence legally ~ in court⟩ **2 :** capable or worthy of being admitted ⟨~ to the university⟩ — **ad·mis·si·bil·i·ty** \-ˌmi-sə-ˈbi-lə-tē\ *n*

ad·mis·sion \əd-ˈmi-shən, ad-\ *n* (15c) **1 a :** the act or process of admitting **b :** the state or privilege of being admitted **c :** a fee paid at or for admission **2 a :** the granting of an argument or position not fully proved **b :** acknowledgment that a fact or statement is true — **ad·mis·sive** \-ˈmi-siv\ *adj*

ad·mit \əd-ˈmit, ad-\ *vb* **ad·mit·ted; ad·mit·ting** [ME *admitten,* fr. L *admittere,* fr. *ad-* + *mittere* to send] *vt* (15c) **1 a :** to allow scope for **:** PERMIT ⟨~s no possibility of misunderstanding⟩ **b :** to concede as true or valid ⟨*admitted* making a mistake⟩ **2 a :** to allow entry (as to a place, fellowship, or privilege) ⟨an open window had *admitted* rain⟩ ⟨*admitted* to the club⟩ **b :** to accept into a hospital as an inpatient ⟨he was *admitted* last night for chest pains⟩ ~ *vi* **1 :** to give entrance or access **2 a :** ALLOW, PERMIT ⟨~s of two interpretations⟩ **b :** to make acknowledgment — used with *to* ***syn*** see ACKNOWLEDGE

ad·mit·tance \əd-ˈmi-tᵊn(t)s, ad-\ *n* (1536) **1 a :** the act or process of admitting **b :** permission to enter **2 :** the reciprocal of the impedance of a circuit

ad·mit·ted·ly \əd-ˈmi-təd-lē, ad-\ *adv* (1804) **1 :** as has been or must be admitted ⟨an ~ inadequate treatment⟩ **2 :** it must be admitted ⟨~, we took a chance⟩

ad·mix \ad-ˈmiks\ *vt* [back-formation fr. obs. *admixt* mingled (with), fr. ME, fr. L *admixtus*] (1533) **:** to mix in

ad·mix·ture \ad-ˈmiks-chər\ *n* [L *admixtus,* pp. of *admiscēre* to mix with, fr. *ad-* + *miscēre* to mix — more at MIX] (1605) **1 a :** the action of mixing **b :** the fact of being mixed **2 a :** something added by mixing **b :** a product of mixing **:** MIXTURE

ad·mon·ish \ad-ˈmä-nish\ *vt* [ME *admonesten,* fr. AF *amonester,* fr. VL **admonestare,* alter. of L *admonēre* to warn, fr. *ad-* + *monēre* to warn — more at MIND] (14c) **1 a :** to indicate duties or obligations to **b :** to express warning or disapproval to esp. in a gentle, earnest, or solicitous manner **2 :** to give friendly earnest advice or encouragement to ***syn*** see REPROVE — **ad·mon·ish·er** *n* — **ad·mon·ish·ing·ly** \-ni-shiŋ-lē\ *adv* — **ad·mon·ish·ment** \-mənt\ *n*

ad·mo·ni·tion \ˌad-mə-ˈni-shən\ *n* [ME *amonicioun,* fr. AF *amonicion,* fr. L *admonition-, admonitio,* fr. *admonēre*] (14c) **1 :** gentle or friendly reproof **2 :** counsel or warning against fault or oversight

ad·mon·i·to·ry \əd-ˈmä-nə-ˌtȯr-ē\ *adj* (1594) **:** expressing admonition **:** WARNING — **ad·mon·i·to·ri·ly** \-ˌmä-nə-ˈtȯr-ə-lē\ *adv*

ad·nate \ˈad-ˌnāt\ *adj* [L *adnatus, adgnatus,* pp. of *adgnasci* to be born in addition, grow later — more at AGNATE] (1661) **:** grown to a usu. unlike part esp. along a margin ⟨a calyx ~ to the ovary⟩ — **ad·na·tion** \ad-ˈnā-shən\ *n*

ad nau·se·am \ad-ˈnȯ-zē-əm *also* -ˌam\ *adv* [L] (1647) **:** to a sickening or excessive degree

ad·nexa \ad-ˈnek-sə\ *n pl* [NL, fr. L *annexa,* neut. pl. of *annexus,* pp. of *annectere* to bind to — more at ANNEX] (1864) **:** conjoined, subordinate, or associated anatomical parts — **ad·nex·al** \-səl\ *adj*

ado \ə-ˈdü\ *n* [ME, fr. *at do,* fr. *at* + *don, do* to do] (14c) **1 :** heightened fuss or concern **:** TO-DO **2 :** time-wasting bother over trivial details ⟨wrote the paper without further ~⟩ **3 :** TROUBLE, DIFFICULTY

ado·be \ə-ˈdō-bē\ *n* [Sp, fr. Ar *al-ṭūb* the brick, fr. Copt *tōbe* brick, fr. Egypt *ḏbt*] (1748) **1 :** a brick or building material of sun-dried earth and straw **2 :** a structure made of adobe bricks **3 :** a heavy clay used in making adobe bricks; *broadly* **:** alluvial or playa clay in desert or arid regions — **ado·be·like** \-ˌlīk\ *adj*

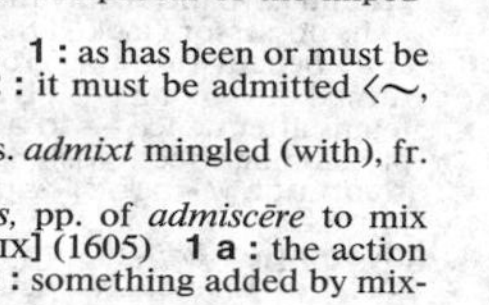

adobe 2

ado·bo \ə-ˈdō-bō, ä-ˈthō-bō\ *n, pl* **-bos** [Sp] (1938) **:** a Philippine dish of fish or meat usu. marinated in a sauce containing vinegar and garlic, browned in fat, and simmered in the marinade

ad·o·les·cence \ˌa-də-ˈle-sᵊn(t)s\ *n* (15c) **1 :** the state or process of growing up **2 :** the period of life from puberty to maturity terminating legally at the age of majority **3 :** a stage of development (as of a language or culture) prior to maturity

[1]**ad·o·les·cent** \-sᵊnt\ *n* [F, fr. L *adolescent-, adolescens,* prp. of *adolescere* to grow up — more at ADULT] (15c) **:** one that is in the state of adolescence

[2]**adolescent** *adj* (1785) **1 :** of, relating to, or being in adolescence **2 :** emotionally or intellectually immature — **ad·o·les·cent·ly** *adv*

Ado·nai \ˌä-də-ˈnȯi, -ˈnī\ *n* [Heb *ʼădhōnāy*] (bef. 12c) — used in place of *YHWH* as a name of the God of the Hebrews during prayer recitation

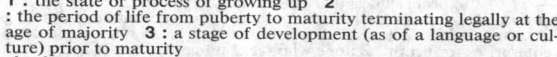

Ado·nis \ə-ˈdä-nəs, -ˈdō-\ *n* [L, fr. Gk *Adōnis*] (1565) **1 :** a youth loved by Aphrodite who is killed at hunting by a wild boar and restored to Aphrodite from Hades for a part of each year **2 :** a very handsome young man

adopt \ə-ˈdäpt\ *vb* [ME, fr. MF or L; MF *adopter,* fr. L *adoptare,* fr. *ad-* + *optare* to choose] *vt* (1500) **1 :** to take by choice into a relationship; *esp* **:** to take voluntarily (a child of other parents) as one's own child **2 :** to take up and practice or use ⟨~*ed* a moderate tone⟩ **3 :** to accept formally and put into effect ⟨~ a constitutional amendment⟩ **4 :** to choose (a textbook) for required study in a course **5 :** to sponsor the care and maintenance of ⟨~ a highway⟩ ~ *vi* **:** to adopt a child ⟨couples choosing to ~⟩ — **adopt·abil·i·ty** \-ˌdäp-tə-ˈbi-lə-tē\ *n* — **adopt·able** \-ˈdäp-tə-bəl\ *adj* — **adopt·er** *n*

syn ADOPT, EMBRACE, ESPOUSE mean to take an opinion, policy, or practice as one's own. ADOPT implies accepting something created by another or foreign to one's nature ⟨forced to *adopt* new policies⟩. EMBRACE implies a ready or happy acceptance ⟨*embraced* the customs of their new homeland⟩. ESPOUSE adds an implication of close attachment to a cause and a sharing of its fortunes ⟨*espoused* the cause of women's rights⟩.

adopt·ee \ə-ˌdäp-ˈtē\ *n* (1851) **:** one who is adopted

adop·tion \ə-ˈdäp-shən\ *n* (14c) **:** the act of adopting **:** the state of being adopted

adop·tion·ism *or* **adop·tian·ism** \-shə-ˌni-zəm\ *n, often cap* (1833) **:** the doctrine that Jesus of Nazareth became the Son of God by adoption — **adop·tion·ist** \-sh(ə-)nist\ *n, often cap*

adop·tive \ə-ˈdäp-tiv\ *adj* (15c) **1 :** made or acquired by adoption ⟨the ~ father⟩ **2 :** of or relating to adoption — **adop·tive·ly** *adv*

ador·able \ə-ˈdȯr-ə-bəl\ *adj* (1611) **1 :** worthy of being adored **2 :** extremely charming ⟨an ~ child⟩ — **ador·abil·i·ty** \-ˌdȯr-ə-ˈbi-lə-tē\ *n* — **ador·able·ness** \-ˈdȯr-ə-bəl-nəs\ *n* — **ador·ably** \-blē\ *adv*

ad·o·ra·tion \ˌa-də-ˈrā-shən\ *n* (15c) **:** the act of adoring **:** the state of being adored

adore \ə-ˈdȯr\ *vt* **adored; ador·ing** [ME *adouren,* fr. AF *aurer, adourer,* fr. L *adorare,* fr. *ad-* + *orare* to speak, pray — more at ORATION] (14c) **1 :** to worship or honor as a deity or as divine **2 :** to regard with loving admiration and devotion ⟨*adored* his wife⟩ **3 :** to be very fond of ⟨~s pecan pie⟩ ***syn*** see REVERE — **ador·er** *n* — **ador·ing·ly** *adv*

adorn \ə-ˈdȯrn\ *vt* [ME, fr. L *adornare,* fr. *ad-* + *ornare* to furnish — more at ORNATE] (14c) **1 :** to enhance the appearance of esp. with beautiful objects **2 :** to enliven or decorate as if with ornaments ⟨people of fashion who ~*ed* the Court⟩

syn ADORN, DECORATE, ORNAMENT, EMBELLISH, BEAUTIFY, DECK, GARNISH mean to enhance the appearance of something by adding something unessential. ADORN implies an enhancing by something beautiful in itself ⟨a diamond necklace *adorned* her neck⟩. DECORATE suggests relieving plainness or monotony by adding beauty of color or design ⟨*decorate* a birthday cake⟩. ORNAMENT and EMBELLISH imply the adding of something extraneous, ORNAMENT stressing the heightening or setting off of the original ⟨a white house *ornamented* with green shutters⟩, EMBELLISH often stressing the adding of superfluous or adventitious ornament ⟨*embellish* a page with floral borders⟩. BEAUTIFY adds to EMBELLISH a suggestion of counterbalancing plainness or ugliness ⟨will *beautify* the grounds with flower beds⟩. DECK implies the addition of something that contributes to gaiety, splendor, or showiness ⟨a house all *decked* out for Christmas⟩. GARNISH suggests decorating with a small final touch and is used esp. in referring to the serving of food ⟨an entrée *garnished* with parsley⟩.

adorn·ment \-mənt\ *n* (14c) **1 :** the action of adorning **:** the state of being adorned **2 :** something that adorns

ADP \ˌā-(ˌ)dē-ˈpē\ *n* [*a*denosine *d*i*p*hosphate] (1943) **:** a nucleotide $C_{10}H_{15}N_5O_{10}P_2$ composed of adenosine and two phosphate groups that is formed in living cells as an intermediate between ATP and AMP and that is reversibly converted to ATP for the storing of energy by the addition of a high-energy phosphate group — called also *adenosine diphosphate*

ad rem \(ˌ)ad-ˈrem\ *adv or adj* [L, to the thing] (1599) **:** to the point or purpose **:** RELEVANTLY

adren- *or* **adreno-** *comb form* [*adrenal*] **1 :** adrenal glands ⟨*adreno*cortical⟩ **2 :** adrenaline ⟨*adren*ergic⟩

[1]**ad·re·nal** \ə-ˈdrē-nᵊl\ *n* [*ad-* + [2]*suprarenal*] (1866) **:** ADRENAL GLAND

[2]**adrenal** *adj* (1868) **:** of, relating to, or derived from the adrenal glands or their secretions ⟨~ steroids⟩

ad·re·nal·ec·to·my \ə-ˌdrē-nə-ˈlek-tə-mē\ *n* (1903) **:** surgical removal of an adrenal gland — **ad·re·nal·ec·to·mized** \-ˌmīzd\ *adj*

adrenal gland *n* (1875) **:** either of a pair of complex endocrine organs near the anterior medial border of the kidney consisting of a mesodermal cortex that produces glucocorticoid, mineralocorticoid, and androgenic hormones and an ectodermal medulla that produces epinephrine and norepinephrine — called also *adrenal, suprarenal gland*

Adren·a·lin \ə-ˈdre-nə-lən\ *trademark* — used for a preparation of levorotatory epinephrine

adren·a·line \ə-ˈdre-nə-lən\ *n* (1890) **:** EPINEPHRINE — often used in nontechnical contexts ⟨the fans were jubilant, raucous, their ~ running high —W. P. Kinsella⟩

adren·al·ized \ə-ˈdre-nə-ˌlīzd\ *adj* (1973) **:** filled with a sudden rush of energy **:** EXCITED

ad·ren·er·gic \ˌa-drə-ˈnər-jik\ *adj* [*adren-* + *-ergic*] (1934) **1 :** liberating, activated by, or involving adrenaline or a substance like adrenaline ⟨an ~ nerve⟩ **2 :** resembling adrenaline esp. in physiological action ⟨~ drugs⟩ — **ad·ren·er·gi·cal·ly** \-ji-k(ə-)lē\ *adv*

ad·re·no·chrome \ə-ˈdrē-nō-ˌkrōm\ *n* (ca. 1913) **:** a red-colored mixture of quinones derived from epinephrine by oxidation

ad·re·no·cor·ti·cal \ə-ˌdrē-nō-ˈkȯr-ti-kəl\ *adj* (1920) **:** of, relating to, or derived from the cortex of the adrenal glands

ad·re·no·cor·ti·co·ste·roid \-ˌkȯr-ti-kō-ˈstir-ˌȯid *also* -ˈster-\ *n* (1960) **:** a steroid obtained from, resembling, or having physiological effects like those of the adrenal cortex

ad·re·no·cor·ti·co·tro·pic \ə-ˈdrē-nō-ˌkȯr-ti-kō-ˈtrō-pik\ *also* **ad·re·no·cor·ti·co·tro·phic** \-ˈtrō-fik\ *adj* (1936) **:** acting on or stimulating the adrenal cortex ⟨~ activity⟩

adrenocorticotropic hormone *n* (1937) **:** ACTH

ad·re·no·cor·ti·co·tro·pin \-ˈtrō-pən\ *also* **ad·re·no·cor·ti·co·tro·phin** \-ˈtrō-fən\ *n* (1952) **:** ACTH

ad·re·no·leu·ko·dys·tro·phy \-ˌlü-kō-ˈdis-trə-fē\ *n* (1976) **:** a rare demyelinating disease of the central nervous system that is inherited as a sex-linked recessive trait chiefly affecting males in childhood and that is characterized by progressive blindness, deafness, tonic spasms, and mental deterioration — abbr. *ALD*

adrift \ə-ˈdrift\ *adv or adj* (1624) **1 :** without motive power and without anchor or mooring ⟨a boat ~ on the sea⟩ **2 :** without ties, guidance, or security ⟨people morally ~⟩ **3 :** free from restraint or support

adroit \ə-ˈdrȯit\ *adj* [F, fr. OF, fr. *a-* (fr. L *ad-*) + *droit* right, droit] (1652) **:** having or showing skill, cleverness, or resourcefulness in handling situations ⟨an ~ leader⟩ ⟨~ maneuvers⟩ ***syn*** see CLEVER, DEXTEROUS — **adroit·ly** *adv* — **adroit·ness** *n*

ad·sci·ti·tious \ˌad-sə-ˈti-shəs\ *adj* [L *adscitus,* fr. pp. of *adsciscere* to admit, adopt, fr. *ad-* + *sciscere* to get to know, fr. *scire* to know — more at SCIENCE] (1620) **:** derived or acquired from something extrinsic

ad·sorb \ad-ˈsȯrb, -ˈzȯrb\ *vb* [*ad-* + ab*sorb*] *vt* (1868) **:** to take up and hold by adsorption ~ *vi* **:** to become adsorbed — **ad·sorb·able** \-ˈsȯr-bə-bəl, -ˈzȯr-\ *adj* — **ad·sorb·er** \-ˈsȯr-bər, -ˈzȯr-\ *n*

ad·sor·bate \ad-ˈsȯr-bət, -ˈzȯr-, -ˌbāt\ *n* (1925) **:** an adsorbed substance

ad·sor·bent \-bənt\ *n* (1917) **:** a usu. solid substance that adsorbs another substance — **adsorbent** *adj*

ad·sorp·tion \ad-ˈsȯrp-shən, -ˈzȯrp-\ *n* [*ad-* + ab*sorption*] (1882) **:** the adhesion in an extremely thin layer of molecules (as of gases, solutes, or liquids) to the surfaces of solid bodies or liquids with which they are in contact — compare ABSORPTION — **ad·sorp·tive** \-ˈsȯrp-tiv, -ˈzȯrp-\ *adj*

ad·u·lar·ia \ˌa-jə-ˈler-ē-ə, ˌa-dyə-\ *n* [It, fr. F *adulaire,* fr. *Adula,* Swiss mountain group] (1798) **:** a transparent or translucent orthoclase

ad·u·la·tion \ˌa-jə-ˈlā-shən, -dyə-, -də-\ *n* [ME *adulacion,* fr. OF, fr. L *adulation-, adulatio,* fr. *adulari* to fawn on (of dogs), flatter] (14c) **:** excessive or slavish admiration or flattery — **ad·u·late** \ˈa-jə-ˌlāt, -dyə-, -də-\ *vt* — **ad·u·la·tor** \-ˌlā-tər\ *n* — **ad·u·la·to·ry** \-lə-ˌtȯr-ē\ *adj*

[1]**adult** \ə-ˈdəlt, ˈa-ˌdəlt\ *adj* [L *adultus,* pp. of *adolescere* to grow up, fr. *ad-* + *-olescere* (fr. *alescere* to grow) — more at OLD] (1531) **1 :** fully developed and mature **:** GROWN-UP **2 :** of, relating to, intended for, or befitting adults ⟨an ~ approach to a problem⟩ **3 :** dealing in or with explicitly sexual material ⟨~ bookstores⟩ ⟨~ movies⟩ — **adult·hood** \ə-ˈdəlt-ˌhu̇d\ *n* — **adult·ly** \ə-ˈdəlt-lē, ˈa-ˌdəlt-\ *adv* — **adult·ness** \ə-ˈdəlt-nəs, ˈa-ˌdəlt-\ *n*

[2]**adult** *n* (1658) **:** one that is adult; *esp* **:** a human being after an age (as 21) specified by law — **adult·like** \ə-ˈdəlt-ˌlīk\ *adj*

adult education *n* (1851) **:** CONTINUING EDUCATION

adul·ter·ant \ə-ˈdəl-t(ə-)rənt\ *n* (ca. 1755) **:** an adulterating substance or agent — **adulterant** *adj*

[1]**adul·ter·ate** \ə-ˈdəl-tə-ˌrāt\ *vt* **-at·ed; -at·ing** [L *adulteratus,* pp. of *adulterare,* fr. *ad-* + *alter* other — more at ELSE] (1531) **:** to corrupt, debase, or make impure by the addition of a foreign or inferior substance or element; *esp* **:** to prepare for sale by replacing more valuable with less valuable or inert ingredients — **adul·ter·a·tor** \-ˌrā-tər\ *n*

[2]**adul·ter·ate** \ə-ˈdəl-t(ə-)rət\ *adj* (1570) **1 :** being adulterated **:** SPURIOUS **2 :** tainted with adultery **:** ADULTEROUS

adul·ter·a·tion \ə-ˌdəl-tə-ˈrā-shən\ *n* (1506) **1 :** the process of adulterating **:** the condition of being adulterated **2 :** an adulterated product

adul·ter·er \ə-ˈdəl-tər-ər\ *n* (15c) **:** a person who commits adultery; *esp* **:** a man who commits adultery

adul·ter·ess \ə-ˈdəl-t(ə-)rəs\ *also* **adul·tress** \-trəs\ *n* (1577) **:** a woman who commits adultery

adul·ter·ine \ə-ˈdəl-tə-ˌrīn, -ˌrēn\ *adj* (1542) **1 a :** marked by adulteration **:** SPURIOUS **b :** ILLEGAL **2 :** born of adultery

adul·ter·ous \ə-ˈdəl-t(ə-)rəs\ *adj* (1558) **:** relating to, characterized by, or given to adultery ⟨an ~ affair⟩ ⟨an ~ wife⟩ — **adul·ter·ous·ly** *adv*

adul·tery \ə-ˈdəl-t(ə-)rē\ *n, pl* **-ter·ies** [ME, alter. of *avoutrie,* fr. AF *avulterie,* fr. L *adulterium,* fr. *adulter* adulterer, back-formation fr. *adulterare*] (15c) **:** voluntary sexual intercourse between a married man and someone other than his wife or between a married woman and someone other than her husband; *also* **:** an act of adultery

adult–on·set diabetes \ə-ˈdəlt-ˈän-ˌset-\ *n* (1975) **:** TYPE 2 DIABETES

ad·um·brate \ˈa-dəm-ˌbrāt, a-ˈdəm-\ *vt* **-brat·ed; -brat·ing** [L *adumbratus,* pp. of *adumbrare,* fr. *ad-* + *umbra* shadow — more at UMBRAGE] (1581) **1 :** to foreshadow vaguely **:** INTIMATE **2 :** to suggest, disclose, or outline partially ⟨~ a plan⟩ **3 :** OVERSHADOW, OBSCURE — **ad·um·bra·tion** \ˌa-(ˌ)dəm-ˈbrā-shən\ *n* — **ad·um·bra·tive** \a-ˈdəm-brə-tiv\ *adj* — **ad·um·bra·tive·ly** *adv*

adust \ə-ˈdəst\ *adj* [ME, fr. L *adustus,* pp. of *adurere* to set fire to, fr. *ad-* + *urere* to burn — more at EMBER] (15c) **1 :** SCORCHED, BURNED **2** *archaic* **:** of a sunburned appearance **3** *archaic* **:** of a gloomy appearance or disposition

adv *abbr* **1** adverb **2** [L *adversus*] against **3** advertisement; advertising **4** advisory

ad val *abbr* ad valorem

ad va·lo·rem \ˌad-və-ˈlȯr-əm\ *adj* [L, according to the value] (1698) **:** imposed at a rate percent of value ⟨*ad valorem* tax on goods⟩ — compare SPECIFIC 5b

[1]**ad·vance** \əd-ˈvan(t)s\ *vb* **ad·vanced; ad·vanc·ing** [ME *advauncen,* fr. AF *avancer,* fr. VL **abantiare,* fr. LL *abante* in front, fr. L *ab-* + *ante* before — more at ANTE-] *vt* (15c) **1 :** to accelerate the growth or progress of ⟨~ a cause⟩ **2 :** to bring or move forward ⟨~ a pawn⟩ **3 :** to raise to a higher rank **4** *archaic* **:** to lift up **:** RAISE **5 :** to bring forward in time; *esp* **:** to make earlier ⟨~ the date of the meeting⟩ **6 :** to bring forward for notice, consideration, or acceptance **:** PROPOSE ⟨~ an idea⟩ **7 :** to supply or furnish in expectation of repayment ⟨~ a loan⟩ **8 :** to raise in rate **:** INCREASE ⟨~ the rent⟩ ~ *vi* **1 :** to move forward **:** PROCEED ⟨an *advancing* army⟩ **2 :** to make progress **:** INCREASE ⟨~ in age⟩ **3 :** to rise in rank, position, or importance ⟨~ through the ranks⟩ **4 :** to rise in rate or price ⟨*advancing* wages⟩ — **ad·vanc·er** *n*

syn ADVANCE, PROMOTE, FORWARD, FURTHER mean to help (someone or something) to move ahead. ADVANCE stresses effective assisting in hastening a process or bringing about a desired end ⟨*advance* the cause of peace⟩. PROMOTE suggests an encouraging or fostering and may denote an increase in status or rank ⟨a campaign to *promote* better health⟩. FORWARD implies an impetus forcing something ahead ⟨a wage increase would *forward* productivity⟩. FURTHER suggests a removing of obstacles in the way of a desired advance ⟨used the marriage to *further* his career⟩.

[2]**advance** *n* (1668) **1 :** a moving forward **2 a :** progress in development ⟨mistaking material ~ for spiritual enrichment —H. J. Laski⟩ **b :** a progressive step **:** IMPROVEMENT ⟨an ~ in medical technique⟩ **3 :** a rise in price, value, or amount **4 :** a first step or approach made ⟨her attitude discouraged all ~*s*⟩ **5 :** a provision of something (as money or goods) before a return is received; *also* **:** the money or goods supplied — **in advance 1 :** to, toward, or in a place or position ahead ⟨sent scouts out *in advance*⟩ **2 :** before a deadline or an anticipated event ⟨made reservations *in advance*⟩ — **in advance of :** AHEAD OF

[3]**advance** *adj* (1701) **1 :** made, sent, or furnished ahead of time ⟨~ sales⟩ **2 :** going or situated before ⟨an ~ party of soldiers⟩

ad·vanced *adj* (1534) **1 :** far on in time or course ⟨a man ~ in years⟩ **2 a :** being beyond others in progress or ideas ⟨tastes a bit too ~ for the times⟩ **b :** being beyond the elementary or introductory ⟨~ chemistry⟩ **c :** greatly developed beyond an initial stage ⟨the most ~ scientific methods⟩ ⟨~ weapons systems⟩ **d :** much evolved from an early ancestral type ⟨bees and other ~ insects⟩ ⟨~ traits⟩

advanced degree *n* (1878) **:** a university degree (as a master's or doctor's degree) higher than a bachelor's

advance directive *n* (1984) **:** a legal document (as a living will) signed by a competent person to provide guidance for medical and health-care decisions (as the termination of life support or organ donation) in the event the person becomes incompetent to make such decisions

Advanced level *n* (1947) **:** A LEVEL

advance man *n* (1906) **:** an employee who makes arrangements and handles publicity in advance of an appearance or engagement by the employer (as a political candidate or a circus)

ad·vance·ment \əd-ˈvan(t)-smənt\ *n* (1553) **1 :** the action of advancing **:** the state of being advanced: **a :** promotion or elevation to a higher rank or position **b :** progression to a higher stage of development **2 :** an improved feature **:** IMPROVEMENT

[1]**ad·van·tage** \əd-ˈvan-tij\ *n* [ME *avantage,* fr. AF, fr. *avant* before, fr. LL *abante*] (1523) **1 :** superiority of position or condition ⟨higher ground gave the enemy the ~⟩ **2 :** a factor or circumstance of benefit to its possessor ⟨lacked the ~*s* of an education⟩ **3 a :** BENEFIT, GAIN; *esp* **:** benefit resulting from some course of action ⟨a mistake which turned out to our ~⟩ **b** *obs* **:** INTEREST 2a **4 :** the first point won in tennis after deuce — **to advantage :** so as to produce a favorable impression or effect ⟨wishing to be seen *to advantage*⟩

[2]**advantage** *vt* **-taged; -tag·ing** (1549) **:** to give an advantage to **:** BENEFIT

advantaged *adj* (1950) **:** having or providing an advantage and esp. a social or financial advantage over others ⟨an ~ position⟩ ⟨~ children⟩

ad·van·ta·geous \ˌad-ˌvan-ˈtā-jəs, -vən-\ *adj* (1593) **:** giving an advantage **:** FAVORABLE ⟨an ~ opportunity⟩ — **ad·van·ta·geous·ly** *adv* — **ad·van·ta·geous·ness** *n*

ad·vec·tion \ad-ˈvek-shən\ *n* [L *advection-, advectio* act of bringing, fr. *advehere* to carry to, fr. *ad-* + *vehere* to carry — more at WAY] (1910) **:** the usu. horizontal movement of a mass of fluid (as air or an ocean current); *also* **:** transport (as of pollutants or plankton) by such movement — **ad·vect** \-ˈvekt\ *vt* — **ad·vec·tive** \-ˈvek-tiv\ *adj*

Ad·vent \ˈad-ˌvent, *chiefly Brit* -vənt\ *n* [ME, fr. ML *adventus,* fr. L, arrival, fr. *advenire*] (12c) **1 :** the period beginning four Sundays before Christmas and observed by some Christians as a season of prayer and fasting **2 a :** the coming of Christ at the Incarnation **b :** SECOND COMING **3** *not cap* **:** a coming into being or use ⟨the ~ of spring⟩ ⟨the ~ of pasteurization⟩ ⟨the ~ of personal computers⟩

Ad·vent·ism \ˈad-ˌven-ˌti-zəm\ *n* (1874) **1 :** the doctrine that the second coming of Christ and the end of the world are near at hand **2 :** the principles and practices of Seventh-Day Adventists — **Ad·vent·ist** \ˈad-ˌven-tist, ad-ˈ, ˈad-ˌ\ *adj or n*

ad·ven·ti·tia \ˌad-vən-ˈti-shə, -(ˌ)ven-\ *n* [NL, alter. of L *adventicia,* neut. pl. of *adventicius* coming from outside, fr. *adventus,* pp.] (1876) **:** an external chiefly connective tissue covering of an organ; *esp* **:** the external coat of a blood vessel — **ad·ven·ti·tial** \-shəl\ *adj*

ad·ven·ti·tious \ˌad-(ˌ)ven-ˈti-shəs, -vən-\ *adj* [L *adventicius*] (1603) **1 :** coming from another source and not inherent or innate ⟨a Federal house without ~ later additions⟩ **2 :** arising or occurring sporadically or in other than the usual location ⟨~ roots⟩ — **ad·ven·ti·tious·ly** *adv*

ad·ven·tive \ad-ˈven-tiv\ *adj* (ca. 1859) **1 :** introduced but not fully naturalized ⟨an ~ weed⟩ **2 :** ADVENTITIOUS 2 — **adventive** *n*

Advent Sunday *n* (15c) **:** the first Sunday in Advent

[1]**ad·ven·ture** \əd-ˈven-chər\ *n* [ME *aventure,* chance, risk, fr. AF, fr. VL **adventura,* fr. L *adventus,* pp. of *advenire* to arrive, fr. *ad-* + *venire* to come — more at COME] (14c) **1 a :** an undertaking usu. involving danger and unknown risks **b :** the encountering of risks ⟨the spirit of ~⟩ **2 :** an exciting or remarkable experience ⟨an ~ in exotic dining⟩ **3 :** an enterprise involving financial risk

[2]**adventure** *vb* **ad·ven·tured; ad·ven·tur·ing** \-ˈven-ch(ə-)riŋ\ *vt* (14c) **1 :** to expose to danger or loss **:** VENTURE **2 :** to venture upon **:** TRY ~ *vi* **1 :** to proceed despite risk **2 :** to take the risk

ad·ven·tur·er \əd-ˈven-ch(ə-)rər\ *n* (15c) **1 :** one that adventures: as **a :** SOLDIER OF FORTUNE **b :** one that engages in risky commercial enterprises for profit **2 :** one who seeks unmerited wealth or position esp. by playing on the credulity or prejudice of others

ad·ven·ture·some \əd-ˈven-chər-səm\ *adj* (ca. 1731) **:** inclined to take risks **:** VENTURESOME — **ad·ven·ture·some·ness** *n*

ad·ven·tur·ess \əd-ˈven-ch(ə-)rəs\ *n* (1754) **:** a female adventurer; *esp* **:** one who seeks position or livelihood by questionable means

ad·ven·tur·ism \əd-ˈven-chə-ˌri-zəm\ *n* (1932) **:** improvisation or experimentation (as in politics or military or foreign affairs) in the absence or in defiance of accepted plans or principles — **ad·ven·tur·ist** \-ˈven-ch(ə-)rist\ *n* — **ad·ven·tur·is·tic** \-ˌven-chə-ˈris-tik\ *adj*

ad·ven·tur·ous \əd-ˈven-ch(ə-)rəs\ *adj* (15c) **1 a :** disposed to seek adventure or to cope with the new and unknown ⟨an ~ explorer⟩ **b :** INNOVATIVE ⟨an ~ artistic style⟩ **2 :** characterized by unknown dangers and risks ⟨an ~ journey⟩ — **ad·ven·tur·ous·ly** *adv* — **ad·ven·tur·ous·ness** *n*

syn ADVENTUROUS, VENTURESOME, DARING, DAREDEVIL, RASH, RECKLESS, FOOLHARDY mean exposing oneself to danger more than required by good sense. ADVENTUROUS implies a willingness to accept risks but not necessarily imprudence ⟨*adventurous* pioneers⟩. VENTURESOME implies eagerness for perilous undertakings ⟨*venturesome* stunt pilots⟩. DARING implies fearlessness in courting danger ⟨*daring* mountain climbers⟩. DAREDEVIL stresses ostentation in daring ⟨*daredevil* motorcyclists⟩. RASH suggests imprudence and lack of forethought ⟨a *rash* decision⟩. RECKLESS implies heedlessness of probable consequences ⟨a *reckless* driver⟩. FOOLHARDY suggests a lack of good sense ⟨the *foolhardy* sailor ventured into the storm⟩.

[1]**ad·verb** \ˈad-ˌvərb\ *n* [ME *adverbe,* fr. MF, fr. L *adverbium,* fr. *ad-* + *verbum* word — more at WORD] (14c) **:** a word belonging to one of the major form classes in any of numerous languages, typically serving as a modifier of a verb, an adjective, another adverb, a preposition, a phrase, a clause, or a sentence, expressing some relation of manner or quality, place, time, degree, number, cause, opposition, affirmation, or denial, and in English also serving to connect and to express comment on clause content — compare ADJUNCT, CONJUNCT, DISJUNCT

[2]**adverb** *adj* (1879) **:** ADVERBIAL

ad·ver·bi·al \ad-ˈvər-bē-əl\ *adj* (1611) **:** of, relating to, or having the function of an adverb — **adverbial** *n* — **ad·ver·bi·al·ly** \-ə-lē\ *adv*

ad ver·bum \(ˌ)ad-ˈvər-bəm\ *adv* [L] (ca. 1580) **:** to a word **:** VERBATIM

ad·ver·sar·i·al \ˌad-və(r)-ˈser-ē-əl, -ˈse-rē-\ *adj* (1871) **:** of, relating to, or characteristic of an adversary or adversary procedures

[1]**ad·ver·sary** \ˈad-və(r)-ˌser-ē, -ˌse-rē\ *n, pl* **-sar·ies** (14c) **:** one that contends with, opposes, or resists **:** ENEMY — **ad·ver·sari·ness** *n*

[2]**adversary** *adj* (14c) **1 :** of, relating to, or involving an adversary **2 :** having or involving antagonistic parties or opposing interests ⟨divorce can be an ~ proceeding⟩

ad·ver·sa·tive \əd-ˈvər-sə-tiv, ad-\ *adj* (15c) **:** expressing antithesis, opposition, or adverse circumstance ⟨the ~ conjunction *but*⟩ — **adversative** *n* — **ad·ver·sa·tive·ly** *adv*

ad·verse \ad-ˈvərs, ˈad-ˌ\ *adj* [ME, fr. AF *advers,* fr. L *adversus,* pp. of *advertere*] (14c) **1 :** acting against or in a contrary direction **:** HOSTILE ⟨hindered by ~ winds⟩ **2 a :** opposed to one's interests ⟨an ~ verdict⟩ ⟨heard testimony ~ to their position⟩; *esp* **:** UNFAVORABLE ⟨~ criticism⟩ **b :** causing harm **:** HARMFUL ⟨~ drug effects⟩ **3** *archaic* **:** opposite in position — **ad·verse·ly** *adv* — **ad·verse·ness** *n*

ad·ver·si·ty \ad-ˈvər-sə-tē\ *n, pl* **-ties** (13c) **:** a state or instance of serious or continued difficulty or misfortune ***syn*** see MISFORTUNE

[1]**ad·vert** \ad-ˈvərt\ *vi* [ME, to perceive, pay heed, fr. AF & L; AF *advertir,* fr. L *advertere,* fr. *ad-* + *vertere* to turn — more at WORTH] (15c) **1 :** to turn the mind or attention — used with *to* ⟨~*ed* to the speaker⟩ **2 :** to call attention in the course of speaking or writing **:** make reference — used with *to* ⟨~*ed* to foreign-language sources⟩

[2]**ad·vert** \ˈad-ˌvərt\ *n* (1860) *chiefly Brit* **:** ADVERTISEMENT

ad·ver·tence \ad-ˈvər-tᵊn(t)s\ *n* (14c) **1 :** the action or process of adverting **:** ATTENTION **2 :** ADVERTENCY 1

ad·ver·ten·cy \-tᵊn(t)-sē\ *n, pl* **-cies** (1646) **1 :** the quality or state of being advertent **:** HEEDFULNESS **2 :** ADVERTENCE 1

ad·ver·tent \-tᵊnt\ *adj* [L *advertent-, advertens,* prp. of *advertere*] (1671) **:** giving attention **:** HEEDFUL — **ad·ver·tent·ly** *adv*

ad·ver·tise \ˈad-vər-ˌtīz\ *vb* **-tised; -tis·ing** [ME, to pay heed to, observe, notify, fr. AF *advertiss-,* stem of *advertir*] *vt* (15c) **1 :** to make something known to **:** NOTIFY **2 a :** to make publicly and generally known ⟨*advertising* their readiness to make concessions⟩ **b :** to announce publicly esp. by a printed notice or a broadcast **c :** to call public attention to esp. by emphasizing desirable qualities so as to arouse a desire to buy or patronize **:** PROMOTE ~ *vi* **:** to issue or sponsor advertising ⟨~ for a secretary⟩ — **ad·ver·tis·er** *n*

ad·ver·tise·ment \ˌad-vər-ˈtīz-mənt; əd-ˈvər-təz-mənt, -tə-smənt\ *n* (15c) **1 :** the act or process of advertising **2 :** a public notice; *esp* **:** one published in the press or broadcast over the air

ad·ver·tis·ing *n* (1751) **1 :** the action of calling something to the attention of the public esp. by paid announcements **2 :** ADVERTISEMENTS ⟨the magazine contains much ~⟩ **3 :** the business of preparing advertisements for publication or broadcast

ad·ver·to·ri·al \ˌad-vər-ˈtȯr-ē-əl\ *n* [blend of *advertisement* and *editorial*] (1946) **:** an advertisement that imitates editorial format

ad·vice \əd-ˈvīs\ *n* [ME *avis, advis* view, opinion, fr. AF, fr. the OF phrase *ce m'est a vis* that appears to me, part trans. of L *mihi visum est* it seemed so to me, I decided] (14c) **1 :** recommendation regarding a decision or course of conduct **:** COUNSEL ⟨he shall have power, by and with the ~ and consent of the Senate, to make treaties —*U.S. Constitution*⟩ **2 :** information or notice given — usu. used in pl. **3 :** an official notice concerning a business transaction

ad·vis·able \əd-ˈvī-zə-bəl\ *adj* (1582) **:** fit to be advised or done **:** PRUDENT ***syn*** see EXPEDIENT — **ad·vis·abil·i·ty** \-ˌvī-zə-ˈbi-lə-tē\ *n* — **ad·vis·able·ness** \-ˈvī-zə-bəl-nəs\ *n* — **ad·vis·ably** \-blē\ *adv*

ad·vise \əd-ˈvīz\ *vb* **ad·vised; ad·vis·ing** [ME, to look at, consider, advise, fr. AF *aviser,* fr. *avis*] *vt* (15c) **1 a :** to give advice to **:** COUNSEL ⟨~ her to try a drier climate⟩ **b :** CAUTION, WARN ⟨~ them of the consequences⟩ **c :** RECOMMEND ⟨~ prudence⟩ **2 :** to give information or notice to **:** INFORM ⟨~ them of their rights⟩ ~ *vi* **1 :** to give advice ⟨~ on legal matters⟩ **2 :** to take counsel **:** CONSULT ⟨~ with friends⟩ — **ad·vis·er** *also* **ad·vi·sor** \-ˈvī-zər\ *n*

ad·vised \əd-ˈvīzd\ *adj* (15c) **:** thought out **:** CONSIDERED — often used in combination ⟨ill-*advised* plans⟩ — **ad·vis·ed·ly** \-ˈvī-zəd-lē\ *adv*

ad·vis·ee \əd-ˌvī-ˈzē\ *n* (1824) **:** one who is advised

ad·vise·ment \əd-ˈvīz-mənt\ *n* (15c) **1 :** careful consideration **:** DELIBERATION ⟨take a matter under ~⟩ **2 :** the act or process of advising (as a college student)

[1]**ad·vi·so·ry** \əd-ˈvīz-rē, -ˈvī-zə-\ *adj* (1731) **1 :** having or exercising power to advise ⟨an ~ council⟩ **2 :** containing or giving advice

[2]**advisory** *n, pl* **-ries** (1920) **:** a report giving information (as on the weather) and often recommending action to be taken

ad·vo·ca·cy \ˈad-və-kə-sē\ *n* (15c) **:** the act or process of advocating or supporting a cause or proposal

advocacy journalism *n* (1969) **:** journalism that advocates a cause or expresses a viewpoint — **advocacy journalist** *n*

[1]**ad·vo·cate** \ˈad-və-kət, -ˌkāt\ *n* [ME *advocat,* fr. AF, fr. L *advocatus,* fr. pp. of *advocare* to summon, fr. *ad-* + *vocare* to call, fr. *voc-, vox* voice — more at VOICE] (14c) **1 :** one that pleads the cause of another; *specif* **:** one that pleads the cause of another before a tribunal or judicial court **2 :** one that defends or maintains a cause or proposal **3 :** one that supports or promotes the interests of another

[2]**ad·vo·cate** \-ˌkāt\ *vt* **-cat·ed; -cat·ing** (1599) **:** to plead in favor of ***syn*** see SUPPORT — **ad·vo·ca·tion** \ˌad-və-ˈkā-shən\ *n* — **ad·vo·ca·tive** \ˈad-və-ˌkā-tiv\ *adj* — **ad·vo·ca·tor** \-ˌkā-tər\ *n*

ad·vow·son \əd-ˈvau̇-zᵊn\ *n* [ME *avoueson,* fr. AF, fr. ML *advocation-, advocatio,* fr. L, act of calling, fr. *advocare*] (15c) **:** the right in English law of presenting a nominee to a benefice

advt *abbr* advertisement

ad·ware \ˈad-ˌwer\ *n* (1992) **:** computer software that is provided usu. for free but contains advertisements

ady·nam·ic \ˌā-(ˌ)dī-ˈna-mik, ˌa-də-ˈna-\ *adj* [Gk *adynamia* lack of strength, fr. *a-* + *dynamis* power, fr. *dynasthai* to be able] (1829) **:** characterized by or causing a loss of strength or function ⟨~ ileus⟩

ad·y·tum \ˈa-də-təm\ *n, pl* **-ta** \-tə\ [L, fr. Gk *adyton,* neut. of *adytos* not to be entered, fr. *a-* + *dyein* to enter] (1611) **:** the innermost sanctuary in an ancient temple open only to priests **:** SANCTUM

adze *also* **adz** \ˈadz\ *n* [ME *adse,* fr. OE *adesa*] (bef. 12c) **:** a cutting tool that has a thin arched blade set at right angles to the handle and is used chiefly for shaping wood

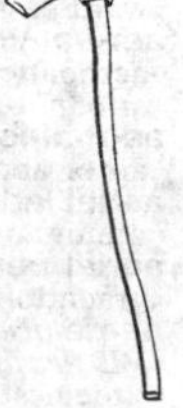

adze

ad·zu·ki \ad-ˈzü-kē\ *or* **azu·ki** \ä-ˈzü-\ *n* [Jp *azuki*] (1727) **:** ADZUKI BEAN

adzuki bean *or* **azuki bean** *n* (1795) **:** an annual bushy leguminous plant (*Vigna angularis* syn. *Phaseolus angularis*) widely grown in Japan and China for its seeds which are used as food and to produce a flour; *also* **:** its seed

ae \ˈā\ *adj* [ME (northern dial.) *a,* alter. of *an*] (1725) *chiefly Scot* **:** ONE

AE *abbr* American English

Ae·a·cus \ˈē-ə-kəs\ *n* [L, fr. Gk *Aiakos*] (1606) **:** a son of Zeus who is given the Myrmidons as followers and becomes on his death a judge of the underworld

AEC *abbr* Atomic Energy Commission

ae·cio·spore \ˈē-shə-ˌspȯr, ˈē-sə-\ *n* (1905) **:** one of the spores arranged within an aecium in a series like a chain

ae·ci·um \ˈē-shē-əm, ˈē-sē-\ *n, pl* **-cia** \-shē-ə, -sē-\ [NL, fr. Gk *aikia* outrage, assault, fr. *aikēs, aeikēs* unseemly, fr. *a-* + *-eikēs,* fr. *eikenai* to seem] (1905) **:** the fruiting body of a rust fungus in which the first binucleate spores are usu. produced — **ae·cial** \-sh(ē-)əl\ *adj*

AED *abbr* automated external defibrillator; automatic external defibrillator

ae·des \ā-ˈē-(ˌ)dēz\ *n, pl* **aedes** [NL, genus name, fr. Gk *aēdēs* unpleasant, fr. *a-* + *ēdos* pleasure; akin to Gk *hēdys* sweet — more at SWEET] (ca. 1909) **:** any of a genus (*Aedes*) of mosquitoes including the vector of yellow fever, dengue, and other diseases — **ae·dine** \-ˈē-ˌdīn\ *adj*

ae·dile \ˈē-ˌdī(-ə)l, ˈē-dᵊl\ *n* [L *aedilis,* fr. *aedes* temple — more at EDIFY] (1538) **:** an official in ancient Rome in charge of public works and games, police, and the grain supply

AEF *abbr* American Expeditionary Force

Ae·ge·an \i-ˈjē-ən\ *adj* [L *Aegaeus,* fr. Gk *Aigaios*] (1513) **1 :** of or relating to the arm of the Mediterranean Sea east of Greece **2 :** of or relating to the chiefly Bronze Age civilization of the islands of the Aegean Sea and the countries adjacent to it

ae·gis *also* **egis** \ˈē-jəs *also* ˈā-\ *n* [L, fr. Gk *aigis,* lit., goatskin, fr. *aig-, aix* goat; akin to Arm *ayc* goat] (1581) **1 :** a shield or breastplate emblematic of majesty that was associated with Zeus and Athena **2 a :** PROTECTION ⟨under the ~ of the Constitution⟩ **b :** controlling or conditioning influence ⟨passed new laws under the ~ of national security⟩ **3 a :** AUSPICES, SPONSORSHIP ⟨under the ~ of the museum⟩ **b :** control or guidance esp. by an individual, group, or system

Ae·gis·thus \i-ˈjis-thəs\ *n* [L, fr. Gk *Aigisthos*] (1567) **:** a lover of Clytemnestra slain with her by her son Orestes

-aemia *chiefly Brit var of* -EMIA

Ae·ne·as \i-ˈnē-əs\ *n* [L, fr. Gk *Aineias*] (14c) **:** a son of Anchises and Aphrodite, defender of Troy, and hero of Virgil's *Aeneid*

Ae·ne·o·lith·ic \ā-ˌē-nē-ō-ˈli-thik\ *adj* [L *aeneus* of copper or bronze, fr. *aes* copper, bronze — more at ORE] (1901) **:** of or relating to a transitional period between the Neolithic and Bronze ages in which some copper was used

[1]**ae·o·lian** \ē-ˈō-lē-ən, ē-ˈōl-yən\ *adj* (1595) **1** *often cap* **:** of or relating to Aeolus **2 :** giving forth or marked by a moaning or sighing sound or musical tone produced by or as if by the wind

[2]**aeolian** *var of* EOLIAN

[1]**Ae·o·lian** \ē-ˈō-lē-ən, ā-, -ˈōl-yən\ *adj* (1567) **:** of or relating to Aeolis or its inhabitants

[2]**Aeolian** *n* (ca. 1726) **1 :** a member of a group of Greek peoples of Thessaly and Boeotia that colonized Lesbos and the adjacent coast of Asia Minor **2 :** AEOLIC

aeolian harp *n* (1750) **:** a box-shaped musical instrument having stretched strings usu. tuned in unison on which the wind produces varying harmonics over the same fundamental tone

[1]**Ae·ol·ic** \ē-ˈä-lik\ *adj* (1641) **:** AEOLIAN

[2]**Aeolic** *n* (1889) **:** a group of ancient Greek dialects used by the Aeolians

Ae·o·lus \ˈē-ə-ləs\ *n* [L, fr. Gk *Aiolos*] (14c) **:** the Greek god of the winds

ae·on *or* **eon** \ˈē-ən, ˈē-ˌän\ *n* [L, fr. Gk *aiōn* — more at AYE] (ca. 1642) **1 :** an immeasurably or indefinitely long period of time **:** AGE **2 a** *usu* **eon :** a very large division of geologic time usu. longer than an era **b :** a unit of geologic time equal to one billion years

\ə\ **abut** \ᵊ\ kitten, F table \ər\ **further** \a\ **ash** \ā\ **ace** \ä\ mop, mar \au̇\ **out** \ch\ **chin** \e\ **bet** \ē\ **easy** \g\ **go** \i\ **hit** \ī\ **ice** \j\ **job** \ŋ\ **sing** \ō\ **go** \ȯ\ **law** \ȯi\ **boy** \th\ **thin** \t͟h\ **the** \ü\ **loot** \u̇\ **foot** \y\ **yet** \zh\ **vision, beige** \k, ⁿ, œ, ue, ʸ\ *see* Guide to Pronunciation

ae·o·ni·an \ē-ˈō-nē-ən\ *or* **ae·on·ic** \-ˈä-nik\ *adj* (1765) **:** lasting for an immeasurably or indefinitely long period of time

ae·py·or·nis \ˌē-pē-ˈȯr-nəs\ *n* [NL, genus name, fr. Gk *aipys* high + *ornis* bird — more at ERNE] (1851) **:** ELEPHANT BIRD

aeq *abbr* [L *aequalis*] equal

aer- *or* **aero-** *comb form* [L, fr. Gk *aer-, aero-,* fr. *aēr*] **1 a :** air **:** atmosphere ⟨*aer*ate⟩ ⟨*aero*biology⟩ **b :** air and ⟨*aero*space⟩ **2 :** gas ⟨*aero*sol⟩ **3 :** aviation ⟨*aero*drome⟩

aer·ate \ˈer-ˌāt\ *vt* **aer·at·ed; aer·at·ing** (1789) **1 :** to supply or impregnate (as the soil or a liquid) with air **2 :** to supply (the blood) with oxygen by respiration **3 a** *Brit* **:** CARBONATE 2 **b :** to make light or sparkling — **aer·a·tion** \ˌa(-ə)r-ˈā-shən, ˌe(-ə)r-\ *n*

aer·a·tor \ˈer-ˌā-tər\ *n* (1861) **:** one that aerates; *esp* **:** an apparatus for aerating something (as sewage)

aer·en·chy·ma \ˌer-ˈeŋ-kə-mə\ *n* [NL] (ca. 1893) **:** modified parenchymatous tissue having large intracellular air spaces that is found esp. in aquatic plants where it facilitates gaseous exchange and maintains buoyancy

[1]**ae·ri·al** \ˈer-ē-əl, ā-ˈir-ē-əl\ *adj* [L *aerius,* fr. Gk *aerios,* fr. *aēr*] (1604) **1 a :** of, relating to, or occurring in the air or atmosphere **b :** existing or growing in the air rather than in the ground or in water **c :** high in the air ⟨~ spires⟩ **d :** operating or operated overhead on elevated cables or rails ⟨an ~ tram⟩ **2 :** suggestive of air: as **a :** lacking substance **b :** FANCIFUL, ETHEREAL ⟨visions of ~ joy —P. B. Shelley⟩ **3 a :** of or relating to aircraft ⟨~ navigation⟩ **b :** designed for use in, taken from, or operating from or against aircraft **c :** effected by means of aircraft ⟨~ transportation⟩ **4 :** of, relating to, or gained by the forward pass in football — **ae·ri·al·ly** \-ə-lē\ *adv*

[2]**aer·i·al** \ˈer-ē-əl\ *n* (1902) **1 :** ANTENNA 2 **2 :** FORWARD PASS **3 :** an acrobatic maneuver performed (as by skiers and gymnasts) in the air; *also, pl* **:** a ski event featuring aerials

ae·ri·al·ist \ˈer-ē-ə-list, ā-ˈir-\ *n* (1905) **:** one who performs feats in the air or above the ground esp. on the trapeze

aerial ladder *n* (1904) **:** a mechanically operated extensible ladder usu. mounted on a fire truck

aerial perspective *n* (1704) **:** the expression of space in painting by gradation of color and distinctness

ae·rie *also* **aery** \ˈer-ē, ˈir-, ˈā-(ə-)rē\ *n* [ML *aerea,* fr. OF *aire,* prob. fr. VL **agrum* origin, nest, lair, fr. L *ager* field — more at ACRE] (1554) **1 :** the nest of a bird on a cliff or a mountaintop **2** *obs* **:** a brood of birds of prey **3 :** an elevated often secluded dwelling, structure, or position

[1]**aero** \ˈer-(ˌ)ō\ *adj* [*aero-*] (1874) **:** of or relating to aircraft or aeronautics ⟨an ~ engine⟩

[2]**aero** *abbr* aerodynamic

aer·o·bat·ics \ˌer-ə-ˈba-tiks\ *n pl but sing or pl in constr* [*aer-* + *acrobatics*] (ca. 1911) **:** spectacular flying feats and maneuvers (as rolls and dives) — **aer·o·bat** \ˈer-ə-ˌbat\ *n* — **aer·o·bat·ic** \ˌer-ə-ˈba-tik\ *adj*

aer·obe \ˈer-ˌōb\ *n* [F *aérobie,* fr. *aéro-* aer- + *-bie* (fr. Gk *-bion,* fr. *bios* life) — more at QUICK] (1886) **:** an organism (as a bacterium) that lives only in the presence of oxygen

aer·o·bic \ˌer-ˈō-bik\ *adj* (1884) **1 :** living, active, or occurring only in the presence of oxygen ⟨~ respiration⟩ **2 :** of, relating to, or induced by aerobes **3 a :** involving, utilizing, or increasing oxygen consumption for metabolic processes in the body ⟨stationary bicycles used for ~ conditioning⟩ **b :** relating to, resulting from, or used in aerobics — **aer·o·bi·cal·ly** \-bi-k(ə-)lē\ *adv*

aer·o·bi·cize \ˌer-ˈō-bə-ˌsīz\ *vb* **-cized; -ciz·ing** *vt* (1981) **:** to bring to good physical condition through aerobics ~ *vi* **:** to engage in aerobics

aer·o·bics \-biks\ *n pl* (1967) **1** *sing or pl in constr* **:** a system of physical conditioning involving exercises (as running, walking, swimming, or calisthenics) strenuously performed so as to cause marked temporary increase in respiration and heart rate **2 :** aerobic exercises

aero·bi·ol·o·gy \ˌer-ō-bī-ˈä-lə-jē\ *n* (ca. 1937) **:** the science dealing with the occurrence, transportation, and effects of airborne materials (as viruses, pollen, or pollutants) — **aero·bi·o·log·i·cal** \-ˌbī-ə-ˈlä-ji-kəl\ *adj*

aero·bi·o·sis \ˌer-ō-bī-ˈō-səs, -bē-\ *n, pl* **-o·ses** \-ˌsēz\ [NL] (ca. 1900) **:** life in the presence of air or oxygen

aero·brake \ˈer-ō-ˌbrāk\ *vt* (1965) **:** to decelerate (as a spacecraft) by passage through a planetary atmosphere

aero·drome \ˈer-ə-ˌdrōm\ *n* (1908) *chiefly Brit* **:** AIRFIELD

aero·dy·nam·i·cist \ˌer-ō-dī-ˈna-mə-sist\ *n* (1926) **:** one who specializes in aerodynamics

aero·dy·nam·ics \-ˈna-miks\ *n pl but sing or pl in constr* (ca. 1837) **:** a branch of dynamics that deals with the motion of air and other gaseous fluids and with the forces acting on bodies in motion relative to such fluids — **aero·dy·nam·ic** \-mik\ *also* **aero·dy·nam·i·cal** \-mi-kəl\ *adj* — **aero·dy·nam·i·cal·ly** \-mi-k(ə-)lē\ *adv*

aero·dyne \ˈer-ə-ˌdīn\ *n* [*aerodynamic*] (ca. 1906) **:** a heavier-than-air aircraft (as an airplane, helicopter, or glider) — compare AEROSTAT

aero·elas·tic·i·ty \ˌer-ō-ˌē-ˌlas-ˈti-sə-tē, -i-ˌlas-\ *n* (1935) **:** distortion (as from bending) in a structure (as an airplane wing or a building) caused by aerodynamic forces — **aero·elas·tic** \-ˈlas-tik\ *adj*

aero·em·bo·lism \ˌer-ō-ˈem-bə-ˌli-zəm\ *n* (ca. 1939) **:** decompression sickness caused by rapid ascent to high altitudes and resulting exposure to rapidly lowered air pressure

aero·foil \ˈer-ə-ˌfȯi(-ə)l\ *n* (1907) *chiefly Brit* **:** AIRFOIL

aero·gram *or* **aero·gramme** \ˈer-ə-ˌgram\ *n* (1920) **:** AIR LETTER 2

aer·og·ra·pher's mate \ˌer-ˈä-grə-fərz-\ *n* (ca. 1952) **:** a navy petty officer specializing in meteorology

aer·o·lite \ˈer-ə-ˌlīt\ *n* (ca. 1815) **:** a stony meteorite

aero·mag·net·ic \ˌer-ō-mag-ˈne-tik\ *adj* (1946) **:** of, relating to, or derived from a study of the earth's magnetic field esp. from the air ⟨an ~ survey⟩

aero·me·chan·ics \-mə-ˈka-niks\ *n pl but sing or pl in constr* (ca. 1909) **:** mechanics that deals with the equilibrium and motion of gases and of solid bodies immersed in them

aero·med·i·cal \-ˈme-di-kəl\ *adj* (1937) **1 :** of or relating to aeromedicine **2 :** relating to or involving air transportation to a hospital

aero·med·i·cine \-ˈme-də-sən\ *n* (1942) **:** a branch of medicine that deals with the diseases and disturbances arising from flying and the associated physiological and psychological problems

aer·om·e·ter \ˌer-ˈä-mə-tər\ *n* [prob. fr. F *aéromètre,* fr. *aér-* + *-mètre* -meter] (1794) **:** an instrument for ascertaining the weight or density of air or other gases

aero·naut \ˈer-ə-ˌnȯt, -ˌnät\ *n* [F *aéronaute,* fr. *aér-* aer- + Gk *nautēs* sailor — more at NAUTICAL] (1784) **:** one who operates or travels in an airship or balloon

aero·nau·tics \ˌer-ə-ˈnȯ-tiks, -ˈnä-\ *n pl but sing in constr* (ca. 1824) **1 :** a science dealing with the operation of aircraft **2 :** the art or science of flight — **aero·nau·ti·cal** \-ti-kəl\ *also* **aero·nau·tic** \-tik\ *adj* — **aero·nau·ti·cal·ly** \-ti-k(ə-)lē\ *adv*

aer·on·o·my \ˌer-ˈä-nə-mē\ *n* (1946) **:** a science that deals with the physics and chemistry of the upper atmosphere of planets — **aer·on·o·mer** \-mər\ *n* — **aer·o·nom·ic** \ˌer-ə-ˈnä-mik\ *adj* — **aer·on·o·mist** \ˌer-ˈä-nə-mist\ *n*

aero·pho·bia \ˌer-ō-ˈfō-bē-ə\ *n* (1911) **:** fear or strong dislike of flying — **aero·phobe** \ˈer-ō-ˌfōb\ *n* — **aero·pho·bic** \ˌer-ō-ˈfō-bik\ *adj or n*

aero·plane \ˈer-ə-ˌplān\ *n* [F *aéroplane,* fr. *aéro-* aer- + *-plane,* prob. fr. fem. of *plan* flat, level, fr. L *planus* — more at FLOOR] (1873) *chiefly Brit* **:** AIRPLANE

aero·sol \ˈer-ə-ˌsäl, -ˌsȯl\ *n* [*aer-* + [4]*sol*] (1923) **1 :** a suspension of fine solid or liquid particles in gas ⟨smoke, fog, and mist are ~*s*⟩; *also, pl* **:** the fine particles of an aerosol ⟨stratospheric ~*s*⟩ **2 :** a substance (as an insecticide or medicine) dispensed from a pressurized container as an aerosol; *also* **:** the container for this

aero·sol·ize \-ˌsä-ˌlīz, -ˌsȯ-, -sə-\ *vt* **-ized; -iz·ing** (1944) **:** to disperse as an aerosol — **aero·sol·i·za·tion** \ˌar-ə-ˌsä-lə-ˈzā-shən, -ˌsȯ-, -sə-\ *n*

[1]**aero·space** \ˈer-ō-ˌspās\ *n* (ca. 1958) **1 :** space comprising the earth's atmosphere and the space beyond **2 :** a physical science that deals with aerospace **3 :** the aerospace industry

[2]**aerospace** *adj* (1958) **:** of or relating to aerospace, to vehicles used in aerospace or the manufacture of such vehicles, or to travel in aerospace ⟨~ research⟩ ⟨~ profits⟩ ⟨~ medicine⟩

aerospace plane *n* (1960) **:** an airplane designed to be able to reach low earth orbit

aero·stat \-ˌstat\ *n* [F *aérostat,* fr. *aér-* + *-stat*] (1784) **:** a lighter-than-air aircraft (as a balloon or blimp) — compare AERODYNE

aero·stat·ics \ˌer-ō-ˈsta-tiks\ *n pl but sing or pl in constr* [modif. of NL *aerostatica,* fr. *aer-* + *statica* statics] (1784) **:** a branch of statics that deals with the equilibrium of gaseous fluids and of solid bodies immersed in them

aero·ther·mo·dy·nam·ics \-ˌthər-mə-(ˌ)dī-ˈna-miks\ *n pl but sing or pl in constr* (1949) **:** the thermodynamics of gases and esp. of air — **aero·ther·mo·dy·nam·ic** \-mik\ *adj*

[1]**aery** \ˈer-ē, ˈā-ə-rē\ *adj* **aer·i·er; -est** [L *aerius* — more at AERIAL] (14c) **:** having an aerial quality **:** ETHEREAL ⟨~ visions⟩ — **aer·i·ly** \ˈer-ə-lē\ *adv*

[2]**aery** *var of* AERIE

Aes·cu·la·pi·an \ˌes-k(y)ə-ˈlā-pē-ən\ *adj* [*Aesculapius,* Greco-Roman god of medicine, fr. L, fr. Gk *Asklēpios*] (1605) **:** of or relating to Aesculapius or the healing art

Ae·sir \ˈā-ˌzir, -ˌsir\ *n pl* [ON *Æsir,* pl. of *āss* god] (1850) **:** the principal race of Norse gods

Ae·so·pi·an \ē-ˈsō-pē-ən, -ˈsä-\ *also* **Ae·sop·ic** \-ˈsä-pik\ *adj* (1728) **1 :** of, relating to, or characteristic of Aesop or his fables **2 :** conveying an innocent meaning to an outsider but a hidden meaning to a member of a conspiracy or underground movement ⟨~ language⟩

aes·thete *also* **es·thete** \ˈes-ˌthēt, *Brit usu* ˈēs-\ *n* [back-formation fr. *aesthetic*] (1881) **:** one having or affecting sensitivity to the beautiful esp. in art

[1]**aes·thet·ic** *also* **es·thet·ic** \es-ˈthe-tik, is-, *Brit usu* ēs-\ *or* **aes·thet·i·cal** *or* **es·thet·i·cal** \-ti-kəl\ *adj* [G *ästhetisch,* fr. NL *aestheticus,* fr. Gk *aisthētikos* of sense perception, fr. *aisthanesthai* to perceive — more at AUDIBLE] (1798) **1 a :** of, relating to, or dealing with aesthetics or the beautiful ⟨~ theories⟩ **b :** ARTISTIC ⟨a work of ~ value⟩ **c :** pleasing in appearance **:** ATTRACTIVE ⟨easy-to-use keyboards, clear graphics, and other ergonomic and ~ features —Mark Mehler⟩ **2 :** appreciative of, responsive to, or zealous about the beautiful; *also* **:** responsive to or appreciative of what is pleasurable to the senses — **aes·thet·i·cal·ly** *also* **es·thet·i·cal·ly** \-ti-k(ə-)lē\ *adv*

[2]**aesthetic** *also* **esthetic** *n* (1822) **1** *pl but sing or pl in constr* **:** a branch of philosophy dealing with the nature of beauty, art, and taste and with the creation and appreciation of beauty **2 :** a particular theory or conception of beauty or art **:** a particular taste for or approach to what is pleasing to the senses and esp. sight ⟨modernist ~*s*⟩ ⟨staging new ballets which reflected the ~ of the new nation —Mary Clarke & Clement Crisp⟩ **3** *pl* **:** a pleasing appearance or effect **:** BEAUTY ⟨appreciated the ~*s* of the gemstones⟩

aesthetic distance *n* (1938) **:** the frame of reference that an artist creates by the use of technical devices in and around the work of art to differentiate it psychologically from reality

aes·the·ti·cian *also* **es·the·ti·cian** \ˌes-thə-ˈti-shən\ *n* (1829) **1 :** a specialist in aesthetics **2 :** COSMETOLOGIST

aes·thet·i·cism *also* **es·thet·i·cism** \es-ˈthe-tə-ˌsi-zəm, is-\ *n* (1855) **1 :** a doctrine that the principles of beauty are basic to other and esp. moral principles **2 :** devotion to or emphasis on beauty or the cultivation of the arts

aes·thet·i·cize *also* **es·thet·i·cize** \-ˌsīz\ *vt* **-cized; -ciz·ing** (1864) **:** to make aesthetic

aestival *var of* ESTIVAL

aestivate, aestivation *var of* ESTIVATE, ESTIVATION

aet *or* **aetat** *abbr* [L *aetatis*] of age; aged

aether *var of* ETHER 2a

aetiology *chiefly Brit var of* ETIOLOGY

af *abbr* affix

AF *abbr* **1** air force **2** audio frequency

af- — see AD-

[1]**afar** \ə-ˈfär\ *adv* [ME *afer,* fr. *on fer* at a distance and *of fer* from a distance] (14c) **:** from, to, or at a great distance ⟨roamed ~⟩

[2]**afar** *n* (14c) **:** a great distance ⟨saw him from ~⟩

AFB *abbr* air force base

AFC *abbr* **1** American Football Conference **2** automatic frequency control

AFDC *abbr* Aid to Families with Dependent Children

afeard *or* **afeared** \ə-ˈfird\ *adj* [ME *afered,* fr. OE *āfǣred,* pp. of *āfǣran* to frighten, fr. *ā-,* perfective prefix + *fǣran* to frighten — more at ABIDE, FEAR] (bef. 12c) *chiefly dial* **:** AFRAID

afe·brile \(ˌ)ā-ˈfe-ˌbrī(-ə)l *also* -ˈfē-\ *adj* (1875) **:** not marked by or having a fever

aff *abbr* affirmative

af·fa·ble \ˈa-fə-bəl\ *adj* [ME *affabyl,* fr. AF, fr. L *affabilis,* fr. *affari* to speak to, fr. *ad-* + *fari* to speak — more at BAN] (15c) **1 :** being pleasant and at ease in talking to others ⟨an ~ host⟩ **2 :** characterized by ease and friendliness ⟨an ~ manner⟩ ***syn*** see GRACIOUS — **af·fa·bil·i·ty** \ˌa-fə-ˈbi-lə-tē\ *n* — **af·fa·bly** \-blē\ *adv*

af·fair \ə-ˈfer\ *n* [ME *afere,* fr. AF *afaire,* fr. *a faire* to do] (14c) **1 a** *pl* **:** commercial, professional, public, or personal business **b :** MATTER, CONCERN **2 :** a procedure, action, or occasion only vaguely specified; *also* **:** an object or collection of objects only vaguely specified ⟨their house was a 2-story ~⟩ **3** *also* **af·faire a :** a romantic or passionate attachment typically of limited duration **:** LIAISON 2b **b :** a matter occasioning public anxiety, controversy, or scandal **:** CASE

[1]**af·fect** \ˈa-ˌfekt\ *n* [ME, fr. AF, fr. L *affectus,* fr. *afficere*] (14c) **1** *obs* **:** FEELING, AFFECTION **2 :** the conscious subjective aspect of an emotion considered apart from bodily changes; *also* **:** a set of observable manifestations of a subjectively experienced emotion ⟨patients . . . showed perfectly normal reactions and ~s —Oliver Sacks⟩ ***usage*** see EFFECT

[2]**af·fect** \ə-ˈfekt, a-\ *vb* [ME, fr. MF & L; MF *affecter,* fr. L *affectare,* freq. of *afficere* to influence, fr. *ad-* + *facere* to do — more at DO] *vt* (15c) **1** *archaic* **:** to aim at **2 a** *archaic* **:** to have affection for **b :** to be given to **:** FANCY ⟨~ flashy clothes⟩ **3 :** to make a display of liking or using **:** CULTIVATE ⟨~ a worldly manner⟩ **4 :** to put on a pretense of **:** FEIGN ⟨~ indifference, though deeply hurt⟩ **5 :** to tend toward ⟨drops of water ~ roundness⟩ **6 :** FREQUENT ~ *vi, obs* **:** INCLINE 2 ***syn*** see ASSUME ***usage*** see EFFECT

[3]**affect** *vt* [ME, fr. *affectus,* pp. of *afficere*] (15c) **:** to produce an effect upon: as **a :** to produce a material influence upon or alteration in ⟨paralysis ~*ed* his limbs⟩ **b :** to act upon (as a person or a person's mind or feelings) so as to effect a response **:** INFLUENCE ***usage*** see EFFECT — **af·fect·abil·i·ty** \-ˌfek-tə-ˈbi-lə-tē\ *n* — **af·fect·able** \-ˈfek-tə-bəl\ *adj*

syn AFFECT, INFLUENCE, TOUCH, IMPRESS, STRIKE, SWAY mean to produce or have an effect upon. AFFECT implies the action of a stimulus that can produce a response or reaction ⟨the sight *affected* her to tears⟩. INFLUENCE implies a force that brings about a change (as in nature or behavior) ⟨our beliefs are *influenced* by our upbringing⟩. TOUCH may carry a vivid suggestion of close contact and may connote stirring, arousing, or harming ⟨plants *touched* by frost⟩ ⟨his emotions were *touched* by her distress⟩. IMPRESS stresses the depth and persistence of the effect ⟨only one of the plans *impressed* him⟩. STRIKE, similar to but weaker than *impress,* may convey the notion of sudden sharp perception or appreciation ⟨*struck* by the solemnity of the occasion⟩. SWAY implies the acting of influences that are not resisted or are irresistible, with resulting change in character or course of action ⟨politicians who are *swayed* by popular opinion⟩.

af·fec·ta·tion \ˌa-ˌfek-ˈtā-shən\ *n* (1548) **1 a :** the act of taking on or displaying an attitude or mode of behavior not natural to oneself or not genuinely felt **b :** speech or conduct not natural to oneself **:** ARTIFICIALITY **2** *obs* **:** a striving after ***syn*** see POSE

af·fect·ed \ə-ˈfek-təd, a-\ *adj* (1587) **1 :** INCLINED, DISPOSED ⟨was well ~ toward her⟩ **2 a :** given to or marked by affectation ⟨spoke in an ~ manner⟩ **b :** assumed artificially or falsely **:** PRETENDED ⟨an ~ interest in art⟩ — **af·fect·ed·ly** *adv* — **af·fect·ed·ness** *n*

af·fect·ing \ə-ˈfek-tiŋ, a-\ *adj* (1720) **:** evoking a strong emotional response ***syn*** see MOVING — **af·fect·ing·ly** \-tiŋ-lē\ *adv*

af·fec·tion \ə-ˈfek-shən\ *n* [ME, fr. AF *affection,* fr. L *affection-, affectio,* fr. *afficere*] (13c) **1 :** a moderate feeling or emotion **2 :** tender attachment **:** FONDNESS ⟨she had a deep ~ for her parents⟩ **3 a (1) :** a bodily condition **(2) :** DISEASE, MALADY **b :** ATTRIBUTE ⟨shape and weight are ~*s* of bodies⟩ **4** *obs* **:** PARTIALITY, PREJUDICE **5 :** the feeling aspect (as in pleasure) of consciousness **6 a :** PROPENSITY, DISPOSITION **b** *archaic* **:** AFFECTATION 1 **7 :** the action of affecting **:** the state of being affected ***syn*** see FEELING — **af·fec·tion·less** \-ləs\ *adj*

af·fec·tion·al \ə-ˈfek-shnəl, -shə-nᵊl\ *adj* (1859) **:** of or relating to the affections — **af·fec·tion·al·ly** *adv*

af·fec·tion·ate \ə-ˈfek-sh(ə-)nət\ *adj* (15c) **1** *obs* **:** INCLINED, DISPOSED **2 :** having affection or warm regard **:** LOVING ⟨~ friends⟩ **3 :** motivated by affection **:** TENDER ⟨~ care⟩ — **af·fec·tion·ate·ly** *adv*

af·fec·tioned \-shənd\ *adj* (1555) *archaic* **:** having a tendency, disposition, or inclination **:** DISPOSED

af·fec·tive \a-ˈfek-tiv\ *adj* (1623) **1 :** relating to, arising from, or influencing feelings or emotions **:** EMOTIONAL ⟨cognitive and ~ symptoms⟩ **2 :** expressing emotion ⟨~ language⟩ — **af·fec·tive·ly** *adv* — **af·fec·tiv·i·ty** \ˌa-ˌfek-ˈti-və-tē\ *n*

affective disorder *n* (1937) **:** MOOD DISORDER

af·fect·less \ˈa-ˌfekt-ləs, a-ˈfekt-\ *adj* (1967) **:** showing or expressing no emotion; *also* **:** UNFEELING ⟨a ruthless ~ society⟩ — **af·fect·less·ness** *n*

af·fen·pin·scher \ˈa-fən-ˌpin-chər\ *n* [G, fr. *Affe* ape + *Pinscher,* a breed of hunting dog] (1903) **:** any of a breed of toy dogs with a wiry black, red, tan, or gray coat, erect ears, large round eyes, and bushy eyebrows, chin tuft, and mustache

[1]**af·fer·ent** \ˈa-fə-rənt, -ˌfer-ənt, -ˌfe-rənt\ *adj* [L *afferent-, afferens,* prp. of *afferre* to bring to, fr. *ad-* + *ferre* to bear — more at BEAR] (ca. 1847) **:** bearing or conducting inward; *specif* **:** conveying impulses toward the central nervous system — compare EFFERENT — **af·fer·ent·ly** *adv*

[2]**afferent** *n* (1949) **:** an afferent anatomical part (as a nerve)

[1]**af·fi·ance** \ə-ˈfī-ən(t)s\ *n* [ME, fr. AF, fr. *affier* to pledge, trust, fr. ML *affidare* to pledge, fr. L *ad-* + VL **fidare* to trust — more at FIANCÉ] (14c) *archaic* **:** TRUST, CONFIDENCE

[2]**affiance** *vt* **-anced; -anc·ing** (1555) **:** to solemnly promise (oneself or another) in marriage **:** BETROTH

af·fi·ant \ə-ˈfī-ənt\ *n* [F, fr. prp. of *affier,* fr. OF] (1807) **:** one who swears to an affidavit; *broadly* **:** DEPONENT

afficionado *var of* AFICIONADO

af·fi·da·vit \ˌa-fə-ˈdā-vət\ *n* [ML, he has made an oath, fr. *affidare*] (1593) **:** a sworn statement in writing made esp. under oath or on affirmation before an authorized magistrate or officer

[1]**af·fil·i·ate** \ə-ˈfi-lē-ˌāt\ *vb* **-at·ed; -at·ing** [ML *affiliatus,* pp. of *affiliare* to adopt as a son, fr. L *ad-* + *filius* son — more at FEMININE] *vt* (1761) **1 a :** to bring or receive into close connection as a member or branch **b :** to associate as a member ⟨~*s* herself with the local club⟩ **2 :** to trace the origin of ~ *vi* **:** to connect or associate oneself **:** COMBINE — **af·fil·i·a·tion** \-ˌfi-lē-ˈā-shən\ *n*

[2]**af·fil·i·ate** \ə-ˈfi-lē-ət, -ˌāt\ *n* (1879) **:** an affiliated person or organization

af·fil·i·at·ed \-lē-ˌā-təd\ *adj* (1795) **:** closely associated with another typically in a dependent or subordinate position ⟨the university and its ~ medical school⟩

[1]**af·fine** \a-ˈfīn, ə-\ *n* [AF *affin,* fr. L *affinis,* fr. *affinis* related] (ca. 1509) **:** a relative by marriage **:** IN-LAW

[2]**affine** *adj* [L *affinis,* adj.] (1918) **:** of, relating to, or being a transformation (as a translation, a rotation, or a uniform stretching) that carries straight lines into straight lines and parallel lines into parallel lines but may alter distance between points and angles between lines ⟨~ geometry⟩ — **af·fine·ly** *adv*

af·fined \a-ˈfīnd, ə-\ *adj* (1597) **1 :** joined in a close relationship **:** CONNECTED **2 :** bound by obligation

af·fin·i·ty \ə-ˈfi-nə-tē\ *n, pl* **-ties** [ME *affinite,* fr. AF or L; AF *affinité,* fr. L *affinitas,* fr. *affinis* bordering on, related by marriage, fr. *ad-* + *finis* end, border] (14c) **1 :** relationship by marriage **2 a :** sympathy marked by community of interest **:** KINSHIP **b (1) :** an attraction to or liking for something ⟨people with an ~ to darkness —Mark Twain⟩ ⟨pork and fennel have a natural ~ for each other —Abby Mandel⟩ **(2) :** an attractive force between substances or particles that causes them to enter into and remain in chemical combination **c :** a person esp. of the opposite sex having a particular attraction for one **3 a :** likeness based on relationship or causal connection ⟨found an ~ between the teller of a tale and the craftsman —Mary McCarthy⟩ ⟨this investigation, with *affinities* to a case history, a psychoanalysis, a detective story —Oliver Sacks⟩ **b :** a relation between biological groups involving resemblance in structural plan and indicating a common origin ***syn*** see ATTRACTION

affinity card *n* (1979) **:** a credit card which is issued in affiliation with a participating organization (as a charity or an airline) and the use of which earns a benefit for the organization or the cardholder

affinity chromatography *n* (1970) **:** chromatography in which a macromolecule (as a protein) is isolated and purified by passing it in solution through a column treated with a substance having a ligand for which the macromolecule has an affinity that causes it to be retained on the column

affinity group *n* (1970) **:** a group of people having a common interest or goal or acting together for a specific purpose (as for a chartered tour)

af·firm \ə-ˈfərm\ *vb* [ME *affermen,* fr. AF *afermer,* fr. L *affirmare,* fr. *ad-* + *firmare* to make firm, fr. *firmus* firm — more at FIRM] *vt* (14c) **1 a :** VALIDATE, CONFIRM **b :** to state positively ⟨he ~*ed* his innocence⟩ **2 :** to assert (as a judgment or decree) as valid or confirmed **3 :** to express dedication to ⟨~ life⟩ ~ *vi* **1 :** to testify or declare by affirmation as distinguished from swearing an oath **2 :** to uphold a judgment or decree of a lower court ***syn*** see ASSERT — **af·firm·able** \ə-ˈfər-mə-bəl\ *adj* — **af·fir·mance** \ə-ˈfər-mən(t)s\ *n*

af·fir·ma·tion \ˌa-fər-ˈmā-shən\ *n* (15c) **1 a :** the act of affirming **b :** something affirmed **:** a positive assertion **2 :** a solemn declaration made under the penalties of perjury by a person who conscientiously declines taking an oath

[1]**af·fir·ma·tive** \ə-ˈfər-mə-tiv\ *adj* (15c) **1 :** asserting a predicate of a subject **2 :** asserting that the fact is so **3 :** POSITIVE ⟨~ approach⟩ **4 :** favoring or supporting a proposition or motion — **af·fir·ma·tive·ly** *adv*

[2]**affirmative** *n* (15c) **1 :** an expression (as the word *yes*) of affirmation or assent **2 :** an affirmative proposition **3 :** the side that upholds the proposition stated in a debate

affirmative action *n* (1965) **:** an active effort to improve the employment or educational opportunities of members of minority groups and women; *also* **:** a similar effort to promote the rights or progress of other disadvantaged persons

[1]**af·fix** \ə-ˈfiks, a-\ *vt* [L *affixus,* pp. of *affigere* to fasten to, fr. *ad-* + *figere* to fasten — more at FIX] (1533) **1 :** to attach physically ⟨~ a stamp to a letter⟩ **2 :** to attach in any way **:** ADD, APPEND ⟨~ a signature to a document⟩ **3 :** IMPRESS ⟨~*ed* my seal⟩ ***syn*** see FASTEN — **af·fix·able** \-ˈfik-sə-bəl\ *adj* — **af·fix·a·tion** \ˌa-ˌfik-ˈsā-shən\ *n* — **af·fix·ment** \ə-ˈfik-smənt, a-\ *n*

[2]**af·fix** \ˈa-ˌfiks\ *n* (1612) **1 :** one or more sounds or letters occurring as a bound form attached to the beginning or end of a word, base, or phrase or inserted within a word or base and serving to produce a derivative word or an inflectional form **2 :** APPENDAGE — **af·fix·al** \-ˌfik-səl\ *or* **af·fix·i·al** \a-ˈfik-sē-əl\ *adj*

af·fla·tus \ə-ˈflā-təs, a-\ *n* [L, act of blowing or breathing on, fr. *afflare* to blow on, fr. *ad-* + *flare* to blow — more at BLOW] (1660) **:** a divine imparting of knowledge or power **:** INSPIRATION

af·flict \ə-ˈflikt\ *vt* [ME, fr. L *afflictus,* pp. of *affligere* to cast down, fr. *ad-* + *fligere* to strike — more at PROFLIGATE] (14c) **1** *obs* **a :** HUMBLE **b :** OVERTHROW **2 a :** to distress so severely as to cause persistent suffering or anguish ⟨~*ed* with arthritis⟩ **b :** TROUBLE, INJURE

syn AFFLICT, TRY, TORMENT, TORTURE, RACK mean to inflict on a person something that is hard to bear. AFFLICT is a general term and applies to the causing of pain or suffering or of acute annoyance, embarrassment, or any distress ⟨ills that *afflict* the elderly⟩. TRY suggests imposing something that strains the powers of endurance or of self-control ⟨children often *try* their parents' patience⟩. TORMENT suggests persecution or the repeated inflicting of suffering or annoyance ⟨a horse *tormented* by flies⟩. TORTURE adds the implication of causing unbearable pain or suffering ⟨*tortured* by a sense of guilt⟩. RACK stresses straining or wrenching ⟨a body *racked* by pain⟩.

\ə\ **abut** \ᵊ\ kitten, F table \ər\ **further** \a\ **ash** \ā\ **ace** \ä\ mop, mar \au̇\ **out** \ch\ **chin** \e\ bet \ē\ **easy** \g\ **go** \i\ hit \ī\ **ice** \j\ **job** \ŋ\ **sing** \ō\ **go** \ȯ\ **law** \ȯi\ **boy** \th\ **thin** \t͟h\ **the** \ü\ **loot** \u̇\ **foot** \y\ yet \zh\ **vision,** beige \k, ⁿ, œ, ue, ʸ\ *see* Guide to Pronunciation

af·flic·tion \ə-ˈflik-shən\ *n* (14c) **1 :** the state of being afflicted **2 :** the cause of persistent pain or distress **3 :** great suffering
af·flic·tive \ə-ˈflik-tiv\ *adj* (1611) **:** causing affliction **:** DISTRESSING, TROUBLESOME ⟨∼ emotions⟩ — **af·flic·tive·ly** *adv*
af·flu·ence \ˈa-(ˌ)flü-ən(t)s *also* a-ˈflü- *or* ə-\ *n* (14c) **1 a :** an abundant flow or supply **:** PROFUSION **b :** abundance of property **:** WEALTH **2 :** a flowing to or toward a point **:** INFLUX
af·flu·en·cy \-ən(t)-sē\ *n, pl* **-cies** (1664) **:** AFFLUENCE
[1]**af·flu·ent** \-ənt\ *adj* [ME, fr. L *affluent-, affluens,* prp. of *affluere* to flow to, flow abundantly, fr. *ad-* + *fluere* to flow — more at FLUID] (15c) **1 :** flowing in abundance ⟨∼ streams⟩ ⟨∼ creativity⟩ **2 :** having a generously sufficient and typically increasing supply of material possessions ⟨our ∼ society⟩ ***syn*** see RICH — **af·flu·ent·ly** *adv*
[2]**af~flu~ent** \ˈa-(ˌ)flü-ənt\ *n* (1818) **1 :** a tributary stream **2 :** an affluent person
af·ford \ə-ˈfȯrd\ *vt* [ME *aforthen,* fr. OE *geforthian* to carry out, fr. *ge-,* perfective prefix + *forthian* to carry out, fr. *forth* — more at CO-, FORTH] (14c) **1 a :** to manage to bear without serious detriment ⟨you can't ∼ to neglect your health⟩ **b :** to be able to bear the cost of ⟨can't ∼ to be out of work long⟩ **2 :** to make available, give forth, or provide naturally or inevitably ⟨the sun ∼*s* warmth to the earth⟩ ***syn*** see GIVE — **af·ford·abil·i·ty** \-ˌfȯr-də-ˈbi-lə-tē\ *n* — **af·ford·able** \-ˈfȯr-də-bəl\ *adj* — **af·ford·ably** \ə-ˈfȯr-də-blē\ *adv*
af·for·es·ta·tion \(ˌ)a-ˌfȯr-ə-ˈstā-shən, ə-, -ˌfär-\ *n* [ML *afforestation-, afforestatio,* fr. *afforestare* to put under forest laws, fr. L *ad-* + ML *foresta, forestis* forest] (1649) **:** the act or process of establishing a forest esp. on land not previously forested — **af·for·est** \a-ˈfȯr-əst, -ˈfär-\ *vt*
[1]**af·fray** \ə-ˈfrā\ *n* [ME, fr. AF, fr. *affraier*] (14c) **1** *archaic* **:** FRAY, BRAWL **2** *chiefly Brit* **:** a fight in a public place that disturbs the peace
[2]**affray** *vt* [ME *affraien* to attack, brawl, disturb, frighten, fr. AF *affraier, effreer,* fr. VL **exfridare,* fr. L *ex-* + VL **-fridare* (of Gmc origin; akin to OHG *fridu* peace, OE *frēo* free) — more at FREE] (14c) *archaic* **:** STARTLE, FRIGHTEN
af·fri·cate \ˈa-fri-kət\ *n* [prob. fr. G *Affrikata,* fr. L *affricata,* fem. of *affricatus,* pp. of *affricare* to rub against, fr. *ad-* + *fricare* to rub — more at FRICTION] (1880) **:** a stop and its immediately following release into a fricative that are considered to constitute a single phoneme (as the \t\ and \sh\ of \ch\ in *choose*) — **af·fric·a·tive** \a-ˈfri-kə-tiv, ə-\ *n or adj*
[1]**af·fright** \ə-ˈfrīt\ *vt* [ME *afyrht, afright* frightened, fr. OE *āfyrht,* pp. of *āfyrhtan* to frighten, fr. *ā-,* perfective prefix + *fyrhtan* to fear; akin to OE *fyrhto* fright — more at ABIDE, FRIGHT] (bef. 12c) *archaic* **:** FRIGHTEN, ALARM
[2]**affright** *n* (1596) *archaic* **:** sudden and great fear **:** TERROR
[1]**af·front** \ə-ˈfrənt\ *vt* [ME *afronten,* fr. AF *afrunter* to defy, fr. VL **affrontare,* fr. L *ad-* + *front-, frons* forehead] (14c) **1 a :** to insult esp. to the face by behavior or language **b :** to cause offense to ⟨laws that ∼ society⟩ **2 :** to face in defiance **:** CONFRONT ⟨∼ death⟩ **3 :** to appear directly before ***syn*** see OFFEND
[2]**affront** *n* (1533) **1** *obs* **:** a hostile encounter **2 :** a deliberate offense **:** INSULT ⟨an ∼ to his dignity⟩
afft *abbr* affidavit
af·fu·sion \a-ˈfyü-zhən\ *n* [LL *affusion-, affusio,* fr. L *affundere* to pour on, fr. *ad-* + *fundere* to pour — more at FOUND] (1615) **:** an act of pouring a liquid on (as in baptism)
Af·ghan \ˈaf-ˌgan *also* -gən\ *n* [Pers *afghān* Pashtun] (1742) **1 a** (1) **:** PASHTUN (2) **:** PASHTO **b :** a native or inhabitant of Afghanistan **2** *not cap* **:** a blanket or shawl of colored yarn knitted or crocheted in strips or squares **3** *not cap* **:** a Turkoman carpet of large size and long pile woven in geometric designs **4 :** AFGHAN HOUND — **Afghan** *or* **Af·ghani** \af-ˈga-nē, -ˈgä-\ *adj*
Afghan hound *n* (1925) **:** any of a breed of tall slim swift hunting dogs originating in Afghanistan with a coat of silky thick hair and a long silky topknot

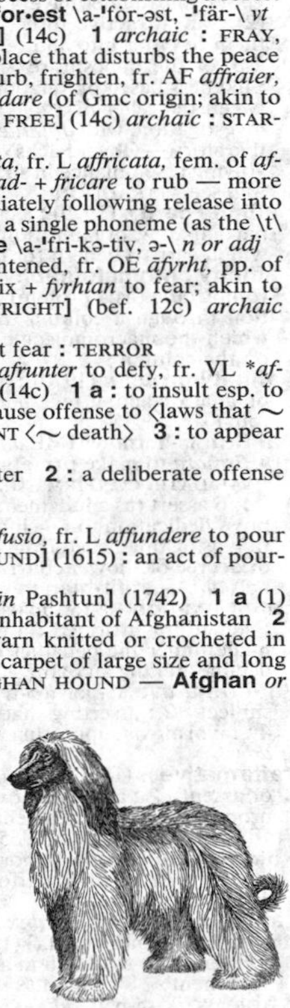

Afghan hound

af·ghani \af-ˈga-nē, -ˈgä-\ *n* [Pers *afghānī,* lit., of the Pashtuns] (1927) — see MONEY table
A–fib \ˈā-ˈfib\ *also* **AFib** *or* **Afib** *n* [by shortening] (1988) ATRIAL FIBRILLATION
afi·cio·na·da \ə-ˌfi-sh(ē-)ə-ˈnä-də, -fē-, -sē-ə-, -ˌdä\ *n* [Sp, fem. of *aficionado*] (1866) **:** a woman who is an aficionado
afi·cio·na·do *also* **af·fi·cio·na·do** \-ˈnä-(ˌ)dō\ *n, pl* **-dos** [Sp, fr. pp. of *aficionar* to inspire affection, fr. *afición* affection, fr. L *affection-, affectio* — more at AFFECTION] (1802) **:** a person who likes, knows about, and appreciates a usu. fervently pursued interest or activity **:** DEVOTEE ⟨∼*s* of the bullfight⟩ ⟨movie ∼*s*⟩
afield \ə-ˈfēld\ *adv or adj* (bef. 12c) **1 :** to, in, or on the field ⟨was weak at bat but strong ∼⟩ **2 :** away from home **:** ABROAD **3 :** out of the way **:** ASTRAY ⟨irrelevant remarks that carried us far ∼⟩
afire \ə-ˈfī(-ə)r\ *adj or adv* (13c) **1 :** being on fire **:** BLAZING **2 :** being in a state of great excitement or energy ⟨her music set the audience ∼⟩
afk *abbr* away from keyboard
AFL *abbr* American Football League
aflame \ə-ˈflām\ *adj or adv* (1555) **:** AFIRE
af·la·tox·in \ˌa-flə-ˈtäk-sən\ *n* [NL *Aspergillus flavus,* species of mold + E *toxin*] (1962) **:** any of several carcinogenic mycotoxins that are produced esp. in stored agricultural crops (as peanuts) by molds (as *Aspergillus flavus*)
AFL–CIO *abbr* American Federation of Labor and Congress of Industrial Organizations
afloat \ə-ˈflōt\ *adj or adv* [ME *aflot,* fr. OE *on flot,* fr. *on* + *flot,* fr. *flot* deep water, sea; akin to OE *flēotan* to float — more at FLEET] (bef. 12c) **1 a :** borne on or as if on the water **b :** being at sea **2 :** free of difficulties **:** SELF-SUFFICIENT ⟨the inheritance kept them ∼ for years⟩ **3 a :** circulating about ⟨nasty stories were ∼⟩ **b :** ADRIFT
aflut·ter \ə-ˈflə-tər\ *adj* (1830) **1 :** being in a flutter **:** FLUTTERING **2 :** nervously excited ⟨all ∼ at the news⟩ **3 :** filled with or marked by the presence of fluttering things ⟨roofs ∼ with flags⟩
AFM *abbr* atomic force microscope
afoot \ə-ˈfu̇t\ *adv or adj* (13c) **1 :** on foot **2 :** in the process of development **:** UNDER WAY ⟨a plan is ∼ to build a new school⟩
afore \ə-ˈfȯr\ *adv or conj or prep* [ME, fr. OE *onforan,* fr. *on* + *foran* before — more at BEFORE] (bef. 12c) *chiefly dial* **:** BEFORE
afore·men·tioned \-ˈmen(t)-shənd\ *adj* (1587) **:** mentioned previously
afore·said \-ˌsed\ *adj* (14c) **:** said or named before or above
afore·thought \-ˌthȯt\ *adj* (15c) **:** previously in mind **:** PREMEDITATED, DELIBERATE ⟨with malice ∼⟩
a for·ti·o·ri \ˌä-ˌfȯr-shē-ˈȯr-ˌī, ˌä-ˌfȯr-shē-ˈȯr-ē, -ˌfȯr-tē-\ *adv* [NL, lit., from the stronger (argument)] (1561) **:** with greater reason or more convincing force — used in drawing a conclusion that is inferred to be even more certain than another ⟨the man of prejudice is, *a fortiori,* a man of limited mental vision⟩
afoul of \ə-ˈfau̇-ləv\ *prep* (1819) **1 :** in or into conflict with ⟨ran *afoul of* the law⟩ **2 :** in or into collision or entanglement with
AFP *abbr* alpha-fetoprotein
Afr *abbr* Africa; African
Afr- *or* **Afro-** *comb form* [L *Afr-, Afer*] **:** African ⟨*Afro*-American⟩ **:** African and ⟨*Afro*-Asiatic⟩
afraid \ə-ˈfrād, *Southern also* ə-ˈfred\ *adj* [ME *affraied,* fr. pp. of *affraien* to frighten — more at AFFRAY] (14c) **1 :** filled with fear or apprehension ⟨∼ of machines⟩ ⟨∼ for his job⟩ **2 :** filled with concern or regret over an unwanted situation ⟨I'm ∼ I won't be able to go⟩ **3 :** having a dislike for something ⟨∼ of hard work⟩ ***syn*** see FEARFUL
A–frame \ˈā-ˌfrām\ *n* (ca. 1909) **1 :** a support structure shaped like the letter A **2 :** a building typically having triangular front and rear walls and a roof reaching to or nearly to the ground
afreet *or* **afrit** \ˈa-ˌfrēt, ə-ˈfrēt\ *n* [Ar *ʿifrīt*] (1786) **:** a powerful evil jinni, demon, or monstrous giant in Arabic mythology
afresh \ə-ˈfresh\ *adv* (15c) **:** from a fresh beginning **:** ANEW, AGAIN
[1]**Af·ri·can** \ˈa-fri-kən *also* ˈä-\ *n* (bef. 12c) **1 :** a native or inhabitant of Africa **2 :** a person and esp. a black person of African ancestry
[2]**African** *adj* (1564) **:** of, relating to, or characteristic of the continent of Africa or its people — **Af·ri·can·ness** \-kə(n)-nəs\ *n*
Af·ri·ca·na \ˌa-fri-ˈka-nə, -ˈkä-, -ˈkā- *also* ˌä-\ *n pl* (1908) **:** materials (as books, documents, or artifacts) relating to African history and culture
Af·ri·can–Amer·i·can \ˌa-fri-kə-nə-ˈmer-ə-kən, -ˈme-rə- *also* ˌä-\ *n* (1831) **:** an American of African and esp. of black African descent — **African–American** *adj*
African buffalo *n* (1784) **:** CAPE BUFFALO
African daisy *n* (1731) **:** any of a genus (*Arctotis*) of widely cultivated composite herbs native to southern Africa
Af·ri·can·der *or* **Af·ri·kan·der** \ˌa-fri-ˈkan-dər\ *n* [Afrik *Afrikaner, Afrikaander,* lit., Afrikaner] (1837) **:** any of a breed of tall red large-horned humped southern African cattle used chiefly for meat or draft
African elephant *n* (1607) **:** ELEPHANT 1a
African gray *n* (1858) **:** a parrot (*Psittacus erithacus*) native to equatorial Africa that has gray plumage, a red tail, and a whitish face and is commonly domesticated esp. for its ability in learning to talk
Af·ri·can·ise *Brit var of* AFRICANIZE
Af·ri·can·ism \ˈa-fri-kə-ˌni-zəm *also* ˈä-\ *n* (1641) **1 :** a characteristic feature of African culture **2 :** a characteristic feature of an African language occurring in a non-African language **3 :** allegiance to the traditions, interests, or ideals of Africa — **Af·ri·can·ist** \-nist\ *adj*
Africanist *n* (1852) **:** a specialist in African languages or cultures
Af·ri·can·ize \-ˌnīz\ *vt* **-ized; -iz·ing** (1817) **1 :** to cause to acquire a distinctively African trait **2 :** to bring under the influence, control, or cultural or civil supremacy of Africans and esp. black Africans — **Af·ri·can·i·za·tion** \ˌa-fri-kə-nə-ˈzā-shən *also* ˌä-\ *n*
Africanized bee *n* (1970) **:** a honeybee that originated in Brazil as an accidental hybrid between an aggressive African subspecies (*Apis mellifera scutellata*) and previously established European honeybees and has spread to Mexico and the southernmost U.S. by breeding with local bees producing populations retaining most of the African bee's traits — called also *Africanized honeybee, killer bee*
African mahogany *n* (1831) **:** MAHOGANY 1b
African swine fever *n* (1948) **:** SWINE FEVER 2
African violet *n* (ca. 1897) **:** any of several tropical African gesneriads (esp. *Saintpaulia ionantha*) widely grown as houseplants for their velvety fleshy leaves and showy purple, pink, or white flowers
African wild dog *n* (1827) **:** a powerful canid (*Lycaon pictus*) that has a mottled coat of black, white, and reddish yellow, lives and hunts in packs, and was formerly common in sub-Saharan Africa but is now restricted to small populations in southern and eastern Africa — called also *African hunting dog*
[1]**Af·ri·kaans** \ˌa-fri-ˈkän(t)s, ˌä-, -ˈkänz, ˈa-fri-ˌ, ˈä-\ *n* [Afrik, fr. *afrikaans,* adj., African, fr. obs. Afrik *afrikanisch,* ultim. fr. L *africanus*] (1892) **:** a language developed from 17th century Dutch that is one of the official languages of the Republic of So. Africa
[2]**Afrikaans** *adj* (1923) **:** of or relating to Afrikaners or Afrikaans
Af·ri·ka·ner \ˌa-fri-ˈkä-nər\ *n, often attrib* [Afrik, lit., African, fr. L *africanus*] (1824) **:** a South African of European descent whose native language is Afrikaans — **Af·ri·ka·ner·dom** \-dəm\ *n*
Af·ro \ˈa-(ˌ)frō\ *n, pl* **Afros** (1966) **:** a hairstyle of tight curls in a full evenly rounded shape — **Af·roed** \-(ˌ)frōd\ *adj*

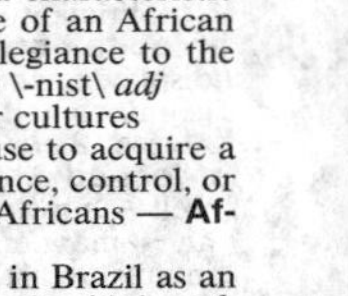

Afro

Af·ro–Amer·i·can \ˌa-frō-ə-ˈmer-ə-kən, -ˈme-rə-\ *n* (1889) **:** AFRICAN-AMERICAN — **Afro–American** *adj*
Af·ro–Asi·at·ic \ˌa-frō-ˌā-zhē-ˈa-tik, -zē- *also* -shē-\ *adj* (1922) **:** of, relating to, or being a family of languages widely distributed over southwestern Asia and Africa including the Semitic, Egyptian, Berber, Cushitic, and Chadic subfamilies
Af·ro·cen·tric \ˌa-frō-ˈsen-trik\ *adj* (1966) **1 :** centered on or derived from Africa or the Africans **2 :** emphasizing or promoting emphasis on African culture and the contributions of Africans to the development of Western civilization — **Af·ro·cen·tric·i·ty** \-ˌsen-ˈtri-sə-tē\ *n* — **Af·ro·cen·trism** \-ˈsen-ˌtri-zəm\ *n* — **Af·ro·cen·trist** \-ˈsen-trist\ *n or adj*
[1]**aft** \ˈaft\ *adv* [ME *afte* back, fr. OE *æftan* from behind, behind; akin to OE *æfter*] (1580) **:** near, toward, or in the stern of a ship or the tail of an aircraft ⟨called all hands ∼⟩
[2]**aft** *adj* (1667) **:** REARWARD, AFTER 2 ⟨the ∼ decks⟩
[3]**aft** *Scot var of* OFT
[4]**aft** *abbr* afternoon

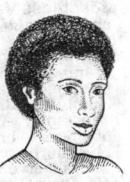

AFT abbr **1** American Federation of Teachers **2** automatic fine-tuning

¹af·ter \'af-tər\ adv [ME, fr. OE æfter; akin to OHG aftar after, and prob. to OE of of] (bef. 12c) **:** following in time or place **:** AFTERWARD, BEHIND, LATER ⟨we arrived shortly ∼⟩ ⟨returned 20 years ∼⟩

²after prep (bef. 12c) **1 a :** behind in place ⟨people lined up one ∼ another⟩ **b** (1) **:** subsequent to in time or order ⟨20 minutes ∼ 6⟩ (2) **:** subsequent to and in view of ⟨∼ all our advice⟩ **2** — used as a function word to indicate the object of a stated or implied action ⟨go ∼ gold⟩ ⟨was asking ∼ you⟩ **3 :** so as to resemble: as **a :** in accordance with **b :** with the name of or a name derived from that of ⟨named ∼ his father⟩ **c :** in the characteristic manner of **:** in imitation of ⟨writing ∼ the manner of Hemingway⟩

³after conj (bef. 12c) **:** subsequently to the time when ⟨we will come ∼ we make plans⟩

⁴after adj (bef. 12c) **1 :** later in time ⟨in ∼ years⟩ **2 :** located toward the rear and esp. toward the stern of a ship or tail of an aircraft

⁵af·ter \'äf-tər\ verbal auxiliary (1792) chiefly Irish — used with a present participle to indicate action completed and esp. just completed ⟨the poor old man is ∼ dying on me —J. M. Synge⟩

⁶after n (ca. 1902) **:** AFTERNOON

after all adv (1641) **1 :** in spite of considerations or expectations to the contrary **:** NEVERTHELESS ⟨decided to take the train after all⟩ ⟨didn't rain after all⟩ **2 :** in view of all circumstances ⟨literature which is after all only a special department of reading —W. W. Watt⟩

af·ter·birth \'af-tər-,bərth\ n (1587) **:** the placenta and fetal membranes that are expelled after delivery

af·ter·burn·er \-,bər-nər\ n (1947) **1 :** a device incorporated into the tailpipe of a turbojet engine for injecting fuel into the hot exhaust gases and burning it to provide extra thrust **2 :** a device for burning or catalytically destroying unburned or partially burned carbon compounds in exhaust (as from an automobile)

af·ter·care \-,ker\ n (1843) **:** the care, treatment, help, or supervision given to persons discharged from an institution (as a hospital)

af·ter·clap \-,klap\ n (14c) **:** an unexpected damaging or unsettling event following a supposedly closed affair

af·ter·deck \-,dek\ n (1797) **:** the part of a deck abaft amidships

af·ter·ef·fect \'af-tər-ə-,fekt\ n (1659) **:** an effect that follows its cause after an interval

af·ter·glow \'af-tər-,glō\ n (1832) **1 :** a glow remaining where a light has disappeared **2 :** a pleasant effect or feeling that lingers after something is done, experienced, or achieved ⟨basking in the ∼ of success⟩

af·ter·guard \-,gärd\ n (1750) **1 :** the sailors stationed on the poop or after part of a ship **2 :** the decision-making members of a sailboat racing team usu. including a helmsman, tactician, and navigator

af·ter–hours \'af-tər-'au̇(-ə)rz\ adj (1902) **:** engaged in or operating after a legal or conventional closing time ⟨∼ drinking⟩ ⟨an ∼ club⟩

af·ter·im·age \'af-tər-,i-mij\ n (1840) **:** a usu. visual sensation occurring after stimulation by its external cause has ceased

af·ter·life \'af-tər-,līf\ n (ca. 1593) **1 :** an existence after death **2 :** a later period in one's life **3 :** a period of continued or renewed use, existence, or popularity beyond what is normal, primary, or expected ⟨a TV show with a long ∼ in syndication⟩

af·ter·mar·ket \-,mär-kət\ n (1940) **1 :** the market for parts and accessories used in the repair or enhancement of a product (as an automobile) **2 :** a secondary market available after sales in the original market are finished ⟨a movie in the videocassette ∼⟩

af·ter·math \-,math\ n [¹after + math (mowing, crop)] (1523) **1 :** a second-growth crop — called also rowen **2 :** CONSEQUENCE, RESULT ⟨stricken with guilt as an ∼ of the accident⟩ **3 :** the period immediately following a usu. ruinous event ⟨in the ∼ of the war⟩

af·ter·most \-,mōst\ adj (1773) **:** farthest aft

af·ter·noon \,af-tər-'nün\ n (13c) **1 :** the part of the day between noon and sunset **2 :** a relatively late period (as of time or life) ⟨in the ∼ of the 19th century⟩ — **afternoon** adj

af·ter·noons \-'nünz\ adv (ca. 1697) **:** in the afternoon repeatedly **:** on any afternoon

af·ter–par·ty \'af-tər-,pär-tē\ n (1961) **:** a party for invited guests that follows a main party or event

af·ter·piece \'af-tər-,pēs\ n (1770) **:** a short usu. comic entertainment performed after a play

af·ters \'af-tərz\ n pl (ca. 1909) Brit **:** DESSERT

af·ter·shave \'af-tər-,shāv\ n (1946) **:** a usu. scented lotion for use on the face after shaving

af·ter·shock \-,shäk\ n (1847) **1 :** an aftereffect of a distressing or traumatic event **2 :** a minor shock following the main shock of an earthquake

af·ter·taste \-,tāst\ n (ca. 1754) **:** persistence of a sensation (as of flavor or an emotion) after the stimulating agent or experience has gone

af·ter–tax \-'taks\ adj (1947) **:** remaining after payment of taxes and esp. of income tax ⟨an ∼ profit⟩

af·ter·thought \-,thȯt\ n (1644) **1 :** an idea occurring later **2 :** something (as a part or feature) not thought of originally **:** something secondary

af·ter·time \-,tīm\ n (1597) **:** FUTURE

af·ter·ward \'af-tə(r)-wərd\ or **af·ter·wards** \-wərdz\ adv (13c) **:** at a later or succeeding time **:** SUBSEQUENTLY, THEREAFTER

af·ter·word \-,wərd\ n (1890) **:** EPILOGUE 1

af·ter·world \-,wərld\ n (1596) **:** a future world **:** a world after death

AFTRA abbr American Federation of Television and Radio Artists

ag \'ag\ adj (ca. 1918) **:** of or relating to agriculture ⟨∼ schools⟩

Ag symbol [L argentum] silver

AG abbr **1** adjutant general **2** [G Aktiengesellschaft] joint stock company **3** attorney general

ag- — see AD-

again \ə-'gen, -'gin, -'gān\ adv [ME, opposite, again, fr. OE ongēan opposite, back, fr. on + gēn, gēan still, again; akin to OE gēan- against, OHG gegin again, toward] (13c) **1 :** in return **:** BACK ⟨swore he would pay him ∼ when he was able —Shak.⟩ **2 :** another time **:** once more **:** ANEW ⟨I shall not look upon his like ∼ —Shak.⟩ **3 :** on the other hand ⟨he might go, and ∼ he might not⟩ **4 :** in addition **:** BESIDES ⟨∼, there is another matter to consider⟩

again and again adv (1604) **:** at frequent intervals **:** OFTEN, REPEATEDLY

¹against \ə-'gen(t)st, -'gin(t)st, -'gān(t)st\ prep [ME, alter. of againes, fr. again] (13c) **1 a :** in opposition or hostility to ⟨spoke ∼ his enemies⟩ **b :** contrary to ⟨∼ the law⟩ **c :** in competition with ⟨racing ∼ each other⟩ **d :** as a basis for disapproval of ⟨had nothing ∼ him⟩ **2 a :** directly opposite **:** FACING ⟨she sat down just over ∼ me —Daniel Defoe⟩ **b** obs **:** exposed to **3 :** compared or contrasted with ⟨profits are up ∼ last year⟩ **4 a :** in preparation or provision for ⟨saving ∼ an uncertain future⟩ **b :** as a defense or protection from ⟨a shelter ∼ the cold⟩ **5 a :** in the direction of and into contact with ⟨knocked ∼ the ropes⟩ **b :** in contact with ⟨leaning ∼ the wall⟩ **6 :** in a direction opposite to the motion or course of **:** counter to ⟨sail ∼ the wind⟩ **7 a :** as a counterbalance to ⟨weighing risk ∼ profit⟩ **b :** in exchange for ⟨a lower rate ∼ the dollar⟩ **c :** as a charge on ⟨charged ∼ her account⟩ **8 :** before the background of ⟨viewed ∼ the sky⟩

²against conj (14c) archaic **:** in preparation for the time when ⟨throw on another log of wood ∼ father comes home —Charles Dickens⟩

Ag·a·mem·non \,a-gə-'mem-,nän, -nən\ n [L, fr. Gk Agamemnōn] (14c) **:** a king of Mycenae and leader of the Greeks in the Trojan War

agam·ic \(,)ā-'ga-mik\ adj [Gk agamos unmarried, fr. a- + gamos marriage] (1816) **:** ASEXUAL, PARTHENOGENETIC

agam·ma·glob·u·lin·emia \,ā-,ga-mə-,glä-byə-lə-'nē-mē-ə\ n [NL, fr. a- + ISV gamma globulin + NL -emia] (ca. 1952) **:** a condition in which the body forms few or no gamma globulins or antibodies — **agam·ma·glob·u·lin·emic** \-'nē-mik\ adj

aga·mo·sper·my \(,)ā-'ga-mə-,spər-mē, 'a-gə-mō-,spər-\ n [Gk agamos + E -spermy] (1944) **:** APOGAMY; specif **:** apogamy in which sexual union is not completed and the embryo is produced from the innermost layer of the integument of the female gametophyte

ag·a·pan·thus \,a-gə-'pan(t)-thəs\ n, pl **-thus** also **-thuses** [NL, genus name, fr. Gk agapē + anthos flower — more at ANTHOLOGY] (ca. 1789) **:** any of several African plants (genus Agapanthus) of the lily family cultivated for their umbels of showy blue, purple, or white flowers

¹aga·pe \ä-'gä-(,)pā, 'ä-gə-,pā\ n [LL, fr. Gk agapē, lit., love] (1607) **1 :** LOVE FEAST **2 :** LOVE 4a

²agape \ə-'gāp also -'gap\ adj or adv (1667) **1 :** wide open **:** GAPING ⟨with mouth ∼⟩ **2 :** being in a state of wonder

agar \'ä-gər\ n [Malay agar-agar] (ca. 1813) **1 :** a gelatinous colloidal extractive of a red alga (as of the genera Gelidium, Gracilaria, and Eucheuma) used esp. in culture media or as a gelling and stabilizing agent in foods **2 :** a culture medium containing agar

agar–agar \,ä-gər-'ä-gər\ n [Malay] (1820) **:** AGAR

agar·ic \'a-gə-rik, ə-'ger-ik, -'ga-rik\ n [L agaricum, a fungus, fr. Gk agarikon] (15c) **1 :** the dried fruiting body of a fungus (Fomes officinalis syn. Polyporus officinalis) formerly used in medicine **2 :** any of a family (Agaricaceae) of fungi with the sporophore usu. resembling an umbrella and with numerous gills on the underside of the cap

aga·rose \'a-gə-,rōs, 'ä-, -,rōz\ n (1953) **:** a polysaccharide obtained from agar and used esp. as a supporting medium in gel electrophoresis

ag·ate \'a-gət\ n, often attrib [MF, fr. L achates, fr. Gk achatēs] (1570) **1 :** a fine-grained variegated chalcedony having its colors arranged in stripes, blended in clouds, or showing mosslike forms **2 :** something made of or fitted with agate: as **a :** a drawplate used by gold-wire drawers **b :** a playing marble of agate **3 a :** a size of type approximately 5½ point **b :** condensed information (as advertisements or box scores) set esp. in agate type

agate line n (1870) **:** a space one column wide and 1/14 inch deep used as a unit of measurement in classified advertising

agate ware n (1817) **1 :** an enameled iron or steel ware for household utensils **2 :** pottery veined and mottled to resemble agate

aga·ve \ə-'gä-vē\ n [NL Agave, genus name, fr. L, a daughter of Cadmus, fr. Gk Agauē] (1763) **:** any of a genus (Agave of the family Agavaceae, the agave family) of plants having spiny-margined leaves and flowers in tall spreading panicles and including some cultivated for their fiber or sap or for ornament

agave

agaze \ə-'gāz\ adj (1720) **:** engaged in the act of gazing

AGC abbr advanced graduate certificate

agcy abbr agency

¹age \'āj\ n [ME, fr. AF aage, age, fr. VL *aetaticum, fr. L aetat-, aetas, fr. aevum lifetime — more at AYE] (13c) **1 a :** the time of life at which some particular qualification, power, or capacity arises or rests ⟨the voting ∼ is 18⟩; specif **:** MAJORITY **b :** one of the stages of life **c :** the length of an existence extending from the beginning to any given time ⟨a boy 10 years of ∼⟩ **d :** LIFETIME **e :** an advanced stage of life **2 :** a period of time dominated by a central figure or prominent feature ⟨the ∼ of Pericles⟩: as **a :** a period in history or human progress ⟨the ∼ of reptiles⟩ ⟨the ∼ of exploration⟩ **b :** a cultural period marked by the prominence of a particular item ⟨entering the atomic ∼⟩ **c :** a division of geologic time that is usu. shorter than an epoch **3 a :** the period contemporary with a person's lifetime or with his or her active life **b :** a long time — usu. used in pl. ⟨haven't seen him in ∼s⟩ **c :** GENERATION **4 :** an individual's development measured in terms of the years requisite for like development of an average individual **syn** see PERIOD

²age vb **aged; ag·ing** or **age·ing** vi (14c) **1 :** to become old **:** show the effects or the characteristics of increasing age **2 :** to acquire a desirable quality (as mellowness or ripeness) by standing undisturbed for some time ⟨letting cheese ∼⟩ ∼ vt **1 :** to cause to become old **2 :** to bring to a state fit for use or to maturity — **ag·er** \'ā-jər\ n

-age n suffix [ME, fr. OF, fr. L -aticum] **1 :** aggregate **:** collection ⟨trackage⟩ **2 a :** action **:** process ⟨haulage⟩ **b :** cumulative result of ⟨breakage⟩ **c :** rate of ⟨dosage⟩ **3 :** house or place of ⟨orphanage⟩ **4 :** state **:** rank ⟨peonage⟩ **5 :** charge ⟨postage⟩

\ə\ abut \ᵊ\ kitten, F table \ər\ further \a\ ash \ā\ ace \ä\ mop, mar \au̇\ out \ch\ chin \e\ bet \ē\ easy \g\ go \i\ hit \ī\ ice \j\ job \ŋ\ sing \ō\ go \ȯ\ law \ȯi\ boy \th\ thin \t̷h\ the \ü\ loot \u̇\ foot \y\ yet \zh\ vision, beige \k̲, ⁿ, œ, ᵫ, �златᵊ\ see Guide to Pronunciation

aged \ˈā-jəd, ˈājd; ˈājd *for 1b*\ *adj* (15c) **1 :** grown old: as **a :** of an advanced age ⟨an ~ man⟩ **b :** having attained a specified age ⟨a man ~ 40 years⟩ **2 :** typical of old age — **aged·ness** \ˈā-jəd-nəs\ *n*
age–group \ˈāj-ˌgrüp\ *n* (1904) **:** a segment of a population that is of approximately the same age or is within a specified range of ages
age·ism *also* **ag·ism** \ˈā-(ˌ)ji-zəm\ *n* (1969) **:** prejudice or discrimination against a particular age-group and esp. the elderly — **age·ist** *also* **ag·ist** \-jist\ *adj*
age·less \ˈāj-ləs\ *adj* (1651) **1 :** not growing old or showing the effects of age **2 :** TIMELESS, ETERNAL ⟨~ truths⟩ — **age·less·ly** *adv* — **age·less·ness** *n*
age·long \ˈāj-ˌlȯŋ\ *adj* (1810) **:** lasting for an age **:** EVERLASTING
age–mate \-ˌmāt\ *n* (1583) **:** one who is of about the same age as another
agen·cy \ˈā-jən(t)-sē\ *n, pl* **-cies** (1640) **1 a :** the office or function of an agent **b :** the relationship between a principal and that person's agent **2 :** the capacity, condition, or state of acting or of exerting power **:** OPERATION **3 :** a person or thing through which power is exerted or an end is achieved **:** INSTRUMENTALITY ⟨communicated through the ~ of the ambassador⟩ **4 :** an establishment engaged in doing business for another ⟨an advertising ~⟩ **5 :** an administrative division (as of a government) ⟨the ~ for consumer protection⟩
agency shop *n* (ca. 1946) **:** an establishment in which the union serves as the agent for and receives dues and assessments from all employees in the bargaining unit regardless of union membership
agen·da \ə-ˈjen-də\ *n* [L, neut. pl. of *agendum,* gerundive of *agere*] (1871) **1 :** a list or outline of things to be considered or done ⟨~*s* of faculty meetings⟩ **2 :** an underlying often ideological plan or program ⟨a political ~⟩ — **agen·da·less** \-də-ləs\ *adj*
agen·dum \-dəm\ *n, pl* **-da** \-də\ *or* **-dums** [L] (ca. 1847) **1 :** AGENDA **2 :** an item on an agenda
agen·e·sis \(ˌ)ā-ˈje-nə-səs\ *n* [NL] (ca. 1879) **:** lack or failure of development (as of a body part)
agent \ˈā-jənt\ *n* [ME, fr. ML *agent-, agens,* fr. L, prp. of *agere* to drive, lead, act, do; akin to ON *aka* to travel in a vehicle, Gk *agein* to drive, lead] (15c) **1 :** one that acts or exerts power **2 a :** something that produces or is capable of producing an effect **:** an active or efficient cause **b :** a chemically, physically, or biologically active principle **3 :** a means or instrument by which a guiding intelligence achieves a result **4 :** one who is authorized to act for or in the place of another: as **a :** a representative, emissary, or official of a government ⟨crown ~⟩ ⟨federal ~⟩ **b :** one engaged in undercover activities (as espionage) **:** SPY ⟨secret ~⟩ **c :** a business representative (as of an athlete or entertainer) ⟨a theatrical ~⟩ **5 :** a computer application designed to automate certain tasks (as gathering information online)
agent–general *n, pl* **agents–general** (1833) **:** a chief agent; *specif* **:** the representative in England of a British dominion
agent·ing \ˈā-jən-tiŋ\ *n* (1681) **:** the business or activities of an agent
Agent Orange *n* [so called fr. the identifying color stripe on its container] (1970) **:** an herbicide widely used as a defoliant in the Vietnam War that is composed of 2,4-D and 2,4,5-T and contains dioxin as a contaminant
agent pro·vo·ca·teur \ˈä-ˌzhäⁿ-prō-ˌvä-kə-ˈtər, ˈā-jənt-\ *n, pl* **agents provocateurs** \ˈä-ˌzhäⁿ-prō-ˌvä-kə-ˈtər, ˈā-jən(t)s-prō-\ [F, lit., provoking agent] (1877) **:** one employed to associate with suspected persons and by pretending sympathy with their aims to incite them to some incriminating action
agent·ry \ˈā-jən-trē\ *n, pl* **-ries** (1913) **:** the office, duties, or activities of an agent
age of consent (1504) **:** the age at which one is legally competent to give consent esp. to marriage or to sexual intercourse
age of reason (1650) **1 :** the time of life when one begins to be able to distinguish right from wrong **2 :** a period characterized by a prevailing belief in the use of reason; *esp* **:** the 18th century in England and France
age–old \ˈāj-ˈōld\ *adj* (1886) **:** having existed for ages **:** ANCIENT
ag·er·a·tum \ˌa-jə-ˈrā-təm\ *n, pl* **-tum** *also* **-tums** [NL, genus name, fr. Gk *agēratos* ageless, fr. *a-* + *gēras* old age — more at GERONT-] (1866) **:** any of a genus (*Ageratum*) of annual tropical American composite herbs often cultivated for their small showy heads of usu. blue or white flowers; *also* **:** a related blue-flowered perennial (*Eupatorium coelestinum*)
age spots *n pl* (1955) **:** benign flat spots of dark pigmentation on the skin (as from exposure to the sun) occurring esp. among older people — called also *liver spots*
Ag·ga·dah \ə-ˈgä-də, -ˈgȯ-\ *n, pl* **Ag·ga·dot** \-ˌdōt, -ˌdōth, -ˌdōs\ [Heb *haggādhāh*] (1856) **:** ancient Jewish lore forming esp. the nonlegal part of the Talmud
Ag·ge·us \a-ˈgē-əs\ *n* [LL *Aggaeus,* fr. Gk *Aggaios,* fr. Heb *Ḥaggai*] (bef. 12c) **:** HAGGAI
1**ag·gie** \ˈa-gē\ *n, often cap* [*ag*ricultural + *-ie*] (1902) **:** an agricultural school or college; *also* **:** a student at such an institution
2**aggie** *n* [*ag*ate + *-ie*] (1915) **:** a playing marble; *specif* **:** AGATE 2b
ag·gior·na·men·to \ə-ˌjȯr-nə-ˈmen-(ˌ)tō\ *n, pl* **-tos** [It, fr. *aggiornare* to bring up to date, fr. *a* to (fr. L *ad-*) + *giorno* day, fr. LL *diurnum* day — more at JOURNEY] (1963) **:** a bringing up to date **:** MODERNIZATION ⟨dedicated to the ~ of the church⟩
1**ag·glom·er·ate** \ə-ˈglä-mə-ˌrāt\ *vt* **-at·ed; -at·ing** [L *agglomeratus,* pp. of *agglomerare* to heap up, join, fr. *ad-* + *glomer-, glomus* ball — more at CLAM] (1684) **:** to gather into a ball, mass, or cluster
2**ag·glom·er·ate** \-rət\ *adj* (1828) **:** gathered into a ball, mass, or cluster; *specif* **:** clustered or growing together but not coherent ⟨an ~ flower head⟩
3**ag·glom·er·ate** \-rət\ *n* (1830) **1 :** a rock composed of volcanic fragments of various sizes and degrees of angularity **2 :** a jumbled mass or collection **:** AGGLOMERATION
ag·glom·er·a·tion \ə-ˌglä-mə-ˈrā-shən\ *n* (1774) **1 :** the action or process of collecting in a mass **2 :** a heap or cluster of usu. disparate elements ⟨urban ~*s* knit together by the new railways —*Times Lit. Supp.*⟩ — **ag·glom·er·a·tive** \-ˈglä-mə-ˌrā-tiv\ *adj*
ag·glu·ti·na·bil·i·ty \ə-ˌglü-tᵊn-ə-ˈbi-lə-tē\ *n* (1901) **:** capacity (as of red blood cells) to be agglutinated — **ag·glu·ti·na·ble** \ə-ˈglü-tᵊn-ə-bəl\ *adj*
1**ag·glu·ti·nate** \ə-ˈglü-tᵊn-ˌāt\ *vb* **-nat·ed; -nat·ing** [L *agglutinatus,* pp. of *agglutinare* to glue to, fr. *ad-* + *glutinare* to glue, fr. *glutin-, gluten* glue — more at CLAY] *vt* (1586) **1 :** to cause to adhere **:** FASTEN **2 :** to combine into a compound **:** attach to a base as an affix **3 :** to cause to undergo agglutination ~ *vi* **1 :** to unite or combine into a group or mass **2 :** to form words by agglutination
2**ag·glu·ti·nate** \-tᵊn-ət, -tᵊn-ˌāt\ *n* (1952) **:** a clump of agglutinated material (as blood cells or mineral particles in soil)
ag·glu·ti·na·tion \ə-ˌglü-tᵊn-ˈā-shən\ *n* (1541) **1 :** the action or process of agglutinating **2 :** a mass or group formed by the union of separate elements **3 :** the formation of derivational or inflectional words by putting together constituents of which each expresses a single definite meaning **4 :** a reaction in which particles (as red blood cells or bacteria) suspended in a liquid collect into clumps and which occurs esp. as a serologic response to a specific antibody
ag·glu·ti·na·tive \ə-ˈglü-tᵊn-ˌā-tiv, -ə-tiv\ *adj* (1634) **1 :** ADHESIVE **2 :** characterized by linguistic agglutination
ag·glu·ti·nin \ə-ˈglü-tᵊn-ən\ *n* [ISV *agglutin*ation + *-in*] (1902) **:** a substance (as an antibody) producing agglutination
ag·glu·ti·no·gen \ə-ˈglü-tᵊn-ə-jən\ *n* [*agglutin*in + *-o-* + *-gen*] (1904) **:** an antigen whose presence results in the formation of an agglutinin — **ag·glu·ti·no·gen·ic** \-ˌglü-tᵊn-ə-ˈje-nik\ *adj*
ag·gra·da·tion \ˌa-grə-ˈdā-shən\ *n* [*ad-* + *gradation*] (1898) **:** a modification of the earth's surface in the direction of uniformity of grade by deposition — **ag·gra·da·tion·al** \-shnəl, -shə-nᵊl\ *adj*
ag·gran·dise *Brit var of* AGGRANDIZE
ag·gran·dize \ə-ˈgran-ˌdīz *also* ˈa-grən-\ *vt* **-dized; -diz·ing** [F *agrandiss-,* stem of *agrandir,* fr. *a-* (fr. L *ad-*) + *grandir* to increase, fr. L *grandire,* fr. *grandis* great] (1634) **1 :** to make great or greater **:** INCREASE, ENLARGE ⟨~ an estate⟩ **2 :** to make appear great or greater **:** praise highly **3 :** to enhance the power, wealth, position, or reputation of ⟨exploited the situation to ~ himself⟩ — **ag·gran·dize·ment** \ə-ˈgran-dəz-mənt, -ˌdīz- *also* ˌa-grən-ˈdīz-\ *n* — **ag·gran·diz·er** \ə-ˈgran-ˌdī-zər *also* ˈa-grən-\ *n*
ag·gra·vate \ˈa-grə-ˌvāt\ *vt* **-vat·ed; -vat·ing** [L *aggravatus,* pp. of *aggravare* to make heavier, fr. *ad-* + *gravare* to burden, fr. *gravis* heavy — more at GRIEVE] (1530) **1** *obs* **a :** to make heavy **:** BURDEN **b :** INCREASE **2 :** to make worse, more serious, or more severe **:** intensify unpleasantly ⟨problems have been *aggravated* by neglect⟩ **3 a :** to rouse to displeasure or anger by usu. persistent and often petty goading **b :** to produce inflammation in
usage Although *aggravate* has been used in sense 3a since the 17th century, it has been the object of disapproval only since about 1870. It is used in expository prose ⟨when his silly conceit . . . about his not-very-good early work has begun to *aggravate* us —William Styron⟩ but seems to be more common in speech and casual writing ⟨a good profession for him, because bus drivers get *aggravated* —Jackie Gleason (interview, 1986)⟩ ⟨& now this letter comes to *aggravate* me a thousand times worse —Mark Twain (letter, 1864)⟩. Sense 2 is far more common than sense 3a in published prose. Such is not the case, however, with *aggravation* and *aggravating. Aggravation* is used in sense 3 somewhat more than in its earlier senses; *aggravating* has practically no use other than to express annoyance.
aggravated assault *n* (1845) **:** an assault that is more serious than a common assault: as **a :** an assault combined with an intent to commit a crime **b :** any of various assaults so defined by statute
aggravating *adj* (1673) **:** arousing displeasure, impatience, or anger ⟨an ~ habit⟩ ***usage*** see AGGRAVATE
ag·gra·va·tion \ˌa-grə-ˈvā-shən\ *n* (ca. 1555) **1 :** an act or circumstance that intensifies or makes worse **2 :** the act, action, or result of aggravating; *esp* **:** an increasing in seriousness or severity ⟨~ of an injury⟩ **3 :** IRRITATION, PROVOCATION ***usage*** see AGGRAVATE
1**ag·gre·gate** \ˈa-gri-gət\ *adj* [ME *aggregat,* fr. L *aggregatus,* pp. of *aggregare* to add to, fr. *ad-* + *greg-, grex* flock] (15c) **:** formed by the collection of units or particles into a body, mass, or amount **:** COLLECTIVE: as **a** (1) **:** clustered in a dense mass or head ⟨an ~ flower⟩ (2) **:** formed from several separate ovaries of a single flower ⟨~ fruit⟩ **b :** composed of mineral crystals of one or more kinds or of mineral rock fragments **c :** taking all units as a whole ⟨~ sales⟩ — **ag·gre·gate·ly** *adv* — **ag·gre·gate·ness** *n*
2**ag·gre·gate** \-ˌgāt\ *vt* **-gat·ed; -gat·ing** (15c) **1 :** to collect or gather into a mass or whole **2 :** to amount in the aggregate to **:** TOTAL
3**ag·gre·gate** \-gət\ *n* (15c) **1 :** a mass or body of units or parts somewhat loosely associated with one another **2 :** the whole sum or amount **:** SUM TOTAL **3 a :** an aggregate rock **b :** any of several hard inert materials (as sand, gravel, or slag) used for mixing with a cementing material to form concrete, mortar, or plaster **c :** a clustered mass of individual soil particles varied in shape, ranging in size from a microscopic granule to a small crumb, and considered the basic structural unit of soil **4 :** SET 21 **5 :** MONETARY AGGREGATE — **in the aggregate :** considered as a whole **:** COLLECTIVELY ⟨dividends for the year amounted *in the aggregate* to 25 million dollars⟩
ag·gre·ga·tion \ˌa-gri-ˈgā-shən\ *n* (1547) **1 :** a group, body, or mass composed of many distinct parts or individuals **2 a :** the collecting of units or parts into a mass or whole **b :** the condition of being so collected — **ag·gre·ga·tion·al** \-shnəl, -shə-nᵊl\ *adj*
ag·gre·ga·tive \ˈa-gri-ˌgā-tiv\ *adj* (1644) **1 :** of or relating to an aggregate **2 :** tending to aggregate — **ag·gre·ga·tive·ly** *adv*
ag·gress \ə-ˈgres\ *vi* (ca. 1714) **:** to commit aggression **:** act aggressively
ag·gres·sion \ə-ˈgre-shən\ *n* [L *aggression-, aggressio* attack, fr. *aggredi* to attack, fr. *ad-* + *gradi* to step, go — more at GRADE] (1611) **1 :** a forceful action or procedure (as an unprovoked attack) esp. when intended to dominate or master **2 :** the practice of making attacks or encroachments; *esp* **:** unprovoked violation by one country of the territorial integrity of another **3 :** hostile, injurious, or destructive behavior or outlook esp. when caused by frustration
ag·gres·sive \ə-ˈgre-siv\ *adj* (1824) **1 a :** tending toward or exhibiting aggression ⟨~ behavior⟩ **b :** marked by combative readiness ⟨an ~ fighter⟩ **2 a :** marked by obtrusive energy **b :** marked by driving forceful energy or initiative **:** ENTERPRISING ⟨an ~ salesman⟩ **3 :** strong or emphatic in effect or intent ⟨~ colors⟩ ⟨~ flavors⟩ **4 :** growing, developing, or spreading rapidly ⟨~ bone tumors⟩ **5 :** more severe, intensive, or comprehensive than usual esp. in dosage or

extent ⟨~ chemotherapy⟩ — **ag·gres·sive·ly** *adv* — **ag·gres·sive·ness** *n* — **ag·gres·siv·i·ty** \ˌa-ˌgre-ˈsi-və-tē\ *n*

syn AGGRESSIVE, MILITANT, ASSERTIVE, SELF-ASSERTIVE mean obtrusively energetic esp. in pursuing particular goals. AGGRESSIVE implies a disposition to dominate often in disregard of others' rights or in determined and energetic pursuit of one's ends ⟨*aggressive* in his business dealings⟩. MILITANT also implies a fighting disposition but suggests not self-seeking but devotion to a cause, movement, or principle ⟨*militant* protesters rallied against the new law⟩. ASSERTIVE suggests bold self-confidence in expression of opinion ⟨the more *assertive* speakers dominated the forum⟩. SELF-ASSERTIVE connotes forwardness or brash self-confidence ⟨a *self-assertive* young upstart⟩.

ag·gres·sor \ə-ˈgre-sər\ *n* (1646) **:** one that commits or practices aggression

ag·grieve \ə-ˈgrēv\ *vt* **ag·grieved; ag·griev·ing** [ME *agreven,* fr. AF *agrever,* fr. L *aggravare* to make heavier] (14c) **1 :** to give pain or trouble to **:** DISTRESS **2 :** to inflict injury on ***syn*** see WRONG

ag·grieved \ə-ˈgrēvd\ *adj* (14c) **1 :** troubled or distressed in spirit **2 a :** suffering from an infringement or denial of legal rights ⟨~ minority groups⟩ **b :** showing or expressing grief, injury, or offense ⟨an ~ plea⟩ — **ag·griev·ed·ly** \-ˈgrē-vəd-lē\ *adv*

ag·grieve·ment \ə-ˈgrēv-mənt\ *n* (1847) **:** the quality or state of being aggrieved

1**ag·gro** \ˈa-(ˌ)grō\ *n, pl* **aggros** [prob. *agg*ravation + 1*-o,* later taken as short for *aggression*] (1969) **1** *Brit* **:** deliberately aggressive, provoking, or violent behavior **2** *Brit* **:** EXASPERATION, IRRITATION

2**aggro** *adj* (1970) **:** aggressive or aggressively daring in style or manner

aghast \ə-ˈgast\ *adj* [ME *agast,* fr. pp. of *agasten* to frighten, fr. *a-* (perfective prefix) + *gasten* to frighten — more at ABIDE, GAST] (13c) **:** struck with terror, amazement, or horror **:** SHOCKED

ag·ile \ˈa-jəl, -ˌjī(-ə)l\ *adj* [MF, fr. L *agilis,* fr. *agere* to drive, act — more at AGENT] (1581) **1 :** marked by ready ability to move with quick easy grace ⟨an ~ dancer⟩ **2 :** having a quick resourceful and adaptable character ⟨an ~ mind⟩ — **ag·ile·ly** \-jə(l)-lē, -ˌjī(l)-lē\ *adv*

agil·i·ty \ə-ˈji-lə-tē\ *n, pl* **-ties** (15c) **:** the quality or state of being agile **:** NIMBLENESS, DEXTERITY ⟨played with increasing ~⟩

agin \ə-ˈgin\ *dial var of* AGAINST

aging *pres part of* AGE

agism *var of* AGEISM

ag·i·ta \ˈa-jə-tə\ *n* [S It dial. pron. of It *acido,* lit., heartburn, acid, fr. L *acidus*] (1982) **:** a feeling of agitation or anxiety

ag·i·tate \ˈa-jə-ˌtāt\ *vb* **-tat·ed; -tat·ing** [L *agitatus,* pp. of *agitare,* freq. of *agere* to drive — more at AGENT] *vt* (15c) **1 a** *obs* **:** to give motion to **b :** to move with an irregular, rapid, or violent action ⟨the storm *agitated* the sea⟩ **2 :** to excite and often trouble the mind or feelings of **:** DISTURB **3 a :** to discuss excitedly and earnestly **b :** to stir up public discussion of ~ *vi* **:** to attempt to arouse public feeling ⟨*agitated* for better schools⟩ ***syn*** see SHAKE, DISCOMPOSE — **ag·i·tat·ed·ly** *adv* — **ag·i·ta·tion** \ˌa-jə-ˈtā-shən\ *n* — **ag·i·ta·tion·al** \-shnəl, -shə-nᵊl\ *adj*

ag·i·ta·tive \ˈa-jə-ˌtā-tiv\ *adj* (1687) **:** causing agitation

ag·i·ta·to \ˌa-jə-ˈtä-(ˌ)tō\ *adv or adj* [It, lit., agitated, fr. L *agitatus*] (ca. 1801) **:** in a restless and agitated manner — used as a direction in music

ag·i·ta·tor \ˈa-jə-ˌtā-tər\ *n* (1663) **:** one that agitates: as **a :** one who stirs up public feeling on controversial issues ⟨political ~*s*⟩ **b :** a device or an apparatus for stirring or shaking

ag·it·prop \ˈa-jət-ˌpräp\ *n* [Russ, ultim. fr. *agitatsiya* agitation + *propaganda*] (1935) **:** PROPAGANDA; *esp* **:** political propaganda promulgated chiefly in literature, drama, music, or art — **agitprop** *adj*

AGL *abbr* above ground level

Aglaia \ə-ˈglī-ə, -ˈglā-ə\ *n* [L, fr. Gk] (1579) **:** one of the three Graces

aglare \ə-ˈgler\ *adj* (1866) **:** GLARING ⟨his eyes ~ with fury⟩

agleam \ə-ˈglēm\ *adj* (1854) **:** gleaming esp. with reflected light

ag·let \ˈa-glət\ *n* [ME, fr. MF *aguillette, aiguillette,* fr. OF, dim. of *aguille, aiguille* needle, fr. LL *acicula, acucula* ornamental pin, dim. of L *acus* needle, pin — more at ACUTE] (15c) **1 :** the plain or ornamental tag covering the ends of a lace or point **2 :** any of various ornamental studs, cords, or pins worn on clothing

agley \ə-ˈglā, -ˈglē, -ˈglī\ *adv* [Sc, fr. 1*a-* + *gley* to squint] (1785) *chiefly Scot* **:** AWRY, WRONG ⟨the best-laid schemes o' mice an' men gang aft ~ —Robert Burns⟩

aglit·ter \ə-ˈgli-tər\ *adj* (1865) **:** glittering esp. with reflected light

aglow \ə-ˈglō\ *adj* (1817) **:** glowing esp. with warmth or excitement

agly·cone \a-ˈglī-ˌkōn\ *also* **agly·con** \-ˌkän\ *n* [ISV *a-* (fr. Gk *ha-,* together) + *glyc-* + *-one, -on*] (1925) **:** an organic compound (as a phenol or alcohol) combined with the sugar portion of a glycoside

AGN *abbr* active galactic nucleus; active galactic nuclei

1**ag·nate** \ˈag-ˌnāt\ *n* [L *agnatus,* fr. pp. of *agnasci* to be born in addition to, fr. *ad-* + *nasci* to be born — more at NATION] (1534) **1 :** a relative whose kinship is traceable exclusively through males **2 :** a paternal kinsman

2**agnate** *adj* (1782) **1 :** ALLIED, AKIN **2 :** related through male descent or on the father's side — **ag·nat·ic** \ag-ˈna-tik\ *adj*

Ag·ne·an \ˈäg-nē-ən\ *n* [*Agni,* ancient kingdom in Turkestan] (1939) **:** TOCHARIAN A

ag·nize \ag-ˈnīz\ *vt* **ag·nized; ag·niz·ing** [L *agnoscere* to acknowledge (fr. *ad-* + *noscere* to know) + E *-ize* (as in *recognize*) — more at KNOW] (1535) *archaic* **:** RECOGNIZE, ACKNOWLEDGE

ag·no·lot·ti \ˌän-yə-ˈlä-tē, -ˈlȯ-\ *n, pl* **agnolotti** [It, pl. of *agnolotto, agnellotto,* alter. of *anellotto,* dim. of *anello* ring, fr. L *anellus,* dim. of *anus* ring — more at ANUS] (1953) **:** pasta in the form of semicircular cases containing a filling (as of meat, cheese, or vegetables)

ag·no·men \ag-ˈnō-mən\ *n, pl* **-nom·i·na** \-ˈnä-mə-nə\ *or* **-no·mens** [L, irreg. fr. *ad-* + *nomen* name — more at NAME] (1665) **:** an additional cognomen given to a person by the ancient Romans (as in honor of some achievement)

ag·no·sia \ag-ˈnō-zhə, -shə\ *n* [NL, fr. Gk *agnōsia* ignorance, fr. *a-* + *gnōsis* knowledge, fr. *gignōskein*] (ca. 1900) **:** loss or diminution of the ability to recognize familiar objects or stimuli usu. as a result of brain damage

1**ag·nos·tic** \ag-ˈnäs-tik, əg-\ *n* [Gk *agnōstos* unknown, unknowable, fr. *a-* + *gnōstos* known, fr. *gignōskein* to know — more at KNOW] (1869) **1 :** a person who holds the view that any ultimate reality (as God) is unknown and prob. unknowable; *broadly* **:** one who is not committed to believing in either the existence or the nonexistence of God or a god **2 :** a person unwilling to commit to an opinion about something ⟨political ~*s*⟩ — **ag·nos·ti·cism** \-tə-ˌsi-zəm\ *n*

2**agnostic** *adj* (1873) **1 :** of, relating to, or being an agnostic or the beliefs of agnostics **2 :** NONCOMMITTAL, UNDOGMATIC

Ag·nus Dei \ˌäg-ˌnu̇s-ˈdā(-ˌē), -ˌnüs-; ˌän-yu̇s-; ˌag-nəs-\ *n* [ME, fr. LL, lamb of God; fr. its opening words] (14c) **1 :** a liturgical prayer addressed to Christ as Savior **2 :** an image of a lamb often with a halo and a banner and cross used as a symbol of Christ

ago \ə-ˈgō\ *adj or adv* [ME *agon, ago,* fr. pp. of *agon* to pass away, fr. OE *āgān,* fr. *ā-* (perfective prefix) + *gān* to go — more at ABIDE, GO] (14c) **:** earlier than the present time ⟨10 years ~⟩

agog \ə-ˈgäg\ *adj* [MF *en gogues* in mirth] (1559) **:** full of intense interest or excitement **:** EAGER ⟨kids all ~ over new toys⟩

1**a–go–go** \ä-ˈgō-(ˌ)gō, ə-\ *n* [*Whisky à Gogo,* café and discotheque in Paris, France, fr. F *à gogo* galore, fr. MF] (1965) **:** a nightclub for dancing to popular music **:** DISCO

2**a–go–go** *adj* (1965) **1 :** GO-GO 1 **2 :** being in a whirl of motion **3 :** being up-to-date — often used postpositively

-agogue *n comb form* [F & NL; F, fr. LL *-agogus* promoting the expulsion of, fr. Gk *-agōgos,* fr. *agein* to lead; NL *-agogon,* fr. Gk, neut. of *-agōgos* — more at AGENT] **:** substance that promotes the secretion or expulsion of ⟨emmen*agogue*⟩

agon \ˈä-ˌgän, ˈa-, ä-ˈgōn\ *n* [Gk *agōn*] (1600) **:** CONFLICT; *esp* **:** the dramatic conflict between the chief characters in a literary work

ag·o·nal \ˈa-gə-nᵊl\ *adj* (1901) **:** of, relating to, or associated with agony and esp. the death agony

agone \ə-ˈgȯn *also* -ˈgän\ *adj or adv* (14c) *archaic* **:** AGO

ag·o·nise, agonised, agonising *Brit var of* AGONIZE, AGONIZED, AGONIZING

ag·o·nist \ˈa-gə-nist\ *n* [LL *agonista* competitor, fr. Gk *agōnistēs,* fr. *agōnizesthai* to contend, fr. *agōn*] (ca. 1623) **1 :** one that is engaged in a struggle **2** [fr. *antagonist*] **a :** a muscle that is controlled by the action of an antagonist with which it is paired **b :** a chemical substance capable of combining with a specific receptor on a cell and initiating the same reaction or activity typically produced by the binding endogenous substance ⟨dopaminergic ~*s*⟩ — compare ANTAGONIST 2b

ag·o·nis·tic \ˌa-gə-ˈnis-tik\ *adj* (1648) **1 :** of or relating to the athletic contests of ancient Greece **2 :** ARGUMENTATIVE **3 :** striving for effect **:** STRAINED **4 :** of, relating to, or being aggressive or defensive social interaction (as fighting, fleeing, or submitting) between individuals usu. of the same species — **ag·o·nis·ti·cal·ly** \-ti-k(ə-)lē\ *adv*

ag·o·nize \ˈa-gə-ˌnīz\ *vb* **-nized; -niz·ing** *vt* (1583) **:** to cause to suffer agony **:** TORTURE ~ *vi* **1 :** to suffer agony, torture, or anguish ⟨~*s* over every decision⟩ **2 :** STRUGGLE

agonized *adj* (1583) **:** characterized by, suffering, or expressing agony

agonizing *adj* (1593) **:** causing agony — **ag·o·niz·ing·ly** *adv*

ag·o·ny \ˈa-gə-nē\ *n, pl* **-nies** [ME *agonie,* fr. LL *agonia,* fr. Gk *agōnia* struggle, anguish, fr. *agōn* gathering, contest for a prize, fr. *agein* to lead, celebrate — more at AGENT] (14c) **1 a :** intense pain of mind or body **:** ANGUISH, TORTURE **b :** the struggle that precedes death **2 :** a violent struggle or contest **3 :** a strong sudden display (as of joy or delight) **:** OUTBURST ***syn*** see DISTRESS

agony aunt *n* (1975) *chiefly Brit* **:** one who writes an agony column

agony column *n* (1863) **1** *chiefly Brit* **:** a newspaper column of personal advertisements relating esp. to missing relatives or friends **2** *chiefly Brit* **:** a newspaper column that includes letters from readers seeking personal advice and the columnist's replies

1**ag·o·ra** \ˈa-gə-rə\ *n, pl* **-ras** *or* **-rae** \-ˌrē, -ˌrī\ [Gk, fr. *ageirein* to gather] (1598) **:** a gathering place; *esp* **:** the marketplace in ancient Greece

2**ago·ra** \ˌä-gə-ˈrä\ *n, pl* **ago·rot** \-ˈrōt\ [ModHeb *ăgōrāh,* fr. Heb, a small coin] (1963) — see *shekel* at MONEY table

ag·o·ra·pho·bia \ˌa-g(ə-)rə-ˈfō-bē-ə\ *n* [NL, fr. Gk *agora* + NL *-phobia*] (1873) **:** abnormal fear of being helpless in an embarrassing or unescapable situation that is characterized esp. by the avoidance of open or public places — **ag·o·ra·phobe** \ˈa-g(ə-)rə-ˌfōb\ *n* — **ag·o·ra·pho·bic** \-ˈfō-bik\ *adj or n*

agou·ti \ə-ˈgü-tē\ *n* [F, fr. Sp *agutí,* ultim. fr. Tupi *akutí*] (1625) **1 :** any of a genus (*Dasyprocta*) of tropical American rodents about the size of a rabbit **2 :** a grizzled color of fur resulting from the barring of each hair in several alternate dark and light bands

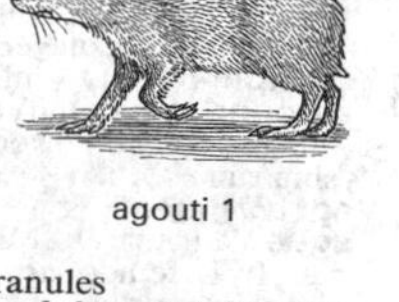

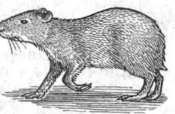

agouti 1

agr *or* **agric** *abbr* agricultural; agriculture

agrafe *or* **agraffe** \ə-ˈgraf\ *n* [F *agrafe*] (1643) **:** a hook-and-loop fastening; *esp* **:** an ornamental clasp used on armor or costumes

agran·u·lo·cyte \(ˌ)ā-ˈgran-yə-lō-ˌsīt\ *n* (ca. 1923) **:** a white blood cell without cytoplasmic granules

agran·u·lo·cy·to·sis \ˌā-ˌgran-yə-lō-ˌsī-ˈtō-səs\ *n, pl* **-to·ses** \-ˈtō-ˌsēz\ [NL] (1927) **:** an acute febrile condition marked by severe decrease in blood granulocytes and often associated with the use of certain drugs

ag·ra·pha \ˈa-grə-fə\ *n pl* [Gk, neut. pl. of *agraphos* unwritten, fr. *a-* + *graphein* to write — more at CARVE] (1890) **:** sayings of Jesus not in the canonical gospels but found in other New Testament or early Christian writings

agraph·ia \(ˌ)ā-ˈgra-fē-ə\ *n* [NL, fr. 2*a-* + Gk *graphein* to write] (1871) **:** the pathologic loss of the ability to write

1**agrar·i·an** \ə-ˈgrer-ē-ən\ *adj* [L *agrarius,* fr. *agr-, ager* field — more at ACRE] (1600) **1 :** of or relating to fields or lands or their tenure **2 a :** of, relating to, or characteristic of farmers or their way of life ⟨~ values⟩ **b :** organized or designed to promote agricultural interests

2**agrarian** *n* (1818) **:** a member of an agrarian party or movement

agrar·i·an·ism \-ē-ə-ˌni-zəm\ *n* (1830) **:** a social or political movement designed to bring about land reforms or to improve the economic status of the farmer

agree \ə-ˈgrē\ *vb* **agreed; agree·ing** [ME, fr. AF *agreer,* fr. *a gre* at will, fr. *a* (fr. L *ad*) + *gre* will, pleasure, fr. L *gratum,* neut. of *gratus*

\ə\ **abut** \ᵊ\ **kitten, F table** \ər\ **further** \a\ **ash** \ā\ **ace** \ä\ **mop, mar** \au̇\ **out** \ch\ **chin** \e\ **bet** \ē\ **easy** \g\ **go** \i\ **hit** \ī\ **ice** \j\ **job** \ŋ\ **sing** \ō\ **go** \ȯ\ **law** \ȯi\ **boy** \th\ **thin** \t͟h\ **the** \ü\ **loot** \u̇\ **foot** \y\ **yet** \zh\ **vision, beige** \k, ⁿ, œ, ue, ʸ\ *see* **Guide to Pronunciation**

pleasing, agreeable — more at GRACE] *vt* (15c) **1 a :** to concur in (as an opinion) **:** ADMIT, CONCEDE ⟨~*s* that he is right⟩ **b :** to consent to as a course of action ⟨*agreed* to sell him the house⟩ **2** *chiefly Brit* **:** to settle on by common consent **:** ARRANGE ⟨I *agreed* rental terms with him —Eric Bennett⟩ ~ *vi* **1 :** to accept or concede something (as the views or wishes of another) ⟨~ to a plan⟩ **2 a :** to achieve or be in harmony (as of opinion, feeling, or purpose) ⟨we ~ in our taste in music⟩ **b :** to get along together **c :** to come to terms ⟨~ on a fair division of profits⟩ **3 a :** to be similar **:** CORRESPOND ⟨both copies ~⟩ **b :** to be consistent ⟨the story ~*s* with the facts⟩ **4 :** to be fitting, pleasing, or healthful **:** SUIT ⟨this climate ~*s* with him⟩ **5 :** to have an inflectional form denoting identity or other regular correspondence in a grammatical category (as gender, number, case, or person)

syn AGREE, CONCUR, COINCIDE mean to come into or be in harmony regarding a matter of opinion. AGREE implies complete accord usually attained by discussion and adjustment of differences ⟨on some points we all can *agree*⟩. CONCUR often implies approval of someone else's statement or decision ⟨if my wife *concurs,* it's a deal⟩. COINCIDE, used more often of opinions, judgments, wishes, or interests than of people, implies total agreement ⟨their wishes *coincide* exactly with my desire⟩. ***syn*** see in addition ASSENT

agree·able \ə-ˈgrē-ə-bəl\ *adj* (14c) **1 :** pleasing to the mind or senses esp. as according well with one's tastes or needs ⟨an ~ companion⟩ ⟨an ~ change⟩ **2 :** ready or willing to agree or consent **3 :** being in harmony **:** CONSONANT — **agree·abil·i·ty** \-ˌgrē-ə-ˈbi-lə-tē\ *n* — **agree·able·ness** \-ˈgrē-ə-bəl-nəs\ *n* — **agree·ably** \-blē\ *adv*

agree·ment \ə-ˈgrē-mənt\ *n* (14c) **1 a :** harmony of opinion, action, or character **:** CONCORD **b :** the act or fact of agreeing **2 a :** an arrangement as to a course of action **b :** COMPACT, TREATY **3 a :** a contract duly executed and legally binding **b :** the language or instrument embodying such a contract

ag·ri·busi·ness \ˈa-grə-ˌbiz-nəs, -nəz\ *n* [*agri*culture + *business*] (ca. 1955) **:** an industry engaged in the producing operations of a farm, the manufacture and distribution of farm equipment and supplies, and the processing, storage, and distribution of farm commodities

ag·ri·busi·ness·man \ˌa-grə-ˈbiz-nəs-ˌman, -mən, -nəz-\ *n* (1958) **:** a person who works in or manages an agribusiness

ag·ri·cul·tur·al \ˌa-gri-ˈkəl-ch(ə-)rəl\ *adj* (1776) **:** of, relating to, used in, or concerned with agriculture — **ag·ri·cul·tur·al·ly** *adv*

ag·ri·cul·ture \ˈa-gri-ˌkəl-chər\ *n* [ME, fr. MF, fr. L *agricultura,* fr. *ager* field + *cultura* cultivation — more at ACRE, CULTURE] (15c) **:** the science, art, or practice of cultivating the soil, producing crops, and raising livestock and in varying degrees the preparation and marketing of the resulting products **:** FARMING — **ag·ri·cul·tur·ist** \ˌa-gri-ˈkəl-ch(ə-)rist\ *or* **ag·ri·cul·tur·al·ist** \-ch(ə-)rə-list\ *n*

ag·ri·mo·ny \ˈa-grə-ˌmō-nē\ *n, pl* **-nies** [ME, fr. AF & L; AF *egremoine,* fr. L *agrimonia,* MS var. of *argemonia,* fr. Gk *argemōnē*] (14c) **:** any of a genus (*Agrimonia* and esp. *A. eupatoria*) of herbs of the rose family having compound leaves, slender spikes of small yellow flowers, and fruits like burs

ag·ri·tour·ism \ˌa-gri-ˈtu̇r-ˌi-zəm\ *n* [*agri*culture + *tourism*] (1978) **:** the practice of touring agricultural areas to see farms and often to participate in farm activities

agro- *comb form* [F, fr. Gk, fr. *agros* field — more at ACRE] **1 :** of or belonging to fields or soil **:** agricultural ⟨*agro*chemical⟩ **2 :** agricultural and ⟨*agro*-industrial⟩

ag·ro·chem·i·cal \ˌa-grō-ˈke-mi-kəl\ *also* **ag·ri·chem·i·cal** \ˌa-gri-\ *n* (1956) **:** an agricultural chemical (as an herbicide or an insecticide)

ag·ro·ecol·o·gy \ˌa-grō-ē-ˈkä-lə-jē, -i-ˈkä-, -e-ˈkä-\ *n* (1967) **:** an ecological approach to agriculture that views agricultural areas as ecosystems and is concerned with the ecological impact of agricultural practices — **ag·ro·eco·log·i·cal** \-ˌē-kə-ˈlä-ji-kəl, -ˌe-kə-\ *adj*

ag·ro·for·est·ry \ˌa-grō-ˈfȯr-ə-strē, -ˈfär-\ *n* (1977) **:** land management involving the growing of trees in association with food crops or pastures — **ag·ro·for·est·er** \-stər\ *n*

ag·ro–in·dus·tri·al \ˌa-grō-in-ˈdəs-trē-əl\ *adj* (1907) **:** of or relating to production (as of power for industry and water for irrigation) for both industrial and agricultural purposes

agron·o·my \ə-ˈgrä-nə-mē\ *n* [prob. fr. F *agronomie,* fr. *agro-* + *-nomie* -nomy] (1814) **:** a branch of agriculture dealing with field-crop production and soil management — **ag·ro·nom·ic** \ˌa-grə-ˈnä-mik\ *adj* — **ag·ro·nom·i·cal·ly** \-mi-k(ə-)lē\ *adv* — **agron·o·mist** \ə-ˈgrä-nə-mist\ *n*

aground \ə-ˈgrau̇nd\ *adv or adj* (13c) **1 :** on the ground ⟨planes aloft and ~⟩ **2 :** on or onto the shore or the bottom of a body of water ⟨a ship run ~⟩

agt *abbr* agent

ague \ˈā-(ˌ)gyü\ *n* [ME, fr. AF *ague,* fr. ML (*febris*) *acuta,* lit., sharp fever, fr. L, fem. of *acutus* sharp — more at ACUTE] (14c) **1 :** a fever (as malaria) marked by paroxysms of chills, fever, and sweating that recur at regular intervals **2 :** a fit of shivering — **agu·ish** \ˈā-ˌgyü-ish\ *adj*

[1]**ah** \ˈä\ *interj* [ME] (13c) — used to express delight, relief, regret, or contempt

[2]**ah** *var of* AAH

AH *abbr* **1** ampere-hour **2** anno hegirae **3** arts and humanities

aha \ä-ˈhä\ *interj* [ME] (14c) — used to express surprise, triumph, or derision

AHA \ˌā-(ˌ)āch-ˈā\ *n* (1991) **:** ALPHA HYDROXY ACID

Ahab \ˈā-ˌhab\ *n* [Heb *Aḥʼābh*] (1540) **:** a king of Israel in the ninth century B.C. and husband of Jezebel

aha moment *n* (1939) **:** a moment of sudden realization, inspiration, insight, recognition, or comprehension

ahchoo *var of* ACHOO

ahead \ə-ˈhed\ *adv or adj* (1596) **1 a :** in a forward direction or position **:** FORWARD **b :** in front **2 :** in, into, or for the future ⟨plan ~⟩ **3 :** in or toward a more advantageous position ⟨helped others to get ~⟩ **4 :** at or to an earlier time **:** in advance ⟨make payments ~⟩

ahead of *prep* (1613) **1 :** in front or advance of **2 :** in excess of

ahem *a throat-clearing sound; often read as* ə-ˈhem\ *interj* [imit.] (1603) — used esp. to attract attention or to express disapproval or embarrassment

ahi \ˈä-hē\ *n* [Hawaiian *ʻahi*] (1898) **1 :** YELLOWFIN TUNA **2 :** BIGEYE TUNA

ahim·sa \ə-ˈhim-ˌsä\ *n* [Skt *ahiṁsā* noninjury] (1875) **:** the Hindu and Buddhist doctrine of refraining from harming any living being

ahis·tor·i·cal \ˌā-hi-ˈstȯr-i-kəl, -ˈtär-\ *or* **ahis·tor·ic** \-ik\ *adj* (1911) **:** not concerned with or related to history, historical development, or tradition ⟨an ~ attitude⟩; *also* **:** historically inaccurate or ignorant ⟨an ~ version of events⟩ — **ahis·tor·i·cal·ly** \-i-k(ə-)lē\ *adv* — **ahis·tor·i·cism** \-ə-ˌsi-zəm\ *n* — **ahis·to·ric·i·ty** \-ˌhis-tə-ˈri-sə-tē\ *n*

ahold \ə-ˈhōld\ *n* [prob. fr. the phrase *a hold*] (1854) **:** HOLD ⟨if you could get ~ of a representative —Norman Mailer⟩

-aholic *also* **-oholic** *n comb form* [*alcoholic*] **1 :** one who feels compulsively the need to (do something) ⟨work*aholic*⟩ **2 :** one who likes (something) to excess ⟨choc*oholic*⟩

A horizon \ˈā-\ *n* (1907) **:** the uppermost dark-colored layer of a soil consisting largely of partly disintegrated organic debris

ahoy \ə-ˈhȯi\ *interj* [*a-* (as in *aha*) + *hoy*] (1748) — used in hailing ⟨ship ~⟩

Ah·ri·man \ˈär-i-mən, -ˌmän\ *n* [Pers, modif. of Av *aṅrō mainyuš* hostile spirit] (1728) **:** Ahura Mazda's antagonist who is a spirit of darkness and evil in Zoroastrianism

Ahu·ra Maz·da \ə-ˌhu̇r-ə-ˈmaz-də, ä-ˌhu̇r-\ *n* [Av *Ahuramazda,* lit., wise god] (1850) **:** the Supreme Being represented as a deity of goodness and light in Zoroastrianism

AI *abbr* **1** ad interim **2** airborne intercept **3** air interception **4** artificial insemination **5** artificial intelligence

AIA *abbr* American Institute of Architects

Ai·as \ˈī-əs\ *n* [Gk] (1833) **:** AJAX

ai·blins \ˈā-blənz\ *adv* [*able* + *-lings, -lins* -lings] (ca. 1605) *chiefly Scot* **:** PERHAPS

[1]**aid** \ˈād\ *vb* [ME *eyden,* fr. AF *aider,* fr. L *adjutare,* freq. of *adjuvare,* fr. *ad-* + *juvare* to help] *vt* (15c) **:** to provide with what is useful or necessary in achieving an end ~ *vi* **:** to give assistance — **aid·er** *n*

[2]**aid** *n* (15c) **1 :** a subsidy granted to the king by the English parliament until the 18th century for an extraordinary purpose **2 a :** the act of helping **b :** help given **:** ASSISTANCE ⟨providing ~ and comfort⟩; *specif* **:** tangible means of assistance (as money or supplies) **3 a :** AIDE **b :** something by which assistance is given **:** an assisting device ⟨an ~ to understanding⟩ ⟨a visual ~⟩; *esp* **:** HEARING AID **4 :** a tribute paid by a vassal to his lord

AID *abbr* **1** Agency for International Development **2** artificial insemination by donor

aide \ˈād\ *n* [short for *aide-de-camp*] (1777) **:** a person who acts as an assistant; *specif* **:** a military officer who acts as an assistant to a superior officer

aide–de–camp \ˌād-di-ˈkamp, -ˈkäⁿ\ *n, pl* **aides–de–camp** \ˌād(z)-di-\ [F *aide de camp,* lit., camp assistant] (1670) **:** a military aide; *also* **:** a civilian aide usu. to an executive

aide–mé·moire \ˌād-mām-ˈwär\ *n, pl* **aide–mémoire** [F, fr. *aider* to aid + *mémoire* memory] (1836) **1 :** an aid to the memory; *esp* **:** a mnemonic device **2 :** a written summary or outline of important items of a proposed agreement or diplomatic communication

aid·man \ˈād-ˌman\ *n* (1941) **:** an army medical corpsman attached to a field unit

AIDS \ˈādz\ *n* [*a*cquired *i*mmuno*d*eficiency *s*yndrome] (1982) **:** a disease of the human immune system that is characterized cytologically esp. by reduction in the numbers of CD4-bearing helper T cells to 20 percent or less of normal thereby rendering the subject highly vulnerable to life-threatening conditions (as Pneumocystis carinii pneumonia) and to some (as Kaposi's sarcoma) that become life-threatening and that is caused by infection with HIV commonly transmitted in infected blood esp. during illicit intravenous drug use and in bodily secretions (as semen) during sexual intercourse

AIDS–related complex *n* (1984) **:** a group of symptoms (as fever, weight loss, and lymphadenopathy) that is associated with the presence of antibodies to HIV and is followed by the development of AIDS in a certain proportion of cases

AIDS virus *n* (1983) **:** HIV

ai·grette \ā-ˈgret, ˈā-ˌ\ *n* [F, plume, egret, fr. MF — more at EGRET] (1630) **1 :** a spray of feathers (as of the egret) for the head **2 :** a spray of gems worn on a hat or in the hair

ai·guille \ā-ˈgwēl, -ˈgwē\ *n* [F, lit., needle — more at AGLET] (1809) **:** a sharp-pointed pinnacle of rock

ai·guil·lette \ˌā-gwi-ˈlet\ *n* [F — more at AGLET] (1812) **:** AGLET; *specif* **:** a shoulder cord worn by designated military aides — compare FOURRAGÈRE

ai·ki·do \ˌī-ki-ˈdō, ī-ˈkē-(ˌ)dō\ *n* [Jp *aikidō,* fr. *ai-* match, coordinate + *ki* breath, spirit + *dō* art, way] (1956) **:** a Japanese art of self-defense employing locks and holds and utilizing the principle of nonresistance to cause an opponent's own momentum to work against him

[1]**ail** \ˈāl\ *vb* [ME *eilen,* fr. OE *eglan;* akin to Goth *agljan* to harm] *vt* (bef. 12c) **:** to give physical or emotional pain, discomfort, or trouble to ~ *vi* **:** to have something the matter; *esp* **:** to suffer ill health

[2]**ail** *n* (13c) **:** AILMENT

ai·lan·thus \ā-ˈlan(t)-thəs\ *n* [NL, fr. Kamarian (Austronesian language of the Piru Bay region, Seram) *ai lanito,* lit., the sky tree, or fr. a cognate phrase in a related central Moluccan language] (1789) **:** any of a small Asian genus (*Ailanthus* of the family Simaroubaceae, the ailanthus family) of chiefly tropical trees and shrubs with bitter bark, pinnate leaves, and terminal panicles of ill-scented greenish flowers; *esp* **:** TREE OF HEAVEN

ai·le·ron \ˈā-lə-ˌrän\ *n* [F, fr. dim. of *aile* wing — more at AISLE] (1909) **:** a movable airfoil at the trailing edge of an airplane wing that is used for imparting a rolling motion esp. in banking for turns — see AIRPLANE illustration

ail·ment \ˈāl-mənt\ *n* (1657) **1 :** a bodily disorder or chronic disease **2 :** UNREST, UNEASINESS

ai·lu·ro·phile \ī-ˈlu̇r-ə-ˌfī(-ə)l, ā-\ *n* [Gk *ailouros* cat] (1914) **:** a cat fancier **:** a lover of cats

ai·lu·ro·phobe \-ˌfōb\ *n* (1905) **:** a person who hates or fears cats

[1]**aim** \ˈām\ *vb* [ME, fr. AF *aesmer & esmer;* AF *aesmer,* fr. *a-* (fr. L *ad-*) + *esmer* to estimate, fr. L *aestimare*] *vi* (14c) **1 :** to direct a course; *specif* **:** to point a weapon at an object **2 :** ASPIRE, INTEND ⟨she ~*s* to win⟩ ~ *vt* **1** *obs* **:** GUESS, CONJECTURE **2 a :** POINT ⟨~ a gun⟩ **b :** to direct toward a specified object or goal ⟨a story ~*ed* at children⟩

[2]**aim** *n* (14c) **1** *obs* **:** MARK, TARGET **2 a :** the pointing of a weapon at a mark ⟨take careful ~⟩ **b :** the ability to hit a target ⟨a shooter with good ~⟩ **c :** a weapon's accuracy or effectiveness ⟨the gun's ~ is

off⟩ 3 *obs* **a** : CONJECTURE, GUESS **b** : the directing of effort toward a goal **4** : a clearly directed intent or purpose ⟨our ~ is to win⟩ ***syn*** see INTENTION — **aim·less** \-ləs\ *adj* — **aim·less·ly** *adv* — **aim·less·ness** *n*

AIM *abbr* American Indian Movement

ain \ˈān\ *adj* [prob. fr. ON *eiginn*] (1721) *Scot* : OWN

ain't \ˈānt\ [contr. of *are not*] (1749) **1** : am not : are not : is not **2** : have not : has not **3** : do not : does not : did not — used in some varieties of Black English

usage Although widely disapproved as nonstandard and more common in the habitual speech of the less educated, *ain't* in senses 1 and 2 is flourishing in American English. It is used in both speech and writing to catch attention and to gain emphasis ⟨the wackiness of movies, once so deliciously amusing, *ain't* funny anymore —Richard Schickel⟩ ⟨I am telling you—there *ain't* going to be any blackmail —R. M. Nixon⟩. It is used esp. in journalistic prose as part of a consistently informal style ⟨the creative process *ain't* easy —Mike Royko⟩. This informal *ain't* is commonly distinguished from habitual *ain't* by its frequent occurrence in fixed constructions and phrases ⟨well—class it *ain't* —Cleveland Amory⟩ ⟨for money? say it *ain't* so, Jimmy! —Andy Rooney⟩ ⟨you *ain't* seen nothing yet⟩ ⟨that *ain't* hay⟩ ⟨two out of three *ain't* bad⟩ ⟨if it *ain't* broke, don't fix it⟩. In fiction *ain't* is used for purposes of characterization; in familiar correspondence it tends to be the mark of a warm personal friendship. It is also used for metrical reasons in popular songs ⟨*Ain't* She Sweet⟩ ⟨It *Ain't* Necessarily So⟩. Our evidence shows British use to be much the same as American.

Ai·nu \ˈī-(ˌ)nü\ *n, pl* **Ainu** *or* **Ainus** [Ainu *aynu* person] (1817) **1** : a member of an indigenous people of the Japanese archipelago, the Kuril Islands, and part of Sakhalin Island **2** : the language of the Ainu people

ai·o·li \(ˌ)ī-ˈō-lē, (ˌ)ā-\ *n* [Occitan, fr. *ai* garlic + *oli* oil] (1896) : a mayonnaise flavored with garlic and sometimes other ingredients (as red pepper)

[1]**air** \ˈer\ *n, often attrib* [ME, fr. AF, fr. L *aer*, fr. Gk *aēr*] (14c) **1 a** *archaic* : BREATH **b** : the mixture of invisible odorless tasteless gases (as nitrogen and oxygen) that surrounds the earth **c** : a light breeze **2 a** : empty space **b** : NOTHINGNESS ⟨vanished into thin ~⟩ **c** : a sudden severance of relations ⟨she gave me the ~⟩ **3** [prob. trans. of It *aria*] **a** : TUNE, MELODY **b** *Elizabethan & Jacobean music* : an accompanied song or melody in usu. strophic form **c** : the chief voice part or melody in choral music **4 a** : outward appearance of a thing ⟨an ~ of luxury⟩ **b** : a surrounding or pervading influence : ATMOSPHERE ⟨an ~ of mystery⟩ **c** : the look, appearance, or bearing of a person esp. as expressive of some personal quality or emotion : DEMEANOR ⟨an ~ of dignity⟩ **d** : an artificial or affected manner ⟨put on ~*s*⟩ **5** : public utterance ⟨he gave ~ to his opinion⟩ **6** : COMPRESSED AIR **7 a** (1) : AIRCRAFT ⟨go by ~⟩ (2) : AVIATION ⟨~ safety⟩ ⟨~ rights⟩ (3) : AIR FORCE ⟨~ headquarters⟩ **b** (1) : the medium of transmission of radio waves; *also* : RADIO, TELEVISION ⟨went on the ~⟩ (2) : AIRTIME **8** : a football offense utilizing primarily the forward pass ⟨trailing by 20 points, the team took to the ~⟩ **9** : an air-conditioning system **10** : the height achieved in performing an aerial maneuver ⟨a snowboarder catching big ~⟩; *also* : the maneuver itself ***syn*** see POSE — **air·less** \-ləs\ *adj* — **air·less·ness** *n* — **in the air** : in wide circulation : ABOUT — **up in the air** : not yet settled

[2]**air** *vt* (1530) **1** : to expose to the air for drying, purifying, or refreshing : VENTILATE — often used with *out* **2** : to expose to public view or bring to public notice **3** : to transmit by radio or television ⟨~ a program⟩ ~ *vi* **1** : to become exposed to the open air **2** : to become broadcast ⟨the program ~*s* daily⟩ ***syn*** see EXPRESS

air bag *n* (1969) : an automobile safety device consisting of a bag designed to inflate automatically esp. in front of an occupant in case of collision

air ball *n* (1981) : a missed shot in basketball that fails to touch the rim and backboard

air base *n* (1915) : a military base chiefly for the operation of aircraft

air bladder *n* (1731) : a sac containing gas and esp. air; *esp* : a hydrostatic organ present in most fishes that serves as an accessory respiratory organ

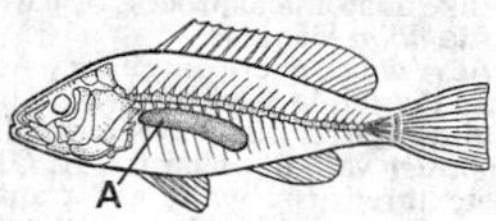

A air bladder

air·boat \ˈer-ˌbōt\ *n* (1914) : a shallow-draft boat driven by an airplane propeller and steered by an airplane rudder

air·borne \-ˌbȯrn\ *adj* (1637) **1** : done or being in the air : being off the ground: as **a** : carried through the air (as by an aircraft) **b** : supported esp. by aerodynamic forces or propelled through the air by force ⟨a plane becoming ~⟩ **c** : transported or carried by the air ⟨~ allergens⟩ **2** : trained for deployment by air and esp. by parachute ⟨~ troops⟩

air brake *n* (1846) **1** : a brake operated by a piston driven by compressed air **2** : a surface that may be projected into the airstream for increasing drag and lowering the speed of an airplane

air–breath·ing \ˈer-ˌbrē-thiŋ\ *adj* (1938) : of, employing, or being an engine that requires air for combustion

[1]**air·brush** \-ˌbrəsh\ *n* (1884) : an atomizer for applying by compressed air a fine spray (as of paint or liquid color)

[2]**airbrush** *vt* (1907) : to paint, treat, or alter (as to conceal imperfections) with or as if with an airbrush ⟨~ a photograph⟩

air·burst \-ˌbərst\ *n* (1914) : the burst of a shell or bomb in the air

Air·bus \-ˌbəs\ *trademark* — used for a subsonic jet passenger airplane

air chief marshal *n* (1919) : a commissioned officer in the British air force who ranks with a general in the army

air commodore *n* (1919) : a commissioned officer in the British air force who ranks with a brigadier in the army

air–con·di·tion \ˌer-kən-ˈdi-shən\ *vt* [back-formation fr. *air conditioning*] (1914) : to equip (as a building) with an apparatus for washing air and controlling its humidity and temperature; *also* : to subject (air) to these processes — **air conditioner** *n* — **air–con·di·tion·ing** \-ˈdi-sh(ə-)niŋ\ *n*

air·craft \ˈer-ˌkraft\ *n, pl* **aircraft** *often attrib* (1845) : a vehicle (as an airplane or balloon) for traveling through the air

aircraft carrier *n* (1917) : a warship with a flight deck on which aircraft can be launched and landed

air·crew \ˈer-ˌkrü\ *n* (1918) : the crew manning an airplane

air–cush·ion vehicle *n* (1958) : HOVERCRAFT

air dam *n* (1970) : a device attached to the underside of the front of an automobile to improve stability, aerodynamic performance, and engine cooling by redirecting the flow of air

air·date \-ˌdāt\ *n* (1950) : the scheduled date of a broadcast

air·drome \ˈer-ˌdrōm\ *n* [alter. of *aerodrome*] (1917) : AIRPORT

air·drop \-ˌdräp\ *n* (1943) : delivery of cargo, emergency supplies, or personnel by parachute from an airplane in flight — **air–drop** *vt* — **air–drop·pa·ble** \-ˌdrä-pə-bəl\ *adj*

[1]**air–dry** \-ˈdrī\ *adj* (1846) : dry to such a degree that no further moisture is given up on exposure to air

[2]**air–dry** *vt* (1886) : to dry by exposure to air ~ *vi* : to become dry by exposure to air

Aire·dale terrier \ˈer-ˌdāl-\ *n* [*Airedale*, valley of the Aire River, England] (1880) : any of a breed of large terriers with a hard, wiry, black-and-tan coat — called also *Airedale*

air·er \ˈer-ər\ *n* (1817) *Brit* : a frame on which clothes are aired or dried

air·fare \ˈer-ˌfer\ *n* (1917) : fare for travel by airplane

air·field \-ˌfēld\ *n* (1919) : an area of land from which aircraft operate: as **a** : AIRPORT **b** : AIR BASE

air·flow \-ˌflō\ *n* (1878) : a flow of air; *esp* : the motion of air (as around parts of an airplane in flight) relative to the surface of a body immersed in it

air·foil \-ˌfȯi(-ə)l\ *n* (1919) : a body (as an airplane wing or propeller blade) designed to provide a desired reaction force when in motion relative to the surrounding air

air force *n* (1911) **1** : the military organization of a nation for air warfare **2** : a unit of the U.S. Air Force higher than a division and lower than a command

air·frame \-ˌfrām\ *n* (1930) : the structure of an aircraft, rocket vehicle, or missile without the power plant; *also* : AIRCRAFT

air·freight \-ˈfrāt\ *n* (1918) : freight transport by air in volume; *also* : the charge for this service — **airfreight** *vt*

air·glow \-ˌglō\ *n* (1949) : light that is observed esp. during the night, that originates in the high atmosphere of a planet (as the earth), and that is associated with photochemical reactions of gases caused by solar radiation

air guitar *n* (1980) : an imaginary guitar that one pretends to play; *also* : the action of playing air guitar

air gun *n* (ca. 1753) **1** : a gun from which a projectile is propelled by compressed air **2** : any of various hand tools that work by compressed air; *esp* : AIRBRUSH

[1]**air·head** \-ˌhed\ *n* [[1]*air* + *-head* (as in *beachhead*)] (ca. 1943) : an area in hostile territory secured usu. by airborne troops for further use in bringing in troops and matériel by air

[2]**airhead** *n* (1971) : a mindless or stupid person — **air·head·ed** \-ˌhe-dəd\ *adj*

air·hole \-ˌhōl\ *n* (1601) : a hole to admit or discharge air

air·ing \ˈer-iŋ\ *n* (1587) **1** : exposure to air or heat for drying or freshening ⟨give the room an ~⟩ **2** : exposure to or exercise in the open air esp. to promote health or fitness **3** : exposure to public view or notice **4** : a radio or television broadcast

air–kiss \ˈer-ˌkis\ *vt* (1975) : to greet from a distance with a kissing motion of the lips — **air–kiss** *n*

air lane *n* (1909) : a path customarily followed by airplanes

air letter *n* (1918) **1** : an airmail letter **2** : a sheet of airmail stationery that can be folded and sealed with the message inside and the address outside

air·lift \ˈer-ˌlift\ *n* (1943) : a system of transporting cargo or passengers by aircraft often to or from an otherwise inaccessible area — **airlift** *vt*

air·line \-ˌlīn\ *n* (1901) : an air transportation system including its equipment, routes, operating personnel, and management

air line *n* (1813) : a straight line through the air between two points

air·lin·er \-ˌlī-nər\ *n* (1908) : an airplane operated by an airline

air lock *n* (1840) **1** : an intermediate chamber with two airtight doors or openings to permit passage between two dissimilar spaces (as two places of unequal atmospheric pressure) **2** : a stoppage of flow caused by air being in a part where liquid ought to circulate

air·mail \ˈer-ˌmāl\ *n* (1911) : the system of transporting mail by aircraft; *also* : the mail thus transported — **airmail** *vt*

air·man \-mən\ *n* (1873) **1** : a civilian or military pilot, aviator, or aviation technician **2** : an enlisted man in the air force: as **a** : an enlisted man of one of the three ranks below sergeant **b** : an enlisted man ranking above an airman basic and below an airman first class

airman basic *n* (1952) : an enlisted man of the lowest rank in the air force

airman first class *n* (1952) : an enlisted man in the air force ranking above an airman and below a sergeant

air·man·ship \ˈer-mən-ˌship\ *n* (1859) : skill in piloting or navigating aircraft

air marshal *n* (1919) **1** : a commissioned officer in the British air force who ranks with a lieutenant general in the army **2** : SKY MARSHAL

air mass *n* (1882) : a body of air extending hundreds or thousands of miles horizontally and sometimes as high as the stratosphere and maintaining as it travels nearly uniform conditions of temperature and humidity at any given level

air mattress *n* (1832) : MATTRESS 1b

Air Medal *n* (1942) : a U.S. military decoration awarded for meritorious achievement while participating in an aerial flight

air mile *n* (1907) : a mile in air travel

air–mind·ed \ˈer-ˈmīn-dəd\ *adj* (1924) : interested in aviation or in air travel — **air–mind·ed·ness** *n*

\ə\ **abut** \ᵊ\ kitten, F table \ər\ **further** \a\ **ash** \ā\ **ace** \ä\ mop, mar \au̇\ **out** \ch\ **chin** \e\ **bet** \ē\ **easy** \g\ **go** \i\ **hit** \ī\ **ice** \j\ **job** \ŋ\ **sing** \ō\ **go** \ȯ\ **law** \ȯi\ **boy** \th\ **thin** \t͟h\ **the** \ü\ **loot** \u̇\ **foot** \y\ yet \zh\ **vision**, beige \k̲, ⁿ, œ, ue, ʸ\ *see* Guide to Pronunciation

air·mo·bile \-ˌmō-bəl, -ˌbēl, -ˌbī(-ə)l\ *adj* (1959) **:** of, relating to, or being a military unit whose members are transported to combat areas usu. by helicopter
air·park \-ˌpärk\ *n* (1908) **:** a small airport usu. near an industrial area
air piracy *n* (1948) **:** the hijacking of a flying airplane **:** SKYJACKING
air·plane \ˈer-ˌplān\ *n* [alter. of *aeroplane*] (1906) **:** a powered heavier-than-air aircraft with fixed wings from which it derives most of its lift

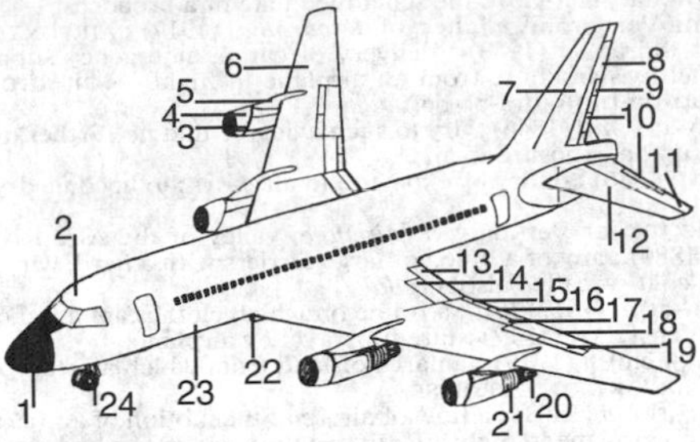

airplane: *1* weather radar, *2* cockpit, *3* jet engine, *4* engine pod, *5* pylon, *6* wing, *7* vertical stabilizer, *8* rudder, *9, 10* tabs, *11* elevator, *12* horizontal stabilizer, *13* inboard flap, *14* inboard spoiler, *15, 16* tabs, *17* aileron, *18* outboard flap, *19* outboard spoiler, *20* sound suppressor, *21* thrust reverser, *22* cabin air intake, *23* fuselage, *24* nose landing gear

air plant *n* (1798) **1 :** EPIPHYTE **2 :** any of several kalanchoes (esp. *Kalanchoe pinnata*)
air·play \-ˌplā\ *n* (1942) **:** the playing of a musical recording on the air by a radio station ⟨a song getting a lot of ~⟩
air pocket *n* (1912) **:** a condition of the atmosphere (as a local downdraft) that causes an airplane to drop suddenly
air police *n* (1927) **:** the military police of an air force
air·port \ˈer-ˌpȯrt\ *n* (1902) **:** a place from which aircraft operate that usu. has paved runways and maintenance facilities and often serves as a terminal
air·post \-ˈpōst\ *n* (1911) **:** AIRMAIL
air·pow·er \-ˌpau̇(-ə)r\ *n* (1908) **:** the military strength of a nation's air force
air pump *n* (1653) **:** a pump for exhausting air from a closed space or for compressing air or forcing it through other apparatus
air quotes *n pl* (1989) **:** a gesture made by raising and flexing the index and middle fingers of both hands that is used to call attention to a spoken word or expression
air rage *n* (1997) **:** an airline passenger's uncontrolled anger that is usu. expressed in aggressive or violent behavior
air raid *n* (1909) **:** an attack by armed airplanes on a surface target — usu. hyphenated when used attributively ⟨*air-raid* shelter⟩
air rifle *n* (1801) **:** a rifle whose projectile (as a BB or pellet) is propelled by compressed air or carbon dioxide
air right *n* (1922) **:** a property right to the space above a surface area or object
air sac *n* (ca. 1805) **1 :** one of the air-filled spaces in the body of a bird connected with the air passages of the lungs **2 :** ALVEOLUS 1b **3 :** a thin-walled dilation of a trachea occurring in many insects
air·screw \ˈer-ˌskrü\ *n* (1859) *chiefly Brit* **:** an airplane propeller
air·ship \-ˌship\ *n* (1826) **:** a lighter-than-air aircraft having propulsion and steering systems
air show *n* (1912) **:** an exhibition of aircraft and aviation skills
air·sick \-ˌsik\ *adj* (ca. 1785) **:** affected with motion sickness associated with flying — **air·sick·ness** *n*
air·space \-ˌspās\ *n* (1911) **:** the space lying above the earth or above a certain area of land or water; *esp* **:** the space lying above a nation and coming under its jurisdiction
air·speed \-ˌspēd\ *n* (1909) **:** the speed (as of an airplane) with relation to the air — compare GROUND SPEED
air·stream \-ˌstrēm\ *n* (1719) **:** a current of air; *specif* **:** AIRFLOW
air·strip \-ˌstrip\ *n* (1911) **:** a runway without normal air base or airport facilities
[1]**airt** \ˈärt, ˈert\ *n* [ME (Sc) *art,* fr. ScGael *àirt*] (15c) *chiefly Scot* **:** compass point **:** DIRECTION
[2]**airt** *vt* (ca. 1782) *chiefly Scot* **:** DIRECT, GUIDE
air taxi *n* (1919) **:** a small commercial airplane used for short flights between localities not served by scheduled airlines
air·tight \ˈer-ˌtīt\ *adj* (1728) **1 :** impermeable to air or nearly so ⟨an ~ seal⟩ **2 a :** having no noticeable weakness, flaw, or loophole ⟨an ~ argument⟩ **b :** permitting no opportunity for an opponent to score ⟨an ~ defense⟩ — **air·tight·ness** *n*
air·time \-ˌtīm\ *n* (1924) **1 :** the time or any part thereof that a radio or television station is on the air **2 :** the time at which a radio or television broadcast is scheduled to begin
air–to–air \ˌer-tə-ˈ(w)er\ *adj* (1939) **:** launched from one airplane in flight at another ⟨~ missiles⟩; *also* **:** involving aircraft in flight ⟨~ combat⟩
air vice–marshal *n* (1919) **:** a commissioned officer in the British air force who ranks with a major general in the army
air·wave \ˈer-ˌwāv\ *adj* (1944) **:** of, created for, or heard on the airwaves
air·waves \-ˌwāvz\ *n pl* (1900) **:** the medium of radio and television transmission — not used technically
air·way \-ˌwā\ *n* (1800) **1 :** a passage for a current of air (as in a mine or to the lungs) **2 :** a designated route along which airplanes fly from airport to airport; *esp* **:** such a route equipped with navigational aids **3 :** AIRLINE **4 :** a channel of a designated radio frequency for broadcasting or other radio communication
air·wor·thy \-ˌwər-t͟hē\ *adj* (1829) **:** fit for operation in the air ⟨kept the historic aircraft in ~ condition⟩ — **air·wor·thi·ness** *n*
airy \ˈer-ē\ *adj* **air·i·er; -est** (14c) **1 a :** of or relating to air **:** ATMOSPHERIC **b :** high in the air **:** LOFTY ⟨~ perches⟩ **c :** performed in air **:** AERIAL ⟨~ leaps⟩ **2 :** UNREAL, ILLUSORY ⟨~ romances⟩ **3 a :** being light and graceful in movement or manner **:** SPRIGHTLY, VIVACIOUS ⟨an ~ dance⟩ **b :** exceptionally light, delicate, or refined ⟨an ~ fragrance⟩ **4 a :** open to the free circulation of air ⟨an ~ room⟩ **b :** having openings or spaces ⟨~ lacework⟩ **5 :** AFFECTED, PROUD ⟨~ condescension⟩ — **air·i·ly** \ˈer-ə-lē\ *adv* — **air·i·ness** \-ē-nəs\ *n*
airy–fairy \-ˈfer-ē\ *adj* (1837) **1** *chiefly Brit* **:** DELICATE, FAIRYLIKE **2** *chiefly Brit* **:** lacking substance or purpose ⟨in . . . an ~, unserious, insufficiently careful fashion —*Times Lit. Supp.*⟩
aisle \ˈī(-ə)l\ *n* [ME *ile,* alter. of *ele,* fr. AF, lit., wing, fr. L *ala;* akin to OE *eaxl* shoulder, L *axis* axletree — more at AXIS] (15c) **1 :** the side of a church nave separated by piers from the nave proper **2 a** (1) **:** a passage (as in a theater or railroad passenger car) separating sections of seats (2) **:** such a passage regarded as separating opposing parties in a legislature ⟨supported by members on both sides of the ~⟩ **b :** a passage (as in a store or warehouse) for inside traffic
aisle·way \-ˌwā\ *n* (1872) **:** AISLE 2b
ait \ˈāt\ *n* [ME *eyt,* fr. OE **ēget,* by-form of *īggoth, igeoth,* fr. *īg* island — more at ISLAND] (bef. 12c) *Brit* **:** a little island
aitch \ˈāch\ *n* [F *hache,* fr. VL **hacca*] (ca. 1580) **:** the letter *h*
aitch·bone \ˈāch-ˌbōn\ *n* [ME *hachbon,* alter. (resulting from incorrect division of *a nachebon*) of ME **nachebon,* fr. ME *nache* buttock (fr. AF, fr. LL *natica,* fr. L *natis*) + *bon* bone] (15c) **1 :** the hipbone esp. of cattle **2 :** the cut of beef containing the aitchbone
ajar \ə-ˈjär\ *adj or adv* [earlier *on char,* fr. ME, fr. *on* + *char* turn — more at CHARE] (15c) **:** slightly open ⟨left the door ~⟩
Ajax \ˈā-ˌjaks\ *n* [L, fr. Gk *Aias*] (15c) **1 :** a Greek hero in the Trojan War who kills himself because the armor of Achilles is awarded to Odysseus **2 :** a fleet-footed Greek hero in the Trojan War
aji \ä-ˈhē\ *n* [AmerSp *ají,* fr. Taino *axí*] (1822) a chili pepper that ranges in pungency from mild to very hot
aju·ga \ˈa-jə-gə\ *n, pl* **-ga** *or* **-gas** [NL, fr. [2]*a-* + L *jugum* yoke — more at YOKE] (1806) **:** [1]BUGLE
AK *abbr* Alaska
aka *abbr* also known as
Akan \ˈä-ˌkän\ *n, pl* **Akan** *or* **Akans** (1694) **1 :** a member of any of the Akan-speaking peoples (as the Ashanti) **2 :** a Kwa language of southern Ghana and the southeast Ivory Coast
AKC *abbr* American Kennel Club
akee *var of* ACKEE
AK–47 \ˈā-ˈkā-ˌfȯr-tē-ˈse-vᵊn\ *n* [Russ *avtomat Kalashnikova 1947* Kalashnikov automatic rifle of 1947] (1962) **:** a Soviet-designed 7.62 mm (.30 cal.) gas-operated magazine-fed rifle for automatic or semiautomatic fire
akim·bo \ə-ˈkim-(ˌ)bō\ *adj or adv* [ME *in kenebowe*] (15c) **1 :** having the hand on the hip and the elbow turned outward **2 :** set in a bent position ⟨a tailor sitting with legs ~⟩
akin \ə-ˈkin\ *adj* (1567) **1 :** related by blood **:** descended from a common ancestor or prototype **2 :** essentially similar, related, or compatible ⟨his interests are ~ to mine⟩
Aki·ta \ə-ˈkē-tə, ä-\ *n* [fr. *Akita,* Japan] (1928) **:** any of a breed of large muscular dogs of Japanese origin
Ak·ka·di·an \ə-ˈkā-dē-ən\ *n* [*Akkad,* Babylonia] (1867) **1 :** an extinct Semitic language of ancient Mesopotamia **2 :** a Semitic inhabitant of central Mesopotamia before 2000 B.C. — **Akkadian** *adj*
akvavit *var of* AQUAVIT
Al *symbol* aluminum
AL *abbr* **1** Alabama **2** American League **3** American Legion
al- — see AD-
[1]**-al** *adj suffix* [ME, fr. AF & L; AF, fr. L *-alis*] **:** of, relating to, or characterized by ⟨direction*al*⟩ ⟨fiction*al*⟩
[2]**-al** *n suffix* [ME *-aille,* fr. AF, fr. L *-alia,* neut. pl. of *-alis*] **:** action **:** process ⟨rehears*al*⟩
[3]**-al** *n suffix* [F, fr. *alcool* alcohol, fr. ML *alcohol*] **:** aldehyde ⟨furfur*al*⟩
ala \ˈā-lə\ *n, pl* **alae** \-ˌlē\ [L — more at AISLE] (1731) **:** a wing or a winglike anatomical process or part — **alar** \ˈā-lər\ *adj* — **ala·ry** \-lə-rē\ *adj*
Ala *abbr* Alabama
ALA *abbr* American Library Association
à la *also* **a la** \ˌä-(ˌ)lä, ˌä-lə, ˌa-lə\ *prep* [F *à la*] (1589) **:** in the manner of
al·a·bas·ter \ˈa-lə-ˌbas-tər\ *n* [ME *alabastre,* fr. AF *albastre,* fr. L *alabaster* vase of alabaster, fr. Gk *alabastros*] (14c) **1 :** a compact fine-textured usu. white and translucent gypsum often carved into vases and ornaments **2 :** a hard calcite or aragonite that is translucent and sometimes banded — **alabaster** *or* **al·a·bas·trine** \ˌa-lə-ˈbas-trən\ *adj*
à la carte *also* **a la carte** \ˌä-lə-ˈkärt, ˌa-lə-\ *adv or adj* [F, by the bill of fare] (1816) **:** according to a menu or list that prices items separately
al·a·chlor \ˈa-lə-ˌklȯr\ *n* [*ala-* (perh. fr. rearranged letters of *acetanilide*) + *chlor-*] (1970) **:** an herbicide $C_{14}H_{20}ClNO_2$ derived from aniline and used to control grasses and broadleaved weeds among crop plants
alack \ə-ˈlak\ *interj* [ME] (15c) — used to express sorrow or regret
alac·ri·ty \ə-ˈla-krə-tē\ *n* [L *alacritas,* fr. *alacr-, alacer* lively, eager] (15c) **:** promptness in response **:** cheerful readiness ⟨accepted the invitation with ~⟩ — **alac·ri·tous** \-krə-təs\ *adj*
Alad·din \ə-ˈla-dᵊn\ *n* (1747) **:** a youth in the *Arabian Nights' Entertainments* who comes into possession of a magic lamp
à la grecque \ˌä-lə-ˈgrek, ˌa-lə-\ *adj, often cap G* [F, in the Greek manner] (1895) **:** served in a sauce made of olive oil, lemon juice, and several seasonings (as fennel, coriander, sage, and thyme)
à la king \ˌä-lə-ˈkiŋ, ˌa-lə-\ *adj* (1893) **:** served in a cream sauce with mushrooms and pimiento or green peppers ⟨chicken *à la king*⟩
al·a·me·da \ˌa-lə-ˈmē-də, -ˈmā-\ *n* [Sp, fr. *álamo* poplar] (1777) **:** a public promenade bordered with trees
à la mode *also* **a la mode** \ˌä-lə-ˈmōd, ˌa-lə-\ *adj* [F, according to the fashion] (1641) **1 :** FASHIONABLE, STYLISH **2 :** topped with ice cream
al·a·nine \ˈa-lə-ˌnēn\ *n* [G *Alanin,* irreg. fr. *Aldehyd* aldehyde] (1850) **:** a simple nonessential crystalline amino acid $C_3H_7NO_2$
al·a·nyl \ˈa-lə-ˌnil\ *n* [ISV *alan*ine + *-yl*] (1904) **:** the amino acid radical or residue of alanine
[1]**alarm** \ə-ˈlärm\ *also* **ala·rum** \ə-ˈlär-əm *also* -ˈler-; -ˈla-rəm\ *n* [ME *alarme, alarom,* fr. MF *alarme,* fr. OIt *all'arme,* lit., to the arms] (14c) **1** *usu alarum, archaic* **:** a call to arms ⟨the angry trumpet sounds

alarum —Shak.) **2 :** a signal (as a loud noise or flashing light) that warns or alerts; *also* **:** a device that signals ⟨set the ~ to wake me at seven⟩ **3 :** sudden sharp apprehension and fear resulting from the perception of imminent danger **4 :** a warning notice ***syn*** see FEAR

[2]**alarm** *also* **alarum** *vt* (1586) **1 :** to strike with fear **2 :** DISTURB, EXCITE **3 :** to give warning to **4 :** to equip with an alarm — **alarm·ing·ly** \-ˈlär-miŋ-lē\ *adv*

alarm clock *n* (1662) **:** a clock that can be set to sound an alarm at a desired time

alarm·ism \ə-ˈlär-ˌmi-zəm\ *n* (1842) **:** the often unwarranted exciting of fears or warning of danger — **alarm·ist** \-mist\ *n or adj*

alarm reaction *n* (1936) **:** the initial reaction of an organism (as increased hormonal activity) to stress

alarums and excursions *n pl* (1605) **1 :** martial sounds and the movement of soldiers across the stage — used as a stage direction in Elizabethan drama **2 :** clamor, excitement, and feverish or disordered activity

alas \ə-ˈlas\ *interj* [ME, fr. AF, fr. *a* ah + *las* weary, fr. L *lassus* — more at LASSITUDE] (13c) — used to express unhappiness, pity, or concern

Alas *abbr* Alaska

Alas·kan malamute \ə-ˈlas-kən-\ *n* (1913) **:** any of a breed of powerful heavy-coated deep-chested dogs of Alaskan origin that have erect ears, heavily cushioned feet, and a bushy tail

Alas·ka time \ə-ˈlas-kə-\ *n* (1901) **:** the time of the ninth time zone west of Greenwich that includes most of Alaska

[1]**alate** \ˈā-ˌlāt\ *adj* [L *alatus,* fr. *ala*] (1653) **:** having wings or a winglike part

[2]**alate** *n* (1941) **:** a winged insect (as an ant or termite) of a kind having winged and wingless forms

A·la·wi \ˈä-lä-wē\ *also* **Al·a·wite** \ˌa-lə-ˈwēt\ *n* [Ar *ʿalawī,* fr. the caliph *ʿAlī* ibn Abī Ṭālib, central figure in Shia Islam] (1930) **:** a member of a religious sect living mainly in Syria that originated in Shiite Islam but separated from other Shiite groups in the ninth and tenth centuries

alb \ˈalb\ *n* [ME *albe,* fr. OE, fr. ML *alba,* fr. L, fem. of *albus* white; akin to Gk *alphos* white leprous spot] (bef. 12c) **:** a full-length white linen ecclesiastical vestment with long sleeves that is gathered at the waist with a cincture

Alb *abbr* Albania; Albanian

al·ba·core \ˈal-bə-ˌkȯr\ *n, pl* **-core** *or* **-cores** [Pg *albacor,* fr. Ar *al-bakūra* the albacore] (1579) **:** a large pelagic tuna (*Thunnus alalunga*) with long pectoral fins that is a source of canned tuna; *broadly* **:** any of various tunas (as a bonito)

Al·ba·nian \al-ˈbā-nē-ən, -nyən *also* ȯl-\ *n* (1579) **1 :** a native or inhabitant of Albania **2 :** the Indo-European language of the Albanian people — see INDO-EUROPEAN LANGUAGES table — **Albanian** *adj*

al·ba·tross \ˈal-bə-ˌtrȯs, -ˌträs\ *n, pl* **-tross** *or* **-tross·es** [prob. alter. of obs. *alcatrace* frigate bird, fr. Sp or Pg *alcatraz* pelican, fr. Ar *al-ghaṭṭās,* a kind of sea eagle] (1672) **1 :** any of a family (Diomedeidae) of large web-footed seabirds that have long slender wings, are excellent gliders, and include the largest seabirds **2 a :** something that causes persistent deep concern or anxiety **b :** something that greatly hinders accomplishment **:** ENCUMBRANCE

al·be·do \al-ˈbē-(ˌ)dō\ *n, pl* **-dos** [LL, whiteness, fr. L *albus*] (ca. 1859) **:** reflective power; *specif* **:** the fraction of incident radiation (as light) that is reflected by a surface or body (as the moon or a cloud)

al·be·it \ȯl-ˈbē-ət, al-\ *conj* [ME, lit., all though it be] (14c) **:** conceding the fact that **:** even though **:** ALTHOUGH

Al·bi·gen·ses \ˌal-bə-ˈjen-ˌsēz\ *n pl* [ML, pl. of *Albigensis,* lit., inhabitant of Albi, fr. *Albiga* (Albi), France] (1580) **:** members of a Catharistic sect of southern France flourishing primarily in the 12th and 13th centuries — **Al·bi·gen·sian** \-ˈjen(t)-shən, -ˈjen(t)-sē-ən\ *adj or n* — **Al·bi·gen·sian·ism** \-shə-ˌni-zəm, -sē-ə-ˌ\ *n*

al·bi·nism \ˈal-bə-ˌni-zəm, al-ˈbī-\ *n* (1836) **:** the condition of an albino — **al·bi·nis·tic** \ˌal-bə-ˈnis-tik\ *adj*

al·bi·no \al-ˈbī-(ˌ)nō\ *n, pl* **-nos** [Pg, fr. Sp, fr. *albo* white, fr. L *albus*] (1777) **:** an organism exhibiting deficient pigmentation; *esp* **:** a human being that is congenitally deficient in pigment and usu. has a milky or translucent skin, white or colorless hair, and eyes with pink or blue iris and deep-red pupil — **albino** *adj*

al·bi·not·ic \ˌal-bə-ˈnä-tik\ *adj* [*albino* + *-tic* (as in *melanotic*)] (1872) **1 :** of, relating to, or affected with albinism **2 :** tending toward albinism

Al·bi·on \ˈal-bē-ən\ *n* [L] (bef. 12c) **1 :** Great Britain **2 :** England

al·bite \ˈal-ˌbīt\ *n* [Sw *albit,* fr. L *albus*] (ca. 1843) **:** a triclinic usu. white mineral of the feldspar group consisting of a sodium aluminum silicate — **al·bit·ic** \al-ˈbit-ik\ *adj*

al·bum \ˈal-bəm\ *n* [L, a white tablet, fr. neut. of *albus*] (1612) **1 a :** a book with blank pages used for making a collection (as of autographs, stamps, or photographs) **b :** a cardboard container for a phonograph record **:** JACKET **c :** one or more recordings (as on tape or disc) produced as a single unit ⟨a 2-CD ~⟩ **2 :** a collection usu. in book form of literary selections, musical compositions, or pictures **:** ANTHOLOGY

al·bu·men \al-ˈbyü-mən; ˈal-ˌbyü-, -byə-\ *n* [LL, fr. L *albus*] (1599) **1 :** the white of an egg — see EGG illustration **2 :** ALBUMIN

al·bu·min \al-ˈbyü-mən; ˈal-ˌbyü-, -byə-\ *n* [ISV *albumen* + *-in*] (1802) **:** any of numerous simple heat-coagulable water-soluble proteins that occur in blood plasma or serum, muscle, the whites of eggs, milk, and other animal substances and in many plant tissues and fluids

al·bu·min·ous \al-ˈbyü-mə-nəs\ *adj* (1738) **:** relating to, containing, or having the properties of albumen or albumin

al·bu·min·uria \(ˌ)al-ˌbyü-mə-ˈnu̇r-ē-ə, -ˈnyu̇r-\ *n* [NL] (1830) **:** the presence of albumin in the urine often symptomatic of kidney disease — **al·bu·min·uric** \-ˈnu̇r-ik, -ˈnyu̇r-\ *adj*

al·bu·te·rol \al-ˈbyü-tə-ˌrȯl, -ˌrōl\ *n* [prob. fr. [2]*alpha* + *butyl* + *tertiary* + *diol*] (1972) **:** a drug $C_{13}H_{21}NO_3$ used to treat asthma as an aerosol or as the sulfate in tablet form

alc *abbr* alcohol

al·ca·ic \al-ˈkā-ik\ *adj, often cap* [LL *Alcaicus* of Alcaeus, fr. Gk *Alkaïkos,* fr. *Alkaios* Alcaeus, *fl ab* 600 B.C. Greek poet] (ca. 1637) **:** relating to or written in a verse or strophe marked by complicated variation of a dominant iambic pattern — **alcaic** *n, often cap*

al·cai·de *or* **al·cay·de** \al-ˈkī-dē\ *n* [Sp *alcaide,* fr. Ar *al-qāʾid* the captain] (1502) **:** a commander of a castle or fortress (as among Spaniards, Portuguese, or Moors)

al·cal·de \al-ˈkäl-dē\ *n* [Sp, fr. Ar *al-qāḍī* the judge] (1565) **:** the chief administrative and judicial officer or the mayor of a town in a Spanish-speaking country or region

al·ca·zar \al-ˈkä-zər, -ˈka-\ *n* [Sp *alcázar,* fr. Ar *al-qaṣr* the castle] (ca. 1615) **:** a Spanish fortress or palace

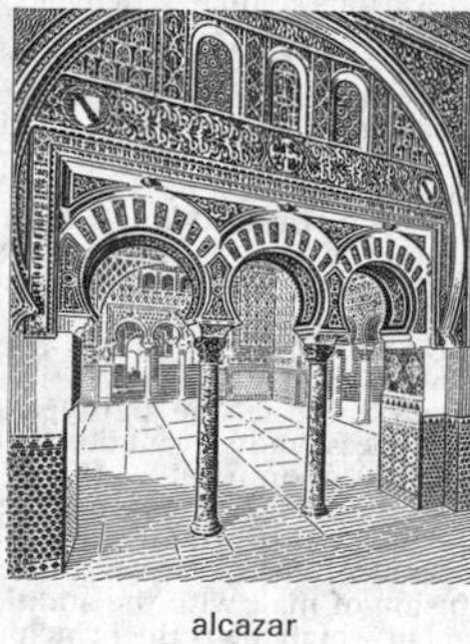

alcazar

Al·ces·tis \al-ˈses-təs\ *n* [L, fr. Gk *Alkēstis*] (14c) **:** the wife of Admetus who dies for her husband and is restored to him by Hercules

al·che·mist \ˈal-kə-mist\ *n* (14c) **:** a person who studies or practices alchemy — **al·che·mis·tic** \ˌal-kə-ˈmis-tik\ *also* **al·che·mis·ti·cal** \-ti-kəl\ *adj*

al·che·mize \ˈal-kə-ˌmīz\ *vt* **-mized; -miz·ing** (1597) **:** to change by alchemy **:** TRANSMUTE

al·che·my \ˈal-kə-mē\ *n* [ME *alkamie, alquemie,* fr. MF or ML; MF *alkimie,* fr. ML *alchymia,* fr. Ar *al-kīmiyāʾ,* fr. *al* the + *kīmiyāʾ* alchemy, fr. LGk *chēmeia*] (14c) **1 :** a medieval chemical science and speculative philosophy aiming to achieve the transmutation of the base metals into gold, the discovery of a universal cure for disease, and the discovery of a means of indefinitely prolonging life **2 :** a power or process of transforming something common into something special **3 :** an inexplicable or mysterious transmuting — **al·chem·i·cal** \-mi-kəl\ *also* **al·chem·ic** \al-ˈke-mik\ *adj* — **al·chem·i·cal·ly** \-mi-k(ə-)lē\ *adv*

al·cid \ˈal-səd\ *n* [NL *Alcidae,* fr. *Alca* type, genus, fr. Sw *alka* auk, fr. Norw — more at AUK] (1885) **:** any of a family (Alcidae, the alcid family) of web-footed diving birds with short legs and wings that includes the auks, murres, and puffins

Alc·me·ne \alk-ˈmē-nē\ *n* [Gk *Alkmēnē*] (14c) **:** the mother of Hercules by Zeus in the form of her husband Amphitryon

al·co·hol \ˈal-kə-ˌhȯl\ *n* [NL, fr. ML, powdered antimony, fr. OSp, fr. Ar *al-kuḥul* the powdered antimony, fr. *kuḥl* kohl] (1672) **1 a :** ethanol esp. when considered as the intoxicating agent in fermented and distilled liquors **b :** drink (as whiskey or beer) containing ethanol **c :** a mixture of ethanol and water that is usu. 95 percent ethanol **2 :** any of a class of organic compounds that are analogous to ethanol and that are hydroxyl derivatives of hydrocarbons

[1]**al·co·hol·ic** \ˌal-kə-ˈhȯ-lik, -ˈhä-\ *adj* (1790) **1 a :** of, relating to, or caused by alcohol **b :** containing alcohol **2 :** affected with alcoholism — **al·co·hol·i·cal·ly** \-li-k(ə-)lē\ *adv*

[2]**alcoholic** *n* (1864) **:** a person affected with alcoholism

al·co·hol·ism \ˈal-kə-ˌhȯ-ˌli-zəm, -kə-hə-\ *n* (1850) **1 :** continued excessive or compulsive use of alcoholic drinks **2 a :** poisoning by alcohol **b :** a chronic disorder marked by excessive and usu. compulsive drinking of alcohol leading to psychological and physical dependence or addiction

al·co·pop \ˈal-kə-ˌpäp\ *n* [*alc*ohol + soda *pop*] (1996) **:** a flavored beverage containing usu. 4 to 6 percent alcohol

Al·co·ran \ˌal-kə-ˈran\ *n* [ME, fr. MF or ML; MF & ML, fr. Ar *al-qurʾān,* lit., the reading] (14c) *archaic* **:** KORAN

al·cove \ˈal-ˌkōv\ *n* [F *alcôve,* fr. Sp *alcoba,* fr. Ar *al-qubba* the arch] (1655) **1 a :** a small recessed section of a room **:** NOOK **b :** an arched opening (as in a wall) **:** NICHE **2 :** SUMMERHOUSE 2 — **al·coved** \-ˌkōvd\ *adj*

ALCS *abbr* American League Championship Series

al·cy·o·nar·ian \ˌal-sē-ə-ˈner-ē-ən\ *n* [ultim. fr. Gk *alkyoneion,* a zoophyte, fr. neut. of *alkyoneios* of a kingfisher, fr. *alkyon* kingfisher; fr. its resemblance to a kingfisher's nest] (1878) **:** any of a subclass (Alcyonaria) of colonial anthozoans (as the sea pens) having polyps with eight branched tentacles and eight septa

Al·cy·o·ne \al-ˈsī-ə-(ˌ)nē\ *n* [L, fr. Gk *Alkyonē*] (14c) **:** the brightest star in the Pleiades

ald *abbr* alderman

ALD *abbr* adrenoleukodystrophy

Al·deb·a·ran \al-ˈde-bə-rən\ *n* [Ar *al-dabarān,* lit., the follower] (14c) **:** a red star of the first magnitude that is seen in the eye of Taurus and is the brightest star in the Hyades

al·de·hyde \ˈal-də-ˌhīd\ *n* [G *Aldehyd,* fr. NL *al. dehyd.,* abbr. of *alcohol dehydrogenatum* dehydrogenated alcohol] (1833) **:** ACETALDEHYDE; *broadly* **:** any of a class of highly reactive organic compounds that are analogous to acetaldehyde and characterized by a carbonyl group attached to a hydrogen atom — **al·de·hy·dic** \ˌal-də-ˈhī-dik\ *adj*

al den·te \äl-ˈden-(ˌ)tā, al-\ *adj* [It; lit., to the tooth] (1920) **:** cooked just enough to retain a somewhat firm texture — **al dente** *adv*

al·der \ˈȯl-dər\ *n* [ME, fr. OE *alor;* akin to OHG *elira* alder, L *alnus*] (14c) **:** any of a genus (*Alnus*) of toothed-leaved trees or shrubs of the birch family that have catkins which become woody, that typically grow in cool moist ground, and that have wood used esp. in turnery; *also* **:** its wood

al·der·man \ˈȯl-dər-mən\ *n* [ME, fr. OE *ealdorman,* fr. *ealdor* parent (fr. *eald* old) + *man* — more at OLD] (bef. 12c) **1 :** a person governing a kingdom, district, or shire as viceroy for an Anglo-Saxon king **2 a :** a magistrate formerly ranking next below the mayor in an English or Irish city or borough **b :** a high-ranking member of a borough or county council in Ireland or formerly in England chosen by elected members **3 :** a member of a city legislative body — **al·der·man·ic** \ˌȯl-dər-ˈma-nik\ *adj*

al·der·wom·an \ˈȯl-dər-ˌwu̇-mən\ *n* [*alder-* (as in *alderman*) + *woman*] (1768) **:** a female member of a city legislative body

al·di·carb \ˈal-də-ˌkärb\ *n* [prob. fr. *alde*hyde + *-i-* + *carb*amate] (1970) **:** a persistent highly toxic agricultural carbamate pesticide $C_7H_{14}N_2O_2S$ used against insects, mites, and nematodes

\ə\ **abut** \ᵊ\ kitten, F table \ər\ **further** \a\ **ash** \ā\ **ace** \ä\ **mop, mar**
\au̇\ **out** \ch\ **chin** \e\ **bet** \ē\ **easy** \g\ **go** \i\ **hit** \ī\ **ice** \j\ **job**
\ŋ\ **sing** \ō\ **go** \ȯ\ **law** \ȯi\ **boy** \th\ **thin** \t͟h\ **the** \ü\ **loot** \u̇\ **foot**
\y\ **yet** \zh\ **vision, beige** \k, ⁿ, œ, ue, ʸ\ *see* Guide to Pronunciation

al·dol \ˈal-ˌdȯl, -ˌdōl\ *n* [ISV *alde*hyde + [1]*-ol*] (1874) : a colorless beta-hydroxy aldehyde $C_4H_8O_2$ used esp. in organic synthesis; *broadly* : any of various similar aldehydes — **al·dol·i·za·tion** \ˌal-ˌdȯ-lə-ˈzā-shən, -ˌdō-\ *n*
al·dol·ase \ˈal-də-ˌlās, -ˌlāz\ *n* [*aldol* + *-ase*] (1940) : a crystalline enzyme that occurs widely in living systems and catalyzes reversibly the cleavage of a phosphorylated fructose into triose sugars
al·dose \ˈal-ˌdōs, -ˌdōz\ *n* [ISV *alde*hyde + *-ose*] (1894) : a sugar containing in its acyclic form one aldehyde group per molecule
al·do·ste·rone \al-ˈdäs-tə-ˌrōn; ˌal-dō-ˈster-ˌōn, -ˈstir-; ˈal-dō-stə-ˌrōn\ *n* [*alde*hyde + *-o-* + *-sterone*] (1954) : a steroid hormone $C_{21}H_{28}O_5$ of the adrenal cortex that functions in the regulation of the salt and water balance of the body
al·do·ste·ron·ism \al-ˈdäs-tə-rə-ˌni-zəm; ˌal-dō-ˈster-(ˌ)ō-, -ˈstir-; ˌal-dō-stə-ˈrō-\ *n* (1955) : a condition that is characterized by excessive secretion of aldosterone and typically by loss of body potassium, muscular weakness, and elevated blood pressure
al·drin \ˈȯl-drən, ˈal-\ *n* [Kurt *Alder* †1958 Ger. chemist + E [1]*-in*] (1949) : a very poisonous formerly used cyclodiene insecticide $C_{12}H_8Cl_6$
ale \ˈāl\ *n* [ME, fr. OE *ealu*; akin to ON *ǫl* ale, Lith *alus*] (bef. 12c) **1** : an alcoholic beverage brewed esp. by rapid fermentation from an infusion of malt with the addition of hops **2** : an English country festival at which ale is the principal beverage
ale·a·tor·ic \ˌā-lē-ə-ˈtȯr-ik, -ˈtär-\ *adj* [L *aleatorius*] (1961) : characterized by chance or indeterminate elements ⟨~ music⟩
ale·a·to·ry \ˈā-lē-ə-ˌtȯr-ē\ *adj* [L *aleatorius* of a gambler, fr. *aleator* gambler, fr. *alea* a dice game] (1693) **1** : depending on an uncertain event or contingency as to both profit and loss ⟨an ~ contract⟩ **2** : relating to luck and esp. to bad luck **3** : ALEATORIC
alee \ə-ˈlē\ *adv* (14c) : on or toward the lee — compare AWEATHER
ale·house \ˈāl-ˌhau̇s\ *n* (bef. 12c) : a place where ale is sold to be drunk on the premises
Al·e·man·nic \ˌa-lə-ˈma-nik\ *n* [ultim. fr. LL *Alemanni, Alamanni* a confederation of Germanic tribes, fr. Gmc **ala-* all + **mann-* man — more at ALL, MAN] (ca. 1797) : the group of dialects of German spoken in Alsace, Switzerland, and southwestern Germany
alem·bic \ə-ˈlem-bik\ *n* [ME, fr. MF & ML; MF *alambic* & ML *alembicum*, fr. Ar *al-anbīq*, fr. *al* the + *anbīq* still, fr. LGk *ambik-, ambix* alembic, fr. Gk, cap of a still] (14c) **1** : an apparatus used in distillation **2** : something that refines or transmutes as if by distillation ⟨philosophy . . . filtered through the ~ of Plato's mind —B. T. Shropshire⟩
alen·çon \ə-ˈlen-ˌsän, -ˈlen(t)-sən\ *n, often cap* [*Alençon*, France] (1865) : a delicate needlepoint lace
aleph \ˈä-ˌlef, -ləf\ *n* [Heb *āleph*, prob. fr. *eleph* ox] (14c) : the 1st letter of the Hebrew alphabet — see ALPHABET table
aleph–null \-ˈnəl\ *n* (ca. 1909) : the number of elements in the set of all integers which is the smallest transfinite cardinal number
[1]**alert** \ə-ˈlərt\ *adj* [It *all'erta*, on the watch, lit., on the height] (1618) **1 a** : watchful and prompt to meet danger or emergency **b** : quick to perceive and act **2** : ACTIVE, BRISK ***syn*** see WATCHFUL, INTELLIGENT — **alert·ly** *adv* — **alert·ness** *n*
[2]**alert** *n* (1803) **1** : a state of careful watching and readiness esp. for danger or opportunity ⟨on 24-hour ~⟩ **2 a** : an alarm or other signal of danger **b** : an urgent notice ⟨an ~ to parents . . . about new immunization requirements —Ann Schrader⟩ **3** : the period during which an alert is in effect
[3]**alert** *vt* (ca. 1868) **1** : to call to a state of readiness : WARN **2** : to make aware of ⟨~*ed* the public to the dangers of pesticides⟩
-ales *n pl suffix* [NL, fr. L, pl. of *-alis* -al] : plants consisting of or related to — in the names of orders of plants ⟨Coniferales⟩
al·eu·rone \ˈal-yə-ˌrōn\ *n* [G *Aleuron*, fr. Gk, flour; akin to Arm *ałam* I grind] (1869) : protein matter in the form of minute granules or grains occurring in seeds in endosperm or in a special peripheral layer
Aleut \ˌa-lē-ˈüt, ˈa-lē-ˌ; ə-ˈlüt\ *n* [Russ] (1780) **1** : a member of a people of the Aleutian and Shumagin islands and the western part of Alaska Peninsula **2** : the language of the Aleuts
A level *n* (1951) **1** : the second of three standardized British examinations in a secondary school subject used as a qualification for university entrance; *also* : successful completion of an A-level examination in a particular subject — called also *Advanced level*; compare O LEVEL, S LEVEL **2 a** : the level of education required to pass an A-level examination **b** : a course leading to an A-level examination
al·e·vin \ˈa-lə-vən\ *n* [F, fr. OF, fr. *alever* to lift up, rear (offspring), fr. L *allevare*, fr. *ad-* + *levare* to raise — more at LEVER] (1868) : a young fish; *esp* : a newly hatched salmon when still attached to the yolk sac
[1]**ale·wife** \ˈāl-ˌwīf\ *n* (15c) : a woman who keeps an alehouse
[2]**alewife** *n, pl* **ale·wives** \-ˌwīvz\ [perh. alter. of obs. *allowes*, a kind of shad, fr. F *alose* shad, fr. OF, fr. LL *alausa*] (1633) : a food fish (*Alosa pseudoharengus*) of the herring family that is very abundant along the Atlantic coast; *also* : any of several related fishes (as the menhaden)
al·ex·an·der \ˌa-lig-ˈzan-dər, ˌe-\ *n, often cap* (1929) : an iced cocktail made from crème de cacao, sweet cream, and gin or brandy
Al·ex·an·dri·an \ˌa-lig-ˈzan-drē-ən, ˌe-\ *adj* (1840) **1** : HELLENISTIC **2** : of or relating to Alexander the Great
al·ex·an·drine \-ˈzan-ˌdrēn, -drən, -ˌdrīn\ *n, often cap* [F *alexandrin*, adj., fr. *Alexandre* Alexander the Great; fr. its use in a poem on Alexander] (1667) : a line of verse of 12 syllables consisting regularly of 6 iambs with a caesura after the third iamb — **alexandrine** *adj*
al·ex·an·drite \-ˈzan-ˌdrīt\ *n* [G *Alexandrit*, fr. *Alexander I* Russ. emperor] (ca. 1880) : a grass-green chrysoberyl that shows a red color by transmitted or artificial light
alex·ia \ə-ˈlek-sē-ə\ *n* [NL, fr. *a-* + Gk *lexis* speech, fr. *legein* to speak — more at LEGEND] (1878) : aphasia marked by loss of ability to read
Al·fa \ˈal-fə\ (1952) — a communications code word for the letter *a*
al·fal·fa \al-ˈfal-fə\ *n* [Sp, modif. of Ar dial. *al-faṣfaṣa* the alfalfa] (1845) : a deep-rooted leguminous perennial plant (*Medicago sativa*) of southwestern Asia that is widely grown for hay and forage
alfalfa weevil *n* (1912) : a small dark brown European weevil (*Hypera postica*) that is now a widespread pest of alfalfa in No. America
al·for·ja \al-ˈfȯr-(ˌ)hä\ *n* [Sp, fr. Ar *al-khurj*] (1611) *West* : SADDLEBAG
al·fres·co \al-ˈfres-(ˌ)kō\ *adj or adv* [It] (1753) : taking place or located in the open air : OUTDOOR, OUTDOORS ⟨an ~ lunch⟩ ⟨an ~ café⟩ ⟨dining ~⟩

alg *abbr* algebra
al·ga \ˈal-gə\ *n, pl* **al·gae** \ˈal-(ˌ)jē\ *also* **algas** [L, seaweed] (1551) : a plant or plantlike organism of any of several phyla, divisions, or classes of chiefly aquatic usu. chlorophyll-containing nonvascular organisms of polyphyletic origin that usu. include the green, yellow-green, brown, and red algae in the eukaryotes and esp. formerly the cyanobacteria in the prokaryotes — **al·gal** \-gəl\ *adj*
al·ga·ro·ba *or* **al·gar·ro·ba** \ˌal-gə-ˈrō-bə\ *or* **al·gar·ro·bo** \-bō\ *n* [Sp *algarroba*, fr. Ar *al-kharrūba* the carob] (1577) **1** : CAROB 1 **2** [MexSp, fr. Sp] : MESQUITE; *also* : its pods
al·ge·bra \ˈal-jə-brə\ *n* [ML, fr. Ar *al-jabr*, lit., the reduction] (1551) **1** : a generalization of arithmetic in which letters representing numbers are combined according to the rules of arithmetic **2** : any of various systems or branches of mathematics or logic concerned with the properties and relationships of abstract entities (as complex numbers, matrices, sets, vectors, groups, rings, or fields) manipulated in symbolic form under operations often analogous to those of arithmetic — compare BOOLEAN ALGEBRA — **al·ge·bra·ist** \-ˌbrā-ist\ *n*
al·ge·bra·ic \ˌal-jə-ˈbrā-ik\ *adj* (1662) **1** : relating to, involving, or according to the laws of algebra **2** : involving only a finite number of repetitions of addition, subtraction, multiplication, division, extraction of roots, and raising to powers ⟨~ equation⟩ — compare TRANSCENDENTAL — **al·ge·bra·i·cal·ly** \-ˈbrā-ə-k(ə-)lē\ *adv*
algebraic number *n* (1904) : a root of an algebraic equation with rational coefficients
-algia *n comb form* [Gk, fr. *algos* pain] : pain ⟨neur*algia*⟩
al·gi·cide *or* **al·gae·cide** \ˈal-jə-ˌsīd\ *n* (1904) : an agent used to kill algae — **al·gi·cid·al** \ˌal-jə-ˈsī-dᵊl\ *adj*
al·gid \ˈal-jəd\ *adj* [L *algidus*, fr. *algēre* to feel cold] (ca. 1623) : COLD
al·gin \ˈal-jən\ *n* [*alga* + [1]*-in*] (1883) : any of various colloidal substances (as an alginate or alginic acid) derived from marine brown algae and used esp. as emulsifiers or thickeners
al·gi·nate \ˈal-jə-ˌnāt\ *n* (ca. 1909) : a salt or ester of alginic acid
al·gin·ic acid \(ˌ)al-ˈji-nik-\ *n* [ISV *algin* + [1]*-ic*] (1885) : an insoluble colloidal acid $(C_6H_8O_6)_n$ that in the form of its salts is a constituent of the cell walls of brown algae
Al·gol \ˈal-ˌgäl, -ˌgȯl\ *n* [Ar *al-ghūl*, lit., the ghoul] (14c) : a binary star in the constellation Perseus whose larger member orbits and eclipses the smaller brighter star causing periodic variation in brightness
AL·GOL *or* **Al·gol** \ˈal-ˌgäl, -ˌgȯl\ *n* [*algo*rithmic *l*anguage] (1959) : an algebraic computer programming language used esp. in mathematical and scientific applications
al·go·lag·nia \ˌal-gō-ˈlag-nē-ə\ *n* [NL, fr. Gk *algos* pain + *lagneia* lust, fr. *lagnos* lustful — more at SLACK] (ca. 1900) : a perversion (as sadism or masochism) characterized by pleasure and esp. sexual gratification in inflicting or suffering pain — **al·go·lag·ni·ac** \-ˈlag-nē-ˌak\ *n*
al·gol·o·gy \al-ˈgä-lə-jē\ *n* (1849) : PHYCOLOGY — **al·go·log·i·cal** \ˌal-gə-ˈlä-ji-kəl\ *adj* — **al·gol·o·gist** \al-ˈgä-lə-jist\ *n*
Al·gon·qui·an \al-ˈgän-kwē-ən, -ˈgäŋ-\ *or* **Al·gon·quin** \-kwən\ *or* **Al·gon·ki·an** \-ˈgäŋ-kē-ən\ *also* **Al·gon·kin** \-ˈgäŋ-kən\ *n* [CanF *Algoumequin, Algonquin*, perh. fr. Malecite-Passamaquoddy (Algonquian language of Maine and New Brunswick) *elakómkwik* they are our relatives] (1625) **1** *usu Algonquin* **a** : an American Indian people of the Ottawa River valley **b** : the dialect of Ojibwa spoken by these people **2** *usu Algonquian* **a** : a family of American Indian languages spoken by peoples from Labrador to Carolina and westward into the Great Plains **b** : a member of the peoples speaking Algonquian languages
al·go·rithm \ˈal-gə-ˌri-t͟həm\ *n* [alter. of ME *algorisme*, fr. OF & ML; OF, fr. ML *algorismus*, fr. Ar *al-khuwārizmi*, fr. *al-Khwārizmī fl* A.D. 825 Islamic mathematician] (1926) : a procedure for solving a mathematical problem (as of finding the greatest common divisor) in a finite number of steps that frequently involves repetition of an operation; *broadly* : a step-by-step procedure for solving a problem or accomplishing some end esp. by a computer — **al·go·rith·mic** \ˌal-gə-ˈrit͟h-mik\ *adj* — **al·go·rith·mi·cal·ly** \-mi-k(ə-)lē\ *adv*
Al·ham·bra \al-ˈham-brə\ *n* [Sp, fr. Ar *al-ḥamrā'* the red house] (1612) : the palace of the Moorish kings at Granada, Spain
[1]**ali·as** \ˈā-lē-əs, ˈāl-yəs\ *adv* [L, otherwise, fr. *alius* other — more at ELSE] (15c) : otherwise called : otherwise known as
[2]**alias** *n* (1605) : an assumed or additional name
Ali Ba·ba \ˌa-lē-ˈbä-bə, ˌä-lē-\ *n* (1812) : a woodcutter in the *Arabian Nights' Entertainments* who enters the cave of the Forty Thieves by using the password *Sesame*
[1]**al·i·bi** \ˈa-lə-ˌbī\ *n* [L, elsewhere, fr. *alius*] (1743) **1** : the plea of having been at the time of the commission of an act elsewhere than at the place of commission; *also* : the fact or state of having been elsewhere at the time **2** : an excuse usu. intended to avert blame or punishment (as for failure or negligence) ***syn*** see APOLOGY
[2]**alibi** *vb* **-bied; -bi·ing** *vt* (1909) : to exonerate by an alibi : furnish an excuse for ~ *vi* : to offer an excuse
Al·ice–in–Won·der·land \ˈa-lə-sən-ˈwən-dər-ˌland\ *adj* [fr. *Alice's Adventures in Wonderland* (1865) by Lewis Carroll] (1925) : suitable to a world of fantasy or illusion : UNREAL
ali·cy·clic \ˌa-lə-ˈsī-klik, -ˈsi-klik\ *adj* [ISV *ali*phatic + *cyclic*] (1891) : of, relating to, or being an organic compound that contains a ring but is not aromatic — compare ALIPHATIC
al·i·dade \ˈa-lə-ˌdād\ *n* [ME *allidatha*, fr. ML *alhidada*, fr. Ar *al-ʿiḍāda* the revolving radius of a circle] (15c) : a rule equipped with simple or telescopic sights and used for determination of direction: as **a** : a part of an astrolabe **b** : a part of a surveying instrument consisting of the telescope and its attachments
[1]**alien** \ˈā-lē-ən, ˈāl-yən\ *adj* [ME, fr. AF, fr. L *alienus*, fr. *alius*] (14c) **1 a** : belonging or relating to another person, place, or thing : STRANGE **b** : relating, belonging, or owing allegiance to another country or government : FOREIGN **c** : EXOTIC 1 **2** : differing in nature or character typically to the point of incompatibility ***syn*** see EXTRINSIC — **alien·ly** *adv* — **alien·ness** \-lē-ən-nəs, -yən-nəs\ *n*
[2]**alien** *n* (14c) **1** : a person of another family, race, or nation **2** : a foreign-born resident who has not been naturalized and is still a subject or citizen of a foreign country; *broadly* : a foreign-born citizen **3** : EXTRATERRESTRIAL **4** : EXOTIC 1
[3]**alien** *vt* (14c) **1** : ALIENATE, ESTRANGE **2** : to make over (as property)
alien·able \ˈāl-yə-nə-bəl, ˈā-lē-ə-nə-\ *adj* (1611) : transferable to another's ownership — **alien·abil·i·ty** \ˌāl-yə-nə-ˈbi-lə-tē, ˌā-lē-ə-nə-\ *n*

alien·age \ˈāl-yə-nij, ˈā-lē-ə-nij\ *n* (1809) **:** the status of an alien
alien·ate \ˈā-lē-ə-ˌnāt, ˈāl-yə-\ *vt* **-at·ed; -at·ing** (ca. 1509) **1 :** to make unfriendly, hostile, or indifferent esp. where attachment formerly existed **2 :** to convey or transfer (as property or a right) usu. by a specific act rather than the due course of law **3 :** to cause to be withdrawn or diverted ***syn*** see ESTRANGE — **alien·ator** \-ˌnā-tər\ *n*
alien·ation \ˌā-lē-ə-ˈnā-shən, ˌāl-yə-\ *n* (14c) **1 :** a withdrawing or separation of a person or a person's affections from an object or position of former attachment **:** ESTRANGEMENT ⟨~ . . . from the values of one's society and family —S. L. Halleck⟩ **2 :** a conveyance of property to another
alien·ee \-ˈnē\ *n* (1531) **:** one to whom property is transferred
alien·ism \ˈā-lē-ə-ˌni-zəm, ˈāl-yə-\ *n* (1808) **:** ALIENAGE
alien·ist \-nist\ *n* [F *aliéniste,* fr. *aliéné* insane, fr. L *alienatus,* pp. of *alienare* to estrange, fr. *alienus*] (1864) **:** PSYCHIATRIST
alien·or \ˌā-lē-ə-ˈnȯr, ˌāl-yə-\ *n* (ca. 1552) **:** one who transfers property to another
¹**alight** \ə-ˈlīt\ *vi* **alight·ed** *also* **alit** \ə-ˈlit\; **alight·ing** [ME, fr. OE *ālihtan,* fr. *ā-* (perfective prefix) + *līhtan* to alight — more at ABIDE, LIGHT] (bef. 12c) **1 :** to come down from something (as a vehicle): as **a :** DISMOUNT **b :** DEPLANE **2 :** to descend from or as if from the air and come to rest **:** LAND, SETTLE **3** *archaic* **:** to come by chance — **alight·ment** *n*
²**alight** *adj* (15c) **1** *chiefly Brit* **:** being on fire **2 :** lighted up
align *also* **aline** \ə-ˈlīn\ *vb* [F *aligner,* fr. OF, fr. *a-* (fr. L *ad-*) + *ligne* line, fr. L *linea*] *vt* (ca. 1693) **1 :** to bring into line or alignment **2 :** to array on the side of or against a party or cause ⟨he ~*ed* himself with the protesters⟩ ~ *vi* **1 :** to get or fall into line **2 :** to be in or come into precise adjustment or correct relative position — **align·er** *n*
align·ment *also* **aline·ment** \ə-ˈlīn-mənt\ *n* (1790) **1 :** the act of aligning or state of being aligned; *esp* **:** the proper positioning or state of adjustment of parts (as of a mechanical or electronic device) in relation to each other **2 a :** a forming in line **b :** the line thus formed **3 :** the ground plan (as of a railroad or highway) in distinction from the profile **4 :** an arrangement of groups or forces in relation to one another ⟨new ~*s* within the political party⟩
¹**alike** \ə-ˈlīk\ *adv* (14c) **:** in the same manner, form, or degree **:** EQUALLY ⟨was denounced by teachers and students ~⟩
²**alike** *adj* [ME *ilik, ilich* (fr. OE *gelīc*) & *alik,* alter. of OE *onlīc,* fr. *on* + *līc* body — more at LIKE] (15c) **:** exhibiting close resemblance without being identical ⟨~ in their beliefs⟩ — **alike·ness** *n*
¹**al·i·ment** \ˈa-lə-mənt\ *n* [ME, fr. L *alimentum,* fr. *alere* to nourish — more at OLD] (15c) **:** FOOD, NUTRIMENT; *also* **:** SUSTENANCE ⟨there was nothing there of conversational ~ —Kingsley Amis⟩
²**al·i·ment** \-ˌment\ *vt* (15c) **:** to give aliment to **:** NOURISH, SUSTAIN
al·i·men·ta·ry \ˌa-lə-ˈmen-t(ə-)rē\ *adj* (1615) **1 :** of or relating to nourishment or nutrition **2 :** furnishing sustenance or maintenance
alimentary canal *n* (1764) **:** the tubular passage that extends from mouth to anus and functions in digestion and absorption of food and elimination of residual waste
al·i·men·ta·tion \ˌa-lə-mən-ˈtā-shən, -ˌmen-\ *n* (ca. 1656) **:** the act or process of affording nutriment or nourishment ⟨intravenous ~⟩
al·i·mo·ny \ˈa-lə-ˌmō-nē\ *n, pl* **-nies** [L *alimonia* sustenance, fr. *alere*] (1656) **1 :** an allowance made to one spouse by the other for support pending or after legal separation or divorce **2 :** the means of living **:** MAINTENANCE
A–line \ˈā-ˌlīn\ *adj* (1964) **:** having a flared bottom and a close-fitting top — used of a garment ⟨an ~ skirt⟩
al·i·phat·ic \ˌa-lə-ˈfa-tik\ *adj* [ISV, fr. Gk *aleiphat-, aleiphar* oil, fr. *aleiphein* to smear; perh. akin to Gk *lipos* fat — more at LEAVE] (1889) **:** of, relating to, or being an organic compound (as an alkane) having an open-chain structure — compare ALICYCLIC, AROMATIC 2
al·i·quot \ˈa-lə-ˌkwät, -kwət\ *adj* [ML *aliquotus,* fr. L *aliquot* some, several, fr. *alius* other + *quot* how many — more at ELSE, QUOTE] (1570) **1 :** contained an exact number of times in something else — used of a divisor or part ⟨5 is an ~ part of 15⟩ ⟨an ~ portion of a solution⟩ **2 :** FRACTIONAL ⟨an ~ part of invested capital⟩ — **aliquot** *n*
A–list \ˈā-ˌlist\ *n* (1980) **:** a list or group of individuals of the highest level of society, excellence, or eminence
alit·er·a·cy \ˌā-ˈli-tər-ə-sē, ə-ˈl-\ *n* (1984) **:** the quality or state of being able to read but uninterested in doing so — **alit·er·ate** \-ˈli-tər-ət\ *adj or n*
alive \ə-ˈlīv\ *adj* [ME, fr. OE *on life,* fr. *on* + *līf* life] (bef. 12c) **1 :** having life **:** not dead or inanimate **2 a :** still in existence, force, or operation **:** ACTIVE ⟨kept hope ~⟩ **b :** still active in competition with a chance of victory ⟨must win to stay ~ in the playoffs⟩ **3 :** knowing or realizing the existence of **:** SENSITIVE ⟨~ to the danger⟩ **4 :** marked by alertness, energy, or briskness ⟨his face came ~ at the mention of food⟩ **5 :** marked by much life, animation, or activity **:** SWARMING ⟨streets ~ with traffic⟩ **6** — used as an intensive following the noun ⟨the proudest boy ~⟩ ***syn*** see AWARE — **alive·ness** *n*
ali·yah *or* **ali·ya** \ä-ˈlē-(ˌ)yä, ˌä-lē-ˈyä\ *n* [ModHeb *ʿălīyāh,* fr. Heb, ascent] (ca. 1934) **:** the immigration of Jews to Israel
aliz·a·rin \ə-ˈli-zə-rən\ *n* [prob. fr. F *alizarine*] (ca. 1835) **1 :** an orange or red crystalline compound $C_{14}H_8O_4$ formerly prepared from madder and now made synthetically and used esp. to dye Turkey reds and in making red pigments **2 :** any of various acid, mordant, and solvent dyes derived like alizarin proper from anthraquinone
alk *abbr* alkaline
al·ka·hest \ˈal-kə-ˌhest\ *n* [NL *alchahest*] (1641) **:** the universal solvent believed by alchemists to exist — **al·ka·hes·tic** \ˌal-kə-ˈhes-tik\ *adj*
al·ka·li \ˈal-kə-ˌlī\ *n, pl* **-lies** *or* **-lis** [ME, fr. ML, fr. Ar *al-qili* the ashes of the plant saltwort] (14c) **1 :** a soluble salt obtained from the ashes of plants and consisting largely of potassium or sodium carbonate; *broadly* **:** a substance (as a hydroxide or carbonate of an alkali metal) having marked basic properties — compare BASE 7a **2 :** ALKALI METAL **3 :** a soluble salt or a mixture of soluble salts present in some soils of arid regions in quantity detrimental to agriculture
alkali metal *n* (1860) **:** any of the monovalent mostly basic metals of group I of the periodic table comprising lithium, sodium, potassium, rubidium, cesium, and francium — see PERIODIC TABLE table
al·ka·line \ˈal-kə-lən, -ˌlīn\ *adj* (1675) **:** of, relating to, containing, or having the properties of an alkali or alkali metal **:** BASIC; *esp, of a solution* **:** having a pH of more than 7 — **al·ka·lin·i·ty** \ˌal-kə-ˈli-nə-tē\ *n*
alkaline battery *n* (1941) **:** a long-lived dry cell with an alkaline electrolyte that decreases corrosion of the cell — called also *alkaline cell*
alkaline earth metal *n* (1869) **:** any of the divalent strongly basic metals of group II of the periodic table comprising beryllium, magnesium, calcium, strontium, barium, and radium — called also *alkaline earth;* see PERIODIC TABLE table
alkaline phosphatase *n* (1948) **:** any of the phosphatases that are optimally active in alkaline medium and occur in esp. high concentrations in bone, the liver, the kidneys, and the placenta
al·ka·lin·ize \ˈal-kə-lə-ˌnīz\ *vt* **-ized; -iz·ing** (1800) **:** to make alkaline — **al·ka·lin·i·za·tion** \ˌal-kə-ˌli-nə-ˈzā-shən, -lə-nə-\ *n*
al·ka·loid \ˈal-kə-ˌlȯid\ *n* (ca. 1831) **:** any of numerous usu. colorless, complex, and bitter organic bases (as morphine or caffeine) containing nitrogen and usu. oxygen that occur esp. in seed plants and are typically physiologically active — **al·ka·loi·dal** \ˌal-kə-ˈlȯi-dᵊl\ *adj*
al·ka·lo·sis \ˌal-kə-ˈlō-səs\ *n* (1911) **:** an abnormal condition of increased alkalinity of the blood and tissues — **al·ka·lot·ic** \-ˈlä-tik\ *adj*
al·kane \ˈal-ˌkān\ *n* [*alk*yl + *-ane*] (1899) **:** any of numerous saturated hydrocarbons; *specif* **:** any of a series of open-chain hydrocarbons C_nH_{2n+2} (as methane and butane) — called also *paraffin*
al·ka·net \ˈal-kə-ˌnet\ *n* [ME, fr. ML *alcannetta,* fr. Ar *al-hanna, al-ḥinnāʾ* the henna] (14c) **1 a :** a European plant (*Alkanna tinctoria*) of the borage family; *also* **:** its root **b :** a red dyestuff prepared from the root **2 :** a Eurasian plant (*Anchusa officinalis*) of the borage family with delicate usu. blue flowers
al·kene \ˈal-ˌkēn\ *n* [ISV *alk*yl + *-ene*] (1899) **:** any of numerous unsaturated hydrocarbons having one double bond; *specif* **:** any of a series of open-chain hydrocarbons C_nH_{2n} (as ethylene)
al·kie *or* **al·ky** \ˈal-kē\ *n, pl* **alkies** [by shortening & alter.] (1948) *slang* **:** ALCOHOLIC
alk·ox·ide \al-ˈkäk-ˌsīd, -səd\ *n* [*alk*yl + *oxide*] (ca. 1889) **:** a basic salt derived from an alcohol by the replacement of the hydroxyl hydrogen with a metal
alk·oxy \ˈal-ˌkäk-sē\ *adj* [ISV *alk*yl + *oxy*gen] (ca. 1925) **:** of, relating to, or containing a monovalent radical RO– composed of an alkyl group united with oxygen — often used in combination
alky *abbr* alkalinity
al·kyd \ˈal-kəd\ *n* [blend of *alkyl* and *acid*] (1929) **1 :** any of numerous synthetic resins that are used esp. for protective coatings and in paint **2 :** a paint in which the vehicle is an alkyd resin
¹**al·kyl** \ˈal-kəl\ *adj* (1879) **:** having a monovalent organic group and esp. one C_nH_{2n+1} (as methyl) derived from an alkane (as methane)
²**alkyl** *n* [prob. fr. G, fr. *Alkohol* alcohol] (1889) **:** a compound of one or more alkyl groups with a metal ⟨mercury ~*s*⟩
alkylating agent *n* (1900) **:** a substance that causes replacement of hydrogen by an alkyl group esp. in a biologically important molecule; *specif* **:** one with mutagenic activity that inhibits cell division and growth and is used to treat some cancers
al·kyl·ation \ˌal-kə-ˈlā-shən\ *n* (1895) **:** the act or process of introducing one or more alkyl groups into a compound (as to increase octane number in a motor fuel) — **al·kyl·ate** \ˈal-kə-ˌlāt\ *vt*
al·kyne \ˈal-ˌkīn\ *n* [*alk*yl + *-yne,* alter. of *-ine*] (ca. 1909) **:** any of a series of open-chain hydrocarbons C_nH_{2n-2} (as acetylene) having one triple bond
¹**all** \ˈȯl\ *adj* [ME *all, al,* fr. OE *eall;* akin to OHG *all* all] (bef. 12c) **1 a :** the whole amount, quantity, or extent of ⟨needed ~ the courage they had⟩ ⟨sat up ~ night⟩ **b :** as much as possible ⟨spoke in ~ seriousness⟩ **2 :** every member or individual component of ⟨~ men will go⟩ ⟨~ five children were present⟩ **3 :** the whole number or sum of ⟨~ the angles of a triangle are equal to two right angles⟩ **4 :** EVERY ⟨~ manner of hardship⟩ **5 :** any whatever ⟨beyond ~ doubt⟩ **6 :** nothing but **:** ONLY: **a :** completely taken up with, given to, or absorbed by ⟨became ~ attention⟩ **b :** having or seeming to have (some physical feature) in conspicuous excess or prominence ⟨~ legs⟩ **c :** paying full attention with ⟨~ ears⟩ **7** *dial* **:** used up **:** entirely consumed — used esp. of food and drink **8 :** being more than one person or thing ⟨who ~ is coming⟩ ***syn*** see WHOLE — **all the :** as much of . . . as **:** as much of a . . . as ⟨*all the* home I ever had⟩
²**all** *adv* (bef. 12c) **1 a :** WHOLLY, QUITE ⟨sat ~ alone⟩ — often used as an intensive ⟨~ out of proportion⟩ ⟨~ over the yard⟩ ⟨it wasn't ~ that funny⟩ **b :** selected as the best (as at a sport) within an area or organization — used in combination ⟨*all*-league halfback⟩ **2** *obs* **:** ONLY, EXCLUSIVELY **3** *archaic* **:** JUST **4 :** so much ⟨~ the better for it⟩ **5 :** for each side **:** APIECE ⟨the score is two ~⟩
³**all** *pron, sing or pl in constr* (bef. 12c) **1 a :** the whole number, quantity, or amount **:** TOTALITY ⟨~ that I have⟩ ⟨~ of us⟩ ⟨~ of the books⟩ **b** — used in such phrases as *for all I know, for all I care,* and *for all the good it does* to indicate a lack of knowledge, interest, or effectiveness **2 :** EVERYBODY, EVERYTHING ⟨gave equal attention to ~⟩ ⟨that is ~⟩ — **all in all :** on the whole **:** GENERALLY ⟨*all in all,* things might have been worse⟩ — **and all :** and everything else esp. of a kind suggested by a previous context ⟨cards to fill out with . . . numbers *and all* —Sally Quinn⟩
⁴**all** *n* (1593) **:** the whole of one's possessions, resources, or energy ⟨gave his ~ for the cause⟩
all- *or* **allo-** *comb form* [Gk, fr. *allos* other — more at ELSE] **1 :** other **:** different **:** atypical ⟨*allo*gamous⟩ ⟨*allo*tropy⟩ **2** *allo-* **:** isomeric form or variety of (a specified chemical compound) ⟨*allo*purinol⟩ **3** *allo-* **:** being one of a group whose members together constitute a structural unit esp. of a language ⟨*allo*phone⟩
¹**al·la breve** \ˌa-lə-ˈbrev, ˌä-lə-ˈbre-(ˌ)vā\ *n* [It, lit., according to the breve] (ca. 1740) **:** the sign marking a piece or passage to be played alla breve; *also* **:** a passage so marked

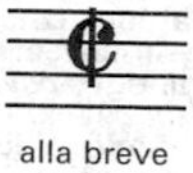
alla breve

²**alla breve** *adv or adj* (ca. 1823) **:** in duple or quadruple time with the beat represented by the half note

\ə\ **abut** \ᵊ\ kitten, F table \ər\ **fur**ther \a\ **ash** \ā\ **ace** \ä\ **mop, mar** \au̇\ **out** \ch\ **chin** \e\ **bet** \ē\ **easy** \g\ **go** \i\ **hit** \ī\ **ice** \j\ **job** \ŋ\ **sing** \ō\ **go** \ȯ\ **law** \ȯi\ **boy** \th\ **thin** \t͟h\ **the** \ü\ **loot** \u̇\ **foot** \y\ **yet** \zh\ **vi**sion, beige \k̲, ⁿ, œ, ue, ʸ\ *see* Guide to Pronunciation

Al·lah \ˈä-lə, ˈa-lə, ˈä-ˌlä, ä-ˈlä\ *n* [Ar *allāh*] (1584) **:** GOD 1a — used in Islam

all along *adv* (1630) **:** all the time ⟨knew the truth *all along*⟩

[1]**all–Amer·i·can** \ˌȯl-ə-ˈmer-ə-kən, -ˈme-rə-\ *adj* (1888) **1 a** *also* **all–Amer·i·ca** \-ə-kə\ **:** selected (as by a poll of journalists) as one of the best in the U.S. in a particular category at a particular time ⟨an ~ quarterback⟩ **b :** having only all-American participants ⟨an ~ basketball team⟩ **2 :** composed wholly of American elements **3 :** representative or typical of the U.S. or its ideals ⟨an ~ boy⟩ ⟨her ~ optimism⟩ **4 :** of or relating to the American nations as a group

[2]**all–American** *n* (1920) **1** *also* **all–Amer·i·ca :** one (as an athlete) that is voted all-American **2 :** one that has all-American qualities or characteristics ⟨a clean-cut ~⟩

al·lan·to·in \ə-ˈlan-tə-wən\ *n* [prob. fr. G, fr. NL *allantois* + G *-in*] (ca. 1844) **:** a crystalline oxidation product $C_4H_6N_4O_3$ of uric acid used to promote healing of local wounds and infections

al·lan·to·is \ə-ˈlan-tə-wəs\ *n, pl* **al·lan·to·ides** \ˌa-lən-ˈtō-ə-ˌdēz, ˌa-ˌlan-\ [NL, ultim. fr. Gk *allant-, allas* sausage] (1646) **:** a vascular fetal membrane of reptiles, birds, and mammals that is formed as a pouch from the hindgut and that in placental mammals is intimately associated with the chorion in formation of the placenta — **al·lan·to·ic** \ˌa-lən-ˈtō-ik, ˌa-ˌlan-\ *adj*

al·lar·gan·do \ˌä-lär-ˈgän-(ˌ)dō\ *adj or adv* [It, widening, verbal of *allargare* to widen, fr. *al-* (fr. L *ad-*) + *largare* to widen] (1877) **:** becoming gradually slower and more stately — used as a direction in music

all–around \ˌȯl-ə-ˈrau̇nd\ *also* **all–round** \ˈȯl-ˈrau̇nd\ *adj* (1867) **1 :** considered in or encompassing all aspects **:** COMPREHENSIVE ⟨the best ~ performance so far⟩ **2 :** competent in many fields ⟨an ~ performer⟩ **3 :** having general utility or merit ⟨an ~ tool⟩ — **all around** *adv*

al·lay \ə-ˈlā, a-\ *vb* [ME *alayen,* fr. OE *ālecgan,* fr. *ā-* (perfective prefix) + *lecgan* to lay — more at ABIDE, LAY] *vt* (14c) **1 :** to subdue or reduce in intensity or severity **:** ALLEVIATE ⟨expect a breeze to ~ the heat⟩ **2 :** to make quiet **:** CALM ⟨trying to ~ their fears⟩ ~ *vi, obs* **:** to diminish in strength **:** SUBSIDE ***syn*** see RELIEVE

all but *adv* (1598) **:** very nearly **:** ALMOST ⟨would be *all but* impossible⟩

all clear *n* (1865) **:** a signal that a danger has passed

all–day \ˈȯl-ˈdā\ *adj* (ca. 1870) **:** lasting for, occupying, or appearing throughout an entire day ⟨an ~ trip⟩

al·lée \ä-ˈlā, a-\ *n* [F, fr. MF *alee* — more at ALLEY] (1759) **:** a walkway lined with trees or tall shrubs

al·le·ga·tion \ˌa-li-ˈgā-shən\ *n* (15c) **1 :** the act of alleging **2 :** a positive assertion; *specif* **:** a statement by a party to a legal action of what the party undertakes to prove **3 :** an assertion unsupported and by implication regarded as unsupportable ⟨vague ~*s* of misconduct⟩

al·lege \ə-ˈlej\ *vt* **al·leged; al·leg·ing** [ME *alleggen* to submit in evidence or as justification, adduce, fr. AF *aleger, allegger,* prob. in part modif. of ML *allegare,* fr. L, to send as a representative, adduce in support of a plea (fr. *ad-* + *legare* to depute), in part fr. AF *aleger* to lighten, free, exculpate, fr. LL *alleviare* to relieve — more at LEGATE, ALLEVIATE] (14c) **1** *archaic* **:** to adduce or bring forward as a source or authority **2 :** to assert without proof or before proving ⟨the newspaper ~*s* the mayor's guilt⟩ **3 :** to bring forward as a reason or excuse

al·leged \ə-ˈlejd, -ˈle-jəd\ *adj* (15c) **1 :** asserted to be true or to exist ⟨an ~ miracle⟩ **2 :** questionably true or of a specified kind **:** SUPPOSED, SO-CALLED ⟨bought an ~ antique vase⟩ **3 :** accused but not proven or convicted ⟨an ~ burglar⟩ — **al·leg·ed·ly** \-ˈle-jəd-lē\ *adv*

Al·le·ghe·ny spurge \ˈa-lə-ˌgā-nē- *also* -ˌge-nē-\ *n* [*Allegheny* Mountains, U.S.A.] (ca. 1936) **:** a low herb or subshrub (*Pachysandra procumbens*) of the box family widely grown as a ground cover

al·le·giance \ə-ˈlē-jən(t)s\ *n* [ME *aligeaunce,* fr. AF *allegeance,* alter. of *ligeance,* fr. *lige* liege] (14c) **1 a :** the obligation of a feudal vassal to his liege lord **b (1) :** the fidelity owed by a subject or citizen to a sovereign or government **(2) :** the obligation of an alien to the government under which the alien resides **2 :** devotion or loyalty to a person, group, or cause ***syn*** see FIDELITY — **al·le·giant** \-jənt\ *adj*

al·le·gor·i·cal \ˌa-lə-ˈgȯr-i-kəl, -ˈgär-\ *adj* (1528) **1 :** of, relating to, or having the characteristics of allegory **2 :** having hidden spiritual meaning that transcends the literal sense of a sacred text — **al·le·gor·i·cal·ly** \-k(ə-)lē\ *adv* — **al·le·gor·i·cal·ness** \-kəl-nəs\ *n*

al·le·go·rise *Brit var of* ALLEGORIZE

al·le·go·rist \ˈa-lə-ˌgȯr-əst\ *n* (1684) **:** a creator of allegory

al·le·go·rize \ˈa-lə-ˌgȯr-ˌīz, -gər-\ *vb* **-rized; -riz·ing** *vi* (1579) **1 :** to give allegorical explanations **2 :** to compose or use allegory ~ *vt* **1 :** to treat or explain as an allegory **2 :** to make into allegory — **al·le·go·ri·za·tion** \ˌa-lə-ˌgȯr-ə-ˈzā-shən, -gər-\ *n* — **al·le·go·riz·er** *n*

al·le·go·ry \ˈa-lə-ˌgȯr-ē\ *n, pl* **-ries** [ME *allegorie,* fr. L *allegoria,* fr. Gk *allēgoria,* fr. *allēgorein* to speak figuratively, fr. *allos* other + *-ēgorein* to speak publicly, fr. *agora* assembly — more at ELSE, AGORA] (14c) **1 :** the expression by means of symbolic fictional figures and actions of truths or generalizations about human existence; *also* **:** an instance (as in a story or painting) of such expression **2 :** a symbolic representation **:** EMBLEM 2

[1]**al·le·gret·to** \ˌa-lə-ˈgre-(ˌ)tō, ˌä-lə-\ *adv or adj* [It, dim. of *allegro*] (ca. 1740) **:** faster than andante but not so fast as allegro — used as a direction in music

[2]**allegretto** *n, pl* **-tos** (ca. 1846) **:** a musical composition or movement in allegretto tempo

[1]**al·le·gro** \ə-ˈle-(ˌ)grō, -ˈlā-\ *n, pl* **-gros** (1683) **:** a musical composition or movement in allegro tempo

[2]**allegro** *adv or adj* [It, merry, fr. VL **alecrus* lively, alter. of L *alacr-, alacer*] (ca. 1721) **:** at a brisk lively tempo — used as a direction in music

al·lele \ə-ˈlēl\ *n* [G *Allel,* short for *Allelomorph*] (1928) **1 :** any of the alternative forms of a gene that may occur at a given locus **2 :** either of a pair of alternative Mendelian characters (as smooth and wrinkled seed in the pea) — **al·le·lic** \-ˈlē-lik, -ˈle-\ *adj* — **al·lel·ism** \-ˈlē-ˌli-zəm, -ˈle-\ *n*

allelo- *comb form* [Gk *allēlon* of each other, fr. *allos . . . allos* one . . . the other, fr. *allos* other — more at ELSE] **1 :** alternative ⟨*allelo*morph⟩ **2 :** reciprocal ⟨*allelo*pathy⟩

al·le·lo·morph \ə-ˈlē-lə-ˌmȯrf, -ˈle-lə-\ *n* (1902) **:** ALLELE — **al·le·lo·mor·phic** \ə-ˌlē-lə-ˈmȯr-fik, -ˌle-lə-\ *adj* — **al·le·lo·mor·phism** \ə-ˈlē-lə-ˌmȯr-ˌfi-zəm, -ˈle-lə-\ *n*

al·le·lop·a·thy \ə-ˈlē-lə-ˌpa-thē, -ˈle-lə-; *also* ˌa-lə-ˈlä-pə-thē\ *n* [ISV] (1948) **:** the suppression of growth of one plant species by another due to the release of toxic substances — **al·le·lo·path·ic** \ə-ˌlē-lə-ˈpa-thik, -ˌle-lə-\ *adj*

al·le·lu·ia \ˌa-lə-ˈlü-yə\ *interj* [ME, fr. LL, fr. Gk *allēlouia,* fr. Heb *halălūyāh* praise ye Jehovah] (14c) **:** HALLELUJAH

al·le·mande \ˈa-lə-ˌman(d), -mən, -ˌmänd, *1a & 2 also* ˌa-lə-ˈ\ *n, often cap* [F, fr. fem. of *allemand* German] (1685) **1 :** a musical composition or movement (as in a baroque suite) in moderate tempo and duple or quadruple time **2 a :** a 17th and 18th century court dance developed in France from a German folk dance **b :** a dance step with arms interlaced

all–em·brac·ing \ˌȯ-lim-ˈbrā-siŋ\ *adj* (ca. 1649) **:** COMPLETE, SWEEPING ⟨an ~ theory⟩

Al·len wrench \ˈa-lən-\ *n* [*Allen* Manufacturing Co., Hartford, Conn.] (1943) **:** an L-shaped hexagonal metal bar either end of which fits the socket of a screw or bolt

al·ler·gen \ˈa-lər-jən\ *n* [ISV *allergy* + *-gen*] (1910) **:** a substance (as pollen) that induces allergy — **al·ler·gen·ic** \ˌa-lər-ˈje-nik\ *adj* — **al·ler·ge·nic·i·ty** \ˌa-lər-jə-ˈni-sə-tē\ *n*

al·ler·gic \ə-ˈlər-jik\ *adj* (1911) **1 :** of, relating to, affected with, or caused by allergy **2 :** having an aversion ⟨~ to work⟩

allergic rhinitis *n* (1924) **:** rhinitis caused by exposure to an allergen; *esp* **:** HAY FEVER

al·ler·gist \ˈa-lər-jist\ *n* (1928) **:** a specialist in allergy

al·ler·gy \ˈa-lər-jē\ *n, pl* **-gies** [G *Allergie,* fr. *all-* + Gk *ergon* work — more at WORK] (1910) **1 :** altered bodily reactivity (as hypersensitivity) to an antigen in response to a first exposure ⟨a bee venom ~ so severe that a second sting may be fatal⟩ **2 :** exaggerated or pathological immunological reaction (as by sneezing, difficult breathing, itching, or skin rashes) to substances, situations, or physical states that are without comparable effect on the average individual **3 :** medical practice concerned with allergies **4 :** a feeling of antipathy or aversion

al·le·thrin \ˈa-lə-thrən\ *n* [*all*yl + pyr*ethrin*] (1950) **:** a light yellow viscous oily synthetic pyrethroid insecticide $C_{19}H_{26}O_3$ used esp. in household aerosols

al·le·vi·ate \ə-ˈlē-vē-ˌāt\ *vt* **-at·ed; -at·ing** [LL *alleviatus,* pp. of *alleviare,* fr. L *ad-* + *levis* light — more at LIGHT] (15c) **:** RELIEVE, LESSEN: as **a :** to make (as suffering) more bearable ⟨her sympathy *alleviated* his distress⟩ **b :** to partially remove or correct ⟨measures taken to ~ a labor shortage⟩ ***syn*** see RELIEVE — **al·le·vi·a·tion** \-ˌlē-vē-ˈā-shən\ *n* — **al·le·vi·a·tor** \-ˈlē-vē-ˌā-tər\ *n*

[1]**al·ley** \ˈa-lē\ *n, pl* **alleys** [ME, fr. AF *alee,* fr. *aler* to go] (14c) **1 :** a garden or park walk bordered by trees or bushes **2 a (1) :** a grassed enclosure for bowling or skittles **(2) :** a hardwood lane for bowling; *also* **:** a room or building housing a group of such lanes **b :** the space on each side of a tennis doubles court between the sideline and the service sideline **c :** an area in a baseball outfield between two outfielders when they are in normal positions **3 :** a narrow street; *esp* **:** a thoroughfare through the middle of a block giving access to the rear of lots or buildings — **up one's alley** *also* **down one's alley :** suited to one's own tastes or abilities

[2]**alley** *n, pl* **alleys** [by shortening and alter. fr. *alabaster*] (1720) **:** a playing marble; *esp* **:** one of superior quality

alley cat *n* (1904) **:** a stray cat

al·ley–oop \ˌa-lē-ˈyüp\ *n* [alter. of *allez-oop,* cry of a circus acrobat about to leap, prob. fr. F *allez,* 2d pers. pl. imper. of *aller* to go + E *-oop,* perh. alter. of *up*] (1967) **:** a basketball play in which a leaping player catches a pass above the basket and immediately dunks the ball; *also* **:** the usu. looping pass thrown on such a play

al·ley·way \ˈa-lē-ˌwā\ *n* (1788) **1 :** a narrow passageway **2 :** ALLEY 3

all–fired \ˈȯl-ˌfī(-ə)rd\ *adv* [alter. of *hell-fired* damned, fr. *hellfire*] (1837) **:** EXTREMELY, EXCESSIVELY ⟨~ stubborn⟩

All Fools' Day *n* (1712) **:** APRIL FOOLS' DAY

all fours *n pl* (15c) **1 a :** all four legs of a quadruped **b :** the two legs and two arms of a person when used to support the body ⟨down on *all fours*⟩ **2** *sing in constr* **:** any of various card games in which points are scored for the high trump, low trump, jack of trumps, and game

all get–out \ˌȯl-ˈget-ˌau̇t, -ˈgit-\ *n* (1879) **:** the utmost conceivable degree — used in comparisons to suggest something superlative ⟨is busy as *all get-out*⟩

all hail *interj* (14c) — used to express greeting, welcome, or acclamation

All·hal·lows \ȯl-ˈha-(ˌ)lōz, -ləz\ *n, pl* **Allhallows** [short for *All Hallows' Day*] (15c) **:** ALL SAINTS' DAY

all hours *n pl* (1816) **:** a very late time ⟨stayed up until *all hours*⟩

al·li·a·ceous \ˌa-lē-ˈā-shəs\ *adj* [L *allium* garlic] (1792) **:** resembling garlic or onion esp. in smell or taste

al·li·ance \ə-ˈlī-ən(t)s\ *n* (14c) **1 a :** the state of being allied **:** the action of allying **b :** a bond or connection between families, states, parties, or individuals ⟨a closer ~ between government and industry⟩ **2 :** an association to further the common interests of the members; *specif* **:** a confederation of nations by treaty **3 :** union by relationship in qualities **:** AFFINITY **4 :** a treaty of alliance

al·li·cin \ˈa-lə-sən\ *n* [NL *Alli*um (genus name of garlic, fr. L, garlic) + *-cin* (as in *-mycin*)] (1944) **:** a pungent compound $C_6H_{10}OS_2$ formed enzymatically in crushed garlic cloves that imparts the distinctive smell to garlic and possesses antimicrobial properties

al·lied \ə-ˈlīd, ˈa-ˌlīd\ *adj* (14c) **1 :** having or being in close association **:** CONNECTED ⟨two families ~ by marriage⟩ **2 :** joined in alliance by compact or treaty; *specif, cap* **:** of or relating to the nations united against Germany and its allies in World War I or those united against the Axis powers in World War II **3 a :** related esp. by common properties or qualities ⟨heraldry and ~ subjects⟩ **b :** related genetically

allies *pl of* ALLY

al·li·ga·tor \ˈa-lə-ˌgā-tər\ *n* [Sp *el lagarto* the lizard, fr. *el* the (fr. L *ille* that) + *lagarto* lizard, fr. VL **lacartus,* fr. L *lacertus, lacerta* — more at LIZARD] (1579) **1 a :** either of two crocodilians (*Alligator mississippiensis* of the southeastern U.S. and *A. sinensis* of China) having broad heads not tapering to the snout and a special pocket in the upper jaw for reception of the enlarged lower fourth tooth **b :** CROCODILIAN **2 :** leather made from alligator hide

alligator clip *n* (ca. 1941) : a spring-loaded clip that has jaws resembling an alligator's and is used for making temporary electrical connections

alligator pear *n* [by folk etymology fr. Sp *aguacate* — more at AVOCADO] (1763) : AVOCADO

alligator snapping turtle *n* (1882) : a turtle (*Macroclemys temminckii*) of southeastern U.S. rivers that may reach nearly 150 pounds (68 kilograms) in weight and 31 inches (79 centimeters) in length — called also *alligator snapper*

all–im·por·tant \ˌȯl-im-ˈpȯr-tᵊnt, -tənt\ *adj* (1787) : of very great or greatest importance ⟨an ~ question⟩

all–in \ˌȯl-ˈin\ *adj* (1890) **1** *chiefly Brit* : ALL-INCLUSIVE **2** *chiefly Brit* : being almost without restrictions ⟨~ wrestling⟩

all in *adj* (1903) : TIRED, EXHAUSTED ⟨after a day of wood-splitting he was *all in*⟩

all–in·clu·sive \ˌȯl-in-ˈklü-siv, -ziv\ *adj* (1850) : including everything ⟨a broader and more nearly ~ view⟩ — **all–in·clu·sive·ness** *n*

al·lit·er·ate \ə-ˈli-tə-ˌrāt\ *vb* **-at·ed; -at·ing** [back-formation fr. *alliteration*] *vi* (1776) **1** : to form an alliteration **2** : to write or speak alliteratively ~ *vt* : to arrange or place so as to make alliteration ⟨~ syllables in a sentence⟩

al·lit·er·a·tion \ə-ˌli-tə-ˈrā-shən\ *n* [*ad-* + L *littera* letter] (ca. 1624) : the repetition of usu. initial consonant sounds in two or more neighboring words or syllables (as *w*ild and *w*oolly, *thr*eatening *thr*ongs) — called also *head rhyme, initial rhyme*

al·lit·er·a·tive \ə-ˈli-tər-ə-tiv, -tə-ˌrā-tiv\ *adj* (1764) : of, relating to, or marked by alliteration — **al·lit·er·a·tive·ly** *adv*

al·li·um \ˈa-lē-əm\ *n* [NL, genus name, fr. L, garlic] (1597) : any of a large genus (*Allium*) of bulbous herbs of the lily family including the onion, garlic, chive, leek, and shallot

all–night \ˈȯl-ˈnīt\ *adj* (1886) **1** : lasting throughout the night ⟨an ~ poker game⟩ **2** : open throughout the night ⟨an ~ diner⟩

all–night·er \ˈȯl-ˈnī-tər\ *n* (1964) : something that lasts all night; *specif* : an all-night study session

allo- — see ALL-

al·lo·an·ti·body \ˌa-lō-ˈan-ti-ˌbä-dē\ *n* (1964) : an antibody produced following introduction of an alloantigen into the system of an individual of a species lacking that particular antigen

al·lo·an·ti·gen \ˌa-lō-ˈan-ti-jən\ *n* (1964) : an antigen present only in some individuals (as of a particular blood group) of a species and capable of inducing the production of an alloantibody by individuals which lack it

al·lo·ca·ble \ˈa-lə-kə-bəl\ *adj* (1916) : capable of being allocated

al·lo·cate \ˈa-lə-ˌkāt\ *vt* **-cat·ed; -cat·ing** [ML *allocatus*, pp. of *allocare*, fr. L *ad-* + *locare* to place, fr. *locus* place — more at STALL] (ca. 1641) **1** : to apportion for a specific purpose or to particular persons or things : DISTRIBUTE ⟨~ tasks among human and automated components⟩ **2** : to set apart or earmark : DESIGNATE ⟨~ a section of the building for special research purposes⟩ — **al·lo·cat·able** \-ˌkā-tə-bəl\ *adj* — **al·lo·ca·tion** \ˌa-lə-ˈkā-shən\ *n* — **al·lo·ca·tor** \ˈa-lə-ˌkā-tər\ *n*

al·lo·cu·tion \ˌa-lə-ˈkyü-shən\ *n* [L *allocution-, allocutio*, fr. *alloqui* to speak to, fr. *ad-* + *loqui* to speak] (1615) : a formal speech; *esp* : an authoritative or hortatory address

all of *adv* (1829) : FULLY ⟨she's *all of* 20 years old⟩

al·log·a·mous \ə-ˈlä-gə-məs\ *adj* (ca. 1890) : reproducing by cross-fertilization — **al·log·a·my** \-mē\ *n*

al·lo·ge·ne·ic \ˌa-lō-jə-ˈnē-ik\ *also* **al·lo·gen·ic** \-ˈje-nik\ *adj* [*all-* + *-geneic* (as in *syngeneic*)] (1961) : involving, derived from, or being individuals of the same species that are sufficiently unlike genetically to interact antigenically ⟨~ skin grafts⟩ — compare SYNGENEIC

al·lo·graft \ˈa-lə-ˌgraft\ *n* (1961) : a homograft between allogeneic individuals — **allograft** *vt*

al·lo·graph \ˈa-lə-ˌgraf\ *n* (1951) **1** : a letter of an alphabet in a particular shape (as A or a) **2** : a letter or combination of letters that is one of several ways of representing one phoneme (as *pp* in *hopping* representing the phoneme \p\) — **al·lo·graph·ic** \ˌa-lə-ˈgra-fik\ *adj*

al·lom·e·try \ə-ˈlä-mə-trē\ *n* (1936) : relative growth of a part in relation to an entire organism or to a standard; *also* : the measure and study of such growth — **al·lo·me·tric** \ˌa-lə-ˈme-trik\ *adj*

al·lo·morph \ˈal-ə-ˌmȯrf\ *n* [*allo-* + *morph*eme] (1945) : one of a set of forms that a morpheme may take in different contexts ⟨the *-s* of *cats*, the *-en* of *oxen*, and the zero suffix of *sheep* are ~*s* of the English plural morpheme⟩ — **al·lo·mor·phic** \ˌa-lə-ˈmȯr-fik\ *adj* — **al·lo·mor·phism** \ˈa-lə-ˌmȯr-ˌfi-zəm\ *n*

al·longe \a-ˈlōⁿzh\ *n* [F, lit., lengthening] (ca. 1859) : RIDER 2a

al·lo·path·ic \ˌa-lə-ˈpa-thik\ *adj* [G *allopatisch*, fr. *Allopathie* an allopathic system of medicine, fr. *allo-* all- + *-pathie* -pathy] (1830) : relating to or being a system of medicine that aims to combat disease by using remedies (as drugs or surgery) which produce effects that are different from or incompatible with those of the disease being treated

al·lo·pat·ric \ˌa-lə-ˈpa-trik\ *adj* [*all-* + Gk *patra* fatherland, fr. *patēr* father — more at FATHER] (1942) : occurring in different geographical areas or in isolation ⟨~ speciation⟩ — compare SYMPATRIC — **al·lo·pat·ri·cal·ly** \-tri-k(ə-)lē\ *adv* — **al·lop·a·try** \ə-ˈlä-pə-trē\ *n*

al·lo·phane \ˈa-lə-ˌfān\ *n* [Gk *allophanēs* appearing otherwise, fr. *all-* + *phainesthai* to appear, middle voice of *phainein* to show — more at FANCY] (ca. 1821) : an amorphous translucent mineral of various colors often occurring in incrustations and stalactite forms and consisting of a hydrous aluminum silicate

al·lo·phone \ˈa-lə-ˌfōn\ *n* [*allo-* + *phone*] (1938) : one of two or more variants of the same phoneme ⟨the aspirated \p\ of *pin* and the unaspirated \p\ of *spin* are ~*s* of the phoneme \p\⟩ — **al·lo·phon·ic** \ˌa-lə-ˈfä-nik\ *adj*

al·lo·poly·ploid \ˌa-lō-ˈpä-li-ˌplȯid\ *n* (1928) : a polyploid individual or strain having a chromosome set composed of two or more chromosome sets derived more or less complete from different species — **allopolyploid** *adj* — **al·lo·poly·ploi·dy** \-ˌplȯi-dē\ *n*

al·lo·pu·ri·nol \ˌa-lō-ˈpyu̇r-ə-ˌnȯl, -ˌnōl\ *n* [*all-* + *purine* + [1]*-ol*] (1964) : a drug $C_5H_4N_4O$ used to promote excretion of uric acid

all–or–none \ˌȯl-ər-ˈnən\ *adj* (1900) : marked either by entire or complete operation or effect or by none at all ⟨~ response of a nerve cell⟩

all–or–noth·ing \-ˈnə-thiŋ\ *adj* (1765) **1** : ALL-OR-NONE **2 a** : accepting no less than everything ⟨he's an ~ perfectionist⟩ **b** : risking everything ⟨an ~ combat strategy⟩

al·lo·saur \ˈa-lə-ˌsȯr\ *n* (ca. 1934) : any of a family (Allosauridae) of large theropod dinosaurs usu. having three clawed digits on each arm and leg and living from the late Jurassic to the early Cretaceous period; *esp* : ALLOSAURUS

al·lo·sau·rus \ˌa-lə-ˈsȯr-əs\ *n* [NL, fr. Gk *all-* + *sauros* lizard] (1886) : any of a genus (*Allosaurus*) of very large carnivorous No. American theropod dinosaurs of the late Jurassic period

al·lo·ste·ric \ˌa-lō-ˈster-ik, -ˈstir-\ *adj* [*all-* + *steric*] (1962) : of, relating to, undergoing, or being a change in the shape and activity of a protein (as an enzyme) that results from combination with another substance at a point other than the chemically active site — **al·lo·ste·ri·cal·ly** \-i-k(ə-)lē\ *adv* — **al·lo·ste·ry** \ˈa-lō-ˌster-ē, -ˌstir-\ *n*

al·lot \ə-ˈlät\ *vt* **al·lot·ted; al·lot·ting** [ME *alotten*, fr. AF *aloter*, fr. *a-* (fr. L *ad-*) + *lot*, of Gmc origin; akin to OE *hlot* lot] (15c) **1** : to assign as a share or portion ⟨~ 10 minutes for the speech⟩ **2** : to distribute by or as if by lot ⟨~ seats to the press⟩ — **al·lot·ter** *n*

al·lo·te·tra·ploid \ˌa-lō-ˈte-trə-ˌplȯid\ *n* (1930) : AMPHIDIPLOID — **al·lo·te·tra·ploi·dy** \-ˌplȯi-dē\ *n*

al·lot·ment \ə-ˈlät-mənt\ *n* (1574) **1** : the act of allotting : APPORTIONMENT **2** : something that is allotted; *esp, chiefly Brit* : a plot of land let to an individual for cultivation

al·lo·trope \ˈa-lə-ˌtrōp\ *n* [ISV, back-formation fr. *allotropy*] (1876) : a form showing allotropy

al·lot·ro·py \ə-ˈlä-trə-pē\ *n, pl* **-pies** (1850) : the existence of a substance and esp. an element in two or more different forms (as of crystals) usu. in the same phase — **al·lo·trop·ic** \ˌa-lə-ˈträ-pik\ *adj*

all' ot·ta·va \ˌa-lə-ˈtä-və, ˌä-lō-\ *adv or adj* [It, at the octave] (ca. 1823) : OTTAVA

al·lot·tee \ə-ˌlä-ˈtē\ *n* (1846) : one to whom an allotment is made

al·lo·type \ˈa-lə-ˌtīp\ *n* (1960) : an alloantigen that is part of a plasma protein (as an antibody) — **al·lo·typ·ic** \ˌa-lə-ˈti-pik\ *adj* — **al·lo·typ·i·cal·ly** \-pi-k(ə-)lē\ *adv* — **al·lo·typy** \ˈa-lə-ˌtī-pē\ *n*

all–out \ˈȯl-ˈau̇t\ *adj* (1908) **1** : made with maximum effort : THOROUGHGOING ⟨an ~ effort to win the contest⟩ **2** : FULL-BLOWN 2

all out *adv* (1895) : with full determination or enthusiasm : with maximum effort — used chiefly in the phrase *go all out*

[1]**all·over** \ˈȯl-ˌō-vər\ *adj* (1796) : covering the whole extent or surface ⟨a sweater with an ~ pattern⟩

[2]**allover** *n* (1838) **1** : an embroidered, printed, or lace fabric with a design covering most of the surface **2** : a pattern or design in which a single unit is repeated so as to cover an entire surface

[1]**all over** *adv* (15c) **1** : over the whole extent ⟨decorated *all over* with a flower pattern⟩ **2** : EVERYWHERE ⟨looked *all over* for the book⟩ **3** : in every respect : THOROUGHLY ⟨she is her mother *all over*⟩

[2]**all over** *prep* (1912) **1** : in eagerly affectionate, attentive, or aggressive pursuit of ⟨the band's fans were *all over* them⟩ **2** : in or into a state marked by all-out criticism of ⟨the press was *all over* the coach after the loss⟩

al·low \ə-ˈlau̇\ *vb* [ME, fr. AF *aluer, alouer* to place, apportion, allow, fr. MF *allocare* — more at ALLOCATE] *vt* (14c) **1 a** : to assign as a share or suitable amount (as of time or money) ⟨~ an hour for lunch⟩ **b** : to reckon as a deduction or an addition ⟨~ a gallon for leakage⟩ **2 a** *chiefly Southern & Midland* : to be of the opinion : THINK **b** *dial* : SAY, STATE **c** : to express an opinion — usu. used with *as how* or *that* **3** *chiefly Southern & Midland* : INTEND, PLAN **4** : ADMIT, CONCEDE ⟨must ~ that money causes problems in marriage⟩ **5 a** : PERMIT ⟨doesn't ~ people to smoke in his home⟩ **b** : to forbear or neglect to restrain or prevent ⟨~ the dog to roam⟩ ~ *vi* **1** : to make a possibility : ADMIT — used with *of* ⟨evidence that ~*s* of only one conclusion⟩ **2** : to give consideration to circumstances or contingencies — used with *for* ⟨~ for expansion⟩

al·low·able \ə-ˈlau̇-ə-bəl\ *adj* (15c) : PERMISSIBLE ⟨~ income tax deductions⟩ — **al·low·ably** \-blē\ *adv*

[1]**al·low·ance** \ə-ˈlau̇-ən(t)s\ *n* (14c) **1 a** : a share or portion allotted or granted **b** : a sum granted as a reimbursement or bounty or for expenses ⟨salary includes cost-of-living ~⟩; *esp* : a sum regularly provided for personal or household expenses ⟨each child has an ~⟩ **c** : a fixed or available amount ⟨provide an ~ of time for recreation⟩ **d** : a reduction from a list price or stated price ⟨a trade-in ~⟩ **2** : an imposed handicap (as in a horse race) **3** : an allowed dimensional difference between mating parts of a machine **4** : the act of allowing : PERMISSION **5** : a taking into account of mitigating circumstances or contingencies ⟨the plan makes no ~ for bad weather⟩

[2]**allowance** *vt* **-anced; -anc·ing** (1758) **1** *archaic* : to put on a fixed allowance (as of food and drink) **2** *archaic* : to supply in a fixed or regular quantity

al·low·ed·ly \ə-ˈlau̇-əd-lē\ *adv* (1602) : by allowance : ADMITTEDLY

al·lox·an \ə-ˈläk-sən\ *n* [G, fr. *All*antoin + *Ox*alsäure oxalic acid + *-an*] (1853) : a crystalline compound $C_4H_2N_2O_4$ causing diabetes mellitus when injected into experimental animals

[1]**al·loy** \ˈa-ˌlȯi *also* ə-ˈlȯi\ *n* [F *aloi*, fr. OF *alei*, fr. *aleir* to combine, fr. L *alligare* to bind — more at ALLY] (1604) **1** : the degree of mixture with base metals : FINENESS **2** : a substance composed of two or more metals or of a metal and a nonmetal intimately united usu. by being fused together and dissolving in each other when molten; *also* : the state of union of the components **3 a** : an admixture that lessens value **b** : an impairing alien element **4** : a compound, mixture, or union of different things ⟨an ethnic ~ of many peoples⟩ **5** *archaic* : a metal mixed with a more valuable metal to give durability or some other desired quality

[2]**al·loy** \ə-ˈlȯi *also* ˈa-ˌlȯi\ *vt* (1661) **1 a** : TEMPER, MODERATE **b** : to impair or debase by admixture **2** : to reduce the purity of by mixing with a less valuable metal **3** : to mix so as to form an alloy ~ *vi* : to lend itself to being alloyed ⟨iron ~*s* well⟩

all–pow·er·ful \ˈȯl-ˈpau̇(-ə)r-fəl\ *adj* (1667) : having complete or sole power ⟨an ~ leader⟩

all–pur·pose \-ˈpər-pəs\ *adj* (1928) : suited for many purposes or uses

[1]**all right** *adj* (1808) **1 :** SATISFACTORY, AGREEABLE ⟨whatever you decide is *all right* with me⟩ **2 :** SAFE, WELL ⟨he was ill but he's *all right* now⟩ **3 :** GOOD, PLEASING — often used as a generalized term of approval ⟨an *all right* guy⟩ ***usage*** see ALRIGHT

[2]**all right** *adv* (ca. 1811) **1 :** beyond doubt **:** CERTAINLY ⟨she has pneumonia *all right*⟩ **2** — used interjectionally esp. to express agreement or resignation or to indicate the resumption of a discussion ⟨*all right,* we can do that if you want⟩ ⟨*all right,* let's go⟩ **3 :** well enough **:** SATISFACTORILY ⟨does *all right* in school⟩ ***usage*** see ALRIGHT

all–round *var of* ALL-AROUND

all–round·er \ˈȯl-ˈrau̇n-dər\ *n* (1875) *Brit* **:** one having many skills or uses

All Saints' Day *n* (1622) **:** November 1 observed in Western liturgical churches as a Christian feast in honor of all the saints

All Souls' Day *n* (14c) **:** November 2 observed in some Christian churches as a day of prayer for the souls of the faithful departed

all·spice \ˈȯl-ˌspīs\ *n* (1621) **1 :** the berry of a West Indian tree (*Pimenta dioica*) of the myrtle family; *also* **:** the allspice tree **2 :** a mildly pungent and aromatic spice prepared from dried allspice berries

[1]**all–star** \ˈȯl-ˌstär\ *adj* (1888) **:** composed wholly or chiefly of stars or of outstanding performers or participants ⟨an ~ cast⟩

[2]**all–star** \ˈȯl-ˌstär\ *n* (1905) **:** a member of an all-star team

all–ter·rain vehicle *n* (1969) **:** a small motor vehicle with three or four wheels that is designed for use on various types of terrain — called also *ATV*

all that *adv* (1945) **:** to an indicated or suggested extent or degree **:** SO ⟨didn't take his threats *all that* seriously⟩

all–time \ˈȯl-ˌtīm\ *adj* (1914) **1 :** FULL-TIME 1 **2 :** being for or of all time up to and including the present; *esp* **:** exceeding all others of all time ⟨an ~ best seller⟩

all told *adv* (1814) **:** with everything or everyone taken into account **:** in all ⟨expecting eight guests *all told*⟩

al·lude \ə-ˈlüd\ *vi* **al·lud·ed; al·lud·ing** [L *alludere,* lit., to play with, fr. *ad-* + *ludere* to play — more at LUDICROUS] (1533) **:** to make indirect reference ⟨comments *alluding* to an earlier discussion⟩; *broadly* **:** REFER

[1]**al·lure** \ə-ˈlu̇r\ *vt* **al·lured; al·lur·ing** [ME *aluren,* fr. MF *alurer,* fr. OF, fr. *a-* (fr. L *ad-*) + *lure, leure* lure — more at LURE] (15c) **:** to entice by charm or attraction ***syn*** see ATTRACT — **al·lure·ment** \-ˈlu̇r-mənt\ *n* — **al·lur·ing·ly** *adv*

[2]**allure** *n* (1548) **:** power of attraction or fascination **:** CHARM

al·lu·sion \ə-ˈlü-zhən\ *n* [LL *allusion-, allusio,* fr. L *alludere*] (1612) **1 :** an implied or indirect reference esp. in literature; *also* **:** the use of such references **2 :** the act of alluding to or hinting at something — **al·lu·sive** \-ˈlü-siv, -ziv\ *adj* — **al·lu·sive·ly** *adv* — **al·lu·sive·ness** *n*

[1]**al·lu·vi·al** \ə-ˈlü-vē-əl\ *adj* (1781) **:** relating to, composed of, or found in alluvium ⟨~ soil⟩ ⟨~ diamonds⟩

[2]**alluvial** *n* (1816) **:** an alluvial deposit

alluvial fan *n* (1862) **:** the alluvial deposit of a stream where it issues from a gorge upon a plain or of a tributary stream at its junction with the main stream

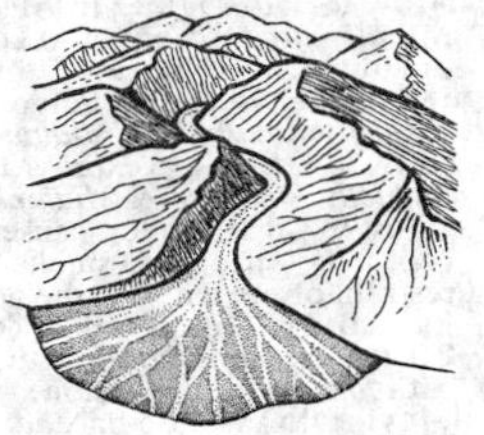

alluvial fan

al·lu·vi·on \ə-ˈlü-vē-ən\ *n* [L *alluvion-, alluvio,* fr. *alluere* to flow past, deposit (of water), fr. *ad-* + *lavere* to wash — more at LYE] (1536) **1 :** the wash or flow of water against a shore **2 :** FLOOD, INUNDATION **3 :** ALLUVIUM **4 :** an accession to land by the gradual addition of matter (as by deposit of alluvium) that then belongs to the owner of the land to which it is added; *also* **:** the land so added

al·lu·vi·um \-vē-əm\ *n, pl* **-vi·ums** *or* **-via** \-vē-ə\ [ML, alter. of L *alluvio*] (ca. 1656) **:** clay, silt, sand, gravel, or similar detrital material deposited by running water

all–wheel drive \ˈȯl-ˈwēl-\ *n* (1934) **:** an automobile drive mechanism that acts on all four wheels of the vehicle

[1]**al·ly** \ə-ˈlī, ˈa-ˌlī\ *vb* **al·lied; al·ly·ing** [ME *allien,* fr. AF *alier,* fr. L *alligare* to bind to, fr. *ad-* + *ligare* to bind — more at LIGATURE] *vt* (14c) **:** to unite or form a connection or relation between **:** ASSOCIATE ⟨*allied* himself with a wealthy family by marriage⟩ ~ *vi* **:** to form or enter into an alliance ⟨two factions *~ing* with each other⟩

[2]**al·ly** \ˈa-ˌlī, ə-ˈlī\ *n, pl* **allies** (1598) **1 :** a sovereign or state associated with another by treaty or league **2 :** a plant or animal linked to another by genetic or taxonomic proximity **3 :** one that is associated with another as a helper **:** AUXILIARY

-ally *adv suffix* [ˈ-*al* + -*ly*] **:** ²-LY ⟨terrifi*cally*⟩ — in adverbs formed from adjectives in *-ic* with no alternative form in *-ical*

al·lyl \ˈa-ləl\ *adj* [ISV, fr. L *allium* garlic] (1854) **:** being or containing the unsaturated monovalent radical CH_2CHCH_2–

al·lyl·ic \ə-ˈli-lik, a-\ *adj* (1856) **:** involving or characteristic of an allyl radical

al·ma·gest \ˈal-mə-ˌjest\ *n* [ME *almageste,* fr. AF & ML, fr. Ar *al-majusti,* the Arabic version of Ptolemy's astronomy treatise, fr. *al* the + Gk *megistē* (*syntaxis*), lit., greatest (composition)] (14c) **:** any of several early medieval treatises on a branch of knowledge

al·ma ma·ter \ˌal-mə-ˈmä-tər\ *n* [L, fostering mother] (1651) **1 :** a school, college, or university which one has attended or from which one has graduated **2 :** the song or hymn of a school, college, or university

al·ma·nac \ˈȯl-mə-ˌnak, ˈal-\ *n* [ME *almenak,* fr. ML *almanach,* prob. fr. Ar *al-manākh* the almanac] (14c) **1 :** a publication containing astronomical and meteorological data for a given year and often including a miscellany of other information **2 :** a usu. annual publication containing statistical, tabular, and general information

al·man·dine \ˈal-mən-ˌdēn, -ˌdīn\ *n* [ME *alemaundine,* fr. AF *alamandine,* alter. of OF *alabandine,* fr. ML *alabandina,* fr. *Alabanda,* ancient city in Asia Minor] (15c) **:** ALMANDITE

al·man·dite \ˈal-mən-ˌdīt\ *n* [alter. of *almandine*] (ca. 1868) **:** a deep red garnet consisting of an iron aluminum silicate

[1]**al·mighty** \ȯl-ˈmī-tē\ *adj* [ME, fr. OE *ealmihtig,* fr. *eall* all + *mihtig* mighty] (bef. 12c) **1** *often cap* **:** having absolute power over all ⟨*Almighty* God⟩ **2 a :** relatively unlimited in power ⟨an ~ board of directors⟩ **b :** having or regarded as having great power or importance ⟨the ~ dollar⟩ **3 :** MIGHTY — used as an intensive ⟨an ~ shock⟩ — **al·mighti·ness** *n*

[2]**almighty** *adv* (1833) **:** to a great degree **:** EXTREMELY ⟨although he did not precisely starve, he was ~ hungry —W. A. Swanberg⟩

Almighty *n* (bef. 12c) **:** GOD 1 — used with *the*

al·mond \ˈä-mənd, ˈa-, ˈäl-, ˈal-\ *n* [ME *almande,* fr. AF *alemande* fr. LL *amandula,* alter. of L *amygdala,* fr. Gk *amygdalē*] (14c) **1 a :** the drupaceous fruit of a small tree (*Prunus dulcis* syn. *P. amygdalus*) of the rose family with flowers and young fruit resembling those of the peach; *esp* **:** its ellipsoidal edible kernel used as a nut **b :** any of several similar fruits **2 :** a tree that produces almonds

al·mond–eyed \-ˌīd\ *adj* (1849) **:** having narrow slant almond-shaped eyes

al·mo·ner \ˈal-mə-nər, ˈä-mə-\ *n* [ME *almoiner,* fr. AF *aumoner, almener,* fr. *aumone* alms, fr. LL *eleemosyna*] (14c) **1 :** one who distributes alms **2** *Brit* **:** a social-service worker in a hospital

[1]**al·most** \ˈȯl-ˌmōst, ȯl-ˈ\ *adv* [ME, fr. OE *ealmǣst,* fr. *eall* + *mǣst* most] (bef. 12c) **:** very nearly but not exactly or entirely ⟨we're ~ there⟩

[2]**almost** *adj* (1709) **:** very near but not quite ⟨an ~ failure⟩

alms \ˈä(l)mz\ *n, pl* **alms** [ME *almesse, almes,* fr. OE *ælmesse, ælmes,* fr. LL *eleemosyna* alms, fr. Gk *eleēmosynē* pity, alms, fr. *eleēmōn* merciful, fr. *eleos* pity] (bef. 12c) **1** *archaic* **:** CHARITY **2 :** something (as money or food) given freely to relieve the poor — **alms·giv·er** \-ˌgi-vər\ *n* — **alms·giv·ing** \-ˌgi-viŋ\ *n*

alms·house \-ˌhau̇s\ *n* (14c) **1** *Brit* **:** a privately financed home for the poor **2 :** POORHOUSE

alms·man \-mən\ *n* (bef. 12c) **:** a recipient of alms

al·ni·co \ˈal-ni-ˌkō\ *n* [*al*uminum + *ni*ckel + *co*balt] (1935) **:** a powerful permanent-magnet alloy containing iron, nickel, aluminum, and one or more of the elements cobalt, copper, and titanium

al·oe \ˈa-(ˌ)lō\ *n* [ME, fr. LL, fr. L, dried juice of aloe leaves, fr. Gk *aloē*] (bef. 12c) **1** *pl* **:** the fragrant wood of an East Indian tree (*Aquilaria agallocha*) of the mezereon family **2 a :** any of a large genus (*Aloe*) of succulent chiefly southern African plants of the lily family with basal leaves and spicate flowers **b :** the dried juice of the leaves of various aloes used esp. formerly as a purgative — usu. used in pl. but sing. in constr. **c :** ALOE VERA

aloe vera \-ˈver-ə, -ˈvir-\ *n* [NL, species name, fr. *Aloe* + L *vera,* fem. of *verus* true — more at VERY] (1766) **:** an aloe (*Aloe barbadensis* syn. *A. vera*) whose leaves furnish a gelatinous emollient extract used esp. in cosmetics and skin creams; *also* **:** such an extract or a preparation composed primarily of such an extract

[1]**aloft** \ə-ˈlȯft\ *adv* [ME, fr. ON *ā lopt,* fr. *ā* on, in + *lopt* air — more at ON, LOFT] (13c) **1 :** at or to a great height ⟨measuring the winds ~⟩ **2 :** in the air; *esp* **:** in flight (as in an airplane) ⟨meals served ~⟩ **3 :** at, on, or to the masthead or the higher rigging

[2]**aloft** *prep* (14c) **:** on top of **:** ABOVE ⟨bright signs ~ hotels⟩

alog·i·cal \(ˌ)ā-ˈlä-ji-kəl\ *adj* (1694) **:** being outside the bounds of that to which logic can apply — **alog·i·cal·ly** \-k(ə-)lē\ *adv*

alo·ha \ə-ˈlō-(h)ä, ä-, -(h)ə\ *interj* [Hawaiian, fr. *aloha* love] (1820) — used as a greeting or farewell

aloha shirt *n* (1937) **:** HAWAIIAN SHIRT

[1]**alone** \ə-ˈlōn\ *adj* [ME, fr. *al* all + *one* one] (13c) **1 :** separated from others **:** ISOLATED **2 :** exclusive of anyone or anything else **:** ONLY ⟨she ~ knows why⟩ **3 a :** considered without reference to any other ⟨the children ~ would eat that much⟩ **b :** INCOMPARABLE, UNIQUE ⟨~ among their contemporaries in this respect⟩ — **alone·ness** \-ˈlōn-nəs\ *n*

syn ALONE, SOLITARY, LONELY, LONESOME, LONE, FORLORN, DESOLATE mean isolated from others. ALONE stresses the objective fact of being by oneself with slighter notion of emotional involvement than most of the remaining terms ⟨everyone needs to be *alone* sometimes⟩. SOLITARY may indicate isolation as a chosen course ⟨glorying in the calm of her *solitary* life⟩ but more often it suggests sadness and a sense of loss ⟨left *solitary* by the death of his wife⟩. LONELY adds to SOLITARY a suggestion of longing for companionship ⟨felt *lonely* and forsaken⟩. LONESOME heightens the suggestion of sadness and poignancy ⟨an only child often leads a *lonesome* life⟩. LONE may replace LONELY or LONESOME but typically is as objective as ALONE ⟨a *lone* robin pecking at the lawn⟩. FORLORN stresses dejection, woe, and listlessness at separation from one held dear ⟨a *forlorn* lost child⟩. DESOLATE implies inconsolable grief at loss or bereavement ⟨*desolate* after her brother's death⟩.

[2]**alone** *adv* (13c) **1 :** SOLELY, EXCLUSIVELY ⟨the blame is his ~⟩ **2 :** without aid or support ⟨said he could do it ~⟩

[1]**along** \ə-ˈlȯŋ\ *prep* [ME, fr. OE *andlang,* fr. *and-* against + *lang* long — more at ANTE-] (bef. 12c) **1 :** in a line matching the length or direction of ⟨walking ~ the road⟩; *also* **:** at a point or points on ⟨a house ~ the river⟩ **2 :** in the course of ⟨made stops ~ the way⟩ **3 :** in accordance with **:** IN ⟨a new agreement ~ the lines of the first⟩

[2]**along** *adv* (14c) **1 :** FORWARD, ON ⟨move ~⟩ **2 :** from one to another ⟨word was passed ~⟩ **3 a :** in company **:** as a companion ⟨brought his wife ~⟩ — often used with *with* ⟨walked to school ~ with her friends⟩ **b :** in association — used with *with* ⟨work ~ with colleagues⟩ **4 a :** sometime within a specified or implied extent of time — usu. used with *about* ⟨~ about July 17⟩ **b :** at or to an advanced point ⟨plans are far ~⟩ **5 :** in addition **:** ALSO — usu. used with *with* ⟨a bill came ~ with the package⟩ **6 :** at hand **:** as a necessary or useful item ⟨brought an extra one ~⟩ ⟨had his gun ~⟩ **7 :** on hand **:** THERE ⟨tell him I'll be ~ to see him⟩

along of *prep* [ME *ilong on,* fr. OE *gelang on,* fr. *ge-,* associative prefix + *lang* — more at CO-] (bef. 12c) *dial* **:** BECAUSE OF

along·shore \ə-ˈlȯŋ-ˈshȯr\ *adv or adj* (ca. 1689) **:** along the shore or coast ⟨walked ~⟩ ⟨~ currents⟩

[1]**along·side** \-ˈsīd\ *adv* (1707) **1 :** along the side **:** in parallel position **2 :** at the side **:** close by ⟨a guard with a prisoner ~⟩

[2]**alongside** *prep* (1735) **1 a :** along the side of ⟨the boat docked ~ the pier⟩ **b :** BESIDE 1 ⟨standing ~ me⟩ **2 a :** in company with ⟨men she has been working ~ —Richard Halloran⟩ **b :** in addition to ⟨a special category ~ the awards it annually presents —*Horizon*⟩

alongside of *prep* (1737) **:** ALONGSIDE

[1]**aloof** \ə-ˈlüf\ *adv* [obs. *aloof* to windward, fr. ¹*a-* + *louf, luf* luff] (1523) : at a distance
[2]**aloof** *adj* (1608) : removed or distant either physically or emotionally ⟨he stood ~ from worldly success —John Buchan⟩ ***syn*** see INDIFFERENT — **aloof·ly** *adv* — **aloof·ness** *n*
al·o·pe·cia \ˌa-lə-ˈpē-sh(ē-)ə\ *n* [ME *allopicia,* fr. L *alopecia,* fr. Gk *alōpekia,* fr. *alōpek-, alōpēx* fox; akin to Arm *aluēs* fox, Skt *lopāśa*] (14c) : loss of hair, wool, or feathers — **al·o·pe·cic** \-ˈpē-sik\ *adj*
aloud \ə-ˈlau̇d\ *adv* [ME, fr. ¹*a-* + *loud*] (13c) **1** *archaic* : in a loud manner : LOUDLY **2** : with the speaking voice ⟨read ~⟩
alow \ə-ˈlō\ *adv* [ME, fr. ¹*a-* + *low*] (13c) : BELOW ⟨~ in the ship's hold⟩
alp \ˈalp\ *n* [back-formation fr. *Alps,* mountain system of Europe] (15c) **1** : a high rugged mountain **2** : something suggesting an alp in height, size, or ruggedness
al·paca \al-ˈpa-kə\ *n* [Sp, fr. Aymara *allpaqa*] (1747) **1** : a domesticated mammal (*Vicugna pacos* syn. *Lama pacos*) esp. of Peru that is prob. descended from the vicuña **2 a** : wool of the alpaca **b (1)** : a thin cloth made of or containing this wool **(2)** : a rayon or cotton imitation of this cloth
al·pen·glow \ˈal-pən-ˌglō\ *n* [part trans. of G *Alpenglühen,* fr. *Alpen* Alps + *Glühen* glow] (1870) : a reddish glow seen near sunset or sunrise on the summits of mountains
al·pen·horn \ˈal-pən-ˌhȯrn\ *or* **alp·horn** \ˈalp-ˌhȯrn\ *n* [G, fr. *Alpen* + *Horn* horn] (1811) : a straight wooden horn 5 to 14 feet (about 1.5 to 4.3 meters) in length used chiefly by Swiss herdsmen
al·pen·stock \ˈal-pən-ˌstäk\ *n* [G, fr. *Alpen* + *Stock* staff] (1811) : a long iron-pointed staff used in mountain climbing
[1]**al·pha** \ˈal-fə\ *n* [ME, fr. L, fr. Gk, of Sem origin; akin to Heb *āleph* aleph] (13c) **1** : the 1st letter of the Greek alphabet — see ALPHABET table **2** : something that is first : BEGINNING **3** : ALPHA WAVE **4** : ALPHA PARTICLE

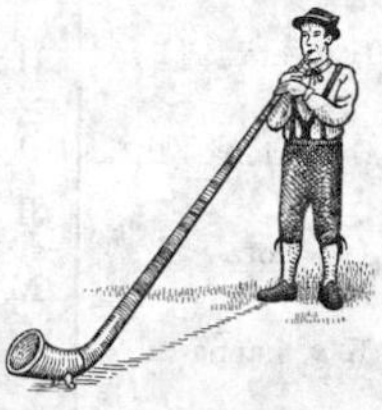
alpenhorn

[2]**alpha** *adj* (1842) **1** : closest in the structure of an organic molecule to a particular group or atom — symbol α ⟨α-substitution⟩ **2** : socially dominant esp. in a group of animals ⟨an ~ male⟩ **3** : ALPHABETIC
al·pha–ad·ren·er·gic \ˈal-fə-ˌa-drə-ˈnər-jik\ *adj* (1965) : of, relating to, or being an alpha-receptor ⟨~ blocking action⟩
alpha and omega *n* [fr. the fact that alpha and omega are respectively the first and last letters of the Greek alphabet] (1526) **1** : the beginning and ending **2** : the principal element
al·pha·bet \ˈal-fə-ˌbet, -bət\ *n* [ME *alphabete,* fr. LL *alphabetum,* fr. Gk *alphabētos,* fr. *alpha* + *bēta* beta] (1513) **1 a** : a set of letters or other characters with which one or more languages are written esp. if arranged in a customary order **b** : a system of signs or signals that serve as equivalents for letters **2** : RUDIMENTS, ELEMENTS
☞ The Alphabet Table is on the following page.
al·pha·bet·ic \ˌal-fə-ˈbe-tik\ *or* **al·pha·bet·i·cal** \-ti-kəl\ *adj* (1567) **1** *usu alphabetical* : arranged in the order of the letters of the alphabet **2** : of, relating to, or employing an alphabet — **al·pha·bet·i·cal·ly** \-ti-k(ə-)lē\ *adv*
al·pha·bet·i·za·tion \ˌal-fə-ˌbe-tə-ˈzā-shən\ *n* (1864) **1** : the act or process of alphabetizing **2** : an alphabetically arranged series, list, or file
al·pha·bet·ize \ˈal-fə-bə-ˌtīz\ *vt* **-ized; -iz·ing** (1691) **1** : to arrange alphabetically **2** : to furnish with an alphabet — **al·pha·bet·iz·er** *n*
alphabet soup *n* (1934) : a hodgepodge esp. of initials (as of the names of organizations)
al·pha–fe·to·pro·tein \ˌal-fə-ˌfē-tō-ˈprō-ˌtēn, -ˈprō-tē-ən\ *n* (1968) : a fetal blood protein present abnormally in adults with some cancers (as of the liver) and normally in the amniotic fluid of pregnant women with high or low levels tending to be associated with certain birth defects (as spina bifida or Down syndrome)
alpha globulin *n* [ISV] (1922) : any of several globulins of plasma or serum that have at alkaline pH the greatest electrophoretic mobility next to albumin — compare BETA GLOBULIN, GAMMA GLOBULIN
al·pha–he·lix \ˌal-fə-ˈhē-liks\ *n* (1955) : the coiled structural arrangement of many proteins consisting of a single chain of amino acids stabilized by hydrogen bonds — **al·pha–he·li·cal** \-ˈhe-li-kəl, -ˈhē-li-\ *adj*
alpha hydroxy acid *n* (1899) : any of various carboxylic acids with a hydroxyl group attached at the alpha position; *specif* : one (as malic acid or lactic acid) that occurs in natural products (as fruits, sugarcane, or yogurt) and is used in cosmetics for its exfoliating effect on the surface layer of skin — called also *AHA*
alpha interferon *n* (1980) : an interferon produced by white blood cells that inhibits viral replication, suppresses cell proliferation, and regulates immune response and that is used in a form obtained from recombinant DNA to treat various diseases — compare BETA INTERFERON, GAMMA INTERFERON
alpha iron *n* (1902) : the form of iron stable below 910°C (1670°F)
al·pha·mer·ic \ˌal-fə-ˈmer-ik\ *adj* [*alpha*betic + nu*meric*] (ca. 1952) : ALPHANUMERIC
al·pha·nu·mer·ic \-nu̇-ˈmer-ik, -nyu̇-\ *also* **al·pha·nu·mer·i·cal** \-i-kəl\ *adj* [*alpha*betic + *numeric, numerical*] (1950) **1** : consisting of both letters and numbers and often other symbols (as punctuation marks and mathematical symbols) ⟨an ~ code⟩; *also* : being a character in an alphanumeric system **2** : capable of using or displaying alphanumeric characters — **al·pha·nu·mer·i·cal·ly** \-i-k(ə-)lē\ *adv* — **al·pha·nu·mer·ics** \-iks\ *n pl*
alpha particle *n* (1903) : a positively charged nuclear particle identical with the nucleus of a helium atom that consists of two protons and two neutrons and is ejected at high speed in certain radioactive transformations — called also *alpha, alpha radiation, alpha ray*
alpha privative *n* (1568) : the prefix *a-* or *an-* expressing negation in Greek and in English
al·pha–re·cep·tor \ˈal-fə-ri-ˌsep-tər\ *n* (1961) : any of a group of receptors that are present on cell surfaces of some effector organs and tissues innervated by the sympathetic nervous system and that mediate certain physiological responses (as vasoconstriction, relaxation of intestinal muscle, and contraction of most smooth muscle) when bound by specific adrenergic agents — compare BETA-RECEPTOR
alpha test *n* (1964) : a test of a nearly complete prototype of a product esp. by employees of the company developing the product
al·pha–to·coph·er·ol \-tō-ˈkä-fə-ˌrȯl, -ˌrōl\ *n* (1941) : a tocopherol $C_{29}H_{50}O_2$ with high vitamin E potency : VITAMIN E
alpha wave *n* (1936) : an electrical rhythm of the brain with a frequency of approximately 8 to 13 cycles per second that is often associated with a state of wakeful relaxation — called also *alpha, alpha rhythm*
Al·phe·us \al-ˈfē-əs\ *n* [L, fr. Gk *Alpheios*] (1567) : a Greek river-god who pursues the nymph Arethusa and is finally united with her
al·pine \ˈal-ˌpīn\ *n* (ca. 1828) **1** : a plant native to alpine or boreal regions that is often grown for ornament **2** *cap* : a person possessing Alpine physical characteristics
Alpine *adj* (15c) **1** *often not cap* : of, relating to, or resembling the Alps or any mountains **2** *often not cap* : of, relating to, or growing in the biogeographic zone including the elevated slopes above timberline **3** : of or relating to a physical type characterized by a broad head, stockiness, medium height, and brown hair or eyes often regarded as constituting a branch of the Caucasian race **4** : of or relating to competitive ski events consisting of slalom and downhill racing — compare NORDIC
al·pin·ism \ˈal-pə-ˌni-zəm\ *n, often cap* (1873) : mountain climbing in the Alps or other high mountains — **al·pin·ist** \-nist\ *n*
al·praz·o·lam \al-ˈpra-zə-ˌlam\ *n* [*alprazol-* (perh. fr. rearrangement of letters in *triazole* — compound with a ring composed of two carbon and three nitrogen atoms — and *benzodiazepine*) + *-am* (as in *diazepam*)] (1973) : a benzodiazepine tranquilizer $C_{17}H_{13}ClN_4$ used esp. to treat mild to moderate anxiety
al·pros·ta·dil \al-ˈpräs-tə-dil\ *n* [prob. fr. ²*al*pha + *prosta*glandin + *-il,* alter. of *-yl*] (1981) : a prostaglandin $C_{20}H_{34}O_5$ that promotes vasodilation and is used esp. to treat erectile dysfunction
al·ready \ȯl-ˈre-dē, ˈȯl-ˌ\ *adv* [ME *al redy,* fr. *al redy,* adj., wholly ready, fr. *al* all + *redy* ready] (14c) **1** : prior to a specified or implied past, present, or future time : by this time : PREVIOUSLY ⟨he had ~ left when I called⟩ **2** — used as an intensive ⟨all right ~⟩ ⟨enough ~⟩
al·right \(ˌ)ȯl-ˈrīt, ˈȯl-ˌ\ *adv or adj* (1810) : ALL RIGHT
usage Although the spelling *alright* is nearly as old as *all right,* some critics have insisted *alright* is all wrong. Nevertheless it has its defenders and its users, who perhaps have been influenced by analogy with *altogether* and *already.* It is less frequent than *all right* but remains common esp. in informal writing. It is quite common in fictional dialogue and is sometimes found in more formal writing ⟨the first two years of medical school were *alright* —Gertrude Stein⟩.
ALS *abbr* **1** amyotrophic lateral sclerosis **2** autographed letter signed
Al·sa·tian \al-ˈsā-shən\ *n* [ML *Alsatia* Alsace] (1917) : GERMAN SHEPHERD
al·sike clover \ˈal-ˌsak-, -ˌsīk-\ *n* [*Alsike,* Sweden] (1835) : a European perennial clover (*Trifolium hybridum*) much used as a forage plant
al·so \ˈȯl(t)-(ˌ)sō, ˈȯ-\ *adv* [ME, fr. OE *eallswā,* fr. *eall* all + *swā* so — more at SO] (bef. 12c) **1** : LIKEWISE 1 **2** : in addition : BESIDES, TOO
al·so–ran \-ˌran\ *n* (1896) **1** : a horse or dog that finishes out of the money in a race **2** : a contestant that does not win **3** : one that is of little importance esp. competitively ⟨was just an ~ in the scramble for . . . privileges —C. A. Buss⟩
al·stroe·me·ria \ˌal-strə-ˈmir-ē-ə\ *n* [NL, fr. Klas von *Alstroemer* †1794 Swed. botanist] (1833) : any of a genus (*Alstroemeria*) of tropical South American herbs of the lily family that are often cultivated for their clusters of showy variegated flowers
alt *abbr* **1** alternate **2** altitude **3** alto
Alta *abbr* Alberta
Al·ta·ic \al-ˈtā-ik\ *adj* (1757) **1** : of or relating to the Altai Mountains **2** : of, relating to, or constituting the Turkic, Tungusic, and Mongolian language families collectively
Al·tair \al-ˈtī(-ə)r, -ˈter, ˈal-ˌ\ *n* [Ar *al-ṭā'ir,* lit., the flier] (1759) : the brightest star in the constellation Aquila
al·tar \ˈȯl-tər\ *n, often attrib* [ME *alter,* fr. OE *altar,* fr. L *altare;* prob. akin to L *adolēre* to burn up] (bef. 12c) **1** : a usu. raised structure or place on which sacrifices are offered or incense is burned in worship — often used figuratively to describe a thing given great or undue precedence or value esp. at the cost of something else ⟨sacrificed his family life on the ~ of career advancement⟩ **2** : a table on which the eucharistic elements are consecrated or which serves as a center of worship or ritual
altar boy *n* (1772) : a boy who assists the celebrant in a liturgical service
altar call *n* (1899) : an appeal by an evangelist to worshipers to come forward to signify their decision to commit their lives to Christ
altar of repose *often cap A&R* (1853) : REPOSITORY 2
al·tar·piece \ˈȯl-tər-ˌpēs\ *n* (1644) : a work of art that decorates the space above and behind an altar
altar rail *n* (1705) : a railing in front of an altar separating the chancel from the body of the church
altar server *n* (1826) : a boy or girl who assists the celebrant in a liturgical service
altar stone *n* (14c) : a stone slab with a compartment containing the relics of martyrs that forms an essential part of a Roman Catholic altar
alt·az·i·muth \(ˌ)al-ˈtaz-məth, -ˈta-zə-\ *n, often attrib* [ISV *alt*itude + *azimuth*] (1851) : a telescope mounted so that it can swing horizontally and vertically; *also* : any of several other similarly mounted instruments
al·ter \ˈȯl-tər\ *vb* **al·tered; al·ter·ing** \-t(ə-)riŋ\ [ME, fr. ML *alterare,* fr. L *alter* other (of two); akin to L *alius* other — more at ELSE] *vt* (14c) **1** : to make different without changing into something else **2** : CASTRATE, SPAY ~ *vi* : to become different ***syn*** see CHANGE — **al·ter·abil·i·ty** \ˌȯl-t(ə-)rə-ˈbi-lə-tē\ *n* — **al·ter·able** \ˈȯl-t(ə-)rə-bəl\ *adj* — **al·ter·ably** \-blē\ *adv* — **al·ter·er** \-tər-ər\ *n*
al·ter·a·tion \ˌȯl-tə-ˈrā-shən\ *n* (14c) **1** : the act or process of altering : the state of being altered **2** : the result of altering : MODIFICATION

\ə\ **abut** \ᵊ\ kitten, F table \ər\ **fur**ther \a\ ash \ā\ ace \ä\ mop, mar \au̇\ **out** \ch\ **chin** \e\ **bet** \ē\ **easy** \g\ **go** \i\ **hit** \ī\ **ice** \j\ **job** \ŋ\ **sing** \ō\ **go** \ȯ\ **law** \ȯi\ **boy** \th\ **thin** \t͟h\ **the** \ü\ **loot** \u̇\ **foot** \y\ yet \zh\ vision, beige \k̲, ⁿ, œ, ue, ʸ\ *see* Guide to Pronunciation

ALPHABET TABLE

Showing the letters of five non-Roman alphabets and the transliterations used in the etymologies

HEBREW[1,4]

Letter	Name	Translit.
א	aleph	', [2]
ב	beth	b, bh
ג	gimel	g, gh
ד	daleth	d, dh
ה	he	h
ו	waw	w
ז	zayin	z
ח	heth	ḥ
ט	teth	ṭ
י	yod	y
כ ך	kaph	k, kh
ל	lamed	l
מ ם	mem	m
נ ן	nun	n
ס	samekh	s
ע	ayin	'
פ ף	pe	p, ph
צ ץ	sadhe	ṣ
ק	qoph	q
ר	resh	r
שׂ	sin	ś
שׁ	shin	sh
ת	taw	t, th

ARABIC[3,4]

Name	Translit.
alif	[5]
bā	b
tā	t
thā	th
jīm	j
ḥā	ḥ
khā	kh
dāl	d
dhāl	dh
rā	r
zāy	z
sīn	s
shīn	sh
ṣād	ṣ
ḍād	ḍ
ṭā	ṭ
ẓā	ẓ
'ayn	'
ghayn	gh
fā	f
qāf	q
kāf	k
lām	l
mīm	m
nūn	n
hā	h[6]
wāw	w
yā	y

GREEK[7]

Letter	Name	Translit.
A α	alpha	a
B β	beta	b
Γ γ	gamma	g, n
Δ δ	delta	d
E ε	epsilon	e
Z ζ	zeta	z
H η	eta	ē
Θ θ	theta	th
I ι	iota	i
K κ	kappa	k
Λ λ	lambda	l
M μ	mu	m
N ν	nu	n
Ξ ξ	xi	x
O o	omicron	o
Π π	pi	p
P ρ	rho	r, rh
Σ σ s	sigma	s
T τ	tau	t
Υ υ	upsilon	y, u
Φ φ	phi	ph
X χ	chi	ch
Ψ ψ	psi	ps
Ω ω	omega	ō

RUSSIAN[8]

Letter	Translit.
A a	a
Б б	b
В в	v
Г г	g
Д д	d
E e	e
Ж ж	zh
З з	z
И и Й й	i, ĭ
К к	k
Л л	l
М м	m
Н н	n
O o	o
П п	p
P p	r
C c	s
T т	t
У у	u
Ф ф	f
X x	kh
Ц ц	ts
Ч ч	ch
Ш ш	sh
Щ щ	shch
Ъ ъ[9]	"
Ы ы	y
Ь ь[10]	'
Э э	e
Ю ю	yu
Я я	ya

SANSKRIT[11]

Letter	Translit.	Letter	Translit.
अ	a	ञ	ñ
आ	ā	ट	ṭ
इ	i	ठ	th
ई	ī	ड	ḍ
उ	u	ढ	dh
ऊ	ū	ण	ṇ
ऋ	ṛ	त	t
ॠ	r̄	थ	th
ऌ	ḷ	द	d
ॡ	ḹ	ध	dh
ए	e	न	n
ऐ	ai	प	p
ओ	o	फ	ph
औ	au	ब	b
ं	ṁ	भ	bh
ः	ḥ	म	m
क	k	य	y
ख	kh	र	r
ग	g	ल	l
घ	gh	व	v
ङ	ṅ	श	ś
च	c	ष	ṣ
छ	ch	स	s
ज	j	ह	h
झ	jh		

1 See ALEPH, BETH, etc., in the vocabulary. Where two forms of a letter are given, the one at the right is the form used at the end of a word. 2 Not represented in transliteration when initial. 3 The left column shows the form of each Arabic letter that is used when it stands alone, the second column its form when it is joined to the preceding letter, the third column its form when it is joined to both the preceding and the following letter, and the right column its form when it is joined to the following letter only. In the names of the Arabic letters, ā, ī, and ū respectively are pronounced like a in *father*, i in *machine*, u in *rude*. 4 Hebrew and Arabic are written from right to left. The Hebrew and Arabic letters are all primarily consonants; a few of them are also used secondarily to represent certain vowels, but full indication of vowels, when provided at all, is by means of a system of dots or strokes adjacent to the consonantal characters. 5 Alif represents no sound in itself, but is used principally as an indicator of the presence of a glottal stop (transliterated ' medially and finally; not represented in transliteration when initial) and as the sign of a long *a*. 6 When ة has two dots above it (ة), it is called *tā marbūta* and, if it immediately precedes a vowel, is transliterated *t* instead of *h*. 7 See ALPHA, BETA, GAMMA, etc., in the vocabulary. The letter gamma is transliterated *n* only before velars; the letter upsilon is transliterated *u* only as the final element in diphthongs. 8 See CYRILLIC in the vocabulary. 9 This sign indicates that the immediately preceding consonant is not palatalized even though immediately followed by a palatal vowel. 10 This sign indicates that the immediately preceding consonant is palatalized even though not immediately followed by a palatal vowel. 11 The alphabet shown here is the Devanagari. When vowels are combined with preceding consonants they are indicated by various strokes or hooks instead of by the signs here given, or, in the case of short *a*, not written at all. Thus the character क represents *ka;* the character का, *kā;* the character कि, *ki;* the character की, *kī;* the character कु, *ku;* the character कू, *kū;* the character कृ, *kṛ;* the character कॄ, *kṝ;* the character के, *ke;* the character कै, *kai;* the character को, *ko;* the character कौ, *kau;* and the character क्, *k* without any following vowel. There are also many compound characters representing combinations of two or more consonants.

al·ter·cate \ˈȯl-tər-ˌkāt\ *vi* **-cat·ed; -cat·ing** [L *altercatus,* pp. of *altercari,* fr. *alter*] (1530) **:** to dispute angrily or noisily **:** WRANGLE

al·ter·ca·tion \ˌȯl-tər-ˈkā-shən\ *n* (14c) **:** a noisy heated angry dispute; *also* **:** noisy controversy ***syn*** see QUARREL

al·ter ego \ˌȯl-tər-ˈē-(ˌ)gō *also* -ˈe-(ˌ)gō\ *n* [L, lit., second I] (1537) **:** a second self: as **a :** a trusted friend **b :** the opposite side of a personality **c :** COUNTERPART 3

al·ter·i·ty \ȯl-ˈter-ə-tē, -ˈte-rə-\ *n* [LL *alteritat-, alteritas,* fr. *alter*] (1642) **:** OTHERNESS; *specif* **:** the quality or state of being radically alien to the conscious self or a particular cultural orientation

[1]**al·ter·nate** *US & Canad* ˈȯl-tər-nət *also* ˈal-; *chiefly Brit* ȯl-ˈtər-\ *adj* [L *alternatus,* pp. of *alternare,* fr. *alternus* alternate, fr. *alter*] (1513) **1 :** occurring or succeeding by turns ⟨a day of ~ sunshine and rain⟩ **2 a :** arranged first on one side and then on the other at different levels or points along an axial line ⟨~ leaves⟩ — compare OPPOSITE **b :** arranged one above or alongside the other **3 :** every other **:** every second ⟨he works on ~ days⟩ **4 :** constituting an alternative ⟨took the ~ route home⟩ **5 :** ALTERNATIVE 3 — **al·ter·nate·ly** *adv*

[2]**al·ter·nate** \ˈȯl-tər-ˌnāt *also* ˈal-\ *vb* **-nat·ed; -nat·ing** *vt* (1599) **1 :** to perform by turns or in succession **2 :** to cause to alternate ~ *vi* **:** to change from one to another repeatedly ⟨rain *alternated* with sun⟩

[3]**al·ter·nate** *same as* [1]\ *n* (1717) **1 :** ALTERNATIVE **2 :** one that substitutes for or alternates with another

alternate angle *n* (1610) **:** one of a pair of angles with different vertices and on opposite sides of a transversal at its intersection with two other lines: **a :** one of a pair of angles inside the two intersected lines — called also *alternate interior angle* **b :** one of a pair of angles outside the two intersected lines — called also *alternate exterior angle*

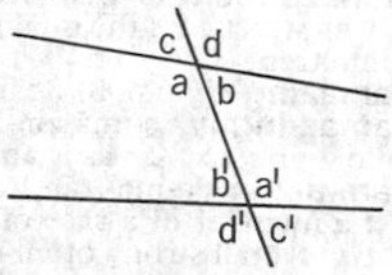

alternate interior angles *a, a', b, b'*; alternate exterior angles *c, c', d, d'*

alternating current *n* (1833) **:** an electric current that reverses its direction at regularly recurring intervals — abbr. *AC*

alternating group *n* (1901) **:** a permutation group whose elements comprise those permutations of *n* objects which can be formed from the original order by making an even number of interchanges of pairs of objects

alternating series *n* (1817) **:** a mathematical series in which consecutive terms are alternatively positive and negative

al·ter·na·tion \ˌȯl-tər-ˈnā-shən *also* ˌal-\ *n* (15c) **1 a :** the act or process of alternating or causing to alternate **b :** alternating occurrence **:** SUCCESSION **2 :** INCLUSIVE DISJUNCTION **3 :** the occurrence of different allomorphs or allophones

alternation of generations (1813) **:** the occurrence of two or more forms differently produced in the life cycle of a plant or animal usu. involving the regular alternation of a sexual with an asexual generation

[1]**al·ter·na·tive** \ȯl-ˈtər-nə-tiv, al-\ *adj* (1540) **1 :** ALTERNATE 1 **2 :** offering or expressing a choice ⟨several ~ plans⟩ **3 :** different from the usual or conventional: as **a :** existing or functioning outside the established cultural, social, or economic system ⟨an ~ newspaper⟩ ⟨~ lifestyles⟩ **b :** of, relating to, or being rock music that is regarded as an alternative to conventional rock and is typically influenced by punk rock, hard rock, hip-hop, or folk music **c :** of or relating to alternative medicine ⟨~ therapies⟩ — **al·ter·na·tive·ly** *adv* — **al·ter·na·tive·ness** *n*

[2]**alternative** *n* (1576) **1 a :** a proposition or situation offering a choice between two or more things only one of which may be chosen **b :** an opportunity for deciding between two or more courses or propositions **2 a :** one of two or more things, courses, or propositions to be chosen **b :** something which can be chosen instead ⟨the only ~ to intervention⟩ **3 :** alternative rock music ***syn*** see CHOICE

alternative medicine *n* (1977) **:** any of various systems of healing or treating disease (as chiropractic, homeopathy, or faith healing) not included in the traditional medical curricula of the U.S. and Britain

alternative school *n* (1972) **:** an elementary or secondary school with a nontraditional curriculum

al·ter·na·tor \ˈȯl-tər-ˌnā-tər *also* ˈal-\ *n* (1883) **:** an electric generator for producing alternating current

alt·horn \ˈalt-ˌhȯrn\ *n* [G, fr. *alt* alto + *Horn* horn] (1854) **:** an alto saxhorn

al·though *also* **al·tho** \ȯl-ˈt͟hō\ *conj* [ME *although,* fr. *al* all + *though*] (14c) **:** in spite of the fact that **:** even though

al·tim·e·ter \al-ˈti-mə-tər, ˈal-tə-ˌmē-tər\ *n* [L *altus* + E *-meter*] (1768) **:** an instrument for measuring altitude; *esp* **:** an aneroid barometer designed to register changes in atmospheric pressure accompanying changes in altitude — **al·tim·e·try** \al-ˈti-mə-trē\ *n*

al·ti·pla·no \ˌal-ti-ˈplä-(ˌ)nō\ *n, pl* **-nos** [AmerSp, fr. L *altus* + *planum* plain] (1919) **:** a high plateau or plain **:** TABLELAND

al·ti·tude \ˈal-tə-ˌtüd *also* -ˌtyüd\ *n* [ME, fr. L *altitudo* height, depth, fr. *altus* high, deep — more at OLD] (14c) **1 a :** the angular elevation of a celestial object above the horizon **b :** the vertical elevation of an object above a surface (as sea level or land) of a planet or natural satellite **c (1) :** a perpendicular line segment from a vertex of a geometric figure (as a triangle or a pyramid) to the opposite side or the opposite side extended or from a side or face to a parallel side or face or the side or face extended **(2) :** the length of an altitude **2 :** a high level (as of quality or feeling) ⟨the ~*s* of his anger⟩ **3 a :** vertical distance or extent **b :** position at a height **c :** an elevated region **:** EMINENCE — usu. used in pl. ***syn*** see HEIGHT — **al·ti·tu·di·nal** \ˌal-tə-ˈtü-dᵊn-əl, -ˈtyü-\ *adj* — **al·ti·tu·di·nous** \-dᵊn-əs\ *adj*

altitude sickness *n* (1901) **:** the effects (as headache, nausea, or swelling of the brain) of oxygen deficiency in the blood and tissues developed at high altitudes having reduced atmospheric pressure

[1]**al·to** \ˈal-(ˌ)tō\ *n, pl* **altos** [It, lit., high, fr. L *altus*] (ca. 1724) **1 a :** COUNTERTENOR **b :** CONTRALTO **2 :** the second highest voice part in a 4-part chorus **3 :** a member of a family of instruments having a range lower than that of the treble or soprano; *esp* **:** an alto saxophone

[2]**alto** *adj* (ca. 1724) **:** relating to or having the range or part of an alto

al·to·cu·mu·lus \ˌal-tō-ˈkyü-myə-ləs\ *n, pl* **-li** \-ˌlī, -ˌlē\ [NL, fr. L *altus* + NL *-o-* + *cumulus*] (1884) **:** a fleecy mid-altitude cloud formation consisting of large whitish globular masses with shaded portions — see CLOUD illustration

[1]**al·to·geth·er** \ˌȯl-tə-ˈge-t͟hər\ *adv* [ME *altogedere,* fr. *al* all + *togedere* together] (13c) **1 :** WHOLLY, COMPLETELY ⟨an ~ different problem⟩ ⟨stopped raining ~⟩ **2 :** in all **:** ALL TOLD ⟨spent a hundred dollars ~⟩ **3 :** on the whole ⟨~ their efforts were successful⟩

[2]**altogether** *n* (1893) **:** NUDE — used with *the* ⟨posed in the ~⟩

al·to–re·lie·vo *or* **al·to–ri·lie·vo** \ˌal-(ˌ)tō-ri-ˈlē-(ˌ)vō, ˌäl-(ˌ)tō-rēl-ˈyā-(ˌ)vō\ *n, pl* **alto–relievos** *or* **al·to–ri·lie·vi** \ˌäl-(ˌ)tō-rēl-ˈyā-(ˌ)vē\ [It *altorilievo*] (1664) **1 :** HIGH RELIEF **2 :** a sculpture in high relief

al·to·stra·tus \ˌal-tō-ˈstrā-təs, -ˈstra-\ *n, pl* **-ti** \-ˌtī\ [NL, fr. L *altus* + NL *-o-* + *stratus*] (1890) **:** a fairly uniform mid-altitude layer of gray cloud darker than cirrostratus — see CLOUD illustration

al·tri·cial \al-ˈtri-shəl\ *adj* [L *altric-, altrix,* fem. of *altor* one who nourishes, fr. *alere* to nourish — more at OLD] (1869) **:** being hatched or born or having young that are hatched or born in a very immature and helpless condition so as to require care for some time ⟨~ birds⟩ — compare PRECOCIAL

alt–rock \ˈȯlt-ˌräk\ *n* [by shortening] (1989) **:** alternative rock music — **alt–rock·er** \-ˌrä-kər\ *n*

al·tru·ism \ˈal-trü-ˌi-zəm\ *n* [F *altruisme,* fr. *autrui* other people, fr. OF, oblique case form of *autre* other, fr. L *alter*] (1853) **1 :** unselfish regard for or devotion to the welfare of others **2 :** behavior by an animal that is not beneficial to or may be harmful to itself but that benefits others of its species — **al·tru·ist** \-trü-ist\ *n* — **al·tru·is·tic** \ˌal-trü-ˈis-tik\ *adj* — **al·tru·is·ti·cal·ly** \-ti-k(ə-)lē\ *adv*

al·u·la \ˈal-yə-lə\ *n, pl* **-lae** \-ˌlē, -ˌlī\ [NL, fr. L, dim. of *ala* wing — more at AISLE] (1772) **:** the process of a bird's wing corresponding to the thumb and bearing a few short quills — called also *bastard wing*

[1]**al·um** \ˈa-ləm\ *n* [ME, fr. AF *alum, alun,* fr. L *alumen*] (14c) **1 :** a potassium aluminum sulfate $KAl(SO_4)_2{\cdot}12H_2O$ or an ammonium aluminum sulfate $NH_4Al(SO_4)_2{\cdot}12H_2O$ used esp. as an emetic and as an astringent and styptic **2 :** any of various double salts isomorphous with potassium aluminum sulfate **3 :** ALUMINUM SULFATE

[2]**alum** \ə-ˈləm\ *n* [by shortening] (1910) **:** ALUMNUS, ALUMNA

[3]**alum** *abbr* aluminum

alu·mi·na \ə-ˈlü-mə-nə\ *n* [NL, fr. L *alumin-, alumen* alum] (ca. 1790) **:** the oxide of aluminum Al_2O_3 occurring native as corundum and in hydrated forms (as in bauxite)

alu·mi·nate \-nət\ *n* (1814) **:** a compound of alumina with a metallic oxide

al·u·min·i·um \ˌal-yə-ˈmi-nē-əm\ *n* [NL, fr. *alumina*] (1805) *chiefly Brit* **:** ALUMINUM

alu·mi·nize \ə-ˈlü-mə-ˌnīz\ *vt* **-nized; -niz·ing** (1888) **:** to treat or coat with aluminum

alu·mi·no·sil·i·cate \ə-ˌlü-mə-nō-ˈsi-lə-ˌkāt, -ˈsi-li-kət\ *n* [L *alumin-, alumen* + *-o-* + ISV *silicate*] (1842) **:** a combined silicate and aluminate

alu·mi·nous \ə-ˈlü-mə-nəs\ *adj* (15c) **:** of, relating to, or containing alum or aluminum

alu·mi·num \ə-ˈlü-mə-nəm\ *n, often attrib* [NL, fr. *alumina*] (1810) **:** a bluish silver-white malleable ductile light trivalent metallic element that has good electrical and thermal conductivity, high reflectivity, and resistance to oxidation and is the most abundant metal in the earth's crust where it always occurs in combination — see ELEMENT table

aluminum oxide *n* (1869) **:** ALUMINA

aluminum sulfate *n* (1868) **:** a white salt $Al_2(SO_4)_3$ usu. made by treating bauxite with sulfuric acid and used in making paper, in water purification, and in tanning

alum·na \ə-ˈləm-nə\ *n, pl* **-nae** \-(ˌ)nē *also* -ˌnī\ [L, fem. of *alumnus*] (1843) **1 :** a girl or woman who has attended or has graduated from a particular school, college, or university **2 :** a girl or woman who is a former member, employee, contributor, or inmate

alum·nus \ə-ˈləm-nəs\ *n, pl* **-ni** \-ˌnī\ [L, foster son, pupil, fr. *alere* to nourish — more at OLD] (1645) **1 :** a person who has attended or has graduated from a particular school, college, or university **2 :** a person who is a former member, employee, contributor, or inmate

al·um·root \ˈa-ləm-ˌrüt, -ˌru̇t\ *n* (1799) **:** any of a genus (*Heuchera*) of No. American herbs of the saxifrage family having basal rounded or lobed toothed leaves; *esp* **:** one (*H. americana*) of eastern No. America

al·u·nite \ˈal-yə-ˌnīt, ˈa-lə-\ *n* [F, fr. *alun* alum] (1823) **:** a mineral that consists of a hydrous potassium aluminum sulfate and occurs in massive form or in rhombohedral crystals

al·ve·o·lar \al-ˈvē-(ə-)lər\ *adj* (1778) **1 :** of, relating to, resembling, or having alveoli; *esp* **:** of, relating to, or constituting the part of the jaws where the teeth arise, the air-containing compartments of the lungs, or glands with secretory cells about a central space **2 :** articulated with the tip of the tongue touching or near the teethridge — **al·ve·o·lar·ly** *adv*

al·ve·o·late \-lət\ *adj* (ca. 1796) **:** pitted like a honeycomb ⟨~ pollen⟩

al·ve·o·lus \al-ˈvē-ə-ləs\ *n, pl* **-li** \-ˌlī, -(ˌ)lē\ [NL, fr. L, dim. of *alveus* cavity, hollow, fr. *alvus* belly, beehive; akin to Lith *aulys* beehive, Gk *aulos* tube, flute] (1702) **1 :** a small cavity or pit: as **a :** a socket in the jaw for a tooth **b :** a small air-containing compartment of the lungs in which the bronchioles terminate and from which respiratory gases are exchanged with the pulmonary capillaries **c :** an acinus of a compound gland **d :** a cell of a honeycomb **2 :** TEETHRIDGE

al·way \ˈȯl-(ˌ)wā\ *adv* [ME *alwey, alneway,* fr. OE *ealne weg,* lit., all the way, fr. *ealne* (acc. of *eall* all) + *weg* (acc.) way — more at WAY] (14c) *archaic* **:** ALWAYS

al·ways \ˈȯl-wēz, -wəz, -(ˌ)wāz *also* ˈȯ-\ *adv* [ME *alwayes,* fr. *alwey*] (14c) **1 :** at all times **:** INVARIABLY ⟨~ smiling⟩ **2 :** FOREVER ⟨will love you ~⟩ **3 :** at any rate **:** in any event ⟨you can ~ try again⟩

Al·yce clover \ˈa-ləs-\ *n* [prob. by folk etymology fr. NL *Alysicarpus,* genus name, fr. Gk *halysis* chain + *karpos* fruit] (1941) **:** a low spreading legume (*Alysicarpus vaginalis*) native to tropical Asia that is planted in the southern U.S. as a cover crop and for hay and forage

alys·sum \ə-ˈli-səm\ *n* [NL, fr. Gk *alysson,* plant believed to cure rabies, fr. neut. of *alyssos* curing rabies, fr. *a-* + *lyssa* rabies] (1548) **1 :** any of a genus (*Alyssum*) of Eurasian herbs of the mustard family with

\ə\ **abut** \ᵊ\ kitten, F table \ər\ **further** \a\ **ash** \ā\ **ace** \ä\ **mop, mar** \au̇\ **out** \ch\ **chin** \e\ **bet** \ē\ **easy** \g\ **go** \i\ **hit** \ī\ **ice** \j\ **job** \ŋ\ **sing** \ō\ **go** \ȯ\ **law** \ȯi\ **boy** \th\ **thin** \t͟h\ **the** \ü\ **loot** \u̇\ **foot** \y\ **yet** \zh\ **vision, beige** \ḵ, ⁿ, œ, ue, ʸ\ *see* Guide to Pronunciation

small usu. yellow racemose flowers — called also *madwort* **2 :** SWEET ALYSSUM

Alz·hei·mer's disease \ˈälts-ˌhī-mərz-, ˈalts-\ *n* [Alois *Alzheimer* †1915 Ger. physician] (1911) **:** a degenerative brain disease of unknown cause that is the most common form of dementia, that usu. starts in late middle age or in old age, that results in progressive memory loss, impaired thinking, disorientation, and changes in personality and mood, and that is marked histologically by the degeneration of brain neurons esp. in the cerebral cortex and by the presence of neurofibrillary tangles and plaques containing beta-amyloid — called also *Alzheimer's*

am [ME, fr. OE *eom;* akin to ON *em* am, L *sum,* Gk *eimi*] *pres 1st sing of* BE

[1]**Am** *abbr* America; American

[2]**Am** *symbol* americium

[1]**AM** \ˈā-ˌem\ *n, often attrib* [*a*mplitude *m*odulation] (1940) **:** a broadcasting system using amplitude modulation; *also* **:** a radio receiver of such a system

[2]**AM** *abbr* **1** airmail **2** Air Medal **3** [L *anno mundi*] in the year of the world — often printed in small capitals **4** ante meridiem — often not cap and often punctuated **5** [NL *artium magister*] master of arts

ama \ˈä-(ˌ)mä\ *n, pl* **amas** *or* **ama** [Jp] (1906) **:** a Japanese diver esp. for pearls or food

AMA *abbr* American Medical Association

amah \ˈä-(ˌ)mä\ *n* [Pg *ama* wet nurse, fr. ML *amma*] (1839) **:** a female servant in eastern Asia; *esp* **:** a Chinese nurse

amain \ə-ˈmān\ *adv* (1540) **1 :** with all one's might ⟨the soul strives ~ to live and work —R. W. Emerson⟩ **2** *archaic* **a :** at full speed **b :** in great haste **3** *archaic* **:** to a high degree **:** EXCEEDINGLY ⟨they whom I favour thrive in wealth ~ —John Milton⟩

Ama·le·kite \ˈa-mə-ˌle-ˌkīt, ə-ˈma-lə-ˌkīt\ *n* [Heb *ʽĀmālēqī,* pl. fr. *ʽĂmālēq* Amalek, grandson of Esau] (1537) **:** a member of an ancient nomadic people living south of Canaan

amal·gam \ə-ˈmal-gəm\ *n* [ME *amalgame,* fr. MF, fr. ML *amalgama*] (15c) **1 :** an alloy of mercury with another metal that is solid or liquid at room temperature according to the proportion of mercury present and is used esp. in making tooth cements **2 :** a mixture of different elements

amal·gam·ate \-gə-ˌmāt\ *vt* **-at·ed; -at·ing** (1617) **:** to unite in or as if in an amalgam; *esp* **:** to merge into a single body ***syn*** see MIX — **amal·gam·ator** \-ˌmā-tər\ *n*

amal·gam·ation \ə-ˌmal-gə-ˈmā-shən\ *n* (1612) **1 a :** the action or process of amalgamating **:** UNITING **b :** the state of being amalgamated **2 :** the result of amalgamating **:** AMALGAM **3 :** MERGER ⟨~ of two corporations⟩

aman·dine \ˌä-ˌmän-ˈdēn\ *adj* [F] (1941) **:** prepared or served with almonds ⟨sole of sole ~⟩

am·a·ni·ta \ˌa-mə-ˈnī-tə, -ˈnē-\ *n* [NL, genus name, fr. Gk *amanitai,* pl., a kind of fungus] (1899) **:** any of a genus (*Amanita*) of white-spored basidiomycetous fungi that typically have a volva and an annulus about the stipe and include some deadly poisonous forms

am·a·ni·tin \-ˈnī-tᵊn, -ˈnē-\ *n* [*amanita* + *-in*] (1836) **:** a highly toxic peptide that is produced by the death cap and that selectively inhibits mammalian RNA polymerase

aman·ta·dine \ə-ˈman-tə-ˌdēn\ *n* [ISV *amantad-* (alter. of *adamantane,* $C_{10}H_{16}$) + *amine*] (1964) **:** a drug used esp. as the hydrochloride $C_{10}H_{17}N \cdot HCl$ to prevent infection (as by an influenza virus) by interfering with virus penetration into host cells

aman·u·en·sis \ə-ˌman-yə-ˈwen(t)-səs\ *n, pl* **-en·ses** \-(ˌ)sēz\ [L, fr. (*servus*) *a manu* slave with secretarial duties] (1619) **:** one employed to write from dictation or to copy manuscript

am·a·ranth \ˈa-mə-ˌran(t)th\ *n* [L *amarantus,* a flower, fr. Gk *amaranton,* fr. neut. of *amarantos* unfading, fr. *a-* + *marainein* to waste away] (1616) **1 :** any of a large genus (*Amaranthus* of the family Amaranthaceae, the amaranth family) of coarse annual herbs including forms cultivated as food crops and various pigweeds **2 :** a flower that never fades **3 :** a red azo dye

am·a·ran·thine \ˌa-mə-ˈran(t)-thən, -ˈran-ˌthīn\ *adj* (1667) **1 a :** of or relating to an amaranth **b :** UNDYING **2 :** of the color amaranth

am·a·ret·to \ˌa-mə-ˈre-(ˌ)tō, ˌä-\ *n* [It, dim. of *amaro* bitter, fr. L *amarus*] (1873) **1 am·a·ret·ti** \-(ˌ)tē\ *pl* **:** macaroons made with bitter almonds **2** *often cap* **:** an almond-flavored liqueur

ama·ro·ne \ˌä-mä-ˈrō-nā\ *n* [It, fr. It dial. (Veneto), lit., tart, very dry, aug. of *amaro* tart, bitter, fr. L *amarus* bitter] (1973) **:** a robust dry red Italian wine with a high alcohol content

am·a·ryl·lis \ˌa-mə-ˈri-ləs\ *n* [NL, genus name, prob. fr. L, name of a shepherdess in Virgil's *Eclogues*] (1754) **:** an autumn-flowering So. African bulbous herb (*Amaryllis belladonna* of the family Amaryllidaceae, the amaryllis family) widely grown for its large deep red to whitish umbellate flowers; *also* **:** a plant of any of several related genera (as *Hippeastrum* or *Sprekelia*)

amass \ə-ˈmas\ *vb* [AF *amasser,* fr. *a-* (fr. L *ad-*) + *masser* to gather into a mass, fr. *masse* mass] *vt* (15c) **1 :** to collect for oneself **:** ACCUMULATE ⟨~ a great fortune⟩ **2 :** to collect into a mass **:** GATHER ⟨must select rather than simply ~ details⟩ ~ *vi* **:** to come together **:** ASSEMBLE — **amass·er** *n* — **amass·ment** \-mənt\ *n*

am·a·teur \ˈa-mə-(ˌ)tər, -ˌtu̇r, -ˌtyu̇r, -ˌchu̇r, -chər\ *n* [F, fr. L *amator* lover, fr. *amare* to love] (1777) **1 :** DEVOTEE, ADMIRER **2 :** one who engages in a pursuit, study, science, or sport as a pastime rather than as a profession **3 :** one lacking in experience and competence in an art or science — **amateur** *adj* — **am·a·teur·ish** \ˌa-mə-ˈtər-ish, -ˈt(y)u̇r-, -ˈchu̇r-, -ˈchər-\ *adj* — **am·a·teur·ish·ly** *adv* — **am·a·teur·ish·ness** *n* — **am·a·teur·ism** \ˈa-mə-ˌtər-ˌi-zəm, -ˌt(y)u̇r-, -ˌchu̇r-, -ˌchər-; -ˌtə-ˌri-, -ˌchə-ˌri-\ *n*

syn AMATEUR, DILETTANTE, DABBLER, TYRO mean a person who follows a pursuit without attaining proficiency or professional status. AMATEUR often applies to one practicing an art without mastery of its essentials ⟨a painting obviously done by an *amateur*⟩; in sports it may also suggest not so much lack of skill but avoidance of direct remuneration ⟨remained an *amateur* despite lucrative offers⟩. DILETTANTE may apply to the lover of an art rather than its skilled practitioner but usu. implies elegant trifling in the arts and an absence of serious commitment ⟨had no patience for *dilettantes*⟩. DABBLER suggests desultory habits of work and lack of persistence ⟨a *dabbler* who started novels but never finished them⟩. TYRO implies inexperience often combined with audacity with resulting crudeness or blundering ⟨shows talent but is still a mere *tyro*⟩.

Ama·ti \ä-ˈmä-tē, ə-\ *n, pl* **Amatis** (1816) **:** a violin made by a member of the Amati family of Cremona

am·a·tive \ˈa-mə-tiv\ *adj* [ML *amativus,* fr. L *amatus,* pp. of *amare*] (1636) **1 :** AMOROUS 1 **2 :** AMOROUS 3 — **am·a·tive·ly** *adv* — **am·a·tive·ness** *n*

am·a·to·ry \ˈa-mə-ˌtȯr-ē\ *adj* (1599) **:** of, relating to, or expressing sexual love ⟨~ adventures⟩

am·au·ro·sis \ˌa-mȯ-ˈrō-səs\ *n, pl* **-ro·ses** \-ˌsēz\ [NL, fr. Gk *amaurōsis,* lit., dimming, fr. *amauroun* to dim, fr. *amauros* dim] (ca. 1657) **:** partial or complete loss of sight occurring esp. without an externally perceptible change in the eye — **am·au·rot·ic** \-ˈrä-tik\ *adj*

amaurotic idiocy *n* (1896) **:** any of several recessive genetic conditions characterized by the accumulation of lipid-containing cells in the viscera and nervous system, mental retardation, and impaired vision or blindness; *esp* **:** TAY-SACHS DISEASE

[1]**amaze** \ə-ˈmāz\ *vb* **amazed; amaz·ing** [ME *amasen,* fr. OE *āmasian,* fr. *ā-* (perfective prefix) + **masian* to confuse — more at ABIDE] *vt* (bef. 12c) **1** *obs* **:** BEWILDER, PERPLEX **2 :** to fill with wonder **:** ASTOUND ~ *vi* **:** to show or cause astonishment ***syn*** see SURPRISE — **amaz·ed·ly** \-ˈmā-zəd-lē\ *adv*

[2]**amaze** *n* (15c) **:** AMAZEMENT

amaze·ment \ə-ˈmāz-mənt\ *n* (1592) **1** *obs* **:** CONSTERNATION, BEWILDERMENT **2 :** the quality or state of being amazed **3 :** something that amazes

amazing *adj* (1593) **:** causing amazement, great wonder, or surprise

amaz·ing·ly \ə-ˈmā-ziŋ-lē\ *adv* (1673) **1 :** to an amazing degree ⟨~ low prices⟩ **2 :** as is amazing ⟨~, she wasn't hurt by the fall⟩

am·a·zon \ˈa-mə-ˌzän, -zən\ *n* [ME, fr. L, fr. Gk *Amazōn*] (14c) **1** *cap* **:** a member of a race of female warriors of Greek mythology **2** *often cap* **:** a tall strong often masculine woman **3** *often cap* **:** any of a genus (*Amazona*) of tropical American parrots typically having green plumage marked with other bright colors

Am·a·zo·nian \ˌa-mə-ˈzō-nē-ən, -nyən\ *adj* (1594) **1 :** relating to, resembling, or befitting an Amazon or an amazon **2 :** of or relating to the Amazon River or its valley

am·a·zon·ite \ˈa-mə-zə-ˌnīt\ *n* [*Amazon* River] (ca. 1879) **:** an apple-green or bluish-green variety of microcline

am·a·zon·stone \-zən-ˌstōn\ *n* (1800) **:** AMAZONITE

amb *abbr* ambassador

am·bage \ˈam-bij\ *n, pl* **am·ba·ges** \am-ˈbā-(ˌ)jēz, ˈam-bi-jəz\ [back-formation fr. ME *ambages,* fr. AF or L; AF, fr. L, fr. *ambi-* + *agere* to drive — more at AGENT] (14c) **1** *archaic* **:** AMBIGUITY, CIRCUMLOCUTION — usu. used in pl. **2** *pl, archaic* **:** indirect ways or proceedings

am·bas·sa·dor \am-ˈba-sə-dər, əm-, im-, -ˌdȯr, -ˈbas-dər\ *n* [ME *ambassadour,* fr. AF *ambassateur,* ultim. of Gmc origin; akin to OHG *ambaht* service] (14c) **1 :** an official envoy; *esp* **:** a diplomatic agent of the highest rank accredited to a foreign government or sovereign as the resident representative of his or her own government or sovereign or appointed for a special and often temporary diplomatic assignment **2 a :** an authorized representative or messenger **b :** an unofficial representative ⟨traveling abroad as ~s of goodwill⟩ — **am·bas·sa·do·ri·al** \-ˌba-sə-ˈdȯr-ē-əl\ *adj* — **am·bas·sa·dor·ship** \-ˈba-sə-dər-ˌship\ *n*

ambassador–at–large *n, pl* **ambassadors–at–large** (1820) **:** a minister of the highest rank not accredited to a particular foreign government or sovereign

am·bas·sa·dress \am-ˈba-sə-drəs, əm-, im-\ *n* (1594) **1 :** a woman who is an ambassador **2 :** the wife of an ambassador

am·beer \ˈam-ˌbir\ *n* [prob. alter. of *amber;* fr. its color] (1848) *chiefly Southern & southern Midland* **:** TOBACCO JUICE

[1]**am·ber** \ˈam-bər\ *n* [ME *ambre,* fr. AF, fr. ML *ambra,* fr. Ar *ʽanbar* ambergris] (14c) **1 :** a hard yellowish to brownish translucent fossil resin that takes a fine polish and is used chiefly in making ornamental objects (as beads) **2 :** a variable color averaging a dark orange yellow

[2]**amber** *adj* (15c) **1 :** consisting of amber **2 :** resembling amber; *esp* **:** having the color amber

Amber Alert *n* [fr. the U.S. Justice Dept. AMBER Alert Program that issues such bulletins, orig. fr. *Amber* Hagerman †1996 U.S. victim of an abduction, later read as an acronym for *A*merica's *M*issing *B*roadcast *E*mergency *R*esponse] (1997) **:** a widely publicized bulletin that alerts the public to a recently abducted or missing child

am·ber·gris \ˈam-bər-ˌgris, -ˌgrē(s)\ *n* [ME *ambregris,* fr. MF *ambre gris,* fr. *ambre* + *gris* gray — more at GRIZZLE] (15c) **:** a waxy substance found floating in or on the shores of tropical waters, believed to originate in the intestines of the sperm whale, and used in perfumery as a fixative

am·ber·i·na \ˌam-bə-ˈrē-nə\ *n* [fr. *Amberina,* a trademark] (1885) **:** a late 19th century American clear glassware of a graduated color that shades from ruby to amber

am·ber·jack \ˈam-bər-ˌjak\ *n* [fr. its color] (1873) **:** any of several carangid fishes (genus *Seriola*); *esp* **:** a large vigorous sport fish (*S. dumerili*) of the western Atlantic

ambi- *prefix* [L *ambi-, amb-* both, around; akin to L *ambo* both, Gk *amphō* both, *amphi* around — more at BY] **:** both ⟨*ambi*valence⟩

am·bi·dex·ter·i·ty \ˌam-bi-(ˌ)dek-ˈster-ə-tē, -ˈste-rə-\ *n* (1593) **:** the quality or state of being ambidextrous

am·bi·dex·trous \ˌam-bi-ˈdek-strəs\ *adj* [LL *ambidexter,* fr. L *ambi-* + *dexter* right-hand — more at DEXTER] (1646) **1 :** using both hands with equal ease **2 :** unusually skillful **:** VERSATILE **3 :** characterized by duplicity **:** DOUBLE-DEALING — **am·bi·dex·trous·ly** *adv*

am·bi·ence *or* **am·bi·ance** \ˈam-bē-ən(t)s, ˈäm-bē-än(t)s\ *n* [F *ambiance,* fr. *ambiant* ambient] (1815) **:** a feeling or mood associated with a particular place, person, or thing **:** ATMOSPHERE

[1]**am·bi·ent** \ˈam-bē-ənt\ *adj* [L *ambient-, ambiens,* prp. of *ambire* to go around, fr. *ambi-* + *ire* to go — more at ISSUE] (1596) **:** existing or present on all sides **:** ENCOMPASSING

[2]**ambient** *n* (1624) **1 :** an encompassing atmosphere **:** ENVIRONMENT **2 :** music intended to serve as an unobtrusive accompaniment to other activities (as in a public place) and characterized esp. by quiet and repetitive instrumental melodies

am·bi·gu·i·ty \ˌam-bə-ˈgyü-ə-tē\ *n, pl* **-ties** (15c) **1 a :** the quality or state of being ambiguous esp. in meaning **b :** an ambiguous word or expression **2 :** UNCERTAINTY

am·big·u·ous \am-ˈbi-gyə-wəs\ *adj* [L *ambiguus,* fr. *ambigere* to be undecided, fr. *ambi-* + *agere* to drive — more at AGENT] (1528) **1 a** : doubtful or uncertain esp. from obscurity or indistinctness ⟨eyes of an ~ color⟩ **b** : INEXPLICABLE **2** : capable of being understood in two or more possible senses or ways ⟨an ~ smile⟩ ⟨an ~ term⟩ ⟨a deliberately ~ reply⟩ ***syn*** see OBSCURE — **am·big·u·ous·ly** *adv* — **am·big·u·ous·ness** *n*

am·bi·sex·u·al \ˌam-bi-ˈsek-sh(ə-)wəl, -shü-əl, -ˈsek-shəl\ *adj* (1912) : BISEXUAL — **ambisexual** *n* — **am·bi·sex·u·al·i·ty** \-ˌsek-shə-ˈwa-lə-tē, -shü-ˈa-\ *n*

am·bit \ˈam-bət\ *n* [ME, fr. L *ambitus,* fr. *ambire*] (1597) **1** : CIRCUIT, COMPASS **2** : the bounds or limits of a place or district **3** : a sphere of action, expression, or influence : SCOPE

[1]**am·bi·tion** \am-ˈbi-shən\ *n* [ME, fr. MF or L; MF, fr. L *ambition-, ambitio,* lit., act of soliciting for votes, fr. *ambire*] (14c) **1 a** : an ardent desire for rank, fame, or power **b** : desire to achieve a particular end **2** : the object of ambition ⟨her ~ is to start her own business⟩ **3** : a desire for activity or exertion ⟨felt sick and had no ~⟩ — **am·bi·tion·less** \-ləs\ *adj*

syn AMBITION, ASPIRATION, PRETENSION mean strong desire for advancement. AMBITION applies to the desire for personal advancement or preferment and may suggest equally a praiseworthy or an inordinate desire ⟨driven by *ambition*⟩. ASPIRATION implies a striving after something higher than oneself ⟨an *aspiration* to become president someday⟩. PRETENSION suggests ardent desire for recognition of accomplishment often without actual possession of the necessary ability and therefore may imply presumption ⟨has literary *pretensions*⟩.

[2]**ambition** *vt* (1664) : to have as one's ambition : DESIRE

am·bi·tious \am-ˈbi-shəs\ *adj* (14c) **1 a** : having or controlled by ambition ⟨an ~ young executive⟩ **b** : having a desire to achieve a particular goal : ASPIRING ⟨~ for power⟩ **2** : resulting from, characterized by, or showing ambition ⟨an ~ film⟩ — **am·bi·tious·ly** *adv* — **am·bi·tious·ness** *n*

am·biv·a·lence \am-ˈbi-və-lən(t)s\ *n* [ISV] (1909) **1** : simultaneous and contradictory attitudes or feelings (as attraction and repulsion) toward an object, person, or action **2 a** : continual fluctuation (as between one thing and its opposite) **b** : uncertainty as to which approach to follow — **am·biv·a·lent** \-lənt\ *adj* — **am·biv·a·lent·ly** *adv*

am·bi·ver·sion \ˌam-bi-ˈvər-zhən, -shən\ *n* [*ambi-* + *-version* (as in *introversion*)] (1927) : the personality configuration of an ambivert

am·bi·vert \ˈam-bi-ˌvərt\ *n* [*ambi-* + *-vert* (as in *introvert*)] (1927) : a person having characteristics of both extrovert and introvert

[1]**am·ble** \ˈam-bəl\ *vi* **am·bled; am·bling** \-b(ə-)liŋ\ [ME, fr. AF *ambler,* fr. L *ambulare* to walk, fr. *ambi-* + *-ulare* (verb base akin to MW *el* he may go, Gk *ēlythe* he went) — more at ELASTIC] (14c) : to go at or as if at an amble : SAUNTER — **am·bler** \-b(ə-)lər\ *n*

[2]**amble** *n* (14c) **1 a** : an easy gait of a horse in which the legs on the same side of the body move together **b** : [7]RACK b **2** : an easy gait **3** : a leisurely walk

am·bly·opia \ˌam-blē-ˈō-pē-ə\ *n* [NL, fr. Gk *amblyōpia,* fr. *amblys* blunt, dull + *-ōpia* -opia — more at MOLLIFY] (ca. 1706) : dimness of sight esp. in one eye without apparent change in the eye structures — called also *lazy eye* — **am·bly·opic** \-ˈō-pik, -ˈä-pik\ *adj*

am·boy·na *or* **am·boi·na** \am-ˈbȯi-nə\ *n* [*Amboina,* Moluccas, Indonesia] (1770) : a mottled curly-grained wood of a southeast Asian tree (*Pterocarpus indicus*) of the legume family

am·bro·sia \am-ˈbrō-zh(ē-)ə\ *n* [L, fr. Gk, lit., immortality, fr. *ambrotos* immortal, fr. *a-* + *-mbrotos* (akin to *brotos* mortal) — more at MURDER] (15c) **1 a** : the food of the Greek and Roman gods **b** : the ointment or perfume of the gods **2** : something extremely pleasing to taste or smell **3** : a dessert made of oranges and shredded coconut — **am·bro·sial** \-zh(ē-)əl\ *adj* — **am·bro·sial·ly** \-zh(ē-)ə-lē\ *adv*

ambrosia beetle *n* (1897) : any of various small wood-boring beetles (family Scolytidae) that cultivate a fungus on which they feed and raise their larvae

am·bro·type \ˈam-brə-ˌtīp\ *n* [Gk *ambrotos* + E *type*] (1854) : a positive picture made of a photographic negative on glass backed by a dark surface

am·bry \ˈam-brē; ˈäm-rē, ˈȯm-\ *n, pl* **ambries** [ME *almery,* fr. AF *almarie,* fr. L *armarium,* fr. *arma* weapons — more at ARM] (14c) **1** *dial chiefly Brit* : PANTRY **2** : a recess in a church wall (as for holding sacramental vessels)

ambs·ace \ˈām-ˌzās\ *n* [ME *ambes as,* fr. AF, fr. *ambes* both + *as* aces] (13c) *archaic* : the lowest throw at dice; *also* : something worthless or unlucky

am·bu·la·cral \ˌam-byə-ˈla-krəl, -ˈlā-\ *adj* (1811) : of, relating to, or being any of the radial areas of echinoderms along which run the principal nerves, blood vessels, and elements of the water-vascular system ⟨~ grooves⟩

am·bu·la·crum \-krəm\ *n, pl* **-cra** \-krə\ [NL, fr. L, alley, fr. *ambulare* to walk — more at AMBLE] (1802) : an ambulacral area or part

am·bu·lance \ˈam-byə-lən(t)s, -bə- *also* -ˌlan(t)s\ *n* [F, fr. (*hôpital*) *ambulant,* lit., ambulant field hospital, fr. *ambulant* itinerant, fr. L *ambulant-, ambulans,* prp. of *ambulare*] (1809) : a vehicle equipped for transporting the injured or sick

ambulance chaser *n* (1896) : a lawyer or lawyer's agent who incites accident victims to sue for damages — **ambulance chasing** *n*

am·bu·lant \ˈam-byə-lənt\ *adj* (1619) : moving about : AMBULATORY

am·bu·late \-ˌlāt\ *vi* **-lat·ed; -lat·ing** [L *ambulatus,* pp. of *ambulare*] (ca. 1623) : to move from place to place : WALK — **am·bu·la·tion** \ˌam-byə-ˈlā-shən\ *n*

[1]**am·bu·la·to·ry** \ˈam-byə-lə-ˌtȯr-ē\ *adj* (1598) **1** : of, relating to, or adapted to walking; *also* : occurring during a walk **2** : moving from place to place : ITINERANT **3** : capable of being altered ⟨a will is ~ until the testator's death⟩ **4 a** : able to walk about and not bedridden ⟨~ patients⟩ **b** : performed on or involving an ambulatory patient or an outpatient ⟨~ medical care⟩ ⟨an ~ electrocardiogram⟩ — **am·bu·la·to·ri·ly** \ˌam-byə-lə-ˈtȯr-ə-lē\ *adv*

[2]**ambulatory** *n, pl* **-ries** (ca. 1616) : a sheltered place (as in a cloister or church) for walking

am·bus·cade \ˈam-bə-ˌskād, ˌam-bə-ˈ\ *n* [MF *embuscade,* modif. of OIt *imboscata,* fr. *imboscare* to place in ambush, fr. *in* (fr. L) + *bosco* forest, of Gmc origin; akin to OHG *busc* forest — more at IN, BUSH] (ca. 1588) : AMBUSH — **ambuscade** *vb* — **am·bus·cad·er** *n*

[1]**am·bush** \ˈam-ˌbu̇sh\ *vb* [ME *embushen,* fr. AF *embuscher,* fr. *en* in (fr. L *in*) + *busche* log, firewood] *vt* (14c) **1** : to station in ambush **2** : to attack from an ambush : WAYLAY ~ *vi* : to lie in wait : LURK — **am·bush·er** *n* — **am·bush·ment** \-mənt\ *n*

[2]**ambush** *n* (15c) **1** : a trap in which concealed persons lie in wait to attack by surprise **2** : the persons stationed in ambush; *also* : their concealed position **3** : an attack esp. from an ambush

amdt *abbr* amendment

AmE *abbr* American English

ameba, amebic, ameboid *var of* AMOEBA, AMOEBIC, AMOEBOID

am·e·bi·a·sis *or* **am·oe·bi·a·sis** \ˌa-mi-ˈbī-ə-səs\ *n, pl* **-a·ses** \-ˌsēz\ [NL] (1903) : infection with or disease caused by amoebas (esp. *Entamoeba histolytica*)

ame·bic dysentery \ə-ˈmē-bik-\ *n* (1883) : acute human intestinal amebiasis caused by an amoeba (*Entamoeba histolytica*) and marked by dysentery, abdominal pain, and erosion of the intestinal wall

amebocyte *var of* AMOEBOCYTE

ameer *var of* EMIR

ame·lio·rate \ə-ˈmēl-yə-ˌrāt, -ˈmē-lē-ə-\ *vb* **-rat·ed; -rat·ing** [alter. of *meliorate*] *vt* (1656) : to make better or more tolerable ~ *vi* : to grow better ***syn*** see IMPROVE — **ame·lio·ra·tion** \-ˌmēl-yə-ˈrā-shən, -ˌmē-lē-ə-\ *n* — **ame·lio·ra·tive** \-ˈmēl-yə-ˌrā-tiv, -ˈmē-lē-ə-\ *adj* — **ame·lio·ra·tor** \-ˌrā-tər\ *n* — **ame·lio·ra·to·ry** \-rə-ˌtȯr-ē\ *adj*

am·e·lo·blast \ˈa-mə-lō-ˌblast\ *n* [obs. *amel* enamel (ME, ultim. fr. OF *esmail*) + *-o-* + *-blast* — more at ENAMEL] (1878) : one of a group of columnar epithelial cells that produce and deposit enamel on the surface of a developing vertebrate tooth

amen \(ˈ)ä-ˈmen, (ˈ)ā-; ˈä- *when sung*\ *interj* [ME, fr. OE, fr. LL, fr. Gk *amēn,* fr. Heb *āmēn*] (bef. 12c) — used to express solemn ratification (as of an expression of faith) or hearty approval (as of an assertion)

ame·na·ble \ə-ˈmē-nə-bəl, -ˈme-\ *adj* [AF, fr. *amener* to bring, compel, fr. *a-* (fr. L *ad-*) + *mener* to lead, fr. LL *minare* to drive, fr. L *minari* to threaten — more at MOUNT] (1596) **1** : liable to be brought to account : ANSWERABLE ⟨citizens ~ to the law⟩ **2 a** : capable of submission (as to judgment or test) : SUITED ⟨the data is ~ to analysis⟩ **b** : readily brought to yield, submit, or cooperate ⟨a government not ~ to change⟩ **c** : WILLING 1 ⟨was ~ to spending more time at home⟩ ***syn*** see RESPONSIBLE, OBEDIENT — **ame·na·bil·i·ty** \-ˌmē-nə-ˈbil-ət-ē, -ˌme-\ *n* — **ame·na·bly** \-ˈmē-nə-blē, -ˈme-\ *adv*

amen corner \ˈā-ˌmen-\ *n* (ca. 1848) : a conspicuous corner in a church occupied by fervent worshipers

amend \ə-ˈmend\ *vb* [ME, fr. AF *amender,* modif. of L *emendare,* fr. *e, ex* out + *menda* fault; akin to L *mendax* lying, *mendicus* beggar, and perh. to Skt *mindā* physical defect] *vt* (13c) **1** : to put right; *esp* : to make emendations in (as a text) **2 a** : to change or modify for the better : IMPROVE ⟨~ the situation⟩ **b** : to alter esp. in phraseology; *esp* : to alter formally by modification, deletion, or addition ⟨~ a constitution⟩ ~ *vi* : to reform oneself ***syn*** see CORRECT — **amend·able** \-ˈmen-də-bəl\ *adj* — **amend·er** *n*

amen·da·to·ry \ə-ˈmen-də-ˌtȯr-ē\ *adj* [*amend* + *-atory* (as in *emendatory*)] (1764) : CORRECTIVE

amend·ment \ə-ˈmen(d)-mənt\ *n* (13c) **1** : the act of amending : CORRECTION **2** : a material (as compost or sand) that aids plant growth indirectly by improving the condition of the soil **3 a** : the process of amending by parliamentary or constitutional procedure **b** : an alteration proposed or effected by this process ⟨a constitutional ~⟩

amends \ə-ˈmen(d)z\ *n pl but sing or pl in constr* [ME *amendes,* fr. AF, pl. of *amende* reparation, fr. *amender*] (14c) : compensation for a loss or injury : RECOMPENSE ⟨make ~⟩

ame·ni·ty \ə-ˈme-nə-tē, -ˈmē-\ *n, pl* **-ties** [ME *amenite,* fr. L *amoenitat-, amoenitas,* fr. *amoenus* pleasant] (14c) **1 a** : the quality of being pleasant or agreeable **b** (1) : the attractiveness and value of real estate or of a residential structure (2) : a feature conducive to such attractiveness and value **2** *usu pl* : something (as a conventional social gesture) that conduces to smoothness or pleasantness of social relationships ⟨maintaining social *amenities*⟩ **3** : something that conduces to comfort, convenience, or enjoyment ⟨hotels with modern *amenities*⟩

amen·or·rhea \ˌā-ˌme-nə-ˈrē-ə, ˌä-\ *n* [NL, fr. *a-* + Gk *mēn* month + NL *-o-* + *-rrhea* — more at MOON] (ca. 1771) : abnormal absence or suppression of menses — **amen·or·rhe·ic** \-ˈrē-ik\ *adj*

ament \ˈa-mənt, ˈā-\ *n* [NL *amentum,* fr. L, thong, strap] (1783) : CATKIN — **amen·tif·er·ous** \-mən-ˈti-f(ə-)rəs\ *adj*

amen·tia \(ˌ)ā-ˈmen(t)-sh(ē-)ə, (ˌ)ä-\ *n* [NL, fr. L, madness, fr. *ament-, amens* mad, fr. *a-* (fr. *ab-*) + *ment-, mens* mind — more at MIND] (14c) : MENTAL RETARDATION; *specif* : a condition of lack of development of intellectual capacity

Amer *abbr* America; American

Am·er·asian \ˈa-mə-ˈrā-zhən, -shən\ *n* [*Amer*ican + *Asian*] (1953) : a person of mixed American and Asian descent; *esp* : one fathered by an American and esp. an American serviceman in Asia

amerce \ə-ˈmərs\ *vt* **amerced; amerc·ing** [ME *amercien,* fr. AF *amercier,* fr. OF *a merci* at (one's) mercy] (15c) : to punish by a fine whose amount is fixed by the court; *broadly* : PUNISH — **amerce·ment** \-ˈmər-smənt\ *n* — **amer·cia·ble** \-ˈmər-sē-ə-bəl, -ˈmər-shə-bəl\ *adj*

[1]**Amer·i·can** \ə-ˈmer-ə-kən, -ˈmər-, -ˈme-rə-\ *n* (1568) **1** : an American Indian of No. America or So. America **2** : a native or inhabitant of No. America or So. America **3** : a citizen of the U.S. **4** : AMERICAN ENGLISH

[2]**American** *adj* (1580) **1** : of or relating to America **2** : of or relating to the U.S. or its possessions or original territory — **Amer·i·can·ness** \-kə(n)-nəs\ *n*

Amer·i·ca·na \ə-ˌmer-ə-ˈkä-nə, -ˌmər-, -ˌme-rə-, -ˈka-nə\ *n pl* (1841) **1** : materials concerning or characteristic of America, its civilization, or its culture; *broadly* : things typical of America **2** : American culture **3** : a genre of American music having roots in early folk and country music

American chameleon *n* (1881) : an anole (*Anolis carolinensis*) of the southeastern U.S. that can vary its skin color from green to brown and is often kept as a pet

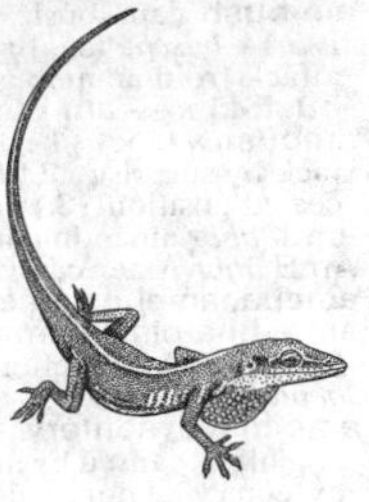

American chameleon

American cheese *n* (1763) : a process cheese made from American cheddar
American dog tick *n* (1927) : a common No. American ixodid tick (*Dermacentor variabilis*) esp. of dogs and humans that is an important vector of Rocky Mountain spotted fever and tularemia — called also *dog tick*
American dream *n, often cap D* (1931) : an American social ideal that stresses egalitarianism and esp. material prosperity; *also* : the prosperity or life that is the realization of this ideal
American eel *n* (1923) : a yellow to greenish-brown catadromous eel (*Anguilla rostrata*) that is lighter below, has 103 to 111 vertebrae, is found in fresh and coastal waters along the Atlantic coasts of No. America, and is held to spawn in or near the Sargasso Sea
American elm *n* (1785) : a large elm (*Ulmus americana*) with gradually spreading branches and pendulous branchlets that is common in eastern No. America
American English *n* (1805) : the English language as spoken in the U.S. — used esp. with the implication that it is clearly distinguishable from British English yet not so divergent as to be a separate language
Amer·i·ca·nese \ə-ˌmer-ə-kə-ˈnēz, -ˌmər-, -ˌme-rə-, -ˈnēs\ *n* (1870) : AMERICAN ENGLISH
American foxhound *n* (ca. 1891) : any of a breed of foxhounds developed in the U.S. that are smaller than the English foxhound but with longer ears and a short glossy coat usu. of black, tan, and white
American Indian *n* (1732) : a member of any of the aboriginal peoples of the western hemisphere except often the Eskimos; *esp* : an American Indian of No. America and esp. the U.S. — compare NATIVE AMERICAN — **American Indian** *adj*
Amer·i·can·i·sa·tion, Amer·i·can·ise *Brit var of* AMERICANIZATION, AMERICANIZE
Amer·i·can·ism \ə-ˈmer-ə-kə-ˌni-zəm, -ˈmər-, -ˈme-rə-\ *n* (1781) **1** : a characteristic feature of American English esp. as contrasted with British English **2** : attachment or allegiance to the traditions, interests, or ideals of the U.S. **3 a** : a custom or trait peculiar to America **b** : the political principles and practices essential to American culture
Amer·i·can·ist \-kə-nist\ *n* (1881) **1** : a specialist in American culture or history **2** : a specialist in the languages or cultures of the aboriginal inhabitants of America
Amer·i·can·i·za·tion \ə-ˌmer-ə-kə-nə-ˈzā-shən, -ˌmər-, -ˌme-rə-\ *n* (1853) **1** : the act or process of Americanizing **2** : instruction of foreigners (as immigrants) in English and in U.S. history, government, and culture
Amer·i·can·ize \ə-ˈmer-ə-kə-ˌnīz, -ˈmər-, -ˈme-rə-\ *vb* **-ized; -iz·ing** *vt* (1797) **1** : to cause to acquire or conform to American characteristics **2** : to bring (as an area) under the political, cultural, or commercial influence of the U.S. ~ *vi* : to acquire or conform to American traits
American pit bull terrier *n* (1950) : any of a breed of dogs developed to combine the traits of terriers and bulldogs that have extremely powerful jaws and great strength and tenacity and that were orig. bred for dog fighting — called also *pit bull terrier*
American plan *n* (1852) : a hotel plan whereby the daily rates cover the costs of the room and three meals — compare EUROPEAN PLAN
American saddlebred *n* (1948) : any of a breed of 3-gaited or 5-gaited saddle horses developed chiefly in Kentucky from Thoroughbreds and smooth-gaited stock — called also *American saddle horse*
American shad *n* (ca. 1929) : a shad (*Alosa sapidissima*) of the Atlantic coast of No. America that has a greenish back and silvery sides
American shorthair *n* (1974) : any of a breed of cats with a short thick coat of variable color and pattern that are descended from cats brought to America by European settlers
American Sign Language *n* (1960) : a sign language for the deaf in which meaning is conveyed by a system of articulated hand gestures and their placement relative to the upper body
American Staffordshire terrier *n* (1971) : any of a breed of strong stocky dogs that are of similar ancestry to but are larger and heavier than the related American pit bull terrier and Staffordshire bull terrier
American Standard Version *n* (1901) : an American version of the Bible based on the Revised Version and published in 1901 — called also *American Revised Version*
American trotter *n* (1857) : STANDARDBRED
American water spaniel *n* (1947) : any of a breed of medium-sized spaniels of U.S. origin that have a thick curly chocolate or liver-colored coat
American wigeon *n* (1788) : a No. American wigeon (*Anas americana*) with a large white patch on each wing and in the male a white crown — called also *baldpate*
am·er·i·ci·um \ˌa-mə-ˈri-shē-əm, -sē-\ *n* [NL, fr. *America* + NL *-ium*] (1946) : a radioactive metallic element produced artificially by bombarding plutonium with high-energy neutrons — see ELEMENT table
AmerInd *abbr* American Indian
Am·er·in·di·an \ˌa-mə-ˈrin-dē-ən\ *n* [*Amer*ican + *Indian*] (ca. 1898) : AMERICAN INDIAN — **Am·er·ind** \ˈa-mə-ˌrind\ *n or adj* — **Amerindian** *adj*
Ame·slan \ˈa-məs-ˌlan, ˈam-ˌslan\ *n* (1972) : AMERICAN SIGN LANGUAGE
Ames test \ˈāmz-\ *n* [Bruce N. *Ames b*1928 Am. biochemist] (1976) : a test for identifying potential carcinogens by studying their mutagenic effect on bacteria
am·e·thyst \ˈa-mə-thəst, -(ˌ)thist\ *n* [ME *amatiste,* fr. AF & L; AF, fr. L *amethystus,* fr. Gk *amethystos,* lit., remedy against drunkenness, fr. *a-* + *methyein* to be drunk, fr. *methy* wine — more at MEAD] (13c) **1 a** : a clear purple or bluish-violet variety of crystallized quartz that is often used as a jeweler's stone **b** : a deep purple variety of corundum **2** : a moderate purple — **am·e·thys·tine** \ˌa-mə-ˈthis-tən\ *adj*
am·e·tro·pia \ˌa-mə-ˈtrō-pē-ə\ *n* [NL, fr. Gk *ametros* without measure (fr. *a-* + *metron* measure) + NL *-opia* — more at MEASURE] (1875) : an abnormal refractive condition (as myopia, hyperopia, or astigmatism) of the eye in which images fail to focus upon the retina — **am·e·tro·pic** \-ˈtrō-pik, -ˈträ-\ *adj*
AMG *abbr* allied military government
Am·har·ic \am-ˈher-ik, -ˈha-rik; am-ˈhär-, äm-\ *n* [part trans. of Amharic *amarəñña,* fr. *Amara* region of highland Ethiopia] (1813) : a Semitic language that is an official language of Ethiopia — **Amharic** *adj*
ami·a·ble \ˈā-mē-ə-bəl\ *adj* [ME, fr. AF, fr. LL *amicabilis* friendly, fr. L *amicus* friend; akin to L *amare* to love] (14c) **1** *archaic* : PLEASING, ADMIRABLE **2 a** : generally agreeable ⟨an ~ comedy⟩ **b** : being friendly, sociable, and congenial — **ami·a·bil·i·ty** \ˌā-mē-ə-ˈbi-lə-tē\ *n* — **ami·a·ble·ness** \ˈā-mē-ə-bəl-nəs\ *n* — **ami·a·bly** \-blē\ *adv*
syn AMIABLE, GOOD-NATURED, OBLIGING, COMPLAISANT mean having the desire or disposition to please. AMIABLE implies having qualities that make one liked and easy to deal with ⟨an *amiable* teacher not easily annoyed⟩. GOOD-NATURED implies cheerfulness or helpfulness and sometimes a willingness to be imposed upon ⟨a *good-natured* girl who was always willing to pitch in⟩. OBLIGING stresses a friendly readiness to be helpful ⟨our *obliging* innkeeper found us a bigger room⟩. COMPLAISANT often implies passivity or a yielding to others because of weakness ⟨was too *complaisant* to protest a decision he thought unfair⟩.
am·i·ca·ble \ˈa-mi-kə-bəl\ *adj* [ME, fr. LL *amicabilis*] (15c) : characterized by friendly goodwill : PEACEABLE — **am·i·ca·bil·i·ty** \ˌa-mi-kə-ˈbi-lə-tē\ *n* — **am·i·ca·ble·ness** \ˈa-mi-kə-bəl-nəs\ *n* — **am·i·ca·bly** \-blē\ *adv*
syn AMICABLE, NEIGHBORLY, FRIENDLY mean exhibiting goodwill and an absence of antagonism. AMICABLE implies a state of peace and a desire on the part of the parties not to quarrel ⟨maintained *amicable* relations⟩. NEIGHBORLY implies a disposition to live on good terms with others and to be helpful on principle ⟨*neighborly* concern⟩. FRIENDLY stresses cordiality and often warmth or intimacy of personal relations ⟨sought *friendly* advice⟩.
am·ice \ˈa-məs\ *n* [ME *amis,* modif. of AF *amit,* fr. ML *amictus,* fr. L, cloak, fr. *amicire* to wrap around, fr. *am-, amb-* around + *jacere* to throw — more at AMBI-, JET] (13c) : a liturgical vestment made of an oblong piece of cloth usu. of white linen and worn about the neck and shoulders and partly under the alb
ami·cus \ə-ˈmē-kəs, -ˈmī-\ *n, pl* **ami·ci** \-ˈmē-ˌkē, -ˈmī-ˌsī\ (1951) : AMICUS CURIAE
amicus cu·ri·ae \-ˈkyu̇r-ē-ˌī, -ˈku̇r-, -i-ˌē\ *n, pl* **amici curiae** [NL, lit., friend of the court] (1612) : one (as a professional person or organization) that is not a party to a particular litigation but that is permitted by the court to advise it in respect to some matter of law that directly affects the case in question
amid \ə-ˈmid\ *or* **amidst** \-ˈmidst, -ˈmitst\ *prep* [*amid* fr. ME *amidde,* fr. OE *onmiddan,* fr. *on* + *middan,* dat. of *midde* mid; *amidst* fr. ME *amiddes,* fr. *amidde* + *-es* -s] (bef. 12c) **1** : in or into the middle of : surrounded by : AMONG ⟨~ the crowd⟩ **2 a** : DURING ⟨~ the fighting⟩ **b** : with the accompaniment of ⟨resigned ~ rumors of misconduct⟩
am·i·dase \ˈa-mə-ˌdās, -ˌdāz\ *n* [ISV] (1921) : an enzyme that hydrolyzes acid amides usu. with the liberation of ammonia
am·ide \ˈa-ˌmīd, -məd\ *n* [ISV, fr. NL *ammonia*] (1838) **1** : an inorganic compound derived from ammonia by replacement of an atom of hydrogen with another element (as a metal) **2** : any of a class of organic compounds derived from ammonia or an amine by replacement of hydrogen with an acyl group — compare AMINE, IMIDE
ami·do \ə-ˈmē-(ˌ)dō, ˈa-mə-ˌdō\ *adj* [ISV *amide* + *-o-*] (1877) : relating to or containing an organic amide group — often used in combination
amid·ships \ə-ˈmid-ˌships\ *adv* (1692) **1** : in or toward the part of a ship midway between bow and stern **2** : in or toward the middle
ami·go \ə-ˈmē-(ˌ)gō, ä-\ *n, pl* **-gos** [Sp, fr. L *amicus* — more at AMIABLE] (1835) : FRIEND
amine \ə-ˈmēn, ˈa-ˌmēn\ *n* [ISV, fr. NL *ammonia*] (1863) : any of a class of basic organic compounds derived from ammonia by replacement of hydrogen with one or more monovalent hydrocarbon radicals — compare AMIDE 2
ami·no \ə-ˈmē-(ˌ)nō\ *adj* [ISV *amine* + *-o-*] (1900) : relating to, being, or containing an amine group — often used in combination
amino acid *n* (1898) : an amphoteric organic acid containing the amino group NH_2; *esp* : any of the various amino acids having the amino group in the alpha position that are the chief components of proteins and are synthesized by living cells or are obtained as essential components of the diet
ami·no·ac·id·uria \ə-ˌmē-nō-ˌa-sə-ˈdu̇r-ē-ə, -ˈdyu̇r-\ *n* [NL] (ca. 1923) : a condition in which one or more amino acids are excreted in excessive amounts
ami·no·ben·zo·ic acid \ə-ˌmē-nō-ben-ˈzō-ik-\ *n* [ISV] (1904) : any of three crystalline derivatives $C_7H_7NO_2$ of benzoic acid; *esp* : PARA-AMINOBENZOIC ACID
ami·no·pep·ti·dase \ə-ˌmē-nō-ˈpep-tə-ˌdās, -ˌdāz\ *n* (1935) : an enzyme that hydrolyzes peptides by acting on the peptide bond next to a terminal amino acid containing a free amino group
am·i·noph·yl·line \ˌa-mə-ˈnä-fə-lən\ *n* [*amino* + theo*phylline*] (1934) : a theophylline derivative $C_{16}H_{24}N_{10}O_4$ used esp. to stimulate the heart in congestive heart failure and to dilate the air passages in respiratory disorders (as asthma)
am·i·nop·ter·in \ˌa-mə-ˈnäp-tə-rən\ *n* [*amino* + *pter*oylglutamic acid + *-in*] (1948) : a derivative $C_{19}H_{20}N_8O_5$ of glutamic acid that is a folic acid antagonist and has been used as a rodenticide and antileukemic agent
ami·no·py·rine \ə-ˌmē-nō-ˈpī-(ə)r-ˌēn\ *n* [ISV, fr. *amino* + anti*pyrine*] (ca. 1936) : a crystalline compound $C_{13}H_{17}N_3O$ formerly used to relieve pain and fever but now largely abandoned for this purpose because of the occurrence of fatal agranulocytosis as a side effect in some users
ami·no·sal·i·cyl·ic acid \ə-ˌmē-nō-ˌsa-lə-ˈsi-lik-\ *n* (1925) : any of four isomeric derivatives $C_7H_7NO_3$ of salicylic acid that have a single amino group; *esp* : PARA-AMINOSALICYLIC ACID
ami·no·trans·fer·ase \-ˈtran(t)s-fə-ˌrās, -ˌrāz\ *n* (ca. 1965) : TRANSAMINASE
amir *var of* EMIR
Amish \ˈä-mish, ˈa-, ˈā-\ *adj* [prob. fr. G *amisch,* fr. Jacob *Amman* or

*Amen fl*1693 Swiss Mennonite bishop] (1844) : of or relating to a strict sect of Mennonites who were followers of Amman and settled in America chiefly in the 18th century — **Amish** *n*

[1]**amiss** \ə-ˈmis\ *adv* (13c) **1 a :** in a mistaken way : WRONGLY ⟨if you think he is guilty, you judge ~⟩ **b :** ASTRAY ⟨something had gone ~⟩ **2 :** in a faulty way : IMPERFECTLY

[2]**amiss** *adj* (14c) **1 :** not being in accordance with right order **2 :** FAULTY, IMPERFECT **3 :** out of place in given circumstances — usu. used with a negative ⟨a few remarks may not be ~ here⟩

ami·to·sis \ˌā-mī-ˈtō-səs\ *n* [NL, fr. [2]*a-* + *mitosis*] (1894) : cell division by simple cleavage of the nucleus and division of the cytoplasm without spindle formation or appearance of chromosomes — **ami·tot·ic** \-ˈtä-tik\ *adj* — **ami·tot·i·cal·ly** \-ti-k(ə-)lē\ *adv*

am·i·trip·ty·line \ˌa-mə-ˈtrip-tə-ˌlēn\ *n* [*amino* + *tryptophan* + *-yl* + [2]*-ine*] (1961) : a tricyclic aromatic antidepressant drug $C_{20}H_{23}N$ used in the form of its hydrochloride salt

am·i·trole \ˈa-mə-ˌtrōl\ *n* [*amino* + *triazole*] (ca. 1960) : a systemic herbicide $C_2H_4N_4$ used in areas other than food croplands

am·i·ty \ˈa-mə-tē\ *n, pl* **-ties** [ME *amite,* fr. AF *amyté,* fr. ML *amicitas,* fr. L *amicus* friend — more at AMIABLE] (15c) : FRIENDSHIP; *esp* : friendly relations between nations

am·me·ter \ˈa-ˌmē-tər\ *n* [*ampere* + *-meter*] (1882) : an instrument for measuring electric current esp. in amperes

am·mine \ˈa-ˌmēn, a-ˈmēn\ *n* [ISV *ammonia* + [2]*-ine*] (1897) **1 :** a molecule of ammonia as it exists in a coordination complex ⟨hex*ammine*cobalt chloride $Co(NH_3)_6Cl_3$⟩ **2 :** a compound that contains an ammine

am·mo \ˈa-(ˌ)mō\ *n* [by shortening & alter.] (1911) : AMMUNITION

am·mo·nia \ə-ˈmō-nyə\ *n* [NL, fr. L *sal ammoniacus* sal ammoniac, lit., salt of Ammon, fr. Gk *ammōniakos* of Ammon, fr. *Ammōn* Ammon, Amun, an Egyptian god near whose temple at the Siwa oasis it was extracted] (1789) **1 :** a pungent colorless gaseous alkaline compound of nitrogen and hydrogen NH_3 that is very soluble in water and can easily be condensed to a liquid by cold and pressure **2 :** AMMONIA WATER

am·mo·ni·ac \ə-ˈmō-nē-ˌak\ *n* [ME & L; ME, fr. L *ammoniacum,* fr. Gk *ammōniakon,* fr. neut. of *ammōniakos* of Ammon] (15c) : the aromatic gum resin of a southwest Asian herb (*Dorema ammoniacum*) of the carrot family used as an expectorant and stimulant and in plasters

am·mo·ni·a·cal \ˌa-mə-ˈnī-ə-kəl\ *also* **am·mo·ni·ac** \ə-ˈmō-nē-ˌak\ *adj* (1646) : of, relating to, containing, or resembling ammonia

am·mo·ni·ate \ə-ˈmō-nē-ˌāt\ *vt* **-at·ed; -at·ing** (ca. 1928) **1 :** to combine or impregnate with ammonia or an ammonium compound **2 :** to subject to ammonification — **am·mo·ni·a·tion** \-ˌmō-nē-ˈā-shən\ *n*

ammonia water *n* (1852) : a water solution of ammonia

am·mo·ni·fi·ca·tion \ə-ˌmä-nə-fə-ˈkā-shən, -ˌmō-nə-\ *n* (1886) **1 :** the act or process of ammoniating **2 :** decomposition with production of ammonia or ammonium compounds esp. by the action of bacteria on nitrogenous organic matter — **am·mo·ni·fy** \-ˌfī\ *vb*

am·mo·nite \ˈa-mə-ˌnīt\ *n* [NL *ammonites,* fr. L *cornu Ammonis,* lit., horn of Ammon] (1758) : any of a subclass (Ammonoidea) of extinct cephalopods esp. abundant in the Mesozoic age that had flat spiral shells with the interior divided by septa into chambers — **am·mo·nit·ic** \ˌa-mə-ˈni-tik\ *adj*

Am·mon·ite \ˈa-mə-ˌnīt\ *n* [LL *Ammonites,* fr. Heb *ʿAmmōn* Ammon (son of Lot), descendant of Ammon] (1530) : a member of a Semitic people who in Old Testament times lived east of the Jordan between the Jabbok and the Arnon — **Ammonite** *adj*

am·mo·ni·um \ə-ˈmō-nē-əm\ *n* [NL, fr. *ammonia*] (1808) : an ion NH_4^+ derived from ammonia by combination with a hydrogen ion and known in compounds (as salts) that resemble in properties the compounds of the alkali metals

ammonium carbonate *n* (ca. 1829) : a carbonate of ammonium; *specif* : the commercial mixture of the bicarbonate and carbamate used esp. in smelling salts

ammonium chloride *n* (1869) : a white crystalline volatile salt NH_4Cl that is used in dry cells and as an expectorant — called also *sal ammoniac*

ammonium cyanate *n* (ca. 1881) : an inorganic white crystalline salt NH_4CNO that can be converted into organic urea

ammonium hydroxide *n* (1899) : a weakly basic compound NH_4OH that is formed when ammonia dissolves in water and that exists only in solution

ammonium nitrate *n* (1869) : a colorless crystalline salt NH_4NO_3 used in explosives and fertilizers and in veterinary medicine

ammonium phosphate *n* (1880) : a phosphate of ammonium; *esp* : DIAMMONIUM PHOSPHATE

ammonium sulfate *n* (1869) : a colorless crystalline salt $(NH_4)_2SO_4$ used chiefly as a fertilizer

am·mo·noid \ˈa-mə-ˌnȯid\ *n* (1884) : AMMONITE ⟨Mesozoic ~*s*⟩

am·mu·ni·tion \ˌam-yə-ˈni-shən\ *n* [obs. F *amunition,* fr. MF, alter. of *munition*] (1607) **1 a :** the projectiles with their fuses, propelling charges, or primers fired from guns **b :** CARTRIDGES **c :** explosive military items (as grenades or bombs) **2 :** material for use in attacking or defending a position ⟨~ for the defense lawyers⟩

Amn *abbr* airman

am·ne·sia \am-ˈnē-zhə\ *n* [NL, fr. Gk *amnēsia* forgetfulness, alter. of *amnēstia*] (1618) **1 :** loss of memory due usu. to brain injury, shock, fatigue, repression, or illness **2 :** a gap in one's memory **3 :** the selective overlooking or ignoring of events or acts that are not favorable or useful to one's purpose or position — **am·ne·si·ac** \-zhē-ˌak, -zē-\ *or* **am·ne·sic** \-zik, -sik\ *adj or n*

am·nes·ty \ˈam-nə-stē\ *n, pl* **-ties** [Gk *amnēstia* forgetfulness, fr. *amnēstos* forgotten, fr. *a-* + *mnasthai* to remember — more at MIND] (1580) : the act of an authority (as a government) by which pardon is granted to a large group of individuals — **amnesty** *vt*

am·nio \ˈam-nē-ō\ *n, pl* **am·ni·os** (1983) : AMNIOCENTESIS

am·nio·cen·te·sis \ˌam-nē-ō-(ˌ)sen-ˈtē-səs\ *n, pl* **-te·ses** \-ˌsēz\ [NL, fr. *amnion* + *centesis* puncture, fr. Gk *kentesis,* fr. *kentein* to prick — more at CENTER] (1957) : the surgical insertion of a hollow needle through the abdominal wall and into the uterus to obtain amniotic fluid esp. for the determination of fetal sex or chromosomal abnormality

am·ni·on \ˈam-nē-ˌän, -ən\ *n, pl* **amnions** *or* **am·nia** \-nē-ə\ [NL, fr. Gk, caul, fr. *amnos* lamb — more at YEAN] (1667) **1 :** a thin membrane forming a closed sac about the embryos or fetuses of reptiles, birds, and mammals and containing the amniotic fluid **2 :** a membrane analogous to the amnion and occurring in various invertebrates — **am·ni·ot·ic** \ˌam-nē-ˈä-tik\ *adj*

am·ni·ote \ˈam-nē-ˌōt\ *n* [NL *Amniota,* fr. *amnion*] (1887) : any of a group (Amniota) of vertebrates that undergo embryonic or fetal development within an amnion and include the birds, reptiles, and mammals — **amniote** *adj*

amniotic fluid *n* (ca. 1855) : the serous fluid in which the embryo or fetus is suspended within the amnion

amniotic sac *n* (ca. 1881) : AMNION

amn't \ˈänt, ˈant, ˈa-mənt\ (1618) *chiefly Scot & Irish* : am not

amo·bar·bi·tal \ˌa-mō-ˈbär-bə-ˌtȯl\ *n* [*amyl* + *-o-* + *barbital*] (1949) : a barbiturate $C_{11}H_{18}N_2O_3$ used as a hypnotic and sedative; *also* : its sodium salt

amoe·ba *also* **ame·ba** \ə-ˈmē-bə\ *n, pl* **-bas** *or* **-bae** \-(ˌ)bē\ [NL, genus name, fr. Gk *amoibē* change, fr. *ameibein* to change — more at MIGRATE] (1855) : any of a large genus (*Amoeba*) of naked rhizopod protozoans with lobed and never anastomosing pseudopodia, without permanent organelles or supporting structures, and of wide distribution in fresh and salt water and moist terrestrial environments; *broadly* : a naked rhizopod or other amoeboid protozoan — **amoe·bic** *also* **amebic** \-bik\ *adj*

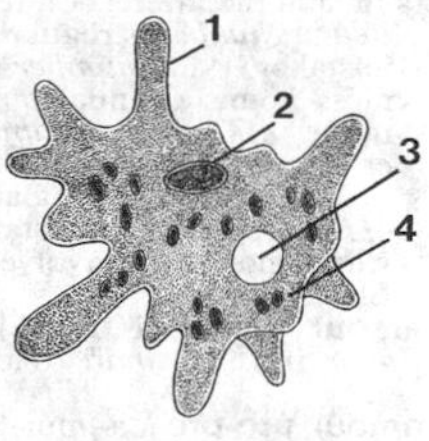

amoeba: *1* pseudopodium, *2* nucleus, *3* contractile vacuole, *4* food vacuole

amoebiasis *var of* AMEBIASIS

amoe·bo·cyte *also* **ame·bo·cyte** \ə-ˈmē-bə-ˌsīt\ *n* (1892) : a cell (as a phagocyte) having amoeboid form or movements

amoe·boid *also* **ame·boid** \ə-ˈmē-ˌbȯid\ *adj* (1856) : resembling an amoeba specif. in moving or changing in shape by means of protoplasmic flow

[1]**amok** \ə-ˈmək, -ˈmäk\ *also* **amuck** \ə-ˈmək\ *n* [Malay *amok*] (1665) : a murderous frenzy that has traditionally been regarded as occurring esp. in Malaysian culture

[2]**amok** *also* **amuck** *adv* (1672) **1 :** in a murderously frenzied state **2 a :** in a violently raging manner **b :** in an undisciplined, uncontrolled, or faulty manner ⟨films . . . about computers run ~ —*People*⟩

[3]**amok** *also* **amuck** *adj* (1944) : possessed with or motivated by a murderous or violently uncontrollable frenzy

amo·le \ə-ˈmō-lē\ *n* [AmerSp, fr. Nahuatl *ahmōlli* soap] (1831) : a plant part (as a root) possessing detergent properties and serving as a substitute for soap; *also* : a plant (as a yucca or agave) so used

among \ə-ˈməŋ\ *also* **amongst** \-ˈməŋ(k)st\ *prep* [*among* fr. ME, fr. OE *on gemonge,* fr. *on* + *gemonge,* dat. of *gemong* crowd, fr. *ge-* (associative prefix) + *-mong* (akin to OE *mengan* to mix); *amongst* fr. ME *amonges,* fr. *among* + *-es* -s — more at CO-, MINGLE] (bef. 12c) **1 :** in or through the midst of : surrounded by ⟨hidden ~ the trees⟩ **2 :** in company or association with ⟨living ~ artists⟩ **3 :** by or through the aggregate of ⟨discontent ~ the poor⟩ **4 :** in the number or class of ⟨wittiest ~ poets⟩ ⟨~ other things she was president of her college class⟩ **5 :** in shares to each of ⟨divided ~ the heirs⟩ **6 a :** through the reciprocal acts of ⟨quarrel ~ themselves⟩ **b :** through the joint action of ⟨made a fortune ~ themselves⟩ ***usage*** see BETWEEN

amon·til·la·do \ə-ˌmän-tə-ˈlä-(ˌ)dō, -ti(l)-ˈyä-(ˌ)thō\ *n, pl* **-dos** [Sp, lit., done in the manner of *Montilla,* town in Andalusia] (1825) : a medium dry sherry

amor·al \(ˌ)ā-ˈmȯr-əl, (ˌ)a-, -ˈmär-\ *adj* (1779) **1 a :** being neither moral nor immoral; *specif* : lying outside the sphere to which moral judgments apply ⟨science as such is completely ~ —W. S. Thompson⟩ **b :** lacking moral sensibility ⟨infants are ~⟩ **2 :** being outside or beyond the moral order or a particular code of morals ⟨~ customs⟩ — **amor·al·ism** \-ə-ˌli-zəm\ *n* — **amo·ral·i·ty** \ˌā-mə-ˈra-lə-tē, ˌa-, -(ˌ)mȯ-\ *n* — **amor·al·ly** \ˌā-ˈmȯr-ə-lē, (ˌ)a-, -ˈmär-\ *adv*

amo·ret·to \ˌa-mə-ˈre-(ˌ)tō, ˌä-\ *n, pl* **-ti** \-(ˌ)tē\ *or* **-tos** [It, dim. of *amore* love, cupid, fr. L *amor*] (1622) : CUPID, CHERUB 2

am·or·ist \ˈa-mə-rist\ *n* (1581) **1 :** a devotee of love and esp. sexual love : GALLANT **2 :** one who writes about romantic love — **am·or·is·tic** \ˌa-mə-ˈris-tik\ *adj*

Am·o·rite \ˈa-mə-ˌrīt\ *n* [Heb *Ĕmōrī*] (1535) : a member of one of various Semitic peoples living in Mesopotamia, Syria, and Palestine during the third and second millennia B.C. — **Amorite** *adj*

am·o·rous \ˈa-mə-rəs, ˈam-rəs\ *adj* [ME, fr. AF, fr. ML *amorosus,* fr. L *amor* love, fr. *amare* to love] (14c) **1 :** strongly moved by love and esp. sexual love ⟨~ couples⟩ **2 :** being in love : ENAMORED — usu. used with *of* ⟨~ of the girl⟩ **3 a :** indicative of love ⟨received ~ glances from her partner⟩ **b :** of or relating to love ⟨an ~ novel⟩ — **am·o·rous·ly** *adv* — **am·o·rous·ness** *n*

amor·phous \ə-ˈmȯr-fəs\ *adj* [Gk *amorphos,* fr. *a-* + *morphē* form] (ca. 1731) **1 a :** having no definite form : SHAPELESS ⟨an ~ cloud mass⟩ **b :** being without definite character or nature : UNCLASSIFIABLE ⟨an ~ segment of society⟩ **c :** lacking organization or unity ⟨an ~ style of writing⟩ **2 :** having no real or apparent crystalline form ⟨an ~ mineral⟩ — **amor·phous·ly** *adv* — **amor·phous·ness** *n*

amort \ə-ˈmȯrt\ *adj* [short for *all-a-mort,* by folk etymology fr. MF *a la mort* to the death] (1546) *archaic* : being at the point of death

am·or·ti·za·tion \ˌa-mər-tə-ˈzā-shən *also* ə-ˌmȯr-\ *n* (1851) **1 :** the act or process of amortizing **2 :** the result of amortizing

am·or·tize \ˈa-mər-ˌtīz *also* ə-ˈmȯr-\ *vt* **-tized; -tiz·ing** [ME *amortisen* to kill, alienate in mortmain, fr. AF *amorteser,* alter. of *amortir,* fr. VL *admortire* to kill, fr. L *ad-* + *mort-, mors* death — more at MURDER] (1867) **1 :** to pay off (as a mortgage) gradually usu. by periodic payments of principal and interest or by payments to a sinking fund **2 :** to gradually reduce or write off the cost or value of (as an asset) ⟨~ goodwill⟩ ⟨~ machinery⟩ — **am·or·tiz·able** \-ˌtī-zə-bəl\ *adj*

\ə\ **a**but \ᵊ\ kitten, F table \ər\ **fur**ther \a\ **a**sh \ā\ **a**ce \ä\ m**o**p, m**a**r \au̇\ **ou**t \ch\ **ch**in \e\ b**e**t \ē\ **ea**sy \g\ **g**o \i\ h**i**t \ī\ **i**ce \j\ **j**ob \ŋ\ si**ng** \ō\ g**o** \ȯ\ l**aw** \ȯi\ b**oy** \th\ **th**in \t͟h\ **th**e \ü\ l**oo**t \u̇\ f**oo**t \y\ **y**et \zh\ vi**s**ion, beige \k, ⁿ, œ, ue, ʸ\ *see* Guide to Pronunciation

Amos \ˈā-məs\ *n* [Heb *ʿĀmōs*] (bef. 12c) **1 :** a Hebrew prophet of the eighth century B.C. **2 :** a prophetic book of canonical Jewish and Christian Scripture — see BIBLE table

am·o·site \ˈa-mə-ˌsīt, -ˌzīt\ *n* [*Amosa* (fr. *A*sbestos *M*ines *o*f *S*outh *A*frica) + ¹*-ite*] (ca. 1918) **:** an iron-rich amphibole that is a variety of asbestos

¹**amount** \ə-ˈmau̇nt\ *vi* [ME, fr. AF *amounter*, fr. *amount* upward, fr. *a-* (fr. L *ad-*) + *mont* mountain — more at MOUNT] (14c) **1 a :** to be equivalent ⟨acts that ~ to treason⟩ **b :** to reach in kind or quality ⟨wants her son to ~ to something⟩ ⟨doesn't ~ to much⟩ **2 :** to reach a total **:** add up ⟨the bill ~*s* to $10⟩

²**amount** *n* (1595) **1 a :** the total number or quantity **:** AGGREGATE **b :** the quantity at hand or under consideration ⟨has an enormous ~ of energy⟩ **2 :** the whole effect, significance, or import **3 :** a principal sum and the interest on it
usage *Number* is regularly used with count nouns ⟨a large *number* of mistakes⟩ ⟨any *number* of times⟩ while *amount* is mainly used with mass nouns ⟨annual *amount* of rainfall⟩ ⟨a substantial *amount* of money⟩. The use of *amount* with count nouns has been frequently criticized; it usu. occurs when the number of things is thought of as a mass or collection ⟨glad to furnish any *amount* of black pebbles —*New Yorker*⟩ ⟨a substantial *amount* of film offers —Lily Tomlin⟩ or when money is involved ⟨a substantial *amount* of loans —E. R. Black⟩.

amour \ə-ˈmu̇r, ä-, a-\ *n* [ME, love, affection, fr. AF, fr. Old Occitan *amor*, fr. L, fr. *amare* to love] (14c) **:** a usu. illicit love affair; *also* **:** LOVER

amour pro·pre \ˌa-ˌmu̇r-ˈprōprᵊ, ˌä-, -ˈpro̅prᵊ\ *n* [F *amour-propre*, lit., love of oneself] (1775) **:** SELF-ESTEEM

amox·i·cil·lin \ə-ˌmäk-sē-ˈsi-lən\ *n* [*am*ino + *ox-* + peni*cillin*] (1971) **:** a semisynthetic penicillin $C_{16}H_{19}N_3O_5S$ derived from ampicillin

amox·y·cil·lin *Brit var of* AMOXICILLIN

Amoy \ä-ˈmȯi, a-, ə-\ *n* (1904) **:** the dialect of Chinese spoken in and near Xiamen (Amoy) in southeastern China

¹**amp** \ˈamp\ *n* [by shortening] (1886) **1 :** AMPERE **2 :** AMPLIFIER; *also* **:** a unit consisting of an electronic amplifier and a loudspeaker

²**amp** *vt* (1972) **:** EXCITE, ENERGIZE — often used with *up* ⟨trying to ~ up the crowd⟩; *also* **:** HEIGHTEN, INTENSIFY — often used with *up* ⟨~ up the drama⟩

AMP \ˌā-ˌem-ˈpē\ *n* [*a*denosine *m*ono*p*hosphate] (1951) **:** a nucleotide $C_{10}H_{12}N_5O_3H_2PO_4$ composed of adenosine and one phosphate group that is reversibly convertible to ADP and ATP in metabolic reactions — called also *adenosine monophosphate, adenylic acid*; compare CYCLIC AMP

am·per·age \ˈam-p(ə-)rij, -ˌpir-ij\ *n* (1893) **:** the strength of a current of electricity expressed in amperes

am·pere \ˈam-ˌpir *also* -ˌper\ *n* [André-Marie *Ampère*] (1881) **1 :** the practical meter-kilogram-second unit of electric current that is equivalent to a flow of one coulomb per second or to the steady current produced by one volt applied across a resistance of one ohm **2 :** the base unit of electric current in the International System of Units that is equal to a constant current which when maintained in two straight parallel conductors of infinite length and negligible circular sections one meter apart in a vacuum produces between the conductors a force equal to 2×10^{-7} newton per meter of length

ampere–hour *n* (1883) **:** a unit quantity of electricity equal to the quantity carried past any point of a circuit in one hour by a steady current of one ampere

ampere–turn *n* (1884) **:** the meter-kilogram-second unit of magnetomotive force equal to the magnetomotive force around a path that links with one turn of wire carrying an electric current of one ampere

am·per·o·met·ric \ˌam-pir-ə-ˈme-trik\ *adj* [*ampere* + *-o-* + *-metric*] (1940) **:** relating to or being a chemical titration in which the measurement of the electric current flowing under an applied potential difference between two electrodes in a solution is used for detecting the end point

am·per·sand \ˈam-pər-ˌsand\ *n* [alter. of *and* (&) *per se and*, lit., (the character) & by itself (is the word) *and*] (1835) **:** a character typically & standing for the word *and*

am·phet·amine \am-ˈfe-tə-ˌmēn, -mən\ *n* [ISV *a*lpha + *m*ethyl + *phen-* + *et*hyl + *amine*] (1938) **:** a racemic compound $C_9H_{13}N$ or one of its derivatives (as dextroamphetamine or methamphetamine) frequently abused as a stimulant of the central nervous system but used clinically esp. as the sulfate or hydrochloride salt to treat hyperactive children and the symptoms of narcolepsy and as a short-term appetite suppressant in dieting

amphi- *or* **amph-** *prefix* [L *amphi-* around, on both sides, fr. Gk *amphi-, amph-*, fr. *amphi* — more at AMBI-] **:** on both sides **:** of both kinds **:** both ⟨*amphi*brach⟩ ⟨*amphi*diploid⟩

am·phib·ia \am-ˈfi-bē-ə\ *n pl* (1607) **:** AMPHIBIANS

am·phib·i·an \-bē-ən\ *n* [ultim. fr. Gk *amphibion* amphibious being, fr. neut. of *amphibios*] (1835) **1 :** an amphibious organism; *esp* **:** any of a class (Amphibia) of cold-blooded vertebrates (as frogs, toads, or salamanders) intermediate in many characters between fishes and reptiles and having gilled aquatic larvae and air-breathing adults **2 :** an amphibious vehicle; *esp* **:** an airplane designed to take off from and land on either land or water — **amphibian** *adj*

am·phib·i·ous \am-ˈfi-bē-əs\ *adj* [Gk *amphibios*, lit., living a double life, fr. *amphi-* + *bios* mode of life — more at QUICK] (1643) **1 :** combining two characteristics **2 a :** relating to or adapted for both land and water ⟨~ vehicles⟩ **b :** executed by coordinated action of land, sea, and air forces organized for invasion ⟨an ~ landing⟩; *also* **:** trained or organized for such action ⟨~ forces⟩ **3 :** able to live both on land and in water ⟨~ plants⟩ — **am·phib·i·ous·ly** *adv* — **am·phib·i·ous·ness** *n*

am·phi·bole \ˈam(p)-fə-ˌbōl\ *n* [F, fr. LL *amphibolus*, fr. Gk *amphibolos* ambiguous, fr. *amphiballein* to throw round, doubt, fr. *amphi-* + *ballein* to throw — more at DEVIL] (ca. 1823) **1 :** HORNBLENDE **2 :** any of a group of complex silicate minerals with like crystal structures that contain calcium, sodium, magnesium, aluminum, or iron ions or a combination of them

am·phib·o·lite \am-ˈfi-bə-ˌlīt\ *n* (1826) **:** a usu. metamorphic rock consisting essentially of amphibole

am·phi·bol·o·gy \ˌam(p)-fə-ˈbä-lə-jē\ *n, pl* **-gies** [ME *amphibologie*, fr. LL *amphibologia*, alter. of L *amphibolia*, fr. Gk, fr. *amphibolos*] (14c) **:** a sentence or phrase (as "nothing is good enough for you") that can be interpreted in more than one way

am·phib·o·ly \am-ˈfi-bə-lē\ *n, pl* **-lies** [LL *amphibolia*] (ca. 1588) **:** AMPHIBOLOGY

am·phi·brach \ˈam(p)-fə-ˌbrak\ *n* [L *amphibrachys*, fr. Gk, lit., short at both ends, fr. *amphi-* + *brachys* short — more at BRIEF] (1858) **:** a metrical foot consisting of a long syllable between two short syllables in quantitative verse or of a stressed syllable between two unstressed syllables in accentual verse ⟨*romantic* is an accentual ~⟩ — **am·phi·brach·ic** \ˌam(p)-fə-ˈbra-kik\ *adj*

am·phic·ty·o·ny \am-ˈfik-tē-ə-nē\ *n, pl* **-nies** [Gk *amphiktyonia*, fr. *amphiktiones* neighbors, fr. *amphi-* + *-ktiones*, fr. *ktizein* to found, inhabit — more at HOME] (1835) **:** an association of neighboring states in ancient Greece to defend a common religious center; *broadly* **:** an association of neighboring states for their common interest — **am·phic·ty·on·ic** \(ˌ)am-ˌfik-tē-ˈä-nik\ *adj*

am·phi·dip·loid \ˌam(p)-fi-ˈdi-ˌplȯid\ *n* (1930) **:** an interspecific hybrid having a complete diploid chromosome set from each parent form — called also *allotetraploid* — **amphidiploid** *adj* — **am·phi·dip·loi·dy** \-ˌplȯi-dē\ *n*

am·phi·mix·is \ˌam(p)-fi-ˈmik-səs\ *n, pl* **-mix·es** \-ˌsēz\ [NL, fr. *amphi-* + Gk *mixis* mingling, fr. *mignynai* to mix — more at MIX] (1893) **:** the union of gametes in sexual reproduction

Am·phi·on \am-ˈfī-ən\ *n* [L, fr. Gk *Amphiōn*] (15c) **:** a musician of Greek mythology who builds the walls of Thebes by charming the stones into place with his lyre

am·phi·ox·us \ˌam(p)-fē-ˈäk-səs\ *n, pl* **-oxi** \-ˌsī\ *or* **-ox·us·es** [NL, fr. *amphi-* + Gk *oxys* sharp] (1847) **:** any of a genus (*Branchiostoma*) of lancelets; *broadly* **:** LANCELET

am·phi·path·ic \ˌam(p)-fə-ˈpa-thik\ *adj* [*amphi-* + *-pathic* (as in *empathic*)] (1936) **:** AMPHIPHILIC

am·phi·phil·ic \-ˈfi-lik\ *adj* (1948) **:** of, relating to, or being a compound (as a surfactant) consisting of molecules having a polar water-soluble group attached to a water-insoluble hydrocarbon chain; *also* **:** being a molecule of such a compound — **am·phi·phile** \ˈam(p)-fə-ˌfīl\ *n*

am·phi·ploid \ˈam(p)-fi-ˌplȯid\ *adj* (1945) *of an interspecific hybrid* **:** having at least one complete diploid set of chromosomes derived from each parent species — **amphiploid** *n* — **am·phi·ploi·dy** \-ˌplȯi-dē\ *n*

am·phi·pod \-ˌpäd\ *n* [ultim. fr. Gk *amphi-* + *pod-, pous* foot — more at FOOT] (1835) **:** any of a large order (Amphipoda) of small crustaceans (as the sand flea) with a laterally compressed body — **amphipod** *adj*

am·phi·pro·style \ˌam(p)-fi-ˈprō-ˌstī(-ə)l\ *adj* [L *amphiprostylos*, fr. Gk, fr. *amphi-* + *prostylos* having pillars in front, fr. *pro-* + *stylos* pillar — more at STEER] (1850) **:** having columns at each end only ⟨an ~ building⟩ — **amphiprostyle** *n*

am·phis·bae·na \ˌam(p)-fəs-ˈbē-nə\ *n* [L, fr. Gk *amphisbaina*, fr. *amphis* on both sides (fr. *amphi* around) + *bainein* to walk, go — more at BY, COME] (14c) **:** a serpent in classical mythology having a head at each end and capable of moving in either direction — **am·phis·bae·nic** \-nik\ *adj*

am·phi·the·ater \ˈam(p)-fə-ˌthē-(-ə)-tər *also* ˈam-pə-ˌthē-\ *n* [L *amphitheatrum*, fr. Gk *amphitheatron*, fr. *amphi-* + *theatron* theater] (14c) **1 :** an oval or circular building with rising tiers of seats ranged about an open space and used in ancient Rome esp. for contests and spectacles **2 a :** a very large auditorium **b :** a room with a gallery from which doctors and students may observe surgical operations **c :** a rising gallery in a modern theater **d :** a flat or gently sloping area surrounded by abrupt slopes **3 :** a place of public entertainment (as for games or concerts) — **am·phi·the·at·ric** \ˌam(p)-fə-thē-ˈa-trik *also* ˌam-pə-thē-\ *or* **am·phi·the·at·ri·cal** \-tri-kəl\ *adj* — **am·phi·the·at·ri·cal·ly** \-tri-k(ə-)lē\ *adv*

Am·phit·ry·on \am-ˈfi-trē-ən\ *n* [Gk *Amphitryōn*] (1567) **:** the husband of Alcmene

am·pho·ra \ˈam(p)-fə-rə\ *n, pl* **-rae** \-ˌrē, -ˌrī\ *or* **-ras** [L, modif. of Gk *amphoreus, amphiphoreus*, fr. *amphi-* + *phoreus* bearer, fr. *pherein* to bear — more at BEAR] (14c) **1 :** an ancient Greek jar or vase with a large oval body, narrow cylindrical neck, and two handles that rise almost to the level of the mouth; *broadly* **:** such a jar or vase used elsewhere in the ancient world **2 :** a 2-handled vessel shaped like an amphora

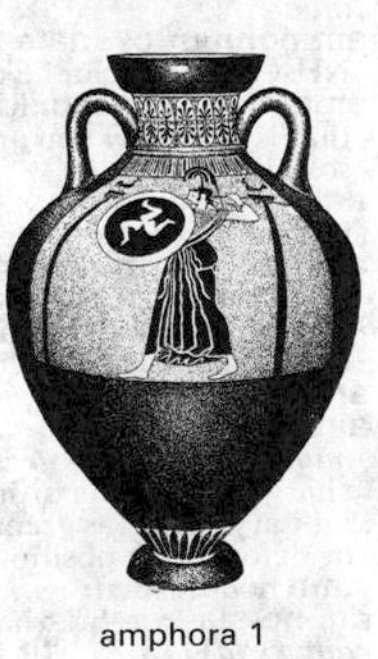
amphora 1

am·pho·ter·ic \ˌam(p)-fə-ˈter-ik\ *adj* [ISV, fr. Gk *amphoteros* each of two, fr. *amphō* both — more at AMBI-] (ca. 1849) **:** partly one and partly the other; *specif* **:** capable of reacting chemically either as an acid or as a base

am·pho·ter·i·cin B \ˌam(p)-fə-ˈter-ə-sən-ˈbē\ *n* [*amphoteric* + ¹*-in*] (1955) **:** an antifungal antibiotic obtained from a soil streptomycete (*Streptomyces nodosus*) and used esp. to treat systemic fungal infections

amp hr *abbr* ampere-hour

am·pi·cil·lin \ˌam-pə-ˈsi-lən\ *n* [*am*ino + *penicillin*] (1961) **:** a penicillin $C_{16}H_{19}N_3O_4S$ that is effective against gram-negative and gram-positive bacteria and is used to treat various infections of the urinary, respiratory, and intestinal tracts

am·ple \ˈam-pəl\ *adj* **am·pler** \-p(ə-)lər\; **am·plest** \-p(ə-)ləst\ [ME, fr. AF, fr. L *amplus*] (15c) **1 :** generous or more than adequate in size, scope, or capacity ⟨there was room for an ~ garden⟩ **2 :** generously sufficient to satisfy a requirement or need ⟨they had ~ money for the trip⟩ **3 :** BUXOM, PORTLY ⟨an ~ figure⟩ ***syn*** see SPACIOUS, PLENTIFUL — **am·ple·ness** \-pəl-nəs\ *n* — **am·ply** \-plē\ *adv*

am·plex·us \am-ˈplek-səs\ *n* [NL, fr. L, embrace, fr. *amplecti* to embrace, fr. *am-, amb-* around + *plectere* to braid — more at AMBI-, PLY] (ca. 1927) **:** the mating embrace of a frog or toad during which eggs are shed into the water and there fertilized

am·pli·fi·ca·tion \ˌam-plə-fə-ˈkā-shən\ *n* (1546) **1 a :** an act, example, or product of amplifying **b :** a usu. massive replication of genetic material and esp. of a gene or DNA sequence (as in a polymerase chain reaction) **2 a :** the particulars by which a statement is expanded **b :** an expanded statement

am·pli·fi·er \ˈam-plə-ˌfī(-ə)r\ *n* (1546) **:** one that amplifies; *specif* **:** an electronic device (as in a stereo system) for amplifying voltage, current, or power

am·pli·fy \-ˌfī\ *vb* **-fied; -fy·ing** [ME *amplifien,* fr. MF *amplifier,* fr. L *amplificare,* fr. *amplus*] *vt* (14c) **1 :** to expand (as a statement) by the use of detail or illustration or by closer analysis **2 a :** to make larger or greater (as in amount, importance, or intensity) **:** INCREASE **b :** to increase the strength or amount of; *esp* **:** to make louder **c :** to cause (a gene or DNA sequence) to undergo amplification ~ *vi* **:** to expand one's remarks or ideas ***syn*** see EXPAND

am·pli·tude \-ˌtüd, -ˌtyüd\ *n* (1542) **1 :** extent of dignity, excellence, or splendor **2 :** the quality or state of being ample **:** FULLNESS, ABUNDANCE **3 :** the extent or range of a quality, property, process, or phenomenon: as **a :** the extent of a vibratory movement (as of a pendulum) measured from the mean position to an extreme **b :** the maximum departure of the value of an alternating current or wave from the average value **4 :** the angle assigned to a complex number when it is plotted in a complex plane using polar coordinates — called also *argument*; compare ABSOLUTE VALUE 2

amplitude modulation *n* (1921) **:** modulation of the amplitude of a radio carrier wave in accordance with the strength of the audio or other signal; *also* **:** a broadcasting system using such modulation — compare FREQUENCY MODULATION

am·poule *or* **am·pule** *also* **am·pul** \ˈam-ˌpyül, -ˌpül\ *n* [ME *ampulle* flask, fr. OE & AF; OE *ampulle* & AF *ampuille,* fr. L *ampulla*] (1886) **1 :** a hermetically sealed small bulbous glass vessel that is used to hold a solution for hypodermic injection **2 :** a vial resembling an ampoule

am·pul·la \am-ˈpu̇-lə, ˈam-ˌpyü-lə\ *n, pl* **-lae** \-(ˌ)lē, -ˌlī\ [ME, fr. OE, fr. L, dim. of *amphora*] (bef. 12c) **1 :** a glass or earthenware flask with a globular body and two handles used esp. by the ancient Romans to hold ointment, perfume, or wine **2 :** a saccular anatomical swelling or pouch — **am·pul·la·ry** \am-ˈpu̇-lər-ē, ˈam-pyə-ˌler-ē\ *adj*

ampulla of Lo·ren·zi·ni \-ˌlȯr-ən-ˈzē-nē\ [Stefano *Lorenzini fl*1678 Ital. physician] (1898) **:** any of the pores on the snouts of marine sharks and rays that contain receptors highly sensitive to weak electric fields

am·pu·tate \ˈam-pyə-ˌtāt\ *vt* **-tat·ed; -tat·ing** [L *amputatus,* pp. of *amputare,* fr. *am-, amb-* around + *putare* to cut, prune — more at AMBI-] (1612) **:** to remove by or as if by cutting; *esp* **:** to cut (as a limb) from the body — **am·pu·ta·tion** \ˌam-pyə-ˈtā-shən\ *n*

am·pu·tee \ˌam-pyə-ˈtē\ *n* (1910) **:** one that has had a limb amputated

amt *abbr* amount

am·trac *or* **am·track** \ˈam-ˌtrak\ *n* [*am*phibious + *trac*tor] (1944) **:** a flat-bottomed military vehicle that moves on tracks on land or water

amu *abbr* atomic mass unit

amuck *var of* AMOK

am·u·let \ˈam-yə-lət\ *n* [L *amuletum*] (1584) **:** a charm (as an ornament) often inscribed with a magic incantation or symbol to aid the wearer or protect against evil (as disease or witchcraft)

Amur tiger \ä-ˈmu̇r-\ *n* [*Amur* River, Asia] (1917) **:** SIBERIAN TIGER

amuse \ə-ˈmyüz\ *vb* **amused; amus·ing** [MF *amuser,* fr. OF, fr. *a-* (fr. L *ad-*) + *muser* to muse] *vt* (15c) **1 a** *archaic* **:** to divert the attention of so as to deceive **b** *obs* **:** to occupy the attention of **:** ABSORB **c** *obs* **:** DISTRACT, BEWILDER **2 a :** to entertain or occupy in a light, playful, or pleasant manner ⟨~ the child with a story⟩ **b :** to appeal to the sense of humor of ⟨the joke doesn't ~ me⟩ ~ *vi, obs* **:** MUSE — **amus·ed·ly** \-ˈmyü-zəd-lē\ *adv* — **amus·er** *n*

syn AMUSE, DIVERT, ENTERTAIN mean to pass or cause to pass the time pleasantly. AMUSE suggests that one's attention is engaged lightly ⟨*amuse* yourselves while I make dinner⟩. DIVERT implies distracting attention from worry or routine occupation esp. by something funny ⟨a light comedy to *divert* the tired businessman⟩. ENTERTAIN suggests supplying amusement by specially contrived methods ⟨a magician *entertaining* children at a party⟩.

amuse–bouche \ä-ˌmüz-ˈbüsh, -ˌmœz-\ *n* [F, lit., (it) entertains (the) mouth] (1984) **:** a small complimentary appetizer offered at some restaurants

amuse·ment \ə-ˈmyüz-mənt\ *n* (1586) **1 :** a means of amusing or entertaining ⟨what are her favorite ~*s*⟩ **2 :** the condition of being amused ⟨could not hide his ~⟩ **3 :** pleasurable diversion **:** ENTERTAINMENT ⟨plays the piano for ~⟩

amusement park *n* (1896) **:** a commercially operated park having various devices for entertainment (as a merry-go-round and roller coaster) and usu. booths for the sale of food and drink

amus·ing \ə-ˈmyü-ziŋ\ *adj* (1676) **:** giving amusement **:** DIVERTING — **amus·ing·ly** \-ziŋ-lē\ *adv* — **amus·ing·ness** *n*

AMVETS *abbr* American Veterans (of World War II)

amyg·da·la \ə-ˈmig-də-lə\ *n, pl* **-lae** \-ˌlē, -ˌlī\ [NL, fr. L, almond, fr. Gk *amygdalē*] (1845) **:** the one of the four basal ganglia in each cerebral hemisphere that is part of the limbic system and consists of an almond-shaped mass of gray matter in the anterior extremity of the temporal lobe — called also *amygdaloid nucleus*

amyg·da·lin \-lən\ *n* [L *amygdala*] (1651) **:** a white crystalline cyanogenetic glucoside $C_{20}H_{27}NO_{11}$ found esp. in the seeds of the apricot, peach, and bitter almond — compare LAETRILE

amyg·da·loid \-ˌlȯid\ *adj* [Gk *amygdaloeidēs,* fr. *amygdalē*] (1836) **1 :** almond-shaped **2 :** of, relating to, or affecting an amygdala

amyg·da·loi·dal \ə-ˌmig-də-ˈlȯi-dᵊl\ *adj* (1797) **:** of, being, or containing small cavities in igneous rock that are filled with deposits of different minerals (as chalcedony) — **amyg·da·loid** \ə-ˈmig-də-ˌlȯid\ *n*

am·yl \ˈa-məl\ *n* [L *amylum* + E *-yl*] (1841) **:** any of various isomeric alkyl radicals C_5H_{11}– derived from pentane

amyl- *or* **amylo-** *comb form* [L *amylum,* fr. Gk *amylon,* fr. neut. of *amylos* unmilled (of grain), fr. *a-* + *mylē* mill — more at MEAL] **:** starch ⟨*amylo*plast⟩

amyl acetate *n* (1863) **:** a colorless liquid acetate $C_7H_{14}O_2$ of amyl alcohol that has a pleasant fruity odor and is used esp. as a solvent and in the manufacture of artificial fruit essences — called also *banana oil*

amyl alcohol *n* (1849) **:** any of eight isomeric alcohols $C_5H_{12}O$ used esp. as solvents and in making esters; *also* **:** a commercially produced mixture of amyl alcohols used esp. as a solvent

am·y·lase \ˈa-mə-ˌlās, -ˌlāz\ *n* (1883) **:** any of a group of enzymes (as amylopsin) that catalyze the hydrolysis of starch and glycogen or their intermediate hydrolysis products

amyl nitrate *n* (1867) **1 :** a colorless liquid ester $C_5H_{11}NO_3$ of amyl alcohol and nitric acid **2 :** AMYL NITRITE — not used technically

amyl nitrite *n* (1867) **:** a pale yellow pungent flammable liquid ester $C_5H_{11}NO_2$ of commercial amyl alcohol and nitrous acid that is used in medicine as a vasodilator and inhaled illicitly esp. as an aphrodisiac — compare POPPER 2

am·y·loid \-ˌlȯid\ *n* (1866) **:** a waxy translucent substance consisting primarily of protein that is deposited in some animal organs and tissues under abnormal conditions (as Alzheimer's disease) — compare BETA-AMYLOID — **amyloid** *adj*

am·y·loid·osis \ˌa-mə-ˌlȯi-ˈdō-səs\ *n* [NL] (1886) **:** a disorder characterized by the deposition of amyloid in bodily organs and tissues

am·y·lo·lyt·ic \ˌa-mə-lō-ˈli-tik\ *adj* [NL *amylolysis,* fr. *amyl-* + *-lysis*] (1876) **:** characterized by or capable of the enzymatic splitting of starch into soluble products ⟨~ enzymes⟩ ⟨~ activity⟩

am·y·lo·pec·tin \ˌa-mə-lō-ˈpek-tən\ *n* (1905) **:** a component of starch that has a high molecular weight and branched structure and does not tend to gel in aqueous solutions

am·y·lo·plast \ˈa-mə-(ˌ)lō-ˌplast\ *n* (1882) **:** a colorless plastid that forms and stores starch

am·y·lop·sin \ˌa-mə-ˈläp-sən\ *n* [*amyl-* + *-psin* (as in *trypsin*)] (1878) **:** the amylase of the pancreatic juice

am·y·lose \ˈa-mə-ˌlōs, -ˌlōz\ *n* (1833) **:** a component of starch characterized by its straight chains of glucose units

amyo·to·nia \ˌā-ˌmī-ə-ˈtō-nē-ə\ *n* [NL] (1908) **:** deficiency of muscle tone

amyo·tro·phic lateral sclerosis \ˌā-ˌmī-ə-ˈtrō-fik-, -ˈträ-\ *n* [2*a-* + *my-* + *-trophic*] (1875) **:** a rare progressive degenerative fatal disease affecting the motor neurons, usu. beginning in middle age, and characterized esp. by increasing and spreading muscular weakness and atrophy — abbr. *ALS*; called also *Lou Gehrig's disease*

Am·y·tal \ˈa-mə-ˌtȯl\ *trademark* — used for amobarbital

1an \ən, (ˈ)an\ *indefinite article* [ME, fr. OE *ān* one — more at ONE] (bef. 12c) **:** 2A ***usage*** see 2A

2an \ən, an\ *prep* (bef. 12c) **:** 3A 2 ***usage*** see 2A

3an *or* **an'** *conj* (12c) **1** *see* AND\ **:** AND **2** \ˈan\ *archaic* **:** IF

4an *abbr* [L *annum; annus*] year

an- — see 2A-

1-an *or* **-ian** *also* **-ean** *n suffix* [*-an* & *-ian* fr. ME *-an, -ian,* fr. AF & L; AF *-ien,* fr. L *-ianus,* fr. *-i-* + *-anus,* fr. *-anus,* adj. suffix; *-ean* fr. such words as *Mediterranean, European*] **1 :** one that is of or relating to ⟨American⟩ **2 :** one skilled in or specializing in ⟨phonetic*ian*⟩

2-an *or* **-ian** *also* **-ean** *adj suffix* **1 :** of or belonging to ⟨Americ*an*⟩ ⟨Florid*ian*⟩ **2 :** characteristic of **:** resembling ⟨Mozart*ean*⟩

3-an *n suffix* [ISV *-an, -ane,* alter. of *-ene, -ine,* & *-one*] **1 :** unsaturated organic compound ⟨fur*an*⟩ **2 :** anhydride of a carbohydrate ⟨dex*tran*⟩

AN *abbr* airman (Navy)

1ana \ˈa-nə\ *adv* [ME, fr. ML, fr. Gk, at the rate of, lit., up] (14c) **:** of each an equal quantity

2ana \ˈa-nə, ˈä-, ˈā-\ *n, pl* **ana** *or* **anas** [*-ana*] (ca. 1751) **1 :** a collection of the memorable sayings of a person **2 :** a collection of anecdotes or interesting information about a person or a place

ANA *abbr* American Nurses Association

ana- *or* **an-** *prefix* [L, fr. Gk, up, back, again, fr. *ana* up — more at ON] **1 :** up **:** upward ⟨*ana*bolism⟩ **2 :** back **:** backward ⟨*ana*tropous⟩

-ana *or* **-iana** *n pl suffix* [NL, fr. L, neut. pl. of *-anus* -an & *-ianus* -ian] **:** collected items of information esp. anecdotal or bibliographical concerning ⟨Americ*ana*⟩

ana·bap·tism \ˌa-nə-ˈbap-ˌti-zəm\ *n* [NL *anabaptismus,* fr. LGk *anabaptismos* rebaptism, fr. *anabaptizein* to rebaptize, fr. Gk *ana-* again + *baptizein* to baptize] (1575) **1** *cap* **a :** the doctrine or practices of the Anabaptists **b :** the Anabaptist movement **2 :** the baptism of one previously baptized

Ana·bap·tist \-ˈbap-tist\ *n* (1532) **:** a Protestant sectarian of a radical movement arising in the 16th century and advocating the baptism and church membership of adult believers only, nonresistance, and the separation of church and state — **Anabaptist** *adj*

anab·a·sis \ə-ˈna-bə-səs\ *n, pl* **-a·ses** \-ˌsēz\ [Gk, inland march, fr. *anabainein* to go up or inland, fr. *ana-* + *bainein* to go — more at COME] (ca. 1706) **1 :** a going or marching up **:** ADVANCE; *esp* **:** a military advance **2** [fr. the retreat of Greek mercenaries in Asia Minor described in the *Anabasis* of Xenophon] **:** a difficult and dangerous military retreat

an·a·bat·ic \ˌa-nə-ˈba-tik\ *adj* [Gk *anabatos,* verbal of *anabainein*] (ca. 1918) **:** moving upward **:** RISING ⟨an ~ wind⟩

anabolic steroid *n* (1946) **:** any of a group of usu. synthetic hormones that are derivatives of testosterone, are used medically esp. to promote tissue growth, and are sometimes abused by athletes to increase the size and strength of their muscles and improve endurance

anab·o·lism \ə-ˈna-bə-ˌli-zəm\ *n* [ISV *ana-* + meta*bolism*] (1886) **:** the constructive part of metabolism concerned esp. with macromolecular synthesis — compare CATABOLISM — **an·a·bol·ic** \ˌa-nə-ˈbä-lik\ *adj*

anach·ro·nism \ə-ˈna-krə-ˌni-zəm\ *n* [prob. fr. MGk *anachronismos,* fr. *anachronizesthai* to be an anachronism, fr. LGk *anachronizein* to be late, fr. Gk *ana-* + *chronos* time] (1617) **1 :** an error in chronology; *esp* **:** a chronological misplacing of persons, events, objects, or customs in regard to each other **2 :** a person or a thing that is chronologically out of place; *esp* **:** one from a former age that is incongruous in the present **3 :** the state or condition of being chronologically out of place — **anach·ro·nis·tic** \ə-ˌna-krə-ˈnis-tik\ *also* **ana·chron·ic** \ˌa-nə-ˈkrä-nik\ *adj* — **anach·ro·nis·ti·cal·ly** \ə-ˌna-krə-ˈnis-ti-k(ə-)lē\ *adv* — **anach·ro·nous** \ə-ˈna-krə-nəs\ *adj* — **anach·ro·nous·ly** *adv*

an·a·clit·ic \ˌa-nə-ˈkli-tik\ *adj* [Gk *anaklitos,* verbal of *anaklinein* to lean upon, fr. *ana-* + *klinein* to lean — more at LEAN] (1922) **:** of, relat-

\ə\ **abut** \ᵊ\ **kitten,** F **table** \ər\ **further** \a\ **ash** \ā\ **ace** \ä\ **mop, mar**
\au̇\ **out** \ch\ **chin** \e\ **bet** \ē\ **easy** \g\ **go** \i\ **hit** \ī\ **ice** \j\ **job**
\ŋ\ **sing** \ō\ **go** \ȯ\ **law** \ȯi\ **boy** \th\ **thin** \t͟h\ **the** \ü\ **loot** \u̇\ **foot**
\y\ **yet** \zh\ **vision, beige** \k͟, ⁿ, œ, ue, ʸ\ *see* Guide to Pronunciation

ing to, or characterized by the direction of love toward an object (as the mother) that satisfies nonsexual needs (as hunger)

an·a·co·lu·thon \ˌa-nə-kə-ˈlü-ˌthän\ *n, pl* **-tha** \-thə\ *also* **-thons** [LL, fr. LGk *anakolouthon* inconsistency in logic, fr. Gk, neut. of *anakolouthos* inconsistent, fr. *an-* + *akolouthos* following, fr. *ha-, a-* together + *keleuthos* path] (ca. 1706) **:** syntactical inconsistency or incoherence within a sentence; *esp* **:** a shift in an unfinished sentence from one syntactic construction to another (as in "you really ought—well, do it your own way") — **an·a·co·lu·thic** \-thik\ *adj* — **an·a·co·lu·thi·cal·ly** \-thi-k(ə-)lē\ *adv*

an·a·con·da \ˌa-nə-ˈkän-də\ *n* [prob. modif. of Sinhalese *henakandayā*, a slender green snake] (1768) **:** a large semiaquatic constricting snake (*Eunectes murinus*) of the boa family of tropical So. America that may reach a length of 30 feet (9.1 meters); *broadly* **:** any of the large constricting snakes

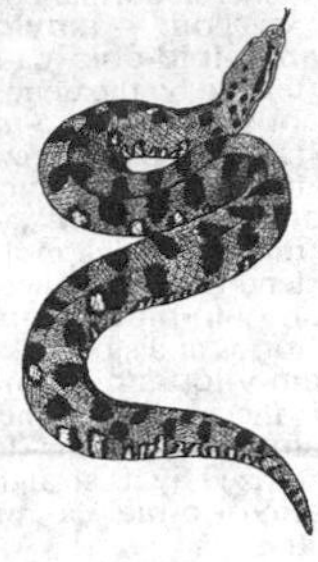

anaconda

anac·re·on·tic \ə-ˌna-krē-ˈän-tik\ *n* (1656) **:** a poem in the manner of Anacreon; *esp* **:** a drinking song or light lyric

Anacreontic *adj* [L *anacreonticus*, fr. *Anacreont-, Anacreon* Anacreon, fr. Gk *Anakreont-, Anakreōn*] (1611) **1 :** of, relating to, or resembling the poetry of Anacreon **2 :** convivial or amatory in tone or theme

an·a·cru·sis \ˌa-nə-ˈkrü-səs\ *n, pl* **-cru·ses** \-ˌsēz\ [NL, fr. Gk *anakrousis* beginning of a song, fr. *anakrouein* to begin a song, fr. *ana-* + *krouein* to strike, beat; akin to Lith *kraušyti* to strike] (1830) **1 :** one or more syllables at the beginning of a line of poetry that are regarded as preliminary to and not a part of the metrical pattern **2 :** UPBEAT; *specif* **:** one or more notes or tones preceding the first downbeat of a musical phrase

an·a·dama bread \ˌa-nə-ˈda-mə-\ *n* [origin unknown] (1954) **:** a leavened bread made with flour, cornmeal, and molasses

an·a·dem \ˈa-nə-ˌdem\ *n* [L *anadema*, fr. Gk *anadēma*, fr. *anadein* to wreathe, fr. *ana-* + *dein* to bind — more at DIADEM] (1598) *archaic* **:** a wreath for the head **:** GARLAND

ana·di·plo·sis \ˌa-nə-də-ˈplō-səs, ˌa-nə-(ˌ)dī-ˈplō-\ *n, pl* **-plo·ses** \-ˌsēz\ [LL, fr. Gk *anadiplōsis*, lit., repetition, fr. *anadiploun* to double, fr. *ana-* + *diploun* to double — more at DIPLOMA] (ca. 1550) **:** repetition of a prominent and usu. the last word in one phrase or clause at the beginning of the next (as in "rely on his honor—honor such as his?")

anad·ro·mous \ə-ˈna-drə-məs\ *adj* [Gk *anadromos* running upward, fr. *anadramein* to run upward, fr. *ana-* + *dramein* to run — more at DROMEDARY] (ca. 1753) **:** ascending rivers from the sea for breeding ⟨shad are ~⟩ — compare CATADROMOUS

anae·mia, anae·mic *chiefly Brit var of* ANEMIA, ANEMIC

an·aer·obe \ˈa-nə-ˌrōb; (ˌ)an-ˈer-ˌōb\ *n* [ISV] (1884) **:** an anaerobic organism

an·aer·o·bic \ˌa-nə-ˈrō-bik; ˌan-ˌer-ˈō-\ *adj* (ca. 1881) **1 a :** living, active, occurring, or existing in the absence of free oxygen ⟨~ respiration⟩ ⟨~ bacteria⟩ **b :** of, relating to, or being activity in which the body incurs an oxygen debt ⟨~ exercise⟩ **2 :** relating to or induced by anaerobes — **an·aer·o·bi·cal·ly** \-bi-k(ə-)lē\ *adv*

an·aero·bi·o·sis \ˌa-nə-rō-(ˌ)bī-ˈō-səs, -bē-; ˌan-ˌer-ō-\ *n, pl* **-o·ses** \-ˈō-ˌsēz\ [NL] (ca. 1889) **:** life in the absence of air or free oxygen

an·aes·the·sia, an·aes·the·si·ol·o·gist, an·aes·the·si·ol·o·gy, an·aes·thet·ic, anaes·the·tise, anaes·the·tist *chiefly Brit var of* ANESTHESIA, ANESTHESIOLOGIST, ANESTHESIOLOGY, ANESTHETIC, ANESTHETIZE, ANESTHETIST

ana·gen·e·sis \ˌa-nə-ˈje-nə-səs\ *n* [NL] (1889) **:** evolutionary change producing a single lineage in which one taxon replaces another without branching — compare CLADOGENESIS

ana·glyph \ˈa-nə-ˌglif\ *n* [LL *anaglyphus* embossed, fr. Gk *anaglyphos*, fr. *anaglyphein* to emboss, fr. *ana-* + *glyphein* to carve — more at CLEAVE] (1651) **1 :** a sculptured, chased, or embossed ornament worked in low relief **2 :** a stereoscopic motion or still picture in which the right component of a composite image usu. red in color is superposed on the left component in a contrasting color to produce a three-dimensional effect when viewed through correspondingly colored filters in the form of spectacles — **ana·glyph·ic** \ˌa-nə-ˈgli-fik\ *adj*

an·ag·no·ri·sis \ˌa-ˌnag-ˈnȯr-ə-səs\ *n, pl* **-ri·ses** \-ˌsēz\ [Gk *anagnōrisis*, fr. *anagnōrizein* to recognize, fr. *ana-* + *gnōrizein* to make known; akin to Gk *gnōrimos* well-known, *gignōskein* to come to know — more at KNOW] (ca. 1800) **:** the point in the plot esp. of a tragedy at which the protagonist recognizes his or her or some other character's true identity or discovers the true nature of his or her own situation

an·a·go·ge *or* **an·a·go·gy** \ˈa-nə-ˌgō-jē\ *n, pl* **-ges** *or* **-gies** [LL *anagoge*, fr. LGk *anagōgē*, fr. Gk, reference, fr. *anagein* to refer, fr. *ana-* + *agein* to lead — more at AGENT] (15c) **:** interpretation of a word, passage, or text (as of Scripture or poetry) that finds beyond the literal, allegorical, and moral senses a fourth and ultimate spiritual or mystical sense — **an·a·gog·ic** \ˌa-nə-ˈgä-jik\ *or* **an·a·gog·i·cal** \-ji-kəl\ *adj* — **an·a·gog·i·cal·ly** \-ji-k(ə-)lē\ *adv*

[1]**an·a·gram** \ˈa-nə-ˌgram\ *n* [prob. fr. MF *anagramme*, fr. NL *anagrammat-, anagramma*, modif. of Gk *anagrammatismos*, fr. *anagrammatizein* to transpose letters, fr. *ana-* + *grammat-, gramma* letter — more at GRAM] (1589) **1 :** a word or phrase made by transposing the letters of another word or phrase **2** *pl but sing in constr* **:** a game in which words are formed by rearranging the letters of other words or by arranging letters taken (as from a stock of cards or blocks) at random — **an·a·gram·mat·ic** \ˌa-nə-grə-ˈma-tik\ *also* **an·a·gram·mat·i·cal** \-ti-kəl\ *adj* — **an·a·gram·mat·i·cal·ly** \-ti-k(ə-)lē\ *adv*

[2]**anagram** *vt* **-grammed; -gram·ming** (1630) **1 :** ANAGRAMMATIZE **2 :** to rearrange (the letters of a text) in order to discover a hidden message

an·a·gram·ma·tize \ˌa-nə-ˈgra-mə-ˌtīz\ *vt* **-tized; -tiz·ing** (1588) **:** to transpose (as letters in a word) so as to form an anagram — **an·a·gram·ma·ti·za·tion** \-ˌgra-mə-tə-ˈzā-shən\ *n*

An·a·heim \ˈa-nə-ˌhīm\ *n* [*Anaheim*, Calif.] (1936) **:** a long tapered reen usu. mild chili pepper

\ˈā-nᵊl\ *adj* (1769) **1 :** of, relating to, situated near, or involving us ⟨an ~ fin⟩ **2 a :** of, relating to, characterized by, or being the stage of psychosexual development in psychoanalytic theory which follows the oral stage and during which the child is concerned esp. with its feces **b :** of, relating to, characterized by, or being personality traits (as parsimony, meticulousness, and ill humor) considered typical of fixation at the anal stage of development ⟨an ~ disposition⟩ ⟨~ neatness⟩ — **anal·ly** \-nᵊl-ē\ *adv*

[2]**anal** *abbr* **1** analogy **2** analysis; analytic

anal·cime \ə-ˈnal-ˌsēm\ *n* [F, fr. Gk *analkimos* weak, fr. *an-* + *alkimos* strong, fr. *alkē* strength] (1803) **:** a white or slightly colored mineral that consists of hydrated silicate of sodium and aluminum and occurs in various igneous rocks in massive form or in crystals

an·a·lects \ˈa-nə-ˌlek(t)s\ *also* **an·a·lec·ta** \ˌa-nə-ˈlek-tə\ *n pl* [NL *analecta*, fr. Gk *analekta*, neut. pl. of *analektos*, verbal of *analegein* to collect, fr. *ana-* + *legein* to gather — more at LEGEND] (1652) **:** selected miscellaneous written passages

an·a·lem·ma \ˌa-nə-ˈle-mə\ *n* [L, sundial on a pedestal, fr. Gk *analēmma*, lofty structure, sundial, fr. *analambanein* to take up, restore, fr. *ana-* + *lambanein* to take — more at LATCH] (1832) **:** a plot or graph of the position of the sun in the sky at a certain time of day (as noon) at one locale measured throughout the year that has the shape of a figure 8; *also* **:** a scale (as on a globe or sundial) based on such a plot that shows the sun's position for each day of the year or that allows local mean time to be determined — **an·a·lem·mat·ic** \ˌa-nə-le-ˈma-tik, -lə-\ *adj*

an·a·lep·tic \ˌa-nə-ˈlep-tik\ *n* [Gk *analēptikos*, fr. *analambanein*] (1671) **:** a drug that stimulates the central nervous system — **analeptic** *adj*

an·al·ge·sia \ˌa-nᵊl-ˈjē-zh(ē-)ə, -zē-ə\ *n* [NL, fr. Gk *analgēsia*, fr. *an-* + *algēsis* sense of pain, fr. *algein* to suffer pain, fr. *algos* pain] (ca. 1706) **:** insensibility to pain without loss of consciousness

an·al·ge·sic \ˌa-nᵊl-ˈjē-zik, -sik\ *n* (1875) **:** an agent for producing analgesia — **analgesic** *adj*

anal·i·ty \ā-ˈna-lə-tē\ *n, pl* **-ties** (1939) **:** the psychological state or quality of being anal

an·a·log \ˈa-nə-ˌlȯg, -ˌläg\ *adj* (1946) **1 :** of, relating to, or being an analogue **2 a :** of, relating to, or being a mechanism in which data is represented by continuously variable physical quantities **b :** of or relating to an analog computer **c :** being a timepiece having hour and minute hands

analog computer *n* (1948) **:** a computer that operates with numbers represented by directly measurable quantities (as voltages or rotations) — compare DIGITAL COMPUTER, HYBRID COMPUTER

an·a·log·i·cal \ˌa-nə-ˈlä-ji-kəl\ *also* **an·a·log·ic** \-jik\ *adj* (1609) **1 :** of, relating to, or based on analogy **2 :** expressing or implying analogy — **an·a·log·i·cal·ly** \-ji-k(ə-)lē\ *adv*

anal·o·gist \ə-ˈna-lə-jist\ *n* (1788) **:** one who searches for or reasons from analogies

anal·o·gize \-ˌjīz\ *vb* **-gized; -giz·ing** *vi* (1655) **:** to use or exhibit analogy ~ *vt* **:** to compare by analogy

anal·o·gous \ə-ˈna-lə-gəs\ *adj* [L *analogus*, fr. Gk *analogos*, lit., proportionate, fr. *ana-* + *logos* reason, ratio, fr. *legein* to gather, speak — more at LEGEND] (1646) **1 :** showing an analogy or a likeness that permits one to draw an analogy **2 :** being or related to as an analogue ***syn*** see SIMILAR — **anal·o·gous·ly** *adv* — **anal·o·gous·ness** *n*

[1]**an·a·logue** *or* **an·a·log** \ˈa-nə-ˌlȯg, -ˌläg\ *n* [F *analogue*, fr. *analogue* analogous, fr. Gk *analogos*] (1826) **1 :** something that is analogous or similar to something else **2 :** an organ or part similar in function to an organ or part of another animal or plant but different in structure and origin **3** *usu analog* **:** a chemical compound that is structurally similar to another but differs slightly in composition (as in the replacement of one atom by an atom of a different element or in the presence of a particular functional group) **4 :** a food product made by combining a less expensive food (as soybeans or whitefish) with additives to give the appearance and taste of a more expensive food (as beef or crab)

[2]**an·a·logue** *chiefly Brit var of* ANALOG

anal·o·gy \ə-ˈna-lə-jē\ *n, pl* **-gies** (15c) **1 :** inference that if two or more things agree with one another in some respects they will prob. agree in others **2 a :** resemblance in some particulars between things otherwise unlike **:** SIMILARITY **b :** comparison based on such resemblance **3 :** correspondence between the members of pairs or sets of linguistic forms that serves as a basis for the creation of another form **4 :** correspondence in function between anatomical parts of different structure and origin — compare HOMOLOGY ***syn*** see LIKENESS

an·al·pha·bet \(ˌ)an-ˈal-fə-ˌbet, -bət\ *n* [Gk *analphabētos* not knowing the alphabet, fr. *an-* + *alphabētos* alphabet] (1881) **:** a person who cannot read **:** ILLITERATE — **an·al·pha·bet·ic** \ˌan-ˌal-fə-ˈbe-tik\ *adj or n* — **an·al·pha·bet·ism** \(ˌ)an-ˈal-fə-bə-ˌti-zəm\ *n*

anal–re·ten·tive \ˈā-nᵊl-ri-ˈten-tiv\ *adj* (1953) **:** exhibiting or typifying personality traits (as frugality and obstinacy) held to be psychological consequences of toilet training — **anal–retentive** *n* — **anal–re·ten·tive·ness** *n*

anal·y·sand \ə-ˈna-lə-ˌsand\ *n* [*analyse* + *-and* (as in *multiplicand*)] (1917) **:** a person who is undergoing psychoanalysis

an·a·lyse *chiefly Brit var of* ANALYZE

anal·y·sis \ə-ˈna-lə-səs\ *n, pl* **-y·ses** \-ˌsēz\ [NL, fr. Gk, fr. *analyein* to break up, fr. *ana-* + *lyein* to loosen — more at LOSE] (1581) **1 :** separation of a whole into its component parts **2 a :** the identification or separation of ingredients of a substance **b :** a statement of the constituents of a mixture **3 a :** proof of a mathematical proposition by assuming the result and deducing a valid statement by a series of reversible steps **b (1) :** a branch of mathematics concerned mainly with limits, continuity, and infinite series **(2) :** CALCULUS 1b **4 a :** an examination of a complex, its elements, and their relations **b :** a statement of such an analysis **5 a :** a method in philosophy of resolving complex expressions into simpler or more basic ones **b :** clarification of an expression by an elucidation of its use in discourse **6 :** the use of function words instead of inflectional forms as a characteristic device of a language **7 :** PSYCHOANALYSIS

analysis of variance (1918) **:** analysis of variation in an experimental outcome and esp. of a statistical variance in order to determine the contributions of given factors or variables to the variance

analysis si·tus \-ˈsī-təs, -ˈsē-, -ˌtüs\ *n* [NL, lit., analysis of situation] (ca. 1909) **:** TOPOLOGY 2a(1)

an·a·lyst \ˈa-nə-ləst\ *n* [F *analyste*, fr. *analyse* analysis] (1656) **1 :** a person who analyzes or who is skilled in analysis **2 :** PSYCHOANALYST

an·a·lyte \ˈa-nə-ˌlīt\ *n* (1978) : a chemical substance that is the subject of chemical analysis

an·a·lyt·ic \ˌa-nə-ˈli-tik\ *or* **an·a·lyt·i·cal** \-ti-kəl\ *adj* [LL *analyticus,* fr. Gk *analytikos,* fr. *analyein*] (1601) **1 :** of or relating to analysis or analytics; *esp* **:** separating something into component parts or constituent elements **2 :** being a proposition (as "no bachelor is married") whose truth is evident from the meaning of the words it contains — compare SYNTHETIC **3 :** skilled in or using analysis esp. in thinking or reasoning ⟨a keenly ~ person⟩ **4 :** characterized by analysis rather than inflection ⟨~ languages⟩ **5 :** PSYCHOANALYTIC **6 :** treated or treatable by or using the methods of algebra and calculus **7 a** *of a function of a real variable* **:** capable of being expanded in a Taylor's series in powers of $x - h$ in some neighborhood of the point h **b** *of a function of a complex variable* **:** differentiable at every point in some neighborhood of a given point — **an·a·lyt·i·cal·ly** \-ti-k(ə-)lē\ *adv* — **an·a·lyt·ic·i·ty** \ˌa-nə-lə-ˈti-sə-tē\ *n*

analytic geometry *n* (1835) : the study of geometric properties by means of algebraic operations upon symbols defined in terms of a coordinate system — called also *coordinate geometry*

analytic philosophy *n* (1891) : a philosophical movement that seeks the solution of philosophical problems in the analysis of propositions or sentences — called also *philosophical analysis;* compare ORDINARY-LANGUAGE PHILOSOPHY

an·a·lyt·ics \ˌa-nə-ˈli-tiks\ *n pl but sing or pl in constr* (ca. 1590) : the method of logical analysis

an·a·ly·za·tion \ˌa-nə-lə-ˈzā-shən\ *n* (1742) : ANALYSIS

an·a·lyze \ˈa-nə-ˌlīz\ *vt* **-lyzed; -lyz·ing** [prob. irreg. fr. *analysis*] (1587) **1 :** to study or determine the nature and relationship of the parts of by analysis **2 :** to subject to scientific or grammatical analysis **3 :** PSYCHOANALYZE — **an·a·lyz·abil·i·ty** \ˌa-nə-ˌlī-zə-ˈbi-lə-tē\ *n* — **an·a·lyz·able** \ˈa-nə-ˌlī-zə-bəl\ *adj* — **an·a·lyz·er** \-ˌlī-zər\ *n*

syn ANALYZE, DISSECT, BREAK DOWN mean to divide a complex whole into its parts or elements. ANALYZE suggests separating or distinguishing the component parts of something (as a substance, a process, a situation) so as to discover its true nature or inner relationships ⟨*analyzed* the collected data⟩. DISSECT suggests a searching analysis by laying bare parts or pieces for individual scrutiny ⟨commentators *dissected* every word of the speech⟩. BREAK DOWN implies a reducing to simpler parts or divisions ⟨*break down* the budget⟩.

an·am·ne·sis \ˌa-ˌnam-ˈnē-səs\ *n, pl* **-ne·ses** \-ˌsēz\ [NL, fr. Gk *anamnēsis,* fr. *anamimnēskesthai* to remember, fr. *ana-* + *mimnēskesthai* to remember — more at MIND] (ca. 1593) **1 :** a recalling to mind : REMINISCENCE **2 :** a preliminary case history of a medical or psychiatric patient

an·am·nes·tic \-ˈnes-tik\ *adj* [Gk *anamnēstikos* easily recalled, fr. *anamimnēskesthai*] (ca. 1753) **1 :** of or relating to an anamnesis **2 :** of or relating to a secondary response to an immunogenic substance after serum antibodies can no longer be detected in the blood

ana·mor·phic \ˌa-nə-ˈmȯr-fik\ *adj* [NL *anamorphosis* distorted optical image] (ca. 1925) : producing, relating to, or marked by intentional distortion (as by unequal magnification along perpendicular axes) of an image ⟨an ~ lens⟩

anan·da·mide \ə-ˈnan-də-ˌmīd\ *n* [Skt *ānanda* joy, bliss + E *amide*] (1992) : a derivative of arachidonic acid that occurs naturally in the brain and in some foods (as chocolate) and that binds to the same brain receptors as the cannabinoids (as THC)

An·a·ni·as \ˌa-nə-ˈnī-əs\ *n* [Gk, prob. fr. Heb *Ḥănanyāh*] (14c) **1 :** an early Christian struck dead for lying **2 :** LIAR

an·a·pest \ˈa-nə-ˌpest\ *n* [L *anapaestus,* fr. Gk *anapaistos,* lit., struck back (a dactyl reversed), fr. *ana-* + *-paistos,* verbal of *paiein* to strike] (ca. 1678) : a metrical foot consisting of two short syllables followed by one long syllable or of two unstressed syllables followed by one stressed syllable (as *unaware*) — **an·a·pes·tic** \ˌa-nə-ˈpes-tik\ *adj or n*

ana·phase \ˈa-nə-ˌfāz\ *n* [ISV] (1887) : the stage of mitosis and meiosis in which the chromosomes move toward the poles of the spindle — **ana·pha·sic** \ˌa-nə-ˈfā-zik\ *adj*

ana·phor \ˈa-nə-ˌfȯr\ *n, pl* **anaphors** *also* **anaph·o·ra** \ə-ˈna-f(ə-)rə\ [back-formation fr. *anaphoric*] (1975) : a word or phrase with an anaphoric function

anaph·o·ra \ə-ˈna-f(ə-)rə\ *n* [LL, fr. LGk, fr. Gk, act of carrying back, reference, fr. *anapherein* to carry back, refer, fr. *ana-* + *pherein* to carry — more at BEAR] (ca. 1589) **1 :** repetition of a word or expression at the beginning of successive phrases, clauses, sentences, or verses esp. for rhetorical or poetic effect ⟨Lincoln's "we cannot dedicate—we cannot consecrate—we cannot hallow—this ground" is an example of ~⟩ — compare EPISTROPHE **2 :** use of a grammatical substitute (as a pronoun or a pro-verb) to refer to the denotation of a preceding word or group of words; *also* **:** the relation between a grammatical substitute and its antecedent

an·a·phor·ic \ˌa-nə-ˈfȯr-ik, -ˈfär-\ *adj* (1904) : of or relating to anaphora ⟨an ~ usage⟩; *esp* **:** being a word or phrase that takes its reference from another word or phrase and esp. from a preceding word or phrase — compare CATAPHORIC — **ana·phor·i·cal·ly** \-i-k(ə-)lē\ *adv*

an·aph·ro·di·si·ac \ˌa-ˌna-frə-ˈdē-zē-ˌak, -zhē-, -ˈdi-zē-\ *adj* (1823) : inhibiting or discouraging sexual desire — **anaphrodisiac** *n*

ana·phy·lac·tic \ˌa-nə-fə-ˈlak-tik\ *adj* (1907) : of, relating to, affected by, or causing anaphylaxis or anaphylactic shock — **ana·phy·lac·ti·cal·ly** \-ti-k(ə-)lē\ *adv* — **ana·phy·lac·toid** \-ˈlak-ˌtȯid\ *adj*

anaphylactic shock *n* (1910) : an often severe and sometimes fatal systemic reaction in a susceptible individual upon exposure to a specific antigen (as wasp venom or penicillin) after previous sensitization that is characterized esp. by respiratory symptoms, fainting, itching, and hives

ana·phy·lax·is \-ˈlak-səs\ *n, pl* **-lax·es** \-ˌsēz\ [NL, fr. *ana-* + *prophylaxis*] (1907) **1 :** hypersensitivity (as to foreign proteins or drugs) resulting from sensitization following prior contact with the causative agent **2 :** ANAPHYLACTIC SHOCK

an·a·pla·sia \ˌa-nə-ˈplā-zh(ē-)ə\ *n* [NL] (ca. 1909) : reversion of cells to a more primitive or undifferentiated form — **an·a·plas·tic** \-ˈplas-tik\ *adj*

an·a·plas·mo·sis \ˌa-nə-ˌplaz-ˈmō-səs\ *n, pl* **-mo·ses** \-ˌsēz\ [NL, fr. *Anaplasma,* genus name, fr. *ana-* + *plasma* (protoplasm)] (1920) : a tick-borne disease of cattle and sheep caused by a bacterium (*Anaplasma marginale*) and characterized esp. by anemia and by jaundice

an·arch \ˈa-ˌnärk\ *n* [back-formation fr. *anarchy*] (1667) : a leader or advocate of revolt or anarchy

an·ar·chic \a-ˈnär-kik, ə-\ *also* **an·ar·chi·cal** \-ki-kəl\ *adj* (1649) **1 a :** of, relating to, or advocating anarchy **b :** likely to bring about anarchy ⟨~ violence⟩ **2 :** lacking order, regularity, or definiteness ⟨~ art forms⟩ — **an·ar·chi·cal·ly** \-k(ə-)lē\ *adv*

an·ar·chism \ˈa-nər-ˌki-zəm, -ˌnär-\ *n* (1642) **1 :** a political theory holding all forms of governmental authority to be unnecessary and undesirable and advocating a society based on voluntary cooperation and free association of individuals and groups **2 :** the advocacy or practice of anarchistic principles

an·ar·chist \ˈa-nər-kist, -ˌnär-\ *n* (1678) **1 :** a person who rebels against any authority, established order, or ruling power **2 :** a person who believes in, advocates, or promotes anarchism or anarchy; *esp* **:** one who uses violent means to overthrow the established order — **anarchist** *or* **an·ar·chis·tic** \ˌa-nər-ˈkis-tik, -(ˌ)när-\ *adj*

an·ar·cho–syn·di·cal·ism \a-ˌnär-kō-ˈsin-di-kə-ˌli-zəm, ˌa-nər-kō-\ *n* (ca. 1928) : SYNDICALISM — **an·ar·cho–syn·di·cal·ist** \-kə-list\ *n or adj*

an·ar·chy \ˈa-nər-kē, -ˌnär-\ *n* [ML *anarchia,* fr. Gk, fr. *anarchos* having no ruler, fr. *an-* + *archos* ruler — more at ARCH-] (1539) **1 a :** absence of government **b :** a state of lawlessness or political disorder due to the absence of governmental authority **c :** a utopian society of individuals who enjoy complete freedom without government **2 a :** absence or denial of any authority or established order **b :** absence of order : DISORDER ⟨not manicured plots but a wild ~ of nature —Israel Shenker⟩ **3 :** ANARCHISM

ana·sar·ca \ˌa-nə-ˈsär-kə\ *n* [NL, fr. *ana-* + Gk *sark-, sarx* flesh — more at SARCASM] (14c) : generalized edema with accumulation of serum in the connective tissue — **ana·sar·cous** \-kəs\ *adj*

An·a·sa·zi \ˌä-nə-ˈsä-zē\ *n, pl* **Anasazi** [Navajo *anaasází,* lit., enemy ancestors] (1938) : a prehistoric American Indian inhabitant of the canyons of northern Arizona and New Mexico and southwestern Colorado

an·as·tig·mat \a-ˈnas-tig-ˌmat, ˌa-nə-ˈstig-\ *n* [G, back-formation fr. *anastigmatisch* anastigmatic] (1890) : an anastigmatic lens

an·a·stig·mat·ic \ˌa-nə-(ˌ)stig-ˈma-tik, ˌa-ˌnas-tig-\ *adj* [ISV] (1890) : not astigmatic — used esp. of lenses that are able to form approximately point images of object points

anas·to·mose \ə-ˈnas-tə-ˌmōz, -ˌmōs\ *vb* **-mosed; -mos·ing** [prob. back-formation fr. *anastomosis*] *vt* (1697) : to connect or join by anastomosis ~ *vi* : to communicate or be joined by anastomosis

anas·to·mo·sis \ə-ˌnas-tə-ˈmō-səs\ *n, pl* **-mo·ses** \-ˌsēz\ [LL, fr. Gk *anastomōsis,* fr. *anastomoun* to provide with an outlet, fr. *ana-* + *stoma* mouth, opening — more at STOMACH] (1541) **1 :** the union of parts or branches (as of streams, blood vessels, or leaf veins) so as to intercommunicate or interconnect **2 :** a product of anastomosis : NETWORK — **anas·to·mot·ic** \-ˈmä-tik\ *adj*

anas·tro·phe \ə-ˈnas-trə-(ˌ)fē\ *n* [ML, fr. Gk *anastrophē,* lit., turning back, fr. *anastrephein* to turn back, fr. *ana-* + *strephein* to turn] (ca. 1550) : inversion of the usual syntactical order of words for rhetorical effect — compare HYSTERON PROTERON

anat *abbr* anatomical; anatomy

an·a·tase \ˈa-nə-ˌtās, -ˌtāz\ *n* [F, fr. Gk *anatasis* extension, fr. *anateinein* to extend, fr. *ana-* + *teinein* to stretch — more at THIN] (ca. 1828) : a tetragonal mineral consisting of titanium dioxide and used esp. as a white pigment

anath·e·ma \ə-ˈna-thə-mə\ *n* [LL *anathemat-, anathema,* fr. Gk, thing devoted to evil, curse, fr. *anatithenai* to set up, dedicate, fr. *ana-* + *tithenai* to place, set — more at DO] (1526) **1 a :** one that is cursed by ecclesiastical authority **b :** someone or something intensely disliked or loathed — usu. used as a predicate nominative ⟨this notion was ~ to most of his countrymen —S. J. Gould⟩ **2 a :** a ban or curse solemnly pronounced by ecclesiastical authority and accompanied by excommunication **b :** the denunciation of something as accursed **c :** a vigorous denunciation : CURSE

anath·e·ma·tize \-ˌtīz\ *vt* **-tized; -tiz·ing** (1566) : to pronounce an anathema upon

An·a·to·lian \ˌa-nə-ˈtō-lē-ən, -ˈtōl-yən\ *n* (1590) **1 :** a native or inhabitant of Anatolia and specif. of the western plateau lands of Turkey in Asia **2 :** a branch of the Indo-European language family that includes a group of extinct languages of ancient Anatolia — see INDO-EUROPEAN LANGUAGES table — **Anatolian** *adj*

Anatolian shepherd *n* (1970) : any of a breed of large rugged working dogs of Turkish origin

anat·o·mise *Brit var of* ANATOMIZE

anat·o·mist \ə-ˈna-tə-mist\ *n* (1543) **1 :** a specialist in anatomy **2 :** one who analyzes minutely and critically ⟨an ~ of urban society⟩

anat·o·mize \-ˌmīz\ *vt* **-mized; -miz·ing** (15c) **1 :** to cut in pieces in order to display or examine the structure and use of the parts : DISSECT **2 :** ANALYZE

anat·o·my \ə-ˈna-tə-mē\ *n, pl* **-mies** [LL *anatomia* dissection, fr. Gk *anatomē,* fr. *anatemnein* to dissect, fr. *ana-* + *temnein* to cut] (14c) **1 :** a branch of morphology that deals with the structure of organisms **2 :** a treatise on anatomical science or art **3 :** the art of separating the parts of an organism in order to ascertain their position, relations, structure, and function : DISSECTION **4** *obs* **:** a body dissected or to be dissected **5 :** structural makeup esp. of an organism or any of its parts **6 :** a separating or dividing into parts for detailed examination : ANALYSIS **7 a (1) :** SKELETON **(2) :** MUMMY **b :** the human body — **an·a·tom·i·cal** \ˌa-nə-ˈtä-mi-kəl\ *or* **an·a·tom·ic** \-ˈtä-mik\ *adj* — **an·a·tom·i·cal·ly** \-mi-k(ə-)lē\ *adv*

anat·ro·pous \ə-ˈna-trə-pəs\ *adj* (ca. 1846) : having or being a plant ovule inverted so that the micropyle is bent down to the funiculus to which the body of the ovule is united

anc *abbr* ancient

ANC *abbr* African National Congress

\ə\ **abut** \ᵊ\ **kitten,** F table \ər\ **further** \a\ **ash** \ā\ **ace** \ä\ **mop, mar** \au̇\ **out** \ch\ **chin** \e\ **bet** \ē\ **easy** \g\ **go** \i\ **hit** \ī\ **ice** \j\ **job** \ŋ\ **sing** \ō\ **go** \ȯ\ **law** \ȯi\ **boy** \th\ **thin** \t͟h\ **the** \ü\ **loot** \u̇\ **foot** \y\ **yet** \zh\ **vision, beige** \k̲, ⁿ, œ, ue, ʸ\ *see* Guide to Pronunciation

-ance *n suffix* [ME, fr. AF, fr. L *-antia,* fr. *-ant-, -ans* -ant + *-ia* -y] **1** : action or process ⟨further*ance*⟩ : instance of an action or process ⟨perform*ance*⟩ **2** : quality or state : instance of a quality or state ⟨protuber*ance*⟩ **3** : amount or degree ⟨conduct*ance*⟩
an·ces·tor \ˈan-ˌses-tər *also* -səs-\ *n* [ME *ancestre,* fr. AF, fr. L *antecessor* predecessor, fr. *antecedere* to go before, fr. *ante-* + *cedere* to go] (13c) **1 a** : one from whom a person is descended and who is usu. more remote in the line of descent than a grandparent **b** : FOREFATHER 2 **2** : FORERUNNER, PROTOTYPE **3** : a progenitor of a more recent or existing species or group
ancestor worship *n* (1854) : the custom of venerating deceased ancestors who are considered still a part of the family and whose spirits are believed to have the power to intervene in the affairs of the living
an·ces·tral \an-ˈses-trəl\ *adj* (15c) : of, relating to, or inherited from an ancestor ⟨~ estates⟩ — **an·ces·tral·ly** \-trə-lē\ *adv*
an·ces·tress \ˈan-ˌses-trəs\ *n* (1580) : a female ancestor
an·ces·try \ˈan-ˌses-trē\ *n* (14c) **1** : line of descent : LINEAGE; *esp* : honorable, noble, or aristocratic descent **2** : persons initiating or comprising a line of descent : ANCESTORS
An·chi·ses \an-ˈkī-(ˌ)sēz, aŋ-\ *n* [L, fr. Gk *Anchisēs*] (14c) : the father of Aeneas rescued by his son from the burning city of Troy
an·cho \ˈän-chō\ *n, pl* **anchos** [AmerSp (*chile*) *ancho,* lit., wide chili] (1902) : a poblano chili pepper esp. when mature and dried to a reddish black — compare POBLANO
[1]**an·chor** \ˈaŋ-kər\ *n, often attrib* [ME *ancre,* fr. OE *ancor,* fr. L *anchora,* fr. Gk *ankyra;* akin to OE *anga* hook — more at ANGLE] (bef. 12c) **1** : a device usu. of metal attached to a ship or boat by a cable and cast overboard to hold it in a particular place by means of a fluke that digs into the bottom **2** : a reliable or principal support : MAINSTAY **3** : something that serves to hold an object firmly **4** : an object shaped like a ship's anchor **5** : an anchorman or anchorwoman **6** : the member of a team (as a relay team) that competes last **7** : a large business (as a department store) that attracts customers and other businesses to a shopping center or mall **8** : a fixed object (as a tree or a piton) to which a climber's rope is secured — **an·chor·less** \-ləs\ *adj* — **at anchor** : being anchored
[2]**anchor** *vb* **an·chored; an·chor·ing** \-k(ə-)riŋ\ *vt* (13c) **1** : to hold in place in the water by an anchor ⟨~ a ship⟩ **2** : to secure firmly : FIX ⟨~ a post in concrete⟩ **3** : to act or serve as an anchor for ⟨it is she who is *~ing* the rebuilding campaign —G. D. Boone⟩ ⟨*~ing* the evening news⟩ ~ *vi* **1** : to cast anchor **2** : to become fixed

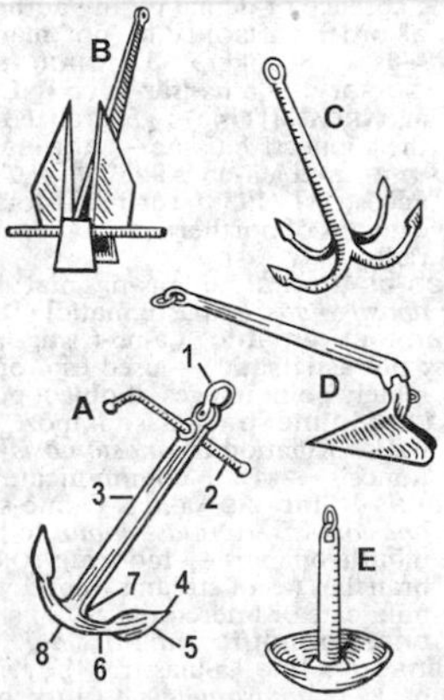

anchor 1: *A* yachtsman's: *1* ring, *2* stock, *3* shank, *4* bill, *5* fluke, *6* arm, *7* throat, *8* crown; *B* fluke; *C* grapnel; *D* plow; *E* mushroom

an·chor·age \ˈaŋ-k(ə-)rij\ *n* (15c) **1 a** : a place where vessels anchor : a place suitable for anchoring **b** : the act of anchoring : the condition of being anchored **2** : a means of securing : a source of reassurance ⟨this ~ of Christian hope —T. O. Wedel⟩ **3** : something that provides a secure hold
an·cho·ress \ˈaŋ-k(ə-)rəs\ *or* **an·cress** \-krəs\ *n* [ME *ankeresse,* fr. *anker* hermit, fr. OE *ancor,* fr. OIr *anchara,* fr. LL *anachoreta*] (14c) : a woman who is an anchorite
an·cho·rite \ˈaŋ-kə-ˌrīt\ *also* **an·cho·ret** \-ˌret\ *n* [ME, fr. ML *anchorita,* alter. of LL *anachoreta,* fr. LGk *anachōrētēs,* fr. Gk *anachōrein* to withdraw, fr. *ana-* + *chōrein* to make room, fr. *chōros* place] (15c) : a person who lives in seclusion usu. for religious reasons — **an·cho·rit·ic** \ˌaŋ-kə-ˈri-tik\ *adj* — **an·cho·rit·i·cal·ly** \-ti-k(ə-)lē\ *adv*
an·chor·man \ˈaŋ-kər-ˌman\ *n* (1911) **1** : a person who is last: as **a** : the member of a team who competes last ⟨the ~ on a relay team⟩ **b** : the student who has the lowest scholastic standing in a graduating class **2** : a broadcaster (as on a news program) who introduces reports by other broadcasters and usu. reads the news **3** : MODERATOR 2c
an·chor·peo·ple \-ˌpē-pəl\ *n pl* (1974) : ANCHORPERSONS
an·chor·per·son \-ˌpər-sᵊn\ *n* (1973) : an anchorman or anchorwoman
an·chor·wom·an \-ˌwu̇-mən\ *n* (1973) : a woman who anchors a broadcast
an·cho·veta *also* **an·cho·vet·ta** \ˌan-chō-ˈve-tə\ *n* [Sp *anchoveta,* dim. of *anchova*] (1940) : a small anchovy (*Cetengraulis mysticetus*) of the Pacific coast of America from southern California to Peru
an·cho·vy \ˈan-ˌchō-vē, an-ˈ\ *n, pl* **-vies** *or* **-vy** [Sp *anchova*] (1595) : any of a family (Engraulidae) of small fishes resembling herrings that includes several (as *Engraulis encrasicholus*) that are important food fishes used esp. in appetizers, as a garnish, and for making sauces and relishes
an·cien ré·gime \äⁿs-yaⁿ-rā-ˈzhēm\ *n* [F, lit., old regime] (1794) **1** : the political and social system of France before the Revolution of 1789 **2** : a system or mode no longer prevailing
[1]**an·cient** \ˈān(t)-shənt, ˈāŋ(k)-shənt\ *adj* [ME *ancien,* fr. AF, fr. VL **anteanus,* fr. L *ante* before — more at ANTE-] (14c) **1** : having had an existence of many years **2** : of or relating to a remote period, to a time early in history, or to those living in such a period or time; *esp* : of or relating to the historical period beginning with the earliest known civilizations and extending to the fall of the western Roman Empire in A.D. 476 **3** : having the qualities of age or long existence: as **a** : VENERABLE **b** : OLD-FASHIONED, ANTIQUE ***syn*** see OLD — **an·cient·ness** *n*
[2]**ancient** *n* (1502) **1** : an aged living being ⟨a penniless ~⟩ **2** : a person who lived in ancient times: **a** *pl* : the civilized people of antiquity; *esp* : those of the classical nations **b** : one of the classical authors ⟨Plutarch and other ~*s*⟩ **3** : an ancient coin
[3]**ancient** *n* [alter. of *ensign*] (1554) **1** *archaic* : ENSIGN, STANDARD, FLAG **2** *obs* : the bearer of an ensign
ancient history *n* (1555) **1** : the history of ancient times **2** : knowledge or information that is widespread and has lost its initial freshness or importance : common knowledge
an·cient·ly *adv* (15c) : in ancient times : long ago
an·cient·ry \-shən-trē\ *n* (1580) : ANTIQUITY, ANCIENTNESS
an·cil·la \an-ˈsi-lə\ *n, pl* **-lae** \-(ˌ)lē\ [L, female servant] (1902) : an aid to achieving or mastering something difficult
an·cil·lary \ˈan(t)-sə-ˌler-ē, -ˌle-rē, *esp Brit* an-ˈsi-lə-rē\ *adj* (1667) **1** : SUBORDINATE, SUBSIDIARY ⟨the main factory and its ~ plants⟩ **2** : AUXILIARY, SUPPLEMENTARY ⟨the need for ~ evidence⟩ — **ancillary** *n*
-ancy *n suffix* [L *-antia* — more at -ANCE] : quality or state ⟨piqu*ancy*⟩
an·cy·lo·sto·mi·a·sis \ˌaŋ-ki-ˌlō-stə-ˈmī-ə-səs, ˌan(t)-sə-\ *also* **an·ky·lo·sto·mi·a·sis** \ˌaŋ-ki-\ *n, pl* **-a·ses** \-ˌsēz\ [NL, fr. *Ancylostoma,* genus of hookworms, fr. Gk *ankylos* hooked (akin to OE *anga* hook) + *stoma* mouth — more at ANGLE, STOMACH] (1887) : HOOKWORM 2
and \ən(d), (ˈ)an(d), *usu* ᵊn(d) *after* t, d, s *or* z, *often* ᵊm *after* p *or* b, *sometimes* ᵊŋ *after* k *or* g\ *conj* [ME, fr. OE; akin to OHG *unti* and] (bef. 12c) **1** — used as a function word to indicate connection or addition esp. of items within the same class or type; used to join sentence elements of the same grammatical rank or function **2 a** — used as a function word to express logical modification, consequence, antithesis, or supplementary explanation **b** — used as a function word to join one finite verb (as *go, come, try*) to another so that together they are logically equivalent to an infinitive of purpose ⟨come ~ see me⟩ **3** *obs* : IF **4** — used in logic to form a conjunction — **and so forth** \ən-ˈsō-ˌfȯrth\ **1** : and others or more of the same or similar kind **2** : further in the same or similar manner **3** : and the rest **4** : and other things — **and so on** \ən-ˈsō-ˌȯn, -ˌän\ : and so forth
AND \ˈand\ *n* (1949) : a logical operator that requires both of two inputs to be present or two conditions to be met for an output to be made or a statement to be executed
An·da·lu·sian \ˌan-də-ˈlü-zhən\ *n* [*Andalusia,* Spain] (1966) : any of a breed of horses of Spanish origin that have a high-stepping gait
an·da·lu·site \ˌan-də-ˈlü-ˌsīt\ *n* [F *andalousite,* fr. *Andalousie* Andalusia, region in Spain] (ca. 1828) : a mineral consisting of a silicate of aluminum usu. in thick orthorhombic prisms of various colors
[1]**an·dan·te** \än-ˈdän-(ˌ)tā, -ˈdän-tē; an-ˈdan-tē\ *adv or adj* [It, lit., going, prp. of *andare* to go] (1724) : moderately slow — usu. used as a direction in music
[2]**andante** *n* (1784) : a musical composition or movement in andante tempo
[1]**an·dan·ti·no** \ˌän-ˌdän-ˈtē-(ˌ)nō\ *adv or adj* [It, dim. of *andante*] (1819) : slightly faster than andante — used as a direction in music
[2]**andantino** *n, pl* **-nos** (1845) : a musical composition or movement in andantino tempo
An·de·an condor \ˈan-(ˌ)dē-ən-, an-ˈ\ *n* (1980) : CONDOR 1a
an·des·ite \ˈan-di-ˌzīt\ *n* [G *Andesit,* fr. *Andes*] (1850) : an extrusive usu. dark grayish rock consisting essentially of oligoclase or feldspar — **an·des·it·ic** \ˌan-di-ˈzi-tik\ *adj*
and how *adv* (1865) — used to emphasize the preceding idea ⟨having a great time—*and how!*⟩
and·iron \ˈand-ˌī(-ə)rn\ *n* [ME *aundiren,* modif. of AF *aundyre,* alter. of OF *andier*] (14c) : either of a pair of metal supports for firewood used on a hearth and made of a horizontal bar mounted on short legs with usu. a vertical shaft surmounting the front end
and/or \ˈand-ˈȯr\ *conj* (1853) — used as a function word to indicate that two words or expressions are to be taken together or individually ⟨language comprehension *and/or* production —David Crystal⟩
an·dou·ille \än-ˈdü-ē, ˈän-dü-ē\ *n* [F, fr. OF *andoille,* fr. VL **inductilia,* neut. pl. of **inductilis* made by insertion, fr. L *inductus,* pp. of *inducere* to insert, bring in — more at INDUCE] (1605) : a highly spiced smoked pork sausage
an·douill·ette \ˌän-dü-ˈyet\ *n* [F, dim. of *andouille*] (1611) : a fresh pork sausage made with tripe or chitterlings
andr- *or* **andro-** *comb form* [L, fr. Gk, fr. *andr-, anēr;* akin to Oscan *ner-* man, Skt *nar-,* OIr *nert* strength] **1** : male human being ⟨*andro*centric⟩ **2** : male ⟨*andro*ecium⟩
an·dra·dite \an-ˈdrä-ˌdīt, ˈan-drə-ˌdīt\ *n* [José B. de *Andrada* e Silva †1838 Brazilian geologist] (1868) : a calcium-iron garnet occurring in various colors ranging from yellow and green to brown and black
an·dro \ˈan-drō\ *n* (1997) : ANDROSTENEDIONE
an·dro·cen·tric \ˌan-drə-ˈsen-trik\ *adj* (1903) : dominated by or emphasizing masculine interests or a masculine point of view — **an·dro·cen·trism** \-ˌtri-zəm\ *n*
An·dro·cles \ˈan-drə-ˌklēz\ *n* [L, fr. Gk *Androklēs*] (1607) : a fabled Roman slave spared in the arena by a lion from whose foot he had years before extracted a thorn
an·droe·ci·um \an-ˈdrē-shē-əm, -sē-əm\ *n, pl* **-cia** \-shē-ə, -sē-ə\ [NL, fr. *andr-* + Gk *oikion,* dim. of *oikos* house — more at VICINITY] (ca. 1839) : the aggregate of stamens in the flower of a seed plant
an·dro·gen \ˈan-drə-jən\ *n* [ISV] (1936) : a male sex hormone (as testosterone) — **an·dro·gen·ic** \ˌan-drə-ˈje-nik\ *adj*
an·dro·gen·e·sis \ˌan-drō-ˈje-nə-səs\ *n* [NL] (ca. 1900) : development of an embryo containing only paternal chromosomes due to failure of the egg to participate in fertilization — **an·dro·ge·net·ic** \-jə-ˈne-tik\ *adj*
an·dro·gyne \ˈan-drə-ˌjīn\ *n* [ME *androgine,* fr. L *androgynus*] (12c) : one that is androgynous
an·drog·y·nous \an-ˈdrä-jə-nəs\ *adj* [L *androgynus* hermaphrodite, fr. Gk *androgynos,* fr. *andr-* + *gynē* woman — more at QUEEN] (1651) **1** : having the characteristics or nature of both male and female **2 a** : neither specifically feminine nor masculine ⟨the ~ pronoun *them*⟩ **b** : suitable to or for either sex ⟨~ clothing⟩ **3** : having traditional male and female roles obscured or reversed ⟨an ~ marriage⟩ — **an·drog·y·nous·ly** *adv* — **an·drog·y·ny** \-nē\ *n*
an·droid \ˈan-ˌdrȯid\ *n* [LGk *androeidēs* manlike, fr. Gk *andr-* + *-oeidēs* -oid] (ca. 1751) : a mobile robot usu. with a human form
an·drol·ogy \an-ˈdrä-lə-jē\ *n* [ISV] (ca. 1899) : a branch of medicine concerned with male diseases and esp. with those affecting the male reproductive system

An·drom·a·che \an-ˈdrä-mə-(ˌ)kē\ *n* [L, fr. Gk *Andromachē*] (14c) **:** the wife of Hector

an·drom·eda \an-ˈdrä-mə-də\ *n* [NL *Andromeda,* genus name, fr. L] (1754) **:** any of several evergreen shrubs (genera *Pieris* and *Andromeda*) of the heath family; *esp* **:** JAPANESE ANDROMEDA

An·drom·e·da \an-ˈdrä-mə-də\ *n* [L, fr. Gk *Andromedē*] (1551) **1 :** an Ethiopian princess of Greek mythology rescued from a monster by her future husband Perseus **2** [L (gen. *Andromedae*)] **:** a northern constellation directly south of Cassiopeia between Pegasus and Perseus

an·dro·pause \ˈan-drə-ˌpȯz\ *n* (1967) **:** a gradual and highly variable decline in the production of androgenic hormones and esp. testosterone in the human male together with its associated effects that is held to occur during and after middle age — called also *climacteric, male menopause*

an·dro·stene·di·one \ˌan-drə-ˌstēn-ˈdī-ōn, -ˈstēn-dē-ˌōn\ *n* [ISV *androsterone* + *-ene* + *di-* + *-one*] (1935) **:** a steroid sex hormone $C_{19}H_{26}O_2$ that is secreted by the testes, ovaries, and adrenal cortex and is an intermediate in the biosynthesis of testosterone and estrogen

an·dros·ter·one \an-ˈdräs-tə-ˌrōn\ *n* [ISV] (1934) **:** an androgenic hormone that is a hydroxy ketone $C_{19}H_{30}O_2$ found esp. in male urine

ane \ˈān\ *adj or n or pron* (bef. 12c) *chiefly Scot* **:** ONE

-ane *n suffix* [ISV *-an, -ane,* alter. of *-ene, -ine, & -one*] **1 :** [3]-AN 1 ⟨fur*ane*⟩ **2 :** saturated hydrocarbon ⟨alk*ane*⟩ ⟨meth*ane*⟩

an·ec·dot·age \ˈa-nik-ˌdō-tij\ *n* (1798) **1 :** garrulous old age **2 :** the telling of anecdotes; *also* **:** ANECDOTES

an·ec·dot·al \ˌa-nik-ˈdō-tᵊl\ *adj* (1747) **1 a :** of, relating to, or consisting of anecdotes ⟨an ~ biography⟩ **b :** ANECDOTIC 2 ⟨my ~ uncle⟩ **2 :** based on or consisting of reports or observations of usu. unscientific observers ⟨~ evidence⟩ **3 :** of, relating to, or being the depiction of a scene suggesting a story ⟨~ details⟩ — **an·ec·dot·al·ly** \-tᵊl-ē\ *adv*

an·ec·dot·al·ist \ˌa-nik-ˈdō-tᵊl-ist\ *or* **an·ec·dot·ist** \ˈa-nik-ˌdō-tist\ *n* (1837) **:** a person who is given to or is skilled in telling anecdotes — **an·ec·dot·al·ism** \-tᵊl-ˌi-zəm\ *n*

an·ec·dote \ˈa-nik-ˌdōt\ *n, pl* **anecdotes** *also* **an·ec·dota** \ˌa-nik-ˈdō-tə\ [F, fr. Gk *anekdota* unpublished items, fr. neut. pl. of *anekdotos* unpublished, fr. *a-* + *ekdidonai* to publish, fr. *ex* out + *didonai* to give — more at EX-, DATE] (ca. 1721) **:** a usu. short narrative of an interesting, amusing, or biographical incident

an·ec·dot·ic \ˌa-nik-ˈdä-tik\ *or* **an·ec·dot·i·cal** \-ˈdä-ti-kəl\ *adj* (ca. 1744) **1 :** ANECDOTAL 1a **2 :** given to or skilled in telling anecdotes — **an·ec·dot·i·cal·ly** \-ˈdä-ti-k(ə-)lē\ *adv*

an·echo·ic \ˌa-ni-ˈkō-ik\ *adj* (1946) **:** free from echoes and reverberations ⟨an ~ chamber⟩

an·elas·tic \ˌa-nə-ˈlas-tik\ *adj* (1947) **:** relating to the property of a substance in which there is no definite relation between stress and strain — **an·elas·tic·i·ty** \-nə-ˌlas-ˈti-sə-tē, -ˈtis-tē\ *n*

anem- *or* **anemo-** *comb form* [Gk, fr. *anemos* — more at ANIMATE] **:** wind ⟨*anemo*meter⟩

ane·mia \ə-ˈnē-mē-ə\ *n* [NL, fr. Gk *anaimia* bloodlessness, fr. *a-* + *-aimia* -emia] (1800) **1 a :** a condition in which the blood is deficient in red blood cells, in hemoglobin, or in total volume **b :** ISCHEMIA **2 :** lack of vitality

ane·mic \ə-ˈnē-mik\ *adj* (1826) **1 :** relating to or affected with anemia **2 a :** lacking force, vitality, or spirit ⟨an ~ rendition of the song⟩ ⟨~ efforts at enforcement⟩ **b :** lacking interest or savor **:** INSIPID ⟨~ wines⟩ **c :** lacking in substance or quantity ⟨~ returns on an investment⟩ ⟨~ attendance⟩ — **ane·mi·cal·ly** \-mi-k(ə-)lē\ *adv*

anemo·graph \ə-ˈne-mə-ˌgraf\ *n* (1855) **:** a recording anemometer

an·e·mom·e·ter \ˌa-nə-ˈmä-mə-tər\ *n* (1749) **:** an instrument for measuring and indicating the force or speed and sometimes direction of the wind

an·e·mom·e·try \ˌa-nə-ˈmä-mə-trē\ *n* (1831) **:** the process of ascertaining the force, speed, and direction of wind or an airflow

anem·o·ne \ə-ˈne-mə-nē\ *n* [L, fr. Gk *anemōnē*] (1548) **1 :** any of a large genus (*Anemone*) of perennial herbs of the buttercup family having lobed or divided leaves and showy flowers without petals but with conspicuous sepals — called also *windflower* **2 :** SEA ANEMONE

an·e·moph·i·lous \ˌa-nə-ˈmä-fə-ləs\ *adj* (ca. 1872) **:** pollinated by wind

an·en·ceph·a·ly \ˌan-(ˌ)en-ˈse-fə-lē\ *n, pl* **-lies** [[2]*a-* + *encephal-* + [2]*-y*] (1831) **:** congenital absence of all or a major part of the brain — **an·en·ce·phal·ic** \-ˌen(t)-sə-ˈfa-lik\ *adj*

anent \ə-ˈnent\ *prep* [ME *onevent, anent,* fr. OE *on efen* alongside, fr. *on* + *efen* even] (13c) **:** ABOUT, CONCERNING

an·er·gy \ˈa-(ˌ)nər-jē\ *n* [ISV [2]*a-* + *-ergy* (as in *allergy*)] (1890) **:** a condition in which the body fails to react to an antigen

an·er·oid \ˈa-nə-ˌrȯid\ *adj* [F *anéroïde,* fr. Gk *a-* + LGk *nēron* water, fr. Gk, neut. of *nearos, nēros* fresh; akin to Gk *neos* new — more at NEW] (ca. 1842) **:** using no liquid; *specif* **:** operating by the effect of outside air pressure on a diaphragm forming one wall of an evacuated container ⟨~ barometer⟩

an·es·the·sia \ˌa-nəs-ˈthē-zhə\ *n* [NL, fr. Gk *anaisthēsia* insensibility, fr. *a-* + *aisthēsis* perception, fr. *aisthanesthai* to perceive — more at AUDIBLE] (ca. 1721) **:** loss of sensation with or without loss of consciousness

an·es·the·si·ol·o·gist \-ˌthē-zē-ˈä-lə-jist\ *n* (1922) **:** ANESTHETIST; *specif* **:** a physician specializing in anesthesiology

an·es·the·si·ol·o·gy \-jē\ *n* (1911) **:** a branch of medical science dealing with anesthesia and anesthetics

[1]**an·es·thet·ic** \ˌa-nəs-ˈthe-tik\ *adj* (1823) **1 :** of, relating to, or capable of producing anesthesia **2 :** lacking awareness or sensitivity ⟨was ~ to their feelings⟩ — **an·es·thet·i·cal·ly** \-ti-k(ə-)lē\ *adv*

[2]**anesthetic** *n* (1845) **1 :** a substance that produces anesthesia **2 :** something that brings relief **:** PALLIATIVE

anes·the·tist \ə-ˈnes-thə-tist, *Brit* -ˈnēs-\ *n* (1860) **:** one who administers anesthetics

anes·the·tize \-thə-ˌtīz\ *vt* **-tized; -tiz·ing** (1848) **:** to subject to anesthesia

an·es·trous \(ˌ)an-ˈes-trəs\ *adj* (1902) **1 :** not exhibiting estrus **2 :** of or relating to anestrus

an·es·trus \-trəs\ *n* [NL] (1923) **:** the period of sexual quiescence between two periods of sexual activity in cyclically breeding mammals

an·eu·ploid \ˈan-yu̇-ˌplȯid\ *adj* (1926) **:** having or being a chromosome number that is not an exact multiple of the usu. haploid number — compare EUPLOID — **aneuploid** *n* — **an·eu·ploi·dy** \-ˌplȯi-dē\ *n*

an·eu·rysm *also* **an·eu·rism** \ˈan-yə-ˌri-zəm\ *n* [Gk *aneurysma,* fr. *aneurynein* to dilate, fr. *ana-* + *eurynein* to stretch, fr. *eurys* wide — more at EURY-] (15c) **:** an abnormal blood-filled bulge of a blood vessel and esp. an artery resulting from weakening (as from disease) of the vessel wall — **an·eu·rys·mal** \ˌan-yə-ˈriz-məl\ *adj*

anew \ə-ˈnü, -ˈnyü\ *adv* [ME *of newe,* fr. OE *of nīwe,* fr. *of* + *nīwe* new] (bef. 12c) **1 :** for an additional time **:** AGAIN ⟨begin ~⟩ **2 :** in a new or different form ⟨a story told ~ on film⟩

ANFO \ˈan-(ˌ)fō\ *n* [*a*mmonium *n*itrate/*f*uel *o*il] (1965) **:** a compound made from ammonium nitrate and fuel oil that is used both as a commercial explosive and in the manufacture of improvised bombs

an·frac·tu·os·i·ty \(ˌ)an-ˌfrak-chə-ˈwä-sə-tē, -shə-; -chü-ˈä-, -shü-\ *n, pl* **-ties** (1596) **1 :** the quality or state of being anfractuous **2 :** a winding channel or course; *esp* **:** an intricate path or process (as of the mind)

an·frac·tu·ous \an-ˈfrak-chə-wəs, -shə-; -chü-əs, -shü-\ *adj* [F *anfractueux,* fr. LL *anfractuosus,* fr. L *anfractus* coil, bend, fr. *an-* (fr. *ambi-* around) + *-fractus,* fr. *frangere* to break — more at AMBI-, BREAK] (1619) **:** full of windings and intricate turnings **:** TORTUOUS

an·gel \ˈān-jəl\ *n* [ME, fr. OE *engel* & AF *angele;* both fr. LL *angelus,* fr. Gk *angelos,* lit., messenger] (bef. 12c) **1 a :** a spiritual being superior to humans in power and intelligence; *esp* **:** one in the lowest rank in the celestial hierarchy **b** *pl* **:** an order of angels — see CELESTIAL HIERARCHY **2 :** an attendant spirit or guardian **3 :** a usu. white-robed winged figure of human form in fine art **4 :** MESSENGER, HARBINGER ⟨~ of death⟩ **5 :** a person like an angel (as in looks or behavior) **6** *Christian Science* **:** inspiration from God **7 :** one (as a backer of a theatrical venture) who aids or supports with money or influence **8 :** ANGELFISH — **an·gel·ic** \an-ˈje-lik\ *or* **an·gel·i·cal** \-li-kəl\ *adj* — **an·gel·i·cal·ly** \-li-k(ə-)lē\ *adv*

angel dust *n* (1969) **:** PHENCYCLIDINE

An·ge·le·no \ˌan-jə-ˈlē-(ˌ)nō\ *n, pl* **-nos** [AmerSp *angeleño,* fr. Los *Angeles,* Calif.] (1885) **:** a native or resident of Los Angeles, Calif.

an·gel·fish \ˈān-jəl-ˌfish\ *n* (1668) **1 :** any of several laterally compressed brightly colored bony fishes (family Pomacanthidae) of warm seas **2 :** a black and silver laterally compressed So. American cichlid fish (*Pterophyllum scalare*) popular in aquariums — called also *scalare*

angel food cake *n* (1908) **:** a usu. white sponge cake made of flour, sugar, and whites of eggs

angel–hair pasta \ˈān-jəl-ˌher-\ *n* (1975) **:** pasta made in long thin strings smaller in diameter than vermicelli

an·gel·i·ca \an-ˈje-li-kə\ *n* [NL, genus name, fr. ML, fr. LL, fem. of *angelicus* angelic, fr. LGk *angelikos,* fr. Gk, of a messenger, fr. *angelos*] (1527) **1 a :** any of a genus (*Angelica*) of herbs of the carrot family; *esp* **:** a Eurasian biennial or perennial (*A. archangelica*) whose roots and seeds yield a flavoring oil and whose young stems are often candied **b :** a confection prepared from angelica **2** *cap* **:** a sweet fortified wine

angelica tree *n* (1785) **:** HERCULES'-CLUB 1

an·gel·ol·o·gy \ˌān-jə-ˈlä-lə-jē\ *n, often cap* (ca. 1805) **:** the theological doctrine of angels or its study — **an·gel·ol·o·gist** \-jist\ *n*

An·ge·lus \ˈan-jə-ləs\ *n* [ML, fr. LL, angel; fr. the first word of the opening versicle] (1658) **1 :** a devotion of the Western church that commemorates the Incarnation and is said in the morning, at noon, and in the evening **2 :** a bell announcing the time for the Angelus

[1]**an·ger** \ˈaŋ-gər\ *vb* **an·gered; an·ger·ing** \-g(ə-)riŋ\ *vt* (13c) **:** to make angry ⟨he was ~*ed* by the decision⟩ ~ *vi* **:** to become angry

[2]**anger** *n* [ME, affliction, anger, fr. ON *angr* grief; akin to OE *enge* narrow, L *angere* to strangle, Gk *anchein*] (14c) **1 :** a strong feeling of displeasure and usu. of antagonism **2 :** RAGE 2 — **an·ger·less** \-ləs\ *adj*

syn ANGER, IRE, RAGE, FURY, INDIGNATION, WRATH mean an intense emotional state induced by displeasure. ANGER, the most general term, names the reaction but by itself does not convey cause or intensity ⟨tried to hide his *anger*⟩. IRE, more frequent in literary contexts, suggests an intense anger, often with an evident display of feeling ⟨cheeks flushed with *ire*⟩. RAGE and FURY suggest loss of self-control from violence of emotion ⟨shook with *rage*⟩ ⟨could not contain his *fury*⟩. INDIGNATION stresses righteous anger at what one considers unfair, mean, or shameful ⟨a comment that caused general *indignation*⟩. WRATH is likely to suggest a desire or intent to punish or get revenge ⟨I feared her *wrath* if I was discovered⟩.

An·ge·vin \ˈan-jə-vən\ *adj* [F, fr. OF, fr. ML *andegavinus,* fr. *Andegavia* Anjou] (1702) **:** of, relating to, or characteristic of Anjou or the Plantagenets — **Angevin** *n*

angi- *or* **angio-** *comb form* [NL, fr. Gk *angei-, angeio-,* fr. *angeion* vessel, blood vessel, dim. of *angos* vessel] **1 :** blood or lymph vessel **:** blood vessels and ⟨*angio*cardiography⟩ **2 :** pericarp ⟨*angio*sperm⟩

an·gi·na \an-ˈjī-nə, ˈan-jə-\ *n* [L, throat inflammation, fr. Gk *anchonē* strangling, fr. *anchein* to strangle] (1578) **:** a disease marked by spasmodic attacks of intense suffocative pain: as **a :** a severe inflammatory or ulcerated condition of the mouth or throat **b :** ANGINA PECTORIS — **an·gi·nal** \an-ˈjī-nᵊl, ˈan-jə-\ *adj*

angina pec·to·ris \-ˈpek-t(ə-)rəs\ *n* [NL, lit., angina of the chest] (1768) **:** a disease marked by brief paroxysmal attacks of chest pain precipitated by deficient oxygenation of the heart muscles

an·gio·car·di·og·ra·phy \ˈan-jē-ō-ˌkär-dē-ˈä-grə-fē\ *n* (1938) **:** the radiographic visualization of the heart and its blood vessels after injection of a radiopaque substance — **an·gio·car·dio·graph·ic** \-dē-ə-ˈgra-fik\ *adj*

an·gio·gen·e·sis \ˌan-jē-ō-ˈje-nə-səs\ *n* [NL] (ca. 1895) **:** the formation and differentiation of blood vessels — **an·gio·gen·ic** \-ˈje-nik\ *adj*

an·gio·gram \ˈan-jē-ə-ˌgram\ *n* (1933) **1 :** a radiograph made by angiography **2 :** ANGIOGRAPHY

an·gi·og·ra·phy \ˌan-jē-ˈä-grə-fē\ *n* (1933) **:** the radiographic visualization of the blood vessels after injection of a radiopaque substance — **an·gio·graph·ic** \ˌan-jē-ə-ˈgra-fik\ *adj* — **an·gio·graph·ic·al·ly** \-fi-k(ə-)lē\ *adv*

\ə\ **a**but \ᵊ\ kitten, F table \ər\ **fur**ther \a\ **a**sh \ā\ **a**ce \ä\ m**o**p, m**a**r
\au̇\ **ou**t \ch\ **ch**in \e\ b**e**t \ē\ **ea**sy \g\ **g**o \i\ h**i**t \ī\ **i**ce \j\ **j**ob
\ŋ\ si**ng** \ō\ g**o** \ȯ\ l**aw** \ȯi\ b**oy** \th\ **th**in \t͟h\ **th**e \ü\ l**oo**t \u̇\ f**oo**t
\y\ **y**et \zh\ vi**s**ion, beige \k, ⁿ, œ, ue, ʸ\ *see* Guide to Pronunciation

an·gi·o·ma \ˌan-jē-ˈō-mə\ *n, pl* **-mas** *also* **-ma·ta** \-mə-tə\ [NL] (1871) **:** a tumor composed chiefly of blood vessels or lymph vessels — **an·gi·o·ma·tous** \-mə-təs\ *adj*

an·gio·plas·ty \ˈan-jē-ə-ˌplas-tē\ *n, pl* **-ties** (ca. 1919) **:** surgical repair or recanalization of a blood vessel; *esp* **:** BALLOON ANGIOPLASTY

an·gio·sperm \ˈan-jē-ə-ˌspərm\ *n* [ultim. fr. NL *angi-* + Gk *sperma* seed — more at SPERM] (ca. 1828) **:** any of a class (Angiospermae) or division (Magnoliophyta) of vascular plants (as magnolias, grasses, oaks, roses, and daisies) that have the ovules and seeds enclosed in an ovary, form the embryo and endosperm by double fertilization, and typically have each flower surrounded by a perianth composed of two sets of floral envelopes comprising the calyx and corolla — called also *flowering plant* — **an·gio·sper·mous** \ˌan-jē-ə-ˈspər-məs\ *adj*

an·gio·ten·sin \ˌan-jē-ō-ˈten(t)-sən\ *n* [*angi-* + hyper*tension* + *-in*] (1958) **:** either of two forms of a kinin of which one has marked vasoconstrictive action; *also* **:** a synthetic amide derivative of the physiologically active form used to treat some forms of hypotension

angiotensin converting enzyme *n* (1960) **:** a proteolytic enzyme that converts the physiologically inactive form of angiotensin to the active vasoconstrictive form

Angl *abbr* Anglican

[1]**an·gle** \ˈaŋ-gəl\ *n* [ME, fr. AF, fr. L *angulus*] (14c) **1 :** a corner whether constituting a projecting part or a partially enclosed space ⟨they sheltered in an ~ of the building⟩ **2 a :** the figure formed by two lines extending from the same point; *also* **:** DIHEDRAL ANGLE **b :** a measure of an angle or of the amount of turning necessary to bring one line or plane into coincidence with or parallel to another **3 a :** the precise viewpoint from which something is observed or considered ⟨a camera ~⟩ ⟨consider the question from all ~*s*⟩; *also* **:** the aspect seen from such an angle ⟨discuss all ~*s* of the question⟩ **b (1) :** a special approach, point of attack, or technique for accomplishing an objective ⟨try a new ~⟩ **(2) :** an often improper or illicit method of obtaining advantage ⟨a salesman always looking for an ~⟩ **4 :** a sharply divergent course ⟨the road went off at an ~⟩ **5 :** a position to the side of an opponent in football from which a player may block his opponent more effectively or without penalty — usu. used in the phrases *get an angle* or *have an angle* — **an·gled** \-gəld\ *adj*

[2]**angle** *vb* **an·gled; an·gling** \-g(ə-)liŋ\ *vi* (1621) **:** to turn or proceed at an angle ~ *vt* **1 :** to turn, move, or direct at an angle **2 :** to present (as a news story) from a particular or prejudiced point of view **:** SLANT

[3]**angle** *vi* **an·gled; an·gling** \-g(ə-)liŋ\ [ME *angelen,* fr. *angel* fishhook, fr. OE, fr. *anga* hook; akin to OHG *ango* hook, L *uncus,* Gk *onkos* barbed hook, *ankos* glen] (15c) **1 :** to fish with a hook **2 :** to use artful means to attain an objective ⟨*angled* for an invitation⟩

An·gle \ˈaŋ-gəl\ *n* [L *Angli,* pl., of Gmc origin; akin to OE *Engle* Angles] (bef. 12c) **:** a member of a Germanic people that invaded England along with the Saxons and Jutes in the fifth century A.D. and merged with them to form the Anglo-Saxon peoples

angle bracket *n* (ca. 1956) **:** BRACKET 3b

angle iron *n* (ca. 1846) **1 :** an iron cleat for joining parts of a structure at an angle **2 :** a piece of structural steel rolled with an L-shaped section

angle of attack (1908) **:** the acute angle between the direction of the relative wind and the chord of an airfoil

angle of depression (1773) **:** the angle formed by the line of sight and the horizontal plane for an object below the horizontal

angle of elevation (ca. 1737) **:** the angle formed by the line of sight and the horizontal plane for an object above the horizontal

angle of incidence (1626) **:** the angle that a line (as a ray of light) falling on a surface or interface makes with the normal drawn at the point of incidence

angle of reflection (1638) **:** the angle between a reflected ray and the normal drawn at the point of incidence to a reflecting surface

angle of refraction (1636) **:** the angle between a refracted ray and the normal drawn at the point of incidence to the interface at which refraction occurs

an·gler \ˈaŋ-glər\ *n* (15c) **1 :** one that angles **2 :** ANGLERFISH

ang·ler·fish \-ˌfish\ *n* (ca. 1889) **:** any of several pediculate fishes (as the goosefishes); *esp* **:** MONKFISH

angle shot *n* (ca. 1922) **:** a picture taken with the camera pointed at an angle from the horizontal

an·gle·site \ˈaŋ-gəl-ˌsīt, -glə-\ *n* [F *anglésite,* fr. *Anglesey* Island, Wales] (ca. 1841) **:** a mineral consisting of lead sulfate formed by the oxidation of galena

an·gle·worm \ˈaŋ-gəl-ˌwərm\ *n* (1653) **:** EARTHWORM

An·gli·an \ˈaŋ-glē-ən\ *n* (ca. 1711) **1 :** a member of the Angles **2 :** the Old English dialects of Mercia and Northumbria — **Anglian** *adj*

An·gli·can \ˈaŋ-gli-kən\ *adj* [ML *anglicanus,* fr. *anglicus* English, fr. L *Angli* Angles] (1635) **1 :** of or relating to the established episcopal Church of England and churches of similar faith and order in communion with it **2 :** of or relating to England or the English nation — **Anglican** *n* — **An·gli·can·ism** \-kə-ˌni-zəm\ *n*

an·gli·ce \ˈaŋ-glə-(ˌ)sē\ *adv, often cap* [ML, adv. of *anglicus*] (1602) **:** in English; *esp* **:** in readily understood English ⟨the city of Napoli, ~ Naples⟩

an·gli·cise *often cap, chiefly Brit, var of* ANGLICIZE

an·gli·cism \ˈaŋ-glə-ˌsi-zəm\ *n, often cap* [ML *anglicus* English] (1642) **1 :** a characteristic feature of English occurring in another language **2 :** adherence or attachment to English customs or ideas

An·gli·cist \ˈaŋ-glə-sist\ *n* (1801) **:** a specialist in English linguistics

an·gli·cize \ˈaŋ-glə-ˌsīz\ *vt* **-cized; -ciz·ing** *often cap* (1710) **1 :** to make English in quality or characteristics **2 :** to adapt (a foreign word, name, or phrase) to English usage: as **a :** to alter to a characteristic English form, sound, or spelling **b :** to convert (a name) to its English equivalent ⟨~ *Juan* as *John*⟩ — **an·gli·ci·za·tion** \ˌaŋ-glə-sə-ˈzā-shən\ *n, often cap*

an·gling \ˈaŋ-gliŋ\ *n* (15c) **:** the action of one who angles; *esp* **:** the action or sport of fishing with hook and line

An·glist \ˈaŋ-glist\ *n* (1888) **:** ANGLICIST

An·glo \ˈaŋ-(ˌ)glō\ *n, pl* **Anglos** [in sense 2, fr. AmerSp, short for Sp *angloamericano* Anglo-American] (1800) **1 :** ANGLO-AMERICAN **2 :** a white inhabitant of the U.S. of non-Hispanic descent — **Anglo** *adj*

Anglo- *comb form* [NL, fr. LL *Angli*] **1** \ˈaŋ-(ˌ)glō, -glə\ **:** English ⟨*Anglo*-Norman⟩ **2** \-(ˌ)glō\ **:** English and ⟨*Anglo*-Japanese⟩

An·glo–Amer·i·can \ˌaŋ-glō-ə-ˈmer-ə-kən\ *n* (ca. 1782) **1 :** an inhabitant of the U.S. of English origin or descent **2 :** a North American whose native language is English and esp. whose culture or ethnic background is of European origin — **Anglo–American** *adj*

An·glo–Cath·o·lic \-ˈkath-lik, -ˈka-thə-\ *adj* (1838) **:** of or relating to a High Church movement in Anglicanism emphasizing its continuity with historic Catholicism and fostering Catholic dogmatic and liturgical traditions — **Anglo–Catholic** *n* — **An·glo–Ca·thol·i·cism** \-kə-ˈthä-lə-ˌsi-zəm\ *n*

An·glo·cen·tric \-ˈsen-trik\ *adj* (1886) **:** centered on or giving priority to England or things English ⟨an ~ view of history⟩

An·glo–French \-ˈfrench\ *n* (1876) **:** the French language used in medieval England

An·glo·ma·nia \-ˈmā-nē-ə, -nyə\ *n* (1787) **:** an absorbing or pervasive interest in England or things English

An·glo–Nor·man \-ˈnȯr-mən\ *n* (1735) **1 :** any of the Normans living in England after the Norman conquest of 1066 **2 :** the form of Anglo-French used by Anglo-Normans — **Anglo–Norman** *adj*

An·glo·phile \ˈaŋ-glə-ˌfī(-ə)l\ *also* **An·glo·phil** \-ˌfil\ *n* [F, fr. *anglo-* + *-phile*] (1883) **:** a person who greatly admires or favors England and things English — **Anglophile** *or* **An·glo·phil·ic** \ˌaŋ-glə-ˈfi-lik\ *adj*

An·glo·phil·ia \ˌaŋ-glə-ˈfi-lē-ə\ *n* (1896) **:** unusual admiration of partiality for England, English ways, or things English — **An·glo·phil·i·ac** \-lē-ˌak\ *adj*

An·glo·phobe \ˈaŋ-glə-ˌfōb\ *n* [prob. fr. F, fr. *anglo-* + *-phobe*] (1866) **:** a person who is averse to or dislikes England and things English — **An·glo·pho·bia** \ˌaŋ-glə-ˈfō-bē-ə\ *n* — **An·glo·pho·bic** \-bik\ *adj*

an·glo·phone \ˈaŋ-glə-ˌfōn\ *adj, often cap* (1900) **:** consisting of or belonging to an English-speaking population esp. in a country where two or more languages are spoken — **Anglophone** *n*

An·glo–Sax·on \ˌaŋ-glō-ˈsak-sən\ *n* [NL *Anglo-Saxones,* pl., alter. of ML *Angli Saxones,* fr. L *Angli* Angles + LL *Saxones* Saxons] (bef. 12c) **1 :** a member of the Germanic peoples conquering England in the fifth century A.D. and forming the ruling class until the Norman conquest — compare ANGLE, JUTE, SAXON **2 a :** ENGLISHMAN; *specif* **:** a person descended from the Anglo-Saxons **b :** a white gentile of an English-speaking nation **3 :** OLD ENGLISH 1 **4 :** direct plain English; *esp* **:** English using words considered crude or vulgar — **Anglo–Saxon** *adj*

An·glo·sphere \ˈaŋ-glə-ˌsfir\ *n* (1995) **:** the countries of the world in which the English language and cultural values predominate

an·go·ra \aŋ-ˈgȯr-ə, an-\ *n* (1812) **1 :** the hair of the Angora rabbit or Angora goat — called also *angora wool* **2 :** a yarn of Angora rabbit hair used esp. for knitting **3** *cap* **a :** ANGORA CAT **b :** ANGORA GOAT **c :** ANGORA RABBIT

Angora cat *n* [*Angora* (Ankara), Turkey] (1819) **:** any of a breed of cats having a long graceful body and silky medium-length hair with no undercoat; *broadly* **:** a long-haired domestic cat

Angora goat *n* (1833) **:** any of a breed of domestic goats raised for their long silky hair which is the true mohair

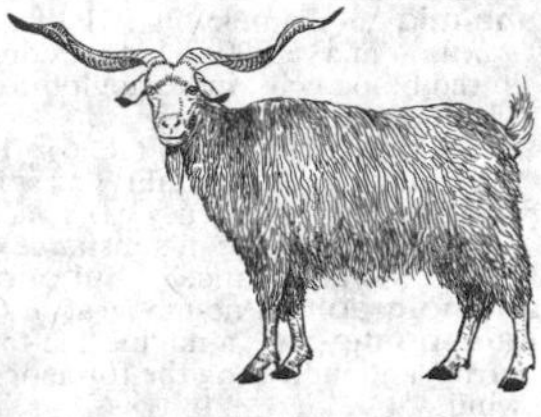
Angora goat

Angora rabbit *n* (1849) **:** any of several breeds of long-haired rabbits raised for their abundant fine wool; *esp* **:** any of a breed having usu. white wool and red eyes

an·gry \ˈaŋ-grē\ *adj* **an·gri·er; -est** (14c) **1 :** feeling or showing anger **2 a :** indicative of or proceeding from anger ⟨~ words⟩ **b :** seeming to show anger or to threaten in an angry manner ⟨an ~ sky⟩ **3 :** painfully inflamed ⟨an ~ rash⟩ — **an·gri·ly** \-grə-lē\ *adv* — **an·gri·ness** \-grē-nəs\ *n*

angry young man *n* (1941) **1 :** an outspoken critic of or protester against an economic condition or social injustice **2 :** one of a group of mid-20th century British authors whose works express the bitterness of the lower classes toward the established sociopolitical system and toward the mediocrity and hypocrisy of the middle and upper classes

angst \ˈäŋ(k)st, ˈaŋ(k)st\ *n* [Dan & G; Dan, fr. G] (ca. 1942) **:** a feeling of anxiety, apprehension, or insecurity ⟨teenage ~⟩

ang·strom \ˈaŋ-strəm *also* ˈȯŋ-\ *n* [Anders J. *Ångström*] (1892) **:** a unit of length equal to one ten-billionth of a meter

[1]**an·guish** \ˈaŋ-gwish\ *n* [ME *angwisshe,* fr. AF *anguisse, angoisse,* fr. L *angustiae,* pl., straits, distress, fr. *angustus* narrow; akin to OE *enge* narrow — more at ANGER] (13c) **:** extreme pain, distress, or anxiety ***syn*** see SORROW

[2]**anguish** *vi* (14c) **:** to suffer anguish ~ *vt* **:** to cause to suffer anguish

an·guished *adj* (14c) **1 :** suffering anguish **:** TORMENTED ⟨the ~ martyrs⟩ **2 :** expressing anguish **:** AGONIZED ⟨~ cries⟩

an·gu·lar \ˈaŋ-gyə-lər\ *adj* [MF or L; MF *angulaire,* fr. L *angularis,* fr. *angulus* angle] (15c) **1 a :** forming an angle **:** sharp-cornered **b :** having one or more angles **2 :** measured by an angle ⟨~ distance⟩ **3 a :** stiff in character or manner **:** lacking smoothness or grace **b :** lean and having prominent bone structure — **an·gu·lar·ly** *adv*

angular acceleration *n* (1883) **:** the rate of change per unit time of angular velocity

an·gu·lar·i·ty \ˌaŋ-gyə-ˈler-ə-tē, -ˈla-rə-\ *n, pl* **-ties** (1642) **1 :** the quality of being angular **2** *pl* **:** angular outlines or characteristics

angular momentum *n* (1870) **:** a vector quantity that is a measure of the rotational momentum of a rotating body or system, that is equal in classical physics to the product of the angular velocity of the body or system and its moment of inertia with respect to the rotation axis, and that is directed along the rotation axis

angular velocity *n* (1672) **:** the rate of rotation around an axis usu. expressed in radians or revolutions per second or per minute

an·gu·la·tion \ˌaŋ-gyə-ˈlā-shən\ *n* (1869) **1 :** the action of making angular **2 :** an angular position, formation, or shape

An·gus \ˈaŋ-gəs\ *n* [*Angus,* county in Scotland] (1842) **:** any of a breed of usu. black hornless beef cattle originating in Scotland

an·he·do·nia \ˌan-(ˌ)hē-ˈdō-nē-ə, -nyə\ *n* [NL, fr. [2]*a-* + Gk *hēdonē* pleasure — more at HEDONISM] (1897) **:** a psychological condition characterized by inability to experience pleasure in normally pleasurable acts — **an·he·don·ic** \-ˈdä-nik\ *adj*

an·hin·ga \an-ˈhiŋ-gə\ *n* [NL, prob. ultim. fr. Tupi **ajíŋa*] (1769) **:** any of a genus (*Anhinga*) of fish-eating birds related to the cormorants but distinguished by a longer neck and sharply pointed rather than hooked bill; *esp* **:** one (*A. anhinga*) occurring from the southern U.S. to Argentina

anhyd *abbr* anhydrous

an·hy·dride \(ˌ)an-ˈhī-ˌdrīd\ *n* (1863) **:** a compound derived from another (as an acid) by removal of the elements of water

an·hy·drite \-ˌdrīt\ *n* [G *Anhydrit,* fr. Gk *anydros*] (ca. 1823) **:** a mineral consisting of an anhydrous calcium sulfate that is usu. massive and white or slightly colored

an·hy·drous \-drəs\ *adj* [Gk *anydros,* fr. *a-* + *hydōr* water — more at WATER] (1819) **:** free from water and esp. water of crystallization

ani \ä-ˈnē, ˈä-nē\ *n* [NL, prob. modif. of Pg *anuí,* fr. Tupi *anúˀí,* fr. *anú* ani + *-ˀí* small] (ca. 1823) **:** any of a genus (*Crotophaga*) of black cuckoos of the warmer parts of America

anile \ˈa-ˌnīl(-ə)l, ˈā-\ *adj* [L *anilis,* fr. *anus* old woman] (1652) **:** of or resembling a doddering old woman; *esp* **:** SENILE — **anil·i·ty** \a-ˈni-lə-tē, ā-, ə-\ *n*

an·i·line \ˈa-nᵊl-ən\ *n* [G *Anilin,* fr. *Anil* indigo, fr. F, fr. Pg, fr. Ar *al-nīl* the indigo plant, fr. Skt *nīlī* indigo, fr. fem. of *nīla* dark blue] (1849) **:** an oily liquid poisonous amine $C_6H_5NH_2$ obtained esp. by the reduction of nitrobenzene and used chiefly in organic synthesis (as of dyes)

aniline dye *n* (1864) **:** a dye made by the use of aniline or one chemically related to such a dye; *broadly* **:** a synthetic organic dye

ani·lin·gus \ˌā-ni-ˈliŋ-gəs\ *or* **ani·linc·tus** \-ˈliŋ(k)-təs\ *n* [NL, fr. *anus* + *-i-* + *-lingus, -linctus* (as in *cunnilingus, cunnilinctus*)] (1949) **:** erotic stimulation achieved by contact between mouth and anus

an·i·ma \ˈa-nə-mə\ *n* [NL, fr. L, soul] (1923) **:** an individual's true inner self that in the analytic psychology of C. G. Jung reflects archetypal ideals of conduct; *also* **:** an inner feminine part of the male personality — compare ANIMUS, PERSONA

an·i·mad·ver·sion \ˌa-nə-ˌmad-ˈvər-zhən, -məd-, -ˈvər-shən\ *n* [L *animadversion-, animadversio,* fr. *animadvertere*] (1599) **1 :** a critical and usu. censorious remark — often used with *on* **2 :** adverse criticism

an·i·mad·vert \-ˈvərt\ *vb* [L *animadvertere* to pay attention to, censure, fr. *animum advertere,* lit., to turn the mind to] *vt* (15c) *archaic* **:** NOTICE, OBSERVE ~ *vi* **:** to make an animadversion

[1]**an·i·mal** \ˈa-nə-məl\ *n* [L, fr. *animale,* neut. of *animalis* animate, fr. *anima* soul — more at ANIMATE] (14c) **1 :** any of a kingdom (Animalia) of living things including many-celled organisms and often many of the single-celled ones (as protozoans) that typically differ from plants in having cells without cellulose walls, in lacking chlorophyll and the capacity for photosynthesis, in requiring more complex food materials (as proteins), in being organized to a greater degree of complexity, and in having the capacity for spontaneous movement and rapid motor responses to stimulation **2 a :** one of the lower animals as distinguished from human beings **b :** MAMMAL; *broadly* **:** VERTEBRATE **3 :** a human being considered chiefly as physical or nonrational; *also* **:** this nature **4 :** a person with a particular interest or aptitude ⟨a political ~⟩ **5 :** MATTER, THING ⟨the theater . . . is an entirely different ~ —Arthur Miller⟩; *also* **:** CREATURE 1c — **an·i·mal·like** \-mə(l)-ˌlīk\ *adj*

[2]**animal** *adj* (1615) **1 :** of, relating to, resembling, or derived from animals **2 a :** of or relating to the physical or sentient as contrasted with the intellectual or rational **b :** SENSUAL, FLESHLY **3 :** of or relating to the animal pole of an egg or to the part from which ectoderm normally develops ***syn*** see CARNAL — **an·i·mal·ly** \-mə-lē\ *adv*

animal control *n* (1957) **:** an office or department responsible for enforcing ordinances relating to the control, impoundment, and disposition of animals

animal cracker *n* (1892) **:** a small cookie in the shape of an animal

an·i·mal·cule \ˌa-nə-ˈmal-(ˌ)kyü(ə)l\ *also* **an·i·mal·cu·lum** \-ˈmal-kyə-ləm\ *n, pl* **-cules** *also* **-cu·la** \-kyə-lə\ [NL *animalculum,* dim. of L *animal*] (1662) **:** a minute usu. microscopic organism

animal heat *n* (1748) **:** heat produced in the body of a living animal by functional chemical and physical activities

animal husbandry *n* (1898) **:** a branch of agriculture concerned with the production and care of domestic animals

an·i·mal·ier \ˌa-nə-mə-ˈlir\ *n* [F, fr. *animal* animal, fr. L] (1912) **:** a sculptor or painter of animal subjects

an·i·mal·ism \ˈa-nə-mə-ˌli-zəm\ *n* (1831) **:** ANIMALITY — **an·i·mal·is·tic** \ˌa-nə-mə-ˈlis-tik\ *adj*

an·i·mal·i·ty \ˌa-nə-ˈma-lə-tē\ *n* (1615) **1 :** a quality or nature associated with animals: **a :** VITALITY **b :** a natural unrestrained unreasoned response to physical drives or stimuli **2 :** the animal nature of human beings

an·i·mal·ize \ˈa-nə-mə-ˌlīz\ *vt* **-ized; -iz·ing** (1741) **1 :** to represent in animal form **2 :** to cause to be or act like an animal — **an·i·mal·iza·tion** \ˌa-nə-mə-lə-ˈzā-shən\ *n*

animal kingdom *n* (ca. 1766) **:** a basic group of natural objects that includes all living and extinct animals — compare MINERAL KINGDOM, PLANT KINGDOM

animal magnetism *n* (1784) **1 :** a mysterious force claimed by Mesmer to enable him to hypnotize patients **2 :** a magnetic charm or appeal; *esp* **:** SEX APPEAL

animal model *n* (1973) **:** an animal sufficiently like humans in its anatomy, physiology, or response to a pathogen to be used in medical research in order to obtain results that can be extrapolated to human medicine; *also* **:** a pathological or physiological condition that occurs in such an animal and is similar to one occurring in humans

animal pole *n* (1887) **:** the point on the surface of an egg that is diametrically opposite to the vegetal pole and usu. marks the most active part of the protoplasm or the part containing least yolk

animal rights *n pl* (1879) **:** rights (as to fair and humane treatment) regarded as belonging fundamentally to all animals — **animal right·ist** \-ˈrī-tist\ *n*

animal spirits *n pl* (1543) **1** *sometimes* **animal spirit,** *obs* **:** the nervous energy that is the source of physical sensation and movement **2 :** vivacity arising from physical health and energy **3 :** a willingness to take esp. economic risks

animal starch *n* (ca. 1860) **:** GLYCOGEN

[1]**an·i·mate** \ˈa-nə-mət\ *adj* [ME, fr. L *animatus,* pp. of *animare* to give life to, fr. *anima* breath, soul; akin to OE *ōthian* to breathe, L *animus* spirit, Gk *anemos* wind, Skt *aniti* he breathes] (15c) **1 :** possessing or characterized by life **:** ALIVE **2 :** full of life **:** ANIMATED **3 :** of or relating to animal life as opposed to plant life **4 :** referring to a living thing ⟨an ~ noun⟩ — **an·i·mate·ly** *adv* — **an·i·mate·ness** *n*

[2]**an·i·mate** \-ˌmāt\ *vt* **-mat·ed; -mat·ing** (15c) **1 :** to give spirit and support to **:** ENCOURAGE **2 a :** to give life to **b :** to give vigor and zest to **3 :** to move to action ⟨a criminal *animated* by greed⟩ **4 a :** to make or design in such a way as to create apparently spontaneous lifelike movement ⟨~ a cartoon⟩ **b :** to produce in the form of an animated cartoon ⟨~ a story⟩ ***syn*** see QUICKEN

an·i·mat·ed \-ˌmā-təd\ *adj* (1534) **1 a :** endowed with life or the qualities of life **:** ALIVE **b :** full of movement and activity ⟨an ~ crowd⟩ **c :** full of vigor and spirit **:** LIVELY ⟨an ~ discussion⟩ **2 :** having the appearance of something alive ⟨an unusually ~ piece of sculpture⟩ **3 :** made in the form of an animated cartoon ⟨an ~ film⟩ ***syn*** see LIVELY — **an·i·mat·ed·ly** *adv*

animated cartoon *n* (1915) **:** a motion picture that is made from a series of drawings, computer graphics, or photographs of inanimate objects (as puppets) and that simulates movement by slight progressive changes in each frame

an·i·ma·tion \ˌa-nə-ˈmā-shən\ *n* (1597) **1 :** the act of animating **:** the state of being animate or animated **2 :** ANIMATED CARTOON **3 :** the preparation of animated cartoons

an·i·ma·to \ˌä-nə-ˈmä-(ˌ)tō, ˌa-\ *adv or adj* [It, fr. L *animatus*] (ca. 1724) **:** with animation — used as a direction in music

an·i·ma·tor \ˈa-nə-ˌmā-tər\ *n* (1611) **1 :** one that animates ⟨prime ~ of the movement⟩ **2 :** an artist who creates drawings for an animated cartoon

an·i·ma·tron·ic \ˌa-nə-mə-ˈträ-nik\ *adj* [short for *audio-animatronic*] (1978) **:** of, relating to, or being a puppet or similar figure that is animated by means of electromechanical devices — **an·i·ma·tron·i·cal·ly** \-ni-k(ə-)lē\ *adv*

an·i·ma·tron·ics \-ˈträ-niks\ *n pl but sing or pl in constr* (1971) **:** technology dealing with animatronic animation

an·i·me \ˈa-nə-ˌmā, ˈä-nē-\ *n* [Jp, animation, short for *animēshiyon,* fr. E] (1988) **:** a style of animation originating in Japan that is characterized by stark colorful graphics depicting vibrant characters in action-filled plots often with fantastic or futuristic themes

an·i·mism \ˈa-nə-ˌmi-zəm\ *n* [G *Animismus,* fr. L *anima* soul] (1832) **1 :** a doctrine that the vital principle of organic development is immaterial spirit **2 :** attribution of conscious life to objects in and phenomena of nature or to inanimate objects **3 :** belief in the existence of spirits separable from bodies — **an·i·mist** \-mist\ *n* — **an·i·mis·tic** \ˌa-nə-ˈmis-tik\ *adj*

an·i·mos·i·ty \ˌa-nə-ˈmä-sə-tē\ *n, pl* **-ties** [ME *animosite,* fr. MF or LL; MF *animosité,* fr. LL *animositat-, animositas,* fr. L *animosus* spirited, fr. *animus*] (1605) **:** ill will or resentment tending toward active hostility **:** an antagonistic attitude ***syn*** see ENMITY

an·i·mus \ˈa-nə-məs\ *n* [L, spirit, mind, courage, anger] (1816) **1 :** basic attitude or governing spirit **:** DISPOSITION, INTENTION **2 :** a usu. prejudiced and often spiteful or malevolent ill will **3 :** an inner masculine part of the female personality in the analytic psychology of C. G. Jung — compare ANIMA ***syn*** see ENMITY

an·ion \ˈa-ˌnī-ən\ *n* [Gk, neut. of *aniōn,* prp. of *anienai* to go up, fr. *ana-* + *ienai* to go — more at ISSUE] (1834) **:** the ion in an electrolyzed solution that migrates to the anode; *broadly* **:** a negatively charged ion

an·ion·ic \ˌa-(ˌ)nī-ˈä-nik\ *adj* (ca. 1920) **1 :** of or relating to anions **2 :** characterized by an active and esp. surface-active anion

anis- *or* **aniso-** *comb form* [NL, fr. Gk, fr. *anisos,* fr. *a-* + *isos* equal] **:** unequal ⟨*aniso*tropic⟩

an·ise \ˈa-nəs\ *n* [ME *anis,* fr. AF, fr. L *anisum,* fr. Gk *annēson, anison*] (14c) **:** a Eurasian annual herb (*Pimpinella anisum*) of the carrot family having carminative and aromatic seeds; *also* **:** ANISEED

ani·seed \ˈa-nə(s)-ˌsēd\ *n* [ME *anis seed,* fr. *anis* + *seed*] (14c) **:** the seed of anise often used as a flavoring in liqueurs and in cooking

an·is·ei·ko·nia \ˌa-ˌnī-ˌsī-ˈkō-nē-ə\ *n* [NL, fr. *anis-* + Gk *eikōn* image — more at ICON] (1934) **:** a defect of binocular vision in which the two retinal images of an object differ in size — **an·is·ei·kon·ic** \-ˈkä-nik\ *adj*

an·is·ette \ˌa-nə-ˈset, -ˈzet\ *n* [F, fr. *anis*] (1836) **:** a usu. colorless sweet liqueur flavored with aniseed

Anish·i·na·be *also* **Anish·i·naa·be** \ä-ni-shi-ˈnō-bā\ *or* **Anish·i·na·beg** \-bāg, -bāk\ *n* [Ojibwa *aniššina·pe·* (pl. *aniššina·pe·k*) Ojibwa, Indian] (1902) **:** OJIBWA 1

an·isog·a·mous \ˌa-(ˌ)nī-ˈsä-gə-məs\ *adj* (1891) **:** characterized by fusion of heterogamous gametes or of individuals that usu. differ chiefly in size ⟨~ reproduction⟩ — **an·isog·a·my** \-(ˌ)nī-ˈsä-gə-mē\ *n*

an·iso·me·tro·pia \ˌa-ˌnī-sə-mə-ˈtrō-pē-ə\ *n* [NL, fr. Gk *anisometros* of unequal measure (fr. *anis-* + *metron* measure) + NL *-opia* — more at MEASURE] (ca. 1880) **:** unequal refractive power in the two eyes — **an·iso·me·tro·pic** \-ˈträ-pik, -ˈtrō-\ *adj*

an·iso·trop·ic \ˌa-ˌnī-sə-ˈträ-pik\ *adj* (1879) **:** exhibiting properties with different values when measured in different directions ⟨an ~ crystal⟩ — **an·iso·trop·i·cal·ly** \-pi-k(ə-)lē\ *adv* — **an·isot·ro·py** \-(ˌ)nī-ˈsä-trə-pē\ *also* **an·isot·ro·pism** \-ˌpi-zəm\ *n*

An·jou \ˈan-jü, -zhü\ *n* [*Anjou,* France] (1941) **:** a large sweet ovoid pear having a usu. yellowish-green skin

an·ker·ite \ˈaŋ-kə-ˌrīt\ *n* [G *Ankerit,* fr. M. J. *Anker* †1843 Austrian mineralogist] (ca. 1843) **:** a yellowish to brown mineral consisting of a carbonate of calcium and iron

ankh \ˈäŋk\ *n* [Egypt *ʿnḫ* live] (1888) **:** a cross having a loop for its upper vertical arm and serving esp. in ancient Egypt as an emblem of life

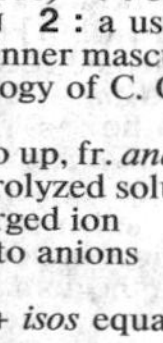

ankh

an·kle \ˈaŋ-kəl\ *n* [ME *ankel,* fr. OE *anclēow;* akin to OHG *anchlāo* ankle] (bef. 12c) **1 :** the joint between the foot

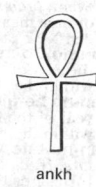

and the leg; *also* : the region of this joint **2** : the joint between the cannon bone and pastern (as in the horse)
an·kle·bone \'aŋ-kəl-ˌbōn, ˌaŋ-kəl-'\ *n* (14c) : ²TALUS 1
an·klet \'aŋ-klət\ *n* (1793) **1** : something (as an ornament) worn around the ankle **2** : a short sock reaching slightly above the ankle
an·ky·lo·saur \'aŋ-kə-lō-ˌsȯr\ *n* [NL *Ankylosauria,* fr. *Ankylosaurus*] (1908) : any of a suborder (Ankylosauria) of herbivorous Cretaceous ornithischian dinosaurs having a long low-lying thickset body covered dorsally with bony plates
an·ky·lo·sau·rus \ˌaŋ-kə-lō-'sȯr-əs\ *n* [NL, genus name, fr. Gk *ankylos* + *sauros* lizard] (1907) : any of a No. American genus (*Ankylosaurus*) of large ankylosaurs having a bony club at the end of the tail
an·ky·lose \'aŋ-ki-ˌlōs, -ˌlōz\ *vb* **-losed; -los·ing** [back-formation fr. *ankylosis*] *vt* (1771) : to unite or stiffen by ankylosis ~ *vi* : to undergo ankylosis
an·ky·lo·sis \ˌaŋ-ki-'lō-səs\ *n, pl* **-lo·ses** \-ˌsēz\ [NL, fr. Gk *ankylōsis,* fr. *ankyloun* to make crooked, fr. *ankylos* crooked — more at ANGLE] (1713) **1** : stiffness or fixation of a joint by disease or surgery **2** : union of separate bones or hard parts to form a single bone or part — **an·ky·lot·ic** \-'lä-tik\ *adj*
ankylostomiasis *var of* ANCYLOSTOMIASIS
an·la·ge \'än-ˌlä-gə\ *n, pl* **-gen** \-gən\ *also* **-ges** \-gəz\ [G, lit., act of laying on] (1874) : the foundation of a subsequent development; *esp* : PRIMORDIUM
ann *abbr* **1** annals **2** annual
an·na \'ä-nə\ *n* [Hindi & Urdu *ānā*] (1708) **1** : a former monetary unit of Burma, India, and Pakistan equal to ¹⁄₁₆ rupee **2** : a coin representing one anna
an·nal·ist \'a-nᵊl-ist\ *n* (ca. 1611) : a writer of annals : CHRONICLER — **an·nal·is·tic** \ˌa-nᵊl-'is-tik\ *adj*
an·nals \'a-nᵊlz\ *n pl* [L *annales,* fr. pl. of *annalis* yearly — more at ANNUAL] (1542) **1** : a record of events arranged in yearly sequence **2** : historical records : CHRONICLES **3** : records of the activities of an organization
An·nam·ese \ˌa-nə-'mēz, -'mēs\ *n, pl* **Annamese** (1825) **1** *or* **An·nam·ite** \'a-nə-ˌmīt\ : a native or inhabitant of Annam **2** : VIETNAMESE 2 — **Annamese** *adj* — **Annamite** *adj*
an·nat·to \ə-'nä-(ˌ)tō\ *n* [Carib *annoto* tree producing annatto] (1629) **1** : a yellowish-red dyestuff made from the pulp around the seeds of a tropical American tree (*Bixa orellana*) **2** : the tree from which annatto is derived; *also* : its dried seed used to color and flavor food
an·neal \ə-'nēl\ *vb* [ME *anelen* to set on fire, fr. OE *onǣlan,* fr. *on* + *ǣlan* to set on fire, burn, fr. *āl* fire; akin to OE *ǣled* fire, ON *eldr*] *vt* (1664) **1 a** : to heat and then cool (as steel or glass) usu. for softening and making less brittle; *also* : to cool slowly usu. in a furnace **b** : to heat and then cool (double-stranded nucleic acid) in order to separate strands and induce combination at lower temperature with complementary strands **2** : STRENGTHEN, TOUGHEN ~ *vi* : to be capable of combining with complementary nucleic acid by a process of heating and cooling
an·ne·lid \'a-nə-ˌlid\ *n* [ultim. fr. L *anellus* little ring — more at ANNULET] (1813) : any of a phylum (Annelida) of usu. elongated segmented coelomate invertebrates (as earthworms and leeches) — **annelid** *adj* — **an·nel·i·dan** \ə-'ne-lə-dən, a-\ *adj or n*
¹**an·nex** \ə-'neks, 'a-ˌneks\ *vt* [ME, fr. AF *annexer,* fr. *annexe* attached, fr. L *annexus,* pp. of *annectere* to bind to, fr. *ad-* + *nectere* to bind] (14c) **1** : to attach as a quality, consequence, or condition **2** *archaic* : to join together materially : UNITE **3** : to add to something earlier, larger, or more important **4** : to incorporate (a country or other territory) within the domain of a state **5** : to obtain or take for oneself — **an·nex·a·tion** \ˌa-ˌnek-'sā-shən\ *n* — **an·nex·a·tion·al** \-shnəl, -shə-nᵊl\ *adj* — **an·nex·a·tion·ist** \-sh(ə-)nist\ *n*
²**an·nex** \'a-ˌneks, -niks\ *n* (1501) : something annexed as an expansion or supplement: as **a** : an added stipulation or statement : APPENDIX **b** : a subsidiary or supplementary building or structure : WING
an·nexe *chiefly Brit var of* ²ANNEX
An·nie Oak·ley \ˌa-nē-'ō-klē\ *n, pl* **Annie Oakleys** [*Annie Oakley* †1926 Am. markswoman; fr. the resemblance of a punched pass to a playing card with bullet holes through the spots] (ca. 1910) : a free ticket
an·ni·hi·late \ə-'nī-ə-ˌlāt\ *vb* **-lat·ed; -lat·ing** [LL *annihilatus,* pp. of *annihilare* to reduce to nothing, fr. L *ad-* + *nihil* nothing — more at NIL] *vt* (1525) **1 a** : to cause to be of no effect : NULLIFY **b** : to destroy the substance or force of **2** : to regard as of no consequence **3** : to cause to cease to exist; *esp* : KILL **4 a** : to destroy a considerable part of ⟨bombs *annihilated* the city⟩ **b** : to vanquish completely : ROUT ⟨*annihilated* the visitors 56–0⟩ **5** : to cause (a particle and its antiparticle) to vanish by annihilating ~ *vi, of a particle and its antiparticle* : to vanish or cease to exist by coming together and changing into other forms of energy (as photons) — **an·ni·hi·la·tion** \-ˌnī-ə-'lā-shən\ *n* — **an·ni·hi·la·tor** \-ˌlā-tər\ *n* — **an·ni·hi·la·to·ry** \-'nī-ə-lə-ˌtȯr-ē\ *adj*
an·ni·ver·sa·ry \ˌa-nə-'vərs-rē, -'vər-sə-\ *n, pl* **-ries** [ME *anniversarie,* fr. ML *anniversarium,* fr. L, neut. of *anniversarius* returning annually, fr. *annus* year + *versus,* pp. of *vertere* to turn — more at ANNUAL, WORTH] (13c) **1** : the annual recurrence of a date marking a notable event; *broadly* : a date that follows such an event by a specified period of time measured in units other than years ⟨the 6-month ~ of the accident⟩ **2** : the celebration of an anniversary
an·no Do·mi·ni \ˌa-(ˌ)nō-'dä-mə-nē, -'dō-, -ˌnī\ *adv, often cap A* [ML, in the year of the Lord] (1512) — used to indicate that a time division falls within the Christian era
an·no he·gi·rae \-hi-'jī-(ˌ)rē, -'he-jə-ˌrē\ *adv, often cap A&H* [NL, in the year of the Hegira] (1613) — used to indicate that a time division falls within the Islamic era
an·no·tate \'a-nə-ˌtāt\ *vb* **-tat·ed; -tat·ing** [L *annotatus,* pp. of *annotare,* fr. *ad-* + *notare* to mark — more at NOTE] *vi* (1710) : to make or furnish critical or explanatory notes or comment ~ *vt* : to make or furnish annotations for (as a literary work or subject) — **an·no·ta·tive** \-ˌtā-tiv\ *adj* — **an·no·ta·tor** \-ˌtā-tər\ *n*
an·no·ta·tion \ˌa-nə-'tā-shən\ *n* (15c) **1** : a note added by way of comment or explanation **2** : the act of annotating
an·nounce \ə-'nau̇n(t)s\ *vb* **an·nounced; an·nounc·ing** [ME, fr. AF *annuncier,* fr. L *annuntiare,* fr. *ad-* + *nuntiare* to report, fr. *nuntius* messenger] *vt* (15c) **1** : to make known publicly : PROCLAIM ⟨*announced* the deal⟩ **2 a** : to give notice of the arrival, presence, or readiness of ⟨~ dinner⟩ **b** : to indicate beforehand : FORETELL **3** : to serve as an announcer of ⟨~ a football game⟩ ~ *vi* **1** : to serve as an announcer **2 a** : to declare one's candidacy ⟨~ for president⟩ **b** : to declare oneself politically ⟨~ against a nominee⟩ ***syn*** see DECLARE
an·nounce·ment \ə-'nau̇n(t)-smənt\ *n* (1781) **1** : the act of announcing or of being announced **2** : a public notification or declaration **3** : a piece of formal stationery designed for a social or business announcement
an·nounc·er \ə-'nau̇n(t)-sər\ *n* (ca. 1611) : one who announces: as **a** : a person who introduces television or radio programs, makes commercial announcements, or gives station identification **b** : a person who describes and comments on the action in a broadcast sports event
an·noy \ə-'nȯi\ *vb* [ME *anoien,* fr. AF *anuier, ennoier,* fr. LL *inodiare* to make loathsome, fr. L *in* + *odium* hatred — more at ODIUM] *vt* (13c) **1** : to disturb or irritate esp. by repeated acts **2** : to harass esp. by quick brief attacks ~ *vi* : to cause annoyance — **an·noy·er** *n*
syn ANNOY, VEX, IRK, BOTHER mean to upset a person's composure. ANNOY implies a wearing on the nerves by persistent petty unpleasantness ⟨their constant complaining *annoys* us⟩. VEX implies greater provocation and stronger disturbance and usu. connotes anger but sometimes perplexity or anxiety ⟨*vexed* by her son's failure to clean his room⟩. IRK stresses difficulty in enduring and the resulting weariness or impatience of spirit ⟨careless waste *irks* the boss⟩. BOTHER suggests interference with comfort or peace of mind ⟨don't *bother* me while I'm reading⟩. ***syn*** see in addition WORRY
an·noy·ance \ə-'nȯi-ən(t)s\ *n* (14c) **1** : the act of annoying or of being annoyed **2** : the state or feeling of being annoyed : VEXATION **3** : a source of vexation or irritation : NUISANCE ⟨the delay was a minor ~⟩
an·noy·ing \-iŋ\ *adj* (14c) : causing vexation : IRRITATING ⟨an ~ habit⟩ ⟨~ questions⟩ — **an·noy·ing·ly** \-iŋ-lē\ *adv*
¹**an·nu·al** \'an-yə(-wə)l, -yü-əl\ *adj* [ME, fr. AF & LL; AF *annuel,* fr. LL *annualis,* blend of L *annuus* yearly (fr. *annus* year) and L *annalis* yearly (fr. *annus* year); prob. akin to Goth *athnam* (dat. pl.) years, Skt *atati* he walks, goes] (14c) **1** : covering the period of a year ⟨~ rainfall⟩ **2** : occurring or happening every year or once a year : YEARLY ⟨an ~ reunion⟩ **3** : completing the life cycle in one growing season or single year ⟨~ plants⟩ — **an·nu·al·ly** *adv*
²**annual** *n* (14c) **1** : an event that occurs yearly **2** : a publication appearing yearly **3** : something that lasts one year or season; *specif* : a plant that completes its life cycle in one growing season
an·nu·al·ize \'an-yə(-wə)-ˌlīz, -yü-ə-\ *vt* **-ized; -iz·ing** (1906) : to calculate or adjust to reflect a rate based on a full year ⟨quarterly returns yielding at an *annualized* rate of seven percent⟩
annual report *n* (1815) : a usu. lengthy report issued yearly by an organization giving an account of its internal workings and esp. its finances
annual ring *n* (1681) : the layer of wood produced by a single year's growth of a woody plant
an·nu·itant \ə-'nü-ə-tənt, -'nyü-\ *n* (1716) : a beneficiary of an annuity
an·nu·ity \ə-'nü-ə-tē, -'nyü-\ *n, pl* **-ities** [ME *annuite,* fr. AF *annuité,* fr. ML *annuitat-, annuitas,* fr. L *annuus* yearly] (15c) **1** : a sum of money payable yearly or at other regular intervals **2** : the right to receive an annuity **3** : a contract or agreement providing for the payment of an annuity
an·nul \ə-'nəl\ *vt* **an·nulled; an·nul·ling** [ME *annullen,* fr. AF *annuller,* fr. LL *annullare,* fr. L *ad-* + *nullus* not any — more at NULL] (15c) **1** : to reduce to nothing : OBLITERATE **2** : to make ineffective or inoperative : NEUTRALIZE ⟨~ the drug's effect⟩ **3** : to declare or make legally invalid or void ⟨wants the marriage *annulled*⟩ ***syn*** see NULLIFY
an·nu·lar \'an-yə-lər\ *adj* [MF or ML; MF *annulaire,* fr. ML *anularis,* fr. L *anulus*] (1571) : of, relating to, or forming a ring ⟨an ~ skin lesion⟩
annular eclipse *n* (1731) : an eclipse in which a thin outer ring of the sun's disk is not covered by the smaller dark disk of the moon
an·nu·late \'an-yə-lət, -ˌlāt\ *adj* (ca. 1656) : furnished with or composed of rings : RINGED
an·nu·la·tion \ˌan-yə-'lā-shən\ *n* (1794) : a ringlike anatomical structure
an·nu·let \'an-yə-lət\ *n* [modif. of MF *annelet,* dim. of *anel,* fr. L *anellus,* dim. of *anulus*] (1598) **1** : a little ring **2** : a small architectural molding or ridge forming a ring
an·nul·ment \ə-'nəl-mənt\ *n* (15c) **1** : the act of annulling : the state of being annulled **2** : a judicial or ecclesiastical pronouncement declaring a marriage invalid
an·nu·lus \'an-yə-ləs\ *n, pl* **-li** \-ˌlī, -(ˌ)lē\ *also* **-lus·es** [ML, fr. L *anulus* finger ring, fr. *anus* ring — more at ANUS] (1563) **1** : RING **2** : a part, structure, or marking resembling a ring: as **a** : a line of cells around a fern sporangium that ruptures the sporangium by contracting **b** : a growth ring (as on the scale of a fish) that is used in estimating age
an·nun·ci·ate \ə-'nən(t)-sē-ˌāt\ *vt* **-at·ed; -at·ing** (ca. 1536) : ANNOUNCE
an·nun·ci·a·tion \ə-ˌnən(t)-sē-'ā-shən\ *n* [ME *annunciacioun,* fr. AF *annuntiatun,* fr. LL *annuntiation-, annuntiatio,* fr. L *annuntiare* — more at ANNOUNCE] (14c) **1** *cap* : March 25 observed as a church festival in commemoration of the announcement of the Incarnation to the Virgin Mary **2** : the act of announcing or of being announced : ANNOUNCEMENT
an·nun·ci·a·tor \ə-'nən(t)-sē-ˌā-tər\ *n* (ca. 1753) : one that annunciates; *specif* : a usu. electrically controlled signal board or indicator — **an·nun·ci·a·to·ry** \-sē-ə-ˌtȯr-ē\ *adj*
an·nus hor·ri·bi·lis \'a-nəs-hȯr-'i-bə-ləs, 'ä-\ *n, pl* **an·ni hor·ri·bi·les** \'a-ˌnī-hȯr-'i-bə-ˌlēz, 'ä-\ [NL, lit., horrible year] (1983) : a disastrous or unfortunate year
an·nus mi·ra·bi·lis \'a-nəs-mə-'rä-bə-ləs, 'ä-\ *n, pl* **an·ni mi·ra·bi·les** \'a-ˌnī-mə-'rä-bə-ˌlēz, 'ä-\ [NL, lit., wonderful year] (1660) : a remarkable or notable year
an·ode \'a-ˌnōd\ *n* [Gk *anodos* way up, fr. *ana-* + *hodos* way] (1834) **1** : the electrode of an electrochemical cell at which oxidation occurs: as **a** : the positive terminal of an electrolytic cell **b** : the negative terminal of a galvanic cell **2** : the electron-collecting electrode of an electron tube; *broadly* : the positive electrode of a diode — compare CATHODE — **an·od·ic** \a-'nä-dik\ *also* **an·od·al** \-'nō-dᵊl\ *adj* — **an·od·i·cal·ly** \-di-k(ə-)lē\ *also* **an·od·al·ly** \-dᵊl-ē\ *adv*

an·od·ize \'a-nə-ˌdīz\ *vt* **-ized; -iz·ing** (1931) **:** to subject (a metal) to electrolytic action as the anode of a cell in order to coat with a protective or decorative film — **an·od·i·za·tion** \ˌa-ˌnō-də-'zā-shən, ˌa-nə-\ *n*

1**an·o·dyne** \'a-nə-ˌdīn\ *adj* [L *anodynos,* fr. Gk *anōdynos,* fr. *a-* + *odynē* pain; prob. akin to OE *etan* to eat] (1543) **1 :** serving to alleviate pain **2 :** not likely to offend or arouse tensions **:** INNOCUOUS

2**anodyne** *n* (ca. 1550) **1 :** something that soothes, calms, or comforts ⟨the ~ of bridge, a comfortable book, or sport —Harrison Smith⟩ **2 :** a drug that allays pain

anoint \ə-'nȯint\ *vt* [ME, fr. AF *enoint,* pp. of *enoindre,* fr. L *inunguere,* fr. *in-* + *unguere* to smear — more at OINTMENT] (14c) **1 :** to smear or rub with oil or an oily substance **2 a :** to apply oil to as a sacred rite esp. for consecration **b :** to choose by or as if by divine election; *also* **:** to designate as if by a ritual anointment ⟨critics ~*ed* the author as the bright new talent⟩ — **anoint·er** *n* — **anoint·ment** \-mənt\ *n*

anointing of the sick (1649) **:** EXTREME UNCTION

ano·le \ə-'nō-lē\ *n* [prob. fr. F *anolis,* fr. Arawak of the Lesser Antilles] (1745) **:** any of a genus (*Anolis*) of arboreal American lizards (as the American chameleon) of the iguana family that have a brightly colored dewlap and the ability to change color

anom·a·lous \ə-'nä-mə-ləs\ *adj* [LL *anomalus,* fr. Gk *anōmalos,* lit., uneven, fr. *a-* + *homalos* even, fr. *homos* same — more at SAME] (1655) **1 :** inconsistent with or deviating from what is usual, normal, or expected **:** IRREGULAR, UNUSUAL **2 a :** of uncertain nature or classification **b :** marked by incongruity or contradiction **:** PARADOXICAL ***syn*** see IRREGULAR — **anom·a·lous·ly** *adv* — **anom·a·lous·ness** *n*

anom·a·ly \ə-'nä-mə-lē\ *n, pl* **-lies** (1603) **1 :** the angular distance of a planet from its perihelion as seen from the sun **2 :** deviation from the common rule **:** IRREGULARITY **3 :** something anomalous **:** something different, abnormal, peculiar, or not easily classified

an·o·mie *also* **an·o·my** \'a-nə-mē\ *n* [F *anomie,* fr. MF, fr. Gk *anomia* lawlessness, fr. *anomos* lawless, fr. *a-* + *nomos* law, fr. *nemein* to distribute — more at NIMBLE] (1933) **:** social instability resulting from a breakdown of standards and values; *also* **:** personal unrest, alienation, and uncertainty that comes from a lack of purpose or ideals — **ano·mic** \ə-'nä-mik, -'nō-\ *adj*

1**anon** \ə-'nän\ *adv* [ME, fr. OE *on ān,* fr. *on* in + *ān* one — more at ON, ONE] (bef. 12c) **1** *archaic* **:** at once **:** IMMEDIATELY **2 :** SOON, PRESENTLY ⟨tomorrow will be here ~ —Nathaniel Hawthorne⟩ **3 :** after a while **:** LATER ⟨more of that ~⟩

2**anon** *abbr* anonymous; anonymously

an·o·nym \'a-nə-ˌnim\ *n* (1793) **1 :** an anonymous person **2 :** PSEUDONYM

an·o·nym·i·ty \ˌa-nə-'ni-mə-tē\ *n, pl* **-ties** (1820) **1 :** the quality or state of being anonymous **2 :** one that is anonymous

anon·y·mous \ə-'nä-nə-məs\ *adj* [LL *anonymus,* fr. Gk *anōnymos,* fr. *a-* + *onyma* name — more at NAME] (1563) **1 :** of unknown authorship or origin ⟨an ~ tip⟩ **2 :** not named or identified ⟨an ~ author⟩ ⟨they wish to remain ~⟩ **3 :** lacking individuality, distinction, or recognizability ⟨the ~ faces in the crowd⟩ ⟨the gray ~ streets —William Styron⟩ — **anon·y·mous·ly** *adv* — **anon·y·mous·ness** *n*

anoph·e·les \ə-'nä-fə-ˌlēz\ *n* [NL, genus name, fr. Gk *anōphelēs* useless, fr. *a-* + *ophelos* advantage, help; akin to Gk *ophellein* to increase, Arm *aweli* more] (1824) **:** any of a genus (*Anopheles*) of mosquitoes that includes all mosquitoes which transmit malaria to humans — **anoph·e·line** \-ˌlīn\ *adj or n*

an·o·rak \'a-nə-ˌrak\ *n* [Dan, fr. Inuit (Greenland) *annoraaq*] (1877) **:** a usu. pullover hooded jacket long enough to cover the hips

1**an·o·rec·tic** \ˌa-nə-'rek-tik\ *also* **an·o·ret·ic** \-'re-tik\ *adj* [Gk *anorektos,* fr. *a-* + *oregein* to reach after — more at RIGHT] (1832) **1 a :** lacking appetite **b :** ANOREXIC 2 **2 :** causing loss of appetite

2**anorectic** *also* **anoretic** *n* (1957) **1 :** an anorectic agent **2 :** ANOREXIC

an·orex·ia \ˌa-nə-'rek-sē-ə, -'rek-shə\ *n* [NL, fr. Gk, fr. *a-* + *orexis* appetite, fr. *oregein*] (1598) **1 :** loss of appetite esp. when prolonged **2 :** ANOREXIA NERVOSA

anorexia ner·vo·sa \-(ˌ)nər-'vō-sə, -zə\ *n* [NL, nervous anorexia] (1873) **:** a serious disorder in eating behavior primarily of young women in their teens and early twenties that is characterized esp. by a pathological fear of weight gain leading to faulty eating patterns, malnutrition, and usu. excessive weight loss

1**an·orex·ic** \ˌa-nə-'rek-sik\ *adj* (1875) **1 :** ANORECTIC **2 :** relating to, characteristic of, or affected with anorexia nervosa; *also* **:** seemingly affected with anorexia nervosa as by being excessively skinny

2**anorexic** *n* (1907) **:** a person affected with or as if with anorexia nervosa

an·orex·i·gen·ic \ˌa-nə-ˌrek-sə-'je-nik\ *adj* (1948) **:** ANORECTIC 2

an·or·thite \ə-'nȯr-ˌthīt\ *n* [F, fr. *a-* + Gk *orthos* straight] (1823) **:** a white, grayish, or reddish feldspar occurring in many igneous rocks — **an·or·thit·ic** \ˌa-nȯr-'thi-tik\ *adj*

an·or·tho·site \ə-'nȯr-thə-ˌsīt\ *n* [F *anorthose,* a feldspar, fr. *a-* + Gk *orthos* — more at ORTH-] (1863) **:** a granular plutonic igneous rock composed almost exclusively of a soda-lime feldspar (as labradorite) — **an·or·tho·si·tic** \ə-ˌnȯr-thə-'si-tik\ *adj*

an·os·mia \a-'näz-mē-ə\ *n* [NL, fr. *a-* + Gk *osmē* smell — more at ODOR] (1797) **:** loss or impairment of the sense of smell — **an·os·mic** \-mik\ *adj*

1**an·oth·er** \ə-'nə-t͟hər *also* a- *or* ā-\ *adj* (12c) **1 :** different or distinct from the one first considered ⟨the same scene viewed from ~ angle⟩ **2 :** some other ⟨do it ~ time⟩ **3 :** being one more in addition to one or more of the same kind ⟨have ~ piece of pie⟩

2**another** *pron* (13c) **1 :** an additional one of the same kind **:** one more **2 :** one that is different from the first or present one **3 :** one of a group of unspecified or indefinite things ⟨in one way or ~⟩

anoth·er–guess \ə-'nə-t͟hər-ˌges\ *adj* [alter. of *anothergates,* fr. *1another* + *gate*] (1625) *archaic* **:** of another sort

ANOVA *abbr* analysis of variance

an·ovu·la·to·ry \(ˌ)an-'äv-yə-lə-ˌtȯr-ē, -'ōv-\ *adj* (1934) **1 :** not involving or accompanied by ovulation ⟨~ bleeding⟩ **2 :** suppressing ovulation

an·ox·emia \ˌa-ˌnäk-'sē-mē-ə\ *n* [NL] (1861) **:** a condition of subnormal oxygenation of the arterial blood — **an·ox·emic** \-mik\ *adj*

an·ox·ia \a-'näk-sē-ə\ *n* [NL] (1931) **:** hypoxia esp. of such severity as to result in permanent damage

an·ox·ic \(ˌ)a-'näk-sik\ *adj* (1920) **1 :** of, relating to, or affected with anoxia **2 :** greatly deficient in oxygen **:** OXYGENLESS ⟨~ water⟩

ans *abbr* answer

ANSI *abbr* American National Standards Institute

1**an·swer** \'an(t)-sər\ *n* [ME, fr. OE *andswaru* (akin to ON *andsvar* answer); akin to OE *and-* against, *swerian* to swear — more at ANTE-] (bef. 12c) **1 a :** something spoken or written in reply to a question **b :** a correct response ⟨knows the ~⟩ **2 :** a reply to a legal charge or suit **:** PLEA; *also* **:** DEFENSE **3 :** something done in response or reaction ⟨his only ~ was to walk out⟩ **4 :** a solution of a problem ⟨more money is not the ~⟩ **5 :** one that imitates, matches, or corresponds to another ⟨television's ~ to the newsmagazines⟩

syn ANSWER, RESPONSE, REPLY, REJOINDER, RETORT mean something spoken, written, or done in return. ANSWER implies the satisfying of a question, demand, call, or need ⟨had *answers* to all their questions⟩. RESPONSE may imply a quick or spontaneous reaction to a person or thing that serves as a stimulus ⟨a *response* to the call for recruits⟩. REPLY often suggests a thorough response to all issues, points, or questions raised ⟨a point-by-point *reply* to the accusation⟩. REJOINDER can be a response to a reply or to an objection ⟨a salesman with a quick *rejoinder* to every argument⟩. RETORT implies a reaction to an implicit or explicit charge, criticism, or attack which contains a countercharge or counterattack ⟨she made a cutting *retort* to her critics⟩.

2**answer** *vb* **an·swered; an·swer·ing** \'an(t)s-riŋ, 'an(t)-sə-\ *vi* (bef. 12c) **1 :** to speak or write in reply **2 a :** to be or make oneself responsible or accountable ⟨~ for a debt⟩ **b :** to make amends **:** ATONE ⟨must ~ for his crimes⟩ **3 :** to be in conformity or correspondence ⟨~*ed* to the description⟩ **4 :** to act in response to an action performed elsewhere or by another ⟨the home team scored first but the visitors ~*ed* quickly⟩ **5 :** to be adequate **:** SERVE ⟨an old bucket ~*ed* for a sink⟩ ~ *vt* **1 a :** to speak or write in reply to ⟨~ a question⟩ ⟨~ me⟩ **b :** to say or write by way of reply ⟨~ yes or no⟩ **2 :** to reply to in rebuttal, justification, or explanation ⟨~ an accusation⟩ **3 a :** to correspond to ⟨~*s* the description⟩ **b :** to be adequate or usable for **:** FULFILL ⟨~ a need⟩ **4** *obs* **:** to atone for **5 :** to act in response to ⟨~*ed* the call to arms⟩ **6 :** to offer a solution for; *esp* **:** SOLVE ⟨~ a riddle⟩ — **an·swer·er** \'an(t)-sər-ər\ *n*

an·swer·able \'an(t)-s(ə-)rə-bəl\ *adj* (1536) **1** *archaic* **:** SUITABLE, ADEQUATE **2 :** liable to be called to account **:** RESPONSIBLE **3** *archaic* **:** CORRESPONDING, SIMILAR **4 :** capable of being refuted ***syn*** see RESPONSIBLE — **an·swer·abil·i·ty** \ˌan(t)-s(ə-)rə-'bi-lə-tē\ *n*

answering machine *n* (1924) **:** a machine that receives telephone calls by playing a recorded message and usu. by recording messages from callers

answering service *n* (1921) **:** a commercial service that answers telephone calls for its clients

1**ant** \'ant\ *n* [ME *ante, emete,* fr. OE *æmette;* akin to OHG *āmeiza* ant] (bef. 12c) **:** any of a family (Formicidae) of colonial hymenopterous insects with a complex social organization and various castes performing special duties — **ants in one's pants :** impatience for action or activity **:** RESTLESSNESS

2**ant** *abbr* **1** antenna **2** antonym

Ant *abbr* Antarctica

ant- — see ANTI-

1**-ant** *n suffix* [ME, fr. AF, fr. *-ant,* prp. suffix, fr. L *-ant-, -ans,* prp. suffix of first conjugation, fr. *-a-* (stem vowel of first conjugation) + *-nt-, -ns,* prp. suffix; akin to OE *-nde,* prp. suffix, Gk *-nt-, -n,* part. suffix] **1 a :** one that performs (a specified action) **:** personal or impersonal agent ⟨claim*ant*⟩ ⟨cool*ant*⟩ **b :** thing that promotes (a specified action or process) ⟨expector*ant*⟩ **2 :** one connected with ⟨annuit*ant*⟩ **3 :** thing acted upon (in a specified manner) ⟨inhal*ant*⟩

2**-ant** *adj suffix* **1 :** performing (a specified action) or being (in a specified condition) ⟨somnambul*ant*⟩ **2 :** promoting (a specified action or process) ⟨expector*ant*⟩

an·ta \'an-tə\ *n, pl* **antas** *or* **an·tae** \-ˌtē, -ˌtī\ [L; akin to ON *ǫnd* anteroom] (1598) **:** a pier produced by thickening a wall at its termination

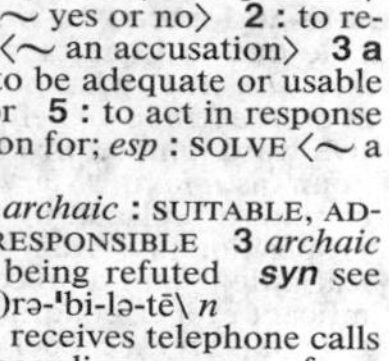

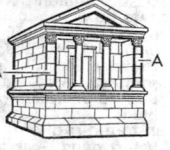

A anta

ant·ac·id \(ˌ)ant-'a-səd, 'ant-ˌa-\ *n* (1715) **:** an agent that counteracts or neutralizes acidity — **antacid** *adj*

An·tae·an \an-'tē-ən\ *adj* [*Antaeus,* a giant overcome by Hercules] (1782) **1 :** MAMMOTH **2 :** having superhuman strength

an·tag·o·nism \an-'ta-gə-ˌni-zəm\ *n* (1752) **1 :** opposition in physiological action; *esp* **:** interaction of two or more substances such that the action of any one of them on living cells or tissues is lessened **2 a :** opposition of a conflicting force, tendency, or principle ⟨the ~ of democracy to dictatorship⟩ **b :** actively expressed opposition or hostility ⟨~ between factions⟩ ***syn*** see ENMITY

an·tag·o·nist \-nist\ *n* (1575) **1 :** one that contends with or opposes another **:** ADVERSARY, OPPONENT **2 :** an agent of physiological antagonism: as **a :** a muscle that contracts with and limits the action of an agonist with which it is paired — called also *antagonistic muscle* **b :** a chemical that acts within the body to reduce the physiological activity of another chemical substance (as an opiate); *esp* **:** one that opposes the action on the nervous system of a drug or a substance occurring naturally in the body by combining with and blocking its nervous receptor — compare AGONIST 2b

an·tag·o·nis·tic \(ˌ)an-ˌta-gə-'nis-tik\ *adj* (1632) **:** marked by or resulting from antagonism — **an·tag·o·nis·ti·cal·ly** \-ti-k(ə-)lē\ *adv*

an·tag·o·nize \an-'ta-gə-ˌnīz\ *vt* **-nized; -niz·ing** [Gk *antagōnizesthai,* fr. *anti-* + *agōnizesthai* to struggle, fr. *agōn* contest — more at AGONY] (ca. 1742) **1 :** to act in opposition to **:** COUNTERACT **2 :** to incur or provoke the hostility of ⟨his criticism *antagonized* his friends⟩

\ə\ **abut** \ᵊ\ **kitten,** F **table** \ər\ **further** \a\ **ash** \ā\ **ace** \ä\ **mop, mar** \au̇\ **out** \ch\ **chin** \e\ **bet** \ē\ **easy** \g\ **go** \i\ **hit** \ī\ **ice** \j\ **job** \ŋ\ **sing** \ō\ **go** \ȯ\ **law** \ȯi\ **boy** \th\ **thin** \t͟h\ **the** \ü\ **loot** \u̇\ **foot** \y\ **yet** \zh\ **vision, beige** \k, ⁿ, œ, ue, ʸ\ *see* Guide to Pronunciation

ant·arc·tic \(ˌ)ant-ˈärk-tik, -ˈär-tik\ *adj, often cap* [ME *antartik,* fr. L *antarcticus,* fr. Gk *antarktikos,* fr. *anti-* + *arktikos* arctic] (14c) **:** of or relating to the south pole or to the region near it

antarctic circle *n, often cap A&C* (1556) **:** the parallel of latitude that is approximately 66½ degrees south of the equator and that circumscribes the southern frigid zone

An·tar·es \an-ˈter-(ˌ)ēz\ *n* [Gk *Antarēs*] (1842) **:** a giant red star of very low density that is the brightest star in Scorpio

ant·bear \ˈant-ˌber\ *n* (1796) **:** AARDVARK

ant cow *n* (1875) **:** an aphid from which ants obtain honeydew

¹an·te \ˈan-tē\ *n* [*ante-*] (1821) **1 :** a poker stake usu. put up before the deal to build the pot ⟨the dealer called for a dollar ~⟩ **2 a :** COST, PRICE ⟨these improvements would raise the ~⟩ **b :** RISK, STAKES ⟨the new law ups the ~ on tax cheats⟩ **c :** a level (as of achievement or intensity) regarded esp. as a goal or standard ⟨the film ups the ~ on special effects⟩

²ante *vb* **an·ted; an·te·ing** *vt* (1775) **:** to put up (an ante); *also* **:** PAY, PRODUCE — often used with *up* ~ *vi* **:** PAY UP — often used with *up*

ante- *prefix* [ME, fr. L, fr. *ante* before, in front of; akin to OE *and-* against, Gk *anti* before, against — more at END] **1 a :** prior **:** earlier ⟨*ante*date⟩ **b :** anterior **:** forward ⟨*ante*room⟩ **2 :** prior to **:** earlier than ⟨*ante*diluvian⟩

ant·eat·er \ˈant-ˌē-tər\ *n* (1764) **:** any of several mammals that feed largely or entirely on ants or termites: as **a :** any of a family (Myrmecophagidae) of New World edentates with a long narrow snout, a long tongue, and large salivary glands that includes the giant anteater and tamandua **b :** PANGOLIN **c :** ECHIDNA **d :** AARDVARK

an·te·bel·lum \ˌan-ti-ˈbe-ləm\ *adj* [L *ante bellum* before the war] (ca. 1847) **:** existing before a war; *esp* **:** existing before the American Civil War

an·te·cede \ˌan-tə-ˈsēd\ *vt* **-ced·ed; -ced·ing** [L *antecedere*] (1624) **:** PRECEDE

an·te·ced·ence \-ˈsē-dᵊn(t)s\ *n* (1599) **:** PRIORITY, PRECEDENCE

¹an·te·ced·ent \ˌan-tə-ˈsē-dᵊnt\ *n* [ME, fr. ML & L; ML *antecedent-, antecedens,* fr. L, what precedes, fr. neut. of *antecedent-, antecedens,* prp. of *antecedere* to go before, fr. *ante-* + *cedere* to go] (14c) **1 :** a substantive word, phrase, or clause whose denotation is referred to by a pronoun (as *John* in "Mary saw John and called to him"); *broadly* **:** a word or phrase replaced by a substitute **2 :** the conditional element in a proposition (as *if A* in "if A, then B") **3 :** the first term of a mathematical ratio **4 a :** a preceding event, condition, or cause **b** *pl* **:** the significant events, conditions, and traits of one's earlier life **5 a :** PREDECESSOR; *esp* **:** a model or stimulus for later developments **b** *pl* **:** ANCESTORS, PARENTS

²antecedent *adj* (14c) **:** PRIOR ***syn*** see PRECEDING — **an·te·ced·ent·ly** *adv*

an·te·ces·sor \ˌan-ti-ˈse-sər\ *n* [ME *antecessour,* fr. L *antecessor* — more at ANCESTOR] (14c) **:** one that goes before **:** PREDECESSOR

an·te·cham·ber \ˈan-ti-ˌchām-bər\ *n* [F *antichambre,* fr. MF, fr. It *anti-* (fr. L *ante-*) + MF *chambre* room] (1655) **:** ANTEROOM

an·te·chap·el \-ˌcha-pəl\ *n* (1703) **:** a vestibule or anteroom to a chapel or church

¹an·te·date \ˈan-ti-ˌdāt\ *n* (15c) **:** a date assigned to an event or document earlier than the actual date of the event or document

²an·te·date \ˈan-ti-ˌdāt, ˌan-ti-ˈ\ *vt* (1572) **1 a :** to date as of a time prior to that of execution **b :** to assign to a date prior to that of actual occurrence **2** *archaic* **:** ANTICIPATE **3 :** to precede in time

an·te·di·lu·vi·an \ˌan-ti-də-ˈlü-vē-ən, -(ˌ)dī-\ *adj* [*ante-* + L *diluvium* flood — more at DELUGE] (1646) **1 :** of or relating to the period before the flood described in the Bible **2 a :** made, evolved, or developed a long time ago ⟨an ~ automobile⟩ **b :** extremely primitive or outmoded ⟨an ~ prejudice⟩ — **antediluvian** *n*

an·te·fix \ˈan-ti-ˌfiks\ *n, pl* **-fix·ae** \-ˌfik-ˌsē\ *or* **-fix·es** \-ˌfik-səz\ [L *antefixum,* fr. neut. of *antefixus,* pp. of *antefigere* to fasten before, fr. *ante-* + *figere* to fasten — more at FIX] (1832) **:** an ornament at the eaves of a classical building concealing the ends of the joint tiles of the roof

an·te·lope \ˈan-tə-ˌlōp\ *n, pl* **-lope** *or* **-lopes** [ME, fabulous heraldic beast, prob. fr. MF *antelop* savage animal with sawlike horns, fr. ML *anthalopus,* fr. LGk *antholop-, antholops*] (15c) **1 a :** any of various ruminant deerlike mammals (family Bovidae) chiefly of Africa and southwest Asia that have a slender lean build and usu. horns directed upward and backward **b :** PRONGHORN **2 :** leather from antelope hide

an·te me·ri·di·em \ˌan-ti-mə-ˈri-dē-əm, -dē-ˌem\ *adj* [L] (1563) **:** being before noon — abbr. *a.m.*

an·te·mor·tem \-ˈmȯr-təm\ *adj* [L *ante mortem*] (1862) **:** preceding death

an·te·na·tal \-ˈnā-tᵊl\ *adj* (1806) **:** PRENATAL ⟨~ diagnosis of birth defects⟩ — **an·te·na·tal·ly** \-ē\ *adv*

an·ten·na \an-ˈte-nə\ *n, pl* **-nae** \-(ˌ)nē\ *or* **-nas** [ML, fr. L, sail yard] (1646) **1** *pl* **-nae :** one of a pair of slender movable segmented sensory organs on the head of insects, myriapods, and crustaceans — see INSECT illustration **2 :** a usu. metallic device (as a rod or wire) for radiating or receiving radio waves **3** *antennae pl* **:** a special sensitivity or receptiveness ⟨his political *antennae* proved to be shrewder than ever —Erich Segal⟩ — **an·ten·nal** \-ˈte-nᵊl\ *adj*

an·ten·nule \an-ˈten-(ˌ)yül\ *n* (1843) **:** a small antenna or similar appendage — **an·ten·nu·lar** \-ˈten-yə-lər\ *adj*

an·te·nup·tial \ˌan-ti-ˈnəp-shəl, -chəl; ÷-shə-wəl, ÷-chə-\ *adj* (1696) **:** PRENUPTIAL

an·te·pen·di·um \ˌan-ti-ˈpen-dē-əm\ *n, pl* **-di·ums** *or* **-dia** \-dē-ə\ [ML, fr. L *ante-* + *pendēre* to hang — more at PENDANT] (1635) **:** a hanging for the front of an altar, pulpit, or lectern

an·te·pe·nult \ˌan-ti-ˈpē-ˌnəlt, -pi-ˈ\ *also* **an·te·pen·ul·ti·ma** \-pi-ˈnəl-tə-mə\ *n* [LL *antepaenultima,* fem. of *antepaenultimus* preceding the next to last, fr. L *ante-* + *paenultimus* penultimate] (1552) **:** the third syllable of a word counting from the end (as *cu* in *accumulate*) — **an·te·pen·ul·ti·mate** \-pi-ˈnəl-tə-mət\ *adj or n*

an·te–post \ˈan-ti-ˌpōst\ *adj* (1902) *Brit* **:** relating to or being wagers on a horse race made esp. before the day of the race

an·te·ri·or \an-ˈtir-ē-ər\ *adj* [L, compar. of *ante* before — more at ANTE-] (1541) **1 a :** situated before or toward the front **b :** situated near or toward the head or part most nearly corresponding to a head **2 :** coming before in time or development ***syn*** see PRECEDING — **an·te·ri·or·ly** *adv*

anterior cruciate ligament *n* (1974) **:** a cruciate ligament of each knee that attaches the front of the tibia with the back of the femur and functions esp. to prevent hyperextension of the knee and is subject to injury esp. by tearing — called also *ACL*

an·ter·o·grade \ˈan-tə-(ˌ)rō-ˌgrād\ *adj* [NL *antero-* from front to (fr. L *anterior*) + E *-grade*] (1923) **1 :** occurring or performed in the normal or forward direction of conduction or flow ⟨~ axonal transport⟩ **2 :** affecting memories of a period immediately following a shock or seizure ⟨~ amnesia⟩

an·te·room \ˈan-ti-ˌrüm, -ˌrům\ *n* (1762) **:** an outer room that leads to another room and that is often used as a waiting room

anth- — see ANTI-

an·thel·min·tic \ˌant-ˌhel-ˈmin-tik, ˌan-ˌthel-\ *adj* [*anti-* + Gk *helminth-, helmis* worm] (1684) **:** expelling or destroying parasitic worms esp. of the intestine — **anthelmintic** *n*

an·them \ˈan(t)-thəm\ *n* [ME *antem,* fr. OE *antefn,* fr. LL *antiphona,* fr. LGk *antiphōna,* pl. of *antiphōnon,* fr. Gk, neut. of *antiphōnos* responsive, fr. *anti-* + *phōnē* sound — more at BAN] (bef. 12c) **1 a :** a psalm or hymn sung antiphonally or responsively **b :** a sacred vocal composition with words usu. from the Scriptures **2 :** a song or hymn of praise or gladness **3 :** a usu. rousing popular song that typifies or is identified with a particular subculture, movement, or point of view ⟨~*s* of teenage angst⟩ — **an·the·mic** \ˌan(t)-ˈthē-mik, -ˈthe-\ *adj*

an·the·mi·on \an-ˈthē-mē-ən\ *n, pl* **-mia** \-mē-ə\ [Gk, fr. dim. of *anthemon* flower, fr. *anthos* — more at ANTHOLOGY] (1865) **:** a flat ornament of floral form (as in relief sculpture or in painting)

an·ther \ˈan(t)-thər\ *n* [NL *anthera,* fr. L, medicine made fr. flowers, fr. Gk *anthēra,* fr. fem. of *anthēros* flowery, fr. *anthos*] (ca. 1706) **:** the part of a stamen that produces and contains pollen and is usu. borne on a stalk — see FLOWER illustration — **an·ther·al** \-thə-rəl\ *adj*

an·ther·id·i·um \ˌan(t)-thə-ˈri-dē-əm\ *n, pl* **-id·ia** \-dē-ə\ [NL, fr. *anthera*] (1839) **:** the male reproductive organ of some cryptogamous plants — **an·ther·id·i·al** \-dē-əl\ *adj*

an·the·sis \an-ˈthē-səs\ *n* [NL, fr. Gk *anthēsis* bloom, fr. *anthein* to flower, fr. *anthos*] (ca. 1823) **:** the action or period of opening of a flower

ant·hill \ˈant-ˌhil\ *n* (14c) **:** a mound of debris thrown up by ants or termites in digging their nest

an·tho·cy·a·nin \ˌan(t)-thə-ˈsī-ə-nən\ *n* [Gk *anthos* + *kyanos* dark blue] (1839) **:** any of various soluble glycoside pigments producing blue to red coloring in flowers and plants

an·thol·o·gist \an-ˈthä-lə-jist\ *n* (1805) **:** a compiler of an anthology

an·thol·o·gize \-ˌjīz\ *vt* **-gized; -giz·ing** (1892) **:** to compile, publish, or include in an anthology — **an·thol·o·giz·er** \-ˌjī-zər\ *n*

an·thol·o·gy \an-ˈthä-lə-jē\ *n, pl* **-gies** [NL *anthologia* collection of epigrams, fr. MGk, fr. Gk, flower gathering, fr. *anthos* flower + *logia* collecting, fr. *legein* to gather; akin to Skt *andha* herb — more at LEGEND] (1621) **1 :** a collection of selected literary pieces or passages or works of art or music **2 :** ASSORTMENT ⟨an ~ of threadbare clichés of . . . bistro cuisine —Jay Jacobs⟩ — **an·tho·log·i·cal** \ˌan(t)-thə-ˈlä-ji-kəl\ *adj*

an·thoph·i·lous \an-ˈthä-fə-ləs\ *adj* [ISV, fr. Gk *anthos* + E *-philous*] (1883) **:** feeding upon or living among flowers ⟨~ insects⟩

an·tho·phyl·lite \ˌan(t)-thə-ˈfi-ˌlīt, (ˌ)an-ˈthä-fə-\ *n* [G *Anthophyllit,* fr. NL *anthophyllum,* fr. Gk *anthos* + *phyllon* leaf — more at BLADE] (ca. 1828) **:** an orthorhombic mineral of the amphibole group that is essentially a silicate of magnesium and iron and is usu. lamellar or fibrous and when fibrous is one of the less common forms of asbestos

an·tho·zo·an \ˌan(t)-thə-ˈzō-ən\ *n* [ultim. fr. Gk *anthos* + *zōion* animal; akin to Gk *zōē* life — more at QUICK] (1877) **:** any of a class (Anthozoa) of marine coelenterates (as the corals and sea anemones) having polyps with radial partitions — **anthozoan** *adj*

an·thra·cene \ˈan(t)-thrə-ˌsēn\ *n* (1863) **:** a crystalline tricyclic aromatic hydrocarbon $C_{14}H_{10}$ obtained from coal-tar distillation

an·thra·cite \ˈan(t)-thrə-ˌsīt\ *n* [Gk *anthrakitis,* fr. *anthrak-, anthrax* coal] (1811) **:** a hard natural coal of high luster differing from bituminous coal in containing little volatile matter and in burning very cleanly — called also *hard coal* — **an·thra·cit·ic** \ˌan(t)-thrə-ˈsi-tik\ *adj*

an·thrac·nose \an-ˈthrak-ˌnōs\ *n* [F, fr. Gk *anthrak-, anthrax* + *nosos* disease] (1886) **:** any of numerous destructive plant diseases caused by imperfect fungi and characterized esp. by necrotic lesions

an·thra·ni·late \an-ˈthra-nə-ˌlāt, ˌan-thrə-ˈni-ˌlāt\ *n* (1845) **:** a salt or ester of anthranilic acid

an·thra·nil·ic acid \ˌan(t)-thrə-ˈni-lik-\ *n* [ISV *anthra*cene + *anil*ine] (1845) **:** a crystalline acid $NH_2C_6H_4COOH$ used as an intermediate in the manufacture of dyes (as indigo), pharmaceuticals, and perfumes

an·thra·qui·none \ˌan(t)-thrə-kwi-ˈnōn, -ˈkwi-ˌnōn\ *n* [prob. fr. F, fr. *anthra*cene + *quinone*] (1869) **:** a yellow crystalline ketone $C_{14}H_8O_2$ often derived from anthracene and used esp. in the manufacture of dyes

an·thrax \ˈan-ˌthraks\ *n* [ME *antrax* carbuncle, fr. L *anthrax,* fr. Gk, coal, carbuncle] (1861) **:** an infectious disease of warm-blooded animals (as cattle and sheep) caused by a spore-forming bacterium (*Bacillus anthracis*), transmissible to humans esp. by the handling of infected products (as wool), and characterized by cutaneous ulcerating nodules or by often fatal lesions in the lungs; *also* **:** the bacterium causing anthrax

anthrop *abbr* anthropological; anthropology

anthrop- *or* **anthropo-** *comb form* [L *anthropo-,* fr. Gk *anthrōp-, anthrōpo-,* fr. *anthrōpos*] **:** human being ⟨*anthropo*genic⟩

an·throp·ic \an-ˈthrä-pik\ *or* **an·throp·i·cal** \-pi-kəl\ *adj* [Gk *anthrōpikos,* fr. *anthrōpos*] (ca. 1806) **:** of or relating to human beings or the period of their existence on earth

anthropic principle *n* (1974) **:** either of two principles in cosmology: **a :** conditions that are observed in the universe must allow the observer to exist — called also *weak anthropic principle* **b :** the universe must have properties that make inevitable the existence of intelligent life — called also *strong anthropic principle*

an·thro·po·cen·tric \ˌan(t)-thrə-pə-ˈsen-trik\ *adj* (1863) **1 :** considering human beings as the most significant entity of the universe **2 :** interpreting or regarding the world in terms of human values and experi-

ences — **an·thro·po·cen·tri·cal·ly** \-tri-k(ə-)lē\ *adv* — **an·thro·po·cen·tric·i·ty** \-pō-(ˌ)sen-ˈtri-sə-tē\ *n* — **an·thro·po·cen·trism** \-ˈsen-ˌtri-zəm\ *n*
an·thro·po·gen·ic \-pə-ˈje-nik\ *adj* (1923) : of, relating to, or resulting from the influence of human beings on nature ⟨~ pollutants⟩ — **an·thro·po·gen·ic·al·ly** \-ni-k(ə-)lē\ *adv*
an·thro·poid \ˈan(t)-thrə-ˌpóid\ *n* [Gk *anthrōpoeidēs* resembling a human, fr. *anthrōpos*] (1832) **1** : any of a suborder (Anthropoidea) of higher primates (as macaques and marmosets); *esp* : APE 1b **2** : a person resembling an ape ⟨the howling ~s of the Hookworm Belt —H. L. Mencken⟩ — **anthropoid** *adj*
anthropoid ape *n* (ca. 1837) : APE 1b
an·thro·pol·o·gy \ˌan(t)-thrə-ˈpä-lə-jē\ *n* [NL *anthropologia*, fr. *anthrōp-* + *-logia* -logy] (1593) **1** : the science of human beings; *esp* : the study of human beings and their ancestors through time and space and in relation to physical character, environmental and social relations, and culture **2** : theology dealing with the origin, nature, and destiny of human beings — **an·thro·po·log·i·cal** \-pə-ˈlä-ji-kəl\ *adj* — **an·thro·po·log·i·cal·ly** \-ji-k(ə-)lē\ *adv* — **an·thro·pol·o·gist** \ˌan(t)-thrə-ˈpä-lə-jist\ *n*
an·thro·pom·e·try \ˌan(t)-thrə-ˈpä-mə-trē\ *n* [F *anthropométrie*, fr. *anthrop-* + *-métrie* -metry] (ca. 1839) : the study of human body measurements esp. on a comparative basis — **an·thro·po·met·ric** \-pə-ˈme-trik\ *adj*
an·thro·po·morph \ˈan(t)-thrə-pə-ˌmórf\ *n* (1894) : a stylized human figure (as in prehistoric art)
an·thro·po·mor·phic \ˌan(t)-thrə-pə-ˈmór-fik\ *adj* [LL *anthropomorphus* of human form, fr. Gk *anthrōpomorphos*, fr. *anthrōp-* + *-morphos* -morphous] (1827) **1** : described or thought of as having a human form or human attributes ⟨~ deities⟩ **2** : ascribing human characteristics to nonhuman things ⟨~ supernaturalism⟩ — **an·thro·po·mor·phi·cal·ly** \-fi-k(ə-)lē\ *adv*
an·thro·po·mor·phism \-ˌfi-zəm\ *n* (1753) : an interpretation of what is not human or personal in terms of human or personal characteristics : HUMANIZATION — **an·thro·po·mor·phist** \-fist\ *n*
an·thro·po·mor·phize \-ˌfīz\ *vb* **-phized; -phiz·ing** *vt* (1845) : to attribute human form or personality to ~ *vi* : to attribute human form or personality to things not human — **an·thro·po·mor·phi·za·tion** \-ˌmòr-fə-ˈzā-shən\ *n*
an·thro·po·pa·thism \ˌan(t)-thrə-ˈpä-pə-ˌthi-zəm, -pō-ˈpa-ˌthi-\ *n* [LGk *anthrōpopatheia* humanity, fr. Gk *anthrōpopathēs* having human feelings, fr. *anthrōp-* + *pathos* experience — more at PATHOS] (1847) : the ascription of human feelings to something not human
an·thro·poph·a·gous \ˌan(t)-thrə-ˈpä-fə-gəs\ *adj* (ca. 1828) : feeding on human flesh — **an·thro·poph·a·gy** \-fə-jē\ *n*
an·thro·poph·a·gus \-fə-gəs\ *n, pl* **-a·gi** \-fə-ˌgī, -ˌjī, -ˌgē\ [L, fr. Gk *anthrōpophagos*, fr. *anthrōp-* + *-phagos* -phagous] (1552) : MAN-EATER, CANNIBAL
an·thro·pos·o·phy \ˌan(t)-thrə-ˈpä-sə-fē\ *n* (1916) : a 20th century religious system growing out of theosophy and centering on human development — **an·thro·pos·o·phist** \-sə-fist\ *n*
an·thu·ri·um \an-ˈthür-ē-əm, -ˈthyür-\ *n* [NL, fr. Gk *anthos* flower + *oura* tail — more at ANTHOLOGY, ASS] (ca. 1839) : any of a genus (*Anthurium*) of tropical American plants of the arum family with large often brightly colored leaves, a cylindrical spadix, and a colored spathe
¹an·ti \ˈan-ˌtī, ˈan-tē\ *also* **an·ti** *before consonants\ or* **ant-** *or* **anth-** *prefix* [anti- fr. ME, fr. AF & L; AF, fr. L, against, fr. Gk, fr. *anti; ant-* fr. ME, fr. L, against, fr. Gk, fr. *anti; anth-* fr. L, against, fr. Gk, fr. *anti* — more at ANTE-] **1 a** : of the same kind but situated opposite, exerting energy in the opposite direction, or pursuing an opposite policy ⟨*anti*clinal⟩ **b** : one that is opposite in kind to ⟨*anti*climax⟩ **2 a** : opposing or hostile to in opinion, sympathy, or practice ⟨*anti*-Semite⟩ **b** : opposing in effect or activity ⟨*ant*acid⟩ **3** : serving to prevent, cure, or alleviate ⟨*anti*anxiety⟩ **4** : combating or defending against ⟨*anti*aircraft⟩ ⟨*anti*missile⟩
²anti *adj* (1857) : OPPOSED
³anti *prep* (1953) : opposed to : AGAINST

an·ti·ac·a·dem·ic
an·ti·ac·ne
an·ti·ad·min·is·tra·tion
an·ti·ag·gres·sion
an·ti·ag·ing
an·ti–AIDS
an·ti·al·co·hol
an·ti·al·co·hol·ism
an·ti·alien
an·ti·al·ler·gen·ic
an·ti·al·ler·gy
an·ti·ane·mia
an·ti·apart·heid
an·ti·aph·ro·di·si·ac
an·ti–Ar·ab
an·ti·aris·to·crat·ic
an·ti·ar·mor
an·ti·ar·thrit·ic
an·ti·ar·thri·tis
an·ti–Asian
an·ti·as·sim·i·la·tion
an·ti·asth·ma
an·ti·au·thor·i·tar·i·an
an·ti·au·thor·i·tar·i·an·ism
an·ti·au·thor·i·ty
an·ti·aux·in
an·ti·back·lash
an·ti·bac·te·ri·al
an·ti·bi·as
an·ti·bill·board
an·ti–Bol·she·vik
an·ti·boss
an·ti·bour·geois
an·ti·boy·cott

an·ti–Brit·ish
an·ti·bug
an·ti·bu·reau·crat·ic
an·ti·bur·glar
an·ti·bur·glary
an·ti·cak·ing
an·ti·cap·i·tal·ism
an·ti·cap·i·tal·ist
an·ti·car·cin·o·gen
an·ti·car·ci·no·gen·ic
an·ti·car·ies
an·ti–Cath·o·lic
an·ti–Cath·ol·i·cism
an·ti·cel·lu·lite
an·ti·cen·sor·ship
an·ti·cho·les·ter·ol
an·ti–Chris·tian
an·ti–Chris·tian·i·ty
an·ti·church
an·ti·cig·a·rette
an·ti·city
an·ti·clas·si·cal
an·ti·cling
an·ti·clot·ting
an·ti·cold
an·ti·col·li·sion
an·ti·co·lo·nial
an·ti·co·lo·nial·ism
an·ti·co·lo·nial·ist
an·ti·com·mer·cial
an·ti·com·mer·cial·ism
an·ti·com·mu·nism
an·ti·com·mu·nist
an·ti·con·glom·er·ate
an·ti·con·ser·va·tion

an·ti·con·ser·va·tion·ist
an·ti·con·sum·er
an·ti·con·ven·tion·al
an·ti·cor·po·rate
an·ti·cor·ro·sion
an·ti·cor·ro·sive
an·ti·cor·rup·tion
an·ti·coun·ter·feit·ing
an·ti·crack
an·ti·cre·ative
an·ti·crime
an·ti·cru·el·ty
an·ti·cult
an·ti·cul·tur·al
an·ti·dan·druff
an·ti–Dar·win·i·an
an·ti–Dar·win·ism
an·ti·def·a·ma·tion
an·ti·de·pres·sion
an·ti·de·seg·re·ga·tion
an·ti·de·sert·i·fi·ca·tion
an·ti·des·ic·cant
an·ti·de·vel·op·ment
an·ti·di·a·bet·ic
an·ti·di·ar·rhe·al
an·ti·di·lu·tion
an·ti·dis·crim·i·na·tion
an·ti·dog·mat·ic
an·ti·draft
an·ti·eco·nom·ic
an·ti·ed·u·ca·tion·al
an·ti·egal·i·tar·i·an
an·ti·elite
an·ti·elit·ism

an·ti·elit·ist
an·ti·emet·ic
an·ti–En·glish
an·ti·en·tro·pic
an·ti·en·vi·ron·men·tal
an·ti·ep·i·lep·sy
an·ti·ep·i·lep·tic
an·ti·erot·ic
an·ti·es·sen·tial·ist
an·ti·es·tab·lish·ment
an·ti·es·tro·gen
an·ti·evo·lu·tion
an·ti·evo·lu·tion·ary
an·ti·evo·lu·tion·ism
an·ti·evo·lu·tion·ist
an·ti·fam·i·ly
an·ti·fas·cism
an·ti·fas·cist
an·ti·fash·ion
an·ti·fash·ion·able
an·ti·fa·tigue
an·ti·fe·male
an·ti·fem·i·nine
an·ti·fem·i·nism
an·ti·fem·i·nist
an·ti·fil·i·bus·ter
an·ti·flu
an·ti·foam
an·ti·foam·ing
an·ti·fog·ging
an·ti·for·eign
an·ti·for·eign·er
an·ti·for·mal·ist
an·ti·fraud
an·ti–French
an·ti·fric·tion
an·ti·fur
an·ti·gam·bling
an·ti·gang
an·ti·gay
an·ti–Ger·man
an·ti·glare
an·ti·glob·al·iza·tion
an·ti·gov·ern·ment
an·ti·growth
an·ti·guer·ril·la
an·ti·gun
an·ti·ha·rass·ment
an·ti·her·pes
an·ti·hi·er·ar·chi·cal
an·ti·hi·jack·ing
an·ti·his·tor·i·cal
an·ti–HIV
an·ti·ho·mo·sex·u·al
an·ti·hu·man·ism
an·ti·hu·man·ist
an·ti·hu·man·i·tar·i·an
an·ti·hun·ger
an·ti·hunt·er
an·ti·hunt·ing
an·ti·hys·ter·ic
an·ti·ic·ing
an·ti·ideo·log·i·cal
an·ti·im·mi·grant
an·ti·im·mi·gra·tion
an·ti·im·pe·ri·al·ism
an·ti·im·pe·ri·al·ist
an·ti·in·cum·bent
an·ti·in·fec·tive
an·ti·in·flam·ma·tion
an·ti·in·fla·tion
an·ti·in·fla·tion·ary
an·ti·in·sti·tu·tion·al
an·ti·in·te·gra·tion
an·ti·in·tru·sion
an·ti–Irish
an·ti–Ital·ian
an·ti·jam
an·ti·jam·ming
an·ti–Jap·a·nese
an·ti–Jew·ish
an·ti–Ju·da·ism
an·ti·kick·back
an·ti·knock
an·ti·la·bor
an·ti·lep·ro·sy
an·ti·lib·er·al
an·ti·lib·er·al·ism
an·ti·lib·er·tar·i·an
an·ti·lit·er·ary
an·ti·lit·er·ate
an·ti·lit·ter
an·ti·lit·ter·ing
an·ti·log·i·cal
an·ti·lynch·ing

an·ti·ma·cho
an·ti·ma·lar·ia
an·ti·male
an·ti·man
an·ti·man·age·ment
an·ti·mar·i·jua·na
an·ti·mar·ket
an·ti·ma·te·ri·al·ism
an·ti·ma·te·ri·al·ist
an·ti·mech·a·nist
an·ti·merg·er
an·ti·met·a·bol·ic
an·ti·meta·phys·i·cal
an·ti·mil·i·ta·rism
an·ti·mil·i·ta·rist
an·ti·mil·i·ta·ris·tic
an·ti·mil·i·tary
an·ti·mine
an·ti·mis·ce·ge·na·tion
an·ti·mis·sile
an·ti·mod·ern
an·ti·mod·ern·ism
an·ti·mod·ern·ist
an·ti·mo·nar·chi·cal
an·ti·mo·nop·o·list
an·ti·mo·nop·o·ly
an·ti·mos·qui·to
an·ti·mu·si·cal
an·ti·nar·cot·ics
an·ti·nar·ra·tive
an·ti·na·tion·al
an·ti·na·tion·al·ist
an·ti·nat·u·ral
an·ti·na·ture
an·ti·nau·sea
an·ti–Na·zi
an·ti–Ne·gro
an·ti·nep·o·tism
an·ti·noise
an·ti·obe·si·ty
an·ti·ob·scen·i·ty
an·ti·or·ga·ni·za·tion
an·ti·pa·pal
an·ti·par·a·sit·ic
an·ti·par·ty
an·ti·pes·ti·cide
an·ti·pi·ra·cy
an·ti·plague
an·ti·plaque
an·ti·plate·let
an·ti·plea·sure
an·ti·poach·ing
an·ti·po·lice
an·ti·po·lit·i·cal
an·ti·pol·i·tics
an·ti·pop·u·lar
an·ti·porn
an·ti·por·no·graph·ic
an·ti·por·nog·ra·phy
an·ti·pot
an·ti·pov·er·ty
an·ti·pred·a·tor
an·ti·press
an·ti·prof·i·teer·ing
an·ti·pro·gres·sive
an·ti·pros·ti·tu·tion
an·ti·pru·rit·ic
an·ti·ra·bies
an·ti·ra·chit·ic
an·ti·rac·ism
an·ti·rac·ist
an·ti·rack·e·teer·ing
an·ti·ra·dar
an·ti·rad·i·cal
an·ti·rad·i·cal·ism
an·ti·rape
an·ti·ra·tio·nal
an·ti·ra·tio·nal·ism
an·ti·ra·tio·nal·ist
an·ti·ra·tio·nal·i·ty
an·ti·re·al·ism
an·ti·re·al·ist
an·ti·re·ces·sion
an·ti·re·ces·sion·ary
an·ti·red
an·ti·re·duc·tion·ism
an·ti·re·duc·tion·ist
an·ti·re·flec·tion
an·ti·re·flec·tive
an·ti·re·form
an·ti·reg·u·la·to·ry
an·ti·re·li·gion
an·ti·re·li·gious
an·ti·re·pub·li·can
an·ti·rev·o·lu·tion·ary
an·ti·ri·ot

an·ti·rit·u·al·ism
an·ti·rock
an·ti·roll
an·ti·ro·man·tic
an·ti–ro·man·ti·cism
an·ti·roy·al·ist
an·ti–Rus·sian
an·ti·rust
an·ti·sat·el·lite
an·ti·schizo·phre·nia
an·ti·schiz·o·phren·ic
an·ti·sci·ence
an·ti·sci·en·tif·ic
an·ti·se·cre·cy
an·ti·seg·re·ga·tion
an·ti·sei·zure
an·ti·sen·ti·men·tal
an·ti·sep·a·rat·ist
an·ti·sex
an·ti·sex·ist
an·ti·sex·u·al
an·ti·sex·u·al·i·ty
an·ti·shark
an·ti·ship
an·ti·shock
an·ti·shop·lift·ing
an·ti·skid
an·ti·slav·ery
an·ti·sleep
an·ti·slip
an·ti·smog
an·ti·smoke
an·ti·smok·er
an·ti·smok·ing
an·ti·smug·gling
an·ti·smut
an·ti·snob
an·ti·so·cial·ist
an·ti·sod·omy
an·ti–So·vi·et
an·ti–So·vi·et·ism
an·ti·spam
an·ti·spec·u·la·tion
an·ti·spec·u·la·tive
an·ti·spend·ing
an·ti–Sta·lin·ist
an·ti·state
an·ti·stat·ist
an·ti·stick
an·ti·stress
an·ti·strike
an·ti·stu·dent
an·ti·sub·ma·rine
an·ti·sub·si·dy
an·ti·sub·ver·sion
an·ti·sub·ver·sive
an·ti·sui·cide
an·ti·syph·i·lit·ic
an·ti·take·over
an·ti·tank
an·ti·tar·nish
an·ti·tax
an·ti·tech·no·log·i·cal
an·ti·tech·nol·o·gy
an·ti·ter·ror·ism
an·ti·ter·ror·ist
an·ti·theft
an·ti·the·o·ret·i·cal
an·ti·to·bac·co
an·ti·to·tal·i·tar·i·an
an·ti·tra·di·tion·al
an·ti·tu·ber·cu·lar
an·ti·tu·ber·cu·lo·sis
an·ti·tu·ber·cu·lous
an·ti·tu·mor
an·ti·tu·mor·al
an·ti·ty·phoid
an·ti·ul·cer
an·ti·un·em·ploy·ment
an·ti·union
an·ti·uni·ver·si·ty
an·ti·ur·ban
an·ti·vi·o·lence
an·ti·vi·ral
an·ti·vi·rus
an·ti·vivi·sec·tion
an·ti·vivi·sec·tion·ist
an·ti·war
an·ti·wear
an·ti·wel·fare
an·ti–West
an·ti–West·ern
an·ti·whal·ing
an·ti·wom·an
an·ti·wrin·kle
an·ti–Zi·on·ism
an·ti–Zi·on·ist

an·ti·abor·tion \ˌan-tē-ə-ˈbȯr-shən, ˌan-ˌtī-\ *adj* (1866) **:** opposed to abortion and esp. to the legalization of abortion ⟨~ lobbyists⟩ — **an·ti·abor·tion·ist** \-sh(ə-)nist\ *n*

an·ti·air \ˌan-tē-ˈer, -ˌtī-\ *adj* (1915) **:** ANTIAIRCRAFT

[1]**an·ti·air·craft** \-ˈer-ˌkraft\ *adj* (1913) **:** designed for or concerned with defense against air attack

[2]**antiaircraft** *n* (1926) **:** antiaircraft guns or their fire

an·ti·ali·as·ing \-ˈā-lē-ə-siŋ, -ˈāl-yə-\ *n* [*alias* (spurious frequency generated during digital processing of a signal)] (1981) **:** a procedure in computer graphics for smoothing lines and removing visual distortions

an·ti–Amer·i·can \-ə-ˈmer-ə-kən, -ˈmər-, -ˈme-rə-\ *adj* (1765) **:** opposed or hostile to the people or the government policies of the U.S. — **an·ti–Amer·i·can·ism** \-kə-ˌni-zəm\ *n*

an·ti·anx·i·ety \-(ˌ)aŋ-ˈzī-ə-tē\ *adj* (1962) **:** tending to prevent or relieve anxiety ⟨~ drugs⟩

an·ti·ar·rhyth·mic \ˌan-tē-(ˌ)ā-ˈrith-mik, ˌan-ˌtī-\ *adj* (1954) **:** tending to prevent or relieve cardiac arrhythmia ⟨an ~ agent⟩

an·ti–art \-ˈärt\ *n* (1937) **:** art based on premises antithetical to traditional or popular art forms; *specif* **:** DADA

an·ti·bal·lis·tic missile \ˌan-tē-bə-ˈlis-tik-, ˌan-ˌtī-\ *n* (ca. 1957) **:** a missile for intercepting and destroying ballistic missiles

an·ti·bi·o·sis \-bī-ˈō-səs, -bē-\ *n* [NL] (1889) **:** antagonistic association between organisms to the detriment of one of them or between one organism and a metabolic product of another

[1]**an·ti·bi·ot·ic** \ˌan-tē-bī-ˈä-tik, -ˌtī-; -bē-ˈä-\ *adj* (1891) **1 :** tending to prevent, inhibit, or destroy life **2 :** of or relating to antibiotics or to antibiosis — **an·ti·bi·ot·i·cal·ly** \-ti-k(ə-)lē\ *adv*

[2]**antibiotic** *n* (1943) **:** a substance produced by or a semisynthetic substance derived from a microorganism and able in dilute solution to inhibit or kill another microorganism

an·ti·black \-ˈblak\ *adj* (1836) **:** opposed or hostile to black people

an·ti·body \ˈan-ti-ˌbä-dē\ *n* (1894) **:** any of a large number of proteins of high molecular weight that are produced normally by specialized B cells after stimulation by an antigen and act specifically against the antigen in an immune response, that are produced abnormally by some cancer cells, and that typically consist of four subunits including two heavy chains and two light chains — called also *immunoglobulin*

an·ti·bond·ing \ˌan-tē-ˈbän-diŋ\ *adj* (1936) **:** tending to inhibit bonding between atoms ⟨~ orbitals⟩ ⟨an ~ electron⟩

an·ti·busi·ness \ˌan-tē-ˈbiz-nəs, ˌan-ˌtī-, -nəz\ *adj* (1858) **:** antagonistic toward business and esp. big business

an·ti·bus·ing \-ˈbə-siŋ\ *adj* (1964) **:** opposed to the busing of schoolchildren ⟨~ parents⟩ ⟨~ campaign⟩

[1]**an·tic** \ˈan-tik\ *n* [It *antico* ancient thing or person, fr. *antico* ancient, fr. L *antiquus* — more at ANTIQUE] (1529) **1 :** an attention-drawing often wildly playful or funny act or action **:** CAPER ⟨childish ~*s*⟩ **2** *archaic* **:** a performer of a grotesque or ludicrous part **:** BUFFOON

[2]**antic** *adj* (1548) **1** *archaic* **:** GROTESQUE, BIZARRE **2 a :** characterized by clownish extravagance or absurdity **b :** whimsically gay **:** FROLICSOME — **an·ti·cal·ly** \-ti-k(ə-)lē\ *adv*

an·ti·can·cer \ˌan-ˌtī-ˈkan(t)-sər, ˌan-tē-\ *adj* (1847) **:** used against or tending to arrest or prevent cancer ⟨~ drugs⟩ ⟨~ activity⟩ ⟨~ effects⟩

an·ti·choice \ˌan-tē-ˈchȯis, ˌan-ˌtī-\ *adj* (1978) **:** ANTIABORTION — **an·ti·choic·er** \-ˈchȯi-sər\ *n*

an·ti·cho·lin·er·gic \-ˌkō-lə-ˈnər-jik\ *adj* (1942) **:** opposing or blocking the physiologic action of acetylcholine — **anticholinergic** *n*

an·ti·cho·lin·es·ter·ase \-ˈnes-tə-ˌrās, -ˌrāz\ *n* (1942) **:** a substance (as neostigmine) that inhibits a cholinesterase by combination with it

An·ti·christ \ˈan-tē-ˌkrīst, -ˌtī-\ *n* [ME *anticrist,* fr. OE & LL; OE *antecrist,* fr. LL *Antichristus,* fr. Gk *Antichristos,* fr. *anti-* + *Christos* Christ] (bef. 12c) **1 :** one who denies or opposes Christ; *specif* **:** a great antagonist expected to fill the world with wickedness but to be conquered forever by Christ at his second coming **2 :** a false Christ

an·tic·i·pant \an-ˈti-sə-pənt\ *adj* (1626) **:** EXPECTANT, ANTICIPATING — usu. used with *of* — **anticipant** *n*

an·tic·i·pate \an-ˈti-sə-ˌpāt\ *vb* **-pat·ed; -pat·ing** [L *anticipatus,* pp. of *anticipare,* fr. *ante-* + *-cipare* (fr. *capere* to take) — more at HEAVE] *vt* (1532) **1 :** to give advance thought, discussion, or treatment to **2 :** to meet (an obligation) before a due date **3 :** to foresee and deal with in advance **:** FORESTALL **4 :** to use or expend in advance of actual possession **5 :** to act before (another) often so as to check or counter **6 :** to look forward to as certain **:** EXPECT ~ *vi* **:** to speak or write in knowledge or expectation of later matter ***syn*** see FORESEE, PREVENT — **an·tic·i·pat·able** \-ˌpā-tə-bəl\ *adj* — **an·tic·i·pa·tor** \-ˌpā-tər\ *n*

an·tic·i·pa·tion \(ˌ)an-ˌti-sə-ˈpā-shən\ *n* (14c) **1 a :** a prior action that takes into account or forestalls a later action **b :** the act of looking forward; *esp* **:** pleasurable expectation **2 :** the use of money before it is available **3 a :** visualization of a future event or state **b :** an object or form that anticipates a later type **4 :** the early sounding of one or more tones of a succeeding chord to form a temporary dissonance — compare SUSPENSION ***syn*** see PROSPECT

an·tic·i·pa·to·ry \an-ˈti-sə-pə-ˌtȯr-ē\ *adj* (1669) **:** characterized by anticipation **:** ANTICIPATING ⟨took ~ measures to prevent floods⟩

an·ti·cler·i·cal \ˌan-tē-ˈkler-i-kəl, ˌan-ˌtī-\ *adj* (1759) **:** opposed to clericalism or to the interference or influence of the clergy in secular affairs — **anticlerical** *n* — **an·ti·cler·i·cal·ism** \-kə-ˌli-zəm\ *n*

an·ti·cli·mac·tic \-klī-ˈmak-tik, -klə-\ *also* **an·ti·cli·mac·ti·cal** \-ti-kəl\ *adj* (1831) **:** of, relating to, or marked by anticlimax — **an·ti·cli·mac·ti·cal·ly** \-ti-k(ə-)lē\ *adv*

an·ti·cli·max \-ˈklī-ˌmaks\ *n* (1696) **1 :** the usu. sudden transition in discourse from a significant idea to a trivial or ludicrous idea; *also* **:** an instance of this transition **2 :** an event, period, or outcome that is strikingly less important or dramatic than expected

an·ti·cli·nal \ˌan-ti-ˈklī-nᵊl\ *adj* [*anti-* + Gk *klinein* to lean — more at LEAN] (1879) **:** occurring at right angles to the surface or circumference of a plant organ ⟨an ~ pattern of cell walls⟩

an·ti·cline \ˈan-ti-ˌklīn\ *n* (1845) **:** an arch of stratified rock in which the layers bend downward in opposite directions from the crest — compare SYNCLINE

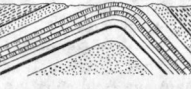

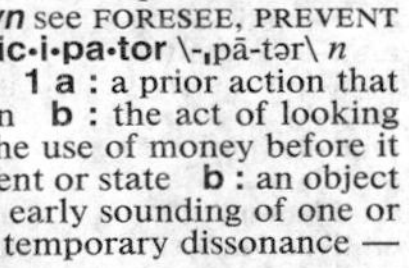
cross section of strata showing anticline

an·ti·clock·wise \ˌan-tē-ˈkläk-ˌwīz, ˌan-ˌtī-\ *adj or adv* (1879) *chiefly Brit* **:** COUNTERCLOCKWISE

an·ti·co·ag·u·lant \-kō-ˈa-gyə-lənt\ *n* (1886) **:** a substance that hinders the clotting of blood **:** BLOOD THINNER — **anticoagulant** *adj*

an·ti·co·don \-ˈkō-ˌdän\ *n* (1965) **:** a triplet of nucleotide bases in transfer RNA that identifies the amino acid carried and binds to a complementary codon in messenger RNA during protein synthesis at a ribosome

an·ti·com·pet·i·tive \-kəm-ˈpe-tə-tiv\ *adj* (1854) **:** tending to reduce or discourage competition

an·ti·con·vul·sant \-kən-ˈvəl-sənt\ *also* **an·ti·con·vul·sive** \-siv\ *adj* (1733) **:** used or tending to control or to prevent convulsions (as in epilepsy) — **anticonvulsant** *also* **anticonvulsive** *n*

an·ti·cy·clone \ˌan-ti-ˈsī-ˌklōn\ *n* (1862) **1 :** a system of winds that rotates about a center of high atmospheric pressure clockwise in the northern hemisphere and counterclockwise in the southern, that usu. advances at 20 to 30 miles (about 30 to 50 kilometers) per hour, and that usu. has a diameter of 1500 to 2500 miles (2400 to 4000 kilometers) **2 :** HIGH 2 — **an·ti·cy·clon·ic** \-sī-ˈklä-nik\ *adj*

an·ti·dem·o·crat·ic \ˌan-tē-ˌde-mə-ˈkra-tik, ˌan-ˌtī-\ *adj* (1791) **:** opposed or hostile to the theories or policies of democracy

[1]**an·ti·de·pres·sant** \-di-ˈpre-sᵊnt\ *adj* (1961) **:** used or tending to relieve or prevent psychic depression

[2]**antidepressant** *n* (1962) **:** an antidepressant drug — compare TRICYCLIC ANTIDEPRESSANT

an·ti·de·riv·a·tive \-di-ˈri-və-tiv\ *n* (1887) **:** INDEFINITE INTEGRAL

an·ti·di·uret·ic hormone \ˌan-ti-ˌdī-yu̇-ˈre-tik-\ *n* (1942) **:** VASOPRESSIN

an·ti·dot·al \ˌan-ti-ˈdō-tᵊl\ *adj* (1646) **:** of, relating to, or acting as an antidote — **an·ti·dot·al·ly** \-tᵊl-ē\ *adv*

an·ti·dote \ˈan-ti-ˌdōt\ *n* [ME *antidot,* fr. L *antidotum,* fr. Gk *antidotos,* fr. fem. of *antidotos* given as an antidote, fr. *antididonai* to give as an antidote, fr. *anti-* + *didonai* to give — more at DATE] (15c) **1 :** a remedy to counteract the effects of poison **2 :** something that relieves, prevents, or counteracts ⟨an ~ to the mechanization of our society⟩ — **antidote** *vt*

an·ti·drom·ic \ˌan-ti-ˈdrä-mik\ *adj* [*anti-* + Gk *dromos* racecourse, running — more at DROMEDARY] (1895) **:** proceeding or conducting in a direction opposite to the usual one — used esp. of a nerve impulse or fiber — **an·ti·drom·i·cal·ly** \-mi-k(ə-)lē\ *adv*

an·ti·drug \ˈan-ˌtī-ˌdrəg, ˌan-tī-ˈ\ *adj* (1906) **:** acting against or opposing illicit drugs or their use ⟨~ activists⟩ ⟨an ~ program⟩

an·ti·dump·ing \ˌan-tē-ˈdəm-piŋ, ˌan-ˌtī-\ *adj* (1894) **:** designed to discourage the importation and sale of foreign goods at prices well below domestic prices ⟨~ tariffs⟩

an·ti·elec·tron \ˌan-tē-ə-ˈlek-ˌträn, ˌan-ˌtī-\ *n* (1931) **:** POSITRON

an·ti–fed·er·al·ist \ˌan-tē-ˈfe-d(ə-)rə-list, ˌan-ˌtī-\ *n, often cap A&F* (1787) **:** a person who opposed the adoption of the U.S. Constitution

an·ti·fer·ro·mag·net·ic \-ˌfer-ō-mag-ˈne-tik\ *adj* (1936) **:** FERRIMAGNETIC — **an·ti·fer·ro·mag·net** \-ˈmag-nət\ *n* — **an·ti·fer·ro·mag·net·i·cal·ly** \-mag-ˈne-ti-k(ə-)lē\ *adv* — **an·ti·fer·ro·mag·net·ism** \-ˈmag-nə-ˌti-zəm\ *n*

an·ti·fer·til·i·ty \-fər-ˈti-lə-tē\ *adj* (1953) **:** capable of or tending to reduce or destroy fertility **:** CONTRACEPTIVE ⟨~ agents⟩

an·ti·flu·o·ri·da·tion·ist \-ˌflu̇r-ə-ˈdā-sh(ə-)nist, -ˌflȯr-\ *n* (1953) **:** a person opposed to the fluoridation of public water supplies

an·ti·foul·ing \-ˈfau̇-liŋ\ *adj* (1855) **:** intended to prevent fouling of underwater structures (as the bottoms of ships) ⟨~ paint⟩

an·ti·freeze \ˈan-ti-ˌfrēz\ *n* (1903) **1 :** a substance added to a liquid (as the water in an automobile engine) to lower its freezing point **2 :** any of various substances (as proteins or alcohols) that are found in some living organisms (as certain fish and insects) and serve to lower the freezing point of body fluids esp. by limiting ice crystal growth

an·ti·fun·gal \ˌan-tē-ˈfəŋ-gəl, ˌan-ˌtī-\ *adj* (1945) **:** destroying fungi or inhibiting their growth **:** FUNGICIDAL, FUNGISTATIC — **antifungal** *n*

an·ti·gen \ˈan-ti-jən, -ˌjen\ *n* [G, fr. F *antigène,* fr. *anticorps* antibody + *-gène* -gen] (1908) **:** any substance (as an immunogen or a hapten) foreign to the body that evokes an immune response either alone or after forming a complex with a larger molecule (as a protein) and that is capable of binding with a product (as an antibody or T cell) of the immune response — **an·ti·gen·ic** \ˌan-ti-ˈje-nik\ *adj* — **an·ti·gen·i·cal·ly** \-ni-k(ə-)lē\ *adv* — **an·ti·ge·nic·i·ty** \-jə-ˈni-sə-tē\ *n*

antigenic determinant *n* (1950) **:** EPITOPE

an·ti·gen–pre·sent·ing cell \ˈan-ti-jən-pri-ˈzen-tiŋ-, -ˌjen-\ *n* (1975) **:** any of various cells (as a macrophage or a B cell) that take up an antigen and process it into a form recognized by and serving to activate a specific helper T cell

an·ti·glob·u·lin \ˌan-tē-ˈglä-byə-lən, ˌan-ˌtī-\ *n* (1902) **:** an antibody that combines with and precipitates globulin

An·tig·o·ne \an-ˈti-gə-(ˌ)nē\ *n* [Gk *Antigonē*] (1570) **:** a daughter of Oedipus and Jocasta who buries her brother Polynices' body against the order of her uncle Creon

[1]**an·ti·grav·i·ty** \ˌan-tē-ˈgra-və-tē, ˌan-ˌtī-\ *adj* (1944) **:** reducing, canceling, or protecting against the effect of gravity

[2]**antigravity** *n* (1949) **:** a hypothetical effect resulting from cancellation or reduction of a gravitational field

an·ti·he·mo·phil·ic factor \-ˌhē-mə-ˈfi-lik-\ *n* (1947) **:** FACTOR VIII

an·ti·he·ro \ˈan-tē-ˌhē-(ˌ)rō, ˈan-ˌtī-, -ˌhir-(ˌ)ō\ *n* (1714) **:** a protagonist or notable figure who is conspicuously lacking in heroic qualities — **an·ti·he·ro·ic** \ˌan-tē-hi-ˈrō-ik, ˌan-ˌtī-\ *adj*

an·ti·her·o·ine \ˌan-tē-ˈher-ə-wən, ˌan-ˌtī-\ *n* (1823) **:** a female antihero

an·ti·his·ta·mine \-ˈhis-tə-ˌmēn, -mən\ *n* (1933) **:** any of various compounds that counteract histamine in the body and that are used for treating allergic reactions (as hay fever) and cold symptoms — **antihistamine** *adj* — **an·ti·his·ta·min·ic** \-ˌhis-tə-ˈmi-nik\ *adj or n*

an·ti·hor·mone \-ˈhȯr-ˌmōn\ *n* (1908) **:** a substance (as tamoxifen) that blocks the action or inhibits the production of a hormone

an·ti·hu·man \-ˈhyü-mən, -ˈyü-\ *adj* (1738) **1 :** acting or being against humanity **2 :** reacting strongly with human antigens ⟨~ antibodies⟩

an·ti·hy·per·ten·sive \-ˌhī-pər-ˈten(t)-siv\ *n* (1941) **:** a substance that is effective against high blood pressure — **antihypertensive** *adj*

an·ti–id·io·type \ˌan-tē-ˈi-dē-ə-ˌtīp, ˌan-ˌtī-\ *n* (1973) **:** an antibody that binds to the antigen-combining site of another antibody either suppressing or enhancing the immune response — **an·ti–id·io·typ·ic** \-ˌi-dē-ə-ˈti-pik\ *adj*

an·ti–in·flam·ma·to·ry \-in-ˈfla-mə-ˌtȯr-ē\ *adj* (1736) : counteracting inflammation — **anti–inflammatory** *n*

an·ti–in·tel·lec·tu·al \-ˌin-tə-ˈlek-ch(ə-w)əl, -ˈlek-shwəl\ *adj* (1821) : opposing or hostile to intellectuals or to an intellectual view or approach — **anti–intellectual** *n* — **an·ti–in·tel·lec·tu·al·ism** \-ˈlek-chə(-wə)-ˌli-zəm, -ˈlek-shwə-\ *n*

an·ti·leu·ke·mic \-lü-ˈkē-mik\ *adj* (1905) : counteracting the effects of leukemia

an·ti·life \-ˈlīf\ *adj* (1929) : antagonistic or antithetical to life or to normal human values

an·ti·lock \ˈan-ˌtē-ˌläk, ˈan-tē-, ˈan-ˌtī-\ *adj* (1963) : being a braking system designed to keep a vehicle's wheels from locking by electronically controlled pulsed application of the brake for each wheel

an·ti·log \ˈan-tē-ˌlȯg, ˈan-ˌtī-, -ˌläg\ *n* (1910) : ANTILOGARITHM

an·ti·log·a·rithm \ˌan-ti-ˈlȯ-gə-ˌri-t͟həm, ˌan-ˌtī-, -ˈlä-\ *n* (1618) : the number corresponding to a given logarithm

an·ti·ma·cas·sar \ˌan-ti-mə-ˈka-sər\ *n* [*anti-* + *Macassar* (*oil*) (a hairdressing)] (1844) : a cover to protect the back or arms of furniture

an·ti·mag·net·ic \ˌan-tē-mag-ˈne-tik, ˌan-ˌtī-\ *adj* (1883) *of a watch* : having a balance unit composed of alloys that will not remain magnetized

an·ti·ma·lar·i·al \-mə-ˈler-ē-əl\ *adj* (1843) : serving to prevent, control, or cure malaria — **antimalarial** *n*

an·ti·mat·ter \ˈan-tē-ˌma-tər, ˈan-ˌtī-\ *n* (1950) : matter composed of antiparticles

an·ti·me·tab·o·lite \ˌan-tē-mə-ˈta-bə-ˌlīt, ˌan-ˌtī-\ *n* (1945) : a substance that replaces or inhibits an organism's utilization of a metabolite

an·ti·mi·cro·bi·al \ˌan-ti-mī-ˈkrō-bē-əl\ *adj* (1891) : destroying or inhibiting the growth of microorganisms and esp. pathogenic microorganisms — **antimicrobial** *n*

an·ti·mi·tot·ic \ˌan-tē-mī-ˈtä-tik, ˌan-ˌtī-\ *adj* (1948) : inhibiting or disrupting mitosis ⟨~ agents⟩ ⟨~ activity⟩ — **antimitotic** *n*

an·ti·mo·ni·al \ˌan-tə-ˈmō-nē-əl\ *adj* (1605) : of, relating to, or containing antimony — **antimonial** *n*

an·ti·mo·nide \ˈan-ti-mə-ˌnīd\ *n* (1825) : a binary compound of antimony with a more electropositive element

an·ti·mo·ny \ˈan-tə-ˌmō-nē\ *n* [ME *antimonie,* fr. ML *antimonium*] (15c) **1** : STIBNITE **2** : a trivalent and pentavalent metalloid element that is commonly metallic silvery white, crystalline, and brittle and that is used esp. in alloys, semiconductors, and flame-retardant substances — see ELEMENT table

an·ti·my·cin A \ˌan-ti-ˈmī-sᵊn-ˈā\ *n* [*anti-* + *-mycin*] (1949) : a crystalline antibiotic $C_{28}H_{40}N_2O_9$ used esp. as a fungicide, insecticide, and miticide — called also *antimycin*

an·ti·neo·plas·tic \ˌan-tē-ˌnē-ə-ˈplas-tik, ˌan-ˌtī-\ *adj* (1898) : inhibiting or preventing the growth and spread of tumors or malignant cells

an·ti·neu·tri·no \-nü-ˈtrē-(ˌ)nō, -nyü-\ *n* (1934) : the antiparticle of the neutrino

an·ti·neu·tron \-ˈnü-ˌträn, -ˈnyü-\ *n* (1942) : the antiparticle of the neutron

ant·ing \ˈan-tiŋ\ *n* (1936) : bird behavior in which ants are rubbed on the feathers to obtain chemicals (as formic acid) from the ants

an·ti·node \ˈan-tē-ˌnōd, ˈan-ˌtī-\ *n* [ISV] (1875) : a region of maximum amplitude situated between adjacent nodes in a vibrating body — **an·ti·nod·al** \ˌan-tē-ˈnō-dᵊl, ˌan-ˌtī-\ *adj*

an·ti·no·mi·an \ˌan-ti-ˈnō-mē-ən\ *n* [ML *antinomus,* fr. L *anti-* + Gk *nomos* law] (1565) **1** : one who holds that under the gospel dispensation of grace the moral law is of no use or obligation because faith alone is necessary to salvation **2** : one who rejects a socially established morality — **antinomian** *adj* — **an·ti·no·mi·an·ism** \-mē-ə-ˌni-zəm\ *n*

an·tin·o·my \an-ˈti-nə-mē\ *n, pl* **-mies** [G *Antinomie,* fr. L *antinomia* conflict of laws, fr. Gk, fr. *anti-* + *nomos* law — more at NIMBLE] (1592) **1** : a contradiction between two apparently equally valid principles or between inferences correctly drawn from such principles **2** : a fundamental and apparently unresolvable conflict or contradiction ⟨*antinomies* of beauty and evil, freedom and slavery —Stephen Holden⟩ — **an·ti·nom·ic** \ˌan-ti-ˈnä-mik\ *adj*

an·ti·nov·el \ˈan-tē-ˌnä-vəl, ˈan-ˌtī-\ *n* (1899) : a work of fiction that lacks most or all of the traditional features of the novel — **an·ti·nov·el·ist** \-ˌnäv-list, -ˌnä-və-\ *n*

an·ti·nu·cle·ar \ˌan-tē-ˈnü-klē-ər, ˌan-ˌtī-, -ˈnyü-, ÷-kyə-lər\ *adj* (1958) **1** : opposing the use or production of nuclear power **2** : tending to react with cell nuclei or their components (as DNA) ⟨~ antibodies⟩

an·ti·nu·cle·on \-ˈn(y)ü-klē-ˌän\ *n* (1946) : the antiparticle of a nucleon

an·ti·nuke \-ˈnük, -ˈnyük\ *adj* (1975) : ANTINUCLEAR 1

an·ti·ox·i·dant \ˌan-tē-ˈäk-sə-dənt, ˌan-ˌtī-\ *n* (1919) : a substance (as beta-carotene or vitamin C) that inhibits oxidation or reactions promoted by oxygen, peroxides, or free radicals — **antioxidant** *adj*

an·ti·ozon·ant \-ˈō-(ˌ)zō-nənt\ *n* (1954) : a substance that opposes ozonization or protects against it

an·ti·par·al·lel \ˌan-tē-ˈper-ə-ˌlel, ˌan-ˌtī-, -ləl\ *adj* (ca. 1660) : parallel but oppositely directed or oriented ⟨~ electron spins⟩ ⟨two ~ chains of nucleotides comprise DNA⟩

an·ti·par·ti·cle \ˈan-tē-ˌpär-ti-kəl, ˈan-ˌtī-\ *n* (1934) : a subatomic particle identical to another subatomic particle in mass but opposite to it in electric and magnetic properties (as sign of charge) that when brought together with its counterpart produces mutual annihilation; *esp* : a subatomic particle not found in ordinary matter

an·ti·pas·to \ˌan-tē-ˈpas-(ˌ)tō, ˌän-tē-, -ˈpäs-\ *n, pl* **-ti** \-(ˌ)tē\ [It, fr. *anti-* (fr. L *ante-*) + *pasto* food, fr. L *pastus,* fr. *pascere* to feed — more at FOOD] (1590) : any of various typically Italian hors d'oeuvres; *also* : a plate of these served esp. as the first course of a meal

an·ti·pa·thet·ic \ˌan-ti-pə-ˈthe-tik, (ˌ)an-ˌti-pə-\ *adj* (1640) **1** : having a natural aversion; *also* : not sympathetic : HOSTILE ⟨a government ~ to democracy⟩ **2** : arousing antipathy — **an·ti·pa·thet·i·cal·ly** \-ti-k(ə-)lē\ *adv*

an·tip·a·thy \an-ˈti-pə-thē\ *n, pl* **-thies** [L *antipathia,* fr. Gk *antipatheia,* fr. *antipathēs* of opposite feelings, fr. *anti-* + *pathos* experience — more at PATHOS] (1592) **1** *obs* : opposition in feeling **2** : settled aversion or dislike **3** : an object of aversion ***syn*** see ENMITY

an·ti·per·son·nel \ˌan-tē-ˌpər-sə-ˈnel, ˌan-ˌtī-\ *adj* (1939) : designed for use against military personnel ⟨an ~ mine⟩

an·ti·per·spi·rant \-ˈpər-sp(ə-)rənt\ *n* (1920) : a preparation used to reduce perspiration

an·ti·phlo·gis·tic \-flə-ˈjis-tik\ *adj* (1715) : ANTI-INFLAMMATORY

an·ti·phon \ˈan-tə-fən, -ˌfän\ *n* [ME *antiphone,* fr. MF, fr. LL *antiphona* — more at ANTHEM] (15c) **1** : a psalm, anthem, or verse sung responsively **2** : a verse usu. from Scripture said or sung before and after a canticle, psalm, or psalm verse as part of the liturgy

1**an·tiph·o·nal** \an-ˈti-fə-nᵊl\ *n* (1537) : ANTIPHONARY

2**antiphonal** *adj* (1704) : of, relating to, or suggesting an antiphon or antiphony — **an·tiph·o·nal·ly** \-nᵊl-ē\ *adv*

an·tiph·o·nary \an-ˈti-fə-ˌner-ē\ *n, pl* **-nar·ies** (15c) **1** : a book containing a collection of antiphons **2** : a book containing the choral parts of the Divine Office

an·tiph·o·ny \an-ˈti-fə-nē\ *n, pl* **-nies** (1592) : responsive alternation between two groups esp. of singers

an·tiph·ra·sis \an-ˈti-frə-səs\ *n, pl* **-ra·ses** \-ˌsēz\ [LL, fr. Gk, fr. *anti-* + *phrasis* diction — more at PHRASE] (1533) : the usu. ironic or humorous use of words in senses opposite to the generally accepted meanings (as in "this giant of 3 feet 4 inches")

1**an·tip·o·dal** \an-ˈti-pə-dᵊl\ *adj* (1646) **1** : of or relating to the antipodes; *specif* : situated at the opposite side of the earth or moon ⟨an ~ meridian⟩ ⟨an ~ continent⟩ **2** : diametrically opposite ⟨an ~ point on a sphere⟩ **3** : entirely opposed ⟨a system ~ to democracy⟩

2**antipodal** *n* (1880) : any of three haploid cells in most angiosperms that are grouped at the end of the embryo sac farthest from the micropyle — called also *antipodal cell*

an·ti·pode \ˈan-tə-ˌpōd\ *n, pl* **an·tip·o·des** \an-ˈti-pə-ˌdēz\ [ME *antipodes,* pl., persons dwelling at opposite points on the globe, fr. L, fr. Gk, fr. pl. of *antipod-, antipous* with feet opposite, fr. *anti-* + *pod-, pous* foot — more at FOOT] (1549) **1** : the parts of the earth diametrically opposite — usu. used in pl.; often used of Australia and New Zealand as contrasted to the western hemisphere **2** : the exact opposite or contrary — **an·tip·o·de·an** \(ˌ)an-ˌti-pə-ˈdē-ən\ *adj or n*

an·ti·po·et·ic \ˌan-tē-pō-ˈe-tik, ˌan-ˌtī-\ *adj* (1847) : of, relating to, or characterized by opposition to traditional poetic technique or style

an·ti·pol·lu·tion \-pə-ˈlü-shən\ *adj* (1872) : designed to prevent, reduce, or eliminate pollution ⟨~ laws⟩ — **antipollution** *n*

an·ti·pope \ˈan-ti-ˌpōp\ *n* [ME *antepope,* fr. MF *antipape,* fr. ML *antipapa,* fr. *anti-* + *papa* pope] (15c) : one elected or claiming to be pope in opposition to the pope canonically chosen

an·ti·pro·ton \ˌan-tē-ˈprō-ˌtän, ˌan-ˌtī-\ *n* (1940) : the antiparticle of the proton

an·ti·psy·chot·ic \ˌan-tē-sī-ˈkä-tik\ *n* (1958) : any of the powerful tranquilizers (as the phenothiazines and butyrophenones) used esp. to treat psychosis and believed to act by blocking dopamine nervous receptors — called also *neuroleptic* — **antipsychotic** *adj*

an·ti·py·ret·ic \-pī-ˈre-tik\ *n* (ca. 1681) : an agent that reduces fever — **antipyretic** *adj*

an·ti·py·rine \-ˈpī-ˌrēn\ *n* [fr. *Antipyrine,* a trademark] (1884) : an analgesic and antipyretic $C_{11}H_{12}N_2O$ formerly widely used but now largely replaced in oral use by less toxic substances (as aspirin)

antiq *abbr* antiquarian; antiquary

1**an·ti·quar·i·an** \ˌan-tə-ˈkwer-ē-ən\ *n* (1610) : one who collects or studies antiquities

2**antiquarian** *adj* (1771) **1** : of or relating to antiquarians or antiquities **2** : dealing in old or rare books — **an·ti·quar·i·an·ism** \-ē-ə-ˌni-zəm\ *n*

an·ti·quark \ˈan-tē-ˌkwärk, ˈan-ˌtī-\ *n* (1964) : the antiparticle of the quark

an·ti·quary \ˈan-tə-ˌkwer-ē\ *n, pl* **-quar·ies** (1586) : ANTIQUARIAN

an·ti·quate \ˈan-tə-ˌkwāt\ *vt* **-quat·ed; -quat·ing** [LL *antiquatus,* pp. of *antiquare,* fr. L *antiquus*] (1596) : to make old or obsolete — **an·ti·qua·tion** \ˌan-tə-ˈkwā-shən\ *n*

an·ti·quat·ed *adj* (1601) **1** : OBSOLETE ⟨an ~ calendar⟩ **2** : outmoded or discredited by reason of age : being out of style or fashion ⟨~ methods of farming⟩ **3** : advanced in age ***syn*** see OLD

1**an·tique** \(ˌ)an-ˈtēk, *in verse often* ˈan-tik\ *adj* [MF, fr. L *antiquus,* fr. *ante* before — more at ANTE-] (1527) **1** : existing since or belonging to earlier times : ANCIENT ⟨~ trade routes to India⟩ **2 a** : being in the style or fashion of former times ⟨~ manners and graces⟩ **b** : made in or representative of the work of an earlier period ⟨~ mirrors⟩; *also* : being an antique **3** : selling or exhibiting antiques ⟨an ~ show⟩ ***syn*** see OLD

2**an·tique** \(ˌ)an-ˈtēk\ *n* (1530) **1** : a relic or object of ancient times **2 a** : a work of art, piece of furniture, or decorative object made at an earlier period and according to various customs laws at least 100 years ago **b** : a manufactured product (as an automobile) from an earlier period

3**an·tique** \(ˌ)an-ˈtēk\ *vb* **-tiqued; -tiqu·ing** *vt* (1884) : to finish or refinish in antique style : give an appearance of age to ⟨~ a table⟩ ~ *vi* : to shop around for antiques — **an·tiqu·er** \an-ˈtē-kər\ *n*

an·tiq·ui·ty \an-ˈti-kwə-tē\ *n, pl* **-ties** (13c) **1** : ancient times; *esp* : those before the Middle Ages **2** : the quality of being ancient **3** *pl* **a** : relics or monuments (as coins, statues, or buildings) of ancient times **b** : matters relating to the life or culture of ancient times **4** : the people of ancient times

an·ti·re·jec·tion \ˌan-tē-ri-ˈjek-shən, ˌan-ˌtī-\ *adj* (1964) : used or tending to prevent organ or tissue transplant rejection ⟨~ drugs⟩ ⟨~ treatment⟩

an·ti·re·tro·vi·ral \-ˈre-trō-ˌvī-rəl\ *adj* (1979) : acting, used, or effective against retroviruses ⟨~ drugs⟩ ⟨~ therapy⟩ — **antiretroviral** *n*

an·ti·rheu·mat·ic \-rü-ˈma-tik\ *adj* (1758) : alleviating or preventing rheumatism ⟨~ therapy⟩ ⟨~ drugs⟩ — **antirheumatic** *n*

an·ti–roll bar \ˈan-ˌtī-ˌrōl-\ *n* (1951) : SWAY BAR

an·tir·rhi·num \ˌan-tə-ˈrī-nəm\ *n* [NL, genus name, fr. L, snapdragon, fr. Gk *antirrhinon,* fr. *anti-* like (fr. *anti* against, equivalent to) + *rhin-, rhis* nose — more at ANTI-] (1548) : SNAPDRAGON

antis *pl of* ANTI

an·ti·scor·bu·tic \ˌan-tē-skȯr-ˈbyü-tik, ˌan-ˌtī-\ *adj* (1725) **:** counteracting scurvy ⟨the ~ vitamin is vitamin C⟩ — **antiscorbutic** *n*
an·ti–Sem·i·tism \ˌan-tē-ˈse-mə-ˌti-zəm, ˌan-ˌtī-\ *n* (1882) **:** hostility toward or discrimination against Jews as a religious, ethnic, or racial group — **an·ti–Se·mit·ic** \-sə-ˈmi-tik\ *adj* — **an·ti–Sem·ite** \-ˈse-ˌmīt\ *n*
an·ti·sense \ˈan-ˌtī-ˌsen(t)s, ˈan-tē-\ *adj* [*anti-* + non*sense*] (1977) **:** having a sequence complementary to a segment of genetic material; *specif* **:** of, being, relating to, or possessing a sequence of DNA or RNA that is complementary to and pairs with a specific messenger RNA blocking it from being translated into protein and serving to inhibit gene function ⟨~ drug therapy⟩ ⟨~ RNA⟩ — compare MISSENSE, NONSENSE
an·ti·sep·sis \ˌan-tə-ˈsep-səs\ *n* (1875) **:** the inhibiting of the growth and multiplication of microorganisms by antiseptic means
[1]**an·ti·sep·tic** \ˌan-tə-ˈsep-tik\ *adj* [*anti-* + Gk *sēptikos* putrefying, septic] (1751) **1 a :** opposing sepsis, putrefaction, or decay; *esp* **:** preventing or arresting the growth of microorganisms (as on living tissue) **b :** acting or protecting like an antiseptic **2 :** relating to or characterized by the use of antiseptics **3 a :** scrupulously clean **:** ASEPTIC **b :** extremely neat or orderly; *esp* **:** neat to the point of being bare or uninteresting **c :** free from what is held to be contaminating **4 a :** coldly impersonal ⟨an ~ greeting⟩ **b :** of, relating to, or being warfare conducted with cold precision from a safe distance with few or no casualties on one's side ⟨~ bombings⟩ — **an·ti·sep·ti·cal·ly** \-ti-k(ə-)lē\ *adv*
[2]**antiseptic** *n* (1751) **:** a substance that inhibits the growth or action of microorganisms esp. in or on living tissue; *also* **:** GERMICIDE
an·ti·se·rum \ˈan-tē-ˌsir-əm, ˈan-ˌtī-, -ˌser-\ *n* [ISV] (1901) **:** a serum containing antibodies
an·ti·so·cial \ˌan-tē-ˈsō-shəl, ˌan-ˌtī-\ *adj* (1797) **1 :** averse to the society of others **:** UNSOCIABLE **2 :** hostile or harmful to organized society; *esp* **:** being or marked by behavior deviating sharply from the social norm — **an·ti·so·cial·ly** \-shə-lē\ *adv*
antisocial personality disorder *n* (1979) **:** a personality disorder that is characterized by antisocial behavior exhibiting pervasive disregard for and violation of the rights, feelings, and safety of others starting in childhood or the early teenage years and continuing into adulthood — called also *psychopathic personality disorder*
an·ti·so·lar \-ˈsō-lər\ *adj* (ca. 1890) **:** being or having a direction away from the sun ⟨the ~ point⟩
an·ti·spas·mod·ic \-spaz-ˈmä-dik\ *adj* (1763) **:** capable of preventing or relieving spasms or convulsions — **antispasmodic** *n*
an·ti·stat·ic \-ˈsta-tik\ *also* **an·ti·stat** \-ˈstat\ *adj* (1952) **:** reducing, removing, or preventing the buildup of static electricity
an·tis·tro·phe \an-ˈtis-trə-(ˌ)fē\ *n* [LL, fr. Gk *antistrophē*, fr. *anti-* + *strophē* strophe] (ca. 1550) **1 a :** the repetition of words in reversed order **b :** the repetition of a word or phrase at the end of successive clauses **2 a :** a returning movement in Greek choral dance exactly answering to a previous strophe **b :** the part of a choral song delivered during the antistrophe — **an·ti·stroph·ic** \ˌan-tə-ˈsträ-fik\ *adj* — **anti·stroph·i·cal·ly** \-fi-k(ə-)lē\ *adv*
an·ti·style \ˈan-tē-ˌstī(-ə)l, ˈan-ˌtī-\ *n* (1964) **:** a style (as of dress) based on the rejection of current or established styles
an·ti·sym·met·ric \ˌan-tē-sə-ˈme-trik, ˌan-ˌtī-\ *adj* (1923) **:** relating to or being a relation (as "is a subset of") that implies equality of any two quantities for which it holds in both directions ⟨the relation *R* is ~ if *aRb* and *bRa* implies *a* = *b*⟩
an·tith·e·sis \an-ˈti-thə-səs\ *n, pl* **-e·ses** \-ˌsēz\ [LL, fr. Gk, lit., opposition, fr. *antitithenai* to oppose, fr. *anti-* + *tithenai* to set — more at DO] (1529) **1 a (1) :** the rhetorical contrast of ideas by means of parallel arrangements of words, clauses, or sentences (as in "action, not words" or "they promised freedom and provided slavery") **(2) :** OPPOSITION, CONTRAST ⟨the ~ of prose and verse⟩ **b (1) :** the second of two opposing constituents of an antithesis **(2) :** the direct opposite ⟨her temperament is the very ~ of mine⟩ **2 :** the second stage of a dialectic process
an·ti·thet·i·cal \ˌan-tə-ˈthe-ti-kəl\ *also* **an·ti·thet·ic** \-ˈthe-tik\ *adj* (1583) **1 :** constituting or marked by antithesis **2 :** being in direct and unequivocal opposition ***syn*** see OPPOSITE — **an·ti·thet·i·cal·ly** \-ti-k(ə-)lē\ *adv*
an·ti·throm·bin \ˌan-tē-ˈthräm-bən, ˌan-ˌtī-\ *n* (ca. 1911) **:** any of a group of substances that inhibit blood clotting by inactivating thrombin
an·ti·thy·roid \ˌan-ti-ˈthī-ˌrȯid\ *adj* (1908) **:** able to counteract excessive thyroid activity ⟨~ drugs⟩
an·ti·tox·ic \-ˈtäk-sik\ *adj* (ca. 1890) **1 :** counteracting toxins **2 :** being or containing antitoxins ⟨~ serum⟩
an·ti·tox·in \ˌan-ti-ˈtäk-sən\ *n* [ISV] (ca. 1890) **:** an antibody that is capable of neutralizing the specific toxin (as a specific causative agent of disease) that stimulated its production in the body and is produced in animals for medical purposes by injection of a toxin or toxoid with the resulting serum being used to counteract the toxin in other individuals; *also* **:** an antiserum containing antitoxins
an·ti·trust \ˌan-tē-ˈtrəst, ˌan-ˌtī-\ *adj* (1890) **:** of, relating to, or being legislation against or opposition to trusts or combinations; *specif* **:** consisting of laws to protect trade and commerce from unlawful restraints and monopolies or unfair business practices
an·ti·trust·er \-ˈtrəs-tər\ *n* (1947) **:** one who advocates or enforces antitrust provisions of the law
an·ti·tus·sive \-ˈtə-siv\ *n* (ca. 1909) **:** a cough suppressant — **antitussive** *adj*
an·ti–uto·pia \ˌan-tē-yü-ˈtō-pē-ə, ˌan-ˌtī-\ *n* (1966) **1 :** DYSTOPIA 1 **2 :** a work describing an anti-utopia — **an·ti–uto·pi·an** \-pē-ən\ *adj or n*
an·ti·ven·in \ˌan-tē-ˈve-nən, ˌan-ˌtī-\ *n* [ISV] (1895) **:** an antitoxin to a venom; *also* **:** an antiserum containing such antitoxin
an·ti·ven·om \-ˈve-nəm\ *n* (1904) **:** ANTIVENIN
an·ti·vi·ta·min \ˈan-ti-ˌvī-tə-mən, *Brit usu* -ˌvi-\ *n* (1927) **:** a substance that makes a vitamin metabolically ineffective
an·ti·white \ˌan-tē-ˈhwīt, ˌan-ˌtī-, -ˈwīt\ *adj* (1906) **:** opposed or hostile to white people
ant·ler \ˈant-lər\ *n* [ME *aunteler*, fr. AF *antiler*, fr. VL **anteoculare*, fr. neut. of **anteocularis* located before the eye, fr. L *ante-* + *oculus* eye — more at EYE] (14c) **:** one of the paired deciduous solid bony processes that arise from the frontal bone on the head of an animal of the deer family; *also* **:** a branch of an antler — **ant·lered** \-lərd\ *adj* — **ant·ler·less** \-ləs\ *adj*
ant lion *n* (1815) **:** any of various neuropterous insects (as of the genus *Myrmeleon*) having long-jawed larvae that feed on insects (as ants) and including some that dig conical pits to capture prey
An·to·ni·an \an-ˈtō-nē-ən\ *n* [L *Antonius* Anthony] (ca. 1907) **:** a member of one of several monastic communities (as the Armenian Antonians) that follow a rule devised by St. Anthony
an·ton·o·ma·sia \ˌan-tə-nō-ˈmā-zh(ē-)ə, (ˌ)an-ˌtä-nə-\ *n* [L, use of an epithet for a proper name, fr. Gk, fr. *antonomazein* to call by a new name, fr. *anti-* + *onomazein* to name, fr. *onoma* name — more at NAME] (ca. 1550) **:** the use of a proper name to designate a member of a class (as a *Solomon* for a *wise ruler*); *also* **:** the use of an epithet or title in place of a proper name (as *the Bard* for *Shakespeare*)
an·to·nym \ˈan-tə-ˌnim\ *n* (1870) **:** a word of opposite meaning ⟨the usual ~ of *good* is *bad*⟩ — **an·to·nym·ic** \ˌan-tə-ˈni-mik\ *adj* — **an·ton·y·mous** \an-ˈtä-nə-məs\ *adj* — **an·ton·y·my** \-mē\ *n*
an·tre \ˈan-tər\ *n* [F, fr. L *antrum*] (1604) **:** CAVE 1
an·trum \ˈan-trəm\ *n, pl* **an·tra** \-trə\ [LL, fr. L, cave, fr. Gk *antron;* akin to Arm *ayr* cave] (ca. 1751) **:** an anatomical cavity within a bone (as the maxilla) or hollow organ (as the stomach) — **an·tral** \-trəl\ *adj*
ant·sy \ˈant-sē\ *adj* (1838) **1 :** RESTLESS, FIDGETY ⟨~ children⟩; *also* **:** IMPATIENT, EAGER ⟨~ for a new challenge⟩ **2 :** NERVOUS, APPREHENSIVE ⟨~ investors⟩
Anu·bis \ə-ˈnü-bəs, -ˈnyü-\ *n* [L, fr. Gk *Anoubis,* fr. Egypt *inpw*] (1708) **:** a jackal-headed god in Egyptian mythology who leads the dead to judgment
an·uran \ə-ˈnyu̇r-ən, a-, -ˈnu̇r-\ *n* [ultim. fr. Gk *a-* + *oura* tail — more at ASS] (1900) **:** any of an order (Anura) of amphibians comprising the frogs, toads, and tree frogs all of which lack a tail in the adult stage and have long hind limbs often suited to leaping and swimming — **anuran** *adj*
an·uria \ə-ˈnyu̇r-ē-ə, a-, -ˈnu̇r-\ *n* [NL] (1838) **:** absence or defective excretion of urine — **an·uric** \-ˈnyu̇r-ik, -ˈnu̇r-\ *adj*
anus \ˈā-nəs\ *n* [L, ring, anus; perh. akin to OIr *ánne* ring] (15c) **:** the posterior opening of the alimentary canal
an·vil \ˈan-vəl\ *n* [ME *anfilt*, fr. OE; akin to OHG *anafalz* anvil; akin to L *pellere* to beat — more at FELT] (bef. 12c) **1 :** a heavy usu. steel-faced iron block on which metal is shaped (as by hand hammering) **2 :** INCUS **3 :** the anvil-shaped top of a cumulonimbus

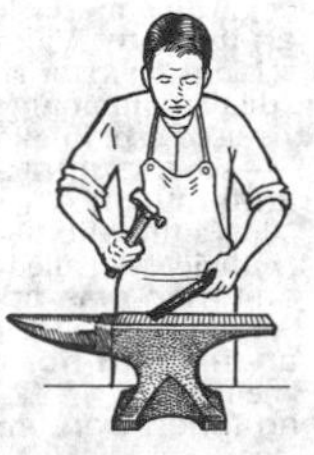

anvil 1

anx·i·ety \aŋ-ˈzī-ə-tē\ *n, pl* **-eties** [L *anxietas,* fr. *anxius*] (ca. 1525) **1 a :** painful or apprehensive uneasiness of mind usu. over an impending or anticipated ill **b :** fearful concern or interest **c :** a cause of anxiety **2 :** an abnormal and overwhelming sense of apprehension and fear often marked by physiological signs (as sweating, tension, and increased pulse), by doubt concerning the reality and nature of the threat, and by self-doubt about one's capacity to cope with it ***syn*** see CARE
an·xi·o·lyt·ic \ˌaŋ-zē-ō-ˈli-tik, ˌaŋ(k)-sē-\ *n* [*anxi*ety + *-o-* + *-lytic*] (1965) **:** a drug that relieves anxiety — **anxiolytic** *adj*
anx·ious \ˈaŋ(k)-shəs\ *adj* [L *anxius;* akin to L *angere* to strangle, distress — more at ANGER] (ca. 1616) **1 :** characterized by extreme uneasiness of mind or brooding fear about some contingency **:** WORRIED ⟨~ parents⟩ **2 :** characterized by, resulting from, or causing anxiety **:** WORRYING ⟨an ~ night⟩ **3 :** ardently or earnestly wishing ⟨~ to learn more⟩ ***syn*** see EAGER — **anx·ious·ly** *adv* — **anx·ious·ness** *n*
[1]**any** \ˈe-nē\ *adj* [ME, fr. OE *ǣnig;* akin to OHG *einag* any, OE *ān* one — more at ONE] (bef. 12c) **1 :** one or some indiscriminately of whatever kind: **a :** one or another taken at random ⟨ask ~ man you meet⟩ **b :** EVERY — used to indicate one selected without restriction ⟨~ child would know that⟩ **2 :** one, some, or all indiscriminately of whatever quantity: **a :** one or more — used to indicate an undetermined number or amount ⟨have you ~ money⟩ **b :** ALL — used to indicate a maximum or whole ⟨needs ~ help he can get⟩ **c :** a or some without reference to quantity or extent ⟨grateful for ~ favor at all⟩ **3 a :** unmeasured or unlimited in amount, number, or extent ⟨~ quantity you desire⟩ **b :** appreciably large or extended ⟨could not endure it ~ length of time⟩
[2]**any** *pron, sing or pl in constr* (bef. 12c) **1 :** any person or persons **:** ANYONE **2 a :** any thing or things **b :** any part, quantity, or number
[3]**any** *adv* (14c) **:** to any extent or degree **:** AT ALL ⟨was never ~ good⟩ ⟨no, it doesn't help me ~⟩
any·body \-ˌbä-dē, -bə-\ *pron* (14c) **:** any person **:** ANYONE
any·how \-ˌhau̇\ *adv* (1690) **1 a :** in any manner whatever **b :** in a haphazard manner **2 a :** at any rate **b :** in any event
any·more \ˌe-nē-ˈmȯr\ *adv* (14c) **1 :** any longer ⟨I was not moving ~ with my feet —Anaïs Nin⟩ **2 :** at the present time **:** NOW ⟨hardly a day passes without rain ~⟩
usage Although both *anymore* and *any more* are found in written use, in the 20th century *anymore* is the more common styling. *Anymore* is regularly used in negative ⟨no one can be natural *anymore* —May Sarton⟩, interrogative ⟨do you read much *anymore*?⟩, and conditional ⟨if you do that *anymore*, I'll leave⟩ contexts and in certain positive constructions ⟨the Washingtonian is too sophisticated to believe *anymore* in solutions —Russell Baker⟩. In many regions of the U.S. the use of *anymore* in sense 2 is quite common in positive constructions, esp. in speech ⟨everybody's cool *anymore* —Bill White⟩ ⟨every time we leave the house *anymore*, I play a game called "Stump the Housebreaker" —Erma Bombeck⟩. The positive use appears to have been of Midland origin, but it is now reported to be widespread in all speech areas of the U.S. except New England.
any·one \ˈe-nē-(ˌ)wən\ *pron* (ca. 1500) **:** any person at all
any·place \-ˌplās\ *adv* (1916) **:** in any place **:** ANYWHERE
[1]**any·thing** \-ˌthiŋ\ *pron* (bef. 12c) **:** any thing whatever **:** any such thing
[2]**anything** *adv* (bef. 12c) **:** AT ALL — **anything like :** in any way **:** AT ALL ⟨it's not *anything like* as good as it used to be⟩
any·time \ˈe-nē-ˌtīm\ *adv* (1926) **:** at any time whatever
any·way \-ˌwā\ *adv* (13c) **1 :** ANYWISE **2 :** in any case **:** ANYHOW

any·ways \ˈe-nē-ˌwāz\ *adv* (13c) **1 a** *archaic* : ANYWISE **b** *dial* : to any degree at all **2** *chiefly dial* : ANYHOW, ANYWAY

[1]**any·where** \-ˌ(h)wer, -(h)wər\ *adv* (14c) **1** : at, in, or to any place or point **2** : to any extent : AT ALL ⟨we're not ~ near to being finished⟩ **3** — used as a function word to indicate limits of variation ⟨~ from 40 to 60 students⟩

[2]**anywhere** *n* (1775) : any place

any·wheres \-ˌ(h)werz, -(h)wərz\ *adv* (1775) *chiefly dial* : ANYWHERE

any·wise \ˈe-nē-ˌwīz\ *adv* (13c) : in any way whatever : AT ALL

An·zac \ˈan-ˌzak\ *n* [*A*ustralian and *N*ew *Z*ealand *A*rmy *C*orps] (1915) : a soldier from Australia or New Zealand

AO *abbr* **1** account of **2** and others

A–OK \ˌā-(ˌ)ō-ˈkā\ *adv or adj* (1961) : very definitely OK

A1 \ˈā-ˈwən\ *adj* (1801) **1** : having the highest possible classification — used of a ship **2** : of the finest quality : FIRST-RATE

A1C *abbr* airman first class

aor *abbr* aorist

ao·rist \ˈā-ə-rəst\ *n* [LL & Gk; LL *aoristos,* fr. Gk, fr. *aoristos* undefined, fr. *a-* + *horistos* definable, fr. *horizein* to define — more at HORIZON] (1566) : an inflectional form of a verb typically denoting simple occurrence of an action without reference to its completeness, duration, or repetition — **aorist** *or* **ao·ris·tic** \ˌā-ə-ˈris-tik\ *adj* — **ao·ris·ti·cal·ly** \-ti-k(ə-)lē\ *adv*

aor·ta \ā-ˈȯr-tə\ *n, pl* **-tas** *or* **-tae** \-tē\ [NL, fr. Gk *aortē,* fr. *aeirein* to lift] (1543) : the great arterial trunk that carries blood from the heart to be distributed by branch arteries through the body — see HEART illustration — **aor·tic** \-ˈȯr-tik\ *adj*

aortic arch *n* (1802) : one of the arterial branches in vertebrate embryos that exist in a series of pairs with one on each side of the embryo, connect the ventral arterial system lying anterior to the heart to the dorsal arterial system above the alimentary tract, and persist in adult fishes but are reduced or much modified in the adult of higher forms

aor·tog·ra·phy \ˌā-ˌȯr-ˈtä-grə-fē\ *n* (ca. 1935) : arteriography of the aorta — **aor·to·graph·ic** \(ˌ)ā-ˌȯr-tə-ˈgra-fik\ *adj*

aou·dad \ˈau̇-ˌdad, ˈä-ü-\ *n* [F, fr. Berber *audad*] (1809) : a wild bovine (*Ammotragus lervia*) of No. Africa that is closely related to goats and sheep and has been introduced into the southwestern U.S. — called also *aoudad sheep, Barbary sheep*

à ou·trance \ˌä-ˌü-ˈträ^{n}s\ *adv* [F] (1819) : to the limit : UNSPARINGLY

ap *abbr* **1** apostle **2** apothecaries'

AP *abbr* **1** additional premium **2** adjective phrase **3** airplane **4** American plan **5** antipersonnel **6** arithmetic progression **7** armor-piercing **8** Associated Press **9** author's proof

[1]**ap-** — see AD-

[2]**ap-** — see APO-

APA *abbr* **1** American Psychiatric Association **2** American Psychological Association

apace \ə-ˈpās\ *adv* [ME, prob. fr. MF *à pas* on step] (14c) **1** : at a quick pace : SWIFTLY ⟨growing ~⟩ **2** : ABREAST — used with *of* or *with* ⟨trying to keep ~ with changes in technology⟩

Apache \ə-ˈpa-chē, *in sense 3* ə-ˈpash\ *n, pl* **Apache** *or* **Apach·es** \-ˈpa-chēz; -ˈpash, -ˈpa-shəz\ [AmerSp, perh. fr. Zuni *ʔaʼpaču* Navajo, Apachean] (1703) **1** : a member of a group of American Indian peoples of the southwestern U.S. **2** : any of the Athabascan languages of the Apache people **3** *not cap* [F, fr. *Apache* Apache Indian] **a** : a member of a gang of criminals esp. in Paris **b** : RUFFIAN — **Apach·e·an** \ə-ˈpa-chē-ən\ *adj or n*

apanage *var of* APPANAGE

ap·a·re·jo \ˌa-pə-ˈrā-(ˌ)(h)ō\ *n, pl* **-jos** [AmerSp] (1828) : a packsaddle of stuffed leather or canvas

[1]**apart** \ə-ˈpärt\ *adv* [ME, fr. AF *a part,* lit., to one side] (14c) **1 a** : at a little distance ⟨tried to keep ~ from the family squabbles⟩ **b** : away from one another in space or time ⟨towns 20 miles ~⟩ **2 a** : as a separate unit : INDEPENDENTLY ⟨viewed ~, his arguments were unsound⟩ **b** : so as to separate one from another ⟨found it hard to tell the twins ~⟩ **3** : excluded from consideration : ASIDE ⟨a few blemishes ~, the novel is excellent⟩ **4** : in or into two or more parts : to pieces ⟨coming ~ at the seams⟩

[2]**apart** *adj* (1680) **1** : SEPARATE, ISOLATED ⟨those athletes are a breed ~⟩ **2** : holding different opinions : DIVIDED — **apart·ness** *n*

apart from *prep* (1724) : other than : BESIDES, EXCEPT FOR

apart·heid \ə-ˈpär-ˌtāt, -ˌtīt\ *n* [Afrik, fr. *apart* apart + *-heid* -hood] (1947) **1** : racial segregation; *specif* : a former policy of segregation and political and economic discrimination against non-European groups in the Republic of So. Africa **2** : SEPARATION, SEGREGATION ⟨cultural ~⟩ ⟨gender ~⟩

apart·ment \ə-ˈpärt-mənt\ *n* [F *appartement,* fr. It *appartamento*] (1641) **1** : a room or set of rooms fitted esp. with housekeeping facilities and usu. leased as a dwelling **2** : a building containing several individual apartments — **apart·men·tal** \ə-ˌpärt-ˈmen-t^{ə}l\ *adj*

apartment building *n* (1845) : a building containing separate residential apartments — called also *apartment house*

apartment hotel *n* (1874) : a hotel containing apartments as well as accommodations for transients

ap·a·thet·ic \ˌa-pə-ˈthe-tik\ *adj* (1744) **1** : having or showing little or no feeling or emotion : SPIRITLESS **2** : having little or no interest or concern : INDIFFERENT ***syn*** see IMPASSIVE — **ap·a·thet·i·cal·ly** \-ti-k(ə-)lē\ *adv*

ap·a·thy \ˈa-pə-thē\ *n* [Gk *apatheia,* fr. *apathēs* without feeling, fr. *a-* + *pathos* emotion — more at PATHOS] (1594) **1** : lack of feeling or emotion : IMPASSIVENESS **2** : lack of interest or concern : INDIFFERENCE

ap·a·tite \ˈa-pə-ˌtīt\ *n* [G *Apatit,* fr. Gk *apatē* deceit] (1794) : any of a group of calcium phosphate minerals occurring in various colors as hexagonal crystals, as granular masses, or in fine-grained masses as the chief constituent of phosphate rock and of bones and teeth; *esp* : calcium phosphate fluoride

apato·sau·rus \ə-ˌpa-tə-ˈsȯr-əs\ *n* [NL, fr. Gk *apatē* + *sauros* lizard] (1878) : BRONTOSAURUS

APB *abbr* all points bulletin

APC \ˌā-(ˌ)pē-ˈsē\ *n* [*a*rmored *p*ersonnel *c*arrier] (1952) : an armored vehicle used to transport military personnel

[1]**ape** \ˈāp\ *n* [ME, fr. OE *apa;* akin to OHG *affo* ape] (bef. 12c) **1 a** : MONKEY; *esp* : one of the larger tailless or short-tailed Old World forms **b** : any of various large tailless semierect primates of Africa and southeastern Asia (as the chimpanzee, gorilla, orangutan, or gibbon) — called also *anthropoid, anthropoid ape*; compare GREAT APE **2 a** : MIMIC **b** : a large uncouth person — **ape·like** \ˈāp-ˌlīk\ *adj*

[2]**ape** *vt* **aped; ap·ing** (1632) : to copy closely but often clumsily and ineptly ***syn*** see COPY — **ap·er** *n*

[3]**ape** *adj* (1955) : CRAZY, WILD — usu. used in the phrase *go ape*

apeak \ə-ˈpēk\ *adj or adv* [alter. of earlier *apike,* prob. fr. F *à pic* vertically] (1596) : being in a vertical position ⟨with oars ~⟩

ape–man \ˈāp-ˌman, -ˈman\ *n* (1869) : a primate (as an australopithecine) intermediate in character between Homo sapiens and the higher apes

aper·çu \ä-per-ˈsue\ *n, pl* **aperçus** \-ˈsuez\ [F, fr. *aperçu,* pp. of *apercevoir* to perceive, fr. OF *aperceivre,* fr. *a-* (fr. L *ad-*) + *perceivre* to perceive — more at PERCEIVE] (1809) **1** : a brief survey or sketch : OUTLINE **2** : an immediate impression; *esp* : INSIGHT 2

ape·ri·ent \ə-ˈpir-ē-ənt\ *adj* [L *aperient-, aperiens,* prp. of *aperire*] (1626) : gently moving the bowels : LAXATIVE — **aperient** *n*

ape·ri·od·ic \ˌā-ˌpir-ē-ˈä-dik\ *adj* (1870) **1** : of irregular occurrence : not periodic ⟨~ floods⟩ **2** : not having periodic vibrations : not oscillatory — **ape·ri·od·i·cal·ly** \-di-k(ə-)lē\ *adv* — **ape·ri·o·dic·i·ty** \-ē-ə-ˈdi-sə-tē\ *n*

aper·i·tif \ə-ˌper-ə-ˈtēf, a-; ˌä-pər-(ə-)ˈtēf\ *n* [F *apéritif* aperient, aperitif, fr. MF *aperitif,* adj., aperient, fr. ML *aperitivus,* irreg. fr. L *aperire*] (1894) : an alcoholic drink taken before a meal as an appetizer

ap·er·ture \ˈa-pə(r)-ˌchu̇r, -chər, -ˌtyu̇r, -ˌtu̇r\ *n* [ME, fr. L *apertura,* fr. *apertus,* pp. of *aperire* to open] (15c) **1** : an opening or open space : HOLE **2 a** : the opening in a photographic lens that admits the light **b** : the diameter of the stop in an optical system that determines the diameter of the bundle of rays traversing the instrument **c** : the diameter of the objective lens or mirror of a telescope

apet·al·ous \(ˌ)ā-ˈpe-t^{ə}l-əs\ *adj* (ca. 1706) : having no petals

apex \ˈā-ˌpeks\ *n, pl* **apex·es** *or* **api·ces** \ˈā-pə-ˌsēz, ˈa-\ [L] (1601) **1 a** : the uppermost point : VERTEX ⟨the ~ of a mountain⟩ **b** : the narrowed or pointed end : TIP ⟨the ~ of the tongue⟩ **2** : the highest or culminating point ⟨the ~ of his career⟩ ***syn*** see SUMMIT

Ap·gar score \ˈap-ˌgär-\ *n* [Virginia *Apgar* †1974 Am. anesthesiologist] (1959) : an index used to evaluate the condition of a newborn infant based on a rating of 0, 1, or 2 for each of the five characteristics of color, heart rate, response to stimulation of the sole of the foot, muscle tone, and respiration with 10 being a perfect score

aphaer·e·sis \ə-ˈfer-ə-səs\ *n, pl* **-e·ses** \-ˌsēz\ [LL, fr. Gk *aphairesis,* lit., taking off, fr. *aphairein* to take away, fr. *apo-* + *hairein* to take] (ca. 1550) : the loss of one or more sounds or letters at the beginning of a word (as in *round* for *around* and *coon* for *raccoon*) — **aph·ae·ret·ic** \ˌa-fə-ˈre-tik\ *adj*

apha·sia \ə-ˈfā-zh(ē-)ə\ *n* [NL, fr. Gk, fr. *a-* + *-phasia*] (1864) : loss or impairment of the power to use or comprehend words usu. resulting from brain damage — **apha·sic** \-zik\ *n or adj*

aph·elion \a-ˈfēl-yən, ˌap-ˈhē-l-\ *n, pl* **-elia** \-yə\ [NL, fr. *apo-* + Gk *hēlios* sun — more at SOLAR] (1656) : the point in the path of a celestial body (as a planet) that is farthest from the sun — compare PERIHELION

aphe·re·sis \ˌa-fə-ˈrē-səs\ *n, pl* **-re·ses** \-ˌsēz\ [fr. *-apheresis* (as in *plasmapheresis*)] (1977) : withdrawal of blood from a donor's body, removal of one or more blood components (as plasma, platelets, or white blood cells), and transfusion of the remaining blood back into the donor — called also *pheresis*

aph·e·sis \ˈa-fə-səs\ *n, pl* **-e·ses** \-ˌsēz\ [NL, fr. Gk, release, fr. *aphienai* to let go, fr. *apo-* + *hienai* to send — more at JET] (1880) : aphaeresis consisting of the loss of a short unaccented vowel (as in *lone* for *alone*) — **aphet·ic** \ə-ˈfe-tik\ *adj* — **aphet·i·cal·ly** \-ti-k(ə-)lē\ *adv*

aphid \ˈā-fəd *also* ˈa-fəd\ *n* (1827) : any of numerous very small soft-bodied homopterous insects (superfamily Aphidoidea) that suck the juices of plants

aphid lion *n* (1949) : any of several insect larvae (as a lacewing or ladybug larva) that feed on aphids — called also *aphis lion*

aphis \ˈā-fəs *also* ˈa-fəs\ *n, pl* **aphi·des** \ˈā-fə-ˌdēz, ˈa-fə-\ [NL *Aphid-, Aphis,* genus name] (1763) : any of a genus (*Aphis*) of aphids; *broadly* : APHID

apho·nia \(ˌ)ā-ˈfō-nē-ə\ *n* [NL, fr. Gk *aphōnia,* fr. *aphōnos* voiceless, fr. *a-* + *phōnē* sound — more at BAN] (1654) : loss of voice and of all but whispered speech — **apho·nic** \-ˈfä-nik, -ˈfō-\ *adj*

aph·o·rism \ˈa-fə-ˌri-zəm\ *n* [MF *aphorisme,* fr. LL *aphorismus,* fr. Gk *aphorismos* definition, aphorism, fr. *aphorizein* to define, fr. *apo-* + *horizein* to bound — more at HORIZON] (1528) **1** : a concise statement of a principle **2** : a terse formulation of a truth or sentiment : ADAGE — **aph·o·rist** \-rist\ *n* — **aph·o·ris·tic** \ˌa-fə-ˈris-tik\ *adj* — **aph·o·ris·ti·cal·ly** \-ti-k(ə-)lē\ *adv*

aph·o·rize \ˈa-fə-ˌrīz\ *vi* **-rized; -riz·ing** (1669) : to write or speak in or as if in aphorisms

apho·tic \(ˌ)ā-ˈfō-tik\ *adj* (1894) : being the deep zone of an ocean or lake receiving too little light to permit photosynthesis

aph·ro·di·si·ac \ˌa-frə-ˈdē-zē-ˌak, -ˈdi-zē-\ *n* [Gk *aphrodisiakos* sexual, gem with aphrodisiac properties, fr. *aphrodisia* heterosexual pleasures, fr. neut. pl. of *aphrodisios* of Aphrodite, fr. *Aphroditē*] (1711) : an agent (as a food or drug) that arouses or is held to arouse sexual desire — **aphrodisiac** *also* **aph·ro·di·si·a·cal** \ˌa-frə-di-ˈsī-ə-kəl, -ˈzī-\ *adj*

Aph·ro·di·te \ˌa-frə-ˈdī-tē\ *n* [Gk *Aphroditē*] (1565) : the Greek goddess of love and beauty — compare VENUS

api·ar·i·an \ˌā-pē-ˈer-ē-ən\ *adj* (1790) : of or relating to beekeeping or bees

api·a·rist \ˈā-pē-ə-rist, -pē-ˌer-ist\ *n* (1785) : BEEKEEPER

api·ary \ˈā-pē-ˌer-ē, -ˌe-rē\ *n, pl* **-ar·ies** [L *apiarium,* fr. *apis* bee] (1654) : a place where bees are kept; *esp* : a collection of hives or colonies of bees kept for their honey

api·cal \ˈā-pi-kəl *also* ˈa-pi-\ *adj* [prob. fr. NL *apicalis,* fr. L *apic-, apex*] (1806) **1** : of, relating to, or situated at an apex **2** : of, relating to, or

\ə\ **abut** \$^{ə}$\ kitten, F table \ər\ **fur**ther \a\ **ash** \ā\ **ace** \ä\ **mop, mar**
\au̇\ **out** \ch\ **chin** \e\ **bet** \ē\ **easy** \g\ **go** \i\ **hit** \ī\ **ice** \j\ **job**
\ŋ\ **sing** \ō\ **go** \ȯ\ **law** \ȯi\ **boy** \th\ **thin** \t͟h\ **the** \ü\ **loot** \u̇\ **foot**
\y\ **yet** \zh\ **vision, beige** \k̲, ^{n}, œ, ue, ^{y}\ *see* Guide to Pronunciation

formed with the tip of the tongue ⟨*n, l,* and *r* are ~ consonants⟩ — **api·cal·ly** \-k(ə-)lē\ *adv*
apical dominance *n* (1947) : inhibition of the growth of lateral buds by the terminal bud of a shoot
apical meristem *n* (ca. 1934) : a meristem at the apex of a root or shoot that is responsible for increase in length
apic·u·late \ə-ˈpi-kyə-lət, ā-\ *adj* [NL *apiculus,* dim. of L *apic-, apex*] (1830) : ending abruptly in a small distinct point ⟨an ~ leaf⟩
api·cul·ture \ˈā-pə-ˌkəl-chər\ *n* [prob. fr. F, fr. L *apis* bee + F *culture*] (1864) : the keeping of bees esp. on a large scale — **api·cul·tur·al** \ˌā-pə-ˈkəl-ch(ə-)rəl\ *adj* — **api·cul·tur·ist** \-ch(ə-)rist\ *n*
apiece \ə-ˈpēs\ *adv* (15c) : for each one : INDIVIDUALLY
Apis \ˈā-pəs\ *n* [L, fr. Gk, fr. Egypt *ḥp*] (14c) : a sacred bull worshipped by the ancient Egyptians
ap·ish \ˈā-pish\ *adj* (ca. 1527) : resembling an ape: as **a** : extremely silly or affected ⟨~ antics⟩ **b** : given to slavish imitation — **ap·ish·ly** *adv* — **ap·ish·ness** *n*
APL \ˌā-(ˌ)pē-ˈel\ *n* [*a programming language*] (1966) : a computer programming language designed esp. for the concise representation of algorithms
ap·la·nat·ic \ˌa-plə-ˈna-tik\ *adj* [*a-* + Gk *planasthai* to wander — more at PLANET] (1794) : free from or corrected for spherical aberration ⟨an ~ lens⟩
aplas·tic anemia \(ˌ)ā-ˈplas-tik-\ *n* (1928) : anemia that is characterized by defective function of the blood-forming organs (as the bone marrow) and is caused by toxic agents (as chemicals or X-rays) or is idiopathic in origin
[1]**aplen·ty** \ə-ˈplen-tē\ *adj* (1830) : being in plenty or abundance — used postpositively ⟨money ~ for all their needs⟩
[2]**aplenty** *adv* (1846) **1** : in abundance : PLENTIFULLY **2** : very much : EXTREMELY ⟨scared ~⟩
ap·lite \ˈa-ˌplīt\ *n* [prob. fr. G *Aplit,* fr. Gk *haploos* simple — more at HAPL-] (1879) : a fine-grained light-colored granite consisting almost entirely of quartz and feldspar — **ap·lit·ic** \a-ˈpli-tik\ *adj*
aplomb \ə-ˈpläm, -ˈpləm\ *n* [F, lit., perpendicularity, fr. MF, fr. *a plomb,* lit., according to the plummet] (1823) : complete and confident composure or self-assurance : POISE ***syn*** see CONFIDENCE
ap·nea \ˈap-nē-ə\ *n* [NL, fr. *a-* + *-pnea*] (ca. 1719) **1** : transient cessation of respiration; *esp* : SLEEP APNEA **2** : ASPHYXIA — **ap·ne·ic** \-nē-ik\ *adj*
ap·noea *chiefly Brit var of* APNEA
apo \ˈa-pō\ *n, pl* **apos** (1983) : APOLIPOPROTEIN — usu. used with a letter or letter and number
APO *abbr* army post office
apo- *or* **ap-** *prefix* [L, fr. Gk, fr. *apo* — more at OF] **1** : away from : off ⟨*ap*helion⟩ **2** : detached : separate ⟨*apo*gamy⟩ **3** : formed from : related to ⟨*apo*morphine⟩
Apoc *abbr* **1** Apocalypse **2** Apocrypha **3** apocryphal
apoc·a·lypse \ə-ˈpä-kə-ˌlips\ *n* [ME, revelation, Revelation, fr. AF *apocalipse,* fr. LL *apocalypsis,* fr. Gk *apokalypsis,* fr. *apokalyptein* to uncover, fr. *apo-* + *kalyptein* to cover — more at HELL] (13c) **1 a** : one of the Jewish and Christian writings of 200 B.C. to A.D. 150 marked by pseudonymity, symbolic imagery, and the expectation of an imminent cosmic cataclysm in which God destroys the ruling powers of evil and raises the righteous to life in a messianic kingdom **b** *cap* : REVELATION 3 **2 a** : something viewed as a prophetic revelation **b** : ARMAGEDDON **3** : a great disaster ⟨an environmental ~⟩
apoc·a·lyp·tic \ə-ˌpä-kə-ˈlip-tik\ *also* **apoc·a·lyp·ti·cal** \-ti-kəl\ *adj* (1663) **1** : of, relating to, or resembling an apocalypse **2** : forecasting the ultimate destiny of the world : PROPHETIC **3** : foreboding imminent disaster or final doom : TERRIBLE **4** : wildly unrestrained : GRANDIOSE **5** : ultimately decisive : CLIMACTIC ⟨an ~ battle⟩ — **apoc·a·lyp·ti·cal·ly** \-ti-k(ə-)lē\ *adv*
apoc·a·lyp·ti·cism \-tə-ˌsi-zəm\ *or* **apoc·a·lyp·tism** \ə-ˈpä-kə-ˌlip-ˌti-zəm\ *n* (1884) : apocalyptic expectation; *esp* : a doctrine concerning an imminent end of the world and an ensuing general resurrection and final judgment
apoc·a·lyp·tist \ə-ˈpä-kə-ˌlip-tist\ *n* (1835) : the writer of an apocalypse
apo·chro·mat·ic \ˌa-pə-krō-ˈma-tik\ *adj* [ISV] (1886) : free from chromatic and spherical aberration ⟨an ~ lens⟩
apoc·o·pe \ə-ˈpä-kə-(ˌ)pē\ *n* [LL, fr. Gk *apokopē,* lit., cutting off, fr. *apokoptein* to cut off, fr. *apo-* + *koptein* to cut — more at CAPON] (ca. 1550) : the loss of one or more sounds or letters at the end of a word (as in *sing* from Old English *singan*)
apo·crine \ˈa-pə-krən, -ˌkrīn, -ˌkrēn\ *adj* [ISV *apo-* + Gk *krinein* to separate — more at CERTAIN] (1926) : producing a fluid secretion by pinching off one end of the secretory cell while leaving the rest intact ⟨an ~ gland⟩; *also* : produced by an apocrine gland
apoc·ry·pha \ə-ˈpä-krə-fə\ *n pl but sing or pl in constr* [ML, fr. LL, neut. pl. of *apocryphus* secret, not canonical, fr. Gk *apokryphos* obscure, fr. *apokryptein* to hide away, fr. *apo-* + *kryptein* to hide — more at CRYPT] (14c) **1** : writings or statements of dubious authenticity **2** *cap* **a** : books included in the Septuagint and Vulgate but excluded from the Jewish and Protestant canons of the Old Testament — see BIBLE table **b** : early Christian writings not included in the New Testament
apoc·ry·phal \-fəl\ *adj* (1590) **1** : of doubtful authenticity : SPURIOUS **2** *often cap* : of or resembling the Apocrypha ***syn*** see FICTITIOUS — **apoc·ry·phal·ly** \-fə-lē\ *adv* — **apoc·ry·phal·ness** *n*
apo·dic·tic \ˌa-pə-ˈdik-tik\ *also* **apo·deic·tic** \-ˈdīk-tik\ *adj* [L *apodicticus,* fr. Gk *apodeiktikos,* fr. *apodeiknynai* to demonstrate, fr. *apo-* + *deiknynai* to show — more at DICTION] (ca. 1645) : expressing or of the nature of necessary truth or absolute certainty — **apo·dic·ti·cal·ly** \-ti-k(ə-)lē\ *adv*
apod·o·sis \ə-ˈpä-də-səs\ *n, pl* **-o·ses** \-ˌsēz\ [NL, fr. Gk, fr. *apodidonai* to give back, deliver, fr. *apo-* + *didonai* to give — more at DATE] (1604) : the main clause of a conditional sentence — compare PROTASIS
apo·en·zyme \ˌa-pō-ˈen-ˌzīm\ *n* [ISV] (1936) : a protein that forms an active enzyme system by combination with a coenzyme and determines the specificity of this system for a substrate
apog·a·my \ə-ˈpä-gə-mē\ *n* [ISV] (ca. 1878) : development of a sporophyte from a gametophyte without fertilization
apo·gee \ˈa-pə-(ˌ)jē\ *n* [F *apogée,* fr. NL *apogaeum,* fr. Gk *apogaion,* fr. neut. of *apogeios, apogaios* far from the earth, fr. *apo-* + *gē, gaia* earth] (1594) **1** : the point in the orbit of an object (as a satellite) orbiting the earth that is at the greatest distance from the center of the earth; *also* : the point farthest from a planet or a satellite (as the moon) reached by an object orbiting it — compare PERIGEE **2** : the farthest or highest point : CULMINATION ⟨Aegean civilization reached its ~ in Crete⟩ — **apo·ge·an** \ˌa-pə-ˈjē-ən\ *adj*

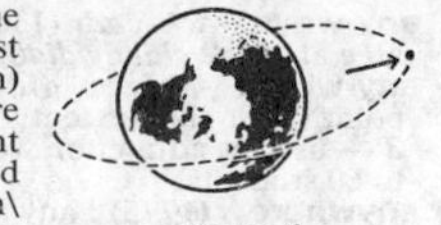

apogee 1

apo·li·po·pro·tein \ˌa-pō-ˌlī-pō-ˈprō-ˌtēn, -ˌli-, -ˌtē-ən\ *n* (1970) : a protein that combines with a lipid to form a lipoprotein — often used with a letter or letter and number
apo·lit·i·cal \ˌā-pə-ˈli-ti-kəl\ *adj* (1935) **1** : having no interest or involvement in political affairs; *also* : having an aversion to politics or political affairs **2** : having no political significance — **apo·lit·i·cal·ly** \-k(ə-)lē\ *adv* — **apo·lit·i·cism** \-tə-ˌsi-zəm\ *n*
Ap·ol·lin·i·an \ˌa-pə-ˈli-nē-ən\ *adj* (1924) : APOLLONIAN
Apol·lo \ə-ˈpä-(ˌ)lō\ *n* [L *Apollin-, Apollo,* fr. Gk *Apollōn*] (13c) **1** : the Greek and Roman god of sunlight, prophecy, music, and poetry **2** [*Apollo,* an asteroid of this class] : any of a class of asteroids having an orbit that extends from inside to beyond the earth's orbit
Ap·ol·lo·ni·an \ˌa-pə-ˈlō-nē-ən\ *adj* (1663) **1** : of, relating to, or resembling the god Apollo **2** : harmonious, measured, ordered, or balanced in character — compare DIONYSIAN
Apol·lyon \ə-ˈpäl-yən, -ˈpä-lē-ən\ *n* [Gk *Apollyōn*] (14c) : the angel of the bottomless pit in the Book of Revelation
[1]**apol·o·get·ic** \ə-ˌpä-lə-ˈje-tik\ *n* (15c) : APOLOGETICS 1
[2]**apologetic** *adj* [Gk *apologētikos,* fr. *apologeisthai* to defend, fr. *apo-* + *logos* speech] (1649) **1 a** : offered in defense or vindication ⟨the ~ writings of the early Christians⟩ **b** : offered by way of excuse or apology ⟨an ~ smile⟩ **2** : regretfully acknowledging fault or failure : CONTRITE ⟨replied in an ~ tone⟩ — **apol·o·get·i·cal·ly** \-ti-k(ə-)lē\ *adv*
apol·o·get·ics \-tiks\ *n pl but sing or pl in constr* (ca. 1733) **1** : systematic argumentative discourse in defense (as of a doctrine) **2** : a branch of theology devoted to the defense of the divine origin and authority of Christianity
ap·o·lo·gia \ˌa-pə-ˈlō-j(ē-)ə\ *n* [LL] (1784) : a defense esp. of one's opinions, position, or actions ⟨the finest ~ or explanation of what drives a man to devote his life to pure mathematics —*Brit. Book News*⟩ ***syn*** see APOLOGY
apol·o·gise *Brit var of* APOLOGIZE
apol·o·gist \ə-ˈpä-lə-jist\ *n* (1640) : one who speaks or writes in defense of someone or something
apol·o·gize \-ˌjīz\ *vi* **-gized; -giz·ing** (1596) : to make an apology — **apol·o·giz·er** *n*
ap·o·logue \ˈa-pə-ˌlȯg, -ˌläg\ *n* [F, fr. L *apologus,* fr. Gk *apologos,* fr. *apo-* + *logos* speech, narrative] (ca. 1555) : an allegorical narrative usu. intended to convey a moral
apol·o·gy \ə-ˈpä-lə-jē\ *n, pl* **-gies** [MF or LL; MF *apologie,* fr. LL *apologia,* fr. Gk, fr. *apo-* + *logos* speech — more at LEGEND] (1533) **1 a** : a formal justification : DEFENSE **b** : EXCUSE 2a **2** : an admission of error or discourtesy accompanied by an expression of regret ⟨a public ~⟩ **3** : a poor substitute : MAKESHIFT
syn APOLOGY, APOLOGIA, EXCUSE, PLEA, PRETEXT, ALIBI mean matter offered in explanation or defense. APOLOGY usu. applies to an expression of regret for a mistake or wrong with implied admission of guilt or fault and with or without reference to mitigating or extenuating circumstances ⟨said by way of *apology* that he would have met them if he could⟩. APOLOGIA implies not admission of guilt or regret but a desire to make clear the grounds for some course, belief, or position ⟨his speech was an *apologia* for his foreign policy⟩. EXCUSE implies an intent to avoid or remove blame or censure ⟨used illness as an *excuse* for missing the meeting⟩. PLEA stresses argument or appeal for understanding or sympathy or mercy ⟨her usual *plea* that she was nearsighted⟩. PRETEXT suggests subterfuge and the offering of false reasons or motives in excuse or explanation ⟨used any *pretext* to get out of work⟩. ALIBI implies a desire to shift blame or evade punishment and imputes mere plausibility to the explanation ⟨his *alibi* failed to stand scrutiny⟩.
apo·lune \ˈa-pə-ˌlün\ *n* [*apo-* + L *luna* moon — more at LUNAR] (ca. 1968) : the point in the path of a body orbiting the moon that is farthest from the center of the moon — compare PERILUNE
apo·mict \ˈa-pə-ˌmikt\ *n* [prob. back-formation fr. ISV *apomictic,* fr. *apo-* + Gk *mignynai* to mix — more at MIX] (ca. 1938) : one produced or reproducing by apomixis — **apo·mic·tic** \ˌa-pə-ˈmik-tik\ *adj* — **apo·mic·ti·cal·ly** \-ti-k(ə-)lē\ *adv*
apo·mix·is \ˌa-pə-ˈmik-səs\ *n, pl* **-mix·es** \-ˌsēz\ [NL, fr. *apo-* + Gk *mixis* act of mixing, fr. *mignynai*] (1913) : reproduction (as apogamy or parthenogenesis) involving specialized generative tissues but not dependent on fertilization
apo·mor·phine \ˌa-pə-ˈmȯr-ˌfēn\ *n* [ISV] (1888) : a crystalline morphine derivative $C_{17}H_{17}NO_2$ that is a dopamine agonist and is administered in the form of its hydrochloride for its powerful emetic action
apo·neu·ro·sis \ˌa-pə-nu̇-ˈrō-səs, -nyu̇-\ *n* [NL, fr. Gk *aponeurōsis,* fr. *aponeurousthai* to pass into a tendon, fr. *apo-* + *neuron* sinew — more at NERVE] (1676) : a broad flat sheet of dense fibrous collagenous connective tissue that covers, invests, and forms the terminations and attachments of various muscles — **apo·neu·rot·ic** \-ˈrä-tik\ *adj*
apoph·a·sis \ə-ˈpä-fə-səs\ *n* [LL, repudiation, fr. Gk, denial, negation, fr. *apophanai* to deny, fr. *apo-* + *phanai* to say — more at BAN] (1657) : the raising of an issue by claiming not to mention it (as in "we won't discuss his past crimes")
ap·o·phthegm *chiefly Brit var of* APOTHEGM
apo·phyl·lite \ə-ˈpä-fə-ˌlīt, ˌa-pə-ˈfi-ˌlīt\ *n* [F, fr. *apo-* + Gk *phyllon* leaf — more at BLADE] (1810) : a mineral composed of a hydrous silicate of potassium, calcium, and fluorine that is related to the zeolites and is usu. found in transparent square prisms or white or grayish masses
apoph·y·sis \ə-ˈpä-fə-səs\ *n, pl* **-y·ses** \-ˌsēz\ [NL, fr. Gk, fr. *apo-* + *phyein* to bring forth — more at BE] (1646) : an expanded or projecting part esp. of an organism — **apoph·y·se·al** \ə-ˌpä-fə-ˈsē-əl\ *adj*
ap·o·plec·tic \ˌa-pə-ˈplek-tik\ *adj* [F or LL; F *apoplectique,* fr. LL *apoplecticus,* fr. Gk *apoplēktikos,* fr. *apoplēssein*] (1611) **1** : of, relating to, or causing stroke **2** : affected with, inclined to, or showing symptoms of stroke **3** : of a kind to cause or apparently cause stroke ⟨an ~

rage⟩; *also* : greatly excited or angered ⟨was ∼ over the news⟩ — **ap·o·plec·ti·cal·ly** \-ti-k(ə-)lē\ *adv*

ap·o·plexy \ˈa-pə-ˌplek-sē\ *n* [ME *apoplexie,* fr. MF & LL; MF, fr. LL *apoplexia,* fr. Gk *apoplēxia,* fr. *apoplēssein* to cripple by a stroke, fr. *apo-* + *plēssein* to strike — more at PLAINT] (15c) : STROKE 5

ap·o·pto·sis \ˌa-pəp-ˈtō-səs, -pə-ˈtō-\ *n, pl* **-pto·ses** \-ˌsēz\ [NL, fr. Gk *apoptōsis* a falling off, fr. *apopiptein* to fall off, fr. *apo-* + *piptein* to fall — more at FEATHER] (1972) : a genetically directed process of cell self-destruction that is marked by the fragmentation of nuclear DNA, is activated either by the presence of a stimulus or removal of a suppressing agent or stimulus, and is a normal physiological process eliminating DNA-damaged, superfluous, or unwanted cells — called also *programmed cell death* — **ap·o·pto·tic** \-ˈtä-tik\ *adj*

apo·ria \ə-ˈpȯr-ē-ə\ *n* [F *aporie,* ultim. fr. Gk *aporia* difficulty, perplexity, fr. *aporos* impassable, fr. *a-* + *poros* passage — more at FARE] (ca. 1550) **1** : an expression of real or pretended doubt or uncertainty esp. for rhetorical effect **2** : a logical impasse or contradiction; *esp* : a radical contradiction in the import of a text or theory that is seen in deconstruction as inevitable

aport \ə-ˈpȯrt\ *adv* (1627) : on or toward the left side of a ship ⟨put the helm hard ∼⟩

apos *pl of* APO

apo·se·mat·ic \ˌa-pə-si-ˈma-tik\ *adj* [*apo-* + Gk *sēmat-, sēma* sign] (1890) : being conspicuous and serving to warn ⟨∼ coloration in butterflies⟩ — **apo·se·mat·i·cal·ly** \-ti-k(ə-)lē\ *adv*

ap·o·si·o·pe·sis \ˌa-pə-ˌsī-ə-ˈpē-səs\ *n, pl* **-pe·ses** \-ˌsēz\ [LL, fr. Gk *aposiōpēsis,* fr. *aposiōpan* to be fully silent, fr. *apo-* + *siōpan* to be silent, fr. *siōpē* silence] (1555) : the leaving of a thought incomplete usu. by a sudden breaking off (as in "his behavior was—but I blush to mention that") — **ap·o·si·o·pet·ic** \-ˈpe-tik\ *adj*

apos·po·ry \ˈa-pə-ˌspȯr-ē, ə-ˈpäs-pə-rē\ *n* (1884) : production of gametophytes directly from diploid cells of the sporophytes without spore formation (as in certain ferns and mosses)

apos·ta·sy \ə-ˈpäs-tə-sē\ *n, pl* **-sies** [ME *apostasie,* fr. LL *apostasia,* fr. Gk, lit., revolt, fr. *aphistasthai* to revolt, fr. *apo-* + *histasthai* to stand — more at STAND] (14c) **1** : renunciation of a religious faith **2** : abandonment of a previous loyalty : DEFECTION

apos·tate \ə-ˈpäs-ˌtāt, -tət\ *n* (14c) : one who commits apostasy — **apostate** *adj*

apos·ta·tise *Brit var of* APOSTATIZE

apos·ta·tize \ə-ˈpäs-tə-ˌtīz\ *vi* **-tized; -tiz·ing** (1611) : to commit apostasy

a pos·te·ri·o·ri \ˌä-(ˌ)pō-ˌstir-ē-ˈȯr-ē, -ˌster-; ˌā-(ˌ)pä-ˌstir-ē-ˈȯr-ˌī, -(ˌ)pō-, -ˈȯr-ē\ *adj* [L, lit., from the latter] (1588) **1** : INDUCTIVE **2** : relating to or derived by reasoning from observed facts — compare A PRIORI — **a posteriori** *adv*

apos·tle \ə-ˈpä-səl\ *n* [ME, fr. AF & OE; AF *apostle* & OE *apostol,* both fr. LL *apostolus,* fr. Gk *apostolos,* fr. *apostellein* to send away, fr. *apo-* + *stellein* to send] (bef. 12c) **1** : one sent on a mission: as **a** : one of an authoritative New Testament group sent out to preach the gospel and made up esp. of Christ's 12 original disciples and Paul **b** : the first prominent Christian missionary to a region or group **2 a** : a person who initiates a great moral reform or who first advocates an important belief or system **b** : an ardent supporter : ADHERENT **3** : the highest ecclesiastical official in some church organizations **4** : one of a Mormon administrative council of 12 men — **apos·tle·ship** \-ˌship\ *n*

Apostles' Creed *n* (1602) : a Christian statement of belief ascribed to the Twelve Apostles and used esp. in public worship

apos·to·late \ə-ˈpäs-tə-ˌlāt, -lət\ *n* [LL *apostolatus,* fr. *apostolus*] (14c) **1** : the office or mission of an apostle **2** : an association of persons dedicated to the propagation of a religion or a doctrine

ap·os·tol·ic \ˌa-pə-ˈstä-lik\ *adj* (13c) **1 a** : of or relating to an apostle **b** : of, relating to, or conforming to the teachings of the New Testament apostles **2 a** : of or relating to a succession of spiritual authority from the apostles held (as by Roman Catholics, Anglicans, and Eastern Orthodox) to be perpetuated by successive ordinations of bishops and to be necessary for valid sacraments and orders **b** : PAPAL — **apos·to·lic·i·ty** \ə-ˌpäs-tə-ˈli-sə-tē\ *n*

apostolic delegate *n* (ca. 1907) : an ecclesiastical representative of the Holy See to the Catholic hierarchy of another country

Apostolic Father *n* (1828) : a church father of the first or second century A.D.

[1]**apos·tro·phe** \ə-ˈpäs-trə-(ˌ)fē\ *n* [L, fr. Gk *apostrophē,* lit., act of turning away, fr. *apostrephein* to turn away, fr. *apo-* + *strephein* to turn] (1533) : the addressing of a usu. absent person or a usu. personified thing rhetorically ⟨Carlyle's "O Liberty, what things are done in thy name!" is an example of ∼⟩ — **ap·os·troph·ic** \ˌa-pə-ˈsträ-fik\ *adj*

[2]**apostrophe** *n* [F & LL; F, fr. LL *apostrophus,* fr. Gk *apostrophos,* fr. *apostrophos* turned away, fr. *apostrephein*] (1727) : a mark ' used to indicate the omission of letters or figures, the possessive case, or the plural of letters or figures — **apostrophic** *adj*

apos·tro·phise *Brit var of* APOSTROPHIZE

apos·tro·phize \ə-ˈpäs-trə-ˌfīz\ *vb* **-phized; -phiz·ing** *vt* (1718) : to address by or in apostrophe ∼ *vi* : to make use of apostrophe

apothecaries' measure *n* (ca. 1900) : a system of liquid units of measure used chiefly by pharmacists — called also *apothecary measure*

apothecaries' weight *n* (1765) : a system of weights used chiefly by pharmacists — called also *apothecary weight;* see WEIGHT table

apoth·e·cary \ə-ˈpä-thə-ˌker-ē, -ˌke-rē\ *n, pl* **-car·ies** [ME *apothecarie,* fr. ML *apothecarius,* fr. LL, shopkeeper, fr. L *apotheca* storehouse, fr. Gk *apothēkē,* fr. *apotithenai* to put away, fr. *apo-* + *tithenai* to put — more at DO] (14c) **1** : one who prepares and sells drugs or compounds for medicinal purposes **2** : PHARMACY

apo·the·ci·um \ˌa-pə-ˈthē-shē-əm, -sē-\ *n, pl* **-cia** \-shē-ə, -sē-\ [NL, fr. L *apotheca*] (1830) : a spore-bearing structure in many lichens and fungi consisting of a discoid or cupped body bearing asci on the exposed flat or concave surface — **apo·the·cial** \-sh(ē-)əl, -sē-əl\ *adj*

ap·o·thegm \ˈa-pə-ˌthem\ *n* [Gk *apophthegmat-, apophthegma,* fr. *apophthengesthai* to speak out, fr. *apo-* + *phthengesthai* to utter] (ca. 1587) : a short, pithy, and instructive saying or formulation : APHORISM — **ap·o·theg·mat·ic** \ˌa-pə-theg-ˈma-tik\ *adj*

ap·o·them \ˈa-pə-ˌthem\ *n* [ISV *apo-* + *-them* (fr. Gk *thema* something laid down, theme)] (ca. 1856) : the perpendicular from the center of a regular polygon to one of the sides

apo·the·o·sis \ə-ˌpä-thē-ˈō-səs, ˌa-pə-ˈthē-ə-səs\ *n, pl* **-o·ses** \-ˌsēz\ [LL, fr. Gk *apotheōsis,* fr. *apotheoun* to deify, fr. *apo-* + *theos* god] (ca. 1580) **1** : elevation to divine status : DEIFICATION **2** : the perfect example : QUINTESSENCE ⟨this is the literary ∼ of the shaggy dog story —Thomas Sutcliffe⟩ — **apo·the·o·size** \ˌa-pə-ˈthē-ə-ˌsīz, ə-ˈpä-thē-ə-\ *vt*

apo·tro·pa·ic \ˌa-pə-trō-ˈpā-ik\ *adj* [Gk *apotropaios,* fr. *apotrepein* to avert, fr. *apo-* + *trepein* to turn] (1883) : designed to avert evil ⟨an ∼ ritual⟩ — **apo·tro·pa·i·cal·ly** \-ˈpā-ə-k(ə-)lē\ *adv*

[1]**app** \ˈap\ *n* (1987) : APPLICATION 1a(3)

[2]**app** *abbr* **1** apparatus **2** appendix **3** appliance

Ap·pa·la·chian \ˌa-pə-ˈlā-ch(ē-)ən, -ˈla-, -sh(ē-)ən\ *n* (1949) : a native or resident of the Appalachian mountain area

Appalachian dulcimer *n* (1962) : DULCIMER 2

ap·pall *also* **ap·pal** \ə-ˈpȯl\ *vb* **ap·palled; ap·pall·ing** [ME, fr. MF *apalir,* fr. OF, fr. *a-* (fr. L *ad-*) + *palir* to grow pale, fr. L *pallescere,* incho. of *pallēre* to be pale — more at FALLOW] *vi* (14c) *obs* : WEAKEN, FAIL ∼ *vt* : to overcome with consternation, shock, or dismay ⟨we were ∼*ed* by his behavior⟩ ***syn*** see DISMAY

ap·pall·ing *adj* (1817) : inspiring horror, dismay, or disgust ⟨living under ∼ conditions⟩ — **ap·pall·ing·ly** *adv*

Ap·pa·loo·sa \ˌa-pə-ˈlü-sə\ *n* [origin unknown] (1947) : any of a breed of rugged saddle horses developed in western No. America and usu. having a white or solid-colored coat with small spots

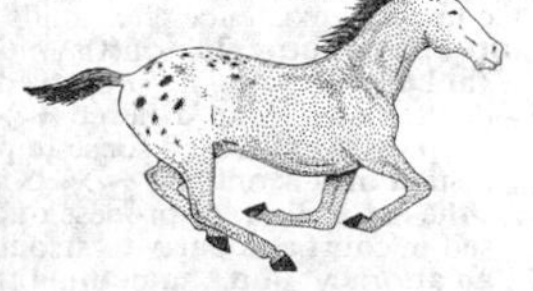
Appaloosa

ap·pa·nage *also* **a·pa·nage** \ˈa-pə-nij\ *n* [F *apanage,* fr. OF, fr. *apaner* to provide for a younger offspring, fr. ML *appanare,* fr. L *ad-* + *panis* bread — more at FOOD] (1602) **1 a** : a grant (as of land or revenue) made by a sovereign or a legislative body to a dependent member of the royal family or a principal vassal **b** : a property or privilege appropriated to or by a person as something due **2** : a rightful endowment or adjunct

ap·pa·rat \ˈa-pə-ˌrat, ˌä-pə-ˈrät\ *n* [Russ] (1941) : APPARATUS 2

ap·pa·rat·chik \ˌä-pə-ˈrä(t)-chik\ *n, pl* **-chiks** *also* **-chi·ki** \-chi-kē\ [Russ, fr. *apparat*] (1941) **1** : a member of a Communist apparat **2** : a blindly devoted official, follower, or member of an organization (as a corporation or political party) ⟨a movie studio ∼⟩

ap·pa·ra·tus \ˌa-pə-ˈra-təs, -ˈrā-\ *n, pl* **-tus·es** *or* **-tus** [L, fr. *apparare* to prepare, fr. *ad-* + *parare* to prepare — more at PARE] (ca. 1628) **1 a** : a set of materials or equipment designed for a particular use **b** : a group of anatomical or cytological parts functioning together ⟨mitotic ∼⟩ **c** : an instrument or appliance designed for a specific operation **2** : the functional processes by means of which a systematized activity is carried out ⟨the ∼ of society⟩: as **a** : the machinery of government **b** : the organization of a political party or an underground movement

[1]**ap·par·el** \ə-ˈper-əl, -ˈpa-rəl\ *vt* **-eled** *or* **-elled; -el·ing** *or* **-el·ling** [ME *appareillen,* fr. AF *appareiller* to prepare, fr. VL **appariculare,* fr. L *apparare*] (14c) **1** : to put clothes on : DRESS **2** : ADORN, EMBELLISH ⟨accused of ∼*ing* the truth⟩

[2]**apparel** *n* (14c) **1** : the equipment (as sails and rigging) of a ship **2** : personal attire : CLOTHING **3** : something that clothes or adorns ⟨the bright ∼ of spring⟩

ap·par·ent \ə-ˈper-ənt, -ˈpa-rənt\ *adj* [ME, fr. AF *apparant,* fr. L *apparent-, apparens,* prp. of *apparēre* to appear] (14c) **1** : open to view : VISIBLE **2** : clear or manifest to the understanding ⟨reasons that are readily ∼⟩ **3** : appearing as actual to the eye or mind **4** : having an indefeasible right to succeed to a title or estate **5** : manifest to the senses or mind as real or true on the basis of evidence that may or may not be factually valid ⟨the air of spontaneity is perhaps more ∼ than real —J. R. Sutherland⟩ — **ap·par·ent·ness** \-nəs\ *n*

syn APPARENT, ILLUSORY, SEEMING, OSTENSIBLE mean not actually being what appearance indicates. APPARENT suggests appearance to unaided senses that may or may not be borne out by more rigorous examination or greater knowledge ⟨the *apparent* cause of the accident⟩. ILLUSORY implies a false impression based on deceptive resemblance or faulty observation, or influenced by emotions that prevent a clear view ⟨an *illusory* sense of security⟩. SEEMING implies a character in the thing observed that gives it the appearance, sometimes through intent, of something else ⟨the *seeming* simplicity of the story⟩. OSTENSIBLE suggests a discrepancy between an openly declared or naturally implied aim or reason and the true one ⟨the *ostensible* reason for their visit⟩. ***syn*** see in addition EVIDENT

ap·par·ent·ly \-lē\ *adv* (1566) : it seems apparent ⟨the window had ∼ been forced open⟩ ⟨∼, we're supposed to wait here⟩

apparent magnitude *n* (1785) : the luminosity of a celestial body (as a star) as observed from the earth — compare ABSOLUTE MAGNITUDE

apparent time *n* (1694) : the time of day indicated by the hour angle of the sun or by a sundial

ap·pa·ri·tion \ˌa-pə-ˈri-shən\ *n* [ME *apparicioun,* fr. AF *aparicion,* fr. LL *apparition-, apparitio* appearance, fr. L *apparēre*] (15c) **1 a** : an unusual or unexpected sight : PHENOMENON **b** : a ghostly figure **2** : the act of becoming visible : APPEARANCE — **ap·pa·ri·tion·al** \-ˈrish-nəl, -ˈri-shə-nᵊl\ *adj*

ap·par·i·tor \ə-ˈper-ə-tər, -ˈpa-rə-\ *n* [L, fr. *apparēre*] (15c) : an official formerly sent to carry out the orders of a magistrate, judge, or court

[1]**ap·peal** \ə-ˈpēl\ *n* [ME *appel,* fr. AF *apel,* fr. *apeler*] (13c) **1** : a legal proceeding by which a case is brought before a higher court for review of the decision of a lower court **2** : a criminal accusation **3 a** : an application (as to a recognized authority) for corroboration, vindication, or decision **b** : an earnest plea : ENTREATY ⟨an ∼ for help⟩ **c** : an organized request for donations ⟨the annual ∼⟩ **4** : the power of

\ə\ **abut** \ᵊ\ kitten, F table \ər\ **fur**ther \a\ **ash** \ā\ **ace** \ä\ mop, mar \au̇\ **out** \ch\ **chin** \e\ bet \ē\ **easy** \g\ **go** \i\ **hit** \ī\ **ice** \j\ **job** \ŋ\ **sing** \ō\ **go** \ȯ\ **law** \ȯi\ **boy** \th\ **thin** \t͟h\ **the** \ü\ **loot** \u̇\ **foot** \y\ yet \zh\ **vision, beige** \ḵ, ⁿ, œ, ue, ʸ\ *see* Guide to Pronunciation

arousing a sympathetic response : ATTRACTION ⟨movies had a great ~ for him⟩
[2]**appeal** *vb* [ME *appelen* to accuse, appeal, fr. AF *apeler,* lit., to call, summon, fr. L *appellare,* fr. *appellere* to drive to, fr. *ad-* + *pellere* to drive — more at FELT] *vt* (14c) **1 :** to charge with a crime : ACCUSE **2 :** to take proceedings to have (a lower court's decision) reviewed in a higher court ~ *vi* **1 :** to take a lower court's decision to a higher court for review **2 :** to call upon another for corroboration, vindication, or decision **3 :** to make an earnest request ⟨~*ed* to them for help⟩ **4 :** to arouse a sympathetic response ⟨that idea ~*s* to him⟩ — **ap·peal·abil·i·ty** \-ˌpē-lə-ˈbi-lə-tē\ *n* — **ap·peal·able** \-ˈpē-lə-bəl\ *adj* — **ap·peal·er** *n*
ap·peal·ing \ə-ˈpē-liŋ\ *adj* (1813) **1 :** marked by earnest entreaty : IMPLORING **2 :** having appeal : PLEASING ⟨an ~ design⟩ — **ap·peal·ing·ly** \-liŋ-lē\ *adv*
ap·pear \ə-ˈpir\ *vi* [ME *apperen,* fr. AF *aparer, aparoir,* fr. L *apparēre,* fr. *ad-* + *parēre* to show oneself] (13c) **1 a :** to be or come in sight ⟨the sun ~*s* on the horizon⟩ **b :** to show up ⟨~*s* promptly at eight each day⟩ **2 :** to come formally before an authoritative body ⟨must ~ in court today⟩ **3 :** to have an outward aspect : SEEM ⟨~*s* happy enough⟩ **4 :** to become evident or manifest ⟨there ~*s* to be evidence to the contrary⟩ **5 :** to come into public view ⟨first ~*ed* on a television variety show⟩ ⟨the book ~*ed* in print a few years ago⟩ **6 :** to come into existence ⟨hominids ~*ed* late in the evolutionary chain⟩
ap·pear·ance \ə-ˈpir-ən(t)s\ *n* (14c) **1 a :** external show : SEMBLANCE ⟨although hostile, he preserved an ~ of neutrality⟩ **b :** outward aspect : LOOK ⟨had a fierce ~⟩ **c** *pl* **:** outward indication ⟨trying to keep up ~*s*⟩ **2 a :** a sense impression or aspect of a thing ⟨the blue of distant hills is only an ~⟩ **b :** the world of sensible phenomena **3 a :** the act, action, or process of appearing **b :** the presentation of oneself in court as a party to an action often through the representation of an attorney **4 a :** something that appears : PHENOMENON **b :** an instance of appearing : OCCURRENCE
ap·pease \ə-ˈpēz\ *vt* **ap·peased; ap·peas·ing** [ME *appesen,* fr. AF *apeser, apaiser,* fr. *a-* (fr. L *ad-*) + *pais* peace — more at PEACE] (14c) **1 :** to bring to a state of peace or quiet : CALM **2 :** to cause to subside : ALLAY ⟨*appeased* my hunger⟩ **3 :** PACIFY, CONCILIATE; *esp* **:** to buy off (an aggressor) by concessions usu. at the sacrifice of principles ***syn*** see PACIFY — **ap·peas·able** \-ˈpē-zə-bəl\ *adj* — **ap·pease·ment** \-ˈpēz-mənt\ *n* — **ap·peas·er** *n*
[1]**ap·pel·lant** \ə-ˈpe-lənt\ *adj* (14c) **:** of or relating to an appeal : APPELLATE ⟨an ~ court⟩
[2]**appellant** *n* (15c) **:** one that appeals; *specif* **:** one that appeals from a judicial decision or decree
ap·pel·late \ə-ˈpe-lət\ *adj* [L *appellatus,* pp. of *appellare*] (1768) **:** of, relating to, or recognizing appeals; *specif* **:** having the power to review the judgment of another tribunal ⟨an ~ court⟩
ap·pel·la·tion \ˌa-pə-ˈlā-shən\ *n* (15c) **1 :** an identifying name or title : DESIGNATION **2** *archaic* **:** the act of calling by a name **3 :** a geographical name (as of a region, village, or vineyard) under which a winegrower is authorized to identify and market wine; *also* **:** the area designated by such a name
ap·pel·la·tive \ə-ˈpe-lə-tiv\ *adj* (15c) **1 :** of or relating to a common noun **2 :** of, relating to, or inclined to the giving of names — **ap·pel·la·tive** *n* — **ap·pel·la·tive·ly** *adv*
ap·pel·lee \ˌa-pə-ˈlē\ *n* (1531) **:** one against whom an appeal is taken
ap·pend \ə-ˈpend\ *vt* [L *appendere,* to hang, weigh out, fr. *ad-* + *pendere* to weigh — more at PENDANT] (1646) **1 :** ATTACH, AFFIX **2 :** to add as a supplement or appendix (as in a book)
ap·pend·age \ə-ˈpen-dij\ *n* (1647) **1 :** an adjunct to something larger or more important : APPURTENANCE **2 :** a usu. projecting part of an animal or plant body that is typically smaller and of less functional importance than the main part to which it is attached; *esp* **:** a limb or analogous part (as a seta) **3** [*appendant*] **:** a dependent or subordinate person
ap·pen·dant \ə-ˈpen-dənt\ *adj* [ME, fr. AF *apendaunt,* prp. of *apendre* to belong, be subject, fr. ML *appendēre* to be attached, belong to, fr. L, to be pending, fr. *ad-* + *pendēre* to hang (vi.)] (15c) **1 :** belonging as a right by prescription — used of annexed land in English law **2 :** associated as an attendant circumstance **3** [*append*] **:** attached as an appendage ⟨a seal ~ to a document⟩ — **appendant** *n*
ap·pen·dec·to·my \ˌa-pən-ˈdek-tə-mē, ˌa-ˌpen-\ *n, pl* **-mies** [L *appendic-, appendix* + E *-ectomy*] (ca. 1895) **:** surgical removal of the vermiform appendix
ap·pen·di·cec·to·my \ə-ˌpen-də-ˈsek-tə-mē\ *n, pl* **-mies** (1894) *Brit* **:** APPENDECTOMY
ap·pen·di·ci·tis \ə-ˌpen-də-ˈsī-təs\ *n* [NL] (1886) **:** inflammation of the vermiform appendix
ap·pen·dic·u·lar \ˌa-pən-ˈdi-kyə-lər\ *adj* (1651) **:** of or relating to an appendage and esp. a limb ⟨the ~ skeleton⟩
ap·pen·dix \ə-ˈpen-diks\ *n, pl* **-dix·es** *or* **-di·ces** \-də-ˌsēz\ [L *appendic-, appendix,* fr. *appendere*] (1542) **1 a :** APPENDAGE **b :** supplementary material usu. attached at the end of a piece of writing **2 :** a bodily outgrowth or process; *specif* **:** VERMIFORM APPENDIX
ap·per·ceive \ˌa-pər-ˈsēv\ *vt* **-ceived; -ceiv·ing** [F *apercevoir*] (1843) **:** to have apperception of
ap·per·cep·tion \-ˈsep-shən\ *n* [F *aperception,* fr. *apercevoir,* fr. MF *aperceivre,* fr. *a-* (fr. L *ad-*) + *perceivre* to perceive] (1753) **1 :** introspective self-consciousness **2 :** mental perception; *esp* **:** the process of understanding something perceived in terms of previous experience — **ap·per·cep·tive** \-ˈsep-tiv\ *adj*
ap·per·tain \ˌa-pər-ˈtān\ *vi* [ME *apperteinen,* fr. AF *apurtenir,* fr. LL *appertinēre,* fr. L *ad-* + *pertinēre* to belong — more at PERTAIN] (14c) **:** to belong or be connected as a rightful part or attribute : PERTAIN
ap·pe·tence \ˈa-pə-tən(t)s\ *n* (1598) **:** APPETENCY
ap·pe·ten·cy \-tən(t)-sē\ *n, pl* **-cies** [L *appetentia,* fr. *appetent-, appetens,* prp. of *appetere*] (1611) **:** a fixed and strong desire : APPETITE — **ap·pe·tent** \-tənt\ *adj*
ap·pe·tis·er, ap·pe·tis·ing *Brit var of* APPETIZER, APPETIZING
ap·pe·tite \ˈa-pə-ˌtīt\ *n* [ME *apetit,* fr. AF, fr. L *appetitus,* fr. *appetere* to strive after, fr. *ad-* + *petere* to go to — more at FEATHER] (14c) **1 :** any of the instinctive desires necessary to keep up organic life; *esp* **:** the desire to eat **2 a :** an inherent craving ⟨an insatiable ~ for work⟩ **b :** TASTE, PREFERENCE ⟨the cultural ~*s* of the time —J. D. Hart⟩ — **ap·pe·ti·tive** \-ˌtī-tiv\ *adj*
ap·pe·tiz·er \ˈa-pə-ˌtī-zər\ *n* (1820) **1 :** a food or drink that stimulates the appetite and is usu. served before a meal **2 :** something that stimulates a desire for more ⟨a literary ~⟩
ap·pe·tiz·ing \-ˌtī-ziŋ\ *adj* (1653) **:** appealing to the appetite esp. in appearance or aroma; *also* **:** appealing to one's taste ⟨an ~ display of merchandise⟩ ***syn*** see PALATABLE — **ap·pe·tiz·ing·ly** \-ziŋ-lē\ *adv*
appl *abbr* applied
ap·plaud \ə-ˈplȯd\ *vb* [ME, fr. MF or L; MF *aplaudir,* fr. L *applaudere,* fr. *ad-* + *plaudere* to applaud] *vi* (15c) **:** to express approval esp. by clapping the hands ~ *vt* **1 :** to express approval of : PRAISE ⟨~ her efforts to lose weight⟩ **2 :** to show approval of esp. by clapping the hands — **ap·plaud·able** \-ˈplȯ-də-bəl\ *adj* — **ap·plaud·ably** \-blē\ *adv* — **ap·plaud·er** *n*
ap·plause \ə-ˈplȯz\ *n* [ML *applausus,* fr. L, beating of wings, fr. *applaudere*] (15c) **1 :** marked commendation : ACCLAIM ⟨the kind of ~ every really creative writer wants —Robert Tallant⟩ **2 :** approval publicly expressed (as by clapping the hands)
ap·ple \ˈa-pəl\ *n, often attrib* [ME *appel,* fr. OE *æppel;* akin to OHG *apful* apple, OIr *ubull,* OCS *ablŭko*] (bef. 12c) **1 :** the fleshy usu. rounded red, yellow, or green edible pome fruit of a usu. cultivated tree (genus *Malus*) of the rose family; *also* **:** an apple tree — compare CRAB APPLE **2 :** a fruit (as a star apple) or other vegetative growth (as an oak apple) suggestive of an apple — **apple of one's eye :** one that is highly cherished ⟨his daughter is the *apple of his eye*⟩
apple butter *n* (ca. 1774) **:** a thick brown spread made by cooking apples with sugar and spices usu. in cider
ap·ple·cart \-ˌkärt\ *n* (1788) **:** a plan, system, situation, or undertaking that may be disrupted or terminated ⟨upset the ~⟩
ap·ple–cheeked \ˈa-pəl-ˌchēkt\ *adj* (1847) **:** having cheeks the color of red apples ⟨~ youngsters⟩
ap·ple·jack \-ˌjak\ *n* (1816) **:** brandy distilled from hard cider; *also* **:** an alcoholic beverage traditionally made by freezing hard cider and siphoning off the concentrated liquor
ap·ple–knock·er \-ˌnä-kər\ *n* (1919) **:** RUSTIC
apple maggot *n* (1867) **:** a dipteran fly (*Rhagoletis pomonella*) whose larva burrows in and feeds esp. on apples
ap·ple–pie \ˈa-pəl-ˈpī\ *adj* (1780) **1 :** EXCELLENT, PERFECT ⟨~ order⟩ **2 :** of, relating to, or characterized by traditionally American values (as honesty or simplicity) ⟨is the epitome of ~ wholesomeness⟩
ap·ple–pol·ish \ˈa-pəl-ˌpä-lish\ *vb* [fr. the traditional practice of schoolchildren bringing a shiny apple as a gift to their teacher] *vi* (1935) **:** to attempt to ingratiate oneself : TOADY ~ *vt* **:** to curry favor with (as by flattery) — **ap·ple–pol·ish·er** *n*
ap·ple·sauce \-ˌsȯs\ *n* (1704) **1 :** a relish or dessert made of apples stewed to a pulp and sweetened **2** *slang* **:** BUNKUM, NONSENSE
apple scab *n* (ca. 1899) **:** a disease of apple trees caused by a fungus (*Venturia inaequalis*) producing dark blotches or lesions on the leaves, fruit, and sometimes the young twigs
ap·plet \ˈa-plət, -(ˌ)plet\ *n* [*appl*ication + [1]*-et*] (1990) **:** a short computer application esp. for performing a simple specific task
ap·pli·ance \ə-ˈplī-ən(t)s\ *n* (1561) **1 :** an act of applying **2 a :** a piece of equipment for adapting a tool or machine to a special purpose : ATTACHMENT **b :** an instrument or device designed for a particular use or function ⟨an orthodontic ~⟩; *specif* **:** a household or office device (as a stove, fan, or refrigerator) operated by gas or electric current **c** *Brit* **:** FIRE ENGINE **3** *obs* **:** COMPLIANCE ***syn*** see IMPLEMENT
ap·pli·ca·ble \ˈa-pli-kə-bəl *also* ə-ˈpli-kə-\ *adj* (1655) **:** capable of or suitable for being applied : APPROPRIATE ⟨statutes ~ to the case⟩ ***syn*** see RELEVANT — **ap·pli·ca·bil·i·ty** \ˌa-pli-kə-ˈbi-lə-tē *also* ə-ˌpli-kə-\ *n*
ap·pli·cant \ˈa-pli-kənt\ *n* (1776) **:** one who applies ⟨a job ~⟩
ap·pli·ca·tion \ˌa-plə-ˈkā-shən\ *n* [ME *applicacioun,* fr. L *application-, applicatio* inclination, fr. *applicare*] (15c) **1 :** an act of applying: **a** (1) **:** an act of putting to use ⟨~ of new techniques⟩ (2) **:** a use to which something is put ⟨new ~*s* for old remedies⟩ (3) **:** a program (as a word processor or a spreadsheet) that performs one of the major tasks for which a computer is used **b :** an act of administering or superposing ⟨~ of paint to a house⟩ **c :** assiduous attention ⟨succeeds by ~ to her studies⟩ **2 a :** REQUEST, PETITION ⟨an ~ for financial aid⟩ **b :** a form used in making a request **3 :** the practical inference to be derived from a discourse (as a moral tale) **4 :** a medicated or protective layer or material ⟨an oily ~ for dry skin⟩ **5 :** capacity for practical use ⟨words of varied ~⟩
ap·pli·ca·tive \ˈa-plə-ˌkā-tiv, ə-ˈpli-kə-\ *adj* (1638) **1 :** APPLICABLE, PRACTICAL **2 :** put to use : APPLIED — **ap·pli·ca·tive·ly** *adv*
ap·pli·ca·tor \ˈa-plə-ˌkā-tər\ *n* (1659) **:** one that applies; *specif* **:** a device for applying a substance (as medicine or polish)
ap·pli·ca·to·ry \ˈa-pli-kə-ˌtȯr-ē, ə-ˈpli-kə-\ *adj* (1649) **:** capable of being applied
ap·plied \ə-ˈplīd\ *adj* (1656) **1 :** put to practical use ⟨~ art⟩; *esp* **:** applying general principles to solve definite problems ⟨~ sciences⟩ **2 :** working in an applied science ⟨an ~ physicist⟩
[1]**ap·pli·qué** \ˌa-plə-ˈkā\ *n* [F, pp. of *appliquer* to put on, fr. L *applicare*] (1801) **:** a cutout decoration fastened to a larger piece of material
[2]**appliqué** *vt* **-quéd; -qué·ing** (1864) **:** to apply (as a decoration or ornament) to a larger surface : OVERLAY
ap·ply \ə-ˈplī\ *vb* **ap·plied; ap·ply·ing** [ME *applien,* fr. AF *aplier,* fr. L *applicare,* fr. *ad-* + *plicare* to fold — more at PLY] *vt* (14c) **1 a :** to put to use esp. for some practical purpose ⟨*applies* pressure to get what he wants⟩ **b :** to bring into action ⟨~ the brakes⟩ **c :** to lay or spread on ⟨~ varnish⟩ **d :** to put into operation or effect ⟨~ a law⟩ **2 :** to employ diligently or with close attention ⟨should ~ yourself to your work⟩ ~ *vi* **1 :** to have relevance or a valid connection ⟨this rule *applies* to freshmen only⟩ **2 :** to make an appeal or request esp. in the form of a written application ⟨~ for a job⟩ — **ap·pli·er** \-ˈplī(-ə)r\ *n*
ap·pog·gia·tu·ra \ə-ˌpä-jə-ˈtu̇r-ə\ *n* [It, lit., support] (1753) **:** an embellishing note or tone preceding an essential melodic note or tone and usu. written as a note of smaller size
ap·point \ə-ˈpȯint\ *vb* [ME, fr. AF *appointer,* fr. *a-* (fr. L *ad-*) + *point* point] *vt* (14c) **1 a :** to fix or set officially ⟨~ a trial date⟩ **b :** to name officially ⟨will ~ her director of the program⟩ **c** *archaic* **:** ARRANGE **d :** to determine the disposition of (an estate) to someone by

virtue of a power of appointment **2 :** to provide with complete and usu. appropriate or elegant furnishings or equipment ⟨a beautifully ~*ed* room⟩ ~ *vi* **:** to exercise a power of appointment ***syn*** see FURNISH

ap·poin·tee \ə-ˌpȯin-ˈtē, ˌa-\ *n* (1768) **1 :** one who is appointed **2 :** one to whom an estate is appointed

ap·point·ive \ə-ˈpȯin-tiv\ *adj* (1880) **:** of, relating to, or filled by appointment ⟨an ~ office⟩

ap·point·ment \ə-ˈpȯint-mənt\ *n* (15c) **1 a :** an act of appointing **:** DESIGNATION **b :** the designation by virtue of a vested power of a person to enjoy an estate **2 :** an arrangement for a meeting **:** ENGAGEMENT ⟨an ~ for an interview⟩ **3 :** EQUIPMENT, FURNISHINGS — usu. used in pl. ⟨expensive homes with luxurious ~*s*⟩ **4 :** a nonelective office or position ⟨holds an academic ~⟩

ap·por·tion \ə-ˈpȯr-shən\ *vt* **-tioned; -tion·ing** \-sh(ə-)niŋ\ [MF *apportionner,* fr. *a-* (fr. L *ad-*) + *portionner* to portion] (1574) **:** to divide and share out according to a plan; *esp* **:** to make a proportionate division or distribution of — **ap·por·tion·able** \-shə-nə-bəl\ *adj*

ap·por·tion·ment \-shən-mənt\ *n* (1579) **:** an act or result of apportioning; *esp* **:** the apportioning of representatives or taxes among the states according to U.S. law

ap·pose \a-ˈpōz\ *vt* **ap·posed; ap·pos·ing** [MF *aposer,* fr. OF, fr. *a-* + *poser* to put — more at POSE] (1596) **1** *archaic* **:** to put before **:** apply (one thing) to another **2 :** to place in juxtaposition or proximity

ap·po·site \ˈa-pə-zət\ *adj* [L *appositus,* fr. pp. of *apponere* to place near, fr. *ad-* + *ponere* to put — more at POSITION] (1621) **:** highly pertinent or appropriate **:** APT ⟨~ remarks⟩ ***syn*** see RELEVANT — **ap·po·site·ly** *adv* — **ap·po·site·ness** *n*

ap·po·si·tion \ˌa-pə-ˈzi-shən\ *n* (15c) **1 a :** a grammatical construction in which two usu. adjacent nouns having the same referent stand in the same syntactical relation to the rest of a sentence (as *the poet* and *Burns* in "a biography of the poet Burns") **b :** the relation of one of such a pair of nouns or noun equivalents to the other **2 a :** an act or instance of apposing; *specif* **:** the deposition of successive layers upon those already present (as in cell walls) **b :** the state of being apposed — **ap·po·si·tion·al** \-ˈzish-nəl, -ˈzi-shə-nᵊl\ *adj*

ap·pos·i·tive \ə-ˈpä-zə-tiv, a-\ *adj* (1693) **:** of, relating to, or standing in grammatical apposition — **appositive** *n* — **ap·pos·i·tive·ly** *adv*

ap·prais·al \ə-ˈprā-zəl\ *n* (1817) **:** an act or instance of appraising; *esp* **:** a valuation of property by the estimate of an authorized person

ap·praise \ə-ˈprāz\ *vt* **ap·praised; ap·prais·ing** [ME *appraysen,* prob. fr. AF **appreiser,* fr. *a-* (fr. L *ad-*) + *preiser* to prize, praise] (15c) **1 :** to set a value on **:** estimate the amount of ⟨~ the damage⟩ **2 :** to evaluate the worth, significance, or status of; *esp* **:** to give an expert judgment of the value or merit of ⟨~ an actor's career⟩ ***syn*** see ESTIMATE — **ap·prais·ee** \ə-ˌprā-ˈzē\ *n* — **ap·praise·ment** \-ˈprāz-mənt\ *n* — **ap·prais·er** *n* — **ap·prais·ing·ly** \-ˈprā-ziŋ-lē\ *adv* — **ap·prais·ive** \-ˈprā-ziv\ *adj*

ap·pre·cia·ble \ə-ˈprē-shə-bəl, -ˈpri-sh(ē-)ə-bəl\ *adj* (1818) **:** capable of being perceived or measured ⟨no ~ difference⟩ ***syn*** see PERCEPTIBLE — **ap·pre·cia·bly** \-blē\ *adv*

ap·pre·ci·ate \ə-ˈprē-shē-ˌāt, -ˈpri- *also* -ˈprē-sē-\ *vb* **-at·ed; -at·ing** [LL *appretiatus,* pp. of *appretiare,* fr. L *ad-* + *pretium* price — more at PRICE] *vt* (1655) **1 a :** to grasp the nature, worth, quality, or significance of ⟨~ the difference between right and wrong⟩ **b :** to value or admire highly ⟨~*s* our work⟩ **c :** to judge with heightened perception or understanding **:** be fully aware of ⟨must see it to ~ it⟩ **d :** to recognize with gratitude ⟨certainly ~*s* your kindness⟩ **2 :** to increase the value of ~ *vi* **:** to increase in number or value — **ap·pre·ci·a·tor** \-ˌā-tər\ *n* — **ap·pre·cia·to·ry** \-ˈprē-shə-ˌtȯr-ē, -ˈpri-shə-\ *adj*

syn APPRECIATE, VALUE, PRIZE, TREASURE, CHERISH mean to hold in high estimation. APPRECIATE often connotes sufficient understanding to enjoy or admire a thing's excellence ⟨*appreciates* fine wine⟩. VALUE implies rating a thing highly for its intrinsic worth ⟨*values* our friendship⟩. PRIZE implies taking a deep pride in something one possesses ⟨Americans *prize* their freedom⟩. TREASURE emphasizes jealously safeguarding something considered precious ⟨a *treasured* memento⟩. CHERISH implies a special love and care for something ⟨*cherishes* her children above all⟩. ***syn*** see in addition UNDERSTAND

ap·pre·ci·a·tion \ə-ˌprē-shē-ˈā-shən, -ˌpri- *also* -ˌprē-sē-\ *n* (1604) **1 a :** JUDGMENT, EVALUATION; *esp* **:** a favorable critical estimate **b :** sensitive awareness; *esp* **:** recognition of aesthetic values **c :** an expression of admiration, approval, or gratitude **2 :** increase in value

ap·pre·cia·tive \ə-ˈprē-shə-tiv, -ˈpri- *also* -ˈprē-shē-ˌā-\ *adj* (ca. 1698) **:** having or showing appreciation ⟨an ~ audience⟩ ⟨was ~ of his good luck⟩ — **ap·pre·cia·tive·ly** *adv* — **ap·pre·cia·tive·ness** *n*

ap·pre·hend \ˌa-pri-ˈhend\ *vb* [ME, fr. L *apprehendere,* lit., to seize, fr. *ad-* + *prehendere* to seize — more at GET] *vt* (15c) **1 :** ARREST, SEIZE ⟨~ a thief⟩ **2 a :** to become aware of **:** PERCEIVE **b :** to anticipate esp. with anxiety, dread, or fear **3 :** to grasp with the understanding **:** recognize the meaning of ~ *vi* **:** UNDERSTAND, GRASP

ap·pre·hen·si·ble \ˌa-pri-ˈhen(t)-sə-bəl\ *adj* (15c) **:** capable of being apprehended ⟨an easily ~ truth⟩ — **ap·pre·hen·si·bly** \-blē\ *adv*

ap·pre·hen·sion \ˌa-pri-ˈhen(t)-shən\ *n* [ME, fr. LL *apprehension-, apprehensio,* fr. L *apprehendere*] (14c) **1 a :** the act or power of perceiving or comprehending ⟨a person of dull ~⟩ **b :** the result of apprehending mentally **:** CONCEPTION ⟨according to popular ~⟩ **2 :** seizure by legal process **:** ARREST ⟨~ of a criminal⟩ **3 :** suspicion or fear esp. of future evil **:** FOREBODING ⟨an atmosphere of nervous ~⟩

ap·pre·hen·sive \-ˈhen(t)-siv\ *adj* (14c) **1 :** capable of apprehending or quick to do so **:** DISCERNING **2 :** having apprehension **:** COGNIZANT **3 :** viewing the future with anxiety or alarm ***syn*** see FEARFUL — **ap·pre·hen·sive·ly** *adv* — **ap·pre·hen·sive·ness** *n*

[1]**ap·pren·tice** \ə-ˈpren-təs\ *n, often attrib* [ME *aprentis,* fr. AF *apprentiz,* fr. *aprendre* to learn, fr. L *apprendere, apprehendere*] (14c) **1 a :** one bound by indenture to serve another for a prescribed period with a view to learning an art or trade **b :** one who is learning by practical experience under skilled workers a trade, art, or calling **2 :** an inexperienced person **:** NOVICE ⟨an ~ in cooking⟩ — **ap·pren·tice·ship** \-tə(sh)-ˌship, -təs-ˌship\ *n*

[2]**apprentice** *vb* **-ticed; -tic·ing** *vt* (1596) **:** to set at work as an apprentice; *esp* **:** to bind to an apprenticeship by contract or indenture ~ *vi* **:** to serve as an apprentice

ap·pressed \a-ˈprest\ *adj* [L *appressus,* pp. of *apprimere* to press to, fr. *ad-* + *premere* to press — more at PRESS] (1613) **:** pressed close to or lying flat against something ⟨leaves ~ against the stem⟩

ap·pres·so·ri·um \ˌa-pre-ˈsȯr-ē-əm\ *n, pl* **-ria** \-ē-ə\ [NL, fr. L *apprimere*] (1897) **:** the flattened thickened tip of a hyphal branch by which some parasitic fungi attach to and penetrate their host

ap·prise \ə-ˈprīz\ *vt* **ap·prised; ap·pris·ing** [F *appris,* pp. of *apprendre* to learn, teach, fr. OF *aprendre*] (1694) **:** to give notice to **:** TELL ⟨they *apprised* him of his rights⟩ ***syn*** see INFORM

ap·prize \ə-ˈprīz\ *vt* **ap·prized; ap·priz·ing** [ME *apprisen,* fr. AF **appriser,* fr. *a-* (fr. L *ad-*) + *preiser, priser* to value, prize — more at PRIZE] (14c) **:** VALUE, APPRECIATE

appro *abbr* approval

[1]**ap·proach** \ə-ˈprōch\ *vb* [ME *approchen,* fr. AF *aprocher,* fr. LL *appropiare,* fr. L *ad-* + *prope* near; akin to L *pro* before — more at FOR] *vt* (13c) **1 a :** to draw closer to **:** NEAR ⟨~ a destination⟩ **b :** to come very near to **:** be almost the same as ⟨its mathematics ~*es* mysticism —Theodore Sturgeon⟩ ⟨as the quantity *x* ~*es* zero⟩ **2 a :** to make advances to esp. in order to create a desired result ⟨was ~*ed* by several Broadway producers⟩ **b :** to take preliminary steps toward accomplishment or full knowledge or experience of ⟨~ the subject with an open mind⟩ ~ *vi* **1 :** to draw nearer ⟨the time is fast ~*ing*⟩ **2 :** to make an approach in golf

[2]**approach** *n* (15c) **1 a :** an act or instance of approaching ⟨the ~ of summer⟩ **b :** APPROXIMATION ⟨in this book he makes his closest ~ to greatness⟩ **2 a :** the taking of preliminary steps toward a particular purpose ⟨experimenting with new lines of ~⟩ **b :** a particular manner of taking such steps ⟨a highly individual ~ to language⟩ **3 :** a means of access **:** AVENUE **4 a :** a golf shot from the fairway toward the green **b :** the steps taken by a bowler before delivering the ball; *also* **:** the part of the alley behind the foul line from which the bowler delivers the ball **5 :** the descent of an aircraft toward a landing place

ap·proach·able \ə-ˈprō-chə-bəl\ *adj* (1571) **:** capable of being approached **:** ACCESSIBLE; *specif* **:** easy to meet or deal with ⟨friendly and ~ people⟩ — **ap·proach·abil·i·ty** \-ˌprō-chə-ˈbi-lə-tē\ *n*

ap·pro·bate \ˈa-prə-ˌbāt\ *vt* **-bat·ed; -bat·ing** [ME, fr. L *approbatus,* pp. of *approbare* — more at APPROVE] (15c) **:** APPROVE, SANCTION

ap·pro·ba·tion \ˌa-prə-ˈbā-shən\ *n* (14c) **1** *obs* **:** PROOF **2 a :** an act of approving formally or officially **b :** COMMENDATION, PRAISE — **ap·pro·ba·to·ry** \ˈa-prə-bə-ˌtȯr-ē, ə-ˈprō-bə-\ *adj*

[1]**ap·pro·pri·ate** \ə-ˈprō-prē-ˌāt\ *vt* **-at·ed; -at·ing** [ME, fr. LL *appropriatus,* pp. of *appropriare,* fr. L *ad-* + *proprius* own] (15c) **1 :** to take exclusive possession of **:** ANNEX ⟨no one should ~ a common benefit⟩ **2 :** to set apart for or assign to a particular purpose or use ⟨~ money for the research program⟩ **3 :** to take or make use of without authority or right — **ap·pro·pri·a·ble** \-prē-ə-bəl\ *adj* — **ap·pro·pri·a·tor** \-prē-ˌā-tər\ *n*

[2]**ap·pro·pri·ate** \ə-ˈprō-prē-ət\ *adj* (15c) **:** especially suitable or compatible **:** FITTING ⟨an ~ response⟩ ⟨remarks ~ to the occasion⟩ ***syn*** see FIT — **ap·pro·pri·ate·ly** *adv* — **ap·pro·pri·ate·ness** *n*

ap·pro·pri·a·tion \ə-ˌprō-prē-ˈā-shən\ *n* (14c) **1 :** an act or instance of appropriating **2 :** something that has been appropriated; *specif* **:** money set aside by formal action for a specific use — **ap·pro·pri·a·tive** \-ˈprō-prē-ˌā-tiv\ *adj*

ap·prov·able \ə-ˈprü-və-bəl\ *adj* (15c) **:** capable or worthy of being approved ⟨an ~ plan⟩ — **ap·prov·ably** \-blē\ *adv*

ap·prov·al \ə-ˈprü-vəl\ *n* (1613) **:** an act or instance of approving **:** APPROBATION — **on approval :** subject to a prospective buyer's acceptance or refusal ⟨stamps sent to collectors *on approval*⟩

ap·prove \ə-ˈprüv\ *vb* **ap·proved; ap·prov·ing** [ME, fr. AF *apruer, approver,* fr. L *approbare,* fr. *ad-* + *probare* to prove — more at PROVE] *vt* (14c) **1** *obs* **:** PROVE, ATTEST **2 :** to have or express a favorable opinion of ⟨couldn't ~ such conduct⟩ **3 a :** to accept as satisfactory ⟨hopes she will ~ the date of the meeting⟩ **b :** to give formal or official sanction to **:** RATIFY ⟨Congress *approved* the proposed budget⟩ ~ *vi* **:** to take a favorable view ⟨doesn't ~ of fighting⟩ — **ap·prov·ing·ly** \-ˈprü-viŋ-lē\ *adv*

syn APPROVE, ENDORSE, SANCTION, ACCREDIT, CERTIFY mean to have or express a favorable opinion of. APPROVE often implies no more than this but may suggest considerable esteem or admiration ⟨the parents *approve* of the marriage⟩. ENDORSE suggests an explicit statement of support ⟨publicly *endorsed* her for Senator⟩. SANCTION implies both approval and authorization ⟨the President *sanctioned* covert operations⟩. ACCREDIT and CERTIFY usu. imply official endorsement attesting to conformity to set standards ⟨the board voted to *accredit* the college⟩ ⟨must be *certified* to teach⟩.

approved school *n* (1932) *Brit* **:** a school for juvenile delinquents

approx *abbr* approximate; approximately

[1]**ap·prox·i·mate** \ə-ˈpräk-sə-mət\ *adj* [LL *approximatus,* pp. of *approximare* to come near, fr. L *ad-* + *proximare* to come near — more at PROXIMATE] (15c) **1 :** located close together ⟨~ leaves⟩ **2 :** nearly correct or exact ⟨an ~ solution⟩ — **ap·prox·i·mate·ly** *adv*

[2]**ap·prox·i·mate** \-ˌmāt\ *vb* **-mat·ed; -mat·ing** *vt* (15c) **1 a :** to bring near or close **b :** to bring (cut edges of tissue) together **2 :** to come near to or be close to in position, value, or characteristics ⟨a child tries to ~ his parents' speech⟩ ~ *vi* **:** to come close — usu. used with *to*

ap·prox·i·ma·tion \ə-ˌpräk-sə-ˈmā-shən\ *n* (15c) **1 :** the act or process of drawing together **2 :** the quality or state of being close or near ⟨an ~ to the truth⟩ ⟨an ~ of justice⟩ **3 :** something that is approximate; *esp* **:** a mathematical quantity that is close in value to but not the same as a desired quantity — **ap·prox·i·ma·tive** \-ˈpräk-sə-ˌmā-tiv\ *adj*

appt *abbr* appoint; appointed; appointment

apptd *abbr* appointed

ap·pur·te·nance \ə-ˈpərt-nən(t)s, -ˈpər-tə-nən(t)s\ *n* (14c) **1 :** an incidental right (as a right-of-way) attached to a principal property right and passing in possession with it **2 :** a subordinate part or adjunct

⟨the ~ of welcome is fashion and ceremony —Shak.⟩ **3** *pl* **:** accessory objects **:** APPARATUS ⟨the ~*s* of wealth⟩
ap·pur·te·nant \ə-ˈpərt-nənt, -ˈpər-tə-nənt\ *adj* [ME *apertenant,* fr. AF *appurtenant,* prp. of *apurtenir* to belong — more at APPERTAIN] (14c) **1 :** constituting a legal accompaniment **2 :** AUXILIARY, ACCESSORY ⟨~ equipment⟩ — **appurtenant** *n*
Apr *abbr* April
APR *abbr* annual percentage rate
aprax·ia \(ˌ)ā-ˈprak-sē-ə\ *n* [NL, fr. Gk, inaction, fr. *a-* + *praxis* action, fr. *prassein* to do — more at PRACTICAL] (ca. 1881) **:** loss or impairment of the ability to execute complex coordinated movements without muscular or sensory impairment — **aprac·tic** \-ˈprak-tik\ *or* **aprax·ic** \-ˈprak-sik\ *adj*
après \(ˌ)ä-ˈprā, ˈä-ˌprā; ˈa-ˌ\ *prep* [F *après-,* fr. *après* after] (1889) **:** AFTER ⟨~ tennis⟩ — usu. used in combination ⟨*après*-theater party⟩
après–ski \ˌä-ˌprā-ˈskē, ˌa-\ *n, often attrib* [F *après* after + *ski* ski, skiing] (1951) **:** social activity (as at a ski lodge) after a day's skiing
apri·cot \ˈa-prə-ˌkät, ˈā-\ *n, often attrib* [alter. of earlier *abrecock,* ultim. fr. Ar *al-birqūq* the apricot, ultim. fr. L (*persicum*) *praecox,* lit., early ripening (peach) — more at PRECOCIOUS] (1580) **1 a :** the oval orange-colored fruit of a temperate-zone tree (*Prunus armeniaca*) resembling the related peach and plum in flavor **b :** a tree that bears apricots **2 :** a variable color averaging a moderate orange
April \ˈā-prəl\ *n* [ME, fr. AF & L; AF *avrill,* fr. L *Aprilis*] (bef. 12c) **:** the fourth month of the Gregorian calendar
April fool *n* (1693) **:** the butt of a joke or trick played on April Fools' Day; *also* **:** such a joke or trick
April Fools' Day *also* **April Fool's Day** *n* (1753) **:** April 1 characteristically marked by the playing of practical jokes
a pri·o·ri \ˌä-prē-ˈōr-ē, ˌa-; ˌā-(ˌ)prī-ˈōr-ˌī, -ˌprē-ˈōr-ē\ *adj* [L, lit., from the former] (1652) **1 a :** DEDUCTIVE **b :** relating to or derived by reasoning from self-evident propositions — compare A POSTERIORI **c :** presupposed by experience **2 a :** being without examination or analysis **:** PRESUMPTIVE **b :** formed or conceived beforehand — **a priori** *adv* — **apri·or·i·ty** \-ˈōr-ə-tē\ *n*
apron \ˈā-prən, -pərn\ *n, often attrib* [ME, alter. (resulting fr. false division of *a napron*) of *napron,* fr. MF *naperon,* dim. of *nape* cloth, modif. of L *mappa* napkin] (15c) **1 :** a garment usu. of cloth, plastic, or leather usu. tied around the waist and used to protect clothing or adorn a costume **2 :** something that suggests or resembles an apron in shape, position, or use: as **a :** the lower member under the sill of the interior casing of a window **b :** an upward or downward vertical extension of a bathroom fixture (as a sink or tub) **c :** an endless belt for carrying material **d :** an extensive fan-shaped deposit of detritus **e :** the part of the stage in front of the proscenium arch **f :** the area along the waterfront edge of a pier or wharf **g :** a shield (as of concrete or gravel) to protect against erosion (as of a waterway) by water **h :** the extensive paved part of an airport immediately adjacent to the terminal area or hangars — **aproned** \-prənd, -pərnd\ *adj*
apron string *n* (1542) **:** the string of an apron — usu. used in pl. as a symbol of dominance or complete control ⟨though 40 years old he was still tied to his mother's *apron strings*⟩
[1]**ap·ro·pos** \ˌa-prə-ˈpō, ˈa-prə-ˌ\ *adv* [F *à propos,* lit., to the purpose] (1668) **1 :** at an opportune time **:** SEASONABLY **2 :** by way of interjection or further comment **:** with regard to the present topic
[2]**apropos** *adj* (1686) **:** being both relevant and opportune ⟨~ comments⟩ ***syn*** see RELEVANT
[3]**apropos** *prep* (1751) **:** APROPOS OF
apropos of *prep* (1732) **:** with regard to **:** CONCERNING
apro·tic \(ˌ)ā-ˈprō-tik\ *adj* [[2]*a-* + *proton* + [1]*-ic*] (1931) *of a solvent* **:** incapable of acting as a proton donor
apse \ˈaps\ *n* [ML & L; ML *apsis,* fr. L] (1715) **1 :** APSIS 1 **2 :** a projecting part of a building (as a church) that is usu. semicircular in plan and vaulted
ap·si·dal \ˈap-sə-dᵊl\ *adj* (1807) **:** of or relating to an apse or apsis
ap·sis \ˈap-səs\ *n, pl* **ap·si·des** \-sə-ˌdēz\ [NL *apsid-, apsis,* fr. L, arch, orbit, fr. Gk *hapsid-, hapsis,* fr. *haptein* to fasten] (1601) **1 :** the point in an astronomical orbit at which the distance of the body from the center of attraction is either greatest or least **2 :** APSE 2
[1]**apt** \ˈapt\ *adj* [ME, fr. L *aptus,* lit., fastened, fr. pp. of *apere* to fasten; akin to L *apisci* to grasp, obtain, *apud* near, Hitt *ḫap-* to attach] (14c) **1 :** unusually fitted or qualified **:** READY ⟨proved an ~ tool in the hands of the conspirators⟩ **2 a :** having a tendency **:** LIKELY ⟨plants ~ to suffer from drought⟩ **b :** ordinarily disposed **:** INCLINED ⟨~ to accept what is plausible as true⟩ **3 :** suited to a purpose; *esp* **:** being to the point ⟨an ~ quotation⟩ **4 :** keenly intelligent and responsive ⟨an ~ pupil⟩ ***syn*** see FIT, QUICK ***usage*** see LIABLE — **apt·ly** \ˈap(t)-lē\ *adv* — **apt·ness** \ˈap(t)-nəs\ *n*
[2]**apt** *abbr* **1** apartment **2** aptitude
ap·ter·ous \ˈap-tə-rəs\ *adj* [Gk *apteros,* fr. *a-* + *pteron* wing — more at FEATHER] (1775) **:** lacking wings ⟨~ insects⟩
ap·ter·yx \ˈap-tə-riks\ *n* [NL, fr. *a-* + Gk *pteryx* wing; akin to Gk *pteron*] (1813) **:** KIWI 1
ap·ti·tude \ˈap-tə-ˌtüd, -ˌtyüd\ *n* [ME, fr. ML *aptitudo,* fr. LL, fitness, fr. L *aptus*] (15c) **1 a :** INCLINATION, TENDENCY ⟨an ~ for hard work⟩ **b :** a natural ability **:** TALENT **2 :** capacity for learning ⟨an ~ for languages⟩ **3 :** general suitability **:** APTNESS ***syn*** see GIFT — **ap·ti·tu·di·nal** \ˌap-tə-ˈtü-dᵊn-əl, -ˈtyü-\ *adj* — **ap·ti·tu·di·nal·ly** *adv*
aptitude test *n* (1919) **:** a standardized test designed to predict an individual's ability to learn certain skills
APU *abbr* auxiliary power unit
ap·y·rase \ˈa-pə-ˌrās, -ˌrāz\ *n* [*a*denosine + *py*rophosphate + *-ase*] (1945) **:** any of several enzymes that catalyze the hydrolysis of ATP to AMP with the liberation of phosphate and energy
aq *abbr* **1** aqua **2** aqueous
aqua \ˈä-kwə *also* ˈa-\ *n* [L — more at ISLAND] (14c) **1** *pl* **aquae** \ˈä-ˌkwī *also* ˈa-(ˌ)kwē\ **:** WATER; *esp* **:** WATER 5a(2) **2** *pl* **aquas :** a light greenish-blue color
aqua·cade \ˈä-kwə-ˌkād, ˈa-\ *n* [*Aquacade,* a water spectacle orig. at Cleveland, Ohio] (1937) **:** a water spectacle that consists usu. of exhibitions of swimming and diving with musical accompaniment
aqua·cul·ture *also* **aqui·cul·ture** \ˈä-kwə-ˌkəl-chər, ˈa-\ *n* [L *aqua* + E *-culture* (as in *agriculture*)] (1864) **:** the cultivation of aquatic organisms (as fish or shellfish) esp. for food — **aqua·cul·tur·al** \ˌä-kwə-ˈkəl-ch(ə-)rəl, ˌa-\ *adj* — **aquaculture** *vt* — **aqua·cul·tur·ist** \-ch(ə-)rist\ *n*
aqua for·tis \ˈä-kwə-ˈfȯr-təs, ˈa-\ *n* [NL *aqua fortis,* lit., strong water] (15c) **:** NITRIC ACID
Aqua–Lung \ˈä-kwə-ˌləŋ, ˈa-\ *trademark* — used for an underwater breathing apparatus
aqua·ma·rine \ˌä-kwə-mə-ˈrēn, ˌa-\ *n* [NL *aqua marina,* fr. L, sea water] (1677) **1 :** a transparent blue, blue-green, or green variety of beryl used as a gem **2 :** a pale blue to light greenish blue
aqua·naut \ˈä-kwə-ˌnȯt, ˈa-, -ˌnät\ *n* [L *aqua* + E *-naut* (as in *aeronaut*)] (1881) **:** a scuba diver who lives and operates both inside and outside an underwater shelter for an extended period
[1]**aqua·plane** \ˈä-kwə-ˌplān, ˈa-\ *n* (1912) **:** a board on which a standing rider is towed behind a speeding motorboat — **aqua·plan·er** *n*
[2]**aquaplane** *vi* (1919) **1 :** to ride an aquaplane **2** *Brit* **:** HYDROPLANE
aqua·pon·ics \ˌa-kwə-ˈpä-niks, ˌä-\ *n pl but sing in constr* [L *aqua* + *-ponics* (in *hydroponics*)] (1981) **:** a system of growing plants in the water that has been used to cultivate aquatic organisms
aqua re·gia \-ˈrē-j(ē-)ə\ *n* [NL, lit., royal water] (1617) **:** a mixture of nitric and hydrochloric acids that dissolves gold or platinum
aqua·relle \ˌa-kwə-ˈrel, ˌä-\ *n* [F, fr. obs. It *acquarella* (now *acquerello*), fr. *acqua* water, fr. L *aqua*] (1821) **:** a drawing usu. in transparent watercolor — **aqua·rell·ist** \-ˈre-list\ *n*
Aquar·i·an \ə-ˈkwa-rē-ən, -ˈkwer-ē-\ *n* (1899) **:** AQUARIUS 1b — **Aquarian** *adj*
aquar·ist \ə-ˈkwa-rist, -ˈkwer-ist\ *n* (1863) **:** a person who keeps or maintains an aquarium
aquar·i·um \ə-ˈkwer-ē-əm\ *n, pl* **-i·ums** *or* **-ia** \-ē-ə\ [prob. alter. of *aquatic vivarium*] (ca. 1847) **1 :** a container (as a glass tank) or an artificial pond in which living aquatic animals or plants are kept **2 :** an establishment where aquatic organisms are kept and exhibited
Aquar·i·us \-ē-əs\ *n* [L (gen. *Aquarii*), lit., water carrier] (14c) **1 a :** the 11th sign of the zodiac in astrology — see ZODIAC table **b :** one born under the sign of Aquarius **2 :** a constellation south of Pegasus pictured as a man pouring water
aqua·scape \ˈä-kwə-ˌskāp, ˈa-\ *n* (1954) **1 :** a scenic view of a body of water **2 :** an area having an aquatic feature (as a pond or fountain)
[1]**aquat·ic** \ə-ˈkwä-tik, -ˈkwa-\ *adj* (1610) **1 :** growing or living in or frequenting water ⟨~ mosquito larvae⟩ **2 :** taking place in or on water ⟨~ sports⟩ — **aquat·i·cal·ly** \-ti-k(ə-)lē\ *adv*
[2]**aquatic** *n* (ca. 1600) **1 :** an aquatic animal or plant **2** *pl but sing or pl in constr* **:** water sports
aqua·tint \ˈa-kwə-ˌtint, ˈä-\ *n* [It *acqua tinta* dyed water] (1782) **:** a method of etching a printing plate so that tones similar to watercolor washes can be reproduced; *also* **:** a print made from a plate so etched — **aquatint** *vt* — **aqua·tint·er** *n* — **aqua·tint·ist** \-ˌtin-tist\ *n*
aqua·vit \ˈä-kwə-ˌvēt\ *also* **ak·va·vit** \ˈä-kwə-ˌvēt, ˈäk-vä-\ *n* [Sw, Dan, & Norw *akvavit,* fr. ML *aqua vitae*] (1864) **:** a clear Scandinavian liquor flavored with caraway seeds
aqua vi·tae \ˌa-kwə-ˈvī-tē, ˌä-\ *n* [ME, fr. ML, lit., water of life] (15c) **:** a strong alcoholic liquor (as brandy)
aq·ue·duct \ˈa-kwə-ˌdəkt\ *n* [L *aquaeductus,* fr. *aquae* (gen. of *aqua*) + *ductus* act of leading — more at DUCT] (1538) **1 a :** a conduit for water; *esp* **:** one for carrying a large quantity of flowing water **b :** a structure for conveying a canal over a river or hollow **2 :** a canal or passage in a part or organ
aque·ous \ˈā-kwē-əs, ˈa-\ *adj* [ML *aqueus,* fr. L *aqua*] (1646) **1 a :** of, relating to, or resembling water **b :** made from, with, or by water ⟨an ~ solution⟩ **2 :** of or relating to the aqueous humor
aqueous humor *n* (1638) **:** a transparent fluid occupying the space between the crystalline lens and the cornea of the eye
aqui·fer \ˈa-kwə-fər, ˈä-\ *n* [NL, fr. L *aqua* + *-fer*] (1897) **:** a water-bearing stratum of permeable rock, sand, or gravel — **aquif·er·ous** \ə-ˈkwi-fə-rəs, ä-\ *adj*
Aq·ui·la \ˈa-kwə-lə *also* ə-ˈkwi-lə\ *n* [L (gen. *Aquilae*), lit., eagle] (14c) **:** a constellation in the northern hemisphere represented by the figure of an eagle
aq·ui·le·gia \ˌa-kwə-ˈlē-j(ē-)ə\ *n* [NL] (1706) **:** COLUMBINE
aq·ui·line \ˈa-kwə-ˌlīn, -lən\ *adj* [L *aquilinus,* fr. *aquila* eagle] (1646) **1 :** curving like an eagle's beak ⟨an ~ nose⟩ **2 :** of, relating to, or resembling an eagle — **aq·ui·lin·i·ty** \ˌa-kwə-ˈli-nə-tē\ *n*
aquiv·er \ə-ˈkwi-vər\ *adj* (1864) **:** marked by trembling or quivering
[1]**ar** \ˈär\ *n* [ME] (15c) **:** the letter *r*
[2]**ar** *abbr* arrival; arrive
[1]**Ar** *abbr* Arabic
[2]**Ar** *symbol* argon
AR *abbr* **1** accounts receivable **2** acknowledgment of receipt **3** all rail **4** all risks **5** annual return **6** Arkansas **7** army regulation **8** autonomous republic
-ar *adj suffix* [ME, fr. L *-aris,* alter. of *-alis* -al] **:** of or relating to ⟨molecular⟩ **:** being ⟨spectacular⟩ **:** resembling ⟨oracular⟩
[1]**Ar·ab** \ˈa-rəb, ˈer-əb; *dial also* ˈā-ˌrab\ *n* [ME, fr. L *Arabus, Arabs,* fr. Gk *Arab-, Araps,* of Sem origin; akin to Akkadian *Arabu, Aribi* desert nomads, Ar *A'rāb* Bedouins] (14c) **1 a :** a member of the Semitic people of the Arabian Peninsula **b :** a member of an Arabic-speaking people **2 :** ARABIAN HORSE — **Arab** *adj*
[2]**Arab** *abbr* Arabian; Arabic
[1]**ar·a·besque** \ˌa-rə-ˈbesk, ˌer-ə-\ *adj* [F, fr. It *arabesco* Arabian in fashion, fr. *arabo* Arab, fr. L *Arabus*] (ca. 1656) **:** of, relating to, or being in the style of arabesque or an arabesque
[2]**arabesque** *n* (ca. 1720) **1 :** an ornament or style that employs flower, foliage, or fruit and sometimes animal and figural outlines to produce an intricate pattern of interlaced lines **2 :** a posture (as in ballet) in which the body is bent forward from the hip on one leg with one arm extended forward and the other arm and leg backward **3 :** an elaborate or intricate pattern

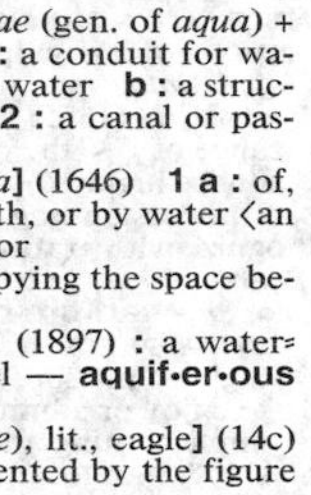
arabesque 1

[1]**Ara·bi·an** \ə-ˈrā-bē-ən\ *n* (14c) **1 :** a native or inhabitant of Arabia **2 :** ARABIAN HORSE
[2]**Arabian** *adj* (14c) **:** ARABIC 1
Arabian horse *n* (1588) **:** any of an ancient breed of swift compact horses developed in Arabia and usu. having gray or chestnut silky hair

[1]**Ar·a·bic** \ˈa-rə-bik, ˈer-ə-\ *n* (14c) : a Semitic language orig. of the Arabs of the Hejaz and Nejd that is now the prevailing speech of a wide region of southwestern Asia and northern Africa

[2]**Arabic** *adj* (14c) **1** : of, relating to, or characteristic of Arabia or the Arabs **2** : of, relating to, or constituting Arabic **3** : expressed in or utilizing Arabic numerals

arab·i·ca \ə-ˈra-bə-kə\ *n, often attrib* [NL, specific epithet of *Coffea arabica,* fr. L, fem. of *Arabicus* Arabian] (1882) **1** : an evergreen shrub or tree (*Coffea arabica*) yielding seeds that produce a high-quality coffee and form a large portion of the coffee of commerce **2** : the seeds of arabica esp. roasted and often ground

Arabic alphabet *n* (1732) : an alphabet of 28 letters derived from the Aramaic alphabet which is used for writing Arabic and also with adaptations for other languages of the Islamic world

arab·i·cize \ə-ˈra-bə-ˌsīz\ *vt* **-cized; -ciz·ing** *often cap* (1826) **1** : to adapt (a language or elements of a language) to the phonetic or structural pattern of Arabic **2** : ARABIZE 1 — **arab·i·ci·za·tion** \ə-ˌra-bə-sə-ˈzā-shən\ *n*

Arabic numeral *n* (1756) : any of the number symbols 0, 1, 2, 3, 4, 5, 6, 7, 8, 9 — see NUMBER table

arab·i·nose \ə-ˈra-bə-ˌnōs, -ˌnōz\ *n* [ISV *arabin* (the solid principle in gum arabic, fr. *gum arabic* + [1]*-in*) + *-ose*] (1889) : a white crystalline aldose sugar $C_5H_{10}O_5$ occurring esp. in vegetable gums

ara·bi·no·side \ˌa-rə-ˈbi-nə-ˌsīd, ə-ˈra-bə-nō-ˌsīd\ *n* (1927) : a glycoside that yields arabinose on hydrolysis

Ar·ab·ise *Brit var of* ARABIZE

Ar·ab·ism \ˈa-rə-ˌbi-zəm, ˈer-ə-\ *n* (1614) **1** : a characteristic feature of Arabic occurring in another language **2** : devotion to Arab interests, culture, aspirations, or ideals

Ar·ab·ist \-bist\ *n* (1753) **1** : a specialist in the Arabic language or in Arabic culture **2** : a person who favors Arab interests and positions in international affairs

Ar·ab·ize \-ˌbīz\ *vt* **-ized; -iz·ing** (1883) **1 a** : to cause to acquire Arabic customs, manners, speech, or outlook **b** : to modify (a population) by intermarriage with Arabs **2** : ARABICIZE 1 — **Ar·ab·i·za·tion** \ˌar-ə-bə-ˈzā-shən\ *n*

[1]**ar·a·ble** \ˈa-rə-bəl, ˈer-ə-\ *adj* [AF or L; AF, fr. L *arabilis,* fr. *arare* to plow; akin to OE *erian* to plow, Gk *aroun*] (15c) **1** : fit for or used for the growing of crops **2** *Brit* : engaged in, produced by, or being the cultivation of arable land — **ar·a·bil·i·ty** \ˌa-rə-ˈbi-lə-tē, ˌer-ə-\ *n*

[2]**arable** *n* (1576) *chiefly Brit* : land fit or used for the growing of crops; *also* : a plot of such land ⟨the village ~ of Anglo-Saxon times⟩

Arab Spring *noun* (2010) : a series of antigovernment uprisings affecting Arab countries of North Africa and the Middle East beginning in 2010

ar·a·chi·don·ic acid \ˌar-ə-kə-ˈdä-nik-\ *n* [NL *Arachid-, Arachis* + E *-onic* (as in *gluconic acid*)] (1913) : a liquid unsaturated fatty acid $C_{20}H_{32}O_2$ that occurs in most animal fats, is a precursor of prostaglandins, and is considered essential in animal nutrition

ar·a·chis oil \ˈar-ə-kəs-\ *n* [NL *Arachis,* genus that includes the peanut, fr. Gk *arakis,* dim. of *arakos,* a legume] (1811) : PEANUT OIL

arachn- *or* **arachno-** *comb form* [NL & Gk; NL, fr. Gk, fr. *arachnē* spider, spiderweb; perh. akin to L *aranea* spider, Gk *arkys* net] : spider : arachnid ⟨*arachno*logy⟩

arach·nid \ə-ˈrak-nəd, -ˌnid\ *n* (1826) : any of a class (Arachnida) of arthropods comprising chiefly terrestrial invertebrates, including the spiders, scorpions, mites, and ticks, and having a segmented body divided into two regions of which the anterior bears four pairs of legs but no antennae — **arachnid** *adj*

[1]**arach·noid** \ə-ˈrak-ˌnȯid\ *adj* (1789) **1** : of or relating to a thin membrane of the brain and spinal cord that lies between the dura mater and the pia mater **2** : covered with or composed of soft loose hairs or fibers

[2]**arachnoid** *n* [NL *arachnoides,* fr. Gk *arachnoeidēs,* like a cobweb, fr. *arachnē* spiderweb] (1804) : an arachnoid membrane

[3]**arachnoid** *adj* [NL *Arachn*ida + E *-oid*] (1825) : resembling or related to the arachnids

arach·nol·o·gist \ˌa-ˌrak-ˈnä-lə-jist, ˌer-ˌak-\ *n* (1816) : a person who specializes in the study of spiders and other arachnids — **arach·no·log·i·cal** \-nə-ˈlä-ji-kəl\ *adj* — **arach·nol·ogy** \-ˈnä-lə-jē\ *n*

arach·no·pho·bia \ə-ˌrak-nə-ˈfō-bē-ə\ *n* (1863) : pathological fear or loathing of spiders — **arach·no·phobe** \-ˈrak-nə-ˌfōb\ *n* — **arach·no·pho·bic** \-ˌrak-nə-ˈfō-bik\ *adj or n*

ara·go·nite \ə-ˈra-gə-ˌnīt, ˈa-rə-gə-, ˈer-ə-\ *n* [G *Aragonit,* fr. *Aragon,* Spain] (1801) : a mineral similar to calcite in consisting of calcium carbonate but differing from calcite in its orthorhombic crystallization, greater density, and less distinct cleavage — **ara·go·nit·ic** \ə-ˌra-gə-ˈni-tik, ˌer-ə-gə-, ˌa-rə-\ *adj*

arak *var of* ARRACK

Ar·a·mae·an *also* **Ar·a·me·an** \ˌa-rə-ˈmē-ən, ˌer-ə-\ *n* [L *Aramaeus,* fr. Gk *Aramaios,* fr. Heb *ʿĀrām* Aram, ancient name for Syria] (1689) **1** : ARAMAIC **2** : a member of a Semitic people of the second millennium B.C. in Syria and Upper Mesopotamia — **Aramaean** *adj*

Ar·a·ma·ic \-ˈmā-ik\ *n* (1813) : a Semitic language known since the ninth century B.C. as the speech of the Aramaeans and later used extensively in southwest Asia as a commercial and governmental language and adopted as their customary speech by various non-Aramaean peoples including the Jews after the Babylonian exile

Aramaic alphabet *n* (1835) **1** : an extinct North Semitic alphabet dating from the ninth century B.C. which was for several centuries the commercial alphabet of southwest Asia and the parent of other alphabets (as Syriac and Arabic) **2** : the square Hebrew alphabet as distinguished from the early Hebrew alphabet

ar·a·mid \ˈa-rə-məd, -ˌmid, ˈer-ə-\ *n* [*ar*omatic poly*amide*] (1972) : any of a group of lightweight but very strong heat-resistant synthetic aromatic polyamide materials that are fashioned into fibers, filaments, or sheets and used esp. in textiles and plastics

Arap·a·ho *or* **Arap·a·hoe** \ə-ˈra-pə-ˌhō\ *n, pl* **-ho** *or* **-hos** *or* **-hoe** *or* **-hoes** [prob. fr. Hidatsa *arúpahu* Arapaho, or a cognate word in another Siouan language] (1812) **1** : a member of an American Indian people of the plains region ranging from Saskatchewan and Manitoba to New Mexico and Texas **2** : the Algonquian language of the Arapaho people

Arau·ca·ni·an \ə-ˌrau̇-ˈkä-nē-ən, ˌa-ˌrȯ-ˈkā-\ *also* **Arau·can** \ə-ˈrau̇-kən\ *n* [Sp *araucano,* fr. *Arauco,* former province in Chile] (1777) **1** : a member of a group of Indian peoples of south central Chile and adjacent regions of Argentina **2** : the language of the Araucanian people that constitutes an independent language family — **Araucanian** *adj*

ar·au·car·ia \ˌa-ˌrȯ-ˈka-rē-ə\ *n* [NL, fr. *Arauco*] (1806) : any of a genus (*Araucaria* of the family Araucariaceae, the araucaria family) of So. American or Australian coniferous trees that resemble pines and are often grown as ornamentals; *esp* : MONKEY PUZZLE — **ar·au·car·i·an** \-ē-ən\ *adj*

Ar·a·wak \ˈa-rə-ˌwäk, -ˌwak\ *n, pl* **Arawak** *or* **Arawaks** [earlier *Arwaca, Aroaca,* an Arawak subgroup of 16th cent. Trinidad, perh. fr. an Arawak name for the subgroup] (1769) **1** : a member of an Indian people of the Arawakan group now living chiefly along the coast of Guyana **2** : the language of the Arawak people

Ar·a·wak·an \ˌa-rə-ˈwä-kən, -ˈwa-\ *n, pl* **Arawakan** *or* **Arawakans** (1848) **1** : a member of a group of Indian peoples of So. America and the West Indies **2** : the language family of the Arawakan peoples

arb \ˈärb\ *n* (1979) : ARBITRAGEUR

ar·ba·lest *or* **ar·ba·list** \ˈär-bə-list\ *n* [ME *arblast,* fr. AF *arblaste, arcbaleste,* fr. LL *arcuballista,* fr. L *arcus* bow + *ballista* — more at ARROW] (bef. 12c) : a crossbow esp. of medieval times

ar·bi·ter \ˈär-bə-tər\ *n* [ME *arbitre,* fr. AF, fr. L *arbitr-, arbiter*] (14c) **1** : a person with power to decide a dispute : JUDGE **2** : a person or agency whose judgment or opinion is considered authoritative ⟨~*s* of taste⟩

arbiter el·e·gan·ti·a·rum \-ˌe-lə-ˌgan-shē-ˈa-rəm, -ˈer-əm\ *n* [L, lit., arbiter of refinements] (1728) : a person who prescribes, rules on, or is a recognized authority on matters of social behavior and taste

ar·bi·tra·ble \ˈär-bə-trə-bəl, är-ˈbi-\ *adj* (1531) : subject to decision by arbitration

[1]**ar·bi·trage** \ˈär-bə-ˌträzh\ *n* [F, fr. MF, arbitration, fr. OF, fr. *arbitrer* to render judgment, fr. L *arbitrari,* fr. *arbitr-, arbiter*] (1875) **1** : the nearly simultaneous purchase and sale of securities or foreign exchange in different markets in order to profit from price discrepancies **2** : the purchase of the stock of a takeover target esp. with a view to selling it profitably to the raider

[2]**arbitrage** *vi* **-traged; -trag·ing** (ca. 1896) : to engage in arbitrage

ar·bi·tra·geur \ˌär-bə-(ˌ)trä-ˈzhər\ *or* **ar·bi·trag·er** \ˈär-bə-ˌträ-zhər\ *n* [F *arbitrageur,* fr. *arbitrage*] (1870) : one that practices arbitrage

ar·bi·tral \ˈär-bə-trəl\ *adj* (1609) : relating to arbiters or arbitration

ar·bit·ra·ment \är-ˈbi-trə-mənt\ *n* [ME, fr. AF *arbitrement,* fr. *arbitrer*] (14c) **1** *archaic* : the right or power of deciding **2** : the settling of a dispute by an arbiter **3** : the judgment given by an arbitrator

ar·bi·trary \ˈär-bə-ˌtrer-ē, -ˌtre-rē\ *adj* (15c) **1** : depending on individual discretion (as of a judge) and not fixed by law ⟨the manner of punishment is ~⟩ **2 a** : not restrained or limited in the exercise of power : ruling by absolute authority ⟨an ~ government⟩ **b** : marked by or resulting from the unrestrained and often tyrannical exercise of power ⟨protection from ~ arrest and detention⟩ **3 a** : based on or determined by individual preference or convenience rather than by necessity or the intrinsic nature of something ⟨an ~ standard⟩ ⟨take any ~ positive number⟩ ⟨~ division of historical studies into watertight compartments —A. J. Toynbee⟩ **b** : existing or coming about seemingly at random or by chance or as a capricious and unreasonable act of will ⟨when a task is not seen in a meaningful context it is experienced as being ~ —Nehemiah Jordan⟩ — **ar·bi·trari·ly** \ˌär-bə-ˈtrer-ə-lē, -ˈtre-rə-\ *adv* — **ar·bi·trar·i·ness** \ˈär-bə-ˌtrer-ē-nəs, -ˌtre-rē-\ *n*

ar·bi·trate \ˈär-bə-ˌtrāt\ *vb* **-trat·ed; -trat·ing** *vt* (1588) **1** *archaic* : DECIDE, DETERMINE **2** : to act as arbiter upon **3** : to submit or refer for decision to an arbiter ⟨agreed to ~ their differences⟩ ~ *vi* : to act as arbiter — **ar·bi·tra·tive** \-ˌtrā-tiv\ *adj*

ar·bi·tra·tion \ˌär-bə-ˈtrā-shən\ *n* (15c) : the action of arbitrating; *esp* : the hearing and determination of a case in controversy by an arbiter — **ar·bi·tra·tion·al** \-sh(ə-)nəl\ *adj*

ar·bi·tra·tor \ˈär-bə-ˌtrā-tər\ *n* (15c) : one that arbitrates : ARBITER

[1]**ar·bor** \ˈär-bər\ *n* [ME *erber, herber* garden, fr. AF, fr. *herbe* herb, grass] (14c) : a shelter of vines or branches or of latticework covered with climbing shrubs or vines

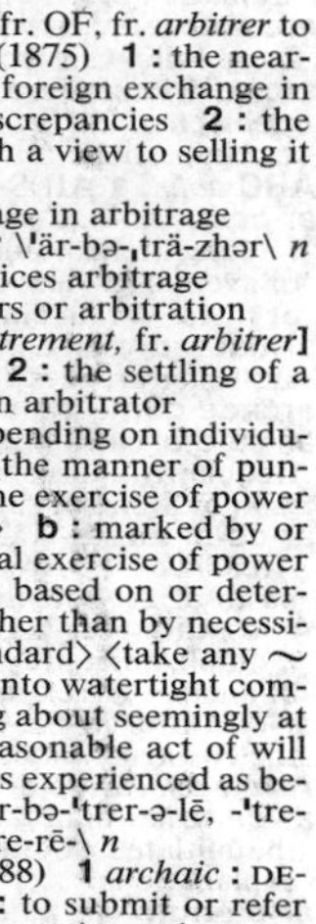

[1]arbor

[2]**arbor** *n* [L, tree, shaft] (1659) **1** : a spindle or axle of a wheel **2** : a main shaft or beam **3** : a shaft on which a revolving cutting tool is mounted **4** : a spindle on a cutting machine that holds the work to be cut

arbor- *or* **arbori-** *comb form* [L *arbor*] : tree ⟨*arbori*culture⟩

Arbor Day *n* [L *arbor* tree] (1863) : a day designated for planting trees

ar·bo·re·al \är-ˈbȯr-ē-əl\ *adj* [L *arboreus* of a tree, fr. *arbor*] (ca. 1667) **1** : of, relating to, or resembling a tree **2** : inhabiting or frequenting trees ⟨~ monkeys⟩ — **ar·bo·re·al·ly** \-ə-lē\ *adv*

ar·bo·re·ous \-ē-əs\ *adj* (1646) : ARBOREAL ⟨an ~ palm⟩

ar·bo·res·cent \ˌär-bə-ˈre-sᵊnt\ *adj* (1675) : resembling a tree in properties, growth, structure, or appearance — **ar·bo·res·cence** \-sᵊn(t)s\ *n*

ar·bo·re·tum \ˌär-bə-ˈrē-təm\ *n, pl* **-retums** *or* **-re·ta** \-ˈrē-tə\ [NL, fr. L, plantation of trees, fr. *arbor*] (1796) : a place where trees, shrubs, and herbaceous plants are cultivated for scientific and educational purposes

ar·bor·i·cul·ture \ˈär-bər-ə-ˌkəl-chər, är-ˈbȯr-ə-\ *n* [*arbori-* + *-culture* (as in *agriculture*)] (ca. 1778) : the cultivation of trees and shrubs esp. for ornamental purposes — **ar·bor·i·cul·tur·al** \ˌär-bər-ə-ˈkəl-chər-əl, är-ˌbȯr-ə-\ *adj*

ar·bo·rio rice \ˌär-ˈbȯr-ē-ō-\ *n, often cap A* [*Arborio,* village in Piedmont region of Italy] (1976) : a short-grain rice that has a creamy texture when cooked and is typically used in risotto

ar•bor•ist \ˈär-bə-rist\ *n* (1578) **:** a specialist in the care and maintenance of trees

ar•bor•i•za•tion \ˌär-bə-rə-ˈzā-shən\ *n* (1794) **:** formation of or into an arborescent figure arrangement; *also* **:** such a figure or arrangement (as a dendritic process of a neuron)

ar•bor•ize \ˈär-bə-ˌrīz\ *vi* **-ized; -iz•ing** (1847) **:** to branch freely and repeatedly

ar•bor•vi•tae \ˌär-bər-ˈvī-tē\ *n* [NL *arbor vitae,* lit., tree of life] (1646) **:** any of various evergreen trees and shrubs (esp. genus *Thuja*) of the cypress family that usu. have closely overlapping or compressed scale leaves and are often grown for ornament and in hedges

ar•bour *chiefly Brit var of* ARBOR

ar•bo•vi•rus \ˌär-bə-ˈvī-rəs\ *n* [*ar*thropod-*bo*rne *virus*] (1957) **:** any of various RNA viruses (as the causative agents of equine encephalitis, sandfly fever, and West Nile fever) transmitted chiefly by arthropods

ar•bu•tus \är-ˈbyü-təs\ *n* [NL, fr. L, strawberry tree] (1548) **1 :** any of a genus (*Arbutus*) of shrubs and trees of the heath family with white or pink flowers and red or orange berries **2 :** a creeping plant (*Epigaea repens*) of the heath family that occurs in eastern No. America and bears fragrant pink or white flowers in early spring

[1]**arc** \ˈärk\ *n* [ME *ark,* fr. AF *arc* bow, fr. L *arcus* bow, arch, arc — more at ARROW] (14c) **1 :** the apparent path described above and below the horizon by a celestial body (as the sun) **2 a :** something arched or curved **b :** a curved path ⟨the ~ of a fly ball⟩ **3 :** a sustained luminous discharge of electricity across a gap in a circuit or between electrodes; *also* **:** ARC LAMP **4 :** a continuous portion (as of a circle or ellipse) of a curved line **5 :** degree measurement on the circumference of a circle — used esp. in the phrase *of arc* ⟨11 minutes 3 seconds of ~⟩ **6 :** a continuous progression or line of development ⟨a story's dramatic ~⟩

[2]**arc** *vi* **arced** \ˈärkt\; **arc•ing** \ˈär-kiŋ\ (1893) **1 :** to form an electric arc **2 :** to follow an arc-shaped course

[3]**arc** *adj* [*arc sine* arc or angle (corresponding to the) sine (of so many degrees)] (ca. 1949) **:** INVERSE 2 — used with the trigonometric functions and hyperbolic functions

ARC *abbr* **1** AIDS-related complex **2** American Red Cross

ar•cade \är-ˈkād\ *n* [F, fr. It *arcata,* fr. *arco* arch, fr. L *arcus*] (1725) **1 :** a long arched building or gallery **2 :** an arched covered passageway or avenue (as between shops) **3 :** a series of arches with their columns or piers **4 :** an amusement center having coin-operated games

ar•cad•ed \-ˈkā-dəd\ *adj* (1805) **:** having, formed in, or decorated with arches or arcades ⟨~ streets⟩ ⟨an ~ bowl⟩

arcade game *n* (1978) **:** VIDEO GAME

ar•ca•dia \är-ˈkā-dē-ə\ *n, often cap* [*Arcadia,* region of ancient Greece frequently chosen as background for pastoral poetry] (ca. 1890) **:** a region or scene of simple pleasure and quiet

ar•ca•di•an \är-ˈkā-dē-ən\ *adj, often cap* (1565) **1 a :** of or relating to Arcadia or the Arcadians **b :** of or relating to Arcadian **2 :** idyllically pastoral; *esp* **:** idyllically innocent, simple, or untroubled

Ar•ca•di•an \är-ˈkā-dē-ən\ *n* (1573) **1** *often not cap* **:** a person who lives a simple quiet life **2 :** a native or inhabitant of Arcadia **3 :** the dialect of ancient Greek used in Arcadia

ar•cad•ing \är-ˈkā-diŋ\ *n* (1849) **:** a series of arches or arcades used in the construction or decoration esp. of a building

Ar•ca•dy \ˈär-kə-dē\ *n* (14c) **:** ARCADIA

ar•cane \är-ˈkān\ *adj* [L *arcanus*] (1547) **:** known or knowable only to the initiate **:** SECRET ⟨~ rites⟩; *broadly* **:** MYSTERIOUS, OBSCURE ⟨~ explanations⟩

ar•ca•num \är-ˈkā-nəm\ *n, pl* **-na** \-nə\ [L, fr. neut. of *arcanus* secret, fr. *arca* chest — more at ARK] (15c) **1 :** mysterious or specialized knowledge, language, or information accessible or possessed only by the initiate — usu. used in pl. **2 :** ELIXIR 1

arc•co•sine \(ˌ)är(k)-ˈkō-ˌsīn\ *n* (ca. 1884) **:** the inverse function of the cosine ⟨if *y* is the cosine of *θ,* then *θ* is the ~ of *y*⟩

[1]**arch** \ˈärch\ *n* [ME *arche,* fr. AF, fr. VL **arca,* fr. L *arcus* — more at ARROW] (14c) **1 :** a typically curved structural member spanning an opening and serving as a support (as for the wall or other weight above the opening) **2 a :** something resembling an arch in form or function; *esp* **:** either of two vaulted portions of the bony structure of the foot that impart elasticity to it **b :** a curvature having the form of an arch **3 :** ARCHWAY

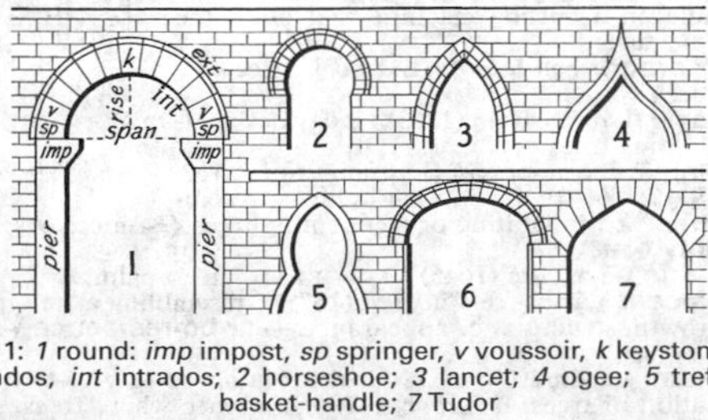

arch 1: *1* round: *imp* impost, *sp* springer, *v* voussoir, *k* keystone, *ext* extrados, *int* intrados; *2* horseshoe; *3* lancet; *4* ogee; *5* trefoil; *6* basket-handle; *7* Tudor

[2]**arch** *vt* (15c) **1 :** to cover or provide with an arch **2 :** to form into an arch ~ *vi* **1 :** to form an arch **2 :** to take an arch-shaped course

[3]**arch** *adj* [ˈarch-] (1547) **1 :** PRINCIPAL, CHIEF ⟨your ~ opponent⟩ **2 a :** MISCHIEVOUS, SAUCY **b :** marked by a deliberate and often forced playfulness, irony, or impudence ⟨known for her ~ comments⟩ ⟨decided to answer them by being teacherly in a sort of ~, Olympian way —Gerald Early⟩ — **arch•ness** *n*

[4]**arch** *abbr* **1** archaic **2** archery **3** architect; architectural; architecture

Arch *abbr* Archbishop

[1]**arch-** *prefix* [ME *arche-, arch-,* fr. OE & AF; OE *arce-,* fr. LL *arch-* & L *archi-;* AF *arch-,* fr. LL *arch-* & L *archi-,* fr. Gk *arch-, archi-,* fr. *archein* to begin, rule; akin to Gk *archē* beginning, rule, *archos* ruler] **1 :** chief **:** principal ⟨*arch*fiend⟩ **2 :** extreme **:** most fully embodying the qualities of the kind ⟨*arch*conservative⟩

[2]**arch-** — see ARCHI-

[1]**-arch** *n comb form* [ME *-arche,* fr. AF & LL & L; AF *-arche,* fr. LL *-archa,* fr. L *-arches, -archus,* fr. Gk *-archēs, -archos,* fr. *archein*] **:** ruler **:** leader ⟨matri*arch*⟩

[2]**-arch** *adj comb form* [prob. fr. G, fr. Gk *archē* beginning] **:** having (such) a point or (so many) points of origin ⟨end*arch*⟩

archae- *or* **archaeo-** *also* **archeo-** *comb form* [Gk *archaio-,* fr. *archaios* ancient, fr. *archē* beginning] **:** ancient **:** primitive ⟨*archaeo*pteryx⟩

ar•chaea \är-ˈkē-ə\ *n pl* [NL, fr. Gk *archaios*] (1990) **:** microorganisms of a domain (Archaea) including esp. methane-producing forms, some red halophilic forms, and others of harsh hot acidic environments (as a hot spring) — compare BACTERIUM, EUKARYOTE — **ar•chae•al** \-əl\ *adj* — **ar•chae•an** \-ən\ *adj or n*

ar•chae•bac•te•ri•um \ˌär-kē-ˌbak-ˈtir-ē-əm\ *n* [NL] (1977) **:** any of the microorganisms comprising the archaea

ar•chaeo•as•tron•o•my \ˌär-kē-(ˌ)ō-ə-ˈsträ-nə-mē\ *n* (1971) **:** the study of the astronomy of ancient cultures

ar•chae•ol•o•gy *or* **ar•che•ol•o•gy** \ˌär-kē-ˈä-lə-jē\ *n* [F *archéologie,* fr. LL *archaeologia* antiquarian lore, fr. Gk *archaiologia,* fr. *archaio-* + *-logia* -logy] (1837) **1 :** the scientific study of material remains (as fossil relics, artifacts, and monuments) of past human life and activities **2 :** remains of the culture of a people **:** ANTIQUITIES — **ar•chae•o•log•i•cal** \ˌär-kē-ə-ˈlä-ji-kəl\ *adj* — **ar•chae•o•log•i•cal•ly** \-k(ə-)lē\ *adv* — **ar•chae•ol•o•gist** \ˌär-kē-ˈä-lə-jist\ *n*

ar•chae•op•ter•yx \ˌär-kē-ˈäp-tə-riks\ *n* [NL, fr. *archae-* + Gk *pteryx* wing; akin to Gk *pteron* wing — more at FEATHER] (1859) **:** a primitive crow-sized bird (genus *Archaeopteryx*) of the Upper Jurassic period of Europe having reptilian characteristics (as teeth and a long bony tail)

ar•cha•ic \är-ˈkā-ik\ *adj* [F or Gk; F *archaïque,* fr. Gk *archaïkos,* fr. *archaios*] (1832) **1 :** having the characteristics of the language of the past and surviving chiefly in specialized uses ⟨an ~ word⟩ **2 :** of, relating to, or characteristic of an earlier or more primitive time **:** ANTIQUATED ⟨~ legal traditions⟩ **3** *cap* **:** of or belonging to the early or formative phases of a culture or a period of artistic development; *esp* **:** of or belonging to the period leading up to the classical period of Greek culture **4 :** surviving from an earlier period; *specif* **:** typical of a previously dominant evolutionary stage **5** *cap* **:** of or relating to the period from about 8000 B.C. to 1000 B.C. and the North American cultures of that time ***syn*** see OLD — **ar•cha•i•cal•ly** \-i-k(ə-)lē\ *adv*

archaic smile *n* (ca. 1902) **:** an expression that resembles a smile and is characteristic of early Greek sculpture

ar•cha•ism \ˈär-kē-ˌi-zəm, -(ˌ)kā-ˌi-\ *n* [NL *archaïsmus,* fr. Gk *archaïsmos,* fr. *archaios*] (1643) **1 :** the use of archaic diction or style **2 :** an instance of archaic usage **3 :** something archaic; *esp* **:** something (as a practice or custom) that is outmoded or old-fashioned — **ar•cha•ist** \-ist\ *n* — **ar•cha•is•tic** \ˌär-kē-ˈis-tik, -(ˌ)kā-\ *adj* — **ar•cha•ize** \ˈär-kē-ˌīz, -(ˌ)kā-\ *vb*

arch•an•gel \ˈärk-ˌān-jəl\ *n* [ME, fr. AF or LL; AF *archangle,* fr. LL *archangelus,* fr. Gk *archangelos,* fr. *archi-* + *angelos* angel] (12c) **1 :** a chief angel **2** *pl* **:** an order of angels — see CELESTIAL HIERARCHY — **arch•an•gel•ic** \ˌärk-(ˌ)an-ˈje-lik\ *adj*

arch•bish•op \(ˌ)ärch-ˈbi-shəp\ *n* [ME, fr. OE *arcebiscop,* fr. LL *archiepiscopus,* fr. LGk *archiepiskopos,* fr. *archi-* + *episkopos* bishop — more at BISHOP] (bef. 12c) **:** a bishop at the head of an ecclesiastical province or one of equivalent honorary rank

arch•bish•op•ric \-shə-(ˌ)prik\ *n* (bef. 12c) **1 :** the see or province over which an archbishop exercises authority **2 :** the jurisdiction or office of an archbishop

arch•con•ser•va•tive \(ˌ)ärch-kən-ˈsər-və-tiv\ *n* (1934) **:** an extreme conservative — **archconservative** *adj*

arch•dea•con \(ˌ)ärch-ˈdē-kən\ *n* [ME *archedeken,* fr. OE *arcediacon,* fr. LL *archidiaconus,* fr. LGk *archidiakonos,* fr. Gk *archi-* + *diakonos* deacon] (bef. 12c) **:** a clergyman having the duty of assisting a diocesan bishop in ceremonial functions or administrative work

arch•dea•con•ry \-kən-rē\ *n, pl* **-ries** (1529) **:** the district or residence of an archdeacon

arch•di•o•cese \(ˌ)ärch-ˈdī-ə-səs, -ˌsēs, -ˌsēz\ *n, pl* **-ces•es** \-ˈdī-ə-sə-səz, -ˌsē-zəz, -ˈdī-ə-ˌsēz\ (1844) **:** the diocese of an archbishop — **arch•di•oc•e•san** \ˌärch-dī-ˈä-sə-sən *also* -ˈdī-ə-ˌsē-sᵊn\ *adj*

arch•du•cal \(ˌ)ärch-ˈdü-kəl, -ˈdyü-\ *adj* [F *archiducal,* fr. *archiduc*] (1665) **:** of or relating to an archduke or archduchy

arch•duch•ess \-ˈdə-chəs\ *n* [F *archiduchesse,* fem. of *archiduc* archduke, fr. MF *archeduc*] (1555) **1 :** the wife or widow of an archduke **2 :** a woman having in her own right a rank equal to that of an archduke

arch•duchy \-ˈdə-chē\ *n* [F *archiduché,* fr. MF *archeduché,* fr. *arche-* arch- + *duché* duchy] (1530) **:** the territory of an archduke or archduchess

arch•duke \-ˈdük, -ˈdyük\ *n* [MF *archeduc,* fr. *arche-* arch- + *duc* duke] (15c) **1 :** a sovereign prince **2 :** a prince of the imperial family of Austria — **arch•duke•dom** \-dəm\ *n*

Ar•che•an *or* **Ar•chae•an** \är-ˈkē-ən\ *adj* [Gk *archaios*] (1872) **1 :** of, relating to, or being the earliest eon of geological history or the corresponding system of rocks — see GEOLOGIC TIME table **2 :** PRECAMBRIAN — **Archean** *n*

ar•che•go•ni•um \ˌär-ki-ˈgō-nē-əm\ *n, pl* **-nia** \-nē-ə\ [NL, fr. Gk *archegonos* originator, fr. *archein* to begin + *gonos* procreation; akin to Gk *gignesthai* to be born — more at ARCH-, KIN] (1854) **:** the flask-shaped female sex organ of bryophytes, lower vascular plants (as ferns), and some gymnosperms — **ar•che•go•ni•al** \-nē-əl\ *adj*

arch•en•e•my \(ˌ)ärch-ˈe-nə-mē\ *n, pl* **-mies** (1550) **:** a principal enemy

arch•en•ter•on \är-ˈken-tə-ˌrän, -rən\ *n* [NL] (1877) **:** the cavity of a gastrula forming a primitive gut

archeol *abbr* archeology

Ar•cheo•zo•ic *also* **Ar•chaeo•zo•ic** \ˌär-kē-ə-ˈzō-ik\ *adj* (1872) **:** ARCHEAN 1 — **Archeozoic** *n*

ar•cher \ˈär-chər\ *n* [ME, fr. AF, fr. LL *arcarius,* alter. of *arcuarius,* fr. *arcuarius* of a bow, fr. L *arcus* bow — more at ARROW] (14c) **1 :** a person who uses a bow and arrow **2** *cap* **:** SAGITTARIUS

ar•cher•fish \ˈär-chər-ˌfish\ *n* (ca. 1889) **:** any of several small East Indian bony fishes (genus *Toxotes* and esp. *T. ejaculator* of the family Toxotidae) that catch insects by stunning them with water ejected from their mouths

ar·chery \ˈär-chə-rē\ *n* (15c) **1 :** the art, practice, or skill of shooting with bow and arrow **2 :** an archer's weapons **3 :** a body of archers

ar·che·type \ˈär-ki-ˌtīp\ *n* [L *archetypum,* fr. Gk *archetypon,* fr. neut. of *archetypos* archetypal, fr. *archein* + *typos* type] (1545) **1 :** the original pattern or model of which all things of the same type are representations or copies : PROTOTYPE; *also* : a perfect example **2 :** IDEA 1a **3 :** an inherited idea or mode of thought in the psychology of C. G. Jung that is derived from the experience of the race and is present in the unconscious of the individual — **ar·che·typ·al** \ˌär-ki-ˈtī-pəl\ *also* **ar·che·typ·i·cal** \-ˈti-pi-kəl\ *adj* — **ar·che·typ·al·ly** \-pə-lē\ *also* **ar·che·typ·i·cal·ly** \-ˈti-pi-k(ə-)lē\ *adv*

arch·fiend \(ˌ)ärch-ˈfēnd\ *n* (1667) : a chief fiend; *esp* : SATAN

arch·foe \-ˈfō\ *n* (1595) : a principal foe : ARCHENEMY

archi- *or* **arch-** *prefix* [F or L; F, fr. L, fr. Gk — more at ARCH-] : primitive : original : primary ⟨*arch*enteron⟩

ar·chi·di·ac·o·nal \ˌär-ki-dī-ˈa-kə-nᵊl\ *adj* [LL *archidiaconus* archdeacon] (15c) : of or relating to an archdeacon

ar·chi·epis·co·pal \ˌär-kē-ə-ˈpis-kə-pəl\ *adj* [ML *archiepiscopalis,* fr. LL *archiepiscopus* archbishop — more at ARCHBISHOP] (ca. 1600) : of or relating to an archbishop — **ar·chi·epis·co·pal·ly** \-p(ə-)lē\ *adv*

ar·chi·epis·co·pate \-pət, -ˌpāt\ *n* (1792) : ARCHBISHOPRIC

ar·chil \ˈär-chəl\ *n* [ME *orchell*] (15c) **1 :** a violet dye obtained from lichens (genera *Roccella* and *Lecanora*) **2 :** a lichen that yields archil

ar·chi·man·drite \ˌär-kə-ˈman-ˌdrīt\ *n* [LL *archimandrites,* fr. LGk *archimandritēs,* fr. Gk *archi-* + LGk *mandra* monastery, fr. Gk, fold, pen] (1591) : a dignitary in an Eastern church ranking below a bishop; *specif* : the superior of a large monastery or group of monasteries

Ar·chi·me·des' screw \ˌär-kə-ˈmē-dēz-\ *n* [*Archimedes*] (1728) : a device made of a tube bent spirally around an axis or of a broad-threaded screw encased by a cylinder and used to raise water

ar·chi·pe·lag·ic \ˌär-kə-pə-ˈla-jik, ˌär-chə-\ *adj* (1841) : of, relating to, or located in an archipelago

ar·chi·pel·a·go \ˌär-kə-ˈpe-lə-ˌgō, ˌär-chə-\ *n, pl* **-goes** *or* **-gos** [*Archipelago* Aegean Sea, fr. It *Arcipelago,* lit., chief sea, fr. *arci-* (fr. L *archi-*) + Gk *pelagos* sea — more at PLAGAL] (1589) **1 :** an expanse of water with many scattered islands **2 :** a group of islands **3 :** something resembling an archipelago; *esp* : a group or scattering of similar things ⟨an ~ of small parks within the city⟩

ar·chi·tect \ˈär-kə-ˌtekt\ *n* [MF *architecte,* fr. L *architectus,* fr. Gk *architektōn* master builder, fr. *archi-* + *tektōn* builder, carpenter — more at TECHNICAL] (1563) **1 :** a person who designs buildings and advises in their construction **2 :** a person who designs and guides a plan or undertaking ⟨the ~ of American foreign policy⟩

ar·chi·tec·ton·ic \ˌär-kə-ˌtek-ˈtä-nik\ *adj* [L *architectonicus,* fr. Gk *architektonikos,* fr. *architektōn*] (1645) **1 :** of, relating to, or according with the principles of architecture : ARCHITECTURAL **2 :** having an organized and unified structure that suggests an architectural design — **ar·chi·tec·ton·i·cal·ly** \-ni-k(ə-)lē\ *adv*

ar·chi·tec·ton·ics \-ˈtä-niks\ *n pl but sing or pl in constr* (1660) **1** *also* **architectonic :** the science of architecture **2 a** *also* **architectonic :** the unifying structural design of something **b** *also* **architectonic :** the system of structure

ar·chi·tec·tur·al \ˌär-kə-ˈtek-chə-rəl, -ˈtek-shrəl\ *adj* (1786) **1 :** of or relating to architecture : conforming to the rules of architecture **2 :** having or conceived of as having a single unified overall design, form, or structure — **ar·chi·tec·tur·al·ly** *adv*

ar·chi·tec·ture \ˈär-kə-ˌtek-chər\ *n* (1555) **1 :** the art or science of building; *specif* : the art or practice of designing and building structures and esp. habitable ones **2 a :** formation or construction resulting from or as if from a conscious act ⟨the ~ of the garden⟩ **b :** a unifying or coherent form or structure ⟨the novel lacks ~⟩ **3 :** architectural product or work **4 :** a method or style of building **5 :** the manner in which the components of a computer or computer system are organized and integrated

ar·chi·trave \ˈär-kə-ˌtrāv\ *n* [MF, fr. OIt, fr. *archi-* + *trave* beam, fr. L *trab-, trabs* — more at THORP] (1563) **1 :** the lowest division of an entablature resting in classical architecture immediately on the capital of the column — see COLUMN illustration **2 :** the molding around a rectangular opening (as a door)

ar·chi·val \är-ˈkī-vəl\ *adj* (ca. 1828) : of, relating to, contained in, suitable for, or constituting archives — **ar·chi·val·ly** \-və-lē\ *adv*

[1]**ar·chive** \ˈär-ˌkīv\ *n* [F & L; F, fr. L *archivum,* fr. Gk *archeion* government house (in pl., official documents), fr. *archē* rule, government — more at ARCH-] (1603) **1 :** a place in which public records or historical documents are preserved; *also* : the material preserved — often used in pl. **2 :** a repository or collection esp. of information

[2]**archive** *vt* **ar·chived; ar·chiv·ing** (1855) : to file or collect in or as if in an archive ⟨~ documents⟩ ⟨*archived* tissue samples⟩

ar·chi·vist \ˈär-kə-vist, -ˌkī-\ *n* (1753) : a person in charge of archives

ar·chi·volt \ˈär-kə-ˌvōlt\ *n* [It *archivolto,* fr. ML *archivoltum*] (1723) : an ornamental molding around an arch corresponding to an architrave

arch·ly \ˈärch-lē\ *adv* (1662) **1 :** in an arch manner **2 :** EXTREMELY ⟨~ conservative⟩

ar·chon \ˈär-ˌkän, -kən\ *n* [L, fr. Gk *archōn,* fr. prp. of *archein*] (1579) **1 :** a chief magistrate in ancient Athens **2 :** a presiding officer

ar·cho·saur \ˈär-kə-ˌsȯr\ *n* [NL *Archosauria,* fr. Gk *archōn* + *sauros* lizard] (1933) : any of a subclass (Archosauria) of reptiles comprising the dinosaurs, pterosaurs, and crocodilians — **ar·cho·sau·ri·an** \ˌär-kə-ˈsȯr-ē-ən\ *adj or n*

arch·priest \(ˌ)ärch-ˈprēst\ *n* (14c) : a priest of preeminent rank

arch·ri·val \-ˈrī-vəl\ *n* (1941) : a principal rival

arch·way \ˈärch-ˌwā\ *n* (1751) : a way or passage under an arch; *also* : an arch over a passage

-archy *n comb form, pl* **-archies** [L *-archia,* fr. Gk, fr. *archein* to rule — more at ARCH-] : rule : government ⟨squire*archy*⟩

arc lamp *n* (1879) : an electric lamp that produces light by an arc made when a current passes between two incandescent electrodes surrounded by gas — called also *arc light*

arcmin *abbr* arc minute

arc minute *n* (1971) : MINUTE 1b

ar·co \ˈär-(ˌ)kō\ *adv or adj* [It, fr. *arco* bow, fr. L *arcus* — more at ARROW] (1806) : with the bow — usu. used as a direction in music for players of stringed instruments; compare PIZZICATO

arcsec *abbr* arc second

arc second *n* (1968) : [3]SECOND 1a

arc·sine \(ˌ)ärk-ˈsīn\ *n* (ca. 1889) : the inverse function of the sine ⟨if *y* is the sine of *θ*, then *θ* is the ~ of *y*⟩

arc·tan·gent \(ˌ)ärk-ˈtan-jənt\ *n* (ca. 1889) : the inverse function of the tangent ⟨if *y* is the tangent of *θ*, then *θ* is the ~ of *y*⟩

[1]**arc·tic** \ˈärk-tik, ˈär-tik\ *adj* [ME *artik,* fr. L *arcticus,* fr. Gk *arktikos,* fr. *arktos* bear, Ursa Major, north; akin to L *ursus* bear, Skt *ṛkṣa*] (14c) **1** *often cap* : of, or relating to, or suitable for use at the north pole or the region near it ⟨~ waters⟩ ⟨~ animals⟩ ⟨~ clothing⟩ **2 a :** bitter cold : FRIGID ⟨~ air⟩ **b :** cold in temper or mood ⟨an ~ smile⟩ — **arc·ti·cal·ly** \-ti-k(ə-)lē\ *adv*

[2]**arc·tic** \ˈär-tik, ˈärk-tik\ *n* (1867) : a rubber overshoe reaching to the ankle or above

arctic char *n* (ca. 1902) : a Holarctic char (*Salvelinus alpinus*) of arctic waters occurring in freshwater or anadromous populations

arctic circle *n, often cap A&C* (1622) : the parallel of latitude that is approximately 66½ degrees north of the equator and that circumscribes the northern frigid zone

arctic fox *n* (1772) : a small migratory Holarctic fox (*Alopex lagopus*) esp. of coastal arctic and alpine tundra

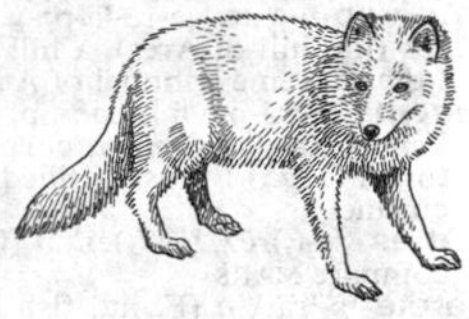
arctic fox

arctic hare *n* (1842) : a gregarious hare (*Lepus arcticus*) of the tundra of Greenland and northern Canada that turns white in winter and is a major food source for arctic predators (as wolves and snowy owls)

arctic tern *n* (1844) : a Holarctic tern (*Sterna paradisaea*) that breeds in arctic regions and migrates to southern Africa and So. America

Arc·tu·rus \ärk-ˈtu̇r-əs, -ˈtyu̇r-\ *n* [L, fr. Gk *Arktouros,* lit., bear watcher] : a giant fixed star of the first magnitude in Boötes

ar·cu·ate \ˈär-kyə-wət, -ˌwāt\ *adj* [L *arcuatus,* pp. of *arcuare* to bend like a bow, fr. *arcus* bow] (1626) : curved like a bow ⟨an ~ cloud⟩ — **ar·cu·ate·ly** *adv*

-ard *also* **-art** *n suffix* [ME, fr. AF, of Gmc origin; akin to OHG *-hart* (in personal names such as *Gērhart* Gerard), OE *heard* hard] : one that is characterized by performing some action, possessing some quality, or being associated with some thing esp. conspicuously or excessively ⟨bragg*art*⟩ ⟨dull*ard*⟩ ⟨poll*ard*⟩

ar·den·cy \ˈär-dᵊn(t)-sē\ *n* (1549) : the quality or state of being ardent

ar·dent \ˈär-dᵊnt\ *adj* [ME, fr. MF, fr. L *ardent-, ardens,* prp. of *ardēre* to burn, fr. *ardor*] (14c) **1 :** characterized by warmth of feeling typically expressed in eager zealous support or activity ⟨~ proponents of the bill⟩ **2 :** FIERY, HOT ⟨an ~ sun⟩ **3 :** SHINING, GLOWING ⟨~ eyes⟩ ***syn*** see IMPASSIONED — **ar·dent·ly** *adv*

ardent spirits *n pl* (1684) : strong distilled liquors

ar·dor \ˈär-dər\ *n* [ME *ardour,* fr. AF & L; AF, fr. L *ardor* burning, heat, ardor, fr. *aridus* dry — more at ARID] (14c) **1 a :** an often restless or transitory warmth of feeling ⟨the sudden ~*s* of youth⟩ **b :** extreme vigor or energy : INTENSITY **c :** ZEAL **d :** LOYALTY **2 :** sexual excitement ***syn*** see PASSION

ar·dour *chiefly Brit var of* ARDOR

ar·du·ous \ˈär-jə-wəs, -dyü-, -jü-əs\ *adj* [L *arduus* high, steep, difficult; akin to OIr *ard* high] (1538) **1 a :** hard to accomplish or achieve : DIFFICULT ⟨years of ~ training⟩ **b :** marked by great labor or effort : STRENUOUS ⟨a life of ~ toil —A. C. Cole⟩ **2 :** hard to climb : STEEP ⟨an ~ path⟩ ***syn*** see HARD — **ar·du·ous·ly** *adv* — **ar·du·ous·ness** *n*

[1]**are** [ME, fr. OE *earun;* akin to ON *eru, erum* are, OE *is* is] *pres 2d sing or pres pl of* BE

[2]**are** \ˈer, ˈär\ *n* [F, fr. L *area*] (ca. 1819) — see METRIC SYSTEM table

ar·ea \ˈer-ē-ə, ˈā-rē-ə\ *n* [L, open space, threshing floor; perh. akin to L *arēre* to be dry — more at ARID] (1538) **1 :** a level piece of ground **2 :** the surface included within a set of lines; *specif* : the number of unit squares equal in measure to the surface — see METRIC SYSTEM table, WEIGHT table **3 :** the scope of a concept, operation, or activity : FIELD ⟨the whole ~ of foreign policy⟩ **4 :** AREAWAY **5 :** a particular extent of space or surface or one serving a special function: as **a :** a part of the surface of the body **b :** a geographic region **6 :** a part of the cerebral cortex having a particular function — **ar·e·al** \-ē-əl\ *adj* — **ar·e·al·ly** \-ə-lē\ *adv*

area code *n* (1961) : a usu. 3-digit number that identifies each telephone service area in a country (as the U.S. or Canada)

ar·ea·way \ˈer-ē-ə-ˌwā, ˈā-rē-\ *n* (1867) : a sunken space affording access, air, and light to a basement

are·ca \ə-ˈrē-kə, ˈa-ri-kə\ *n* [NL, fr. Pg, fr. Malayalam *aṭaykka*] (1510) : any of several tropical Asian palms (*Areca* or related genera); *esp* : BETEL PALM

arec·o·line \ə-ˈre-kə-ˌlēn\ *n* [ISV *areca* + [1]*-ol* + [2]*-ine*] (1894) : a toxic parasympathomimetic alkaloid $C_8H_{13}NO_2$ that is used as a veterinary anthelmintic and occurs naturally in betel nuts

are·na \ə-ˈrē-nə\ *n* [L *harena, arena* sand, sandy place] (1600) **1 :** an area in a Roman amphitheater for gladiatorial combats **2 a :** an enclosed area used for public entertainment **b :** a building containing an arena **3 a :** a sphere of interest, activity, or competition ⟨the political ~⟩ **b :** a place or situation for controversy ⟨in the public ~⟩

ar·e·na·ceous \ˌa-rə-ˈnā-shəs\ *adj* [L *arenaceus,* fr. *arena*] (1646) **1 :** resembling, made of, or containing sand or sandy particles **2 :** growing in sandy places

arena football *n* (1986) : a game resembling American football that is played on a shorter indoor field between two teams of eight players each

arena theater *n* (1943) : THEATER-IN-THE-ROUND

ar·e·na·vi·rus \ˌa-rə-nə-ˈvī-rəs, ˌer-ə-\ *n* [NL, ultim. fr. L *arena* sand + NL *virus;* fr. the fine granules seen in cross sections of the virion]

\ə\ **abut** \ᵊ\ **kitten,** F table \ər\ **further** \a\ **ash** \ā\ **ace** \ä\ **mop, mar**
\au̇\ **out** \ch\ **chin** \e\ **bet** \ē\ **easy** \g\ **go** \i\ **hit** \ī\ **ice** \j\ **job**
\ŋ\ **sing** \ō\ **go** \ȯ\ **law** \ȯi\ **boy** \th\ **thin** \t͟h\ **the** \ü\ **loot** \u̇\ **foot**
\y\ **yet** \zh\ **vision, beige** \k̲, ^{n}, œ, ue, ^{y}\ *see* Guide to Pronunciation

(1971) : any of a family (*Arenaviridae*) of single-stranded RNA viruses having a dense outer lipid envelope covered by numerous club-shaped projections and including the causative agents of lymphocytic choriomeningitis and Lassa fever

ar·ene \ˈa-ˌrēn, ˈer-ˌēn\ *n* [*aromatic* + *-ene*] (1956) : an aromatic hydrocarbon (as benzene or naphthalene)

ar·e·nic·o·lous \ˌar-ə-ˈni-kə-ləs\ *adj* [L *arena* + E *-i-* + *-colous*] (ca. 1859) : living, burrowing, or growing in sand

aren't \ˈärnt, ˈär-ənt\ (1675) **1** : are not ⟨they ~ here yet⟩ **2** : am not — used in questions ⟨I'm right, ~ I?⟩

are·o·la \ə-ˈrē-ə-lə; ˌer-ē-ˈō-, ˌa-rē-\ *n, pl* **-lae** \-ˌlē\ *or* **-las** [NL, fr. L, small open space, dim. of *area*] (1664) : a small area between things or about something; *esp* : a colored ring (as about the nipple, a vesicle, or a pustule) — **are·o·lar** \-lər\ *adj* — **are·o·late** \-lət\ *adj*

ar·e·ole \ˈer-ē-ˌōl, ˈa-rē-\ *n* (ca. 1934) : a round or elongated often raised or depressed area on a cactus which is equivalent to a bud and from which spines, flowers, stems, or roots grow

Ar·e·op·a·gite \ˌa-rē-ˈä-pə-ˌgīt, -ˌjīt\ *n* (14c) : a member of the Areopagus — **Ar·e·op·a·git·ic** \-ˌä-pə-ˈji-tik\ *adj*

Ar·e·op·a·gus \ˌa-rē-ˈä-pə-gəs\ *n* [L, fr. Gk *Areios pagos,* fr. *Areios pagos* (lit., hill of Ares), a hill in Athens where the tribunal met] (1586) : the supreme tribunal of Athens

are·pa \ə-ˈrā-pə\ *n* [AmerSp, prob. fr. Cumaná (Cariban language of the Venezuela coast) *erepa* corn, cornmeal cake, or fr. a cognate Cariban form] (1925) : a usu. grilled cornmeal cake served in Latin-American cuisine

Ar·es \ˈa-(ˌ)rēz, ˈer-(ˌ)ēz\ *n* [Gk *Arēs*] (1681) : the Greek god of war — compare MARS

arête \ə-ˈrāt\ *n* [F, lit., fish bone, fr. LL *arista,* fr. L, beard of grain] (1838) : a sharp-crested ridge in rugged mountains

Ar·e·thu·sa \ˌa-rə-ˈthü-zə, -ˈthyü-\ *n* [L, fr. Gk *Arethousa*] (1513) : a wood nymph who is changed into a spring while fleeing the advances of the river-god Alpheus

arg *abbr* **1** argent **2** argument

Arg *abbr* Argentina

ar·ga·li \ˈär-gə-lē\ *n* [Mongolian] (ca. 1774) : a large wild sheep (*Ovis ammon*) of central Asia with the ram having massive horns

Ar·gand diagram \ˌär-ˈgän-, -ˈgan-\ *n* [Jean Robert *Argand* †1825 Swiss mathematician] (1908) : a system of rectangular coordinates in which the complex number $x + iy$ is represented by the point whose coordinates are x and y

ar·gent \ˈär-jənt\ *n* [ME, fr. AF & L; AF, fr. L *argentum;* akin to Gk *argyros* silver, *argos* white, Skt *rajata* whitish, silvery] (15c) **1** *archaic* : the metal silver; *also* : WHITENESS **2** : the heraldic color silver or white — **argent** *adj*

ar·gen·tif·er·ous \ˌär-jən-ˈti-f(ə-)rəs\ *adj* (1801) : containing silver

[1]**ar·gen·tine** \ˈär-jən-ˌtīn, -ˌtēn\ *adj* (15c) : SILVER, SILVERY

[2]**argentine** *n* (1577) : SILVER; *also* : any of various similar materials

ar·gen·tite \ˈär-jən-ˌtīt\ *n* (ca. 1868) : a dark gray or black mineral of metallic luster that consists of native sulfide of silver and is a valuable silver ore

ar·gil \ˈär-jəl\ *n* [ME, fr. L *argilla,* fr. Gk *argillos;* akin to Gk *argos* white] (14c) : CLAY; *esp* : POTTER'S CLAY

ar·gil·la·ceous \ˌär-jə-ˈlā-shəs\ *adj* (ca. 1731) : of, relating to, or containing clay or clay minerals : CLAYEY

ar·gil·lite \ˈär-jə-ˌlīt\ *n* (1795) : a compact argillaceous rock cemented by silica and having no slaty cleavage

ar·gi·nase \ˈär-jə-ˌnās, -ˌnāz\ *n* [ISV] (1904) : a crystalline enzyme that converts naturally occurring arginine into ornithine and urea

ar·gi·nine \ˈär-jə-ˌnēn\ *n* [G *Arginin*] (1886) : a crystalline basic amino acid $C_6H_{14}N_4O_2$ derived from guanidine

Ar·give \ˈär-ˌjīv, -ˌgīv\ *adj* [L *Argivus,* fr. Gk *Argeios,* lit., of Argos, fr. *Argos* city-state of ancient Greece] (1598) : of or relating to the Greeks or Greece and esp. the Achaean city of Argos or the surrounding territory of Argolis — **Argive** *n*

ar·gle–bar·gle \ˌär-gəl-ˈbär-gəl\ *n* [redupl. of Sc & E *argle,* alter. of *argue*] (1872) *chiefly Brit* : ARGY-BARGY

Ar·go \ˈär-(ˌ)gō\ *n* [L (gen. *Argus*), fr. Gk *Argō*] (1565) : a large constellation in the southern hemisphere lying principally between Canis Major and the Southern Cross

ar·gol \ˈär-ˌgȯl\ *n* [ME *argoile,* fr. AF *argoil*] (14c) : crude tartar deposited in wine casks during aging

ar·gon \ˈär-ˌgän\ *n* [Gk, neut. of *argos* idle, lazy, fr. *a-* + *ergon* work; fr. its relative inertness — more at WORK] (1894) : a colorless odorless inert gaseous element found in the air and in volcanic gases and used esp. in welding, lasers, and electric bulbs — see ELEMENT table

ar·go·naut \ˈär-gə-ˌnȯt, -ˌnät\ *n* [L *Argonautes,* fr. Gk *Argonautēs,* fr. *Argō,* ship in which the Argonauts sailed + *nautēs* sailor — more at NAUTICAL] (14c) **1 a** *cap* : any of a band of heroes sailing with Jason in quest of the Golden Fleece **b** : an adventurer engaged in a quest **2** : PAPER NAUTILUS

ar·go·sy \ˈär-gə-sē\ *n, pl* **-sies** [modif. of It *ragusea* Ragusan vessel, fr. *Ragusa,* Dalmatia (now Dubrovnik, Croatia)] (1581) **1** : a large ship; *esp* : a large merchant ship ⟨three of your *argosies* are . . . come to harbor —Shak.⟩ **2** : a fleet of ships **3** : a rich supply ⟨an ~ of railway folklore —F. P. Donovan⟩

ar·got \ˈär-gət, -(ˌ)gō\ *n* [F] (1842) : an often more or less secret vocabulary and idiom peculiar to a particular group ⟨shoved into a taxi by a porter whose ~ I couldn't understand —Allen Tate⟩

ar·gu·able \ˈär-gyü-ə-bəl\ *adj* (ca. 1611) **1** : open to argument, dispute, or question **2** : that can be plausibly or convincingly argued

ar·gu·ably \ˈär-gyü-(ə-)blē\ *adv* (1890) : as may be argued or shown by argument ⟨an ~ effective strategy⟩ ⟨~ the greatest writer of his era⟩

ar·gue \ˈär-(ˌ)gyü\ *vb* **ar·gued; ar·gu·ing** [ME, fr. AF *arguer* to reprove, argue & L *arguere* to demonstrate, prove; AF *arguer,* fr. L *argutare* to prate, freq. of *arguere;* akin to Hitt *arkuwai-* to plead, respond] *vi* (14c) **1** : to give reasons for or against something : REASON ⟨~ for a new policy⟩ **2** : to contend or disagree in words : DISPUTE ⟨~ about money⟩ ~ *vt* **1** : to give evidence of : INDICATE ⟨the facts ~ his innocence⟩ **2** : to consider the pros and cons of : DISCUSS ⟨~ an issue⟩ **3** : to prove or try to prove by giving reasons : MAINTAIN ⟨asking for a chance to ~ his case⟩ **4** : to persuade by giving reasons : INDUCE ⟨couldn't ~ her out of going⟩ ***syn*** see DISCUSS — **ar·gu·er** \-gyə-wər, -gyü-ər\ *n*

ar·gu·fy \ˈär-gyə-ˌfī\ *vb* **-fied; -fy·ing** *vt* (1698) : DISPUTE, DEBATE ~ *vi* : WRANGLE — **ar·gu·fi·er** \-ˌfī(-ə)r\ *n*

ar·gu·ment \ˈär-gyə-mənt\ *n* [ME, fr. AF, fr. L *argumentum,* fr. *arguere*] (14c) **1** *obs* : an outward sign : INDICATION **2 a** : a reason given in proof or rebuttal **b** : discourse intended to persuade **3 a** : the act or process of arguing : ARGUMENTATION **b** : a coherent series of statements leading from a premise to a conclusion **c** : QUARREL, DISAGREEMENT **4** : an abstract or summary esp. of a literary work ⟨an ~ preceded the poem⟩ **5** : the subject matter esp. of a literary work **6 a** : one of the independent variables upon whose value that of a function depends **b** : a substantive (as the direct object of a transitive verb) that is required by a predicate in grammar **c** : AMPLITUDE 4

ar·gu·men·ta·tion \ˌär-gyə-mən-ˈtā-shən, -ˌmen-\ *n* (15c) **1** : the act or process of forming reasons and of drawing conclusions and applying them to a case in discussion **2** : DEBATE, DISCUSSION

ar·gu·men·ta·tive \ˌär-gyə-ˈmen-tə-tiv\ *also* **ar·gu·men·tive** \-ˈmen-tiv\ *adj* (15c) **1** : characterized by argument : CONTROVERSIAL **2** : given to argument : DISPUTATIOUS — **ar·gu·men·ta·tive·ly** *adv*

ar·gu·men·tum \ˌär-gyə-ˈmen-təm\ *n, pl* **-men·ta** \-ˈmen-tə\ [L] (1550) : ARGUMENT 3b

Ar·gus \ˈär-gəs\ *n* [L, fr. Gk *Argos*] (14c) **1** : a hundred-eyed monster of Greek mythology **2** : a watchful guardian

Ar·gus–eyed \ˈär-gəs-ˌīd\ *adj* (1603) : vigilantly observant

ar·gy–bar·gy \ˌär-jē-ˈbär-jē, ˌär-gē-ˈbär-gē\ *n* [redupl. of Sc & E dial. *argy,* alter. of *argue*] (1887) *chiefly Brit* : a lively discussion : ARGUMENT, DISPUTE

ar·gyle *also* **ar·gyll** \ˈär-ˌgī(-ə)l, är-ˈ\ *n, often cap* [*Argyle, Argyll,* branch of the Scottish clan of Campbell, fr. whose tartan the design was adapted] (1899) : a geometric knitting pattern of varicolored diamonds in solid and outline shapes on a single background color; *also* : a sock knit in this pattern

ar·hat \ˈär-(ˌ)hət\ *n* [Skt, fr. prp. of *arhati* he deserves; akin to Gk *alphein* to gain] (1870) : a Buddhist who has reached the stage of enlightenment — **ar·hat·ship** \-ˌship\ *n*

aria \ˈär-ē-ə\ *n* [It, lit., atmospheric air, modif. of L *aer*] (1723) **1** : AIR, MELODY, TUNE; *specif* : an accompanied elaborate melody sung (as in an opera) by a single voice **2** : a striking solo performance (as in a movie)

Ar·i·ad·ne \ˌa-rē-ˈad-nē\ *n* [L, fr. Gk *Ariadnē*] (14c) : a daughter of Minos who helps Theseus escape from the labyrinth

[1]**Ar·i·an** \ˈa-rē-ən, ˈer-ē-\ *adj* (14c) : of or relating to Arius or his doctrines esp. that the Son is not of the same substance as the Father but was created as an agent for creating the world — **Ar·i·an·ism** \-ə-ˌni-zəm\ *n*

[2]**Arian** *n* (14c) : a supporter of Arian doctrines

[3]**Ar·i·an** \ˈer-ē-ən, ˈa-rē-\ *n* (1917) : ARIES 1b

-ar·i·an *n suffix* [L *-arius* -ary] **1** : believer ⟨necessit*arian*⟩ : advocate ⟨latitudin*arian*⟩ **2** : producer ⟨disciplin*arian*⟩

ari·a·ry \ˌä-rē-ˈä-rē\ *n, pl* **ariary** [Malagasy, five-franc note] (1979) — see MONEY table

ari·bo·fla·vin·osis \ˌā-ˌrī-bə-ˌflā-və-ˈnō-səs\ *n* [NL] (1939) : a deficiency disease due to inadequate intake of riboflavin and characterized by sores on the mouth

ar·id \ˈa-rəd, ˈer-əd\ *adj* [F or L; F *aride,* fr. L *aridus,* fr. *arēre* to be dry; akin to Skt *āsa* ash, OE *asce*] (1652) **1** : excessively dry; *specif* : having insufficient rainfall to support agriculture **2** : lacking in interest and life : JEJUNE — **arid·i·ty** \ə-ˈri-də-tē, a-\ *n* — **ar·id·ness** \ˈa-rəd-nəs, ˈer-əd-\ *n*

Ar·i·el \ˈa-rē-əl, ˈer-ē-\ *n* (ca. 1612) : a prankish spirit in Shakespeare's *The Tempest*

Ar·i·es \ˈer-ˌēz, -ē-ˌēz, ˈa-rēz, -rē-ˌēz\ *n* [L (gen. *Arietis*), lit., ram; perh. akin to Gk *eriphos* kid, OIr *heirp* she-goat] (bef. 12c) **1 a** : the first sign of the zodiac in astrology — see ZODIAC table **b** : one born under the sign of Aries **2** : a constellation between Pisces and Taurus pictured as a ram

ari·et·ta \ˌär-ē-ˈe-tə, ˌa-rē-\ *n* [It, dim. of *aria*] (ca. 1724) : a short aria

aright \ə-ˈrīt\ *adv* [ME, fr. OE *ariht,* fr. ˈa- + *riht* right] (bef. 12c) : RIGHT, CORRECTLY ⟨if I remember ~⟩

Arik·a·ra \ə-ˈri-kə-rə\ *n, pl* **Arikara** [prob. fr. a Pawnee name for an Arikara band] (1811) **1** : a member of an American Indian people of the Missouri River valley in No. Dakota **2** : the language of the Arikara

ar·il \ˈa-rəl, ˈer-əl\ *n* [prob. fr. NL *arillus,* fr. ML, raisin, grape seed] (1794) : an exterior covering or appendage of some seeds (as of the yew) that develops after fertilization as an outgrowth from the ovule stalk — **ar·il·late** \ˈa-rə-ˌlāt, ˈer-ə-\ *adj*

ari·o·so \ˌär-ē-ˈō-(ˌ)sō, -(ˌ)zō\ *n, pl* **-sos** *also* **-si** \-(ˌ)sē, -(ˌ)zē\ [It, fr. *aria*] (ca. 1724) : a musical passage or composition having a mixture of free recitative and metrical song

arise \ə-ˈrīz\ *vi* **arose** \-ˈrōz\; **aris·en** \-ˈri-zᵊn\; **aris·ing** \-ˈrī-ziŋ\ [ME, fr. OE *ārīsan,* fr. *ā-,* perfective prefix + *rīsan* to rise — more at ABIDE] (bef. 12c) **1** : to get up : RISE **2 a** : to originate from a source **b** : to come into being or to attention **3** : ASCEND ***syn*** see SPRING

aris·ta \ə-ˈris-tə\ *n, pl* **-tae** \-(ˌ)tē, -ˌtī\ *or* **-tas** [NL, fr. L, beard of grain] (1691) : a bristlelike structure or appendage — **aris·tate** \-ˌtāt\ *adj*

aris·to \ə-ˈris-(ˌ)tō\ *n, pl* **-tos** [by shortening] (1864) : ARISTOCRAT

ar·is·toc·ra·cy \ˌa-rə-ˈstä-krə-sē, ˌer-ə-\ *n, pl* **-cies** [MF & LL; MF *aristocratie,* fr. LL *aristocratia,* fr. Gk *aristokratia,* fr. *aristos* best + *-kratia* -cracy] (1561) **1** : government by the best individuals or by a small privileged class **2 a** : a government in which power is vested in a minority consisting of those believed to be best qualified **b** : a state with such a government **3** : a governing body or upper class usu. made up of a hereditary nobility **4** : the aggregate of those believed to be superior

aris·to·crat \ə-ˈris-tə-ˌkrat, a-; ˈa-rə-stə-\ *n* (1789) **1** : a member of an aristocracy; *esp* : NOBLE **2 a** : one who has the bearing and viewpoint typical of the aristocracy **b** : one who favors aristocracy **3** : one believed to be superior of its kind ⟨the ~ of Southern resorts —*Southern Living*⟩

aris·to·crat·ic \ə-ˌris-tə-ˈkra-tik, (ˌ)a-ˌris-tə-, ˌa-rə-stə-\ *adj* [MF *aristocratique,* fr. ML *aristocraticus,* fr. Gk *aristokratikos,* fr. *aristokratia*] (1602) **1** : belonging to, having the qualities of, or favoring aristocracy **2 a** : socially exclusive ⟨an ~ neighborhood⟩ **b** : SNOBBISH — **aris·to·crat·i·cal·ly** \-ti-k(ə-)lē\ *adv*

Ar·is·to·te·lian *also* **Ar·is·to·te·lean** \ˌa-rə-stə-ˈtēl-yən\ *adj* [L *Aristoteles* Aristotle, fr. Gk *Aristotelēs*] (1581) **:** of or relating to the Greek philosopher Aristotle or his philosophy — **Aristotelian** *n* — **Ar·is·to·te·lian·ism** \-yə-ˌni-zəm\ *n*
arith *abbr* arithmetic; arithmetical
arith·me·tic \ə-ˈrith-mə-ˌtik\ *n* [ME *arsmetrik,* fr. AF *arismatike,* fr. L *arithmetica,* fr. Gk *arithmētikē,* fr. fem. of *arithmētikos* arithmetical, fr. *arithmein* to count, fr. *arithmos* number; akin to OE *rīm* number, and perh. to Gk *arariskein* to fit] (15c) **1 a :** a branch of mathematics that deals usu. with the nonnegative real numbers including sometimes the transfinite cardinals and with the application of the operations of addition, subtraction, multiplication, and division to them **b :** a treatise on arithmetic **2 :** COMPUTATION, CALCULATION — **ar·ith·met·ic** \ˌer-ith-ˈme-tik, ˌa-rith\ *or* **ar·ith·met·i·cal** \-ti-kəl\ *adj* — **ar·ith·met·i·cal·ly** \-ti-k(ə-)lē\ *adv* — **arith·me·ti·cian** \ə-ˌrith-mə-ˈti-shən\ *n*
arithmetic mean *n* (1743) **:** a value that is computed by dividing the sum of a set of terms by the number of terms
arithmetic progression *n* (1704) **:** a progression (as 3, 5, 7, 9) in which the difference between any term and its predecessor is constant
arithmetic scale *n* (1897) **:** a scale on which the value of a point corresponds to the number of graduations the point is from the scale's zero — compare LOGARITHMIC SCALE
-arium *n suffix, pl* **-ariums** *or* **-aria** [L, fr. neut. of *-arius* -ary] **:** thing or place relating to or connected with ⟨planet*arium*⟩
Ariz *abbr* Arizona
ark \ˈärk\ *n* [ME, fr. OE *arc,* fr. L *arca* chest; akin to L *arcēre* to hold off, defend, Gk *arkein,* Hitt *ḫark-* to have, hold] (bef. 12c) **1 a :** a boat or ship held to resemble that in which Noah and his family were preserved from the Flood **b :** something that affords protection and safety **2 a :** the sacred chest representing to the Hebrews the presence of God among them **b :** a repository traditionally in or against the wall of a synagogue for the scrolls of the Torah
Ark *abbr* Arkansas
ar·kose \ˈär-ˌkōs, -ˌkōz\ *n* [F] (1829) **:** a sandstone characterized by feldspar fragments that is derived from granite or gneiss which has disintegrated rapidly — **ar·ko·sic** \(ˌ)är-ˈkō-sik, -zik\ *adj*
1**arm** \ˈärm\ *n* [ME, fr. OE *earm;* akin to L *armus* shoulder, Skt *īrma* arm] (bef. 12c) **1 :** a human upper limb; *esp* **:** the part between the shoulder and the wrist **2 :** something like or corresponding to an arm: as **a :** the forelimb of a vertebrate **b :** a limb of an invertebrate animal **c :** a branch or lateral shoot of a plant **d :** a slender part of a structure, machine, or an instrument projecting from a main part, axis, or fulcrum **e :** the end of a ship's yard; *also* **:** the part of an anchor from the crown to the fluke — see ANCHOR illustration **f :** any of the usu. two parts of a chromosome lateral to the centromere **3 :** an inlet of water (as from the sea) **4 :** a narrow extension of a larger area, mass, or group **5 :** POWER, MIGHT ⟨the long ∼ of the law⟩ **6 :** a support (as on a chair) for the elbow and forearm **7 :** SLEEVE **8 :** the ability to throw or pitch a ball well; *also* **:** a player having such ability **9 :** a functional division of a group, organization, institution, or activity ⟨the logistical ∼ of the air force⟩ — **arm·less** \ˈärm-ləs\ *adj* — **arm·like** \-ˌlīk\ *adj* — **arm in arm :** with arms linked together
2**arm** *vb* [ME *armen,* fr. AF *armer,* fr. L *armare,* fr. *arma* weapons, tools; akin to L *ars* skill, Gk *harmos* joint, *arariskein* to fit] *vt* (12c) **1 :** to furnish or equip with weapons **2 :** to furnish with something that strengthens or protects ⟨∼*ing* citizens with the right to vote⟩ **3 :** to equip or ready for action or operation ⟨∼ a bomb⟩ ∼ *vi* **:** to prepare oneself for struggle or resistance ⟨∼ for combat⟩
3**arm** *n, often attrib* [ME *armes* (pl.) weapons, fr. AF, fr. L *arma*] (13c) **1 a :** a means (as a weapon) of offense or defense; *esp* **:** FIREARM **b :** a combat branch (as of an army) **c :** an organized branch of national defense (as the navy) **2** *pl* **a :** the hereditary heraldic devices of a family **b :** heraldic devices adopted by a government **3** *pl* **a :** active hostilities **:** WARFARE ⟨a call to ∼*s*⟩ **b :** military service — **up in arms :** aroused and ready to undertake a fight or conflict
Arm *abbr* Armenian
ARM *abbr* adjustable rate mortgage
ar·ma·da \är-ˈmä-də, -ˈmā- *also* -ˈma-\ *n* [Sp, fr. ML *armata* army, fleet, fr. L, fem. of *armatus,* pp. of *armare* to arm, fr. *arma*] (1533) **1 :** a fleet of warships **2 :** a large force or group usu. of moving things
ar·ma·dil·lo \ˌär-mə-ˈdi-(ˌ)lō\ *n, pl* **-los** [Sp, fr. dim. of *armado* armed one, fr. L *armatus*] (1577) **:** any of a family (Dasypodidae) of burrowing edentate mammals found from the southern U.S. to Argentina and having the body and head encased in an armor of small bony plates

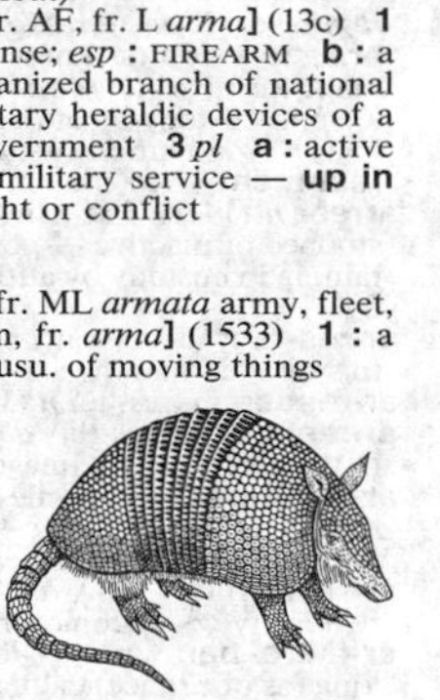
armadillo

Ar·ma·ged·don \ˌär-mə-ˈge-dᵊn\ *n* [Gk *Armageddōn, Harmagedōn,* scene of the battle foretold in Rev 16:14–16] (14c) **1 a :** the site or time of a final and conclusive battle between the forces of good and evil **b :** the battle taking place at Armageddon **2 :** a usu. vast decisive conflict or confrontation
Ar·ma·gnac \ˈär-mən-ˌyak\ *n* [F, fr. *Armagnac,* region in southwest France] (1831) **:** a brandy produced in the Gers department of France
ar·ma·ment \ˈär-mə-mənt *also* ˈärm-mənt\ *n* [F *armement,* fr. L *armamenta* (pl.) utensils, military or naval equipment, fr. *armare*] (1632) **1 :** a military or naval force **2 a :** the aggregate of a nation's military strength **b :** WEAPONS, ARMS **3 :** the process of preparing for war
ar·ma·men·tar·i·um \ˌär-mə-ˌmen-ˈter-ē-əm, -mən-\ *n, pl* **-tar·ia** \-ē-ə\ [L, armory, fr. *armamenta*] (ca. 1860) **:** a collection of resources available or utilized for an undertaking or field of activity; *esp* **:** the equipment, methods, and pharmaceuticals used in medicine
arm and a leg *n* (1956) **:** an exorbitant price
ar·ma·ture \ˈär-mə-ˌchu̇r, -chər, -ˌtyu̇r, -ˌtu̇r\ *n* [ME, armor, fr. L *armatura* armor, equipment, fr. *armatus*] (15c) **1 :** an organ or structure (as teeth or thorns) for offense or defense **2 a :** a piece of soft iron or steel that connects the poles of a magnet or of adjacent magnets **b :** a usu. rotating part of an electric machine (as a generator or motor) which consists essentially of coils of wire around a metal core and in which electric current is induced or in which the input current interacts with a magnetic field to produce torque **c :** the movable part of an electromagnetic device (as a loudspeaker) **d :** a framework used by a sculptor to support a figure being modeled in a plastic material **e :** FRAMEWORK 1a ⟨events that serve as the ∼ of the book⟩
arm·band \ˈärm-ˌband\ *n* (1797) **:** a band worn around the arm; *esp* **:** a band worn around the arm for identification or in mourning
arm candy *n* (1992) **:** a young attractive person who accompanies a usu. older person at social events
1**arm·chair** \ˈärm-ˌcher\ *n* (1633) **:** a chair with armrests
2**armchair** *adj* (1858) **1 :** remote from direct dealing with problems **:** theoretical rather than practical ⟨∼ strategists⟩ **2 :** sharing vicariously in another's experiences ⟨an ∼ traveler⟩
1**armed** \ˈärmd\ *adj* (13c) **1 a :** furnished with weapons ⟨an ∼ guard⟩; *also* **:** using or involving a weapon **b :** furnished with something that provides security, strength, or efficacy ⟨∼ with knowledge⟩ **2 :** marked by the maintenance of armed forces in readiness
2**armed** *adj* (1606) **:** having an arm or arms esp. of a specified kind or number — usu. used in combination ⟨long-*armed*⟩ ⟨two-*armed*⟩
armed forces *n pl* (1625) **:** the combined military, naval, and air forces of a nation — called also *armed services*
Ar·me·nian \är-ˈmē-nē-ən, -nyən\ *n* (ca. 1537) **1 :** a member of a people dwelling chiefly in Armenia and neighboring areas (as Turkey or Azerbaijan) **2 :** the Indo-European language of the Armenians — see INDO-EUROPEAN LANGUAGES table **3 :** a member of the Armenian church established by St. Gregory the Illuminator that adheres to the decisions of the first three ecumenical councils — **Armenian** *adj*
arm·ful \ˈärm-ˌfu̇l\ *n, pl* **arm·fuls** \-ˌfu̇lz\ *also* **arms·ful** \ˈärmz-ˌfu̇l\ (1579) **:** as much as the arm or arms can hold
arm·hole \ˈärm-ˌhōl\ *n* (ca. 1775) **:** an opening for the arm in a garment
ar·mi·ger \ˈär-mi-jər\ *n* [ML, fr. L, armor-bearer, fr. *armiger* bearing arms, fr. *arma* arms + *gerere* to carry] (1577) **1 :** SQUIRE **2 :** one entitled to bear heraldic arms — **ar·mig·er·al** \är-ˈmi-jə-rəl\ *adj*
ar·mig·er·ous \är-ˈmi-jər-əs\ *adj* (ca. 1731) **:** bearing heraldic arms
ar·mil·la·ry sphere \ˈär-mə-ˌler-ē-, är-ˈmi-lə-rē-\ *n* [F *sphère armillaire,* fr. ML *armilla,* fr. L, bracelet, iron ring, fr. *armus* shoulder — more at ARM] (1664) **:** an old astronomical instrument composed of rings showing the positions of important circles of the celestial sphere
Ar·min·i·an \är-ˈmi-nē-ən\ *adj* (1617) **:** of or relating to Arminius or his doctrines opposing the absolute predestination of strict Calvinism and maintaining the possibility of salvation for all — **Arminian** *n* — **Ar·min·i·an·ism** \-nē-ə-ˌni-zəm\ *n*
ar·mi·stice \ˈär-mə-stəs\ *n* [F or NL; F, fr. NL *armistitium,* fr. L *arma* + *-stitium* (as in *solstitium* solstice)] (1706) **:** temporary suspension of hostilities by agreement between the opponents **:** TRUCE
Armistice Day *n* [fr. the armistice terminating World War I on November 11, 1918] (1918) **:** VETERANS DAY — used before the official adoption of *Veterans Day* in 1954
arm·let \ˈärm-lət\ *n* (1535) **1 :** a band (as of cloth or metal) worn around the upper arm **2 :** a small arm (as of the sea)
arm·load \ˈärm-ˌlōd\ *n* (1823) **:** ARMFUL
arm·lock \-ˌläk\ *n* (1853) **:** HAMMERLOCK
ar·moire \ärm-ˈwär, *Southern also* ˈär-mər\ *n* [MF, fr. OF *armaire,* fr. L *armarium,* fr. *arma*] (1571) **:** a usu. tall cupboard or wardrobe
ar·mor \ˈär-mər\ *n* [ME *armure,* fr. AF, fr. L *armatura* — more at ARMATURE] (13c) **1 :** defensive covering for the body; *esp* **:** covering (as of metal) used in combat **2 :** a quality or circumstance that affords protection ⟨the ∼ of prosperity⟩ **3 :** a protective outer layer (as of a ship, a plant or animal, or a cable) **4 :** armored forces and vehicles (as tanks) — **armor** *vt* — **ar·mor·less** \-mər-ləs\ *adj*

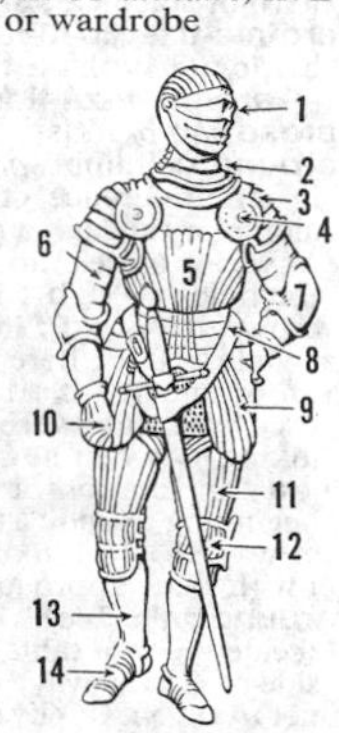

armor 1: *1* helmet, *2* gorget, *3* shoulder piece, *4* pallette, *5* breastplate, *6* brassard, *7* elbow piece, *8* skirt of tasses, *9* tuille, *10* gauntlet, *11* cuisse, *12* knee piece, *13* jambeau, *14* solleret

ar·mored \ˈär-mərd\ *adj* (1594) **1 a :** equipped or protected with armor **b :** equipped with armored fighting vehicles ⟨an ∼ division⟩ **2 :** marked by the use of armor ⟨∼ combat⟩
armored scale *n* (1888) **:** any of a family (Diaspididae) of scale insects having a firm covering of wax best developed in the female
ar·mor·er \ˈär-mər-ər\ *n* (14c) **1 :** one that makes armor or arms **2 :** one that repairs, assembles, and tests firearms
ar·mo·ri·al \är-ˈmȯr-ē-əl\ *adj* [*armory* (heraldry)] (1576) **:** of, relating to, or bearing heraldic arms — **ar·mo·ri·al·ly** \-ē-ə-lē\ *adv*
Ar·mor·i·can \är-ˈmȯr-i-kən, -ˈmär-\ *or* **Ar·mor·ic** \-ik\ *n* (1606) **:** a native or inhabitant of Armorica; *esp* **:** BRETON — **Armorican** *or* **Armoric** *adj*
ar·mory \ˈärm-rē, ˈär-mə-\ *n, pl* **ar·mor·ies** (14c) **1 a :** a supply of arms for defense or attack **b :** a collection of available resources **2 :** a place where arms and military equipment are stored; *esp* **:** one used for training reserve military personnel **3 :** a place where arms are manufactured
ar·mour, ar·moury *chiefly Brit var of* ARMOR, ARMORY
arm·pit \ˈärm-ˌpit\ *n* (14c) **1 :** the hollow beneath the junction of the arm and shoulder **2 :** the least desirable place **:** PIT ⟨77th Street Station . . . was the ∼ of detective duty —Joseph Wambaugh⟩
arm·rest \-ˌrest\ *n* (1849) **:** a support for the arm
arm's length *n* (1707) **1 :** a distance discouraging personal contact or familiarity ⟨kept former friends at *arm's length* now⟩ **2 :** the condition or fact that the parties to a transaction are independent and on an equal footing — **arm's–length** *adj*
arms race *n* (1924) **:** a race between hostile nations to accumulate or develop weapons; *broadly* **:** an ever escalating race or competition
arm–twist·ing \-ˌtwis-tiŋ\ *n* (1948) **:** the use of direct personal pressure in order to achieve a desired end ⟨for all the ∼, the . . . vote on the

measure was unexpectedly tight —*Newsweek*〉 — **arm–twist** \-ˌtwist\ *vb*

arm wrestling *n* (1973) **:** a form of wrestling in which two opponents sit face to face gripping usu. their right hands, set corresponding elbows firmly on a surface (as a tabletop), and attempt to force each other's arm down — called also *Indian wrestling*

ar·my \ˈär-mē\ *n, pl* **armies** [ME *armee,* fr. AF, fr. ML *armata* — more at ARMADA] (14c) **1 a :** a large organized body of armed personnel trained for war esp. on land **b :** a unit capable of independent action and consisting usu. of a headquarters, two or more corps, and auxiliary troops **c** *often cap* **:** the complete military organization of a nation for land warfare **2 :** a great multitude 〈an ~ of birds〉 **3 :** a body of persons organized to advance a cause

army ant *n* (1874) **:** any of a subfamily (Dorylinae) of aggressive nomadic tropical ants that prey on insects and spiders

ar·my·worm \ˈär-mē-ˌwərm\ *n* (1816) **:** any of numerous moths whose larvae travel in multitudes from field to field destroying grass, grain, and other crops; *esp* **:** the common armyworm (*Pseudaletia unipuncta*) of the eastern and central U.S. and Canada

ar·ni·ca \ˈär-ni-kə\ *n* [NL] (ca. 1753) **:** any of a genus (*Arnica*) of composite herbs including some with bright yellow ray flowers

ar·oid \ˈa-ˌrȯid, ˈer-ˌȯid\ *adj* [NL *Arum*] (1886) **:** of or relating to the arum family — **aroid** *n*

aroint \ə-ˈrȯint\ *vb imper* [origin unknown] (1605) *archaic* **:** BEGONE 〈~ thee, witch —Shak.〉

aro·ma \ə-ˈrō-mə\ *n* [ME *aromat* spice, fr. AF, fr. L *aromat-, aroma,* fr. Gk *arōmat-, arōma*] (1796) **1 a :** a distinctive pervasive and usu. pleasant or savory smell; *broadly* **:** ODOR **b :** the odor of a wine imparted by the grapes from which it is made **2 :** a distinctive quality or atmosphere **:** FLAVOR 〈the ~ of enjoyment —Stella D. Gibbons〉 ***syn*** see SMELL

aro·ma·tase \ə-ˈrō-mə-ˌtās, -ˌtāz\ *n* [*aromat*ic + *-ase*] (1984) **:** an enzyme or complex of enzymes that promotes the conversion of an androgen into estrogen

aro·ma·ther·a·py \ə-ˌrō-mə-ˈther-ə-pē\ *n* [F *aromathérapie,* fr. L *aroma* + F *thérapie* therapy] (1949) **:** massage of the body and esp. of the face with a preparation of fragrant essential oils extracted from herbs, flowers, and fruits; *broadly* **:** the use of aroma to enhance a feeling of well-being — **aro·ma·ther·a·peu·tic** \-ˌther-ə-ˈpyü-tik\ *adj* — **aro·ma·ther·a·pist** \-ˈther-ə-pist\ *n*

[1]ar·o·mat·ic \ˌa-rə-ˈma-tik, ˌer-ə-\ *adj* (14c) **1 :** of, relating to, or having aroma: **a :** FRAGRANT **b :** having a strong smell **c :** having a distinctive quality **2** *of an organic compound* **:** characterized by increased chemical stability resulting from the delocalization of electrons in a ring system (as benzene) containing usu. multiple conjugated double bonds — compare ALICYCLIC, ALIPHATIC ***syn*** see ODOROUS — **ar·o·mat·i·cal·ly** \-ti-k(ə-)lē\ *adv* — **aro·ma·tic·i·ty** \ˌa-rə-mə-ˈti-sə-tē, ˌer-ə-, ə-ˌrō-mə-\ *n*

[2]aromatic *n* (15c) **1 :** an aromatic plant or plant part; *esp* **:** an aromatic herb or spice **2 :** an aromatic organic compound

aro·ma·tize \ə-ˈrō-mə-ˌtīz\ *vt* **-tized; -tiz·ing** (15c) **1 :** to make aromatic **:** FLAVOR **2 :** to convert into one or more aromatic compounds — **aro·ma·ti·za·tion** \-ˌrō-mə-tə-ˈzā-shən\ *n*

arose *past of* ARISE

[1]around \ə-ˈrau̇nd\ *adv* [ME, fr. [1]*a-* + [2]*round*] (14c) **1 a :** in a circle or in circumference 〈the wheel goes ~〉 〈a tree five feet ~〉 **b :** in, along, or through a circuit 〈the road goes ~ by the lake〉 **2 a :** on all or various sides **:** in every or any direction 〈papers lying ~〉 〈nothing for miles ~〉 **b :** in close from all sides so as to surround 〈people crowded ~〉 **c :** in or near one's present place or situation 〈wait ~ awhile〉 **3 a :** here and there **:** from one place to another 〈travels ~ on business〉 **b :** to a particular place 〈come ~ for dinner〉 **c** — used with some verbs to indicate repeated or continued action 〈always joking ~ when he should be serious〉 〈don't play ~ with your food〉 **4 a :** in rotation or succession 〈another winter comes ~〉 **b :** from beginning to end **:** THROUGH 〈mild the year ~〉 **c :** in order 〈the other way ~〉 **5 :** in or to an opposite direction or position 〈turn ~〉 **6 :** with some approach to exactness **:** APPROXIMATELY 〈cost ~ $5〉

[2]around *prep* (14c) **1 a :** on all sides of **b :** so as to encircle or enclose 〈seated ~ the table〉 **c :** so as to avoid or get past **:** on or to another side of 〈find a way ~ their objections〉 〈went ~ the lake〉 〈~ the corner〉 **d :** NEAR 〈lives ~ Chicago〉 〈~ the turn of the century〉 **2 :** in all directions outward from 〈look ~ you〉 **3 :** here and there in or throughout 〈barnstorming ~ the country〉 **4 :** so as to have a center or basis in 〈a society organized ~ kinship ties〉

[3]around *adj* (1849) **1 :** ABOUT 1 〈has been up and ~ for two days〉 **2 :** being in existence, evidence, or circulation 〈the most intelligent of the artists ~ today —R. M. Coates〉 — **been around :** gone through many varied experiences **:** become worldly-wise

around–the–clock *adj* (1853) **:** being in effect, continuing, or lasting 24 hours a day **:** CONSTANT 〈~ surveillance〉

arouse \ə-ˈrau̇z\ *vb* **aroused; arous·ing** [*a-* (as in *arise*) + *rouse*] *vt* (1593) **1 :** to awaken from sleep **2 :** to rouse or stimulate to action or to physiological readiness for activity **:** EXCITE 〈the book *aroused* debate〉 ~ *vi* **:** to awake from sleep **:** STIR — **arous·al** \ə-ˈrau̇-zəl\ *n*

ar·peg·gi·ate \är-ˈpe-jē-ˌāt\ *vt* **-at·ed; -at·ing** (1953) **:** to play (as a chord or passage) in arpeggio

ar·peg·gio \är-ˈpe-jē-ˌō, -ˈpe-jō\ *n, pl* **-gios** [It, fr. *arpeggiare* to play on the harp, fr. *arpa* harp, of Gmc origin; akin to OHG *harpha* harp] (ca. 1724) **1 :** production of the tones of a chord in succession and not simultaneously **2 :** a chord played in arpeggio

ar·pent \är-ˈpäⁿ\ *n, pl* **ar·pents** \-ˈpäⁿ(z)\ [MF] (1580) **1 :** any of various old French units of land area; *esp* **:** one used in French sections of Canada and the U.S. equal to about 0.85 acre (0.34 hectare) **2 :** a unit of length equal to one side of a square arpent

arquebus *var of* HARQUEBUS

arr *abbr* **1** arranged **2** arrival; arrive

ar·rack *or* **ar·ak** \ˈa-rək, ə-ˈrak\ *n* [ultim. fr. Ar *ʿaraq* sweet juice, liquor] (1521) **:** an Asian alcoholic beverage like rum that is distilled from a fermented mash of malted rice with toddy or molasses

ar·raign \ə-ˈrān\ *vt* [ME *arreinen,* fr. AF *areisner, arener,* fr. *a-* (fr. L *ad-*) + *raisner* to address, fr. VL **rationare,* fr. L *ration-, ratio* reason — more at REASON] (14c) **1 :** to call (a defendant) before a court to answer to an indictment **:** CHARGE **2 :** to accuse of wrong, inadequacy, or imperfection — **ar·raign·ment** \-mənt\ *n*

ar·range \ə-ˈrānj\ *vb* **-ranged; -rang·ing** [ME *arangen,* fr. MF *arenger,* fr. *a-* + *renger* to set in ranks, fr. *renc, ranc* row — more at RANK] *vt* (1638) **1 :** to put into a proper order or into a correct or suitable sequence, relationship, or adjustment 〈~ flowers in a vase〉 〈~ cards alphabetically〉 **2 :** to make preparations for **:** PLAN 〈*arranged* a reception for the visitor〉 **3 a :** to adapt (a musical composition) by scoring for voices or instruments other than those for which orig. written **b :** ORCHESTRATE **4 :** to bring about an agreement or understanding concerning **:** SETTLE 〈~ an exchange of war prisoners〉 ~ *vi* **1 :** to bring about an agreement or understanding 〈*arranged* to have a table at the restaurant〉 **2 :** to make preparations **:** PLAN 〈*arranged* for a vacation with his family〉 ***syn*** see ORDER — **ar·rang·er** \ə-ˈrān-jər\ *n*

ar·range·ment \ə-ˈrānj-mənt\ *n* (1690) **1 a :** the state of being arranged **:** ORDER 〈everything in neat ~〉 **b :** the act of arranging 〈the ~ of the details was quickly accomplished〉 **2 :** something arranged: as **a :** a preliminary measure **:** PREPARATION 〈travel ~*s*〉 **b :** an adaptation of a musical composition by rescoring **c :** an informal agreement or settlement esp. on personal, social, or political matters 〈~*s* under the new regime〉 **3 :** something made by arranging parts or things together 〈a floral ~〉

ar·rant \ˈa-rənt, ˈer-ənt\ *adj* [alter. of *errant*] (14c) **:** being notoriously without moderation **:** EXTREME 〈we are ~ knaves, all; believe none of us —Shak.〉 — **ar·rant·ly** *adv*

ar·ras \ˈa-rəs, ˈer-əs\ *n, pl* **arras** [ME, fr. *Arras,* France] (15c) **1 :** a tapestry of Flemish origin used esp. for wall hangings and curtains **2 :** a wall hanging or screen of tapestry

[1]ar·ray \ə-ˈrā\ *vt* [ME, fr. AF *arraier,* fr. VL **arredare,* fr. L *ad-* + a base of Gmc origin; akin to Goth *garaiths* arranged — more at READY] (14c) **1 :** to dress or decorate esp. in splendid or impressive attire **:** ADORN 〈he had already ~*ed* himself in his best clothes —Thomas Hardy〉 **2 a :** to set or place in order **:** DRAW UP, MARSHAL 〈the forces ~*ed* against us〉 **b :** to set or set forth in order (as a jury) for the trial of a cause **3 :** to arrange or display in or as if in an array 〈the . . . data are ~*ed* in descending order —Ed Burnett〉 — **ar·ray·er** *n*

[2]array *n* (14c) **1 a :** a regular and imposing grouping or arrangement **:** ORDER 〈lined up . . . in soldierly ~ —Donald Barthelme〉 **b :** an orderly listing of jurors impaneled **2 a :** CLOTHING, ATTIRE **b :** rich or beautiful apparel **:** FINERY **3 :** a body of soldiers **:** MILITIA 〈the baron and his feudal ~〉 **4 :** an imposing group **:** large number 〈faced a whole ~ of problems〉; *also* **:** VARIETY, ASSORTMENT 〈a broad ~ of styles〉 **5 a (1) :** a number of mathematical elements arranged in rows and columns **(2) :** a data structure in which similar elements of data are arranged in a table **b :** a series of statistical data arranged in classes in order of magnitude **6 :** a group of elements forming a complete unit 〈an antenna ~〉

ar·rear \ə-ˈrir\ *n* [ME *arrere* behind, backward, fr. AF *arere,* fr. VL **ad retro* backward, fr. L *ad* to + *retro* backward, behind — more at AT, RETRO-] (1620) **1 :** the state of being behind in the discharge of obligations — usu. used in pl. 〈in ~*s* with the rent〉 **2 a :** an unfinished duty — usu. used in pl. 〈~*s* of work that have piled up〉 **b :** an unpaid and overdue debt — usu. used in pl. 〈paying off the ~*s* of the past several months〉

ar·rear·age \-ij\ *n* (14c) **1 :** the condition of being in arrears **2 :** something that is in arrears; *esp* **:** something unpaid and overdue

[1]ar·rest \ə-ˈrest\ *vt* [ME *aresten,* fr. AF *arester* to stop, arrest, fr. VL **arrestare,* fr. L *ad-* + *restare* to remain — more at REST] (14c) **1 a :** to bring to a stop 〈sickness ~*ed* his activities〉 **b :** CHECK, SLOW **c :** to make inactive 〈an ~*ed* tumor〉 **2 :** SEIZE, CAPTURE; *specif* **:** to take or keep in custody by authority of law **3 :** to catch suddenly and engagingly 〈~ attention〉 — **ar·rest·er** *also* **ar·res·tor** \-ˈres-tər\ *n* — **ar·rest·ment** \-ˈres(t)-mənt\ *n*

[2]arrest *n* (14c) **1 a :** the act of stopping **b :** the condition of being stopped or inactive — compare CARDIAC ARREST **2 :** the taking or detaining in custody by authority of law — **under arrest :** in legal custody

ar·res·tant \ə-ˈres-tənt\ *n* (1962) **:** a substance that stimulates an insect to stop locomotion

ar·rest·ee \ə-ˌres-ˈtē\ *n* (1944) **:** a person who is under arrest

ar·rest·ing \ə-ˈres-tiŋ\ *adj* (1792) **:** catching the attention **:** STRIKING, IMPRESSIVE 〈an ~ image〉 — **ar·rest·ing·ly** \-tiŋ-lē\ *adv*

ar·rhyth·mia \ā-ˈrith-mē-ə\ *n* [NL, fr. Gk, lack of rhythm, fr. *arrhythmos* unrhythmical, fr. *a-* + *rhythmos* rhythm] (ca. 1860) **:** an alteration in rhythm of the heartbeat either in time or force

ar·rhyth·mic \-mik\ *adj* [Gk *arrhythmos*] (1853) **:** lacking rhythm or regularity 〈~ locomotor activity〉

ar·ri·ère–ban \ˌar-ē-ˌer-ˈbän, -ˈban\ *n* [F] (1523) **:** a proclamation of a king (as of France) calling his vassals to arms; *also* **:** the body of vassals summoned

ar·ri·ère–pen·sée \-päⁿ-ˈsā\ *n* [F, fr. *arrière* in back + *pensée* thought] (1824) **:** mental reservation

ar·ris \ˈa-rəs, ˈer-əs\ *n, pl* **arris** *or* **ar·ris·es** [prob. modif. of MF *areste,* lit., fishbone, fr. LL *arista* — more at ARÊTE] (1677) **:** the sharp edge or salient angle formed by the meeting of two surfaces esp. in moldings

ar·riv·al \ə-ˈrī-vəl\ *n* (14c) **1 :** the act of arriving **2 :** the attainment of an end or state **3 :** one that has recently arrived 〈new ~*s*〉

ar·rive \ə-ˈrīv\ *vi* **ar·rived; ar·riv·ing** [ME *ariven,* fr. AF *ariver,* fr. VL **arripare* to come to shore, fr. L *ad-* + *ripa* shore — more at RIVE] (13c) **1 a :** to reach a destination **b :** to make an appearance 〈the guests have *arrived*〉 **2 a** *archaic* **:** HAPPEN **b :** to be near in time **:** COME 〈the moment has *arrived*〉 **3 :** to achieve success — **ar·riv·er** *n* — **arrive at :** to reach by effort or thought 〈*arrived at* a decision〉

ar·ri·vé \ˌa-ri-ˈvā\ *n* [F, fr. pp. of *arriver* to arrive, fr. OF *ariver*] (1925) **:** one who has risen rapidly to success, power, or fame

ar·ri·viste \-ˈvēst\ *n* [F, fr. *arriver*] (1901) **:** one that is a new and uncertain arrival (as in social position or artistic endeavor)

ar·ro·ba \ə-ˈrō-bə\ *n* [Sp & Pg, fr. Ar *al-rubʿ,* lit., the quarter] (1555) **1 :** an old Spanish unit of weight equal to about 25 pounds **2 :** an old Portuguese unit of weight equal to about 32 pounds

ar·ro·gance \ˈer-ə-gən(t)s, ˈa-rə-\ *n* (14c) **:** an attitude of superiority manifested in an overbearing manner or in presumptuous claims or assumptions

ar·ro·gant \-gənt\ *adj* [ME, fr. L *arrogant-, arrogans,* prp. of *arrogare*] (14c) **1 :** exaggerating or disposed to exaggerate one's own worth or importance often by an overbearing manner ⟨an ~ official⟩ **2 :** proceeding from or characterized by arrogance ⟨an ~ reply⟩ ***syn*** see PROUD — **ar·ro·gant·ly** *adv*

ar·ro·gate \-ˌgāt\ *vt* **-gat·ed; -gat·ing** [L *arrogatus,* pp. of *arrogare,* fr. *ad-* + *rogare* to ask — more at RIGHT] (1537) **1 a :** to claim or seize without justification **b :** to make undue claims to having : ASSUME **2 :** to claim on behalf of another : ASCRIBE — **ar·ro·ga·tion** \ˌer-ə-ˈgā-shən, ˌa-rə-\ *n*

ar·ron·disse·ment \ə-ˈrän-də-smənt, ˌa-ˌrōⁿ-(ˌ)dē-ˈsmäⁿ\ *n* [F] (1807) **1 :** an administrative district of some large French cities **2 :** the largest division of a French department

[1]**ar·row** \ˈer-(ˌ)ō, ˈa-(ˌ)rō\ *n* [ME *arwe,* fr. OE; akin to Goth *arhwazna* arrow, L *arcus* bow, arch, arc] (bef. 12c) **1 :** a missile shot from a bow and usu. having a slender shaft, a pointed head, and feathers at the butt **2 :** something shaped like an arrow; *esp* **:** a mark (as on a map or signboard) to indicate direction

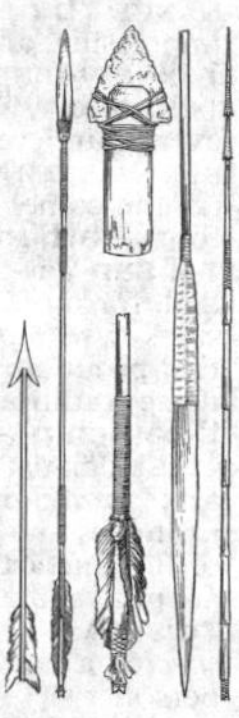

arrow 1

[2]**arrow** *vi* (1827) **:** to move fast and straight like an arrow in flight : DART

ar·row·head \ˈer-ō-ˌhed, ˈer-ə-, ˈa-rō-, ˈa-rə-\ *n* (14c) **1 :** a wedge-shaped piercing tip usu. fixed to an arrow **2 :** something resembling an arrowhead **3 :** any of a genus (*Sagittaria*) of marsh or aquatic plants of the water-plantain family with leaves shaped like arrowheads

ar·row·root \-ˌrüt, -ˌru̇t\ *n* (1696) **1 a :** any of a genus (*Maranta* of the family Marantaceae, the arrowroot family) of tropical American plants with tuberous roots; *esp* **:** one (*M. arundinacea*) whose roots yield an easily digested edible starch **b :** any of several plants (as coontie) that yield starch **2 :** starch yielded by an arrowroot

ar·row·wood \-ˌwu̇d\ *n* (1709) **:** any of several common viburnums (esp. *Viburnum dentatum*) of eastern No. America

ar·row·worm \-ˌwərm\ *n* (ca. 1889) **:** any of a phylum (Chaetognatha) of small planktonic wormlike marine organisms having curved bristles on either side of the head for seizing prey

ar·rowy \ˈer-ə-wē, ˈa-rə-\ *adj* (1616) **1 :** resembling or suggesting an arrow ⟨~ pines⟩; *esp* **:** swiftly moving ⟨the sky was radiant with ~ bolts —Mark Twain⟩ **2 :** consisting of arrows ⟨~ showers⟩

ar·royo \ə-ˈrȯi-(ˌ)ō, -ə\ *n, pl* **-royos** [Sp] (1843) **1 :** a watercourse (as a creek) in an arid region **2 :** a water-carved gully or channel

ar·roz con po·llo \ä-ˈrōth-(ˌ)kȯn-ˈpōl-(ˌ)yō, -ˈpō-(ˌ)yō\ *n* [Sp, lit., rice with chicken] (1938) **:** a dish of chicken cooked with rice and usu. flavored with saffron

ARRT *abbr* American Registry of Radiologic Technologists

arse *var of* ASS

ar·se·nal \ˈärs-nəl, ˈär-sə-\ *n* [It *arsenale,* ultim. fr. Ar *dār ṣināʻa* house of manufacture] (1555) **1 a :** an establishment for the manufacture or storage of arms and military equipment **b :** a collection of weapons **2 :** STORE, REPERTOIRE ⟨the team's ~ of veteran players⟩

ar·se·nate \ˈärs-nət, ˈär-sə-, -ˌnāt\ *n* (1800) **:** a salt or ester of an arsenic acid

[1]**ar·se·nic** \ˈärs-nik, ˈär-sə-\ *n* [ME *arsenik* orpiment, fr. AF & L; AF, fr. L *arsenicum,* fr. Gk *arsenikon, arrhenikon,* fr. Syr *zarnīg,* of Iranian origin; akin to Av *zaranya* gold, Skt *hari* yellowish — more at YELLOW] (14c) **1 :** a trivalent and pentavalent metalloid poisonous element that is commonly metallic steel gray, crystalline, and brittle and is used esp. in wood preservatives, alloys, and semiconductors — see ELEMENT table **2 :** a poisonous trioxide As_2O_3 or As_4O_6 of arsenic used esp. as an insecticide or weed killer — called also *arsenic trioxide*

[2]**ar·sen·ic** \är-ˈse-nik\ *adj* (1801) **:** of, relating to, or containing arsenic esp. with a valence of five

ar·sen·i·cal \är-ˈse-ni-kəl\ *adj* (1605) **:** of, relating to, containing, or caused by arsenic ⟨~ poisoning⟩ — **arsenical** *n*

ar·se·nide \ˈär-sə-ˌnīd\ *n* (1854) **:** a binary compound of arsenic with a more electropositive element

ar·se·ni·ous \är-ˈsē-nē-əs\ *adj* (1810) **:** of, relating to, or containing arsenic esp. when trivalent

ar·se·nite \ˈär-sə-ˌnīt\ *n* (1800) **:** a salt or ester of an arsenious acid

ar·se·no·py·rite \ˌär-sə-nō-ˈpī-ˌrīt\ *n* (1868) **:** a silver-white mineral consisting of a combined sulfide and arsenide of iron that occurs in prismatic orthorhombic crystals or in masses or grains and that is the principal source of arsenic

ar·sine \är-ˈsēn, ˈär-ˌ\ *n* [ISV, fr. *arsenic*] (1869) **:** a colorless flammable extremely poisonous gas AsH_3 with an odor like garlic; *also* **:** a derivative of arsine

ar·sis \ˈär-səs\ *n, pl* **ar·ses** \-ˌsēz\ [LL & Gk; LL, raising of the voice, accented part of foot, fr. Gk, upbeat, less important part of foot, lit., act of lifting, fr. *aeirein, airein* to lift] (14c) **1 a :** the lighter or shorter part of a poetic foot esp. in quantitative verse **b :** the accented or longer part of a poetic foot esp. in accentual verse **2 :** the unaccented part of a musical measure — compare THESIS

ar·son \ˈär-sᵊn\ *n* [AF *arsoun,* fr. *ars,* pp. of *arder, ardre* to burn, fr. L *ardēre* — more at ARDOR] (ca. 1680) **:** the willful or malicious burning of property (as a building) esp. with criminal or fraudulent intent — **ar·son·ist** \-ist\ *n* — **ar·son·ous** \-əs\ *adj*

ars·phen·a·mine \ärs-ˈfe-nə-ˌmēn, -mən\ *n* [ISV *arsenic* + *phenamine*] (1917) **:** a light-yellow toxic hygroscopic powder $C_{12}Cl_2H_{14}As_2N_2O_2 \cdot 2H_2O$ formerly used in the treatment esp. of syphilis and yaws

[1]**art** \ˈärt, ərt\ [ME, fr. OE *eart;* akin to ON *est, ert* (thou) art, OE *is* is] *archaic pres 2d sing of* BE

[2]**art** \ˈärt\ *n* [ME, fr. AF, fr. L *art-, ars* — more at ARM] (13c) **1 :** skill acquired by experience, study, or observation ⟨the ~ of making friends⟩ **2 a :** a branch of learning: (1) **:** one of the humanities (2) *pl* **:** LIBERAL ARTS **b** *archaic* **:** LEARNING, SCHOLARSHIP **3 :** an occupation requiring knowledge or skill ⟨the ~ of organ building⟩ **4 a :** the conscious use of skill and creative imagination esp. in the production of aesthetic objects; *also* **:** works so produced **b** (1) **:** FINE ARTS (2) **:** one of the fine arts (3) **:** a graphic art **5 a** *archaic* **:** a skillful plan **b :** the quality or state of being artful **6 :** decorative or illustrative elements in printed matter

syn ART, SKILL, CUNNING, ARTIFICE, CRAFT mean the faculty of executing well what one has devised. ART implies a personal, unanalyzable creative power ⟨the *art* of choosing the right word⟩. SKILL stresses technical knowledge and proficiency ⟨the *skill* of a glassblower⟩. CUNNING suggests ingenuity and subtlety in devising, inventing, or executing ⟨a mystery plotted with great *cunning*⟩. ARTIFICE suggests technical skill esp. in imitating things in nature ⟨believed realism in film could be achieved only by *artifice*⟩. CRAFT may imply expertness in workmanship ⟨the *craft* of a master goldsmith⟩.

[3]**art** *adj* (1868) **:** produced as an artistic effort or for decorative purposes ⟨an ~ film⟩ ⟨~ dolls⟩ ⟨~ music⟩

[4]**art** *abbr* **1** article **2** artificial **3** artillery

-art — see -ARD

art de·co \ˌärt-ˈde-ˌkō; ˌär(t)-dā-ˈkō, ˈär(t)-ˈdā-(ˌ)\ *n, often cap A&D* [F *Art Déco,* fr. *Exposition Internationale des Arts Décoratifs et Industriels Modernes,* an exposition of modern decorative and industrial arts held in Paris, France, in 1925] (1966) **:** a popular design style of the 1920s and 1930s characterized esp. by bold outlines, geometric and zigzag forms, and the use of new materials (as plastic)

ar·te·fact *chiefly Brit var of* ARTIFACT

Ar·te·mis \ˈär-tə-məs\ *n* [Gk] **:** a Greek moon goddess often portrayed as a virgin huntress — compare DIANA

ar·te·mi·sia \ˌär-tə-ˈmi-zh(ē-)ə, -zē-ə\ *n* [NL, fr. L, artemisia, fr. Gk, wormwood] (14c) **:** any of a genus (*Artemisia*) of aromatic composite herbs and shrubs (as sagebrush) — compare WORMWOOD 1

arteri- *or* **arterio-** *comb form* [Gk *artēri-, artērio-,* fr. *artēria* artery] **1 :** artery ⟨*arterio*gram⟩ **2 :** arterial and ⟨*arterio*venous⟩

[1]**ar·te·ri·al** \är-ˈtir-ē-əl\ *adj* (15c) **1 a :** of or relating to an artery **b :** relating to or being the bright red blood present in most arteries that has been oxygenated in lungs or gills **2 :** of, relating to, or constituting through traffic — **ar·te·ri·al·ly** \-ē-ə-lē\ *adv*

[2]**arterial** *n* (1932) **:** a through street or highway

ar·te·rio·gram \är-ˈtir-ē-ə-ˌgram\ *n* [ISV] (1929) **:** a radiograph of an artery made by arteriography

ar·te·ri·og·ra·phy \är-ˌtir-ē-ˈä-grə-fē\ *n, pl* **-phies** [ISV] (1929) **:** the radiographic visualization of an artery after injection of a radiopaque substance — **ar·te·rio·graph·ic** \-ē-ə-ˈgra-fik\ *adj*

ar·te·ri·ole \är-ˈtir-ē-ˌōl\ *n* [F or NL; F *artériole,* prob. fr. NL *arteriola,* dim. of L *arteria*] (1830) **:** any of the small terminal twigs of an artery that ends in capillaries — **ar·te·ri·o·lar** \-ˌtir-ē-ˈō-ˌlär, -lər\ *adj*

ar·te·rio·scle·ro·sis \är-ˌtir-ē-ō-sklə-ˈrō-səs\ *n* [NL] (1881) **:** a chronic disease characterized by abnormal thickening and hardening of the arterial walls with resulting loss of elasticity — compare ATHEROSCLEROSIS — **ar·te·rio·scle·rot·ic** \-ˈrä-tik\ *adj or n*

ar·te·rio·ve·nous \-ˈvē-nəs\ *adj* [ISV] (ca. 1880) **:** of, relating to, or connecting the arteries and veins ⟨an ~ fistula⟩

ar·ter·i·tis \ˌär-tə-ˈrī-təs\ *n, pl* **-ter·i·ti·des** \-ˈri-tə-ˌdēz\ [NL] (1836) **:** arterial inflammation

ar·tery \ˈär-tə-rē, ˈär-trē\ *n, pl* **-ter·ies** [ME *arterie,* fr. L *arteria,* fr. Gk *artēria;* akin to Gk *aortē* aorta] (14c) **1 :** any of the tubular branching muscular- and elastic-walled vessels that carry blood from the heart through the body **2 :** a channel (as a river or highway) of transportation or communication; *esp* **:** the main channel in a branching system

ar·te·sian well \är-ˈtē-zhən-\ *n* [F *artésien,* lit., of Artois, fr. OF, fr. *Arteis* Artois, France] (1835) **1 :** a well in which water is under pressure; *esp* **:** one in which the water flows to the surface naturally **2 :** a deep well

art form *n* (1868) **1 :** a form or medium of expression recognized as fine art ⟨sees dance as both an *art form* and an entertainment⟩ **2 a :** an unconventional form or medium in which impulses regarded as artistic may be expressed ⟨describe pinball as a great American *art form* —Tom Buckley⟩ **b :** an undertaking or activity enhanced by a high level of skill or refinement ⟨easy conversation—an *art form* in peril of being lost to contemporary schedules —Joanna Pruess⟩

art·ful \ˈärt-fəl\ *adj* (1609) **1 :** performed with or showing art or skill ⟨an ~ performance on the violin⟩ **2 a :** using or characterized by art and skill **:** DEXTEROUS ⟨an ~ prose stylist⟩ **b :** adroit in attaining an end usu. by insinuating or indirect means **:** WILY ⟨an ~ cross-examiner⟩ **3 :** ARTIFICIAL ⟨trim walks and ~ bowers —William Wordsworth⟩ ***syn*** see SLY — **art·ful·ly** \-fə-lē\ *adv* — **art·ful·ness** *n*

art glass *n* (1886) **:** articles of glass designed primarily for decorative purposes; *esp* **:** novelty glassware

art historical *adj* (1933) **:** of or relating to the history of art — **art historically** *adv*

art house *n* (1951) **:** ART THEATER

arthr- *or* **arthro-** *comb form* [L, fr. Gk, fr. *arthron;* akin to Gk *arariskein* to fit — more at ARM] **:** joint ⟨*arthro*pathy⟩

ar·thral·gia \är-ˈthral-j(ē-)ə\ *n* [NL] (ca. 1848) **:** pain in one or more joints — **ar·thral·gic** \-jik\ *adj*

ar·thrit·ic \är-ˈthri-tik\ *adj* (14c) **1 :** of, relating to, or affected with arthritis ⟨~ hands⟩ **2 :** seemingly affected with or caused by arthritis ⟨an ~ legal system⟩ ⟨a story moving with ~ slowness⟩ — **arthritic** *n* — **ar·thrit·i·cal·ly** \-ti-k(ə-)lē\ *adv*

ar·thri·tis \är-ˈthrī-təs\ *n, pl* **-thrit·i·des** \-ˈthri-tə-ˌdēz\ [L, fr. Gk, fr. *arthron*] (1543) **:** inflammation of joints due to infectious, metabolic, or constitutional causes; *also* **:** a specific arthritic condition

ar·throd·e·sis \är-ˈthrä-də-səs\ *n, pl* **-e·ses** \-ˌsēz\ [NL, fr. *arthr-* + Gk *desis* binding, fr. *dein* to bind] (ca. 1901) **:** the surgical immobilization of a joint so that the bones grow solidly together

ar·throp·a·thy \är-ˈthrä-pə-thē\ *n, pl* **-thies** (ca. 1860) **:** a disease of a joint

ar·thro·pod \ˈär-thrə-ˌpäd\ *n* [NL *Arthropoda,* fr. *arthr-* + Gk *pod-, pous* foot — more at FOOT] (1876) **:** any of a phylum (Arthropoda) of invertebrate animals (as insects, arachnids, and crustaceans) that have a segmented body and jointed appendages, a usu. chitinous exoskeleton

\ə\ **abut** \ᵊ\ **kitten**, F table \ər\ **further** \a\ **ash** \ā\ **ace** \ä\ **mop**, **mar** \au̇\ **out** \ch\ **chin** \e\ **bet** \ē\ **easy** \g\ **go** \i\ **hit** \ī\ **ice** \j\ **job** \ŋ\ **sing** \ō\ **go** \ȯ\ **law** \ȯi\ **boy** \th\ **thin** \t͟h\ **the** \ü\ **loot** \u̇\ **foot** \y\ **yet** \zh\ **vision, beige** \k, ⁿ, œ, ue, ʸ\ *see* Guide to Pronunciation

molted at intervals, and a dorsal anterior brain connected to a ventral chain of ganglia — **arthropod** *adj* — **ar·throp·o·dan** \är-ˈthrä-pə-dən\ *adj*

ar·thro·scope \ˈär-thrə-ˌskōp\ *n* (1925) **:** a fiber-optic instrument surgically inserted through an incision near a joint (as the knee) and used to visually examine the joint interior — **ar·thro·scop·ic** \ˌär-thrə-ˈskä-pik\ *adj*

ar·thros·co·py \är-ˈthräs-kə-pē\ *n* (1931) **:** examination of a joint with an arthroscope; *also* **:** surgery on a joint using an arthroscope

ar·thro·sis \är-ˈthrō-səs\ *n, pl* **-thro·ses** \-ˌsēz\ [NL, fr. Gk *arthrōsis* jointing, articulation, fr. *arthroun* to articulate, fr. *arthron*] (1634) **1 :** an articulation between bones **2 :** a degenerative disease of a joint

ar·thro·spore \ˈär-thrə-ˌspȯr\ *n* (1895) **:** OIDIUM 1b

Ar·thur \ˈär-thər\ *n* (13c) **:** a legendary king of the Britons whose story is based on traditions of a sixth century military leader

Ar·thu·ri·an \är-ˈthu̇r-ē-ən, -ˈthyu̇r-\ *adj* (1612) **:** of or relating to King Arthur and his court

ar·ti·choke \ˈär-tə-ˌchōk\ *n* [It dial. *articiocco,* ultim. fr. Ar *al-khurshūf* the artichoke] (1530) **1 :** a tall Mediterranean composite herb (*Cynara scolymus*) resembling a thistle with coarse pinnately incised leaves; *also* **:** its edible immature flower head which is cooked as a vegetable **2 :** JERUSALEM ARTICHOKE

[1]**ar·ti·cle** \ˈär-ti-kəl\ *n* [ME, fr. AF, fr. L *articulus* joint, division, dim. of *artus* joint, limb; akin to Gk *arariskein* to fit — more at ARM] (13c) **1 a :** a distinct often numbered section of a writing **b :** a separate clause **c :** a stipulation in a document (as a contract or a creed) ⟨~*s* of indenture⟩ **d :** a nonfictional prose composition usu. forming an independent part of a publication (as a magazine) **2 :** an item of business **:** MATTER **3 :** any of a small set of words or affixes (as *a, an,* and *the*) used with nouns to limit or give definiteness to the application **4 :** a member of a class of things; *esp* **:** an item of goods ⟨~*s* of value⟩ **5 :** a thing or person of a particular and distinctive kind or class ⟨the genuine ~⟩

[2]**article** *vt* **-cled; -cling** \-k(ə-)liŋ\ (1820) **:** to bind by articles (as of apprenticeship)

article of faith (15c) **:** a basic belief

ar·tic·u·la·ble \är-ˈti-kyə-lə-bəl\ *adj* (1833) **:** capable of being articulated

ar·tic·u·la·cy \är-ˈti-kyə-lə-sē\ *n* (1918) *chiefly Brit* **:** the quality or state of being articulate

ar·tic·u·lar \är-ˈti-kyə-lər\ *adj* [ME *articuler,* fr. L *articularis,* fr. *articulus*] (15c) **:** of or relating to a joint ⟨~ cartilage⟩

[1]**ar·tic·u·late** \är-ˈti-kyə-lət\ *adj* [L *articulatus* jointed, pp. of *articulare,* fr. *articulus*] (1586) **1 a :** divided into syllables or words meaningfully arranged **:** INTELLIGIBLE **b :** able to speak **c :** expressing oneself readily, clearly, or effectively ⟨an ~ teacher⟩; *also* **:** expressed in this manner ⟨an ~ argument⟩ **2 a :** consisting of segments united by joints **:** JOINTED ⟨~ animals⟩ **b :** distinctly marked off — **ar·tic·u·late·ly** *adv* — **ar·tic·u·late·ness** *n*

[2]**ar·tic·u·late** \-ˌlāt\ *vb* **-lat·ed; -lat·ing** *vt* (1551) **1 a :** to give clear and effective utterance to **:** put into words ⟨~ one's grievances⟩ **b :** to utter distinctly ⟨*articulating* each note in the musical phrase⟩ **c :** to give definition to (as a shape or object) ⟨shades of gray were chosen to ~ different spaces —Carol Vogel⟩ **d :** to give shape or expression to (as a theme or concept) ⟨a drama that uses eerie props to ~ a sense of foreboding⟩ **2 a :** to unite by or as if by means of a joint **:** JOINT **b :** to form or fit into a systematic whole ⟨*articulating* a program for all school grades⟩ ~ *vi* **1 :** to utter articulate sounds **2 :** to become united or connected by or as if by a joint — **ar·tic·u·la·tive** \-lə-tiv, -ˌlā-\ *adj* — **ar·tic·u·la·tor** \-ˌlā-tər\ *n*

ar·tic·u·lat·ed \-ˌlā-təd\ *adj* (1899) *of a vehicle* **:** having a hinge or pivot connection esp. to allow negotiation of sharp turns ⟨~ lorry⟩ ⟨~ bus⟩

ar·tic·u·la·tion \(ˌ)är-ˌti-kyə-ˈlā-shən\ *n* (15c) **1 a :** a joint or juncture between bones or cartilages in the skeleton of a vertebrate **b :** a movable joint between rigid parts of an animal **2 a :** the action or manner of jointing or interrelating **b :** the state of being jointed or interrelated **3 a :** the act of giving utterance or expression **b :** the act or manner of articulating sounds **c :** an articulated utterance or sound; *specif* **:** CONSONANT **4 :** OCCLUSION 1b

ar·tic·u·la·to·ry \är-ˈti-kyə-lə-ˌtȯr-ē\ *adj* (1818) **:** of or relating to articulation

ar·ti·fact \ˈär-ti-ˌfakt\ *n* [L *arte* by skill (abl. of *art-, ars* skill) + *factum,* neut. of *factus,* pp. of *facere* to do — more at ARM, DO] (1821) **1 a :** something created by humans usu. for a practical purpose; *esp* **:** an object remaining from a particular period ⟨caves containing prehistoric ~*s*⟩ **b :** something characteristic of or resulting from a particular human institution, period, trend, or individual ⟨self-consciousness . . . turns out to be an ~ of our education system —*Times Lit. Supp.*⟩ **2 :** a product of artificial character (as in a scientific test) due usu. to extraneous (as human) agency — **ar·ti·fac·tu·al** \ˌär-ti-ˈfak-chə(-wə)l, -ˈfak-shwəl, -chü-əl\ *adj*

ar·ti·fice \ˈär-tə-fəs\ *n* [MF, fr. L *artificium,* fr. *artific-, artifex* artificer, fr. L *art-, ars + facere*] (ca. 1604) **1 a :** clever or artful skill **:** INGENUITY ⟨believing that characters had to be created from within rather than with ~ —Garson Kanin⟩ **b :** an ingenious device or expedient **2 a :** an artful stratagem **:** TRICK **b :** false or insincere behavior ⟨social ~⟩ ***syn*** see TRICK, ART

ar·ti·fi·cer \är-ˈti-fə-sər, ˈär-tə-fə-sər\ *n* (14c) **1 :** a skilled or artistic worker or craftsman **2 :** one that makes or contrives **:** DEVISER ⟨had been the ~ of his own fortunes —*Times Lit. Supp.*⟩

ar·ti·fi·cial \ˌär-tə-ˈfi-shəl\ *adj* (14c) **1 :** humanly contrived often on a natural model **:** MAN-MADE ⟨an ~ limb⟩ ⟨~ diamonds⟩ **2 a :** having existence in legal, economic, or political theory **b :** caused or produced by a human and esp. social or political agency ⟨an ~ price advantage⟩ ⟨~ barriers of discrimination —R. C. Weaver⟩ **3** *obs* **:** ARTFUL, CUNNING **4 a :** lacking in natural or spontaneous quality ⟨an ~ smile⟩ ⟨an ~ excitement⟩ **b :** IMITATION, SHAM ⟨~ flavor⟩ **5 :** based on differential morphological characters not necessarily indicative of natural relationships ⟨an ~ key for plant identification⟩ — **ar·ti·fi·ci·al·i·ty** \ˌär-tə-ˌfi-shē-ˈa-lə-tē\ *n* — **ar·ti·fi·cial·ly** \-ˈfi-shᵊl-ē\ *adv* — **ar·ti·fi·cial·ness** \-ˈfi-shəl-nəs\ *n*

artificial horizon *n* (1920) **:** a gyroscopic flight instrument designed to indicate aircraft attitude with respect to the true horizon

artificial insemination *n* (1897) **:** introduction of semen into the uterus or oviduct by other than natural means

artificial intelligence *n* (1956) **1 :** a branch of computer science dealing with the simulation of intelligent behavior in computers **2 :** the capability of a machine to imitate intelligent human behavior

artificial respiration *n* (1817) **:** the rhythmic forcing of air into and out of the lungs of a person whose breathing has stopped

ar·til·ler·ist \är-ˈti-lə-rist\ *n* (1757) **:** GUNNER, ARTILLERYMAN

ar·til·lery \är-ˈti-lər-ē, -ˈtil-rē\ *n, pl* **-ler·ies** [ME *artillerie,* fr. AF, fr. *artiller* to equip, arm, alter. of OF *atillier,* fr. VL **apticulare,* fr. L *aptare* to don, prepare, fit — more at ADAPT] (15c) **1 :** weapons (as bows, slings, and catapults) for discharging missiles **2 a :** large bore crew-served mounted firearms (as guns, howitzers, and rockets) **:** ORDNANCE **b :** a branch of an army armed with artillery **3 :** means of impressing, arguing, or persuading

ar·til·lery·man \-mən\ *n* (1635) **:** a soldier in the artillery

ar·tio·dac·tyl \ˌär-tē-ō-ˈdak-tᵊl\ *n* [NL *Artiodactyla,* fr. Gk *artios* fitting, even-numbered + *daktylos* finger, toe; akin to Gk *arariskein* to fit — more at ARM] (ca. 1879) **:** any of an order (Artiodactyla) of ungulates (as the camel or pig) with an even number of functional toes on each foot — **artiodactyl** *adj*

ar·ti·san \ˈär-tə-zən, -sən, *chiefly Brit* ˌär-tə-ˈzan\ *n* [MF, fr. northern It dial. form of Tuscan *artigiano,* fr. *arte* art, fr. L *art-, ars*] (1538) **1 :** a worker who practices a trade or handicraft **:** CRAFTSPERSON **2 :** one that produces something (as cheese or wine) in limited quantities often using traditional methods — **ar·ti·san·al** \-zə-nᵊl, -sə-, -ˈza-\ *adj* — **ar·ti·san·ship** \-ˌship\ *n*

art·ist \ˈär-tist\ *n* (ca. 1507) **1 a** *obs* **:** one skilled or versed in learned arts **b** *archaic* **:** PHYSICIAN **c** *archaic* **:** ARTISAN 1 **2 a :** one who professes and practices an imaginative art **b :** a person skilled in one of the fine arts **3 :** a skilled performer; *esp* **:** ARTISTE **4 :** one who is adept at something ⟨con ~⟩ ⟨strikeout ~⟩

ar·tiste \är-ˈtēst\ *n* [F] (1823) **1 :** a skilled adept public performer; *specif* **:** a musical or theatrical entertainer **2 :** an artistic or creative person

ar·tis·tic \är-ˈtis-tik\ *adj* (ca. 1753) **1 :** of, relating to, or characteristic of art or artists ⟨~ subjects⟩ ⟨an ~ success⟩ **2 :** showing imaginative skill in arrangement or execution ⟨~ photography⟩ — **ar·tis·ti·cal·ly** \-ti-k(ə-)lē\ *adv*

art·ist·ry \ˈär-tə-strē\ *n* (1868) **1 :** artistic quality of effect or workmanship ⟨the ~ of his novel⟩ **2 :** artistic ability ⟨the ~ of the violinist⟩ ⟨a lawyer's ~ in persuading juries⟩

art·less \ˈärt-ləs\ *adj* (1589) **1 :** lacking art, knowledge, or skill **:** UNCULTURED ⟨an ~ brute⟩ **2 a :** made without skill **:** CRUDE ⟨an ~ attempt to win votes⟩ **b :** free from artificiality **:** NATURAL ⟨~ grace⟩ **3 :** free from guile or craft **:** sincerely simple ⟨an ~ young woman⟩ ***syn*** see NATURAL — **art·less·ly** *adv* — **art·less·ness** *n*

art mo·derne \ˌär(t)-mō-ˈdern\ *n, often cap A&M* [F — more at ART DECO] (1931) **:** ART DECO

art nou·veau \ˌär(t)-nü-ˈvō\ *n, often cap A&N* [F, lit., new art] (1908) **:** a design style of late 19th century origin characterized esp. by sinuous lines and foliate forms

art–rock \ˈärt-ˌräk\ *n* (1968) **:** rock music that incorporates elements of traditional or classical music — **art–rock·er** \ˈärt-ˌrä-kər\ *n*

arts and crafts *n, often cap A&C* (1888) **:** a movement in European and American design during the late 19th and early 20th centuries promoting handcraftsmanship over industrial mass production

art song *n* (1890) **:** a usu. through-composed song for solo voice and accompaniment — compare FOLK SONG

art·sy \ˈärt-sē\ *adj* (1902) **:** ARTY

artsy–craftsy \ˌärt-sē-ˈkraf(t)-sē\ *also* **arty–crafty** \är-tē-ˈkraf-tē\ *adj* [fr. the phrase *arts and crafts*] (1902) **:** ARTY

art theater *n* (1923) **:** a theater that specializes in the presentation of art films

art·work \ˈärt-ˌwərk\ *n* (1877) **1 a :** an artistic production ⟨an 8-foot metal ~⟩ **b :** artistic work ⟨~ being sold on the sidewalk⟩ **2 a :** ART 6 **b :** material (as a drawing or photograph) prepared for reproduction in printed matter

[1]**arty** \ˈär-tē\ *adj* **art·i·er; -est** (1901) **:** showily or pretentiously artistic ⟨~ lighting and photography⟩ — **art·i·ly** \ˈär-tᵊl-ē\ *adv* — **art·i·ness** \ˈär-tē-nəs\ *n*

[2]**arty** *abbr* artillery

aru·gu·la \ə-ˈrü-gə-lə, -gyə-\ *n* [prob. fr. It dial.; akin to It dial. (Lombardy) *arigola* arugula, It *ruca* — more at ROCKET] (1967) **:** a yellowish-flowered Mediterranean herb (*Eruca vesicaria sativa*) of the mustard family cultivated for its foliage which is used esp. in salads — called also *garden rocket, rocket, roquette, rugola*

ar·um \ˈa-rəm, ˈer-əm\ *n* [NL, fr. L *arum,* fr. Gk *aron*] (14c) **:** any of a genus (*Arum* of the family Araceae, the arum family) of Eurasian plants having usu. arrow-shaped leaves and a showy spathe partially enclosing a spadix; *broadly* **:** a plant of the arum family

ARV *abbr* American Revised Version

ARVN *abbr* Army of the Republic of Vietnam (South Vietnam)

[1]**-ary** *US usu* ˌer-ē *or* ˌe-rē *when an unstressed syllable precedes,* ə-rē *or* rē *when a stressed syllable precedes; Brit usu* ə-rē *or* rē *in all cases*\ *n suffix* [ME *-arie,* fr. AF & L; AF *-aire, -arie,* fr. L *-arius, -aria, -arium,* fr. *-arius,* adj. suffix] **1 :** thing belonging to or connected with; *esp* **:** place of ⟨ov*ary*⟩ **2 :** person belonging to, connected with, or engaged in ⟨function*ary*⟩

[2]**-ary** *adj suffix* [ME *-arie,* fr. AF & L; AF *-aire,* fr. L *-arius*] **:** of, relating to, or connected with ⟨budget*ary*⟩

[1]**Ary·an** \ˈa-rē-ən, ˈer-ē-; ˈär-yən\ *adj* [Skt *ārya* noble, belonging to an ancient people of northern India speaking an Indo-European dialect] (1839) **1 :** INDO-EUROPEAN **2 a :** of or relating to a hypothetical ethnic type illustrated by or descended from early speakers of Indo-European languages **b :** NORDIC **c —** used in Nazism to designate a supposed master race of non-Jewish Caucasians usu. having Nordic features **3 :** of or relating to Indo-Iranian or its speakers

[2]**Aryan** *n* (1851) **1 :** INDO-EUROPEAN **2 a :** NORDIC **b :** GENTILE

ar·yl \ˈa-rəl, ˈer-əl\ *adj* [ISV *aromatic* + *-yl*] (1906) **:** having or being a monovalent organic radical (as phenyl) derived from an aromatic hydrocarbon by the removal of one hydrogen atom — often used in combination

ar·y·te·noid \ˌa-rə-ˈtē-ˌnȯid, ə-ˈri-tᵊn-ˌȯid\ *adj* [NL *arytaenoides,* fr. Gk *arytainoeidēs,* lit., ladle-shaped, fr. *arytaina* ladle] (ca. 1751) **1 :** relating to or being either of two small laryngeal cartilages to which the vocal cords are attached **2 :** relating to or being either of a pair of small muscles or an unpaired muscle of the larynx — **arytenoid** *n*

¹**as** \əz, (ˌ)az\ *adv* [ME, fr. OE *eallswā* likewise, just as — more at ALSO] (bef. 12c) **1 :** to the same degree or amount ⟨~ soft as silk⟩ ⟨twice ~ long⟩ **2 :** for instance ⟨various trees, ~ oak or pine⟩ **3 :** when considered in a specified form or relation — usu. used before a preposition or a participle ⟨my opinion ~ distinguished from his⟩

²**as** *conj* (12c) **1 :** AS IF ⟨looks ~ he had seen a ghost —S. T. Coleridge⟩ **2 :** in or to the same degree in which ⟨soft ~ silk⟩ — usu. used as a correlative after an adjective or adverb modified by adverbial *as* or *so* ⟨as cool ~ a cucumber⟩ **3 :** in the way or manner that ⟨do ~ I do⟩ **4 :** in accordance with what or the way in which ⟨quite good ~ boys go⟩ **5 :** WHILE, WHEN ⟨spilled the milk ~ she got up⟩ **6 :** regardless of the degree to which : THOUGH ⟨improbable ~ it seems, it's true⟩ **7 :** for the reason that : BECAUSE, SINCE ⟨stayed home ~ she had no car⟩ **8 :** that the result is ⟨so clearly guilty ~ to leave no doubt⟩ ***usage*** see LIKE — **as is :** in the presently existing condition without modification ⟨bought the clock at an auction *as is*⟩ — **as it were :** as if it were so : in a manner of speaking

³**as** *pron* (12c) **1 :** THAT, WHO, WHICH — used after *same* or *such* ⟨in the same building ~ my brother⟩ ⟨tears such ~ angels weep —John Milton⟩ and chiefly dial. after a substantive not modified by *same* or *such* ⟨that kind of fruit ~ maids call medlars —Shak.⟩ **2 :** a fact that ⟨is a foreigner, ~ is evident from his accent⟩

⁴**as** *prep* (13c) **1 a :** LIKE 2 ⟨all rose ~ one man⟩ **b :** LIKE 1a ⟨his face was ~ a mask —Max Beerbohm⟩ **2 :** in the capacity, character, condition, or role of ⟨works ~ an editor⟩

⁵**as** \ˈas\ *n, pl* **as·ses** \ˈa-ˌsēz, ˈa-səz\ [L] (1540) **1 a :** a bronze coin of the ancient Roman republic **b :** a unit of value equivalent to an as coin **2 :** LIBRA 2a

¹**As** *abbr* altostratus

²**As** *symbol* arsenic

AS *abbr* **1** after sight **2** airspeed **3** American Samoa **4** Anglo-Saxon **5** antisubmarine **6** associate in science

as- — see AD-

asa·fet·i·da *or* **asa·foe·ti·da** \ˌa-sə-ˈfe-tə-də, -ˈfē-; *Southern also* -ˈfi-tə-dē\ *n* [ME *asafetida,* fr. ML *asafoetida,* fr. Pers *azā* mastic + L *foetida,* fem. of *foetidus* fetid] (14c) : the dried fetid gum resin of the root of several west Asian plants (genus *Ferula*) of the carrot family used as a flavoring esp. in Indian cooking and formerly used in medicine esp. as an antispasmodic and in folk medicine as a general prophylactic against disease

asa·na \ˈä-sə-nə\ *n* [Skt *āsana* manner of sitting, fr. *āste* he sits; akin to Gk *hēsthai* to sit, Hitt *es-*] (ca. 1934) : any of various yogic postures

Asan·te \ə-ˈsan-tē, -ˈsän-\ *n, pl* **Asante** (1721) : ASHANTI

ASAP *abbr* as soon as possible

asb *abbr* asbestos

as·bes·tos \as-ˈbes-təs, az-\ *n* [ME *albeston* mineral supposed to be inextinguishable when set on fire, prob. fr. MF *abeston,* fr. ML *asbeston,* alter. of L *asbestos,* fr. Gk, unslaked lime, fr. *asbestos* inextinguishable, fr. *a-* + *sbennynai* to quench] (1607) : any of several minerals (as chrysotile) that readily separate into long flexible fibers, that cause asbestosis and have been implicated as causes of certain cancers, and that have been used esp. formerly as fireproof insulating materials

as·bes·to·sis \ˌas-ˌbes-ˈtō-səs, ˌaz-\ *n, pl* **-to·ses** \-ˌsēz\ (1927) : a pneumoconiosis due to asbestos particles that is marked by thickening and scarring of lung tissue

asc- *or* **asco-** *comb form* [NL, fr. *ascus*] : ascus ⟨*ascocarp*⟩

ASCAP *abbr* American Society of Composers, Authors and Publishers

as·ca·ri·a·sis \ˌas-kə-ˈrī-ə-səs\ *n, pl* **-a·ses** \-ˌsēz\ [NL] (ca. 1888) : infestation with or disease caused by ascarids

as·ca·rid \ˈas-kə-rəd\ *n* [ultim. fr. LL *ascarid-, ascaris* intestinal worm, fr. Gk *askarid-, askaris,* prob. by back-formation fr. *askarizein* to jump, throb, alter. of *skarizein,* fr. *skairein* to gambol] (14c) : any of a family (Ascaridae) of nematode worms that includes the common roundworm (*Ascaris lumbricoides*) parasitic in the human intestine

as·ca·ris \ˈas-kə-rəs\ *n, pl* **as·car·i·des** \a-ˈska-rə-ˌdēz\ (14c) : ASCARID

as·cend \ə-ˈsend\ *vb* [ME, fr. L *ascendere,* fr. *ad-* + *scandere* to climb — more at SCAN] *vi* (14c) **1 a :** to move upward ⟨the balloon ~*ed*⟩ **b :** to slope upward **2 a :** to rise from a lower level or degree ⟨~ to power⟩ **b :** to go back in time or in order of genealogical succession ~ *vt* **1 :** to go or move up ⟨~ a staircase⟩ **2 :** to succeed to : OCCUPY ⟨~ the throne⟩ — **as·cend·able** *or* **as·cend·ible** \-ˈsen-də-bəl\ *adj*

as·cen·dance *also* **as·cen·dence** \ə-ˈsen-dən(t)s\ *n* (1715) : ASCENDANCY

as·cen·dan·cy *also* **as·cen·den·cy** \ə-ˈsen-dən(t)-sē\ *n* (1677) : governing or controlling influence : DOMINATION

¹**as·cen·dant** *also* **as·cen·dent** \ə-ˈsen-dənt\ *n* [ME *ascendent,* fr. ML *ascendent-, ascendens,* fr. L, prp. of *ascendere*] (14c) **1 :** the point of the ecliptic or degree of the zodiac that rises above the eastern horizon at any moment **2 :** a state or position of dominant power or importance **3 :** a lineal or collateral relative in the ascending line

²**ascendant** *also* **ascendent** *adj* (1591) **1 a :** moving upward : RISING **b :** directed upward ⟨an ~ stem⟩ **2 a :** SUPERIOR **b :** DOMINANT 1a — **as·cen·dant·ly** *adv*

as·cend·er \ə-ˈsen-dər, ˈa-\ *n* (ca. 1867) **1 :** the part of a lowercase letter (as b) that rises above the main body of the letter; *also* : a letter that has such a part **2 :** a device used for climbing rope that slides freely in one direction and grips the rope when pulled in the opposite direction

as·cend·ing \ə-ˈsen-diŋ\ *adj* (1581) **1 a :** rising or increasing to higher levels, values, or degrees ⟨~ powers of *x*⟩ **b :** mounting or sloping upward **2 :** rising upward usu. from a more or less prostrate base or point of attachment

as·cen·sion \ə-ˈsen(t)-shən\ *n* [ME, fr. L *ascension-, ascensio,* fr. *ascendere*] (14c) : the act or process of ascending

as·cen·sion·al \ə-ˈsench-nəl, ə-ˈsen(t)-shə-nᵊl\ *adj* (1594) : of or relating to ascension or ascent

Ascension Day *n* (14c) : the Thursday 40 days after Easter observed in commemoration of Christ's ascension into Heaven

as·cen·sive \ə-ˈsen(t)-siv\ *adj* (1602) : rising or tending to rise

as·cent \ə-ˈsent, a-\ *n* [irreg. fr. *ascend*] (ca. 1596) **1 a :** the act of rising or mounting upward : CLIMB **b :** an upward slope or rising grade : ACCLIVITY **c :** the degree of elevation : INCLINATION, GRADIENT **2 :** an advance in social status or reputation : PROGRESS **3 :** a going back in time or upward in order of genealogical succession

as·cer·tain \ˌa-sər-ˈtān\ *vt* [ME *acertainen* to inform, give assurance to, fr. AF *acerteiner,* fr. *a-* (fr. L *ad-*) + *certein, certain* certain] (15c) **1** *archaic* : to make certain, exact, or precise **2 :** to find out or learn with certainty ***syn*** see DISCOVER — **as·cer·tain·able** \-ˈtā-nə-bəl\ *adj* — **as·cer·tain·ment** \-ˈtān-mənt\ *n*

as·ce·sis \ə-ˈsē-səs\ *also* **as·ke·sis** \ə-ˈskē-səs\ *n, pl* **as·ce·ses** \-ˈsē-(ˌ)sēz\ *also* **as·ke·ses** \-ˈskē-(ˌ)sēz\ [LL or Gk; LL, fr. Gk *askēsis,* lit., exercise, fr. *askein*] (1873) : SELF-DISCIPLINE, ASCETICISM

as·cet·ic \ə-ˈse-tik, a-\ *also* **as·cet·i·cal** \-ti-kəl\ *adj* [Gk *askētikos,* lit., laborious, fr. *askētēs* one that exercises, hermit, fr. *askein* to work, exercise] (1646) **1 :** practicing strict self-denial as a measure of personal and esp. spiritual discipline **2 :** austere in appearance, manner, or attitude ***syn*** see SEVERE — **ascetic** *n* — **as·cet·i·cal·ly** \-ti-k(ə-)lē\ *adv* — **as·cet·i·cism** \-ˈse-tə-ˌsi-zəm\ *n*

as·cid·i·an \ə-ˈsi-dē-ən\ *n* [NL *Ascidia,* group comprising tunicates, fr. *Ascidium,* genus name, fr. Gk *askidion,* dim. of *askos* wineskin, bladder] (1835) : any of a class (Ascidiacea) of solitary or colonial sessile tunicates having an incurrent and excurrent siphon — called also *sea squirt*

ASCII \ˈas-(ˌ)kē\ *n* [*A*merican *S*tandard *C*ode for *I*nformation *I*nterchange] (1963) : a code for representing alphanumeric information

as·ci·tes \ə-ˈsī-tēz\ *n, pl* **ascites** [ME *aschytes,* fr. LL *ascites,* fr. Gk *askitēs,* fr. *askos*] (14c) : abnormal accumulation of serous fluid in the spaces between tissues and organs in the cavity of the abdomen — **as·cit·ic** \-ˈsi-tik\ *adj*

as·cle·pi·ad \ə-ˈsklē-pē-əd, a-, -ˌad\ *n* [ultim. fr. Gk *asklēpiad-, asklēpias* celandine, fr. *Asklēpios,* Greek god of medicine] (1859) : MILKWEED

as·co·carp \ˈas-kə-ˌkärp\ *n* (ca. 1887) : the mature fruiting body of an ascomycetous fungus; *broadly* : such a body with its enclosed asci, spores, and paraphyses — **as·co·car·pic** \ˌas-kə-ˈkär-pik\ *adj*

as·co·go·ni·um \ˌas-kə-ˈgō-nē-əm\ *n, pl* **-nia** \-nē-ə\ [NL] (1875) : the female sex organ in ascomycetous fungi

as·co·my·cete \ˌas-kō-ˈmī-ˌsēt, -ˌmī-ˈsēt\ *n* [ultim. fr. Gk *askos* + *mykēt-, mykēs* fungus; akin to Gk *myxa* mucus — more at MUCUS] (1872) : any of a group (as class Ascomycetes or subdivision Ascomycotina) of higher fungi (as yeasts or molds) with septate hyphae and spores formed in asci — **as·co·my·ce·tous** \-ˌmī-ˈsē-təs\ *adj*

ascor·bate \ə-ˈskȯr-ˌbāt, -bət\ *n* (1941) : a salt of ascorbic acid

ascor·bic acid \ə-ˈskȯr-bik-\ *n* [ISV *a-* + NL *scorbutus* scurvy — more at SCORBUTIC] (1933) : VITAMIN C

as·co·spore \ˈas-kə-ˌspȯr\ *n* (1875) : any of the spores contained in an ascus — **as·co·spor·ic** \ˌas-kə-ˈspȯr-ik\ *adj*

as·cot \ˈas-kət, -ˌkät\ *n* [*Ascot* Heath, racetrack near Ascot, England] (1898) : a broad neck scarf that is looped under the chin

as·cribe \ə-ˈskrīb\ *vt* **as·cribed; as·crib·ing** [ME, fr. L *ascribere,* fr. *ad-* + *scribere* to write — more at SCRIBE] (15c) : to refer to a supposed cause, source, or author — **as·crib·able** \-ˈskrī-bə-bəl\ *adj*

syn ASCRIBE, ATTRIBUTE, ASSIGN, IMPUTE, CREDIT mean to lay something to the account of a person or thing. ASCRIBE suggests an inferring or conjecturing of cause, quality, authorship ⟨forged paintings formerly *ascribed* to masters⟩. ATTRIBUTE suggests less tentativeness than ASCRIBE, less definiteness than ASSIGN ⟨*attributed* to Rembrandt but possibly done by an associate⟩. ASSIGN implies ascribing with certainty or after deliberation ⟨*assigned* the bones to the Cretaceous period⟩. IMPUTE suggests ascribing something that brings discredit by way of accusation or blame ⟨tried to *impute* sinister motives to my actions⟩. CREDIT implies ascribing a thing or esp. an action to a person or other thing as its agent, source, or explanation ⟨*credited* his teammates for his success⟩.

ascribed *adj* (1969) : acquired or assigned arbitrarily (as at birth) ⟨~ social status⟩

as·crip·tion \ə-ˈskrip-shən\ *n* [LL *ascription-, ascriptio,* fr. L, written addition, fr. *ascribere*] (1598) **1 :** the act of ascribing : ATTRIBUTION **2 :** arbitrary placement (as at birth) in a particular social status

as·crip·tive \ə-ˈskrip-tiv\ *adj* (1650) : relating to, marked by, or involving ascription

as·cus \ˈas-kəs\ *n, pl* **as·ci** \ˈas-ˌkī, -ˌkē, ˈa-ˌsī\ [NL, fr. Gk *askos* wineskin, bladder] (1830) : the membranous oval or tubular spore case of an ascomycete

as·dic \ˈaz-(ˌ)dik\ *n* [fr. *asdics* underwater echo ranging, prob. fr. *A*nti-*S*ubmarine *D*ivision (British Admiralty department 1916–18) + *-ics*] (1939) *chiefly Brit* : SONAR

ASE *abbr* American Stock Exchange

-ase *n suffix* [F, fr. *diastase*] : enzyme ⟨prote*ase*⟩

ASEAN *abbr* Association of Southeast Asian Nations

asep·sis \(ˌ)ā-ˈsep-səs, ə-\ *n* [NL] (1892) **1 :** the condition of being aseptic **2 :** the methods of making or keeping aseptic

asep·tic \(ˌ)ā-ˈsep-tik, ə-\ *adj* [ISV] (ca. 1859) **1 a :** preventing infection ⟨~ techniques⟩ **b :** free or freed from pathogenic microorganisms ⟨an ~ operating room⟩ **2 :** lacking vitality, emotion, or warmth ⟨~ essays⟩ — **asep·ti·cal·ly** \-ti-k(ə-)lē\ *adv*

asex·u·al \(ˌ)ā-ˈsek-sh(ə-)wəl, -shü-əl, -ˈsek-shəl\ *adj* (1830) **1 :** lacking sex or functional sex organs ⟨~ plants⟩ **2 a :** involving or reproducing by reproductive processes (as cell division, spore formation, fission, or budding) that do not involve the union of individuals or gametes ⟨~ reproduction⟩ ⟨an ~ generation⟩ **b :** produced by asexual reproduction ⟨~ spores⟩ **3 :** devoid of sexuality ⟨an ~ relationship⟩ — **asex·u·al·i·ty** \ˌā-ˌsek-shə-ˈwa-lə-tē, -shü-ˈa-\ *n* — **asex·u·al·ly** \(ˌ)ā-ˈsek-sh(ə-)wə-lē, -shü-ə-, -ˌsek-sh(ə-)lē\ *adv*

\ə\ **a**but \ᵊ\ kitt**e**n, F ta**ble** \ər\ f**ur**th**er** \a\ **a**sh \ā\ **a**ce \ä\ m**o**p, m**ar** \au̇\ **ou**t \ch\ **ch**in \e\ b**e**t \ē\ **ea**sy \g\ **g**o \i\ h**i**t \ī\ **i**ce \j\ **j**ob \ŋ\ si**ng** \ō\ g**o** \ȯ\ l**aw** \ȯi\ b**oy** \th\ **th**in \t͟h\ **th**e \ü\ l**oo**t \u̇\ f**oo**t \y\ **y**et \zh\ vi**si**on, bei**ge** \k͟, ⁿ, œ, ue, ʸ\ *see* Guide to Pronunciation

[1]**as far as** *conj* (14c) **:** to the extent or degree that ⟨is safe, *as far as* we know⟩ — often used in expressions like "as far as (something) goes" and "as far as (something) is concerned" to mean "with regard to (something)" ⟨we felt pretty safe *as far as* the fire was concerned —Mark Twain⟩ or in expressions like "as far as (someone) is concerned" to mean "in (someone's) opinion" ⟨*as far as* I'm concerned, it's a mistake⟩
[2]**as far as** *prep* (1523) **:** with regard to **:** CONCERNING ⟨neatly groomed and, *as far as* clothes, casual looking —*N.Y. Times*⟩ ⟨*as far as* being mentioned in the Ten Commandments, I think it is —Billy Graham⟩ — chiefly in oral use
as for *prep* (15c) **:** with regard to **:** CONCERNING ⟨*as for* the others, they'll arrive later⟩
As·gard \ˈas-ˌgärd, ˈaz-\ *n* [ON *āsgarthr*] (1806) **:** the home of the Norse gods
asgd *abbr* assigned
[1]**ash** \ˈash\ *n* [ME *asshe,* fr. OE *æsc;* akin to OHG *ask* ash, L *ornus* mountain ash] (bef. 12c) **1 :** any of a genus (*Fraxinus*) of trees of the olive family with pinnate leaves, thin furrowed bark, and gray branchlets **2 :** the tough elastic wood of an ash **3** [OE *æsc,* name of the corresponding runic letter] **:** the ligature æ used in Old English and some phonetic alphabets to represent a low front vowel \a\

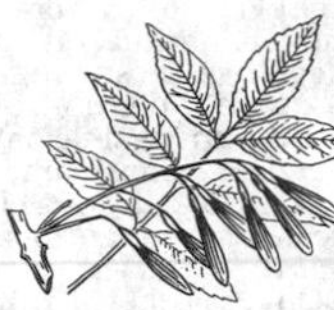
[1]ash 1

[2]**ash** *n, often attrib* [ME *asshe,* fr. OE *asce* — more at ARID] (bef. 12c) **1 :** something that symbolizes grief, repentance, or humiliation **2 a :** the solid residue left when combustible material is thoroughly burned or is oxidized by chemical means **b :** fine particles of mineral matter from a volcanic vent **3** *pl* **:** the remains of the dead human body after cremation or disintegration **4** *pl* **:** deathly pallor ⟨the lip of ~*es* and the cheek of flame —Lord Byron⟩ **5** *pl* **:** RUINS — **ash·less** \-ləs\ *adj*
[3]**ash** *vt* (ca. 1894) **:** to convert into ash
ashamed \ə-ˈshāmd\ *adj* [ME, fr. OE *āscamod,* pp. of *āscamian* to shame, fr. *ā-* (perfective prefix) + *scamian* to shame — more at ABIDE, SHAME] (bef. 12c) **1 a :** feeling shame, guilt, or disgrace **b :** feeling inferior or unworthy **2 :** restrained by anticipation of shame ⟨was ~ to beg⟩ — **asham·ed·ly** \-ˈshā-məd-lē\ *adv*
Ashan·ti \ə-ˈshan-tē, -ˈshän-\ *n, pl* **Ashanti** *or* **Ashantis** [ultim. fr. Twi *asànté*] (1721) **1 :** a member of a people of southern Ghana **2 :** the dialect of Akan spoken by the Ashanti people
ash–blond *or* **ash–blonde** \ˈash-ˈbländ\ *adj* (1865) **:** pale or grayish blond ⟨~ hair⟩
Ash·can \ˈash-ˌkan\ *adj* (1939) **:** of or relating to a group of 20th century American painters who depicted city life realistically ⟨~ school⟩
ash can *n* (1894) **1 :** a metal receptacle for refuse **2** *slang* **:** DEPTH CHARGE
[1]**ash·en** \ˈa-shən\ *adj* (bef. 12c) **:** of, relating to, or made from ash wood
[2]**ashen** *adj* (14c) **:** resembling ashes (as in color); *esp* **:** deathly pale ⟨a face ~ and haggard⟩
Ash·er \ˈa-shər\ *n* [Heb *Āshēr*] (14c) **:** a son of Jacob and the traditional eponymous ancestor of one of the tribes of Israel
ash·fall \ˈash-ˌfȯl\ *n* (1923) **:** a deposit of volcanic ash
Ash·ke·nazi \ˌäsh-kə-ˈnä-zē, ˌash-kə-ˈna-\ *n, pl* **-naz·im** \-ˈnä-zəm, -ˈna-\ [LHeb *Ashkĕnāzī,* fr. *Ashkĕnāz,* medieval rabbinical name for Germany] (1839) **:** a member of one of the two great divisions of Jews comprising the eastern European Yiddish-speaking Jews — compare SEPHARDI — **Ash·ke·naz·ic** \-ˈnä-zik, -ˈna-\ *adj*
ash·lar \ˈash-lər\ *n* [ME *asheler,* fr. AF *aiseler,* fr. OF, traverse beam, fr. *aissele,* dim. of *ais* plank, fr. L *axis,* alter. of *assis*] (14c) **1 :** hewn or squared stone; *also* **:** masonry of such stone **2 :** a thin squared and dressed stone for facing a wall of rubble or brick
ashore \ə-ˈshȯr\ *adv* (ca. 1536) **:** on or to the shore
as how *conj* (1741) **:** THAT ⟨allowed *as how* she was glad to be here⟩
ash·ram \ˈäsh-rəm, -ˌräm; ˈash-ˌram\ *n* [Skt *āśrama,* fr. *śrama* religious exercise] (1917) **1 :** a secluded dwelling of a Hindu sage; *also* **:** the group of disciples instructed there **2 :** a religious retreat
Ash·to·reth \ˈash-tə-ˌreth\ *n* [Heb *ʿAshtōreth*] (1855) **:** ASTARTE
ash·tray \ˈash-ˌtrā\ *n* (1876) **:** a receptacle for tobacco ashes and for cigar and cigarette butts
Ashur \ˈä-ˌshu̇r\ *n* [Akkadian *Ashūr*] (1589) **:** the chief deity of the Assyrians
Ash Wednesday *n* (14c) **:** the first day of Lent — see EASTER table
ashy \ˈa-shē\ *adj* **ash·i·er; -est** (14c) **1 :** of or relating to ashes **2 :** ASHEN
ASI *abbr* airspeed indicator
Asi·a·go \ˌä-zhē-ˈä-(ˌ)gō, ˌä-sē, -shē-\ *n* [*Asiago,* town in Italy] (1938) **:** a pungent hard yellow cheese of Italian origin suitable for grating
[1]**Asian** \ˈā-zhən *also* -shən\ *adj* (1550) **:** of, relating to, or characteristic of the continent of Asia or its people
[2]**Asian** *n* (1555) **1 :** a native or inhabitant of Asia **2 :** a person of Asian descent
Asian–Amer·i·can \-ə-ˈmer-ə-kən\ *n* (1973) **:** an American of Asian descent — **Asian–American** *adj*
Asian elephant *n* (1818) **:** ELEPHANT 1b
Asian flu *n* (1957) **:** influenza that is caused by a subtype (H2N2) of the orthomyxovirus causing influenza A and that was responsible for about 70,000 deaths in the U.S. in the influenza pandemic of 1957–58 — called also *Asian influenza*
Asian pear *n* (1983) **:** any of various pears chiefly of Japanese and Chinese origin that have crisp juicy flesh, usu. resemble an apple in shape, and typically have yellow, brown, or green skin
Asian tiger mosquito *n* (1986) **:** a black-and-white striped Asian mosquito (*Aedes albopictus*) that is a vector of several diseases (as dengue) and has been introduced into the U.S.
Asi·at·ic \ˌā-zhē-ˈa-tik, -zē-\ *adj* (1602) *sometimes offensive* **:** ASIAN — **Asiatic** *n, sometimes offensive*
Asiatic cholera *n* (1831) **:** cholera of Asian origin that is caused by virulent strains of the cholera vibrio (*Vibrio cholerae*)
Asiatic elephant *n* (1803) **:** ELEPHANT 1b
[1]**aside** \ə-ˈsīd\ *adv* (14c) **1 :** to or toward the side ⟨stepped ~⟩ **2 :** away from others or into privacy ⟨pulled him ~⟩ **3 :** out of the way esp. for future use **:** AWAY ⟨putting ~ savings⟩ **4 :** away from one's thought or consideration ⟨jesting ~⟩
[2]**aside** *prep* (1592) *obs* **:** BEYOND, PAST
[3]**aside** *n* (ca. 1751) **1 :** an utterance meant to be inaudible to someone; *esp* **:** an actor's speech heard by the audience but supposedly not by other characters **2 :** a straying from the theme **:** DIGRESSION
aside from *prep* (1818) **1 :** in addition to **:** BESIDES **2 :** EXCEPT FOR
as if *conj* (13c) **1 :** as it would be if ⟨it was *as if* he had lost his last friend⟩ **2 :** as one would do if ⟨he ran *as if* ghosts were chasing him⟩ **3 :** THAT ⟨it seemed *as if* the day would never end⟩
as·i·nine \ˈa-sə-ˌnīn\ *adj* [L *asininus,* fr. *asinus* ass] (15c) **1 :** extremely or utterly foolish ⟨an ~ excuse⟩ **2 :** of, relating to, or resembling an ass ***syn*** see SIMPLE — **as·i·nine·ly** *adv* — **as·i·nin·i·ty** \ˌa-sə-ˈni-nə-tē\ *n*
ask \ˈask, ˈäsk; *dial* ˈaks\ *vb* **asked** \ˈas(k)t, ˈäs(k)t, ˈask; *dial* ˈakst\; **ask·ing** [ME, fr. OE *āscian;* akin to OHG *eiscōn* to ask, Lith *ieškoti* to seek, Skt *icchati* he seeks] *vt* (bef. 12c) **1 a :** to call on for an answer ⟨she ~*ed* him about his trip⟩ **b :** to put a question about ⟨~*ing* her whereabouts⟩ **c :** SPEAK, UTTER ⟨~ a question⟩ **2 a :** to make a request of ⟨she ~*ed* her teacher for help⟩ **b :** to make a request for ⟨she ~*ed* help from her teacher⟩ **3 :** to call for **:** REQUIRE ⟨a challenge that will ~ much of us⟩ **4 :** to set as a price ⟨~*ed* $3000 for the car⟩ **5 :** INVITE ~ *vi* **1 :** to seek information **2 :** to make a request ⟨~*ed* for food⟩ **3 :** LOOK — often used in the phrase *ask for trouble* — **ask·er** *n*
syn ASK, QUESTION, INTERROGATE, QUERY, INQUIRE mean to address a person in order to gain information. ASK implies no more than the putting of a question ⟨*ask* for directions⟩. QUESTION usu. suggests the asking of series of questions ⟨*questioned* them about every detail of the trip⟩. INTERROGATE suggests formal or official systematic questioning ⟨the prosecutor *interrogated* the witness all day⟩. QUERY implies a desire for authoritative information or confirmation ⟨*queried* a librarian about the book⟩. INQUIRE implies a searching for facts or for truth often specifically by asking questions ⟨began to *inquire* of friends and teachers what career she should pursue⟩.
syn ASK, REQUEST, SOLICIT mean to seek to obtain by making one's wants known. ASK implies no more than the statement of the desire ⟨*ask* a favor of a friend⟩. REQUEST implies greater formality and courtesy ⟨*requests* the pleasure of your company⟩. SOLICIT suggests a calling attention to one's wants or desires by public announcement or advertisement ⟨a letter *soliciting* information⟩.
askance \ə-ˈskan(t)s\ *also* **askant** \-ˈskant\ *adv* [origin unknown] (ca. 1530) **1 :** with a side-glance **:** OBLIQUELY **2 :** with disapproval or distrust **:** SCORNFULLY ⟨they eyed the stranger ~⟩
askesis *var of* ASCESIS
askew \ə-ˈskyü\ *adv or adj* [prob. fr. [1]*a-* + *skew*] (1567) **:** out of line **:** AWRY ⟨the picture hung ~⟩ — **askew·ness** *n*
asking price *n* (1755) **:** the price at which something is offered for sale
ASL *abbr* American Sign Language
[1]**aslant** \ə-ˈslant\ *adv or adj* (14c) **:** in a slanting direction **:** OBLIQUELY
[2]**aslant** *prep* (1596) **:** over or across in a slanting direction
[1]**asleep** \ə-ˈslēp\ *adj* [ME *aslepe,* fr. OE *on slæpe*] (13c) **1 :** being in a state of sleep **2 :** DEAD **3 :** lacking sensation **:** NUMB **4 a :** INACTIVE, DORMANT **b :** not alert **:** INDIFFERENT
[2]**asleep** *adv* (13c) **1 :** into a state of sleep **2 :** into the sleep of death **3 :** into a state of inactivity, sluggishness, or indifference
as long as *conj* (15c) **1 :** provided that ⟨can do as they like *as long as* they have a B average⟩ **2 :** INASMUCH AS, SINCE ⟨*as long as* you're going, I'll go too⟩
aslope \ə-ˈslōp\ *adj or adv* (14c) **:** being in a sloping or slanting position or direction
aso·cial \(ˌ)ā-ˈsō-shəl\ *adj* (1883) **:** not social: as **a :** rejecting or lacking the capacity for social interaction **b :** ANTISOCIAL
as of *prep* (1900) **:** ON, AT, FROM — used to indicate a time or date at which something begins or ends ⟨takes effect *as of* July 1⟩
[1]**asp** \ˈasp\ *n* [ME, fr. OE *æspe*] (bef. 12c) **:** ASPEN
[2]**asp** *n* [ME *aspis,* fr. L, fr. Gk] (14c) **:** a small venomous snake of Egypt usu. held to be a cobra (*Naja haje*)
as·par·a·gine \ə-ˈsper-ə-ˌjēn, -ˈspa-rə-\ *n* [F, fr. L *asparagus*] (1813) **:** a nonessential amino acid $C_4H_8N_2O_3$ that is an amide of aspartic acid
as·par·a·gus \ə-ˈsper-ə-gəs, -ˈspa-rə-\ *n, pl* **-gus** [NL, genus name, fr. L, asparagus plant, fr. Gk *asparagos;* perh. akin to Gk *spargan* to swell] (1545) **:** any of a genus (*Asparagus*) of Old World perennial plants of the lily family having much-branched stems, minute scalelike leaves, and narrow usu. filiform branchlets that function as leaves; *esp* **:** one (*A. officinalis*) widely cultivated for its edible young shoots
as·par·tame \ˈas-pər-ˌtām, ə-ˈspär-ˌtām\ *n* [*aspart*ic acid + phenyl*ala*nine + *m*ethyl + *e*ster] (1972) **:** a crystalline compound $C_{14}H_{18}N_2O_5$ that is a diamide synthesized from phenylalanine and aspartic acid and that is used as a low-calorie sweetener
as·par·tate \ə-ˈspär-ˌtāt\ *n* (1863) **:** a salt or ester of aspartic acid
as·par·tic acid \ə-ˈspär-tik-\ *n* [ISV, irreg. fr. L *asparagus*] (1863) **:** a crystalline amino acid $C_4H_7NO_4$ found esp. in plants
ASPCA *abbr* American Society for the Prevention of Cruelty to Animals
as·pect \ˈas-ˌpekt\ *n* [ME, fr. L *aspectus,* fr. *aspicere* to look at, fr. *ad-* + *specere* to look — more at SPY] (14c) **1 a :** the position of planets or stars with respect to one another held by astrologers to influence human affairs; *also* **:** the apparent position (as conjunction) of a body in the solar system with respect to the sun **b :** a position facing a particular direction **:** EXPOSURE ⟨the house has a southern ~⟩ **c :** the manner of presentation of a plane to a fluid through which it is moving or to a current **2 a** (1) **:** appearance to the eye or mind (2) **:** a particular appearance of the face **:** MIEN **b :** a particular status or phase in which something appears or may be regarded ⟨studied every ~ of the question⟩ **3** *archaic* **:** an act of looking **:** GAZE **4 a :** the nature of the action of a verb as to its beginning, duration, completion, or repetition and without reference to its position in time **b :** a set of inflected verb forms that indicate aspect — **as·pec·tu·al** \a-ˈspek-chə(-wə)l, -chü(-ə)l\ *adj*

aspect ratio *n* (1907) **:** a ratio of one dimension to another: as **a :** the ratio of span to mean chord of an airfoil **b :** the ratio of the width of a television or motion-picture image to its height

as·pen \ˈas-pən\ *n* [ME, of an aspen, fr. *asp* aspen, fr. OE *æspe;* akin to OHG *aspa* aspen, Russ *osina*] (1593) **:** any of several poplars (esp. *Populus tremula* of Europe and *P. tremuloides* and *P. grandidentata* of No. America) with leaves that flutter in the lightest wind because of their flattened petioles

as per \ˈaz-ˌpər\ *prep* (1782) **:** in accordance with **:** ACCORDING TO ⟨*as per* your instructions⟩ — **as per usual :** as usual

As·per·ger's syndrome \ˈäs-ˌpər-gərz-\ *n* [Hans *Asperger* †1980 Austrian pediatrician] (1989) **:** a developmental disorder resembling autism that is characterized by impaired social interaction, by restricted and repetitive behaviors and activities, and by normal language and cognitive development — called also *Asperger's disorder*

as·per·ges \ə-ˈspər-(ˌ)jēz\ *n* [L, thou wilt sprinkle, fr. *aspergere*] (ca. 1587) **:** a ceremony of sprinkling altar and people with holy water

as·per·gil·lo·sis \ˌas-pər-(ˌ)ji-ˈlō-səs\ *n, pl* **-lo·ses** \-ˌsēz\ (1898) **:** infection with or disease caused (as in poultry) by aspergillus molds

as·per·gil·lum \ˌas-pər-ˈji-ləm\ *n, pl* **-la** \-lə\ *or* **-lums** [NL, fr. L *aspergere*] (1649) **:** a brush or small perforated container with a handle that is used for sprinkling holy water in a liturgical service

as·per·gil·lus \-ˈji-ləs\ *n, pl* **-gil·li** \-ˈji-ˌlī\ [NL, genus name, fr. *aspergillum*] (1862) **:** any of a genus (*Aspergillus*) of ascomycetous fungi with branched radiate sporophores including many common molds

as·per·i·ty \a-ˈsper-ə-tē, ə-, -ˈspe-rə-\ *n, pl* **-ties** [ME *asprete,* fr. AF *aspreté,* fr. *aspre* rough, fr. L *asper,* fr. OL **absperos,* fr. *ab-* ab- + *-speros;* akin to Skt *apasphura* repelling, L *spernere* to spurn — more at SPURN] (13c) **1 :** RIGOR, SEVERITY **2 a :** roughness of surface **:** UNEVENNESS; *also* **:** a tiny projection from a surface **b :** roughness of sound **3 :** roughness of manner or of temper **:** HARSHNESS ⟨asked with some ~ just what they were implying⟩

as·perse \ə-ˈspərs, a-\ *vt* **as·persed; as·pers·ing** [L *aspersus,* pp. of *aspergere,* fr. *ad-* + *spargere* to scatter — more at SPARK] (15c) **1 :** SPRINKLE; *esp* **:** to sprinkle with holy water **2 :** to attack with evil reports or false or injurious charges ***syn*** see MALIGN

as·per·sion \ə-ˈspər-zhən, -shən\ *n* (ca. 1587) **1 :** a sprinkling with water esp. in religious ceremonies **2 a :** a false or misleading charge meant to harm someone's reputation ⟨cast ~*s* on her integrity⟩ **b :** the act of making such a charge **:** DEFAMATION

[1]**as·phalt** \ˈas-ˌfȯlt *also* ˈash-, *esp Brit* -ˌfalt\ *also* **as·phal·tum** \as-ˈfȯl-təm, *esp Brit* -ˈfal-\ *n* [ME *aspalt,* fr. LL *aspaltus,* fr. Gk *asphaltos*] (14c) **1 :** a dark bituminous substance that is found in natural beds and is also obtained as a residue in petroleum refining and that consists chiefly of hydrocarbons **2 :** an asphaltic composition used for pavements and as a waterproof cement — **as·phal·tic** \as-ˈfȯl-tik, *esp Brit* -ˈfal-\ *adj*

[2]**asphalt** *vt* (ca. 1859) **:** to cover with asphalt **:** PAVE 1

asphalt jungle *n* (1920) **:** a big city or a specified part of a big city

aspher·ic \(ˌ)ā-ˈsfir-ik, -ˈsfer-\ *or* **aspher·i·cal** \-i-kəl\ *adj* (ca. 1922) **:** departing slightly from the spherical form esp. in order to correct for spherical aberration ⟨an ~ lens⟩

as·pho·del \ˈas-fə-ˌdel\ *n* [L *asphodelus,* fr. Gk *asphodelos*] (1597) **:** any of various Old World herbs (esp. genera *Asphodelus* and *Asphodeline*) of the lily family with flowers in usu. long erect racemes

as·phyx·ia \as-ˈfik-sē-ə, əs-\ *n* [NL, fr. Gk, stopping of the pulse, fr. *a-* + *sphyzein* to throb] (1778) **:** a lack of oxygen or excess of carbon dioxide in the body that results in unconsciousness and often death and is usu. caused by interruption of breathing or inadequate oxygen supply

as·phyx·i·ate \-sē-ˌāt\ *vb* **-at·ed; -at·ing** *vt* (1836) **:** to cause asphyxia in ~ *vi* **:** to become asphyxiated — **as·phyx·i·a·tion** \-ˌfik-sē-ˈā-shən\ *n*

[1]**as·pic** \ˈas-pik\ *n* [MF, alter. of *aspe,* fr. L *aspis*] (1530) *obs* **:** [2]ASP

[2]**aspic** *n* [F, lit., asp] (1789) **:** a clear savory jelly (as of fish or meat stock) used as a garnish or to make a meat, fish, or vegetable mold

as·pi·dis·tra \ˌas-pə-ˈdis-trə\ *n* [NL, irreg. fr. Gk *aspid-, aspis* shield] (1822) **:** an Asian plant (*Aspidistra elatior*) of the lily family that has large pointed basal leaves and is often grown as a foliage plant

[1]**as·pi·rant** \ˈas-p(ə-)rənt, ə-ˈspī-rənt\ *n* (1738) **:** one who aspires ⟨presidential ~*s*⟩

[2]**aspirant** *adj* (1800) **:** seeking to attain a desired position or status ⟨the pilot was an ~ astronaut⟩

[1]**as·pi·rate** \ˈas-p(ə-)rət\ *n* (1617) **1 :** an independent sound \h\ or a character (as the letter *h*) representing it **2 :** a consonant having aspiration as its final component ⟨in English the \p\ of *pit* is an ~⟩ **3 :** material removed by aspiration

[2]**as·pi·rate** \ˈas-pə-ˌrāt\ *vt* **-rat·ed; -rat·ing** [L *aspiratus,* pp. of *aspirare*] (ca. 1700) **1 :** to pronounce (a vowel or a consonant) with aspiration (sense 1a) **2 a :** to draw by suction **b :** to remove (as blood) by aspiration **c :** to take into the lungs by aspiration

as·pi·ra·tion \ˌas-pə-ˈrā-shən\ *n* (14c) **1 a :** audible breath that accompanies or comprises a speech sound **b :** the pronunciation or addition of an aspiration; *also* **:** the symbol of an aspiration **2 :** a drawing of something in, out, up, or through by or as if by suction: as **a :** the act of breathing and esp. of breathing in **b :** the withdrawal of fluid or tissue from the body **c :** the taking of foreign matter into the lungs with the respiratory current **3 a :** a strong desire to achieve something high or great **b :** an object of such desire ***syn*** see AMBITION — **as·pi·ra·tion·al** \-ˈrā-sh(ə-)nəl\ *adj*

as·pi·ra·tor \ˈas-pə-ˌrā-tər\ *n* (1804) **:** an apparatus for producing suction or moving or collecting materials by suction; *esp* **:** a hollow tubular instrument connected with a partial vacuum and used to remove fluid or tissue or foreign bodies from the body

as·pire \ə-ˈspī(-ə)r\ *vi* **as·pired; as·pir·ing** [ME, fr. MF or L; MF *aspirer,* fr. L *aspirare,* lit., to breathe upon, fr. *ad-* + *spirare* to breathe] (14c) **1 :** to seek to attain or accomplish a particular goal ⟨*aspired* to a career in medicine⟩ **2 :** ASCEND, SOAR — **as·pir·er** *n*

as·pi·rin \ˈas-p(ə-)rən\ *n, pl* **aspirin** *or* **aspirins** [ISV, fr. acetyl + *spiraeic* acid (former name of salicylic acid), fr. NL *Spiraea,* genus of shrubs — more at SPIREA] (1899) **1 :** a white crystalline derivative $C_9H_8O_4$ of salicylic acid used for relief of pain and fever **2 :** a tablet of aspirin

ASR *abbr* **1** airport surveillance radar **2** air-sea rescue

as regards *also* **as respects** *prep* (1633) **:** in regard to **:** with respect to ⟨*as regards* our previous discussion⟩

[1]**ass** \ˈas\ *n* [ME, fr. OE *assa,* prob. fr. OIr *asan,* fr. L *asinus*] (bef. 12c) **1 :** any of several hardy gregarious African or Asian perissodactyl mammals (genus *Equus*) smaller than the horse and having long ears; *esp* **:** an African mammal (*E. asinus*) that is the ancestor of the donkey **2** *sometimes vulgar* **:** a stupid, obstinate, or perverse person ⟨made an ~ of himself⟩ — often compounded with a preceding adjective ⟨don't be a smart-*ass*⟩

[2]**ass** \ˈas\ *or* **arse** \ˈas, ˈärs\ *n* [ME *ars, ers,* fr. OE *ærs, ears;* akin to OHG & ON *ars* buttocks, Gk *orrhos* buttocks, *oura* tail] (bef. 12c) **1 a** *often vulgar* **:** BUTTOCKS — often used in emphatic reference to a specific person ⟨get your ~ over here⟩ ⟨saved my ~⟩ **b** *often vulgar* **:** ANUS **2** *usu vulgar* **:** SEXUAL INTERCOURSE

[3]**ass** *adv* [[2]*ass*] (ca. 1920) *often vulgar* — used as a postpositive intensive esp. with words of derogatory implication ⟨fancy-*ass*⟩

as·sai \ä-ˈsī\ *adv* [It, fr. VL **ad satis* enough — more at ASSET] (ca. 1724) **:** VERY — used with tempo direction in music ⟨allegro ~⟩

as·sail \ə-ˈsāl\ *vt* [ME, fr. AF *assaillir,* fr. VL **assalire,* alter. of L *assilire* to leap upon, fr. *ad-* + *salire* to leap — more at SALLY] (13c) **:** to attack violently with blows or words ***syn*** see ATTACK — **as·sail·able** \-ˈsā-lə-bəl\ *adj* — **as·sail·ant** \-ˈsā-lənt\ *n*

As·sam \ə-ˈsam, a-\ *n* [*Assam,* India] (1842) **:** a black tea grown in northeastern India

As·sam·ese \ˌa-sə-ˈmēz, -ˈmēs\ *n, pl* **Assamese** (1826) **1 :** a native or inhabitant of Assam, India **2 :** the Indo-Aryan language of Assam — **Assamese** *adj*

as·sas·sin \ə-ˈsa-sᵊn\ *n* [ML *assassinus,* fr. Ar *ḥashshāshīn,* pl. of *ḥashshāsh* worthless person, lit., hashish user, fr. *hashīsh* hashish] (ca. 1520) **1** *cap* **:** a member of a Shia Muslim sect who at the time of the Crusades was sent out on a suicidal mission to murder prominent enemies **2 :** a person who commits murder; *esp* **:** one who murders a politically important person either for hire or from fanatical motives

as·sas·si·nate \ə-ˈsa-sə-ˌnāt\ *vt* **-nat·ed; -nat·ing** (1607) **1 :** to injure or destroy unexpectedly and treacherously **2 :** to murder (a usu. prominent person) by sudden or secret attack often for political reasons ***syn*** see KILL — **as·sas·si·na·tion** \-ˌsa-sə-ˈnā-shən\ *n* — **as·sas·si·na·tor** \-ˈsa-sə-ˌnā-tər\ *n*

assassin bug *n* (1895) **:** any of a family (Reduviidae) of bugs that are usu. predatory on insects though some (as a kissing bug) suck the blood of mammals — called also *reduviid*

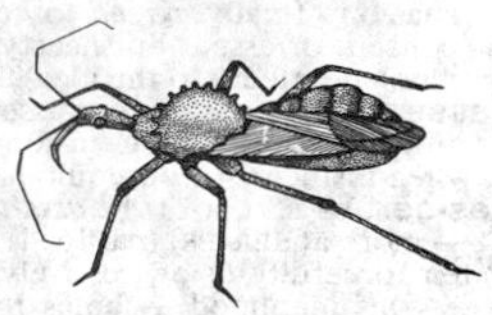

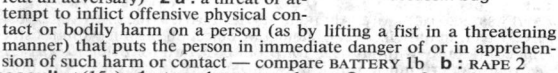

assassin bug

[1]**as·sault** \ə-ˈsȯlt\ *n* [ME *assaut,* fr. AF, fr. VL **assaltus,* fr. *assalire*] (14c) **1 a :** a violent physical or verbal attack **b :** a military attack usu. involving direct combat with enemy forces **c :** a concerted effort (as to reach a goal or defeat an adversary) **2 a :** a threat or attempt to inflict offensive physical contact or bodily harm on a person (as by lifting a fist in a threatening manner) that puts the person in immediate danger of or in apprehension of such harm or contact — compare BATTERY 1b **b :** RAPE 2

[2]**assault** *vt* (15c) **1 :** to make an assault on **2 :** RAPE 2 ~ *vi* **:** to make an assault ***syn*** see ATTACK — **as·sault·er** *n*

assault boat *n* (1941) **:** a small portable boat used in an amphibious military attack or in land warfare for crossing rivers or lakes

as·sault·ive \ə-ˈsȯl-tiv\ *adj* (1946) **1 :** of, relating to, or tending toward assault ⟨~ behavior⟩ **2 :** having an intense or abrasive effect on the senses or emotions ⟨loud and ~ music⟩ — **as·sault·ive·ly** *adv* — **as·sault·ive·ness** *n*

assault rifle *n* (1972) **:** any of various automatic or semiautomatic rifles with large capacity magazines designed for military use

assault weapon *n* (1973) **:** any of various automatic or semiautomatic firearms; *esp* **:** ASSAULT RIFLE

[1]**as·say** \ˈa-ˌsā, a-ˈsā\ *n* [ME, fr. AF *assai, essai* — more at ESSAY] (14c) **1** *archaic* **:** TRIAL, ATTEMPT **2 :** examination and determination as to characteristics (as weight, measure, or quality) **3 :** analysis (as of an ore or drug) to determine the presence, absence, or quantity of one or more components; *also* **:** a test used in this analysis **4 :** a substance to be assayed; *also* **:** the tabulated result of assaying

[2]**as·say** \a-ˈsā, ˈa-ˌsā\ *vt* (14c) **1 :** TRY, ATTEMPT **2 a :** to analyze (as an ore) for one or more specific components **b :** to judge the worth of **:** ESTIMATE ~ *vi* **:** to prove up in an assay — **as·say·er** *n*

assed \ˈast\ *adv* (1923) *often vulgar* **:** [3]ASS — used in combination ⟨sorry-*assed* state of affairs⟩

as·se·gai *or* **as·sa·gai** \ˈa-si-ˌgī\ *n* [ultim. fr. Ar *al-zaghāya* the assegai, fr. *al-* the + Berber *zaghāya* spear] (1600) **:** a slender hardwood spear or light javelin usu. tipped with iron and used in southern Africa

as·sem·blage \ə-ˈsem-blij, *for 3 also* ˌa-ˌsäm-ˈbläzh\ *n* (1690) **1 :** a collection of persons or things **:** GATHERING **2 :** the act of assembling **:** the state of being assembled **3 a :** an artistic composition made from scraps, junk, and odds and ends (as of paper, cloth, wood, stone, or metal) **b :** the art of making assemblages

as·sem·blag·ist \-bli-jist, -ˈblä-zhist\ *n* (1965) **:** an artist who specializes in assemblages

as·sem·ble \ə-ˈsem-bəl\ *vb* **as·sem·bled; as·sem·bling** \-b(ə-)liŋ\ [ME, fr. AF *assembler,* fr. VL **assimulare,* fr. L *ad-* + *simul* together — more at SAME] *vt* (13c) **1 :** to bring together (as in a particular place or for a particular purpose) **2 :** to fit together the parts of ~ *vi* **:** to meet together **:** CONVENE ***syn*** see GATHER

as·sem·bler \-b(ə-)lər\ *n* (1616) **1 :** one that assembles **2 a :** a computer program that automatically converts instructions written in assembly language into machine language **b :** ASSEMBLY LANGUAGE

as·sem·bly \ə-ˈsem-blē\ *n, pl* **-blies** [ME *assemblee,* fr. AF, fr. *assembler*] (14c) **1 :** a company of persons gathered for deliberation and leg-

\ə\ **abut** \ᵊ\ kitten, F table \ər\ **further** \a\ **ash** \ā\ **ace** \ä\ **mop, mar** \au̇\ **out** \ch\ **chin** \e\ **bet** \ē\ **easy** \g\ **go** \i\ **hit** \ī\ **ice** \j\ **job** \ŋ\ **sing** \ō\ **go** \ȯ\ **law** \ȯi\ **boy** \th\ **thin** \t͟h\ **the** \ü\ **loot** \u̇\ **foot** \y\ **yet** \zh\ **vision, beige** \k̲, ⁿ, œ, ue, ʸ\ *see* Guide to Pronunciation

islation, worship, or entertainment **2** *cap* **:** a legislative body; *specif* **:** the lower house of a legislature **3 :** a meeting of a student body and usu. faculty for administrative, educational, or recreational purposes **4 a :** ASSEMBLAGE 1 **b :** ASSEMBLAGE 2 **5 :** a signal for troops to assemble or fall in **6 a :** the fitting together of manufactured parts into a complete machine, structure, or unit of a machine **b :** a collection of parts so assembled **7 :** the translation of assembly language to machine language by an assembler

assembly language *n* (ca. 1964) **:** a programming language that consists of instructions that are mnemonic codes for corresponding machine language instructions

as·sem·bly–line \ə-ˈsem-blē-ˌlīn\ *adj* (1939) **:** made by or as if by an assembly line; *esp* **:** lacking originality or creativity ⟨bored by the novel's ~ plot⟩

assembly line *n* (1914) **1 :** an arrangement of machines, equipment, and workers in which work passes from operation to operation in direct line until the product is assembled **2 :** a process for turning out a finished product in a mechanically efficient manner ⟨academic *assembly lines*⟩

as·sem·bly·man \ə-ˈsem-blē-mən\ *n* (1647) **:** a member of an assembly

Assembly of God (1952) **:** a congregation belonging to a Pentecostal body founded in the U.S. in 1914

as·sem·bly·wom·an \-ˌwu̇-mən\ *n* (1869) **:** a woman who is a member of an assembly

1**as·sent** \ə-ˈsent, a-\ *vi* [ME, fr. AF *assentir, assenter,* fr. L *assentari,* fr. *assentire,* fr. *ad-* + *sentire* to feel — more at SENSE] (14c) **:** to agree to something esp. after thoughtful consideration **:** CONCUR — **as·sen·tor** *or* **as·sent·er** \-ˈsen-tər\ *n*

syn ASSENT, CONSENT, ACCEDE, ACQUIESCE, AGREE, SUBSCRIBE mean to concur with what has been proposed. ASSENT implies an act involving the understanding or judgment and applies to propositions or opinions ⟨voters *assented* to the proposal⟩. CONSENT involves the will or feelings and indicates compliance with what is requested or desired ⟨*consented* to their daughter's going⟩. ACCEDE implies a yielding, often under pressure, of assent or consent ⟨officials *acceded* to the prisoners' demands⟩. ACQUIESCE implies tacit acceptance or forbearance of opposition ⟨*acquiesced* to his boss's wishes⟩. AGREE sometimes implies previous difference of opinion or attempts at persuasion ⟨finally *agreed* to come along⟩. SUBSCRIBE implies not only consent or assent but hearty approval and active support ⟨*subscribes* wholeheartedly to the idea⟩.

2**assent** *n* (14c) **:** an act of assenting **:** ACQUIESCENCE, AGREEMENT

as·sen·ta·tion \ˌa-sᵊn-ˈtā-shən, ˌa-ˌsen-\ *n* (15c) **:** ready assent esp. when insincere or obsequious

as·sert \ə-ˈsərt, a-\ *vt* [L *assertus,* pp. of *asserere,* fr. *ad-* + *serere* to join — more at SERIES] (ca. 1604) **1 :** to state or declare positively and often forcefully or aggressively **2 a :** to demonstrate the existence of ⟨~ his manhood —James Joyce⟩ **b :** POSIT, POSTULATE — **assert oneself :** to speak or act in a manner that compels recognition esp. of one's rights

syn ASSERT, DECLARE, AFFIRM, PROTEST, AVOW mean to state positively usu. in anticipation of denial or objection. ASSERT implies stating confidently without need for proof or regard for evidence ⟨*asserted* that modern music is just noise⟩. DECLARE stresses open or public statement ⟨*declared* her support for the candidate⟩. AFFIRM implies conviction based on evidence, experience, or faith ⟨*affirmed* the existence of an afterlife⟩. PROTEST emphasizes affirming in the face of denial or doubt ⟨*protested* that he really had been misquoted⟩. AVOW stresses frank declaration and acknowledgment of personal responsibility for what is declared ⟨*avowed* that all investors would be repaid in full⟩. ***syn*** see in addition MAINTAIN

as·sert·ed·ly \ə-ˈsər-təd-lē, a-\ *adv* (1937) **:** by positive and usu. unsubstantiated assertion **:** ALLEGEDLY

as·ser·tion \ə-ˈsər-shən, a-\ *n* (15c) **:** the act of asserting; *also* **:** DECLARATION, AFFIRMATION

as·ser·tive \ə-ˈsər-tiv, a-\ *adj* (ca. 1619) **1 :** disposed to or characterized by bold or confident assertion ⟨an ~ leader⟩ **2 :** having a strong or distinctive flavor or aroma ⟨~ wines⟩ ***syn*** see AGGRESSIVE — **as·ser·tive·ly** *adv* — **as·ser·tive·ness** *n*

assertiveness training *n* (1975) **:** a method of training individuals to act in a bold self-confident manner

asses *pl of* AS *or of* ASS

as·sess \ə-ˈses, a-\ *vt* [ME, prob. fr. ML *assessus,* pp. of *assidēre,* fr. L, to sit beside, assist in the office of a judge — more at ASSIZE] (15c) **1 :** to determine the rate or amount of (as a tax) **2 a :** to impose (as a tax) according to an established rate **b :** to subject to a tax, charge, or levy **3 :** to make an official valuation of (property) for the purposes of taxation **4 :** to determine the importance, size, or value of ⟨~ a problem⟩ **5 :** to charge (a player or team) with a foul or penalty ***syn*** see ESTIMATE — **as·sess·able** \-ˈse-sə-bəl\ *adj*

as·sess·ment \ə-ˈses-mənt, a-\ *n* (1534) **1 :** the action or an instance of assessing **:** APPRAISAL **2 :** the amount assessed

as·ses·sor \ə-ˈse-sər\ *n* (14c) **1 :** an official who assists a judge or magistrate **2 :** one that assesses; *esp* **:** an official who assesses property for taxation

as·set \ˈa-ˌset *also* -sət\ *n* [back-formation fr. *assets,* sing., sufficient property to pay debts and legacies, fr. AF *assetz,* fr. *asez* enough, fr. VL **ad satis,* fr. L *ad* to + *satis* enough — more at AT, SAD] (1531) **1** *pl* **a :** the property of a deceased person subject by law to the payment of his or her debts and legacies **b :** the entire property of a person, association, corporation, or estate applicable or subject to the payment of debts **2 :** ADVANTAGE, RESOURCE ⟨his wit is his chief ~⟩ **3 a :** an item of value owned **b** *pl* **:** the items on a balance sheet showing the book value of property owned **4 :** something useful in an effort to foil or defeat an enemy: as **a :** a piece of military equipment **b :** SPY

as·sev·er·ate \ə-ˈse-və-ˌrāt\ *vt* **-at·ed; -at·ing** [L *asseveratus,* pp. of *asseverare,* fr. *ad-* + *severus* severe] (1749) **:** to affirm or declare positively or earnestly ⟨he always *asseverated* that he did not know —G. K. Chesterton⟩ — **as·sev·er·a·tion** \-ˌse-və-ˈrā-shən\ *n* — **as·sev·er·a·tive** \-ˈse-və-ˌrā-tiv\ *adj*

ass·hole \ˈas-ˌ(h)ōl\ *n* (14c) **1** *usu vulgar* **:** ANUS **2 a** *usu vulgar* **:** a stupid, incompetent, or detestable person **b** *usu vulgar* **:** the worst place — used in phrases like *asshole of the world*

as·si·du·ity \ˌa-sə-ˈdü-ə-tē, -ˈdyü-\ *n, pl* **-ities** (1596) **1 :** the quality or state of being assiduous **:** DILIGENCE **2 :** persistent personal attention — usu. used in pl.

as·sid·u·ous \ə-ˈsij-wəs, -ˈsi-jə-\ *adj* [L *assiduus,* fr. *assidēre*] (1622) **:** marked by careful unremitting attention or persistent application ⟨an ~ book collector⟩ ⟨tended her garden with ~ attention⟩ ***syn*** see BUSY — **as·sid·u·ous·ly** *adv* — **as·sid·u·ous·ness** *n*

1**as·sign** \ə-ˈsīn\ *vt* [ME, fr. AF *assigner,* fr. L *assignare,* fr. *ad-* + *signare* to mark, fr. *signum* mark, sign] (13c) **1 :** to transfer (property) to another esp. in trust or for the benefit of creditors **2 a :** to appoint to a post or duty ⟨~*ed* them to light duty⟩ ⟨~*ed* me two clerks⟩ **b :** to appoint as a duty or task ⟨~*s* 20 pages for homework⟩ **3 :** to fix or specify in correspondence or relationship ⟨~ counsel to the defendant⟩ ⟨~ a value to the variable⟩ **4 a :** to ascribe as a motive, reason, or cause esp. after deliberation **b :** to consider to belong to (a specified period of time) ***syn*** see ASCRIBE — **as·sign·abil·i·ty** \-ˌsī-nə-ˈbi-lə-tē\ *n* — **as·sign·able** \-ˈsī-nə-bəl\ *adj* — **as·sign·er** \ə-ˈsī-nər\ *or* **as·sign·or** \ˌa-sə-ˈnȯr, ˌa-ˌsī-, ə-ˌsī-\ *n*

2**assign** *n* (15c) **:** ASSIGNEE 3 ⟨heirs and ~*s*⟩

as·si·gnat \ˌa-(ˌ)sēn-ˈyä, ˈa-sig-ˌnat\ *n* [F, fr. L *assignatus,* pp. of *assignare*] (1790) **:** a bill issued as currency by the French Revolutionary government (1789–96) on the security of expropriated lands

as·sig·na·tion \ˌa-sig-ˈnā-shən\ *n* (15c) **1 :** the act of assigning or the assignment made **2 :** an appointment of time and place for a meeting; *esp* **:** TRYST ⟨returned from an ~ with his mistress —W. B. Yeats⟩

assigned risk *n* (1946) **:** a poor risk (as an accident-prone motorist) that insurance companies would normally reject but are forced to insure by state law

as·sign·ee \ˌa-sə-ˈnē, ˌa-ˌsī-, ə-ˌsī-\ *n* (14c) **1 :** a person to whom an assignment is made **2 :** a person appointed to act for another **3 :** a person to whom a right or property is legally transferred

as·sign·ment \ə-ˈsīn-mənt\ *n* (14c) **1 :** the act of assigning **2 a :** a position, post, or office to which one is assigned **b :** a specified task or amount of work assigned or undertaken as if assigned by authority **3 :** the transfer of property; *esp* **:** the transfer of property to be held in trust or to be used for the benefit of creditors ***syn*** see TASK

as·sim·i·la·ble \ə-ˈsi-mə-lə-bəl\ *adj* (1667) **:** capable of being assimilated ⟨provides . . . information in a clear, ~ fashion —*Times Lit. Supp.*⟩ — **as·sim·i·la·bil·i·ty** \-ˌsi-mə-lə-ˈbi-lə-tē\ *n*

1**as·sim·i·late** \ə-ˈsi-mə-ˌlāt\ *vb* **-lat·ed; -lat·ing** [ME, fr. ML *assimilatus,* pp. of *assimilare,* fr. L *assimulare* to make similar, fr. *ad-* + *simulare* to make similar, simulate] *vt* (15c) **1 a :** to take in and utilize as nourishment **:** absorb into the system **b :** to take into the mind and thoroughly comprehend **2 a :** to make similar **b :** to alter by assimilation **c :** to absorb into the culture or mores of a population or group **3 :** COMPARE, LIKEN ~ *vi* **:** to become assimilated — **as·sim·i·la·tor** \-ˌlā-tər\ *n*

usage When *assimilate* is followed by a preposition, transitive senses 2a and 2c commonly take *to* and *into* and less frequently *with;* 2b regularly takes *to;* sense 3 most often takes *to* and sometimes *with.* The most frequent prepositions used with the intransitive sense are *to* and *into.*

2**as·sim·i·late** \-lət, -ˌlāt\ *n* (1935) **:** something that is assimilated

as·sim·i·la·tion \ə-ˌsi-mə-ˈlā-shən\ *n* (15c) **1 a :** an act, process, or instance of assimilating **b :** the state of being assimilated **2 :** the incorporation or conversion of nutrients into protoplasm that in animals follows digestion and absorption and in higher plants involves both photosynthesis and root absorption **3 :** change of a sound in speech so that it becomes identical with or similar to a neighboring sound ⟨the usual ~ of \z\ to \sh\ in the phrase *his shoe*⟩ **4 :** the process of receiving new facts or of responding to new situations in conformity with what is already available to consciousness

as·sim·i·la·tion·ist \-sh(ə-)nist\ *n* (1899) **:** a person who advocates a policy of assimilating differing racial or cultural groups — **as·sim·i·la·tion·ism** \-shə-ˌni-zəm\ *n* — **as·sim·i·la·tion·ist** *adj*

as·sim·i·la·tive \ə-ˈsi-mə-ˌlā-tiv, -lə-tiv\ *adj* (14c) **:** of, relating to, or causing assimilation

as·sim·i·la·to·ry \ə-ˈsi-mə-lə-ˌtȯr-ē\ *adj* (ca. 1847) **:** ASSIMILATIVE

As·sin·i·boin *or* **As·sin·i·boine** \ə-ˈsi-nə-ˌbȯin\ *n, pl* **-boin** *or* **-boins** *or* **-boine** *or* **-boines** [Ojibwa dial. *assini·pwa·n,* lit., stone Sioux] (1794) **:** a member of an American Indian people orig. of the area between the upper Missouri and middle Saskatchewan rivers

1**as·sist** \ə-ˈsist\ *vb* [MF or L; MF *assister* to help, stand by, fr. L *assistere,* fr. *ad-* + *sistere* to cause to stand; akin to L *stare* to stand — more at STAND] *vt* (15c) **:** to give usu. supplementary support or aid to ⟨~*ed* the boy with his lessons⟩ ~ *vi* **1 :** to give support or aid ⟨~*ed* at the stove⟩ ⟨another surgeon ~*ed* on the operation⟩ **2 :** to be present as a spectator ⟨the ideal figures ~*ing* at Italian holy scenes —Mary McCarthy⟩

2**assist** *n* (1597) **1 :** an act of assistance **:** AID **2 :** the action (as a throw or pass) of a player who enables a teammate to make a putout or score a goal; *also* **:** official credit given for such an action **3 :** a mechanical or electromechanical device that provides assistance

as·sis·tance \ə-ˈsis-tən(t)s\ *n* (14c) **:** the act of assisting or the help supplied **:** AID ⟨financial and technical ~⟩

as·sis·tant \-tənt\ *n* (15c) **:** a person who assists **:** HELPER; *also* **:** a person holding an assistantship — **assistant** *adj*

assistant professor *n* (1827) **:** a member of a college or university faculty who ranks above an instructor and below an associate professor — **assistant professorship** *n*

as·sis·tant·ship \ə-ˈsis-tən(t)-ˌship\ *n* (1948) **:** a paid appointment awarded annually to a qualified graduate student that requires part-time teaching, research, or residence hall duties

as·sis·ted living \ə-ˈsis-təd-\ *n* (1981) **:** a system of housing and limited care that is designed for senior citizens who need some assistance with daily activities but do not require care in a nursing home — usu. hyphenated when used attributively ⟨an *assisted-living* facility⟩

assisted suicide *n* (1976) **:** suicide committed by someone with assistance from another person; *esp* **:** PHYSICIAN-ASSISTED SUICIDE

as·sis·tive \ə-ˈsis-tiv\ *adj* (1829) **:** providing aid or assistance; *specif* **:** designed or intended to assist disabled persons ⟨~ technology⟩

as·size \ə-ˈsīz\ *n* [ME *assise,* fr. AF, session, legal action, fr. *asseer, aseoir* to seat, fr. VL **assedēre,* fr. L *assidēre* to sit beside, assist in the office of a judge, fr. *ad-* + *sedēre* to sit — more at SIT] (14c) **1 a :** a judicial inquest **b** : an action to be decided by such an inquest, the writ for instituting it, or the verdict or finding rendered by the jury **2 a** : the former periodical sessions of the superior courts in English counties for trial of civil and criminal cases — usu. used in pl. **b** : the time or place of holding such a court, the court itself, or a session of it — usu. used in pl.

assn *abbr* association

assoc *abbr* associate; associated; association

[1]**as·so·ci·ate** \ə-ˈsō-shē-ˌāt, -sē-\ *vb* **-at·ed; -at·ing** [ME *associat* associated, fr. L *associatus,* pp. of *associare* to unite, fr. *ad-* + *sociare* to join, fr. *socius* companion — more at SOCIAL] *vt* (14c) **1** : to join as a partner, friend, or companion **2** *obs* : to keep company with : ATTEND **3** : to join or connect together : COMBINE **4** : to bring together or into relationship in any of various intangible ways (as in memory or imagination) ~ *vi* **1** : to come or be together as partners, friends, or companions **2** : to combine or join with other parts : UNITE ***syn*** see JOIN

[2]**as·so·ciate** \ə-ˈsō-shē-ət, -sē-, -ˌāt, -shət\ *adj* (14c) **1** : closely connected (as in function or office) with another **2** : closely related esp. in the mind **3** : having secondary or subordinate status ⟨~ membership in a society⟩

[3]**as·so·ciate** *same as* [2]\ *n* (1533) **1** : one associated with another: as **a** : PARTNER, COLLEAGUE **b** : COMPANION, COMRADE **2 a** : an entry-level member (as of a learned society, professional organization, or profession) **b** : EMPLOYEE, WORKER **3** *often cap* : a degree conferred esp. by a junior college ⟨~ in arts⟩ — **as·so·ciate·ship** \-ˌship\ *n*

associate professor *n* (1819) : a member of a college or university faculty who ranks above an assistant professor and below a professor — **associate professorship** *n*

as·so·ci·a·tion \ə-ˌsō-sē-ˈā-shən, -shē-\ *n* (1535) **1 a** : the act of associating **b** : the state of being associated : COMBINATION, RELATIONSHIP **2** : an organization of persons having a common interest : SOCIETY **3** : something linked in memory or imagination with a thing or person **4** : the process of forming mental connections or bonds between sensations, ideas, or memories **5** : the aggregation of chemical species to form (as with hydrogen bonds) loosely bound complexes **6** : a major unit in ecological community organization characterized by essential uniformity and usu. by two or more dominant species — **as·so·ci·a·tion·al** \-sh(ə-)nᵊl\ *adj*

association area *n* (ca. 1909) : an area of the cerebral cortex that functions in linking and coordinating the sensory and motor areas

association football *n* (1873) : SOCCER

as·so·ci·a·tion·ism \ə-ˌsō-sē-ˈā-shə-ˌni-zəm, -ˌsō-shē-\ *n* (1875) : a reductionist school of psychology that holds that the content of consciousness can be explained by the association and reassociation of irreducible sensory and perceptual elements — **as·so·ci·a·tion·ist** \-ˈā-sh(ə-)nist\ *n* — **as·so·ci·a·tion·is·tic** \-ˌā-shə-ˈnis-tik\ *adj*

as·so·cia·tive \ə-ˈsō-shē-ˌā-tiv, -sē-, -shə-tiv\ *adj* (1804) **1** : of or relating to association esp. of ideas or images **2** : dependent on or acquired by association or learning **3** : of, having, or being the property of combining to the same mathematical result regardless of the grouping of an expression's elements given that the order of those elements is preserved ⟨addition is ~ since $(a + b) + c = a + (b + c)$⟩ — **as·so·cia·tive·ly** *adv* — **as·so·cia·tiv·i·ty** \-ˌsō-shē-ə-ˈti-və-tē, -sē-, -shə-ˈti-\ *n*

associative learning *n* (1957) : a learning process in which discrete ideas and percepts become linked to one another

associative neuron *n* (1935) : INTERNEURON

as·soil \ə-ˈsȯi(-ə)l\ *vt* [ME, fr. AF *assoilé,* pp. of *assoudre* to absolve, fr. L *absolvere*] (13c) **1** *archaic* : ABSOLVE, PARDON **2** *archaic* : ACQUIT, CLEAR **3** *archaic* : EXPIATE — **as·soil·ment** \-mənt\ *n, archaic*

as·so·nance \ˈa-sə-nən(t)s\ *n* [F, fr. L *assonare* to answer with the same sound, fr. *ad-* + *sonare* to sound, fr. *sonus* sound — more at SOUND] (1727) **1** : resemblance of sound in words or syllables **2 a** : relatively close juxtaposition of similar sounds esp. of vowels **b** : repetition of vowels without repetition of consonants (as in *stony* and *holy*) used as an alternative to rhyme in verse — **as·so·nant** \-nənt\ *adj or n* — **as·so·nant·al** \ˌa-sə-ˈnan-tᵊl\ *adj*

as soon as *conj* (14c) : immediately at or shortly after the time that ⟨call *as soon as* you get there⟩

as·sort \ə-ˈsȯrt\ *vb* [MF *assortir,* fr. *a-* (fr. L *ad-*) + *sorte* sort] *vt* (15c) **1** : to distribute into groups of a like kind : CLASSIFY **2** : to supply with an assortment (as of goods) ~ *vi* **1** : to agree in kind : HARMONIZE **2** : to keep company : ASSOCIATE — **as·sort·er** *n*

as·sor·ta·tive \ə-ˈsȯr-tə-tiv\ *adj* (1897) : being nonrandom mating based on like or unlike characteristics — **as·sor·ta·tive·ly** \-lē\ *adv*

as·sort·ed \-ˈsȯr-təd\ *adj* (ca. 1797) **1** : suited esp. by nature or character ⟨an ill-*assorted* pair⟩ **2** : consisting of various kinds ⟨~ chocolates⟩

as·sort·ment \-ˈsȯrt-mənt\ *n* (1611) **1 a** : the act of assorting **b** : the state of being assorted **2** : a collection of assorted things or persons

ASSR *abbr* Autonomous Soviet Socialist Republic

asst *abbr* **1** assistant **2** assorted

asstd *abbr* **1** assented **2** assorted

as·suage \ə-ˈswāj *also* -ˈswāzh *or* -ˈswäzh\ *vt* **as·suaged; as·suag·ing** [ME *aswagen,* fr. AF *asuager,* fr. VL **assuaviare,* fr. L *ad-* + *suavis* sweet — more at SWEET] (14c) **1** : to lessen the intensity of (something that pains or distresses) : EASE ⟨unable to ~ their grief⟩ **2** : PACIFY, QUIET ⟨vainly strove . . . to ~ an implacable foe —Edward Gibbon⟩ **3** : to put an end to by satisfying : APPEASE, QUENCH ⟨*assuaging* his thirst⟩ ***syn*** see RELIEVE — **as·suage·ment** \-mənt\ *n*

as·sua·sive \ə-ˈswā-siv, -ziv\ *adj* (1708) : SOOTHING, CALMING

as·sume \ə-ˈsüm\ *vt* **as·sumed; as·sum·ing** [ME, fr. L *assumere,* fr. *ad-* + *sumere* to take — more at CONSUME] (15c) **1 a** : to take up or in : RECEIVE **b** : to take into partnership, employment, or use **2 a** : to take to or upon oneself : UNDERTAKE ⟨~ responsibility⟩ **b** : PUT ON, DON **c** : to place oneself in ⟨~ a position⟩ **3** : SEIZE, USURP ⟨~ control⟩ **4** : to pretend to have or be : FEIGN ⟨*assumed* an air of confidence in spite of her dismay⟩ **5** : to take as granted or true : SUPPOSE ⟨I ~ he'll be there⟩ **6** : to take over (the debts of another) as one's own — **as·sum·abil·i·ty** \-ˌsü-mə-ˈbi-lə-tē\ *n* — **as·sum·able** \-ˈsü-mə-bəl\ *adj* — **as·sum·ably** \-blē\ *adv*

syn ASSUME, AFFECT, PRETEND, SIMULATE, FEIGN, COUNTERFEIT, SHAM mean to put on a false or deceptive appearance. ASSUME often implies a justifiable motive rather than an intent to deceive ⟨*assumed* an air of cheerfulness around the patients⟩. AFFECT implies making a false show of possessing, using, or feeling ⟨*affected* an interest in art⟩. PRETEND implies an overt and sustained false appearance ⟨*pretended* that nothing had happened⟩. SIMULATE suggests a close imitation of the appearance of something ⟨cosmetics that *simulate* a suntan⟩. FEIGN implies more artful invention than PRETEND, less specific mimicry than SIMULATE ⟨*feigned* sickness⟩. COUNTERFEIT implies achieving the highest degree of verisimilitude of any of these words ⟨an actor *counterfeiting* drunkenness⟩. SHAM implies an obvious falseness that fools only the gullible ⟨*shammed* a most unconvincing limp⟩.

as·sum·ing *adj* (1692) : PRETENTIOUS, PRESUMPTUOUS

as·sump·sit \ə-ˈsəm(p)-sət\ *n* [NL, he undertook, fr. L *assumere* to undertake] (1590) **1** : an express or implied promise or contract not under seal on which an action may be brought **2 a** : a former common-law action brought to recover damages alleged from the breach of an assumpsit **b** : an action to recover damages for breach of a contract

as·sump·tion \ə-ˈsəm(p)-shən\ *n* [ME, fr. LL *assumption-, assumptio* taking up, fr. L *assumere*] (13c) **1 a** : the taking up of a person into heaven **b** *cap* : August 15 observed in commemoration of the Assumption of the Virgin Mary **2** : a taking to or upon oneself ⟨the ~ of a new position⟩ **3** : the act of laying claim to or taking possession of something ⟨the ~ of power⟩ **4** : ARROGANCE, PRETENSION **5 a** : an assuming that something is true **b** : a fact or statement (as a proposition, axiom, postulate, or notion) taken for granted **6** : the taking over of another's debts

as·sump·tive \ə-ˈsəm(p)-tiv\ *adj* (1611) : of, relating to, or based on assumption

as·sur·ance \ə-ˈshu̇r-ən(t)s\ *n* (14c) **1** : the act or action of assuring: as **a** : PLEDGE, GUARANTEE **b** : the act of conveying real property; *also* : the instrument by which it is conveyed **c** *chiefly Brit* : INSURANCE **2** : the state of being assured: as **a** : SECURITY **b** : a being certain in the mind ⟨the puritan's ~ of salvation⟩ **c** : confidence of mind or manner : easy freedom from self-doubt or uncertainty; *also* : excessive self-confidence : BRASHNESS, PRESUMPTION **3** : something that inspires or tends to inspire confidence ⟨gave repeated ~*s* of goodwill⟩ ***syn*** see CONFIDENCE

as·sure \ə-ˈshu̇r\ *vt* **as·sured; as·sur·ing** [ME, fr. AF *asseurer, assurer,* fr. ML *assecurare,* fr. L *ad-* + *securus* secure] (14c) **1** : to make safe (as from risks or against overthrow) : INSURE **2** : to give confidence to ⟨and hereby we know that we are of the truth, and shall ~ our hearts —1 Jn 3:19(AV)⟩ **3** : to make sure or certain : CONVINCE ⟨glancing back to ~ himself no one was following⟩ **4** : to inform positively ⟨I ~ you that we can do it⟩ **5** : to make certain the coming or attainment of : GUARANTEE ⟨worked hard to ~ accuracy⟩ ***syn*** see ENSURE

[1]**as·sured** \ə-ˈshu̇rd\ *adj* (15c) **1** : characterized by certainty or security : GUARANTEED ⟨an ~ market⟩ **2 a** : SELF-ASSURED **b** : SELF-SATISFIED **3** : satisfied as to the certainty or truth of a matter ⟨rest ~ we won't be late⟩ — **as·sured·ness** \-ˈshu̇r-əd-nəs, -ˈshu̇rd-\ *n*

[2]**assured** *n, pl* **assured** *or* **assureds** (1755) : INSURED

as·sured·ly \ə-ˈshu̇r-əd-lē\ *adv* (14c) **1** : without a doubt : CERTAINLY **2** : in an assured manner : CONFIDENTLY

as·sur·er \ə-ˈshu̇r-ər\ *or* **as·sur·or** \ə-ˈshu̇r-ər, ə-ˌshu̇r-ˈȯr\ *n* (1607) : one that assures : INSURER

as·sur·gent \ə-ˈsər-jənt\ *adj* [L *assurgent-, assurgens,* prp. of *assurgere* to rise, fr. *ad-* + *surgere* to rise — more at SURGE] (1578) : moving upward : RISING; *esp* : ASCENDANT 1b

assy *abbr* assembly

Assyr *abbr* Assyrian

As·syr·i·an \ə-ˈsir-ē-ən\ *n* (15c) **1** : a native or inhabitant of ancient Assyria **2** : the dialect of Akkadian spoken by the Assyrians — **Assyrian** *adj*

As·syr·i·ol·o·gy \ə-ˌsir-ē-ˈä-lə-jē\ *n* (1828) : the science or study of the history, language, and antiquities of ancient Assyria and Babylonia — **As·syr·i·o·log·i·cal** \-ˌsir-ē-ə-ˈlä-ji-kəl\ *adj* — **As·syr·i·ol·o·gist** \-ˈä-lə-jist\ *n*

AST *abbr* Alaska standard time

-ast *n suffix* [ME, fr. L *-astes,* fr. Gk *-astēs,* fr. verbs in *-azein*] : one connected with ⟨ecdysi*ast*⟩

astar·board \ə-ˈstär-bərd\ *adv* (ca. 1630) : toward or on the starboard side of a ship ⟨put the helm hard ~⟩

As·tar·te \ə-ˈstär-tē\ *n* [L, fr. Gk *Astartē*] (1599) : the Phoenician goddess of fertility and of sexual love

as·ta·tine \ˈas-tə-ˌtēn\ *n* [Gk *astatos* unsteady, fr. *a-* + *statos* standing, fr. *histanai* to cause to stand — more at STAND] (1947) : a radioactive halogen element discovered by bombarding bismuth with alpha particles and also formed by radioactive decay — see ELEMENT table

as·ter \ˈas-tər\ *n* (1664) **1** [NL, fr. L, aster, fr. Gk *aster-, astēr* star, aster — more at STAR] **a** : any of various chiefly fall-blooming leafy-stemmed composite herbs (*Aster* and closely related genera) with often showy heads containing disk flowers or both disk and ray flowers **b** : CHINA ASTER **2** [NL, fr. Gk *aster-, astēr*] : a system of microtubules arranged radially about a centriole at either end of the mitotic or meiotic spindle

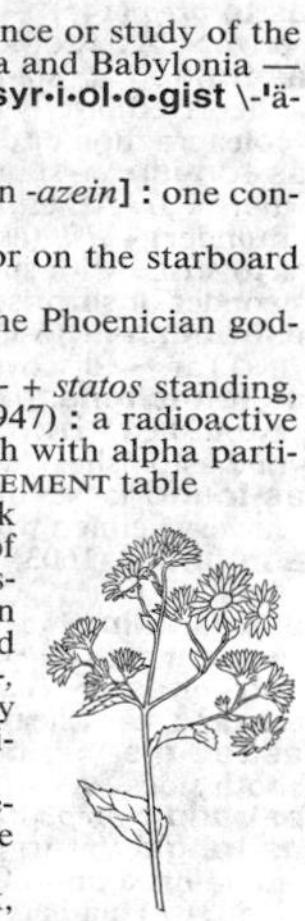
aster 1a

-aster *n suffix* [ME, fr. L, suffix denoting partial resemblance] : one that is inferior or not genuine ⟨critic*aster*⟩

as·te·ria \a-ˈstir-ē-ə\ *n* [L, a precious stone, fr. Gk, fem. of *asterios* starry, fr. *aster-, astēr*] (1903) : a gemstone cut to show asterism

as·te·ri·at·ed \-ē-ˌā-təd\ *adj* [Gk *asterios*] (1816) : exhibiting asterism ⟨~ sapphire⟩

[1]**as·ter·isk** \ˈas-tə-ˌrisk, *esp in plural also* -ˌrik\ *n* [ME, *astarisc,* fr. LL *asteriscus,* fr. Gk *asteriskos,* lit., little star, dim. of *aster-, astēr*] (14c) : the character * used in printing or writing as a reference mark, as an indication of the omission of letters or words, to denote a hypothetical

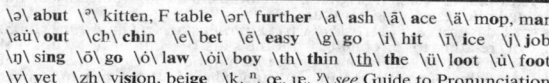

or unattested linguistic form, or for various arbitrary meanings — **as·ter·isk·less** \-ləs\ *adj*

[2]asterisk *vt* (ca. 1733) : to mark with an asterisk : STAR

as·ter·ism \ˈas-tə-ˌri-zəm\ *n* [Gk *asterismos,* fr. *asterizein* to arrange in constellations, fr. *aster-, astēr*] (1598) **1 a** : CONSTELLATION **b** : a small group of stars **2** : a star-shaped figure exhibited by some crystals by reflected light (as in a star sapphire) or by transmitted light (as in some mica)

astern \ə-ˈstərn\ *adv or adj* (ca. 1571) **1** : behind a ship **2** : at or toward the stern of a ship **3** : with the stern in advance : BACKWARD

[1]as·ter·oid \ˈas-tə-ˌrȯid\ *n* [Gk *asteroeidēs* starlike, fr. *aster-, astēr*] (1802) **1** : any of the small rocky celestial bodies found esp. between the orbits of Mars and Jupiter **2** : STARFISH — **as·ter·oi·dal** \ˌas-tə-ˈrȯi-dᵊl\ *adj*

[2]asteroid *adj* (1854) **1** : resembling a star ⟨~ bodies in sporotrichosis⟩ **2** : of or resembling a starfish

asteroid belt *n* (1952) : the region of interplanetary space between the orbits of Mars and Jupiter in which most asteroids are found

aster yellows *n pl* (1922) : a widespread disease affecting more than 40 families of plants, characterized esp. by yellowing and stunting, and caused by a phytoplasma transmitted by leafhoppers

as·the·nia \as-ˈthē-nē-ə\ *n* [NL, fr. Gk *astheneia,* fr. *asthenēs* weak, fr. *a-* + *sthenos* strength] (1802) : lack or loss of strength : DEBILITY

as·then·ic \as-ˈthe-nik\ *adj* (1789) **1** : of, relating to, or exhibiting asthenia : WEAK **2** : ECTOMORPHIC 2

as·theno·sphere \as-ˈthe-nə-ˌsfir\ *n* [Gk *asthenēs* weak + E *-o-* + *sphere*] (1914) : a zone of a celestial body (as the earth) which lies beneath the lithosphere and within which the material is believed to yield readily to persistent stresses — **as·theno·spher·ic** \-ˌthe-nə-ˈsfir-ik, -ˈsfer-\ *adj*

asth·ma \ˈaz-mə, *Brit* ˈas-\ *n* [ME *asma,* fr. ML, modif. of Gk *asthma*] (14c) : a chronic lung disorder that is marked by recurring episodes of airway obstruction (as from bronchospasm) manifested by labored breathing accompanied esp. by wheezing and coughing and by a sense of constriction in the chest, and that is triggered by hyperreactivity to various stimuli (as allergens or rapid change in air temperature) — **asth·mat·ic** \az-ˈma-tik, *Brit* as-\ *adj or n* — **asth·mat·i·cal·ly** \-ti-k(ə-)lē\ *adv*

as though *conj* (13c) : AS IF

as·tig·mat·ic \ˌas-tig-ˈma-tik\ *adj* [*a-* + Gk *stigmat-, stigma* stigma] (1849) **1** : affected with, relating to, or correcting astigmatism **2** : showing incapacity for observation or discrimination ⟨an ~ fanaticism, a disregard for the facts —*N.Y. Herald Tribune*⟩ — **astigmatic** *n*

astig·ma·tism \ə-ˈstig-mə-ˌti-zəm\ *n* (1846) **1** : a defect of an optical system (as a lens) causing rays from a point to fail to meet in a focal point resulting in a blurred and imperfect image **2** : a defect of vision due to astigmatism of the refractive system of the eye and esp. to corneal irregularity **3** : distorted understanding suggestive of the blurred vision of an astigmatic person

astil·be \ə-ˈstil-(ˌ)bē\ *n* [NL, fr. [2]*a-* + Gk *stilbē,* fem. of *stilbos* sparkling] (1843) : any of a genus (*Astilbe*) of chiefly Asian perennials of the saxifrage family that have simple or usu. compound leaves and are widely cultivated for their panicles of usu. white or reddish flowers

astir \ə-ˈstər\ *adj* (1765) **1** : exhibiting activity ⟨streets ~ with shoppers⟩ **2** : being out of bed : UP ⟨no one was ~⟩

As·ti Spu·man·te \ˈäs-tē-spü-ˈmän-(ˌ)tē, ˈas-tē-, -spü-ˈman-\ *n* [It, fr. *Asti,* Italy + It *spumante* effervescent, lit., foaming] (1908) : a sweet sparkling white wine made in and around the village of Asti in Piedmont

ASTM *abbr* American Society for Testing Materials

as to *prep* (14c) **1** : AS FOR, ABOUT ⟨at a loss *as to* how to explain the error⟩ **2** : ACCORDING TO, BY ⟨graded *as to* size and color⟩

as·ton·ied \ə-ˈstä-nēd\ *adj* [ME, fr. pp. of *astonien*] (14c) **1** *archaic* : deprived briefly of the power to act : DAZED **2** *archaic* : filled with consternation or dismay

as·ton·ish \ə-ˈstä-nish\ *vt* [prob. fr. earlier *astony* (fr. ME *astonen, astonien,* fr. AF *estoner* to stun, fr. VL **extonare,* fr. L *ex-* + *tonare* to thunder) + *-ish* (as in *abolish*) — more at THUNDER] (ca. 1534) **1** *obs* : to strike with sudden fear **2** : to strike with sudden and usu. great wonder or surprise ⟨was too *astonished* to speak⟩ ***syn*** see SURPRISE

as·ton·ish·ing \-ni-shiŋ\ *adj* (1593) : causing astonishment : SURPRISING ⟨an ~ discovery⟩ — **as·ton·ish·ing·ly** \-shiŋ-lē\ *adv*

as·ton·ish·ment \ə-ˈstä-nish-mənt\ *n* (1566) **1 a** : the state of being astonished **b** : CONSTERNATION **c** : AMAZEMENT **2** : something that astonishes : a cause of amazement or wonder

[1]as·tound \ə-ˈstau̇nd\ *adj* [ME *astoned,* fr. pp. of *astonen*] (14c) *archaic* : overwhelmed with astonishment or amazement : ASTOUNDED

[2]astound *vt* (1603) : to fill with bewilderment or wonder ***syn*** see SURPRISE

as·tound·ing \ə-ˈstau̇n-diŋ\ *adj* (1586) : causing astonishment or amazement ⟨an ~ revelation⟩ — **as·tound·ing·ly** \-diŋ-lē\ *adv*

astr- *or* **astro-** *comb form* [L *astr-, astro-,* fr. Gk, fr. *astron* — more at STAR] : star : heavens : outer space : astronomical ⟨*astro*physics⟩

[1]astrad·dle \ə-ˈstra-dᵊl\ *adv* (1697) : on or above and extending onto both sides : ASTRIDE

[2]astraddle *prep* (1935) : with one leg on each side of : ASTRIDE

as·tra·gal \ˈas-tri-gəl\ *n* [L *astragalus,* fr. Gk *astragalos* neck vertebra, molding; akin to Gk *astakos* lobster, *osteon* bone — more at OSSEOUS] (1563) **1** : a narrow half-round molding **2** : a projecting strip on the edge of a folding door

as·trag·a·lus \ə-ˈstra-gə-ləs\ *n* [NL, fr. L, fr. Gk *astragalos* neck vertebra, ankle joint, milk vetch (fr. the vertebra-like appearance of the flower clusters)] (1541) **1** *pl* **as·trag·a·li** \-ˌlī, -ˌlē\ : [2]TALUS 1 **2** : the dried root of an Asian milk vetch (*Astragalus membranaceus*) used esp. as a remedy in Chinese herbal medicine; *also* : a preparation or extract of this root

as·tra·khan \ˈas-trə-kən, -ˌkan\ *n, often cap* [*Astrakhan,* Russia] (1766) **1** : karakul of Russian origin **2** : a cloth with a usu. wool, curled, and looped pile resembling karakul

as·tral \ˈas-trəl\ *adj* [LL *astralis,* fr. L *astrum* star, fr. Gk *astron*] (1605) **1** : of, relating to, or coming from the stars ⟨~ influences⟩ ⟨unusual ~ occurrences⟩ **2** : of or relating to a mitotic or meiotic aster **3** : of or consisting of a supersensible substance held in theosophy to be next above the tangible world in refinement **4 a** : VISIONARY **b** : elevated in station or position : EXALTED — **as·tral·ly** \-trə-lē\ *adv*

astray \ə-ˈstrā\ *adv or adj* [ME, fr. AF *estraié* wandering, fr. *estraier* to stray — more at STRAY] (14c) **1** : off the right path or route : STRAYING **2** : in error : away from what is proper or desirable

[1]astride \ə-ˈstrīd\ *adv* (1610) **1** : with one leg on each side : astride a horse ⟨she rode ~, not sidesaddle⟩ **2** : with the legs stretched wide apart ⟨standing ~⟩

[2]astride *prep* (1653) **1** : on or above and with one leg on each side of ⟨~ a horse⟩ **2** : placed or lying on both sides of ⟨towns lying ~ a river⟩ **3** : extending over or across : SPANNING, BRIDGING

as·trin·gen·cy \ə-ˈstrin-jən(t)-sē\ *n* (1601) : the quality or state of being astringent

[1]as·trin·gent \-jənt\ *adj* [prob. fr. MF, fr. L *astringent-, astringens,* prp. of *astringere* to bind fast, fr. *ad-* + *stringere* to bind tight — more at STRAIN] (1541) **1** : causing contraction of soft organic tissues : STYPTIC, PUCKERY ⟨~ lotions⟩ ⟨an ~ fruit⟩ **2** : suggestive of an astringent effect upon tissue : rigidly severe : AUSTERE ⟨dry ~ comments⟩; *also* : PUNGENT, CAUSTIC — **as·trin·gent·ly** *adv*

[2]astringent *n* (1626) : an astringent agent or substance

as·tro·bi·ol·o·gy \ˌas-trō-(ˌ)bī-ˈä-lə-jē\ *n* (1955) : EXOBIOLOGY — **as·tro·bi·ol·o·gist** \-(ˌ)bī-ˈä-lə-jist\ *n*

as·tro·cyte \ˈas-trə-ˌsīt\ *n* [ISV] (1898) : a large star-shaped cell of the glia — **as·tro·cyt·ic** \ˌas-trə-ˈsi-tik\ *adj*

as·tro·cy·to·ma \ˌas-trə-sī-ˈtō-mə\ *n, pl* **-mas** *also* **-ma·ta** \-mə-tə\ [NL] (ca. 1923) : a nerve-tissue tumor composed of astrocytes

as·tro·dome \ˈas-trə-ˌdōm\ *n* [ISV] (1941) : a transparent dome in the upper surface of an airplane from within which the navigator makes celestial observations

astrol *abbr* astrologer; astrology

as·tro·labe \ˈas-trə-ˌlāb *also* -ˌlab\ *n* [ME, fr. AF & ML; AF *astrelabe,* fr. ML *astrolabium,* fr. LGk *astrolabion,* fr. Gk *astrolabos,* fr. *astr-* + *lambanein* to take — more at LATCH] (14c) : a compact instrument used to observe and calculate the position of celestial bodies before the invention of the sextant

as·trol·o·ger \ə-ˈsträ-lə-jər\ *n* (14c) : a person who practices astrology

as·trol·o·gy \ə-ˈsträ-lə-jē\ *n* [ME *astrologie,* fr. MF, fr. L *astrologia,* fr. Gk, fr. *astr-* + *-logia* -logy] (14c) **1** *archaic* : ASTRONOMY **2** : the divination of the supposed influences of the stars and planets on human affairs and terrestrial events by their positions and aspects — **as·tro·log·i·cal** \ˌas-trə-ˈlä-ji-kəl\ *adj* — **as·tro·log·i·cal·ly** \-k(ə-)lē\ *adv*

as·trom·e·try \ə-ˈsträ-mə-trē\ *n* (ca. 1859) : a branch of astronomy that deals with measurements (as of positions and movements) of celestial bodies — **as·tro·me·tric** \ˌas-trə-ˈme-trik\ *adj*

astron *abbr* astronomer; astronomy

as·tro·naut \ˈas-trə-ˌnȯt, -ˌnät\ *n* [*astr-* + *-naut* (as in *aeronaut*)] (1929) : a person who travels beyond the earth's atmosphere; *also* : a trainee for spaceflight

as·tro·nau·tics \ˌas-trə-ˈnȯ-tiks, -ˈnä-\ *n pl but sing or pl in constr* (1928) : the science of the construction and operation of vehicles for travel in space beyond the earth's atmosphere — **as·tro·nau·tic** \-tik\ *or* **as·tro·nau·ti·cal** \-ti-kəl\ *adj* — **as·tro·nau·ti·cal·ly** \-ti-k(ə-)lē\ *adv*

as·tron·o·mer \ə-ˈsträ-nə-mər\ *n* (14c) : a person who is skilled in astronomy or who makes observations of celestial phenomena

as·tro·nom·i·cal \ˌas-trə-ˈnä-mi-kəl\ *also* **as·tro·nom·ic** \-mik\ *adj* (1556) **1** : of or relating to astronomy ⟨~ observations⟩ **2** : enormously or inconceivably large or great ⟨~ numbers⟩ — **as·tro·nom·i·cal·ly** \-mi-k(ə-)lē\ *adv*

astronomical unit *n* (1903) : a unit of length used in astronomy equal to the mean distance of the earth from the sun or about 93 million miles (150 million kilometers)

as·tron·o·my \ə-ˈsträ-nə-mē\ *n, pl* **-mies** [ME *astronomie,* fr. AF, fr. L *astronomia,* fr. Gk, fr. *astr-* + *-nomia* -nomy] (13c) : the study of objects and matter outside the earth's atmosphere and of their physical and chemical properties

as·tro·pho·tog·ra·phy \ˌas-(ˌ)trō-fə-ˈtä-grə-fē\ *n* [ISV] (ca. 1858) : photography involving astronomical objects and events — **as·tro·pho·to·graph** \-ˈfō-tə-ˌgraf\ *n* — **as·tro·pho·tog·ra·pher** \-fə-ˈtä-grə-fər\ *n*

as·tro·phys·ics \ˌas-trə-ˈfi-ziks\ *n pl but sing or pl in constr* [ISV] (1890) : a branch of astronomy dealing esp. with the behavior, physical properties, and dynamic processes of celestial objects and phenomena — **as·tro·phys·i·cal** \-zi-kəl\ *adj* — **as·tro·phys·i·cal·ly** \-zi-k(ə-)lē\ *adv* — **as·tro·phys·i·cist** \-ˈfi-zə-sist, -ˈfiz-sist\ *n*

As·tro·turf \ˈas-trə-ˌtərf, -ˌtrō-\ *trademark* — used for artificial turf

as·tute \ə-ˈstüt, a-, -ˈstyüt\ *adj* [L *astutus,* fr. *astus* craft] (1565) : having or showing shrewdness and perspicacity ⟨an ~ observer⟩ ⟨~ remarks⟩; *also* : CRAFTY, WILY ***syn*** see SHREWD — **as·tute·ly** *adv* — **as·tute·ness** *n*

As·ty·a·nax \ə-ˈstī-ə-ˌnaks\ *n* [Gk] (1567) : a son of Hector and Andromache hurled by the Greeks from the walls of Troy

asun·der \ə-ˈsən-dər\ *adv or adj* (14c) **1** : into parts ⟨torn ~⟩ **2** : apart from each other in position ⟨wide ~⟩

ASV *abbr* American Standard Version

ASW *abbr* antisubmarine warfare

aswarm \ə-ˈswȯrm\ *adj* (1830) : filled to overflowing : SWARMING ⟨streets ~ with people⟩

[1]as well as *conj* (15c) : and in addition : AND ⟨brave *as well as* loyal⟩

[2]as well as *prep* (1589) : in addition to : BESIDES ⟨the coach, *as well as* the team, is ready⟩

aswirl \ə-ˈswər(-ə)l\ *adj* (1877) : being in a swirl : SWIRLING

aswoon \ə-ˈswün\ *adj* (14c) : being in a swoon : DAZED

asy·lum \ə-ˈsī-ləm\ *n* [ME, fr. L, fr. Gk *asylon,* neut. of *asylos* inviolable, fr. *a-* + *sylon* right of seizure] (15c) **1** : an inviolable place of refuge and protection giving shelter to criminals and debtors : SANCTUARY **2** : a place of retreat and security : SHELTER **3 a** : the protection or inviolability afforded by an asylum : REFUGE **b** : protection from arrest and extradition given esp. to political refugees by a nation or by an embassy or other agency enjoying diplomatic immunity **4** : an institution for the care of the destitute or sick and esp. the insane

asym·met·ri·cal \ˌā-sə-ˈme-tri-kəl\ *or* **asym·met·ric** \-trik\ *adj* [Gk *asymmetria* lack of proportion, fr. *asymmetros* ill-proportioned, fr. *a-* + *symmetros* symmetrical] (1690) **1** : not symmetrical **2** *usu asymmetric, of a carbon atom* : bonded to four different atoms or groups —

asym·met·ri·cal·ly \-tri-k(ə-)lē\ *adv* — **asym·me·try** \(ˌ)ā-ˈsi-mə-trē\ *n*
asymp·tom·at·ic \ˌā-ˌsim(p)-tə-ˈma-tik\ *adj* (1856) : presenting no symptoms of disease — **asymp·tom·at·i·cal·ly** \-ti-k(ə-)lē\ *adv*
as·ymp·tote \ˈa-səm(p)-ˌtōt\ *n* [prob. fr. NL **asymptotus,* fr. Gk *asymptōtos* not meeting, fr. *a-* + *sympiptein* to meet — more at SYMPTOM] (1656) : a straight line associated with a curve such that as a point moves along an infinite branch of the curve the distance from the point to the line approaches zero and the slope of the curve at the point approaches the slope of the line — **as·ymp·tot·ic** \ˌa-səm(p)-ˈtä-tik\ *adj* — **as·ymp·tot·i·cal·ly** \-ti-k(ə-)lē\ *adv*
asyn·ap·sis \ˌā-sə-ˈnap-səs\ *n, pl* **-ap·ses** \-ˌsēz\ [NL *2a-* + *synapsis*] (1930) : failure of pairing of homologous chromosomes in meiosis
asyn·chro·nous \(ˌ)ā-ˈsiŋ-krə-nəs, -ˈsin-\ *adj* (1748) **1** : not synchronous **2** : of, used in, or being digital communication (as between computers) in which there is no timing requirement for transmission and in which the start of each character is individually signaled by the transmitting device — **asyn·chro·nous·ly** *adv*
asyn·chro·ny \-krə-nē\ *or* **asyn·chro·nism** \-krə-ˌni-zəm\ *n* (1875) : the quality or state of being asynchronous : absence or lack of concurrence in time
as·yn·det·ic \ˌa-sᵊn-ˈde-tik\ *adj* (ca. 1864) : marked by asyndeton — **as·yn·det·i·cal·ly** \-ti-k(ə-)lē\ *adv*
asyn·de·ton \ə-ˈsin-də-ˌtän, (ˌ)ā-ˈsin-\ *n, pl* **-tons** *or* **-ta** \-də-tə\ [LL, fr. Gk, fr. neut. of *asyndetos* unconnected, fr. *a-* + *syndetos* bound together, fr. *syndein* to bind together, fr. *syn-* + *dein* to bind — more at DIADEM] (1555) : omission of the conjunctions that ordinarily join coordinate words or clauses (as in "I came, I saw, I conquered")
1**at** \ət, ˈat\ *prep* [ME, fr. OE *æt;* akin to OHG *az* at, L *ad*] (bef. 12c) **1** — used as a function word to indicate presence or occurrence in, on, or near ‹staying ~ a hotel› ‹~ a party› ‹sick ~ heart› **2** — used as a function word to indicate the goal of an indicated or implied action or motion ‹aim ~ the target› ‹creditors are ~ him again› **3** — used as a function word to indicate that with which one is occupied or employed ‹~ work› ‹~ the controls› ‹good ~ chess› **4** — used as a function word to indicate situation in an active or passive state or condition ‹~ liberty› ‹~ rest› **5** — used as a function word to indicate the means, cause, or manner ‹sold ~ auction› ‹laughed ~ my joke› ‹act ~ your own discretion› **6 a** — used as a function word to indicate the rate, degree, or position in a scale or series ‹the temperature ~ 90› ‹~ first› **b** — used as a function word to indicate age or position in time ‹will retire ~ 65›
2**at** *also* **att** \ˈät\ *n, pl* **at** *also* **att** [Lao] (1955) — see *kip* at MONEY table
3**at** *abbr* **1** airtight **2** atmosphere **3** atomic
At *symbol* astatine
AT *abbr* **1** air temperature **2** ampere-turn **3** automatic transmission
at- — see AD-
at·a·brine \ˈa-tə-brən\ *n* [fr. *Atabrine,* a trademark] (1933) : QUINACRINE
atac·tic \(ˌ)ā-ˈtak-tik\ *adj* [ISV *2a-* + *-tactic*] (1957) : of, relating to, or being a polymer exhibiting no stereochemical regularity of structure ‹~ polypropylene› — compare ISOTACTIC
At·a·lan·ta \ˌa-tə-ˈlan-tə\ *n* [L, fr. Gk *Atalantē*] (14c) : a fleet-footed huntress in Greek mythology who challenges her suitors to a race and is defeated by Hippomenes when she stops to pick up three golden apples he has dropped
at all *adv* (14c) : in any way or respect : to the least extent or degree : under any circumstances ‹doesn't smoke *at all*›
at·a·man \ˌa-tə-ˈman\ *n* [Russ] (1835) : HETMAN
at·a·mas·co lily \ˌa-tə-ˈmas-(ˌ)kō-\ *n* [Virginia Algonquian *attamusco*] (1743) : any of a genus (*Zephyranthes*) of American bulbous herbs of the amaryllis family with pink, white, or yellowish flowers; *esp* : one (*Z. atamasco*) of the southeastern U.S. with white flowers usu. tinged with purple
at·a·vism \ˈa-tə-ˌvi-zəm\ *n* [F *atavisme,* fr. L *atavus* ancestor, fr. *at-* (prob. akin to *atta* daddy) + *avus* grandfather — more at UNCLE] (1833) **1 a** : recurrence in an organism of a trait or character typical of an ancestral form and usu. due to genetic recombination **b** : recurrence of or reversion to a past style, manner, outlook, approach, or activity ‹architectural ~› **2** : one that manifests atavism : THROWBACK — **at·a·vis·tic** \ˌa-tə-ˈvis-tik\ *adj* — **at·a·vis·ti·cal·ly** \-ti-k(ə-)lē\ *adv*
atax·ia \ə-ˈtak-sē-ə, (ˌ)ā-\ *n* [Gk, fr. *a-* + *tassein* to put in order] (1670) : an inability to coordinate voluntary muscular movements that is symptomatic of some central nervous system disorders and injuries and not due to muscle weakness — called also *incoordination* — **atax·ic** \-sik\ *adj*
atax·ia–tel·an·gi·ec·ta·sia \-ˌte-ˌlan-jē-ˌek-ˈtā-zh(ē-)ə, -tē-, -tə-\ *n* (1961) : an inherited systemic disorder marked esp. by progressive pathological changes in the nervous system resulting in loss of motor coordination and by increased susceptibility to cancer esp. of lymphoid tissue
at bat *n* (1941) : an official turn at batting charged to a baseball player except when the player walks, sacrifices, is hit by a pitched ball, or is interfered with by the catcher ‹three hits in five *at bats*›
ATC *abbr* air traffic control
ate *past of* EAT
Ate \ˈā-tē, ˈā-(ˌ)tē; ˈä-ˌtā\ *n* [Gk *Atē*] (1583) : a Greek goddess personifying foolhardy and ruinous impulse
1**-ate** *n suffix* [ME *-at,* fr. AF, fr. L *-atus, -atum,* masc. & neut. of *-atus,* pp. ending] **1** : one acted upon (in a specified way) ‹distill*ate*› **2** [NL *-atum,* fr. L] : chemical compound or complex anion derived from a (specified) compound or element ‹phenol*ate*›; *esp* : salt or ester of an acid with a name ending in *-ic* and not beginning with *hydro-* ‹bor*ate*›
2**-ate** *n suffix* [ME *-at,* fr. AF, fr. L *-atus,* fr. *-a-,* stem vowel of 1st conj. + *-tus,* suffix of verbal nouns] **1** : office : function : rank : group of persons holding a (specified) office or rank or having a (specified) function ‹vicar*ate*› **2** : state : dominion : jurisdiction ‹emir*ate*› ‹khan*ate*›
3**-ate** *adj suffix* [ME *-at,* fr. L *-atus,* fr. pp. ending of 1st conj. verbs, fr. *-a-,* stem vowel of 1st conj. + *-tus,* pp. suffix — more at -ED] : marked by having ‹crani*ate*›
4**-ate** *vb suffix* [ME *-aten,* fr. L *-atus,* pp. ending] : act on (in a specified way) ‹insul*ate*› : cause to be modified or affected by ‹camphor*ate*› : cause to become ‹activ*ate*› : furnish with ‹capacit*ate*›
-ated *adj suffix* : 3-ATE ‹pile*ated*›
at·el·ec·ta·sis \ˌa-tə-ˈlek-tə-səs\ *n, pl* **-ta·ses** \-ˌsēz\ [NL, fr. Gk *atelēs* incomplete, defective (fr. *a-* *2a-* + *telos* end) + *ektasis* extension, fr. *ekteinein* to stretch out, fr. *ex-* + *teinein* to stretch — more at TELOS, THIN] (1859) : collapse of the expanded lung; *also* : defective expansion of the pulmonary alveoli at birth
ate·lier \ˌa-tᵊl-ˈyā\ *n* [F, fr. MF *astelier* woodpile, fr. *astele* splinter, fr. LL *astella,* dim. of L *astula*] (1699) **1** : an artist's or designer's studio or workroom **2** : WORKSHOP
ate·moya \ˌä-tə-ˈmȯi-ə, ˌa-\ *n* [*ates* sweetsop (fr. Tag) + cheri*moya*] (1914) : a white-pulped tropical fruit of a tree that is a hybrid of the sweetsop and the cherimoya
a tem·po \ä-ˈtem-(ˌ)pō\ *adv or adj* [It] (1834) : in time — used as a direction in music to return to the original tempo
atem·po·ral \(ˌ)ā-ˈtem-p(ə-)rəl\ *adj* (1870) : independent of or unaffected by time : TIMELESS
aten·o·lol \ə-ˈte-nə-ˌlȯl, -ˌlōl\ *n* [perh. fr. antihyper*ten*sive + *-olol* (as in *propranolol*)] (1972) : a beta blocker $C_{14}H_{22}N_2O_3$ used in the treatment of hypertension
ATF *abbr* [Bureau of] Alcohol, Tobacco, Firearms and Explosives
Ath·a·bas·can \ˌa-thə-ˈbas-kən\ *or* **Ath·a·bas·kan** \-ˈbas-\ *also* **Ath·a·pas·kan** \-ˈpas-\ *or* **Ath·a·pas·can** \-ˈpas-\ *n* [*Athabasca,* a Cree band, fr. Cree dial. *aδapaska·w,* name for the area east of Lake Athabasca, lit., (where) there are reeds one after another] (1846) **1** : a family of American Indian languages spoken primarily in western Canada, Alaska, and the U.S. Southwest **2** : a member of a people speaking an Athabascan language
Ath·a·na·sian \ˌa-thə-ˈnā-zhən, -shən\ *adj* (1586) : of or relating to Athanasius or his advocacy of the homoousian doctrine against Arianism
Athanasian Creed *n* (1586) : a Christian creed originating in Europe about A.D. 400 and relating esp. to the Trinity and Incarnation
athe·ism \ˈā-thē-ˌi-zəm\ *n* [MF *athéisme,* fr. *athée* atheist, fr. Gk *atheos* godless, fr. *a-* + *theos* god] (1546) **1** *archaic* : UNGODLINESS, WICKEDNESS **2 a** : a disbelief in the existence of deity **b** : the doctrine that there is no deity
athe·ist \ˈā-thē-ist\ *n* (1551) : one who believes that there is no deity — **athe·is·tic** \ˌā-thē-ˈis-tik\ *or* **athe·is·ti·cal** \ˌā-thē-ˈis-ti-kəl\ *adj* — **athe·is·ti·cal·ly** \-ti-k(ə-)lē\ *adv*
ath·e·ling \ˈa-thə-liŋ, -*th*ə-\ *n* [ME, fr. OE *ætheling,* fr. *æthelu* nobility, akin to OHG *adal* nobility] (bef. 12c) : an Anglo-Saxon prince or nobleman; *esp* : the heir apparent or a prince of the royal family
Athe·na \ə-ˈthē-nə\ *or* **Athe·ne** \-nē\ *n* [L *Athena,* fr. Gk *Athēnē*] (14c) : the Greek goddess of wisdom — compare MINERVA
ath·e·nae·um *or* **ath·e·ne·um** \ˌa-thə-ˈnē-əm\ *n* [L *Athenaeum,* a school in ancient Rome for the study of arts, fr. Gk *Athēnaion,* a temple of Athena, fr. *Athēnē*] (1799) **1** : a building or room in which books, periodicals, and newspapers are kept for use **2** : a literary or scientific association
athe·o·ret·i·cal \ˌā-ˌthē-ə-ˈre-ti-kəl, -ˌthir-ˈe-\ *adj* (1969) : not based on or concerned with theory
athero- *comb form* [Gk *athēra*] : atheroma ‹*athero*genic›
ath·ero·gen·e·sis \ˌa-thə-rō-ˈje-nə-səs\ *n* (1953) : the formation of atheroma
ath·ero·gen·ic \-ˈje-nik\ *adj* (1954) : relating to or causing atherogenesis ‹an ~ diet›
ath·er·o·ma \ˌa-thə-ˈrō-mə\ *n, pl* **-mas** *also* **-ma·ta** \-mə-tə\ [NL *atheromat-, atheroma,* fr. L, a tumor containing matter resembling gruel, fr. Gk *athērōma,* fr. *athēra* gruel] (1875) **1** : fatty degeneration of the inner coat of the arteries **2** : an abnormal fatty deposit in an artery — **ath·er·o·ma·tous** \-ˈrō-mə-təs\ *adj*
ath·ero·scle·ro·sis \ˌa-thə-ˌrō-sklə-ˈrō-səs\ *n* [NL] (1910) : an arteriosclerosis characterized by atheromatous deposits in and fibrosis of the inner layer of the arteries — **ath·ero·scle·rot·ic** \-sklə-ˈrä-tik\ *adj*
athirst \ə-ˈthərst\ *adj* [ME, fr. OE *ofthyrst,* pp. of *ofthyrstan* to suffer from thirst, fr. *of* off, from + *thyrstan* to thirst — more at OF] (bef. 12c) **1** *archaic* : THIRSTY **2** : having a strong eager desire ‹I that for ever feel ~ for glory —John Keats› ***syn*** see EAGER
ath·lete \ˈath-ˌlēt, ÷ˈa-thə-ˌlēt\ *n* [ME, fr. L *athleta,* fr. Gk *athlētēs,* fr. *athlein* to contend for a prize, fr. *athlon* prize, contest] (15c) : a person who is trained or skilled in exercises, sports, or games requiring physical strength, agility, or stamina
athlete's foot *n* (1928) : ringworm of the feet
ath·let·ic \ath-ˈle-tik, ÷ˌa-thə-ˈle-\ *adj* (1636) **1** : of or relating to athletes or athletics **2** : characteristic of an athlete; *esp* : VIGOROUS, ACTIVE **3** : MESOMORPHIC **4** : used by athletes — **ath·let·i·cal·ly** \-ti-k(ə-)lē\ *adv* — **ath·let·i·cism** \-ˈle-tə-ˌsi-zəm\ *n*
ath·let·ics \ath-ˈle-tiks, ÷ˌa-thə-ˈle-\ *n pl but sing or pl in constr* (1749) **1** : exercises, sports, or games engaged in by athletes **2** : the practice or principles of athletic activities
athletic supporter *n* (1927) : a supporter (as of elasticized fabric) for the genitals worn by men participating in sports or strenuous activities
at–home \ət-ˈhōm, ˈat-ˌhōm\ *adj* (1951) **1** : intended or suitable for one's home ‹an ~ dress› **2** : being or occurring at one's home ‹~ entertainment›
at home *n* (1745) : a reception given at one's home
-athon *n comb form* [*marathon*] : event or activity lasting a long time or involving a great deal of something ‹talk*athon*›
1**athwart** \ə-ˈthwȯrt, *naut often* -ˈthȯrt\ *prep* (15c) **1** : ACROSS **2** : in opposition to ‹a procedure directly ~ the New England prejudices —R. G. Cole›
2**athwart** *adv* (ca. 1500) **1** : across esp. in an oblique direction **2** : in opposition to the right or expected course ‹and quite ~ goes all decorum —Shak.›
athwart·ship \-ˌship\ *adj* (1775) : being across the ship from side to side ‹~ and longitudinal framing›
athwart·ships \-ˌships\ *adv* (1718) : across the ship from side to side

\ə\ **a**but \ᵊ\ kitten, F table \ər\ **fur**ther \a\ **a**sh \ā\ **a**ce \ä\ m**o**p, m**a**r
\au̇\ **ou**t \ch\ **ch**in \e\ b**e**t \ē\ **ea**sy \g\ **g**o \i\ h**i**t \ī\ **i**ce \j\ **j**ob
\ŋ\ si**ng** \ō\ g**o** \ȯ\ l**aw** \ȯi\ b**oy** \th\ **th**in \th\ **th**e \ü\ l**oo**t \u̇\ f**oo**t
\y\ **y**et \zh\ vi**si**on, bei**ge** \k, ⁿ, œ, ue, ʸ\ *see* Guide to Pronunciation

atilt \ə-ˈtilt\ *adv or adj* (1562) **1 :** in a tilted position **2 :** with lance in hand ⟨run ~ at death —Shak.⟩
atin·gle \ə-ˈtiŋ-gəl\ *adj* (1855) **:** tingling esp. with excitement
-ation *n suffix* [L *-ation-, -atio,* fr. *-a-,* stem vowel of 1st conj. + *-tion-, -tio,* n. suffix] **:** action or process ⟨flirt*ation*⟩ **:** something connected with an action or process ⟨discolor*ation*⟩
-ative *adj suffix* [L *-ativus,* fr. *-atus* -ate + *-ivus* -ive] **:** of, relating to, or connected with ⟨authorit*ative*⟩ **:** tending to ⟨talk*ative*⟩
At·ka mackerel \ˈat-kə-, ˈät-\ *n* [*Atka* Island, Alaska] (1888) **:** a greenling (*Pleurogrammus monopterygius*) that is a food fish found in Alaska and adjacent regions
Atl *abbr* Atlantic
[1]**At·lan·te·an** \ˌat-ˌlan-ˈtē-ən, ət-ˈlan-tē-\ *adj* (1667) **:** of, relating to, or resembling Atlas **:** STRONG
[2]**Atlantean** *adj* (ca. 1828) **:** of or relating to Atlantis
At·lan·tic \ət-ˈlan-tik, at-\ *adj* (1594) **1 a :** of, relating to, or found in, on, or near the Atlantic Ocean **b :** of, relating to, or found on or near the east coast of the U.S. **2 :** of or relating to the nations that border the Atlantic Ocean ⟨the ~ community⟩
Atlantic croaker *n* (ca. 1949) **:** a small croaker (*Micropogonias undulatus*) of the Gulf coast and the Atlantic coast
At·lan·ti·cism \-ˈlan-tə-ˌsi-zəm\ *n* (1950) **:** a policy of military cooperation between European powers and the U.S. — **At·lan·ti·cist** \-sist\ *n*
Atlantic puffin *n* (1931) **:** a small black-and-white puffin (*Fratercula arctica*) of the northern coastal parts of the No. Atlantic Ocean that has a triangular bill with a broad red or yellow tip
Atlantic salmon *n* (1884) **:** SALMON 1a
Atlantic time *n* (1880) **:** the time of the fourth time zone west of Greenwich that includes the Canadian Maritime Provinces, Puerto Rico, and the Virgin Islands
Atlantic white cedar *n* (1948) **:** WHITE CEDAR 1
At·lan·tis \ət-ˈlan-təs, at-\ *n* [L, fr. Gk, fr. *Atlas*] (1602) **:** a fabled island in the Atlantic that according to legend sank beneath the sea
at–large \ˈat-ˈlärj\ *adj* (1969) **:** relating to or being a political representative who is elected to serve an entire area rather than one of its subdivisions ⟨an ~ city councilor⟩ ⟨an ~ election⟩
at·las \ˈat-ləs\ *n* [L *Atlant-, Atlas,* fr. Gk] (1513) **1** *cap* **:** a Titan who for his part in the Titans' revolt against the gods is forced by Zeus to support the heavens on his shoulders **2** *cap* **:** one who bears a heavy burden **3 a :** a bound collection of maps often including illustrations, informative tables, or textual matter **b :** a bound collection of tables, charts, or plates **4 :** the first vertebra of the neck **5** *pl usu* **at·lan·tes** \ət-ˈlan-(ˌ)tēz, at-\ **:** a male figure used like a caryatid as a supporting column or pilaster — called also *telamon*
at·latl \ˈät-ˌlä-tᵊl\ *n* [Nahuatl *ahtlatl*] (1871) **:** a device for throwing a spear or dart that consists of a rod or board with a projection (as a hook) at the rear end to hold the weapon in place until released

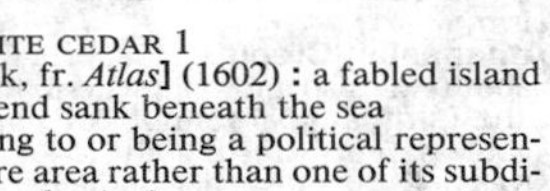

A atlatl

At·li \ˈät-lē\ *n* [ON] (1876) **:** a king of the Huns figuring in Germanic legend and corresponding to the historical Attila
atm *abbr* atmosphere; atmospheric
[1]**ATM** \ˌā-(ˌ)tē-ˈem\ *n* (1976) **:** a computerized electronic machine that performs basic banking functions (as handling check deposits or issuing cash withdrawals) — called also *automated teller machine, automatic teller, automatic teller machine*
[2]**ATM** *abbr* asynchronous transfer mode
at·man \ˈät-mən, -ˌmän\ *n, often cap* [Skt *ātman,* lit., breath, soul; akin to OE *ǣthm* breath] (1785) **1** *Hinduism* **:** the innermost essence of each individual **2** *Hinduism* **:** the supreme universal self **:** BRAHMA 2
at·mo·sphere \ˈat-mə-ˌsfir\ *n* [NL *atmosphaera,* fr. Gk *atmos* vapor + L *sphaera* sphere] (1677) **1 a :** the gaseous envelope of a celestial body (as a planet) **b :** the whole mass of air surrounding the earth **2 :** the air of a locality **3 :** a surrounding influence or environment ⟨an ~ of hostility⟩ **4 :** a unit of pressure equal to the pressure of the air at sea level or approximately 14.7 pounds per square inch (101,325 pascals) **5 a :** the overall aesthetic effect of a work of art **b :** an intriguing or singular tone, effect, or appeal ⟨an inn with ~⟩ — **at·mo·sphered** \-ˌsfird\ *adj*
at·mo·spher·ic \ˌat-mə-ˈsfir-ik, -ˈsfer-\ *adj* (ca. 1735) **1 a :** of, relating to, or occurring in the atmosphere ⟨~ dust⟩ **b :** resembling the atmosphere **:** AIRY **2 :** having, marked by, or contributing aesthetic or emotional atmosphere ⟨an ~ inn⟩; *also* **:** marked by an emphasis on impression or tone — **at·mo·spher·i·cal·ly** \-i-k(ə-)lē\ *adv*
at·mo·spher·ics \-iks\ *n pl* (1905) **1 :** audible disturbances produced in radio receiving apparatus by atmospheric electrical phenomena (as lightning); *also* **:** the electrical phenomena causing these disturbances **2 :** actions (as official statements) intended to create or suggest a particular atmosphere or mood in politics and esp. international relations; *also* **:** the mood so created or suggested **3 :** realistic detail added (as to a literary work) to create a mood
at no *abbr* atomic number
atoll \ˈa-ˌtȯl, -ˌtäl, -ˌtōl, ˈā-\ *n* [Divehi (Indo-Aryan language of the Maldive Islands) *atolu*] (1625) **:** a coral island consisting of a reef surrounding a lagoon
at·om \ˈa-təm\ *n* [ME, fr. L *atomus,* fr. Gk *atomos,* fr. *atomos* indivisible, fr. *a-* + *temnein* to cut] (15c) **1 :** one of the minute indivisible particles of which according to ancient materialism the universe is composed **2 :** a tiny particle **:** BIT **3 :** the smallest particle of an element that can exist either alone or in combination **4 :** the atom considered as a source of vast potential energy
atom·ic \ə-ˈtä-mik\ *adj* (1678) **1 a :** of, relating to, or concerned with atoms ⟨~ physics⟩ **b :** NUCLEAR 2 ⟨~ energy⟩ **2 a :** marked by acceptance of the theory of atomism **b :** ATOMISTIC 2 **3 :** MINUTE **4** *of a chemical element* **:** existing in the state of separate atoms — **atom·i·cal·ly** \-mi-k(ə-)lē\ *adv*
atomic bomb *n* (1917) **1 :** a bomb whose violent explosive power is due to the sudden release of energy resulting from the splitting of nuclei of a heavy chemical element (as plutonium or uranium) by neutrons in a very rapid chain reaction — called also *atom bomb* **2 :** a nuclear weapon (as a hydrogen bomb)
atomic clock *n* (1938) **:** a precision clock that depends for its operation on an electrical oscillator regulated by the natural vibration frequencies of an atomic system (as a beam of cesium atoms)
atomic force microscope *n* (1986) **:** an instrument used for mapping the atomic-scale topography of a surface by means of the repulsive electronic forces between the surface and the tip of a microscopic probe moving above the surface — abbr. *AFM*
atomic mass *n* (1874) **:** the mass of an atom usu. expressed in atomic mass units; *also* **:** ATOMIC WEIGHT
atomic mass unit *n* (ca. 1942) **:** a unit of mass for expressing masses of atoms, molecules, or nuclear particles equal to $1/12$ the mass of a single atom of the most abundant carbon isotope ^{12}C — called also *dalton*
atomic number *n* (1821) **:** an experimentally determined number characteristic of a chemical element that represents the number of protons in the nucleus which in a neutral atom equals the number of electrons outside the nucleus and that determines the place of the element in the periodic table — see ELEMENT table
atomic reactor *or* **atomic pile** *n* (1945) **:** REACTOR 3b
atomic theory *n* (1814) **1 :** a theory of the nature of matter: all material substances are composed of minute particles or atoms of a comparatively small number of kinds and all the atoms of the same kind are uniform in size, weight, and other properties **2 :** any of several theories of the structure of the atom; *esp* **:** one based on experimentation and theoretical considerations holding that the atom is composed essentially of a small positively charged comparatively heavy nucleus surrounded by a comparatively large arrangement of electrons
atomic weight *n* (1820) **:** the mass of one atom of an element; *specif* **:** the average mass of an atom of an element as it occurs in nature that is expressed in atomic mass units — see ELEMENT table
at·om·ise, at·om·is·er *Brit var of* ATOMIZE, ATOMIZER
at·om·ism \ˈa-tə-ˌmi-zəm\ *n* (1678) **1 :** a doctrine that the physical or physical and mental universe is composed of simple indivisible minute particles **2 :** INDIVIDUALISM 1 — **at·om·ist** \-mist\ *n*
at·om·is·tic \ˌa-tə-ˈmis-tik\ *adj* (1809) **1 :** of or relating to atoms or atomism **2 :** composed of many simple elements; *also* **:** characterized by or resulting from division into unconnected or antagonistic fragments ⟨an ~ society⟩ — **at·om·is·ti·cal·ly** \-ti-k(ə-)lē\ *adv*
at·om·ize \ˈa-tə-ˌmīz\ *vt* **-ized; -iz·ing** (1845) **1 :** to treat as made up of many discrete units **2 :** to reduce to minute particles or to a fine spray **3 :** DIVIDE, FRAGMENT ⟨an *atomized* society⟩; *also* **:** to deprive of meaningful ties to others ⟨*atomized* individuals⟩ **4 :** to subject to attack by nuclear weapons — **at·om·i·za·tion** \ˌa-tə-mə-ˈzā-shən\ *n*
at·om·iz·er \ˈa-tə-ˌmī-zər\ *n* (1865) **:** an instrument for atomizing usu. a perfume, disinfectant, or medicament
atom smasher *n* (1937) **:** ACCELERATOR d
at·o·my \ˈa-tə-mē\ *n, pl* **-mies** [irreg. fr. L *atomi,* pl. of *atomus* atom] (1591) **:** a tiny particle **:** ATOM, MITE
aton·al \(ˌ)ā-ˈtō-nᵊl, (ˌ)a-\ *adj* [²*a-* + *tonal*] (1922) **:** marked by avoidance of traditional musical tonality; *esp* **:** organized without reference to key or tonal center and using the tones of the chromatic scale impartially — **aton·al·ism** \-nə-ˌli-zəm\ *n* — **aton·al·ist** \-list\ *n* — **ato·nal·i·ty** \ˌā-tō-ˈna-lə-tē, ˌa-\ *n* — **aton·al·ly** \(ˌ)ā-ˈtō-nə-lē, (ˌ)a-\ *adv*
atone \ə-ˈtōn\ *vb* **atoned; aton·ing** [ME, to become reconciled, fr. *at on* in harmony, fr. *at* + *on* one] *vt* (1574) **1** *obs* **:** RECONCILE **2 :** to supply satisfaction for **:** EXPIATE ~ *vi* **:** to make amends ⟨~ for sins⟩
atone·ment \ə-ˈtōn-mənt\ *n* (1513) **1** *obs* **:** RECONCILIATION **2 :** the reconciliation of God and humankind through the sacrificial death of Jesus Christ **3 :** reparation for an offense or injury **:** SATISFACTION **4** *Christian Science* **:** the exemplifying of human oneness with God
aton·ic \(ˌ)ā-ˈtä-nik, (ˌ)a-\ *adj* (1792) **1 :** characterized by atony **2 :** uttered without accent or stress
at·o·ny \ˈa-tə-nē\ *n* [LL *atonia,* fr. Gk, fr. *atonos* without tone, fr. *a-* + *tonos* tone] (1693) **:** lack of physiological tone esp. of a contractile organ
[1]**atop** \ə-ˈtäp\ *adv or adj* (1650) **:** on, to, or at the top
[2]**atop** *prep* (1655) **:** on top of
at·o·py \ˈa-tə-pē\ *n* [Gk *atopia* uncommonness, fr. *atopos* out of the way, uncommon, fr. *a-* + *topos* place] (1923) **:** a prob. hereditary allergy characterized by symptoms (as asthma, hay fever, or hives) produced upon exposure esp. by inhalation to the exciting environmental antigen — **atop·ic** \(ˌ)ā-ˈtä-pik, -ˈtō-\ *adj*
-ator *n suffix* [L *-ator,* fr. *-a-,* stem vowel of 1st conj. + *-tor,* agent suffix] **:** one that does ⟨totaliz*ator*⟩
ator·va·stat·in \ə-ˌtȯr-və-ˈsta-tᵊn, -ˈtȯr-və-ˌsta-\ *n* [*ator-* (perh. alter. of lip*id* cont*rol*) + *-vastatin* (as in *lovastatin*)] (1994) **:** a statin administered orally in the form of its hydrated calcium salt $(C_{33}H_{34}FN_2O_5)_2{\cdot}Ca_3H_2O$ to lower lipid levels in the blood
ATP \ˌā-ˌtē-ˈpē\ *n* [*a*denosine *tri*phosphate] (1939) **:** a phosphorylated nucleotide $C_{10}H_{16}N_5O_{13}P_3$ composed of adenosine and three phosphate groups that supplies energy for many biochemical cellular processes by undergoing enzymatic hydrolysis esp. to ADP — called also *adenosine triphosphate*
ATPase \ˌā-ˌtē-ˈpē-ˌās, -ˌāz\ *n* (1946) **:** an enzyme that hydrolyzes ATP; *esp* **:** one that hydrolyzes ATP to ADP and inorganic phosphate
at·ra·bil·ious \ˌa-trə-ˈbil-yəs\ *adj* [L *atra bilis* black bile] (1651) **1 :** given to or marked by melancholy **:** GLOOMY **2 :** ILL-NATURED, PEEVISH — **at·ra·bil·ious·ness** *n*
at·ra·zine \ˈa-trə-ˌzēn\ *n* [perh. fr. *a*mino + *triazine*] (1962) **:** a photosynthesis-inhibiting persistent herbicide $C_8H_{14}ClN_5$ used esp. to kill annual weeds and quack grass
atrem·ble \ə-ˈtrem-bəl\ *adj* (1862) **:** shaking involuntarily **:** TREMBLING ⟨he was white as death and all ~ —Robert Coover⟩
atre·sia \ə-ˈtrē-zhə\ *n* [NL, fr. ²*a-* + Gk *trēsis* perforation, fr. *tetrainein* to pierce — more at THROW] (ca. 1807) **1 :** absence or closure of a natural passage of the body **2 :** absence or disappearance of an anatomical part (as an ovarian follicle) by degeneration
Atreus \ˈā-ˌtrüs, -trē-əs\ *n* [Gk] (15c) **:** a king of Mycenae and father of Agamemnon and Menelaus
atrial natriuretic peptide *n* (1984) **:** a peptide hormone secreted by the cardiac atria that in pharmacological doses promotes salt and water excretion and lowers blood pressure — called also *atrial natriuretic factor*
atrio·ven·tric·u·lar \ˌā-trē-ō-ven-ˈtri-kyə-lər, -vən-\ *adj* [NL *atrium* + E *ventricular*] (ca. 1860) **:** of, relating to, or located between an atrium and ventricle of the heart

atrioventricular node *n* (ca. 1934) : a small mass of tissue in the right atrioventricular region of higher vertebrates through which impulses from the sinoatrial node are passed to the ventricles

atrip \ə-ˈtrip\ *adj* (1796) *of an anchor* : AWEIGH

atri·um \ˈā-trē-əm\ *n, pl* **atria** \-trē-ə\ *also* **atri·ums** [L] (1577) **1** : the central room of a Roman house **2** *pl usu atriums* **a** : a rectangular open patio around which a house is built **b** : a many-storied court in a building (as a hotel) usu. with a skylight **3** [NL, fr. L] : an anatomical cavity or passage; *esp* : the chamber or either of the chambers of the heart that receives blood from the veins and forces it into the ventricle or ventricles — see HEART illustration — **atri·al** \-trē-əl\ *adj*

atro·cious \ə-ˈtrō-shəs\ *adj* [L *atroc-, atrox* gloomy, atrocious, fr. *atr-, ater* black + *-oc-, -ox* (akin to Gk *ōps* eye) — more at EYE] (1658) **1** : extremely wicked, brutal, or cruel : BARBARIC **2** : APPALLING, HORRIFYING ⟨the ∼ weapons of modern war⟩ **3 a** : utterly revolting : ABOMINABLE ⟨∼ working conditions⟩ **b** : of very poor quality ⟨∼ handwriting⟩ — **atro·cious·ly** *adv* — **atro·cious·ness** *n*

atroc·i·ty \ə-ˈträ-sə-tē\ *n, pl* **-ties** (1534) **1** : the quality or state of being atrocious **2** : an atrocious act, object, or situation ⟨the . . . sufferings and *atrocities* of trench warfare —Aldous Huxley⟩

at·ro·phy \ˈa-trə-fē\ *n, pl* **-phies** [LL *atrophia,* fr. Gk, fr. *atrophos* ill fed, fr. *a-* + *trephein* to nourish] (1601) **1** : decrease in size or wasting away of a body part or tissue; *also* : arrested development or loss of a part or organ incidental to the normal development or life of an animal or plant **2** : a wasting away or progressive decline ⟨was not a solitude of ∼, of negation, but of perpetual flowering —Willa Cather⟩ — **atro·phic** \(ˌ)ā-ˈtrō-fik\ *adj* — **atrophy** \ˈa-trə-fē, -ˌfī\ *vb*

at·ro·pine \ˈa-trə-ˌpēn\ *n* [G *Atropin,* fr. NL *Atropa,* genus name of belladonna, fr. Gk *Atropos,* one of the three Fates] (1836) : a racemic mixture of hyoscyamine obtained from any of various solanaceous plants (as belladonna) and used esp. in the form of its sulfate for its anticholinergic effects (as pupil dilation or inhibition of smooth muscle spasms)

at sign *n* (1982) : the symbol @ esp. when used as part of an Internet user's e-mail address

1**att** *var of* AT

2**att** *abbr* **1** attached **2** attention **3** attorney

at·ta·boy \ˈa-tə-ˌbȯi\ *interj* [prob. alter. of *that's the boy*] (1909) — used to express encouragement, approval, or admiration

at·tach \ə-ˈtach\ *vb* [ME, fr. AF *attacher,* alter. of OF *estachier,* fr. *estache* stake, of Gmc origin; akin to OE *staca* stake] *vt* (14c) **1** : to take by legal authority esp. under a writ ⟨∼*ed* the property⟩ **2 a** : to bring (oneself) into an association ⟨∼*ed* herself to their cause⟩ **b** : to assign (an individual or unit in the military) temporarily **3** : to bind by personal ties (as of affection or sympathy) ⟨was strongly ∼*ed* to his family⟩ **4** : to make fast (as by tying or gluing) ⟨∼ a label to a package⟩ **5** : to associate esp. as a property or an attribute : ASCRIBE ⟨∼*ed* great importance to public opinion polls⟩ ∼ *vi* : to become attached : ADHERE ***syn*** see FASTEN — **at·tach·able** \-ˈta-chə-bəl\ *adj*

at·ta·ché \ˌa-tə-ˈshā, ˌa-ˌta-, ə-ˌta-\ *n* [F, pp. of *attacher*] (1826) **1** : a technical expert on a country's diplomatic staff at a foreign capital ⟨a military ∼⟩ **2** : ATTACHÉ CASE

at·ta·ché case \ˌa-ˌta-ˈshā-, ˌa-tə-; ə-ˈta-(ˌ)shā-\ *n* (1904) **1** : a small thin suitcase used esp. for carrying business papers **2** : BRIEFCASE

at·tached \ə-ˈtacht\ *adj* (1854) : permanently fixed when adult ⟨∼ barnacles⟩

at·tach·ment \ə-ˈtach-mənt\ *n* (14c) **1** : a seizure by legal process; *also* : the writ or precept commanding such seizure **2 a** : the state of being personally attached : FIDELITY ⟨∼ to a cause⟩ **b** : affectionate regard ⟨a deep ∼ to nature⟩ **3** : a device attached to a machine or implement **4** : the physical connection by which one thing is attached to another **5** : the process of physically attaching

1**at·tack** \ə-ˈtak\ *vb* [MF *attaquer,* fr. OIt **estaccare* to attach, fr. *stacca* stake, of Gmc origin; akin to OE *staca*] *vt* (1562) **1** : to set upon or work against forcefully **2** : to assail with unfriendly or bitter words **3** : to begin to affect or to act on injuriously ⟨plants ∼*ed* by aphids⟩ **4** : to set to work on ⟨∼ a problem⟩ **5** : to threaten (a piece in chess) with immediate capture ∼ *vi* : to make an attack — **at·tack·er** *n*

syn ATTACK, ASSAIL, ASSAULT, BOMBARD, STORM mean to make an onslaught upon. ATTACK implies taking the initiative in a struggle ⟨plan to *attack* the town at dawn⟩. ASSAIL implies attempting to break down resistance by repeated blows or shots ⟨*assailed* the enemy with artillery fire⟩. ASSAULT suggests a direct attempt to overpower by suddenness and violence of onslaught ⟨commandos *assaulted* the building from all sides⟩. BOMBARD applies to attacking with bombs or shells ⟨*bombarded* the city nightly⟩. STORM implies attempting to break into a defended position ⟨preparing to *storm* the fortress⟩.

2**attack** *n* (1655) **1** : the act of attacking with physical force or unfriendly words : ASSAULT **2** : a belligerent or antagonistic action **3 a** : a fit of sickness; *esp* : an active episode of a chronic or recurrent disease **b** : a period of being strongly affected by something (as a desire or mood) **4 a** : an offensive or scoring action ⟨won the game with an 8-hit ∼⟩ **b** : offensive players or the positions taken up by them **5** : the setting to work on some undertaking ⟨made a new ∼ on the problem⟩ **6** : the beginning of destructive action (as by a chemical agent) **7** : the act or manner of beginning a musical tone or phrase

3**attack** *adj* (1899) : designed, planned, or used for carrying out a military attack ⟨an ∼ helicopter⟩

attack dog *n* (1970) **1** : a dog trained to attack on command or on sight **2** : a person noted for harsh, personal, and usu. public verbal attacks against others ⟨a political *attack dog*⟩

at·tack·man \-ˌman\ *n* (1940) : a player (as in lacrosse) assigned to an offensive zone or position

at·tain \ə-ˈtān\ *vb* [ME *atteynen,* fr. AF *ateign-,* stem of *ateindre* to reach, accomplish, convict, fr. VL **attangere,* alter. of L *attingere,* fr. *ad-* + *tangere* to touch — more at TANGENT] *vt* (14c) **1** : to reach as an end : GAIN, ACHIEVE ⟨∼ a goal⟩ **2** : to come into possession of : OBTAIN ⟨he ∼*ed* preferment over his fellows⟩ **3** : to come to as the end of a progression or course of movement ⟨they ∼*ed* the top of the hill⟩ ⟨∼ a ripe old age⟩ ∼ *vi* : to come or arrive by motion, growth, or effort — usu. used with *to* — **at·tain·abil·i·ty** \-ˌtā-nə-ˈbi-lə-tē\ *n* — **attain·able** \-ˈtā-nə-bəl\ *adj*

at·tain·der \ə-ˈtān-dər\ *n* [ME *attaynder,* fr. AF *ateindre* conviction, fr. infin. of *ateindre*] (15c) **1** : extinction of the civil rights and capacities of a person upon sentence of death or outlawry usu. after a conviction of treason **2** *obs* : DISHONOR

at·tain·ment \ə-ˈtān-mənt\ *n* (1549) **1** : the act of attaining : the condition of being attained **2** : something attained : ACCOMPLISHMENT

1**at·taint** \ə-ˈtānt\ *vt* [ME *attaynten,* fr. AF *ateint,* pp. of *ateindre*] (14c) **1** : to affect by attainder **2 a** : INFECT, CORRUPT **b** *archaic* : TAINT, SULLY **3** *archaic* : ACCUSE

2**attaint** *n* (1592) *obs* : a stain upon honor or purity : DISGRACE

at·tar \ˈa-tər, ˈa-ˌtär\ *also* **ot·to** \ˈä-(ˌ)tō\ *n* [Pers *ʿaṭir* perfumed, fr. Ar, fr. *ʿiṭr* perfume] (1798) : a fragrant essential oil (as from rose petals); *also* : FRAGRANCE

1**at·tempt** \ə-ˈtem(p)t\ *vt* [ME, fr. AF & L; AF *attempter,* fr. L *attemptare,* fr. *ad-* + *temptare* to touch, try — more at TEMPT] (14c) **1** : to make an effort to do, accomplish, solve, or effect ⟨∼*ed* to swim the swollen river⟩ **2** *archaic* : TEMPT **3** *archaic* : to try to subdue or take by force : ATTACK — **at·tempt·able** \-ˈtem(p)-tə-bəl\ *adj*

syn ATTEMPT, TRY, ENDEAVOR, ESSAY, STRIVE mean to make an effort to accomplish an end. ATTEMPT stresses the initiation or beginning of an effort ⟨will *attempt* to photograph the rare bird⟩. TRY is often close to ATTEMPT but may stress effort or experiment made in the hope of testing or proving something ⟨*tried* to determine which was the better procedure⟩. ENDEAVOR heightens the implications of exertion and difficulty ⟨*endeavored* to find crash survivors in the mountains⟩. ESSAY implies difficulty but also suggests tentative trying or experimenting ⟨will *essay* a dramatic role for the first time⟩. STRIVE implies great exertion against great difficulty and specifically suggests persistent effort ⟨continues to *strive* for peace⟩.

2**attempt** *n* (1534) **1 a** : the act or an instance of attempting; *esp* : an unsuccessful effort **b** : something resulting from or representing an attempt ⟨surrounded by . . . a few ∼*s* at rose bushes —Marian Engel⟩ **2** : ATTACK, ASSAULT ⟨an ∼ on the life of the president⟩

at·tend \ə-ˈtend\ *vb* [ME, fr. AF *atendre,* fr. L *attendere,* lit., to stretch to, fr. *ad-* + *tendere* to stretch — more at THIN] *vt* (14c) **1** : to pay attention to **2** : to look after : take charge of ⟨campsites . . . ∼*ed* by park rangers —Jackson Rivers⟩ **3 a** : to go or stay with as a companion, nurse, or servant **b** : to visit professionally esp. as a physician **4** *archaic* **a** : to wait for **b** : to be in store for **5** : to be present with : ACCOMPANY **6** : to be present at : go to ⟨∼ law school⟩ ∼ *vi* **1** : to apply oneself ⟨∼ to your work⟩ **2** : to apply the mind or pay attention : HEED **3 a** : to be ready for service ⟨ministers who ∼ upon the king⟩ **b** : to be present **4** *obs* : WAIT, STAY **5** : to direct one's attention : SEE ⟨I'll ∼ to that⟩ — **at·tend·er** *n*

at·ten·dance \ə-ˈten-dən(t)s\ *n* (14c) **1** : the act or fact of attending ⟨a physician in ∼⟩ **2 a** : the persons or number of persons attending; *also* : an account of persons attending ⟨the teacher took ∼ before starting class⟩ **b** : the number of times a person attends

attendance officer *n* (1884) : TRUANT OFFICER

1**at·ten·dant** \ə-ˈten-dənt\ *n* (15c) **1** : one who attends another to perform a service; *esp* : an employee who waits on customers **2** : something that accompanies : CONCOMITANT **3** : ATTENDEE

2**attendant** *adj* (15c) **1** : accompanying, waiting upon, or following in order to perform service ⟨Cherub and Seraph . . . ∼ on their Lord —John Milton⟩ **2** : accompanying or following as a consequence or result ⟨problems ∼ on pollution⟩ ⟨civilization and its ∼ morality —Robert Stone⟩

at·tend·ee \ə-ˌten-ˈdē, ˌa-\ *n* (1937) : a person who is present on a given occasion or at a given place ⟨∼*s* at a convention⟩

1**at·tend·ing** \ə-ˈten-diŋ\ *adj* (ca. 1923) : serving as a physician on the staff of a teaching hospital ⟨an ∼ surgeon⟩

2**attending** *n* (1951) : an attending physician or surgeon

at·ten·tion \ə-ˈten(t)-shən; *sense 4 often* (ə-)ˌten(ch)-ˈhət\ *n* [ME *attencioun,* fr. L *attention-, attentio,* fr. *attendere*] (14c) **1 a** : the act or state of applying the mind to something **b** : a condition of readiness for such attention involving esp. a selective narrowing or focusing of consciousness and receptivity **2** : OBSERVATION, NOTICE; *esp* : consideration with a view to action ⟨a problem requiring prompt ∼⟩ **3 a** : an act of civility or courtesy esp. in courtship ⟨she welcomed his ∼*s*⟩ **b** : sympathetic consideration of the needs and wants of others : ATTENTIVENESS **4** : a position assumed by a soldier with heels together, body erect, arms at the sides, and eyes to the front — often used as a command — **at·ten·tion·al** \-ˈten(t)-sh(ə-)nəl\ *adj*

attention deficit disorder *n* (1978) : a syndrome of disordered learning and disruptive behavior that is not caused by any serious underlying physical or mental disorder and that has several subtypes characterized primarily by symptoms of inattentiveness or primarily by symptoms of hyperactivity and impulsive behavior (as speaking out of turn) or by the significant expression of all three — abbr. *ADD*

attention–deficit/hyperactivity disorder *n* (1987) : ATTENTION DEFICIT DISORDER — abbr. *ADHD*

attention line *n* (1925) : a line usu. placed above the salutation in a business letter directing the letter to one specified

attention span *n* (1934) : the length of time during which one (as an individual or a group) is able to concentrate or remain interested

at·ten·tive \ə-ˈten-tiv\ *adj* (14c) **1** : MINDFUL, OBSERVANT ⟨∼ to what he is doing⟩ **2** : heedful of the comfort of others : SOLICITOUS ⟨an ∼ waitress⟩ **3** : offering attentions in or as if in the role of a suitor — **atten·tive·ly** *adv* — **at·ten·tive·ness** *n*

1**at·ten·u·ate** \ə-ˈten-yə-wət, -yü-ət\ *adj* [ME *attenuat,* fr. L *attenuatus,* pp. of *attenuare* to make thin, fr. *ad-* + *tenuis* thin — more at THIN] (15c) **1** : reduced esp. in thickness, density, or force **2** : tapering gradually usu. to a long slender point ⟨∼ leaves⟩

2**at·ten·u·ate** \ə-ˈten-yə-ˌwāt, -yü-ˌāt\ *vb* **-at·ed; -at·ing** *vt* (1530) **1** : to make thin or slender **2** : to make thin in consistency : RAREFY **3** : to lessen the amount, force, magnitude, or value of : WEAKEN **4** : to reduce the severity, virulence, or vitality of ⟨an *attenuated* virus⟩ ∼ *vi* : to become thin, fine, or less — **at·ten·u·a·tion** \-ˌten-yə-ˈwā-shən, -yü-ˈā-\ *n*

\ə\ **abut** \ᵊ\ kitten, F table \ər\ **further** \a\ **ash** \ā\ **ace** \ä\ **mop, mar**
\au̇\ **out** \ch\ **chin** \e\ **bet** \ē\ **easy** \g\ **go** \i\ **hit** \ī\ **ice** \j\ **job**
\ŋ\ **sing** \ō\ **go** \ȯ\ **law** \ȯi\ **boy** \th\ **thin** \t͟h\ **the** \ü\ **loot** \u̇\ **foot**
\y\ **yet** \zh\ **vision, beige** \k̲, ⁿ, œ, ue, ʸ\ *see* Guide to Pronunciation

at·ten·u·a·tor \-yə-ˌwā-tər, -yü-ˌā-\ *n* (1924) **:** a device for attenuating; *esp* **:** one for reducing the amplitude of an electrical signal without appreciable distortion

at·test \ə-ˈtest\ *vb* [MF *attester,* fr. L *attestari,* fr. *ad-* + *testis* witness — more at TESTAMENT] *vt* (ca. 1500) **1 a :** to affirm to be true or genuine; *specif* **:** to authenticate by signing as a witness **b :** to authenticate officially **2 :** to establish or verify the usage of **3 :** to be proof of **:** MANIFEST ⟨her record ~*s* her integrity⟩ **4 :** to put on oath ~ *vi* **:** to bear witness **:** TESTIFY ⟨~ to a belief⟩ ***syn*** see CERTIFY — **at·tes·ta·tion** \ˌa-ˌtes-ˈtā-shən, ˌa-tə-ˈstā-\ *n* — **at·test·er** \ə-ˈtes-tər\ *n*

at·tic \ˈa-tik\ *n* [F *attique,* fr. *attique* of Attica, fr. L *Atticus*] (ca. 1696) **1 :** a low story or wall above the main order of a facade in the classical styles **2 :** a room behind an attic **3 :** a room or a space immediately below the roof of a building **:** GARRET **4 :** something resembling an attic (as in being used for storage)

[1]**At·tic** \ˈa-tik\ *adj* [L *Atticus* of Attica, fr. Gk *Attikos,* fr. *Attikē* Attica, Greece] (1599) **1 :** of, relating to, or having the characteristics of Athens or its ancient civilization **2 :** marked by simplicity, purity, and refinement ⟨an ~ prose style⟩

[2]**Attic** *n* (ca. 1771) **:** a dialect of ancient Greek orig. used in Attica and later the literary language of the Greek-speaking world

at·ti·cism \ˈa-tə-ˌsi-zəm\ *n, often cap* (1593) **1 :** a witty or well-turned phrase **2 :** a characteristic feature of Attic Greek occurring in another language or dialect

[1]**at·tire** \ə-ˈtī(-ə)r\ *vt* **at·tired; at·tir·ing** [ME, fr. AF *atirer* to equip, prepare, attire, fr. *a-* (fr. L *ad-*) + *tire* order, rank, of Gmc origin; akin to OE *tīr* glory, ornament] (14c) **:** to put garments on **:** DRESS, ARRAY; *esp* **:** to clothe in fancy or rich garments

[2]**attire** *n* (14c) **1 :** DRESS, CLOTHES; *esp* **:** splendid or decorative clothing **2 :** the antlers or antlers and scalp of a stag or buck

at·ti·tude \ˈa-tə-ˌtüd, -ˌtyüd\ *n* [F, fr. It *attitudine,* lit., aptitude, fr. LL *aptitudin-, aptitudo* fitness — more at APTITUDE] (1668) **1 :** the arrangement of the parts of a body or figure **:** POSTURE **2 :** a position assumed for a specific purpose ⟨a threatening ~⟩ **3 :** a ballet position similar to the arabesque in which the raised leg is bent at the knee **4 a :** a mental position with regard to a fact or state ⟨a helpful ~⟩ **b :** a feeling or emotion toward a fact or state **5 :** the position of an aircraft or spacecraft determined by the relationship between its axes and a reference datum (as the horizon or a particular star) **6 :** an organismic state of readiness to respond in a characteristic way to a stimulus (as an object, concept, or situation) **7 a :** a negative or hostile state of mind **b :** a cool, cocky, defiant, or arrogant manner

at·ti·tu·di·nal \ˌa-tə-ˈtü-də-nəl, -ˈtyü-\ *adj* [*attitude* + *-inal* (as in *aptitudinal,* fr. L *aptitudin-, aptitudo*)] (1831) **:** relating to, based on, or expressive of personal attitudes or feelings ⟨~ judgment⟩ — **at·ti·tu·di·nal·ly** \-ə-lē\ *adv*

at·ti·tu·di·nise *Brit var of* ATTITUDINIZE

at·ti·tu·di·nize \ˌa-tə-ˈtü-də-ˌnīz, -ˈtyü-\ *vi* **-nized; -niz·ing** (1784) **:** to assume an affected mental attitude **:** POSE

attn *abbr* attention

at·to- \ˈa-(ˌ)tō\ *comb form* [ISV, fr. Dan or Norw *atten* eighteen, fr. ON *āttjān;* akin to OE *eahtatīene* eighteen] **:** one quintillionth (10^{-18}) part of ⟨*atto*gram⟩

at·torn \ə-ˈtərn\ *vi* [ME *attournen,* fr. AF *aturner* to prepare, designate, attorn, fr. *a-* (fr. L *ad-*) + *turner* to turn] (15c) **:** to agree to be tenant to a new owner or landlord of the same property — **at·torn·ment** \-mənt\ *n*

at·tor·ney \ə-ˈtər-nē\ *n, pl* **-neys** [ME *attourney,* fr. AF *aturné,* pp. of *aturner*] (14c) **:** one who is legally appointed to transact business on another's behalf; *esp* **:** LAWYER — **at·tor·ney·ship** \-ˌship\ *n*

attorney–at–law *n, pl* **attorneys–at–law** (1768) **:** a practitioner in a court of law who is legally qualified to prosecute and defend actions in such court on the retainer of clients

attorney general *n, pl* **attorneys general** *or* **attorney generals** (1585) **:** the chief law officer of a nation or state who represents the government in litigation and serves as its principal legal adviser

at·tract \ə-ˈtrakt\ *vb* [ME, fr. L *attractus,* pp. of *attrahere,* fr. *ad-* + *trahere* to pull, draw] *vt* (15c) **:** to cause to approach or adhere: as **a :** to pull to or draw toward oneself or itself ⟨a magnet ~*s* iron⟩ **b :** to draw by appeal to natural or excited interest, emotion, or aesthetic sense **:** ENTICE ⟨~ attention⟩ ~ *vi* **:** to exercise attraction — **at·trac·tor** \-ˈtrak-tər\ *n*

syn ATTRACT, ALLURE, CHARM, CAPTIVATE, FASCINATE, ENCHANT mean to draw another by exerting a powerful influence. ATTRACT applies to any degree or kind of ability to exert influence over another ⟨students *attracted* by the school's locale⟩. ALLURE implies an enticing by what is fair, pleasing, or seductive ⟨an *alluring* smile⟩. CHARM implies the power of casting a spell over the person or thing affected and so compelling a response ⟨*charmed* by their hospitality⟩, but it may, like CAPTIVATE, suggest no more than evoking delight or admiration ⟨her performances *captivated* audiences⟩. FASCINATE suggests a magical influence and tends to stress the ineffectiveness of attempts to resist ⟨a story that continues to *fascinate* children⟩. ENCHANT is perhaps the strongest of these terms in stressing the appeal of the agent and the degree of delight evoked in the subject ⟨hopelessly *enchanted* by her beauty⟩.

at·trac·tant \ə-ˈtrak-tənt\ *n* (1920) **:** a substance (as a pheromone) that attracts specific animals (as insects or individuals of the opposite sex)

at·trac·tion \ə-ˈtrak-shən\ *n* (14c) **1 a :** the act, process, or power of attracting **b :** personal charm **2 :** the action or power of drawing forth a response **:** an attractive quality **3 :** a force acting mutually between particles of matter, tending to draw them together, and resisting their separation **4 :** something that attracts or is intended to attract people by appealing to their desires and tastes ⟨coming ~*s*⟩

syn ATTRACTION, AFFINITY, SYMPATHY mean the relationship existing between things or persons that are naturally or involuntarily drawn together. ATTRACTION implies the possession by one thing of a quality that pulls another to it ⟨felt an *attraction* to danger⟩. AFFINITY implies a susceptibility or predisposition on the part of the one drawn ⟨an *affinity* for mathematics⟩. SYMPATHY implies a reciprocal or natural relation between two things that are both susceptible to the same influence ⟨two minds in *sympathy*⟩.

at·trac·tive \ə-ˈtrak-tiv\ *adj* (14c) **1 :** having or relating to the power to attract ⟨~ forces between molecules⟩ **2 a :** arousing interest or pleasure **:** CHARMING ⟨an ~ smile⟩ **b :** APPEALING ⟨an ~ offer⟩ — **at·trac·tive·ly** *adv* — **at·trac·tive·ness** *n*

attrib *abbr* attributive; attributively

[1]**at·tri·bute** \ˈa-trə-ˌbyüt\ *n* [ME, fr. L *attributus,* pp. of *attribuere* to attribute, fr. *ad-* + *tribuere* to bestow — more at TRIBUTE] (14c) **1 :** an inherent characteristic; *also* **:** an accidental quality **2 :** an object closely associated with or belonging to a specific person, thing, or office ⟨a scepter is the ~ of power⟩; *esp* **:** such an object used for identification in painting or sculpture **3 :** a word ascribing a quality; *esp* **:** ADJECTIVE ***syn*** see QUALITY

[2]**at·trib·ute** \ə-ˈtri-ˌbyüt, -byət\ *vt* **-ut·ed; -ut·ing** (1530) **1 :** to explain by indicating a cause ⟨*attributed* his success to his coach⟩ **2 a :** to regard as a characteristic of a person or thing **b :** to reckon as made or originated in an indicated fashion ⟨*attributed* the invention to a Russian⟩ **c :** CLASSIFY, DESIGNATE ***syn*** see ASCRIBE — **at·trib·ut·able** \-byü-tə-bəl, -byə-\ *adj*

at·tri·bu·tion \ˌa-trə-ˈbyü-shən\ *n* (1651) **1 :** the act of attributing; *esp* **:** the ascribing of a work (as of literature or art) to a particular author or artist **2 :** an ascribed quality, character, or right — **at·tri·bu·tion·al** \-sh(ə-)n^{ə}l\ *adj*

at·trib·u·tive \ə-ˈtri-byə-tiv\ *adj* (1606) **1 :** relating to or of the nature of an attribute **:** ATTRIBUTING **2 :** joined directly to a modified noun without a linking verb (as *city* in *city streets*) — **attributive** *n* — **at·trib·u·tive·ly** *adv*

at·trit·ed \ə-ˈtrī-təd\ *adj* (1760) **:** worn by attrition

at·tri·tion \ə-ˈtri-shən, a-\ *n* [L *attrition-, attritio,* fr. *atterere* to rub against, fr. *ad-* + *terere* to rub — more at THROW] (14c) **1** [ME *attricioun,* fr. ML *attrition-, attritio,* fr. L] **:** sorrow for one's sins that arises from a motive other than that of the love of God **2 :** the act of rubbing together **:** FRICTION; *also* **:** the act of wearing or grinding down by friction **3 :** the act of weakening or exhausting by constant harassment, abuse, or attack ⟨a war of ~⟩ **4 :** a reduction in numbers usu. as a result of resignation, retirement, or death ⟨a company with a high rate of ~⟩ — **at·tri·tion·al** \-ˈtri-sh(ə-)n^{ə}l\ *adj*

at·tune \ə-ˈtün, -ˈtyün\ *vt* (1596) **1 :** to bring into harmony **:** TUNE **2 :** to make aware or responsive ⟨~ businesses to changing trends⟩ — **at·tune·ment** \-mənt\ *n*

atty *abbr* attorney

atty gen *abbr* attorney general

ATV \ˌā-(ˌ)tē-ˈvē\ *n* (1969) **:** ALL-TERRAIN VEHICLE

atwit·ter \ə-ˈtwi-tər\ *adj* (1833) **:** nervously concerned **:** EXCITED ⟨gossips ~ with speculation —*Time*⟩

at wt *abbr* atomic weight

atyp·i·cal \(ˌ)ā-ˈti-pi-kəl\ *adj* (1885) **:** not typical **:** IRREGULAR, UNUSUAL ⟨an ~ form of a disease⟩ — **atyp·i·cal·i·ty** \ˌā-ˌti-pə-ˈka-lə-tē\ *n* — **atyp·i·cal·ly** \(ˌ)ā-ˈti-pi-k(ə-)lē\ *adv*

[1]**Au** *abbr* author

[2]**Au** *symbol* [L *aurum*] gold

AU *abbr* **1** angstrom unit **2** astronomical unit

au·bade \ō-ˈbäd\ *n* [F, fr. MF, fr. Old Occitan *aubada,* fr. *alba, auba* dawn, fr. VL **alba,* fr. L, fem. of *albus* white — more at ALB] (ca. 1678) **1 :** a song or poem greeting the dawn **2 a :** a morning love song **b :** a song or poem of lovers parting at dawn **3 :** morning music — compare NOCTURNE

au·berge \ō-ˈberzh\ *n* [F, fr. MF, of Gmc origin; akin to OHG *heriberga* military quarters — more at HARBOR] (1599) **:** INN 1a

au·ber·gine \ˈō-bər-ˌzhēn\ *n* [F, fr. Catal *albergínia,* fr. Ar *al-bādhinjān* the eggplant, ultim. fr. Middle Indo-Aryan **vātiṅjaṇa-, vātiṅgaṇa-*] (1794) **1** *chiefly Brit* **:** EGGPLANT 1 **2 :** EGGPLANT 2

[1]**au·burn** \ˈȯ-bərn\ *adj* [ME *auborne* blond, fr. MF, fr. ML *alburnus* whitish, fr. L *alburnum* sapwood] (15c) **1 :** of the color auburn **2 :** of a reddish-brown color

[2]**auburn** *n* (1613) **:** a moderate brown

Au·bus·son \ˌō-bə-ˈsō^{n}\ *n* [*Aubusson,* town in France] (1900) **:** a figured scenic tapestry used for wall hangings and upholstery; *also* **:** a rug woven to resemble Aubusson tapestry

AUC *abbr* [L *ab urbe condita*] from the year of the founding of the city (of Rome)

au cou·rant \ˌō-kü-ˈrä^{n}\ *adj* [F, lit., in the current] (1762) **1 a :** fully informed **:** UP-TO-DATE ⟨trying to stay *au courant*⟩ **b :** FASHIONABLE, STYLISH ⟨*au courant* outfits⟩ **2 :** fully familiar **:** CONVERSANT

[1]**auc·tion** \ˈȯk-shən\ *n* [L *auction-, auctio,* fr. *augēre* to increase — more at EKE] (1595) **1 :** a sale of property to the highest bidder **2 :** the act or process of bidding in some card games

[2]**auction** *vt* **auc·tioned; auc·tion·ing** \-sh(ə-)niŋ\ (ca. 1798) **:** to sell at auction ⟨~*ed* off his library⟩

auction bridge *n* (1903) **:** a bridge game differing from contract bridge in that tricks made in excess of the contract are scored toward game

auc·tion·eer \ˌȯk-shə-ˈnir\ *n* (ca. 1708) **:** an agent who sells goods at auction

auc·to·ri·al \ȯk-ˈtȯr-ē-əl\ *adj* [L *auctor* author — more at AUTHOR] (1821) **:** of or relating to an author

aud *abbr* audit; auditor

au·da·cious \ȯ-ˈdā-shəs\ *adj* [MF *audacieux,* fr. *audace* boldness, fr. L *audacia,* fr. *audac-, audax* bold, fr. *audēre* to dare, fr. *avidus* eager — more at AVID] (1550) **1 a :** intrepidly daring **:** ADVENTUROUS ⟨an ~ mountain climber⟩ **b :** recklessly bold **:** RASH ⟨an ~ maneuver⟩ **2 :** contemptuous of law, religion, or decorum **:** INSOLENT **3 :** marked by originality and verve ⟨~ experiments⟩ — **au·da·cious·ly** *adv* — **au·da·cious·ness** *n*

au·dac·i·ty \ȯ-ˈda-sə-tē\ *n, pl* **-ties** [ME *audacite,* fr. L *audac-, audax*] (15c) **1 :** the quality or state of being audacious: as **a :** intrepid boldness **b :** bold or arrogant disregard of normal restraints ⟨had the ~ to defy his boss⟩ **2 :** an audacious act — usu. used in pl. ⟨her worst *audacities* did not seem to surprise him —Edith Wharton⟩ ***syn*** see TEMERITY

au·di·al \ˈȯ-dē-əl\ *adj* [*audio* + [1]*-al*] (1966) **:** of, relating to, or affecting the sense of hearing **:** AURAL

au·di·bi·lize \ˈȯ-də-bə-ˌlīz\ *vi* **-ized; -iz·ing** (1971) **:** AUDIBLE

[1]**au·di·ble** \ˈȯ-də-bəl\ *adj* [LL *audibilis,* fr. L *audire* to hear; akin to Gk *aisthanesthai* to perceive, Skt *āvis* evidently] (1529) **:** heard or capable of being heard — **au·di·bil·i·ty** \ˌȯ-də-ˈbi-lə-tē\ *n* — **au·di·bly** \ˈȯ-də-blē\ *adv*

2**audible** *n* (1961) : a substitute offensive or defensive play called at the line of scrimmage in football
3**audible** *vi* **-bled; -bling** \-b(ə-)liŋ\ (1974) : to call an audible ⟨*audibled* to a pass play —Peter King⟩
au·di·ence \'ȯ-dē-ən(t)s, 'ä-\ *n* [ME, fr. AF, fr. L *audientia,* fr. *audient-, audiens,* prp. of *audire*] (14c) **1 :** the act or state of hearing **2 a :** a formal hearing or interview ⟨an ~ with the pope⟩ **b :** an opportunity of being heard **3 a :** a group of listeners or spectators **b :** a reading, viewing, or listening public **4 :** a group of ardent admirers or devotees
au·dile \'ȯ-ˌdī(-ə)l\ *adj* [*aud*itory + *-ile* (as in *tactile*)] (1887) : AUDITORY
aud·ing \'ȯ-diŋ\ *n* [L *audire* + E 1*-ing*] (ca. 1949) : the process of hearing, recognizing, and interpreting spoken language
1**au·dio** \'ȯ-dē-ˌō\ *adj* [*audio-*] (1907) **1 :** of or relating to acoustic, mechanical, or electrical frequencies corresponding to normally audible sound waves which are of frequencies approximately from 15 to 20,000 hertz **2 a :** of or relating to sound or its reproduction and esp. high-fidelity reproduction **b :** relating to or used in the transmission or reception of sound — compare VIDEO **c :** of, relating to, or utilizing recorded sound
2**audio** *n* (1934) **1 :** an audio signal; *broadly* : SOUND **2 :** the section of television or motion-picture equipment that deals with sound **3 :** the transmission, reception, or reproduction of sound
audio- *comb form* [L *audire* to hear — more at AUDIBLE] **1 :** hearing ⟨*audio*meter⟩ **2 :** sound ⟨*audio*phile⟩ **3 :** auditory and ⟨*audio*visual⟩
au·dio–an·i·ma·tron·ic \ˌȯ-dē-ō-ˌa-nə-mə-'trä-nik\ *adj* [fr. *Audio-Animatronics,* a trademark] (1963) : being or consisting of a lifelike electromechanical figure of a person or animal that has synchronized movement and sound
au·dio·book \'ȯ-dē-ō-ˌbu̇k\ *n* (1953) : a recording of a book or magazine being read
au·dio·cas·sette \ˌȯ-dē-(ˌ)ō-kə-'set, -ka-\ *n* (1967) : an audiotape recording mounted in a cassette
au·dio·gen·ic \ˌȯ-dē-ō-'je-nik\ *adj* (1941) : produced by frequencies corresponding to sound waves — used esp. of epileptoid responses
au·dio·gram \'ȯ-dē-ō-ˌgram\ *n* (1927) : a graphic representation of the relation of vibration frequency and the minimum sound intensity for hearing
au·dio–lin·gual \ˌȯ-dē-ō-'liŋ-gwəl *also* -gyə-wəl\ *adj* (1959) : involving a drill routine of listening and speaking in language learning
au·di·ol·o·gy \ˌȯ-dē-'ä-lə-jē\ *n* (1946) : a branch of science dealing with hearing; *specif* : therapy of individuals having impaired hearing — **au·di·o·log·i·cal** \-ē-ə-'lä-ji-kəl\ *also* **au·di·o·log·ic** \-ē-ə-'lä-jik\ *adj* — **au·di·ol·o·gist** \-ē-'ä-lə-jist\ *n*
au·di·om·e·ter \ˌȯ-dē-'ä-mə-tər\ *n* (1879) : an instrument used in measuring the acuity of hearing — **au·dio·met·ric** \-dē-ō-'me-trik\ *adj* — **au·di·om·e·try** \-dē-'ä-mə-trē\ *n*
au·dio·phile \'ȯ-dē-ō-ˌfī(-ə)l\ *n* (1951) : a person who is enthusiastic about high-fidelity sound reproduction
au·dio·tape \'ȯ-dē-ō-ˌtāp\ *n* (1951) : a tape recording of sound
au·dio·vi·su·al \ˌȯ-dē-(ˌ)ō-'vi-zhə-wəl, -zhəl, -zhü(-ə)l\ *adj* (1902) **1 :** designed to aid in learning or teaching by making use of both hearing and sight **2 :** of or relating to both hearing and sight
au·dio·vi·su·als \-zhə-wəlz, -zhəlz, -zhü(-ə)lz\ *n pl* (1948) : audiovisual teaching materials (as filmstrips accompanied by recordings)
1**au·dit** \'ȯ-dət\ *n* [ME, fr. L *auditus* act of hearing, fr. *audire*] (15c) **1 a :** a formal examination of an organization's or individual's accounts or financial situation **b :** the final report of an audit **2 :** a methodical examination and review
2**audit** *vt* (15c) **1 :** to perform an audit of or for ⟨~ the books⟩ ⟨~ the company⟩ **2 :** to attend (a course) without working for or expecting to receive formal credit — **au·dit·abil·i·ty** \ˌȯ-də-tə-'bi-lə-tē\ *n* — **au·dit·able** \-ˌȯ-di-tə-bəl\ *adj* — **au·dit·ee** \ˌȯ-də-'tē\ *n*
1**au·di·tion** \ȯ-'di-shən\ *n* [MF or L; MF, fr. L *audition-, auditio,* fr. *audire*] (1599) **1 :** the power or sense of hearing **2 :** the act of hearing; *esp* : a critical hearing ⟨an ~ of new recordings⟩ **3 :** a trial performance to appraise an entertainer's merits
2**audition** *vb* **au·di·tioned; au·di·tion·ing** \-'di-sh(ə-)niŋ\ *vt* (1931) : to test or try out esp. in an audition ~ *vi* : to give a trial performance
au·di·tor \'ȯ-də-tər\ *n* (14c) **1 :** a person authorized to examine and verify accounts **2 :** one who hears or listens; *esp* : one who is a member of an audience **3 :** a person who audits a course of study **4 :** a person who hears (as a court case) in the capacity of judge
au·di·to·ri·um \ˌȯ-də-'tȯr-ē-əm\ *n, pl* **-riums** *or* **-ria** \-ē-ə\ [L, lit., lecture room] (1640) **1 :** the part of a public building where an audience sits **2 :** a room, hall, or building used for public gatherings
1**au·di·to·ry** \'ȯ-də-ˌtȯr-ē\ *n* [ME *auditorie,* fr. L *auditorium*] (14c) **1** *archaic* : AUDIENCE **2** *archaic* : AUDITORIUM
2**auditory** *adj* [LL *auditorius*] (1578) : of, relating to, or experienced through hearing ⟨~ stimuli⟩ — **au·di·to·ri·ly** *adv*
auditory nerve *n* (1713) : either of the eighth pair of cranial nerves connecting the inner ear with the brain and transmitting impulses concerned with hearing and balance — see EAR illustration
auditory tube *n* (ca. 1705) : EUSTACHIAN TUBE
audit trail *n* (1954) : a record of a sequence of events (as actions performed by a computer) from which a history may be reconstructed
Auf·klä·rung \'au̇f-ˌkler-əŋ, -u̇ŋ\ *n* [G] (1842) : ENLIGHTENMENT 2
auf Wie·der·seh·en \au̇f-'vē-dər-ˌzā(-ə)n\ *interj* [G, lit., on seeing again] (1845) — used to express farewell
aug *abbr* augmentative
Aug *abbr* August
Au·ge·an \ȯ-'jē-ən\ *adj* [L *Augeas,* king of Elis, fr. Gk *Augeias;* fr. the legend that his stable, left neglected for 30 years, was finally cleaned by Hercules] (1676) : extremely formidable or difficult and occas. distasteful ⟨an ~ task⟩
Augean stable *n* (1622) : a condition or place marked by great accumulation of filth or corruption
au·ger \'ȯ-gər\ *n* [ME, alter. (resulting from false division of *a nauger*) of *nauger,* fr. OE *nafogār;* akin to OHG *nabugēr* auger, OE *nafu* nave, *gār* spear — more at NAVE, GORE] (bef. 12c) : any of various tools or devices with a helical shaft or part that are used for boring holes (as in wood) or moving loose material (as snow)

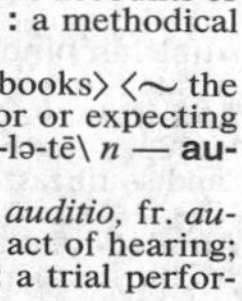

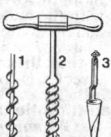

auger: *1, 2* screw, *3* tapering pod

Au·ger effect \(ˌ)ō-'zhā-\ *n* [Pierre V. *Auger* †1993 Fr. physicist] (1928) : a process in which an atom that has been ionized through the emission of an electron with energy in the X-ray range undergoes a transition in which a second electron is emitted rather than an X-ray photon — called also *Auger process*
Auger electron *n* (1939) : an electron emitted from an atom in the Auger effect
Auger electron spectroscopy *n* (1970) : an instrumental method for determining the chemical composition of a material's surface by means of analysis of the energies of Auger electrons emitted from the surface — called also *Auger spectroscopy*
1**aught** \'ȯt, 'ät\ *pron* [ME, fr. OE *āwiht,* fr. *ā* ever + *wiht* creature, thing — more at AYE, WIGHT] (bef. 12c) **1 :** ANYTHING **2 :** ALL, EVERYTHING ⟨for ~ I care⟩ ⟨for ~ we know⟩
2**aught** *adv* (13c) *archaic* : AT ALL
3**aught** *n* [alter. (resulting from false division of *a naught*) of *naught*] (1872) **1 :** ZERO, CIPHER **2** *archaic* : NONENTITY, NOTHING **3** *pl* : the first decade of a century
au·gite \'ȯ-ˌjīt\ *n* [L *augites,* a precious stone, fr. Gk *augitēs*] (1804) **1 :** a usu. black or dark green mineral that consists of aluminous pyroxene and is found esp. in igneous rocks **2 :** PYROXENE — **au·git·ic** \ȯ-'ji-tik\ *adj*
1**aug·ment** \ȯg-'ment\ *vb* [ME, fr. AF *augmenter,* fr. LL *augmentare,* fr. L *augmentum* increase, fr. *augēre* to increase — more at EKE] *vt* (14c) **1 :** to make greater, more numerous, larger, or more intense ⟨the impact of the report was ~*ed* by its timing⟩ **2 :** to add an augment to **3 :** SUPPLEMENT ⟨~*ed* her income⟩ ~ *vi* : to become augmented ***syn*** see INCREASE — **aug·ment·er** *or* **aug·men·tor** \-'men-tər\ *n*
2**aug·ment** \'ȯg-ˌment\ *n* (1671) : a vowel prefixed or a lengthening of the initial vowel to mark past time esp. in Greek and Sanskrit verbs
aug·men·ta·tion \ˌȯg-mən-'tā-shən, -ˌmen-\ *n* (14c) **1 a :** the act or process of augmenting **b :** the state of being augmented **2 :** something that augments : ADDITION
1**aug·men·ta·tive** \ȯg-'men-tə-tiv\ *adj* (15c) **1 :** able to augment **2 :** indicating large size and sometimes awkwardness or unattractiveness — used of words and affixes; compare DIMINUTIVE
2**augmentative** *n* (1804) : an augmentative word or affix
aug·ment·ed \ȯg-'men-təd\ *adj* (15c) *of a musical interval* : made one half step greater than major or perfect ⟨an ~ fifth⟩
augmented matrix *n* (1861) : a matrix whose elements are the coefficients of a set of simultaneous linear equations with the constant terms of the equations entered in an added column
augmented reality *n* (1993) : an enhanced version of reality created by the use of technology to overlay digital information on an image of something being viewed through a device (as a smartphone camera); *also* : the technology used to create augmented reality
au gra·tin \ō-'grä-tᵊn, ȯ-, -'gra-\ *adj* [F, lit., with the burnt scrapings from the pan] (1806) : covered with bread crumbs or grated cheese and browned (as under a broiler) — **au gratin** *adv*
1**au·gur** \'ȯ-gər\ *n* [L; akin to L *augēre*] (14c) **1 :** an official diviner of ancient Rome **2 :** one held to foretell events by omens
2**augur** *vt* (1593) **1 :** to foretell esp. from omens **2 :** to give promise of : PRESAGE ~ *vi* : to predict the future esp. from omens
au·gu·ry \'ȯ-gyə-rē, -gə-\ *n, pl* **-ries** (14c) **1 :** divination from auspices or omens; *also* : an instance of this **2 :** OMEN, PORTENT
au·gust \ȯ-'gəst, 'ȯ-(ˌ)gəst\ *adj* [L *augustus;* akin to L *augur*] (1581) : marked by majestic dignity or grandeur ⟨her ~ lineage⟩ — **au·gust·ly** *adv* — **au·gust·ness** \ȯ-'gəs(t)-nəs, 'ȯ-(ˌ)gəs(t)-\ *n*
Au·gust \'ȯ-gəst\ *n* [ME, fr. OE, fr. L *Augustus,* fr. *Augustus* Caesar] (bef. 12c) : the eighth month of the Gregorian calendar
Au·gus·tan \ȯ-'gəs-tən, ə-\ *adj* (1704) **1 :** of, relating to, or characteristic of Augustus Caesar or his age **2 :** of, relating to, or characteristic of the neoclassical period in England — **Augustan** *n*
1**Au·gus·tin·i·an** \ˌȯ-gə-'sti-nē-ən\ *n* (1534) **1 :** a member of an Augustinian order; *specif* : a friar of the Hermits of St. Augustine founded in 1256 and devoted to educational, missionary, and parish work **2 :** a follower of St. Augustine
2**Augustinian** *adj* (1653) **1 :** of or relating to St. Augustine or his doctrines **2 :** of or relating to any of several orders under a rule ascribed to St. Augustine — **Au·gus·tin·i·an·ism** \-nē-ə-ˌni-zəm\ *n*
au jus \ō-'zhü(s), -'jüs; ō-zhœ\ *adj* [F, lit., with juice] (1865) *of meat* : served in the juice obtained from roasting
auk \'ȯk\ *n* [Norw or Icel *alk, alka,* fr. ON *ālka*] (1674) : any of several black-and-white short-necked diving seabirds of the alcid family that breed in colder parts of the northern hemisphere — compare GREAT AUK
auk·let \'ȯ-klət\ *n* (1883) : any of several small seabirds (esp. genera *Aethia* and *Ptychorhamphus*) of the alcid family that occur along No. Pacific coasts
auld \'ȯl(d), 'äl(d)\ *adj* (14c) *chiefly Scot* : OLD
auld lang syne \ˌōl(d)-ˌ(l)aŋ-'zīn, ˌȯl(d)-\ *n* [Sc, lit., old long ago] (1720) : the good old times
au na·tu·rel \ˌō-ˌna-tə-'rel, -ˌna-chə-\ *adj* [F] (1812) **1 :** cooked or served plainly **2 a :** being in natural style or condition **b :** NUDE
aunt \'ant, 'änt\ *n* [ME, fr. OF *ante,* fr. L *amita;* akin to OHG *amma* mother, nurse, Gk *amma* nurse] (13c) **1 :** the sister of one's father or mother **2 :** the wife of one's uncle — **aunt·hood** \-ˌhu̇d\ *n* — **aunt·like** \-ˌlīk\ *adj* — **aunt·ly** *adj*
aunt·ie \'an-tē, 'än-\ *n* (1724) : AUNT
Aunt Sal·ly \-'sa-lē\ *n, pl* **Aunt Sallies** [*Aunt Sally,* name given to an effigy of a woman smoking a pipe set up as an amusement attraction at English fairs for patrons to throw missiles at] (1879) *Brit* : an object of criticism or contention; *esp* : one that is set up to invite criticism or be easily refuted
au pair \'ō-'per\ *n, pl* **au pairs** \-'perz\ [F, on even terms] (1918) : a usu. young foreign person who cares for children and does domestic work for a family in return for room and board and the opportunity to learn the family's language

\ə\ **abut** \ᵊ\ kitten, F table \ər\ **fur**ther \a\ **a**sh \ā\ **a**ce \ä\ **mop, mar**
\au̇\ **out** \ch\ **chin** \e\ bet \ē\ **easy** \g\ **go** \i\ **hit** \ī\ **ice** \j\ **job**
\ŋ\ **sing** \ō\ **go** \ȯ\ **law** \ȯi\ **boy** \th\ **thin** \t͟h\ **the** \ü\ **loot** \u̇\ **foot**
\y\ yet \zh\ vision, beige \k, ⁿ, œ, ue, ʸ\ *see* Guide to Pronunciation

au poivre \ō-ˈpwäv(rᵊ)\ *adj* [F, with pepper] (1953) **:** prepared or served with a generous amount of usu. coarsely ground black pepper ⟨steak *au poivre*⟩

au·ra \ˈȯr-ə\ *n* [ME, fr. L, puff of air, breeze, fr. Gk; prob. akin to Gk *aēr* air] (1694) **1 a :** a subtle sensory stimulus (as an aroma) **b :** a distinctive atmosphere surrounding a given source ⟨the place had an ~ of mystery⟩ **2 :** a luminous radiation **:** NIMBUS **3 :** a subjective sensation (as of lights) experienced before an attack of some disorders (as epilepsy or a migraine) **4 :** an energy field that is held to emanate from a living being

au·ral \ˈȯr-əl\ *adj* [L *auris* ear — more at EAR] (1773) **:** of or relating to the ear or to the sense of hearing — **au·ral·i·ty** \ȯ-ˈra-lə-tē\ *n* — **au·ral·ly** \ˈȯr-ə-lē\ *adv*

aurar *pl of* EYRIR

au·re·ate \ˈȯr-ē-ət\ *adj* [ME *aureat,* fr. ML *aureatus* decorated with gold, fr. L *aureus*] (15c) **1 :** of a golden color or brilliance ⟨~ light⟩ **2 :** marked by grandiloquent and rhetorical style ⟨~ diction⟩

au·re·ole \ˈȯr-ē-ˌōl\ *or* **au·re·o·la** \ȯ-ˈrē-ə-lə, ə-\ *n* [ME *aureole* heavenly crown worn by saints, fr. ML *aureola,* fr. L, fem. of *aureolus* golden, dim. of *aureus*] (13c) **1 a :** a radiant light around the head or body of a representation of a sacred personage **b :** something resembling an aureole ⟨an ~ of hair⟩ **2 :** RADIANCE, AURA ⟨an ~ of youth and health⟩ **3 :** the luminous area surrounding the sun or other bright light when seen through thin cloud or mist **:** CORONA **4 :** a ring-shaped zone around an igneous intrusion — **aureole** *vt*

au·re·us \ˈȯr-ē-əs\ *n, pl* **-rei** \-ē-ˌī\ [L, lit., golden, fr. *aurum* gold; akin to OPruss *ausis* gold] (1609) **:** a gold coin of ancient Rome varying in weight from 1/30 to 1/70 libra

au re·voir \ˌōr-ə-ˈvwär, ˌȯr-, *F* ōr-(ə)-vwȧr\ *n* [F, lit., till seeing again] (1676) **:** GOOD-BYE — often used interjectionally

au·ric \ˈȯr-ik\ *adj* [L *aurum*] (ca. 1828) **:** of, relating to, or derived from gold

au·ri·cle \ˈȯr-i-kəl\ *n* [L *auricula,* fr. dim. of *auris* ear — more at EAR] (15c) **1 a :** an atrium of a heart **b :** PINNA 1 **c :** an anterior ear-shaped pouch in each atrium of the human heart **2 :** an angular or ear-shaped lobe, process, or appendage

au·ric·u·la \ȯ-ˈri-kyə-lə\ *n* [NL, fr. L, external ear] (1655) **:** a yellow-flowered Alpine primrose (*Primula auricula*)

au·ric·u·lar \ȯ-ˈri-kyə-lər\ *adj* (15c) **1 :** told privately ⟨an ~ confession⟩ **2 :** understood or recognized by the sense of hearing **3 :** of, relating to, or using the ear or the sense of hearing ⟨~ therapy⟩ **4 :** of or relating to an auricle ⟨~ tachycardia⟩

au·ric·u·late \ȯ-ˈri-kyə-lət\ *adj* (1711) **:** having auricles ⟨an ~ leaf⟩

au·rif·er·ous \ȯ-ˈri-f(ə-)rəs\ *adj* [L *aurifer,* fr. *aurum* + *-fer* -ferous] (1655) **:** containing gold

Au·ri·ga \ȯ-ˈrī-gə\ *n* [L, lit., charioteer] **:** a constellation between Perseus and Gemini

Au·ri·gna·cian \ˌȯr-ēn-ˈyā-shən\ *adj* [F *aurignacien,* fr. *Aurignac,* France] (1909) **:** of or relating to an Upper Paleolithic culture marked by finely made artifacts of stone and bone, paintings, and engravings

au·rochs \ˈau̇-ˌräks, ˈȯr-ˌäks\ *n, pl* **aurochs** [G, fr. OHG *ūrohso,* fr. *ūro* aurochs + *ohso* ox; akin to OE *ūr* aurochs — more at OX] (1766) **:** an extinct large long-horned wild ox (*Bos primigenius*) of Europe that is the ancestor of domestic cattle

au·ro·ra \ə-ˈrȯr-ə, ȯ-\ *n, pl* **auroras** *or* **au·ro·rae** \-(ˌ)ē\ [L — more at EAST] (14c) **1 :** DAWN **2** *cap* **:** the Roman goddess of dawn — compare EOS **3 :** a luminous phenomenon that consists of streamers or arches of light appearing in the upper atmosphere of a planet's magnetic polar regions and is caused by the emission of light from atoms excited by electrons accelerated along the planet's magnetic field lines — **au·ro·ral** \-əl\ *adj* — **au·ro·re·an** \-ē-ən\ *adj*

aurora aus·tra·lis \-ȯ-ˈstrā-ləs, -ä-ˈstrā-\ *n* [NL, lit., southern dawn] (1741) **:** an aurora that occurs in earth's southern hemisphere — called also *southern lights*

aurora bo·re·al·is \-ˌbȯr-ē-ˈa-ləs\ *n* [NL, lit., northern dawn] (1717) **:** an aurora that occurs in earth's northern hemisphere — called also *northern lights*

Aus *abbr* Austria; Austrian

AUS *abbr* Army of the United States

aus·cul·tate \ˈȯ-skəl-ˌtāt\ *vt* **-tat·ed; -tat·ing** [back-formation fr. *auscultation*] (1846) **:** to examine by auscultation ⟨~ the patient's heart for a murmur⟩ — **aus·cul·ta·to·ry** \ȯ-ˈskəl-tə-ˌtȯr-ē\ *adj*

aus·cul·ta·tion \ˌȯ-skəl-ˈtā-shən\ *n* [L *auscultation-, auscultatio* act of listening, fr. *auscultare* to listen; akin to L *auris* ear — more at EAR] (1821) **:** the act of listening to sounds arising within organs (as the lungs) as an aid to diagnosis and treatment

aus·land·er \ˈau̇s-ˌlen-dər, -ˌlan-\ *n* [G *Ausländer*] (1936) **:** OUTSIDER, FOREIGNER

aus·pice \ˈȯs-pəs\ *n, pl* **aus·pic·es** \-pə-səz, -ˌsēz\ [L *auspicium,* fr. *auspic-, auspex* diviner by birds, fr. *avis* bird + *specere* to look, look at — more at AVIARY, SPY] (1533) **1 :** observation by an augur esp. of the flight and feeding of birds to discover omens **2** *pl* **:** kindly patronage and guidance ⟨doing research under the *auspices* of the local historical society⟩ **3 :** a prophetic sign; *esp* **:** a favorable sign

aus·pi·cious \ȯ-ˈspi-shəs\ *adj* (1593) **1 :** affording a favorable auspice **:** PROPITIOUS ⟨made an ~ beginning⟩ **2 :** attended by good auspices **:** PROSPEROUS ⟨an ~ year⟩ ***syn*** see FAVORABLE — **aus·pi·cious·ly** *adv* — **aus·pi·cious·ness** *n*

Aus·sie \ˈȯ-sē, ˈä-sē, *Brit & Austral usu* ˈȯ-zē\ *n* [*Australian* + *-ie*] (1917) **:** a native or inhabitant of Australia

aus·ten·ite \ˈȯs-tə-ˌnīt, ˈäs-\ *n* [F, fr. Sir W. C. Roberts-*Austen* †1902 Eng. metallurgist] (1901) **:** a solid solution in iron of carbon and sometimes other solutes that occurs as a constituent of steel under certain conditions — **aus·ten·it·ic** \ˌȯs-tə-ˈni-tik, ˌäs-\ *adj*

aus·tere \ȯ-ˈstir *also* -ˈster\ *adj* [ME, fr. AF, fr. L *austerus,* fr. Gk *austēros* harsh, severe; akin to Gk *hauos* dry — more at SERE] (14c) **1 a :** stern and cold in appearance or manner **b :** SOMBER, GRAVE ⟨an ~ critic⟩ **2 :** morally strict **:** ASCETIC **3 :** markedly simple or unadorned ⟨an ~ office⟩ ⟨an ~ style of writing⟩ **4 :** giving little or no scope for pleasure ⟨~ diets⟩ **5** *of a wine* **:** having the flavor of acid or tannin predominant over fruit flavors usu. indicating a capacity for aging ***syn*** see SEVERE — **aus·tere·ly** *adv* — **aus·tere·ness** *n*

aus·ter·i·ty \ȯ-ˈster-ə-tē, -ˈste-rə- *also* -ˈstir-ə-\ *n, pl* **-ties** (14c) **1 :** the quality or state of being austere **2 a :** an austere act, manner, or attitude **b :** an ascetic practice **3 :** enforced or extreme economy

[1]**Austr-** *or* **Austro-** *comb form* [L, fr. *Austr-, Auster* south wind] **:** south **:** southern ⟨*Austro*asiatic⟩

[2]**Austr-** *or* **Austro-** *comb form* [prob. fr. NL, fr. *Austria*] **:** Austrian and ⟨*Austro*-Hungarian⟩

[1]**aus·tral** \ˈȯs-trəl, ˈäs-\ *adj* [ME, fr. L *australis,* fr. *Austr-, Auster*] (14c) **1 :** of or relating to the Southern hemisphere **2** *cap* **:** AUSTRALIAN

[2]**aus·tral** \au̇-ˈsträl\ *n, pl* **aus·tral·es** \-ˈsträ-lās\ *also* **australs** [Sp] (1985) **:** the basic monetary unit of Argentina from 1985 to 1991

Austral *abbr* Australia

Aus·tra·lia Day \ȯ-ˈstrāl-yə-, ä-, ə-\ *n* (1911) **:** a national holiday in Australia commemorating the landing of the British at Sydney Cove in 1788 and observed on the Monday of or next following Jan. 26

[1]**Aus·tra·lian** \ȯ-ˈstrāl-yən, ä-, ə-\ *adj* (1814) **1 :** of, relating to, or characteristic of the continent or commonwealth of Australia, its inhabitants, or the languages spoken there **2 :** of, relating to, or being a biogeographic region that comprises Australia, the islands north of it from Celebes eastward, Tasmania, New Zealand, and Polynesia

[2]**Australian** *n* (1814) **1 :** a native or inhabitant of the Australian commonwealth **2 :** a group of about 200 languages spoken by the aboriginal inhabitants of Australia

Australian ballot *n* (1888) **:** an official ballot printed at public expense on which the names of all the candidates and proposals appear and which is distributed only at the polling place and marked in secret

Australian cattle dog *n* (1926) **:** any of a breed of medium-sized dogs that were developed in Australia to herd cattle and that have upright ears and a red or blue mottled coat

Australian cattle dog

Aus·tra·lian·ism \ȯ-ˈstrāl-yə-ˌni-zəm, ˌä-, ə-\ *n* (1883) **:** a characteristic feature of Australian English

Australian pine *n* (1891) **:** any of several casuarinas (esp. *Casuarina equisetifolia*) now widely grown as ornamentals in warm regions

Australian Rules football *n* (1904) **:** a game resembling rugby that is played between two teams of 18 players on a field 180–190 yards long that has four goalposts at each end

Australian shepherd *n* (1964) **:** any of a breed of agile intelligent short-tailed working dogs developed in the U.S. for herding livestock

Australian terrier *n* (1903) **:** any of a breed of small rather short-legged wirehaired terriers of Australian origin usu. having a tan and blue or sandy coat

Aus·tra·loid \ˈȯs-trə-ˌlȯid, ˈäs-\ *adj* [*Austral*ia + E *-oid*] (1864) *in some classifications* **:** of or relating to a racial group including the Australian aborigines and other peoples of southern Asia and Pacific islands — **Australoid** *n*

aus·tra·lo·pith·e·cine \ȯ-ˌstrā-lō-ˈpi-thə-ˌsīn, ä-; ˌȯs-trə-, ˌäs-\ *n* [ultim. fr. L *australis* + Gk *pithēkos* ape] (1943) **:** any of a genus (*Australopithecus*) of extinct southern and eastern African hominids that include gracile and robust forms with near-human dentition and a relatively small brain — **australopithecine** *adj*

Austrian pine *n* (1857) **:** a tall European pine (*Pinus nigra*) widely cultivated for ornament and having needles in clusters of two

Aus·tro·asi·at·ic \ˈȯs-(ˌ)trō-ˌā-zhē-ˈa-tik, -zē-ˈa-, ˈäs- *also* -ˌā-shē-\ *adj* (1922) **:** of, relating to, or constituting a family of languages of south and southeast Asia that includes Mon-Khmer and Munda as subfamilies

Aus·tro·ne·sian \ˌȯs-trə-ˈnē-zhən, ˌäs-, -shən\ *adj* [*Austronesia,* islands of the southern Pacific] (1925) **:** of, relating to, or constituting a family of languages spoken in the area extending from Madagascar eastward through the Malay Peninsula and Archipelago to Hawaii and Easter Island and including practically all the native languages of the Pacific islands with the exception of the Australian and Papuan languages

aut- *or* **auto-** *comb form* [Gk, fr. *autos* same, -self, self] **1 :** self **:** same one ⟨*autism*⟩ ⟨*auto*biography⟩ **2 :** automatic **:** self-acting ⟨*auto*pilot⟩

au·ta·coid \ˈȯ-tə-ˌkȯid\ *n* [*aut-* + Gk *akos* remedy; prob. akin to OIr *ícc* cure] (1914) **:** a physiologically active substance (as serotonin, bradykinin, or angiotensin) produced by and acting within the body

au·tar·chic \ȯ-ˈtär-kik\ *adj* (1883) **:** AUTARKIC — **au·tar·chi·cal** \-ki-kəl\ *adj*

[1]**au·tar·chy** \ˈȯ-ˌtär-kē\ *n* [by alter.] (1617) **:** AUTARKY

[2]**autarchy** *n, pl* **-chies** [Gk *autarchia,* fr. *aut-* + *-archia* -archy] (1665) **:** absolute sovereignty **:** AUTOCRACY — **au·tarch** \ˈȯ-ˌtärk\ *n*

au·tar·kic \ȯ-ˈtär-kik\ *adj* (1936) **:** of, relating to, or marked by autarky — **au·tar·ki·cal** \-ki-kəl\ *adj*

au·tar·ky \ˈȯ-ˌtär-kē\ *n* [G *Autarkie,* fr. Gk *autarkeia,* fr. *autarkēs* self-sufficient, fr. *aut-* + *arkein* to defend, suffice — more at ARK] (1657) **1 :** SELF-SUFFICIENCY, INDEPENDENCE; *specif* **:** national economic self-sufficiency and independence **2 :** a policy of establishing a self-sufficient and independent national economy

aut·ecol·o·gy \ˌȯ-ti-ˈkä-lə-jē, ˌȯt-ē-\ *n* [ISV] (1910) **:** ecology dealing with individual organisms or individual species of organisms — **aut·eco·log·i·cal** \ˌȯt-ˌē-kə-ˈlä-ji-kəl, -ˌe-kə-\ *adj*

au·teur \ō-ˈtər\ *n* [F, originator, author, fr. OF *autor,* fr. L *auctor* — more at AUTHOR] (1967) **1 :** a film director whose practice accords with the auteur theory; *broadly* **:** DIRECTOR C **2 :** an artist (as a musician or writer) whose style and practice are distinctive — **au·teur·ist** \-ist\ *adj or n*

au·teur theory \ō-ˈtər-\ *n* (1962) **:** a view of filmmaking in which the director is considered the primary creative force in a motion picture

auth *abbr* **1** authentic **2** author **3** authorized

au·then·tic \ə-ˈthen-tik, ȯ-\ *adj* [ME *autentik,* fr. AF, fr. LL *authenticus,* fr. Gk *authentikos,* fr. *authentēs* perpetrator, master, fr. *aut-* + *-hentēs* (akin to Gk *anyein* to accomplish, Skt *sanoti* he gains)] (14c) **1** *obs* **:** AUTHORITATIVE **2 a :** worthy of acceptance or belief as conforming to or based on fact ⟨paints an ~ picture of our society⟩ **b :** conforming to an original so as to reproduce essential features ⟨an ~ reproduction of a colonial farmhouse⟩ **c :** made or done the same way as an original ⟨~ Mexican fare⟩ **3 :** not false or imitation **:** REAL, ACTUAL ⟨an ~ cockney accent⟩ **4 a** *of a church mode* **:** ranging upward from the keynote — compare PLAGAL 1 **b** *of a cadence* **:** progressing from the dominant chord to the tonic — compare PLAGAL 2 **5 :** true to one's own personality, spirit, or character — **au·then·ti·cal·ly** \-ti-k(ə-)lē\ *adv* — **au·then·tic·i·ty** \ˌȯ-ˌthen-ˈti-sə-tē, -thən-\ *n*

syn AUTHENTIC, GENUINE, BONA FIDE mean being actually and exactly what is claimed. AUTHENTIC implies being fully trustworthy as according with fact ⟨an *authentic* account of the perilous journey⟩; it can also stress painstaking or faithful imitation of an original ⟨an *authentic* reproduction⟩ ⟨*authentic* Vietnamese cuisine⟩. GENUINE implies actual character not counterfeited, imitated, or adulterated ⟨*genuine* piety⟩ ⟨*genuine* maple syrup⟩; it also connotes definite origin from a source ⟨a *genuine* Mark Twain autograph⟩. BONA FIDE implies good faith and sincerity of intention ⟨a *bona fide* offer for the stock⟩.

au·then·ti·cate \ə-ˈthen-ti-ˌkāt, ȯ-\ *vt* **-cat·ed; -cat·ing** (1651) **:** to prove or serve to prove the authenticity of ⟨~ a document⟩ ***syn*** see CONFIRM — **au·then·ti·ca·tion** \-ˌthen-ti-ˈkā-shən\ *n* — **au·then·ti·ca·tor** \-ˈthen-ti-ˌkā-tər\ *n*

[1]**au·thor** \ˈȯ-thər\ *n* [ME *auctour,* fr. AF *auctor, autor,* fr. L *auctor* promoter, originator, author, fr. *augēre* to increase — more at EKE] (14c) **1 a :** one that originates or creates **:** SOURCE ⟨software ~*s*⟩ ⟨film ~*s*⟩ ⟨the ~ of this crime⟩ **b** *cap* **:** GOD 1 **2 :** the writer of a literary work (as a book) — **au·tho·ri·al** \ȯ-ˈthȯr-ē-əl\ *adj*

[2]**author** *vt* (1596) **:** to be the author of **:** WRITE ⟨has ~*ed* several books⟩

au·thor·ess \ˈȯ-th(ə-)rəs\ *n* (15c) **:** a woman or girl who is an author

au·tho·ri·sa·tion, au·tho·rise *Brit var of* AUTHORIZATION, AUTHORIZE

au·thor·i·tar·i·an \ȯ-ˌthär-ə-ˈter-ē-ən, ə-, -ˌthȯr-\ *adj* (1861) **1 :** of, relating to, or favoring blind submission to authority ⟨had ~ parents⟩ **2 :** of, relating to, or favoring a concentration of power in a leader or an elite not constitutionally responsible to the people ⟨an ~ regime⟩ — **authoritarian** *n* — **au·thor·i·tar·i·an·ism** \-ē-ə-ˌni-zəm\ *n*

au·thor·i·ta·tive \ə-ˈthär-ə-ˌtā-tiv, ȯ-, -ˈthȯr-\ *adj* (1605) **1 a :** having or proceeding from authority **:** OFFICIAL ⟨~ church doctrines⟩ **b :** clearly accurate or knowledgeable ⟨an ~ critique⟩ **2 :** DICTATORIAL 2 — **au·thor·i·ta·tive·ly** *adv* — **au·thor·i·ta·tive·ness** *n*

au·thor·i·ty \ə-ˈthär-ə-tē, ȯ-, -ˈthȯr-\ *n, pl* **-ties** [ME *auctorite,* fr. AF *auctorité,* fr. L *auctoritat-, auctoritas* opinion, decision, power, fr. *auctor*] (13c) **1 a (1) :** a citation (as from a book or file) used in defense or support **(2) :** the source from which the citation is drawn **b (1) :** a conclusive statement or set of statements (as an official decision of a court) **(2) :** a decision taken as a precedent **(3) :** TESTIMONY **c :** an individual cited or appealed to as an expert **2 a :** power to influence or command thought, opinion, or behavior **b :** freedom granted by one in authority **:** RIGHT **3 a :** persons in command; *specif* **:** GOVERNMENT **b :** a governmental agency or corporation to administer a revenue-producing public enterprise ⟨the transit ~⟩ **4 a :** GROUNDS, WARRANT ⟨had excellent ~ for believing the claim⟩ **b :** convincing force ⟨lent ~ to the performance⟩ ***syn*** see INFLUENCE, POWER

au·tho·ri·za·tion \ˌȯ-th(ə-)rə-ˈzā-shən\ *n* (15c) **1 :** the act of authorizing **2 :** an instrument that authorizes **:** SANCTION

au·tho·rize \ˈȯ-thə-ˌrīz\ *vt* **-rized; -riz·ing** (14c) **1 :** to establish by or as if by authority **:** SANCTION ⟨a custom *authorized* by time⟩ **2 :** to invest esp. with legal authority **:** EMPOWER ⟨*authorized* to act for her husband⟩ **3** *archaic* **:** JUSTIFY 1a — **au·tho·riz·er** *n*

Authorized Version *n* (1814) **:** a revision of the English Bishops' Bible carried out under James I, published in 1611, and widely used by Protestants — called also *King James Version*

au·thor·ship \ˈȯ-thər-ˌship\ *n* (1710) **1 :** the profession of writing **2 :** the source (as the author) of a piece of writing, music, or art **3 :** the state or act of writing, creating, or causing

au·tism \ˈȯ-ˌti-zəm\ *n* (1946) **:** a variable developmental disorder that appears by age three and is characterized by impairment of the ability to form normal social relationships, by impairment of the ability to communicate with others, and by stereotyped behavior patterns — **au·tis·tic** \ȯ-ˈtis-tik\ *adj or n* — **au·tis·ti·cal·ly** \-ti-k(ə-)lē\ *adv*

autism spectrum disorder *n* (1992) **:** any of a group of developmental disorders (as autism and Asperger's syndrome) marked by impairments in the ability to communicate and interact socially and by the presence of repetitive behaviors or restricted interests — called also *autistic spectrum disorder, pervasive developmental disorder*

[1]**au·to** \ˈȯ-(ˌ)tō, ˈä-\ *n, pl* **autos** (1899) **:** AUTOMOBILE

[2]**auto** *adj* (1876) **:** AUTOMATIC

auto- — see AUT-

au·to·an·ti·body \ˌȯ-(ˌ)tō-ˈan-ti-ˌbä-dē\ *n* (1905) **:** an antibody active against a tissue constituent of the individual producing it

au·to·bahn \ˈȯ-tō-ˌbän, ˈau̇-\ *n* [G, fr. *Auto* + *Bahn* road] (1939) **:** a German, Swiss, or Austrian expressway

au·to·bi·og·ra·phy \ˌȯ-tə-bī-ˈä-grə-fē, -bē-\ *n* (1797) **:** the biography of a person narrated by himself or herself — **au·to·bi·og·ra·pher** \-fər\ *n* — **au·to·bio·graph·i·cal** \-ˌbī-ə-ˈgra-fi-kəl\ *also* **au·to·bio·graph·ic** \-fik\ *adj* — **au·to·bio·graph·i·cal·ly** \-fi-k(ə-)lē\ *adv*

au·to·bus \ˈȯ-tō-ˌbəs\ *n* [*auto* + *bus*] (1899) **:** OMNIBUS 1

au·to·ca·tal·y·sis \ˌȯ-tō-kə-ˈta-lə-səs\ *n, pl* **-y·ses** \-ˌsēz\ [NL] (1891) **:** catalysis of a reaction by one of its products — **au·to·cat·a·lyt·ic** \-ˌka-tə-ˈli-tik\ *adj* — **au·to·cat·a·lyt·i·cal·ly** \-ti-k(ə-)lē\ *adv*

au·to·ceph·a·lous \ˌȯ-tō-ˈse-f(ə-)ləs\ *adj* [LGk *autokephalos,* fr. Gk *aut-* + *kephalē* head — more at CEPHALIC] (1845) **:** independent of external and esp. patriarchal authority — used esp. of Eastern national churches — **au·to·ceph·a·ly** \-fə-lē\ *n*

au·toch·thon \ȯ-ˈtäk-thən\ *n, pl* **-thons** *or* **-tho·nes** \-thə-ˌnēz\ [Gk *autochthōn,* fr. *aut-* + *chthōn* earth — more at HUMBLE] (1579) **:** one (as a person, plant, or animal) that is autochthonous

au·toch·tho·nous \ȯ-ˈtäk-thə-nəs\ *adj* (1893) **1 :** INDIGENOUS, NATIVE ⟨an ~ people⟩ **2 :** formed or originating in the place where found ⟨~ rock⟩ ⟨an ~ infection⟩ — **au·toch·tho·nous·ly** *adv*

[1]**au·to·clave** \ˈȯ-tō-ˌklāv\ *n* [F, fr. *aut-* + L *clavis* key — more at CLAVICLE] (1820) **:** an apparatus in which special conditions (as high or low pressure or temperature) can be established for a variety of applications; *esp* **:** an apparatus (as for sterilizing) using steam under high pressure

[2]**autoclave** *vt* **-claved; -clav·ing** (1911) **:** to treat in an autoclave

au·to·cor·re·la·tion \ˌȯ-tō-ˌkȯr-ə-ˈlā-shən, -ˌkär-\ *n* (1933) **:** the correlation between paired values of a function of a mathematical or statistical variable taken at usu. constant intervals that indicates the degree of periodicity of the function

au·toc·ra·cy \ȯ-ˈtä-krə-sē\ *n, pl* **-cies** (1655) **1 :** the authority or rule of an autocrat **2 :** government in which one person possesses unlimited power **3 :** a community or state governed by autocracy

au·to·crat \ˈȯ-tə-ˌkrat\ *n* [F *autocrate,* fr. Gk *autokratēs* ruling by oneself, absolute, fr. *aut-* + *-kratēs* ruling — more at -CRAT] (1800) **1 :** a person (as a monarch) ruling with unlimited authority **2 :** one who has undisputed influence or power

au·to·crat·ic \ˌȯ-tə-ˈkra-tik\ *also* **au·to·crat·i·cal** \-ti-kəl\ *adj* (1772) **1 :** of, relating to, or being an autocracy **:** ABSOLUTE ⟨an ~ government⟩ **2 :** characteristic of or resembling an autocrat **:** DESPOTIC ⟨an ~ ruler⟩ — **au·to·crat·i·cal·ly** \-ti-k(ə-)lē\ *adv*

au·to·crine \ˈȯ-tō-ˌkrin\ *adj* [*aut-* + *-crine* (as in *endocrine*)] (1980) **:** of, relating to, promoted by, or being a substance secreted by a cell and acting on surface receptors of the same cell — compare PARACRINE

au·to·cross \ˈȯ-tō-ˌkrȯs, ˈä-tō-\ *n* [*auto* + motocross] (1957) **:** an automobile gymkhana

au·to–da–fé \ˌau̇-tō-də-ˈfā, ˌȯ-tō-\ *n, pl* **au·tos–da–fé** \-tōz-də-\ [Pg *auto da fé,* lit., act of the faith] (1697) **:** the ceremony for pronouncing judgment by the Inquisition which was followed by the execution of sentence by secular authorities; *broadly* **:** the burning of a heretic

au·to·di·dact \ˌȯ-tō-ˈdī-ˌdakt, -dī-ˈ, -də-ˈ\ *n* [Gk *autodidaktos* self-taught, fr. *aut-* + *didaktos* taught, fr. *didaskein* to teach] (1748) **:** a self-taught person — **au·to·di·dac·tic** \-dī-ˈdak-tik, -də-\ *adj*

au·toe·cious \ȯ-ˈtē-shəs\ *adj* [*aut-* + Gk *oikia* house — more at VICINITY] (ca. 1877) **:** passing through all life stages on the same host ⟨~ rusts⟩ — **au·toe·cious·ly** *adv* — **au·toe·cism** \-ˈtē-ˌsi-zəm\ *n*

autoerotic asphyxiation *n* (1973) **:** a state of asphyxia intentionally induced (as by smothering or strangling oneself) so as to heighten sexual arousal during masturbation

au·to·erot·i·cism \ˌȯ-tō-i-ˈrä-tə-ˌsi-zəm\ *also* **au·to·er·o·tism** \-ˈer-ə-ˌti-zəm\ *n* (1898) **1 :** sexual feeling arising without known external stimulation **2 :** sexual gratification obtained solely through stimulation by oneself of one's own body — **au·to·erot·ic** \-i-ˈrä-tik\ *adj*

au·to·ex·po·sure \-ik-ˈspō-zhər\ *n* (1957) **:** a camera system that automatically adjusts the exposure according to ambient lighting

au·to·fo·cus \ˈȯ-tō-ˌfō-kəs\ *n* (ca. 1937) **:** an automatic focusing system (as on a camera) — **autofocus** *vb*

au·tog·a·my \ȯ-ˈtä-gə-mē\ *n* [ISV] (1877) **:** SELF-FERTILIZATION: as **a :** pollination of a flower by its own pollen **b :** conjugation of two sister cells or sister nuclei of protozoans or fungi — **au·tog·a·mous** \-məs\ *adj*

au·tog·e·nous \ȯ-ˈtä-jə-nəs\ *also* **au·to·gen·ic** \ˌȯ-tə-ˈje-nik\ *adj* [Gk *autogenēs,* fr. *aut-* + *-genēs* born, produced — more at -GEN] (1826) **1 :** produced independently of external influence or aid **:** ENDOGENOUS **2 :** originating or derived from sources within the same individual ⟨an ~ graft⟩ **3 :** not requiring a meal of blood to produce eggs ⟨~ mosquitoes⟩ — **au·tog·e·nous·ly** *adv* — **au·tog·e·ny** \ȯ-ˈtä-jə-nē\ *n*

au·to·gi·ro *or* **au·to·gy·ro** \ˌȯ-tō-ˈjī-(ˌ)rō\ *n, pl* **-ros** [fr. *Autogiro,* a trademark] (1907) **:** a rotary-wing aircraft that employs a propeller for forward motion and a freely rotating rotor for lift

au·to·graft \ˈȯ-tō-ˌgraft\ *n* (1881) **:** a tissue or organ that is transplanted from one part to another of the same body — **autograft** *vt*

[1]**au·to·graph** \ˈȯ-tə-ˌgraf\ *n* [LL *autographum,* fr. L, neut. of *autographus* written with one's own hand, fr. Gk *autographos,* fr. *aut-* + *-graphos* written — more at -GRAPH] (1623) **:** something written or made with one's own hand: **a :** an original manuscript or work of art **b :** a person's handwritten signature — **au·tog·ra·phy** \ȯ-ˈtä-grə-fē\ *n*

[2]**autograph** *adj* (ca. 1676) **:** being in the writer's own handwriting **:** not copied or duplicated ⟨an ~ letter⟩

[3]**autograph** *vt* (1817) **1 :** to write with one's own hand **2 :** to write one's signature in or on ⟨~ a book⟩

au·to·graph·ic \ˌȯ-tə-ˈgra-fik\ *adj* (1807) **:** of, relating to, or constituting an autograph — **au·to·graph·i·cal·ly** \-fi-k(ə-)lē\ *adv*

Au·to·harp \ˈȯ-tō-ˌhärp\ *trademark* — used for a zither with button-controlled dampers for selected strings

au·to·hyp·no·sis \ˌȯ-tō-hip-ˈnō-səs\ *n* [NL] (1889) **:** self-induced and usu. automatic hypnosis — **au·to·hyp·not·ic** \-ˈnä-tik\ *adj*

au·to·im·mune \-im-ˈyün\ *adj* (1952) **:** of, relating to, or caused by autoantibodies or T cells that attack molecules, cells, or tissues of the organism producing them ⟨~ diseases⟩ — **au·to·im·mu·ni·ty** \-ˈyü-nə-tē\ *n* — **au·to·im·mu·ni·za·tion** \-ˌim-yə-nə-ˈzā-shən *also* -im-ˌyü-\ *n*

au·to·in·fec·tion \-in-ˈfek-shən\ *n* [ISV] (1879) **:** reinfection with larvae produced by parasitic worms already in the body

au·to·in·tox·i·ca·tion \-in-ˌtäk-sə-ˈkā-shən\ *n* [ISV] (1884) **:** a state of being poisoned by toxic substances produced within the body

au·tol·o·gous \ȯ-ˈtä-lə-gəs\ *adj* [*aut-* + *-ologous* (as in *homologous*)] (ca. 1911) **1 :** derived from the same individual ⟨incubated lymphoid cells with ~ tumor cells⟩ **2 :** involving one individual as both donor and recipient ⟨an ~ blood transfusion⟩ ⟨an ~ bone marrow transplant⟩

au·tol·y·sate \ȯ-ˈtä-lə-ˌsāt, -ˌzāt\ *also* **au·tol·y·zate** \-ˌzāt\ *n* (1906) **:** a product of autolysis

au·to·lyse *Brit var of* AUTOLYZE

au·tol·y·sis \-lə-səs\ *n* [NL] (1900) **:** breakdown of all or part of a cell or tissue by self-produced enzymes — **au·to·lyt·ic** \ˌȯ-tə-ˈli-tik\ *adj*

au·to·lyze \ˈȯ-tə-ˌlīz\ *vb* **-lyzed; -lyz·ing** [back-formation fr. *autolysis*] *vi* (1903) **:** to undergo autolysis ~ *vt* **:** to subject to autolysis

au·to·mak·er \ˈȯ-tō-ˌmā-kər, ˈä-tō-\ *n* (1903) **:** a manufacturer of automobiles

Au·to·mat \ˈȯ-tə-ˌmat\ *service mark* — used for a cafeteria in which food is obtained esp. from vending machines

au·to·mate \ˈȯ-tə-ˌmāt\ *vb* **-mat·ed; -mat·ing** [back-formation fr. *automation*] *vt* (1952) **1 :** to operate by automation **2 :** to convert to largely automatic operation ⟨~ a process⟩ ~ *vi* **:** to undergo automation — **au·to·mat·able** \-ˌmā-tə-bəl\ *adj*

automated teller *n* (1972) **:** ATM

automated teller machine *n* (1973) : ATM

[1]**au·to·mat·ic** \ˌȯ-tə-ˈma-tik\ *adj* [Gk *automatos* self-acting, fr. *aut-* + *-matos* (akin to L *ment-, mens* mind) — more at MIND] (1748) **1 a** : largely or wholly involuntary; *esp* : REFLEX 5 ⟨~ blinking of the eyelids⟩ **b** : acting or done spontaneously or unconsciously **c** : done or produced as if by machine : MECHANICAL ⟨the answers were ~⟩ **2** : having a self-acting or self-regulating mechanism ⟨an ~ transmission⟩ **3** *of a firearm* : firing repeatedly until the trigger is released *syn* see SPONTANEOUS — **au·to·mat·i·cal·ly** \-ti-k(ə-)lē\ *adv* — **au·to·ma·tic·i·ty** \-mə-ˈti-sə-tē, -ma-\ *n*

[2]**automatic** *n* (1897) **1** : a machine or apparatus that operates automatically: as **a** : an automatic firearm **b** : an automatic transmission **2** : a semiautomatic firearm **3** : AUDIBLE

automatic pilot *n* (1915) **1** : AUTOPILOT 1 **2** : a state or condition in which activity or behavior is regulated automatically in a predetermined or instinctive manner ⟨doing his job on *automatic pilot*⟩

automatic teller *n* (1971) : ATM

automatic teller machine *n* (1977) : ATM

automatic writing *n* (1855) : writing produced without conscious intention as if of telepathic or spiritualistic origin

au·to·ma·tion \ˌȯ-tə-ˈmā-shən\ *n* [[1]*automatic*] (1912) **1** : the technique of making an apparatus, a process, or a system operate automatically **2** : the state of being operated automatically **3** : automatically controlled operation of an apparatus, process, or system by mechanical or electronic devices that take the place of human labor

au·tom·a·tism \ȯ-ˈtä-mə-ˌti-zəm\ *n* [F *automatisme,* fr. *automate* automaton, fr. L *automaton*] (1776) **1 a** : the quality or state of being automatic **b** : an automatic action **2** : the moving or functioning (as of an organ, tissue, or a body part) without conscious control that occurs either independently of external stimuli (as in the beating of the heart) or under the influence of external stimuli (as in pupil dilation) **3** : a theory that views the body as a machine and consciousness as a noncontrolling adjunct of the body **4** : suspension of the conscious mind to release subconscious images ⟨~ —the surrealist trend toward spontaneity and intuition —*Elle*⟩ — **au·tom·a·tist** \-ˈtä-mə-tist\ *n or adj*

au·tom·a·tize \ȯ-ˈtä-mə-ˌtīz\ *vt* **-tized; -tiz·ing** [[1]*automatic*] (1910) : to make (an action) reflexive — **au·tom·a·ti·za·tion** \ȯ-ˌtä-mə-tə-ˈzā-shən, -ˌtī-ˈzā-\ *n*

au·tom·a·ton \ȯ-ˈtä-mə-tən, -mə-ˌtän\ *n, pl* **-atons** *or* **-a·ta** \-mə-tə, -mə-ˌtä\ [L, fr. Gk, neut. of *automatos*] (1611) **1** : a mechanism that is relatively self-operating; *esp* : ROBOT **2** : a machine or control mechanism designed to follow automatically a predetermined sequence of operations or respond to encoded instructions **3** : an individual who acts in a mechanical fashion

[1]**au·to·mo·bile** \ˈȯ-tə-mō-ˌbēl, ˌȯ-tə-mō-ˈbēl, ˌȯ-tə-ˈmō-ˌbēl\ *adj* [F, fr. *aut-* + *mobile*] (1876) : AUTOMOTIVE

[2]**automobile** *n* (1881) : a usu. four-wheeled automotive vehicle designed for passenger transportation — **automobile** *vi* — **au·to·mo·bil·ist** \-ˈbē-list, -ˌbē-\ *n*

au·to·mo·bil·i·ty \ˌȯ-tō-mə-ˈbi-lə-tē, -mō-\ *n* (1896) : the use of automobiles as the major means of transportation

au·to·mor·phism \ˌȯ-tə-ˈmȯr-ˌfi-zəm\ *n* [*aut-* + is*omorphism*] (1862) : an isomorphism of a set (as a group) with itself

au·to·mo·tive \ˌȯ-tə-ˈmō-tiv\ *adj* (1852) **1** : SELF-PROPELLED **2** : of, relating to, or concerned with self-propelled vehicles or machines

au·to·nom·ic \ˌȯ-tə-ˈnä-mik\ *adj* (1888) **1** : acting or occurring involuntarily ⟨~ reflexes⟩ **2** : relating to, affecting, or controlled by the autonomic nervous system or its effects or activity ⟨~ drugs⟩ — **au·to·nom·i·cal·ly** \-mi-k(ə-)lē\ *adv*

autonomic nervous system *n* (1898) : a part of the vertebrate nervous system that innervates smooth and cardiac muscle and glandular tissues and governs involuntary actions (as secretion and peristalsis) and that consists of the sympathetic nervous system and the parasympathetic nervous system

au·ton·o·mist \ȯ-ˈtä-nə-mist\ *n* (1819) : one who advocates autonomy

au·ton·o·mous \ȯ-ˈtä-nə-məs\ *adj* [Gk *autonomos* independent, fr. *aut-* + *nomos* law — more at NIMBLE] (1799) **1** : of, relating to, or marked by autonomy **2 a** : having the right or power of self-government **b** : undertaken or carried on without outside control : SELF-CONTAINED ⟨an ~ school system⟩ **3 a** : existing or capable of existing independently ⟨an ~ zooid⟩ **b** : responding, reacting, or developing independently of the whole ⟨an ~ growth⟩ **4** : controlled by the autonomic nervous system *syn* see FREE — **au·ton·o·mous·ly** *adv*

au·ton·o·my \-mē\ *n, pl* **-mies** (ca. 1623) **1** : the quality or state of being self-governing; *esp* : the right of self-government **2** : self-directing freedom and esp. moral independence **3** : a self-governing state

au·to·pi·lot \ˈȯ-tō-ˌpī-lət\ *n* (1916) **1** : a device for automatically steering ships, aircraft, and spacecraft **2** : AUTOMATIC PILOT 2

au·to·poly·ploid \ˌȯ-tō-ˈpä-lē-ˌplȯid\ *n* (1928) : an individual or strain whose chromosome complement consists of more than two complete copies of the genome of a single ancestral species — **autopolyploid** *adj* — **au·to·poly·ploi·dy** \-ˌplȯi-dē\ *n*

au·top·sy \ˈȯ-ˌtäp-sē, ˈȯ-təp-\ *n, pl* **-sies** [Gk *autopsia* act of seeing with one's own eyes, fr. *aut-* + *opsis* sight, appearance — more at OPTIC] (1678) **1** : an examination of a body after death to determine the cause of death or the character and extent of changes produced by disease — called also *necropsy* **2** : a critical examination, evaluation, or assessment of someone or something past — **autopsy** *vt*

au·to·ra·dio·gram \ˌȯ-tō-ˈrā-dē-ə-ˌgram\ *n* (1931) : AUTORADIOGRAPH

au·to·ra·dio·graph \ˌȯ-tō-ˈrā-dē-ə-ˌgraf\ *n* [ISV] (1903) : an image produced on a photographic film or plate by the radiations from a radioactive substance in an object which is in close contact with the emulsion — **au·to·ra·dio·graph·ic** \-ˌrā-dē-ə-ˈgra-fik\ *adj* — **au·to·ra·di·og·ra·phy** \-ˌrā-dē-ˈä-grə-fē\ *n*

au·to·ro·ta·tion \-rō-ˈtā-shən\ *n* (1926) : the turning of the rotor of an autogiro or a helicopter with the resulting lift caused solely by the aerodynamic forces induced by motion of the rotor along its flight path — **au·to·ro·tate** \-ˈrō-ˌtāt\ *vi*

au·to·route \ˈȯ-tō-ˌrüt, -ˌrau̇t\ *n* [F, fr. *automobile* + *route*] (1951) : an expressway esp. in France

autos–da–fé *pl of* AUTO-DA-FÉ

au·to·sex·ing \ˈȯ-tō-ˌsek-siŋ\ *adj* (1936) : exhibiting different characters in the two sexes at birth or hatching ⟨~ chickens⟩

au·to·some \ˈȯ-tə-ˌsōm\ *n* (1906) : a chromosome other than a sex chromosome — **au·to·so·mal** \ˌȯ-tə-ˈsō-məl\ *adj* — **au·to·so·mal·ly** \-mə-lē\ *adv*

au·to·stra·da \ˌau̇-tō-ˈsträ-də, ˌȯ-tō-\ *n, pl* **-stradas** *or* **-stra·de** \-ˈsträ-(ˌ)dā\ [It, fr. *automobile* + *strada* street, fr. LL *strata* paved road — more at STREET] (1927) : an expressway esp. in Italy

au·to·sug·ges·tion \ˌȯ-tō-sə(g)-ˈjes-chən, -ˈjesh-\ *n* [ISV] (1880) : an influencing of one's own attitudes, behavior, or physical condition by mental processes other than conscious thought : SELF-HYPNOSIS — **au·to·sug·gest** \-sə(g)-ˈjest\ *vt*

au·to·te·lic \ˌȯ-tō-ˈte-lik, -ˈtē-\ *adj* [Gk *autotelēs,* fr. *aut-* + *telos* end — more at TELOS] (1900) : having a purpose in and not apart from itself

au·to·tet·ra·ploid \ˌȯ-tō-ˈte-trə-ˌplȯid\ *n* (1930) : an individual or strain whose chromosome complement consists of four copies of a single genome due to doubling of an ancestral chromosome complement — **autotetraploid** *adj* — **au·to·tet·ra·ploi·dy** \-ˌplȯi-dē\ *n*

au·tot·o·my \ȯ-ˈtä-tə-mē\ *n* [ISV] (1887) : reflex separation of a part (as an appendage) from the body : division of the body into two or more pieces — **au·tot·o·mous** \-məs\ *adj* — **au·tot·o·mize** \-ˌmīz\ *vb*

au·to·trans·fu·sion \ˌȯ-tō-tran(t)s-ˈfyü-zhən\ *n* (1886) : return of autologous blood to the patient's own circulatory system

au·to·troph \ˈȯ-tə-ˌtrōf, -ˌträf\ *n* [G, fr. *autotroph,* adj.] (1938) : an autotrophic organism

au·to·tro·phic \ˌȯ-tə-ˈtrō-fik\ *adj* [prob. fr. G *autotroph,* fr. Gk *autotrophos* supplying one's own food, fr. *aut-* + *trephein* to nourish] (1893) **1** : requiring only carbon dioxide or carbonates as a source of carbon and a simple inorganic nitrogen compound for metabolic synthesis of organic molecules (as glucose) ⟨~ plants⟩ — compare HETEROTROPHIC **2** : not requiring a specified exogenous factor for normal metabolism — **au·to·tro·phi·cal·ly** \-fi-k(ə-)lē\ *adv* — **au·tot·ro·phy** \ȯ-ˈtä-trə-fē\ *n*

Au·to–Tune *or* **auto–tune** \ˈȯ-ˌtō-ˌt(y)ün\ *vt* [*Auto-Tune,* proprietary signal processor] (2003) : to adjust or alter (a recording of a voice) with Auto-Tune software or other audio-editing software esp. to correct sung notes that are out of tune

au·to·work·er \ˈȯ-tō-ˌwər-kər, ˈä-\ *n* (1901) : a person employed in the automobile manufacturing industry

au·tox·i·da·tion \ȯ-ˌtäk-sə-ˈdā-shən\ *n* (1883) : oxidation by direct combination with oxygen (as in air) at ordinary temperatures

au·tumn \ˈȯ-təm\ *n* [ME *autumpne,* fr. L *autumnus*] (14c) **1** : the season between summer and winter comprising in the northern hemisphere usu. the months of September, October, and November or as reckoned astronomically extending from the September equinox to the December solstice — called also *fall* **2** : a period of maturity or incipient decline ⟨in the ~ of life⟩ — **au·tum·nal** \ȯ-ˈtəm-nəl\ *adj* — **au·tum·nal·ly** \-nə-lē\ *adv*

autumn crocus *n* (1822) : an autumn-blooming colchicum (*Colchicum autumnale*)

au·tun·ite \ō-ˈtə-ˌnīt, ˈȯ-tə-\ *n* [*Autun,* town in France] (ca. 1852) : a radioactive usu. lemon-yellow calcium phosphate mineral that occurs in tabular crystals and in scales and that is an ore of uranium

aux *abbr* auxiliary verb

[1]**aux·il·ia·ry** \ȯg-ˈzil-yə-rē, -ˈzil-rē, -ˈzi-lə-\ *adj* [L *auxiliaris,* fr. *auxilium* help; akin to L *augēre* to increase — more at EKE] (15c) **1 a** : offering or providing help **b** : functioning in a subsidiary capacity ⟨an ~ branch of the state university⟩ **2** *of a verb* : accompanying another verb and typically expressing person, number, mood, or tense **3 a** : SUPPLEMENTARY **b** : constituting a reserve ⟨an ~ power plant⟩ **4** : equipped with sails and a supplementary inboard engine ⟨an ~ sloop⟩

[2]**auxiliary** *n, pl* **-ries** (1567) **1 a** : an auxiliary person, group, or device; *specif* : a member of a foreign force serving a nation at war **b** : a Roman Catholic titular bishop assisting a diocesan bishop and not having the right of succession — called also *auxiliary bishop* **2** : an auxiliary boat or ship **3** : an auxiliary verb

aux·in \ˈȯk-sən\ *n* [ISV, fr. Gk *auxein* to increase — more at EKE] (1933) **1** : any of various usu. acidic organic substances that promote cell elongation in plant shoots and usu. regulate other growth processes (as root initiation): as **a** : INDOLEACETIC ACID **b** : any of various synthetic substances (as 2,4-D) resembling indoleacetic acid in activity and used esp. in research and agriculture **2** : PLANT HORMONE — **aux·in·ic** \ȯk-ˈsi-nik\ *adj*

auxo·troph \ˈȯk-sə-ˌtrōf, -ˌträf\ *n* (1950) : an auxotrophic strain or individual

auxo·tro·phic \ˌȯk-sə-ˈtrō-fik\ *adj* [Gk *auxein* to increase + *-o-* + E *-trophic*] (1944) : requiring a specific growth substance beyond the minimum required for normal metabolism and reproduction by the parental or wild-type strain ⟨~ mutants of bacteria⟩ — **aux·ot·ro·phy** \ȯk-ˈsä-trə-fē\ *n*

av *abbr* **1** avenue **2** average **3** avoirdupois

AV *abbr* **1** ad valorem **2** audiovisual **3** Authorized Version

A/V *abbr* audio/video

[1]**avail** \ə-ˈvāl\ *vb* [ME, AF *availler,* prob. fr. *a-* (fr. L *ad-*) + *valer, valoir* to be of worth, fr. L *valēre* — more at WIELD] *vi* (14c) : to be of use or advantage : SERVE ⟨our best efforts did not ~⟩ ~ *vt* : to produce or result in as a benefit or advantage : GAIN ⟨his efforts ~*ed* him nothing⟩ — **avail oneself of** *also* **avail of** : to make use of : take advantage of ⟨they *availed themselves of* his services⟩

[2]**avail** *n* (15c) : advantage toward attainment of a goal or purpose : USE ⟨effort was of little ~⟩

avail·abil·i·ty \ə-ˌvā-lə-ˈbi-lə-tē\ *n, pl* **-ties** (1803) **1** : the quality or state of being available **2** : an available person or thing

avail·able \ə-ˈvā-lə-bəl\ *adj* (15c) **1** *archaic* : having a beneficial effect **2** : VALID — used of a legal plea or charge **3** : present or ready for immediate use ⟨~ resources⟩ **4** : ACCESSIBLE, OBTAINABLE ⟨articles ~ in any drugstore⟩ **5** : qualified or willing to do something or to assume a responsibility ⟨~ candidates⟩ **6** : present in such chemical or physical form as to be usable (as by a plant) ⟨~ nitrogen⟩ ⟨~ water⟩ — **avail·able·ness** *n* — **avail·ably** \-blē\ *adv*

[1]**av·a·lanche** \ˈa-və-ˌlanch\ *n* [F, fr. F dial. (Franco-Provençal) *lavantse, avalantse*] (1744) **1** : a large mass of snow, ice, earth, rock, or other material in swift motion down a mountainside or over a precipice **2** : a sudden great or overwhelming rush or accumulation of something ⟨hit by an ~ of paperwork⟩ **3** : a cumulative process in which pho-

tons or accelerated charge carriers produce additional photons or charge carriers through collisions (as with gas molecules)

2**avalanche** *vb* **-lanched; -lanch·ing** *vi* (1855) **:** to descend in an avalanche ~ *vt* **:** OVERWHELM, FLOOD

Av·a·lon \ˈa-və-ˌlän\ *n* (13c) **:** a paradise to which Arthur is carried after his death

avant \ˈä-ˌvän(t), ˈa-, -ˌvȯn(t), -ˌvō^n\ *adj* [F *avant-* fore-, front, fr. *avant* before, fr. L *abante*] (1965) **:** culturally or stylistically advanced **:** AVANT-GARDE ⟨~ jazz⟩

1**avant–garde** \ˌä-ˌvän(t)-ˈgärd, ˌa-; ə-ˈvänt-ˌ; ˌa-ˌvō^n-ˈ, ˌa-ˌvȯn(t)-ˈ\ *n* [F, vanguard] (1910) **:** an intelligentsia that develops new or experimental concepts esp. in the arts — **avant–gard·ism** \-ˈgär-ˌdi-zəm\ *n* — **avant–gard·ist** \-ˈgär-dist\ *n*

2**avant–garde** *adj* (1925) **:** of or relating to an avant-garde ⟨~ writers⟩

av·a·rice \ˈa-və-rəs, ˈav-rəs\ *n* [ME, fr. AF, fr. L *avaritia,* fr. *avarus* avaricious, fr. *avēre* to crave — more at AVID] (14c) **:** excessive or insatiable desire for wealth or gain **:** GREEDINESS, CUPIDITY

av·a·ri·cious \ˌa-və-ˈri-shəs\ *adj* (15c) **:** greedy of gain **:** excessively acquisitive esp. in seeking to hoard riches ***syn*** see COVETOUS — **av·a·ri·cious·ly** *adv* — **av·a·ri·cious·ness** *n*

avas·cu·lar \(ˌ)ā-ˈvas-kyə-lər\ *adj* (ca. 1900) **:** having few or no blood vessels ⟨~ tissue⟩ — **avas·cu·lar·i·ty** \ˌā-ˌvas-kyə-ˈlar-ə-tē\ *n*

avascular necrosis *n* (1953) **:** necrosis of bone tissue due to impaired or disrupted blood supply (as from traumatic injury or disease)

avast \ə-ˈvast\ *vb imper* [perh. fr. D *houd vast* hold fast] (1681) — a nautical command to stop or cease

av·a·tar \ˈa-və-ˌtär\ *n* [Skt *avatāraḥ* descent, fr. *avatarati* he descends, fr. *ava-* away + *tarati* he crosses over — more at UKASE, THROUGH] (1784) **1 :** the incarnation of a Hindu deity (as Vishnu) **2 a :** an incarnation in human form **b :** an embodiment (as of a concept or philosophy) often in a person **3 :** a variant phase or version of a continuing basic entity **4 :** an electronic image that represents and is manipulated by a computer user (as in a computer game)

avaunt \ə-ˈvȯnt, -ˈvänt\ *adv* [ME, lit., forward, fr. AF *avant,* fr. L *abante* forward, before, fr. *ab* from + *ante* before — more at OF, ANTE-] (15c) **:** AWAY, HENCE

AVC *abbr* automatic volume control

avdp *abbr* avoirdupois

1**ave** \ˈä-(ˌ)vā\ *n* [ME, fr. L, hail] (13c) **1 :** an expression of greeting or of leave-taking **:** HAIL, FAREWELL **2** *often cap* **:** AVE MARIA

2**ave** *abbr* avenue

avel·lan \ə-ˈve-lən\ *or* **avel·lane** \ə-ˈve-ˌlān, ˈa-və-ˌlān\ *adj* [L *abellana, avellana* filbert, fr. fem. of *Abellanus* of Abella, fr. *Abella,* ancient town in Italy] (1610) *of a heraldic cross* **:** having the four arms shaped like conventionalized filberts — see CROSS illustration

Ave Ma·ria \ˌä-(ˌ)vā-mə-ˈrē-ə\ *n* [ME, fr. ML, hail, Mary] (13c) **:** HAIL MARY 1

avenge \ə-ˈvenj\ *vt* **avenged; aveng·ing** [ME, fr. AF *avenger,* fr. *a-* (fr. L *ad-*) + *venger* to avenge — more at VENGEANCE] (14c) **1 :** to take vengeance for or on behalf of **2 :** to exact satisfaction for (a wrong) by punishing the wrongdoer — **aveng·er** *n*

av·ens \ˈa-vənz\ *n, pl* **avens** [ME *avence,* fr. AF *avance, avence*] (13c) **:** any of a genus (*Geum*) of perennial herbs of the rose family with white, purple, red, or yellow flowers

av·en·tail \ˈa-vən-ˌtāl\ *n* [ME, fr. AF *aventaille,* alter. of *ventaille*] (14c) **:** VENTAIL

aven·tu·rine \ə-ˈven-chə-ˌrēn, -rən\ *n* [F, fr. *aventure* chance — more at ADVENTURE] (1811) **1 :** glass containing opaque sparkling particles of foreign material (as copper or chromic oxide) **2 :** a translucent quartz spangled throughout with scales of mica or other mineral

av·e·nue \ˈa-və-ˌnü, -ˌnyü\ *n* [MF, fr. fem. of *avenu,* pp. of *avenir* to come to, fr. L *advenire* — more at ADVENTURE] (1600) **1 :** a way of access **:** ROUTE **2 :** a channel for pursuing a desired object ⟨~*s* of communication⟩ **3 a** *chiefly Brit* **:** the principal walk or driveway to a house situated off a main road **b :** a broad passageway bordered by trees **4 :** an often broad street or road

aver \ə-ˈvər\ *vt* **averred; aver·ring** [ME *averren,* fr. AF *averer,* fr. ML *adverare* to confirm as authentic, fr. L *ad-* + *verus* true — more at VERY] (15c) **1 a :** to verify or prove to be true in pleading a cause **b :** to allege or assert in pleading **2 :** to declare positively

1**av·er·age** \ˈa-v(ə-)rij\ *n* [fr. earlier *average* proportionally distributed charge for damage at sea, modif. of MF *avarie* damage to ship or cargo, fr. OIt *avaria,* fr. Ar *ʽawārīya* damaged merchandise] (1732) **1 a :** a single value (as a mean, mode, or median) that summarizes or represents the general significance of a set of unequal values **b :** MEAN 1b **2 a :** an estimation of or approximation to an arithmetic mean **b :** a level (as of intelligence) typical of a group, class, or series ⟨above the ~⟩ **3 :** a ratio expressing the average performance esp. of an athletic team or an athlete computed according to the number of opportunities for successful performance — **on average** *or* **on the average :** taking the typical example of the group under consideration ⟨prices have increased *on average* by five percent⟩

syn AVERAGE, MEAN, MEDIAN, NORM mean something that represents a middle point. AVERAGE is the quotient obtained by dividing the sum total of a set of figures by the number of figures ⟨scored an *average* of 85 on tests⟩. MEAN may be the simple average or it may represent value midway between two extremes ⟨a high of 70° and a low of 50° give a *mean* of 60°⟩. MEDIAN applies to the value that represents the point at which there are as many instances above as there are below ⟨*average* of a group of persons earning 3, 4, 5, 8, and 10 dollars an hour is 6 dollars, whereas the *median* is 5 dollars⟩. NORM means the average of performance of a significantly large group, class, or grade ⟨scores about the *norm* for fifth grade arithmetic⟩.

2**average** *adj* (1770) **1 :** equaling an arithmetic mean **2 a :** being about midway between extremes ⟨a man of ~ height⟩ **b :** not out of the ordinary **:** COMMON ⟨the ~ person⟩ — **av·er·age·ly** *adv* — **av·er·age·ness** *n*

3**average** *vb* **av·er·aged; av·er·ag·ing** *vi* (1769) **1 a :** to be or come to an average ⟨the gain *averaged* out to 20 percent⟩ **b :** to have a medial value of ⟨a color *averaging* a pale purple⟩ **2 :** to buy on a falling market or sell on a rising market additional shares or commodities so as to obtain a more favorable average price — usu. used with *down* or *up* ~ *vt* **1 :** to do, get, or have on the average or as an average sum or quantity ⟨~*s* 12 hours of work a day⟩ **2 :** to find the arithmetic mean of (a series of unequal quantities) **3 a :** to bring toward the average **b :** to divide among a number proportionately

aver·ment \ə-ˈvər-mənt\ *n* (15c) **1 :** the act of averring **2 :** something that is averred **:** AFFIRMATION

averse \ə-ˈvərs\ *adj* [L *aversus,* pp. of *avertere*] (1597) **:** having an active feeling of repugnance or distaste — usu. used with *to* ⟨~ to strenuous exercise⟩ ***syn*** see DISINCLINED — **averse·ly** *adv* — **averse·ness** *n*

aver·sion \ə-ˈvər-zhən, -shən\ *n* (1596) **1** *obs* **:** the act of turning away **2 a :** a feeling of repugnance toward something with a desire to avoid or turn from it ⟨regards drunkenness with ~⟩ **b :** a settled dislike **:** ANTIPATHY ⟨expressed an ~ to parties⟩ **c :** a tendency to extinguish a behavior or to avoid a thing or situation and esp. a usu. pleasurable one because it is or has been associated with a noxious stimulus **3 :** an object of aversion ⟨inconstancy is my ~ —Jane Austen⟩

aversion therapy *n* (1946) **:** therapy intended to suppress an undesirable habit or behavior (as smoking) by associating the habit or behavior with a noxious or punishing stimulus (as electric shock)

aver·sive \ə-ˈvər-siv, -ziv\ *adj* (1923) **:** tending to avoid or causing avoidance of a noxious or punishing stimulus ⟨behavior modification by ~ stimulation⟩ — **aver·sive·ly** *adv* — **aver·sive·ness** *n*

avert \ə-ˈvərt\ *vt* [ME, fr. MF *avertir,* fr. L *avertere,* fr. *ab-* + *vertere* to turn — more at WORTH] (15c) **1 :** to turn away or aside (as the eyes) in avoidance **2 :** to see coming and ward off **:** AVOID ⟨~ disaster⟩

Aves·ta \ə-ˈves-tə\ *n* [MPers *abestāg,* lit., text] (1856) **:** the book of the sacred writings of Zoroastrianism

Aves·tan \-tən\ *n* (1856) **:** an ancient Iranian language in which the sacred books of Zoroastrianism were written — see INDO-EUROPEAN LANGUAGES table — **Avestan** *adj*

avg *abbr* average

av·gas \ˈav-ˌgas\ *n* [*aviation gasoline*] (1943) **:** gasoline for airplanes

av·go·lem·o·no \ˌäv-gō-ˈle-mə-(ˌ)nō\ *n* [ModGk *augolemono,* fr. *augo* egg + *lemoni* lemon] (1961) **:** a soup or sauce made with chicken stock, egg yolks, and lemon juice

avi·an \ˈā-vē-ən\ *adj* [L *avis*] (1870) **:** of, relating to, or derived from birds ⟨~ behavior⟩ ⟨~ species⟩

avian influenza *n* (1980) **:** highly variable influenza A of birds caused by any of the subtypes of the causative orthomyxovirus of which some strains have been or may be transmitted to other vertebrates including humans esp. after undergoing mutation — called also *avian flu*; compare BIRD FLU

avi·ary \ˈā-vē-ˌer-ē, -ˌe-rē\ *n, pl* **-ar·ies** [L *aviarium,* fr. *avis* bird; akin to Gk *aetos* eagle] (1577) **:** a place for keeping birds confined

avi·ate \ˈā-vē-ˌāt, ˈa-\ *vi* **-at·ed; -at·ing** [back-formation fr. *aviation*] (1887) **:** to navigate the air (as in an airplane)

avi·a·tion \ˌā-vē-ˈā-shən, ˌa-\ *n, often attrib* [F, fr. L *avis*] (1866) **1 :** the operation of heavier-than-air aircraft **2 :** military airplanes **3 :** airplane manufacture, development, and design

avi·a·tor \ˈā-vē-ˌā-tər, ˈa-\ *n* (1887) **:** the operator or pilot of an aircraft and esp. an airplane

aviator glasses *n pl* (1968) **:** eyeglasses having a lightweight metal frame and relatively large usu. tinted lenses

avi·a·trix \ˌā-vē-ˈā-triks, ˌa-\ *n, pl* **-trix·es** \-trik-səz\ *or* **-tri·ces** \-trə-ˌsēz\ (1910) **:** a woman who is an aviator

avi·cul·ture \ˈā-və-ˌkəl-chər, ˈa-\ *n* [L *avis* + E *culture*] (ca. 1879) **:** the raising and care of birds and esp. of wild birds in captivity — **avi·cul·tur·ist** \ˌā-və-ˈkəl-ch(ə-)rist, ˌa-\ *n*

av·id \ˈa-vəd\ *adj* [F or L; F *avide,* fr. L *avidus,* fr. *avēre* to desire, crave; akin to W *ewyllys* desire, OIr *con-oí* he protects] (1769) **1 :** desirous to the point of greed **:** urgently eager **:** GREEDY ⟨~ for publicity⟩ **2 :** characterized by enthusiasm and vigorous pursuit ⟨~ readers⟩ ***syn*** see EAGER — **av·id·ly** *adv* — **av·id·ness** *n*

av·i·din \ˈa-və-dən\ *n* [fr. its avidity for biotin] (1941) **:** a protein found in egg white that inactivates biotin by combining with it

avid·ity \ə-ˈvi-də-tē, a-\ *n, pl* **-ities** (15c) **1 :** the quality or state of being avid: **a :** keen eagerness **b :** consuming greed **2 :** AFFINITY 2b(2)

avi·fau·na \ˌā-və-ˈfȯ-nə, ˌa-, -ˈfä-nə\ *n* [NL, fr. L *avis* + NL *fauna*] (1873) **:** the birds or the kinds of birds of a region, period, or environment — **avi·fau·nal** \-ˈfȯ-nᵊl, -ˈfä-\ *adj*

avi·on·ics \ˌā-vē-ˈä-niks, ˌa-\ *n pl* [*aviation electronics*] (1949) **:** electronics designed for use in aerospace vehicles — **avi·on·ic** \-nik\ *adj*

avir·u·lent \(ˌ)ā-ˈvir-(y)ə-lənt\ *adj* [ISV] (ca. 1900) **:** not virulent — compare NONPATHOGENIC

avi·ta·min·osis \ˌā-ˌvī-tə-mə-ˈnō-səs\ *n, pl* **-o·ses** \-ˌsēz\ [NL] (1914) **:** disease (as pellagra) resulting from a deficiency of one or more vitamins — **avi·ta·min·ot·ic** \-mə-ˈnä-tik\ *adj*

A–V node \ˌā-ˈvē-, ˈā-ˌ\ *n* (1949) **:** ATRIOVENTRICULAR NODE

avo \ˈa-(ˌ)vü\ *n, pl* **avos** [Pg, fr. *avo* fractional part, fr. *-avo* ordinal suffix (as in *oitavo* eighth, fr. L *octavus*) — more at OCTAVE] (ca. 1909) — see *pataca* at MONEY table

av·o·ca·do \ˌä-və-ˈkä-(ˌ)dō, ˌa-\ *n, pl* **-dos** *also* **-does** [modif. of Sp *aguacate,* fr. Nahuatl *āhuacatl* avocado, testicle] (1697) **1 :** a pulpy green- to purple-skinned nutty-flavored fruit of any of various tropical American trees (genus *Persea* esp. *P. americana*) of the laurel family; *also* **:** a tree bearing avocados **2 :** a light yellowish green

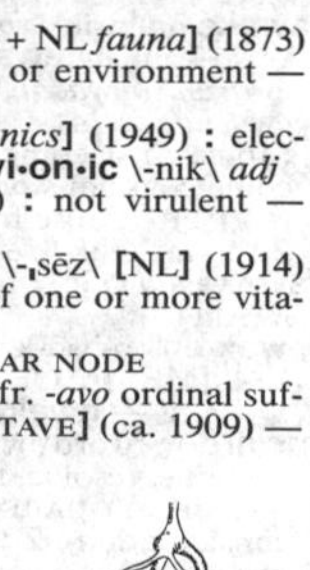

avocado 1

avocado pear *n* (1830) *chiefly Brit* **:** AVOCADO 1

av·o·ca·tion \ˌa-və-ˈkā-shən\ *n* [L *avocation-, avocatio,* fr. *avocare* to call away, fr. *ab-* + *vocare* to call, fr. *voc-, vox* voice — more at VOICE] (ca. 1617) **1** *archaic* **:** DIVERSION, DISTRACTION **2 :** customary employment **:** VOCATION **3 :** a subordinate occupation pursued in addition to one's vocation esp. for enjoyment **:** HOBBY

av·o·ca·tion·al \ˌa-və-ˈkā-sh(ə-)nəl\ *adj* (1921) **1 :** of or relating to an avocation ⟨an ~ interest in sports⟩ **2 :** being

such by avocation ⟨an ~ musician⟩ — **av·o·ca·tion·al·ly** \-sh(ə-)nə-lē\ *adv*
av·o·cet \ˈa-və-ˌset\ *n* [F & It; F *avocette,* fr. It *avocetta*] (1766) **:** any of a genus (*Recurvirostra*) of rather large long-legged shorebirds with webbed feet and slender upward-curving bill
Avo·ga·dro's number \ˌa-və-ˈgä-(ˌ)drōz-, ˌa-və-, -ˈga-\ *n* [Count Amedeo *Avogadro*] (1924) **:** the number 6.022×10^{23} indicating the number of atoms or molecules in a mole of any substance — called also *Avogadro number*
avoid \ə-ˈvȯid\ *vt* [ME, fr. AF *avoider,* alter. of OF *esvuider,* fr. *es-* (fr. L *ex-*) + *vuider* to empty — more at VOID] (14c) **1 :** to make legally void **:** ANNUL ⟨~ a plea⟩ **2** *obs* **:** VOID, EXPEL **3 a :** to keep away from **:** SHUN ⟨have been ~*ing* me⟩ **b :** to prevent the occurrence or effectiveness of ⟨~ further delays⟩ **c :** to refrain from ⟨~ overeating⟩ **4** *archaic* **:** to depart or withdraw from **:** LEAVE ***syn*** see ESCAPE — **avoid·able** \-ˈvȯi-də-bəl\ *adj* — **avoid·ably** \-blē\ *adv* — **avoid·er** *n*
avoid·ance \ə-ˈvȯi-dᵊn(t)s\ *n* (14c) **1** *obs* **a :** an action of emptying, vacating, or clearing away **b :** OUTLET **2 :** ANNULMENT 1 **3 :** an act or practice of avoiding or withdrawing from something
[1]**av·oir·du·pois** \ˌa-vər-də-ˈpȯiz, ˈa-vər-də-ˌ\ *n* [ME *avoir de pois* goods sold by weight, fr. AF, lit., goods of weight] (15c) **1 :** AVOIRDUPOIS WEIGHT **2 :** WEIGHT, HEAVINESS; *esp* **:** personal weight
[2]**avoirdupois** *adj* (1755) **:** expressed in avoirdupois weight ⟨one ounce ~⟩
avoirdupois weight *n* (1619) **:** the series of units of weight based on the pound of 16 ounces and the ounce of 16 drams — see WEIGHT table
avouch \ə-ˈvau̇ch\ *vt* [ME, to cite as authority, fr. MF *avochier* to summon, fr. L *advocare* — more at ADVOCATE] (15c) **1 :** to declare as a matter of fact or as a thing that can be proved **:** AFFIRM **2 :** to vouch for **:** CORROBORATE **3 a :** to acknowledge (as an act) as one's own **b :** CONFESS, AVOW
avouch·ment \-mənt\ *n* (1574) **:** an act of avouching **:** AVOWAL
avow \ə-ˈvau̇\ *vt* [ME, fr. AF *avuer, avouer,* fr. L *advocare*] (14c) **1 :** to declare assuredly ⟨she ~*ed* her innocence⟩ **2 :** to declare openly, bluntly, and without shame ⟨ever ready to ~ his reactionary outlook⟩ ***syn*** see ACKNOWLEDGE, ASSERT — **avow·er** \-ˈvau̇(-ə)r\ *n*
avow·al \-ˈvau̇(-ə)l\ *n* (ca. 1686) **:** an open declaration or acknowledgment
avow·ed·ly \ə-ˈvau̇-əd-lē\ *adv* (1656) **1 :** with open acknowledgment **:** FRANKLY ⟨an ~ hostile review⟩ **2 :** by unsupported assertion or profession alone **:** ALLEGEDLY ⟨politicians remain skeptical of . . . ~ democratic intentions —Jerry Kirshenbaum⟩
avulse \ə-ˈvəls\ *vt* **avulsed; avuls·ing** [L *avulsus,* pp. of *avellere* to tear off, fr. *ab-* + *vellere* to pluck — more at VULNERABLE] (ca. 1765) **:** to separate by avulsion
avul·sion \ə-ˈvəl-shən\ *n* (1622) **:** a forcible separation or detachment: as **a :** a tearing away of a body part accidentally or surgically **b :** a sudden cutting off of land by flood, currents, or change in course of a body of water; *esp* **:** one separating land from one person's property and joining it to another's
avun·cu·lar \ə-ˈvəŋ-kyə-lər\ *adj* [L *avunculus* maternal uncle — more at UNCLE] (1831) **1 :** of or relating to an uncle **2 :** suggestive of an uncle esp. in kindliness or geniality ⟨~ indulgence⟩ — **avun·cu·lar·i·ty** \ə-ˌvəŋ-kyə-ˈla-rə-tē, -ˈler-ə-\ *n* — **avun·cu·lar·ly** \ə-ˈvəŋ-kyə-lər-lē\ *adv*
aw \ˈȯ\ *interj* (1852) — used to express mild disappointment, gentle entreaty, or real or mock sympathy or sentiment
AW *abbr* **1** actual weight **2** aircraft warning **3** articles of war **4** automatic weapon
AWACS *abbr* airborne warning and control system
await \ə-ˈwāt\ *vb* [ME, fr. AF *aweiter, aguaiter,* fr. *a-* (fr. L *ad-*) + *guaiter* to watch — more at WAIT] *vt* (13c) **1** *obs* **:** to lie in wait for **2 a :** to wait for ⟨~*ing* his arrival⟩ **b :** to remain in abeyance until ⟨a treaty ~*ing* ratification⟩ **3 :** to be in store for ⟨wonders what ~*s* him next⟩ ~ *vi* **1** *obs* **:** ATTEND **2 :** to stay or be in waiting **:** WAIT **3 :** to be in store
[1]**awake** \ə-ˈwāk\ *vb* **awoke** \-ˈwōk\ *also* **awaked** \-ˈwākt\; **awo·ken** \-ˈwō-kən\ *or* **awaked** *also* **awoke; awak·ing** [ME *awaken* (fr. OE *awacan, onwacan,* fr. [1]*a-, on* + *wacan* to awake) & *awakien,* fr. OE *awacian,* fr. [1]*a-* + *wacian* to be awake — more at WAKE] *vi* (bef. 12c) **1 :** to cease sleeping **2 :** to become aroused or active again **3 :** to become conscious or aware of something ⟨*awoke* to the possibilities⟩ ~ *vt* **1 :** to arouse from sleep or a sleeplike state ⟨*awoken* by the storm⟩ **2 :** to make active **:** stir up ⟨*awoke* old memories⟩
[2]**awake** *adj* (13c) **:** fully conscious, alert, and aware **:** not asleep ***syn*** see AWARE
awak·en \ə-ˈwā-kən\ *vb* **awak·ened; awak·en·ing** \-ˈwāk-niŋ, -ˈwā-kə-\ [ME, fr. OE *awæcnian,* fr. *a-* + *wæcnian* to waken] (bef. 12c) **:** AWAKE — **awak·en·er** \-ˈwāk-nər, -ˈwā-kə-\ *n*
[1]**award** \ə-ˈwȯrd\ *vt* [ME, to decide, fr. AF *awarder, agarder* to look at, examine, resolve, fr. *a-* (fr. L *ad-*) + *warder, garder* to look after, guard — more at GUARD] (14c) **1 :** to give by judicial decree or after careful consideration **2 :** to confer or bestow as being deserved or merited or needed ⟨~ scholarships to disadvantaged students⟩ ***syn*** see GRANT — **award·able** \-ˈwȯr-də-bəl\ *adj* — **award·ee** \-ˌwȯr-ˈdē\ *n* — **award·er** \-ˈwȯr-dər\ *n*
[2]**award** *n* (14c) **1 a :** a judgment or final decision; *esp* **:** the decision of arbitrators in a case submitted to them **b :** the document containing the decision of arbitrators **2 :** something that is conferred or bestowed esp. on the basis of merit or need
aware \ə-ˈwer\ *adj* [ME *iwar,* fr. OE *gewær,* fr. *ge-* (associative prefix) + *wær* wary — more at CO-, WARY] (bef. 12c) **1** *archaic* **:** WATCHFUL, WARY **2 :** having or showing realization, perception, or knowledge — **aware·ness** *n*
syn AWARE, COGNIZANT, CONSCIOUS, SENSIBLE, ALIVE, AWAKE mean having knowledge of something. AWARE implies vigilance in observing or alertness in drawing inferences from what one experiences ⟨*aware* of changes in climate⟩. COGNIZANT implies having special or certain knowledge as from firsthand sources ⟨not fully *cognizant* of the facts⟩. CONSCIOUS implies that one is focusing one's attention on something or is even preoccupied by it ⟨*conscious* that my heart was pounding⟩. SENSIBLE implies direct or intuitive perceiving esp. of intangibles or of emotional states or qualities ⟨*sensible* of a teacher's influence⟩. ALIVE adds to SENSIBLE the implication of acute sensitivity to something ⟨*alive* to the thrill of danger⟩. AWAKE implies that one has become alive to something and is on the alert ⟨a country always *awake* to the threat of invasion⟩.
awash \ə-ˈwȯsh, -ˈwäsh\ *adj* (1831) **1 a :** alternately covered and exposed by waves or tide **b :** washing about **:** AFLOAT **c :** covered with water **:** FLOODED **2 :** filled, covered, or completely overrun as if by a flood ⟨a movie ~ in sentimentality⟩
[1]**away** \ə-ˈwā\ *adv* (bef. 12c) **1 :** on the way **:** ALONG ⟨get ~ early⟩ **2 :** from this or that place ⟨go ~⟩ **3 a :** in a secure place or manner ⟨locked ~⟩ **b :** in another direction ⟨look ~⟩ **4 :** out of existence **:** to an end ⟨echoes dying ~⟩ **5 :** from one's possession ⟨gave ~ a fortune⟩ **6 :** steadily onward **:** UNINTERRUPTEDLY ⟨clocks ticking ~⟩ **7 :** by a long distance or interval **:** FAR ⟨~ back in 1910⟩
[2]**away** *adj* (14c) **1 :** absent from a place **:** GONE ⟨~ for the weekend⟩ **2 :** distant in space or time ⟨a lake 10 miles ~⟩ ⟨the season is two months ~⟩ **3 :** played on an opponent's grounds ⟨home and ~ games⟩ **4** *baseball* **:** OUT ⟨two ~ in the ninth⟩ — **away·ness** *n*
awd *abbr* all-wheel drive
[1]**awe** \ˈȯ\ *n* [ME, fr. ON *agi;* akin to OE *ege* awe, Gk *achos* pain] (13c) **1 :** an emotion variously combining dread, veneration, and wonder that is inspired by authority or by the sacred or sublime ⟨stood in ~ of the king⟩ ⟨regard nature's wonders with ~⟩ **2** *archaic* **a :** DREAD, TERROR **b :** the power to inspire dread
[2]**awe** *vt* **awed; aw·ing** (13c) **:** to inspire with awe ⟨we were *awed* by the beauty of the mountains⟩
aweary \ə-ˈwir-ē\ *adj* (1537) *archaic* **:** being weary
aweath·er \ə-ˈwe-t͟hər\ *adv* (1599) **:** on or toward the weather or windward side — compare ALEE
awed \ˈȯd\ *adj* (1592) **:** showing awe ⟨~ respect⟩
aweigh \ə-ˈwā\ *adj* (1670) **:** raised just clear of the bottom — used of an anchor
awe·less *also* **aw·less** \ˈȯ-ləs\ *adj* (14c) **1 :** feeling no awe **2** *obs* **:** inspiring no awe
awe·some \ˈȯ-səm\ *adj* (1598) **1 :** expressive of awe ⟨~ tribute⟩ **2 a :** inspiring awe ⟨an ~ task⟩ **b :** TERRIFIC, EXTRAORDINARY ⟨had an ~ time⟩ — **awe·some·ly** *adv* — **awe·some·ness** *n*
awe·struck \-ˌstrək\ *also* **awe·strick·en** \-ˌstri-kən\ *adj* (1634) **:** filled with awe
[1]**aw·ful** \ˈȯ-fəl\ *adj* (13c) **1 :** inspiring awe **2 :** filled with awe: as **a** *obs* **:** AFRAID, TERRIFIED **b :** deeply respectful or reverential **3 :** extremely disagreeable or objectionable ⟨~ food⟩ **4 :** exceedingly great — used as an intensive ⟨an ~ lot of money⟩ — **aw·ful·ly** \ˈȯ-fə-lē, *esp as adv of adj senses 3 & 4* -flē\ *adv* — **aw·ful·ness** \-fəl-nəs\ *n*
usage Many grammarians take issue with the senses of *awful* and *awfully* that do not convey the etymological connection with *awe.* However, senses 3 and 4 of the adjective were used in speech and casual writing by the late 18th century ⟨it is an *awful* while since you have heard from me —John Keats (letter)⟩ ⟨there was an *awful* crowd —Sir Walter Scott (letter)⟩ ⟨this is an *awful* thing to say to oil painters —William Blake⟩. Adverbial use of *awful* as an intensifier began to appear in print in the early 19th century, as did the senses of *awfully* corresponding to senses 3 and 4 of the adjective. Both adverbs remain in widespread use ⟨a sad state of affairs and *awful* tough on art —H. L. Mencken⟩ ⟨the *awfully* rich young American —Henry James⟩ ⟨decided to play it so *awfully* safe —A. M. Schlesinger *b*1917⟩.
[2]**awful** *adv* (1818) **:** VERY, EXTREMELY ⟨~ tired⟩
awhile \ə-ˈhwī(-ə)l, ə-ˈwī(-ə)l\ *adv* (bef. 12c) **:** for a while
usage Although considered a solecism by many commentators, *awhile,* like several other adverbs of time and place, is often used as the object of a preposition ⟨for *awhile* there is a silence —Lord Dunsany⟩.
awhirl \ə-ˈhwər(-ə)l, -ˈwər(-ə)l\ *adj* (1843) **:** being in a whirl
awk·ward \ˈȯ-kwərd\ *adj* [ME *awkeward* in the wrong direction, fr. *awke* turned the wrong way, fr. ON *ǫfugr;* akin to OHG *abuh* turned the wrong way] (1530) **1** *obs* **:** PERVERSE **2** *archaic* **:** UNFAVORABLE, ADVERSE **3 a :** lacking dexterity or skill (as in the use of hands) ⟨~ with a needle and thread⟩ **b :** showing the result of a lack of expertness ⟨~ pictures⟩ **4 a :** lacking ease or grace (as of movement or expression) ⟨~ writing⟩ **b :** lacking the right proportions, size, or harmony of parts **:** UNGAINLY ⟨an ~ design⟩ **5 a :** lacking social grace and assurance ⟨an ~ newcomer⟩ **b :** causing embarrassment ⟨an ~ moment⟩ **6 :** not easy to handle or deal with **:** requiring great skill, ingenuity, or care ⟨an ~ load⟩ ⟨an ~ diplomatic situation⟩ — **awk·ward·ly** *adv* — **awk·ward·ness** *n*
syn AWKWARD, CLUMSY, MALADROIT, INEPT, GAUCHE mean not marked by ease (as of performance, movement, or social conduct). AWKWARD is widely applicable and may suggest unhandiness, inconvenience, lack of muscular control, embarrassment, or lack of tact ⟨periods of *awkward* silence⟩. CLUMSY implies stiffness and heaviness and so may connote inflexibility, unwieldiness, or lack of ordinary skill ⟨a *clumsy* mechanic⟩. MALADROIT suggests a tendency to create awkward situations ⟨a *maladroit* politician⟩. INEPT often implies complete failure or inadequacy ⟨a hopelessly *inept* defense attorney⟩. GAUCHE implies the effects of shyness, inexperience, or ill breeding ⟨felt *gauche* and unsophisticated at formal parties⟩.
awl \ˈȯl\ *n* [ME *al,* fr. OE *æl;* akin to OHG *āla* awl, Skt *ārā*] (bef. 12c) **:** a pointed tool for marking surfaces or piercing small holes (as in leather or wood)

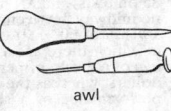

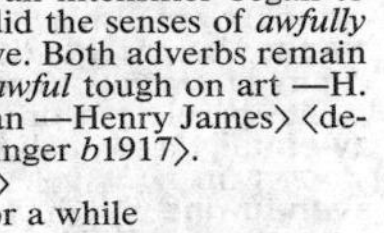
awl

awn \ˈȯn\ *n* [ME, fr. OE *agen,* fr. ON *ǫgn;* akin to OHG *agana* awn, OE *ecg* edge — more at EDGE] (12c) **:** one of the slender bristles that terminate the glumes of the spikelet in some cereal and other grasses — **awned** \ˈȯnd\ *adj* — **awn·less** \ˈȯn-ləs\ *adj*
aw·ning \ˈȯ-niŋ, ˈä-niŋ\ *n* [origin unknown] (1582) **:** a rooflike cover extending over or in front of a place (as over the deck or in front of a door or window) as a shelter — **aw·ninged** \-niŋd\ *adj*
awoke *past and past part of* AWAKE
awoken *past part of* AWAKE
[1]**AWOL** \ˈā-ˌwȯl, ˌā-ˌdə-bəl-yü-ˌō-ˈel\ *adj or adv, sometimes not cap* [*a*bsent *w*ith*o*ut *l*eave] (1918) **:** ABSENT WITHOUT LEAVE; *broadly* **:** absent often without notice or permission ⟨the place looked as if its caretaker had been ~ for some time —Daniel Ford⟩

[2]**AWOL** *n, sometimes not cap* (1918) : a person who is AWOL

awry \ə-ˈrī\ *adv or adj* (14c) **1** : in a turned or twisted position or direction : ASKEW **2** : off the correct or expected course : AMISS

aw–shucks \ˈȯ-ˌshəks\ *adj* (1951) : being or marked by an unsophisticated, self-conscious, or self-effacing manner ⟨an ~ grin⟩

[1]**ax** *or* **axe** \ˈaks\ *n* [ME, fr. OE *æcs;* akin to OHG *ackus* ax, L *ascia,* Gk *axinē*] (bef. 12c) **1** : a cutting tool that consists of a heavy edged head fixed to a handle with the edge parallel to the handle and that is used esp. for felling trees and chopping and splitting wood **2** : a hammer with a sharp edge for dressing or spalling stone **3** : abrupt removal (as from employment or from a budget) — sometimes used in the phrase *get the ax* **4** : a musical instrument (as a guitar or a saxophone) — **ax to grind** : an ulterior often selfish underlying purpose ⟨claims that he has no *ax to grind* in criticizing the proposed law⟩

[2]**ax** *or* **axe** *vt* **axed; ax·ing** (1677) **1 a** : to shape, dress, or trim with an ax **b** : to chop, split, or sever with an ax **2** : to remove abruptly (as from employment or from a budget)

[3]**ax** *abbr* **1** axiom **2** axis

ax·el \ˈak-səl, ˈäk-\ *n, often cap* [*Axel* Paulsen †1938 Norw. figure skater] (1930) : a jump in figure skating from the outer forward edge of one skate with 1½ turns taken in the air and a return to the outer backward edge of the other skate

axe·nic \(ˌ)ā-ˈze-nik, -ˈzē-\ *adj* [[2]*a-* + Gk *xenos* strange] (1942) : free from other living organisms — **axe·ni·cal·ly** \-ni-k(ə-)lē\ *adv*

ax·i·al \ˈak-sē-əl\ *adj* (ca. 1847) **1** : of, relating to, or having the characteristics of an axis **2 a** : situated around, in the direction of, on, or along an axis **b** : extending in a direction essentially perpendicular to the plane of a cyclic structure (as of cyclohexane) ⟨~ hydrogens⟩ — compare EQUATORIAL — **ax·i·al·i·ty** \ˌak-sē-ˈa-lə-tē\ *n* — **ax·i·al·ly** \ˈak-sē-ə-lē\ *adv*

axial skeleton *n* (1872) : the skeleton of the trunk and head

ax·il \ˈak-səl, -ˌsil\ *n* [NL *axilla,* fr. L] (1794) : the angle between a branch or leaf and the axis from which it arises

ax·il·la \ag-ˈzi-lə, ak-ˈsi-\ *n, pl* **-lae** \-(ˌ)lē, -ˌlī\ *or* **-las** [L, dim. of *ala* wing, upper arm, armpit, axil — more at AISLE] (1616) : the cavity beneath the junction of a forelimb and the body; *esp* : ARMPIT

ax·il·lar \ag-ˈzi-lər, ak-ˈsi-, ˈag-zə-, ˈak-sə-, -ˌlär\ *n* (1541) : an axillary part (as a feather)

[1]**ax·il·lary** \ˈak-sə-ˌler-ē, -ˌle-rē\ *adj* (1615) **1** : of, relating to, or located near the axilla **2** : situated in or growing from an axil ⟨~ buds⟩

[2]**axillary** *n, pl* **-lar·ies** (ca. 1889) : one of the feathers arising from the axilla and closing the space between the flight feathers and body of a flying bird

ax·i·ol·o·gy \ˌak-sē-ˈä-lə-jē\ *n* [Gk *axios* + ISV *-logy*] (1908) : the study of the nature, types, and criteria of values and of value judgments esp. in ethics — **ax·i·o·log·i·cal** \ˌak-sē-ə-ˈlä-ji-kəl\ *adj* — **ax·i·o·log·i·cal·ly** \-ji-k(ə-)lē\ *adv*

ax·i·om \ˈak-sē-əm\ *n* [L *axioma,* fr. Gk *axiōma,* lit., something worthy, fr. *axioun* to think worthy, fr. *axios* worth, worthy; akin to Gk *agein* to weigh, drive — more at AGENT] (15c) **1** : a maxim widely accepted on its intrinsic merit **2** : a statement accepted as true as the basis for argument or inference : POSTULATE 1 **3** : an established rule or principle or a self-evident truth

ax·i·om·at·ic \ˌak-sē-ə-ˈma-tik\ *adj* [MGk *axiōmatikos,* fr. Gk, honorable, fr. *axiōmat-, axiōma*] (1797) **1** : taken for granted : SELF-EVIDENT ⟨an ~ truth⟩ **2** : based on or involving an axiom or system of axioms ⟨~ set theory⟩ — **ax·i·om·at·i·cal·ly** \-ti-k(ə-)lē\ *adv*

ax·i·omat·i·sa·tion *chiefly Brit var of* AXIOMATIZATION

ax·i·omat·i·za·tion \ˌak-sē-ə-ˌma-tə-ˈzā-shən, -sē-ˌä-mə-tə-\ *n* (1931) : the act or process of reducing to a system of axioms — **ax·i·om·a·tize** \-sē-ˈä-mə-ˌtīz\ *vt*

axiom of choice (1942) : an axiom in set theory that is equivalent to Zorn's lemma: for every collection of nonempty sets there is a function which chooses an element from each set

ax·ion \ˈak-sē-(ˌ)än\ *n* [*axial* + [2]*-on*] (1978) : a hypothetical subatomic particle of low mass and energy that is postulated to exist because of certain properties of the strong force

ax·is \ˈak-səs\ *n, pl* **ax·es** \-ˌsēz\ [L, axis, axle; akin to OE *eax* axis, axle, Gk *axōn,* Lith *ašis,* Skt *akṣaḥ*] (14c) **1 a** : a straight line about which a body or a geometric figure rotates or may be supposed to rotate **b** : a straight line with respect to which a body or figure is symmetrical — called also *axis of symmetry* **c** : a straight line that bisects at right angles a system of parallel chords of a curve and divides the curve into two symmetrical parts **d** : one of the reference lines of a coordinate system **2 a** : the second vertebra of the neck on which the head and first vertebra turn as on a pivot **b** : any of various central, fundamental, or axial parts **3** : a plant stem **4** : one of several imaginary lines assumed in describing the positions of the planes by which a crystal is bounded and the positions of atoms in the structure of the crystal **5** : a main line of direction, motion, growth, or extension **6 a** : an implied line in painting or sculpture through a composition to which elements in the composition are referred **b** : a line actually drawn and used as the basis of measurements in an architectural or other working drawing **7** : any of three fixed lines of reference in an aircraft that run in the longitudinal, lateral, and vertical directions, are mutually perpendicular, and usu. pass through the aircraft's center of gravity **8** : PARTNERSHIP, ALLIANCE **9** : a point or continuum on which something centers ⟨an ~ of social power⟩

Axis *adj* (1938) : of or relating to the three powers Germany, Italy, and Japan engaged against the Allied nations in World War II

axis deer *n* [NL *Axis,* genus name, fr. L *axis,* a wild quadruped of India] (1817) : a deer (*Axis axis*) of India and surrounding areas having brownish hair with white spots

axi·sym·met·ric \ˌak-si-sə-ˈme-trik\ *also* **axi·sym·met·ri·cal** \-tri-kəl\ *adj* [*axis* + *symmetric*] (1893) : symmetric in respect to an axis — **axi·sym·me·try** \-ˈsi-mə-trē\ *n*

ax·le \ˈak-səl\ *n* [ME *axel-* (as in *axeltre*)] (14c) **1 a** : a pin or shaft on or with which a wheel or pair of wheels revolves **b (1)** : a fixed bar or beam with bearings at its ends on which wheels (as of a cart) revolve **(2)** : the spindle of such a beam **2** *archaic* : AXIS

axle·tree \-(ˌ)trē\ *n* [ME *axeltre,* fr. ON *ǫxultrē,* fr. *ǫxull* axle + *trē* tree] (14c) : AXLE 1b(1)

ax·man \ˈaks-mən\ *n* (1671) : one who wields an ax

Ax·min·ster \ˈaks-ˌmin(t)-stər\ *n* [*Axminster,* town in England] (1844) : a machine-woven carpet with pile tufts inserted mechanically in a variety of textures and patterns

ax·o·lotl \ˈak-sə-ˌlä-tᵊl\ *n* [Nahuatl *āxōlōtl*] (ca. 1768) : any of several salamanders (genus *Ambystoma* esp. *A. mexicanum* and *A. tigrinum*) of mountain lakes of Mexico and the western U.S. that ordinarily live and breed in the larval form without metamorphosing

ax·on \ˈak-ˌsän\ *also* **ax·one** \-ˌsōn\ *n* [NL *axon,* fr. Gk *axōn*] (ca. 1899) : a usu. long and single nerve-cell process that usu. conducts impulses away from the cell body — see NEURON illustration — **ax·o·nal** \ˈak-sə-nᵊl; ak-ˈsä-, -ˈsō-\ *adj*

ax·o·neme \ˈak-sə-ˌnēm\ *n* [Gk *axōn* axis + *nēma* thread, fr. *nēn* to spin — more at NEEDLE] (1901) : the fibrillar bundle of a flagellum or cilium that usu. consists of nine pairs of microtubules arranged in a ring around a single central pair — **ax·o·ne·mal** \ˌak-sə-ˈnē-məl\ *adj*

ax·o·no·met·ric \ˌak-sə-nō-ˈme-trik\ *adj* [Gk *axōn* axis + E *-metric*] (1908) : being or prepared by the projection of objects on the drawing surface so that they appear inclined with three sides showing and with horizontal and vertical distances drawn to scale but diagonal and curved lines distorted ⟨an ~ drawing⟩

axo·plasm \ˈak-sə-ˌpla-zəm\ *n* [*axon* + *-plasm*] (1900) : the protoplasm of an axon — **axo·plas·mic** \ˌak-sə-ˈplaz-mik\ *adj*

ay \ˈī\ *interj* [MF *aymi* ay me] (14c) — usu. used with following *me* to express sorrow or regret

ayah \ˈī-ə; ˈä-yə, -(ˌ)yä\ *n* [Hindi & Urdu *āyā,* fr. Pg *aia,* fr. L *avia* grandmother] (1779) : a nurse or maid native to India

aya·hua·sca \ˌī-yə-ˈhwäs-kə, -ˈwäs-\ *n* [AmerSp] (1949) : a hallucinogenic beverage prepared from the bark of a So. American woody vine (*Banisteriopsis caapi* of the family Malpighiaceae)

aya·tol·lah \ˌī-ə-ˈtō-lə, -ˈtä-, -ˈtə-, ˈī-ə-ˌ\ *n* [Pers *āyatollāh,* lit., sign of God, fr. Ar *āyatallāh,* fr. *āya* sign, miracle + *allāh* God] (1950) : a religious leader among Shiite Muslims — used as a title of respect esp. for one who is not an imam

[1]**aye** *also* **ay** \ˈā\ *adv* [ME, fr. ON *ei;* akin to OE *ā* always, L *aevum* age, lifetime, Gk *aiōn* age] (13c) : ALWAYS, CONTINUALLY, EVER ⟨love that will ~ endure —W. S. Gilbert⟩

[2]**aye** *also* **ay** \ˈī\ *adv* [perh. fr. ME *ye, yie* — more at YEA] (1576) : YES ⟨~, ~, sir⟩

[3]**aye** *also* **ay** \ˈī\ *n, pl* **ayes** (1589) : an affirmative vote or voter ⟨the ~*s* have it⟩

aye–aye \ˈī-ˌī\ *n* [F, fr. Malagasy *aiay*] (ca. 1781) : a small primitive nocturnal forest-dwelling primate (*Daubentonia madagascariensis*) of northern Madagascar that has a round head, large eyes and ears, and long thin fingers

AYH *abbr* American Youth Hostels

ayin \ˈī-ən\ *n* [Heb *ʿayin,* lit., eye] (1823) : the 16th letter of the Hebrew alphabet — see ALPHABET table

Ay·ma·ra \ˌī-mə-ˈrä\ *n, pl* **Aymara** *or* **Aymaras** [Sp *aymará*] (1842) **1** : a member of an Indian people of Bolivia, Peru, and northern Chile **2** : the language of the Aymara people

Ayr·shire \ˈer-ˌshir, -shər; ˈash-ˌir\ *n* [*Ayrshire,* Scotland] (1856) : any of a breed of hardy dairy cattle developed in Ayr and usu. marked with blotches of red or brown with white

ay·ur·ve·da \ˌī-ər-ˈvā-də, -ˈve-\ *n, often cap* [Skt *āyurvedaḥ,* fr. *āyuḥ* life, vital power + *vedaḥ* knowledge] (1788) : a form of holistic alternative medicine that is the traditional system of medicine of India — **ay·ur·ve·dic** \-dik\ *adj, often cap*

az *abbr* **1** azimuth **2** azure

AZ *abbr* Arizona

az- *or* **azo-** *comb form* [ISV, fr. F *azote* nitrogen, fr. *a-* [2]*a-* + *-zote,* prob. fr. Gk *zōtikos* maintaining life, fr. *zōē* life — more at QUICK] : containing nitrogen esp. as the divalent group N=N ⟨*azine*⟩

aza- *or* **az-** *comb form* [ISV *az-* + *-a-*] : containing nitrogen in place of carbon and usu. the divalent group NH for the group CH_2 or a single trivalent nitrogen atom for the group CH ⟨*aza*thioprine⟩

aza·lea \ə-ˈzāl-yə\ *n* [NL, genus name, fr. Gk, fem. of *azaleos* dry, fr. *azein* to parch, dry; akin to Hitt *ḫat-* to dry up and prob. to L *ador* emmer] (1760) : any of a subgenus (*Azalea*) of rhododendrons with funnel-shaped corollas and usu. deciduous leaves including many species and hybrid forms cultivated as ornamentals

aza·thi·o·prine \ˌa-zə-ˈthī-ə-ˌprēn\ *n* [*aza-* + *thi-* + *purine*] (1962) : a purine antimetabolite $C_9H_7N_7O_2S$ used esp. as an immunosuppressant

Aza·zel \ə-ˈzā-zəl, ˈa-zə-ˌzel\ *n* [Heb *ʿăzāzēl*] (1674) : an evil spirit of the wilderness to which a scapegoat was sent by the ancient Hebrews in a ritual of atonement

azeo·trope \ˈā-zē-ə-ˌtrōp\ *n* [[2]*a-* + *zeo-* (fr. Gk *zein* to boil) + *-trope* something changed, fr. Gk *tropos* turn — more at YEAST, TROPE] (1938) : a liquid mixture that is characterized by a constant minimum or maximum boiling point which is lower or higher than that of any of the components

Azer·bai·ja·ni \ˌa-zər-ˌbī-ˈjä-nē, ˌä-\ *n, pl* **Azerbaijanis** *also* **Azerbaijani** [Pers *āzarbāyjānī,* fr. *Āzarbāyjān* Azerbaijan] (ca. 1909) **1** : a member of a Turkic-speaking people of Azerbaijan and northwest Iran **2** : the Turkic language of the Azerbaijanis — **Azerbaijani** *adj*

Azeri \ə-ˈze-rē, -ˈzer-ē; ˈä-zə-rē\ *n* [Turk *Azeri* & Azerbaijani *azäri,* ultim. fr. Ar *ādhar-,* short for *Ādharbayjān* Azerbaijan] (1979) : AZERBAIJANI

azide \ˈā-ˌzīd, ˈa-\ *n* (ca. 1904) : a compound containing the group N_3 combined with an element or radical

az·i·do \ˈa-zə-(ˌ)dō\ *adj* [ISV *azide* + *-o-*] (ca. 1926) : relating to or containing the monovalent group N_3 — often used in combination

az·i·do·thy·mi·dine \ə-ˌzi-dō-ˈthī-mə-ˌdēn\ *n* (1974) : AZT

az·i·muth \ˈaz-məth, ˈa-zə-\ *n* [ME, fr. ML *azimut,* fr. Ar *al-sumūt* the azimuth, pl. of *al-samt* the way] (14c) **1** : an arc of the horizon measured between a fixed point (as true north) and the vertical circle passing through the center of an object usu. in astronomy and navigation clockwise from the north point through 360 degrees **2** : horizontal direction expressed as the angular distance between the direction of a fixed point (as the observer's heading) and the direction of the object — **az·i·muth·al** \ˌa-zə-'məthəl\ *adj* — **az·i·muth·al·ly** \-'məthə-lē\ *adv*

azimuthal equidistant projection *n* (1942) : a map projection of the surface of the earth so centered at any given point that a straight line radiating from the center to any other point represents the shortest distance and can be measured to scale

azine \'ā-ˌzēn, 'a-\ *n* (1887) : a compound of the general formula RCH=NN=CHR or R₂C=NN=CR₂ formed by the action of hydrazine on aldehydes or ketones

azo \'ā-(ˌ)zō, 'a-\ *adj* [*az-*] (ca. 1879) : relating to or containing the divalent group N=N united at both ends to carbon

azo dye *n* (1884) : any of numerous dyes containing azo groups

azo·ic \(ˌ)ā-'zō-ik\ *adj* [*ᵃa-* + Gk *zōē* life — more at QUICK] (1845) : having no living beings; *esp* : of or relating to the part of geologic time that antedates life — compare ARCHEAN 1

azole \'ā-ˌzōl, 'a-\ *n* (ca. 1899) : any of numerous compounds characterized by a 5-membered ring containing at least one nitrogen atom

azon·al \(ˌ)ā-'zō-n°l\ *adj* (1938) : of, relating to, or being a soil or a major group of soils lacking well-developed horizons often because of immaturity — compare INTRAZONAL, ZONAL

azo·o·sper·mia \(ˌ)ā-ˌzō-ə-'spər-mē-ə\ *n* [NL, fr. Gk *azoos* lifeless (fr. *a-* ²a- + *zōē* life) + *sperma* semen, seed — more at SPERM] (ca. 1881) : absence of spermatozoa from the seminal fluid

azo·te·mia \ˌā-zō-'tē-mē-ə\ *n* [ISV *azote* nitrogen + NL *-emia* — more at AZ-] (ca. 1900) : an excess of urea or other nitrogenous wastes in the

blood as a result of kidney insufficiency — compare UREMIA — **azo·te·mic** \-mik\ *adj*

az·oth \'a-ˌzȯth\ *n* [ML, alter. of *azoc*, fr. Ar *al-zāʾūq* the mercury] (15c) **1** : mercury regarded by alchemists as the first principle of metals **2** : the universal remedy of Paracelsus

azo·to·bac·ter \ā-ˌzō-tə-ˌbak-tər\ *n* [NL, genus name, fr. ISV *azote* + NL *bacterium*] (1910) : any of a genus (*Azotobacter*) of large rod-shaped or spherical bacteria occurring in soil and sewage and fixing atmospheric nitrogen

azo·tu·ria \ˌā-zō-'tür-ē-ə, -'tyür-\ *n* [ISV *azote* + NL *-uria*] (ca. 1838) : an abnormal condition of horses characterized by muscle damage esp. to the hindquarters and dark-colored urine containing nitrogenous substances from muscle tissue breakdown

AZT \ˌā-(ˌ)zē-'tē\ *n* (1985) : an antiviral drug $C_{10}H_{13}N_5O_4$ that inhibits replication of some retroviruses (as HIV) and is used to treat AIDS — called also *azidothymidine, zidovudine*

Az·tec \'az-ˌtek\ *n* [Sp *azteca*, fr. Nahuatl *aztēcah*, pl. of *aztēcatl*] (1814) **1 a** : a member of a Nahuatl-speaking people that founded the Mexican empire conquered by Cortes in 1519 **b** : a member of any people under Aztec influence **2** : NAHUATL — **Az·tec·an** \'az-ˌte-kən, ˌaz-'te-\ *adj*

azuki, azuki bean *var of* ADZUKI, ADZUKI BEAN

azu·le·jo \ˌä-sü-'lā-(ˌ)hō, -zü-, -thü-\ *n, pl* **-jos** [Pg or Sp] (ca. 1889) : a glazed usu. blue ceramic tile orig. of Portugal and Spain

azure \'a-zhər\ *n* [ME *asur*, fr. AF *azeure*, prob. fr. OSp, modif. of Ar *lāzaward*, fr. Pers *lāzhuward*] (14c) **1** *archaic* : LAPIS LAZULI **2 a** : the blue color of the clear sky **b** : the heraldic color blue **3** : the unclouded sky — **azure** *adj*

azur·ite \'a-zhə-ˌrīt\ *n* [F, fr. *azur* azure] (ca. 1868) **1** : a mineral that consists of blue basic carbonate of copper and is a minor copper ore **2** : a semiprecious stone derived from azurite

¹azy·gos \ā-'zī-gəs\ *n* [NL, fr. Gk, unyoked, fr. *a-* + *zygon* yoke — more at YOKE] (1646) : an azygos anatomical part

²azy·gos *also* **azy·gous** \(ˌ)ā-'zī-gəs\ *adj* (1681) : not being one of a pair : SINGLE ⟨an ∼ vein⟩

B

¹b \'bē\ *n, pl* **b's** *or* **bs** \'bēz\ *often cap, often attrib* (bef. 12c) **1 a** : the second letter of the English alphabet **b** : a graphic representation of this letter **c** : a speech counterpart of orthographic *b* **2** : the seventh tone of a C-major scale **3** : a graphic device for reproducing the letter *b* **4** : one designated *b* esp. as the second in order or class **5 a** : a grade rating a student's work as good but short of excellent **b** : one graded or rated with a B **6** : something shaped like the letter B **7** *cap* : the one of the four ABO blood groups characterized by the presence of antigens designated by the letter B and by the presence of antibodies against the antigens present in the A blood group

²b *abbr* **1** bachelor **2** bacillus **3** back **4** bag **5** bale **6** bass **7** basso **8** bat **9** Baumé **10** before **11** Bible **12** billion **13** bishop **14** black **15** blue **16** bolivar **17** book **18** born **19** bottom **20** brick **21** brightness **22** British **23** bulb **24** butut

B *symbol* boron

Ba *symbol* barium

BA *abbr* **1** bachelor of arts **2** batting average **3** Buenos Aires

baa \'ba, 'bä\ *vi* **baaed; baa·ing** [imit.] (ca. 1586) : to make the bleat of a sheep — **baa** *n*

BAA *abbr* bachelor of applied arts

BAAE *abbr* bachelor of aeronautical and astronautical engineering

baal \'bā(-ə)l, 'bäl\ *n, pl* **baals** *or* **baa·lim** \'bā-(ə-)ləm, 'bä-ə-ˌlim\ *often cap* [Heb *baʿal* lord] (14c) : any of numerous Canaanite and Phoenician local deities — **baal·ism** \'bā-(ə-)li-zəm\ *n, often cap* — **baal·ist** \-list\ *or* **baal·ite** \-ˌlīt\ *n*

baas \'bäs\ *n* [Afrik, fr. D] (1785) *SoAfr* : BOSS, MASTER — used esp. by nonwhites when speaking to or about Europeans in positions of authority

Baath·ism *or* **Ba'ath·ism** \'bä-thi-zəm\ *n* [*Baath* (*Party*) (part trans. of Ar *ḥizb al-baʿath*, lit., Renaissance Party) + *-ism*] (1963) : the principles and policies of the Baath political party of Iraq and Syria characterized esp. by promotion of pan-Arab socialism — **Baath·ist** *or* **Ba'ath·ist** \-thist\ *n or adj*

ba·ba \'bä-(ˌ)bä, -bə\ *n* [F, fr. Pol, lit., old woman] (1826) : a rich cake soaked in a rum and sugar syrup — called also *baba au rhum* \-ō-'rəm\

ba·ba gha·noush \ˌbä-bə-gə-'nüsh\ *or* **baba gha·nouj** \-'nüzh\ *n* [Ar dial. *bābaghanūj*] (1977) : an appetizer or spread made chiefly of eggplant, tahini, garlic, olive oil, and lemon

ba·bas·su \ˌbä-bə-'sü\ *n* [Pg *babaçú*, fr. Tupi *ʷiβáwasú*, fr. *iβá* fruit + *-wasú* large] (1917) : a tall pinnate-leaved palm (*Orbignya phalerata* syn. *O. barbosiana*) of Brazil with hard-shelled nuts yielding a valuable oil

Bab·bitt \'ba-bət\ *n* [George F. *Babbitt*, character in the novel *Babbitt* (1922) by Sinclair Lewis] (1923) : a person and esp. a business or professional man who conforms unthinkingly to prevailing middle-class standards — **Bab·bit·ry** \-bə-trē\ *n* — **Bab·bit·ty** \-bi-tē\ *adj*

bab·ble \'ba-bəl\ *vb* **bab·bled; bab·bling** \-b(ə-)liŋ\ [ME *babelen*, prob. of imit. origin] *vi* (13c) **1 a** : to talk enthusiastically or excessively **b** : to utter meaningless or unintelligible sounds **2** : to make

sounds as though babbling ∼ *vt* **1** : to utter in an incoherently or meaninglessly repetitious manner **2** : to reveal by talk that is too free — **babble** *n* — **bab·ble·ment** \-bəl-mənt\ *n* — **bab·bler** \-b(ə-)lər\ *n*

babe \'bāb\ *n* [ME, prob. of imit. origin] (14c) **1 a** : INFANT, BABY **b** *slang* : GIRL, WOMAN **c** *slang* : a person and esp. a young woman who is sexually attractive **2** : a naive inexperienced person — used esp. in the phrase *babe in the woods*

Ba·bel \'bā-bəl, 'ba-\ *n* [ME, fr. Heb *Bābhel*, fr. Akkadian *bāb-ilu* gate of god] (14c) **1** : a city in Shinar where the building of a tower is held in Genesis to have been halted by the confusion of tongues **2** *often not cap* **a** : a confusion of sounds or voices **b** : a scene of noise or confusion

ba·be·sia \bə-'bē-zh(ē-)ə\ *n* [NL, fr. Victor *Babeş* †1926 Rom. bacteriologist] (1911) : any of a genus (*Babesia*) of sporozoans parasitic in mammalian red blood cells (as in Texas fever) and transmitted by the bite of a tick — called also *piroplasm*

ba·be·si·o·sis \bə-ˌbē-zh(ē-)'ō-səs\ *n* [NL] (1911) : an infection with or disease caused by babesias

Ba·bin·ski reflex \bə-'bin(t)-skē-\ *n* [J.F.F. *Babinski* †1932 Fr. neurologist] (1900) : a reflex movement in which when the sole is tickled the big toe turns upward instead of downward and which is normal in infancy but indicates damage to the central nervous system (as in the pyramidal tracts) later in life — called also *Babinski sign, Ba·bin·ski's reflex* \-skēz-\

bab·i·ru·sa \ˌba-bə-'rü-sə, ˌbä-\ *n* [Malay, fr. *babi* pig + *rusa* deer] (1673) : a large wild swine (*Babyrousa babyrussa*) of Indonesia

ba·boon \ba-'bün, chiefly Brit bə-\ *n* [ME *babewin*, fr. MF *babouin*, fr. *baboue* grimace] (15c) : any of a genus (*Papio*) of large gregarious primates of Africa and southwestern Asia having a long square naked muzzle; *also* : any of several closely related primates

baboon

ba·bu *also* **ba·boo** \'bä-(ˌ)bü\ *n, often attrib* [Hindi *bābū*, lit., father] (1776) **1** : a Hindu gentleman — a form of address corresponding to *Mr.* **2 a** : an Indian clerk who writes English **b** *often disparaging* : an Indian having some education in English

ba·bul \bə-'bül\ *n* [Pers *babūl*] (1780) : an acacia tree (*Acacia nilotica* syn. *A. arabica*) widespread in India and northern Africa that yields gum arabic and tannins as well as fodder and timber

ba·bush·ka \bə-'büsh-kə, -'bùsh-\ *n* [Russ, grandmother, dim. of *baba* old woman] (1938) **1 a** : a usu. triangularly folded kerchief for the head **b** : a head covering (as a scarf) resembling a babushka **2** : an elderly Russian woman

¹ba·by \'bā-bē\ *n, pl* **babies** [ME, fr. *babe*] (14c) **1 a** (1) : an extremely young child; *esp* : INFANT (2) : an extremely young animal **b** : the youngest of a group **2 a** : one that is like a baby (as in behavior) **b** : something that is one's special responsibility, achievement, or interest **3** *slang* **a** : GIRL, WOMAN — often used in address **b** : BOY, MAN —

often used in address **4 :** PERSON, THING ⟨is one tough ~⟩ — **ba·by·hood** \-bē-ˌhu̇d\ *n* — **ba·by·ish** \-ish\ *adj*

[2]**baby** *adj* (1591) **1 :** of, relating to, or being a baby **2 :** much smaller than the usual ⟨~ carrots⟩ ⟨a ~ flattop⟩ ⟨take two ~ steps⟩

[3]**baby** *vt* **ba·bied; ba·by·ing** (1744) **1 :** to tend to indulge with often excessive or inappropriate care and solicitude ⟨~*ing* their only child⟩ **2 :** to use or treat with care ⟨~*ing* a sore knee⟩ ***syn*** see INDULGE

baby back ribs *n pl* (1954) **:** meaty pork ribs cut from the lower back rib section

baby blue *n* (1859) **1 :** a pale blue **2** *pl* **:** blue eyes

baby blue eyes *n pl but sing or pl in constr* (1887) **:** a delicate blue-flowered California herb (*Nemophila menziesii*) of the waterleaf family

baby boom *n* (1880) **:** a marked rise in birthrate (as in the U.S. immediately following the end of World War II) — **baby boomer** *n*

baby boomlet *n* (1968) **:** a small or secondary baby boom (as in the U.S. in the 1980s and 1990s)

baby bump *n* (2003) **:** the enlarged abdomen of a pregnant woman

baby bust *n* (1966) **:** a marked decline in birthrate — **baby buster** *n*

baby carriage *n* (1825) **:** a small four-wheeled carriage often with a folding top for pushing a baby around in — called also *baby buggy*

baby grand *n* (1879) **:** a small grand piano

Bab·y·lon \ˈba-bə-ˌlän, -lən\ *n* [*Babylon,* ancient city of Babylonia] (14c) **:** a city devoted to materialism and sensual pleasure

[1]**Bab·y·lo·nian** \ˌba-bə-ˈlō-nyən, -nē-ən\ *n* (1530) **1 :** a native or inhabitant of ancient Babylonia or Babylon **2 :** the form of the Akkadian language used in ancient Babylonia

[2]**Babylonian** *adj* (1553) **1 :** of, relating to, or characteristic of Babylonia or Babylon, the Babylonians, or Babylonian **2 :** marked by luxury, extravagance, or the pursuit of sensual pleasure ⟨the ~ halls of the big hotel —G. K. Chesterton⟩ ⟨the ~ delights of the city⟩

baby oil *n* (1950) **:** a usu. fragrant mineral oil that is used esp. to moisturize and cleanse the skin; *also* **:** any of various oils used similarly

baby powder *n* (1853) **:** a fine powder composed mainly of talc or cornstarch that is sprinkled or rubbed on the skin esp. to absorb moisture and relieve chafing

baby's breath *n* (1866) **:** GYPSOPHILA; *esp* **:** a perennial herb (*Gypsophila paniculata*) or an annual herb (*G. elegans*) commonly used in floral arrangements

ba·by·sit \ˈbā-bē-ˌsit\ *vb* **-sat** \-ˌsat\; **-sit·ting** [back-formation fr. *babysitter*] *vi* (1944) **:** to care for children usu. during a short absence of the parents; *broadly* **:** to give care ⟨~ for a neighbor's pets⟩ ~ *vt* **:** to babysit for; *broadly* **:** TEND ⟨~ house plants⟩ — **ba·by·sit·ter** *n*

baby talk *n* (1788) **1 a :** the consciously imperfect or altered speech used by adults in speaking to small children **b :** the syntactically imperfect speech or phonetically modified forms used by small children learning to talk **2 :** oversimplified speech or writing

baby tooth *n* (1834) **:** MILK TOOTH

BAC *abbr* blood alcohol concentration

bac·ca·lau·re·ate \ˌba-kə-ˈlȯr-ē-ət, -ˈlär-\ *n* [ML *baccalaureatus,* fr. *baccalaureus* bachelor, alter. of *baccalarius*] (ca. 1649) **1 :** the degree of bachelor conferred by universities and colleges **2 a :** a sermon to a graduating class **b :** the service at which this sermon is delivered

bac·ca·rat \ˌbä-kə-ˈrä, ˌba-\ *n* [F *baccara*] (1848) **:** a card game resembling chemin de fer in which three hands are dealt and players may bet either or both hands against the dealer's; *also* **:** a two-handed version in which players may bet on or against either hand

Bac·chae \ˈba-ˌkē, -ˌkī\ *n pl* [L, fr. Gk *Bakchai,* fr. *Bakchos* Bacchus] (1639) **1 :** the female attendants or priestesses of Bacchus **2 :** the women participating in the Bacchanalia

[1]**bac·cha·nal** \ˈba-kə-nᵊl, ˈbä-; ˌba-kə-ˈnal, ˌbä-kə-ˈnäl\ *n* [L, shrine of Bacchus, prob. back-formation fr. *Bacchanalia*] (1594) **1 a :** ORGY 2 **b :** ORGY 3 **2 a :** a devotee of Bacchus; *esp* **:** one who celebrates the Bacchanalia **b :** REVELER

[2]**bac·cha·nal** \ˈba-kə-nᵊl\ *adj* (1550) **:** of, relating to, or suggestive of the Bacchanalia **:** BACCHANALIAN

bac·cha·na·lia \ˌba-kə-ˈnāl-yə, ˌbä-\ *n, pl* **bacchanalia** [L, fr. *Bacchus*] (1591) **1** *pl, cap* **:** a Roman festival of Bacchus celebrated with dancing, song, and revelry **2 a :** ORGY 2 **b :** ORGY 3 — **bac·cha·na·lian** \-ˈnāl-yən\ *adj or n*

bac·chant \bə-ˈkant, -ˈkänt; ˈba-kənt, ˈbä-\ *n, pl* **bac·chants** *or* **bac·chantes** \bə-ˈkants, -ˈkänts, -ˈkan-tēz, -ˈkän-tēz\ [L *bacchant-, bacchans,* fr. prp. of *bacchari* to take part in the orgies of Bacchus] (1699) **:** BACCHANAL — **bacchant** *adj*

bac·chante \bə-ˈkant, -ˈkänt; -ˈkan-tē, -ˈkän-\ *n* [F, fr. L *bacchant-, bacchans*] (1579) **:** a priestess or female follower of Bacchus

bac·chic \ˈba-kik, ˈbä-\ *adj, often cap* (1669) **:** of, relating to, or suggestive of Bacchus or the Bacchanalia **:** BACCHANALIAN

Bac·chus \ˈba-kəs, ˈbä-\ *n* [L, fr. Gk *Bakchos*] (14c) **:** the Greek god of wine — called also *Dionysus*

[1]**bach** *also* **batch** \ˈbach\ *vi* (1865) **:** to live as a bachelor — often used with *it*

[2]**bach** *n* [ˈbach] (1925) *NewZeal* **:** a small house or weekend cottage

[1]**bach·e·lor** \ˈbach-lər, ˈba-chə-\ *n* [ME *bacheler,* fr. AF] (14c) **1 :** a young knight who follows the banner of another **2 :** a person who has received a degree from a college, university, or professional school usu. after four years of study ⟨~ of arts⟩; *also* **:** the degree itself ⟨received a ~ of laws⟩ **3 a :** an unmarried man **b :** a male animal without a mate during breeding time — **bach·e·lor·dom** \-dəm\ *n* — **bach·e·lor·hood** \-ˌhu̇d\ *n*

[2]**bachelor** *adj* (1840) **1 :** suitable for or occupied by a single person ⟨a ~ apartment⟩ **2 :** UNMARRIED ⟨~ women⟩ ⟨~ parents⟩

bach·e·lor·ette \ˌbach-lə-ˈret, ˌba-chə-\ *n* (1896) **:** a young unmarried woman

bachelor's button *n* (1847) **:** a European composite (*Centaurea cyanus*) having flower heads with usu. blue, pink, or white rays that is often cultivated in No. America — called also *cornflower*

ba·cil·la·ry \ˈba-sə-ˌler-ē, bə-ˈsi-lə-rē\ *also* **ba·cil·lar** \bə-ˈsi-lər, ˈba-sə-lər\ *adj* [ML & NL *bacillus*] (1814) **1 :** shaped like a rod; *also* **:** consisting of small rods **2 :** of, relating to, or caused by bacilli

ba·cil·lus \bə-ˈsi-ləs\ *n, pl* **-li** \-ˌlī *also* -lē\ [NL, fr. ML, small staff, rod, dim. of L *baculus* staff, alter. of *baculum*] (1868) **1 :** any of a genus (*Bacillus*) of rod-shaped gram-positive usu. aerobic bacteria producing endospores and including many saprophytes and some parasites (as *B. anthracis* of anthrax); *broadly* **:** a straight rod-shaped bacterium **2 :** BACTERIUM; *esp* **:** a disease-producing bacterium

bac·i·tra·cin \ˌba-sə-ˈtrā-sᵊn\ *n* [NL *Bacillus subtilis* (species of bacillus producing the toxin) + Margaret *Tracy b ab* 1936 Am. child in whose tissues it was found] (1945) **:** a polypeptide antibiotic isolated from a bacillus (*Bacillus subtilis* or *B. licheniformis*) and usu. used topically esp. against gram-positive bacteria

[1]**back** \ˈbak\ *n* [ME, fr. OE *bæc;* akin to OHG *bah* back, ON *bak*] (bef. 12c) **1 a** (1) **:** the rear part of the human body esp. from the neck to the end of the spine (2) **:** the body considered as the wearer of clothes (3) **:** capacity for labor, effort, or endurance (4) **:** the back considered as the seat of one's awareness of duty or failings ⟨get off my ~⟩ (5) **:** the back considered as an area of vulnerability ⟨the police officer's partner always watches his ~⟩ **b :** the part of a lower animal (as a quadruped) corresponding to the human back **c :** SPINAL COLUMN **d :** SPINE 1c **2 a :** the side or surface opposite the front or face **:** the rear part; *also* **:** the farther or reverse side **b :** something at or on the back for support ⟨~ of a chair⟩ **c :** a place away from the front ⟨sat in ~⟩ **3 :** a position in some games behind the front line of players; *also* **:** a player in this position — **backed** \ˈbakt\ *adj* — **back·less** \ˈbak-ləs\ *adj* — **back of one's hand** *or* **back of the hand :** a show of contempt — **back of one's mind :** the part of one's mind where thoughts and memories are stored to be drawn on — **behind one's back :** without one's knowledge — **in back of :** BEHIND

[2]**back** *adv* (13c) **1 a :** to, toward, or at the rear **b :** in or into the past **:** backward in time; *also* **:** AGO **c :** to or at an angle off the vertical **d** (1) **:** under restraint (2) **:** in a delayed or retarded condition **2 a :** to, toward, or in a place from which a person or thing came **b :** to or toward a former state **c :** in return or reply

[3]**back** *adj* (15c) **1 a :** being at or in the back ⟨~ door⟩ **b :** distant from a central or main area ⟨~ roads⟩ **c :** articulated at or toward the back of the oral passage ⟨~ vowels⟩ **2 :** having returned or been returned **3 :** being in arrears **:** OVERDUE **4 :** moving or operating backward **:** REVERSE **5 :** not current ⟨~ issues of a magazine⟩ **6 :** constituting the final 9 holes of an 18-hole golf course

[4]**back** *vt* (1548) **1 a :** to support by material or moral assistance **b :** SUBSTANTIATE **c :** to assume financial responsibility for **d :** to provide musical accompaniment for — often used with *up* **2 a :** to cause to go back or in reverse **b :** to articulate (a sound) with the tongue farther back **3 a :** to furnish with a back **b :** to be at the back of ~ *vi* **1 :** to move backward — often used with *up* **2** *of the wind* **:** to shift counterclockwise — compare VEER **3 :** to have the back in the direction of something ***syn*** see SUPPORT, RECEDE — **back·er** \ˈba-kər\ *n* — **back and fill 1 :** to manage the sails of a ship so as to keep it clear of obstructions as it floats down with the current of a river or channel **2 :** to take opposite positions alternately **:** SHILLY-SHALLY — **back into :** to get into inadvertently ⟨*backed into* the antiques business⟩

back·ache \ˈbak-ˌāk\ *n* (1601) **:** a pain in the lower back

back–and–forth *n* (1941) **:** DISCUSSION 1, GIVE-AND-TAKE

back and forth *adv* (1613) **:** backward and forward; *also* **:** between two places or persons

back away *vi* (1833) **:** to move away (as from a stand on an issue or from a commitment)

back bacon *n* (1902) *chiefly Brit* **:** CANADIAN BACON

back·beat \ˈbak-ˌbēt\ *n* (1928) **:** a steady pronounced rhythm stressing the second and fourth beats of a four-beat measure

back·bench \-ˈbench\ *n, often attrib* (1799) **:** a bench in a British legislature (as the House of Commons) occupied by rank-and-file members — compare FRONT BENCH — **back·bench·er** \-ˈben-chər\ *n*

back·bite \-ˌbīt\ *vb* **-bit; -bit·ten; -bit·ing** *vt* (12c) **:** to say mean or spiteful things about (as one not present) ~ *vi* **:** to backbite a person — **back·bit·er** *n*

back·block \-ˌbläk\ *n* (1868) *Austral & NewZeal* **:** BOONDOCKS 2 — usu. used in pl.

back·board \-ˌbȯrd\ *n* (1761) **1 :** a board placed at or serving as the back of something; *esp* **:** a rounded or rectangular board behind the basket on a basketball court which serves to keep missed shots from going out-of-bounds and from which the ball can be made to rebound into the basket **2 :** a stiff board on which an injured person and esp. one with neck or spinal injuries is placed and immobilized in order to prevent further injury during transport

back·bone \-ˈbōn, -ˌbōn\ *n* (14c) **1 :** SPINAL COLUMN, SPINE **2 :** something that resembles a backbone: as **a :** a chief mountain ridge, range, or system **b :** the foundation or most substantial or sturdiest part of something **c :** the longest chain of atoms or groups of atoms in a usu. long molecule (as a polymer or protein) **d :** the primary high-speed hardware and transmission lines of a telecommunications network (as the Internet) **3 :** firm and resolute character **4 :** SPINE 1c — **back·boned** \-ˌbōnd\ *adj*

back·break·ing \-ˌbrā-kiŋ\ *adj* (1766) **:** extremely arduous, exhausting, or demoralizing ⟨~ labor⟩ ⟨~ rents⟩ — **back·break·er** \-kər\ *n*

back burner *n* (1943) **:** the condition of being out of active consideration or development — usu. used in the phrase *on the back burner* — **back–burner** *vt*

back channel *n* (1975) **:** a secret, unofficial, or irregular means of communication — **back–channel** *adj*

back·chat \ˈbak-ˌchat\ *n* (1894) **1 :** BACK TALK **2 :** gossipy or bantering conversation

back–check \-ˌchek\ *vi* (1913) **:** to skate back toward one's own goal while closely defending against the offensive rushes of an opposing player in ice hockey — **back–check·er** \-ˌche-kər\ *n*

back·cloth \-ˌklȯth\ *n* (1874) *chiefly Brit* **:** BACKDROP

back·coun·try \-ˌkən-trē\ *n, often attrib* (1746) **:** a remote undeveloped rural area

back·court \-ˈkȯrt\ *n* (1884) **1 :** the area near or nearest the back boundary lines or back wall of the playing area in a net or court game **2 a :** a basketball team's defensive half of the court **b :** the positions

of the guards on a basketball team; *also* : the guards themselves ⟨a team with a strong ~⟩
back·court·man \-mən\ *n* (1954) : a guard on a basketball team
1**back·cross** \ˈbak-ˌkrȯs\ *vt* (1904) : to cross (a first-generation hybrid) with one of the parental types
2**backcross** *n* (1918) : a mating that involves backcrossing; *also* : an individual produced by backcrossing
back·date \ˈbak-ˌdāt\ *vt* (1944) : to put a date earlier than the actual one on ⟨~ a memo⟩; *also* : to make retroactive ⟨~ pension rights⟩
back dive *n* (ca. 1934) : a dive from a position facing the diving board
back·door \ˈbak-ˈdȯr\ *adj* (1805) **1** : INDIRECT, DEVIOUS **2** : involving or being a play in basketball in which a player moves behind the defense and toward the basket to receive a quick pass ⟨a ~ layup⟩
back down *vi* (1849) : to withdraw from a commitment or position
back·drop \ˈbak-ˌdräp\ *n* (1913) **1** : a painted cloth hung across the rear of a stage **2** : BACKGROUND — **backdrop** *vt*
back·field \-ˌfēld\ *n* (1903) : the football players whose positions are behind the line of scrimmage; *also* : the positions themselves
back·fill \-ˌfil\ *vt* (1908) : to refill (as an excavation) usu. with excavated material ~ *vi* : to backfill an excavation — **backfill** *n*
1**back·fire** \-ˌfī(-ə)r\ *n* (1839) **1** : a fire started to check an advancing fire by clearing an area **2** : a loud noise caused by the improperly timed explosion of fuel mixture in the cylinder of an internal combustion engine
2**backfire** *vi* (1886) **1** : to make or undergo a backfire **2** : to have the reverse of the desired or expected effect ⟨their plans *backfired*⟩
back·fit \ˈbak-ˌfit\ *vt* (1967) : RETROFIT — **backfit** *n*
back·flip \-ˌflip\ *n* (1935) : a backward somersault esp. in the air
back·flow \-ˌflō\ *n* (1878) : a flowing back or returning esp. toward a source
back–formation *n* (1889) **1** : a word formed by subtraction of a real or supposed affix from an already existing longer word (as *burgle* from *burglar*) **2** : the formation of back-formations
back·gam·mon \ˈbak-ˌga-mən, ˌbak-ˈ\ *n* [perh. fr. 3*back* + ME *gamen, game* game] (ca. 1645) : a board game played with dice and counters in which players try to be the first to gather their pieces into one corner and then systematically remove them from the board
1**back·ground** \ˈbak-ˌ(g)rau̇nd\ *n, often attrib* (1672) **1 a** : the scenery or ground behind something **b** : the part of a painting representing what lies behind objects in the foreground **2** : an inconspicuous position **3 a** : the conditions that form the setting within which something is experienced **b (1)** : the circumstances or events antecedent to a phenomenon or development **(2)** : information essential to understanding of a problem or situation **c** : the total of a person's experience, knowledge, and education **4 a** : intrusive sound or radiation that interferes with received or recorded electronic signals **b** : a more or less steady level of noise above which the effect (as radioactivity) being measured by an apparatus (as a Geiger counter) is detected; *esp* : a somewhat steady level of radiation in the natural environment (as from cosmic rays) **5** : a level of computer processing at which the processor uses time not required for a primary task to work on an additional task — compare FOREGROUND — **on background** : with the understanding that information offered for publication will not be attributed to a specific source ⟨an official speaking *on background*⟩
syn BACKGROUND, SETTING, ENVIRONMENT, MILIEU, MISE-EN-SCÈNE mean the place, time, and circumstances in which something occurs. BACKGROUND often refers to the circumstances or events that precede a phenomenon or development ⟨the shocking decision was part of the *background* of the riots⟩. SETTING suggests looking at real-life situations in literary or dramatic terms ⟨a militant reformer who was born into an unlikely social *setting*⟩. ENVIRONMENT applies to all the external factors that have a formative influence on one's physical, mental, or moral development ⟨the kind of *environment* that produces juvenile delinquents⟩. MILIEU applies esp. to the physical and social surroundings of a person or group of persons ⟨an intellectual *milieu* conducive to artistic experimentation⟩. MISE-EN-SCÈNE strongly suggests the use of properties to achieve a particular atmosphere or theatrical effect ⟨a gothic thriller with a carefully crafted *mise-en-scène*⟩.
2**background** *vt* (1768) : to provide with background
back·ground·er \ˈbak-ˌ(g)rau̇n-dər\ *n* (1960) : an off-the-record briefing for reporters
background music *n* (1928) : music to accompany the dialogue or action of a motion picture or radio or television drama
background radiation *n* (1968) : the microwave radiation pervading the universe that exhibits a corresponding blackbody temperature of 2.7 K and that is the principal evidence supporting the big bang theory — called also *cosmic background radiation*
1**back·hand** \ˈbak-ˌhand\ *n* (1657) **1 a** : a stroke (as in tennis) made with the back of the hand turned in the direction of movement; *also* : the side on which such strokes are made **b** : a catch (as in baseball) made to the side of the body opposite the hand being used **2** : handwriting whose strokes slant downward from left to right

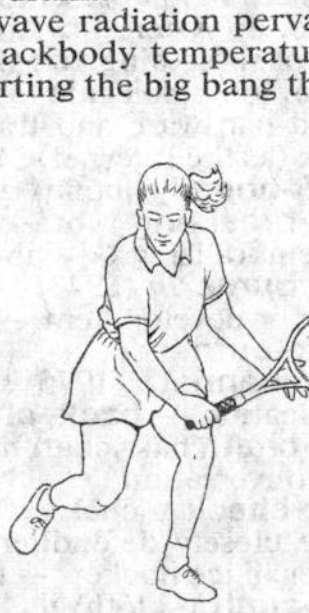
backhand 1a

2**backhand** *adj* (1695) : made with a backhand ⟨a ~ tennis stroke⟩
3**backhand** *or* **back·hand·ed** \-ˈhan-dəd\ *adv* (1889) : with a backhand
4**backhand** *vt* (ca. 1935) : to do, hit, or catch backhand
back·hand·ed \ˈbak-ˈhan-dəd\ *adj* (1800) **1** : INDIRECT, DEVIOUS; *esp* : SARCASTIC ⟨a ~ compliment⟩ **2** : using or made with a backhand — **back·hand·ed·ly** *adv*
back·hand·er \-dər\ *n* (1960) **1** *Brit* : BRIBE **2** : a backhand shot
back·hoe \-ˌhō\ *n* (1928) : an excavating machine having a bucket that is attached to a rigid bar hinged to a boom and that is drawn toward the machine in operation
back·house \-ˌhau̇s\ *n* (1836) : PRIVY 1a
back·ing \ˈba-kiŋ\ *n* (1793) **1** : something forming a back **2 a** : SUPPORT, AID **b** : endorsement esp. of a warrant by a magistrate
back judge *n* (ca. 1966) : a football official whose duties include keeping the game's official time and identifying eligible pass receivers
back·land \ˈbak-ˌland\ *n* (1681) : BACKCOUNTRY, HINTERLAND — usu. used in pl.
back·lash \ˈbak-ˌlash\ *n* (1815) **1 a** : a sudden violent backward movement or reaction **b** : the play between adjacent movable parts (as in a series of gears); *also* : the jar caused by this when the parts are put into action **2** : a snarl in that part of a fishing line wound on the reel **3** : a strong adverse reaction (as to a recent political or social development) — **back·lash·er** *n*
back·light \-ˌlīt\ *n* (ca. 1846) : illumination from behind; *also* : the source of such illumination — **backlight** *vt*
back·list \ˈbak-ˌlist\ *n* (1964) : a list of books kept in print as distinguished from books newly published
1**back·log** \-ˌlȯg, -ˌläg\ *n* (1684) **1** : a large log at the back of a hearth fire **2** : an accumulation of tasks unperformed or materials not processed ⟨a ~ of court cases⟩
2**backlog** *vb* (1963) : ACCUMULATE
back matter *n* (1947) : matter following the main text of a book
back mutation *n* (1939) : mutation of a previously mutated gene to its former condition
back of *prep* (1694) : BEHIND ⟨out *back of* the barn⟩
back of beyond (1816) : a remote place
back off *vi* (1850) : BACK DOWN
back–office \ˈbak-ˈä-fəs, -ˈȯ-fəs\ *adj* (1953) : of or relating to the inner workings of a business or institution : INTERNAL ⟨~ operations⟩
back–order *vt* (1950) : to assign to the status of back order
back order *n* (ca. 1929) : a business order yet to be fulfilled because stock is unavailable
back out *vi* (1807) : to withdraw esp. from a commitment or contest
1**back·pack** \ˈbak-ˌpak\ *n* (1914) **1 a** : a load carried on the back **b** : a camping pack (as of canvas or nylon) supported by a usu. aluminum frame and carried on the back **c** : KNAPSACK **2** : a piece of equipment designed for use while being carried on the back
2**backpack** *vt* (1927) : to carry (food or equipment) on the back esp. in hiking ~ *vi* : to hike with a backpack — **back·pack·er** *n*
back·ped·al \ˈbak-ˌpe-dᵊl\ *vi* (1901) : to retreat or move backward
back·rest \-ˌrest\ *n* (1859) : a rest for the back
back·room \ˈbak-ˈrüm, -ˈru̇m\ *adj* (1940) : made or operating in an inconspicuous way : BEHIND-THE-SCENES ⟨~ deals⟩ ⟨a ~ politician⟩
back room *n* (1592) **1** : a room situated in the rear **2** : the meeting place of a directing group that exercises its authority in an inconspicuous and indirect way
back·saw \ˈbak-ˌsȯ\ *n* (ca. 1876) : a saw with a metal rib along its back
back·scat·ter \-ˌska-tər\ *also* **back·scat·ter·ing** \-tə-riŋ\ *n* (1940) : the scattering of radiation or particles in a direction opposite to that of the incident radiation due to reflection from particles of the medium traversed; *also* : the radiation or particles so reversed in direction — **backscatter** *vb*
back–scratch·ing \ˈbak-ˌskra-chiŋ\ *n* (1904) : the reciprocal exchange of favors, services, assistance, or praise
back·seat \-ˈsēt\ *n* (1780) **1** : a seat in the back (as of an automobile) **2** : an inferior position ⟨won't take a ~ to anyone⟩
back·set \ˈbak-ˌset\ *n* (1721) : SETBACK
back·side \-ˌsīd\ *n* (ca. 1500) : BUTTOCKS — often used in pl.
back·slap \-ˌslap\ *vt* (1777) : to display excessive or effusive goodwill for ~ *vi* : to display excessive cordiality or goodwill — **backslap** *n* — **back·slap·per** *n*
back·slash \-ˌslash\ *n* (1982) : a mark \ used esp. in computer programming
back·slide \-ˌslīd\ *vi* **-slid** \-ˌslid\; **-slid** *or* **-slid·den** \-ˌsli-dᵊn\; **-slid·ing** \-ˌslī-diŋ\ (1552) **1** : to lapse morally or in the practice of religion **2** : to revert to a worse condition : RETROGRESS — **backslide** *n* — **back·slid·er** \-ˌslī-dər\ *n*
1**back·space** \-ˌspās\ *vi* (1911) : to move back a space in a text with the press of a key
2**backspace** *n* (1983) : an instance of backspacing; *also* : the key pressed in backspacing
back·spin \-ˌspin\ *n* (ca. 1909) : a backward rotary motion of a ball
back·splash \ˈbak-ˌsplash\ *n* (1947) : a vertical surface (as of tiles) designed to protect the wall behind a stove or countertop
back·stab·bing \-ˌsta-biŋ\ *n* (1946) : betrayal (as by a verbal attack against one not present) esp. by a false friend — **back·stab** \-ˌstab\ *vb* — **back·stab·ber** \-ˌsta-bər\ *n*
1**back·stage** \ˈbak-ˌstāj\ *adj* (1916) **1** : of, relating to, or occurring in the area behind the stage and esp. in the dressing rooms **2** : of or relating to the private lives of theater people **3** : of or relating to the inner working or operation (as of an organization)
2**back·stage** \ˈbak-ˈstāj\ *adv* (1922) **1** : in or to a backstage area **2** : in private : SECRETLY
back·stairs \-ˌsterz\ *adj* (1663) **1** : SECRET, FURTIVE ⟨~ political deals⟩ **2** : SORDID, SCANDALOUS ⟨~ gossip⟩
back·stay \-ˌstā\ *n* (1626) **1** : a stay extending aft from a masthead **2** : a strengthening or supporting device at the back (as of a carriage or a shoe)
back·stitch \-ˌstich\ *n* (1611) : a stitch sewn one stitch length backward on the front side and two stitch lengths forward on the reverse side to form a solid line of stitching on both sides — **backstitch** *vb*
1**back·stop** \-ˌstäp\ *n* (1851) **1** : something at the back serving as a stop: as **a** : a screen or fence for keeping a ball from leaving the field of play **b** : a stop (as a pawl) that prevents a backward movement (as of a wheel) **2** : a player (as the catcher) positioned behind the batter
2**backstop** *vt* (1941) **1** : SUPPORT, BOLSTER **2** : to serve as a backstop to **3** : to play the position of goalkeeper for ⟨~ a hockey team⟩
back·story \-ˌstȯr-ē\ *n* (1984) : a story that tells what led up to the main story or plot (as of a film)
back·street \ˈbak-ˈstrēt\ *n, often attrib* (15c) : a street away from the main thoroughfares
back·stretch \ˈbak-ˌstrech\ *n* (1839) : the side opposite the homestretch on a racecourse
back·stroke \-ˌstrōk\ *n* (1879) : a swimming stroke executed on the back and usu. consisting of alternating circular arm pulls and a flutter kick — **back·strok·er** \-ˌstrō-kər\ *n*
back·swept \-ˌswept\ *adj* (ca. 1918) : swept or slanting backward
back·swim·mer \-ˌswi-mər\ *n* (1862) : an aquatic bug (family Notonectidae) that swims on its back

back·swing \ˈbak-ˌswiŋ\ *n* (1892) **:** the movement of a club, racket, bat, or arm backward to a position from which the forward or downward swing is made
back·sword \-ˌsȯrd\ *n* (1597) **:** a single-edged sword
back talk *n* (1858) **:** impudent, insolent, or argumentative replies
back–to–back *adj or adv* (15c) **1 :** facing in opposite directions and often touching **2 :** coming one after the other **:** CONSECUTIVE
back·track \ˈbak-ˌtrak\ *vi* (1904) **1 a :** to retrace one's course **b :** to go back to an earlier point in a sequence **2 :** to reverse a position
back·up \-ˌəp\ *n, often attrib* (1951) **1 a :** one that serves as a substitute or support ⟨a ~ plan⟩ **b :** musical accompaniment **c :** additional personnel who provide assistance **2 :** an accumulation caused by a stoppage in the flow ⟨traffic ~⟩ **3 :** a copy of computer data (as a file or the contents of a hard drive); *also* **:** the act or an instance of making a backup
back up *vi* (1837) **:** to accumulate in a congested state ⟨traffic *backed up* for miles⟩ ~ *vt* **1 :** to move into a position behind (a teammate) in order to assist on a play **2 :** HOLD BACK 1 **3 :** to make a copy of (a computer file or data) to protect against accidental loss; *also* **:** to make copies of all the files on (a hard drive)
[1]**back·ward** \ˈbak-wərd\ *or* **back·wards** \-wərdz\ *adv* (14c) **1 a :** toward the back **b :** with the back foremost **2 a :** in a reverse or contrary direction or way **b :** toward the past **c :** toward a worse state — **bend over backward** *or* **lean over backward :** to make extreme efforts (as at concession)
[2]**backward** *adj* (14c) **1 a :** directed or turned backward **b :** done or executed backward **2 :** DIFFIDENT, SHY **3 :** retarded in development — **back·ward·ly** *adv* — **back·ward·ness** *n*
[3]**backward** *n* (1610) **:** the part behind or past
back·wash \ˈbak-ˌwȯsh, -ˌwäsh\ *n* (1869) **1 :** a backward flow or movement (as of water or air) produced esp. by a propelling force; *also* **:** the fluid that is moving backward **2 :** CONSEQUENCE, AFTERMATH
back·wa·ter \-ˌwȯ-tər, -ˌwä-\ *n* (1629) **1 a :** water backed up in its course by an obstruction, an opposing current, or the tide **b :** a body of water (as an inlet or tributary) that is out of the main current of a larger body **2 a :** an isolated or backward place or condition **b :** an unpopular or unimportant field (as of study or business)
[1]**back·woods** \-ˈwu̇dz\ *n pl but sing or pl in constr* (1709) **1 :** wooded or partly cleared areas far from cities **2 :** a remote or culturally backward area — **back·woodsy** \-ˈwu̇d-zē\ *adj*
[2]**backwoods** *adj* (1784) **:** of, relating to, or suggesting backwoods; *esp* **:** culturally backward or unsophisticated ⟨a ~ sentimentality⟩
back·woods·man \ˌbak-ˈwu̇dz-mən, ˈbak-ˌ\ *n* (1774) **:** a person who lives in or is a native of the backwoods
back·wrap \ˈbak-ˌrap\ *n* (1951) **:** a wraparound garment (as a skirt) that fastens in the back
[1]**back·yard** \-ˈyärd\ *n* (1659) **1 :** an area at the rear of a house **2 :** a nearby area **:** NEIGHBORHOOD ⟨crimes committed in our own ~⟩
[2]**backyard** *adj* (1740) **:** located or occurring in a backyard ⟨a ~ barbecue⟩; *also* **:** lacking professional training **:** AMATEUR ⟨a ~ breeder⟩
bac·lo·fen \ˈbak-lō-ˌfen\ *n* [origin unknown] (1978) **:** a gamma-aminobutyric acid analog $C_{10}H_{12}ClNO_2$ used as a relaxant of skeletal muscle esp. in treating spasticity (as in multiple sclerosis)
ba·con \ˈbā-kən *sometimes* -kᵊŋ\ *n* [ME, fr. AF, of Gmc origin; akin to OHG *bahho* side of bacon, *bah* back — more at BACK] (14c) **1 :** a side of a pig cured and smoked **2 :** MONEY; *specif* **:** money gained through employment or legislation — usu. used in the phrase *bring home the bacon*
Ba·co·ni·an \bā-ˈkō-nē-ən\ *adj* (1812) **1 :** of, relating to, or characteristic of Francis Bacon or his doctrines **2 :** of or relating to those who believe that Francis Bacon wrote the works usu. attributed to Shakespeare — **Baconian** *n*
bact *abbr* **1** bacterial **2** bacteriology **3** bacterium
bac·ter·emia \ˌbak-tə-ˈrē-mē-ə\ *n* [NL, alter. of *bacteriemia,* fr. *bacteri-* + *-emia*] (ca. 1890) **:** the usu. transient presence of bacteria in the blood — **bac·ter·emic** \-mik\ *adj*
bacteri- *or* **bacterio-** *comb form* [NL *bacterium*] **:** bacteria ⟨*bacteriolysis*⟩
bac·te·ria \bak-ˈtir-ē-ə\ *n, pl* **bacteria** *also* **-ri·as** [pl. of *bacterium*] (1881) **:** BACTERIUM — not usu. used technically
usage *Bacteria* is regularly a plural in scientific and pedagogical use; in speech and in journalism it is also used as a singular, and it is sometimes pluralized as *bacterias* ⟨caused by a ~ borne by certain tiny ticks —*Wall Street Jour.*⟩ ⟨more resistant to chlorine and elevated water temperatures than other ~*s* —Allan Bruckheim, M.D., *Chicago Tribune*⟩. These journalistic uses are found in British as well as American sources.
bac·te·ri·al \bak-ˈtir-ē-əl\ *adj* (1871) **:** of, relating to, or caused by bacteria ⟨~ infection⟩ — **bac·te·ri·al·ly** \-ə-lē\ *adv*
bacterial vaginosis *n* (1985) **:** vaginitis that is marked by a grayish vaginal discharge usu. of foul odor and that is associated with the presence of excessive amounts of some bacteria (esp. *Gardnerella vaginalis*) — called also *nonspecific vaginitis*
bac·te·ri·cid·al \bak-ˌtir-ə-ˈsī-dᵊl\ *also* **bac·te·ri·o·cid·al** \-ˌtir-ē-ə-ˈsī-\ *adj* (1877) **:** destroying bacteria — **bac·te·ri·cide** \-ˈtir-ə-ˌsīd\ *also* **bac·te·ri·o·cide** \-ˈtir-ē-ə-ˌsīd\ *n*
bac·ter·in \ˈbak-tə-rən\ *n* (ca. 1912) **:** a suspension of killed or attenuated bacteria for use as a vaccine
bac·te·ri·o·chlo·ro·phyll \bak-ˌtir-ē-ō-ˈklȯr-ə-ˌfil, -fəl\ *n* (1938) **:** a pyrrole derivative in photosynthetic bacteria related to the chlorophyll of higher plants
bac·te·ri·o·cin \bak-ˈtir-ē-ə-sən\ *n* [ISV *bacteri-* + *-cin* (as in *colicin*)] (1954) **:** an antibiotic (as colicin) produced by bacteria
bac·te·ri·ol·o·gy \(ˌ)bak-ˌtir-ē-ˈä-lə-jē\ *n* [ISV] (1884) **1 :** a science that deals with bacteria and their relations to medicine, industry, and agriculture **2 :** bacterial life and phenomena — **bac·te·ri·o·log·ic** \bak-ˌtir-ē-ə-ˈlä-jik\ *or* **bac·te·ri·o·log·i·cal** \-ˈlä-ji-kəl\ *adj* — **bac·te·ri·o·log·i·cal·ly** \-ji-k(ə-)lē\ *adv* — **bac·te·ri·ol·o·gist** \(ˌ)bak-ˌtir-ē-ˈä-lə-jist\ *n*
bac·te·ri·ol·y·sis \(ˌ)bak-ˌtir-ē-ˈä-lə-səs\ *n* [NL] (1900) **:** destruction or dissolution of bacterial cells — **bac·te·ri·o·lyt·ic** \bak-ˌtir-ē-ə-ˈli-tik\ *adj*
bac·te·ri·o·phage \bak-ˈtir-ē-ə-ˌfāj *also* -ˌfäzh\ *n* [ISV] (1920) **:** a virus that infects bacteria — **bac·te·ri·oph·a·gy** \(ˌ)bak-ˌtir-ē-ˈä-fə-jē\ *n*
bac·te·ri·o·rho·dop·sin \bak-ˌtir-ē-ə-rō-ˈdäp-sin\ *n* (1971) **:** a purple-pigmented protein that is found in the outer membrane of a bacterium (*Halobacterium salinarium* syn. *H. halobium*) and that converts light energy into chemical energy in the synthesis of ATP
bac·te·ri·o·sta·sis \bak-ˌtir-ē-ō-ˈstā-səs\ *n* [NL] (1920) **:** inhibition of the growth of bacteria without destruction
bac·te·ri·o·stat \-ˈtir-ē-ō-ˌstat\ *n* (1920) **:** an agent that causes bacteriostasis — **bac·te·ri·o·stat·ic** \-ˌtir-ē-ō-ˈsta-tik\ *adj*
bac·te·ri·um \bak-ˈtir-ē-əm\ *n, pl* **-ria** \-ē-ə\ [NL, fr. Gk *baktērion* staff] (ca. 1849) **:** any of a domain (Bacteria) of prokaryotic round, spiral, or rod-shaped single-celled microorganisms that may lack cell walls or are gram-positive or gram-negative if they have cell walls, that are often aggregated into colonies or motile by means of flagella, that typically live in soil, water, organic matter, or the bodies of plants and animals, that are usu. autotrophic, saprophytic, or parasitic in nutrition, and that are noted for their biochemical effects and pathogenicity; *broadly* **:** PROKARYOTE — compare ARCHAEA, EUKARYOTE
bac·te·ri·uria \bak-ˌtir-ē-ˈyu̇r-ē-ə\ *n* [NL] (1900) **:** the presence of bacteria in the urine
bac·te·rize \ˈbak-tə-ˌrīz\ *vt* **-rized; -riz·ing** (1914) **:** to subject to bacterial action — **bac·te·ri·za·tion** \ˌbak-tə-rə-ˈzā-shən\ *n*
bac·te·roid \ˈbak-tə-ˌrȯid\ *n* (1878) **:** an irregularly shaped form of a nitrogen-fixing bacterium (as a rhizobium) found esp. in root nodules of legumes
Bac·tri·an camel \ˈbak-trē-ən-\ *n* (1609) **:** CAMEL 1b
[1]**bad** \ˈbad\ *adj* **worse** \ˈwərs\; **worst** \ˈwərst\ [ME] (14c) **1 a :** failing to reach an acceptable standard **:** POOR ⟨a ~ repair job⟩ **b :** UNFAVORABLE ⟨make a ~ impression⟩ **c :** not fresh **:** SPOILED ⟨~ fish⟩ **d :** not sound **:** DILAPIDATED ⟨the house was in ~ condition⟩ **2 a :** morally objectionable **:** EVIL ⟨~ men⟩ **b :** MISCHIEVOUS, DISOBEDIENT ⟨a ~ dog⟩ **3 :** inadequate or unsuited to a purpose ⟨a ~ plan⟩ ⟨~ lighting⟩ **4 :** DISAGREEABLE, UNPLEASANT ⟨~ news⟩ **5 a :** INJURIOUS, HARMFUL ⟨a ~ influence⟩ **b :** SERIOUS, SEVERE ⟨in ~ trouble⟩ ⟨a ~ cough⟩ **6 :** INCORRECT, FAULTY ⟨~ grammar⟩ **7 a :** suffering pain or distress ⟨felt generally ~⟩ **b :** UNHEALTHY, DISEASED ⟨~ teeth⟩ **8 :** SORROWFUL, SORRY ⟨feels ~ about forgetting to call⟩ **9 a :** INVALID, VOID ⟨a ~ check⟩ **b :** not able to be collected ⟨a ~ debt⟩ **10 bad·der; bad·dest** *slang* **a :** GOOD, GREAT **b :** TOUGH, MEAN — **bad·ness** *n*
[2]**bad** *n* (15c) **1 :** something that is bad **2 :** an evil or unhappy state **3 :** FAULT 4 ⟨the mistake was my ~⟩
[3]**bad** *adv* (1681) **:** BADLY ⟨not doing so ~⟩ ⟨doesn't want it ~ enough⟩
[1]**bad·ass** \-ˌas\ *adj* (1955) **1** *often vulgar* **:** ready to cause or get into trouble **:** MEAN ⟨pretending to be a ~ gunslinger —L. L. King⟩ **2** *often vulgar* **:** of formidable strength or skill ⟨such a ~ guitar player —N'Gai Croal⟩
[2]**badass** *n* (1956) *often vulgar* **:** a person who is badass
bad blood *n* (1825) **:** ill feeling **:** BITTERNESS
bad boy *n* (1945) **:** a person who flouts convention ⟨a literary *bad boy*⟩
bad cholesterol *n* (1980) **:** LDL
bad·die *or* **bad·dy** \ˈba-dē\ *n, pl* **baddies** (1937) **:** one that is bad; *esp* **:** an opponent of the hero (as in fiction or motion pictures)
bade *past and past part of* BID
badge \ˈbaj\ *n* [ME *bage, bagge*] (14c) **1 :** a device or token esp. of membership in a society or group **2 :** a characteristic mark **3 :** an emblem awarded for a particular accomplishment — **badge** *vt*
[1]**bad·ger** \ˈba-jər\ *n* [prob. fr. *badge;* fr. the white mark on its forehead] (1523) **1 a :** any of various burrowing mammals (esp. *Taxidea taxus* and *Meles meles*) of the weasel family that are widely distributed in the northern hemisphere **b :** the pelt or fur of a badger **2** *cap* **:** a native or resident of Wisconsin — used as a nickname
[2]**badger** *vt* [fr. the sport of baiting badgers] (1794) **:** to harass or annoy persistently ***syn*** see BAIT
ba·di·nage \ˌba-də-ˈnäzh\ *n* [F] (ca. 1658) **:** playful repartee **:** BANTER
bad·land \ˈbad-ˌland\ *n* (1851) **:** a region marked by intricate erosional sculpturing, scanty vegetation, and fantastically formed hills — usu. used in pl.
bad·ly \ˈbad-lē\ *adv* (14c) **1 :** in a bad manner ⟨played ~⟩ **2 :** to a great or intense degree ⟨want something ~⟩
bad·min·ton \ˈbad-ˌmi-tᵊn, -ˌmin-tᵊn\ *n* [*Badminton,* residence of the Duke of Beaufort, England] (1874) **:** a court game played with light long-handled rackets and a shuttlecock volleyed over a net
bad–mouth \ˈbad-ˌmau̇th, -ˌmau̇t͟h\ *vt* (1941) **:** to criticize severely
bad news *n pl but sing in constr* (1917) **:** one that is troublesome, unwelcome, or dangerous ⟨stay away from him, he's *bad news*⟩
BAE *abbr* **1** bachelor of aeronautical engineering **2** bachelor of agricultural engineering **3** bachelor of architectural engineering **4** bachelor of art education **5** bachelor of arts in education
BAEd *abbr* bachelor of arts in education
Bae·de·ker \ˈbā-di-kər, ˈbe-\ *n* [Karl *Baedeker* †1859 Ger. publisher of guidebooks] (1924) **:** GUIDEBOOK
BAeE *abbr* bachelor of aeronautical engineering
BAEE *abbr* bachelor of arts in elementary education
[1]**baf·fle** \ˈba-fəl\ *vt* **baf·fled; baf·fling** \-f(ə-)liŋ\ [prob. alter. of ME (Sc) *bawchillen* to denounce, discredit publicly] (1675) **1 :** to defeat or check (as a person) by confusing or puzzling **:** DISCONCERT **2 :** to check or break the force or flow of by or as if by a baffle ***syn*** see FRUSTRATE — **baf·fle·ment** \-fəl-mənt\ *n* — **baf·fler** \-f(ə-)lər\ *n* — **baf·fling·ly** \ˈba-fliŋ-lē\ *adv*
[2]**baffle** *n* (1881) **:** a device (as a plate, wall, or screen) to deflect, check, or regulate flow or passage (as of a fluid, light, or sound) — **baf·fled** \ˈba-fəld\ *adj*
baf·fle·gab \ˈba-fəl-ˌgab\ *n* (1952) **:** GOBBLEDYGOOK
[1]**bag** \ˈbag *also* ˈbāg\ *n* [ME *bagge,* fr. ON *baggi*] (13c) **1 a :** a usu. flexible container that may be closed for holding, storing, or carrying something: as **a :** PURSE; *esp* **:** HANDBAG **b :** a bag for game **c :** SUIT-

\ə\ abut \ᵊ\ kitten, F table \ər\ further \a\ ash \ā\ ace \ä\ mop, mar \au̇\ out \ch\ chin \e\ bet \ē\ easy \g\ go \i\ hit \ī\ ice \j\ job \ŋ\ sing \ō\ go \ȯ\ law \ȯi\ boy \th\ thin \t͟h\ the \ü\ loot \u̇\ foot \y\ yet \zh\ vision, beige \k, ⁿ, œ, ue, ʸ\ *see* Guide to Pronunciation

CASE **2 :** something resembling a bag: as **a** (1) **:** a pouched or pendulous bodily part or organ; *esp* **:** UDDER (2) **:** a puffy or sagging protuberance of flabby skin **b :** a puffed-out sag or bulge in cloth **c :** a square white stuffed canvas bag used to mark a base in baseball **3 :** the amount contained in a bag **4 a :** a quantity of game taken; *also* **:** the maximum legal quantity of game **b :** an assortment or collection esp. of nonmaterial things ⟨a ~ of tricks⟩ **5 :** an unattractive woman **6 :** something one likes or does regularly or well; *also* **:** one's characteristic way of doing things — **in the bag 1 :** SURE, CERTAIN ⟨her nomination was *in the bag*⟩; *also* **:** assured of a successful conclusion **:** sewn up ⟨have the game *in the bag*⟩ **2** *slang* **:** DRUNK 1a

2**bag** *vb* **bagged; bag·ging** *vi* (15c) **1 :** to swell out **:** BULGE **2 :** to hang loosely ~ *vt* **1 :** to cause to swell **2 :** to put into a bag **3 a :** to take (animals) as game **b :** to get possession of esp. by strategy or stealth **c :** CAPTURE, SEIZE **d :** to shoot down **:** DESTROY **4 :** to achieve in or as if in competition **:** WIN ⟨~ a play-off berth⟩ **5 :** to give up, forgo, or abandon esp. for something more desirable or attainable ⟨decided to ~ her job and move to the country⟩ — often used with *it* ***syn*** see CATCH — **bag·ger** *n*

BAg *abbr* bachelor of agriculture

ba·gasse \bə-ˈgas\ *n* [F] (ca. 1826) **:** plant residue (as of sugarcane or grapes) left after a product (as juice) has been extracted

bag·a·telle \ˌba-gə-ˈtel\ *n* [F, fr. It *bagattella*] (1633) **1 :** TRIFLE 1 **2 :** any of various games involving the rolling of balls into scoring areas **3 :** a short literary or musical piece in light style

ba·gel \ˈbā-gəl\ *n* [Yiddish *beygl,* fr. MHG **böugel* ring, fr. *bouc* ring, fr. OHG; akin to OE *bēag* ring, *būgan* to bend — more at BOW] (1916) **:** a firm doughnut-shaped roll traditionally made by boiling and then baking

bag·ful \ˈbag-ˌfu̇l\ *n* (15c) **1 :** as much or as many as a bag will hold **2 :** a large number or amount ⟨had a ~ of tricks⟩

1**bag·gage** \ˈba-gij\ *n* [ME *bagage,* fr. MF, fr. *bagues* belongings, baggage] (15c) **1 :** suitcases, trunks, and personal belongings of travelers **:** LUGGAGE **2 :** transportable equipment esp. of a military force **3 :** intangible things (as feelings, circumstances, or beliefs) that get in the way ⟨emotional ~⟩

2**baggage** *n* [prob. modif. of MF *bagasse,* fr. Old Occitan *bagassa*] (1594) **1 :** a contemptible woman; *esp* **:** PROSTITUTE **2 :** a young woman

baggage claim *n* (1972) **:** the area in an airport where arriving passengers pick up their checked baggage

bag·gies \ˈba-gēz\ *n pl* (1963) **:** baggy pants or shorts

Bag·gies \ˈba-gēz\ *trademark* — used for transparent plastic bags

bag·ging \ˈba-giŋ\ *n* (1732) **:** material (as cloth) for bags

bag·gy \ˈba-gē\ *adj* **bag·gi·er; -est** (1831) **1 :** loose, puffed out, or hanging like a bag ⟨~ trousers⟩ **2 :** loosely constructed and inflated with inessential elements ⟨a ~ novel⟩ — **bag·gi·ly** \ˈba-gə-lē\ *adv* — **bag·gi·ness** \ˈba-gē-nəs\ *n*

bag·house \ˈbag-ˌhau̇s\ *n* (1914) **:** a device or facility in which particulates are removed from a stream of exhaust gases (as from a blast furnace) as the stream passes through a large cloth bag; *also* **:** the bag used to filter the gas stream

bag lady *n* (1972) **:** a homeless woman who roams the streets of a city carrying her possessions in shopping bags

bag·man \ˈbag-mən\ *n* (1765) **1** *chiefly Brit* **:** TRAVELING SALESMAN **2 :** a person who on behalf of another collects or distributes illicitly gained money; *broadly* **:** an intermediary in an illicit or unethical transaction

ba·gnio \ˈban-(ˌ)yō, ˈbän-\ *n, pl* **bagnios** [It *bagno,* lit., public baths (fr. the Turks' use of Roman baths at Constantinople as prisons), fr. L *balneum,* fr. Gk *balaneion*] (1599) **1** *obs* **:** PRISON **2 :** BORDELLO

bag of waters (ca. 1881) **:** the double-walled fluid-filled sac that encloses and protects the fetus in the womb and that breaks releasing its fluid during the birth process

bag·pipe \ˈbag-ˌpīp\ *n* (14c) **:** a wind instrument consisting of a reed melody pipe and from one to five drones with air supplied continuously either by a bag with valve-stopped mouth tube or by bellows — often used in pl. — **bag·pip·er** \-ˌpī-pər\ *n*

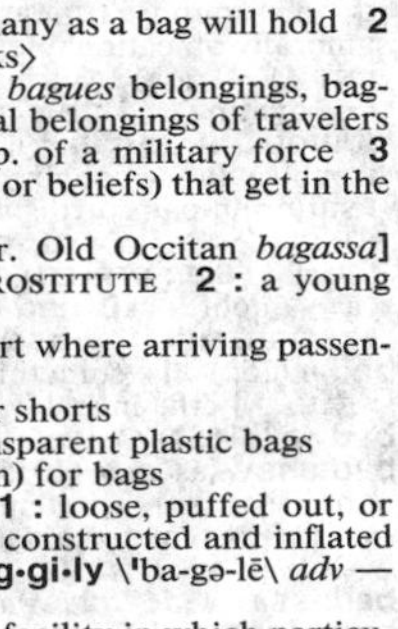

bagpipe

ba·guette \ba-ˈget\ *n* [F, lit., rod, fr. MF, fr. It *bacchetta,* ultim. fr. L *baculum* staff] (1926) **1 :** a gem having the shape of a narrow rectangle; *also* **:** the shape itself **2 :** a long thin loaf of French bread

bag·wig \ˈbag-ˌwig\ *n* (1717) **:** an 18th century wig with the back hair enclosed in a small silk bag

bag·worm \-ˌwərm\ *n* (1862) **:** any of a family (Psychidae) of moths with wingless females and plant-feeding larvae that live in a silk case covered with plant debris; *esp* **:** one (*Thyridopteryx ephemeraeformis*) often destructive to deciduous and evergreen trees of the eastern U.S.

bah \ˈbä, ˈba\ *interj* (1600) — used to express disdain or contempt

Ba·ha'i \bä-ˈhä-ˌē, -ˈhī, bə-\ *n, pl* **Baha'is** [Pers *bahā'ī,* lit., follower of *Bahā' Allāh* (fr. Ar, splendor of God)] (1889) **:** an adherent of a religious movement originating in Iran in the 19th century and emphasizing the spiritual unity of humankind — **Baha'i** *adj* — **Ba·ha·ism** \-ˈhä-ˌi-zəm, -ˈhī-ˌi-\ *n* — **Ba·ha·ist** \-ˈhä-(ˌ)ist\ *n or adj*

Ba·ha·sa In·do·ne·sia \bə-ˌhä-sə-ˌin-də-ˈnē-zhə, -shə\ *n* [Indonesian *bahasa indonésia,* lit., Indonesian language] (1952) **:** INDONESIAN 2b

Ba·hia grass \bə-ˈhē-ə-\ *n* [*Bahia,* state in Brazil] (ca. 1927) **:** a perennial tropical American grass (*Paspalum notatum*) used in the southern U.S. as a lawn grass

baht \ˈbät\ *n, pl* **baht** *also* **bahts** [Thai *bàad*] (1828) — see MONEY table

1**bail** \ˈbāl\ *n* [ME *baille,* fr. AF, bucket, fr. ML *bajula* water vessel, fr. fem. of L *bajulus* porter, carrier] (14c) **:** a container used to remove water from a boat

2**bail** *vt* (1613) **1 :** to clear (water) from a boat by dipping and throwing over the side — usu. used with *out* **2 :** to clear water from by dipping and throwing — usu. used with *out* ~ *vi* **:** BAIL OUT 2 — **bail·er** *n*

3**bail** *n* [ME, custody, bail, fr. AF, lit., handing over, delivery, fr. *baillier* to give, entrust, hand over, fr. L *bajulare* to carry a burden, fr. *bajulus* porter, carrier] (15c) **1 :** the temporary release of a prisoner in exchange for security given for the due appearance of the prisoner **2 :** security given for the release of a prisoner on bail **3 :** one who provides bail

4**bail** *vt* (1548) **1 :** to release under bail **2 :** to procure the release of by giving bail — often used with *out* **3 :** to help from a predicament — used with *out* ⟨~*ing* out impoverished countries⟩ — **bail·able** *adj*

5**bail** *n* [ME *beil, baile,* prob. fr. OE **begel,* **bygel*; akin to MD *beughel* iron ring, hilt guard; akin to OE *būgan* to bend — more at BOW] (15c) **1 a :** a supporting half hoop **b :** a hinged bar for holding paper against the platen of a typewriter **2 :** a usu. arched handle (as of a kettle or pail)

6**bail** *vt* [AF *baillier*] (1768) **:** to deliver (personal property) in trust to another for a special purpose and for a limited period

7**bail** *n* [perh. fr. 5*bail*] (1844) *chiefly Brit* **:** a device for confining or separating animals

bail·ee \bā-ˈlē\ *n* (1528) **:** the person to whom personal property is bailed

bai·ley \ˈbā-lē\ *n, pl* **baileys** [ME *bailli,* palisade, bailey, fr. AF *baille, balie*] (13c) **1 :** the outer wall of a castle or any of several walls surrounding the keep **2 :** a courtyard within the external wall or between two outer walls of a castle

bai·lie \ˈbā-lē\ *n* [ME] (14c) **1** *chiefly dial* **:** BAILIFF **2 :** a Scottish municipal magistrate corresponding to an English alderman

bai·liff \ˈbā-ləf\ *n* [ME *baillif, bailie,* fr. AF *baillif,* fr. *bail* power, authority, office, fr. *baillier* to govern, administer, fr. ML *bajulare* to care for, support, fr. L, to carry a burden — more at BAIL] (14c) **1 a :** an official employed by a British sheriff to serve writs and make arrests and executions **b :** a minor officer of some U.S. courts usu. serving as a messenger or usher **2** *chiefly Brit* **:** one who manages an estate or farm — **bai·liff·ship** \-ˌship\ *n*

bai·li·wick \ˈbā-li-ˌwik, -lē-\ *n* [ME *baillifwik,* fr. *baillif* + *wik* dwelling place, village, fr. OE *wīc,* fr. L *vicus* village — more at VICINITY] (15c) **1 :** the office or jurisdiction of a bailiff **2 :** a special domain

bail·ment \ˈbā(ə)l-mənt\ *n* (1554) **:** the act of bailing a person or personal property

bail·or \bā-ˈlȯr, ˈbā-lər\ *or* **bail·er** \ˈbā-lər\ *n* (1602) **:** a person who delivers personal property to another in trust

bail·out \ˈbā-ˌlau̇t\ *n* (1951) **:** a rescue from financial distress

bail out *vi* (1930) **1 :** to parachute from an aircraft **2 :** to abandon a harmful or difficult situation; *also* **:** LEAVE, DEPART

bails·man \ˈbālz-mən\ *n* (1862) **:** one who gives bail for another

bain–ma·rie \ˌban-mə-ˈrē, ˌbaⁿ-\ *n, pl* **bains–marie** *same*\ [F, fr. MF, trans. of ML *balneum Mariae,* lit., Mary's bath, after *Maria Hebraea,* Mary the Jewess, legendary inventor of apparatus used in alchemy] (1822) **:** a cooking utensil containing heated water in which food in smaller pots is cooked — compare DOUBLE BOILER

bairn \ˈbern\ *n* [ME *bern, barn,* fr. OE *bearn* & ON *barn;* akin to OHG *barn* child] (bef. 12c) *chiefly Scot* **:** CHILD

1**bait** \ˈbāt\ *vb* [ME, fr. ON *beita;* akin to OE *bǣtan* to bait, *bītan* to bite — more at BITE] *vt* (13c) **1 a :** to persecute or exasperate with unjust, malicious, or persistent attacks **b :** TEASE **2 a :** to harass (as a chained animal) with dogs usu. for sport **b :** to attack by biting and tearing **3 a :** to furnish with bait **b :** ENTICE, LURE **4 :** to give food and drink to (an animal) esp. on the road ~ *vi, archaic* **:** to stop for food and rest when traveling — **bait·er** *n*

syn BAIT, BADGER, HECKLE, HECTOR, CHIVY, HOUND mean to harass by efforts to break down. BAIT implies wanton cruelty or delight in persecuting a helpless victim ⟨*baited* the chained dog⟩. BADGER implies pestering so as to drive a person to confusion or frenzy ⟨*badgered* her father for a car⟩. HECKLE implies persistent annoying or belligerent interruptions of a speaker ⟨drunks *heckled* the stand-up comic⟩. HECTOR carries an implication of bullying and domineering ⟨football players *hectored* by their coach⟩. CHIVY suggests persecution by teasing or nagging ⟨*chivied* the new student mercilessly⟩. HOUND implies unrelenting pursuit and harassing ⟨*hounded* by creditors⟩.

2**bait** *n* [ME, fr. ON *beit* pasturage & *beita* food; akin to OE *bītan* to bite] (14c) **1 a :** something (as food) used in luring esp. to a hook or trap **b :** a poisonous material placed where it will be eaten by harmful or objectionable animals **2 :** LURE, TEMPTATION

bait and switch *n* (1967) **1 :** a sales tactic in which a customer is attracted by the advertisement of a low-priced item but is then encouraged to buy a higher-priced one **2 :** the ploy of offering a person something desirable to gain favor (as political support) then thwarting expectations with something less desirable

bait·fish \ˈbāt-ˌfish\ *n* (1820) **:** a small fish (as a golden shiner or menhaden) that attracts and is a food source for a larger game fish; *also* **:** a fish used for bait

bai·za \ˈbī-(ˌ)zä\ *n, pl* **baiza** *or* **baizas** [Ar *baisa,* prob. fr. Gujarati *paisɔ,* fr. Hindi *paisā* quarter-anna coin — more at PAISA] (1970) — see *rial* at MONEY table

baize \ˈbāz\ *n* [MF *baies,* pl. of *baie* baize, fr. fem. of *bai* bay-colored — more at BAY] (1578) **:** a coarse woolen or cotton fabric napped to imitate felt

1**bake** \ˈbāk\ *vb* **baked; bak·ing** [ME, fr. OE *bacan;* akin to OHG *bahhan* to bake, Gk *phōgein* to roast] *vt* (bef. 12c) **1 :** to cook (as food) by dry heat esp. in an oven **2 :** to dry or harden by subjecting to heat ~ *vi* **1 :** to prepare food by baking it **2 :** to become baked **3 :** to be or become extremely hot ⟨sidewalks *baking* in the sun⟩ — **bak·er** *n*

2**bake** *n* (1565) **1 :** the act or process of baking **2 :** a social gathering at which a baked food is served

Ba·ke·lite \ˈbā-kə-ˌlīt, -ˌklīt\ *trademark* — used for any of various synthetic resins and plastics

baker's dozen *n* (1596) **:** THIRTEEN

baker's yeast *n* (1847) **:** a yeast (as *Saccharomyces cerevisiae*) used or suitable for use as a leavening agent

bak·ery \ˈbā-k(ə-)rē\ *n, pl* **-er·ies** (1758) **:** a place for baking or selling baked goods

bake sale *n* (1903) **:** a fund-raising event at which usu. homemade foods (as cakes and cookies) are sold

bake·shop \ˈbāk-ˌshäp\ *n* (1789) **:** BAKERY

bake·ware \-ˌwer\ *n* (1946) **:** dishes used for baking and serving food

baking powder *n* (1850) **:** a powder used as a leavening agent in making baked goods (as quick breads) that typically consists of sodium bicarbonate, an acidic substance (as cream of tartar), and starch or flour

baking soda *n* (1862) **:** SODIUM BICARBONATE

bak·la·va \ˈbä-klə-ˌvä, ˌbä-klə-ˈvä\ *n* [Turk] (1653) **:** a dessert made of thin pastry, nuts, and honey

bak·sheesh \ˈbak-ˌshēsh, bak-ˈ\ *n* [Pers *bakhshīsh,* fr. *bakhshīdan* to give; akin to Gk *phagein* to eat, Skt *bhajati* he allots] (ca. 1760) **:** payment (as a tip or bribe) to expedite service

bal *abbr* balance

BAL \ˌbē-(ˌ)ā-ˈel\ *n* [British *Anti-Lewisite*] (1942) **:** DIMERCAPROL

Ba·laam \ˈbā-ləm\ *n* [Gk, fr. Heb *Bilʿām*] (bef. 12c) **:** an Old Testament prophet who is reproached by the ass he is riding and rebuked by God's angel while on the way to meet with an enemy of Israel

bal·a·cla·va \ˌba-lə-ˈklä-və, -ˈkla-\ *n* [*Balaclava,* Crimea, site of a British encampment during the Crimean War] (1941) **:** a knit cap for the head and neck — called also *balaclava helmet*

bal·a·lai·ka \ˌba-lə-ˈlī-kə\ *n* [Russ] (1780) **:** a usu. 3-stringed instrument of Russian origin with a triangular body played by plucking or strumming

[1]**bal·ance** \ˈba-lən(t)s\ *n* [ME, fr. AF, fr. VL **bilancia,* fr. LL *bilanc-, bilanx* having two scalepans, fr. L *bi-* + *lanc-, lanx* plate] (13c) **1 :** an instrument for weighing: as **a :** a beam that is supported freely in the center and has two pans of equal weight suspended from its ends **b :** a device that uses the elasticity of a spiral spring for measuring weight or force **2 :** a means of judging or deciding **3 :** a counterbalancing weight, force, or influence **4 :** an oscillating wheel operating with a hairspring to regulate the movement of a timepiece **5 a :** stability produced by even distribution of weight on each side of the vertical axis **b :** equipoise between contrasting, opposing, or interacting elements **c :** equality between the totals of the two sides of an account **6 a :** an aesthetically pleasing integration of elements **b :** the juxtaposition in writing of syntactically parallel constructions containing similar or contrasting ideas **7 a :** physical equilibrium **b :** the ability to retain one's balance **8 a :** weight or force of one side in excess of another **b :** something left over **:** REMAINDER **c :** an amount in excess esp. on the credit side of an account **9 :** mental and emotional steadiness — **bal·anced** \-lən(t)st\ *adj* — **in the balance** *or* **in balance :** with the fate or outcome about to be determined ⟨our future hangs *in the balance* as we await his decision⟩ — **on balance :** with all things considered ⟨the meeting went well *on balance*⟩

[2]**balance** *vb* **bal·anced; bal·anc·ing** *vt* (1588) **1 a** (1) **:** to compute the difference between the debits and credits of (an account) (2) **:** to pay the amount due on **:** SETTLE **b** (1) **:** to arrange so that one set of elements exactly equals another ⟨~ a mathematical equation⟩ (2) **:** to complete (a chemical equation) so that the same number of atoms and electric charges of each kind appears on each side **2 a :** COUNTERBALANCE, OFFSET **b :** to equal or equalize in weight, number, or proportion **3 :** to weigh in or as if in a balance **4 a :** to bring to a state or position of equipoise **b :** to poise in or as if in balance **c :** to bring into harmony or proportion ~ *vi* **1 :** to become balanced or established in balance **2 :** to be an equal counterpoise **3 :** WAVER 1 ⟨~*s* and temporizes on matters that demand action⟩

balance beam *n* (ca. 1949) **1 :** a narrow wooden beam supported in a horizontal position approximately four feet above the floor and used for balancing feats in gymnastics **2 :** an event in gymnastics competition in which the balance beam is used

balance of payments (1844) **:** a summary of the international transactions of a country or region over a period of time including commodity and service transactions, capital transactions, and gold movements

balance of power (1701) **:** an equilibrium of power sufficient to discourage or prevent one nation or party from imposing its will on or interfering with the interests of another

balance of trade (1668) **:** the difference in value over a period of time between a country's imports and exports

bal·anc·er \ˈba-lən(t)-sər\ *n* (15c) **:** one that balances; *specif* **:** HALTERE

balance sheet *n* (ca. 1771) **:** a statement of financial condition at a given date

balance wheel *n* (1669) **1 :** a wheel that regulates or stabilizes the motion of a mechanism **2 :** a balancing or stabilizing force

balancing act *n* (1954) **:** an attempt to cope with several often conflicting factors or situations at the same time

bal·as \ˈba-ləs\ *n* [ME, fr. MF *balais,* fr. ML *balagius, balascius,* fr. Ar *balakhsh,* fr. *Balakhshān,* ancient region of Afghanistan] (15c) **:** a ruby spinel of a pale rose-red or orange

ba·la·ta \bə-ˈlä-tə\ *n* [Sp, fr. Carib] (1860) **:** the dried latex of a tropical American tree (genus *Manilkara* and esp. *M. bidentata*) of the sapodilla family that is similar to gutta-percha and is used esp. in belting and golf balls; *also* **:** a tree yielding it

bal·boa \bal-ˈbō-ə\ *n* [Sp, fr. Vasco Núñez de *Balboa*] (ca. 1909) — see MONEY table

bal·brig·gan \bal-ˈbri-gən\ *n* [*Balbriggan,* town in Ireland] (1885) **:** a knitted cotton fabric used esp. for underwear or hosiery

bal·co·ny \ˈbal-kə-nē\ *n, pl* **-nies** [It *balcone,* fr. OIt, large window, of Gmc origin; akin to OHG *balko* beam — more at BALK] (1618) **1 :** a platform that projects from the wall of a building and is enclosed by a parapet or railing **2 :** an interior projecting gallery in a public building (as a theater) — **bal·co·nied** \-nēd\ *adj*

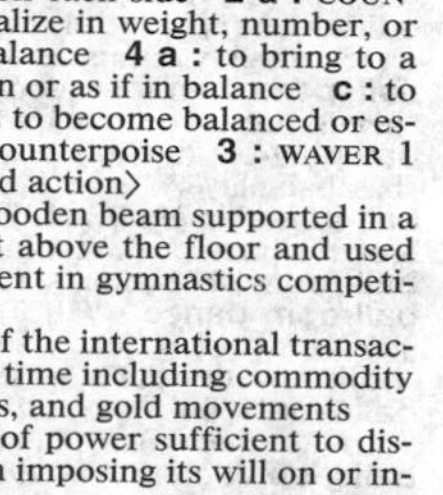

balcony 1

[1]**bald** \ˈbȯld\ *adj* [ME *balled;* prob. akin to Dan dial. *bældet* bald, L *fulica* coot, Gk *phalios* having a white spot, OE *bǣl* fire, pyre] (14c) **1 a :** lacking a natural or usual covering (as of hair, vegetation, or nap) **b :** having little or no tread ⟨~ tires⟩ **2 :** marked with white **3 :** lacking adornment or amplification ⟨a ~ assertion⟩ **4 :** UNDISGUISED, PALPABLE ⟨~ arrogance⟩ ***syn*** see BARE — **bald·ish** \ˈbȯl-dish\ *adj* — **bald·ly** \ˈbȯl(d)-lē\ *adv* — **bald·ness** \ˈbȯl(d)-nəs\ *n*

[2]**bald** *vt* (1602) **:** to make bald ~ *vi* **:** to become bald

bal·da·chin \ˈbȯl-də-kən, ˈbal-\ *or* **bal·da·chi·no** \ˌbal-də-ˈkē-(ˌ)nō, ˌbäl-\ *n, pl* **baldachins** *or* **baldachinos** [It *baldacchino,* fr. *Baldacco* Baghdad, Iraq] (1537) **1 :** a cloth canopy fixed or carried over an important person or a sacred object **2 :** a rich embroidered fabric of silk and gold **3 :** an ornamental structure resembling a canopy used esp. over an altar

bald cypress *n* (1709) **1 :** a large deciduous conifer (*Taxodium distichum* of the family Taxodiaceae, the bald cypress family) of southern U.S. swamps that has flexible flat needles and is related to the sequoias; *also* **:** a related tree (*T. mucronatum*) of Mexico and southern Texas — see CONE illustration **2 :** the hard red wood of bald cypress that is much used for shingles

bald eagle *n* (1688) **:** an eagle (*Haliaeetus leucocephalus*) of No. America that is brown when young with white only on the undersides of the wings but in full adult plumage has white head and neck feathers and a white tail

Bal·der \ˈbȯl-dər\ *n* [ON *Baldr*] (1552) **:** the son of Odin and Frigga and Norse god of light and peace slain through the trickery of Loki by a mistletoe sprig

bal·der·dash \ˈbȯl-dər-ˌdash\ *n* [origin unknown] (1674) **:** NONSENSE

bald–faced \ˈbȯl(d)-ˈfāst\ *adj* (1943) **:** BAREFACED ⟨a ~ lie⟩

bald·head \ˈbȯld-ˌhed\ *n* (1535) **:** a bald-headed person

balding *adj* (1938) **:** becoming bald ⟨bespectacled and ~⟩

bald·pate \ˈbȯl(d)-ˌpāt\ *n* (1577) **1 :** BALDHEAD **2 :** AMERICAN WIGEON

bal·dric \ˈbȯl-drik\ *n* [ME *baudry, baudrik,* fr. MF *baudré,* fr. OF *baldrei*] (14c) **:** an often ornamented belt worn over one shoulder to support a sword or bugle

[1]**bale** \ˈbāl\ *n* [ME, fr. OE *bealu;* akin to OHG *balo* evil, OCS *bolĭ* sick person] (bef. 12c) **1 :** great evil **2 :** WOE, SORROW

[2]**bale** *n* [ME, fr. MF, of Gmc origin; akin to OHG *balla* ball] (14c) **:** a large bundle of goods; *specif* **:** a large closely pressed package of merchandise bound and usu. wrapped ⟨a ~ of paper⟩ ⟨a ~ of hay⟩

[3]**bale** *vt* **baled; bal·ing** (1760) **:** to make up into a bale — **bal·er** *n*

ba·leen \bə-ˈlēn, ˈbā-ˌlēn\ *n* [ME *baleine* whale, baleen, fr. L *balaena* whale; akin to Gk *phallaina* whale] (14c) **:** a horny keratinous substance found in two rows of transverse plates which hang down from the upper jaws of baleen whales

baleen whale *n* (1874) **:** any of a suborder (Mysticeti) of usu. large whales lacking teeth but having baleen which is used to filter chiefly small crustaceans (as krill) out of large quantities of seawater

bale·fire \ˈbāl-ˌfī(-ə)r\ *n* [ME, fr. OE *bǣlfȳr* funeral fire, fr. *bǣl* pyre + *fȳr* fire] (16c) **:** an outdoor fire often used as a signal fire

bale·ful \-fəl\ *adj* (bef. 12c) **1 :** deadly or pernicious in influence ⟨~ effects⟩ **2 :** foreboding or threatening evil ⟨a ~ look⟩ ***syn*** see SINISTER — **bale·ful·ly** \-fə-lē\ *adv* — **bale·ful·ness** \-fəl-nəs\ *n*

Ba·li·nese \ˌbä-li-ˈnēz, ˌba-, -ˈnēs\ *n* [D *Balinees,* fr. *Bali* island of Indonesia] (1820) **1 :** a native or inhabitant of Bali **2 :** any of a breed of slender longhaired cats that originated as a spontaneous mutation of the Siamese — **Balinese** *adj*

[1]**balk** \ˈbȯk *sometimes* ˈbȯlk\ *n* [ME *balke,* fr. OE *balca;* akin to OHG *balko* beam, L *fulcire* to prop, Gk *phalanx* log, phalanx] (bef. 12c) **1 :** a ridge of land left unplowed as a dividing line or through carelessness **2 :** BEAM, RAFTER **3 :** HINDRANCE, CHECK **4 a :** the space behind the balkline on a billiard table **b :** any of the outside divisions made by the balklines **5 :** failure of a player to complete a motion; *esp* **:** an illegal motion of the pitcher in baseball while in position

[2]**balk** *vt* (15c) **1** *archaic* **:** to pass over or by **2 :** to check or stop by or as if by an obstacle **:** BLOCK ~ *vi* **1 :** to stop short and refuse to proceed **2 :** to refuse abruptly — used with *at* ⟨Congress ~*ed* at putting up the money —Thomas Fleming⟩ **3 :** to commit a balk in sports ***syn*** see FRUSTRATE — **balk·er** *n*

bal·kan·ize \ˈbȯl-kə-ˌnīz\ *vt* **-ized; -iz·ing** *often cap* [*Balkan* Peninsula] (1919) **1 :** to break up (as a region or group) into smaller and often hostile units **2 :** DIVIDE, COMPARTMENTALIZE ⟨now pop culture has been *balkanized;* it is full of niches, with different groups watching and playing their own things —Richard Corliss⟩ — **bal·kan·i·za·tion** \ˌbȯl-kə-nə-ˈzā-shən\ *n, often cap*

balk·line \ˈbȯ-ˌklīn\ *n* (1839) **1 :** a line across a billiard table near one end behind which the cue balls are placed in making opening shots **2 a :** one of four lines parallel to the cushions of a billiard table dividing it into nine compartments **b :** a billiards game that sets restrictions in scoring caroms according to these lines

balky \ˈbȯ-kē *sometimes* ˈbȯl-\ *adj* **balk·i·er; -est** (1847) **:** refusing or likely to refuse to proceed, act, or function as directed or expected ⟨a ~ mule⟩ ⟨a ~ engine⟩ ***syn*** see CONTRARY — **balk·i·ness** *n*

[1]**ball** \ˈbȯl\ *n, often attrib* [ME *bal,* prob fr. OE **beall;* akin to OE *beallucs* testis, OHG *balla* ball, ON *bǫllr,* OE *blāwan* to blow — more at BLOW] (13c) **1 :** a round or roundish body or mass: as **a :** a spherical or ovoid body used in a game or sport ⟨a tennis ~⟩ — used figuratively in phrases like *the ball is in your court* to indicate who has the responsibility or opportunity for further action **b :** EARTH, GLOBE **c :** a spherical or conical projectile; *also* **:** projectiles used in firearms **d :** a roundish protuberant anatomical structure (as near the tip of a human finger or toe or at the base of a thumb); *esp* **:** the part of the sole of the human foot between the toes and arch on which the main weight of the body rests in normal walking **2 a** *often vulgar* **:** TESTIS **b** *pl* (1) *often vulgar* **:** NONSENSE — often used interjectionally (2) *often vulgar* **:** NERVE 3 **3 :** a game in which a ball is thrown, kicked, or struck; *also* **:** quality of play in such a game **4 a :** a pitch not swung at by the batter that fails to pass through the strike zone **b :** a hit or thrown ball in various games ⟨foul ~⟩ — **on the ball 1 :** COMPETENT, KNOWLEDGEABLE, ALERT ⟨the other introductory essay . . . is much more *on the ball* —*Times Lit. Supp.*⟩ ⟨keep *on the ball*⟩ **2 :** of ability or competence ⟨if the teacher has something *on the ball,* the pupils won't squirm much —*New Yorker*⟩

\ə\ **abut** \ᵊ\ kitten, F table \ər\ **further** \a\ **ash** \ā\ **ace** \ä\ **mop, mar** \au̇\ **out** \ch\ **chin** \e\ **bet** \ē\ **easy** \g\ **go** \i\ **hit** \ī\ **ice** \j\ **job** \ŋ\ **sing** \ō\ **go** \ȯ\ **law** \ȯi\ **boy** \th\ **thin** \t͟h\ **the** \ü\ **loot** \u̇\ **foot** \y\ **yet** \zh\ **vision, beige** \k, ⁿ, œ, ue, ʸ\ *see* Guide to Pronunciation

[2]**ball** *vt* (1658) **1 :** to form or gather into a ball ⟨~*ed* the paper into a wad⟩ **2** *usu vulgar* **:** to have sexual intercourse with ~ *vi* **1 :** to form or gather into a ball **2** *usu vulgar* **:** to engage in sexual intercourse

[3]**ball** *n* [F *bal,* fr. OF, fr. *baller* to dance, fr. LL *ballare,* fr. Gk *ballizein*] (ca. 1639) **1 :** a large formal gathering for social dancing **2 :** a very pleasant experience **:** a good time ⟨everyone had a ~ at the wedding⟩

bal·lad \ˈba-ləd\ *n* [ME *balade* ballade, song, fr. MF, fr. Old Occitan *balada* dance, song sung while dancing, fr. *balar* to dance, fr. LL *ballare*] (14c) **1 a :** a narrative composition in rhythmic verse suitable for singing **b :** an art song accompanying a traditional ballad **2 :** a simple song **:** AIR **3 :** a popular song; *esp* **:** a slow romantic or sentimental song — **bal·lad·ic** \bə-ˈla-dik, ba-\ *adj*

bal·lade \bə-ˈläd, ba-\ *n* [ME *balade,* fr. MF, ballad, ballade] (14c) **1 :** a fixed verse form consisting usu. of three stanzas with recurrent rhymes, an envoi, and an identical refrain for each part **2 :** a musical composition usu. for piano suggesting the epic ballad

bal·lad·eer \ˌba-lə-ˈdir\ *n* (1830) **:** a singer of ballads

bal·lad·ist \ˈba-lə-dist\ *n* (1848) **:** a person who writes or sings ballads

bal·lad·ry \ˈba-lə-drē\ *n* (1596) **1 :** the composing or performing of ballads **2 :** BALLADS

ballad stanza *n* (1856) **:** a stanza consisting of four lines with the first and third lines unrhymed iambic tetrameters and the second and fourth lines rhymed iambic trimeters

ball–and–socket joint *n* (1809) **1 :** a joint in which a ball moves within a socket so as to allow rotary motion in every direction within certain limits **2 :** an articulation (as the hip joint) in which the rounded head of one bone fits into a cuplike cavity of the other and admits movement in any direction

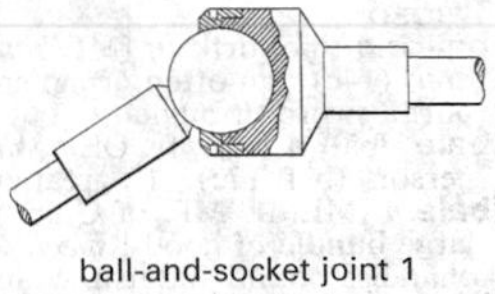
ball-and-socket joint 1

[1]**bal·last** \ˈba-ləst\ *n* [prob. fr. LG, of Scand origin; akin to Dan & Sw *barlast* ballast; perh. akin to OE *bær* bare & to OE *hlæst* load, *hladan* to load — more at LADE] (1530) **1 :** a heavy substance placed in such a way as to improve stability and control (as of the draft of a ship or the buoyancy of a balloon or submarine) **2 :** something that gives stability (as in character or conduct) **3 :** gravel or broken stone laid in a railroad bed or used in making concrete **4 :** a device used to provide the starting voltage or to stabilize the current in a circuit (as of a fluorescent lamp) — **in ballast** *of a ship* **:** having only ballast for a load

[2]**ballast** *vt* (1538) **1 :** to steady or equip with or as if with ballast **2 :** to fill in (as a railroad bed) with ballast

ball bearing *n* (1883) **:** a bearing in which the journal turns upon loose hardened steel balls that roll easily in a race; *also* **:** one of the balls in such a bearing

ball boy *n* (1903) **:** a male attendant who retrieves balls for players or officials (as in a tennis match or a baseball or basketball game)

ball·bust·er \ˈbȯl-ˌbəs-tər\ *n* (ca. 1944) *sometimes vulgar* **:** a person who is relentlessly aggressive, intimidating, or domineering

ball·car·ri·er \ˈbȯl-ˌker-ē-ər, -ˌka-rē-\ *n* (1934) **:** a football player who carries the ball on offense

ball cock *n* (1790) **:** an automatic valve whose opening and closing are controlled by a hollow float at the end of a lever

ball control *n* (1928) **:** an offensive strategy (as in football) in which a team tries to keep possession of the ball for extended periods of time

ball·er \ˈbȯ-lər\ *n* (1945) **:** an implement for shaping food into a ball or removing a core ⟨a melon ~⟩

bal·le·ri·na \ˌba-lə-ˈrē-nə\ *n* [It, fr. *ballare* to dance, fr. LL — more at BALL] (1815) **:** a woman who is a ballet dancer **:** DANSEUSE

bal·let \ˈba-ˌlā, ba-ˈ\ *n* [F, fr. It *balletto,* dim. of *ballo* dance, fr. *ballare*] (1634) **1 a :** a theatrical art form using dancing, music, and scenery to convey a story, theme, or atmosphere **b :** dancing in which conventional poses and steps are combined with light flowing figures (as leaps and turns) **2 :** music for a ballet **3 :** a group that performs ballets — **bal·let·ic** \ba-ˈle-tik\ *adj*

bal·let·o·mane \ba-ˈle-tə-ˌmān\ *n* [Russ *baletoman,* fr. *balet* ballet + *-o-* + *-man,* fr. *maniya* mania] (1930) **:** a devotee of ballet — **bal·let·o·ma·nia** \-ˌle-tə-ˈmā-nē-ə, -nyə\ *n*

ball–flow·er \ˈbȯl-ˌflau̇(-ə)r\ *n* (1845) **:** an architectural ornament consisting of a ball in the flower-shaped hollow of a circular mold

ball game *n* (1848) **1 :** a game played with a ball **2 a :** a set of circumstances **:** SITUATION ⟨a whole new *ball game*⟩ **b :** CONTEST 1

ball girl *n* (1926) **:** a female attendant who retrieves balls for players or officials (as in a tennis match or a baseball or basketball game)

ball handler *n* (1948) **:** a player who controls the ball in any of various games; *esp* **:** a player who is skilled at handling the ball (as in basketball) — **ball·han·dling** *n*

bal·lis·ta \bə-ˈlis-tə\ *n, pl* **-tae** \-ˌtē\ [L, fr. Gk **ballistēs,* fr. *ballein* to throw — more at DEVIL] (14c) **:** an ancient military engine often in the form of a crossbow for hurling large missiles

bal·lis·tic \bə-ˈlis-tik\ *adj* [L *ballista*] (ca. 1775) **1 :** of or relating to ballistics or to a body in motion according to the laws of ballistics **2 :** being or characterized by repeated bouncing ⟨~ stretching⟩ **3 :** extremely and usu. suddenly excited, upset, or angry **:** WILD ⟨went ~⟩ — **bal·lis·ti·cal·ly** \-ti-k(ə-)lē\ *adv*

ballistic missile *n* (1954) **:** a missile guided in the ascent of a high-arch trajectory and freely falling in the descent

bal·lis·tics \bə-ˈlis-tiks\ *n pl but sing or pl in constr* (ca. 1737) **1 a :** the science of the motion of projectiles in flight **b :** the flight characteristics of a projectile **2 a :** the study of the processes within a firearm as it is fired **b :** the firing characteristics of a firearm or cartridge

ball joint *n* (ca. 1849) **:** BALL-AND-SOCKET JOINT 1

ball lightning *n* (1857) **:** a rare form of lightning consisting of luminous balls that may move along solid objects or float in the air

ball mill *n* (1903) **:** a pulverizing machine consisting of a rotating drum which contains pebbles or metal balls as the grinding implements

ball of fire (ca. 1900) **:** a person of unusual energy, vitality, or drive

ball of wax (ca. 1953) **:** AFFAIR, CONCERN ⟨the whole *ball of wax*⟩

bal·lon \ba-ˈlōⁿ\ *n* [F, lit., balloon] (1830) **:** lightness of movement that exaggerates the duration of a ballet dancer's jump

bal·lo·net \ˌba-lə-ˈnā\ *n* [F *ballonnet,* dim. of *ballon*] (1902) **:** a compartment of variable volume within the interior of a balloon or airship used to control ascent and descent

[1]**bal·loon** \bə-ˈlün\ *n* [F *ballon* large football, balloon, fr. It dial. *ballone* large football, aug. of *balla* ball, of Gmc origin; akin to OHG *balla* ball — more at BALL] (1783) **1 :** a nonporous bag of light material that can be inflated esp. with air or gas: as **a :** a bag that is filled with heated air or a gas lighter than air so as to rise and float in the atmosphere and that usu. carries a suspended load (as a gondola with passengers) **b :** an inflatable bag (as of rubber or plastic) usu. used as a toy or for decoration **2 :** the outline enclosing words spoken or thought by a figure esp. in a cartoon

[2]**balloon** *adj* (ca. 1786) **1 :** relating to, resembling, or suggesting a balloon ⟨a ~ sleeve⟩ **2 :** being or having a final installment that is much larger than preceding ones in a term or installment note

[3]**balloon** *vi* (1841) **1 :** to swell or puff out **:** EXPAND ⟨~*ed* to 200 pounds⟩ **2 :** to ascend or travel in or as if in a balloon **3 :** to increase rapidly ⟨~*ing* prices⟩ ~ *vt* **:** INFLATE, INCREASE

balloon angioplasty *n* (1980) **:** dilation of an obstructed atherosclerotic artery by the passage of a balloon catheter through the vessel to the area of disease where inflation of the catheter's tip compresses the plaque against the vessel wall

balloon catheter *n* (1952) **:** a catheter with an inflatable tip that serves esp. to hold the catheter in place or to expand a partly closed or obstructed bodily passage or tube (as a coronary artery) — called also *balloon-tipped catheter*

balloon flower *n* (ca. 1900) **:** a perennial Asian herb (*Platycodon grandiflorus*) cultivated for its star-shaped flowers which open from buds resembling balloons

bal·loon·ing \bə-ˈlü-niŋ\ *n* (1784) **:** the act or sport of riding in a balloon

bal·loon·ist \-nist\ *n* (1784) **:** a person who operates or rides in a balloon

balloon tire *n* (1923) **:** a flexible low-pressure pneumatic tire with a large cross section designed to provide cushioning

balloon vine *n* (1836) **:** a tropical American vine (*Cardiospermum halicacabum*) of the soapberry family bearing large ornamental pods

[1]**bal·lot** \ˈba-lət\ *n* [It *ballotta,* fr. It dial., dim. of *balla* ball — more at BALLOON] (1549) **1 a :** a small ball used in secret voting **b :** a sheet of paper used to cast a secret vote **2 a :** the action or system of secret voting **b :** the right to vote **c :** VOTE 1a **3 :** the number of votes cast **4 :** the drawing of lots

[2]**ballot** *vi* (1580) **:** to vote or decide by ballot — **bal·lot·er** *n*

ballot box *n* (ca. 1680) **1 :** a box for receiving ballots **2 :** BALLOT 2a

[1]**ball·park** \ˈbȯl-ˌpärk\ *n* (1897) **1 :** a park in which ball games (as baseball) are played **2 :** a range (as of prices or views) within which comparison or compromise is possible — **in the ballpark :** approximately correct ⟨my first guess wasn't even *in the ballpark*⟩

[2]**ballpark** *adj* [fr. the phrase *in the ballpark*] (1964) **:** approximately correct **:** roughly estimated ⟨a ~ price⟩ ⟨a ~ figure⟩

ball–peen hammer \ˈbȯl-ˈpēn-\ *n* (ca. 1876) **:** a hammer having a hemispherical peen at one end of its head

ball·play·er \ˈbȯl-ˌplā-ər\ *n* (1619) **:** a person who plays ball; *esp* **:** a baseball player

ball·point \-ˌpȯint\ *n* (1953) **:** a pen having as the writing point a small rotating metal ball that inks itself by contact with an inner magazine

ball·room \ˈbȯl-ˌrüm, -ˌru̇m\ *n* (1736) **:** a large room used for dances

ballroom dance *n* (1927) **:** any of various usu. social dances (as the tango, two-step, and waltz) in which couples perform set moves — **ballroom dancer** *n* — **ballroom dancing** *n*

balls–out \ˈbȯlz-ˌau̇t\ *adj* (ca. 1945) **1** *often vulgar* **:** ALL-OUT, FULL-OUT **2** *often vulgar* **:** boldly aggressive or competitive

balls–up \ˈbȯlz-ˌəp\ *n* (1900) *Brit, sometimes vulgar* **:** FOUL-UP

ball·sy \ˈbȯl-zē\ *adj* **ball·si·er; -est** [[1]*ball*] (1935) *sometimes vulgar* **:** aggressively bold **:** GUTSY, NERVY — **ball·si·ness** *n*

ball up *vt* (1884) **:** to make a mess of **:** CONFUSE, MUDDLE ~ *vi* **:** to become badly muddled or confused

ball valve *n* (1839) **:** a valve in which a ball regulates the aperture esp. by its rise and fall due to fluid pressure, a spring, or its own weight

bally \ˈba-lē\ *adj or adv* [euphemism for *bloody,* adj., adv.] (1885) *Brit* — used as an intensive

ball·yard \ˈbȯl-ˌyärd\ *n* (1927) **:** BALLPARK 1

bal·ly·hoo \ˈba-lē-ˌhü\ *n, pl* **-hoos** [origin unknown] (1901) **1 :** a noisy attention-getting demonstration or talk **2 :** flamboyant, exaggerated, or sensational promotion or publicity **3 :** excited commotion — **ballyhoo** *vt*

ballyrag *var of* BULLYRAG

balm \ˈbä(l)m\ *n* [ME *basme, baume,* fr. AF, fr. L *balsamum* balsam] (13c) **1 :** a balsamic resin; *esp* **:** one from small tropical evergreen trees (genus *Commiphora* of the family Burseraceae) **2 :** an aromatic preparation (as a healing ointment) **3 :** any of several aromatic plants of the mint family; *esp* **:** LEMON BALM **4 :** a spicy aromatic odor **5 :** a soothing restorative agency

bal·ma·caan \ˌbal-mə-ˈkan, -ˈkän\ *n* [*Balmacaan,* estate near Inverness, Scotland] (1919) **:** a loose single-breasted overcoat usu. having raglan sleeves and a short turnover collar

balm of Gil·e·ad \-ˈgi-lē-əd\ [*Gilead,* region of ancient Palestine known for its balm] (1629) **1 :** an agency that soothes, relieves, or heals **2 :** a small evergreen African and Asian tree (*Commiphora opobalsamum* syn. *C. meccanensis* of the family Burseraceae) with aromatic leaves; *also* **:** a fragrant oleoresin from this tree **3 :** any of several poplars having resinous buds: as **a :** a hybrid No. American tree (*Populus gileadensis*) with broadly cordate leaves that are pubescent esp. on the underside **b :** BALSAM POPLAR

bal·mor·al \bal-ˈmȯr-əl, -ˈmär-\ *n* [*Balmoral* Castle, Scotland] (1859) **1 :** a laced boot or shoe **2** *often cap* **:** a round flat cap with a top projecting all around

balmy \ˈbä-mē, ˈbäl-mē\ *adj* **balm·i·er; -est** (15c) **1 a :** having the qualities of balm **:** SOOTHING **b :** MILD 3 ⟨~ weather⟩ **2 :** CRAZY, FOOLISH — **balm·i·ly** \-mə-lē\ *adv* — **balm·i·ness** \-mē-nəs\ *n*

bal·ne·ol·o·gy \ˌbal-nē-ˈä-lə-jē\ *n* [ISV, fr. L *balneum* bath — more at BAGNIO] (ca. 1879) **:** the science of the therapeutic use of baths

Balochi *var of* BALUCHI

[1]**baloney** *var of* BOLOGNA

[2]**ba·lo·ney** *also* **bo·lo·ney** \bə-ˈlō-nē\ *n* [*bologna*] (1922) **:** pretentious nonsense **:** BUNKUM — often used as a generalized expression of disagreement

bal·sa \ˈbȯl-sə\ *n* [Sp] (ca. 1600) **1 :** a small raft or boat; *specif* **:** one made of tightly bundled reeds and used on Lake Titicaca **2 :** a tropical American tree (*Ochroma pyramidale* syn. *O. lagopus*) of the silk-cotton family with extremely light strong wood used esp. for floats; *also* **:** its wood

bal·sam \ˈbȯl-səm\ *n* [L *balsamum*, fr. Gk *balsamon*, prob. of Sem origin; akin to Heb *bāshām* balsam] (bef. 12c) **1 a :** an aromatic and usu. oily and resinous substance flowing from various plants; *esp* **:** any of several resinous substances containing benzoic or cinnamic acid and used esp. in medicine **b :** a preparation containing resinous substances and having a balsamic odor **2 a :** a balsam-yielding tree; *esp* **:** BALSAM FIR **b :** IMPATIENS; *esp* **:** a common garden ornamental (*Impatiens balsamina*) **3 :** BALM 5

balsam fir *n* (1805) **:** a resinous No. American fir (*Abies balsamea*) that is widely used for pulpwood and as a Christmas tree and is the source of Canada balsam

bal·sam·ic \bȯl-ˈsa-mik, -ˈsä-\ *adj* (1705) **1 :** of, relating to, yielding, or containing balsam **2 :** made with balsamic vinegar ⟨a ~ vinaigrette⟩

balsamic vinegar *n* [trans. of It *aceto balsamico*, lit., curative vinegar] (1980) **:** an aged Italian vinegar made from the must of white grapes

balsam poplar *n* (1786) **:** a No. American poplar (*Populus balsamifera*) that is often cultivated as a shade tree and has buds thickly coated with an aromatic resin — called also *balm of Gilead, tacamahac*

Balt \ˈbȯlt\ *n* [ML *Balthae* Balts] (1937) **:** a native or inhabitant of Lithuania, Latvia, or Estonia

Bal·ti \ˈbəl-tē, ˈbȯl-\ *n* (1901) **:** a Tibeto-Burman language of northern Kashmir

Bal·tic \ˈbȯl-tik\ *adj* [ML (*mare*) *balticum* Baltic Sea] (ca. 1590) **1 :** of or relating to the Baltic Sea or to the states of Lithuania, Latvia, and Estonia **2 :** of or relating to a branch of the Indo-European language family containing Latvian, Lithuanian, and Old Prussian — see INDO-EUROPEAN LANGUAGES table

Bal·ti·more oriole \ˈbȯl-tə-ˌmȯr-, -mər-\ *n* [George Calvert, Lord *Baltimore*] (1808) **:** an oriole (*Icterus galbula*) of the eastern and central U.S. and southern Canada in which the male has a solid black head and the female usu. has an olive-brown back and orange-yellow underside and that was formerly considered to be a subspecies of northern oriole

Bal·to–Sla·vic \ˌbȯl-(ˌ)tō-ˈslä-vik, -ˈsla-\ *n* (1896) **:** a subgroup of Indo-European languages consisting of the Baltic and the Slavic branches — see INDO-EUROPEAN LANGUAGES table

Ba·lu·chi \bə-ˈlü-chē\ *also* **Ba·lo·chi** \-ˈlō-\ *n* [Pers *Balūchī* of the Baluchis, fr. *Balūch, Baloch* Baluchi] (1616) **1 :** a member of an Indo-Iranian people of Baluchistan **2 :** the Iranian language of the Baluchis

bal·us·ter \ˈba-lə-stər\ *n* [F *balustre*, fr. It *balaustro*, fr. *balausta* wild pomegranate flower, fr. L *balaustium*, fr. Gk *balaustion*; fr. its shape] (1602) **1 :** an object or vertical member (as the leg of a table, a round in a chair back, or the stem of a glass) having a vaselike or turned outline **2 :** an upright often vase-shaped support for a rail

bal·us·trade \ˈba-lə-ˌstrād\ *n* [F, fr. It *balaustrata*, fr. *balaustro*] (1644) **1 :** a row of balusters topped by a rail **2 :** a low parapet or barrier — **bal·us·trad·ed** \-ˌstrā-dəd\ *adj*

bam \ˈbam\ *n* [imit.] (1772) **:** a sudden loud noise — often used interjectionally to indicate a sudden impact or occurrence ⟨was fine, then ~, he lost his job⟩

BAM *abbr* **1** bachelor of applied mathematics **2** bachelor of arts in music

Bam·ba·ra \bam-ˈbär-ə\ *n, pl* **Bambara** *or* **Bambaras** [Ar *bambāra*, prob. ultim. fr. Bambara *bamana*, a self-designation] (1851) **1 :** a member of an African people of the upper Niger **2 :** a Mande language of the Bambara people

bam·bi·no \bam-ˈbē-(ˌ)nō, bäm-\ *n, pl* **-nos** *or* **-ni** \-(ˌ)nē\ [It, dim. of *bambo* child] (1722) **1** *pl usu bambini* **:** a representation of the infant Christ **2 :** CHILD, BABY

bam·boo \(ˌ)bam-ˈbü, ˈbam-ˌ\ *n, pl* **bamboos** *often attrib* [Malay *bambu*] (1586) **:** any of various woody or arborescent grasses (as of the genera *Bambusa, Arundinaria,* and *Dendrocalamus* of the subfamily Bambusoideae) of tropical and temperate regions having hollow stems, thick rhizomes, and shoots that are used for food; *also* **:** the jointed stem of bamboo used esp. for building, furniture, and utensils

bamboo curtain *n, often cap B&C* (1949) **:** a political, military, and ideological barrier isolating an area of eastern Asia

bam·boo·zle \bam-ˈbü-zəl\ *vt* **-boo·zled; -boo·zling** \-ˈbüz-liŋ, -ˈbü-zə-\ [origin unknown] (1703) **1 :** to deceive by underhanded methods **:** DUPE, HOODWINK **2 :** to confuse, frustrate, or throw off thoroughly or completely ⟨a quarterback *bamboozled* by an unexpected defense⟩ — **bam·boo·zle·ment** \-ˈbü-zəl-mənt\ *n*

[1]**ban** \ˈban\ *vb* **banned; ban·ning** [ME *bannen* to summon, curse, fr. OE *bannan* to summon; akin to OHG *bannan* to command, L *fari* to speak, Gk *phanai* to say, *phōnē* sound, voice] *vt* (12c) **1** *archaic* **:** CURSE **2 :** to prohibit esp. by legal means ⟨~ discrimination⟩; *also* **:** to prohibit the use, performance, or distribution of ⟨~ a book⟩ ⟨~ a pesticide⟩ **3 :** BAR 3c ⟨*banned* from the U.N.⟩ ~ *vi, archaic* **:** to utter curses or maledictions

[2]**ban** *n* [ME, partly fr. *bannen* & partly fr. OF *ban*, of Gmc origin; akin to OHG *bannan* to command] (14c) **1 :** the summoning in feudal times of the king's vassals for military service **2 :** ANATHEMA, EXCOMMUNICATION **3 :** MALEDICTION, CURSE **4 :** legal or formal prohibition ⟨a ~ on beef exports⟩ **5 :** censure or condemnation esp. through social pressure

[3]**ban** \ˈbän\ *n, pl* **ba·ni** \ˈbä-(ˌ)nē\ [Rom, money, coin, small coin] (1880) — see *leu* at MONEY table

Ba·nach space \ˈbä-ˌnäk-, -nək-, -ˌnäk-, -nək-\ *n* [Stefan *Banach* †1945 Pol. mathematician] (1938) **:** a complete normed vector space

ba·nal \bə-ˈnal, ba-, -ˈnäl; bā-ˈnal; ˈbā-nᵊl\ *adj* [F, fr. MF, of compulsory feudal service, possessed in common, commonplace, fr. *ban*] (1825) **:** lacking originality, freshness, or novelty **:** TRITE ***syn*** see INSIPID — **ba·nal·ize** \bə-ˈna-ˌlīz, ba-, -ˈnä-; bā-ˈna-; ˈbā-nᵊl-ˌīz\ *vt* — **ba·nal·ly** \bə-ˈnal-lē, ba-, -ˈnäl-; bā-ˈnal-; ˈbā-nᵊl-(l)ē\ *adv*

ba·nal·i·ty \bə-ˈna-lə-tē, bā-, *also* ba-\ *n, pl* **-ties** (1861) **1 :** something banal **:** COMMONPLACE **2 :** the quality or state of being banal

ba·nana \bə-ˈna-nə, *esp Brit* -ˈnä-\ *n, often attrib* [Sp or Pg; Sp, fr. Pg, of African origin; akin to Wolof *banaana* banana] (1597) **1 :** an elongated usu. tapering tropical fruit with soft pulpy flesh enclosed in a soft usu. yellow rind **2 :** any of several widely cultivated perennial herbs (genus *Musa* of the family Musaceae, the banana family) bearing bananas in compact pendent bunches

banana oil *n* (1926) **:** AMYL ACETATE

banana pepper *n* (1973) **:** a long tapered yellow pepper occurring in several varieties from mild and sweet tasting to hot and pungent

banana republic *n* (1904) **:** a small dependent country usu. of the tropics; *esp* **:** one run despotically

ba·nan·as \bə-ˈna-nəz, *esp Brit* -ˈnä-\ *adj* (1957) **:** CRAZY ⟨drives me ~⟩ ⟨the crowd went ~⟩

banana seat *n* (1965) **:** an elongated bicycle saddle

bananas Fos·ter \-ˈfȯs-tər, -ˈfäs-\ *n* [Richard *Foster*, friend of New Orleans restaurateur Owen E. Brennan, at whose restaurant the dish was first made] (1976) **:** a dessert of bananas flamed (as with rum) and served with ice cream

banana split *n* (1915) **:** ice cream served on a banana sliced in half lengthwise and usu. garnished with flavored syrups, fruits, nuts, and whipped cream

ba·nau·sic \bə-ˈnȯ-sik, -zik\ *adj* [Gk *banausikos* of an artisan, nonintellectual, vulgar, fr. *banausos* artisan] (1845) **:** relating to or concerned with earning a living — used pejoratively ⟨contempt for the ~ occupations —T. S. Eliot⟩; *also* **:** UTILITARIAN, PRACTICAL ⟨such mundane and ~ considerations as comfort and durability —G. B. Boyer⟩

[1]**band** \ˈband\ *n* [in senses 1 & 2, fr. ME *band, bond* something that constricts, fr. ON *band;* akin to OE *bindan* to bind; in other senses, fr. ME *bande* strip, fr. MF, fr. VL **binda*, of Gmc origin; akin to OHG *binta* fillet; akin to OE *bindan* to bind, *bend* fetter — more at BIND] (12c) **1 :** something that confines or constricts while allowing a degree of movement **2 :** something that binds or restrains legally, morally, or spiritually **3 :** a strip serving to join or hold things together: as **a :** BELT 2 **b :** a cord or strip across the back of a book to which the sections are sewn **4 :** a thin flat encircling strip: as **a :** a close-fitting strip that confines material at the waist, neck, or cuff of clothing **b :** a strip of cloth used to protect a newborn baby's navel — called also *bellyband* **c :** a ring of elastic **5 a :** a strip (as of living tissue or rock) or a stripe (as on an animal) differentiable (as by color, texture, or structure) from the adjacent material or area **b :** a more or less well-defined range of wavelengths, frequencies, or energies **c :** RANGE 7a **6 :** a narrow strip serving chiefly as decoration: as **a :** a narrow strip of material applied as trimming to an article of dress **b** *pl* **:** a pair of strips hanging at the front of the neck as part of a clerical, legal, or academic dress **c :** a ring without raised portions **7 :** TRACK 1e(2)

[2]**band** *vt* (15c) **1 :** to affix a band to or tie up with a band **2 :** to finish or decorate with a band **3 :** to gather together **:** UNITE ⟨~*ed* themselves together for protection⟩ ~ *vi* **:** to unite for a common purpose — often used with *together* ⟨have ~*ed* together in hopes of attacking the blight that is common to them all —J. B. Conant⟩ — **band·er** *n*

[3]**band** *n* [MF *bande* troop, fr. Old Occitan *banda*, of Gmc origin; akin to Goth *bandwo* sign, standard — more at BANNER] (15c) **:** a group of persons, animals, or things; *esp* **:** a group of musicians organized for ensemble playing

[1]**ban·dage** \ˈban-dij\ *n* [MF, fr. *bande*] (1599) **1 :** a strip of fabric used esp. to cover, dress, and bind up wounds **2 :** a flexible strip or band used to cover, strengthen, or compress something

[2]**bandage** *vt* **ban·daged; ban·dag·ing** (1774) **:** to bind, dress, or cover with a bandage ⟨~ a wound⟩ ⟨a *bandaged* ankle⟩

[1]**Band–Aid** \ˈban-ˈdād\ *adj* (1970) **:** offering, making use of, or serving as a temporary or expedient remedy or solution

[2]**Band–Aid** *trademark* — used for a small adhesive strip with a gauze pad for covering minor wounds

ban·dan·na *or* **ban·dana** \ban-ˈda-nə\ *n* [Hindi *bā̃dhnū* & Urdu *bāndhnū* tie-dyeing, cloth so dyed, ultim. fr. Skt *badhnāti* he ties — more at BIND] (1741) **:** a large often colorfully patterned handkerchief

B and B *n* (1953) **:** BED-AND-BREAKFAST

[1]**band·box** \ˈban(d)-ˌbäks\ *n* (1631) **1 :** a usu. cylindrical box of cardboard or thin wood for holding light articles of attire **2 :** a structure (as a baseball park) having relatively small interior dimensions

[2]**bandbox** *adj* (1844) **:** exquisitely neat, clean, or ordered as if just taken from a bandbox ⟨a ~ perfection of appearance⟩ — **bandbox** *adv*

B and E *abbr* breaking and entering

ban·deau \ban-ˈdō\ *n, pl* **ban·deaux** *also* **ban·deaus** \-ˈdōz\ [F, dim. of *bande*] (1706) **1 :** a fillet or band esp. for the hair **2 :** BRASSIERE; *also* **:** a band-shaped covering for the breasts

band·ed \ˈban-dəd\ *adj* (1787) **:** having or marked with bands

ban·de·ri·lla \ˌban-də-ˈrē(l)-yə\ *n* [Sp, dim. of *bandera* banner, prob. fr. Old Occitan *bandiera*] (1789) **:** a decorated barbed dart that the banderillero thrusts into the neck or shoulders of the bull in a bullfight

ban·de·ri·lle·ro \ˌban-də-(ˌ)rē(l)-ˈyer-(ˌ)ō\ *n, pl* **-ros** [Sp, fr. *banderilla*] (1789) **:** a person who thrusts in the banderillas in a bullfight

ban·de·role *or* **ban·de·rol** \ˈban-də-ˌrōl\ *n* [F *banderole*, fr. It *banderuola*, dim. of *bandiera* banner, fr. Old Occitan *bandiera*, fr. OF *baniere* — more at BANNER] (1562) **1 :** a long narrow forked flag or streamer **2 :** a long scroll bearing an inscription or a device

ban·di·coot \ˈban-di-ˌküt\ *n* [Telugu *pandikokku*] (1813) **1 :** any of several very large rats (genera *Bandicota* and *Nesokia*) of southern Asia destructive to crops **2 :** any of various small chiefly insectivorous and herbivorous marsupial mammals (family Peramelidae or family Peroryctidae) of Australia, Tasmania, and New Guinea

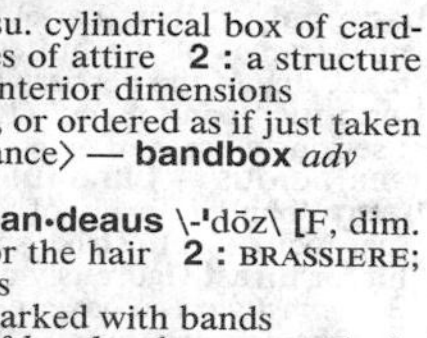

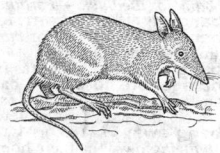

bandicoot 2

ban·dit \ˈban-dət\ *n* [It *bandito,* fr. pp. of *bandire* to banish, of Gmc origin; akin to OHG *bannan* to command — more at BAN] (1611) **1** *pl also* **ban·dit·ti** \ban-ˈdi-tē\ : an outlaw who lives by plunder; *esp* : a member of a band of marauders **2** : ROBBER **3** : an enemy plane — **ban·dit·ry** \ˈban-də-trē\ *n*

ban·di·to \ban-ˈdē-(ˌ)tō\ *n* [It] (1591) : an outlaw esp. of Mexican extraction or origin

band·lead·er \ˈband-ˌlē-dər\ *n* (1894) : the conductor of a band (as a dance band)

band·mas·ter \ˈban(d)-ˌmas-tər\ *n* (1858) : BANDLEADER; *esp* : a conductor of a military or concert band

band·mate \ˈban(d)-ˌmāt\ *n* (1956) : a fellow member of a band

ban·dog \ˈban-ˌdȯg\ *n* [ME *bandogge,* fr. *band* + *dogge* dog] (14c) : a dog kept tied to serve as a watchdog or because of its ferocity

ban·do·lier *or* **ban·do·leer** \ˌban-də-ˈlir\ *n* [MF *bandouliere,* ultim. fr. OSp *bando* band, of Gmc origin; akin to Goth *bandwo* — more at BANNER] (ca. 1577) : a belt worn over the shoulder and across the breast often for the suspending or supporting of some article (as cartridges) or as a part of an official or ceremonial dress

ban·dore \ˈban-ˌdȯr\ *or* **ban·do·ra** \ban-ˈdȯr-ə\ *n* [Sp *bandurria* or Pg *bandurra,* fr. LL *pandura* 3-stringed lute, fr. Gk *pandoura*] (1566) : a bass stringed instrument resembling a guitar

band–pass filter \ˈban(d)-ˌpas-\ *n* (1926) : a filter that transmits only frequencies within a selected band

band saw *n* (1858) : a saw in the form of an endless steel belt running over pulleys; *also* : a power saw using this device usu. with the blade in a vertical position

band shell *n* (1926) : a bandstand having at the rear a sounding board shaped like a huge concave seashell

bands·man \ˈban(d)z-mən\ *n* (ca. 1842) : a member of a musical band

band·stand \ˈban(d)-ˌstand\ *n* (1859) **1** : a usu. roofed platform on which a band or orchestra performs outdoors **2** : a platform in a ballroom or nightclub on which musicians perform

b and w *abbr* black and white

band·wag·on \ˈband-ˌwa-gən\ *n, often attrib* (1855) **1** : a usu. ornate and high wagon for a band of musicians esp. in a circus parade **2** : a popular party, faction, or cause that attracts growing support — often used in such phrases as *jump on the bandwagon* **3** : a current or fashionable trend

band·width \ˈband-ˌwidth\ *n* (1930) **1** : a range within a band of wavelengths, frequencies, or energies; *esp* : a range of radio frequencies which is occupied by a modulated carrier wave, which is assigned to a service, or over which a device can operate **2** : the capacity for data transfer of an electronic communications system ⟨graphics consume more ~ than text does⟩; *esp* : the maximum data transfer rate of such a system ⟨a ~ of 56 kilobits per second⟩

[1]**ban·dy** \ˈban-dē\ *vb* **ban·died; ban·dy·ing** [origin unknown] *vt* (1577) **1** : to bat (as a tennis ball) to and fro **2 a** : to toss from side to side or pass about from one to another often in a careless or inappropriate manner **b** : EXCHANGE; *esp* : to exchange (words) argumentatively **c** : to discuss lightly or banteringly **d** : to use in a glib or offhand manner — often used with *about* ⟨~ these statistics about with considerable bravado —Richard Pollak⟩ **3** *archaic* : to band together ~ *vi* **1** *obs* : CONTEND **2** *archaic* : UNITE

[2]**bandy** *n* (1693) : a game similar to hockey and believed to be its prototype

[3]**bandy** *adj* [perh. fr. [2]*bandy* (hockey stick)] (1687) **1** *of legs* : BOWED **2** : BOWLEGGED — **ban·dy–legged** \ˈban-dē-ˌlegd; ˌban-dē-ˈle-gəd, -ˈlā-\ *adj*

[1]**bane** \ˈbān\ *n* [ME, fr. OE *bana;* akin to OHG *bano* death] (bef. 12c) **1 a** *obs* : KILLER, SLAYER **b** : POISON **c** : DEATH, DESTRUCTION ⟨stop the way of those that seek my ~ —Philip Sidney⟩ **d** : WOE **2** : a source of harm or ruin : CURSE ⟨national frontiers have been more of a ~ than a boon for mankind —D. C. Thomson⟩

[2]**bane** *vt* **baned; ban·ing** (1578) *obs* : to kill esp. with poison

[3]**bane** *n* [ME (northern dial.) *ban,* fr. OE *bān* — more at BONE] (bef. 12c) *chiefly Scot* : BONE

bane·ber·ry \ˈbān-ˌber-ē\ *n* (1755) : any of several perennial herbs (genus *Actaea*) of the buttercup family having acrid poisonous berries; *also* : one of the berries

bane·ful \ˈbān-fəl\ *adj* (1579) **1** : productive of destruction or woe : seriously harmful ⟨a ~ influence⟩ **2** *archaic* : POISONOUS ***syn*** see PERNICIOUS — **bane·ful·ly** \-fə-lē\ *adv*

[1]**bang** \ˈbaŋ\ *vb* [prob. of Scand origin; akin to ON *bang* hammering] *vt* (ca. 1550) **1** : to strike sharply : BUMP ⟨~*ed* his knee⟩ **2** : to knock, hit, or thrust vigorously often with a sharp noise ⟨~*ed* the door shut⟩ **3** *often vulgar* : to have sexual intercourse with ~ *vi* **1** : to strike with a sharp noise or thump **2** : to produce a sharp often metallic explosive or percussive noise or series of such noises **3** : to play a sport (as basketball) in a very aggressive and forceful manner ⟨~ for rebounds⟩

[2]**bang** *n* (ca. 1550) **1** : a resounding blow **2** : a sudden loud noise — often used interjectionally **3 a** : a sudden striking effect **b** : a quick burst of energy ⟨start off with a ~⟩ **c** : THRILL ⟨I get a ~ out of all this —W. H. Whyte⟩ — **bang for the buck** *also* **bang for one's buck** : value received from outlay or effort ⟨investment is yielding less *bang for the buck* —*Fortune*⟩

[3]**bang** *adv* (1828) : RIGHT, DIRECTLY ⟨ran ~ up against more trouble⟩

[4]**bang** *n* [prob. short for *bangtail* short tail] (1878) : a fringe of banged hair — usu. used in pl.

[5]**bang** *vt* (1878) : to cut (as front hair) short and squarely across

ban·ga·lore torpedo \ˈbaŋ-gə-ˌlȯr-\ *n* [*Bangalore,* India] (1913) : a metal tube that contains explosives and a firing mechanism and is used to cut barbed wire and detonate buried mines

bang away *vi* (1839) **1** : to work with determined effort ⟨students *banging away* at their homework⟩ **2** : to attack persistently ⟨police are going to keep *banging away* at you —Erle Stanley Gardner⟩

bang–bang \ˈbaŋ-ˌbaŋ\ *adj* (1972) **1 a** : having a sudden, forceful, or attention-grabbing effect : PUNCHY ⟨~ headlines⟩ **b** : executed or happening so quickly as to make judgment (as by an umpire or referee) difficult ⟨a ~ play at first base⟩ **2** : characterized by violent or fast-paced action ⟨a ~ movie⟩

bang·er \ˈbaŋ-ər\ *n* (ca. 1919) **1** *Brit* : SAUSAGE **2** *Brit* : FIRECRACKER **3** *Brit* : JALOPY **4** : a forceful and aggressive athlete

bang·kok \ˈbaŋ-ˌkäk, baŋ-ˈ\ *n* [earlier *bangkok,* a fine straw, fr. *Bangkok,* Thailand] (1916) : a hat woven of fine palm fiber in the Philippines

ban·gle \ˈbaŋ-gəl\ *n* [Hindi *baṅglī*] (1787) **1** : a stiff usu. ornamental bracelet or anklet slipped or clasped on **2** : an ornamental disk that hangs loosely (as on a bracelet)

bang on *adj* (1936) *chiefly Brit* : exactly correct or appropriate

Bang's disease \ˈbaŋz-\ *n* [Bernhard L. F. *Bang* †1932 Dan. veterinarian] (ca. 1929) : BRUCELLOSIS; *specif* : contagious abortion of cattle caused by a brucella (*Brucella abortus*)

bang·tail \ˈbaŋ-ˌtāl\ *n* [*bangtail* short tail] (1921) : RACEHORSE

bang–up \ˈbaŋ-ˌəp\ *adj* [[3]*bang*] (1810) : FIRST-RATE ⟨a ~ job⟩

bang up *vt* [[1]*bang*] (1886) : to cause extensive damage to

bani *pl of* [3]BAN

ban·ish \ˈba-nish\ *vt* [ME, fr. AF *baniss-,* stem of *banir,* of Gmc origin; akin to OHG *bannan* to command — more at BAN] (14c) **1** : to require by authority to leave a country **2** : to drive out or remove from a home or place of usual resort or continuance **3** : to clear away : DISPEL ⟨his discovery ~*es* anxiety —Stringfellow Barr⟩ — **ban·ish·er** *n* — **ban·ish·ment** \-nish-mənt\ *n*

syn BANISH, EXILE, DEPORT, TRANSPORT mean to remove by authority from a state or country. BANISH implies compulsory removal from a country not necessarily one's own ⟨*banished* for seditious activities⟩. EXILE may imply compulsory removal or an enforced or voluntary absence from one's own country ⟨a writer who *exiled* himself for political reasons⟩. DEPORT implies sending out of the country an alien who has illegally entered or whose presence is judged inimical to the public welfare ⟨illegal aliens will be *deported*⟩. TRANSPORT implies sending a convicted criminal to an overseas penal colony ⟨a convict who was *transported* to Australia⟩.

ban·is·ter *also* **ban·nis·ter** \ˈba-nəs-tər\ *n* [alter. of *baluster*] (1641) **1 a** : a handrail with its supporting posts **b** : HANDRAIL **2** : BALUSTER 2 — **ban·is·tered** \-tərd\ *adj*

ban·jax \ˈban-ˌjaks\ *vt* [origin unknown] (1939) *chiefly Irish* : DAMAGE, RUIN; *also* : SMASH

ban·jo \ˈban-(ˌ)jō\ *n, pl* **banjos** *also* **banjoes** [prob. of African origin; akin to Kimbundu *mbanza,* a similar instrument] (1739) : a musical instrument with a drumlike body, a fretted neck, and usu. four or five strings which may be plucked or strummed — **ban·jo·ist** \-ˌjō-ist\ *n*

banjo clock *n* (1903) : a pendulum clock whose shape suggests a banjo

[1]**bank** \ˈbaŋk\ *n* [ME, prob. of Scand origin; akin to ON *bakki* bank; akin to OE *benc* bench — more at BENCH] (13c) **1** : a mound, pile, or ridge raised above the surrounding level: as **a** : a piled-up mass of cloud or fog **b** : an undersea elevation rising esp. from the continental shelf **2** : the rising ground bordering a lake, river, or sea or forming the edge of a cut or hollow **3 a** : a steep slope (as of a hill) **b** : the lateral inward tilt of a surface along a curve or of a vehicle (as an airplane) when turning **4** : a protective or cushioning rim or piece

[2]**bank** *vt* (1590) **1 a** : to raise a bank about **b** : to cover (as a fire) with fresh fuel and adjust the draft of air so as to keep in an inactive state **c** : to build (a curve) with the roadbed or track inclined laterally upward from the inside edge **2** : to heap or pile in a bank **3 a** : to drive (a ball in billiards) into a cushion **b** : to bounce (a ball or shot) off a surface (as a backboard) into or toward a goal ⟨~ in a rebound⟩ **4** : to form or group in a tier ~ *vi* **1** : to rise in or form a bank — often used with *up* ⟨clouds would ~ up about midday, and showers fall —William Beebe⟩ **2 a** : to incline an airplane laterally **b** (1) : to incline laterally (2) : to follow a curve or incline ⟨skiers ~*ing* around the turn⟩

[3]**bank** *n* [ME, fr. MF or OIt; MF *banque,* fr. OIt *banca,* lit., bench, of Gmc origin; akin to OE *benc*] (15c) **1 a** : an establishment for the custody, loan, exchange, or issue of money, for the extension of credit, and for facilitating the transmission of funds **b** *obs* : the table, counter, or place of business of a money changer **2** : a person conducting a gambling house or game; *specif* : DEALER **3** : a supply of something held in reserve: as **a** : the fund of supplies (as money, chips, or pieces) held by the banker or dealer for use in a game **b** : a fund of pieces belonging to a game (as dominoes) from which the players draw **4** : a place where something is held available ⟨memory ~*s*⟩; *esp* : a depot for the collection and storage of a biological product ⟨a blood ~⟩

[4]**bank** *vi* (ca. 1751) **1** : to manage a bank **2** : to deposit money or have an account in a bank ~ *vt* : to deposit or store in a bank — **bank on** : to depend or rely on ⟨can always *bank on* her friendship⟩

[5]**bank** *n* [ME *banc* bench, fr. AF, of Gmc origin; akin to OE *benc*] (1614) **1** : a group or series of objects arranged together in a row or a tier: as **a** : a set of elevators **b** : a row or tier of telephones **2** : one of the horizontal and usu. secondary or lower divisions of a headline

bank·able \ˈbaŋ-kə-bəl\ *adj* (1818) **1** : acceptable to or at a bank ⟨~ currency⟩ **2** : sure to bring in a profit ⟨Hollywood's most ~ star —Sidney Sheldon⟩ — **bank·abil·i·ty** \ˌbaŋ-kə-ˈbi-lə-tē\ *n*

bank·book \ˈbaŋk-ˌbu̇k\ *n* (1714) : the depositor's book in which a bank records deposits and withdrawals — called also *passbook*

bank card *n* (1970) : a card (as a credit card or an ATM card) issued by a bank

bank discount *n* (1841) : the interest discounted in advance on a note and computed on the face value of the note

[1]**bank·er** \ˈbaŋ-kər\ *n* (1534) **1** : one that engages in the business of banking **2** : the player who keeps the bank in various games — **bank·er·ly** \-lē\ *adj*

[2]**banker** *n* (1666) : a person or boat employed in the cod fishery on the Newfoundland banks

banker's acceptance *n* (ca. 1924) : a short-term credit instrument issued by an importer's bank that guarantees payment of an exporter's invoice

bank holiday *n* (1871) **1** *Brit* : LEGAL HOLIDAY **2** : a period when banks in general are closed often by government fiat

bank·ing *n* (1735) : the business of a bank or a banker

bank money *n* (1904) : a medium of exchange consisting chiefly of checks and drafts

bank·note \ˈbaŋk-ˌnōt\ *n* (1695) : a promissory note issued by a bank payable to bearer on demand without interest and acceptable as money

[1]**bank·roll** \ˈbaŋk-ˌrōl\ *n* (1887) : supply of money : FUNDS

[2]**bankroll** *vt* (1928) : to supply money for (a business, project, or person) — **bank·roll·er** *n*

[1]**bank•rupt** \ˈbaŋk-(ˌ)rəpt\ *n* [modif. of MF & OIt; MF *banqueroute* bankruptcy, fr. OIt *bancarotta,* fr. *banca* bank + *rotta* broken, fr. L *rupta,* fem. of *ruptus,* pp. of *rumpere* to break — more at BANK, REAVE] (1533) **1 a :** a person who has done any of the acts that by law entitle creditors to have his or her estate administered for their benefit **b :** a person judicially declared subject to having his or her estate administered under the bankrupt laws for the benefit of creditors **c :** a person who becomes insolvent **2 :** a person who is completely lacking in a particular desirable quality or attribute ⟨a moral ~⟩

[2]**bankrupt** *adj* (1566) **1 a :** reduced to a state of financial ruin : IMPOVERISHED; *specif* : legally declared a bankrupt ⟨the company went ~⟩ **b :** of or relating to bankrupts or bankruptcy ⟨~ laws⟩ **2 a :** BROKEN, RUINED ⟨a ~ professional career⟩ **b :** exhausted of valuable qualities : STERILE ⟨a ~ old culture⟩ **c :** DESTITUTE — used with *of* or *in* ⟨~ of all merciful feelings⟩

[3]**bankrupt** *vt* (1588) **1 :** to reduce to bankruptcy **2 :** IMPOVERISH ⟨defections had *~ed* the party of its brainpower⟩ ***syn*** see DEPLETE

bank•rupt•cy \ˈbaŋk-(ˌ)rəp(t)-sē\ *n, pl* **-cies** (1700) **1 :** the quality or state of being bankrupt **2 :** utter failure or impoverishment

bank shot *n* (1800) **1 :** a shot in billiards and pool in which a player banks the cue ball or the object ball **2 :** a shot in basketball played to rebound from the backboard into the basket

bank•sia \ˈbaŋ(k)-sē-ə\ *n* [NL, genus name, fr. Sir Joseph *Banks*] (1783) **:** any of a genus (*Banksia*) of Australian evergreen trees or shrubs of the protea family with alternate leathery leaves and flowers in dense cylindrical heads

bank•side \ˈbaŋk-ˌsīd\ *n* (15c) **:** the slope of a bank esp. of a stream

[1]**ban•ner** \ˈba-nər\ *n* [ME *banere,* fr. AF, of Gmc origin; akin to Goth *bandwo* sign; prob. akin to Gk *phainein* to show — more at FANCY] (13c) **1 a :** a piece of cloth attached by one edge to a staff and used by a leader (as a monarch or feudal lord) as his standard **b :** [2]FLAG 1 **c :** an ensign displaying a distinctive or symbolic device or legend; *esp* : one presented as an award of honor or distinction **2 :** a headline in large type running across a newspaper page **3 :** a strip of cloth on which a sign is painted ⟨welcome *~s* stretched across the street⟩ **4 :** a name, slogan, or goal associated with a particular group or ideology ⟨the new ~ is "community control" —F. M. Hechinger⟩ — often used with *under* ⟨every new administration arrives . . . under the ~ of change —John Cogley⟩ **5 :** an advertisement graphic that runs usu. across the top of a World Wide Web page

[2]**banner** *vt* (1809) **1 :** to furnish with a banner **2 :** to print (as a news story) under a banner usu. on the front page

[3]**banner** *adj* (1840) **1 :** prominent in support of a political party ⟨a ~ Democratic county⟩ **2 :** distinguished from all others esp. in excellence ⟨a ~ year for business⟩

[1]**ban•ner•et** \ˈba-nə-rət, ˌba-nə-ˈret\ *n, often cap* [ME *baneret,* fr. AF, fr. *banere*] (14c) **:** a knight leading his vassals into the field under his own banner

[2]**banneret** *also* **ban•ner•ette** *n* (14c) **:** a small banner

ban•ne•rol \ˈba-nə-ˌrōl\ *n* (1548) **:** BANDEROLE

bannister *var of* BANISTER

ban•nock \ˈba-nək\ *n* [ME *bannok,* fr. OE *bannuc*] (bef. 12c) **1 :** a usu. unleavened flat bread or biscuit made with oatmeal or barley meal **2** *chiefly NewEng* : CORN BREAD; *esp* : a thin cake baked on a griddle

banns \ˈbanz\ *n pl* [pl. of *bann,* fr. ME *bane, ban* proclamation, ban] (14c) **:** public announcement esp. in church of a proposed marriage

[1]**ban•quet** \ˈbaŋ-kwət, ˈban- *also* -ˌkwet\ *n* [MF, fr. OIt *banchetto,* fr. dim. of *banca* bench, bank] (15c) **1 :** a sumptuous feast; *esp* : an elaborate and often ceremonious meal for numerous people often in honor of a person ⟨a state ~⟩ **2 :** a meal held in recognition of some occasion or achievement ⟨an awards ~⟩

[2]**banquet** *vi* (ca. 1500) **:** to partake of a banquet ~ *vt* **:** to treat with a banquet : FEAST — **ban•quet•er** *n*

banquet room *n* (1717) **:** a large room (as in a restaurant or hotel) suitable for banquets

ban•quette \baŋ-ˈket, ban-, *1b is also* ˈbaŋ-kət\ *n* [F, fr. MF, fr. Old Occitan *banqueta,* dim. of *banc* bench, of Gmc origin; akin to OE *benc* bench] (1629) **1 a :** a raised way along the inside of a parapet or trench for gunners or guns **b** *Southern* : SIDEWALK **2 a :** a long upholstered bench **b :** a sofa having one roll-over arm **c :** a built-in usu. upholstered bench along a wall

Ban•quo \ˈbaŋ-(ˌ)kwō, ˈban-\ *n* (1607) **:** a murdered Scottish thane in Shakespeare's *Macbeth* whose ghost appears to Macbeth

ban•shee \ˈban-(ˌ)shē, ban-ˈ\ *n* [Ir *bean sídhe* & ScGael *bean sìth,* lit., woman of fairyland] (1771) **:** a female spirit in Gaelic folklore whose appearance or wailing warns a family that one of them will soon die

[1]**ban•tam** \ˈban-təm\ *n* [*Bantam,* former residency in Java] (1740) **1 :** any of numerous small domestic fowls that are often miniatures of members of the standard breeds **2 :** a person of diminutive stature and often combative disposition

[2]**bantam** *adj* (1881) **1 :** SMALL, DIMINUTIVE **2 :** pertly combative

ban•tam•weight \-ˌwāt\ *n* (1884) **:** a boxer in a weight division having a maximum limit of 118 pounds for professionals and 119 pounds for amateurs — compare FEATHERWEIGHT, FLYWEIGHT

ban•teng \ˈbän-ˌteŋ\ *n* [Malay of Indonesia, fr. Jav *banṭéng*] (1817) **:** a wild ox (*Bos javanicus* syn. *B. banteng*) of southeastern Asia sometimes domesticated for use as a draft animal or for its meat

[1]**ban•ter** \ˈban-tər\ *vb* [origin unknown] *vt* (1653) **1 :** to speak to or address in a witty and teasing manner **2** *archaic* : DELUDE **3** *chiefly Southern & Midland* : CHALLENGE ~ *vi* **:** to speak or act playfully or wittily — **ban•ter•er** \-tər-ər\ *n* — **ban•ter•ing•ly** \ˈban-tə-riŋ-lē\ *adv*

[2]**banter** *n* (1688) **:** good-natured and usu. witty and animated joking

bant•ling \ˈbant-liŋ\ *n* [perh. modif. of G *Bänkling* bastard, fr. *Bank* bench, fr. OHG — more at BENCH] (1593) **:** a very young child

Ban•tu \ˈban-(ˌ)tü, ˈbän-\ *n, pl* **Bantu** *or* **Bantus** [*ba-,* a pl. noun classifier + *-ntu,* noun base meaning "person" in several Bantu languages] (1862) **1 :** a family of Niger-Congo languages spoken in central and southern Africa **2 :** a member of any of a group of African peoples who speak Bantu languages

Ban•tu•stan \ˌban-tü-ˈstan, ˌbän-tü-ˈstän, ˈban-tü-ˌ, ˈbän-tü-ˌ, -tə-\ *n* [*Bantu* + *-stan* land (as in *Hindustan*)] (1949) **:** any of several all-black enclaves formerly in the Republic of So. Africa that had a limited degree of self-government

ban•yan \ˈban-yən, -ˌyan\ *n* [earlier *banyan* Gujarati trader, fr. Pg *banean,* prob. fr. Tamil *vāṇiyan* trader, fr. Skt *vāṇija;* fr. a tree of the species in Iran under which such traders conducted business] (1634) **:** an East Indian fig tree (*Ficus benghalensis*) of the mulberry family with branches that send out roots which grow down to the soil and form secondary trunks

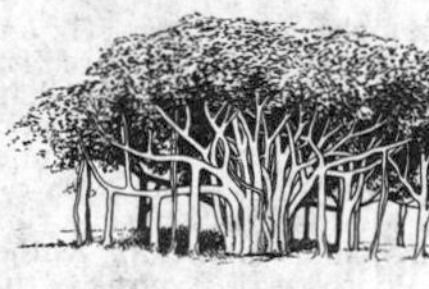

banyan

ban•zai \(ˌ)bän-ˈzī, ˈbän-ˌ\ *n* [Jp] (1892) **:** a Japanese cheer or war cry

banzai attack *n* (1944) **:** a mass attack by Japanese soldiers in World War II; *also* : an all-out usu. desperate attack

banzai charge *n* (1942) **1 :** BANZAI ATTACK **2 :** a determined often reckless act

bao•bab \ˈbau̇-ˌbab, ˈbā-ə-\ *n* [NL *bahobab*] (1640) **:** a broad-trunked tropical tree (*Adansonia digitata*) of the silk-cotton family that is native to Africa and has an edible acidic fruit resembling a gourd and bark used in making paper, cloth, and rope; *also* : any of several related trees chiefly of Madagascar and Australia

bap \ˈbap\ *n* [origin unknown] (ca. 1575) *Brit* : a small bun or roll

Bap *or* **Bapt** *abbr* Baptist

bap•ti•sia \bap-ˈti-zh(ē-)ə\ *n* [NL, genus name, fr. Gk *baptisis* a dipping, fr. *baptein*] (ca. 1868) **:** any of a genus (*Baptisia*) of No. American plants of the legume family having showy papilionaceous flowers similar in form to those of the pea plant

bap•tism \ˈbap-ˌti-zəm, *esp Southern* ˈbab-\ *n* [ME *baptisme*] (14c) **1 a :** a Christian sacrament marked by ritual use of water and admitting the recipient to the Christian community **b :** a non-Christian rite using water for ritual purification **c** *Christian Science* : purification by or submergence in Spirit **2 :** an act, experience, or ordeal by which one is purified, sanctified, initiated, or named — **bap•tis•mal** \bap-ˈtiz-məl, *esp Southern* bab-\ *adj* — **bap•tis•mal•ly** \-mə-lē\ *adv*

baptismal name *n* (1711) **:** a name given at christening or confirmation

baptism of fire (1625) **1 :** an introductory or initial experience that is a severe ordeal; *esp* : a soldier's first exposure to enemy fire **2 :** a spiritual baptism by a gift of the Holy Spirit — often used in allusion to Acts 2:3–4; Mt 3:11(RSV)

bap•tist \ˈbap-tist, *esp Southern* ˈbab- *also* ˈbab-dist\ *n* (13c) **1 :** one that baptizes **2** *cap* **:** a member or adherent of an evangelical Protestant denomination marked by congregational polity and baptism by immersion of believers only — **Baptist** *adj*

bap•tis•tery *or* **bap•tis•try** \ˈbap-tə-strē, *esp Southern* ˈbab-\ *n, pl* **-teries** *or* **-tries** (14c) **:** a part of a church or formerly a separate building used for baptism

bap•tize *also* **bap•tise** \bap-ˈtīz, ˈbap-ˌ, *esp Southern* bab- *or* ˈbab-\ *vb* **bap•tized** *also* **bap•tised; bap•tiz•ing** *also* **bap•tis•ing** [ME, fr. AF *baptiser,* fr. LL *baptizare,* fr. Gk *baptizein* to dip, baptize, fr. *baptein* to dip, dye; akin to ON *kvefja* to quench] *vt* (13c) **1 :** to administer baptism to **2 a :** to purify or cleanse spiritually esp. by a purging experience or ordeal **b :** INITIATE **3 :** to give a name to (as at baptism) **:** CHRISTEN ~ *vi* **:** to administer baptism — **bap•tiz•er** *n*

[1]**bar** \ˈbär\ *n, often attrib* [ME *barre,* fr. AF, fr. VL **barra*] (12c) **1 a :** a straight piece (as of wood or metal) that is longer than it is wide and has any of various uses (as for a lever, support, barrier, or fastening) **b :** a solid piece or block of material that is longer than it is wide ⟨a ~ of gold⟩ ⟨a candy ~⟩ **c :** a usu. rigid piece (as of wood or metal) longer than it is wide that is used as a handle or support; *esp* : a handrail used by ballet dancers to maintain balance while exercising **2 :** something that obstructs or prevents passage, progress, or action: as **a :** the destruction of an action or claim in law; *also* : a plea or objection that effects such destruction **b :** an intangible or nonphysical impediment **c :** a submerged or partly submerged bank (as of sand) along a shore or in a river often obstructing navigation **3 a (1) :** the railing in a courtroom that encloses the place about the judge where prisoners are stationed or where the business of the court is transacted in civil cases **(2) :** COURT, TRIBUNAL **(3) :** a particular system of courts **(4) :** an authority or tribunal that hands down judgment **b (1) :** the barrier in the English Inns of Court that formerly separated the seats of the benchers or readers from the body of the hall occupied by the students **(2) :** the whole body of barristers or lawyers qualified to practice in the courts of any jurisdiction **(3) :** the profession of barrister or lawyer **4 :** a straight stripe, band, or line much longer than it is wide: as **a :** one of two or more horizontal stripes on a heraldic shield **b :** a metal or embroidered strip worn on a usu. military uniform esp. to indicate rank (as of a company officer) or service **5 a :** a counter at which food or esp. alcoholic beverages are served **b :** BARROOM **c :** SHOP 2b **6 a :** a vertical line across the musical staff before the initial measure accent **b :** MEASURE **7 :** a lace and embroidery joining covered with buttonhole stitch for connecting various parts of the pattern in needlepoint lace and cutwork **8 :** STANDARD ⟨wants to raise the ~ for approving new drugs⟩ — **behind bars :** in jail

[2]**bar** *vt* **barred; bar•ring** (13c) **1 a :** to fasten with a bar **b :** to place bars across to prevent ingress or egress ⟨~ the door⟩ **2 :** to mark with bars **:** STRIPE **3 a :** to confine or shut in by or as if by bars **b :** to set aside **:** RULE OUT ⟨did not ~ the possibility of further measures⟩ **c :** to keep out **:** EXCLUDE ⟨*barring* him from the club⟩ **4 a :** to interpose legal objection to or to the claim of **b :** PREVENT, FORBID ⟨a decision *barring* his participation⟩

[3]**bar** *prep* (1714) **:** EXCEPT ⟨the country's most popular actor, ~ none⟩

[4]**bar** *n* [G, fr. Gk *baros*] (1910) **:** a unit of pressure equal to 100,000 pascals

[5]**bar** *abbr* **1** barometer; barometric **2** barrel

Bar *abbr* Baruch

BAr *abbr* bachelor of architecture

BAR *abbr* Browning automatic rifle

bar- *or* **baro-** *comb form* [Gk *baros;* akin to Gk *barys* heavy — more at GRIEVE] **:** weight **:** pressure ⟨*baro*meter⟩

Ba·rab·bas \bə-ˈra-bəs\ *n* [Gk, fr. Aram *Bar-abba*] (bef. 12c) **:** a prisoner according to Matthew, Mark, and John released in preference to Christ at the demand of the multitude

bar·a·thea \ˌber-ə-ˈthē-ə, ˌba-rə-\ *n* [fr. *Barathea,* a trademark] (1862) **:** a fabric that has a broken rib weave and a pebbly texture and that is made of silk, worsted, or synthetic fiber or a combination of these

[1]**barb** \ˈbärb\ *n* [ME *barbe* barb, beard, fr. AF, fr. L *barba* — more at BEARD] (14c) **1 :** a medieval cloth headdress passing over or under the chin and covering the neck **2 a :** a sharp projection extending backward (as from the point of an arrow or fishhook) and preventing easy extraction; *also* **:** a sharp projection with its point similarly oblique to something else **b :** a biting or pointedly critical remark or comment **3 :** [2]BARBEL **4 :** any of the side branches of the shaft of a feather — see FEATHER illustration **5 :** a plant hair or bristle ending in a hook — **barb·less** \-ləs\ *adj*

[2]**barb** *vt* (1759) **:** to furnish with a barb

[3]**barb** *n* [F *barbe,* fr. It *barbero,* fr. *barbero* of Barbary, fr. *Barberia* Barbary, coastal region in Africa] (1636) **:** any of a northern African breed of horses that are noted for speed and endurance

[4]**barb** *n* (1967) *slang* **:** BARBITURATE

bar·bar·i·an \bär-ˈber-ē-ən\ *adj* [L *barbarus* — more at BARBAROUS] (14c) **1 :** of or relating to a land, culture, or people alien and usu. believed to be inferior to another land, culture, or people **2 :** lacking refinement, learning, or artistic or literary culture — **barbarian** *n* — **bar·bar·i·an·ism** \-ē-ə-ˌni-zəm\ *n*

bar·bar·ic \bär-ˈber-ik, -ˈba-rik\ *adj* (15c) **1 a :** of, relating to, or characteristic of barbarians **b :** possessing or characteristic of a cultural level more complex than primitive savagery but less sophisticated than advanced civilization **2 a :** marked by a lack of restraint **:** WILD **b :** having a bizarre, primitive, or unsophisticated quality **3 :** BARBAROUS 3 — **bar·bar·i·cal·ly** \-i-k(ə-)lē\ *adv*

bar·ba·rism \ˈbär-bə-ˌri-zəm\ *n* (15c) **1 a :** a barbarian or barbarous social or intellectual condition **:** BACKWARDNESS **b :** the practice or display of barbarian acts, attitudes, or ideas **2 :** an idea, act, or expression that in form or use offends against contemporary standards of good taste or acceptability

bar·bar·i·ty \bär-ˈber-ə-tē, -ˈba-rə-\ *n, pl* **-ties** (ca. 1570) **1 :** BARBARISM **2 a :** barbarous cruelty **:** INHUMANITY **b :** an act or instance of such cruelty

bar·ba·rize \ˈbär-bə-ˌrīz\ *vb* **-rized; -riz·ing** *vt* (1602) **:** to make barbarian or barbarous ~ *vi* **:** to become barbarous — **bar·ba·ri·za·tion** \ˌbär-bə-rə-ˈzā-shən\ *n*

bar·ba·rous \ˈbär-b(ə-)rəs\ *adj* [L *barbarus,* fr. Gk *barbaros* foreign, ignorant] (15c) **1 a :** UNCIVILIZED **b :** lacking culture or refinement **:** PHILISTINE **2 :** characterized by the occurrence of barbarisms ⟨~ language⟩ **3 :** mercilessly harsh or cruel ⟨~ crimes⟩ ***syn*** see FIERCE — **bar·ba·rous·ly** *adv* — **bar·ba·rous·ness** *n*

Bar·ba·ry ape \ˈbär-b(ə-)rē-\ *n* [*Barbary,* Africa] (1791) **:** a tailless monkey (*Macaca sylvanus*) of northern Africa and Gibraltar — called also *Barbary macaque*

Barbary sheep *n* (ca. 1898) **:** AOUDAD

[1]**bar·be·cue** \ˈbär-bi-ˌkyü\ *vt* **-cued; -cu·ing** [[2]*barbecue*] (1690) **1 :** to roast or broil on a rack or revolving spit over or before a source of heat (as hot coals) **2 :** to cook in a highly seasoned vinegar sauce — **bar·be·cu·er** *n*

[2]**barbecue** *also* **bar·be·que** *n* [AmerSp *barbacoa* framework for supporting meat over a fire, prob. fr. Taino] (1709) **1 a :** a large animal (as a steer) roasted whole or split over an open fire or a fire in a pit **b :** barbecued food ⟨eat ~⟩ **2 :** a social gathering esp. in the open air at which barbecued food is eaten **3 :** an often portable fireplace over which meat and fish are roasted

barbed \ˈbärbd\ *adj* (1611) **1 :** having barbs **2 :** characterized by pointed and biting criticism or sarcasm ⟨~ witticisms⟩

barbed wire \ˈbärb(d)-ˈwī(-ə)r, ˈbäb(d)-\ *n* (1866) **:** twisted wires armed with barbs or sharp points — called also *barbwire*

[1]**bar·bel** \ˈbär-bəl\ *n* [ME, fr. AF, fr. VL **barbellus,* dim. of L *barbus* barbel, fr. *barba* beard — more at BEARD] (14c) **:** a European freshwater cyprinid fish (*Barbus barbus*) with four barbels on its upper jaw; *also* **:** any of various closely related fishes

[2]**barbel** *n* [obs. F, fr. MF, dim. of *barbe* barb, beard] (1601) **:** a slender tactile process on the lips of certain fishes (as catfishes)

bar·bell \ˈbär-ˌbel\ *n* (1887) **:** a bar with adjustable weighted disks attached to each end that is used for exercise and in weight lifting

[1]**bar·ber** \ˈbär-bər\ *n* [ME, fr. AF *barbour,* fr. *barbe* beard — more at BARB] (14c) **:** one whose business is cutting and dressing hair, shaving and trimming beards, and performing related services

[2]**barber** *vb* **bar·bered; bar·ber·ing** \-b(ə-)riŋ\ *vt* (1606) **:** to perform the services of a barber for **:** trim or groom the hair or beard of ~ *vi* **:** to perform the services of a barber

bar·ber·ry \ˈbär-ˌber-ē, -ˌbe-rē\ *n* [ME *berberie,* fr. ML *berberis,* fr. Ar *barbārīs*] (14c) **:** any of a genus (*Berberis* of the family Berberidaceae, the barberry family) of shrubs usu. having spines, usu. yellow flowers, and oblong red or blackish berries

[1]**bar·ber·shop** \ˈbär-bər-ˌshäp\ *n* (1579) **:** a barber's place of business

[2]**barbershop** *adj* [fr. the old custom of men in barbershops forming quartets for impromptu singing of sentimental songs] (1910) **:** of a style of unaccompanied group singing of popular songs usu. marked by highly conventionalized close harmony

bar·bet \ˈbär-bət\ *n* [prob. fr. [1]*barb*] (1824) **:** any of various often brightly colored nonpasserine tropical birds (families Capitonidae, Lybiidae, and Megalaimidae) having a stout bill bearing bristles at the base

bar·bette \bär-ˈbet\ *n* [F, dim. of *barbe* headdress] (1772) **1 :** a mound of earth or a protected platform from which guns fire over a parapet **2 :** an armored structure protecting a gun turret on a warship

bar·bi·can \ˈbär-bi-kən\ *n* [ME, fr. AF *barbecane,* fr. ML *barbacana*] (13c) **:** an outer defensive work; *esp* **:** a tower at a gate or bridge

bar·bi·cel \ˈbär-bə-ˌsel\ *n* [NL *barbicella,* dim. of L *barba*] (1869) **:** any of the small hook-bearing processes on a barbule of a feather — see FEATHER illustration

bar·bie \ˈbär-bē\ *n* [by shortening & alter.] (1976) *chiefly Austral* **1 :** BARBECUE 2 **2 :** BARBECUE 3

bar·bi·tal \ˈbär-bə-ˌtȯl\ *n* [*barbit*uric + *-al* (as in *Veronal,* trademark for barbital)] (1919) **:** a crystalline barbiturate $C_8H_{12}N_2O_3$ used as a sedative and hypnotic often in the form of its soluble sodium salt

bar·bi·tone \ˈbär-bə-ˌtōn\ *n* [*barbit*uric + *-one*] (1914) *Brit* **:** BARBITAL

bar·bi·tu·rate \bär-ˈbi-chə-rət, -ˌrāt; ˌbär-bə-ˈtyu̇r-ət, -ˈtu̇r-, -ˌāt; ÷bär-ˈbi-chə-wət\ *n* (1928) **1 :** a salt or ester of barbituric acid **2 :** any of various derivatives of barbituric acid (as phenobarbital) that are used esp. as sedatives, hypnotics, and antispasmodics and are often addictive

bar·bi·tu·ric acid \ˌbär-bə-ˈt(y)u̇r-ik-\ *n* [part trans. of G *Barbitursäure,* irreg. fr. the name *Barbara* + ISV *uric* + G *Säure* acid] (1866) **:** a synthetic crystalline acid $C_4H_4N_2O_3$ derived from pyrimidine

Bar·bi·zon \ˌbär-bə-ˈzōn, -ˈzän\ *adj* [*Barbizon,* France] (1889) **:** of, relating to, or being a school of mid-19th century French landscape painters whose naturalistic canvases were based on direct observation of nature

bar·bule \ˈbär-(ˌ)byü(ə)l\ *n* (1835) **:** a minute barb; *esp* **:** one of the processes that fringe the barbs of a feather — see FEATHER illustration

barb·wire \ˈbärb-ˈwī(-ə)r, ˈbäb-\ *n* (1880) **:** BARBED WIRE

bar car *n* (1945) **:** CLUB CAR

bar·ca·role *or* **bar·ca·rolle** \ˈbär-kə-ˌrōl\ *n* [F *barcarolle,* fr. It dial. (Venice) *barcarola,* fr. *barcarolo* gondolier, fr. *barca* bark, fr. LL] (ca. 1779) **1 :** a Venetian boat song usu. in 6/8 or 12/8 time characterized by the alternation of a strong and weak beat that suggests a rowing rhythm **2 :** music imitating a barcarole

Bar·ce·lo·na chair \ˌbär-sə-ˈlō-nə-\ *n* [*Barcelona,* Spain] (1970) **:** an armless chair with leather-covered cushions on a stainless steel frame

bar·chan \(ˌ)bär-ˈkän, -ˈkän\ *n* [Russ *barkhan,* fr. Kazakh] (1888) **:** a moving crescent-shaped sand dune

bar chart *n* (1914) **:** BAR GRAPH

bar code *n* (1963) **:** a code consisting of a group of printed and variously patterned bars and spaces and sometimes numerals that is designed to be scanned and read into computer memory and that contains information (as identification) about the object it labels — **bar–cod·ed** \ˈbär-ˌkō-dəd\ *adj* — **bar coding** *n*

[1]**bard** \ˈbärd\ *n* [ME, fr. ScGael & Ir] (15c) **1 a :** a tribal poet-singer skilled in composing and reciting verses on heroes and their deeds **b :** a composer, singer, or declaimer of epic or heroic verse **2 :** POET — **bard·ic** \ˈbär-dik\ *adj*

[2]**bard** *or* **barde** \ˈbärd\ *n* [MF *barde,* fr. OIt *barda,* fr. Ar dial. *barḏʿa* packsaddle, saddle cover] (15c) **:** a piece of armor or ornament for a horse's neck, breast, or flank

[3]**bard** *vt* (ca. 1521) **1 :** to furnish with bards **2 :** to dress meat for cooking by covering with strips of fat

bard·ol·a·ter \bär-ˈdä-lə-tər\ *n* [*Bard* (*of Avon*), epithet of Shakespeare + *-o-* + *-later*] (1903) **:** a person who idolizes Shakespeare — **bard·ol·a·try** \-lə-trē\ *n*

Bar·do·li·no \ˌbär-də-ˈlē-(ˌ)nō\ *n, pl* **-nos** [*Bardolino,* village on Lake Garda, Italy] (1934) **:** a light red Italian wine

[1]**bare** \ˈber\ *adj* **bar·er; bar·est** [ME, fr. OE *bær;* akin to OHG *bar* naked, Lith *basas* barefoot] (bef. 12c) **1 a :** lacking a natural, usual, or appropriate covering **b** (1) **:** lacking clothing ⟨~ feet⟩ (2) *obs* **:** BAREHEADED **c :** lacking any tool or weapon ⟨opened the box with his ~ hands⟩ **2 :** open to view **:** EXPOSED ⟨laying ~ their secrets⟩ **3 a :** unfurnished or scantily supplied ⟨a ~ room⟩ **b :** DESTITUTE ⟨~ of all safeguards⟩ **4 a :** having nothing left over or added ⟨the ~ necessities of life⟩ **b :** MERE ⟨a ~ two hours away⟩ **c :** devoid of amplification or adornment ⟨the ~ facts⟩ **5** *obs* **:** WORTHLESS — **bare·ness** *n*

syn BARE, NAKED, NUDE, BALD, BARREN mean deprived of naturally or conventionally appropriate covering. BARE implies the removal of what is additional, superfluous, ornamental, or dispensable ⟨an apartment with *bare* walls⟩. NAKED suggests absence of protective or ornamental covering but may imply a state of nature, of destitution, or of defenselessness ⟨poor half-*naked* children⟩. NUDE applies esp. to the unclothed human figure ⟨a *nude* model posing for art students⟩. BALD implies actual or seeming absence of natural covering and may suggest a conspicuous bareness ⟨a *bald* mountain peak⟩. BARREN often suggests aridity or impoverishment or sterility ⟨*barren* plains⟩.

[2]**bare** *vt* **bared; bar·ing** (bef. 12c) **:** to make or lay bare **:** UNCOVER

[3]**bare** *archaic past of* BEAR

bare·back \-ˌbak\ *or* **bare·backed** \-ˈbakt\ *adv or adj* (1562) **:** on the bare back of a horse **:** without a saddle ⟨likes riding ~⟩ ⟨~ riding⟩

bare·boat \-ˌbōt\ *n* (ca. 1949) **:** a boat chartered without its crew

bare bones *n pl* (1647) **:** the barest essentials, facts, or elements ⟨the *bare bones* of her life⟩ — **bare–bones** *adj*

bare·faced \ˈber-ˈfāst\ *adj* (1590) **1 :** having the face uncovered: **a :** having no whiskers **:** BEARDLESS **b :** wearing no mask **2 a :** OPEN, UNCONCEALED ⟨~ impudence⟩ **b :** having or showing a lack of scruples ⟨a ~ lie⟩ — **bare·faced·ly** \-ˈfā-səd-lē, -ˈfāst-lē\ *adv* — **bare·faced·ness** \-ˈfā-səd-nəs, -ˈfās(t)-nəs\ *n*

bare·foot \-ˌfu̇t\ *or* **bare·foot·ed** \-ˈfu̇-təd\ *adv or adj* (bef. 12c) **:** with the feet bare ⟨walked ~⟩ ⟨~ boy, with cheek of tan —J. G. Whittier⟩

bare·hand \ˈber-ˌhand\ *vt* (1973) **:** to catch or retrieve (a baseball) with a bare hand

bare–hand·ed \ˈber-ˈhan-dəd\ *adv or adj* (15c) **1 :** without gloves **2 :** without tools or weapons ⟨fight an animal ~⟩

bare·head·ed \-ˈhe-dəd\ *adv or adj* (14c) **:** without a covering for the head ⟨went ~ in the hot sun⟩ ⟨a ~ boy who had lost his cap⟩

bare–knuck·le \-ˈnə-kəl\ *also* **bare–knuck·led** \-kəld\ *or* **bare–knuck·les** \-kəlz\ *adj or adv* (1903) **1 :** not using boxing gloves ⟨champion ~ prizefighter of England —Dennis Craig⟩ ⟨when men fought ~⟩ **2 :** having a fierce unrelenting character ⟨~ politics⟩

bare·ly *adv* (bef. 12c) **1 :** in a meager manner **:** PLAINLY ⟨a ~ furnished room⟩ **2 :** SCARCELY, HARDLY ⟨~ enough money for lunch⟩

barf \ˈbärf\ *vi* [origin unknown] (1956) **:** VOMIT

bar·fly \ˈbär-ˌflī\ *n* (1910) **:** a person who spends much time in bars

[1]**bar·gain** \ˈbär-gən\ *n, often attrib* [ME, fr. AF, fr. *bargaigner*] (14c) **1 :** an agreement between parties settling what each gives or receives in a transaction between them or what course of action or policy each pursues in respect to the other **2 :** something acquired by or as if by bargaining; *esp* **:** an advantageous purchase ⟨at that price the car is a ~⟩ **3 :** a transaction, situation, or event regarded in the light of its results ⟨a bad ~⟩ — **into the bargain** *also* **in the bargain :** BESIDES ⟨tastes good and is good for you, *into the bargain*⟩

[2]**bargain** *vb* [ME, fr. AF *bargaigner*, prob. of Gmc origin; akin to OE *borgian* to borrow — more at BURY] *vi* (14c) **1 :** to negotiate over the terms of a purchase, agreement, or contract : HAGGLE **2 :** to come to terms : AGREE ~ *vt* **1 :** to bring to a desired level by bargaining ⟨~ a price down⟩ **2 :** to sell or dispose of by bargaining — **bar·gain·er** *n* — **bargain for :** EXPECT ⟨more work than I *bargained for*⟩

bar·gain–base·ment \ˈbär-gən-ˈbās-mənt\ *adj* (1948) **1 :** of inferior quality or worth **2 :** markedly inexpensive ⟨~ rates⟩

bargain basement *n* (1899) **:** a section of a store (as the basement) where merchandise is sold at reduced prices

[1]**barge** \ˈbärj\ *n* [ME, fr. AF, fr. LL *barca*] (14c) **:** any of various boats: as **a :** a roomy usu. flat-bottomed boat used chiefly for the transport of goods on inland waterways and usu. propelled by towing **b :** a large motorboat supplied to the flag officer of a flagship **c :** a roomy pleasure boat; *esp* **:** a boat of state elegantly furnished and decorated

[2]**barge** *vb* **barged; barg·ing** *vt* (1649) **:** to carry by barge ~ *vi* **1 :** to move ponderously or clumsily **2 :** to thrust oneself heedlessly or unceremoniously ⟨*barged* into the meeting⟩

barge·board \ˈbärj-ˌbȯrd\ *n* [origin unknown] (1827) **:** an often ornamented board that conceals roof timbers projecting over gables

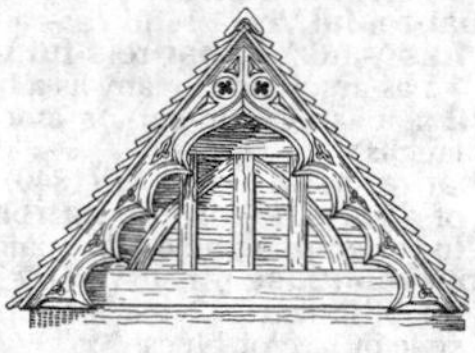

bargeboard

barg·ee \bär-ˈjē\ *n* (1666) *Brit* **:** BARGEMAN

bar·gel·lo \bär-ˈje-(ˌ)lō\ *n* [*Bargello*, museum in Florence, Italy; fr. the use of this stitch in the upholstery of 17th cent. chairs at the Bargello] (ca. 1924) **:** a needlework stitch that produces a zigzag pattern

barge·man \ˈbärj-mən\ *n* (14c) **:** the master or a deckhand of a barge

bar graph *n* (1924) **:** a graphic means of quantitative comparison by rectangles with lengths proportional to the measure of the data or things being compared — called also *bar chart*

bar·hop \ˈbär-ˌhäp\ *vi* (1947) **:** to visit and drink at a series of bars in the course of an evening

bar·iat·ric \ˌber-ē-ˈa-trik, ˌba-rē-\ *adj* [*bar-* + *-iatric*] (1977) **:** relating to or specializing in the treatment of obesity

ba·ris·ta \bə-ˈrēs-tə, bä-ˈrēs-tä\ *n* [It, person working behind a bar, fr. *bar* bar (fr. E) + *-ista* [1]-ist] (1982) **:** a person who makes and serves coffee (as espresso) to the public

bar·ite \ˈber-ˌīt\ *n* [Gk *barytēs* weight, fr. *barys*] (1837) **:** barium sulfate occurring as a mineral

[1]**bari·tone** *also* **bary·tone** \ˈber-ə-ˌtōn, ˈba-rə-\ *n* [F *baryton* or It *baritono*, fr. Gk *barytonos* deep sounding, fr. *barys* heavy + *tonos* tone — more at GRIEVE] (1609) **1 :** a male singing voice of medium compass between bass and tenor; *also* **:** a person having this voice **2 :** a member of a family of instruments having a range between tenor and bass; *esp* **:** the baritone saxhorn or baritone saxophone — **bari·ton·al** \ˌbar-ə-ˈtō-nᵊl\ *adj*

[2]**baritone** *also* **barytone** *adj* (1729) **:** relating to or having the range or part of a baritone

bar·i·um \ˈber-ē-əm\ *n* [NL, fr. *bar-*] (1808) **1 :** a silver-white malleable toxic divalent metallic element of the alkaline-earth group that occurs only in combination — see ELEMENT table **2 :** BARIUM SULFATE

barium sulfate *n* (1866) **:** a crystalline insoluble compound $BaSO_4$ that is used esp. as a pigment and extender, as a filler (as in fluids used in gas and oil drilling), and as a substance opaque to X rays in medical photography of the alimentary canal

[1]**bark** \ˈbärk\ *vb* [ME *berken*, fr. OE *beorcan*; akin to ON *berkja* to bark, Lith *burgėti* to growl] *vi* (bef. 12c) **1 a :** to make the characteristic short loud cry of a dog **b :** to make a noise resembling a bark **2 :** to speak in a curt loud and usu. angry tone : SNAP ~ *vt* **1 :** to utter in a curt loud usu. angry tone ⟨an officer ~*ing* orders⟩ **2 :** to advertise by persistent outcry ⟨~*ing* their wares⟩ — **bark up the wrong tree :** to promote or follow a mistaken course (as in doing research)

[2]**bark** *n* (bef. 12c) **1 a :** the sound made by a barking dog **b :** a similar sound **2 :** a short sharp peremptory tone of speech or utterance — **bark·less** \ˈbärk-ləs\ *adj*

[3]**bark** *n* [ME, fr. ON *bark-*, *bǫrkr*; akin to MD & MLG *borke* bark] (14c) **1 :** the tough exterior covering of a woody root or stem; *specif* **:** the tissues outside the cambium that include an inner layer esp. of secondary phloem and an outer layer of periderm **2 :** CINCHONA 2 **3 :** a candy containing chocolate and nuts that is made in a sheet and broken into pieces — **bark·less** \ˈbärk-ləs\ *adj*

[4]**bark** *vt* (14c) **1 :** to treat with an infusion of tanbark **2 a :** to strip the bark from **b :** to rub off or abrade the skin of ⟨~*ed* a shin on the desk⟩

[5]**bark** *or* **barque** *n* [ME, fr. MF *barque*, fr. Old Occitan *barca*, fr. LL] (15c) **1 a :** a small sailing ship **b :** a sailing ship of three or more masts with the aftmost mast fore-and-aft rigged and the others square-rigged **2 :** a craft propelled by sails or oars

bark beetle *n* (1862) **:** any of numerous beetles (family Scolytidae) that bore under the bark of trees both as a larva and as an adult

bar·keep \ˈbär-ˌkēp\ *also* **bar·keep·er** \-ˌkē-pər\ *n* (1671) **:** BARTENDER

bar·ken·tine *or* **bar·quen·tine** \ˈbär-kən-ˌtēn\ *n* [[5]*bark* + *-entine*, alter. of *-antine* (as in *brigantine*)] (1693) **:** a sailing ship of three or more masts with the foremast square-rigged and the others fore-and-aft rigged

[1]**bark·er** \ˈbär-kər\ *n* (14c) **:** one that barks; *esp* **:** a person who advertises by hawking at an entrance to a show

[2]**barker** *n* (1611) **:** one that removes or prepares bark

barking deer *n* (1880) **:** MUNTJAC

barky \ˈbär-kē\ *adj* **bark·i·er; -est** (1590) **:** covered with or resembling bark

bar·ley \ˈbär-lē\ *n* [ME *barly*, fr. OE *bærlic* of barley; akin to OE *bere* barley, L *far* spelt] (bef. 12c) **:** a cereal grass (genus *Hordeum* and esp. *H. vulgare*) having the flowers in dense spikes with long awns and three spikelets at each joint of the rachis; *also* **:** its seed used esp. in malt beverages, breakfast foods, and stock feeds

bar·ley–bree \-ˌbrē\ *also* **bar·ley–broo** \-ˌbrü\ *n* [*barley* + Sc *bree* or *broo* (bree)] (1724) *chiefly Scot* **:** WHISKY; *also* **:** MALT LIQUOR

bar·ley·corn \-ˌkȯrn\ *n* (1500) **1 :** a grain of barley **2 :** an old unit of length equal to a third of an inch

bar·low \ˈbär-ˌlō\ *n* [*Barlow*, family of 18th cent. Eng. knife makers] (1884) **:** a sturdy inexpensive jackknife

barm \ˈbärm\ *n* [ME *berme*, fr. OE *beorma*; akin to MLG *berm* yeast, L *fermentum* yeast, *fervēre* to boil, OIr *berbaid* he boils] (bef. 12c) **:** yeast formed on fermenting malt liquors

bar·maid \ˈbär-ˌmād\ *n* (ca. 1658) **:** a woman who serves liquor at a bar

bar·man \-mən\ *n* (1837) *chiefly Brit* **:** BARTENDER

Bar·me·cid·al \ˌbär-mə-ˈsī-dᵊl\ *or* **Bar·me·cide** \ˈbär-mə-ˌsīd\ *adj* [*Barmecide*, a wealthy Persian, who, in a tale of *The Arabian Nights' Entertainments*, invited a beggar to a feast of imaginary food] (1842) **:** providing only the illusion of abundance ⟨a ~ feast⟩

[1]**bar mitz·vah** \bär-ˈmits-və\ *n, often cap B&M* [Heb *bar miṣwāh*, lit., son of the (divine) law] (1816) **1 :** a Jewish boy who reaches his 13th birthday and attains the age of religious duty and responsibility **2 :** the initiatory ceremony recognizing a boy as a bar mitzvah

[2]**bar mitzvah** *vt* **bar mitz·vahed; bar mitz·vah·ing** (1947) **:** to administer the ceremony of bar mitzvah to

[1]**barmy** \ˈbär-mē\ *adj* **barm·i·er; -est** (15c) **:** full of froth or ferment

[2]**barmy** *adj* **barm·i·er; -est** [alter. of *balmy*] (1892) *chiefly Brit* **:** BALMY 2

barn \ˈbärn\ *n* [ME *bern*, fr. OE *bereærn*, fr. *bere* barley + *ærn* house, store] (bef. 12c) **1 a :** a usu. large building for the storage of farm products or feed and usu. for the housing of farm animals or farm equipment **b :** an unusually large and usu. bare building ⟨a great ~ of a hotel —W. A. White⟩ **2 :** a large building for the housing of a fleet of vehicles (as trolley cars or trucks) — **barn·like** \-ˌlīk\ *adj* — **barny** \ˈbär-nē\ *adj*

Bar·na·bas \ˈbär-nə-bəs\ *n* [Gk, fr. Aram *Barnebhūʾāh*] (14c) **:** a companion of the apostle Paul on his first missionary journey

bar·na·cle \ˈbär-ni-kəl\ *n* [ME *barnakille*, alter. of *bernake*, *bernekke*] (15c) **1 :** BARNACLE GOOSE **2** [fr. a popular belief that the goose grew from the crustacean] **:** any of numerous marine crustaceans (subclass Cirripedia) with feathery appendages for gathering food that are free-swimming as larvae but permanently fixed (as to rocks, boat hulls, or whales) as adults — **bar·na·cled** \-kəld\ *adj*

barnacle goose *n* (1768) **:** a European goose (*Branta leucopsis*) that has a whitish face and black breast and breeds in the arctic

barn burner *n* (ca. 1960) **:** one that arouses much interest or excitement ⟨the game should be a real *barn burner*⟩

barn dance *n* (1831) **:** an American social dance orig. held in a barn and featuring several dance forms (as square dancing)

barn lot *n* (1724) *chiefly Southern & Midland* **:** BARNYARD

barn owl *n* (1674) **:** a widely distributed owl (*Tyto alba*) that has plumage mottled buff brown and gray above and chiefly white below, frequents barns and other buildings, and preys esp. on rodents

barn raising *n* (1856) **:** a gathering for the purpose of erecting a barn — compare [3]BEE

barn·storm \ˈbärn-ˌstȯrm\ *vi* (1883) **1 :** to tour through rural districts staging usu. theatrical performances **2 :** to travel from place to place making brief stops (as in a political campaign or a promotional tour) **3 :** to pilot one's airplane in sight-seeing flights with passengers or in exhibition stunts in an unscheduled course esp. in rural districts ~ *vt* **:** to travel across while barnstorming — **barn·storm·er** *n*

barn swallow *n* (1851) **:** a swallow (*Hirundo rustica* of the family Hirundinidae) that is widespread in the northern hemisphere, has a deeply forked tail, and often nests in or near buildings

[1]**barn·yard** \-ˌyärd\ *n* (14c) **:** a usu. fenced area adjoining a barn

[2]**barnyard** *adj* (1927) **:** SMUTTY, EARTHY, SCATOLOGICAL ⟨~ humor⟩

barnyard grass *n* (1843) **:** a coarse annual panicled grass (*Echinochloa crusgalli*) that has flowers borne on only one side of the raceme and is nearly cosmopolitan as a weed in cultivated ground

baro- — see BAR-

baro·gram \ˈber-ə-ˌgram, ˈba-rə-\ *n* [ISV] (1875) **:** a barographic tracing

baro·graph \-ˌgraf\ *n* [ISV] (ca. 1864) **:** a recording barometer — **baro·graph·ic** \ˌber-ə-ˈgra-fik, ˌba-rə-\ *adj*

Ba·ro·lo \bä-ˈrō-(ˌ)lō, bə-\ *n, pl* **-los** [*Barolo*, village in the Piedmont region, Italy] (1875) **:** a dry red Italian wine

ba·rom·e·ter \bə-ˈrä-mə-tər\ *n* (ca. 1666) **1 :** an instrument for determining the pressure of the atmosphere and hence for assisting in forecasting weather and for determining altitude **2 :** something that indicates fluctuations (as in public opinion) ⟨housing sales and other economic ~*s*⟩ **3 :** STANDARD, TEST ⟨a ~ to measure high school talent —Jeff Fellenzer⟩ — **baro·met·ric** \ˌber-ə-ˈme-trik, ˌba-rə-\ *adj* — **baro·met·ri·cal·ly** \-tri-k(ə-)lē\ *adv* — **ba·rom·e·try** \bə-ˈrä-mə-trē\ *n*

barometric pressure *n* (1807) **:** the pressure of the atmosphere usu. expressed in terms of the height of a column of mercury

bar·on \ˈber-ən, ˈba-rən\ *n* [ME, fr. AF, of Gmc origin; akin to OHG *baro* freeman] (13c) **1 a :** one of a class of tenants holding his rights and title by military or other honorable service directly from a feudal superior (as a king) **b :** a lord of the realm : NOBLE, PEER **2 a :** a member of the lowest grade of the peerage in Great Britain **b :** a nobleman on the continent of Europe of varying rank **c :** a member of the lowest order of nobility in Japan **3 :** a joint of meat consisting of two sirloins or loins and legs not cut apart at the backbone ⟨a ~ of beef⟩ **4 :** a man who possesses great power or influence in some field of activity ⟨a cattle ~⟩

bar·on·age \-ə-nij\ *n* (13c) **:** the whole body of barons or peers : NOBILITY 2

bar·on·ess \ˈber-ə-nəs, ˈba-rə-, -ˌnes, *US also* ˌber-ə-ˈnes, ˌba-rə-\ *n* (15c) **1 :** the wife or widow of a baron **2 :** a woman who holds a baronial title in her own right

bar·on·et \ˈber-ə-nət, ˈba-rə-, *US also* ˌber-ə-ˈnet, ˌba-rə-\ *n* (1614) **:** the holder of a rank of honor below a baron and above a knight

bar·on·et·age \ˈber-ə-nə-(ˌ)tij, ˌba-rə-; ˌber-ə-ˈne-tij, ˌba-rə-\ *n* (1760) **1 :** BARONETCY **2 :** the whole body of baronets

---

\ə\ **a**but \ᵊ\ kitten, F table \ər\ f**ur**ther \a\ **a**sh \ā\ **a**ce \ä\ m**o**p, m**ar** \au̇\ **ou**t \ch\ **ch**in \e\ b**e**t \ē\ **ea**sy \g\ **g**o \i\ h**i**t \ī\ **i**ce \j\ **j**ob \ŋ\ si**ng** \ō\ g**o** \ȯ\ l**aw** \ȯi\ b**oy** \th\ **th**in \t͟h\ **th**e \ü\ l**oo**t \u̇\ f**oo**t \y\ **y**et \zh\ vi**si**on, bei**ge** \k, ⁿ, œ, ue, ʸ\ *see* Guide to Pronunciation

bar·on·et·cy \ˈber-ə-nət-sē, ˈba-rə-; ˌber-ə-ˈnet-sē, ˌba-rə-\ *n* (1795) : the rank of a baronet

ba·rong \bə-ˈrȯŋ, -ˈräŋ\ *n* [prob. fr. Maranao (Austronesian language of southern Mindanao)] (1898) : a thick-backed thin-edged knife or sword used by the Moros

ba·ro·ni·al \bə-ˈrō-nē-əl\ *adj* (1767) **1** : of or relating to a baron or the baronage **2** : STATELY, AMPLE ⟨a ~ room⟩

bar·ony \ˈber-ə-nē, ˈba-rə-\ *n, pl* **-on·ies** (14c) **1** : the domain, rank, or dignity of a baron **2** : a vast private landholding **3** : a field of activity under the sway of an individual or a special group

[1]**ba·roque** \bə-ˈrōk, ba-, -ˈräk, -ˈrȯk\ *adj, often cap* [F, fr. MF *barroque* irregularly shaped (of a pearl), fr. Pg *barroco* irregularly shaped pearl] (1765) **1** : of, relating to, or having the characteristics of a style of artistic expression prevalent esp. in the 17th century that is marked generally by use of complex forms, bold ornamentation, and the juxtaposition of contrasting elements often conveying a sense of drama, movement, and tension **2** : characterized by grotesqueness, extravagance, complexity, or flamboyance **3** : irregularly shaped — used of gems ⟨a ~ pearl⟩ — **ba·roque·ly** *adv*

[2]**baroque** *n, often cap* (1877) : the baroque style or the period in which it flourished

baro·re·cep·tor \ˌber-ō-ri-ˈsep-tər, ˌba-rə-\ *also* **baro·cep·tor** \ˈber-ō-ˌsep-tər, ˈba-rō-\ *n* (1948) : a sensory nerve ending esp. in the walls of large arteries (as the carotid sinus) that is sensitive to changes in blood pressure

baro·trau·ma \-ˈtrau̇-mə, -ˈtrȯ-\ *n* (1937) : injury of a body part or organ as a result of changes in barometric pressure

ba·rouche \bə-ˈrüsh\ *n* [G *Barutsche,* fr. It *biroccio,* ultim. fr. LL *birotus* two-wheeled, fr. L *bi-* + *rota* wheel — more at ROLL] (1801) : a four-wheeled carriage with a driver's seat high in front, two double seats inside facing each other, and a folding top over the back seat

barque, barquentine *var of* BARK, BARKENTINE

bar·quette \bär-ˈket\ *n* [F, dim. of *barque* bark (ship)] (ca. 1949) : a small boat-shaped pastry shell

[1]**bar·rack** \ˈber-ək, -ik; ˈba-rək, -rik\ *n* [F *baraque* hut, fr. Catal *barraca*] (1686) **1** : a building or set of buildings used esp. for lodging soldiers in garrison **2 a** : a structure resembling a shed or barn that provides temporary housing **b** : housing characterized by extreme plainness or dreary uniformity — usu. used in pl. in all senses

[2]**barrack** *vt* (1701) : to lodge in barracks

[3]**barrack** *vb* [perh. fr. dial. (northern Ireland) *barrack* to brag] *vt* (1887) *chiefly Brit* : to shout at derisively or sarcastically ~ *vi* **1** *chiefly Austral* : ROOT, CHEER — usu. used with *for* **2** *chiefly Brit* : JEER, SCOFF — **bar·rack·er** *n*

barracks bag *n* (1938) : a fabric bag for carrying personal equipment; *esp* : DUFFEL BAG

bar·ra·coon \ˌber-ə-ˈkün, ˌba-rə-\ *n* [Sp *barracón,* aug. of *barraca* hut, fr. Catal] (1848) : an enclosure or barracks formerly used for temporary confinement of slaves or convicts — often used in pl.

bar·ra·cou·ta \ˌber-ə-ˈkü-tə, ˌba-rə-\ *n* [modif. of AmerSp *barracuda*] (1770) : a large elongate marine bony fish (*Thyrsites atun* of the family Gempylidae) used for food and caught commercially in the waters off New Zealand and southern Australia

bar·ra·cu·da \ˌber-ə-ˈkü-də, ˌba-rə-\ *n, pl* **-da** *or* **-das** [AmerSp] (1678) **1** : any of a genus (*Sphyraena* of the family Sphyraenidae) of elongate predaceous often large bony fishes of warm seas that includes food and sport fishes as well as some forms frequently causing ciguatera poisoning **2** : one that uses aggressive, selfish, and sometimes unethical methods to obtain a goal esp. in business

[1]**bar·rage** \ˈbär-ij\ *n* [F, fr. *barrer* to bar, fr. *barre* bar] (1845) : a dam placed in a watercourse to increase the depth of water or to divert it into a channel for navigation or irrigation

[2]**bar·rage** \bə-ˈräzh, -ˈräj\ *n* [F (*tir de*) *barrage* barrier fire] (1916) **1** : artillery fire laid on a line close to friendly troops to screen and protect them **2** : a vigorous or rapid outpouring or projection of many things at once ⟨a ~ of protests⟩

[3]**bar·rage** \bə-ˈräzh, -ˈräj\ *vt* **bar·raged; bar·rag·ing** (1918) : to deliver a barrage against

barrage balloon *n* (ca. 1920) : a small captive balloon used to support wires or nets as protection against air attacks

bar·ra·mun·di \ˌber-ə-ˈmən-dē, ˌba-rə-\ *n, pl* **-di** *also* **-dis** [prob. fr. an Australian aboriginal language of Queensland] (1864) : a catadromous bony fish (*Lates calcarifer* of the family Centropomidae) with a greenish-bronze back and silvery sides that is found from the Persian Gulf to southern China and Australia and is valued as a sport and food fish

bar·ran·ca \bə-ˈraŋ-kə\ *also* **bar·ran·co** \-(ˌ)kō\ *n, pl* **-cas** *also* **-cos** [Sp] (1648) **1** : a deep gully or arroyo with steep sides **2** : a steep bank or bluff

bar·ra·tor *also* **bar·ra·ter** \ˈber-ə-tər, ˈba-rə-\ *n* (15c) : one who engages in barratry

bar·ra·try \ˈber-ə-trē, ˈba-rə-\ *n, pl* **-tries** [ME (Sc) *barratrie,* fr. AF **baraterie,* lit., deception, fr. OF *barater* to be active, do business, cause strife, deceive, perh. fr. VL **prattare,* fr. Gk *prattein, prassein* to do — more at PRACTICAL] (15c) **1** : the purchase or sale of office or preferment in church or state **2** : an unlawful act or fraudulent breach of duty by a master of a ship or by the mariners to the injury of the owner of the ship or cargo **3** : the persistent incitement of litigation

Barr body \ˈbär-\ *n* [Murray Llewellyn *Barr* †1995 Canad. anatomist] (1961) : a densely staining inactivated condensed X chromosome that is present in each somatic cell of most female mammals and is used as a test of genetic femaleness (as in a fetus) — called also *sex chromatin*

barre \ˈbär\ *n* [F, fr. ML *barra*] (1936) : BAR 1c

barred \ˈbärd\ *adj* (14c) : marked by or divided off by bars; *esp* : having alternate bands of different color ⟨a ~ feather⟩

barred owl *n* (1811) : a large No. American owl (*Strix varia*) with brown eyes and bars of dark brown on the breast

[1]**bar·rel** \ˈber-əl, ˈba-rəl\ *n* [ME *barel,* fr. AF *baril*] (14c) **1** : a round bulging vessel of greater length than breadth that is usu. made of staves bound with hoops and has flat ends of equal diameter **2 a** : the amount contained in a barrel; *esp* : the amount (as 31 gallons of fermented beverage or 42 gallons of petroleum) fixed for a certain commodity used as a unit of measure **b** : a great quantity **3** : a drum or cylindrical part: as **a** : the discharging tube of a gun **b** : the part of a fountain pen or of a pencil containing the ink or lead **c** : a cylindrical or tapering housing containing the optical components of a photographic-lens system and the iris diaphragm **d** : the fuel outlet from the carburetor on a gasoline engine **4** : the trunk of a quadruped — **bar·reled** \-əld\ *adj* — **on the barrel** : asking for or granting no credit — **over a barrel** : at a disadvantage : in an awkward position

[2]**barrel** *vb* **-reled** *or* **-relled; -rel·ing** *or* **-rel·ling** *vt* (15c) : to put or pack in a barrel ~ *vi* : to move at a high speed or without hesitation

bar·rel·age \ˈber-ə-lij, ˈba-rə-\ *n* (1890) : amount (as of beer) in barrels

barrel cactus *n* (1881) : any of a genus (*Ferocactus*) of nearly globular deeply ribbed spiny cacti of Mexico and the adjacent U.S.; *also* : any of several similar cacti (genus *Echinocactus*)

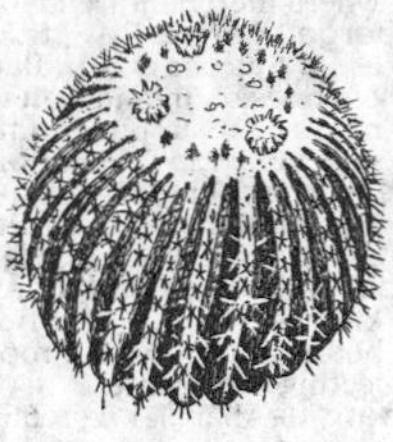
barrel cactus

bar·rel–chest·ed \ˈber-əl-ˌches-təd, ˈba-rəl-\ *adj* (1926) : having a large rounded chest ⟨a ~ athlete⟩

barrel cuff *n* (1926) : an unfolded cuff (as on a shirt) usu. fastened by a button

bar·rel·ful \ˈber-əl-ˌfu̇l, ˈba-rəl-\ *n, pl* **barrel·fuls** \-ˌfu̇lz\ *or* **bar·rels·ful** \-əlz-ˌfu̇l\ (14c) **1** : as much or as many as a barrel will hold **2** : a large number or amount ⟨a ~ of laughs⟩

bar·rel·head \-ˌhed\ *n* (1840) : the flat end of a barrel — **on the barrelhead** : asking for or granting no credit ⟨paid cash *on the barrelhead*⟩

bar·rel·house \-ˌhau̇s\ *n* (1883) **1** : a cheap drinking and usu. dancing establishment **2** : a strident, uninhibited, and forcefully rhythmic style of jazz or blues

barrel organ *n* (1772) : an instrument for producing music by the action of a revolving cylinder studded with pegs on a series of valves that admit air from a bellows to a set of pipes

barrel racing *n* (1941) : a rodeo event for women in which a mounted rider makes a series of sharp turns around three barrels in a cloverleaf pattern — **barrel race** *n* — **barrel racer** *n*

barrel roll *n* (1917) : an airplane maneuver in which a complete revolution about the longitudinal axis is made

barrel vault *n* (1842) : a semicylindrical vault — **bar·rel–vault·ed** \-ˌvȯl-təd\ *adj*

[1]**bar·ren** \ˈber-ən, ˈba-rən\ *adj* [ME *bareine,* fr. AF *barain,* perh. of Celt origin; akin to MW *brynar* fallow land] (13c) **1** : not reproducing: as **a** : incapable of producing offspring — used esp. of females or matings **b** : not yet or not recently pregnant **c** : habitually failing to fruit **2** : not productive: as **a** : producing little or no vegetation : DESOLATE ⟨~ deserts⟩ **b** : producing inferior crops ⟨~ soil⟩ **c** : unproductive of results or gain : FRUITLESS ⟨a ~ scheme⟩ **3** : DEVOID, LACKING — used with *of* ⟨~ of excitement⟩ **4** : lacking interest or charm ⟨a ~ routine⟩ **5** : lacking inspiration or ideas ⟨a ~ mind⟩ ***syn*** see BARE — **bar·ren·ly** *adv* — **bar·ren·ness** \-ə(n)-nəs\ *n*

[2]**barren** *n* (1651) **1** *pl* : an extent of usu. level land having an inferior growth of trees or little vegetation **2** : a tract of barren land

bar·rette \bä-ˈret, bə-\ *n* [F, dim. of *barre* bar] (1901) : a clip or bar for holding hair in place

[1]**bar·ri·cade** \ˈber-ə-ˌkād, ˈba-rə-, ˌber-ə-ˈ, ˌba-rə-ˈ\ *vt* **-cad·ed; -cad·ing** [[2]*barricade*] (1592) **1** : to block off or stop up with a barricade ⟨~ a street⟩ **2** : to prevent access to by means of a barricade

[2]**barricade** *n* [F, fr. MF, fr. *barriquer* to barricade, fr. *barrique* barrel] (1642) **1a** : an obstruction or rampart thrown up across a way or passage to check the advance of the enemy **b** : BARRIER 1a **2** : BARRIER 3, OBSTACLE **3** *pl* : a field of combat or dispute

bar·ri·ca·do \ˌber-ə-ˈkā-(ˌ)dō, ˌba-rə-\ *n, pl* **-does** [modif. of MF *barricade*] (1590) *archaic* : BARRICADE — **barricado** *vt, archaic*

bar·ri·er \ˈber-ē-ər, ˈba-rē-\ *n* [ME *barrere,* fr. AF, fr. *barre* bar] (14c) **1 a** : something material that blocks or is intended to block passage ⟨highway ~s⟩ ⟨a ~ contraceptive⟩ **b** : a natural formation or structure that prevents or hinders movement or action ⟨geographic ~s to species dissemination⟩ ⟨~ beaches⟩ ⟨drugs that cross the placental ~⟩ **2** *pl, often cap* : a medieval war game in which combatants fight on foot with a fence or railing between them **3** : something immaterial that impedes or separates : OBSTACLE ⟨behavioral ~s⟩ ⟨trade ~s⟩

barrier island *n* (1943) : a long broad sandy island lying parallel to a shore that is built up by the action of waves, currents, and winds and that protects the shore from the effects of the ocean

barrier reef *n* (1805) : a coral reef roughly parallel to a shore and separated from it usu. by a lagoon

bar·ring \ˈbär-iŋ\ *prep* (15c) : excluding by exception : EXCEPTING

bar·rio \ˈbär-ē-ˌō, ˈber-, ˈba-rē-\ *n, pl* **-ri·os** [Sp, fr. Ar *barrī* of the open country, fr. *barr* outside, open country] (1833) **1** : a ward, quarter, or district of a city or town in a Spanish-speaking country **2** : a Spanish-speaking quarter or neighborhood in a city or town in the U.S. esp. in the Southwest

bar·ris·ter \ˈber-ə-stər, ˈba-rə-\ *n* [ME *barrester,* fr. *barre* bar + *-ster* (as in *legister* lawyer)] (15c) : a counsel admitted to plead at the bar and undertake the public trial of causes in an English superior court — compare SOLICITOR

bar·room \ˈbär-ˌrüm, -ˌru̇m\ *n* (1797) : a room or establishment whose main feature is a bar for the sale of liquor

[1]**bar·row** \ˈber-(ˌ)ō, ˈba-(ˌ)rō\ *n* [ME *bergh,* fr. OE *beorg;* akin to OHG *berg* mountain, Skt *bṛhant* high] (bef. 12c) **1** : MOUNTAIN, MOUND — used only in the names of hills in England **2** : a large mound of earth or stones over the remains of the dead : TUMULUS

[2]**barrow** *n* [ME *barow,* fr. OE *bearg;* akin to OHG *barug* barrow] (bef. 12c) : a male hog castrated before sexual maturity

[3]**barrow** *n* [ME *barew,* fr. OE *bearwe;* akin to OE *beran* to carry — more at BEAR] (bef. 12c) **1 a** : HANDBARROW **b** : WHEELBARROW **2** : a cart with a shallow box body, two wheels, and shafts for pushing it

barrow boy *n* (1939) *Brit* : COSTERMONGER

bar sinister *n* (1823) **1** : a heraldic charge held to be a mark of bastardy **2** : the fact or condition of being of illegitimate birth

Bart *abbr* baronet

bar·tend·er \ˈbär-ˌten-dər\ *n* (1836) : a person who serves drinks at a bar — **bar·tend** \ˈbär-ˌtend\ *vi*

[1]**bar·ter** \ˈbär-tər\ *vb* [ME *bartren,* fr. AF **bareter* to do business, ex-

change, alter. of OF *barater* — more at BARRATRY] *vi* (15c) **:** to trade by exchanging one commodity for another ~ *vt* **:** to trade or exchange by or as if by bartering — **bar·ter·er** \ˈtər-ər\ *n*
[2]**barter** *n* (15c) **1 :** the act or practice of carrying on trade by bartering **2 :** the thing given in exchange in bartering
Bar·tho·lin's gland \ˈbär-thə-lənz-, ˈbär-tᵊl-ənz-\ *n* [Kaspar *Bartholin* †1738 Dan. physician] (1901) **:** either of two oval racemose glands lying one to each side of the lower part of the vagina and secreting a lubricating mucus — compare COWPER'S GLAND
bar·ti·zan \ˈbär-tə-zən, ˌbär-tə-ˈzan\ *n* [alter. of ME *bretasinge,* fr. *bretais* parapet — more at BRATTICE] (1801) **:** a small structure (as a turret) projecting from a building and serving esp. for lookout or defense
Bart·lett \ˈbärt-lət\ *n* [Enoch *Bartlett* †1860 Am. orchardist] (1847) **:** a pear that has yellowish-green or sometimes red skin and whitish flesh and is the principal commercially produced pear in the U.S.
Ba·ruch \bə-ˈrük, ˈbär-ˌük, ˈber-\ *n* [LL, fr. Gk *Barouch,* fr. Heb *Bārūkh*] **:** a homiletic book included in the Roman Catholic canon of the Old Testament and in the Protestant Apocrypha — see BIBLE table
bar·ware \ˈbär-ˌwer\ *n* (1941) **:** glassware or utensils used in preparing and serving alcoholic beverages
bary·on \ˈber-ē-ˌän, ˈba-rē-\ *n* [ISV *bary-* (fr. Gk *barys* heavy) + [2]*-on* — more at GRIEVE] (1953) **:** any of a group of subatomic particles (as nucleons) that are subject to the strong force and are composed of three quarks — **bary·on·ic** \ˌber-ē-ˈä-nik, ˌba-rē-\ *adj*
ba·ry·tes \bə-ˈrī-tēz\ *also* **bar·yte** \ˈber-ˌīt\ *chiefly Brit var of* BARITE
barytone *var of* BARITONE
BAS *abbr* **1** bachelor of applied science **2** bachelor of arts and sciences
bas·al \ˈbā-səl, -zəl\ *adj* (1645) **1 a :** relating to, situated at, or forming the base **b :** arising from the base of a stem ⟨~ leaves⟩ **2 a :** of or relating to the foundation, base, or essence **:** FUNDAMENTAL **b :** of, relating to, or being essential for maintaining the fundamental vital activities of an organism **:** MINIMAL ⟨a ~ diet⟩ **c :** used for teaching beginners ⟨~ readers⟩ — **ba·sal·ly** *adv*
basal body *n* (1902) **:** a minute distinctively staining cell organelle found at the base of a flagellum or cilium and identical to a centriole in structure — called also *basal granule, kinetosome*
basal cell *n* (ca. 1903) **:** one of the innermost cells of the deeper epidermis of the skin
basal ganglion *n* (ca. 1889) **:** any of four deeply placed masses of gray matter (as the amygdala) in each cerebral hemisphere — called also *basal nucleus*
basal metabolic rate *n* (1922) **:** the rate at which heat is given off by an organism at complete rest
basal metabolism *n* (1913) **:** the turnover of energy in a fasting and resting organism using energy solely to maintain vital cellular activity, respiration, and circulation as measured by the basal metabolic rate
ba·salt \bə-ˈsȯlt, ˈbā-ˌ\ *n* [L *basaltes,* MS var. of *basanites* touchstone, fr. Gk *basanitēs* (*lithos*), fr. *basanos* touchstone, fr. Egypt *bḫnw*] (1601) **:** a dark gray to black dense to fine-grained igneous rock that consists of basic plagioclase, augite, and usu. magnetite — **ba·sal·tic** \bə-ˈsȯl-tik\ *adj*
bas·cule \ˈbas-(ˌ)kyül\ *n* [F, seesaw] (1678) **:** an apparatus or structure (as a drawbridge) in which one end is counterbalanced by the other on the principle of the seesaw or by weights
[1]**base** \ˈbās\ *n, pl* **bas·es** \ˈbā-səz\ [ME, fr. AF, fr. L *basis,* fr. Gk, step, base, fr. *bainein* to go — more at COME] (13c) **1 a** (1) **:** the lower part of a wall, pier, or column considered as a separate architectural feature (2) **:** the lower part of a complete architectural design **b :** the bottom of something considered as its support **:** FOUNDATION **c** (1) **:** a side or face of a geometrical figure from which an altitude can be constructed; *esp* **:** one on which the figure stands (2) **:** the length of a base **d :** that part of a bodily organ by which it is attached to another more central structure of the organism **2 a :** a main ingredient ⟨paint having a latex ~⟩ **b :** a supporting or carrying ingredient (as of a medicine) **3 a :** the fundamental part of something **:** GROUNDWORK, BASIS **b :** the economic factors on which in Marxist theory all legal, social, and political relations are formed **4 :** the lower part of a heraldic field **5 a :** the starting point or line for an action or undertaking **b :** a baseline in surveying **c :** a center or area of operations: as (1) **:** the place from which a military force draws supplies (2) **:** a place where military operations begin (3) **:** a permanent military installation **d** (1) **:** a number (as 5 in $5^{6.44}$ or 5^7) that is raised to a power; *esp* **:** the number that when raised to a power equal to the logarithm of a number yields the number itself ⟨the logarithm of 100 to the ~ 10 is 2 since $10^2 = 100$⟩ (2) **:** a number equal to the number of units in a given digit's place that for a given system of writing numbers is required to give the numeral 1 in the next higher place ⟨the decimal system uses a ~ of 10⟩; *also* **:** such a system of writing numbers using an indicated base ⟨convert from ~ 10 to ~ 2⟩ (3) **:** a number that is multiplied by a rate or of which a percentage or fraction is calculated ⟨to find the interest on $90 at 10 percent multiply the ~ 90 by .10⟩ **e :** ROOT 6 **6 a :** the starting place or goal in various games **b :** any one of the four stations at the corners of a baseball infield **c :** a point to be considered ⟨his opening remarks touched every ~⟩ **7 a :** any of various typically water-soluble and bitter tasting compounds that in solution have a pH greater than 7, are capable of reacting with an acid to form a salt, and are molecules or ions able to take up a proton from an acid or able to give up an unshared pair of electrons to an acid **b :** any of the five purine or pyrimidine bases of DNA and RNA that include cytosine, guanine, adenine, thymine, and uracil **8 :** a price level at which a security previously declining in price resists further decline **9 :** the part of a transformational grammar that consists of rules and a lexicon and generates the deep structures of a language — **based** \ˈbāst\ *adj* — **base·less** \ˈbā-sləs\ *adj* — **off base 1 :** WRONG, MISTAKEN ⟨estimates were way *off base*⟩ **2 :** UNAWARES ⟨caught *off base* by the charges⟩
[2]**base** *vt* **based; bas·ing** (1587) **1 :** to make, form, or serve as a base for **2 :** to find a base or basis for — usu. used with *on* or *upon*
[3]**base** *adj* [ME *bas,* fr. AF, fr. LL *bassus* fat, short, low] (14c) **1** *archaic* **:** of little height **2** *obs* **:** low in place or position **3** *obs* **:** BASS **4** *archaic* **:** BASEBORN **5 a :** resembling a villein **:** SERVILE ⟨a ~ tenant⟩ **b :** held by villenage ⟨~ tenure⟩ **6 a :** being of comparatively low value and having relatively inferior properties (as lack of resistance to corrosion) ⟨a ~ metal such as iron⟩ — compare NOBLE **b :** containing a larger than usual proportion of base metals ⟨~ silver denarii⟩ **7 a :** lacking or indicating the lack of higher qualities of mind or spirit **:** IGNOBLE **b :** lacking higher values **:** DEGRADING ⟨a drab ~ way of life⟩ — **base·ly** *adv* — **base·ness** *n*
syn BASE, LOW, VILE mean deserving of contempt because of the absence of higher values. BASE stresses the ignoble and may suggest cruelty, treachery, greed, or grossness ⟨*base* motives⟩. LOW may connote crafty cunning, vulgarity, or immorality and regularly implies an outraging of one's sense of decency or propriety ⟨refused to listen to such *low* talk⟩. VILE, the strongest of these words, tends to suggest disgusting depravity or filth ⟨a *vile* remark⟩.
base angle *n* (ca. 1949) **:** either of the angles of a triangle that have one side in common with the base
base·ball \ˈbās-ˌbȯl\ *n, often attrib* (ca. 1815) **:** a game played with a bat and ball between two teams of nine players each on a large field having four bases that mark the course a runner must take to score; *also* **:** the ball used in this game
baseball cap *n* (1944) **:** a cap of the kind worn by baseball players that has a rounded crown and a long visor
base·board \-ˌbȯrd\ *n* (1847) **:** a board situated at or forming the base of something; *specif* **:** a molding covering the joint of a wall and the adjoining floor
base·born \-ˈbȯrn\ *adj* (1591) **1 :** MEAN, IGNOBLE **2 a :** of humble birth **b :** of illegitimate birth
base exchange *n* (ca. 1956) **:** a post exchange at a naval or air force base
base hit *n* (1874) **:** a hit in baseball that enables the batter to reach base safely without benefit of an error or fielder's choice
BASE jumping \ˈbās-\ *n* [*b*uilding, *a*ntenna, *s*pan, *e*arth] (1982) **:** the activity or sport of parachuting from a high structure (as a building, tower, or bridge) or cliff — **BASE jumper** *n*
base·line \ˈbās-ˌlīn\ *n, often attrib* (1610) **1 :** a line serving as a basis; *esp* **:** one of known measure or position used (as in surveying or navigation) to calculate or locate something **2 a :** either of the lines on a baseball field that lead from home plate to first base and third base and are extended into the outfield as foul lines **b :** BASE PATH **3 :** a boundary line at either end of a court (as in tennis or basketball) **4 :** a usu. initial set of critical observations or data used for comparison or a control **5 :** a starting point ⟨the ~ of this discussion⟩
base·lin·er \ˈbās-ˌlī-nər\ *n* (ca. 1929) **:** a tennis player who stays on or near the baseline and seldom moves to the net
base·ment \ˈbās-mənt\ *n* [prob. fr. [1]*base*] (1613) **1 :** the part of a building that is wholly or partly below ground level **2 :** the ground floor facade or interior in Renaissance architecture **3 :** the lowest or fundamental part of something; *specif* **:** the rocks underlying stratified rocks **4** *chiefly NewEng* **:** a toilet or washroom esp. in a school — **base·ment·less** \-ləs\ *adj*
basement membrane *n* (1847) **:** a thin membranous layer of connective tissue that separates a layer of epithelial cells from the underlying lamina propia
ba·sen·ji \bə-ˈsen-jē, -ˈzen-\ *n* [prob. modif. of Lingala *mbwa na basenji,* lit., dogs of the bushland people] (1937) **:** any of a breed of small curly-tailed dogs of African origin that do not bark
base on balls (1884) **:** an advance to first base awarded a baseball player who during a turn at bat takes four pitches that are balls
base–pair *vi* (1973) **:** to participate in formation of a base pair ⟨adenine ~*s* with thymine⟩
base pair *n* (1956) **:** one of the pairs of nucleotide bases on complementary strands of nucleic acid that consist of a purine on one strand joined to a pyrimidine on the other strand by hydrogen bonds holding together the two strands much like the rungs of a ladder and that include adenine linked to thymine in DNA or to uracil in RNA and guanine linked to cytosine in both DNA and RNA
base path *n* (1935) **:** the area between the bases of a baseball field used by a base runner
base pay *n* (1920) **:** a rate or amount of pay for a standard work period, job, or position exclusive of additional payments or allowances
base·plate \ˈbās-ˌplāt\ *n* (1876) **:** a plate that serves as a base or support
base runner *n* (1867) **:** a baseball player of the team at bat who is on base or is attempting to reach a base — **base·run·ning** *n*
bases *pl of* BASE *or of* BASIS
[1]**bash** \ˈbash\ *vb* [origin unknown] *vt* (1750) **1 :** to strike violently **:** HIT; *also* **:** to injure or damage by striking **:** SMASH — often used with *in* **2 :** to attack physically or verbally ⟨media ~*ing*⟩ ⟨celebrity ~*ing*⟩ ~ *vi* **:** CRASH — **bash·er** *n*
[2]**bash** *n* (1805) **1 :** a forceful blow **2 :** a festive social gathering **:** PARTY **3** *chiefly Brit* **:** TRY, ATTEMPT ⟨have a ~ at it⟩
bashaw *var of* PASHA
bash·ful \ˈbash-fəl\ *adj* [obs. *bash* (to be abashed)] (1548) **1 :** socially shy or timid **:** DIFFIDENT, SELF-CONSCIOUS **2 :** resulting from or typical of a bashful nature ⟨a ~ smile⟩ ***syn*** see SHY — **bash·ful·ly** \-fə-lē\ *adv* — **bash·ful·ness** \-fəl-nəs\ *n*
[1]**ba·sic** \ˈbā-sik *also* -zik\ *adj* (1842) **1 a :** of, relating to, or forming the base or essence **:** FUNDAMENTAL ⟨~ truths⟩ **b :** concerned with fundamental scientific principles **:** not applied ⟨~ research⟩ **2 :** constituting or serving as the basis or starting point ⟨a ~ set of tools⟩ **3 a :** of, relating to, containing, or having the character of a chemical base **b :** having an alkaline reaction **4 :** containing relatively little silica ⟨~ rocks⟩ **5 :** relating to, made by, used in, or being a process of making steel done in a furnace lined with basic material and under basic slag — **ba·sic·i·ty** \bā-ˈsi-sə-tē\ *n*
[2]**basic** *n* (1926) **1 :** something that is basic **:** FUNDAMENTAL ⟨get back to ~*s*⟩ **2 :** BASIC TRAINING
BA·SIC \ˈbā-sik\ *n* [*B*eginner's *A*ll-purpose *S*ymbolic *I*nstruction *C*ode] (1964) **:** a simplified high-level language for programming a computer
ba·si·cal·ly \ˈbā-si-k(ə-)lē *also* -zi-\ *adv* (1903) **1 a :** at a basic level **:** in

fundamental disposition or nature ⟨~ correct⟩ ⟨~, they are simple people⟩ **b :** for the most part ⟨they ~ play zone defense⟩ **2 :** in a basic manner : SIMPLY ⟨live ~⟩

basic slag *n* (1869) **:** a slag low in silica and high in base-forming oxides that is used in the basic process of steelmaking and that is subsequently useful as a fertilizer

basic training *n* (1943) **:** the initial period of training of a military recruit

ba·sid·io·my·cete \bə-ˌsi-dē-ō-ˈmī-ˌsēt, -ˌmī-ˈsēt\ *n* [ultim. fr. NL *basidium* + Gk *mykēt-, mykēs* fungus; akin to Gk *myxa* mucus — more at MUCUS] (1899) **:** any of a group of higher fungi that have septate hyphae and spores borne on a basidium, that include rusts, smuts, mushrooms, and puffballs, and that are variously considered to comprise a class (Basidiomycetes), a subdivision (Basidiomycotina), or a division (Basidiomycota) — **ba·sid·io·my·ce·tous** \-dē-ō-ˌmī-ˈsē-təs\ *adj*

ba·sid·io·spore \bə-ˈsi-dē-ə-ˌspȯr\ *n* [NL *basidium* + E *-o-* + *spore*] (1859) **:** a spore produced by a basidium

ba·sid·i·um \bə-ˈsi-dē-əm\ *n, pl* **-ia** \-dē-ə\ [NL, fr. L *basis*] (1859) **:** a structure on a basidiomycete in which karyogamy occurs followed by meiosis to form usu. four basidiospores

ba·si·fy \ˈbā-sə-ˌfī\ *vt* **-fied; -fy·ing** (ca. 1847) **:** to convert into a base or make alkaline — **ba·si·fi·ca·tion** \ˌbā-sə-fə-ˈkā-shən\ *n*

ba·sil \ˈba-zəl, ˈbā-, -səl\ *n* [MF *basile,* fr. LL *basilicum,* fr. Gk *basilikon,* fr. neut. of *basilikos*] (15c) **1 :** any of several aromatic herbs (genus *Ocimum*) of the mint family; *esp* **:** SWEET BASIL **2 :** the dried or fresh leaves of a basil used esp. as a seasoning

bas·i·lar \ˈba-zə-lər, -sə- *also* ˈbā-\ *adj* [MF *basilaire,* irreg. fr. *base* base] (1541) **:** of, relating to, or situated at the base

basilar membrane *n* (1867) **:** a membrane extending from the bony shelf of the cochlea to the outer wall and supporting the organ of Corti

Ba·sil·i·an \bə-ˈzi-lē-ən\ *n* (1780) **:** a member of the monastic order founded by St. Basil in the fourth century in Cappadocia — **Basilian** *adj*

ba·sil·i·ca \bə-ˈsi-li-kə *also* -ˈzi-\ *n* [L, fr. Gk *basilikē,* fr. fem. of *basilikos* royal, fr. *basileus* king] (1541) **1 :** an oblong building ending in a semicircular apse used in ancient Rome esp. for a court of justice and place of public assembly **2 :** an early Christian church building consisting of nave and aisles with clerestory and a large high transept from which an apse projects **3 :** a Roman Catholic church given ceremonial privileges — **ba·sil·i·can** \-kən\ *adj*

[1]**bas·i·lisk** \ˈba-sə-ˌlisk, ˈba-zə-\ *n* [ME, fr. L *basiliscus,* fr. Gk *basiliskos,* fr. dim. of *basileus*] (14c) **1 :** a legendary reptile with fatal breath and glance **2 :** any of several crested tropical American lizards (genus *Basiliscus* of the family Iguanidae) related to the iguanas and noted for their ability to run on their hind legs

[2]**basilisk** *adj* (1821) **:** suggesting a basilisk **:** BALEFUL, SPELLBINDING ⟨the eyes . . . with all their blaze of ~ horror —Bram Stoker⟩

ba·sin \ˈbā-sᵊn\ *n* [ME, fr. AF *bacin,* fr. LL *bacchinon*] (13c) **1 a :** an open usu. circular vessel with sloping or curving sides used typically for holding water for washing **b** *chiefly Brit* **:** a bowl used esp. in cooking **c :** the quantity contained in a basin **2 a :** a dock built in a tidal river or harbor **b :** an enclosed or partly enclosed water area **3 a :** a large or small depression in the surface of the land or in the ocean floor **b :** the entire tract of country drained by a river and its tributaries **c :** a great depression in the surface of the lithosphere occupied by an ocean **4 :** a broad area of the earth beneath which the strata dip usu. from the sides toward the center — **ba·sin·al** \-sᵊn-əl\ *adj* — **ba·sined** \-sᵊnd\ *adj* — **ba·sin·ful** \-ˌfu̇l\ *n*

bas·i·net \ˌba-sə-ˈnet\ *n* [ME *bacinet,* fr. AF, dim. of *bacin*] (14c) **:** a light typically pointed steel helmet often having a visor

ba·sip·e·tal \bā-ˈsi-pə-tᵊl, -ˈzi-\ *adj* [L *basis* + *petere* to go toward — more at FEATHER] (1869) **:** proceeding from the apex toward the base or from above downward ⟨~ maturation of an inflorescence⟩ — **ba·sip·e·tal·ly** \-tᵊl-ē\ *adv*

ba·sis \ˈbā-səs\ *n, pl* **ba·ses** \-ˌsēz\ [L — more at BASE] (14c) **1 :** the bottom of something considered as its foundation **2 :** the principal component of something **3 a :** something on which something else is established or based **b :** an underlying condition or state of affairs ⟨hired on a trial ~⟩ ⟨on a first-name ~⟩ **4 :** the basic principle **5 :** a set of linearly independent vectors in a vector space such that any vector in the vector space can be expressed as a linear combination of them with appropriately chosen coefficients

basis point *n* (1967) **:** one hundredth of one percent (as in the yield of an investment)

bask \ˈbask\ *vb* [ME, prob. fr. ON *bathask,* refl. of *batha* to bathe; akin to OE *bæth* bath] *vi* (14c) **1 :** to lie or relax in a pleasant warmth or atmosphere **2 :** to take pleasure or derive enjoyment ⟨~*ed* in the spotlight⟩ ~ *vt, obs* **:** to warm by continued exposure to heat

bas·ket \ˈbas-kit, *Brit also* ˈbäs-\ *n* [ME, fr. AF; akin to OF *baschoue* wooden vessel; both fr. L *bascauda* kind of basin, of Celt origin; akin to MIr *basc* necklace — more at FASCIA] (14c) **1 a :** a receptacle made of interwoven material (as osiers) **b :** any of various lightweight usu. wood containers **c :** the quantity contained in a basket **2 :** something that resembles a basket esp. in shape or use **3 a :** a net open at the bottom and suspended from a metal ring that constitutes the goal in basketball **b :** a field goal in basketball **4 a :** an aggregate of values (as of selected currencies) the average of which serves as a monetary standard **b :** a selection of financial instruments (as equities, futures, or options) the values of which reflect market fluctuations **5 :** a ring around the lower end of a ski pole that keeps the pole from sinking too deep in snow — **bas·ket·like** \-ˌlīk\ *adj*

bas·ket·ball \-ˌbȯl\ *n, often attrib* (1892) **:** a usu. indoor court game between two teams of usu. five players each who score by tossing an inflated ball through a raised goal; *also* **:** the ball used in this game

bas·ket·bal·ler \-ˌbȯ-lər\ *n* (1928) **:** a basketball player

basket case *n* (1919) **1 :** a person who has all four limbs amputated **2 :** a person who is mentally incapacitated or worn out (as from nervous tension); *also* **:** one that is not functioning well or is in a run-down condition ⟨an economic *basket case*⟩

basket catch *n* (1964) **:** a catch of a fly ball made with the glove held palm up at waist level

bas·ket·ful \ˈbas-kit-ˌfu̇l\ *n, pl* **bas·ket·fuls** \-ˌfu̇lz\ *also* **bas·kets·ful** \-kits-ˌfu̇l\ (14c) **:** as much or as many as a basket will hold; *also* **:** a considerable quantity

basket hilt *n* (ca. 1550) **:** a hilt with a basket-shaped guard to protect the hand — **bas·ket–hilt·ed** \ˌbas-kit-ˈhil-təd\ *adj*

Basket Maker *n* (1897) **:** any of three stages of an ancient culture of the plateau area of southwestern U.S.; *also* **:** a member of the people who produced the Basket Maker culture

basket–of–gold *n* (ca. 1889) **:** a European perennial herb (*Aurinia saxatilis* syn. *Alyssum saxatile*) of the mustard family widely cultivated for its grayish foliage and yellow flowers

bas·ket·ry \ˈbas-ki-trē\ *n, pl* **-ries** (1851) **1 :** BASKETWORK **2 :** the art or craft of making baskets or objects woven like baskets

basket star *n* (ca. 1902) **:** any of various brittle stars with slender complexly branched interlacing arms

basket weave *n* (1897) **:** a textile weave resembling the checkered pattern of a plaited basket; *also* **:** something resembling this weave

bas·ket·work \ˈbas-kit-ˌwərk\ *n* (1665) **:** objects produced by basketry

bask·ing shark \ˈbas-kiŋ-\ *n* (ca. 1769) **:** a large plankton-feeding shark (*Cetorhinus maximus*) that has an oil-rich liver and may attain a length of up to 45 feet (13.7 meters)

bas·ma·ti rice \ˌbäz-ˈmä-tē-, ˌbäs- *also* ˌbaz-, ˌbas-\ *n* [Hindi *bāsmatī* kind of rice, lit., something fragrant] (1845) **:** a cultivated aromatic long-grain rice originating in southern Asia — called also *basmati*

bas mitzvah *often cap B&M, var of* BAT MITZVAH

ba·so·phil \ˈbā-sə-ˌfil, -zə-\ *also* **ba·so·phile** \-ˌfī(-ə)l\ *n* (ca. 1890) **:** a basophilic substance or structure; *esp* **:** a white blood cell containing basophilic granules that is similar in function to a mast cell

ba·so·phil·ia \ˌbā-sə-ˈfi-lē-ə, -zə-\ *n* [NL] (1905) **1 :** tendency to stain with basic dyes **2 :** an abnormal condition in which some tissue element has increased basophilia

ba·so·phil·ic \-ˈfi-lik\ *adj* [ISV *base* + *-o-* + *-philic*] (ca. 1894) **:** staining readily with basic stains

Ba·so·tho \bä-ˈsō-ˌtō, -ˈsü-ˌtü\ *n, pl* **Basotho** *also* **Basothos** [Sotho, pl. of *Mosotho* Basotho person, fr. *mo-,* class prefix + *-sotho,* perh. alter. of *motho* human being] (1895) **:** a Bantu-speaking people of Lesotho; *also* **:** a member of this people

Basque \ˈbask, ˈbäsk\ *n* [F, fr. MF, ultim. fr. L *Vasco* member of a group of ancient peoples inhabiting the present Basque country] (1667) **1 :** a member of a people inhabiting the western Pyrenees on the Bay of Biscay **2 :** the language of the Basques of unknown relationship **3** *not cap* **:** a tight-fitting bodice for women — **Basque** *adj*

bas–re·lief \ˌbä-ri-ˈlēf, ˌbas-, bäs-; ˈbä-ri-ˌ, ˈbas-, ˈbäs-\ *n* [F, fr. *bas* low + *relief* raised work] (1667) **:** sculptural relief in which the projection from the surrounding surface is slight and no part of the modeled form is undercut; *also* **:** sculpture executed in bas-relief

[1]**bass** \ˈbas\ *n, pl* **bass** *or* **bass·es** [ME *base, bærs,* fr. OE *bærs;* akin to OHG *bersich* perch] (bef. 12c) **:** any of numerous edible marine or freshwater bony fishes (esp. families Centrarchidae, Serranidae, and Percichthyidae of the order Perciformes)

[2]**bass** \ˈbās\ *adj* [ME *bas* base — more at BASE] (15c) **1 :** deep or grave in tone **2 a :** of low pitch **b :** relating to or having the range or part of a bass

[3]**bass** \ˈbās\ *n* (15c) **1 a :** the lowest voice part in a 4-part chorus **b :** the lower half of the whole vocal or instrumental tonal range — compare TREBLE **c :** the lowest adult male singing voice; *also* **:** a person having this voice **d :** a member of a family of instruments having the lowest range; *esp* **:** DOUBLE BASS **2 :** a deep or grave tone **:** a low-pitched sound

[4]**bass** \ˈbas\ *n* [alter. of *bast*] (1691) **1 :** BASSWOOD 1 **2 :** a coarse tough fiber from palms

bass clef *n* (ca. 1771) **1 :** a clef placing the F below middle C on the fourth line of the staff **2 :** the bass staff

bass drum *n* (1804) **:** a large drum having two heads and giving a booming sound of low indefinite pitch — see DRUM illustration

bas·set hound \ˈba-sət-\ *n* [F *basset,* fr. MF, fr. *basset* short, fr. *bas* low — more at BASE] (1883) **:** any of an old breed of short-legged hunting dogs of French origin having very long ears and a short smooth coat — called also *basset*

bass fiddle *n* (1836) **:** DOUBLE BASS

bass horn *n* (ca. 1825) **:** an obsolete wind instrument shaped like a bassoon but with a cup-shaped mouthpiece

bas·si·net \ˌba-sə-ˈnet, ˈba-sə-ˌ\ *n* [prob. modif. of F *barcelonnette,* dim. of *berceau* cradle] (1854) **:** a baby's basketlike bed (as of wickerwork or plastic) often with a hood over one end

bass·ist \ˈbā-sist\ *n* (ca. 1909) **:** a person who plays an acoustic or electric bass

bas·so \ˈba-(ˌ)sō, ˈbä-\ *n, pl* **bassos** *or* **bas·si** \ˈbä-ˌsē\ [It, fr. ML *bassus,* fr. *bassus* short, low] (ca. 1724) **1 :** a bass singer; *esp* **:** an operatic bass **2 :** a low deep voice

bas·soon \bə-ˈsün, ba-\ *n* [F *basson,* fr. It *bassone,* fr. *basso*] (1724) **:** a double-reed woodwind instrument having a long U-shaped conical tube connected to the mouthpiece by a thin metal tube and a usual range two octaves lower than that of the oboe — **bas·soon·ist** \-ˈsü-nist\ *n*

bas·so pro·fun·do \ˌba-(ˌ)sō-prə-ˈfən-(ˌ)dō, ˌbä-, -ˈfu̇n-\ *n, pl* **basso profundos** [It, lit., deep bass] (1853) **:** a deep heavy bass voice with an exceptionally low range; *also* **:** a person having this voice

bas·so–re·lie·vo *also* **bas·so–ri·lie·vo** \ˌba-(ˌ)sō-ri-ˈlē-(ˌ)vō, ˌbä-(ˌ)sō-rēl-ˈyā-(ˌ)vō\ *n* [It *bassorilievo,* fr. *basso* low + *rilievo* relief] (ca. 1639) **:** BAS-RELIEF

bass viol *n* (1590) **1 :** VIOLA DA GAMBA **2 :** DOUBLE BASS

bass·wood \ˈbas-ˌwu̇d\ *n* (1670) **1 :** any of several New World lindens; *esp* **:** LINDEN 1b **2 :** the straight-grained soft white wood of a basswood

bast \ˈbast\ *n* [ME, fr. OE *bæst;* akin to OHG & ON *bast* bast] (bef. 12c) **1 :** PHLOEM **2 :** BAST FIBER

[1]**bas·tard** \ˈbas-tərd\ *n* [ME, fr. AF, prob. of Gmc origin; akin to OFris *bost* marriage, OE *bindan* to bind] (14c) **1 :** an illegitimate child **2 :** something that is spurious, irregular, inferior, or of questionable origin **3 a :** an offensive or disagreeable person — used as a generalized term of abuse **b :** MAN, FELLOW — **bas·tard·ly** *adj*

[2]**bastard** *adj* (14c) **1 :** ILLEGITIMATE **2 :** of mixed or ill-conceived origin ⟨known for coining ~ words⟩ **3 :** of abnormal shape or irregular size **4 :** of a kind similar to but inferior to or less typical than some standard **5 :** lacking genuineness or authority **:** FALSE

bas·tard·ise *Brit var of* BASTARDIZE

bas·tard·ize \ˈbas-tər-ˌdīz\ *vt* **-ized; -iz·ing** (1587) **1 :** to reduce from a higher to a lower state or condition : DEBASE **2 :** to declare or prove to be a bastard **3 :** to modify esp. by introducing discordant or disparate elements — **bas·tard·i·za·tion** \ˌbas-tər-də-ˈzā-shən\ *n*

bastard wing *n* (1772) : ALULA

bas·tardy \ˈbas-tər-dē\ *n, pl* **-tard·ies** (15c) **1 :** the quality or state of being a bastard **2 :** the begetting of an illegitimate child

[1]**baste** \ˈbāst\ *vt* **bast·ed; bast·ing** [ME, fr. MF *bastir,* of Gmc origin; akin to OHG *besten* to patch, OE *bæst* bast] (15c) : to sew with long loose stitches in order to hold something in place temporarily — **bast·er** *n*

[2]**baste** *vt* **bast·ed; bast·ing** [ME *baisten*] (15c) : to moisten (as meat) at intervals with a liquid (as melted butter, fat, or pan drippings) esp. during cooking — **bast·er** *n*

[3]**baste** *vt* **bast·ed; bast·ing** [prob. fr. ON *beysta;* akin to OE *bēatan* to beat] (1533) **1 :** to beat severely or soundly : THRASH **2 :** to scold vigorously : BERATE

bast fiber *n* (1852) : a strong woody fiber obtained chiefly from the phloem of plants and used esp. in cordage, matting, and fabrics

bas·tille \ba-ˈstēl\ *n* [F *bastille,* fr. the *Bastille,* fortress in Paris, fr. MF *bastille,* modif. of Old Occitan *bastida* fortified town, fr. *bastir* to build, of Gmc origin; akin to OHG *besten* to patch] (1741) : PRISON, JAIL

Bastille Day *n* (1837) : July 14 observed in France as a national holiday in commemoration of the fall of the Bastille in 1789

[1]**bas·ti·na·do** \ˌbas-tə-ˈnā-(ˌ)dō, -ˈnä-\ *or* **bas·ti·nade** \ˌbas-tə-ˈnād, -ˈnäd\ *n, pl* **-na·does** *or* **-nades** [Sp *bastonada,* fr. *bastón* stick, fr. LL *bastum*] (1572) **1 :** a blow with a stick or cudgel **2 a :** a beating esp. with a stick **b :** a punishment consisting of beating the soles of the feet with a stick **3 :** STICK, CUDGEL

[2]**bastinado** *vt* **-doed; -do·ing** (1599) : to subject to repeated blows

[1]**basting** *n* (15c) **1 :** the action of a sewer who bastes **2 a :** the thread used in basting **b :** the stitching made by basting

[2]**basting** *n* (1530) **1 :** the action of one that bastes food **2 :** the liquid used in basting

[3]**basting** *n* (ca. 1616) : a severe beating

bas·tion \ˈbas-chən\ *n* [MF, fr. OIt *bastione,* aug. of *bastia* fortress, derivative fr. dial. form of *bastire* to build, of Gmc origin; akin to OHG *besten* to patch] (1562) **1 :** a projecting part of a fortification **2 :** a fortified area or position **3 :** STRONGHOLD 2 ⟨the last ~ of academic standards —*Amer. Scientist*⟩ — **bas·tioned** \-chənd\ *adj*

Ba·su·to \bə-ˈsü-(ˌ)tō\ *n, pl* **Basuto** *or* **Basutos** (1834) : BASOTHO

[1]**bat** \ˈbat\ *n* [ME, fr. OE *batt*] (bef. 12c) **1 :** a stout solid stick : CLUB **2 :** a sharp blow : STROKE **3 a :** a usu. wooden implement used for hitting the ball in various games **b :** a paddle used in various games (as table tennis) **c :** the short whip used by a jockey **4 a :** BATSMAN, BATTER ⟨a right-handed ~⟩ **b :** a turn at batting — usu. used in the phrase *at bat* **c :** hitting ability ⟨we need his ~ in the lineup⟩ **5 :** BATT **6** *Brit* : rate of speed : GAIT **7 :** BINGE — **off one's own bat** *chiefly Brit* : through one's own efforts — **off the bat** : without delay : IMMEDIATELY ⟨recognized him right *off the bat*⟩

[2]**bat** *vb* **bat·ted; bat·ting** *vt* (13c) **1 :** to strike or hit with or as if with a bat **2 a :** to advance (a base runner) by batting **b :** to have a batting average of **3 :** to discuss at length : consider in detail ~ *vi* **1 a :** to strike or hit a ball with a bat **b :** to take one's turn at bat **2 :** to wander aimlessly

[3]**bat** *n* [prob. alter. of ME *bakke,* of Scand origin; akin to OSw natt*bakka* bat] (1580) : any of a widely distributed order (Chiroptera) of nocturnal usu. frugivorous or insectivorous flying mammals that have wings formed from four elongated digits of the forelimb covered by a cutaneous membrane and that have adequate visual capabilities but often rely on echolocation

[4]**bat** *vt* **bat·ted; bat·ting** [prob. alter. of [2]*bate*] (ca. 1787) : to wink esp. in surprise or emotion ⟨never *batted* an eye⟩; *also* : FLUTTER ⟨*batted* his eyelashes⟩

BAT *abbr* bachelor of arts in teaching

bat·boy \ˈbat-ˌbȯi\ *n* (1897) : a boy employed to look after the equipment (as bats) of a baseball team

[1]**batch** \ˈbach\ *n* [ME *bache;* akin to OE *bacan* to bake] (15c) **1 :** the quantity baked at one time : BAKING **2 a :** the quantity of material prepared or required for one operation; *specif* : a mixture of raw materials ready for fusion into glass **b :** the quantity produced at one operation **c :** a group of jobs (as programs) that are submitted for processing on a computer and whose results are obtained at a later time ⟨~ processing⟩ — compare TIME-SHARING **3 :** a quantity (as of persons or things) considered as a group

[2]**batch** *vt* (1863) : to bring together or process as a batch — **batch·er** *n*

[3]**batch** *var of* BACH

[1]**bate** \ˈbāt\ *vb* **bat·ed; bat·ing** [ME, short for *abaten* to abate] *vt* (14c) **1 :** to reduce the force or intensity of : RESTRAIN ⟨with *bated* breath⟩ **2 :** to take away : DEDUCT **3** *archaic* : to lower esp. in amount or estimation **4** *archaic* : BLUNT ~ *vi, obs* : DIMINISH, DECREASE

[2]**bate** *vi* **bat·ed; bat·ing** [ME, fr. MF *batre* to beat, fr. L *battuere*] (14c) *of a falcon or hawk* : to attempt to fly off something (as a gauntlet) in fear

bat–eared fox \ˈbat-ˌird-\ *n* (1930) : a large-eared yellowish-gray fox (*Otocyon megalotis*) that inhabits arid unforested areas of eastern and southern Africa

ba·teau *also* **bat·teau** \ba-ˈtō\ *n, pl* **ba·teaux** *also* **bat·teaux** [CanF, fr. F, fr. OF *batel,* fr. OE *bāt* boat — more at BOAT] (1711) : any of various small craft; *esp* : a flat-bottomed boat with raked bow and stern and flaring sides

Bates·ian \ˈbāt-sē-ən\ *adj* [Henry Walter *Bates* †1892 Eng. naturalist] (1895) : characterized by or being mimicry involving resemblance of an innocuous species to another that is protected from predators by repellent qualities (as unpalatability) ⟨a ~ mimic⟩

bat·fish \ˈbat-ˌfish\ *n* (1808) : any of several fishes with winglike processes; *esp* : any of a family (Ogcocephalidae of the order Lophiiformes) of flattened pediculate bony fishes

bat·fowl \-ˌfau̇(-ə)l\ *vi* (15c) : to catch birds at night by blinding them with a light and knocking them down with a stick or netting them

bat girl *n* (1937) : a girl or woman employed to look after the equipment (as bats) of a baseball team

[1]**bath** \ˈbath, ˈbäth\ *n, pl* **baths** \ˈbat͟hz, ˈbaths, ˈbät͟hz, ˈbäths\ [ME, fr. OE *bæth;* akin to OHG *bad* bath, OHG *bāen* to warm] (bef. 12c) **1 :** a washing or soaking (as in water or steam) of all or part of the body **2 a :** water used for bathing **b (1) :** a contained liquid for a special purpose **(2) :** a receptacle holding the liquid **c (1) :** a medium for regulating the temperature of something placed in or on it **(2) :** a vessel containing this medium **3 a :** BATHROOM **b :** a building containing an apartment or a series of rooms designed for bathing **c :** SPA 1 — usu. used in pl. **d** *Brit* : SWIMMING POOL — often used in pl. **4 a :** the quality or state of being covered with a liquid **b :** FLOOD 3 **5 :** BATHTUB **6 :** a financial setback : LOSS ⟨took a ~ in the market⟩

[2]**bath** *vt* (15c) *Brit* : to give a bath to ~ *vi, Brit* : to take a bath

[3]**bath** *n* [Heb] (14c) : an ancient Hebrew liquid measure corresponding to the ephah of dry measure

bath chair \ˈbath-, ˈbäth-\ *n* [*Bath,* England] (1765) : a hooded and sometimes glassed wheeled chair used esp. by invalids; *broadly* : WHEELCHAIR

[1]**bathe** \ˈbāt͟h\ *vb* **bathed; bath·ing** [ME, fr. OE *bathian;* akin to OE *bæth* bath] *vt* (bef. 12c) **1 :** MOISTEN, WET **2 :** to wash in a liquid (as water) **3 :** to apply water or a liquid medicament to **4 :** to flow along the edge of : LAVE **5 :** to suffuse with or as if with light ~ *vi* **1 :** to take a bath **2 :** to go swimming **3 :** to become immersed or absorbed — **bath·er** \ˈbā-t͟hər\ *n*

[2]**bathe** *n* (1747) **1** *Brit* : [1]BATH 1 **2** *Brit* : SWIM, DIP

ba·thet·ic \bə-ˈthe-tik\ *adj* [*bathos* + *-etic* (as in *pathetic*)] (1845) : characterized by bathos — **ba·thet·i·cal·ly** \-ti-k(ə-)lē\ *adv*

bath·house \ˈbath-ˌhau̇s, ˈbäth-\ *n* (1705) **1 :** a building equipped for bathing **2 :** a building containing dressing rooms for bathers

bathing beauty *n* (1916) : a woman in a bathing suit who is a contestant in a beauty contest

bathing suit *n* (1852) : SWIMSUIT

bath mat *n* (1867) : a usu. washable mat used in a bathroom

bath·o·lith \ˈba-thə-ˌlith\ *n* [Gk *bathos* depth + ISV *-lith*] (1884) : a great mass of intruded igneous rock that for the most part stopped in its rise a considerable distance below the surface — **bath·o·lith·ic** \ˌba-thə-ˈli-thik\ *adj*

ba·thos \ˈbā-ˌthäs\ *n* [Gk, lit., depth] (1727) **1 a :** the sudden appearance of the commonplace in otherwise elevated matter or style **b :** ANTICLIMAX **2 :** exceptional commonplaceness : TRITENESS **3 :** insincere or overdone pathos : SENTIMENTALISM

bath·robe \ˈbath-ˌrōb, ˈbäth-\ *n* (1834) : a loose often absorbent robe worn before and after bathing or as a dressing gown

bath·room \-ˌrüm, -ˌru̇m\ *n* (1780) **1 :** a room containing a bathtub or shower and usu. a sink and toilet **2 :** LAVATORY 2

bath salts *n pl* (1899) **1 :** a usu. colored crystalline compound for perfuming and softening bathwater **2 :** any of various synthetic illicit drugs with stimulant and sometimes hallucinogenic properties that are used (as by being injected or snorted) typically in the form of a white or brown crystalline powder

bath·tub \-ˌtəb\ *n* (1821) : a usu. fixed tub for bathing

bathtub gin *n* (1923) : a homemade spirit concocted from raw alcohol, water, essences, and essential oils

bath·wa·ter \ˈbath-ˌwȯ-tər, ˈbäth-, -ˌwä-tər\ *n* (14c) : water for a bath

bathy- *comb form* [ISV, fr. Gk, fr. *bathys* deep] **1 :** deep : depth ⟨*bathy*al⟩ **2 :** deep-sea ⟨*bathy*sphere⟩

bathy·al \ˈba-thē-əl\ *adj* (1907) : of or relating to the ocean depths or floor usu. from 600 to 6000 feet (180 to 1800 meters)

ba·thym·e·try \bə-ˈthi-mə-trē\ *n, pl* **-tries** [ISV] (ca. 1855) : the measurement of water depth at various places in a body of water; *also* : the information derived from such measurements — **bathy·met·ric** \ˌba-thi-ˈme-trik\ *also* **bathy·met·ri·cal** \-tri-kəl\ *adj* — **bathy·met·ri·cal·ly** \-tri-k(ə-)lē\ *adv*

bathy·pe·lag·ic \ˌba-thi-pə-ˈla-jik\ *adj* (1891) : of, relating to, or living in the ocean depths esp. between approximately 2000 and 12,000 feet (600 and 3600 meters)

bathy·scaphe \ˈba-thi-ˌskaf, -ˌskāf\ *or* **bathy·scaph** \-ˌskaf\ *n* [ISV *bathy-* + Gk *skaphē* light boat] (1947) : a navigable submersible for deep-sea exploration having a spherical watertight cabin attached to its underside

bathy·sphere \-ˌsfir\ *n* (1930) : a strongly built steel diving sphere for deep-sea observation

bathy·ther·mo·graph \-ˈthər-mə-ˌgraf\ *n* (1938) : an instrument designed to record water temperature as a function of depth

ba·tik \bə-ˈtēk, ˈba-tik\ *n* [Jav *baṭik*] (1830) **1 :** a fabric printed by an Indonesian method of hand-printing textiles by coating with wax the parts not to be dyed; *also* : the method itself **2 :** a design executed in batik

bat·ing \ˈbā-tiŋ\ *prep* (1568) *archaic* : with the exception of

ba·tiste \bə-ˈtēst, ba-\ *n* [F] (1697) : a fine soft sheer fabric of plain weave made of various fibers

bat·man \ˈbat-mən\ *n* [F *bât* packsaddle] (1755) : an orderly of a British military officer

bat·ing \ˈbā-tiŋ\ *prep* (1568) *archaic* : with the exception of

[1]**bat mitz·vah** \bät-ˈmits-və\ *also* **bas mitz·vah** \bäs-\ *n, often cap B&M* [Heb *bath miṣwāh,* lit., daughter of the (divine) law] (1910) **1 :** a Jewish girl who at 12 or more years of age assumes religious responsibilities **2 :** the initiatory ceremony recognizing a girl as a bat mitzvah

[2]**bat mitzvah** *also* **bas mitzvah** *vt* **bat mitz·vahed** *also* **bas mitz·vahed; bat mitz·vah·ing** *also* **bas mitz·vah·ing** (1976) : to administer the ceremony of bat mitzvah to

ba·ton \bə-ˈtän, ba- *also* ˈba-tᵊn\ *n* [F *bâton,* fr. OF *baston,* ultim. fr. LL *bastum* stick] (1520) **1 :** CUDGEL, TRUNCHEON; *specif* : BILLY CLUB **2 :** a staff borne as a symbol of office **3 :** a narrow heraldic bend **4 :** a slender rod with which a leader directs a band or orchestra **5 :** a hollow cylinder carried by each member of a relay team and passed to the succeeding runner **6 :** a hollow metal rod with a weighted bulb at one or both ends that is flourished by a drum major or drum majorette

bat out *vt* (1941) : to compose esp. in a casual, careless, or hurried manner ⟨*batted out* a first draft of the memo⟩

\ə\ **abut** \ᵊ\ **kitten**, F table \ər\ **further** \a\ **ash** \ā\ **ace** \ä\ **mop**, **mar**
\au̇\ **out** \ch\ **chin** \e\ **bet** \ē\ **easy** \g\ **go** \i\ **hit** \ī\ **ice** \j\ **job**
\ŋ\ **sing** \ō\ **go** \ȯ\ **law** \ȯi\ **boy** \th\ **thin** \t͟h\ **the** \ü\ **loot** \u̇\ **foot**
\y\ **yet** \zh\ **vision**, **beige** \k̲, ^{n}, œ, ue, ^{y}\ *see* Guide to Pronunciation

ba·tra·chi·an \bə-ˈtrā-kē-ən\ *n* [ultim. fr. Gk *batrachos* frog] (ca. 1828) : AMPHIBIAN 1; *esp* : FROG, TOAD — **batrachian** *adj*
bat ray *n* (ca. 1933) : a stingray (*Myliobatis californica*) of coastal waters from Oregon to the Gulf of California having two long pectoral fins and a large protruding head
bats \ˈbats\ *adj* (1919) : BATTY 2
bats·man \ˈbats-mən\ *n* (1756) : a batter esp. in cricket
batt \ˈbat\ *n* (1836) : BATTING 2; *also* : an often square piece of batting
bat·tai·lous \ˈba-tᵊl-əs\ *adj* [ME *bataillous,* fr. AF **bataillos,* fr. *bataille* battle] (14c) *archaic* : ready for battle : WARLIKE
bat·ta·lia \bə-ˈtāl-yə, -ˈtal-\ *n* [It *battaglia*] (1569) **1** *archaic* : order of battle **2** *obs* : a large body of men in battle array
bat·tal·ion \bə-ˈtal-yən\ *n* [MF *bataillon,* fr. OIt *battaglione,* aug. of *battaglia* company of soldiers, battle, fr. LL *battalia* combat — more at BATTLE] (1579) **1** : a considerable body of troops organized to act together : ARMY **2** : a military unit composed of a headquarters and two or more companies, batteries, or similar units **3** : a large group
batteau *var of* BATEAU
bat·te·ment \ˌbat-ˈmäⁿ\ *n* [F, fr. *battre* to beat, fr. L *battuere*] (1802) : a ballet movement in which the foot is extended in any direction usu. followed by a beat against the supporting foot
[1]**bat·ten** \ˈba-tᵊn\ *vb* **bat·tened; bat·ten·ing** \ˈbat-niŋ, ˈba-tᵊn-iŋ\ [prob. fr. ON *batna* to improve; akin to OE *betera* better] *vi* (ca. 1540) **1 a** : to grow fat **b** : to feed gluttonously **2** : to grow prosperous esp. at the expense of another — usu. used with *on* ~ *vt* : FATTEN
[2]**batten** *n* [alter. of ME *batent, bataunt* finished board, fr. AF **bataunt,* fr. prp. of *batre* to beat, fr. L *battuere*] (1658) **1 a** *Brit* : a piece of lumber used esp. for flooring **b** : a thin narrow strip of lumber used esp. to seal or reinforce a joint **2** : a strip, bar, or support resembling or used similarly to a batten (as in a sail)
[3]**batten** *vb* **bat·tened; bat·ten·ing** \ˈbat-niŋ, ˈba-tᵊn-iŋ\ *vt* (1663) **1** : to furnish with battens **2** : to fasten with or as if with battens — often used with *down* ~ *vi* : to make one secure by or as if by battens ⟨~*ing* down for the hurricane⟩ — **batten down the hatches** : to prepare for a difficult or dangerous situation
[1]**bat·ter** \ˈba-tər\ *vb* [ME *bateren,* prob. freq. of *batten* to bat, fr. *bat*] *vt* (14c) **1 a** : to beat with successive blows so as to bruise, shatter, or demolish **b** : BOMBARD **2** : to subject to strong, overwhelming, or repeated attack ⟨~*ed* by forces of change⟩ **3** : to wear or damage by hard usage or blows ⟨a ~*ed* old hat⟩ ~ *vi* : to strike heavily and repeatedly : BEAT ***syn*** see MAIM — **bat·ter·er** \-tər-ər\ *n*
[2]**batter** *n* [ME *bater,* prob. fr. *bateren*] (14c) **1 a** : a mixture consisting chiefly of flour, egg, and milk or water and being thin enough to pour or drop from a spoon **b** : a mixture (as of flour and egg) used as a coating for food that is to be fried **2** : an instance of battering
[3]**batter** *vt* (1973) : to coat (food) with batter for frying
[4]**batter** *n* [origin unknown] (1743) : a receding upward slope of the outer face of a structure
[5]**batter** *vt* (ca. 1882) : to give a receding upward slope to (as a wall)
[6]**batter** *n* (1773) : one that bats; *esp* : the player whose turn it is to bat
battered child syndrome *n* (1962) : the complex of physical injuries sustained by a grossly abused child
battered woman syndrome *n* (1984) : the highly variable symptom complex of physical and psychological injuries exhibited by a woman repeatedly abused esp. physically by her mate — called also *battered woman's syndrome, battered wife syndrome, battered women's syndrome*
bat·te·rie \ˌba-tə-ˈrē\ *n* [F, lit., beating — more at BATTERY] (1712) : a ballet movement consisting of beating together the feet or calves of the legs during a leap
battering ram *n* (1593) **1** : a military siege engine consisting of a large wooden beam with a head of iron used in ancient times to beat down the walls of a besieged place **2** : a heavy metal bar with handles used (as by firefighters) to batter down doors and walls
bat·tery \ˈba-t(ə-)rē\ *n, pl* **-ter·ies** [AF *baterie,* fr. *batre* to beat, fr. L *battuere*] (1531) **1 a** : the act of battering or beating **b** : an offensive touching or use of force on a person without the person's consent — compare ASSAULT 2a **2** [MF *batterie,* fr. *battre* to beat] **a** : a grouping of artillery pieces for tactical purposes **b** : the guns of a warship **3** : an artillery unit in the army equivalent to a company **4 a** : a combination of apparatus for producing a single electrical effect **b** : a group of two or more cells connected together to furnish electric current; *also* : a single cell that furnishes electric current ⟨a flashlight ~⟩ **c** *pl* : level of energy or enthusiasm ⟨needs a vacation to recharge her *batteries*⟩ **5 a** : a number of similar articles, items, or devices arranged, connected, or used together : SET, SERIES ⟨a ~ of tests⟩ **b** : a usu. impressive or imposing group : ARRAY **6** : the position of readiness of a gun for firing **7** : the pitcher and catcher of a baseball team
bat·ting \ˈba-tiŋ\ *n* (1773) **1 a** : the action of one who bats **b** : the use of or ability with a bat **2** : layers or sheets of raw cotton or wool or of synthetic fibrous material used for lining quilts or for stuffing or packaging; *also* : a blanket of thermal insulation (as fiberglass)
batting average *n* (1867) **1** : a ratio (as a rate per thousand) of base hits to official times at bat for a baseball player **2** : a record of achievement or accomplishment
batting cage *n* (1952) : a screen placed around the back and sides of the home plate area to stop baseballs during batting practice
[1]**bat·tle** \ˈba-tᵊl\ *n, often attrib* [ME *batel,* fr. AF *bataille* battle, battalion, fr. LL *battalia* combat, alter. of *battualia* fencing exercises, fr. L *battuere* to beat] (13c) **1** *archaic* : BATTALION **2** : a combat between two persons **3** : a general encounter between armies, ships of war, or aircraft **4** : an extended contest, struggle, or controversy ⟨a ~ of wits⟩
[2]**battle** *vb* **bat·tled; bat·tling** \ˈbat-liŋ, ˈba-tᵊl-iŋ\ *vi* (14c) **1** : to engage in battle : FIGHT **2** : to contend with full strength, vigor, skill, or resources : STRUGGLE ~ *vt* **1** : to fight or struggle against **2** : to force (as one's way) by battling — **bat·tler** \-lər, ˈba-tᵊl-ər\ *n*
[3]**battle** *vt* **bat·tled; bat·tling** [ME *batailen,* fr. AF *bataillier* to fortify with battlements, fr. OF *batailles* battlemented tower, prob. fr. pl. of *bataille* battle] (14c) *archaic* : to fortify with battlements
bat·tle–ax *or* **bat·tle–axe** \ˈba-tᵊl-ˌaks\ *n* (14c) **1** : a broadax formerly used as a weapon of war **2** : a usu. older woman who is sharp-tongued, domineering, or combative
battle cruiser *n* (1911) : a large heavily armed warship that is lighter, faster, and more maneuverable than a battleship
battle cry *n* (1814) : WAR CRY
battle dress uniform *n* (1982) : a military uniform for field service
battle fatigue *n* (1944) : COMBAT FATIGUE — **bat·tle–fa·tigued** *adj*
bat·tle·field \ˈba-tᵊl-ˌfēld\ *n* (1769) **1** : a place where a battle is fought **2** : an area of conflict
bat·tle·front \-ˌfrənt\ *n* (1824) : the military sector in which actual combat takes place
bat·tle·ground \-ˌgrau̇nd\ *n* (1573) : BATTLEFIELD
battle line *n* (1814) **1** : a line along which a battle is fought **2** : a line defining the positions of opposing groups in a conflict or controversy — usu. used in pl. ⟨*battle lines* were drawn over economic policies⟩
bat·tle·ment \ˈba-tᵊl-mənt\ *n* [ME *batelment,* fr. AF **bataillement,* fr. *batailler* to fortify with battlements — more at BATTLE] (14c) : a parapet with open spaces that surmounts a wall and is used for defense or decoration — **bat·tle·ment·ed** \-ˌmen-təd\ *adj*

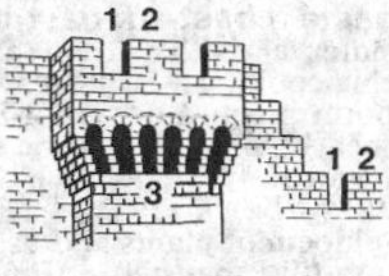

battlement: *1* crenellations, *2* merlons, *3* machicolations

battle royal *n, pl* **battles royal** *or* **battle royals** (1671) **1 a** : a fight participated in by more than two combatants; *esp* : one in which the last man in the ring or on his feet is declared the winner **b** : a violent struggle **2** : a heated dispute
bat·tle·ship \ˈba-tᵊl-ˌship\ *n* [short for *line-of-battle ship*] (1794) : a warship of the largest and most heavily armed and armored class
bat·tle·wag·on \-ˌwa-gən\ *n* (1918) : BATTLESHIP
bat·tu \ba-ˈtü, -ˈtyü\ *adj* [F, fr. pp. of *battre* to beat] (1947) *of a ballet movement* : performed with a striking together of the legs
bat·tue \ba-ˈtü, -ˈtyü\ *n* [F, fr. fem. of *battu,* pp. of *battre* to beat] (1816) : the beating of woods and bushes to flush game; *also* : a hunt in which this procedure is used
bat·ty \ˈba-tē\ *adj* **bat·ti·er; -est** (1590) **1** : of, relating to, or resembling a bat **2** : mentally unstable : CRAZY — **bat·ti·ness** *n*
bau·ble \ˈbȯ-bəl, ˈbä-\ *n* [ME *babel,* fr. MF] (14c) **1** : TRINKET 1 **2** : a fool's scepter **3** : something of trifling appeal
Bau·cis \ˈbȯ-səs\ *n* [L, fr. Gk *Baukis*] (1567) : the wife of Philemon
baud \ˈbȯd, ˈbäd, *Brit* ˈbōd\ *n, pl* **baud** *also* **bauds** [*baud* (telegraphic transmission speed unit), fr. J. M. E. *Baudot* †1903 Fr. inventor] (1931) : a variable unit of data transmission speed (as one bit per second)
Bau·haus \ˈbau̇-ˌhau̇s\ *adj* [G *Bauhaus,* lit., architecture house, school founded by Walter Gropius] (1923) : of, relating to, or influenced by a school of design noted esp. for a program that synthesized technology, craftsmanship, and design aesthetics
bau·hin·ia \bō-ˈi-nē-ə, -ˈhi-, bȯ-\ *n* [NL, fr. Jean *Bauhin* †1613 and Gaspard *Bauhin* †1624 Swiss botanists] (1725) : any of a genus (*Bauhinia*) of leguminous vines, shrubs, and trees of the legume family that grow in tropical and subtropical regions and include some that are grown esp. for their fragrant orchid-like flowers
baulk *chiefly Brit var of* BALK
Bau·mé \bō-ˈmā\ *adj* [Antoine *Baumé*] (1877) : being, calibrated in accordance with, or according to either of two arbitrary hydrometer scales for liquids lighter than water or for liquids heavier than water that indicate specific gravity in degrees
baum marten \ˈbau̇m-ˌmär-tᵊn\ *n* [part trans. of G *Baummarder,* fr. *Baum* tree + *Marder* marten] (ca. 1879) : the pelt or fur of the European marten (*Martes martes*)
baux·ite \ˈbȯk-ˌsīt, ˈbäk-\ *n* [F *bauxite,* fr. Les *Baux,* near Arles, France] (1861) : an impure mixture of earthy hydrous aluminum oxides and hydroxides that is the principal source of aluminum — **baux·it·ic** \bȯk-ˈsi-tik, bäk-\ *adj*
Bav *abbr* Bavaria; Bavarian
Ba·var·i·an \bə-ˈver-ē-ən\ *n* (1634) **1** : a native or inhabitant of Bavaria **2** : the High German dialect of southern Bavaria and Austria — **Bavarian** *adj*
Bavarian cream *n* (1847) : flavored custard or pureed fruit combined with gelatin and whipped cream
baw·bee \ˈbȯ-(ˌ)bē, bȯ-ˈ\ *n* [prob. fr. Alexander Orrok, laird of Sillebawbe *fl* 1538 Scot. master of the mint] (1542) **1** : any of various Scottish coins of small value **2** : an English halfpenny
baw·cock \ˈbȯ-ˌkäk\ *n* [F *beau coq,* fr. *beau* fine + *coq* fellow, cock] (1599) *archaic* : a fine fellow
bawd \ˈbȯd\ *n* [ME *bawde*] (14c) **1** *obs* : PANDER **2 a** : one who keeps a house of prostitution : MADAM **b** : PROSTITUTE
bawd·ry \ˈbȯ-drē\ *n* [ME *bawderie,* fr. *bawde*] (15c) **1** *obs* : UNCHASTITY **2** : suggestive, coarse, or obscene language
[1]**bawdy** \ˈbȯ-dē\ *adj* **bawd·i·er; -est** [*bawd*] (1513) **1** : OBSCENE, LEWD **2** : boisterously or humorously indecent — **bawd·i·ly** \ˈbȯ-də-lē\ *adv* — **bawd·i·ness** \ˈbȯ-dē-nəs\ *n*
[2]**bawdy** *n* [prob. fr. [1]*bawdy*] (1656) : BAWDRY 2
bawdy house *n* (1552) : BORDELLO
[1]**bawl** \ˈbȯl\ *vb* [ME, to bark, prob. of Gmc origin; akin to Icel *baula* to low] *vi* (1533) **1** : to cry out loudly and unrestrainedly **2** : to cry loudly : WAIL ~ *vt* : to cry out at the top of one's voice — **bawl·er** *n*
[2]**bawl** *n* (1566) : a loud prolonged cry : OUTCRY
bawl out *vt* (1899) : to reprimand loudly or severely
[1]**bay** \ˈbā\ *adj* [ME, fr. AF *bai,* fr. L *badius;* akin to OIr *buide* yellow] (14c) : reddish brown ⟨a ~ mare⟩
[2]**bay** *n* (1535) **1** : a bay-colored animal; *specif* : a horse with a bay-colored body and black mane, tail, and points — compare CHESTNUT 4, [1]SORREL 1 **2** : a reddish brown
[3]**bay** *n* [ME, fr. AF *baee* opening, fr. fem. of *baé,* pp. of *baer* to be wide open, gape, fr. VL **batare*] (14c) **1** : a principal compartment of the walls, roof, or other part of a building or of the whole building **2** : a main division of a structure **3** : any of various compartments or sections used for a special purpose (as in an airplane, spacecraft, or service station) ⟨a bomb ~⟩ ⟨a cargo ~⟩ **4** : BAY WINDOW 1 **5** : a support or housing for electronic equipment
[4]**bay** *vb* [ME *baien, abaien,* fr. AF *abaier,* of imit. origin] *vi* (14c) **1** : to bark with prolonged tones ⟨dogs ~*ing* at the moon⟩ **2** : to cry out : SHOUT ~ *vt* **1** : to bark at **2** : to bring to bay **3** : to pursue with barking **4** : to utter in deep prolonged tones
[5]**bay** *n* (14c) **1** : a baying of dogs **2** : the position of one unable to retreat and forced to face danger ⟨brought his quarry to ~⟩ **3** : the position of one checked ⟨police kept the rioters at ~⟩

6**bay** *n, often attrib* [ME *baye,* fr. AF *bai,* perh. fr. *baer* to be wide open] (14c) **1 :** an inlet of the sea or other body of water usu. smaller than a gulf **2 :** a small body of water set off from the main body **3 :** any of various terrestrial formations resembling a bay of the sea

7**bay** *n* [ME, berry, laurel berry, fr. AF *bai,* fr. L. *baca*] (15c) **1 a :** LAUREL 1 **b :** any of several shrubs or trees (as the red bay or sweet bay) resembling the laurel — compare BAY RUM **2 a :** a garland or crown esp. of laurel given as a prize for victory or excellence **b :** HONOR, FAME — usu. used in pl.

ba·ya·dere \ˈbī-ə-ˌdir, -ˌder\ *n* [F *bayadère* professional female dancer in India] (1851) **:** a fabric with horizontal stripes in strongly contrasted colors

bay·ber·ry \ˈbā-ˌber-ē, -ˌbe-rē\ *n* (1575) **1 :** any of several wax myrtles; *esp* **:** a hardy shrub (*Myrica pensylvanica*) of coastal eastern No. America bearing dense clusters of small berries covered with grayish-white wax **2 :** the fruit of a bayberry

Bayes·ian \ˈbā-zē-ən, -zhən\ *adj* (1950) **:** being, relating to, or involving statistical methods that assign probabilities or distributions to events (as rain tomorrow) or parameters (as a population mean) based on experience or best guesses before experimentation and data collection and that apply Bayes' theorem to revise the probabilities and distributions after obtaining experimental data

Bayes' theorem \ˈbāz-\ *n* [Thomas *Bayes* †1761 Eng. mathematician] (1830) **:** a theorem about conditional probabilities: the probability that an event A occurs given that another event B has already occurred is equal to the probability that the event B occurs given that A has already occurred multiplied by the probability of occurrence of event A and divided by the probability of occurrence of event B

bay leaf *n* (15c) **:** the dried leaf of the European laurel (*Laurus nobilis*) used in cooking

bay·man \ˈbā-mən, -ˌman\ *n* (1641) **:** a person and esp. a fisherman who lives or works on or about a bay

1**bay·o·net** \ˈbā-ə-nət, -ˌnet, ˌbā-ə-ˈnet\ *n* [F *baïonnette,* fr. *Bayonne,* France] (1680) **:** a steel blade attached at the muzzle end of a shoulder arm (as a rifle) and used in hand-to-hand combat

2**bayonet** *vb* **-net·ed** *also* **-net·ted; -net·ing** *also* **-net·ting** *vt* (1778) **1 :** to stab with a bayonet **2 :** to compel or drive by or as if by the bayonet ~ *vi* **:** to use a bayonet

bay·ou \ˈbī-(ˌ)ü, -(ˌ)ō\ *n* [LaF, fr. Choctaw *bayuk*] (1763) **1 :** a creek, secondary watercourse, or minor river that is tributary to another body of water **2 :** any of various usu. marshy or sluggish bodies of water

bay rum *n* (1816) **:** a fragrant cosmetic and medicinal liquid distilled from the leaves of a West Indian bay tree (*Pimenta racemosa*) of the myrtle family or usu. prepared from essential oils, alcohol, and water

bay scallop *n* (1943) **:** a scallop (*Argopecten irradians*) of U.S. coastal and estuarine waters of the Atlantic Ocean and the Gulf of Mexico that is harvested commercially for food

Bay Stat·er \ˈbā-ˌstā-tər\ *n* (1845) **:** a native or resident of Massachusetts — used as a nickname

bay window *n* (15c) **1 :** a window or series of windows forming a bay in a room and projecting outward from the wall **2 :** POTBELLY 1

ba·zaar \bə-ˈzär\ *n* [Pers *bāzār*] (1612) **1 :** a market (as in the Middle East) consisting of rows of shops or stalls selling miscellaneous goods **2 a :** a place for the sale of goods **b :** DEPARTMENT STORE **3 :** a fair for the sale of articles esp. for charitable purposes

ba·zoo·ka \bə-ˈzü-kə\ *n* [*bazooka* (a crude musical instrument made of pipes and a funnel)] (1943) **:** a light portable antitank weapon consisting of an open-breech smoothbore firing tube that launches an armor-piercing rocket and is fired from the shoulder

1**BB** \ˈbē-(ˌ)bē\ *n* (1832) **1 :** a shot pellet 0.18 inch in diameter for use in a shotgun cartridge **2 :** a shot pellet 0.175 inch in diameter for use in an air gun

2**BB** *abbr* **1** bachelor of business **2** ball bearing **3** base on balls **4** blue book **5** B'nai B'rith

BBA *abbr* bachelor of business administration

b–ball \ˈbē-ˌbȯl\ *n, often cap first B* [by shortening] (1967) **:** BASKETBALL — **b–ball·er** \-ˌbȯ-lər\ *n, often cap first B*

BBB *abbr* Better Business Bureau

BBC *abbr* British Broadcasting Corporation

BBE *abbr* bachelor of business education

bbl *abbr* barrel; barrels

B–boy \ˈbē-ˌbȯi\ *n* [*b* prob. fr. *b*reak (solo instrumental passage) or *b*reak beat] (1981) **:** a male who engages in the pursuit of hip-hop culture or adopts its styles

BBQ *abbr* barbecue

BBS *abbr* bulletin board system

BC *abbr* **1** before Christ — often printed in small capitals and often punctuated **2** British Columbia

1**bcc** \ˌbē-ˌsē-ˈsē\ *vt* **bcc'd; bcc'·ing** (1989) **1 :** to send a blind carbon copy to **2 :** to send as a blind carbon copy

2**bcc** *abbr* blind carbon copy

1**BCD** \ˌbē-(ˌ)sē-ˈdē\ *n* [*b*inary *c*oded *d*ecimal] (ca. 1962) **:** a system of writing numbers in which each decimal digit is represented by its 4-digit binary equivalent ⟨51 in ~ is 0101 0001⟩

2**BCD** *abbr* bad conduct discharge

BCE *abbr* **1** bachelor of chemical engineering **2** bachelor of civil engineering **3** before the Christian Era — often punctuated; before the Common Era — often punctuated

B cell *n* [*B* prob. fr. *b*ursa-derived (produced by the bursa of Fabricius)] (1962) **:** any of the lymphocytes that have antigen-binding antibody molecules on the surface, that comprise the antibody-secreting plasma cells when mature, and that in mammals differentiate in the bone marrow — called also *B lymphocyte;* compare T CELL

bcf *abbr* billion cubic feet

BCG vaccine \ˌbē-(ˌ)sē-ˈjē-\ *n* [*B*acillus *C*almette-*G*uérin (an attenuated strain of tubercle bacilli), fr. Albert *Calmette* †1933 and Camille *Guérin* †1961 Fr. bacteriologists] (1925) **:** a vaccine prepared from a living attenuated strain of tubercle bacilli and used to vaccinate human beings against tuberculosis — called also *BCG*

BCh *abbr* bachelor of chemistry

BChE *abbr* bachelor of chemical engineering

BCL *abbr* **1** bachelor of canon law **2** bachelor of civil law

BCN *abbr* beacon

B complex *n* (1933) **:** VITAMIN B COMPLEX

BCS *abbr* **1** bachelor of chemical science **2** Bowl Championship Series

bd *abbr* **1** barrels per day **2** board **3** bound **4** boundary **5** bundle

BD *abbr* **1** bachelor of divinity **2** bank draft **3** bills discounted **4** bomb disposal **5** brought down

bdel·li·um \ˈde-lē-əm\ *n* [ME, fr. L, fr. Gk *bdellion*] (14c) **:** a gum resin similar to myrrh obtained from various trees (genus *Commiphora*) of the East Indies and Africa

bd ft *abbr* board foot

bdl *or* **bdle** *abbr* bundle

bdrm *abbr* bedroom

BDU *abbr* battle dress uniform

be \ˈbē\ *vb, past 1st & 3d sing* **was** \ˈwəz, ˈwäz\; *2d sing* **were** \ˈwər\; *pl* **were**; *past subjunctive* **were**; *past part* **been** \ˈbin, ˈben, *chiefly Brit* ˈbēn\; *pres part* **be·ing** \ˈbē(-i)ŋ\; *pres 1st sing* **am** \əm, ˈam\; *2d sing* **are** \ˈär, ər\; *3d sing* **is** \ˈiz, əz\; *pl* **are**; *pres subjunctive* **be** [ME, fr. OE *bēon;* akin to OHG *bim* am, L *fui* I have been, *futurus* about to be, *fieri* to become, be done, Gk *phynai* to be born, be by nature, *phyein* to produce] *vi* (bef. 12c) **1 a :** to equal in meaning **:** have the same connotation as **:** SYMBOLIZE ⟨God *is* love⟩ ⟨January *is* the first month⟩ ⟨let *x* ~ 10⟩ **b :** to have identity with ⟨the first person I met *was* my brother⟩ **c :** to constitute the same class as **d :** to have a specified qualification or characterization ⟨the leaves *are* green⟩ **e :** to belong to the class of ⟨the fish *is* a trout⟩ — used regularly in senses 1a through 1e as the copula of simple predication **2 a :** to have an objective existence **:** have reality or actuality **:** LIVE ⟨I think, therefore I *am*⟩ **b :** to have, maintain, or occupy a place, situation, or position ⟨the book *is* on the table⟩ **c :** to remain unmolested, undisturbed, or uninterrupted — used only in infinitive form ⟨let him ~⟩ **d :** to take place **:** OCCUR ⟨the concert *was* last night⟩ **e :** to come or go ⟨has already *been* and gone⟩ ⟨has never *been* to the circus⟩ **f** *archaic* **:** BELONG, BEFALL ~ *verbal auxiliary* **1** — used with the past participle of transitive verbs as a passive-voice auxiliary ⟨the money *was* found⟩ ⟨the house is *being* built⟩ **2** — used as the auxiliary of the present participle in progressive tenses expressing continuous action ⟨he *is* reading⟩ ⟨I have *been* sleeping⟩ **3** — used with the past participle of some intransitive verbs as an auxiliary forming archaic perfect tenses ⟨Christ *is* risen from the dead —1 Cor 15:20(DV)⟩ **4** — used with the infinitive with *to* to express futurity, arrangement in advance, or obligation ⟨I *am* to interview him today⟩ ⟨she *was* to become famous⟩

Be *symbol* beryllium

Bé *abbr* Baumé

BE *abbr* **1** bachelor of education **2** bachelor of engineering **3** bill of exchange **4** Black English

be- *prefix* [ME, fr. OE *bi-, be-;* akin to OE *bī* by, near — more at BY] **1 :** on **:** around **:** over ⟨*be*smear⟩ **2 :** to a great or greater degree **:** thoroughly ⟨*be*fuddle⟩ **3 :** excessively **:** ostentatiously — in intensive verbs formed from simple verbs ⟨*be*deck⟩ and in adjectives based on adjectives ending in *-ed* ⟨*be*ribboned⟩ **4 :** about **:** to **:** at **:** upon **:** against **:** across ⟨*be*stride⟩ **5 :** make **:** cause to be **:** treat as ⟨*be*little⟩ ⟨*be*friend⟩ **6 :** call or dub esp. excessively ⟨*be*doctor⟩ **7 :** affect, afflict, treat, provide, or cover with esp. excessively ⟨*be*devil⟩ ⟨*be*fog⟩

1**beach** \ˈbēch\ *n* [origin unknown] (ca. 1535) **1 :** shore pebbles **:** SHINGLE **2 a :** a shore of a body of water covered by sand, gravel, or larger rock fragments **b :** a seashore area

2**beach** *vt* (1799) **1 :** to run or drive ashore **2 :** to strand on or as if on a beach

beach ball *n* (1940) **:** a large inflated ball for use at the beach

beach·boy \-ˌbȯi\ *n* (1938) **:** a male beach attendant (as at a hotel)

beach buggy *n* (1943) **:** DUNE BUGGY

beach·comb·er \ˈbēch-ˌkō-mər\ *n* (1840) **1 :** a white man living as a drifter or loafer esp. on the islands of the So. Pacific **2 :** a person who searches along a shore (as for salable refuse or for seashells) — **beach·comb** \-ˌkōm\ *vb*

beach flea *n* (1843) **:** SAND FLEA 2

beach·front \ˈbēch-ˌfrənt\ *n* (1921) **:** a strip of land that fronts a beach

beach·go·er \-ˌgō-ər\ *n* (1954) **:** a person who frequently goes to the beach

beach grass *n* (1681) **:** any of several tough strongly rooted grasses that grow on exposed sandy shores; *esp* **:** any of a genus (*Ammophila*) of rhizomatous perennials widely planted to bind sandy slopes

beach·head \ˈbēch-ˌhed\ *n* (1940) **1 :** an area on a hostile shore occupied to secure further landing of troops and supplies **2 :** FOOTHOLD

beach pea *n* (1802) **:** a wild pea (*Lathyrus japonicus* syn. *L. maritimus*) having tough roots and purple flowers that is found along sandy shores

beach plum *n* (1741) **:** a shrubby plum (*Prunus maritima*) having white flowers and growing chiefly along the northeastern coast of No. America; *also* **:** its edible usu. dark purple fruit that is used esp. in preserves

beach·side \ˈbēch-ˌsīd\ *adj* (1952) **:** located at a beach ⟨~ property⟩

beach towel *n* (1958) **:** a very large usu. brightly colored towel designed for use at the beach

beach·wear \-ˌwer\ *n* (1928) **:** clothing for wear at a beach

beachy \ˈbē-chē\ *adj* **beach·i·er; -est** (1597) **1 :** covered with pebbles or shingle **2 :** characterized by beaches ⟨a ~ island⟩

1**bea·con** \ˈbē-kən\ *n* [ME *beken,* fr. OE *bēacen* sign; akin to OHG *bouhhan* sign] (14c) **1 :** a signal fire commonly on a hill, tower, or pole **2 a :** a lighthouse or other signal for guidance **b :** a radio transmitter emitting signals to guide aircraft **3 :** a source of light or inspiration

2**beacon** *vi* (1650) **:** to shine as a beacon ~ *vt* **:** to furnish with a beacon

1**bead** \ˈbēd\ *n* [ME *bede* prayer, prayer bead, fr. OE *bed, gebed* prayer; akin to OE *biddan* to entreat, pray — more at BID] (bef. 12c) **1 a** *obs* **:** PRAYER — usu. used in pl. **b** *pl* **:** a series of prayers and meditations made with a rosary **2 :** a small piece of material pierced for threading on a string or wire (as in a rosary) **3** *pl* **a :** ROSARY **b :** a necklace of beads or pearls **4 :** a small ball-shaped body: as **a :** a drop of sweat or blood **b :** a bubble formed in or on a beverage **c :** a small metal knob on a firearm used as a front sight **d :** a blob or a line of weld

\ə\ **abut** \ᵊ\ **kitten,** F **table** \ər\ **further** \a\ **ash** \ā\ **ace** \ä\ **mop, mar** \au̇\ **out** \ch\ **chin** \e\ **bet** \ē\ **easy** \g\ **go** \i\ **hit** \ī\ **ice** \j\ **job** \ŋ\ **sing** \ō\ **go** \ȯ\ **law** \ȯi\ **boy** \th\ **thin** \t͟h\ **the** \ü\ **loot** \u̇\ **foot** \y\ **yet** \zh\ **vision, beige** \k̲, ⁿ, œ, ue, ʸ\ *see* Guide to Pronunciation

metal **5 :** a projecting rim, band, or molding **6 :** a precise knowledge or understanding — used in such phrases as *get a bead on*

[2]**bead** *vt* (1577) **1 :** to furnish, adorn, or cover with beads or beading **2 :** to string together like beads ~ *vi* **:** to form into a bead — **bead•er** *n*

bead•ing *n* (1845) **1 :** a beaded molding **2 :** material or a part or a piece consisting of a bead **3 :** an openwork trimming **4 :** BEADWORK

bea•dle \ˈbē-dᵊl\ *n* [ME *bedel* messenger, fr. OE *bydel;* akin to OHG *butil* bailiff, OE *bēodan* to command — more at BID] (1581) **:** a minor parish official whose duties include ushering and preserving order at services and sometimes civil functions

bead•roll \ˈbēd-ˌrōl\ *n* [fr. the reading in church of a list of names of persons for whom prayers are to be said] (1529) **1 :** a list of names **:** CATALOG **2 :** ROSARY

beads•man \ˈbēdz-mən\ *n* (13c) *archaic* **:** one who prays for another

bead•work \ˈbēd-ˌwərk\ *n* (1751) **1 :** ornamental work in beads **2 :** joinery beading

beady \ˈbē-dē\ *adj* **bead•i•er; -est** (1826) **1 a :** resembling beads **b :** small, round, and shiny with interest or greed ⟨~ eyes⟩ **2 :** marked by bubbles or beads ⟨a ~ liquor⟩ — **bead•i•ly** \ˈbē-də-lē\ *adv*

bea•gle \ˈbē-gəl\ *n* [ME *begle*] (15c) **:** any of a breed of small short-legged smooth-coated often black, white, and tan hounds

beak \ˈbēk\ *n* [ME *bec,* fr. AF, fr. L *beccus,* of Gaulish origin] (13c) **1 a :** the bill of a bird; *esp* **:** a strong short broad bill **b** (1) **:** the elongated sucking mouth of some insects (as the true bugs) (2) **:** any of various rigid projecting mouth structures (as of a turtle) **c :** the human nose **2 :** a pointed structure or formation: **a :** a metal-pointed beam projecting from the bow esp. of an ancient galley for piercing an enemy ship **b :** the spout of a vessel **c :** a continuous slight architectural projection ending in an arris — see MOLDING illustration **d :** a process suggesting the beak of a bird **3** *chiefly Brit* **a :** MAGISTRATE **b :** HEADMASTER — **beaked** \ˈbēkt\ *adj* — **beaky** \ˈbē-kē\ *adj*

beaked whale *n* (1755) **:** any of a widely distributed family (Ziphiidae) of medium-sized toothed whales that have an elongated snout and a small dorsal fin

bea•ker \ˈbē-kər\ *n* [ME *biker,* fr. ON *bikarr,* prob. fr. OS *bikeri,* fr. ML *bicarium*] (14c) **1 :** a large drinking cup that has a wide mouth and is sometimes supported on a standard **2 :** a deep widemouthed thin-walled vessel usu. with a lip for pouring that is used esp. in science laboratories

be–all and end–all \ˈbē-ˌȯl-ən(d)-ˈend-ˌȯl\ *n* (1605) **1 :** prime cause **:** essential element **2 :** TOTALITY 1

[1]**beam** \ˈbēm\ *n* [ME *beem,* fr. OE *bēam* tree, beam; akin to OHG *boum* tree] (bef. 12c) **1 a :** a long piece of heavy often squared timber suitable for use in construction **b :** a wood or metal cylinder in a loom on which the warp is wound **c :** the part of a plow to which handles, standard, and coulter are attached **d :** the bar of a balance from which scales hang **e :** one of the principal horizontal supporting members (as of a building or ship) ⟨a steel ~ supporting a floor⟩; *also* **:** BOOM, SPAR ⟨the ~ of a crane⟩ **f :** the extreme width of a ship at the widest part **g :** an oscillating lever on a central axis receiving motion at one end from an engine connecting rod and transmitting it at the other **2 a :** a ray or shaft of light **b :** a collection of nearly parallel rays (as X rays) or a stream of particles (as electrons) **c :** a constant directional radio signal transmitted for the guidance of pilots; *also* **:** the course indicated by a radio beam **3 :** the main stem of a deer's antler **4 :** the width of the buttocks — **on the beam 1 :** following a guiding beam **2 :** proceeding or operating correctly

[2]**beam** *vt* (15c) **1 :** to emit in beams or as a beam **2 :** to support with beams **3 a :** to transmit esp. by satellite **:** BROADCAST **b :** to transmit (data) electronically **c :** to direct to a particular audience ~ *vi* **1 :** to send out beams of light **2 :** to smile with joy

beam–ends \ˈbēm-ˈen(d)z\ *n pl* (1750) **:** the ends of a ship's beams — **on her beam–ends :** inclined so much on one side that the beams approach a vertical position

beam•ish \ˈbē-mish\ *adj* (1870) **:** beaming and bright with optimism, promise, or achievement ⟨a ~ boy⟩ — **beam•ish•ly** *adv*

beam sea *n* (1861) **:** a sea whose surface motion is approximately at a right angle to the course of a vessel

beam splitter *n* (1935) **:** a mirror or prism or a combination of the two that is used to divide a beam of radiation into two or more parts

beamy \ˈbē-mē\ *adj* (14c) **1 :** emitting beams of light **:** RADIANT **2 :** broad in the beam ⟨a ~ cargo ship⟩

[1]**bean** \ˈbēn\ *n* [ME *bene,* fr. OE *bēan;* akin to OHG *bōna* bean] (bef. 12c) **1 a :** BROAD BEAN **b :** the seed of any of various erect or climbing plants (as of the genera *Phaseolus* and *Vigna*) of the legume family other than the broad bean **c :** a plant bearing beans **d :** an immature bean pod used as a vegetable **2 a :** a valueless item **b** *pl* **:** the least amount ⟨didn't know ~*s* about it⟩ **3 :** any of various seeds or fruits that resemble beans or bean pods ⟨coffee ~*s*⟩; *also* **:** a plant producing these **4 a** *pl* **:** EXUBERANCE — used in the phrase *full of beans* **b** *pl* **:** NONSENSE, BUNKUM — used in the phrase *full of beans* **5 :** HEAD, BRAIN **6 :** a protuberance on the upper mandible of waterfowl — see DUCK illustration

[2]**bean** *vt* (1910) **:** to strike (a person) on the head with an object

bean•bag \ˈbēn-ˌbag\ *n* (1871) **1 :** a cloth bag partially filled typically with dried beans and used as a toy **2 :** any of various pellet-filled bags used as furniture (as a chair) or household articles (as an ashtray base)

bean•ball \-ˌbȯl\ *n* (ca. 1905) **:** a pitch thrown at a batter's head

bean counter *n* (1975) **:** a person involved in corporate or government financial decisions and esp. one reluctant to spend money

bean curd *n* (ca. 1885) **:** TOFU

bean•ery \ˈbēn-rē, ˈbē-nə-\ *n, pl* **-er•ies** (1887) **:** RESTAURANT

bean•ie \ˈbē-nē\ *n* [prob. fr. [1]*bean* (head) + *-ie*] (1904) **:** a small round tight-fitting skullcap

[1]**beano** \ˈbē-(ˌ)nō\ *n, pl* **beanos** [alter. of *beanfeast* festive occasion] (1891) *Brit* **:** a noisy festive celebration

[2]**beano** *n, pl* **beanos** [by alter.] (1935) **:** BINGO

bean•pole \ˈbēn-ˌpō(ə)l\ *n* (1798) **1 :** a pole up which bean vines may climb **2 :** a tall thin person

bean sprouts *n pl* (1921) **:** the sprouts of bean seeds esp. of the mung bean used as a vegetable

bean thread *n* (1977) **:** CELLOPHANE NOODLE

[1]**bear** \ˈber\ *n, pl* **bears** *often attrib* [ME *bere,* fr. OE *bera;* akin to OE *brūn* brown — more at BROWN] (bef. 12c) **1** *or pl* **bear :** any of a family (Ursidae of the order Carnivora) of large heavy mammals of America and Eurasia that have long shaggy hair, rudimentary tails, and plantigrade feet and feed largely on fruit, plant matter, and insects as well as on flesh **2 :** a surly, uncouth, burly, or shambling person ⟨a tall, friendly ~ of a man⟩ **3** [prob. fr. the proverb about *selling the bearskin before catching the bear*] **:** one that sells securities or commodities in expectation of a price decline — compare BULL **4 :** something difficult to do or deal with ⟨the oven is a ~ to clean⟩ — **bear•like** \-ˌlīk\ *adj*

[2]**bear** *vb* **bore** \ˈbȯr\; **borne** *also* **born** \ˈbȯrn\; **bear•ing** [ME *beren* to carry, bring forth, fr. OE *beran;* akin to OHG *beran* to carry, L *ferre,* Gk *pherein*] *vt* (bef. 12c) **1 a :** to move while holding up and supporting **b :** to be equipped or furnished with **c :** BEHAVE, CONDUCT ⟨~*ing* himself well⟩ **d :** to have as a feature or characteristic ⟨~*s* a likeness to her grandmother⟩ **e :** to give as testimony ⟨~ false witness⟩ **f :** to have as an identification ⟨*bore* the name of John⟩ **g :** to hold in the mind or emotions ⟨~ malice⟩ **h :** DISSEMINATE **i :** LEAD, ESCORT **j :** RENDER, GIVE **2 a :** to give birth to **b :** to produce as yield **c** (1) **:** to permit growth of (2) **:** CONTAIN ⟨oil-*bearing* shale⟩ **3 a :** to support the weight of **:** SUSTAIN **b :** to accept or allow oneself to be subjected to esp. without giving way ⟨couldn't ~ the pain⟩ ⟨I can't ~ seeing you cry⟩ **c :** to call for as suitable or essential ⟨it ~*s* watching⟩ **d :** to hold above, on top, or aloft **e :** to admit of **:** ALLOW **f :** ASSUME, ACCEPT **4 :** THRUST, PRESS ~ *vi* **1 :** to produce fruit **:** YIELD **2 a :** to force one's way **b :** to extend in a direction indicated or implied **c :** to be situated **:** LIE **d :** to become directed **e :** to go or incline in an indicated direction **3 :** to support a weight or strain — often used with *up* **4 a :** to exert influence or force **b :** APPLY, PERTAIN — often used with *on* or *upon* ⟨facts ~*ing* on the question⟩ — **bear a hand :** to join in and help out — **bear arms 1 :** to carry or possess arms **2 :** to serve as a soldier — **bear fruit :** to come to satisfying fruition, production, or development — **bear in mind :** to think of esp. as a warning **:** REMEMBER — **bear with :** to be indulgent, patient, or forbearing with

syn BEAR, SUFFER, ENDURE, ABIDE, TOLERATE, STAND mean to put up with something trying or painful. BEAR usu. implies the power to sustain without flinching or breaking ⟨forced to *bear* a tragic loss⟩. SUFFER often suggests acceptance or passivity rather than courage or patience in bearing ⟨*suffering* many insults⟩. ENDURE implies continuing firm or resolute through trials and difficulties ⟨*endured* years of rejection⟩. ABIDE suggests acceptance without resistance or protest ⟨cannot *abide* their rudeness⟩. TOLERATE suggests overcoming or successfully controlling an impulse to resist, avoid, or resent something injurious or distasteful ⟨refused to *tolerate* such treatment⟩. STAND emphasizes even more strongly the ability to bear without discomposure or flinching ⟨unable to *stand* teasing⟩.

bear•able \ˈber-ə-bəl\ *adj* (ca. 1550) **:** capable of being borne — **bear•abil•i•ty** \ˌber-ə-ˈbi-lə-tē\ *n* — **bear•ably** \-blē\ *adv*

bear•bait•ing \ˈber-ˌbā-tiŋ\ *n* (14c) **:** the practice of setting dogs on a chained bear

bear•ber•ry \-ˌber-ē, -ˌbe-rē\ *n* (1625) **:** a trailing evergreen plant (*Arctostaphylos uva-ursi*) of the heath family with astringent foliage and red berries

bear claw *n* (1936) **:** a filled pastry that is cut and fanned to resemble a bear's foot

[1]**beard** \ˈbird\ *n* [ME *berd,* fr. OE *beard;* akin to OHG *bart* beard, L *barba*] (bef. 12c) **1 :** the hair that grows on a man's face often excluding the mustache **2 :** a hairy or bristly appendage or tuft **3 :** FRONT 7a — **beard•ed** \ˈbir-dəd\ *adj* — **beard•ed•ness** *n* — **beard•less** \ˈbird-ləs\ *adj*

[2]**beard** *vt* (15c) **1 :** to confront and oppose with boldness, resolution, and often effrontery **:** DEFY **2 :** to furnish with a beard

bearded collie *n* (1880) **:** any of a breed of large herding dogs of Scottish origin that have a long rough coat and drooping ears

bearded iris *n* (1923) **:** any of numerous wild or cultivated irises with a growth of short hairs on each fall

bearded seal *n* (1853) **:** a large arctic hair seal (*Erignathus barbatus*) with a tuft of long whiskers on each side of the muzzle

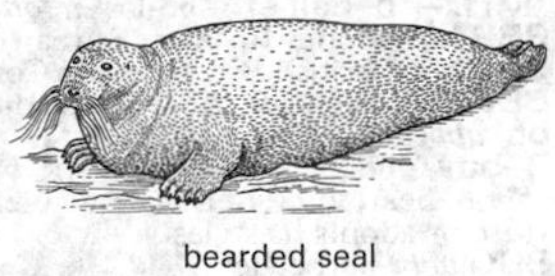
bearded seal

bear down *vt* (14c) **:** OVERCOME, OVERWHELM ~ *vi* **:** to exert full strength and concentrated attention — **bear down on 1 :** EMPHASIZE **2 :** to weigh heavily on **:** BURDEN

beard•tongue \ˈbird-ˌtəŋ\ *n* (1821) **:** PENSTEMON

bear•er \ˈber-ər\ *n* (13c) **:** one that bears: as **a :** PORTER 1 **b :** a plant yielding fruit **c :** PALLBEARER **d :** one holding a check, draft, bond, or other order for payment esp. if marked payable to bearer — often used attributively ⟨~ bonds⟩

bear grass *n* (1750) **:** any of several plants (genera *Yucca, Nolina,* or *Xerophyllum*) of the lily or agave families chiefly of the southern and western U.S. with foliage resembling coarse blades of grass

bear–hug \ˈber-ˌhəg\ *vt* (1927) **:** to embrace in a bear hug

bear hug *n* (1921) **:** a rough tight embrace

bear•ing *n* (13c) **1 :** the manner in which one bears or comports oneself **2 a :** the act, power, or time of bringing forth offspring or fruit **b :** a product of bearing **:** CROP **3 a :** an object, surface, or point that supports **b :** a machine part in which another part (as a journal or pin) turns or slides **4 :** a figure borne on a heraldic field **5 :** PRESSURE, THRUST **6 a :** the situation or horizontal direction of one point with respect to another or to the compass **b :** a determination of position **c** *pl* **:** comprehension of one's position, environment, or situation **d :** RELATION, CONNECTION; *also* **:** PURPORT **7 :** the part of a structural member that rests on its supports

syn BEARING, DEPORTMENT, DEMEANOR, MIEN, MANNER, CARRIAGE mean the outward manifestation of personality or attitude. BEARING is the most general of these words but now usu. implies characteristic posture ⟨a woman of regal *bearing*⟩. DEPORTMENT suggests actions or behavior as formed by breeding or training ⟨your *deportment* was atrocious⟩. DEMEANOR suggests one's attitude toward others as expressed in outward behavior ⟨the haughty *demeanor* of the headwaiter⟩. MIEN is a literary term referring both to bearing and demeanor ⟨a *mien* of supreme self-satisfaction〉. MANNER implies characteristic or customary way of moving and gesturing and addressing others 〈the imperious *manner* of a man used to giving orders〉. CARRIAGE applies chiefly to habitual posture in standing or walking 〈the kind of *carriage* learned at boarding school〉.

bearing rein *n* (1795) : CHECKREIN 1

bear·ish \ˈber-ish\ *adj* (1744) **1** : resembling a bear in build or in roughness, gruffness, or surliness 〈a ~ man〉 **2 a** : marked by, tending to cause, or fearful of falling prices (as in a stock market) 〈~ investors〉 **b** : PESSIMISTIC — **bear·ish·ly** *adv* — **bear·ish·ness** *n*

bear market *n* [[1]*bear* (one that sells in expectation of a price decline)] (1858) : a market in which securities or commodities are persistently declining in value — compare BULL MARKET

bé·ar·naise sauce \ˈbā-är-ˌnāz-, -ər-; ˈber-\ *n* [F *béarnaise,* fem. of *béarnais* of Béarn, France] (1869) : a sauce of egg yolks and butter flavored with shallots, wine, vinegar, and seasonings

bear out *vt* (15c) : CONFIRM, VERIFY 〈a theory *borne out* by data〉

bear·skin \ˈber-ˌskin\ *n* (14c) : an article made of the skin of a bear; *esp* : a military hat made of the skin of a bear

bear up *vt* (1606) : SUPPORT, ENCOURAGE ~ *vi* : to summon up courage, resolution, or strength 〈*bearing up* under the strain〉

beast \ˈbēst\ *n* [ME *beste,* fr. AF, fr. L *bestia*] (13c) **1 a** : a four-footed mammal as distinguished from a human being, a lower vertebrate, and an invertebrate **b** : a lower animal as distinguished from a human being **c** : an animal as distinguished from a plant **d** : an animal under human control **2** : a contemptible person **3** : something formidably difficult to control or deal with

beast epic *n* (1843) : a poem with epic conventions in which animals speak and act like human beings

beast fable *n* (1840) : a usu. didactic prose or verse fable in which animals speak and act like human beings

beast·ie \ˈbē-stē\ *n* (1714) : BEAST, ANIMAL, CRITTER

beastings *var of* BEESTINGS

[1]**beast·ly** \ˈbēst-lē\ *adj* **beast·li·er; -est** (14c) **1** : BESTIAL 1 **2** : ABOMINABLE, DISAGREEABLE 〈~ weather〉 — **beast·li·ness** *n*

[2]**beastly** *adv* (15c) : VERY 〈a ~ cold day〉

beast of burden (1740) : an animal employed to carry heavy loads or to perform other heavy work (as pulling a plow)

[1]**beat** \ˈbēt\ *vb* **beat; beat·en** \ˈbē-tᵊn\ *or* **beat; beat·ing** [ME *beten,* fr. OE *bēatan;* akin to OHG *bōzan* to beat] *vt* (bef. 12c) **1** : to strike repeatedly: **a** : to hit repeatedly so as to inflict pain — often used with *up* **b** : to walk on : TREAD 〈~ the pavement looking for work〉 **c** : to strike directly against forcefully and repeatedly : dash against **d** : to flap or thrash at vigorously **e** : to strike at in order to rouse game; *also* : to range over in or as if in quest of game **f** : to mix by stirring : WHIP — often used with *up* **g** : to strike repeatedly in order to produce music or a signal 〈~ a drum〉 **2 a** : to drive or force by blows 〈~ back his attackers〉 **b** : to pound into a powder, paste, or pulp **c** : to make by repeated treading or driving over 〈~ a path〉 **d** (1) : to dislodge by repeated hitting 〈~ dust from the carpet〉 (2) : to lodge securely by repeated striking 〈~ a stake into the ground〉 **e** : to shape by beating 〈~ swords into plowshares〉; *esp* : to flatten thin by blows **f** : to sound or express esp. by drumbeat **3** : to cause to strike or flap repeatedly 〈a bird ~*ing* its wings〉 **4 a** : OVERCOME, DEFEAT; *also* : SURPASS — often used with *out* **b** : to prevail despite 〈~ the odds〉 **c** : BEWILDER, BAFFLE 〈it ~*s* me how she does it〉 **d** (1) : FATIGUE, EXHAUST (2) : to leave dispirited, irresolute, or hopeless **e** : CHEAT, SWINDLE **5 a** (1) : to act ahead of usu. so as to forestall (2) : to report a news item in advance of **b** : to come or arrive before **c** : CIRCUMVENT 〈~ the system〉 **d** : to outmaneuver (a defender) and get free **e** : to score against (a goalkeeper) **6** : to indicate by beating 〈~ the tempo〉 ~ *vi* **1 a** : to become forcefully impelled : DASH **b** : to glare or strike with oppressive intensity **c** : to sustain distracting activity **d** : to beat a drum **2 a** (1) : PULSATE, THROB (2) : TICK **b** : to sound upon being struck **3 a** : to strike repeated blows 〈~*ing* on the door〉 **b** : to strike the air : FLAP **c** : to strike cover in order to rouse game; *also* : to range or scour for or as if for game **4** : to progress with much difficulty **5** : to sail to windward by a series of tacks — **beat·able** \ˈbē-tə-bəl\ *adj* — **beat about the bush** *or* **beat around the bush** : to fail or refuse to come to the point in discourse — **beat a retreat** : to leave in haste — **beat it 1** : to hurry away : SCRAM **2** : HURRY, RUSH — **beat one's brains out** : to try intently to resolve something difficult by thinking — **beat the bushes** : to search thoroughly through all possible areas — **beat the drum** : to proclaim as meritorious or significant : publicize vigorously — **beat the pants off** : to defeat or surpass overwhelmingly — **beat the rap** : to evade the penalties connected with an accusation or charge — **beat up on** : to attack physically or verbally — **to beat the band** : in a very energetic or forceful manner 〈talking away *to beat the band*〉

[2]**beat** *n* (ca. 1625) **1 a** : a single stroke or blow esp. in a series; *also* : PULSATION, TICK **b** : a sound produced by or as if by beating **c** : a driving impact or force **2** : one swing of the pendulum or balance of a timepiece **3 a** : a regularly traversed round 〈the cop on the ~〉 **b** : a group of news sources that a reporter covers regularly **4 a** : a metrical or rhythmic stress in poetry or music or the rhythmic effect of these stresses **b** : the tempo indicated (as by a conductor) to a musical performer **c** : the pronounced rhythm that is the characteristic driving force in some types of music (as jazz or rock); *also* : [2]ROCK 2 **5 a** : one that excels 〈I've never seen the ~ of it〉 **b** : the reporting of a news story ahead of competitors **6** : DEADBEAT **7 a** : an act of beating to windward **b** : one of the reaches so traversed : TACK **8** : each of the pulsations of amplitude produced by the union of sound or radio waves or electric currents having different frequencies **9** : an accented stroke (as of one leg or foot against the other) in dancing **10** : MOMENT 〈waited a ~ before responding〉 — **beat·less** \-ləs\ *adj*

[3]**beat** *adj* [ME *beten, bete,* fr. pp. of *beten*] (1800) **1 a** : being in a state of exhaustion : EXHAUSTED **b** : sapped of resolution or morale **2** *often cap* : of, relating to, or being beatniks 〈~ poets〉

[4]**beat** *n, often cap* (1957) : BEATNIK

beat·box \ˈbēt-ˌbäks\ *n* (1971) : an electronic device that adds a backbeat, manipulates sounds, and mimics musical instruments

beat·en \ˈbē-tᵊn\ *adj* (13c) **1** : hammered into a desired shape 〈~ gold〉 **2** : much trodden and worn smooth; *also* : FAMILIAR 〈a ~ path〉 **3** : being in a state of exhaustion : EXHAUSTED

beaten biscuit *n* (1836) : a biscuit whose dough is lightened by beating and folding

beat·er \ˈbē-tər\ *n* (14c) **1** : one that beats: as **a** : EGGBEATER **b** : a rotary blade attached to an electric mixer **c** : DRUMSTICK 1 **2** : one who strikes bushes or other cover to rouse game **3** : a dilapidated old automobile : CLUNKER

be·atif·ic \ˌbē-ə-ˈti-fik\ *adj* [L *beatificus* making happy, fr. *beatus* happy, fr. pp. of *beare* to bless; perh. akin to L *bonus* good — more at BOUNTY] (1640) **1** : of, possessing, or imparting beatitude **2** : having a blissful appearance 〈a ~ smile〉 — **be·atif·i·cal·ly** \-fi-k(ə-)lē\ *adv*

beatific vision *n* (1702) : the direct knowledge of God enjoyed by the blessed in heaven

be·at·i·fy \bē-ˈa-tə-ˌfī\ *vt* **-fied; -fy·ing** [MF *beatifier,* fr. LL *beatificare,* fr. L *beatus* + *facere* to make — more at DO] (1535) **1** : to make supremely happy **2** : to declare to have attained the blessedness of heaven and authorize the title "Blessed" and limited public religious honor — **be·at·i·fi·ca·tion** \-ˌa-tə-fə-ˈkā-shən\ *n*

beat·ing \ˈbē-tiŋ\ *n* (13c) **1** : an act of striking with repeated blows so as to injure or damage; *also* : the injury or damage thus inflicted **2** : PULSATION **3** : DEFEAT, SETBACK

beating reed *n* (1851) : a reed in a musical instrument that vibrates against the edges of an air opening (as in a clarinet or organ pipe) to which it is attached — compare FREE REED

be·at·i·tude \bē-ˈa-tə-ˌtüd, -ˌtyüd\ *n* [L *beatitudo,* fr. *beatus*] (15c) **1 a** : a state of utmost bliss **b** — used as a title for a primate esp. of an Eastern church **2** : any of the declarations made in the Sermon on the Mount (Mt 5:3–11) beginning in the AV "Blessed are"

beat·nik \ˈbēt-nik\ *n* [[3]*beat* + *-nik*] (1958) : a person who participated in a social movement of the 1950s and early 1960s which stressed artistic self-expression and the rejection of the mores of conventional society; *broadly* : a usu. young and artistic person who rejects the mores of conventional society

beat off *vt* (15c) : REPEL ~ *vi, usu vulgar* : MASTURBATE — used of a male

beat out *vt* (1588) **1** : to make or perform by or as if by beating **2** : to mark or accompany by beating **3** : to turn (a routine ground ball or a bunt) into a hit in baseball by fast running to first base

Be·atrice \ˌbā-ä-ˈtrē-(ˌ)chā, ˈbē-ə-trəs\ *n* [It] (1642) : a Florentine woman idealized in Dante's *Vita Nuova* and *Divina Commedia*

beat–up \ˈbēt-ˌəp, -ˈəp\ *adj* (1863) : DILAPIDATED, SHABBY

beau \ˈbō\ *n, pl* **beaux** \ˈbōz\ *or* **beaus** [F, fr. *beau* beautiful, fr. L *bellus* pretty] (1653) **1** : DANDY 1 **2** : BOYFRIEND 2

Beau Brum·mell \ˈbō-ˈbrə-məl\ *n* [nickname of G. B. *Brummell*] (1834) : DANDY 1

beau·coup \ˈbō-(ˌ)kü\ *adj* [F] (ca. 1918) *slang* : great in quantity or amount : MANY, MUCH 〈spent ~ dollars〉

Beau·fort scale \ˈbō-fərt-\ *n* [Sir Francis *Beaufort*] (1856) : a scale in which the force of the wind is indicated by numbers from 0 to 12

BEAUFORT SCALE

BEAUFORT NUMBER	NAME	WIND SPEED MPH	KPH	DESCRIPTION
0	calm	<1	<1	calm; smoke rises vertically
1	light air	1-3	1-5	direction of wind shown by smoke but not by wind vanes
2	light breeze	4-7	6-11	wind felt on face; leaves rustle; wind vane moves
3	gentle breeze	8-12	12-19	leaves and small twigs in constant motion; wind extends light flag
4	moderate breeze	13-18	20-29	wind raises dust and loose paper; small branches move
5	fresh breeze	19-24	30-39	small trees with leaves begin to sway; crested wavelets form on inland waters
6	strong breeze	25-31	40-50	large branches move; overhead wires whistle; umbrellas difficult to control
7	moderate gale *or* near gale	32-38	51-61	whole trees sway; walking against wind is difficult
8	fresh gale *or* gale	39-46	62-74	twigs break off trees; moving cars veer
9	strong gale	47-54	75-87	slight structural damage occurs; shingles may blow away
10	whole gale *or* storm	55-63	88-102	trees uprooted; considerable structural damage occurs
11	storm *or* violent storm	64-72	103-117	widespread damage occurs
12	hurricane*	≥73	≥118	widespread damage occurs

*The U.S. uses 74 statute mph as the speed criterion for a hurricane.

\ə\ **abut** \ᵊ\ **kitten, F table** \ər\ **further** \a\ **ash** \ā\ **ace** \ä\ **mop, mar** \au̇\ **out** \ch\ **chin** \e\ **bet** \ē\ **easy** \g\ **go** \i\ **hit** \ī\ **ice** \j\ **job** \ŋ\ **sing** \ō\ **go** \ȯ\ **law** \ȯi\ **boy** \th\ **thin** \t͟h\ **the** \ü\ **loot** \u̇\ **foot** \y\ **yet** \zh\ **vision, beige** \k͟, ⁿ, œ, ue, ʸ\ *see* Guide to Pronunciation

beau geste \bō-ˈzhest\ *n, pl* **beaux gestes** *or* **beau gestes** \bō-ˈzhest\ [F, lit., beautiful gesture] (1900) **1 :** a graceful or magnanimous gesture **2 :** an ingratiating conciliatory gesture
beau ide·al \ˌbō-ī-ˈdē(-ə)l, ˌbō-ˌē-dā-ˈäl\ *n, pl* **beau ideals** [F *beau idéal* ideal beauty] (1786) **:** the perfect type or model
Beau·jo·lais \ˌbō-zhō-ˈlā, -zhə-\ *n, pl* **Beaujolais** [F, fr. *Beaujolais,* region of eastern France] (1836) **:** a light fruity red burgundy wine made from the Gamay grape
Beaujolais nouveau *n* [F, lit., new Beaujolais] (1971) **:** a Beaujolais wine that is released shortly after a grape harvest and is sold for immediate consumption
beau monde \bō-ˈmänd, -mōⁿd\ *n, pl* **beau mondes** \-ˈmän(d)z\ *or* **beaux mondes** \bō-mōⁿd\ [F, lit., fine world] (1673) **:** the world of high society and fashion
[1]**beaut** \ˈbyüt\ *n* (1866) **:** BEAUTY 4
[2]**beaut** *adj* (1918) *Austral & NewZeal* **:** EXCELLENT 2
beau·te·ous \ˈbyü-tē-əs\ *adj* [ME, fr. *beaute*] (15c) **:** BEAUTIFUL — **beau·te·ous·ly** *adv* — **beau·te·ous·ness** *n*
beau·ti·cian \byü-ˈti-shən\ *n* [*beauty* + *-ician*] (1924) **:** COSMETOLOGIST
beau·ti·ful \ˈbyü-ti-fəl\ *adj* (15c) **1 :** having qualities of beauty **:** exciting aesthetic pleasure **2 :** generally pleasing **:** EXCELLENT — **beau·ti·ful·ly** \-f(ə-)lē\ *adv* — **beau·ti·ful·ness** \-fəl-nəs\ *n*
syn BEAUTIFUL, LOVELY, HANDSOME, PRETTY, COMELY, FAIR mean exciting sensuous or aesthetic pleasure. BEAUTIFUL applies to whatever excites the keenest of pleasure to the senses and stirs emotion through the senses ⟨*beautiful* mountain scenery⟩. LOVELY is close to BEAUTIFUL but applies to a narrower range of emotional excitation in suggesting the graceful, delicate, or exquisite ⟨a *lovely* melody⟩. HANDSOME suggests aesthetic pleasure due to proportion, symmetry, or elegance ⟨a *handsome* Georgian mansion⟩. PRETTY often applies to superficial or insubstantial attractiveness ⟨a painter of conventionally *pretty* scenes⟩. COMELY is like HANDSOME in suggesting what is coolly approved rather than emotionally responded to ⟨the *comely* grace of a dancer⟩. FAIR suggests beauty because of purity, flawlessness, or freshness ⟨*fair* of face⟩.
beautiful people *n pl, often cap B&P* (1963) **:** wealthy or famous people whose lifestyle is usu. expensive and well-publicized
beau·ti·fy \ˈbyü-tə-ˌfī\ *vb* **-fied; -fy·ing** *vt* (1526) **:** to make beautiful or add beauty to ~ *vi* **:** to grow beautiful ***syn*** see ADORN — **beau·ti·fi·ca·tion** \ˌbyü-tə-fə-ˈkā-shən\ *n* — **beau·ti·fi·er** \ˈbyü-tə-ˌfī(-ə)r\ *n*
beau·ty \ˈbyü-tē\ *n, pl* **beauties** [ME *beute, bealte,* fr. AF, fr. *bel, beau* beautiful, fr. L *bellus* pretty; akin to L *bonus* good — more at BOUNTY] (14c) **1 :** the quality or aggregate of qualities in a person or thing that gives pleasure to the senses or pleasurably exalts the mind or spirit **:** LOVELINESS **2 :** a beautiful person or thing; *esp* **:** a beautiful woman **3 :** a particularly graceful, ornamental, or excellent quality **4 :** a brilliant, extreme, or egregious example or instance ⟨that mistake was a ~⟩ **5 :** BOTTOM 9
beau·ty·ber·ry \-ˌber-ē, -ˌbe-rē\ *n* (1918) **:** any of a genus (*Callicarpa*) of deciduous shrubs and trees of the vervain family that bear dense clusters of small usu. purple berries and are often cultivated as ornamentals
beauty bush *n* (1926) **:** a Chinese shrub (*Kolkwitzia amabilis*) of the honeysuckle family with pinkish flowers and bristly fruit
beauty contest *n* (1886) **1 :** an assemblage of girls or women at which judges select the most beautiful — called also *beauty pageant* **2 :** a presidential primary election in which the popular vote does not determine the number of convention delegates a candidate receives
beauty mark *n* (1849) **:** a small dark mark (as a mole) on the skin esp. of the face
beauty part *n* (1951) **:** the most desirable or beneficial aspect of something
beauty queen *n* (1893) **:** a beautiful and glamorous woman or girl; *specif* **:** a winner of a beauty contest
beauty shop *n* (1890) **:** an establishment or department where hairdressing, facials, and manicures are done — called also *beauty parlor, beauty salon*
beauty spot *n* (1650) **1 :** [1]PATCH 2 **2 :** BEAUTY MARK
[1]**beaux arts** \ˈbō-ˈzär\ *n pl* [F *beaux-arts*] (1753) **:** FINE ARTS
[2]**beaux arts** *adj, often cap B&A* [F *École des Beaux-Arts* School of Fine Arts, in Paris] (1878) **:** characterized by the use of historic forms, rich decorative detail, and a tendency toward monumental conception in architecture
[1]**bea·ver** \ˈbē-vər\ *n, pl* **beavers** [ME *bever,* fr. OE *beofor;* akin to OHG *bibar* beaver, and prob. to OE *brūn* brown — more at BROWN] (bef. 12c) **1** *or pl* **beaver a :** either of two large semiaquatic herbivorous rodents comprising a family (Castoridae including *Castor canadensis* of No. America and *C. fiber* of Eurasia), having webbed hind feet and a broad flat scaly tail, and constructing dams and partially submerged lodges **b :** the fur or pelt of the beaver **2 a :** a hat made of beaver fur or a fabric imitation **b :** SILK HAT **3 :** a heavy fabric of felted wool or of cotton napped on both sides **4** *usu vulgar* **:** the pudenda of a woman
[2]**beaver** *n* [ME *baviere,* fr. MF] (15c) **1 :** a piece of armor protecting the lower part of the face **2 :** a helmet visor
[3]**beaver** *vi* (1946) **:** to work energetically ⟨~*ing* away at the problem⟩
bea·ver·board \ˈbē-vər-ˌbȯrd\ *n* [fr. *Beaver Board,* a trademark] (1903) **:** a fiberboard used for partitions and ceilings
bea·ver·tail \-ˌtāl\ *n* (1919) **:** a low-growing prickly pear cactus (*Opuntia basilaris*) of the southwestern U.S. and northern Mexico having large usu. pink or red flowers
be·bop \ˈbē-ˌbäp\ *n* [imit.] (1942) **:** [3]BOP 1 — **be·bop·per** *n*
BEC *abbr* Bureau of Employees' Compensation
be·calm \bi-ˈkä(l)m\ *vt* (1582) **1 a :** to keep motionless by lack of wind **b :** to stop the progress of **2 :** to make calm **:** SOOTHE
be·cause \bi-ˈkȯz, -ˈkəz, -ˈkȯs, bē-\ *conj* [ME *because that, because,* fr. *by cause that*] (14c) **1 :** for the reason that **:** SINCE ⟨rested ~ he was tired⟩ **2 :** the fact that **:** THAT ⟨the reason I haven't been fired is ~ my boss hasn't got round to it yet —E. B. White⟩
because of *prep* (14c) **:** by reason of **:** on account of
bé·cha·mel \ˌbā-shə-ˈmel\ *n* [F *sauce béchamelle,* fr. Louis de *Béchamel* †1703 Fr. courtier] (1789) **:** a rich white sauce
be·chance \bi-ˈchan(t)s, bē-\ *vb* (1527) *archaic* **:** BEFALL
bêche–de–mer \ˌbesh-də-ˈmer, ˌbäsh-\ *n* [F, alter. of *biche de mer,* fr. Pg *bicho do mar,* lit., sea worm] (1783) **1** *pl* **bêche–de–mer** *or* **bêches–de–mer** \ˌbesh-də-, ˌbe-shəz-, ˌbäsh-\ **:** TREPANG **2** *cap B&M* **:** any of several English-based pidgins spoken on islands of the western Pacific
[1]**beck** *vt* [ME, alter. of *beknen*] (13c) *archaic* **:** BECKON
[2]**beck** *n* (14c) **1** *chiefly Scot* **:** BOW, CURTSY **2 a :** a beckoning gesture **b :** SUMMONS, BIDDING — **at one's beck and call :** ready to obey one's command immediately
[3]**beck** \ˈbek\ *n* [ME *bek,* fr. ON *bekkr;* akin to OE *bæc* brook, OHG *bah,* Lith *bėgti* to flee — more at PHOBIA] (14c) *Brit* **:** CREEK 2
Beck·er muscular dystrophy \ˈbe-kər-\ *n* [Peter Emil *Becker* b1908 Ger. geneticist] (1972) **:** a less severe form of Duchenne muscular dystrophy marked by later onset and slower progression of the disease — called also *Beck·er's muscular dystrophy* \-kərz-\
beck·et \ˈbe-kət\ *n* [origin unknown] (ca. 1769) **:** a device for holding something in place: as **a :** a grommet or a loop of rope with a knot at one end to catch in an eye at the other **b :** a ring of rope or metal **c :** a loop of rope (as for a handle)
beck·on \ˈbe-kən\ *vb* **beck·oned; beck·on·ing** [ME *beknen,* fr. OE *bīecnan,* fr. *bēacen* sign — more at BEACON] *vi* (bef. 12c) **1 :** to summon or signal typically with a wave or nod **2 :** to appear inviting **:** ATTRACT ⟨the frontier ~*s*⟩ ~ *vt* **:** to beckon to — **beckon** *n*
be·cloud \bi-ˈklau̇d, bē-\ *vt* (1600) **1 :** to obscure with or as if with a cloud **2 :** to prevent clear perception or realization of **:** MUDDLE ⟨prejudices that ~ his judgment⟩
be·come \bi-ˈkəm, bē-\ *vb* **-came** \-ˈkām\; **-come; -com·ing** [ME, to come to, become, fr. OE *becuman,* fr. *be-* + *cuman* to come] *vi* (bef. 12c) **1 a :** to come into existence **b :** to come to be ⟨~ sick⟩ **2 :** to undergo change or development ~ *vt* **:** to be suitable to ⟨seriousness *becoming* the occasion⟩; *esp* **:** to be becoming to ⟨her clothes ~ her⟩ — **become of :** to happen to ⟨wondering whatever *became of* old friends⟩
be·com·ing \-ˈkə-miŋ\ *adj* (15c) **:** SUITABLE, FITTING; *esp* **:** attractively suitable ⟨~ modesty⟩ — **be·com·ing·ly** \-miŋ-lē\ *adv*
[1]**bed** \ˈbed\ *n* [ME, fr. OE *bedd;* akin to OHG *betti* bed, L *fodere* to dig] (bef. 12c) **1 a :** a piece of furniture on or in which to lie and sleep **b** (1) **:** a place of sex relations (2) **:** marital relationship (3) **:** close association **:** CAHOOTS ⟨a legislator in ~ with lobbyists⟩ **c :** a place for sleeping **d :** SLEEP; *also* **:** a time for sleeping ⟨took a walk before ~⟩ **e** (1) **:** a mattress filled with soft material (2) **:** BEDSTEAD **f :** the equipment and services needed to care for one hospitalized patient or hotel guest **2 :** a flat or level surface: as **a :** a plot of ground prepared for plants; *also* **:** the plants grown in such a plot **b :** the bottom of a body of water; *esp* **:** an area of sea bottom supporting a heavy growth of a particular organism ⟨an oyster ~⟩ **3 :** a supporting surface or structure **:** FOUNDATION **4 :** LAYER, STRATUM **5 a :** the place or material in which a block or brick is laid **b :** the lower surface of a brick, slate, or tile **6 :** a mass or heap resembling a bed ⟨a ~ of ashes⟩ ⟨served on a ~ of lettuce⟩ — **in bed :** in the act of sexual intercourse
[2]**bed** *vb* **bed·ded; bed·ding** *vi* (bef. 12c) **1 a :** to find or make sleeping accommodations — usu. used with *down* ⟨a place to ~ down⟩ **b :** to go to bed — usu. used with *down* ⟨~ down at midnight⟩ **2 :** to form a layer **3 :** to lie flat or flush ~ *vt* **1 a :** to furnish with a bed or bedding **:** settle in sleeping quarters — often used with *down* **b :** to put, take, or send to bed **2 a :** EMBED **b :** to plant or arrange in beds **c :** BASE, ESTABLISH **3 a :** to lay flat or in a layer **b :** to make a bed in or of **4 :** to have sexual intercourse with
BEd *abbr* bachelor of education
be·dab·ble \bi-ˈda-bəl, bē-\ *vt* (1590) *archaic* **:** to wet or soil by dabbling
bed–and–breakfast *n* (1978) **:** an establishment (as an inn) offering lodging and breakfast
be·daub \bi-ˈdȯb, -ˈdäb, bē-\ *vt* (1558) **1 :** to daub over **:** BESMEAR **2 :** to ornament with vulgar excess
be·daz·zle \bi-ˈda-zəl, bē-\ *vt* (ca. 1616) **1 :** to confuse by a strong light **2 :** to impress forcefully **:** ENCHANT — **be·daz·zle·ment** \-mənt\ *n*
bed·bug \ˈbed-ˌbəg\ *n* (1708) **:** a wingless bloodsucking hemipterous bug (*Cimex lectularius*) sometimes infesting houses and esp. beds and feeding on human blood

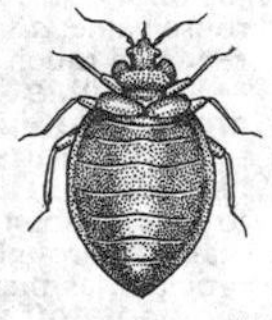
bedbug

bed·cham·ber \-ˌchām-bər\ *n* (14c) **:** BEDROOM
bed check *n* (1919) **:** a night inspection to check the presence of persons (as soldiers) required by regulations to be in bed or in quarters
bed·clothes \ˈbed-ˌklō(th)z\ *n pl* (14c) **:** the covering (as sheets and blankets) used on a bed
bed·cov·er \-ˌkə-vər\ *also* **bed·cov·er·ing** \-ˌkə-v(ə-)riŋ\ *n* (ca. 1656) **1 :** BEDSPREAD **2 :** BEDCLOTHES — usu. used in pl.
bed·ded \ˈbe-dəd\ *adj* (1773) **:** having a bed or beds of a specified kind or number — used in combination ⟨a twin-*bedded* room⟩
bed·der \ˈbe-dər\ *n* (1849) **1 :** a bedding plant **2 :** a person who makes up beds
[1]**bed·ding** \ˈbe-diŋ\ *n* [ME, fr. OE, fr. *bedd*] (bef. 12c) **1 :** BEDCLOTHES **2 :** a bottom layer **:** FOUNDATION **3 :** material to provide a bed for livestock **4 :** STRATIFICATION
[2]**bedding** *adj* [fr. gerund of [2]*bed*] (1836) **:** suitable for planting in large groups in flower beds to produce a mass display ⟨~ plants⟩
be·deck \bi-ˈdek, bē-\ *vt* (1565) **1 :** to clothe with finery **:** DECK **2 :** DECORATE 2
be·dev·il \bi-ˈde-vəl, bē-\ *vt* (1574) **1 :** to possess with or as if with a devil **2 :** to cause distress **:** TROUBLE **3 :** to change for the worse **:** SPOIL **4 :** to confuse utterly — **be·dev·il·ment** \-mənt\ *n*
be·dew \bi-ˈdü, -ˈdyü, bē-\ *vt* (14c) **:** to wet with or as if with dew
bed·fast \ˈbed-ˌfast\ *adj* (1560) **:** BEDRIDDEN
bed·fel·low \-ˌfe-(ˌ)lō\ *n* (15c) **1 :** one who shares a bed with another **2 :** ASSOCIATE, ALLY ⟨political ~*s*⟩
Bed·ford cord \ˈbed-fərd-\ *n* [perh. fr. New *Bedford,* Massachusetts] (1860) **:** a clothing fabric with lengthwise ribs that resembles corduroy; *also* **:** the weave used in making this fabric
bed–hop \ˈbed-ˌhäp\ *vi* (1943) **:** SLEEP AROUND
be·dight \bi-ˈdīt, bē-\ *vt* **be·dight·ed** *or* **bedight; be·dight·ing** (15c) *archaic* **:** EQUIP, ARRAY
be·dim \bi-ˈdim, bē-\ *vt* (1565) **1 :** to make less bright **2 :** to make indistinct **:** OBSCURE

Bed·i·vere \ˈbe-də-ˌvir\ *n* (15c) : a knight of the Round Table
be·di·zen \bi-ˈdī-zᵊn, -ˈdi-, bē-\ *vt* (1661) : to dress or adorn gaudily — **be·di·zen·ment** \-mənt\ *n*
bed·lam \ˈbed-ləm\ *n* [*Bedlam,* popular name for the Hospital of St. Mary of Bethlehem, London, an insane asylum, fr. ME *Bedlem* Bethlehem] (ca. 1529) **1** *obs* : MADMAN, LUNATIC **2** *often cap* : a lunatic asylum **3** : a place, scene, or state of uproar and confusion — **bedlam** *adj*
bed·lam·ite \ˈbed-lə-ˌmīt\ *n* (1589) : MADMAN, LUNATIC — **bedlamite** *adj*
Bed·ling·ton terrier \ˈbed-liŋ-tən-\ *n* [*Bedlington,* parish in Northumberland, England] (1867) : a swift lightly built terrier of English origin with a long narrow head, arched back, and usu. curly coat — called also *Bedlington*
bed·mate \ˈbed-ˌmāt\ *n* (1582) : one who shares one's bed; *esp* : a sexual partner
bed of roses (1576) : a place or situation of agreeable ease
bed·ou·in *also* **bed·u·in** \ˈbe-də-wən, -dü-ən, ˈbed-wən\ *n, pl* **bedouin** *or* **bedouins** *also* **beduin** *or* **beduins** *often cap* [ME *Bedoyne,* fr. MF *bedoïn,* fr. Ar *badawī* desert dweller, fr. *badw* desert, desert dwellers] (14c) : a nomadic Arab of the Arabian, Syrian, or northern African deserts
bed·pan \ˈbed-ˌpan\ *n* (1678) : a shallow vessel used by a bedridden person for urination or defecation
bed·plate \-ˌplāt\ *n* (1817) : a plate or framing used as a support
bed·post \-ˌpōst\ *n* (1598) : the usu. turned or carved post of a bed
be·drag·gle \bi-ˈdra-gəl\ *vt* (1727) : to wet thoroughly
be·drag·gled \bi-ˈdra-gəld; bē-\ *adj* (ca. 1775) **1** : soiled and stained by or as if by trailing in mud **2** : left wet and limp by or as if by rain **3** : DILAPIDATED ⟨~ buildings⟩
bed rest *n* (1902) : confinement of a sick person to bed
bed·rid·den \ˈbed-ˌri-dᵊn\ *also* **bed·rid** \-ˌrid\ *adj* [alter. of ME *bedrede, bedreden,* fr. OE *bedreda,* fr. *bedreda* one confined to bed, fr. *bedd* bed + *-rida, -reda,* fr. *rīdan* to ride — more at BED, RIDE] (bef. 12c) : confined (as by illness) to bed
[1]**bed·rock** \-ˈräk, -ˌräk\ *n* (1839) **1** : the solid rock underlying unconsolidated surface materials (as soil) **2 a** : lowest point **b** : BASIS
[2]**bedrock** *adj* (1873) : solidly fundamental, basic, or reliable ⟨traditional ~ values⟩ ⟨a ~ constituency⟩
bed·roll \-ˌrōl\ *n* (1849) : bedding rolled up for carrying
[1]**bed·room** \-ˌrüm, -ˌru̇m\ *n* (1600) : a room furnished with a bed and intended primarily for sleeping — **bed·roomed** \-ˌrümd, -ˌru̇md\ *adj*
[2]**bedroom** *adj* (1900) **1** : dealing with, suggestive of, or inviting sexual relations ⟨a ~ farce⟩ ⟨~ eyes⟩ **2** : inhabited or used by commuters ⟨a ~ community⟩
Beds *abbr* Bedfordshire
bed·sheet \ˈbed-ˌshēt\ *n* (15c) : an oblong piece of usu. cotton or linen cloth used as an article of bedding
[1]**bed·side** \ˈbed-ˌsīd\ *n* (14c) : the side of a bed : a place beside a bed
[2]**bedside** *adj* (1787) **1** : of, relating to, or conducted at the bedside ⟨a ~ diagnosis⟩ **2** : suitable for reading in bed ⟨a ~ book⟩
bedside manner *n* (1848) : the manner that a physician assumes toward patients
bed–sit·ter \ˈbed-ˌsi-tər\ *n* [*bed-sitt*ing room + *-er* (as in *fresher* freshman, *rugger* rugby)] (1899) *Brit* : a one-room apartment serving as both bedroom and sitting room — called also *bedsit, bed-sitting-room*
bed·sore \ˈbed-ˌsȯr\ *n* (1826) : an ulceration of tissue deprived of adequate blood supply by prolonged pressure — called also *decubitus ulcer*
bed·spread \-ˌspred\ *n* (1820) : a usu. ornamental cloth cover for a bed
bed·spring \-ˌspriŋ\ *n* (1858) : a spring supporting a mattress
bed·stead \ˈbed-ˌsted\ *n* [ME *bedstede,* fr. *bed* + *stede* stead, place — more at STEAD] (15c) : the framework of a bed
bed·straw \-ˌstrȯ\ *n* [fr. its use for mattresses] (1527) : any of a genus (*Galium*) of herbs of the madder family having squarish stems, whorled leaves, and small flowers
bed table *n* (1811) **1** : an adjustable table used (as for eating or writing) by a person in bed **2** : a small table beside a bed
bed·time \-ˌtīm\ *n* (13c) : a time for going to bed
bedtime story *n* (1868) : a story read or recounted to someone (as a child) at bedtime
be·du \ˈbe-(ˌ)dü\ *n, pl* **bedu** *often cap* [Ar *badw* desert, desert dwellers] (1871) : BEDOUIN
bed warmer *n* (1740) : a covered pan containing hot coals used to warm a bed
bed–wet·ting \-ˌwe-tiŋ\ *n* (1890) : enuresis esp. when occurring in bed during sleep — **bed wetter** *n*
[1]**bee** \ˈbē\ *n* [ME, fr. OE *bēo;* akin to OHG *bīa* bee, OIr *bech,* Lith *bitis*] (bef. 12c) **1** : any of numerous hymenopterous insects (superfamily Apoidea) that differ from the related wasps esp. in the heavier hairier body and in having sucking as well as chewing mouthparts, that feed on pollen and nectar, and that store both and often also honey — see AFRICANIZED BEE, BUMBLEBEE, CARPENTER BEE, HONEYBEE, SWEAT BEE **2** : an eccentric notion : FANCY — **bee·like** \-ˌlīk\ *adj* — **bee in one's bonnet** : [1]BEE 2
[2]**bee** *n* (14c) : the letter *b*
[3]**bee** *n* [perh. fr. E dial. *been* help given by neighbors, fr. ME *bene* prayer, boon, fr. OE *bēn* prayer — more at BOON] (1769) : a gathering of people for a specific purpose ⟨a quilting ~⟩
BEE *abbr* bachelor of electrical engineering
bee balm *n* (1836) **1** : any of several monardas; *esp* : OSWEGO TEA **2** : LEMON BALM
bee·bread \ˈbē-ˌbred\ *n* (1657) : bitter yellowish-brown pollen stored up in honeycomb cells and used mixed with honey by bees as food
beech \ˈbēch\ *n, pl* **beech·es** *or* **beech** [ME *beche,* fr. OE *bēce;* akin to OE *bōc* beech, OHG *buohha,* L *fagus,* Gk *phēgos* oak] (bef. 12c) : any of a genus (*Fagus* of the family Fagaceae, the beech family) of hardwood trees with smooth gray bark and small edible nuts; *also* : its wood — **beech·en** \ˈbē-chən\ *adj*
beech·drops \ˈbēch-ˌdräps\ *n pl but sing or pl in constr* (1813) : a plant (*Epifagus virginiana*) of the broomrape family parasitic on the roots of beeches
beech·nut \-ˌnət\ *n* (1661) : the nut of the beech
bee–eat·er \ˈbē-ˌē-tər\ *n* (1668) : any of a family (Meropidae) of brightly colored slender-billed insectivorous chiefly tropical Old World birds
[1]**beef** \ˈbēf\ *n, pl* **beefs** \ˈbēfs\ *or* **beeves** \ˈbēvz\ [ME, fr. AF *beof, bef* ox, beef, fr. L *bov-, bos* head of cattle — more at COW] (13c) **1** : the flesh of an adult domestic bovine (as a steer or cow) used as food **2 a** : an ox, cow, or bull in a full-grown or nearly full-grown state; *esp* : a steer or cow fattened for food ⟨quality Texas *beeves*⟩ ⟨a herd of good ~⟩ **b** : a dressed carcass of a beef animal **3** : muscular flesh : BRAWN **4** *pl beefs* : COMPLAINT
[2]**beef** *vt* (1860) : to increase or add substance, strength, or power to — usu. used with *up* ⟨money to ~ up its staff of professional economists —John Fischer⟩ ~ *vi* : COMPLAIN ⟨always ~*ing* about something⟩

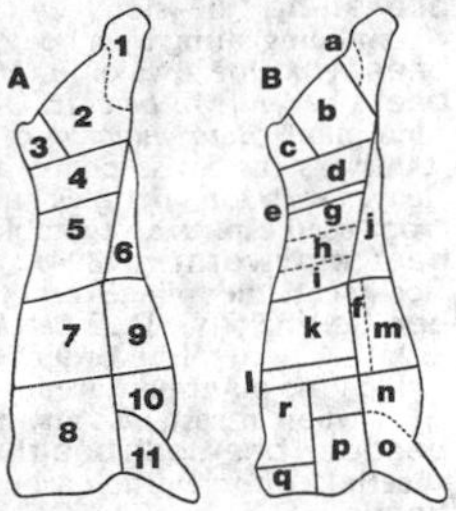

beef 2b: *A* wholesale cuts: *1* shank, *2* round with rump and shank cut off, *3* rump, *4* sirloin, *5* short loin, *6* flank, *7* rib, *8* chuck, *9* plate, *10* brisket, *11* shank; *B* retail cuts: *a* heel pot roast, *b* round steak, *c* rump roast, *d* sirloin steak, *e* pinbone steak, *f* short ribs, *g* porterhouse, *h* T-bone, *i* club steak, *j* flank steak, *k* rib roast, *l* blade rib roast, *m* plate, *n* brisket, *o* crosscut shank, *p* arm pot roast, *q* boneless neck, *r* blade roast

beef·a·lo \ˈbē-fə-ˌlō\ *n, pl* **-lo** *or* **-loes** *also* **-los** [blend of [1]*beef* and *buffalo*] (1973) : any of a breed of beef cattle developed in the U.S. that is genetically 3/8 No. American bison and 5/8 domestic bovine
beef·cake \ˈbēf-ˌkāk\ *n, often attrib* (1949) : a usu. photographic display of muscular male physiques; *also* : a man of the type featured in such a display or such men in general — compare CHEESECAKE
beef cattle *n pl* (1758) : cattle developed primarily for the efficient production of meat and marked by capacity for rapid growth, heavy well-fleshed body, and stocky build
beef·eat·er \ˈbēf-ˌē-tər\ *n, often cap* (1671) **1** : a yeoman of the guard that forms part of an English monarch's train on state occasions **2** : a warder of the tower of London uniformed like a beefeater
bee fly *n* (1751) : any of a family (Bombyliidae) of dipteran flies many of which resemble bees
beef·steak \ˈbēf-ˌstāk\ *n* (ca. 1706) : a steak of beef usu. from the hindquarter
beefsteak tomato *n* (1869) : a very large globe-shaped red tomato with dense flesh
beef Stro·ga·noff \-ˈstrȯ-gə-ˌnȯf, -ˈstrō-\ *n* [prob. fr. *Stroganov,* surname of a prominent line of Russian nobility] (1932) : beef sliced thin and cooked in a sour-cream sauce
beef Wel·ling·ton \-ˈwe-liŋ-tən\ *n* [prob. fr. the name *Wellington*] (1930) : a fillet of beef covered with pâté de foie gras and baked in a casing of pastry
beef·wood \ˈbēf-ˌwu̇d\ *n* (1805) **1** : the hard heavy reddish wood of any of various chiefly Australian trees **2** : AUSTRALIAN PINE
beefy \ˈbē-fē\ *adj* **beef·i·er; -est** (1743) **1 a** : heavily and powerfully built ⟨a ~ thug⟩ **b** : SUBSTANTIAL, STURDY ⟨~ shock absorbers⟩ **2 a** : of or suggesting beef ⟨a ~ flavor⟩ **b** : full of beef ⟨a ~ steak⟩
bee·hive \ˈbē-ˌhīv\ *n* (14c) **1** : HIVE 1 **2** : something resembling a hive for bees: as **a** : a scene of crowded activity **b** : a woman's hairdo that is conical in shape — **beehive** *adj*
beehive oven *n* (1872) : an arched oven used esp. for baking food and formerly for coking coal
bee·keep·er \-ˌkē-pər\ *n* (1783) : a person who raises bees — **bee·keep·ing** *n*
[1]**bee·line** \-ˌlīn\ *n* [fr. the belief that nectar-laden bees return to their hives in a direct line] (1830) : a straight direct course
[2]**beeline** *vi* (1882) : to go quickly in a straight direct course
Beel·ze·bub \bē-ˈel-zi-ˌbəb, ˈbēl-zi-, ˈbel-\ *n* [*Beelzebub,* prince of devils, fr. L, fr. Gk *Beelzeboub,* fr. Heb *Baʿal zĕbhūbh,* a Philistine god, lit., lord of flies] (bef. 12c) **1** : DEVIL **2** : a fallen angel in Milton's *Paradise Lost* ranking next to Satan
been *past part of* BE
[1]**beep** *vt* (1936) : to cause (as a horn) to sound ~ *vi* **1** : to sound a horn **2** : to make a beep
[2]**beep** \ˈbēp\ *n* [imit.] (1943) : a short usu. high-pitched sound (as from a horn or an electronic device) that serves as a signal or warning
beep·er \ˈbē-pər\ *n* (1970) : PAGER; *specif* : one that beeps
beer \ˈbir\ *n* [ME *ber,* fr. OE *bēor;* akin to OHG *bior* beer] (bef. 12c) **1** : an alcoholic beverage usu. made from malted cereal grain (as barley), flavored with hops, and brewed by slow fermentation **2** : a carbonated nonalcoholic or a fermented slightly alcoholic beverage with flavoring from roots or other plant parts ⟨birch ~⟩ **3** : fermented mash **4** : a drink of beer
beer and skittles *n pl but sing or pl in constr* (1855) : a situation of agreeable ease ⟨won't be all *beer and skittles*⟩
beer belly *n* (1829) : POTBELLY — **beer–bel·lied** \ˈbir-ˌbe-lēd\ *adj*
beer goggles *n pl* (1987) : the effects of alcohol thought of metaphorically as a pair of goggles that alter a person's perceptions esp. by making others appear more attractive than they actually are
beer pong \-ˈpäŋ, -ˈpȯŋ\ *n* [*beer* + Ping-Pong] (1972) : a game in which a set of beer-containing cups is placed at two ends of a table and in which a player scores by bouncing or tossing a Ping-Pong ball into an opponent's cup from which the opponent then has to drink the beer
beery \ˈbir-ē\ *adj* **beer·i·er; -est** (1764) **1** : affected or caused by beer ⟨~ voices⟩ **2** : smelling or tasting of beer ⟨~ tavern⟩
bee's knees *n* (1921) : a highly admired person or thing : CAT'S MEOW
bees·tings *or* **beas·tings** \ˈbē-stiŋz\ *n pl but sing or pl in constr* [ME *bestynge,* fr. OE *bȳsting,* fr. *bēost* beestings; akin to OHG *biost* beestings] (bef. 12c) : the colostrum esp. of a cow

bee–stung \ˈbē-ˌstəŋ\ *adj* (1822) **:** having a red puffy appearance as if from being stung by a bee ⟨∼ lips⟩
bees·wax \ˈbēz-ˌwaks\ *n* (1655) **:** WAX 1
beet \ˈbēt\ *n* [ME *bete,* fr. OE *bēte,* fr. L *beta*] (bef. 12c) **:** a biennial garden plant (*Beta vulgaris*) of the goosefoot family that includes several cultivars (as Swiss chard and sugar beet) and that has thick edible leaves with long petioles and often swollen purplish-red roots; *also* **:** its root used esp. as a vegetable, as a source of sugar, or for forage
beet armyworm *n* (1894) **:** an armyworm (*Spodoptera exigua*) that typically eats the foliage of beets, alfalfa, and vegetables
[1]**bee·tle** \ˈbē-tᵊl\ *n* [ME *betylle,* fr. OE *bitula;* akin to *bītan* to bite] (bef. 12c) **1 :** any of an order (Coleoptera) of insects having four wings of which the outer pair are modified into stiff elytra that protect the inner pair when at rest **2 :** any of various insects resembling a beetle
[2]**beetle** *vi* **bee·tled; bee·tling** \ˈbē-tᵊl-iŋ\ (ca. 1919) **:** to scurry like a beetle ⟨editors *beetled* around the office⟩
[3]**beetle** *n* [ME *betel,* fr. OE *bīetel;* akin to OE *bēatan* to beat] (bef. 12c) **1 :** a heavy wooden hammering or ramming instrument **2 :** a wooden pestle or bat for domestic tasks
[4]**beetle** *adj* [ME *bitel-browed* having overhanging brows, prob. fr. *betylle, bitel* beetle] (14c) **:** being prominent and overhanging ⟨∼ brows⟩
[5]**beetle** *vi* **bee·tled; bee·tling** \ˈbē-tᵊl-iŋ\ (1602) **:** PROJECT, JUT ⟨to scale the *beetling* crags —R. L. Stevenson⟩
beet leafhopper *n* (1906) **:** a leafhopper (*Circulifer tenellus*) that transmits curly top virus to sugar beets and other garden plants
bee tree *n* (1773) **:** a hollow tree in which honeybees nest
beet·root \ˈbēt-ˌrüt\ *n* (1579) *chiefly Brit* **:** a beet grown for its edible usu. red root; *also* **:** the root
beeves *pl of* BEEF
bee·yard \ˈbē-ˌyärd\ *n* (15c) **:** APIARY
bef *abbr* before
BEF *abbr* British Expeditionary Force
be·fall \bi-ˈfȯl, bē-\ *vb* **-fell** \-ˈfel\; **-fall·en** \-ˈfȯ-lən\ *vi* (13c) **:** to happen esp. as if by fate ∼ *vt* **:** to happen to ⟨the fate that *befell* them⟩
be·fit \bi-ˈfit, bē-\ *vt* **be·fit·ted; be·fit·ting** (15c) **:** to be proper or becoming to ⟨clothing that ∼*s* the occasion⟩
be·fit·ting \-ˈfi-tiŋ\ *adj* (ca. 1612) **1 :** SUITABLE, APPROPRIATE **2 :** PROPER, DECENT — **be·fit·ting·ly** \-tiŋ-lē\ *adv*
be·fog \bi-ˈfȯg, -ˈfäg, bē-\ *vt* (1601) **1 :** CONFUSE **2 :** FOG, OBSCURE
be·fool \bi-ˈfül, bē-\ *vt* (14c) **1 :** to make a fool of **2 :** DELUDE 1
[1]**be·fore** \bi-ˈfȯr, bē-\ *adv or adj* [ME, adv. & prep., fr. OE *beforan,* fr. *be-* + *foran* before, fr. *fore*] (bef. 12c) **1 :** in advance **:** AHEAD ⟨marching on ∼⟩ **2 :** at an earlier time ⟨the night ∼⟩ ⟨knew her ∼⟩
[2]**before** *prep* (bef. 12c) **1 a (1) :** forward of **:** in front of ⟨stood ∼ the fire⟩ **(2) :** in the presence of ⟨speaking ∼ the conference⟩ **b :** under the jurisdiction or consideration of ⟨the case ∼ the court⟩ **c (1) :** at the disposal of ⟨the great sums placed ∼ him⟩ **(2) :** in store for ⟨got the whole summer ∼ you⟩ **2 :** preceding in time **:** earlier than ⟨just ∼ noon⟩ **3 :** in a higher or more important position than ⟨put quantity ∼ quality⟩
[3]**before** *conj* (13c) **1 a (1) :** earlier than the time that ⟨call me ∼ you go⟩ **(2) :** sooner or quicker than ⟨I'll be done ∼ you know it⟩ **(3) :** so that . . . do not ⟨get out of there ∼ you get dirty⟩ **b :** until the time that ⟨miles to go ∼ I sleep —Robert Frost⟩ **c (1) :** or else . . . not ⟨must be convicted ∼ he can be removed from office⟩ **(2) :** or else ⟨get out of here ∼ I call a cop⟩ **2 :** rather or sooner than ⟨would starve ∼ he'd steal⟩
be·fore·hand \bi-ˈfȯr-ˌhand, bē-\ *adv or adj* (13c) **1 a :** in anticipation **b :** in advance **2 :** ahead of time **:** EARLY
before long *adv* (1585) **:** in the near future **:** SOON
be·fore·time \-ˌtīm\ *adv* (13c) *archaic* **:** FORMERLY
be·foul \bi-ˈfau̇(-ə)l, bē-\ *vt* (12c) **1 :** to make foul (as with dirt or waste) **2 :** SULLY, SOIL, BESMIRCH ⟨scandal ∼*ed* his reputation⟩
be·friend \bi-ˈfrend\ *vt* (1559) **:** to become or act as a friend to
be·fud·dle \bi-ˈfə-dᵊl, bē-\ *vt* (1801) **1 :** to muddle or stupefy with or as if with drink **2 :** CONFUSE, PERPLEX — **be·fud·dle·ment** \-mənt\ *n*
[1]**beg** \ˈbeg\ *vb* **begged; beg·ging** [ME *beggen*] *vt* (13c) **1 :** to ask for as a charity **2 a :** to ask earnestly for **:** ENTREAT **b :** to require as necessary or appropriate **3 :** EVADE, SIDESTEP ⟨*begged* the real problems⟩ ∼ *vi* **1 :** to ask for alms **2 :** to ask earnestly ⟨*begged* for mercy⟩ — **beg the question 1 :** to pass over or ignore a question by assuming it to be established or settled **2 :** to elicit a question logically as a reaction or response ⟨the quarterback's injury *begs the question* of who will start in his place⟩
syn BEG, ENTREAT, BESEECH, IMPLORE, SUPPLICATE, ADJURE, IMPORTUNE mean to ask urgently. BEG suggests earnestness or insistence in the asking ⟨they *begged* for help⟩. ENTREAT implies an effort to persuade or to overcome resistance ⟨*entreated* me to join them⟩. BESEECH and IMPLORE imply a deeply felt anxiety ⟨I *beseech* you to have mercy⟩ ⟨*implored* her not to leave⟩. SUPPLICATE suggests a posture of humility ⟨with bowed heads they *supplicated* their Lord⟩. ADJURE implies advising as well as pleading ⟨we were *adjured* to tell the truth⟩. IMPORTUNE suggests an annoying persistence in trying to break down resistance ⟨*importuning* viewers for donations⟩.
[2]**beg** *abbr* begin; beginning
be·get \bi-ˈget, bē-\ *vt* **-got** \-ˈgät\ *also* **-gat** \-ˈgat\; **-got·ten** \-ˈgä-tᵊn\ *or* **-got; -get·ting** [ME *begeten,* alter. of *beyeten,* fr. OE *bigietan* — more at GET] (13c) **1 :** to procreate as the father **:** SIRE **2 :** to produce esp. as an effect or outgrowth — **be·get·ter** *n*
[1]**beg·gar** \ˈbe-gər\ *n* [ME *beggere, beggare,* fr. *beggen* to beg + *-ere, -are* [2]-er] (13c) **1 :** one that begs; *esp* **:** a person who lives by asking for gifts **2 :** PAUPER **3 :** FELLOW 4c
[2]**beggar** *vt* **beg·gared; beg·gar·ing** \ˈbe-gə-riŋ\ (15c) **1 :** to reduce to beggary **2 :** to exceed the resources or abilities of **:** DEFY ⟨∼*s* description⟩ ⟨so outrageous as to ∼ belief⟩
beg·gar·ly \ˈbe-gər-lē\ *adj* (1526) **1 :** contemptibly mean, scant, petty, or paltry **2 :** befitting or resembling a beggar; *esp* **:** marked by extreme poverty — **beg·gar·li·ness** *n*
beggar–my–neighbour *adj* (1815) *chiefly Brit* **:** BEGGAR-THY-NEIGHBOR
beg·gar's–lice \ˈbe-gərz-ˌlīs\ *or* **beg·gar–lice** \-gər-ˌlīs\ *n pl but sing or pl in constr* (1835) **:** any of various plants (as of the genera *Hackelia* and *Cynoglossum* of the borage family) with prickly or adhesive fruits; *also* **:** one of these fruits
beggar–thy–neighbor *adj* (1945) **:** relating to or being an action or policy that produces gains for one group at the expense of another ⟨followed ∼ policies in imposing taxes⟩
beg·gar–ticks \ˈbe-gər-ˌtiks\ *also* **beg·gar's–ticks** \-gərz-\ *n pl but sing or pl in constr* (ca. 1818) **1 :** BUR MARIGOLD; *also* **:** its prickly achenes **2 :** BEGGAR'S-LICE
beg·gar·weed \ˈbe-gər-ˌwēd\ *n* (1789) **1 :** any of various plants (as knotgrass or dodder) that grow in waste ground **2 :** any of several tick trefoils (genus *Desmodium*); *esp* **:** a West Indian forage plant (*D. tortuosum*) cultivated in the southern U.S.
beg·gary \ˈbe-gə-rē\ *n* (14c) **1 :** POVERTY, PENURY **2 :** the class of beggars **3 :** the practice of begging
be·gin \bi-ˈgin, bē-\ *vb* **be·gan** \-ˈgan\; **be·gun** \-ˈgən\; **be·gin·ning** [ME *beginnen,* fr. OE *beginnan;* akin to OHG *biginnan* to begin, OE *onginnan*] *vi* (bef. 12c) **1 :** to do the first part of an action **:** go into the first part of a process **:** START **2 a :** to come into existence **:** ARISE **b :** to have a starting point **3 :** to do or succeed in the least degree ⟨I can't ∼ to tell you how pleased I am⟩ ∼ *vt* **1 :** to set about the activity of **:** START **2 a :** to bring into being **:** FOUND **b :** ORIGINATE, INVENT — **to begin with :** as the first thing to be considered
syn BEGIN, COMMENCE, START, INITIATE, INAUGURATE, USHER IN mean to take the first step in a course, process, or operation. BEGIN, START, and COMMENCE are often interchangeable. BEGIN, opposed to *end,* is the most general ⟨*begin* a trip⟩ ⟨*began* dancing⟩. START, opposed to *stop,* applies esp. to first actions, steps, or stages ⟨the work *started* slowly⟩. COMMENCE can be more formal or bookish than BEGIN or START ⟨*commence* firing⟩ ⟨*commenced* a conversation⟩. INITIATE implies taking a first step in a process or series that is to continue ⟨*initiated* diplomatic contacts⟩. INAUGURATE suggests a beginning of some formality or notion of significance ⟨the discovery of penicillin *inaugurated* a new era in medicine⟩. USHER IN is somewhat less weighty than INAUGURATE ⟨*ushered in* a period of economic decline⟩.
be·gin·ner \bi-ˈgi-nər, bē-\ *n* (15c) **:** one that begins something; *esp* **:** an inexperienced person
[1]**be·gin·ning** \bi-ˈgi-niŋ, bē-\ *n* (12c) **1 :** the point at which something begins **:** START **2 :** the first part **3 :** ORIGIN, SOURCE **4 :** a rudimentary stage or early period — usu. used in pl.
[2]**beginning** *adj* (1576) **1 :** just starting out ⟨a ∼ writer⟩ **2 a :** being first or the first part ⟨the ∼ chapters⟩ **b :** INTRODUCTORY ⟨∼ chemistry⟩
beginning rhyme *n* (1886) **1 :** rhyme at the beginning of successive lines of verse **2 :** ALLITERATION
be·gird \bi-ˈgərd, bē-\ *vt* **-girt** \-ˈgərt\ *also* **-gird·ed; -gird·ing** (bef. 12c) **1 :** GIRD 1a **2 :** SURROUND, ENCOMPASS
be·glam·our *also* **be·glam·or** \bi-ˈgla-mər, bē-\ *vt* (1822) **:** to impress or deceive with glamour
beg off *vi* (1788) **:** to ask to be excused from something ∼ *vt* **:** to ask or gain permission to be excused from ⟨*begged off* attending the party⟩ — **beg–off** \ˈbeg-ˌȯf\ *n*
be·gog·gled \bi-ˈgä-gəld, bē-\ *adj* (1852) **:** wearing goggles ⟨a helmeted ∼ motorcycle rider⟩
be·gone \bi-ˈgȯn, -ˈgän, bē-\ *vi* [ME, fr. *be gone* (imper.)] (14c) **:** to go away **:** DEPART — used esp. in the imperative
be·go·nia \bi-ˈgō-nyə\ *n* [NL, fr. Michel *Bégon* †1710 Fr. governor of Santo Domingo] (1751) **:** any of a large genus (*Begonia* of the family Begoniaceae, the begonia family) of tropical or subtropical herbs and shrubs that have asymmetrical leaves and are widely cultivated as ornamentals
be·gor·ra \bi-ˈgȯr-ə, -ˈgär-\ *interj* [euphemism for *by God*] (1715) *Irish* — used as a mild usu. jocular oath
be·grime \bi-ˈgrīm, bē-\ *vt* **be·grimed; be·grim·ing** (ca. 1556) **1 :** to make dirty with grime **2 :** SULLY, CORRUPT
be·grudge \bi-ˈgrəj, bē-\ *vt* (14c) **1 :** to give or concede reluctantly or with displeasure ⟨∼ money⟩ ⟨∼*d* the weeks spent away from home⟩ **2 :** to look upon with disapproval ⟨∼ their rivals' success⟩ — **be·grudg·er** \-ˈgrə-jər\ *n* — **be·grudg·ing·ly** \-ˈgrə-jiŋ-lē\ *adv*
be·guile \bi-ˈgī(-ə)l, bē-\ *vb* **be·guiled; be·guil·ing** *vt* (13c) **1 :** to lead by deception **2 :** HOODWINK **3 :** to while away esp. by some agreeable occupation; *also* **:** DIVERT 2 **4 :** to engage the interest of by or as if by guile ∼ *vi* **:** to deceive by wiles ***syn*** see DECEIVE — **be·guile·ment** \-ˈgī(-ə)l-mənt\ *n* — **be·guil·er** \-ˈgī-lər\ *n* — **be·guil·ing·ly** \-ˈgī-liŋ-lē\ *adv*
[1]**be·guine** \ˈbā-ˌgēn, ˌbā-ˈ\ *n, often cap* [MF] (15c) **:** a member of one of various ascetic and philanthropic communities of women not under vows founded chiefly in the Netherlands in the 13th century
[2]**be·guine** \bi-ˈgēn\ *n* [AmerF *béguine,* fr. F *béguin* flirtation] (1935) **:** a vigorous popular dance of the islands of Saint Lucia and Martinique that somewhat resembles the rumba
be·gum \ˈbā-gəm, ˈbē-\ *n* [Hindi & Urdu *begam*] (1617) **:** a Muslim woman of high rank (as in India or Pakistan)
be·half \bi-ˈhaf, -ˈhäf, bē-\ *n* [ME, fr. *by* + *half* half, side] (14c) **:** INTEREST, BENEFIT; *also* **:** SUPPORT, DEFENSE ⟨argued in his ∼⟩ — **on behalf of** *or* **in behalf of :** in the interest of; *also* **:** as a representative of
usage A body of opinion favors *in* with the "interest, benefit" sense of *behalf* and *on* with the "support, defense" sense. This distinction has been observed by some writers but overall has never had a sound basis in actual usage. In current British use, *on behalf* (*of*) has replaced *in behalf* (*of*); both are still used in American English, but the distinction is frequently not observed.
be·have \bi-ˈhāv, bē-\ *vb* **be·haved; be·hav·ing** [ME *behaven,* fr. *be-* + *haven* to have, hold] *vt* (15c) **1 :** to manage the actions of (oneself) in a particular way **2 :** to conduct (oneself) in a proper manner ∼ *vi* **1 :** to act, function, or react in a particular way **2 :** to conduct oneself properly — **be·hav·er** *n*
syn BEHAVE, CONDUCT, DEPORT, COMPORT, ACQUIT mean to act or to cause oneself to do something in a certain way. BEHAVE may apply to the meeting of a standard of what is proper or decorous ⟨the children *behaved* in church⟩. CONDUCT implies action or behavior that shows the extent of one's power to control or direct oneself ⟨*conducted* herself with unfailing good humor⟩. DEPORT implies behaving so as to show how far one conforms to conventional rules of discipline or propriety ⟨the hero *deported* himself in accord with the code of chivalry⟩. COMPORT suggests conduct measured by what is expected or required of one in a certain class or position ⟨*comported* themselves as gentle-

men⟩. ACQUIT applies to action under stress that deserves praise or meets expectations ⟨*acquitted* herself well in her first assignment⟩.

be·hav·ior \bi-ˈhā-vyər, bē-\ *n* [alter. of ME *behavour,* fr. *behaven*] (15c) **1 a :** the manner of conducting oneself **b :** anything that an organism does involving action and response to stimulation **c :** the response of an individual, group, or species to its environment **2 :** the way in which someone behaves; *also* **:** an instance of such behavior **3 :** the way in which something functions or operates — **be·hav·ior·al** \-vyə-rəl\ *adj* — **be·hav·ior·al·ly** \-rə-lē\ *adv*

behavioral science *n* (1951) **:** a branch of science (as psychology, sociology, or anthropology) that deals primarily with human action and often seeks to generalize about human behavior in society — **behavioral scientist** *n*

be·hav·ior·ism \bi-ˈhā-vyə-ˌri-zəm, bē-\ *n* (1913) **:** a school of psychology that takes the objective evidence of behavior (as measured responses to stimuli) as the only concern of its research and the only basis of its theory without reference to conscious experience — compare INTROSPECTIONISM — **be·hav·ior·is·tic** \-ˌhā-vyə-ˈris-tik\ *adj*

be·hav·ior·ist \-vyə-rist\ *n* (1913) **1 :** a person who advocates or practices behaviorism **2 :** a person who specializes in the study of behavior ⟨an animal ~⟩ — **behaviorist** *adj*

behavior modification *n* (1970) **:** psychotherapy that is concerned with the treatment (as by desensitization or aversion therapy) of observable behaviors rather than underlying psychological processes and that applies principles of learning to substitute desirable responses for undesirable ones (as phobias or obsessions) — called also *behavioral therapy, behavior therapy*

be·hav·iour, be·hav·iour·ism, be·hav·iour·ist *chiefly Brit var of* BEHAVIOR, BEHAVIORISM, BEHAVIORIST

be·head \bi-ˈhed, bē-\ *vt* (bef. 12c) **:** to cut off the head of **:** DECAPITATE

be·he·moth \bi-ˈhē-məth, ˈbē-ə-məth, -ˌmäth, -ˌmȯth\ *n, often attrib* [ME, fr. LL, fr. Heb *bĕhēmōth*] (14c) **1** *often cap* **:** a mighty animal described in Job 40:15–24 as an example of the power of God **2 :** something of monstrous size, power, or appearance ⟨a ~ truck⟩

be·hest \bi-ˈhest, bē-\ *n* [ME, promise, command, fr. OE *behǣs* promise, fr. *behātan* to promise, fr. *be-* + *hātan* to command, promise — more at HIGHT] (12c) **1 :** an authoritative order **:** COMMAND **2 :** an urgent prompting ⟨called at the ~ of my friends⟩

[1]**be·hind** \bi-ˈhīnd, bē-\ *adv or adj* [ME *behinde,* fr. OE *behindan,* fr. *be-* + *hindan* from behind; akin to OE *hinder* behind — more at HIND] (bef. 12c) **1 a :** in the place or situation that is being or has been departed from ⟨stay ~⟩ **b :** in, to, or toward the back ⟨look ~⟩ ⟨came from ~⟩ **c :** later in time ⟨can spring be far ~⟩ **2 a :** in a secondary or inferior position **b :** in arrears ⟨~ in the rent⟩ **c :** SLOW **3** *archaic* **:** still to come

[2]**behind** *prep* (bef. 12c) **1 a :** in or to a place or situation in back of or to the rear of ⟨look ~ you⟩ ⟨put ~ bars⟩ **b** — used as a function word to indicate something that screens an observer ⟨the sun went ~ a cloud⟩ **c :** following in order ⟨marched ~ the band⟩ **2** — used as a function word to indicate backwardness, delay, or deficiency ⟨~ the times⟩ ⟨~ schedule⟩ ⟨lagged ~ last year's sales⟩ **3 a :** in the background of ⟨the conditions ~ the strike⟩ **b :** out of the mind or consideration of ⟨put our troubles ~ us⟩ **c :** beyond in depth or time ⟨the story ~ the story⟩ ⟨go back ~ St. Augustine⟩ **4 a :** in support of **:** on the side of ⟨solidly ~ the candidate⟩ **b :** with the support of ⟨won 1–0 ~ brilliant pitching⟩

[3]**be·hind** \ˈbē-ˌhīnd; bi-ˈhīnd, bē-\ *n* [[1]*behind*] (ca. 1830) **:** BUTTOCKS — often used as a euphemism for *ass* in idiomatic expressions ⟨get your ~ over here⟩

be·hind·hand \bi-ˈhīnd-ˌhand, bē-\ *adj* (1535) **1 :** being in arrears **2 a :** being in an inferior position **b :** being behind schedule

behind–the–scenes *adj* (1850) **1 :** being or working out of public view or in secret ⟨~ lobbying for more money⟩ ⟨a ~ player⟩ **2 :** revealing or reporting the hidden workings ⟨a ~ account⟩ ⟨a ~ glimpse⟩

be·hold \bi-ˈhōld, bē-\ *vb* **-held** \-ˈheld\; **-hold·ing** [ME, to keep, behold, fr. OE *behealdan,* fr. *be-* + *healdan* to hold] *vt* (bef. 12c) **1 :** to perceive through sight or apprehension **:** SEE **2 :** to gaze upon **:** OBSERVE ~ *vi* — used in the imperative esp. to call attention — **be·hold·er** *n*

be·hold·en \bi-ˈhōl-dən, bē-\ *adj* [ME, fr. pp. of *beholden*] (14c) **:** being under obligation for a favor or gift **:** INDEBTED ⟨I'm ~ to you⟩

be·hoof \bi-ˈhüf, bē-\ *n* [ME *behof,* fr. OE *behōf* profit, need; akin to OE *hebban* to raise — more at HEAVE] (bef. 12c) **:** ADVANTAGE, PROFIT ⟨for his own ~⟩

be·hoove \bi-ˈhüv, bē-\ *vb* **be·hooved; be·hoov·ing** [ME *behoven,* fr. OE *behōfian,* fr. *behōf*] *vt* (bef. 12c) **:** to be necessary, proper, or advantageous for ⟨it ~*s* us to go⟩ ~ *vi* **:** to be necessary, fit, or proper

be·hove \bi-ˈhōv, bē-\ *chiefly Brit var of* BEHOOVE

[1]**beige** \ˈbāzh\ *n* [F] (ca. 1858) **1 :** cloth made of natural undyed wool **2 a :** a variable color averaging light grayish-yellowish brown **b :** a pale to grayish yellow — **beigy** \ˈbā-zhē\ *adj*

[2]**beige** *adj* (1879) **1 :** of the color beige **2 :** lacking distinction **:** VANILLA 2

bei·gnet \ˌbān-ˈyā, ˌben-\ *n* [AmerF & F; AmerF, fr. F, fr. MF *bignet,* fr. *buyne* bump, bruise] (1835) **1 :** FRITTER **2 :** a light square doughnut usu. sprinkled with powdered sugar

[1]**be·ing** \ˈbē-(i)ŋ\ *n* (14c) **1 a :** the quality or state of having existence **b** (1) **:** something conceivable as existing (2) **:** something that actually exists (3) **:** the totality of existing things **c :** conscious existence **:** LIFE **2 :** the qualities that constitute an existent thing **:** ESSENCE; *esp* **:** PERSONALITY **3 :** a living thing; *esp* **:** PERSON

[2]**being** *adj* [prp. of *be*] (14c) **:** PRESENT — used in the phrase *for the time being*

[3]**being** *conj* (1528) *chiefly dial* **:** SINCE, BECAUSE — usu. used with *as, as how,* or *that*

Be·ja \ˈbā-jə\ *n, pl* **Beja** [Ar dial. *beja, bega,* prob. ultim. fr. Geez *bega*] (1819) **1 :** a member of a pastoral people living between the Nile and the Red Sea **2 :** the Cushitic language of the Beja people

be·jab·bers \bi-ˈja-bərz\ *or* **be·jee·bers** \-ˈjē-\ *interj* [euphemism for *by Jesus*] (1890) **:** BEJESUS

be·je·sus *also* **be·jee·zus** \bi-ˈjē-zəs, -ˈjā-, -zəz\ *interj* [alter. of *by Jesus*] (1861) — used as a mild oath; used as a noun for emphasis ⟨scares the ~ out of me⟩

be·jew·eled *or* **be·jew·elled** \bi-ˈjü-əld, -ˈjüld, bē- *also* -ˈju̇(ə)ld\ *adj* (1557) **:** ornamented with or as if with jewels

bel \ˈbel\ *n* [Alexander Graham *Bell*] (1929) **:** ten decibels

be·la·bor \bi-ˈlā-bər, bē-\ *vt* (1596) **1 a :** to attack verbally **b :** to beat soundly **2 :** to explain or insist on excessively ⟨~ the obvious⟩

be·la·bour *chiefly Brit var of* BELABOR

Be·la·rus·ian \ˌb(y)e-lä-ˈrü-sē-ən, ˌb(y)ä-\ *or* **Be·la·rus·sian** \-ˈrə-shən\ *also* **Be·la·rus·an** \-ˈrü-sən\ *n* (1993) **1 :** a native or inhabitant of Belarus **2 :** the Slavic language of the Belarusians — **Belarusian** *or* **Belarussian** *also* **Belarusan** *adj*

be·lat·ed \bi-ˈlā-təd, bē-\ *adj* [pp. of *belate* (to make late)] (1670) **1 :** delayed beyond the usual time **2 :** existing or appearing past the normal or proper time — **be·lat·ed·ly** *adv* — **be·lat·ed·ness** *n*

be·laud \bi-ˈlȯd, bē-\ *vt* (ca. 1849) **:** to praise usu. to excess

[1]**be·lay** \bi-ˈlā, bē-\ *vb* **be·layed; be·lay·ing** [ME *beleggen* to beset, fr. OE *belecgan,* fr. *be-* + *lecgan* to lay] *vt* (1549) **1 a :** to secure (as a rope) by turns around a cleat, pin, or bitt **b :** to make fast **2 :** STOP **3 a :** to secure (a person) at the end of a rope **b :** to secure (a rope) to a person or object ~ *vi* **1 :** to be made fast **2 :** STOP, QUIT — used in the imperative ⟨~ there⟩ **3 :** to make a line fast by turns around a cleat, pin, or bitt — **be·lay·er** \-ər\ *n*

[2]**belay** *n* (1908) **1 :** the securing of a person or a safety rope to an anchor point (as during mountain climbing); *also* **:** a method of so securing a person or rope **2 :** something (as a projection of rock) to which a person or rope is anchored

bel can·to \bel-ˈkän-(ˌ)tō, -ˈkan-\ *n* [It, lit., beautiful singing] (1893) **:** operatic singing originating in 17th century and 18th century Italy and stressing ease, purity, and evenness of tone production and an agile and precise vocal technique

belch \ˈbelch\ *vb* [ME, fr. OE *bealcan*] *vi* (bef. 12c) **1 :** to expel gas suddenly from the stomach through the mouth **2 :** to erupt, explode, or detonate violently **3 :** to issue forth spasmodically **:** GUSH ~ *vt* **1 :** to eject or emit violently ⟨angrily ~*ed* insults⟩ **2 :** to expel (gas) from the stomach suddenly **:** ERUCT — **belch** *n*

bel·dam *or* **bel·dame** \ˈbel-dəm\ *n* [ME *beldam* grandmother, fr. AF *bel* beautiful + ME *dam*] (1520) **:** an old woman

be·lea·guer \bi-ˈlē-gər, bē-\ *vt* **-guered; -guer·ing** \-g(ə-)riŋ\ [D *belegeren,* fr. *be-* (akin to OE *be-*) + *leger* camp; akin to OHG *legar* bed — more at LAIR] (1587) **1 :** BESIEGE **2 :** TROUBLE, HARASS ⟨~*ed* parents⟩ ⟨an economically ~*ed* city⟩ — **be·lea·guer·ment** \-mənt\ *n*

bel·em·nite \ˈbe-ləm-ˌnīt\ *n* [NL *belemnites,* fr. Gk *belemnon* dart; akin to Gk *ballein* to throw — more at DEVIL] (1646) **:** any of various extinct cephalopods (order Belemnoidea) that had large internal shells and were esp. abundant in the Mesozoic era

bel·fry \ˈbel-frē\ *n, pl* **belfries** [ME *belfrey, berfrey,* bell tower, siege tower, fr. AF **berfrei, *belfrei,* of Gmc origin (akin to MHG *bërvrit* siege tower); akin to OHG *bergan* to shelter and to OE *frith* peace, refuge — more at BURY] (15c) **1 :** a bell tower; *esp* **:** one surmounting or attached to another structure **2 :** a room or framework for enclosing a bell **3 :** HEAD 2a ⟨batty in the ~⟩

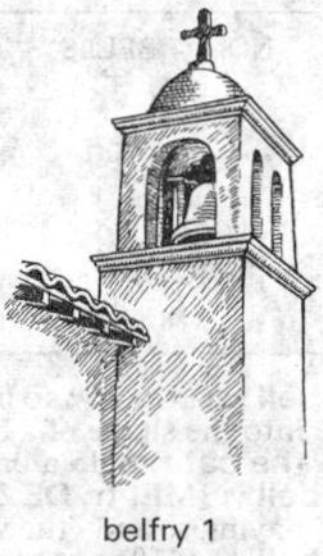

belfry 1

Belg *abbr* Belgian; Belgium

Bel·gae \ˈbel-ˌgī, -ˌjē\ *n pl* [L, pl. of *Belga*] (1627) **:** a people occupying parts of northern Gaul and Britain in Caesar's time — **Bel·gic** \-jik\ *adj*

Bel·gian \ˈbel-jən\ *n* (ca. 1623) **1 :** a native or inhabitant of Belgium **2 :** any of a breed of heavy muscular usu. roan or chestnut draft horses developed in Belgium — **Belgian** *adj*

Belgian endive *n* (1931) **:** the developing crown of chicory when blanched for use as a vegetable or in salads by growing in darkness or semidarkness — called also *endive, witloof*

Belgian hare *n* (1885) **:** any of a breed of slender chestnut-colored domestic rabbits

Belgian Ma·li·nois \-ˌma-lən-ˈwä\ *n, pl* **Belgian Malinois** (1968) **:** any of a breed of working dogs closely related to the Belgian sheepdog and having relatively short straight fawn or reddish-brown hair with black tips and a dense undercoat — called also *Malinois*

Belgian sheepdog *n* (1929) **:** any of a breed of hardy dogs developed in Belgium esp. for herding sheep and having abundant long straight black hair with a dense undercoat

Belgian Ter·vu·ren \-(ˌ)tər-ˈvyu̇r-ən, -ter-\ *n* [*Tervuren,* commune in Brabant, Belgium] (1964) **:** any of a breed of working dogs closely related to the Belgian sheepdog and having abundant long straight fawn or reddish-brown hair with black tips and a dense undercoat

Belgian waffle *n* (1969) **:** a waffle having large depressions that is usu. topped with fruit and whipped cream

Be·lial \ˈbē-lē-əl, ˈbēl-yəl\ *n* [Gk, fr. Heb *bĕlīyaʻal* worthlessness] (13c) **1** — a biblical name of the devil or one of the fiends **2 :** one of the fallen angels in Milton's *Paradise Lost*

be·lie \bi-ˈlī, bē-\ *vt* **-lied; -ly·ing** (bef. 12c) **1 a :** to give a false impression of **b :** to present an appearance not in agreement with **2 a :** to show (something) to be false or wrong **b :** to run counter to **:** CONTRADICT **3 :** DISGUISE 3 — **be·li·er** \-ˈlī(-ə)r\ *n*

be·lief \bə-ˈlēf\ *n* [ME *beleave,* prob. alter. of OE *gelēafa,* fr. *ge-,* associative prefix + *lēafa;* akin to OE *lȳfan* — more at BELIEVE] (12c) **1 :** a state or habit of mind in which trust or confidence is placed in some person or thing **2 :** something believed; *esp* **:** a tenet or body of tenets held by a group **3 :** conviction of the truth of some statement or the reality of some being or phenomenon esp. when based on examination of evidence

syn BELIEF, FAITH, CREDENCE, CREDIT mean assent to the truth of something offered for acceptance. BELIEF may or may not imply certitude in the believer ⟨my *belief* that I had caught all the errors⟩. FAITH almost always implies certitude even where there is no evidence or proof ⟨an unshakable *faith* in God⟩. CREDENCE suggests intellectual assent without implying anything about grounds for assent ⟨a theory now given *credence* by scientists⟩. CREDIT may imply assent on grounds other than direct proof ⟨gave full *credit* to the statement of a reputable witness⟩. ***syn*** see in addition OPINION

be·liev·able \-ˈlē-və-bəl\ *adj* (14c) **:** capable of being believed esp. as within the range of known possibility or probability — **be·liev·abil·i·ty** \-ˌlē-və-ˈbi-lə-tē\ *n* — **be·liev·ably** \-ˈlē-və-blē\ *adv*

be·lieve \bə-ˈlēv\ *vb* **be·lieved; be·liev·ing** [ME *beleven,* fr. OE *belēfan,* fr. *be-* + *lȳfan, lēfan* to allow, believe; akin to OHG *gilouben* to believe, OE *lēof* dear — more at LOVE] *vi* (bef. 12c) **1 a :** to have a firm religious faith **b :** to accept as true, genuine, or real ⟨ideals we ~ in⟩ ⟨~*s* in ghosts⟩ **2 :** to have a firm conviction as to the goodness, efficacy, or ability of something ⟨~ in exercise⟩ **3 :** to hold an opinion **:** THINK ⟨I ~ so⟩ ~ *vt* **1 a :** to consider to be true or honest ⟨~ the reports⟩ ⟨you wouldn't ~ how long it took⟩ **b :** to accept the word or evidence of ⟨I ~ you⟩ ⟨couldn't ~ my ears⟩ **2 :** to hold as an opinion **:** SUPPOSE ⟨I ~ it will rain soon⟩ — **be·liev·er** *n* — **not believe :** to be astounded at ⟨I could*n't believe* my luck⟩

be·like \bi-ˈlīk\ *adv* (ca. 1500) *archaic* **:** most likely **:** PROBABLY

be·lit·tle \bi-ˈli-tᵊl, bē-\ *vt* **-lit·tled; -lit·tling** \-ˈli-tᵊl-iŋ, -ˈlit-liŋ\ (1797) **1 :** to speak slightingly of **:** DISPARAGE ⟨~*s* her efforts⟩ **2 :** to cause (a person or thing) to seem little or less ⟨a curiosity so vast that it almost *belittled* the main matter —Mark Twain⟩ ***syn*** see DECRY — **be·lit·tle·ment** \-ˈli-tᵊl-mənt\ *n* — **be·lit·tler** \-ˈli-tᵊl-ər, -ˈlit-lər\ *n*

be·live \bi-ˈlīv\ *adv* [ME *bilive* vigorously, fr. *by* + *live,* dat. of *lif* life] (1594) *Scot* **:** in due time **:** BY AND BY

¹bell \ˈbel\ *n* [ME *belle,* fr. OE; perh. akin to OE *bellan* to roar — more at BELLOW] (bef. 12c) **1 a :** a hollow metallic device that gives off a reverberating sound when struck **b :** DOORBELL **2 a :** the sounding of a bell as a signal **b :** a stroke of a bell (as on shipboard) to indicate the time; *also* **:** the time so indicated **c :** a half hour period of a watch on shipboard indicated by the strokes of a bell — see SHIP'S BELLS table below **3 :** something having the form of a bell: as **a :** the corolla of a flower **b :** a bell-shaped organ or part (as the umbrella of a jellyfish or the dewlap of a moose) **c :** the part of the capital of a column between the abacus and neck molding **d :** the flared end of a wind instrument **4 a :** a percussion instrument consisting of metal bars or tubes that when struck give out tones resembling bells — usu. used in pl. **b :** GLOCKENSPIEL

SHIP'S BELLS

NO. OF BELLS	HOUR (A.M. OR P.M.)		
1	12:30	4:30	8:30
2	1:00	5:00	9:00
3	1:30	5:30	9:30
4	2:00	6:00	10:00
5	2:30	6:30	10:30
6	3:00	7:00	11:00
7	3:30	7:30	11:30
8	4:00	8:00	12:00

²bell *vt* (14c) **1 :** to provide with a bell **2 :** to flare the end of (as a tube) into the shape of a bell ~ *vi* **:** to take the form of a bell **:** FLARE — **bell the cat :** to do a daring or risky deed

³bell *vi* [ME, fr. OE *bellan*] (bef. 12c) **:** to make a resonant bellowing or baying sound ⟨the wild buck ~*s* from ferny brake —Sir Walter Scott⟩

⁴bell *n* (1510) **:** BELLOW, ROAR

bel·la·don·na \ˌbe-lə-ˈdä-nə\ *n* [It, lit., beautiful lady] (1597) **1 :** an Old World poisonous plant (*Atropa belladonna*) of the nightshade family having purple or green bell-shaped flowers, glossy black berries, and root and leaves that yield atropine — called also *deadly nightshade* **2 :** a medicinal extract (as atropine) from the belladonna plant

belladonna lily *n* (1734) **:** AMARYLLIS

bell·bird \ˈbel-ˌbərd\ *n* (1802) **:** any of various birds (as flycatchers of the genus *Procnias* and the honeyeater of the genus *Anthornis*) whose notes suggest the sound of a bell

bell–bot·toms \ˈbel-ˈbä-təmz\ *n pl* (1904) **:** pants with wide flaring bottoms — **bell–bottom** *adj*

bell·boy \ˈbel-ˌbȯi\ *n* (1857) **:** BELLHOP

bell buoy *n* (1823) **:** a buoy with a bell rung by the action of the waves

bell captain *n* (1900) **:** CAPTAIN 2c

bell curve *n* [fr. the shape] (1938) **:** NORMAL CURVE

belle \ˈbel\ *n* [F, fr. fem. of *beau* beautiful — more at BEAU] (1622) **:** a popular and attractive girl or woman; *esp* **:** a girl or woman whose charm and beauty make her a favorite ⟨the ~ of the ball⟩

Bel·leek \bə-ˈlēk\ *trademark* — used for a very thin translucent porcelain with a lustrous pearly glaze produced in Ireland

belle epoque *or* **belle époque** \ˈbel-ā-ˈpȯk\ *n, often cap B&E* [F, lit., beautiful age] (1904) **:** a period of high artistic or cultural development; *esp* **:** such a period in fin de siècle France

Bel·ler·o·phon \bə-ˈler-ə-fən, -ˌfän\ *n* [L, fr. Gk *Bellerophōn*] (1561) **:** a legendary Greek hero noted for killing the Chimera

belles let·tres \bel-letrᵊ\ *n pl but sing in constr* [F, lit., fine letters] (1665) **:** literature that is an end in itself and not merely informative; *specif* **:** light, entertaining, and often sophisticated literature

bel·le·trist *also* **belle–let·trist** \bel-ˈle-trist\ *n* [*belles lettres*] (1801) **:** a writer of belles lettres — **bel·le·tris·tic** *also* **belle–let·tris·tic** \ˌbe-lə-ˈtris-tik\ *adj*

bell·flow·er \ˈbel-ˌflau̇(-ə)r\ *n* (1578) **:** any of a genus (*Campanula* of the family Campanulaceae, the bellflower family) of widely cultivated herbs having alternate leaves and usu. showy bell-shaped flowers

bell·hop \-ˌhäp\ *n* [short for *bell-hopper*] (1897) **:** a hotel or club employee who escorts guests to rooms, assists them with luggage, and runs errands

bel·li·cose \ˈbe-li-ˌkōs\ *adj* [ME, fr. L *bellicosus,* fr. *bellicus* of war, fr. *bellum* war] (15c) **:** favoring or inclined to start quarrels or wars ***syn*** see BELLIGERENT — **bel·li·cos·i·ty** \ˌbe-li-ˈkä-sə-tē\ *n*

bel·lied \ˈbe-lēd\ *adj* (15c) **:** having a belly of a specified kind — used in combination ⟨a big-*bellied* man⟩

bel·lig·er·ence \bə-ˈlij-rən(t)s, -ˈli-jə-\ *n* (1814) **:** an aggressive or truculent attitude, atmosphere, or disposition

bel·lig·er·en·cy \-rən(t)-sē\ *n* (1815) **1 :** the state of being at war or in conflict; *specif* **:** the status of a legally recognized belligerent state or nation **2 :** BELLIGERENCE

bel·lig·er·ent \-rənt\ *adj* [modif. of L *belligerant-, belligerans,* prp. of *belligerare* to wage war, fr. *belliger* waging war, fr. *bellum* + *gerere* to wage] (1577) **1 :** waging war; *specif* **:** belonging to or recognized as a state at war and protected by and subject to the laws of war **2 :** inclined to or exhibiting assertiveness, hostility, or combativeness — **belligerent** *n* — **bel·lig·er·ent·ly** *adv*

syn BELLIGERENT, BELLICOSE, PUGNACIOUS, QUARRELSOME, CONTENTIOUS mean having an aggressive or fighting attitude. BELLIGERENT often implies being actually at war or engaged in hostilities ⟨*belligerent* nations⟩. BELLICOSE suggests a disposition to fight ⟨a drunk in a *bellicose* mood⟩. PUGNACIOUS suggests a disposition that takes pleasure in personal combat ⟨a *pugnacious* gangster⟩. QUARRELSOME stresses an ill-natured readiness to fight without good cause ⟨the heat made us all *quarrelsome*⟩. CONTENTIOUS implies perverse and irritating fondness for arguing and quarreling ⟨wearied by his *contentious* disposition⟩.

Bel·li·ni \be-ˈlē-nē, bə-\ *n* [prob. fr. Giovanni *Bellini* †1516 Venetian painter] (1962) **:** a cocktail of champagne and usu. peach juice

bell jar *n* (1806) **:** a bell-shaped usu. glass vessel designed to cover objects or to contain gases or a vacuum

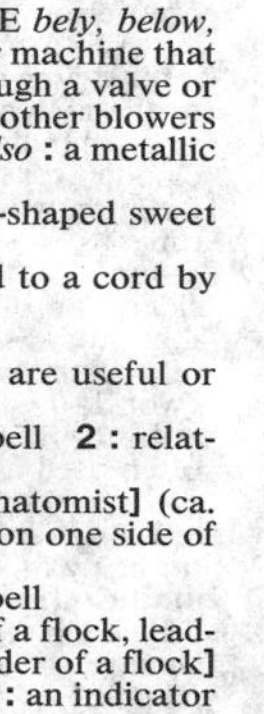

bell jar

bell–ly·ra \ˈbel-ˈlī-rə\ *or* **bell lyre** \-ˌlī(-ə)r\ *n* [*lyra* fr. L, lyre] (1934) **:** a glockenspiel mounted in a portable lyre-shaped frame and used esp. in marching bands

bell·man \ˈbel-mən\ *n* (14c) **1 :** a man (as a town crier) who rings a bell **2 :** BELLHOP

bell metal *n* (ca. 1523) **:** bronze that consists usu. of three to four parts of copper to one of tin and that is used for making bells

Bel·lo·na \bə-ˈlō-nə\ *n* [L] (14c) **:** the Roman goddess of war

bel·low \ˈbe-(ˌ)lō\ *vb* [ME *belwen,* fr. OE *bylgian;* akin to OE & OHG *bellan* to roar] *vi* (bef. 12c) **1 :** to make the loud deep hollow sound characteristic of a bull **2 :** to shout in a deep voice ~ *vt* **:** BAWL ⟨~*s* the orders⟩ — **bellow** *n*

bel·lows \ˈbe-(ˌ)lōz, -ləz\ *n pl but sing or pl in constr* [ME *bely, below, belwes* — more at BELLY] (bef. 12c) **1 :** an instrument or machine that by alternate expansion and contraction draws in air through a valve or orifice and expels it through a tube; *also* **:** any of various other blowers **2 :** LUNGS **3 :** the pleated expansible part in a camera; *also* **:** a metallic or plastic flexible and expansible vessel

bell pepper *n* (1707) **:** SWEET PEPPER; *esp* **:** a large bell-shaped sweet pepper

bell·pull \ˈbel-ˌpu̇l\ *n* (1764) **:** a handle or knob attached to a cord by which one rings a bell; *also* **:** the cord itself

bell push *n* (1870) **:** a button that is pushed to ring a bell

bells and whistles *n pl* (1968) **:** items or features that are useful or decorative but not essential **:** FRILLS

bell–shaped \ˈbel-ˌshāpt\ *adj* (1744) **1 :** shaped like a bell **2 :** relating to or being a normal curve or a normal distribution

Bell's palsy \ˈbelz-\ *n* [Sir Charles *Bell* †1842 Scot. anatomist] (ca. 1845) **:** paralysis of the facial nerve producing distortion on one side of the face

bell tower *n* (1596) **:** a tower that supports or shelters a bell

bell·weth·er \ˈbel-ˈwe-t͟hər, -ˌwe-\ *n* [ME, leading sheep of a flock, leader, fr. *belle* bell + *wether;* fr. the practice of belling the leader of a flock] (13c) **:** one that takes the lead or initiative **:** LEADER; *also* **:** an indicator of trends

bell·wort \ˈbel-ˌwərt, -ˌwȯrt\ *n* (1737) **:** any of a small genus (*Uvularia*) of herbs of the lily family with yellow bell-shaped flowers

¹bel·ly \ˈbe-lē\ *n, pl* **bellies** [ME *bely* bellows, belly, fr. OE *belg* bag, skin; akin to OHG *balg* bag, skin, OE *blāwan* to blow — more at BLOW] (bef. 12c) **1 a :** ABDOMEN 1; *also* **:** POTBELLY 1 **b :** the stomach and its adjuncts **c :** the undersurface of an animal's body; *also* **:** hide from this part **d :** WOMB, UTERUS **2 :** an internal cavity **:** INTERIOR **3 :** appetite for food **4 :** a surface or object curved or rounded like a human belly **5 a :** the enlarged fleshy body of a muscle **b :** the part of a sail that swells out when filled with wind **6 :** GUT 1a(2)

²belly *vb* **bel·lied; bel·ly·ing** *vt* (1606) **:** to cause to swell or fill out ⟨wind ~*ing* the sails⟩ ~ *vi* **1 :** SWELL, FILL **2 a :** to slide or crawl on one's belly **b :** BELLY-LAND

¹bel·ly·ache \ˈbe-lē-ˌāk\ *n* (1552) **:** pain in the abdomen and esp. in the stomach **:** STOMACHACHE

²bellyache *vi* (1881) **:** to complain whiningly or peevishly **:** find fault — **bel·ly·ach·er** *n*

bel·ly·band \ˈbe-lē-ˌband\ *n* (15c) **:** a band around or across the belly: as **a :** GIRTH 1 **b :** BAND 4b

belly button *n* (ca. 1877) **:** the human navel

belly dance *n* (1899) **:** a usu. solo dance emphasizing movements of the belly — **belly dance** *vi* — **belly dancer** *n*

belly flop *n* (ca. 1890) **:** a dive (as into water or in coasting prone on a sled) in which the front of the body strikes flat against another surface — called also *belly flopper* — **belly flop** *vi*

bel·ly·ful \ˈbe-lē-ˌfu̇l\ *n* (1535) **:** an excessive amount ⟨a ~ of advice⟩

bel·ly–land \-ˌland\ *vi* (1942) **:** to land an airplane on its undersurface without use of landing gear — **belly landing** *n*

belly laugh *n* (1916) **:** a deep hearty laugh

bel·ly–up \-ˈəp\ *adj* [fr. the floating position of a dead fish] (1918) **:** hopelessly ruined or defeated; *esp* **:** BANKRUPT ⟨the business went ~⟩

belly up *vi* (1880) **:** to move close or next to ⟨*bellied up* to the bar⟩

be·lon \bā-ˈlōn, -ˈlōⁿ\ *n, often cap* [F, fr. *Bélon,* river in Brittany] (1940) **:** EUROPEAN FLAT; *specif* **:** a European flat oyster of coastal waters of northwestern France

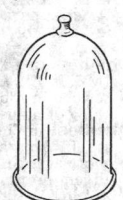

be·long \bi-ˈlȯŋ, bē-\ *vb* [ME *belongen*, fr. *be-* + *longen* to be suitable — more at LONG] *vi* (14c) **1 a** : to be suitable, appropriate, or advantageous ⟨a dictionary ~*s* in every home⟩ **b** : to be in a proper situation ⟨a man of his ability ~*s* in teaching⟩ **2 a** : to be the property of a person or thing — used with *to* ⟨the book ~*s* to me⟩ **b** : to be attached or bound by birth, allegiance, or dependency — usu. used with *to* ⟨they ~ to their homeland⟩ **c** : to be a member of a club, organization, or set — usu. used with *to* ⟨she ~*s* to a country club⟩ **3** : to be an attribute, part, adjunct, or function of a person or thing ⟨nuts and bolts ~ to a car⟩ **4** : to be properly classified ~ *verbal auxiliary, chiefly Southern & southern Midland* : OUGHT, MUST

be·long·ing \-ˈlȯŋ-iŋ\ *n* (1782) **1** : POSSESSION — usu. used in pl. **2** : close or intimate relationship ⟨a sense of ~⟩ — **be·long·ing·ness** *n*

Be·lo·rus·sian \ˌbe-lō-ˈrə-shən, ˌbye-\ *n* (1943) : BELARUSIAN — **Belorussian** *adj*

be·loved \bi-ˈləvd, -ˈlə-vəd, bē-\ *adj* [ME, fr. pp. of *beloven* to love, fr. *be-* + *loven* to love] (14c) : dearly loved : dear to the heart — **beloved** *n*

[1]**be·low** \bi-ˈlō\ *adv* [ME *bilooghe*, fr. *bi* by + *looghe* low, adj.] (14c) **1** : in or to a lower place **2 a** : on earth **b** : in or to Hades or hell **3** : on or to a lower floor or deck **4 a** : in, to, at, or by a lower rank or number **b** : below zero ⟨the temperature was 20 ~⟩ **5** : lower on the same page or on a following page **6** : under the surface of the water

[2]**below** *prep* (1575) **1 a** : lower in place, rank, or value than : UNDER **b** : down river from **c** : south of **2** : inferior to (as in rank) **3** : not suitable to the rank of : BENEATH

[3]**below** *n* (1697) : something that is below

[4]**below** *adj* (1916) : written or discussed lower on the same page or on a following page

be·low·decks \bi-ˌlō-ˈdeks; -ˈlō-ˌdeks\ *adv* (1897) : inside or into the superstructure of a boat : down to a lower deck

be·low·ground \-ˈgrau̇nd; -ˌgrau̇nd\ *adv or adj* (1617) : beneath the surface of the earth

Bel·shaz·zar \bel-ˈsha-zər\ *n* [Heb *Bēlshaṣṣar*] (1587) : a son of Nebuchadnezzar and king of Babylon in the book of Daniel

[1]**belt** \ˈbelt\ *n* [ME, fr. OE; akin to OHG *balz* belt; both fr. L *balteus* belt] (bef. 12c) **1 a** : a strip of flexible material worn esp. around the waist as an item of clothing or a means of carrying something (as tools) **b** : a similar article worn as a corset or for protection or safety or as a symbol of distinction **2** : a continuous band of tough flexible material for transmitting motion and power or conveying materials **3 a** : an area characterized by some distinctive feature (as of culture, habitation, geology, or life forms); *esp* : one suited to a particular crop ⟨the corn ~⟩ **b** : ASTEROID BELT **4** : BELTWAY 1 — **belt·ed** \ˈbel-təd\ *adj* — **belt·less** \ˈbelt-ləs\ *adj* — **below the belt** : UNFAIR, UNFAIRLY — **under one's belt** : in one's possession : as part of one's experience

[2]**belt** *vt* (14c) **1 a** : to encircle or fasten with a belt **b** : to strap on **2 a** : to beat with or as if with a belt : THRASH **b** : STRIKE, HIT **3** : to mark with a band **4** : to sing in a forceful manner or style ⟨~*ing* out popular songs⟩ **5** : to drink quickly ⟨~*ed* down a shot of whisky⟩ ~ *vi* **1** : to move or act in a speedy, vigorous, or violent manner **2** : to sing loudly

[3]**belt** *n* (1899) **1** : a jarring blow : WHACK **2** : DRINK ⟨a ~ of gin⟩

Bel·tane \ˈbel-ˌtān, -tin\ *n* [ME (Sc), May 1 or 2, fr. ScGael *bealltain*] (15c) : the Celtic May Day festival

belted kingfisher *n* (1811) : a No. American kingfisher (*Ceryle alcyon* syn. *Megaceryle alcyon*) that is slate blue above and white below with a slate-blue breast band and an additional chestnut-colored band in the female

belt·er \ˈbel-tər\ *n* (1953) : a singer with a powerful voice

belt·ing \ˈbel-tiŋ\ *n* (1567) **1** : BELTS **2** : material for belts

belt–tight·en·ing \ˈbelt-ˌtīt-niŋ, -ˌtī-tᵊn-iŋ\ *n* (1937) : a reduction in spending

belt up *vi* (1949) *Brit* : SHUT UP

belt·way \ˈbelt-ˌwā\ *n, often attrib* (ca. 1952) **1** : a highway skirting an urban area **2** *cap* : the political and social world of Washington, D.C., viewed esp. as insular and exclusive ⟨understanding better than *Beltway* insiders what really interests voters —L. I. Barrett⟩

be·lu·ga \bə-ˈlü-gə\ *n* [Russ, fr. *belyĭ* white; akin to Gk *phalios* having a white spot — more at BALD] (1772) **1** : a large white sturgeon (*Huso huso* syn. *Acipenser huso*) of the Black Sea, Caspian Sea, and their tributaries; *also* : caviar processed from beluga roe — compare OSETRA, SEVRUGA **2** [Russ *belukha*, fr. *belyĭ*] : a toothed whale (*Delphinapterus leucas*) of arctic and subarctic waters having a fusiform body that is about 10 to 15 feet (3.0 to 5.0 meters) long and white when mature — called also *white whale*

bel·ve·dere \ˈbel-və-ˌdir\ *n* [It, lit., beautiful view] (1593) : a structure (as a cupola or a summerhouse) designed to command a view

BEM *abbr* **1** bachelor of engineering of mines **2** British Empire Medal

be·ma \ˈbē-mə\ *n* [LL & LGk; LL, fr. LGk *bēma*, fr. Gk, step, tribunal, fr. *bainein* to go — more at COME] (1683) **1** : the usu. raised part of an Eastern church containing the altar **2** : BIMAH

Bem·ba \ˈbem-bə\ *n, pl* **Bemba** *or* **Bembas** [Bemba, stem of *ulúbembá*, a self-designation] (1940) **1** : a member of a primarily agricultural Bantu-speaking people of northeastern Zambia **2** : a Bantu language of the Bemba people

be·med·aled *or* **be·med·alled** \bi-ˈme-dᵊld, bē-\ *adj* (1880) : wearing or decorated with medals

be·mire \bi-ˈmīr, bē-\ *vt* (ca. 1532) **1** : to soil with mud or dirt **2** : to drag through or sink in mire

be·moan \bi-ˈmōn, bē-\ *vt* (bef. 12c) **1** : to express deep grief or distress over **2** : to regard with displeasure, disapproval, or regret ***syn*** see DEPLORE

be·mock \bi-ˈmäk, -ˈmȯk\ *vt* (1607) *archaic* : MOCK

be·muse \bi-ˈmyüz, bē-\ *vt* (1735) **1** : to make confused : PUZZLE, BEWILDER **2** : to occupy the attention of : DISTRACT, ABSORB **3** : to cause to have feelings of wry or tolerant amusement ⟨seems truly ~*ed* that people beyond his circle in Seattle would be interested in his ruminations —Ruth B. Smith⟩ — **be·mus·ed·ly** \-ˈmyü-zəd-lē\ *adv* — **be·muse·ment** \-ˈmyüz-mənt\ *n*

[1]**ben** \ˈben\ *adv* [ME, fr. OE *binnan*, fr. *be-* + *innan* within, from within, fr. *in*] (bef. 12c) *Scot* : WITHIN

[2]**ben** *prep* (bef. 12c) *Scot* : WITHIN

[3]**ben** *n* (1766) *Scot* : the inner room or parlor of a 2-room cottage

Bence–Jones protein \ˈben(t)s-ˈjōnz-\ *n* [Henry *Bence-Jones* †1873 Eng. physician and chemist] (ca. 1923) : a polypeptide composed of one or two antibody light chains that is found esp. in the urine of persons affected with multiple myeloma

[1]**bench** \ˈbench\ *n* [ME, fr. OE *benc;* akin to OHG *bank* bench] (bef. 12c) **1 a** : a long seat for two or more persons **b** : a thwart in a boat **c** (1) : a seat on which the members of an athletic team await a turn or opportunity to play (2) : the reserve players on a team; *broadly* : a reserve force **2 a** : the seat where a judge sits in court **b** : the place where justice is administered : COURT **c** : the office or dignity of a judge ⟨sat on the ~ for 20 years⟩ **d** : the persons who sit as judges **3 a** : the office or dignity of an official **b** : a seat for an official **c** : the officials occupying a bench **4 a** : a long worktable; *also* : LABORATORY ⟨~ chemist⟩ ⟨~ test⟩ **b** : a table forming part of a machine **5** : TERRACE, SHELF: as **a** : a former wave-cut shore of a sea or lake or floodplain of a river **b** : a shelf or ridge formed in working an open excavation on more than one level **6** : a compartmented platform on which dogs or cats are kept at a show when not being judged

[2]**bench** *vt* (14c) **1** : to furnish with benches **2 a** : to seat on a bench **b** (1) : to remove from or keep out of a game; *broadly* : to remove from use or from a position (2) : to remove from the starting lineup **3** : to exhibit (dogs or cats) to the public on a bench **4** : to lift (a weight) in a bench press ⟨~ 200 pounds⟩ ~ *vi* : to form a bench by natural processes

bench·er \ˈben-chər\ *n* (15c) : one who sits on or presides at a bench

bench jockey *n* (1939) : BENCHWARMER; *esp* : one who rides members of the opposing team from the bench

bench·land \ˈbench-ˌland\ *n* (1857) : BENCH 5a

[1]**bench·mark** \ˈbench-ˌmärk\ *n* (ca. 1842) **1** *usu* **bench mark** : a mark on a permanent object indicating elevation and serving as a reference in topographic surveys and tidal observations **2 a** : a point of reference from which measurements may be made **b** : something that serves as a standard by which others may be measured or judged **c** : a standardized problem or test that serves as a basis for evaluation or comparison (as of computer system performance)

[2]**benchmark** *vt* (1972) : to study (as a competitor's product or business practices) in order to improve the performance of one's own company

bench press *n* (ca. 1965) : a lift or exercise in which a weight is raised by extending the arms upward while lying on a bench — **bench–press** *vt*

bench seat *n* (1952) : a seat in an automotive vehicle that extends the full width of the passenger section

bench·top \ˈbench-ˌtäp\ *adj* (1965) : suitable (as in size or configuration) for convenient use on a laboratory workbench ⟨a ~ centrifuge⟩

bench·warm·er \ˈbench-ˌwȯr-mər\ *n* (1892) : a reserve player on an athletic team

bench warrant *n* (1696) : a warrant issued by a presiding judge or by a court against a person guilty of contempt or indicted for a crime

[1]**bend** \ˈbend\ *vb* **bent** \ˈbent\; **bend·ing** [ME, fr. OE *bendan;* akin to OE *bend* fetter — more at BAND] *vt* (bef. 12c) **1** : to constrain or strain to tension by curving ⟨~ a bow⟩ **2 a** : to turn or force from straight or even to curved or angular **b** : to force from a proper shape **c** : to force back to an original straight or even condition **3** : FASTEN ⟨~ a sail to its yard⟩ **4 a** : to cause to turn from a straight course : DEFLECT **b** : to guide or turn toward : DIRECT **c** : INCLINE, DISPOSE **d** : to adapt to one's purpose : DISTORT ⟨~ the rules⟩ **5** : to direct strenuously or with interest : APPLY ⟨*bent* himself to the task⟩ **6** : to make submissive : SUBDUE ~ *vi* **1** : to curve out of a straight line or position; *specif* : to incline the body in token of submission **2** : to apply oneself vigorously ⟨~*ing* to their work⟩ **3** : INCLINE, TEND **4** : COMPROMISE 2 — **bend·a·ble** \ˈben-də-bəl\ *adj* — **bend one's ear** : to talk to someone at length — **bend over backward** *or* **bend over backwards** : to make extreme efforts

[2]**bend** *n* (15c) **1** : the act or process of bending : the state of being bent **2** : something that is bent: as **a** : a curved part of a path (as of a stream or road) **b** : [1]WALE 2 — usu. used in pl. **3** *pl but sing or pl in constr* : the painful manifestations (as joint pain) of decompression sickness; *also* : DECOMPRESSION SICKNESS — usu. used with *the* — **around the bend** : MAD, CRAZY

[3]**bend** *n* [ME, fr. MF *bende*, of Gmc origin; akin to OHG *binta, bant* band — more at BAND] (15c) **1** : a diagonal band that runs from the dexter chief to the sinister base on a heraldic shield — compare BEND SINISTER **2** [ME, band, fr. OE *bend* fetter — more at BAND] : a knot by which one rope is fastened to another or to some object

ben·day \ˈben-ˈdā\ *adj, often cap* [*Ben*jamin *Day* †1916 Am. printer] (1903) : involving a process for adding shaded or tinted areas made up of dots for reproduction by line engraving — **benday** *vt*

bend·er \ˈben-dər\ *n* (15c) **1** : one that bends **2** : SPREE ⟨hungover after a weekend ~⟩

bend sinister *n* (1612) : a diagonal band that runs from the sinister chief to the dexter base on a heraldic shield

bendy \ˈben-dē\ *adj* (1928) *chiefly Brit* : FLEXIBLE, PLIABLE

[1]**be·neath** \bi-ˈnēth, bē-\ *adv* [ME *benethe*, fr. OE *beneothan*, fr. *be-* + *neothan* below; akin to OE *nithera* nether — more at NETHER] (bef. 12c) **1** : in or to a lower position : BELOW ⟨the mountains and the towns ~⟩ **2** : directly under : UNDERNEATH

[2]**beneath** *prep* (bef. 12c) **1 a** : in or to a lower position than : BELOW ⟨~ the surface⟩ **b** : directly under ⟨the ground ~ her feet⟩ **c** : at the foot of ⟨a camp ~ a hill⟩ **2** : not suitable to the rank of : unworthy of ⟨~ his dignity⟩ **3** : under the control, pressure, or influence of ⟨the chair sagged ~ his weight⟩ **4** : concealed by : under the guise of ⟨a warm heart ~ a gruff manner⟩

ben·e·dict \ˈbe-nə-ˌdikt\ *n* [alter. of *Benedick*, character in Shakespeare's *Much Ado About Nothing*] (1821) : a newly married man who has long been a bachelor

Ben•e•dic•tine \ˌbe-nə-ˈdik-tən, -ˌtēn\ *n* (15c) **:** a monk or a nun of one of the congregations following the rule of St. Benedict and devoted esp. to scholarship and liturgical worship — **Benedictine** *adj*
bene•dic•tion \ˌbe-nə-ˈdik-shən\ *n* [ME *benediccioun,* fr. LL *benediction-, benedictio,* fr. *benedicere* to bless, fr. L, to speak well of, fr. *bene* well (akin to L *bonus* good) + *dicere* to say — more at BOUNTY, DICTION] (15c) **1 :** the invocation of a blessing; *esp* **:** the short blessing with which public worship is concluded **2 :** something that promotes goodness or well-being **3** *often cap* **:** a Roman Catholic or Anglo-Catholic devotion including the exposition of the eucharistic Host in the monstrance and the blessing of the people with it **4 :** an expression of good wishes
bene•dic•to•ry \-ˈdik-t(ə-)rē\ *adj* (1710) **:** of or expressing benediction
Ben•e•dict's solution \ˈbe-nə-ˌdik(t)s-\ *n* [Stanley Rossiter *Benedict* †1936 Am. chemist] (1921) **:** a blue solution containing a carbonate, citrate, and sulfate which yields a red, yellow, or orange precipitate upon warming with a sugar (as glucose) that is a reducing agent
Ben•e•dic•tus \ˌbe-nə-ˈdik-təs\ *n* [LL, blessed, fr. pp. of *benedicere;* fr. its first word] (1552) **1 :** a canticle from Lk 1:68 beginning "Blessed be the Lord God of Israel" **2 :** a canticle from Mt 21:9 beginning "Blessed is he that cometh in the name of the Lord"
ben•e•fac•tion \ˌbe-nə-ˈfak-shən\ *n* [LL *benefaction-, benefactio,* fr. L *bene facere* to do good to, fr. *bene* + *facere* to do — more at DO] (1635) **1 :** the act of benefiting **2 :** a benefit conferred; *esp* **:** a charitable donation
ben•e•fac•tor \ˈbe-nə-ˌfak-tər\ *n* (15c) **:** one that confers a benefit; *esp* **:** one that makes a gift or bequest
ben•e•fac•tress \ˈbe-nə-ˌfak-tris\ *n* (1711) **:** a woman who is a benefactor
be•nef•ic \bə-ˈne-fik\ *adj* [L *beneficus,* fr. *bene* + *facere*] (1641) **:** BENEFICENT
ben•e•fice \ˈbe-nə-fəs\ *n* [ME, fr. AF, fr. ML *beneficium,* fr. L, favor, promotion, fr. *beneficus*] (14c) **1 :** an ecclesiastical office to which the revenue from an endowment is attached **2 :** a feudal estate in lands **:** FIEF — **benefice** *vt*
be•nef•i•cence \bə-ˈne-fə-sən(t)s\ *n* [L *beneficentia,* fr. *beneficus*] (15c) **1 :** the quality or state of being beneficent **2 :** BENEFACTION
be•nef•i•cent \-sənt\ *adj* [back-formation fr. *beneficence*] (1616) **1 :** doing or producing good; *esp* **:** performing acts of kindness and charity **2 :** BENEFICIAL — **be•nef•i•cent•ly** *adv*
ben•e•fi•cial \ˌbe-nə-ˈfi-shəl\ *adj* [L *beneficium* favor, benefit] (15c) **1 :** conferring benefits **:** conducive to personal or social well-being **2 :** receiving or entitling one to receive advantage, use, or benefit ⟨a ~ legacy⟩ — **ben•e•fi•cial•ly** \-ˈfi-sh(ə-)lē\ *adv* — **ben•e•fi•cial•ness** *n*
beneficials *n pl* (1989) **:** organisms (as ladybugs, lacewings, and bacteria) that feed on or parasitize pests of crops, gardens, and turf
ben•e•fi•cia•ry \ˌbe-nə-ˈfi-shē-ˌer-ē, -e-rē, -ˈfi-sh(ə-)rē\ *n, pl* **-ries** (1662) **1 :** one that benefits from something **2 a :** the person designated to receive the income of a trust estate **b :** the person named (as in an insurance policy) to receive proceeds or benefits — **beneficiary** *adj*
ben•e•fi•ci•a•tion \ˌbe-nə-ˌfi-shē-ˈā-shən\ *n* (1871) **:** the treatment of raw material (as iron ore) to improve physical or chemical properties esp. in preparation for smelting — **ben•e•fi•ci•ate** \-ˈfi-shē-ˌāt\ *vt*
[1]**ben•e•fit** \ˈbe-nə-ˌfit\ *n* [ME, fr. AF *benfet,* fr. L *bene factum,* fr. neut. of *bene factus,* pp. of *bene facere*] (14c) **1** *archaic* **:** an act of kindness **:** BENEFACTION **2 a :** something that promotes well-being **:** ADVANTAGE **b :** useful aid **:** HELP **3 a :** financial help in time of sickness, old age, or unemployment **b :** a payment or service provided for under an annuity, pension plan, or insurance policy **c :** a service (as health insurance) or right (as to take vacation time) provided by an employer in addition to wages or salary **4 :** an entertainment or social event to raise funds for a person or cause
[2]**benefit** *vb* **-fit•ed** \-ˌfi-təd\ *also* **-fit•ted; -fit•ing** *also* **-fit•ting** *vt* (15c) **:** to be useful or profitable to ~ *vi* **:** to receive benefit ⟨has ~*ed* from his experience⟩ — **ben•e•fit•er** \-ˌfi-tər\ *n*
benefit of clergy (15c) **1 :** clerical exemption from trial in a civil court **2 :** the ministration or sanction of the church
be•nev•o•lence \bə-ˈnev-lən(t)s, -ˈne-və-\ *n* (14c) **1 :** disposition to do good **2 a :** an act of kindness **b :** a generous gift **3 :** a compulsory levy by certain English kings with no other authority than the claim of prerogative
be•nev•o•lent \-lənt\ *adj* [ME, fr. L *benevolent-, benevolens,* fr. *bene* + *volent-, volens,* prp. of *velle* to wish — more at WILL] (15c) **1 a :** marked by or disposed to doing good ⟨a ~ donor⟩ **b :** organized for the purpose of doing good ⟨a ~ society⟩ **2 :** marked by or suggestive of goodwill ⟨~ smiles⟩ — **be•nev•o•lent•ly** *adv* — **be•nev•o•lent•ness** *n*
Ben•gali \ben-ˈgȯ-lē, beŋ-, -ˈgä-\ *n* [Hindi *baṅgālī,* fr. *Baṅgāl* Bengal] (ca. 1841) **1 :** a native or resident of Bengal **2 :** the modern Indo-Aryan language of Bengal — **Bengali** *adj*
ben•ga•line \ˈbeŋ-gə-ˌlēn\ *n* [F, fr. *Bengal*] (1884) **:** a fabric with a crosswise rib made from textile fibers (as rayon, nylon, cotton, or wool) often in combination
Ben•gal light \ˈben-ˌgȯl-, ˌbeŋ-, -ˌgäl-, -gəl-\ *n* (1818) **:** a usu. blue light or flare used formerly esp. for signaling and illumination
Bengal tiger *n* (1826) **:** a tiger (*Panthera tigris tigris*) occurring esp. in India

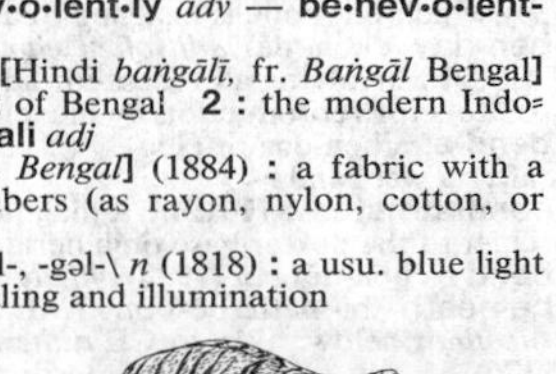
Bengal tiger

BEngr *abbr* bachelor of engineering
BEngS *abbr* bachelor of engineering science
be•night•ed \bi-ˈnī-təd, bē-\ *adj* (15c) **1 :** overtaken by darkness or night **2 :** existing in a state of intellectual, moral, or social darkness **:** UNENLIGHTENED — **be•night•ed•ly** *adv* — **be•night•ed•ness** *n*
be•nign \bi-ˈnīn\ *adj* [ME *benigne,* fr. AF, fr. L *benignus,* fr. *bene* + *gignere* to beget — more at KIN] (14c) **1 :** of a gentle disposition **:** GRACIOUS ⟨a ~ teacher⟩ **2 a :** showing kindness and gentleness ⟨~ faces⟩ **b :** FAVORABLE, WHOLESOME ⟨a ~ climate⟩ **3 a :** of a mild type or character that does not threaten health or life; *esp* **:** not becoming cancerous ⟨a ~ lung tumor⟩ **b :** having no significant effect **:** HARMLESS ⟨environmentally ~⟩ — **be•nig•ni•ty** \-ˈnig-nə-tē\ *n* — **be•nign•ly** \-ˈnīn-lē\ *adv*
be•nig•nan•cy \bi-ˈnig-nən(t)-sē\ *n* (1876) **:** the quality or state of being benignant or benign
be•nig•nant \-nənt\ *adj* [*benign* + *-ant* (as in *malignant*)] (ca. 1782) **1 :** serenely mild and kindly **:** BENIGN **2 :** FAVORABLE, BENEFICIAL ⟨a ~ power⟩ — **be•nig•nant•ly** *adv*
benign neglect *n* (1970) **:** an attitude or policy of ignoring an often delicate or undesirable situation that one is held to be responsible for dealing with
benign prostatic hyperplasia *n* (1968) **:** enlargement of the prostate gland caused by a benign overgrowth of chiefly glandular tissue that occurs esp. in some men over 50 years old and that tends to obstruct urination by constricting the urethra — abbr. *BPH*; called also *benign prostatic hypertrophy*
ben•i•son \ˈbe-nə-sən, -zən\ *n* [ME *beneson,* fr. AF *beneiçon,* fr. LL *benediction-, benedictio*] (14c) **:** BLESSING, BENEDICTION
Ben•ja•min \ˈben-jə-mən\ *n* [Heb *Binyāmīn*] (14c) **:** a son of Jacob and the traditional eponymous ancestor of one of the tribes of Israel
ben•ne *also* **bene** \ˈbe-nē\ *n* [of African origin; akin to Malinke *bĕne* sesame] (1769) **:** SESAME 1
ben•ny \ˈbe-nē\ *n, pl* **bennies** [*Benzedrine* + *-ie*] (1945) **1** *slang* **:** AMPHETAMINE **2** *slang* **:** a tablet of amphetamine taken as a stimulant
ben•o•myl \ˈbe-nə-ˌmil\ *n* [*benz-* + *-o-* + *methyl*] (1969) **:** a derivative $C_{14}H_{18}N_4O_3$ of carbamate and benzimidazole used esp. as a systemic agricultural fungicide
[1]**bent** \ˈbent\ *n* [ME, grassy place, bent grass, fr. OE *beonot-;* akin to OHG *binuz* rush] (14c) **1 :** unenclosed grassland **2 a (1) :** a reedy grass **(2) :** a stalk of stiff coarse grass **b :** BENT GRASS
[2]**bent** *adj* [ME, fr. pp. of *benden* to bend] (14c) **1 :** changed by bending out of an orig. straight or even condition ⟨~ twigs⟩ **2 :** strongly inclined **:** DETERMINED — usu. used with *on* ⟨was ~ on going⟩ **3** *slang* **a :** different from the normal or usual **b** *chiefly Brit* **:** DISHONEST, CORRUPT — **bent out of shape :** extremely upset or angry
[3]**bent** *n* [irreg. fr. [1]*bend*] (1586) **1 a :** a strong inclination or interest **:** BIAS **b :** a special inclination or capacity **:** TALENT **2 :** capacity of endurance **3 :** a transverse framework (as in a bridge) to carry lateral as well as vertical loads ***syn*** see GIFT
bent grass *n* (1677) **:** any of a genus (*Agrostis*) of grasses including important chiefly perennial and rhizomatous pasture and lawn grasses with fine velvety or wiry herbage
Ben•tham•ism \ˈben(t)-thə-ˌmi-zəm\ *n* (1829) **:** the utilitarian philosophy of Jeremy Bentham and his followers — **Ben•tham•ite** \-ˌmīt\ *n or adj*
ben•thic \ˈben(t)-thik\ *adj* [*benthos*] (1902) **1 :** of, relating to, or occurring at the bottom of a body of water **2 :** of, relating to, or occurring in the depths of the ocean
ben•thon•ic \ben-ˈthä-nik\ *adj* [irreg. fr. *benthos*] (1897) **:** BENTHIC
ben•thos \ˈben-ˌthäs\ *n* [NL, fr. Gk, depth, deep sea; akin to Gk *bathys* deep] (1891) **:** organisms that live on or in the bottom of a body of water
ben•ton•ite \ˈben-tə-ˌnīt\ *n* [Fort *Benton,* Mont.] (1898) **:** an absorptive and colloidal clay used esp. as a sealing agent or suspending agent (as of drugs) — **ben•ton•it•ic** \ˌben-tə-ˈni-tik\ *adj*
ben tro•va•to \ˌben-trō-ˈvä-(ˌ)tō\ *adj* [It, lit., well found] (1874) **:** characteristic or appropriate even if not true ⟨the story is *ben trovato*⟩
bent•wood \ˈbent-ˌwu̇d\ *adj* (1862) **:** made of wood that is bent rather than cut into shape ⟨~ furniture⟩ — **bentwood** *n*
be•numb \bi-ˈnəm, bē-\ *vt* [ME *benomen,* fr. *benomen,* pp. of *benimen* to deprive, fr. OE *beniman,* fr. *be-* + *niman* to take — more at NIMBLE] (14c) **1 :** to make inactive **:** DEADEN **2 :** to make numb esp. by cold
benz- *or* **benzo-** *comb form* [ISV, fr. *benzoin*] **:** related to benzene or benzoic acid ⟨*benzo*phenone⟩ ⟨*benz*yl⟩
benz•al•de•hyde \ben-ˈzal-də-ˌhīd\ *n* [ISV] (ca. 1860) **:** a colorless nontoxic aromatic liquid C_6H_5CHO found in essential oils (as in peach kernels) and used in flavoring and perfumery, in pharmaceuticals, and in synthesis of dyes
benz•an•thra•cene \ben-ˈzan(t)-thrə-ˌsēn\ *n* [ISV] (1932) **:** a crystalline carcinogenic cyclic hydrocarbon $C_{18}H_{12}$ that is found in small amounts in coal tar
Ben•ze•drine \ˈben-zə-ˌdrēn\ *n* [fr. *Benzedrine,* a trademark] (1933) **:** a preparation of the sulfate of amphetamine $(C_9H_{13}N)_2 \cdot H_2SO_4$ formerly used in medicine
ben•zene \ˈben-ˌzēn, ben-ˈ\ *n* [ISV *benz-* + *-ene*] (1835) **:** a colorless volatile flammable toxic liquid aromatic hydrocarbon C_6H_6 used in organic synthesis, as a solvent, and as a motor fuel — **ben•ze•noid** \ˈben-zə-ˌnȯid\ *adj or n*
benzene hexa•chlo•ride \-ˌhek-sə-ˈklȯr-ˌīd\ *n* (1884) **:** BHC
benzene ring *n* (1877) **:** a structural arrangement of atoms in benzene and other aromatic compounds that consists of a planar symmetrical hexagon of six carbon atoms which derives added stability from the delocalization of certain bonding electrons over the entire ring — compare META- 4a, ORTH- 4b, PARA- 2b
ben•zi•dine \ˈben-zə-ˌdēn\ *n* [ISV *benz-* + *-idine*] (ca. 1855) **:** a crystalline diamine base $C_{12}H_{12}N_2$ prepared from nitrobenzene and used esp. in making dyes
benz•imid•azole \ˌben-ˌzi-mə-ˈda-ˌzōl, ˌben-zə-ˈmi-də-ˌzōl\ *n* [ISV] (1912) **:** a crystalline base $C_7H_6N_2$ used esp. to inhibit the growth of various viruses, parasitic worms, or fungi; *also* **:** one of its derivatives
ben•zine \ˈben-ˌzēn, ben-ˈ\ *n* [G *Benzin,* fr. *benz-*] (1835) **:** any of various volatile flammable petroleum distillates used esp. as solvents or as motor fuels
ben•zo•ate \ˈben-zə-ˌwāt, -zō-ˌāt\ *n* (1788) **:** a salt or ester of benzoic acid
ben•zo•caine \ˈben-zə-ˌkān\ *n* [ISV *benz-* + *-caine*] (1922) **:** a white crystalline ester $C_9H_{11}NO_2$ used as a local anesthetic
ben•zo•di•az•e•pine \ˌben-zō-dī-ˈa-zə-ˌpēn\ *n* [*benz-* + *di-* + *az-* + *-epine* (fr. *hepta-* + [2]*-ine*)] (1934) **:** any of a group of aromatic lipophilic amines (as diazepam and chlordiazepoxide) used esp. as tranquilizers
ben•zo•ic acid \ben-ˈzō-ik-\ *n* [ISV, fr. *benzoin*] (1791) **:** a white crystalline acid C_6H_5COOH found naturally (as in benzoin or in cranberries) or made synthetically and used esp. as a preservative of foods, in medicine, and in organic synthesis

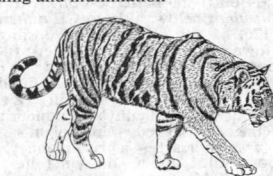

ben·zo·in \'ben-zə-wən, -zō-, -ˌwēn; -ˌzȯin\ *n* [modif. of MF *benjoin,* fr. Catal *benjuí,* fr. Ar *lubān jāwī,* lit., frankincense of Java] (1562) **1 :** a hard fragrant yellowish balsamic resin from trees (genus *Styrax*) of southeastern Asia used esp. as a fixative in perfumes, as incense, and in medicine as an expectorant and skin protectant **2 :** a white crystalline hydroxy ketone $C_{14}H_{12}O_2$ made from benzaldehyde

ben·zo·phe·none \ˌben-zō-fi-'nōn, -'fē-ˌnōn\ *n* [ISV *benz-* + *phen-* + *-one*] (1877) **:** a colorless crystalline ketone $C_{13}H_{10}O$ used esp. as a perfume fixative and in sunscreens; *also* **:** a derivative of benzophenone

ben·zo·py·rene \ˌben-zō-'pī-ˌrēn, -pī-'rēn\ *n* [ISV *benz-* + *pyrene* a crystalline hydrocarbon $C_{16}H_{10}$, fr. *pyr-* + *-ene*] (1936) **:** a yellow crystalline carcinogenic hydrocarbon $C_{20}H_{12}$ found in coal tar — called also *benzo[a]pyrene*

ben·zo·qui·none \ˌben-zō-kwi-'nōn, -'kwi-ˌ\ *n* [ISV] (1903) **:** QUINONE 1

ben·zo·yl \'ben-zə-ˌwil, -zō-ˌil, -ˌzȯil\ *n* [G, fr. *Benzoësäure* benzoic acid + Gk *hylē* matter, lit., wood] (ca. 1855) **:** the acyl radical of benzoic acid

benzoyl peroxide *n* (1924) **:** a white crystalline compound $C_{14}H_{10}O_4$ used in bleaching and in medicine esp. in the treatment of acne

ben·zyl \'ben-ˌzēl, -zəl\ *n* [ISV *benz-* + *-yl*] (1868) **:** a monovalent radical $C_6H_5CH_2$– derived from toluene — **ben·zyl·ic** \ben-'zi-lik\ *adj*

Be·o·wulf \'bā-ə-ˌwu̇lf\ *n* (bef. 12c) **:** a legendary Geatish warrior and hero of the Old English poem *Beowulf* — **Be·o·wulf·ian** \ˌbā-ə-'wu̇l-fē-ən\ *adj*

be·paint \bi-'pānt\ *vt* (ca. 1555) *archaic* **:** TINGE

be·queath \bi-'kwēth, -'kwē*th*, bē-\ *vt* [ME *bequethen,* fr. OE *becwethan,* fr. *be-* + *cwethan* to say — more at QUOTH] (bef. 12c) **1 :** to give or leave by will — used esp. of personal property **2 :** to hand down **:** TRANSMIT — **be·queath·al** \-'kwē-thəl, -*th*əl\ *n*

be·quest \bi-'kwest, bē-\ *n* [ME, irreg. fr. *bequethen*] (14c) **1 :** the act of bequeathing **2 :** something bequeathed **:** LEGACY

be·rate \bi-'rāt, bē-\ *vt* (1548) **:** to scold or condemn vehemently and at length ***syn*** see SCOLD

Ber·ber \'bər-bər\ *n* [ultim. fr. Ar *barbar*] (1732) **1 :** a member of any of various peoples living in northern Africa west of Tripoli **2 a :** a branch of the Afro-Asiatic language family comprising languages spoken by various peoples of northern Africa and the Sahara (as the Tuaregs and the Kabyles) **b :** any one of the Berber languages

ber·ber·ine \'bər-bə-ˌrēn\ *n* [G *Berberin,* fr. NL *berberis*] (ca. 1847) **:** a bitter crystalline yellow alkaloid $C_{20}H_{19}NO_5$ obtained from the roots of various plants (as barberry) and used in medicine esp. for its antimicrobial properties

ber·ber·is \'bər-bər-əs\ *n* [NL, the genus including barberry, alter. of ML *barberis* barberry, fr. Ar *barbārīs*] (ca. 1868) **:** BARBERRY

ber·ceuse \ber-'sœz, -'süz\ *n, pl* **ber·ceuses** \-'sœz; -'süz, -'sü-zəz\ [F, fr. *bercer* to rock, fr. OF *bercier,* fr. *bers* cradle] (1858) **1 :** a musical composition usu. in ⁶⁄₈ time that resembles a lullaby **2 :** LULLABY

ber·dache \bər-'dash\ *n* [AmerF, alter. of F *bardache* catamite, fr. It dial. (southern Italy) *bardascio,* fr. Ar *bardaj* slave, fr. Pers *bardag* prisoner, fr. MPers *vartak*] (1806) *sometimes offensive* **:** an American Indian who assumes the dress, social status, and role of the opposite sex

be·reave \bi-'rēv, bē-\ *vt* **-reaved** *or* **-reft** \-'reft\; **-reav·ing** [ME *bereven,* fr. OE *berēafian,* fr. *be-* + *rēafian* to rob — more at REAVE] (bef. 12c) **1 :** to deprive of something — usu. used with *of* ⟨madam, you have *bereft* me of all words —Shak.⟩ **2 :** to take away (a valued or necessary possession) esp. by force

¹be·reaved \bi-'rēvd, bē-\ *adj* (1799) **:** suffering the death of a loved one

²bereaved *n, pl* **bereaved** (1815) **:** one who is bereaved

be·reave·ment \bi-'rēv-mənt, bē-\ *n* (ca. 1731) **:** the state or fact of being bereaved; *esp* **:** the loss of a loved one by death

be·reft \-'reft\ *adj* (1565) **1 a :** deprived or robbed of the possession or use of something — usu. used with *of* ⟨both players are instantly ~ of their poise —A. E. Wier⟩ **b :** lacking something needed, wanted, or expected — used with *of* ⟨the book is . . . completely ~ of an index —*Times Lit. Supp.*⟩ **2 :** BEREAVED ⟨a ~ mother⟩

be·ret \bə-'rā\ *n* [F *béret,* fr. Gascon *berret,* fr. Old Occitan, cap — more at BIRETTA] (1827) **:** a visorless usu. woolen cap with a tight headband and a soft full flat top

berg \'bərg\ *n* (1818) **:** ICEBERG

ber·ga·mot \'bər-gə-ˌmät\ *n* [F *bergamote,* fr. It *bergamotta,* modif. of Turk *bey armudu,* lit., the bey's pear] (1650) **1 :** a pear-shaped orange of a Mediterranean tree (*Citrus aurantium bergamia*) having a rind that yields an essential oil used esp. in perfumery; *also* **:** this oil **2 :** any of several mints (genus *Monarda*) — compare WILD BERGAMOT

ber·gère *also* **ber·gere** \ber-'zher, bər-\ *n* [F, lit., shepherdess, fem. of *berger* shepherd, fr. OF *bergier,* fr. VL **berbicarius,* fr. L. *vervec-, vervex, verbex, berbex* wether] (1762) **:** an upholstered armchair of an 18th century style having an exposed wood frame

be·rib·boned \bi-'ri-bənd, bē-\ *adj* (1853) **:** adorned with ribbons

beri·beri \'ber-ē-'ber-ē, 'be-rē-'be-rē\ *n* [Sinhalese *bæribæri*] (1703) **:** a deficiency disease marked by inflammatory or degenerative changes of the nerves, digestive system, and heart and caused by a lack of or inability to assimilate thiamine

berk \'bərk\ *n* [prob. short for *Berkeley* (or *Berkshire*) *hunt,* rhyming slang for *cunt*] (1936) *Brit* **:** FOOL

Berke·le·ian *or* **Berke·ley·an** \'bär-klē-ən, 'bər-; bär-', ˌbər-'\ *adj* (1813) **:** of, relating to, or suggestive of Bishop Berkeley or his system of philosophical idealism — **Berkeleian** *n* — **Berke·le·ian·ism** \-ə-ˌni-zəm\ *n*

berke·li·um \'bər-klē-əm\ *n* [NL, fr. *Berkeley,* Calif.] (1950) **:** a radioactive metallic element produced artificially (as by bombarding americium 241 with alpha particles) — see ELEMENT table

Berk·shire \'bərk-ˌshir, -shər\ *n* [*Berkshire,* England] (1831) **:** any of a breed of medium-sized black swine with white markings

berm \'bərm\ *n* [F *berme,* fr. D *berm* strip of ground along a dike; akin to ME *brimme* brim] (1704) **1 :** a narrow shelf, path, or ledge typically at the top or bottom of a slope; *also* **:** a mound or wall of earth or sand ⟨a landscaped ~⟩ **2 :** the shoulder of a road

Ber·mu·da bag \(ˌ)bər-'myü-də-, *esp Southern* -'mü-də-\ *n* [*Bermuda* islands, No. Atlantic] (1979) **:** a round or oval-shaped handbag with a wooden handle and removable cloth covers

Bermuda grass *n* (1808) **:** a creeping stoloniferous southern European grass (*Cynodon dactylon*) often used as a lawn and pasture grass

Bermuda onion *n* (1876) **:** a large flattened onion that has a mild flavor and yellow, white, or red skin

Bermuda rig *n* (1853) **:** MARCONI RIG

Ber·mu·das \(ˌ)bər-'myü-dəz, *esp Southern* -'mü-dəz\ *n pl* (1961) **:** BERMUDA SHORTS

Bermuda shorts *n pl* (1951) **:** knee-length walking shorts

Ber·nese mountain dog \'bər-ˌnēz-, -ˌnēs-\ *n* [*Bern,* Switzerland] (1935) **:** any of a breed of large powerful long-coated black dogs of Swiss origin that have tan and white markings and were developed as draft animals

Ber·noul·li's principle \bər-'nü-lēz-, ˌber-ˌnü-'lēz-\ *n* [Daniel *Bernoulli* †1782 Swiss physicist] (1940) **:** a principle in hydrodynamics: the pressure in a stream of fluid is reduced as the speed of the flow is increased

Ber·noul·li trial \bər-'nü-lē-, ˌber-ˌnü-'lē-\ *n* [Jacques *Bernoulli* †1705 Swiss mathematician] (1951) **:** one of the repetitions of a statistical experiment having exactly two mutually exclusive outcomes each with a constant probability of occurrence

ber·ried \'ber-ēd, 'be-rēd\ *adj* (1785) **1 :** having or covered with berries ⟨~ shrubs⟩ **2 :** bearing eggs ⟨a ~ lobster⟩

¹ber·ry \'ber-ē, 'be-rē\ *n, pl* **berries** [ME *berye,* fr. OE *berie;* akin to OHG *beri* berry] (bef. 12c) **1 a :** a pulpy and usu. edible fruit (as a strawberry, raspberry, or checkerberry) of small size irrespective of its structure **b :** a simple fruit (as a grape, blueberry, tomato, or cucumber) with a pulpy or fleshy pericarp **c :** the dry seed of some plants (as wheat) **2 :** an egg of a fish or lobster

²berry *vi* **ber·ried; ber·ry·ing** (ca. 1780) **1 :** to bear or produce berries ⟨a ~*ing* shrub⟩ **2 :** to gather or seek berries

ber·ry·like \'ber-ē-ˌlīk, 'be-rē-\ *adj* (1847) **1 :** resembling a berry esp. in size or structure **2 :** being small and rounded **:** COCCOID

ber·seem \(ˌ)bər-'sēm\ *n* [Ar *barsīm,* fr. Copt *bersīm*] (ca. 1902) **:** a succulent annual clover (*Trifolium alexandrinum*) cultivated as a forage plant and green-manure crop esp. in the alkaline soils of the Nile valley and in the southwestern U.S. — called also *Egyptian clover*

¹ber·serk \bə(r)-'sərk, ˌbər-, -'zərk; 'bər-ˌ\ *or* **ber·serk·er** \-'sər-kər, -'zər-; 'bər-ˌ\ *n* [ON *berserkr,* prob. fr. *ber-* bear + *serkr* shirt] (1818) **1 :** an ancient Scandinavian warrior frenzied in battle and held to be invulnerable **2 :** one whose actions are recklessly defiant

²berserk *adj* (1851) **:** FRENZIED, CRAZED — usu. used in the phrase *go berserk* ⟨sinister ravings of an imagination gone ~ —John Gruen⟩ — **berserk** *adv* — **ber·serk·ly** *adv*

¹berth \'bərth\ *n* [ME *birth,* prob. fr. *beren* to bear + *-th*] (15c) **1 a :** sufficient distance for maneuvering a ship **b :** an amount of distance maintained for safety ⟨give the fire a wide ~⟩ **2 a :** the place where a ship lies when at anchor or at a wharf **b :** a space for an automotive vehicle at rest ⟨a truck-loading ~⟩ **3 :** a place to sit or sleep esp. on a ship or vehicle **:** ACCOMMODATION **4 a :** a billet on a ship **b :** JOB, POSITION, PLACE ⟨a starting ~ on the team⟩

²berth *vt* (1667) **1 :** to bring into a berth **2 :** to allot a berth to ~ *vi* **:** to come into a berth

ber·tha \'bər-thə\ *n* [F *berthe,* fr. *Berthe* (Bertha) †783 queen of the Franks] (1842) **:** a wide round collar covering the shoulders

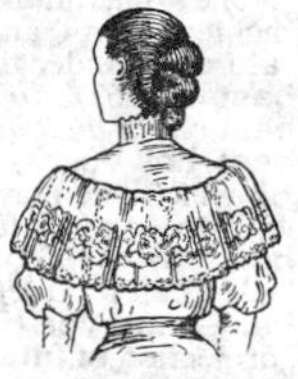

bertha

Ber·til·lon system \'bər-tᵊl-ˌän-, 'ber-tē-ˌyōⁿ-\ *n* [Alphonse *Bertillon* †1914 Fr. criminologist] (1893) **:** a system for identifying persons based on bodily measurements, photographs, and notation of data (as markings, color, and thumb line impressions)

ber·yl \'ber-əl, 'be-rəl\ *n* [ME, fr. MF *beril,* fr. L *beryllus,* fr. Gk *bēryllos,* back-formation fr. *bēryllion* beryl, of Indo-Aryan origin; akin to Prakrit *verulia, veluriya* beryl] (13c) **:** a mineral consisting of a silicate of beryllium and aluminum of great hardness that occurs in colorless hexagonal prisms when pure and in various colors (as green, blue, yellow, or pink) when not pure, that is valued as a source of gems, and that is the principal source of beryllium

be·ryl·li·um \bə-'ri-lē-əm\ *n* [NL, fr. Gk *bēryllion*] (ca. 1847) **:** a steel-gray light strong brittle toxic divalent metallic element used chiefly as a hardening agent in alloys — see ELEMENT table

be·seech \bi-'sēch, bē-\ *vb* **-seeched** *or* **-sought** \-'sȯt\; **-seech·ing** [ME *besechen,* fr. *be-* + *sechen* to seek] *vt* (12c) **1 :** to beg for urgently or anxiously **2 :** to request earnestly **:** IMPLORE ~ *vi* **:** to make supplication ***syn*** see BEG — **be·seech·ing·ly** \-'sē-chiŋ-lē\ *adv*

be·seem \bi-'sēm\ *vi* (13c) *archaic* **:** to be fitting or becoming ~ *vt, archaic* **:** to be suitable to **:** BEFIT

be·set \bi-'set, bē-\ *vt* **-set; -set·ting** [ME *besetten,* fr. OE *besettan,* fr. *be-* + *settan* to set] (bef. 12c) **1 :** to set or stud with or as if with ornaments **2 :** TROUBLE, HARASS ⟨inflation ~*s* the economy⟩ **3 a :** to set upon **:** ASSAIL ⟨the settlers were ~ by savages⟩ **b :** to hem in **:** SURROUND — **be·set·ment** \-mənt\ *n*

be·set·ting *adj* (1634) **:** constantly present or attacking **:** OBSESSIVE

be·shrew \bi-'shrü, bē-, *esp Southern* -'srü\ *vt* (14c) *archaic* **:** CURSE

¹be·side \bi-'sīd, bē-\ *prep* [ME, adv. & prep., fr. OE *be sīdan* at or to the side, fr. *be* at (fr. *bī*) + *sīdan,* dat. & acc. of *sīde* side — more at BY] (13c) **1 a :** by the side of ⟨walk ~ me⟩ **b :** in comparison with **c :** on a par with **2 :** BESIDES **3 :** not relevant to ⟨~ the point⟩ — **beside oneself :** in a state of extreme excitement

²beside *adv* (14c) **1** *archaic* **:** NEARBY **2** *archaic* **:** BESIDES

¹be·sides \bi-'sīdz, bē-\ *prep* (14c) **1 :** OTHER THAN, EXCEPT ⟨no one ~ us⟩ **2 :** together with ⟨a decision that, ~ being practical, is morally right⟩

²besides *adv* (1564) **1 :** as well **:** ALSO **2 :** MOREOVER, FURTHERMORE

³besides *adj* (1594) **:** ELSE

be·siege \bi-'sēj, bē-\ *vt* **-sieged; -sieg·ing** (14c) **1 :** to surround with armed forces **2 a :** to press with requests **:** IMPORTUNE **b :** to cause worry or distress to : BESET ⟨doubts *besieged* him⟩ — **be·sieg·er** *n*

be·smear \bi-ˈsmir, bē-\ *vt* (bef. 12c) : SMEAR

be·smirch \bi-ˈsmərch, bē-\ *vt* (1599) : SULLY, SOIL

be·som \ˈbē-zəm\ *n* [ME *beseme,* fr. OE *besma;* akin to OHG *besmo* broom] (bef. 12c) : BROOM 2; *esp* : one made of twigs

besom pocket *n* [origin unknown] (1966) : a pocket with a welted slit opening

be·sot \bi-ˈsät, bē-\ *vt* **be·sot·ted; be·sot·ting** [*be-* + *sot* (to stultify)] (1567) **1** : INFATUATE 2 **2** : to make dull or stupid; *esp* : to muddle with drunkenness — **be·sot·ted·ly** *adv*

be·spat·ter \bi-ˈspa-tər, bē-\ *vt* (1600) : SPATTER

be·speak \bi-ˈspēk, bē-\ *vt* **-spoke** \-ˈspōk\; **-spo·ken** \-ˈspō-kən\; **-speak·ing** (1533) **1** : to hire, engage, or claim beforehand **2** : to speak to esp. with formality : ADDRESS **3** : REQUEST ⟨~ a favor⟩ **4 a** : INDICATE, SIGNIFY ⟨her performance ~*s* considerable practice⟩ **b** : to show beforehand : FORETELL

be·spec·ta·cled \bi-ˈspek-(ˌ)ti-kəld, bē-\ *adj* (1742) : wearing spectacles

be·spoke \bi-ˈspōk, bē-\ *also* **be·spo·ken** \-ˈspō-kən\ *adj* [pp. of *bespeak*] (1607) **1 a** : CUSTOM-MADE ⟨a ~ suit⟩ **b** : dealing in or producing custom-made articles **2** *dial* : ENGAGED

be·sprent \bi-ˈsprent\ *adj* [ME *bespreynt,* fr. pp. of *besprengen* to besprinkle, fr. OE *besprengan,* fr. *be-* + *sprengan* to scatter; akin to OE *springan* to spring] (14c) *archaic* : sprinkled over

be·sprin·kle \bi-ˈspriŋ-kəl, bē-\ *vt* [ME *besprengeln,* freq. of *besprengen*] (15c) : SPRINKLE

Bes·sel function \ˈbe-səl-\ *n* [Friedrich W. *Bessel* †1846 Prussian astronomer] (1872) : one of a class of transcendental functions expressible as infinite series and occurring in the solution of the differential equation

$$x^2 \frac{d^2y}{dx^2} + x\frac{dy}{dx} = (n^2 - x^2)y$$

Bes·se·mer process \ˈbe-sə-mər-\ *n* [Sir Henry *Bessemer*] (1856) : a process of making steel from pig iron by burning out carbon and other impurities by means of a blast of air forced through the molten metal

1**best** \ˈbest\ *adj, superlative of* GOOD [ME, fr. OE *betst;* akin to OE *bōt* remedy — more at BETTER] (bef. 12c) **1** : excelling all others ⟨the ~ student⟩ **2** : most productive of good : offering or producing the greatest advantage, utility, or satisfaction ⟨what is the ~ thing to do⟩ **3** : MOST, LARGEST ⟨it rained for the ~ part of their vacation⟩

2**best** *adv, superlative of* WELL (bef. 12c) **1** : in the best way : to greatest advantage ⟨some things are ~ left unsaid⟩ **2** : MOST ⟨those ~ able will provide needed support⟩ — **as best** : as well, skillfully, or accurately as ⟨try to do it *as best* you can⟩

3**best** *n, pl* **best** (bef. 12c) **1** : the best state or part **2** : one that is best ⟨the ~ falls short⟩ **3** : the greatest degree of good or excellence **4 a** : one's maximum effort ⟨do your ~⟩ **b** : a best performance or achievement ⟨ran a new personal ~⟩ **5** : best clothes ⟨Sunday ~⟩ — **at best** : under the most favorable circumstances

4**best** *vt* (1863) : to get the better of : OUTDO

5**best** *verbal auxiliary* (1914) : had best ⟨you ~ listen⟩

best–ball \ˈbes(t)-ˈbȯl\ *adj* (1909) **1** : relating to or being a golf match in which one player competes against the best individual score of two or more players for each hole **2** : FOUR-BALL

best boy *n* (1937) : the chief assistant to the gaffer in motion-picture or television production

best–case \ˈbes(t)-ˈkās\ *adj* (1973) : being, relating to, or based on a projection of future events that assumes only the best possible circumstances ⟨a ~ scenario⟩

1**be·stead** *or* **be·sted** \bi-ˈsted\ *adj* [ME *bested,* fr. *be-* + *sted,* pp. of *steden* to place, fr. *stede* place — more at STEAD] (14c) *archaic* : SITUATED

2**bestead** *vt* **be·stead·ed; be·stead; be·stead·ing** [*be-* + *stead*] (1578) **1** *archaic* : HELP **2** *archaic* : to be useful to : AVAIL

bes·tial \ˈbes-chəl, ˈbesh-, ˈbēs-, ˈbēsh-\ *adj* [ME, fr. MF, fr. L *bestialis,* fr. *bestia* beast] (14c) **1 a** : of or relating to beasts **b** : resembling a beast **2 a** : lacking intelligence or reason **b** : marked by base or inhuman instincts or desires : BRUTAL ***syn*** see BRUTAL — **bes·tial·ize** \-chə-ˌlīz\ *vt* — **bes·tial·ly** \-chə-lē\ *adv*

bes·ti·al·i·ty \ˌbes-chē-ˈa-lə-tē, ˌbesh-, ˌbēs-, ˌbēsh-\ *n, pl* **-ties** (14c) **1** : the condition or status of a lower animal **2** : display or gratification of bestial traits or impulses **3** : sexual relations between a human being and a lower animal

bes·ti·ary \ˈbes-chē-ˌer-ē, -ˌe-rē, ˈbesh-, ˈbēs-, ˈbēsh-\ *n, pl* **-ar·ies** [ML *bestiarium,* fr. L, neut. of *bestiarius* of beasts, fr. *bestia*] (1840) **1** : a medieval allegorical or moralizing work on the appearance and habits of real or imaginary animals **2 a** : a collection of descriptions or representations of real or imaginary animals **b** : an array of real humans or literary characters often having symbolic significance **3** : an unusual or whimsical collection ⟨a truly astounding ~ of airplane designs —Peter Garrison⟩

be·stir \bi-ˈstər, bē-\ *vt* (14c) : to rouse to action : get going

best man *n* (ca. 1782) : the principal groomsman at a wedding

be·stow \bi-ˈstō, bē-\ *vt* [ME, fr. *be-* + *stowe* place — more at STOW] (14c) **1** : to put to use : APPLY ⟨~*ed* his spare time on study⟩ **2** : to put in a particular or appropriate place : STOW **3** : to provide with quarters : PUT UP **4** : to convey as a gift — usu. used with *on* or *upon* ***syn*** see GIVE — **be·stow·al** \-ˈstō(-ə)l\ *n* — **be·stow·er** \-ˈstō(-ə)r\ *n*

be·strew \bi-ˈstrü, bē-\ *vt* **-strewed; -strewed** *or* **-strewn** \-ˈstrün\; **-strew·ing** (bef. 12c) **1** : STREW **2** : to lie scattered over

be·stride \bi-ˈstrīd, bē-\ *vt* **-strode** \-ˈstrōd\; **-strid·den** \-ˈstri-dᵊn\; **-strid·ing** \-ˈstrī-diŋ\ (bef. 12c) **1** : to ride, sit, or stand astride : STRADDLE **2** : to tower over : DOMINATE ⟨the bloated bureaucracy that ~*s* us all —Edward Ney⟩ **3** *archaic* : to stride across

best sell·er \ˈbes(t)-ˈse-lər\ *n* (1889) : an article (as a book) whose sales are among the highest of its class — **best–sell·er·dom** \-dəm\ *n* — **best–sell·ing** \-ˈse-liŋ\ *adj*

1**bet** \ˈbet\ *n* [origin unknown] (1592) **1 a** : something that is laid, staked, or pledged typically between two parties on the outcome of a contest or a contingent issue : WAGER — often used figuratively in such phrases as *all bets are off* to stress the uncertainty of an outcome **b** : the act of giving such a pledge **2** : something to wager on **3** : a choice made by consideration of probabilities ⟨your best ~ is the back road⟩

2**bet** *vb* **bet** *also* **bet·ted; bet·ting** *vt* (1597) **1 a** : to stake on the outcome of an issue or the performance of a contestant **b** : to be able to be sure that — usu. used in the expression *you bet* ⟨you ~ I'll be there⟩ **2 a** : to maintain with or as if with a bet **b** : to make a bet with **c** : to make a bet on ~ *vi* : to lay a bet

3**bet** *abbr* between

1**be·ta** \ˈbā-tə, *chiefly Brit* ˈbē-\ *n* [ME *betha,* fr. L *beta,* fr. Gk *bēta,* of Sem origin; akin to Heb *bēth* beth] (14c) **1** : the 2d letter of the Greek alphabet — see ALPHABET table **2** : BETA PARTICLE **3** : a measure of the risk potential of a stock or an investment portfolio expressed as a ratio of the stock's or portfolio's volatility to the volatility of the market as a whole **4** : a nearly complete prototype of a product (as software) ⟨released in ~⟩ ⟨the ~ version⟩

2**beta** *adj* (1862) : second in position in the structure of an organic molecule from a particular group or atom ⟨~ substitution⟩ — often used in combination; symbol β

be·ta–ad·ren·er·gic \-ˌa-drə-ˈnər-jik\ *adj* (1959) : of, relating to, or being a beta-receptor ⟨~ blocking action⟩

be·ta–am·y·loid \-ˈa-mə-ˌlȯid\ *n* (1987) : an amyloid that is derived from a larger precursor protein and is the primary component of plaques characteristic of Alzheimer's disease

be·ta–block·er \-ˌblä-kər\ *n* (1968) : any of a class of drugs (as propranolol) that decrease the rate and force of heart contractions and lower high blood pressure by blocking the activity of beta-receptors — **be·ta–block·ing** \-kiŋ\ *adj*

be·ta–car·o·tene \-ˈker-ə-ˌtēn, -ˈka-rə-\ *n* (1934) : an isomer of carotene found in dark green and dark yellow vegetables and fruits

beta cell *n* (1926) : any of the insulin-secreting pancreatic cells in the islets of Langerhans

beta decay *n* (1931) : a radioactive nuclear transformation governed by the weak force in which a nucleon (as a neutron) changes into a nucleon (as a proton) of the other type with the emission of either an electron and an antineutrino or a positron and a neutrino

be·ta–en·dor·phin \-en-ˈdȯr-fən\ *n* (1976) : an endorphin of the pituitary gland having a much greater analgesic potency than morphine

beta globulin *n* [ISV] (1943) : any of several globulins of plasma or serum that have at alkaline pH electrophoretic mobilities intermediate between those of the alpha globulins and gamma globulins

beta–glu·can \-ˈglü-ˌkan, -kən\ *n* (1966) : any of several polysaccharides consisting of glucose units and including one found in endosperm cell walls of cereal grains (as barley and oats)

be·ta·ine \ˈbē-tə-ˌēn\ *n* [ISV, fr. L *beta* beet] (1875) : a sweet crystalline quaternary ammonium salt $C_5H_{11}NO_2$ obtained esp. from sugar beets; *also* : its hydrate or its hydrochloride

beta interferon *n* (1980) : an interferon produced esp. by fibroblasts that is used in a form obtained from recombinant DNA esp. in the treatment of multiple sclerosis marked by recurrent attacks alternating with periods of remission — compare ALPHA INTERFERON, GAMMA INTERFERON

be·take \bi-ˈtāk\ *vt* **-took** \-ˈtu̇k\; **-tak·en** \-ˈtā-kən\; **-tak·ing** (14c) **1** *archaic* : COMMIT **2** : to cause (oneself) to go

be·ta–lac·ta·mase \ˈbā-tə-ˈlak-tə-ˌmās, -ˌmāz\ *n* [*lactam,* a cyclic amide (fr. ISV *lact-* + *am*ide) + *-ase*] (1965) : an enzyme found esp. in staphylococcal bacteria that inactivates the penicillins by hydrolyzing them

be·ta–ox·i·da·tion \ˈbā-tə-ˌäk-sə-ˈdā-shən\ *n* (ca. 1935) : stepwise catabolism of fatty acids in which two-carbon fragments are successively removed from the carboxyl end of the chain

beta particle *n* (1904) : a high-speed electron; *specif* : one emitted by a radioactive nucleus in beta decay

beta ray *n* (1902) **1** : BETA PARTICLE **2** : a stream of beta particles — called also *beta radiation*

be·ta–re·cep·tor \ˈbā-tə-ri-ˈsep-tər\ *n* (1948) : any of a group of receptors that are present on cell surfaces of some effector organs and tissues innervated by the sympathetic nervous system and that mediate certain physiological responses (as vasodilation, relaxation of bronchial and uterine smooth muscle, and increased heart rate) when bound by specific adrenergic agents — compare ALPHA-RECEPTOR

beta test *n* (1978) : a field test of the beta version of a product (as software) esp. by testers outside the company developing it that is conducted prior to commercial release — **beta test** *vt* — **beta tester** *n*

be·ta–thal·as·se·mia \-ˌtha-lə-ˈsē-mē-ə\ *n* (1962) : thalassemia in which the longer hemoglobin chain is affected and which comprises Cooley's anemia in the homozygous condition and thalassemia minor in the heterozygous condition

be·ta·tron \ˈbā-tə-ˌträn\ *n* [ISV] (1941) : an accelerator in which electrons are propelled by the inductive action of a rapidly varying magnetic field

beta wave *n* (1936) : an electrical rhythm of the brain with a frequency of 13 to 30 cycles per second that is associated with normal conscious waking experience — called also *beta, beta rhythm*

be·tel \ˈbē-tᵊl\ *n* [Pg *bétele,* fr. Tamil *verrilai*] (1553) : a climbing pepper (*Piper betle*) of southeastern Asia whose leaves are chewed together with betel nut and mineral lime as a stimulant masticatory

Be·tel·geuse \ˈbē-tᵊl-ˌjüs, ˈbe-, -ˌjüz\ *n* [F *Bételgeuse,* fr. Ar *bayt al-jawzā'* Gemini, lit., the house of the twins (confused with Orion & Betelgeuse)] (1769) : a variable red supergiant star of the first magnitude near the eastern shoulder of Orion

betel nut *n* [fr. its being chewed with betel leaves] (1673) : the astringent seed of the betel palm

betel palm *n* (1875) : an Asian pinnate-leaved palm (*Areca catechu*) that has an orange-colored drupe with an outer fibrous husk

bête noire \ˌbet-ˈnwär, ˌbāt-\ *n, pl* **bêtes noires** \ˌbet-ˈnwär(z), ˌbāt-\ [F, lit., black beast] (1828) : a person or thing strongly detested or avoided : BUGBEAR

beth \ˈbāth, ˈbāt, ˈbās\ *n* [Heb *bēth,* fr. *bayith* house] (1650) : the 2d letter of the Hebrew alphabet — see ALPHABET table

beth·el \ˈbe-thəl\ *n* [Heb *bēth'ēl* house of God] (ca. 1617) **1** : a hallowed spot **2 a** : a chapel for Nonconformists **b** : a place of worship for seamen

be·think \bi-ˈthiŋk, bē-\ *vt* **-thought** \-ˈthȯt\; **-think·ing** (bef. 12c) **1 a** : REMEMBER, RECALL **b** : to cause (oneself) to be reminded **2** : to cause (oneself) to consider
be·tide \bi-ˈtīd, bē-\ *vi* (12c) : to happen esp. as if by fate ~ *vt* : to happen to : BEFALL — used chiefly in the phrase *woe betide* ⟨woe ~ our enemies⟩
be·times \bi-ˈtīmz, bē-\ *adv* (13c) **1** : in good time : EARLY **2** *archaic* : in a short time : SPEEDILY **3** : at times : OCCASIONALLY
bê·tise \bā-ˈtēz\ *n, pl* **bê·tises** \-ˈtēz\ [F, fr. *bête* idiot, fool, lit., beast] (1798) **1** : an act of foolishness or stupidity **2** : lack of good sense : STUPIDITY
be·to·ken \bi-ˈtō-kən, bē-\ *vt* **-to·kened; -to·ken·ing** \-ˈtōk-niŋ, -ˈtō-kə-\ (15c) **1** : to typify beforehand : PRESAGE **2** : to give evidence of : SHOW
be·tray \bi-ˈtrā, bē-\ *vb* [ME, fr. *be-* + *trayen* to betray, fr. AF *trahir,* fr. L *tradere* — more at TRAITOR] *vt* (13c) **1** : to lead astray; *esp* : SEDUCE **2** : to deliver to an enemy by treachery **3** : to fail or desert esp. in time of need ⟨~*ed* his family⟩ **4 a** : to reveal unintentionally ⟨~ one's true feelings⟩ **b** : SHOW, INDICATE **c** : to disclose in violation of confidence ⟨~ a secret⟩ ~ *vi* : to prove false ***syn*** see REVEAL — **be·tray·al** \-ˈtrā(-ə)l\ *n* — **be·tray·er** \-ˈtrā-ər\ *n*
be·troth \bi-ˈtrōth, -ˈtrȯth, bē-\ *vt* [ME, fr. *be-* + *trouthe* truth, troth] (14c) **1** : to promise to marry **2** : to give in marriage
be·troth·al \-ˈtrō-thəl, -ˈtrȯ-, -thəl\ *n* (1831) **1** : the act of betrothing or fact of being betrothed **2** : a mutual promise or contract for a future marriage
be·trothed \bi-ˈtrōthd, -ˈtrȯtht\ *n* (1588) : the person to whom one is betrothed
bet·ta \ˈbe-tə\ *n* [NL, prob. fr. Jav *wadĕr,* a freshwater fish] (1927) : any of a genus (*Betta* of the family Anabantidae) of small brilliantly colored long-finned freshwater bony fishes of southeastern Asia; *esp* : SIAMESE FIGHTING FISH
1bet·ter \ˈbe-tər\ *adj, comparative of* GOOD [ME *bettre,* fr. OE *betera;* akin to OE *bōt* remedy, Skt *bhadra* fortunate] (bef. 12c) **1** : greater than half ⟨for the ~ part of an hour⟩ **2** : improved in health or mental attitude ⟨feeling ~⟩ **3** : more attractive, favorable, or commendable ⟨in ~ circumstances⟩ **4** : more advantageous or effective ⟨a ~ solution⟩ **5** : improved in accuracy or performance ⟨building a ~ engine⟩
2better *vt* (bef. 12c) **1** : to make better: as **a** : to make more tolerable or acceptable ⟨trying to ~ the lot of slum dwellers⟩ **b** : to make more complete or perfect ⟨looked forward to ~*ing* her acquaintance with the new neighbors⟩ **2** : to surpass in excellence : EXCEL ~ *vi* : to become better ***syn*** see IMPROVE
3better *adv, comparative of* WELL (12c) **1 a** : in a more excellent manner ⟨sings ~ than I do⟩ **b** : to greater advantage : PREFERABLY ⟨some things are ~ left unsaid⟩ **2 a** : to a higher or greater degree ⟨he knows the story ~ than you do⟩ **b** : MORE ⟨it is ~ than nine miles to the next town⟩
4better *n* (12c) **1 a** : something better ⟨I expected ~ from them⟩ **b** : a superior esp. in merit or rank ⟨was respectful of his ~*s*⟩ **2** : ADVANTAGE, VICTORY ⟨get the ~ of her⟩
5better *verbal auxiliary* (1831) : had better ⟨you ~ hurry⟩
better half *n* (1580) : SPOUSE
bet·ter·ment \ˈbe-tər-mənt\ *n* (1598) **1** : a making or becoming better **2** : an improvement that adds to the value of a property or facility
bet·ter–off \ˌbe-tə-ˈrȯf\ *adj* (ca. 1859) **1** : being in comfortable economic circumstances ⟨the ~ people live in the older section of town⟩ **2** : being in a more advantageous position
betting shop *n* (1852) *Brit* : a shop where bets are taken
bet·tor *or* **bet·ter** \ˈbe-tər\ *n* (1609) : one that bets
1be·tween \bi-ˈtwēn, bē-\ *prep* [ME *betwene,* prep. & adv., fr. OE *betwēonum,* fr. *be-* + *-twēonum* (dat. pl.) (akin to Goth *tweihnai* two each); akin to OE *twā* two] (bef. 12c) **1 a** : by the common action of : jointly engaging ⟨shared the work ~ the two of them⟩ ⟨talks ~ the three —*Time*⟩ **b** : in common to : shared by ⟨divided ~ his four grandchildren⟩ **2 a** : in the time, space, or interval that separates **b** : in intermediate relation to **3 a** : from one to another of ⟨air service ~ Miami and Chicago⟩ **b** : serving to connect or unite in a relationship (as difference, likeness, or proportion) ⟨a one-to-one correspondence ~ sets⟩ **c** : setting apart ⟨the line ~ fact and fancy⟩ **4 a** : in preference for one or the other of ⟨had no difficulty deciding ~ the two⟩ **b** : in point of comparison of ⟨not much to choose ~ the two coats⟩ **5** : in confidence restricted to ⟨a secret ~ you and me⟩ **6** : taking together the combined effect of ⟨~ work and family life, they have no time for hobbies⟩
usage There is a persistent but unfounded notion that *between* can be used only of two items and that *among* must be used for more than two. *Between* has been used of more than two since Old English; it is esp. appropriate to denote a one-to-one relationship, regardless of the number of items. It can be used when the number is unspecified ⟨economic cooperation *between* nations⟩, when more than two are enumerated ⟨*between* you and me and the lamppost⟩ ⟨partitioned *between* Austria, Prussia, and Russia —Nathaniel Benchley⟩, and even when only one item is mentioned (but repetition is implied) ⟨pausing *between* every sentence to rap the floor —George Eliot⟩. *Among* is more appropriate where the emphasis is on distribution rather than individual relationships ⟨discontent *among* the peasants⟩. When *among* is automatically chosen for more than two, English idiom may be strained ⟨a worthy book that nevertheless falls *among* many stools —John Simon⟩ ⟨the author alternates *among* mod slang, clichés and quotes from literary giants —A. H. Johnston⟩.
2between *adv* (bef. 12c) : in an intermediate space or interval
be·tween·ness \-nəs\ *n* (1884) : the quality or state of being between two others in an ordered mathematical set
be·tween·times \-ˌtīmz\ *adv* (1580) : at or during intervals
be·tween·whiles \-ˌhwī(-ə)lz, -ˌwī(-ə)lz\ *adv* (1656) : BETWEENTIMES
be·twixt \bi-ˈtwikst, bē-\ *adv or prep* [ME, fr. OE *betwux,* fr. *be-* + *-twux* (akin to Goth *tweihnai* two each) — more at BETWEEN] (bef. 12c) : BETWEEN
betwixt and between *adv or adj* (1789) : in a midway position : neither one thing nor the other
Beu·lah \ˈbyü-lə\ *n* (1684) : an idyllic land near the end of life's journey in Bunyan's *Pilgrim's Progress*
beurre blanc \ˈbər-ˈblä^n\ *n* [F, lit., white butter] (1931) : a seasoned butter sauce (as for fish) flavored with white wine, shallots, and vinegar or lemon juice
beurre ma·nié \-män-ˈyā\ *n* [F, lit., handled butter] (1939) : flour and butter kneaded together used as a thickener in sauces
beurre noir \-ˈnwär\ *n* [F, lit., black butter] (1830) : butter heated until brown or black and often flavored with vinegar or lemon juice
BeV *abbr* billion electron volts
BEV *abbr* Black English vernacular
1bev·el \ˈbe-vəl\ *adj* (ca. 1600) : OBLIQUE, BEVELED ⟨a ~ edge⟩
2bevel *n* [MF **bevel,* fr. OF **baivel,* fr. *baïf* with open mouth, fr. *baer* to yawn — more at ABEYANCE] (1610) **1** : an instrument consisting of two rules or arms jointed together and opening to any angle for drawing angles or adjusting surfaces to be cut at an angle **2 a** : the angle that one surface or line makes with another when they are not at right angles **b** : the slant of such a surface or line **3** : the part of printing type extending from face to shoulder
3bevel *vb* **-eled** *or* **-elled; -el·ing** *or* **-el·ling** \ˈbev-liŋ, ˈbe-və-\ *vt* (1677) : to cut or shape to a bevel ~ *vi* : INCLINE, SLANT
bevel gear *n* (ca. 1790) : either of a pair of toothed wheels whose working surfaces are inclined to nonparallel axes
bev·er·age \ˈbev-rij, ˈbe-və-\ *n* [ME, fr. AF, fr. *beivre* to drink, fr. L *bibere* — more at POTABLE] (14c) : a drinkable liquid
bevy \ˈbe-vē\ *n, pl* **bev·ies** [ME *bevey*] (15c) **1** : a large group or collection ⟨a ~ of girls⟩ **2** : a group of animals and esp. quail
be·wail \bi-ˈwā(ə)l\ *vt* (14c) **1** : to wail over **2** : to express deep sorrow for usu. by wailing and lamentation ***syn*** see DEPLORE
be·ware \bi-ˈwer, bē-\ *vb* [ME *been war,* fr. *been* to be + *war* careful — more at BE, WARE] *vi* (14c) : to be on one's guard ⟨~ of the dog⟩ ~ *vt* **1** : to take care of ⟨~ your wallet⟩ **2** : to be wary of ⟨we must . . . ~ the exceedingly tenuous generalization —Matthew Lipman⟩
be·whis·kered \-ˈhwis-kərd, -ˈwis-\ *adj* (1820) : having whiskers
be·wigged \bi-ˈwigd, bē-\ *adj* (1774) : wearing a wig
be·wil·der \bi-ˈwil-dər, bē-\ *vt* **-wil·dered; -wil·der·ing** \-d(ə-)riŋ\ (1684) **1** : to cause to lose one's bearings **2** : to perplex or confuse esp. by a complexity, variety, or multitude of objects or considerations ***syn*** see PUZZLE — **be·wil·dered·ly** *adv* — **be·wil·dered·ness** *n* — **be·wil·der·ing·ly** \-d(ə-)riŋ-lē\ *adv*
be·wil·der·ment \-dər-mənt\ *n* (1811) **1** : the quality or state of being bewildered **2** : a bewildering tangle or confusion
be·witch \bi-ˈwich, bē-\ *vt* (13c) **1 a** : to influence or affect esp. injuriously by witchcraft **b** : to cast a spell over **2** : to attract as if by the power of witchcraft : ENCHANT, FASCINATE ⟨~*ed* by her beauty⟩ ~ *vi* : to bewitch someone or something — **be·witch·ery** \-ˈwi-ch(ə-)rē\ *n* — **be·witch·ing·ly** \-ˈwi-chiŋ-lē\ *adv*
be·witch·ment \-ˈwich-mənt\ *n* (1607) **1 a** : the act or power of bewitching **b** : a spell that bewitches **2** : the state of being bewitched
be·wray \bi-ˈrā\ *vt* [ME, fr. *be-* + *wreyen* to accuse, fr. OE *wrēgan;* akin to OHG *ruogen* to accuse] (13c) *archaic* : DIVULGE, BETRAY
bey \ˈbā\ *n* [Turk, gentleman, chief] (1537) **1 a** : a provincial governor in the Ottoman Empire **b** : the former native ruler of Tunis or Tunisia **2** — used as a courtesy title in Turkey and Egypt
1be·yond \bē-ˈänd\ *adv* [ME, prep. & adv., fr. OE *begeondan,* fr. *be-* + *geondan* beyond, fr. *geond* yond — more at YOND] (bef. 12c) **1** : on or to the farther side : FARTHER **2** : in addition : BESIDES
2beyond *prep* (bef. 12c) **1** : on or to the farther side of : at a greater distance than ⟨~ the horizon⟩ **2 a** : out of the reach or sphere of ⟨a task ~ his strength⟩ **b** : in a degree or amount surpassing ⟨beautiful ~ measure⟩ **c** : out of the comprehension of ⟨his reasoning is ~ me⟩ **3** : in addition to : BESIDES ⟨doing work ~ his regular duties⟩
3beyond *n* (14c) **1** : something that lies beyond **2** : something that lies outside the scope of ordinary experience; *specif* : HEREAFTER
be·zant \ˈbe-zᵊnt, bə-ˈzant\ *n* [ME *besant,* fr. AF, fr. ML *Byzantius* Byzantine, fr. *Byzantium,* ancient name of Istanbul] (13c) **1** : SOLIDUS 1 **2** : a flat disk used in architectural ornament
be·zel \ˈbē-zəl, ˈbe-\ *n* [prob. fr. dial. form of F *biseau* bezel, fr. MF] (1611) **1** : a rim that holds a transparent covering (as on a watch, clock, or headlight) or that is rotatable and has special markings (as on a watch) **2** : the oblique side or face of a cut gem; *specif* : the upper faceted portion of a brilliant projecting from the setting — see BRILLIANT illustration **3** : a usu. metal rim of a piece of jewelry in which an ornament (as a gem) is set
be·zique \bə-ˈzēk\ *n* [F *bésique*] (1861) : a card game similar to pinochle that is played with a pack of 64 cards
be·zoar \ˈbē-ˌzȯr\ *n* [MF, fr. ML, fr. Ar dial. *bezuwār,* fr. Ar *bāzahr,* fr. Pers *pād-zahr,* fr. *pād* protecting (against) + *zahr* poison] (1577) : any of various calculi found chiefly in the gastrointestinal organs and formerly believed to possess magical properties — called also *bezoar stone*
bf *abbr* boldface
BF *abbr* **1** bachelor of forestry **2** board foot **3** brought forward
BFA *abbr* bachelor of fine arts
BFF *abbr* best friends forever
bg *abbr* **1** background **2** bag **3** beige **4** being
BG *or* **B Gen** *abbr* brigadier general
BGH *abbr* bovine growth hormone
B–girl *n* [prob. fr. *bar* + *girl*] (1936) : a woman who entertains bar patrons and encourages them to spend freely
BGS *abbr* bachelor of general studies
Bh *symbol* bohrium
BH *abbr* **1** bill of health **2** Brinell hardness
BHA \ˌbē-(ˌ)ā-ˈchā\ *n* [*b*utylated *h*ydroxy*a*nisole] (1950) : a phenolic antioxidant $C_{11}H_{16}O_2$ used esp. to preserve fats and oils in food
Bha·ga·vad Gi·ta \ˌbä-gə-ˌväd-ˈgē-tə\ *n* [Skt *Bhagavadgītā,* lit., song of the blessed one (Krishna)] (ca. 1785) : a Hindu devotional work in poetic form
bhak·ti \ˈbək-tē\ *n* [Skt, lit., portion] (1832) : devotion to a deity constituting a way to salvation in Hinduism

\ə\ **abut** \ᵊ\ **kitten, F table** \ər\ **further** \a\ **ash** \ā\ **ace** \ä\ **mop, mar** \au̇\ **out** \ch\ **chin** \e\ **bet** \ē\ **easy** \g\ **go** \i\ **hit** \ī\ **ice** \j\ **job** \ŋ\ **sing** \ō\ **go** \ȯ\ **law** \ȯi\ **boy** \th\ **thin** \th\ **the** \ü\ **loot** \u̇\ **foot** \y\ **yet** \zh\ **vision, beige** \k, ^n, œ, ue, ^y\ *see* Guide to Pronunciation

bhang \\'baŋ, 'bäŋ\\ *n* [Hindi *bhāṅg* & Urdu *bhang* hemp] (1563) : a mildly intoxicating preparation of the leaves and flowering tops of uncultivated hemp; *also* : HEMP 1a, c — compare MARIJUANA, HASHISH

bhan·gra \\'bäŋgrä, -rə\\ *n* [Panjabi *bhaṁgrā,* a kind of folk dance] (1965) : popular dance music originating chiefly in England that combines traditional Punjabi music with elements of disco and hip-hop

bha·ral \\'bər-əl, 'bä-rəl\\ *n* [Hindi] (1838) : any of a genus (*Pseudois*) of goatlike bovid mammals of the Himalayas and western China having a bluish-gray coat

BHC \\'bē-,ach-'sē\\ *n* [benzene *h*exachloride] (1946) **1** : any of several stereoisomeric chlorine derivatives $C_6H_6Cl_6$ of cyclohexane in which the chlorine atoms are all attached to different carbon atoms **2** : LINDANE

bhd *abbr* bulkhead

BHL *abbr* **1** bachelor of Hebrew letters **2** bachelor of Hebrew literature

BHN *abbr* Brinell hardness number

Bhoj·pu·ri \\'bōj-,pu̇r-ē, 'bäj-, -pə-rē\\ *n* [Hindi *bhojpurī,* fr. *Bhojpur,* village in Bihar] (1884) : an Indo-Aryan language spoken in western Bihar and eastern Uttar Pradesh, India

B horizon *n* (1938) : a subsurface soil layer that is immediately beneath the A horizon from which it obtains organic matter chiefly by illuviation and is usu. distinguished by less weathering

bhp *abbr* bishop

BHT \\'bē-,ach-'tē\\ *n* [*b*utylated *h*ydroxy*t*oluene] (1961) : a phenolic antioxidant $C_{15}H_{24}O$ used esp. to preserve fats and oils in food

¹bi \\'bī\\ *n or adj* (1956) : BISEXUAL

²bi- *prefix* [ME, fr. L — more at TWI-] **1 a** : two 〈*bi*lateral〉 **b** : coming or occurring every two 〈*bi*centennial〉 **c** : into two parts 〈*bi*sect〉 **2 a** : twice : doubly : on both sides 〈*bi*convex〉 **b** : coming or occurring two times 〈*bi*annual〉 — compare SEMI- **3** : between, involving, or affecting two (specified) symmetrical parts 〈*bi*labial〉 **4 a** : containing one (specified) constituent in double the proportion of the other constituent or in double the ordinary proportion 〈*bi*carbonate〉 **b** : DI-2 〈*bi*phenyl〉

usage Many people are puzzled about *bimonthly* and *biweekly,* which are often ambiguous because they are formed from both senses 1b and 2b of *bi-.* This ambiguity has been in existence for nearly a century and a half and cannot be eliminated by the dictionary. The chief difficulty is that many users of these words assume that others know exactly what they mean, and they do not bother to make their context clear. So if you need *bimonthly* or *biweekly,* you should leave some clues in your context to the sense of *bi-* you mean. And if you need the meaning "twice a," you can substitute *semi-* for *bi-. Biannual* and *biennial* are usu. differentiated.

²bi- or bio- *comb form* [Gk, fr. *bios* mode of life — more at QUICK] **1** : life : living organisms or tissue 〈*bio*luminescence〉 〈*bio*sphere〉 **2** : biographical 〈*bio*pic〉

Bi *symbol* bismuth

BIA *abbr* **1** bachelor of industrial administration **2** Bureau of Indian Affairs

bi·aly \\bē-'a-lē\\ *n, pl* **bialys** [Yiddish, short for *bialystoker,* fr. *bialystoker* of Bialystok, city in Poland] (1965) : a flat breakfast roll that has a depressed center and is usu. covered with onion flakes

bi·an·nu·al \\(,)bī-'an-yə(-wə)l\\ *adj* (1877) **1** : occurring twice a year **2** : BIENNIAL 1 *usage* see BI- — **bi·an·nu·al·ly** *adv*

¹bi·as \\'bī-əs\\ *n* [MF *biais*] (1530) **1 a** : a line diagonal to the grain of a fabric; *esp* : a line at a 45 degree angle to the selvage often utilized in the cutting of garments for smoother fit **2 a** : a peculiarity in the shape of a bowl that causes it to swerve when rolled on the green in lawn bowling **b** : the tendency of a bowl to swerve; *also* : the impulse causing this tendency **c** : the swerve of the bowl **3 a** : BENT, TENDENCY **b** : an inclination of temperament or outlook; *esp* : a personal and sometimes unreasoned judgment : PREJUDICE **c** : an instance of such prejudice **d** (1) : deviation of the expected value of a statistical estimate from the quantity it estimates (2) : systematic error introduced into sampling or testing by selecting or encouraging one outcome or answer over others **4 a** : a voltage applied to a device (as a transistor control electrode) to establish a reference level for operation **b** : a high-frequency voltage combined with an audio signal to reduce distortion in tape recording *syn* see PREDILECTION — **on the bias** : ASKEW, OBLIQUELY

²bias *adj* (1551) : DIAGONAL, SLANTING — used chiefly of fabrics and their cut — **bi·as·ness** *n*

³bias *adv* (1575) **1** : DIAGONALLY 〈cut cloth ∼〉 **2** *obs* : AWRY

⁴bias *vt biased or bi·assed; bi·as·ing or bi·as·sing* (ca. 1628) **1** : to give a settled and often prejudiced outlook to 〈his background ∼es him against foreigners〉 **2** : to apply a slight negative or positive voltage to (as a transistor) *syn* see INCLINE

bi·as–belt·ed tire \\'bī-əs-,bel-təd-\\ *n* (1968) : a pneumatic tire with a belt (as of steel or fiberglass) to help prevent punctures that is under the tread and on top of the plies of cords which form the tire's carcass and which are set diagonally to the center line of the tread

bias crime *n* (1982) : HATE CRIME

bi·ased *adj* (1657) **1** : exhibiting or characterized by bias; *esp* : PREJUDICED **2** : tending to yield one outcome more frequently than others in a statistical experiment 〈a ∼ coin〉 **3** : having an expected value different from the quantity or parameter estimated 〈a ∼ estimate〉

bi·as–ply tire \\'bī-əs-,plī-\\ *n* (1968) : a pneumatic tire having crossed plies of cords set diagonally to the center line of the tread

bias tape *n* (1915) : a narrow strip of cloth cut on the bias, folded, and used for finishing or decorating clothing

bi·ath·lete \\bī-'ath-,lēt\\ *n* [blend of *athlete* and *biathlon*] (1968) : an athlete who competes in a biathlon

bi·ath·lon \\bī-'ath-lən, -,län\\ *n* [*¹bi-* + *-athlon* (as in *decathlon*)] (1958) : a composite athletic contest consisting of cross-country skiing and rifle sharpshooting

bi·ax·i·al \\(,)bī-'ak-sē-əl\\ *adj* (1854) : having or relating to two axes or optic axes 〈a ∼ crystal〉 — **bi·ax·i·al·ly** \\-ə-lē\\ *adv*

¹bib \\'bib\\ *vb* **bibbed; bib·bing** [ME *bibben*] (14c) : DRINK

²bib *n* (1580) **1** : a cloth or plastic shield tied under the chin to protect the clothes **2** : the part of an apron or of overalls extending above the waist **3** : a patch of differently colored feathers or fur immediately below the bill or chin of a bird or mammal — **bibbed** \\'bibd\\ *adj* — **bib·less** \\'bib-ləs\\ *adj*

³bib *abbr* **1** Bible **2** biblical

bib and tucker *n* (1747) : an outfit of clothing — usu. used in the phrase *best bib and tucker*

bib·ber \\'bi-bər\\ *n* (1536) : a person who regularly drinks alcoholic beverages — **bib·bery** \\'bi-bə-rē\\ *n*

Bibb lettuce \\'bib-\\ *n* [*Major John Bibb,* 19th cent. Am. grower] (1961) : a butter lettuce of a variety that has a small head and dark green color — called also *Bibb*

bi·be·lot \\'bē-bə-,lō\\ *n, pl* **bibelots** \\-,lō(z)\\ [F] (1873) : a small household ornament or decorative object : TRINKET

bi·ble \\'bī-bəl\\ *n* [ME, fr. OF, fr. ML *biblia,* fr. Gk, pl. of *biblion* book, dim. of *byblos* papyrus, book, fr. *Byblos,* ancient Phoenician city from which papyrus was exported] (14c) **1** *cap* **a** : the sacred scriptures of Christians comprising the Old Testament and the New Testament **b** : the sacred scriptures of some other religion (as Judaism) **2** *obs* : BOOK **3** *cap* : a copy or an edition of the Bible **4** : a publication that is preeminent esp. in authoritativeness or wide readership 〈the fisherman's ∼〉 〈the ∼ of the entertainment industry〉

BOOKS OF THE BIBLE

HEBREW BIBLE

Law	1 & 2 Kings	Nahum	Song of Songs
Genesis	Isaiah	Habakkuk	Ruth
Exodus	Jeremiah	Zephaniah	Lamentations
Leviticus	Ezekiel	Haggai	Ecclesiastes
Numbers	Hosea	Zechariah	Esther
Deuteronomy	Joel	Malachi	Daniel
Prophets	Amos	*Writings*	Ezra
Joshua	Obadiah	Psalms	Nehemiah
Judges	Jonah	Proverbs	1 & 2 Chronicles
1 & 2 Samuel	Micah	Job	

CHRISTIAN CANON—OLD TESTAMENT

ROMAN CATHOLIC	PROTESTANT	ROMAN CATHOLIC	PROTESTANT
Genesis	Genesis	Wisdom	
Exodus	Exodus	Sirach	
Leviticus	Leviticus	Isaiah	Isaiah
Numbers	Numbers	Jeremiah	Jeremiah
Deuteronomy	Deuteronomy	Lamentations	Lamentations
Joshua	Joshua	Baruch	
Judges	Judges	Ezekiel	Ezekiel
Ruth	Ruth	Daniel	Daniel
1 & 2 Samuel	1 & 2 Samuel	Hosea	Hosea
1 & 2 Kings	1 & 2 Kings	Joel	Joel
1 & 2 Chronicles	1 & 2 Chronicles	Amos	Amos
Ezra	Ezra	Obadiah	Obadiah
Nehemiah	Nehemiah	Jonah	Jonah
Tobit		Micah	Micah
Judith		Nahum	Nahum
Esther	Esther	Habakkuk	Habakkuk
Job	Job	Zephaniah	Zephaniah
Psalms	Psalms	Haggai	Haggai
Proverbs	Proverbs	Zechariah	Zechariah
Ecclesiastes	Ecclesiastes	Malachi	Malachi
Song of Songs	Song of Solomon	1 & 2 Maccabees	

PROTESTANT APOCRYPHA

1 & 2 Esdras	Ecclesiasticus or the Wisdom of Jesus Son of Sirach	Prayer of Azariah and the Song of the Three Holy Children	Bel and the Dragon
Tobit			The Prayer of Manasses
Judith			
Additions to Esther		Susanna	1 & 2 Maccabees
Wisdom of Solomon	Baruch		

CHRISTIAN CANON—NEW TESTAMENT

Matthew	Romans	1 & 2 Thessalonians	James
Mark	1 & 2 Corinthians	1 & 2 Timothy	1 & 2 Peter
Luke	Galatians	Titus	1, 2, 3 John
John	Ephesians	Philemon	Jude
Acts of the Apostles	Philippians	Hebrews	Revelation *or* Apocalypse
	Colossians		

Bible Belt *n* (1925) : an area chiefly in the southern U.S. whose inhabitants are believed to hold uncritical allegiance to the literal accuracy of the Bible; *broadly* : an area characterized by ardent religious fundamentalism

Bible paper *n* (1903) : INDIA PAPER 2

Bi·ble–thump·er \\'bī-bəl-,thəm-pər\\ *n* (ca. 1923) : an overzealous advocate of Christian fundamentalism — **Bi·ble–thump·ing** \\-piŋ\\ *adj*

bibli- or biblio- *comb form* [MF, fr. L, fr. Gk, fr. *biblion*] : book 〈*bibli*ology〉

bib·li·cal \\'bi-bli-kəl\\ *adj* [ML *biblicus,* fr. *biblia*] (1756) **1** : of, relating to, or being in accord with the Bible **2** : suggestive of the Bible or Bible times — **bib·li·cal·ly** \\-k(ə-)lē\\ *adv*

bib·li·cism \\'bi-blə-,si-zəm\\ *n, often cap* (1850) : adherence to the letter of the Bible — **bib·li·cist** \\-sist\\ *n, often cap*

bib·li·og·ra·pher \\,bi-blē-'ä-grə-fər\\ *n* (1775) **1** : an expert in bibliography **2** : a compiler of bibliographies

bib·li·og·ra·phy \\,bi-blē-'ä-grə-fē\\ *n, pl* **-phies** [prob. fr. NL *bibliographia,* fr. Gk, the copying of books, fr. *bibli-* + *-graphia* -graphy] (1802) **1** : the history, identification, or description of writings or publications **2 a** : a list often with descriptive or critical notes of writings relating to a particular subject, period, or author **b** : a list of works written by an author or printed by a publishing house **3** : the works or a list of the works referred to in a text or consulted by the author in its production — **bib·lio·graph·ic** \ˌbi-blē-ə-ˈgra-fik\ *also* **bib·lio·graph·i·cal** \-fi-kəl\ *adj* — **bib·lio·graph·i·cal·ly** \-k(ə-)lē\ *adv*

bib·li·ol·a·ter \ˌbi-blē-ˈä-lə-tər\ *n* (1847) **1 :** one having excessive reverence for the letter of the Bible **2 :** one overly devoted to books — **bib·li·ol·a·trous** \-ˈä-lə-trəs\ *adj* — **bib·li·ol·a·try** \-trē\ *n*

bib·li·ol·o·gy \ˌbi-blē-ˈä-lə-jē\ *n* (1806) **1 :** the history and science of books as physical objects : BIBLIOGRAPHY **2** *often cap* **:** the study of the theological doctrine of the Bible

bib·lio·ma·nia \ˌbi-blē-ə-ˈmā-nē-ə, -nyə\ *n* [F *bibliomanie,* fr. *bibli-* + *manie* mania, fr. LL *mania*] (1734) **:** extreme preoccupation with collecting books — **bib·lio·ma·ni·ac** \-nē-ˌak\ *n or adj* — **bib·lio·ma·ni·a·cal** \-lē-ō-mə-ˈnī-ə-kəl\ *adj*

bib·li·op·e·gy \ˌbi-blē-ˈä-pə-jē\ *n* [ultim. fr. Gk *bibli-* + *pēgnynai* to fasten together — more at PACT] (ca. 1859) **:** the art of binding books — **bib·li·o·pe·gic** \ˌbi-blē-ə-ˈpe-jik, -ˈpē-\ *adj* — **bib·li·op·e·gist** \ˌbi-blē-ˈä-pə-jist\ *n*

bib·lio·phile \ˈbi-blē-ə-ˌfī(-ə)l\ *n* [F, fr. *bibli-* + *-phile*] (1824) **:** a lover of books esp. for qualities of format; *also* **:** a book collector — **bib·lio·phil·ic** \ˌbi-blē-ə-ˈfi-lik\ *adj* — **bib·li·oph·i·lism** \-ˈä-fə-ˌli-zəm\ *n* — **bib·li·oph·i·ly** \-lē\ *n*

bib·li·o·pole \ˈbi-blē-ə-ˌpōl\ *or* **bib·li·op·o·list** \ˌbi-blē-ˈä-pə-list\ *n* [L *bibliopola* bookseller, fr. Gk *bibliopōlēs,* fr. *bibli-* + *pōlein* to sell] (1775) **:** a dealer esp. in rare or curious books

bib·lio·the·ca \ˌbi-blē-ə-ˈthē-kə\ *n, pl* **-cas** *or* **-cae** \-ˌsē, -ˌkē\ [L, fr. Gk *bibliothēkē,* fr. *bibli-* + *thēkē* case; akin to Gk *tithenai* to put, place — more at DO] (ca. 1824) **1 :** a collection of books **2 :** a list of books — **bib·lio·the·cal** \-ˈthē-kəl\ *adj*

bib·lio·ther·a·py \ˌbi-blē-ə-ˈther-ə-pē, -ˈthe-rə-\ *n* (1919) **:** the use of reading materials for help in solving personal problems or for psychiatric therapy; *also* **:** the reading materials so used

bib·u·lous \ˈbi-byə-ləs\ *adj* [L *bibulus,* fr. *bibere* to drink — more at POTABLE] (1675) **1 :** highly absorbent **2 a :** fond of alcoholic beverages **b :** of, relating to, or marked by the consumption of alcoholic beverages — **bib·u·lous·ly** *adv* — **bib·u·lous·ness** *n*

bi·cam·er·al \(ˌ)bī-ˈkam-rəl, -ˈka-mə-\ *adj* [[1]*bi-* + LL *camera* chamber — more at CHAMBER] (1856) **:** having, consisting of, or based on two legislative chambers ⟨a ~ legislature⟩ — **bi·cam·er·al·ism** \-rə-ˌli-zəm\ *n*

bi·carb \(ˌ)bī-ˈkärb, ˈbī-ˌ\ *n* (1922) **:** SODIUM BICARBONATE

bi·car·bon·ate \(ˌ)bī-ˈkär-bə-ˌnāt, -nət\ *n* [ISV] (1814) **:** an acid carbonate

bicarbonate of soda (1814) **:** SODIUM BICARBONATE

bi·cen·te·na·ry \ˌbī-(ˌ)sen-ˈte-nə-rē, (ˌ)bī-ˈsen-tᵊn-ˌer-ē, ˌbī-(ˌ)sen-ˈtē-nə-rē\ *n* (1872) **:** BICENTENNIAL — **bicentenary** *adj*

bi·cen·ten·ni·al \ˌbī-(ˌ)sen-ˈte-nē-əl\ *n* (1883) **:** a 200th anniversary or its celebration — **bicentennial** *adj*

bi·cep \ˈbī-ˌsep\ *n* [back-formation fr. *biceps*] (1939) **:** BICEPS a

bi·ceps \ˈbī-ˌseps\ *n, pl* **biceps** *also* **bi·ceps·es** [NL *bicipit-, biceps,* fr. L, two-headed, fr. *bi-* + *capit-, caput* head — more at HEAD] (1634) **:** a muscle having two heads: as **a :** the large flexor muscle of the front of the upper arm **b :** the large flexor muscle of the back of the upper leg

biceps bra·chii \-ˈbrā-kē-ˌī, -kē-ˌē\ *n* [NL, lit., biceps of the arm] (ca. 1860) **:** BICEPS a

biceps fe·mo·ris \-ˈfe-mə-rəs\ *n* [NL, lit., biceps of the femur] (ca. 1860) **:** BICEPS b

bi·chlo·ride of mercury \(ˌ)bī-ˈklȯr-ˌīd-\ [ISV] (1810) **:** MERCURIC CHLORIDE

bi·chon fri·se \bē-ˌshō^{n}-frē-ˈzā\ *n, pl* **bi·chons fri·ses** \-ˌshō^{n}-frē-ˈzā(z)\ [modif. of F *bichon à poil frisé* curly-haired lapdog] (1966) **:** any of a breed of small sturdy dogs of Mediterranean origin having a thick wavy white coat

bi·chro·mate \(ˌ)bī-ˈkrō-ˌmāt, ˈbī-krō-\ *n* (1836) **:** a dichromate esp. of sodium or potassium — **bi·chro·mat·ed** \-ˌmā-təd\ *adj*

bi·chrome \ˈbī-ˌkrōm\ *adj* (1921) **:** two-colored

bi·cip·i·tal \bī-ˈsi-pə-tᵊl\ *adj* (1646) **:** of, relating to, or being a biceps

[1]bick·er \ˈbi-kər\ *n* [ME *biker*] (14c) **1 :** petulant quarreling **:** ALTERCATION **2 :** a sound of or as if of bickering

[2]bicker *vi* **bick·ered; bick·er·ing** \ˈbi-k(ə-)riŋ\ (15c) **1 :** to engage in a petulant or petty quarrel ⟨~*ing* over money⟩ **2 a :** to move with a rapidly repeated noise ⟨a ~*ing* stream⟩ **b :** QUIVER, FLICKER — **bick·er·er** \-kə-rər\ *n*

bi·coast·al \(ˌ)bī-ˈkōs-təl\ *adj* (1972) **:** of or relating to or living or working on both the east and west coasts of the U.S. ⟨a ~ couple⟩

bi·col·ored \ˈbī-ˌkə-lərd\ *or* **bi·col·or** \-lər\ *adj* [L *bicolor,* fr. *bi-* + *color*] (ca. 1843) **:** two-colored — **bicolor** *n*

bi·com·po·nent \(ˌ)bī-kəm-ˈpō-nənt, -käm-, -ˈkäm-ˌ\ *adj* (1962) **:** being a fiber made of two polymers having slightly different physical properties so that the fiber has a permanent crimp and fabrics made from it have inherent bulk and stretchability

bi·con·cave \ˌbī-(ˌ)kän-ˈkāv, -ˈkän-ˌ\ *adj* (1833) **:** concave on both sides — **bi·con·cav·i·ty** \ˌbī-(ˌ)kän-ˈka-və-tē\ *n*

bi·con·di·tion·al \ˌbī-kən-ˈdish-nəl, -ˈdi-shə-\ *n* (1940) **:** a relation between two propositions that is true only when both propositions are simultaneously true or false — see TRUTH TABLE table

bi·con·vex \ˌbī-(ˌ)kän-ˈveks, (ˌ)bī-ˈkän-ˌ\ *adj* [ISV] (ca. 1852) **:** convex on both sides — **bi·con·vex·i·ty** \ˌbī-kən-ˈvek-sə-tē, -(ˌ)kän-\ *n*

bi·corne \ˈbī-ˌkȯrn\ *n* [F, fr. L *bicornis* two-horned, fr. *bi-* + *cornu* horn — more at HORN] (1936) **:** COCKED HAT 2

bi·cul·tur·al \(ˌ)bī-ˈkəl-chər-əl\ *adj* (1940) **:** of, relating to, or including two distinct cultures ⟨~ education⟩ — **bi·cul·tur·al·ism** \-ə-ˌli-zəm\ *n*

[1]bi·cus·pid \(ˌ)bī-ˈkəs-pəd\ *adj* [NL *bicuspid-, bicuspis,* fr. *bi-* + L *cuspid-, cuspis* point] (ca. 1839) **:** having or ending in two points ⟨~ teeth⟩

[2]bicuspid *n* (1852) **:** a human premolar tooth — see TOOTH illustration

bicuspid valve *n* (ca. 1903) **:** MITRAL VALVE

[1]bi·cy·cle \ˈbī-si-kəl, -ˌsi- *also* -ˌsī-\ *n* [F, fr. *bi-* + *-cycle* (as in *tricycle*)] (1863) **:** a vehicle with two wheels tandem, handlebars for steering, a saddle seat, and pedals by which it is propelled; *also* **:** a stationary exercise machine that resembles such a vehicle

[2]bicycle *vi* **bi·cy·cled; bi·cy·cling** \-k(ə-)liŋ\ (1869) **:** to ride a bicycle — **bi·cy·cler** \-klər\ *n* — **bi·cy·clist** \-klist\ *n*

bicycle shorts *n pl* (1982) **:** tight-fitting shorts made usu. of spandex with inner lining or padding and worn chiefly by bicyclists

bi·cy·clic \(ˌ)bī-ˈsī-klik, -ˈsi-\ *adj* [ISV] (ca. 1909) **1 :** consisting of or arranged in two cycles **2 :** containing two usu. fused rings in the structure of the molecule

[1]bid \ˈbid\ *vb* **bade** \ˈbad, ˈbād\ *or* **bid; bid·den** \ˈbi-dᵊn\ *or* **bid** *also* **bade; bid·ding** [partly fr. ME *bidden,* fr. OE *biddan;* akin to OHG *bitten* to entreat, and perh. to Skt *bādhate* he presses; partly fr. ME *beden* to offer, command, fr. OE *bēodan;* akin to OHG *biotan* to offer, Gk *pynthanesthai* to examine, Skt *bodhi* enlightenment] *vt* (bef. 12c) **1 a** *obs* **:** BESEECH, ENTREAT **b :** to issue an order to **:** TELL ⟨did as I was *bid*⟩ **c :** to request to come **:** INVITE **2 :** to give expression to ⟨*bade* a tearful farewell⟩ **3 a :** OFFER — usu. used in the phrase *to bid defiance* **b** *past and past part* **bid** (1) **:** to offer (a price) whether for payment or acceptance (2) **:** to make a bid of or in (a suit at cards) ~ *vi* **:** to make a bid ***syn*** see COMMAND — **bid·der** *n* — **bid fair :** to seem likely ⟨a movie that *bids fair* to become a big hit⟩

[2]bid *n* (1788) **1 a :** the act of one who bids **b :** a statement of what one will give or take for something; *esp* **:** an offer of a price **c :** something offered as a bid **2 :** an opportunity to bid **3 :** INVITATION **4 a :** an announcement of what a cardplayer proposes to undertake **b :** the amount of such a bid **c :** a biddable bridge hand **5 :** an attempt or effort to win, achieve, or attract ⟨a ~ for reelection⟩

[3]bid *abbr* [L *bis in die*] twice a day

BID *abbr* bachelor of industrial design

bid·da·ble \ˈbi-də-bəl\ *adj* (ca. 1768) **1 :** easily led, taught, or controlled **:** DOCILE **2 :** capable of being bid — **bid·da·bil·i·ty** \ˌbi-də-ˈbi-lə-tē\ *n* — **bid·da·bly** \ˈbi-də-blē\ *adv*

[1]bid·dy \ˈbi-dē\ *n, pl* **biddies** [perh. imit.] (1601) **:** HEN 1a; *also* **:** a young chicken

[2]biddy *n, pl* **biddies** [dim. of the name *Bridget*] (ca. 1861) **1 :** a hired girl or cleaning woman **2** *usu disparaging* **:** WOMAN; *esp* **:** an elderly woman

bide \ˈbīd\ *vb* **bode** \ˈbōd\ *or* **bid·ed; bided; bid·ing** [ME, fr. OE *bīdan;* akin to OHG *bītan* to wait, L *fidere* to trust, Gk *peithesthai* to believe] *vt* (bef. 12c) **1** *past usu* **bided :** to wait for — used chiefly in the phrase *bide one's time* **2** *archaic* **:** WITHSTAND ⟨two men . . . might ~ the winter storm —W. C. Bryant⟩ **3** *chiefly dial* **:** to put up with **:** TOLERATE ~ *vi* **1 :** to continue in a state or condition **2 :** to wait awhile **:** TARRY **3 :** to continue in a place **:** SOJOURN — **bid·er** *n*

bi·det \bi-ˈdā\ *n* [F, small horse, bidet, fr. MF, fr. *bider* to trot] (1766) **:** a bathroom fixture used esp. for bathing the external genitals and the anal region

bi·di \ˈbē-dē\ *n* [Hindi & Urdu *bīṛī* hand-rolled cigarette with a leaf wrapper] (ca. 1885) **:** a small hand-rolled often flavored cigarette made chiefly in India

bi·di·a·lec·tal·ism \ˌbī-ˌdī-ə-ˈlek-tᵊl-ˌi-zəm\ *n* (1958) **:** facility in using two dialects of the same language; *also* **:** the teaching of Standard English to pupils who normally use a nonstandard dialect — **bi·di·a·lec·tal** *adj*

bi·di·rec·tion·al \ˌbī-də-ˈrek-shnəl, -dī-, -shə-nᵊl\ *adj* (1928) **:** involving, moving, or taking place in two usu. opposite directions ⟨~ flow⟩ ⟨~ replication of DNA⟩ — **bi·di·rec·tion·al·ly** *adv*

bi·don·ville \bē-ˌdō^{n}-ˈvēl\ *n* [F, fr. *bidon* metal can or drum + *ville* city] (1952) **:** a settlement of jerry-built dwellings on the outskirts of a city (as in France or No. Africa)

bid up *vt* (1864) **:** to raise the price of (as property at auction) by a succession of offers

BIE *abbr* bachelor of industrial engineering

Bie·der·mei·er \ˈbē-dər-ˌmī(-ə)r\ *adj* [after Gottlieb *Biedermeier,* satirical name for an uninspired Ger. bourgeois] (1905) **:** of a style of unostentatious furniture and interior decoration popular esp. with the middle class in early 19th century Germany

bi·en·ni·al \(ˌ)bī-ˈe-nē-əl\ *adj* (1562) **1 :** occurring every two years **2 :** continuing or lasting for two years; *specif* **:** growing vegetatively during the first year and fruiting and dying during the second ***usage*** see BI- — **biennial** *n* — **bi·en·ni·al·ly** \-ə-lē\ *adv*

bi·en·ni·um \bī-ˈe-nē-əm\ *n, pl* **-ni·ums** *or* **-nia** \-nē-ə\ [L, fr. *bi-* + *annus* year — more at ANNUAL] (1899) **:** a period of two years

bier \ˈbir\ *n* [ME *bere,* fr. OE *bǣr;* akin to OE *beran* to carry — more at BEAR] (bef. 12c) **1** *archaic* **:** a framework for carrying **2 :** a stand on which a corpse or coffin is placed; *also* **:** a coffin together with its stand

bi·face \ˈbī-ˌfās\ *n* (1934) **:** a bifacial stone tool

bi·fa·cial \(ˌ)bī-ˈfā-shəl\ *adj* (ca. 1847) **:** having opposite sides or faces worked on to form an edge for cutting or scraping — **bi·fa·cial·ly** *adv*

biff \ˈbif\ *n* [prob. imit.] (ca. 1887) **:** WHACK, BLOW — **biff** *vt*

bi·fid \ˈbī-ˌfid, -fəd\ *adj* [L *bifidus,* fr. *bi-* + *-fidus* -fid] (1661) **:** divided into two equal lobes or parts by a median cleft ⟨a ~ leaf⟩

bi·fi·lar \(ˌ)bī-ˈfī-lər\ *adj* [ISV *bi-* + L *filum* thread — more at FILE] (1846) **1 :** involving two threads or wires ⟨~ suspension of a pendulum⟩ **2 :** involving a single thread or wire doubled back upon itself ⟨a ~ resistor⟩ — **bi·fi·lar·ly** *adv*

bi·fla·gel·late \(ˌ)bī-ˈfla-jə-lət, -ˌlāt; -flə-ˈje-lət\ *adj* (1856) **:** having two flagella ⟨~ gametes⟩

[1]bi·fo·cal \ˈbī-ˌfō-kəl\ *adj* [ISV] (1888) **1 :** having two focal lengths **2 :** having one part that corrects for near vision and one for distant vision ⟨a ~ eyeglass lens⟩

[2]bifocal *n* (1899) **1** *pl* **:** eyeglasses with bifocal lenses **2 :** a bifocal glass or lens

bi·fold \ˈbī-ˌfōld\ *adj* (1929) **:** designed to fold twice ⟨~ doors⟩ ⟨a ~ wallet⟩

bi·func·tion·al \(ˌ)bī-ˈfəŋ(k)-shnəl, -shə-nᵊl\ *adj* (1929) **:** having two functions; *esp* **:** DIFUNCTIONAL

bi·fur·cate \ˈbī-(ˌ)fər-ˌkāt, bī-ˈfər-\ *vb* **-cat·ed; -cat·ing** [ML *bifurcatus,* pp. of *bifurcare,* fr. L *bifurcus* two-pronged, fr. *bi-* + *furca* fork] *vt* (1615) **:** to cause to divide into two branches or parts ~ *vi* **:** to divide into two branches or parts — **bi·fur·cate** \(ˌ)bī-ˈfər-kət, -ˌkāt; ˈbī-(ˌ)fər-ˌkāt\ *adj*

bi·fur·ca·tion \ˌbī-(ˌ)fər-ˈkā-shən\ *n* (1615) **1 a :** the point at which bifurcating occurs **b :** BRANCH **2 :** the act of bifurcating **:** the state of being bifurcated

[1]**big** \ˈbig\ *adj* **big·ger; big·gest** [ME, perh. of Scand origin; akin to Norw dial. *bugge* important man] (14c) **1 a** *obs* **:** of great strength **b :** of great force ⟨a ~ storm⟩ **2 a :** large or great in dimensions, bulk, or extent ⟨a ~ house⟩; *also* **:** large or great in quantity, number, or amount ⟨a ~ fleet⟩ **b :** operating on a large scale ⟨~ government⟩ **c :** CAPITAL 1 **3 a :** PREGNANT; *esp* **:** nearly ready to give birth **b :** full to bursting **:** SWELLING ⟨~ with rage⟩ **c** *of the voice* **:** full and resonant **4 a :** CHIEF, PREEMINENT ⟨the ~ issue of the campaign⟩ **b :** outstandingly worthy or able ⟨a truly ~ man⟩ **c :** of great importance or significance ⟨the ~ moment⟩ **d :** IMPOSING, PRETENTIOUS; *also* **:** marked by or given to boasting ⟨~ talk⟩ **e :** MAGNANIMOUS, GENEROUS ⟨was ~ about it⟩ **5 :** POPULAR ⟨soft drinks are very ~ in Mexico —Russ Leadabrand⟩ **6 :** full-bodied and flavorful — used of wine — **big·ly** *adv* — **big·ness** *n* — **big on :** strongly favoring or liking; *also* **:** noted for ⟨she is *big on* blushing —Arnold Hano⟩

[2]**big** *adv* (1556) **1 :** in a loud or declamatory manner; *also* **:** in a boasting manner ⟨talk ~⟩ **2 a :** to a large amount or extent ⟨won ~⟩ **b :** on a large scale ⟨think ~⟩ **3 :** HARD ⟨hits her forehand ~⟩

[3]**big** *n* (1833) **:** an individual or organization of outstanding importance or power; *esp* **:** MAJOR LEAGUE — usu. used in pl. ⟨playing in the ~*s*⟩

big·a·mous \ˈbi-gə-məs\ *adj* (1671) **1 :** guilty of bigamy ⟨a ~ man⟩ **2 :** involving bigamy ⟨a ~ marriage⟩ — **big·a·mous·ly** *adv*

big·a·my \ˈbi-gə-mē\ *n* [ME *bigamie,* fr. ML *bigamia,* fr. L *bi-* + LL *-gamia* -gamy] (14c) **:** the act of entering into a marriage with one person while still legally married to another — **big·a·mist** \-mist\ *n*

bi·ga·rade \ˌbē-gä-ˈräd\ *n* [F, fr. Occitan *bigarrado,* fr. *bigarra* to variegate] (1658) **1 :** SOUR ORANGE **2 :** a brown sauce flavored with the juice and grated rind of oranges

big band *n* (1917) **:** a band that is larger than a combo and that usu. features a mixture of ensemble playing and solo improvisation typical of jazz or swing

big bang *n* (1950) **:** the cosmic explosion that marked the beginning of the universe according to the big bang theory — compare BIG CRUNCH

big bang theory *n* (1955) **:** a theory in astronomy: the universe originated billions of years ago in an explosion from a single point of nearly infinite energy density — compare STEADY STATE THEORY

big beat *n, often cap both Bs* (1957) **:** music (as rock) characterized by a heavy persistent beat

Big Ben \-ˈben\ *n* [Sir *Benjamin* Hall †1867 Eng. Chief Commissioner of Works] (1859) **1 :** a large bell in the clock tower of the Houses of Parliament in London **2 :** the tower that houses Big Ben; *also* **:** the clock in the tower

big bluestem *n* (1887) **:** BLUESTEM 1

big–box \ˈbig-ˌbäks\ *adj* (1990) **:** of, relating to, or being a large chain store having a boxlike structure — **big box** *n*

big boy *n* (1916) **:** BIG GUN — usu. used in pl.

big brother *n* (1809) **1 :** an older brother **2 :** a man who serves as a companion, father figure, and role model for a boy **3** *cap both Bs* [*Big Brother,* personification of the power of the state in *1984* (1949) by George Orwell] **a :** the leader of an authoritarian state or movement **b :** an all-powerful government or organization monitoring and directing people's actions

Big Broth·er·ism \-ˈbrə-t͟hər-ˌi-zəm\ *n* (1950) **:** authoritarian attempts at complete control (as of a person or a nation)

big brown bat *n* (1898) **:** an insectivorous medium-sized bat (*Eptesicus fuscus*) having brownish fur that is found from southern Canada to northern South America and that often roosts in buildings

big buck *n* (1941) **:** a large sum of money — usu. used in pl. ⟨signed a contract for *big bucks*⟩

big business *n* (1905) **1 :** an economic group consisting of large profit-making corporations esp. with regard to their influence on social or political policy **2 :** a very profitable enterprise

big C *n, often cap B* (1964) **:** CANCER 2

big cheese *n* (1912) **:** BOSS, BIG GUN

big crunch *n, often cap B&C* (1977) **:** a hypothetical cosmological event in which all matter in the universe collapses to a singularity and which is posited to be a possible fate of the universe if the density of matter in it is sufficiently high — compare BIG BANG

big daddy *n, often cap B&D* (1881) **:** one preeminent esp. by reason of power, size, or seniority **:** one representing paternalistic authority

big data *n* (1980) **:** an accumulation of data that is too large and complex for processing by traditional database management tools

big deal *n* (1915) **:** something of special importance ⟨what's the *big deal?*⟩ — sometimes used ironically as an interjection

Big Dipper *n* (1853) **:** the seven principal stars in the constellation of Ursa Major

bi·gem·i·ny \bī-ˈje-mə-nē\ *n* [*bigeminal* (double, paired), fr. LL *bigeminus,* fr. *bi-* + *geminus* twin] (ca. 1923) **:** the state of having a pulse characterized by two beats close together with a pause following each pair of beats — **bi·gem·i·nal** \-mə-nᵊl\ *adj*

big·eye \ˈbig-ˌī\ *n* (1861) **:** any of several small widely distributed reddish to silvery bony fishes (genus *Priacanthus* of the family Priacanthidae) of tropical seas

bigeye tuna *n* (1944) **:** a large-eyed tuna (*Thunnus obesus*) that has long pectoral fins and often a bluish stripe on the side and is found in warm ocean waters worldwide

big·foot \ˈbig-ˌfu̇t\ *n, pl* **big·feet** \-ˌfēt\ *or* **big·foots** *often cap* (1958) **1** [fr. the size of the footprints ascribed to it] **:** SASQUATCH **2 :** BIG SHOT

big game *n* (1773) **1 :** relatively large animals sought or taken by hunting or fishing esp. for sport **2 :** an important objective esp. when involving risk

big·ge·ty *or* **big·gi·ty** \ˈbi-gə-tē\ *adj* [*big* + *-ety* (as in *persnickety*)] (1880) **1** *Southern & Midland* **:** CONCEITED, VAIN **2** *Southern & Midland* **:** rudely self-important **:** IMPUDENT ⟨never acted ~ in court, but she would bow her head only so low —Claude Brown⟩

big·gie \ˈbi-gē\ *n* (ca. 1926) **:** one that is big and often important

[1]**big·gin** *or* **big·ging** \ˈbi-gən\ *n* [ME *bigging,* fr. *biggen* to dwell, fr. ON *byggja;* akin to OE *bēon* to be] (14c) *archaic* **:** BUILDING

[2]**biggin** *n* [MF *beguin*] (1511) *archaic* **:** CAP: **a :** a child's cap **b :** NIGHTCAP

big·gish \ˈbi-gish\ *adj* (1611) **:** somewhat big

big gun *n* (1830) **:** one having preeminent status or power in a field

big hair *n* (1966) **:** hair that is styled and teased to occupy an unusually large amount of space above and around the head

big·head \ˈbig-ˌhed\ *n* (1784) **1 :** any of several diseases of animals marked by swelling about the head **2 :** an exaggerated opinion of one's importance — usu. used with *the* — **big·head·ed** \-ˈhe-dəd\ *adj*

big·heart·ed \-ˈhär-təd\ *adj* (1846) **:** GENEROUS, CHARITABLE — **big·heart·ed·ly** *adv* — **big·heart·ed·ness** *n*

big·horn sheep \ˈbig-ˌhȯrn-\ *n* (1817) **:** a usu. grayish-brown wild sheep (*Ovis canadensis*) of mountainous and desert regions of western No. America — called also *bighorn*

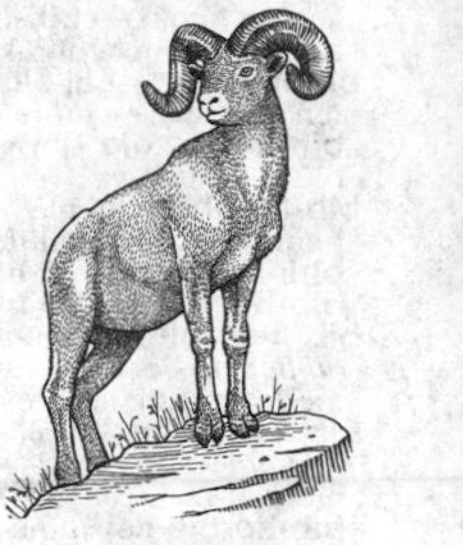

bighorn sheep

big house *n, often cap B&H* (1913) *slang* **:** PENITENTIARY

bight \ˈbīt\ *n* [ME, fr. OE *byht* bend, bay; akin to OE *būgan* to bend — more at BOW] (15c) **1 :** a bend in a coast forming an open bay; *also* **:** a bay formed by such a bend **2 :** a slack part or loop in a rope

big league *n* (1882) **1 :** MAJOR LEAGUE **2 :** BIG TIME 2 — often used in pl. — **big–league** *adj* — **big leaguer** *n*

big lie *n, sometimes cap B&L* (1824) **:** a deliberate gross distortion of the truth used esp. as a propaganda tactic

big·mouthed \ˈbig-ˌmau̇t͟hd, ˈbig-ˌmau̇tht, ˈbig-ˈ\ *adj* (1602) **1 :** having a large mouth **2 :** LOUDMOUTHED

big name *n* (1881) **:** a performer or personage of top rank in popular recognition ⟨a *big name* in the business world⟩ — **big–name** *adj*

big·no·nia \big-ˈnō-nē-ə\ *n* [NL, genus name, fr. J. P. *Bignon* †1743 Fr. royal librarian] (1785) **:** a woody evergreen vine (*Bignonia capreolata* of the family Bignoniaceae, the bignonia family) of the southern and central U.S. that has compound leaves and tubular flowers

big·ot \ˈbi-gət\ *n* [F, hypocrite, bigot] (1660) **:** a person obstinately or intolerantly devoted to his or her own opinions and prejudices; *esp* **:** one who regards or treats the members of a group (as a racial or ethnic group) with hatred and intolerance — **big·ot·ed** \-gə-təd\ *adj* — **big·ot·ed·ly** *adv*

big·ot·ry \ˈbi-gə-trē\ *n, pl* **-ries** (1632) **1 :** the state of mind of a bigot **2 :** acts or beliefs characteristic of a bigot

big picture *n, often cap B&P* (1904) **:** the entire perspective on a situation or issue — used with *the*

big science *n, often cap B&S* (1914) **:** large-scale scientific research consisting of projects funded usu. by a national government or group of governments

big screen *n* (1914) **:** the motion-picture medium often as contrasted to television ⟨a story adapted for the *big screen*⟩ — **big–screen** *adj*

big shot \ˈbig-ˌshät\ *n* (1929) **:** a person of consequence or prominence

big stick *n* (1893) **:** threat esp. of military or political intervention

big–tick·et \ˈbig-ˈti-kət\ *adj* (1945) **:** having a high price ⟨the car was a ~ item⟩

[1]**big–time** \ˈbig-ˌtīm\ *adj* (1910) **:** relating to or involved in the big time ⟨~ sports⟩; *also* **:** MAJOR 4 ⟨~ operators⟩

[2]**big–time** *adv* (1957) **:** in a major or large-scale way ⟨the new show bombed ~⟩; *also* **:** to a great extent or degree ⟨owes me ~⟩

big time \-ˌtīm\ *n* (1910) **1 :** a high-paying vaudeville circuit requiring only two performances a day **2 :** the top rank of an activity or enterprise — **big–tim·er** \-ˌtī-mər\ *n*

big toe *n* (1699) **:** the innermost and largest toe of the foot

big top *n* (1763) **1 :** the main tent of a circus **2 :** CIRCUS 2a, b, c

big tree *n* (1853) **:** GIANT SEQUOIA

big wheel *n* (1942) **:** BIGWIG, BIG SHOT

big·wig \ˈbig-ˌwig\ *n* (1703) **:** an important person

Bi·ha·ri \bi-ˈhär-ē\ *n* (1878) **1 a :** a native or inhabitant of Bihar **b :** a Muslim born in Bihar who emigrated after the partition of India in 1947; *also* **:** a descendant of such a person **2 :** a group of Indo-Aryan languages (as Bhojpuri) spoken in Bihar, India, and adjacent areas

bi·jec·tion \(ˌ)bī-ˈjek-shən\ *n* [[1]*bi-* + *-jection* (as in *injection*)] (1956) **:** a mathematical function that is a one-to-one and onto mapping — compare INJECTION, SURJECTION — **bi·jec·tive** \-ˈjek-tiv\ *adj*

bi·jou \ˈbē-ˌzhü\ *n, pl* **bijous** *or* **bi·joux** \-ˌzhü(z)\ [F, fr. Bret *bizou* ring, fr. *biz* finger] (1668) **1 :** a small dainty usu. ornamental piece of delicate workmanship **:** JEWEL **2 :** something delicate, elegant, or highly prized — **bijou** *adj*

bi·jou·te·rie \bi-ˈzhü-tə-(ˌ)rē\ *n* [F, fr. *bijou*] (1735) **:** a collection of trinkets or ornaments **:** JEWELS; *also* **:** DECORATION

[1]**bike** \ˈbīk\ *n* [ME] (14c) **1** *chiefly Scot* **:** a nest of wild bees, wasps, or hornets **2** *chiefly Scot* **:** a crowd or swarm of people

[2]**bike** *n* [by shortening & alter.] (1880) **1 :** BICYCLE **2 :** MOTORCYCLE **3 :** MOTORBIKE **4 :** STATIONARY BICYCLE

[3]**bike** *vi* **biked; bik·ing** (1885) **:** to ride a bike

bik·er \ˈbī-kər\ *n* (1883) **1 :** BICYCLIST **2 :** MOTORCYCLIST; *esp* **:** one who is a member of an organized club or gang

bike·way \ˈbīk-ˌwā\ *n* (1895) **:** a thoroughfare for bicycles

bik·ie \ˈbī-kē\ *n* [[2]*bike* + *-ie*] (1967) **:** BIKER 2

bi·ki·ni \bə-ˈkē-nē\ *n* [F, fr. *Bikini,* atoll of the Marshall Islands] (1947) **1 a :** a woman's scanty two-piece bathing suit **b :** a man's brief swimsuit **2 :** a man's or woman's low-cut briefs — **bi·ki·nied** *also* **bi·ki·ni'd** \-nēd\ *adj*

bikini wax *n* (1973) **:** a procedure for removing pubic hair from the skin near the edge of the bottom half of a bikini by applying hot wax, covering the wax with a cloth to which the wax and hair adhere, and then peeling it off quickly

bil *abbr* billion

[1]**bi·la·bi·al** \(ˌ)bī-ˈlā-bē-əl\ *adj* [ISV] (1878) *of a consonant* **:** produced with both lips

[2]**bilabial** *n* (1829) **:** a bilabial consonant

bi·la·bi·ate \-bē-ət\ *adj* (1720) **:** having two lips ⟨a ~ corolla⟩

bi·lat·er·al \(ˌ)bī-ˈla-t(ə-)rəl\ *adj* (1751) **1 :** affecting reciprocally two nations or parties ⟨a ~ treaty⟩ ⟨a ~ trade agreement⟩ **2 :** having two sides **3 a :** of, relating to, or affecting the right and left sides of the body or the right and left members of paired organs ⟨~ nephrectomy⟩ **b** : having bilateral symmetry — **bi·lat·er·al·ism** \-t(ə-)rə-ˌli-zəm\ *n* — **bi·lat·er·al·ly** *adv*

bilateral symmetry *n* (1860) : symmetry in which similar anatomical parts are arranged on opposite sides of a median axis so that only one plane can divide the individual into essentially identical halves

bi·lay·er \ˈbī-ˌlā-ər, -ˌler\ *n* (1963) : a film or membrane with two molecular layers ⟨a ~ of phospholipid molecules⟩ — **bilayer** *adj*

bil·ber·ry \ˈbil-ˌber-ē, -ˌbe-rē\ *n* [*bil-* (prob. of Scand origin; akin to Dan *bølle* whortleberry) + *berry*] (1577) **1** : any of several ericaceous shrubs (genus *Vaccinium*) that resemble blueberries but have flowers which arise solitary or in very small clusters from axillary buds; *esp* : a Eurasian shrub (*Vaccinium myrtillus*) **2** : the sweet edible fruit of the bilberry; *also* : an extract of this fruit used in medicine

[1]**bil·bo** \ˈbil-(ˌ)bō\ *n, pl* **bilboes** [perh. fr. *Bilboa*, Spain] (1557) : a long bar of iron with sliding shackles used to confine the feet of prisoners esp. on shipboard

[2]**bilbo** *or* **bil·boa** \ˈbil-(ˌ)bō\ *n, pl* **bilboes** *or* **bilboas** [*Bilboa, Bilbao*, Spain] (1565) : SWORD

bil·by \ˈbil-bē\ *n, pl* **bilbies** [Yuwaalaraay (Australian aboriginal language of northern New South Wales) *bilbi*] (1888) : either of two burrowing nocturnal bandicoots (*Macrotis lagotis* and *M. leucura*) having a long tapered muzzle and large pointed ears — called also *rabbit-eared bandicoot*

bil·dungs·ro·man \ˈbil-dúŋ(k)s-rō-ˌmän, -dúŋz-\ *n* [G, fr. *Bildung* education + *Roman* novel] (1910) : a novel about the moral and psychological growth of the main character

bile \ˈbī(-ə)l\ *n* [L *bilis;* akin to W *bustl* bile] (1547) **1 a** : either of two humors associated in old physiology with irascibility and melancholy **b** : a yellow or greenish viscid alkaline fluid secreted by the liver and passed into the duodenum where it aids esp. in the emulsification and absorption of fats **2 a** : inclination to anger **b** : ACRIMONY, VITRIOL

bile acid *n* (ca. 1881) : any of several steroid acids (as cholic acid) of or derived from bile

bile duct *n* (1774) : a duct by which bile passes from the liver or gallbladder to the duodenum

bile salt *n* (1881) **1** : a salt of bile acid **2** *pl* : a dry mixture of the principal salts of the gall of the ox used as a liver stimulant and as a laxative

[1]**bi–lev·el** \ˈbī-ˈle-vəl\ *adj* (1960) **1** : having two levels of freight or passenger space **2** : having two floors with a ground-level entry situated between the floors

[2]**bi–level** \ˈbī-ˌ\ *n* (1966) : a bi-level house

[1]**bilge** \ˈbilj\ *n* [prob. modif. of MF *boulge, bouge* leather bag, curved part — more at BUDGET] (1513) **1** : the bulging part of a cask or barrel **2 a** : the part of the underwater body of a ship between the flat of the bottom and the vertical topsides **b** : the lowest point of a ship's inner hull **3** : stale or worthless remarks or ideas

[2]**bilge** *vi* **bilged; bilg·ing** (1728) : to become damaged in the bilge

bilge keel *n* (1850) : a projection like a fin extending from the hull near the turn of the bilge on either side to check rolling

bilge·wa·ter \ˈbilj-ˌwó-tər, -ˌwä-\ *n* (1706) : water that collects in the bilge of a ship

bil·har·zia \bil-ˈhär-zē-ə; -ˈhärt-sē-\ *n* [NL, genus name, fr. Theodor *Bilharz* †1862 Ger. zoologist] (ca. 1881) **1** : SCHISTOSOMIASIS **2** : SCHISTOSOME — **bil·har·zi·al** \-zē-əl; -sē-\ *adj*

bil·har·zi·a·sis \ˌbil-ˌhär-ˈzī-ə-səs; -ˌhärt-ˈsī-\ *n, pl* **-a·ses** \-ˌsēz\ [NL] (ca. 1900) : SCHISTOSOMIASIS

bil·i·ary \ˈbi-lē-ˌer-ē, -e-rē\ *adj* [F *biliare*, fr. L *bilis*] (1731) : of, relating to, or conveying bile; *also* : affecting the bile-conveying structures

bi·lin·ear \(ˌ)bī-ˈli-nē-ər\ *adj* (1886) : linear with respect to each of two mathematical variables; *specif* : of or relating to an algebraic form each term of which involves one variable to the first degree from each of two sets of variables

bi·lin·gual \(ˌ)bī-ˈliŋ-gwəl *also* -gyə-wəl\ *adj* [L *bilinguis*, fr. *bi-* + *lingua* tongue — more at TONGUE] (1829) **1** : having or expressed in two languages ⟨a ~ document⟩ ⟨an officially ~ nation⟩ **2** : using or able to use two languages esp. with equal fluency ⟨~ in English and Japanese⟩ **3** : of or relating to bilingual education — **bilingual** *n* — **bi·lin·gual·ly** *adv*

bilingual education *n* (1972) : education in an English-language school system in which students with little fluency in English are taught in both their native language and English

bi·lin·gual·ism \-gwə-ˌli-zəm\ *n* (1873) **1** : the ability to speak two languages **2** : the frequent use (as by a community) of two languages **3** : the political or institutional recognition of two languages

bi·lin·gual·i·ty \ˌbī-liŋ-ˈgwa-lə-tē\ *n* (1930) : BILINGUALISM

bil·ious \ˈbil-yəs\ *adj* [MF *bilieux*, fr. L *biliosus*, fr. *bilis*] (1541) **1 a** : of or relating to bile **b** : marked by or suffering from liver dysfunction and esp. excessive secretion of bile **c** : appearing as if affected by a bilious disorder **2** : of or indicative of a peevish ill-natured disposition **3** : sickeningly unpleasant ⟨with clapboards painted red and ~ yellow —Sinclair Lewis⟩ — **bil·ious·ly** *adv* — **bil·ious·ness** *n*

bil·i·ru·bin \ˌbi-li-ˈrü-bən, ˈbi-li-ˌ\ *n* [L *bilis* + *ruber* red — more at RED] (1871) : a reddish-yellow water insoluble pigment occurring esp. in bile and blood and causing jaundice if accumulated in excess

bil·i·ver·din \-ˈvər-dᵊn, -ˌvər-\ *n* [Sw, fr. L *bilis* + obs. F *verd* green] (1845) : a green pigment that occurs in bile and is an intermediate in the degradation of hemoglobin heme groups to bilirubin

[1]**bilk** \ˈbilk\ *vt* [perh. alter. of [2]*balk*] (1647) **1** : to block the free development of : FRUSTRATE ⟨fate ~*s* their hopes⟩ **2 a** : to cheat out of something valuable : DEFRAUD **b** : to evade payment of or to ⟨~*s* his creditors⟩ **3** : to slip away from ⟨~*ed* her pursuers⟩ — **bilk·er** *n*

[2]**bilk** *n* (1790) : an untrustworthy tricky individual : CHEAT

[1]**bill** \ˈbil\ *n* [ME *bile*, fr. OE; akin to OE *bill*] (bef. 12c) **1** : the jaws of a bird together with their horny covering **2** : a mouthpart (as the beak of a turtle) that resembles a bird's bill **3** : the point of an anchor fluke — see ANCHOR illustration **4** : the visor of a cap or hood

[2]**bill** *vi* (1584) **1** : to touch and rub bill to bill **2** : to caress affectionately ⟨~*ing* and cooing⟩

[3]**bill** *n* [ME *bil*, fr. OE *bill* sword; akin to OHG *bill* pickax] (14c) **1** : a weapon in use up to the 18th century that consists of a long staff ending in a hook-shaped blade **2** : BILLHOOK

[4]**bill** *n* [ME, fr. AF & ML; AF *bille*, fr. ML *billa*, perh. alter. of *bulla*, papal seal, bull — more at BULL] (14c) **1** : an itemized list or a statement

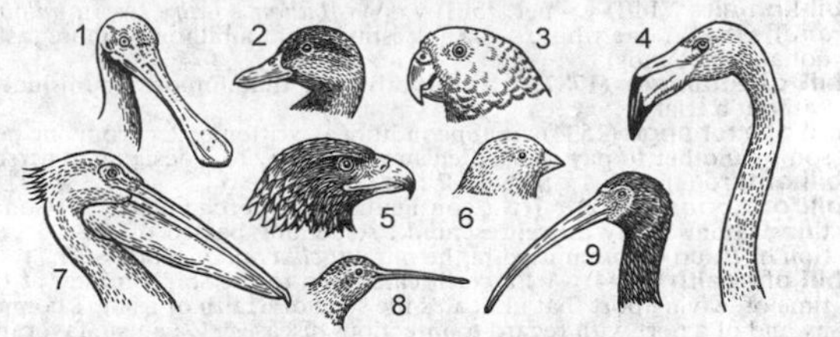

[1]bill 1: *1* spoonbill, *2* duck, *3* parrot, *4* flamingo, *5* eagle, *6* finch, *7* pelican, *8* hummingbird, *9* ibis

of particulars (as a list of materials or of members of a ship's crew) **2** : a written document or note **3** *obs* : a formal petition **4 a** : an itemized account of the separate cost of goods sold, services performed, or work done : INVOICE **b** : an amount expended or owed **c** : a statement of charges for food or drink : CHECK **5 a** : a written or printed advertisement posted or otherwise distributed to announce an event of interest to the public; *esp* : an announcement of a theatrical entertainment **b** : a programmed presentation (as a motion picture, play, or concert) **6** : a draft of a law presented to a legislature for enactment; *also* : the law itself ⟨the GI ~⟩ **7** : a declaration in writing stating a wrong a complainant has suffered from a defendant or stating a breach of law by some person ⟨a ~ of complaint⟩ **8 a** : a piece of paper money **b** : an individual or commercial note ⟨~*s* receivable⟩ **c** *slang* : one hundred dollars — **fill the bill** *or* **fit the bill** : to be exactly what is needed : be suitable

[5]**bill** *vt* (14c) **1 a** : to enter in an accounting system : prepare a bill of (charges) **b** : to submit a bill of charges to **c** : to enter (as freight) in a waybill **d** : to issue a bill of lading to or for **2** : to announce (as a performance) esp. by posters or placards **3** : ADVERTISE, PROMOTE ⟨the book is ~*ed* as a "report" —P. G. Altbach⟩ — **bill·able** *adj*

bil·la·bong \ˈbi-lə-ˌbóŋ, -ˌbäŋ\ *n* [Wiradhuri (Australian aboriginal language of central New South Wales) *bilabaŋ*] (1861) **1** *Austral* **a** : a blind channel leading out from a river **b** : a usu. dry streambed that is filled seasonally **2** *Austral* : a backwater forming a stagnant pool

[1]**bill·board** \ˈbil-ˌbórd\ *n* (1851) : a flat surface (as of a panel, wall, or fence) on which bills are posted; *specif* : a large panel designed to carry outdoor advertising

[2]**billboard** *vt* (1950) : to promote by a conspicuous display on or as if on a billboard

bill·bug \ˈbil-ˌbəg\ *n* [[1]*bill* + *bug*] (1861) : any of various weevils (as of the genus *Sphenophorus*) having larvae that eat the roots of cereal and other grasses

billed \ˈbild\ *adj* : having a bill esp. of a specified kind — usu. used in combination ⟨spoon-*billed*⟩

bill·er \ˈbi-lər\ *n* (1920) : one that bills; *esp* : one that makes out bills

[1]**bil·let** \ˈbi-lət\ *n* [ME *bylet*, fr. AF *billette*, dim. of *bille* bill] (15c) **1** *archaic* : a brief letter : NOTE **2 a** : an official order directing that a member of a military force be provided with board and lodging (as in a private home) **b** : quarters assigned by or as if by a billet **3** : POSITION, JOB ⟨a lucrative ~⟩

[2]**billet** *vt* (1594) **1** : to assign lodging to (as soldiers) by or as if by a billet **2** : to serve with a billet ⟨~ a householder⟩

[3]**billet** *n* [ME *bylet*, fr. AF *billete*, dim. of *bille* log, of Celt origin; akin to OIr *bile* landmark tree] (15c) **1 a** : a chunky piece of wood (as for firewood) **b** *obs* : CUDGEL **2 a** : a bar of metal **b** : a piece of semifinished iron or steel nearly square in section made by rolling an ingot or bloom **c** : a section of nonferrous metal ingot hot-worked by forging, rolling, or extrusion **d** : a nonferrous casting suitable for rolling or extrusion

bil·let–doux \ˌbi-lā-ˈdü, ˌbi-(ˌ)lā-\ *n, pl* **bil·lets–doux** \-ˈdü(z)\ [F *billet doux*, lit., sweet letter] (1673) : a love letter

bill·fish \ˈbil-ˌfish\ *n* (1782) : a fish with long slender jaws; *esp* : any of various bony fishes (families Istiophoridae and Xiphiidae) with an elongated tapering upper jaw including marlins, spearfishes, and sailfishes

bill·fold \-ˌfōld\ *n* [short for earlier *billfolder*] (1895) : a folding pocketbook for paper money : WALLET

bill·hook \-ˌhük\ *n* (1604) : a cutting or pruning tool with a hooked blade

bil·liard \ˈbi(l)-yərd\ *n* (1580) — used as an attributive form of *billiards* ⟨a ~ ball⟩

bil·liards \-yərdz\ *n pl but sing in constr* [MF *billard* billiard cue, billiards, fr. *bille* wooden stick, log — more at BILLET] (1580) : any of several games played on an oblong table by driving small balls against one another or into pockets with a cue; *specif* : a game in which one scores by causing a cue ball to hit in succession two object balls — compare POOL

bil·li–bi *also* **bil·ly–bi** \ˈbi-lē-ˌbē, ˌbi-lē-ˈ\ *n* [F, alter. of *Billy B.*, perh. fr. William B. Leeds, Jr. †1972 Am. industrialist] (1961) : a soup of mussel stock, white wine, and cream served hot or cold

bill·ing \ˈbi-liŋ\ *n* [[5]*bill*] (1875) **1** : advertising or public promotion (as of a product or personality); *also* : relative prominence of a name in such promotion ⟨got top ~⟩ **2** : total amount of business or investments (as of an advertising agency) within a given period

bil·lings·gate \ˈbi-liŋz-ˌgāt, *Brit usu* -git\ *n* [*Billingsgate*, old gate and fish market, London, England] (1652) : coarsely abusive language ***syn*** see ABUSE

bil·lion \ˈbi(l)-yən\ *n* [F, fr. *bi-* + *-illion* (as in *million*)] (1834) **1** — see NUMBER table **2** : a very large number — **billion** *adj* — **bil·lionth** \-yən(t)th\ *adj or n*

\ə\ **abut** \ᵊ\ kitten, F table \ər\ **further** \a\ **ash** \ā\ **ace** \ä\ **mop, mar**
\au̇\ **out** \ch\ **chin** \e\ **bet** \ē\ **easy** \g\ **go** \i\ **hit** \ī\ **ice** \j\ **job**
\ŋ\ **sing** \ō\ **go** \ó\ **law** \ói\ **boy** \th\ **thin** \t͟h\ **the** \ü\ **loot** \u̇\ **foot**
\y\ **yet** \zh\ **vision, beige** \k͟, ⁿ, œ, ue, ʸ\ *see* Guide to Pronunciation

bil·lion·aire \ˌbi(l)-yə-ˈner, ˈbi(l)-yə-ˌ\ *n* [*billion* + *-aire* (as in *millionaire*)] (1844) : one whose wealth is estimated at a billion or more (as of dollars or pounds)
bill of attainder (1787) : a legislative act that imposes punishment without a trial
bill of exchange (1534) : an unconditional written order from one person to another to pay a specified sum of money to a designated person
bill of fare (1631) **1** : MENU **2** : PROGRAM
bill of goods (1842) **1** : a consignment of merchandise **2** : something intentionally misrepresented : something passed off in a deception or fraud — often used in the phrase *sell a bill of goods*
bill of health (1644) **1** : a certificate given to the ship's master at the time of leaving port that indicates the state of health of a ship's company and of a port with regard to infectious diseases **2** : a usu. favorable report following an examination or investigation ⟨gave the criticized textbook a clean *bill of health*⟩
bill of indictment (ca. 1530) : an indictment before it is found or ignored by the grand jury
bill of lading (1532) : a document issued by a carrier that lists goods being shipped and specifies the terms of their transport
bill of particulars (1831) : a detailed listing of charges or claims brought in a legal action or of a defendant's response or counterclaim
bill of rights *often cap B&R* (1701) : a document containing a formal statement of rights ⟨a patients' *bill of rights*⟩; *specif* : a summary of fundamental rights and privileges guaranteed to a people against violation by the state — used esp. of the first 10 amendments to the U.S. Constitution
bill of sale (1550) : a formal instrument for the conveyance or transfer of title to goods and chattels
bil·lon \ˈbi-lən\ *n* [F, fr. MF, fr. *bille* log — more at BILLET] (ca. 1727) **1** : gold or silver heavily alloyed with a less valuable metal **2** : an alloy of silver containing more than 50 percent of copper by weight
[1]**bil·low** \ˈbi-(ˌ)lō\ *n* [ON *bylgja;* akin to OHG *balg* bag — more at BELLY] (1552) **1** : WAVE; *esp* : a great wave or surge of water **2** : a rolling mass (as of flame or smoke) that resembles a high wave — **bil·lowy** \ˈbi-lə-wē\ *adj*
[2]**billow** *vi* (1585) **1** : to rise or roll in waves or surges **2** : to bulge or swell out (as through action of the wind) ~ *vt* : to cause to billow
[1]**bil·ly** \ˈbi-lē\ *n, pl* **billies** [Sc *billy-pot* cooking utensil] (1839) *chiefly Austral & NewZeal* : a metal or enamelware pail or pot with a lid and wire bail — called also *billycan*
[2]**billy** *n, pl* **billies** [prob. fr. the name *Billy*] (1848) **1** : BILLY CLUB **2** : BILLY GOAT
billy club *n* [[2]*billy*] (1949) : a heavy usu. wooden club; *specif* : a police officer's club
bil·ly·cock \ˈbi-lē-ˌkäk\ *n* [origin unknown] (1721) *Brit* : DERBY 3
billy goat *n* [fr. the name *Billy*] (1820) : a male goat
bi·lobed \ˈbī-ˈlōbd\ *adj* (1756) : divided into two lobes ⟨a ~ nucleus⟩
bi·lo·ca·tion \ˈbī-lō-ˌkā-shən\ *n* (1858) : the state of being or ability to be in two places at the same time
bil·tong \ˈbil-ˌtȯŋ, -ˌtäŋ\ *n* [Afrik, fr. *bil* rump + *tong* tongue] (1815) *chiefly SoAfr* : jerked meat
bi·mah *also* **bi·ma** \ˈbē-mə\ *n* [Yiddish & LHeb; Yiddish *bime,* fr. LHeb *bīmāh,* fr. LGk *bēma* raised platform — more at BEMA] (1941) : a raised platform in a synagogue from which the Torah is read
bi·man·u·al \(ˌ)bī-ˈman-yə-wəl, -yəl\ *adj* (ca. 1889) : done with or requiring the use of both hands — **bi·man·u·al·ly** *adv*
bim·bette \ˌbim-ˈbet\ *n* [*bimbo* + *-ette*] (1982) *slang* : an attractive but vacuous woman
bim·bo \ˈbim-(ˌ)bō\ *n, pl* **bimbos** [perh. fr. It *bimbo* baby] (1918) **1** *slang* : MAN, WOMAN ⟨telling a thickheaded pitcher that the ~ at the plate hasn't hit a curve in three seasons —Jay Stuller⟩ — used as a generalized term of disapproval esp. for an attractive but vacuous person ⟨we didn't want a blond ~ in that role . . . we wanted her to be smart —Hugh Wilson⟩ **2** *slang* : TRAMP 1c ⟨evidence of how her hubby's been cheating on her with various ~*s* —Dan Greenburg⟩
bi·met·al \ˈbī-ˌme-tᵊl\ *adj* (1893) : BIMETALLIC — **bimetal** *n*
bi·me·tal·lic \ˌbī-mə-ˈta-lik\ *adj* (1876) **1** : relating to, based on, or using bimetallism **2** : composed of two different metals — often used of devices having a part in which two metals that expand differently are bonded together — **bimetallic** *n*
bi·met·al·lism \(ˌ)bī-ˈme-tᵊl-ˌi-zəm\ *n* [F *bimétallisme,* fr. *bi-* + *métal* metal] (1876) : the use of two metals (as gold and silver) jointly as a monetary standard with both constituting legal tender at a predetermined ratio — **bi·met·al·list** \-tᵊl-ist\ *n* — **bi·met·al·lis·tic** \ˌbī-ˌme-tᵊl-ˈis-tik\ *adj*
bi·mil·le·na·ry \(ˌ)bī-ˈmi-lə-ˌner-ē, -ˌne-rē, ˌbī-mə-ˈle-nə-rē\ *or* **bi·mil·len·ni·al** \ˌbī-mə-ˈle-nē-əl\ *n* (1850) **1** : a period of 2000 years **2** : a 2000th anniversary — **bimillenary** *adj*
bi·mod·al \(ˌ)bī-ˈmō-dᵊl\ *adj* (1903) : having or relating to two modes; *esp* : having or occurring with two statistical modes — **bi·mo·dal·i·ty** \ˌbī-mō-ˈda-lə-tē\ *n*
bi·mo·lec·u·lar \ˌbī-mə-ˈle-kyə-lər\ *adj* [ISV] (1899) **1** : relating to or formed from two molecules **2** : being two molecules thick ⟨~ lipid layers⟩ — **bi·mo·lec·u·lar·ly** *adv*
[1]**bi·month·ly** \(ˌ)bī-ˈmən(t)th-lē\ *adj* (1845) **1** : occurring every two months **2** : occurring twice a month : SEMIMONTHLY ***usage*** see BI-
[2]**bimonthly** *adv* (1858) **1** : once every two months **2** : twice a month
[3]**bimonthly** *n* (ca. 1890) : a bimonthly publication
bi·mor·phe·mic \ˌbī-mȯr-ˈfē-mik\ *adj* (1942) : consisting of two morphemes
[1]**bin** \ˈbin\ *n* [ME *binn,* fr. OE] (bef. 12c) : a box, frame, crib, or enclosed place used for storage
[2]**bin** *vt* **binned; bin·ning** (1841) : to put into a bin
bin- *prefix* [ME, fr. LL, fr. L *bini* two by two; akin to OE *twinn* twofold — more at TWIN] : [1]BI- ⟨*binaural*⟩
bi·na·rism \ˈbī-nə-ˌriz-əm\ *n* [F *binarisme*] (1983) : a mode of thought predicated on stable oppositions (as good and evil or male and female) that is seen in post-structuralist analysis as an inadequate approach to areas of difference; *also* : a specific dichotomy subscribed to or reinforced in such thought ⟨the ~ of West and East⟩
[1]**bi·na·ry** \ˈbī-nə-rē, -ˌner-ē, -ˌne-rē\ *n, pl* **-ries** (15c) : something made of or based on two things or parts: as **a** : BINARY STAR **b** : a binary number system
[2]**binary** *adj* [LL *binarius,* fr. L *bini* two by two — more at BIN-] (1597) **1** : compounded or consisting of or marked by two things or parts **2 a** : DUPLE — used of measure or rhythm **b** : having two musical subjects or two complementary sections **3 a** : relating to, being, or belonging to a system of numbers having 2 as its base ⟨the ~ digits 0 and 1⟩ **b** : involving a choice or condition of two alternatives (as on-off or yes-no) **4 a** : composed of two chemical elements, an element and a radical that acts as an element, or two such radicals **b** : utilizing two harmless ingredients that upon combining form a lethal substance (as a gas) ⟨~ weapons⟩ **5** : relating two logical or mathematical elements ⟨a ~ operation⟩ **6** : of or relating to the use of stable oppositions (as good and evil) to analyze a subject or create a structural model ⟨the ~ opposition of male and female —Joan W. Scott⟩
binary fission *n* (1897) : reproduction of a cell by division into two approximately equal parts ⟨the *binary fission* of protozoans⟩
binary star *n* (ca. 1844) : a system of two stars that revolve around each other under their mutual gravitation
binary system *n* (1844) : BINARY STAR; *also* : a similar system containing bodies (as black holes) other than stars
bi·na·tion·al \(ˌ)bī-ˈna-sh(ə-)nəl\ *adj* (1888) : of or relating to two nations ⟨a ~ board of directors⟩
bin·au·ral \(ˌ)bī-ˈnȯr-əl, (ˌ)bi-\ *adj* [ISV] (1861) **1** : of, relating to, or involving two or both ears **2** : STEREOPHONIC — **bin·au·ral·ly** \-ə-lē\ *adv*
[1]**bind** \ˈbīnd\ *vb* **bound** \ˈbau̇nd\; **bind·ing** [ME, fr. OE *bindan;* akin to OHG *bintan* to bind, Gk *peisma* cable, Skt *badhnāti* he ties] *vt* (bef. 12c) **1 a** : to make secure by tying **b** : to confine, restrain, or restrict as if with bonds **c** : to put under an obligation ⟨~*s* himself with an oath⟩ **d** : to constrain with legal authority **2 a** : to wrap around with something so as to enclose or cover **b** : BANDAGE **3** : to fasten round about **4** : to tie together (as stocks of wheat) **5 a** : to cause to stick together **b** : to take up and hold (as by chemical forces) : combine with **6** : CONSTIPATE **7** : to make a firm commitment for ⟨a handshake ~*s* the deal⟩ **8** : to protect, strengthen, or decorate by a band or binding **9** : to apply the parts of the cover to (a book) **10** : to set at work as an apprentice : INDENTURE **11** : to cause to have an emotional attachment **12** : to fasten together ⟨a pin *bound* the ends of the scarf⟩ ~ *vi* **1 a** : to form a cohesive mass **b** : to combine or be taken up esp. by chemical action ⟨antibody ~*s* to a specific antigen⟩ **2** : to hamper free movement or natural action **3** : to become hindered from free operation **4** : to exert a restraining or compelling effect ⟨a promise that ~*s*⟩
[2]**bind** *n* (bef. 12c) **1 a** : something that binds **b** : the act of binding : the state of being bound **c** : a place where binding occurs **2** : TIE 3 **3** : a position or situation in which one is hampered, constrained, or prevented from free movement or action — **in a bind** : in trouble
bind·er \ˈbīn-dər\ *n* (bef. 12c) **1** : a person or machine that binds something (as books) **2 a** : something used in binding **b** : a usu. detachable cover (as for holding sheets of paper) **3** : something (as tar or cement) that produces or promotes cohesion in loosely assembled substances **4** : a temporary insurance contract that provides coverage until the policy is issued **5** : something (as money) given in earnest; *also* : the agreement arrived at **6** : a tobacco leaf wrapped between the filler and wrapper of a cigar
bind·ery \ˈbīn-d(ə-)rē\ *n, pl* **-er·ies** (1793) : a place where books are bound
[1]**bind·ing** \ˈbīn-diŋ\ *n* (13c) **1** : the action of one that binds **2** : a material or device used to bind: as **a** : the cover and materials that hold a book together **b** : a narrow fabric used to finish raw edges **c** : a set of ski fastenings for holding the boot firm on the ski
[2]**binding** *adj* (14c) **1** : that binds **2** : imposing an obligation — **bind·ing·ly** \-diŋ-lē\ *adv* — **bind·ing·ness** *n*
binding energy *n* (1932) : the energy required to break up a molecule, atom, or atomic nucleus completely into its constituent particles
bin·dle \ˈbin-dᵊl\ *n* [perh. alter. of *bundle*] (1897) : a bundle of clothes or bedding
bindle stiff *n* (1897) : HOBO; *esp* : one who carries his clothes or bedding in a bundle
bind off *vt* (ca. 1939) : to cast off in knitting
bind over *vt* (1610) : to put under a bond to do something (as appear in court)
bind·weed \ˈbīnd-ˌwēd\ *n* (1548) : any of various twining plants (esp. genus *Convolvulus* of the morning-glory family) that mat or interlace with plants among which they grow
bine \ˈbīn\ *n* [alter. of [2]*bind*] (1727) : a twining stem or flexible shoot (as of the hop); *also* : a plant (as woodbine) whose stems are bines
bi·ner \ˈbē-nər\ *n* (1973) : CARABINER
Bi·net–Si·mon scale \bi-ˌnā-sē-ˈmōⁿ-\ *n* [Alfred *Binet* †1911 and Théodore *Simon* †1961 Fr. psychologists] (1914) : an intelligence test consisting orig. of tasks graded from the level of the average 3-year-old to that of the average 12-year-old but later extended in range
bing cherry \ˈbiŋ-\ *n, often cap B* [Ah *Bing* *fl*1875 Am. (Chinese-born) horticulturist] (1925) : a widely cultivated large sweet cherry having glossy dark red skin and firm juicy flesh
[1]**binge** \ˈbinj\ *n* [E dial. *binge* (to drink heavily)] (1854) **1 a** : a drunken revel : SPREE **b** : an unrestrained and often excessive indulgence ⟨a buying ~⟩ **c** : an act of excessive or compulsive consumption (as of food) **2** : a social gathering : PARTY
[2]**binge** *vi* **binged; binge·ing** *or* **bing·ing** (1910) : to go on a binge — **bing·er** \ˈbin-jər\ *n*
[1]**bin·go** \ˈbiŋ-(ˌ)gō\ *interj* [alter. of *bing* (interj. suggestive of a ringing sound)] (1925) **1** — used to announce an unexpected event or instantaneous result **2** — used to announce a winning position in bingo **3** — used to express endorsement of a correct assertion
[2]**bingo** *n, pl* **bingos** (1923) : a game of chance played with cards having numbered squares corresponding to numbered balls drawn at random and won by covering five such squares in a row; *also* : a social gathering at which bingo is played
Bin·ky \ˈbiŋ-kē\ *trademark* — used for an infant's pacifier
bin·na·cle \ˈbi-ni-kəl\ *n* [alter. of ME *bitakle,* fr. OPg or OSp; OPg *bitácola* & OSp *bitácula,* fr. L *habitaculum* dwelling place, fr. *habitare* to inhabit — more at HABITATION] (1762) : a housing for a ship's compass and a lamp
bi·nocs \bə-ˈnäks\ *n pl* (1970) : BINOCULARS

[1]**bin·oc·u·lar** \bī-ˈnä-kyə-lər, bə-\ *adj* (1738) : of, relating to, using, or adapted to the use of both eyes — **bin·oc·u·lar·i·ty** \(ˌ)bī-ˌnä-kyə-ˈler-ə-tē, -ˈla-rə-, bə-\ *n* — **bin·oc·u·lar·ly** \bī-ˈnä-kyə-lər-lē, bə-\ *adv*

[2]**bin·oc·u·lar** \bə-ˈnä-kyə-lər, bī-\ *n* (1871) **1 :** a binocular optical instrument **2 :** a handheld optical instrument composed of two telescopes and a focusing device and usu. having prisms to increase magnifying ability — usu. used in pl.

bi·no·mi·al \bī-ˈnō-mē-əl\ *n* [NL *binomium,* fr. ML, neut. of *binomius* having two names, alter. of L *binominis,* fr. *bi-* + *nomin-, nomen* name — more at NAME] (1557) **1 :** a mathematical expression consisting of two terms connected by a plus sign or minus sign **2 :** a biological species name consisting of two terms — **binomial** *adj* — **bi·no·mi·al·ly** \-mē-ə-lē\ *adv*

binomial coefficient *n* (1876) : a coefficient of a term in the expansion of the binomial $(x + y)^n$ according to the binomial theorem

binomial distribution *n* (1911) : a probability function each of whose values gives the probability that an outcome with constant probability of occurrence in a statistical experiment will occur a given number of times in a succession of repetitions of the experiment

binomial nomenclature *n* (1880) : a system of nomenclature in which each species of animal or plant receives a name of two terms of which the first identifies the genus to which it belongs and the second the species itself

binomial theorem *n* (1753) : a theorem that specifies the expansion of a binomial of the form $(x + y)^n$ as the sum of $n + 1$ terms of which the general term is of the form

$$\frac{n!}{(n-k)!\,k!}x^{(n-k)}y^k$$

where k takes on values from 0 to n

bint \ˈbint\ *n* [Ar, girl, daughter] (1855) *Brit* : GIRL, WOMAN

bi·nu·cle·ate \(ˌ)bī-ˈnü-klē-ət *also* -ˈnyü-\ *also* **bi·nu·cle·at·ed** \-klē-ˌā-təd\ *adj* (1881) : having two cellular nuclei ⟨~ hepatocytes⟩

bio \ˈbī-(ˌ)ō\ *n, pl* **bi·os** (1947) : a biography or biographical sketch

bio- — see BI-

bio·acous·tics \ˌbī-(ˌ)ō-ə-ˈkü-stiks\ *n pl but sing in constr* (1957) : a branch of science concerned with the production of sound by and its effects on living organisms — **bio·ac·ous·ti·cian** \-ˌa-ˌkü-ˈsti-shən, -ə-ˌkü-\ *n*

bio·ac·tive \ˌbī-ō-ˈak-tiv\ *adj* (1965) : having an effect on a living organism ⟨~ molecules⟩ — **bio·ac·tiv·i·ty** \-ak-ˈti-və-tē\ *n*

bio·as·say \ˌbī-(ˌ)ō-ˈa-ˌsā, -a-ˈsā\ *n* (1912) : determination of the relative strength of a substance (as a drug) by comparing its effect on a test organism with that of a standard preparation — **bio·as·say** \-a-ˈsā, -ˈa-ˌsā\ *vt*

bio·avail·abil·i·ty \-ə-ˌvā-lə-ˈbi-lə-tē\ *n* (1971) : the degree and rate at which a substance (as a drug) is absorbed into a living system or is made available at the site of physiological activity — **bio·avail·able** \-ˈvā-lə-bəl\ *adj*

bio·be·hav·ior·al \-bi-ˈhā-vyə-rəl\ *adj* (1970) : of, relating to, or involving the interaction of behavior and biological processes

bio·cat·a·lyst \-ˈka-tə-ləst\ *n* (ca. 1925) : a catalyst (as an enzyme) of biological origin — **bio·ca·tal·y·sis** \-kə-ˈta-lə-sis\ *n* — **bio·cat·a·lyt·ic** \-ˌka-tə-ˈli-tik\ *adj*

bio·ce·no·sis *or* **bio·coe·no·sis** \ˌbī-ō-sə-ˈnō-səs\ *n, pl* **-no·ses** \-ˌsēz\ [NL, fr. [2]*bi-* + Gk *koinōsis* sharing, fr. *koinoun* to make common, fr. *koinos* common] (1883) : an ecological community esp. when forming a self-regulating unit

bio·cen·tric \-ˈsen-trik\ *adj* (ca. 1889) : considering all forms of life as having intrinsic value — **bio·cen·trism** \-ˌtri-zəm\ *n*

bio·chem·i·cal \ˌbī-ō-ˈke-mi-kəl\ *adj* [ISV] (1851) **1 :** of or relating to biochemistry **2 :** characterized by, produced by, or involving chemical reactions in living organisms ⟨a ~ defect in the brain⟩ — **biochemical** *n* — **bio·chem·i·cal·ly** \-k(ə-)lē\ *adv*

biochemical oxygen demand *n* (ca. 1927) : the oxygen used in meeting the metabolic needs of aerobic microorganisms in water rich in organic matter (as water polluted with sewage)

bio·chem·is·try \ˌbī-ō-ˈke-mə-strē\ *n* [ISV] (1848) **1 :** chemistry that deals with the chemical compounds and processes occurring in organisms **2 :** the chemical characteristics and reactions of a particular living organism or biological substance — **bio·chem·ist** \-mist\ *n*

bio·chip \ˈbī-ō-ˌchip\ *n* (1980) **1 :** a hypothetical computer logic circuit or storage device in which the physical or chemical properties of large biological molecules (as proteins) are used to process information **2 :** MICROARRAY

bio·cid·al \ˌbī-ə-ˈsī-dᵊl\ *adj* (1949) : destructive to life

bio·cide \ˈbī-ə-ˌsīd\ *n* (1947) : a substance (as DDT) that is destructive to many different organisms

bio·cli·mat·ic \ˌbī-ō-klī-ˈma-tik\ *adj* (1918) : of or relating to the relations of climate and living matter ⟨~ adaptations⟩

bio·com·pat·i·bil·i·ty \-kəm-ˌpa-tə-ˈbi-lə-tē\ *n* (1971) : compatibility with living tissue or a living system by not being toxic, injurious, or physiologically reactive and not causing immunological rejection — **bio·com·pat·i·ble** \-ˈpa-tə-bəl\ *adj*

bio·con·tain·ment \-kən-ˈtān-mənt\ *n* (1985) : the containment of extremely pathogenic organisms (as viruses) usu. by isolation in secure facilities to prevent their accidental release esp. during research

bio·con·trol \ˌbī-ō-kən-ˈtrōl\ *n* (1967) : BIOLOGICAL CONTROL

bio·con·ver·sion \ˌbī-(ˌ)ō-kən-ˈvər-zhən, -shən\ *n* (1960) : the conversion of organic materials (as wastes) into an energy source (as methane) by processes (as fermentation) involving living organisms

bio·de·fense \ˌbī-(ˌ)ō-di-ˈfen(t)s\ *n, often attrib* (1987) : the means or methods of preventing, detecting, or managing an attack involving biological weapons

bio·de·grad·able \-di-ˈgrā-də-bəl\ *adj* (1961) : capable of being broken down esp. into innocuous products by the action of living things (as microorganisms) ⟨~ trash bags⟩ — **bio·de·grad·abil·i·ty** \-ˌgrā-də-ˈbi-lə-tē\ *n* — **biodegradable** *n* — **bio·deg·ra·da·tion** \-ˌde-grə-ˈdā-shən\ *n* — **bio·de·grade** \-di-ˈgrād\ *vb*

bio·de·te·ri·o·ra·tion \-di-ˌtir-ē-ə-ˈrā-shən\ *n* (1953) : the breakdown of materials by microbial action

bio·die·sel \-ˈdē-zəl, -səl\ *n* (1986) : a fuel that is similar to diesel fuel and is derived from usu. vegetable sources (as soybean oil)

bio·di·ver·si·ty \-də-ˈvər-sə-tē, -dī-\ *n* (1985) : biological diversity in an environment as indicated by numbers of different species of plants and animals — **bio·di·verse** \-dī-ˈvərs, -də-\ *adj*

bio·dy·nam·ic \-di-ˈna-mik, -dī-\ *adj* (1939) : of or relating to a system of farming that uses only organic materials for fertilizing and soil conditioning — **bio·dy·nam·ics** \-miks\ *n pl but sing in constr*

bio·elec·tric \-i-ˈlek-trik\ *also* **bio·elec·tri·cal** \-tri-kəl\ *adj* (1914) : of or relating to electric phenomena in living organisms — **bio·elec·tric·i·ty** \-ˌlek-ˈtri-sə-tē, -ˈtris-tē\ *n*

bio·en·er·get·ics \-ˌe-nər-ˈje-tiks\ *n pl but sing in constr* (1912) **1 :** the biology of energy transformations and energy exchanges (as in photosynthesis) within and between living things and their environments **2 :** a system of physical and psychological therapy that is held to increase well-being by releasing blocked physical and psychic energy — **bio·en·er·get·ic** \-ˈje-tik\ *adj*

bio·en·gi·neer \-ˌen-jə-ˈnir\ *vt* (1951) : to modify or produce by bioengineering ⟨~*ed* insulin⟩ — **bioengineer** *n*

bio·en·gi·neer·ing \-ˌen-jə-ˈnir-iŋ\ *n* (ca. 1954) **1 :** biological or medical application of engineering principles or engineering equipment — called also *biomedical engineering* **2 :** the application of biological techniques (as genetic recombination) to create modified versions of organisms (as crops); *esp* : GENETIC ENGINEERING

bio·equiv·a·lence \-i-ˈkwiv-lən(t)s, -ˈkwi-və-\ *n* (1977) : the property wherein two drugs with identical active ingredients or two different dosage forms of the same drug possess similar bioavailability and produce the same effect at the site of physiological activity — **bio·equiv·a·lent** \-lənt\ *adj*

bio·eth·ics \-ˈe-thiks\ *n pl but sing in constr* (1971) : a discipline dealing with the ethical implications of biological research and applications esp. in medicine — **bio·eth·i·cal** \-ˈe-thi-kəl\ *adj* — **bio·eth·i·cist** \-ˈe-thə-sist\ *n*

bio·feed·back \-ˈfēd-ˌbak\ *n* (1970) : the technique of making unconscious or involuntary bodily processes (as heartbeats or brain waves) perceptible to the senses (as by the use of an oscilloscope) in order to manipulate them by conscious mental control

bio·film \-ˈfilm\ *n* (1981) : a thin usu. resistant layer of microorganisms (as bacteria) that form on and coat various surfaces

bio·fla·vo·noid \-ˈflā-və-ˌnȯid\ *n* (1952) : any of various biologically active flavonoids (as hesperidin and quercetin) derived from plants and found esp. in fruits and vegetables (as citrus fruits)

bio·foul·ing \-ˈfau̇-liŋ\ *n* (1943) : the gradual accumulation of waterborne organisms (as bacteria and protozoa) on the surfaces of engineering structures in water that contributes to corrosion of the structures and to a decrease in the efficiency of moving parts

bio·fu·el \-ˈfyü(-ə)l\ *n* (1970) : a fuel (as wood or ethanol) composed of or produced from biological raw materials — compare FOSSIL FUEL

biog *abbr* biographer; biographical; biography

bio·gas \ˈbī-ō-ˌgas\ *n* (1971) : a mixture of methane and carbon dioxide produced by the bacterial decomposition of organic wastes and used as a fuel

bio·gen·e·sis \ˌbī-ō-ˈje-nə-səs\ *n* [NL] (1870) **1 :** the development of life from preexisting life **2 :** the synthesis of chemical compounds or structures in the living organism — compare BIOSYNTHESIS — **bio·ge·net·ic** \-jə-ˈne-tik\ *adj* — **bio·ge·net·i·cal·ly** \-ti-k(ə-)lē\ *adv*

biogenetic law *n* (1882) : the theory of ontogenetic recapitulation

bio·gen·ic \-ˈje-nik\ *also* **bi·og·e·nous** \bī-ˈä-jə-nəs\ *adj* (1903) : produced by living organisms ⟨~ methane formation⟩

bio·geo·chem·i·cal \-ˌjē-ə-ˈke-mi-kəl\ *n* (1938) : of or relating to the partitioning and cycling of chemical elements and compounds between the living and nonliving parts of an ecosystem — **bio·geo·chem·is·try** \-mə-strē\ *n*

bio·ge·og·ra·phy \-jē-ˈä-grə-fē\ *n* [ISV] (1894) : a science that deals with the geographical distribution of animals and plants — **bio·ge·og·ra·pher** \-grə-fər\ *n* — **bio·geo·graph·ic** \-ˌjē-ə-ˈgra-fik\ *or* **bio·geo·graph·i·cal** \-fi-kəl\ *adj*

bi·og·ra·phee \bī-ˌä-grə-ˈfē *also* bē-\ *n* (1841) : a person about whom a biography is written

bi·og·ra·pher \-ˈä-grə-fər\ *n* (1702) : a writer of a biography

bio·graph·i·cal \ˌbī-ə-ˈgra-fi-kəl\ *also* **bio·graph·ic** \-fik\ *adj* (1714) **1 :** of, relating to, or constituting biography **2 :** consisting of biographies ⟨a ~ dictionary⟩ **3 :** relating to a list briefly identifying persons ⟨~ notes⟩ — **bio·graph·i·cal·ly** \-fi-k(ə-)lē\ *adv*

bi·og·ra·phy \bī-ˈä-grə-fē *also* bē-\ *n, pl* **-phies** [LGk *biographia,* fr. Gk *bi-* + *-graphia* -graphy] (1683) **1 :** a usu. written history of a person's life **2 :** biographical writings as a whole **3 :** an account of the life of something (as an animal, a coin, or a building)

bio·haz·ard \ˈbī-ō-ˌha-zərd\ *n* (1967) : a biological agent or condition that is a hazard to humans or the environment; *also* : a hazard posed by such an agent or condition — **bio·haz·ard·ous** \ˌbī-ō-ˈha-zər-dəs\ *adj*

bio·iden·ti·cal \ˌbī-ō-ī-ˈden-ti-kəl\ *adj* (1997) : having the same molecular structure as a substance produced in the body ⟨~ estrogens⟩

bio·in·for·mat·ics \ˌbī-ō-in-fər-ˈma-tiks\ *n pl but sing in constr* (1988) : the collection, classification, storage, and analysis of biochemical and biological information using computers esp. as applied to molecular genetics and genomics — **bio·in·for·mat·ic** \-tik\ *adj*

biol *abbr* biologic; biological; biologist; biology

bi·o·log·ic \ˌbī-ə-ˈlä-jik\ *or* **bi·o·log·i·cal** \-ji-kəl\ *n* (1921) : a biological product (as a vaccine or blood serum) used in medicine

biological *also* **biologic** *adj* (1847) **1 :** of or relating to biology or to life and living processes **2 :** used in or produced by applied biology **3 :** connected by direct genetic relationship rather than by adoption or marriage ⟨her ~ father⟩ — **bi·o·log·i·cal·ly** \-ji-k(ə-)lē\ *adv*

biological clock *n* (1955) : an inherent timing mechanism in a living system that is inferred to exist in order to explain the timing or periodicity of various behaviors and physiological states and processes

biological control *n* (1921) **1 :** the reduction in numbers or elimination of pest organisms by interference with their ecology (as by the in-

troduction of parasites or diseases) **2 :** an agent used in biological control
biological oxygen demand *n* (1930) : BIOCHEMICAL OXYGEN DEMAND
biological warfare *n* (1946) : warfare involving the use of biological weapons; *also* : warfare involving the use of herbicides
biological weapon *n* (1947) : a harmful biological agent (as a pathogenic microorganism or a neurotoxin) used as a weapon to cause death or disease usu. on a large scale
bi·ol·o·gism \bī-ˈä-lə-ˌji-zəm\ *n* (1920) : the use of biological explanations in the analysis of social situations — **bi·ol·o·gis·tic** \-ˌä-lə-ˈjis-tik\ *adj*
bi·ol·o·gy \bī-ˈä-lə-jē\ *n* [G *Biologie,* fr. *bi-* + *-logie* -logy] (1819) **1 :** a branch of knowledge that deals with living organisms and vital processes **2 a :** the plant and animal life of a region or environment **b :** the life processes esp. of an organism or group; *broadly* : ECOLOGY — **bi·ol·o·gist** \-jist\ *n*
bio·lu·mi·nes·cence \ˌbī-ō-ˌlü-mə-ˈne-sᵊn(t)s\ *n* [ISV] (1916) : the emission of light from living organisms; *also* : the light so produced — **bio·lu·mi·nes·cent** \-sᵊnt\ *adj*
bio·mark·er \ˈbī-ō-ˌmär-kər\ *n* (1982) : a distinctive biological or biologically derived indicator (as a metabolite) of a process, event, or condition (as aging, disease, or oil formation)
bio·mass \ˈbī-ō-ˌmas\ *n* (1934) **1 :** the amount of living matter (as in a unit area or volume of habitat) **2 :** plant materials and animal waste used esp. as a source of fuel
bio·ma·te·ri·al \ˌbī-ō-mə-ˈtir-ē-əl\ *n* (1966) : a natural or synthetic material (as a metal or polymer) that is suitable for introduction into living tissue esp. as part of a medical device (as an artificial joint)
bio·math·e·mat·ics \-ˌma-thə-ˈma-tiks, -math-ˈma-\ *n pl but usu sing in constr* (1923) : mathematics of special use in biology and medicine — **bio·math·e·mat·i·cal** \-ti-kəl\ *adj* — **bio·math·e·ma·ti·cian** \-ˌmath-mə-ˈti-shən, -ˌma-thə-\ *n*
bi·ome \ˈbī-ˌōm\ *n* [²*bi-* + *-ome*] (1916) : a major ecological community type (as tropical rain forest, grassland, or desert)
bio·me·chan·ics \ˈbī-ō-mə-ˈka-niks\ *n pl but sing or pl in constr* (ca. 1933) : the mechanics of biological and esp. muscular activity (as in locomotion or exercise); *also* : the scientific study of this — **bio·me·chan·i·cal** \-ni-kəl\ *adj* — **bio·me·chan·i·cal·ly** \-ni-k(ə-)lē\ *adv*
bio·med·i·cal \ˌbī-ō-ˈme-di-kəl\ *adj* (1926) **1 :** of or relating to biomedicine **2 :** of, relating to, or involving biological, medical, and physical science
biomedical engineering *n* (1961) : BIOENGINEERING 1 — **biomedical engineer** *n*
bio·med·i·cine \-ˈme-də-sən, *Brit usu* -ˈmed-sən\ *n* (1923) : medicine based on the application of the principles of the natural sciences and esp. biology and biochemistry
bio·me·te·o·rol·o·gy \-ˌmē-tē-ə-ˈrä-lə-jē\ *n* (1946) : a science that deals with the relationship between living things and atmospheric phenomena — **bio·me·te·o·ro·log·i·cal** \-rə-ˈlä-ji-kəl\ *adj* — **bio·me·te·o·rol·o·gist** \-ˈrä-lə-jist\ *n*
bio·met·ric \ˌbī-ō-ˈme-trik\ *also* **bio·met·ri·cal** \-tri-kəl\ *adj* (1901) : of, relating to, or utilizing biometrics or biometry
biometrics \-ˈme-triks\ *n pl but sing or pl in constr* (1902) **1 :** BIOMETRY **2 :** the measurement and analysis of unique physical or behavioral characteristics (as fingerprint or voice patterns) esp. as a means of verifying personal identity
bi·om·e·try \bī-ˈä-mə-trē\ *n* [ISV] (1901) : the statistical analysis of biological observations and phenomena — **bio·me·tri·cian** \ˌbī-ō-me-ˈtri-shən\ *n*
bio·mi·met·ics \ˌbī-ō-mə-ˈme-tiks, -mī-\ *n pl but sing in constr* (1974) : the study of the formation, structure, or function of biologically produced substances and materials (as enzymes or silk) and biological mechanisms and processes (as protein synthesis or photosynthesis) esp. for the purpose of synthesizing similar products by artificial mechanisms which mimic natural ones — **bio·mi·met·ic** \-tik\ *adj*
bio·min·er·al·i·za·tion \-ˌmin-rə-lə-ˈzā-shən, -ˌmi-nə-\ *n* (1973) : the formation or accumulation of minerals by organisms esp. into biological tissues or structures (as bones, teeth, and shells) — **bio·min·er·al** \-ˈmin-rəl, -ˈmi-nə-\ *n*
bio·mol·e·cule \ˌbī-ō-ˈmä-li-ˌkyül\ *n* (1901) : an organic molecule and esp. a macromolecule (as a protein or nucleic acid) in living organisms — **bio·mo·lec·u·lar** \-mə-ˈle-kyə-lər\ *adj*
bio·mor·phic \ˌbī-ō-ˈmȯr-fik\ *adj* (1895) : resembling or suggesting the forms of living organisms ⟨∼ sculptures⟩ ⟨∼ images⟩
bi·on·ic \bī-ˈä-nik\ *adj* (1963) **1 :** of or relating to bionics **2 :** having normal biological capability or performance enhanced by or as if by electronic or electromechanical devices
bi·on·ics \bī-ˈä-niks\ *n pl but sing or pl in constr* [²*bi-* + *-onics* (as in *electronics*)] (1960) : a science concerned with the application of data about the functioning of biological systems to the solution of engineering problems
bi·o·nom·ics \ˌbī-ə-ˈnä-miks\ *n pl but sing or pl in constr* [*bionomic,* adj., prob. fr. F *bionomique,* fr. *bionomie* ecology, fr. *bi-* + *-nomie* -nomy] (1888) : ECOLOGY — **bi·o·nom·ic** \-mik\ *adj*
bio·pes·ti·cide \ˌbī-ō-ˈpes-tə-ˌsīd\ *n* (1980) : a pesticide consisting of naturally occurring or genetically engineered microorganisms (as bacteria)
bio·phar·ma·ceu·ti·cal \ˌbī-ō-ˌfär-mə-ˈsü-ti-kəl\ *n* (1985) : a pharmaceutical derived from biological sources and esp. one produced by biotechnology — **biopharmaceutical** *adj*
bio·phil·ia \ˌbī-ō-ˈfi-lē-ə, -ˈfēl-yə\ *n* [NL] (1979) : a hypothetical human tendency to interact or be closely associated with other forms of life in nature
bio·phys·ics \ˌbī-ō-ˈfi-ziks\ *n pl but sing or pl in constr* (1892) : a branch of science concerned with the application of physical principles and methods to biological problems — **bio·phys·i·cal** \-zi-kəl\ *adj* — **bio·phys·i·cist** \-ˈfi-zə-sist, -ˈfiz-sist\ *n*
bio·pic \ˈbī-(ˌ)ō-ˌpik\ *n* [²*bi-* + ¹*pic*] (1951) : a biographical movie
bio·poly·mer \ˌbī-ō-ˈpä-lə-mər\ *n* (1961) : a polymeric substance (as a protein or polysaccharide) formed in a biological system
bio·pros·pect \-ˈprä-ˌspekt\ *vt* (1996) : to search for substances that are produced by living organisms and may be of medicinal or commercial value — **bio·pros·pec·tor** \-ˌspek-tər\ *n*
bi·op·sy \ˈbī-ˌäp-sē\ *n, pl* **-sies** [ISV ²*bi-* + *-opsy* (as in *autopsy*)] (1895) : the removal and examination of tissue, cells, or fluids from the living body — **biopsy** *vt*
bio·psy·chol·o·gy \ˌbī-ō-sī-ˈkä-lə-jē\ *n* (1909) : PSYCHOBIOLOGY — **bio·psy·cho·log·i·cal** \-ˌsī-kə-ˈlä-ji-kəl\ *adj* — **bio·psy·chol·o·gist** \-sī-ˈkä-lə-jist\ *n*
bio·re·ac·tor \ˌbī-ō-rē-ˈak-tər\ *n* (1974) : a device or apparatus in which living organisms and esp. bacteria synthesize useful substances (as interferon) or break down harmful ones (as in sewage)
bio·re·gion \ˈbī-ō-ˌrē-jən\ *n* (1978) : a region whose limits are naturally defined by topographic and biological features (as mountain ranges and ecosystems) — **bio·re·gion·al** \ˌbī-ō-ˈrēj-nəl, -ˈrē-jə-nᵊl\ *adj*
bio·re·gion·al·ism \ˌbī-ō-ˈrēj-nə-ˌli-zəm, -ˈrē-jə-nᵊl-i-\ *n* (1981) : an environmentalist movement to make political boundaries coincide with bioregions — **bio·re·gion·al·ist** \-list, -ist\ *n or adj*
bio·re·me·di·a·tion \-ri-ˌmē-dē-ˈā-shən\ *n* (1986) : the treatment of pollutants or waste (as in an oil spill, contaminated groundwater, or an industrial process) by the use of microorganisms (as bacteria) that break down the undesirable substances
bio·rhythm \ˈbī-ō-ˌri-thəm\ *n* (1960) : an innately determined rhythmic biological process or function (as sleep behavior); *also* : the internal mechanism that determines such a process or function — **bio·rhyth·mic** \-ˈrith-mik\ *adj*
BIOS *abbr* Basic Input/Output System
bio·safe·ty \ˌbī-ō-ˈsāf-tē\ *n* (1977) : safety with respect to the effects of biological research on humans and the environment
bio·sci·ence \-ˈsī-ən(t)s\ *n* (1941) : BIOLOGY 1; *also* : LIFE SCIENCE — **bio·sci·en·tif·ic** \-ˌsī-ən-ˈti-fik\ *adj* — **bio·sci·en·tist** \-ˈsī-ən-tist\ *n*
bio·se·cu·ri·ty \ˌbī-(ˌ)ō-si-ˈkyu̇r-ə-tē\ *n* (1985) : security from exposure to harmful biological agents; *also* : measures taken to ensure this security
bio·sen·sor \-ˈsen-ˌsȯr, -ˈsen(t)-sər\ *n* (1962) : a device that monitors and transmits information about a life process; *esp* : a device consisting of a biological component (as an enzyme or bacterium) that reacts with a target substance and a signal-generating electrochemical component that detects the resulting products or by-products
-biosis *n comb form, pl* **-bioses** [NL, fr. Gk *biōsis,* fr. *bioun* to live, fr. *bios* life — more at QUICK] : mode of life ⟨para*biosis*⟩
bio·so·cial \ˌbī-ō-ˈsō-shəl\ *adj* (1897) : of, relating to, or concerned with the interaction of the biological aspects and social relationships of living organisms ⟨∼ science⟩ — **bio·so·cial·ly** \-ˈsōsh-lē, -ˈsō-shə-\ *adv*
bio·sol·id \ˈbī-ō-ˌsä-ləd\ *n* (1990) : solid organic matter recovered from a sewage treatment process and used esp. as fertilizer — usu. used in pl.
bio·sphere \ˈbī-ə-ˌsfir\ *n* (1899) **1 :** the part of the world in which life can exist **2 :** living organisms together with their environment — **bio·spher·ic** \ˌbī-ə-ˈsfir-ik, -ˈsfer-, -ˈsfe-rik\ *adj*
bio·sta·tis·tics \ˌbī-ō-stə-ˈtis-tiks\ *n pl but sing in constr* (1949) : statistics applied to the analysis of biological data — **bio·sta·tis·ti·cal** \-ti-kəl\ *adj* — **bio·stat·is·ti·cian** \-ˌsta-tə-ˈsti-shən\ *n*
bio·stra·tig·ra·phy \-strə-ˈti-grə-fē\ *n* [ISV] (1926) **1 :** the identification of fossils found within sedimentary rock strata as a method of determining the relative geologic age of the rock; *also* : the branch of paleontology involving such identification **2 :** the arrangement of fossils in rock strata — **bio·strat·i·graph·ic** \-ˌstra-tə-ˈgra-fik\ *adj*
bio·syn·the·sis \-ˈsin(t)-thə-səs\ *n* [NL] (1930) : the production of a chemical compound by a living organism — **bio·syn·thet·ic** \-sin-ˈthe-tik\ *adj* — **bio·syn·thet·i·cal·ly** \-ti-k(ə-)lē\ *adv*
bio·sys·te·mat·ics \-ˌsis-tə-ˈma-tiks\ *n pl but sing or pl in constr* (1945) : taxonomy esp. as based on cytogenetics and genetics — **bio·sys·te·mat·ic** \-tik\ *adj* — **bio·sys·tem·atist** \-ˈsis-tə-mə-tist, -sis-ˈte-mə-\ *n*
bi·o·ta \bī-ˈō-tə\ *n* [NL, fr. Gk *biotē* life; akin to Gk *bios*] (1901) : the flora and fauna of a region
bio·tech \ˈbī-ō-ˌtek\ *n* (1974) : BIOTECHNOLOGY 1
bio·tech·ni·cal \ˌbī-ō-ˈtek-ni-kəl\ *adj* (1938) : of or relating to biotechnology
bio·tech·nol·o·gy \ˌbī-ō-tek-ˈnä-lə-jē\ *n* (1941) **1 :** the manipulation (as through genetic engineering) of living organisms or their components to produce useful usu. commercial products (as pest resistant crops, new bacterial strains, or novel pharmaceuticals); *also* : any of various applications of biological science used in such manipulation **2 :** ERGONOMICS 1 — **bio·tech·no·log·i·cal** \-ˌtek-nə-ˈlä-ji-kəl\ *adj* — **bio·tech·no·log·i·cal·ly** \-ji-k(ə-)lē\ *adv* — **bio·tech·nol·o·gist** \-ˈnä-lə-jist\ *n*
bio·te·lem·e·try \-tə-ˈle-mə-trē\ *n* (1963) : the remote detection and measurement of a human or animal function, activity, or condition (as heart rate or body temperature) — **bio·tel·e·met·ric** \-ˌte-lə-ˈme-trik\ *adj*
bio·ter·ror \-ˈter-ər, -ˈte-rər\ *n, often attrib* (1996) : BIOTERRORISM
bio·ter·ror·ism \-ˈter-ər-ˌi-zəm, -ə-ˌri-\ *n* (1991) : terrorism involving the use of biological weapons — **bio·ter·ror·ist** \-ər-ist, -ə-rist\ *adj or n*
bi·ot·ic \bī-ˈä-tik\ *adj* [Gk *biōtikos,* fr. *bioun*] (1868) : of, relating to, or caused by living organisms ⟨∼ diversity⟩
-biotic *adj comb form* [prob. fr. NL *-bioticus,* fr. Gk *biōtikos*] : having a (specified) mode of life ⟨endo*biotic*⟩
biotic potential *n* (1928) : the inherent capacity of an organism or species to reproduce and survive
bi·o·tin \ˈbī-ə-tən\ *n* [ISV, fr. Gk *biotos* life, sustenance; akin to Gk *bios*] (1936) : a colorless crystalline growth vitamin $C_{10}H_{16}N_2O_3S$ of the vitamin B complex found esp. in yeast, liver, and egg yolk
bi·o·tite \ˈbī-ə-ˌtīt\ *n* [G *Biotit,* fr. Jean B. *Biot* †1862 Fr. mathematician] (1862) : a generally black or dark green form of mica that is a constituent of crystalline rocks and consists of a silicate of iron, magnesium, potassium, and aluminum — **bi·o·tit·ic** \ˌbī-ə-ˈti-tik\ *adj*
bio·tope \ˈbī-ə-ˌtōp\ *n* [²*bi-* + Gk *topos* place] (1927) : a region uniform in environmental conditions and in its populations of animals and plants for which it is the habitat
bio·tox·in \ˈbī-ō-ˌtäk-sən\ *n* (1927) : a toxic substance of biological origin
bio·trans·for·ma·tion \ˈbī-ō-ˌtran(t)s-fər-ˈmā-shən, -ˌfȯr-\ *n* (1955) : the transformation of chemical compounds within a living system
bio·tur·ba·tion \ˌbī-ō-tər-ˈbā-shən\ *n* [ISV] (1967) : the restructuring of sedimentary deposits (as in a lake bottom or seabed) by moving organisms (as worms and burrowing clams) — **bio·tur·bat·ed** \-ˈbā-təd\ *adj*

bio·type \-ˌtīp\ *n* [ISV] (1906) : the organisms sharing a specified genotype; *also* : the genotype shared or its distinguishing peculiarity — **bio·typ·ic** \ˌbī-ə-'ti-pik\ *adj*

bio·war·fare \ˌbī-ō-'wȯr-ˌfer\ *n* (ca. 1966) : BIOLOGICAL WARFARE

bio·waste \'bī-ō-ˌwāst\ *n* (1968) : waste (as manure, sawdust, or food scraps) that is composed chiefly of organic matter

bio·weap·on \'bī-ō-ˌwe-pən\ *n* (1973) : BIOLOGICAL WEAPON

bi·pa·ren·tal \ˌbī-pə-'ren-t³l\ *adj* (1900) : of, relating to, involving, or derived from two parents — **bi·pa·ren·tal·ly** \-t³l-ē\ *adv*

bi·par·ti·san \(ˌ)bī-'pär-tə-zən, -sən, -ˌzan, *chiefly Brit* ˌbī-ˌpär-tə-'zan\ *adj* (1895) : of, relating to, or involving members of two parties; *specif* : marked by or involving cooperation, agreement, and compromise between two major political parties — **bi·par·ti·san·ism** \-zə-ˌni-zəm, -sə-\ *n* — **bi·par·ti·san·ship** \-zən-ˌship, -sən-\ *n*

bi·par·tite \(ˌ)bī-'pär-ˌtīt\ *adj* [L *bipartitus*, pp. of *bipartire* to divide in two, fr. *bi-* + *partire* to divide, fr. *part-, pars* part] (1574) **1 a** : being in two parts **b** : having a correspondent part for each of two parties **c** : shared by two **2** : divided into two parts almost to the base ⟨a ~ leaf⟩ — **bi·par·tite·ly** *adv* — **bi·par·ti·tion** \ˌbī-(ˌ)pär-'ti-shən\ *n*

bi·ped \'bī-ˌped\ *n* [L *biped-, bipes*, fr. *bi-* + *ped-, pes* foot — more at FOOT] (1646) : a two-footed animal — **bi·ped·al** \(ˌ)bī-'pe-d³l\ *adj* — **bi·ped·al·ly** \-ē\ *adv*

bi·ped·al·ism \(ˌ)bī-'pe-d³l-ˌi-zəm\ *n* (1907) : the condition of having two feet or of using only two feet for locomotion

bi·pe·dal·i·ty \ˌbī-pə-'da-lə-tē\ *n* (1847) : BIPEDALISM

bi·phas·ic \ˌbī-'fā-zik\ *adj* (ca. 1909) : having two phases

bi·phe·nyl \(ˌ)bī-'fe-n³l, -'fē-\ *n* [ISV] (ca. 1923) : a white crystalline hydrocarbon C₆H₅·C₆H₅ used esp. as a heat-transfer medium and in organic synthesis; *also* : a derivative of biphenyl

bi·pin·nate \ˌbī-ˌpi-ˌnāt\ *adj* (1760) : twice pinnate — **bi·pin·nate·ly** *adv*

bi·plane \'bī-ˌplān\ *n* (1874) : an aircraft with two main supporting surfaces usu. placed one above the other

bi·pod \'bī-ˌpäd\ *n* [*bi-* + *-pod* (as in *tripod*)] (1922) : a 2-legged support

bi·po·lar \(ˌ)bī-'pō-lər\ *adj* (1810) **1** : having or marked by two mutually repellent forces or diametrically opposed natures or views **2 a** : having or involving the use of two poles or polarities **b** : relating to, being, or using a transistor in which both electrons and holes are utilized as charge carriers **3** : relating to, associated with, or occurring in both polar regions ⟨~ species of birds⟩ **4** : being, characteristic of, or affected with a bipolar disorder — **bi·po·lar·i·ty** \ˌbī-pō-'ler-ə-tē, -'la-rə-\ *n* — **bi·po·lar·i·za·tion** \(ˌ)bī-ˌpō-lə-rə-'zā-shən\ *n* — **bi·po·lar·ize** \(ˌ)bī-'pō-lə-ˌrīz\ *vt*

bipolar disorder *n* (1980) : any of several psychological disorders of mood characterized usu. by alternating episodes of depression and mania — called also *manic depression, manic-depressive illness*

bi·pro·pel·lant \ˌbī-prə-'pe-lənt\ *n* (1947) : a rocket propellant consisting of separate fuel and oxidizer that come together only in a combustion chamber

bi·pyr·a·mid \(ˌ)bī-'pir-ə-mid\ *n* (1897) : a crystal consisting of two identical pyramids base to base — **bi·py·ra·mi·dal** \-pə-'ra-mə-d³l\ *adj*

bi·qua·drat·ic \ˌbī-kwä-'dra-tik\ *adj or n* (1668) : QUARTIC

bi·ra·cial \(ˌ)bī-'rā-shəl\ *adj* (1922) : of, relating to, or involving members of two races — **bi·ra·cial·ism** \-shə-ˌli-zəm\ *n*

bi·ra·di·al \(ˌ)bī-'rā-dē-əl\ *adj* (ca. 1909) : having both bilateral and radial symmetry

bi·rad·i·cal \-'ra-di-kəl\ *n* (1943) : a free radical or compound with two unpaired electrons

bi·ra·mous \(ˌ)bī-'rā-məs\ *adj* [*bi-* + L *ramus* branch] (1877) : having two branches

¹birch \'bərch\ *n* [ME, fr. OE *beorc*; akin to OHG *birka* birch, OE *beorht* bright, and prob. to L *fraxinus* ash tree — more at BRIGHT] (bef. 12c) **1** : any of a genus (*Betula* of the family Betulaceae, the birch family) of monoecious deciduous trees or shrubs having simple petioled leaves and typically a layered membranous outer bark that peels readily **2** : the hard pale close-grained wood of a birch **3** : a birch rod or bundle of twigs for flogging — **birch** *or* **birch·en** \'bər-chən\ *adj*

²birch *vt* (1830) : to beat with or as if with a birch : WHIP

Birch·er \'bər-chər\ *n* (1961) : a member or adherent of the John Birch Society — **Birch·ism** \'bər-ˌchi-zəm\ *n* — **Birch·ist** \-chist\ *or* **Birch·ite** \-ˌchīt\ *n or adj*

¹bird \'bərd\ *n, often attrib* [ME *brid, bird*, fr. OE *bridd*] (bef. 12c) **1** *archaic* : the young of a feathered vertebrate **2** : any of a class (Aves) of warm-blooded vertebrates distinguished by having the body more or less completely covered with feathers and the forelimbs modified as wings **3** : a game bird **4** : CLAY PIGEON **5** : FELLOW **b** : a peculiar person **c** *chiefly Brit* : GIRL **6** : SHUTTLECOCK **7** *chiefly Brit* **a** : a hissing or jeering sound expressive of disapproval **b** : dismissal from employment **8** : a thin piece of meat rolled up with stuffing and

cooked **9** : a man-made object (as an aircraft, rocket, or satellite) that resembles a bird esp. by flying or being aloft **10** : an obscene gesture of contempt made by pointing the middle finger upward while keeping the other fingers down — usu. used with *the*; called also *finger* **11** : BIRDIE 2 — **bird·like** \-ˌlīk\ *adj* — **for the birds** : WORTHLESS, RIDICULOUS

²bird *vi* (1918) : to observe or identify wild birds in their habitats

bird·bath \'bərd-ˌbath, -ˌbäth\ *n* (1895) : a usu. ornamental basin set up for birds to bathe in

bird·brain \-ˌbrān\ *n* (1933) **1** : a stupid person **2** : SCATTERBRAIN — **bird·brained** \-ˌbrānd\ *adj*

bird·cage \-ˌkāj\ *n* (15c) : a cage for confining birds

bird·call \-ˌkȯl\ *n* (ca. 1625) **1** : a device for imitating the cry of a bird **2** : the note or cry of a bird; *also* : a sound imitative of it

bird colonel *n* [fr. the eagle serving as insignia for this rank] (ca. 1946) *slang* : COLONEL 1a

bird–dog \'bərd-ˌdȯg\ *vi* (1943) : to watch closely ~ *vt* : to seek out : FOLLOW, DETECT

bird dog *n* (ca. 1854) **1** : a gundog trained to hunt or retrieve birds **2 a** : one (as a canvasser or talent scout) who seeks out something for another **3** : one who steals another's date

bird–dog·ging \-ˌdȯ-giŋ\ *n* (ca. 1941) **1** : the stealing of another's date (as at a party) **2** : the action of one that bird-dogs

bird·er \'bər-dər\ *n* (15c) **1** : a catcher or hunter of birds esp. for market **2** : a person who birds

bird flu *n* (1995) : AVIAN INFLUENZA; *specif* : severe often fatal influenza A caused by strains of a subtype (H5N1) of the causative orthomyxovirus that have produced epidemics in domestic birds esp. in Asia with sporadic associated human infections

bird·house \'bərd-ˌhau̇s\ *n* (1858) : an artificial nesting site for birds; *also* : AVIARY

¹bird·ie \'bər-dē\ *n* (1768) **1** : a little bird **2** : a golf score of one stroke less than par on a hole — compare EAGLE

²birdie *vt* **bird·ied; bird·ie·ing** (1921) : to score a birdie on

bird·life \'bərd-ˌlīf\ *n* (1860) : AVIFAUNA

bird·lime \'bərd-ˌlīm\ *n* (15c) **1** : a sticky substance usu. made from the bark of a holly (*Ilex aquifolium*) that is smeared on twigs to snare small birds **2** : something that ensnares — **birdlime** *vt*

bird louse *n* (1826) : BITING LOUSE

bird·man \'bərd-mən, *esp for 1 also* -ˌman\ *n* (1697) **1** : a person who deals with birds **2** : a person who flies (as in an aircraft)

bird–of–paradise *n* (ca. 1884) : an ornamental plant (*Strelitzia reginae* of the family Strelitziaceae) native to southern Africa that has scapes terminating in a horizontal bract from which emerges an upright flower having three orange or yellow sepals and three irregular blue petals

bird of paradise (1595) : any of numerous brilliantly colored plumed oscine birds (family Paradisaeidae) chiefly of New Guinea and neighboring islands

bird of passage (1678) **1** : a migratory bird **2** : a person who leads a wandering or unsettled life

bird of prey (14c) : a carnivorous bird (as a hawk, falcon, or vulture) that feeds wholly or chiefly on meat taken by hunting or on carrion

bird pepper *n* (1696) : CHILTEPIN

bird·seed \'bərd-ˌsēd\ *n* (1840) : a mixture of seeds (as of hemp, millet, and sunflowers) used for feeding caged and wild birds

¹bird's–eye \'bərdz-ˌī\ *n* (1597) **1** : any of numerous plants with small bright-colored flowers; *esp* : a speedwell (*Veronica chamaedrys*) **2 a** : an allover pattern for textiles consisting of a small diamond with a center dot **b** : a fabric woven with this pattern **3** : a small spot in wood surrounded with an ellipse of concentric fibers

²bird's–eye *adj* (1665) **1** : marked with spots resembling birds' eyes **2** : having or involving a bird's-eye view ⟨~ perspective⟩

bird's–eye maple *n* (1793) : wood of the sugar maple having a wavy grain that causes markings resembling eyes

bird's–eye view *n* (1762) **1** : a view from a high angle as if seen by a bird in flight **2** : an overall or cursory look at something

bird's–foot trefoil \'bərdz-ˌfut-\ *n* (1833) : a yellow-flowered European herb (*Lotus corniculatus*) of the legume family that has claw-shaped pods and is widely grown for forage and for erosion control

bird's–foot violet *n* (1839) : a common violet (*Viola pedata*) of the eastern U.S. with deeply cleft leaves and pale blue to purple flowers

bird's–nest fern \'bərdz-ˌnest-\ *n* (1858) : a large epiphytic spleenwort (*Asplenium nidus*) of tropical Asia and Polynesia that has large lance-shaped leaves and is often grown as a houseplant

bird's nest soup *n* (1818) : a soup made with the nest of a swiftlet (esp. *Collocalia fuciphaga*) that builds it using a glutinous secretion from its salivary glands

bird·song \'bərd-ˌsȯŋ\ *n* (1896) : the song of one or more birds

bird–watch·er \'bərd-ˌwä-chər\ *n* (1891) : BIRDER 2 — **bird–watch** \-ˌwäch\ *vi*

bi·re·frin·gence \ˌbī-ri-'frin-jən(t)s\ *n* [ISV ¹*bi-* + *refringent* refracting, fr. L *refringent-, refringens,* prp. of *refringere* to break up — more at REFRACT] (1898) : the refraction of light in an anisotropic material (as calcite) in two slightly different directions to form two rays — **bi·re·frin·gent** \-jənt\ *adj*

bi·reme \'bī-ˌrēm\ *n* [L *biremis,* fr. *bi-* + *remus* oar — more at ROW] (1662) : a galley with two banks of oars used esp. by the ancient Greeks and Phoenicians

bi·ret·ta \bə-'re-tə\ *n* [It *berretta,* fr. Old Occitan *berret* cap, fr. ML *birretum,* fr. LL *birrus* cloak with a hood, perh. of Celt origin; akin to MIr *berr* short] (1598) : a square cap with three ridges on top worn by clergymen esp. of the Roman Catholic Church

birk \'birk\ *n* [ME *birch, birk*] (14c) *chiefly Scot* : BIRCH

birk·ie \'bir-kē, 'bər-\ *n* [origin unknown] (1724) **1** *Scot* : a lively smart assertive person **2** *Scot* : FELLOW, BOY

¹birl \'bər(-ə)l, *Scot also* 'bir(-ə)l\ *vi* [ME, fr. OE *byrlian;* prob. akin to OE *beran* to carry — more at BEAR] (ca. 1585) *chiefly Scot* : CAROUSE

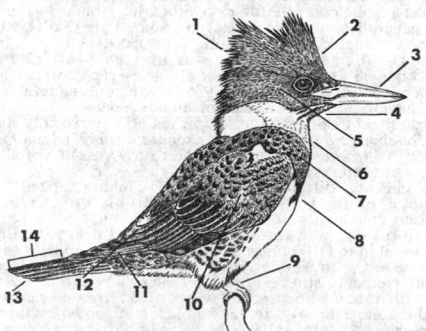

bird 2 (kingfisher): *1* crest, *2* crown, *3* bill, *4* throat, *5* auricular region, *6* breast, *7* scapulars, *8* abdomen, *9* tarsus, *10* upper wing coverts, *11* primaries, *12* secondaries, *13* rectrix, *14* tail

[2]**birl** *vb* [perh. imit.] *vt* (1724) **1 :** SPIN **2 :** to cause (a floating log) to rotate by treading ~ *vi* **:** to progress by whirling — **birl·er** \ˈbər-lər, ˈbir-\ *n*

Bir·man \ˈbər-mən\ *n* [var. of *Burman*] (1973) **:** a long-haired domestic cat of a breed originating in Burma (Myanmar) and resembling the Siamese in eye color and coat pattern but much stockier in build with paws symmetrically marked with white

Bi·ro \ˈbī-(ˌ)rō\ *trademark* — used for a ballpoint pen

birr \ˈbər, ˈbir\ *n, pl* **birr** [Amharic *bərr,* lit., silver] (ca. 1978) — see MONEY table

birse \ˈbirs, ˈbərs\ *n* [ME **birst,* fr. OE *byrst* — more at BRISTLE] (bef. 12c) **1** *chiefly Scot* **:** a bristle or tuft of bristles **2** *chiefly Scot* **:** ANGER

[1]**birth** \ˈbərth\ *n, often attrib* [ME, fr. ON *byrth;* akin to OE *beran*] (13c) **1 a :** the emergence of a new individual from the body of its parent **b :** the act or process of bringing forth young from the womb **2 :** a state resulting from being born esp. at a particular time or place ⟨a Southerner by ~⟩ **3 a :** LINEAGE, EXTRACTION **b :** high or noble birth **4 a** *archaic* **:** one that is born **b :** BEGINNING, START

[2]**birth** *vt* (1855) **1** *chiefly dial* **:** to bring forth **2 a :** to give rise to **:** ORIGINATE **b :** to give birth to ~ *vi* **:** to bring forth or be brought forth as a child or young

[3]**birth** *adj* (1975) **:** BIOLOGICAL 3 ⟨his ~ mother⟩

birth canal *n* (1927) **:** the channel formed by the cervix, vagina, and vulva through which the fetus passes during birth

birth certificate *n* (1860) **:** a copy of an official record of a person's date and place of birth and parentage

birth control *n* (1914) **1 :** control of the number of children born esp. by preventing or lessening the frequency of conception **:** CONTRACEPTION **2 :** contraceptive devices or preparations

birth control pill *n* (1966) **:** any of various preparations that usu. contain both a progestin (as norethindrone) and an estrogen (as ethinyl estradiol), are taken orally esp. on a daily basis, and act as contraceptives typically preventing ovulation by suppressing secretion of gonadotropins (as luteinizing hormone) — called also *oral contraceptive*

birth·day \ˈbərth-ˌdā\ *n* (14c) **1 a :** the day of a person's birth **b :** a day of origin **2 :** an anniversary of a birth ⟨her 21st ~⟩

birthday suit *n* (1753) **:** unclothed skin **:** NAKEDNESS

birth defect *n* (1971) **:** a physical or biochemical defect that is present at birth and may be inherited or environmentally induced

birthing room *n* (1978) **:** a comfortably furnished hospital room where both labor and delivery take place and in which the baby usu. remains during the hospital stay

birth·mark \ˈbərth-ˌmärk\ *n* (1580) **:** an unusual mark or blemish on the skin at birth **:** NEVUS

birth pang *n* (1721) **1 :** one of the regularly recurrent pains that are characteristic of childbirth — usu. used in pl. **2** *pl* **:** disorder and distress incident esp. to a major social change

birth·place \ˈbərth-ˌplās\ *n* (1607) **:** place of birth or origin

birth·rate \ˈbərth-ˌrāt\ *n* (1859) **:** the ratio between births and individuals in a specified population and time

birth·right \ˈbərth-ˌrīt\ *n* (1530) **:** a right, privilege, or possession to which a person is entitled by birth

birth·root \ˈbərth-ˌrüt, -ˌru̇t\ *n* (1822) **:** any of several trilliums with astringent roots used in folk medicine

birth·stone \ˈbərth-ˌstōn\ *n* (1907) **:** a gemstone associated symbolically with the month of one's birth

birth·wort \-ˌwərt, -ˌwȯrt\ *n* (1551) **:** any of several herbs or woody vines (genus *Aristolochia* of the family Aristolochiaceae, the birthwort family) with aromatic roots used in folk medicine to aid childbirth

bis \ˈbis\ *adv* [L, fr. OL *dvis;* akin to OHG *zwiro* twice, L *duo* two — more at TWO] (1609) **1 :** AGAIN — used in music as a direction to repeat **2 :** TWICE

Bisayan *var of* VISAYAN

bis·cot·to \bi-ˈskät-ō\ *n, pl* **bis·cot·ti** \-ē\ [It, biscuit, cookie, fr. (*pane*) *biscotto,* lit., bread baked twice] (1946) **:** a crisp cookie or biscuit of Italian origin that is flavored usu. with anise and filberts or almonds — usu. used in pl.

bis·cuit \ˈbis-kət\ *n, pl* **biscuits** *also* **biscuit** [ME *bisquite,* fr. AF *besquit,* fr. (*pain*) *besquit* twice-cooked bread] (14c) **1 a :** any of various hard or crisp dry baked products: as (1) *Brit* **:** CRACKER 4 (2) *Brit* **:** COOKIE **b :** a small quick bread made from dough that has been rolled out and cut or dropped from a spoon **2 :** earthenware or porcelain after the first firing and before glazing **3 a :** a light grayish-yellowish brown **b :** a grayish yellow — **bis·cuity** \ˈbis-kə-tē\ *adj*

bi·sect \ˈbī-ˌsekt, bī-ˈ\ *vb* [[1]*bi-* + inter*sect*] *vt* (ca. 1645) **:** to divide into two usu. equal parts ~ *vi* **:** CROSS, INTERSECT — **bi·sec·tion** \ˈbī-ˌsek-shən, bī-ˈ\ *n* — **bi·sec·tion·al** \-shnəl, -shə-nᵊl\ *adj* — **bi·sec·tion·al·ly** *adv*

bi·sec·tor \ˈbī-ˌsek-tər, bī-ˈ\ *n* (1864) **:** one that bisects; *esp* **:** a straight line that bisects an angle or a line segment

bi·sex·u·al \(ˌ)bī-ˈsek-sh(ə-)wəl, -shəl\ *adj* (1824) **1 a :** possessing characters of both sexes **:** HERMAPHRODITIC **b :** of, relating to, or characterized by a tendency to direct sexual desire toward both sexes **2 :** of, relating to, or involving both sexes — **bisexual** *n* — **bi·sex·u·al·i·ty** \ˌbī-ˌsek-shə-ˈwa-lə-tē\ *n* — **bi·sex·u·al·ly** \(ˌ)bī-ˈsek-sh(ə-)wə-lē, -sh(ə-)lē\ *adv*

bish·op \ˈbi-shəp\ *n* [ME *bisshop,* fr. OE *bisceop,* fr. LL *episcopus,* fr. Gk *episkopos,* lit., overseer, fr. *epi-* + *skeptesthai* to look — more at SPY] (bef. 12c) **1 :** one having spiritual or ecclesiastical supervision: as **a :** an Anglican, Eastern Orthodox, or Roman Catholic clergyman ranking above a priest, having authority to ordain and confirm, and typically governing a diocese **b :** any of various Protestant clerical officials who superintend other clergy **c :** a Mormon high priest presiding over a ward or over all other bishops and over the Aaronic priesthood **2 :** either of two pieces of each color in a set of chessmen having the power to move diagonally across any number of adjoining unoccupied squares **3 :** mulled port wine flavored with oranges and cloves

bish·op·ric \ˈbi-shə-(ˌ)prik\ *n* [ME *bisshopriche,* fr. OE *bisceoprīce,* fr. *biscеop* + *rīce* kingdom — more at RICH] (bef. 12c) **1 :** DIOCESE **2 :** the office of bishop **3 :** the administrative body of a Mormon ward consisting of a bishop and two high priests as counselors

Bishops' Bible *n* (1835) **:** an officially commissioned English translation of the Bible published in 1568

bis·muth \ˈbiz-məth\ *n* [NL *bismuthum,* modif. of G *Wismut*] (1668) **:** a heavy brittle grayish-white chiefly trivalent metallic element that is chemically like arsenic and antimony and that is used in alloys and pharmaceuticals — see ELEMENT table — **bis·mu·thic** \biz-ˈmə-thik, -ˈmyü-\ *adj*

bismuth sub·sa·lic·y·late \-ˌsəb-sə-ˈli-sə-ˌlāt\ *n* (1941) **:** a drug $C_7H_5BiO_4$ taken orally to relieve diarrhea, nausea, and indigestion

bi·son \ˈbī-sᵊn, -zᵊn\ *n, pl* **bison** [L *bisont-, bison,* of Gmc origin; akin to OHG *wisant* aurochs; akin to OPruss *wis*sambrs aurochs] (ca. 1611) **:** any of several large shaggy-maned usu. gregarious recent or extinct bovine mammals (genus *Bison*) having a large head with short horns and heavy forequarters surmounted by a large fleshy hump: as **a :** WISENT **b :** BUFFALO 1c(1) — **bi·son·tine** \-sᵊn-ˌtīn, -zᵊn-\ *adj*

bis·phe·nol A \ˌbis-ˈfē-nōl-, -ˌnȯl-\ *n* [*bis* + *phenol*] (1951) **:** an industrial chemical compound $C_{15}H_{16}O_2$ that is a component of several commercially useful types of plastic

bis·phos·pho·nate \ˌbis-ˈfäs-fə-ˌnāt\ *n* [*bis* + *phosphon*ic acid (an acid obtained from phosphine) + [1]*-ate*] (1982) **:** any of a group of drugs that slow the breakdown of bone by osteoclasts

[1]**bisque** \ˈbisk\ *n* [F] (1647) **1 a :** a thick cream soup made with shellfish or game **b :** a cream soup of pureed vegetables **2 :** ice cream containing powdered nuts or macaroons

[2]**bisque** *n* [F] (ca. 1656) **:** odds allowed an inferior player: as **a :** a point taken when desired in a set of tennis **b :** an extra turn in croquet **c :** one or more strokes off a golf score

[3]**bisque** *n* [by shortening & alter.] (1664) **:** BISCUIT 2; *esp* **:** unglazed china that is not to be glazed but is hard-fired and vitreous

bi·state \ˈbī-ˌstāt\ *adj* (1928) **:** of or relating to two states

bis·ter *or* **bis·tre** \ˈbis-tər\ *n* [F *bistre*] (ca. 1751) **1 :** a yellowish-brown to dark brown pigment used in art **2 :** a grayish to yellowish brown — **bis·tered** \-tərd\ *adj*

bis·tort \ˈbis-ˌtȯrt, bis-ˈ\ *n* [MF *bistorte,* fr. ML **bistorta,* fr. L *bis* + *torta,* fem. of *tortus,* pp. of *torquēre* to twist — more at TORTURE] (1578) **:** any of several polygonums; *esp* **:** a Eurasian perennial herb (*Polygonum bistorta*) with twisted roots used as astringents

bis·tro \ˈbēs-(ˌ)trō, ˈbis-\ *n, pl* **bistros** [F] (1921) **1 :** a small or unpretentious restaurant **2 a :** a small bar or tavern **b :** NIGHTCLUB

bi·sul·fate \(ˌ)bī-ˈsəl-ˌfāt\ *n* (1814) **:** an acid sulfate

bi·sul·fide \-ˌfīd\ *n* [ISV] (1863) **:** DISULFIDE

bi·sul·fite \-ˌfīt\ *n* [F, fr. *bi-* + *sulfite*] (ca. 1846) **:** an acid sulfite

bi–swing \ˈbī-ˈswiŋ\ *adj* [[1]*bi-* + *swing;* perh. fr. the freedom of movement allowed by this jacket] (1937) **:** made with a pleat or gusset at the back of the arms ⟨~ jacket⟩

[1]**bit** \ˈbit\ *n* [ME *bitt,* fr. OE *bite* act of biting; akin to OE *bītan* bite] (14c) **1 a** (1) **:** the biting or cutting edge or part of a tool (2) **:** a replaceable part of a compound tool that actually performs the function (as drilling or boring) for which the whole tool is designed **b** *pl* **:** the jaws of tongs or pincers **2 :** something bitten or held with the teeth: **a :** the usu. steel part of a bridle inserted in the mouth of a horse **b :** the rimmed mouth end on the stem of a pipe or cigar holder **3 :** something that curbs or restrains **4 :** the part of a key that enters the lock and acts on the bolt and tumblers

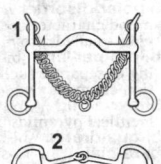

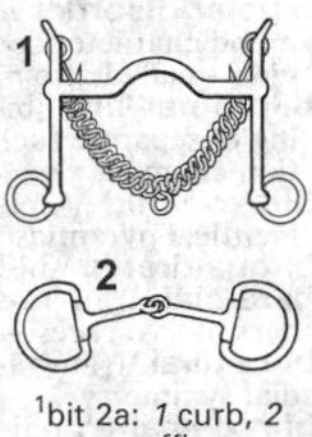

[1]bit 2a: *1* curb, *2* snaffle

[2]**bit** *vt* **bit·ted; bit·ting** (1583) **1 a :** to put a bit in the mouth of (a horse) **b :** to control as if with a bit **2 :** to form a bit on (a key)

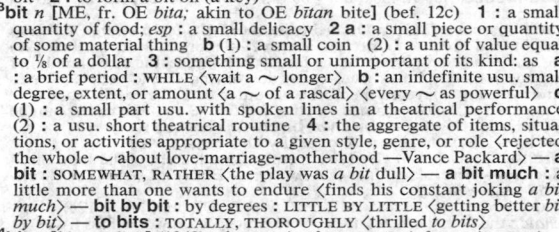

[3]**bit** *n* [ME, fr. OE *bita;* akin to OE *bītan* bite] (bef. 12c) **1 :** a small quantity of food; *esp* **:** a small delicacy **2 a :** a small piece or quantity of some material thing **b** (1) **:** a small coin (2) **:** a unit of value equal to ⅛ of a dollar **3 :** something small or unimportant of its kind: as **a :** a brief period **:** WHILE ⟨wait a ~ longer⟩ **b :** an indefinite usu. small degree, extent, or amount ⟨a ~ of a rascal⟩ ⟨every ~ as powerful⟩ **c** (1) **:** a small part usu. with spoken lines in a theatrical performance (2) **:** a usu. short theatrical routine **4 :** the aggregate of items, situations, or activities appropriate to a given style, genre, or role ⟨rejected the whole ~ about love-marriage-motherhood —Vance Packard⟩ — **a bit :** SOMEWHAT, RATHER ⟨the play was *a bit* dull⟩ — **a bit much :** a little more than one wants to endure ⟨finds his constant joking *a bit much*⟩ — **bit by bit :** by degrees **:** LITTLE BY LITTLE ⟨getting better *bit by bit*⟩ — **to bits :** TOTALLY, THOROUGHLY ⟨thrilled *to bits*⟩

[4]**bit** *n* [*b*inary dig*it*] (1948) **1 :** a unit of computer information equivalent to the result of a choice between two alternatives (as *yes* or *no, on* or *off*) **2 :** the physical representation of a bit by an electrical pulse, a magnetized spot, or a hole whose presence or absence indicates data

bi·tar·trate \(ˌ)bī-ˈtär-ˌtrāt\ *n* [ISV] (1827) **:** an acid tartrate

[1]**bitch** \ˈbich\ *n* [ME *bicche,* fr. OE *bicce*] (bef. 12c) **1 :** the female of the dog or some other carnivorous mammals **2 a :** a lewd or immoral woman **b :** a malicious, spiteful, or overbearing woman — sometimes used as a generalized term of abuse **3 :** something that is extremely difficult, objectionable, or unpleasant **4 :** COMPLAINT

[2]**bitch** *vt* (1823) **1 :** SPOIL, BOTCH ⟨~*ed* up their lives⟩ **2 :** CHEAT, DOUBLE-CROSS **3 :** to complain of or about ~ *vi* **:** COMPLAIN

bitch·ery \ˈbi-chə-rē\ *n, pl* **-er·ies** (1936) **:** malicious, spiteful, or overbearing behavior; *also* **:** an instance of such behavior

bitch goddess *n* (1906) **:** SUCCESS; *esp* **:** material or worldly success

bitch·in' \ˈbi-chən\ *adj* [prob. short for *sonofabitching,* fr. *son of a bitch* + [3]*-ing*] (1957) **1** *slang* **:** remarkably bad **:** DETESTABLE ⟨of all the ~ luck⟩ **2** *slang* **:** remarkably good or cool ⟨a ~ car⟩

bitchy \ˈbi-chē\ *adj* **bitch·i·er; -est** (1937) **:** characterized by malicious, spiteful, or arrogant behavior — **bitch·i·ly** \ˈbi-chə-lē\ *adv* — **bitch·i·ness** \ˈbi-chē-nəs\ *n*

[1]**bite** \ˈbīt\ *vb* **bit** \ˈbit\; **bit·ten** \ˈbi-tᵊn\ *also* **bit; bit·ing** \ˈbī-tiŋ\ [ME, fr. OE *bītan;* akin to OHG *bīzan* to bite, L *findere* to split] *vt* (bef. 12c) **1 a :** to seize esp. with teeth or jaws so as to enter, grip, or wound **b :** to wound, pierce, or sting esp. with a fang or a proboscis **2 :** to cut or pierce with or as if with an edged weapon **3 :** to cause sharp pain or stinging discomfort to **4 :** to take hold of **5** *archaic* **:** to take in **:** CHEAT ~ *vi* **1 :** to bite or have the habit of biting something **2** *of a weapon or tool* **:** to cut, pierce, or take hold **3 :** to cause irritation or smarting **4 :** CORRODE **5 a** *of fish* **:** to take a bait **b :** to respond so as to be caught (as by a trick) **c :** to accept a suggestion or an offer ⟨offered them a deal but they wouldn't ~⟩ **6 :** to take or maintain a

firm hold **7** : to produce a negative effect ⟨the recession began to ~⟩ **8** *slang* : to be objectionable or extremely bad in quality : STINK, SUCK — **bit·er** \ˈbī-tər\ *n* — **bite off more than one can chew** : to undertake more than one can handle — **bite one's tongue** : to hold back (as from a reluctance to offend) a remark one would like to make — **bite the bullet** : to enter with resignation upon a difficult or distressing course of action — **bite the dust** **1** : to fall dead esp. in battle **2 a** : to suffer humiliation or defeat **b** : to come to an end — **bite the hand that feeds one** : to injure a benefactor maliciously

[2]**bite** *n* (15c) **1 a** : the act of biting **b** : the manner of biting; *esp* : OCCLUSION 1b **2** : FOOD: as **a** : the amount of food taken at a bite : MORSEL **b** : a small amount of food : SNACK ⟨have a ~ to eat⟩ **3** *archaic* **a** : CHEAT, TRICK **b** : SHARPER **4** : a wound made by biting **5** : the hold or grip by which friction is created or purchase is obtained **6** : a surface that creates friction or is brought into contact with another for the purpose of obtaining a hold **7 a** : a keen incisive quality **b** : a sharp penetrating effect **8** : a single exposure of an etcher's plate to the corrosive action of acid **9** : an amount taken usu. in one operation for one purpose : SHARE **10** : SOUND BITE

bite plate *n* (ca. 1922) : a removable usu. plastic dental appliance used in orthodontics and prosthodontics: as **a** : a device worn in the upper or lower jaw and used esp. to reposition the jaw or prevent bruxism **b** : RETAINER 3b

bite–size \ˈbīt-ˌsīz\ *also* **bite–sized** \-ˌsīzd\ *adj* (1947) **1** : of a size that can be eaten in one bite ⟨~ pieces of chicken⟩ **2** : being or made small or brief esp. so as to be easily manageable ⟨~ tasks⟩ ⟨~ essays⟩

bite·wing \ˈbīt-ˌwiŋ\ *n* (1938) : a dental X-ray film designed to show the crowns of the upper and lower teeth simultaneously

bit·ing \ˈbī-tiŋ\ *adj* (14c) : having the power to bite ⟨a ~ wind⟩; *esp* : able to grip and impress deeply ⟨a ~ wit⟩ — **bit·ing·ly** \-tiŋ-lē\ *adv*

biting louse *n* (1896) : any of numerous wingless insects (order Mallophaga) that are parasitic esp. on birds — called also *bird louse*

biting midge *n* (1945) : any of a family (Ceratopogonidae) of tiny biting dipteran flies of which some are vectors of filarial worms

bit·map \ˈbit-ˌmap\ *n* (1982) **1** : an array of binary data representing a bitmapped image or display; *also* : a file containing such data **2** : a bitmapped image or display

bit·mapped \ˈbit-ˌmapt\ *adj* (1978) : of, relating to, or being a digital image or display for which an array of binary data specifies the value of each pixel ⟨~ graphics⟩

bit·stock \ˈbit-ˌstäk\ *n* (1869) : BRACE 3

bit·sy \ˈbit-sē\ *adj* [*itsy-bitsy*] (1905) : TINY

[1]**bitt** \ˈbit\ *n* [prob. fr. MF *bitte,* ultim. fr. ON *biti* beam] (1593) **1** : a post or pair of posts fixed on the deck of a ship for securing lines **2** : BOLLARD 1

[2]**bitt** *vt* (1769) : to make (a cable) fast about a bitt

[1]**bit·ter** \ˈbi-tər\ *adj* [ME, fr. OE *biter;* akin to OHG *bittar* bitter, OE *bītan* to bite — more at BITE] (bef. 12c) **1 a** : being or inducing the one of the four basic taste sensations that is peculiarly acrid, astringent, or disagreeable and suggestive of an infusion of hops — compare SALT, SOUR, SWEET **b** : distasteful or distressing to the mind : GALLING ⟨a ~ sense of shame⟩ **2** : marked by intensity or severity: **a** : accompanied by severe pain or suffering ⟨a ~ death⟩ **b** : being relentlessly determined : VEHEMENT ⟨a ~ partisan⟩ **c** : exhibiting intense animosity ⟨~ enemies⟩ **d (1)** : harshly reproachful ⟨~ complaints⟩ (2) : marked by cynicism and rancor ⟨~ contempt⟩ **e** : intensely unpleasant esp. in coldness or rawness ⟨a ~ wind⟩ **3** : expressive of severe pain, grief, or regret ⟨~ tears⟩ — **bit·ter·ish** \ˈbi-tə-rish\ *adj* — **bit·ter·ly** *adv* — **bit·ter·ness** *n*

[2]**bitter** *n* (bef. 12c) **1** : bitter quality **2 a** *pl* : a usu. alcoholic solution of bitter and often aromatic plant products used esp. in preparing mixed drinks or as a mild tonic **b** *Brit* : a very dry heavily hopped ale

[3]**bitter** *vt* (12c) : to make bitter ⟨~*ed* ale⟩

[4]**bitter** *adv* (1749) : to a bitter degree ⟨it's ~ cold⟩

bitter almond *n* (1601) : an almond with a bitter taste that contains amygdalin; *also* : a tree (*Prunus dulcis amara*) producing bitter almonds

bit·ter·brush \ˈbi-tər-ˌbrəsh\ *n* (1910) : a much-branched shrub (*Purshia tridentata*) of the rose family that grows in arid western No. America, that has 3-lobed leaves and yellow flowers, and is valuable for forage

bitter cress *n* (ca. 1890) : any of a genus (*Cardamine*) of herbs of the mustard family that produce flat pods and wingless seeds

[1]**bitter end** *n* [perh. fr. [2]*bitter end*] (1827) : the last extremity however painful or calamitous — **bit·ter–end·er** \ˌbi-tər-ˈen-dər\ *n*

[2]**bitter end** *n* [*bitter* (a turn of cable around the bitts)] (ca. 1862) : the inboard end of a ship's anchoring cable

[1]**bit·tern** \ˈbi-tərn\ *n* [ME *bitoure,* fr. AF *butor,* fr. VL **butitaurus,* fr. L *buteo* hawk + *taurus* bull] (1515) : any of various small or medium-sized usu. secretive herons (esp. genera *Botaurus* and *Ixobrychus*)

[2]**bittern** *n* [irreg. fr. [1]*bitter*] (1682) : the bitter water solution of salts that remains after sodium chloride has crystallized out of a brine

bitter orange *n* (1849) : SOUR ORANGE

bit·ter·root \ˈbi-tə(r)-ˌrüt, -ˌru̇t\ *n* (1838) : a succulent herb (*Lewisia rediviva*) of the purslane family that grows in western No. America and has starchy roots and pink or white flowers

[1]**bit·ter·sweet** \ˈbi-tər-ˌswēt\ *n* (14c) **1** : something that is bittersweet; *esp* : pleasure alloyed with pain **2 a** : a poisonous Eurasian woody vine (*Solanum dulcamara*) of the nightshade family that has purple flowers and oval reddish berries and is naturalized in No. America **b** : a No. American poisonous woody vine (*Celastrus scandens*) of the staff-tree family having clusters of small greenish flowers succeeded by yellow capsules that open when ripe and disclose the scarlet aril

[2]**bittersweet** *adj* (1576) **1** : being at once bitter and sweet; *esp* : pleasant but including or marked by elements of suffering or regret ⟨a ~ ballad⟩ **2** : of or relating to a prepared chocolate containing little sugar — **bit·ter·sweet·ly** *adv* — **bit·ter·sweet·ness** *n*

bit·ter·weed \ˈbi-tər-ˌwēd\ *n* (1819) : any of several American plants containing a bitter substance: as **a** : either of two ragweeds: (1) : a low-growing common ragweed (*Ambrosia artemisiifolia*) (2) : HORSEWEED **b** : an annual yellow-flowered sneezeweed (*Helenium amarum* syn. *H. tenuifolium*) **c** : an erect annual composite herb (*Hymenoxys odorata*) of the southwestern U.S. that has yellow flowers and is poisonous to livestock

bit·tock \ˈbi-tək\ *n* (ca. 1802) *chiefly Scot* : a little bit

[1]**bit·ty** \ˈbi-tē\ *adj* (1892) *chiefly Brit* : made up of or containing bits; *esp* : not cohesive or flowing

[2]**bitty** *adj* (1905) : SMALL, TINY ⟨a little ~ room⟩

bi·tu·men \bə-ˈtyü-mən, bī-, -ˈtü-, *esp Brit also* ˈbit-yə-\ *n* [ME *bithumen* mineral pitch, fr. L *bitumin-, bitumen*] (15c) **1** : an asphalt of Asia Minor used in ancient times as a cement and mortar **2** : any of various mixtures of hydrocarbons (as tar) often together with their nonmetallic derivatives that occur naturally or are obtained as residues after heat-refining natural substances (as petroleum); *specif* : such a mixture soluble in carbon disulfide — **bi·tu·mi·ni·za·tion** \bə-ˌtyü-mə-nə-ˈzā-shən, bī-, -ˌtü-\ *n* — **bi·tu·mi·nize** \-ˈtyü-mə-ˌnīz, -ˈtü-\ *vt*

bi·tu·mi·nous \bə-ˈtyü-mə-nəs, bī-, -ˈtü-\ *adj* (1620) **1** : containing or impregnated with bitumen **2** : of or relating to bituminous coal

bituminous coal *n* (1827) : a coal that when heated yields considerable volatile bituminous matter — called also *soft coal*

bi·unique \ˌbī-yu̇-ˈnēk, -yü-\ *adj* (1941) : being a correspondence between two sets that is one-to-one in both directions — **bi·unique·ness** *n*

[1]**bi·va·lent** \(ˌ)bī-ˈvā-lənt, ˈbi-və-\ *adj* (1869) **1** : DIVALENT **2** : associated in pairs in synapsis

[2]**bivalent** *n* (ca. 1934) : a pair of synaptic chromosomes

[1]**bi·valve** \ˈbī-ˌvalv\ *adj* (1661) : being or having a shell composed of two valves

[2]**bivalve** *n* (1683) : any of a class (Bivalvia syn. Pelecypoda) of typically marine mollusks (as clams, oysters, or scallops) that have a 2-valved hinged shell, are usu. filter feeders, and lack a distinct head

bi·var·i·ate \(ˌ)bī-ˈver-ē-ət, -ˈva-rē-\ *adj* (1920) : of, relating to, or involving two variables ⟨a ~ frequency distribution⟩

[1]**biv·ouac** \ˈbi-və-ˌwak, ˈbiv-ˌwak\ *n* [F, fr. LG *biwacht,* fr. *bi* by + *wacht* guard] (1819) **1** : a usu. temporary encampment under little or no shelter **2 a** : encampment usu. for a night **b** : a temporary or casual shelter or lodging

[2]**bivouac** *vb* **-ouacked; -ouack·ing** *vi* (1809) **1** : to make a bivouac : CAMP **2** : to take shelter often temporarily ~ *vt* : to provide temporary quarters for ⟨they were *bivouacked* in the gym during the storm⟩

[1]**bi·week·ly** \(ˌ)bī-ˈwē-klē\ *adj* (1832) **1** : occurring twice a week **2** : occurring every two weeks : FORTNIGHTLY ***usage*** see BI- — **bi·weekly** *adv*

[2]**biweekly** *n* (ca. 1890) **1** : a publication issued every two weeks **2** : SEMIWEEKLY

bi·year·ly \(ˌ)bī-ˈyir-lē\ *adj* (ca. 1909) **1** : BIANNUAL 1 **2** : BIENNIAL 1

biz \ˈbiz\ *n* (1861) : BUSINESS

[1]**bi·zarre** \bə-ˈzär\ *adj* [F, fr. It *bizzarro*] (ca. 1648) : strikingly out of the ordinary: as **a** : odd, extravagant, or eccentric in style or mode **b** : involving sensational contrasts or incongruities ***syn*** see FANTASTIC — **bi·zarre·ly** *adv* — **bi·zarre·ness** *n*

[2]**bizarre** *n* (ca. 1753) : a flower with atypical striped marking

bi·zar·re·rie \bi-ˌzär-ə-ˈrē\ *n* [F] (1747) **1** : a bizarre quality **2** : something bizarre

bi·zar·ro \bə-ˈzär-ō\ *adj* [alter. of *bizarre*] (1971) : characterized by a bizarre, fantastic, or unconventional approach — **bizarro** *n*

bi·zon·al \(ˌ)bī-ˈzō-nᵊl\ *adj* (1946) : of or relating to the affairs of a zone governed or administered by two powers acting together — **bi·zone** \ˈbī-ˌzōn\ *n*

BJ *abbr* bachelor of journalism

bk *abbr* **1** bank **2** book **3** break **4** brook

Bk *symbol* berkelium

bkg *abbr* **1** banking **2** bookkeeping

bkgd *abbr* background

bkt *abbr* **1** basket **2** bracket

bl *abbr* **1** bale **2** barrel **3** black **4** block **5** blue

BL *abbr* **1** bachelor of letters **2** baseline **3** bill of lading **4** breadth-length

[1]**blab** \ˈblab\ *n* [ME *blabbe;* akin to ME *blaberen*] (14c) **1** *archaic* : one that blabs : TATTLETALE **2** : idle or excessive talk : CHATTER — **blab·by** \ˈbla-bē\ *adj*

[2]**blab** *vb* **blabbed; blab·bing** *vi* (15c) **1** : to talk idly or thoughtlessly **2** : to reveal a secret esp. by indiscreet chatter ~ *vt* : to reveal esp. without reserve or discretion ⟨*blabbed* the whole affair to the press⟩

[1]**blab·ber** \ˈbla-bər\ *vb* **blab·bered; blab·ber·ing** \-b(ə-)riŋ\ [ME *blaberen*] *vi* (14c) : to talk foolishly or excessively ~ *vt* : to say indiscreetly

[2]**blabber** *n* (ca. 1913) : idle talk : BABBLE

[3]**blabber** *n* [[2]*blab*] (1557) : a person who blabs

blab·ber·mouth \ˈbla-bər-ˌmau̇th\ *n* (1936) : a person who talks too much; *esp* : TATTLETALE

[1]**black** \ˈblak\ *adj* [ME *blak,* fr. OE *blæc;* akin to OHG *blah* black, and prob. to L *flagrare* to burn, Gk *phlegein*] (bef. 12c) **1 a** : of the color black **b (1)** : very dark in color ⟨his face was ~ with rage⟩ (2) : having a very deep or low register ⟨a bass with a ~ voice⟩ (3) : HEAVY, SERIOUS ⟨the play was a ~ intrigue⟩ **2 a** : having dark skin, hair, and eyes : SWARTHY ⟨the ~ Irish⟩ **b (1)** *often cap* : of or relating to any of various population groups having dark pigmentation of the skin ⟨~ Americans⟩ (2) : of or relating to the African-American people or their culture ⟨~ literature⟩ ⟨a ~ college⟩ ⟨~ pride⟩ ⟨~ studies⟩ (3) : typical or representative of the most readily perceived characteristics of black culture ⟨trying to sound ~⟩ ⟨tried to play ~*er* jazz⟩ **3** : dressed in black **4** : DIRTY, SOILED ⟨hands ~ with grime⟩ **5 a** : characterized by the absence of light ⟨a ~ night⟩ **b** : reflecting or transmitting little or no light ⟨~ water⟩ **c** : served without milk or cream ⟨~ coffee⟩ **6 a** : thoroughly sinister or evil : WICKED ⟨a ~ deed⟩ **b** : indicative of condemnation or discredit ⟨got a ~ mark for being late⟩ **7** : connected with or invoking the supernatural and esp. the devil ⟨~ magic⟩ **8 a** : very sad, gloomy, or calamitous ⟨~ despair⟩ **b** : marked by the occurrence of disaster ⟨~ Friday⟩ **9** : characterized by hostility or angry discontent : SULLEN ⟨~ resent-

\ə\ **abut** \ᵊ\ kitten, F table \ər\ **fur**ther \a\ **ash** \ā\ **ace** \ä\ **mop, mar** \au̇\ **out** \ch\ **chin** \e\ **bet** \ē\ **easy** \g\ **go** \i\ **hit** \ī\ **ice** \j\ **job** \ŋ\ **sing** \ō\ **go** \ȯ\ **law** \ȯi\ **boy** \th\ **thin** \t͟h\ **the** \ü\ **loot** \u̇\ **foot** \y\ **yet** \zh\ **vision, beige** \k̲, ⁿ, œ, ue, ʸ\ *see* Guide to Pronunciation

ment filled his heart⟩ **10** *chiefly Brit* **:** subject to boycott by trade-union members as employing or favoring nonunion workers or as operating under conditions considered unfair by the trade union **11 a** *of propaganda* **:** conducted so as to appear to originate within an enemy country and designed to weaken enemy morale **b :** characterized by or connected with the use of black propaganda ⟨∼ radio⟩ **12 :** characterized by grim, distorted, or grotesque satire ⟨∼ humor⟩ **13 :** of or relating to covert intelligence operations ⟨∼ government programs⟩ — **black·ish** \ˈbla-kish\ *adj* — **black·ly** *adv* — **black·ness** *n*

[2]**black** *n* (bef. 12c) **1 :** a black pigment or dye; *esp* **:** one consisting largely of carbon **2 :** the achromatic color of least lightness characteristically perceived to belong to objects that neither reflect nor transmit light **3 :** something that is black: as **a :** black clothing ⟨looks good in ∼⟩ **b :** a black animal (as a horse) **4 a :** a person belonging to any of various population groups having dark pigmentation of the skin **b :** AFRICAN-AMERICAN **5 :** the pieces of a dark color in a board game for two players (as chess) **6 :** total or nearly total absence of light ⟨the ∼ of night⟩ **7 :** the condition of making a profit — usu. used with *the* ⟨operating in the ∼⟩; compare RED

[3]**black** *vi* (13c) **:** to become black ∼ *vt* **1 :** to make black **2** *chiefly Brit* **:** to declare (as a business or industry) subject to boycott by trade-union members

black alder *n* (1805) **:** WINTERBERRY 1

black·a·moor \ˈbla-kə-ˌmu̇r\ *n* [irreg. fr. *black* + *Moor*] (1547) **:** a dark-skinned person; *esp* **:** BLACK 4a

black–and–blue \ˌbla-kən-ˈblü\ *adj* (14c) **:** darkly discolored from blood effused by bruising

black–and–tan \-kən-ˈtan\ *adj* (1850) **1 :** having a predominantly black color pattern with deep red or rusty tan usu. on the feet, breeching, and cheek patches, above the eyes, and inside the ears **2 :** favoring or practicing proportional representation of whites and blacks in politics **3 :** frequented by both blacks and whites ⟨a ∼ bar⟩

black and tan *n* (1870) **1 :** a black-and-tan animal (as a dog) **2** *chiefly Brit* **:** a drink consisting of a dark beer (as stout or porter) and ale or beer of a paler color **3** *cap B&T* [fr. the color of his uniform] **:** a recruit enlisted in England in 1920–21 for service in the Royal Irish Constabulary against the armed movement for Irish independence **4 :** a member of a black-and-tan political organization (as in the southern U.S.) — compare LILY-WHITE

black–and–tan coonhound *n* (1948) **:** any of a breed of strong vigorous coonhounds of U.S. origin with black-and-tan markings

[1]**black–and–white** \ˌbla-kən-ˈhwīt, -ˈwīt\ *adj* (1612) **1 :** partly black and partly white in color **2 :** being in writing or print **3 :** executed in dark pigment on a light background or in light pigment on a dark ground ⟨a ∼ drawing⟩ **4 :** MONOCHROME 2 ⟨∼ film⟩ ⟨∼ television⟩ **5 a :** sharply divided into good and evil **b :** evaluating or viewing things as either all good or all bad ⟨∼ morality⟩ **c :** sharply defined **:** CLEAR-CUT ⟨the truth is not always ∼⟩

[2]**black–and–white** *n* [fr. a common color scheme for such cars] (1958) **:** SQUAD CAR

black and white *n* (1571) **1 :** WRITING, PRINT **2 :** a drawing or print done in black and white or in monochrome **3 :** monochrome reproduction of visual images (as by photography or television)

Black Angus *n* (1948) **:** ANGUS

black–a–vised \ˈbla-kə-ˌvīst\ *adj* [*black* + F *à vis* as to face] (ca. 1758) **:** having a dark complexion

[1]**black·ball** \ˈblak-ˌbȯl\ *vt* (1770) **1 :** to vote against; *esp* **:** to exclude from membership by casting a negative vote **2 a :** to exclude socially **:** OSTRACIZE **b :** BOYCOTT

[2]**blackball** *n* (1777) **1 :** a small black ball for use as a negative vote in a ballot box **2 :** an adverse vote esp. against admitting someone to membership in an organization

black bass *n* (1815) **:** any of a genus (*Micropterus*) of freshwater sunfishes native to eastern and central No. America and including the largemouth bass and smallmouth bass

black bean *n* (1668) **1 :** a black kidney bean commonly used in Latin American cuisine **2 :** a black soybean commonly used usu. fermented in east Asian cuisine

black bear *n* (1705) **:** the common No. American bear (*Ursus americanus*) ranging in color from brown or typical black to white

black beast *n* (1862) **:** BÊTE NOIRE

[1]**black belt** \ˈblak-ˌbelt\ *n* (1870) **1 :** an area characterized by rich black soil **2** *often cap both Bs* **:** an area densely populated by blacks

[2]**black belt** *n* (1939) **:** one who holds the rating of expert in various arts of self-defense (as judo and karate); *also* **:** the rating itself

black·ber·ry \ˈblak-ˌber-ē, -ˈbe-rē\ *n* (bef. 12c) **1 :** the usu. black or dark purple juicy but seedy edible aggregate fruit of various brambles (genus *Rubus*) of the rose family **2 :** a plant that bears blackberries

black bile *n* (1681) **:** a humor of medieval physiology believed to be secreted by the kidneys or spleen and to cause melancholy

black birch *n* (1674) **:** SWEET BIRCH

[1]**black·bird** \ˈblak-ˌbərd\ *n* (14c) **1 :** any of various birds of which the males are largely or entirely black: as **a :** a common thrush (*Turdus merula*) of Eurasia and northern Africa having an orange bill and eye rim **b :** any of several American oscine birds (family Icteridae) **2 :** a Pacific islander kidnapped for use as a plantation laborer

[2]**blackbird** *vi* (ca. 1873) **:** to engage in the slave trade esp. in the So. Pacific

black·bird·er *n* (1880) **1 :** a person who blackbirds **2 :** a ship used in blackbirding

black·board \ˈblak-ˌbȯrd\ *n* (1823) **:** a hard smooth usu. dark surface used esp. in a classroom for writing or drawing on with chalk

black·body \ˈblak-ˈbä-dē\ *n* (1710) **:** an ideal body or surface that completely absorbs all radiant energy falling upon it with no reflection and that radiates at all frequencies with a spectral energy distribution dependent on its absolute temperature

black book *n* (1592) **:** a book containing a blacklist

[1]**black box** *n* (ca. 1945) **1 :** a usu. complicated electronic device whose internal mechanism is usu. hidden from or mysterious to the user; *broadly* **:** anything that has mysterious or unknown internal functions or mechanisms **2 :** a crashworthy device in aircraft for recording cockpit conversations and flight data

[2]**black box** *adj* (1988) **:** being or containing a warning of a serious or life-threatening side effect (as stroke or muscle damage) that is highlighted by a black border on a prescription drug's label or accompanying literature

black·buck \ˈblak-ˌbək\ *n* (1850) **:** an antelope (*Antilope cervicapra*) native to India and adjacent regions in which the male has spirally twisted horns and a chiefly dark brown coat and the female a chiefly yellowish-fawn coat

black·cap \ˈblak-ˌkap\ *n* (1667) **1 :** any of several birds with black heads or crowns: as **a :** a small gray European warbler (*Sylvia atricapilla*) with a black crown **b :** CHICKADEE **2 :** BLACK RASPBERRY

black–capped \-ˈkapt\ *adj* (1781) *of a bird* **:** having the top of the head black

Black Carib *n* (1901) **:** GARIFUNA

black cherry *n* (1720) **1 :** a large cherry (*Prunus serotina*) of eastern and central No. America having drooping clusters of small white flowers and astringent black or dark purple fruits; *also* **:** the fruit **2 :** the strong reddish-brown wood of the black cherry used esp. for cabinetwork

black·cock \-ˌkäk\ *n* (15c) *chiefly Brit* **:** BLACK GROUSE; *specif* **:** the male black grouse

black cod *n* (1887) **:** a large gray to blackish bony fish (*Anoplopoma fimbria* of the family Anoplomatidae) of the Pacific coast that is an important food fish and has a liver rich in vitamins — called also *sablefish*

black cohosh *n* (1828) **:** a bugbane (*Cimicifuga racemosa*) of the eastern U.S.

black crappie *n* (ca. 1827) **:** a silvery black-mottled sunfish (*Pomoxis nigromaculatus*) of eastern and central No. America having seven or eight protruding spines on the dorsal fins

black–crowned night heron \ˈblak-ˌkrau̇nd-\ *n* (1844) **:** a widely distributed night heron (*Nycticorax nycticorax*) having a black crown and back, gray wings, and white underparts

black currant *n* (1629) **:** a European perennial currant (*Ribes nigrum*) bearing aromatic edible black berries that are used esp. in flavoring liqueur (as cassis); *also* **:** the fruit

black damp *n* (1836) **:** a carbon dioxide mixture occurring as a mine gas and incapable of supporting life or flame

black death *n, often cap B&D* [fr. the black patches formed on the skin of its victims] (1758) **1 :** PLAGUE 2b **2 :** a severe epidemic of plague and esp. bubonic plague that occurred in Asia and Europe in the 14th century

black diamond *n* (1763) **1 :** dense black hematite **2** *pl* **:** COAL 3a **3 :** [3]CARBONADO

black duck *n* (1637) **:** any of several ducks that are dark in color; *esp* **:** a common brown duck (*Anas rubripes*) of eastern No. America

black dwarf *n, pl* **black dwarfs** (1945) **:** a very small cooled remnant of white dwarf that emits no detectable light

black·en \ˈbla-kən\ *vb* **black·ened; black·en·ing** \ˈblak-niŋ, ˈbla-kə-\ *vi* (14c) **:** to become dark or black ⟨the sky ∼*s*⟩ ∼ *vt* **1 :** to make black **2 :** DEFAME, SULLY ⟨∼*ed* her reputation⟩ — **black·en·er** \ˈblak-nər, ˈbla-kə-\ *n*

black·ened \-kənd\ *adj* (1979) **:** coated with a mixture of spices (as garlic powder and cayenne pepper) and fried over extremely high heat

Black English *n* (1968) **:** a nonstandard variety of English spoken by some African-Americans — called also *Black English vernacular*

black·en·ing \ˈblak-niŋ, ˈbla-kə-\ *n* (ca. 1909) **:** BLACKING

black eye *n* (1604) **1 :** a discoloration of the skin around the eye from bruising **2 a :** DEFEAT, SETBACK **b :** a bad reputation

black–eyed pea \ˈblak-ˌīd-\ *n* (1728) **:** COWPEA

black–eyed Su·san \-ˈsü-zᵊn\ *n* (1884) **:** a No. American coneflower (*Rudbeckia hirta* syn. *R. serotina*) having flower heads with deep yellow to orange rays and dark conical disks

black·face \ˈblak-ˌfās\ *n* (1869) **:** makeup applied to a performer playing a black person esp. in a minstrel show; *also* **:** a performer wearing such makeup

black·fish \-ˌfish\ *n* (1754) **1 :** any of numerous dark-colored fishes: as **a :** TAUTOG **b :** a small bony fish (*Dallia pectoralis* of the family Umbridae) of Alaska and Siberia that is used for food and is noted for its resistance to cold **2 :** any of several small toothed whales; *esp* **:** PILOT WHALE

black–flag \-ˈflag\ *vt* (1963) **:** to signal (a race-car driver) to go immediately to the pits

black flag *n* (1720) **:** a pirate's flag usu. bearing a skull and crossbones

black·fly \ˈblak-ˌflī\ *n, pl* **-flies** *or* **-fly** (1608) **:** any of various small dark-colored insects; *esp* **:** any of a family (Simuliidae and esp. genus *Simulium*) of bloodsucking dipteran flies whose larvae usu. live in flowing streams

Black·foot \ˈblak-ˌfu̇t\ *n, pl* **Blackfeet** *or* **Blackfoot** (1790) **1 :** a member of an American Indian people of Montana, Alberta, and Saskatchewan **2 :** the Algonquian language of the Blackfeet

black–foot·ed albatross \ˈblak-ˌfu̇-təd-\ *n* (1839) **:** an albatross (*Diomedea nigripes*) of the Pacific that is chiefly blackish with dusky bill and black feet and legs — called also *gooney*

black–footed ferret *n* (1846) **:** a rare weasel (*Mustela nigripes*) of western No. American prairies having a yellowish coat, dark feet and facial mask, and a dark-tipped tail

black gold *n* (1910) **:** PETROLEUM

black grouse *n* (1678) **:** a large grouse (*Tetrao tetrix* syn. *Lyrurus tetrix*) of western Asia and Europe of which the male is black with white wing patches and the female is barred and mottled

[1]**black·guard** \ˈbla-gərd, -ˌgärd; ˈblak-ˌgärd\ *n* (1535) **1** *obs* **:** the kitchen servants of a household **2 a :** a rude or unscrupulous person **b :** a person who uses foul or abusive language — **black·guard·ism** \-gər-ˌdi-zəm, -ˌgär-\ *n* — **black·guard·ly** \-gərd-lē, -ˌgärd-\ *adj or adv*

[2]**blackguard** *vt* (1769) **:** to talk about or address in abusive terms

black gum *n* (1709) **:** a tupelo (*Nyssa sylvatica*) of the eastern U.S. with light and soft but tough wood

black hand *n, often cap B&H* [*Black Hand,* a Sicilian and Italian-American secret society of the late 19th and 20th centuries] (1904) **:** a lawless secret society engaged in criminal activities (as terrorism or extortion) — **black·hand·er** \ˈblak-ˌhan-dər\ *n*

black·head \ˈblak-ˌhed\ *n* (ca. 1837) **1 :** a small plug of sebum blocking the duct of a sebaceous gland esp. on the face **2 :** a destructive disease of turkeys and related birds caused by a protozoan (*Histomonas meleagridis*) that invades the intestinal ceca and liver **3 :** a larval clam or mussel attached to the skin or gills of a freshwater fish

black·heart \-ˌhärt\ *n* (1909) **:** a plant disease in which the central tissues blacken

black hole *n* (1964) **1 :** a celestial object that has a gravitational field so strong that light cannot escape it and that is believed to be created esp. in the collapse of a very massive star **2 :** something resembling a black hole: as **a :** something that consumes a resource continually ⟨a financial *black hole*⟩ **b :** an empty space **:** VOID

black ice *n* (1961) **:** a nearly transparent film of ice on a dark surface (as a paved road or a body of water) that is difficult to see

black·ing \ˈbla-kiŋ\ *n* (1571) **:** a substance (as a paste or polish) that is applied to an object to make it black

[1]**black·jack** \-ˌjak\ *n* (1591) **1** [*black* + *jack* (vessel)] **:** a tankard for beer or ale usu. of tar-coated leather **2 :** SPHALERITE **3 :** a hand weapon typically consisting of a piece of leather-enclosed metal with a strap or springy shaft for a handle **4 :** an often scrubby oak (*Quercus marilandica*) chiefly of the southeastern U.S. — called also *blackjack oak* **5 :** a card game the object of which is to be dealt cards having a higher count than those of the dealer up to but not exceeding 21 — called also *twenty-one, vingt-et-un*

[2]**blackjack** *vt* (1905) **1 :** to strike with a blackjack **2 :** to coerce with threats or pressure

black·land \ˈblak-ˌland\ *n* (1803) **1 :** a heavy sticky black soil such as that covering large areas in Texas **2** *pl* **:** a region of blackland

black·lead \ˈblak-ˌled\ *n* (1580) *chiefly Brit* **:** GRAPHITE 1

black·leg \ˈblak-ˌleg, -ˌlāg\ *n* (ca. 1722) **1 :** a usu. fatal toxemia esp. of young cattle caused by a soil bacterium (*Clostridium chauvoei*) **2 :** a cheating gambler **:** SWINDLER **3** *chiefly Brit* **:** a worker hostile to trade unionism or acting in opposition to union policies **:** SCAB

black–legged tick \ˈblak-ˈlegd-, -ˈlāgd-; -ˈle-gəd-, -ˈlā-\ *n* (1944) **:** either of two ixodid ticks: **a :** DEER TICK **b :** a tick (*Ixodes pacificus*) of the western U.S. and British Columbia that is the vector of several diseases (as Lyme disease)

black letter *n* (ca. 1644) **:** a heavy angular condensed typeface used esp. by the earliest European printers and based on handwriting used chiefly in the 13th to 15th centuries; *also* **:** this style of handwriting

black light *n* (1927) **1 :** invisible ultraviolet light **2 :** a lamp that radiates black light

black·light trap \ˈblak-ˌlīt-\ *n* (1961) **:** a trap for insects that uses a form of black light perceptible to particular insects as an attractant

[1]**black·list** \-ˌlist\ *n* (ca. 1619) **:** a list of persons who are disapproved of or are to be punished or boycotted

[2]**blacklist** *vt* (1702) **:** to put on a blacklist — **black·list·er** *n*

black locust *n* (1787) **:** a tall tree (*Robinia pseudoacacia*) of eastern No. America with pinnately compound leaves, drooping racemes of fragrant white flowers, and strong stiff wood

black lung *n* (1837) **:** pneumoconiosis caused by habitual inhalation of coal dust

black·mail \ˈblak-ˌmāl\ *n* [*black* + [1]*mail*] (1552) **1 :** a tribute anciently exacted on the Scottish border by plundering chiefs in exchange for immunity from pillage **2 a :** extortion or coercion by threats esp. of public exposure or criminal prosecution **b :** the payment that is extorted — **blackmail** *vt* — **black·mail·er** *n*

Black Ma·ria \ˌblak-mə-ˈrī-ə\ *n* (1843) **:** PADDY WAGON

black–mar·ket *vi* (1943) **:** to buy or sell goods in the black market ∼ *vt* **:** to sell in the black market — **black marketer** *or* **black marketeer** \-ˌmär-kə-ˈtir\ *n* — **black mar·ke·teer·ing** \-ˈtir-iŋ\ *n*

black market *n* (1931) **:** illicit trade in goods or commodities in violation of official regulations; *also* **:** a place where such trade is carried on

Black Mass *n* (1820) **:** a travesty of the Christian Mass ascribed to worshipers of Satan

Black Muslim *n* (1960) **:** a member of a chiefly black group that professes Islamic religious belief

black nationalist *n, often cap B&N* (1963) **:** a member of a group of militant blacks who advocate separatism from the whites and the formation of self-governing black communities — **black nationalism** *n, often cap B&N*

black–on–black *adj* (1975) **:** involving a black person against another black person ⟨∼ crime⟩

black·out \ˈblak-ˌau̇t\ *n* (1913) **1 a :** a turning off of the stage lighting to separate scenes in a play or end a play or skit; *also* **:** a skit that ends with a blackout **b :** a period of darkness enforced as a precaution against air raids **c :** a period of darkness (as in a city) caused by a failure of electrical power **2 :** a transient dulling or loss of vision, consciousness, or memory ⟨an alcoholic ∼⟩ **3 a :** a wiping out **:** OBLITERATION **b :** a blotting out by censorship **:** SUPPRESSION ⟨a news ∼⟩ **4 :** a usu. temporary loss of a radio signal **5 :** the prohibition or restriction of the telecasting of a sports event **6 :** a time during which a special commercial offer (as of tickets) is not valid — usu. used attributively ⟨∼ dates⟩

black out *vt* (1850) **1 a :** BLOT OUT, ERASE ⟨*blacked out* the event from his mind⟩ **b :** to suppress by censorship ⟨*black out* the news⟩ **2 :** to envelop in darkness ⟨*black out* the stage⟩ **3 :** to make inoperative (as by a power failure) **4 :** to impose a blackout on ⟨*blacked out* the local game⟩ ∼ *vi* **1 :** to become enveloped in darkness **2 :** to undergo a temporary loss of vision, consciousness, or memory

Black Panther *n* (1965) **:** a member of an organization of militant American blacks

black pepper *n* (bef. 12c) **:** a spice that consists of the dried berry of an Indian vine ground with the black husk still on; *also* **:** the plant (*Piper nigrum*) that yields black pepper

black·poll \ˈblak-ˌpōl\ *n* (1783) **:** a No. American warbler (*Dendroica striata*) with the male having a black cap when in breeding plumage

black powder *n* (1861) **:** an explosive mixture of potassium nitrate or sodium nitrate, charcoal, and sulfur used esp. in fireworks and as a propellant in antique firearms — compare GUNPOWDER

black power *n, often cap B&P* (1954) **:** the mobilization of the political and economic power of American blacks esp. to compel respect for their rights and improve their condition

black pudding *n* (1568) *chiefly Brit* **:** BLOOD SAUSAGE

black racer *n* (1836) **:** either of two common black colubrid snakes of the U.S.: **a :** a snake (*Coluber constrictor constrictor*) chiefly of the eastern U.S. **b :** a snake (*C. constrictor priapus*) of the southeastern U.S.

black raspberry *n* (ca. 1782) **:** a raspberry (*Rubus occidentalis*) of eastern No. America that has a purplish-black fruit and is the source of several cultivated varieties — called also *blackcap*

black rhinoceros *n* (1848) **:** a rhinoceros (*Diceros bicornis*) of sub-Saharan Africa having a prehensile upper lip that protrudes in the middle — called also *black rhino*

Black Rod *n* (ca. 1607) **:** the principal usher of the House of Lords

black rot *n* (1849) **:** a bacterial or fungal rot of plants marked by dark brown discoloration

black sheep *n* (1657) **:** a disfavored or disreputable member of a group

Black·shirt \ˈblak-ˌshərt\ *n* (1922) **:** a member of a fascist organization having a black shirt as a distinctive part of its uniform; *esp* **:** a member of the Italian Fascist party

black·smith \ˈblak-ˌsmith\ *n* [fr. a distinction between black metal (iron) and white metal (tin)] (15c) **:** a smith who forges iron — **black·smith·ing** \-ˌsmi-thiŋ\ *n*

black smoker *n* (1980) **:** a vent in a geologically active region of the sea floor from which issues superheated water laden with minerals (as sulfide precipitates); *also* **:** a rock chimney covering such a vent

black·snake \-ˌsnāk\ *n* (1634) **1 :** any of several snakes that are largely black or very dark in color: as **a :** a black racer (*Coluber constrictor constrictor*) **b :** a rat snake (*Elaphe obsoleta obsoleta*) **2 :** a long tapering braided whip of rawhide or leather

black spot *n* (ca. 1889) **:** any of several bacterial or fungal diseases of plants characterized by black spots or blotches esp. on the leaves

black spruce *n* (1744) **:** a widely distributed spruce (*Picea mariana*) of northern No. America that grows chiefly in moist soils and bogs

black·strap molasses \ˈblak-ˌstrap-\ *n* [*blackstrap* cheap wine, mixture of rum and molasses] (1880) **:** a thick dark molasses obtained from successive processing of raw sugar

black swallowtail *n* (1889) **:** a usu. dark-colored New World swallowtail (*Papilio polyxenes*) having yellow spots on the wing margins and a black spot centered within a larger orange spot on the hindwing inner edge

black·tail \ˈblak-ˌtāl\ *n* (1805) **:** BLACK-TAILED DEER

black–tailed deer \ˈblak-ˌtāl(d)-\ *n* (1806) **:** MULE DEER; *esp* **:** one of a subspecies (*Odocoileus hemionus columbianus*) esp. of British Columbia, Oregon, and Washington

black tea *n* (1789) **:** tea that is dark in color from complete oxidation of the leaf before firing

black·thorn \ˈblak-ˌthȯrn\ *n* (14c) **:** a European spiny plum (*Prunus spinosa*) with hard wood and small white flowers

black–tie *adj* (1933) **:** characterized by or requiring the wearing of semiformal evening clothes consisting of a usu. black tie and tuxedo for men and a formal dress for women ⟨a ∼ dinner⟩ — compare WHITE-TIE

black tie *n* (1935) **:** semiformal clothing ⟨gentlemen in *black tie* for the banquet⟩

black·top \ˈblak-ˌtäp\ *n* (1931) **:** a bituminous material used esp. for surfacing roads; *also* **:** a surface paved with blacktop — **blacktop** *vt*

Blackwall hitch \ˈblak-ˌwȯl-\ *n* [*Blackwall*, shipyard in London, England] (ca. 1862) **:** a hitch knot for securing a rope to a hook — see KNOT illustration

black walnut *n* (1612) **:** a walnut (*Juglans nigra*) of eastern No. America with hard strong heavy dark brown wood and oily edible nuts; *also* **:** its wood or nut

black·wa·ter \ˈblak-ˌwȯ-tər, -ˌwä-\ *n* (1800) **:** any of several diseases (as blackwater fever) characterized by dark-colored urine

blackwater fever *n* (1884) **:** a febrile complication of repeated malarial attacks that is characterized esp. by extensive kidney damage and urine discolored by heme from blood

black widow *n* (1915) **:** a venomous New World spider (*Latrodectus mactans*) the female of which is black with an hourglass-shaped red mark on the underside of the abdomen

black·wood \ˈblak-ˌwu̇d\ *n* (1631) **:** any of several hardwood trees (as *Acacia melanoxylon* and *Dalbergia latifolia* of the legume family) or their dark-colored wood

blad·der \ˈbla-dər\ *n* [ME, fr. OE *blǣdre;* akin to OHG *blātara* bladder, OE *blāwan* to blow] (bef. 12c) **1 a :** a membranous sac in animals that serves as the receptacle of a liquid or contains gas; *esp* **:** URINARY BLADDER **b :** CYST 2b **2 :** something (as the rubber bag inside a football) resembling a bladder — **blad·der·like** \-ˌlīk\ *adj*

bladder campion *n* (1783) **:** an Old World campion (*Silene vulgaris* syn. *S. cucubalus*) with an inflated calyx introduced into temperate No. America

blad·der·nut \ˈbla-dər-ˌnət\ *n* (1578) **:** any of a genus (*Staphylea* of the family Staphyleaceae, the bladdernut family) of ornamental shrubs or small trees with panicles of small white flowers followed by inflated capsules; *also* **:** one of the capsules

bladder worm *n* (1858) **:** a bladderlike larval tapeworm (as a cysticercus)

blad·der·wort \ˈbla-dər-ˌwərt, -ˌwȯrt\ *n* (ca. 1815) **:** any of a genus (*Utricularia* of the family Lentibulariaceae, the bladderwort family) of chiefly aquatic plants with leaves usu. having insect-trapping bladders

bladder wrack *n* (1810) **:** a common rockweed (*Fucus vesiculosus*) used in preparing kelp and as a manure

[1]**blade** \ˈblād\ *n* [ME, fr. OE *blæd;* akin to OHG *blat* leaf, L *folium*, Gk *phyllon*, OE *blōwan* to blossom — more at BLOW] (bef. 12c) **1 a :** LEAF 1a(1); *esp* **:** the leaf of an herb or a grass **b :** the flat expanded part of a leaf as distinguished from the petiole **2 :** something resembling the blade of a leaf: as **a :** the broad flattened part of an oar or paddle **b :** an arm of a screw propeller, electric fan, or steam turbine **c :** the broad flat or concave part of a machine (as a bulldozer or snowplow) that comes into contact with the material to be moved **d :** a broad flat body part; *specif* **:** SCAPULA — used chiefly in naming cuts of meat **e :** the flat portion of the tongue immediately behind the tip; *also* **:** this portion together with the tip **3 a :** the cutting part of an im-

plement **b** (1) : SWORD (2) : SWORDSMAN (3) : a dashing lively man **c** : the runner of an ice skate — **blade·like** \-ˌlīk\ *adj*

2blade *vi* **blad·ed; blad·ing** (1989) : to skate on in-line skates — **blad·er** \ˈblā-dər\ *n*

blad·ed \ˈblā-dəd\ *adj* (1600) : having blades — often used in combination ⟨5-*bladed* propeller⟩

blae \ˈblā\ *adj* [ME *bla, blo,* fr. ON *blār;* akin to OHG *blāo* blue — more at BLUE] (13c) *chiefly Scot* : dark blue or bluish gray

blae·ber·ry \ˈblā-ˌber-ē, -ˌb(ə-)rē\ *n* (14c) *chiefly Scot* : BILBERRY

1blah \ˈblä\ *n* [imit.] (1918) **1** *also* **blah–blah** \-ˌblä\ : silly or pretentious chatter or nonsense **2** *pl* [perh. influenced in meaning by *blasé*] : a feeling of boredom, lethargy, or general dissatisfaction

2blah *adj* (1922) : lacking interest : DULL : BORING ⟨a ~ winter day⟩

blain \ˈblān\ *n* [ME, fr. OE *blegen;* akin to MLG *bleine* blain, OE *blāwan* to blow] (bef. 12c) : an inflammatory swelling or sore

blam·able \ˈblā-mə-bəl\ *adj* (14c) : deserving blame : REPREHENSIBLE *syn* see BLAMEWORTHY — **blam·ably** \-blē\ *adv*

1blame \ˈblām\ *vt* **blamed; blam·ing** [ME, fr. AF *blamer, blasmer,* fr. LL *blasphemare* to blaspheme, fr. Gk *blasphēmein*] (13c) **1** : to find fault with : CENSURE ⟨the right to praise or ~ a literary work⟩ **2 a** : to hold responsible ⟨they ~ me for everything⟩ **b** : to place responsibility for ⟨~*s* it on me⟩ — **blam·er** *n* — **to blame** : at fault : RESPONSIBLE ⟨says he's not *to blame* for the accident⟩

usage Use of *blame* in sense 2b with *on* has occas. been disparaged as wrong. Such disparagement is without basis; *blame on* occurs as frequently in carefully edited prose as *blame for.* Both are standard.

2blame *n* (13c) **1** : an expression of disapproval or reproach : CENSURE **2 a** : a state of being blameworthy : CULPABILITY **b** *archaic* : FAULT, SIN **3** : responsibility for something believed to deserve censure ⟨they must share the ~⟩ — **blame·less** \-ləs\ *adj* — **blame·less·ly** *adv* — **blame·less·ness** *n*

blame·ful \ˈblām-fəl\ *adj* (14c) : BLAMABLE — **blame·ful·ly** \-fə-lē\ *adv*

blame·wor·thy \-ˌwər-thē\ *adj* (14c) : being at fault : deserving blame — **blame·wor·thi·ness** *n*

syn BLAMEWORTHY, BLAMABLE, GUILTY, CULPABLE mean deserving reproach or punishment. BLAMEWORTHY and BLAMABLE apply to any degree of reprehensibility ⟨conduct adjudged *blameworthy*⟩ ⟨an accident for which no one is *blamable*⟩. GUILTY implies responsibility for or consciousness of crime, sin, or, at the least, grave error or misdoing ⟨*guilty* of a breach of etiquette⟩. CULPABLE is weaker than *guilty* and is likely to connote malfeasance or errors of ignorance, omission, or negligence ⟨*culpable* neglect⟩.

blanc de chine \ˌbläⁿ-də-ˈshēn\ *n, often cap C* [F, lit., white of China] (1888) : white Chinese porcelain usu. used for making figurines

blanch \ˈblanch\ *vb* [ME *blaunchen,* fr. AF *blanchir,* fr. *blanc,* adj., white — more at BLANK] *vt* (14c) : to take the color out of: as **a** : to scald or parboil in water or steam in order to remove the skin from, whiten, or stop enzymatic action in (as food for freezing) **b** : to bleach by excluding light **c** : to make ashen or pale ⟨fear ~*es* the cheek⟩ ~ *vi* : to become white or pale — **blanch·er** *n*

blanc·mange \blə-ˈmänj, -ˈmäⁿzh\ *n* [ME *blancmanger,* fr. AF **blanc manger,* lit., white food] (1717) : a usu. sweetened and flavored dessert made from gelatinous or starchy ingredients and milk

bland \ˈbland\ *adj* [L *blandus*] (1565) **1 a** : smooth and soothing in manner or quality ⟨a ~ smile⟩ **b** : exhibiting no personal concern or embarrassment : UNPERTURBED ⟨a ~ confession of guilt⟩ **2 a** : not irritating, stimulating, or invigorating : SOOTHING **b** : DULL, INSIPID ⟨~ stories with little plot or action⟩ *syn* see SUAVE — **bland·ly** \ˈblan(d)-lē\ *adv* — **bland·ness** \ˈblan(d)-nəs\ *n*

blan·dish \ˈblan-dish\ *vb* [ME, fr. AF *blandiss-,* stem of *blandir,* fr. L *blandiri,* fr. *blandus* mild, flattering] *vt* (14c) : to coax with flattery : CAJOLE ~ *vi* : to act or speak in a flattering or coaxing manner *syn* see CAJOLE — **blan·dish·er** *n*

blan·dish·ment \-dish-mənt\ *n* (ca. 1553) : something that tends to coax or cajole : ALLUREMENT — often used in pl.

1blank \ˈblaŋk\ *adj* [ME, fr. AF *blanc* colorless, white, of Gmc origin; akin to OHG *blanch* white; prob. akin to L *flagrare* to burn — more at BLACK] (14c) **1** *archaic* : COLORLESS **2 a** : appearing or causing to appear dazed, confounded, or nonplussed ⟨stared in ~ dismay⟩ **b** : EXPRESSIONLESS ⟨a ~ stare⟩ **3 a** : devoid of covering or content; *esp* : free from writing or marks ⟨~ paper⟩ **b** : having spaces to be filled in **c** : lacking interest, variety, or change ⟨~ hours⟩ **4** : ABSOLUTE, UNQUALIFIED ⟨a ~ refusal⟩ **5** : UNFINISHED; *esp* : having a plain or unbroken surface where an opening is usual ⟨a ~ key⟩ ⟨a ~ arch⟩ *syn* see EMPTY — **blank·ly** *adv* — **blank·ness** *n*

2blank *n* (ca. 1570) **1** *obs* : the bull's-eye of a target **2 a** : an empty space (as on a paper) **b** : a paper with spaces for the entry of data ⟨an order ~⟩ **3 a** : a piece of material prepared to be made into something (as a key) by a further operation **b** : a cartridge loaded with propellant and a seal but no projectile **4 a** : an empty or featureless place or space ⟨my mind was a ~⟩ **b** : a vacant or uneventful period ⟨a long ~ in history⟩ **5** : a dash substituting for an omitted word

3blank *vt* (1764) **1 a** : OBSCURE, OBLITERATE ⟨~ out a line⟩ **b** : to stop access to : SEAL ⟨~ off a tunnel⟩ **2** : to keep (an opponent) from scoring ⟨were ~*ed* for eight innings⟩ ~ *vi* **1** : FADE — usu. used with *out* ⟨the music ~*ed* out⟩ **2** : to become confused or abstracted — often used with *out* ⟨his mind ~*ed* out momentarily⟩

blank check *n* (1793) **1** : a signed check with the amount unspecified **2** : complete freedom of action or control : CARTE BLANCHE

1blan·ket \ˈblaŋ-kət\ *n* [ME, white woolen cloth, bed covering, fr. AF *blankete,* fr. *blanc* white — more at BLANK] (14c) **1 a** : a large usu. oblong piece of woven fabric used as a bed covering **b** : a similar piece of fabric used as a body covering (as for an animal) ⟨a horse ~⟩ **2** : something that resembles a blanket ⟨a ~ of fog⟩ ⟨a ~ of gloom⟩ **3** : a rubber or plastic sheet on the cylinder in an offset press that transfers the image to the surface being printed — **blan·ket·like** \-ˌlīk\ *adj*

2blanket *vt* (1605) **1** : to cover with or as if with a blanket ⟨new grass ~*s* the slope⟩ **2 a** : to cover so as to obscure, interrupt, suppress, or extinguish ⟨~ a fire with foam⟩ **b** : to interrupt the smooth flow of wind to (as a downwind ship) **c** : to apply or cause to apply to uniformly despite wide separation or diversity among the elements included ⟨freight rates that ~ a region⟩ **d** : to cause to be included ⟨automatically ~*ed* into the program⟩ ⟨towns ~*ed* into the district⟩

3blanket *adj* (1886) **1** : effective or applicable in all instances **2** : covering all members of a group or class ⟨a ~ wage increase⟩

blanket chest *n* (1849) : a piece of furniture with a hinged lid, a deep well, and usu. one or two drawers underneath

blan·ket·flow·er \ˈblaŋ-kət-ˌflau̇(-ə)r\ *n* (1878) : GAILLARDIA

blanket stitch *n* (1873) : a buttonhole stitch with spaces of variable width used on materials too thick to hem — **blanket–stitch** *vt*

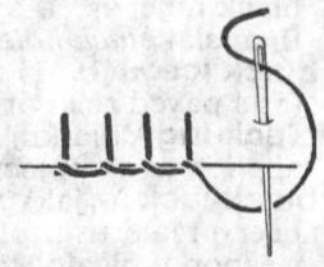

blanket stitch

blank·ie \ˈblaŋ-kē\ *n* [ˈ*blank*et + *-ie*] (1921) : a child's blanket

blank slate *n* (1980) : TABULA RASA

blank verse *n* (1588) : unrhymed verse; *specif* : unrhymed iambic pentameter verse

blan·quette \bläⁿ-ˈket\ *n* [F, fr. Occitan *blanqueto,* fr. *blanc* white, of Gmc origin; akin to OHG *blanch* white — more at BLANK] (1717) : a stew of light meat or seafood in a white sauce ⟨~ of veal⟩ ⟨~ of lobster⟩

1blare \ˈbler\ *vb* **blared; blar·ing** [ME *bleren;* akin to MD *blēren* to shout] *vi* (15c) : to sound loud and strident ⟨radios *blaring*⟩ ~ *vt* **1** : to sound or utter raucously ⟨sat *blaring* the car horn⟩ **2** : to proclaim flamboyantly ⟨headlines *blared* his defeat⟩

2blare *n* (1796) **1** : a loud strident noise **2** : dazzling often garish brilliance **3** : FLAMBOYANCE

blar·ney \ˈblär-nē\ *n* [*Blarney stone,* a stone in Blarney Castle, near Cork, Ireland, held to bestow skill in flattery on those who kiss it] (1780) **1** : skillful flattery : BLANDISHMENT **2** : NONSENSE, HUMBUG — **blarney** *vb*

bla·sé \blä-ˈzā\ *also* **bla·se** *adj* [F] (1819) **1** : apathetic to pleasure or excitement as a result of excessive indulgence or enjoyment : WORLD-WEARY **2** : SOPHISTICATED, WORLDLY-WISE **3** : UNCONCERNED *syn* see SOPHISTICATED

blas·pheme \blas-ˈfēm, ˈblas-ˌ\ *vb* **blas·phemed; blas·phem·ing** [ME *blasfemen,* fr. LL *blasphemare* — more at BLAME] *vi* (14c) : to utter blasphemy ~ *vt* **1** : to speak of or address with irreverence **2** : REVILE, ABUSE — **blas·phem·er** \-ˈfē-mər; ˈblas-ˌfē-mər, -fə-mər\ *n*

blas·phe·mous \ˈblas-fə-məs\ *adj* (15c) : impiously irreverent : PROFANE — **blas·phe·mous·ly** *adv* — **blas·phe·mous·ness** *n*

blas·phe·my \ˈblas-fə-mē\ *n, pl* **-mies** (13c) **1 a** : the act of insulting or showing contempt or lack of reverence for God **b** : the act of claiming the attributes of deity **2** : irreverence toward something considered sacred or inviolable

1blast \ˈblast\ *n* [ME, fr. OE *blǣst;* akin to OHG *blāst* blast, *blāsan* to blow, OE *blāwan* — more at BLOW] (bef. 12c) **1 a** : a violent gust of wind **b** : the effect or accompaniment (as sleet) of such a gust **2** : the sound produced by an impulsion of air through a wind instrument or whistle **3** : something resembling a gust of wind: as **a** : a stream of air or gas forced through a hole **b** : a vehement outburst **c** : the continuous blowing to which a charge of ore or metal is subjected in a blast furnace **4 a** : a sudden pernicious influence or effect ⟨the ~ of a huge epidemic⟩ **b** : a disease of plants marked by the formation of destructive lesions on leaves and inflorescences **5 a** : an explosion or violent detonation **b** : the shock wave of an explosion **c** : a forceful hit (as in baseball) or shot (as in soccer or golf); *esp* : HOME RUN **6** : SPEED, CAPACITY, OPERATION ⟨go full ~⟩ ⟨in full ~⟩ **7** : an enjoyably exciting experience, occasion, or event ⟨I had a ~⟩; *esp* : PARTY — **blast from the past** : a striking reminder of an earlier time : something that excites nostalgia

2blast *vi* (14c) **1** : BLARE ⟨music ~*ing* from the radio⟩ **2** : to make a vigorous attack **3 a** : to use an explosive **b** : SHOOT **4** : to hit a golf ball out of a sand trap with explosive force **5** : to proceed rapidly or aggressively ⟨~*ing* down the ski slope⟩ ~ *vt* **1 a** : to injure by or as if by the action of wind **b** : BLIGHT **2 a** : to shatter by or as if by an explosive **b** : to remove, open, or form by or as if by an explosive **c** : SHOOT **3** : to attack vigorously **4** : to cause to blast off ⟨will ~ themselves from the moon's surface⟩ **5** : to hit vigorously and effectively ⟨~*ed* a home run⟩ **6** : to play loudly ⟨~*ing* rock music on the stereo⟩ — **blast·er** *n*

blast- *or* **blasto-** *comb form* [G, fr. Gk, fr. *blastos*] : bud : budding : germ ⟨*blasto*disc⟩ ⟨*blast*ula⟩

-blast \ˌblast\ *n comb form* [NL *-blastus,* fr. Gk *blastos* bud, shoot, fr. *blastanein* to bud, sprout] : formative unit esp. of living matter : germ : cell : cell layer ⟨epi*blast*⟩

blast·ed *adj* (1540) **1** : damaged by or as if by an explosive, lightning, wind, or supernatural force ⟨upon this ~ heath —Shak.⟩ ⟨a ~ apple tree⟩ **2** : DAMNED, DETESTABLE ⟨this ~ weather⟩ **3** *slang* : intoxicated from drugs or alcohol

blas·te·ma \bla-ˈstē-mə\ *n, pl* **-mas** *or* **-ma·ta** \-mə-tə\ [NL, fr. Gk *blastēma* offshoot, fr. *blastanein*] (ca. 1823) : a mass of undifferentiated cells capable of growth and formation of new structures — **blas·te·mal** \-məl\ *or* **blas·te·mat·ic** \ˌblas-tə-ˈma-tik\ *adj*

blast furnace *n* (1706) : a furnace in which combustion is forced by a current of air under pressure; *esp* : one for the reduction of iron ore

-blastic *adj comb form* [ISV, fr. *-blast*] : having (such or so many) buds, germs, cells, or cell layers ⟨diplo*blastic*⟩

blast·ie \ˈblas-tē\ *n* [Sc *blast* to wither, fr. ²*blast*] (1786) *Scot* : an ugly little creature

blasting cap *n* (1879) : a small explosive device that is combined with a fuse to detonate a larger explosive

blast·ment \ˈblas(t)-mənt\ *n* (1604) *archaic* : a blighting influence

blas·to·coel *or* **blas·to·coele** \ˈblas-tə-ˌsēl\ *n* [ISV] (1875) : the fluid-filled cavity of a blastula — see BLASTULA illustration — **blas·to·coe·lic** \ˌblas-tə-ˈsē-lik\ *adj*

blas·to·cyst \ˈblas-tə-ˌsist\ *n* (1876) : the modified blastula of a placental mammal having an outer layer composed of the trophoblast

blas·to·derm \-ˌdərm\ *n* [G, fr. *blast-* + *-derm*] (1837) : a blastodisc after completion of cleavage and formation of the blastocoel

blas·to·der·mic vesicle \ˈblas-tə-ˌdər-mik-\ *n* (1836) : BLASTOCYST

blas·to·disc \ˈblas-tə-ˌdisk\ *n* (1878) : the embryo-forming portion of an egg with discoidal cleavage usu. appearing as a small disc on the upper surface of the yolk mass — see EGG illustration

blast·off \ˈblast-ˌȯf\ *n* (1939) : a blasting off (as of a rocket)

blast off *vi* (1950) : TAKE OFF 2d — used esp. of rocket-propelled missiles and vehicles

blas·to·mere \ˈblas-tə-ˌmir\ *n* [ISV] (1877) **:** one of the cells that are produced during cleavage of a zygote and that form the morula

blas·to·my·co·sis \ˌblas-tə-ˌmī-ˈkō-səs\ *n* [NL, fr. *Blastomyces,* fungus genus, fr. *blast-* + Gk *mykēs* fungus; akin to Gk *myxa* mucus — more at MUCUS] (ca. 1900) **:** any of several fungal infections; *esp* **:** an infectious disease caused by a yeast fungus (*Blastomyces dermititidis*) that affects esp. the lungs and skin

blas·to·pore \ˈblas-tə-ˌpȯr\ *n* (1880) **:** the opening of the archenteron — **blas·to·por·ic** \-ˈpȯr-ik\ *adj*

blas·to·spore \ˈblas-tə-ˌspȯr\ *n* [*blast-* + *spore*] (ca. 1927) **:** a fungal spore produced by budding

blas·tu·la \ˈblas-chə-lə\ *n, pl* **-las** *or* **-lae** \-ˌlē\ [NL, fr. Gk *blastos* bud — more at -BLAST] (1879) **:** an early metazoan embryo typically having the form of a hollow fluid-filled rounded cavity bounded by a single layer of cells — compare GASTRULA, MORULA — **blas·tu·la·tion** \ˌblas-chə-ˈlā-shən\ *n*

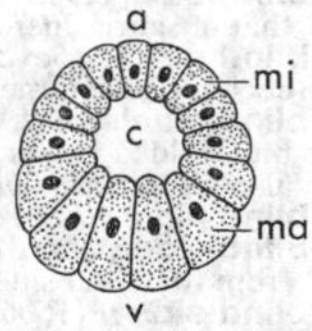

section of blastula: *c* blastocoel, *ma* macromere, *mi* micromere, *a* animal pole, *v* vegetal pole

blat \ˈblat\ *vb* **blat·ted; blat·ting** [perh. alter. of *bleat*] *vi* (1846) **1 :** to cry like a calf or sheep **:** BLEAT **2 a :** to make a raucous noise **b :** BLAB ~ *vt* **:** to utter loudly or foolishly **:** BLURT — **blat** *n*

bla·tan·cy \ˈblā-tᵊn(t)-sē\ *n, pl* **-cies** (1610) **1 :** the quality or state of being blatant **2 :** something that is blatant

bla·tant \ˈblā-tᵊnt\ *adj* [perh. fr. L *blatire* to chatter] (1596) **1 :** noisy esp. in a vulgar or offensive manner **:** CLAMOROUS **2 :** completely obvious, conspicuous, or obtrusive esp. in a crass or offensive manner **:** BRAZEN ⟨~ disregard for the rules⟩ ***syn*** see VOCIFEROUS — **bla·tant·ly** *adv*

blate \ˈblāt\ *adj* [ME] (1535) *chiefly Scot* **:** TIMID, SHEEPISH

[1]**blath·er** \ˈbla-t͟hər\ *vi* **blath·ered; blath·er·ing** \-t͟h(ə-)riŋ\ [ON *blathra;* akin to MHG *blōdern* to chatter] (1524) **:** to talk foolishly at length — often used with *on* — **blath·er·er** \-t͟hər-ər\ *n*

[2]**blather** *n* (1719) **1 :** voluble nonsensical or inconsequential talk or writing **2 :** STIR, COMMOTION

blath·er·skite \ˈbla-t͟hər-ˌskīt\ *n* [Sc, alter. of *blather skate,* fr. *blather, blether* blather + *skate* a contemptible person] (ca. 1650) **1 :** a person who blathers a lot **2 :** NONSENSE, BLATHER

blat·ter \ˈbla-tər\ *vi* [perh. fr. L *blaterare* to chatter] (ca. 1555) *dial* **:** to talk noisily and fast

blaw \ˈblȯ\ *vb* **blawed; blawn** \ˈblȯn\; **blaw·ing** \ˈblȯ(-)iŋ\ [ME (northern dial.) *blawen,* fr. OE *blāwan*] (bef. 12c) *chiefly Scot* **:** BLOW

blax·ploi·ta·tion \ˌblak-(ˌ)splȯi-ˈtā-shən\ *n, often attrib* [blend of *blax-* (alter. of *blacks*) and *exploitation*] (1972) **:** the exploitation of blacks by producers of black-oriented films ⟨~ movies⟩

[1]**blaze** \ˈblāz\ *n* [ME *blase,* fr. OE *blæse* torch; prob. akin to OE *bǣl* fire — more at BALD] (bef. 12c) **1 a :** an intensely burning fire **b :** intense direct light often accompanied by heat ⟨the ~ of TV lights⟩ **c :** an active burning; *esp* **:** a sudden bursting forth of flame **2 :** something that resembles the blaze of a fire: as **a :** a dazzling display ⟨a ~ of color⟩ **b :** a sudden outburst ⟨a ~ of fury⟩ ⟨went down in a ~ of glory⟩ **c** *pl* **:** HELL ⟨go to ~*s*⟩ ⟨as hot as ~*s*⟩

[2]**blaze** *vi* **blazed; blaz·ing** (13c) **1 a :** to burn brightly ⟨the sun *blazed* overhead⟩ **b :** to flare up **:** FLAME ⟨inflation *blazed* up⟩ **2 :** to be conspicuously brilliant or resplendent ⟨fields *blazing* with flowers⟩ **3 :** to shoot rapidly and repeatedly — usu. used with *away* **4 :** to proceed extremely rapidly **:** BLAST ⟨*blazing* down the highway⟩

[3]**blaze** *vt* **blazed; blaz·ing** [ME *blasen,* fr. MD *blāsen* to blow; akin to OHG *blāst* blast] (1541) **:** to make public or conspicuous

[4]**blaze** *n* [perh. fr. D or LG *bles;* akin to ON *blesi* white stripe on an animal and prob. to OE *blæse* torch] (1639) **1 a :** a usu. white stripe down the center of the face of an animal **b :** a white or gray streak in the hair of the head **2 :** a trail marker; *esp* **:** a mark made on a tree by chipping off a piece of the bark

[5]**blaze** *vt* **blazed; blaz·ing** (1750) **1 :** to mark (as a trail) with blazes **2 :** to lead in some direction or activity ⟨~ new trails in education⟩

blaze orange *n* (1959) **:** a very bright orange used in clothing esp. by hunters for visibility

blaz·er \ˈblā-zər\ *n* (15c) **1 :** one that blazes **2 :** a sports jacket often with notched collar and patch pockets — **blaz·ered** \-zərd\ *adj*

blaz·ing *adj* (1567) **:** of outstanding power, speed, heat, or intensity ⟨~ eyes⟩ ⟨a ~ fastball⟩ ⟨~ gunfire⟩ — **blaz·ing·ly** *adv*

blazing star *n* (15c) **1** *archaic* **:** COMET **2 :** any of various plants having conspicuous flower clusters or star-shaped flowers: as **a :** any of a genus (*Liatris*) of No. American composite herbs with spikes of rosy-purple rayless flowers — called also *button snakeroot* **b :** any of several No. American rough-leaved herbs (genus *Mentzelia* of the family Losaceae)

[1]**bla·zon** \ˈblā-zᵊn\ *n* [ME *blason,* fr. AF] (14c) **1 a :** armorial bearings **:** COAT OF ARMS **b :** the proper description or representation of heraldic or armorial bearings **2 :** ostentatious display

[2]**blazon** *vt* **bla·zoned; bla·zon·ing** \ˈblāz-niŋ; ˈblā-zᵊn-iŋ\ (1534) **1 :** to publish widely **:** PROCLAIM **2 a :** to describe (heraldic or armorial bearings) in technical terms **b :** to represent (armorial bearings) in drawing or engraving **3 a :** DISPLAY **b :** DECK, ADORN ⟨the town was ~*ed* with flags⟩ — **bla·zon·er** \-nər; -zᵊn-ər\ *n* — **blazoning** *n*

bla·zon·ry \ˈblā-zᵊn-rē\ *n, pl* **-ries** (1622) **1 a :** BLAZON 1b **b :** BLAZON 1a **2 :** a dazzling display

bld *abbr* **1** blond **2** blood

bldg *abbr* building

bldr *abbr* builder

[1]**bleach** \ˈblēch\ *vb* [ME *blechen,* fr. OE *blǣcean;* akin to OE *blāc* pale; prob. akin to L *flagrare* to burn — more at BLACK] *vt* (bef. 12c) **1 :** to remove color or stains from **2 a :** to make whiter or lighter esp. by physical or chemical removal of color ⟨~ clothing⟩ ⟨the sun had ~*ed* her hair⟩ **b :** to remove, make dull, or sanitize as if by removing color ⟨~*es* colonialism of its genocidal legacy —H. A. Giroux⟩ ~ *vi* **1 :** to grow white or lose color **2** *of coral* **:** to expel symbiotic zooxanthellae exposing a white skeleton — **bleach·able** \ˈblē-chə-bəl\ *adj*

[2]**bleach** *n* (1887) **1 :** the act or process of bleaching **2 :** a preparation used in bleaching **3 :** the degree of whiteness obtained by bleaching

bleach·er \ˈblē-chər\ *n* (1550) **1 :** one that bleaches or is used in bleaching **2 :** a usu. uncovered stand of tiered planks providing seating for spectators — usu. used in pl. — **bleach·er·ite** \-chə-ˌrīt\ *n*

bleaching powder *n* (ca. 1830) **:** a white powder consisting chiefly of calcium hydroxide, calcium chloride, and calcium hypochlorite and used as a bleach, disinfectant, or deodorant

bleak \ˈblēk\ *adj* [ME *bleke* pale; prob. akin to OE *blāc*] (1574) **1 :** exposed and barren and often windswept **2 :** COLD, RAW ⟨a ~ November evening⟩ **3 a :** lacking in warmth, life, or kindliness **:** GRIM **b :** not hopeful or encouraging **:** DEPRESSING ⟨a ~ outlook⟩ **c :** severely simple or austere ***syn*** see DISMAL — **bleak·ly** *adv* — **bleak·ness** *n*

[1]**blear** \ˈblir\ *vt* [ME *bleren,* prob. fr. OE **blerian;* akin to LG *bleer-oged* bleary-eyed] (14c) **1 :** to make (the eyes) sore or watery **2 :** DIM, BLUR

[2]**blear** *adj* (14c) **1 :** dim with water or tears **2 :** obscure to the view or imagination

blear–eyed \-ˈīd\ *adj* (14c) **:** BLEARY-EYED

bleary \ˈblir-ē\ *adj* (14c) **1** *of the eyes or vision* **:** dull or dimmed esp. from fatigue or sleep **2 :** poorly outlined or defined **:** DIM ⟨a ~ view⟩ **3 :** very tired ⟨~ travelers⟩ — **blear·i·ly** \ˈblir-ə-lē\ *adv* — **blear·i·ness** \ˈblir-ē-nəs\ *n*

bleary–eyed \-ˈīd\ *adj* (ca. 1927) **:** having the eyes dimmed and watery (as from fatigue, drink, or emotion)

[1]**bleat** \ˈblēt, *Northern also* ˈblat, *Southern usu* ˈblāt\ *vb* [ME *bleten,* fr. OE *blǣtan;* akin to L *flēre* to weep, OE *bellan* to roar — more at BELLOW] *vi* (bef. 12c) **1 a :** to make the natural cry of a sheep or goat; *also* **:** to utter a similar sound **b :** WHIMPER **2 a :** to talk complainingly or with a whine **b :** BLATHER ~ *vt* **:** to utter in a bleating manner — **bleat·er** *n*

[2]**bleat** *n* (ca. 1505) **1 :** the cry of a sheep or goat; *also* **:** a similar sound ⟨the ~ of a cell phone⟩ **2 :** a feeble outcry, protest, or complaint

bleb \ˈbleb\ *n* [perh. alter. of *blob*] (1607) **1 :** a small blister **2 :** BUBBLE; *also* **:** a small particle **3 :** something resembling a bleb; *esp* **:** a vesicular outgrowth of a plasma or nuclear membrane — **bleb·bing** \ˈble-biŋ\ *n* — **bleb·by** \ˈble-bē\ *adj*

[1]**bleed** \ˈblēd\ *vb* **bled** \ˈbled\; **bleed·ing** [ME *bleden,* fr. OE *blēdan,* fr. *blōd* blood] *vi* (bef. 12c) **1 a :** to emit or lose blood **b :** to sacrifice one's blood esp. in battle **2 :** to feel anguish, pain, or sympathy ⟨a heart that ~*s* at a friend's misfortune⟩ **3 a :** to escape by oozing or flowing (as from a wound) **b :** to spread into or through something gradually **:** SEEP ⟨foreign policy ~*s* into economic policy —J. B. Judis⟩ **4 :** to give up some constituent (as sap or dye) by exuding or diffusing it **5 a :** to pay out or give money **b :** to have money extorted **6 :** to be printed so as to run off one or more edges of the page after trimming ~ *vt* **1 :** to remove or draw blood from **2 :** to get or extort money from esp. over a prolonged period **3 :** to draw sap from (a tree) **4 a :** to extract or let out some or all of a contained substance from ⟨~ a brake line⟩ **b :** to extract or cause to escape from a container **c :** to diminish gradually — usu. used with *off* ⟨a pilot ~*ing* off airspeed⟩ **d :** to lose rapidly and uncontrollably ⟨the company was ~*ing* money⟩ **e :** SAP ⟨cost overruns . . . ~ other programs —Alex Roland⟩ **5 :** to cause (as a printed illustration) to bleed — **bleed white :** to drain of blood or resources

[2]**bleed** *n* (ca. 1937) **1 :** printed matter (as an illustration) that bleeds; *also* **:** the part of a bleed trimmed off **2 :** the escape of blood from vessels **:** HEMORRHAGE

bleed·er *n* (1803) **1 :** one that bleeds; *esp* **:** HEMOPHILIAC **2** *Brit* **:** ROTTER; *also* **:** BLOKE

bleed·ing \ˈblē-diŋ, -dᵊn\ *adj or adv* (1858) *chiefly Brit* **:** BLOODY — used as an intensive

bleeding heart *n* (1691) **1 :** a garden plant (*Dicentra spectabilis*) of the fumitory family with racemes of usu. deep pink or white drooping heart-shaped flowers; *broadly* **:** any of several plants (genus *Dicentra*) **2 :** a person who shows extravagant sympathy esp. for an object of alleged persecution

[1]**bleep** \ˈblēp\ *n* [imit.] (1953) **1 :** a short high-pitched sound (as from electronic equipment) **2** — used in place of an obscene or vulgar expletive

[2]**bleep** *vt* (1968) **:** BLIP

[3]**bleep** *interj* (1970) — used in place of an expletive

[1]**blem·ish** \ˈble-mish\ *vt* [ME *blemisshen,* to damage, injure, sully, fr. AF *blemiss-,* stem of *blemir, blesmir,* fr. OF, lit., to make pale by wounding, of Gmc origin; akin to OHG *blas*ros horse with a blaze, ON *blesi* blaze — more at BLAZE] (14c) **:** to spoil by a flaw

[2]**blemish** *n* (1535) **:** a noticeable imperfection; *esp* **:** one that seriously impairs appearance

[1]**blench** \ˈblench\ *vi* [ME, to deceive, blench, fr. OE *blencan* to deceive; akin to ON *blekkja* to impose on] (13c) **:** to draw back or turn aside from lack of courage **:** FLINCH ***syn*** see RECOIL

[2]**blench** *vb* [alter. of *blanch*] (1813) **:** BLEACH, WHITEN

[1]**blend** \ˈblend\ *vb* **blend·ed** *also* **blent** \ˈblent\; **blend·ing** [ME, prob. fr. ON *blend-,* pres. stem of *blanda* to mix; akin to OE *blandan* to mix, Lith *blandus* impure, cloudy] *vt* (14c) **1 :** MIX; *esp* **:** to combine or associate so that the separate constituents or the line of demarcation cannot be distinguished **2 :** to prepare by thoroughly intermingling different varieties or grades ~ *vi* **1 a :** to mingle intimately or unobtrusively **b :** to combine into an integrated whole **2 :** to produce a harmonious effect ***syn*** see MIX

[2]**blend** *n* (1883) **1 :** something produced by blending: as **a :** a product prepared by blending **b :** a word (as *brunch*) produced by combining other words or parts of words **2 :** a group of two or more consecutive consonants that begin a syllable

blende \ˈblend\ *n* [G, fr. *blenden* to deceive, lit., to blind, fr. OHG *blenten;* akin to OE *blind*] (ca. 1753) **:** SPHALERITE

blended family *n* (1975) **:** a family that includes children of a previous marriage of one spouse or both

\ə\ **a**but \ᵊ\ **k**itten, F ta**ble** \ər\ **fur**ther \a\ **a**sh \ā\ **a**ce \ä\ m**o**p, m**a**r \au̇\ **ou**t \ch\ **ch**in \e\ b**e**t \ē\ **ea**sy \g\ **g**o \i\ h**i**t \ī\ **i**ce \j\ **j**ob \ŋ\ si**ng** \ō\ g**o** \ȯ\ l**aw** \ȯi\ b**oy** \th\ **th**in \t͟h\ **th**e \ü\ l**oo**t \u̇\ f**oo**t \y\ **y**et \zh\ vi**si**on, bei**ge** \k, ⁿ, œ, ue, ʸ\ *see* Guide to Pronunciation

blended whiskey *n* (1940) **:** whiskey blended from two or more straight whiskeys or from whiskey and neutral spirits

blend•er \ˈblen-dər\ *n* (ca. 1611) **:** one that blends; *esp* **:** an electric appliance for grinding or mixing ⟨a food ~⟩

blending inheritance *n* (1922) **:** the expression in offspring of phenotypic characters (as pink flower color from red and white parents) intermediate between those of the parents; *also* **:** inheritance in a now discarded theory in which the genetic material of offspring was held to be a uniform blend of that of the parents

blen•ny \ˈble-nē\ *n, pl* **blennies** [L *blennius,* a sea fish, fr. Gk *blennos*] (1769) **:** any of numerous usu. small and elongated marine fishes (esp. families Blenniidae and Clinidae) including scaled and scaleless forms

blephar- *or* **blepharo-** *comb form* [NL, fr. Gk, fr. *blepharon*] **1 :** eyelid ⟨*blepharo*spasm⟩ **2 :** cilium **:** flagellum ⟨*blepharo*plast⟩

bleph•a•ro•plast \ˈble-fə-rō-ˌplast\ *n* (1897) **:** a basal body esp. of a flagellated cell

bleph•a•ro•plas•ty \-ˌplas-tē\ *n* (1842) **:** plastic surgery on the eyelid esp. to remove fatty or excess tissue

bleph•a•ro•spasm \-ˌspa-zəm\ *n* (1872) **:** spasmodic winking of the eyelids due to contraction of the muscle encircling the orbit

bles•bok \ˈbles-ˌbäk\ *n* [Afrik, fr. *bles* blaze + *bok* male antelope] (1824) **:** a So. African antelope (*Damaliscus dorcas* syn. *D. pygargus*) having a large white patch down the center of the face

bless \ˈbles\ *vt* **blessed** \ˈblest\ *also* **blest** \ˈblest\; **bless•ing** [ME, fr. OE *blētsian,* fr. *blōd* blood; fr. the use of blood in consecration] (bef. 12c) **1 :** to hallow or consecrate by religious rite or word **2 :** to hallow with the sign of the cross **3 :** to invoke divine care for ⟨~ your heart⟩ — used in the phrase *bless you* to wish good health esp. to one who has just sneezed **4 a :** PRAISE, GLORIFY ⟨~ his holy name⟩ **b :** to speak well of **:** APPROVE **5 :** to confer prosperity or happiness upon **6** *archaic* **:** PROTECT, PRESERVE **7 :** ENDOW, FAVOR ⟨~*ed* with athletic ability⟩

bless•ed \ˈble-səd\ *also* **blest** \ˈblest\ *adj* (bef. 12c) **1 a :** held in reverence **:** VENERATED ⟨the ~ saints⟩ **b :** honored in worship **:** HALLOWED ⟨the ~ Trinity⟩ **c :** BEATIFIC ⟨a ~ visitation⟩ **2 :** of or enjoying happiness; *specif* **:** enjoying the bliss of heaven — used as a title for a beatified person **3 :** bringing pleasure, contentment, or good fortune **4** — used as an intensive ⟨never had one ~ minute of instruction —Charles Scribner Jr.⟩ — **bless•ed•ly** *adv* — **bless•ed•ness** *n*

Bless•ed Sacrament \ˈble-səd-\ *n* (15c) **:** the Communion elements; *specif* **:** the consecrated host

bless•ing *n* (bef. 12c) **1 a :** the act or words of one that blesses **b :** APPROVAL, ENCOURAGEMENT **2 :** a thing conducive to happiness or welfare **3 :** grace said at a meal

bleth•er \ˈble-t͟hər\ *chiefly Brit, var of* BLATHER

BLEVE *abbr* boiling liquid expanding vapor explosion

blew *past of* BLOW

[1]**blight** \ˈblīt\ *n* [origin unknown] (1578) **1 a :** a disease or injury of plants marked by the formation of lesions, withering, and death of parts (as leaves and tubers) **b :** an organism (as an insect or a fungus) that causes blight **2 :** something that frustrates plans or hopes **3 :** something that impairs or destroys **4 :** a deteriorated condition ⟨urban ~⟩

[2]**blight** *vt* (1664) **1 :** to affect (as a plant) with blight **2 :** to impair the quality or effect of ⟨the condition that has ~*ed* his son's life —Patricia Guthrie⟩ ~ *vi* **:** to suffer from or become affected with blight

blight•er \ˈblī-tər\ *n* (1822) **1 :** one that blights **2** *chiefly Brit* **a :** a disliked or contemptible person **b :** FELLOW, GUY

Blighty \ˈblī-tē\ *n* [modif. of Hindi & Urdu *bilātī* foreign, English, alter. of *vilāyatī,* fr. *vilāyat* province, realm, country beyond India, fr. Pers, dominion, province, fr. Ar *wilāya*] (1915) *chiefly Brit* **:** one's native land (as England)

blimp \ˈblimp\ *n* [imit.; perh. fr. the sound made by striking the gas bag with the thumb] (1916) **1 :** an airship that maintains its form by pressure from contained gas **2** *cap* **:** COLONEL BLIMP

blimp•ish \ˈblim-pish\ *adj, often cap* (1938) **:** of, relating to, or suggesting a Colonel Blimp — **blimp•ish•ly** *adv* — **blimp•ish•ness** *n*

blin \ˈblin\ *n, pl* **bli•ni** \ˈblē-nē, ˈbli-; blə-ˈnē\ *or* **bli•nis** \ˈblē-nēz, ˈbli-; blə-ˈnēz\ [Russ] (1888) **:** a thin often buckwheat pancake usu. filled (as with sour cream) and folded

[1]**blind** \ˈblīnd\ *adj* [ME, fr. OE; akin to OHG *blint* blind, OE *blandan* to mix — more at BLEND] (bef. 12c) **1 a (1) :** SIGHTLESS **(2) :** having less than 1/10 of normal vision in the more efficient eye when refractive defects are fully corrected by lenses **b :** of or relating to sightless persons **2 a :** unable or unwilling to discern or judge ⟨~ to a lover's faults⟩ **b :** UNQUESTIONING ⟨~ loyalty⟩ **3 a :** having no regard to rational discrimination, guidance, or restriction ⟨~ choice⟩ **b :** lacking a directing or controlling consciousness ⟨~ chance⟩ **c :** DRUNK 1a **4 a :** made or done without sight of certain objects or knowledge of certain facts that could serve for guidance or cause bias ⟨a ~ taste test⟩ — compare DOUBLE-BLIND, SINGLE-BLIND **b :** having no knowledge of information that may cause bias during the course of an experiment or test ⟨physicians ~ to whether the test drug is administered⟩ **5 :** DEFECTIVE: as **a :** lacking a growing point or producing leaves instead of flowers **b :** lacking a complete or legible address ⟨~ mail⟩ **6 a :** difficult to discern, make out, or discover **b :** hidden from sight **:** COVERED ⟨~ seam⟩ **7 :** having but one opening or outlet ⟨~ sockets⟩ **8 :** having no opening for light or passage **:** BLANK ⟨~ wall⟩ — **blind•ly** \ˈblīn(d)-lē\ *adv* — **blind•ness** \ˈblīn(d)-nəs\ *n*

[2]**blind** *vt* (bef. 12c) **1 a :** to make blind **b :** DAZZLE **2 a :** to withhold light from **b :** HIDE, CONCEAL — **blind•ing•ly** \ˈblīn-diŋ-lē\ *adv*

[3]**blind** *n* (1678) **1 :** something to hinder sight or keep out light: as **a :** a window shutter **b :** a roller window shade **c :** VENETIAN BLIND **d :** BLINDER **2 :** a place of concealment; *esp* **:** a concealing enclosure from which one may shoot game or observe wildlife **3 a :** something put forward for the purpose of misleading **:** SUBTERFUGE **b :** a person who acts as a decoy or distraction

[4]**blind** *adv* (ca. 1775) **1 :** BLINDLY: as **a :** to the point of insensibility ⟨~ drunk⟩ **b :** without seeing outside an airplane ⟨fly ~⟩ **c :** without knowledge of certain facts that could serve for guidance or cause bias ⟨tasted the wine ~⟩ **2** — used as an intensive ⟨was robbed ~⟩

blind alley *n* (1583) **:** a fruitless or mistaken course or direction

blind carbon copy *n* (1973) **:** a copy of a message (as an e-mail) that is sent without the knowledge of the other recipients

blind date *n* (1925) **1 :** a date between two persons who have not previously met **2 :** either participant in a blind date

blind•er \ˈblīn-dər\ *n* (1809) **1 :** either of two flaps on a horse's bridle to keep it from seeing objects at its sides **2** *pl* **:** a limitation or obstruction to sight or discernment

blind•fish \ˈblīn(d)-ˌfish\ *n* (1843) **:** any of several small fishes with vestigial functionless eyes found usu. in the waters of caves

[1]**blind•fold** \-ˌfōld\ *vt* [alter. of ME *blindfellen, blindfelden* to strike blind, blindfold, fr. *blind* + *fellen* to fell] (1533) **1 :** to cover the eyes of with or as if with a bandage **2 :** to hinder from seeing; *esp* **:** to keep from comprehension — **blindfold** *adj*

[2]**blindfold** *n* (1715) **1 :** a bandage for covering the eyes **2 :** something that obscures mental or physical vision

blind gut *n* (15c) **:** a digestive cavity open at only one end; *esp* **:** the cecum of the large intestine

blind•man's buff \ˈblīn(d)-ˈmanz-\ *n* (1599) **:** a group game in which a blindfolded player tries to catch and identify another player — called also *blindman's bluff*

blind pig *n* (1886) **:** BLIND TIGER

blind•side \ˈblīn(d)-ˌsīd\ *vt* (1968) **1 :** to hit unexpectedly from or as if from the blind side ⟨~ the quarterback⟩ **2 :** to surprise unpleasantly

blind side *n* (1606) **1 :** the side away from which one is looking **2 :** the side on which one that is blind in one eye cannot see

blind spot *n* (1872) **1 a :** the small circular area at the back of the retina where the optic nerve enters the eyeball and which is devoid of rods and cones and is not sensitive to light — called also *optic disk;* see EYE illustration **b :** a portion of a field that cannot be seen or inspected with available equipment **2 :** an area in which one fails to exercise judgment or discrimination

blind tiger *n* (1857) **:** a place that sells intoxicants illegally

blind trust *n* (1969) **:** an arrangement in which the financial holdings of a person in an influential position are placed in the control of a fiduciary in order to avoid a possible conflict of interest

blind•worm \ˈblīnd-ˌwərm\ *n* (15c) **:** SLOWWORM

bling–bling \ˈbliŋ-ˌbliŋ\ *also* **bling** \ˈbliŋ\ *n* [imit.] (1999) **:** flashy jewelry worn esp. as an indication of wealth; *broadly* **:** expensive and ostentatious possessions

[1]**blink** \ˈbliŋk\ *vb* [ME, to open one's eyes] *vi* (14c) **1 a** *obs* **:** to look glancingly **:** PEEP **b :** to look with half-shut eyes **c :** to close and open the eyes involuntarily **2 :** to shine dimly or intermittently **3 a :** to look with too little concern **b :** to look with surprise or dismay **4 :** YIELD, GIVE IN ⟨each side waiting for the other to ~⟩ ~ *vt* **1 a :** to cause to blink **b :** to remove (as tears) from the eye by blinking **2 :** to deny recognition to

[2]**blink** *n* (1578) **1** *chiefly Scot* **:** GLIMPSE, GLANCE **2 :** GLIMMER, SPARKLE **3 :** a usu. involuntary shutting and opening of the eye **4 :** ICEBLINK — **in the blink of an eye :** in an instant — **on the blink :** in or into a disabled or useless condition ⟨the TV is *on the blink*⟩

[1]**blink•er** \ˈbliŋ-kər\ *n* (1636) **1 :** one that blinks; *esp* **:** a light that flashes off and on as a warning or a signal **2 a :** BLINDER 1 **b :** a cloth hood with shades projecting at the sides of the eye openings used on skittish racehorses — usu. used in pl. **3** *pl* **:** BLINDER 2

[2]**blinker** *vt* (1865) **:** to put blinders on

blink•ered \ˈbliŋ-kərd\ *adj* (1867) **1 :** limited in scope or understanding **:** NARROW-MINDED **2 :** fitted with blinders

blin•tze \ˈblin(t)-sə\ *or* **blintz** \ˈblin(t)s\ *n* [Yiddish *blintse,* of Slavic origin; akin to Ukrainian *mlynets',* dim. of *mlyn* pancake] (1903) **:** a thin usu. wheat-flour pancake folded to form a casing (as for cheese or fruit) and then sautéed or baked

[1]**blip** \ˈblip\ *n* [imit.] (1945) **1 :** a trace on a display screen (as an oscilloscope); *esp* **:** a spot on a radar screen **2 :** a short crisp sound **3 :** an interruption of the sound received in a radio or television program or occurring in a recording as a result of blipping **4 :** a transient sharp movement up or down (as of a quantity commonly shown on a graph) **5 :** something relatively small or inconsequential within a larger context ⟨made only a ~ on the political scene⟩

[2]**blip** *vt* **blipped; blip•ping** (1968) **:** to remove (recorded sound) from a recording so that there is an interruption of the sound in the reproduction ⟨a censor *blipped* the swearwords⟩

bliss \ˈblis\ *n* [ME *blisse,* fr. OE *bliss;* akin to OE *blīthe* blithe] (bef. 12c) **1 :** complete happiness **2 :** PARADISE, HEAVEN

blissed–out \ˈblist-ˈau̇t\ *adj* (1973) **:** experiencing bliss **:** ECSTATIC

bliss•ful \ˈblis-fəl\ *adj* (12c) **1 :** full of, marked by, or causing bliss ⟨a ~ marriage⟩ **2 :** happily benighted ⟨~ ignorance⟩ — **bliss•ful•ly** \-fə-lē\ *adv* — **bliss•ful•ness** *n*

B–list \ˈbē-ˌlist\ *n* (1935) **:** a list or group of individuals who are prominent but not important or popular enough to be on the A-list

[1]**blis•ter** \ˈblis-tər\ *n* [ME *blister, blester,* prob. fr. OE **blȳster, *blǣster;* akin to ON *blāstr* swelling, OE *blǣst* blast] (14c) **1 :** an elevation of the epidermis containing watery liquid **2 :** an enclosed raised spot (as in paint) resembling a blister **3 :** an agent (as lewisite) that causes blistering **4 :** a fungal disease of plants marked by raised patches on the leaves **5 :** any of various structures that bulge out (as a gunner's compartment on a bomber) — **blis•tery** \-t(ə-)rē\ *adj*

[2]**blister** *vb* **blis•tered; blis•ter•ing** \-t(ə-)riŋ\ *vi* (15c) **:** to become affected with a blister ~ *vt* **1 :** to raise a blister on **2 :** LAMBASTE 2

blister beetle *n* (1816) **:** a beetle (as the Spanish fly) used medicinally dried and powdered to raise blisters on the skin; *broadly* **:** any of a family (Meloidae) of soft-bodied beetles whose blood contains cantharidin

blis•ter•ing *adj* (1562) **1 :** extremely intense or severe **2 :** very rapid ⟨a ~ pace⟩ — **blistering** *adv* — **blis•ter•ing•ly** \-t(ə-)riŋ-lē\ *adv*

blister pack *n* (1955) **:** a package holding and displaying merchandise in a clear plastic case sealed to a sheet of cardboard

blister rust *n* (1916) **:** any of several diseases of pines that are caused by rust fungi (genus *Cronartium*) in the aecial stage and that affect the sapwood and inner bark and produce blisters externally

blithe \ˈblīth, ˈblīt͟h\ *adj* **blith•er; blith•est** [ME, fr. OE *blīthe;* akin to OHG *blīdi* joyous] (bef. 12c) **1 :** of a happy lighthearted character or disposition **2 :** lacking due thought or consideration **:** CASUAL, HEEDLESS ⟨~ unconcern⟩ ***syn*** see MERRY — **blithe•ly** *adv*

blith•er \ˈbli-t͟hər\ *vi* (1868) **:** BLATHER — **blither** *n* — **blith•er•ing•ly** \ˈbli-t͟h-riŋ-lē, ˈbli-t͟hə-\ *adv*

blithe•some \ˈblīth-səm, ˈblīt͟h-\ *adj* (1724) **:** GAY, MERRY — **blithe•some•ly** *adv*

BLitt *or* **BLit** *abbr* [ML *baccalaureus litterarum*] bachelor of letters; bachelor of literature
blitz \ˈblits\ *n* (ca. 1939) **1 a :** BLITZKRIEG 1 **b** (1) **:** an intensive aerial military campaign (2) **:** AIR RAID **2 a :** a fast intensive nonmilitary campaign or attack ⟨an advertising ~⟩ **b :** a rush of the passer by a defensive linebacker, back, or end in football — **blitz** *vb*
blitzed \ˈblitst\ *adj* (1966) *slang* **:** intoxicated by drugs or alcohol
blitz·krieg \-ˌkrēg\ *n* [G, fr. *Blitz* lightning + *Krieg* war] (1939) **1 :** war conducted with great speed and force; *specif* **:** a violent surprise offensive by massed air forces and mechanized ground forces in close coordination **2 :** BLITZ 2a — **blitzkrieg** *vt*
bliz·zard \ˈbli-zərd\ *n* [origin unknown] (1870) **1 :** a long severe snowstorm **2 :** an intensely strong cold wind filled with fine snow **3 :** an overwhelming rush or deluge ⟨a ~ of mail around the holidays⟩ — **bliz·zardy** \ˈbli-zər-dē\ *also* **bliz·zard·ly** \-ˌzərd-lē\ *adj*
blk *abbr* **1** black **2** block **3** bulk
BLM *abbr* Bureau of Land Management
[1]**bloat** \ˈblōt\ *adj* [ME *blout, blote* soft, pliable, fr. ON *blautr* soft, weak; akin to OE *blēat* miserable] (14c) **:** BLOATED, PUFFY
[2]**bloat** *vt* (1677) **1 a :** to make turgid or swollen **b :** to cause abdominal distension in **2 :** to fill to capacity or overflowing ~ *vi* **:** SWELL
[3]**bloat** *n* (1836) **1 a :** one that is bloated **b :** unwarranted or excessive growth or enlargement ⟨bureaucratic ~⟩ **2 :** digestive disturbance of ruminant animals and esp. cattle marked by accumulation of gas in one or more stomach compartments **3 :** a condition of large dogs marked by distension and usu. life-threatening rotation of the stomach
bloat·ed *adj* (1656) **1 :** obnoxiously vain ⟨a ~ ego⟩ **2 a :** being much larger than what is warranted ⟨a ~ estimate⟩ **b :** INFLATED 1
[1]**bloat·er** \ˈblō-tər\ *n* [obs. *bloat* (to cure)] (1824) **:** a large fat herring or mackerel lightly salted and briefly smoked
[2]**bloater** *n* [[2]*bloat*] (1888) **:** a small silvery cisco (*Coregonus hoyi*) of the Great Lakes having oily flesh
[1]**blob** \ˈbläb\ *n* [ME (Sc)] (15c) **1 a :** a small drop or lump of something viscid or thick **b :** a daub or spot of color **2 :** something shapeless
[2]**blob** *vt* **blobbed; blob·bing** (15c) **:** to mark with blobs **:** SPLOTCH
bloc \ˈbläk\ *n* [F, lit., block] (1903) **1 a :** a temporary combination of parties in a legislative assembly **b :** a group of legislators who act together for some common purpose irrespective of party lines **2 a :** a combination of persons, groups, or nations forming a unit with a common interest or purpose ⟨a ~ of voters⟩ **b :** a group of nations united by treaty or agreement for mutual support or joint action
[1]**block** \ˈbläk\ *n, often attrib* [ME *blok,* fr. MF & MD; MF *bloc,* fr. MD *blok;* akin to OHG *bloh* block] (14c) **1 :** a compact usu. solid piece of substantial material esp. when worked or altered to serve a particular purpose: as **a :** the piece of wood on which the neck of a person condemned to be beheaded is laid for execution **b :** a mold or form on which articles are shaped or displayed **c :** a hollow rectangular building unit usu. of artificial material **d :** a lightweight usu. cubical and solid wooden or plastic building toy that is usu. provided in sets **e :** the casting that contains the cylinders of an internal combustion engine **f :** STARTING BLOCK **2 a :** OBSTACLE **b :** an obstruction of an opponent's play in sports; *esp* **:** a halting or impeding of the progress or movement of an opponent in football by use of the body **c** (1) **:** interruption of normal physiological function (as of a tissue or organ); *esp* **:** HEART BLOCK (2) **:** local anesthesia (as by injection) produced by interruption of the flow of impulses along a nerve **d :** interruption or cessation esp. of train of thought by competing thoughts or psychological suppression — compare WRITER'S BLOCK **3** *slang* **:** HEAD 1 ⟨threatened to knock his ~ off⟩ **4 :** a wooden or metal case enclosing one or more pulleys and having a hook, eye, or strap by which it may be attached **5 :** a piece of material (as wood or linoleum) having on its surface a hand-cut design from which impressions are to be printed **6 a** (1) **:** a usu. rectangular space (as in a city) enclosed by streets and occupied by or intended for buildings (2) **:** the distance along one of the sides of such a block **b** (1) **:** a large building divided into separate functional units (2) **:** a line of row houses (3) **:** a distinctive part of a building or integrated group of buildings **7 :** a platform from which property is sold at auction **8 a :** a quantity, number, or section of things dealt with as a unit **b :** BLOC 2 — **on the block :** for sale
[2]**block** *vt* (1580) **1 a :** to make unsuitable for passage or progress by obstruction **b** *archaic* **:** BLOCKADE **c :** to hinder the passage, progress, or accomplishment of by or as if by interposing an obstruction **d :** to shut off from view **e :** to interfere usu. legitimately with (as an opponent) in various games or sports **f :** to prevent normal functioning or action of **g :** to restrict the exchange of (as currency or checks) **2 :** to mark or indicate the outline or chief lines of ⟨~ out a design⟩ **3 :** to shape on, with, or as if with a block ⟨~ a hat⟩ **4 :** to secure, support, or provide with a block **5 :** to work out or chart the movements of (as stage performers) — often used with *out* **6 :** to make (two or more lines of writing or type) flush at the left or at both left and right ~ *vi* **:** to block an opponent in sports ***syn*** see HINDER — **block·er** *n*
[1]**block·ade** \blä-ˈkād\ *vt* **block·ad·ed; block·ad·ing** (1563) **1 :** to subject to a blockade **2 :** BLOCK, OBSTRUCT — **block·ad·er** *n*
[2]**blockade** *n* (1683) **1 :** the isolation by a warring nation of an enemy area (as a harbor) by troops or warships to prevent passage of persons or supplies; *broadly* **:** a restrictive measure designed to obstruct the commerce and communications of an unfriendly nation **2 :** something that blocks **3 :** interruption of normal physiological function (as transmission of nerve impulses) of a cellular receptor, tissue, or organ; *also* **:** inhibition of a physiologically active substance (as a hormone)
block·ade–run·ner \-ˈkād-ˌrə-nər\ *n* (1861) **:** a ship or person that runs through a blockade — **block·ade–run·ning** \-ˌrə-niŋ\ *n*
block·age \ˈblä-kij\ *n* (1759) **:** an act or instance of obstructing **:** the state of being blocked ⟨a ~ in a coronary artery⟩
block and tackle *n* (1717) **:** pulley blocks with associated rope or cable for hoisting or hauling
block·bust·er \ˈbläk-ˌbəs-tər\ *n, often attrib* (1942) **1 :** a very large high-explosive bomb **2 :** one that is notably expensive, effective, successful, large, or extravagant **3 :** one who engages in blockbusting
block·bust·ing \-tiŋ\ *n* (1954) **:** profiteering by inducing property owners to sell hastily and often at a loss by appeals to fears of depressed values because of threatened minority encroachment and then reselling at inflated prices
block diagram *n* (1944) **:** a diagram (as of a system, process, or program) in which labeled figures (as rectangles) and interconnecting lines represent the relationship of parts
blocked \ˈbläkt\ *adj* (1898) **:** affected by a psychological block
block grant *n* (1966) **:** an unrestricted federal grant
block·head \ˈbläk-ˌhed\ *n* (1549) **:** a stupid person
block·house \-ˌhau̇s\ *n* (1512) **1 a :** a structure of heavy timbers formerly used for military defense with sides loopholed and pierced for gunfire and often with a projecting upper story **b :** a small easily defended building for protection from enemy fire **2 :** a building usu. of reinforced concrete serving as an observation point for an operation likely to be accompanied by heat, blast, or radiation hazard

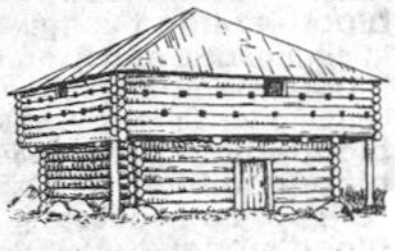

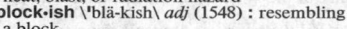

blockhouse 1a

block·ish \ˈblä-kish\ *adj* (1548) **:** resembling a block
block letter *n* (1849) **:** an often hand-drawn simple capital letter composed of strokes of uniform thickness
block party *n* (1907) **:** an outdoor public party put on by the residents of a city block or neighborhood
block plane *n* (1837) **:** a small plane made with the blade set at a lower pitch than other planes and used chiefly on end grains of wood
blocky \ˈblä-kē\ *adj* **block·i·er; -est** (ca. 1816) **1 :** resembling a block in form **:** CHUNKY **2 :** filled with or made up of blocks or patches
blog \ˈblȯg, ˈbläg\ *n* [short for *Weblog*] (1999) **:** a Web site that contains online personal reflections, comments, and often hyperlinks provided by the writer; *also* **:** the contents of such a site — **blog** *vb* — **blog·ger** *n* — **blog·ging** *n*
blog·o·sphere \ˈblä-gə-ˌsfir\ *n* (1999) **:** all of the blogs on the Internet as a collective whole
bloke \ˈblōk\ *n* [origin unknown] (ca. 1829) *chiefly Brit* **:** MAN, FELLOW
[1]**blond** *or* **blonde** \ˈbländ\ *adj* [AF *blunt, blound,* masc., *blounde,* fem.] (15c) **1 :** of a flaxen, golden, light auburn, or pale yellowish-brown color ⟨~ hair⟩; *also* **:** having blond hair ⟨a ~ man⟩ — spelled *blond* when used of a boy or man and often *blonde* when used of a girl or woman **2 a :** of a light color **b :** of the color blond **c :** made light-colored by bleaching ⟨~ wood table⟩ — **blond·ish** \ˈblän-dish\ *adj*
[2]**blond** *or* **blonde** *n* (1819) **1 :** a person having blond hair — spelled *blond* when used of a boy or man and usu. *blonde* when used of a girl or woman **2 :** a light yellowish brown to dark grayish yellow
[1]**blood** \ˈbləd\ *n, often attrib* [ME, fr. OE *blōd;* akin to OHG *bluot* blood] (bef. 12c) **1 a** (1) **:** the fluid that circulates in the heart, arteries, capillaries, and veins of a vertebrate animal carrying nourishment and oxygen to and bringing away waste products from all parts of the body (2) **:** a comparable fluid of an invertebrate **b :** a fluid resembling blood **2 :** the shedding of blood; *also* **:** the taking of life **3 a :** LIFEBLOOD; *broadly* **:** LIFE **b :** human stock or lineage; *esp* **:** royal lineage ⟨a prince of the ~⟩ **c :** relationship by descent from a common ancestor **:** KINSHIP **d :** persons related through common descent **:** KINDRED **e** (1) **:** honorable or high birth or descent (2) **:** descent from parents of recognized breed or pedigree **4 a :** blood regarded as the seat of the emotions **:** TEMPER **b** *obs* **:** LUST **c :** a showy foppish man **:** RAKE **5 :** members of a team, staff, or organization **:** PERSONNEL ⟨a company in need of new ~⟩ **6 :** a black American male — used esp. among black people — **in one's blood :** ingrained in one's nature **:** occurring as an innate or seemingly hereditary principle, inclination, or talent ⟨with two parents who are painters, art is *in her blood*⟩
[2]**blood** *vt* (1590) **1 :** to stain or wet with blood **2** *archaic* **:** BLEED 1 **3 :** to expose (a hunting dog) to sight, scent, or taste of the blood of its prey **4 :** to give experience to ⟨troops ~*ed* in battle⟩
blood–and–guts \ˈblə-dᵊn-ˈgəts\ *adj* (1975) **:** marked by great vigor, violence, or fierceness ⟨~ competition⟩
blood·bath \ˈbləd-ˌbath, -ˌbäth\ *n* (1814) **1 :** a great slaughter **2 a :** a notably fierce, violent, or destructive contest or struggle ⟨the campaign has become a ~⟩ **b :** a major economic disaster ⟨a market ~⟩
blood–borne \ˈbləd-ˌbȯrn\ *adj* (1885) **:** carried or transmitted by the blood ⟨a ~ disease⟩ ⟨~ pathogens⟩
blood–brain barrier \ˈbləd-ˈbrān-\ *n* (1934) **:** a naturally occurring barrier created by the modification of brain capillaries (as by reduction in fenestration and formation of tight cell-to-cell contacts) that prevents many substances from leaving the blood and crossing the capillary walls into the brain tissues
blood brother *n* (1799) **1 :** a brother by birth **2 :** one of two men pledged to mutual loyalty by a ceremonial use of each other's blood — **blood brotherhood** *n*
blood cell *n* (1834) **:** a cell normally present in blood
blood count *n* (1876) **:** the determination of the blood cells in a definite volume of blood; *also* **:** the number of cells so determined
blood·cur·dling \ˈbləd-ˌkərd-liŋ, -ˌkər-dᵊl-iŋ\ *adj* (1724) **:** arousing fright or horror ⟨~ screams⟩
blood doping *n* (1971) **:** a technique for temporarily improving athletic performance in which oxygen-carrying red blood cells from blood previously withdrawn from an athlete are reinjected just before an event — called also *blood packing*
blood·ed \ˈblə-dəd\ *adj* (1572) **1 :** having blood of a specified kind — used in combination ⟨cold-*blooded*⟩ **2 :** being entirely or largely purebred ⟨a herd of ~ stock⟩
blood feud *n* (1815) **:** a feud between different clans or families
blood fluke *n* (1871) **:** SCHISTOSOME
blood group *n* (1916) **:** one of the classes (as those designated A, B, AB, or O) into which individuals or their blood can be separated on the basis of the presence or absence of specific antigens in the blood — called also *blood type*
blood·guilt \ˈbləd-ˌgilt\ *n* (1593) **:** guilt resulting from bloodshed — **blood·guilt·i·ness** \-ˌgil-tē-nəs\ *n* — **blood·guilty** \-tē\ *adj*

\ə\ abut \ᵊ\ kitten, F table \ər\ further \a\ ash \ā\ ace \ä\ mop, mar
\au̇\ out \ch\ chin \e\ bet \ē\ easy \g\ go \i\ hit \ī\ ice \j\ job
\ŋ\ sing \ō\ go \ȯ\ law \ȯi\ boy \th\ thin \t͟h\ the \ü\ loot \u̇\ foot
\y\ yet \zh\ vision, beige \k, ⁿ, œ, ue, ʸ\ *see* Guide to Pronunciation

blood·hound \ˈbləd-ˌhau̇nd\ *n* (14c) **1 :** any of a breed of large powerful hounds of European origin remarkable for acuteness of smell **2 :** a person keen in pursuit
blood·less \ˈbləd-ləs\ *adj* (bef. 12c) **1 :** deficient in or free from blood **2 :** not accompanied by loss or shedding of blood ⟨a ~ victory⟩ **3 :** lacking in spirit or vitality **4 :** lacking in human feeling ⟨~ statistics⟩ — **blood·less·ly** *adv* — **blood·less·ness** *n*
blood·let·ting \-ˌle-tiŋ\ *n* (13c) **1 :** PHLEBOTOMY **2 :** BLOODSHED **3 :** elimination of personnel or resources
blood·line \-ˌlīn\ *n* (1896) **:** a sequence of direct ancestors esp. in a pedigree; *also* **:** FAMILY, STRAIN
blood·lust \-ˌləst\ *n* (1848) **:** desire for bloodshed
blood·mo·bile \-mō-ˌbēl\ *n* (1948) **:** an automotive vehicle staffed and equipped for collecting blood from donors
blood money *n* (1535) **1 :** money obtained at the cost of another's life **2 :** money paid (as by a killer or the killer's clan) to the family of a person who has been killed
blood orange *n* (1851) **:** a cultivated sweet orange having fruit with usu. red pulp; *also* **:** its fruit
blood plasma *n* (1858) **:** the pale yellow fluid of whole blood that consists of water and its dissolved constituents including esp. proteins (as albumin, fibrinogen, and globulins)
blood platelet *n* (1896) **:** PLATELET
blood poisoning *n* (1863) **:** SEPTICEMIA
blood pressure *n* (1873) **:** pressure that is exerted by the blood upon the walls of the blood vessels and esp. arteries and that varies with the muscular efficiency of the heart, the blood volume and viscosity, the age and health of the individual, and the state of the vascular wall
blood·red \ˈbləd-ˈred\ *adj* (bef. 12c) **:** having the color of blood
blood·root \-ˌrüt, -ˌru̇t\ *n* (1722) **:** a plant (*Sanguinaria canadensis*) of the poppy family having a red root and sap and bearing a solitary lobed leaf and white flower in early spring — called also *sanguinaria*
blood sausage *n* (1868) **:** very dark sausage containing a large proportion of blood — called also *blood pudding*
blood serum *n* (1863) **:** the clear yellowish fluid that remains from blood plasma after clotting factors (as fibrinogen and prothrombin) have been removed by clot formation
blood·shed \ˈbləd-ˌshed\ *n* (15c) **1 :** the shedding of blood **2 :** the taking of life **:** SLAUGHTER
blood·shot \-ˌshät\ *adj* (1552) *of an eye* **:** inflamed to redness
blood sport *n* (1895) **:** a sport or contest (as hunting or cockfighting) involving bloodshed
blood·stain \-ˌstān\ *n* (1820) **:** a discoloration caused by blood
blood·stained \-ˌstānd\ *adj* (1596) **1 :** stained with blood **2 :** involved with slaughter ⟨a ~ chronicle of war⟩
blood·stock \-ˌstäk\ *n* (1830) **:** horses of Thoroughbred breeding
blood·stone \-ˌstōn\ *n* (1551) **:** a green chalcedony sprinkled with red spots resembling blood — called also *heliotrope*
blood·stream \-ˌstrēm\ *n* (1630) **1 :** the flowing blood in a circulatory system **2 :** a mainstream of power or vitality ⟨introduce into the economic ~ a large amount of money —*Harper's*⟩
blood·suck·er \-ˌsə-kər\ *n* (14c) **1 :** an animal that sucks blood; *esp* **:** LEECH **2 :** a person who sponges or preys on another — **blood·suck·ing** \-kiŋ\ *adj*
blood sugar *n* (1918) **:** the glucose in the blood; *also* **:** its concentration (as in milligrams per 100 milliliters)
blood test *n* (1912) **:** a test of the blood; *esp* **:** a serologic test for the presence of substances indicative of disease (as syphilis) or disease-causing agents (as HIV)
blood thinner *n* (1969) **:** a drug used to prevent the formation of blood clots by hindering coagulation of the blood — **blood–thin·ning** *adj*
blood·thirsty \ˈbləd-ˌthər-stē\ *adj* (1535) **:** eager for or marked by the shedding of blood, violence, or killing — **blood·thirst·i·ly** \-stə-lē\ *adv* — **blood·thirst·i·ness** \-stē-nəs\ *n*
blood–typ·ing \-ˌtī-piŋ\ *n* (1925) **:** the action or process of determining an individual's blood group
blood vessel *n* (1694) **:** any of the vessels through which blood circulates in the body
blood·worm \ˈbləd-ˌwərm\ *n* (1714) **1 :** any of various reddish annelid worms (as of genera *Glycera* or *Tubifex*) often used as bait **2 :** any of several strongyle worms (genus *Strongylus*) that are parasitic in the large intestine of horses
[1]**bloody** \ˈblə-dē\ *adj* **blood·i·er; -est** (bef. 12c) **1 a :** containing or made up of blood **b :** of or contained in the blood **2 :** smeared or stained with blood **3 :** accompanied by or involving bloodshed; *esp* **:** marked by great slaughter **4 a :** MURDEROUS **b :** MERCILESS, CRUEL **5 :** BLOODRED **6** *sometimes vulgar* **:** DAMNED — often used as an intensive — **blood·i·ly** \ˈblə-dᵊl-ē\ *adv* — **blood·i·ness** \ˈblə-dē-nəs\ *n*

syn BLOODY, SANGUINARY, GORY mean affected by or involving the shedding of blood. BLOODY is applied esp. to things that are actually covered with blood or are made up of blood ⟨*bloody* hands⟩. SANGUINARY applies esp. to something attended by, or someone inclined to, bloodshed ⟨the Civil War was America's most *sanguinary* conflict⟩. GORY suggests a profusion of blood and slaughter ⟨exceptionally *gory*, even for a horror movie⟩.

[2]**bloody** *vt* **blood·ied; bloody·ing** (1530) **1 :** to make bloody or bloodred **2 :** HARM, DAMAGE ⟨an administration *bloodied* by scandal⟩
[3]**bloody** *adv* (1661) *sometimes vulgar* — used as an intensive
Bloody Mary *n, pl* **Bloody Marys** [prob. fr. *Bloody Mary,* appellation of Mary I of England] (1939) **:** a cocktail consisting essentially of vodka and usu. spiced tomato juice
bloody–mind·ed \ˌblə-dē-ˈmīn-dəd\ *adj* (1584) **1 :** inclined towards violence or bloodshed **2** *chiefly Brit* **:** stubbornly contrary or obstructive **:** CANTANKEROUS — **bloody–mind·ed·ness** *n*
bloody murder *adv* (1833) **:** in a loud and violent manner ⟨ran off, screaming *bloody murder*⟩; *also* **:** in vehement protest ⟨screaming *bloody murder* over the pay cut⟩
bloody shirt *n* (1586) **:** something intended to stir up or revive partisan animosity — usu. used in the phrase *wave the bloody shirt*
bloo·ey \ˈblü-ē\ *adj or adv* [*blooey,* interj. representing an explosive sound (of imit. origin)] (1920) *slang* **:** HAYWIRE, AWRY ⟨the engine went ~⟩
[1]**bloom** \ˈblüm\ *n* [ME *blome* lump of metal, fr. OE *blōma*] (bef. 12c) **1 :** a mass of wrought iron from the forge or puddling furnace **2 :** a bar of iron or steel hammered or rolled from an ingot
[2]**bloom** *n* [ME *blome,* fr. ON *blōm;* akin to OE *blōwan* to blossom — more at BLOW] (13c) **1 a :** FLOWER **b :** the flowering state ⟨the roses in ~⟩ **c :** a period of flowering ⟨the spring ~⟩ **d :** a rapid and excessive growth of a plankton population (as of algae or dinoflagellates) — compare RED TIDE **2 a :** a state or time of beauty, freshness, and vigor **b :** a state or time of high development or achievement ⟨a career in full ~⟩ **3 :** a surface coating or appearance: as **a :** a delicate powdery coating on some fruits and leaves **b :** a rosy appearance of the cheeks; *broadly* **:** an outward evidence of freshness or healthy vigor **c :** a cloudiness on a film of varnish or lacquer **d :** a grayish discoloration on chocolate **e :** glare caused by an object reflecting too much light into a television camera
[3]**bloom** *vi* (13c) **1 a :** to produce or yield flowers **b :** to support abundant plant life ⟨make the desert ~⟩ **2 a** (1) **:** to mature into achievement of one's potential (2) **:** to flourish in youthful beauty, freshness, or excellence **b :** to shine out **:** GLOW **3 :** to appear or occur unexpectedly or in remarkable quantity or degree **4 :** to become densely populated with microorganisms and esp. plankton — used of bodies of water ~ *vt* **1** *obs* **:** to cause to bloom **2 :** to give bloom to
[1]**bloom·er** \ˈblü-mər\ *n* (1727) **1 :** a plant that blooms **2 :** a person who reaches full competence or maturity ⟨he was a late ~ as a writer⟩ **3** [*blooming*] **:** a stupid blunder
[2]**bloo·mer** \ˈblü-mər\ *n* [Amelia *Bloomer*] (1851) **1 :** a costume for women consisting of a skirt over long loose trousers gathered closely about the ankles **2** *pl* **a :** full loose trousers gathered at the knee formerly worn by women for athletics **b :** underpants of similar design worn chiefly by girls and women
bloom·ing \ˈblü-mən, -miŋ\ *adj or adv* [prob. euphemism for *bloody*] (1879) *chiefly Brit* — used as a generalized intensive ⟨~ fool⟩
bloomy \ˈblü-mē\ *adj* (1583) **1 :** full of bloom **2 :** covered with bloom ⟨~ plums⟩ **3 :** showing freshness or vitality ⟨all the ~ flush of life is fled —Oliver Goldsmith⟩
bloop \ˈblüp\ *n* [back-formation fr. *blooper*] (1947) **:** BLOOPER 1a — **bloop** *vt*
bloop·er \ˈblü-pər\ *n* [*bloop* (an unpleasant sound)] (1937) **1 a :** a fly ball hit barely beyond a baseball infield **b :** a high baseball pitch lobbed to the batter **2 :** an embarrassing public blunder
[1]**blos·som** \ˈblä-səm\ *n* [ME *blosme,* fr. OE *blōstm;* akin to OE *blōwan*] (bef. 12c) **1 a :** the flower of a seed plant; *also* **:** the mass of such flowers on a single plant **b :** the state of bearing flowers **2 :** a peak period or stage of development — **blos·somy** \-sə-mē\ *adj*
[2]**blossom** *vi* (bef. 12c) **1 :** BLOOM **2 a :** to come into one's own **:** DEVELOP ⟨a ~*ing* talent⟩ **b :** to become evident **c :** to make an appearance
[1]**blot** \ˈblät\ *n* [ME] (14c) **1 :** a soiling or disfiguring mark **:** SPOT **2 :** a mark of reproach **:** moral flaw **3 :** a usu. nitrocellulose or nylon sheet that contains spots of immobilized macromolecules (as of DNA, RNA, or protein) or their fragments and is used to identify specific components of the spots by applying a molecular probe (as a complementary nucleic acid or a radio labeled antibody) — compare SOUTHERN BLOT, WESTERN BLOT
[2]**blot** *vb* **blot·ted; blot·ting** *vt* (15c) **1 :** to spot, stain, or spatter with a discoloring substance **2** *obs* **:** MAR; *esp* **:** to stain with infamy **3 a :** to dry (as writing) with an absorbing agent **b :** to remove with absorbing material ⟨*blotting* up spilled water⟩ ~ *vi* **1 :** to make a blot **2 :** to become marked with a blot
[3]**blot** *n* [perh. fr. D *bloot* naked, exposed, fr. MD; akin to MHG *bloz* bare] (1595) **1 :** a lone backgammon man exposed to capture **2** *archaic* **:** a weak or exposed point
[1]**blotch** \ˈbläch\ *vt* (1604) **:** to mark or mar with blotches
[2]**blotch** *n* [perh. blend of [1]*blot* and [3]*botch*] (1619) **1 :** IMPERFECTION, BLEMISH **2 :** a spot or mark (as of color or ink) esp. when large or irregular — **blotch·i·ly** \ˈblä-chə-lē\ *adv* — **blotchy** \ˈblä-chē\ *adj*
blot out *vt* (1530) **1 :** to make obscure, insignificant, or inconsequential **2 :** WIPE OUT, DESTROY
blot·ter \ˈblä-tər\ *n* (1591) **1 :** a piece of blotting paper **2 :** a book in which entries (as of transactions or occurrences) are made temporarily pending their transfer to permanent record books ⟨police ~⟩
blotting paper *n* (15c) **:** a spongy unsized paper for absorbing ink
blot·to \ˈblä-(ˌ)tō\ *adj* [prob. irreg. fr. [2]*blot*] (1917) *slang* **:** DRUNK 1a
[1]**blouse** \ˈblau̇s *also* ˈblau̇z\ *n, pl* **blous·es** \ˈblau̇-səz, -zəz\ [F] (1823) **1 a :** a long loose overgarment that resembles a shirt or smock and is worn esp. by workmen, artists, and peasants **b :** the jacket of a uniform **2 :** a usu. loose-fitting garment esp. for women that covers the body from the neck to the waist — **blousy** \ˈblau̇-sē, -zē\ *adj*
[2]**blouse** \ˈblau̇s, ˈblau̇z\ *vb* **bloused; blous·ing** *vi* (1897) **:** to fall in a fold ⟨coats that ~ above the hip⟩ ~ *vt* **:** to cause to blouse
blou·son \ˈblau̇-ˌsän, ˈblü-ˌzän\ *n* [F, fr. *blouse*] (1904) **:** a garment (as a dress) having a close waistband with blousing of material over it
blo·vi·ate \ˈblō-vē-ˌāt\ *vi* **-at·ed; -at·ing** [perh. irreg. fr. [1]*blow*] (ca. 1879) **:** to speak or write verbosely and windily — **blo·vi·a·tion** \ˌblō-vē-ˈā-shən\ *n*
[1]**blow** \ˈblō\ *vb* **blew** \ˈblü\; **blown** \ˈblōn\; **blow·ing** [ME, fr. OE *blāwan;* akin to OHG *blāen* to blow, L *flare,* Gk *phallos* penis] *vi* (bef. 12c) **1 a** *of air* (1) **:** to be in motion ⟨a breeze *blew* gently⟩ (2) **:** to move with speed or force ⟨the wind was ~*ing*⟩ **b :** to move or run quickly ⟨the linebacker *blew* past the tackle⟩ **2 :** to send forth a current of air or other gas ⟨don't ~ on your soup⟩ **3 a :** to make a sound by or as if by blowing **b** *of a wind instrument* **:** SOUND **4 a :** BOAST **b :** to talk windily **5 a :** PANT, GASP ⟨the horse *blew* heavily⟩ **b** *of a cetacean* **:** to eject moisture-laden air from the lungs through the blowhole **6 :** to move or be carried by or as if by wind ⟨just *blew* into town⟩ **7 a :** ERUPT, EXPLODE **b** *of an electric fuse* **:** to melt when overloaded — often used with *out* **c** *of a tire* **:** to release the contained air through a spontaneous rupture — usu. used with *out* ~ *vt* **1 a :** to set (gas or vapor) in motion ⟨the fan *blew* hot air on us⟩ **b :** to act on with a current of gas or vapor ⟨the breeze *blew* my hair dry⟩ **2 a :** to play or sound on (a wind instrument) **b :** to play (as a note) on a wind instrument **3 a :** to spread by report **b** *past participle* **blowed** \ˈblōd\ **:** DAMN ⟨~ the expense⟩ **4 a :** to drive with a current of gas or vapor ⟨the storm *blew* the boat off course⟩ **b :** to clear of contents by forc-

ible passage of a current of air ⟨~ your nose⟩ **c :** to project (a gesture or sound made with the mouth) by blowing ⟨*blew* him a kiss⟩ **5 a :** to distend with or as if with gas **b :** to produce or shape by the action of blown or injected air ⟨~*ing* bubbles⟩ **6** *of insects* **:** to deposit eggs or larvae on or in **7 :** to shatter, burst, or destroy by explosion ⟨~ the safe open⟩ **8 a :** to put out of breath with exertion **b :** to let (as a horse) pause to catch the breath **9 a :** to expend (as money) extravagantly **b :** to treat with unusual expenditure ⟨I'll ~ you to a steak⟩ **10 :** to cause (a fuse) to blow **11 :** to rupture by too much pressure ⟨*blow* a seal⟩ **12 a :** BOTCH 1 ⟨*blew* her lines⟩ **b :** to fail to keep or hold ⟨they *blew* a big lead⟩ **13 :** to leave hurriedly ⟨*blew* town⟩ **14 :** to propel with great force or speed ⟨*blew* a fastball by the batter⟩ — **blow a gasket :** to become enraged — **blow hot and cold :** to be favorable at one moment and adverse the next — **blow off steam :** to release pent-up emotions — **blow one's cool :** to lose one's composure — **blow one's cover :** to reveal one's real identity — **blow one's mind :** to overwhelm one with wonder or bafflement — **blow one's top** *or* **blow one's stack 1 :** to become violently angry **2 :** to go crazy — **blow smoke :** to speak idly, misleadingly, or boastfully — **blow the whistle :** to call public or official attention to something (as a wrongdoing) kept secret — usu. used with *on*

[2]**blow** *n* (1651) **1 :** a blowing of wind esp. when strong or violent **2 :** BRAG, BOASTING **3 :** an act or instance of blowing **4 a :** the time during which air is forced through molten metal to refine it **b :** the quantity of metal refined during that time **5** *slang* **:** COCAINE

[3]**blow** *vi* **blew** \ˈblü\; **blown** \ˈblōn\; **blow·ing** [ME, fr. OE *blōwan;* akin to OHG *bluoen* to bloom, L *florēre* to bloom, *flor-, flos* flower] (bef. 12c) **:** FLOWER, BLOOM

[4]**blow** *n* (1710) **1 :** BLOSSOMS **2 :** [2]BLOOM 1b ⟨lilacs in full ~⟩

[5]**blow** *n* [ME (northern dial.) *blaw;* prob. akin to OHG *bliuwan* to beat] (15c) **1 :** a forcible stroke delivered with a part of the body or with an instrument **2 :** a hostile act or state **:** COMBAT ⟨come to ~*s*⟩ **3 :** a forcible or sudden act or effort **:** ASSAULT **4 :** an unfortunate or calamitous happening ⟨failure to land the job came as a ~⟩

blow away *vt* (1579) **1 :** to dissipate or remove as if with a current of air ⟨their doubts were *blown away*⟩ **2 :** to kill by gunfire **:** shoot dead **3 :** to impress very strongly and usu. favorably **4 :** to defeat soundly ⟨*blew* their rivals *away* in the first game⟩

blow·back \ˈblō-ˌbak\ *n* (1973) **:** an unforeseen and unwanted effect, result, or set of repercussions

blow·by \ˈblō-ˌbī\ *n* (1926) **:** leakage of combustion gases between a piston and the cylinder wall into the crankcase in an automobile

blow–by–blow \ˈblō-bī-ˈblō, -bə-\ *adj* (1933) **:** minutely detailed ⟨a ~ account⟩

blow·down \ˈblō-ˌdau̇n\ *n* (1895) **1 :** an instance of trees being blown down by the wind **2 :** a tree blown down; *also* **:** an area of such trees

blow–dried \ˈblō-ˌdrīd\ *adj* (1976) **:** having blow-dried hair; *also* **:** being or appearing well-groomed but superficial or vacuous

blow–dry \-ˌdrī\ *vt* (1966) **:** to dry and usu. style (hair) with a blow-dryer ~ *vi* **:** to dry hair with a blow-dryer — **blow–dry** *n*

blow–dry·er \-ˌdrī(-ə)r\ *n* (1950) **:** a handheld hair dryer

blow·er \ˈblō(-ə)r\ *n* (bef. 12c) **1 :** one that blows **2 :** a device for producing a current of air or gas **3 :** BRAGGART **4** *chiefly Brit* **:** TELEPHONE

blow·fish \ˈblō-ˌfish\ *n* (1872) **:** PUFFER FISH 1

blow·fly \-ˌflī\ *n* (1812) **:** any of a family (Calliphoridae) of dipteran flies (as the bluebottle or screwworm) that deposit their eggs esp. on meat or in wounds

blow·gun \-ˌgən\ *n* (1810) **:** a tube through which a projectile (as a dart) may be impelled by the force of the breath

blow·hard \-ˌhärd\ *n* (1848) **1 :** BRAGGART **2 :** WINDBAG

blow·hole \-ˌhōl\ *n* (1691) **1 :** a hole in metal caused by a bubble of gas captured during solidification **2 :** a nostril in the top of the head of a cetacean and esp. a whale

blow in *vi* (1882) **:** to arrive casually or unexpectedly

blow job *n* (1942) *usu vulgar* **:** an act of fellatio

blown \ˈblōn\ *adj* [ME *blowen,* fr. pp. of *blowen* to blow] (14c) **1 a :** SWOLLEN **b :** affected with bloat **2 :** being out of breath

blow off *vt* (1856) **1 a :** to refuse to take notice of, honor, or deal with **:** IGNORE ⟨decided to *blow off* two billion viewers —Harry Homburg⟩ **b :** to end a relationship with **2 :** to outperform in a contest **3 :** to fail to attend or show up for ⟨*blew off* an official dinner⟩

blow·out \ˈblō-ˌau̇t\ *n* (1822) **1 :** a festive social affair **2 :** a bursting of a container (as a tire) by pressure of the contents on a weak spot **3 :** an uncontrolled eruption of an oil or gas well **4 :** an easy or one-sided victory **5 :** a valley or depression created by the wind in areas of shifting sand or of light cultivated soil

blow out *vt* (14c) **1 :** to extinguish by a gust **2 :** to dissipate (itself) by blowing — used of storms **3 :** to defeat easily **4 :** to damage severely ⟨she *blew out* her knee in the race⟩ ~ *vi* **1 :** to become extinguished by a gust **2 :** to erupt out of control — used of an oil or gas well

blow over *vi* (1617) **:** to pass away without effect

blow·pipe \ˈblō-ˌpīp\ *n* (1685) **1 :** a small tubular instrument for directing a jet of air or other gas into a flame so as to concentrate and increase the heat **2 :** BLOWGUN **3 :** a tubular instrument used for revealing or cleaning a bodily cavity by forcing air into it **4 :** a long metal tube on the end of which a glassmaker gathers a quantity of molten glass and through which he blows to expand and shape it

blow·sy *also* **blow·zy** \ˈblau̇-zē\ *adj* [E dial. *blowse, blowze* wench] (ca. 1712) **1 :** having a sloppy or unkempt appearance or aspect **:** FROWSY **2 :** being coarse and ruddy of complexion

blow·torch \ˈblō-ˌtȯrch\ *n* (1897) **:** a small burner having a device to intensify combustion by means of a blast of air or oxygen, usu. including a fuel tank pressurized by a hand pump, and used esp. in plumbing

blow·up \ˈblō-ˌəp\ *n* (1757) **:** a blowing up: as **a :** EXPLOSION **b :** an outburst of temper **c :** ENLARGEMENT 2

blow–up \ˈblō-ˌəp\ *adj* (1969) **:** INFLATABLE

blow up *vt* (1536) **1 :** to build up or tout to an unreasonable extent ⟨advertisers *blowing up* their products⟩ **2 :** to rend apart, shatter, or destroy by explosion **3 :** to fill up with a gas (as air) ⟨*blow up* a balloon⟩ **4 :** to make a photographic enlargement of **5 :** to bring into existence by blowing of wind ⟨it may *blow up* a storm⟩ ~ *vi* **1 a :** EXPLODE **b :** to be disrupted or destroyed (as by explosion) **c :** to lose self-control; *esp* **:** to become violently angry **2 :** to become or come into being by or as if by blowing of wind **3 a :** to become filled with a gas **b :** to become expanded to unreasonable proportions

blowy \ˈblō-ē\ *adj* (1746) **1 :** [1]WINDY ⟨a ~ March day⟩ **2 :** readily blown about ⟨~ desert sand⟩

BLS *abbr* **1** bachelor of liberal studies **2** bachelor of library science **3** Bureau of Labor Statistics

BLT \ˌbē-(ˌ)el-ˈtē\ *n* (1952) **:** a bacon, lettuce, and tomato sandwich

blub \ˈbləb\ *vi* **blubbed; blub·bing** (1559) *chiefly Brit* **:** BLUBBER

[1]**blub·ber** \ˈblə-bər\ *vb* **blub·bered; blub·ber·ing** \ˈblə-b(ə-)riŋ\ [ME *blubren* to make a bubbling sound, fr. *bluber*] *vi* (15c) **:** to weep noisily ~ *vt* **1 :** to swell, distort, or wet with weeping **2 :** to utter while weeping

[2]**blubber** *n* [ME *bluber* bubble, foam, prob. of imit. origin] (15c) **1 a :** the fat of whales and other large marine mammals **b :** excessive fat on the body **2 :** the action of blubbering

blub·bery \ˈblə-b(ə-)rē\ *adj* (1791) **1 :** having or characterized by blubber **2 :** puffed out **:** THICK

blu·cher \ˈblü-chər *also* -kər\ *n* [G. L. von *Blücher*] (1831) **:** a shoe having the tongue and vamp cut in one piece and the quarters lapped over the vamp and laced together for closing

bludge \ˈbləj\ *vb* **bludged; bludg·ing** [back-formation fr. Brit. argot *bludger* pimp, prob. contr. of *bludgeoner* one wielding a bludgeon, fr. *bludgeon*] *vi* (ca. 1919) **1** *chiefly Austral & NewZeal* **:** to avoid work or responsibility **2** *chiefly Austral & NewZeal* **:** SPONGE 2 ~ *vt, chiefly Austral & NewZeal* **:** SPONGE 3 — **bludg·er** *n, chiefly Austral & NewZeal*

[1]**blud·geon** \ˈblə-jən\ *n* [origin unknown] (1730) **1 :** a short stick that usu. has one thick or loaded end and is used as a weapon **2 :** something used to attack or bully ⟨the ~ of satire⟩

[2]**bludgeon** *vt* (1868) **1 :** to hit with heavy impact **2 :** to attack or overcome by aggressive argument **:** BULLY ⟨mental ~*ing*⟩

[1]**blue** \ˈblü\ *adj* **blu·er; blu·est** [ME, fr. AF *blef, blew,* of Gmc origin; akin to OHG *blāo* blue; akin to L *flavus* yellow] (13c) **1 :** of the color blue **2 a :** BLUISH ⟨the ~ haze of tobacco smoke⟩ **b :** discolored by or as if by bruising ⟨~ with cold⟩ **c :** bluish gray ⟨a ~ cat⟩ **3 a :** low in spirits **:** MELANCHOLY **b :** marked by low spirits **:** DEPRESSING ⟨a ~ funk⟩ ⟨things looked ~⟩ **4 :** wearing blue **5** *of a woman* **:** LEARNED, INTELLECTUAL **6 :** PURITANICAL **7 a :** PROFANE, INDECENT ⟨~ movie⟩ **b :** OFF-COLOR, RISQUÉ ⟨~ jokes⟩ **8 :** of, relating to, or used in blues ⟨a ~ song⟩ **9 :** tending to support Democrats in a general election ⟨~ states⟩ — **blue·ly** *adv* — **blue·ness** *n* — **blue in the face :** extremely exasperated

[2]**blue** *n* (13c) **1 :** a color whose hue is that of the clear sky or that of the portion of the color spectrum lying between green and violet **2 a :** a pigment or dye that colors blue **b :** BLUING **3 a :** blue clothing or cloth **b** *pl* **:** a blue costume or uniform **4 a :** a Union soldier in the American Civil War **b** *often cap* **:** the Union army **5 a (1) :** SKY **(2) :** the far distance ⟨disappeared into the ~⟩ **b :** SEA **6 :** a blue object **7 :** BLUESTOCKING **8 :** any of numerous small chiefly blue butterflies (family Lycaenidae) **9 :** BLUEFISH **10 :** BLUE CHEESE — **out of the blue :** without advance notice **:** UNEXPECTEDLY ⟨the job offer came *out of the blue*⟩

[3]**blue** *vb* **blued; blue·ing** *or* **blu·ing** *vt* (1606) **:** to make blue ~ *vi* **:** to turn blue

blue baby *n* (ca. 1899) **:** an infant with cyanosis usu. from a congenital heart defect in which venous and arterial blood are mingled

blue·back herring \ˈblü-ˌbak-\ *n* (1873) **:** an anadromous clupeid fish (*Alosa aestivalis*) of the Atlantic coast of No. America having a dark blue or bluish-gray back

blue·beard \ˈblü-ˌbird\ *n, often cap* [*Bluebeard,* a fairy-tale character] (1822) **:** a man who marries and kills one wife after another

blue·bell \-ˌbel\ *n* (1578) **1 :** any of various bellflowers; *esp* **:** HAREBELL **2 :** any of various plants bearing blue bell-shaped flowers: as **a :** a European herb (*Hyacinthoides nonscripta* syn. *Scilla nonscripta*) of the lily family having scapose racemes of drooping bell-shaped flowers — called also *wild hyacinth* **b** *pl* **:** a glabrous erect eastern U.S. herb (*Mertensia virginica*) of the borage family with entire leaves and showy blue flowers pink in the bud — called also *Virginia bluebells*

blue·ber·ry \ˈblü-ˌber-ē, -ˌbe-rē, -b(ə-)rē\ *n* (1709) **:** the edible blue or blackish berry of any of several No. American plants (genus *Vaccinium*) of the heath family; *also* **:** a low or tall shrub producing these berries

blue·bird \-ˌbərd\ *n* (1688) **:** any of three small No. American thrushes (*Sialia currucoides, S. mexicana,* and *S. sialis*) that are blue above and reddish brown or pale blue below

blue blood *n* (1832) **1** \ˈblü-ˈbləd\ **:** membership in a noble or socially prominent family **2** \-ˌbləd\ **:** a member of a noble or socially prominent family — **blue–blood·ed** \-ˈblə-dəd\ *adj*

blue·bon·net \ˈblü-ˌbä-nət\ *n* (1682) **1 a :** a wide flat round cap of blue wool formerly worn in Scotland **b :** one that wears such a cap; *specif* **:** SCOT **2 :** either of two low-growing annual lupines (*Lupinus subcarnosus* or *L. texensis*) of Texas with silky foliage and blue flowers

blue book *n* (1835) **1 :** a register esp. of socially prominent persons **2 :** a book of specialized information often published under government auspices **3 :** a blue-covered booklet used for writing examinations **4 :** a periodically issued price list (as of used cars)

blue·bot·tle \ˈblü-ˌbä-tᵊl\ *n* (15c) **1 :** BACHELOR'S BUTTON **2 :** any of several blowflies (genus *Calliphora*) that have the abdomen or the whole body iridescent blue in color and that make a loud buzzing noise in flight

blue catfish *n* (1833) **:** a large bluish catfish (*Ictalurus furcatus*) of the Mississippi valley that may weigh over 100 pounds (45 kilograms)

blue cheese *n* (1925) **:** cheese having veins of greenish-blue mold

blue chip *n* (1927) **1 a :** a stock issue of high investment quality that usu. pertains to a substantial well-established company and enjoys public confidence in its worth and stability; *also* **:** a company that offers such stocks **b :** a business or undertaking with an outstanding record

\ə\ **abut** \ᵊ\ **kitten, F table** \ər\ **further** \a\ **ash** \ā\ **ace** \ä\ **mop, mar**
\au̇\ **out** \ch\ **chin** \e\ **bet** \ē\ **easy** \g\ **go** \i\ **hit** \ī\ **ice** \j\ **job**
\ŋ\ **sing** \ō\ **go** \ȯ\ **law** \ȯi\ **boy** \th\ **thin** \t͟h\ **the** \ü\ **loot** \u̇\ **foot**
\y\ **yet** \zh\ **vision, beige** \k̲, ⁿ, œ, ue, ʸ\ *see* Guide to Pronunciation

or likelihood of profitability **2 :** one that is outstanding: as **a :** an outstandingly worthwhile or valuable property or asset **b :** an athlete rated as excellent or as an excellent prospect — **blue–chip** *adj*

blue–chip·per \ˈblü-ˌchi-pər\ *n* (1968) **:** BLUE CHIP

blue·coat \ˈblü-ˌkōt\ *n* (1593) **:** a person who wears a blue coat: as **a :** a Union soldier during the American Civil War **b :** POLICE OFFICER

blue cohosh *n* (1821) **:** a perennial No. American herb (*Caulophyllum thalictroides*) of the barberry family that has greenish-yellow or purplish flowers and large blue berrylike fruits

blue–col·lar \ˈblü-ˈkä-lər\ *adj* (1946) **1 :** of, relating to, or constituting the class of wage earners whose duties call for the wearing of work clothes or protective clothing — compare WHITE-COLLAR **2 :** having characteristics associated with blue-collar workers: as **a :** having, showing, or appealing to unpretentious or unsophisticated tastes ⟨a new ~ serial . . . woven around a minor-league baseball team —Steven Flax⟩ **b :** dependable and hard-working rather than showy or spectacular ⟨a ~ athlete⟩

blue corn *n* (1945) **:** Indian corn that has bluish kernels used to make flour and is grown esp. in the southwestern U.S.

blue crab *n* (1883) **:** a large bluish-green edible crab (*Callinectes sapidus* of the family Portunidae) of the Atlantic and Gulf coasts

blue curls *n pl but sing or pl in constr* (1817) **:** any of several mints (genus *Trichostema*) with irregular blue flowers

blue devils *n pl* (1781) **:** low spirits **:** DESPONDENCY

blue–eyed \ˈblü-ˌīd\ *adj* (1603) **1 :** having blue eyes **2 :** performed by whites ⟨~ soul⟩; *also* **:** WHITE ⟨a ~ imitator of R&B stars⟩

blue–eyed grass *n* (1783) **:** any of a genus (*Sisyrinchium*) of New World herbs of the iris family having grasslike foliage and blue, yellow, or white flowers

blue·fin tuna \ˈblü-ˌfin-\ *n* (1922) **:** a very large tuna (*Thunnus thynnus*) that is an important food and game fish — called also *bluefin*

blue·fish \-ˌfish\ *n* (ca. 1622) **1 :** an active food and game marine fish (*Pomatomus saltatrix*) that is bluish above with silvery sides **2 :** any of various dark or bluish fishes (as the pollack)

blue flag *n* (1784) **:** a blue-flowered iris; *esp* **:** a common iris (*Iris versicolor*) chiefly of the eastern U.S. with a root formerly used medicinally

blue flu *n* [fr. the color of a police uniform] (1967) **:** a sick-out staged by police officers

blue·gill \ˈblü-ˌgil\ *n* (1881) **:** a common sunfish (*Lepomis macrochirus*) of the eastern and central U.S. sought for food and sport

blue grama *n* (1898) **:** a low-growing perennial grama (*Bouteloua gracilis*) having slender curly leaves that is an important forage grass esp. in the Great Plains

blue·grass \-ˌgras\ *n* (1751) **1 :** any of several grasses (genus *Poa*) of which some have bluish-green culms; *esp* **:** KENTUCKY BLUEGRASS **2** [fr. the *Blue Grass Boys*, performing group, fr. *Bluegrass state*, nickname of Kentucky] **:** country music played on unamplified stringed instruments (as banjo, fiddle, guitar, and mandolin) and characterized by free improvisation and close usu. high-pitched harmony

blue–green alga \ˈblü-ˈgrēn-\ *n* (1899) **:** CYANOBACTERIUM

blue gum *n* (1799) **:** any of several Australian trees (genus *Eucalyptus*) that yield valuable timber

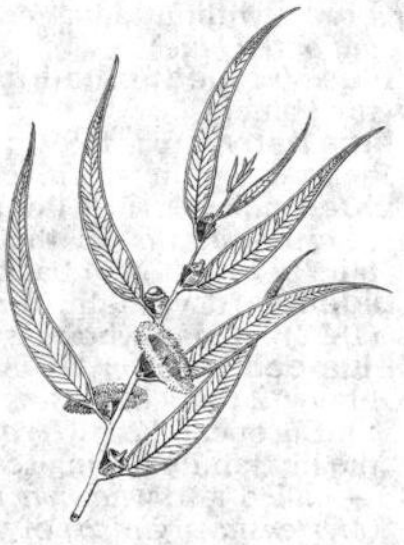
blue gum

blue heeler *n* (1908) **:** AUSTRALIAN CATTLE DOG

blue heron *n* (ca. 1730) **:** either of two herons with bluish or slaty plumage; *esp* **:** GREAT BLUE HERON

blue·jack·et \-ˌja-kət\ *n* (1830) **:** an enlisted man in the navy **:** SAILOR

blue jay \-ˌjā\ *n* (1709) **:** a crested bright blue No. American jay (*Cyanocitta cristata*)

blue jeans *n pl* (1901) **:** pants usu. made of blue denim — **blue–jeaned** \-ˌjēnd\ *adj*

blue law *n* (1762) **1 :** one of numerous extremely rigorous laws designed to regulate morals and conduct in colonial New England **2 :** a statute regulating work, commerce, and amusements on Sundays

blue line *n* (1925) **:** either of two blue lines that divide an ice-hockey rink into three equal zones and that separate the offensive and defensive zones from the center-ice neutral zone

blue·lin·er \ˈblü-ˌlī-nər\ *n* (1974) **:** a defenseman in ice hockey

blue marlin *n* (1940) **:** a large marlin (*Makaira nigricans*) that is widely distributed in warm seas and is valued as a sport fish

blue mold *n* (1664) **:** any of various fungi (genera *Penicillium* and *Peronospora*) that produce blue or blue-green surface growths

blue moon *n* (1821) **1 :** a very long period of time — usu. used in the phrase *once in a blue moon* ⟨such people happen along only once in a *blue moon* —*Saturday Rev.*⟩ **2 :** a second full moon in a calendar month

blue mussel *n* (1977) **:** a widely distributed edible mussel (*Mytilus edulis*) having a usu. blue or brownish shell

blue·nose \ˈblü-ˌnōz\ *n* (1903) **:** a person who advocates a rigorous moral code — **blue·nosed** \-ˌnōzd\ *adj*

blue note *n* [fr. its frequent use in blues music] (1919) **:** a variable microtonal lowering of the third, seventh, and occas. fifth degrees of the major scale

blue–pen·cil \ˈblü-ˈpen(t)-səl\ *vt* (1888) **:** to edit esp. by shortening or deletion — **blue penciller** *n*

blue pencil *n* (1886) **:** a writing instrument used for editing; *also* **:** the act or practice of blue-penciling

blue pe·ter \-ˈpē-tər\ *n* [prob. fr. the name *Peter*] (1823) **:** a blue signal flag with a white square in the center used to indicate that a merchant vessel is ready to sail

blue pike *n* (1842) **:** a grayish-blue walleye (*Stizostedion vitreum glaucum*) of the Great Lakes region now considered to be extinct

blue plate *adj* (1919) **:** being a main course usu. offered at a special price in a restaurant ⟨a *blue plate* luncheon⟩

blue·point \ˈblü-ˌpȯint\ *n* [*Blue Point*, Long Island] (1854) **:** a small oyster (*Crassostrea virginica*) typically from the south shore of Long Island

blue point \-ˌpȯint\ *adj* (1944) *of a domestic cat* **:** having a bluish-cream body coat with dark gray points — **blue point** *n*

blue·print \-ˌprint\ *n* (1886) **1 :** a photographic print in white on a bright blue ground or blue on a white ground used esp. for copying maps, mechanical drawings, and architects' plans **2 :** something resembling a blueprint (as in serving as a model or providing guidance); *esp* **:** a detailed plan or program of action ⟨a ~ for victory⟩ — **blueprint** *vt*

blue racer *n* (1886) **:** a blue or greenish-blue colubrid snake (*Coluber constrictor foxii*) occurring chiefly from southern Ontario to Missouri

blue–ribbon *adj* (1926) **:** of outstanding quality; *esp* **:** consisting of individuals selected for quality, reputation, or authority ⟨a ~ panel⟩

blue ribbon *n* (1651) **1 :** an honor or award gained for preeminence **2 :** a blue ribbon awarded as an honor (as to the first-place winner in a competition)

blues \ˈblüz\ *n pl but sing or pl in constr* [*blue devils*] (1741) **1 :** low spirits **:** MELANCHOLY ⟨suffering a case of the ~⟩ **2 :** a song often of lamentation characterized by usu. 12-bar phrases, 3-line stanzas in which the words of the second line usu. repeat those of the first, and continual occurrence of blue notes in melody and harmony **3 :** jazz or popular music using harmonic and phrase structures of blues

blue screen *n* (1977) **:** a photographic technique in which a subject is filmed in front of a blue background so as to allow matte compositing of the film with other footage; *also* **:** the blue background

blue shark *n* (ca. 1672) **:** a chiefly pelagic shark (*Prionace glauca*) found in all tropical and temperate seas that occas. attacks humans

blue sheep *n* (1910) **:** BHARAL

blue·shift \ˈblü-ˈshift\ *n* (1951) **:** the displacement of the spectrum of an approaching celestial body toward shorter wavelengths — **blueshift·ed** *adj*

blue–sky \ˈblü-ˈskī\ *adj* (1906) **1 :** having little or no value ⟨~ stock⟩ **2 :** not grounded in the realities of the present **:** VISIONARY ⟨~ thinking⟩

blue–sky law *n* (1912) **:** a law providing for the regulation of the sale of securities (as stock)

blues·man \ˈblüz-mən\ *n* (1966) **:** a man who plays or sings the blues

blue spruce *n* (1884) **:** a spruce (*Picea pungens*) native to the Rocky Mountains that has sharp usu. bluish-gray needles and is often planted as an ornamental

blue·stem \ˈblü-ˌstem\ *n* (ca. 1852) **1 :** a tall No. American grass (*Andropogon gerardii* syn. *A. furcatus*) that has smooth bluish leaf sheaths and slender spikes borne in pairs or clusters, is a dominant grass of the orig. tallgrass prairies, and is used for hay and forage — called also *big bluestem*; compare SAND BLUESTEM **2 :** LITTLE BLUESTEM

blue·stock·ing \-ˌstä-kiŋ\ *n* [*Bluestocking* society, 18th cent. literary clubs] (1790) **:** a woman having intellectual or literary interests

blue·stone \-ˌstōn\ *n* (1709) **:** a building stone of bluish-gray color

blue streak *n* (1830) **1 :** something that moves very fast **2 :** a constant stream of words ⟨talked a *blue streak*⟩

bluesy \ˈblü-zē\ *adj* **blues·i·er; -est** (1946) **:** resembling, characteristic of, or suited to the blues

blu·et \ˈblü-ət\ *n* [prob. fr. [1]*blue*] (ca. 1821) **:** any of several perennial No. American herbs (genus *Hedyotis* syn. *Houstonia*) of the madder family; *esp* **:** one (*Hedyotis caerulea* syn. *Houstonia caerulea*) having tufted stems and bluish, white, or purplish flowers with yellow centers

blue tang *n* [[1]*tang* (surgeonfish)] (ca. 1902) **:** a surgeonfish (*Acanthurus coeruleus*) that is bright blue with darker longitudinal stripes when mature and occurs chiefly from Bermuda to Brazil

blue·tick \-ˌtik\ *n* (1945) **:** any of a breed of tricolor coonhounds of American origin having the white areas of the coat usu. heavily ticked with black

blue·tongue \ˈblü-ˌtəŋ\ *n* (1863) **:** a virus disease chiefly of sheep that is marked by hyperemia, cyanosis, and by swelling and sloughing of the mucous membranes esp. about the mouth and tongue and is caused by a reovirus (species *Bluetongue virus* of the genus *Orbivirus*)

blue vitriol *n* (1728) **:** a hydrated copper sulfate $CuSO_4 \cdot 5H_2O$

blue water *n* (1582) **:** the open sea — **blue–wa·ter** \ˈblü-ˌwȯ-tər, -ˌwä-\ *adj*

blue·weed \ˈblü-ˌwēd\ *n* (ca. 1837) **1 :** VIPER'S BUGLOSS **2 :** a small weedy sunflower (*Helianthus ciliaris*) of the southwestern U.S. with blue-green or gray-green foliage

blue whale *n* (1851) **:** a very large baleen whale (*Balaenoptera musculus* syn. *Sibbaldus musculus*) that may reach a weight of 150 tons (135 metric tons) and a length of 100 feet (30 meters) and is generally considered the largest living animal

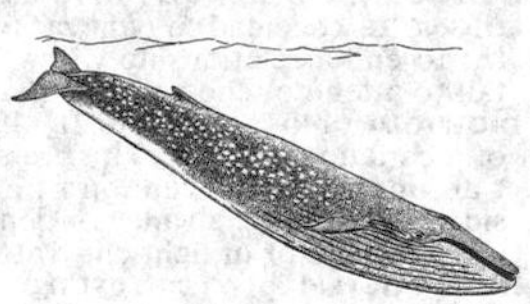
blue whale

blue–winged teal \ˈblü-ˌwiŋ(d)-\ *n* (1789) **:** a No. American dabbling duck (*Anas discors*) with a blue patch on each wing and in the male a white crescent on each cheek

bluey \ˈblü-ē\ *adj* (1802) **:** BLUISH

[1]**bluff** \ˈbləf\ *adj* [obs. D *blaf* flat; akin to MLG *blaff* smooth] (1627) **1 a :** having a broad flattened front **b :** rising steeply with a broad flat or rounded front **2 :** good-naturedly frank and outspoken — **bluff·ly** *adv* — **bluff·ness** *n*

syn BLUFF, BLUNT, BRUSQUE, CURT, CRUSTY, GRUFF mean abrupt and unceremonious in speech and manner. BLUFF connotes good-natured outspokenness and unconventionality ⟨a *bluff* manner⟩. BLUNT suggests directness of expression in disregard of others' feelings ⟨a *blunt* appraisal⟩. BRUSQUE applies to a sharpness or ungraciousness ⟨a *brusque* response⟩. CURT implies disconcerting shortness or rude conciseness ⟨a *curt* command⟩. CRUSTY suggests a harsh or surly manner sometimes concealing an inner kindliness ⟨a *crusty* exterior⟩. GRUFF suggests a hoarse or husky speech which may imply bad temper but more often implies embarrassment or shyness ⟨puts on a *gruff* pose⟩.

[2]**bluff** *n* (1666) **:** a high steep bank **:** CLIFF

[3]**bluff** *vb* [prob. fr. D *bluffen* to boast, play a kind of card game] *vt* (1791) **1 a :** to deter or frighten by pretense or a mere show of strength **b :** DECEIVE **c :** FEIGN ⟨the catcher ~*ed* a throw to first⟩ **2 :** to deceive (an opponent) in cards by a bold bet on an inferior hand ~ *vi* **:** to bluff someone **:** act deceptively — **bluff·er** *n*

[4]**bluff** *n* (1845) **1 a :** an act or instance of bluffing **b :** the practice of bluffing **2 :** one who bluffs
blu·ing *or* **blue·ing** \ˈblü-iŋ\ *n* (1669) **:** a preparation used in laundering to counteract yellowing of white fabrics
blu·ish \ˈblü-ish\ *adj* (14c) **:** somewhat blue **:** having a tinge of blue — **blu·ish·ness** *n*
[1]**blun·der** \ˈblən-dər\ *vb* **blun·dered; blun·der·ing** \-d(ə-)riŋ\ [ME *blundren,* prob. of Scand origin; akin to ON *blunda* to shut one's eyes, doze, Norw dial. *blundra*] *vi* (14c) **1 :** to move unsteadily or confusedly **2 :** to make a mistake through stupidity, ignorance, or carelessness ∼ *vt* **1 :** to utter stupidly, confusedly, or thoughtlessly **2 :** to make a stupid, careless, or thoughtless mistake in — **blun·der·er** \-dər-ər\ *n* — **blun·der·ing·ly** \-d(ə-)riŋ-lē\ *adv*
[2]**blunder** *n* (1693) **:** a gross error or mistake resulting usu. from stupidity, ignorance, or carelessness ***syn*** see ERROR
blun·der·buss \ˈblən-dər-ˌbəs\ *n* [by folk etymology fr. obs. D *donderbus,* fr. D *donder* thunder + obs. D *bus* gun] (1654) **1 :** a muzzle-loading firearm with a short barrel and flaring muzzle to facilitate loading **2 :** a blundering person
[1]**blunt** \ˈblənt\ *adj* [ME] (13c) **1 a :** slow or deficient in feeling **:** INSENSITIVE **b :** obtuse in understanding or discernment **:** DULL **2 :** having an edge or point that is not sharp ⟨a ∼ instrument⟩ **3 a :** abrupt in speech or manner **b :** being straight to the point **:** DIRECT ***syn*** see DULL, BLUFF — **blunt·ly** *adv* — **blunt·ness** *n*
[2]**blunt** *vt* (14c) **:** to make less sharp, definite, or forceful ∼ *vi* **:** to become blunt
[3]**blunt** *n* [*blunt* a short, thick cigar, fr. [1]*blunt*] (1990) **:** a cigar that has been hollowed out and filled with marijuana
blunt trauma *n* (1962) **:** a usu. serious injury caused by a blunt object or surface ⟨died of *blunt trauma* to the head⟩
[1]**blur** \ˈblər\ *n* [perh. akin to ME *bleren* to blear] (1519) **1 :** a smear or stain that obscures **2 :** something vaguely or indistinctly perceived; *esp* **:** something moving or occurring too quickly to be clearly seen
[2]**blur** *vb* **blurred; blur·ring** *vt* (1520) **1 :** to obscure or blemish by smearing **2 :** SULLY **3 :** to make dim, indistinct, or vague in outline or character **4 :** to make cloudy or confused ∼ *vi* **1 :** to make blurs **2 :** to become vague or indistinct — **blur·ring·ly** \ˈblər-iŋ-lē\ *adv*
[1]**blurb** \ˈblərb\ *n* [coined by Gelett Burgess] (1914) **:** a short publicity notice (as on a book jacket)
[2]**blurb** *vt* (1915) **:** to describe or praise in a blurb
blur·ry \ˈblər-ē\ *adj* **blur·ri·er; -est** (1884) **:** lacking definition or focus — **blur·ri·ly** \ˈblər-ə-lē\ *adv* — **blur·ri·ness** \ˈblər-ē-nəs\ *n*
blurt \ˈblərt\ *vt* [prob. imit.] (1573) **:** to utter abruptly and impulsively — usu. used with *out* — **blurt·er** *n*
[1]**blush** \ˈbləsh\ *n* [ME, prob. fr. *blusshen*] (14c) **1 :** outward appearance **:** VIEW ⟨at first ∼⟩ **2 :** a reddening of the face esp. from shame, modesty, or confusion **3 :** a red or rosy tint **4 :** a cosmetic applied to the face to give a usu. pink color or to accent the cheekbones — **blush·ful** \-fəl\ *adj*
[2]**blush** *vi* [ME *blusshen,* fr. OE *blyscan* to redden; akin to OE *blȳsa* flame, OHG *bluhhen* to burn brightly] (15c) **1 :** to become red in the face esp. from shame, modesty, or confusion **2 :** to feel shame or embarrassment **3 :** to have a rosy or fresh color **:** BLOOM — **blush·ing·ly** \ˈblə-shiŋ-lē\ *adv*
blush·er \ˈblə-shər\ *n* (1659) **1 :** one who blushes **2 :** BLUSH 4
blush wine *n* (1985) **:** any of various pinkish table wines
[1]**blus·ter** \ˈbləs-tər\ *vb* **blus·tered; blus·ter·ing** \-t(ə-)riŋ\ [ME *blustren,* prob. fr. MLG *blüsteren*] *vi* (15c) **1 :** to talk or act with noisy swaggering threats **2 a :** to blow in stormy noisy gusts **b :** to be windy and boisterous ∼ *vt* **1 :** to utter with noisy self-assertiveness **2 :** to drive or force by blustering — **blus·ter·er** \-tər-ər\ *n* — **blus·ter·ing·ly** \-t(ə-)riŋ-lē\ *adv*
[2]**bluster** *n* (1583) **1 :** a violent boisterous blowing **2 :** violent commotion **3 :** loudly boastful or threatening speech — **blus·ter·ous** \-t(ə-)rəs\ *adj* — **blus·tery** \-t(ə-)rē\ *adj*
blvd *abbr* boulevard
B lymphocyte *n* (1971) **:** B CELL
bm *abbr* beam
BM *abbr* **1** bachelor of medicine **2** bachelor of music **3** basal metabolism **4** bill of material **5** board measure **6** bowel movement **7** bronze medal
BME *abbr* **1** bachelor of mechanical engineering **2** bachelor of mining engineering **3** bachelor of music education
BMI *abbr* body mass index
BMOC *abbr* big man on campus
B movie *n* (1948) **:** a cheaply produced motion picture
BMR *abbr* basal metabolic rate
BMS *abbr* bachelor of marine science
BMT *abbr* bachelor of medical technology
BMX \ˌbē-(ˌ)em-ˈeks\ *n* [*b*icycle *m*otocross + *X* as symbol for *-cross*] (1975) **:** bicycle racing that resembles motocross with dirt tracks and jumps and the use of special heavy-duty bicycles
bn *abbr* **1** baron **2** battalion **3** beacon **4** been
BN *abbr* **1** bachelor of nursing **2** banknote **3** Bureau of Narcotics
BNDD *abbr* Bureau of Narcotics and Dangerous Drugs
BNS *abbr* bachelor of naval sciences
BO *abbr* **1** back order **2** best offer **3** body odor **4** box office **5** branch office **6** buyer's option
boa \ˈbō-ə\ *n* [L, a water snake] (14c) **1 :** any of a family (Boidae) of large snakes that kill by constriction and that includes the boa constrictor, anaconda, and python **2 :** a long fluffy scarf
boa constrictor *n* (1809) **:** a tropical American boa (*Boa constrictor* syn. *Constrictor constrictor*) that is light brown barred or mottled with darker brown and reaches a length of 10 feet (3 meters) or more; *broadly* **:** BOA 1
boar \ˈbȯr\ *n* [ME *bor,* fr. OE *bār;* akin to OHG & OS *bēr* boar] (bef. 12c) **1 a :** an uncastrated male swine **b :** the male of any of several mammals (as a guinea pig) **2 :** WILD BOAR — **boar·ish** \-ish\ *adj*
[1]**board** \ˈbȯrd\ *n* [ME *bord* piece of sawed lumber, border, ship's side, fr. OE; akin to OHG *bort* ship's side] (bef. 12c) **1** *obs* **:** BORDER, EDGE **2 :** the side of a ship **3 a :** a piece of sawed lumber of little thickness and a length greatly exceeding its width **b** *pl* **:** STAGE 2a(2) **c** *pl* **:** SKIS **4 a** *archaic* **:** TABLE 3a **b :** a table spread with a meal **c :** daily meals esp. when furnished for pay **d :** a table at which a council or magistrates sit **e** (1) **:** a group of persons having managerial, supervisory, investigatory, or advisory powers ⟨∼ of directors⟩ ⟨∼ of examiners⟩ (2) **:** an examination given by an examining board — often used in pl. ⟨pass the medical ∼*s*⟩ **f :** LEAGUE, ASSOCIATION **g** (1) **:** the exposed hands of all the players in a stud poker game (2) **:** an exposed dummy hand in bridge **5 a :** a flat usu. rectangular piece of material (as wood) designed for a special purpose: as (1) **:** SPRINGBOARD 1 (2) **:** SURFBOARD **b :** BACKBOARD 1; *also* **:** a rebound in basketball **c :** a surface, frame, or device for posting notices **d :** BLACKBOARD **e :** SWITCHBOARD **6 a :** CARDBOARD **b :** the stiff foundation piece for the side of a book cover **7 :** a securities or commodities exchange **8** *pl* **:** the low wooden wall enclosing a hockey rink **9 :** a sheet of insulating material carrying circuit elements and terminals so that it can be inserted in an electronic apparatus (as a computer) **10 :** BULLETIN BOARD 2 — **board·like** \-ˌlīk\ *adj* — **across the board :** so as to include or affect all classes or categories ⟨cut spending *across the board*⟩; *also* **:** in all areas or respects ⟨considered an average player *across the board*⟩ — **on board 1 :** ABOARD **2 :** in support of a particular objective ⟨needed to get more senators *on board* for the bill to pass⟩
[2]**board** *vt* (15c) **1** *archaic* **:** to come up against or alongside (a ship) usu. to attack **2 :** ACCOST, ADDRESS **3 a :** to go aboard (as a ship, train, airplane, or bus) **b :** to put aboard ⟨an airliner ∼*ing* passengers⟩ **4 :** to cover or seal off with boards ⟨∼ up a window⟩ ⟨∼ up a house⟩ **5 :** to provide with regular meals and often also lodging usu. for compensation **6 :** to check (a player) into the boards in hockey ∼ *vi* **:** to receive meals or lodging; *specif* **:** to live at a boarding school
board·er \ˈbȯr-dər\ *n* (1530) **1 :** one that boards; *esp* **:** one that is provided with regular meals or regular meals and lodging **2 :** a person who rides a snowboard **:** SNOWBOARDER
board foot *n* (1896) **:** a unit of quantity for lumber equal to the volume of a board 12 × 12 × 1 inches — abbr. *bd ft*
board game *n* (1889) **:** a game of strategy (as checkers, chess, or backgammon) played by moving pieces on a board
board·ing·house \ˈbȯr-diŋ-ˌhau̇s\ *n* (1680) **:** a lodging house at which meals are provided
boarding school *n* (1665) **:** a school that provides meals and lodging
board·man \ˈbȯrd-ˌman, *esp for 2* -mən\ *n* (ca. 1923) **1 :** a member of a board **2 :** one who works at a board
board of trade (1780) **1** *cap B&T* **:** a British governmental department concerned with commerce and industry **2 :** a commodities exchange
board·room \ˈbȯrd-ˌrüm, -ˌru̇m\ *n* (1836) **:** a room that is designated for meetings of a board
board·sail·ing \-ˌsā-liŋ\ *n* (1980) **:** WINDSURFING — **board·sail·or** \-ˌsā-lər\ *n*
board·walk \-ˌwȯk\ *n* (1872) **1 :** a walk constructed of planking **2 :** a walk constructed along a beach
boart *var of* BORT
[1]**boast** \ˈbōst\ *n* [ME *boost*] (14c) **1 :** the act or an instance of boasting **:** BRAG **2 :** a cause for pride — **boast·ful** \ˈbōst-fəl\ *adj* — **boast·ful·ly** \-fə-lē\ *adv* — **boast·ful·ness** *n*
[2]**boast** *vi* (14c) **1 :** to puff oneself up in speech **:** speak vaingloriously **2** *archaic* **:** GLORY, EXULT ∼ *vt* **1 :** to speak of or assert with excessive pride **2 a :** to possess and often call attention to (something that is a source of pride) ⟨∼*s* a new stadium⟩ **b :** HAVE, CONTAIN ⟨a room ∼*ing* no more than a desk and a chair⟩ — **boast·er** *n*

syn BOAST, BRAG, VAUNT, CROW mean to express pride in oneself or one's accomplishments. BOAST often suggests ostentation and exaggeration ⟨*boasts* of every trivial success⟩, but it may imply a claiming with proper and justifiable pride ⟨the town *boasts* one of the best museums in the area⟩. BRAG suggests crudity and artlessness in glorifying oneself ⟨*bragging* of their exploits⟩. VAUNT usu. connotes more pomp and bombast than BOAST and less crudity or naïveté than BRAG ⟨*vaunted* his country's military might⟩. CROW usu. implies exultant boasting or bragging ⟨*crowed* after winning the championship⟩.

[3]**boast** *vt* [origin unknown] (1823) **:** to shape (stone) roughly in sculpture and stonecutting as a preliminary to finer work
[1]**boat** \ˈbōt\ *n* [ME *boot,* fr. OE *bāt;* akin to ON *beit* boat] (bef. 12c) **1 a :** a small vessel for travel on water **b :** SHIP **2 :** a boat-shaped container, utensil, or device ⟨a gravy ∼⟩ ⟨a laboratory ∼⟩ — **boat·ful** \-ˌfu̇l\ *n* — **boat·like** \-ˌlīk\ *adj* — **in the same boat :** in the same situation or predicament
[2]**boat** *vt* (1613) **:** to place in or bring into a boat ∼ *vi* **:** to go by boat
boat·build·er \-ˌbil-dər\ *n* (1679) **:** one that builds boats — **boat·build·ing** \-ˌbil-diŋ\ *n*
boat·er \ˈbō-tər\ *n* (1605) **1 :** one who travels in a boat **2 :** a stiff hat usu. made of braided straw with a brim, hatband, and flat crown
boat hook *n* (ca. 1599) **:** a pole-handled hook with a point or knob on the back used esp. to pull or push a boat, raft, or log into place
boat·house \-ˌhau̇s\ *n* (1722) **:** a building to house and protect boats
boat·load \ˈbōt-ˌlōd\ *n* (1664) **1 :** a load that fills a boat **2 :** an indefinitely large number ⟨a ∼ of money⟩
boat·man \ˈbōt-mən\ *n* (14c) **:** a man who works on, deals in, or operates boats
boat·neck \ˈbōt-ˌnek\ *n* (1940) **:** a wide neckline that extends toward the tips of the shoulders
boat people *n pl* (1977) **:** refugees fleeing by boat
boat shoe *n* (1977) **:** a low-cut shoe with a slip-resistant sole
boat·swain *or* **bosun** *also* **bos'n** *or* **bo's'n** *or* **bo'sun** \ˈbō-sᵊn\ *n* [ME *bootswein,* fr. *boot* boat + *swein* boy, servant — more at SWAIN] (14c) **1 :** a petty officer on a merchant ship having charge of hull maintenance and related work **2 :** a naval warrant officer in charge of the hull and all related equipment
boat train *n* (1864) **:** an express train for transporting passengers between a port and a city
boat·yard \ˈbōt-ˌyärd\ *n* (1795) **:** a yard where boats are built, repaired, and stored and often sold or rented

\ə\ **abut** \ᵊ\ **kitten, F table** \ər\ **further** \a\ **ash** \ā\ **ace** \ä\ **mop, mar** \au̇\ **out** \ch\ **chin** \e\ **bet** \ē\ **easy** \g\ **go** \i\ **hit** \ī\ **ice** \j\ **job** \ŋ\ **sing** \ō\ **go** \ȯ\ **law** \ȯi\ **boy** \th\ **thin** \t͟h\ **the** \ü\ **loot** \u̇\ **foot** \y\ **yet** \zh\ **vision, beige** \k̲, ⁿ, œ, ue, ʸ\ *see* Guide to Pronunciation

[1]**bob** \ˈbäb\ *vb* **bobbed; bob·bing** [ME *boben*] *vt* (13c) **1 :** to strike with a quick light blow **:** RAP **2 :** to move up and down in a short quick movement ⟨~ the head⟩ **3 :** to polish with a bob **:** BUFF ~ *vi* **1 a :** to move up and down briefly or repeatedly **b :** to emerge, arise, or appear suddenly or unexpectedly **2 :** to nod or curtsy briefly **3 :** to try to seize a suspended or floating object with the teeth
[2]**bob** *n* (ca. 1550) **1 a :** a short quick down-and-up motion **b** *Scot* **:** any of several folk dances **2** *obs* **:** a blow or tap esp. with the fist **3 a :** a modification of the order in change ringing **b :** a method of change ringing using a bob **4 :** a small polishing wheel of solid felt or leather with rounded edges
[3]**bob** *vt* **bobbed; bob·bing** [ME *bobben,* fr. OF *bober*] (14c) **1** *obs* **:** DECEIVE, CHEAT **2** *obs* **:** to take by fraud **:** FILCH
[4]**bob** *n* [ME *bobbe*] (14c) **1 a** (1) **:** BUNCH, CLUSTER (2) *Scot* **:** NOSEGAY **b :** a knob, knot, twist, or curl esp. of ribbons, yarn, or hair **c :** a short haircut on a woman or child **2 :** FLOAT 2a **3 :** a hanging ball or weight (as on a plumb line) **4 :** TRIFLE 1 ⟨bits and ~*s*⟩
[5]**bob** *vt* **bobbed; bob·bing** (1675) **1 :** to cut shorter **:** CROP ⟨~ a horse's tail⟩ **2 :** to cut (hair) in the style of a bob
[6]**bob** *n, pl* **bob** [perh. fr. the name *Bob*] (1789) *slang Brit* **:** SHILLING
[7]**bob** *n* (1856) **:** BOBSLED
[1]**bob·ber** \ˈbä-bər\ *n* (1593) **:** one that bobs
[2]**bobber** *n* (1904) **:** a person who rides or races on a bobsled
bob·bery \ˈbä-b(ə-)rē\ *n, pl* **-ber·ies** [Hindi *bāp re,* lit., oh father!] (1800) **:** HUBBUB
bob·bin \ˈbä-bən\ *n* [origin unknown] (1530) **1 a :** a cylinder or spindle on which yarn or thread is wound (as in a sewing machine) **b :** any of various small round devices on which threads are wound for working handmade lace **c :** a coil of insulated wire; *also* **:** the reel it is wound on **2 :** a cotton cord formerly used by dressmakers for piping
bob·bi·net \ˌbä-bə-ˈnet\ *n* [blend of *bobbin* and *net*] (1814) **:** a machine-made net of cotton, silk, or nylon usu. with hexagonal mesh
[1]**bob·ble** \ˈbä-bəl\ *vb* **bob·bled; bob·bling** \-b(ə-)liŋ\ [freq. of [1]*bob*] (1812) **1 :** [1]BOB **2 :** FUMBLE
[2]**bobble** *n* (1880) **1 :** a repeated bobbing movement **2 :** a small ball of fabric; *esp* **:** one in a series used on an edging **3 :** ERROR, MISTAKE; *esp* **:** a mishandling of the ball in baseball or football
bob·ble·head doll \ˈbä-bəl-ˌhed-\ *n* (1964) **:** a doll having a head that makes repeated bobbing movements
bob·by \ˈbä-bē\ *n, pl* **bobbies** [*Bobby,* nickname for *Robert,* after Sir *Robert* Peel, who organized the London police force] (1844) *Brit* **:** POLICE OFFICER
bobby pin *n* [perh. fr. [4]*bob*] (1926) **:** a flat wire hairpin with prongs that press close together
bobby socks *or* **bobby sox** *n pl* [perh. fr. *bobby* pin] (1927) **:** girls' socks reaching above the ankle
bob·by–sox·er \-ˌsäk-sər\ *n* (1944) **:** an adolescent girl
bob·cat \ˈbäb-ˌkat\ *n* [[4]*bob;* fr. the stubby tail] (1864) **:** a common No. American lynx (*Lynx rufus*) reddish in base color with dark markings
bo·beche \bō-ˈbesh, -ˈbāsh\ *n* [F *bobèche*] (1855) **:** a usu. glass collar on a candle socket to catch drippings or on a candlestick or chandelier to hold suspended glass prisms
bo·bo \ˈbō-(ˌ)bō\ *n, pl* **bobos** [*bo*urgeois + *Bo*hemian] (2000) **:** a member of a social class of well-to-do professionals who espouse bohemian values and lead bourgeois lives
bob·o·link \ˈbä-bə-ˌliŋk\ *n* [imit.] (ca. 1801) **:** an American migratory songbird (*Dolichonyx oryzivorus*) with the breeding male chiefly black
bob·sled \ˈbäb-ˌsled\ *n* [perh. fr. [4]*bob*] (1837) **1 :** a short sled usu. used as one of a pair joined by a coupling **2 :** a large usu. metal sled used in racing and equipped with two pairs of runners in tandem, a long seat for two or more people, a steering wheel, and a hand brake — **bobsled** *vi* — **bob·sled·der** *n*
bob·sled·ding \-ˌsle-diŋ\ *n* (1883) **:** the act, skill, or sport of riding or racing on a bobsled
bob·stay \ˈbäb-ˌstā\ *n* [prob. fr. [2]*bob*] (1744) **:** a stay to hold a ship's bowsprit down
bob·tail \ˈbäb-ˌtāl\ *n* [[4]*bob*] (1605) **1 a :** a bobbed tail **b :** a horse, dog, or cat with a bobbed or very short tail; *esp* **:** OLD ENGLISH SHEEPDOG **2 :** something curtailed — **bobtail** *or* **bob·tailed** \-ˌtāld\ *adj*
bob veal \ˈbäb-\ *n* [E dial. *bob* young calf] (1855) **:** the veal of a very young or unborn calf
bob·white \ˈbäb-ˈhwīt, -ˈwīt\ *n* [imit.] (1819) **:** any of a genus (*Colinus*) of quail; *esp* **:** a popular game bird (*C. virginianus*) of eastern and central No. America having mottled chiefly reddish-brown plumage
bo·cac·cio \bə-ˈkä-chē-ˌō, -chō\ *n* [perh. modif. of Sp *bocacha,* aug. of *boca* mouth] (ca. 1890) **:** a large rockfish (*Sebastes paucispinis*) of the Pacific coast locally important as a market fish
boc·cie *or* **boc·ci** *or* **boc·ce** \ˈbä-chē\ *n* [It *bocce,* pl. of *boccia* ball, fr. VL **bottia* boss] (1860) **:** a game of Italian origin similar to lawn bowling played on a long narrow usu. dirt court
bock \ˈbäk\ *n* [G, short for *Bockbier,* by shortening & alter. fr. *Einbecker Bier,* lit., beer from Einbeck, fr. *Einbeck,* Germany] (1856) **:** a strong dark rich beer usu. sold in the early spring
bod \ˈbäd\ *n* (1933) **1** *Brit* **:** FELLOW, GUY **2 :** BODY
BOD *abbr* **1** biochemical oxygen demand **2** biological oxygen demand
bo·da·cious \bō-ˈdā-shəs\ *adj* [prob. blend of *bold* and *audacious*] (1832) **1** *Southern & Midland* **:** OUTRIGHT, UNMISTAKABLE **2 :** REMARKABLE, NOTEWORTHY ⟨a ~ bargain⟩ **3 :** SEXY, VOLUPTUOUS ⟨~ babes⟩ — **bo·da·cious·ly** *adv*
[1]**bode** \ˈbōd\ *vt* **bod·ed; bod·ing** [ME, fr. OE *bodian;* akin to OE *bēodan* to proclaim — more at BID] (bef. 12c) **1** *archaic* **:** to announce beforehand **:** FORETELL **2 :** to indicate by signs **:** PRESAGE
[2]**bode** *past of* BIDE
bo·de·ga \bō-ˈdā-gə\ *n* [Sp, fr. L *apotheca* storehouse — more at APOTHECARY] (1846) **1 :** a storehouse for maturing wine **2 a :** WINESHOP **b** (1) **:** [1]BAR 5a (2) **:** BARROOM **3 :** a usu. small grocery store in an urban area; *specif* **:** one specializing in Hispanic groceries
bode·ment \ˈbōd-mənt\ *n* (1605) **1 :** OMEN **2 :** PREDICTION 2
bo·dhi·satt·va *or* **bod·dhi·satt·va** \ˌbō-di-ˈsət-və, -ˈsät-\ *n* [Skt *bodhisattva* one whose essence is enlightenment, fr. *bodhi* enlightenment + *sattva* being — more at BID] (1828) **:** a being that compassionately refrains from entering nirvana in order to save others and is worshipped as a deity in Mahayana Buddhism
bodh·ran \ˈbò-(ˌ)rän, -rən\ *n* [Ir *bodhrán*] (1972) **:** a shallow handheld Irish drum
bod·ice \ˈbä-dəs\ *n* [alter. of *bodies,* pl. of [1]*body*] (1566) **1 :** the upper part of a woman's dress **2** *archaic* **:** CORSET, STAYS
bodice ripper *n* (1980) **:** a historical or Gothic romance typically featuring scenes in which the heroine is subjected to violence
bod·ied \ˈbä-dēd\ *adj* (ca. 1547) **:** having a body of a specified kind — used in combination ⟨full-*bodied*⟩ ⟨glass-*bodied*⟩
bodi·less \ˈbä-di-ləs, ˈbä-dᵊl-əs\ *adj* (14c) **:** having no body
[1]**bodi·ly** \ˈbä-dᵊl-ē\ *adj* (14c) **1 :** having a body **:** PHYSICAL **2 :** of or relating to the body ⟨~ comfort⟩ ⟨~ organs⟩
[2]**bodily** *adv* (14c) **1 :** in the flesh **2 :** as a whole **:** ALTOGETHER
bod·ing \ˈbō-diŋ\ *n* (13c) **:** FOREBODING
bod·kin \ˈbäd-kən\ *n* [ME *bodekin*] (14c) **1 a :** DAGGER, STILETTO **b :** a sharp slender instrument for making holes in cloth **c :** an ornamental hairpin shaped like a stiletto **2 :** a blunt needle with a large eye for drawing tape or ribbon through a loop or hem
[1]**body** \ˈbä-dē\ *n, pl* **bod·ies** [ME, fr. OE *bodig;* akin to OHG *boteh* corpse] (bef. 12c) **1 a :** the main part of a plant or animal body esp. as distinguished from limbs and head **:** TRUNK **b :** the main, central, or principal part: as (1) **:** the nave of a church (2) **:** the bed or box of a vehicle on or in which the load is placed (3) **:** the enclosed or partly enclosed part of an automobile **2 a :** the organized physical substance of an animal or plant either living or dead: as (1) **:** the material part or nature of a human being (2) **:** a dead organism **:** CORPSE **b :** a human being **:** PERSON **3 a :** a mass of matter distinct from other masses ⟨a ~ of water⟩ **b :** something that embodies or gives concrete reality to a thing; *also* **:** a sensible object in physical space **c :** AGGREGATE, QUANTITY ⟨a ~ of evidence⟩ **4 a :** the part of a garment covering the body or trunk **b :** the main part of a literary or journalistic work **:** TEXT 2b **c :** the sound box or pipe of a musical instrument **5 :** a group of persons or things: as **a :** a fighting unit **:** FORCE **b :** a group of individuals organized for some purpose ⟨a legislative ~⟩ **6 a :** fullness and richness of flavor (as of wine) **b :** VISCOSITY, CONSISTENCY — used esp. of oils and grease **c :** denseness, fullness, or firmness of texture **d :** fullness or resonance of a musical tone
[2]**body** *vt* **bod·ied; body·ing** (15c) **1 :** to give form or shape to **:** EMBODY **2 :** REPRESENT, SYMBOLIZE — usu. used with *forth*
body bag *n* (1954) **:** a large zippered bag (as of rubber or vinyl) in which a human corpse is placed esp. for transportation
body blow *n* (1792) **1 :** a blow to the body **2 :** a damaging or deeply felt blow ⟨an economic *body blow*⟩
body·board \ˈbä-dē-ˌbòrd\ *n* (1982) **:** a short surfboard on which the rider lies prone — **bodyboard** *vi* — **bodyboarder** *n*
body·build·ing \-ˌbil-diŋ\ *n* (1904) **:** the developing of the body through exercise and diet; *specif* **:** the developing of the physique for competitive exhibition — **body·build·er** *n*
body cavity *n* (1875) **:** a cavity in an animal body; *specif* **:** COELOM
body–cen·tered \ˈbä-dē-ˌsen-tərd\ *adj* (1921) **:** relating to or being a crystal space lattice in which each cubic unit cell has an atom at its center and at each vertex — compare FACE-CENTERED
body check *n* (1892) **:** a blocking of an opposing player with the body (as in ice hockey or lacrosse) — **body·check** \ˈbä-dē-ˌchek\ *vt*
body clock *n* (1968) **:** the internal mechanisms that schedule periodic bodily functions and activities — usu. not used technically
body corporate *n* (15c) **:** CORPORATION
body count *n* (1965) **1 :** a count of the bodies of killed enemy soldiers **2 :** the number of persons involved in a particular activity
body double *n* (1981) **:** a double who takes the place of an actor esp. in scenes calling for nudity
body English *n* (1908) **:** bodily motions made in a usu. unconscious effort to influence the progress of a propelled object (as a ball)
body·guard \ˈbä-dē-ˌgärd\ *n* (1704) **:** a usu. armed attendant or group of attendants whose duty is to protect a person
body language *n* (1926) **:** the gestures, movements, and mannerisms by which a person or animal communicates with others
body louse *n* (1575) **:** a louse feeding primarily on the body; *esp* **:** a sucking louse (*Pediculus humanus humanus*) feeding on the body and living in the clothing of humans — called also *cootie*
body mass index *n* (1983) **:** a measure of body fat that is the ratio of the weight of the body in kilograms to the square of its height in meters
body mechanics *n pl but sing or pl in constr* (ca. 1970) **:** systematic exercises designed esp. to develop coordination, endurance, and poise
body piercing *n* (1989) **:** the practice or an instance of adorning the body with jewelry or ornamentation that penetrates the flesh
body politic *n* (15c) **1 :** a group of persons politically organized under a single governmental authority **2** *archaic* **:** CORPORATION 2 **3 :** a people considered as a collective unit
body shirt *n* (1967) **1 :** a close-fitting shirt or blouse **2 :** a woman's close-fitting top made with a sewn-in or snapped crotch
body shop *n* (1954) **:** a shop where automotive bodies are made or repaired
body snatcher *n* (1812) **:** one who steals corpses from graves
body stocking *n* (1965) **:** a usu. sheer close-fitting one-piece garment for the torso that often has sleeves and legs
body·suit \ˈbä-dē-ˌsüt\ *n* (1969) **:** a close-fitting one-piece garment for the torso
body·surf \ˈbä-dē-ˌsərf\ *vi* (1943) **:** to ride on a wave without a surfboard by planing on the chest and stomach — **body·surf·er** *n*
body wall *n* (1862) **:** the external surface of the animal body consisting of ectoderm and mesoderm and enclosing the body cavity
body·wash \ˈbä-dē-ˌwòsh, -ˌwäsh\ *n* (1988) **:** a liquid product for cleansing the body
body·work \ˈbä-dē-ˌwərk\ *n* (1908) **1 :** a vehicle body **2 :** the act or process of making or repairing vehicle bodies **3 :** therapeutic touching or manipulation of the body by using specialized techniques — **body·work·er** \-ˌwər-kər\ *n*
body wrap *n* (1974) **:** a body treatment involving the application of usu. oils or gels followed by a wrapping of the body with a sheet
boehm·ite \ˈbā-ˌmīt, ˈbə(r)-\ *n* [G *Böhmit,* fr. Johann *Böhm* (*Boehm*) †1952 Ger. chemist] (ca. 1929) **:** a mineral consisting of an orthorhombic form of aluminum oxide and hydroxide AlO(OH) found in bauxite
Boer \ˈbȯr, ˈbu̇r\ *n* [D, lit., farmer — more at BOOR] (1800) **:** a South African of Dutch or Huguenot descent

[1]**boff** \ˈbäf\ *vt* [fr. *boff* blow, punch, perh. imit.] (1937) *sometimes vulgar* : to have sexual intercourse with

[2]**boff** *or* **bof·fo** \ˈbä-(ˌ)fō\ *n, pl* **boffs** *or* **boffos** [perh. fr. *box office*] (1946) **1** : a hearty laugh **2** : a gag or line that produces a hearty laugh **3** : something that is conspicuously successful : HIT

bof·fin \ˈbä-fən\ *n* [origin unknown] (1945) *chiefly Brit* : a scientific expert; *esp* : one involved in technological research

bof·fo \ˈbä-(ˌ)fō\ *adj* (1949) : extremely successful : SENSATIONAL

bof·fo·la \bä-ˈfō-lə\ *n* [irreg. fr. *boff*] (1947) : BOFF

Bo·fors gun \ˈbō-ˌfȯrz-, ˈbü-\ *n* [*Bofors,* munition works in Sweden] (1939) : a double-barreled automatic antiaircraft gun

[1]**bog** \ˈbäg, ˈbȯg\ *n* [ME (Sc), fr. ScGael & Ir *bog-* (as in *bogluachair* bulrushes), fr. *bog* marshy, lit., soft, fr. MIr *bocc;* prob. akin to OE *būgan* to bend — more at BOW] (14c) : wet spongy ground; *esp* : a poorly drained usu. acid area rich in accumulated plant material, frequently surrounding a body of open water, and having a characteristic flora (as of sedges, heaths, and sphagnum) — **bog·gy** \ˈbä-gē, ˈbȯ-\ *adj*

[2]**bog** *vb* **bogged; bog·ging** *vt* (1599) : to cause to sink into or as if into a bog : IMPEDE, MIRE — usu. used with *down* ~ *vi* : to become impeded or stuck — usu. used with *down*

[3]**bog** *n* [short for *boghouse,* fr. Brit. argot *bog* to defecate] (ca. 1789) *Brit* : LAVATORY 2

bo·gart \ˈbō-ˌgärt\ *vt* [prob. fr. Humphrey *Bogart* †1957 Am. film actor] (1966) **1** : BULLY 2 **2** : to use or consume without sharing

bog asphodel *n* (1857) : either of two bog herbs (*Narthecium ossifragum* of Europe and *N. americanum* of the U.S.) of the lily family

[1]**bo·gey** *also* **bo·gie** *or* **bo·gy** *n, pl* **bogeys** *also* **bogies** [prob. alter. of *bogle*] (1826) **1** \ˈbu̇-gē, ˈbō-, ˈbü-\ : SPECTER, PHANTOM **2** \ˈbō-gē *also* ˈbu̇- *or* ˈbü-\ : a source of fear, perplexity, or harassment **3** \ˈbō-gē\ **a** *chiefly Brit* : an average golfer's score used as a standard for a particular hole or course **b** : one stroke over par on a hole in golf **4** \ˈbō-gē\ : a numerical standard of performance set up as a mark to be aimed at esp. in competition **5** \ˈbō-gē\ : an unidentified aircraft; *esp* : one not positively identified as friendly and so assumed to be hostile

[2]**bo·gey** \ˈbō-gē\ *vt* **bo·geyed; bo·gey·ing** (1948) : to shoot (a hole in golf) in one over par

bo·gey·man *also* **bo·gy·man** \ˈbu̇-gē-ˌman, ˈbō-, ˈbü-, ˈbu̇-gər-\ *n* (1890) **1** : a monstrous imaginary figure used in threatening children **2** : a terrifying or dreaded person or thing : BUGBEAR

bog·gle \ˈbä-gəl\ *vb* **bog·gled; bog·gling** \-g(ə-)liŋ\ [perh. fr. *bogle*] *vi* (1598) **1** : to start with fright or amazement : be overwhelmed ⟨the mind ~*s* at the research needed⟩ **2** : to hesitate because of doubt, fear, or scruples ~ *vt* **1** : MISHANDLE, BUNGLE **2** : to overwhelm with wonder or bewilderment ⟨~ the mind⟩ — **boggle** *n*

bo·gie *also* **bo·gey** \ˈbō-gē\ *n, pl* **bogies** *also* **bogeys** [origin unknown] (1835) **1** : a low strongly built cart **2 a** *chiefly Brit* : a swiveling railway truck **b** : the driving-wheel assembly consisting of the rear four wheels of a 6-wheel automotive truck **3** : a small supporting or aligning wheel (as on the inside perimeter of a tank tread)

bo·gle \ˈbō-gəl\ *also* **bog·gle** \ˈbä-gəl\ *n* [origin unknown] (ca. 1505) *dial Brit* : GOBLIN, SPECTER; *also* : an object of fear or loathing

Bo·go·mil *also* **Bo·go·mile** \ˌbə-gə-ˈmēl\ *n* [MGk *Bogomilos,* fr. *Bogomilos* Bogomil, 10th cent. Bulg. priest, founder of the sect] (1841) : a member of a medieval Bulgarian sect holding that God has two sons, the rebellious Satan and the obedient Jesus

bo·gus \ˈbō-gəs\ *adj* [obs. argot *bogus* counterfeit money] (1825) : not genuine : COUNTERFEIT, SHAM — **bo·gus·ly** *adv* — **bo·gus·ness** *n*

bo·hea \bō-ˈhē\ *n, often cap* [Chin (Fujian) *Bú-î,* hills in China where it was grown] (1692) : a black tea

bo·he·mia \bō-ˈhē-mē-ə\ *n, often cap* [trans. of F *bohème*] (1861) : a community of bohemians : the world of bohemians

Bo·he·mi·an \-mē-ən\ *n* (1555) **1 a** : a native or inhabitant of Bohemia **b** : the group of Czech dialects used in Bohemia **2** *often not cap* **a** : VAGABOND, WANDERER; *esp* : GYPSY **b** : a person (as a writer or an artist) living an unconventional life usu. in a colony with others — **bohemian** *adj, often cap*

Bohemian Brethren *n pl* (1857) : a Christian body originating in Bohemia in 1467 and forming a parent body of the Moravian Church

bo·he·mi·an·ism \bō-ˈhē-mē-ə-ˌni-zəm\ *n, often cap* (1858) : the unconventional way of life of bohemians

bo·ho \ˈbō-hō\ *n, pl* **bohos** [by shortening & alter.] : BOHEMIAN 2b — **boho** *adj*

Bohr effect \ˈbȯr-\ *n* [Christian *Bohr* †1911 Dan. physiologist] (1939) : the decrease in the oxygen affinity of a respiratory pigment (as hemoglobin) in response to decreased blood pH resulting from increased carbon dioxide concentration in the blood

bohr·i·um \ˈbȯr-ē-əm\ *n* [NL, fr. Niels *Bohr*] (1994) : a short-lived radioactive element produced artificially — see ELEMENT table

Bohr theory *n* [Niels *Bohr*] (1923) : a theory in early quantum physics: an atom consists of a positively charged nucleus about which revolves one or more electrons of quantized energy

bo·hunk \ˈbō-ˌhəŋk\ *n* [*Bohemian* + *Hunk* person of central European descent, by shortening & alter. fr. *Hungarian*] (ca. 1903) *usu disparaging* : a person of central European descent or birth

[1]**boil** \ˈbȯi(-ə)l\ *vb* [ME, fr. AF *buillir, boillir,* fr. L *bullire* to bubble, fr. *bulla* bubble] *vi* (13c) **1 a** : to come to the boiling point **b** : to generate bubbles of vapor when heated — used of a liquid **c** : to cook in boiling water **2** : to become agitated : SEETHE **3** : to be moved, excited, or stirred up **4 a** : to rush headlong **b** : to burst forth **5** : to undergo the action of a boiling liquid ~ *vt* **1** : to subject to the action of a boiling liquid **2** : to heat to the boiling point **3** : to form or separate (as sugar or salt) by boiling — **boil·able** \ˈbȯi-lə-bəl\ *adj*

[2]**boil** *n* [ME, alter. of *bile,* fr. OE *bȳl;* akin to OHG *pūlla* bladder] (15c) : a localized swelling and inflammation of the skin resulting from infection of a hair follicle and adjacent tissue, having a hard central core, and forming pus

[3]**boil** *n* (15c) **1** : the act or state of boiling **2** : a swirling upheaval (as of water) **3** : a boiled dish of seafood, vegetables, and seasonings ⟨a crab ~⟩; *also* : a gathering at which this dish is served

boil down *vt* (1731) **1** : to reduce in bulk by boiling **2** : CONDENSE, SUMMARIZE ⟨*boil down* a report⟩ ~ *vi* **1** : to undergo reduction in bulk by boiling **2 a** : to be equivalent in summary : AMOUNT ⟨his speech *boiled down* to a plea for more money⟩ **b** : to reduce ultimately ⟨your choices *boil down* to three⟩

boil·er \ˈbȯi-lər\ *n* (ca. 1540) **1** : one that boils **2 a** : a vessel used for boiling **b** : the part of a steam generator in which water is converted into steam and which consists usu. of metal shells and tubes **c** : a tank in which water is heated or hot water is stored

boil·er·mak·er \ˈbȯi-lər-ˌmā-kər\ *n* (1865) **1** : a worker who makes, assembles, or repairs boilers **2** : whiskey with a beer chaser

boil·er·plate \-ˌplāt\ *n* (1897) **1** : syndicated material supplied esp. to weekly newspapers in matrix or plate form **2 a** : standardized text **b** : formulaic or hackneyed language ⟨bureaucratic ~⟩ **3** : tightly packed icy snow

boiler room *n* (1903) **1** : a room in which a boiler is located **2** : a room equipped with telephones used for making high-pressure usu. fraudulent sales pitches

boil·er·suit \-ˌsüt\ *n* (1928) : COVERALL

[1]**boil·ing** \ˈbȯi(-ə)-liŋ\ *adj* (14c) **1 a** : heated to the boiling point **b** : TORRID ⟨a ~ sun⟩ **2** : intensely agitated ⟨a ~ sea⟩ ⟨~ with anger⟩

[2]**boiling** *adv* (1607) : to an extreme degree : VERY ⟨~ mad⟩ ⟨~ hot⟩

boiling point *n* (1773) **1** : the temperature at which a liquid boils **2 a** : the point at which a person becomes uncontrollably angry **b** : the point of crisis : HEAD 17b ⟨matters had reached the *boiling point*⟩

boil over *vi* (15c) **1** : to overflow while boiling **2** : to become so incensed as to lose one's temper — **boil·over** \ˈbȯi(-ə)l-ˌō-vər\ *n*

boink \ˈbȯiŋk\ *vt* [*boink, boing,* interjections imit. of a reverberating sound] (1987) *sometimes vulgar* : to copulate with

bois d'arc \ˈbō-ˌdä(r)k, *dial also* ˈbwä-, ˈbȯr-\ *n, pl* **bois d'arcs** *or* **bois d'arc** [AmerF, lit., bow wood] (1805) : OSAGE ORANGE; *also* : its wood

boi·se·rie \ˌbwä-zə-ˈrē\ *n* [F, fr. *bois* wood, fr. OF, of Gmc origin; akin to OHG *busk* forest] (1832) : a panel or paneling of carved wood

bois·ter·ous \ˈbȯi-st(ə-)rəs\ *adj* [ME *boistous* crude, clumsy, fr. AF] (14c) **1** *obs* **a** : COARSE **b** : DURABLE, STRONG **c** : MASSIVE **2 a** : noisily turbulent : ROWDY **b** : marked by or expressive of exuberance and high spirits **3** : STORMY, TUMULTUOUS ***syn*** see VOCIFEROUS — **bois·ter·ous·ly** *adv* — **bois·ter·ous·ness** *n*

boîte \ˈbwät\ *n* [F, lit., box] (1922) : NIGHTCLUB

bok choy *also* **bok choi** \ˈbäk-ˈchȯi\ *or* **pak choi** \ˈpäk-ˈchȯi, ˈpak-\ *n* [Chin (Guangdong) *baahk-choi,* lit., white vegetable] (1847) : a Chinese cabbage (*Brassica rapa chinensis*) forming an open head with long white stalks and green leaves

Bo·kha·ra \bō-ˈkär-ə\ *n* [*Bokhara* (Bukhara), Uzbekistan] (1900) : an Oriental rug characterized by fine knotting and a design of usu. three rows of octagonal medallions

Bok·mål \ˈbu̇k-ˌmȯl, ˈbōk-\ *n* [Norw, lit., book language] (1931) : a literary form of Norwegian developed by the gradual reform of written Danish — compare NYNORSK

bo·la \ˈbō-lə\ *or* **bo·las** \-ləs\ *n, pl* **bolas** \-ləz\ *also* **bo·las·es** [AmerSp *bolas,* fr. Sp *bola* ball] (1818) : a cord with weights attached to the ends for throwing at and entangling an animal

[1]**bold** \ˈbōld\ *adj* [ME, fr. OE *beald;* akin to OHG *bald* bold] (bef. 12c) **1 a** : fearless before danger : INTREPID **b** : showing or requiring a fearless daring spirit **2** : IMPUDENT, PRESUMPTUOUS **3** *obs* : ASSURED, CONFIDENT **4** : SHEER, STEEP ⟨~ cliffs⟩ **5** : ADVENTUROUS, FREE ⟨a ~ thinker⟩ **6** : standing out prominently **7** : being or set in boldface — **bold·ly** \ˈbōl(d)-lē\ *adv* — **bold·ness** \ˈbōl(d)-nəs\ *n*

[2]**bold** *n* (ca. 1871) : BOLDFACE

bold·face \ˈbōl(d)-ˌfās\ *n* (ca. 1889) : a heavy-faced type; *also* : printing in boldface

bold–faced \ˈbōl(d)-ˈfāst\ *adj* (1591) **1** : bold in manner or conduct : IMPUDENT **2** *usu* **bold·faced** : being or set in boldface

bole \ˈbōl\ *n* [ME, fr. ON *bolr*] (14c) : TRUNK 1a

bo·le·ro \bə-ˈler-(ˌ)ō, -ˈle-rō\ *n, pl* **-ros** [Sp] (1787) **1** : a Spanish dance characterized by sharp turns, stamping of the feet, and sudden pauses in a position with one arm arched over the head; *also* : music in ¾ time for a bolero **2** : a loose waist-length jacket open at the front

bo·lete \bō-ˈlēt\ *n* [NL *Boletus*] (1914) : any of a family (Boletaceae) of fleshy stalked pore fungi that usu. grow on the ground in wooded areas; *esp* : BOLETUS

bo·le·tus \bō-ˈlē-təs\ *n, pl* **-tus** *or* **-ti** \-ˈlē-ˌtī\ [NL, genus name, fr. L, mushroom] (1601) : any of a genus (*Boletus*) of boletes (as a porcini) some of which are poisonous and others edible

bo·lide \ˈbō-ˌlīd, -lid\ *n* [F, fr. L *bolid-, bolis,* fr. Gk, fr. *bolē* throw, stroke] (1834) : a large meteor : FIREBALL; *esp* : one that explodes

bo·li·var \bə-ˈlē-ˌvär, ˈbä-lə-vər\ *n, pl* **-va·res** \ˌbä-lə-ˈvär-ˌās, ˌbō-lē-\ *or* **-vars** [AmerSp *bolívar,* fr. Simón *Bolívar*] (ca. 1895) — see MONEY table

bo·li·vi·a·no \bə-ˌli-vē-ˈä-(ˌ)nō\ *n, pl* **-nos** [AmerSp, fr. *boliviano,* adj., Bolivian] (ca. 1872) — see MONEY table

boll \ˈbōl\ *n* [ME] (15c) : the pod or capsule of a plant (as cotton)

bol·lard \ˈbä-lərd, *Brit also* -ˌlärd\ *n* [perh. fr. *bole*] (ca. 1775) **1** : a post of metal or wood on a wharf around which to fasten mooring lines **2** : BITT 1 **3** *chiefly Brit* : any of a series of short posts set at intervals to delimit an area (as a traffic island) or to exclude vehicles

bol·lix \ˈbä-liks\ *vt* [alter. of *bollocks*] (1937) : to throw into disorder; *also* : BUNGLE — usu. used with *up* — **bollix** *n*

bol·locks \ˈbä-ləks\ *n pl* [alter. of *ballocks,* pl. of *ballock* testis, fr. ME, fr. OE *beallucc* — more at BALL] (1774) **1** *chiefly Brit, usu vulgar* : TESTICLES **2** *chiefly Brit, usu vulgar* : NONSENSE

boll weevil *n* (1895) : a usu. grayish or brown weevil (*Anthonomus grandis grandis*) that feeds on the squares and bolls of the cotton plant

boll·worm \ˈbōl-ˌwərm\ *n* (1847) : CORN EARWORM; *also* : any of several other moths that feed on cotton bolls as larvae

Bol·ly·wood \ˈbä-lē-ˌwu̇d\ *n* [*Bombay* (Mumbai), traditional center of the Indian film industry + *Hollywood*] (1976) : the motion-picture industry in India

bo·lo \ˈbō-(ˌ)lō\ *n, pl* **bolos** [PhilSp] (ca. 1900) : a long heavy single-edged knife of Philippine origin used to cut vegetation and as a weapon

bo·lo·gna \bə-ˈlō-nē *also* -nyə, -nə\ *also* **ba·lo·ney** \bə-ˈlō-nē\ *n* [short for *Bologna sausage,* fr. *Bologna,* Italy] (1596) : a large smoked sausage of beef, veal, and pork; *also* : a sausage made (as of turkey) to resemble bologna

Bo·lo·gnese \ˌbō-lə-ˈn(y)ēz, -ˈn(y)āz, -ˈn(y)ēs, -ˈn(y)ās; -ˈn(y)ā-zē, -sē\ *adj* (1754) **1** : of, relating to, or characteristic of Bologna, Italy **2** : being or prepared with tomato sauce flavored with meat

bo·lom·e·ter \bō-ˈlä-mə-tər\ *n* [Gk *bolē* stroke, beam of light (fr. *ballein* to throw) + E *-o-* + *-meter* — more at DEVIL] (1881) : a very sensitive thermometer whose electrical resistance varies with temperature and which is used in the detection and measurement of feeble thermal radiation and is esp. adapted to the study of infrared spectra — **bo·lo·met·ric** \ˌbō-lə-ˈme-trik\ *adj* — **bo·lo·met·ri·cal·ly** \-tri-k(ə-)lē\ *adv*

boloney *var of* 2BALONEY

bo·lo tie \ˈbō-lō-\ *or* **bo·la tie** \-lə-\ *n* [prob. fr. *bola*] (1964) : a cord fastened around the neck with an ornamental clasp and worn as a necktie — called also *bolo*

Bol·she·vik \ˈbōl-shə-ˌvik, ˈbȯl-, ˈbäl-, -ˌvēk\ *n, pl* **Bolsheviks** *also* **Bol·she·vi·ki** \ˌbōl-shə-ˈvi-kē, ˌbȯl-, ˌbäl-, -ˈvē-kē\ [Russ *bol'shevik,* fr. *bol'shiĭ* greater] (1917) **1** : a member of the extremist wing of the Russian Social Democratic party that seized power in Russia by the Revolution of November 1917 **2** : COMMUNIST 3 — **Bolshevik** *adj*

bol·she·vism \ˈbōl-shə-ˌvi-zəm, ˈbȯl-, ˈbäl-\ *n, often cap* (1917) **1** : the doctrine or program of the Bolsheviks advocating violent overthrow of capitalism **2** : Russian communism

Bol·she·vist \-vist\ *n or adj* (1917) : BOLSHEVIK

bol·she·vize \-ˌvīz\ *vt* **-vized; -viz·ing** (1919) : to make Bolshevist — **Bol·she·vi·za·tion** \ˌbōl-shə-və-ˈzā-shən, ˌbȯl-, ˌbäl-\ *n*

bol·shie *or* **bol·shy** \ˈbōl-shē, ˈbȯl-, ˈbäl-\ *n or adj* [by shortening & alter.] (1918) **1** *often cap* : BOLSHEVIK **2** *Brit* : refusing to obey or help : defiant and uncooperative

1bol·ster \ˈbōl-stər\ *n* [ME, fr. OE; akin to OE *belg* bag — more at BELLY] (bef. 12c) **1** : a long pillow or cushion **2** : a structural part designed to eliminate friction or provide support or bearing

2bolster *vt* **bol·stered; bol·ster·ing** \-st(ə-)riŋ\ (15c) **1** : to support with or as if with a bolster : REINFORCE **2** : to give a boost to ⟨news that ~*ed* his spirits⟩ — **bol·ster·er** \-stər-ər\ *n*

1bolt \ˈbōlt\ *n* [ME, fr. OE; akin to OHG *bolz* crossbow bolt, and perh. to Lith *beldėti* to beat] (bef. 12c) **1 a** : a shaft or missile designed to be shot from a crossbow or catapult; *esp* : a short stout usu. blunt-headed arrow **b** : a lightning stroke; *also* : THUNDERBOLT **2 a** : a wood or metal bar or rod used to fasten a door **b** : the part of a lock that is shot or withdrawn by the key **3** : a roll of cloth or wallpaper of specified length **4** : a metal rod or pin for fastening objects together that usu. has a head at one end and a screw thread at the other and is secured by a nut **5 a** : a block of timber to be sawed or cut **b** : a short round section of a log **6** : a metal cylinder that drives the cartridge into the chamber of a firearm, locks the breech, and usu. contains the firing pin and extractor

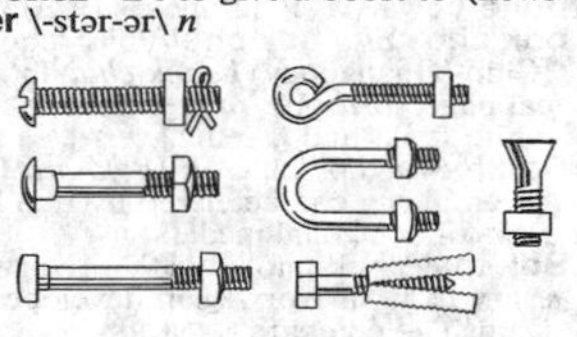

bolt 4

2bolt *vi* (13c) **1** : to move suddenly or nervously : START **2** : to move or proceed rapidly : DASH **3 a** : to dart off or away : FLEE **b** : to break away from control or a set course **4** : to break away from or oppose one's previous affiliation (as with a political party or sports team) **5** : to produce seed prematurely ~ *vt* **1 a** *archaic* : SHOOT, DISCHARGE **b** : FLUSH, START ⟨~ rabbits⟩ **2** : to say impulsively : BLURT **3** : to secure with a bolt ⟨~ the door⟩ **4** : to attach or fasten with bolts **5** : to eat hastily or without chewing ⟨~*ed* his breakfast⟩ **6** : to break away from or refuse to support (as a political party)

3bolt *adv* (14c) **1** : in an erect or straight-backed position : RIGIDLY ⟨sat ~ upright⟩ **2** *archaic* : DIRECTLY, STRAIGHT

4bolt *n* (1550) : the act or an instance of bolting

5bolt *vt* [ME *bulten,* fr. AF *buleter,* of Gmc origin; akin to MHG *biuteln* to sift, fr. *biutel* bag, fr. OHG *būtil*] (13c) **1** : to sift (as flour) usu. through fine-meshed cloth **2** *archaic* : SIFT 2

bolt–ac·tion \ˈbōlt-ˈak-shən\ *adj* (1896) *of a firearm* : loaded by means of a manually operated bolt

bolt·er \ˈbōl-tər\ *n* (ca. 1699) : one that bolts: as **a** : a horse given to running away **b** : a voter who bolts from a political party

bolt from the blue (1907) : a complete surprise : something totally unexpected — called also *bolt out of the blue*

bolt–hole \ˈbōlt-ˌhōl\ *n* (ca. 1851) *chiefly Brit* : a place of escape or refuge

bolt·rope \ˈbōlt-ˌrōp\ *n* (14c) : a strong rope stitched to the edges of a sail to strengthen it

bo·lus \ˈbō-ləs\ *n, pl* **bo·lus·es** [LL, fr. Gk *bōlos* lump] (1562) **1** : a rounded mass: as **a** : a large pill **b** : a soft mass of chewed food **2 a** : a dose of a substance (as a drug) given intravenously **b** : a large dose of a substance given by injection for the purpose of rapidly achieving the needed therapeutic concentration in the bloodstream

1bomb \ˈbäm\ *n* [F *bombe,* fr. It *bomba,* prob. fr. L *bombus* deep hollow sound, fr. Gk *bombos,* of imit. origin] (1684) **1 a** : an explosive device fused to detonate under specified conditions **b** : ATOMIC BOMB; *also* : nuclear weapons in general — usu. used with *the* **2** : a vessel for compressed gases: as **a** : a pressure vessel for conducting chemical experiments **b** : a container for an aerosol (as an insecticide) : SPRAY CAN **3** : a rounded mass of lava exploded from a volcano **4** : a lead-lined container for radioactive material **5** : FAILURE, FLOP ⟨the play was a ~⟩ **6** *Brit* : a large sum of money **7 a** *Brit* : a great success : HIT **b** *slang* : one that is striking or extraordinary — used with *the* ⟨their new album is the ~⟩ **8 a** : a long pass in football **b** : a very long shot (as in basketball) ⟨shooting 3-point ~*s*⟩; *also* : HOME RUN **9** : something unexpected and unpleasant — often used with *drop* ⟨dropped a ~ with her resignation⟩

2bomb *vt* (1688) **1** : to attack with or as if with bombs : BOMBARD **2** : to defeat decisively **3** : to hit (as a baseball or a golf shot) very hard ~ *vi* **1** : to fall flat : FAIL **2** *slang* : to move rapidly ⟨~*ed* down the hill⟩ — **bomb·ing** *n*

1bom·bard \ˈbäm-ˌbärd\ *n* [ME *bombarde,* fr. MF, prob. fr. L *bombus*] (15c) : a late medieval cannon used to hurl large stones

2bom·bard \bäm-ˈbärd *also* bəm-\ *vt* (1686) **1** : to attack esp. with artillery or bombers **2** : to assail vigorously or persistently (as with questions) **3** : to subject to the impact of rapidly moving particles (as electrons) ***syn*** see ATTACK — **bom·bard·ment** \-mənt\ *n*

bom·bar·dier \ˌbäm-bə-ˈdir, -bər-\ *n* (1560) **1 a** *archaic* : ARTILLERYMAN **b** : a noncommissioned officer in the British artillery **2** : a bomber-crew member who releases the bombs

bom·bar·don \ˈbäm-bər-ˌdōn, bäm-ˈbär-dᵊn\ *n* [F, fr. It *bombardone*] (1856) **1** : a bass tuba **2** : the bass member of the shawm family

bom·bast \ˈbäm-ˌbast\ *n* [ME *bombast* cotton padding, fr. MF *bombace,* fr. ML *bombac-, bombax* cotton, alter. of L *bombyc-, bombyx* silkworm, silk, fr. Gk *bombyk-, bombyx*] (1583) : pretentious inflated speech or writing

bom·bas·tic \bäm-ˈbas-tik\ *adj* (1704) : marked by or given to bombast : POMPOUS, OVERBLOWN — **bom·bas·ti·cal·ly** \-ti-k(ə-)lē\ *adv*

bom·ba·zine \ˌbäm-bə-ˈzēn\ *n* [MF *bombasin,* fr. ML *bombacinum, bombycinum* silken texture, fr. L, neut. of *bombycinus* of silk, fr. *bombyc-, bombyx*] (1572) **1** : a twilled fabric with silk warp and worsted filling **2** : a silk fabric in twill weave dyed black

bombe \ˈbäm, ˈbōⁿ(m)b\ *n* [F, lit., bomb] (1892) : a frozen dessert usu. containing ice cream and formed in layers in a mold

bom·bé *or* **bom·be** \(ˌ)bäm-ˈbā, (ˌ)bōⁿ-\ *adj* [F, fr. *bombe*] (1904) : having outward curving lines — usu. used of furniture

bombed \ˈbämd\ *adj* (1956) : affected by alcohol or drugs : DRUNK, HIGH

bombed–out \ˈbämd-ˌau̇t, -ˈau̇t\ *adj* (1972) **1** : destroyed by bombing ⟨a ~ factory⟩ **2** : extremely dilapidated or run-down ⟨a ~ inner-city neighborhood⟩

bomb·er \ˈbä-mər\ *n* (1862) **1** : one that bombs; *specif* : an airplane designed for bombing **2** : BOMBER JACKET **3** : a skilled long-distance shooter in basketball

bomber jacket *n* (1952) : a zippered usu. leather jacket with front pockets and knitted cuffs and waistband

bom·bi·nate \ˈbäm-bə-ˌnāt\ *vi* **-nat·ed; -nat·ing** [NL *bombinatus,* pp. of *bombinare,* alter. of L *bombilare,* fr. *bombus*] (1880) : BUZZ, DRONE — **bom·bi·na·tion** \ˌbäm-bə-ˈnā-shən\ *n*

bomb·let \ˈbäm-lət\ *n* (1937) : a small bomb; *esp* : one of the many small bombs that make up a cluster bomb

bomb·proof \ˈbäm-ˌprüf\ *adj* (1702) **1** : safe from the force of bombs **2** : extremely sturdy or durable ⟨a ~ parka⟩ ⟨a ~ horse⟩

bomb·shell \ˈbäm-ˌshel\ *n* (1708) **1** : BOMB 1a **2** : one that is stunning, amazing, or devastating ⟨the book was a political ~⟩

bomb·sight \-ˌsīt\ *n* (1917) : a sighting device for aiming bombs

bo·na fide \ˈbō-nə-ˌfīd, ˈbä-; ˌbō-nə-ˈfī-dē, -ˈfī-də\ *adj* [L, lit., in good faith] (1632) **1** : made in good faith without fraud or deceit ⟨a *bona fide* offer to buy a farm⟩ **2** : made with earnest intent : SINCERE **3** : neither specious nor counterfeit : GENUINE ***syn*** see AUTHENTIC

bo·na fi·des \ˌbō-nə-ˈfī-ˌdēz, ÷ˈbō-nə-ˌfīdz\ *n* [L, lit., good faith] (1665) **1** : good faith : SINCERITY **2** : the fact of being genuine — often pl. in constr. **3** : evidence of one's good faith or genuineness — often pl. in constr. **4** : evidence of one's qualifications or achievements — often pl. in constr.

bo·nan·za \bə-ˈnan-zə\ *n* [Sp, lit., calm sea, fr. ML *bonacia,* alter. of L *malacia,* fr. Gk *malakia,* lit., softness, fr. *malakos* soft] (1829) **1** : an exceptionally large and rich mineral deposit (as of an ore, precious metal, or petroleum) **2 a** : something that is very valuable, profitable, or rewarding ⟨a box-office ~⟩ **b** : a very large amount ⟨a ~ of sympathy⟩ **c** : EXTRAVAGANZA ⟨channels planning all-day viewing ~*s* —William Borders⟩

Bo·na·part·ism \ˈbō-nə-ˌpär-ˌti-zəm\ *n* (1815) **1** : support of the French emperors Napoleon I, Napoleon III, or their dynasty **2** : a political movement associated chiefly with authoritarian rule usu. by a military leader ostensibly supported by a popular mandate — **Bo·na·part·ist** \-ˌpär-tist\ *n or adj*

bon·bon \ˈbän-ˌbän\ *n* [F, redupl. of *bon* good, fr. L *bonus* — more at BOUNTY] (1770) **1** : a candy with chocolate or fondant coating and fondant center that sometimes contains fruits and nuts **2** : something that is pleasing in a light or frivolous way ⟨singing pop ~*s*⟩

1bond \ˈbänd\ *n* [ME *band, bond* — more at BAND] (12c) **1** : something that binds or restrains : FETTER **2** : a binding agreement : COVENANT **3 a** : a band or cord used to tie something **b** : a material or device for binding **c** : an attractive force that holds together the atoms, ions, or groups of atoms in a molecule or crystal **d** : an adhesive, cementing material, or fusible ingredient that combines, unites, or strengthens **4** : a uniting or binding element or force : TIE ⟨the ~*s* of friendship⟩ **5 a** : an obligation made binding by a money forfeit; *also* : the amount of the money guarantee **b** : one who acts as bail or surety **c** : an interest-bearing certificate of public or private indebtedness **d** : an insurance agreement pledging surety for financial loss caused to another by the act or default of a third person or by some contingency over which the third person may have no control **6** : the systematic lapping of brick in a wall **7** : the state of goods made, stored, or transported under the care of bonded agencies until the duties or taxes on them are paid **8** : a 100-proof straight whiskey aged at least four years under government supervision before being bottled — called also *bonded whiskey* **9** : BOND PAPER

2bond *vt* (1677) **1** : to lap (as brick) for solidity of construction **2 a** : to secure payment of duties and taxes on (goods) by giving a bond **b** : to convert into a debt secured by bonds **c** : to provide a bond for or cause to provide such a bond ⟨~ an employee⟩ **3 a** : to cause to adhere firmly **b** : to embed in a matrix **c** : to hold together in a molecule or crystal by chemical bonds ~ *vi* **1** : to hold together or solidify by or as if by means of a bond or binder **2** : to form a close relationship esp. through frequent association ⟨the new mother ~*ed* with her child⟩ — **bond·able** \ˈbän-də-bəl\ *adj* — **bond·er** *n*

3bond *adj* [ME *bonde,* fr. *bonde* customary tenant, fr. OE *bōnda* householder, fr. ON *bōndi*] (14c) *archaic* : bound in slavery

bond·age \ˈbän-dij\ *n* [ME, fr. AF, fr. *bonde* customary tenant, fr. ME] (14c) **1** : the tenure or service of a villein, serf, or slave **2** : a state of being bound usu. by compulsion (as of law or mastery): as **a** : CAPTIVITY, SERFDOM **b** : servitude or subjugation to a controlling person or force ⟨young people in ~ to drugs⟩ **3** : sadomasochistic sexual practices involving the physical restraint of one partner

bond·ed \ˈbän-dəd\ *adj* (1945) : composed of two or more layers of the same or different fabrics held together by an adhesive ⟨~ jersey⟩

bond·hold·er \ˈbänd-ˌhōl-dər\ *n* (1823) **:** one that holds a government or corporation bond

bond·ing \ˈbän-diŋ\ *n* (1969) **1 :** the formation of a close relationship (as between a mother and child or between a person and an animal) esp. through frequent or constant association **2 :** the attaching of a material (as porcelain) to a tooth surface esp. for cosmetic purposes

bond·maid \ˈbän(d)-ˌmād\ *n* (1526) *archaic* **:** a female bond servant

bond·man \ˈbän(d)-mən\ *also* **bonds·man** \ˈbän(d)z-\ *n* (13c) **:** SLAVE, SERF

bond paper *n* (1869) **:** a durable paper orig. used for documents

bond servant *n* (15c) **:** one bound to service without wages; *also* **:** SLAVE

[1]**bonds·man** \ˈbän(d)z-mən\ *n* (1713) **:** one who assumes the responsibility of a bond **:** SURETY

[2]**bondsman** *var of* BONDMAN

bond·stone \ˈbän(d)-ˌstōn\ *n* (1823) **:** a stone long enough to extend through the full thickness of a wall to bind it together

bond·wom·an \ˈbänd-ˌwu̇-mən\ *also* **bonds·wom·an** \ˈbän(d)z-\ *n* (14c) **:** a female slave

[1]**bone** \ˈbōn\ *n, often attrib* [ME *bon,* fr. OE *bān;* akin to OHG & ON *bein* bone, and perh. to OIr *benaid* he hews] (bef. 12c) **1 a :** one of the hard parts of the skeleton of a vertebrate **b :** any of various hard animal substances or structures (as baleen or ivory) akin to or resembling bone **c :** the hard largely calcareous connective tissue of which the adult skeleton of most vertebrates is chiefly composed **2 a :** ESSENCE, CORE ⟨cut costs to the ~⟩ ⟨a liberal to the ~⟩ **b :** the most deeply ingrained part **:** HEART — usu. used in pl. ⟨knew in his ~*s* that it was wrong⟩ **3** *pl* **a** (1) **:** SKELETON (2) **:** BODY ⟨rested my weary ~*s*⟩ (3) **:** CORPSE ⟨inter a person's ~*s*⟩ **b :** the basic design or framework (as of a play or novel) **4 :** MATTER, SUBJECT ⟨a ~ of contention⟩ **5 a** *pl* **:** thin bars of bone, ivory, or wood held in pairs between the fingers and used to produce musical rhythms **b :** a strip of material (as whalebone or steel) used to stiffen a garment (as a corset) **c** *pl* **:** DICE **6 :** something that is designed to placate **:** SOP **7 :** a light beige **8 :** INCLINATION 1b ⟨hadn't a political ~ in his body —John Hersey⟩ **9** *slang* **:** DOLLAR — **boned** \ˈbōnd\ *adj* — **bone·less** \ˈbōn-ləs\ *adj* — **bone to pick :** a matter to argue or complain about

[2]**bone** *vb* **boned; bon·ing** *vt* (15c) **1 :** to remove the bones from ⟨~ a fish⟩ **2 :** to provide (a garment) with stays **3 :** to rub (as a boot or baseball bat) with something hard (as a piece of bone) in order to smooth the surface ~ *vi* **:** to study hard **:** GRIND ⟨~ through medical school⟩

[3]**bone** *adv* (ca. 1825) **:** EXTREMELY, VERY ⟨~ tired⟩; *also* **:** TOTALLY

bone ash *n* (1622) **:** the white porous residue chiefly of tribasic calcium phosphate from bones calcined in air used esp. in making pottery and glass and in cleaning jewelry

bone black *n* (1815) **:** the black residue chiefly of tribasic calcium phosphate and carbon from bones calcined in closed vessels used esp. as a pigment or as a decolorizing adsorbent in sugar manufacturing — called also *bone char*

bone–chill·ing \ˈbōn-ˌchi-liŋ\ *adj* (1883) **:** intensely cold ⟨~ weather⟩; *also* **:** penetrating, disturbing, or intense in emotional or physical effect ⟨~ drama⟩ ⟨a ~ wind⟩

bone china *n* (1879) **:** translucent white china made with bone ash or calcium phosphate and characterized by whiteness

bone–dry \ˈbōn-ˈdrī\ *adj* (ca. 1825) **1 :** very dry **2 :** DRY 5

bone·fish \ˈbōn-ˌfish\ *n* (1884) **1 :** a slender silvery small-scaled fish (*Albula vulpes*) that is a notable sport and food fish of warm seas **2 :** LADYFISH 2 — **bone·fish·ing** *n*

[1]**bone·head** \-ˌhed\ *n* (1908) **:** a stupid person **:** NUMSKULL — **bone·head·ed** \-ˈhe-dəd\ *adj* — **bone·head·ed·ness** *n*

[2]**bonehead** *adj* (1911) **1 :** of, relating to, or characteristic of a bonehead **:** performed in a stupid or clumsy manner ⟨the shortstop made a ~ play⟩ **2 :** being a college course for students lacking fundamental skills ⟨teaches ~ English⟩

bone marrow *n* (1893) **:** a soft highly vascular modified connective tissue that occupies the cavities of most bones and occurs in two forms: **a :** one that is yellowish, consists chiefly of fat cells, and is found esp. in the cavities of long bones **b :** one that is reddish, is the chief site of blood cell formation, and occurs in the normal adult in cancellous tissue esp. of certain flat bones — called also *red marrow*

bone·meal \ˈbōn-ˌmēl\ *n* (1850) **:** crushed or ground bone used esp. as fertilizer or feed

bon·er \ˈbō-nər\ *n* (ca. 1899) **1 :** one that bones **2 :** a clumsy or stupid mistake; *also* **:** HOWLER 2 **3** *usu vulgar* **:** an erect penis

bone·set \ˈbōn-ˌset\ *n* (1764) **:** any of several composite herbs (genus *Eupatorium*); *esp* **:** a perennial (*E. perfoliatum*) of central and eastern No. America with opposite perfoliate leaves and white-rayed flower heads used in folk medicine

bone·set·ter \-ˌse-tər\ *n* (15c) **:** a person who sets broken or dislocated bones usu. without being a licensed physician

bone up *vi* (1887) **1 :** to try to master necessary information quickly **:** CRAM ⟨*bone up* for the exam⟩ **2 :** to renew one's skill or refresh one's memory ⟨*boned up* on the speech just before giving it⟩

bone·yard \-ˌyärd\ *n* (1851) **1 :** CEMETERY **2 :** a place where worn-out or damaged objects (as cars) are collected to await disposal

bon·fire \ˈbän-ˌfī(-ə)r\ *n* [ME *bonefire* a fire of bones, fr. *bon* bone + *fire*] (15c) **:** a large fire built in the open air

[1]**bong** \ˈbäŋ, ˈbȯŋ\ *n* [imit.] (1853) **:** the deep resonant sound esp. of a bell — **bong** *vb*

[2]**bong** *n* [Thai *bɔ̄ɔŋ* hollow piece of wood or bamboo] (1971) **:** a simple water pipe consisting of a bottle or vertical tube partially filled with a liquid (as water or liqueur) and a smaller offset tube ending in a bowl

[1]**bon·go** \ˈbäŋ-(ˌ)gō, ˈbȯŋ-\ *n, pl* **bongos** *also* **bongoes** [AmerSp *bongó*] (1920) **:** one of a pair of small connected drums of different sizes and pitches played with the hands — **bon·go·ist** \-ˌgō-ist\ *n*

[2]**bongo** *n, pl* **bongo** *or* **bongos** [prob. fr. Kele (Bantu language of Gabon)] (1861) **:** an African antelope (*Tragelaphus euryceros* syn. *Boocerus euryceros*) that is chestnut red with narrow white vertical stripes and is found in forests from Sierra Leone to Kenya

bon·ho·mie \ˌbä-nə-ˈmē, ˌbō-\ *n* [F *bonhomie,* fr. *bonhomme* good-natured man, fr. *bon* good + *homme* man] (1779) **:** good-natured easy friendliness — **bon·ho·mous** \ˈbä-nə-məs\ *adj*

bo·ni·a·to \ˌbō-nē-ˈä-tō\ *n, pl* **-tos** [AmerSp, perh. fr. Taino] (1980) **:** a sweet potato having white dry flesh with little sweetness that is usu. grown in subtropical regions

bon·i·face \ˈbä-nə-fəs, -ˌfās\ *n* [*Boniface,* innkeeper in *The Beaux' Stratagem* (1707) by George Farquhar] (1742) **:** the proprietor of a hotel, nightclub, or restaurant

bo·ni·to \bə-ˈnē-(ˌ)tō, -ˈnē-tə\ *n, pl* **-tos** *or* **-to** [Sp, fr. *bonito* pretty, dim. of *bueno* good, fr. L *bonus*] (1565) **:** any of several scombroid fishes (esp. genera *Sarda* and *Euthynnus*) intermediate between the smaller mackerels and the larger tunas

bonk \ˈbäŋk, ˈbȯŋk\ *vt* [imit.] (1931) **:** HIT ⟨~*ed* him over the head⟩

bon·kers \ˈbäŋ-kərz, ˈbȯŋ-\ *adj* [perh. fr. *bonk* + *-ers* (as in *crackers*)] (ca. 1948) **:** CRAZY, MAD ⟨fans went ~ when their team won⟩

bon mot \bō^{n}-ˈmō\ *n, pl* **bons mots** \bō^{n}-ˈmō(z)\ *or* **bon mots** \-ˈmō(z)\ [F, lit., good word] (ca. 1730) **:** a clever remark **:** WITTICISM

bonne \ˈbȯn\ *n* [F, fr. fem. of *bon*] (1771) **:** a French nursemaid or maidservant

[1]**bon·net** \ˈbä-nət\ *n* [ME *bonet* auxiliary sail, kind of cap, fr. AF, prob. of Gmc origin; akin to OS *gibund* bundle, OE *bindan* to bind] (14c) **1 a** (1) *chiefly Scot* **:** a man's or boy's cap (2) **:** a brimless Scottish cap of seamless woolen fabric — compare TAM-O'-SHANTER 2 **b :** a cloth or straw hat tied under the chin and worn by women and children **2 a** *Brit* **:** an automobile hood **b :** a metal covering or cowl (as for a fireplace, valve chamber, or ventilator)

[2]**bonnet** *vt* (1858) **:** to provide with or dress in a bonnet

bon·ny *also* **bon·nie** \ˈbä-nē\ *adj* **bon·ni·er; -est** [ME (Sc) *bonie,* perh. ultim. fr. AF *bon* good, fr. L *bonus* — more at BOUNTY] (15c) *chiefly Brit* **:** ATTRACTIVE, FAIR; *also* **:** FINE, EXCELLENT — **bon·ni·ly** \ˈbä-nə-lē\ *adv*

bon·ny·clab·ber \ˈbä-nē-ˌkla-bər\ *n* [Ir *bainne clabair,* fr. *bainne* milk + *clabair,* gen. of *clabar* sour thick milk] (1605) *Northern & Midland* **:** CLABBER

bo·no·bo \bə-ˈnō-bō; ˈbä-nə-bō, -nō-\ *n, pl* **-bos** [origin unknown] (1954) **:** a rare anthropoid ape (*Pan paniscus*) that has a more slender build and longer limbs than the related common chimpanzee (*P. troglodytes*) and that inhabits a small geographic region in equatorial Africa south of the Congo River — called also *pygmy chimpanzee*

bon·sai \(ˌ)bōn-ˈsī, ˈbōn-ˌ, ˈbän-ˌ *also* ˈbän-ˌzī\ *n, pl* **bonsai** [Jp, lit., tray planting] (1900) **:** a potted plant (as a tree) dwarfed (as by pruning) and trained to an artistic shape; *also* **:** the art of growing such a plant

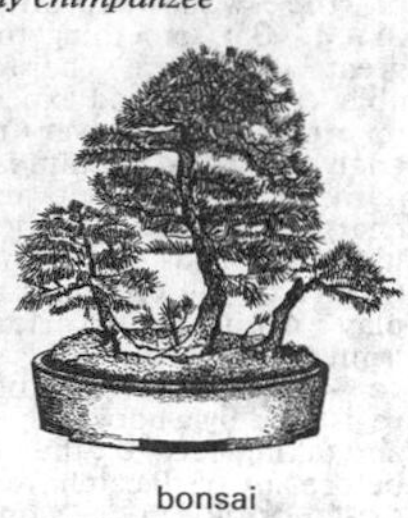
bonsai

bon·spiel \ˈbän-ˌspēl\ *n* [perh. fr. D *bond* league + *spel* game] (ca. 1772) **:** a match or tournament between curling clubs

bon ton \(ˌ)bän-ˈtän, ˈbän-ˌ\ *n* [F, lit., good tone] (1747) **1 a :** fashionable manner or style **b :** the fashionable or proper thing **2 :** high society

bo·nus \ˈbō-nəs\ *n* [L, lit., good — more at BOUNTY] (1773) **:** something in addition to what is expected or strictly due: as **a :** money or an equivalent given in addition to an employee's usual compensation **b :** a premium (as of stock) given by a corporation to a purchaser of its securities, to a promoter, or to an employee **c :** a government payment to war veterans **d :** a sum in excess of salary given an athlete for signing with a team

bon vi·vant \ˌbän-vē-ˈvänt, ˌbō^{n}-vē-ˈvä^{n}\ *n, pl* **bons vivants** \ˌbän-vē-ˈvän(t)s, ˌbō^{n}-vē-ˈvä^{n}(z)\ *or* **bon vivants** *same*\ [F, lit., good liver] (ca. 1695) **:** a person having cultivated, refined, and sociable tastes esp. with respect to food and drink

bon voy·age \ˌbō^{n}-vȯi-ˈäzh, ˌbän-; ˌbō^{n}-ˌvwī-ˈäzh, -ˌvwä-ˈyäzh\ *n* [F, lit., good journey!] (15c) **:** FAREWELL — often used interjectionally

bony *also* **bon·ey** \ˈbō-nē\ *adj* **bon·i·er; -est** (14c) **1 a :** consisting of bone **b :** resembling bone **2 a :** full of bones ⟨a ~ piece of fish⟩ **b :** having prominent bones ⟨a rugged ~ face⟩ **3 a :** SKINNY, SCRAWNY **b :** BARREN, LEAN

bony fish *n* (1691) **:** any of a major taxon (class Osteichthyes or superclass Teleostomi) comprising fishes (as sturgeons, eels, mackerels, and sunfish) with a bony rather than a cartilaginous skeleton — called also *teleost;* compare CARTILAGINOUS FISH, JAWLESS FISH

bonze \ˈbänz\ *n* [F, fr. Pg *bonzo,* fr. Jp *bonsō*] (1653) **:** a Buddhist monk

[1]**boo** \ˈbü\ *interj* [ME *bo*] (15c) — used to express contempt or disapproval or to startle or frighten

[2]**boo** *n, pl* **boos** (1801) **1 :** a shout of disapproval or contempt **2 :** any utterance at all — usu. used in negative constructions ⟨never said ~⟩

[3]**boo** *vi* (1884) **:** to deride esp. by uttering a prolonged *boo* ~ *vt* **:** to express disapproval of by booing ⟨the crowd ~*ed* the referee⟩

[1]**boob** \ˈbüb\ *n* [short for [1]*booby*] (1907) **1 :** a stupid awkward person **:** SIMPLETON **2 :** BOOR, PHILISTINE — **boob·ish** \ˈbü-bish\ *adj*

[2]**boob** *n* [[3]*boob*] (1934) *Brit* **:** MISTAKE, BLUNDER

[3]**boob** *vi* [[1]*boob*] (1935) *Brit* **:** GOOF 2

[4]**boob** *n* [short for [2]*booby*] (ca. 1931) *sometimes vulgar* **:** BREAST

boo·bird \ˈbü-ˌbərd\ *n* (1975) **:** a home fan at a sporting event who boos one or more members of the home team

boob·oi·sie \ˌbüb-ˌwä-ˈzē\ *n* [blend of [1]*boob* and *bourgeoisie*] (1922) **:** the general public regarded as consisting of boobs

boo–boo \ˈbü-(ˌ)bü\ *n, pl* **boo–boos** [prob. baby-talk alter. of *boohoo,* imitation of the sound of weeping] (1953) **1 :** a usu. trivial injury (as a bruise or scratch) — used esp. by or of a child **2 :** MISTAKE, BLUNDER

boob tube *n* (1966) **:** TELEVISION

[1]**boo·by** \ˈbü-bē\ *n, pl* **boobies** [modif. of Sp *bobo,* fr. L *balbus* stammering, prob. of imit. origin] (1602) **1 :** an awkward foolish person **:** DOPE **2 :** any of several tropical seabirds (genus *Sula*) of the gannet family

[2]**boo·by** \ˈbü-bē, ˈbu̇-\ *n, pl* **boobies** [alter. of *bubby*] (1916) *sometimes vulgar* : BREAST
booby hatch *n* (1840) **1** : a raised framework with a sliding cover over a small hatch on a ship **2** : a psychiatric hospital
booby prize *n* (1889) **1** : an award for the poorest performance in a game or competition **2** : an acknowledgment of notable inferiority
booby trap *n* (1850) **1** : a trap for the unwary or unsuspecting : PITFALL **2** : a concealed explosive device contrived to go off when some harmless-looking object is touched — **boo·by–trap** *vt*
boo·dle \ˈbü-dᵊl\ *n* [D *boedel* estate, lot, fr. MD; akin to ON *būth* booth] (1833) **1** : a collection or lot of persons : CABOODLE **2 a** : bribe money **b** : a large amount esp. of money
boog·er \ˈbu̇-gər, ˈbü-\ *n* [alter. of E dial. *buggard, boggart,* fr. [1]*bug* + *-ard*] (1866) **1** : BOGEYMAN **2** : a piece of dried nasal mucus
boo·gey·man \ˈbu̇-gē-ˌman, ˈbü-\ *also* **boog·er·man** \ˈbu̇-gər-, ˈbü-\ *n* [by alter.] (ca. 1850) : BOGEYMAN
[1]**boo·gie** \ˈbu̇-gē, ˈbü-\ *n* (1929) **1** : BOOGIE-WOOGIE **2** : earthy and strongly rhythmic rock music conducive to dancing; *also* : a period of or occasion for dancing to this music
[2]**boogie** *also* **boo·gy** *or* **boo·gey** \ˈbu̇-gē, ˈbü-\ *vi* **boo·gied** *also* **boo·geyed; boo·gy·ing** *also* **boo·gey·ing** (1930) **1** : to dance to rock music; *also* : REVEL, PARTY **2 a** : to move quickly **b** : to get going
boo·gie–woo·gie \ˌbu̇-gē-ˈwu̇-gē, ˌbü-gē-ˈwü-gē\ *n* [origin unknown] (1928) : a percussive style of playing blues on the piano characterized by a steady rhythmic ground bass of eighth notes in quadruple time and a series of improvised melodic variations
boo·jum \ˈbü-jəm\ *n* [perh. fr. *boojum,* an imaginary creature in *The Hunting of the Snark* by Lewis Carroll; fr. its grotesque appearance] (1951) : a tall spiny long-lived desert tree (*Fouquieria columnaris* syn. *Idria columnaris*) native to northwestern Mexico and related to the ocotillo
[1]**book** \ˈbu̇k\ *n* [ME, fr. OE *bōc;* akin to OHG *buoh* book, Goth *boka* letter] (bef. 12c) **1 a** : a set of written sheets of skin or paper or tablets of wood or ivory **b** : a set of written, printed, or blank sheets bound together into a volume **c** : a long written or printed literary composition **d** : a major division of a treatise or literary work **e** : a record of a business's financial transactions or financial condition — often used in pl. ⟨the *~s* show a profit⟩ **f** : MAGAZINE 4a **g** : E-BOOK **2** *cap* : BIBLE 1 **3** : something that yields knowledge or understanding ⟨the great ~ of nature⟩ ⟨her face was an open ~⟩ **4 a (1)** : the total available knowledge and experience that can be brought to bear on a task or problem ⟨tried every trick in the ~⟩ **(2)** : inside information or analysis ⟨the ~ on him is that he can't hit a curveball⟩ **b** : the standards or authority relevant in a situation ⟨run by the ~⟩ **5 a** : all the charges that can be made against an accused person ⟨threw the ~ at him⟩ **b** : a position from which one must answer for certain acts : ACCOUNT ⟨bring criminals to ~⟩ **6 a** : LIBRETTO **b** : the script of a play **c** : a book of arrangements for a musician or dance orchestra : musical repertory **7** : a packet of items bound together like a book ⟨a ~ of stamps⟩ ⟨a ~ of matches⟩ **8 a** : BOOKMAKER **b** : the bets registered by a bookmaker; *also* : the business or activity of giving odds and taking bets **9** : the number of tricks a cardplayer or side must win before any trick can have scoring value — **book·ful** \ˈbu̇k-ˌfu̇l\ *n* — **in one's book** : in one's own opinion — **in one's good books** : in favor with one — **one for the book** : an act or occurrence worth noting — **on the books** : on the records
[2]**book** *adj* (13c) **1** : derived from books and not from practical experience ⟨~ learning⟩ **2** : shown by books of account ⟨~ assets⟩
[3]**book** *vt* (1807) **1 a** : to register (as a name) for some future activity or condition (as to engage transportation or reserve lodgings) ⟨he was *~ed* to sail on Monday⟩ **b** : to schedule engagements for ⟨~ the band for a week⟩ **c** : to set aside time for **d** : to reserve in advance ⟨~ two seats at the theater⟩ ⟨were all *~ed* up⟩ **2 a** : to enter charges against in a police register **b** *of a referee* : to note the name or number of (as a soccer player) for a serious infraction of the rules **~** *vi* **1** : to make a reservation ⟨~ through your travel agent⟩ **2** *chiefly Brit* : to register in a hotel — usu. used with *in* **3** *slang* : LEAVE, GO; *esp* : to depart quickly — **book·able** \ˈbu̇-kə-bəl\ *adj, chiefly Brit* — **book·er** *n*
book·bind·ing \ˈbu̇k-ˌbīn-diŋ\ *n* (1707) **1** : the art or trade of binding books **2** : the binding of a book — **book·bind·er** \-ˌbīn-dər\ *n* — **book·bind·ery** \-d(ə-)rē\ *n*
book·case \-ˌkās\ *n* (1726) : a piece of furniture consisting of shelves to hold books
book club *n* (1905) **1** : an organization that ships selected books to members usu. on a regular schedule and often at discount prices **2** : a group of people who meet regularly to discuss books they are reading
book·end \-ˌend\ *n* (1907) : a support placed at the end of a row of books
book·ie \ˈbu̇-kē\ *n* [by shortening & alter.] (1885) : BOOKMAKER 2
book·ing \ˈbu̇-kiŋ\ *n* (1823) **1** : the act of one that books **2** : an engagement or scheduled performance **3** : RESERVATION 1c
booking office *n* (ca. 1837) *chiefly Brit* : a ticket office; *esp* : one in a railroad station
book·ish \ˈbu̇-kish\ *adj* (1566) **1 a** : of or relating to books **b** : fond of books and reading **2 a** : inclined to rely on book knowledge **b** *of words* : literary and formal as opposed to colloquial and informal **c** : given to literary or scholarly pursuits; *also* : affectedly learned — **book·ish·ly** *adv* — **book·ish·ness** *n*
book·keep·er \ˈbu̇k-ˌkē-pər\ *n* (1555) : a person who records the accounts or transactions of a business — **book·keep·ing** \-piŋ\ *n*
book·let \ˈbu̇k-lət\ *n* (1856) : a little book; *esp* : PAMPHLET
book louse *n* (1867) : any of various tiny usu. wingless insects (order Psocoptera and esp. genus *Liposcelis*) that feed on organic matter (as paper) and usu. inhabit damp areas
book lung *n* (1897) : a saccular breathing organ in many arachnids containing thin folds of membrane arranged like the leaves of a book
book·mak·er \ˈbu̇k-ˌmā-kər\ *n* (1515) **1** : a printer, binder, or designer of books **2** : a person who determines odds and receives and pays off bets — **book·mak·ing** \-kiŋ\ *n*
book·man \-mən\ *n* (1583) **1** : a person who has a love of books and esp. of reading **2** : a person who is involved in the writing, publishing, or selling of books
[1]**book·mark** \-ˌmärk\ *n* (1838) **1** *or* **book·mark·er** \-ˌmär-kər\ : a marker for finding a place in a book **2** : a menu entry or icon on a computer that is usu. created by the user and that serves as a shortcut to a previously viewed location (as an Internet site)
[2]**bookmark** *vt* (1985) : to create a computer bookmark for ⟨~ a Web site⟩
book–match \-ˌmach\ *vt* (1942) : to match the grains of (as two sheets of veneer) so that one sheet seems to be the mirror image of the other
book·mo·bile \ˈbu̇k-mō-ˌbēl\ *n* (1926) : a truck that serves as a traveling library
Book of Common Prayer (1549) : the service book of the Anglican Communion
book off *vi* (1971) *chiefly Canad* : to notify an employer that one is not reporting for work (as because of sickness)
book·plate \ˈbu̇k-ˌplāt\ *n* (1791) : a book owner's identification label that is usu. pasted to the inside front cover of a book
book·sell·er \ˈbu̇k-ˌse-lər\ *n* (15c) : one that sells books; *esp* : the proprietor of a bookstore — **book·sell·ing** \-ˌse-liŋ\ *n*
book·shelf \-ˌshelf\ *n* (1623) : an open shelf for holding books
book·shop \-ˌshäp\ *n* (1765) : BOOKSTORE
book·stall \-ˌstȯl\ *n* (1800) **1** : a stall where books are sold **2** *chiefly Brit* : NEWSSTAND
book·store \-ˌstȯr\ *n* (1760) : a place of business where books are the main item offered for sale — called also *bookshop*
book value *n* (1899) : the value of something as shown on bookkeeping records as distinguished from market value: **a** : the value of an asset equal to cost minus depreciation **b** : the value of a corporation's stock equal to its book value minus its liabilities
book·worm \ˈbu̇k-ˌwərm\ *n* (1592) : a person unusually devoted to reading and study
Bool·ean \ˈbü-lē-ən\ *adj* [George *Boole* †1864 Eng. mathematician] (1851) : of, relating to, or being a logical combinatorial system (as Boolean algebra) that represents symbolically relationships (as those implied by the logical operators AND, OR, and NOT) between entities (as sets, propositions, or on-off computer circuit elements) ⟨~ expression⟩ ⟨~ search strategy for information retrieval⟩
Boolean algebra *n* (ca. 1889) : an algebraic system that consists of a set closed under two binary operations and that can be described by any of various systems of postulates all of which can be deduced from the postulates that each operation is commutative, that each operation is distributive over the other, that an identity element exists for each operation, and that for every element in the set there exists another element which when combined with the first under either one of the operations yields the identity element of the other operation
[1]**boom** \ˈbüm\ *vb* [ME *bomben, bummen,* of imit. origin] *vi* (15c) **1** : to make a deep hollow sound **2 a** : to increase in importance, popularity, or esteem **b** : to experience a sudden rapid growth and expansion usu. with an increase in prices ⟨business was *~ing*⟩ **c** : to develop rapidly in population and importance ⟨California *~ed* when gold was discovered there⟩ **d** : to increase greatly in size or number ⟨the population *~ed*⟩ **~** *vt* **1** : to cause to resound — often used with *out* ⟨his voice *~s* out the lyrics⟩ **2** : to cause a rapid growth or increase of : BOOST **3** : to hit or kick forcefully ⟨~ a punt⟩
[2]**boom** *n* (15c) **1** : a booming sound or cry — often used interjectionally to indicate suddenness ⟨then ~, he was fired⟩ **2** : a rapid expansion or increase: as **a** : a general movement in support of a candidate for office **b** : rapid settlement and development of a town or district **c** : a rapid widespread expansion of economic activity **d** : an upsurge in activity, interest, or popularity ⟨a folk music ~⟩
[3]**boom** *n* [D, tree, beam; akin to OHG *boum* tree — more at BEAM] (1627) **1** : a long spar used to extend the foot of a sail **2 a** : a chain or line of connected floating timbers extended across a river, lake, or harbor (as to obstruct passage or catch floating objects) **b** : a temporary floating barrier used to contain an oil spill **3 a** : a long beam projecting from the mast of a derrick to support or guide cargo **b** : a long more or less horizontal supporting arm or brace (as for holding a microphone) **4** : a spar or outrigger connecting the tail surfaces and the main supporting structure of an aircraft
boom box *n* (1981) : a usu. large portable stereophonic radio and tape or CD player
boom·er *n* (1880) **1** : one that booms **2** : one that joins a rush of settlers to a boom area **3** : a transient worker (as a bridge builder) **4** : a person born during a baby boom : BABY BOOMER
boo·mer·ang \ˈbü-mə-ˌraŋ\ *n* [Dharuk (Australian aboriginal language of the Port Jackson area) *bumariny*] (1825) **1** : a bent or angular throwing club typically flat on one side and rounded on the other so that it soars or curves in flight; *esp* : one designed to return near the thrower **2** : an act or utterance that backfires on its originator — **boomerang** *vi*
boomerang child *n* (1988) : a young adult who returns to live at his or her family home esp. for financial reasons
boom·ing \ˈbü-miŋ\ *adj* (1682) **1** : making a loud deep sound ⟨his ~ voice⟩ **2** : forcefully or powerfully executed ⟨hit a ~ serve⟩
boom·let \ˈbüm-lət\ *n* (1880) : a small boom; *specif* : a sudden increase in business activity ⟨a stock market ~⟩
boom·town \ˈbüm-ˌtau̇n\ *n* (1896) : a town enjoying a business and population boom
boomy \ˈbü-mē\ *adj* **boom·i·er; -est** (1888) **1** : of, relating to, or characterized by an economic boom **2** : having an excessive accentuation on the tones of lower pitch in reproduced sound
[1]**boon** \ˈbün\ *n* [ME *bone* prayer, request, the favor requested, fr. ON *bōn* request; akin to OE *bēn* prayer, *bannan* to summon — more at BAN] (12c) **1** : BENEFIT, FAVOR; *esp* : one that is given in answer to a request **2** : a timely benefit : BLESSING
[2]**boon** *adj* [ME *bon,* fr. AF, good — more at BOUNTY] (14c) **1** *archaic* : FAVORABLE **2** : CONVIVIAL ⟨a ~ companion⟩
boon·docks \ˈbün-ˌdäks\ *n pl* [Tag *bundok* mountain] (1930) **1** : rough country filled with dense brush **2** : a rural area : STICKS
boon·dog·gle \ˈbün-ˌdä-gəl, -ˌdȯ-\ *n* [coined by Robert H. Link †1957 Am. scoutmaster] (1929) **1** : a braided cord worn by Boy Scouts as a neckerchief slide, hatband, or ornament **2** : a wasteful or impractical project or activity often involving graft — **boondoggle** *vi* — **boon·dog·gler** \-g(ə-)lər\ *n*
boon·ies \ˈbü-nēz\ *n pl* (1956) *slang* : BOONDOCKS 2
boor \ˈbu̇r\ *n* [D *boer;* akin to OE *būan* to dwell — more at BOWER] (1551) **1** : PEASANT **2** : a rude or insensitive person

boor·ish \ˈbu̇r-ish\ *adj* (1562) **:** resembling or befitting a boor (as in crude insensitivity) — **boor·ish·ly** *adv* — **boor·ish·ness** *n*
syn BOORISH, CHURLISH, LOUTISH, CLOWNISH mean uncouth in manners or appearance. BOORISH implies rudeness of manner due to insensitiveness to others' feelings and unwillingness to be agreeable ⟨a drunk's *boorish* behavior⟩. CHURLISH suggests surliness, unresponsiveness, and ungraciousness ⟨*churlish* remarks⟩. LOUTISH implies bodily awkwardness together with stupidity ⟨a *loutish* oaf⟩. CLOWNISH suggests ill-bred awkwardness, ignorance or stupidity, ungainliness, and often a propensity for absurd antics ⟨an adolescent's *clownish* conduct⟩.

[1]**boost** \ˈbüst\ *vb* [origin unknown] *vt* (1801) **1 :** to push or shove up from below **2 :** INCREASE, RAISE ⟨plans to ~ production⟩ ⟨an extra holiday to ~ morale⟩ **3 :** to promote the cause or interests of **:** PLUG ⟨a campaign to ~ the new fashions⟩ **4 :** to raise the voltage of or across (an electric circuit) **5** *slang* **:** STEAL, SHOPLIFT ~ *vi, slang* **:** SHOPLIFT *syn* see LIFT

[2]**boost** *n* (1801) **1 :** a push upward **2 :** an act that brings help or encouragement **:** ASSIST **3 :** an increase in amount

boost·er \ˈbü-stər\ *n* (1888) **:** one that boosts: as **a :** an enthusiastic supporter **b :** an auxiliary device for increasing force, power, pressure, or effectiveness **c** *slang* **:** SHOPLIFTER **d :** a radio-frequency amplifier for a radio or television receiving set **e :** the first stage of a multistage rocket providing thrust for the launching and the initial part of the flight **f :** a substance that increases the effectiveness of a medicament; *esp* **:** BOOSTER SHOT

boost·er·ism \-stər-ˌi-zəm\ *n* (ca. 1913) **:** the activities and attitudes characteristic of boosters

booster seat *n* (1973) **:** a seat used to elevate a sitting child

booster shot *n* (1944) **:** a supplementary dose of an immunizing agent — called also *booster, booster dose*

[1]**boot** \ˈbüt\ *n* [ME, fr. OE *bōt* remedy — more at BETTER] (bef. 12c) **1** *archaic* **:** DELIVERANCE **2 :** something to equalize a trade **3** *obs* **:** AVAIL — **to boot :** BESIDES

[2]**boot** *vb* (15c) *archaic* **:** AVAIL, PROFIT

[3]**boot** *n* [ME, fr. AF *bote*] (14c) **1 :** a fitted covering (as of leather or rubber) for the foot and usu. reaching above the ankle **2 :** an instrument of torture used to crush the leg and foot **3 :** something that resembles or is likened to a boot; *esp* **:** an enclosing or protective casing or sheath (as for a rifle or over an electrical or mechanical connection) **4 :** a navy or marine corps recruit undergoing basic training **5** *Brit* **:** an automobile trunk **6 a :** a kick with the foot **b :** summary dismissal — used with *the* ⟨gave him the ~⟩ **c :** momentary pleasure or enjoyment **:** BANG ⟨got a big ~ out of the joke⟩ **7 :** a sheath enclosing the inflorescence **8 :** DENVER BOOT

[4]**boot** *vt* (15c) **1 :** to put boots on **2 a :** KICK **b :** to eject or discharge summarily — often used with *out* ⟨was ~*ed* out of office⟩ **3 :** to make an error on (a grounder in baseball); *broadly* **:** BOTCH **4 :** to ride (a horse) in a race ⟨~*ed* home three winners⟩ **5** [[2]*bootstrap*] **a :** to load (a program) into a computer from a disk **b :** to start or ready for use esp. by booting a program ⟨~ a computer⟩ — often used with *up* ~ *vi* **1 :** to become loaded into a computer's memory from a disk ⟨the program ~*s* automatically⟩ **2 :** to become ready for use esp. by booting a program ⟨the computer ~*s* quickly⟩ — often used with *up* — **boot·able** \ˈbü-tə-bəl\ *adj*

[5]**boot** *n* [[1]*boot*] (1593) *archaic* **:** BOOTY, PLUNDER

boot·black \ˈbüt-ˌblak\ *n* (1817) **:** one who shines shoes

boot camp *n* (1916) **1 :** a navy or marine corps camp for basic training **2 :** a disciplinary facility or program in which young offenders are forced to participate in a rigidly structured routine

boot·ed \ˈbü-təd\ *adj* (1552) **:** wearing boots

boo·tee *or* **boo·tie** \bü-ˈtē, *of infants' footwear* ˈbü-tē\ *n* (1799) **:** a usu. ankle-length boot, slipper, or sock; *esp* **:** an infant's knitted or crocheted sock

Bo·ö·tes \bō-ˈō-tēz\ *n* [L (gen. *Boötis*), fr. Gk *Boōtēs*, lit., plowman, fr. *bous* head of cattle — more at COW] **:** a northern constellation containing the bright star Arcturus

booth \ˈbüth, *esp Brit* ˈbüth\ *n, pl* **booths** \ˈbüthz, ˈbüths\ [ME *bothe*, of Scand origin; akin to ON *būth* booth; akin to OE *būan* to dwell — more at BOWER] (13c) **1 :** a temporary shelter for livestock or field workers **2 a :** a stall or stand (as at a fair) for the sale or exhibition of goods **b** (1) **:** a small enclosure affording privacy for one person at a time ⟨a telephone ~⟩ ⟨polling ~*s*⟩ (2) **:** a small enclosure that isolates its occupant esp. from patrons or customers ⟨a ticket ~⟩ (3) **:** an isolated enclosure used in sound recording or in broadcasting ⟨a radio ~⟩ **c :** a restaurant seating arrangement consisting of a table between two high-back benches

bootie *var of* BOOTEE, [2]BOOTY

boot·jack \ˈbüt-ˌjak\ *n* (1798) **:** a device (as with a V-shaped notch) used for pulling off boots

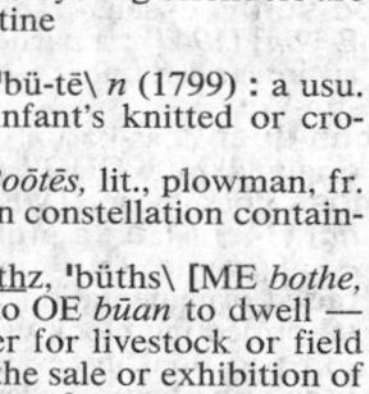

bootjack

boot·lace \-ˌlās\ *n* (1832) *Brit* **:** SHOELACE

[1]**boot·leg** \-ˌleg, -ˌlāg\ *n* (1634) **1 :** the upper part of a boot **2 :** something bootlegged: as **a :** MOONSHINE **b :** an unauthorized audio or video recording **3 :** a football play in which the quarterback fakes a handoff, hides the ball against his hip, and rolls out — compare DRAW 8 — **bootleg** *adj*

[2]**bootleg** *vt* (1889) **1 a :** to carry (alcoholic liquor) on one's person illegally **b :** to manufacture, sell, or transport for sale (alcoholic liquor) illegally **2 a :** to produce, reproduce, or distribute illicitly or without authorization **b :** SMUGGLE ~ *vi* **1 :** to engage in bootlegging **2 :** to run a bootleg play in football — **boot·leg·ger** *n*

boot·less \ˈbüt-ləs\ *adj* [[1]*boot*] (1559) **:** USELESS, UNPROFITABLE ⟨a ~ attempt⟩ — **boot·less·ly** *adv* — **boot·less·ness** *n*

boot·lick \-ˌlik\ *vt* (1845) **:** to try to gain favor with through a servile or obsequious manner ~ *vi* **:** to act obsequiously — **boot·lick·er** *n*

boots \ˈbüts\ *n pl but sing or pl in constr* [fr. pl. of [3]*boot*] (ca. 1837) *Brit* **:** a servant who shines shoes esp. in a hotel

[1]**boot·strap** \ˈbüt-ˌstrap\ *n* (1875) **1 :** a looped strap sewed at the side or the rear top of a boot to help in pulling it on **2** *pl* **:** unaided efforts — often used in the phrase *by one's own bootstraps*

[2]**bootstrap** *adj* (1926) **1 :** designed to function independently of outside direction **:** capable of using one internal function or process to control another ⟨a ~ operation to load a computer⟩ **2 :** carried out with minimum resources or advantages ⟨~ efforts⟩

[3]**bootstrap** *vt* (1951) **:** to promote or develop by initiative and effort with little or no assistance ⟨*bootstrapped* herself to the top⟩ — **boot·strap·per** *n*

[1]**boo·ty** \ˈbü-tē\ *n, pl* **booties** [modif. of MF *butin*, fr. MLG *būte* exchange] (15c) **1 :** plunder taken (as in war); *esp* **:** plunder taken on land as distinguished from prizes taken at sea **2 :** a rich gain or prize *syn* see SPOIL

[2]**booty** *also* **boo·tie** \ˈbü-tē\ *n, pl* **booties** [alter. of an English-based creole word, ultim. fr. Early Mod E **bottie* buttocks, perh. fr. [1]*bottom* + *-ie*] (1928) *slang* **:** BUTTOCKS

booty call *n* (1993) *slang* **:** a phone call made to arrange a sexual encounter with someone; *also* **:** the person to whom such a call is made

[1]**booze** \ˈbüz\ *vi* **boozed; booz·ing** [ME *bousen*, fr. MD *būsen*] (14c) **:** to drink intoxicating liquor esp. to excess — often used in the phrase *booze it up*

[2]**booze** *n* (14c) **:** intoxicating drink; *esp* **:** hard liquor — **booz·i·ly** \-zə-lē\ *adv* — **boozy** \-zē\ *adj*

booze·hound \ˈbüz-ˌhau̇nd\ *n* (1911) **:** BOOZER, DRUNK

booz·er \ˈbü-zər\ *n* (1816) **1 :** a person who boozes **:** DRUNK **2** *Brit* **:** a drinking place **:** PUB

[1]**bop** \ˈbäp\ *vt* **bopped; bop·ping** [imit.] (1928) **:** HIT, SOCK

[2]**bop** *n* (1932) **:** a blow (as with the fist or a club) that strikes a person

[3]**bop** *n* [short for *bebop*] (1947) **1 :** jazz characterized by harmonic complexity, convoluted melodic lines, and constant shifting of accent and often played at very rapid tempos **2 :** JIVE 2 — **bop·per** *n*

[4]**bop** *vi* **bopped; bop·ping** (1952) **1 :** to go quickly or unceremoniously **:** POP ⟨~ into the corner store⟩ — often used with *off* **2 :** to dance or shuffle along to or as if to bop music

BOQ *abbr* bachelor officers' quarters

bor *abbr* borough

bo·ra \ˈbȯr-ə\ *n* [It, fr. It dial. (Trieste), fr. L *boreas*] (1839) **:** a violent cold northerly wind of the Adriatic

bo·rac·ic acid \bə-ˈra-sik-\ *n* [ML *borac-, borax* borax] (1801) **:** BORIC ACID

bor·age \ˈbȯr-ij, ˈbär-\ *n* [ME, fr. AF *bourage*, fr. ML *borrago*, prob. fr. Ar dial. **bū'araq*, alter. of Ar *abū 'araq*, lit., source of sweat; fr. its use as a diaphoretic] (14c) **:** a coarse hairy blue-flowered European herb (*Borago officinalis* of the family Boraginaceae, the borage family) used medicinally and in salads

bo·rane \ˈbȯr-ˌān\ *n* [ISV, fr. *boron*] (1916) **1 :** a compound of boron and hydrogen; *specif* **:** a compound BH_3 known only in the form of its derivatives **2 :** a derivative of borane

bo·rate \-ˌāt\ *n* (1788) **:** a salt or ester of a boric acid

bo·rat·ed \-ˌā-təd\ *adj* (ca. 1901) **:** mixed or impregnated with borax or boric acid

[1]**bo·rax** \ˈbȯr-ˌaks, -əks\ *n* [ME *boras*, fr. AF *boreis*, fr. ML *borac-, borax*, fr. Ar *būraq*, fr. Pers *būrah*] (14c) **:** a white crystalline compound that consists of a hydrated sodium borate $Na_2B_4O_7{\cdot}10H_2O$, that occurs as a mineral or is prepared from other minerals, and that is used esp. as a flux, cleansing agent, and water softener, as a preservative, and as a fireproofing agent

[2]**borax** *n* [origin unknown] (1932) **:** cheap shoddy merchandise

bor·bo·ryg·mus \ˌbȯr-bə-ˈrig-məs\ *n, pl* **-mi** \-ˌmī\ [NL, fr. Gk *borborygmos*, fr. *borboryzein* to rumble] (ca. 1724) **:** intestinal rumbling caused by moving gas

Bor·deaux \bȯr-ˈdō\ *n, pl* **Bor·deaux** \-ˈdōz\ *often not cap* (ca. 1570) **1 :** white or red wine of the Bordeaux region of France **2 :** CLARET 2

bor·deaux mixture \bȯr-ˈdō-, ˈbȯr-ˌ\ *n, often cap B* (1892) **:** a fungicide made by combination of copper sulfate, lime, and water

bor·de·laise sauce \ˈbȯr-dᵊl-ˈāz-\ *n, often cap B* [F *bordelaise*, fem. of *bordelais* of Bordeaux] (1902) **:** a sauce consisting of stock thickened with roux and flavored typically with red wine and shallots

bor·del·lo \bȯr-ˈde-(ˌ)lō\ *n, pl* **-los** [It, fr. OF *bordel*, fr. *borde* hut, of Gmc origin; akin to OE *bord* board] (1593) **:** a building in which prostitutes are available

[1]**bor·der** \ˈbȯr-dər\ *n* [ME *bordure*, fr. AF, fr. *border* to border, fr. OF *bort* border, of Gmc origin; prob. akin to OE *bord* board] (14c) **1 :** an outer part or edge **2 :** an ornamental design at the edge of a fabric or rug **3 :** a narrow bed of planted ground along the edge of a lawn or walk **4 :** BOUNDARY ⟨crossed the ~ into Italy⟩ **5 :** a plain or decorative margin around printed matter — **bor·dered** \-dərd\ *adj*

[2]**border** *vb* **bor·dered; bor·der·ing** \ˈbȯr-d(ə-)riŋ\ *vt* (14c) **1 :** to put a border on **2 :** to touch at the edge or boundary **:** BOUND ⟨~*s* the city on the south⟩ ~ *vi* **1 :** to lie on the border ⟨the U.S. ~*s* on Canada⟩ **2 :** to approach the nature of a specified thing **:** VERGE ⟨~*s* on the ridiculous⟩ — **bor·der·er** \-dər-ər\ *n*

border collie *n, often cap B* (1938) **:** any of a breed of medium-sized sheepdogs of British origin noted for their herding abilities

bor·de·reau \ˌbȯr-də-ˈrō\ *n, pl* **-reaux** \-ˈrō(z)\ [F, fr. MF *bordrel*, prob. fr. *bord* border, fr. OF *bort* — more at BORDER] (ca. 1858) **:** a detailed note or memorandum of account; *esp* **:** one containing an enumeration of documents

bor·der·land \ˈbȯr-dər-ˌland\ *n* (1811) **1 a :** territory at or near a border **b :** FRINGE 3a ⟨lives on the ~ of society⟩ **2 :** a vague intermediate state or region ⟨the ~ between fantasy and reality⟩

[1]**bor·der·line** \-ˌlīn\ *adj* (1907) **1 a :** being in an intermediate position or state **:** not fully classifiable as one thing or its opposite ⟨a ~ state between waking and sleeping⟩ **b :** not quite up to, typical of, or as severe as what is usual, standard, or expected ⟨~ intelligence⟩ ⟨~ hypertension⟩ **c :** characterized by psychological instability in several areas (as interpersonal relations, behavior, and identity) but only with brief or no psychotic episodes ⟨a ~ personality disorder⟩ **2 :** situated at or near a border ⟨a ~ town⟩ — **borderline** *n*

2borderline *adv* (1925) : ALMOST, NEARLY ⟨~ tacky⟩ ⟨~ suicidal⟩
border terrier *n, often cap B* (1894) : any of a breed of small terriers of British origin having a harsh dense coat and close undercoat
bor·dure \ˈbȯr-jər\ *n* [ME] (14c) : a border on a heraldic shield
1bore \ˈbȯr\ *vb* **bored; bor·ing** [ME, fr. OE *borian;* akin to OHG *borōn* to bore, L *forare* to bore, *ferire* to strike] *vt* (bef. 12c) **1** : to pierce with a turning or twisting movement of a tool **2** : to make (as a cylindrical hole) by boring or digging away material ⟨*bored* a tunnel⟩ ~ *vi* **1 a** : to make a hole by or as if by boring **b** : to sink a mine shaft or well **2** : to make one's way steadily esp. against resistance ⟨we *bored* through the jostling crowd⟩
2bore *n* (14c) **1 a** : a usu. cylindrical hole made by or as if by boring **b** *chiefly Austral & NewZeal* : a borehole drilled esp. to make an artesian well **2 a** : the long usu. cylindrical hollow part of something (as a tube or gun barrel) **b** : the inner surface of a hollow cylindrical object **3** : the size of a bore: as **a** : the interior diameter of a gun barrel; *esp, chiefly Brit* : GAUGE 1a(2) **b** : the diameter of an engine cylinder
3bore *past of* BEAR
4bore *n* [ME *bore wave, fr. ON *bāra*] (1601) : a tidal flood with a high abrupt front
5bore *n* [origin unknown] (1766) : one that causes boredom: as **a** : a tiresome person **b** : something that is devoid of interest
6bore *vt* **bored; bor·ing** (1768) : to cause to feel boredom
bo·re·al \ˈbȯr-ē-əl\ *adj* [ME *boriall,* fr. LL *borealis,* fr. L *boreas* north wind, north, fr. Gk, fr. *Boreas*] (15c) **1** : of, relating to, or located in northern regions ⟨~ waters⟩ **2** : of, relating to, or comprising the northern biotic area characterized esp. by dominance of coniferous forests
Bo·re·as \-ē-əs\ *n* [L, fr. Gk] **1** : the Greek god of the north wind **2** : the north wind personified
bore·dom \ˈbȯr-dəm\ *n* (1852) : the state of being weary and restless through lack of interest
bo·reen \bȯr-ˈēn\ *n* [Ir *bóthrín,* dim. of *bóthar* road] (1836) *Irish* : a narrow country lane
bore·hole \ˈbȯr-ˌhōl\ *n* (1708) : a hole bored or drilled in the earth: as **a** : an exploratory well **b** *chiefly Brit* : a small-diameter well drilled esp. to obtain water
bor·er \ˈbȯr-ər\ *n* (14c) **1** : a tool used for boring **2 a** : SHIPWORM **b** : an insect that bores in the woody parts of plants
bore·scope \ˈbȯr-ˌskōp\ *n* (1941) : an optical device (as a prism or optical fiber) used to inspect an inaccessible space (as an engine cylinder)
bo·ric acid \ˈbȯr-ik-\ *n* [*boron*] (1869) : a white crystalline acid $B(OH)_3$ obtained from its salts and used esp. as a weak antiseptic and fire-retardant
bo·ride \ˈbȯr-ˌīd\ *n* (1863) : a binary compound of boron with a more electropositive element or radical
bor·ing \ˈbȯr-iŋ\ *adj* (1785) : causing boredom : TIRESOME ⟨a ~ lecture⟩ — **bor·ing·ly** \-iŋ-lē\ *adv* — **bor·ing·ness** *n*
born \ˈbȯrn\ *adj* [ME, fr. OE *boren,* pp. of *beran* to carry — more at BEAR] (bef. 12c) **1 a** : brought forth by or as if by birth **b** : NATIVE — usu. used in combination ⟨American-*born*⟩ **c** : deriving or resulting from — usu. used in combination ⟨poverty-*born* crime⟩ **2 a** : having from birth specified qualities ⟨a ~ leader⟩ **b** : being in specified circumstances from birth ⟨nobly ~⟩ ⟨~ to wealth⟩ **3** : destined from or as if from birth ⟨~ to succeed⟩
born–again \-ə-ˈgen, -ˈgin, -ˈgān\ *adj* [fr. the verse "Except a man be *born again,* he cannot see the Kingdom of God" (Jn 3:3–AV)] (1861) **1** : of, relating to, or being a usu. Christian person who has made a renewed or confirmed commitment of faith esp. after an intense religious experience **2** : having returned to or newly adopted an activity, a conviction, or a persona esp. with a proselytizing zeal ⟨a ~ conservative⟩
1borne \ˈbȯrn\ *past part of* BEAR
2borne *adj* (ca. 1559) : transported or transmitted by — used in combination ⟨soil*borne*⟩ ⟨air*borne*⟩
bor·ne·ol \ˈbȯr-nē-ˌȯl, -ˌōl\ *n* [ISV, fr. *Borneo,* island of Indonesia] (1876) : a crystalline cyclic alcohol $C_{10}H_{17}OH$ that occurs in two enantiomeric forms, is found in essential oils, and is used esp. in perfumery
born·ite \ˈbȯr-ˌnīt\ *n* [G *Bornit,* fr. Ignaz von *Born* †1791 Austrian mineralogist] (ca. 1847) : a brittle metallic-looking mineral that consists of a sulfide of copper and iron and is a valuable copper ore
boro- *comb form* : boron ⟨*boro*silicate⟩
bo·ro·hy·dride \ˌbȯr-ō-ˈhī-ˌdrīd\ *n* (1940) : the anion BH_4^- of boron and hydrogen that is used esp. as a reducing agent and as a source of hydrogen atoms; *also* : any of various compounds (as of metals) containing the borohydride anion
bo·ron \ˈbȯr-ˌän\ *n* [*bor*ax + *-on* (as in *carbon*)] (1812) : a trivalent metalloid element found in nature only in combination and used esp. in glass and detergents — see ELEMENT table — **bo·ron·ic** \bȯr-ˈä-nik\ *adj*
boron carbide *n* (ca. 1909) : a refractory shiny black crystalline compound B_4C that is one of the hardest known materials and is used esp. in abrasives and as a structural reinforcing material
bo·ro·sil·i·cate \ˌbȯr-ō-ˈsi-lə-ˌkāt, -ˈsi-li-kət\ *n* [ISV] (1817) **1** : a silicate containing boron in the anion and occurring naturally **2** : BOROSILICATE GLASS
borosilicate glass *n* (1933) : a silicate glass that is composed of at least five percent oxide of boron and is used esp. in heat-resistant glassware
bor·ough \ˈbər-(ˌ)ō, ˈbə-(ˌ)rō\ *n* [ME *burgh,* fr. OE *burg* fortified town; akin to OHG *burg* fortified place, and prob. to OE *beorg* hill — more at BARROW] (bef. 12c) **1 a** : a medieval fortified group of houses forming a town with special duties and privileges **b** : a town or urban constituency in Great Britain that sends a member to Parliament **c** : an urban area in Great Britain incorporated for purposes of self-government **2 a** : a municipal corporation proper in some states (as New Jersey and Minnesota) corresponding to the incorporated town or village of the other states **b** : one of the five constituent political divisions of New York City **3** : a civil division of the state of Alaska corresponding to a county in most other states
borough English *n* (14c) : a custom formerly existing in parts of England by which the lands of an intestate descended to the youngest son
borough hall *n* (1938) : the chief administrative building of a borough
bor·row \ˈbär-(ˌ)ō, ˈbȯr-\ *vb* [ME *borwen,* fr. OE *borgian;* akin to OE *beorgan* to preserve — more at BURY] *vt* (bef. 12c) **1 a** : to receive with the implied or expressed intention of returning the same or an equivalent ⟨~ a book⟩ ⟨~*ed* a dollar⟩ **b** : to borrow (money) with the intention of returning the same plus interest **2 a** : to appropriate for one's own use ⟨~ a metaphor⟩ **b** : DERIVE, ADOPT **3** : to take (one) from a digit of the minuend in arithmetical subtraction in order to add as 10 to the digit holding the next lower place **4** : to adopt into one language from another **5** *dial* : LEND ~ *vi* : to borrow something — **bor·row·er** \-ə-wər\ *n* — **borrow trouble** : to do something unnecessarily that may result in adverse reaction or repercussions
bor·rowed time *n* (1664) : an uncertain and usu. uncontrolled postponement of something inevitable — used with *living on*
bor·row·ing \ˈbär-ə-wiŋ, ˈbȯr-\ *n* (1609) : something borrowed; *esp* : a word or phrase adopted from one language into another
borrow pit *n* (1863) : an excavated area where material has been dug for use as fill at another location
Bors \ˈbȯrz\ *n* [ME, fr. MF *Bohort*] (15c) : a knight of the Round Table and nephew of Lancelot
borscht *or* **borsch** \ˈbȯrsh(t)\ *n* [Yiddish *borsht* & Ukrainian & Russ *borshch*] (1808) : a soup made primarily of beets and served hot or cold often with sour cream
borscht belt *also* **borsch belt** *n* (1936) : BORSCHT CIRCUIT
borscht circuit *or* **borsch circuit** *n, often cap B&C* [fr. the popularity of borscht on menus of the resorts] (1936) : the theaters and nightclubs associated with the Jewish summer resorts in the Catskills
Bor·stal \ˈbȯr-stᵊl\ *n* [*Borstal,* Eng. village where the first such institution was set up] (1907) *Brit* : REFORMATORY
bort *also* **boart** \ˈbȯrt\ *n* [prob. fr. D *boort*] (1622) : imperfectly crystallized diamond or diamond fragments used as an abrasive
bor·zoi \ˈbȯr-ˌzȯi\ *n* [Russ *borzoĭ,* fr. *borzoĭ* swift] (1887) : any of a breed of large dogs developed in Russia esp. for pursuing wolves that have a long silky usu. white coat with darker markings — called also *Russian wolfhound*
Bosc \ˈbäsk\ *n* [short for *Beurré Bosc,* fr. F, fr. *beurré,* any of various soft-fleshed pear varieties + *bosc,* perh. fr. L.-A.-G. *Bosc* d'Antic †1828 Fr. naturalist] (1850) : a pear with firm flesh and brown or dark yellow skin
bos·cage *also* **bosk·age** \ˈbäs-kij\ *n* [ME *boskage,* fr. AF *boscage,* fr. *bois* forest, of Gmc origin; akin to OHG *busk* forest, bush] (14c) : a growth of trees or shrubs : THICKET
bosh \ˈbäsh\ *n* [Turk *boş* empty] (1834) : foolish talk or activity : NONSENSE — often used interjectionally
bosk *or* **bosque** \ˈbäsk\ *n* [prob. back-formation fr. *bosky*] (1814) : a small wooded area
bosky \ˈbäs-kē\ *adj* [E dial. *bosk* bush, fr. ME *bush, bosk*] (1593) **1** : having abundant trees or shrubs **2** : of or relating to a woods
1bos·om \ˈbu̇-zəm *also* ˈbü-\ *n* [ME, fr. OE *bōsm;* akin to OHG *buosam* bosom] (bef. 12c) **1 a** : the human chest and esp. the front part of the chest ⟨hugged the child to his ~⟩ **b** : a woman's breasts regarded esp. as a single feature ⟨a woman with an ample ~⟩; *also* : BREAST **2 a** : the chest conceived of as the seat of the emotions and intimate feelings ⟨a story you will take to your ~⟩ **b** : the security and intimacy of or like that of being hugged to someone's bosom ⟨the ~ of her family⟩ **3** : the part of a garment that covers the chest or the breasts
2bosom *vt* (1587) **1** : EMBRACE **2** : to enclose or carry in the bosom
3bosom *adj* (1590) : CLOSE, INTIMATE ⟨~ friends⟩
bos·omed \-zəmd\ *adj* (1603) : having a bosom of a specified kind — used in combination ⟨full-*bosomed*⟩
bos·omy \ˈbu̇-zə-mē *also* ˈbü-\ *adj* (1860) **1** : swelling upward or outward ⟨~ hills⟩ **2** : having prominent breasts
bo·son \ˈbō-ˌsän, -ˌzän\ *n* [Satyendranath *Bose* †1974 Indian physicist + E 2*-on*] (1947) : a particle (as a photon or meson) whose spin is zero or an integral number — compare FERMION — **bo·son·ic** \ˌbō-ˈsä-nik, -ˈzä-\ *adj*
bos·quet \ˈbäs-kət\ *n* [F, fr. It *boschetto,* dim. of *bosco* forest, of Gmc origin; akin to OHG *busk* forest, bush] (ca. 1737) : THICKET
1boss \ˈbäs, ˈbȯs\ *n* [ME *boce,* fr. AF, fr. VL **bottia*] (14c) **1 a** : a protuberant part or body ⟨a ~ of granite⟩ ⟨a ~ on an animal's horn⟩ **b** : a raised ornamentation : STUD **c** : an ornamental projecting block used in architecture **2** : a soft pad used in ceramics and glassmaking **3** : the hub of a propeller

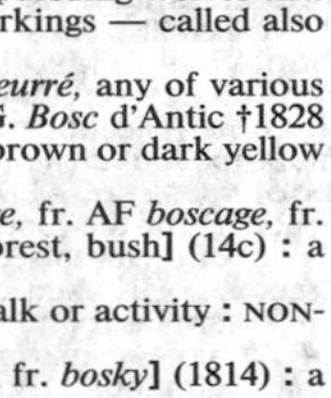
boss 1c

2boss *vt* (15c) **1** : to ornament with bosses : EMBOSS **2** : to treat (as the surface of porcelain) with a boss
3boss *n* [D *baas* master] (1653) **1** : a person who exercises control or authority; *specif* : one who directs or supervises workers **2** : a politician who controls votes in a party organization or dictates appointments or legislative measures — **boss·dom** \-dəm\ *n* — **boss·ism** \ˈbä-ˌsi-zəm, ˈbȯ-\ *n*
4boss \ˈbȯs\ *adj* (1836) *slang* : EXCELLENT, FIRST-RATE
5boss \ˈbȯs\ *vt* (1856) **1** : to act as boss of **2** : to give usu. arbitrary orders to — usu. used with *around*
6boss \ˈbȯs, ˈbäs\ *n* [E dial., young cow] (1790) : COW, CALF
bos·sa no·va \ˌbä-sə-ˈnō-və\ *n* [Pg, lit., new trend] (1962) **1** : popular music of Brazilian origin that is rhythmically related to the samba but with complex harmonies and improvised jazzlike passages **2** : a dance performed to bossa nova music
boss man *n* (1909) : 3BOSS
1bossy \ˈbä-sē, ˈbȯ-\ *adj* (1543) **1** : marked by a swelling or roundness **2** : marked by bosses : STUDDED
2bossy \ˈbȯ-sē, ˈbä-\ *n, pl* **boss·ies** [6*boss*] (1843) : COW, CALF
3bossy \ˈbȯ-sē, ˈbä-\ *adj* **boss·i·er; -est** (1882) : inclined to domineer : DICTATORIAL — **boss·i·ness** *n*
Bos·ton \ˈbȯs-tən\ *n* [F, fr. *Boston,* Mass.] (1800) **1** : a variation of whist played with two decks of cards **2** [*Boston,* Mass.] : a dance somewhat like a waltz
Boston cream pie *n* (1908) : a round cake that is split and filled with a custard or cream filling and usu. frosted with chocolate
Boston fern *n* (ca. 1900) : a luxuriant fern (*Nephrolepis exaltata bostoniensis*) often with drooping much-divided fronds
Boston ivy *n* (ca. 1900) : a woody Asian vine (*Parthenocissus tricuspidata*) of the grape family typically having 3-lobed leaves

Boston lettuce *n* (1880) **:** butter lettuce of a variety that is larger than the closely related Bibb lettuce
Boston marriage *n* (1980) **:** a long-term loving relationship between two women
Boston rocker *n* (1843) **:** a wooden rocking chair with a high spindle back, a decorative top panel, and a seat and arms that curve down at the front
Boston terrier *n* (1894) **:** any of a breed of small smooth-coated terriers originating as a cross of the bulldog and bull terrier and being brindled or black with white markings — called also *Boston bull*
bosun *also* **bos'n** *or* **bo's'n** *or* **bo'sun** *var of* BOATSWAIN
Bos·well \ˈbäz-ˌwel, -wəl\ *n* [James *Boswell*] (1858) **:** a person who records in detail the life of a usu. famous contemporary — **Bos·well·ian** \bäz-ˈwe-lē-ən\ *adj* — **Bos·well·ize** \ˈbäz-wə-ˌlīz, -ˌwe-\ *vb*
[1]**bot** *also* **bott** \ˈbät\ *n* [ME; akin to D leverbot liver fluke] (15c) **:** the larva of a botfly; *esp* **:** one infesting the horse
[2]**bot** *abbr* **1** botanical; botanist; botany **2** bottle **3** bottom **4** bought **5** robot
bo·ta \ˈbō-tə\ *n* [Sp, fr. LL *buttis* cask] (1832) **:** a leather bottle (as for wine)
botan *abbr* botanical
bo·tan·i·ca \bə-ˈta-ni-kə\ *n* [AmerSp *botánica,* fr. fem. of Sp *botánico* botanical] (1969) **:** a shop that deals in herbs and charms used esp. by adherents of Santeria
[1]**bo·tan·i·cal** \bə-ˈta-ni-kəl\ *adj* [F *botanique,* fr. Gk *botanikos* of herbs, fr. *botanē* pasture, herb, fr. *boskein* to feed, graze; prob. akin to Lith *guotas* flock] (1658) **1 :** of or relating to plants or botany **2 :** derived from plants **3 :** SPECIES ⟨~ tulips⟩ — **bo·tan·i·cal·ly** \-k(ə-)lē\ *adv*
[2]**botanical** *n* (ca. 1926) **:** a plant part or extract used esp. in skin and hair care products; *also* **:** a medicinal preparation derived from a plant
botanical garden *n* (1775) **:** a garden often with greenhouses for the culture, study, and exhibition of special plants — called also *bo·tan·ic garden* \bə-ˈta-nik-\
bot·an·ise *Brit var of* BOTANIZE
bot·a·nize \ˈbä-tə-ˌnīz\ *vb* **-nized; -niz·ing** *vi* (1751) **:** to collect plants for botanical investigation; *also* **:** to study plants esp. on a field trip ~ *vt* **:** to explore for botanical purposes — **bot·a·niz·er** \-ˌnī-zər\ *n*
bot·a·ny \ˈbä-tə-nē, ˈbät-nē\ *n, pl* **-nies** [*botan*ic botanical + [2]-*y*] (1696) **1 :** a branch of biology dealing with plant life **2 a :** plant life **b :** the properties and life phenomena exhibited by a plant, plant type, or plant group **3 :** a botanical treatise or study; *esp* **:** a particular system of botany — **bot·a·nist** \-nist\ *n*
[1]**botch** \ˈbäch\ *n* [ME *boche,* fr. AF, fr. VL **bottia* boss] (14c) **:** an inflammatory sore
[2]**botch** *vt* [ME *bocchen*] (1530) **1 :** to foul up hopelessly — often used with *up* **2 :** to put together in a makeshift way — **botch·er** *n*
[3]**botch** *n* (1605) **1 :** something that is botched **:** MESS **2 :** PATCHWORK, HODGEPODGE — **botchy** \ˈbä-chē\ *adj*
bot·fly \ˈbät-ˌflī\ *n* (1819) **:** any of various stout dipteran flies (family Oestridae) with larvae parasitic in cavities or tissues of various mammals including humans
[1]**both** \ˈbōth\ *pron, pl in constr* [ME *bothe,* prob. fr. ON *bāthir;* akin to OHG *beide* both] (12c) **:** the one as well as the other ⟨~ of us⟩
[2]**both** *conj* (12c) — used as a function word to indicate and stress the inclusion of each of two or more things specified by coordinated words, phrases, or clauses ⟨prized ~ for its beauty and for its utility⟩ ⟨he . . . who loveth well ~ man and bird and beast —S. T. Coleridge⟩
[3]**both** *adj* (13c) **:** being the two **:** affecting or involving the one and the other ⟨~ feet⟩ ⟨~ his eyes⟩ ⟨~ these armies⟩
[1]**both·er** \ˈbä-t͟hər\ *vb* **both·ered; both·er·ing** \ˈbät͟h-riŋ, ˈbä-t͟hə-\ [origin unknown] *vt* (1728) **1 :** to annoy esp. by petty provocation **:** IRK **2 :** to intrude upon **:** PESTER **3 :** to cause to be somewhat anxious or concerned ⟨my stomach is ~*ing* me⟩ — often used interjectionally ~ *vi* **1 :** to become concerned ⟨wouldn't ~ with details⟩ **2 :** to take pains **:** take the trouble ⟨never ~*ed* to ask⟩ ***syn*** see ANNOY
[2]**bother** *n* (1788) **1 a :** a state of petty discomfort, annoyance, or worry **b :** something that causes petty annoyance or worry **2 :** FUSS
both·er·a·tion \ˌbä-t͟hə-ˈrā-shən\ *n* (1797) **1 :** the act of bothering **:** the state of being bothered **2 :** something that bothers — often used interjectionally
both·er·some \ˈbä-t͟hər-səm\ *adj* (1834) **:** causing bother **:** VEXING
bo·thy \ˈbä-thē, ˈbō-\ *n* [Sc, prob. fr. obs. Sc *both* booth] (1771) *chiefly Scot* **:** HUT
bot·o·née *or* **bot·on·née** \ˌbä-tᵊn-ˈā\ *adj* [MF *botonné*] (15c) *of a heraldic cross* **:** having a cluster of three balls or knobs at the end of each arm — see CROSS illustration
Botox \ˈbō-ˌtäks\ *trademark* — used for a preparation of botulinum toxin
bo tree \ˈbō-\ *n* [Sinhalese *bō,* fr. Skt *bodhi* enlightenment; fr. Buddha receiving enlightenment under this tree — more at BID] (1860) **:** PIPAL
bot·ry·oi·dal \ˌbä-trē-ˈȯi-dᵊl\ *adj* [Gk *botryoeidēs,* fr. *botrys* bunch of grapes] (1816) **:** having the form of a bunch of grapes ⟨~ garnets⟩
bo·try·tis \bō-ˈtrī-təs\ *n* [NL, fr. Gk *botrys*] (1863) **:** any of a genus (*Botrytis*) of imperfect fungi having botryoidal conidia and including several serious plant pathogens
[1]**bot·tle** \ˈbä-tᵊl\ *n, often attrib* [ME *botel,* fr. OF *botele,* fr. ML *butticula,* dim. of LL *buttis* cask] (14c) **1 a :** a rigid or semirigid container typically of glass or plastic having a comparatively narrow neck or mouth and usu. no handle **b :** a usu. bottle-shaped container made of skin for storing a liquid **2 :** the quantity held by a bottle **3 a :** intoxicating drink **:** the practice of drinking ⟨slipped deeper and deeper into the ~ —Anne Bernays⟩ **b :** liquid food (as milk) used in place of mother's milk **4** *slang Brit* **:** METTLE, COURAGE — **bot·tle·ful** \-ˌfu̇l\ *n*
[2]**bottle** *vt* **bot·tled; bot·tling** \ˈbä-tᵊl-iŋ, ˈbät-liŋ\ (1594) **1 a :** to confine as if in a bottle **:** RESTRAIN — usu. used with *up* ⟨*bottling* up their anger⟩ **b :** to put or keep in a position or situation that makes free activity, progress, or escape difficult or impossible — usu. used with *up* ⟨~ up legislation in committee⟩ **2 :** to put into or as if into a bottle ⟨wished she could ~ their energy⟩ — **bot·tler** \ˈbä-tᵊl-ər, ˈbät-lər\ *n*
bottle blond *n* (1963) **:** a person whose hair has been bleached blond
bot·tle·brush \ˈbä-tᵊl-ˌbrəsh\ *n* [fr. the shape of the flowers] (ca. 1841) **:** any of a genus (*Callistemon*) of Australian trees and shrubs of the myrtle family widely cultivated in warm regions esp. for their spikes of brightly colored flowers
bottle club *n* (1943) **:** a club serving patrons previously purchased or reserved alcoholic drinks after normal legal closing hours
bottled gas *n* (1858) **:** gas under pressure in portable cylinders
bot·tle–feed \ˈbä-tᵊl-ˌfēd\ *vt* **-fed; -feed·ing** (ca. 1865) **:** to feed (as an infant) with a bottle
bottle gourd *n* (1652) **:** a common cultivated gourd (*Lagenaria siceraria*) having a variably shaped fruit with a hard shell that is sometimes used as a container
bottle green *n* (1795) **:** a dark green
[1]**bot·tle·neck** \ˈbä-tᵊl-ˌnek\ *adj* (1896) **:** NARROW ⟨~ harbors⟩
[2]**bottleneck** *n* (1907) **1 a :** a narrow route **b :** a point of traffic congestion **2 a :** someone or something that retards or halts free movement and progress **b :** IMPASSE **c :** a dramatic reduction in the size of a population (as of a species) that results in a decrease in genetic variation **3 :** a style of guitar playing in which glissando effects are produced by sliding an object (as a knife blade or the neck of a bottle) along the strings — called also *bottleneck guitar*
[3]**bottleneck** *vt* (1933) **:** to slow or halt by causing a bottleneck
bot·tle–nosed dolphin \ˈbä-tᵊl-ˌnōz-\ *n* (ca. 1909) **:** BOTTLENOSE DOLPHIN
bottlenose dolphin *n* (1940) **:** a relatively small stout-bodied chiefly gray toothed whale (*Tursiops truncatus*) with a prominent beak and falcate dorsal fin
bot·tling \ˈbä-tᵊl-iŋ, ˈbät-liŋ\ *n* (1954) **:** a beverage and esp. a wine that is bottled at a particular time
[1]**bot·tom** \ˈbä-təm\ *n* [ME *botme,* fr. OE *botm;* akin to OHG *bodam* bottom, L *fundus,* Gk *pythmēn*] (bef. 12c) **1 a :** the underside of something **b :** a surface (as the seat of a chair) designed to support something resting on it — used figuratively in phrases like *the bottom dropped out* to describe a sudden collapse or downturn ⟨lost millions when the ~ dropped out of the stock market⟩ **c :** the posterior end of the trunk **:** BUTTOCKS, RUMP **2 :** the surface on which a body of water lies **3 a :** the part of a ship's hull lying below the water **b :** BOAT, SHIP **4 a :** the lowest part or place ⟨the ~ of the page⟩ **b :** the remotest or inmost point **c :** the lowest or last place in point of precedence ⟨started work at the ~⟩ **d :** the part of a garment worn on the lower part of the body; *esp* **:** the pants of pajamas — usu. used in pl. **e :** the last half of an inning of baseball **f :** the bass or baritone instruments of a band **5 :** BOTTOMLAND — usu. used in pl. **6 :** BASIS, SOURCE ⟨trying to get to the ~ of these rumors⟩ **7 :** capacity (as of a horse) to endure strain **8 :** a foundation color applied to textile fibers before dyeing **9 :** a fundamental quark that accounts for the existence and lifetime of upsilon particles and has an electric charge of −⅓ and a measured energy of approximately 5 GeV; *also* **:** the flavor characterizing this particle — **bot·tomed** \-təmd\ *adj* — **at bottom :** REALLY, BASICALLY
[2]**bottom** *vt* (1520) **1 :** to furnish with a bottom **2 :** to provide a foundation for **3 :** to bring to the bottom **4 :** to get to the bottom of ~ *vi* **1 :** to become based **2 :** to reach the bottom **3 :** to reach a point where a decline is halted or reversed — usu. used with *out* ⟨the team *bottomed* out in last place⟩ — **bot·tom·er** *n*
[3]**bottom** *adj* (1561) **1 :** of, relating to, or situated at the bottom ⟨~ rock⟩ **2 :** frequenting the bottom ⟨~ fish⟩
bot·tom–feed·er \ˈbä-təm-ˌfē-dər\ *n* (1885) **1 :** a fish that feeds at the bottom **2 :** one that is of the lowest status or rank **3 :** an opportunist who seeks quick profit usu. at the expense of others or from their misfortune — **bot·tom–feed·ing** \-diŋ\ *adj*
bot·tom–fish·ing \-ˌfi-shiŋ\ *n* (1975) **:** the practice of making purchases (as of stocks) when prices appear to be at their lowest point — **bot·tom–fish·er** \-shər\ *n*
bot·tom·land \ˈbä-təm-ˌland\ *n* (1728) **:** low-lying land along a watercourse — often used in pl. ⟨the fertile ~*s*⟩
bot·tom·less \-ləs\ *adj* (14c) **1 :** having no bottom ⟨a ~ chair⟩ **2 a :** extremely deep **b :** impossible to comprehend **:** UNFATHOMABLE ⟨a ~ mystery⟩ **c :** BOUNDLESS, UNLIMITED **3 a** [fr. the absence of lower as well as upper garments] **:** NUDE ⟨~ dancers⟩ **b :** featuring nude entertainers — **bot·tom·less·ly** *adv* — **bot·tom·less·ness** *n*
bot·tom–line \ˈbä-təm-ˌlīn\ *adj* (1972) **1 :** concerned only with cost or profits **2 :** PRAGMATIC, REALISTIC — **bot·tom–lin·er** \-ˌlī-nər\ *n*
bottom line *n* (1967) **1 a :** the essential or salient point **:** CRUX **b :** the primary or most important consideration **2 a :** the line at the bottom of a financial report that shows the net profit or loss **b :** financial considerations (as cost or profit or loss) **c :** the final result
bot·tom·most \ˈbä-tə(m)-ˌmōst\ *adj* (1855) **1 a :** situated at the very bottom **:** LOWEST, DEEPEST **b :** LAST ⟨the ~ part of the day —Alfred Kazin⟩ **2 :** most basic ⟨the ~ problems facing the world⟩
bottom round *n* (1923) **:** meat (as steak) from the outer part of a round of beef
bot·tom–up \ˈbä-təm-ˈəp\ *adj* (1976) **:** progressing upward from the lowest levels (as of a stratified organization or system) ⟨~ management⟩
bot·u·lin \ˈbä-chə-lən\ *n* [prob. fr. NL *botulinum*] (ca. 1900) **:** BOTULINUM TOXIN
bot·u·li·num \ˌbä-chə-ˈlī-nəm\ *also* **bot·u·li·nus** \-nəs\ *n* [NL, fr. L *botulus* sausage] (1902) **:** a spore-forming bacterium (*Clostridium botulinum*) that secretes botulinum toxin — **bot·u·li·nal** \-ˈlī-nᵊl\ *adj*
botulinum toxin *n* (1928) **:** a neurotoxin formed by botulinum that causes botulism and that is injected in a purified form for therapeutic and cosmetic purposes (as to treat blepharospasm and reduce wrinkles)
bot·u·lism \ˈbä-chə-ˌli-zəm\ *n* (1887) **:** an acute paralytic disease caused by botulinum toxin esp. in food
bou·bou \ˈbü-ˌbü\ *n* [F, fr. Malinke *bubu*] (1961) **:** a long flowing garment worn in parts of Africa
bou·chée \bü-ˈshā\ *n* [F, lit., mouthful, fr. OF *buchiee,* fr. VL **buccata,* fr. L *bucca* cheek, mouth] (1846) **:** a small patty shell usu. containing a creamed filling

\ə\ **a**but \ᵊ\ kitten, F table \ər\ **fur**ther \a\ **a**sh \ā\ **a**ce \ä\ m**o**p, m**a**r \au̇\ **ou**t \ch\ **ch**in \e\ b**e**t \ē\ **ea**sy \g\ **g**o \i\ h**i**t \ī\ **i**ce \j\ **j**ob \ŋ\ si**ng** \ō\ g**o** \ȯ\ l**aw** \ȯi\ b**oy** \th\ **th**in \t͟h\ **th**e \ü\ l**oo**t \u̇\ f**oo**t \y\ **y**et \zh\ vi**s**ion, bei**ge** \k, ⁿ, œ, ue, ʸ\ *see* Guide to Pronunciation

bou·clé *or* **bou·cle** \bü-ˈklā\ *n* [F *bouclé* curly, fr. pp. of *boucler* to curl, fr. *bocle* buckle, curl] (1886) **1 :** an uneven yarn of three plies one of which forms loops at intervals **2 :** a fabric of bouclé yarn

bou·din \bü-ˈdan, -ˈda^n\ *n, pl* **bou·dins** \-ˈdanz, -ˈda^n\ [LaF & F, sausage] (1845) **1 :** BLOOD SAUSAGE **2 :** a spicy Cajun sausage containing rice and meat (as pork) or seafood

bou·doir \ˈbü-ˌdwär, ˈbu̇-, ˌbü-ˈ, ˌbu̇-ˈ\ *n* [F, fr. *bouder* to pout] (1781) **:** a woman's dressing room, bedroom, or private sitting room

bouf·fant \bü-ˈfänt, ˈbü-ˌ\ *adj* [F, fr. MF, fr. prp. of *bouffer* to puff] (1832) **:** puffed out ⟨~ hairdos⟩ ⟨a ~ veil⟩

bou·gain·vil·lea *also* **bou·gain·vil·laea** \ˌbü-gən-ˈvil-yə, ˌbō-, ˌbu̇-, -ˈvē-ə\ *n* [NL, fr. Louis Antoine de *Bougainville*] (1849) **:** any of a genus (*Bougainvillaea*) of the four-o'clock family of ornamental tropical American woody vines and shrubs with brilliant purple or red floral bracts

bough \ˈbau̇\ *n* [ME, shoulder, bough, fr. OE *bōg;* akin to OHG *buog* shoulder, Gk *pēchys* forearm] (bef. 12c) **:** a branch of a tree; *esp* **:** a main branch — **boughed** \ˈbau̇d\ *adj*

[1]**bought** \ˈbȯt\ *past and past part of* BUY

[2]**bought** *adj* [pp. of *buy*] (1599) **:** STORE 2 ⟨~ clothes⟩

bought·en \ˈbȯ-tᵊn\ *adj* [*bought* + *-en* (as in *forgotten*)] (1738) *chiefly dial* **:** BOUGHT ⟨the only ~ carpet in the region —H. W. Thompson⟩

bou·gie \ˈbü-ˌzhē, -ˌjē\ *n* [F, fr. *Bougie,* seaport in Algeria] (1755) **1 :** a wax candle **2 a :** a tapering cylindrical instrument for introduction into a tubular passage of the body **b :** SUPPOSITORY

bouil·la·baisse \ˌbü-yə-ˈbās, -ˈbāz, ˈbü-yə-ˌ, -ˌbāz\ *n* [F] (1855) **1 :** a highly seasoned fish stew made with at least two kinds of fish **2 :** POTPOURRI 2

bouil·lon \ˈbü(l)-ˌyän, ˈbu̇(l)-; ˈbu̇l-yən; ˈbü-ˌyō^n\ *n* [F, fr. OF *boillon,* fr. *boillir* to boil] (ca. 1656) **:** a clear seasoned soup made usu. from lean beef; *broadly* **:** BROTH

bouillon cube *n* (ca. 1922) **:** a cube of evaporated meat extract

boul·der *also* **bowl·der** \ˈbōl-dər\ *n* [short for *boulder stone,* fr. ME *bulder ston,* part trans. of a word of Scand origin; akin to Sw dial. *bullersten* large stone in a stream, fr. *buller* noise + *sten* stone] (1617) **:** a detached and rounded or much-worn mass of rock — **boul·dered** \-dərd\ *adj* — **boul·dery** \-d(ə-)rē\ *adj*

boul·der·ing \-d(ə-)riŋ\ *n* (1920) **:** the sport of rock climbing on large boulders or low cliffs — **boulder** *vi* — **boul·der·er** \-d(ə-)rər\ *n*

[1]**bou·le** \ˈbü-(ˌ)lē, bü-ˈlā\ *n* [Gk *boulē,* lit., will, fr. *boulesthai* to wish] (1840) **:** a legislative council of ancient Greece consisting first of an aristocratic advisory body and later of a representative senate

[2]**boule** \ˈbül\ *n* [F, ball — more at BOWL] (1918) **:** a synthetically formed mass (as of sapphire) with the atomic structure of a single crystal

bou·le·vard \ˈbu̇-lə-ˌvärd, ˈbü- *also* ˈbə-\ *n* [F, modif. of MD *bolwerc* bulwark] (1768) **:** a broad often landscaped thoroughfare

bou·le·vard·ier \ˌbu̇-lə-ˌvär-ˈdyā, ˌbü-, -ˈdir\ *n* [F, fr. *boulevard*] (1871) **:** a frequenter of the Parisian boulevards; *broadly* **:** MAN-ABOUT-TOWN

bou·le·ver·se·ment \bül-ver-sə-mä^n\ *n* [F] (1782) **1 :** REVERSAL **2 :** a violent disturbance **:** DISORDER

boulle *or* **buhl** \ˈbül, ˈbyül\ *n* [André Charles *Boulle* †1732 Fr. cabinetmaker] (1823) **:** inlaid decoration of tortoiseshell, yellow metal, and white metal in cabinetwork

[1]**bounce** \ˈbau̇n(t)s\ *vb* **bounced; bounc·ing** [ME *bounsen*] *vt* (13c) **1** *obs* **:** BEAT, BUMP **2 :** to cause to rebound or be reflected ⟨~ a ball⟩ ⟨~ a light ray off a reflector⟩ **3 a :** DISMISS, FIRE **b :** to expel precipitately from a place **c :** to eliminate from a competition by defeating ⟨was *bounced* from the tournament in the first round⟩ **4 :** to issue (a check) drawn on an account with insufficient funds **5 :** to present (as an idea) to another person to elicit comments or to gain approval — usu. used with *off* ~ *vi* **1 :** to rebound or reflect after striking a surface (as the ground) **2 :** to recover from a blow or a defeat quickly — usu. used with *back* **3 :** to be returned by a bank because of insufficient funds in a checking account ⟨his checks ~⟩ **4 a :** to leap suddenly **:** BOUND **b :** to walk with springing steps **5 :** to hit a baseball so that it hits the ground before it reaches an infielder

[2]**bounce** *n* (1523) **1 a :** a sudden leap or bound **b :** REBOUND **2 :** BLUSTER **3 :** VERVE, LIVELINESS

bounc·er \ˈbau̇n(t)-sər\ *n* (1865) **:** one that bounces: as **a :** one employed to restrain or eject disorderly persons **b :** a bouncing ground ball

bounc·ing \-siŋ\ *adj* (ca. 1563) **1 :** LIVELY, ANIMATED **2 :** enjoying good health **:** ROBUST — **bounc·ing·ly** \-siŋ-lē\ *adv*

bouncing bet \-ˈbet\ *n, often cap 2d B* [fr. *Bet,* nickname for *Elizabeth*] (ca. 1818) **:** a European perennial herb (*Saponaria officinalis*) of the pink family that is widely naturalized in the U.S. and has pink or white flowers and leaves which yield a detergent when bruised — called also *soapwort*

bouncy \ˈbau̇n(t)-sē\ *adj* **bounc·i·er; -est** (1921) **1 :** BUOYANT, EXUBERANT **2 :** RESILIENT **3 :** marked by or producing bounces — **bounc·i·ly** \-sə-lē\ *adv*

[1]**bound** \ˈbau̇nd\ *adj* [ME *boun,* fr. ON *būinn,* pp. of *būa* to dwell, prepare; akin to OHG *būan* to dwell — more at BOWER] (13c) **1** *archaic* **:** READY **2 :** intending to go **:** GOING ⟨~ for home⟩ ⟨college-*bound*⟩

[2]**bound** *n* [ME, fr. AF *bounde, bodne,* fr. ML *bodina*] (13c) **1 a :** a limiting line **:** BOUNDARY — usu. used in pl. **b :** something that limits or restrains ⟨beyond the ~*s* of decency⟩ **2** *usu pl* **a :** BORDERLAND **b :** the land within certain bounds **3 :** a number greater than or equal to every number in a set (as the range of a function); *also* **:** a number less than or equal to every number in a set

[3]**bound** *past and past part of* BIND

[4]**bound** *vt* (14c) **1 :** to set limits or bounds to **:** CONFINE **2 :** to form the boundary of **:** ENCLOSE **3 :** to name the boundaries of

[5]**bound** *adj* [ME *bounden,* fr. pp. of *binden* to bind] (14c) **1 :** placed under legal or moral restraint or obligation **:** OBLIGED ⟨duty-*bound*⟩ **2 a :** fastened by or as if by a band **:** CONFINED ⟨desk-*bound*⟩ **b :** very likely **:** SURE ⟨~ to rain soon⟩ **3 :** made costive **:** CONSTIPATED **4** *of a book* **:** secured to the covers by cords, tapes, or glue **5 :** DETERMINED, RESOLVED **6 :** held in chemical or physical combination **7 :** always occurring in combination with another linguistic form ⟨*un-* in *unknown* and *-er* in *speaker* are ~ forms⟩ — compare FREE 11d

[6]**bound** *n* [MF *bond,* fr. *bondir* to leap, fr. VL **bombitire* to hum, fr. L *bombus* deep hollow sound — more at BOMB] (ca. 1553) **1 :** LEAP, JUMP **2 :** the action of rebounding **:** BOUNCE

[7]**bound** *vi* (1592) **1 :** to move by leaping **2 :** REBOUND, BOUNCE

bound·ary \ˈbau̇n-d(ə-)rē\ *n, pl* **-aries** [[2]*bound* + [1]*-ary*] (1598) **:** something that indicates or fixes a limit or extent — **bound·ary·less** \-ləs\ *adj* — **bound·ary·less·ness** *n*

boundary layer *n* (1921) **:** a region of retarded fluid near the surface of a body which moves through a fluid or past which a fluid moves

bound·ed \ˈbau̇n-dəd\ *adj* (1956) **:** having a mathematical bound or bounds ⟨a set ~ above by 25 and ~ below by −10⟩

bound·ed·ness \ˈbau̇n-dəd-nəs\ *n* (1674) **:** the quality or state of being bounded

bound·en \ˈbau̇n-dən\ *adj* [ME] (14c) **1** *archaic* **:** being under obligation **:** BEHOLDEN **2 :** made obligatory **:** BINDING ⟨our ~ duty⟩

bound·er \-dər\ *n* (1505) **1 :** one that bounds **2 :** a man of objectionable social behavior **:** CAD — **bound·er·ish** \-d(ə-)rish\ *adj*

bound·less \ˈbau̇n(d)-ləs\ *adj* (1592) **:** having no boundaries **:** VAST ⟨~ possibilities⟩ — **bound·less·ly** *adv* — **bound·less·ness** *n*

bound up *adj* (1611) **:** closely involved or associated — usu. used with *with* ⟨his life was *bound up* with the town's history⟩

boun·te·ous \ˈbau̇n-tē-əs\ *adj* [ME *bountevous, bounteuous,* fr. AF *bontive* kind, fr. *bunté*] (14c) **1 :** giving or disposed to give freely **2 :** liberally bestowed — **boun·te·ous·ly** *adv* — **boun·te·ous·ness** *n*

boun·tied \ˈbau̇n-tēd\ *adj* (1788) **1 :** having the benefit of a bounty **2 :** rewarded or rewardable by a bounty

boun·ti·ful \ˈbau̇n-ti-fəl\ *adj* (1508) **1 :** liberal in bestowing gifts or favors **2 :** given or provided abundantly ⟨a ~ harvest⟩ ***syn*** see LIBERAL — **boun·ti·ful·ly** \-f(ə-)lē\ *adv* — **boun·ti·ful·ness** \-fəl-nəs\ *n*

boun·ty \ˈbau̇n-tē\ *n, pl* **bounties** [ME *bounte* goodness, fr. AF *bunté, bountee,* fr. L *bonitat-, bonitas,* fr. *bonus* good, fr. OL *duenos;* akin to Skt *duva* reverence, favor] (13c) **1 :** something that is given generously **2 :** liberality in giving **:** GENEROSITY **3 :** yield esp. of a crop **4 :** a reward, premium, or subsidy esp. when offered or given by a government: as **a :** an extra allowance to induce entry into the armed services **b :** a grant to encourage an industry **c :** a payment to encourage the destruction of noxious animals **d :** a payment for the capture of or assistance in the capture of an outlaw

bounty hunter *n* (1930) **1 :** one who tracks down and captures outlaws for whom a reward is offered **2 :** one who hunts predatory animals for the reward offered

bou·quet \bō-ˈkā, bü-\ *n* [F, fr. MF, thicket, bunch of flowers, fr. OF (Norman-Picard dial.) *bosquet* thicket, fr. OF *bosc* forest — more at BOSCAGE] (1701) **1 a :** flowers picked and fastened together in a bunch **:** NOSEGAY **b :** MEDLEY ⟨a ~ of songs⟩ **2 :** COMPLIMENT **3 a :** a distinctive and characteristic fragrance (as of wine) **b :** a subtle aroma or quality (as of an artistic performance)

bou·quet gar·ni \-gär-ˈnē\ *n, pl* **bou·quets gar·nis** \-ˈkā(z)-gär-ˈnē\ [F, lit., garnished bouquet] (ca. 1852) **:** an herb mixture that is either tied together or enclosed in a porous container and is cooked with a dish but removed before serving

bour·bon \ˈbu̇r-bən, ˈbȯr-; *usu* ˈbər- *in sense 3*\ *n* [*Bourbon,* seigniory in France] (1596) **1** *cap* **:** a member of a French family founded in 1272 to which belong the rulers of France from 1589 to 1793 and from 1814 to 1830, of Spain from 1700 to 1808, from 1814 to 1868, from 1875 to 1931, and from 1975, of Naples from 1735 to 1805, and of the Two Sicilies from 1815 to 1860 **2** [*Bourbon* (now Réunion), French island in the Indian Ocean] **:** a rose (*Rosa borboniana*) of upright growth with shining leaves, prickly branches, and clustered large flowers **3** [*Bourbon* County, Kentucky] **:** a whiskey distilled from a mash made up of not less than 51 percent corn plus malt and rye — compare CORN WHISKEY **4** *often cap* **:** a person who clings obstinately to old social and political ideas; *specif* **:** an extremely conservative member of the U.S. Democratic party usu. from the South — **bour·bon·ism** \-bə-ˌnizəm\ *n, often cap*

bourg \ˈbu̇r(g)\ *n* [ME, fr. AF *burc, borghe,* fr. L *burgus* fortified place, of Gmc origin; akin to OHG *burg* fortified place — more at BOROUGH] (12c) **:** TOWN, VILLAGE: as **a :** one neighboring a castle **b :** a market town

[1]**bour·geois** \ˈbu̇rzh-ˌwä *also* ˈbu̇zh- *or* ˈbüzh- *or* bu̇rzh-ˈ\ *adj* [MF, fr. OF *burgeis* townsman, fr. *burc, borg* town, fr. L *burgus*] (ca. 1565) **1 :** of, relating to, or characteristic of the townsman or of the social middle class **2 :** marked by a concern for material interests and respectability and a tendency toward mediocrity **3 :** dominated by commercial and industrial interests **:** CAPITALISTIC — **bour·geois·ifi·ca·tion** \ˌbu̇(r)zh-ˌwä-zə-fə-ˈkā-shən\ *n* — **bour·geois·ify** \bu̇(r)zh-ˈwä-zə-ˌfī\ *vb*

[2]**bourgeois** *n, pl* **bourgeois** \-ˌwä(z), -ˈwä(z)\ (ca. 1674) **1 a :** BURGHER **b :** a middle-class person **2 :** a person with social behavior and political views held to be influenced by private-property interest **:** CAPITALIST **3** *pl* **:** BOURGEOISIE

bour·geoise \ˈbu̇rzh-ˌwäz *also* ˈbu̇zh- *or* ˈbüzh- *or* bu̇rzh-ˈ\ *n* [F, fem. of *bourgeois*] (1794) **:** a woman of the middle class

bour·geoi·sie \ˌbu̇(r)zh-ˌwä-ˈzē\ *n* [F, fr. *bourgeois*] (1707) **1 :** MIDDLE CLASS; *also, pl in constr* **:** members of the middle class **2 :** a social order dominated by bourgeois

bourgeon *var of* BURGEON

bour·gui·gnonne \ˌbu̇r-gēn-ˈyȯn\ *or* **bour·gui·gnon** \-ˈyō^n\ *adj, often cap* [F, fr. *Bourgogne* Burgundy] (1936) **:** prepared or served in the manner of Burgundy (as with a sauce made with red wine) ⟨beef ~⟩

bourn *or* **bourne** \ˈbȯrn, ˈbu̇rn\ *n* [ME *burn, bourne* — more at BURN] (12c) **:** STREAM, BROOK

bourne *also* **bourn** *n* [MF *bourne,* fr. OF *bodne* — more at BOUND] (1523) **1 :** BOUNDARY, LIMIT **2 :** GOAL, DESTINATION

bour·rée \bu̇-ˈrā, ˈbü-ˌ\ *n* [F] (1706) **1 :** a 17th century French dance usu. in quick duple time; *also* **:** a musical composition with the rhythm of this dance **2 :** PAS DE BOURRÉE

bour·ride \bu̇-ˈrēd, bə-\ *n* [F, fr. Occitan *bourrido,* alter. of *boulido* something boiled, fr. *bouli* to boil, fr. L *bullire* — more at BOIL] (1872) **:** a fish stew similar to bouillabaisse that is usu. thickened with egg yolks and strongly flavored with garlic

bourse \ˈbu̇rs\ *n* [MF, lit., purse, fr. ML *bursa* — more at PURSE] (1597) **1 :** EXCHANGE 5a; *specif* **:** a European stock exchange **2 :** a sale of numismatic or philatelic items on tables (as at a convention)

bou·stro·phe·don \ˌbü-strə-ˈfē-ˌdän, -dᵊn\ *n* [Gk *boustrophēdon,* adv., lit., turning like oxen in plowing, fr. *bous* ox, cow + *strephein* to turn — more at COW] (1699) **:** the writing of alternate lines in opposite directions (as from left to right and from right to left) — **boustrophedon** *adj or adv* — **bou·stro·phe·don·ic** \-fē-ˈdä-nik\ *adj*

bout \ˈbau̇t\ *n* [E dial., a trip going and returning in plowing, fr. ME *bought* bend] (1575) **:** a spell of activity: as **a :** an athletic match (as of boxing) **b :** OUTBREAK, ATTACK ⟨a ~ of pneumonia⟩ **c :** SESSION

bou·tique \bü-ˈtēk\ *n, often attrib* [F, shop, prob. fr. Old Occitan *botica,* ultim. fr. Gk *apothēkē* storehouse — more at APOTHECARY] (1767) **1 a :** a small fashionable shop **b :** a small shop within a large department store **2 :** a small company that offers highly specialized services or products ⟨~ wineries⟩ ⟨an independent investment ~⟩ — **bou·tiqu·ey** \-ˈtē-kē\ *adj*

bou·ton·niere \ˌbü-t^{ə}n-ˈir, ˌbü-tən-ˈyer\ *n* [F *boutonnière* buttonhole, fr. MF, fr. *bouton* button] (ca. 1867) **:** a flower or bouquet worn in a buttonhole

Bou·vi·er des Flan·dres \ˌbü-vē-ˌā-də-ˈflan-dərz, -ˈflä^{n}dr^ə\ *n, pl* **Bouvier des Flandres** *or* **Bou·vi·ers des Flandres** \ˌbü-vē-ˌāz-\ [F, lit., cowherd of Flanders] (1929) **:** any of a breed of large powerfully built rough-coated dogs of Belgian origin used esp. for herding and in guard work — called also *Bouvier*

bou·zou·ki \bü-ˈzü-kē\ *n, pl* **-kis** *also* **-kia** \-kē-ə\ [ModGk *mpouzouki*] (1952) **:** a long-necked stringed instrument of Greek origin that resembles a mandolin

bo·vid \ˈbō-vəd\ *n* [NL *Bovidae,* fr. *Bov-, Bos,* type genus, fr. L *bov-, bos*] (1939) **:** any of a family (Bovidae) of ruminants that have hollow unbranched permanently attached horns present in usu. both sexes and that include antelopes, oxen, sheep, and goats

[1]**bo·vine** \ˈbō-ˌvīn, -ˌvēn\ *adj* [LL *bovinus,* fr. L *bov-, bos* ox, cow — more at COW] (1776) **1 :** of, relating to, or resembling bovines and esp. the ox or cow **2 :** having qualities (as placidity or dullness) characteristic of oxen or cows — **bo·vine·ly** *adv* — **bo·vin·i·ty** \bō-ˈvi-nə-tē\ *n*

[2]**bovine** *n* (1852) **:** any of a subfamily (Bovinae) of bovids including oxen, bison, buffalo, and their close relatives

bovine spongiform encephalopathy *n* (1987) **:** a fatal prion disease of cattle that affects the nervous system, resembles or is identical to scrapie of sheep and goats, and is prob. transmitted by infected tissue in food — abbr. *BSE*; called also *mad cow disease*

[1]**bow** \ˈbau̇\ *vb* [ME, fr. OE *būgan;* akin to OHG *biogan* to bend, Skt *bhujati* he bends] *vi* (bef. 12c) **1 :** to cease from competition or resistance **:** SUBMIT, YIELD ⟨refusing to ~ to the inevitable —John O'Hara⟩; *also* **:** to suffer defeat ⟨~*ed* to the champion⟩ **2 :** to bend the head, body, or knee in reverence, submission, or shame **3 :** to incline the head or body in salutation or assent or to acknowledge applause **4 :** DEBUT ⟨the play will ~ next month⟩ ~ *vt* **1 :** to cause to incline **2 :** to incline (as the head) esp. in respect or submission **3 :** to crush with a heavy burden **4 a :** to express by bowing **b :** to usher in or out with a bow

[2]**bow** *n* (ca. 1656) **:** a bending of the head or body in respect, submission, assent, or salutation; *also* **:** a show of respect or submission

[3]**bow** \ˈbō\ *n* [ME *bowe,* fr. OE *boga;* akin to OE *būgan*] (bef. 12c) **1 a :** something bent into a simple curve **b :** RAINBOW **2 :** a weapon that is made of a strip of flexible material (as wood) with a cord connecting the two ends and holding the strip bent and that is used to propel an arrow **3 :** ARCHER **4 a :** a metal ring or loop forming a handle (as of a key) **b :** a knot formed by doubling a ribbon or string into two or more loops **c :** BOW TIE 1 **d :** a frame for the lenses of eyeglasses; *also* **:** the sidepiece of the frame passing over the ear **5 a :** a wooden rod with horsehairs stretched from end to end used in playing an instrument of the viol or violin family **b :** a stroke of such a bow

[4]**bow** \ˈbō\ *vi* (bef. 12c) **1 :** to bend into a curve **2 :** to play a stringed musical instrument with a bow ~ *vt* **1 :** to cause to bend into a curve **2 :** to play (a stringed instrument) with a bow

[5]**bow** \ˈbau̇\ *n* [ME *bowe, bowgh,* prob. fr. MD *boech* bow, shoulder; akin to OE *bōg* bough] (15c) **1 :** the forward part of a ship — often used in pl. ⟨crossing the ~*s*⟩ **2 :** [2]BOWMAN

Bow bells \ˈbō-\ *n pl* (1567) **:** the bells of the Church of St. Mary-le-Bow in London

bowd·ler·ise *Brit var of* BOWDLERIZE

bowd·ler·ize \ˈbōd-lə-ˌrīz, ˈbau̇d-\ *vt* **-ized; -iz·ing** [Thomas *Bowdler* †1825 Eng. editor] (1836) **1 :** to expurgate (as a book) by omitting or modifying parts considered vulgar **2 :** to modify by abridging, simplifying, or distorting in style or content — **bowd·ler·i·za·tion** \ˌbōd-lə-rə-ˈzā-shən, ˌbau̇d-\ *n* — **bowd·ler·iz·er** *n*

[1]**bowed** \ˈbau̇d\ *adj* [pp. of [1]*bow*] (14c) **1 :** bent downward and forward ⟨listened with ~ heads⟩ **2 :** having the back and head inclined

[2]**bowed** \ˈbōd\ *adj* [partly fr. [3]*bow* + *-ed;* partly fr. pp. of [4]*bow*] (15c) **:** furnished with or shaped like a bow

bow·el \ˈbau̇(-ə)l\ *n* [ME, fr. AF *buel, boel,* fr. ML *botellus,* fr. L, dim. of *botulus* sausage] (14c) **1 :** INTESTINE, GUT; *also* **:** one of the divisions of the intestines — usu. used in pl. except in medical use ⟨the large ~⟩ ⟨move your ~*s*⟩ **2** *archaic* **:** the seat of pity, tenderness, or courage — usu. used in pl. **3** *pl* **:** the interior parts; *esp* **:** the deep or remote parts ⟨~*s* of the earth⟩ — **bow·el·less** \ˈbau̇(-ə)l-ləs\ *adj*

[1]**bow·er** \ˈbau̇(-ə)r\ *n* [ME *bour* dwelling, fr. OE *būr;* akin to OE & OHG *būan* to dwell, OE *bēon* to be — more at BE] (bef. 12c) **1 :** an attractive dwelling or retreat **2 :** a lady's private apartment in a medieval hall or castle **3 :** a shelter (as in a garden) made with tree boughs or vines twined together **:** ARBOR — **bow·ery** \-ē\ *adj*

[2]**bower** *vt* (1592) **:** EMBOWER, ENCLOSE

[3]**bower** *n* (1652) **:** an anchor carried at the bow of a ship

bow·er·bird \ˈbau̇(-ə)r-ˌbərd\ *n* (1845) **:** any of a family (Ptilonorhynchidae) of passerine birds of Australia and New Guinea in which the male builds a chamber or passage arched over with twigs and grasses, often adorned with bright-colored objects, and used esp. to attract the female

bow·ery \ˈbau̇(-ə)r-ē\ *n, pl* **-er·ies** [D *bouwerij,* fr. *bouwer* farmer, fr. *bouwen* to till; akin to OHG *būan* to dwell] (1650) **1 :** a colonial Dutch plantation or farm **2** [*Bowery,* street in New York City] **:** a city district known for cheap bars and derelicts

bow·fin \ˈbō-ˌfin\ *n* (1845) **:** a predaceous dull-green iridescent No. American freshwater fish (*Amia calva*) that is the only surviving member of an order (Amiiformes) dating back to the Jurassic

bow·front \-ˌfrənt\ *adj* (1918) **1 :** having an outward curving front ⟨~ furniture⟩ **2 :** having a bow window in front ⟨~ houses⟩

bow·head whale \-ˌhed-\ *n* (1887) **:** a baleen whale (*Balaena mysticetus*) of arctic and subarctic seas — called also *bowhead*

bow·ie knife \ˈbü-ē-, ˈbō-\ *n* [James *Bowie*] (1836) **:** a stout single-edged hunting knife with part of the back edge curved concavely to a point and sharpened

bow·ing \ˈbō-iŋ\ *n* (1838) **:** the technique or manner of managing the bow in playing a stringed musical instrument

bow·knot \ˈbō-ˌnät\ *n* (1547) **:** a knot with decorative loops

[1]**bowl** \ˈbōl\ *n* [ME *bolle,* fr. OE *bolla;* akin to OHG *bolla* blister] (bef. 12c) **1 :** a concave usu. nearly hemispherical vessel; *specif* **:** a drinking vessel (as for wine) **2 :** the contents of a bowl **3 :** a bowl-shaped or concave part: as **a :** the hollow of a spoon or tobacco pipe **b :** the receptacle of a toilet **4 a :** a natural formation or geographical region shaped like a bowl **b :** a bowl-shaped structure; *esp* **:** an athletic stadium **5 :** a postseason football game between specially invited teams — **bowled** \ˈbōld\ *adj* — **bowl·ful** \-ˌfu̇l\ *n*

[2]**bowl** *n* [ME *boule,* fr. MF, fr. L *bulla* bubble] (15c) **1 a :** a ball (as of lignum vitae) weighted or shaped to give it a bias when rolled in lawn bowling **b** *pl but sing in constr* **:** LAWN BOWLING **2 :** a delivery of the ball in bowling **3 :** a cylindrical roller or drum (as for a machine)

[3]**bowl** *vi* (15c) **1 a :** to participate in a game of bowling **b :** to roll a ball in bowling **2 :** to travel smoothly and rapidly (as in a wheeled vehicle) ~ *vt* **1 a :** to roll (a ball) in bowling **b (1) :** to complete by bowling ⟨~ a string⟩ **(2) :** to score by bowling ⟨~*s* 150⟩ **2 :** to strike with a swiftly moving object

bowlder *var of* BOULDER

bow·leg \ˈbō-ˌleg, -ˌlāg, ˈbō-ˈ\ *n* (1656) **:** a leg bowed outward at or below the knee — **bow·legged** \ˈbō-ˌle-gəd, -ˌlā-; -ˌlegd, -ˌlāgd\ *adj*

[1]**bowl·er** \ˈbō-lər\ *n* (ca. 1500) **:** a person who bowls; *specif* **:** the player who delivers the ball to the batsman in cricket

[2]**bow·ler** \ˈbō-lər\ *n* [*Bowler,* 19th cent. family of Eng. hatters] (1861) **:** DERBY 3

bow·line \ˈbō-lən, -ˌlīn\ *n* [ME *boweline,* prob. fr. *bowe* bow + *line*] (13c) **1 :** a rope used to keep the weather edge of a square sail taut forward **2 :** a knot used to form a loop that neither slips nor jams — see KNOT illustration

bowl·ing \ˈbō-liŋ\ *n* (1535) **:** any of several games in which balls are rolled on a green or down an alley at an object or group of objects

bowl over *vt* (1867) **1 :** to take unawares **2 :** [1]IMPRESS 2

[1]**bow·man** \ˈbō-mən\ *n* (13c) **:** ARCHER 1

[2]**bow·man** \ˈbau̇-mən\ *n* (1829) **:** a boatman, oarsman, or paddler stationed in the front of a boat

Bow·man's capsule \ˈbō-mənz-\ *n* [Sir William *Bowman* †1892 Eng. surgeon] (ca. 1860) **:** a thin membranous double-walled capsule surrounding the glomerulus of a vertebrate nephron

bow out *vi* (1942) **:** RETIRE, WITHDRAW; *also* **:** LOSE ⟨*bowed out* in the first round of the tournament⟩

bow saw \ˈbō-\ *n* (1677) **:** a saw having a narrow blade held under tension by a light bow-shaped frame

bowse \ˈbau̇z\ *vb* **bowsed; bows·ing** [origin unknown] *vt* (1593) **:** to haul by means of a tackle ~ *vi* **:** to bowse something

bow shock \ˈbau̇-\ *n* (1950) **:** the shock wave formed by the collision of a stellar wind with another medium (as the magnetosphere of a planet)

bow·sprit \ˈbau̇-ˌsprit, *Brit usu* ˈbō-\ *n* [ME *bouspret,* prob. fr. MLG *boochspreet,* fr. *booch* bow + *spreet* pole] (13c) **:** a large spar projecting forward from the stem of a ship

bow·string \ˈbō-ˌstriŋ\ *n* (14c) **:** a waxed or sized cord joining the ends of a shooting bow

bowstring hemp *n* (ca. 1858) **:** any of various Asian and African sansevierias; *also* **:** its soft tough leaf fiber used esp. in cordage

bow tie \ˈbō-\ *n* (1897) **1 :** a short necktie tied in a bowknot **2 :** something (as pasta) resembling a bow tie in shape

bow window \ˈbō-\ *n* (1679) **:** a usu. curved bay window

bow·wow \ˈbau̇-ˌwau̇, bau̇-ˈ\ *n* [imit.] (1576) **1 :** the bark of a dog; *also* **:** DOG **2 :** noisy clamor **3 :** arrogant dogmatic manner

bow·yer \ˈbō-yər\ *n* [ME *bowyere*] (14c) **:** a maker of shooting bows

[1]**box** \ˈbäks\ *n, pl* **box** *or* **box·es** [ME, fr. OE, fr. L *buxus,* fr. Gk *pyxos*] (bef. 12c) **:** an evergreen shrub or small tree (genus *Buxus* of the family Buxaceae, the box family) with opposite entire leaves and capsular fruits; *esp* **:** a widely cultivated shrub (*B. sempervirens*) used for hedges, borders, and topiary figures

[2]**box** *n* [ME, fr. OE, fr. LL *buxis,* fr. Gk *pyxis,* fr. *pyxos* box tree] (bef. 12c) **1 :** a rigid typically rectangular container with or without a cover ⟨a cigar ~⟩: as **a :** an open cargo container of a vehicle **b :** COFFIN **2 :** the contents of a box esp. as a measure of quantity **3 :** a box or boxlike container and its contents: as **a** *Brit* **:** a gift in a box **b :** an automobile transmission **c :** TELEVISION **d :** a signaling apparatus ⟨alarm ~⟩ **e :** a usu. self-contained piece of electronic equipment **f :** BOOM BOX **4 :** an often small space, compartment, or enclosure: as **a :** an enclosed group of seats for spectators (as in a theater or stadium) **b :** a driver's seat on a carriage or coach **c :** a cell for holding mail **d** *Brit* **:** BOX STALL **e :** PENALTY BOX **5 :** a usu. rectangular space that is frequently outlined or demarcated on a surface: as **a :** any of six spaces on a baseball diamond where the batter, coaches, pitcher, and catcher stand **b :** a space on a page for printed matter or in which to make a mark **6 :** PREDICAMENT, FIX **7 :** a cubical building **8 :** the limitations of conventionality ⟨trying to think outside the ~⟩ — **box·ful** \-ˌfu̇l\ *n* — **box·like** \-ˌlīk\ *adj*

[3]**box** *vt* (15c) **1 :** to enclose in or as if in a box **2 :** to hem in (as an opponent) — usu. used with *in, out,* or *up* ⟨~*ed* out the tackle⟩

[4]**box** *n* [ME] (14c) **:** a punch or slap esp. on the ear

[5]**box** *vt* (1519) **1 :** to hit (as the ears) with the hand **2 :** to engage in boxing with ~ *vi* **:** to fight with the fists **:** engage in boxing

[6]**box** *vt* [prob. fr. Sp *bojar* to circumnavigate, fr. Catal *vogir* to turn, fr. L *volvere* to roll — more at VOLUBLE] (1713) **:** to name the 32 points of (the compass) in their order — used figuratively in the phrase *box the compass* to describe making a complete reversal

\ə\ **abut** \$^ə$\ kitten, F table \ər\ **further** \a\ **ash** \ā\ **ace** \ä\ mop, mar
\au̇\ **out** \ch\ **chin** \e\ bet \ē\ **easy** \g\ **go** \i\ **hit** \ī\ **ice** \j\ **job**
\ŋ\ **sing** \ō\ **go** \ȯ\ **law** \ȯi\ **boy** \th\ **thin** \th\ **the** \ü\ **loot** \u̇\ **foot**
\y\ yet \zh\ vision, beige \k, ^{n}, œ, ue, ^{y}\ *see* Guide to Pronunciation

box·board \ˈbäks-ˌbȯrd\ *n* (1841) **:** cardboard used for making boxes and cartons

box camera *n* (1902) **:** a box-shaped camera with a simple lens and rotary shutter

[1]**box·car** \ˈbäks-ˌkär\ *n* (1856) **:** a roofed freight car usu. with sliding doors in the sides

[2]**boxcar** *adj* [fr. the high numbers stenciled on the sides of boxcars] (1903) **:** very large ⟨the judge awarded her a ~ figure⟩

box coat *n* (1822) **1 :** a heavy overcoat formerly worn for driving **2 :** a loose coat usu. fitted at the shoulders

box cutter *n* (1977) **:** a small cutting tool that is designed for opening cardboard boxes and typically consists of a retractable razor blade in a thin metal sheath

box elder *n* (1787) **:** a rapidly growing No. American maple (*Acer negundo*) with compound leaves

[1]**box·er** \ˈbäk-sər\ *n* (1671) **1 :** a person who engages in the sport of boxing **2** *pl* **:** BOXER SHORTS

[2]**boxer** *n* (1871) **:** one that makes boxes or packs things in boxes

[3]**boxer** *n* [G, fr. E [1]*boxer*] (ca. 1904) **:** any of a German breed of compact medium-sized dogs with a short usu. fawn or brindled coat

Box·er \ˈbäk-sər\ *n* [approx. trans. of Chin (Beijing) *yìhé juǎn*, lit., righteous harmonious fist] (1899) **:** a member of a Chinese secret society that in 1900 attempted by violence to drive foreigners out of China and to force Chinese converts to renounce Christianity

boxer shorts *n pl* (1944) **:** men's underwear shorts characterized by loose fit

[1]**box·ing** \ˈbäk-siŋ\ *n* (1605) **:** the art of attack and defense with the fists practiced as a sport

[2]**boxing** *n* (1607) **1 :** an act of enclosing in a box **2 :** a boxlike enclosure **:** CASING **3 :** material used for boxes and casings

Boxing Day *n* (1743) **:** the first weekday after Christmas observed as a legal holiday in parts of the Commonwealth of Nations and marked by the giving of Christmas boxes to service workers (as postal workers)

boxing glove *n* (ca. 1841) **:** one of a pair of leather mittens heavily padded on the back and worn in boxing

box jellyfish *n* [fr. its square shape] (1981) **:** SEA WASP

box kite *n* (1897) **:** a tailless kite consisting of two or more open-ended connected boxes

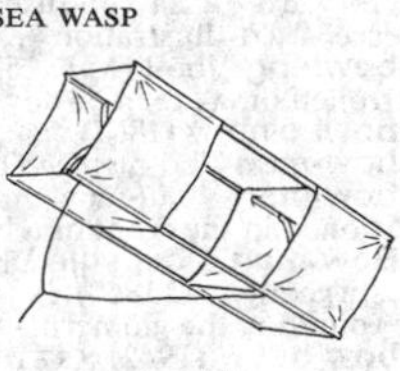
box kite

box lunch *n* (1890) **:** a lunch packed in a container (as a box)

box office *n* (1786) **1 a :** an office (as in a theater) where tickets of admission are sold **b :** income from ticket sales (as for a film) **2 :** the ability (as of a show) to attract ticket buyers; *also* **:** something that enhances that ability ⟨any publicity is good *box office*⟩

box pleat *n* (1877) **:** a pleat made by forming two folded edges one facing right and the other left

box score *n* [fr. its arrangement in a newspaper box] (1913) **:** a printed score of a game (as baseball) giving the names and positions of the players and a record of the play arranged in tabular form; *broadly* **:** total count **:** SUMMARY

box seat *n* (1801) **1 a :** a seat in a box (as in a theater or grandstand) **b :** a position favorable for viewing something **2 :** [2]BOX 4b

box social *n* (1891) **:** a fund-raising affair at which box lunches are auctioned to the highest bidder

box spring *n* (1865) **:** a bedspring that consists of spiral springs attached to a foundation and enclosed in a cloth-covered frame

box stall *n* (1885) **:** an individual enclosure within a barn or stable in which an animal may move about freely without a restraining device

box·thorn \ˈbäks-ˌthȯrn\ *n* (1678) **:** MATRIMONY VINE

box turtle *n* (ca. 1804) **:** any of several No. American land turtles (genus *Terrapene*) capable of withdrawing into their shell and closing it by hinged joints in the lower half — called also *box tortoise*

box·wood \ˈbäks-ˌwu̇d\ *n* (1652) **1 :** the close-grained heavy hard tough wood of the box (genus *Buxus*); *also* **:** a wood of similar properties **2 :** a tree producing boxwood

boxy \ˈbäk-sē\ *adj* **box·i·er; -est** (ca. 1861) **:** resembling a box — **box·i·ness** *n*

boy \ˈbȯi\ *n, often attrib* [ME] (13c) **1** *often offensive* **:** a male servant **2 a :** a male child from birth to adulthood **b :** SON **c :** an immature male ⟨separate the men from the ~*s*⟩ ⟨~ genius⟩ **d :** SWEETHEART, BEAU **3 a :** one native to a given place ⟨local ~⟩ **b :** FELLOW, PERSON ⟨the ~*s* at the office⟩ **c** — used interjectionally to express intensity of feeling ⟨~, what a game⟩ — **boy·hood** \-ˌhu̇d\ *n* — **boy·ish** \-ish\ *adj* — **boy·ish·ly** *adv* — **boy·ish·ness** *n*

bo·yar *also* **bo·yard** \bō-ˈyär\ *n* [Russ *boyarin*] (1591) **:** a member of a Russian aristocratic order next in rank below the ruling princes until its abolition by Peter the Great

boy band *n* (1985) **:** a small ensemble of males in their teens or twenties who play pop songs geared esp. to a young female audience

boy·chick *or* **boy·chik** \ˈbȯi-ˌchik\ *n* [Amer Yiddish *boytshik*, fr. E *boy* + Yiddish *-tshik*, dim. suffix] (ca. 1951) **:** a young man **:** BOY

boy·cott \ˈbȯi-ˌkät\ *vt* [Charles C. *Boycott* †1897 Eng. land agent in Ireland who was ostracized for refusing to reduce rents] (1880) **:** to engage in a concerted refusal to have dealings with (as a person, store, or organization) usu. to express disapproval or to force acceptance of certain conditions — **boycott** *n* — **boy·cott·er** *n*

boy·friend \ˈbȯi-ˌfrend\ *n* (1845) **1 :** a male friend **2 :** a frequent or regular male companion in a romantic or sexual relationship

Boyle's law \ˈbȯi(-ə)lz-\ *n* [Robert *Boyle*] (ca. 1860) **:** a statement in physics: the volume of a gas at constant temperature varies inversely with the pressure exerted on it

boyo \ˈbȯi-(ˌ)ō\ *n, pl* **boy·os** [*boy* + [1]*-o*] (ca. 1870) *Irish* **:** BOY, LAD

Boy Scout *n* (1908) **1 :** a member of any of various national scouting programs (as the Boy Scouts of America) for boys usu. 11 to 17 years of age **2 :** a person whose values or actions are characteristic of a Boy Scout

boy·sen·ber·ry \ˈbȯi-zᵊn-ˌber-ē, -be-rē, -sᵊn-, -zᵊm-\ *n* [Rudolph *Boysen* †1950 Am. horticulturist + E *berry*] (1935) **:** a large reddish black fruit with a raspberry flavor; *also* **:** the trailing hybrid bramble yielding this fruit and developed by crossing several blackberries and raspberries

boy toy *n* (1982) **:** a usu. young man considered as an object of sexual desire

boy wonder *n* (1923) **:** a young man of noteworthy achievements

bo·zo \ˈbō-(ˌ)zō\ *n, pl* **bozos** [origin unknown] (1916) **:** a foolish or incompetent person

bp *abbr* **1** baptized **2** base pair **3** birthplace **4** bishop

BP *abbr* **1** batting practice **2** beautiful people **3** before the present **4** bills payable **5** blood pressure **6** blueprint **7** boiling point

bpd *abbr* barrels per day

BPE *abbr* bachelor of physical education

BPh *abbr* bachelor of philosophy

BPH *abbr* benign prostatic hyperplasia; benign prostatic hypertrophy

BPharm *abbr* bachelor of pharmacy

bpi *abbr* bits per inch; bytes per inch

B picture *n* (ca. 1937) **:** B MOVIE

bpm *abbr* beats per minute

BPOE *abbr* Benevolent and Protective Order of Elks

bps *abbr* bits per second

BPW *abbr* **1** Board of Public Works **2** Business and Professional Women

br *abbr* **1** branch **2** brass **3** brown

[1]**Br** *abbr* Britain; British

[2]**Br** *symbol* bromine

BR *abbr* **1** bedroom **2** bills receivable

bra \ˈbrä\ *n* (1936) **:** BRASSIERE — **bra·less** *adj*

brab·ble \ˈbra-bəl\ *vi* **brab·bled; brab·bling** \-b(ə-)liŋ\ [perh. fr. MD *brabbelen*, of imit. origin] (ca. 1530) **:** SQUABBLE — **brabble** *n*

[1]**brace** \ˈbrās\ *vb* **braced; brac·ing** [ME, fr. AF *bracer* to embrace, fr. *brace*] *vt* (14c) **1** *archaic* **:** to fasten tightly **:** BIND **2 a :** to prepare for use by making taut **b :** PREPARE, STEEL ⟨~ yourself for the shock⟩ **c :** INVIGORATE, FRESHEN **3 :** to turn (a sail yard) by means of a brace **4 a :** to furnish or support with a brace **b :** to make stronger **:** REINFORCE **5 :** to put or plant firmly ⟨~*s* his foot in the stirrup⟩ **6 :** to waylay esp. with demands or questions ~ *vi* **1 :** to take heart — used with *up* **2 :** to get ready (as for an attack)

[2]**brace** *n, pl* **brac·es** [ME, clasp, pair, fr. AF, pair of arms, pair, support, fr. L *bracchia*, pl. of *bracchium* arm, fr. Gk *brachiōn*, fr. compar. of *brachys* short — more at BRIEF] (14c) **1 :** something (as a clasp) that connects or fastens **2** *or pl* **brace :** two of a kind **:** PAIR ⟨several ~ of quail⟩ **3 :** a crank-shaped instrument for turning a bit **4 :** something that transmits, directs, resists, or supports weight or pressure: as **a :** a diagonal piece of structural material that serves to strengthen something (as a framework) **b :** a rope rove through a block at the end of a ship's yard to swing it horizontally **c** *pl* **:** SUSPENDERS **d :** an appliance for supporting a body part **e** *pl* **:** an orthodontic appliance usu. of metallic wire that is used esp. to exert pressure to straighten misaligned teeth **5 a :** one of two marks { } used to connect words or items to be considered together **b :** one of these marks connecting two or more musical staffs carrying parts to be performed simultaneously **c :** BRACKET 3a **6 :** a position of rigid attention **7 :** something that arouses energy or strengthens morale

brace·let \ˈbrās-lət\ *n* [ME, fr. MF, dim. of *bras* arm, fr. L *bracchium*] (15c) **1 :** an ornamental band or chain worn around the wrist **2 :** something (as handcuffs) resembling a bracelet

[1]**bra·cer** \ˈbrā-sər\ *n* [ME, fr. AF *bracer, fr. *braz* arm, fr. L *bracchium*] (14c) **:** an arm or wrist protector esp. for use by an archer

[2]**brac·er** \ˈbrā-sər\ *n* (1579) **1 :** one that braces, binds, or makes firm **2 :** a drink (as of liquor) taken as a stimulant

bra·ce·ro \brä-ˈser-(ˌ)ō, -ˈse-(ˌ)rō\ *n, pl* **-ros** [Sp, laborer, fr. *brazo* arm, fr. L *bracchium*] (1920) **:** a Mexican laborer admitted to the U.S. esp. for seasonal contract labor in agriculture

brace root *n* (1885) **:** PROP ROOT

brachi- *or* **brachio-** *comb form* [L *bracchium, brachium*] **1 :** arm ⟨*brachial*⟩ **2 :** brachial and ⟨*brachio*cephalic⟩

bra·chi·al \ˈbrā-kē-əl\ *adj* (1578) **:** of, relating to, or situated in the arm or an armlike process ⟨the ~ artery of the upper arm⟩

brachial plexus *n* (ca. 1860) **:** a network of nerves lying mostly in the armpit and supplying nerves to the chest, shoulder, and arm

bra·chi·ate \ˈbrā-kē-ˌāt\ *vi* **-at·ed; -at·ing** (1928) **:** to progress by swinging from hold to hold by the arms ⟨a *brachiating* gibbon⟩ — **bra·chi·a·tion** \ˌbrā-kē-ˈā-shən\ *n* — **bra·chi·a·tor** \ˈbrā-kē-ˌā-tər\ *n*

bra·chio·ce·phal·ic artery \ˌbrā-kē-(ˌ)ō-sə-ˈfa-lik-\ *n* (ca. 1839) **:** a short artery that arises from the arch of the aorta and divides into the carotid and subclavian arteries of the right side — called also *innominate artery*

brachiocephalic vein *n* (ca. 1852) **:** either of two large veins that occur one on each side of the neck, receive blood from the head and neck, and unite to form the superior vena cava — called also *innominate vein*

bra·chio·pod \ˈbrā-kē-ə-ˌpäd\ *n* [ultim. fr. L *bracchium* + Gk *pod-, pous* foot — more at FOOT] (1836) **:** any of a phylum (Brachiopoda) of marine invertebrates with bivalve shells within which is a pair of arms bearing tentacles by which a current of water is made to bring microscopic food to the mouth — called also *lampshell* — **brachiopod** *adj*

brach·i·o·saur \ˈbra-kē-ō-ˌsȯr\ *n* [NL *Brachiosaurs*, fr. *brachi-* + Gk *sauros* lizard] (1903) **:** any of a genus (*Brachiosaurus*) of very large sauropod dinosaurs of the Late Jurassic period having a massive body, a very long neck, and forelegs longer than hind legs

brachy- *comb form* [Gk, fr. *brachys* — more at BRIEF] **:** short ⟨*brachy*cephalic⟩

brachy·ce·phal·ic \ˌbra-ki-sə-ˈfa-lik\ *adj* [NL *brachycephalus*, fr. Gk *brachy-* + *kephalē* head — more at CEPHALIC] (ca. 1852) **:** short-headed or broad-headed with a cephalic index of over 80 — **brachy·ceph·a·ly** \-ˈse-fə-lē\ *n*

bra·chyp·ter·ous \bra-ˈkip-tə-rəs\ *adj* [Gk *brachypteros*, fr. *brachy-* + *pteron* wing — more at FEATHER] (1842) **:** having rudimentary or abnormally small wings ⟨~ insects⟩

brachy·ther·a·py \ˌbra-ki-ˈther-ə-pē, -ˈthe-rə-\ *n* [ISV] (1954) **:** radiotherapy in which the source of radiation is placed (as by implantation) in or close to the area being treated

brac·ing \ˈbrā-siŋ\ *adj* (1750) **:** giving strength, vigor, or freshness ⟨a ~ breeze⟩ — **brac·ing·ly** *adv*

bra·ci·o·la \ˌbrä-chē-ˈō-lə, -ˈchō-lə\ *or* **bra·ci·o·le** \-ˈō-ˌlā\ *n* [It, lit., slice of meat roasted over coals, fr. *brace* live coals, prob. of Gmc origin; akin to Sw *brasa* fire] (ca. 1945) : a thin slice of meat wrapped around a seasoned filling and often cooked in wine

brack·en \'bra-kən\ *n* [ME *braken,* prob. of Scand origin; akin to OSw *brækne* fern] (14c) 1 : a large coarse fern; *esp* : a nearly cosmopolitan brake (*Pteridium aquilinum*) found in most tropical and temperate regions 2 : a growth of brakes

¹**brack·et** \'bra-kət\ *n* [perh. fr. MF *braguette* codpiece, fr. dim. of *brague* breeches, fr. Old Occitan *braga,* fr. L *braca,* of Celt origin — more at BREECH] (1580) 1 : an overhanging member that projects from a structure (as a wall) and is usu. designed to support a vertical load or to strengthen an angle 2 a : a fixture (as for holding a lamp) projecting from a wall or column 3 a : one of a pair of marks [ ] used in writing and printing to enclose matter or in mathematics and logic as signs of aggregation — called also *square bracket* b : one of the pair of marks ⟨ ⟩ used to enclose matter — called also *angle bracket* c : PARENTHESIS 3 d : BRACE 5b 4 : a section of a continuously numbered or graded series (as age ranges or income levels) 5 : a pairing of opponents in an elimination tournament

²**bracket** *vt* (ca. 1847) 1 a : to place within or as if within brackets ⟨editorial comments are ∼*ed*⟩ ⟨news stories ∼*ed* by commercials⟩ b : to eliminate from consideration ⟨∼ off politics⟩ c : to extend around so as to encompass : INCLUDE ⟨test pressures . . . which ∼ virtually the entire range of passenger-car tire pressures —*Consumer Reports*⟩ 2 : to furnish or fasten with brackets 3 : to put in the same category or group ⟨∼*ed* in a tie for third⟩ 4 a : to get the range on (a target) by firing over and short b : to establish the limits of ⟨∼*ed* the problem neatly⟩ c : to take photographs of at more than one exposure in order to ensure that the desired exposure is obtained

bracket creep *n* (1978) : movement into a higher tax bracket as a result of income rises intended to offset the effects of inflation

brack·et·ed \'bra-kə-təd\ *adj* (1885) *of a serif* : joined to the stroke by a curved line

bracket fungus *n* (1899) : a basidiomycete that forms shelflike sporophores

brack·ish \'bra-kish\ *adj* [D *brac* salty; akin to MLG *brac* salty] (1538) 1 : somewhat salty ⟨∼ water⟩ 2 a : not appealing to the taste ⟨∼ tea⟩ b : REPULSIVE — **brack·ish·ness** *n*

brac·o·nid \'bra-kə-(‚)nid\ *n* [ultim. fr. Gk *brachys*] (ca. 1893) : any of a large family (Braconidae) of small usu. black or brown parasitoid hymenopterous insects related to the ichneumon wasp — **braconid** *adj*

bract \'brakt\ *n* [NL *bractea,* fr. L, thin metal plate] (1770) 1 : a leaf from the axil of which a flower or floral axis arises 2 : a leaf borne on a floral axis; *esp* : one subtending a flower or flower cluster — **brac·te·al** \'brak-tē-əl\ *adj* — **brac·te·ate** \-tē-ət, -‚āt\ *adj* — **bract·ed** \-təd\ *adj*

brac·te·ole \'brak-tē-‚ōl\ *n* [NL *bracteola,* fr. L, dim. of *bractea*] (ca. 1828) : a small bract esp. on a floral axis

¹**brad** \'brad\ *n* [ME, fr. ON *broddr* spike; perh. akin to OE *byrst* bristle — more at BRISTLE] (13c) 1 : a thin nail of the same thickness throughout but tapering in width and having a slight projection at the top of one side instead of a head 2 : a slender wire nail with a small barrel-shaped head

²**brad** *vt* **brad·ded; brad·ding** (1794) : to fasten with brads

brad·awl \'brad-‚ol\ *n* (1823) : an awl with chisel edge used to make holes for brads or screws

brady- *comb form* [Gk *bradys*] : slow ⟨*brady*kinin⟩

bra·dy·car·dia \‚brā-di-'kär-dē-ə *also* ‚bra-\ *n* [NL] (ca. 1890) : relatively slow heart action — compare TACHYCARDIA

bra·dy·ki·nin \-'kī-nən\ *n* (1949) : a kinin that is formed locally in injured tissue, acts in vasodilation of small arterioles, is considered to play a part in inflammatory processes, and is composed of a chain of nine amino acid residues

brae \'brā\ *n* [ME *bra,* fr. ON *brā* eyelid; akin to OE *brǣw* eyebrow, and prob. to OE *bregdan* to move quickly — more at BRAID] (13c) *chiefly Scot* : a hillside esp. along a river

¹**brag** \'brag\ *n* [ME] (14c) 1 : a pompous or boastful statement 2 : arrogant talk or manner : COCKINESS 3 : BRAGGART

²**brag** *vb* **bragged; brag·ging** *vi* (14c) : to talk boastfully ⟨always *bragging* about his successes⟩ ∼ *vt* : to assert boastfully **syn** see BOAST — **brag·ger** \'bra-gər\ *n* — **brag·gy** \'bra-gē\ *adj*

³**brag** *adj* **brag·ger; brag·gest** (1836) : FIRST-RATE

brag·ga·do·cio \‚bra-gə-'dō-sē-‚ō, -shē-, -shō, -(‚)shō, -(‚)chō\ *n, pl* **-cios** [Braggadochio, personification of boasting in *Faerie Queene* by Edmund Spenser] (1594) 1 : BRAGGART 2 a : empty boasting b : arrogant pretension : COCKINESS

brag·gart \'bra-gərt\ *n* (ca. 1577) : a loud arrogant boaster — **braggart** *adj*

bragging rights *n* (1977) : entitlement to boast about something

¹**Brah·ma** \'brä-mə\ *n* [Skt *brahman*] (1690) 1 : the creator god of the Hindu sacred triad — compare SHIVA, VISHNU 2 : the ultimate ground of all being in Hinduism

²**Brah·ma** \'brä-mə, 'bra-, 'bra-\ *n* (1938) : BRAHMAN 2

Brah·man *or* **Brah·min** \'brä-mən; *2 is* 'brä-, 'bra-, 'bra-\ *n* [ME *Brahman* inhabitant of India, fr. L *Bracmanus,* fr. Gk *Brachman,* fr. Skt *brāhmaṇa* of the Brahman caste, fr. *brahman* Brahman] (15c) 1 a : a Hindu of the highest caste traditionally assigned to the priesthood b : ¹BRAHMA 2 2 : any of an Indian breed of humped cattle : ZEBU; *esp* : a large vigorous heat- and tick-resistant usu. silvery-gray animal developed in the southern U.S. from the zebu and now used chiefly for crossbreeding 3 *usu* **Brahmin** : a person of high social standing and cultivated intellect and taste ⟨Boston ∼s⟩ — **Brah·man·ic** \brä-'ma-nik\ *or* **Brah·man·i·cal** \-ni-kəl\ *adj*

Brah·man·ism \'brä-mə-‚ni-zəm\ *n* (1816) : orthodox Hinduism adhering to the pantheism of the Vedas and to the ancient sacrifices and family ceremonies

¹**braid** \'brād\ *vt* [ME *breyden* to move suddenly, snatch, plait, fr. OE *bregdan;* akin to OHG *brettan* to draw (a sword)] (bef. 12c) 1 a : to make from braids ⟨∼ a rug⟩ b : to form (three or more strands) into a braid 2 : to do up (the hair) by interweaving three or more strands 3 : MIX, INTERMINGLE ⟨∼ fact with fiction⟩ 4 : to ornament esp. with ribbon or braid — **braid·er** *n*

²**braid** *n* (1530) 1 a : length of braided hair b : a cord or ribbon having usu. three or more component strands forming a regular diagonal pattern down its length; *esp* : a narrow fabric of intertwined threads

used esp. for trimming 2 : high-ranking naval officers

braid·ed \'brā-dəd\ *adj* (15c) 1 a : made by intertwining three or more strands b : ornamented with braid 2 : forming an interlacing network of channels ⟨a ∼ river⟩

braid·ing \'brā-diŋ\ *n* (15c) : something made of braided material

¹**brail** \'brāl\ *n* [ME *brayle,* fr. AF *braiel* belt, strap, brail, alter. of OF *braiuel* belt, prob. ultim. fr. L *braca* pants — more at BREECH] (15c) 1 : a rope fastened to the leech of a sail and used for hauling the sail up or in 2 : a dip net with which fish are hauled aboard a boat from a purse seine or trap

²**brail** *vt* (1625) 1 : to take in (a sail) by the brails 2 : to hoist (fish) by means of a brail

braille \'brā(ə)l\ *n, often cap* [Louis *Braille*] (1853) : a system of writing for the blind that uses characters made up of raised dots — **braille** *vt* — **braill·ist** \'brā-list\ *n*

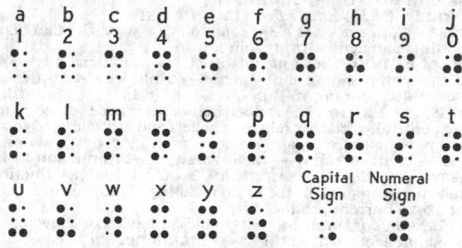

braille alphabet

braille·writ·er \-‚rī-tər\ *n, often cap* (1942) : a machine for writing braille

¹**brain** \'brān\ *n* [ME, fr. OE *brægen;* akin to MLG *bregen* brain, and perh. to Gk *brechmos* front part of the head] (bef. 12c) 1 a : the portion of the vertebrate central nervous system enclosed in the skull and continuous with the spinal cord through the foramen magnum that is composed of neurons and supporting and nutritive structures (as glia) and that integrates sensory information from inside and outside the body in controlling autonomic function (as heartbeat and respiration), in coordinating and directing correlated motor responses, and in the process of learning — compare FOREBRAIN, HINDBRAIN, MIDBRAIN b : a nervous center in invertebrates comparable in position and function to the vertebrate brain 2 a (1) : INTELLECT, MIND ⟨has a clever ∼⟩ (2) : intellectual endowment : INTELLIGENCE — often used in pl. ⟨plenty of ∼s in that family⟩ b (1) : a very intelligent or intellectual person (2) : the chief planner within a group — usu. used in pl. ⟨she's the ∼s behind their success⟩ 3 : something that performs the functions of a brain; *esp* : an automatic device (as a computer) for control or computation

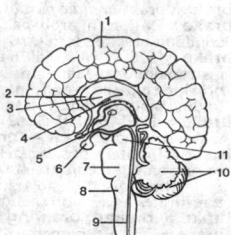

brain 1a: *1* cerebral hemisphere, *2* corpus callosum, *3* ventricle, *4* fornix, *5* thalamus, *6* pituitary gland, *7* pons, *8* medulla oblongata, *9* spinal cord, *10* cerebellum, *11* midbrain

²**brain** *vt* (14c) 1 : to kill by smashing the skull 2 : to hit on the head

brain attack *n* (1990) : STROKE 5

brain·case \'brān-‚kās\ *n* (1741) : the cranium enclosing the brain

brain·child \-‚chī(-ə)ld\ *n* (1628) : a product of one's creative imagination

brain coral *n* (ca. 1711) : a massive reef-building coral (as genus *Diploria*) having the surface covered by ridges and furrows

brain cramp *n* (1982) : a mental lapse caused esp. by carelessness, forgetfulness, or inattention — called also *brain fart*

brain–dead \'brān-‚ded\ *adj* (1974) 1 : characterized by brain death 2 : lacking intelligence or vitality ⟨∼ fools⟩

brain death *n* (1964) : final cessation of activity in the central nervous system esp. as indicated by a flat electroencephalogram for a predetermined length of time

brain drain *n* (1963) : the departure of educated or professional people from one country, economic sector, or field for another usu. for better pay or living conditions

brained \'brānd\ *adj* (15c) : having a brain of a specified kind — used in combination ⟨feather*brained*⟩

brain fog (1853) : a usu. temporary state of diminished mental capacity marked by inability to concentrate or to think or reason clearly

brain freeze *n* (1991) : a sudden shooting pain in the head caused by ingesting very cold food (as ice cream) or drink

brain hormone *n* (1957) 1 : a hormone that is secreted by neurosecretory cells of the insect brain and that stimulates the prothoracic glands to secrete ecdysone 2 : any of various hormones (as serotonin) produced in or acting on the vertebrate brain or central nervous system — not usu. used technically

brain·i·ac \'brā-nē-‚ak\ *n* [prob. fr. *Brainiac,* superintelligent villain in the *Superman* comic-book series] (1982) : a very intelligent person

brain·ish \'brā-nish\ *adj* (ca. 1530) *archaic* : IMPETUOUS, HOTHEADED ⟨and in this ∼ apprehension kills the unseen good old man —Shak.⟩

brain·less \'brān-ləs\ *adj* (15c) : devoid of intelligence : STUPID ⟨a ∼ decision⟩ — **brain·less·ly** *adv* — **brain·less·ness** *n*

brain·pan \'brān-‚pan\ *n* (14c) : BRAINCASE

\ə\ **abut** \ᵊ\ **kitten,** F **table** \ər\ **further** \a\ **ash** \ā\ **ace** \ä\ **mop, mar** \au̇\ **out** \ch\ **chin** \e\ **bet** \ē\ **easy** \g\ **go** \i\ **hit** \ī\ **ice** \j\ **job** \ŋ\ **sing** \ō\ **go** \ȯ\ **law** \ȯi\ **boy** \th\ **thin** \t͟h\ **the** \ü\ **loot** \u̇\ **foot** \y\ **yet** \zh\ **vision, beige** \k, ⁿ, œ, ᴜ, ᵕ\ *see* Guide to Pronunciation

brain–pick·ing \-ˌpi-kiŋ\ *n* (1954) **:** the act of gathering information from another's mind — **brain–pick·er** \-kər\ *n*

brain·pow·er \-ˌpau̇(-ə)r\ *n* (1853) **1 :** intellectual ability **2 :** people with developed intellectual ability

brain·sick \-ˌsik\ *adj* (15c) **1 :** mentally disordered **2 :** arising from mental disorder ⟨a ~ frenzy⟩ — **brain·sick·ly** *adv*

brain stem *n* (1879) **:** the part of the brain composed of the midbrain, pons, and medulla oblongata and connecting the spinal cord with the forebrain and cerebrum

brain·storm \-ˌstȯrm\ *n* (ca. 1894) **1 :** a violent transient fit of insanity **2 a :** a sudden bright idea **b :** a harebrained idea

brain·storm·ing \-ˌstȯr-miŋ\ *n* (1953) **:** a group problem-solving technique that involves the spontaneous contribution of ideas from all members of the group; *also* **:** the mulling over of ideas by one or more individuals in an attempt to devise or find a solution to a problem — **brain·storm** *vb* — **brain·storm·er** *n*

brains trust *n* (1934) *chiefly Brit* **:** BRAIN TRUST

brain·teas·er \-ˌtē-zər\ *n* (1923) **:** something (as a puzzle) that demands mental effort and acuity for its solution

brain trust *n* (1910) **:** a group of official or unofficial advisers concerned esp. with planning and strategy — **brain trust·er** \-ˌtrəs-tər\ *n*

brain·wash·ing \ˈbrān-ˌwȯ-shiŋ, -ˌwä-\ *n* [trans. of Chin (Beijing) *xǐnǎo*] (1950) **1 :** a forcible indoctrination to induce someone to give up basic political, social, or religious beliefs and attitudes and to accept contrasting regimented ideas **2 :** persuasion by propaganda or salesmanship — **brain·wash** *vt* — **brainwash** *n* — **brain·wash·er** *n*

brain wave *n* (1890) **1 :** BRAINSTORM 2a **2 a :** rhythmic fluctuations of voltage between parts of the brain resulting in the flow of an electric current **b :** a current produced by brain waves

brainy \ˈbrā-nē\ *adj* **brain·i·er; -est** (1867) **:** having or showing a well-developed intellect **:** INTELLIGENT — **brain·i·ness** *n*

[1]**braise** \ˈbrāz\ *vt* **braised; brais·ing** [F *braiser,* fr. *braise* live coals, fr. OF *breze,* prob. of Gmc origin; akin to Sw *brasa* fire] (1797) **:** to cook slowly in fat and little moisture in a closed pot

[2]**braise** *n* (ca. 1885) **:** an item of braised food

[1]**brake** \ˈbrāk\ *archaic past of* BREAK

[2]**brake** *n* [ME, fern, prob. back-formation fr. *braken* bracken] (14c) **:** the common bracken fern (*Pteridium aquilinum*)

[3]**brake** *n* [ME, fr. MLG; akin to OE *brecan* to break] (15c) **1 :** a toothed instrument or machine for separating out the fiber of flax or hemp by breaking up the woody parts **2 :** a machine for bending, flanging, folding, and forming sheet metal

[4]**brake** *n* [ME *-brake*] (1562) **:** rough or marshy land overgrown usu. with one kind of plant — **braky** \ˈbrā-kē\ *adj*

[5]**brake** *n* [perh. fr. obs. *brake* bridle] (ca. 1782) **1 :** a device for arresting or preventing the motion of a mechanism usu. by means of friction **2 :** something used to slow down or stop movement or activity ⟨use interest rates as a ~ on spending⟩ — **brake·less** \ˈbrā-kləs\ *adj*

[6]**brake** *vb* **braked; brak·ing** *vt* (1868) **:** to retard or stop by or as if by a brake ~ *vi* **1 :** to operate or manage a brake; *esp* **:** to apply the brake on a vehicle **2 :** to become checked by a brake

brake·man \ˈbrāk-mən\ *n* (1833) **1 :** a freight or passenger train crew member who inspects the train and assists the conductor **2 :** the member of a bobsled team who operates the brake

bram·ble \ˈbram-bəl\ *n* [ME *brembel,* fr. OE *brēmel;* akin to OE *brōm* broom] (bef. 12c) **1 :** any of a genus (*Rubus*) of usu. prickly shrubs of the rose family including the raspberries and blackberries; *also* **:** the fruit of a bramble **2 :** a rough prickly shrub or vine — **bram·bly** \-b(ə-)lē\ *adj*

bran \ˈbran\ *n* [ME, fr. AF *bren, bran*] (14c) **:** the edible broken seed coats of cereal grain separated from the flour or meal by sifting or bolting

[1]**branch** \ˈbranch\ *n, often attrib* [ME, fr. AF *branche,* fr. LL *branca* paw] (14c) **1 :** a natural subdivision of a plant stem; *esp* **:** a secondary shoot or stem (as a bough) arising from a main axis (as of a tree) **2 :** something that extends from or enters into a main body or source: as **a** (1) **:** a stream that flows into another usu. larger stream **:** TRIBUTARY (2) *Southern & Midland* **:** CREEK 2 **b :** a side road or way **c :** a slender projection (as the tine of an antler) **d :** a distinctive part of a mathematical curve **e :** a part of a computer program executed as a result of a program decision **3 :** a part of a complex body: as **a :** a division of a family descending from a particular ancestor **b :** an area of knowledge that may be considered apart from related areas ⟨pathology is a ~ of medicine⟩ **c** (1) **:** a division of an organization (2) **:** a separate but dependent part of a central organization ⟨the neighborhood ~ of the city library⟩ **d :** a language group less inclusive than a family ⟨the Germanic ~ of the Indo-European language family⟩ — **branched** \ˈbrancht\ *adj* — **branch·less** \ˈbranch-ləs\ *adj* — **branchy** \ˈbran-chē\ *adj*

[2]**branch** *vi* (14c) **1 :** to put forth branches **:** RAMIFY **2 :** to spring out (as from a main stem) **:** DIVERGE **3 :** to be an outgrowth — used with *from* ⟨poetry that ~*ed* from religious prose⟩ **4 :** to extend activities — usu. used with *out* ⟨the business is ~*ing* out⟩ **5 :** to follow one of two or more branches (as in a computer program) ~ *vt* **1 :** to ornament with designs of branches **2 :** to divide up **:** SECTION

bran·chi·al \ˈbraŋ-kē-əl\ *adj* [Gk *branchia* gills] (1801) **:** of, relating to, or supplying the gills or associated structures or their embryonic precursors

bran·chio·pod \ˈbraŋ-kē-ə-ˌpäd\ *n* [ultim. fr. Gk *branchia* gills + *pod-, pous* foot — more at FOOT] (1836) **:** any of a group (Branchiopoda) of small usu. freshwater crustaceans (as fairy shrimp or water fleas) with usu. many pairs of setae-bearing appendages — **branchiopod** *adj*

branch·let \ˈbranch-lət\ *n* (ca. 1731) **:** a small usu. terminal branch

branch line *n* (1845) **:** a secondary line usu. of a railroad

branch water *n* [[1]*branch* (creek)] (1835) **:** plain water ⟨bourbon and *branch water*⟩

[1]**brand** \ˈbrand\ *n* [ME, torch, sword, fr. OE; akin to OE *bærnan* to burn] (bef. 12c) **1 a :** a charred piece of wood **b :** FIREBRAND 1 **c :** something (as lightning) that resembles a firebrand **2 :** SWORD **3 a** (1) **:** a mark made by burning with a hot iron to attest manufacture or quality or to designate ownership (2) **:** a printed mark made for similar purposes **:** TRADEMARK **b** (1) **:** a mark put on criminals with a hot iron (2) **:** a mark of disgrace **:** STIGMA ⟨the ~ of poverty⟩ **4 a :** a class of goods identified by name as the product of a single firm or manufacturer **:** MAKE **b :** a characteristic or distinctive kind ⟨a lively ~ of theater⟩ **c :** BRAND NAME 2 **5 :** a tool used to produce a brand

[2]**brand** *vt* (15c) **1 :** to mark with a brand **2 :** to mark with disapproval **:** STIGMATIZE ⟨he was ~*ed* a coward⟩ **3 :** to impress indelibly ⟨~ the lesson on his mind⟩ — **brand·er** *n*

brand·ed \ˈbran-dəd\ *adj* (1897) **:** having a brand name ⟨~ products⟩

brand·ing \ˈbran-diŋ\ *n* (1913) **:** the promoting of a product or service by identifying it with a particular brand

[1]**bran·dish** \ˈbran-dish\ *vt* [ME *braundisshen,* fr. AF *brandiss-,* stem of *brandir,* fr. *brant, braund* sword, of Gmc origin; akin to OE *brand*] (14c) **1 :** to shake or wave (as a weapon) menacingly **2 :** to exhibit in an ostentatious or aggressive manner ***syn*** see SWING

[2]**brandish** *n* (1599) **:** an act or instance of brandishing

brand–name \ˈbran(d)-ˈnām\ *adj* (1949) **1 :** of or relating to a brand name ⟨~ products⟩ **2 :** having a well-known and usu. highly regarded or marketable name ⟨~ authors⟩ ⟨the . . . party lacks ~ guests or good food —Ryan Lizza⟩

brand name *n* (1922) **1 :** an arbitrarily adopted name that is given by a manufacturer or merchant to an article or service to distinguish it as produced or sold by that manufacturer or merchant and that may be used and protected as a trademark **2 :** one having a well-known and usu. highly regarded or marketable name

brand–new \-ˈnü, -ˈnyü\ *adj* [ˈ*brand*] (ca. 1570) **:** conspicuously new and unused; *also* **:** recently introduced ⟨a ~ executive officer⟩

[1]**bran·dy** \ˈbran-dē\ *n, pl* **brandies** [short for *brandywine,* fr. D *brandewijn,* fr. MD *brantwijn,* fr. *brant* distilled + *wijn* wine] (1657) **:** an alcoholic beverage distilled from wine or fermented fruit juice

[2]**brandy** *vt* **bran·died; bran·dy·ing** (ca. 1848) **:** to flavor, blend, or preserve with brandy

bran·ni·gan \ˈbra-ni-gən\ *n* [prob. fr. the name *Brannigan*] (1927) **1 :** a drinking spree **2 :** SQUABBLE

brant \ˈbrant\ *n, pl* **brant** *or* **brants** [ME *brand gos*] (14c) **:** a small goose (*Branta bernicla*) about the size of a mallard having a black head, neck, and chest

[1]**brash** \ˈbrash\ *adj* [origin unknown] (1566) **1 :** BRITTLE ⟨~ wood⟩ **2 a :** heedless of the consequences **:** AUDACIOUS ⟨a ~ adventurer⟩ **b :** done in haste without regard for consequences **:** RASH ⟨~ acts⟩ **3 a :** full of fresh raw vitality ⟨a ~ frontier town⟩ **b :** uninhibitedly energetic or demonstrative **:** BUMPTIOUS ⟨a ~ comedian⟩ **4 a :** lacking restraint and discernment **:** TACTLESS ⟨~ remarks⟩ **b :** aggressively self-assertive **:** IMPUDENT ⟨~ to the point of arrogance⟩ **5 :** piercingly sharp **:** HARSH ⟨a ~ squeal of brakes⟩ **6 :** marked by vivid contrast **:** BOLD ⟨~ colors⟩ — **brash·ly** *adv* — **brash·ness** *n*

[2]**brash** *n* [obs. E *brash* to breach a wall] (1787) **:** a mass of fragments (as of ice)

brass \ˈbras\ *n* [ME *bras,* fr. OE *bræs;* akin to MLG *bras* metal] (bef. 12c) **1 :** an alloy consisting essentially of copper and zinc in variable proportions **2 a :** the brass instruments of an orchestra or band — often used in pl. **b :** a usu. brass memorial tablet **c :** bright metal fittings, utensils, or ornaments **d :** empty cartridge shells **3 :** brazen self-assurance **:** GALL **4** *sing or pl in constr* **a :** high-ranking members of the military **b :** persons in high positions (as in a business or the government) — **brass** *adj*

bras·sard \brə-ˈsärd, ˈbra-ˌ\ *n* [F *brassard,* fr. MF *brassal,* fr. OIt *bracciale,* fr. *braccio* arm, fr. L *bracchium* — more at BRACE] (1830) **1 :** armor for protecting the arm — see ARMOR illustration **2 :** a cloth band worn around the upper arm usu. bearing an identifying mark

brass band *n* (1834) **:** a band consisting chiefly or solely of brass and percussion instruments

brass·bound \ˈbras-ˌbau̇nd, -ˈbau̇nd\ *adj* (1767) **1 :** having trim made of brass or a metal resembling brass **2 a** (1) **:** tradition-bound and opinionated (2) **:** making no concessions **:** INFLEXIBLE **b :** BRAZEN, PRESUMPTUOUS

bras·se·rie \ˌbras-ˈrē, ˌbra-sə-\ *n* [F, lit., brewery, fr. MF *brasser* to brew, fr. OF *bracier,* fr. VL **braciare,* of Celt origin; akin to W *brag* malt] (1864) **:** an informal usu. French restaurant serving simple hearty food

brass hat *n* [fr. the gold braid worn on the cap] (1893) **:** a member of the brass

bras·si·ca \ˈbra-si-kə\ *n* [NL, genus name, fr. L, cabbage] (1727) **:** any of a large genus (*Brassica*) of Old World temperate-zone herbs (as broccoli and cabbage) of the mustard family with cylindrical pods

bras·siere \brə-ˈzir *also* ˌbra-sē-ˈer\ *n* [obs. F *brassière* bodice, fr. OF *braciere* arm protector, fr. *bras* arm — more at BRACELET] (1894) **:** a woman's undergarment to cover and support the breasts

brass instrument *n* (1843) **:** any of a group of wind instruments (as a French horn, trombone, trumpet, or tuba) that is usu. characterized by a long cylindrical or conical metal tube commonly curved two or more times and ending in a flared bell, that produces tones by the vibrations of the player's lips against a usu. cup-shaped mouthpiece, and that usu. has valves or a slide by which the player may produce all the tones within the instrument's range

brass knuckles *n pl but sing or pl in constr* (1855) **:** KNUCKLE 4

brass ring *n* (1950) **:** a rich opportunity **:** PRIZE

brass tacks *n pl* (1867) **:** details of immediate practical importance — usu. used in the phrase *get down to brass tacks*

brassy \ˈbra-sē\ *adj* **brass·i·er; -est** (1576) **1 a :** shamelessly bold ⟨a ~ reporter⟩ **b :** OBSTREPEROUS **2 :** resembling brass esp. in color **3 :** resembling the sound of a brass instrument — **brass·i·ly** \ˈbra-sə-lē\ *adv* — **brass·i·ness** \ˈbra-sē-nəs\ *n*

[1]**brat** \ˈbrat\ *n* [perh. fr. E dial. *brat* coarse garment] (ca. 1505) **1 a :** CHILD; *specif* **:** an ill-mannered annoying child ⟨a spoiled ~⟩ **b :** an ill-mannered immature person **2 :** the child of a career military person ⟨army ~*s*⟩; *also* **:** the child of a person whose career is in a specified and typically unusual field ⟨Hollywood ~*s*⟩ — **brat·ti·ness** \ˈbra-tē-nəs\ *n* — **brat·tish** \ˈbra-tish\ *adj* — **brat·ty** \-tē\ *adj*

[2]**brat** \ˈbrät, ˈbrat\ *n* [by shortening] (1949) **:** BRATWURST

brat·tice \ˈbra-təs, ˈbra-tish\ *n* [ME *bretais* parapet, fr. AF *bretesche,* fr. ML *breteschia*] (ca. 1846) **:** an often temporary partition of planks or cloth used esp. to control mine ventilation — **brattice** *vt*

[1]**brat·tle** \ˈbra-tᵊl\ *n* [prob. imit.] (ca. 1500) *chiefly Scot* **:** CLATTER

[2]**brattle** *vi* **brat·tled; brat·tling** (1513) *chiefly Scot* **:** to make a clattering or rattling sound

brat·wurst \ˈbrät-(ˌ)wərst *also* ˈbrat- *also* -ˌvu̇(r)st; *sometimes* -ˌvu̇sht\ *n* [G, fr. OHG *brātwurst,* fr. *brāt* meat without waste + *wurst* sausage] (1851) **:** fresh pork sausage for frying

braun·schweig·er \ˈbrau̇n-ˌshwī-gər, -ˌshvī- *also* ˈbrän-\ *n* [G *Braunschweiger (Wurst),* lit., Brunswick sausage] (1934) **:** smoked liverwurst

bra·va \ˈbrä-(ˌ)vä, brä-ˈvä\ *n* [It, fem. of *bravo*] (1741) **:** BRAVO — used interjectionally in applauding a woman

bra·va·do \brə-ˈvä-(ˌ)dō\ *n, pl* **-does** *or* **-dos** [MF *bravade* & OSp *bravata,* fr. OIt *bravata,* fr. *bravare* to challenge, show off, fr. *bravo*] (ca. 1580) **1 a :** blustering swaggering conduct **b :** a pretense of bravery **2 :** the quality or state of being foolhardy

[1]brave \ˈbrāv\ *adj* **brav·er; brav·est** [MF, fr. OIt & OSp *bravo* courageous, wild, prob. fr. L *barbarus* barbarous] (15c) **1 :** having or showing courage ⟨a ~ soldier⟩ ⟨a ~ smile⟩ **2 :** making a fine show **:** COLORFUL ⟨~ banners flying in the wind⟩ **3 :** EXCELLENT, SPLENDID ⟨the ~ fire I soon had going —J. F. Dobie⟩ — **brave·ly** *adv*

[2]brave *vb* **braved; brav·ing** *vt* (1546) **1 :** to face or endure with courage **2** *obs* **:** to make showy ~ *vi, archaic* **:** to show courage **:** to make a brave show — **brav·er** *n*

[3]brave *n* (1590) **1** *archaic* **:** BRAVADO **2 :** one who is brave; *specif* **:** an American Indian warrior **3** *archaic* **:** BULLY, ASSASSIN

brave new world *n* [fr. the dystopian novel *Brave New World* (1932) by Aldous Huxley] (1933) **:** a future world, situation, or development; *also* **:** a recent development or recently changed situation

brav·ery \ˈbrāv-rē, ˈbrā-və-\ *n, pl* **-er·ies** (1548) **1 :** the quality or state of being brave **:** COURAGE **2 a :** fine clothes **b :** showy display

[1]bra·vo \ˈbrä-(ˌ)vō\ *n, pl* **bravos** *or* **bravoes** [It, fr. *bravo* brave] (1597) **:** VILLAIN, DESPERADO; *esp* **:** a hired assassin

[2]bra·vo \ˈbrä-(ˌ)vō, brä-ˈvō\ *n, pl* **bravos** (1761) **:** a shout of approval — often used interjectionally in applauding a performance

[3]bra·vo *same as* [2]\ *vt* **bra·voed; bra·vo·ing** (1831) **:** to applaud by shouts of *bravo*

Bra·vo \ˈbrä-(ˌ)vō\ (1952) — a communications code word for the letter *b*

[1]bra·vu·ra \brə-ˈvyu̇r-ə, brä-, -ˈvu̇r-\ *n* [It, lit., bravery, fr. *bravare* to show off — more at BRAVADO] (1757) **1 :** a musical passage requiring exceptional agility and technical skill in execution **2 :** a florid brilliant style **3 :** a show of daring or brilliance

[2]bravura *adj* (1920) **1 :** marked by a dazzling display of skill ⟨a ~ performance⟩ **2 :** ORNATE, SHOWY

braw \ˈbrȯ, ˈbrä\ *adj* [modif. of MF *brave*] (ca. 1565) **1** *chiefly Scot* **:** GOOD, FINE **2** *chiefly Scot* **:** well dressed

[1]brawl \ˈbrȯl\ *vi* [ME] (14c) **1 :** to quarrel or fight noisily **:** WRANGLE **2 :** to make a loud confused noise — **brawl·er** *n*

[2]brawl *n* (15c) **1 :** a noisy quarrel or fight **2 :** a loud tumultuous noise

brawly \ˈbrȯ-lē\ *adj* **brawl·i·er; -est** (1940) **1 :** inclined to brawl **2 :** characterized by brawls or brawling

brawn \ˈbrȯn\ *n* [ME, fr. AF *braon* flesh, muscle, of Gmc origin; akin to OE *brǣd* flesh] (13c) **1 a** *Brit* **:** the flesh of a boar **b :** HEADCHEESE **2 a :** full strong muscles **b :** muscular strength

brawny \ˈbrȯ-nē\ *adj* **brawn·i·er; -est** (1581) **1 :** MUSCULAR; *also* **:** STRONG, POWERFUL **2 :** being swollen and hard ⟨a ~ infected foot⟩ — **brawn·i·ly** \-nə-lē\ *adv* — **brawn·i·ness** \-nē-nəs\ *n*

[1]bray \ˈbrā\ *vb* [ME, fr. AF *braire* to cry, bellow, roar, fr. VL **bragere,* of Celt origin; akin to OIr *braigid* he breaks wind] *vi* (14c) **:** to utter the characteristic loud harsh cry of a donkey; *also* **:** to utter a sound like a donkey's ~ *vt* **:** to utter or play loudly or harshly — **bray** *n*

[2]bray *vt* [ME, fr. AF *braier, breier,* of Gmc origin; akin to OHG *brehhan* to break — more at BREAK] (14c) **1 :** to crush or grind fine ⟨~ seeds in a mortar⟩ **2 :** to spread thin ⟨~ printing ink⟩

bray·er \ˈbrā-ər\ *n* (1683) **:** a printer's hand inking roller

Braz *abbr* Brazil; Brazilian

[1]braze \ˈbrāz\ *vt* **brazed; braz·ing** [irreg. fr. *brass*] (1602) *archaic* **:** HARDEN

[2]braze *vt* **brazed; braz·ing** [F *braser,* fr. OF, to burn, fr. *breze* hot coals — more at BRAISE] (ca. 1574) **:** to solder with a nonferrous alloy having a lower melting point than the metals being joined — **braz·er** *n*

[1]bra·zen \ˈbrā-zᵊn\ *adj* [ME *brasen,* fr. OE *bræsen,* fr. *bræs* brass] (bef. 12c) **1 :** made of brass **2 a :** sounding harsh and loud like struck brass **b :** of the color of polished brass **3 :** marked by contemptuous boldness — **bra·zen·ly** *adv* — **bra·zen·ness** \ˈbrā-zᵊn-(n)əs\ *n*

[2]brazen *vt* **bra·zened; bra·zen·ing** \ˈbrāz-niŋ, ˈbrā-zᵊn-iŋ\ (ca. 1555) **:** to face with defiance or impudence — usu. used in the phrase *brazen it out*

bra·zen–faced \ˈbrā-zᵊn-ˌfāst\ *adj* (1567) **:** marked by insolence and bold disrespect ⟨~ assertions⟩

[1]bra·zier \ˈbrā-zhər\ *n* [ME *brasier,* fr. *bras* brass] (14c) **:** one who works in brass

[2]brazier *n* [F *brasier,* fr. OF, fire of hot coals, fr. *breze* hot coals — more at BRAISE] (1658) **1 :** a pan for holding burning coals **2 :** a utensil in which food is exposed to heat through a wire grill

Bra·zil nut \brə-ˈzil-\ *n* [*Brazil,* So. America] (1830) **:** a tall So. American tree (*Bertholletia excelsa* of the family Lecythidaceae) that bears large globular capsules each containing several closely packed roughly triangular oily edible nuts; *also* **:** its nut

bra·zil·wood \brə-ˈzil-ˌwu̇d\ *n* [Sp *brasil,* fr. *brasa* live coals (fr. the wood's color), prob. of Gmc origin; akin to Sw *brasa* fire] (1559) **:** the heavy wood of any of various tropical leguminous trees (esp. genus *Caesalpinia*) that is used esp. as red and purple dyewood and in violin bows, gun stocks, and cabinetwork

brb *abbr* be right back

BRE *abbr* **1** bachelor of religious education **2** business reply envelope

[1]breach \ˈbrēch\ *n* [ME *breche,* fr. OE *brǣc* act of breaking; akin to OE *brecan* to break] (bef. 12c) **1 :** infraction or violation of a law, obligation, tie, or standard **2 a :** a broken, ruptured, or torn condition or area **b :** a gap (as in a wall) made by battering **3 a :** a break in accustomed friendly relations **b :** a temporary gap in continuity **:** HIATUS **4 :** a leap esp. of a whale out of water

[2]breach *vt* (1547) **1 :** to make a breach in ⟨~ a wall⟩ **2 :** BREAK, VIOLATE ⟨~ an agreement⟩ ~ *vi* **:** to leap out of water ⟨a whale ~*ing*⟩

breach of promise (1590) **:** violation of a promise esp. to marry

[1]bread \ˈbred\ *n* [ME *breed,* fr. OE *brēad;* akin to OHG *brōt* bread, OE *brēowan* to brew] (bef. 12c) **1 :** a usu. baked and leavened food made of a mixture whose basic constituent is flour or meal **2 :** FOOD, SUSTENANCE ⟨our daily ~⟩ **3 a :** LIVELIHOOD ⟨earns his ~ as a laborer⟩ **b** *slang* **:** MONEY — **bready** \ˈbre-dē\ *adj* — **bread upon the waters :** resources risked or charitable deeds performed without expectation of return

[2]bread *vt* (1629) **:** to cover with bread crumbs ⟨a ~*ed* pork chop⟩

bread–and–butter *adj* (ca. 1837) **1 a :** being as basic as the earning of one's livelihood ⟨~ issues⟩ **b** (1) **:** RELIABLE ⟨our ~ repertoire⟩ (2) **:** dependable as a source of income ⟨a company's ~ products⟩ **2 :** sent or given as thanks for hospitality ⟨a ~ letter⟩

bread and butter *n* (1732) **:** a means of sustenance or livelihood

bread and circuses *n pl* [trans. of L *panis et circenses*] (1894) **:** a palliative offered esp. to avert potential discontent

bread·bas·ket \ˈbred-ˌbas-kət\ *n* (1753) **1** *slang* **:** STOMACH **2 :** a major cereal-producing region

[1]bread·board \ˈbred-ˌbȯrd\ *n* (1847) **1 :** a board on which dough is kneaded or bread cut **2 :** a board on which mounted components are breadboarded

[2]breadboard *vt* (1956) **:** to make an experimental arrangement of (as an electronic circuit or a mechanical system) to test feasibility

bread·fruit \ˈbred-ˌfrüt\ *n* (1697) **:** a round starchy usu. seedless fruit that resembles bread in color and texture when baked; *also* **:** a tall tropical evergreen tree (*Artocarpus altilis*) of the mulberry family that bears this fruit

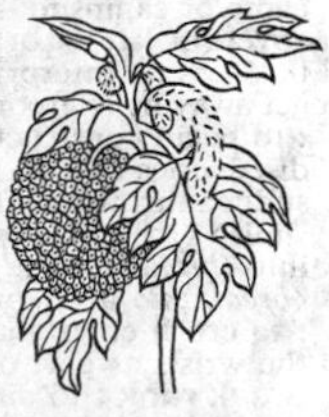

breadfruit

bread·line \-ˌlīn\ *n* (1900) **:** a line of people waiting to receive free food

bread mold *n* (1914) **:** any of various molds found esp. on bread; *esp* **:** a rhizopus (*Rhizopus nigricans* syn. *R. stolonifer*)

bread·stuff \-ˌstəf\ *n* (1793) **1 :** a cereal product (as grain or flour) **2 :** BREAD

breadth \ˈbretth, ˈbredth, ÷ˈbreth\ *n* [ME *breadeth, breth,* fr. *brede* breadth (fr. OE *brǣdu,* fr. *brād* broad) + *-th* (as in *lengthe* length)] (15c) **1 :** distance from side to side **:** WIDTH **2 :** something of full width **3 a :** comprehensive quality **:** SCOPE ⟨the ~ of his learning⟩ **b :** liberality of views or taste ⟨~ of mind⟩ — **breadth·wise** \-ˌwīz\ *adv or adj*

bread·win·ner \ˈbred-ˌwi-nər\ *n* (1771) **1 :** a means (as a tool or craft) of livelihood **2 :** a member of a family whose wages supply its livelihood — **bread·win·ning** \-ˌwi-niŋ\ *n*

[1]break \ˈbrāk\ *vb* **broke** \ˈbrōk\; **bro·ken** \ˈbrō-kən\; **break·ing** [ME *breken,* fr. OE *brecan;* akin to OHG *brehhan* to break, L *frangere*] *vt* (bef. 12c) **1 a :** to separate into parts with suddenness or violence **b :** FRACTURE ⟨~ an arm⟩ **c :** RUPTURE ⟨~ the skin⟩ **d :** to cut into and turn over the surface of ⟨~ the soil⟩ **e :** to render inoperable ⟨*broke* his watch⟩ **2 a :** VIOLATE, TRANSGRESS ⟨~ the law⟩ ⟨~ a promise⟩ **b :** to invalidate (a will) by action at law **3 a** *archaic* **:** to force entry into **b :** to burst and force a way through ⟨~ the sound barrier⟩ ⟨~ a racial barrier⟩ **c :** to escape by force from ⟨~ jail⟩ **d :** to make or effect by cutting, forcing, or pressing through ⟨~ a trail through the woods⟩ **4 :** to disrupt the order or compactness of ⟨~ formation⟩ **5 :** to make ineffective as a binding force ⟨~ the spell⟩ **6 a :** to defeat utterly and end as an effective force **:** DESTROY ⟨used starvation to ~ the enemy⟩ **b :** to crush the spirit of ⟨brutal methods *broke* the prisoner⟩ **c :** to make tractable or submissive: as (1) *past part often* **broke :** to train (an animal) to adjust to the service or convenience of humans ⟨a halter-*broke* horse⟩ (2) **:** INURE, ACCUSTOM **d :** to exhaust in health, strength, or capacity ⟨*broken* by his struggle for power⟩ **7 a :** to stop or bring to an end suddenly **:** HALT ⟨~ a deadlock⟩ **b :** INTERRUPT, SUSPEND ⟨~ the silence with a cry⟩ **c :** to open and bring about suspension of operation ⟨~ an electric circuit⟩ **d :** to destroy unity or completeness of ⟨~ a dining room set by buying a chair⟩ **e :** to change the appearance of uniformity of ⟨a dormer ~*s* the level roof⟩ **f :** to split the surface of ⟨fish ~*ing* water⟩ **g :** to cause to discontinue a habit ⟨tried to ~ him of smoking⟩ **8 a :** to make known **:** TELL ⟨~ the bad news gently⟩ **b :** to bring to attention or prominence initially ⟨radio stations ~*ing* new musicians⟩ ⟨~ a news story⟩ **9 a :** to ruin financially ⟨~ the bank⟩ **b :** to reduce in rank ⟨*broken* from sergeant to private⟩ **10 a :** to split into smaller units, parts, or processes **:** DIVIDE **b** (1) **:** to give or get the equivalent of (a bill) in smaller denominations (2) **:** to use as the denomination in paying a bill ⟨didn't want to ~ a $20 bill⟩ — often used with *into, up,* or *down* **11 a :** to check the speed, force, or intensity of ⟨the bushes will ~ his fall⟩ ⟨without ~*ing* her stride⟩ **b :** to cause failure and discontinuance of (a strike) by measures outside bargaining processes **12 :** to cause a sudden significant decrease in the price, value, or volume of ⟨news likely to ~ the market sharply⟩ **13 a :** EXCEED, SURPASS ⟨~ the record⟩ **b :** to score less than (a specified total) ⟨a golfer trying to ~ 90⟩ **c :** to win against (an opponent's service) in tennis **d :** to make (a run) in football by getting past defenders ⟨*broke* a 20-yard run⟩ **14 :** to open the action of (a breechloader) **15 a :** to find an explanation or solution for **:** SOLVE ⟨the detective *broke* the case⟩ **b :** to discover the essentials of (a code or cipher system) **16 :** to demonstrate the falsity of ⟨~ an alibi⟩ **17 :** to ruin the prospects of ⟨could make or ~ her career⟩ **18 :** to produce visibly ⟨barely ~*s* a sweat⟩ ~ *vi* **1 a :** to escape with sudden forceful effort ⟨the attacker *broke* from the throng⟩ **b :** to come into being by or as if by bursting forth ⟨day was ~*ing*⟩ **c :** to effect a penetration ⟨~ through security lines⟩ **d :** to emerge through the surface of the water **e :** to start abruptly ⟨when the storm *broke*⟩ **f :** to become known or published ⟨when the news *broke*⟩ **g :** to make a sudden dash ⟨~ for cover⟩ **h :** to separate after a clinch in boxing **i :** to achieve initial success in usu. a sudden or striking way ⟨her song *broke* nationally⟩ **j :** to begin a race ⟨the horse *broke* poorly⟩ **2 a :** to come apart or split into pieces **:** FRAGMENT, SHATTER ⟨the cup *broke* when it fell⟩ **b :** to open spon-

\ə\ **abut** \ᵊ\ kitten, F table \ər\ **fur**ther \a\ **ash** \ā\ **ace** \ä\ **mop, mar** \au̇\ **out** \ch\ **chin** \e\ **bet** \ē\ **easy** \g\ **go** \i\ **hit** \ī\ **ice** \j\ **job** \ŋ\ **sing** \ō\ **go** \ȯ\ **law** \ȯi\ **boy** \th\ **thin** \t͟h\ **the** \ü\ **loot** \u̇\ **foot** \y\ **yet** \zh\ **vision, beige** \k̲, ⁿ, œ, ue, ʸ\ *see* Guide to Pronunciation

taneously or by pressure from within ⟨the blister *broke*⟩ **c** *of a wave* : to curl over and fall apart in surf or foam **3** : to interrupt one's activity or occupation for a brief period ⟨~ for lunch⟩ **4** : to alter sharply in tone, pitch, or intensity ⟨a voice ~*ing* with emotion⟩ **5** : to become fair : CLEAR ⟨when the weather ~*s*⟩ **6** : to make the opening shot of a game of pool **7** : to end a relationship, connection, or agreement — usu. used with *with* or *from* **8** : to give way in disorderly retreat **9 a** : to swerve suddenly **b** : to curve from a straight path ⟨a pitch that ~*s* away from the batter⟩ ⟨a putt that ~*s* left⟩ **10 a** : to fail in health, strength, vitality, resolve, or control ⟨may ~ under questioning⟩ **b** : to become inoperative because of damage, wear, or strain ⟨the pump *broke*⟩ **11** : to fail to keep a prescribed gait — used of a horse **12** : to undergo a sudden significant decrease in price, value, or volume ⟨transportation stocks may ~ sharply⟩ **13** : HAPPEN, DEVELOP ⟨for the team to succeed, everything has to ~ right⟩ **14** : to win against an opponent's service in tennis **15 a** : to divide into classes, categories, or types — usu. used with *into* ⟨the rose is *broken* into several varieties⟩ **b** : to fold, bend, lift, or come apart at a seam, groove, or joint **c** *of cream* : to separate during churning into liquid and fat — **break a leg** — used to wish good luck esp. to a performer — **break bread** : to dine together — **break camp** : to pack up gear and leave a camp or campsite — **break cover** *also* **break covert** : to start from a covert or lair — **break even** : to achieve a balance; *esp* : to operate a business or enterprise without either loss or profit — **break free** : to get away by overcoming restraints or constraints — **break ground 1** : to begin construction **2** *or* **break new ground** : to make or show discoveries : PIONEER — **break into 1** : to begin with or as if with a sudden throwing off of restraint ⟨*broke into* tears⟩ ⟨face *breaking into* a smile⟩ ⟨the horse *breaks into* a gallop⟩ **2** : to make entry or entrance into ⟨*broke into* the house⟩ ⟨*break into* show business⟩ **3** : INTERRUPT ⟨*break into* a TV program with a news flash⟩ — **break one's heart** : to crush emotionally with sorrow — **break one's wrists** : to turn the wrists as part of the swing of a club or bat — **break ranks** *also* **break rank** : to differ in opinion or action from one's peers — often used with *with* — **break the back of** : to subdue the main force of ⟨*break the back of* inflation⟩ — **break the ice 1** : to make a beginning **2** : to get through the first difficulties in starting a conversation or discussion — **break wind** : to expel gas from the intestine

²**break** *n* (14c) **1 a** : an act or action of breaking **b** : the opening shot in a game of pool or billiards **2 a** : a condition produced by or as if by breaking : GAP ⟨a ~ in the clouds⟩ **b** : a gap in an otherwise continuous electric circuit **3** : the action or act of breaking in, out, or forth ⟨at ~ of day⟩ ⟨a jail ~⟩ **4** : a place or situation at which a break occurs: as **a** : the place at which a word is divided esp. at the end of a line of print or writing **b** : the point or location at which waves break for surfing **5** : an interruption in continuity ⟨a ~ in the weather⟩: as **a** : a notable change of subject matter, attitude, or treatment **b** (1) : an abrupt, significant, or noteworthy change or interruption in a continuous process, trend, or surface (2) : a respite from work, school, or duty ⟨coffee ~⟩ ⟨spring ~⟩ (3) : relief from annoyance — often used to express exasperation or irritation in phrases like *give me a break* (4) : a planned interruption in a radio or television program ⟨a ~ for the commercial⟩ **c** : deviation of a pitched baseball from a straight line **d** *mining* : FAULT, DISLOCATION **e** : failure of a horse to maintain the prescribed gait **f** : an abrupt change in musical or vocal pitch or quality **g** : the action or an instance of breaking service in tennis **h** : a usu. solo instrumental passage in jazz, folk, or popular music **6 a** : DASH, RUSH ⟨a base runner making a ~ for home⟩ **b** : FAST BREAK **7** : a sudden and abrupt decline of prices or values **8 a** : the start of a race **b** : the act of separating after a clinch in boxing **9 a** : a stroke of luck and esp. of good luck ⟨a bad ~⟩ ⟨got the ~*s*⟩ **b** : a favorable or opportune situation : CHANCE ⟨waiting for a big ~ in show business⟩ **c** : favorable consideration or treatment ⟨a tax ~⟩ ⟨a ~ on the price⟩ **10 a** : a rupture in previously agreeable relations ⟨a ~ between the two countries⟩ **b** : an abrupt split or difference with something previously adhered to or followed ⟨a sharp ~ with tradition⟩ **11** : BREAKDOWN 1c ⟨suffered a mental ~⟩

break·able \ˈbrā-kə-bəl\ *adj* (1570) : capable of being broken — **breakable** *n*

break·age \ˈbrā-kij\ *n* (1769) **1** : loss due to things broken **2 a** : the action or an instance of breaking **b** : a quantity broken

¹**break·away** \ˈbrā-kə-ˌwā\ *n* (1881) **1 a** : one that breaks away **b** : a departure from or rejection of (as a group or tradition) **2 a** : a play (as in hockey) in which an offensive player breaks free of the defenders and rushes toward the goal **b** : a sudden acceleration by one or more bicyclists pulling away from the pack in a race **3** : an object made to shatter or collapse under pressure or impact

²**breakaway** *adj* (1927) **1** : favoring independence from an affiliation : SECEDING ⟨a ~ faction formed a new party⟩ **2** : made to break, shatter, or bend easily ⟨~ road signs for highway safety⟩ **3 a** : of, relating to, or resulting from a breakaway ⟨a ~ goal⟩ **b** : allowing or having an ability to execute a breakaway ⟨~ speed⟩

break away *vi* (1535) **1** : to detach oneself esp. from a group : get away **2** : to depart from or accustomed ways **3** : to pull away with a burst of speed

break beat *n* [²*break* (solo musical passage)] (1985) : a repetitive drum pattern in hip-hop and dance music; *also* : music based on break beats

break·bone fever \ˈbrāk-ˈbōn-\ *n* (1855) : DENGUE

break dancing *n* [²*break* (solo passage) or *break beat*] (1982) : dancing in which solo dancers perform acrobatics that involve touching various parts of the body (as the back or head) to the ground — **break–dance** \ˈbrāk-ˌdan(t)s\ *vb* — **break–danc·er** \-ˌdan(t)-sər\ *n*

break·down \ˈbrāk-ˌdau̇n\ *n* (1827) **1** : the action or result of breaking down: as **a** : a failure to function **b** : failure to progress or have effect : DISINTEGRATION ⟨a ~ of negotiations⟩ **c** : a physical, mental, or nervous collapse **d** : the process of decomposing **e** : division into categories : CLASSIFICATION; *also* : an account analyzed into categories **2** : a fast shuffling dance; *also* : music for such a dance

break down *vt* (14c) **1 a** : to cause to fall or collapse by breaking or shattering **b** : to make ineffective ⟨*break down* legal barriers⟩ **2 a** : to divide into parts or categories **b** : to separate (as a chemical compound) into simpler substances : DECOMPOSE **c** : to take apart esp. for storage or shipment and for later reassembling ~ *vi* **1 a** : to stop functioning because of breakage or wear **b** : to become inoperative or ineffective : FAIL ⟨negotiations *broke down*⟩ **c** : to fail in strength or vitality ⟨her health *broke down*⟩ **d** : to succumb to mental or emotional stress ⟨*broke down* and cried⟩ **e** : to lose one's resolve : GIVE IN ⟨finally *broke down* and bought a computer⟩ **2** *of horses* : to severely injure the supporting ligament or bones of the fetlock joint **3 a** : to be susceptible to or undergo analysis or subdivision ⟨the statistics *break down* like this⟩ **b** : to undergo decomposition *syn* see ANALYZE

¹**break·er** \ˈbrā-kər\ *n* (12c) **1 a** : one that breaks **b** : a machine or plant for breaking rocks or coal **c** *chiefly Brit* : one who breaks up ships or cars for salvage **d** : a device for opening a circuit; *specif* : CIRCUIT BREAKER **2** : a wave breaking into foam (as against the shore)

²**brea·ker** \ˈbrā-kər\ *n* [by folk etymology fr. Sp *barrica*] (1833) : a small water cask

break·even \ˈbrāk-ˈē-vən\ *n* (1958) : the point at which cost and income are equal and there is neither profit nor loss; *also* : a financial result reflecting neither profit nor loss

break–even \ˈbrāk-ˈē-vən\ *adj* (1931) : having equal cost and income

break·fast \ˈbrek-fəst\ *n* (15c) **1** : the first meal of the day esp. when taken in the morning **2** : the food prepared for a breakfast ⟨eat your ~⟩ — **breakfast** *vb* — **break·fast·er** *n*

break·front \ˈbrāk-ˌfrənt\ *n* (1928) : a large cabinet or bookcase whose center section projects beyond the flanking end sections

break–in \ˈbrāk-ˌin\ *n* (1856) **1** : the act or action of breaking in ⟨a rash of ~*s* at the new apartment house⟩ **2** : a performance or a series of performances serving as a trial run **3** : an initial period of operation during which working parts begin to function efficiently

break in *vi* (ca. 1535) **1** : to enter something (as a building or computer system) without consent or by force **2 a** : INTRUDE ⟨*break in* upon his privacy⟩ **b** : to interrupt a conversation **3** : to start in an activity or enterprise ⟨*breaking in* as a cub reporter⟩ ~ *vt* **1** : to accustom to a certain activity or occurrence ⟨*break in* the new clerk⟩ **2** : to overcome the stiffness or newness of ⟨*break in* a pair of shoes⟩

breaking and entering *n* (1778) : the act of forcing or otherwise gaining unlawful passage into and entering another's building

breaking point *n* (1865) **1** : the point at which a person gives way under stress **2** : the point at which a situation becomes critical **3** : the point at which something loses force or validity ⟨stretch the rules to the *breaking point*⟩

break·neck \ˈbrāk-ˈnek\ *adj* (1562) : very fast or dangerous ⟨~ speed⟩

break off *vi* (14c) **1** : to stop abruptly ⟨*break off* in the middle of a sentence⟩ **2** : to become detached ⟨branches that *broke off* in the storm⟩ **3** : to end a relationship ⟨*broke off* with his business partner⟩ ~ *vt* **1** : DISCONTINUE ⟨*break off* diplomatic relations⟩ **2** : to remove by or as if by breaking ⟨*break off* a chunk of bread⟩

¹**break·out** \ˈbrāk-ˌau̇t\ *n* (1820) : a violent or forceful break from a restraining condition or situation; *esp* : a military attack to break from encirclement

²**breakout** *adj* (1978) : being or relating to a sudden or smashing success esp. in comparison to previous efforts ⟨a ~ book⟩

break out *vi* (bef. 12c) **1** : to develop or emerge with suddenness or force ⟨fire *broke out*⟩ ⟨a riot *broke out*⟩ **2 a** : to become covered ⟨*break out* in a sweat⟩ **b** : to become affected with a skin eruption **3** : to make a break from a restraining condition or situation ⟨*broke out* of a slump⟩ ⟨*broke out* of jail⟩ ~ *vt* **1 a** : to make ready for action or use ⟨*break out* the tents and make camp⟩ **b** : to produce for consumption ⟨*break out* a bottle of champagne⟩ **2** : to display flying and unfurled **3** : to separate from a mass of data ⟨*break out* newsstand sales⟩

break point *n* (1969) : a situation in tennis in which the receiving player can win the game by scoring the next point; *also* : the point so scored

break·through \ˈbrāk-ˌthrü\ *n, often attrib* (1918) **1** : an offensive thrust that penetrates and carries beyond a defensive line in warfare **2** : an act or instance of breaking through an obstacle ⟨a ~ agreement⟩ **3 a** : a sudden advance esp. in knowledge or technique ⟨a medical ~⟩ **b** : a person's first notable success ⟨a ~ novel⟩

break through *vi* (1955) : to make a breakthrough

break·up \ˈbrāk-ˌəp\ *n* (1794) **1** : an act or instance of breaking up **2** : the breaking, melting, and loosening of ice in the spring

break up *vi* (15c) **1 a** : to cease to exist as a unified whole : DISPERSE ⟨their partnership *broke up*⟩ **b** : to end a romance **2** : to lose morale, composure, or resolution; *esp* : to become abandoned to laughter ⟨*breaks up* completely, laughing himself into a coughing fit —Gene Williams⟩ ~ *vt* **1** : to break into pieces **2** : to bring to an end ⟨*broke up* the fight⟩ **3** : to do away with : DESTROY ⟨*break up* a monopoly⟩ **4** : to disrupt the continuity or flow of ⟨*break up* a dull routine⟩ **5** : DECOMPOSE ⟨*break up* a chemical⟩ **6** : to cause to laugh heartily

breakup value *n* (1902) : the value esp. of shares of stock of a corporation liquidating its assets

break·wa·ter \ˈbrāk-ˌwȯ-tər, -ˌwä-\ *n* (ca. 1769) : an offshore structure (as a wall) protecting a harbor or beach from the force of waves

¹**bream** \ˈbrim, ˈbrēm\ *n, pl* **bream** *or* **breams** [ME *breme*, fr. AF, of Gmc origin; akin to OHG *brahsima* bream, MHG *brehen* to shine] (14c) **1** : a bronze-colored European freshwater cyprinid fish (*Abramis brama*); *broadly* : any of various related fishes **2 a** : any of various marine fish (family Sparidae) related to the porgy — called also *sea bream* **b** : any of various freshwater sunfishes (*Lepomis* and related genera); *esp* : BLUEGILL

²**bream** \ˈbrēm\ *vt* [prob. fr. D *brem* furze; fr. the use of burning furze in the cleaning] (1626) : to clean (a ship's bottom) by heating and scraping

¹**breast** \ˈbrest\ *n* [ME *brest*, fr. OE *brēost*; akin to OHG *brust* breast, OIr *brú* belly, Russ *bryukho*] (bef. 12c) **1** : either of the pair of mammary glands extending from the front of the chest in pubescent and adult human females and some other mammals; *also* : either of the analogous but rudimentary organs of the male chest esp. when enlarged **2 a** : the fore or ventral part of the body between the neck and the abdomen **b** : the part of an article of clothing covering the breast **3** : the seat of emotion and thought : BOSOM **4 a** : something (as a front, swelling, or curving part) resembling a breast **b** : FACE 6 — **breast·ed** \ˈbres-təd\ *adj*

²**breast** *vt* (1599) **1** : to contend with resolutely : CONFRONT ⟨~*ing* the waves⟩ **2** *chiefly Brit* : CLIMB, ASCEND **3** : to thrust the chest against ⟨the sprinter ~*ed* the tape⟩

breast–beat·ing \ˈbres(t)-ˌbē-tiŋ\ *n* (1938) : noisy demonstrative protestation (as of grief, anger, or self-recrimination)

breast·bone \ˈbres(t)-ˌbōn\ *n* (bef. 12c) : STERNUM

breast drill *n* (1857) **:** a portable drill with a plate that is pressed by the breast in forcing the drill against the work
breast–feed \ˈbrest-ˌfēd\ *vt* (1903) **:** to feed (a baby) from a mother's breast ~ *vi* **:** to breast-feed a baby
breast·plate \ˈbres(t)-ˌplāt\ *n* (14c) **1 :** a usu. metal plate worn as defensive armor for the breast — see ARMOR illustration **2 :** a vestment worn in ancient times by a Jewish high priest and set with 12 gems bearing the names of the tribes of Israel **3 :** a piece against which a worker's breast is pressed in operating a tool (as a breast drill)
breast·stroke \ˈbres(t)-ˌstrōk\ *n* (1867) **:** a swimming stroke executed in a prone position by coordinating a kick in which the legs are brought forward with the knees together and the feet are turned outward and whipped back with a glide and a backward sweeping movement of the arms — **breast·strok·er** \-ˌstrō-kər\ *n*
breast·work \ˈbrest-ˌwərk\ *n* (1642) **:** a temporary fortification
breath \ˈbreth\ *n* [ME *breth,* fr. OE *brǣth;* akin to OHG *brādam* breath, and perh. to OE *beorma* yeast — more at BARM] (bef. 12c) **1 a :** air filled with a fragrance or odor **b :** a slight indication **:** SUGGESTION ⟨the faintest ~ of scandal⟩ **2 a :** the faculty of breathing ⟨recovering his ~ after the race⟩ **b :** an act of breathing ⟨fought to the last ~⟩ **c :** opportunity or time to breathe **:** RESPITE **3 :** a slight breeze **4 a :** air inhaled and exhaled in breathing ⟨bad ~⟩ **b :** something (as moisture on a cold surface) produced by breath or breathing **c :** INHALATION **5 :** a spoken sound **:** UTTERANCE **6 :** SPIRIT, ANIMATION — **breath of fresh air :** a welcome or refreshing change — **in one breath** *or* **in the same breath :** almost simultaneously — **out of breath :** breathing very rapidly (as from strenuous exercise) — **under one's breath :** so as to be barely audible ⟨mumbled something *under his breath*⟩
breath·able \ˈbrē-thə-bəl\ *adj* (ca. 1731) **1 :** suitable for breathing ⟨~ air⟩ **2 :** allowing air to pass through **:** POROUS ⟨a ~ synthetic fabric⟩ — **breath·abil·i·ty** \ˌbrē-thə-ˈbi-lə-tē\ *n*
Breath·a·lyz·er \ˈbre-thə-ˌlī-zər\ *trademark* — used for a device that is used to determine the alcohol content of a breath sample
breathe \ˈbrēth\ *vb* **breathed; breath·ing** [ME *brethen,* fr. *breth*] *vi* (14c) **1 a :** to draw air into and expel it from the lungs **:** RESPIRE; *broadly* **:** to take in oxygen and give out carbon dioxide through natural processes **b :** to inhale and exhale freely **2 :** LIVE **3 a** *obs* **:** to emit a fragrance or aura **b :** to become perceptible **:** be expressed ⟨a personality that ~*s* and that distinguishes his work —Bennett Schiff⟩ **4 :** to pause and rest before continuing **5 :** to blow softly **6 :** to feel free of restraint ⟨needs room to ~⟩ **7** *of wine* **:** to develop flavor and bouquet by exposure to air **8 a :** to permit passage of air or vapor ⟨a fabric that ~*s*⟩ **b** *of an internal combustion engine* **:** to use air to support combustion ~ *vt* **1 a :** to send out by exhaling **b :** to instill by or as if by breathing ⟨~ new life into the movement⟩ **2 :** to give rest from exertion to **3 :** to take in in breathing ⟨~ the scent of pines⟩ **4 :** to inhale and exhale ⟨~ air⟩ **5 a :** UTTER, EXPRESS ⟨don't ~ a word of it to anyone⟩ **b :** to make manifest **:** EVINCE ⟨the novel ~*s* despair⟩ — **breathe down one's neck 1 :** to threaten esp. in attack or pursuit **2 :** to keep one under close or constant surveillance ⟨parents always *breathing down his neck*⟩ — **breathe easy** *or* **breathe easier** *or* **breathe easily** *or* **breathe freely :** to enjoy relief (as from pressure or danger)
breathed \ˈbretht\ *adj* (1580) **1 :** having breath esp. of a specified kind — usu. used in combination ⟨sweet-*breathed*⟩ **2 :** VOICELESS 2
breath·er \ˈbrē-thər\ *n* (14c) **1 :** one that breathes **2 :** a break in activity for rest or relief **3 :** a small vent in an otherwise airtight enclosure
breath·ing \ˈbrē-thiŋ\ *n* (1746) **:** either of the marks ʽ and ʼ used in writing Greek to indicate aspiration or its absence
breathing space *n* (1599) **:** some time in which to recover, get organized, or get going — called also *breathing room, breathing spell*
breathing tube *n* (1969) **:** a tube inserted (as through the nose or mouth) into the trachea to maintain an unobstructed passageway esp. to deliver oxygen or anesthesia to the lungs
breath·less \ˈbreth-ləs\ *adj* (14c) **1 a :** not breathing **b :** DEAD **2 a :** panting or gasping for breath **b :** gripped with emotion ⟨~ in anticipation⟩ **c :** INTENSE, GRIPPING ⟨~ eagerness⟩ ⟨~ prose⟩ **d :** very rapid or strenuous ⟨go at a ~ pace⟩ **e :** marked by intense or unremitting activity ⟨a ~ schedule⟩ **3 :** oppressive because of no fresh air or breeze — **breath·less·ly** *adv* — **breath·less·ness** *n*
breath·tak·ing \ˈbreth-ˌtā-kiŋ\ *adj* (1877) **1 :** making one out of breath **2 a :** EXCITING, THRILLING ⟨a ~ race⟩ **b :** very great **:** ASTONISHING ⟨his ~ ignorance⟩ — **breath·tak·ing·ly** \-kiŋ-lē\ *adv*
breathy \ˈbre-thē\ *adj* **breath·i·er; -est** (1883) **:** characterized or accompanied by or as if by the audible passage of breath — **breath·i·ly** \-thə-lē\ *adv* — **breath·i·ness** \-thē-nəs\ *n*
brec·cia \ˈbre-ch(ē-)ə\ *n* [It] (1774) **:** a rock composed of sharp fragments embedded in a fine-grained matrix (as sand or clay)
brec·ci·ate \ˈbre-chē-ˌāt\ *vt* **-at·ed; -at·ing** (1772) **1 :** to form (rock) into breccia **2 :** to break (rock) into fragments — **brec·ci·a·tion** \ˌbre-chē-ˈā-shən\ *n*
brede \ˈbrēd\ *n* [var. of *braid*] (1640) *archaic* **:** EMBROIDERY
bred–in–the–bone \ˈbre-dᵊn-thə-ˌbōn\ *adj* (15c) **1 :** DEEP-ROOTED ⟨~ honesty⟩ **2 :** INVETERATE ⟨a ~ gambler⟩
breech \ˈbrēch\ *n* [ME, breeches, fr. OE *brēc,* pl. of *brōc* leg covering; akin to OHG *bruoh* breeches, L *braca* pants] (bef. 12c) **1** *pl* \ˈbri-chəz *also* ˈbrē-\ **a :** short pants covering the hips and thighs and fitting snugly at the lower edges at or just below the knee **b :** PANTS **2 a :** the hind end of the body **:** BUTTOCKS **b :** BREECH PRESENTATION; *also* **:** a fetus that is presented breech first **3 :** the part of a firearm at the rear of the barrel
breech·block \ˈbrēch-ˌbläk\ *n* (1881) **:** the block in breech-loading firearms that closes the rear of the barrel against the force of the charge and prevents gases from escaping
breech·cloth \ˈbrēch-ˌklȯth, ˈbrich-\ *n* (1793) **:** LOINCLOTH
breech·clout \-ˌklau̇t\ *n* (1757) **:** LOINCLOTH
breech delivery *n* (1882) **:** delivery of a fetus by breech presentation — called also *breech birth*
breech·es buoy \ˈbrē-chəz- *also* ˈbri-\ *n* (1880) **:** a canvas seat in the form of breeches hung from a life buoy running on a hawser and used to haul persons from one ship to another or from ship to shore esp. in rescue operations
breech·ing \ˈbrē-chiŋ, ˈbri-\ *n* (ca. 1524) **1 :** the part of a harness that passes around the rump of a draft animal **2 :** the short coarse wool on the rump and hind legs of a sheep or goat; *also* **:** the hair on the corresponding part of a dog
breech·load·er \ˈbrēch-ˈlō-dər\ *n* (1855) **:** a firearm that loads at the breech — **breech–load·ing** \-ˈlō-diŋ\ *adj*
breech presentation *n* (1811) **:** presentation of the fetus in which the breech is the first part to appear at the uterine cervix
[1]**breed** \ˈbrēd\ *vb* **bred** \ˈbred\; **breed·ing** [ME *breden,* fr. OE *brēdan;* akin to OE *brōd* brood] *vt* (bef. 12c) **1 :** to produce (offspring) by hatching or gestation **2 a :** BEGET 1 **b :** PRODUCE, ENGENDER ⟨despair often ~*s* violence⟩ **3 :** to propagate (plants or animals) sexually and usu. under controlled conditions ⟨*bred* several strains of corn together to produce a superior variety⟩ **4 a :** BRING UP, NURTURE ⟨born and *bred* in the country⟩ **b :** to inculcate by training ⟨~ good manners into one's children⟩ **5 a :** [4]MATE 3 **b :** to mate with **:** INSEMINATE **c :** IMPREGNATE 2 **6 :** to produce (a fissionable element) by bombarding a nonfissionable element with neutrons from a radioactive element ~ *vi* **1 a :** to produce offspring by sexual union **b :** COPULATE, MATE **2 :** to propagate animals or plants
[2]**breed** *n* (1553) **1 :** a group of usu. domesticated animals or plants presumably related by descent from common ancestors and visibly similar in most characters **2 :** a number of persons of the same stock **3 :** CLASS, KIND ⟨a new ~ of athlete⟩
breed·er \ˈbrē-dər\ *n* (1531) **:** one that breeds: as **a :** an animal or plant kept for propagation **b :** one engaged in the breeding of a specified organism **c :** a nuclear reactor designed to produce more fissionable material than it uses as fuel — called also *breeder reactor*
breed·ing *n* (14c) **1 :** the action or process of bearing or generating **2 :** ANCESTRY **3 a** *archaic* **:** EDUCATION ⟨she had her ~ at my father's charge —Shak.⟩ **b :** training in or observance of the proprieties **4 :** the sexual propagation of plants or animals
breeding ground *n* (1630) **1 :** the place to which animals go to breed **2 :** a place or set of circumstances suitable for or favorable to growth and development ⟨hurricane *breeding grounds*⟩
breeks \ˈbrēks, ˈbriks\ *n pl* [ME (northern dial.) *breke,* fr. OE *brēc*] (14c) *chiefly Scot* **:** BREECHES
[1]**breeze** \ˈbrēz\ *n* [prob. fr. Sp *brisa* northeast wind] (1626) **1 a :** a light gentle wind **b :** a wind of from 4 to 31 miles (6 to 50 kilometers) an hour **2 :** something easily done **:** CINCH — **breeze·less** \-ləs\ *adj* — **in a breeze :** EASILY
[2]**breeze** *vi* **breezed; breez·ing** (1907) **1 :** to move swiftly and airily ⟨*breezed* past the protesters⟩ **2 :** to make progress quickly and easily ⟨*breezed* through the exam⟩ ⟨*breezed* to victory⟩
[3]**breeze** *n* [prob. modif. of F *braise* cinders — more at BRAISE] (1726) **:** residue from the making of coke or charcoal
breeze·way \ˈbrēz-ˌwā\ *n* (1931) **:** a roofed often open passage connecting two buildings (as a house and garage) or halves of a building
breezy \ˈbrē-zē\ *adj* **breez·i·er; -est** (1637) **1 :** swept by breezes ⟨~ beaches⟩ ⟨a ~ day⟩ **2 a :** briskly informal ⟨a ~ essay⟩ **b :** AIRY, NONCHALANT ⟨~ indifference⟩ — **breez·i·ly** \-zə-lē\ *adv* — **breez·i·ness** \-zē-nəs\ *n*
breg·ma \ˈbreg-mə\ *n, pl* **-ma·ta** \-mə-tə\ [NL *bregmat-, bregma,* fr. LL, front part of the head, fr. Gk; akin to Gk *brechmos* front part of the head — more at BRAIN] (1578) **:** the point of junction of the coronal and sagittal sutures of the skull
brems·strah·lung \ˈbrem(p)-ˌshträ-ləŋ\ *n* [G, lit., decelerated radiation] (1939) **:** the electromagnetic radiation produced by the sudden retardation of a charged particle in an intense electric field (as of an atomic nucleus); *also* **:** the process that produces such radiation
brent goose \ˈbrent-\ *n* (1570) *chiefly Brit* **:** BRANT
breth·ren \ˈbreth-rən; ˈbre-thə-, -thərn\ *pl of* BROTHER (bef. 12c) — used chiefly in formal or solemn address or in referring to the members of a profession, society, or sect
Brethren *n pl* (1822) **:** members of various sects originating chiefly in 18th century German Pietism; *esp* **:** DUNKERS
Bret·on \ˈbre-tᵊn\ *n* [F, fr. ML *Briton-, Brito,* fr. L, Briton] (1653) **1 :** a native or inhabitant of Brittany **2 :** the Celtic language of the Breton people — **Breton** *adj*
breve \ˈbrēv, ˈbrev\ *n* [ME *brefe,* fr. ML, fr. neut. of *brevis* brief — more at BRIEF] (15c) **1 :** a note equivalent to two whole notes **2 :** a curved mark ˘ used to indicate a short vowel or a short or unstressed syllable
[1]**bre·vet** \bri-ˈvet, *chiefly Brit* ˈbre-vit\ *n* [ME, document, fr. AF, dim. of *bref* letter — more at BRIEF] (1689) **:** a commission giving a military officer higher nominal rank than that for which pay is received
[2]**brevet** *vt* **bre·vet·ted** *or* **brev·et·ed; bre·vet·ting** *or* **brev·et·ing** (1819) **:** to confer rank upon by brevet
bre·via·ry \ˈbrē-və-rē, -vyə-, -vē-ˌer-ē, -ˌe-rē *also* ˈbre-\ *n, pl* **-ries** [ME *breviarie,* fr. ML *breviarium,* fr. L, summary, fr. *brevis*] (15c) **1** *often cap* **a :** a book of the prayers, hymns, psalms, and readings for the canonical hours **b :** DIVINE OFFICE **2** [L *breviarium*] **:** a brief summary
brev·i·ty \ˈbre-və-tē\ *n, pl* **-ties** [L *brevitas,* fr. *brevis*] (15c) **:** shortness of duration; *esp* **:** shortness or conciseness of expression
[1]**brew** \ˈbrü\ *vb* [ME, fr. OE *brēowan;* akin to L *fervēre* to boil — more at BARM] *vt* (bef. 12c) **1 :** to prepare (as beer or ale) by steeping, boiling, and fermentation or by infusion and fermentation **2 a :** to bring about **:** FOMENT ⟨~ trouble⟩ **b :** CONTRIVE **3 :** to prepare (as tea) by infusion in hot water ~ *vi* **1 :** to brew beer or ale **2 :** to be in the process of forming ⟨a storm is ~*ing*⟩ — **brew·er** \ˈbrü-ər, ˈbru̇(-ə)r\ *n*
[2]**brew** *n* (ca. 1510) **1 a :** a brewed beverage (as beer) **b :** a serving of a brewed beverage ⟨quaff a few ~*s*⟩ **c :** something produced by or as if by brewing **2 :** the process of brewing
brew·age \ˈbrü-ij\ *n* (1542) **1 :** BREW 1a **2 :** BREW 2
brewer's yeast *n* (1855) **:** a yeast used or suitable for use in brewing; *specif* **:** the dried pulverized cells of such a yeast (*Saccharomyces cerevisiae*) used esp. as a source of B-complex vitamins

\ə\ **abut** \ᵊ\ kitten, F table \ər\ **further** \a\ **ash** \ā\ **ace** \ä\ **mop, mar**
\au̇\ **out** \ch\ **chin** \e\ **bet** \ē\ **easy** \g\ **go** \i\ **hit** \ī\ **ice** \j\ **job**
\ŋ\ **sing** \ō\ **go** \ȯ\ **law** \ȯi\ **boy** \th\ **thin** \th\ **the** \ü\ **loot** \u̇\ **foot**
\y\ **yet** \zh\ **vision, beige** \k, ⁿ, œ, ue, ʸ\ *see* Guide to Pronunciation

brew·ery \ˈbrü-ə-rē, ˈbrü(-ə)r-ē\ *n, pl* **-er·ies** (1658) **:** a plant where malt liquors are produced
brew·mas·ter \ˈbrü-ˌmas-tər\ *n* (1904) **:** a person who supervises the brewing process of malt liquors
brew·pub \ˈbrü-ˌpəb\ *n* (1984) **:** a restaurant that sells beverages brewed on the premises
brew·ski \ˈbrü-skē\ *n* [[2]*brew* + *-ski,* suffix in Slavic surnames] (1978) *slang* **:** BEER 4
[1]**bri·ar** *also* **bri·er** \ˈbrī(-ə)r\ *n* [ME *brere,* fr. OE *brēr*] (15c) **:** a plant (as a rose, blackberry, or greenbrier) having a usu. woody and thorny or prickly stem; *also* **:** a mass or twig of these — **bri·ary** \ˈbrī(-ə)r-ē\ *adj*
[2]**briar** *n* [short for *briar pipe,* fr. *briar* wood of the European heath, fr. F *bruyère* heath, fr. MF *bruiere,* fr. VL **brucaria,* fr. LL *brucus* heather, of Celt origin; akin to OIr *froech* heather; akin to Gk *ereikē* heather] (1882) **:** a tobacco pipe made from the root or stem of a European heath (*Erica arborea*)
bri·ard \brē-ˈär(d)\ *n* [F, fr. *Brie,* district in France] (ca. 1929) **:** any of an old French breed of large long-coated sheepdogs
[1]**bribe** \ˈbrīb\ *n* [ME, morsel given to a beggar, bribe, fr. AF, morsel] (15c) **1 :** money or favor given or promised in order to influence the judgment or conduct of a person in a position of trust **2 :** something that serves to induce or influence
[2]**bribe** *vb* **bribed; brib·ing** *vt* (1528) **:** to induce or influence by or as if by bribery ~ *vi* **:** to practice bribery — **brib·able** \ˈbrī-bə-bəl\ *adj* — **brib·ee** \ˌbrī-ˈbē\ *n* — **brib·er** *n*
brib·ery \ˈbrī-b(ə-)rē\ *n, pl* **-er·ies** (1549) **:** the act or practice of giving or taking a bribe
bric–a–brac \ˈbri-kə-ˌbrak\ *n, pl* **bric–a–brac** [F *bric-à-brac*] (1840) **1 :** a miscellaneous collection of small articles commonly of ornamental or sentimental value **:** CURIOS **2 :** something suggesting bric-a-brac esp. in extraneous decorative quality
[1]**brick** \ˈbrik\ *n, often attrib* [ME *bryke,* fr. MD *bricke*] (15c) **1** *pl* **bricks** *or* **brick :** a handy-sized unit of building or paving material typically being rectangular and about 2¼ × 3¾ × 8 inches (57 × 95 × 203 millimeters) and of moist clay hardened by heat **2 :** a good-hearted person **3 :** a rectangular compressed mass (as of ice cream) **4 :** a semisoft cheese with numerous small holes, smooth texture, and often mild flavor **5 :** GAFFE, BLUNDER — used esp. in the phrase *drop a brick* **6 :** a badly missed shot in basketball ⟨he threw up a ~⟩
[2]**brick** *vt* (1592) **1 :** to close, face, or pave with bricks — usu. used with *up, in,* or *over* **2 :** to render (an electronic device, such as a smartphone) nonfunctional (as by accidental damage, malicious hacking, or software changes)
brick–and–mortar *or* **bricks–and–mortar** *adj* (1988) **:** relating to or being a traditional business serving customers in a building as contrasted to an online business ⟨a ~ store⟩
brick·bat \ˈbrik-ˌbat\ *n* [*brick* + [1]*bat* (lump, fragment)] (1579) **1 :** a fragment of a hard material (as a brick); *esp* **:** one used as a missile **2 :** an uncomplimentary remark
brick·lay·er \ˈbrik-ˌlā-ər, -ˌler\ *n* (15c) **:** a person who lays brick — **brick·lay·ing** \-ˌlā-iŋ\ *n*
brick red *n* (1810) **:** a moderate reddish brown
brick wall *n* (15c) **1 :** a wall made of brick **2 :** an immovable block or obstruction ⟨the plan ran into a *brick wall*⟩
brick·work \ˈbrik-ˌwərk\ *n* (1580) **:** work of or with bricks and mortar
brick·yard \-ˌyärd\ *n* (1731) **:** a place where bricks are made
bri·co·lage \ˌbrē-kō-ˈläzh, ˌbri-\ *n* [F, fr. *bricoler* to putter about] (1960) **:** construction (as of a sculpture or a structure of ideas) achieved by using whatever comes to hand; *also* **:** something constructed in this way
bri·co·leur \ˌbrē-kō-ˈlər, -ˈlœr, bri-\ *n* [F, one who putters about, fr. *bricoler*] (1965) **:** one who engages in bricolage
[1]**brid·al** \ˈbrī-dᵊl\ *n* [ME *bridale,* fr. OE *brȳdealu,* fr. *brȳd* + *ealu* ale — more at ALE] (bef. 12c) **:** a marriage festival or ceremony
[2]**bridal** *adj* (13c) **1 :** of or relating to a bride or a wedding **:** NUPTIAL **2 :** intended for a newly married couple ⟨a ~ suite⟩
bridal wreath *n* (ca. 1889) **:** a spirea (*Spiraea prunifolia*) widely grown for its umbels of small white flowers borne in spring
bride \ˈbrīd\ *n* [ME, fr. OE *brȳd;* akin to OHG *brūt* bride] (bef. 12c) **:** a woman just married or about to be married
bride·groom \ˈbrīd-ˌgrüm, -ˌgrum\ *n* [ME (Sc) *brydegrome,* by folk etymology fr. ME *bridegome,* fr. OE *brȳdguma,* fr. *brȳd* + *guma* man; akin to OHG *brūtgomo* bridegroom — more at HOMAGE] (14c) **:** a man just married or about to be married
bride–price \ˈbrīd-ˌprīs\ *n* (1876) **:** a payment given by or in behalf of a prospective husband to the bride's family in many cultures
brides·maid \ˈbrīdz-ˌmād\ *n* (1552) **1 :** a woman who is an attendant of a bride **2 :** one that finishes just behind the winner
bride·well \ˈbrīd-ˌwel, -wəl\ *n* [*Bridewell,* London jail] (ca. 1593) **:** PRISON
[1]**bridge** \ˈbrij\ *n* [ME *brigge,* fr. OE *brycg;* akin to OHG *brucka* bridge, OCS *brŭvŭno* beam] (bef. 12c) **1 a :** a structure carrying a pathway or roadway over a depression or obstacle **b :** a time, place, or means of connection or transition **2 :** something resembling a bridge in form or function: as **a :** the upper bony part of the nose; *also* **:** the part of a pair of glasses that rests upon it **b :** a piece raising the strings of a musical instrument — see VIOLIN illustration **c :** the forward part of a ship's superstructure from which the ship is navigated **d :** GANTRY 2b **e :** the hand as a rest for a billiards or pool cue; *also* **:** a device used as a cue rest **3 a :** a musical passage linking two sections of a composition **b :** a partial denture anchored to adjacent teeth **c :** a connection (as an atom or group of atoms) that joins two different parts of a molecule (as opposite sides of a ring) **4 :** an electrical instrument or network for measuring or comparing resistances, inductances, capacitances, or impedances by comparing the ratio of two opposing voltages to a known ratio — **bridge·less** \-ləs\ *adj*
[2]**bridge** *vt* **bridged; bridg·ing** (bef. 12c) **1 :** to make a bridge over or across ⟨~ the gap⟩; *also* **:** to join by a bridge **2 :** to provide with a bridge — **bridge·able** \ˈbri-jə-bəl\ *adj*
[3]**bridge** *n* [alter. of earlier *biritch,* of unknown origin] (ca. 1897) **:** any of various card games for usu. four players in two partnerships that bid for the right to declare a trump suit, seek to win tricks equal to the final bid, and play with the hand of declarer's partner exposed and played by declarer; *esp* **:** CONTRACT BRIDGE
bridge·head \-ˌhed\ *n* (1812) **1 a :** a fortification protecting the end of a bridge nearest an enemy **b :** an area around the end of a bridge **2 :** an advanced position seized in hostile territory

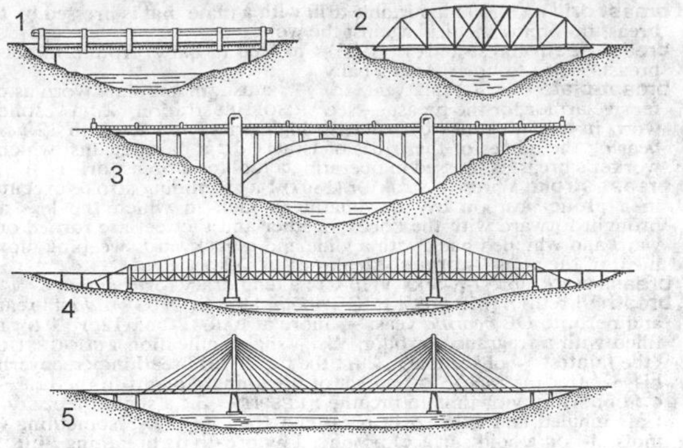

bridge 1a: *1* beam, *2* truss, *3* arch, *4* suspension, *5* cable-stayed

bridge loan *n* (1975) **:** a short-term loan used to finance an enterprise, investment, or government pending the receipt of other funds
bridge·work \-ˌwərk\ *n* (1883) **:** dental bridges
[1]**bri·dle** \ˈbrī-dᵊl\ *n* [ME *bridel,* fr. OE *brīdel;* akin to OE *bregdan* to move quickly — more at BRAID] (bef. 12c) **1 :** the headgear with which a horse is governed and which carries a bit and reins **2 :** a length of line or cable attached to two parts of something to spread the force of a pull; *esp* **:** rigging on a kite for attaching line **3 :** CURB, RESTRAINT ⟨set a ~ on his power⟩
[2]**bridle** *vb* **bri·dled; bri·dling** \ˈbrīd-liŋ, ˈbrī-dᵊl-iŋ\ *vt* (bef. 12c) **1 :** to put a bridle on **2 :** to restrain, check, or control with or as if with a bridle ⟨~ your tongue⟩ ~ *vi* **:** to show hostility or resentment (as to an affront to one's pride or dignity) esp. by drawing back the head and chin ***syn*** see RESTRAIN
bridle path *n* (1811) **:** a trail suitable for horseback riding
Brie \ˈbrē\ *n* [F, fr. *Brie,* district in France] (1835) **:** a soft surface-ripened cheese with a whitish rind and a pale yellow interior
[1]**brief** \ˈbrēf\ *adj* [ME *bref, breve,* fr. AF *bref, brief,* fr. L *brevis;* akin to OHG *murg* short, Gk *brachys*] (14c) **1 :** short in duration, extent, or length **2 a :** CONCISE **b :** CURT, ABRUPT — **brief·ness** *n*
[2]**brief** *n* [ME *bref,* fr. AF, fr. ML *brevis,* fr. LL, summary, fr. L *brevis,* adj.] (14c) **1 a :** an official letter or mandate; *esp* **:** a papal letter less formal than a bull **b :** a specific instruction or responsibility ⟨his ~ was to strengthen the army⟩ **2** [[1]*brief*] **a :** a concise article **b :** SYNOPSIS, SUMMARY **c :** a concise statement of a client's case made out for the instruction of counsel in a trial at law **3 :** an outline of an argument; *esp* **:** a formal outline esp. in law that sets forth the main contentions with supporting statements or evidence **4** *pl* **:** short snug pants or underpants — **in brief :** in a few words **:** BRIEFLY
[3]**brief** *vt* (15c) **1 :** to make an abstract or abridgment of **2 a :** to give final precise instructions to **b :** to coach thoroughly in advance **c :** to give essential information to **3 :** to discuss (as a military operation) in a briefing ⟨~*ed* the mission⟩ — **brief·er** *n*
brief·case \ˈbrēf-ˌkās\ *n* (1917) **:** a flat flexible case for carrying papers or books
brief·ing \ˈbrē-fiŋ\ *n* (1910) **:** an act or instance of giving precise instructions or essential information
brief·ly \ˈbrē-flē\ *adv* (14c) **1 a :** in a brief way ⟨~ mentioned⟩ **b :** in brief ⟨the food, ~, was awful⟩ **2 :** for a short time ⟨~ married⟩
brier *var of* BRIAR
[1]**brig** \ˈbrig\ *n* [short for *brigantine*] (1712) **:** a 2-masted square-rigged ship
[2]**brig** *n* [prob. fr. [1]*brig*] (1832) **1 :** a place (as on a ship) for temporary confinement of offenders in the U.S. Navy **2 :** GUARDHOUSE, PRISON
[3]**brig** *abbr* brigade; brigadier
[1]**bri·gade** \bri-ˈgād\ *n* [F, fr. It *brigata,* fr. *brigare* to fight — more at BRIGAND] (1634) **1 a :** a large body of troops **b :** a tactical and administrative unit composed of a headquarters, one or more units of infantry or armor, and supporting units **2 :** a group of people organized for special activity
[2]**brigade** *vt* **bri·gad·ed; bri·gad·ing** (1781) **:** to form or unite into a brigade
brig·a·dier \ˌbri-gə-ˈdir\ *n* [F, fr. *brigade*] (1678) **1 :** an officer in the British army commanding a brigade and ranking immediately below a major general **2 :** BRIGADIER GENERAL
brigadier general *n* (1690) **:** a commissioned officer in the army, air force, or marine corps who ranks above a colonel and whose insignia is one star
Brig·a·doon \ˌbri-gə-ˈdün\ *n* [fr. *Brigadoon,* village in the musical *Brigadoon* (1947) by A. J. Lerner and F. Loewe] (1968) **:** a place that is idyllic, unaffected by time, or remote from reality
brig·and \ˈbri-gənd\ *n* [ME *brigaunt,* fr. MF *brigand,* fr. OIt *brigante,* fr. *brigare* to fight, fr. *briga* strife, of Celt origin; akin to OIr *bríg* strength] (14c) **:** one who lives by plunder usu. as a member of a band **:** BANDIT — **brig·and·age** \-gən-dij\ *n*
brig·an·dine \ˈbri-gən-ˌdēn\ *n* [ME, fr. MF, fr. *brigand*] (15c) **:** medieval body armor of scales or plates
brig·an·tine \ˈbri-gən-ˌtēn\ *n* [MF *brigantin,* fr. OIt *brigantino,* fr. *brigante*] (1525) **:** a 2-masted sailing ship that is square-rigged except for a fore-and-aft mainsail
Brig Gen *abbr* brigadier general
[1]**bright** \ˈbrīt\ *adj* [ME, fr. OE *beorht;* akin to OHG *beraht* bright, Skt *bhrājate* it shines] (bef. 12c) **1 a :** radiating or reflecting light **:** SHINING, SPARKLING ⟨~ lights⟩ ⟨~ eyes⟩ **b :** SUNNY ⟨a ~ day⟩; *also* **:** radiant with happiness ⟨~ smiling faces⟩ ⟨~ moments⟩ **2 :** ILLUSTRIOUS, GLORIOUS ⟨~*est* star of the opera⟩ **3 :** BEAUTIFUL **4 :** of high

saturation or lightness ⟨∼ colors⟩ **5 a :** LIVELY, CHEERFUL ⟨be ∼ and jovial among your guests —Shak.⟩ **b :** INTELLIGENT, CLEVER ⟨a ∼ idea⟩ ⟨∼ children⟩ **6 :** AUSPICIOUS, PROMISING ⟨∼ prospects for the future⟩ — **bright** *adv* — **bright·ly** *adv*

syn BRIGHT, BRILLIANT, RADIANT, LUMINOUS, LUSTROUS mean shining or glowing with light. BRIGHT implies emitting or reflecting a high degree of light. BRILLIANT implies intense often sparkling brightness. RADIANT stresses the emission or seeming emission of rays of light. LUMINOUS implies emission of steady, suffused, glowing light by reflection or in surrounding darkness. LUSTROUS stresses an even, rich light from a surface that reflects brightly without glittering.

[2]**bright** *n* (1969) **:** a bright color — usu. used in pl. ⟨rich earth tones and crisp ∼*s* —Patricia Peterson⟩

bright·en \ˈbrī-tᵊn\ *vb* **bright·ened; bright·en·ing** \ˈbrīt-niŋ, ˈbrī-tᵊn-iŋ\ *vi* (14c) **:** to become bright or brighter ∼ *vt* **:** to make bright or brighter ⟨you ∼*ed* my day⟩ — **bright·en·er** \ˈbrīt-nər, ˈbrī-tᵊn-ər\ *n*

bright–line \ˈbrīt-ˌlīn\ *adj* (1982) **:** providing an unambiguous criterion or guideline esp. in law ⟨a ∼ distinction⟩

bright·ness *n* (bef. 12c) **1 a :** the quality or state of being bright; *also* **:** an instance of such a quality or state **b :** LUMINANCE **2 :** the attribute of light-source colors by which emitted light is ordered continuously from light to dark in correlation with its intensity — compare HUE 2c, [1]LIGHTNESS 2, SATURATION 4

Bright's disease \ˈbrīts-\ *n* [Richard *Bright* †1858 Eng. physician] (1831) **:** any of several kidney diseases marked esp. by albumin in the urine

bright·work \ˈbrīt-ˌwərk\ *n* (1841) **1 :** polished or plated metalwork **2 :** varnished woodwork on a boat

brill \ˈbril\ *n, pl* **brill** [ME *brell*] (15c) **:** a European flatfish (*Scophthalmus rhombus* syn. *Bothus rhombus* of the family Bothidae); *broadly* **:** TURBOT

bril·liance \ˈbril-yən(t)s\ *n* (1755) **:** the quality or state of being brilliant

bril·lian·cy \-yən(t)-sē\ *n, pl* **-cies** (1747) **1 :** BRILLIANCE **2 :** an instance of brilliance

[1]**bril·liant** \ˈbril-yənt\ *adj* [F *brillant,* prp. of *briller* to shine, fr. It *brillare*] (1696) **1 :** very bright **:** GLITTERING ⟨a ∼ light⟩ **2 a :** STRIKING, DISTINCTIVE ⟨a ∼ example⟩ **b :** distinguished by unusual mental keenness or alertness **3** *Brit* **:** very good **:** EXCELLENT ***syn*** see BRIGHT — **bril·liant·ly** *adv*

[2]**brilliant** *n* (1690) **:** a gem (as a diamond) cut in a particular form with numerous facets so as to have special brilliance

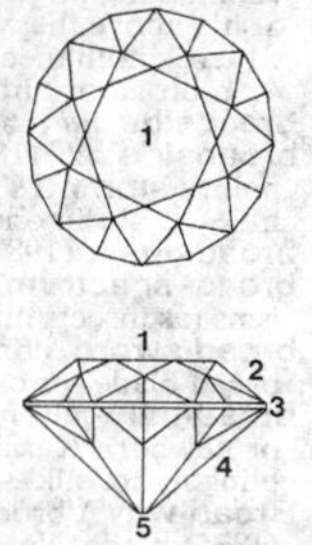

brilliant, top and side view: *1* table, *2* bezel, *3* girdle, *4* pavilion, *5* culet

bril·lian·tine \ˈbril-yən-ˌtēn\ *n* (1873) **1 :** a light lustrous fabric that is similar to alpaca and is woven usu. with a cotton warp and mohair or worsted filling **2 :** a preparation for making hair glossy

[1]**brim** \ˈbrim\ *n* [ME *brimme;* akin to MHG *brem* edge] (13c) **1 a** (1) **:** an upper or outer margin **:** VERGE (2) *archaic* **:** the upper surface of a body of water **b :** the edge or rim of a hollow vessel, a natural depression, or a cavity **2 :** the projecting rim of a hat — **brim·less** \-ləs\ *adj*

[2]**brim** *vb* **brimmed; brim·ming** *vt* (1598) **:** to fill to the brim ∼ *vi* **1 :** to be or become full often to overflowing ⟨eyes *brimming* with tears⟩ **2 :** to reach or overflow a brim

brim·ful \brim-ˈfu̇l, -ˌfu̇l\ *adj* (ca. 1530) **:** full to the brim **:** ready to overflow

brimmed \ˈbrimd\ *adj* (1606) **:** having a brim of a specified nature — used in combination ⟨a wide-*brimmed* hat⟩

brim·mer \ˈbri-mər\ *n* (1650) **:** a brimming cup or glass

brim·stone \ˈbrim-ˌstōn\ *n* [ME *brinston,* prob. fr. *birnen* to burn + *ston* stone] (12c) **:** SULFUR

brind·ed \ˈbrin-dəd\ *adj* [ME *brended*] (15c) *archaic* **:** BRINDLED

brin·dle \ˈbrin-dᵊl\ *n* [*brindle,* adj.] (1696) **1 :** a brindled color **2 :** a brindled animal

brin·dled \-dᵊld\ *or* **brindle** *adj* [alter. of *brinded*] (1620) **:** having obscure dark streaks or flecks on a usu. gray or tawny ground ⟨a ∼ cow⟩

[1]**brine** \ˈbrīn\ *n* [ME, fr. OE *brȳne;* akin to MD *brīne* brine] (bef. 12c) **1 a :** water saturated or strongly impregnated with common salt **b :** a strong saline solution (as of calcium chloride) **2 :** the water of a sea or salt lake

[2]**brine** *vt* **brined; brin·ing** (1552) **:** to treat (as by steeping) with brine — **brin·er** *n*

Bri·nell hardness \brə-ˈnel-\ *n* [Johann A. *Brinell* †1925 Swed. engineer] (1915) **:** the hardness of a metal or alloy measured by hydraulically pressing a hard ball under a standard load into the specimen

Brinell hardness number *n* (1915) **:** a number expressing Brinell hardness and denoting the load applied in testing in kilograms divided by the spherical area of indentation produced in the specimen in square millimeters — called also *Brinell number*

brine shrimp *n* (1836) **:** any of a genus (*Artemia*) of branchiopod crustaceans that can exist in strongly saline environments

bring \ˈbriŋ\ *vb* **brought** \ˈbrȯt\; **bring·ing** \ˈbriŋ-iŋ\ [ME, fr. OE *bringan;* akin to OHG *bringan* to bring, W *hebrwng* to accompany] *vt* (bef. 12c) **1 a :** to convey, lead, carry, or cause to come along with one toward the place from which the action is being regarded **b :** to cause to be, act, or move in a special way: as (1) **:** ATTRACT ⟨her screams *brought* the neighbors⟩ (2) **:** PERSUADE, INDUCE (3) **:** FORCE, COMPEL (4) **:** to cause to come into a particular state or condition ⟨∼ water to a boil⟩ **c** *dial* **:** ESCORT, ACCOMPANY **d :** to bear as an attribute or characteristic ⟨∼*s* years of experience to the position⟩ **2 :** to cause to exist or occur: as **a :** to be the occasion of ⟨winter ∼*s* snow⟩ **b :** to result in ⟨the drug *brought* immediate relief⟩ **c :** INSTITUTE ⟨∼ legal action⟩ **d :** ADDUCE ⟨∼ an argument⟩ **3 :** PREFER ⟨∼ charges⟩ **4 :** to procure in exchange **:** sell for ∼ *vi, chiefly Midland* **:** YIELD, PRODUCE — **bring·er** *n* — **bring forth 1 :** BEAR ⟨*brought forth* fruit⟩ **2 :** to give birth to **:** PRODUCE **3 :** ADDUCE ⟨*bring forth* persuasive arguments⟩ — **bring forward 1 :** to produce to view **:** INTRODUCE ⟨*brought* new evidence *forward*⟩ **2 :** to carry (a total) forward — **bring home :** to make unmistakably clear — **bring to account 1 :** to bring to book **2 :** REPRIMAND — **bring to bear :** to use with effect ⟨*bring* pressure *to bear*⟩ — **bring to book :** to compel to give an account — **bring to light :** DISCLOSE, REVEAL — **bring to mind :** RECALL — **bring to terms :** to compel to agree, assent, or submit — **bring up the rear :** to come last or behind

bring about *vt* (14c) **:** to cause to take place **:** EFFECT

bring around *vt* (1862) **1 :** to restore to consciousness **:** REVIVE **2 :** PERSUADE

bring·down \ˈbriŋ-ˌdau̇n\ *n* (ca. 1944) **:** COMEDOWN, LETDOWN

bring down *vt* (14c) **1 :** to cause to fall by or as if by shooting **2 :** to carry (a total) forward — **bring down the house** *or* **bring the house down :** to win the enthusiastic approval of the audience

bring in *vt* (14c) **1 :** INCLUDE, INTRODUCE **2 :** to produce as profit or return ⟨each sale *brought in* $5⟩ **3 :** to enable (a base runner) to reach home plate by hitting the ball **4 :** to report to a court ⟨the jury *brought in* a verdict⟩ **5 a :** to cause (as an oil well) to be productive **b :** to win tricks with the cards of (a long suit) in bridge **6 :** EARN ⟨*brings in* a good salary⟩

bring off *vt* (1606) **1 :** to cause to escape **:** RESCUE **2 :** to carry to a successful conclusion **:** ACHIEVE, ACCOMPLISH

bring on *vt* (1592) **:** to cause to appear or occur

bring out *vt* (1579) **1 a :** to make apparent **b :** to effectively develop (as a quality) **2 a :** to present to the public **b :** to introduce formally to society **3 :** UTTER

bring to *vt* (1720) **1 :** to cause (a boat) to lie to or come to a standstill **2 :** to restore to consciousness **:** REVIVE

bring up *vt* (14c) **1 :** to bring (a person) to maturity through nurturing care and education **2 :** to cause to stop suddenly **3 :** to bring to attention **:** INTRODUCE **4 :** VOMIT ∼ *vi* **:** to stop suddenly

brink \ˈbriŋk\ *n* [ME, of Scand origin; akin to ON *brekka* slope; akin to MD *brink* grassland] (13c) **1 :** EDGE; *esp* **:** the edge at the top of a steep place **2 :** a bank esp. of a river **3 :** the point of onset **:** VERGE ⟨on the ∼ of war⟩ **4 :** the threshold of danger

brink·man·ship \ˈbriŋk-mən-ˌship\ *also* **brinks·man·ship** \ˈbriŋ(k)s-mən-\ *n* (1956) **:** the art or practice of pushing a dangerous situation or confrontation to the limit of safety esp. to force a desired outcome

briny \ˈbrī-nē\ *adj* **brin·i·er; -est** (1581) **:** of, relating to, or resembling brine or the sea **:** SALTY — **brin·i·ness** *n*

brio \ˈbrē-(ˌ)ō\ *n* [It] (1734) **:** enthusiastic vigor **:** VIVACITY, VERVE

bri·oche \brē-ˈōsh, -ˈȯsh\ *n* [F, fr. MF dial., fr. *brier* to knead, of Gmc origin; akin to OHG *brehhan* to break — more at BREAK] (1826) **:** light slightly sweet bread made with a rich yeast dough

bri·o·lette \ˌbrē-ə-ˈlet\ *n* [F] (1865) **:** an oval or pear-shaped gemstone cut in triangular facets

bri·quette *or* **bri·quet** \bri-ˈket\ *n* [F *briquette,* dim. of *brique* brick] (1883) **:** a compacted often brick-shaped mass of usu. fine material ⟨a charcoal ∼⟩ — **briquette** *vt*

bris *also* **briss** \ˈbris\ *n* [Yiddish *bris,* short for *bris-mile,* fr. Heb *bĕrīth mīlāh,* lit., covenant of circumcision] (ca. 1934) **:** the Jewish rite of circumcision

[1]**brisk** \ˈbrisk\ *adj* [prob. modif. of MF *brusque*] (1560) **1 :** keenly alert **:** LIVELY **2 a :** pleasingly tangy ⟨∼ tea⟩ **b :** FRESH, INVIGORATING ⟨∼ weather⟩ **3 :** sharp in tone or manner **4 a :** ENERGETIC, QUICK ⟨a ∼ pace⟩ **b :** marked by much activity ⟨business was ∼⟩ — **brisk·ly** *adv* — **brisk·ness** *n*

[2]**brisk** *vt* (1598) **:** to make brisk ∼ *vi* **:** to become brisk — usu. used with *up* ⟨business ∼*ed up*⟩

bris·ket \ˈbris-kət\ *n* [ME *brusket;* akin to OE *brēost* breast] (14c) **:** the breast or lower chest of a quadruped animal; *also* **:** a cut of beef from the brisket — see BEEF illustration

bris·ling \ˈbriz-liŋ, ˈbris-\ *n* [Norw *brisling,* fr. LG *bretling,* fr. *bret* broad; akin to OE *brād* broad] (ca. 1868) **:** SPRAT 1a

[1]**bris·tle** \ˈbri-səl\ *n* [ME *bristil,* fr. *brust* bristle, fr. OE *byrst;* akin to OHG *burst* bristle, and perh. to L *fastigium* top] (14c) **:** a short stiff coarse hair or filament — **bris·tle·like** \ˈbri-sə(l)-ˌlīk\ *adj*

[2]**bristle** *vb* **bris·tled; bris·tling** \ˈbris-liŋ, ˈbri-sə-\ *vt* (15c) **1 :** to furnish with bristles **2 :** to make bristly **:** RUFFLE ∼ *vi* **1 a :** to rise and stand stiffly erect ⟨quills *bristling*⟩ **b :** to raise the bristles (as in anger) **2 :** to take on an aggressively defensive attitude (as in response to a slight or criticism) ⟨he *bristled* at the accusations of corruption⟩ **3 a :** to be full of or covered with esp. something suggestive of bristles ⟨roofs *bristled* with chimneys⟩ **b :** to be full of something specified ⟨book ∼*s* with detail and irony —W. J. Broad⟩

bris·tle·cone pine \ˈbri-səl-ˌkōn-\ *n* (1893) **:** either of two pines (*Pinus longaeva* and *P. aristata*) of the western U.S. that include the oldest living trees — called also *bristlecone*

bris·tle·tail \-ˌtāl\ *n* (1706) **:** any of various primitive wingless insects (order Thysanura syn. Archaeognatha) with three slender caudal bristles

bris·tly \ˈbris-lē, ˈbri-sə-\ *adj* **bris·tli·er; -est** (1589) **1 a :** thickly set with bristles ⟨a ∼ shrub⟩ **b :** consisting of or resembling bristles ⟨a ∼ mustache⟩ **2 :** inclined to or showing aggressiveness or anger ⟨a ∼ temperament⟩

bris·tol board \ˈbris-tᵊl-\ *n* [*Bristol,* England] (1809) **:** a cardboard with a smooth surface suitable esp. for artwork — called also *bristol*

Bristol fashion *adj* [*Bristol,* England] (1803) **:** being in good order **:** SHIPSHAPE

brit *also* **britt** \ˈbrit\ *n* [perh. fr. Corn *brȳthel* mackerel] (1851) **:** minute marine animals (as crustaceans and pteropods) on which right whales feed

[1]**Brit** \ˈbrit\ *n* (1898) **:** BRITON 2

[2]**Brit** *abbr* Britain; British

Bri·tan·nia metal \bri-ˈtan-yə-, -ˈta-nē-ə-\ *n* [*Britannia,* poetic name for Great Britain, fr. L] (1817) **:** a silver-white alloy largely of tin, antimony, and copper that is similar to pewter

Bri·tan·nic \bri-ˈta-nik\ *adj* (1641) **:** BRITISH

britch·es \ˈbri-chəz\ *n pl* [alter. of *breeches*] (1571) **:** BREECHES, TROUSERS

\ə\ **abut** \ᵊ\ kitten, F table \ər\ **further** \a\ **ash** \ā\ **ace** \ä\ **mop, mar** \au̇\ **out** \ch\ **chin** \e\ **bet** \ē\ **easy** \g\ **go** \i\ **hit** \ī\ **ice** \j\ **job** \ŋ\ **sing** \ō\ **go** \ȯ\ **law** \ȯi\ **boy** \th\ **thin** \t͟h\ **the** \ü\ **loot** \u̇\ **foot** \y\ **yet** \zh\ **vision, beige** \k̲, ⁿ, œ, ue, ʸ\ *see* Guide to Pronunciation

Brit·i·cism \ˈbri-tə-ˌsi-zəm\ *n* [*Brit*ish + *-icism* (as in *gallicism*)] (1868) **:** a characteristic feature of British English

Brit·ish \ˈbri-tish\ *n* [ME *Bruttische* of Britain, fr. OE *Brettisc,* fr. *Brettas* Britons, of Celt origin; akin to W *Brython* Briton] (13c) **1 a :** the Celtic language of the ancient Britons **b :** BRITISH ENGLISH **2** *pl in constr* **:** the people of Great Britain or the Commonwealth of Nations — **Brit·ish** *adj* — **Brit·ish·ism** \ˈbri-ti-ˌshi-zəm\ *n* — **Brit·ish·ness** *n*

British English *n* (1866) **:** the native language of most inhabitants of England; *esp* **:** English characteristic of England and clearly distinguishable from that used elsewhere (as in the U.S. or Australia)

Brit·ish·er \ˈbri-ti-shər\ *n* (1829) **:** BRITON 2

British thermal unit *n* (1876) **:** the quantity of heat required to raise the temperature of one pound of water one degree Fahrenheit at a specified temperature (as 39°F)

Brit Mi·lah \ˈbrit-mē-ˈlä, -ˈmē-(ˌ)lä\ *also* **Brith Milah** \ˈbrit-, ˈbrith-, ˈbris-\ *n* [Heb *bĕrīth mīlāh,* lit., covenant of circumcision] (ca. 1902) **:** BRIS

Brit·on \ˈbri-tᵊn\ *n* [ME *Breton,* fr. MF & L; MF, fr. L *Britton-, Britto,* of Celt origin; akin to W *Brython*] (13c) **1 :** a member of one of the peoples inhabiting Britain prior to the Anglo-Saxon invasions **2 :** a native or subject of Great Britain; *esp* **:** ENGLISHMAN

Brit·ta·ny \ˈbri-tə-nē\ *n, pl* **Brittanys** *also* **Brittanies** [*Brittany,* region in France] (1967) **:** any of a breed of medium-sized pointers of French origin that resemble the spaniels in appearance — called also *Brittany spaniel*

[1]**brit·tle** \ˈbri-tᵊl\ *adj* **brit·tler** \ˈbrit-lər, ˈbri-tᵊl-ər\; **brit·tlest** \-ləst, -tᵊl-əst\ [ME *britil;* akin to OE *brēotan* to break, ON *brjōta*] (14c) **1 a :** easily broken, cracked, or snapped ⟨~ clay⟩ ⟨~ glass⟩ **b :** easily disrupted, overthrown, or damaged **:** FRAIL ⟨a ~ friendship⟩ **2 a :** PERISHABLE, MORTAL **b :** TRANSITORY, EVANESCENT **3 :** easily hurt or offended **:** SENSITIVE ⟨a ~ personality⟩ **4 :** SHARP ⟨the ~ staccato of snare drums⟩ **5 :** lacking warmth, depth, or generosity of spirit **:** COLD ⟨a ~ selfish person⟩ **6 :** affected with or being a form of type 1 diabetes characterized by large and unpredictable fluctuations in blood glucose level ***syn*** see FRAGILE — **brit·tle·ly** \ˈbri-tᵊl-(l)ē\ *adv* — **brit·tle·ness** \ˈbri-tᵊl-nəs\ *n*

[2]**brittle** *n* (1913) **:** a candy made with caramelized sugar and nuts spread in thin sheets ⟨peanut ~⟩

brit·tle·bush \ˈbri-tᵊl-ˌbu̇sh\ *n* (1903) **:** any of a genus (*Encelia*) of composite plants having brittle stems; *esp* **:** a perennial desert shrub (*E. farinosa*) of the southwestern U.S. and adjacent Mexico with yellow flowers blooming above dense usu. grayish-green foliage

brittle star *n* (1843) **:** any of a class or subclass (Ophiuroidea) of echinoderms that have slender flexible arms distinct from the central disk

Brit·ton·ic \bri-ˈtä-nik\ *adj* [L *Britton-, Britto* Briton] (1923) **:** BRYTHONIC

Brix \ˈbriks\ *adj* (1897) **:** of or relating to a Brix scale

Brix scale *n* [Adolf F. *Brix* †1870 Austrian scientist] (1897) **:** a hydrometer scale for sugar solutions so graduated that its readings at a specified temperature represent percentages by weight of sugar in the solution — called also *Brix*

brl *abbr* barrel

bro \ˈbrō\ *n, pl* **bros** [by alter.] (1838) **1 :** BROTHER 1 **2 :** SOUL BROTHER — often used informally as a term of address

[1]**broach** \ˈbrōch\ *n* [ME *broche,* fr. AF, fr. VL **brocca,* fr. L, fem. of *broccus* projecting] (13c) **1 :** BROOCH **2 :** any of various pointed or tapered tools, implements, or parts: as **a :** a spit for roasting meat **b :** a tool for tapping casks **c :** a cutting tool for removing material from metal or plastic to shape an outside surface or a hole

[2]**broach** *vt* (15c) **1 a :** to pierce (as a cask) in order to draw the contents; *also* **:** to open for the first time **b :** to open up or break into (as a mine or stores) **2 :** to shape or enlarge (a hole) with a broach **3 a :** to make known for the first time **b :** to open up (a subject) for discussion **~** *vi* **:** to break the surface from below ***syn*** see EXPRESS — **broach·er** *n*

[3]**broach** *vi* [perh. fr. [2]*broach*] (1705) **:** to veer or yaw dangerously so as to lie broadside to the waves — often used with *to*

[1]**broad** \ˈbrȯd\ *adj* [ME *brood,* fr. OE *brād;* akin to OHG *breit* broad] (bef. 12c) **1 a :** having ample extent from side to side or between limits ⟨~ shoulders⟩ **b :** having a specified extension from side to side ⟨made the path 10 feet ~⟩ **2 :** extending far and wide **:** SPACIOUS ⟨the ~ plains⟩ **3 a :** OPEN, FULL ⟨~ daylight⟩ **b :** PLAIN, OBVIOUS ⟨a ~ hint⟩ **4 :** dialectal esp. in pronunciation **5 :** marked by lack of restraint, delicacy, or subtlety: **a** *obs* **:** OUTSPOKEN **b :** COARSE, RISQUÉ ⟨~ humor⟩ **6** *of a vowel* **:** OPEN — used specif. of *a* pronounced as in *father* **7 a :** LIBERAL, TOLERANT ⟨~ views⟩ **b :** widely applicable or applied **:** GENERAL ⟨a ~ rule⟩ **8 :** relating to the main or essential points ⟨~ outlines⟩ — **broad·ly** *adv* — **broad·ness** *n*

syn BROAD, WIDE, DEEP mean having horizontal extent. BROAD and WIDE apply to a surface measured or viewed from side to side ⟨a *broad* avenue⟩. WIDE is more common when units of measurement are mentioned ⟨rugs eight feet *wide*⟩ or applied to unfilled space between limits ⟨a *wide* doorway⟩. BROAD is preferred when full horizontal extent is considered ⟨*broad* shoulders⟩. DEEP may indicate horizontal extent away from the observer or from a front or peripheral point ⟨a *deep* cupboard⟩ ⟨*deep* woods⟩.

[2]**broad** *adv* (bef. 12c) **:** in a broad manner **:** FULLY ⟨~ awake⟩

[3]**broad** *n* (1659) **1** *Brit* **:** an expansion of a river — often used in pl. **2** *often offensive* **:** WOMAN

broad arrow *n* (14c) **1 :** an arrow with a flat barbed head **2** *Brit* **:** a mark shaped like a broad arrow that identifies government property including clothing formerly worn by convicts

broad·ax *or* **broad·axe** \ˈbrȯd-ˌaks\ *n* (bef. 12c) **:** a large ax with a broad blade

broad·band \ˈbrȯd-ˌband\ *adj* (1960) **1 :** operating at, responsive to, or comprising a wide band of frequencies ⟨a ~ radio antenna⟩ **2 :** of, relating to, or being a high-speed communications network and esp. one in which a frequency range is divided into multiple independent channels for simultaneous transmission of signals (as voice, data, or video) — **broadband** *n*

broad bean *n* (1783) **:** the large flat edible seed of an Old World upright vetch (*Vicia faba*); *also* **:** this plant widely grown for its seeds and as fodder — called also *fava bean*; compare FAVISM

broad–brush \ˈbrȯd-ˌbrəsh\ *adj* (1967) **:** GENERAL, NONSPECIFIC

[1]**broad·cast** \ˈbrȯd-ˌkast\ *adj* (1767) **1 :** cast or scattered in all directions **2 :** made public by means of radio or television **3 :** of or relating to radio or television broadcasting

[2]**broadcast** *vb* **broadcast** *also* **broad·cast·ed; broad·cast·ing** *vt* (1813) **1 :** to scatter or sow (as seed) over a broad area **2 :** to make widely known **3 :** to transmit or make public by means of radio or television **~** *vi* **1 :** to transmit a broadcast **2 :** to speak or perform on a broadcast program — **broad·cast·er** *n*

[3]**broadcast** *adv* (1814) **:** to or over a broad area

[4]**broadcast** *n* (1922) **1 :** the act of transmitting sound or images by radio or television **2 :** a single radio or television program

Broad Church *adj* (1853) **:** of or relating to a liberal party in the Anglican communion esp. in the later 19th century

broad·cloth \ˈbrȯd-ˌklȯth\ *n* (15c) **1 :** a twilled napped woolen or worsted fabric with smooth lustrous face and dense texture **2 :** a fabric usu. of cotton, silk, or rayon made in plain and rib weaves with soft semigloss finish

broad·en \ˈbrȯ-dᵊn\ *vb* **broad·ened; broad·en·ing** \ˈbrȯd-niŋ, ˈbrȯ-dᵊn-iŋ\ *vt* (1726) **:** to make broader **~** *vi* **:** to become broad

broad–gauge \ˈbrȯd-ˈgāj\ *or* **broad–gauged** \-ˈgājd\ *adj* (1858) **1 :** wide in area or scope ⟨a ~ effort⟩ **2 :** comprehensive in outlook, range, or capability ⟨a ~ statesman⟩

broad jump *n* (1867) **:** LONG JUMP — **broad jumper** *n*

broad–leaved \-ˈlēvd\ *or* **broad·leaf** \-ˈlēf\ *also* **broad–leafed** \-ˈlēft\ *adj* (1552) **1 :** having broad leaves; *specif* **:** having leaves that are not needles **2 :** composed of broad-leaved plants ⟨~ forests⟩

[1]**broad·loom** \-ˌlüm\ *adj* (1925) **:** woven on a wide loom; *also* **:** so woven in solid color

[2]**broadloom** *n* (1926) **:** a broadloom carpet

broad–mind·ed \ˈbrȯd-ˈmīn-dəd, -ˌmīn-\ *adj* (1850) **1 :** tolerant of varied views **2 :** inclined to condone minor departures from conventional behavior — **broad–mind·ed·ly** *adv* — **broad–mind·ed·ness** *n*

broad·scale \-ˌskāl\ *adj* (1939) **:** broad in extent, range, or effect

broad·sheet \-ˌshēt\ *n* (1705) **1 :** BROADSIDE 1 **2** *chiefly Brit* **:** a newspaper with pages of a size larger than those of a tabloid

[1]**broad·side** \-ˌsīd\ *n* (1575) **1 a** (1) **:** a sizable sheet of paper printed on one side (2) **:** a sheet printed on one or both sides and folded **b :** something (as a ballad) printed on a broadside **2** *archaic* **:** the side of a ship above the waterline **3 a :** all the guns on one side of a ship; *also* **:** their simultaneous discharge **b :** a volley of abuse or denunciation **4 :** a broad or unbroken surface

[2]**broadside** *adj* (1646) **:** directed or placed broadside ⟨a ~ attack⟩

[3]**broadside** *adv* (1870) **1 a :** with the side forward or toward a given point **:** SIDEWAYS ⟨turned ~⟩ **b :** directly from the side ⟨the car was hit ~⟩ **2 :** in one volley **3 :** at random

[4]**broadside** *vt* (1981) **:** to hit broadside ⟨the car was *broadsided*⟩

broad–spectrum *adj* (1952) **:** effective against a wide range of organisms (as insects or bacteria) ⟨a ~ antibiotic⟩

broad·sword \ˈbrȯd-ˌsȯrd\ *n* (bef. 12c) **:** a large heavy sword with a broad blade for cutting rather than thrusting

broad·tail \-ˌtāl\ *n* (1892) **1 :** KARAKUL 1 **2 :** the pelt of a premature or newborn Karakul lamb having a flat and wavy appearance resembling moiré silk — compare KARAKUL 2, PERSIAN LAMB 1

Broad·way \ˈbrȯd-ˌwā, -ˈwā\ *n* [*Broadway,* street in New York City] (1835) **:** the New York commercial theater and amusement world; *specif* **:** playhouses located in the area between the Avenue of the Americas and Ninth Avenue and from W. 41st Street to W. 53d Street — **Broadway** *adj* — **Broad·way·ite** \-ˌīt\ *n*

Brob·ding·nag·ian \ˌbräb-diŋ-ˈna-gē-ən, -dig-ˈna-\ *adj* [*Brobdingnag,* imaginary land of giants in *Gulliver's Travels,* by Jonathan Swift] (1728) **:** marked by tremendous size — **Brobdingnagian** *n*

bro·cade \brō-ˈkād\ *n* [Sp *brocado,* fr. Catal *brocat,* fr. It *broccato,* fr. *broccare* to spur, brocade, fr. *brocco* small nail, fr. L *broccus* projecting] (1588) **1 :** a rich silk fabric with raised patterns in gold and silver **2 :** a fabric characterized by raised designs — **brocade** *vt* — **bro·cad·ed** *adj*

Bro·ca's area \ˈbrō-kəz-\ *n* [Paul P. *Broca* †1880 Fr. surgeon] (ca. 1903) **:** a brain center associated with the motor control of speech and usu. located in the left side of the frontal lobe

broc·a·telle \ˌbrä-kə-ˈtel\ *n* [F, fr. It *broccatello,* dim. of *broccato*] (1669) **:** a stiff decorating fabric with patterns in high relief

broc·co·li \ˈbrä-kə-lē, ˈbräk-lē\ *n* [It, pl. of *broccolo* flowering top of a cabbage, dim. of *brocco* small nail, sprout] (1699) **1** *chiefly Brit* **:** a large hardy cauliflower **2 a :** either of two garden vegetable plants closely related to the cabbage: (1) **:** one with a thick central stem and a compact head of dense usu. green florets that is classified with the cauliflower (2) **:** one (*Brassica oleracea italica*) with slender stems and usu. green or purple florets not arranged in a central head **b :** the stems and immature florets of broccoli used as food

broccoli rabe \-ˌräb\ *n* [perh. modif. of It *broccoli di rapa,* lit., flowering tops of the turnip] (1938) **:** a garden brassica (*Brassica rapa ruvo*) that is related to the turnip and produces edible leafy branching stalks and compact clusters of yellow florets — called also *broccoli raab* \-ˌräb, -ˌrab\, *rapini*

bro·chette \brō-ˈshet\ *n* [F, fr. OF *brochete,* fr. *broche* pointed tool — more at BROACH] (15c) **:** SKEWER; *also* **:** food broiled on a skewer

bro·chure \brō-ˈshu̇r, *Brit esp* ˈbrō-ˌ\ *n* [F, fr. *brocher* to sew, fr. MF, to prick, fr. OF *brochier,* fr. *broche*] (1748) **:** PAMPHLET, BOOKLET; *esp* **:** one containing descriptive or advertising material

brock \ˈbräk\ *n* [ME, fr. OE *broc,* of Celt origin; akin to W *broch* badger] (bef. 12c) *Brit* **:** BADGER

brock·age \ˈbrä-kij\ *n* [E dial. *brock* rubbish + E *-age*] (1879) **:** an imperfectly minted coin

brock·et \ˈbrä-kət\ *n* [*brocket* (two-year-old male red deer), fr. ME *broket,* fr. AF; akin to OF *broche* tine of an antler, pointed tool — more at BROACH] (1837) **:** any of several small deer (genus *Mazama*) of Central and So. America with unbranched antlers

bro·gan \ˈbrō-gən, -ˌgan; brō-ˈgan\ *n* [Ir *brógán,* dim. of *bróg*] (1835) **:** a heavy shoe; *esp* **:** a coarse work shoe reaching to the ankle

[1]**brogue** \ˈbrōg\ *n* [Ir *bróg* & ScGael *bròg,* fr. MIr *bróc,* prob. fr. ON *brōk* leg covering; akin to OE *brōc* leg covering — more at BREECH] (1584) **1 :** a stout coarse shoe worn formerly in Ireland and the Scottish High-

lands **2 :** a heavy shoe often with a hobnailed sole **:** BROGAN **3 :** a stout oxford shoe with perforations and usu. a wing tip

[2]**brogue** *n* [Ir *barróg* accent, speech impediment, lit., wrestling hold, tight grip] (1703) **:** a dialect or regional pronunciation; *esp* **:** an Irish accent

broi·der \ˈbrȯi-dər\ *vt* [alter. of ME *brouderen,* modif. of AF *brouder* — more at EMBROIDER] (14c) **:** EMBROIDER — **broi·dery** \ˈbrȯi-d(ə-)rē\ *n*

[1]**broil** \ˈbrȯi(-ə)l\ *vb* [ME, fr. AF *bruiller* to burn, broil, modif. of L *ustulare* to singe, fr. *urere* to burn] *vt* (14c) **:** to cook by direct exposure to radiant heat **:** GRILL ~ *vi* **:** to be subjected to great or oppressive heat ⟨~*ing* in the sun⟩

[2]**broil** *n* (1563) **:** the act or state of broiling

[3]**broil** *vb* [ME, fr. AF *broiller* to jumble, mix, fr. VL **brodiculare,* fr. **brod-,* of Gmc origin; akin to OHG *brod* broth — more at BROTH] *vi* (15c) **:** BRAWL ~ *vt* **:** EMBROIL

[4]**broil** *n* (1525) **:** a noisy disturbance **:** TUMULT; *esp* **:** BRAWL ⟨a tavern row . . . widens into a general ~ —J. R. Green⟩

broil·er \ˈbrȯi-lər\ *n* (14c) **1 :** one that broils **2 :** a bird fit for broiling; *esp* **:** a chicken that is younger and smaller than a roaster

broil·ing \ˈbrȯi(-ə)-liŋ\ *adj* (1555) **:** extremely hot ⟨a ~ sun⟩

[1]**broke** \ˈbrōk\ *past of* BREAK

[2]**broke** *adj* [ME, alter. of *broken*] (1710) **:** PENNILESS

bro·ken \ˈbrō-kən\ *adj* [ME, fr. OE *brocen,* fr. pp. of *brecan* to break] (13c) **1 :** violently separated into parts **:** SHATTERED **2 :** damaged or altered by breaking: as **a :** having undergone or been subjected to fracture ⟨a ~ leg⟩ **b** *of land surfaces* **:** being irregular, interrupted, or full of obstacles **c :** violated by transgression ⟨a ~ promise⟩ **d :** DISCONTINUOUS, INTERRUPTED **e :** disrupted by change **f** *of a tulip flower* **:** having an irregular, streaked, or blotched pattern esp. from virus infection **3 a :** made weak or infirm **b :** subdued completely **:** CRUSHED, SORROWFUL ⟨a ~ heart⟩ ⟨a ~ spirit⟩ **c :** BANKRUPT **d :** reduced in rank **4 a :** cut off **:** DISCONNECTED **b :** imperfectly spoken or written ⟨~ English⟩ **5 :** not complete or full ⟨a ~ bale of hay⟩ **6 :** disunited by divorce, separation, or desertion of one parent ⟨children from ~ homes⟩ ⟨a ~ family⟩ — **bro·ken·ly** *adv* — **bro·ken·ness** \-kə(n)-nəs\ *n*

broken–down *adj* (1792) **:** WORN-OUT, DEBILITATED ⟨a ~ old car⟩

bro·ken–field \-ˌfēld\ *adj* (1903) **:** characterized by or making quick changes in direction to avoid widely scattered tacklers ⟨a halfback known for ~ running⟩ ⟨a ~ runner⟩

bro·ken·heart·ed \-ˈhär-təd\ *adj* (1526) **:** overcome by grief or despair

bro·ken–wind·ed \-ˈwin-dəd\ *adj* (1580) **:** affected with or as if with heaves ⟨a ~ horse⟩

bro·ker \ˈbrō-kər\ *n* [ME, negotiator, fr. AF *brocour*] (14c) **1 :** one who acts as an intermediary: as **a :** an agent who arranges marriages **b :** an agent who negotiates contracts of purchase and sale (as of real estate, commodities, or securities) **2 :** POWER BROKER **3 :** one who sells or distributes something ⟨an information ~⟩ — **broker** *vb*

bro·ker·age \ˈbrō-k(ə-)rij\ *n* (15c) **1 :** the business or establishment of a broker **2 :** a broker's fee or commission

bro·kered \-kərd\ *adj* (1967) **:** arranged or controlled by brokers and esp. power brokers ⟨a ~ political convention⟩

bro·king \-kiŋ\ *n* (1569) *chiefly Brit* **:** the business of a broker **:** BROKERAGE

brol·ly \ˈbrä-lē\ *n, pl* **brollies** [by shortening & alter.] (ca. 1874) *chiefly Brit* **:** UMBRELLA

brom- *or* **bromo-** *comb form* [prob. fr. F *brome,* fr. Gk *brōmos* bad smell] **:** bromine ⟨*brom*ide⟩

bro·mance \ˈbrō-ˌman(t)s\ *n* [blend of *bro* and [1]*romance*] (2004) **:** a close nonsexual friendship between men — **bro·man·tic** \brō-ˈman-tik\ *adj*

bro·mate \ˈbrō-ˌmāt\ *n* (1830) **:** a salt of bromic acid

brome·grass \ˈbrōm-ˌgras\ *n* [NL *Bromus,* fr. L *bromos* oats, fr. Gk] (ca. 1791) **:** any of a large genus (*Bromus*) of tall grasses often having drooping spikelets — called also *brome*

bro·me·lain \ˈbrō-mə-lən, -ˌlān\ *also* **bro·me·lin** \ˈbrō-mə-lən, brō-ˈmē-\ *n* [*bromelain* by alter. of *bromelin,* fr. NL *Bromelia*] (1894) **:** a protease obtained esp. from the pineapple

bro·me·li·ad \brō-ˈmē-lē-ˌad\ *n* [NL *Bromelia,* genus of tropical American plants, fr. Olaf *Bromelius* †1705 Swed. botanist] (1866) **:** any of the chiefly tropical American usu. epiphytic plants comprising the pineapple family and including Spanish moss and various ornamentals

bro·mic acid \ˈbrō-mik-\ *n* (1828) **:** an unstable strongly oxidizing acid $HBrO_3$ known only in solution or in the form of its salts

bro·mide \ˈbrō-ˌmīd\ *n* (1830) **1 :** a binary compound of bromine with another element or a radical including some (as potassium bromide) used as sedatives **2 a :** a commonplace or tiresome person **:** BORE **b :** a commonplace or hackneyed statement or notion

bro·mid·ic \brō-ˈmi-dik\ *adj* (1906) **:** lacking in originality **:** TRITE

bro·mi·nate \ˈbrō-mə-ˌnāt\ *vt* **-nat·ed; -nat·ing** (1873) **:** to treat or cause to combine with bromine or a compound of bromine — **bro·mi·na·tion** \ˌbrō-mə-ˈnā-shən\ *n*

bro·mine \ˈbrō-ˌmēn\ *n* [F *brome* bromine + E [2]*-ine*] (1827) **:** a nonmetallic halogen element that is isolated as a deep red corrosive toxic volatile liquid of disagreeable odor — see ELEMENT table

bro·mo \ˈbrō-(ˌ)mō\ *n, pl* **bromos** [*brom-*] (1923) **:** a dose of a proprietary effervescent headache remedy and antacid

bro·mo·crip·tine \ˌbrō-mō-ˈkrip-ˌtēn, -tən\ *n* [by shortening & alter. fr. *bromoergocryptine,* fr. *brom-* + *ergocryptine,* an ergot derivative, fr. *ergo-* + Gk *kryptos* hidden — more at CRYPT] (1975) **:** a polypeptide ergot derivative $C_{32}H_{40}BrN_5O_5$ that mimics the activity of dopamine in inhibiting prolactin secretion

bro·mo·ura·cil \ˌbrō-mō-ˈyu̇r-ə-ˌsil, -səl\ *n* (1960) **:** a mutagenic uracil derivative $C_4H_3N_2O_2Br$ that is an analog of thymine and pairs readily with adenine and sometimes with guanine

brom·thy·mol blue \ˌbrōm-ˈthī-ˌmȯl-\ *n* (1920) **:** a dye derived from thymol that is an acid-base indicator — called also *bro·mo·thy·mol blue* \ˌbrō-mō-ˈthī-ˌmȯl-\

bronc \ˈbräŋk\ *n* [short for *bronco*] (1893) **:** an unbroken or imperfectly broken range horse of western No. America; *broadly* **:** MUSTANG

bronch- *or* **broncho-** *comb form* [LL, fr. Gk, fr. *bronchos* windpipe] **:** bronchial tube **:** bronchial ⟨*bronch*itis⟩

bronchi- *or* **bronchio-** *comb form* [NL, fr. *bronchia,* pl., branches of the bronchi, fr. LL, fr. Gk, dim. of *bronchos*] **:** bronchial tubes ⟨*bronchi*ectasis⟩

bron·chi·al \ˈbräŋ-kē-əl\ *adj* (ca. 1735) **:** of or relating to the bronchi or their ramifications in the lungs — **bron·chi·al·ly** \-kē-ə-lē\ *adv*

bronchial asthma *n* (ca. 1881) **:** asthma resulting from spasmodic contraction of bronchial muscles

bronchial tube *n* (ca. 1722) **:** a primary bronchus or any of its branches

bron·chi·ec·ta·sis \ˌbräŋ-kē-ˈek-tə-səs\ *n, pl* **bron·chi·ec·ta·ses** \-ˌsēz\ [NL, fr. *bronchi-* + Gk *ektasis* extension — more at ATELECTASIS] (ca. 1860) **:** a chronic dilatation of bronchi or bronchioles

bron·chi·ole \ˈbräŋ-kē-ˌōl\ *n* [NL *bronchiolum,* dim. of *bronchia*] (ca. 1860) **:** a minute thin-walled branch of a bronchus — **bron·chi·o·lar** \ˌbräŋ-kē-ˈō-lər\ *adj*

bron·chi·ol·i·tis \ˌbräŋ-kē-ō-ˈlī-təs\ *n* [NL] (1887) **:** inflammation of the bronchioles

bron·chi·tis \brän-ˈkī-təs, bräŋ-\ *n* [NL] (1808) **:** acute or chronic inflammation of the bronchial tubes; *also* **:** a disease marked by this — **bron·chit·ic** \-ˈki-tik\ *adj*

bron·cho·di·la·tor \ˌbräŋ-(ˌ)kō-dī-ˈlā-tər, -ˈdī-ˌ\ *n* (1903) **:** a drug that relaxes bronchial muscle resulting in expansion of the bronchial air passages — **bronchodilator** *adj*

bron·cho·gen·ic \ˌbräŋ-kə-ˈje-nik\ *adj* (1927) **:** of, relating to, or arising in or by way of the air passages of the lungs ⟨~ carcinoma⟩

bron·cho·pneu·mo·nia \ˌbräŋ-(ˌ)kō-n(y)u̇-ˈmō-nyə, -n(y)ü\ *n* [NL] (1858) **:** pneumonia involving many relatively small areas of lung tissue

bron·cho·scope \ˈbräŋ-kə-ˌskōp\ *n* [ISV] (1899) **:** a usu. flexible endoscope for inspecting or passing instruments into the bronchi (as to obtain tissue for biopsy) — **bron·cho·scop·ic** \ˌbräŋ-kə-ˈskä-pik\ *adj* — **bron·chos·co·pist** \brän-ˈkäs-kə-pist, bräŋ-\ *n* — **bron·chos·co·py** \-pē\ *n*

bron·cho·spasm \ˈbräŋ-kə-ˌspa-zəm\ *n* (ca. 1901) **:** constriction of the air passages of the lung (as in asthma) by spasmodic contraction of the bronchial muscles — **bron·cho·spas·tic** \ˌbräŋ-kə-ˈspas-tik\ *adj*

bron·chus \ˈbräŋ-kəs\ *n, pl* **bron·chi** \ˈbräŋ-ˌkī, -ˌkē\ [NL, fr. Gk *bronchos*] (ca. 1706) **:** either of the two primary divisions of the trachea that lead respectively into the right and the left lung; *broadly* **:** BRONCHIAL TUBE

bron·co *also* **bron·cho** \ˈbräŋ-(ˌ)kō\ *n, pl* **broncos** *also* **bronchos** [MexSp, fr. Sp, lit., rough, wild] (1850) **:** BRONC

bron·co·bust·er \-ˌbəs-tər\ *n* (1887) **:** one who breaks wild horses to the saddle

bron·to·sau·rus \ˌbrän-tə-ˈsȯr-əs\ *also* **bron·to·saur** \ˈbrän-tə-ˌsȯr\ *n* [NL, fr. Gk *brontē* thunder + *sauros* lizard; akin to Gk *bremein* to roar] (1892) **:** any of a genus (*Apatosaurus* syn. *Brontosaurus*) of large sauropod dinosaurs of the Jurassic — called also *apatosaurus*

Bronx cheer \ˈbräŋ(k)s-\ *n* [*Bronx,* borough of New York City] (1924) **:** RASPBERRY 2

[1]**bronze** \ˈbränz\ *vt* **bronzed; bronz·ing** (1645) **:** to give the appearance of bronze to ⟨a *bronzed* sculpture⟩; *also* **:** TAN 2 — **bronz·er** *n*

[2]**bronze** *n, often attrib* [F, fr. It *bronzo*] (1739) **1 a :** an alloy of copper and tin and sometimes other elements **b :** any of various copper-base alloys with little or no tin **2 :** a sculpture or artifact of bronze **3 :** a moderate yellowish brown **4 :** a bronze medal awarded as the third prize in a competition — **bronzy** \ˈbrän-zē\ *adj*

Bronze Age *n* (1860) **:** the period of ancient human culture characterized by the use of bronze that began between 4000 and 3000 B.C. and ended with the advent of the Iron Age

Bronze Star *n* (1944) **:** a U.S. military decoration awarded for valor or for meritorious service not involving aerial flights — called also *Bronze Star Medal*

bronz·ing *n* (1848) **:** a bronze coloring or discoloration (as of leaves)

brooch \ˈbrōch *also* ˈbrüch\ *n* [ME *broche* pointed tool, brooch — more at BROACH] (13c) **:** an ornament that is held by a pin or clasp and is worn at or near the neck

[1]**brood** \ˈbrüd\ *n* [ME, fr. OE *brōd;* akin to MHG *bruot* brood and perh. to OE *beorma* yeast — more at BARM] (bef. 12c) **1 :** the young of an animal or a family of young; *esp* **:** the young (as of a bird or insect) hatched or cared for at one time **2 :** a group having a common nature or origin **3 :** the children of a family

[2]**brood** *adj* (15c) **:** kept for breeding ⟨a ~ flock⟩

[3]**brood** *vt* (15c) **1 a :** to sit on or incubate (eggs) **b :** to produce by or as if by incubation **:** HATCH **2** *of a bird* **:** to cover (young) with the wings **3 :** to think anxiously or gloomily about **:** PONDER ~ *vi* **1 a** *of a bird* **:** to brood eggs or young **b :** to sit quietly and thoughtfully **:** MEDITATE **2 :** HOVER, LOOM **3 a :** to dwell gloomily on a subject **b :** to be in a state of depression — **brood·ing·ly** \ˈbrü-diŋ-lē\ *adv*

brood·er \ˈbrü-dər\ *n* (1599) **1 :** one that broods **2 :** a heated structure used for raising young fowl

brood·mare \ˈbrüd-ˌmer\ *n* (1792) **:** a mare kept for breeding

broody \ˈbrü-dē\ *adj* (1523) **1 :** being in a state of readiness to brood eggs that is characterized by cessation of laying and by marked changes in behavior and physiology ⟨a ~ hen⟩ **2 :** given or conducive to introspection **:** CONTEMPLATIVE, MOODY — **brood·i·ness** *n*

[1]**brook** \ˈbru̇k\ *n* [ME, fr. OE *brōc;* akin to OHG *bruoh* marshy ground] (bef. 12c) **:** CREEK 2

[2]**brook** *vt* [ME *brouken* to use, enjoy, fr. OE *brūcan;* akin to OHG *brūhhan* to use, L *frui* to enjoy] (15c) **:** to stand for **:** TOLERATE ⟨he would ~ no interference with his plans⟩

brook·ie \ˈbru̇-kē\ *n* (1933) **:** BROOK TROUT

brook·ite \ˈbru̇-ˌkīt\ *n* [Henry J. *Brooke* †1857 Eng. mineralogist] (1825) **:** titanium dioxide TiO_2 occurring as a mineral in orthorhombic crystals commonly translucent brown or opaque brown to black

brook·let \ˈbru̇-klət\ *n* (1807) **:** a small brook

Brook·lyn·ese \ˌbru̇-klə-ˈnēz, -ˈnēs\ *n* [*Brooklyn,* borough of New York City] (1939) **:** the vernacular speech of greater New York City and environs

brook trout *n* (ca. 1825) : the common speckled cold-water char (*Salvelinus fontinalis*) of No. America

[1]**broom** \ˈbrüm, ˈbru̇m\ *n* [ME, fr. OE *brōm;* akin to OHG *brāmo* bramble] (bef. 12c) **1** : any of various leguminous shrubs (esp. genera *Cytisus* and *Genista*) with long slender branches, small leaves, and usu. showy yellow flowers; *esp* : SCOTCH BROOM **2** : a bundle of firm stiff twigs or fibers bound together on a long handle esp. for sweeping

[2]**broom** *vt* (1838) **1** : to sweep with or as if with a broom **2** : to finish (as a concrete surface) by means of a broom

broom•ball \-ˌbȯl\ *n* (1933) : a variation of ice hockey played on ice without skates and with brooms and a soccer ball used instead of sticks and a puck — **broom•ball•er** \-ˌbȯ-lər\ *n*

broom•corn \-ˌkȯrn\ *n* (ca. 1782) : any of several tall cultivated sorghums having stiff-branched panicles used in brooms and brushes

broom•rape \-ˌrāp\ *n* (1578) : any of a genus (*Orobanche* of the family Orobanchaceae, the broomrape family) of herbs that have leaves modified to scales and that grow as parasites on the roots of other plants

broom•stick \-ˌstik\ *n* (1663) : the long thin handle of a broom

bros *pl of* BRO

brose \ˈbrōz\ *n* [perh. alter. of Sc *bruis* broth, fr. ME *brewes,* fr. AF *broués,* pl. of *bruet, broué* broth, mash, of Gmc origin; akin to OHG *brod* broth] (1515) : a chiefly Scottish dish made with a boiling liquid and meal

broth \ˈbrȯth\ *n, pl* **broths** \ˈbrȯths, ˈbrȯt͟hz\ [ME, fr. OE; akin to OHG *brod* broth, OE *brēowan* to brew — more at BREW] (bef. 12c) **1** : liquid in which meat, fish, cereal grains, or vegetables have been cooked : STOCK ⟨chicken ~⟩ **2** : a fluid culture medium

broth•el \ˈbrä-thəl, ˈbrȯ- *also* -t͟həl\ *n* [ME, worthless fellow, prostitute, fr. *brothen,* pp. of *brethen* to waste away, go to ruin, fr. OE *brēothan* to waste away; akin to OE *brēotan* to break — more at BRITTLE] (ca. 1566) : BORDELLO

broth•er \ˈbrə-t͟hər\ *n, pl* **brothers** *also* **breth•ren** \ˈbreth-rən; ˈbre-t͟hə-rən, -t͟hərn\ [ME, fr. OE *brōthor;* akin to OHG *bruodor* brother, L *frater,* Gk *phratēr* member of the same clan] (bef. 12c) **1** : a male who has the same parents as another or one parent in common with another **2** : one related to another by common ties or interests **3** : a fellow member — used as a title for ministers in some evangelical denominations **4** : one of a type similar to another **5 a** : KINSMAN **b** : one who shares with another a common national or racial origin; *esp* : SOUL BROTHER **6 a** *cap* : a member of a congregation of men not in holy orders and usu. in hospital or school work **b** : a member of a men's religious order who is not preparing for or is not ready for holy orders ⟨a lay ~⟩

broth•er•hood \ˈbrə-t͟hər-ˌhu̇d\ *n* [ME *brotherhede, brotherhod,* alter. of *brotherrede,* fr. OE *brōthorrǣden,* fr. *brōthor* + *rǣden* condition — more at KINDRED] (14c) **1** : the quality or state of being brothers **2** : FELLOWSHIP, ALLIANCE **3** : an association (as a labor union or monastic society) for a particular purpose **4** : the whole body of persons engaged in a business or profession

broth•er–in–law \ˈbrə-t͟hər-ən-ˌlȯ, ˈbreth-rən-, ˈbrə-t͟hərn-\ *n, pl* **broth•ers–in–law** \ˈbrə-t͟hərz-ən-\ (14c) **1** : the brother of one's spouse **2 a** : the husband of one's sister **b** : the husband of one's spouse's sister

broth•er•ly \ˈbrə-t͟hər-lē\ *adj* (bef. 12c) **1** : of or relating to brothers **2** : natural or becoming to brothers : AFFECTIONATE ⟨~ love⟩ — **broth•er•li•ness** *n* — **brotherly** *adv*

brougham \ˈbrü(-ə)m, ˈbrō(-ə)m\ *n* [Henry Peter *Brougham,* Baron Brougham and Vaux †1868 Scot. jurist] (1851) : a light closed horse-drawn carriage with the driver outside in front

brought *past and past part of* BRING

brou•ha•ha \ˈbrü-ˌhä-ˌhä, ˌbrü-ˈhä-ˈhä, brü-ˈhä-ˌhä\ *n* [F] (1890) : HUBBUB, UPROAR

[1]**brow** \ˈbrau̇\ *n* [ME, fr. OE *brū;* akin to ON *brūn* eyebrow, Gk *ophrys,* Skt *bhrū*] (bef. 12c) **1 a** : EYEBROW **b** : FOREHEAD **2** : the projecting upper part or margin of a steep place **3** : EXPRESSION, MIEN

[2]**brow** *n* [perh. fr. Dan or Sw *bro* bridge; akin to OE *brycg* bridge] (1867) : GANGPLANK

bro•wal•lia \brə-ˈwä-lē-ə\ *n* [NL, fr. J. *Browallius* †1755 Swed. naturalist] (1782) : any of a genus (*Browallia*) of tropical American herbs of the nightshade family cultivated for their blue, violet, or white flowers

brow•beat \ˈbrau̇-ˌbēt\ *vt* **-beat; -beat•en** \-ˈbē-tᵊn\ *or* **-beat; -beat•ing** (1581) : to intimidate or disconcert by a stern manner or arrogant speech : BULLY ***syn*** see INTIMIDATE

browed \ˈbrau̇d\ *adj* (15c) : having brows of a specified nature — used in combination ⟨smooth-*browed*⟩

[1]**brown** \ˈbrau̇n\ *adj* [ME *broun,* fr. OE *brūn;* akin to OHG *brūn* brown, Gk *phrynē* toad] (bef. 12c) : of the color brown; *esp* : of dark or tanned complexion

[2]**brown** *n* (13c) **1** : any of a group of colors between red and yellow in hue, of medium to low lightness, and of moderate to low saturation **2** : a brown-skinned person **3** : BROWN TROUT — **brown•ish** \ˈbrau̇-nish\ *adj* — **browny** \-nē\ *adj*

[3]**brown** *vi* (14c) : to become brown ~ *vt* : to make brown

brown alga *n* (ca. 1899) : any of a division (Phaeophyta) of variable mostly marine algae with chlorophyll masked by brown pigment

brown bagging *n* (1959) **1** : the practice of carrying (as to work) one's lunch usu. in a brown paper bag **2** : the practice of carrying a bottle of liquor into a restaurant or club where setups are available — **brown–bag** \ˈbrau̇n-ˌbag\ *vb or adj* — **brown bagger** *n*

brown bear *n* (1774) : any of several bears predominantly brown in color that are usu. considered a single species (*Ursus arctos*) including the grizzly bear and that formerly inhabited western No. America from the barrens of Alaska to northern Mexico and much of Europe and Asia but are now much restricted in range

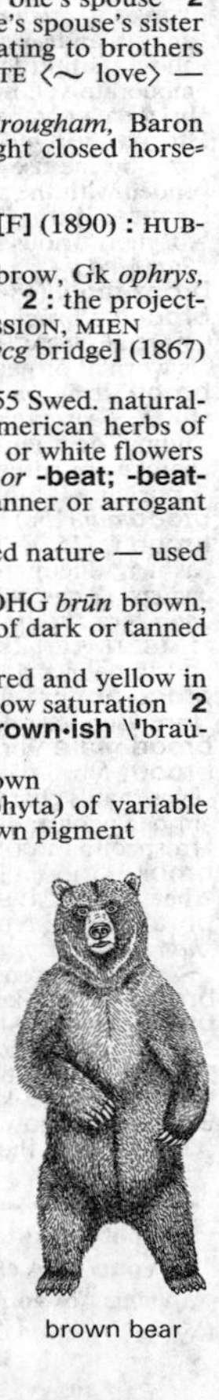

brown bear

brown Bet•ty \-ˈbe-tē\ *n* (1864) : a baked pudding of apples, bread crumbs, and spices

brown bread \-ˌbred\ *n* (14c) **1** : bread made of whole wheat flour **2** : a dark brown steamed bread made usu. of cornmeal, white or whole wheat flours, molasses, soda, and milk or water

brown coal *n* (1821) : LIGNITE

brown dwarf *n* (1978) : a celestial object that is much smaller than a normal star and has insufficient mass to sustain nuclear fusion but that is hot enough to radiate energy esp. at infrared wavelengths

brown earth *n* (1932) : any of a group of intrazonal soils developed in temperate humid regions under deciduous forests and characterized by a dark brown mull horizon that grades through lighter colored soil

brown–eyed Su•san \ˈbrau̇-ˌnīd-ˈsü-zᵊn\ *n* [*brown-eyed* + *Susan* (as in *black-eyed Susan*)] (1896) : a dark-centered coneflower (*Rudbeckia triloba*) of eastern No. America often having tripartite lower leaves

brown fat *n* (1951) : a mammalian heat-producing tissue occurring esp. in human fetuses and newborn infants and in hibernating animals — called also *brown adipose tissue*

brown•field \ˈbrau̇n-ˌfē(ə)ld\ *n, often attrib* (1977) : a tract of land that has been developed for industrial purposes, polluted, and then abandoned

brown–headed cowbird \ˈbrau̇n-ˌhe-dəd-\ *n* (1972) : COWBIRD

Brown•ian motion \ˈbrau̇-nē-ən-\ *n* [Robert *Brown* †1858 Scot. botanist] (1871) : a random movement of microscopic particles suspended in liquids or gases resulting from the impact of molecules of the surrounding medium — called also *Brownian movement*

brown•ie \ˈbrau̇-nē\ *n* [[1]*brown*] (ca. 1500) **1** : a legendary good-natured elf that performs helpful services at night **2** *cap* : a member of a program of the Girl Scouts for girls in the first through third grades in school **3** : a small square or rectangle of rich usu. chocolate cake often containing nuts

brownie point *n, often cap B* (ca. 1962) : a credit regarded as earned esp. by currying favor (as with a superior)

Brow•ning automatic rifle \ˈbrau̇-niŋ-\ *n* [John M. *Browning* †1926 Am. designer of firearms] (1920) : a .30 caliber gas-operated air-cooled magazine-fed automatic rifle often provided with a rest for the barrel

Browning machine gun *n* (1918) : a .30 or .50 caliber recoil-operated air- or water-cooled machine gun fed by a cartridge belt

brown lung *n* (1969) : BYSSINOSIS

brown•nose \ˈbrau̇(n)-ˌnōz\ *vt* [fr. the implication that servility is equivalent to having one's nose in the anus of the person from whom advancement is sought] (ca. 1939) : to ingratiate oneself with : curry favor with — **brownnose** *n* — **brown•nos•er** *n*

brown•out \ˈbrau̇-ˌnau̇t\ *n* [*brown* + black*out*] (1942) : a period of reduced voltage of electricity caused esp. by high demand and resulting in reduced illumination

brown pelican *n* (1823) : a pelican (*Pelecanus occidentalis*) of American coasts that has a brownish body and a chiefly white or white with yellow head

brown rat *n* (1781) : a common domestic rat (*Rattus norvegicus*) that has been introduced worldwide — called also *Norway rat*

brown recluse spider *n* (1964) : a venomous spider (*Loxosceles reclusa*) esp. of the southern and central U.S. that has a violin-shaped mark on the cephalothorax and produces a dangerous cytotoxin which can cause necrotic lesions

brown rice *n* (1916) : hulled but unpolished rice that retains most of the bran layers, endosperm, and germ

brown rot *n* (1863) : a disease of stone fruits (as peaches) caused by a fungus (genus *Monilinia* and esp. *M. fructicola*)

brown sauce *n* (1723) : a sauce consisting typically of stock thickened with flour browned in fat

brown•shirt \ˈbrau̇n-ˌshərt\ *n, often cap* (1932) : NAZI; *esp* : STORM TROOPER

brown•stone \-ˌstōn\ *n* (1846) **1** : a reddish-brown sandstone used for building **2** : a dwelling faced with brownstone

brown study *n* (1532) : a state of serious absorption or abstraction

brown sugar *n* (1697) : soft sugar whose crystals are covered by a film of refined dark syrup

Brown Swiss *n* (1902) : any of a breed of large hardy brown dairy cattle originating in Switzerland

brown–tail moth \ˈbrau̇n-ˌtāl-\ *n* (1782) : a European tussock moth (*Euproctis chrysorrhoea*) introduced in the U.S. and having larvae which feed on foliage and have hairs irritating to the skin

brown tree snake *n* (1947) : a large venomous arboreal colubrid snake (*Boiga irregularis*) of northern Australia, New Guinea, and the Solomon Islands that has been accidentally introduced into other areas (as Guam)

brown trout *n* (1862) : a speckled European trout (*Salmo trutta*) widely introduced as a game fish

brow•ridge \ˈbrau̇-ˌrij\ *n* (1887) : a prominence of the frontal bone above the eye caused by the projection of the frontal air sinuses

[1]**browse** \ˈbrau̇z\ *vb* **browsed; brows•ing** [ME *brouusen,* prob. fr. AF *brouts*] *vt* (15c) **1 a** : to consume as browse **b** : GRAZE **2** : to look over casually : SKIM **3** : to access (a network) by means of a browser ~ *vi* **1 a** : to feed on or as if on browse **b** : GRAZE **2 a** : to skim through a book reading passages that catch the eye **b** : to look over or through an aggregate of things casually esp. in search of something of interest — **brows•able** \ˈbrau̇-zə-bəl\ *adj*

[2]**browse** *n* [prob. modif. of AF *brouts,* pl. of *brout* sprout, of Gmc origin; akin to OS *brustian* to sprout, and perh. to OE *brēost* breast — more at BREAST] (1523) **1** : tender shoots, twigs, and leaves of trees and shrubs used by animals for food **2** : an act or instance of browsing

brows•er \ˈbrau̇-zər\ *n* (1845) **1** : one that browses **2** : a computer program used for accessing sites or information on a network (as the World Wide Web)

bru•cel•la \brü-ˈse-lə\ *n, pl* **-cel•lae** \-ˈse-(ˌ)lē\ *or* **-cel•las** [NL, fr. Sir David *Bruce*] (1930) : any of a genus (*Brucella*) of nonmotile pleomorphic bacteria that cause disease in humans and domestic animals

bru•cel•lo•sis \ˌbrü-sə-ˈlō-səs\ *n, pl* **-lo•ses** \-ˌsēz\ [NL] (1930) : infection with or disease caused by brucellae

bru•cine \ˈbrü-ˌsēn\ *n* [prob. fr. F, fr. NL *Brucea,* genus name of *Brucea antidysenterica,* a shrub] (1823) : a poisonous alkaloid $C_{23}H_{26}N_2O_4$ found with strychnine esp. in nux vomica

bru•in \ˈbrü-ən\ *n* [MD, name of the bear in *Reynard the Fox*] (15c) : BEAR 1

[1]**bruise** \ˈbrüz\ *vb* **bruised; bruis•ing** [ME *brusen, brisen,* fr. AF & OE; AF *bruiser, briser* to break, of Celt origin; akin to OIr *bruid* he shatters; OE *brȳsan* to bruise; akin to OIr *bruid,* L *frustum* piece] *vt* (14c) **1 a** *archaic* : DISABLE **b** : BATTER, DENT **2** : to inflict a bruise on : CONTUSE **3** : to break down (as leaves or berries) by pounding : CRUSH **4**

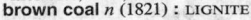

: WOUND, INJURE; *esp* : to inflict psychological hurt on ⟨a *bruised* ego⟩ ~ *vi* **1** : to inflict a bruise **2** : to undergo bruising ⟨her skin ~*s* easily⟩

[2]**bruise** *n* (1541) **1 a** : an injury involving rupture of small blood vessels and discoloration without a break in the overlying skin : CONTUSION **b** : a similar injury to plant tissue **2** : ABRASION, SCRATCH **3** : an injury esp. to the feelings

bruis·er \ˈbrü-zər\ *n* (1744) : a big husky man

bruising *adj* (1872) : ARDUOUS, TAXING ⟨a long and ~ courtroom battle⟩

[1]**bruit** *n* [ME, fr. AF, noise] (15c) **1** \ˈbrüt\ *archaic* **a** : NOISE, DIN **b** : REPORT, RUMOR **2** \brü-ē\ [F, lit., noise] : any of several generally abnormal sounds heard on auscultation

[2]**bruit** \ˈbrüt\ *vt* (15c) : REPORT, RUMOR — usu. used with *about* ⟨word of his imminent dismissal was ~*ed* about⟩

bru·mal \ˈbrü-məl\ *adj* [L *brumalis,* fr. *bruma* winter] (1513) *archaic* : indicative of or occurring in the winter

brum·by \ˈbrəm-bē\ *n, pl* **brumbies** [origin unknown] (1880) *Austral* : a wild or unbroken horse

brume \ˈbrüm\ *n* [F, mist, winter, fr. Old Occitan *bruma,* fr. L, winter solstice, winter; akin to L *brevis* short — more at BRIEF] (1808) : MIST, FOG — **bru·mous** \ˈbrü-məs\ *adj*

brum·ma·gem \ˈbrə-mi-jəm\ *adj* [alter. of *Birmingham,* England, the source in the 17th cent. of counterfeit groats] (1637) : SPURIOUS; *also* : cheaply showy : TAWDRY — **brummagem** *n*

brunch \ˈbrənch\ *n* [*breakfast* + *lunch*] (1896) : a meal usu. taken late in the morning that combines a late breakfast and an early lunch

[1]**bru·net** *or* **bru·nette** \brü-ˈnet\ *n* (ca. 1539) : a person having brown or black hair and often a relatively dark complexion — spelled *brunet* when used of a boy or man and usu. *brunette* when used of a girl or woman

[2]**brunet** *or* **brunette** *adj* [F *brunet,* masc., *brunette,* fem., brownish, fr. OF, fr. *brun* brown, fr. ML *brunus,* of Gmc origin; akin to OHG *brūn* brown] (1709) : of a dark brown or black color ⟨~ hair⟩; *also* : having brunet hair ⟨a ~ woman⟩ — spelled *brunet* when used of a boy or man and usu. *brunette* when used of a girl or woman

brung \ˈbrəŋ\ *chiefly dial past and past part of* BRING

Brun·hild \ˈbrün-ˌhilt\ *n* [G] (1842) : a queen in Germanic legend won by Siegfried for Gunther

Bruns·wick stew \ˈbrənz-(ˌ)wik-\ *n* [*Brunswick* county, Va.] (1856) : a stew made of vegetables and usu. two meats (as chicken and squirrel)

brunt \ˈbrənt\ *n* [ME] (15c) **1** : the principal force, shock, or stress (as of an attack) **2** : the greater part : BURDEN

bru·schet·ta \brü-ˈshe-tə, -ˈske-\ *n* [It, fr. It dial. (Tuscany), fr. *bruscare* to toast, burn, prob. fr. VL **brusicare,* freq. of **brusare,* **brusiare* to burn] (1954) : thick slices of bread grilled, rubbed with garlic, drizzled with olive oil, often topped with tomatoes and herbs, and usu. served as an appetizer

[1]**brush** \ˈbrəsh\ *n* [ME *brusch,* fr. an AF form akin to OF *broce* brushwood, ML *brusca*] (14c) **1** : BRUSHWOOD **2 a** : scrub vegetation **b** : land covered with scrub vegetation

[2]**brush** *n* [ME *brusshe,* fr. an AF form akin to MF *broisse*] (14c) **1** : a device composed of bristles typically set into a handle and used esp. for sweeping, smoothing, scrubbing, or painting **2** : something resembling a brush: as **a** : a bushy tail **b** : a feather tuft worn on a hat **3** : an electrical conductor that makes sliding contact between a stationary and a moving part (as of a generator or a motor) **4 a** : an act of brushing **b** : a quick light touch or momentary contact in passing

[3]**brush** *vt* (15c) **1 a** : to apply a brush to **b** : to apply with a brush **2 a** : to remove with passing strokes (as of a brush) **b** : to dispose of in an offhand way : DISMISS ⟨~*ed* him off⟩ **3** : to pass lightly over or across : touch gently against in passing — **brush·er** *n*

[4]**brush** *n* [ME *brusche* rush, hostile collision, fr. *bruschen*] (14c) : a brief encounter or skirmish ⟨a ~ with disaster⟩ ⟨a ~ with the law⟩

[5]**brush** *vi* [ME *bruschen* to rush, prob. fr. MF *brosser* to dash through underbrush, fr. *broce*] (1674) : to move lightly or heedlessly ⟨~*ed* past the well-wishers waiting to greet him⟩

brush·abil·i·ty \ˌbrə-shə-ˈbi-lə-tē\ *n* (1936) : ease of application with a brush ⟨~ of a paint⟩

brush·back \ˈbrəsh-ˌbak\ *n* (1954) : a pitch intentionally thrown near the batter's head or body in baseball — **brush back** *vt*

brush border *n* (1903) : a stria of microvilli on the plasma membrane of an epithelial cell (as in a kidney tubule) that is specialized for absorption

brush cut *n* (1945) : CREW CUT

brush discharge *n* (1849) : a faintly luminous relatively slow electrical discharge having no spark

brushed \ˈbrəsht\ *adj* (1926) **1** : finished with a nap ⟨a ~ fabric⟩ **2** : polished but not shiny ⟨~ aluminum⟩

brush·fire \ˈbrəsh-ˌfī(-ə)r\ *adj* (1954) : involving mobilization only on a small and local scale ⟨~ border wars⟩

brush fire *n* (1850) **1** : a fire involving low-growing plants (as scrub and brush) **2** : a minor conflict or crisis ⟨putting out political *brush fires*⟩

brush·land \-ˌland\ *n* (1853) : an area covered with brush growth

brush–off \-ˌȯf\ *n* (1941) : a quietly curt or disdainful dismissal

brush·stroke \-ˌstrōk\ *n* (1879) : the configuration given to paint by contact with the bristles of a brush; *also* : the paint left on a surface by a single application of a brush or palette knife — often used figuratively to describe the quality esp. of a narrative or description ⟨a story told in broad ~*s*⟩

brush up *vt* (ca. 1600) **1** : to improve or polish as if by brushing **2** : to renew one's skill in ⟨*brush up* your Spanish⟩ ~ *vi* : to refresh one's memory : renew one's skill ⟨*brush up* on math⟩ — **brush·up** \ˈbrəsh-ˌəp\ *n*

brush·wood \ˈbrəsh-ˌwu̇d\ *n* (ca. 1613) **1** : wood of small branches esp. when cut or broken **2** : a thicket of shrubs and small trees

brush·work \-ˌwərk\ *n* (1868) : work done with a brush (as in painting); *esp* : the characteristic work of an artist using a brush

[1]**brushy** \ˈbrə-shē\ *adj* **brush·i·er; -est** (1567) : covered with or abounding in brush or brushwood ⟨~ hills⟩ ⟨a ~ habitat⟩

[2]**brushy** *adj* **brush·i·er; -est** (1665) : SHAGGY, ROUGH ⟨a ~ moustache⟩

brusque *also* **brusk** \ˈbrəsk\ *adj* [F *brusque,* fr. It *brusco,* fr. ML *bruscus* butcher's-broom (plant with bristly twigs)] (1651) **1** : markedly short and abrupt **2** : blunt in manner or speech often to the point of ungracious harshness ***syn*** see BLUFF — **brusque·ly** *adv* — **brusque·ness** *n*

brus·que·rie \ˌbrəs-kə-ˈrē\ *n* [F, fr. *brusque*] (1752) : abruptness of manner

Brus·sels carpet \ˈbrə-səlz-\ *n* [*Brussels,* Belgium] (1799) : a carpet made of colored worsted yarns first fixed in a foundation web of strong linen thread and then drawn up in loops to form the pattern

Brussels griffon *n* (1904) : any of a breed of short-faced compact rough- or smooth-coated toy dogs of Belgian origin — called also *griffon*

Brussels lace *n* (1732) **1** : any of various fine needlepoint or bobbin laces with floral designs made orig. in or near Brussels **2** : a machine-made net of hexagonal mesh

brus·sels sprout \ˈbrə-səl-\ *n, often cap B* (1796) **1** *pl* : a plant (*Brassica oleracea gemmifera*) of the mustard family that bears small edible green heads on its stem **2** : any of the edible green heads borne on brussels sprouts — usu. used in pl.

brut \ˈbrüt, ˈbrœt\ *adj* [F, lit., rough] (1891) *of champagne* : very dry; *specif* : being the driest made by the producer — **brut** *n*

bru·tal \ˈbrü-tᵊl\ *adj* [ME, fr. MF or ML; MF, fr. ML *brutalis,* fr. L *brutus* — more at BRUTE] (15c) **1** *archaic* : typical of beasts : ANIMAL **2** : befitting a brute: as **a** : grossly ruthless or unfeeling ⟨a ~ slander⟩ **b** : CRUEL, COLD-BLOODED ⟨a ~ attack⟩ **c** : HARSH, SEVERE ⟨~ weather⟩ **d** : unpleasantly accurate and incisive ⟨the ~ truth⟩ **e** : very bad or unpleasant ⟨a ~ mistake⟩ — **bru·tal·ly** \-tᵊl-ē\ *adv*

syn BRUTAL, BRUTISH, BESTIAL, FERAL mean characteristic of an animal in nature, action, or instinct. BRUTAL applies to people, their acts, or their words and suggests a lack of intelligence, feeling, or humanity ⟨a senseless and *brutal* war⟩. BRUTISH stresses likeness to an animal in low intelligence, in base appetites, and in behavior based on instinct ⟨*brutish* stupidity⟩. BESTIAL suggests a state of degradation unworthy of humans and fit only for beasts ⟨*bestial* depravity⟩. FERAL suggests the savagery or ferocity of wild animals ⟨the struggle to survive unleashed their *feral* impulses⟩.

bru·tal·ise *Brit var of* BRUTALIZE

bru·tal·i·ty \brü-ˈta-lə-tē\ *n, pl* **-ties** (1549) **1** : the quality or state of being brutal **2** : a brutal act or course of action

bru·tal·ize \ˈbrü-tᵊl-ˌīz\ *vt* **-ized; -iz·ing** (ca. 1704) **1** : to make brutal, unfeeling, or inhuman ⟨temperaments *brutalized* by poverty and disease⟩ **2** : to treat brutally ⟨an accord not to ~ prisoners of war⟩ — **bru·tal·i·za·tion** \ˌbrü-tᵊl-ə-ˈzā-shən\ *n*

[1]**brute** \ˈbrüt\ *adj* [ME, fr. MF *brut* rough, fr. L *brutus* brutish, lit., heavy; akin to L *gravis* heavy — more at GRIEVE] (15c) **1** : of or relating to beasts ⟨the ways of the ~ world⟩ **2** : INANIMATE 1a **3** : characteristic of an animal in quality, action, or instinct: as **a** : CRUEL, SAVAGE ⟨~ violence⟩ **b** : not working by reason ⟨~ instinct⟩ **4** : purely physical ⟨~ strength⟩ ⟨~ force⟩ **5** : unrelievedly harsh ⟨~ facts⟩ ⟨~ necessity⟩

[2]**brute** *n* (1611) **1** : BEAST **2** : a brutal person

brut·ish \ˈbrü-tish\ *adj* (1534) **1** : resembling, befitting, or typical of a brute or beast ⟨lived a short and ~ life as a slave⟩ **2 a** : strongly and grossly sensual ⟨~ gluttony⟩ **b** : showing little intelligence or sensibility ⟨a ~ lack of understanding⟩ ***syn*** see BRUTAL — **brut·ish·ly** *adv* — **brut·ish·ness** *n*

brux·ism \ˈbrək-ˌsi-zəm\ *n* [irreg. fr. Gk *brychein* to gnash the teeth + E *-ism*] (1932) : the habit of unconsciously gritting or grinding the teeth esp. in situations of stress or during sleep

Bryn·hild \ˈbrin-ˌhild\ *n* [ON *Brynhildr*] (1590) : a Valkyrie who is waked from an enchanted sleep by Sigurd and later has him killed when he forgets her

bry·ol·o·gy \brī-ˈä-lə-jē\ *n* [Gk *bryon* moss (akin to Gk *bryein* to grow luxuriantly) + ISV *-logy*] (1856) **1** : moss life or biology **2** : a branch of botany that deals with the bryophytes — **bry·o·log·i·cal** \brī-ə-ˈlä-ji-kəl\ *adj* — **bry·ol·o·gist** \brī-ˈä-lə-jist\ *n*

bry·o·ny \ˈbrī-ə-nē\ *n, pl* **-nies** [ME, fr. L *bryonia,* fr. Gk *bryōnia;* akin to Gk *bryein*] (14c) : any of a genus (*Bryonia*) of tendril-bearing vines of the gourd family with large leaves and red or black fruit

bryo·phyl·lum \ˌbrī-ə-ˈfi-ləm\ *n* [NL, fr. Gk *bryon* + *phyllon* leaf — more at BLADE] (ca. 1868) : KALANCHOE

bryo·phyte \ˈbrī-ə-ˌfīt\ *n* [ultim. fr. Gk *bryon* + *phyton* plant; akin to Gk *phyein* to bring forth — more at BE] (1878) : any of a division (Bryophyta) of nonflowering plants comprising the mosses, liverworts, and hornworts — **bryo·phyt·ic** \ˌbrī-ə-ˈfi-tik\ *adj*

bryo·zo·an \ˌbrī-ə-ˈzō-ən\ *n* [NL *Bryozoa,* fr. Gk *bryon* + NL *-zoa*] (ca. 1864) : any of a phylum (Bryozoa) of aquatic mostly marine invertebrate animals that reproduce by budding and usu. form permanently attached branched or mossy colonies — **bryozoan** *adj*

[1]**Bry·thon·ic** \bri-ˈthä-nik\ *adj* [W *Brython* Briton, Britons (fr. British Celt **britton-*) + [1]*-ic*] (1884) : of, relating to, or characteristic of the division of the Celtic languages that includes Welsh, Cornish, and Breton

[2]**Brythonic** *n* (1884) : the Brythonic branch of the Celtic languages — see INDO-EUROPEAN LANGUAGES table

BS *abbr* **1** bachelor of science **2** balance sheet **3** bill of sale **4** bishop suffragan **5** British standard **6** *often not cap, sometimes vulgar* bullshit

BSA *abbr* Boy Scouts of America

BSAE *abbr* **1** bachelor of science in aeronautical engineering **2** bachelor of science in agricultural engineering **3** bachelor of science in architectural engineering

BSArch *abbr* bachelor of science in architecture

BSB *abbr* bachelor of science in business

BSc *abbr* bachelor of science

BSCE *abbr* bachelor of science in chemical engineering

BSCh *abbr* bachelor of science in chemistry

B–school \ˈbē-ˌskül\ *n* [*business school*] (1967) **:** a school of business within a university
BSE *abbr* bovine spongiform encephalopathy
BSEc *or* **BSEcon** *abbr* bachelor of science in economics
BSEd *or* **BSE** *abbr* bachelor of science in education
BSEE *abbr* **1** bachelor of science in electrical engineering **2** bachelor of science in elementary education
BSET *abbr* bachelor of science in engineering technology
BSFor *abbr* bachelor of science in forestry
BSI *abbr* British Standards Institution
bskt *abbr* basket
BSL *abbr* bachelor of science in linguistics
BSME *abbr* bachelor of science in mechanical engineering
bsmt *abbr* basement
BSN *abbr* bachelor of science in nursing
BSW *abbr* bachelor of social work
[1]**Bt** \ˈbē-ˈtē\ *n* [NL *Bacillus thuringiensis,* species name, lit., Thuringian bacillus] (1971) **:** a preparation of a bacterium (*Bacillus thuringiensis*) often modified by genetic engineering for use as a biopesticide against insects and esp. lepidopteran larvae; *also* **:** the bacterium itself
[2]**Bt** *abbr* baronet
btry *abbr* battery
Btu \ˌbē-ˌtē-ˈyü\ *n* (1899) **:** BRITISH THERMAL UNIT
BTW *abbr* by the way
bu *abbr* **1** bureau **2** bushel
Bu *abbr* butyl
bub \ˈbəb\ *n* [prob. short for *bubby* little boy] (1839) **:** FELLOW, BUDDY — used in informal address ⟨come on, ~, get moving⟩
Bub·ba \ˈbə-bə\ *n* [fr. *Bubba,* a stereotypical nickname of Southern white males] (1979) *often disparaging* **:** REDNECK
[1]**bub·ble** \ˈbə-bəl\ *n, often attrib* [ME *bobel*] (14c) **1 :** a small globule typically hollow and light: as **a :** a small body of gas within a liquid **b :** a thin film of liquid inflated with air or gas **c :** a globule in a transparent solid **d :** something (as a plastic or inflatable structure) that is hemispherical or semicylindrical **2 a :** something that lacks firmness, solidity, or reality **b :** a delusive scheme **3 :** a sound like that of bubbling **4 :** MAGNETIC BUBBLE **5 :** a state of booming economic activity (as in a stock market) that often ends in a sudden collapse **6 :** the condition of being at risk of exclusion or replacement (as from a tournament) — usu. used in the phrase *on the bubble* ⟨teams still on the ~ for the play-offs⟩
[2]**bubble** *vb* **bub·bled; bub·bling** \ˈbə-b(ə-)liŋ\ *vi* (15c) **1 a :** to form or produce bubbles **b :** to rise in or as if in bubbles — usu. used with *up* **2 :** to flow with a gurgling sound ⟨a brook *bubbling* over rocks⟩ **3 a :** to become lively or effervescent ⟨*bubbling* with good humor⟩ **b :** to speak in a lively and fluent manner ~ *vt* **1 :** to utter (as words) effervescently **2 :** to cause to bubble
bubble and squeak *n* (ca. 1785) **:** a British dish consisting of usu. leftover potatoes, greens (as cabbage), and sometimes meat fried together
bubble chamber *n* (1953) **:** a chamber of superheated liquid in which the path of an ionizing particle is made visible by a string of vapor bubbles
bub·ble–gum \ˈbə-bəl-ˌgəm\ *adj* (1969) **:** appealing to or characteristic of preteens or adolescents ⟨~ fashions⟩
bubble gum *n* (1937) **1 :** a chewing gum that can be blown into large bubbles **2** *usu* **bub·ble·gum** \ˈbə-bəl-ˌgəm\ **:** rock music having simple repetitive phrasings and intended esp. for young teenagers
bub·ble·head \ˈbə-bəl-ˌhed\ *n* (1949) **:** a foolish or stupid person — **bub·ble·head·ed** \-ˌhe-dəd\ *adj*
bubble memory *n* (1969) **:** a computer memory that uses magnetic bubbles to store information
bub·bler \ˈbə-b(ə-)lər\ *n* (1914) **1 :** a drinking fountain from which a stream of water bubbles upward **2 :** one that bubbles
Bubble Wrap *trademark* — used for packing material composed of sheets of plastic with bubbles of entrapped gases
[1]**bub·bly** \ˈbə-b(ə-)lē\ *adj* **bub·bli·er; -est** (1599) **1 :** full of bubbles **:** EFFERVESCENT ⟨a ~ bottle of pop⟩ **2 :** full of or showing good spirits **:** LIVELY, EFFUSIVE **3 :** resembling a bubble ⟨a ~ dome⟩
[2]**bubbly** *n* (1920) **:** CHAMPAGNE 1
bub·by \ˈbə-bē\ *n, pl* **bubbies** [prob. of imit. origin] (1675) *sometimes vulgar* **:** BREAST 1
bub·kes *also* **bup·kes** *or* **bup·kus** \ˈbəp-kəs, ˈbu̇p-\ *n pl but sing in constr* [Yiddish (prob. short for *kozebubkes,* lit., goat droppings), pl. of *bubke, bobke,* dim. of *bub, bob* bean, of Slav origin; akin to Pol *bób* bean] (1937) **:** the least amount **:** BEANS ⟨won't win ~ this year —Ivan Maisel⟩; *also* **:** NOTHING ⟨received ~ for their efforts⟩
bu·bo \ˈbyü-(ˌ)bō, ˈbü-\ *n, pl* **buboes** [ML *bubon-, bubo,* fr. Gk *boubōn*] (14c) **:** an inflammatory swelling of a lymph gland esp. in the groin — **bu·bon·ic** \byü-ˈbä-nik, bü-\ *adj*
bubonic plague *n* (1885) **:** plague caused by a bacterium (*Yersinia pestis*) and characterized esp. by the formation of buboes
buc·cal \ˈbə-kəl\ *adj* [L *bucca* cheek] (1720) **1 :** of, relating to, near, involving, or supplying a cheek ⟨the ~ surface of a tooth⟩ ⟨the ~ branch of the facial nerve⟩ **2 :** of, relating to, involving, or lying in the mouth ⟨the ~ cavity⟩ — **buc·cal·ly** *adv*
buc·ca·neer \ˌbə-kə-ˈnir\ *n* [F *boucanier* woodsman, pirate (in the 17th cent. West Indies), fr. *boucaner* to smoke meat, fr. *boucan* wooden frame for smoking meat, fr. Tupi *mokaʔẽ, mbokaʔẽ,* fr. *mo-, mbo-* causative marker + *kaʔẽ* to be roasted, dried] (1686) **1 :** any of the freebooters preying on Spanish ships and settlements esp. in 17th century West Indies; *broadly* **:** PIRATE **2 :** an unscrupulous adventurer esp. in politics or business — **buccaneer** *vi* — **buc·ca·neer·ish** \-ish\ *adj*
buc·ci·na·tor \ˈbək-sə-ˌnā-tər\ *n* [NL, fr. L *bucinator* trumpeter, fr. *bucinare* to sound on the trumpet, fr. *bucina* trumpet, fr. *bov-, bos* cow + *canere* to sing, play — more at COW, CHANT] (1615) **:** a thin broad muscle forming the wall of the cheek
[1]**buck** \ˈbək\ *n, pl* **bucks** [ME, fr. OE *bucca* stag, he-goat; akin to OHG *boc* he-goat, MIr *bocc*] (bef. 12c) **1** *or pl* **buck :** a male animal; *esp* **:** a male deer or antelope **2 a :** a male human being **:** MAN **b :** a dashing fellow **:** DANDY **3** *or pl* **buck :** ANTELOPE **4 a :** BUCKSKIN; *also* **:** an article (as a shoe) made of buckskin **b (1) :** DOLLAR 3b **(2) :** a sum of money esp. to be gained ⟨make a quick ~⟩; *also* **:** MONEY — usu. used in pl. **5** [short for *sawbuck* sawhorse] **a :** a supporting rack or frame **b :** a short thick leather-covered block for gymnastic vaulting
[2]**buck** *vt* (1750) **1 a** *archaic* **:** [1]BUTT **b :** OPPOSE, RESIST ⟨~*ing* the system⟩ **2 :** to throw (as a rider) by bucking **3 :** to charge into (as a headwind) **4 a :** to pass esp. from one person to another **b :** to move or load (as heavy objects) esp. with mechanical equipment ~ *vi* **1** *of a horse or mule* **:** to spring into the air with the back arched **2 :** to charge against something **3 a :** to move or react jerkily **b :** to refuse assent **:** BALK **4 :** to strive for advancement sometimes without regard to ethical behavior ⟨~*ing* for a promotion⟩ — **buck·er** *n*
[3]**buck** *n* (ca. 1877) **:** an act or instance of bucking
[4]**buck** *n* [short for earlier *buckhorn knife*] (1865) **1 :** an object formerly used in poker to mark the next player to deal; *broadly* **:** a token used as a mark or reminder **2 :** RESPONSIBILITY — used esp. in the phrases *pass the buck* and *the buck stops here*
[5]**buck** *adj* [prob. fr. [1]*buck*] (1918) **:** of the lowest grade within a military category ⟨a ~ private⟩
[6]**buck** *adv* [origin unknown] (1928) **:** STARK, COMPLETELY ⟨~ naked⟩
buck–and–wing \ˌbə-kᵊn-ˈwiŋ\ *n* (1895) **:** a solo tap dance with sharp foot accents, springs, leg flings, and heel clicks
buck·a·roo *also* **buck·er·oo** \ˌbə-kə-ˈrü, ˈbə-kə-ˌ\ *n, pl* **-aroos** *also* **-eroos** [prob. by folk etymology fr. Sp *vaquero,* fr. *vaca* cow, fr. L *vacca* — more at VACCINE] (1827) **1 :** COWBOY **2 :** BRONCOBUSTER
buck·bean \ˈbək-ˌbēn\ *n* (1578) **:** a perennial herbaceous plant (*Menyanthes trifoliata* of the family Menyanthaceae) growing in bogs and having racemes of white or pinkish flowers
buck·board \-ˌbȯrd\ *n* [obs. E *buck* body of a wagon + E *board*] (1839) **:** a four-wheeled vehicle with a floor made of long springy boards

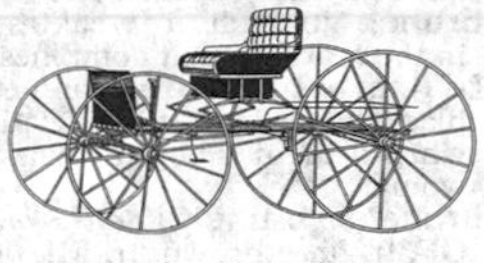
buckboard

[1]**buck·et** \ˈbə-kət\ *n* [ME, fr. AF *buket,* fr. OE *būc* pitcher, belly; akin to OHG *būh* belly] (13c) **1 :** a typically cylindrical vessel for catching, holding, or carrying liquids or solids **2 :** something resembling a bucket: as **a :** the scoop of an excavating machine **b :** one of the receptacles on the rim of a waterwheel **c :** one of the cups of an endless-belt conveyor **d :** one of the vanes of a turbine rotor **3 :** BUCKETFUL **4 :** BUCKET SEAT **5 :** BASKET 3b
[2]**bucket** *vt* (1621) **1 :** to draw or lift in buckets **2** *Brit* **a :** to ride (a horse) hard **b :** to drive hurriedly or roughly **3 :** to deal with in a bucket shop ~ *vi* **1 :** HUSTLE, HURRY **2 a :** to move about haphazardly or irresponsibly **b :** to move roughly or jerkily
bucket brigade *n* (1899) **:** a chain of persons acting to put out a fire by passing buckets of water from hand to hand
buck·et·ful \ˈbə-kət-ˌfu̇l\ *n, pl* **bucketfuls** \-ˌfu̇lz\ *or* **buck·ets·ful** \-kəts-ˌfu̇l\ (ca. 1563) **:** as much as a bucket will hold; *broadly* **:** a large quantity
bucket list *n* [fr. the phrase *kick the bucket* (to die)] (2006) **:** a list of things that one has not done before but wants to do before dying
bucket seat *n* (1908) **:** a low separate seat for one person (as in an automobile or an airplane)
bucket shop *n* (1875) **1 :** a saloon in which liquor was formerly sold from or dispensed in open containers (as buckets or pitchers) **2 a :** a gambling establishment that formerly used market fluctuations (as in securities or commodities) as a basis for gaming **b :** a dishonest brokerage firm; *esp* **:** one that formerly failed to execute customers' margin orders in expectation of making a profit from market fluctuations adverse to the customers' interests
buck·eye \ˈbək-ˌī\ *n* (1763) **1 :** any of various shrubs or trees (genus *Aesculus*) of the horse-chestnut family; *also* **:** the large nutlike seed of such a shrub or tree **2** *cap* **:** a native or resident of Ohio — used as a nickname
buck fever *n* (1841) **:** nervous excitement of an inexperienced hunter at the sight of game
[1]**buck·le** \ˈbə-kəl\ *n* [ME *bocle,* fr. AF, boss of a shield, buckle, fr. L *buccula,* dim. of *bucca* cheek] (14c) **1 :** a fastening for two loose ends that is attached to one and holds the other by a catch **2 :** an ornamental device that suggests a buckle **3** *archaic* **:** a crisp curl
[2]**buckle** *vb* **buck·led; buck·ling** \ˈbə-k(ə-)liŋ\ *vt* (14c) **1 :** to fasten with a buckle **2 :** to prepare with vigor **3 :** to cause to bend, give way, or crumple ~ *vi* **1 :** to become fastened with a buckle **2 :** to apply oneself with vigor — usu. used with *down* ⟨~ down to the job⟩ **3 :** to bend or move usu. under the influence of some external agency ⟨wheat *buckling* in the wind⟩ **4 :** COLLAPSE ⟨the props *buckled* under the strain⟩ **5 :** to give way **:** YIELD ⟨he *buckled* under pressure⟩
[3]**buckle** *n* (ca. 1876) **1 :** a product of buckling **:** BEND, FOLD **2 :** a coffee cake baked with berries and a crumbly topping ⟨blueberry ~⟩
[1]**buck·ler** \ˈbə-klər\ *n* [ME *bocler,* fr. AF *bucler,* fr. *bocle*] (13c) **1 a :** a small round shield held by a handle at arm's length **b :** a shield worn on the left arm **2 :** one that shields and protects
[2]**buckler** *vt* (1590) **:** to shield or defend with a buckler
buckle up *vi* (1971) **:** to fasten one's seat belt
buck·min·ster·ful·ler·ene \ˈbək-(ˌ)min-stər-ˌfu̇-lə-ˈrēn\ *n* [R. *Buckminster Fuller*] (1985) **:** a spherical fullerene C_{60} that is an extremely stable form of pure carbon, consists of interconnected pentagons and hexagons suggestive of the geometry of a geodesic dome, and is believed to be a major constituent of soot
bucko \ˈbə-(ˌ)kō\ *n, pl* **buck·oes** (1883) **1 :** a person who is domineering and bullying **:** SWAGGERER **2** *chiefly Irish* **:** young fellow **:** LAD
buck passer *n* (1920) **:** a person who habitually passes the buck — **buck–pass·ing** \ˈbək-ˌpa-siŋ\ *n*
[1]**buck·ram** \ˈbə-krəm\ *n* [ME *bukeram,* fr. AF *bokeram,* fr. OF *bougherant,* prob. ultim. fr. *Bokhara* (Bukhara, Uzbekistan)] (15c) **1 :** a stiff-finished heavily sized fabric of cotton or linen used for interlinings in garments, for stiffening in millinery, and in bookbinding **2** *archaic* **:** STIFFNESS, RIGIDITY
[2]**buckram** *adj* (ca. 1589) **:** suggesting buckram esp. in stiffness
[3]**buckram** *vt* (1783) **1 :** to give strength or stiffness to (as with buckram) **2** *archaic* **:** to make pretentious
Buck Rogers \ˈbək-ˈrä-jərz\ *adj* [*Buck Rogers,* hero of a science-fiction comic strip created by Phil Nowlan] (1941) **:** marked by futuristic and high-tech qualities **:** suggestive of science fiction
Bucks *abbr* Buckinghamshire

buck·saw \ˈbək-ˌsȯ\ *n* (1856) **:** a saw set in a usu. H-shaped frame for sawing wood

buck·shee \ˈbək-(ˌ)shē, ˌbək-ˈ\ *n* [Hindi *bakhśiś* & Urdu *bakhshish,* fr. Pers *bakhshīsh* — more at BAKSHEESH] (ca. 1760) **1** *Brit* **:** something extra obtained free; *esp* **:** extra rations **2** *Brit* **:** WINDFALL, GRATUITY

^{1}**buck·shot** \ˈbək-ˌshät\ *n* (1775) **:** lead shot that is from .24 to .33 inch (about 6.1 to 8.4 millimeters) in diameter

^{2}**buckshot** *adj* (1941) **:** SCATTERSHOT

buck·skin \-ˌskin\ *n, often attrib* (14c) **1 a :** the skin of a buck **b :** a soft pliable usu. suede-finished leather **2 a** *pl* **:** buckskin breeches **b** *archaic* **:** a person dressed in buckskin; *esp* **:** an early American backwoodsman **3 :** a horse of a light yellowish-dun color with black mane and tail

buck·skinned \-ˌskind\ *adj* (1829) **:** dressed in buckskin

buck·tail \-ˌtāl\ *n* (1911) **:** an angler's lure made typically of hairs from the tail of a deer

buck·thorn \-ˌthȯrn\ *n* (1578) **1 :** any of a genus (*Rhamnus* of the family Rhamnaceae, the buckthorn family) of often thorny trees or shrubs some of which yield purgatives or pigments **2 :** a shrub or small tree (*Bumelia lycioides*) of the sapodilla family of the southern U.S.

buck·tooth \-ˈtüth\ *n* (1753) **:** a large protruding front tooth — **buck-toothed** \-ˌtütht\ *adj*

buck up *vb* [^{2}*buck*] *vi* (1844) **:** to become encouraged **:** brace up ~ *vt* **1 :** IMPROVE, SMARTEN **2 :** to raise the morale of

buck·wheat \ˈbək-ˌhwēt, -ˌwēt\ *n* [D *boekweit,* fr. MD *boecweit,* fr. *boec-* (akin to OHG *buohha* beech tree) + *weit* wheat — more at BEECH] (1548) **1 :** any of a genus (*Fagopyrum* of the family Polygonaceae, the buckwheat family) of Eurasian herbs with alternate leaves, clusters of apetalous pinkish-white flowers, and triangular seeds; *esp* **:** either of two plants (*F. esculentum* and *F. tartaricum*) cultivated for their edible seeds **2 :** the seed of a buckwheat used as a cereal grain

bucky·ball \ˈbə-kē-ˌbȯl\ *n* [R. *Buck*minster Fuller + ^{4}*-y*] (1985) **:** a molecule of buckminsterfullerene; *broadly* **:** FULLERENE

bucky·tube \-ˌtüb, -ˌtyüb\ *n* [*bucky*ball + *tube*] (1991) **:** a nanotube composed of pure carbon with a molecular arrangement similar to that of a fullerene

bu·col·ic \byü-ˈkä-lik\ *adj* [L *bucolicus,* fr. Gk *boukolikos,* fr. *boukolos* cowherd, fr. *bous* head of cattle + *-kolos* (akin to L *colere* to cultivate) — more at COW, WHEEL] (ca. 1609) **1 :** of or relating to shepherds or herdsmen **:** PASTORAL **2 a :** relating to or typical of rural life **b :** IDYLLIC — **bu·col·i·cal·ly** \-li-k(ə-)lē\ *adv*

^{1}**bud** \ˈbəd\ *n* [ME *budde*] (14c) **1 :** a small lateral or terminal protuberance on the stem of a plant that may develop into a flower, leaf, or shoot **2 :** something not yet mature or at full development: as **a :** an incompletely opened flower **b :** CHILD, YOUTH **c** (1) **:** an outgrowth of an organism that differentiates into a new individual **:** GEMMA (2) **:** an outgrowth having the potential to differentiate and grow into a definitive organ or part **:** PRIMORDIUM ⟨an embryonic limb ~⟩ **3 :** BUDDY — **in the bud :** in an early stage of development ⟨nipped the rebellion *in the bud*⟩

^{2}**bud** *vb* **bud·ded; bud·ding** *vi* (14c) **1** *of a plant* **a :** to set or put forth buds **b :** to commence growth from buds **2 :** to grow or develop from or as if from a bud **3 :** to reproduce asexually esp. by the pinching off of a small part of the parent ~ *vt* **1 :** to produce or develop from buds **2 :** to cause (as a plant) to bud **3 :** to insert a bud from a plant of one kind into an opening in the bark of (a plant of another kind) usu. in order to propagate a desired variety — **bud·der** *n*

Bud·dha \ˈbü-də, ˈbu̇-\ *n* [Skt, enlightened; akin to Skt *bodhi* enlightenment — more at BID] (1681) **1 :** a person who has attained Buddhahood **2 :** a representation of Gautama Buddha

Bud·dha·hood \-ˌhu̇d\ *n* (1837) **:** a state of perfect enlightenment sought in Buddhism

Bud·dhism \ˈbü-ˌdi-zəm, ˈbu̇-\ *n* (1801) **:** a religion of eastern and central Asia growing out of the teaching of Gautama Buddha that suffering is inherent in life and that one can be liberated from it by mental and moral self-purification — **Bud·dhist** \ˈbü-dist, ˈbu̇-\ *n or adj* — **Bud·dhis·tic** \bü-ˈdis-tik, bu̇-\ *adj*

bud·ding \ˈbə-diŋ\ *adj* (1581) **:** being in an early stage of development ⟨~ novelists⟩

bud·dle·ia \ˈbəd-lē-ə, ˌbəd-ˈlē-\ *n* [NL, genus name, fr. Adam *Buddle* †1715 Eng. botanist] (1791) **:** any of a genus (*Buddleia* of the family Loganiaceae) of shrubs or small trees of warm regions with showy terminal clusters of usu. purple or white flowers — called also *butterfly bush*

^{1}**bud·dy** \ˈbə-dē\ *n, pl* **buddies** [prob. baby talk alter. of *brother*] (1850) **1 a :** COMPANION, PARTNER **b :** FRIEND 1 **2 :** FELLOW — used esp. in informal address

^{2}**buddy** *vi* **bud·died; bud·dy·ing** (1918) **:** to become friendly — usu. used with *up* or *with*

^{3}**buddy** *adj* (1976) **:** featuring a friendship or partnership between the two main usu. male characters ⟨a ~ movie⟩

bud·dy–bud·dy \ˌbə-dē-ˈbə-dē\ *adj* (1951) **:** familiarly friendly

buddy system *n* (1942) **:** an arrangement in which two individuals are paired (as for mutual safety in a hazardous situation)

^{1}**budge** \ˈbəj\ *n* [ME *bugee,* fr. AF *buge*] (14c) **:** a fur formerly prepared from lambskin dressed with the wool outward

^{2}**budge** *vb* **budged; budg·ing** [AF *bouger,* fr. VL **bullicare,* fr. L *bullire* to boil — more at BOIL] *vi* (1578) **1 :** MOVE, SHIFT ⟨the mule wouldn't ~⟩ **2 :** to give way **:** YIELD ⟨wouldn't ~ on the issue⟩ ~ *vt* **:** to cause to move or change

^{3}**budge** *adj* [origin unknown] (1599) *archaic* **:** POMPOUS, SOLEMN

bud·ger·i·gar \ˈbə-jə-rē-ˌgär\ *n* [modif. of Yuwaalaraay (Australian aboriginal language of northern New South Wales) *gijirrigaa*] (1840) **:** a small Australian parrot (*Melopsittacus undulatus*) usu. light green with black and yellow markings in the wild but bred under domestication in many colors

^{1}**bud·get** \ˈbə-jət\ *n* [ME *bowgette,* fr. MF *bougette,* dim. of *bouge* leather bag, fr. L *bulga,* of Celt origin; akin to MIr *bolg* bag; akin to OE *belg* bag — more at BELLY] (15c) **1** *chiefly dial* **:** a usu. leather pouch, wallet, or pack; *also* **:** its contents **2 :** STOCK, SUPPLY **3 :** a quantity (as of energy or water) involved in, available for, or assignable to a particular situation; *also* **:** an account of gains and losses of such a quantity ⟨the global carbon ~⟩ **4 a :** a statement of the financial position of an administration for a definite period of time based on estimates of expenditures during the period and proposals for financing them **b :** a plan for the coordination of resources and expenditures **c :** the amount of money that is available for, required for, or assigned to a particular purpose — **bud·get·ary** \ˈbə-jə-ˌter-ē, -ˌte-rē\ *adj*

^{2}**budget** *vt* (1618) **1 a :** to put or allow for in a budget **b :** to require to adhere to a budget **2 a :** to allocate funds for in a budget ⟨~ a new hospital⟩ **b :** to plan or provide for the use of in detail ⟨~*ing* manpower⟩ ~ *vi* **:** to put oneself on a budget ⟨~*ing* for a vacation⟩

^{3}**budget** *adj* (1941) **:** suitable for one on a budget **:** INEXPENSIVE

bud·ge·teer \ˌbə-jə-ˈtir\ *also* **bud·get·er** \ˈbə-jə-tər\ *n* (ca. 1841) **1 :** one who prepares a budget **2 :** one who is restricted to a budget

bud·gie \ˈbə-jē\ *n* [by shortening and alter.] (1935) **:** BUDGERIGAR

bud scale *n* (1845) **:** one of the leaves resembling scales that form the sheath of a plant bud

bud·worm \ˈbəd-ˌwərm\ *n* (1849) **:** a moth larva that feeds on the buds of plants — compare SPRUCE BUDWORM, TOBACCO BUDWORM

^{1}**buff** \ˈbəf\ *n* [MF *buffle* wild ox, fr. OIt *bufalo*] (1570) **1 :** a garment (as a uniform) made of buff leather **2 :** the state of being nude ⟨sunbathing in the ~⟩ **3 a :** a moderate orange yellow **b :** a light to moderate yellow **4 :** a device having a soft absorbent surface (as of cloth) by which polishing material is applied **5** [earlier *buff* an enthusiast about going to fires; perh. fr. the buff overcoats worn by volunteer firefighters in New York City *ab* 1820] **:** FAN, ENTHUSIAST

^{2}**buff** *adj* (1746) **1 :** of the color buff **2** *or* **buffed :** having a physique enhanced by bodybuilding exercises

^{3}**buff** *vt* (1838) **1 :** POLISH, SHINE ⟨waxed and ~*ed* the floor⟩ **2 :** to give a velvety surface to (leather)

^{1}**buf·fa·lo** \ˈbə-fə-ˌlō\ *n, pl* **-lo** *or* **-loes** *also* **-los** *often attrib* [It *bufalo* & Sp *búfalo,* fr. LL *bufalus,* alter. of L *bubalus,* fr. Gk *boubalos* African gazelle] (1562) **1 :** any of several wild bovids: as **a :** WATER BUFFALO **b :** CAPE BUFFALO **c** (1) **:** any of a genus (*Bison*) of bovids; *esp* **:** a large shaggy-maned No. American bovid (*B. bison*) that has short horns and heavy forequarters with a large muscular hump and that was formerly abundant on the central and western plains — compare WISENT (2) **:** the flesh of the buffalo used as food **2 :** any of several suckers (genus *Ictiobus*) found mostly in the Mississippi valley — called also *buffalo fish*

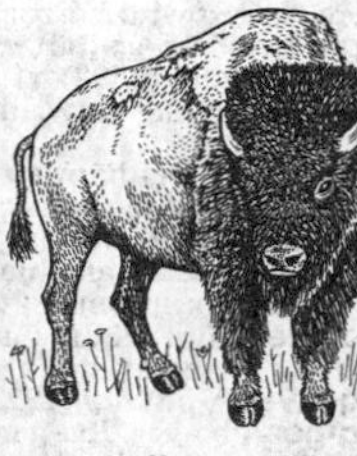

buffalo 1c(1)

^{2}**buffalo** *vt* **-loed; -lo·ing** (1891) **:** BEWILDER, BAFFLE; *also* **:** BAMBOOZLE

buffalo berry *n* (1805) **:** either of two No. American shrubs (*Shepherdia argentea* and *S. canadensis*) of the oleaster family with silvery foliage; *also* **:** their edible scarlet berry

buffalo gourd *n* (ca. 1928) **:** a perennial foul-smelling cucurbit (*Cucurbita foetidissima*) of arid lands of the central and southwest U.S. and Mexico with a large starchy taproot and seeds rich in oil

buffalo grass *n* (1784) **:** a low-growing perennial grass (*Buchloë dactyloides*) native to the Great Plains that has curly grayish-green leaves; *also* **:** GRAMA

buffalo plaid *n* (1979) **:** a broad checkered plaid pattern usu. of two colors

buffalo soldier *n* (1872) **:** an African-American soldier serving in the western U.S. after the Civil War

buffalo wing *n* [*Buffalo,* N.Y.] (1984) **:** a deep-fried chicken wing coated with a spicy sauce and usu. served with a blue cheese dressing

^{1}**buff·er** \ˈbə-fər\ *n* [origin unknown] (1749) *slang Brit* **:** FELLOW, MAN; *esp* **:** an old man

^{2}**buffer** *n, often attrib* [*buff,* v., to react like a soft body when struck] (1835) **1 :** any of various devices or pieces of material for reducing shock or damage due to contact **2 :** a means or device used as a cushion against the shock of fluctuations in business or financial activity **3 :** something that serves as a protective barrier: as **a :** BUFFER STATE **b :** a person who shields another esp. from annoying routine matters **c :** MEDIATOR 1 **4 :** a substance capable in solution of neutralizing both acids and bases and thereby maintaining the original acidity or basicity of the solution; *also* **:** a solution containing such a substance **5 :** a temporary storage unit (as in a computer); *esp* **:** one that accepts information at one rate and delivers it at another — **buff·ered** \-fərd\ *adj*

^{3}**buffer** *vt* **buff·ered; buff·er·ing** \-f(ə-)riŋ\ (1845) **1 :** to lessen the shock of **:** CUSHION **2 :** to treat (as a solution or its acidity) with a buffer; *also* **:** to prepare (aspirin) with an antacid **3 :** to collect (as data) in a buffer

^{4}**buffer** *n* (1854) **:** one that buffs

buffer state *n* (1883) **:** a usu. neutral state lying between two larger potentially rival powers

buffer zone *n* (1908) **:** a neutral area separating conflicting forces; *broadly* **:** an area designed to separate

^{1}**buf·fet** \ˈbə-fət\ *n* [ME, fr. AF, dim. of *buffe* blow] (13c) **1 :** a blow esp. with the hand **2 :** something that strikes with telling force

^{2}**buffet** *vt* (13c) **1 :** to strike sharply esp. with the hand **:** CUFF **2 :** to strike repeatedly **:** BATTER ⟨the waves ~*ed* the shore⟩ **3 :** to drive, force, move, or attack by or as if by repeated blows ~ *vi* **:** to make one's way esp. under difficult conditions

^{3}**buf·fet** \(ˌ)bə-ˈfā, bü-ˈ, *Brit esp* ˈbü-ˌ\ *n* [F] (1718) **1 :** SIDEBOARD **2 a :** a counter for refreshments **b** *chiefly Brit* **:** a restaurant operated as a public convenience (as in a railway station) **c :** a meal set out on a buffet or table for ready access and informal service

^{4}**buf·fet** *same as* ^{3}\ *adj* (1898) **:** served informally (as from a buffet)

buffing wheel *n* (1854) **:** a wheel covered with polishing material

buff leather *n* (1580) **:** a strong supple oil-tanned leather produced chiefly from cattle hides

buf·fle·head \ˈbə-fəl-ˌhed\ *n* [archaic E *buffle* buffalo + E *head*] (1731) **:** a small No. American diving duck (*Bucephala albeola*)

buf•fo \ˈbü-(ˌ)fō\ *n, pl* **buf•fi** \-(ˌ)fē\ *or* **buffos** [It, fr. *buffone*] (1764) : CLOWN, BUFFOON; *specif* : a male singer of comic roles in opera
buf•foon \(ˌ)bə-ˈfün\ *n* [MF *bouffon,* fr. OIt *buffone*] (1585) **1** : a ludicrous figure : CLOWN **2** : a gross and usu. ill-educated or stupid person — **buf•foon•ish** \-ˈfü-nish\ *adj*
buf•foon•ery \-ˈfü-nə-rē, -ˈfün-rē\ *n, pl* **-er•ies** (1621) : foolish or playful behavior or practice
[1]**bug** \ˈbəg\ *n* [ME *bugge* hobgoblin; prob. akin to LG *bögge* goblin] (14c) *obs* : BOGEY, BUGBEAR
[2]**bug** *n* [origin unknown] (1622) **1 a** : an insect or other creeping or crawling invertebrate (as a spider or centipede) **b** : any of several insects (as the bedbug or cockroach) commonly considered obnoxious **c** : any of an order (Hemiptera and esp. its suborder Heteroptera) of insects that have sucking mouthparts, forewings thickened at the base, and incomplete metamorphosis and are often economic pests — called also *true bug* **2** : an unexpected defect, fault, flaw, or imperfection ⟨the software was full of ~*s*⟩ **3 a** : a germ or microorganism esp. when causing disease **b** : an unspecified or nonspecific sickness usu. presumed due to a bug **4** : a sudden enthusiasm **5** : ENTHUSIAST ⟨a camera ~⟩ **6** : a prominent person **7** : a crazy person **8** : a concealed listening device **9** [fr. its designation by an asterisk on race programs] : a weight allowance given apprentice jockeys
[3]**bug** *vb* **bugged; bug•ging** *vt* (1935) **1** : to plant a concealed microphone in **2** : BOTHER, ANNOY ⟨don't ~ me with petty details⟩ ~ *vi* : to lose one's composure : FREAK — often used with *out*
[4]**bug** *vb* **bugged; bug•ging** [prob. fr. [2]*bug*] *vi* (1865) *of the eyes* : PROTRUDE, BULGE — often used with *out* ~ *vt* : to cause to bug ⟨his eyes were *bugged* with horror⟩
bug•a•boo \ˈbə-gə-ˌbü\ *n, pl* **-boos** [earlier *buggybow, bugger-bo,* of unknown origin] (1598) **1** : an imaginary object of fear **2** : BUGBEAR 2; *also* : something that causes fear or distress out of proportion to its importance
bug•bane \ˈbəg-ˌbān\ *n* (1804) : any of several perennial herbs (genus *Cimicifuga*) of the buttercup family; *esp* : BLACK COHOSH
bug•bear \-ˌber\ *n* (1581) **1** : an imaginary goblin or specter used to excite fear **2 a** : an object or source of dread **b** : a continuing source of irritation : PROBLEM
bug•eye \-ˌī\ *n* (1881) : a small boat with a flat bottom, a centerboard, and two raked masts
bug–eyed \-ˌīd\ *adj* (1922) : having the eyes bulging (as with fright)
[1]**bug•ger** \ˈbə-gər, ˈbü-gər\ *n* [ME *bougre* heretic, fr. AF *bugre,* fr. ML *Bulgarus,* lit., Bulgarian; fr. the association of Bulgaria with the Bogomils, who were accused of sodomy] (1555) **1** : SODOMITE **2 a** : a worthless person : RASCAL **b** : FELLOW, CHAP **3** : a small or annoying thing ⟨put down my keys and now I can't find the ~*s*⟩
[2]**bug•ger** \ˈbə-gər\ *vt* (1598) **1** *usu vulgar* : to commit sodomy with **2** : DAMN **3** : to put into disorder : BUNGLE, BOTCH — often used with *up*
[3]**bugger** *n* (1955) : a person who plants electronic bugs
bugger all *n* (1918) *slang Brit* : NOTHING
bugger off *vi* (1922) *slang Brit* : LEAVE, DEPART — often used as a command
bug•gery \ˈbə-gə-rē\ *n* (1514) : SODOMY
[1]**bug•gy** \ˈbə-gē\ *adj* **bug•gi•er; -est** (1714) **1** : infested with bugs ⟨a ~ swamp⟩ **2** : characterized by bugs; *esp* : containing many bugs ⟨a ~ software program⟩
[2]**buggy** *n, pl* **buggies** [origin unknown] (1770) **1** : a light one-horse carriage made with two wheels in England and with four wheels in the U.S. **2** : a small cart or truck for short transportations of heavy materials **3** : BABY CARRIAGE
[1]**bug•house** \ˈbəg-ˌhau̇s\ *adj* (1891) *slang* : mentally deranged : CRAZY
[2]**bughouse** *n* (1899) *slang* : an insane asylum
[1]**bu•gle** \ˈbyü-gəl\ *n* [ME, fr. AF, fr. LL *bugula*] (13c) : any of a genus (*Ajuga*) of plants of the mint family; *esp* : a European annual (*A. reptans*) that has spikes of blue flowers and is naturalized in the U.S.
[2]**bugle** *n* [ME, buffalo, instrument made of buffalo horn, bugle, fr. AF, fr. L *buculus,* dim. of *bos* head of cattle — more at COW] (14c) : a valveless brass instrument that resembles a trumpet and is used esp. for military calls
[3]**bugle** *vi* **bu•gled; bu•gling** \-g(ə-)liŋ\ (1847) **1** : to sound a bugle **2** : to utter the characteristic rutting call of the bull elk
[4]**bugle** *n* [perh. fr. [2]*bugle*] (1579) : a small cylindrical bead of glass or plastic used for trimming esp. on women's clothing
bu•gler \ˈbyü-glər\ *n* (1799) : a person who sounds a bugle
bu•gle•weed \ˈbyü-gəl-ˌwēd\ *n* (ca. 1818) **1** : any of a genus (*Lycopus*) of mints; *esp* : a No. American perennial (*L. virginicus*) that is mildly narcotic and astringent **2** : [1]BUGLE
bu•gloss \ˈbyü-ˌgläs, -ˌglȯs\ *n* [ME *buglosse,* fr. AF, fr. L *buglossa,* irreg. fr. Gk *bouglōssos,* fr. *bous* head of cattle + *glōssa* tongue — more at COW, GLOSS] (14c) : any of several coarse hairy plants (genera *Anchusa, Lycopsis,* and *Echium*) of the borage family — compare VIPER'S BUGLOSS
bug off *vi* [prob. short for *bugger off*] (1971) : LEAVE, DEPART — usu. used as a command
bug out *vi* [origin unknown] (1950) **1** : to retreat during a military action; *esp* : to flee in panic **2** : to depart esp. in a hurry — **bug•out** \ˈbəg-ˌau̇t\ *n*
buhl *var of* BOULLE
[1]**build** \ˈbild\ *vb* **built** \ˈbilt\; **build•ing** [ME *bilden,* fr. OE *byldan;* akin to OE *būan* to dwell — more at BOWER] *vt* (bef. 12c) **1** : to form by ordering and uniting materials by gradual means into a composite whole : CONSTRUCT **2** : to cause to be constructed **3** : to develop according to a systematic plan, by a definite process, or on a particular base **4** : INCREASE, ENLARGE ~ *vi* **1** : to engage in building **2 a** : to progress toward a peak (as of intensity) ⟨~ to a climax⟩ **b** : to develop in extent ⟨a crowd ~*ing*⟩ — **build a fire under** : to stimulate to vigorous action — **build into** : to make an integral part of ⟨*build* quality *into* the product⟩ — **build on** : to use as a foundation ⟨*building on* past experience⟩
[2]**build** *n* (1667) : form or mode of structure : MAKE; *esp* : bodily conformation of a person or animal
build•able \ˈbil-də-bəl\ *adj* (1927) : suitable for building ⟨~ land⟩; *esp* : capable of being built ⟨plans for a ~ house⟩
build•ed \ˈbil-dəd\ *dial past of* BUILD
build•er \ˈbil-dər\ *n* (13c) **1** : one that builds; *esp* : one that contracts to build and supervises building operations **2** : a substance added to or used with detergents to increase their cleansing action
build in *vt* (1933) : to make an integral part of something
build•ing \ˈbil-diŋ\ *n* (14c) **1** : a usu. roofed and walled structure built for permanent use (as for a dwelling) **2** : the art or business of assembling materials into a structure
building block *n* (1756) : a unit of construction or composition; *esp* : something essential on which a larger entity is based
build•up \ˈbild-ˌəp\ *n* (1926) **1** : something produced by building up ⟨fluid ~ in the lungs⟩ **2** : the act or process of building up
build up *vt* (1555) **1** : to develop gradually by increments ⟨*building up* endurance⟩ ⟨*built up* a library⟩ **2** : to promote the health, strength, esteem, or reputation of ~ *vi* : to accumulate or develop appreciably — **build•er–up•per** \ˈbil-dər-ˈə-pər\ *n*
built \ˈbilt\ *adj* (1618) : formed as to physique or bodily contours ⟨slimly ~⟩; *esp* : well or attractively formed
[1]**built–in** \ˈbilt-ˈin\ *adj* (1898) **1 a** : forming an integral part of a structure or object ⟨a camera with a ~ flash⟩; *esp* : constructed as or in a recess in a wall ⟨a ~ bookshelf⟩ **b** : built into the ground ⟨a ~ swimming pool⟩ **2 a** : INHERENT ⟨a ~ advantage⟩ **b** : already established ⟨her best-seller status gave her a ~ audience⟩
[2]**built–in** \-ˌin\ *n* (1930) : a built-in piece of furniture
built–up \ˈbilt-ˈəp\ *adj* (1829) **1** : made of several sections or layers fastened together **2** : covered with buildings
bird•ly \ˈbu̇r(d)-lē\ *adj* [prob. alter. of *burly*] (1773) *Scot* : STURDY
bulb \ˈbəlb\ *n* [ME, fr. L *bulbus,* fr. Gk *bolbos* bulbous plant] (15c) **1 a** : a resting stage of a plant (as the lily, onion, hyacinth, or tulip) that is usu. formed underground and consists of a short stem base bearing one or more buds enclosed in overlapping membranous or fleshy leaves **b** : a fleshy structure (as a tuber or corm) resembling a bulb in appearance **c** : a plant having or developing from a bulb **2** : a bulb-shaped part; *specif* : a glass envelope enclosing the light source of an electric lamp or such an envelope together with the light source it encloses **3** : a rounded or swollen anatomical structure **4** : a camera setting that indicates that the shutter can be opened by pressing on the release and closing by ending the pressure — **bulbed** \ˈbəlbd\ *adj*
bul•bar \ˈbəl-bər, -ˌbär\ *adj* (1876) : of or relating to a bulb; *specif* : involving the medulla oblongata ⟨~ poliomyelitis⟩
bul•bil \ˈbəl-bəl, -ˌbil\ *n* [F *bulbille,* dim. of *bulbe* bulb, fr. L *bulbus*] (1831) : BULBLET
bulb•let \ˈbəlb-lət\ *n* (1842) : a small or secondary bulb; *esp* : an aerial deciduous bud produced in a leaf axil or replacing the flowers and capable when separated of producing a new plant
bul•bo•ure•thral gland \ˌbəl-(ˌ)bō-yu̇-ˈrē-thrəl-\ *n* [L *bulbus* bulb + E *urethral*] (ca. 1903) : COWPER'S GLAND
bul•bous \ˈbəl-bəs\ *adj* (1578) **1** : having a bulb : growing from or bearing bulbs **2** : resembling a bulb esp. in roundness ⟨a ~ nose⟩ — **bul•bous•ly** *adv*
bul•bul \ˈbu̇l-ˌbu̇l\ *n* [Pers, fr. Ar] (1665) **1** : a songbird frequently mentioned in Persian poetry that is prob. a nightingale (*Erithacus megarhynchos*) **2** : any of a group of gregarious passerine birds (family Pycnonotidae) of Asia and Africa
Bulg *abbr* Bulgaria; Bulgarian
Bul•gar \ˈbəl-ˌgär, ˈbu̇l-\ *n* [ME *Bulgare,* fr. ML *Bulgarus*] (14c) : BULGARIAN
Bul•gar•i•an \ˌbəl-ˈger-ē-ən, bu̇l-\ *n* (1555) **1** : a native or inhabitant of Bulgaria **2** : the Slavic language of the Bulgarians — **Bulgarian** *adj*
[1]**bulge** \ˈbəlj *also* ˈbu̇lj\ *vb* **bulged; bulg•ing** [ME *bolgen*] *vt* (15c) : to cause to bulge ~ *vi* **1** *archaic* : BILGE **2 a** : to jut out : SWELL **b** : to bend outward **c** : to become swollen or protuberant ⟨*bulging* eyes⟩ **3** : to be filled to overflowing ⟨a notebook *bulging* with ideas⟩
[2]**bulge** *n* [ME *boulge, bouge* leather bag, curved part, fr. AF *bouge* bag — more at BUDGET] (1622) **1 a** : BILGE 1 **b** : BILGE 2 **2** : a protuberant or swollen part or place **3** : ADVANTAGE, UPPER HAND **4** : sudden expansion ***syn*** see PROJECTION — **bulgy** \ˈbəl-jē *also* ˈbu̇l-\ *adj*
bul•gur \ˈbəl-gər, ˈbu̇l-\ *n* [Turk] (1926) : parched cracked wheat
bu•lim•ia \bü-ˈlē-mē-ə, byü-, -ˈli-\ *n* [NL, fr. Gk *boulimia* great hunger, fr. *bou-,* aug. prefix (fr. *bous* head of cattle) + *limos* hunger — more at COW] (14c) **1** : an abnormal and constant craving for food **2** : a serious eating disorder that occurs chiefly in females, is characterized by compulsive overeating usu. followed by self-induced vomiting or laxative or diuretic abuse, and is often accompanied by guilt and depression — called also *bulimia nervosa* — **bu•lim•ic** \-ˈlē-mik, -ˈli-\ *adj or n*
[1]**bulk** \ˈbəlk *also* ˈbu̇lk\ *n* [ME, heap, bulk, fr. ON *bulki* cargo] (15c) **1 a** : spatial dimension : MAGNITUDE **b** : material that forms a mass in the intestine; *esp* : FIBER 1d **2 a** : BODY; *esp* : a large or corpulent human body **b** : an organized structure esp. when viewed primarily as a mass of material **c** : a ponderous shapeless mass **3** : the main or greater part — **in bulk** **1** : not divided into parts or packaged in separate units **2** : in large quantities
syn BULK, MASS, VOLUME mean the aggregate that forms a body or unit. BULK implies an aggregate that is impressively large, heavy, or numerous ⟨the darkened *bulk* of the skyscrapers⟩. MASS suggests an aggregate made by piling together things of the same kind ⟨a *mass* of boulders⟩. VOLUME applies to an aggregate without shape or outline and capable of flowing or fluctuating ⟨a tremendous *volume* of water⟩.
[2]**bulk** *vt* (1540) **1** : to cause to swell or bulge : STUFF **2** : to gather into a mass or aggregate ~ *vi* **1** : SWELL, EXPAND **2** : to appear as a factor : LOOM ⟨a consideration that ~*s* large in everyone's thinking⟩
[3]**bulk** *adj* (1693) **1** : being in bulk ⟨~ cement⟩ **2** : of or relating to materials in bulk
bulk•head \ˈbəlk-ˌhed, ˈbəl-ˌked\ *n* [*bulk* (structure projecting from a building) + *head*] (15c) **1** : an upright partition separating compartments **2** : a structure or partition to resist pressure or to shut off water, fire, or gas **3** : a retaining wall along a waterfront **4** : a projecting framework with a sloping door giving access to a cellar stairway or a shaft
bulk up *vi* (1979) : to gain weight esp. by becoming more muscular ~ *vt* : to cause to bulk up
bulky \ˈbəl-kē *also* ˈbu̇l-\ *adj* **bulk•i•er; -est** (15c) **1 a** : having bulk **b** (1) : large of its kind (2) : CORPULENT **2** : having great volume in

proportion to weight ⟨a ~ knit sweater⟩ — **bulk·i·ly** \-kə-lē\ *adv* — **bulk·i·ness** \-kē-nəs\ *n*

[1]**bull** \ˈbu̇l, ˈbəl\ *n* [ME *bule,* fr. OE *bula;* akin to ON *boli* bull] (bef. 12c) **1 a :** a male bovine; *esp* : an adult uncastrated male domestic bovine **b :** a usu. adult male of various large animals (as elephants, whales, or seals) **2 :** one who buys securities or commodities in expectation of a price rise or who acts to effect such a rise — compare BEAR **3 :** one that resembles a bull (as in brawny physique) **4 :** BULLDOG **5** *slang* : POLICE OFFICER, DETECTIVE **6** *cap* : TAURUS

[2]**bull** *adj* (13c) **1 a :** of or relating to a bull **b :** MALE ⟨a ~ calf⟩ **c :** suggestive of a bull **2 :** large of its kind ⟨a ~ lathe⟩

[3]**bull** *vi* (1884) : to advance forcefully ~ *vt* **1 :** to act on with violence **2 :** FORCE ⟨~*ed* his way through the crowd⟩

[4]**bull** *n* [ME *bulle,* fr. ML *bulla,* fr. L, bubble, amulet] (14c) **1 :** a solemn papal letter sealed with a bulla or with a red-ink imprint of the device on the bulla **2 :** EDICT, DECREE

[5]**bull** *vt* (1609) *slang* : to fool esp. by fast boastful talk ~ *vi, slang* : to engage in idle and boastful talk

[6]**bull** *n* [perh. fr. obs. *bull* to mock] (1640) **1 :** a grotesque blunder in language **2** *slang* : empty boastful talk **3** *slang* : NONSENSE 2

[7]**bull** *abbr* bulletin

bul·la \ˈbu̇-lə\ *n, pl* **bul·lae** \ˈbu̇-ˌlē, -ˌlī\ (14c) **1** [ML] : the round usu. lead seal attached to a papal bull **2** [NL, fr. L] : a hollow thin-walled rounded bony prominence **3 :** a large vesicle or blister

bul·lace \ˈbu̇-ləs\ *n* [ME *bolace,* fr. AF *bulloce,* fr. ML *bolluca*] (14c) : a European plum (*Prunus domestica insititia*) with small ovoid fruit in clusters

bull·bait·ing \ˈbu̇l-ˌbā-tiŋ, ˈbəl-\ *n* (ca. 1580) : the former practice of baiting bulls with dogs

bull·bat \ˈbu̇l-ˌbat, ˈbəl-\ *n* (1838) : the common nighthawk (*Chordeiles minor*)

[1]**bull·dog** \ˈbu̇l-ˌdȯg *also* ˈbəl-\ *n* (ca. 1500) **1 :** any of a breed of compact muscular short-haired dogs having widely separated forelegs and an undershot lower jaw that were developed in England to fight bulls **2 :** a handgun with a thick usu. short barrel **3 :** a proctor's attendant at an English university

[2]**bulldog** *adj* (1816) : suggestive of a bulldog ⟨~ tenacity⟩

[3]**bulldog** *vt* (1905) : to throw (a steer) by seizing the horns and twisting the neck — **bull·dog·ger** *n* — **bull·dog·ging** *n*

bull·doze \ˈbu̇l-ˌdōz *also* ˈbəl-\ *vb* [perh. fr. [1]*bull* + alter. of *dose*] *vt* (1876) **1 :** to coerce or restrain by threats : BULLY **2 :** to move, clear, gouge out, or level off by pushing with or as if with a bulldozer **3 :** to force insensitively or ruthlessly ~ *vi* **1 :** to operate a bulldozer **2 :** to force one's way like a bulldozer ***syn*** see INTIMIDATE

bull·doz·er \-ˌdō-zər\ *n* (1876) **1 :** one that bulldozes **2 :** a tractor-driven machine usu. having a broad horizontal blade for moving earth

bull dyke *n* (1931) *often disparaging* : an aggressively masculine lesbian

bul·let \ˈbu̇-lət *also* ˈbə-\ *n, often attrib* [MF *boulette* small ball & *boulet* missile, dims. of *boule* ball — more at BOWL] (1579) **1 :** a round or elongated missile (as of lead) to be fired from a firearm; *broadly* : CARTRIDGE 1a **2 a :** something resembling a bullet (as in curved form) **b :** a large dot placed in printed matter to call attention to a particular passage **3 :** a very fast and accurately thrown or hit object (as a ball or puck) — **bul·let·ed** \-lə-təd\ *adj*

[1]**bul·le·tin** \ˈbu̇-lə-tᵊn *also* ˈbə-\ *n* [F, fr. MF, fr. *bullette* seal, notice, dim. of *bulle* seal, fr. ML *bulla*] (1765) **1 :** a brief public notice issuing usu. from an authoritative source; *specif* : a brief news item intended for immediate publication or broadcast **2 :** PERIODICAL; *esp* : the organ of an institution or association

[2]**bulletin** *vt* (1838) : to make public by bulletin

bulletin board *n* (1831) **1 :** a board for posting notices (as at a school) **2 :** a public electronic forum that allows users to post or read messages or to post or download files and that is accessed by computer over a network (as the Internet)

bullet point *n* (1983) : an item in a list that has a large dot in front of it to signify its importance; *broadly* : any point or statement given special emphasis (as in a speech)

bul·let·proof \ˈbu̇-lət-ˌprüf *also* ˈbə-\ *adj* (1693) **1 :** impenetrable to bullets ⟨~ glass⟩ **2 :** not subject to correction, alteration, or modification ⟨a ~ argument⟩ **3 :** INVINCIBLE

bullet train *n* (1966) : a high-speed passenger train esp. of Japan

bull fiddle *n* (1880) : DOUBLE BASS — **bull fiddler** *n*

bull·fight \ˈbu̇l-ˌfīt *also* ˈbəl-\ *n* (1788) : a spectacle in which men ceremonially fight with and in Hispanic tradition kill bulls in an arena for public entertainment — **bull·fight·er** \-ˌfī-tər\ *n*

bull·fight·ing \-tiŋ\ *n* (ca. 1753) : the action involved in a bullfight

bull·finch \ˈbu̇l-ˌfinch *also* ˈbəl-\ *n* (ca. 1570) : a European finch (*Pyrrhula pyrrhula* of the family Fringillidae) having in the male rosy-red underparts, blue-gray back, and black cap, chin, tail, and wings; *also* : any of several other finches

bull·frog \-ˌfrȯg, -ˌfräg\ *n* (1698) : a heavy-bodied deep-voiced frog (*Rana catesbeiana*) of the eastern U.S. and southern Canada that has been introduced elsewhere

bull·head \-ˌhed\ *n* (15c) : any of various large-headed fishes (as a sculpin); *esp* : any of several common freshwater catfishes (genus *Ameiurus* sometimes included in the genus *Ictalurus*) of the U.S.

bull·head·ed \-ˈhe-dəd\ *adj* (1818) : stupidly stubborn : HEADSTRONG — **bull·head·ed·ly** *adv* — **bull·head·ed·ness** *n*

bull·horn \-ˌhȯrn\ *n* (1942) **1 :** a loudspeaker on a naval ship **2 :** a handheld combined microphone and loudspeaker

bul·lion \ˈbu̇l-yən, -ˌyän\ *n* [ME, fr. AF *billion, bullion* melting house, bullion, prob. blend of MF *bille* ingot, piece of money (fr. OF, log) and AF **bulliun, buillun* cauldron, fr. OF *boillon* froth on boiling liquid, broth — more at BILLET, BOUILLON] (14c) **1 a :** gold or silver considered as so much metal; *specif* : uncoined gold or silver in bars or ingots **b :** metal in the mass ⟨lead ~⟩ **2 :** lace, braid, or fringe of gold or silver threads

bull·ish \ˈbu̇-lish *also* ˈbə-\ *adj* (1566) **1 :** suggestive of a bull (as in brawniness) **2 a :** marked by, tending to cause, or hopeful of rising prices (as in a stock market) ⟨a ~ market⟩ ⟨~ policies⟩ ⟨~ investors⟩ **b :** optimistic about something's or someone's prospects ⟨~ on the company's future⟩ — **bull·ish·ly** *adv* — **bull·ish·ness** *n*

bull market *n* (1891) : a market in which securities or commodities are persistently rising in value — compare BEAR MARKET

bull·mas·tiff \ˈbu̇l-ˈmas-təf *also* ˈbəl-\ *n* (1871) : any of a breed of large powerful dogs developed in England by crossing bulldogs with mastiffs

Bull Moose *n* [*bull moose,* emblem of the Progressive party of 1912] (1912) : a follower of Theodore Roosevelt in the U.S. presidential campaign of 1912

Bull Moos·er \-ˈmü-sər\ *n* (1912) : BULL MOOSE

bull neck *n* (1830) : a thick short powerful neck — **bull·necked** \ˈbu̇l-ˈnekt *also* ˈbəl-\ *adj*

bull·ock \ˈbu̇-lək *also* ˈbə-\ *n* (bef. 12c) **1 :** a young bull **2 :** a castrated bull : STEER — **bull·ocky** \-lə-kē\ *adj*

Bul·lock's oriole \ˈbu̇-ləks-\ *n* [William *Bullock fl*1827 Eng. naturalist] (1878) : an oriole (*Icterus bullockii*) of the western U.S. in which the male has a black crown and black line through the eye and the female has a yellowish head and breast and that was formerly considered to be a subspecies of northern oriole

bul·lous \ˈbu̇-ləs\ *adj* (1833) : resembling or characterized by bullae : VESICULAR ⟨~ lesions⟩

bull pen *n* (1809) **1 :** a large cell where prisoners are detained until brought into court **2 a :** a place on a baseball field where pitchers warm up before they start pitching **b :** the relief pitchers of a baseball team **3 :** an open work area not divided into offices

bull·ring \ˈbu̇l-ˌriŋ\ *n* (1802) **1 :** an arena for bullfights **2 :** a short oval track for horse or auto racing

bull rush *n* (1982) : a direct forceful rush by a defensive player in football — **bull–rush** *vb*

bull session *n* [[6]*bull*] (1919) : an informal discursive group discussion

bull's–eye \ˈbu̇lz-ˌī *also* ˈbəlz-\ *n, pl* **bull's–eyes** (1825) **1 :** a very hard globular candy **2 :** a circular piece of glass esp. with a lump in the middle **3 a :** the center of a target; *also* : something central or crucial **b :** a shot that hits the bull's-eye; *broadly* : something that precisely attains a desired end **4 :** a simple lens of short focal distance; *also* : a lantern with such a lens

bull's–eye window *n* (1926) : a circular window; *also* : a window made up of bull's-eyes

[1]**bull·shit** \ˈbu̇l-ˌshit *also* ˈbəl-\ *n* [[1]*bull* & [6]*bull*] (1914) *usu vulgar* : NONSENSE; *esp* : foolish insolent talk

[2]**bullshit** *vi* (1926) **1** *usu vulgar* : to talk foolishly, boastfully, or idly **2** *usu vulgar* : to engage in a discursive discussion ~ *vt, usu vulgar* : to talk nonsense to esp. with the intention of deceiving or misleading

bull·shot \-ˌshät\ *n* (1964) : a drink made of vodka and bouillon

bull snake *n* (1784) : any of several large harmless constricting colubrid snakes (genus *Pituophis*) esp. of the central and western U.S. that feed chiefly on rodents and are classified either as subspecies of the pine snake (P. melanoleucus) or as subspecies of their own species (P. catenifer) — called also *gopher snake*

bull terrier *n* [*bull*dog + *terrier*] (1836) : any of a breed of short-haired terriers developed in England by crossing the bulldog with terriers

bull thistle *n* (1863) : a biennial Eurasian thistle (*Cirsium vulgare*) with purplish flower heads and prickly leaves that is naturalized as a weed in the U.S.

bull tongue *n* (1831) : a wide blade attached to a cultivator or plow to stir the soil, kill weeds, or mark furrows

bull·whip \ˈbu̇l-ˌ(h)wip *also* ˈbəl-\ *n* (1852) : a rawhide whip with a very long plaited lash

[1]**bul·ly** \ˈbu̇-lē, ˈbə-\ *n, pl* **bullies** [prob. fr. MD *boele* lover; akin to MLG *bōle* lover, MHG *buole*] (1538) **1** *archaic* **a :** SWEETHEART **b :** a fine chap **2 a :** a blustering browbeating person; *esp* : one habitually cruel to others who are weaker **b :** PIMP **3 :** a hired ruffian

[2]**bully** *adj* (1609) **1 :** EXCELLENT — often used in interjectional expressions ⟨~ for you⟩ **2 :** resembling or characteristic of a bully

[3]**bully** *vb* **bul·lied; bul·ly·ing** *vt* (1693) **1 :** to treat abusively **2 :** to affect by means of force or coercion ~ *vi* : to use browbeating language or behavior : BLUSTER ***syn*** see INTIMIDATE

[4]**bully** *n* [prob. modif. of F (*bœuf*) *boulli* boiled beef] (1753) : pickled or canned usu. corned beef

bul·ly·boy \ˈbu̇-lē-ˌbȯi, ˈbə-\ *n* (1909) : a swaggering bully

bully pulpit *n* (1976) : a prominent public position (as a political office) that provides an opportunity for expounding one's views; *also* : such an opportunity

bul·ly·rag \-ˌrag\ *also* **bal·ly·rag** \ˈba-lē-\ *vt* [origin unknown] (ca. 1790) **1 :** to intimidate by bullying **2 :** to vex by teasing : BADGER

bul·rush *also* **bull·rush** \ˈbu̇l-ˌrəsh\ *n* [ME *bulrysche*] (15c) : any of several large rushes or sedges growing in wetlands: as **a :** any of a genus (*Scirpus,* esp. *S. lacustris*) of annual or perennial sedges that bear solitary or much-clustered spikelets containing perfect flowers with a perianth of six bristles **b** *Brit* : either of two cattails (*Typha latifolia* and *T. angustifolia*) **c :** PAPYRUS

[1]**bul·wark** \ˈbu̇l-(ˌ)wərk, -ˌwȯrk; ˈbəl-(ˌ)wərk; *sense 3 also* ˈbə-ˌläk\ *n* [ME *bulwerke,* fr. MD *bolwerc,* fr. *bolle* tree trunk + *werc* work] (15c) **1 a :** a solid wall-like structure raised for defense : RAMPART **b :** BREAKWATER, SEAWALL **2 :** a strong support or protection **3 :** the side of a ship above the upper deck — usu. used in pl.

[2]**bulwark** *vt* (15c) : to fortify or safeguard with a bulwark

[1]**bum** \ˈbəm\ *n* [ME *bom*] (14c) : BUTTOCKS

[2]**bum** *adj* [perh. fr. [4]*bum*] (1859) **1 a :** of poor quality or nature ⟨~ advice⟩ **b :** not valid or deserved ⟨a ~ check⟩ **c :** not pleasant or enjoyable ⟨a ~ trip⟩ **2 :** affected or disabled by damage or injury

[3]**bum** *vb* **bummed; bum·ming** [prob. back-formation fr. [1]*bummer*] *vi* (1863) **1 :** LOAF **2 :** to spend time unemployed and often wandering — often used with *around* ~ *vt* : to obtain by asking or begging : CADGE ⟨~ a cigarette⟩

[4]**bum** *n* [prob. short for [1]*bummer*] (1864) **1 a :** one who sponges off others and avoids work **b :** one who performs a function poorly ⟨called the umpire a ~⟩ **c :** one whose time is devoted to a recreational activity ⟨a beach ~⟩ ⟨ski ~*s*⟩ **2 :** VAGRANT, TRAMP — **on the bum :** with no settled residence or means of support

^{5}**bum** *n* [perh. fr. ^{3}*bum*] (1863) **:** a drinking spree **:** BENDER

^{6}**bum** *vt* [prob. back-formation fr. ^{2}*bummer*] (1973) **:** DISAPPOINT, DEPRESS — often used with *out* ‹the news really *bummed* me out›

bum·ber·shoot \ˈbəm-bər-ˌshüt\ *n* [*bumber-* (alter. of *umbr-* in *umbrella*) + *-shoot* (alter. of *-chute* in *parachute*)] (ca. 1896) **:** UMBRELLA

^{1}**bum·ble** \ˈbəm-bəl\ *vi* **bum·bled; bum·bling** \-b(ə-)liŋ\ [ME *bomblen* to boom, of imit. origin] (15c) **1 :** BUZZ **2 :** DRONE, RUMBLE

^{2}**bumble** *vb* **bumbled; bumbling** [perh. alter. of *bungle*] *vi* (1532) **1 :** BLUNDER; *specif* **:** to speak ineptly in a stuttering and faltering manner **2 :** to proceed unsteadily **:** STUMBLE ~ *vt* **:** BUNGLE — **bum·bler** \-b(ə-)lər\ *n* — **bum·bling·ly** \-b(ə-)liŋ-lē\ *adv*

bum·ble·bee \ˈbəm-bəl-ˌbē\ *n* (1530) **:** any of numerous large robust hairy social bees (genus *Bombus*)

bum·boat \ˈbəm-ˌbōt\ *n* [prob. fr. LG *bumboot*, fr. *bum* tree + *boot* boat] (1769) **:** a boat that brings provisions and commodities for sale to larger ships in port or offshore

bumf *also* **bumph** \ˈbəm(p)f\ *n* [fr. *bumf* toilet paper, short for *bumfodder*, fr. ^{1}*bum* + *fodder*] (ca. 1889) *chiefly Brit* **:** PAPERWORK

^{1}**bum·mer** \ˈbə-mər\ *n* [prob. modif. of G *Bummler* loafer, fr. *bummeln* to dangle, loaf] (1855) **:** one that bums

^{2}**bummer** *n* [^{2}*bum* + ^{2}*-er*] (1966) **1 :** an unpleasant experience (as a bad reaction to a hallucinogenic drug) **2 :** FAILURE, FLOP

^{1}**bump** \ˈbəmp\ *n* [prob. imit. of the sound of a blow] (1581) **1 :** a relatively abrupt convexity or protuberance on a surface: as **a :** a swelling of tissue **b :** a cranial protuberance **2 a :** a sudden forceful blow, impact, or jolt **b :** DEMOTION **3 :** an act of thrusting the hips forward in an erotic manner

^{2}**bump** *vt* (1581) **1 :** to strike or knock with force or violence **2 :** to collide with **3 a (1) :** to dislodge with a jolt **(2) :** to subject to a scalar change ‹rates being ~*ed* up› **b :** to oust usu. by virtue of seniority or priority ‹was ~*ed* from the flight› ~ *vi* **1 :** to knock against something with a forceful jolt **2 :** to proceed in or as if in a series of bumps **3 :** to encounter something that is an obstacle or hindrance ‹~*ed* up against a chair› — **bump into :** to encounter esp. by chance

^{1}**bum·per** \ˈbəm-pər\ *n* [prob. fr. *bump* to bulge] (1676) **1 :** a brimming cup or glass **2 :** something unusually large

^{2}**bumper** *adj* (1885) **1 :** unusually large ‹a ~ crop› **2 :** BANNER 2

^{3}**bump·er** \ˈbəm-pər\ *n* (1839) **1 :** a device for absorbing shock or preventing damage (as in collision); *specif* **:** a bar at either end of an automobile **2 :** one that bumps **3 :** a brief interval on radio or television filled with music, video shots, or voice-overs that marks a break between a program and a commercial

bumper car *n* (1959) **:** a small electric car made to be driven around in an enclosure and to be bumped into others (as at an amusement park)

bumper sticker *n* (1967) **:** a strip of adhesive paper or plastic bearing a printed message and designed to be stuck on a vehicle's bumper

bumper–to–bumper *adj* (1938) **:** marked by long closed lines of cars

^{1}**bump·kin** \ˈbəm(p)-kən\ *n* [perh. fr. D *bommekijn* small cask, fr. MD, fr. *bomme* cask] (1570) **:** an awkward and unsophisticated rustic — **bump·kin·ish** \-kə-nish\ *adj* — **bump·kin·ly** \-kən-lē\ *adj*

^{2}**bump·kin** *or* **bum·kin** \ˈbəm(p)-kən\ *n* [prob. fr. D *boomken*, dim. of *boom* tree] (ca. 1632) **:** a spar projecting from a ship esp. at the stern

bump off *vt* (1907) **:** to murder casually or cold-bloodedly

bump·tious \ˈbəm(p)-shəs\ *adj* [^{1}*bump* + *-tious* (as in *fractious*)] (1803) **:** presumptuously, obtusely, and often noisily self-assertive **:** OBTRUSIVE — **bump·tious·ly** *adv* — **bump·tious·ness** *n*

bumpy \ˈbəm-pē\ *adj* **bump·i·er; -est** (1865) **1 :** having or covered with bumps **2 a :** marked by bumps or jolts **b :** marked by or full of difficulties — **bump·i·ly** \-pə-lē\ *adv* — **bump·i·ness** \-pē-nəs\ *n*

bum–rush \ˈbəm-ˈrəsh\ *vt* (1987) **:** to attack or seize with an overpowering rush ‹~ the stage›

bum's rush \ˈbəmz-\ *n* (1904) **:** forcible eviction or dismissal

^{1}**bun** \ˈbən\ *n* [ME *bunne*] (14c) **1 :** a sweet or plain small bread; *esp* **:** a round roll **2 :** a knot of hair shaped like a bun **3** *pl* **:** BUTTOCKS

^{2}**bun** *n* [perh. fr. ^{1}*bun*] (1898) **:** LOAD 4

bu·na \ˈbyü-nə, ˈbü-\ *n* [fr. a trademark] (1936) **:** any of several rubbers made by polymerization or copolymerization of butadiene

^{1}**bunch** \ˈbənch\ *n* [ME *bunche*] (14c) **1 :** PROTUBERANCE, SWELLING **2 a :** a number of things of the same kind ‹a ~ of grapes› **b :** GROUP 2a ‹a ~ of friends› **c :** a considerable amount **:** LOT ‹a ~ of money› — **bunch·i·ly** \ˈbən-chə-lē\ *adv* — **bunchy** \-chē\ *adj*

^{2}**bunch** *vi* (14c) **1 :** SWELL, PROTRUDE **2 :** to form a group or cluster — often used with *up* ~ *vt* **:** to form into a bunch

bunch·ber·ry \ˈbənch-ˌber-ē, -ˌbe-rē\ *n* (1845) **:** a creeping perennial herb (*Cornus canadensis*) of the dogwood family that has whorled leaves and white floral bracts and bears clusters of red berries

bunch·grass \-ˌgras\ *n* (1836) **:** any of various grasses (as of the genus *Andropogon*) esp. of the western U.S. that grow in tufts

bun·co *or* **bun·ko** \ˈbəŋ-(ˌ)kō\ *n, pl* **buncos** *or* **bunkos** [perh. alter. of Sp *banca* bench, banking, bank in gambling, fr. It — more at BANK] (1872) **:** a swindling game or scheme — **bunco** *vt*

^{1}**bund** \ˈbənd\ *n* [Hindi *baṅd* & Urdu *band*, fr. Pers] (1810) **1 :** an embankment used esp. in India to control the flow of water **2 :** an embanked thoroughfare along a river or the sea esp. in the Far East

^{2}**bund** \ˈbu̇nd, ˈbənd, ˈbu̇nt\ *n, often cap* [Yiddish *bund* & G *Bund*, fr. MHG *bunt*; akin to OE *byndel*] (1850) **:** a political association: as **a :** a Jewish socialist organization founded in czarist Russia in 1897 **b :** a pro-Nazi German-American organization of the 1930s — **bund·ist** \ˈbu̇n-dist, ˈbən-\ *n, often cap*

^{1}**bun·dle** \ˈbən-dᵊl\ *n* [ME *bundel*, fr. MD; akin to OE *byndel* bundle, *bindan* to bind] (14c) **1 a :** a group of things fastened together for convenient handling **b :** PACKAGE, PARCEL **c :** a considerable number **:** LOT **d :** a sizable sum of money **e :** a person embodying a specified quality or characteristic **f :** BUNCH 2 **2 a :** a small band of mostly parallel fibers (as of nerve or muscle) **b :** VASCULAR BUNDLE **3 :** a package offering related products or services at a single price

^{2}**bundle** *vb* **bun·dled; bun·dling** \ˈbən(d)-liŋ, ˈbən-dᵊl-iŋ\ *vt* (1611) **1 :** to make into a bundle **2 :** to hustle or hurry unceremoniously ‹*bundled* the children off to school› **3 :** to include (a product or service) with a related product for sale at a single price ~ *vi* **1 :** HURRY, HUSTLE **2 :** to practice bundling — **bun·dler** \-lər, -dᵊl-ər\ *n*

bundle up *vt* (1845) **:** to dress (someone) warmly ~ *vi* **:** to dress warmly

bun·dling \ˈbən(d)-liŋ, ˈbən-dᵊl-iŋ\ *n* (1781) **:** a former custom of an unmarried couple's occupying the same bed without undressing esp. during courtship

Bundt \ˈbənt\ *trademark* — used for a cake pan having a tube in the center and scalloped sides

^{1}**bung** \ˈbəŋ\ *n* [ME, fr. MD *bonne, bonghe*] (15c) **1 :** the stopper esp. in the bunghole of a cask; *also* **:** BUNGHOLE **2 :** the cecum or anus esp. of a slaughtered animal

^{2}**bung** *vt* (1589) **1 :** to plug with or as if with a bung **2** *Brit* **:** THROW 1

bun·ga·low \ˈbəŋ-gə-ˌlō\ *n* [Hindi *baṅglā* & Urdu *banglā*, lit., (house) in the Bengal style] (1676) **:** a one-storied house with a low-pitched roof; *also* **:** a house having one and a half stories and usu. a front porch

bun·gee cord \ˈbən-jē-\ *n* [origin unknown] (1948) **:** an elasticized cord used esp. as a fastening or shock-absorbing device — called also *bungee*

bungee jump *vi* (1990) **:** to jump from a height while attached to an elasticized cord — **bungee jumper** *n*

bung·hole \ˈbəŋ-ˌhōl\ *n* (1571) **:** a hole for emptying or filling a cask

bun·gle \ˈbəŋ-gəl\ *vb* **bun·gled; bun·gling** \-g(ə-)liŋ\ [perh. of Scand origin; akin to Icel *banga* to hammer] *vi* (1549) **:** to act or work clumsily and awkwardly ~ *vt* **:** MISHANDLE, BOTCH ‹~ a job› — **bungle** *n* — **bun·gler** \-g(ə-)lər\ *n* — **bun·gling·ly** \-g(ə-)liŋ-lē\ *adv*

bun·gle·some \-gəl-səm\ *adj* (ca. 1889) **:** AWKWARD, CLUMSY

bung up *vt* (1951) **:** BATTER

bun·ion \ˈbən-yən\ *n* [prob. alter. of *bunny* swelling] (ca. 1718) **:** an inflamed swelling of the small fluid-filled sac on the first joint of the big toe accompanied by enlargement and protrusion of the joint

^{1}**bunk** \ˈbəŋk\ *n* [prob. short for *bunker*] (1758) **1 a :** BUNK BED **b :** a built-in bed (as on a ship) that is often one of a tier of berths **c :** a sleeping place **2 :** a feeding trough for farm animals and esp. cattle

^{2}**bunk** *vi* (1840) **:** to occupy a bunk or bed **:** stay the night ‹~*ed* with a friend for the night› ~ *vt* **:** to provide with a bunk or bed

^{3}**bunk** *n* (1900) **:** BUNKUM, NONSENSE

^{4}**bunk** *n* [origin unknown] (ca. 1870) *Brit* **:** a hurried departure or escape — usu. used in the phrase *do a bunk*

bunk bed *n* (1924) **:** one of two single beds usu. placed one above the other

^{1}**bun·ker** \ˈbəŋ-kər\ *n* [Sc *bonker* chest, box] (1839) **1 :** a bin or compartment for storage; *esp* **:** one on shipboard for the ship's fuel **2 a :** a protective embankment or dugout; *esp* **:** a fortified chamber mostly below ground often built of reinforced concrete and provided with embrasures **b :** a sand trap or embankment constituting a hazard on a golf course — **bun·kered** \-kərd\ *adj*

^{2}**bunker** *vb* **bun·kered; bun·ker·ing** \-k(ə-)riŋ\ *vi* (1891) **:** to fill a ship's bunker with coal or oil ~ *vt* **1 :** to place or store in a bunker **2 :** to hit (a golf ball or shot) into a bunker

bunker mentality *n* (1976) **:** a state of mind esp. among members of a group that is characterized by chauvinistic defensiveness and self-righteous intolerance of criticism

bunk·house \ˈbəŋk-ˌhau̇s\ *n* (1876) **:** a rough simple building providing sleeping quarters

bun·kum *or* **bun·combe** \ˈbəŋ-kəm\ *n* [*Buncombe* county, N.C.; fr. a remark made by its congressman, who defended an irrelevant speech by claiming that he was speaking to Buncombe] (1845) **:** insincere or foolish talk **:** NONSENSE

bun·ny \ˈbə-nē\ *n, pl* **bunnies** [E dial. *bun* rabbit] (ca. 1690) **1 :** RABBIT; *esp* **:** a young rabbit **2 :** a desirable young woman

bunny slope *n* (1966) **:** a gentle incline for skiing used esp. by novice skiers — called also *bunny hill*

Bun·ra·ku \bu̇n-ˈrä-(ˌ)kü\ *n* [Jp] (1920) **:** Japanese puppet theater featuring large costumed wooden puppets, puppeteers who are onstage, and a chanter who speaks all the lines

Bun·sen burner \ˈbən(t)-sən-\ *n* [Robert W. *Bunsen*] (1860) **:** a gas burner consisting typically of a straight tube with small holes at the bottom where air enters and mixes with the gas to produce an intensely hot blue flame

^{1}**bunt** \ˈbənt\ *n* [perh. fr. LG, bundle, fr. MLG; akin to OE *byndel* bundle] (ca. 1582) **1 a :** the middle part of a square sail **b :** the part of a furled sail gathered up in a bunch at the center of the yard **2 :** the bagging part of a fishing net

^{2}**bunt** *vb* [alter. of *butt*] *vt* (1584) **1 :** to strike or push with or as if with the head **:** BUTT **2 :** to push or tap (a baseball) lightly with a bat without swinging ~ *vi* **:** to bunt a baseball — **bunt·er** *n*

^{3}**bunt** *n* (1767) **1 :** an act or instance of bunting **2 :** a bunted ball

^{4}**bunt** *n* [origin unknown] (ca. 1790) **:** a destructive covered smut of wheat caused by a fungus (genus *Tilletia*)

^{1}**bun·ting** \ˈbən-tiŋ\ *n* [ME] (14c) **:** any of various stout-billed passerine birds (families Cardinalidae and Emberizidae) of which some are grouped with the cardinal and some with the New World sparrows — compare INDIGO BUNTING, PAINTED BUNTING

^{2}**bunting** *n* [perh. fr. E dial. *bunt* (to sift)] (1711) **1 :** a lightweight loosely woven fabric used chiefly for flags and festive decorations **2 a :** FLAGS **b :** decorations esp. in the colors of the national flag

^{3}**bunting** *n* [term of endearment in the nursery rhyme "Bye, baby bunting"] (1922) **:** an infant's hooded garment made of napped fabric

bunt·line \ˈbənt-ˌlīn, -lən\ *n* (1627) **:** one of the lines attached to the foot of a square sail to haul the sail up to the yard for furling

Bun·yan·esque \ˌbən-yə-ˈnesk\ *adj* (1888) **1** [John *Bunyan*] **:** of, relating to, or suggestive of the allegorical writings of John Bunyan **2** [Paul *Bunyan*, legendary giant lumberjack of U.S. & Canada] **a :** of, relating to, or suggestive of the tales of Paul Bunyan **b :** of fantastically large size

bun·ya·vi·rus \ˈbən-yə-ˌvī-rəs\ *n* [NL, fr. *bunya-* (fr. *Bunyamwera*, locale in western Uganda where the virus was isolated in 1943) + *virus*] (1985) **:** any of a family (*Bunyaviridae*) of usu. spherical or pleomorphic single-stranded RNA viruses usu. transmitted by the bite of an arthropod (as a mosquito) or in the bodily secretions of rodents and including the hantaviruses and the causative agents of Rift Valley fever, sandfly fever, and some forms of encephalitis and hemorrhagic fever

^{1}**buoy** \ˈbü-ē, ˈbȯi\ *n* [ME *boye*, prob. fr. MD *boeye*; akin to OHG *bouhhan* sign — more at BEACON] (13c) **1 :** FLOAT 2; *esp* **:** a floating object moored to the bottom to mark a channel or something (as a shoal) lying under the water **2 :** LIFE BUOY

^{2}**buoy** *vt* (1596) **1 :** to mark by or as if by a buoy **2 a :** to keep afloat **b :** SUPPORT, UPLIFT ‹an economy ~*ed* by the dramatic postwar growth of industry —*Time*〉 **3 :** to raise the spirits of — usu. used with *up* 〈hope ~*s* him up〉 ~ *vi* **:** FLOAT — usu. used with *up*

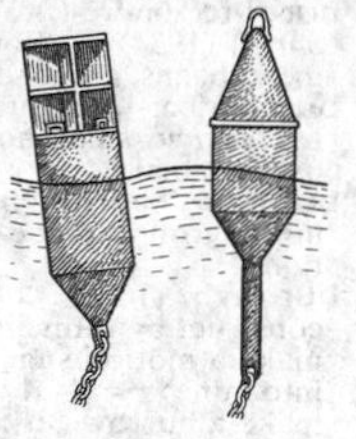

buoy 1

buoy·ance \ˈbȯi-ən(t)s, ˈbü-yən(t)s\ *n* (1793) **:** BUOYANCY

buoy·an·cy \ˈbȯi-ən(t)-sē, ˈbü-yən(t)-\ *n* (1713) **1 a :** the tendency of a body to float or to rise when submerged in a fluid **b :** the power of a fluid to exert an upward force on a body placed in it; *also* **:** the upward force exerted **2 :** the ability to recover quickly from depression or discouragement **:** RESILIENCE **3 :** the property of maintaining a satisfactorily high level (as of prices or economic activity)

buoy·ant \ˈbȯi-ənt, ˈbü-yənt\ *adj* (1578) **:** having buoyancy: as **a :** capable of floating **b :** CHEERFUL, GAY **c :** capable of maintaining a satisfactorily high level 〈a ~ economy〉 — **buoy·ant·ly** *adv*

bupkes *or* **bupkus** *var of* BUBKES

bup·pie \ˈbə-pē\ *n* [ˈ*b*lack + y*uppie*] (1984) **:** a college-educated black adult who is employed in a well-paying profession and who lives or works in or near a large city

[1]**bur** *var of* BURR

[2]**bur** *abbr* bureau

burb \ˈbərb\ *n* [by shortening] (1971) **:** SUBURB — usu. used in pl.

Bur·ber·ry \ˈbər-b(ə-)rē, ˈbər-ˌber-ē, -ˌbe-rē\ *trademark* — used for various fabrics used esp. for coats for outdoor wear

[1]**bur·ble** \ˈbər-bəl\ *vi* **bur·bled; bur·bling** \-b(ə-)liŋ\ [ME] (14c) **1 :** to make a bubbling sound **2 :** BABBLE, PRATTLE — **bur·bler** \-b(ə-)lər\ *n*

[2]**burble** *n* (1898) **1 :** PRATTLE **2 :** the breaking up of the smooth flow of air about a body (as an airplane wing) — **bur·bly** \-b(ə-)lē\ *adj*

bur·bot \ˈbər-bət\ *n, pl* **burbot** *also* **burbots** [ME, fr. AF, fr. OF *borbeter* to stir up mud] (14c) **:** a Holarctic freshwater bony fish (*Lota lota*) of the cod family having barbels on the nose and chin

[1]**bur·den** \ˈbər-dᵊn\ *n* [ME, fr. OE *byrthen;* akin to OE *beran* to carry — more at BEAR] (bef. 12c) **1 a :** something that is carried **:** LOAD **b :** DUTY, RESPONSIBILITY **2 :** something oppressive or worrisome **3 a :** the bearing of a load — usu. used in the phrase *beast of burden* **b :** capacity for carrying cargo 〈a ship of a hundred tons ~〉 **4 :** LOAD 11 〈worm ~〉〈cancer ~〉

[2]**burden** *vt* **bur·dened; bur·den·ing** \ˈbərd-niŋ, ˈbər-dᵊn-iŋ\ (1541) **:** LOAD, OPPRESS 〈I will not ~ you with a lengthy account〉

[3]**burden** *n* [ME *burdoun,* fr. AF *burdun* a drone bass, of imit. origin] (14c) **1** *archaic* **:** a bass or accompanying part **2 a :** CHORUS, REFRAIN **b :** a central topic **:** THEME

burden of proof (1780) **:** the duty of proving a disputed assertion or charge

bur·den·some \ˈbər-dᵊn-səm\ *adj* (1578) **:** imposing or constituting a burden **:** OPPRESSIVE 〈~ restrictions〉 ***syn*** see ONEROUS

bur·dock \ˈbər-ˌdäk\ *n* (15c) **:** any of a genus (*Arctium*) of coarse composite herbs bearing globular flower heads with prickly bracts

bu·reau \ˈbyu̇r-(ˌ)ō, ˈbyər-\ *n, pl* **bureaus** *also* **bu·reaux** \-(ˌ)ōz\ [F, desk, cloth covering for desks, fr. OF *burel* woolen cloth, fr. OF **bure,* fr. LL *burra* shaggy cloth] (1699) **1 a** *Brit* **:** WRITING DESK; *esp* **:** one having drawers and a slant top **b :** a low chest of drawers for use in a bedroom **2 a :** a specialized administrative unit; *esp* **:** a subdivision of an executive department of a government **b :** a branch of a newspaper, newsmagazine, or wire service in an important news center **c :** a usu. commercial agency that serves as an intermediary esp. for exchanging information or coordinating activities 〈credit ~〉

bu·reau·cra·cy \byu̇-ˈrä-krə-sē, byə-, byər-ˈä-\ *n, pl* **-cies** [F *bureaucratie,* fr. *bureau* + *-cratie* -cracy] (1818) **1 a :** a body of nonelective government officials **b :** an administrative policy-making group **2 :** government characterized by specialization of functions, adherence to fixed rules, and a hierarchy of authority **3 :** a system of administration marked by officialism, red tape, and proliferation

bu·reau·crat \ˈbyu̇r-ə-ˌkrat, ˈbyər-\ *n* (1839) **:** a member of a bureaucracy

bu·reau·crat·ese \ˌbyu̇r-ə-(ˌ)kra-ˈtēz, -ˈtēs, ˌbyər-\ *n* (1949) **:** a style of language held to be characteristic of bureaucrats and marked by abstractions, jargon, euphemisms, and circumlocutions

bu·reau·crat·ic \ˌbyu̇r-ə-ˈkra-tik, ˌbyər-\ *adj* (1836) **:** of, relating to, or having the characteristics of a bureaucracy or a bureaucrat 〈~ government〉 — **bu·reau·crat·i·cal·ly** \-ti-k(ə-)lē\ *adv*

bu·reau·cra·tise *Brit var of* BUREAUCRATIZE

bu·reau·crat·ism \ˈbyu̇r-ə-(ˌ)kra-ˌti-zəm, ˈbyər-\ *n* (1880) **:** BUREAUCRACY 3

bu·reau·cra·tize \byu̇-ˈrä-krə-ˌtīz, byə-, byər-ˈä-\ *vt* **-tized; -tiz·ing** (1880) **:** to make bureaucratic — **bu·reau·cra·ti·za·tion** \-ˌrä-krə-tə-ˈzā-shən\ *n*

bu·rette *or* **bu·ret** \byu̇-ˈret\ *n* [F *burette,* fr. OF *bivrete* cruet, fr. *buire* pitcher, perh. of Gmc origin; akin to OE *būr* storehouse, dwelling — more at BOWER] (1836) **:** a graduated glass tube with a small aperture and stopcock for delivering measured quantities of liquid or for measuring the liquid or gas received or discharged

burg \ˈbərg\ *n* [OE — more at BOROUGH] (1753) **1 :** an ancient or medieval fortress or walled town **2** [G *Burg*] **:** CITY, TOWN

bur·gage \ˈbər-gij\ *n* [ME, property held by burgage tenure, fr. AF, fr. *burc, borg* town — more at BOURG] (15c) **:** a tenure by which real property in England and Scotland was held under the king or a lord for a yearly rent or for watching and warding

bur·gee \ˌbər-ˈjē, ˈbər-ˌ\ *n* [perh. fr. F dial. *bourgeais* shipowner] (1750) **1 :** a swallow-tailed flag used esp. by ships for signals or identification **2 :** the usu. triangular identifying flag of a yacht club

bur·geon *also* **bour·geon** \ˈbər-jən\ *vi* [ME *burjonen,* fr. AF *burjuner,* fr. *burjun* bud, fr. VL **burrion-, burrio,* fr. LL *burra* fluff, shaggy cloth] (14c) **1 a :** to send forth new growth (as buds or branches) **:** SPROUT **b :** BLOOM **2 :** to grow and expand rapidly **:** FLOURISH

bur·ger \ˈbər-gər\ *n* (1937) **1 :** HAMBURGER **2 :** a sandwich similar to a hamburger 〈tofu ~*s*〉 — often used in combination

bur·gess \ˈbər-jəs\ *n* [ME *burgeis,* fr. AF, fr. *borc* town — more at BOURG] (13c) **1 a :** a citizen of a British borough **b :** a representative of a borough, corporate town, or university in the British Parliament **2 :** a representative in the popular branch of the legislature of colonial Maryland or Virginia

burgh \ˈbər-(ˌ)ō, ˈbə-(ˌ)rō\ *n* [ME — more at BOROUGH] (12c) **:** BOROUGH; *specif* **:** an incorporated town in Scotland having local jurisdiction of certain services — **burgh·al** \ˈbər-gəl\ *adj*

bur·gher \ˈbər-gər\ *n* (13c) **1 :** an inhabitant of a borough or a town **2 :** a member of the middle class **:** a prosperous solid citizen

bur·glar \ˈbər-glər *also* -gə-lər\ *n* [AF *burgler,* fr. ML *burglator,* prob. alter. of *burgator,* fr. *burgare* to commit burglary] (1541) **:** one who commits burglary

bur·glar·ize \ˈbər-glə-ˌrīz *also* ˈbər-gə-lə-\ *vb* **-ized; -iz·ing** *vt* (1871) **1 :** to break into and steal from 〈~ a house〉 **2 :** to commit burglary against ~ *vi* **:** to commit burglary

bur·glar·proof \ˈbər-glər-ˌprüf\ *adj* (1848) **:** protected against or designed to afford protection against burglary

bur·glary \ˈbər-glə-rē *also* -gə-lə-rē *also* -gəl-rē\ *n, pl* **-glar·ies** (ca. 1523) **:** the act of breaking and entering a dwelling at night to commit a felony (as theft); *broadly* **:** the entering of a building with the intent to commit a crime — **bur·glar·i·ous** \ˌbər-ˈgler-ē-əs\ *adj* — **bur·glar·i·ous·ly** *adv*

bur·gle \ˈbər-gəl\ *vt* **bur·gled; bur·gling** \-g(ə-)liŋ\ [back-formation fr. *burglar*] (1870) **:** BURGLARIZE

bur·go·mas·ter \ˈbər-gə-ˌmas-tər\ *n* [part modif., part trans. of D *burgemeester,* fr. *burg* town + *meester* master] (1592) **:** the chief magistrate of a town in some European countries **:** MAYOR

bur·go·net \ˈbər-gə-nət, ˌbər-gə-ˈnet\ *n* [modif. of MF *bourguignotte*] (ca. 1567) **:** a close-fitting 16th century helmet with cheek guards

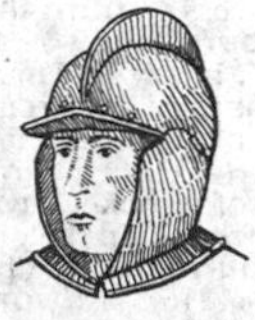

burgonet

bur·goo \ˈbər-ˌgü, (ˌ)bər-ˈ\ *n, pl* **burgoos** [origin unknown] (1700) **1 :** oatmeal gruel **2 :** hardtack and molasses cooked together **3 a :** a stew or thick soup of meat and vegetables orig. served at outdoor gatherings **b :** a picnic at which burgoo is served

bur·gun·dy \ˈbər-gən-dē\ *n, pl* **-dies** [*Burgundy,* region in France] (1664) **1** *often cap* **:** a red or white unblended wine from Burgundy; *also* **:** a blended red wine produced elsewhere **2 :** a reddish-purple color

buri·al \ˈber-ē-əl, ˈbe-rē- *also* ˈbər-\ *n, often attrib* [ME *beriel, berial,* back-formation fr. *beriels* (taken as a plural), fr. OE *byrgels;* akin to OS *burgisli* tomb, OE *byrgan* to bury — more at BURY] (13c) **1 :** GRAVE, TOMB **2 :** the act or process of burying

buri·er \ˈber-ē-ər, ˈbe-rē- *also* ˈbər-\ *n* (bef. 12c) **:** one that buries

bu·rin \ˈbyu̇r-ən, ˈbər-\ *n* [F] (1662) **1 :** an engraver's steel cutting tool having the blade ground obliquely to a sharp point **2 :** a prehistoric flint tool with a beveled point

bur·ka *or* **bur·qa** \ˈbu̇r-kə\ *n* [Urdu, Pers & Ar; Urdu *burqaʿ,* fr. Pers *burqaʿ, burquʿ,* fr. Ar *burquʿ*] (1836) **:** a loose enveloping garment that covers the face and body and is worn in public by certain Muslim women

burke \ˈbərk\ *vt* **burked; burk·ing** [fr. *burke* to suffocate, fr. William *Burke* †1829 Irish criminal executed for smothering victims to sell their bodies for dissection] (1829) **1 :** to suppress quietly or indirectly 〈~ an inquiry〉 **2 :** BYPASS, AVOID 〈~ an issue〉

Bur·kitt's lymphoma \ˈbər-kəts-\ *also* **Bur·kitt lymphoma** \-kət-\ *n* [Denis Parsons *Burkitt* †1993 Brit. surgeon] (1963) **:** a non-Hodgkin's lymphoma of B cell origin that occurs esp. in children of central Africa and is associated with Epstein-Barr virus

burl \ˈbər(-ə)l\ *n* [ME *burle,* fr. AF **bourle* tuft of wool, fr. OF, fr. VL **burrula,* dim. of LL *burra* shaggy cloth] (15c) **1 :** a knot or lump in thread or cloth **2 a :** a hard woody often flattened hemispherical outgrowth on a tree **b :** veneer made from burls

bur·la·de·ro \ˌbu̇r-lə-ˈder-(ˌ)ō, ˌbər-\ *n, pl* **-ros** [Sp, fr. *burlar* to make fun of, elude, fr. *burla* joke] (1890) **:** a wooden shield near the wall in a bullring for bullfighters to take shelter behind if pursued

bur·lap \ˈbər-ˌlap\ *n* [origin unknown] (ca. 1696) **1 :** a coarse heavy plain-woven fabric usu. of jute or hemp used for bagging and wrapping and in furniture and linoleum manufacture **2 :** a lightweight material resembling burlap used in interior decoration or for clothing

burled \ˈbər(-ə)ld\ *adj* (1924) **:** having a distorted grain due to burls

[1]**bur·lesque** \(ˌ)bər-ˈlesk\ *n* [*burlesque,* adj., comic, droll, fr. F, fr. It *burlesco,* fr. *burla* joke, fr. Sp] (1667) **1 :** a literary or dramatic work that seeks to ridicule by means of grotesque exaggeration or comic imitation **2 :** mockery usu. by caricature **3 :** theatrical entertainment of a broadly humorous often earthy character consisting of short turns, comic skits, and sometimes striptease acts ***syn*** see CARICATURE — **burlesque** *adj* — **bur·lesque·ly** *adv*

[2]**burlesque** *vb* **bur·lesqued; bur·lesqu·ing** *vt* (1676) **:** to imitate in a humorous or derisive manner **:** MOCK ~ *vi* **:** to employ burlesque — **bur·lesqu·er** *n*

bur·ley \ˈbər-lē\ *n, often cap* [prob. fr. the name *Burley*] (1874) **:** a thin-bodied air-cured tobacco grown mainly in Kentucky

bur·ly \ˈbər-lē\ *adj* **bur·li·er; -est** [ME] (13c) **:** strongly and heavily built **:** HUSKY 〈a ~ man〉 — **bur·li·ly** \-lə-lē\ *adv* — **bur·li·ness** \-lē-nəs\ *n*

bur marigold *n* (ca. 1818) **:** any of a genus (*Bidens*) of coarse composite herbs with prickly flattened achenes that adhere to clothing and fur

Bur·mese \ˌbər-ˈmēz, -ˈmēs\ *n, pl* **Burmese** (1824) **1 :** a native or inhabitant of Burma (Myanmar) **2 :** the Tibeto-Burman language of the Burmese people **3 :** any of a U.S.-developed breed of slender short-haired cats having gold eyes and a usu. dark brown coat — **Burmese** *adj*

[1]**burn** \ˈbərn\ *n* [ME, fr. OE; akin to OHG *brunno* spring of water] (bef. 12c) *Brit* **:** CREEK 2

[2]**burn** \ˈbərn\ *vb* **burned** \ˈbərnd, ˈbərnt\ *or* **burnt** \ˈbərnt\; **burn·ing** [ME *birnen,* fr. OE *byrnan,* v.i., *bærnan,* v.t.; akin to OHG *brinnan* to burn] *vi* (bef. 12c) **1 a :** to consume fuel and give off heat, light, and gases 〈a small fire ~*s* on the hearth〉 **b :** to undergo combustion; *also*

: to undergo nuclear fission or nuclear fusion **c** : to contain a fire ⟨a little stove ~*ing* in the corner⟩ **d** : to give off light : SHINE, GLOW ⟨a light ~*ing* in the window⟩ **2 a** : to be hot ⟨the ~*ing* sand⟩ **b** : to produce or undergo discomfort or pain ⟨ears ~*ing* from the cold⟩ **c** : to become emotionally excited or agitated: as (1) : to yearn ardently ⟨~*ing* to tell the story⟩ (2) : to be or become very angry or disgusted ⟨the remark made him ~⟩ **3 a** : to undergo alteration or destruction by the action of fire or heat ⟨the house ~*ed* down⟩ ⟨the potatoes ~*ed* to a crisp⟩ **b** : to die in the electric chair **4** : to force or make a way by or as if by burning ⟨her words ~*ed* into his heart⟩ **5** : to suffer sunburn ⟨she ~*s* easily⟩ ~ *vt* **1 a** : to cause to undergo combustion; *esp* : to destroy by fire ⟨~*ed* the trash⟩ **b** : to use as fuel ⟨this furnace ~*s* gas⟩ **c** : to use up : CONSUME ⟨~ calories⟩ **2 a** : to transform by exposure to heat or fire ⟨~ clay to bricks⟩ **b** : to produce by burning ⟨~*ed* a hole in his sleeve⟩ **c** : to record digital data or music on (an optical disk) using a laser ⟨~ a CD⟩; *also* : to record (data or music) in this way ⟨~ songs onto a disk⟩ **3 a** : to injure or damage by or as if by exposure to fire, heat, or radiation : SCORCH ⟨~*ed* his hand⟩ **b** : to execute by burning ⟨~*ed* heretics at the stake⟩; *also* : ELECTROCUTE **4 a** : IRRITATE, ANNOY — often used with *up* ⟨really ~*s* me up⟩ **b** : to subject to misfortune, mistreatment, or deception — often used in passive ⟨has been *burned* in love⟩ **c** : to beat or score on ⟨~*ed* the defense with a touchdown pass⟩ — **burn·able** \ˈbər-nə-bəl\ *adj* — **burn one's bridges** *also* **burn one's boats** : to cut off all means of retreat — **burn one's ears** : to rebuke strongly — **burn the candle at both ends** : to use one's resources or energies to excess — **burn the midnight oil** : to work or study far into the night

[3]**burn** *n* (1594) **1** : an act, process, instance, or result of burning: as **a** : injury or damage resulting from exposure to fire, heat, caustics, electricity, or certain radiations **b** : a burned area ⟨a ~ on the tabletop⟩ **c** : an abrasion (as of the skin) having the appearance of a burn ⟨rope ~*s*⟩ **d** : a burning sensation ⟨the ~ of iodine on a cut⟩ **2** : the firing of a rocket engine in flight **3** : ANGER; *esp* : increasing fury — used chiefly in the phrase *slow burn*

burned–out \ˈbərnd-ˈau̇t, ˈbərnt-ˈau̇t\ *or* **burnt–out** \ˈbərnt-ˈau̇t\ *adj* (1816) **1** : WORN-OUT; *also* : EXHAUSTED **2** : destroyed by fire ⟨a ~ building⟩

burn·er \ˈbər-nər\ *n* (14c) **1** : one that burns : as **a** : the part of a fuel-burning or heat-producing device (as a furnace or stove) where the flame or heat is produced **b** : a device for recording data on an optical disk **2** : an athlete who possesses great speed

bur·net \(ˌ)bər-ˈnet, ˈbər-nət\ *n* [ME, fr. AF *burnete,* fr. *brun* brown — more at BRUNET] (14c) : any of a genus (*Sanguisorba*) of herbs of the rose family with odd-pinnate stipulate leaves and spikes of apetalous flowers

burn–in \ˈbərn-ˌin\ *n* (1966) : the continuous operation of a device (as a computer) as a test for defects or failure prior to putting it to use

burn in *vt* (ca. 1939) : to increase the density of (portions of a photographic print) during enlarging by giving extra exposure

burn·ing \ˈbər-niŋ\ *adj* (bef. 12c) **1 a** : being on fire **b** : ARDENT, INTENSE ⟨~ enthusiasm⟩ **2 a** : affecting with or as if with heat ⟨a ~ fever⟩ **b** : resembling that produced by a burn ⟨a ~ sensation on the tongue⟩ **3** : of fundamental importance : URGENT ⟨one of the ~ issues of our time⟩ — **burn·ing·ly** \-niŋ-lē\ *adv*

burning bush *n* (1785) : any of several plants associated with fire (as by redness): as **a** : [2]WAHOO **b** : SUMMER CYPRESS **c** : a deciduous Asian shrub (*Euonymus alata*) of the spindle tree family having stems with corky wings and leaves that turn a brilliant red in autumn

burning ghat *n* (1877) : a level space at the head of a ghat for cremation

[1]**bur·nish** \ˈbər-nish\ *vt* [ME *burnischen,* fr. AF *burniss-,* stem of *burnir,* alter. of OF *brunir,* lit., to make brown, fr. *brun*] (14c) **1 a** : to make shiny or lustrous esp. by rubbing **b** : POLISH 3 **2** : to rub (a material) with a tool for compacting or smoothing or for turning an edge — **bur·nish·er** *n* — **bur·nish·ing** *adj or n*

[2]**burnish** *n* (ca. 1647) : LUSTER, GLOSS

burn off *vi* (ca. 1925) : to be dissipated by the sun's warmth ⟨waiting for the fog to *burn off*⟩ ~ *vt* : to cause to burn off

bur·noose *or* **bur·nous** \(ˌ)bər-ˈnüs\ *n* [F *burnous,* fr. Ar *burnus*] (1695) : a one-piece hooded cloak worn by Arabs and Berbers — **burnoosed** \-ˈnüst\ *adj*

burn·out \ˈbərn-ˌau̇t\ *n* (1940) **1** : the cessation of operation usu. of a jet or rocket engine; *also* : the point at which burnout occurs **2 a** : exhaustion of physical or emotional strength or motivation usu. as a result of prolonged stress or frustration **b** : a person suffering from burnout **3** : a person showing the effects of drug abuse

burn out *vt* (1710) **1** : to drive out or destroy the property of by fire **2** : to cause to fail, wear out, or become exhausted esp. from overwork or overuse ~ *vi* : to suffer burnout

burn·sides \ˈbərn-ˌsīdz\ *n pl* [Ambrose E. *Burnside*] (1875) : SIDE-WHISKERS; *esp* : full muttonchop whiskers

bur oak *n* (1815) : a usu. large oak (*Quercus macrocarpa*) of eastern No. America having oval acorns enclosed in a fringed cap and tough close-grained wood

[1]**burp** \ˈbərp\ *n* [imit.] (1929) : the act or an instance of belching

[2]**burp** *vi* (ca. 1932) : BELCH ~ *vt* **1** : BELCH **2** : to help (a baby) expel gas from the stomach esp. by patting or rubbing the baby's back

burp gun *n* (1943) : a small submachine gun

burqa *var of* BURKA

[1]**burr** \ˈbər\ *n* [ME *burre;* akin to OE *byrst* bristle — more at BRISTLE] (14c) **1** *usu* **bur a** : a rough or prickly envelope of a fruit **b** : a plant that bears burs **2 a** : something that sticks or clings ⟨a ~ in the throat⟩ **b** : HANGER-ON **3** : an irregular rounded mass; *esp* : a tree burl **4** : a thin ridge or area of roughness produced in cutting or shaping metal **5 a** : a trilled uvular \r\ as used by some speakers of English esp. in northern England and in Scotland **b** : a tongue-point trill that is the usual Scottish \r\ **6 a** : a small rotary cutting tool **b** *usu* **bur** : a bit used on a dental drill **7** : a rough humming sound : WHIR — **burred** \ˈbərd\ *adj*

[2]**burr** *vi* (1798) **1** : to speak with a burr **2** : to make a whirring sound ~ *vt* **1** : to pronounce with a burr **2 a** : to form into a projecting edge **b** : to remove burrs from — **burr·er** *n*

bur reed *n* (1597) : any of a genus (*Sparganium* of the family Sparganiaceae) of herbaceous plants with globose fruits resembling burs

bur·ri·to \bə-ˈrē-(ˌ)tō\ *n, pl* **-tos** [AmerSp, fr. Sp, little donkey, dim. of *burro*] (1934) : a flour tortilla rolled or folded around a filling (as of meat, beans, and cheese)

bur·ro \ˈbər-(ˌ)ō, ˈbu̇r-; ˈbə-(ˌ)rō\ *n, pl* **burros** [Sp, irreg. fr. *borrico,* fr. LL *burricus* small horse] (1775) : DONKEY; *esp* : a small one used as a pack animal

[1]**bur·row** \ˈbər-(ˌ)ō; ˈbə-(ˌ)rō\ *n* [ME *borow*] (13c) : a hole or excavation in the ground made by an animal (as a rabbit) for shelter and habitation

[2]**burrow** *vt* (1602) **1** *archaic* : to hide in or as if in a burrow **2 a** : to construct by tunneling **b** : to penetrate by means of a burrow **3** : to make a motion suggestive of burrowing with : NESTLE ⟨~*s* her hand into mine⟩ ~ *vi* **1** : to conceal oneself in or as if in a burrow **2 a** : to make a burrow **b** : to progress by or as if by digging **3** : to make a motion suggestive of burrowing : SNUGGLE, NESTLE ⟨~*ed* against his back for warmth⟩ — **bur·row·er** *n*

burrowing owl *n* (1823) : a small diurnal chiefly ground-dwelling American owl (*Athene cunicularia*) of grassland and desert regions that roosts and nests in burrows

bur·ry \ˈbər-ē\ *adj* **bur·ri·er; -est** (15c) **1** : containing burs **2** : PRICKLY **3** *of speech* : characterized by a burr

bur·sa \ˈbər-sə\ *n, pl* **bur·sas** \-səz\ *or* **bur·sae** \-ˌsē, -ˌsī\ [NL, fr. ML, bag, purse — more at PURSE] (1803) : a bodily pouch or sac: as **a** : a small serous sac between a tendon and a bone **b** : BURSA OF FABRICIUS — **bur·sal** \-səl\ *adj*

bursa of Fa·bri·cius \-fə-ˈbrē-sh(ē-)əs, -ˈbri-, -s(ē-)əs\ [Johan C. *Fabricius* †1808 Dan. entomologist] (1945) : a lymphoid organ that opens into the cloaca of birds and functions in B cell production

bur·sar \ˈbər-sər, -ˌsär\ *n* [AF & ML; AF *burser,* fr. ML *bursarius,* fr. *bursa*] (13c) : an officer (as of a monastery or college) in charge of funds : TREASURER

bur·sa·ry \ˈbər-sə-rē, ˈbərs-rē\ *n, pl* **-ries** [ML *bursaria,* fr. *bursa*] (1695) **1** : the treasury of a college or monastery **2** *Brit* : a monetary grant to a needy student : SCHOLARSHIP

burse \ˈbərs\ *n* [ME, fr. AF, fr. ML *bursa*] (15c) **1 a** : PURSE **b** : a square cloth case used to carry the corporal in a Communion service **2** *obs* : EXCHANGE, BOURSE

bur·si·tis \(ˌ)bər-ˈsī-təs\ *n* [NL, fr. *bursa*] (1857) : inflammation of a bursa (as of the shoulder or elbow)

[1]**burst** \ˈbərst\ *vb* **burst** *also* **burst·ed; burst·ing** [ME *bersten,* fr. OE *berstan;* akin to OHG *brestan* to burst] *vi* (bef. 12c) **1** : to break open, apart, or into pieces usu. from impact or from pressure from within **2 a** : to give way from an excess of emotion ⟨my heart will ~⟩ **b** : to give vent suddenly to a repressed emotion ⟨~ into tears⟩ ⟨~ out laughing⟩ **3 a** : to emerge or spring suddenly ⟨~ out of the house⟩ ⟨~ onto the scene⟩ **b** : LAUNCH, PLUNGE ⟨~ into song⟩ **4** : to be filled to the breaking point ⟨~*ing* with excitement⟩ ⟨a crate ~*ing* with fruit⟩ ~ *vt* **1** : to cause to burst ⟨~ a balloon⟩ **2 a** : to force open (as a door or a way) by strong or vigorous action **b** : to flood over ⟨the river ~ its banks⟩ **3** : to produce by or as if by bursting — **burst at the seams** : to be larger, fuller, or more crowded than could reasonably have been anticipated

[2]**burst** *n* (1610) **1 a** : a sudden outbreak; *esp* : a vehement outburst (as of emotion) **b** : EXPLOSION, ERUPTION **c** : a sudden intense effort ⟨a ~ of speed⟩ **d** : the duration of fire in one engagement of the mechanism of an automatic firearm **2** : an act of bursting **3** : a result of bursting; *esp* : a visible puff accompanying the explosion of a shell

burst·er \ˈbərs-tər\ *n* (1611) **1** : one that bursts **2** : the celestial source of an outburst of radiation (as X-rays)

bur·then \ˈbər-t͟hən\ *archaic var of* BURDEN

bur·weed \ˈbər-ˌwēd\ *n* (ca. 1783) : any of various plants (as a cocklebur or burdock) having burry fruit

bury \ˈber-ē, ˈbe-rē *also* ˈbər-\ *vt* **bur·ied; bury·ing** [ME *burien,* fr. OE *byrgan;* akin to OHG *bergan* to shelter, Russ *berech'* to spare] (bef. 12c) **1** : to dispose of by depositing in or as if in the earth; *esp* : to inter with funeral ceremonies **2 a** : to conceal by or as if by covering with earth **b** : to cover from view ⟨*buried* her face in her hands⟩ **3 a** : to have done with ⟨~*ing* their differences⟩ **b** : to conceal in obscurity ⟨*buried* the retraction among the classified ads⟩ **c** : SUBMERGE, ENGROSS — usu. used with *in* ⟨*buried* himself in his books⟩ **4** : to put (a playing card) out of play by placing it in or under the dealer's pack **5** : to succeed emphatically or impressively in making (a shot) ⟨~ a jumper⟩ ⟨~ a putt⟩ **6** : to defeat overwhelmingly ***syn*** see HIDE — **bury the hatchet** : to settle a disagreement : become reconciled

burying beetle *n* (1818) : any of various beetles (family Silphidae and esp. genus *Nicrophorus*) that bury and lay eggs on the carcasses of small animals which provide a food source for the developing larvae

[1]**bus** \ˈbəs\ *n, pl* **bus·es** *also* **bus·ses** *often attrib* [short for *omnibus*] (ca. 1909) **1 a** : a large motor vehicle designed to carry passengers usu. along a fixed route according to a schedule **b** : AUTOMOBILE **2** : a small hand truck **3 a** : BUS BAR **b** : a set of parallel conductors in a computer system that forms a main transmission path **4** : a spacecraft or missile that carries one or more detachable devices (as warheads)

[2]**bus** *vb* **bused** *also* **bussed; bus·ing** *also* **bus·sing** *vi* (ca. 1909) **1** : to travel by bus **2** : to work as a busboy ~ *vt* **1** : to transport by bus **2 a** : CLEAR 4d ⟨~ dishes⟩ **b** : to remove dirty dishes from ⟨~ tables⟩

[3]**bus** *abbr* business

bus bar *n* (1893) : a conductor or an assembly of conductors for collecting electric currents and distributing them to outgoing feeders

bus·boy \ˈbəs-ˌbȯi\ *n* [*omnibus* busboy] (1913) : a waiter's assistant; *specif* : one who removes dirty dishes and resets tables in a restaurant

bus·by \ˈbəz-bē\ *n, pl* **busbies** [prob. fr. the name *Busby*] (1853) **1** : a military full-dress fur hat with a pendent bag on one side usu. of the color of regimental facings **2** : the bearskin worn by British guardsmen — not used by the guardsmen themselves

[1]**bush** \ˈbu̇sh\ *n, often attrib* [ME; akin to OHG *busc* forest] (14c) **1 a** : SHRUB; *esp* : a low densely branched shrub **b** : a close thicket of shrubs suggesting a single plant **2** : a large uncleared or sparsely settled area (as in Australia) usu. scrub-covered or forested : WILDERNESS — usu. used with *the* **3 a** *archaic* : a bunch of ivy formerly hung outside a tavern to indicate wine for sale **b** *obs* : TAVERN **c** : ADVERTISING ⟨good wine needs no ~ —Shak.⟩ **4** : a bushy tuft or mass ⟨a ~

of hair⟩; *esp* : ²BRUSH 2a **5 :** MINOR LEAGUE — usu. used in pl. ⟨spent ten years in the ~*es*⟩

²**bush** *vt* (15c) : to support, mark, or protect with bushes ~ *vi* : to extend like a bush : resemble a bush

³**bush** *adj* (1595) **1 :** having a low-growing compact bushy habit — used esp. of cultivated beans ⟨~ snap beans⟩ **2 :** serving, occurring in, or used in the bush ⟨~ planes⟩

⁴**bush** *n* [D *bus* bushing, box, fr. MD *busse* box, fr. LL *buxis* — more at BOX] (1566) *chiefly Brit* : BUSHING

⁵**bush** *adj* [short for *bush-league*] (1959) : falling below acceptable standards : UNPROFESSIONAL ⟨~ behavior⟩

bush baby *n* (1901) : any of several small nocturnal arboreal African primates (*Galago* and related genera of the family Lorisidae) with large eyes, long ears, a long tail, and elongated hind limbs that enable them to leap with great agility — called also *galago*

bush basil *n* (1597) : a sweet basil of a cultivar with small leaves

bush·buck \ˈbu̇sh-ˌbək\ *n, pl* **bushbuck** *or* **bushbucks** [trans. of Afrik *bosbok*] (1852) : a small African striped antelope (*Tragelaphus scriptus*) esp. of sub-Saharan forests that has spirally twisted horns in the male

bush clover *n* (ca. 1818) : any of several usu. shrubby lespedezas

¹**bushed** \ˈbu̇sht\ *adj* (14c) **1 :** covered with or as if with a bushy growth **2** *chiefly Austral* **a :** lost esp. in the bush **b :** PERPLEXED 1, CONFUSED **3 :** TIRED, EXHAUSTED

²**bushed** *adj* (1907) : having a bushing

¹**bush·el** \ˈbu̇-shəl\ *n* [ME *busshel,* fr. AF *bussel, buschelle,* fr. OF *boisse* measure of grain, of Celt origin; akin to MIr *boss* breadth of the hand] (14c) **1 :** any of various units of dry capacity — see WEIGHT table **2 :** a container holding a bushel **3 :** a large quantity ⟨~*s* of money⟩

²**bushel** *vb* **bush·eled; bush·el·ing** \-sh(ə-)liŋ\ [prob. fr. G *bosseln* to do poor work, to patch; akin to OE *bēatan* to beat] (ca. 1877) : REPAIR, RENOVATE — **bush·el·er** \-sh(ə-)lər\ *n*

bush·fire \ˈbu̇sh-ˌfī(-ə)r\ *n* (1832) *Austral* : an uncontrolled fire in a bush area

Bu·shi·do \ˈbü-shi-ˌdō, ˈbü-\ *n* [Jp *bushidō*] (1898) : a feudal-military Japanese code of behavior valuing honor above life

bush·ing \ˈbu̇-shiŋ\ *n* (1839) **1 :** a usu. removable cylindrical lining for an opening (as of a mechanical part) used to limit the size of the opening, resist abrasion, or serve as a guide **2 :** an electrically insulating lining for a hole to protect a through conductor

bush jacket *n* [fr. its use in rough country] (ca. 1939) : a long cotton jacket resembling a shirt and having four patch pockets and a belt

bush·land \ˈbu̇sh-ˌland\ *n* (1827) : ¹BUSH 2

bush–league \-ˌlēg\ *adj* (1908) : being of an inferior class or group of its kind : marked by a lack of sophistication or professionalism

bush league *n* (1902) : MINOR LEAGUE — **bush leaguer** *n*

bush·man \ˈbu̇sh-mən\ *n* (1785) **1** *cap* [modif. of obs. Afrik *boschjesman,* fr. *boschje* (dim. of *bosch* forest) + Afrik *man*] **a :** a member of a group of short-statured peoples of southern Africa who traditionally live by hunting and foraging **b :** the Khoisan languages spoken by these people **2 a :** WOODSMAN **b** *chiefly Austral* : a person who lives in the bush

bush·mas·ter \-ˌmas-tər\ *n* (1826) : a pit viper of Central and So. America that is the largest New World venomous snake

bush·pig \-ˌpig\ *n* (1840) : a wild usu. reddish to black pig (*Potamochoerus porcus*) of forests and scrubland of sub-Saharan Africa and Madagascar that has much facial hair, long pointed ears, and a light-colored mane along the top of the neck and back

bush pilot *n* (1936) : a pilot who flies a small plane into remote areas

bush·rang·er \-ˌrān-jər\ *n* (1801) **1** *Austral* : an outlaw living in the bush **2 :** FRONTIERSMAN, WOODSMAN — **bush·rang·ing** \-jiŋ\ *n*

bush shirt *n* [fr. its use in rough country] (1909) : a usu. loose-fitting cotton shirt with patch pockets

bush·tit \-ˌtit\ *n* (ca. 1889) : a small gray titmouse (*Psaltriparus minimus*) of western No. America with light underparts that occurs in several geographic forms

bush·veld \ˈbu̇sh-ˌfelt\ *n* [part trans. of Afrik *bosveld,* fr. *bos* bush + *veld*] (1879) : veld of southern Africa with abundant shrubby and often thorny vegetation

bush·whack \ˈbu̇sh-ˌhwak, -ˌwak\ *vb* [back-formation fr. *bushwhacker*] *vt* (1866) : AMBUSH; *broadly* : to attack suddenly : ASSAULT ~ *vi* : to clear a path through thick woods esp. by chopping down bushes and low branches — **bush·whack·er** *n*

bushy \ˈbu̇-shē\ *adj* **bush·i·er; -est** (14c) **1 :** full of or overgrown with bushes **2 :** resembling a bush; *esp* : being thick and spreading — **bush·i·ly** \ˈbu̇-shə-lē\ *adv* — **bush·i·ness** \ˈbu̇-shē-nəs\ *n*

busi·ness \ˈbiz-nəs, -nəz, *Southern also* ˈbid-\ *n, often attrib* [ME *bisynesse,* fr. *bisy* busy + *-nesse* -ness] (14c) **1** *archaic* : purposeful activity : BUSYNESS **2 a :** ROLE, FUNCTION ⟨how the human mind went about its ~ of learning —H. A. Overstreet⟩ **b :** an immediate task or objective : MISSION ⟨what is your ~ here⟩ **c :** a particular field of endeavor ⟨the best in the ~⟩ **3 a :** a usu. commercial or mercantile activity engaged in as a means of livelihood : TRADE, LINE ⟨in the restaurant ~⟩ **b :** a commercial or sometimes an industrial enterprise; *also* : such enterprises ⟨the ~ district⟩ **c :** dealings or transactions esp. of an economic nature : PATRONAGE ⟨took their ~ elsewhere⟩ **4 :** AFFAIR, MATTER ⟨the whole ~ got out of hand⟩ ⟨~ as usual⟩ **5 :** CREATION, CONCOCTION **6 :** movement or action (as lighting a cigarette) by an actor intended esp. to establish atmosphere, reveal character, or explain a situation — called also *stage business* **7 a :** personal concern ⟨none of your ~⟩ **b :** RIGHT ⟨you have no ~ speaking to me that way⟩ **8 a :** serious activity requiring time and effort and usu. the avoidance of distractions ⟨got down to ~⟩ **b :** maximum effort **9 a :** a damaging assault **b :** REBUKE, TONGUE-LASHING **c :** DOUBLE CROSS **10 :** a bowel movement — used esp. of pets

syn BUSINESS, COMMERCE, TRADE, INDUSTRY, TRAFFIC mean activity concerned with the supplying and distribution of commodities. BUSINESS may be an inclusive term but specifically designates the activities of those engaged in the purchase or sale of commodities or in related financial transactions. COMMERCE and TRADE imply the exchange and transportation of commodities. INDUSTRY applies to the producing of commodities, esp. by manufacturing or processing, usu. on a large scale. TRAFFIC applies to the operation and functioning of public carriers of goods and persons. ***syn*** see in addition WORK

business administration *n* (ca. 1911) : a program of studies in a college or university providing general knowledge of business principles and practices

business card *n* (1840) : a small card bearing information (as name and address) about a business or business representative

business class *n* (1976) : a class of air transportation at a fare lower than first class and higher than coach

business cycle *n* (1919) : a cycle of economic activity usu. consisting of recession, recovery, growth, and decline

business end *n* (1878) : the end with, from, or through which a thing's function is fulfilled ⟨the *business end* of a revolver⟩

busi·ness·like \ˈbiz-nəs-ˌlīk, -nəz-\ *adj* (1791) **1 :** exhibiting qualities believed to be advantageous in business **2 :** SERIOUS, PURPOSEFUL

busi·ness·man \-ˌman, -mən\ *n* (1826) : a man who transacts business; *esp* : a business executive

busi·ness·peo·ple \-ˌpē-pəl\ *n pl* (1865) : persons active in business

busi·ness·per·son \-ˌpər-sᵊn\ *n* (1974) : a businessman or businesswoman

business suit *n* (1870) : a suit consisting of matching coat and trousers or coat and skirt and sometimes a vest

busi·ness·wom·an \-ˌwu̇-mən\ *n* (1844) : a woman who transacts business; *esp* : one who is a business executive

bus·ing *also* **bus·sing** \ˈbə-siŋ\ *n* (1923) : the act of transporting by bus; *specif* : the transporting of children to a school outside their residential area as a means of achieving racial balance in that school

busk·er \ˈbəs-kər\ *n* [*busk,* prob. fr. It *buscare* to procure, gain, fr. Sp *buscar* to look for] (1857) *chiefly Brit* : a person who entertains in a public place for donations — **busk** \ˈbəsk\ *vi*

bus·kin \ˈbəs-kən\ *n* [prob. modif. of MF *brozequin*] (1503) **1 :** a laced boot reaching halfway or more to the knee **2 a :** COTHURNUS 1 **b :** TRAGEDY; *esp* : tragedy resembling that of ancient Greek drama

bus·load \ˈbəs-ˌlōd\ *n* (1938) : a load that fills a bus ⟨~*s* of tourists⟩

bus·man's holiday \ˈbəs-mənz-\ *n* (1893) : a holiday spent in following or observing the practice of one's usual occupation

buss \ˈbəs\ *n* [perh. alter. of ME *bassen* to kiss] (1570) : KISS — **buss** *vt*

¹**bust** \ˈbəst\ *n* [F *buste,* fr. It *busto,* fr. L *bustum* tomb] (1645) **1 :** a sculptured representation of the upper part of the human figure including the head and neck and usu. part of the shoulders and breast **2 :** the upper part of the human torso between neck and waist; *esp* : the breasts of a woman

²**bust** *vb* **bust·ed** *also* **bust; bust·ing** [alter. of *burst*] *vt* (1806) **1 a :** to break or smash esp. with force; *also* : to make inoperative ⟨~*ed* my watch⟩ **b :** to bring an end to : BREAK UP ⟨helped ~ trusts —*Newsweek*⟩ — often used with *up* ⟨better not try to ~ up his happy marriage —*Forbes*⟩ **c :** to ruin financially **d :** EXHAUST, WEAR OUT — used in phrases like *bust one's butt* to describe making a strenuous effort **e :** to give a hard time to — often used in phrases like *bust one's chops* **2 :** TAME ⟨bronco ~*ing*⟩ **3 :** DEMOTE **4** *slang* **a :** ARREST ⟨~*ed* for carrying guns —Saul Gottlieb⟩ **b :** RAID ⟨~*ed* the apartment⟩ **5 :** HIT, SLUG ~ *vi* **1 :** to go broke **2 a :** BURST ⟨laughing fit to ~⟩ **b :** BREAK DOWN **3 a :** to lose at cards by exceeding a limit (as the count of 21 in blackjack) **b :** to fail to complete a straight or flush in poker

³**bust** *n* (1840) **1 a :** SPREE **b :** a hearty drinking session ⟨a beer ~⟩ **2 a :** a complete failure : FLOP **b :** a business depression **3 :** PUNCH, SOCK **4** *slang* **a :** a police raid **b :** ARREST 2

⁴**bust** *or* **bust·ed** \ˈbəs-təd\ *adj* (1837) : BANKRUPT, BROKE ⟨go ~⟩

bus·tard \ˈbəs-tərd\ *n* [ME, modif. of MF *bistarde,* fr. OIt *bistarda,* fr. L *avis tarda,* lit., slow bird] (15c) : any of a family (Otididae) of large chiefly terrestrial Old World and Australian game birds

bust·er \ˈbəs-tər\ *n* (1831) **1 a** *chiefly Midland* : someone or something extraordinary ⟨a ~ of a breakfast —Harriet B. Stowe⟩ **b :** an unusually sturdy child **c** *often cap* : FELLOW — usu. used as a form of address ⟨hey ~, come here⟩ **2** *chiefly Austral* : a sudden violent wind often coming from the south **3 :** one that breaks, breaks up, or eliminates something ⟨crime ~*s*⟩: as **a :** PLOW **b** [short for *broncobuster*] : a person who breaks horses **4 :** a bad fall

bus·tier \ˌbüs-tē-ˈā, ˌbəs-, -ˈtyā\ *n* [F, fr. *buste*] (1979) : a tight-fitting often strapless top worn as a brassiere or outer garment

¹**bus·tle** \ˈbə-səl\ *vi* **bus·tled; bus·tling** \ˈbəs-liŋ, ˈbə-sə-\ [prob. alter. of obs. *buskle* to prepare, freq. of *busk,* fr. ON *būask* to prepare oneself] (1580) **1 :** to move briskly and often ostentatiously **2 :** to be busily astir : TEEM — **bustling** *adj* — **bus·tling·ly** \-liŋ-lē\ *adv*

²**bustle** *n* (1621) : noisy, energetic, and often obtrusive activity ⟨the hustle and ~ of the big city⟩

³**bustle** *n* [origin unknown] (1786) : a pad or framework expanding and supporting the fullness and drapery of the back of a woman's skirt or dress; *also* : the drapery so supported

bust·line \ˈbəs(t)-ˌlīn\ *n* (1915) **1 :** an arbitrary line encircling the fullest part of the bust **2 :** body circumference at the bust

busty \ˈbəs-tē\ *adj* **bust·i·er; -est** (1944) : having a large bust

bu·sul·fan \byü-ˈsəl-fən\ *n* [*butane* + *sulfonyl* + ³*-an*] (ca. 1958) : an antineoplastic agent $C_6H_{14}O_6S_2$ used in the treatment of chronic myelogenous leukemia

¹**busy** \ˈbi-zē\ *adj* **busi·er; -est** [ME *bisy,* fr. OE *bisig;* akin to MD & MLG *besich* busy] (bef. 12c) **1 a :** engaged in action : OCCUPIED **b :** being in use ⟨found the telephone ~⟩ **2 :** full of activity : BUSTLING ⟨a ~ seaport⟩ **3 :** foolishly or intrusively active : MEDDLING **4 :** full of distracting detail ⟨a ~ design⟩ — **busi·ly** \ˈbi-zə-lē\ *adv* — **busy·ness** \ˈbi-zē-nəs\ *n*

syn BUSY, INDUSTRIOUS, DILIGENT, ASSIDUOUS, SEDULOUS mean actively engaged or occupied. BUSY chiefly stresses activity as opposed to idleness or leisure ⟨too *busy* to spend time with the children⟩. INDUSTRIOUS implies characteristic or habitual devotion to work ⟨*industrious* employees⟩. DILIGENT suggests earnest application to some specific object or pursuit ⟨very *diligent* in her pursuit of a degree⟩. ASSIDUOUS stresses careful and unremitting application ⟨*assiduous* prac-

\ə\ **abut** \ᵊ\ kitten, F table \ər\ **fur**ther \a\ **ash** \ā\ **ace** \ä\ **mop, mar**
\au̇\ **out** \ch\ **ch**in \e\ **bet** \ē\ **easy** \g\ **go** \i\ **hit** \ī\ **ice** \j\ **job**
\ŋ\ **sing** \ō\ **go** \ȯ\ **law** \ȯi\ **boy** \th\ **thin** \t͟h\ **the** \ü\ **loot** \u̇\ **foot**
\y\ **yet** \zh\ **vision, beige** \k͟, ⁿ, œ, ue, ʸ\ *see* Guide to Pronunciation

tice⟩. SEDULOUS implies painstaking and persevering application ⟨a *sedulous* investigation of the murder⟩.

[2]**busy** *vb* **bus·ied; busy·ing** *vt* (bef. 12c) : to make busy : OCCUPY ~ *vi* : BUSTLE ⟨small boats *busied* to and fro —Quentin Crewe⟩

busy·body \ˈbi-zē-ˌbä-dē\ *n* (1526) : an officious or inquisitive person

busy·work \-ˌwərk\ *n* (1910) : work that usu. appears productive or of intrinsic value but actually only keeps one occupied

[1]**but** \ˈbət\ *conj* [ME, fr. OE *būtan,* prep. & conj., outside, without, except, except that; akin to OHG *būzan* without, except; akin to OE *be* by, *ūt* out — more at BY, OUT] (bef. 12c) **1 a :** except for the fact ⟨would have protested ~ that he was afraid⟩ **b :** THAT — used after a negative ⟨there is no doubt ~ he won⟩ **c :** without the concomitant that ⟨it never rains ~ it pours⟩ **d :** if not : UNLESS **e :** THAN ⟨no sooner started ~ it stopped⟩ — not often in formal use **2 a :** on the contrary : on the other hand : NOTWITHSTANDING — used to connect coordinate elements ⟨he was called ~ he did not answer⟩ ⟨not peace ~ a sword⟩ **b :** YET ⟨poor ~ proud⟩ **c :** with the exception of — used before a word often taken to be the subject of a clause ⟨none ~ the brave deserves the fair —John Dryden⟩ — **but that :** THAT — used after a negative ⟨there is no doubt *but that* it must be done⟩ — **but what :** that . . . not — used to indicate possibility or uncertainty ⟨I don't know *but what* I will go⟩

[2]**but** *prep* (bef. 12c) **1 a :** with the exception of : BARRING ⟨no one there ~ me⟩ — compare [1]BUT 2c **b :** other than ⟨this letter is nothing ~ an insult⟩ **2** *Scot* **a :** WITHOUT, LACKING **b :** OUTSIDE

[3]**but** *adv* (12c) **1 :** ONLY, MERELY ⟨he is ~ a child⟩ **2** *Scot* : OUTSIDE **3 :** to the contrary ⟨who knows ~ that she may succeed⟩ **4** — used as an intensive ⟨get there ~ fast⟩

[4]**but** *pron* (1556) : that not : who not ⟨nobody ~ has his fault —Shak.⟩

[5]**but** *n* [Sc *but,* adj. (outer)] (1724) *Scot* : the kitchen or living quarters of a 2-room cottage

bu·ta·di·ene \ˌbyü-tə-ˈdī-ˌēn, -ˌdī-ˈ\ *n* [ISV *butane* + *di-* + *-ene*] (1900) : a flammable gaseous open chain hydrocarbon C_4H_6 used in making synthetic rubbers

bu·tane \ˈbyü-ˌtān\ *n* [ISV *butyric* + *-ane*] (1875) : either of two isomeric flammable gaseous alkanes C_4H_{10} obtained usu. from petroleum or natural gas and used as fuels

bu·ta·nol \ˈbyü-tᵊn-ˌȯl, -ˌōl\ *n* (1894) : either of two flammable isomeric alcohols C_4H_9OH derived from straight-chain butane

butch \ˈbu̇ch\ *adj* [prob. fr. *Butch,* male nickname] (1941) **1 :** notably or deliberately masculine in appearance or manner **2 :** closely cropped ⟨a ~ haircut⟩ — **butch** *n* — **butch·ness** *n*

[1]**butch·er** \ˈbu̇-chər\ *n* [ME *bocher,* fr. AF, fr. *buc* he-goat, prob. of Celt origin; akin to MIr *bocc* he-goat — more at BUCK] (13c) **1 a :** a person who slaughters animals or dresses their flesh **b :** a dealer in meat **2 :** one that kills ruthlessly or brutally **3 :** one that bungles or botches **4 :** a vendor esp. on trains or in theaters

[2]**butcher** *vt* **butch·ered; butch·er·ing** \ˈbu̇ch-riŋ, ˈbu̇-chə-\ (1562) **1 :** to slaughter and dress for market ⟨~ hogs⟩ **2 :** to kill in a barbarous manner **3 :** BOTCH ⟨~*ed* the play⟩

butch·er–bird \ˈbu̇-chər-ˌbərd\ *n* (1668) : any of various shrikes

butcher block *n* (1967) : a block made with thick strips of usu. laminated hardwood — **butcher–block** *adj*

butch·er·ly \ˈbu̇-chər-lē\ *adj* (1513) : resembling a butcher : SAVAGE

butcher paper *n* (1944) : heavy brown or white paper used esp. for wrapping meats

butch·ery \ˈbu̇ch-rē, ˈbu̇-chə-\ *n, pl* **-er·ies** (14c) **1** *chiefly Brit* : SLAUGHTERHOUSE **2 :** the preparation of meat for sale **3 :** cruel and ruthless slaughter of human beings **4 :** BOTCH

bute \ˈbyüt\ *n* (1968) : PHENYLBUTAZONE

bu·tene \ˈbyü-ˌtēn\ *n* [ISV *butyl* + *-ene*] (1885) : a straight-chain butylene

bu·teo \ˈbyü-tē-ˌō\ *n, pl* **-te·os** [NL, genus name, fr. L, a hawk] (1940) : any of a genus (*Buteo*) of hawks with broad rounded wings, relatively short tails, and soaring flight

but for *prep* (12c) : EXCEPT FOR

but·ler \ˈbət-lər\ *n* [ME *buteler,* fr. AF *butiller,* fr. OF *botele* bottle — more at BOTTLE] (13c) **1 :** a manservant having charge of the wines and liquors **2 :** the chief male servant of a household who has charge of other employees, receives guests, directs the serving of meals, and performs various personal services

butler's pantry *n* (1757) : a service room between kitchen and dining room

[1]**butt** \ˈbət\ *vb* [ME, fr. AF *buter, boter,* of Gmc origin; akin to OHG *bōzan* to beat — more at BEAT] *vi* (13c) : to thrust or push headfirst : strike with the head or horns ~ *vt* : to strike or shove with the head or horns — **butt heads :** to come into conflict

[2]**butt** *n* (1647) : a blow or thrust usu. with the head or horns

[3]**butt** *n* [ME, fr. AF *but, bout,* fr. Old Occitan *bota,* fr. LL *buttis*] (14c) **1 :** a large cask esp. for wine, beer, or water **2 :** any of various units of liquid capacity; *esp* : a measure equal to 108 imperial gallons (491 liters)

[4]**butt** *n* [ME, partly fr. MF *but* target, of Gmc origin; akin to ON *būtr* log, LG *butt* blunt; partly fr. MF *bute* goal, target, mound, fr. *but* target] (14c) **1 a :** a backstop (as a mound or bank) for catching missiles shot at a target **b :** TARGET **c** *pl* : RANGE 5c **d :** a blind for shooting birds **2 a** *obs* : LIMIT, BOUND **b** *archaic* : GOAL ⟨here is my journey's end, here is my ~ —Shak.⟩ **3 :** an object of abuse or ridicule : VICTIM ⟨the ~ of all their jokes⟩

[5]**butt** *n* [ME; prob. akin to ME *buttok* buttock, LG *butt* blunt] (15c) **1 :** BUTTOCKS — often used as a euphemism for *ass* in idiomatic expressions ⟨get your ~ over here⟩ ⟨kick ~⟩ ⟨saved our ~*s*⟩ **2 :** the large or thicker end part of something: **a :** a lean upper cut of the pork shoulder **b :** the base of a plant from which the roots spring **c :** the thicker or handle end of a tool or weapon **3 a :** an unused remainder (as of a cigarette or cigar) **b** *slang* : CIGARETTE **4 :** the part of a hide or skin corresponding to the animal's back and sides

[6]**butt** *vb* [partly fr. [4]*butt,* partly fr. [5]*butt*] *vi* (1634) : ABUT — used with *on* or *against* ~ *vt* **1 :** to place end to end or side to side without overlapping **2 :** to trim or square off (as a log) at the end **3 :** to reduce (as a cigarette) to a butt by stubbing or stamping

butte \ˈbyüt\ *n* [F, knoll, fr. MF *bute*] (1805) : an isolated hill or mountain with steep or precipitous sides usu. having a smaller summit area than a mesa

[1]**but·ter** \ˈbə-tər\ *n* [ME, fr. OE *butere,* fr. L *butyrum,* fr. Gk *boutyron,* fr. *bous* cow + *tyros* cheese; akin to Av *tūiri-* curds — more at COW] (bef. 12c) **1 :** a solid emulsion of fat globules, air, and water made by churning milk or cream and used as food **2 :** a buttery substance: as **a :** any of various fatty oils remaining nearly solid at ordinary temperatures **b :** a creamy food spread; *esp* : one made of ground roasted nuts ⟨peanut ~⟩ **3 :** FLATTERY — **but·ter·less** \-ləs\ *adj*

[2]**butter** *vt* (15c) : to spread with or as if with butter

but·ter–and–eggs \ˌbə-tər-ᵊn-ˈegz, -ˈāgz\ *n pl but sing or pl in constr* (1776) : a common Eurasian perennial herb (*Linaria vulgaris*) of the snapdragon family that has showy yellow and orange flowers and is naturalized in much of No. America — called also *toadflax*

but·ter·ball \ˈbə-tər-ˌbȯl\ *n* (1813) **1 :** BUFFLEHEAD **2 :** a chubby person

butter bean *n* (ca. 1819) **1 :** LIMA BEAN: as **a** *chiefly Southern & Midland* : a dried lima bean **b :** SIEVA BEAN **2 :** WAX BEAN **3 :** a green shell bean esp. as opposed to a snap bean

butter clam *n* (1936) : either of two edible clams (*Saxidomus nuttallii* and *S. giganteus*) of the Pacific coast of No. America

but·ter·cream \ˈbə-tər-ˌkrēm\ *n* (1926) : a sweet butter-based mixture used esp. as a filling or frosting

but·ter·cup \-ˌkəp\ *n* (1777) : any of a genus (*Ranunculus* of the family Ranunculaceae, the buttercup family) of herbs with yellow or white flowers and alternate leaves

but·ter·fat \-ˌfat\ *n* (1889) : the natural fat of milk and chief constituent of butter consisting essentially of a mixture of glycerides (as those derived from butyric, capric, caproic, and caprylic acids)

but·ter·fin·gered \-ˌfiŋ-gərd\ *adj* (1615) : apt to let things fall or slip through the fingers : CARELESS — **but·ter·fin·gers** \-gərz\ *n pl but sing or pl in constr*

but·ter·fish \-ˌfish\ *n* (1674) : any of numerous bony fishes (esp. family Stromateidae) with a slippery coating of mucus

[1]**but·ter·fly** \-ˌflī\ *n, often attrib* (bef. 12c) **1 :** any of numerous slender-bodied diurnal lepidopteran insects including one superfamily (Papilionoidea) with broad often brightly colored wings and usu. another superfamily comprising the skippers **2 :** something that resembles or suggests a butterfly; *esp* : a person chiefly occupied with the pursuit of pleasure **3 :** a swimming stroke executed in a prone position by moving both arms in a circular motion while kicking both legs up and down **4** *pl* : a feeling of hollowness or queasiness caused esp. by emotional or nervous tension or anxious anticipation **5 :** a defensive move by a goalie in ice hockey executed by dropping to the knees while spreading the lower legs outward

[2]**butterfly** *vt* **-flied; -fly·ing** (1954) : to split almost entirely and spread apart ⟨a *butterflied* steak⟩ ⟨*butterflied* shrimp⟩

butterfly bush *n* (1923) : BUDDLEIA

butterfly chair *n* (1953) : a chair for lounging consisting of a cloth sling supported by a frame of metal tubing or bars

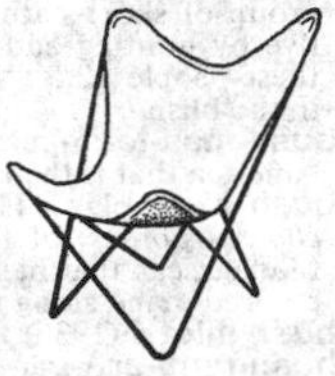

butterfly chair

butterfly effect *n* (1984) : a property of chaotic systems (as the atmosphere) by which small changes in initial conditions can lead to large-scale and unpredictable variation in the future state of the system

but·ter·fly·er \ˈbə-tər-ˌflī(-ə)r\ *n* (1967) : a swimmer who specializes in the butterfly

butterfly fish *n* (1740) **1 :** any of a family (Chaetodontidae) of small brilliantly colored bony fishes of tropical seas with a narrow deep body and scaled fins **2 :** a small brown freshwater bony fish (*Pantodon buchholzi* of the family Pantodontidae) of western Africa that has elongate winglike pectoral fins

butterfly valve *n* (1846) **1 :** a valve consisting of two semicircular clappers hinged to a cross rib that permits fluid flow in only one direction **2 :** a damper or valve in a pipe consisting of a disk turning on a bisecting axis

butterfly weed *n* (1816) : a No. American milkweed (*Asclepias tuberosa*) with showy orange flowers borne on erect leafy stems

but·ter·head \ˈbə-tər-ˌhed\ *n* (ca. 1925) : BUTTER LETTUCE

butter lettuce *n* (1972) : a lettuce (as Bibb or Boston lettuce) with a soft loose head of tender oily mild-flavored leaves

but·ter·milk \ˈbə-tər-ˌmilk\ *n* (15c) **1 :** the liquid left after butter has been churned from milk or cream **2 :** cultured milk made by the addition of suitable bacteria to sweet milk

but·ter·nut \-ˌnət\ *n* (1741) **1 :** an eastern No. American tree (*Juglans cinerea*) of the walnut family with sweet egg-shaped nuts and light brown wood — called also *white walnut* **2 a :** a light yellowish brown **b** *pl* : homespun overalls dyed brown with a butternut extract **c :** a soldier or partisan of the Confederacy during the American Civil War

butternut squash *n* (1945) : a smooth somewhat bottle-shaped buff-colored winter squash (*Cucurbita moschata*) with usu. orange flesh

but·ter·scotch \-ˌskäch\ *n* (1855) **1 :** a candy made from brown sugar, butter, corn syrup, and water; *also* : the flavor of such candy **2 :** a moderate yellowish brown

butter up *vt* (1819) : to charm or beguile with lavish flattery or praise

but·ter·weed \ˈbə-tər-ˌwēd\ *n* (1837) : any of several plants having yellow flowers or smooth soft foliage: as **a :** HORSEWEED 1 **b :** any of several No. American senecios (as *Senecio glabellus*)

but·ter·wort \-ˌwərt, -ˌwȯrt\ *n* (1597) : any of a genus (*Pinguicula*) of herbs of the bladderwort family with fleshy leaves that produce a viscid secretion serving to capture and digest insects

[1]**but·tery** \ˈbə-tə-rē, ˈbə-trē\ *n, pl* **-ter·ies** [ME *boterie,* fr. AF, fr. *but* cask, butt — more at BUTT] (14c) **1 :** a storeroom for liquors **2 a** *chiefly dial* : PANTRY **b :** a room (as in an English college) stocking provisions for sale to students

[2]**but·tery** \ˈbə-tə-rē\ *adj* (14c) **1 a :** having the qualities (as smoothness or richness) of butter ⟨~ flavors⟩ **b :** containing or spread with butter ⟨~ pastry⟩ **2 :** marked by flattery ⟨~ compliments⟩

butt hinge *n* (1815) : a hinge usu. mortised flush into the edge of a door and its jamb

butt in *vi* (1900) : to meddle in the affairs of others : INTERFERE

butt·in·sky *also* **butt·in·ski** \bət-ˈin-skē\ *n, pl* **-skies** [*butt in* + *-sky, -ski* (last element in Slavic surnames)] (1902) : a person given to butting in : a troublesome meddler

butt joint *n* (1823) : a joint made by fastening the parts together end-to-end without overlap and often with reinforcement

but·tock \ˈbə-tək *also* -(ˌ)täk\ *n* [ME *buttok* — more at BUTT] (14c) **1** : the back of a hip that forms one of the fleshy parts on which a person sits **2** *pl* **a** : the seat of the body **b** : RUMP 1a

¹but·ton \ˈbə-tᵊn\ *n, often attrib* [ME *boton,* fr. AF *butun* rose hip, stud, fr. *buter* to thrust — more at BUTT] (14c) **1 a** : a small knob or disk secured to an article (as of clothing) and used as a fastener by passing it through a buttonhole or loop **b** : a usu. circular metal or plastic badge bearing a stamped design or printed slogan ⟨campaign ~⟩ **2** : something that resembles a button: as **a** : any of various parts or growths of a plant or of an animal: as (1) : BUD (2) : an immature whole mushroom; *esp* : BUTTON MUSHROOM (3) : the terminal segment of a rattlesnake's rattle **b** : a small globule of metal remaining after fusion (as in assaying) **c** : a guard on the tip of a fencing foil **3 a** : PUSH BUTTON **b** : something (as a push button) that has the real or symbolic capability of initiating a catastrophe (as a nuclear attack) ⟨has his finger on the ~⟩ **c** : a hidden sensitivity that can be manipulated to produce a desired response ⟨knows how to push my ~*s*⟩ **d** : a usu. box-shaped computer icon that initiates a specific software function **4** : the point of the chin esp. as a target for a knockout blow — **but·ton·less** \-ləs\ *adj* — **on the button** : EXACTLY ⟨arrived at noon *on the button*⟩; *also* : exactly on target : on the nose ⟨the estimate was right *on the button*⟩

²button *vb* **but·toned; but·ton·ing** \ˈbət-niŋ, ˈbə-tᵊn-iŋ\ *vt* (14c) **1** : to furnish or decorate with buttons **2 a** : to pass (a button) through a buttonhole or loop **b** : to close or fasten with buttons — often used with *up* ⟨~ up your overcoat⟩ **3 a** : to close (the lips) to prevent speech ⟨~ your lip⟩ **b** : to close or seal tightly — usu. used with *up* ⟨~ up the house for winter⟩ ~ *vi* : to have buttons for fastening ⟨this dress ~*s* at the back⟩ — **but·ton·er** \ˈbət-nər, ˈbə-tᵊn-ər\ *n*

but·ton·ball \ˈbə-tᵊn-ˌbȯl\ *n* (1821) : ²PLANE

but·ton·bush \-ˌbu̇sh\ *n* (1754) : a No. American shrub (*Cephalanthus occidentalis*) of the madder family with globular flower heads

¹but·ton–down \-ˌdau̇n\ *adj* (1934) **1 a** *of a collar* : having the ends fastened to the garment with buttons **b** *of a garment* : having a button-down collar **2** *or* **but·toned–down** \-tᵊn-ˌdau̇n\ : conservatively traditional or conventional; *esp* : adhering to conventional norms in dress and behavior ⟨~ businessmen⟩

²button–down *n* (1952) : a shirt with a button-down collar

but·toned–up \ˈbə-tᵊnd-ˈəp\ *adj* (1936) : coldly reserved or standoffish ⟨a ~ executive⟩

¹but·ton·hole \ˈbə-tᵊn-ˌhōl\ *n* (1561) **1** : a slit or loop through which a button is passed **2** *chiefly Brit* : BOUTONNIERE

²buttonhole *vt* (1828) **1** : to furnish with buttonholes **2** : to work with buttonhole stitch — **but·ton·hol·er** \-ˌhō-lər\ *n*

³buttonhole *vt* [alter. of *buttonhold*] (1857) : to detain in conversation by or as if by holding on to the outer garments of

buttonhole stitch *n* (1877) : a closely worked loop stitch used to make a firm edge (as on a buttonhole)

but·ton·hook \ˈbə-tᵊn-ˌhu̇k\ *n* (1870) **1** : a hook for drawing small buttons through buttonholes **2** : an offensive play in football in which the pass receiver runs straight downfield and then abruptly cuts back toward the line of scrimmage — **buttonhook** *vi*

button man *n* [perh. fr. *buttons* bellhop] (1966) : a low-ranking member of a criminal underworld organization

button mushroom *n* (1865) : a usu. small white mushroom (*Agaricus bisporus* syn. *A. brunnescens*) in which the pileus has not yet expanded

button quail *n* (1885) : any of a family (Turnicidae) of small terrestrial Old World birds that resemble quails and have only three toes on a foot with the hind toe being absent

button snakeroot *n* (1775) **1** : BLAZING STAR 2a **2** : any of several usu. prickly herbs (genus *Eryngium*) of the carrot family

but·ton·wood \ˈbə-tᵊn-ˌwu̇d\ *n* (1674) : ²PLANE

butt out *vi* (1906) : to cease interference or involvement ⟨told him to *butt out* of my affairs⟩

¹but·tress \ˈbə-trəs\ *n* [ME *butres,* fr. AF (*arche*) *boteraz* thrusting (arch), ultim. fr. *buter* to thrust — more at BUTT] (14c) **1** : a projecting structure of masonry or wood for supporting or giving stability to a wall or building **2** : something that resembles a buttress: as **a** : a projecting part of a mountain or hill **b** : a horny protuberance on a horse's hoof at the heel — see HOOF illustration **c** : the broadened base of a tree trunk or a thickened vertical part of it **3** : something that supports or strengthens ⟨a ~ of the cause of peace⟩ — **but·tressed** \-trəst\ *adj*

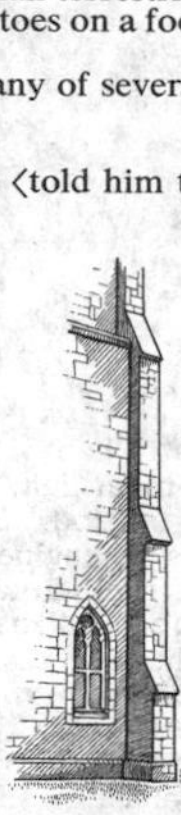

buttress 1

²buttress *vt* (14c) : to furnish or shore up with a buttress; *also* : SUPPORT, STRENGTHEN ⟨arguments ~*ed* by solid facts⟩

butt shaft *n* (1588) : a target arrow without a barb

butt·stock \ˈbət-ˌstäk\ *n* (ca. 1909) : the stock of a firearm in the rear of the breech mechanism

butt weld *n* (ca. 1864) : a butt joint made by welding — **butt–weld** *vt*

but·ty \ˈbə-tē\ *n, pl* **butties** [¹*butter* + ⁴*-y*] (1855) *Brit* : SANDWICH

bu·tut \bu̇-ˈtüt\ *n, pl* **bututs** *or* **butut** [Wolof *butuut,* lit., something small] (1972) — see *dalasi* at MONEY table

bu·tyl \ˈbyü-tᵊl\ *n* [ISV *butyric* + *-yl*] (1869) : any of four isomeric alkyl radicals C_4H_9– derived from butane

butyl alcohol *n* (ca. 1871) : any of four flammable alcohols C_4H_9OH (as butanol) used in organic synthesis and as solvents

bu·tyl·at·ed \ˈbyü-tᵊl-ˌā-təd\ *adj* (1942) : combined with the butyl radical — **bu·tyl·a·tion** \ˌbyü-tᵊl-ˈā-shən\ *n*

butylated hy·droxy·an·i·sole \-(ˌ)hī-ˌdräk-sē-ˈa-nə-ˌsōl\ *n* [*hydroxy* + *anise* + *-ole*] (1950) : BHA

butylated hy·droxy·tol·u·ene \-ˈtäl-yə-ˌwēn\ *n* (1961) : BHT

bu·tyl·ene \ˈbyü-tᵊl-ˌēn\ *n* (1877) : any of three isomeric hydrocarbons C_4H_8 of the ethylene series obtained usu. by cracking petroleum

butyl nitrite *n* (1977) : an oily liquid ester $C_4H_9NO_2$ of butyl alcohol and nitrous acid that is inhaled illicitly esp. as an aphrodisiac — compare POPPER

butyl rubber *n* (1940) : any of a class of synthetic rubbers that are made by copolymerizing isobutylene with a small amount usu. of isoprene at low temperature

butyr- *or* **butyro-** *comb form* [ISV, fr. *butyric*] : butyric ⟨*butyr*aldehyde⟩

bu·tyr·al·de·hyde \ˌbyü-tə-ˈral-də-ˌhīd\ *n* [ISV] (ca. 1885) : either of two aldehydes C_4H_8O used esp. in making synthetic resins

bu·ty·rate \ˈbyü-tə-ˌrāt\ *n* (1873) : a salt or ester of butyric acid

bu·tyr·ic \byü-ˈtir-ik\ *adj* [F *butyrique,* fr. L *butyrum* butter — more at BUTTER] (1854) : relating to or producing butyric acid

butyric acid *n* (1826) : either of two isomeric fatty acids $C_4H_8O_2$; *esp* : the straight-chain acid of unpleasant odor normally found in perspiration and rancid butter

bu·ty·ro·phe·none \ˌbyü-tə-(ˌ)rō-fə-ˈnōn\ *n* [*butyr-* + *phen-* + *-one*] (1970) : any of a class of antipsychotic drugs (as haloperidol) used esp. in the treatment of schizophrenia

bux·om \ˈbək-səm\ *adj* [ME *buxsum,* fr. OE **būhsum;* akin to OE *būgan* to bend — more at BOW] (12c) **1** *obs* **a** : OBEDIENT, TRACTABLE **b** : offering little resistance : FLEXIBLE ⟨wing silently the ~ air —John Milton⟩ **2** *archaic* : full of gaiety **3** : vigorously or healthily plump; *specif* : full-bosomed — **bux·om·ly** *adv* — **bux·om·ness** *n*

¹buy \ˈbī\ *vb* **bought** \ˈbȯt\; **buy·ing** [ME *byen,* fr. OE *bycgan;* akin to Goth *bugjan* to buy] *vt* (bef. 12c) **1** : to acquire possession, ownership, or rights to the use or services of by payment esp. of money : PURCHASE **2 a** : to obtain in exchange for something often at a sacrifice ⟨they *bought* peace with their freedom⟩ **b** : REDEEM 6 **3** : BRIBE, HIRE **4** : to be the purchasing equivalent of ⟨the dollar ~*s* less today than it used to⟩ **5** : ACCEPT, BELIEVE ⟨I don't ~ that hooey⟩ — often used with *into* ~ *vi* : to make a purchase — **buy·er** \ˈbī(-ə)r\ *n* — **buy into** : to purchase a portion of or interest in ⟨the TV network *bought into* its local football team⟩ — **buy it** *or* **buy the farm** : to get killed : DIE — **buy time** : to delay an imminent action or decision : STALL

²buy *n* (1879) **1** : something of value at a favorable price; *esp* : BARGAIN ⟨it's a real ~ at that price⟩ **2** : an act of buying : PURCHASE

buy·back \ˈbī-ˌbak\ *n* (1963) : the act or an instance of buying something back; *esp* : the repurchase by a corporation of shares of its own common stock on the open market

buyer's market *n* (1926) : a market in which goods are plentiful, buyers have a wide range of choice, and prices tend to be low — compare SELLER'S MARKET

buy off *vt* (1629) **1** : to induce to refrain (as from prosecution) by a payment or other consideration **2** : to free (as from military service) by payment

buy·out \ˈbī-ˌau̇t\ *n* (1971) **1** : an act or instance of buying out **2** : a financial incentive offered to an employee in exchange for an early retirement or voluntary resignation

buy out *vt* (1598) **1** : to purchase the share or interest of **2** : to purchase the entire stock-in-trade and the goodwill of (a business)

buy up *vt* (ca. 1534) **1** : to buy freely or extensively **2** : to buy the entire available supply of

¹buzz \ˈbəz\ *vb* [ME *bussen,* of imit. origin] *vi* (14c) **1** : to make a low continuous humming sound like that of a bee **2 a** : MURMUR, WHISPER **b** : to be filled with a confused murmur ⟨the room ~*ed* with excitement⟩ **3** : to make a signal with a buzzer **4** : to go quickly : HURRY ⟨~*ed* around town in a sports car⟩; *also* : SCRAM — usu. used with *off* **5** : to feel high esp. from a drug ~ *vt* **1** : to utter covertly by or as if by whispering **2** : to cause to buzz **3** : to fly fast and close to ⟨planes ~ the crowd⟩ **4** : to summon or signal with a buzzer; *also* : to let in through an electronically controlled entrance — used with *in* or *through* ⟨~*ed* him in⟩ **5** *dial Eng* : to drink to the last drop ⟨get some more port whilst I ~ this bottle —W. M. Thackeray⟩

²buzz *n* (ca. 1600) **1** : a persistent vibratory sound **2 a** : a confused murmur **b** : RUMOR, GOSSIP **c** : a flurry of activity **d** : FAD, CRAZE **e** : speculative or excited talk or attention relating esp. to a new or forthcoming product or event ⟨one of the few new shows that's getting good ~ —*TV Guide*⟩; *also* : an instance of such talk or attention ⟨their first CD created a huge ~⟩ **3** : a signal conveyed by buzzer; *specif* : a telephone call **4** : HIGH 4

buz·zard \ˈbə-zərd\ *n* [ME *busard,* fr. OF, alter. of *buison,* fr. L *buteon, buteo* hawk] (14c) **1** *chiefly Brit* : BUTEO **2** : any of various usu. large birds of prey (as the turkey vulture) **3** : a contemptible or rapacious person

buzz bomb *n* (1944) : an unguided jet-propelled missile used by the Germans against England in World War II

buzz cut *n* (1980) : CREW CUT — **buzz–cut** *adj*

buzz·er \ˈbə-zər\ *n* (1606) **1** : one that buzzes; *specif* : an electric signaling device that makes a buzzing sound **2** : the sound of a buzzer

buzz·kill \ˈbəz-ˌkil\ *n* (1992) : one that has a depressing or negative effect

buzz saw *n* (1847) : CIRCULAR SAW

buzz·word \ˈbəz-ˌwərd\ *n* (1946) **1** : an important-sounding usu. technical word or phrase often of little meaning used chiefly to impress laymen **2** : a voguish word or phrase — called also *buzz phrase*

BVD \ˌbē-(ˌ)vē-ˈdē\ *trademark* — used for underwear

B vitamin *n* (1920) : any vitamin of the vitamin B complex

BVM *abbr* Blessed Virgin Mary

bvt *abbr* brevet

BW *abbr* **1** bacteriological warfare; biological warfare **2** black and white

bwa·na \ˈbwä-nə\ *n* [Swahili, fr. Ar *abūna* our father] (1875) : MASTER, BOSS

BWI *abbr* British West Indies

bx *abbr* box

BX *abbr* base exchange

\ə\ **abut** \ᵊ\ kitten, F table \ər\ **fur**ther \a\ ash \ā\ ace \ä\ mop, mar
\au̇\ **out** \ch\ **chin** \e\ bet \ē\ **easy** \g\ **go** \i\ **hit** \ī\ ice \j\ **job**
\ŋ\ **sing** \ō\ **go** \ȯ\ **law** \ȯi\ **boy** \th\ **thin** \t͟h\ **the** \ü\ **loot** \u̇\ **foot**
\y\ yet \zh\ **vision**, beige \k͟, ⁿ, œ, ue, ʸ\ *see* Guide to Pronunciation

¹by \'bī, *before consonants also* bə\ *prep* [ME, prep. & adv., fr. OE, prep., *be, bī;* akin to OHG *bī* by, near, L *ambi-* on both sides, around, Gk *amphi*] (bef. 12c) **1 :** in proximity to : NEAR ⟨standing ~ the window⟩ **2 a :** through or through the medium of : VIA ⟨enter ~ the door⟩ **b :** in the direction of : TOWARD ⟨north ~ east⟩ **c :** into the vicinity of and beyond : PAST ⟨went right ~ him⟩ **3 a :** during the course of ⟨studied ~ night⟩ **b :** not later than ⟨~ 2 p.m.⟩ **4 a :** through the agency or instrumentality of ⟨~ force⟩ **b :** born or begot of **c :** sired or borne by **5 :** with the witness or sanction of ⟨swear ~ all that is holy⟩ **6 a :** in conformity with ⟨acted ~ the rules⟩ **b :** ACCORDING TO ⟨called her ~ name⟩ **7 a :** on behalf of ⟨did right ~ his children⟩ **b :** with respect to ⟨a lawyer ~ profession⟩ **8 a :** in or to the amount or extent of ⟨win ~ a nose⟩ **b** *chiefly Scot* : in comparison with : BESIDE **9** — used as a function word to indicate successive units or increments ⟨little ~ little⟩ ⟨walk two ~ two⟩ **10** — used as a function word in multiplication, in division, and in measurements ⟨divide *a* ~ *b*⟩ ⟨multiply 10 ~ 4⟩ ⟨a room 15 feet ~ 20 feet⟩ **11 :** in the opinion of : from the point of view of ⟨okay ~ me⟩ — **by the by** *or* **by the bye** : INCIDENTALLY 2

²by \'bī\ *adv* (bef. 12c) **1 a :** close at hand : NEAR **b :** at or to another's home ⟨stop ~⟩ **2 :** PAST ⟨saw him go ~⟩ **3 :** ASIDE, AWAY

³by *or* **bye** \'bī\ *adj* (14c) **1 :** being off the main route : SIDE **2 :** INCIDENTAL

⁴by *or* **bye** \'bī\ *n, pl* **byes** \'bīz\ (1567) : something of secondary importance : a side issue

⁵by *or* **bye** \'bī\ *interj* [short for *goodbye*] (1709) — used to express farewell; often used with following *now*

by-and-by \ˌbī-ən-'bī\ *n* (1591) : a future time or occasion
by and by *adv* (1526) : BEFORE LONG, SOON
by and large *adv* (1706) : on the whole : in general
by-blow \'bī-ˌblō\ *n* (1592) **1 :** an indirect blow **2 :** an illegitimate child
by-catch \-ˌkach, -ˌkech\ *n* (1976) : the portion of a commercial fishing catch that consists of marine animals caught unintentionally
bye \'bī\ *n* [alter. of ²by] (1883) : the position of a participant in a tournament who advances to the next round without playing
¹bye-bye *or* **by-by** \'bī-ˌbī, bī-'bī\ *interj* [baby-talk redupl. of *goodbye*] (ca. 1736) — used to express farewell
²bye-bye *or* **by-by** \'bī-ˌbī\ *adv* (1917) : out esp. for a walk or ride — used with the verb *go*
³bye-bye *or* **by-by** \'bī-ˌbī\ *n* (1867) : BED, SLEEP ⟨lie down . . . and go to ~ —Rudyard Kipling⟩
⁴bye-bye *or* **by-by** \'bī-ˌbī\ *adv* (1920) : to bed or sleep — used with the verb *go*
by-elec-tion *also* **bye-election** \'bī-ə-ˌlek-shən\ *n* (1870) : a special election held between regular elections in order to fill a vacancy
Bye-lo-rus-sian \ˌbē-ˌe-lō-'rə-shən, ˌbye-lō-\ *n* (1944) : BELARUSIAN
by-form \'bī-ˌfȯrm\ *n* (1887) : a parallel and sometimes less important form of a word, stem, or formative element in a given language or dialect
by-gone \'bī-ˌgȯn *also* -ˌgän\ *adj* (15c) : gone by : PAST ⟨~ days⟩; *esp* : OUTMODED ⟨~ styles⟩ — **bygone** *n*
by-law *also* **bye-law** \'bī-ˌlȯ\ *n* [ME *bilawe*, prob. fr. ON *bȳlog,* fr. ON *bȳr* town + *lag-, lǫg* law] (14c) **1 :** a rule adopted by an organization chiefly for the government of its members and the regulation of its affairs **2 :** a local ordinance
¹by-line \'bī-ˌlīn\ *n* (1916) **1 :** a secondary line : SIDELINE **2 :** a line at the beginning of a news story, magazine article, or book giving the writer's name
²byline *vt* (1938) : to write (an article) under a byline — **by-lin-er** \-ˌlī-nər\ *n*

by-name \'bī-ˌnām\ *n* (14c) **1 :** a secondary name **2 :** NICKNAME
BYO *abbr* bring your own
BYOB *abbr* bring your own beer; bring your own booze; bring your own bottle
¹by-pass \'bī-ˌpas\ *n* (1848) **1 :** a passage to one side; *esp* : a deflected route usu. around a town **2 a :** a channel carrying a fluid around a part and back to the main stream **b** (1) : SHUNT 1b (2) : SHUNT 1c; *also* : a surgical procedure for the establishment of a shunt ⟨have a coronary ~⟩
²bypass *vt* (1736) **1 a :** to avoid by means of a bypass ⟨~ a congested area⟩ **b :** to cause to follow a bypass **2 a :** to neglect or ignore usu. intentionally **b :** CIRCUMVENT ⟨attempting to ~ the law⟩
by-past \'bī-ˌpast\ *adj* (15c) : BYGONE
by-path \-ˌpath, -ˌpäth\ *n* (14c) : BYWAY
by-play \-ˌplā\ *n* (1812) : action engaged in on the side while the main action proceeds (as during a dramatic production)
by—prod-uct \-ˌprä-(ˌ)dəkt\ *n* (1857) **1 :** something produced in a usu. industrial or biological process in addition to the principal product **2 :** a secondary and sometimes unexpected or unintended result
byre \'bī-(ə)r\ *n* [ME, fr. OE *bȳre;* akin to OE *būr* dwelling — more at BOWER] *chiefly Brit* : a cow barn
by-road \'bī-ˌrōd\ *n* (1665) : BYWAY
bys-si-no-sis \ˌbi-sə-'nō-səs\ *n, pl* **-no-ses** \-ˌsēz\ [NL, fr. L *byssinus* of fine linen, fr. Gk *byssinos,* fr. *byssos*] (1881) : an occupational respiratory disease associated with inhalation of cotton, flax, or hemp dust and characterized initially by chest tightness, shortness of breath, and cough and eventually by irreversible lung disease
bys-sus \'bi-səs\ *n, pl* **bys-sus-es** *or* **bys-si** \-ˌsī, -(ˌ)sē\ [ME *bissus,* fr. L *byssus,* fr. Gk *byssos* flax, of Sem origin; akin to Heb *būṣ* linen cloth] (14c) **1 :** a fine prob. linen cloth of ancient times **2** [NL, fr. L] : a tuft of long tough filaments by which some bivalve mollusks (as mussels) adhere to a surface
by-stand-er \'bī-ˌstan-dər\ *n* (1584) : one present but not taking part in a situation or event : a chance spectator
by-street \-ˌstrēt\ *n* (1672) : a street off a main thoroughfare
byte \'bīt\ *n* [perh. alter. of ²*bite*] (1962) : a unit of computer information or data-storage capacity that consists of a group of eight bits and that is used esp. to represent an alphanumeric character — compare WORD 2c
by-way \'bī-ˌwā\ *n* (14c) **1 :** a little traveled side road **2 :** a secondary or little known aspect or field ⟨meandering more and more in the fascinating ~s of learning —*Times Lit. Supp.*⟩
by-word \-ˌwərd\ *n* (bef. 12c) **1 :** a proverbial saying : PROVERB **2 a :** one that personifies a type **b :** one that is noteworthy or notorious **3 :** EPITHET **4 :** a frequently used word or phrase
by—your—leave \ˌbī-yər-'lēv\ *n* (1894) : a request for permission ⟨imposed . . . without so much as a ~ —J. L. Granatstein⟩
¹Byz-an-tine \'bi-z°n-ˌtēn, 'bī-, -ˌtīn; bə-'zan-ˌ, bī-\ *adj* (1651) **1 :** of, relating to, or characteristic of the ancient city of Byzantium **2 :** of, relating to, or having the characteristics of a style of architecture developed in the Byzantine Empire esp. in the fifth and sixth centuries featuring the dome carried on pendentives over a square and incrustation with marble veneering and with colored mosaics on grounds of gold **3 :** of or relating to the churches using a traditional Greek rite and subject to Eastern canon law **4** *often not cap* **a :** of, relating to, or characterized by a devious and usu. surreptitious manner of operation ⟨a ~ power struggle⟩ **b :** intricately involved : LABYRINTHINE ⟨rules of ~ complexity⟩
²Byzantine *n* (1651) : a native or inhabitant of Byzantium
By-zan-tin-ist \bi-'zan-ti-nist, bī-\ *n* (1892) : a student of Byzantine culture

¹c \'sē\ *n, pl* **c's** *or* **cs** \'sēz\ *often cap, often attrib* **1 a :** the 3d letter of the English alphabet **b :** a graphic representation of this letter **c :** a speech counterpart of orthographic *c* **2 a :** one hundred — see NUMBER table **b** *slang* : a sum of $100 **3 :** the keynote of a C-major scale **4 :** a graphic device for reproducing the letter *c* **5 :** one designated *c* esp. as the third in order or class **6 a :** a grade rating a student's work as fair or mediocre in quality **b :** one graded or rated with a C **7 :** something shaped like the letter C **8 :** a structured programming language designed to be compact and efficient
²c *abbr* **1** calm **2** calorie **3** canceled **4** candle **5** carat **6** catcher **7** cent **8** centavo **9** centi- **10** centime **11** centimeter **12** century **13** chapter **14** circa **15** circumference **16** cocaine **17** coefficient **18** college **19** [L *congius*] gallon **20** contralto **21** copyright **22** cubic **23** cup **24** curie
¹C *abbr* **1** capacitance **2** Celsius **3** centigrade **4** Coulomb **5** cytosine
²C *symbol* carbon
ca *abbr* circa
Ca *symbol* calcium
CA *abbr* **1** California **2** Central America **3** certified acupuncturist **4** chartered accountant **5** chief accountant **6** chronological age **7** commercial agent **8** controller of accounts **9** current account
ca' \'kȯ, 'kä\ *Scot var of* CALL
¹cab \'kab, 'käb\ *n* [Heb *qabh*] (1535) : an ancient Hebrew unit of capacity equal to about two quarts (2.2 liters)

²cab \'kab\ *n* [short for *cabriolet*] (1826) **1 a** (1) : CABRIOLET (2) : a similar light closed carriage (as a hansom) **b :** a carriage for hire **2 :** TAXICAB **3** [short for *cabin*] **a :** the part of a locomotive that houses the engineer and operating controls **b :** a comparable shelter (as on a truck) housing operating controls
³cab *vi* **cabbed; cab-bing** (1835) : to travel in a cab ⟨*cabbed* back to the hotel⟩
⁴cab \'kab\ *n, often cap* (1986) : CABERNET SAUVIGNON
CAB *abbr* Civil Aeronautics Board
¹ca-bal \kə-'bäl, -'bal\ *n* [F *cabale* cabala, intrigue, cabal, fr. ML *cabbala* cabala, fr. LHeb *qabbālāh,* lit., received (lore)] (1614) **1 :** the artifices and intrigues of a group of persons secretly united in a plot (as to overturn a government); *also* : a group engaged in such artifices and intrigues **2 :** CLUB, GROUP ⟨a ~ of artists⟩ *syn* see PLOT
²cabal *vi* **ca-balled; ca-bal-ling** (1678) : to unite in or form a cabal
cabala *or* **cabbala** *or* **cabbalah** *var of* KABBALAH
ca-ba-let-ta \ˌka-bə-'le-tə, ˌkä-\ *n* [It] (1842) **1 :** an operatic song in simple popular style characterized by a uniform rhythm **2 :** the lively bravura concluding section of an extended aria or duet
¹ca-ba-list \kə-'bä-list, 'ka-bə-\ *n* (ca. 1533) **1** *often cap* : a student, interpreter, or devotee of the Jewish cabala **2 :** one skilled in esoteric doctrine or mysterious art
²ca-bal-ist \kə-'ba-list, -'bä-\ *n* (1569) : a member of a cabal
ca-bal-le-ro \ˌka-bə-'ler-(ˌ)ō, -bə(l)-'yer-\ *n, pl* **-ros** [Sp, fr. LL *caballarius* hostler — more at CAVALIER] (1749) **1 :** KNIGHT, CAVALIER **2** *chiefly Southwest* : HORSEMAN

ca•bana \kə-ˈban-yə, -ˈba-nə\ *n* [Sp *cabaña,* lit., hut, fr. ML *capanna*] (1890) **1 :** a lightweight structure with living facilities **2 :** a tentlike shelter usu. with an open side facing a beach or swimming pool

cab•a•ret \ˌka-bə-ˈrā, ˈka-bə-ˌ\ *n* [F, fr. MF dial. (Picard or Walloon), fr. MD, alter. of *cambret, cameret,* fr. MF dial. (Picard) *camberete* small room, ultim. fr. LL *camera* — more at CHAMBER] (1655) **1** *archaic* **:** a shop selling wines and liquors **2 a :** a restaurant serving liquor and providing entertainment (as by singers or dancers) **:** NIGHTCLUB **b :** the show provided at a cabaret

[1]**cab•bage** \ˈka-bij\ *n, often attrib* [ME *caboche,* fr. MF dial. (Norman & Picard), lit., head, noggin] (15c) **1 a :** any of several brassicas (*Brassica oleracea*) of European origin; *esp* **:** a leafy garden plant (*Brassica oleracea capitata*) with a short stem and a dense globular head of usu. green leaves that is used as a vegetable **b :** any of several plants related to or resembling cabbage **2** *slang* **:** MONEY, CASH — **cab•bagey** *also* **cab•bagy** \-bə-jē\ *adj*

[2]**cabbage** *n* [perh. by folk etymology fr. MF *cabas* cheating, theft] **:** pieces of cloth left in cutting out garments and traditionally kept by tailors as perquisites

[3]**cabbage** *vt* **cab•baged; cab•bag•ing** (1691) **:** STEAL, FILCH

cabbage butterfly *n* (1781) **:** any of several largely white butterflies (family Pieridae) whose green larvae are cabbage worms; *esp* **:** a small cosmopolitan butterfly (*Pieris rapae* syn. *Artogeia rapae*) that is a pest on cabbage — called also *cabbage white*

cabbage looper *n* (1895) **:** a noctuid moth (*Trichoplusia ni*) having pale green white-striped larvae that feed on cruciferous plants

cabbage palm *n* (1770) **:** a palm with terminal buds eaten as a vegetable

cabbage palmetto *n* (1802) **:** a cabbage palm (*Sabal palmetto*) with fan-shaped leaves native to coastal southeastern U.S. and the Bahamas

cabbage rose *n* (1795) **:** a fragrant garden rose (*Rosa centifolia*) with upright branches and large pink flowers

cabbage worm *n* (1688) **:** an insect larva (as of a cabbage butterfly) that feeds on cabbages

cab•bie *or* **cab•by** \ˈka-bē\ *n, pl* **cabbies** (1840) **:** CABDRIVER

cab•driv•er \ˈkab-ˌdrī-vər\ *n* (1825) **:** a driver of a cab

ca•ber \ˈkā-bər, ˈkä-\ *n* [ScGael *cabar*] (1505) **:** POLE; *esp* **:** a young tree trunk used for tossing as a trial of strength in a Scottish sport

cab•er•net franc \ˌka-bər-ˈnā-ˈfräŋk, -ˈfräⁿ\ *n, often cap C&F* [F, lit., pure cabernet] (1952) **:** a dry red wine often used in blends (as with merlot or cabernet sauvignon)

cab•er•net sau•vi•gnon \ˌka-bər-ˈnā-sō-vē-ˈnyōⁿ\ *n, often cap C&S* [F] (1886) **:** a dry red wine made from a single widely cultivated variety of black grape — called also *cabernet*

CABG *abbr* coronary-artery bypass graft

[1]**cab•in** \ˈka-bən\ *n* [ME *cabane,* fr. MF, fr. Old Occitan *cabana* hut, fr. ML *capanna*] (14c) **1 a** (1) **:** a private room on a ship or boat (2) **:** a compartment below deck on a boat used for living accommodations **b :** the passenger or cargo compartment of a vehicle (as an airplane or automobile) **c :** the crew compartment of an exploratory vehicle (as a spacecraft) **2 :** a small one-story dwelling usu. of simple construction **3** *chiefly Brit* **:** CAB 3

[2]**cabin** *vi* (1586) **:** to live in or as if in a cabin ~ *vt* **:** CONFINE, RESTRAIN ⟨significantly ~*s* the discretion of administrators —A. M. Dershowitz⟩

cabin boy *n* (1670) **:** a boy working as servant on a ship

cabin car *n* (1871) **:** CABOOSE

cabin class *n* (1895) **:** a class of accommodations on a passenger ship superior to tourist class and inferior to first class

cabin cruiser *n* (1896) **:** CRUISER 1b

[1]**cab•i•net** \ˈkab-nit, ˈka-bə-\ *n* [MF, small room, dim. of MF dial. (Picard) *cabine* gambling house] (ca. 1550) **1 a :** a case or cupboard usu. having doors and shelves **b :** a collection of specimens esp. of biological or numismatic interest **c :** CONSOLE 4a **d :** a chamber having temperature and humidity controls and used esp. for incubating biological samples **2 a** *archaic* **:** a small room providing seclusion **b :** a small exhibition room in a museum **3 a** *archaic* (1) **:** the private room serving as council chamber of the chief councillors or ministers of a sovereign (2) **:** the consultations and actions of these councillors **b** (1) *often cap* **:** a body of advisers of a head of state (2) **:** a similar advisory council of a governor of a state or a mayor **c** *Brit* **:** a meeting of a cabinet **4** *NewEng* **:** MILK SHAKE

[2]**cabinet** *adj* (1631) **1 :** of or relating to a governmental cabinet **2 :** suitable by reason of size for a small room or by reason of attractiveness or perfection for preservation and display in a cabinet **3 a :** used or adapted for cabinetmaking **b :** done or used by a cabinetmaker

cab•i•net•mak•er \-ˌmā-kər\ *n* (1681) **:** a skilled woodworker who makes fine furniture — **cab•i•net•mak•ing** \-ˌmā-kiŋ\ *n*

cab•i•net•ry \ˈkab-ni-trē, ˈka-bə-\ *n* (1908) **:** CABINETWORK; *also* **:** CABINETS ⟨kitchen ~⟩

cab•i•net•work \-ˌwərk\ *n* (1732) **:** finished woodwork made by a cabinetmaker

cabin fever *n* (1918) **:** extreme irritability and restlessness from living in isolation or a confined indoor area for a prolonged time

cab•in•mate \ˈka-bən-ˌmāt\ *n* (1647) **:** one of two or more persons sharing the same cabin

[1]**ca•ble** \ˈkā-bəl\ *n, often attrib* [ME, fr. AF, fr. ML *capulum* lasso, fr. L *capere* to take — more at HEAVE] (13c) **1 a :** a strong rope esp. of 10 inches (25 centimeters) or more in circumference **b :** a cable-laid rope **c :** a wire rope or metal chain of great tensile strength **d :** a wire or wire rope by which force is exerted to control or operate a mechanism **2 :** CABLE LENGTH **3 a :** an assembly of electrical conductors insulated from each other but laid up together (as by being twisted around a central core) **b :** CABLEGRAM; *also* **:** a radio message or telegram **4 :** something resembling or fashioned like a cable ⟨a fiber-optic ~⟩ **5 :** CABLE TELEVISION ⟨a house with ~⟩

[2]**cable** *vb* **ca•bled; ca•bling** \ˈkā-b(ə-)liŋ\ *vt* (ca. 1500) **1 :** to fasten with or as if with a cable **2 :** to provide with a cable or cables **3 :** to telegraph by submarine cable **4 :** to make into a cable or into a form resembling a cable ~ *vi* **:** to communicate by a submarine cable — **ca•bler** \-b(ə-)lər\ *n*

cable car *n* (1874) **:** a vehicle moved by an endless cable: **a :** one suspended from an overhead cable **b :** one that moves along tracks

ca•ble•cast \ˈkā-bəl-ˌkast\ *n* [[1]*cable* + [4]*broadcast*] (1973) **:** a cable television transmission — **cablecast** *vb*

ca•ble•gram \ˈkā-bəl-ˌgram\ *n* (1867) **:** a message sent by a submarine telegraph cable

ca•ble–knit \ˈkā-bəl-ˌnit\ *adj* (1950) **:** having or made with a knitting stitch that produces a pattern resembling the twist of a usu. two-ply cable ⟨a ~ sweater⟩

ca•ble–laid \ˈkā-bəl-ˈlād\ *adj* (1723) **:** composed of three ropes laid together left-handed with each containing three strands twisted together

cable length *n* (1555) **:** a maritime unit of length variously reckoned as 100 fathoms, 120 fathoms, or 608 feet

cable modem *n* (1983) **:** a modem for connecting a computer to a network over a cable television line

cable television *n* (1951) **:** a system of television reception in which signals from distant stations are picked up by a master antenna and sent by cable to the individual receivers of paying subscribers — called also *cable TV*

ca•ble•way \ˈkā-bəl-ˌwā\ *n* (1891) **:** a suspended cable used as a track along which carriers can be pulled

cab•man \ˈkab-mən\ *n* (1831) **:** CABDRIVER

cab•o•chon \ˈka-bə-ˌshän\ *n* [MF, dim. of MF dial. (Picard) *caboche* head] (1825) **:** a gem or bead cut in convex form and highly polished but not faceted; *also* **:** this style of cutting — **cabochon** *adv*

ca•boo•dle \kə-ˈbü-dᵊl\ *n* [prob. fr. *ca-* (intensive prefix) + *boodle*] (1848) **:** COLLECTION, LOT ⟨sell the whole ~⟩

ca•boose \kə-ˈbüs\ *n* [prob. fr. D *kabuis, kombuis,* fr. MLG *kabūse*] (1732) **1 :** a ship's galley **2 :** a freight-train car attached usu. to the rear mainly for the use of the train crew **3 :** one that follows or brings up the rear **4 :** BUTTOCKS

cab•o•tage \ˈka-bə-ˌtäzh\ *n* [F, fr. *caboter* to sail along the coast] (1801) **1 :** trade or transport in coastal waters or airspace or between two points within a country **2 :** the right to engage in cabotage

ca•bret•ta \kə-ˈbre-tə\ *n* [modif. of Pg and Sp *cabra* goat] (1894) **:** a light soft leather from skins of hairy sheep

ca•bril•la \kə-ˈbrē-ə, -ˈbri-lə\ *n* [Sp, dim. of *cabra* goat, fr. L *capra* she-goat, fem. of *caper* he-goat — more at CAPRIOLE] (ca. 1839) **:** any of various sea basses (esp. of the genera *Epinephelus* and *Paralabrax*) of the Mediterranean, the California coast, and the warmer parts of the western Atlantic

cab•ri•ole \ˈka-brē-ˌōl\ *n* [F, caper] (ca. 1769) **1 :** a ballet leap in which one leg is extended in midair and the other struck against it **2 :** a curved furniture leg ending in an ornamental foot

cab•ri•o•let \ˌka-brē-ə-ˈlā\ *n* [F, fr. dim. of *cabriole* caper, alter. of MF *capriole*] (1770) **1 :** a light 2-wheeled one-horse carriage with a folding leather hood, a large apron, and upward-curving shafts **2 :** a convertible coupe

cab•stand \ˈkab-ˌstand\ *n* (1834) **:** a place where cabs await hire

cac- *or* **caco-** *comb form* [NL, fr. Gk *kak-, kako-,* fr. *kakos* bad] **:** bad ⟨*cacography*⟩

ca•ca \ˈkä-ˌkä\ *n* [baby talk] (1879) **:** EXCREMENT

ca' can•ny \kȯ-ˈka-nē\ *n* [Sc, vb., to proceed cautiously, fr. *ca'* (call) + *canny* careful] (1886) *Brit* **:** SLOWDOWN — **ca' canny** *vi, Brit*

ca•cao \kə-ˈkau̇, kə-ˈkā-(ˌ)ō\ *n, pl* **cacaos** [Sp, fr. Nahuatl *cacahuatl*] (1555) **1 :** the dried partly fermented fatty seeds of a So. American evergreen tree (*Theobroma cacao* of the family Sterculiaceae) that are used in making cocoa, chocolate, and cocoa butter — called also *cacao bean, cocoa bean* **2 :** a tree having small yellowish flowers followed by fleshy pods from which cacao is obtained

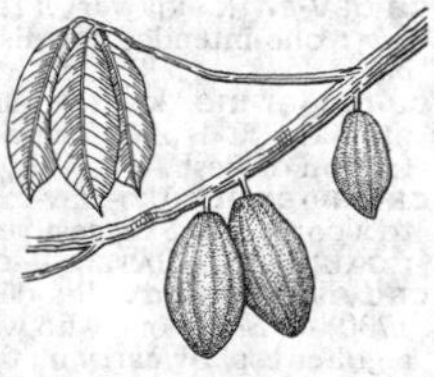

cacao 2

cacao butter *var of* COCOA BUTTER

cac•cia•to•re \ˌkä-chə-ˈtȯr-ē\ *adj* [It, fr. *cacciatore* hunter] (1930) **:** cooked with tomatoes and herbs and sometimes wine ⟨chicken ~⟩

ca•cha•ça \kə-ˈshä-sə\ *n* [Brazilian Pg] (1821) **:** a Brazilian liquor distilled from sugarcane

cach•a•lot \ˈka-shə-ˌlät, -ˌlō\ *n* [F] (1740) **:** SPERM WHALE

[1]**cache** \ˈkash\ *n* [F, fr. *cacher* to press, hide, fr. VL *coacticare* to press together, fr. L *coactare* to compel, freq. of *cogere* to compel — more at COGENT] (1797) **1 a :** a hiding place esp. for concealing and preserving provisions or implements **b :** a secure place of storage **2 :** something hidden or stored in a cache **3 :** a computer memory with very short access time used for storage of frequently or recently used instructions or data — called also *cache memory*

[2]**cache** *vt* **cached; cach•ing** (1805) **:** to place, hide, or store in a cache

ca•chec•tic \kə-ˈkek-tik, ka-\ *adj* [F *cachectique,* fr. L *cachecticus,* fr. Gk *kachektikos,* fr. *kak-* + *echein*] (1634) **:** affected by cachexia

cache•pot \ˈkash-ˌpät, ˈkash-ˌpō, ˈka-shə-\ *n* [F, fr. *cacher* to hide + *pot* pot] (1854) **:** an ornamental receptacle to hold and usu. to conceal a flowerpot

ca•chet \ka-ˈshā\ *n* [F, fr. *cacher*] (ca. 1639) **1 a :** a seal used esp. as a mark of official approval **b :** an indication of approval carrying great prestige **2 a :** a characteristic feature or quality conferring prestige **b :** PRESTIGE ⟨being rich . . . doesn't have the ~ it used to —Truman Capote⟩ **3 :** a medicinal preparation for swallowing consisting of a case usu. of rice-flour paste enclosing a medicine **4 a :** a design or inscription on an envelope to commemorate a postal or philatelic event **b :** an advertisement forming part of a postage meter impression **c :** a motto or slogan included in a postal cancellation

ca•chex•ia \kə-ˈkek-sē-ə, ka-\ *n* [LL *cachexia,* fr. Gk *kachexia* bad condition, fr. *kak-* cac- + *hexis* condition, fr. *echein* to have, be disposed — more at SCHEME] (ca. 1538) **:** general physical wasting and malnutrition usu. associated with chronic disease

cach•in•nate \ˈka-kə-ˌnāt\ *vi* **-nat•ed; -nat•ing** [L *cachinnatus,* pp. of *cachinnare,* of imit. origin] (1824) **:** to laugh loudly or immoderately — **cach•in•na•tion** \ˌka-kə-ˈnā-shən\ *n*

\ə\ **abut** \ᵊ\ **kitten,** F **table** \ər\ **further** \a\ **ash** \ā\ **ace** \ä\ **mop, mar**
\au̇\ **out** \ch\ **chin** \e\ **bet** \ē\ **easy** \g\ **go** \i\ **hit** \ī\ **ice** \j\ **job**
\ŋ\ **sing** \ō\ **go** \ȯ\ **law** \ȯi\ **boy** \th\ **thin** \t͟h\ **the** \ü\ **loot** \u̇\ **foot**
\y\ **yet** \zh\ **vision, beige** \k, ⁿ, œ, ue, ʸ\ *see* Guide to Pronunciation

ca·chou \ka-ˈshü, ˈka-ˌ\ *n* [F, fr. Pg *cachu,* fr. Malayalam *kāccu*] (ca. 1879) : a pill or pastille used to sweeten the breath

ca·cique \kə-ˈsēk\ *n* [Sp, fr. Taino, chief] (1555) **1 :** a native Indian chief in areas dominated primarily by a Spanish culture **2 :** a local political boss in Spain and Latin America — **ca·ciqu·ism** \-ˈsē-ˌki-zəm\ *n*

cack–hand·ed \ˈkak-ˌhan-dəd\ *adj* [E dial. *cack, keck* awkward] (1854) **1** *Brit* **:** LEFT-HANDED 1 **2** *Brit* **:** CLUMSY, AWKWARD

cack·le \ˈka-kəl\ *vi* **cack·led; cack·ling** \-k(ə-)liŋ\ [ME *cakelen,* of imit. origin] (13c) **1 :** to make the sharp broken noise or cry characteristic of a hen esp. after laying **2 :** to laugh esp. in a harsh or sharp manner **3 :** CHATTER — **cackle** *n* — **cack·ler** \-k(ə-)lər\ *n*

caco·de·mon \ˌka-kə-ˈdē-mən\ *n* [Gk *kakodaimōn,* fr. *kak-* cac- + *daimōn* spirit] (1594) **:** DEMON — **caco·de·mon·ic** \-di-ˈmä-nik\ *adj*

cac·o·dyl·ic acid \ˌka-kə-ˈdi-lik-\ *n* [G *Kakodyl* the radical $As(CH_3)_2$, fr. Gk *kakōdēs* foul-smelling, fr. *kak-* + *-ōdēs* (akin to Gk *ozein* to smell) — more at ODOR] (1850) **:** a toxic crystalline compound of arsenic $C_2H_7AsO_2$ used esp. as an herbicide

caco·ë·thes \ˌka-kə-ˈwē-(ˌ)thēz, -kō-ˈē-\ *n* [L, fr. Gk *kakoēthes* wickedness, fr. neut. of *kakoēthēs* malignant, fr. *kak-* cac- + *ēthos* character — more at SIB] (ca. 1587) **:** an insatiable desire **:** MANIA

ca·cog·ra·phy \ka-ˈkä-grə-fē\ *n* (1580) **1 :** bad spelling — compare ORTHOGRAPHY **2 :** bad handwriting — compare CALLIGRAPHY — **caco·graph·i·cal** \ˌka-kə-ˈgra-fi-kəl\ *adj*

cac·o·mis·tle \ˈka-kə-ˌmi-səl, ˌka-kə-ˈmis(t)-lē\ *n* [MexSp, fr. Nahuatl *tlahcomiztli,* fr. *tlahco* half + *miztli* mountain lion] (1869) **:** RINGTAIL 2

ca·coph·o·nous \ka-ˈkä-fə-nəs, -ˈkō- *also* -ˈka-\ *adj* [Gk *kakophōnos,* fr. *kak-* + *phōnē* voice, sound — more at BAN] (1797) **:** marked by cacophony **:** harsh-sounding — **ca·coph·o·nous·ly** *adv*

ca·coph·o·ny \-nē\ *n, pl* **-nies** (ca. 1656) **:** harsh or discordant sound **:** DISSONANCE 2; *specif* **:** harshness in the sound of words or phrases

cac·tus \ˈkak-təs\ *n, pl* **cac·ti** \-ˌtī, -(ˌ)tē\ *or* **cac·tus·es** *also* **cactus** [NL, genus name, fr. L, cardoon, fr. Gk *kaktos*] (1767) **:** any of a family (Cactaceae, the cactus family) of plants that have succulent stems and branches with scales or spines instead of leaves and are found esp. in dry areas (as deserts)

cactus wren *n* (1869) **:** a large harsh-voiced wren (*Campylorhynchus brunneicapillus*) esp. of arid regions of the southwestern U.S. and Mexico

ca·cu·mi·nal \ka-ˈkyü-mə-nᵊl, kə-\ *adj* [ISV, fr. L *cacumin-, cacumen* top, point] (1862) **:** RETROFLEX 2

cad \ˈkad\ *n* [E dial., unskilled assistant, short for Sc *caddie*] (1833) **1 :** an omnibus conductor **2 :** a man who acts with deliberate disregard for another's feelings or rights

CAD *abbr* computer-aided design

ca·das·tral \kə-ˈdas-trəl\ *adj* (1858) **1 :** of or relating to a cadastre **2 :** showing or recording property boundaries, subdivision lines, buildings, and related details — **ca·das·tral·ly** \-trə-lē\ *adv*

ca·das·tre \kə-ˈdas-tər\ *n* [F, fr. It *catastro,* fr. OIt *catastico,* fr. LGk *katastichon* notebook, fr. Gk *kata* by + *stichos* row, line — more at CATA-, DISTICH] (1804) **:** an official register of the quantity, value, and ownership of real estate used in apportioning taxes

ca·dav·er \kə-ˈda-vər\ *n* [L, fr. *cadere* to fall] (ca. 1500) **:** a dead body; *esp* **:** one intended for dissection — **ca·dav·er·ic** \-ˈdav-rik, -ˈda-və-\ *adj*

ca·dav·er·ine \kə-ˈda-və-ˌrēn\ *n* (1887) **:** a syrupy colorless poisonous ptomaine $C_5H_{14}N_2$ formed by decarboxylation of lysine esp. in putrefaction of flesh

ca·dav·er·ous \kə-ˈdav-rəs, -ˈda-vər-əs\ *adj* (1627) **1 a :** of or relating to a corpse **b :** suggestive of corpses or tombs **2 a :** PALLID, LIVID **b :** GAUNT, EMACIATED — **ca·dav·er·ous·ly** *adv*

cad·die *or* **cad·dy** \ˈka-dē\ *n, pl* **caddies** [F *cadet* military cadet] (ca. 1730) **1** *Scot* **:** one who waits about for odd jobs **2 a :** one who assists a golfer esp. by carrying the clubs **b :** a wheeled device for conveying things not readily carried by hand ⟨a luggage ~⟩ — **caddie** *or* **caddy** *vi*

[1]**cad·dis** *also* **cad·dice** \ˈka-dəs\ *n* [ME *cadas* cotton wool, fr. AF *cadaz,* fr. Old Occitan *cadarz*] (1530) **:** worsted yarn; *specif* **:** a worsted ribbon or binding formerly used for garters and girdles

[2]**caddis** *n* (1651) **:** CADDISWORM; *also* **:** CADDIS FLY

caddis fly *n* (1787) **:** any of an order (Trichoptera) of insects with four membranous usu. hairy wings, vestigial mouthparts, slender many-jointed antennae, and aquatic larvae — compare CADDISWORM

cad·dish \ˈka-dish\ *adj* (1868) **:** of, relating to, or being a cad ⟨~ behavior⟩ ⟨her ~ husband⟩ — **cad·dish·ly** *adv* — **cad·dish·ness** *n*

cad·dis·worm \ˈka-dəs-ˌwərm\ *n* [prob. alter. of obs. *codworm;* fr. the case or tube in which it lives] (1622) **:** the larva of a caddis fly that lives in and carries around a silken case covered with bits of debris

Cad·do \ˈka-(ˌ)dō\ *n, pl* **Caddo** *or* **Caddos** [AmerF *Cadaux,* modif. of AmerSp *Cadojodacho,* fr. Caddo *kaduhdā·čuˀ,* a Caddo tribe] (1805) **1 :** a member of a group of American Indian peoples of Louisiana, Arkansas, and eastern Texas **2 :** the language of the Caddo peoples

cad·dy \ˈka-dē\ *n, pl* **caddies** [Malay *kati* catty] (1792) **1 :** a small box, can, or chest used esp. to keep tea in **2 :** a container or device for storing or holding objects when they are not in use

cade \ˈkād\ *adj* [E dial. *cade* pet lamb, fr. ME *cad*] (1551) **:** left by its mother and reared by hand **:** PET ⟨a ~ lamb⟩

-cade *n comb form* [*cavalcade*] **:** procession ⟨motor*cade*⟩

ca·delle \kə-ˈdel\ *n* [F, fr. Occitan *cadello,* fr. L *catella,* fem. of *catellus* little dog, dim. of *catulus* young animal] (ca. 1861) **:** a small cosmopolitan black beetle (*Tenebroides mauritanicus*) destructive to stored grain

ca·dence \ˈkā-dᵊn(t)s\ *n* [ME, fr. OIt *cadenza,* fr. *cadere* to fall, fr. L — more at CHANCE] (14c) **1 a :** a rhythmic sequence or flow of sounds in language **b :** the beat, time, or measure of rhythmical motion or activity **2 a :** a falling inflection of the voice **b :** a concluding and usu. falling strain; *specif* **:** a musical chord sequence moving to a harmonic close or point of rest and giving the sense of harmonic completion **3 :** the modulated and rhythmic recurrence of a sound esp. in nature — **ca·denced** \-dᵊn(t)st\ *adj* — **ca·den·tial** \kā-ˈden(t)-shəl\ *adj*

ca·den·cy \ˈkā-dᵊn(t)-sē\ *n, pl* **-cies** (1627) **:** CADENCE

ca·dent \ˈkā-dᵊnt\ *adj* [L *cadent-, cadens,* prp. of *cadere*] (1605) **1** *archaic* **:** being in the process of falling ⟨with ~ tears fret channels in her cheeks —Shak.⟩ **2 :** having rhythmic cadence ⟨his ~ voice⟩

ca·den·za \kə-ˈden-zə\ *n* [It, cadence, cadenza] (1784) **1 :** a parenthetical flourish in an aria or other solo piece commonly just before a final or other important cadence **2 :** a technically brilliant sometimes improvised solo passage toward the close of a concerto **3 :** an exceptionally brilliant part of an artistic and esp. a literary work

cade oil \ˈkād-\ *n* [*cade* juniper, fr. MF, fr. Old Occitan, fr. ML *catanus*] (1880) **:** JUNIPER TAR

ca·det \kə-ˈdet\ *n, often attrib* [F, fr. Gascon *capdet* chief, fr. LL *capitellum,* dim. of L *capit-, caput* head — more at HEAD] (1610) **1 a :** a younger brother or son **b :** youngest son **c :** a younger branch of a family or a member of it **2 :** one in training for a military or naval commission; *esp* **:** a student in a service academy **3** *slang* **:** PIMP — **ca·det·ship** \-ˌship\ *n*

Ca·dette \kə-ˈdet\ *n* [fr. *cadet*] (1963) **:** a member of a program of the Girl Scouts for girls in the sixth through ninth grades in school

cadge \ˈkaj\ *vb* **cadged; cadg·ing** [back-formation fr. Sc *cadger* carrier, huckster, fr. ME *cadgear*] (ca. 1812) **:** BEG, SPONGE ⟨~ a free cup of coffee⟩ — **cadg·er** *n*

cad·mi·um \ˈkad-mē-əm\ *n* [NL, fr. L *cadmia* zinc oxide, fr. Gk *kadmeia,* lit., Theban (earth), fr. fem. of *kadmeios* Theban, fr. *Kadmos;* fr. the occurrence of its ores together with zinc oxide] (1822) **:** a bluish-white malleable ductile toxic bivalent metallic element used esp. in batteries, pigments, and protective platings — see ELEMENT table

cadmium sulfide *n* (1869) **:** a yellow-brown poisonous salt CdS used esp. in electronic parts, in photoelectric cells, and in medicine

Cad·mus \ˈkad-məs\ *n* [L, fr. Gk *Kadmos*] (14c) **:** the legendary founder of Thebes

cad·re \ˈka-ˌdrā, ˈkä-, -drē; *esp Brit* ˈkä-də(r), ˈkā-, -drə\ *n* [F, fr. It *quadro,* fr. L *quadrum* square — more at QUARREL] (1830) **1 :** FRAME, FRAMEWORK **2 :** a nucleus or core group esp. of trained personnel able to assume control and to train others; *broadly* **:** a group of people having some unifying relationship ⟨a ~ of lawyers⟩ **3 :** a cell of indoctrinated leaders active in promoting the interests of a revolutionary party **4 :** a member of a cadre

ca·du·ceus \kə-ˈdü-sē-əs, -ˈdyü-, -shəs\ *n, pl* **-cei** \-sē-ˌī\ [L, modif. of Gk *karykeion,* fr. *karyx, kēryx* herald; akin to Skt *kāru* singer] (1577) **1 :** the symbolic staff of a herald; *specif* **:** a representation of a staff with two entwined snakes and two wings at the top **2 :** an insignia bearing a caduceus and symbolizing a physician

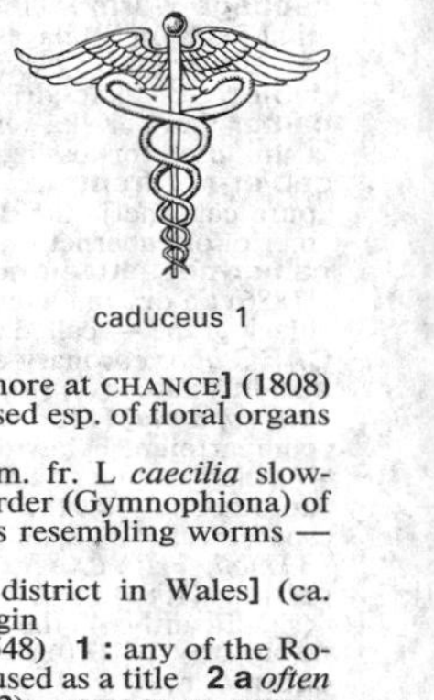

caduceus 1

ca·du·ci·ty \kə-ˈdü-sə-tē, -ˈdyü-\ *n* [F *caducité,* fr. *caduc* transitory, fr. L *caducus*] (1769) **1 :** SENILITY **2 :** the quality of being transitory or perishable

ca·du·cous \kə-ˈdü-kəs, -ˈdyü-\ *adj* [L *caducus* tending to fall, transitory, fr. *cadere* to fall — more at CHANCE] (1808) **:** falling off easily or before the usual time — used esp. of floral organs

caecal, caecum *var of* CECAL, CECUM

cae·cil·ian \si-ˈsil-yən, -ˈsēl-, -ˈsi-lē-ən\ *n* [ultim. fr. L *caecilia* slowworm, fr. *caecus* blind] (ca. 1879) **:** any of an order (Gymnophiona) of chiefly tropical burrowing limbless amphibians resembling worms — **caecilian** *adj*

Caer·phil·ly \kär-ˈfi-lē\ *n* [*Caerphilly,* urban district in Wales] (ca. 1893) **:** a mild white friable cheese of Welsh origin

Cae·sar \ˈsē-zər\ *n* [Gaius Julius *Caesar*] (ca. 1548) **1 :** any of the Roman emperors succeeding Augustus Caesar — used as a title **2 a** *often not cap* **:** a powerful ruler: (1) **:** EMPEROR (2) **:** AUTOCRAT, DICTATOR **b** [fr. the reference in Mt 22:21] **:** the civil power **:** a temporal ruler — **Cae·sar·e·an** *or* **Cae·sar·i·an** \si-ˈzer-ē-ən\ *adj*

caesarean *also* **caesarian** *var of* CESAREAN

caesarean section *var of* CESAREAN SECTION

Cae·sar·ism \ˈsē-zə-ˌri-zəm\ *n* (1857) **:** imperial authority or system **:** political absolutism **:** DICTATORSHIP — **Cae·sar·ist** \-zə-rist\ *n*

Caesar salad *n* [Caesar Cardini †1957 Am. (Ital.-born) restaurateur] (1946) **:** a tossed salad usu. made of romaine, garlic, anchovies, and croutons and dressed with olive oil, coddled egg, lemon juice, and grated cheese

cae·si·um *chiefly Brit var of* CESIUM

caes·pi·tose \ˈses-pə-ˌtōs\ *adj* [NL *caespitosus,* fr. L *caespit-, caespes* turf] (1830) **1 :** growing in clusters or tufts **2 :** forming a dense turf

cae·su·ra \si-ˈzyür-ə, -ˈzhür-\ *n, pl* **-suras** *or* **-su·rae** \-ˈzyür-(ˌ)ē, -ˈzhür-\ [LL, fr. L, act of cutting, fr. *caedere* to cut] (1556) **1** *in modern prosody* **:** a usu. rhetorical break in the flow of sound in the middle of a line of verse **2** *Greek & Latin prosody* **:** a break in the flow of sound in a verse caused by the ending of a word within a foot **3 :** BREAK, INTERRUPTION **4 :** a pause marking a rhythmic point of division in a melody — **cae·su·ral** \-ˈzyür-əl, -ˈzhür-\ *adj*

CAF *abbr* cost and freight

ca·fé *also* **ca·fe** \ka-ˈfā, kə-\ *n, often attrib* [F *café* coffee, café, fr. Turk *kahve* — more at COFFEE] (1802) **1 :** a usu. small and informal establishment serving various refreshments (as coffee); *broadly* **:** RESTAURANT **2 :** BARROOM **3 :** CABARET, NIGHTCLUB

CAFE *abbr* corporate average fuel economy

ca·fé au lait \(ˌ)ka-ˈfā-ō-ˈlā\ *n* [F, coffee with milk] (1763) **1 :** coffee with usu. hot milk in about equal parts **2 :** the color of coffee with milk

ca·fé noir \-ˈnwär\ *n* [F, black coffee] (1845) **:** coffee without milk or cream; *also* **:** DEMITASSE

café society *n* (1937) **:** society of persons who are regular patrons of fashionable cafés

[1]**caf·e·te·ria** \ˌka-fə-ˈtir-ē-ə\ *n* [AmerSp *cafetería* coffeehouse, fr. *cafetera* coffee maker, fr. F *cafetière,* fr. *café*] (1894) **1 :** a restaurant in which the customers serve themselves or are served at a counter and take the food to tables to eat **2 :** LUNCHROOM 2

[2]**cafeteria** *adj* (1951) **:** providing a selection from which a choice may be made ⟨~ benefit plan⟩ ⟨a ~ curriculum⟩

caf·e·te·ria–style \-ˌstī(-ə)l\ *adj* (1952) **:** CAFETERIA ⟨~ benefits⟩

caf·e·to·ri·um \-ˈtȯr-ē-əm\ *n* [blend of *cafeteria* and *auditorium*] (1952) **:** a large room (as in a school building) designed for use both as a cafeteria and an auditorium

caff \ˈkaf\ *n* (1931) *Brit* **:** CAFÉ 1

caf·fein·at·ed \ˈka-fə-ˌnā-təd, -fē-ə-\ *adj* (1970) **1 :** stimulated by or as if by caffeine ⟨~ workers⟩ ⟨~ rhythms of electronic music —Marc Weingarten⟩ **2 :** containing caffeine ⟨~ coffee⟩

caf·feine \ka-ˈfēn, ˈka-ˌ\ *n* [G *Kaffein,* fr. *Kaffee* coffee, fr. F *café*] (ca. 1823) **:** a bitter alkaloid $C_8H_{10}N_4O_2$ found esp. in coffee, tea, cacao, and kola nuts and used medicinally as a stimulant and diuretic
caf·fe lat·te \ˈkä-(ˌ)fā-ˈlä-(ˌ)tā\ *n* [It *caffelatte,* short for *caffè e latte* coffee and milk] (1927) **:** espresso mixed with hot or steamed milk
caf·tan *also* **kaf·tan** \ˈkaf-(ˌ)tan\ *n* [Russ & Turk; Russ *kaftan,* fr. Turk, fr. Pers *qaftān*] (1591) **:** a usu. cotton or silk ankle-length garment with long sleeves that is common throughout the Levant
CAG *abbr* carrier air group
[1]**cage** \ˈkāj\ *n* [ME, fr. AF, fr. L *cavea* cavity, cage, fr. *cavus* hollow — more at CAVE] (13c) **1 :** a box or enclosure having some openwork for confining or carrying animals (as birds) **2 a :** a barred cell for confining prisoners **b :** a fenced area for prisoners of war **3 :** a framework serving as support ⟨the steel ~ of a skyscraper⟩ **4 a :** an enclosure resembling a cage in form or purpose ⟨a cashier's ~⟩ **b :** an arrangement of atoms or molecules so bonded as to enclose a space in which another atom or ion (as of a metal) can reside **5 a :** BATTING CAGE **b :** a goal consisting of posts or a frame with a net attached (as in ice hockey) **6 :** a large building containing an area for practicing outdoor sports and often adapted for indoor events — **cage·ful** \-ˌfu̇l\ *n*
[2]**cage** *vt* **caged; cag·ing** (1556) **1 :** to confine or keep in or as if in a cage **2 :** to drive (as a puck) into a cage and score a goal
cage·ling \ˈkāj-liŋ\ *n* (1823) **:** a caged bird
ca·gey *also* **ca·gy** \ˈkā-jē\ *adj* **ca·gi·er; -est** [origin unknown] (ca. 1893) **1 :** hesitant about committing oneself ⟨officials are ~ about giving out details⟩ **2 a :** wary of being trapped or deceived **:** SHREWD ⟨a ~ consumer⟩ **b :** marked by cleverness ⟨a ~ reply⟩ — **ca·gi·ly** \-jə-lē\ *adv* — **ca·gi·ness** *also* **ca·gey·ness** \-jē-nəs\ *n*
CAGS *abbr* Certificate of Advanced Graduate Study
ca·hier \kä-ˈyā, kī-ˈā\ *n* [F, fr. MF *quaer, caier* quire — more at QUIRE] (1789) **:** a report or memorial concerning policy esp. of a parliamentary body
ca·hoot \kə-ˈhüt\ *n* [perh. fr. F *cahute* cabin, hut] (1829) **:** PARTNERSHIP, LEAGUE — usu. used in pl. ⟨they're in ~*s*⟩
ca·how \kə-ˈhau̇\ *n* [imit.] (1615) **:** a dark-colored petrel (*Pterodroma cahow*) formerly abundant in Bermuda but now nearly extinct
CAI *abbr* computer-aided instruction; computer-assisted instruction
cai·man *also* **cay·man** \ˈkā-mən; kā-ˈman, kī-\ *n* [Sp *caimán,* prob. fr. Carib *caymán*] (1577) **:** any of several Central and So. American crocodilians (genera *Caiman, Melanosuchus,* and *Paleosuchus*) similar to alligators
Cain \ˈkān\ *n* [Heb *Qayin*] (bef. 12c) **:** the brother and murderer of Abel
-caine *n comb form* [G *-kain,* fr. *kokain* cocaine] **:** synthetic alkaloid anesthetic ⟨pro*caine*⟩
cai·pi·ri·nha \ˌkī-pə-ˈrēn-yə\ *n* [Brazilian Pg, fr. *caipira* backwoodsman, rustic] (1973) **:** a cocktail consisting of lime, sugar, and rum
ca·ïque \kä-ˈēk, ˈkīk\ *n* [F, fr. Turk *kayık*] (1625) **1 :** a light skiff used on the Bosporus **2 :** a Levantine sailing vessel
caird \ˈkerd\ *n* [ScGael *ceard* craftsman; akin to Gk *kerdos* profit] (1663) *Scot* **:** a traveling tinker; *also* **:** TRAMP, GYPSY
cairn \ˈkern\ *n* [ME (Sc) *carne,* fr. ScGael *carn;* akin to OIr & W *carn* cairn] (15c) **:** a heap of stones piled up as a memorial or as a landmark — **cairned** \ˈkernd\ *adj*
cairn·gorm \ˈkern-ˌgȯrm\ *n* [*Cairngorm,* mountain in Scotland] (1794) **:** a yellow or smoky-brown crystalline quartz
cairn terrier *n* [fr. its use in hunting among cairns] (1910) **:** any of a breed of small compactly built hard-coated terriers of Scottish origin
cais·son \ˈkā-ˌsän, -sᵊn, *Brit also* kə-ˈsün\ *n* [F, fr. MF, fr. Old Occitan, fr. *caissa* chest, fr. L *capsa* — more at CASE] (ca. 1702) **1 a :** a chest to hold ammunition **b :** a usu. 2-wheeled vehicle for artillery ammunition attachable to a horse-drawn limber; *also* **:** a limber with its attached caisson **2 a :** a watertight chamber used in construction work under water or as a foundation **b :** a hollow floating box or a boat used as a floodgate for a dock or basin **3 :** COFFER 3
caisson disease *n* (1873) **:** DECOMPRESSION SICKNESS
cai·tiff \ˈkā-təf\ *adj* [ME *caitif,* fr. AF *caitif, chaitif* wretched, despicable, fr. L *captivus* captive] (14c) **:** COWARDLY, DESPICABLE — **caitiff** *n*
caj·e·put \ˈka-jə-pət, -ˌpu̇t\ *n* [ultim. fr. Malay *kayu putih,* fr. *kayu* wood, tree + *putih* white] (1822) **:** an Australian and southeast Asian tree (*Melaleuca quinquenervia* syn. *M. leucadendron*) of the myrtle family that yields a pungent medicinal oil and has been introduced into Florida
ca·jole \kə-ˈjōl\ *vt* **ca·joled; ca·jol·ing** [F *cajoler*] (1630) **1 a :** to persuade with flattery or gentle urging esp. in the face of reluctance **:** COAX ⟨had to ~ them into going⟩ **b :** to obtain from someone by gentle persuasion ⟨~*ed* money from his parents⟩ **2 :** to deceive with soothing words or false promises — **ca·jole·ment** \-ˈjōl-mənt\ *n* — **ca·jol·er** *n* — **ca·jol·ery** \-ˈjō-lə-rē\ *n*
syn CAJOLE, COAX, SOFT-SOAP, BLANDISH, WHEEDLE mean to influence or persuade by pleasing words or actions. CAJOLE suggests the deliberate use of flattery to persuade in the face of reluctance or reasonable objections ⟨*cajoled* him into cheating on the final exam⟩. COAX implies gentle and persistent words or actions employed to produce a desired effect ⟨*coaxed* the cat out of the tree⟩. SOFT-SOAP refers to using smooth and somewhat insincere talk usu. for personal gain ⟨politicians *soft-soaping* eligible voters⟩. BLANDISH implies a more open desire to win a person over by effusive praise and affectionate actions ⟨legislators *blandished* with promises of support⟩. WHEEDLE suggests more strongly than *cajole* the use of seductive appeal or artful words in persuading ⟨hucksters *wheedling* her life's savings out of her⟩.
[1]**Ca·jun** *also* **Ca·jan** \ˈkā-jən\ *n* [alter. of *Acadian*] (1868) **:** a Louisianian descended from French-speaking immigrants from Acadia
[2]**Cajun** *adj* (1880) **1 :** of, relating to, or characteristic of the Cajuns **2 :** of, relating to, or prepared in a style of cooking originating among the Cajuns and characterized by the use of hot seasonings (as cayenne pepper)
[1]**cake** \ˈkāk\ *n* [ME, fr. ON *kaka;* akin to OHG *kuocho* cake] (13c) **1 a :** a breadlike food made from a dough or batter that is usu. fried or baked in small flat shapes and is often unleavened **b :** a sweet baked food made from a dough or thick batter usu. containing flour and sugar and often shortening, eggs, and a raising agent (as baking powder) **c :** a flattened usu. round mass of food that is baked or fried ⟨a fish ~⟩ **2 a :** a block of compacted or congealed matter ⟨a ~ of ice⟩ **b :** a hard or brittle layer or deposit **3 :** something easily done ⟨after so much studying, the test was ~⟩ — **cak·ey** \ˈkā-kē\ *adj*
[2]**cake** *vb* **caked; cak·ing** *vt* (1607) **1 :** ENCRUST ⟨*caked* with dust⟩ **2 :** to fill (a space) with a packed mass ~ *vi* **:** to form or harden into a mass
cake·walk \ˈkāk-ˌwȯk\ *n* (1874) **1 :** a black American entertainment having a cake as prize for the most accomplished steps and figures in walking **2 :** a stage dance developed from walking steps and figures typically involving a high prance with backward tilt **3 a :** a one-sided contest **b :** an easy task — **cakewalk** *vi* — **cake·walk·er** *n*
cal *abbr* small calorie
Cal *abbr* **1** California **2** large calorie
Cal·a·bar bean \ˈka-lə-ˌbär-\ *n* [*Calabar,* Nigeria] (1864) **:** the dark brown highly poisonous leguminous seed of a tropical west African woody vine (*Physostigma venenosum*) that is used as a source of physostigmine and was used formerly as an ordeal poison in African witchcraft trials
cal·a·bash \ˈka-lə-ˌbash\ *n* [F & Sp; F *calebasse* gourd, fr. Sp *calabaza*] (1596) **1 :** a tropical American tree (*Crescentia cujete*) of the bignonia family; *also* **:** its large hard-shelled globose fruit **2 :** GOURD; *esp* **:** one whose hard shell is used for a utensil **3 :** a utensil (as a bottle or dipper) made from the shell of a calabash
ca·la·ba·za \ˌka-lə-ˈbä-zə, -sə\ *n* [Sp] (1970) **:** a large winter squash (*Cucurbita moschata*) that resembles a pumpkin and is typically grown in the West Indies and tropical America
cal·a·boose \ˈka-lə-ˌbüs\ *n* [Sp *calabozo* dungeon] (1792) **:** JAIL; *esp* **:** a local jail
ca·la·di·um \kə-ˈlā-dē-əm\ *n* [NL, genus name, fr. Malay *kĕladi,* an aroid plant] (1881) **:** any of a genus (*Caladium* and esp. *C. bicolor*) of tropical American plants of the arum family widely cultivated for their showy variably colored leaves
cal·a·man·der \ˈka-lə-ˌman-dər, ˌka-lə-ˈ\ *n* [prob. fr. D *kalamanderhout* calamander wood] (1804) **:** the hazel-brown black-striped wood of a southeast Asian tree (genus *Diospyros* and esp. *D. quaesita*) that is used in furniture manufacturing
cal·a·mari \ˌkä-lə-ˈmär-ē, ˈka-lə-ˌmer-ē\ *n* [It, pl. of *calamaro, calamaio,* fr. ML *calamarium* ink pot, fr. L *calamus;* fr. the inky substance the squid secretes] (ca. 1961) **:** squid used as food
cal·a·mary \ˈka-lə-ˌmer-ē\ *n, pl* **-mar·ies** [ML *calamarium*] (1567) **:** SQUID
calamata *var of* KALAMATA
cal·a·mine \ˈka-lə-ˌmīn, -mən\ *n* [ME *calamyn* ore of zinc, fr. ML *calamina,* alter. of L *cadmia* — more at CADMIUM] (15c) **:** a mixture of zinc oxide with a small amount of ferric oxide used in lotions, liniments, and ointments
cal·a·mint \ˈka-lə-ˌmint\ *n* [ME *calament,* fr. AF *calamente,* fr. ML *calamentum,* fr. Gk *kalaminthē*] (14c) **:** any of a genus (*Calamintha* syn. *Satureja,* esp. *C. nepeta*) of Eurasian perennial mints
cal·a·mite \ˈka-lə-ˌmīt\ *n* [NL *Calamites,* genus of fossil plants, fr. L *calamus*] (1837) **:** a Paleozoic fossil plant (esp. genus *Calamites*) resembling a giant horsetail
ca·lam·i·tous \kə-ˈla-mə-təs\ *adj* (1545) **:** being, causing, or accompanied by calamity ⟨~ events⟩ — **ca·lam·i·tous·ly** *adv*
ca·lam·i·ty \kə-ˈla-mə-tē\ *n, pl* **-ties** [ME *calamytey,* fr. L *calamitat-, calamitas;* perh. akin to L *clades* destruction] (15c) **1 :** a state of deep distress or misery caused by major misfortune or loss **2 :** a disastrous event marked by great loss and lasting distress and suffering ⟨*calamities* of nature⟩ ⟨an economic ~⟩
cal·a·mon·din \ˌka-lə-ˈmän-dən\ *n* [Tag *kalamunding*] (ca. 1928) **:** a small hybrid citrus tree (*Citrofortunella mitis* syn. *Citrus mitis*); *also* **:** its small tart fruit resembling the mandarin and used esp. in marmalades
cal·a·mus \ˈka-lə-məs\ *n, pl* **-mi** \-ˌmī, -ˌmē\ [L, reed, reed pen, fr. Gk *kalamos* — more at HAULM] (14c) **1 a :** SWEET FLAG **b :** the aromatic peeled and dried rhizome of the sweet flag that is the source of a carcinogenic essential oil **2 :** the hollow basal portion of a feather below the vane **:** QUILL
ca·lash \kə-ˈlash\ *n* [F *calèche,* fr. G *Kalesche,* fr. Czech *kolesa* wheels, carriage; akin to Gk *kyklos* wheel — more at WHEEL] (1679) **1 a :** a light small-wheeled 4-passenger carriage with a folding top **b :** CALÈCHE 1b **2 :** a large hood worn by women in the 18th century
calc *abbr* calculate; calculated
calc- *or* **calci-** *comb form* [L *calc-, calx* lime — more at CHALK] **:** calcium **:** calcium salt ⟨*calc*ic⟩ ⟨*calc*ify⟩
cal·ca·ne·al \kal-ˈkā-nē-əl\ *adj* (ca. 1849) **:** relating to the heel or calcaneus
cal·ca·ne·um \-nē-əm\ *n, pl* **-nea** \-nē-ə\ [L, heel — more at CALK] (ca. 1751) **:** CALCANEUS
cal·ca·ne·us \-nē-əs\ *n, pl* **-nei** \-nē-ˌī\ [LL, heel, alter. of L *calcaneum*] (ca. 1925) **:** a tarsal bone that in humans is the large bone of the heel
cal·car·e·ous \kal-ˈker-ē-əs\ *adj* [L *calcarius* of lime, fr. *calc-, calx*] (1677) **1 a :** resembling calcite or calcium carbonate esp. in hardness **b :** consisting of or containing calcium carbonate; *also* **:** containing calcium **2 :** growing on limestone or in soil impregnated with lime — **cal·car·e·ous·ly** *adv*
cal·cic \ˈkal-sik\ *adj* (1868) **:** derived from or containing calcium or lime **:** rich in calcium
cal·ci·cole \ˈkal-sə-ˌkōl\ *n* [F, calcicolous, fr. *calc-* + *-cole* -colous] (1882) **:** a plant normally growing on calcareous soils — **cal·cic·o·lous** \kal-ˈsi-kə-ləs\ *adj*
cal·cif·er·ol \kal-ˈsi-fə-ˌrȯl, -ˌrōl\ *n* [*calci*ferous + ergoster*ol*] (1931) **:** an alcohol $C_{28}H_{43}OH$ usu. prepared by irradiation of ergosterol and used as a dietary supplement in nutrition and medicinally in the control of rickets and related disorders — called also *vitamin D_2*
cal·cif·er·ous \kal-ˈsi-f(ə-)rəs\ *adj* (1799) **:** producing or containing calcium carbonate
cal·cif·ic \kal-ˈsi-fik\ *adj* [*calcify*] (1861) **:** involving or caused by calcification ⟨~ lesions⟩

\ə\ **abut** \ᵊ\ **kitten,** F **table** \ər\ **further** \a\ **ash** \ā\ **ace** \ä\ **mop, mar** \au̇\ **out** \ch\ **chin** \e\ **bet** \ē\ **easy** \g\ **go** \i\ **hit** \ī\ **ice** \j\ **job** \ŋ\ **sing** \ō\ **go** \ȯ\ **law** \ȯi\ **boy** \th\ **thin** \t͟h\ **the** \ü\ **loot** \u̇\ **foot** \y\ **yet** \zh\ **vision, beige** \k̟, ⁿ, œ, ue, ʸ\ *see* Guide to Pronunciation

cal·ci·fuge \ˈkal-sə-ˌfyüj\ *n* [F, calcifugous, fr. *calc-* + L *fugere* to flee — more at FUGITIVE] (1926) **:** a plant not normally growing on calcareous soils — **calcifuge** *also* **cal·cif·u·gous** \kal-ˈsi-fyə-gəs\ *adj*
cal·ci·fy \ˈkal-sə-ˌfī\ *vb* **-fied; -fy·ing** *vt* (1854) **1 :** to make calcareous by deposit of calcium salts **2 :** to make inflexible or unchangeable ~ *vi* **1 :** to become calcareous **2 :** to become inflexible and changeless **:** HARDEN — **cal·ci·fi·ca·tion** \ˌkal-sə-fə-ˈkā-shən\ *n*
cal·ci·mine \ˈkal-sə-ˌmīn\ *n* [alter. of *kalsomine,* of unknown origin] (ca. 1859) **:** a white or tinted wash of glue, whiting or zinc white, and water that is used esp. on plastered surfaces — **calcimine** *vt*
cal·ci·na·tion \ˌkal-sə-ˈnā-shən\ *n* (14c) **:** the act or process of calcining **:** the state of being calcined
[1]**cal·cine** \kal-ˈsīn, ˈkal-ˌ\ *vb* **cal·cined; cal·cin·ing** [ME *calcenen,* fr. ML *calcinare,* fr. LL *calcina* lime, fr. L *calc-, calx*] *vt* (14c) **:** to heat (as inorganic materials) to a high temperature but without fusing in order to drive off volatile matter or to effect changes (as oxidation or pulverization) ~ *vi* **:** to undergo calcination
[2]**cal·cine** \ˈkal-ˌsīn\ *n* (ca. 1909) **:** a product (as a metal oxide) of calcination or roasting
cal·ci·no·sis \ˌkal-sə-ˈnō-səs\ *n, pl* **-no·ses** \-ˌsēz\ [NL, irreg. (influenced by ISV *calcine*) fr. *calc-* + *-osis*] (ca. 1929) **:** the abnormal deposition of calcium salts in a part or tissue of the body
cal·cite \ˈkal-ˌsīt\ *n* (1849) **:** a mineral $CaCO_3$ consisting of calcium carbonate crystallized in hexagonal form and including common limestone, chalk, and marble — compare ARAGONITE — **cal·cit·ic** \kal-ˈsi-tik\ *adj*
cal·ci·to·nin \ˌkal-sə-ˈtō-nən\ *n* [*calci-* + *-tonin* (as in *serotonin*)] (1961) **:** a polypeptide hormone esp. from the thyroid gland that lowers the level of calcium in the blood plasma — called also *thyrocalcitonin*
cal·ci·um \ˈkal-sē-əm\ *n, often attrib* [NL, fr. L *calc-, calx* lime] (1808) **:** a silver-white divalent metallic element of the alkaline-earth group occurring only in combination — see ELEMENT table
calcium carbide *n* (ca. 1888) **:** a usu. dark gray crystalline compound CaC_2 used esp. for the generation of acetylene and for making calcium cyanamide
calcium carbonate *n* (1869) **:** a compound $CaCO_3$ found in nature as calcite and aragonite and in plant ashes, bones, and shells and used esp. in making lime and portland cement and as a gastric antacid
calcium channel blocker *n* (1980) **:** any of a class of drugs (as verapamil) that prevent or slow the influx of calcium ions into smooth muscle cells and are used esp. to treat some forms of angina pectoris and some cardiac arrhythmias
calcium chloride *n* (1869) **:** a white deliquescent salt $CaCl_2$ used in its anhydrous state as a drying and dehumidifying agent and in a hydrated state for controlling dust and ice on roads
calcium cyanamide *n* (ca. 1893) **:** a compound $CaCN_2$ used as a fertilizer and as a weed killer and as a source of other nitrogen compounds
calcium gluconate *n* (1884) **:** a white powdery salt $CaC_{12}H_{22}O_{14}$ used esp. to supplement bodily calcium stores
calcium hydroxide *n* (ca. 1889) **:** a white crystalline strong alkali $Ca(OH)_2$ that is used esp. to make mortar and plaster and to soften water
calcium hypochlorite *n* (1869) **:** a white powder $CaCl_2O_2$ used esp. as a bleaching agent and disinfectant
calcium oxalate *n* (1873) **:** a crystalline salt CaC_2O_4 normally deposited in many plant cells and in animals sometimes excreted in urine or retained in the form of urinary calculi
calcium oxide *n* (1869) **:** a caustic solid CaO that is white when pure and that is the chief constituent of lime
calcium phosphate *n* (1869) **:** any of various phosphates of calcium: as **a :** the phosphate $CaH_4P_2O_8$ used as a fertilizer and in baking powder **b :** the phosphate $CaHPO_4$ used in pharmaceutical preparations and animal feeds **c :** the phosphate $Ca_3P_2O_8$ used as a fertilizer **d :** the naturally occurring phosphate $Ca_5(F,Cl,OH,½CO_3)(PO_4)_3$ that contains other elements or radicals and is the chief constituent of phosphate rock, bones, and teeth
calcium silicate *n* (1869) **:** any of several silicates of calcium used esp. in construction materials (as portland cement)
calcium sulfate *n* (1869) **:** a white salt $CaSO_4$ that occurs esp. as anhydrite, gypsum, and plaster of paris and that in hydrated form is used as a building material and in anhydrous form is used as a drying agent
cal·cu·la·ble \ˈkal-kyə-lə-bəl\ *adj* (ca. 1734) **1 :** subject to or ascertainable by calculation **2 :** that may be counted on **:** DEPENDABLE
cal·cu·late \ˈkal-kyə-ˌlāt\ *vb* **-lat·ed; -lat·ing** [L *calculatus,* pp. of *calculare,* fr. *calculus* pebble (used in reckoning), perh. irreg. dim. of *calc-, calx* lime — more at CHALK] *vt* (1570) **1 a :** to determine by mathematical processes ⟨~ the rate of acceleration⟩ **b :** to reckon by exercise of practical judgment **:** ESTIMATE ⟨~ the likelihood of success⟩ **c :** to solve or probe the meaning of **:** FIGURE OUT ⟨trying to ~ his expression —Hugh MacLennan⟩ **2 :** to design or adapt for a purpose ⟨he carefully *calculated* the timing of his arrival for maximum impact⟩ **3 a :** to judge to be true or probable **b :** INTEND ⟨I ~ to do it or perish in the attempt —Mark Twain⟩ ~ *vi* **1 a :** to make a calculation **b :** to forecast consequences **2 :** COUNT, RELY
cal·cu·lat·ed \-ˌlā-təd\ *adj* (1722) **1 :** APT, LIKELY **2 a :** worked out by mathematical calculation **b :** engaged in, undertaken, or displayed after reckoning or estimating the statistical probability of success or failure ⟨a ~ risk⟩ **3 a :** planned or contrived to accomplish a purpose **b :** DELIBERATE, INTENDED ⟨a ~ attempt to deceive voters⟩ — **cal·cu·lat·ed·ly** *adv* — **cal·cu·lat·ed·ness** *n*
cal·cu·lat·ing \-ˌlā-tiŋ\ *adj* (1710) **1 :** making calculations ⟨~ machine⟩ **2 :** marked by prudent analysis or by shrewd consideration of self-interest **:** SCHEMING — **cal·cu·lat·ing·ly** \-tiŋ-lē\ *adv*
cal·cu·la·tion \ˌkal-kyə-ˈlā-shən\ *n* (14c) **1 a :** the process or an act of calculating **b :** the result of an act of calculating **2 a :** studied care in analyzing or planning **b :** cold heartless planning to promote self-interest — **cal·cu·la·tion·al** \-ˈlāsh-nəl, -ˈlā-shə-nᵊl\ *adj*
cal·cu·la·tor \ˈkal-kyə-ˌlā-tər\ *n* (14c) **:** one that calculates: as **a :** a usu. electronic device for performing mathematical calculations **b :** a person who operates a calculator
cal·cu·lous \ˈkal-kyə-ləs\ *adj* (1605) **:** caused or characterized by a calculus or calculi
cal·cu·lus \-ləs\ *n, pl* **-li** \-ˌlī, -ˌlē\ *also* **-lus·es** [L, stone (used in reckoning)] (1666) **1 a :** a method of computation or calculation in a special notation (as of logic or symbolic logic) **b :** the mathematical methods comprising differential and integral calculus — often used with *the* **2 :** CALCULATION **3 a :** a concretion usu. of mineral salts around organic material found esp. in hollow organs or ducts **b :** [1]TARTAR 2 **4 :** a system or arrangement of intricate or interrelated parts
calculus of variations (1837) **:** a branch of mathematics concerned with applying the methods of calculus to finding the maxima and minima of a function which depends for its values on another function or a curve
cal·de·ra \kal-ˈder-ə, kȯl-, -ˈdir-\ *n* [Sp, lit., caldron, fr. LL *caldaria* — more at CAULDRON] (1691) **:** a volcanic crater that has a diameter many times that of the vent and is formed by collapse of the central part of a volcano or by explosions of extraordinary violence
caldron *var of* CAULDRON
ca·lèche *or* **ca·leche** \kə-ˈlesh, -ˈlash\ *n* [F *calèche* — more at CALASH] (1666) **1 a :** CALASH 1a **b :** a 2-wheeled horse-drawn vehicle with a driver's seat on the splashboard used in Quebec **2 :** CALASH 2
cal·e·fac·to·ry \ˌka-lə-ˈfak-t(ə-)rē\ *n, pl* **-ries** [ML *calefactorium,* fr. L *calefacere* to warm — more at CHAFE] (ca. 1681) **:** a monastery room warmed and used as a sitting room
[1]**cal·en·dar** \ˈka-lən-dər\ *n* [ME *calender,* fr. AF or ML; AF *kalender,* fr. ML *kalendarium,* fr. L, moneylender's account book, fr. *kalendae* calends] (13c) **1 :** a system for fixing the beginning, length, and divisions of the civil year and arranging days and longer divisions of time (as weeks and months) in a definite order — see MONTH table **2 :** a tabular register of days according to a system usu. covering one year and referring the days of each month to the days of the week **3 :** an orderly list: as **a :** a list of cases to be tried in court **b :** a list of bills or other items reported out of committee for consideration by a legislative assembly **c :** a list or schedule of planned events or activities giving dates and details **4** *Brit* **:** a university catalog
[2]**calendar** *vt* **-dared; -dar·ing** \-d(ə-)riŋ\ (15c) **:** to enter in a calendar
calendar year *n* (ca. 1909) **1 :** a period of a year beginning and ending with the dates that are conventionally accepted as marking the beginning and end of a numbered year **2 :** a period of time equal in length to that of the year in the calendar conventionally in use
[1]**cal·en·der** \ˈka-lən-dər\ *vt* **-dered; -der·ing** \-d(ə-)riŋ\ [MF *calandrer,* fr. *calandre* machine for calendering, fr. VL **colendra* cylinder, modif. of Gk *kylindros* — more at CYLINDER] (1513) **:** to press (as cloth, rubber, or paper) between rollers or plates in order to smooth and glaze or to thin into sheets — **cal·en·der·er** \-dər-ər\ *n*
[2]**calender** *n* (1688) **:** a machine for calendering something
[3]**calender** *n* [Pers *qalandar*] (1621) **:** a member of a Sufic order of wandering mendicant dervishes
ca·len·dri·cal \kə-ˈlen-dri-kəl, ka-\ *also* **ca·len·dric** \-drik\ *adj* (ca. 1843) **:** of, relating to, characteristic of, or used in a calendar
ca·lends *or* **ka·lends** \ˈka-lən(d)z, ˈkā-\ *n pl but sing or pl in constr* [ME *kalendes,* fr. L *kalendae, calendae*] (14c) **:** the first day of the ancient Roman month from which days were counted backward to the ides
ca·len·du·la \kə-ˈlen-jə-lə, -dyu̇-lə\ *n* [NL, genus name, fr. ML, fr. L *calendae* calends] (1789) **:** any of a small genus (*Calendula*) of yellow-rayed composite herbs of temperate regions
cal·en·ture \ˈka-lən-ˌchu̇r\ *n* [Sp *calentura,* fr. *calentar* to heat, fr. L *calent-, calens,* prp. of *calēre* to be warm — more at LEE] (1582) **:** a fever formerly supposed to affect sailors in the tropics
[1]**calf** \ˈkaf, ˈkäf, *dial also* ˈkāf\ *n, pl* **calves** \ˈkavz, ˈka̍vz, ˈkävz\ *also* **calfs** *often attrib* [ME, fr. OE *cealf;* akin to OHG *kalb* calf] (bef. 12c) **1 a :** the young of the domestic cow; *also* **:** that of a closely related mammal (as a bison) **b :** the young of various large animals (as the elephant or whale) **2** *pl* **calfs :** the hide of the domestic calf; *esp* **:** CALFSKIN **3 :** an awkward or silly youth — **calf·like** \ˈkaf-ˌlīk, ˈkäf-, *dial also* ˈkāf-\ *adj* — **in calf :** PREGNANT — used of a cow
[2]**calf** *n, pl* **calves** \ˈkavz, ˈkävz\ [ME, fr. ON *kālfi*] (14c) **:** the fleshy back part of the leg below the knee
calf–love \-ˌləv\ *n* (1823) **:** PUPPY LOVE
calf's–foot jelly \ˈkavz-ˌfu̇t-, ˈkafs-, ˈkävz-, ˈkäfs- *also* ˈkāvz-\ *n* (1775) **:** jelly made from gelatin obtained by boiling calves' feet
calf·skin \ˈkaf-ˌskin, ˈkäf- *also* ˈkāf-\ *n* (15c) **:** leather made of the skin of a calf
Cal·i·ban \ˈka-lə-ˌban\ *n* (ca. 1612) **:** a savage and deformed slave in Shakespeare's *The Tempest*
cal·i·ber *or* **cal·i·bre** \ˈka-lə-bər, *Brit also* kə-ˈlē-\ *n* [MF *calibre,* fr. OIt *calibro,* fr. Ar *qālib* shoemaker's last] (1567) **1 a :** degree of mental capacity or moral quality **b :** degree of excellence or importance **2 a :** the diameter of a bullet or other projectile **b :** the diameter of a bore of a gun usu. expressed in hundredths or thousandths of an inch and typically written as a decimal fraction ⟨.32 ~⟩ **3 :** the diameter of a round or cylindrical body; *esp* **:** the internal diameter of a hollow cylinder
cal·i·brate \ˈka-lə-ˌbrāt\ *vt* **-brat·ed; -brat·ing** (ca. 1864) **1 :** to ascertain the caliber of (as a thermometer tube) **2 :** to determine, rectify, or mark the graduations of (as a thermometer tube) **3 :** to standardize (as a measuring instrument) by determining the deviation from a standard so as to ascertain the proper correction factors **4 :** to adjust precisely for a particular function **5 :** to measure precisely; *esp* **:** to measure against a standard — **cal·i·bra·tor** \-ˌbrā-tər\ *n*
cal·i·bra·tion \ˌka-lə-ˈbrā-shən\ *n* (ca. 1859) **1 :** the act or process of calibrating **:** the state of being calibrated **2 :** a set of graduations to indicate values or positions — usu. used in pl. ⟨~*s* on a gauge⟩
ca·li·che \kə-ˈlē-chē\ *n* [AmerSp, fr. Sp, flake of lime, fr. *cal* lime, fr. L *calx* — more at CHALK] (ca. 1858) **1 :** the nitrate-bearing gravel or rock of the sodium nitrate deposits of Chile and Peru **2 :** a crust of calcium carbonate that forms on the stony soil of arid regions
cal·i·co \ˈka-li-ˌkō\ *n, pl* **-coes** *or* **-cos** [*Calicut,* India] (1578) **1 a :** cotton cloth imported from India **b** *Brit* **:** a plain white cotton fabric that is heavier than muslin **c :** any of various cheap cotton fabrics with figured patterns **2 :** a blotched or spotted animal; *esp* **:** one that is predominantly white with red and black patches — **calico** *adj*
calico bass *n* (ca. 1882) **:** BLACK CRAPPIE
calico bush *n* (1814) **:** MOUNTAIN LAUREL
Calif *abbr* California
Cal·i·for·nia condor \ˌka-lə-ˈfȯr-nyə-\ *n* [*California,* state of U.S.] (1855) **:** a large nearly extinct vulture (*Gymnogyps californianus*) found

most recently in the mountains of southern California that is related to the condor of So. America

California laurel *n* (1868) : an evergreen Pacific coast tree (*Umbellularia californica*) of the laurel family with small umbellate flowers

California poppy *n* (1874) : any of a genus (*Eschscholzia*) of herbs of the poppy family; *esp* : one (*E. californica*) widely cultivated for its usu. yellow or orange flowers

California sea lion *n* (1873) : a small brown sea lion (*Zalophus californianus*) that occurs esp. along the Pacific coast of No. America from Vancouver Island to Baja California and the Gulf of California and in the Galapagos Islands and that is the seal most often trained to perform in circuses

Cal·i·for·nio \ˌka-lə-ˈfȯr-nē-ˌō\ *n, pl* **-nios** [Sp, fr. *California*] (1923) : one of the original Spanish colonists of California or their descendants

cal·i·for·ni·um \ˌka-lə-ˈfȯr-nē-əm\ *n* [NL, fr. *California,* U.S.] (1950) : a radioactive element discovered by bombarding curium 242 with alpha particles — see ELEMENT table

ca·lig·i·nous \kə-ˈli-jə-nəs\ *adj* [MF or L; MF *caligineux,* fr. L *caliginosus,* fr. *caligin-, caligo* darkness] (1548) : MISTY, DARK ⟨a ~ atmosphere⟩

[1]**cal·i·per** \ˈka-lə-pər\ *n* [alter. of *caliber*] (1588) **1 a** : any of various measuring instruments having two usu. adjustable arms, legs, or jaws used esp. to measure diameter or thickness — usu. used in pl. ⟨a pair of ~*s*⟩ **b** : a device for pressing a frictional material (as a brake pad) against the sides of a rotating wheel or disc **2** : thickness esp. of paper, cardboard, or a tree

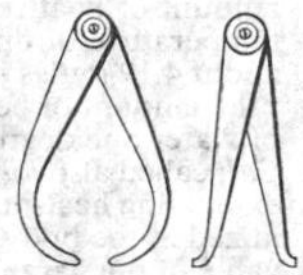
caliper 1a

[2]**caliper** *vt* **-pered; -per·ing** \-p(ə-)riŋ\ (1876) : to measure by or as if by calipers

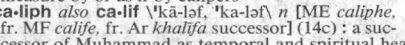

ca·liph *also* **ca·lif** \ˈkā-ləf, ˈka-ləf\ *n* [ME *caliphe,* fr. MF *calife,* fr. Ar *khalīfa* successor] (14c) : a successor of Muhammad as temporal and spiritual head of Islam — used as a title — **ca·liph·al** \-lə-fəl\ *adj*

ca·liph·ate \-lə-ˌfāt, -fət\ *n* (1614) : the office or dominion of a caliph

cal·is·then·ic \ˌka-ləs-ˈthe-nik\ *adj* (1827) : of or relating to calisthenics

cal·is·then·ics \-niks\ *n pl but sing or pl in constr* [Gk *kalos* beautiful + *sthenos* strength] (1827) **1** : systematic rhythmic bodily exercises performed usu. without apparatus **2** *usu sing in constr* : the art or practice of calisthenics

ca·lix \ˈkā-liks, ˈka-\ *n, pl* **ca·li·ces** \ˈkā-lə-ˌsēz, ˈka-\ [L *calic-, calix* — more at CHALICE] (1698) : CUP

[1]**calk** *var of* CAULK

[2]**calk** *or* **caulk** \ˈkȯk\ *n* [prob. alter. of *calkin,* fr. ME *kakun,* fr. MD or MF dial.; MD *calcoen* horse's hoof, fr. MF dial. (Walloon) *calcain* heel, fr. L *calcaneum,* fr. *calc-, calx* heel] (1587) : a cleat on the shoe of a horse to prevent slipping; *also* : a similar device worn on the sole of a shoe

[3]**calk** *or* **caulk** *vt* (1624) **1** : to furnish with calks **2** : to wound with a calk

[1]**call** \ˈkȯl\ *vb* [ME, fr. ON *kalla;* akin to OE hilde*calla* battle herald, OHG *kallōn* to talk loudly, OCS *glasŭ* voice] *vi* (bef. 12c) **1 a** : to speak in a loud distinct voice so as to be heard at a distance : SHOUT ⟨~ for help⟩ **b** : to make a request or demand ⟨~ for an investigation⟩ **c** *of an animal* : to utter a characteristic note or cry **d** : to get or try to get into communication by telephone ⟨just ~*ed* to say hello⟩ — often used with *up* **e** : to make a demand in card games (as for a particular card or for a show of hands) **f** : to give the calls for a square dance **2** : to make a brief visit ⟨~*ed* to pay his respects⟩ ⟨~*ed* on a friend⟩ ~ *vt* **1 a** (1) : to utter in a loud distinct voice — often used with *out* ⟨~ out a number⟩ (2) : to announce or read loudly or authoritatively ⟨~ the roll⟩ ⟨~ off a row of figures⟩ (3) : to announce the play-by-play of (as a football game) **b** (1) : to command or request to come or be present ⟨was ~*ed* to testify⟩ (2) : to cause to come : BRING ⟨~*s* to mind an old saying⟩ **c** : to summon to a particular activity, employment, or office ⟨was ~*ed* to active duty⟩ ⟨was ~*ed* to the bar of justice⟩ **d** : to invite or command to meet : CONVOKE ⟨~ a meeting⟩ **e** : to rouse from sleep or summon to get up **f** (1) : to give the order for : bring into action ⟨~ a strike against the company⟩ ⟨~ a pitchout⟩ (2) : to manage by giving the signals or orders ⟨that catcher ~*s* a good game⟩ **g** (1) : to make a demand in bridge for (a card or suit) (2) : to require (a player) to show the hand in poker by making an equal bet (3) : to challenge to make good on a statement (4) : to charge with or censure for an offense ⟨deserves to be ~*ed* on that⟩ **h** : to attract (as game) by imitating the characteristic cry **i** : to halt (as a baseball game) because of unsuitable conditions **j** : to rule on the status of (as a pitched ball or a player's action) ⟨~ balls and strikes⟩ ⟨~ a base runner safe⟩ **k** : to give the calls for (a square dance) — often used with *off* **l** (1) : to demand payment of esp. by formal notice ⟨~ a loan⟩ (2) : to demand presentation of (as a bond or option) for redemption **m** (1) : to get or try to get in communication with by telephone ⟨~ the doctor to make an appointment⟩ (2) : to generate signals for (a telephone number) in order to reach the party to whom the number is assigned ⟨~ 911⟩ (3) : to make a signal to in order to transmit a message ⟨~ the flagship⟩ **2 a** : to speak of or address by a specified name : give a name to ⟨~ her Kitty⟩ **b** (1) : to regard or characterize as of a certain kind : CONSIDER ⟨can hardly be ~*ed* generous⟩ (2) : to estimate or consider for purposes of an estimate or for convenience ⟨~ it an even dollar⟩ **c** (1) : to describe correctly in advance of or without knowledge of the event : PREDICT (2) : to name or specify in advance ⟨~ the toss of a coin⟩ **3** : to temporarily transfer control of computer processing to (as a subroutine or procedure) ***syn*** see SUMMON — **call a spade a spade 1** : to call a thing by its right name however coarse **2** : to speak frankly — **call for 1** : to call (as at one's house) to get ⟨I'll *call for* you after dinner⟩ **2** : to require as necessary or appropriate ⟨the job *calls for* typing skills⟩ ⟨the design *calls for* three windows⟩ — **call forth** : ELICIT, EVOKE ⟨these events *call forth* great emotions⟩ — **call in question** *or* **call into question** : to cast doubt upon ⟨a report *calling into question* the drug's effectiveness⟩ — **call it a day** : to stop for the remainder of the day or for the present whatever one has been doing — **call it quits** : to call it a day : QUIT — **call names** : to address or speak of a person or thing contemptuously or offensively — **call on 1** : to call upon **2** : to elicit a response from (as a student) ⟨the teacher *called on* her first⟩ — **call one's bluff** : to challenge in order to expose an empty pretense or threat — **call the shots** : to be in charge or control : determine the policy or procedure — **call the tune** : to call the shots — **call time** : to ask for or grant a time-out — **call to account** : to hold responsible : REPRIMAND — **call upon 1** : REQUIRE, OBLIGE ⟨may be *called upon* to do several jobs⟩ **2** : to make a demand on : depend on ⟨universities are *called upon* to produce trained professionals⟩

[2]**call** *n* (14c) **1 a** : an act of calling with the voice : SHOUT **b** : an imitation of the cry of a bird or other animal made to attract it **c** : an instrument used for calling ⟨a duck ~⟩ **d** : the cry of an animal (as a bird) **2 a** : a request or command to come or assemble **b** : a summons or signal on a drum, bugle, or pipe **c** : admission to the bar as a barrister **d** : an invitation to become the minister of a church or to accept a professional appointment **e** : a divine vocation or strong inner prompting to a particular course of action **f** : a summoning of actors to rehearsal ⟨the ~ is for 11 o'clock⟩ **g** : the attraction or appeal of a particular activity, condition, or place ⟨the ~ of the wild⟩ **h** : an order specifying the number of men to be inducted into the armed services during a specified period **i** : the selection of a play in football **3 a** : DEMAND, CLAIM **b** : NEED, JUSTIFICATION ⟨there's no ~ for such behavior⟩ **c** : a demand for payment of money **d** : an option to buy a specified amount of a security (as stock) or commodity (as wheat) at a fixed price at or within a specified time — compare PUT 2 **e** : an instance of asking for something : REQUEST ⟨many ~*s* for Christmas stories⟩ **4** : ROLL CALL **5** : a short usu. formal visit **6** : the name or thing called ⟨the ~ was heads⟩ **7** : the act of calling in a card game **8** : the act of calling on the telephone **9** : a direction or a succession of directions for a square dance rhythmically called to the dancers **10** : a decision or ruling made by an official of a sports contest; *also* : DECISION 1 ⟨a tough ~ to make⟩ **11** : a temporary transfer of control of computer processing to a particular set of instructions (as a subroutine or procedure) — **at call** *or* **on call 1 a** : available for use : at the service of ⟨thousands of men *at* his *call*⟩ **b** : ready to respond to a summons or command ⟨a doctor *on call*⟩ **2** : subject to demand for payment or return without previous notice ⟨money lent *at call*⟩ — **within call** : within hearing or reach of a summons : subject to summons

call·able \ˈkȯ-lə-bəl\ *adj* (1826) : capable of being called; *specif* : subject to a demand for presentation for payment ⟨~ bond⟩

cal·la lily \ˈka-lə-\ *n* [NL, genus name, modif. of Gk *kallaia* rooster's wattles] (1868) : any of several herbs (genus *Zantedeschia*) of the arum family; *esp* : a house or greenhouse plant (*Z. aethiopica*) with a white showy spathe and yellow spadix — called also *calla*

cal·la·loo \ˌka-lə-ˈlü, ˈka-lə-ˌ\ *n* [Caribbean E, perh. ultim. of Afr origin; akin to Caribbean Sp *calalú* callaloo (greens and dish), Brazilian Pg *carurú,* Haitian Creole *kalalou* okra] (1892) **1** : the edible young green leaves of a plant (as taro or a member of the genus *Xanthosoma*) of the arum family used as greens **2** : a soup or stew made with greens, onions, and crabmeat or pork

call–and–response *n* (1879) : a statement quickly followed by an answering statement; *also* : a musical phrase in which the first and often solo part is answered by a second and often ensemble part

cal·lant \ˈka-lənt, ˈkä-\ *n* [D or MF dial.; D *kalant* customer, fellow, fr. MF dial. (Picard) *calland* customer, fr. L *calent-, calens,* prp. of *calēre* to be warm — more at LEE] (ca. 1592) *chiefly Scot* : BOY, LAD

call·back \ˈkȯl-ˌbak\ *n* (1926) **1** : a return call **2 a** : RECALL 5 **b** : a recall of an employee to work after a layoff **c** : a second or additional audition for a theatrical part

call–board \-ˌbȯrd\ *n* (1886) : BULLETIN BOARD 1

call box *n* (1885) **1** *Brit* : a public telephone booth **2** : a telephone usu. located on the side of a road for reporting emergencies (as fires or automobile breakdowns)

call·boy \ˈkȯl-ˌbȯi\ *n* (1794) : BELLHOP, PAGE

call down *vt* (1634) **1** : to cause or entreat to descend ⟨*call down* a blessing⟩ **2** : REPRIMAND ⟨*called* me *down* for being late⟩

called strike *n* (1887) : a pitched baseball not struck at by the batter that passes through the strike zone

call·ee \kȯ-ˈlē\ *n* (1949) : one who receives a telephone call

[1]**cal·ler** \ˈkä-lər\ *adj* [ME (Sc) *callour*] (14c) **1** *Scot* : FRESH **2** *Scot* : COOL

[2]**call·er** \ˈkȯ-lər\ *n* (15c) : one that calls

caller ID \-ˌī-ˈdē\ *n* (1989) : a telephone service that allows a subscriber to identify the telephone number of a caller before answering the call — called also *caller identification*

cal·let \ˈka-lət\ *n* [perh. fr. MF *caillette* frivolous person, fr. *Caillette fl*1500 Fr. court fool] (15c) *chiefly Scot* : PROSTITUTE

call forwarding *n* (1977) : a telephone service that allows a subscriber to have incoming calls forwarded to a different number

call girl *n* (ca. 1940) : a prostitute with whom an appointment may be made by telephone

call house *n* (1929) : a house or apartment where call girls may be procured

cal·li·graphed \ˈka-lə-ˌgraft\ *adj* (1884) : written or printed in calligraphy ⟨a ~ certificate⟩

cal·lig·ra·pher \kə-ˈli-grə-fər\ *n* (1753) **1** : a professional copyist or engrosser **2** : one who practices the art of calligraphy **3** : PENMAN ⟨a fair ~⟩

cal·lig·ra·phist \-fist\ *n* (1816) : CALLIGRAPHER

cal·lig·ra·phy \-fē\ *n* [F or Gk; F *calligraphie,* fr. Gk *kalligraphia,* fr. *kalli-* beautiful (fr. *kallos* beauty) + *-graphia* -graphy] (1604) **1 a** : artistic, stylized, or elegant handwriting or lettering **b** : the art of producing such writing **2** : PENMANSHIP **3** : an ornamental line in drawing or painting — **cal·li·graph·ic** \ˌka-lə-ˈgra-fik\ *adj* — **cal·li·graph·i·cal·ly** \-fi-k(ə-)lē\ *adv*

call–in \ˈkȯl-ˌin\ *adj* (1967) : allowing listeners to engage in broadcast telephone conversations with the host or a guest ⟨a ~ show⟩

call in *vt* (1545) **1 :** to order to return or to be returned: as **a :** to withdraw from an advanced position ⟨*call in* the outposts⟩ **b :** to withdraw from circulation ⟨*call in* bank notes and issue new ones⟩ **2 :** to summon to one's aid or for consultation ⟨*call in* a mediator⟩ **3 :** to deliver (a message) by telephone ⟨*call in* an order for pizza⟩ ~ *vi* **:** to communicate with a person by telephone — **call in sick :** to report by telephone that one will be absent because of illness

call·ing \ˈkȯ-liŋ\ *n* (14c) **1 :** a strong inner impulse toward a particular course of action esp. when accompanied by conviction of divine influence **2 :** the vocation or profession in which one customarily engages **3 :** the characteristic cry of a female cat in heat; *also* **:** the period of heat ***syn*** see WORK

calling card *n* (1846) **1 :** VISITING CARD **2 :** a sign or evidence that someone or something is or has been present; *broadly* **:** an identifying mark **3 :** a card displaying a number that can be used to charge telephone calls to a single account regardless of where the calls are placed

cal·li·ope \kə-ˈlī-ə-(ˌ)pē, *in sense 2 also* ˈka-lē-ˌōp\ *n* [L, fr. Gk *Kalliopē*] (14c) **1** *cap* **:** the Greek Muse of heroic poetry **2 :** a keyboard musical instrument resembling an organ and consisting of a series of whistles sounded by steam or compressed air

cal·li·per *chiefly Brit var of* CALIPER

cal·li·pyg·ian \ˌka-lə-ˈpi-j(ē-)ən\ *also* **cal·li·py·gous** \-ˈpī-gəs\ *adj* [Gk *kallipygos,* fr. *kalli-* + *pygē* buttocks] (ca. 1800) **:** having shapely buttocks

Cal·lis·to \kə-ˈlis-(ˌ)tō\ *n* [L, fr. Gk *Kallistō*] (14c) **:** a nymph loved by Zeus, changed into a she-bear by Hera, and subsequently changed into the Great Bear constellation

cal·li·thump \ˈka-lə-ˌthəmp\ *n* [back-formation fr. *callithumpian,* adj., alter. of E dial. *gallithumpian* disturber of order at elections in 18th cent.] (1950) **:** a noisy boisterous band or parade — **cal·li·thump·ian** \ˌka-lə-ˈthəm-pē-ən\ *adj*

call letters *n pl* (1912) **:** CALL SIGN

call loan *n* (1852) **:** a loan payable at the discretion of the borrower or on demand of the lender

call number *n* (1876) **:** a combination of characters assigned to a library book to indicate its place on a shelf

call off *vt* (1633) **1 :** to draw away **:** DIVERT **2 :** CANCEL

call of nature (1741) **:** the need to urinate or defecate

cal·los·i·ty \ka-ˈlä-sə-tē, kə-\ *n, pl* **-ties** (1578) **1 :** the quality or state of being callous: as **a :** marked or abnormal hardness and thickness **b :** lack of feeling or capacity for emotion **2 :** CALLUS 1

[1]**cal·lous** \ˈka-ləs\ *adj* [ME, fr. L *callosus,* fr. *callum, callus* callous skin] (15c) **1 a :** being hardened and thickened **b :** having calluses ⟨~ hands⟩ **2 a :** feeling no emotion **b :** feeling or showing no sympathy for others **:** HARD-HEARTED — **cal·lous·ly** *adv* — **cal·lous·ness** *n*

[2]**callous** *vt* (1834) **:** to make callous ⟨hands ~*ed* by hard manual labor⟩

call·out \ˈkȯl-ˌau̇t\ *n* (1887) **1 :** the act or an instance of calling out **2 :** an often bordered inset in a printed article or illustration that usu. includes a key excerpt or detail

call out *vt* (15c) **1 :** to summon into action ⟨*call out* troops⟩ **2 :** to challenge to a duel **3 :** to order on strike ⟨*call out* the workers⟩

cal·low \ˈka-(ˌ)lō\ *adj* [ME *calu* bald, fr. OE; akin to OHG *kalo* bald, OCS *golŭ* bare] (1580) **:** lacking adult sophistication **:** IMMATURE ⟨~ youth⟩ — **cal·low·ness** \ˈka-lō-nəs, -lə-nəs\ *n*

call sheet *n* (ca. 1949) **:** a daily schedule of filming for a movie or television show

call sign *n* (1919) **:** the combination of identifying letters, letters and numbers, or words assigned to an operator, office, activity, vehicle, or station for use in communication (as in the address of a message sent by radio)

call slip *n* (1881) **:** a form filled out by a library patron for a desired book

call to arms (1791) **1 :** a summons to engage in active hostilities **2 :** a summons, invitation, or appeal to undertake a particular course of action ⟨a political *call to arms*⟩

call to quarters (1887) **:** a bugle call usu. shortly before taps that summons soldiers to their quarters

call–up \ˈkȯl-ˌəp\ *n* (1940) **1 :** an order to report for military service **2 :** a baseball player brought up to a major league team from the minor leagues

call up *vt* (1549) **1 :** to summon together (as for a united effort) ⟨*call up* all his forces for the attack⟩ **2 :** to bring to mind **:** EVOKE **3 :** to summon before an authority **4 a :** to summon for active military duty **b :** to bring up from a minor league to a major league baseball team **5 :** to bring forward for consideration or action **6 :** to retrieve from the memory of a computer esp. for display and user interaction

[1]**cal·lus** \ˈka-ləs\ *n* [L] (1563) **1 :** a thickening of or a hard thickened area on skin or bark **2 :** a mass of exudate and connective tissue that forms around a break in a bone and is converted into bone in healing **3 :** soft tissue that forms over a wounded or cut plant surface

[2]**callus** *vi* (1864) **:** to form callus ~ *vt* **:** to cause callus to form on

call–waiting *n* (1986) **:** a telephone service that signals (as by a beep) to the user when an incoming call is received during a call in progress

[1]**calm** \ˈkäm, ˈkälm, ˈkam, ˈkȯ(l)m\ *n* [ME *calme,* prob. ultim. fr. OSp *calma,* fr. LL *cauma* heat, fr. Gk *kauma,* fr. *kaiein* to burn] (14c) **1 a :** a period or condition of freedom from storms, high winds, or rough activity of water **b :** complete absence of wind or presence of wind having a speed no greater than one mile (1.6 kilometers) per hour — see BEAUFORT SCALE table **2 :** a state of tranquillity

[2]**calm** *vi* (14c) **:** to become calm — usu. used with *down* ~ *vt* **:** to make calm — often used with *down*

[3]**calm** *adj* (14c) **1 :** marked by calm **:** STILL ⟨a ~ sea⟩ **2 :** free from agitation, excitement, or disturbance — **calm·ly** *adv* — **calm·ness** *n*

syn CALM, TRANQUIL, SERENE, PLACID, PEACEFUL mean quiet and free from disturbance. CALM often implies a contrast with a foregoing or nearby state of agitation or violence ⟨the protests ended, and the streets were *calm* again⟩. TRANQUIL suggests a very deep quietude or composure ⟨the *tranquil* beauty of a formal garden⟩. SERENE stresses an unclouded and lofty tranquillity ⟨watched the sunset of a *serene* summer's evening⟩. PLACID suggests an undisturbed appearance and often implies a degree of complacency ⟨remained *placid* despite the criticism⟩. PEACEFUL implies a state of repose in contrast with or following strife or turmoil ⟨grown *peaceful* in old age⟩.

calm·ative \ˈkä-mə-tiv, ˈkäl-, *also* ˈkȯ(l)-, ˈka-\ *n or adj* [[2]*calm* + *-ative* (as in *sedative*)] (1870) **:** SEDATIVE

cal·mod·u·lin \(ˌ)kal-ˈmä-jə-lin, -dyu̇-lin\ *n* [*calcium* + *modulate* + [1]*-in*] (1978) **:** a calcium-binding protein that mediates cellular metabolic processes (as the contraction of muscle fibers) by regulating the activity of calcium-dependent enzymes

ca·ló \kə-ˈlō\ *n* [Sp, argot, speech of Span. Gypsies, fr. Romany *kalo* Gypsy, lit., black, fr. Skt *kāla*] (1947) **:** any of several Spanish argots; *esp* **:** an argot used by Chicano youths in cities of the U.S. Southwest

cal·o·mel \ˈka-lə-məl, -ˌmel\ *n* [prob. fr. NL **calomelas,* fr. Gk *kalos* beautiful + *melas* black — more at MELAN-] (1676) **:** a white tasteless compound Hg_2Cl_2 used esp. as a component of laboratory electrodes, as a fungicide, and formerly in medicine as a purgative — called also *mercurous chloride*

[1]**ca·lo·ric** \kə-ˈlȯr-ik\ *n* [F *calorique,* fr. L *calor*] (1792) **1 :** a supposed form of matter formerly held responsible for the phenomena of heat and combustion **2** *archaic* **:** HEAT

[2]**caloric** *adj* (ca. 1828) **1 :** of or relating to heat **2 :** of, relating to, or containing calories — **ca·lo·ri·cal·ly** \kə-ˈlȯr-i-k(ə-)lē\ *adv*

cal·o·rie *also* **cal·o·ry** \ˈka-lə-rē, ˈkal-rē\ *n, pl* **-ries** [F *calorie,* fr. L *calor* heat, fr. *calēre* to be warm — more at LEE] (1866) **1 a :** the amount of heat required at a pressure of one atmosphere to raise the temperature of one gram of water one degree Celsius that is equal to about 4.19 joules — abbr. *cal*; called also *gram calorie, small calorie* **b :** the amount of heat required to raise the temperature of one kilogram of water one degree Celsius **:** 1000 gram calories or 3.968 Btu — abbr. *Cal*; called also *large calorie* **2 a :** a unit equivalent to the large calorie expressing heat-producing or energy-producing value in food when oxidized in the body **b :** an amount of food having an energy-producing value of one large calorie

cal·o·rif·ic \ˌka-lə-ˈri-fik\ *adj* [F or L; F *calorifique,* fr. L *calorificus,* fr. *calor*] (1770) **1 :** CALORIC **2 :** of or relating to heat production

cal·o·rim·e·ter \ˌka-lə-ˈri-mə-tər\ *n* [ISV, fr. L *calor*] (1790) **:** an apparatus for measuring quantities of absorbed or emitted heat or for determining specific heats — **ca·lo·ri·met·ric** \ˌka-lə-rə-ˈme-trik; kə-ˌlȯr-ə-\ *adj* — **ca·lo·ri·met·ri·cal·ly** \-tri-k(ə-)lē\ *adv* — **cal·o·rim·e·try** \ˌka-lə-ˈri-mə-trē\ *n*

ca·lotte \kə-ˈlät\ *n* [F] (1632) **:** SKULLCAP 1; *esp* **:** ZUCCHETTO

cal·o·type \ˈka-lə-ˌtīp\ *n* [Gk *kalos* beautiful + *-type* (as in *daguerreotype*)] (1845) **:** a photographic process by which a large number of prints could be produced from a paper negative; *also* **:** a positive print so made

cal·pac *or* **cal·pack** \ˈkal-ˌpak, kal-ˈ\ *n* [Turk *kalpak*] (1598) **:** a high-crowned cap worn in Turkey, Iran, and neighboring countries

calque \ˈkalk\ *n* [F, lit., copy, fr. *calquer* to trace, fr. It *calcare* to trample, trace, fr. L, to trample — more at CAULK] (1937) **:** LOAN TRANSLATION

cal·trop \ˈkal-trəp, ˈkȯl-\ *also* **cal·throp** \-thrəp\ *n* [ME *caltrappe,* alter. of *calketrappe* star thistle, fr. OE *calcatrippe,* fr. ML *calcatrippa*] (15c) **1 a** *pl but sing or pl in constr* **:** STAR THISTLE 1 **b :** PUNCTURE VINE; *also* **:** any of various related herbs (genera *Tribulus* and *Kallstroemia*) of the same family (Zygophyllaceae, the caltrop family) **2 :** a device with four metal points so arranged that when any three are on the ground the fourth projects upward as a hazard to the hooves of horses or to pneumatic tires

cal·u·met \ˈkal-yə-ˌmet, -mət\ *n* [AmerF, fr. F dial., pipe stem, fr. LL *calamellus,* dim. of L *calamus* reed — more at CALAMUS] (1698) **:** a highly ornamented ceremonial pipe of the American Indians

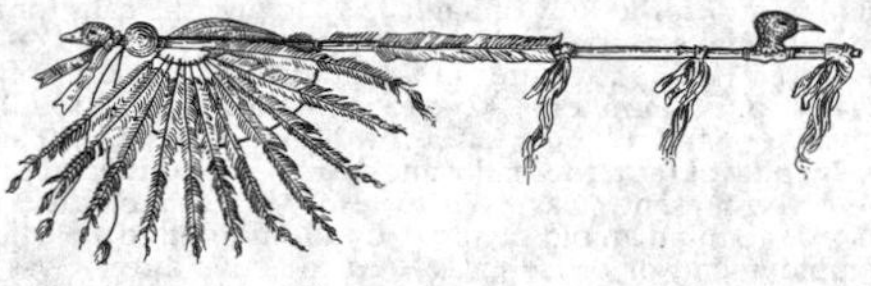

calumet

ca·lum·ni·ate \kə-ˈləm-nē-ˌāt\ *vt* **-at·ed; -at·ing** (1554) **1 :** to utter maliciously false statements, charges, or imputations about **2 :** to injure the reputation of by calumny ***syn*** see MALIGN — **ca·lum·ni·a·tion** \-ˌləm-nē-ˈā-shən\ *n* — **ca·lum·ni·a·tor** \-ˈləm-nē-ˌā-tər\ *n*

cal·um·ny \ˈka-ləm-nē *also* ˈkal-yəm-\ *n, pl* **-nies** [ME *calumnye,* fr. MF & L; MF *calomnie,* fr. L *calumnia,* fr. *calvi* to deceive; perh. akin to OE *hōlian* to slander, Gk *kēlein* to beguile] (15c) **1 :** a misrepresentation intended to harm another's reputation **2 :** the act of uttering false charges or misrepresentations maliciously calculated to harm another's reputation — **ca·lum·ni·ous** \kə-ˈləm-nē-əs\ *adj* — **ca·lum·ni·ous·ly** *adv*

cal·u·tron \ˈkal-yə-ˌträn\ *n* [*Cal*ifornia *U*niversity cyclo*tron*] (1945) **:** an electromagnetic apparatus for separating isotopes according to their masses

cal·va·dos \ˌkal-və-ˈdōs, ˌkäl-\ *n, often cap* [F, fr. *Calvados,* department in Normandy, France] (1906) **:** an applejack made in Calvados

cal·var·i·um \kal-ˈva-rē-əm, -ˈve-rē-\ *n, pl* **-ia** \-ē-ə\ [NL, fr. L *calvaria* skull, fr. *calvus* bald; prob. akin to Skt *kulva* bald] (14c) **:** the portion of a skull including the braincase and excluding the lower jaw or lower jaw and facial portion

cal·va·ry \ˈkal-v(ə-)rē\ *n, pl* **-ries** [*Calvary,* the hill near Jerusalem where Jesus was crucified] (1738) **1 :** an open-air representation of the crucifixion of Jesus **2 :** an experience of usu. intense mental suffering

Calvary cross *n* (1826) **:** a Latin cross usu. mounted on three steps — see CROSS illustration

calve \ˈkav, ˈkäv\ *vb* **calved; calv·ing** [ME, fr. OE *cealfian,* fr. *cealf* calf] *vi* (bef. 12c) **1 :** to give birth to a calf; *also* **:** to produce offspring **2** *of an ice mass* **:** to separate or break so that a part becomes detached ~ *vt* **1 :** to produce by birth **2** *of an ice mass* **:** to let become detached

calves *pl of* CALF

Cal·vin cycle \ˈkal-vən-\ *n* [Melvin *Calvin*] (1957) **:** the cycle of enzyme-catalyzed dark reactions of photosynthesis that occurs in the chloroplasts of plants and in many bacteria and that involves the fixation of carbon dioxide and the formation of a 6-carbon sugar

Cal·vin·ism \ˈkal-və-ˌni-zəm\ *n* [John *Calvin*] (ca. 1570) : the theological system of Calvin and his followers marked by strong emphasis on the sovereignty of God, the depravity of humankind, and the doctrine of predestination — **Cal·vin·ist** \-və-nist\ *n or adj* — **Cal·vin·is·tic** \ˌkal-və-ˈnis-tik\ *adj* — **Cal·vin·is·ti·cal·ly** \-ti-k(ə-)lē\ *adv*

¹**ca·lyp·so** \kə-ˈlip-(ˌ)sō\ *n* [L, fr. Gk *Kalypsō*] (14c) **1** *cap* : a sea nymph in Homer's *Odyssey* who keeps Odysseus seven years on the island of Ogygia **2** *pl* **calypsos** [NL, genus name, prob. fr. L] : a bulbous bog orchid (*Calypso bulbosa*) of northern regions bearing a single white to purplish flower

²**calypso** *n, pl* **-sos** *or* **-soes** [Trinidad E, alter. of *kaiso,* perh. ultim. of Afr origin; akin to eastern Caribbean E *caliso, cariso* satirical song] (1900) : a style of music originating in the West Indies, marked by lively duple meter, and having lyrics that are often improvised and usu. satirize local personalities and events; *also* : a song in this style — **ca·lyp·so·ni·an** \kə-ˌlip-ˈsō-nē-ən, ˌka-(ˌ)lip-\ *n or adj*

ca·lyp·tra \kə-ˈlip-trə\ *n* [NL, fr. Gk *kalyptra* veil, fr. *kalyptein* to cover — more at HELL] (ca. 1753) : a hoodlike structure in a plant; *esp* : haploid tissue forming a membranous hood over the capsule in a moss

ca·lyx \ˈkā-liks *also* ˈka-\ *n, pl* **ca·lyx·es** *or* **ca·ly·ces** \ˈkā-lə-ˌsēz *also* ˈka-\ [L *calyc-, calyx,* fr. Gk *kalyx* — more at CHALICE] (1693) **1** : the usu. green outer whorl of a flower consisting of sepals **2** : a cuplike animal structure (as the body wall of a crinoid)

cal·zo·ne \kal-ˈzōn, -ˈzō-nē, -ˈzō-nā; käl-ˈzō-nā\ *n, pl* **calzone** *or* **calzones** [It, fr. *calzone* (sing. of *calzoni* pants), aug. of *calza* stocking, fr. ML *calcea,* fr. L *calceus* shoe, fr. *calc-, calx* heel] (1947) : a baked or fried turnover of pizza dough stuffed with various fillings usu. including cheese

¹**cam** \ˈkam\ *n* [perh. fr. F *came,* fr. G *Kamm,* lit., comb, fr. OHG *kamb*] (1777) : a rotating or sliding piece (as an eccentric wheel or a cylinder with an irregular shape) in a mechanical linkage used esp. in transforming rotary motion into linear motion or vice versa

²**cam** *n* (1977) : CAMERA; *esp* : VIDEO CAMERA

CAM *abbr* **1** computer-aided manufacturing **2** complementary and alternative medicine

ca·ma·ra·de·rie \ˌkäm-ˈrä-d(ə-)rē, ˌkam-, ˌkä-mə-, ˌka-, -ˈra-\ *n* [F, fr. *camarade* comrade] (1840) : a spirit of friendly good-fellowship

cam·a·ril·la \ˌka-mə-ˈri-lə, -ˈrē-ə\ *n* [Sp, lit., small room] (1834) : a group of unofficial often secret and scheming advisers; *also* : CABAL

cam·as *also* **cam·ass** \ˈka-məs\ *or* **qua·mash** \ˈkwä-mish\ *n* [Nez Percé *qém'es, qém'eš*] (1805) : any of a genus (*Camassia* and esp. *C. quamash*) of plants of the lily family chiefly of the western U.S. with edible bulbs — compare DEATH CAMAS

¹**cam·ber** \ˈkam-bər\ *vb* **cam·bered; cam·ber·ing** \-b(ə-)riŋ\ [F *cambrer,* fr. MF *cambre* curved, fr. L *camur*] *vi* (1627) : to curve upward in the middle ~ *vt* **1** : to arch slightly **2** : to impart camber to

²**camber** *n* (1823) **1** : a slight convexity, arching, or curvature (as of a beam, deck, or road) **2** : the convexity of the curve of an airfoil from the leading edge to the trailing edge **3** : a setting of the wheels of an automotive vehicle closer together at the bottom than at the top

cam·bi·um \ˈkam-bē-əm\ *n, pl* **-bi·ums** *or* **-bia** \-bē-ə\ [NL, fr. ML, exchange, fr. L *cambire* to exchange — more at CHANGE] (1671) : a thin formative layer between the xylem and phloem of most vascular plants that gives rise to new cells and is responsible for secondary growth — **cam·bi·al** \-bē-əl\ *adj*

Cam·bo·di·an \kam-ˈbō-dē-ən\ *n* (1770) **1** : a native or inhabitant of Cambodia **2** : KHMER 2 — **Cambodian** *adj*

Cam·bri·an \ˈkam-brē-ən, ˈkām-\ *adj* [ML *Cambria* Wales, fr. MW *Cymry* Wales, Welshmen] (1604) **1** : WELSH **2** : of, relating to, or being the earliest geologic period of the Paleozoic era or the corresponding system of rocks marked by fossils of nearly every major invertebrate animal group — see GEOLOGIC TIME table — **Cambrian** *n*

cam·bric \ˈkām-brik\ *n* [D *Kamerijk* Cambrai, France] (1530) **1** : a fine thin white linen fabric **2** : a cotton fabric that resembles cambric

cambric tea *n* (1859) : a hot drink of water, milk, sugar, and often a small amount of tea

cam·cord·er \ˈkam-ˌkȯr-dər\ *n* [*camera* + *recorder*] (1981) : a small portable combined camera and video recording device

¹**came** *past of* COME

²**came** \ˈkām\ *n* [origin unknown] (1688) : a slender grooved lead rod used to hold together panes of glass esp. in a stained-glass window

cam·el \ˈka-məl\ *n* [ME, fr. OE & AF, fr. L *camelus,* fr. Gk *kamēlos,* of Sem origin; akin to Heb *gāmāl* camel] (bef. 12c) **1** : either of two large ruminant mammals (genus *Camelus*) used as draft and saddle animals in desert regions esp. of Africa and Asia: **a** : the one-humped camel (*C. dromedarius*) extant only as a domestic or feral animal — called also *dromedary* **b** : the 2-humped camel (*C. bactrianus* syn. *C. ferus*) of Chinese Turkestan and Mongolia — called also *Bactrian camel* **2** : a watertight structure used esp. to lift submerged ships **3** : a light yellowish brown

cam·el·back \ˈkam-əl-ˌbak\ *n* (1860) : the back of a camel

cam·el·eer \ˌka-mə-ˈlir\ *n* (1808) : a camel driver

camel hair *also* **camel's hair** *n* (14c) **1** : the hair of the camel or a substitute for it (as hair from squirrels' tails) **2** : cloth made of camel hair or a mixture of camel hair and wool usu. light tan and of soft silky texture

cam·el·id \ˈka-mə-ˌlid\ *n* [NL *Camelidae,* fr. *Camelus,* genus name, fr. L] (1911) : any of a family (Camelidae) of 2-toed ruminant artiodactyl mammals having a 3-chambered stomach and including the camels, llamas, and vicuña

ca·mel·lia \kə-ˈmēl-yə\ *n* [NL *Camellia,* fr. *Camellus* (Georg Josef Kamel †1706 Moravian Jesuit missionary)] (ca. 1753) : any of a genus (*Camellia*) of shrubs or trees of the tea family; *esp* : an ornamental greenhouse shrub (*C. japonica*) with glossy leaves and roselike flowers

ca·mel·o·pard \kə-ˈme-lə-ˌpärd\ *n* [LL *camelopardus,* alter. of L *camelopardalis,* fr. Gk *kamēlopardalis,* fr. *kamēlos* camel + *pardalis* leopard] (14c) **1** *archaic* : GIRAFFE **2** *cap* : CAMELOPARDALIS

Ca·mel·o·par·da·lis \kə-ˌme-lə-ˈpär-dᵊl-əs\ *n* [L (gen. *Camelopardalis*), camelopard] (1836) : a northern constellation between Cassiopeia and Ursa Major

Cam·e·lot \ˈka-mə-ˌlät\ *n* (15c) **1** : the site of King Arthur's palace and court **2** : a time, place, or atmosphere of idyllic happiness

Cam·em·bert \ˈka-məm-ˌber\ *n* [F, fr. *Camembert,* Normandy, France] (1877) : a soft surface-ripened cheese with a thin grayish-white rind and a yellow interior

cam·eo \ˈka-mē-ˌō\ *n, pl* **-eos** [ME *camew,* fr. MF *camau, kamaheu*] (15c) **1 a** : a gem carved in relief; *esp* : a small piece of sculpture on a stone or shell cut in relief in one layer with another contrasting layer serving as background **b** : a small medallion with a profiled head in relief **2** : a carving or sculpture made in the manner of a cameo **3** : a usu. brief literary or filmic piece that brings into delicate or sharp relief the character of a person, place, or event **4** : a small theatrical role usu. performed by a well-known actor and often limited to a single scene; *broadly* : a brief appearance or role — **cameo** *adj* — **cameo** *vt*

cam·era \ˈkam-rə, ˈka-mər-ə\ *n* [LL, room — more at CHAMBER] (1712) **1** : the treasury department of the papal curia **2 a** : CAMERA OBSCURA **b** : a device that consists of a lightproof chamber with an aperture fitted with a lens and a shutter through which the image of an object is projected onto a surface for recording (as on film) or for translation into electrical impulses (as for television broadcast) — **off camera** **1** : while not being filmed by a television or movie camera ⟨he's a different person *off camera*⟩ **2** : outside the scope of a television or movie camera ⟨sounds of gunfire taking place *off camera*⟩ — **on camera** **1** : before a live television camera ⟨go *on camera*⟩; *also* : while being filmed by a television or movie camera ⟨looked relaxed *on camera*⟩ **2** : within the scope of a television or movie camera ⟨you can hear a dog but he never appears *on camera*⟩

cam·era lu·ci·da \-ˈlü-sə-də\ *n* [NL, lit., light chamber] (1753) : an instrument that by means of a prism or mirrors and often a microscope causes a virtual image of an object to appear as if projected upon a plane surface so that an outline may be traced

cam·era·man \-ˌman, -mən\ *n* (1908) : a person who operates a camera (as for motion pictures or television)

cam·era ob·scu·ra \-əb-ˈskyu̇r-ə\ *n* [NL, lit., dark chamber] (1725) : a darkened enclosure having an aperture usu. provided with a lens through which light from external objects enters to form an image of the objects on the opposite surface

cam·era·per·son \-ˌpər-sᵊn\ *n* (1976) : a man or woman who operates a camera

cam·era·wom·an \-ˌwu̇-mən\ *n* (1971) : a woman who operates a camera

cam·er·len·go \ˌka-mər-ˈleŋ-(ˌ)gō\ *n, pl* **-gos** [It *camarlingo*] (1753) : a cardinal who heads the Apostolic Camera

Cam·er·oo·nian \ˌka-mə-ˈrü-nē-ən, -nyən\ *n* (1965) **1** : a native or inhabitant of Cameroon **2** : a native or inhabitant of the Cameroons — **Cameroonian** *adj*

ca·mion \kä-ˈmyōⁿ\ *n* [F] (1911) : MOTORTRUCK; *also* : BUS

cam·i·sa·do \ˌka-mə-ˈsä-(ˌ)dō, -ˈsā-\ *n, pl* **-does** [prob. fr. obs. Sp *camisada*] (1548) *archaic* : an attack by night

ca·mise \kə-ˈmēz, -ˈmēs\ *n* [Ar *qamīṣ,* ultim. fr. LL *camisia*] (1812) : a light loose long-sleeved shirt, gown, or tunic

cam·i·sole \ˈka-mə-ˌsōl\ *n* [F, fr. Occitan *camisolla,* dim. of *camisa* shirt, fr. LL *camisia*] (1795) **1** : a short negligee jacket for women **2** : a short sleeveless garment for women

cam·let \ˈkam-lət\ *n* [ME *cameloit,* fr. MF *camelot,* fr. Ar *khamlat* woolen plush] (15c) **1 a** : a medieval Asian fabric of camel hair or angora wool **b** : a European fabric of silk and wool **c** : a fine lustrous woolen **2** : a garment made of camlet

¹**camo** \ˈka-(ˌ)mō\ *adj* [by shortening & alter.] (1980) : CAMOUFLAGE

²**camo** *n, pl* **camos** (1980) : a combination of colors and patterns typical of camouflage; *also* : a camouflage garment or outfit

camomile *var of* CHAMOMILE

ca·mor·ra \kə-ˈmȯr-ə, -ˈmär-\ *n* [It] (1865) : a group of persons united for dishonest or dishonorable ends; *esp* : a secret organization formed about 1820 at Naples, Italy

ca·mor·ris·ta \ˌkä-mō-ˈrē-stə\ *n, pl* **-ti** \-(ˌ)stē\ [It, fr. *camorra*] (1897) : a member of a camorra

¹**cam·ou·flage** \ˈka-mə-ˌfläzh, -ˌfläj\ *n* [F, fr. *camoufler* to disguise] (1917) **1** : the disguising esp. of military equipment or installations with paint, nets, or foliage; *also* : the disguise so applied **2 a** : concealment by means of disguise **b** : behavior or artifice designed to deceive or hide — **cam·ou·flag·ic** \ˌka-mə-ˈflä-zhik, -jik\ *adj*

²**camouflage** *vb* **-flaged; -flag·ing** *vt* (1917) : to conceal or disguise by camouflage ~ *vi* : to practice camouflage — **cam·ou·flage·able** \ˈka-mə-ˌflä-zhə-bəl, -jə-bəl\ *adj*

³**camouflage** *adj* (1942) : made in colors or patterns typical of camouflage ⟨a ~ jacket⟩

¹**camp** \ˈkamp\ *n, often attrib* [MF, prob. fr. MF dial. (Picard) or Old Occitan, fr. L *campus* plain, field] (1528) **1 a** : a place usu. away from urban areas where tents or simple buildings (as cabins) are erected for shelter or for temporary residence (as for laborers, prisoners, or vacationers) ⟨migrant labor ~⟩ **b** : a group of tents, cabins, or huts ⟨fishing ~*s* along the river⟩ **c** : a settlement newly sprung up in a lumbering or mining region **d** : a place usu. in the country for recreation or instruction often during the summer ⟨goes to ~ every July⟩; *also* : a program offering access to recreational or educational facilities for a limited period of time ⟨computer ~⟩ ⟨a resort offering boating and hiking ~*s*⟩ **e** : a preseason training session for athletes ⟨the star pitcher injured in ~ this spring⟩ **2 a** : a body of persons encamped **b (1)** : a group of persons; *esp* : a group engaged in promoting or defending a theory, doctrine, position, or person **(2)** : an ideological position **3** : military service or life

²**camp** *vi* (1543) **1** : to make camp or occupy a camp **2** : to live temporarily in a camp or outdoors — often used with *out* **3** : to take up one's quarters : LODGE **4** : to take up one's position : settle down — often used with *out* ⟨~ out in the library for the afternoon⟩ ~ *vt* : to put into a camp; *also* : ACCOMMODATE

³**camp** *n* [origin unknown] (ca. 1909) **1** : exaggerated effeminate mannerisms exhibited esp. by homosexuals **2 a** : something so outra-

\ə\ **abut** \ᵊ\ kitten, F table \ər\ **further** \a\ **ash** \ā\ **ace** \ä\ **mop, mar** \au̇\ **out** \ch\ **chin** \e\ **bet** \ē\ **easy** \g\ **go** \i\ **hit** \ī\ **ice** \j\ **job** \ŋ\ **sing** \ō\ **go** \ȯ\ **law** \ȯi\ **boy** \th\ **thin** \t͟h\ **the** \ü\ **loot** \u̇\ **foot** \y\ **yet** \zh\ **vision, beige** \k, ⁿ, œ, ue, ʸ\ *see* Guide to Pronunciation

geously artificial, affected, inappropriate, or out-of-date as to be considered amusing **b :** a style or mode of personal or creative expression that is absurdly exaggerated and often fuses elements of high and popular culture ⟨a movie that celebrates ~⟩ — **camp·i·ly** \ˈkam-pə-lē\ *adv* — **camp·i·ness** \-pē-nəs\ *n* — **campy** \ˈkam-pē\ *adj*

[4]**camp** *adj* (1909) **:** of, relating to, being, or displaying camp ⟨~ sensibilities of the songs of the fifties and sixties —John Elsom⟩

[5]**camp** *vi* (1925) **:** to engage in camp **:** exhibit the qualities of camp ⟨he . . . was ~*ing,* hands on hips, with a quick eye to notice every man who passed by —R. M. McAlmon⟩

[1]**cam·paign** \(ˌ)kam-ˈpān\ *n* [F *campagne,* prob. fr. It *campagna* level country, campaign, fr. LL *campania* level country, fr. L, the level country around Naples] (ca. 1656) **1 :** a connected series of military operations forming a distinct phase of a war **2 :** a connected series of operations designed to bring about a particular result ⟨election ~⟩

[2]**campaign** *vi* (1701) **:** to go on, engage in, or conduct a campaign ~ *vt* **:** to enter (as a horse or boat) in competition — **cam·paign·er** *n*

cam·pa·ni·le \ˌkam-pə-ˈnē-lē, ˌkäm-, -(ˌ)lā, *esp of US structures also* -ˈnēl\ *n, pl* **-ni·les** *or* **-ni·li** \-ˈnē-lē\ [It, fr. *campana* bell, fr. LL] (1640) **:** a usu. freestanding bell tower

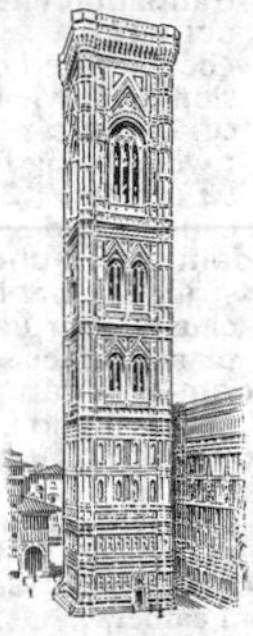
campanile

cam·pa·nol·o·gist \ˌkam-pə-ˈnä-lə-jist\ *n* (1857) **:** one who practices or is skilled in campanology

cam·pa·nol·o·gy \-jē\ *n* [NL *campanologia,* fr. LL *campana* + NL *-o-* + *-logia* -logy] (ca. 1823) **:** the art of bell ringing

cam·pan·u·la \kam-ˈpan-yə-lə\ *n* [NL, dim. of LL *campana*] (1664) **:** BELLFLOWER

cam·pan·u·late \-lət, -ˌlāt\ *adj* [NL *campanula* bell-shaped part, dim. of LL *campana*] (1668) **:** shaped like a bell ⟨~ flowers⟩

Camp·bell·ite \ˈka-mə-ˌlīt *also* ˈkam-bə-\ *n* [Alexander *Campbell*] (1830) *sometimes offensive* **:** DISCIPLE 2

camp·craft \ˈkamp-ˌkraft\ *n* (ca. 1893) **:** skill and practice in the activities relating to camping

camp·er \ˈkam-pər\ *n* (1852) **1 :** one who camps **2 :** a portable dwelling (as a specially equipped trailer or automotive vehicle) for use during casual travel and camping

cam·pe·si·no \ˌkam-pə-ˈsē-(ˌ)nō\ *n, pl* **-nos** [Sp, fr. *campo* field, country, fr. L *campus* field] (1898) **:** a native of a Latin-American rural area; *esp* **:** a Latin-American Indian farmer or farm laborer

cam·pes·tral \kam-ˈpes-trəl\ *adj* [L *campestr-, campester,* fr. *campus*] (ca. 1750) **:** of or relating to fields or open country **:** RURAL

camp·fire \ˈkamp-ˌfī(-ə)r\ *n* (1675) **:** a fire built outdoors (as at a camp or a picnic)

Camp Fire girl *n* [fr. *Camp Fire Girls,* Inc., former name of Camp Fire, Inc.] (1912) **:** a girl who is a member of a national organization of young people from ages 5 to 18

camp follower *n* (1810) **1 :** a civilian (as a prostitute) who follows a military unit to attend or exploit military personnel **2 :** a disciple or follower who is not of the main body of members or adherents; *esp* **:** a politician who joins the party or movement solely for personal gain

camp·ground \ˈkamp-ˌgrau̇nd\ *n* (1805) **:** the area or place (as a field or grove) used for a camp, for camping, or for a camp meeting

cam·phene \ˈkam-ˌfēn\ *n* (ca. 1847) **:** any of several terpenes related to camphor; *esp* **:** a colorless crystalline terpene $C_{10}H_{16}$ used in insecticides

cam·phor \ˈkam(p)-fər\ *n* [ME *caumfre,* fr. AF, fr. ML *camphora,* fr. Ar *kāfūr,* fr. Malay *kapur*] (14c) **:** a tough gummy volatile aromatic crystalline compound $C_{10}H_{16}O$ obtained esp. from the wood and bark of the camphor tree and used as a liniment and mild topical analgesic in medicine, as a plasticizer, and as an insect repellent; *also* **:** any of several similar compounds (as some terpene alcohols and ketones) — **cam·pho·ra·ceous** \ˌkam(p)-fə-ˈrā-shəs\ *adj*

cam·phor·ate \ˈkam(p)-fə-ˌrāt\ *vt* **-at·ed; -at·ing** (1641) **:** to impregnate or treat with camphor

camphor tree *n* (1607) **:** a large Asian evergreen tree (*Cinnamomum camphora*) of the laurel family grown in warm regions

cam·pi·on \ˈkam-pē-ən\ *n* [prob. fr. obs. *campion* (champion)] (1576) **:** any of various plants (genera *Lychnis* and *Silene*) of the pink family

camp meeting *n* (1803) **:** a series of evangelistic meetings usu. held outdoors and attended by persons who often camp nearby

cam·po \ˈkam-(ˌ)pō, ˈkäm-\ *n, pl* **campos** [AmerSp, fr. Sp, field, fr. L *campus*] (1863) **:** a grassland plain in So. America with scattered perennial herbs

camp·o·ree \ˌkam-pə-ˈrē\ *n* [*camp* + *jamboree*] (1927) **:** a gathering of Boy Scouts or Girl Scouts from a given geographic area

camp·out \ˈkamp-ˌau̇t\ *n* (1879) **:** an occasion on which a group camps out

camp shirt *n* (1977) **:** a woman's shirt having a notched collar and often patch pockets

camp·site \ˈkamp-ˌsīt\ *n* (1910) **:** a place suitable for or used as the site of a camp

cam·pus \ˈkam-pəs\ *n, often attrib* [L, plain] (1774) **1 :** the grounds and buildings of a university, college, or school **2 :** a university, college, or school viewed as an academic, social, or spiritual entity **3 :** grounds that resemble a campus ⟨a hospital ~⟩ ⟨a landscaped corporate ~⟩

cam·pylo·bac·ter \ˌkam-pi-lō-ˈbak-tər, kam-ˌpi-lə-\ *n* [NL, fr. Gk *kampylos* bent + NL *bacterium;* akin to Gk *kampē* bend — more at GAMBIT] (1964) **:** any of a genus (*Campylobacter*) of spirally curved motile gram-negative rod-shaped bacteria of which some are pathogenic in domestic animals and humans

cam·py·lot·ro·pous \ˌkam-pi-ˈlä-trə-pəs\ *adj* [Gk *kampylos* + ISV *-tropous* -tropous] (1835) **:** having the ovule curved

cam·shaft \ˈkam-ˌshaft\ *n* (1847) **:** a shaft to which a cam is fastened or of which a cam forms an integral part

cam wheel *n* (1847) **:** a wheel set or shaped to act as a cam

[1]**can** \kən, ˈkan *also* ˈken; *dial* ˈkin\ *vb, past* **could** \kəd, ˈku̇d\ *pres sing & pl* **can** [ME (1st & 3d sing. pres. indic.), fr. OE; akin to OHG *kan* (1st & 3d sing. pres. indic.) know, am able, OE *cnāwan* to know — more at KNOW] *vt* (bef. 12c) **1** *obs* **:** KNOW, UNDERSTAND **2** *archaic* **:** to be able to do, make, or accomplish ~ *vi, archaic* **:** to have knowledge or skill ~ *verbal auxiliary* **1 a :** know how to ⟨she ~ read⟩ **b :** be physically or mentally able to ⟨he ~ lift 200 pounds⟩ **c —** used to indicate possibility ⟨do you think he ~ still be alive⟩ ⟨those things ~ happen⟩; sometimes used interchangeably with *may* **d :** be permitted by conscience or feeling to ⟨~ hardly blame her⟩ **e :** be made possible or probable by circumstances to ⟨he ~ hardly have meant that⟩ **f :** be inherently able or designed to ⟨everything that money ~ buy⟩ **g :** be logically or axiologically able to ⟨2 + 2 ~ also be written 3 + 1⟩ **h :** be enabled by law, agreement, or custom to **2 :** have permission to — used interchangeably with *may* ⟨you ~ go now if you like⟩

usage *Can* and *may* are most frequently interchangeable in senses denoting possibility; because the possibility of one's doing something may depend on another's acquiescence, they have also become interchangeable in the sense denoting permission. The use of *can* to ask or grant permission has been common since the 19th century and is well established, although some commentators feel *may* is more appropriate in formal contexts. *May* is relatively rare in negative constructions (*mayn't* is not common); *cannot* and *can't* are usual in such contexts.

[2]**can** \ˈkan\ *n* [ME *canne,* fr. OE; akin to OHG *channa*] (bef. 12c) **1 a :** a usu. cylindrical receptacle: **a :** a vessel for holding liquids; *specif* **:** a drinking vessel **b :** a usu. metal typically cylindrical receptacle usu. with an open top, often with a removable cover, and sometimes with a spout or side handles (as for holding milk or trash) **c :** a container (as of tinplate) in which products (as perishable foods) are hermetically sealed for preservation until use **d :** a jar for packing or preserving fruit or vegetables **2 :** JAIL **3 a :** TOILET **b :** BATHROOM 1 **4 :** BUTTOCKS **5 :** DESTROYER 2 — **can·ful** \ˈkan-ˌfu̇l\ *n* — **in the can** *of a film or videotape* **:** completed and ready for release

[3]**can** \ˈkan\ *vt* **canned; can·ning** (1859) **1 a :** to put in a can **:** preserve by sealing in airtight cans or jars ⟨~ tomatoes⟩ **b :** to hit (a golf shot) into the cup **c :** to hit (a shot) in basketball **2 :** to discharge from employment **3** *slang* **:** to put a stop or end to — **can·ner** *n*

[4]**can** *abbr* **1** canceled; cancellation **2** cannon **3** canto

Can *or* **Canad** *abbr* Canada; Canadian

Ca·naan·ite \ˈkā-nə-ˌnīt\ *n* [Gk *Kananitēs,* fr. *Kanaan* Canaan, fr. Heb *Kĕnaʿan*] (1535) **:** a member of a Semitic people inhabiting ancient Palestine and Phoenicia from about 3000 B.C. — **Canaanite** *adj*

Can·a·da balsam \ˈka-nə-də-\ *n* [Canada, country in No. America] (1773) **:** a viscid yellowish to greenish oleoresin exudate of the balsam fir (*Abies balsamea*) that solidifies to a transparent mass and is used as a transparent cement esp. in microscopy

Canada Day *n* (1950) **:** July 1 observed as a legal holiday in commemoration of the proclamation of dominion status in 1867

Canada goose *n* (1731) **:** the common wild goose (*Branta canadensis*) of No. America that is chiefly gray and brownish with black head and neck and a white patch running from the sides of the head under the throat

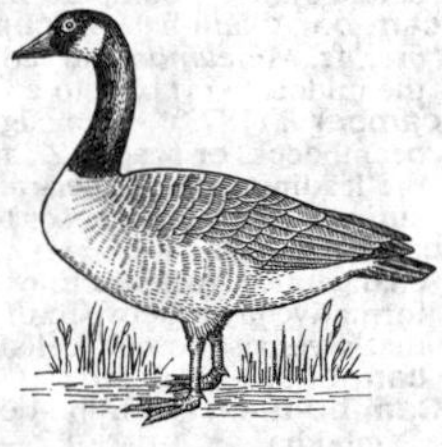
Canada goose

Canada thistle *n* (1799) **:** a European thistle (*Cirsium arvense*) with pinkish-purple or white flowers naturalized as a weed in No. America

Ca·na·di·an \kə-ˈnā-dē-ən\ *n* (1568) **:** a native or inhabitant of Canada — **Canadian** *adj*

Canadian bacon *n* (ca. 1934) **:** bacon cut from the loin that has little fat and is cut into round or oblong slices

Canadian football *n* (1895) **:** a game resembling American football that is played on a turfed field between two teams of 12 players each

Canadian French *n* (1816) **:** the language of the French Canadians

Canadian lynx *or* **Canada lynx** *n* (1822) **:** LYNX c

ca·naille \kə-ˈnī, -ˈnāl\ *n* [F, fr. It *canaglia,* fr. *cane* dog, fr. L *canis* — more at HOUND] (1661) **1 :** RABBLE, RIFFRAFF **2 :** PROLETARIAT

[1]**ca·nal** \kə-ˈnal\ *n* [ME, fr. L *canalis* pipe, channel, fr. *canna* reed — more at CANE] (15c) **1 :** a tubular anatomical passage or channel **:** DUCT **2 :** CHANNEL, WATERCOURSE **3 :** an artificial waterway for navigation or for draining or irrigating land **4 :** any of various faint narrow lines on the planet Mars seen through telescopes and once thought by some to be canals built by Martians

[2]**canal** *vt* **-nalled** *or* **-naled; -nal·ling** *or* **-nal·ing** (1793) **:** to construct a canal through or across

can·a·lic·u·lus \ˌka-nə-ˈli-kyə-ləs\ *n, pl* **-li** \-ˌlī, -ˌlē\ [L, dim. of *canalis*] (ca. 1839) **:** a minute canal in a bodily structure — **can·a·lic·u·lar** \-lər\ *adj*

ca·nal·i·za·tion \ˌka-nə-lə-ˈzā-shən\ *n* (1844) **1 :** an act or instance of canalizing **2 :** a system of channels

ca·na·lize \ˈka-nə-ˌlīz\ *vb* **-lized; -liz·ing** *vt* (1855) **1 a :** to provide with a canal or channel **b :** to make into or similar to a canal **2 :** to provide with an outlet; *esp* **:** to direct into preferred channels ~ *vi* **1 :** to flow in or into a channel **2 :** to establish new channels

can·a·pé \ˈka-nə-pē, -ˌpā\ *n* [F, lit., sofa, fr. ML *canopeum, canapeum* mosquito net — more at CANOPY] (1863) **:** an appetizer consisting of a piece of bread or toast or a cracker topped with a savory spread (as caviar or cheese) — compare HORS D'OEUVRE

ca·nard \kə-ˈnärd *also* -ˈnär\ *n* [F, lit., duck; in sense 1, fr. MF *vendre des canards à moitié* to cheat, lit., to half-sell ducks] (1851) **1 a :** a false or unfounded report or story; *esp* **:** a fabricated report **b :** a groundless rumor or belief **2 :** an airplane with horizontal stabilizing and control surfaces in front of supporting surfaces; *also* **:** a small airfoil in front of the wing of an aircraft that can increase the aircraft's performance

ca·nary \kə-ˈner-ē\ *n, pl* **ca·nar·ies** [MF *canarie,* fr. OSp *canario,* fr. *Islas Canarias* Canary Islands] (1584) **1 :** a Canary Islands usu. sweet wine similar to Madeira **2 :** a lively 16th century court dance **3 :** a small finch (*Serinus canarius* syn. *S. canaria*) of the Canary Islands that is usu. greenish to yellow and is kept as a cage bird and singer **4** *slang* **:** INFORMER 2

canary seed *n* (1597) **:** seed of a Canary Islands grass (*Phalaris canariensis*) used as food for cage birds

canary yellow *n* (1853) **:** a light to a moderate or vivid yellow

ca·nas·ta \kə-'nas-tə\ n [Sp, lit., basket] (1948) **1** : a form of rummy using two full decks in which players or partnerships try to meld groups of three or more cards of the same rank and score bonuses for 7-card melds **2** : a meld of seven cards of the same rank in canasta

canc abbr canceled

can·can \'kan-ˌkan\ n [F] (1848) : a woman's dance of French origin characterized by high kicking usu. while holding up the front of a full ruffled skirt

¹can·cel \'kan(t)-səl\ vb **-celed** or **-celled**; **-cel·ing** or **-cel·ling** \-s(ə-)liŋ\ [ME cancellen, fr. AF canceller, chanceller, fr. LL cancellare, fr. L, to make like a lattice, fr. cancelli (pl.), dim. of cancer lattice, prob. alter. of carcer prison] vt (14c) **1 a** : to destroy the force, effectiveness, or validity of : ANNUL ⟨~ a magazine subscription⟩ ⟨a ~ed check⟩ **b** : to bring to nothingness : DESTROY **c** : to match in force or effect : OFFSET — often used with out ⟨his irritability ~ed out his natural kindness —Osbert Sitwell⟩ **d** : to call off usu. without expectation of conducting or performing at a later time ⟨~ a football game⟩ **2 a** : to mark or strike out for deletion **b** : OMIT, DELETE **3 a** : to remove (a common divisor) from numerator and denominator **b** : to remove (equivalents) on opposite sides of an equation or account **4** : to deface (a postage or revenue stamp) esp. with a set of ink lines so as to invalidate for reuse ~ vi : to neutralize each other's strength or effect : COUNTERBALANCE — **can·cel·able** or **can·cel·la·ble** \-s(ə-)lə-bəl\ adj — **can·cel·er** or **can·cel·ler** \-s(ə-)lər\ n

²cancel n (1806) **1** : CANCELLATION **2 a** : a deleted part or passage **b** (1) : a leaf containing matter to be deleted (2) : a new leaf or slip substituted for matter already printed

can·cel·la·tion also **can·cel·a·tion** \ˌkan(t)-sə-'lā-shən\ n (1535) **1** : the act or an instance of canceling **2** : something (as a hotel room or a ticket) made available by the canceling of an arrangement **3** : a mark made to cancel something (as a postage stamp)

can·cel·lous \kan-'se-ləs, 'kan(t)-sə-ləs\ adj [NL cancelli intersecting osseous plates and bars in cancellous bone, fr. L, lattice] (ca. 1839) of bone : having a porous structure

can·cer \'kan(t)-sər\ n [ME, fr. L (gen. Cancri), lit., crab; akin to Gk karkinos crab, cancer] (14c) **1 cap a** : a northern zodiacal constellation between Gemini and Leo **b** (1) : the fourth sign of the zodiac in astrology — see ZODIAC table (2) : one born under the sign of Cancer **2** [L, crab, cancer] **a** : a malignant tumor of potentially unlimited growth that expands locally by invasion and systemically by metastasis **b** : an abnormal bodily state marked by such tumors **3** : something evil or malignant that spreads destructively ⟨the ~ of hidden resentment —Irish Digest⟩ **4 a** : an enlarged tumorlike plant growth (as that of crown gall) **b** : a plant disease marked by such growths — **can·cer·ous** \'kan(t)s-rəs, 'kan(t)-sə-rəs\ adj — **can·cer·ous·ly** adv

Can·cer·ian \kan-'ser-ē-ən, -'sir-\ n (1911) : CANCER 1b(2)

can·de·la \kan-'dē-lə, -'de-, -'dā-; 'kan-də-lə\ n [L, candle] (1949) : the base unit of luminous intensity in the International System of Units that is equal to the luminous intensity in a given direction of a source which emits monochromatic radiation of frequency 540 × 10¹² hertz and has a radiant intensity in that direction of 1/683 watt per unit solid angle — abbr. cd; called also candle

can·de·la·bra \ˌkan-də-'lä-brə sometimes -'la-\ n [alter. of L candelabrum, fr. candela] (1805) : a branched candlestick or lamp with several lights

can·de·la·brum \-brəm\ n, pl **-bra** \-brə\ also **-brums** [L] (1811) : CANDELABRA

can·dent \'kan-dənt\ adj [L candent-, candens, prp. of candēre] (1577) : glowing from or as if from great heat

can·des·cence \kan-'de-sᵊn(t)s\ n (ca. 1864) : a candescent state : glowing whiteness

can·des·cent \-sᵊnt\ adj [L candescent-, candescens, prp. of candescere, incho. of candēre] (1808) : glowing or dazzling from or as if from great heat

C and F abbr cost and freight

can·did \'kan-dəd\ adj [F & L; F candide, fr. L candidus bright, white, fr. candēre to shine, glow; akin to W can white, Skt candati it shines] (1606) **1** : WHITE ⟨~ flames⟩ **2** : free from bias, prejudice, or malice : FAIR ⟨a ~ observer⟩ **3 a** : marked by honest sincere expression ⟨a ~ discussion⟩ **b** : indicating or suggesting honest honesty and absence of deception ⟨her ~ face⟩ **c** : disposed to criticize severely : BLUNT ⟨~ critics⟩ **4** : relating to or being photography of subjects acting naturally or spontaneously without being posed *syn* see FRANK — **can·did·ly** adv — **can·did·ness** n

can·di·da \'kan-də-də\ n [NL, genus name, fr. L, fem. of candidus] (1939) : any of a genus (Candida) of parasitic fungi that resemble yeasts, occur esp. in the mouth, vagina, and intestinal tract where they are usu. benign but can become pathogenic, and have been grouped with the imperfect fungi but are now often placed with the ascomycetes; esp *one* (C. albicans) causing thrush — **can·di·dal** \-dᵊl\ adj

can·di·da·cy \'kan-də-də-sē, 'kan-nə-\ n, pl **-cies** (1848) : the state of being a candidate ⟨his is the expected to announce his ~⟩

can·di·date \'kan-də-ˌdāt, 'kan-nə-, -dət\ n [L candidatus, fr. candidatus clothed in white, fr. candidus white; fr. the white toga worn by candidates for office in ancient Rome] (1600) **1 a** : one that aspires to or is nominated or qualified for an office, membership, or award ⟨a ~ for governor⟩ **b** : one likely or suited to undergo or be chosen for something specified ⟨a ~ for surgery⟩ **2** : a student in the process of meeting final requirements for a degree

can·di·da·ture \'kan-də-də-ˌchur, 'kan-nə-, -chər\ n (1848) chiefly Brit : CANDIDACY

candid camera n (1929) : a camera used to record subjects in a natural, spontaneous, or unposed manner; also : something likened to a camera used in such a manner — **candid–camera** adj

can·di·di·a·sis \ˌkan-də-'dī-ə-səs\ n, pl **-a·ses** \-ˌsēz\ [NL] (1951) : infection with or disease caused by a candida — called also moniliasis

can·died \'kan-dēd\ adj (1577) **1** : encrusted or coated with sugar ⟨~ fruits⟩ **2** : baked with sugar or syrup until translucent ⟨~ yams⟩

¹can·dle \'kan-dᵊl\ n [ME candel, fr. OE, fr. L candela, fr. candēre] (bef. 12c) **1** : a usu. molded or dipped mass of wax or tallow containing a wick that may be burned (as to give light, heat, or scent or for celebration or votive purposes) **2** : something resembling a candle in shape or use ⟨a sulfur ~ for fumigating⟩ **3** : required effort, expense, or trouble — usu. used in the phrase not worth the candle **4** : CANDELA

²candle vt **can·dled**; **can·dling** \'kan(d)-liŋ, 'kan-dᵊl-iŋ\ (1879) : to examine by holding between the eye and a light; esp : to test (eggs) in this way for staleness, blood clots, fertility, and growth — **can·dler** \'kan(d)-lər, 'kan-dᵊl-ər\ n

can·dle·ber·ry \'kan-dᵊl-ˌber-ē, -ˌbe-rē\ n (ca. 1730) : a wax myrtle (Myrica cerifera); also : a bayberry (Myrica pensylvanica)

can·dle·fish \-ˌfish\ n (1866) : a very oily anadromous marine food fish (Thaleichthys pacificus) of the smelt family that occurs along the No. Pacific coast — called also eulachon

can·dle·hold·er \-ˌhōl-dər\ n (1846) : CANDLESTICK

can·dle·light \'kan-dᵊl-ˌ(l)īt\ n (bef. 12c) **1 a** : the light of a candle **b** : a soft artificial light **2** : the time for lighting candles : TWILIGHT

can·dle·light·er \-ˌ(l)ī-tər\ n (15c) **1** : one who lights the candles for a ceremony **2** : a long-handled implement with a taper and a candlesnuffer that used for the ceremonial lighting and extinguishing of candles

can·dle·lit \-ˌ(l)it\ or **can·dle·light·ed** \-ˌ(l)ī-təd\ adj (1868) : illuminated by candlelight ⟨a ~ dinner⟩

Can·dle·mas \'kan-dᵊl-məs\ n [ME candelmasse, fr. OE candelmæsse, fr. candel + mæsse mass, feast; fr. the candles blessed and carried in celebration of the feast] (bef. 12c) : February 2 observed as a church festival in commemoration of the presentation of Jesus in the temple and the purification of the Virgin Mary

can·dle·nut \-ˌnət\ n (ca. 1836) : the oily seed of a tropical tree (Aleurites moluccana) of the spurge family used locally to make candles and commercially as a source of oil; also : this tree

can·dle·pin \-ˌpin\ n (1901) **1** : a slender cylindrical bowling pin tapering toward top and bottom **2** pl but sing in constr : a bowling game using candlepins and a smaller ball than that used in tenpins

can·dle·pow·er \-ˌpau̇(-ə)r\ n (1869) : luminous intensity expressed in candelas; also : CANDELA

can·dle·snuff·er \-ˌsnə-fər\ n (1552) : an implement for snuffing candles that consists of a small hollow cone attached to a handle

can·dle·stick \-ˌstik\ n (bef. 12c) : a holder with a socket for a candle

can·dle·wick \-ˌwik\ n (bef. 12c) **1** : the wick of a candle **2** : a soft cotton embroidery yarn; also : embroidery made with this yarn usu. in tufts

can·dle·wood \-ˌwu̇d\ n (1712) **1** : any of several trees or shrubs (as ocotillo) chiefly of resinous character **2** : slivers of resinous wood burned for light

can–do \kan-'dü\ adj (1945) : characterized by eager willingness to accept and meet challenges ⟨a ~ attitude⟩ — **can–do–ism** \-ˌi-zəm\ n

can·dor \'kan-dər, -ˌdȯr\ n [F & L; F candeur, fr. L candor, fr. candēre — more at CANDID] (14c) **1 a** : WHITENESS, BRILLIANCE **b** obs : unstained purity **2** : freedom from prejudice or malice : FAIRNESS **3** archaic : KINDLINESS **4** : unreserved, honest, or sincere expression : FORTHRIGHTNESS ⟨the ~ with which he acknowledged a weakness in his own case —Aldous Huxley⟩

can·dour \'kan-dər\ chiefly Brit var of CANDOR

C & W abbr country and western

¹can·dy \'kan-dē\ n, pl **candies** [ME sugre candy, part trans. of MF sucre candi, fr. OF sucre sugar + Ar qandī candied, fr. qand crystallized sugar] (15c) **1** : crystallized sugar formed by boiling down sugar syrup **2 a** : a confection made with sugar and often flavoring and filling **b** : a piece of such confection **3** : something that is pleasant or appealing in a light or frivolous way ⟨visual ~⟩ — **candy** adj

²candy vb **can·died**; **can·dy·ing** vt (1533) **1** : to encrust in or coat with sugar; specif : to cook (as fruit or fruit peel) in a heavy syrup until glazed **2** : to make attractive : SWEETEN **3** : to crystallize into sugar ~ vi : to become coated or encrusted with sugar crystals : become crystallized into sugar

candy floss n (1951) **1** Brit : COTTON CANDY **2** usu **candyfloss**, Brit : something attractive but insubstantial

candy striper n [fr. the striped uniform worn suggesting the stripes on some sticks of candy] (1963) : a teenage volunteer worker at a hospital

can·dy·tuft \'kan-dē-ˌtəft\ n [Candy, alter. of Candia Crete, Greek island + E tuft] (1629) : any of a genus (Iberis) of plants of the mustard family cultivated for their white, pink, or purple flowers

¹cane \'kān\ n [ME, fr. MF, fr. Old Occitan cana, fr. L canna, fr. Gk kanna, of Sem origin; akin to Akkadian qanū reed, Heb qāneh] (14c) **1 a** (1) : a hollow or pithy and usu. slender and flexible jointed stem (as of a reed) (2) : any of various slender woody stems; esp : an elongated flowering or fruiting stem (as of a rose) usu. arising directly from the ground **b** : any of various tall woody grasses or reeds: as : (1) : any of a genus (Arundinaria) of coarse grasses (2) : SUGARCANE (3) : SORGHUM **2** : cane dressed for use: as **a** : a cane walking stick; broadly : WALKING STICK **b** : a cane or rod for flogging **c** : RATTAN; esp : split rattan for wickerwork or basketwork **3** : a tiny glass rod used in decorative glasswork (as in millefiori and paperweights)

²cane vt **caned**; **can·ing** (1662) **1** : to beat with a cane ⟨he sat in a professor's chair and caned sophomores for blowing spitballs —H. L. Mencken⟩ **2** : to weave or furnish with cane ⟨the ~ the seat of a chair⟩

cane·brake \'kān-ˌbrāk\ n (1769) : a thicket of cane

can·er \'kā-nər\ n (1868) : one who canes chairs

ca·nes·cent \kə-'ne-sᵊnt, ka-\ adj [L canescent-, canescens, prp. of canescere, incho. of canēre to be gray, be white, fr. canus white, hoary — more at HARE] (ca. 1828) : growing white, whitish, or hoary; esp : having a fine grayish-white pubescence ⟨~ leaves⟩

cane sugar n (1766) : sugar from sugarcane

cane·ware \'kān-ˌwer\ n [fr. its color] (1856) : a buff or yellowish stoneware

ca·nic·u·lar \kə-'ni-kyə-lər\ adj [ME caniculer of the star Sirius, fr. LL canicularis, fr. L Canicula Sirius, dim. of canis] (12c) : of or relating to the dog days

ca·nid \'kā-nəd, 'kā-\ n [NL Canidae, fr. Canis, type genus, fr. L canis] (ca. 1889) : any of a family (Canidae) of carnivorous animals that includes the wolves, jackals, foxes, coyote, and the domestic dog

---

\ə\ **abut** \ᵊ\ **kitten**, F **table** \ər\ **further** \a\ **ash** \ā\ **ace** \ä\ **mop, mar**
\au̇\ **out** \ch\ **chin** \e\ **bet** \ē\ **easy** \g\ **go** \i\ **hit** \ī\ **ice** \j\ **job**
\ŋ\ **sing** \ō\ **go** \ȯ\ **law** \ȯi\ **boy** \th\ **thin** \th\ **the** \ü\ **loot** \u̇\ **foot**
\y\ **yet** \zh\ **vision, beige** \k, ⁿ, œ, �, ᵛ\ see Guide to Pronunciation

[1]**ca·nine** \ˈkā-ˌnīn, *Brit also* ˈka-\ *n* (15c) **1** [ME, fr. L (*dens*) *caninus* canine tooth] : a conical pointed tooth; *esp* : one situated between the lateral incisor and the first premolar — see TOOTH illustration **2** : DOG 1a; *broadly* : CANID
[2]**canine** *adj* [L *caninus,* fr. *canis* dog — more at HOUND] (1607) **1** : of or resembling that of a dog ⟨~ loyalty⟩ **2** : of or relating to dogs or to the family (Canidae) including the canids
canine distemper *n* (1929) : DISTEMPER 2a
Ca·nis Ma·jor \ˌkā-nəs-ˈmā-jər, ˌka-\ *n* [L (gen. *Canis Majoris*), lit., greater dog] (14c) : a constellation to the southeast of Orion containing Sirius
Canis Mi·nor \-ˈmī-nər\ *n* [L (gen. *Canis Minoris*), lit., lesser dog] (14c) : a constellation to the east of Orion containing Procyon
can·is·ter *also* **can·nis·ter** \ˈka-nə-stər\ *n* [L *canistrum* basket, fr. Gk *kanastron* wicker basket, fr. *kanna* reed — more at CANE] (1692) **1** : an often cylindrical container for holding a usu. specified object or substance ⟨a film ~⟩ **2** : encased shot for close-range artillery fire **3** : a perforated metal box for gas masks with material to adsorb, filter, or detoxify airborne poisons and irritants
[1]**can·ker** \ˈkaŋ-kər\ *n* [ME, fr. AF *cancre, chancre,* fr. L *cancer* crab, cancer] (bef. 12c) **1 a** (1) : an erosive or spreading sore (2) : an area of necrosis in a plant; *also* : a plant disease characterized by cankers **b** : any of various disorders of animals marked by chronic inflammatory changes **2** *archaic* : a caterpillar destructive to plants **3** *chiefly dial* : RUST 1 **4** : a source of corruption or debasement **5** *chiefly dial* : DOG ROSE — **can·ker·ous** \ˈkaŋ-k(ə-)rəs\ *adj*
[2]**canker** *vb* **can·kered; can·ker·ing** \ˈkaŋ-k(ə-)riŋ\ *vt* (14c) **1** *obs* : to infect with a spreading sore **2** : to corrupt the spirit of ~ *vi* **1** : to become infested with canker **2** : to become corrupted
canker sore *n* (ca. 1596) : a painful shallow ulcer of the mouth that has a grayish-white base surrounded by a reddish inflamed area and is of uncertain cause but is not due to the virus causing herpes simplex — compare COLD SORE
can·ker·worm \ˈkaŋ-kər-ˌwərm\ *n* (1530) : either of two geometrid moths (*Alsophila pometaria* and *Paleacrita vernata*) and esp. their larvae which are serious pests of fruit and shade trees
can·na \ˈka-nə\ *n* [NL, genus name, fr. L, reed — more at CANE] (1664) : any of a genus (*Canna* of the family Cannaceae) of tropical herbs with simple stems, large leaves, and a terminal raceme of irregular flowers
can·na·bi·noid \kə-ˈna-bə-ˌnȯid\ *n* [L *cannabis* + [1]*-in* + [1]*-oid*] (1967) : any of various chemical constituents (as THC or cannabinol) of cannabis or marijuana
can·na·bi·nol \-ˌnȯl, -ˌnōl\ *n* [L *cannabis* + [1]*-in* + [1]*-ol*] (1896) : a physiologically inactive crystalline cannabinoid $C_{21}H_{26}O_2$
can·na·bis \ˈka-nə-bəs\ *n* [L, hemp, fr. Gk *kannabis;* akin to OE *hænep* hemp] (1783) **1** : HEMP 1a **2** : any of the preparations (as marijuana or hashish) or chemicals (as THC) that are derived from the hemp and are psychoactive
canned \ˈkand\ *adj* (1904) **1 a** : prepared or recorded in advance; *esp* : prepared in standardized form for nonspecific use or wide distribution ⟨~ laughter⟩ ⟨~ music⟩ **b** : lacking originality or individuality as if mass-produced ⟨~ sales pitch⟩ **2** *slang* : DRUNK 1a
can·nel coal \ˈka-nᵊl-\ *n* [prob. fr. E dial. *cannel* candle, fr. ME *candel*] (1594) : a bituminous coal containing much volatile matter that burns brightly
can·nel·li·ni bean \ˌka-nə-ˈlē-nē-\ *n* [It *cannellini,* pl. of *cannellino* kind of hard candy, variety of white bean resembling the candy, prob. fr. *cannella* cinnamon, lit., small tube, fr. ML *canella,* dim. of L *canna*] (1967) : a usu. large white kidney bean — called also *cannellini*
can·nel·lo·ni \ˌka-nə-ˈlō-nē\ *n pl but sing or pl in constr* [It, pl. of *cannellone,* aug. of *cannello* segment of cane stalk, fr. *canna*] (1892) : boiled tube-shaped or rolled pasta filled with a meat, fish, cheese, or vegetable mixture and baked in a sauce
can·nery \ˈka-nə-rē\ *n, pl* **-ner·ies** (1864) : a factory for the canning of foods
can·ni·bal \ˈka-nə-bəl\ *n* [NL *Canibalis* Carib, fr. Sp *Caníbal,* fr. Taino *Caniba,* of Cariban origin; akin to Carib *kariʔna* Carib, person] (1553) : one that eats the flesh of its own kind
can·ni·bal·ise *Brit var of* CANNIBALIZE
can·ni·bal·ism \ˈka-nə-bə-ˌli-zəm\ *n* (1796) **1** : the usu. ritualistic eating of human flesh by a human being **2** : the eating of the flesh of an animal by another animal of the same kind **3** : an act of cannibalizing something — **can·ni·bal·is·tic** \ˌka-nə-bə-ˈlis-tik\ *adj*
can·ni·bal·ize \ˈka-nə-bə-ˌlīz\ *vb* **-ized; -iz·ing** *vt* (1943) **1 a** : to take salvageable parts from (as a disabled machine) for use in building or repairing another machine **b** : to make use of (a part taken from one thing) in building, repairing, or creating something else **2** : to deprive of an essential part or element in creating or sustaining another facility or enterprise ⟨the energy system has begun *cannibalizing* the economic system it is supposed to fuel —Barry Commoner⟩ **3** : to use or draw on material of (as another writer or an earlier work) ⟨a biography that ~s previous biographies⟩ **4** : to take (sales) away from an existing product by selling or being sold as a similar but new product usu. from the same manufacturer; *also* : to affect (as an existing product) adversely by cannibalizing sales ~ *vi* **1** : to practice cannibalism **2** : to cannibalize one unit for the sake of another of the same kind — **can·ni·bal·i·za·tion** \ˌka-nə-bə-lə-ˈzā-shən\ *n*
can·ni·kin \ˈka-ni-kən\ *n* [prob. fr. obs. D *kanneken,* fr. MD *canneken,* dim. of *canne* can; akin to OE *canne* can] (1570) : a small can or drinking vessel
can·no·li \kə-ˈnō-lē, ka-\ *n pl but sing or pl in constr* [It, pl. of *cannolo* small tube, dim. of *canna*] (1943) : a deep-fried tube of pastry filled with sweetened and flavored ricotta cheese
[1]**can·non** \ˈka-nən\ *n, pl* **cannons** *or* **cannon** [ME *canon,* fr. AF, fr. OIt *cannone,* lit., large tube, aug. of *canna* reed, tube, fr. L, cane, reed — more at CANE] (15c) **1** *pl usu cannon* **a** : a large heavy gun usu. mounted on a carriage **b** : a heavy-caliber automatic aircraft gun firing explosive shells **2** *or* **can·on** : the projecting part of a bell by which it is hung : EAR **3** : the part of the leg in which the cannon bone is found
[2]**cannon** *vi* (1567) : to discharge cannon ~ *vt* : CANNONADE
[1]**can·non·ade** \ˌka-nə-ˈnād\ *n* (1562) **1** : a heavy fire of artillery **2** : an attack (as with words) likened to artillery fire : BOMBARDMENT
[2]**cannonade** *vb* **-ad·ed; -ad·ing** *vt* (1664) : to attack with or as if with artillery ~ *vi* : to deliver artillery fire
[1]**can·non·ball** \ˈka-nən-ˌbȯl\ *n* (1655) **1** : a usu. round solid missile made for firing from a cannon **2** : a jump into water made with the arms holding the knees tight against the chest **3** : a hard flat tennis service **4** : an express train
[2]**cannonball** *vi* (1951) : to travel with great speed
cannon bone *n* [F *canon,* lit., cannon] (1834) : a bone in hoofed mammals that extends from the knee or hock to the fetlock; *esp* : the enlarged metacarpal or metatarsal of the third digit of a horse
can·non·eer \ˌka-nə-ˈnir\ *n* (1562) : an artillery gunner
cannon fodder *n* (ca. 1891) **1** : soldiers regarded or treated as expendable in battle **2** : an expendable or exploitable person, group, or thing ⟨celebrities who have become *cannon fodder* for the tabloids⟩
can·non·ry \ˈka-nən-rē\ *n, pl* **-ries** (1811) : a battery of cannons or cannon fire
can·not \ˈka-(ˌ)nät; kə-ˈnät, ka-\ (15c) : can not — **cannot but** *or* **cannot help but** *also* **cannot help** : to be unable to do otherwise than ⟨we *cannot but* wonder why⟩
can·nu·la \ˈkan-yə-lə\ *n, pl* **-las** *or* **-lae** \-ˌlē, -ˌlī\ [NL, fr. L, dim. of *canna* reed — more at CANE] (1684) : a small tube for insertion into a body cavity or into a duct or vessel
can·nu·lar \ˈkan-yə-lər\ *adj* (1823) : TUBULAR
can·nu·late \ˈkan-yə-ˌlāt\ *vt* **-lated; -lating** (1926) : to insert a cannula into ⟨*cannulated* the femoral artery⟩ — **can·nu·la·tion** \ˌkan-yə-ˈlā-shən\ *n*
[1]**can·ny** \ˈka-nē\ *adj* **can·ni·er; -est** [[1]*can*] (1596) **1** : CLEVER, SHREWD ⟨a ~ lawyer⟩; *also* : PRUDENT ⟨~ investments⟩ **2** *chiefly Scot* **a** : CAREFUL, STEADY; *also* : RESTRAINED **b** : QUIET, SNUG ⟨then ~, in some cozy place, they close the day —Robert Burns⟩ — **can·ni·ly** \ˈka-nᵊl-ē\ *adv* — **can·ni·ness** \ˈka-nē-nəs\ *n*
[2]**canny** *adv* (ca. 1796) *Scot* : in a canny manner : CAREFULLY
[1]**ca·noe** \kə-ˈnü\ *n* [F, fr. NL *canoa,* fr. Sp, fr. Arawakan, of Cariban origin; akin to Carib *kana:wa* canoe] (1555) : a light narrow boat with both ends sharp that is usu. propelled by paddling
[2]**canoe** *vb* **ca·noed; ca·noe·ing** *vt* (1794) : to transport in a canoe; *also* : to travel by canoe down (a river) ~ *vi* : to go or travel in a canoe — **ca·noe·able** \-ə-bəl\ *adj* — **ca·noe·ist** \-ist\ *n* — **ca·no·er** \-ər\ *n*
can of worms (1962) : PANDORA'S BOX
ca·no·la \kə-ˈnō-lə\ *n* [fr. *Canola,* former certification mark] (1979) **1** : a rape plant of an improved variety having seeds that are low in erucic acid and are the source of canola oil **2** : CANOLA OIL
canola oil *n* (1981) : an edible vegetable oil obtained from the seeds of canola that is high in monounsaturated fatty acids
[1]**can·on** \ˈka-nən\ *n* [ME, fr. OE, fr. LL, fr. L, ruler, rule, model, standard, fr. Gk *kanōn*] (bef. 12c) **1 a** : a regulation or dogma decreed by a church council **b** : a provision of canon law **2** [ME, fr. AF, fr. LL, fr. L, model] : the most solemn and unvarying part of the Mass including the consecration of the bread and wine **3** [ME, fr. LL, fr. L, standard] **a** : an authoritative list of books accepted as Holy Scripture **b** : the authentic works of a writer **c** : a sanctioned or accepted group or body of related works ⟨the ~ of great literature⟩ **4 a** : an accepted principle or rule **b** : a criterion or standard of judgment **c** : a body of principles, rules, standards, or norms **5** [LGk *kanōn,* fr. Gk, model] : a contrapuntal musical composition in which each successively entering voice presents the initial theme usu. transformed in a strictly consistent way ***syn*** see LAW
[2]**canon** *n* [ME *canoun,* fr. AF **canoun, chanoun,* fr. LL *canonicus* one living under a rule, fr. L, according to rule, fr. Gk *kanonikos,* fr. *kanōn*] (13c) **1** : a clergyman belonging to the chapter or the staff of a cathedral or collegiate church **2** : CANON REGULAR
cañon *var of* CANYON
can·on·ess \ˈka-nə-nəs\ *n* (1682) **1** : a woman living in community under a religious rule but not under a perpetual vow **2** : a member of a Roman Catholic congregation of women corresponding to canons regular
ca·non·ic \kə-ˈnä-nik\ *adj* (15c) **1** : CANONICAL **2** : of or relating to musical canon
ca·non·i·cal \-ni-kəl\ *adj* (15c) **1** : of, relating to, or forming a canon **2** : conforming to a general rule or acceptable procedure : ORTHODOX **3** : of or relating to a clergyman who is a canon **4** : reduced to the canonical form ⟨a ~ matrix⟩ — **ca·non·i·cal·ly** \-k(ə-)lē\ *adv*
canonical form *n* (1851) : the simplest form of something; *specif* : the form of a square matrix that has zero elements everywhere except along the principal diagonal
canonical hour *n* (15c) **1** : a time of day canonically appointed for an office of devotion **2** : one of the daily offices of devotion that compose the Divine Office and include matins with lauds, prime, terce, sext, none, vespers, and compline
ca·non·i·cals \kə-ˈnä-ni-kəlz\ *n pl* (1748) : the vestments prescribed by canon for an officiating clergyman
can·on·ic·i·ty \ˌka-nə-ˈni-sə-tē\ *n* (1797) : the quality or state of being canonical
can·on·ist \ˈka-nə-nist\ *n* (1542) : a specialist in canon law
can·on·ize \ˈka-nə-ˌnīz\ *vt* **can·on·ized** \-ˌnīzd; *in "Hamlet" usu* kə-ˈnä-ˌnīzd\; **can·on·iz·ing** [ME, fr. ML *canonizare,* fr. LL *canon* catalog of saints, fr. L, standard] (14c) **1** : to declare (a deceased person) an officially recognized saint **2** : to make canonical **3** : to sanction by ecclesiastical authority **4** : to attribute authoritative sanction or approval to **5** : to treat as illustrious, preeminent, or sacred — **can·on·i·za·tion** \ˌka-nə-nə-ˈzā-shən\ *n*
canon law *n* (15c) : the usu. codified law governing a church
canon lawyer *n* (1616) : CANONIST
canon regular *n, pl* **canons regular** (14c) : a member of one of several Roman Catholic religious institutes of regular priests living in community under a usu. Augustinian rule
can·on·ry \ˈka-nən-rē\ *n, pl* **-ries** (15c) : the office of a canon; *also* : the endowment that financially supports a canon
ca·noo·dle \kə-ˈnü-dᵊl\ *vi* **ca·noo·dled; ca·noo·dling** \-ˈnü-dliŋ, -ˈnü-dᵊl-iŋ\ [perh. fr. E dial. *canoodle,* n., donkey, fool, foolish lover] (1859) : PET, FONDLE ⟨lovers *canoodling* in the park⟩
ca·no·pic jar \kə-ˈnō-pik-, -ˈnä-\ *n* [*Canopus,* Egypt] (1893) : a jar in which the ancient Egyptians preserved the viscera of a deceased person usu. for burial with the mummy

Ca·no·pus \kə-ˈnō-pəs\ *n* [L, fr. Gk *Kanōpos*] (1555) : a star of the first magnitude in the constellation Carina not visible north of 37° latitude

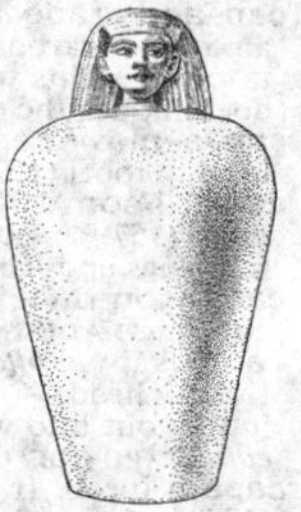
canopic jar

[1]**can·o·py** \ˈka-nə-pē\ *n, pl* **-pies** [ME *canope,* fr. ML *canopeum* mosquito net, fr. L *conopeum,* fr. Gk *kōnōpion,* fr. *kōnōps* mosquito] (14c) **1 a :** a cloth covering suspended over a bed **b :** a cover (as of cloth) fixed or carried above a person of high rank or a sacred object : BALDACHIN **c :** a protective covering: as (1) : the uppermost spreading branchy layer of a forest (2) : AWNING, MARQUEE **2 :** an ornamental rooflike structure **3 a :** the transparent enclosure over an airplane cockpit **b :** the fabric part of a parachute that catches the air

[2]**canopy** *vt* **-pied; -py·ing** (1594) : to cover with or as if with a canopy

ca·no·rous \kə-ˈnȯr-əs, ˈka-nə-rəs\ *adj* [L *canorus,* fr. *canor* melody, fr. *canere* to sing — more at CHANT] (1646) : pleasant sounding : MELODIOUS — **ca·no·rous·ly** *adv* — **ca·no·rous·ness** *n*

canst \kən(t)st, ˈkan(t)st\ *archaic pres 2d sing of* CAN

[1]**cant** \ˈkant\ *adj* [ME, prob. fr. MLG **kant*] (14c) *dial Eng* : LIVELY, LUSTY

[2]**cant** *vt* [3*cant*] (ca. 1543) **1 :** to give a cant or oblique edge to : BEVEL **2 :** to set at an angle : TILT **3** *chiefly Brit* : to throw with a lurch ~ *vi* **1 :** to pitch to one side : LEAN **2 :** SLOPE

[3]**cant** *n* [ME *cant* side, prob. fr. MD or MF dial.; MD, edge, corner, fr. MF dial. (Picard), fr. L *canthus, cantus* iron tire, perh. of Celt origin; akin to W *cant* rim; perh. akin to Gk *kanthos* corner of the eye] (1603) **1** *obs* : CORNER, NICHE **2 :** an external angle (as of a building) **3 :** a log with one or more squared sides **4 a :** an oblique or slanting surface **b :** INCLINATION, SLOPE

[4]**cant** *adj* (1663) **1 :** having canted corners or sides **2 :** INCLINED 2

[5]**cant** *vi* [perh. fr. MF dial. (Norman-Picard) *canter* to tell, lit., to sing, fr. L *cantare* — more at CHANT] (1567) **1 :** to talk or beg in a whining or singsong manner **2 :** to speak in cant or jargon **3 :** to talk hypocritically

[6]**cant** *n* (1640) **1 :** affected singsong or whining speech **2 a :** the private language of the underworld **b** *obs* : the phraseology peculiar to a religious class or sect **c :** JARGON 2 **3 :** a set or stock phrase **4 :** the expression or repetition of conventional or trite opinions or sentiments; *esp* : the insincere use of pious words

Cant *abbr* **1** Canticle of Canticles **2** Cantonese

can't \ˈkant, ˈkänt, *esp Southern* ˈkānt\ (15c) : can not

Can·tab \ˈkan-ˌtab\ *n* [by shortening] (1697) : CANTABRIGIAN

can·ta·bi·le \kän-ˈtä-bi-ˌlā, -lē\ *adv or adj* [It, fr. LL *cantabilis* worthy to be sung, fr. L *cantare*] (ca. 1724) : in a singing manner — often used as a direction in music

Can·ta·brig·i·an \ˌkan-tə-ˈbri-j(ē-)ən\ *n* [ML *Cantabrigia* Cambridge] (ca. 1540) **1 :** a student or graduate of Cambridge University **2 :** a native or resident of Cambridge, Mass. — **Cantabrigian** *adj*

can·tal \kän-ˈtäl\ *n, often cap* [F, fr. *Cantal,* mountain massif and department in Auvergne, France] (1890) : a hard cheddar-type cheese made in the south of France

can·ta·la \kan-ˈtä-lə\ *n* [NL, specific epithet of *Agave cantala,* perh. fr. Skt *kaṇṭala* babul, fr. *kaṇṭa* thorn] (1911) : a hard fiber produced from the leaves of an agave (*Agave cantala*)

can·ta·loupe *also* **can·ta·loup** \ˈkan-tə-ˌlōp *also* -ˌüp\ *n* [*Cantalupo,* former papal villa near Rome, Italy] (1739) **1 :** a small widely cultivated muskmelon (*Cucumis melo reticulatus*) with a heavily netted rind and reddish-orange flesh; *broadly* : MUSKMELON a **2 :** a muskmelon (*Cucumis melo cantalupensis*) with a rough hard warty rind that is not usu. grown in No. America

can·tan·ker·ous \kan-ˈtaŋ-k(ə-)rəs, kən-\ *adj* [perh. irreg. fr. obs. *contack* contention] (1772) : difficult or irritating to deal with ⟨a ~ mule⟩ — **can·tan·ker·ous·ly** *adv* — **can·tan·ker·ous·ness** *n*

can·ta·ta \kən-ˈtä-tə\ *n* [It, fr. *cantare* to sing, fr. L] (1724) : a composition for one or more voices usu. comprising solos, duets, recitatives, and choruses and sung to an instrumental accompaniment

can·ta·trice \ˌkän-tə-ˈtrē-(ˌ)chä, ˌkäⁿ-tə-ˈtrēs\ *n, pl* **-trices** \-ˈtrē-(ˌ)chäz, -ˈtrēs, -ˈtrē-səz\ *or* **-tri·ci** \ˌkän-tə-ˈtrē-(ˌ)chē\ [It & F; F, fr. It, fr. LL *cantatric-, cantatrix,* fem. of L *cantator* singer, fr. *cantare*] (1801) : a woman who is a singer; *esp* : an opera singer

cant dog *n* [3*cant*] (1850) : PEAVEY

can·teen \kan-ˈtēn\ *n* [F *cantine* bottle case, sutler's shop, fr. It *cantina* wine cellar, prob. fr. *canto* corner, fr. L *canthus* iron tire — more at CANT] (1737) **1 a :** a portable chest with compartments for carrying bottles or for cooking and eating utensils **b :** a flask for carrying liquids (as on a hike) **c :** MESS KIT **d** *Brit* : a chest for storing flatware **2 a :** a bar at a military post or camp **b :** a general store at a military post : EXCHANGE **c :** an establishment that serves as an informal social club (as for soldiers or a community's teenagers) **d :** a small cafeteria or snack bar

[1]**cant·er** \ˈkan-tər\ *n* (1609) : one who uses cant: as **a :** BEGGAR, VAGABOND **b :** a user of professional or religious cant

[2]**can·ter** \ˈkan-tər\ *vb* [short for obs. *canterbury,* n. (canter), fr. *Canterbury,* England; fr. the supposed gait of pilgrims riding to Canterbury] *vi* (1706) **1 :** to move at or as if at a canter : LOPE **2 :** to ride a horse at a canter ~ *vt* : to cause to go at a canter

[3]**can·ter** *n* (1755) **1 :** a 3-beat gait resembling but smoother and slower than the gallop **2 :** a ride at a canter

Can·ter·bury bell \ˈkan-tə(r)-ˌber-ē-, -ˌbe-rē-, -ˌb(ə-)rē-\ *n* [*Canterbury,* England] (1565) : any of several bellflowers (as *Campanula medium*) cultivated for their showy flowers

can·thar·i·din \kan-ˈtha-rə-dən, -ˈther-ə-\ *n* (1819) : a bitter crystalline compound $C_{10}H_{12}O_4$ that is the active blister-producing ingredient of cantharides

can·tha·ris \ˈkan(t)-thə-rəs\ *n, pl* **can·thar·i·des** \kan-ˈthar-ə-ˌdēz\ [ME & L; ME *cantharide,* fr. L *cantharid-, cantharis,* fr. Gk *kantharid-, kantharis*] (14c) **1 :** SPANISH FLY 1 **2** *pl but sing or pl in constr* : a preparation of dried beetles (as Spanish flies) used in medicine as a counterirritant and formerly as an aphrodisiac

can·tha·xan·thin \ˌkan(t)-thə-ˈzan-ˌthin\ *n* [ISV *cantha-* (fr. NL *Cantharellus cinnabarinus,* mushroom species from which it was obtained) + *xanth-* + [1]*-in*] (ca. 1951) : a naturally occurring carotenoid $C_{40}H_{52}O_2$ used esp. as a color additive for food

cant hook *n* [3*cant*] (ca. 1848) : a lumberman's lever that has a pivoting hooked arm and a blunt often toothed metal cap at one end — compare PEAVEY

can·thus \ˈkan(t)-thəs\ *n, pl* **can·thi** \ˈkan-ˌthī, -ˌthē\ [LL, fr. Gk *kanthos* — more at CANT] (1646) : either of the angles formed by the meeting of an eye's upper and lower eyelids

can·ti·cle \ˈkan-ti-kəl\ *n* [ME, fr. L *canticulum,* dim. of *canticum* song, fr. *cantus,* pp. of *canere*] (13c) : SONG; *specif* : one of several liturgical songs (as the Magnificat) taken from the Bible

Canticle of Canticles (1609) : SONG OF SOLOMON

Canticles *n pl but sing in constr* (15c) : SONG OF SOLOMON

can·ti·le·na \ˌkan-tə-ˈlā-nə, -ˈlē-\ *n* [It, fr. L, song, fr. *cantus*] (ca. 1740) : a vocal or instrumental passage of sustained lyricism

[1]**can·ti·le·ver** \ˈkan-tə-ˌlē-vər, -ˌle-\ *n* [perh. fr. 3*cant* + *-i-* + *lever*] (1667) : a projecting beam or member supported at only one end: as **a :** a bracket-shaped member supporting a balcony or a cornice **b :** either of the two beams or trusses that project from piers toward each other and that when joined directly or by a suspended connecting member form a span of a cantilever bridge

[2]**cantilever** *vt* (1902) **1 :** to support by a cantilever ⟨a ~*ed* shelf⟩ **2 :** to build as a cantilever ~ *vi* : to project as a cantilever

can·til·late \ˈkan-tə-ˌlāt\ *vt* **-lat·ed; -lat·ing** [L *cantilatus,* pp. of *cantilare* to sing, perh. fr. *cantilena*] (ca. 1828) : to recite with musical tones — **can·til·la·tion** \ˌkan-tə-ˈlā-shən\ *n*

can·ti·na \kan-ˈtē-nə\ *n* [AmerSp, fr. Sp, canteen, fr. It, wine cellar — more at CANTEEN] (1844) **1** *Southwest* : a pouch or bag at the pommel of a saddle **2** *Southwest* : a small barroom : SALOON

cant·ing \ˈkan-tiŋ\ *adj* [5*cant*] (1663) : affectedly pious or righteous ⟨a ~ moralist⟩

can·tle \ˈkan-tᵊl\ *n* [ME *cantel,* fr. AF *cantel, chantel,* dim. of OF *chant* side, edge — more at CANT] (14c) **1 :** a segment cut off or out of something : PART, PORTION **2 :** the upward projecting rear part of a saddle

can't–miss \ˈkant-ˌmis\ *adj* (1975) : certain to have a favorable result, performance, or reception : SUREFIRE ⟨a ~ prospect⟩

can·to \ˈkan-(ˌ)tō\ *n, pl* **cantos** [It, fr. L *cantus* song, fr. *canere* to sing — more at CHANT] (1590) : one of the major divisions of a long poem

[1]**can·ton** \ˈkan-tᵊn, -ˌtän\ *n* [MF, fr. It *cantone,* fr. *canto* corner, fr. L *canthus* iron tire — more at CANT] (1522) **1 :** a small territorial division of a country: as **a :** one of the states of the Swiss confederation **b :** a division of a French arrondissement — **can·ton·al** \ˈkan-tə-nəl, kan-ˈtä-nᵊl\ *adj*

[2]**canton** *n* [MF, fr. Old Occitan, fr. *cant* edge, corner, fr. L *canthus*] (1572) **1** *obs* : DIVISION, SECTION **2 :** the top inner quarter of a flag **3 :** the dexter chief region of a heraldic field

Can·ton·ese \ˌkan-tə-ˈnēz, -ˈnēs\ *n, pl* **Cantonese** [*Canton* Guangzhou, ultim. fr. Pg *Cantão,* fr. Ch (Guangzhou) *Gwóngdūng* Guangdong] (1857) **1 :** a native or inhabitant of Guangzhou, China **2 :** the dialect of Chinese spoken in Guangzhou and Hong Kong **3 :** a style of Chinese cooking that emphasizes fresh ingredients, subtle tastes, and relatively mild sauces — **Cantonese** *adj*

can·ton flannel \ˈkan-ˌtän-, -tᵊn-\ *n, often cap C* [*Canton,* China] (1872) : FLANNEL 1c

can·ton·ment \kan-ˈtōn-mənt, -ˈtän- *also* -ˈtün-\ *n* (1753) **1 :** usu. temporary quarters for troops **2 :** a permanent military station in India

Can·ton ware \ˈkan-ˌtän-\ *n* (ca. 1902) : ceramic ware exported from China esp. during the 18th and 19th centuries by way of Canton (Guangzhou) and including blue-and-white and enameled porcelain and various ornamented stonewares

can·tor \ˈkan-tər\ *n* [L, singer, fr. *canere* to sing] (1538) **1 :** a choir leader : PRECENTOR **2 :** a synagogue official who sings or chants liturgical music and leads the congregation in prayer — **can·to·ri·al** \kan-ˈtȯr-ē-əl\ *adj*

can·trip \ˈkan-trəp\ *n* [prob. alter. of *caltrop*] (1719) **1** *chiefly Scot* : a witch's trick : SPELL **2** *chiefly Brit* : HOCUS-POCUS 2

can·tus \ˈkan-təs\ *n, pl* **can·tus** \ˈkan-təs, ˈkan-ˌtüs\ (1590) **1 :** CANTUS FIRMUS **2 :** the principal melody or voice

cantus fir·mus \-ˈfir-məs, -ˈfər-\ *n* [ML, lit., fixed song] (1847) **1 :** the plainsong or simple Gregorian melody orig. sung in unison and prescribed as to form and use by ecclesiastical tradition **2 :** a melodic theme or subject; *esp* : one for contrapuntal treatment

canty \ˈkan-tē\ *adj* [1*cant*] (1719) *dial Brit* : CHEERFUL, SPRIGHTLY

Ca·nuck \kə-ˈnək *sometimes* -ˈnu̇k\ *n* [origin unknown] (1835) : a Canadian and esp. a French Canadian

[1]**can·vas** *also* **can·vass** \ˈkan-vəs\ *n* [ME *canevas,* fr. AF *canevas, chanevaz,* fr. VL **cannabaceus* hempen, fr. L *cannabis* hemp — more at CANNABIS] (13c) **1 :** a firm closely woven cloth usu. of linen, hemp, or cotton used for clothing and formerly much used for tents and sails **2 :** a set of sails : SAIL **3 :** a piece of canvas used for a particular purpose **4 :** TENT; *also* : a group of tents **5 a :** a piece of cloth backed or framed as a surface for a painting; *also* : the painting on such a surface **b :** the background, setting, or scope of a historical or fictional account or narrative **6 :** a coarse cloth so woven as to form regular meshes for working with the needle **7 :** the canvas-covered floor of a boxing or wrestling ring — **can·vas·like** \-vəs-ˌlīk\ *adj*

[2]**canvas** *vt* **-vased** *or* **-vassed; -vas·ing** *or* **-vass·ing** (1556) : to cover, line, or furnish with canvas

can·vas·back \ˈkan-vəs-ˌbak\ *n* (1782) : a No. American wild duck (*Aythya valisineria*) that has a reddish-brown head, black breast, and whitish body and is characterized esp. by the elongate sloping profile of the bill and head

[1]**can·vass** *also* **can·vas** \ˈkan-vəs\ *vt* **can·vassed; can·vass·ing** (1508) **1** *obs* : to toss in a canvas sheet in sport or punishment **2 a**

: to examine in detail; *specif* : to examine (votes) officially for authenticity **b** : DISCUSS, DEBATE **3** : to go through (a district) or go to (persons) in order to solicit orders or political support or to determine opinions or sentiments ⟨~ voters⟩ ~ *vi* : to seek orders or votes : SOLICIT — **can·vass·er** *also* **can·vas·er** *n*

[2]**canvass** *also* **canvas** *n* (ca. 1611) : the act or an instance of canvassing; *esp* : a personal solicitation of votes or survey of public opinion

can·yon *also* **ca·ñon** \ˈkan-yən\ *n* [AmerSp *cañón,* prob. alter. of obs. Sp *callón,* aug. of *calle* street, fr. L *callis* footpath] (1834) **1** : a deep narrow valley with steep sides and often with a stream flowing through it **2** : something resembling a canyon ⟨the city's concrete ~*s*⟩

can·yon·eer·ing \ˌkan-yə-ˈnir-iŋ\ *n* (1957) : the sport of exploring canyons (as by climbing, rappelling, or rafting) — **can·yon·eer** \-ˈnir\ *n*

can·yon·ing \ˈkan-yə-niŋ\ *n* (1991) *chiefly Brit* : CANYONEERING

can·zo·ne \kan-ˈzō-nē, känt-ˈsō-(ˌ)nā\ *n, pl* **-nes** \-nēz, -(ˌ)nāz\ *or* **-ni** \-nē\ [It, fr. L *cantion-, cantio* song, fr. *canere* to sing — more at CHANT] (1589) **1** : a medieval Italian or Provençal lyric poem **2** : the musical setting of a canzone

can·zo·net \ˌkan-zə-ˈnet\ *n* [It *canzonetta,* dim. of *canzone*] (1588) **1** : a light usu. strophic song **2** : a part-song resembling but less elaborate than a madrigal

caou·tchouc \ˈkau̇-ˌchu̇k, -ˌchük, -ˌchü\ *n* [F, fr. obs. Sp *cauchuc* (now *caucho),* prob. fr. a language of Amazonian Peru or Ecuador] (1775) : [1]RUBBER 2a

[1]**cap** \ˈkap\ *n, often attrib* [ME *cappe,* fr. OE *cæppe,* fr. LL *cappa* head covering, cloak] (bef. 12c) **1 a** : a head covering esp. with a visor and no brim **b** : a distinctive head covering emblematic of a position or office: as (1) : a cardinal's biretta (2) : MORTARBOARD **2** : a natural cover or top: as **a** : an overlying rock layer that is usu. hard to penetrate **b** (1) : PILEUS (2) : CALYPTRA **c** : the top of a bird's head or a patch of distinctively colored feathers in this area **3 a** : something that serves as a cover or protection esp. for a tip, knob, or end ⟨a bottle ~⟩ **b** : a fitting for closing the end of a tube **c** *Brit* : CERVICAL CAP **d** : an artificial crown for a tooth **4** : an overlaying or covering structure **5** : a paper or metal container holding an explosive charge (as for a toy pistol) **6** : an upper limit (as on expenditures) : CEILING **7** : the symbol ∩ indicating the intersection of two sets — compare CUP 9 **8** : a cluster of molecules or chemical groups bound to one end or a region of a cell, virus, or molecule — **cap in hand** : in a respectful, humble, or sometimes fearful manner

[2]**cap** *vb* **capped; cap·ping** *vt* (15c) **1 a** : to provide or protect with a cap **b** : to give a cap to as a symbol of honor, rank, or achievement **2** : to form a cap over : CROWN ⟨mountains *capped* with mist⟩ **3 a** : to follow with something more noticeable or more significant : OUTDO **b** : to bring to a climax or conclusion ⟨~ off the show with a song⟩ **4** : to form a chemical cap on **5** : to prevent from growing or spreading : set an upper limit on ⟨~ oil prices⟩ **6** : to supply (a tooth) with an artificial crown ~ *vi* : to form or produce a chemical cap

[3]**cap** *n* [short for *capsule*] (1942) : a small amount of an illegal or legally regulated drug; *esp* : a small amount of a drug enclosed in a capsule

[4]**cap** *n* (1982) : CAPITALIZATION 1d

[5]**cap** *abbr* **1** capacity **2** capital **3** capitalize; capitalized

CAP *abbr* **1** Civil Air Patrol **2** combat air patrol

ca·pa·bil·i·ty \ˌkā-pə-ˈbi-lə-tē\ *n, pl* **-ties** (1587) **1** : the quality or state of being capable; *also* : ABILITY **2** : a feature or faculty capable of development : POTENTIALITY **3** : the facility or potential for an indicated use or deployment ⟨the ~ of a metal to be fused⟩ ⟨nuclear ~⟩

ca·pa·ble \ˈkā-pə-bəl, *in rapid speech* ˈkāp-bəl\ *adj* [MF or LL; MF *capable,* fr. LL *capabilis,* irreg. fr. L *capere* to take — more at HEAVE] (1579) **1** : SUSCEPTIBLE ⟨a remark ~ of being misunderstood⟩ **2** *obs* : COMPREHENSIVE **3** : having attributes (as physical or mental power) required for performance or accomplishment ⟨is ~ of intense concentration⟩ **4** : having traits conducive to or features permitting ⟨this woman is ~ of murder by violence —Robert Graves⟩ **5** : having legal right to own, enjoy, or perform **6** : having or showing general efficiency and ability ⟨a ~ lawyer⟩ ⟨a ~ performance⟩ — **ca·pa·ble·ness** \ˈkā-pə-bəl-nəs\ *n* — **ca·pa·bly** \-pə-blē\ *adv*

ca·pa·cious \kə-ˈpā-shəs\ *adj* [L *capac-, capax* capacious, capable, fr. L *capere*] (1606) : containing or capable of containing a great deal ***syn*** see SPACIOUS — **ca·pa·cious·ly** *adv* — **ca·pa·cious·ness** *n*

ca·pac·i·tance \kə-ˈpa-sə-tən(t)s\ *n* [*capacity*] (1893) **1 a** : the property of an electric nonconductor that permits the storage of energy as a result of the separation of charge that occurs when opposite surfaces of the nonconductor are maintained at a difference of potential **b** : the measure of this property that is equal to the ratio of the charge on either surface to the potential difference between the surfaces **2** : a part of a circuit or network that possesses capacitance — **ca·pac·i·tive** \-ˈpa-sə-tiv\ *adj* — **ca·pac·i·tive·ly** *adv*

ca·pac·i·tate \kə-ˈpa-sə-ˌtāt\ *vt* **-tat·ed; -tat·ing** (1657) **1** *archaic* : to make capable **2** : to cause (sperm) to undergo capacitation

ca·pac·i·ta·tion \kə-ˌpa-sə-ˈtā-shən\ *n* (1951) : the change undergone by sperm in the female reproductive tract that enables them to penetrate and fertilize an egg

ca·pac·i·tor \kə-ˈpa-sə-tər\ *n* (1925) : a device giving capacitance and usu. consisting of conducting plates or foils separated by thin layers of dielectric (as air or mica) with the plates on opposite sides of the dielectric layers oppositely charged by a source of voltage and the electrical energy of the charged system stored in the polarized dielectric

[1]**ca·pac·i·ty** \kə-ˈpa-sə-tē, -ˈpas-tē\ *n, pl* **-ties** [ME *capacite,* fr. MF *capacité,* fr. L *capacitat-, capacitas,* fr. *capac-, capax*] (15c) **1** : legal competency or fitness ⟨~ to stand trial⟩ **2 a** : the potential or suitability for holding, storing, or accommodating ⟨a large seating ~⟩ **b** : the maximum amount or number that can be contained or accommodated ⟨a jug with a one-gallon ~⟩ ⟨the auditorium was filled to ~⟩ — see METRIC SYSTEM table, WEIGHT table **3 a** : an individual's mental or physical ability : APTITUDE, SKILL **b** : the faculty or potential for treating, experiencing, or appreciating ⟨~ for love⟩ **4** : DUTY, POSITION, ROLE ⟨will be happy to serve in any ~⟩ **5** : the facility or power to produce, perform, or deploy : CAPABILITY ⟨a plan to double the factory's ~⟩; *also* : maximum output ⟨industries running at three-quarter ~⟩ **6 a** : CAPACITANCE **b** : the quantity of electricity that a battery can deliver under specified conditions

[2]**capacity** *adj* (1897) : equaling maximum capacity ⟨a ~ crowd⟩

cap–and–trade *adj* (1995) : relating to or being a system that caps the amount of carbon emissions a given company may produce but allows it to buy rights to produce additional emissions from a company that does not use the equivalent amount of its own allowance

cap–a–pie *or* **cap–à–pie** \ˌka-pə-ˈpē, -ˈpā\ *adv* [MF (*de*) *cap a pé* from head to foot] (1523) : from head to foot ⟨armed ~ for battle⟩

[1]**ca·par·i·son** \kə-ˈper-ə-sən, -ˈpa-rə-\ *n* [MF *caparaçon,* fr. OSp *caparazón*] (1579) **1 a** : an ornamental covering for a horse **b** : decorative trappings and harness **2** : rich clothing : ADORNMENT

[2]**caparison** *vt* (1594) : to provide with or as if with a rich ornamental covering : ADORN

[1]**cape** \ˈkāp\ *n, often attrib* [ME *cap,* fr. AF *cape,* fr. Old Occitan *cap,* fr. L *caput* head — more at HEAD] (14c) **1** : a point or extension of land jutting out into water as a peninsula or as a projecting point **2** *often cap* : CAPE COD COTTAGE

[2]**cape** *n* [prob. fr. Sp *capa* cloak, fr. LL *cappa* head covering, cloak] (1758) **1** : a sleeveless outer garment or part of a garment that fits closely at the neck and hangs loosely over the shoulders **2** : the short feathers covering the shoulders of a fowl — see DUCK illustration

Cape buffalo \ˈkāp-\ *n* [*Cape* of Good Hope, Africa] (1860) : the large reddish-brown to black wild buffalo (*Syncerus caffer*) of sub-Saharan Africa — called also *African buffalo*

Cape Cod cottage \(ˈ)kāp-ˈkäd-\ *n* [*Cape Cod,* Mass.] (1916) : a compact rectangular dwelling of one or one-and-a-half stories usu. with a central chimney and steep gable roof — called also *cape, Cape Cod*

Cape gooseberry *n* [*Cape* of Good Hope] (1807) : any of several ground-cherries (esp. *Physalis peruviana*) bearing edible acid berries; *also* : its berry

Cape Horn·er \ˌkāp-ˈhȯr-nər\ *n* (1840) : a ship that voyages around Cape Horn

cape·let \ˈkāp-lət\ *n* (1912) : a small cape usu. covering the shoulders

cap·e·lin \ˈka-p(ə-)lən\ *n* [CanF *capelan,* fr. F, codfish, fr. Old Occitan, chaplain, codfish, fr. ML *cappellanus* chaplain — more at CHAPLAIN] (1620) : a small northern sea fish (*Mallotus villosus*) of the smelt family

Ca·pel·la \kə-ˈpe-lə\ *n* [L, lit., she-goat, fr. *caper* he-goat — more at CAPRIOLE] (1674) : a star of the first magnitude in Auriga

cap·el·lini \ˌka-pə-ˈlē-nē\ *n* [It, pl. of *capellino,* dim. of *capello* hair, fr. L *capillus*] (1950) : ANGEL-HAIR PASTA

[1]**ca·per** \ˈkā-pər\ *n* [back-formation fr. earlier *capers* (taken as a plural), fr. ME *caperis,* fr. L *capparis,* fr. Gk *kapparis*] (14c) **1** : any of a genus (*Capparis* of the family Capparidaceae, the caper family) of low prickly shrubs of the Mediterranean region; *esp* : one (*C. spinosa*) cultivated for its buds **2** : one of the immature greenish flower buds of the caper pickled and used as a seasoning or garnish

[2]**caper** *vi* **ca·pered; ca·per·ing** \-p(ə-)riŋ\ [prob. by shortening & alter. fr. *capriole*] (1588) : to leap or prance about in a playful manner

[3]**caper** *n* (1592) **1** : a frolicsome leap **2** : a capricious escapade : PRANK **3** : an illegal or questionable act; *esp* : THEFT

cap·er·cail·lie \ˌka-pər-ˈkā-lē, -ˈkāl-yē\ *or* **cap·er·cail·zie** \-ˈkāl-zē\ *n, pl* **-caillie** *or* **-cailzies** *also* **-caillies** *or* **-cailzie** [ScGael *capalcoille,* lit., horse of the woods] (1536) : a very large European grouse (*Tetrao urogallus*) of hilly coniferous woodlands

cape·skin \ˈkāp-ˌskin\ *n* [*Cape* of Good Hope, Africa] (1919) : a light flexible leather made from sheepskins with the natural grain retained and used esp. for gloves and garments

Ca·pe·tian \kə-ˈpē-shən\ *adj* [Hugh *Capet*] (1836) : of or relating to the French royal house that ruled from 987 to 1328 — **Capetian** *n*

cape·work \ˈkāp-ˌwərk\ *n* (1926) : the art of the bullfighter in working a bull with the cape

cap·ful \ˈkap-ˌfu̇l\ *n* (1873) : as much as a cap will hold

ca·pi·as \ˈkā-pē-əs\ *n* [ME, fr. L, lit., you should seize, fr. *capere* to take — more at HEAVE] (15c) : an arrest warrant

cap·il·lar·i·ty \ˌka-pə-ˈler-ə-tē, -ˈla-rə-\ *n, pl* **-ties** (1830) **1** : the property or state of being capillary **2** : the action by which the surface of a liquid where it is in contact with a solid (as in a capillary tube) is elevated or depressed depending on the relative attraction of the molecules of the liquid for each other and for those of the solid

[1]**cap·il·lary** \ˈka-pə-ˌler-ē, -ˌle-rē, *Brit usu* kə-ˈpi-lə-rē\ *adj* [F or L; F *capillaire,* fr. L *capillaris,* fr. *capillus* hair] (14c) **1 a** : resembling a hair esp. in slender elongated form ⟨~ leaves⟩ **b** : having a very small bore ⟨a ~ tube⟩ **2** : involving, held by, or resulting from surface tension ⟨~ water in the soil⟩ **3** : of or relating to capillaries or capillarity

[2]**capillary** *n, pl* **-lar·ies** (1667) **1** : a minute thin-walled vessel of the body; *esp* : any of the smallest blood vessels connecting arterioles with venules and forming networks throughout the body **2** : a tube (as of glass) having a very small bore

capillary attraction *n* (1813) : the force of adhesion between a solid and a liquid in capillarity

[1]**cap·i·tal** \ˈka-pə-tᵊl, ˈkap-tᵊl\ *n* [ME *capitale,* fr. AF *capital, capitel,* fr. LL *capitellum* small head, top of column, dim. of L *capit-, caput* head — more at HEAD] (13c) : the uppermost member of a column or pilaster crowning the shaft and taking the weight of the entablature — see COLUMN illustration

[2]**capital** *adj* [ME, fr. L *capitalis,* fr. *capit-, caput*] (14c) **1** *of a letter* : of or conforming to the series A, B, C, etc. rather than a, b, c, etc. **2 a** : punishable by death ⟨a ~ crime⟩ **b** : involving execution ⟨~ punishment⟩ **c** : most serious ⟨a ~ error⟩ **3 a** : chief in importance or influence ⟨~ ships⟩ ⟨the ~ importance of criticism in the work of creation itself —T. S. Eliot⟩ **b** : being the seat of government **4** : of or relating to capital; *esp* : relating to or being assets that add to the long-term net worth of a corporation ⟨~ improvements⟩ **5** : EXCELLENT ⟨a ~ book⟩ — **with a capital** — used with a following capital letter to emphasize or qualify a preceding word ⟨not an accident but murder *with a capital* M⟩ ⟨desired romance *with a capital* R⟩

[3]**capital** *n* [F or It; F, fr. It *capitale,* fr. *capitale,* adj., chief, principal, fr. L *capitalis*] (ca. 1639) **1 a** (1) : a stock of accumulated goods esp. at a specified time and in contrast to income received during a specified period; *also* : the value of these accumulated goods (2) : accumulated goods devoted to the production of other goods (3) : accumulated possessions calculated to bring in income **b** (1) : net worth (2) : STOCK 7c(1) **c** : persons holding capital **d** : ADVANTAGE, GAIN ⟨make ~ of the situation⟩ **e** : a store of useful assets or advantages ⟨wasted their political ~ on an unpopular cause⟩ ⟨wrote from the ~ of his emotionally desolate boyhood —E. L. Doctorow⟩ **2** [[2]*capital*]

a : a capital letter; *esp* : an initial capital letter **b** : a letter belonging to a style of alphabet modeled on the style customarily used in inscriptions **3** [[2]*capital*] **a** : a city serving as a seat of government **b** : a city preeminent in some special activity ⟨the fashion ~⟩

capital gain *n* (1921) : the increase in value of an asset (as stock or real estate) between the time it is bought and the time it is sold

capital goods *n pl* (1896) : [3]CAPITAL 1a(1), 1a(2)

capital–intensive *adj* (1959) : having a high capital cost per unit of output; *esp* : requiring greater expenditure in the form of capital than of labor

cap·i·tal·ise *Brit var of* CAPITALIZE

cap·i·tal·ism \ˈka-pə-tə-ˌli-zəm, ˈkap-tə-, *Brit also* kə-ˈpi-tə-\ *n* (1826) : an economic system characterized by private or corporate ownership of capital goods, by investments that are determined by private decision, and by prices, production, and the distribution of goods that are determined mainly by competition in a free market

[1]**cap·i·tal·ist** \-ist\ *n* (1776) **1** : a person who has capital esp. invested in business; *broadly* : a person of wealth : PLUTOCRAT **2** : a person who favors capitalism

[2]**capitalist** *or* **cap·i·tal·is·tic** \ˌka-pə-tə-ˈlis-tik, ˌkap-tə-, *Brit also* kə-ˌpi-tə-\ *adj* (1845) **1** : owning capital ⟨the ~ class⟩ **2 a** : practicing or advocating capitalism ⟨~ nations⟩ **b** : marked by capitalism ⟨~ period of history⟩ — **cap·i·tal·is·ti·cal·ly** \-ti-k(ə-)lē\ *adv*

cap·i·tal·i·za·tion \ˌka-pə-tə-lə-ˈzā-shən, ˌkap-tə-, *Brit also* kə-ˌpi-tə-\ *n* (1852) **1 a** : the act or process of capitalizing **b** : a sum resulting from a process of capitalizing **c** : the total liabilities of a business including both ownership capital and borrowed capital **d** : the total par value or the stated value of no-par issues of authorized stock **2** : the use of a capital letter in writing or printing

cap·i·tal·ize \ˈka-pə-tə-ˌlīz, ˈkap-tə-, *Brit also* kə-ˈpi-tə-\ *vb* **-ized; -iz·ing** *vt* (1764) **1** : to write or print with an initial capital or in capitals **2 a** : to convert into capital ⟨~ the company's reserve fund⟩ **b** : to treat as an amortizable investment in long-term capital assets rather than as an ordinary operating expense to be charged against revenue for the period in which it is incurred ⟨~ development costs⟩ **3 a** : to compute the present value of (an income extended over a period of time) **b** : to convert (a periodic payment) into an equivalent capital sum ⟨*capitalized* annuities⟩ **4** : to supply capital for ~ *vi* : to gain by turning something to advantage ⟨~ on an opponent's mistake⟩

cap·i·tal·ly \ˈka-pə-tə-lē, ˈkap-tə-\ *adv* (1619) **1** : in a manner involving capital punishment **2** : in a capital manner : EXCELLENTLY

capital stock *n* (1709) **1** : the outstanding shares of a joint-stock company considered as an aggregate **2** : CAPITALIZATION 1d **3** : STOCK 7c(1)

cap·i·tate \ˈka-pə-ˌtāt\ *adj* [L *capitatus* headed, fr. *capit-, caput* head] (1661) **1** : forming a head **2** : abruptly enlarged and globose

cap·i·tat·ed \ˈka-pə-ˌtā-təd\ *adj* [back-formation fr. *capitation*] (1983) : of, relating to, participating in, or being a health-care system in which a medical provider is given a set fee per patient (as by an HMO) regardless of treatment required

cap·i·ta·tion \ˌka-pə-ˈtā-shən\ *n* [LL *capitation-, capitatio* poll tax, fr. L *capit-, caput*] (1641) **1** : a direct uniform tax imposed on each head or person : POLL TAX **2** : a uniform per capita payment or fee **3** : a capitated health-care system

cap·i·tol \ˈka-pə-tᵊl, ˈkap-tᵊl\ *n* [L *Capitolium,* temple of Jupiter at Rome on the Capitoline hill] (1679) **1 a** : a building in which a state legislative body meets **b** : a group of buildings in which the functions of state government are carried out **2** *cap* : the building in which the U.S. Congress meets at Washington

Capitol Hill *n* [*Capitol Hill,* Washington, site of the U.S. Capitol] (1935) : the legislative branch of the U.S. government

Cap·i·to·line \ˈka-pə-tə-ˌlīn, *Brit usu* kə-ˈpi-tə-ˌlīn\ *adj* [L *capitolinus,* fr. *Capitolium*] (1667) : of or relating to the smallest of the seven hills of ancient Rome, the temple on it, or the gods worshipped there

ca·pit·u·lar \kə-ˈpi-chə-lər\ *adj* [ML *capitularis,* fr. *capitulum*] (ca. 1525) : of or relating to an ecclesiastical chapter

ca·pit·u·lary \-ˌler-ē, -ˌle-rē\ *n, pl* **-lar·ies** [ML *capitulare,* lit., document divided into sections, fr. LL *capitulum* section, chapter — more at CHAPTER] (1650) : a civil or ecclesiastical ordinance; *also* : a collection of ordinances

ca·pit·u·late \kə-ˈpi-chə-ˌlāt\ *vi* **-lat·ed; -lat·ing** [ML *capitulatus,* pp. of *capitulare* to distinguish by heads or chapters, fr. LL *capitulum*] (1596) **1** *archaic* : PARLEY, NEGOTIATE **2 a** : to surrender often after negotiation of terms **b** : to cease resisting : ACQUIESCE ***syn*** see YIELD

ca·pit·u·la·tion \kə-ˌpi-chə-ˈlā-shən\ *n* (1535) **1** : a set of terms or articles constituting an agreement between governments **2 a** : the act of surrendering or yielding **b** : the terms of surrender

ca·pit·u·lum \kə-ˈpi-chə-ləm\ *n, pl* **-la** \-lə\ [NL, fr. L, small head — more at CHAPTER] (ca. 1755) **1** : a rounded protuberance of an anatomical part (as a bone) **2** : a racemose inflorescence (as of the sunflower) with the axis shortened and dilated to form a rounded or flattened cluster of sessile flowers — see INFLORESCENCE illustration

cap·let \ˈka-plət\ *n* [[1]*capsule* + *tablet*] (1937) : a capsule-shaped medicinal tablet

[1]**ca·po** \ˈkā-(ˌ)pō\ *n, pl* **capos** [short for *capotasto,* fr. It, lit., head of fingerboard] (1926) : a movable bar attached to the fingerboard of a fretted instrument to uniformly raise the pitch of all the strings

[2]**ca·po** \ˈkä-(ˌ)pō, ˈka-\ *n, pl* **capos** [It, head, chief, fr. L *caput*] (ca. 1952) : the head of a branch of a crime syndicate

ca·po·ei·ra \ˌkä-pə-ˈwā-rə, ˌkäp-ˈwā-\ *n* [Brazilian Pg, kind of martial art, ruffian skilled in this art, fugitive slave living in the forest, fr. *capão* island of forest in a clear-cut area, fr. Tupi *kaʔapáũ,* fr. *kaʔá* forest + *paũ* round] (1945) : a Brazilian dance of African origin that incorporates martial arts movements such as kicks and chops

ca·pon \ˈkā-ˌpän, -pən\ *n* [ME, fr. OE *capūn,* prob. fr. OF *capon, chapun,* fr. L *capon-, capo;* akin to Lith *kapoti* to mince, Gk *koptein* to cut] (bef. 12c) : a castrated male chicken

ca·po·na·ta \ˌkä-pə-ˈnä-tə\ *n* [It, fr. It dial. (Sicily) *capunata,* sailor's dish of biscuit steeped in oil and vinegar, chopped vegetables served similarly, fr. Catal *caponada* dry bread soaked in oil and vinegar, perh. fr. *capó* capon] (1931) : a relish of chopped eggplant and assorted vegetables

ca·pote \kə-ˈpōt\ *n* [F, fr. *cape* cloak, fr. LL *cappa*] (1799) : a usu. long and hooded cloak or overcoat

cap·pel·let·ti \ˌka-pə-ˈle-tē\ *n pl but sing or pl in constr* [It, pl. of *cappelletto,* dim. of *cappello* hat, fr. ML *cappellus* cap, dim. of LL *cappa* head covering — more at CAP] (1945) : pasta in the form of little peaked hats filled with a savory mixture

cap·per \ˈka-pər\ *n* (1587) **1** : one that caps: as **a** : a device that fits caps on bottles **b** : FINALE, CLIMAX, CLINCHER **2** : a lure or decoy esp. in an illicit or questionable activity : SHILL

cap·ping \ˈka-piŋ\ *n* (14c) : something that caps

cap·puc·ci·no \ˌka-pə-ˈchē-(ˌ)nō, ˌkä-pü-\ *n* [It, lit., Capuchin; fr. the likeness of its color to that of a Capuchin's habit] (1893) : espresso coffee topped with frothed hot milk or cream and often flavored with cinnamon

ca·pre·se \kə-ˈprā-zē, -(ˌ)zā\ *n* [It, short for *insalata caprese,* lit., salad in the manner of Capri] (1978) : a salad consisting of slices of mozzarella and tomatoes, basil, and olive oil or Italian dressing

cap·ric acid \ˈka-prik-\ *n* [ISV, fr. L *capr-, caper* goat; fr. its odor — more at CAPRIOLE] (1830) : a fatty acid $C_{10}H_{20}O_2$ found in fats and oils and used in flavors and perfumes

ca·pric·cio \kə-ˈprē-ch(ē-ˌ)ō\ *n, pl* **-cios** [It] (1665) **1** : FANCY, WHIMSY **2** : CAPER, PRANK **3** : an instrumental piece in free form usu. lively in tempo and brilliant in style

ca·price \kə-ˈprēs\ *n* [F, fr. It *capriccio* caprice, shudder, perh. fr. *capo* head (fr. L *caput*) + *riccio* hedgehog, fr. L *ericius* — more at HEAD, URCHIN] (1667) **1 a** : a sudden, impulsive, and seemingly unmotivated notion or action **b** : a sudden usu. unpredictable condition, change, or series of changes ⟨the ~*s* of the weather⟩ **2** : a disposition to do things impulsively **3** : CAPRICCIO 3

syn CAPRICE, WHIM, VAGARY, CROTCHET mean an irrational or unpredictable idea or desire. CAPRICE stresses lack of apparent motivation and suggests willfulness ⟨by sheer *caprice* she quit her job⟩. WHIM implies a fantastic, capricious turn of mind or inclination ⟨an odd antique that was bought on a *whim*⟩. VAGARY stresses the erratic, irresponsible character of the notion or desire ⟨he had been prone to strange *vagaries*⟩. CROTCHET implies an eccentric opinion or preference ⟨a serious scientist equally known for his bizarre *crotchets*⟩.

ca·pri·cious \kə-ˈpri-shəs, -ˈprē-\ *adj* (1601) : governed or characterized by caprice : IMPULSIVE, UNPREDICTABLE ***syn*** see INCONSTANT — **ca·pri·cious·ly** *adv* — **ca·pri·cious·ness** *n*

Cap·ri·corn \ˈka-pri-ˌkȯrn\ *n* [ME *Capricorne,* fr. L *Capricornus* (gen. *Capricorni*), fr. *caper* goat + *cornu* horn — more at HORN] (14c) **1** : a southern zodiacal constellation between Sagittarius and Aquarius **2 a** : the 10th sign of the zodiac in astrology — see ZODIAC table **b** : one born under the sign of Capricorn

cap·ri·fi·ca·tion \ˌka-prə-fə-ˈkā-shən\ *n* [L *caprification-, caprificatio,* fr. *caprificare* to pollinate by caprification, fr. *caprificus*] (1601) : artificial pollination of figs that usu. bear only pistillate flowers by hanging male flowering branches of the caprifig in the trees to facilitate pollen transfer by a fig wasp

cap·ri·fig \ˈka-prə-ˌfig\ *n* [ME *caprifige,* part trans. of L *caprificus,* fr. *capr-, caper* goat + *ficus* fig — more at FIG] (15c) : a wild fig (*Ficus carica sylvestris*) of southern Europe and southwestern Asia used for caprification of the cultivated fig; *also* : its fruit

cap·rine \ˈka-ˌprīn\ *adj* [ME, fr. L *caprinus,* fr. *capr-, caper*] (15c) : of, relating to, or being a goat ⟨~ serum⟩ ⟨the ~ family⟩

cap·ri·ole \ˈka-prē-ˌōl\ *n* [MF or OIt; MF *capriole,* fr. OIt *capriola,* fr. *capriolo* roebuck, fr. L *capreolus* goat, roebuck, fr. *capr-, caper* he-goat; akin to OE *hæfer* goat, Gk *kapros* wild boar] (1594) **1** : a playful leap : CAPER **2** *of a trained horse* : a vertical leap with a backward kick of the hind legs at the height of the leap — **capriole** *vi*

ca·pri pants \kə-ˈprē-\ *n pl, often cap C* [*Capri,* Italy] (1952) : close-fitting women's pants that end above the ankle — called also *capris*

cap·rock \ˈkap-ˌräk\ *n* (1859) : CAP 2a

ca·pro·ic acid \kə-ˈprō-ik-\ *n* [ISV, fr. L *capr-, caper*] (1830) : a liquid fatty acid $C_6H_{12}O_2$ that is found as a glycerol ester in fats and oils or made synthetically and used in pharmaceuticals and flavorings

cap·ro·lac·tam \ˌka-prō-ˈlak-ˌtam\ *n* [*caproic* acid + *lactone* + *amide*] (1944) : a white crystalline cyclic amide $C_6H_{11}NO$ used esp. in making one type of nylon

ca·pryl·ic acid \kə-ˈpri-lik-\ *n* [ISV *capryl,* a radical contained in it] (1845) : a fatty acid $C_8H_{16}O_2$ of rancid odor occurring in fats and oils and used esp. in the synthesis of esters for perfumes

caps *abbr* **1** capitals **2** capsule

cap·sa·i·cin \kap-ˈsā-ə-sən\ *n* [irreg. fr. NL *Capsicum*] (ca. 1890) : a colorless irritant phenolic amide $C_{18}H_{27}NO_3$ found in various capsicums that gives hot peppers their hotness and that is used in topical creams for its analgesic properties

Cap·si·an \ˈkap-sē-ən\ *adj* [F *capsien,* fr. L *Capsa* Gafsa, Tunisia] (1915) : of or relating to a Paleolithic culture of northern Africa and southern Europe

cap·si·cum \ˈkap-si-kəm\ *n* [NL, perh. fr. L *capsa*] (1588) **1 a** : any of a genus (*Capsicum*) of tropical American herbs and shrubs of the nightshade family widely cultivated for their many-seeded usu. fleshy-walled berries — called also *pepper* **b** : PEPPER 3b **2** : an oleoresin derived from the fruit of some capsicums that contains capsaicin and related compounds and is used medicinally esp. as a topical pain reliever

cap·sid \ˈkap-səd\ *n* [F *capside,* fr. L *capsa* case + F *-ide* [2]-id] (1959) : the protein shell of a virus particle surrounding its nucleic acid

cap·size \ˈkap-ˌsīz, kap-ˈ\ *vb* **cap·sized; cap·siz·ing** [perh. fr. Sp *capuzar* or Catal *cabussar* to thrust (the head) underwater] *vt* (1778) : to cause to overturn ⟨~ a canoe⟩ ~ *vi* : to become upset or overturned : TURN OVER ⟨the canoe *capsized*⟩ — **capsize** *n*

cap sleeve *n* (1926) : a very short sleeve (as on a dress) that hangs over the edge of the shoulder without extending along the underside of the arm

cap·stan \ˈkap-stən, -ˌstan\ *n* [ME, prob. fr. MF *cabestant*] (14c) **1** : a machine for moving or raising heavy weights that consists of a vertical

\ə\ **abut** \ᵊ\ kitten, F table \ər\ **further** \a\ **ash** \ā\ **ace** \ä\ **mop, mar**
\au̇\ **out** \ch\ **chin** \e\ **bet** \ē\ **easy** \g\ **go** \i\ **hit** \ī\ **ice** \j\ **job**
\ŋ\ **sing** \ō\ **go** \ȯ\ **law** \ȯi\ **boy** \th\ **thin** \t͟h\ **the** \ü\ **loot** \u̇\ **foot**
\y\ **yet** \zh\ **vision, beige** \k̲, ⁿ, œ, ue, ʸ\ *see* Guide to Pronunciation

drum which can be rotated and around which cable is turned **2 :** a rotating shaft that drives tape at a constant speed in a recorder
cap·stone \ˈkap-ˌstōn\ *n* [[1]*cap*] (14c) **1 :** a coping stone **:** COPING **2 :** the high point **:** crowning achievement ⟨the ~ of her career⟩
cap·su·lar \ˈkap-sə-lər\ *adj* (1708) **1 :** of, relating to, or resembling a capsule **2 :** CAPSULATED
cap·su·lat·ed \-ˌlā-təd\ *adj* (1646) **:** enclosed in a capsule
[1]**cap·sule** \ˈkap-səl, -(ˌ)sül *also* -ˌsyül\ *n* [F, fr. L *capsula,* dim. of *capsa* box — more at CASE] (ca. 1693) **1 a :** a membrane or sac enclosing a body part (as a knee joint or kidney) **b :** either of two layers of white matter in the cerebrum **2 :** a closed receptacle containing spores or seeds: as **a :** a dry dehiscent usu. many-seeded fruit composed of two or more carpels **b :** the spore case of a moss **3 :** a shell usu. of gelatin for packaging something (as a drug or vitamins); *also* **:** a usu. medicinal or nutritional preparation for oral use consisting of the shell and its contents **4 :** an often polysaccharide envelope surrounding a microorganism **5 :** an extremely brief condensation **:** OUTLINE, SURVEY **6 a :** a compact often sealed and detachable container or compartment **b :** a small pressurized compartment or vehicle (as for space flight)
[2]**capsule** *vt* **cap·suled; cap·sul·ing** (1859) **1 :** to equip with or enclose in a capsule **2 :** to condense into or devise in a compact form
[3]**capsule** *adj* (1938) **1 :** extremely brief **2 :** small and very compact
cap·sul·ize \ˈkap-sə-ˌlīz\ *vt* **-ized; -iz·ing** (1945) **:** CAPSULE
Capt *abbr* captain
[1]**cap·tain** \ˈkap-tən *also* ˈkap-ᵊm\ *n* [ME *capitane,* fr. AF *capitain,* fr. LL *capitaneus,* adj. & n., chief, fr. L *capit-, caput* head — more at HEAD] (14c) **1 a (1) :** a military leader **:** the commander of a unit or a body of troops **(2) :** a subordinate officer commanding under a sovereign or general **(3) :** a commissioned officer in the army, air force, or marine corps ranking above a first lieutenant and below a major **b (1) :** a naval officer who is master or commander of a ship **(2) :** a commissioned officer in the navy ranking above a commander and below a commodore and in the coast guard ranking above a commander and below a rear admiral **c :** a senior pilot who commands the crew of an airplane **d :** an officer in a police department or fire department in charge of a unit (as a precinct or company) and usu. ranking above a lieutenant and below a chief **2 :** one who leads or supervises: as **a :** a leader of a sports team or side **b :** HEADWAITER **c :** a person in charge of hotel bellhops — called also *bell captain* **3 :** a person of importance or influence in a field ⟨~*s* of industry⟩ — **cap·tain·cy** \ˈkap-tən-sē\ *n* — **cap·tain·ship** \-ˌship\ *n*
[2]**captain** *vt* (1598) **:** to be captain of **:** LEAD ⟨~*ed* the football team⟩
captain's chair *n* (1946) **:** an armchair with a saddle seat and a low curved back with vertical spindles
captain's mast *n* (1941) **:** MAST 3
cap·tan \ˈkap-ˌtan\ *n* [short for *mercaptan*] (1952) **:** a fungicide $C_9H_8Cl_3NO_2S$ used on agricultural crops
[1]**cap·tion** \ˈkap-shən\ *n* [prob. short for *certificate of caption* (taking, seizure)] (ca. 1670) **1 :** the part of a legal document that shows where, when, and by what authority it was taken, found, or executed **2 a :** the heading esp. of an article or document **:** TITLE **b :** the explanatory comment or designation accompanying a pictorial illustration **c :** a motion-picture subtitle — **cap·tion·less** \-ləs\ *adj*

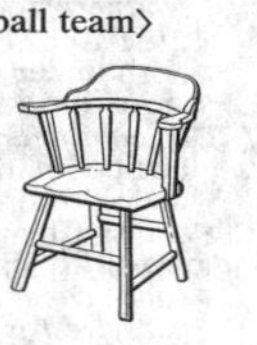
captain's chair

[2]**caption** *vt* **cap·tioned; cap·tion·ing** \-sh(ə-)niŋ\ (1848) **:** to furnish with a caption
cap·tious \ˈkap-shəs\ *adj* [ME *capcious,* fr. MF or L; MF *captieux,* fr. L *captiosus,* fr. *captio* deception, verbal quibble, fr. *capere* to take — more at HEAVE] (14c) **1 :** marked by an often ill-natured inclination to stress faults and raise objections ⟨~ critics⟩ **2 :** calculated to confuse, entrap, or entangle in argument ⟨a ~ question⟩ ***syn*** see CRITICAL — **cap·tious·ly** *adv* — **cap·tious·ness** *n*
cap·ti·vate \ˈkap-tə-ˌvāt\ *vt* **-vat·ed; -vat·ing** (ca. 1555) **1** *archaic* **:** SEIZE, CAPTURE **2 :** to influence and dominate by some special charm, art, or trait and with an irresistible appeal ***syn*** see ATTRACT — **cap·ti·va·tion** \ˌkap-tə-ˈvā-shən\ *n* — **cap·ti·va·tor** \ˈkap-tə-ˌvā-tər\ *n*
cap·tive \ˈkap-tiv\ *adj* [ME, fr. L *captivus,* fr. *captus,* pp. of *capere*] (14c) **1 a :** taken and held as or as if a prisoner of war **b (1) :** kept within bounds **:** CONFINED **(2) :** of or relating to captive animals ⟨~ breeding⟩ **2 :** held under control of another but having the appearance of independence; *esp* **:** owned or controlled by another concern and operated for its needs rather than for an open market ⟨a ~ mine⟩ **3 :** being such involuntarily because of a situation that makes free choice or departure difficult ⟨a ~ audience⟩ — **captive** *n*
cap·tiv·i·ty \kap-ˈti-və-tē\ *n* (14c) **1 :** the state of being captive ⟨some birds thrive in ~⟩ **2** *obs* **:** a group of captives
cap·to·pril \ˈkap-tə-ˌpril\ *n* [mer*captan* + *-o-* + proline + *-il,* alter. of *-yl*] (1978) **:** an antihypertensive drug $C_9H_{15}NO_3S$ that is an ACE inhibitor
cap·tor \ˈkap-tər, -ˌtȯr\ *n* [LL, fr. L *capere*] (ca. 1688) **:** one that has captured a person or thing
[1]**cap·ture** \ˈkap-chər, -shər\ *n* [MF, fr. L *captura,* fr. *captus*] (ca. 1542) **1 :** an act or instance of capturing: as **a :** an act of catching, winning, or gaining control by force, stratagem, or guile **b :** a move in a board game (as chess or checkers) that gains an opponent's piece **c :** the absorption by an atom, nucleus, or particle of a subatomic particle that often results in subsequent emission of radiation or in fission **d :** the act of recording in a permanent file ⟨data ~⟩ **2 :** one that has been taken (as a prize ship)
[2]**capture** *vt* **cap·tured; cap·tur·ing** \ˈkap-chə-riŋ, ˈkap-shriŋ\ (1574) **1 a :** to take captive; *also* **:** to gain control of esp. by force ⟨~ a city⟩ **b :** to gain or win esp. through effort ⟨*captured* 60 percent of the vote⟩ **2 a :** to emphasize, represent, or preserve (as a scene, mood, or quality) in a more or less permanent form ⟨at any such moment as a photograph might ~ —C. E. Montague⟩ **b :** to record in a permanent file (as in a computer) **3 :** to captivate and hold the interest of **4 :** to take according to the rules of a game **5 :** to bring about the capture of (a subatomic particle) ***syn*** see CATCH
capture the flag *n* (ca. 1925) **:** a game in which players on each of two teams seek to capture the other team's flag and return it to their side without being captured and imprisoned
ca·puche \kə-ˈpüch, -ˈpüsh\ *n* [MF, fr. It *cappuccio,* fr. *cappa* cloak, fr. LL] (ca. 1600) **:** HOOD; *esp* **:** the cowl of a Capuchin friar
ca·pu·chin \ˈka-pyə-shən, -pə-, *esp for 3 also* kə-ˈpyü-, -ˈpü-\ *n* [MF, fr. OIt *cappuccino,* fr. *cappuccio;* fr. his cowl] (1589) **1** *cap* **:** a member of the Order of Friars Minor Capuchin forming since 1529 an austere branch of the first order of St. Francis of Assisi engaged in missionary work and preaching **2 :** a hooded cloak for women **3 :** any of a genus (*Cebus*) of So. and Central American monkeys; *esp* **:** one (*C. capucinus*) with the hair on its crown resembling a monk's cowl
Cap·u·let \ˈka-pyə-lət\ *n* (1592) **:** the family of Juliet in Shakespeare's *Romeo and Juliet*
cap·y·bara \ˌka-pi-ˈber-ə, -ˈbär-, -ˈba-rə\ *n* [Pg *capibara, capivara,* alter. of *capiiuara,* fr. Tupi *kapiʔiwara,* fr. *kapiʔi* grass, brush + *-wara* eater] (1774) **:** a tailless semiaquatic So. and Central American rodent (*Hydrochaerus hydrochaeris*) often exceeding four feet (1.2 meters) in length

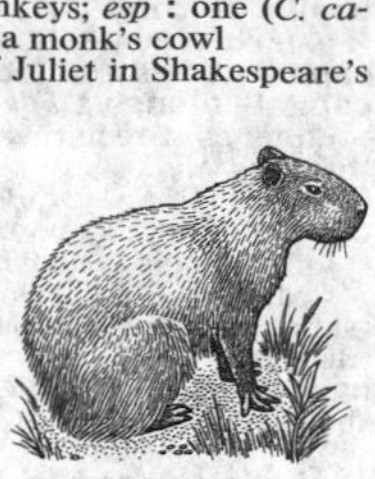
capybara

car \ˈkär, *dial also* ˈkȯr, ˈkyär\ *n* [ME *carre,* fr. AF, fr. L *carra,* pl. of *carrum,* alter. of *carrus,* of Celt origin; akin to OIr & MW *carr* vehicle; akin to L *currere* to run] (14c) **1 :** a vehicle moving on wheels: as **a** *archaic* **:** CARRIAGE, CHARIOT **b :** a vehicle designed to move on rails (as of a railroad) **c :** AUTOMOBILE **2 :** the passenger compartment of an elevator **3 :** the part of an airship or balloon that carries the passengers and cargo
CAR *abbr* civil air regulations
ca·ra·bao \ˌker-ə-ˈbau̇, ˌkär-, ˌka-rə-\ *n, pl* **-bao** *or* **-baos** [PhilSp, fr. Visayan of Samar and Leyte *karabáw*] (1900) **:** WATER BUFFALO
ca·ra·bid \ˈker-ə-bəd, ˈka-rə-, kə-ˈra-bəd\ *n* [ultim. fr. Gk *karabos* horned beetle] (1880) **:** GROUND BEETLE
car·a·bi·neer *or* **car·a·bi·nier** \ˌker-ə-bə-ˈnir, ˌka-rə-\ *n* [F *carabinier,* fr. *carabine* carbine] (1672) **:** a cavalry soldier armed with a carbine
car·a·bi·ner *also* **kar·a·bi·ner** \ˌker-ə-ˈbē-nər, ˌka-rə-\ *n* [G *Karabiner,* short for *Karabinerhaken,* lit., carabineer's hook] (1920) **:** an oblong metal ring with one spring-hinged side that is used esp. in mountain climbing as a connector and to hold a freely running rope
ca·ra·bi·ne·ro \ˌker-ə-bə-ˈner-(ˌ)ō, ˌkär-, ˌka-rə-\ *n, pl* **-ros** [Sp, fr. *carabina* carbine, fr. F *carabine*] (1845) **1 :** a member of a Spanish national police force serving esp. as frontier guards **2 :** a customs or coast guard officer in the Philippines
ca·ra·bi·nie·re \ˌker-ə-bən-ˈyer-(ˌ)ā, ˌkär-, ˌka-rə-\ *n, pl* **-nie·ri** \-ˈyer-ē\ [It, fr. F *carabinier*] (1847) **:** a member of the Italian national police force
car·a·cal \ˈker-ə-ˌkal, ˈka-rə-\ *n* [F, fr. Turk *karakulak,* fr. *kara* black + *kulak* ear] (1760) **:** a long-legged reddish-brown nocturnal cat (*Felis caracal* syn. *Lynx caracal*) of savannas in Africa and parts of Asia that has long pointed ears with a tuft of black hairs at the tip
ca·ra·ca·ra \ˌka-rə-ˈka-rə, -ə-kə-ˈrä\ *n* [Sp *caracara* & Pg *caracará,* fr. Tupi *karakará*] (1838) **:** any of various large long-legged hawks found from the southern U.S. to So. America that are classified with the falcons
car·a·cole \ˈka-rə-ˌkōl\ *n* [F, fr. Sp *caracol* snail, spiral stair, caracole] (1614) **:** a half turn to right or left executed by a mounted horse — **caracole** *vb*
car·a·cul \ˈka-rə-kəl\ *n* [alter. of *karakul*] (1894) **:** the pelt of a karakul lamb after the curl begins to loosen
ca·rafe \kə-ˈraf, -ˈräf\ *n* [F, fr. It *caraffa,* fr. Ar *gharrāfa*] (1767) **1 :** a bottle with a flaring lip used to hold beverages and esp. wine **2 :** a usu. glass container used to hold and serve coffee
car·am·bo·la \ˌka-rəm-ˈbō-lə\ *n* [Pg, fr. Marathi *karambal,* fr. Skt *karmaphala*] (1598) **1 :** a 5-angled green to yellow tropical fruit of star-shaped cross section — called also *star fruit* **2 :** a tropical tree (*Averrhoa carambola*) of the wood-sorrel family that is native to southeastern Asia and is widely cultivated for carambolas
car·a·mel \ˈkär-məl; ˈker-ə-məl, ˈka-rə-, -ˌmel\ *n* [F, fr. Sp *caramelo,* fr. Pg, icicle, caramel, fr. LL *calamellus* small reed — more at SHAWM] (1653) **1 :** an amorphous brittle brown and somewhat bitter substance obtained by heating sugar and used as a coloring and flavoring agent **2 :** a firm chewy usu. caramel-flavored candy
car·a·mel·ise *Brit var of* CARAMELIZE
car·a·mel·ize \-mə-ˌlīz\ *vb* **-ized; -iz·ing** *vt* (1842) **:** to change (as sugar) into caramel ~ *vi* **:** to change to caramel
ca·ran·gid \kə-ˈran-jəd, -ˈraŋ-gəd\ *adj* [ultim. fr. F *carangue* shad, horse mackerel, fr. Sp *caranga*] (1931) **:** of or relating to a large family (Carangidae of the order Perciformes) of marine spiny-finned bony fishes including important food fishes — **carangid** *n*
car·a·pace \ˈker-ə-ˌpās, ˈka-rə-\ *n* [F, fr. Sp *carapacho*] (1836) **1 :** a bony or chitinous case or shield covering the back or part of the back of an animal (as a turtle or crab) **2 :** a protective, decorative, or disguising shell ⟨the ~ of reserve he built around himself —M. M. Mintz⟩
[1]**carat** *var of* KARAT
[2]**car·at** \ˈker-ət, ˈka-rət\ *n* [ME *carrat* measure of fineness in gold, fr. MF *carat* measure of fineness in gold or of weight in gems, fr. It *carato,* fr. Ar *qīrāṭ* bean pod, a small weight, fr. Gk *keration* carob bean, a small weight, fr. dim. of *kerat-, keras* horn — more at HORN] (1555) **:** a unit of weight for precious stones equal to 200 milligrams
[1]**car·a·van** \ˈker-ə-ˌvan, ˈka-rə-\ *n* [It *caravana,* fr. Pers *kārvān*] (1588) **1 a :** a company of travelers on a journey through desert or hostile regions; *also* **:** a train of pack animals **b :** a group of vehicles traveling together (as in a file) **2 a :** a covered wagon or motor vehicle equipped as traveling living quarters **b** *Brit* **:** TRAILER 3b
[2]**caravan** *vi* **-vanned** *or* **-vaned; -van·ning** *or* **-van·ing** (1885) **:** to travel in a caravan
car·a·van·ner *or* **car·a·van·er** \-ˌva-nər\ *n* (1909) **1 :** one that travels in a caravan **2** *Brit* **:** one who goes camping with a trailer
car·a·van·sa·ry \ˌker-ə-ˈvan(t)-sə-rē, ˌka-rə-\ *or* **car·a·van·se·rai** \-sə-ˌrī\ *n, pl* **-ries** *or* **-rais** *or* **-rai** [Pers *kārvānsarāī,* fr. *kārvān* caravan + *sarāī* palace, inn] (1599) **1 :** an inn surrounding a court in eastern countries where caravans rest at night **2 :** HOTEL, INN
car·a·vel \ˈker-ə-ˌvel, ˈka-rə-, -vəl\ *n* [MF *caravelle,* fr. OPg *caravela*] (1527) **:** any of several sailing ships; *specif* **:** a small 15th and 16th century ship that has broad bows, high narrow poop, and usu. three masts with lateen or both square and lateen sails
car·a·way \ˈker-ə-ˌwā, ˈka-rə-\ *n* [ME, prob. fr. ML *carvi,* fr. Ar

karawyā, fr. Gk *karon*] (13c) **1 :** a biennial usu. white-flowered aromatic Old World herb (*Carum carvi*) of the carrot family **2 :** the pungent fruit of the caraway used in seasoning and medicine — called also *caraway seed*
[1]**carb** \ˈkärb\ *n* (ca. 1942) *slang* **:** CARBURETOR
[2]**carb** \ˈkärb\ *or* **car·bo** \ˈkär-(ˌ)bō\ *n* (1965) **:** CARBOHYDRATE; *also* **:** a high-carbohydrate food — usu. used in pl.
carb- *or* **carbo-** *comb form* [F, fr. *carbone*] **:** carbon **:** carbonic **:** carbonyl **:** carboxyl ⟨*carb*ide⟩ ⟨*carbo*hydrate⟩
car·ba·chol \ˈkär-bə-ˌkȯl, -ˌkōl\ *n* [*carb*amic acid + *chol*ine] (ca. 1940) **:** a synthetic parasympathomimetic drug $C_6H_{15}ClN_2O_2$ that is used in veterinary medicine and topically in glaucoma
car·ba·mate \ˈkär-bə-ˌmāt, kär-ˈba-ˌmāt\ *n* (1888) **:** a salt or ester of carbamic acid; *esp* **:** one that is a synthetic organic insecticide
car·ba·maz·e·pine \ˌkär-bə-ˈma-zə-ˌpēn\ *n* [*carbam*oyl (a radical of carbamic acid) + *-azepine* (as in *benzodiazepine*)] (1966) **:** a tricyclic anticonvulsant and analgesic $C_{15}H_{12}N_2O$ used in the treatment of trigeminal neuralgia and epilepsy
car·bam·ic acid \(ˌ)kär-ˈba-mik-\ *n* [ISV *carbam*ide + [1]*-ic*] (1869) **:** an acid CH_3NO_2 known in the form of salts and esters that is a half amide of carbonic acid
car·bam·ide \ˈkär-bə-ˌmīd, kär-ˈba-məd\ *n* [ISV *carb-* + *amide*] (1865) **:** UREA
carb·ami·no \ˌkär-bə-ˈmē-(ˌ)nō\ *adj* (1922) **:** relating to any of various carbamic acid derivatives formed by reaction of carbon dioxide with an amino acid or a protein (as hemoglobin)
carb·an·ion \kär-ˈba-ˌnī-ən, -ˌnī-ˌän\ *n* (1933) **:** an organic ion carrying a negative charge on a carbon atom — compare CARBONIUM
car·barn \ˈkär-ˌbärn\ *n* (1880) **:** a building that houses the cars of a street railway or the buses of a bus system
car·ba·ryl \ˈkär-bə-ˌril\ *n* [*carba*mate + *aryl*] (1963) **:** a carbamate insecticide $C_{12}H_{11}NO_2$ effective esp. against numerous crop, forage, and forest pests
car·ba·zole \ˈkär-bə-ˌzōl\ *n* [ISV *carb-* + *az-* + *-ole*] (1887) **:** a crystalline slightly basic cyclic compound $C_{12}H_9N$ found in anthracene and used in making dyes
car·bide \ˈkär-ˌbīd\ *n* [ISV] (ca. 1865) **1 :** a binary compound of carbon with a more electropositive element; *esp* **:** CALCIUM CARBIDE **2 :** a very hard material made of carbon and one or more heavy metals
car·bine \ˈkär-ˌbēn, -ˌbīn\ *n* [F *carabine,* fr. MF *carabin* carabineer] (1592) **1 :** a short-barreled lightweight firearm orig. used by cavalry **2 :** a light short-barreled repeating rifle that is used as a supplementary military arm or for hunting in dense brush
car·bi·nol \ˈkär-bə-ˌnȯl, -ˌnōl\ *n* [ISV, fr. obs. G *Karbin* methyl, fr. G *karb-* carb-] (ca. 1885) **:** METHANOL; *also* **:** an alcohol derived from it
car·bo·cy·clic \ˌkär-bō-ˈsī-klik, -ˈsi-\ *adj* [ISV] (1899) **:** being or having an organic ring composed of carbon atoms
car·bo·hy·drase \ˌkär-bō-ˈhī-ˌdrās, -bə-, -ˌdrāz\ *n* [ISV] (1910) **:** any of a group of enzymes (as amylase) that promote hydrolysis or synthesis of a carbohydrate (as a disaccharide)
car·bo·hy·drate \-ˌdrāt, -drət\ *n* (1853) **:** any of various neutral compounds of carbon, hydrogen, and oxygen (as sugars, starches, and celluloses) most of which are formed by green plants and which constitute a major class of animal foods
car·bol·ic \kär-ˈbä-lik\ *n* (1884) **:** PHENOL 1
carbolic acid *n* [ISV *carb-* + L *oleum* oil — more at OIL] (ca. 1859) **:** PHENOL 1
car·bo–load \ˈkär-bō-ˌlōd\ *vi* [*carbo*] (1981) **:** to consume a large amount of carbohydrates through food intake usu. in order to improve performance in an upcoming athletic event (as a marathon)
car bomb *n* (1972) **:** an explosive device concealed in an automobile for use as a weapon of terrorism
car·bon \ˈkär-bən\ *n, often attrib* [F *carbone,* fr. L *carbon-, carbo* ember, charcoal] (1789) **1 :** a nonmetallic chiefly tetravalent element found native (as in diamond and graphite) or as a constituent of coal, petroleum, and asphalt, of limestone and other carbonates, and of organic compounds or obtained artificially in varying degrees of purity esp. as carbon black, lampblack, activated carbon, charcoal, and coke — see ELEMENT table **2 :** a carbon rod used in an arc lamp **3 a :** a sheet of carbon paper **b :** CARBON COPY
car·bo·na·ceous \ˌkär-bə-ˈnā-shəs\ *adj* (1791) **1 :** relating to, containing, or composed of carbon **2 :** rich in carbon
[1]**car·bo·na·do** \ˌkär-bə-ˈnā-(ˌ)dō, -ˈnä-\ *n, pl* **-dos** *or* **-does** [Sp *carbonada*] (1584) *archaic* **:** a piece of meat scored before grilling
[2]**carbonado** *vt* (1599) **1** *archaic* **:** to make a carbonado of **2** *archaic* **:** CUT, SLASH
[3]**carbonado** *n, pl* **-dos** [Pg, lit., carbonated] (1853) **:** an impure opaque dark-colored fine-grained aggregate of diamond particles valuable for its superior toughness
car·bo·nara \ˌkär-bə-ˈnär-ə\ *n* [It dial. (*alla*) *carbonara,* lit., in the manner of a charcoal maker] (1963) **:** a dish of hot pasta into which other ingredients (as eggs, bacon or ham, and grated cheese) have been mixed — often used as a postpositive modifier ⟨spaghetti ~⟩
[1]**car·bon·ate** \ˈkär-bə-ˌnāt, -nət\ *n* (1794) **:** a salt or ester of carbonic acid
[2]**car·bon·ate** \-ˌnāt\ *vt* **-at·ed; -at·ing** (1805) **1 :** to convert into a carbonate **2 :** to combine or infuse with carbon dioxide ⟨*carbonated* beverages⟩ — **car·bon·ation** \ˌkär-bə-ˈnā-shən\ *n*
carbon black *n* (ca. 1889) **:** any of various colloidal black substances consisting wholly or principally of carbon obtained usu. as soot and used esp. in tires and as pigments
carbon copy *n* (1895) **1 :** a copy made by carbon paper **2 :** DUPLICATE ⟨is a *carbon copy* of his father⟩
carbon cycle *n* (1912) **1 :** the cycle of carbon in the earth's ecosystems in which carbon dioxide is fixed by photosynthetic organisms to form organic nutrients and is ultimately restored to the inorganic state (as by respiration, protoplasmic decay, or combustion) **2 :** a cycle of thermonuclear reactions in which four hydrogen atoms synthesize into a helium atom by the catalytic action of carbon with the release of nuclear energy and which is held to be the source of most of the energy radiated by the sun and stars
carbon dating *n* (1951) **:** the determination of the age of old material (as an archaeological or paleontological specimen) by means of the content of carbon 14 — **carbon–date** \ˈkär-bən-ˈdāt\ *vt*
carbon dioxide *n* (1869) **:** a heavy colorless gas CO_2 that does not support combustion, dissolves in water to form carbonic acid, is formed esp. in animal respiration and in the decay or combustion of animal and vegetable matter, is absorbed from the air by plants in photosynthesis, and is used in the carbonation of beverages
carbon disulfide *n* (1869) **:** a colorless flammable poisonous liquid CS_2 used as a solvent for rubber and as an insect fumigant — called also *carbon bisulfide*
carbon fiber *n* (1960) **:** a very strong lightweight synthetic fiber made esp. by carbonizing acrylic fiber at high temperatures
carbon footprint *n* (1999) **:** the amount of greenhouse gases and specif. carbon dioxide emitted by something (as a person's activities or a product's manufacture and transport) during a given period
carbon 14 *n* (1936) **:** a heavy radioactive isotope of carbon of mass number 14 used esp. in tracer studies and in dating old materials (as archaeological and geological specimens)
car·bon·ic \kär-ˈbä-nik\ *adj* (1788) **:** of, relating to, or derived from carbon, carbonic acid, or carbon dioxide
carbonic acid *n* (1788) **:** a weak dibasic acid H_2CO_3 known only in solution that reacts with bases to form carbonates
carbonic acid gas *n* (1797) **:** CARBON DIOXIDE
carbonic an·hy·drase \-an-ˈhī-ˌdrās, -ˌdrāz\ *n* [*anhydr*ous + *-ase;* fr. its promotion of dehydration] (1932) **:** a zinc-containing enzyme that occurs in living tissues (as red blood cells) and aids carbon-dioxide transport from the tissues and its release from the blood in the lungs by catalyzing the reversible hydration of carbon dioxide to carbonic acid
car·bon·if·er·ous \ˌkär-bə-ˈni-f(ə-)rəs\ *adj* (1799) **1 :** producing or containing carbon or coal **2** *cap* **:** of, relating to, or being the period of the Paleozoic era between the Devonian and the Permian or the corresponding system of rocks that includes coal beds — see GEOLOGIC TIME table — **Carboniferous** *n*
car·bo·ni·um \kär-ˈbō-nē-əm\ *n* [*carb-* + *-onium*] (1942) **:** an organic ion carrying a positive charge on a carbon atom — compare CARBANION
car·bon·i·za·tion \ˌkär-bə-nə-ˈzā-shən\ *n* (1804) **:** the process of carbonizing; *esp* **:** DESTRUCTIVE DISTILLATION
car·bon·ize \ˈkär-bə-ˌnīz\ *vb* **-ized; -iz·ing** *vt* (1806) **1 :** to convert into carbon or a carbonic residue **2 :** CARBURIZE 1 ~ *vi* **:** to become carbonized **:** CHAR
car·bon·less \ˈkär-bən-ləs\ *adj* (1850) **1 :** being without carbon **2 :** being or composed of paper that makes multiple copies without intervening layers of carbon paper ⟨~ forms⟩
carbon monoxide *n* (1869) **:** a colorless odorless very toxic gas CO that is formed as a product of the incomplete combustion of carbon or a carbon compound
car·bon·nade *also* **car·bo·nade** \ˌkär-bə-ˈnäd\ *n* [F, lit., dish of grilled meat, fr. It *carbonata,* fr. *carbone* charcoal, coal, fr. L *carbon-, carbo*] (1877) **:** a beef stew cooked in beer
carbon paper *n* (1877) **:** a thin paper faced with a waxy pigmented coating so that when placed between two sheets of paper the pressure of writing or typing on the top sheet causes transfer of pigment to the bottom sheet
carbon steel *n* (1903) **:** a strong hard steel that derives its physical properties from the presence of carbon and is used in hand tools and kitchen utensils
carbon tetrachloride *n* (1866) **:** a colorless nonflammable toxic liquid CCl_4 that has an odor resembling that of chloroform and is used as a solvent and a refrigerant
carbon 13 *n* (1939) **:** an isotope of carbon of mass number 13 that constitutes about 1⁄70 of natural carbon and is used as a tracer esp. in spectroscopy utilizing nuclear magnetic resonance
carbon 12 *n* (1946) **:** an isotope of carbon of mass number 12 that is the most abundant carbon isotope and is used as a standard for measurements of atomic weight
car·bon·yl \ˈkär-bə-ˌnil, -ˌnēl\ *n* (1863) **1 :** an organic functional group or radical –CO– occurring in aldehydes, ketones, carboxylic acids, esters, and their derivatives **2 :** a coordination complex involving the neutral radical CO ⟨chromium ~⟩ — **car·bon·yl·ic** \ˌkär-bə-ˈni-lik\ *adj*
car·bon·yl·a·tion \(ˌ)kär-ˌbä-nə-ˈlā-shən\ *n* (1946) **:** the synthesis of a carbonyl compound esp. by a reaction involving carbon monoxide
Car·bo·run·dum \ˌkär-bə-ˈrən-dəm\ *trademark* — used for various abrasives
carboxy- *or* **carbox-** *comb form* **:** carboxyl ⟨*carboxy*peptidase⟩
car·box·yl \kär-ˈbäk-səl\ *n* [ISV] (1869) **:** a monovalent functional group or radical –COOH typical of organic acids — called also *carboxyl group* — **car·box·yl·ic** \ˌkär-(ˌ)bäk-ˈsi-lik\ *adj*
car·box·yl·ase \kär-ˈbäk-sə-ˌlās, -ˌlāz\ *n* [ISV] (1911) **:** an enzyme that catalyzes decarboxylation or carboxylation
[1]**car·box·yl·ate** \-ˌlāt, -lət\ *n* (1884) **:** a salt or ester of a carboxylic acid
[2]**car·box·yl·ate** \-ˌlāt\ *vt* **-at·ed; -at·ing** (1921) **:** to introduce carboxyl or carbon dioxide into (a compound) with formation of a carboxylic acid — **car·box·yl·a·tion** \(ˌ)kär-ˌbäk-sə-ˈlā-shən\ *n*
carboxylic acid *n* (1883) **:** an organic acid (as acetic acid) containing one or more carboxyl groups
car·boxy·meth·yl·cel·lu·lose \kär-ˌbäk-sē-ˌme-thəl-ˈsel-yə-ˌlōs, -ˌlōz\ *n* (1947) **:** an acid ether derivative of cellulose that in the form of its sodium salt is used as a thickening, emulsifying, and stabilizing agent and as a bulk laxative in medicine
car·boxy·pep·ti·dase \-ˈpep-tə-ˌdās, -ˌdāz\ *n* (1935) **:** an enzyme that hydrolyzes peptides and esp. polypeptides by splitting off sequentially the amino acids at the end of the peptide chain which contain free carboxyl groups
car·boy \ˈkär-ˌbȯi\ *n* [Pers *qarāba,* fr. Ar *qarrāba* demijohn] (1753) **:** a large container for liquids
car·bun·cle \ˈkär-ˌbəŋ-kəl\ *n* [ME, fr. AF *charbucle, carbuncule,* fr. L *carbunculus* small coal, carbuncle, dim. of *carbon-, carbo* charcoal, em-

ber] (13c) **1 a** *obs* : any of several red precious stones **b** : the garnet cut cabochon **2** : a painful local purulent inflammation of the skin and deeper tissues with multiple openings for the discharge of pus and usu. necrosis and sloughing of dead tissue — **car·bun·cled** \-kəld\ *adj* — **car·bun·cu·lar** \kär-ˈbəŋ-kyə-lər\ *adj*

car·bu·ret·ed \ˈkär-bə-ˌrā-təd, -byə-, *esp by chemists* -ˌre-təd\ *adj* [back-formation fr. *carburetor*] (1972) : equipped with a carburetor

car·bu·re·tion \ˌkär-bə-ˈrā-shən, -byə-\ *n* [*carburet* to combine chemically with carbon, fr. obs. *carburet* carbide] (1896) : the process of mixing (as in a carburetor) the vapor of a flammable hydrocarbon (as gasoline) with air to form an explosive mixture esp. for use in an internal-combustion engine

car·bu·re·tor \ˈkär-bə-ˌrā-tər, -byə-\ *n* (1896) : a mechanical apparatus for premixing vaporized fuel and air in proper proportions and supplying the mixture to an internal combustion engine

car·bu·ret·tor *also* **car·bu·ret·ter** \ˌkär-byə-ˈre-tər, ˈkär-byə-ˌ\ *chiefly Brit var of* CARBURETOR

car·bu·rise *Brit var of* CARBURIZE

car·bu·rize \ˈkär-bə-ˌrīz, -byə-\ *vt* **-rized; -riz·ing** [obs. *carburet* carbide] (1864) : to combine or impregnate (as metal) with carbon — **car·bu·ri·za·tion** \ˌkär-bə-rə-ˈzā-shən, -byə-\ *n*

car·ca·net \ˈkär-kə-nət\ *n* [MF *carcan*] (ca. 1530) *archaic* : an ornamental necklace, chain, collar, or headband

car·case \ˈkär-kəs\ *Brit var of* CARCASS

car·cass \ˈkär-kəs\ *n* [ME *carcays,* fr. AF *carcas, carkeis*] (14c) **1** : a dead body : CORPSE; *esp* : the dressed body of a meat animal **2** : the living, material, or physical body **3** : the decaying or worthless remains of a structure ⟨the ~ of an abandoned automobile⟩ **4** : the underlying structure or frame of something (as of a piece of furniture)

car·cer·al \ˈkär-sə-rəl\ *adj* [LL, fr. L *carcer* prison] (ca. 1587) : of, relating to, or suggesting a jail or prison

carcin- *or* **carcino-** *comb form* [Gk *karkin-, karkino-,* fr. *karkinos* ulcerous sore, lit., crab — more at CANCER] : tumor : cancer ⟨*carcino*genic⟩

car·ci·no·em·bry·on·ic antigen \ˌkär-sə-nō-ˌem-brē-ˈä-nik-\ *n* (1967) : a glycoprotein present in fetal digestive-tract tissues and in peripheral blood of patients with some forms of cancer

car·cin·o·gen \kär-ˈsi-nə-jən, ˈkär-sə-nə-ˌjen\ *n* (1853) : a substance or agent causing cancer — **car·ci·no·gen·ic** \ˌkär-sə-nō-ˈje-nik\ *adj* — **car·ci·no·ge·nic·i·ty** \-jə-ˈni-sə-tē\ *n*

car·ci·no·gen·e·sis \ˌkär-sə-nō-ˈje-nə-sis\ *n* (ca. 1923) : the production of cancer

car·ci·noid \ˈkär-sə-ˌnȯid\ *n* (1925) : a benign or malignant tumor arising esp. from the mucosa of the gastrointestinal tract

car·ci·no·ma \ˌkär-sə-ˈnō-mə\ *n, pl* **-mas** *also* **-ma·ta** \-mə-tə\ [L, fr. Gk *karkinōma* cancer, fr. *karkinos*] (ca. 1721) : a malignant tumor of epithelial origin — **car·ci·no·ma·tous** \-ˈnō-mə-təs\ *adj*

car·ci·no·ma·to·sis \-ˌnō-mə-ˈtō-səs\ *n* [NL, fr. L *carcinomat-, carcinoma*] (1903) : a condition in which multiple carcinomas develop simultaneously usu. after dissemination from a primary source

car coat *n* (1958) : a three-quarter-length overcoat

[1]**card** \ˈkärd\ *vt* (14c) : to cleanse, disentangle, and collect together (as fibers) by the use of cards preparatory to spinning — **card·er** *n*

[2]**card** *n* [ME *carde,* fr. ML *cardus, carduus,* thistle, carding instrument, fr. L *carduus* thistle — more at CHARD] (15c) **1** : an instrument or machine for carding fibers that consists usu. of bent wire teeth set closely in rows in a thick piece of leather fastened to a back **2** : an implement for raising a nap on cloth

[3]**card** *n* [ME *carde,* fr. AF, alter. of MF *carte,* prob. fr. OIt *carta,* lit., leaf of paper, fr. L *charta* leaf of papyrus, fr. Gk *chartēs*] (15c) **1** : PLAYING CARD **2** *pl but sing or pl in constr* **a** : a game played with cards **b** : card playing **3 a** : something (as an advantage) compared to a valuable playing card in one's hand ⟨holding all the ~*s* in negotiations⟩ **b** : an issue esp. with emotional appeal that is brought into play to achieve a desired end (as winning a political campaign) ⟨played the race ~⟩ **4** : a usu. clownishly amusing person : WAG ⟨he's such a ~⟩ **5** : COMPASS CARD **6 a** : a flat stiff usu. small and rectangular piece of material (as paper, cardboard, or plastic) usu. bearing information: as (1) : POSTCARD (2) : VISITING CARD (3) : BUSINESS CARD (4) : CREDIT CARD (5) : one bearing a picture (as of a baseball player) on one side and usu. statistical data on the other (6) : one on which computer information is stored (as in the form of punched holes or magnetic encoding) (7) : one bearing electronic circuit components for insertion into a larger electronic device (as a computer) **b** : PROGRAM; *esp* : a sports program ⟨three fights on the ~⟩ **c** (1) : a wine list (2) : MENU **d** : GREETING CARD ⟨a birthday ~⟩ — **in the cards** *also* **on the cards** : INEVITABLE ⟨success just wasn't *in the cards* for her⟩

[4]**card** *vt* (1884) **1** : to place or fasten on or by means of a card **2** : to provide with a card **3** : to list or record on a card **4** : SCORE ⟨a golfer ~*ing* a 75⟩ **5** : to ask for identification (as in a bar) ⟨we all got ~*ed*⟩

[5]**card** *abbr* cardinal

car·da·mom \ˈkär-də-məm, -ˌmäm\ *n* [L *cardamomum,* fr. Gk *kardamōmon,* blend of *kardamon* peppergrass and *amōmon,* an Indian spice plant] (1553) : the aromatic capsular fruit of an Indian herb (*Elettaria cardamomum*) of the ginger family with seeds used as a spice or condiment and in medicine; *also* : this plant

[1]**card·board** \ˈkärd-ˌbȯrd\ *n* (1831) : a material made from cellulose fiber (as wood pulp) like paper but usu. thicker — **card·boardy** \-ˌbȯr-dē\ *adj*

[2]**cardboard** *adj* (1852) **1** : made of or as if of cardboard **2** : UNREAL, STEREOTYPED ⟨a play with ~ characters⟩

card–car·ry·ing \ˈkärd-ˌka-rē-iŋ\ *adj* [fr. the assumption that such a person carries an identification card] (1948) **1** : being a full-fledged member of an organization (as a Communist party) **2 a** : strongly identified with a group (as of people with a common interest) ⟨~ members of the ecology movement —R. J. Neuhaus⟩ **b** : being such emphatically or unmistakably ⟨a ~ hippie⟩

card catalog *n* (1854) : a catalog (as of books) in which the entries are arranged systematically on cards

card·hold·er \ˈkärd-ˌhōl-dər\ *n* (1909) : one who possesses a card and esp. a credit card

cardi- *or* **cardio-** *comb form* [Gk *kardi-, kardio-,* fr. *kardia* — more at HEART] : heart : cardiac : cardiac and ⟨*cardio*gram⟩ ⟨*cardio*vascular⟩

car·dia \ˈkär-dē-ə\ *n, pl* **-di·ae** \-dē-ˌē\ *or* **-dias** [NL, fr. Gk *kardia* heart, upper orifice of the stomach] (1782) : the opening of the esophagus into the stomach; *also* : the part of the stomach adjoining this opening

-cardia *n comb form* [NL, fr. Gk *kardia*] : heart action or location (of a specified type) ⟨tachy*cardia*⟩

[1]**car·di·ac** \ˈkär-dē-ˌak\ *adj* [L *cardiacus,* fr. Gk *kardiakos,* fr. *kardia*] (1601) **1 a** : of, relating to, situated near, or acting on the heart **b** : of or relating to the cardia of the stomach **2** : of, relating to, or affected with heart disease ⟨~ patients⟩

[2]**cardiac** *n* (ca. 1929) : a person with heart disease

cardiac arrest *n* (1950) : temporary or permanent cessation of the heartbeat

cardiac muscle *n* (ca. 1881) : the principal involuntary-muscle tissue of the vertebrate heart made up of striated fibers joined at usu. branched ends and functioning in synchronized rhythmic contraction

car·di·gan \ˈkär-di-gən\ *n* [James Thomas Brudenell, 7th Earl of *Cardigan* †1868 Eng. soldier] (1862) : a usu. collarless sweater or jacket that opens the full length of the center front

Cardigan Welsh corgi *n* [*Cardigan,* former county in Wales] (1935) : any of a breed of Welsh corgis with rounded ears, slightly bowed forelegs, and a long tail — called also *Cardigan*

[1]**car·di·nal** \ˈkärd-nəl, ˈkär-də-\ *n* [ME, fr. AF, fr. ML *cardinalis,* fr. LL *cardinalis,* adj.] (12c) **1** : a high ecclesiastical official of the Roman Catholic Church who ranks next below the pope and is appointed by him to assist him as a member of the college of cardinals **2** : CARDINAL NUMBER — usu. used in pl. **3** [fr. its color, resembling that of the cardinal's robes] : a crested finch (*Cardinalis cardinalis* of the family Cardinalidae) of the eastern U.S. and adjacent Canada, the southwestern U.S., and Mexico to Belize which has a black face and heavy red bill in both sexes and is nearly completely red in the male — **car·di·nal·ship** \-ˌship\ *n*

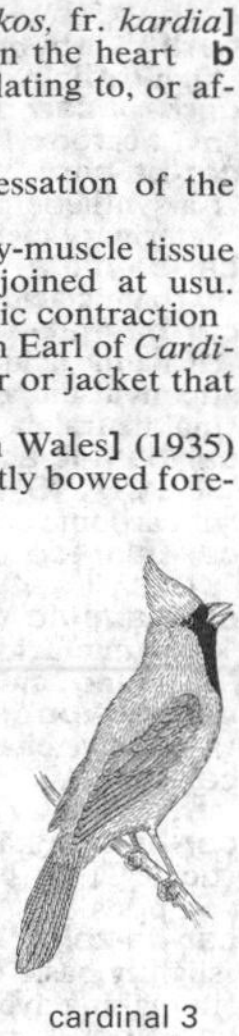
cardinal 3

[2]**cardinal** *adj* [ME, fr. LL *cardinalis,* serving as a hinge, fr. *cardin-, cardo* hinge] (14c) **1** : of basic importance ⟨a ~ principle⟩ **2** : very serious or grave ⟨a ~ sin⟩ ***syn*** see ESSENTIAL — **car·di·nal·ly** *adv*

car·di·nal·ate \ˈkärd-nə-lət, ˈkär-də-, -ˌlāt\ *n* (1645) : the office, rank, or dignity of a cardinal

cardinal flower *n* (1698) : a No. American lobelia (*Lobelia cardinalis*) that bears a spike of brilliant red flowers

car·di·nal·i·ty \ˌkär-də-ˈna-lə-tē\ *n, pl* **-ties** [[1]*cardinal* + *-ity*] (1935) : the number of elements in a given mathematical set

cardinal number *n* (1591) **1** : a number (as 1, 5, 15) that is used in simple counting and that indicates how many elements there are in an assemblage — see NUMBER table **2** : the property that a mathematical set has in common with all sets that can be put in one-to-one correspondence with it

cardinal point *n* (1658) : one of the four principal compass points north, south, east, and west

cardinal virtue *n* (14c) **1** : one of the four classically defined natural virtues prudence, justice, temperance, or fortitude **2** : a quality designated as a major virtue

[1]**car·dio** \ˈkär-dē-(ˌ)ō\ *adj* (1984) : CARDIOVASCULAR

[2]**cardio** *n* (1991) : cardiovascular exercise

car·dio·gram \ˈkär-dē-ə-ˌgram\ *n* [ISV] (1876) : the curve or tracing made by a cardiograph

car·dio·graph \-ˌgraf\ *n* [ISV] (1870) : an instrument that graphically registers movements of the heart — **car·dio·graph·ic** \ˌkär-dē-ə-ˈgra-fik\ *adj* — **car·di·og·ra·phy** \ˌkär-dē-ˈä-grə-fē\ *n*

car·di·oid \ˈkär-dē-ˌȯid\ *n* (1753) : a heart-shaped curve that is traced by a point on the circumference of a circle rolling completely around an equal fixed circle and has an equation in one of the forms $\rho = a(1 \pm \cos\theta)$ or $\rho = a(1 \pm \sin\theta)$ in polar coordinates

car·di·ol·o·gy \ˌkär-dē-ˈä-lə-jē\ *n* [ISV] (1847) : the study of the heart and its action and diseases — **car·di·o·log·i·cal** \-dē-ə-ˈlä-ji-kəl\ *adj* — **car·di·ol·o·gist** \-dē-ˈä-lə-jist\ *n*

car·dio·my·op·a·thy \ˈkär-dē-ō-(ˌ)mī-ˈä-pə-thē\ *n, pl* **-thies** (1957) : any of several structural or functional diseases of heart muscle marked esp. by hypertrophy and obstructive damage to the heart

car·di·op·a·thy \ˌkär-dē-ˈä-pə-thē\ *n, pl* **-thies** (1885) : any disease of the heart

car·dio·pro·tec·tive \ˌkär-dē-ō-prə-ˈtek-tiv\ *adj* (1984) : serving to protect the heart ⟨a drug's ~ effect⟩

car·dio·pul·mo·nary \ˌkär-dē-ō-ˈpu̇l-mə-ˌner-ē, -ˈpəl-\ *adj* (ca. 1881) : of or relating to the heart and lungs

cardiopulmonary resuscitation *n* (1972) : a procedure designed to restore normal breathing after cardiac arrest that includes the clearance of air passages to the lungs, mouth-to-mouth method of artificial respiration, and heart massage by the exertion of pressure on the chest

car·dio·re·spi·ra·to·ry \ˌkär-dē-ō-ˈres-p(ə-)rə-ˌtȯr-ē, -ri-ˈspī-rə-\ *adj* (1892) : of or relating to the heart and the respiratory system

car·dio·tho·rac·ic \-thə-ˈra-sik\ *adj* (1962) : relating to, involving, or specializing in the heart and chest ⟨~ surgery⟩

car·dio·ton·ic \-ˈtä-nik\ *adj* (1927) : tending to increase the tonus of heart muscle — **cardiotonic** *n*

car·dio·vas·cu·lar \-ˈvas-kyə-lər\ *adj* [ISV] (1879) **1** : of, relating to, or involving the heart and blood vessels **2** : used, designed, or performed to cause a temporary increase in heart rate ⟨a ~ workout⟩

car·dio·ver·sion \-ˈvər-zhən\ *n* [*cardi-* + *version* (turning of an organ)] (1963) : application of an electric shock in order to restore normal heartbeat

-cardium *n comb form, pl* **-cardia** [NL, fr. Gk *kardia*] : heart ⟨epi*cardium*⟩

car·doon \kär-ˈdün\ *n* [F *cardon,* fr. LL *cardon-, cardo* thistle, fr. *cardus,* fr. L *carduus* thistle, cardoon] (1611) : a large perennial Mediterranean plant (*Cynara cardunculus*) related to the artichoke and cultivated for its edible root and petioles; *also* : the root and petioles

card·play·er \ˈkärd-ˌplā-ər\ *n* (1589) : one who plays cards

card·sharp \-ˌshärp\ *or* **card·sharp·er** \-ˌshär-pər\ *n* (1858) : a person who habitually cheats at cards

card table *n* (1711) : a table designed for playing cards; *esp* : a square table with folding legs

[1]**care** \ˈker\ *n* [ME, fr. OE *caru;* akin to OHG *kara* lament, OIr *gairm* call, cry, L *garrire* to chatter] (bef. 12c) **1 :** suffering of mind : GRIEF **2 a :** a disquieted state of mixed uncertainty, apprehension, and responsibility **b :** a cause for such anxiety **3 a :** painstaking or watchful attention **b :** MAINTENANCE ⟨floor-*care* products⟩ **4 :** regard coming from desire or esteem **5 :** CHARGE, SUPERVISION ⟨under a doctor's ~⟩ **6 :** a person or thing that is an object of attention, anxiety, or solicitude

syn CARE, CONCERN, SOLICITUDE, ANXIETY, WORRY mean a troubled or engrossed state of mind or the thing that causes this. CARE implies oppression of the mind weighed down by responsibility or disquieted by apprehension ⟨a face worn by years of *care*⟩. CONCERN implies a troubled state of mind because of personal interest, relation, or affection ⟨crimes caused *concern* in the neighborhood⟩. SOLICITUDE implies great concern and connotes either thoughtful or hovering attentiveness toward another ⟨acted with typical maternal *solicitude*⟩. ANXIETY stresses anguished uncertainty or fear of misfortune or failure ⟨plagued by *anxiety* and self-doubt⟩. WORRY suggests fretting over matters that may or may not be real cause for anxiety ⟨financial *worries*⟩.

[2]**care** *vb* **cared; car·ing** *vi* (bef. 12c) **1 a :** to feel trouble or anxiety **b :** to feel interest or concern ⟨~ about freedom⟩ **2 :** to give care ⟨~ for the sick⟩ **3 a :** to have a liking, fondness, or taste ⟨don't ~ for your attitude⟩ **b :** to have an inclination ⟨would you ~ for some pie⟩ ~ *vt* **1 :** to be concerned about or to the extent of ⟨don't ~ what they say⟩ ⟨doesn't ~ a damn⟩ **2 :** WISH ⟨if you ~ to go⟩ — **car·er** *n* — **care less :** not to care — used positively and negatively with the same meaning ⟨I could *care less* what happens⟩ ⟨I couldn't *care less* what happens⟩

care and feeding *n* (1965) **:** the providing of what is needed for sustenance, well-being, or efficient operation ⟨machines that don't need a lot of *care and feeding*⟩

[1]**ca·reen** \kə-ˈrēn\ *vb* [fr. *carine* side of a ship, fr. MF, submerged part of a hull, fr. L *carina* hull, half of a nutshell; perh. akin to Gk *karyon* nut] *vt* (ca. 1583) **1 :** to put (a ship or boat) on a beach esp. in order to clean, caulk, or repair the hull **2 :** to cause to heel over ~ *vi* **1 a :** to careen a boat **b :** to undergo this process **2 :** to heel over **3 :** to sway from side to side : LURCH ⟨a ~*ing* carriage being pulled wildly . . . by a team of runaway horses —J. P. Getty⟩ **4 :** CAREER

[2]**careen** *n* (1712) *archaic* **:** the act or process of careening : the state of being careened

[1]**ca·reer** \kə-ˈrir\ *n* [MF *carriere,* fr. Old Occitan *carriera* street, fr. ML *carraria* road for vehicles, fr. L *carrus* car] (ca. 1534) **1 a :** speed in a course ⟨ran at full ~⟩ **b :** COURSE, PASSAGE **2 :** ENCOUNTER, CHARGE **3 :** a field for or pursuit of consecutive progressive achievement esp. in public, professional, or business life ⟨Washington's ~ as a soldier⟩ **4 :** a profession for which one trains and which is undertaken as a permanent calling ⟨a ~ in medicine⟩ ⟨a ~ diplomat⟩

[2]**career** *vi* (1647) **:** to go at top speed esp. in a headlong manner ⟨a car ~*ed* off the road⟩

ca·reer·ism \-ˌi-zəm\ *n* (1933) **:** the policy or practice of advancing one's career often at the cost of one's integrity — **ca·reer·ist** \-ist\ *n or adj*

care·free \ˈker-ˌfrē\ *adj* (1621) **:** free from care: as **a :** having no worries or troubles **b :** IRRESPONSIBLE ⟨is ~ with his money⟩

care·ful \-fəl\ *adj* **care·ful·ler; care·ful·lest** (bef. 12c) **1** *archaic* **a :** SOLICITOUS, ANXIOUS **b :** filling with care or solicitude **2 :** exercising or taking care **3 a :** marked by attentive concern and solicitude **b :** marked by wary caution or prudence ⟨be very ~ with knives⟩ **c :** marked by painstaking effort to avoid errors or omissions — often used with *of* or an infinitive ⟨~ of money⟩ ⟨~ to adjust the machine⟩ — **care·ful·ly** \-f(ə-)lē\ *adv* — **care·ful·ness** \-fəl-nəs\ *n*

syn CAREFUL, METICULOUS, SCRUPULOUS, PUNCTILIOUS mean showing close attention to detail. CAREFUL implies attentiveness and cautiousness in avoiding mistakes ⟨a *careful* worker⟩. METICULOUS may imply either commendable extreme carefulness or a hampering finicky caution over small points ⟨*meticulous* scholarship⟩. SCRUPULOUS applies to what is proper or fitting or ethical ⟨*scrupulous* honesty⟩. PUNCTILIOUS implies minute, even excessive attention to fine points ⟨*punctilious* observance of ritual⟩.

care·giv·er \-ˌgi-vər\ *n* (1966) **:** a person who provides direct care (as for children, elderly people, or the chronically ill) — **care·giv·ing** \-ˌgi-viŋ\ *n*

care·less \-ləs\ *adj* (bef. 12c) **1 a :** free from care : UNTROUBLED ⟨~ days⟩ **b :** INDIFFERENT, UNCONCERNED ⟨~ of the consequences⟩ **2 :** not taking care **3 :** not showing or receiving care: **a :** NEGLIGENT, SLOVENLY ⟨~ writing⟩ **b :** UNSTUDIED, SPONTANEOUS ⟨a ~ grace⟩ **c** *obs* **:** UNVALUED, DISREGARDED — **care·less·ly** *adv* — **care·less·ness** *n*

care package *n* [fr. *CARE package,* a charity parcel sent to needy Europeans after World War II] (1962) **:** a package of useful or pleasurable items that is sent or given as a gift to another (as a college student)

[1]**ca·ress** \kə-ˈres\ *vt* [F *caresser,* fr. It *carezzare,* fr. *carezza*] (1598) **1 :** to treat with tokens of fondness, affection, or kindness : CHERISH **2 a :** to touch or stroke lightly in a loving or endearing manner **b :** to touch or affect as if with a caress ⟨echoes that ~ the ear⟩ — **ca·ress·er** *n* — **ca·ress·ing·ly** \kə-ˈre-siŋ-lē\ *adv*

[2]**caress** *n* [F *caresse,* fr. It *carezza,* fr. *caro* dear, fr. L *carus* — more at CHARITY] (1609) **1 :** an act or expression of kindness or affection : ENDEARMENT **2 a :** a light stroking, rubbing, or patting **b :** KISS — **ca·res·sive** \-ˈre-siv\ *adj* — **ca·res·sive·ly** *adv*

car·et \ˈker-ət, ˈka-rət\ *n* [L, there is lacking, fr. *carēre* to lack, be without] (1681) **:** a wedge-shaped mark made on written or printed matter to indicate the place where something is to be inserted

care·tak·er \ˈker-ˌtā-kər\ *n* (1801) **1 :** one that gives physical or emotional care and support ⟨served as ~ to the younger children⟩ **2 :** one that takes care of the house or land of an owner who may be absent **3 :** one temporarily fulfilling the function of office ⟨a ~ government⟩ — **care·take** \-ˌtāk\ *vb* — **care·tak·ing** *n*

care·worn \-ˌwȯrn\ *adj* (1790) **:** showing the effect of grief or anxiety ⟨a ~ face⟩

car·fare \ˈkär-ˌfer\ *n* (1863) **:** passenger fare (as on a bus)

car·ful \ˈkär-ˌfu̇l\ *n* (1832) **:** as much or as many as a car will hold

car·go \ˈkär-(ˌ)gō\ *n, pl* **cargoes** *or* **cargos** [Sp, load, charge, fr. *cargar* to load, fr. LL *carricare* — more at CHARGE] (1657) **:** the goods or merchandise conveyed in a ship, airplane, or vehicle : FREIGHT

cargo cult *n* (1949) **:** any of various Melanesian religious groups characterized by the belief that material wealth (as money or manufactured goods) can be obtained through ritual worship

cargo pants *n pl* (1980) **:** pants with cargo pockets typically on the sides of the legs at thigh level

cargo pocket *n* (1974) **:** a large pocket usu. with a flap and a pleat

car·hop \ˈkär-ˌhäp\ *n* [*car* + *-hop* (as in *bellhop*)] (1937) **:** one who serves customers at a drive-in restaurant

Car·ib \ˈka-rəb\ *n* [NL *Caribes* (pl.), fr. Sp *Caribe,* of Cariban origin — more at CANNIBAL] (1555) **1 :** a member of an Indian people of northern So. America and the Lesser Antilles **2 :** the language of the Caribs

Ca·ri·ban \ˈka-rə-bən, kə-ˈrē-bən\ *n* (1901) **1 :** a member of a group of Indian peoples of So. America and the Lesser Antilles **2 :** the language family comprising the languages of the Cariban peoples

Ca·rib·be·an \ˌker-ə-ˈbē-ən, ˌka-rə-, kə-ˈri-bē-ən\ *adj* [NL *Caribbaeus,* fr. *Caribes*] (1772) **:** of or relating to the Caribs, the eastern and southern West Indies, or the Caribbean Sea

ca·ri·be \kə-ˈrē-bē\ *n* [AmerSp, fr. Sp, Carib, cannibal] (1863) **:** PIRANHA

car·i·bou \ˈker-ə-ˌbü, ˈka-rə-\ *n, pl* **-bou** *or* **-bous** [CanF, fr. Micmac *yalipu*] (ca. 1665) **:** a large gregarious deer (*Rangifer tarandus*) of Holarctic taiga and tundra that usu. has palmate antlers in both sexes — used esp. for one of the New World; called also *reindeer*

[1]**car·i·ca·ture** \ˈker-i-kə-ˌchu̇r, -ˌchər, -ˌtyu̇r, -ˌtu̇r, -ˈka-ri-\ *n* [It *caricatura,* lit., act of loading, fr. *caricare* to load, fr. LL *carricare*] (1712) **1 :** exaggeration by means of often ludicrous distortion of parts or characteristics **2 :** a representation esp. in literature or art that has the qualities of caricature **3 :** a distortion so gross as to seem like caricature — **car·i·ca·tur·al** \ˌker-i-kə-ˈchu̇r-əl, -ˈchər-, -ˈtyu̇r-, -ˈtu̇r-, -ˌka-ri-\ *adj* — **car·i·ca·tur·ist** \ˈker-i-kə-ˌchu̇r-ist, -ˌchər-, -ˌtyu̇r-, -ˌtu̇r-, -ˈka-ri-\ *n*

syn CARICATURE, BURLESQUE, PARODY, TRAVESTY mean a comic or grotesque imitation. CARICATURE implies ludicrous exaggeration of the characteristic features of a subject ⟨*caricatures* of politicians in cartoons⟩. BURLESQUE implies mockery esp. through giving a serious or lofty subject a frivolous treatment ⟨a nightclub *burlesque* of a trial in court⟩. PARODY applies esp. to treatment of a trivial or ludicrous subject in the exactly imitated style of a well-known author or work ⟨a witty *parody* of a popular novel⟩. TRAVESTY implies that the subject remains unchanged but that the style is extravagant or absurd ⟨this production is a *travesty* of the opera⟩.

[2]**caricature** *vt* **-tured; -tur·ing** (ca. 1771) **:** to make or draw a caricature of : represent in caricature ⟨the portrait *caricatured* its subject⟩

car·ies \ˈker-ēz\ *n, pl* **caries** [L, decay; akin to OIr ara-*chrinn* it decays] (1634) **:** a progressive destruction of bone or tooth; *esp* **:** tooth decay

car·il·lon \ˈker-ə-ˌlän, -lən, ˈka-rə-; ˈker-ē-ˌän, -ˌōn, ˈka-rē-; kə-ˈril-yən\ *n* [F, fr. OF *quarregnon,* modif. of LL *quaternion-, quaternio* set of four — more at QUATERNION] (1775) **1 a :** a set of fixed chromatically tuned bells sounded by hammers controlled from a keyboard **b :** an electronic instrument imitating a carillon **2 :** a composition for the carillon

car·il·lon·neur \ˌker-ə-lə-ˈnər, ˌka-rə-; ˌker-ē-ə-ˈnər, ˌka-rē-; kə-ˌril-yə-ˈnər\ *n* [F, fr. *carillon*] (1772) **:** a carillon player

ca·ri·na \kə-ˈrī-nə, -ˈrē-\ *n, pl* **-ri·nas** *or* **-ri·nae** \-ˈrī-ˌnē, -ˈrē-ˌnī\ [NL, fr. L, hull, keel — more at CAREEN] (ca. 1704) **1 :** a keel-shaped anatomical part, ridge, or process **2** *cap* **:** a constellation in the southern hemisphere lying near the Southern Cross

car·i·nate \ˈker-ə-ˌnāt, -nət, ˈka-rə-\ *or* **car·i·nat·ed** \-ˌnā-təd\ *adj* (1781) **:** having or shaped like a keel or carina

ca·ri·o·ca \ˌka-rē-ˈō-kə\ *n* [Brazilian Pg] (1830) **1** *cap* **:** a native or resident of Rio de Janeiro **2 a :** a variation of the samba **b :** the music for this dance

car·i·o·gen·ic \ˌker-ē-ə-ˈje-nik, -ˈjē-\ *adj* [*caries* + *-o-* + *-genic*] (1930) **:** producing or promoting the development of tooth decay ⟨~ foods⟩

car·i·ous \ˈker-ē-əs\ *adj* [L *cariosus,* fr. *caries*] (1676) **:** affected with caries

car·jack·ing \ˈkär-ˌja-kiŋ\ *n* [*car* + hi*jack* + *-ing*] (1991) **:** the theft of an automobile from its driver by force or intimidation — **car·jack** \-ˌjak\ *vt* — **car·jack·er** \-ˌja-kər\ *n*

cark·ing \ˈkär-kiŋ\ *adj* [ME, fr. *carken,* lit., to load, burden, fr. AF *carker,* fr. LL *carricare*] (ca. 1565) **:** BURDENSOME, ANNOYING

carl *or* **carle** \ˈkär(-ə)l\ *n* [ME, fr. OE *-carl,* fr. ON *karl* man, carl — more at CHURL] (bef. 12c) **1 :** a man of the common people **2** *chiefly dial* **:** CHURL, BOOR

car·line *or* **car·lin** \ˈkär-lən\ *n* [ME *kerling,* fr. ON, fr. *karl* man] (14c) *chiefly Scot* **:** WOMAN; *esp* **:** an old woman

Car·list \ˈkär-list\ *n* [Sp *carlista,* fr. Don *Carlos*] (1830) **:** a supporter of Don Carlos or his successors as having rightful title to the Spanish throne — **Carlist** *adj*

car·load \ˈkär-ˈlōd, -ˌlōd\ *n* (1824) **1 :** a load (as of occupants) that fills a car ⟨a ~ of tourists⟩ **2 :** the minimum number of tons required for shipping at carload rates **3 :** a large unspecified quantity ⟨a ~ of excuses⟩

carload rate *n* (1906) **:** a rate for large shipments lower than that quoted for less-than-carload lots of the same class

Car·lo·vin·gian \ˌkär-lə-ˈvin-j(ē-)ən\ *adj* [F *carlovingien,* fr. ML *Carl*us Charles + F *-ovingien* (as in *mérovingien* Merovingian)] (1781) **:** CAROLINGIAN

car·ma·gnole \ˈkär-mən-ˌyōl\ *n* [F] (1793) **1 :** a lively song popular at the time of the first French Revolution **2 :** a street dance in a meandering course to the tune of the carmagnole

car·mak·er \ˈkär-ˌmā-kər\ *n* (1954) **:** an automobile manufacturer

Car·mel·ite \ˈkär-mə-ˌlīt\ *n* [ME, fr. ML *carmelita,* fr. *Carmel* Mount Carmel, Palestine] (15c) **:** a member of the Roman Catholic mendicant

Order of Our Lady of Mount Carmel founded in the 12th century — **Carmelite** *adj*

car·mi·na·tive \kär-ˈmi-nə-tiv, ˈkär-mə-ˌnā-\ *adj* [F *carminatif,* fr. L *carminatus,* pp. of *carminare* to card, fr. **carmin-, *carmen* card, fr. *carrere* to card; akin to Lith *karšti* to card] (15c) : expelling gas from the stomach or intestines so as to relieve flatulence or abdominal pain or distension — **carminative** *n*

car·mine \ˈkär-mən, -ˌmīn\ *n* [F *carmin,* fr. ML *carminium,* perh. ultim. fr. Ar *qirmiz* kermes + L *minium* cinnabar] (1712) **1 :** a rich crimson or scarlet lake made from cochineal **2 :** a vivid red

car·nage \ˈkär-nij\ *n* [F, fr. ML *carnaticum* tribute consisting of animals or meat, fr. L *carn-, caro*] (1614) **1 :** the flesh of slain animals or men **2 :** great and usu. bloody slaughter or injury (as in battle)

car·nal \ˈkär-nᵊl\ *adj* [ME, fr. AF or LL; AF *carnel, charnel,* fr. LL *carnalis,* fr. L *carn-, caro* flesh; akin to Gk *keirein* to cut — more at SHEAR] (14c) **1 a :** relating to or given to crude bodily pleasures and appetites **b :** marked by sexuality ⟨~ love⟩ **2 :** BODILY, CORPOREAL ⟨seen with ~ eyes⟩ **3 a :** TEMPORAL ⟨~ weapons⟩ **b :** WORLDLY ⟨a ~ mind⟩ — **car·nal·i·ty** \kär-ˈna-lə-tē\ *n* — **car·nal·ly** \ˈkär-nə-lē\ *adv*

syn CARNAL, FLESHLY, SENSUAL, ANIMAL mean having a relation to the body. CARNAL may mean only this but more often connotes derogatorily an action or manifestation of a person's lower nature ⟨a slave to *carnal* desires⟩. FLESHLY is less derogatory than CARNAL ⟨a saint who had experienced *fleshly* temptations⟩. SENSUAL may apply to any gratification of a bodily desire or pleasure but commonly implies sexual appetite with absence of the spiritual or intellectual ⟨fleshpots providing *sensual* delights⟩. ANIMAL stresses the physical as distinguished from the rational nature of a person ⟨led a mindless *animal* existence⟩.

car·nall·ite \ˈkär-nə-ˌlīt\ *n* [G *Carnallit,* fr. Rudolf von *Carnall* †1874 Ger. mining engineer] (1876) : a mineral consisting of hydrous potassium-magnesium chloride that is an important source of potassium

car·nas·si·al \kär-ˈna-sē-əl\ *adj* [F *carnassier* carnivorous, ultim. fr. L *carn-, caro*] (ca. 1852) : of, relating to, or being a tooth of a carnivore often larger and longer than adjacent teeth and adapted for cutting rather than tearing — **carnassial** *n*

car·na·tion \kär-ˈnā-shən\ *n* [MF, fr. OIt *carnagione,* fr. *carne* flesh, fr. L *carn-, caro*] (ca. 1535) **1 a (1) :** the variable color of human flesh **(2) :** a pale to grayish yellow **b :** a moderate red **2 :** a plant of any of numerous often cultivated and usu. double-flowered varieties or subspecies of an Old World pink (*Dianthus caryophyllus*) orig. flesh-colored but now found in many color variations

car·nau·ba \kär-ˈnò-bə, -ˈnaù-; ˌkär-nə-ˈü-bə\ *n* [Brazilian Pg *carnaúba,* fr. Tupi *karanaʔiβa,* fr. *karanã,* a palm (perh. *Mauritia carana* or *M. flexuosa*) + *iβa* stem, plant, tree] (1866) : a fan-leaved palm (*Copernicia prunifera* syn. *C. cerifera*) of Brazil that has an edible root and yields a useful leaf fiber and carnauba wax

carnauba wax *n* (1854) : a hard brittle high-melting wax obtained from the leaves of the carnauba palm and used chiefly in polishes

car·ne asa·da \ˌkär-nā-ə-ˈsä-də\ *n* [Sp, grilled meat] (1977) : a grilled Mexican dish of spicy marinated steak strips sometimes served in a burrito or taco

car·ne·lian \kär-ˈnēl-yən\ *n* [alter. of *cornelian,* fr. ME *corneline,* fr. AF, perh. fr. OF *cornele* cornel cherry] (1695) : a hard red chalcedony used in jewelry

car·ni·tine \ˈkär-nə-ˌtēn\ *n* [ISV, fr. L *carn-, caro*] (ca. 1922) : a quaternary ammonium compound $C_7H_{15}NO_3$ that is present esp. in vertebrate muscle and that in the levorotatory form is involved in the transfer of fatty acids across mitochondrial membranes

¹car·ni·val \ˈkär-nə-vəl\ *n* [It *carnevale,* alter. of earlier *carnelevare,* lit., removal of meat, fr. *carne* flesh (fr. L *carn-, caro*) + *levare* to remove, fr. L, to raise] (1549) **1 :** a season or festival of merrymaking before Lent **2 a :** an instance of merrymaking, feasting, or masquerading **b :** an instance of riotous excess ⟨a ~ of violence⟩ **3 a :** a traveling enterprise offering amusements **b :** an organized program of entertainment or exhibition : FESTIVAL ⟨a winter ~⟩

²carnival *adj* (1605) : suggestive of or suited to a carnival ⟨a ~ atmosphere⟩ ⟨~ colors⟩

car·ni·val·esque \ˌkär-nə-və-ˈlesk\ *adj* (1791) **1 :** suggestive of a carnival ⟨a ~ celebration⟩ **2 :** marked by an often mocking or satirical challenge to authority and the traditional social hierarchy ⟨a ~ protest⟩

car·niv·o·ra \kär-ˈni-və-rə\ *n pl* [L, neut. pl. of *carnivorus*] (1830) : carnivorous mammals

car·ni·vore \ˈkär-nə-ˌvȯr\ *n* [ultim. fr. L *carnivorus*] (1840) **1 :** any of an order (Carnivora) of typically flesh-eating mammals that includes dogs, foxes, bears, raccoons, and cats; *broadly* : a carnivorous animal **2 :** a carnivorous plant

car·niv·o·rous \kär-ˈni-v(ə-)rəs\ *adj* [L *carnivorus,* fr. *carn-, caro* + *-vorus* -vorous] (1592) **1 :** subsisting or feeding on animal tissues **2** *of a plant* : subsisting on nutrients obtained from the breakdown of animal protoplasm (as of insects) **3 :** of or relating to the carnivores **4 :** RAPACIOUS — **car·niv·o·rous·ly** *adv* — **car·niv·o·rous·ness** *n* — **car·niv·ory** \kär-ˈni-və-rē\ *n*

car·no·saur \ˈkär-nə-ˌsȯr\ *n* [ultim. fr. L *carn-, caro* flesh + Gk *sauros* lizard] (1952) : any of a group (Carnosauria) of very large theropod dinosaurs (as a tyrannosaur)

car·no·tite \ˈkär-nə-ˌtīt\ *n* [F, fr. M. A. *Carnot* †1920 Fr. inspector general of mines] (1899) : a yellow to greenish-yellow mineral consisting of a radioactive hydrous vanadate of uranium and potassium that is a source of radium and uranium

car·ny *or* **car·ney** *or* **car·nie** \ˈkär-nē\ *n, pl* **carnies** *or* **carneys** *often attrib* (ca. 1933) **1 :** CARNIVAL 3a **2 :** a person who works with a carnival

car·ob \ˈker-əb, ˈka-rəb\ *n* [MF *carobe,* fr. ML *carrubium,* fr. Ar *kharrūba*] (1548) **1 :** a Mediterranean evergreen leguminous tree (*Ceratonia siliqua*) with racemose red flowers **2 :** a pod of the carob tree or its sweet pulp having a flavor similar to that of chocolate

ca·roche \kə-ˈrōch, -ˈrōsh\ *n* [MF *carroche,* fr. OIt *carroccio,* aug. of *carro* car, fr. L *carrus*] (1591) : a luxurious horse-drawn carriage

¹car·ol \ˈker-əl, ˈka-rəl\ *n* [ME *carole,* fr. AF, modif. of LL *choraula* choral song, fr. L, choral accompanist, fr. Gk *choraulēs,* fr. *choros* chorus + *aulein* to play a reed instrument, fr. *aulos,* a reed instrument — more at ALVEOLUS] (14c) **1 :** an old round dance with singing **2 :** a song of joy or mirth ⟨the ~ of a bird —Lord Byron⟩ **3 :** a popular song or ballad of religious joy

²carol *vb* **-oled** *or* **-olled; -ol·ing** *or* **-ol·ling** *vi* (14c) **1 :** to sing esp. in a joyful manner **2 :** to sing carols; *specif* : to go about outdoors in a group singing Christmas carols ~ *vt* **1 :** to praise in or as if in song **2 :** to sing esp. in a cheerful manner : WARBLE — **car·ol·er** *or* **car·ol·ler** \-ə-lər\ *n*

Car·o·li·na parakeet \ˌker(-ə)-ˈlī-nə-, ˌka-rə-\ *n* [*Carolina,* English colony] (1893) : an extinct parakeet (*Conuropsis carolinensis*) of the eastern U.S.

Carolina wren *n* (1868) : a large wren (*Thryothorus ludovicianus*) chiefly of eastern No. America having a loud lively song

Car·o·line \ˈka-rə-ˌlīn, -lən\ *or* **Car·o·le·an** \ˌka-rə-ˈlē-ən\ *adj* [NL *carolinus,* fr. ML *Carolus* Charles] (1652) : of or relating to Charles — used esp. with reference to Charles I and Charles II of England

Car·o·lin·gi·an \ˌka-rə-ˈlin-j(ē-)ən\ *adj* [F *carolingien,* fr. ML *Karolingi* Carolingians, fr. *Karolus* Charlemagne + *-ingi* (as in *Merovingi* Merovingians)] (1881) : of or relating to a Frankish dynasty dating from about A.D. 613 and including among its members the rulers of France from 751 to 987, of Germany from 752 to 911, and of Italy from 774 to 961 — **Carolingian** *n*

¹car·om \ˈker-əm, ˈka-rəm\ *n* [by shortening & alter. fr. obs. *carambole,* fr. Sp *carambola*] (1779) **1 a :** a shot in billiards in which the cue ball strikes each of two object balls **b :** a shot in pool in which an object ball strikes another ball before falling into a pocket — compare COMBINATION SHOT **2 :** a rebounding esp. at an angle

²carom *vi* (1860) **1 :** to strike and rebound : GLANCE ⟨the car ~*ed* off a tree⟩ **2 :** to make a carom **3 :** to proceed by or as if by caroms ⟨~ from city to city⟩

car·o·tene \ˈker-ə-ˌtēn, ˈka-rə-\ *n* [ISV, fr. LL *carota* carrot] (1861) : any of several orange or red crystalline hydrocarbon pigments (as $C_{40}H_{56}$) that occur in the chromoplasts of plants and in the fatty tissues of plant-eating animals and are convertible to vitamin A — compare BETA-CAROTENE

ca·rot·en·oid *also* **ca·rot·in·oid** \kə-ˈrä-tə-ˌnȯid\ *n* (1911) : any of various usu. yellow to red pigments (as carotenes) found widely in plants and animals and characterized chemically by a long aliphatic polyene chain composed of eight isoprene units — **carotenoid** *adj*

ca·rot·id \kə-ˈrä-təd\ *adj* [F or Gk; F *carotide,* fr. Gk *karōtides* carotid arteries, fr. *karoun* to stupefy; akin to Gk *kara* head — more at CEREBRAL] (1543) : of, relating to, or being the chief artery or pair of arteries that pass up the neck and supply the head — **carotid** *n*

carotid body *n* (1925) : a small body of vascular tissue that adjoins the carotid sinus, functions as a chemoreceptor sensitive to change in the oxygen content of blood, and mediates reflex changes in respiratory activity

carotid sinus *n* (ca. 1923) : a small but richly innervated arterial enlargement that is located near the point in the neck where either carotid artery divides to form its main branches and that functions in the regulation of heart rate and blood pressure

ca·rous·al \kə-ˈraù-zəl\ *n* (1760) : CAROUSE 2

¹ca·rouse \kə-ˈraùz\ *n* [MF *carrousse,* fr. *carous,* adv., all out (in *boire carous* to empty the cup), fr. G *gar aus*] (1559) **1** *archaic* : a large draft of liquor : TOAST **2 :** a drunken revel

²carouse *vb* **ca·roused; ca·rous·ing** *vi* (1566) **1 :** to drink liquor freely or excessively **2 :** to take part in a carouse : engage in dissolute behavior ~ *vt, obs* : to drink up : QUAFF — **ca·rous·er** *n*

car·ou·sel *also* **car·rou·sel** \ˌker-ə-ˈsel, ˌka-rə- *also* -ˈzel; ˈker-ə-ˌ, ˈka-rə-\ *n* [F *carrousel,* fr. It *carosello*] (1650) **1 :** a tournament or exhibition in which horsemen execute evolutions **2 a :** MERRY-GO-ROUND **b :** a circular conveyor ⟨the luggage ~ at the airport⟩ **c :** a revolving case or tray used for storage or display

¹carp \ˈkärp\ *vi* [ME, of Scand origin; akin to Icel *karpa* to dispute] (14c) : to find fault or complain querulously — **carp·er** *n*

²carp *n* (1904) : COMPLAINT

³carp *n, pl* **carp** *or* **carps** [ME *carpe,* fr. MF, fr. LL *carpa,* prob. of Gmc origin; akin to OHG *karpfo* carp] (15c) **1 :** a large variable Asian soft-finned freshwater cyprinid fish (*Cyprinus carpio*) of sluggish waters that is often raised for food and has been widely introduced into U.S. waters; *also* : any of various related cyprinid fishes (as the grass carp) **2 :** a fish (as the European sea bream) resembling a carp

carp- *or* **carpo-** *comb form* [F & NL, fr. Gk *karp-, karpo-,* fr. *karpos* — more at HARVEST] : fruit ⟨*carpo*gonium⟩

-carp *n comb form* [NL *-carpium,* fr. Gk *-karpion,* fr. *karpos*] : part of a fruit ⟨meso*carp*⟩ : fruit ⟨schizo*carp*⟩

car·pac·cio \kär-ˈpä-ch(ē-)ō\ *n* [Vittore *Carpaccio;* fr. the prominent use of red in his painting] (1969) : thinly sliced raw meat or fish served with a sauce — often used as a postpositive modifier ⟨beef ~⟩

¹car·pal \ˈkär-pəl\ *adj* [NL *carpalis,* fr. *carpus*] (1743) : of or relating to the carpus

²carpal *n* (1855) : a carpal element or bone

carpal tunnel syndrome *n* (1954) : a condition caused by compression of a nerve where it passes through the wrist into the hand and characterized esp. by weakness, pain, and disturbances of sensation in the hand and fingers

car park *n* (1926) *chiefly Brit* : a lot or garage for parking

car·pe di·em \ˈkär-pe-ˈdē-ˌem, -ˈdī-, -əm\ *n* [L, lit., pluck the day] (1817) : the enjoyment of the pleasures of the moment without concern for the future

car·pel \ˈkär-pəl\ *n* [NL *carpellum,* fr. Gk *karpos* fruit] (1835) : one of the ovule-bearing structures in an angiosperm that comprises the innermost whorl of a flower — compare PISTIL — **car·pel·lary** \-pə-ˌler-ē\ *adj* — **car·pel·late** \-ˌlāt, -lət\ *adj*

¹car·pen·ter \ˈkär-pən-tər, ˈkär-pᵊm-tər\ *n* [ME, fr. AF *carpenter, charpenter,* fr. L *carpentarius* carriage maker, fr. *carpentum* carriage, of Celt origin; akin to OIr *carpat* chariot, *carr* vehicle — more at CAR] (14c) : a worker who builds or repairs wooden structures or their structural parts

²carpenter *vb* **-tered; -ter·ing** \-t(ə-)riŋ\ *vi* (ca. 1815) : to follow the trade of a carpenter ⟨~*ed* when he was young⟩ ~ *vt* **1 :** to make by or as if by carpentry **2 :** to put together often in a mechanical manner ⟨~*ed* many television scripts⟩

carpenter ant *n* (1883) **:** an ant (esp. genus *Camponotus*) that gnaws galleries esp. in dead or decaying wood

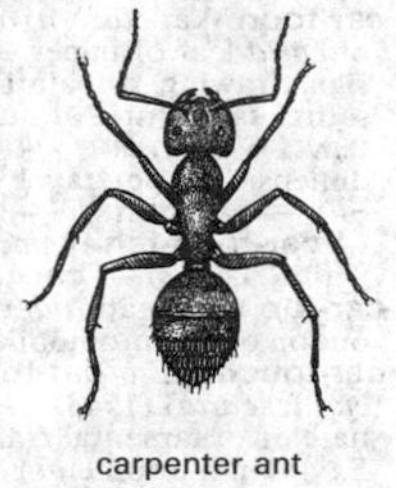

carpenter ant

carpenter bee *n* (1838) **:** any of various solitary bees (genera *Xylocopa* and *Ceratina*) that nest in wood

car·pen·try \-trē\ *n* (14c) **1 :** the art or trade of a carpenter; *specif* **:** the art of shaping and assembling structural woodwork **2 :** timberwork constructed by a carpenter **3 :** the form or manner of putting together the parts (as of a literary or musical composition)

car·pet \ˈkär-pət\ *n* [ME, fr. MF *carpite,* fr. OIt *carpita,* fr. *carpire* to pluck, modif. of L *carpere* to pluck — more at HARVEST] (15c) **1 :** a heavy often tufted fabric used as a floor covering; *also* **:** a floor covering made of this fabric **2 :** a surface or layer resembling or suggesting a carpet — **carpet** *vt* — **on the carpet :** before an authority for censure or reproof ⟨got called *on the carpet* by his boss⟩

[1]**car·pet·bag** \-ˌbag\ *n* (1829) **:** a traveler's bag made of carpet and widely used in the U.S. in the 19th century

[2]**carpetbag** *or* **car·pet·bag·ging** \-ˌba-giŋ\ *adj* (1870) **:** of, relating to, or characteristic of carpetbaggers ⟨a ~ government⟩

car·pet·bag·ger \-ˌba-gər\ *n* [fr. their carrying all their belongings in carpetbags] (1868) **1 :** a Northerner in the South after the American Civil War usu. seeking private gain under the reconstruction governments **2 :** OUTSIDER; *esp* **:** a nonresident or new resident who seeks private gain from an area often by meddling in its business or politics — **car·pet·bag·gery** \-ˌba-g(ə-)rē\ *n*

carpetbag steak *n* (1958) **:** a thick piece of steak in which a pocket is cut and stuffed (as with oysters)

carpet beetle *n* (ca. 1889) **:** any of several small dermestid beetles (genera *Anthrenus* and *Attagenus*) whose larvae are destructive esp. to woolen goods

carpet bomb *vt* (1944) **1 :** to drop large numbers of bombs so as to cause uniform devastation over (a given area) **2 :** to bombard repeatedly, widely, or excessively ⟨*carpet bomb* the country with advertising⟩

car·pet·ing \ˈkär-pə-tiŋ\ *n* (1758) **:** material for carpets; *also* **:** CARPETS

car·pet·weed \ˈkär-pət-ˌwēd\ *n* (1784) **:** a No. American mat-forming weed (*Mollugo verticillata* of the family Aizoaceae, the carpetweed family)

-carpic *adj comb form* [prob. fr. NL *-carpicus,* fr. Gk *karpos* fruit] **:** -CARPOUS ⟨mono*carpic*⟩

carp·ing \ˈkär-piŋ\ *adj* (1567) **:** marked by or inclined to querulous and often perverse criticism ***syn*** see CRITICAL — **carp·ing·ly** \-piŋ-lē\ *adv*

car·po·go·ni·um \ˌkär-pə-ˈgō-nē-əm\ *n, pl* **-nia** \-nē-ə\ [NL] (1882) **:** the egg-bearing portion of the female reproductive organ in some red algae — **car·po·go·ni·al** \-nē-əl\ *adj*

car·pool \ˈkär-ˌpül\ *vi* (1962) **:** to participate in a car pool — **car·pool·er** *n*

car pool *n* (1942) **:** an arrangement in which a group of people commute together by car; *also* **:** the group entering into such an arrangement

car·port \ˈkär-ˌpȯrt\ *n* (1939) **:** an open-sided automobile shelter by the side of a building

car·po·spore \ˈkär-pə-ˌspȯr\ *n* (1881) **:** a diploid spore of a red alga

-carpous *adj comb form* [NL *-carpus,* fr. Gk *-karpos,* fr. *karpos* fruit — more at HARVEST] **:** having (such) fruit or (so many) fruits ⟨syn*carpous*⟩ — **-carpy** *n comb form*

car·pus \ˈkär-pəs\ *n, pl* **car·pi** \-ˌpī, -(ˌ)pē\ [NL, fr. Gk *karpos* — more at WHARF] (1676) **1 :** WRIST 1 **2 :** the bones of the wrist

carr \ˈkä(r)\ *n* [ME *ker,* of Scand origin; akin to ON *kjarr* underbrush] (14c) *chiefly Brit* **:** [1]FEN

car·rack \ˈka-rək, -rik\ *n* [ME *carrake,* fr. AF *carrak,* fr. OSp *carraca,* fr. Ar *qarāqīr,* pl. of *qurqūr* merchant ship, fr. Gk *kerkouros* light vessel] (14c) **:** a beamy sailing ship esp. of the 15th and 16th centuries

car·ra·geen *also* **car·ra·gheen** \ˈka-rə-ˌgēn\ *n* [*Carragheen,* near Waterford, Ireland] (1829) **1 :** IRISH MOSS 2 **2 :** CARRAGEENAN

car·ra·geen·an *or* **car·ra·geen·in** \ˌker-ə-ˈgē-nən, ˌka-rə-\ *n* [*carrageen* + [3]*-an* or [1]*-in*] (ca. 1889) **:** a colloid extracted from various red algae (as Irish moss) and used esp. as a stabilizing or thickening agent

car·re·four \ˌka-rə-ˈfu̇r\ *n* [MF, fr. LL *quadrifurcum,* neut. of *quadrifurcus* having four forks, fr. L *quadri-* + *furca* fork] (15c) **1 :** CROSSROADS **2 :** SQUARE, PLAZA ⟨the farmers . . . preferred the open ~ for their transactions —Thomas Hardy⟩

car·rel \ˈker-əl, ˈka-rəl\ *n* [alter. of ME *caroll,* fr. ML *carola,* perh. fr. *carola* round dance, something circular, fr. LL *choraula* choral song — more at CAROL] (1593) **:** a table that is often partitioned or enclosed and is used for individual study esp. in a library

car·riage \ˈker-ij, ˈka-rij\ *n* [ME *cariage,* fr. AF, fr. *carier* to transport — more at CARRY] (14c) **1 :** the act of carrying **2 a** *archaic* **:** DEPORTMENT **b :** manner of bearing the body **:** POSTURE **3** *archaic* **:** MANAGEMENT **4** *chiefly Brit* **:** the price or expense of carrying **5** *obs* **:** BURDEN, LOAD **6 a :** a wheeled vehicle; *esp* **:** a horse-drawn vehicle designed for private use and comfort **b** *Brit* **:** a railway passenger coach **7 :** a wheeled support carrying a burden **8** *obs* **:** IMPORT, SENSE **9** *obs* **:** a hanger for a sword **10 :** a movable part of a machine for supporting some other movable object or part ⟨a typewriter ~⟩ ***syn*** see BEARING

carriage trade *n* (ca. 1909) **:** trade from well-to-do or upper-class people; *also* **:** well-to-do people

car·riage·way \ˈker-ij-ˌwā, ˈka-rij-\ *n* (1739) *Brit* **:** the part of a road used by vehicular traffic

car·rick bend \ˈka-rik-\ *n* [prob. fr. obs. E *carrick* carrack, fr. ME *carrake, carryk*] (1819) **:** a knot used to join the ends of two large ropes — see KNOT illustration

car·ri·er \ˈker-ē-ər, ˈka-rē-\ *n* (14c) **1 :** one that carries **:** BEARER, MESSENGER **2 a :** an individual or organization engaged in transporting passengers or goods for hire **b :** a transportation line carrying mail between post offices **c :** a postal employee who delivers or collects mail **d :** one that delivers newspapers **e :** an entity (as a hole or an electron) capable of carrying an electric charge **3 a :** a container for carrying **b :** a device or machine that carries **:** CONVEYOR **4 :** AIRCRAFT CARRIER **5 a :** a bearer and transmitter of a causative agent of an infectious disease; *esp* **:** one who carries the causative agent of a disease systemically but is asymptomatic or immune to it **b :** an individual (as one heterozygous for a recessive trait) having a specified gene that is not expressed or only weakly expressed in its phenotype **6 a :** a usu. inactive accessory substance **:** VEHICLE ⟨a ~ for a drug or an insecticide⟩ **b :** a substance (as a catalyst) by whose agency some element or group is transferred from one compound to another **7 a :** an electromagnetic wave or alternating current whose modulations are used as communications signals (as in radio, telephonic, or telegraphic transmissions) **b :** a telecommunication company **8 :** an organization acting as an insurer

carrier pigeon *n* (1647) **1 :** a pigeon used to carry messages; *esp* **:** HOMING PIGEON **2 :** any of a breed of large long-bodied show pigeons

car·ri·on \ˈker-ē-ən, ˈka-rē-\ *n* [ME *caroine,* fr. AF *caroine, charoine,* fr. VL **caronia,* irreg. fr. L *carn-, caro* flesh — more at CARNAL] (14c) **:** dead and putrefying flesh; *also* **:** flesh unfit for food

carrion crow *n* (1528) **:** a uniformly black crow (*Corvus corone corone*) occurring in much of western Europe

car·ron·ade \ˌka-rə-ˈnād\ *n* [*Carron,* Scotland] (1779) **:** a short-barreled gun of the late 18th and 19th centuries that fired large shot at short range and was used esp. on warships

car·rot \ˈker-ət, ˈka-rət\ *n* [MF *carotte,* fr. LL *carota,* fr. Gk *karōton*] (1533) **1 :** a biennial herb (*Daucus carota* of the family Umbelliferae, the carrot family) with a usu. orange spindle-shaped edible root; *also* **:** its root **2 :** a reward or advantage offered esp. as an inducement

car·rot–and–stick \ˌker-ət-ᵊn-ˈstik, ˌka-rət-\ *adj* [fr. the traditional alternatives of driving a donkey on by either holding out a carrot or whipping it with a stick] (1876) **:** characterized by the use of both reward and punishment to induce cooperation ⟨~ foreign policy⟩

car·rot·top \ˈker-ə(t)-ˌtäp, ˈka-rə(t)-\ *n* (1889) **:** REDHEAD 1 — **car·rot-topped** \-ˌtäpt\ *adj*

car·roty \ˈker-ə-tē, ˈka-rə-\ *adj* (1696) **:** resembling carrots in color ⟨~ hair⟩

carrousel *var of* CAROUSEL

[1]**car·ry** \ˈka-rē, ˈker-ē\ *vb* **car·ried; car·ry·ing** [ME *carien,* fr. AF *carier* to transport, fr. *carre* vehicle, fr. L *carrus* — more at CAR] *vt* (14c) **1 :** to move while supporting **:** TRANSPORT ⟨her legs refused to ~ her further —Ellen Glasgow⟩ **2 :** to convey by direct communication ⟨~ tales about a friend⟩ **3** *chiefly dial* **:** CONDUCT, ESCORT **4 :** to influence by mental or emotional appeal **:** SWAY **5 :** to get possession or control of **:** CAPTURE ⟨*carried* off the prize⟩ **6 :** to transfer from one place (as a column) to another ⟨~ a number in adding⟩ **7 :** to contain and direct the course of ⟨the drain *carries* sewage⟩ **8 a :** to wear or have on one's person **b :** to bear upon or within one ⟨is ~*ing* an unborn child⟩ **9 a :** to have or bear esp. as a mark, attribute, or property ⟨~ a scar⟩ **b :** IMPLY, INVOLVE ⟨the crime *carried* a heavy penalty⟩ **10 :** to hold or comport (as one's person) in a specified manner **11 :** to sustain the weight or burden of ⟨pillars ~ an arch⟩ ⟨is ~*ing* a full course load⟩ **12 :** to bear as a crop **13 :** to sing with reasonable correctness of pitch ⟨~ a tune⟩ **14 a :** to keep in stock for sale **b :** to provide sustenance for ⟨land ~*ing* 10 head of cattle⟩ **c :** to have or maintain on a list or record ⟨~ a person on a payroll⟩ ⟨*carried* six guards on the team⟩ **15 :** to be chiefly or solely responsible for the success, effectiveness, or continuation of ⟨a player capable of ~*ing* a team⟩ ⟨her performance *carried* the play⟩ **16 :** to prolong or maintain in space, time, or degree ⟨~ a principle too far⟩ ⟨~ the wall above the eaves⟩ ⟨*carried* a no-hitter into the ninth inning⟩ **17 a :** to gain victory for; *esp* **:** to secure the adoption or passage of **b :** to win a majority or plurality of votes in (as a legislative body or a state) **18 :** to present for public use or consumption ⟨newspapers ~ weather reports⟩ ⟨channel nine will ~ the game⟩ **19 a :** to bear the charges of holding or having (as stocks or merchandise) from one time to another **b :** to keep on one's books as a debtor ⟨a merchant *carries* a customer⟩ **20 :** to hold to and follow after (as a scent) **21 :** to hoist and maintain (a sail) in use **22 :** to pass over (as a hazard) at a single stroke in golf ⟨~ a bunker⟩ **23 :** to propel and control (a puck or ball) along a playing surface ~ *vi* **1 :** to act as a bearer **2 a :** to reach or penetrate to a distance ⟨voices ~ well⟩ ⟨fly balls don't ~ well in cold air⟩ **b :** to convey itself to a reader or audience **3 :** to undergo or admit of carriage in a specified way **4** *of a hunting dog* **:** to keep and follow the scent **5 :** to win adoption ⟨the motion *carried* by a vote of 71–25⟩ — **carry a torch** *or* **carry the torch 1 :** CRUSADE **2 :** to be in love esp. without reciprocation **:** cherish a longing or devotion ⟨still *carrying a torch* for a former lover⟩ — **carry the ball :** to perform or assume the chief role **:** bear the major portion of work or responsibility — **carry the day :** WIN, PREVAIL

[2]**carry** *n, pl* **car·ries** (1858) **1 :** carrying power; *esp* **:** the range of a gun or projectile or of a struck or thrown ball **2 a :** PORTAGE **b :** the act or method of carrying ⟨fireman's ~⟩ **c :** the act of rushing with the ball in football ⟨averaged four yards per ~⟩ **3 :** the position assumed by a color-bearer with the flag or guidon held in position for marching **4 :** a quantity that is transferred in addition from one number place to the adjacent one of higher place value

car·ry·all \ˈka-rē-ˌȯl, ˈker-ē-\ *n* (1714) **1** [by folk etymology fr. F *carriole,* fr. Old Occitan *carriola,* ultim. fr. L *carrus* car] **a :** a light covered carriage for four or more persons **b :** a passenger automobile used as a small bus **2** [[1]*carry* + [3]*all*] **:** a capacious bag or carrying case

carry away *vt* (1562) **1 :** to arouse to a high and often excessive degree of emotion or enthusiasm **2 :** CARRY OFF 1

car·ry·back \ˈka-rē-ˌbak, ˈker-ē-\ *n* (1942) **:** a loss sustained or a portion of a credit not used in a given period that may be deducted from taxable income of a prior period

car·ry–cot \-ˌkät\ *n* (1943) *Brit* **:** a portable bed for an infant

car·ry·for·ward \-ˈfȯr-wərd, -ˌfȯr-, *Southern also* -ˈfär-, -ˌfär-\ *n* (1898) : CARRYOVER

carrying capacity *n* (1889) : the maximum population (as of deer) that an area will support without undergoing deterioration

carrying charge *n* (1914) **1** : expense incident to ownership or use of property **2** : a charge added to the price of merchandise sold on the installment plan

car·ry·ing–on \ˌka-rē-iŋ-ˈȯn, ˌker-ē-, -ˈän\ *n, pl* **carryings–on** (1663) : foolish, excited, or improper behavior; *also* : an instance of such behavior

carry off *vt* (ca. 1680) **1** : to cause the death of ‹the plague *carried off* thousands› **2** : to perform or manage successfully : BRING OFF ‹tried to look suave but couldn't *carry* it *off*›

[1]**car·ry–on** \ˈka-rē-ˌȯn, ˈker-ē-, -ˌän\ *n* (1890) **1** *Brit* : CARRYING-ON **2** : a piece of luggage suitable for being carried aboard an airplane by a passenger

[2]**carry–on** *adj* (1967) : carried or suitable for being carried aboard ‹~ baggage›

carry on *vt* (1600) : to continue doing, pursuing, or operating ‹*carry on* research› ‹*carried on* the business› ~ *vi* **1** : to continue esp. in spite of hindrance or discouragement ‹chose to *carry on* despite the weather› **2** : to behave or speak in a foolish, excited, or improper manner ‹shocked at how he *carries on*›

car·ry·out \ˈka-rē-ˌau̇t, ˈker-ē-\ *n* (1964) : TAKEOUT 3 — **carryout** *adj*

carry out *vt* (1589) **1** : to bring to a successful issue : COMPLETE, ACCOMPLISH ‹*carried out* the assignment› **2** : to put into execution ‹*carry out* a plan› **3** : to continue to an end or stopping point

car·ry·over \ˈka-rē-ˌō-vər, ˈker-ē-\ *n* (1894) **1** : the act or process of carrying over **2** : something retained or carried over

carry over *vt* (1745) **1 a** : to transfer (an amount) to the next column, page, or book relating to the same account **b** : to hold over (as goods) for another time or season **2** : to deduct (a loss or an unused credit) from taxable income of a later period ~ *vi* : to persist from one stage or sphere of activity to another

carry through *vt* (1605) : CARRY OUT ~ *vi* : PERSIST, SURVIVE ‹feelings that *carry through* to the present›

car seat *n* (1968) : a portable seat for an infant or a small child that attaches to an automobile seat and holds the child safely

car·sick \ˈkär-ˌsik\ *adj* (1908) : affected with motion sickness esp. in an automobile — **car sickness** *n*

[1]**cart** \ˈkärt\ *n* [ME, prob. fr. ON *kartr;* akin to OE *cræt* cart] (13c) **1** : a heavy usu. horse-drawn 2-wheeled vehicle used for farming or transporting freight **2** : a lightweight 2-wheeled vehicle drawn by a horse, pony, or dog **3** : a small wheeled vehicle

[2]**cart** *vt* (14c) **1** : to carry or convey in or as if in a cart ‹buses to ~ the kids to and from school —L. S. Gannett› **2** : to take or drag away without ceremony or by force — usu. used with *off* ‹they ~*ed* him off to jail› — **cart·er** *n*

cart·age \ˈkär-tij\ *n* (15c) : the action of or rate charged for carting

carte blanche \ˈkärt-ˈbläⁿsh, -ˈblänch\ *n, pl* **cartes blanches** \ˈkärt(s)-\ [F, lit., blank document] (1751) : full discretionary power ‹was given *carte blanche* to furnish the house›

carte du jour \ˌkärt-də-ˈzhu̇r\ *n, pl* **cartes du jour** \ˌkärt(s)-\ [F, lit., card of the day] (1936) : MENU

car·tel \kär-ˈtel\ *n* [F, letter of defiance, fr. OIt *cartello,* lit., placard, fr. *carta* leaf of paper — more at CARD] (1692) **1** : a written agreement between belligerent nations **2** : a combination of independent commercial or industrial enterprises designed to limit competition or fix prices **3** : a combination of political groups for common action

car·tel·ise *Brit var of* CARTELIZE

car·tel·ize \ˈkär-tə-ˌlīz\ *vt* **-ized; -iz·ing** (1915) : to bring under the control of a cartel — **car·tel·i·za·tion** \ˌkär-tə-lə-ˈzā-shən\ *n*

Car·te·sian \kär-ˈtē-zhən\ *adj* [NL *cartesianus,* fr. *Cartesius* Descartes] (1656) : of or relating to René Descartes or his philosophy — **Cartesian** *n* — **Car·te·sian·ism** \-zhə-ˌni-zəm\ *n*

Cartesian coordinate *n* (1887) **1** : either of two coordinates that locate a point on a plane and measure its distance from either of two intersecting straight-line axes along a line parallel to the other axis **2** : any of three coordinates that locate a point in space and measure its distance from any of three intersecting coordinate planes measured parallel to that one of three straight-line axes that is the intersection of the other two planes

Cartesian plane *n* (1960) : a plane whose points are labeled with Cartesian coordinates

Cartesian product *n* (1958) : a set that is constructed from two given sets and comprises all pairs of elements such that the first element of the pair is from the first set and the second is from the second set

Car·thu·sian \kär-ˈthü-zhən, -ˈthyü-\ *n* [ML *Cartusiensis,* fr. *Cartusia* Chartreuse, motherhouse of the Carthusian order, near Grenoble, France] (1526) : a member of an ascetic contemplative religious order founded by St. Bruno in 1084 — **Carthusian** *adj*

car·ti·lage \ˈkär-tə-lij, ˈkärt-lij\ *n* [ME, fr. L *cartilagin-, cartilago*] (15c) **1** : a usu. translucent somewhat elastic tissue that composes most of the skeleton of vertebrate embryos and except for a small number of structures (as some joints, respiratory passages, and the external ear) is replaced by bone during ossification in the higher vertebrates **2** : a part or structure composed of cartilage

car·ti·lag·i·nous \ˌkär-tə-ˈla-jə-nəs\ *adj* (14c) : composed of, relating to, or resembling cartilage

cartilaginous fish *n* (1769) : any of a class (Chondrichthyes) of fishes (as a shark, ray, or chimaera) having the skeleton wholly or largely composed of cartilage — compare BONY FISH, JAWLESS FISH

cart·load \ˈkärt-ˈlōd, -ˌlōd\ *n* (14c) : as much as a cart will hold

car·tog·ra·pher \kär-ˈtä-grə-fər\ *n* (ca. 1847) : one that makes maps

car·tog·ra·phy \-fē\ *n* [F *cartographie,* fr. *carte* card, map + *-graphie* -graphy — more at CARD] (ca. 1847) : the science or art of making maps — **car·to·graph·ic** \ˌkär-tə-ˈgra-fik\ *also* **car·to·graph·i·cal** \-fi-kəl\ *adj* — **car·to·graph·i·cal·ly** \-fi-k(ə-)lē\ *adv*

[1]**car·ton** \ˈkär-tᵊn\ *n* [F, fr. It *cartone* pasteboard] (1825) : a box or container usu. made of cardboard and often of corrugated cardboard

[2]**carton** *vt* (1921) : to pack or enclose in a carton ~ *vi* : to shape cartons from cardboard sheets

car·toon \kär-ˈtün\ *n, often attrib* [It *cartone* pasteboard, cartoon, aug. of *carta* leaf of paper — more at CARD] (1671) **1** : a preparatory design, drawing, or painting (as for a fresco) **2 a** : a drawing intended as satire, caricature, or humor ‹a political ~› **b** : COMIC STRIP **3** : ANIMATED CARTOON **4** : a ludicrously simplistic, unrealistic, or one-dimensional portrayal or version ‹the film's villain is an entertaining ~› — **cartoon** *vb* — **car·toon·ing** *n* — **car·toon·ish** \-ˈtü-nish\ *adj* — **car·toon·ish·ly** *adv* — **car·toon·ist** \-ˈtü-nist\ *n* — **car·toon·like** \-ˈtün-ˌlīk\ *adj* — **car·toony** \-ˈtü-nē\ *adj*

car·top \ˈkär-ˌtäp\ *adj* (1946) : suitable in size and weight for carrying on top of an automobile ‹a ~ fishing boat› — **car·top·per** \-ˌtä-pər\ *n*

car·touche *also* **car·touch** \kär-ˈtüsh\ *n* [MF *cartouche,* fr. It *cartoccio,* fr. *carta*] (1548) **1** : a gun cartridge with a paper case **2** : an ornate or ornamental frame **3** : an oval or oblong figure (as on ancient Egyptian monuments) enclosing a sovereign's name

car·tridge \ˈkär-trij, *dial* ˈka-trij\ *n* [alter. of earlier *cartage,* modif. of MF *cartouche*] (1626) : a case or container that holds a substance, device, or material which is difficult, troublesome, or awkward to handle and that usu. can be easily changed: as **a** : a tube (as of metal) containing a complete charge for a firearm and usu. an initiating device (as a primer) **b** : a case containing an explosive charge for blasting **c** : an often cylindrical container for insertion into a larger mechanism or apparatus **d** : CASSETTE 2 **e** : a small case that contains a phonograph needle and transducer and is attached to a tonearm **f** : a removable case containing a magnetic tape or one or more disks and used as a computer storage medium **g** : a case for holding printed circuit chips containing a computer program ‹a video-game ~›

cartridge belt *n* (1849) **1** : a belt having a series of loops for holding cartridges **2** : a belt worn around the waist and designed for carrying various attachable equipment

car·tu·lary \ˈkär-chə-ˌler-ē\ *n, pl* **-lar·ies** [ML *chartularium,* fr. *chartula* charter — more at CHARTER] (1541) : a collection of charters; *esp* : a book holding copies of the charters and title deeds of an estate

[1]**cart·wheel** \ˈkärt-ˌhwēl, -ˌwēl\ *n* (1855) **1** : a large coin (as a silver dollar) **2** : a lateral handspring with arms and legs extended

[2]**cartwheel** *vi* (1917) : to move like a turning wheel; *specif* : to perform cartwheels — **cart·wheel·er** *n*

car·un·cle \ˈker-ˌəŋ-kəl, ˈka-ˌrəŋ-, kə-ˈrəŋ-\ *n* [obs. F *caruncule,* fr. L *caruncula* little piece of flesh, dim. of *caro* flesh — more at CARNAL] (1615) **1** : a naked fleshy outgrowth (as a bird's wattle) **2** : an outgrowth on a seed adjacent to the micropyle

car·va·crol \ˈkär-və-ˌkrȯl, -ˌkrōl\ *n* [ISV, fr. NL *carvi* (specific epithet of *Carum carvi* caraway) + L *acr-, acer* sharp — more at CARAWAY, EDGE] (1854) : a liquid phenol $C_{10}H_{14}O$ found in essential oils of various mints (as thyme) and used esp. as a fungicide and disinfectant

carve \ˈkärv\ *vb* **carved; carv·ing** [ME *kerven,* fr. OE *ceorfan;* akin to OHG *kerban* to notch, Gk *graphein* to scratch, write] *vt* (bef. 12c) **1** : to cut with care or precision ‹*carved* fretwork› **2** : to make or get by or as if by cutting — often used with *out* ‹~ out a career› **3** : to cut into pieces or slices ‹*carved* the turkey› ~ *vi* **1** : to cut up and serve meat **2** : to work as a sculptor or engraver — **carv·er** *n*

car·vel–built \ˈkär-vəl-ˌbilt, -ˌvel-\ *adj* [prob. fr. D *karveel-,* fr. *karveel* caravel, fr. MF *carvelle*] (1798) : built with the planks meeting flush at the seams ‹a ~ ship›

carv·en \ˈkär-vən\ *adj* (14c) : wrought or ornamented by carving

carv·ing \ˈkär-viŋ\ *n* (13c) **1** : the act or art of one who carves **2** : a carved object, design, or figure

car wash *n* (1948) : an area or structure equipped with facilities for washing automobiles

cary- *or* **caryo-** — see KARY-

cary·at·id \ˌker-ē-ˈa-təd, ˌka-rē-; ˈker-ē-ə-ˌtid, ˈka-rē-\ *n, pl* **-ids** *or* **-ides** \ˌker-ē-ˈa-tə-ˌdēz, ˌka-rē-\ [L *caryatides,* pl., fr. Gk *karyatides* priestesses of Artemis at Caryae, caryatids, fr. *Karyai* Caryae in Laconia] (1563) : a draped female figure supporting an entablature

cary·op·sis \ˌker-ē-ˈäp-səs, ˌka-rē-\ *n, pl* **-op·ses** \-ˌsēz\ *also* **-si·des** \-sə-ˌdēz\ [NL] (1830) : a small one-seeded dry indehiscent fruit (as of corn or wheat) in which the fruit and seed fuse in a single grain

CAS *abbr* certificate of advanced study

ca·sa \ˈkä-sə\ *n* [Sp & It, fr. L, cottage] (1843) *chiefly Southwest* : DWELLING

ca·sa·ba \kə-ˈsä-bə\ *n* [*Kasaba* (now Turgutlu), Turkey] (1887) : any of several winter melons with usu. yellow rind and sweet white, yellow, or orange flesh

Ca·sa·no·va \ˌka-zə-ˈnō-və, ˌka-sə-\ *n* [Giacomo Girolamo *Casanova*] (1852) : LOVER; *esp* : a man who is a promiscuous and unscrupulous lover

cas·bah *also* **kas·bah** \ˈkaz-ˌbä, ˈkäz-\ *n, often cap* [F, fr. Ar dial. *qaṣba*] (1844) **1** : a No. African castle or fortress **2** : the native section of a No. African city

cas·ca·bel \ˈkas-kə-ˌbel\ *n* [Sp, lit., small bell] (1639) **1** : a projection behind the breech of a muzzle-loading cannon **2** : a small hollow perforated spherical bell enclosing a loose pellet

[1]**cas·cade** \(ˌ)kas-ˈkād\ *n* [F, fr. It *cascata,* fr. *cascare* to fall, fr. VL **casicare,* fr. L *casus* fall] (1641) **1** : a steep usu. small fall of water; *esp* : one of a series **2 a** : something arranged or occurring in a series or in a succession of stages so that each stage derives from or acts upon the product of the preceding ‹blood clotting involves a biochemical ~› **b** : a fall of material (as lace) that hangs in a zigzag line **3** : something falling or rushing forth in quantity ‹a ~ of sound› ‹a ~ of events›

[2]**cascade** *vb* **cas·cad·ed; cas·cad·ing** *vi* (1702) : to fall, pour, or rush in or as if in a cascade ~ *vt* **1** : to cause to fall like a cascade **2** : to connect in a cascade arrangement

cas·cara \ka-ˈska-rə\ *n* [Sp *cáscara* husk, bark, prob. fr. *cascar* to crack, break, fr. VL **quassicare* to shake, fr. L *quassare* — more at QUASH] (1879) **1** : CASCARA BUCKTHORN **2** : CASCARA SAGRADA

cascara buckthorn *n* (ca. 1900) : a buckthorn (*Rhamnus purshiana*) of the Pacific coast of the U.S. yielding cascara sagrada

cascara sa·gra·da \-sə-ˈgrä-də\ *n* [AmerSp *cáscara sagrada,* lit., sacred bark] (1885) : the dried bark of cascara buckthorn used as a laxative

cas·ca·ril·la \ˌkas-kə-ˈri-lə, -ˈrē-ə\ *n* [Sp, dim. of *cáscara*] (1686) : the aromatic bark of a West Indian shrub (*Croton eluteria*) of the spurge family used esp. for making incense and as a tonic; *also* : this shrub

[1]**case** \ˈkās\ *n* [ME *cas,* fr. AF, fr. L *casus* fall, chance, fr. *cadere* to fall — more at CHANCE] (13c) **1 a :** a set of circumstances or conditions ⟨is the statement true in all three ~*s*⟩ **b** (1) **:** a situation requiring investigation or action (as by the police) (2) **:** the object of investigation or consideration **2 :** CONDITION; *specif* **:** condition of body or mind **3** [ME *cas,* fr. AF, fr. L *casus,* trans. of Gk *ptōsis,* lit., fall] **a :** an inflectional form of a noun, pronoun, or adjective indicating its grammatical relation to other words **b :** such a relation whether indicated by inflection or not **4 :** what actually exists or happens **:** FACT ⟨thought he had failed, but that wasn't the ~⟩ **5 a :** a suit or action in law or equity **b** (1) **:** the evidence supporting a conclusion or judgment (2) **:** ARGUMENT; *esp* **:** a convincing argument ⟨makes a good ~ for adopting the proposal⟩ **6 a :** an instance of disease or injury ⟨a ~ of pneumonia⟩; *also* **:** PATIENT **b :** an instance that directs attention to a situation or exhibits it in action **:** EXAMPLE **c :** a peculiar person **:** CHARACTER **7 :** oneself considered as an object of harassment or criticism ⟨get off my ~⟩ ***syn*** see INSTANCE — **in any case :** without regard to or in spite of other considerations **:** whatever else is done or is the case ⟨war is inevitable *in any case*⟩ ⟨*in any case* the report will be made public next month⟩ — **in case :** as a precaution ⟨took an umbrella, just *in case*⟩ — **in case of :** in the event of ⟨*in case of* trouble, yell⟩

[2]**case** *n* [ME *cas,* fr. AF *case, chase,* fr. L *capsa* chest, case, prob. fr. *capere* to take — more at HEAVE] (14c) **1 a :** a box or receptacle for holding something **b :** a box together with its contents **c :** SET; *specif* **:** PAIR **2 a :** an outer covering or housing ⟨a pastry ~⟩ **b :** a tube into which the components of a round of ammunition are loaded **3 :** a divided tray for holding printing type **4 :** the frame of a door or window **:** CASING

[3]**case** *vt* **cased; cas•ing** (1575) **1 :** to enclose in or cover with or as if with a case **:** ENCASE **2 :** to line (as a well) with supporting material (as metal pipe) **3 :** to inspect or study esp. with intent to rob

ca•se•ation \ˌkā-sē-ˈā-shən\ *n* [L *caseus* cheese] (1866) **:** necrosis with conversion of damaged tissue into a soft cheesy substance — **ca•se•ate** \ˈkā-sē-ˌāt\ *vi*

case•bear•er \ˈkās-ˌber-ər\ *n* (ca. 1889) **:** an insect larva that forms a protective case (as of silk)

case•book \-ˌbu̇k\ *n* (1762) **1 :** a book containing records of illustrative cases that is used for reference and instruction (as in law or medicine) **2 :** a compilation of primary and secondary documents relating to a central topic together with scholarly comment, exercises, and study aids that is designed to serve as a sourcebook for short papers (as in a writing course) or as a point of departure for a research paper

cased glass \ˈkāst-\ *n* (1851) **:** glass consisting of two or more fused layers of different colors often decorated by cutting so that the inner layers show through — called also *case glass*

case goods *n pl* (1922) **1 :** furniture (as bureaus or bookcases) that provides interior storage space; *also* **:** dining-room and bedroom furniture sold as sets **2 :** products often sold by the case

case–hard•en \ˈkās-ˌhär-dᵊn\ *vt* (1677) **1 :** to harden (a ferrous alloy) so that the surface layer is harder than the interior **2 :** to make callous or insensible — **case–hard•ened** *adj*

case history *n* (1894) **:** a record of history, environment, and relevant details of a case esp. for use in analysis or illustration

ca•sein \ˈkā-ˌsēn, kā-ˈ\ *n* [prob. fr. F *caséine,* fr. L *caseus* cheese] (1841) **:** a phosphoprotein of milk**:** as **a :** one that is precipitated from milk by heating with an acid or by the action of lactic acid in souring and is used in making paints and adhesives **b :** one that is produced when milk is curdled by rennet, is the chief constituent of cheese, and is used in making plastics

ca•sein•ate \kā-ˈsē-ˌnāt, ˈkā-si-ˌnāt\ *n* (1904) **:** a compound of casein with a metal (as calcium or sodium)

case in point (1722) **:** an illustrative, relevant, or pertinent case

case knife *n* (1673) **1 :** SHEATH KNIFE **2 :** a table knife

case law *n* (1861) **:** law established by judicial decision in cases

case•load \ˈkās-ˌlōd\ *n* (1938) **:** the number of cases handled (as by a court or clinic) usu. in a particular period

case•mate \ˈkās-ˌmāt\ *n* [MF, fr. OIt *casamatta*] (1575) **:** a fortified position or chamber or an armored enclosure on a warship from which guns are fired through embrasures

case•ment \ˈkās-mənt\ *n* [ME, hollow molding] (15c) **:** a window sash that opens on hinges at the side; *also* **:** a window with such a sash

ca•se•ous \ˈkā-sē-əs\ *adj* [L *caseus* cheese] (1661) **:** marked by caseation; *also* **:** CHEESY 1

ca•sern *or* **ca•serne** \kə-ˈzərn\ *n* [F *caserne*] (1696) **:** a military barracks in a garrison town

case study *n* (1875) **1 :** an intensive analysis of an individual unit (as a person or community) stressing developmental factors in relation to environment **2 :** CASE HISTORY

case system *n* (ca. 1889) **:** a system of teaching law in which instruction is chiefly on the basis of leading or selected cases as primary authorities instead of from textbooks — called also *case method*

case•work \ˈkās-ˌwərk\ *n* (1886) **:** social work involving direct consideration of the problems, needs, and adjustments of the individual case (as a person or family) — **case•work•er** \-ˌwər-kər\ *n*

[1]**cash** \ˈkash\ *n* [modif. of MF or OIt; MF *casse* money box, fr. OIt *cassa,* fr. L *capsa* chest — more at CASE] (1593) **1 :** ready money **2 :** money or its equivalent (as a check) paid for goods or services at the time of purchase or delivery

[2]**cash** *adj* (1622) **:** being a method of accounting that includes as income only what has been received and as expenses only those paid — compare ACCRUAL

[3]**cash** *vt* (1811) **1 :** to pay or obtain cash for ⟨~ a check⟩ **2 :** to lead and win a bridge trick with (a card that is the highest remaining card of its suit) — **cash•able** \ˈka-shə-bəl\ *adj*

[4]**cash** *n, pl* **cash** [Pg *caixa,* fr. Tamil *kācu,* a small copper coin, fr. Skt *karṣa,* a weight of gold or silver] (1598) **1 :** any of various coins of small value in China and southern India; *esp* **:** a Chinese coin with a square hole in the center **2 :** a unit of value equivalent to one cash

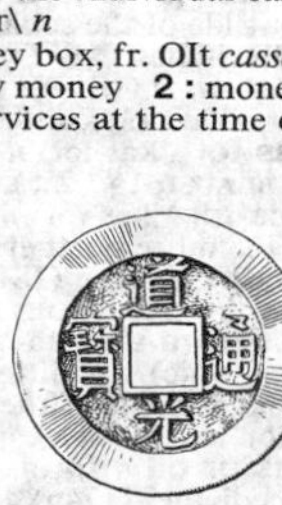

[4]cash 1

[1]**cash–and–car•ry** \ˌka-shᵊn-ˈka-rē, -ˈker-ē\ *adj* (1917) **:** sold or provided for cash and usu. without delivery service

[2]**cash–and–carry** *n* (1921) **:** the policy of selling on a cash-and-carry basis

cash bar *n* (1968) **:** a bar (as at a reception) at which drinks are sold — compare OPEN BAR

cash•book \ˈkash-ˌbu̇k\ *n* (1606) **:** a book in which record is kept of all cash receipts and disbursements

cash cow *n* (1979) **1 :** a consistently profitable business, property, or product whose profits are used to finance a company's investments in other areas **2 :** one regarded or exploited as a reliable source of money ⟨a singer deemed a *cash cow* for the record label⟩

cash crop *n* (1868) **:** a readily salable crop (as cotton or tobacco) produced or gathered primarily for market

cash discount *n* (1917) **:** a discount granted in consideration of immediate payment or payment within a prescribed time

cash•ew \ˈka-(ˌ)shü, kə-ˈshü\ *n* [Pg *cajú, acajú,* fr. Tupi *akajú*] (1598) **:** a tropical American tree (*Anacardium occidentale* of the family Anacardiaceae, the cashew family) grown for a phenolic oil and the edible kernel of its nut and for a gum from its stem; *also* **:** CASHEW NUT

cashew nut *n* (1796) **:** the kidney-shaped kernel of the fruit of the cashew that is edible when roasted

cash flow *n* (1954) **1 :** a measure of an organization's liquidity that usu. consists of net income after taxes plus noncash charges against income **2 :** a flow of cash; *esp* **:** one that provides solvency

[1]**ca•shier** \ka-ˈshir, kə-\ *vt* [D *casseren,* fr. MF *casser* to discharge, annul — more at QUASH] (1592) **1 :** to dismiss from service; *esp* **:** to dismiss dishonorably **2 :** REJECT, DISCARD

[2]**cash•ier** \(ˌ)ka-ˈshir\ *n* [D or MF; D *kassier,* fr. MF *cassier,* fr. *casse* money box] (1593) **:** one that has charge of money**:** as **a :** a high officer in a bank or trust company responsible for moneys received and expended **b :** one who collects and records payments **c :** an employee (as in a store) who handles monetary transactions

cashier's check *n* (1867) **:** a check drawn by a bank on its own funds and signed by the cashier

cash in *vt* (1888) **:** to obtain cash for ⟨*cashed in* the bonds⟩ ~ *vi* **1 a :** to retire from a gambling game **b :** to settle accounts and withdraw from an involvement (as a business deal) **2 :** to obtain advantage or financial profit — often used with *on* ⟨*cash in* on a best seller⟩

cash•less \ˈkash-ləs\ *adj* (1731) **:** not having or involving cash; *specif* **:** relying largely or entirely on monetary transactions that use electronic means rather than cash

cash•mere \ˈkazh-ˌmir, ˈkash-\ *n* [*Cashmere* (Kashmir)] (1684) **1 :** fine wool from the undercoat of the cashmere goat; *also* **:** a yarn of this wool **2 :** a soft twilled fabric made orig. from cashmere

cashmere goat *n* (1850) **:** an Indian goat raised esp. for its undercoat of fine soft wool that constitutes the cashmere wool of commerce

cash out *vt* (1971) **:** to convert (noncash assets) to cash ⟨*cash out* stocks⟩ ~ *vi* **:** to convert noncash assets to cash — **cash–out** *n*

cash register *n* (1879) **:** a business machine that usu. has a money drawer, indicates the amount of each sale, and records the amount of money received

cash–strapped \ˈkash-ˌstrapt\ *adj* (1973) **:** lacking sufficient money

cas•ing \ˈkā-siŋ\ *n* (1791) **1 :** something that encases **:** material for encasing**:** as **a :** an enclosing frame esp. around a door or window opening **b :** a metal pipe used to case a well **c :** [4]TIRE 2 **d :** a membranous case for processed meat **2 :** a space formed between two parallel lines of stitching through at least two layers of cloth into which something (as a rod or string) may be inserted

ca•si•no \kə-ˈsē-(ˌ)nō\ *n, pl* **-nos** [It, fr. *casa* house, fr. L, cottage] (1744) **1 :** a building or room used for social amusements; *specif* **:** one used for gambling **2** *also* **cas•si•no :** a card game in which cards are won by matching or combining cards in a hand with those exposed on the table **3 :** SUMMERHOUSE 2

ca•si•ta \kə-ˈsē-tə\ *n* [Sp, dim. of *casa*] (1868) **:** a small house

cask \ˈkask\ *n* [ME *caske,* perh. fr. MF *casque* helmet, fr. Sp *casco* potsherd, skull, helmet] (15c) **1 :** a barrel-shaped vessel of staves, headings, and hoops usu. for liquids **2 :** a cask and its contents; *also* **:** the quantity contained in a cask

cas•ket \ˈkas-kət\ *n* [ME, perh. modif. of MF *cassette*] (15c) **1 :** a small chest or box (as for jewels) **2 :** a usu. fancy coffin — **casket** *vt*

casque \ˈkask\ *n* [MF — more at CASK] (1580) **1 :** a piece of armor for the head **:** HELMET **2 :** an anatomical structure (as the horny outgrowth on the head of a cassowary) suggestive of a helmet

Cas•san•dra \kə-ˈsan-drə, -ˈsän-\ *n* [L, fr. Gk *Kassandra*] (1542) **1 :** a daughter of Priam endowed with the gift of prophecy but fated never to be believed **2 :** one that predicts misfortune or disaster

cas•sa•va \kə-ˈsä-və\ *n* [Sp *cazabe* cassava bread, fr. Taino *caçábi*] (1555) **:** any of several American plants (genus *Manihot,* esp. *M. esculenta*) of the spurge family grown in the tropics for their edible tuberous roots which yield a nutritious starch; *also* **:** the root — compare TAPIOCA 1

cas•se•role \ˈka-sə-ˌrōl *also* ˈka-zə-\ *n* [F, saucepan, fr. MF, dim. of *casse* ladle, dripping pan, fr. Old Occitan *cassa,* perh. ultim. fr. Gk *kyathos* ladle] (1708) **1 :** a dish in which food may be baked and served **2 :** food cooked and served in a casserole **3 :** a deep round usu. porcelain dish with a handle used for heating substances in the laboratory

cas•sette *also* **ca•sette** \kə-ˈset, ka-\ *n* [F, fr. MF, dim. of dial. F (Norman & Picard) *casse* case] (1793) **1 :** CASKET 1 **2 :** a usu. flat case or cartridge that can be easily loaded or unloaded**:** as **a :** a lightproof magazine for holding film or plates for use in a camera **b :** a plastic cartridge containing magnetic tape with the tape passing from one reel to another **3 :** a cassette tape player

cas•sia \ˈka-shə\ *n* [ME, fr. OE, fr. L, fr. Gk *kassia,* of Sem origin; akin to Heb *qĕṣīʿāh* cassia] (bef. 12c) **1 :** a dried coarse cinnamon bark (as from *Cinnamomum cassia*) **2 :** any of a genus (*Cassia*) of leguminous herbs, shrubs, and trees of warm regions

\ə\ **abut** \ᵊ\ kit**t**en, F ta**ble** \ər\ **fur**ther \a\ **a**sh \ā\ **a**ce \ä\ m**o**p, m**a**r \au̇\ **ou**t \ch\ **ch**in \e\ b**e**t \ē\ **ea**sy \g\ **g**o \i\ h**i**t \ī\ **i**ce \j\ **j**ob \ŋ\ si**ng** \ō\ g**o** \ȯ\ l**aw** \ȯi\ b**oy** \th\ **th**in \t͟h\ **th**e \ü\ l**oo**t \u̇\ f**oo**t \y\ **y**et \zh\ vi**si**on, bei**ge** \k̲, ⁿ, œ, ue, ʸ\ *see* Guide to Pronunciation

cas·si·mere \ˈka-zə-ˌmir, ˈka-sə-\ *n* [obs. *Cassimere* (Kashmir)] (1774) : a closely woven smooth twilled usu. wool fabric (as for suits)
Cas·si·o·pe·ia \ˌka-sē-ə-ˈpē-ə\ *n* [L, fr. Gk *Kassiopeia*] (1596) **1** : the wife of King Cepheus who gives birth to Andromeda and is later changed into a constellation **2** [L (gen. *Cassiopeiae*), fr. Gk *Kassiopeia*] : a northern constellation between Andromeda and Cepheus
cas·sis \kə-ˈsēs\ *n* [F, lit., black currants, perh. fr. L *cassia*] (1899) : a syrupy liquor of low alcoholic strength made from black currants and used chiefly as a flavoring and sweetening agent
cas·sit·er·ite \kə-ˈsi-tə-ˌrīt\ *n* [F *cassitérite,* fr. Gk *kassiteros* tin] (1858) : a brown or black mineral that consists of tin dioxide and is the chief source of metallic tin — called also *tinstone*
cas·sock \ˈka-sək\ *n* [MF *casaque*] (1631) : a close-fitting ankle-length garment worn esp. in Roman Catholic and Anglican churches by the clergy and by laypersons assisting in services
cas·sou·let \ˌka-sə-ˈlā\ *n* [F, fr. Occitan, lit., earthenware dish, dim. of *cassolo* dish, dim. of *casso* ladle, fr. Old Occitan *cassa*] (ca. 1929) : a casserole of white beans baked with herbs and meat (as pork, lamb, and goose or duck)
cas·so·wary \ˈka-sə-ˌwer-ē\ *n, pl* **-war·ies** [Malay *kĕsuari,* fr. an Austronesian language of the Moluccas] (1611) : any of a genus (*Casuarius*) of large ratite birds chiefly of New Guinea and northern Australia that have a horny casque on the head and are closely related to the emu
[1]**cast** \ˈkast\ *vb* **cast; cast·ing** [ME, fr. ON *kasta;* akin to ON *kǫs* heap] *vt* (13c) **1 a** : to cause to move or send forth by throwing ⟨~ a fishing lure⟩ ⟨~ dice⟩ **b** : DIRECT ⟨~ a glance⟩ **c** (1) : to put forth ⟨the fire ~*s* a warm glow⟩ ⟨~ light on the subject⟩ (2) : to place as if by throwing ⟨~ doubt on their reliability⟩ **d** : to deposit (a ballot) formally **e** (1) : to throw off or away ⟨the horse ~ a shoe⟩ (2) : to get rid of : DISCARD ⟨~ off all restraint⟩ (3) : SHED, MOLT (4) : to bring forth; *esp* : to give birth to prematurely **f** : to throw to the ground esp. in wrestling **g** : to build by throwing up earth **2 a** (1) : to perform arithmetical operations on : ADD (2) : to calculate by means of astrology **b** *archaic* : DECIDE, INTEND **3 a** : to dispose or arrange into parts or into a suitable form or order **b** (1) : to assign the parts of (a dramatic production) to actors ⟨~ a movie⟩ (2) : to assign (as an actor) to a role or part ⟨was ~ in the leading role⟩ **4 a** : to give a shape to (a substance) by pouring in liquid or plastic form into a mold and letting harden without pressure ⟨~ steel⟩ **b** : to form by this process **5** : TURN ⟨~ the scale slightly⟩ **6** : to make (a knot or stitch) by looping or catching up **7** : TWIST, WARP ⟨a beam ~ by age⟩ ~ *vi* **1** : to throw something; *specif* : to throw out a lure with a fishing rod **2** *dial Brit* : VOMIT **3** *dial Eng* : to bear fruit : YIELD **4 a** : to perform addition **b** *obs* : ESTIMATE, CONJECTURE **5** : WARP **6** : to range over land in search of a trail — used of hunting dogs or trackers **7** : VEER ***syn*** see DISCARD, THROW — **cast·abil·i·ty** \ˌkas-tə-ˈbi-lə-tē\ *n* — **cast·able** \ˈkas-tə-bəl\ *adj* — **cast lots** : to draw lots to determine a matter by chance
[2]**cast** *n* (14c) **1 a** : an act of casting **b** : something that happens as a result of chance **c** : a throw of dice **d** : a throw of a line (as a fishing line) or net **2 a** : the form in which a thing is constructed **b** (1) : the set of actors in a dramatic production (2) : a set of characters or persons ⟨in both great houses there is the usual ~ of servants —Elizabeth Bowen⟩ **c** : the arrangement of draperies in a painting **3** : the distance to which a thing can be thrown; *specif* : the distance a bow can shoot **4 a** : a turning of the eye in a particular direction; *also* : EXPRESSION ⟨this freakish, elfish ~ came into the child's eye —Nathaniel Hawthorne⟩ **b** : a slight strabismus **5** : something that is thrown or the quantity thrown; *esp, Brit* : the leader of a fishing line **6 a** : something that is formed by casting in a mold or form: as (1) : a reproduction (as of a statue) in metal or plaster : CASTING (2) : a fossil reproduction of the details of a natural object by mineral infiltration **b** : an impression taken from an object with a liquid or plastic substance : MOLD **c** : a rigid casing (as of fiberglass or of gauze impregnated with plaster of paris) used for immobilizing a usu. diseased or broken part **7** : FORECAST, CONJECTURE **8 a** : an overspread of a color or modification of the appearance of a substance by a trace of some added hue : SHADE ⟨gray with a greenish ~⟩ **b** : TINGE, SUGGESTION **9 a** : a ride on one's way in a vehicle : LIFT **b** *Scot* : HELP, ASSISTANCE **10 a** : SHAPE, APPEARANCE ⟨the delicate ~ of her features⟩ **b** : characteristic quality ⟨his father's conservative ~ of mind⟩ **11** : something that is shed, ejected, or thrown out or off: as **a** : the excrement of an earthworm **b** : a mass of soft matter formed in cavities of diseased organs and discharged from the body **c** : the skin of an insect **12** : the ranging in search of a trail by a dog, hunting pack, or tracker
cast about *vi* (1575) : to look around : SEEK ⟨*cast about* for a seat⟩ ~ *vt* : to lay plans concerning : CONTRIVE ⟨*cast about* how he was to go⟩
cas·ta·net \ˌkas-tə-ˈnet\ *n* [Sp *castañeta,* fr. *castaña* chestnut, fr. L *castanea* — more at CHESTNUT] (ca. 1647) : a percussion instrument used esp. by dancers that consists of two small shells of hard wood, ivory, or plastic usu. fastened to the thumb and clicked together by the other fingers — usu. used in pl.
cast around *vi* (1904) : CAST ABOUT
cast·away \ˈkast-ə-ˌwā\ *adj* (1542) **1** : thrown away : REJECTED **2 a** : cast adrift or ashore as a survivor of a shipwreck **b** : thrown out or left without friends or resources — **castaway** *n*
cast down *adj* (14c) : DOWNCAST
caste \ˈkast *also* ˈkäst\ *n* [Pg *casta,* lit., race, lineage, fr. fem. of *casto* pure, chaste, fr. L *castus*] (1613) **1** : one of the hereditary social classes in Hinduism that restrict the occupation of their members and their association with the members of other castes **2 a** : a division of society based on differences of wealth, inherited rank or privilege, profession, occupation, or race **b** : the position conferred by caste standing : PRESTIGE **3** : a system of rigid social stratification characterized by hereditary status, endogamy, and social barriers sanctioned by custom, law, or religion **4** : a specialized form (as the worker of an ant or bee) of a polymorphic social insect that carries out a particular function in the colony — **caste·ism** \ˈkas-ˌti-zəm\ *n*
cas·tel·lan \ˈkas-tə-lən\ *n* [ME *castelleyn,* fr. AF *castelain, chastelein,* fr. L *castellanus* occupant of a fortress, fr. *castellanus* of a fortress, fr. *castellum* fortress — more at CASTLE] (14c) : a governor or warden of a castle or fort
cas·tel·lat·ed \ˈkas-tə-ˌlā-təd\ *adj* [ML *castellatus,* pp. of *castellare* to fortify, fr. L *castellum*] (1679) **1** : having battlements like a castle **2** : having or supporting a castle
cast·er \ˈkas-tər\ *n* (14c) **1** : one that casts; *esp* : a machine that casts type **2** *or* **cas·tor** \-tər\ **a** : a usu. silver table vessel with a perforated top for sprinkling a seasoning (as sugar or spice) **b** : a usu. revolving metal stand bearing condiment containers (as cruets, mustard pot, and often shakers) for table use : a cruet stand **3** : any of a set of wheels or rotating balls mounted in a swivel frame and used for the support and movement of furniture, trucks, and portable equipment **4** : the slight usu. backward tilt from vertical of the axis of the steering mechanism of an automobile for giving directional stability to the front wheels
cas·ti·gate \ˈkas-tə-ˌgāt\ *vt* **-gat·ed; -gat·ing** [L *castigatus,* pp. of *castigare* — more at CHASTEN] (1606) : to subject to severe punishment, reproof, or criticism ***syn*** see PUNISH — **cas·ti·ga·tion** \ˌkas-tə-ˈgā-shən\ *n* — **cas·ti·ga·tor** \ˈkas-tə-ˌgā-tər\ *n*
cas·tile soap \(ˌ)kas-ˈtēl-\ *n, often cap C* [ME *castell sope,* fr. *Castell* Castile] (15c) : a fine hard bland soap made from olive oil and sodium hydroxide; *also* : any of various similar soaps
Cas·til·ian \ka-ˈstil-yən\ *n* (1566) **1** : a native or inhabitant of Castile; *broadly* : SPANIARD **2 a** : the dialect of Castile **b** : the official and literary language of Spain based on this dialect — **Castilian** *adj*
cast·ing *n* (14c) **1** : something (as the excrement of an earthworm) that is cast out or off **2** : the act of one that casts: as **a** : the throwing of a fishing line by means of a rod and reel **b** : the assignment of parts and duties to actors or performers **3** : something cast in a mold
casting couch *n* (1931) : a couch in an entertainment executive's office on which aspiring actresses are reputed to perform sexual acts in exchange for desired roles; *broadly* : the practice of abusing one's power to obtain sexual partners
casting director *n* (1922) : a person who supervises the casting of dramatic productions (as films and plays)
casting vote *n* (1678) : a deciding vote cast by a presiding officer to break a tie
cast–iron *adj* (1692) **1** : made of cast iron **2** : resembling cast iron: as **a** : capable of withstanding great strain ⟨a ~ stomach⟩ **b** : not admitting change, adaptation, or exception : RIGID ⟨a ~ will⟩
cast iron *n* (1664) : a commercial alloy of iron, carbon, and silicon that is cast in a mold and is hard, brittle, nonmalleable, and incapable of being hammer-welded but more easily fusible than steel
[1]**cas·tle** \ˈka-səl\ *n* [ME *castel,* fr. OE, fr. OF & L; OF dial. (Norman-Picard) *castel,* fr. L *castellum* fortress, dim. of *castrum* fortified place; perh. akin to L *castrare* to castrate] (bef. 12c) **1 a** : a large fortified building or set of buildings **b** : a massive or imposing house **2** : a retreat safe against intrusion or invasion **3** : [3]ROOK

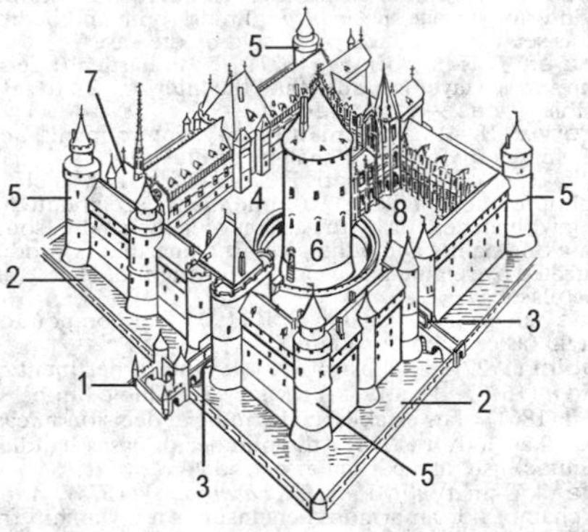

castle 1a: *1* fortified approach, *2* moat, *3* drawbridge, *4* ward, *5* angle tower, *6* donjon *or* keep, *7* chapel, *8* gallery

[2]**castle** *vb* **cas·tled; cas·tling** \ˈka-s(ə-)liŋ\ *vt* (1587) **1** : to establish in a castle **2** : to move (the chess king) in castling ~ *vi* : to move a chess king two squares toward a rook and in the same move the rook to the square next past the king
cas·tled \ˈka-səld\ *adj* (1603) : CASTELLATED
castle in the air (1566) : an impracticable project : DAYDREAM — called also *castle in Spain*
cast–off \ˈkast-ˌȯf\ *adj* (1613) : thrown away or aside — **cast·off** *n*
cast off *vt* (1575) **1** : LOOSE ⟨*cast off* a hunting dog⟩ **2** : UNFASTEN ⟨*cast off* a boat⟩ **3** : to remove (a stitch) from a knitting needle in such a way as to prevent unraveling ~ *vi* **1** : to unfasten or untie a boat or a line **2** : to turn one's partner in a square dance and pass around the outside of the set and back **3** : to finish a knitted fabric by casting off all stitches
cast on *vt* (1840) : to place (stitches) on a knitting needle for beginning or enlarging knitted work
cas·tor \ˈkas-tər\ *n* [ME, fr. L, fr. Gk *kastōr,* fr. *Kastōr* Castor] (14c) **1** : BEAVER 1a **2** : CASTOREUM **3** : a beaver hat
Cas·tor \ˈkas-tər\ *n* [L, fr. Gk *Kastōr*] (15c) **1** : one of the Dioscuri **2** : the more northern of the two bright stars in Gemini
castor bean *n* (1819) : the very poisonous seed of the castor-oil plant; *also* : CASTOR-OIL PLANT
cas·to·re·um \ka-ˈstȯr-ē-əm\ *n* [ME *castorium,* fr. L *castoreum,* fr. *castor*] (14c) : a bitter strong-smelling creamy orange-brown substance that consists of the dried perineal glands of the beaver and their secretion and is used esp. by perfumers — called also *castor*
castor oil *n* [prob. fr. its former use as a substitute for castoreum in medicine] (1746) : a pale viscous fatty oil from castor beans used esp. as a cathartic and as a lubricant and plasticizer
castor–oil plant *n* (1836) : a tropical Old World herb (*Ricinus communis*) widely grown as an ornamental or for its oil-rich castor beans

castor sugar *or* **caster sugar** *n* [*caster*] (1855) *chiefly Brit* **:** finely granulated white sugar

cast out *vt* (14c) **:** to drive out **:** EXPEL

cas·trate \ˈkas-ˌtrāt\ *vt* **cas·trat·ed; cas·trat·ing** [L *castratus,* pp. of *castrare;* akin to Gk *keazein* to split, Skt *śasati* he slaughters] (1554) **1 :** to render impotent or deprive of vitality esp. by psychological means **2 a :** to deprive of the testes **:** GELD **b :** to deprive of the ovaries **:** SPAY — **castrate** *n* — **cas·tra·tion** \kas-ˈtrā-shən\ *n* — **cas·tra·tor** \-ˌtrā-tər\ *n* — **cas·tra·to·ry** \ˈkas-trə-ˌtȯr-ē\ *adj*

cas·tra·to \ka-ˈsträ-(ˌ)tō, kə-\ *n, pl* **-ti** \-tē\ [It, fr. pp. of *castrare* to castrate, fr. L] (1763) **:** a singer castrated before puberty to preserve the soprano or contralto range of his voice

Cas·tro·ism \ˈkas-(ˌ)trō-ˌi-zəm\ *n* (1960) **:** the political, economic, and social principles and policies of Fidel Castro — **Cas·tro·ite** \-ˌīt\ *n*

[1]**ca·su·al** \ˈkazh-wəl, ˈka-zhə-wəl, ˈka-zhəl\ *adj* [ME, fr. AF & LL; AF *casuel,* fr. LL *casualis,* fr. L *casus* fall, chance — more at CASE] (14c) **1 :** subject to, resulting from, or occurring by chance ⟨a ~ meeting⟩ **2 a :** occurring without regularity **:** OCCASIONAL ⟨~ employment⟩ **b :** employed for irregular periods ⟨a ~ worker⟩ **c :** met with on occasion and known only superficially ⟨a ~ friend⟩ **3 a** (1) **:** feeling or showing little concern **:** NONCHALANT ⟨a ~ approach to cooking⟩ (2) **:** lacking a high degree of interest or devotion ⟨~ sports fans⟩ ⟨~ readers⟩ (3) **:** done without serious intent or commitment ⟨~ sex⟩ **b** (1) **:** INFORMAL, NATURAL ⟨a ~ conversation⟩ (2) **:** designed for informal use ⟨~ clothing⟩ ***syn*** see ACCIDENTAL, RANDOM — **ca·su·al·ly** *adv* — **ca·su·al·ness** *n*

[2]**casual** *n* (ca. 1852) **1 :** a casual or migratory worker **2 :** an officer or enlisted person awaiting assignment or transportation to a unit

ca·su·al·ty \ˈka-zhəl-tē, ˈkazh-wəl-, ˈka-zhə-wəl-\ *n, pl* **-ties** (15c) **1** *archaic* **:** CHANCE, FORTUNE ⟨losses that befall them by mere ~ —Sir Walter Raleigh⟩ **2 :** serious or fatal accident **:** DISASTER **3 a :** a military person lost through death, wounds, injury, sickness, internment, or capture or through being missing in action **b :** a person or thing injured, lost, or destroyed **:** VICTIM ⟨the ex-senator was a ~ of the last election⟩

casual water *n* (1899) **:** a temporary accumulation of water not forming a regular hazard of a golf course

ca·su·a·ri·na \ˌka-zhə-(wə-)ˈrē-nə\ *n* [NL, genus name, fr. Malay (*pohon*) *kĕsuari,* lit., cassowary tree; fr. the resemblance of its twigs to cassowary feathers] (1777) **:** any of a genus (*Casuarina* of the family Casuarinaceae) of dicotyledonous chiefly Australian trees which have whorls of scalelike leaves and jointed stems resembling horsetails and some of which yield a heavy hard wood

ca·su·ist \ˈka-zhü-ist, ˈkazh-wist\ *n* [prob. fr. Sp *casuista,* fr. L *casus* fall, chance — more at CASE] (1609) **:** one skilled in or given to casuistry — **ca·su·is·tic** \ˌka-zhə-ˈwis-tik\ *or* **ca·su·is·ti·cal** \-ti-kəl\ *adj*

ca·su·ist·ry \ˈkazh-wə-strē, ˈka-zhə-\ *n, pl* **-ries** (1723) **1 :** a resolving of specific cases of conscience, duty, or conduct through interpretation of ethical principles or religious doctrine **2 :** specious argument **:** RATIONALIZATION

ca·sus bel·li \ˈkä-səs-ˈbe-ˌlē, ˈkā-səs-ˈbe-ˌlī\ *n, pl* **ca·sus belli** \ˈkä-ˌsüs-, ˈkā-ˌsüs-\ [NL, occasion of war] (ca. 1841) **:** an event or action that justifies or allegedly justifies a war or conflict

[1]**cat** \ˈkat\ *n, often attrib* [ME, fr. OE *catt,* prob. fr. LL *cattus, catta* cat] (bef. 12c) **1 a :** a carnivorous mammal (*Felis catus*) long domesticated as a pet and for catching rats and mice **b :** any of a family (Felidae) of carnivorous usu. solitary and nocturnal mammals (as the domestic cat, lion, tiger, leopard, jaguar, cougar, wildcat, lynx, and cheetah) **2 :** a malicious woman **3 :** a strong tackle used to hoist an anchor to the cathead of a ship **4 a :** CATBOAT **b :** CATAMARAN **5 :** CAT-O'-NINE-TAILS **6 :** CATFISH **7 a :** a player or devotee of jazz **b :** GUY

[2]**cat** *vb* **cat·ted; cat·ting** *vi* (1681) **:** to search for a sexual mate — often used with *around* ~ *vt* **:** to bring (an anchor) up to the cathead

[3]**cat** *abbr* **1** catalog **2** catalyst

Cat \ˈkat\ *trademark* — used for a Caterpillar tractor

CAT *abbr* **1** clean-air turbulence **2** computerized axial tomography

cata- *or* **cat-** *or* **cath-** *prefix* [Gk *kata-, kat-, kath-,* fr. *kata* down, in accordance with, by (also as a perfective prefix); akin to OW *cant* with, Hitt *katta*] **:** down ⟨*cat*ion⟩ ⟨*cath*ode⟩

ca·tab·o·lism \kə-ˈta-bə-ˌli-zəm\ *n* [Gk *katabolē* throwing down, fr. *kataballein* to throw down, fr. *kata-* + *ballein* to throw — more at DEVIL] (1876) **:** degradative metabolism involving the release of energy and resulting in the breakdown of complex materials (as proteins or lipids) within the organism — compare ANABOLISM — **cat·a·bol·ic** \ˌka-tə-ˈbä-lik\ *adj* — **cat·a·bol·i·cal·ly** \-li-k(ə-)lē\ *adv*

ca·tab·o·lite \-ˌlīt\ *n* (ca. 1909) **:** a product of catabolism

ca·tab·o·lize \-ˌlīz\ *vb* **-lized; -liz·ing** *vt* (ca. 1926) **:** to subject to catabolism ~ *vi* **:** to undergo catabolism

cat·a·chre·sis \ˌka-tə-ˈkrē-səs\ *n, pl* **-chre·ses** \-ˌsēz\ [L, fr. Gk *katachrēsis* misuse, fr. *katachrēsthai* to use up, misuse, fr. *kata-* + *chrēsthai* to use] (1550) **1 :** use of the wrong word for the context **2 :** use of a forced and esp. paradoxical figure of speech (as *blind mouths*) — **cat·a·chres·tic** \-ˈkres-tik\ *or* **cat·a·chres·ti·cal** \-ti-kəl\ *adj* — **cat·a·chres·ti·cal·ly** \-ti-k(ə-)lē\ *adv*

cat·a·clysm \ˈka-tə-ˌkli-zəm\ *n* [F *cataclysme,* fr. L *cataclysmos,* fr. Gk *kataklysmos,* fr. *kataklyzein* to inundate, fr. *kata-* + *klyzein* to wash — more at CLYSTER] (1599) **1 :** FLOOD, DELUGE **2 :** CATASTROPHE 3a **3 :** a momentous and violent event marked by overwhelming upheaval and demolition; *broadly* **:** an event that brings great changes — **cat·a·clys·mal** \ˌka-tə-ˈkliz-məl\ *or* **cat·a·clys·mic** \-mik\ *adj* — **cat·a·clys·mi·cal·ly** \-mi-k(ə-)lē\ *adv*

cat·a·comb \ˈka-tə-ˌkōm\ *n* [ME *catacumb,* MF *catacombe,* prob. fr. OIt *catacomba,* fr. LL *catacumbae,* pl.] (15c) **1 :** a subterranean cemetery of galleries with recesses for tombs — usu. used in pl. **2 :** something resembling a catacomb: as **a :** an underground passageway or group of passageways **b :** a complex set of interrelated things ⟨the endless ~*s* of formal education —Kingman Brewster †1988⟩

cata·di·op·tric \ˌka-tə-dī-ˈäp-trik\ *adj* (1723) **:** belonging to, produced by, or involving both the reflection and the refraction of light

ca·tad·ro·mous \kə-ˈta-drə-məs\ *adj* [prob. fr. NL *catadromus,* fr. *cata-* + *-dromus* -dromous] (1880) **:** living in freshwater and going to the sea to spawn ⟨~ eels⟩ — compare ANADROMOUS

cat·a·falque \ˈka-tə-ˌfȯ(l)k, -ˌfalk\ *n* [It *catafalco,* fr. VL **catafalicum* scaffold, fr. *cata-* + L *fala* siege tower] (1641) **1 :** an ornamental structure sometimes used in funerals for the lying in state of the body **2 :** a pall-covered coffin-shaped structure used at requiem masses celebrated after burial

Cat·a·lan \ˈka-tə-lən, -ˌlan\ *n* [Sp *catalán*] (15c) **1 :** a native or inhabitant of Catalonia **2 :** the Romance language of Catalonia, Valencia, Andorra, and the Balearic islands — **Catalan** *adj*

cat·a·lase \ˈka-tə-ˌlās, -ˌlāz\ *n* [*catalysis*] (1901) **:** a red crystalline enzyme that consists of a protein complex with hematin groups and catalyzes the decomposition of hydrogen peroxide into water and oxygen — **cat·a·lat·ic** \ˌka-tə-ˈla-tik\ *adj*

cat·a·lec·tic \ˌka-tə-ˈlek-tik\ *adj* [LL *catalecticus,* fr. Gk *katalēktikos,* fr. *katalēgein* to leave off, fr. *kata-* + *lēgein* to stop — more at SLACK] (1589) **:** lacking a syllable at the end of a line in metrical verse or ending in an incomplete foot — **catalectic** *n*

cat·a·lep·sy \ˈka-tə-ˌlep-sē\ *n, pl* **-sies** [ME *catalempsi,* fr. ML *catalepsia,* fr. LL *catalepsis,* fr. Gk *katalēpsis,* lit., act of seizing, fr. *katalambanein* to seize, fr. *kata-* + *lambanein* to take — more at LATCH] (14c) **:** a trancelike state marked by loss of voluntary motion in which the limbs remain in whatever position they are placed — **cat·a·lep·tic** \ˌka-tə-ˈlep-tik\ *adj or n* — **cat·a·lep·ti·cal·ly** \-ti-k(ə-)lē\ *adv*

cat·a·lex·is \ˌka-tə-ˈlek-səs\ *n, pl* **-lex·es** \-ˌsēz\ [NL, fr. Gk *katalēxis* close, cadence, fr. *katalēgein*] (1830) **:** omission or incompleteness usu. in the last foot of a line in metrical verse

[1]**cat·a·log** *or* **cat·a·logue** \ˈka-tə-ˌlȯg, -ˌläg\ *n* [ME *cathaloge, cateloge,* fr. MF *catalogue,* fr. LL *catalogus,* fr. Gk *katalogos,* fr. *katalegein* to list, enumerate, fr. *kata-* + *legein* to gather, speak — more at LEGEND] (15c) **1 :** LIST, REGISTER **2 a :** a complete enumeration of items arranged systematically with descriptive details **b :** a pamphlet or book that contains such a list **c :** material in such a list

[2]**catalog** *or* **catalogue** *vb* **-loged** *or* **-logued; -log·ing** *or* **-logu·ing** *vt* (1598) **1 :** to make a catalog of **2 a :** to enter in a catalog **b :** to classify (as books or information) descriptively ~ *vi* **1 :** to make or work on a catalog **2 :** to become listed in a catalog at a specified price ⟨this stamp ~*s* at $2⟩ — **cat·a·log·er** *or* **cat·a·logu·er** *n*

catalogue rai·son·né \-ˌrā-zə-ˈnā\ *n, pl* **cat·a·logues rai·son·nés** \-ˌlȯg(z)-ˌrā-zə-ˈnā\ [F, lit., reasoned catalog] (1784) **:** a systematic annotated catalog; *esp* **:** a critical bibliography

ca·tal·pa \kə-ˈtal-pə, -ˈtȯl-\ *n* [Creek *katálpa,* fr. *iká* head + *tálpa* wing] (ca. 1730) **:** any of a genus (*Catalpa*) of No. American and Asian trees of the bignonia family with pale showy flowers in terminal clusters

ca·tal·y·sis \kə-ˈta-lə-səs\ *n, pl* **-y·ses** \-ˌsēz\ [Gk *katalysis* dissolution, fr. *katalyein* to dissolve, fr. *kata-* + *lyein* to dissolve, release — more at LOSE] (1836) **:** a modification and esp. increase in the rate of a chemical reaction induced by material unchanged chemically at the end of the reaction

cat·a·lyst \ˈka-tə-ləst\ *n* (1902) **1 :** a substance that enables a chemical reaction to proceed at a usu. faster rate or under different conditions (as at a lower temperature) than otherwise possible **2 :** an agent that provokes or speeds significant change or action

cat·a·lyt·ic \ˌka-tə-ˈli-tik\ *adj* (1836) **:** causing, involving, or relating to catalysis — **cat·a·lyt·i·cal·ly** \-ˈli-ti-k(ə-)lē\ *adv*

catalytic converter *n* (1955) **:** an automobile exhaust-system component containing a catalyst that causes conversion of harmful gases (as carbon monoxide and uncombusted hydrocarbons) into mostly harmless products (as water and carbon dioxide)

catalytic cracker *n* (1947) **:** the unit in a petroleum refinery in which cracking is carried out in the presence of a catalyst

cat·a·lyze \ˈka-tə-ˌlīz\ *vt* **-lyzed; -lyz·ing** (1890) **1 :** to bring about the catalysis of (a chemical reaction) **2 :** BRING ABOUT, INSPIRE **3 :** to alter significantly by or as if by catalysis ⟨innovations in basic chemical theory that have *catalyzed* the field —*Newsweek*⟩ — **cat·a·lyz·er** *n*

cat·a·ma·ran \ˌka-tə-mə-ˈran, ˈka-tə-mə-ˌran\ *n* [Tamil *kaṭṭumaram,* fr. *kaṭṭu* to tie + *maram* tree, wood] (1673) **:** a vessel (as a sailboat) with twin hulls and usu. a deck or superstructure connecting the hulls

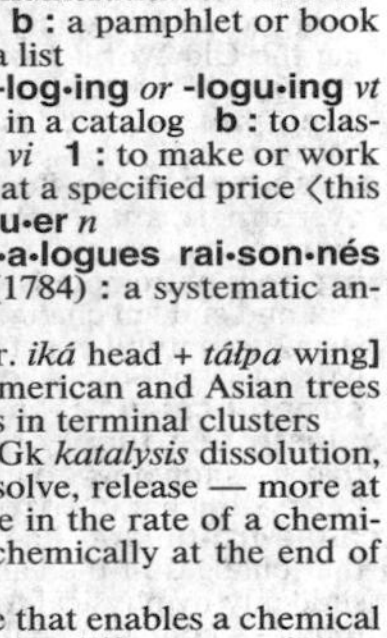
catamaran

cat·a·me·nia \ˌka-tə-ˈmē-nē-ə\ *n pl* [NL, fr. Gk *katamēnia,* fr. neut. pl. of *katamēnios* monthly, fr. *kata* by + *mēn* month — more at CATA-, MOON] (1750) **:** MENSES — **cat·a·me·ni·al** \-nē-əl\ *adj*

cat·a·mite \ˈka-tə-ˌmīt\ *n* [L *catamitus,* fr. *Catamitus* Ganymede, fr. Etruscan *Catmite,* fr. Gk *Ganymēdēs*] (1593) **:** a boy kept by a pederast

cat·a·mount \ˈka-tə-ˌmau̇nt\ *n* [short for *cat-a-mountain*] (1664) **:** any of various wild cats: as **a :** COUGAR 1 **b :** LYNX

cat–a–moun·tain \ˌka-tə-ˈmau̇n-tᵊn\ *n* [ME *cat of the mountaine*] (15c) **:** any of various wild cats

cat and mouse *n* (1675) **:** behavior like that of a cat with a mouse: as **a :** the act of toying with or tormenting something before destroying it **b :** a contrived action involving constant pursuit, near captures, and repeated escapes ⟨played a game of *cat and mouse* with the police⟩; *broadly* **:** an evasive action

ca·taph·o·ra \kə-ˈta-fə-rə\ *n* [*cata-* + *anaphora*] (1976) **:** the use of a grammatical substitute (as a pronoun) that has the same reference as a following word or phrase

cat·a·pho·re·sis \ˌka-tə-fə-ˈrē-səs\ *n, pl* **-re·ses** \-ˌsēz\ [NL] (1889) **:** ELECTROPHORESIS — **cat·a·pho·ret·ic** \-ˈre-tik\ *adj*

cat·a·phor·ic \ˌka-tə-ˈfȯr-ik\ *adj* (1968) **:** of or relating to cataphora; *esp* **:** being a word or phrase (as a pronoun) that takes its reference from a following word or phrase (as *her* in *before her Jane saw nothing but desert*) — compare ANAPHORIC

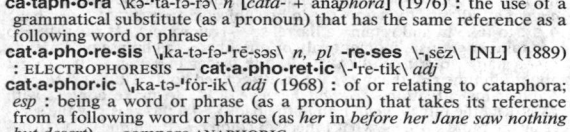

cat·a·plasm \ˈka-tə-ˌpla-zəm\ *n* [MF *cataplasme,* fr. L *cataplasma,* fr. Gk *kataplasma,* fr. *kataplassein* to plaster over, fr. *kata-* + *plassein* to mold — more at PLASTER] (ca. 1540) : POULTICE

cat·a·plexy \ˈka-tə-ˌplek-sē\ *n, pl* **-plex·ies** \-sēz\ [G *Kataplexie,* fr. Gk *kataplēxis,* fr. *kataplēssein* to strike down, terrify, fr. *kata-* + *plēssein* to strike — more at PLAINT] (1883) : sudden loss of muscle power following a strong emotional stimulus

[1]**cat·a·pult** \ˈka-tə-ˌpəlt, -ˌpu̇lt\ *n* [MF or L; MF *catapulte,* fr. L *catapulta,* fr. Gk *katapaltēs,* fr. *kata-* + *pallein* to hurl] (1577) **1 :** an ancient military device for hurling missiles **2 :** a device for launching an airplane at flying speed (as from an aircraft carrier)

[2]**catapult** *vt* (1848) : to throw or launch by or as if by a catapult ~ *vi* : to become catapulted ⟨he ~*ed* to fame⟩

cat·a·ract \ˈka-tə-ˌrakt\ *n* [L *cataracta* waterfall, portcullis, fr. Gk *kataraktēs,* fr. *katarassein* to dash down, fr. *kata-* + *arassein* to strike, dash] (14c) **1** [ME, fr. MF or ML; MF *cataracte,* fr. ML *cataracta,* fr. L, portcullis] : a clouding of the lens of the eye or of its surrounding transparent membrane that obstructs the passage of light **2 a** *obs* : WATERSPOUT **b :** WATERFALL; *esp* : a large one over a precipice **c :** steep rapids in a river **d :** DOWNPOUR, FLOOD ⟨~*s* of rain⟩ ⟨~*s* of information⟩ — **cat·a·rac·tous** \ˌka-tə-ˈrak-təs\ *adj*

ca·tarrh \kə-ˈtär\ *n* [ME *catarre,* fr. MF or LL; MF *catarrhe,* fr. LL *catarrhus,* fr. Gk *katarrhous,* fr. *katarrhein* to flow down, fr. *kata-* + *rhein* to flow — more at STREAM] (15c) : inflammation of a mucous membrane; *esp* : one chronically affecting the human nose and air passages — **ca·tarrh·al** \-əl\ *adj* — **ca·tarrh·al·ly** \-ə-lē\ *adv*

cat·ar·rhine \ˈka-tə-ˌrīn\ *adj* [NL *Catarrhina,* fr. Gk *katarrhina,* neut. pl. of *katarrhin* hook-nosed, fr. *kata-* + *rhin-, rhis* nose] (1863) : of, relating to, or being any of a division (Catarrhina) of primates comprising the Old World monkeys, higher apes, and hominids that have the nostrils close together and directed downward, 32 teeth, and the tail when present never prehensile — compare PLATYRRHINE — **catarrhine** *n*

ca·tas·tro·phe \kə-ˈtas-trə-(ˌ)fē\ *n* [Gk *katastrophē,* fr. *katastrephein* to overturn, fr. *kata-* + *strephein* to turn] (1540) **1 :** the final event of the dramatic action esp. of a tragedy **2 :** a momentous tragic event ranging from extreme misfortune to utter overthrow or ruin **3 a :** a violent and sudden change in a feature of the earth **b :** a violent usu. destructive natural event (as a supernova) **4 :** utter failure : FIASCO ⟨the party was a ~⟩ — **cat·a·stroph·ic** \ˌka-tə-ˈsträ-fik\ *adj* — **cat·a·stroph·i·cal·ly** \-fi-k(ə-)lē\ *adv*

catastrophe theory *n* (1971) : mathematical theory and conjecture that uses topology to explain events (as an earthquake or a stock market crash) characterized by major abrupt changes

ca·tas·tro·phism \kə-ˈtas-trə-ˌfi-zəm\ *n* (1869) : a geological doctrine that changes in the earth's crust have in the past been brought about suddenly by physical forces operating in ways that cannot be observed today — compare UNIFORMITARIANISM — **ca·tas·tro·phist** \-fist\ *n*

cat·a·to·nia \ˌka-tə-ˈtō-nē-ə\ *n* [NL, fr. G *Katatonie,* fr. *kata-* cata- + NL *-tonia*] (ca. 1891) : catatonic schizophrenia

cat·a·ton·ic \-ˈtä-nik\ *adj* (1904) **1 :** of, relating to, being, resembling, or affected by schizophrenia characterized esp. by a marked psychomotor disturbance that may involve stupor or mutism, negativism, rigidity, purposeless excitement, and inappropriate or bizarre posturing **2 :** characterized by a marked lack of movement, activity, or expression — **catatonic** *n* — **cat·a·ton·i·cal·ly** \-ni-k(ə-)lē\ *adv*

Ca·taw·ba \kə-ˈtȯ-bə\ *n* [prob. ultim. fr. Catawba (Sp spelling) *Catapa, Cataba,* name of a 16th cent. Catawba town] (1715) **1** *pl* **Catawba** *or* **Catawbas :** a member of an American Indian people of No. Carolina and So. Carolina **2 :** the language of the Catawba people **3 :** any of various wines produced from a pale red native American grape

cat·bird \ˈkat-ˌbərd\ *n* (1709) : an American songbird (*Dumetella carolinensis*) that is dark gray in color with a black cap and reddish coverts under the tail and is related to the mockingbird

catbird seat *n* (1942) : a position of great prominence or advantage

cat·boat \ˈkat-ˌbōt\ *n* (1860) : a sailboat having a cat rig and usu. a centerboard and being of light draft and broad beam

cat·bri·er \-ˌbrī(-ə)r\ *n* (1839) : any of a genus (*Smilax*) of dioecious often prickly climbing plants of the lily family

cat burglar *n* (1907) : a burglar who is adept at entering and leaving the burglarized place without attracting notice

cat·call \-ˌkȯl\ *n* (1693) **1 :** a loud or raucous cry made esp. to express disapproval (as at a sports event) **2 :** a derisive remark : CRITICISM — **catcall** *vb*

[1]**catch** \ˈkach, ˈkech\ *vb* **caught** \ˈkȯt *also* ˈkät\; **catch·ing** [ME *cacchen,* fr. AF *cacher, chacher, chacer* to hunt, fr. VL **captiare,* alter. of L *captare* to chase, freq. of *capere* to take — more at HEAVE] *vt* (13c) **1 a :** to capture or seize esp. after pursuit ⟨~ a thief⟩ **b :** to take or entangle in or as if in a snare ⟨~ fish in a net⟩ **c :** DECEIVE **d :** to discover unexpectedly : FIND ⟨*caught* in the act⟩ **e :** to check (oneself) suddenly or momentarily **f :** to become suddenly aware of ⟨*caught* me looking at him⟩ **2 a :** to take hold of : SEIZE **b :** to affect suddenly **c :** to grasp and hold on to (something in motion) ⟨~ a fly ball⟩ **d :** to avail oneself of : TAKE ⟨*caught* the first opportunity to leave⟩ **e :** to obtain through effort : GET ⟨~ a ride⟩ **f :** to overtake unexpectedly — usu. used in the passive ⟨was *caught* in a storm⟩ **g :** to get entangled ⟨~ a sleeve on a nail⟩ **3 :** to become affected by: as **a :** CONTRACT ⟨~ a cold⟩ **b :** to respond sympathetically to the point of being imbued with ⟨~ the spirit of an occasion⟩ **c :** to be struck by ⟨he *caught* a bullet in the leg⟩ **d :** to be subjected to : RECEIVE ⟨~ hell⟩ **4 a :** to take in and retain ⟨a barrel to ~ rainwater⟩ **b :** FASTEN **5 :** to take or get usu. momentarily or quickly ⟨~ a glimpse of a friend⟩ ⟨~ a nap⟩ **6 a :** OVERTAKE ⟨~ the leader in a race⟩ **b :** to get aboard in time ⟨~ the bus⟩ **7 :** to attract and hold : ARREST, ENGAGE ⟨*caught* my attention⟩ ⟨*caught* her eye⟩ **8 :** to make contact with : STRIKE ⟨the pitch *caught* him in the back⟩ **9 a :** to grasp by the senses or the mind ⟨you ~ what I mean?⟩ ⟨didn't ~ the name⟩ **b :** to apprehend and fix by artistic means ⟨~ a person's likeness⟩ **10 a :** SEE, WATCH ⟨~ a game on TV⟩ **b :** to listen to **11 :** to serve as a catcher for in baseball **12 :** to meet with ⟨~ you later⟩ ~ *vi* **1 :** to grasp hastily or try to grasp **2 :** to become caught **3 :** to catch fire **4 :** to play the position of catcher on a baseball team **5 :** KICK OVER ⟨the engine *caught*⟩ — **catch·able** \ˈka-chə-bəl, ˈke-\ *adj* — **catch a crab :** to fail to raise an oar clear of the water on recovery of a stroke — **catch dead :** to find or see at any time — used in strongly negative constructions ⟨wouldn't be *caught dead* in that shirt⟩ — **catch fire 1 :** to become ignited **2 :** to become fired with enthusiasm **3 :** to increase greatly in scope, popularity, interest, or effectiveness ⟨this stock has not *caught fire*—yet —*Forbes*⟩ — **catch it :** to incur blame, reprimand, or punishment ⟨he'll really *catch it* from the boss if he's late again⟩ — **catch one's breath :** to rest long enough to restore normal breathing; *broadly* : to rest after a period of intense activity

syn CATCH, CAPTURE, TRAP, SNARE, ENTRAP, ENSNARE, BAG mean to come to possess or control by or as if by seizing. CATCH implies the seizing of something in motion or in flight or in hiding ⟨*caught* the dog as it ran by⟩. CAPTURE suggests taking by overcoming resistance or difficulty ⟨*capture* an enemy stronghold⟩. TRAP, SNARE, ENTRAP, ENSNARE imply seizing by some device that holds the one caught at the mercy of the captor. TRAP and SNARE apply more commonly to physical seizing ⟨*trap* animals⟩ ⟨*snared* butterflies with a net⟩. ENTRAP and ENSNARE more often are figurative ⟨*entrapped* the witness with a trick question⟩ ⟨a sting operation that *ensnared* burglars⟩. BAG implies shooting down a fleeing or distant prey ⟨*bagged* a brace of pheasants⟩.

[2]**catch** *n* (15c) **1 :** something caught; *esp* : the total quantity caught at one time ⟨a large ~ of fish⟩ **2 a :** the act, action, or fact of catching **b :** a game in which a ball is thrown and caught **3 :** something that checks or holds immovable ⟨a safety ~⟩ **4 :** one worth catching esp. as a spouse **5 :** a round for three or more unaccompanied usu. male voices often with suggestive or obscene lyrics **6 :** FRAGMENT, SNATCH **7 :** a concealed difficulty or complication ⟨there must be a ~⟩ **8 :** a momentary audible break in the voice or breath

catch·all \ˈkach-ˌȯl, ˈkech-\ *n, often attrib* (1838) : something that holds or includes odds and ends or a wide variety of things ⟨a ~ tray⟩ ⟨*dyspepsia* is a ~ term for stomach discomfort⟩

catch–as–catch–can *adj* (1764) : using any available means or method : HIT-OR-MISS ⟨a ~ system that relies on borrowed judges —Patricia Nealon⟩

catch·er \ˈka-chər, ˈke-\ *n* (15c) : one that catches; *specif* : a baseball player positioned behind home plate

catch·fly \ˈkach-ˌflī, ˈkech-\ *n* (1597) : any of various plants (as of the genera *Lychnis* and *Silene*) of the pink family often with viscid stems

catch·ing *adj* (1590) **1 :** INFECTIOUS, CONTAGIOUS ⟨the flu is ~⟩ ⟨his spirit is ~⟩ **2 :** CATCHY, ALLURING

catch·ment \ˈkach-mənt, ˈkech-\ *n* (1847) **1 :** something that catches water; *also* : the amount of water caught **2 :** the action of catching water

catchment area *n* (1885) **1 :** an area that serves to catch water **2 :** the geographical area served by an institution

catch on *vi* (ca. 1878) **1 :** to become aware : LEARN; *also* : UNDERSTAND ⟨didn't *catch on* to what was going on⟩ **2 :** to become popular ⟨this idea has already *caught on*⟩

catch out *vt* (1804) **1 :** to detect in error or wrongdoing ⟨*caught* him *out* committing perjury⟩ **2 :** to take unawares or by surprise

catch·pen·ny \ˈkach-ˌpe-nē, ˈkech-\ *adj* (1748) : using sensationalism or cheapness for appeal ⟨a ~ newspaper⟩

catch·phrase \-ˌfrāz\ *n* (1842) **1 :** a word or expression that is used repeatedly and conveniently to represent or characterize a person, group, idea, or point of view **2 :** SLOGAN 2

catch·pole *or* **catch·poll** \-ˌpōl\ *n* [ME *cacchepol,* fr. AF *cachepole,* lit., chicken chaser, fr. *cacher* + *pol* chicken, fr. L *pullus* — more at CATCH, PULLET] (bef. 12c) : a sheriff's deputy; *esp* : one who makes arrests for failure to pay a debt

catch–22 \-ˌtwen-tē-ˈtü\ *n, pl* **catch–22's** *or* **catch–22s** *often cap* [fr. *Catch-22,* paradoxical rule in the novel *Catch-22* (1961) by Joseph Heller] (1971) **1 :** a problematic situation for which the only solution is denied by a circumstance inherent in the problem or by a rule ⟨the show-business ~—no work unless you have an agent, no agent unless you've worked —Mary Murphy⟩; *also* : the circumstance or rule that denies a solution **2 a :** an illogical, unreasonable, or senseless situation **b :** a measure or policy whose effect is the opposite of what was intended **c :** a situation presenting two equally undesirable alternatives **3 :** a hidden difficulty or means of entrapment : CATCH

catchup *var of* KETCHUP

[1]**catch–up** \ˈkach-ˌəp, ˈkech-\ *adj* (1945) : intended to catch up to a theoretical norm or a competitor's accomplishments

[2]**catch–up** *n* (1948) : the act or fact of catching up or trying to catch up (as with a norm or competitor) ⟨had to play ~⟩; *also* : an increase intended to achieve catch-up

catch up *vt* (14c) **1 a :** to pick up often abruptly ⟨the thief *caught* the purse *up* and ran⟩ **b :** ENSNARE, ENTANGLE ⟨education has been *caught up* in a stultifying mythology —N. M. Pusey⟩ **c :** ENTHRALL ⟨the . . . public was *caught up* in the car's magic —D. A. Jedlicka⟩ **2 :** to provide with the latest information ⟨*catch* me *up* on the news⟩ ~ *vi* **1 a :** to travel fast enough to overtake an advance party **b :** to reach a state of parity or of being able to cope ⟨students who miss class have difficulty *catching up*⟩ **2 :** to bring about arrest for illicit activities ⟨the police *caught up* with the thieves⟩ **3 a :** to complete or compensate for something belatedly ⟨*catch up* on lost sleep⟩ **b :** to acquire belated information ⟨*catch up* on the news⟩

catch·word \ˈkach-ˌwərd, ˈkech-\ *n* (ca. 1736) **1 a :** a word under the right-hand side of the last line on a book page that repeats the first word on the following page **b :** GUIDE WORD **2 :** CATCHPHRASE 1

catchy \ˈka-chē, ˈke-chē\ *adj* **catch·i·er; -est** (1831) **1 a :** tending to catch the interest or attention ⟨a ~ title⟩ **b :** easily retained in the memory ⟨a ~ melody⟩ **2 :** FITFUL, IRREGULAR ⟨~ breathing⟩ **3 :** TRICKY ⟨a ~ question⟩

cat·claw \ˈkat-ˌklȯ\ *n* (1898) : a yellow-flowered spiny acacia (*Acacia greggi*) of the southwestern U.S. and Mexico

cat distemper *n* (ca. 1950) : PANLEUKOPENIA

cate \ˈkāt\ *n* [ME, article of purchased food, short for *acate,* fr. AF *acat, achat* purchase, fr. *acater, achater* to buy, fr. VL **accaptare,* fr. L *acceptare* to accept] (15c) *archaic* : a dainty or choice food

cat·e·che·sis \ˌka-tə-ˈkē-səs\ *n, pl* **-che·ses** \-ˌsēz\ [LL, fr. Gk *katēchēsis,* fr. *katēchein* to teach] (1753) : oral instruction of catechumens — **cat·e·chet·i·cal** \-ˈke-ti-kəl\ *adj*

cat·e·chin \ˈka-tə-ˌkin\ *n* [ISV *catechu* + [1]*-in*] (1853) **:** a crystalline flavonoid compound $C_{15}H_{14}O_6$ or its derivatives having antioxidant properties and used in dyeing and tanning

cat·e·chism \ˈka-tə-ˌki-zəm\ *n* (1502) **1 :** oral instruction **2 :** a manual for catechizing; *specif* **:** a summary of religious doctrine often in the form of questions and answers **3 a :** a set of formal questions put as a test **b :** something resembling a catechism esp. in being a rote response or formulaic statement — **cat·e·chis·mal** \ˌka-tə-ˈkiz-məl\ *adj* — **cat·e·chis·tic** \-ˈkis-tik\ *adj*

cat·e·chist \ˈka-tə-kist\ *n* (ca. 1563) **:** one that catechizes: as **a :** a teacher of catechumens **b :** a native in a missionary district who does Christian teaching

cat·e·chize \ˈka-tə-ˌkīz\ *vt* **-chized; -chiz·ing** [LL *catechizare,* fr. Gk *katēchein* to teach, lit., to din into, fr. *kata-* cata- + *ēchein* to resound, fr. *ēchē* sound — more at ECHO] (15c) **1 :** to instruct systematically esp. by questions, answers, and explanations and corrections; *specif* **:** to give religious instruction in such a manner **2 :** to question systematically or searchingly — **cat·e·chi·za·tion** \ˌka-ti-kə-ˈzā-shən\ *n* — **cat·e·chiz·er** \ˈka-tə-ˌkī-zər\ *n*

cat·e·chol \ˈka-tə-ˌkȯl, -ˌkōl\ *n* (1880) **1 :** CATECHIN **2 :** a crystalline phenol $C_6H_6O_2$ obtained from various natural sources but usu. made synthetically and used esp. in organic synthesis

cat·e·chol·amine \ˌka-tə-ˈkō-lə-ˌmēn, -ˈkȯ-\ *n* (1954) **:** any of various amines (as epinephrine, norepinephrine, and dopamine) that function as hormones or neurotransmitters or both

cat·e·chol·amin·er·gic \-ˌkō-lə-mē-ˈnər-jik, -ˌkȯ-, -mi-\ *adj* (1970) **:** involving, liberating, or mediated by catecholamine

cat·e·chu \ˈka-tə-ˌchü, -ˌshü\ *n* [prob. modif. of Malay *kachu,* of Dravidian origin; akin to Tamil & Kannada *kācu* catechu] (1683) **:** any of several dry, earthy, or resinous astringent substances obtained from tropical plants of Asia: as **a :** an extract of the heartwood of an East Indian acacia (*Acacia catechu*) **b :** GAMBIER

cat·e·chu·men \ˌka-tə-ˈkyü-mən\ *n* [ME *cathecumyn,* fr. LL *catechumenus,* fr. Gk *katēchoumenos,* pres. pass. part. of *katēchein*] (15c) **1 :** a convert to Christianity receiving training in doctrine and discipline before baptism **2 :** one receiving instruction in the basic doctrines of Christianity before admission to communicant membership in a church

cat·e·gor·i·cal \ˌka-tə-ˈgȯr-i-kəl, -ˈgär-\ *also* **cat·e·gor·ic** \-ik\ *adj* [LL *categoricus,* fr. Gk *katēgorikos,* fr. *katēgoria*] (1588) **1 :** ABSOLUTE, UNQUALIFIED ⟨a ~ denial⟩ **2 a :** of, relating to, or constituting a category **b :** involving, according with, or considered with respect to specific categories — **cat·e·gor·i·cal·ly** \-i-k(ə-)lē\ *adv*

categorical imperative *n* (1827) **:** a moral obligation or command that is unconditionally and universally binding

cat·e·go·rise *Brit var of* CATEGORIZE

cat·e·go·rize \ˈka-ti-gə-ˌrīz\ *vt* **-rized; -riz·ing** (1705) **:** to put into a category **:** CLASSIFY — **cat·e·go·ri·za·tion** \ˌka-ti-gə-rə-ˈzā-shən\ *n*

cat·e·go·ry \ˈka-tə-ˌgȯr-ē\ *n, pl* **-ries** [LL *categoria,* fr. Gk *katēgoria* predication, category, fr. *katēgorein* to accuse, affirm, predicate, fr. *kata-* + *agora* public assembly, fr. *ageirein* to gather] (1588) **1 :** any of several fundamental and distinct classes to which entities or concepts belong **2 :** a division within a system of classification

ca·te·na \kə-ˈtē-nə\ *n, pl* **-nae** \-(ˌ)nē\ *or* **-nas** [ML, fr. L, chain] (1641) **:** a connected series of related things

cat·e·nary \ˈka-tə-ˌner-ē, -ˌne-rē, *esp Brit* kə-ˈtē-nə-rē\ *n, pl* **-nar·ies** [NL *catenaria,* fr. L, fem. of *catenarius* of a chain, fr. *catena*] (1788) **1 :** the curve assumed by a cord of uniform density and cross section that is perfectly flexible but not capable of being stretched and that hangs freely from two fixed points **2 :** something in the form of a catenary — **catenary** *adj*

cat·e·nate \ˈka-tə-ˌnāt\ *vt* **-nat·ed; -nat·ing** [L *catenatus,* pp. of *catenare,* fr. *catena*] (ca. 1623) **:** to connect in a series **:** LINK — **cat·e·na·tion** \ˌka-tə-ˈnā-shən\ *n*

ca·ter \ˈkā-tər\ *vb* [obs. *cater* buyer of provisions, fr. ME *catour,* short for *acatour,* fr. AF, fr. *acater* to buy — more at CATE] *vi* (1580) **1 :** to provide a supply of food **2 :** to supply what is required or desired ⟨~*ing* to middle-class tastes⟩ ~ *vt* **:** to provide food and service for ⟨~*ed* the banquet⟩ — **ca·ter·er** \-tər-ər\ *n*

cat·er·an \ˈka-tə-rən\ *n* [ME (Sc) *ketharan,* prob. fr. ML *katheranus,* fr. ScGael *ceithearn* band of fighting men] (14c) **:** a former military irregular or brigand of the Scottish Highlands

catercorner *or* **catercornered** *var of* KITTY-CORNER

ca·ter–cous·in \ˈkā-tər-ˌkə-zᵊn\ *n* [perh. fr. obs. *cater* buyer of provisions] (1519) **:** an intimate friend

cat·er·pil·lar \ˈka-tə(r)-ˌpi-lər\ *n, often attrib* [ME *catyrpel,* fr. AF **catepelose,* lit., hairy cat] (15c) **:** the elongated wormlike larva of a butterfly or moth; *also* **:** any of various similar larvae

Caterpillar *trademark* — used for a tractor made for use on rough or soft ground and moved on two endless metal belts

cat·er·waul \ˈka-tər-ˌwȯl\ *vi* [ME *caterwawen*] (14c) **1 :** to make a harsh cry **2 :** to protest or complain noisily — **caterwaul** *n*

cat·fac·ing \ˈkat-ˌfā-siŋ\ *n* (1940) **:** a disfigurement or malformation of fruit suggesting a cat's face in appearance

cat·fight \-ˌfīt\ *n* (1919) **:** an intense fight or argument esp. between two women

cat·fish \-ˌfish\ *n* (1612) **1 :** any of an order (Siluriformes) of chiefly freshwater stout-bodied scaleless bony fishes having long tactile barbels **2 :** a person who sets up a false personal profile on a social networking site for fraudulent or deceptive purposes

cat·gut \-ˌgət\ *n* (1599) **:** a tough cord made usu. from sheep intestines

cath *abbr* **1** cathedral **2** catheter; catheterization **3** cathode

cath- — see CATA-

Cath·ar \ˈka-ˌthär\ *n, pl* **Cath·a·ri** \ˈka-thə-ˌrī, -ˌrē\ *or* **Cathars** [LL *cathari* (pl.), fr. LGk *katharoi,* fr. Gk, pl. of *katharos* pure] (1634) **:** a member of one of various ascetic and dualistic Christian sects esp. of the later Middle Ages teaching that matter is evil and professing faith in an angelic Christ who did not really undergo human birth or death — **Cath·a·rism** \ˈka-thə-ˌri-zəm\ *n* — **Cath·a·rist** \-rist\ *or* **Cath·a·ris·tic** \ˌka-thə-ˈris-tik\ *adj*

ca·thar·sis \kə-ˈthär-səs\ *n, pl* **ca·thar·ses** \-ˌsēz\ [NL, fr. Gk *katharsis,* fr. *kathairein* to cleanse, purge, fr. *katharos*] (ca. 1775) **1 :** PURGATION **2 a :** purification or purgation of the emotions (as pity and fear) primarily through art **b :** a purification or purgation that brings about spiritual renewal or release from tension **3 :** elimination of a complex by bringing it to consciousness and affording it expression

[1]**ca·thar·tic** \kə-ˈthär-tik\ *adj* [LL or Gk; LL *catharticus,* fr. Gk *kathartikos,* fr. *kathairein*] (1612) **:** of, relating to, or producing catharsis ⟨~ drugs⟩ ⟨a ~ experience⟩ — **ca·thar·tic·al·ly** \-ti-k(ə-)lē\ *adv*

[2]**cathartic** *n* (1651) **:** a cathartic medicine **:** PURGATIVE

cat·head \ˈkat-ˌhed\ *n* (1626) **:** a projecting piece of timber or iron near the bow of a ship to which the anchor is hoisted and secured

ca·thect \kə-ˈthekt, ka-\ *vt* [back-formation fr. *cathectic*] (1925) **:** to invest with mental or emotional energy

ca·thec·tic \kə-ˈthek-tik, ka-\ *adj* [NL *cathexis*] (1927) **:** of, relating to, or invested with mental or emotional energy

ca·the·dra \kə-ˈthē-drə\ *n* [L, chair — more at CHAIR] (ca. 1797) **:** a bishop's official throne

[1]**ca·the·dral** \kə-ˈthē-drəl\ *adj* (14c) **1 :** of, relating to, or containing a cathedra **2 :** emanating from a chair of authority **3 :** suggestive of a cathedral ⟨a ~ grove of redwoods⟩

[2]**cathedral** *n* (1587) **1 :** a church that is the official seat of a diocesan bishop **2 :** something that resembles or suggests a cathedral (as in size or importance) ⟨a ~ of business⟩ ⟨the sports ~⟩

cathedral 1

ca·thep·sin \kə-ˈthep-sən\ *n* [Gk *kathepsein* to digest (fr. *kata-* cata- + *hepsein* to boil) + E [2]*-in*] (1929) **:** any of several intracellular proteases of animal tissue that aid in autolysis

Cath·er·ine wheel \ˈka-th(ə-)rin-\ *n* [St. *Catherine* of Alexandria †*ab*307 Christian martyr] (1584) **1 :** a wheel with spikes projecting from the rim **2 :** PINWHEEL 1 **3 :** CARTWHEEL 2

cath·e·ter \ˈka-thə-tər, ˈkath-tər\ *n* [LL, fr. Gk *kathetēr,* fr. *kathienai* to send down, fr. *kata-* cata- + *hienai* to send — more at JET] (1601) **:** a tubular medical device for insertion into canals, vessels, passageways, or body cavities usu. to permit injection or withdrawal of fluids or to keep a passage open — compare BALLOON CATHETER

cath·e·ter·i·za·tion \ˌka-thə-tə-rə-ˈzā-shən, ˌkath-tə-rə-\ *n* (ca. 1852) **:** the use of or introduction of a catheter (as in or into the bladder, trachea, or heart) — **cath·e·ter·ize** \ˈka-thə-tə-ˌrīz, ˈkath-tə-\ *vt*

ca·thex·is \kə-ˈthek-səs, ka-\ *n, pl* **ca·thex·es** \-ˌsēz\ [NL (intended as trans. of G *Besetzung*), fr. Gk *kathexis* holding, fr. *katechein* to hold fast, occupy, fr. *kata-* + *echein* to have, hold — more at SCHEME] (1922) **:** investment of mental or emotional energy in a person, object, or idea

cath·ode \ˈka-ˌthōd\ *n* [Gk *kathodos* way down, fr. *kata-* + *hodos* way] (1834) **1 :** the electrode of an electrochemical cell at which reduction occurs: **a :** the negative terminal of an electrolytic cell **b :** the positive terminal of a galvanic cell **2 :** the electron-emitting electrode of an electron tube; *broadly* **:** the negative electrode of a diode — compare ANODE — **cath·od·al** \ˈka-ˌthō-dᵊl\ *adj* — **cath·od·al·ly** *adv* — **ca·thod·ic** \ka-ˈthä-dik, -ˈthō-\ *adj* — **ca·thod·i·cal·ly** \-di-k(ə-)lē\ *adv*

cathode ray *n* (1880) **1** *pl* **:** the high-speed electrons emitted in a stream from the heated cathode of a vacuum tube **2 :** a stream of electrons emitted from the cathode of a vacuum tube — usu. used in pl.

cathode–ray tube *n* (1905) **:** a vacuum tube in which a beam of electrons is projected on a phosphor-coated screen to produce a luminous spot at a point on the screen determined by the effect on the electron beam of a variable magnetic field within the tube

cathodic protection *n* (1930) **:** the prevention of electrolytic corrosion of a usu. metallic structure (as a pipeline) by causing it to act as the cathode rather than as the anode of an electrochemical cell

cath·o·lic \ˈkath-lik, ˈka-thə-\ *adj* [ME *catholik,* fr. MF & LL; MF *catholique,* fr. LL *catholicus,* fr. Gk *katholikos* universal, general, fr. *katholou* in general, fr. *kata* by + *holos* whole — more at CATA-, SAFE] (14c) **1 a** *often cap* **:** of, relating to, or forming the church universal **b** *often cap* **:** of, relating to, or forming the ancient undivided Christian church or a church claiming historical continuity from it **c** *cap* **:** ROMAN CATHOLIC **2 :** COMPREHENSIVE, UNIVERSAL; *esp* **:** broad in sympathies, tastes, or interests ⟨a ~ taste in music⟩ — **ca·thol·i·cal·ly** \kə-ˈthä-li-k(ə-)lē\ *adv* — **ca·thol·i·cize** \-ˈthä-lə-ˌsīz\ *vb*

Cath·o·lic \ˈkath-lik, ˈka-thə-\ *n* (15c) **1 :** a person who belongs to the universal Christian church **2 :** a member of a Catholic church; *esp* **:** ROMAN CATHOLIC

Catholic Apostolic *adj* (1888) **:** of or relating to a Christian sect founded in 19th century England in anticipation of Christ's second coming

ca·thol·i·cate \kə-ˈthä-lə-ˌkāt, -kət\ *n* (1850) **:** the jurisdiction of a catholicos

Catholic Epistles *n pl* (1582) **:** the five New Testament letters including James, I and II Peter, I John, and Jude addressed to the early Christian churches at large

Ca·thol·i·cism \kə-ˈthä-lə-ˌsi-zəm\ *n* (1582) **1 :** ROMAN CATHOLICISM **2 :** the faith, practice, or system of Catholic Christianity

cath·o·lic·i·ty \ˌka-thə-ˈli-sə-tē, ˌkath-ˈli-\ *n, pl* **-ties** (1704) **1** *cap* **:** the character of being in conformity with a Catholic church **2 a :** liberality of sentiments or views ⟨~ of viewpoint —W. V. O'Connor⟩ **b :** UNIVERSALITY **c :** comprehensive range ⟨~ of topics⟩

ca·thol·i·con \kə-ˈthä-lə-ˌkän\ *n* [ME, fr. ML, fr. Gk *katholikon,* neut. of *katholikos*] (15c) **:** CURE-ALL, PANACEA

ca·thol·i·cos \kə-ˈthä-li-kōs\ *n, pl* **-i·cos·es** \-kō-səz\ *or* **-i·coi** \-ˌkȯi\ *often cap* [LGk *katholikos,* fr. Gk, general] (1878) **:** a primate of certain Eastern churches and esp. of the Armenian or of the Nestorian church

cat·house \ˈkat-ˌhau̇s\ *n* (1882) : BORDELLO

cat·ion \ˈkat-ˌī-ən, ˈka-(ˌ)tī-ən\ *n* [Gk *kation,* neut. of *katiōn,* prp. of *katienai* to go down, fr. *kata-* cata- + *ienai* to go — more at ISSUE] (1834) : the ion in an electrolyzed solution that migrates to the cathode; *broadly* : a positively charged ion

cat·ion·ic \ˌkat-(ˌ)ī-ˈä-nik, ˌka-(ˌ)tī-\ *adj* (ca. 1920) **1** : of, relating to, or being a cation **2** : characterized by an active and esp. surface-active cation ⟨a ~ dye⟩ — **cat·ion·i·cal·ly** \-ni-k(ə-)lē\ *adv*

cat·kin \ˈkat-kən\ *n* [fr. its resemblance to a cat's tail] (1578) : a spicate inflorescence (as of the willow, birch, or oak) bearing scaly bracts and unisexual usu. apetalous flowers — called also *ament*

cat·like \ˈkat-ˌlīk\ *adj or adv* (1554) : resembling a cat; *esp* : STEALTHY ⟨with ~ tread, upon our prey we steal —W. S. Gilbert⟩

cat·mint \-ˌmint\ *n* (13c) : any of a genus (*Nepeta*) of Old World temperate-zone herbs of the mint family; *esp* : CATNIP 1

cat·nap \-ˌnap\ *n* (1823) : a very short light nap — **catnap** *vi*

cat·nap·per *also* **cat·nap·er** \ˈkat-ˌna-pər\ *n* [1cat + -napper (as in *kidnapper*)] (1942) : one who steals cats usu. to sell them for research

cat·nip \-ˌnip\ *n* [1cat + obs. *nep* catnip, fr. ME, fr. OE *nepte,* fr. L *nepeta*] (1712) **1** : a strong-scented perennial mint (*Nepeta cataria*) that has whorls of small pale flowers in terminal spikes and contains a substance attractive to cats **2** : something very attractive

cat–o'–nine–tails \ˌka-tə-ˈnīn-ˌtālz\ *n, pl* **cat–o'–nine–tails** [fr. the resemblance of its scars to the scratches of a cat] (1665) : a whip made of usu. nine knotted lines or cords fastened to a handle

ca·top·tric \kə-ˈtäp-trik\ *adj* [Gk *katoptrikos,* fr. *katoptron* mirror, fr. *katopsesthai* to be going to observe, fr. *kata-* + *opsesthai* to be going to see — more at OPTIC] (ca. 1766) : being or using a mirror to focus light

cat rig *n* (1867) : a rig consisting of a single mast far forward carrying a single large sail extended by a boom — **cat–rigged** \ˈkat-ˈrigd\ *adj*

cats and dogs *adv* (1738) : in great quantities : very hard ⟨it was raining *cats and dogs*⟩

CAT scan \ˈkat-\ *n* [computerized *a*xial *t*omography] (1975) : an image made by computed tomography — **CAT scanning** *n*

CAT scanner *n* (1975) : a medical instrument consisting of integrated X-ray and computing equipment and used for computed tomography

cat's cradle *n* (1754) **1** : a game in which a string looped in a pattern like a cradle on the fingers of one person's hands is transferred to the hands of another so as to form a different figure **2** : something that is intricate, complicated, or elaborate ⟨a *cat's cradle* of red tape⟩

cat scratch disease *n* (1952) : an illness that is characterized by swelling of the lymph glands, fever, and chills and is caused by a bacterium (*Bartonella henselae* syn. *Rochalimaea henselae*) transmitted esp. by a cat scratch — called also *cat scratch fever*

cat's–eye \ˈkat-ˌsī\ *n, pl* **cat's–eyes** (ca. 1599) **1** : any of various gems (as a chrysoberyl or a chalcedony) exhibiting opalescent reflections from within **2** : a marble with eyelike concentric circles

cat's meow *n* (1926) : a highly admired person or thing

cat's–paw \ˈkats-ˌpȯ\ *n, pl* **cat's–paws** (ca. 1769) **1** : a light air that ruffles the surface of the water in irregular patches during a calm **2** [fr. the fable of the monkey that used a cat's paw to draw chestnuts from the fire] : one used by another as a tool : DUPE ⟨the . . . government became the ~ for foreign powers —D. J. Boorstin⟩ **3** : a hitch knot formed with two eyes for attaching a line to a hook — see KNOT illustration

cat·suit \ˈkat-ˌsüt\ *n* (1960) : a close-fitting one-piece garment that covers the torso and the legs and sometimes the arms

catsup *var of* KETCHUP

cat·tail \ˈkat-ˌtāl\ *n* (1548) : any of a genus (*Typha* of the family Typhaceae, the cattail family) of tall reedy marsh plants with brown furry fruiting spikes; *esp* : a plant (*Typha latifolia*) with long flat leaves used esp. for making mats and chair seats

cat·tery \ˈka-tə-rē\ *n, pl* **-ter·ies** (ca. 1843) : an establishment for the breeding and boarding of cats

cat·tle \ˈka-tᵊl\ *n pl* [ME *catel,* fr. AF *katil, chatel* personal property, fr. ML *capitale,* fr. L, neut. of *capitalis* of the head — more at CAPITAL] (14c) **1** : domesticated quadrupeds held as property or raised for use; *specif* : bovine animals on a farm or ranch **2** : human beings esp. en masse

cattle call *n* (1952) : a mass audition (as of actors)

cattle egret *n* (ca. 1899) : a small Old World white egret (*Bubulcus ibis*) introduced into the New World and having a yellow bill and in the breeding season buff on the crown, breast, and back

cattle grub *n* (1926) : either of two warble flies (genus *Hypoderma*) esp. in the larval stage: **a** : COMMON CATTLE GRUB **b** : a related warble fly (*H. bovis*)

cattle guard *n* (1843) : a shallow ditch with rails or bars laid across that are spread far enough apart to prevent livestock from crossing but not people or vehicles

cat·tle·man \-mən, -ˌman\ *n* (1864) : one who tends or raises cattle

cattle prod *n* (1970) : a handheld prodding device that delivers an electric shock (as in controlling cattle)

cattle tick *n* (1869) : either of two ixodid ticks (*Boophilus annulatus* and *B. microplus*) that infest cattle and transmit the protozoan which causes Texas fever

cat·tle·ya \ˈkat-lē-ə; kat-ˈlā-ə, -ˈlē-\ *n* [NL, fr. Wm. *Cattley* †1832 Eng. patron of botany] (1828) : any of a genus (*Cattleya*) of tropical American epiphytic orchids with showy hooded flowers

1**cat·ty** \ˈka-tē\ *n, pl* **catties** [Malay *kati*] (1598) : any of various units of weight of China and southeast Asia varying around 1⅓ pounds (about 600 grams); *also* : a standard Chinese unit equal to 1.1023 pounds (500 grams)

2**catty** *adj* **cat·ti·er; -est** (1886) **1** : resembling a cat; *esp* : slyly spiteful : MALICIOUS ⟨made several ~ comments⟩ **2** : of or relating to a cat — **cat·ti·ly** \ˈka-tə-lē\ *adv* — **cat·ti·ness** \ˈka-tē-nəs\ *n*

catty–corner *or* **catty–cornered** *var of* KITTY-CORNER

CATV *abbr* **1** cable television **2** community antenna television

cat·walk \ˈkat-ˌwȯk\ *n* (1845) : a narrow walkway (as along a bridge)

Cau·ca·sian \kȯ-ˈkā-zhən, kä- *also* -ˈka-zhən\ *adj* (1658) **1** : of or relating to the Caucasus or its inhabitants **2** : of, constituting, or characteristic of a race of humankind native to Europe, No. Africa, and southwest Asia and classified according to physical features — used esp. in referring to persons of European descent having usu. light skin pigmentation — **Caucasian** *n* — **Cau·ca·soid** \ˈkȯ-kə-ˌsȯid\ *adj or n*

Cau·chy sequence \kō-ˈshē-, ˈkō-shē-\ *n* [Augustin-Louis *Cauchy* †1857 Fr. mathematician] (ca. 1949) : a sequence of elements in a metric space such that for any positive number no matter how small there exists a term in the sequence for which the distance between any two terms beyond this term is less than the arbitrarily small number

1**cau·cus** \ˈkȯ-kəs\ *n* [origin unknown] (1760) : a closed meeting of a group of persons belonging to the same political party or faction usu. to select candidates or to decide on policy; *also* : a group of people united to promote an agreed-upon cause

2**caucus** *vi* (1788) : to meet in or hold a caucus

cau·dad \ˈkȯ-ˌdad\ *adv* [L *cauda*] (1888) : toward the tail or posterior end

cau·dal \ˈkȯ-dᵊl\ *adj* [NL *caudalis,* fr. L *cauda* tail] (1661) **1** : of, relating to, or being a tail **2** : directed toward or situated in or near the tail or posterior part of the body — **cau·dal·ly** \-də-lē\ *adv*

cau·date \ˈkȯ-ˌdāt\ *adj* (1600) : having a tail or a taillike appendage

caudate nucleus *n* (1902) : the most medial of the four basal ganglia in each cerebral hemisphere — called also *caudate*

cau·dex \ˈkȯ-ˌdeks\ *n, pl* **cau·di·ces** \ˈkȯ-də-ˌsēz\ *or* **cau·dex·es** [L, tree trunk or stem] (ca. 1797) **1** : the stem of a palm or tree fern **2** : the woody base of a perennial plant

cau·di·llis·mo \ˌkau̇-t͟hē-ˈyēz-(ˌ)mō, -t͟hēl-ˈyēz-\ *n* [Sp, fr. *caudillo*] (1927) : the doctrine or practice of a caudillo

cau·di·llo \kau̇-ˈt͟hē-(ˌ)yō, -ˈt͟hēl-(ˌ)yō\ *n, pl* **-llos** [Sp, chief, leader, fr. LL *capitellum* small head — more at CADET] (1852) : a Spanish or Latin-American military dictator

cau·dle \ˈkȯ-dᵊl\ *n* [ME *caudel,* fr. AF **caudel, chaudel* fr. *calt, chaut* warm, fr. L *calidus* — more at CAULDRON] (14c) : a drink (as for invalids) usu. of warm ale or wine mixed with bread or gruel, eggs, sugar, and spices

1**caught** \ˈkȯt\ *past and past part of* CATCH

2**caught** *adj* (1858) : PREGNANT — often used in the phrase *get caught*

caul \ˈkȯl\ *n* [ME *calle* net, omentum, prob. fr. OE *cawl* basket] (14c) **1** : the large fatty omentum covering the intestines (as of a cow, sheep, or pig) **2** : the inner fetal membrane of higher vertebrates esp. when covering the head at birth

caul·dron *also* **cal·dron** \ˈkȯl-drən\ *n* [ME *caudron, caldron,* fr. AF *cauderon,* dim. of *caldere* basin, fr. LL *caldaria,* fr. fem. of L *caldarius* used for hot water, fr. *calidus* warm, fr. *calēre* to be warm — more at LEE] (14c) **1** : a large kettle or boiler **2** : something resembling a boiling cauldron in intensity or degree of agitation ⟨a ~ of intense emotions⟩

cau·li·flow·er \ˈkȯ-li-ˌflau̇(-ə)r, ˈkä-, -lē-\ *n, often attrib* [It *cavolfiore,* fr. *cavolo* cabbage (fr. LL *caulus,* fr. L *caulis* stem, cabbage) + *fiore* flower, fr. L *flor-, flos* — more at COLE, BLOW] (1597) : a garden plant (*Brassica oleracea botrytis*) related to the cabbage and grown for its compact edible head of usu. white undeveloped flowers; *also* : its flower cluster used as a vegetable

cauliflower ear *n* (1904) : an ear deformed from injury and excessive growth of reparative tissue

cau·li·flow·er·et \ˌkȯ-li-ˌflau̇(-ə)-ˈret, ˌkä-, -lē-\ *n* (1946) : a bite-size piece of cauliflower

cau·line \ˈkȯ-ˌlīn\ *adj* [prob. fr. NL *caulinus,* fr. L *caulis*] (1756) : of, relating to, or growing on a stem and esp. on the upper part

1**caulk** *or* **calk** \ˈkȯk\ *vt* [ME *caulken,* fr. AF *cauker, calcher, chalcher* to trample, fr. L *calcare,* fr. *calc-, calx* heel] (15c) : to stop up and make tight against leakage (as a boat or its seams, the cracks in a window frame, or the joints of a pipe) — **caulk·er** *n*

2**caulk** *or* **calk** *also* **caulk·ing** *or* **calk·ing** \ˈkȯ-kiŋ\ *n* (1954) : material used to caulk

3**caulk** *var of* 2CALK *or of* 3CALK

caus *abbr* causative

caus·al \ˈkȯ-zəl\ *adj* (ca. 1530) **1** : expressing or indicating cause : CAUSATIVE ⟨a ~ clause introduced by *since*⟩ **2** : of, relating to, or constituting a cause ⟨the ~ agent of a disease⟩ **3** : involving causation or a cause : marked by cause and effect ⟨a ~ link⟩ **4** : arising from a cause ⟨a ~ development⟩ — **caus·al·ly** \-zə-lē\ *adv*

cau·sal·gia \kȯ-ˈzal-j(ē-)ə, -ˈsal-\ *n* [NL, fr. Gk *kausos* fever (fr. *kaiein* to burn) + NL *-algia*] (1872) : a constant usu. burning pain resulting from injury to a peripheral nerve — **cau·sal·gic** \-jik\ *adj*

cau·sal·i·ty \kȯ-ˈza-lə-tē\ *n, pl* **-ties** (1603) **1** : a causal quality or agency **2** : the relation between a cause and its effect or between regularly correlated events or phenomena

cau·sa·tion \kȯ-ˈzā-shən\ *n* (1615) **1 a** : the act or process of causing **b** : the act or agency which produces an effect **2** : CAUSALITY

caus·a·tive \ˈkȯ-zə-tiv\ *adj* (15c) **1** : effective or operating as a cause or agent ⟨~ bacteria of cholera⟩ **2** : expressing causation; *specif* : being a linguistic form that indicates that the subject causes an act to be performed or a condition to come into being — **causative** *n* — **caus·a·tive·ly** *adv*

1**cause** \ˈkȯz\ *n* [ME, fr. AF, fr. L *causa*] (13c) **1 a** : a reason for an action or condition : MOTIVE **b** : something that brings about an effect or a result **c** : a person or thing that is the occasion of an action or state; *esp* : an agent that brings something about **d** : sufficient reason ⟨discharged for ~⟩ **2 a** : a ground of legal action **b** : CASE **3** : a matter or question to be decided **4 a** : a principle or movement militantly defended or supported **b** : a charitable undertaking ⟨for a good ~⟩ — **cause·less** \-ləs\ *adj*

2**cause** *vt* **caused; caus·ing** (14c) **1** : to serve as a cause or occasion of ⟨~ an accident⟩ **2** : to compel by command, authority, or force ⟨*caused* him to resign⟩ — **caus·er** *n*

'cause \ˈkȯz, ˈkəz\ *conj* (15c) : BECAUSE

cause cé·lè·bre *also* **cause ce·le·bre** \ˌkȯz-sə-ˈleb, -ˈle-brə, ˌkōz-, -ˈlebrᵊ\ *n, pl* **causes cé·lè·bres** *also* **causes celebres** *same*\ [F, lit., celebrated case] (1763) **1** : a legal case that excites widespread interest **2** : a notorious person, thing, incident, or episode

cause of action (15c) : the grounds (as violation of a right) that entitle a plaintiff to bring a suit

cau·se·rie \ˌkōz-ˈrē, ˌkō-zə-\ *n* [F, fr. *causer* to chat, fr. L *causari* to plead, discuss, fr. *causa*] (1818) **1** : an informal conversation : CHAT **2** : a short informal essay

cause·way \ˈkȯz-ˌwā\ *n* [ME *cauciwey,* fr. *cauci* + *wey* way] (15c) **1** : a raised way across wet ground or water **2** : HIGHWAY; *esp* : one of ancient Roman construction in Britain — **causeway** *vt*

cau·sey \ˈkȯ-zē\ *n, pl* **causeys** [ME *cauci,* fr. AF *causee, chaucee,* fr. ML *calciata* paved highway, prob. fr. L *calc-, calx* limestone — more at CHALK] (14c) **1** : CAUSEWAY 1 **2** *obs* : CAUSEWAY 2

[1]**caus·tic** \ˈkȯs-tik\ *adj* [L *causticus,* fr. Gk *kaustikos,* fr. *kaiein* to burn] (14c) **1** : capable of destroying or eating away by chemical action : CORROSIVE **2** : marked by incisive sarcasm **3** : relating to or being the surface or curve of a caustic — **caus·ti·cal·ly** \-ti-k(ə-)lē\ *adv* — **caus·tic·i·ty** \kȯ-ˈsti-sə-tē\ *n*

syn CAUSTIC, MORDANT, ACRID, SCATHING mean stingingly incisive. CAUSTIC suggests a biting wit ⟨*caustic* comments⟩. MORDANT suggests a wit that is used with deadly effectiveness ⟨*mordant* reviews of the play⟩. ACRID implies bitterness and often malevolence ⟨*acrid* invective⟩. SCATHING implies indignant attacks delivered with fierce severity ⟨a *scathing* satire⟩.

[2]**caustic** *n* (15c) **1** : a caustic agent: as **a** : a substance that burns or destroys organic tissue by chemical action **b** : SODIUM HYDROXIDE **2** : the envelope of rays emanating from a point and reflected or refracted by a curved surface

caustic potash *n* (1839) : POTASSIUM HYDROXIDE

caustic soda *n* (1796) : SODIUM HYDROXIDE

cau·ter·ize \ˈkȯ-tə-ˌrīz\ *vt* **-ized; -iz·ing** (14c) **1** : to sear with a cautery or caustic ⟨∼ a wound⟩ **2** : to make insensible : DEADEN — **cau·ter·i·za·tion** \ˌkȯ-tə-rə-ˈzā-shən\ *n*

cau·tery \ˈkȯ-tə-rē\ *n, pl* **-ter·ies** [L *cauterium,* fr. Gk *kautērion* branding iron, fr. *kaiein*] (14c) **1** : the act or effect of cauterizing : CAUTERIZATION **2** : an agent (as a hot iron or caustic) used to burn, sear, or destroy tissue

[1]**cau·tion** \ˈkȯ-shən\ *n* [L *caution-, cautio* precaution, fr. *cavēre* to be on one's guard — more at HEAR] (1566) **1** : WARNING, ADMONISHMENT **2** : PRECAUTION **3** : prudent forethought to minimize risk **4** : one that astonishes or commands attention ⟨some shoes you see . . . these days are a ∼ —*Esquire*⟩ — **cau·tion·ary** \-shə-ˌner-ē, -ne-rē\ *adj*

[2]**caution** *vt* **cau·tioned; cau·tion·ing** \ˈkȯ-sh(ə-)niŋ\ (1683) : to advise caution to : WARN

cau·tious \ˈkȯ-shəs\ *adj* (1614) : marked by or given to caution ⟨∼ investors⟩ ⟨∼ optimism⟩ — **cau·tious·ly** *adv* — **cau·tious·ness** *n*

syn CAUTIOUS, CIRCUMSPECT, WARY, CHARY mean prudently watchful and discreet in the face of danger or risk. CAUTIOUS implies the exercise of forethought usu. prompted by fear of danger ⟨a *cautious* driver⟩. CIRCUMSPECT suggests less fear and stresses the surveying of all possible consequences before acting or deciding ⟨*circumspect* in his business dealings⟩. WARY emphasizes suspiciousness and alertness in watching for danger and cunning in escaping it ⟨keeps a *wary* eye on the competition⟩. CHARY implies a cautious reluctance to give, act, or speak freely ⟨*chary* of signing papers without having read them first⟩.

cav *abbr* **1** cavalry **2** cavity

cav·al·cade \ˌka-vəl-ˈkād, ˈka-vəl-ˌ\ *n* [F, ride on horseback, fr. OIt *cavalcata,* fr. *cavalcare* to go on horseback, fr. LL *caballicare,* fr. L *caballus* horse; akin to Gk *kaballeion* horse, MIr *capall* workhorse] (1644) **1 a** : a procession of riders or carriages **b** : a procession of vehicles or ships **2** : a dramatic sequence or procession : SERIES

[1]**cav·a·lier** \ˌka-və-ˈlir\ *n* [MF, fr. OIt *cavaliere,* fr. Old Occitan *cavalier,* fr. LL *caballarius* horseman, fr. L *caballus*] (1589) **1** : a gentleman trained in arms and horsemanship **2** : a mounted soldier : KNIGHT **3** *cap* : an adherent of Charles I of England **4** : GALLANT

[2]**cavalier** *adj* (ca. 1641) **1** : DEBONAIR **2** : marked by or given to offhand and often disdainful dismissal of important matters ⟨a ∼ attitude toward money⟩ **3 a** *cap* : of or relating to the party of Charles I of England in his struggles with the Puritans and Parliament **b** : ARISTOCRATIC **c** *cap* : of or relating to the English Cavalier poets of the mid-17th century — **ca·va·lier·ism** \-ˌi-zəm\ *n* — **cav·a·lier·ly** *adv*

Cavalier King Charles spaniel \-ˈchär(-ə)lz-\ *n* [[1]*cavalier* + *King Charles spaniel,* a breed of toy spaniel, fr. *Charles* II of England] (1969) : any of a breed of toy spaniels developed in Great Britain from English toy spaniels and having a tapered muzzle and a long silky coat

ca·val·la \kə-ˈva-lə\ *n, pl* **-la** *or* **-las** [Sp *caballa,* a fish, fr. LL, mare, fem. of L *caballus*] (1624) **1** *also* **ca·val·ly** \-ˈva-lē\ : any of various carangid fishes **2** : KING MACKEREL

cav·al·let·ti *also* **cav·a·let·ti** \ˌka-və-ˈle-tē\ *n pl but sing or pl in constr* [It, pl. of *cavalletto* trestle, dim. of *cavallo* horse, fr. L *caballus*] (1950) : a series of timber jumps that are adjustable in height for schooling horses

cav·al·ry \ˈka-vəl-rē, ÷ˈkal-və-rē\ *n, pl* **-ries** [It *cavalleria* cavalry, chivalry, fr. *cavaliere*] (1546) **1 a** : an army component mounted on horseback **b** : an army component moving in motor vehicles or helicopters and assigned to combat missions that require great mobility **2** : HORSEMEN ⟨a thousand ∼ in flight⟩

cav·al·ry·man \-rē-mən, -ˌman\ *n* (1860) : a cavalry soldier

cavalry twill *n* (1939) : TRICOTINE

cav·a·ti·na \ˌka-və-ˈtē-nə, ˌkä-\ *n* [It, fr. *cavata* production of sound from an instrument, extraction, fr. *cavare* to dig out, fr. L, to make hollow, fr. *cavus*] (1813) **1** : an operatic solo simpler and briefer than an aria **2** : a songlike instrumental piece or movement

[1]**cave** \ˈkāv\ *n* [ME, fr. AF, fr. L *cava,* fr. *cavus* hollow; akin to Gk *koilos* hollow, and prob. to Gk *kyein* to be pregnant — more at CYME] (13c) **1** : a natural chamber or series of chambers in the earth or in the side of a hill or cliff **2** : a usu. underground chamber for storage ⟨a wine ∼⟩; *also* : the articles stored there

[2]**cave** *vb* **caved; cav·ing** *vt* (15c) : to form a cave in or under ∼ *vi* : to explore caves esp. as a sport or hobby — **cav·er** \ˈkā-vər\ *n*

[3]**cave** \ˈkāv\ *vb* **caved; cav·ing** [prob. alter. of *calve*] *vi* (1513) **1** : to fall in or down esp. from being undermined — usu. used with *in* **2** : to cease to resist : SUBMIT — usu. used with *in* ∼ *vt* : to cause to fall or collapse — usu. used with *in*

ca·ve·at \ˈka-vē-ˌät, -ˌat; ˈkä-vē-ˌät; ˈkā-vē-ˌat\ *n* [L, let him beware, fr. *cavēre* — more at HEAR] (1533) **1 a** : a warning enjoining one from certain acts or practices **b** : an explanation to prevent misinterpretation **c** : a modifying or cautionary detail to be considered when evaluating, interpreting, or doing something **2** : a legal warning to a judicial officer to suspend a proceeding until the opposition has a hearing

caveat emp·tor \-ˈem(p)-tər, -ˌtȯr\ *n* [NL, let the buyer beware] (1523) : a principle in commerce: without a warranty the buyer takes the risk

cave bear *n* (1865) : a very large extinct bear (*Ursus spelaeus*) known esp. from Pleistocene deposits in European caves

cave dweller *n* (1865) **1** : one (as a prehistoric human) that dwells in a cave **2** : one that lives in a city apartment building

cave–in \ˈkāv-ˌin\ *n* (1860) **1** : the action of caving in **2** : a place where earth has caved in

cave·man \ˈkāv-ˌman\ *n* (1865) **1** : a cave dweller esp. of the Stone Age **2** : a man who acts in a rough or crude manner

[1]**cav·ern** \ˈka-vərn *also* -vrən\ *n* [ME *caverne,* fr. MF, fr. L *caverna,* fr. *cavus*] (14c) : CAVE; *esp* : one of large or indefinite extent

[2]**cavern** *vt* (ca. 1630) **1** : to place in or as if in a cavern **2** : to form a cavern of : HOLLOW — used with *out*

cav·er·nic·o·lous \ˌka-vər-ˈni-kə-ləs\ *adj* (ca. 1889) : inhabiting caves

cav·ern·ous \ˈka-vər-nəs\ *adj* (15c) **1 a** : having caverns or cavities **b** *of animal tissue* : composed largely of vascular sinuses and capable of dilating with blood to bring about the erection of a body part **2** : constituting or suggesting a cavern ⟨a ∼ warehouse⟩ — **cav·ern·ous·ly** *adv*

ca·vet·to \kə-ˈve-(ˌ)tō, kä-\ *n, pl* **-ti** \-tē\ [It, fr. *cavo* hollow, fr. L *cavus*] (1664) : a concave molding having a curve that approximates a quarter circle — see MOLDING illustration

cav·i·ar *also* **cav·i·are** \ˈka-vē-ˌär *also* ˈkä-\ *n* [earlier *cavery, caviarie,* fr. obs. It *caviari,* pl. of *caviaro,* fr. Turk *havyar*] (ca. 1560) **1** : processed salted roe of large fish (as sturgeon) **2** : something considered too delicate or lofty for mass appreciation — usu. used in the phrase *caviar to the general* **3** : something considered the best of its kind

cav·il \ˈka-vəl\ *vb* **-iled** *or* **-illed; -il·ing** *or* **-il·ling** \ˈka-və-liŋ, ˈkav-liŋ\ [L *cavillari* to jest, cavil, fr. *cavilla* raillery; akin to L *calvi* to deceive — more at CALUMNY] *vi* (1542) : to raise trivial and frivolous objection ∼ *vt* : to raise trivial objections to — **cavil** *n* — **cav·il·er** *or* **cav·il·ler** \ˈka-və-lər, ˈkav-lər\ *n*

cav·ing \ˈkā-viŋ\ *n* (1932) : the sport of exploring caves : SPELUNKING

cav·i·tary \ˈka-və-ˌter-ē, -ˌte-rē\ *adj* (1835) : of, relating to, or characterized by bodily cavitation ⟨∼ tuberculosis⟩ ⟨∼ lesions⟩

cav·i·tate \ˈka-və-ˌtāt\ *vb* **-tat·ed; -tat·ing** *vi* (1909) : to form cavities or bubbles ∼ *vt* : to cavitate in

cav·i·ta·tion \ˌka-və-ˈtā-shən\ *n* [*cavity* + *-ation*] (1895) : the process of cavitating: as **a** : the formation of partial vacuums in a liquid by a swiftly moving solid body (as a propeller) or by high-intensity sound waves; *also* : the pitting and wearing away of solid surfaces (as of metal or concrete) as a result of the collapse of these vacuums in surrounding liquid **b** : the formation of cavities in an organ or tissue esp. in disease

cav·i·ty \ˈka-və-tē\ *n, pl* **-ties** [MF *cavité,* fr. LL *cavitas,* fr. L *cavus*] (1541) **1** : an unfilled space within a mass; *esp* : a hollowed-out space **2** : an area of decay in a tooth : CARIES

ca·vort \kə-ˈvȯrt\ *vi* [perh. alter. of *curvet*] (1794) **1** : to leap or dance about in a lively manner **2** : to engage in extravagant behavior

CAVU *abbr* ceiling and visibility unlimited

ca·vy \ˈkā-vē\ *n, pl* **cavies** [NL *Cavia,* genus name, fr. obs. Pg *çavia* (now *sauiá*) the spiny rat *Makalata* (*Echimys*) *armata,* fr. Tupi *saujá*] (1796) : any of several short-tailed rough-haired So. American rodents (family Caviidae); *esp* : GUINEA PIG

caw \ˈkȯ\ *vi* [imit.] (1589) : to utter the harsh raucous natural call of the crow or a similar cry — **caw** *n*

cay \ˈkē, ˈkā\ *n* [Sp *cayo* — more at KEY] (1707) : a low island or reef of sand or coral

cay·enne \(ˌ)kī-ˈen, (ˌ)kā-; ˈkī-ˌ, ˈkā-ˌ\ *n* (1773) : CAYENNE PEPPER

cayenne pepper *n* [by folk etymology fr. earlier *cayan,* ultim. modif. of Tupi *kiʔijá, kiʔiⁿyá*] (1756) **1** : a pungent condiment consisting of the ground dried fruits or seeds of hot peppers **2** : HOT PEPPER; *esp* : any of several cultivated peppers of a variety (*Capsicum annuum longum*) with very long twisted pungent red fruits **3** : the fruit of a cayenne pepper

cayman *var of* CAIMAN

Ca·yu·ga \kā-ˈyü-gə, kī-\ *n, pl* **Cayuga** *or* **Cayugas** [Cayuga **kayó·kwę,* a 17th cent. Cayuga town] (1743) **1** : a member of an American Indian people of New York **2** : the Iroquoian language of the Cayuga people

Cay·use \ˈkī-ˌyüs, kī-ˈ\ *n, pl* **Cayuse** *or* **Cayuses** [origin unknown] (1825) **1** : a member of an American Indian people of Oregon and Washington **2** *pl cayuses, not cap, West* : a native range horse

[1]**Cb** *abbr* cumulonimbus

[2]**Cb** *symbol* columbium

CB \ˌsē-ˈbē\ *n* (1959) : CITIZENS BAND; *also* : the radio transmitting and receiving set used for citizens-band communications

CBC *abbr* **1** Canadian Broadcasting Corporation **2** complete blood count

CBD *abbr* **1** cash before delivery **2** central business district

CBE *abbr* **1** commander of the Order of the British Empire **2** companion of the Order of the British Empire

CBer \(ˌ)sē-ˈbē-ər, -ˈbir\ *n* (1959) : one that operates a CB radio

CBI *abbr* computer-based instruction

CBO *abbr* Congressional Budget Office

CBS *abbr* Columbia Broadcasting System

CBW *abbr* chemical and biological warfare

[1]**cc** \ˌsē-ˈsē\ *vt* **cc'd; cc'·ing** [fr. *CC* (carbon copy)] (1983) : to send someone a copy of (an e-mail, letter, or memo) ⟨∼ an e-mail to a co-worker⟩; *also* : to send a copy to (someone) ⟨he *cc'd* me on his reply⟩

[2]**cc** *abbr* cubic centimeter

Cc *abbr* cirrocumulus

CC *abbr* **1** carbon copy **2** chief clerk **3** closed-captioned **4** common carrier **5** community college **6** country club

CCC *abbr* Civilian Conservation Corps

[1]**CCD** \ˌsē-(ˌ)sē-ˈdē\ *n* (1971) : CHARGE-COUPLED DEVICE

[2]**CCD** *abbr* Confraternity of Christian Doctrine

C–clamp \ˈsē-ˌklamp\ *n* (1926) : a C-shaped general-purpose clamp

C clef *n* (1596) : a movable clef indicating middle C by its placement on one of the lines of the staff

CCTV *abbr* closed-circuit television

\ə\ **a**but \ᵊ\ kitten, F table \ər\ **fur**ther \a\ **a**sh \ā\ **a**ce \ä\ m**o**p, m**a**r
\au̇\ **ou**t \ch\ **ch**in \e\ b**e**t \ē\ **ea**sy \g\ **g**o \i\ h**i**t \ī\ **i**ce \j\ **j**ob
\ŋ\ si**ng** \ō\ g**o** \ȯ\ l**aw** \ȯi\ b**oy** \th\ **th**in \t͟h\ **th**e \ü\ l**oo**t \u̇\ f**oo**t
\y\ **y**et \zh\ vi**s**ion, beige \k, ⁿ, œ, ue, ʸ\ *see* Guide to Pronunciation

CCU *abbr* **1** cardiac care unit **2** coronary care unit **3** critical care unit
ccw *abbr* counterclockwise
cd *abbr* **1** candela **2** candle **3** cord
Cd *symbol* cadmium
1**CD** \ˌsē-ˈdē\ *n* (1965) : CERTIFICATE OF DEPOSIT
2**CD** *n* [compact *d*isc] (1979) : a small optical disk usu. containing recorded music or computer data; *also* : the content (as music or a computer program) of a CD released as a unit ⟨promoting her latest ~⟩
3**CD** *abbr* **1** carried down **2** civil defense **3** [F *corps diplomatique*] diplomatic corps
CDC *abbr* Centers for Disease Control; Centers for Disease Control and Prevention
CDD *abbr* certificate of disability for discharge
CD4 \ˌsē-(ˌ)dē-ˈfȯr\ *n, often attrib* [cluster of *d*ifferentiation] (1984) : a large glycoprotein that is found on the surface esp. of helper T cells, that is the receptor for HIV, and that usu. functions to facilitate recognition of antigens by helper T cells
Cdn *abbr* Canadian
cDNA \ˈsē-ˌdē-(ˌ)en-ˈā, ˌsē-\ *n* [complementary] (1973) : a DNA that is complementary to a given RNA which serves as a template for synthesis of the DNA in the presence of reverse transcriptase
CDP *abbr* certificate in data processing
CDR *abbr* commander
CD–ROM \ˌsē-ˌdē-ˈräm\ *n* [compact *d*isc *r*ead-*o*nly *m*emory] (1983) : a CD containing computer data that cannot be altered
CDT *abbr* central daylight time
CDW *abbr* collision damage waiver
Ce *symbol* cerium
CE *abbr* **1** chemical engineer **2** civil engineer **3** Christian Era — often punctuated; Common Era — often punctuated **4** Corps of Engineers
CEA *abbr* **1** College English Association **2** Council of Economic Advisors
ce·a·no·thus \ˌsē-ə-ˈnō-thəs\ *n* [NL, fr. Gk *keanōthos,* a thistle] (1785) : any of a genus (*Ceanothus*) of American vines, shrubs, and small trees of the buckthorn family having the calyx disk adherent to the ovary
1**cease** \ˈsēs\ *vb* **ceased; ceas·ing** [ME *cesen,* fr. AF *cesser,* fr. L *cessare* to hold back, be remiss, freq. of *cedere*] *vt* (14c) : to cause to come to an end esp. gradually : no longer continue ⟨they were forced to ~ operations⟩ ⟨~ to exist⟩ ~ *vi* **1 a** : to come to an end ⟨the fighting gradually *ceased*⟩ **b** : to bring an activity or action to an end : DISCONTINUE ⟨they have been ordered to ~ and desist⟩ **2** *obs* : to become extinct : DIE OUT ***syn*** see STOP
2**cease** *n* (14c) : CESSATION — usu. used with *without*
cease and desist order *n* (1926) : an order from an administrative agency to refrain from a method of competition or a labor practice found by the agency to be unfair
cease–fire \ˈsēs-ˈfī(-ə)r\ *n* (1859) **1** : a military order to cease firing **2** : a suspension of active hostilities
cease·less \ˈsēs-ləs\ *adj* (1570) : continuing without cease : CONSTANT ⟨~ efforts⟩ — **cease·less·ly** *adv* — **cease·less·ness** *n*
ce·cro·pia moth \si-ˈkrō-pē-ə-\ *n* [NL *cecropia,* fr. L, fem. of *Cecropius* Athenian, fr. Gk *Kekropios,* fr. *Kekrops* Cecrops, legendary king of Athens] (1885) : a large No. American saturniid moth (*Hyalophora cecropia*) that is brown with red, white, and black markings

cecropia moth

ce·cum *also* **cae·cum** \ˈsē-kəm\ *n, pl* **ce·ca** \-kə\ [NL, fr. L *intestinum caecum,* lit., blind intestine] (ca. 1721) : a cavity open at one end (as the blind end of a duct); *esp* : the blind pouch at the beginning of the large intestine into which the ileum opens from one side and which is continuous with the colon — **ce·cal** *also* **cae·cal** \-kəl\ *adj* — **ce·cal·ly** \-kə-lē\ *adv*
CED *abbr* Committee for Economic Development
ce·dar \ˈsē-dər\ *n* [ME *cedre,* fr. AF, fr. L *cedrus,* fr. Gk *kedros*] (14c) **1 a** : any of a genus (*Cedrus*) of usu. tall coniferous trees (as the cedar of Lebanon or the deodar) of the pine family noted for their fragrant durable wood **b** : any of numerous coniferous trees (as of the genera *Juniperus, Chamaecyparis,* or *Thuja* of the cypress family) that resemble the true cedars esp. in the fragrance and durability of their wood **2** : the wood of a cedar — **ce·dary** \-də-rē, -də-rē\ *adj*
ce·dar–ap·ple rust \ˈsē-dər-ˈa-pəl-\ *n* (1946) : a gall-producing disease esp. of the apple caused by a rust fungus (*Gymnosporangium juniperi-virginianae*) that completes the first part of its life cycle on the common red cedar (*Juniperus virginiana*) and the second on the leaves and fruit of the apple
ce·dar·bird \-ˌbərd\ *n* (1883) : CEDAR WAXWING
ce·darn \ˈsē-dərn\ *adj* (1634) *archaic* : made or suggestive of cedar
cedar of Leb·a·non \-ˈleb-nän, -ˈle-bə-, -nən\ (14c) : a long-lived cedar (*Cedrus libani*) native to Asia Minor with short fascicled leaves and erect cones
cedar waxwing *n* (ca. 1844) : a brown gregarious American waxwing (*Bombycilla cedrorum*) with a yellow band on the tip of the tail and a pale yellow belly
ce·dar·wood \ˈsē-dər-ˌwu̇d\ *n* (14c) : the wood of a cedar that is esp. repellent to insects
cede \ˈsēd\ *vt* **ced·ed; ced·ing** [F or L; F *céder,* fr. L *cedere* to go, withdraw, yield] (1749) **1** : to yield or grant typically by treaty **2** : ASSIGN, TRANSFER — **ced·er** *n*
ce·di \ˈsā-dē\ *n* [Twi *sedi* cowry] (1965) — see MONEY table
ce·dil·la \si-ˈdi-lə\ *n* [Sp, the obs. letter *ç* (actually a medieval form of the letter *z*), cedilla, fr. dim. of *ceda, zeda* the letter *z,* fr. LL *zeta* — more at ZED] (1599) : the diacritical mark ¸ placed under a letter (as *ç* in French) to indicate an alteration or modification of its usual phonetic value (as in the French word *façade*)
cee \ˈsē\ *n* (1542) : the letter *c*
cef·tri·ax·one \ˌsef-ˌtrī-ˈak-ˌsōn\ *n* [*cef-* (alter. of *ceph*alosporin) + *-triaxone,* of unknown origin] (1984) : a broad-spectrum semisynthetic cephalosporin antibiotic $C_{18}H_{18}N_8O_7S_3$ administered parenterally in the form of its sodium salt
cei·ba \ˈsā-bə\ *n* [Sp, prob. fr. Taino *ceíba*] (1764) **1** : a massive tropical tree (*Ceiba pentandra*) of the silk-cotton family with large pods filled with seeds invested with a silky floss that yields the fiber kapok **2** : KAPOK
ceil \ˈsēl\ *vt* [ME *celen,* fr. ML *celare, caelare,* perh. fr. L *caelare* to carve, fr. *caelum* chisel; akin to L *caedere* to cut] (15c) **1** : to furnish (as a wooden ship) with a lining **2** : to furnish with a ceiling
cei·lidh *also* **cei·li** \ˈkā-lē\ *n* [Ir *céilí* & ScGael *cèilidh* visit, social evening, party with music and dancing, fr. OIr *céilide* visit, fr. *céile* servant, companion, neighbor; akin to W *cilydd* companion, Old Bret *kiled*] (1875) *Scot & Irish* : a party with music, dancing, and often storytelling
ceil·ing \ˈsē-liŋ\ *n* [ME *celing,* fr. *celen*] (1535) **1 a** : the overhead inside lining of a room **b** : material used to ceil a wall or roof of a room **2** : something thought of as an overhanging shelter or a lofty canopy ⟨a ~ of stars⟩ **3 a** : the height above the ground from which prominent objects on the ground can be seen and identified **b** : the height above the ground of the base of the lowest layer of clouds when over half of the sky is obscured **4 a** : ABSOLUTE CEILING **b** : SERVICE CEILING **5** : an upper usu. prescribed limit ⟨a ~ on prices, rents, and wages⟩ — **ceil·inged** \-liŋd\ *adj*
ceil·om·e·ter \sē-ˈlä-mə-tər\ *n* [*ceil*ing + *-o-* + *-meter*] (1943) : a photoelectric instrument for determining by triangulation the height of the cloud ceiling above the earth
cein·ture \saⁿ(n)-ˈtyu̇r, -ˈtu̇r, ˈsan-chər\ *n* [ME *seynture,* fr. AF *ceinture,* fr. L *cinctura* — more at CINCTURE] (15c) : a belt or sash for the waist
cel *also* **cell** \ˈsel\ *n* [short for *celluloid*] (1933) : a transparent sheet of celluloid on which objects are drawn or painted in the making of animated cartoons
cel·a·don \ˈse-lə-ˌdän, -lə-dᵊn\ *n* [F *céladon*] (ca. 1768) **1** : a grayish-yellow green **2** : a ceramic glaze originated in China that is greenish in color; *also* : an article with a celadon glaze
cel·an·dine \ˈse-lən-ˌdīn, -ˌdēn\ *n* [ME *celidoine,* fr. AF, fr. L *chelidonia,* fr. fem. of *chelidonius* of the swallow, fr. Gk *chelidonios,* fr. *chelidon-, chelidōn* swallow] (12c) **1** : a yellow-flowered Eurasian biennial herb (*Chelidonium majus*) of the poppy family naturalized in the eastern U.S. **2** : LESSER CELANDINE
-cele *n comb form* [F, fr. L, fr. Gk *kēlē;* akin to OE *hēala* hernia] : tumor : hernia ⟨varico*cele*⟩
ce·leb \sə-ˈleb\ *n* (ca. 1912) : CELEBRITY 2
cel·e·brant \ˈse-lə-brənt\ *n* (1839) : one who celebrates; *specif* : the priest officiating at the Eucharist
cel·e·brate \ˈse-lə-ˌbrāt\ *vb* **-brat·ed; -brat·ing** [ME, fr. L *celebratus,* pp. of *celebrare* to frequent, celebrate, fr. *celebr-, celeber* much frequented, famous; perh. akin to L *celer*] *vt* (15c) **1** : to perform (a sacrament or solemn ceremony) publicly and with appropriate rites **2 a** : to honor (as a holiday) esp. by solemn ceremonies or by refraining from ordinary business **b** : to mark (as an anniversary) by festivities or other deviation from routine **3** : to hold up or play up for public notice ⟨her poetry ~*s* the glory of nature⟩ ~ *vi* **1** : to observe a holiday, perform a religious ceremony, or take part in a festival **2** : to observe a notable occasion with festivities ***syn*** see KEEP — **cel·e·bra·tion** \ˌse-lə-ˈbrā-shən\ *n* — **cel·e·bra·tive** \ˈse-lə-ˌbrā-tiv\ *adj* — **cel·e·bra·tor** \-tər\ *n* — **cel·e·bra·to·ry** \-brə-ˌtȯr-ē, ˌse-lə-ˈbrā-tə-rē\ *adj*
cel·e·brat·ed *adj* (1580) : widely known and often referred to ⟨a ~ author⟩ ***syn*** see FAMOUS — **cel·e·brat·ed·ness** *n*
ce·leb·ri·ty \sə-ˈle-brə-tē\ *n, pl* **-ties** (14c) **1** : the state of being celebrated : FAME **2** : a famous or celebrated person
ce·leb·u·tante \sə-ˈle-byü-ˌtänt\ *n* [blend of *celebrity* and *debutante*] (1939) : a debutante who has attracted such media attention as to be considered a celebrity
ce·le·ri·ac \sə-ˈler-ē-ˌak, -ˈlir-\ *n* [irreg. fr. *celery*] (1743) : a celery (*Apium graveolens rapaceum*) grown for its knobby edible root
ce·ler·i·ty \sə-ˈler-ə-tē, -ˈle-rə-\ *n* [ME *celerite,* fr. AF, fr. L *celeritat-, celeritas,* fr. *celer* swift — more at HOLD] (15c) : rapidity of motion or action
cel·ery \ˈse-lə-rē, ˈsel-rē\ *n, pl* **-er·ies** [obs. F *celeris,* fr. It dial. *seleri,* pl. of *selero,* modif. of LL *selinon,* fr. Gk] (1664) : a European herb (*Apium graveolens*) of the carrot family; *specif* : one of a cultivated variety (*A. graveolens dulce*) with leafstalks eaten raw or cooked
celery cabbage *n* (1930) : CHINESE CABBAGE b
celery root *n* (1947) : CELERIAC
ce·les·ta \sə-ˈles-tə, chə-\ *or* **ce·leste** \sə-ˈlest, chə-\ *n* [F *célesta,* alter. of *céleste,* lit., heavenly, fr. L *caelestis*] (1899) : a keyboard instrument with hammers that strike steel plates producing a tone similar to that of a glockenspiel
1**ce·les·tial** \sə-ˈles-chəl, -ˈlesh-, -ˈles-tē-əl\ *adj* [ME, fr. AF, fr. L *caelestis* celestial, fr. *caelum* sky] (14c) **1** : of, relating to, or suggesting heaven or divinity ⟨~ beings⟩ **2** : of or relating to the sky or visible heavens ⟨the sun, moon, and stars are ~ bodies⟩ **3 a** : ETHEREAL, OTHERWORLDLY ⟨~ music⟩ **b** : OLYMPIAN, SUPREME **4** *cap* [*Celestial* Empire, old name for China] : of or relating to China or the Chinese — **ce·les·tial·ly** \-chə-lē, -tē-ə-lē\ *adv*
2**celestial** *n* (1573) **1** : a heavenly or mythical being **2** *cap* : CHINESE 1a
celestial equator *n* (1848) : the great circle on the celestial sphere midway between the celestial poles
celestial globe *n* (1668) : a globe depicting the celestial bodies
celestial hierarchy *n* (1768) : a traditional hierarchy of angels ranked from lowest to highest into the following nine orders: angels, archangels, principalities, powers, virtues, dominions, thrones, cherubim, and seraphim
celestial marriage *n* (1862) : a special order of Mormon marriage solemnized in a Mormon temple and held to be binding for a future life as well as the present one
celestial navigation *n* (1939) : navigation by observation of the positions of celestial bodies
celestial pole *n* (1848) : either of the two points on the celestial sphere around which the diurnal rotation of the stars appears to take place
celestial sphere *n* (1829) : an imaginary sphere of infinite radius against which the celestial bodies appear to be projected and of which the apparent dome of the visible sky forms half
ce·les·tite \ˈse-ləs-ˌtīt, sə-ˈles-ˌtīt\ *n* [G *Zölestin,* fr. L *caelestis*] (1854) : a usu. white mineral consisting of the sulfate of strontium

ce·li·ac also **coe·li·ac** \'sē-lē-,ak\ adj [L coeliacus, fr. Gk koiliakos, fr. koilia cavity, fr. koilos hollow — more at CAVE] (1662) : of or relating to the abdominal cavity

celiac disease n (1911) : a chronic hereditary intestinal disorder in which an inability to absorb the gliadin portion of gluten results in the gliadin triggering an immune response that damages the intestinal mucosa — called also celiac sprue

cel·i·ba·cy \'se-lə-bə-sē\ n (1646) **1** : the state of not being married **2 a** : abstention from sexual intercourse **b** : abstention by vow from marriage

cel·i·bate \'se-lə-bət\ n [L caelibatus, fr. caelib-, caelebs unmarried] (1680) : a person who lives in celibacy — **celibate** adj

cell \'sel\ n [ME, fr. OE, religious house and AF celle hermit's cell, fr. L cella small room; akin to L celare to conceal — more at HELL] (12c) **1** : a small religious house dependent on a monastery or convent **2 a** : a one-room dwelling occupied by a solitary person (as a hermit) **b** : a single room (as in a convent or prison) usu. for one person **3** : a small compartment, cavity, or bounded space: as **a** : one of the compartments of a honeycomb **b** : a membranous area bounded by veins in the wing of an insect **4** : a small usu. microscopic mass of protoplasm bounded externally by a semipermeable membrane, usu. including one or more nuclei and various other organelles with their products, capable alone or interacting with other cells of performing all the fundamental functions of life, and forming the smallest structural unit of living matter capable of functioning independently **5 a** (1) : a receptacle containing electrodes and an electrolyte either for generating electricity by chemical action or for use in electrolysis (2) : FUEL CELL **b** : a single unit in a device for converting radiant energy into electrical energy or for varying the intensity of an electrical current in accordance with radiation **6** : a unit in a statistical array (as a spreadsheet) formed by the intersection of a column and a row **7** : a basic and usu. small unit of an organization or movement ⟨terrorist ∼s⟩ **8** : a portion of the atmosphere that behaves as a unit ⟨a storm ∼⟩ **9 a** : any of the small sections of a geographic area of a cellular telephone system **b** : CELL PHONE

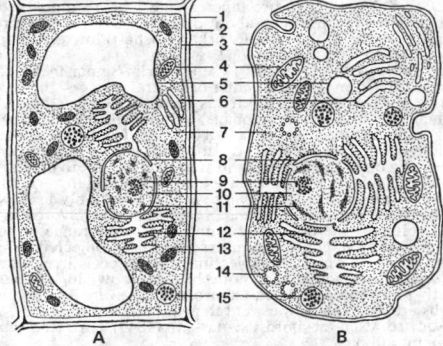

cell 4 (schematic): A plant, B animal; 1 cell wall, 2 middle lamella, 3 plasma membrane, 4 mitochondrion, 5 vacuole, 6 Golgi apparatus, 7 cytoplasm, 8 nuclear membrane, 9 nucleolus, 10 nucleus, 11 chromatin, 12 endoplasmic reticulum with associated ribosomes, 13 chloroplast, 14 centriole, 15 lysosome

¹cel·lar \'se-lər\ n [ME celer, fr. AF, fr. L cellarium storeroom, fr. cella] (13c) **1 a** : basement **b** : the lowest grade or rank; esp : the lowest place in the standings (as of an athletic league) ⟨the team spent most of last year in the ∼⟩ **2** : a stock of wines

²cellar vt (1677) : to put into a cellar (as for storage) ⟨∼ing wine⟩

cel·lar·age \'se-lə-rij\ n (1602) : cellar space esp. for storage

cel·lar·er \'se-lər-ər\ n [ME celerer, fr. AF, fr. LL cellariarius, fr. L cellarium] (13c) : an official (as in a monastery) in charge of provisions

cel·lar·ette or **cel·lar·et** \,se-lə-'ret\ n (ca. 1807) : a case or sideboard for holding bottles of wine or liquor

cellar master n (1955) : a person who supervises the making of wine in a winery

cell body n (1878) : the nucleus-containing central part of a neuron exclusive of its axons and dendrites — see NEURON illustration

cell cycle n (1961) : the complete series of events from one cell division to the next — compare G₁ PHASE, G₂ PHASE, M PHASE, S PHASE

cell division n (1853) : the process by which cells multiply involving both nuclear and cytoplasmic division — compare MEIOSIS, MITOSIS

celled \'seld\ adj : having (such or so many) cells — used in combination ⟨single-celled organisms⟩

cell line n (1951) : a cell culture selected for uniformity from a cell population derived from a usu. homogeneous tissue source (as an organ) ⟨a newly established cell line derived from a human endometrial carcinoma —Biol. Abstracts⟩

cell-me·di·at·ed \'sel-'mē-dē-,ā-təd\ adj (1967) : relating to or being the part of immunity or the immune response that is mediated primarily by T cells

cell membrane n (1852) : a membrane of a cell; esp : PLASMA MEMBRANE

cel·lo \'che-(,)lō\ n, pl **cellos** also **cel·li** \-lē\ [short for violoncello] (1855) : the bass member of the violin family tuned an octave below the viola — **cel·list** \'che-list\ n

cel·lo·bi·ose \,se-lə-'bī-,ōs, -,ōz\ n [ISV cellulose + -o- + biose disaccharide, fr. ¹bi- + ²ose] (1902) : a faintly sweet disaccharide C₁₂H₂₂O₁₁ obtained by partial hydrolysis of cellulose

cel·loi·din \se-'lòi-dᵊn\ n [cellulose + -oid + ¹-in] (1883) : a purified pyroxylin used chiefly in microscopy

cel·lo·phane \'se-lə-,fān\ n [F, fr. cellulose + -phane (as in diaphane diaphanous, fr. ML diaphanus)] (1912) : regenerated cellulose in thin transparent sheets used esp. for packaging

cellophane noodle n (1958) : a translucent noodle made from mung beans

cell phone n (1984) : a portable usu. cordless telephone for use in a cellular system

cell plate n (1882) : a disk formed in the phragmoplast of a dividing plant cell that eventually forms the middle lamella of the wall between the daughter cells

cell sap n (1871) **1** : the liquid contents of a plant cell vacuole **2** : CYTOSOL

cell theory n (1859) : a theory in biology that includes one or both of the statements that the cell is the fundamental structural and functional unit of living matter and that the organism is composed of autonomous cells with its properties being the sum of those of its cells

¹cel·lu·lar \'sel-yə-lər\ adj [NL cellularis, fr. cellula living cell, fr. L, dim. of cella small room] (ca. 1739) **1** : of, relating to, or consisting of cells **2** : containing cavities : having a porous texture ⟨∼ rocks⟩ **3** : of, relating to, or being a radiotelephone system in which a geographical area (as a city) is divided into small sections each served by a transmitter of limited range ⟨∼ phones⟩ — **cel·lu·lar·i·ty** \,sel-yə-'la-rə-tē, -ᵊl'ler-ə-\ n

²cellular n (1987) : CELL PHONE

cel·lu·lase \'sel-yə-,lās, -,lāz\ n [ISV] (1903) : an enzyme that hydrolyzes cellulose

cel·lule \'sel-(,)yül\ n [L cellula] (1652) : a small cell

cel·lu·lite \'sel-yə-,līt, -,lēt\ n [F, lit., accumulation of subcutaneous fat, cellulitis, fr. cellule cell + -ite -itis] (1968) : deposits of subcutaneous fat within fibrous connective tissue (as in the thighs, hips, and buttocks) that give a puckered and dimpled appearance to the skin surface

cel·lu·li·tis \,sel-yə-'lī-təs\ n [NL, fr. cellula] (1861) : diffuse and esp. subcutaneous inflammation of connective tissue

cel·lu·loid \'sel-yə-,lòid\ n [fr. Celluloid, a trademark] (1870) **1** : a tough flammable thermoplastic composed essentially of cellulose nitrate and camphor **2** : a motion-picture film ⟨a work . . . making its third appearance on ∼ —John McCarten⟩ — **celluloid** adj

cel·lu·lo·lyt·ic \,sel-yə-lō-'li-tik\ adj [cellulose + -o- + -lytic] (1943) : hydrolyzing or having the capacity to hydrolyze cellulose

cel·lu·lose \'sel-yə-,lōs, -,lōz\ n [F, fr. cellule living cell, fr. NL cellula] (1848) : a polysaccharide (C₆H₁₀O₅)ₓ of glucose units that constitutes the chief part of the cell walls of plants, occurs naturally in such fibrous products as cotton and kapok, and is the raw material of many manufactured goods (as paper, rayon, and cellophane)

cellulose acetate n (1895) : any of several compounds insoluble in water that are formed esp. by the action of acetic acid, anhydride of acetic acid, and sulfuric acid on cellulose and are used for making textile fibers, packaging sheets, photographic films, and varnishes

cellulose nitrate n (1880) : NITROCELLULOSE

cel·lu·los·ic \,sel-yə-'lō-sik, -zik\ adj (1881) : of, relating to, or made from cellulose — **cellulosic** n

cell wall n (ca. 1849) : the usu. rigid nonliving permeable wall that surrounds the plasma membrane and encloses and supports the cells of most plants, bacteria, fungi, and algae — see CELL illustration

ce·lo·sia \sē-'lō-zh(ē-)ə\ n [NL, irreg. fr. Gk kēleos burning; akin to Gk kaiein to burn] (1807) : any of a genus (Celosia) of tropical annual herbs (as cockscomb) of the amaranth family that have alternate leaves and showy flower spikes often forming feathery clusters in cultivated forms

Cel·si·us \'sel-sē-əs, -shəs\ adj [Anders Celsius] (ca. 1850) : relating to, conforming to, or having the international thermometric scale on which the interval between the triple point of water and the boiling point of water is divided into 99.99 degrees with 0.01° representing the triple point and 100° the boiling point ⟨10° ∼⟩; also : CENTIGRADE — abbr. C

celt \'selt\ n [LL celtis chisel] (1715) : a prehistoric stone or metal implement shaped like a chisel or ax head

Celt \'kelt, 'selt\ n [L Celtae, pl., fr. Gk Keltoi] (1550) **1** : a member of a division of the early Indo-European peoples distributed from the British Isles and Spain to Asia Minor **2** : a modern Gael, Highland Scot, Irishman, Welshman, Cornishman, or Breton

¹Celt·ic \'kel-tik, 'sel-\ adj (1590) : of, relating to, or characteristic of the Celts or their languages

²Celtic n (1739) : a group of Indo-European languages usu. subdivided into Brythonic and Goidelic and now largely confined to Brittany, Wales, Ireland, and the Scottish Highlands — see INDO-EUROPEAN LANGUAGES table

Celtic cross n (1873) : a cross having essentially the form of a Latin cross with a ring about the intersection of the crossbar and upright shaft — see CROSS illustration

Celt·i·cist \'kel-tə-sist, 'sel-\ n (1912) : a specialist in Celtic languages or cultures

cem·ba·lo \'chem-bə-,lō\ n, pl **-ba·li** \-(,)lē\ or **-balos** [It] (ca. 1801) : HARPSICHORD

¹ce·ment \si-'ment\ also 'sē-,ment\ n [ME sement, fr. AF ciment, fr. L caementum stone chips used in making mortar, fr. caedere to cut] (14c) **1 a** : CONCRETE **b** : a powder of alumina, silica, lime, iron oxide, and magnesium oxide burned together in a kiln and finely pulverized and used as an ingredient of mortar and concrete; also : any mixture used for a similar purpose **2** : a binding element or agency: as **a** : a substance to make objects adhere to each other **b** : something serving to unite firmly ⟨justice is the ∼ that holds a political community together —R. M. Hutchins⟩ **3** : CEMENTUM **4** : a plastic composition made esp. of zinc or silica for filling dental cavities **5** : the fine-grained groundmass or glass of a porphyry

²cement vt (14c) **1** : to unite or make firm by or as if by cement **2** : to overlay with concrete ∼ vi : to become cemented — **ce·ment·er** n

ce·men·ta·tion \ˌsē-ˌmen-ˈtā-shən\ *n* (1594) **1 :** a process of surrounding a solid with a powder and heating the whole so that the solid is changed by chemical combination with the powder **2 :** the act or process of cementing **:** the state of being cemented

ce·ment·ite \si-ˈmen-ˌtīt\ *n* [[1]*cement*] (1888) **:** a hard brittle iron carbide Fe_3C that occurs in steel, cast iron, and iron-carbon alloys

ce·men·ti·tious \ˌsē-ˌmen-ˈti-shəs\ *adj* (ca. 1828) **:** having the properties of cement

ce·men·tum \si-ˈmen-təm\ *n* [NL, fr. L *caementum*] (1842) **:** a specialized bony layer of connective tissue covering the dentin of the part of a tooth normally within the gum — see TOOTH illustration

cem·e·tery \ˈse-mə-ˌter-ē, -ˌte-rē\ *n, pl* **-ter·ies** [ME *cimitery,* fr. AF *cimiterie,* fr. LL *coemeterium,* fr. Gk *koimētērion* sleeping chamber, burial place, fr. *koiman* to put to sleep; akin to Gk *keisthai* to lie, Skt *śete* he lies] (15c) **:** a burial ground

CEMF *abbr* counter electromotive force

cen·a·cle \ˈse-ni-kəl\ *n* [LL *cenaculum* the room where Christ and his disciples had the Last Supper, fr. L, top story, prob. fr. *cena* dinner] (1889) **:** a retreat house; *esp* **:** one for Roman Catholic women directed by nuns of the Society of Our Lady of the Cenacle

-cene *adj comb form* [Gk *kainos* new, recent — more at RECENT] **:** recent — in names of geologic periods ⟨Eo*cene*⟩

ce·no·bite *also* **coe·no·bite** \ˈse-nə-ˌbīt, ˈsē-\ *n* [LL *coenobita,* fr. *coenobium* monastery, fr. LGk *koinobion,* ultim. fr. Gk *koin-* coen- + *bios* life — more at QUICK] (15c) **:** a member of a religious group living together in a monastic community — **cen·o·bit·ic** \ˌse-nə-ˈbi-tik, ˌsē-\ *adj*

ceno·taph \ˈse-nə-ˌtaf, -ˌtäf\ *n* [F *cénotaphe,* fr. L *cenotaphium,* fr. Gk *kenotaphion,* fr. *kenos* empty + *taphos* tomb] (1578) **:** a tomb or a monument erected in honor of a person or group of persons whose remains are elsewhere

ce·no·te \si-ˈnō-tē\ *n* [MexSp, fr. Yucatec *ts'onot*] (1841) **:** a deep sinkhole in limestone with a pool at the bottom that is found esp. in Yucatán

Ce·no·zo·ic \ˌsē-nə-ˈzō-ik, ˌse-\ *adj* [Gk *kainos* + E *-zoic*] (1841) **:** of, relating to, or being an era of geological history that extends from the beginning of the Tertiary period to the present time and is marked by a rapid evolution of mammals and birds and of angiosperms and esp. grasses and by little change in the invertebrates; *also* **:** relating to the corresponding system of rocks — see GEOLOGIC TIME table — **Cenozoic** *n*

cense \ˈsen(t)s\ *vt* **censed; cens·ing** [ME, prob. short for *encensen* to offer incense, fr. AF *encenser,* fr. LL *incensare,* fr. *incensum* incense] (14c) **:** to perfume esp. with a censer

cen·ser \ˈsen(t)-sər\ *n* (13c) **:** a vessel for burning incense; *esp* **:** a covered incense burner swung on chains in a religious ritual

[1]**cen·sor** \ˈsen(t)-sər\ *n* [L, Roman magistrate, fr. *censēre* to give as one's opinion, assess; perh. akin to Skt *śaṁsati* he praises] (1526) **1 :** a person who supervises conduct and morals: as **a :** an official who examines materials (as publications or films) for objectionable matter **b :** an official (as in time of war) who reads communications (as letters) and deletes material considered sensitive or harmful **2 :** one of two magistrates of early Rome acting as census takers, assessors, and inspectors of morals and conduct **3 :** a hypothetical psychic agency that represses unacceptable notions before they reach consciousness — **cen·so·ri·al** \sen-ˈsȯr-ē-əl\ *adj*

[2]**censor** *vt* **cen·sored; cen·sor·ing** \ˈsen(t)-sə-riŋ, ˈsen(t)s-riŋ\ (1882) **:** to examine in order to suppress or delete anything considered objectionable ⟨~ the news⟩; *also* **:** to suppress or delete as objectionable ⟨~ out indecent passages⟩

cen·so·ri·ous \sen-ˈsȯr-ē-əs\ *adj* [L *censorius* of a censor, fr. *censor*] (1536) **:** marked by or given to censure ⟨~ comments⟩ ⟨a ~ critic⟩ *syn* see CRITICAL — **cen·so·ri·ous·ly** *adv* — **cen·so·ri·ous·ness** *n*

cen·sor·ship \ˈsen(t)-sər-ˌship\ *n* (ca. 1591) **1 a :** the institution, system, or practice of censoring **b :** the actions or practices of censors; *esp* **:** censorial control exercised repressively **2 :** the office, power, or term of a Roman censor **3 :** exclusion from consciousness by the psychic censor

cen·sur·able \ˈsen(t)-sh(ə-)rə-bəl\ *adj* (1634) **:** deserving or open to censure ⟨~ behavior⟩

[1]**cen·sure** \ˈsen(t)-shər\ *n* [L *censura,* fr. *censēre*] (14c) **1 :** a judgment involving condemnation **2** *archaic* **:** OPINION, JUDGMENT **3 :** the act of blaming or condemning sternly **4 :** an official reprimand

[2]**censure** *vt* **cen·sured; cen·sur·ing** \ˈsen(t)-sh(ə-)riŋ\ (1587) **1** *obs* **:** ESTIMATE, JUDGE **2 :** to find fault with and criticize as blameworthy *syn* see CRITICIZE — **cen·sur·er** \ˈsen(t)-shər-ər\ *n*

cen·sus \ˈsen(t)-səs\ *n* [L, fr. *censēre*] (1634) **1 :** a count of the population and a property evaluation in early Rome **2 :** a usu. complete enumeration of a population; *specif* **:** a periodic governmental enumeration of population **3 :** COUNT, TALLY — **census** *vt*

[1]**cent** \ˈsent\ *n* [F, hundred, fr. L *centum* — more at HUNDRED] (1782) **1 :** a monetary unit equal to 1/100 of a basic unit of value — see *birr, dollar, euro, leone, lilangeni, nakfa, rand, rupee, shilling* at MONEY table **2 :** a coin, token, or note representing one cent **3 :** the fen of the People's Republic of China

[2]**cent** *abbr* **1** centigrade **2** central **3** centum **4** century

Cent *abbr* Central

cen·tal \ˈsen-tᵊl\ *n* [L *centum* + E *-al* (as in *quintal*)] (1870) *chiefly Brit* **:** HUNDREDWEIGHT 1

cen·tas \ˈsen-ˌtäs\ *n, pl* **cen·tai** \-ˌtī\ *or* **cen·tu** \-ˌtü\ [Lith (nom. pl. *centai,* gen. pl. *centų*), prob. fr. F *centime* or E *cent*] (ca. 1934) — see *litas* at MONEY table

cen·taur \ˈsen-ˌtȯr\ *n* [ME, fr. L *Centaurus,* fr. Gk *Kentauros*] (14c) **:** any of a race of creatures fabled to be half human and half horse and to live in the mountains of Thessaly

cen·tau·rea \sen-ˈtȯr-ē-ə\ *n* [NL, genus name, fr. ML] (ca. 1829) **:** any of a large genus (*Centaurea*) of composite herbs (as bachelor's button) including several cultivated for their showy heads of tubular florets

Cen·tau·rus \-ˈtȯr-əs\ *n* [L (gen. *Centauri*)] (1870) **:** a southern constellation between the Southern Cross and Hydra

cen·tau·ry \ˈsen-ˌtȯr-ē\ *n, pl* **-ries** [ME *centaure,* fr. AF *centorie,* fr. ML *centaurea,* fr. L *centaureum,* fr. Gk *kentaureion,* fr. *Kentauros*] (14c) **:** any of a genus (*Centaurium*) of low herbs of the gentian family; *esp* **:** an Old World herb (*C. crythraea* syn. *C. umbellatum*) that produces pink flowers and is used in herbal medicine

[1]**cen·ta·vo** \sen-ˈtä-(ˌ)vō\ *n, pl* **-vos** [Sp, lit., hundredth, fr. *ciento* hundred, fr. L *centum*] (1883) — see *boliviano, córdoba, lempira, peso, quetzal* at MONEY table

[2]**cen·ta·vo** \-ˈtä-(ˌ)vü, -(ˌ)vō\ *n, pl* **-vos** [Pg, fr. Sp] (1913) **1 :** a former monetary unit equal to 1/100 Portuguese escudo **2** — see *escudo, metical* at MONEY table

cen·te·nar·i·an \ˌsen-tə-ˈner-ē-ən, -ˈne-rē-\ *n* (1790) **:** one that is 100 years old or older — **centenarian** *adj*

cen·te·na·ry \sen-ˈte-nə-rē, ˈsen-tə-ˌner-ē, -ˌne-rē, *esp Brit* sen-ˈtē-nə-rē\ *n, pl* **-ries** [LL *centenarium,* fr. L *centenarius* of a hundred, fr. *centeni* one hundred each, fr. *centum* hundred — more at HUNDRED] (1788) **:** CENTENNIAL — **centenary** *adj*

cen·ten·ni·al \sen-ˈte-nē-əl\ *n* [L *cent*um + E *-ennial* (as in *biennial*)] (1876) **:** a 100th anniversary or its celebration — **centennial** *adj* — **cen·ten·ni·al·ly** \-ə-lē\ *adv*

[1]**cen·ter** \ˈsen-tər, ˈse-nər\ *n* [ME *centre,* fr. MF, fr. L *centrum,* fr. Gk *kentron* sharp point, center of a circle, fr. *kentein* to prick; prob. akin to OHG *hantag* pointed] (14c) **1 a :** the point around which a circle or sphere is described; *broadly* **:** a point that is related to a geometrical figure in such a way that for any point on the figure there is another point on the figure such that a straight line joining the two points is bisected by the original point — called also *center of symmetry* **b :** the center of the circle inscribed in a regular polygon **2 a :** a point, area, person, or thing that is most important or pivotal in relation to an indicated activity, interest, or condition ⟨a railroad ~⟩ ⟨the ~ of the controversy⟩ **b :** a source from which something originates ⟨a propaganda ~⟩ **c :** a group of neurons having a common function ⟨respiratory ~⟩ **d :** a region of concentrated population ⟨an urban ~⟩ **e :** a facility providing a place for a particular activity or service ⟨a day-care ~⟩ **3 a :** the middle part (as of the forehead or a stage) **b** *often cap* **(1) :** a grouping of political figures holding moderate views esp. between those of conservatives and liberals **(2) :** the views of such politicians **(3) :** the adherents of such views **4 a :** a player occupying a middle position on a team: as **(1) :** the football player in the middle of a line who passes the ball between his legs to a back to start a down **(2) :** the usu. tallest player on a basketball team who usu. plays near the basket **b :** CENTER FIELD **5 a :** either of two tapered rods which support work in a lathe or grinding machine and about or with which the work revolves **b :** a conical recess in the end of work (as a shaft) for receiving such a center — **cen·ter·less** \-ləs\ *adj*

[2]**center** *vb* **cen·tered; cen·ter·ing** \ˈsen-t(ə-)riŋ, ˈse-nər-iŋ\ *vt* (1590) **1 :** to place or fix at or around a center or central area ⟨~ the picture on the wall⟩ **2 :** to give a central focus or basis ⟨~*s* her hopes on her son⟩ ⟨the plot was ~*ed* on espionage⟩ **3 :** to adjust (as lenses) so that the axes coincide **4 a :** to pass (a ball or puck) from either side toward the middle of the playing area **b :** to hand or pass (a football) backward between one's legs to a back to start a down **5 :** to play center on ⟨~ a line in hockey⟩ ~ *vi* **:** to have a specified center **:** FOCUS

usage The intransitive verb *center* is most commonly used with the prepositions *in, on, at,* and *around. At* appears to be favored in mathematical contexts; the others are found in a broad range of contexts. *Center around,* a standard idiom, has often been objected to as illogical. The logic on which the objections are based is irrelevant, since *center around* is an idiom and idioms have their own logic. *Center on* is currently more common in edited prose, and *revolve around* and similar verbs are available if you want to avoid *center around.*

cen·ter·board \ˈsen-tər-ˌbȯrd, ˈse-nər-\ *n* (1849) **:** a retractable keel used esp. in sailboats

cen·tered \ˈsen-tərd, ˈse-nərd\ *adj* (ca. 1893) **1 :** having a center — often used in combination ⟨a dark-*centered* coneflower⟩ **2 :** having a center of curvature — often used in combination ⟨a 3-*centered* arch⟩ **3 :** emotionally stable and secure — **cen·tered·ness** \-nəs\ *n*

center field *n* (1857) **1 :** the position of the player for defending center field **2 :** the part of the baseball outfield between right and left field — **center fielder** *n*

cen·ter·fold \ˈsen-tər-ˌfōld, ˈse-nər-\ *n* (1952) **1 :** a foldout that is the center spread of a magazine **2 :** a picture (as of a nude) on a centerfold; *also* **:** a model featured in such a picture

cen·ter·line \-ˈlīn, -ˌlīn\ *n* (1807) **:** a real or imaginary line that is equidistant from the surface or sides of something

center of curvature (1850) **:** the center of the circle whose center lies on the concave side of a curve on the normal to a given point of the curve and whose radius is equal to the radius of curvature at that point

center of gravity (1648) **1 :** CENTER OF MASS **2 :** the point at which the entire weight of a body may be considered as concentrated so that if supported at this point the body would remain in equilibrium in any position **3 :** CENTER 2a

center of mass (1862) **:** the point in a body or system of bodies at which the whole mass may be considered as concentrated

cen·ter·piece \-ˌpēs\ *n* (1803) **1 :** an object occupying a central position; *esp* **:** an adornment in the center of a table **2 :** one that is of central importance or interest in a larger whole ⟨the ~ of a political agenda⟩

center punch *n* (1861) **:** a hand punch consisting of a short steel bar with a hardened conical point at one end used for marking the centers of holes to be drilled

center stage *n* (1954) **1 :** the central part of a theatrical stage **2 :** a central or highly prominent position ⟨an issue that has taken *center stage* in the campaign⟩ — **center stage** *adj or adv*

cen·tes·i·mal \sen-ˈte-sə-məl\ *adj* [L *centesimus* hundredth, fr. *centum*] (1809) **:** marked by or relating to division into hundredths

[1]**cen·tes·i·mo** \chen-ˈte-zə-ˌmō\ *n, pl* **-mi** \-(ˌ)mē\ [It] (1851) **:** a former monetary unit equal to 1/100 Italian lira

[2]**cen·tes·i·mo** \sen-ˈte-sə-ˌmō\ *n, pl* **-mos** [Sp *centésimo*] (ca. 1883) — see *balboa, peso* at MONEY table

centi- *comb form* [F & L; F, hundredth, fr. L, hundred, fr. *centum* — more at HUNDRED] **1 :** hundred ⟨*centi*pede⟩ **2 :** one hundredth part of ⟨*centi*meter⟩

cen·ti·grade \ˈsen-tə-ˌgrād, ˈsän-\ *adj* [F, fr. L *centi-* hundred + F *grade*] (1801) **:** relating to, conforming to, or having a thermometric scale on which the interval between the freezing point of water and the boiling point of water is divided into 100 degrees with 0° representing the

freezing point and 100° the boiling point ⟨10° ~⟩ — abbr. *C*; compare CELSIUS
cen·ti·gram \-ˌgram\ *n* (1801) — see METRIC SYSTEM table
cen·ti·li·ter \ˈsen-ti-ˌlē-tər, ˈsän-\ *n* (1801) — see METRIC SYSTEM table
cen·til·lion \sen-ˈtil-yən\ *n, often attrib* [L *cent*um + E *-illion* (as in *million*)] (1852) — see NUMBER table
cen·time \ˈsän-ˌtēm, ˈsen-\ *n* [F, fr. *cent* hundred (fr. L *centum*) + *-ime* (as in *décime* tenth part)] (1801) **1 :** any of several former monetary units equal to ¹⁄₁₀₀ franc (as of Belgium, France, and Luxembourg) **2** — see *dinar, dirham, franc, gourde* at MONEY table
cen·ti·me·ter \ˈsen-tə-ˌmē-tər, ˈsän-\ *n* (1801) — see METRIC SYSTEM table
centimeter–gram–second *adj* (1875) **:** of, relating to, or being a system of units based on the centimeter as the unit of length, the gram as the unit of mass, and the second as the unit of time — abbr. *cgs*
cen·ti·mo \ˈsen-tə-ˌmō\ *n, pl* **-mos** [Sp *céntimo*] (1899) **1 :** a former monetary unit equal to ¹⁄₁₀₀ peseta **2** — see *bolivar, colón, dobra, guarani, sol* at MONEY table
cen·ti·mor·gan \ˈsen-tə-ˌmȯr-gən, ˈsän-\ *n* (1919) **:** a genetic unit equivalent to ¹⁄₁₀₀ of a morgan
cen·ti·pede \ˈsen-tə-ˌpēd\ *n* [L *centipeda*, fr. *centi-* + *ped-, pes* foot — more at FOOT] (1601) **:** any of a class (Chilopoda) of long flattened many-segmented predaceous arthropods with each segment bearing one pair of legs of which the foremost pair is modified into poison fangs

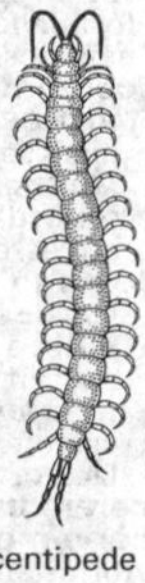
centipede

cent·ner \ˈsent-nər\ *n* [prob. fr. LG] (1683) **:** any of various units of weight used esp. in Europe and usu. equal to about 110 pounds (about 50 kilograms)
cen·to \ˈsen-(ˌ)tō\ *n, pl* **cen·to·nes** \sen-ˈtō-(ˌ)nēz\ [LL, fr. L, patchwork garment; perh. akin to Skt *kanthā* patched garment] (1605) **:** a literary work made up of parts from other works
CENTO *abbr* Central Treaty Organization
centr- *or* **centri-** *or* **centro-** *comb form* [Gk *kentr-, kentro-*, fr. *kentron* center — more at CENTER] **:** center ⟨*centri*fugal⟩ ⟨*centr*oid⟩
centra *pl of* CENTRUM
[1]**cen·tral** \ˈsen-trəl\ *adj* [L *centralis*, fr. *centrum* center] (1647) **1 :** containing or constituting a center **2 :** of primary importance **:** ESSENTIAL, PRINCIPAL ⟨the ~ character of the novel⟩ **3 a :** situated at, in, or near the center **b :** easily accessible from outlying districts ⟨a ~ location for the new theater⟩ **4 a :** centrally placed and superseding separate scattered units ⟨~ heating⟩ **b :** controlling or directing local or branch activities ⟨the ~ committee⟩ **5 :** holding to a middle between extremes **:** MODERATE **6 :** of, relating to, or comprising the brain and spinal cord; *also* **:** originating within the central nervous system ⟨~ deafness⟩ — **cen·tral·ly** \-trə-lē\ *adv*
[2]**central** *n* (1889) **1 :** a telephone exchange or operator **2 :** a central office or bureau usu. controlling others ⟨weather ~⟩ **3 :** a center or hub for a specified activity or group ⟨her house is party ~⟩ ⟨the family room becomes kid ~⟩
central angle *n* (1904) **:** an angle formed by two radii of a circle
central bank *n* (1922) **:** a national bank that operates to establish monetary and fiscal policy and to control the money supply and interest rate — **central banker** *n*
central casting *n* (1957) **:** the department of a movie studio responsible for casting actors esp. viewed as a source of people who are stereotypical of their role in appearance, behavior, or nature ⟨a politician right out of *central casting*⟩
central city *n* (1950) **:** a city that constitutes the densely populated center of a metropolitan area
cen·tral·ise *Brit var of* CENTRALIZE
cen·tral·ism \ˈsen-trə-ˌli-zəm\ *n* (1831) **:** the concentration of power and control in the central authority of an organization (as a political or educational system) — compare FEDERALISM — **cen·tral·ist** \-list\ *n or adj* — **cen·tral·is·tic** \ˌsen-trə-ˈlis-tik\ *adj*
cen·tral·i·ty \sen-ˈtra-lə-tē\ *n, pl* **-ties** (1647) **1 :** the quality or state of being central **2 :** central situation **3 :** tendency to remain in or at the center
cen·tral·ize \ˈsen-trə-ˌlīz\ *vb* **-ized; -iz·ing** *vi* (1800) **:** to form a center **:** cluster around a center ~ *vt* **1 :** to bring to a center **:** CONSOLIDATE ⟨~ all the data in one file⟩ **2 :** to concentrate by placing power and authority in a center or central organization — **cen·tral·i·za·tion** \ˌsen-trə-lə-ˈzā-shən\ *n* — **cen·tral·iz·er** \ˈsen-trə-ˌlī-zər\ *n*
central limit theorem *n* (1951) **:** any of several fundamental theorems of probability and statistics that state the conditions under which the distribution of a sum of independent random variables is approximated by the normal distribution; *esp* **:** one which is much applied in sampling and which states that the distribution of a mean of a sample from a population with finite variance is approximated by the normal distribution as the number in the sample becomes large
central nervous system *n* (ca. 1907) **:** the part of the nervous system which in vertebrates consists of the brain and spinal cord, to which sensory impulses are transmitted and from which motor impulses pass out, and which coordinates the activity of the entire nervous system — compare PERIPHERAL NERVOUS SYSTEM
central processing unit *n* (1961) **:** CPU
central tendency *n* (ca. 1928) **:** the degree of clustering of the values of a statistical distribution that is usu. measured by the arithmetic mean, mode, or median
central time *n, often cap C* (1883) **:** the time of the sixth time zone west of Greenwich that includes the central U.S. — see TIME ZONE illustration
cen·tre *chiefly Brit var of* CENTER
cen·tric \ˈsen-trik\ *adj* [Gk *kentrikos* of the center, fr. *kentron*] (ca. 1590) **1 :** located in or at a center **:** CENTRAL ⟨a ~ point⟩ **2 :** concentrated about or directed to a center ⟨a ~ activity⟩ **3 :** of, relating to, or having a centromere **4 :** of, relating to, or resembling an order (Centrales) of radially symmetrical diatoms — **cen·tri·cal·ly** \-tri-k(ə-)lē\ *adv* — **cen·tric·i·ty** \sen-ˈtri-sə-tē\ *n*
-centric *adj comb form* [ML *-centricus*, fr. L *centrum* center] **1 :** having (such) a center or (such or so many) centers ⟨poly*centric*⟩ **2 :** having (something specified) as its center ⟨helio*centric*⟩

[1]**cen·trif·u·gal** \sen-ˈtri-fyə-gəl, -ˈtri-fi-, *esp Brit* ˌsen-tri-ˈfyü-gəl\ *adj* [NL *centrifugus*, fr. *centr-* + L *fugere* to flee — more at FUGITIVE] (ca. 1721) **1 :** proceeding or acting in a direction away from a center or axis **2 :** using or acting by centrifugal force ⟨a ~ pump⟩ **3 :** EFFERENT **4 :** tending away from centralization **:** SEPARATIST ⟨~ tendencies in modern society⟩ — **cen·trif·u·gal·ly** \-gə-lē\ *adv*
[2]**centrifugal** *n* (1866) **:** a centrifugal machine or a drum in such a machine
centrifugal force *n* (ca. 1721) **:** the apparent force that is felt by an object moving in a curved path that acts outwardly away from the center of rotation — compare CENTRIPETAL FORCE
cen·tri·fu·ga·tion \ˌsen-trə-fyü-ˈgā-shən, -f(y)ə-\ *n* (1903) **:** the process of centrifuging
[1]**cen·tri·fuge** \ˈsen-trə-ˌfyüj\ *n* [F, fr. *centrifuge* centrifugal, fr. NL *centrifugus*] (1887) **:** a machine using centrifugal force for separating substances of different densities, for removing moisture, or for simulating gravitational effects
[2]**centrifuge** *vt* **-fuged; -fug·ing** (ca. 1895) **:** to subject to centrifugal action esp. in a centrifuge
cen·tri·ole \ˈsen-trē-ˌōl\ *n* [G *Zentriol*, fr. *Zentrum* center] (ca. 1896) **:** one of a pair of cellular organelles that occur esp. in animals, are adjacent to the nucleus, function in the formation of the spindle apparatus during cell division, and consist of a cylinder with nine microtubules arranged peripherally in a circle — see CELL illustration
cen·trip·e·tal \sen-ˈtri-pə-tᵊl\ *adj* [NL *centripetus*, fr. *centr-* + L *petere* to go to, seek — more at FEATHER] (1709) **1 :** proceeding or acting in a direction toward a center or axis **2 :** AFFERENT **3 :** tending toward centralization **:** UNIFYING — **cen·trip·e·tal·ly** \-tə-lē\ *adv*
centripetal force *n* (1686) **:** the force that is necessary to keep an object moving in a curved path and that is directed inward toward the center of rotation ⟨a string on the end of which a stone is whirled about exerts *centripetal force* on the stone⟩ — compare CENTRIFUGAL FORCE
cen·trist \ˈsen-trist\ *n* (1872) **1** *often cap* **:** a member of a center party **2 :** a person who holds moderate views — **cen·trism** \-ˌtri-zəm\ *n* — **centrist** *adj*
cen·troid \ˈsen-ˌtrȯid\ *n* (1882) **1 :** CENTER OF MASS **2 :** a point whose coordinates are the averages of the corresponding coordinates of a given set of points and which for a given plane or three-dimensional figure (as a triangle or sphere) corresponds to the center of mass of a thin plate of uniform thickness and consistency or a body of uniform consistency having the same boundary
cen·tro·mere \ˈsen-trə-ˌmir\ *n* [ISV] (ca. 1925) **:** the point or region on a chromosome to which the spindle attaches during mitosis and meiosis — **cen·tro·mer·ic** \ˌsen-trə-ˈmir-ik, -ˈmer-\ *adj*
cen·tro·some \ˈsen-trə-ˌsōm\ *n* [ISV] (1889) **1 :** CENTRIOLE **2 :** the centriole-containing region of clear cytoplasm adjacent to the cell nucleus
cen·tro·sym·met·ric \ˌsen-trə-sə-ˈme-trik\ *adj* (ca. 1909) **:** symmetric with respect to a central point ⟨~ molecules⟩ ⟨a ~ curve⟩
cen·trum \ˈsen-trəm\ *n, pl* **centrums** *or* **cen·tra** \-trə\ [L — more at CENTER] (1854) **1 :** CENTER **2 :** the body of a vertebra ventral to the neural arch
centu *pl of* CENTAS
cen·tum \ˈken-təm, -ˌtu̇m\ *adj* [L, hundred; fr. the fact that its initial sound (a velar stop) is the representative of an IE palatal stop — more at HUNDRED] (1901) **:** of, relating to, or constituting an Indo-European language group in which the palatal stops did not in prehistoric times become palatal or alveolar fricatives — compare SATEM
cen·tu·ri·on \sen-ˈchu̇r-ē-ən, -ˈtyu̇r-, -ˈtu̇r-\ *n* [ME, fr. MF & L; MF, fr. L *centurion-, centurio*, fr. *centuria*] (13c) **:** an officer commanding a Roman century
cen·tu·ry \ˈsen(t)-sh(ə-)rē\ *n, pl* **-ries** [L *centuria*, irreg. fr. *centum* hundred] (1533) **1 :** a subdivision of the Roman legion **2 :** a group, sequence, or series of 100 like things **3 :** a period of 100 years esp. of the Christian era or of the preceding period of human history **4 :** a race over a hundred units (as yards or miles)
century plant *n* (1764) **:** a Mexican agave (*Agave americana*) that takes many years to mature, flowers only once, and then dies
CEO \ˌsē-(ˌ)ē-ˈō\ *n* [*c*hief *e*xecutive *o*fficer] (1975) **:** the executive with the chief decision-making authority in an organization or business
ceorl \ˈchā-ˌȯrl\ *n* [OE — more at CHURL] (bef. 12c) **:** a freeman of the lowest rank in Anglo-Saxon England
cèpe *or* **cepe** \ˈsep, ˈsep\ *also* **cep** \ˈsep\ *n* [F, fr. Gascon *cep* tree trunk, mushroom, fr. L *cippus* stake, post] (1865) **:** PORCINI
cephal- *or* **cephalo-** *comb form* [L, fr. Gk *kephal-, kephalo-*, fr. *kephalē*] **:** head ⟨*cephal*ad⟩ ⟨*cephalo*pod⟩
ceph·a·lad \ˈse-fə-ˌlad\ *adv* (1887) **:** toward the head or anterior end of the body
ceph·a·lex·in \ˌse-fə-ˈlek-sən\ *n* [*cephalo*sporin + *-ex-* (of unknown origin) + [1]*-in*] (1967) **:** a semisynthetic cephalosporin $C_{16}H_{17}N_3O_4S$ with a spectrum of antibiotic activity similar to the penicillins
ce·phal·ic \sə-ˈfa-lik\ *adj* [MF *céphalique*, fr. L *cephalicus*, fr. Gk *kephalikos*, fr. *kephalē* head; akin to OHG *gebal* skull, ON *gafl* gable, Toch A *śpāl* head] (1599) **1 :** of or relating to the head **2 :** directed toward or situated on or in or near the head — **ce·phal·i·cal·ly** \-li-k(ə-)lē\ *adv*
cephalic index *n* (1866) **:** the ratio multiplied by 100 of the maximum breadth from side to side of the head to its maximum length from front to back in living individuals — compare CRANIAL INDEX
ceph·a·lin \ˈke-fə-lən, ˈse-\ *n* [ISV] (ca. 1899) **:** PHOSPHATIDYLETHANOLAMINE
ceph·a·li·za·tion \ˌse-fə-lə-ˈzā-shən\ *n* (1864) **:** a tendency in the evolution of organisms to concentrate the sensory and neural organs in an anterior head
ceph·a·lom·e·try \ˌse-fə-ˈlä-mə-trē\ *n* [ISV] (ca. 1889) **:** the science of measuring the head in living individuals — compare CRANIOMETRY — **ceph·a·lo·met·ric** \-lō-ˈme-trik\ *adj*

\ə\ **abut** \ᵊ\ **kitten**, F **table** \ər\ **further** \a\ **ash** \ā\ **ace** \ä\ **mop**, **mar**
\au̇\ **out** \ch\ **chin** \e\ **bet** \ē\ **easy** \g\ **go** \i\ **hit** \ī\ **ice** \j\ **job**
\ŋ\ **sing** \ō\ **go** \ȯ\ **law** \ȯi\ **boy** \th\ **thin** \t͟h\ **the** \ü\ **loot** \u̇\ **foot**
\y\ **yet** \zh\ **vision, beige** \k̲, ⁿ, œ, ue, ʸ\ *see* Guide to Pronunciation

ceph·a·lo·pod \ˈse-fə-lə-ˌpäd\ *n* [ultim. fr. *cephal-* + Gk *pod-, pous* foot — more at FOOT] (1826) **:** any of a class (Cephalopoda) of marine mollusks including the squids, cuttlefishes, and octopuses that move by expelling water from a tubular siphon under the head and that have a group of muscular usu. sucker-bearing arms around the front of the head, highly developed eyes, and usu. a sac containing ink which is ejected for defense or concealment — **cephalopod** *adj*

ceph·a·lor·i·dine \ˌse-fə-ˈlȯr-ə-ˌdēn, -ˈlär-\ *n* [prob. fr. *cephalo*sporin + *-idine*] (1964) **:** a semisynthetic broad-spectrum antibiotic $C_{19}H_{17}N_3O_4S_2$ derived from cephalosporin

ceph·a·lo·spo·rin \ˌse-fə-lə-ˈspȯr-ən\ *n* [*NL Cephalosporium,* genus of fungi + 1*-in*] (1951) **:** any of several antibiotics produced by an imperfect fungus (genus *Acremonium* syn. *Cephalosporium*)

ceph·a·lo·thin \ˈse-fə-lə-thən, -ˌthin\ *n* [*cephalo*sporin + *thi-* + 1*-in*] (1962) **:** a semisynthetic broad-spectrum antibiotic derived from cephalosporin and used in the form of its sodium salt $C_{16}H_{15}N_2NaO_6S_2$

ceph·a·lo·tho·rax \ˌse-fə-lə-ˈthȯr-ˌaks\ *n* [ISV] (1835) **:** the united head and thorax of an arachnid or higher crustacean

Ce·phe·id \ˈse-f(ē-)id, ˈsē-\ *n* [ISV, fr. *Cepheus*] (ca. 1903) **:** any of a class of variable stars whose very regular light variations are related directly to their intrinsic luminosities and whose apparent luminosities are used to estimate distances in astronomy

Ce·pheus \ˈsē-ˌfyüs; ˈsē-fē-əs, ˈse-\ *n* [L (gen. *Cephei*), fr. Gk *Kēpheus*] (1563) **:** a constellation between Cygnus and the north pole

1**ce·ram·ic** \sə-ˈra-mik, *esp Brit* kə-\ *adj* [Gk *keramikos,* fr. *keramos* potter's clay, pottery] (1850) **:** of or relating to the manufacture of any product (as earthenware, porcelain, or brick) made essentially from a nonmetallic mineral (as clay) by firing at a high temperature; *also* **:** of or relating to such a product

2**ceramic** *n* (1859) **1** *pl but sing in constr* **:** the art or process of making ceramic articles **2 :** a product of ceramic manufacture

cer·amide \ˈsir-ə-ˌmīd, ˈser-\ *n* [*cerebroside* + *amide*] (1958) **:** any of various lipids formed by linking a fatty acid to sphingosine and found widely but in small amounts in plant and animal tissue

ce·ra·mist \sə-ˈra-mist, ˈser-ə-\ *or* **ce·ram·i·cist** \sə-ˈra-mə-sist\ *n* (1855) **:** one who makes ceramic products or works of art

ce·rate \ˈsir-ˌāt\ *n* [ME, fr. L *ceratum* wax salve, fr. *cera* wax — more at CERUMEN] (15c) **:** an unctuous preparation for external use consisting of wax or resin or spermaceti mixed with oil, lard, and medicinal ingredients

cer·a·top·sian \ˌsər-ə-ˈtäp-sē-ən\ *n* [NL *Ceratopsia,* fr. *Ceratops,* a genus, fr. Gk *kerat-, keras* horn + *ōps* face — more at HORN, EYE] (1909) **:** any of a suborder (Ceratopsia) of ornithischian dinosaurs of the Late Cretaceous having horns, a sharp horny beak, and a bony frill projecting backward from the skull — **ceratopsian** *adj*

Cer·ber·us \ˈsər-b(ə-)rəs\ *n* [L, fr. Gk *Kerberos*] (14c) **:** a 3-headed dog that in Greek mythology guards the entrance to Hades — **Cer·ber·e·an** \ˌsər-bə-ˈrē-ən\ *adj*

-cercal *adj comb form* [F *-cerque,* fr. Gk *kerkos* tail] **:** -tailed ⟨homocer*cal*⟩

cer·car·ia \(ˌ)sər-ˈker-ē-ə\ *n, pl* **-i·ae** \-ē-ˌē\ [NL, fr. Gk *kerkos*] (ca. 1871) **:** a usu. tadpole-shaped larval trematode worm that develops in a molluscan host from a redia — **cer·car·i·al** \-ē-əl\ *adj*

cer·cus \ˈsər-kəs\ *n, pl* **cer·ci** \ˈsər-ˌsī, -ˌkī\ [NL, fr. Gk *kerkos*] (1826) **:** either of a pair of simple or segmented appendages at the posterior end of various arthropods that usu. act as sensory organs

1**cere** \ˈsir\ *vt* **cered; cer·ing** [ME, to impregnate with wax, fr. MF *cirer,* fr. L *cerare,* fr. *cera*] (15c) **:** to wrap in or as if in a cerecloth

2**cere** *n* [MF *cere,* fr. ML *cera,* fr. L, wax] (15c) **:** a usu. waxy protuberance or enlarged area at the base of the bill of a bird

1**ce·re·al** \ˈsir-ē-əl\ *adj* [F or L; F *céréale,* fr. L *cerealis* of Ceres, of grain, fr. *Ceres*] (1818) **:** relating to grain or to the plants that produce it; *also* **:** made of grain

2**cereal** *n* (1832) **1 :** a plant (as a grass) yielding starchy grain suitable for food; *also* **:** its grain **2 :** a prepared foodstuff of grain (as oatmeal or cornflakes)

cereal leaf beetle *n* (1962) **:** a small reddish-brown black-headed Old World chrysomelid beetle (*Oulema melanopus*) that feeds on cereal grasses and is a serious pest of U.S. grain crops

cer·e·bel·lum \ˌser-ə-ˈbe-ləm, ˌse-rə-\ *n, pl* **-bellums** *or* **-bel·la** \-ˈbe-lə\ [ML, fr. L, dim. of *cerebrum*] (1543) **:** a large dorsally projecting part of the brain concerned esp. with the coordination of muscles and the maintenance of bodily equilibrium, situated between the brain stem and the back of the cerebrum, and formed in humans of two lateral lobes and a median lobe — see BRAIN illustration — **cer·e·bel·lar** \-ˈbe-lər\ *adj*

cerebr- *or* **cerebro-** *comb form* [*cerebrum*] **1 :** brain **:** cerebrum ⟨*cerebration*⟩ **2 :** cerebral and ⟨*cerebro*spinal⟩

ce·re·bral \sə-ˈrē-brəl, ˈser-ə-, ˈse-rə-\ *adj* [F *cérébral,* fr. L *cerebrum* brain; akin to OHG *hirni* brain, Gk *kara* head, *keras* horn, Skt *śiras* head — more at HORN] (1816) **1 a :** of or relating to the brain or the intellect **b :** of, relating to, affecting, or being the cerebrum **2 a :** appealing to intellectual appreciation ⟨~ drama⟩ **b :** primarily intellectual in nature ⟨a ~ society⟩ — **ce·re·bral·ly** \-brə-lē\ *adv*

cerebral cortex *n* (1926) **:** the convoluted surface layer of gray matter of the cerebrum that functions chiefly in coordination of sensory and motor information — compare NEOCORTEX

cerebral hemisphere *n* (1816) **:** either of the two hollow convoluted lateral halves of the cerebrum — see BRAIN illustration

cerebral palsy *n* (1889) **:** a disability resulting from damage to the brain before, during, or shortly after birth and outwardly manifested by muscular incoordination and speech disturbances — **cerebral-palsied** *adj*

cer·e·brate \ˈser-ə-ˌbrāt, ˈse-rə-\ *vi* **-brat·ed; -brat·ing** [back-formation fr. *cerebration,* fr. *cerebrum*] (1915) **:** to use the mind **:** THINK — **cer·e·bra·tion** \ˌser-ə-ˈbrā-shən, ˈse-rə-\ *n*

ce·re·bro·side \ˈser-ə-brə-ˌsīd, ˈse-rə-, sə-ˈrē-\ *n* [*cerebrose* galactose] (1883) **:** any of various glycolipids found esp. in nerve tissue

ce·re·bro·spi·nal \sə-ˌrē-brō-ˈspī-nᵊl, ˌser-ə-brō-\ *adj* (1826) **:** of or relating to the brain and spinal cord or to these together with the cranial and spinal nerves that innervate voluntary muscles

cerebrospinal fluid *n* (ca. 1889) **:** a colorless liquid that is comparable to serum, is secreted from the blood into the lateral ventricles of the brain, and serves chiefly to maintain uniform pressure within the brain and spinal cord

cerebrospinal meningitis *n* (1873) **:** inflammation of the meninges of both brain and spinal cord; *specif* **:** an infectious often epidemic and fatal meningitis caused by the meningococcus

ce·re·bro·vas·cu·lar \sə-ˌrē-brō-ˈvas-kyə-lər, ˌser-ə-brō-\ *adj* (1935) **:** of or involving the cerebrum and the blood vessels supplying it

cerebrovascular accident *n* (1935) **:** STROKE 5

ce·re·brum \sə-ˈrē-brəm, ˈser-ə-brəm, ˈse-rə-\ *n, pl* **-brums** *or* **-bra** \-brə\ [L] (1615) **1 :** BRAIN 1a **2 :** an enlarged anterior or upper part of the brain; *esp* **:** the expanded anterior portion of the brain that in higher mammals overlies the rest of the brain, consists of cerebral hemispheres and connecting structures, and is considered to be the seat of conscious mental processes **:** TELENCEPHALON

cere·cloth \ˈsir-ˌklȯth\ *n* [alter. of earlier *cered cloth* (waxed cloth)] (1553) **:** cloth treated with melted wax or gummy matter and formerly used esp. for wrapping a dead body

cere·ment \ˈser-ə-mənt, ˈse-rə-, ˈsir-mənt\ *n* (1602) **:** a shroud for the dead; *esp* **:** CERECLOTH — usu. used in pl.

1**cer·e·mo·ni·al** \ˌser-ə-ˈmō-nē-əl, ˌse-rə-\ *adj* (14c) **1 :** marked by, involved in, or belonging to ceremony **:** stressing careful attention to form and detail ⟨~ rites⟩ **2 :** having no real power or influence ⟨his new position is largely ~⟩ — **cer·e·mo·ni·al·ism** \-ə-ˌli-zəm\ *n* — **cer·e·mo·ni·al·ist** \-ə-list\ *n* — **cer·e·mo·ni·al·ly** \-ə-lē\ *adv*

syn CEREMONIAL, CEREMONIOUS, FORMAL, CONVENTIONAL mean marked by attention to or adhering strictly to prescribed forms. CEREMONIAL and CEREMONIOUS both imply strict attention to what is prescribed by custom or by ritual, but CEREMONIAL applies to things that are associated with ceremonies ⟨a *ceremonial* offering⟩, CEREMONIOUS to persons given to ceremony or to acts attended by ceremony ⟨made his *ceremonious* entrance⟩. FORMAL applies both to things prescribed by and to persons obedient to custom and may suggest stiff, restrained, or old-fashioned behavior ⟨a *formal* report⟩ ⟨the headmaster's *formal* manner⟩. CONVENTIONAL implies accord with general custom and usage ⟨*conventional* courtesy⟩ and may suggest a stodgy lack of originality or independence ⟨*conventional* fiction⟩.

2**ceremonial** *n* (14c) **:** a ceremonial act, action, or system

cer·e·mo·ni·ous \ˌser-ə-ˈmō-nē-əs, ˌse-rə-\ *adj* (1553) **1 :** devoted to forms and ceremony ⟨~ courtiers⟩ **2 :** of, relating to, or constituting a ceremony ⟨a ~ occasion⟩ **3 :** according to formal usage or prescribed procedures ⟨the cold and ~ politeness of her curtsey —Jane Austen⟩ **4 :** marked by ceremony ⟨a ~ procession⟩ ***syn*** see CEREMONIAL — **cer·e·mo·ni·ous·ly** *adv* — **cer·e·mo·ni·ous·ness** *n*

cer·e·mo·ny \ˈser-ə-ˌmō-nē, ˈse-rə-\ *n, pl* **-nies** [ME *ceremonie,* fr. MF *ceremonie,* fr. L *caerimonia*] (14c) **1 :** a formal act or series of acts prescribed by ritual, protocol, or convention ⟨the marriage ~⟩ **2 a :** a conventional act of politeness or etiquette ⟨the ~ of introduction⟩ **b :** an action performed only formally with no deep significance **c :** a routine action performed with elaborate pomp **3 a :** prescribed procedures **:** USAGES ⟨the ~ attending an inauguration⟩ **b :** observance of an established code of civility or politeness ⟨opened the door without ~ and strode in⟩

Ce·ren·kov radiation \chə-ˈreŋ-kȯf-, chər-ˈyeŋ-\ *n* [P. A. *Cherenkov*] (1939) **:** light produced by charged particles (as electrons) traversing a transparent medium at a speed greater than that of light in the same medium — called also *Cerenkov light*

Ce·res \ˈsir-(ˌ)ēz\ *n* [L] (15c) **1 :** the Roman goddess of agriculture — compare DEMETER **2 :** a dwarf planet that orbits within the asteroid belt with a mean distance from the sun of 2.7 astronomical units (260 million miles) and a diameter of 590 miles (950 kilometers)

ce·re·us \ˈsir-ē-əs\ *n* [NL, genus name, fr. L, wax candle, fr. *cera* wax — more at CERUMEN] (1730) **:** any of various cacti (as of the genus *Cereus*) of the western U.S. and tropical America

ce·ric \ˈsir-ik, ˈser-\ *adj* (1869) **:** of, relating to, or containing cerium esp. with a valence of four

ce·rise \sə-ˈrēs, -ˈrēz\ *n* [F, lit., cherry, fr. LL *ceresia* — more at CHERRY] (1844) **:** a moderate red

ce·ri·um \ˈsir-ē-əm\ *n* [NL, fr. *Ceres,* an asteroid] (1804) **:** a malleable ductile metallic element that is the most abundant of the rare-earth group — see ELEMENT table

cer·met \ˈsər-ˌmet\ *n* [*ceramic* + *metal*] (1948) **:** a composite structural material of a heat-resistant compound (as titanium carbide) and a metal (as nickel) used esp. for turbine blades

CERN *abbr* [orig. *Conseil Européen pour la Recherche Nucléaire*] European Organization for Nuclear Research

cero \ˈser-(ˌ)ō\ *n, pl* **cero** *or* **ceros** [modif. of Sp *sierra* saw, cero] (1884) **:** a large spotted food and sport fish (*Scomberomorus regalis*) of the warmer parts of the western Atlantic

ce·rous \ˈsir-əs\ *adj* (1869) **:** of, relating to, or containing cerium esp. with a valence of three

cert *abbr* certificate; certification; certified; certify

1**cer·tain** \ˈsər-tᵊn\ *adj* [ME, fr. AF, fr. VL **certanus,* fr. L *certus,* fr. pp. of *cernere* to sift, discern, decide; akin to Gk *krinein* to separate, decide, judge, OIr *criathar* sieve] (13c) **1 :** FIXED, SETTLED ⟨a ~ percentage of the profit⟩ **2 :** of a specific but unspecified character, quantity, or degree ⟨the house has a ~ charm⟩ **3 a :** DEPENDABLE, RELIABLE ⟨a ~ remedy for the disease⟩ **b :** known or proved to be true **:** INDISPUTABLE ⟨it is ~ that we exist⟩ **4 a :** INEVITABLE ⟨the ~ advance of age⟩ **b :** incapable of failing **:** DESTINED — used with a following infinitive ⟨she is ~ to do well⟩ **5 :** assured in mind or action ⟨I am ~ they are right⟩ ***syn*** see SURE — **for certain :** as a certainty **:** ASSUREDLY ⟨the cause is not known *for certain*⟩ — **of a certain age :** of a somewhat advanced age **:** no longer young ⟨remembered by people *of a certain age*⟩

2**certain** *pron, pl in constr* (15c) **:** certain ones

cer·tain·ly \-lē\ *adv* (14c) **1 :** in a manner that is certain **:** with certainty **2 :** it is certain that **:** ASSUREDLY

cer·tain·ty \ˈsər-tᵊn-tē\ *n, pl* **-ties** (14c) **1 :** something that is certain **2 :** the quality or state of being certain esp. on the basis of evidence

syn CERTAINTY, CERTITUDE, CONVICTION mean a state of being free from doubt. CERTAINTY and CERTITUDE are very close; CERTAINTY may stress the existence of objective proof ⟨claims that cannot be confirmed with scientific *certainty*⟩, while CERTITUDE may emphasize a faith in something not needing or not capable of proof ⟨believes with *certitude* in an afterlife⟩. CONVICTION applies esp. to belief strongly held by an individual ⟨holds firm *convictions* on every issue⟩.

cer·tes \ˈsər-tēz, ˈsərts\ *adv* [ME, fr. OF, fr. *cert* certain, fr. L *certus*] (13c) *archaic* : in truth : CERTAINLY

cer·ti·fi·able \ˌsər-tə-ˈfī-ə-bəl\ *adj* (1846) **1 a** : capable of being certified ⟨~ teachers⟩ **b** : GENUINE, AUTHENTIC ⟨a ~ liar⟩ ⟨a ~ movie star⟩ **2** : fit to be certified as insane : CRAZY ⟨downright ~ behavior⟩ — **cer·ti·fi·ably** \-blē\ *adv*

[1]**cer·tif·i·cate** \(ˌ)sər-ˈti-fi-kət\ *n* [ME *certificat,* fr. ML *certificatum,* fr. LL, neut. of *certificatus,* pp. of *certificare* to certify] (15c) **1** : a document containing a certified statement esp. as to the truth of something; *specif* : a document certifying that one has fulfilled the requirements of and may practice in a field **2** : something serving the same end as a certificate **3** : a document evidencing ownership or debt ⟨a stock ~⟩

[2]**cer·tif·i·cate** \-ˈti-fə-ˌkāt\ *vt* **-cat·ed; -cat·ing** (1818) : to testify to or authorize by a certificate; *esp* : CERTIFY 4 — **cer·tif·i·ca·to·ry** \-ˈti-fi-kə-ˌtȯr-ē\ *adj*

certificate of deposit (1846) : a money-market bond of a preset face value paying fixed interest and redeemable without penalty only on maturity

cer·ti·fi·ca·tion \ˌsər-tə-fə-ˈkā-shən\ *n* (15c) **1** : the act of certifying : the state of being certified **2** : a certified statement

certification mark *n* (1947) : a mark or device used to identify a product or service that has been certified to conform to a particular set of standards

certified *adj* (1611) **1** : having earned certification ⟨a ~ gemologist⟩ **2** : GENUINE, AUTHENTIC ⟨a ~ big shot⟩ ⟨~ intellectuals⟩

certified mail *n* (1955) : first class mail for which proof of delivery is secured but no indemnity value is claimed

certified milk *n* (1899) : milk produced in dairies that operate under the rules and regulations of an authorized medical milk commission

certified public accountant *n* (1896) : an accountant who has met the requirements of a state law and has been granted a certificate

cer·ti·fy \ˈsər-tə-ˌfī\ *vt* **-fied; -fy·ing** [ME *certifien,* fr. AF *certefier,* fr. LL *certificare,* fr. L *certus* certain — more at CERTAIN] (14c) **1** : to attest authoritatively: as **a** : CONFIRM **b** : to present in formal communication **c** : to attest as being true or as represented or as meeting a standard **d** : to attest officially to the insanity of **2** : to inform with certainty : ASSURE **3** : to guarantee (a personal check) as to signature and amount by so indicating on the face **4** : to recognize as having met special qualifications (as of a governmental agency or professional board) within a field ⟨agencies that ~ teachers⟩ — **cer·ti·fi·er** \-ˌfī(-ə)r\ *n*

syn CERTIFY, ATTEST, WITNESS, VOUCH mean to testify to the truth or genuineness of something. CERTIFY usu. applies to a written statement, esp. one carrying a signature or seal ⟨*certified* that the candidate had met all requirements⟩. ATTEST applies to oral or written testimony usu. from experts or witnesses ⟨*attested* to the authenticity of the document⟩. WITNESS applies to the subscribing of one's own name to a document as evidence of its genuineness ⟨*witnessed* the signing of the will⟩. VOUCH applies to one who testifies as a competent authority or a reliable person ⟨willing to *vouch* for her integrity⟩. ***syn*** see in addition APPROVE

cer·tio·ra·ri \ˌsər-sh(ē-)ə-ˈrer-ē, -ˈrär-ē, -ˈra-rē\ *n* [ME, fr. L, lit., to be informed; fr. the use of the word in the writ] (15c) : a writ of superior court to call up the records of an inferior court or a body acting in a quasi-judicial capacity

cer·ti·tude \ˈsər-tə-ˌtüd *also* -ˌtyüd\ *n* [ME, fr. LL *certitudo,* fr. L *certus*] (15c) **1** : the state of being or feeling certain **2** : certainty of act or event ***syn*** see CERTAINTY

ce·ru·le·an \sə-ˈrü-lē-ən\ *adj* [L *caeruleus* dark blue] (1662) : resembling the blue of the sky

ce·ru·lo·plas·min \sə-ˌrü-lō-ˈplaz-mən\ *n* [ISV *cerulo-* (fr. L *caeruleus*) + *plasma* + [1]*-in*] (ca. 1952) : a blue copper-binding serum oxidase that is deficient in Wilson's disease

ce·ru·men \sə-ˈrü-mən\ *n* [NL, irreg. fr. L *cera* wax; akin to Gk *kēros* wax] (1741) : EARWAX — **ce·ru·mi·nous** \-mə-nəs\ *adj*

ce·ruse \sə-ˈrüs, ˈsir-ˌüs\ *n* [ME, fr. MF *céruse,* fr. L *cerussa*] (14c) **1** : white lead as a pigment **2** : a cosmetic containing white lead

ce·rus·site \sə-ˈrə-ˌsīt\ *n* [G *Zerussit,* fr. L *cerussa*] (1850) : a colorless or white mineral consisting of a carbonate of lead that occurs in transparent crystals and also in massive form and is a source of white lead

cer·ve·lat \ˈsər-və-ˌlat, -ˌlä\ *n* [obs. F (now *cervelas*)] (1613) : smoked sausage made from a combination of pork and beef

cer·ve·za \sər-ˈvā-sə; ser-ˈbā-sä, ther-ˈbā-thä\ *n* [Sp, fr. L *cervesia,* a kind of beer] (1949) **1** : BEER 1 **2** : BEER 4

cer·vi·cal \ˈsər-vi-kəl\ *adj* (1681) : of or relating to a neck or cervix

cervical cap *n* (1923) : a usu. rubber or plastic contraceptive device in the form of a thimble-shaped molded cap that fits snugly over the uterine cervix and blocks sperm from entering the uterus

cer·vi·ci·tis \ˌsər-və-ˈsī-təs\ *n* [NL] (1889) : inflammation of the uterine cervix

cer·vine \ˈsər-ˌvīn\ *adj* [L *cervinus* of a deer, fr. *cervus* stag, deer — more at HART] (ca. 1828) : of, relating to, or resembling deer

cer·vix \ˈsər-viks\ *n, pl* **cer·vi·ces** \ˈsər-və-ˌsēz, (ˌ)sər-ˈvī-(ˌ)sēz\ *or* **cer·vix·es** [L *cervic-, cervix*] (15c) **1** : NECK; *esp* : the back part of the neck **2** : a constricted portion of an organ or part; *esp* : the narrow outer end of the uterus

ce·sar·e·an *or* **cae·sar·e·an** *also* **ce·sar·i·an** *or* **cae·sar·i·an** \si-ˈzer-ē-ən\ *n, often cap* (ca. 1903) : CESAREAN SECTION — **cesarean** *or* **caesarean** *also* **cesarian** *or* **caesarian** *adj, often cap*

cesarean section *or* **caesarean section** *n, often cap C* [fr. the legendary association of such a delivery with the Roman cognomen *Caesar*] (1615) : surgical incision of the walls of the abdomen and uterus for delivery of offspring

ce·si·um \ˈsē-zē-əm *also* -zhē-\ *n* [NL, fr. L *caesius* bluish gray] (1861) : a silver-white soft ductile element of the alkali metal group that is the most electropositive element known and that is used esp. in photoelectric cells — see ELEMENT table

cesium 133 *n* (1966) : an isotope of cesium used esp. in atomic clocks and one of whose atomic transitions is used as a scientific time standard

cess \ˈses\ *n* [prob. short for *success*] (1830) *chiefly Irish* : LUCK — usu. used in the phrase *bad cess to you*

ces·sa·tion \se-ˈsā-shən\ *n* [ME *cessacioun,* fr. MF *cessation,* fr. L *cessation-, cessatio* delay, idleness, fr. *cessare* to delay, be idle — more at CEASE] (15c) : a temporary or final ceasing (as of action) : STOP

ces·sion \ˈse-shən\ *n* [ME, fr. AF, fr. L *cession-, cessio,* fr. *cedere* to withdraw — more at CEDE] (15c) : a yielding to another : CONCESSION

cess·pit \ˈses-ˌpit\ *n* [*cess*pool + *pit*] (1777) : a pit for the disposal of refuse (as sewage)

cess·pool \-ˌpül\ *n* [perh. by folk etymology fr. ME *suspiral* vent, tap on a main pipe, settling pool, fr. AF *suspirale* vent, fr. *suspirer* to sigh, exhale, fr. L *suspirare,* lit., to draw a long breath — more at SUSPIRE] (1782) **1** : an underground reservoir for liquid waste (as household sewage) **2** : a filthy, evil, or corrupt place or state ⟨a ~ of corruption⟩

ces·ta \ˈses-tə\ *n* [Sp, lit., basket, fr. L *cista* box, basket] (ca. 1902) : a narrow curved wicker basket used to catch and propel the ball in jai alai

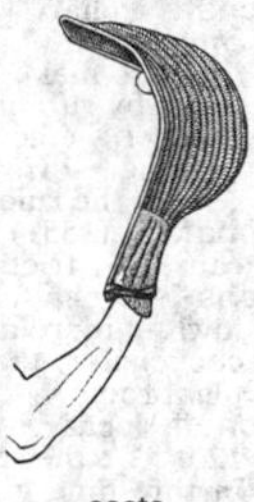
cesta

ces·tode \ˈses-ˌtōd\ *n* [NL *Cestoda,* taxonomic group comprising tapeworms, ultim. fr. Gk *kestos* girdle] (ca. 1890) : TAPEWORM — **cestode** *adj*

[1]**ces·tus** \ˈses-təs\ *n, pl* **ces·ti** \-ˌtī\ [L, girdle, belt, fr. Gk *kestos,* fr. *kestos* stitched, fr. *kentein* to prick — more at CENTER] (1557) : a woman's belt; *esp* : a symbolic one worn by a bride

[2]**cestus** *n* [L *cestus, caestus*] (ca. 1720) : a hand covering of leather bands often loaded with lead or iron and used by boxers in ancient Rome

CETA *abbr* Comprehensive Employment and Training Act

ce·ta·cean \si-ˈtā-shən\ *n* [ultim. fr. L *cetus* whale, fr. Gk *kētos*] (1835) : any of an order (Cetacea) of aquatic mostly marine mammals that includes the whales, dolphins, porpoises, and related forms and that have a torpedo-shaped nearly hairless body, paddle-shaped forelimbs but no hind limbs, one or two nares opening externally at the top of the head, and a horizontally flattened tail used for locomotion — **cetacean** *adj* — **ce·ta·ceous** \-shəs\ *adj*

ce·tane \ˈsē-ˌtān\ *n* [fr. *cetyl,* the radical $C_{16}H_{33}$] (1871) : a colorless oily hydrocarbon $C_{16}H_{34}$ found in petroleum

cetane number *n* (1935) : a measure of the ignition value of a diesel fuel that represents the percentage by volume of cetane in a mixture of liquid methylnaphthalene that gives the same ignition lag as the oil being tested — called also *cetane rating*; compare OCTANE NUMBER

ce·te·ris pa·ri·bus \ˈkā-tər-əs-ˈpa-rə-bəs, ˈke-, ˈse-\ *adv* [NL, other things being equal] (1601) : if all other relevant things, factors, or elements remain unaltered

ce·tol·o·gy \sē-ˈtä-lə-jē\ *n* [L *cetus* whale] (ca. 1828) : a branch of zoology concerned with the cetaceans — **ce·tol·o·gist** \-jist\ *n*

Ce·tus \ˈsē-təs\ *n* [L (gen. *Ceti*), lit., whale] (1825) : an equatorial constellation south of Pisces and Aries

ce·tyl alcohol \ˈsē-tᵊl-\ *n* [ISV *cet-* (fr. L *cetus* whale) + *-yl;* fr. its occurrence in spermaceti] (1863) : a waxy crystalline alcohol $C_{16}H_{34}O$ obtained by the saponification of spermaceti or the hydrogenation of palmitic acid and used esp. in pharmaceutical and cosmetic preparations and in making detergents

CEU *abbr* continuing education unit

ceviche *var of* SEVICHE

cf *abbr* **1** calf **2** [L *confer,* imper. of *conferre* to compare] compare

Cf *symbol* californium

CF *abbr* **1** carried forward **2** centrifugal force **3** cost and freight **4** cystic fibrosis

CFC *abbr* chlorofluorocarbon

CFI *abbr* **1** certified flight instructor; chief flying instructor **2** cost, freight, and insurance

CFL *abbr* **1** Canadian Football League **2** compact fluorescent lamp; compact fluorescent lightbulb

cfm *abbr* cubic feet per minute

CFO *abbr* chief financial officer

CFP *abbr* certified financial planner

cfs *abbr* cubic feet per second

CFS *abbr* chronic fatigue syndrome

cg *abbr* centigram

CG *abbr* **1** center of gravity **2** coast guard **3** commanding general

CGI *abbr* computer-generated images; computer-generated imagery

cgs *abbr* centimeter-gram-second

CGT *abbr* [F *Confédération Générale du Travail*] General Confederation of Labor

ch *abbr* **1** chain **2** champion **3** chaplain **4** chapter **5** chief **6** child; children **7** church

CH *abbr* **1** clearinghouse **2** courthouse **3** customhouse

Cha·blis \sha-ˈblē, shə-, shä-; ˈsha-(ˌ)blē\ *n, pl* **Cha·blis** \-ˈblēz, -(ˌ)blēz\ [F, fr. *Chablis,* town in France] (1668) **1** : a dry sharp white burgundy wine **2** : a semidry soft white California wine

cha–cha \ˈchä-(ˌ)chä\ *n* [AmerSp *cha-cha-cha*] (1954) : a fast rhythmic ballroom dance of Latin-American origin with a basic pattern of three steps and a shuffle

chac·ma baboon \ˈchäk-mə-\ *n* [Khoikhoi] (1896) : a large dusky baboon (*Papio ursinus*) of southern African savannas — called also *chacma*

cha·conne \shä-ˈkȯn, sha-, -ˈkän, -ˈkən\ *n* [F & Sp; F *chaconne,* fr. Sp *chacona*] (1659) **1** : an old Spanish dance tune of Latin-American origin **2** : a musical composition in moderate triple time typically consisting of variations on a repeated succession of chords

chad \ˈchad\ *n* [origin unknown] (1944) : small pieces of paper or cardboard produced in punching paper tape or data cards; *also* : a piece of chad — **chad·less** \-ləs\ *adj*

Chad·ic \ˈcha-dik\ *or* **Chad** \ˈchad\ *n* (ca. 1950) : a subfamily of the Afro-Asiatic language family comprising numerous languages of northern Nigeria, northern Cameroon, and Chad — **Chadic** *adj*

\ə\ **abut** \ᵊ\ **kitten**, F table \ər\ **further** \a\ **ash** \ā\ **ace** \ä\ **mop, mar** \au̇\ **out** \ch\ **chin** \e\ **bet** \ē\ **easy** \g\ **go** \i\ **hit** \ī\ **ice** \j\ **job** \ŋ\ **sing** \ō\ **go** \ȯ\ **law** \ȯi\ **boy** \th\ **thin** \t͟h\ **the** \ü\ **loot** \u̇\ **foot** \y\ **yet** \zh\ **vision, beige** \ᵏ, ⁿ, œ, ue, ʸ\ *see* Guide to Pronunciation

cha·dor \'chə-dər, 'chä-\ *n* [Hindi, Urdu, & Pers; Hindi *caddar, cādar* & Urdu *chaddar,* fr. Pers *chaddar, chādar*] (1525) : a large cloth worn as a combination head covering, veil, and shawl usu. by Muslim women esp. in Iran

chae·bol \'chā-ˌbōl, 'je-ˌbəl\ *n, pl* **chaebol** [Korean *chaebŏl,* fr. *chae* wealth, property + *pŏl* faction, clan] (1984) : a family-controlled industrial conglomerate in South Korea

chae·ta \'kē-tə\ *n, pl* **chae·tae** \'kē-ˌtē\ [NL, fr. Gk *chaitē* long flowing hair] (ca. 1866) : BRISTLE, SETA — **chae·tal** \'kē-tᵊl\ *adj*

chae·to·gnath \'kē-ˌtäg-ˌnath, -tə(g)-\ *n* [NL *Chaetognatha,* class or phylum name, ultim. fr. Gk *chaitē* + *gnathos* jaw — more at -GNATHOUS] (ca. 1889) : ARROWWORM — **chaetognath** *adj*

[1]**chafe** \'chāf\ *vb* **chafed; chaf·ing** [ME *chaufen* to warm, fr. AF *chaufer,* fr. VL **calfare,* alter. of L *calefacere,* fr. *calēre* to be warm + *facere* to make — more at LEE, DO] *vt* (14c) **1** : IRRITATE, VEX **2** : to warm by rubbing esp. with the hands **3 a** : to rub so as to wear away : ABRADE ⟨the strap *chafed* his skin⟩ **b** : to make sore by or as if by rubbing ~ *vi* **1** : to feel irritation, discontent, or impatience : FRET ⟨~*s* at the rules⟩ **2** : to rub and thereby cause wear or irritation

[2]**chafe** *n* (1551) **1** : a state of vexation : RAGE **2** : injury or wear caused by friction; *also* : FRICTION, RUBBING

cha·fer \'chā-fər\ *n* [ME *cheaffer,* fr. OE *ceafor;* prob. akin to OE *ceafl* jowl — more at JOWL] (bef. 12c) : any of various scarab beetles (as a cockchafer) that feed on leaves and flowers and whose larvae feed on plant roots

[1]**chaff** \'chaf\ *n* [ME *chaf,* fr. OE *ceaf;* akin to OHG *cheva* husk] (bef. 12c) **1** : the seed coverings and other debris separated from the seed in threshing grain **2** : something comparatively worthless **3** : the scales borne on the receptacle among the florets in the heads of many composite plants **4** : material (as strips of foil or clusters of fine wires) ejected into the air for reflecting radar waves (as for confusing an enemy's radar detection) — **chaffy** \'cha-fē\ *adj*

[2]**chaff** *n* [prob. fr. [1]*chaff*] (1821) : light jesting talk : BANTER

[3]**chaff** *vt* (1827) : to tease good-naturedly ~ *vi* : JEST, BANTER

[1]**chaf·fer** \'cha-fər\ *n* [ME *chaffare,* fr. *chep* trade + *fare* journey — more at CHEAP, FARE] (13c) *archaic* : a haggling about price

[2]**chaffer** *vb* **chaf·fered; chaf·fer·ing** \'cha-f(ə-)riŋ\ *vi* (14c) **1** : HAGGLE **2** *Brit* : to exchange small talk : CHATTER ~ *vt* **1** : EXCHANGE, BARTER **2** : to bargain for — **chaf·fer·er** \-fər-ər\ *n*

chaf·finch \'cha-(ˌ)finch\ *n* [ME, fr. OE *ceaffinc,* fr. *ceaf* + *finc* finch] (bef. 12c) : a common European finch (*Fringilla coelebs* of the family Frangillidae) of which the male has a pinkish-brown breast

chaf·ing dish \'chā-fiŋ-\ *n* [ME *chafing,* prp. of *chaufen, chafen* to warm] (15c) : a utensil for cooking or keeping food warm at the table

Cha·gas' disease \'shä-gəs-, -gə-səz-\ *n* [Carlos *Chagas* †1934 Braz. physician] (1912) : a tropical American disease that is caused by a trypanosome (*Trypanosoma cruzi*) and is marked by prolonged high fever, edema, and enlargement of the spleen, liver, and lymph nodes

[1]**cha·grin** \shə-'grin\ *n* [F, fr. *chagrin* sad] (ca. 1681) : disquietude or distress of mind caused by humiliation, disappointment, or failure

[2]**chagrin** *vt* **cha·grined** \-'grind\; **cha·grin·ing** \-'gri-niŋ\ (1733) : to vex or unsettle by disappointing or humiliating ⟨he was ~*ed* to learn that his help was not needed⟩

chai \'chī\ *n* [Turk *çay* & Russ, Pers, Hindi, & Urdu *chay* tea] (1974) : a beverage that is a blend of black tea, honey, spices, and milk

[1]**chain** \'chān\ *n, often attrib* [ME *cheyne,* fr. AF *chaene,* fr. L *catena*] (14c) **1 a** : a series of usu. metal links or rings connected to or fitted into one another and used for various purposes (as support, restraint, transmission of mechanical power, or measurement) **b** : a series of links used or worn as an ornament or insignia **c** (1) : a measuring instrument of 100 links used in surveying (2) : a unit of length equal to 66 feet (about 20 meters) **2** : something that confines, restrains, or secures **3 a** : a series of things linked, connected, or associated together ⟨a ~ of events⟩ ⟨a mountain ~⟩ **b** : a group of enterprises or institutions of the same kind or function usu. under a single ownership, management, or control ⟨fast-food ~*s*⟩ **c** : a number of atoms or chemical groups united like links in a chain

[2]**chain** *vt* (14c) **1** : to obstruct or protect by a chain **2** : to fasten, bind, or connect with or as if with a chain; *also* : FETTER

chaî·né \sha-'nā\ *n* [F, fr. pp. of *chaîner* to chain] (1897) : a series of short usu. fast turns by which a ballet dancer moves across the stage

chain gang *n* (1830) : a gang of people (as convicts) chained together esp. as an outside working party

chain letter *n* (1905) : a letter sent to several persons with a request that each send copies of the letter to an equal number of persons

chain–link fence *n* (ca. 1927) : a fence of heavy steel wire woven to form a diamond-shaped mesh

chain mail *n* (1822) : flexible armor of interlinked metal rings

chain of command (1898) : a series of executive positions in order of authority ⟨a military *chain of command*⟩

chain pickerel *n* [fr. the markings resembling chains on the sides] (1887) : a large greenish-black pickerel (*Esox niger*) with dark markings along the sides that is common in quiet waters of eastern No. America

chain reaction *n* (ca. 1902) **1 a** : a series of events so related to each other that each one initiates the next **b** : a number of events triggered by the same initial event **2** : a self-sustaining chemical or nuclear reaction yielding energy or products that cause further reactions of the same kind — **chain–re·act** \'chān-rē-'akt\ *vi*

chain rule *n* (ca. 1937) : a mathematical rule concerning the differentiation of a function of a function (as $f[u(x)]$) by which under suitable conditions of continuity and differentiability one function is differentiated with respect to the second function considered as an independent variable and then the second function is differentiated with respect to its independent variable

chain saw *n* (1944) : a portable power saw that has teeth linked together to form an endless chain — **chain·saw** \'chān-ˌsȯ\ *vt*

chain–smoke \'chān-'smōk\ *vi* (1890) : to smoke esp. cigarettes continually ~ *vt* : to smoke (as cigarettes) almost without interruption — **chain–smok·er** \-ˌsmō-kər\ *n*

chain stitch *n* (1820) **1** : an ornamental stitch like chain links **2** : a machine stitch forming a chain on the underside of the work

chain store *n* (1910) : one of numerous usu. retail stores having the same ownership and selling the same lines of goods

chain·wheel \'chān-ˌhwēl, -ˌwēl\ *n* (1845) : SPROCKET 1

[1]**chair** \'cher\ *n* [ME *chaiere,* fr. AF, fr. L *cathedra,* fr. Gk *kathedra,* fr. *kata-* cata- + *hedra* seat — more at SIT] (13c) **1 a** : a seat typically having four legs and a back for one person **b** : ELECTRIC CHAIR — used with *the* **2 a** : an official seat or a seat of authority, state, or dignity **b** : an office or position of authority or dignity **c** : PROFESSORSHIP ⟨holds a university ~⟩ **d** : CHAIRMAN 1 **3** : a sedan chair **4** : a position of employment usu. of one occupying a chair or desk; *specif* : the position of a player in an orchestra or band **5** : any of various devices that hold up or support

[2]**chair** *vt* (1552) **1** : to install in office **2** *chiefly Brit* : to carry on the shoulders in acclaim ⟨we ~*ed* you through the market place —A. E. Housman⟩ **3** : to preside as chairman of

chair car *n* (1880) **1** : a railroad car having pairs of chairs with individually adjustable backs on each side of the aisle **2** : PARLOR CAR

chair·lift \'cher-ˌlift\ *n* (1940) : a motor-driven conveyor consisting of a series of seats suspended from a cable and used for transporting skiers or sightseers up or down a long slope or mountainside

[1]**chair·man** \-mən\ *n* (1592) **1 a** : the presiding officer of a meeting, organization, committee, or event **b** : the administrative officer of a department of instruction (as in a college) **2** : a carrier of a sedan chair — **chair·man·ship** \-ˌship\ *n*

[2]**chairman** *vt* **-maned** *or* **-manned; -man·ing** *or* **-man·ning** (1888) : CHAIR 3

chair·per·son \-ˌpər-sᵊn\ *n* (1971) : CHAIRMAN 1

chair·wom·an \-ˌwu̇-mən\ *n* (1685) : a woman who serves as chairman

chaise \'shāz\ *n* [F, chair, chaise, alter. of OF *chaiere* chair] (1701) **1** : any of various light horse-drawn vehicles: as **a** : a 2-wheeled carriage for one or two persons with a folding top **b** : POST CHAISE **2** : CHAISE LONGUE

chaise longue \'shāz-'lȯŋ\ *n, pl* **chaise longues** *also* **chaises longues** \'shāz-'lȯŋ(z)\ [F, lit., long chair] (1800) : a long reclining chair

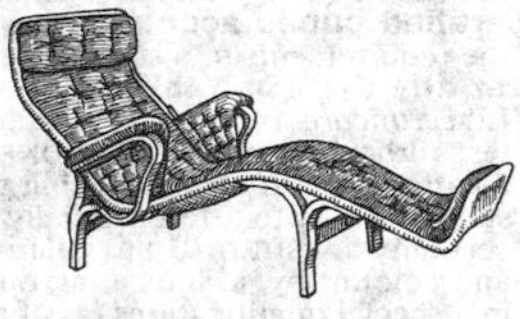
chaise longue

chaise lounge \'shāz-'lau̇nj, 'chās-\ *n* [by folk etymology fr. F *chaise longue*] (ca. 1906) : CHAISE LONGUE

chak·ra \'chä-krə, 'shä-, 'chə-\ *n* [Skt *cakra,* lit., wheel — more at WHEEL] (1888) : any of several points of physical or spiritual energy in the human body according to yoga philosophy

cha·la·za \kə-'lā-zə, -'la-\ *n, pl* **-zae** \-ˌzē\ *or* **-zas** [NL, fr. Gk, hailstone] (ca. 1704) **1** : either of two spiral bands in the white of a bird's egg that extend from the yolk and attach to opposite ends of the lining membrane — see EGG illustration **2** : the basal part of a plant ovule where the nucellus is fused to the surrounding integument and to which the funiculus is usu. attached — **cha·la·zal** \-'lā-zəl, -'la-\ *adj*

Chal·ce·do·ni·an \ˌkal-sə-'dō-nē-ən\ *adj* (1758) : of or relating to Chalcedon or the ecumenical council held there in A.D. 451 declaring Monophysitism heretical — **Chalcedonian** *n*

chal·ce·do·ny \kal-'se-dᵊn-ē, chal-; 'kal-sə-ˌdō-nē, 'chal-, -ˌdä-\ *n, pl* **-nies** [ME *calcedonie,* a precious stone, fr. AF, fr. LL *chalcedonius,* fr. Gk *Chalkēdōn* Chalcedon] (13c) : a translucent variety of quartz of various colors and waxy luster — **chal·ce·don·ic** \ˌkal-sə-'dä-nik\ *adj*

chal·cid \'kal-səd\ *n* [ultim. fr. Gk *chalkos* copper, bronze] (1893) : any of a superfamily (Chalcidoidea) of mostly minute wasps parasitic in the larval state on the larvae or pupae of other insects — **chalcid** *adj*

chal·co·cite \'kal-kə-ˌsīt\ *n* [alter. of *chalcosine,* fr. F, irreg. fr. Gk *chalkos*] (1868) : a black or gray lustrous metallic mineral that consists of a sulfide of copper and is an important copper ore

chal·co·gen \'kal-kə-jən\ *n* [ISV *chalk-* bronze, ore (fr. Gk *chalkos*) + *-gen;* fr. the occurrence of oxygen and sulfur in many ores] (ca. 1961) : any of the elements oxygen, sulfur, selenium, and tellurium

chal·co·gen·ide \-jə-ˌnīd\ *n* (1945) : a binary compound of a chalcogen with a more electropositive element or radical

chal·co·py·rite \ˌkal-kə-'pī-ˌrīt\ *n* [NL *chalcopyrites,* fr. Gk *chalkos* + L *pyrites*] (1835) : a yellow mineral that consists of a sulfide of copper and iron and is an important copper ore

Chal·da·ic \kal-'dā-ik, kȯl-, käl-\ *adj or n* (1655) : CHALDEAN

Chal·de·an \kal-'dē-ən, kȯl-, käl-\ *n* [L *Chaldaeus* Chaldean, astrologer, fr. Gk *Chaldaios,* fr. *Chaldaia* Chaldea, region of ancient Babylonia] (1561) **1 a** : a member of an ancient Semitic people that became dominant in Babylonia **b** : the Semitic language of the Chaldeans **2** : a person versed in the occult arts — **Chaldean** *adj*

Chal·dee \'kal-ˌdē, 'kȯl-, 'käl-\ *n* [ME *Caldey,* prob. fr. MF *chaldée,* fr. L *Chaldaeus*] (14c) **1** : CHALDEAN 1a **2** : the Aramaic vernacular that was the original language of some parts of the Bible

chal·dron \'chȯl-drən, 'chäl-\ *n* [MF *chauderon,* fr. *chaudere* basin, fr. LL *caldaria* — more at CAULDRON] (1615) : any of various old units of measure varying from 32 to 72 imperial bushels

cha·let \sha-'lā, 'sha-(ˌ)lā\ *n* [F] (1782) **1** : a remote herdsman's hut in the Alps **2 a** : a Swiss dwelling with unconcealed structural members and a wide overhang at the front and sides **b** : a cottage or house in chalet style

chal·ice \'cha-ləs\ *n* [ME, fr. AF, fr. L *calic-, calix;* akin to Gk *kalyx* calyx] (14c) **1** : a drinking cup : GOBLET; *esp* : the eucharistic cup **2** : the cup-shaped interior of a flower

[1]**chalk** \'chȯk\ *n* [ME, fr. OE *cealc,* fr. L *calc-, calx* lime; akin to Gk *chalix* pebble] (bef. 12c) **1 a** : a soft white, gray, or buff limestone composed chiefly of the shells of foraminifers **b** : a prepared form of chalk or a material resembling chalk esp. when used (as for writing on blackboards) as a crayon **2 a** : a mark made with chalk **b** *Brit* : a point scored in a game — **chalky** \'chȯ-kē\ *adj*

[2]**chalk** *vt* (1580) **1** : to write or draw with chalk **2** : to rub or mark with chalk **3 a** : to delineate roughly : SKETCH **b** : to set down or add up with or as if with chalk : RECORD — usu. used with *up* ⟨~ up the totals⟩ ~ *vi* : to become chalky ⟨the paint had begun to ~⟩

chalk·board \'chȯk-ˌbȯrd\ *n* (1936) : BLACKBOARD

chalk talk \'chȯk-ˌtȯk\ *n* (1878) : a talk or lecture illustrated at a blackboard

chalk up *vt* (1826) **1** : ASCRIBE, CREDIT ⟨*chalked up* his failures to inexperience⟩ **2** : ATTAIN, ACHIEVE ⟨*chalk up* another victory⟩

chal·lah *also* **chal·la** *or* **hal·lah** \ˈkä-lə, ˈhä-\ *n* [Yiddish *khale,* fr. Heb *ḥallāh*] (1907) **:** egg-rich yeast-leavened bread that is usu. braided or twisted before baking and is traditionally eaten by Jews on the Sabbath and holidays

[1]**chal·lenge** \ˈcha-lənj\ *vb* **chal·lenged; chal·leng·ing** [ME *chalengen* to accuse, fr. AF *chalenger,* fr. L *calumniari* to accuse falsely, fr. *calumnia* calumny] *vt* (13c) **1 :** to demand as due or deserved **:** REQUIRE ⟨an event that ∼*s* explanation⟩ **2 :** to order to halt and prove identity ⟨the sentry *challenged* the stranger⟩ **3 :** to dispute esp. as being unjust, invalid, or outmoded **:** IMPUGN ⟨new data that ∼*s* old assumptions⟩ **4 :** to question formally the legality or legal qualifications of ⟨∼ a juror⟩ **5 a :** to confront or defy boldly **:** DARE ⟨he *challenged* his critics to prove his guilt⟩ **b :** to call out to duel or combat **c :** to invite into competition ⟨he *challenged* his brother to a tennis match⟩ **6 :** to arouse or stimulate esp. by presenting with difficulties ⟨she wants a job that will ∼ her⟩ **7 :** to administer a physiological and esp. an immunologic challenge to (an organism or cell) ∼ *vi* **1 :** to make or present a challenge **2 :** to take legal exception — **chal·leng·er** *n*

[2]**challenge** *n* (14c) **1 a :** a summons that is often threatening, provocative, stimulating, or inciting; *specif* **:** a summons to a duel to answer an affront **b :** an invitation to compete in a sport **2 a :** a calling to account or into question **:** PROTEST **b :** an exception taken to a juror before the juror is sworn **c :** a sentry's command to halt and prove identity **d :** a questioning of the right or validity of a vote or voter **3 :** a stimulating task or problem ⟨looking for new ∼*s*⟩ **4 :** the act or process of provoking or testing physiological activity by exposure to a specific substance; *esp* **:** a test of immunity by exposure to an antigen

challenged *adj* (1983) **:** presented with difficulties (as by a disability) ⟨physically ∼⟩

chal·leng·ing \-lən-jiŋ\ *adj* (1842) **1 :** arousing competitive interest, thought, or action ⟨a ∼ course of study⟩ **2 :** invitingly provocative **:** FASCINATING ⟨a ∼ personality⟩ — **chal·leng·ing·ly** \-jiŋ-lē\ *adv*

chal·lis \ˈsha-lē\ *n, pl* **chal·lises** \ˈsha-lēz\ [prob. fr. the name *Challis*] (1836) **:** a lightweight soft clothing fabric made of cotton, wool, or synthetic yarns

cha·lone \ˈkā-ˌlōn, ˈka-\ *n* [Gk *chalōn,* prp. of *chalan* to slacken] (1914) **:** a substance (as a glycoprotein) that inhibits mitosis only in the specific tissue that secretes it — compare HORMONE

cha·lu·pa \chä-ˈlü-pä, chə-ˈlü-pə\ *n* [MexSp, fr. Sp, boat, skiff, fr. F *chaloupe*] (1895) **:** a fried corn tortilla sometimes shaped like a boat and usu. filled with a savory mixture (as of meat, vegetables, or cheese)

[1]**cha·ly·be·ate** \kə-ˈlē-bē-ət, -ˈli-\ *adj* [prob. fr. NL *chalybeatus,* irreg. fr. L *chalybs* steel, fr. Gk *chalyb-, chalyps,* fr. *Chalybes,* ancient people in Asia Minor] (1634) **:** impregnated with salts of iron; *also* **:** having a taste due to iron ⟨∼ springs⟩

[2]**chalybeate** *n* (1667) **:** a chalybeate liquid or medicine

cham·ae·phyte \ˈka-mi-ˌfīt\ *n* [Gk *chamai* on the ground + E *-phyte* — more at HUMBLE] (1913) **:** a perennial plant that bears its perennating buds just above the surface of the soil

[1]**cham·ber** \ˈchām-bər\ *n* [ME *chambre,* fr. AF, fr. LL *camera,* fr. L, arched roof, fr. Gk *kamara* vault] (13c) **1 :** ROOM; *esp* **:** BEDROOM **2 :** a natural or artificial enclosed space or cavity **3 a :** a hall for the meetings of a deliberative, legislative, or judicial body ⟨the senate ∼⟩ **b :** a room where a judge transacts business — usu. used in pl. **c :** the reception room of a person of rank or authority **4 a :** a legislative or judicial body; *esp* **:** either of the houses of a bicameral legislature **b :** a voluntary board or council **5 a :** the part of the bore of a gun that holds the charge **b :** a compartment in the cartridge cylinder of a revolver — **cham·bered** \-bərd\ *adj*

[2]**chamber** *vt* **cham·bered; cham·ber·ing** \-b(ə-)riŋ\ (1575) **1 :** to place in or as if in a chamber **:** HOUSE **2 :** to serve as a chamber for; *esp* **:** to accommodate in the chamber of a firearm

[3]**chamber** *adj* (1706) **:** being, relating to, or performing chamber music

chambered nautilus *n* (1776) **:** NAUTILUS 1

cham·ber·lain \ˈchām-bər-lən\ *n* [ME, fr. AF *chamberlein,* of Gmc origin; akin to OHG *chamarling* chamberlain, fr. *chamara* chamber, fr. LL *camera*] (13c) **1 :** an attendant on a sovereign or lord in his bedchamber **2 a :** a chief officer in the household of a king or nobleman **b :** TREASURER **3 :** an often honorary papal attendant; *specif* **:** a priest having a rank of honor below domestic prelate

cham·ber·maid \-ˌmād\ *n* (1578) **:** a maid who makes beds and does general cleaning of bedrooms (as in a hotel)

chamber music *n* (1615) **:** music and esp. instrumental ensemble music intended for performance in a private room or small auditorium and usu. having one performer for each part

chamber of commerce (1723) **:** an association of businesspeople to promote commercial and industrial interests in the community

chamber of horrors (1849) **:** a place in which macabre or horrible objects are exhibited; *also* **:** a collection of such exhibits

chamber orchestra *n* (ca. 1927) **:** a small orchestra usu. with one player for each part

chamber pot *n* (1540) **:** a bedroom vessel for urination and defecation

cham·bray \ˈsham-ˌbrā, -brē\ *n* [irreg. fr. *Cambrai,* France] (1814) **:** a lightweight clothing fabric with colored warp and white filling yarns

cha·me·leon \kə-ˈmēl-yən\ *n, often attrib* [ME *camelion,* fr. MF, fr. L *chamaeleon,* fr. Gk *chamaileōn,* fr. *chamai* on the ground + *leōn* lion — more at HUMBLE] (14c) **1 :** any of a family (Chamaeleontidae) of chiefly arboreal Old World lizards with prehensile tail, independently movable eyeballs, and unusual ability to change the color of the skin **2 a :** a person given to often expedient or facile change in ideas or character **b :** one that is subject to quick or frequent change esp. in appearance **3 :** AMERICAN CHAMELEON — **cha·me·le·on·ic** \-ˌmē-lē-ˈä-nik\ *adj* — **cha·me·leon·like** \-ˌlīk\ *adj*

[1]**cham·fer** \ˈcham(p)-fər, ˈcham-pər\ *vt* **cham·fered; cham·fer·ing** \-f(ə-)riŋ, -p(ə-)riŋ\ [back-formation fr. *chamfering,* alter. of MF *chanfreint,* fr. pp. of *chanfraindre* to bevel, fr. *chant* edge (fr. L *canthus* iron tire) + *fraindre* to break, fr. L *frangere* — more at CANT, BREAK] (1567) **1 :** to cut a furrow in (as a column) **:** GROOVE **2 :** to make a chamfer on **:** BEVEL

[2]**chamfer** *n* (ca. 1847) **:** a beveled edge

cham·fron \ˈsham-frən, ˈcham-\ *n* [ME *chaumfreyn,* fr. AF *champfrein*] (15c) **:** the headpiece of a horse's bard

cha·mi·sa \shə-ˈmē-sə, chə-\ *or* **cha·mi·so** \-(ˌ)sō\ *n* [AmerSp *chamiza, chamizo,* ultim. fr. Sp *chamiza* brushwood, kindling, fr. Pg or Galician *chamiça,* fr. *chama* flame, fr. L *flamma* — more at FLAME] (1960) **1 :** a saltbush (*Atriplex canescens*) of the western U.S. and Mexico having winged seeds **2 :** a rabbitbrush (*Chrysothamnus nauseosus*) having yellow flowers

cha·mise \shə-ˈmēs, chə-\ *n* [modif. of AmerSp *chamiza*] (1846) **:** a Californian shrub (*Adenostoma fasciculatum*) of the rose family that forms dense stands in chaparral

cham·ois \ˈsha-mē, *sense 1 also* sham-ˈwä\ *n, pl* **cham·ois** *also* **cham·oix** *sense 1* ˈsha-mē(z) *or* sham-ˈwä(z), *senses 2 & 3* ˈsha-mēz\ [MF, fr. LL *camox*] (1560) **1 :** a small goatlike bovid (*Rupicapra rupicapra*) of mountainous regions from southern Europe to the Caucasus **2** *also* **cham·my** *or* **sham·my** \ˈsha-mē\ **:** a soft pliant leather prepared from the skin of the chamois or from sheepskin **3 :** a cotton fabric made in imitation of chamois leather

cham·o·mile *or* **cam·o·mile** \ˈka-mə-ˌmī(-ə)l, -ˌmēl\ *n* [ME *camemille,* fr. ML *camomilla,* modif. of L *chamaemelon,* fr. Gk *chamaimēlon,* fr. *chamai* + *mēlon* apple] (13c) **1 :** a perennial composite herb (*Chamaemelum nobile* syn. *Anthemis nobilis*) of Europe and No. Africa with aromatic foliage and flower heads **2 :** any of several composite plants (genera *Matricaria* and *Anthemis*) related to chamomile; *esp* **:** an annual Eurasian herb (*M. recutita* syn. *M. chamomilla*) naturalized in No. America **3 :** the dried flower heads of chamomile that are often used in making tea and that yield an essential oil possessing medicinal properties

[1]**champ** \ˈchamp, ˈchämp, ˈchȯmp\ *vb* [ME *chammen, champen*] *vt* (14c) **1 :** CHOMP **2 :** MASH, TRAMPLE ∼ *vi* **1 :** to make biting or gnashing movements **2 :** to show impatience of delay or restraint — usu. used in the phrase *champing at the bit* ⟨he was ∼*ing* at the bit to begin⟩

[2]**champ** \ˈchamp\ *n* (1868) **:** CHAMPION

cham·pac *or* **cham·pak** \ˈcham-ˌpak, ˈchəm-(ˌ)pək\ *n* [Hindi & Skt; Hindi *campak,* fr. Skt *campaka*] (ca. 1770) **:** an Asian tree (*Michelia champaca*) of the magnolia family with fragrant usu. yellow flowers

cham·pagne \sham-ˈpān\ *n* [F, fr. *Champagne,* France] (1664) **1 :** a white sparkling wine made in the old province of Champagne, France; *also* **:** a similar wine made elsewhere **2 :** a pale orange yellow to light grayish-yellowish brown

cham·paign \sham-ˈpān\ *n* [ME *champaine,* fr. AF *champaigne,* fr. LL *campania* — more at CAMPAIGN] (15c) **1 :** an expanse of level open country **:** PLAIN **2** *archaic* **:** BATTLEFIELD — **champaign** *adj*

cham·pers \ˈsham-pərz\ *n pl but sing in constr* [by alter.] (1955) *Brit* **:** CHAMPAGNE 1

cham·per·ty \ˈcham-pər-tē\ *n* [ME *champartie,* fr. AF, fr. *champart* share in litigious property, fr. *champ* field (fr. L *campus*) + *part* portion — more at PART] (15c) **:** a proceeding by which a person not a party in a suit bargains to aid in or carry on its prosecution or defense in consideration of a share of the matter in suit — **cham·per·tous** \-pər-təs\ *adj*

cham·pi·gnon \(ˌ)sham-pē-ˈnyōn, (ˌ)shäm-, -ˈnyō^{n}; sham-ˈpin-yən, cham-\ *n* [F, fr. MF, alter. of *champigneul,* ultim. fr. LL *campania*] (1670) **:** an edible fungus; *esp* **:** BUTTON MUSHROOM

[1]**cham·pi·on** \ˈcham-pē-ən\ *n* [ME, fr. AF, fr. ML *campion-, campio,* of WGmc origin; akin to OE *cempa* warrior] (13c) **1 :** WARRIOR, FIGHTER **2 :** a militant advocate or defender ⟨a ∼ of civil rights⟩ **3 :** one that does battle for another's rights or honor ⟨God will raise me up a ∼ —Sir Walter Scott⟩ **4 :** a winner of first prize or first place in competition; *also* **:** one who shows marked superiority ⟨a ∼ at selling⟩

[2]**champion** *vt* (1605) **1** *archaic* **:** CHALLENGE, DEFY **2 :** to protect or fight for as a champion **3 :** to act as militant supporter of **:** UPHOLD, ADVOCATE ⟨always ∼*s* the cause of the underdog⟩ ***syn*** see SUPPORT

cham·pi·on·ship \-ˌship\ *n* (1825) **1 :** designation as champion **2 :** the act of championing **:** DEFENSE ⟨his ∼ of freedom of speech⟩ **3 :** a contest held to determine a champion

champ·le·vé \ˌshä^{n}-lə-ˈvā\ *adj* [F] (1856) **:** of, relating to, or being a style of enamel decoration in which the enamel is applied and fired in cells depressed (as by incising) into a metal background — compare CLOISONNÉ — **champlevé** *n*

chan *abbr* channel

[1]**chance** \ˈchan(t)s\ *n* [ME, fr. AF, fr. VL **cadentia* fall, fr. L *cadent-, cadens,* prp. of *cadere* to fall; perh. akin to Skt *śad-* to fall off] (14c) **1 a :** something that happens unpredictably without discernible human intention or observable cause **b :** the assumed impersonal purposeless determiner of unaccountable happenings **:** LUCK ⟨an outcome decided by ∼⟩ **c :** the fortuitous or incalculable element in existence **:** CONTINGENCY **2 :** a situation favoring some purpose **:** OPPORTUNITY ⟨needed a ∼ to relax⟩ **3 :** a fielding opportunity in baseball **4 a :** the possibility of a particular outcome in an uncertain situation; *also* **:** the degree of likelihood of such an outcome ⟨a small ∼ of success⟩ **b** *pl* **:** the more likely indications ⟨∼*s* are he's already gone⟩ **5 a :** RISK ⟨not taking any ∼*s*⟩ **b :** a raffle ticket — **chance** *adj* — **by chance :** in the haphazard course of events ⟨they met *by chance*⟩

[2]**chance** *vb* **chanced; chanc·ing** *vi* (14c) **1 a :** to take place, come about, or turn out by chance **:** HAPPEN ⟨it *chanced* to rain that day⟩ **b :** to have the good or bad luck ⟨we *chanced* to meet⟩ **2 :** to come or light by chance ⟨they *chanced* upon a remote inn⟩ ∼ *vt* **1 :** to leave the outcome of to chance **2 :** to accept the hazard of **:** RISK ⟨knew the trip was dangerous but decided to ∼ it⟩ — **chance one's arm** *Brit* **:** to take a risk

chance·ful \ˈchan(t)s-fəl\ *adj* (1594) **1** *archaic* **:** CASUAL **2 :** full of chance or uncertainty

chan·cel \ˈchan(t)-səl\ *n* [ME, fr. AF, fr. LL *cancellus* lattice, fr. L *cancelli;* fr. the latticework enclosing it — more at CANCEL] (14c) **:** the part of a church containing the altar and seats for the clergy and choir

chan·cel·lery *or* **chan·cel·lory** \ˈchan(t)-s(ə-)lə-rē, -səl-rē\ *n, pl* **-ler·ies** *or* **-lor·ies** (14c) **1 a :** the position, court, or department of a chancellor **b :** the building or room where a chancellor's office is located **2 :** the office of secretary of the court of a person high in authority **3 :** the office or staff of an embassy or consulate

\ə\ **abut** \$^{ə}$\ kitten, F table \ər\ **further** \a\ **ash** \ā\ **ace** \ä\ mop, mar
\au̇\ **out** \ch\ **chin** \e\ bet \ē\ **easy** \g\ go \i\ **hit** \ī\ **ice** \j\ **job**
\ŋ\ sing \ō\ go \ȯ\ **law** \ȯi\ **boy** \th\ **thin** \t͟h\ **the** \ü\ **loot** \u̇\ **foot**
\y\ yet \zh\ vision, beige \k̲, ^{n}, œ, ue, ^{y}\ *see* Guide to Pronunciation

chan·cel·lor \ˈchan(t)-s(ə-)lər\ *n* [ME *chanceler,* fr. AF, fr. LL *cancellarius* doorkeeper, secretary, fr. *cancellus*] (14c) **1 a :** the secretary of a nobleman, prince, or king **b :** the lord chancellor of Great Britain **c** *Brit* **:** the chief secretary of an embassy **d :** a Roman Catholic priest heading the office in which diocesan business is transacted and recorded **2 a :** the titular head of a British university **b** (1) **:** a university president (2) **:** the chief executive officer in some state systems of higher education **3 a :** a lay legal officer or adviser of an Anglican diocese **b :** a judge in a court of chancery or equity in various states of the U.S. **4 :** the chief minister of state in some European countries — **chan·cel·lor·ship** \-ˌship\ *n*

chancellor of the exchequer *often cap C&E* (1535) **:** a member of the British cabinet in charge of the public income and expenditure

chance–med·ley \ˈchan(t)s-ˈmed-lē\ *n* [AF *chance medlée* mingled chance] (15c) **1 :** accidental homicide not entirely without fault of the killer but without evil intent **2 :** haphazard action **:** CONFUSION

chanc·er \ˈchan(t)-sər\ *n* (1959) *Brit* **:** a scheming opportunist

chan·cery \ˈchan(t)-sə-rē, ˈchan(t)s-rē\ *n, pl* **-cer·ies** [ME *chancerie,* alter. of *chancelerie* chancellery, fr. AF, fr. *chanceler*] (14c) **1 :** a record office for public archives or those of ecclesiastical, legal, or diplomatic proceedings **2 a** *cap* **:** a high court of equity in England and Wales with common-law functions and jurisdiction over causes in equity **b :** a court of equity in the American judicial system **c :** the principles and practice of judicial equity **3 a :** a chancellor's court or office or the building in which it is located **b :** the office in which the business of a Roman Catholic diocese is transacted and recorded **c :** the office of an embassy **:** CHANCELLERY 3 — **in chancery 1 :** in litigation in a court of chancery; *also* **:** under the superintendence of the lord chancellor ⟨a ward *in chancery*⟩ **2 :** in a hopeless predicament

chan·cre \ˈshaŋ-kər\ *n* [F, fr. OF, fr. L *cancer*] (ca. 1605) **:** a primary sore or ulcer at the site of entry of a pathogen (as in tularemia); *esp* **:** the initial lesion of syphilis — **chan·crous** \-k(ə-)rəs\ *adj*

chan·croid \ˈshaŋ-ˌkrȯid\ *n* (1861) **:** a venereal disease caused by a bacterium (*Hemophilus ducreyi*) and characterized by chancres unlike those of syphilis in lacking firm indurated margins — called also *soft chancre* — **chan·croi·dal** \shaŋ-ˈkrȯi-d^{ə}l\ *adj*

chancy \ˈchan(t)-sē\ *adj* **chanc·i·er; -est** (1513) **1** *Scot* **:** bringing good luck **:** AUSPICIOUS **2 :** uncertain in outcome or prospect **:** RISKY **3 :** occurring by chance **:** HAPHAZARD — **chanc·i·ness** *n*

chan·de·lier \ˌshan-də-ˈlir\ *n* [F, fr. OF, candle holder, modif. of L *candelabrum*] (1736) **:** a branched often ornate lighting fixture suspended from a ceiling — **chan·de·liered** \-ˈlird\ *adj*

chan·delle \shan-ˈdel, shä^n-\ *n* [F, lit., candle] (1918) **:** an abrupt climbing turn of an airplane in which the momentum of the plane is used to attain a higher rate of climb — **chandelle** *vi*

chan·dler \ˈchan(d)-lər\ *n* [ME *chandeler,* fr. AF, fr. *chandele* candle, fr. L *candela*] (14c) **1 :** a maker or seller of tallow or wax candles and usu. soap **2 :** a retail dealer in provisions and supplies or equipment of a specified kind ⟨a yacht ~⟩

chan·dlery \-lə-rē\ *n, pl* **-dler·ies** (15c) **1 :** a place where candles are kept **2 :** the business or shop of a chandler **3 :** the commodities sold by a chandler

[1]**change** \ˈchānj\ *vb* **changed; chang·ing** [ME, fr. AF *changer,* fr. L *cambiare* to exchange, prob. of Celt origin; akin to OIr *camm* crooked] *vt* (13c) **1 a :** to make different in some particular **:** ALTER ⟨never bothered to ~ the will⟩ **b :** to make radically different **:** TRANSFORM ⟨can't ~ human nature⟩ **c :** to give a different position, course, or direction to **2 a :** to replace with another ⟨let's ~ the subject⟩ **b :** to make a shift from one to another **:** SWITCH ⟨always ~*s* sides in an argument⟩ **c :** to exchange for an equivalent sum of money (as in smaller denominations or in a foreign currency) ⟨~ a 20-dollar bill⟩ **d :** to undergo a modification of ⟨foliage *changing* color⟩ **e :** to put fresh clothes or covering on ⟨~ a bed⟩ ~ *vi* **1 :** to become different ⟨her mood ~*s* every hour⟩ **2** *of the moon* **:** to pass from one phase to another **3 :** to shift one's means of conveyance **:** TRANSFER ⟨on the bus trip he had to ~ twice⟩ **4** *of the voice* **:** to shift to lower register **:** BREAK **5 :** to undergo transformation, transition, or substitution ⟨winter *changed* to spring⟩ **6 :** to put on different clothes ⟨need a few minutes to ~ for dinner⟩ **7 :** EXCHANGE, SWITCH ⟨neither liked his seat so they *changed* with each other⟩ — **chang·er** *n* — **change hands :** to pass from the possession of one owner to that of another ⟨money *changes hands* many times⟩

syn CHANGE, ALTER, VARY, MODIFY mean to make or become different. CHANGE implies making either an essential difference often amounting to a loss of original identity or a substitution of one thing for another ⟨*changed* the shirt for a larger size⟩. ALTER implies a difference in some particular respect without suggesting loss of identity ⟨slightly *altered* the original design⟩. VARY stresses a breaking away from sameness, duplication, or exact repetition ⟨*vary* your daily routine⟩. MODIFY suggests a difference that limits, restricts, or adapts to a new purpose ⟨*modified* the building for use by the disabled⟩.

[2]**change** *n* (13c) **1 :** the act, process, or result of changing: as **a :** ALTERATION ⟨a ~ in the weather⟩ **b :** TRANSFORMATION ⟨a time of vast social ~⟩ ⟨going through ~*s*⟩ **c :** SUBSTITUTION ⟨a ~ of scenery⟩ **d :** the passage of the moon from one monthly revolution to another; *also* **:** the passage of the moon from one phase to another **e :** MENOPAUSE **2 :** a fresh set of clothes **3** *Brit* **:** EXCHANGE 5a **4 a :** money in small denominations received in exchange for an equivalent sum in larger denominations **b :** money returned when a payment exceeds the amount due **c :** coins esp. of low denominations ⟨a pocketful of ~⟩ **d :** a negligible additional amount ⟨only six minutes and ~ left in the game⟩ **e :** MONEY 1 ⟨cost a large chunk of ~⟩ **5 :** an order in which a set of bells is struck in change ringing **6 :** CHANGEUP

change·able \ˈchān-jə-bəl\ *adj* (13c) **:** capable of change: as **a :** able or apt to vary ⟨~ weather⟩ **b :** subject to change **:** ALTERABLE ⟨~ plans⟩ **c :** FICKLE ⟨a person ~ in his moods⟩ — **change·abil·i·ty** \ˌchān-jə-ˈbi-lə-tē\ *n* — **change·able·ness** \ˈchān-jə-bəl-nəs\ *n* — **change·ably** \-blē\ *adv*

change·ful \ˈchānj-fəl\ *adj* (1591) **:** notably variable **:** UNCERTAIN ⟨~ times⟩ — **change·ful·ly** \-fə-lē\ *adv* — **change·ful·ness** *n*

change·less \ˈchānj-ləs\ *adj* (1580) **:** never changing **:** CONSTANT ⟨~ truths⟩ — **change·less·ly** *adv* — **change·less·ness** *n*

change·ling \ˈchānj-liŋ\ *n* (1537) **1** *archaic* **:** TURNCOAT **2 :** a child secretly exchanged for another in infancy **3** *archaic* **:** IMBECILE — **changeling** *adj*

change off *vi* (1873) **1 :** to alternate with another at doing an act **2 :** to alternate between two different acts or instruments or between an action and a rest period

change of heart (1649) **:** a reversal in position or attitude

change of life (1834) **1 :** MENOPAUSE **2 :** ANDROPAUSE

change of pace (1788) **1 :** CHANGEUP **2 :** an interruption of continuity by a shift to a different activity

change·over \ˈchānj-ˌō-vər\ *n* (1907) **1 :** CONVERSION, TRANSITION **2 :** a pause in a tennis match during which the players change sides of the court

change ringing *n* (1872) **:** the art or practice of ringing a set of tuned bells (as in the bell tower of a church) in continually varying order

change·up \ˈchānj-ˌəp\ *n* (1943) **:** a slow pitch in baseball thrown with the same motion as a fastball in order to deceive the batter

[1]**chan·nel** \ˈcha-n^{ə}l\ *n* [ME *chanel,* fr. AF, fr. L *canalis* channel — more at CANAL] (14c) **1 a :** the bed where a natural stream of water runs **b :** the deeper part of a river, harbor, or strait **c :** a strait or narrow sea between two close landmasses **d :** a means of communication or expression: as (1) **:** a path along which information (as data or music) in the form of an electrical signal passes (2) *pl* **:** a fixed or official course of communication ⟨went through established military ~*s* with his grievances⟩ **e :** a way, course, or direction of thought or action ⟨new ~*s* of exploration⟩ **f :** a band of frequencies of sufficient width for a single radio or television communication **g :** CHANNELER **2 a :** a usu. tubular enclosed passage **:** CONDUIT **b :** a passage created in a selectively permeable cell membrane by a conformational change in membrane proteins; *also* **:** the proteins of such a passage — compare ION CHANNEL **3 :** a long gutter, groove, or furrow **4 :** a metal bar of flattened U-shaped section

[2]**channel** *vt* **-neled** *or* **-nelled; -nel·ing** *or* **-nel·ling** (15c) **1 a :** to form, cut, or wear a channel in **b :** to make a groove in ⟨~ a chair leg⟩ **2 :** to convey or direct into or through a channel ⟨~ his energy into useful work⟩ **3 :** to serve as a channeler or intermediary for

[3]**channel** *n* [alter. of *chainwale,* fr. [1]*chain* + [1]*wale*] (1769) **:** one of the flat ledges of heavy plank or metal bolted edgewise to the outside of a ship to increase the spread of the shrouds

channel bass *n* (1884) **:** RED DRUM

channel catfish *n* (1820) **:** a large black-spotted catfish (*Ictalurus punctatus*) that is an important freshwater food fish of the U.S. and Canada — called also *channel cat*

chan·nel·er \ˈcha-nə-lər\ *n* (1987) **:** a person who conveys thoughts or energy from a source believed to be outside the person's body or conscious mind; *specif* **:** one who speaks for nonphysical beings or spirits

chan·nel–hop·ping \ˈcha-n^{ə}l-ˌhä-piŋ\ *n* (1979) **:** CHANNEL SURFING — **chan·nel–hop** \-ˌhäp\ *vi*

chan·nel·ize \ˈcha-nə-ˌlīz\ *vt* **-ized; -iz·ing** (1609) **1 :** CHANNEL 1 **2 :** CHANNEL 2 **3 :** to straighten by means of a channel ⟨~ a stream⟩ — **chan·nel·i·za·tion** \ˌcha-nə-lə-ˈzā-shən\ *n*

channel surfing *n* (1988) **:** the action or practice of surfing through television programs usu. by use of a remote control — **channel surf** *vi* — **channel surfer** *n*

chan·son \shä^n-ˈsō^n\ *n, pl* **chan·sons** \-ˈsō^n(z)\ [F, fr. L *cantion-, cantio,* fr. *canere*] (1602) **:** SONG; *specif* **:** a music-hall or cabaret song

chanson de geste \-də-ˈzhest\ *n, pl* **chansons de geste** *same*\ [F, lit., song of heroic deeds] (1833) **:** any of several Old French epic poems of the 11th to the 13th centuries

chan·son·nier \ˌshä^n-sō-ˈnyā\ *n* [F, fr. *chanson*] (1872) **:** a writer or singer of chansons; *esp* **:** a cabaret singer

[1]**chant** \ˈchant\ *vb* [ME *chaunten,* fr. AF *chanter,* fr. L *cantare,* freq. of *canere* to sing; akin to OE *hana* rooster, OIr *canid* he sings] *vi* (14c) **1 :** to make melodic sounds with the voice; *esp* **:** to sing a chant **2 :** to recite something in a monotonous repetitive tone ⟨protesters were ~*ing* outside⟩ ~ *vt* **1 :** to utter as in chanting **2 :** to celebrate or praise in song or chant

[2]**chant** *n* (1671) **1 :** SONG 1 **2 a :** PLAINSONG **b :** a rhythmic monotonous utterance or song **c :** a composition for chanting

chant·er \ˈchan-tər\ *n* (14c) **1 :** one who chants: **a :** CHORISTER **b :** CANTOR **2 :** the chief singer in a chantry **3 :** the reed pipe of a bagpipe with finger holes on which the melody is played

chan·te·relle \ˌshan-tə-ˈrel, ˌshän-\ *n* [F] (1775) **:** a fragrant edible mushroom (*Cantharellus cibarius*) usu. having a yellow to orange color

chan·teuse \shan-ˈtüz, shä^n-ˈtə(r)z\ *n, pl* **chan·teuses** \-ˈtüz, -ˈtü-zəz, -ˈtə(r)z, -ˈtə(r)-zəz\ [F, fem. of *chanteur* singer, fr. *chanter*] (1844) **:** SONGSTRESS; *esp* **:** a woman who is a concert or nightclub singer

chan·tey *or* **chan·ty** \ˈshan-tē, ˈchan-\ *or* **shan·ty** \ˈshan-\ *n, pl* **chanteys** *or* **chanties** *or* **shanties** [modif. of F *chanter*] (1856) **:** a song sung by sailors in rhythm with their work

chan·ti·cleer \ˌchan-tə-ˈklir, ˌshan-\ *n* [ME *Chantecleer,* rooster in verse narratives, fr. OF *Chantecler,* rooster in the *Roman de Renart*] (14c) **:** ROOSTER

Chan·til·ly lace \shan-ˈti-lē-\ *n* [*Chantilly,* France] (1848) **:** a delicate silk, linen, or synthetic lace having a 6-sided mesh ground and a floral or scrolled design — called also *Chantilly*

chan·try \ˈchan-trē\ *n, pl* **chantries** [ME *chanterie,* fr. AF, lit., singing, fr. *chanter*] (14c) **1 :** an endowment for the chanting of masses commonly for the founder **2 :** a chapel endowed by a chantry

Chanukah *var of* HANUKKAH

cha·os \ˈkā-ˌäs\ *n* [L, fr. Gk — more at GUM] (15c) **1** *obs* **:** CHASM, ABYSS **2 a** *often cap* **:** a state of things in which chance is supreme; *esp* **:** the confused unorganized state of primordial matter before the creation of distinct forms — compare COSMOS **b :** the inherent unpredictability in the behavior of a complex natural system (as the atmosphere, boiling water, or the beating heart) **3 a :** a state of utter confusion ⟨the blackout caused ~ throughout the city⟩ **b :** a confused mass or mixture ⟨a ~ of television antennas⟩ — **cha·ot·ic** \kā-ˈä-tik\ *adj* — **cha·ot·i·cal·ly** \-ti-k(ə-)lē\ *adv*

chaos theory *n* (1984) **:** a branch of mathematical and physical theory that deals with the nature and consequences of chaos and chaotic systems

[1]**chap** \ˈchap\ *n* [ME *chappes,* pl., fr. *chappen*] (14c) **:** a crack in or a sore roughening of the skin caused by exposure to wind or cold

[2]**chap** *vb* **chapped; chap·ping** [ME *chappen;* akin to MD *cappen* to cut down] *vi* (15c) **:** to open in cracks, slits, or chinks; *also* **:** to become cracked, roughened, or reddened esp. by the action of wind or cold ⟨hands often ~ in winter⟩ ~ *vt* **:** to cause to chap ⟨wind-*chapped* lips⟩

[3]**chap** \ˈchäp, ˈchap\ *n* [origin unknown] (1555) **1 :** the fleshy covering of a jaw; *also* **:** JAW — usu. used in pl. ⟨a wolf's ~*s*⟩ **2 :** the forepart of the face — usu. used in pl.

[4]**chap** \ˈchap\ *n* [short for *chapman*] (1705) **1** *chiefly Brit* **:** FELLOW 4c **2** *Southern & Midland* **:** BABY, CHILD

[5]**chap** *abbr* chapter

chap·a·ra·jos *or* **chap·a·re·jos** \ˌsha-pə-ˈrā-(ˌ)ōs, -ˈrä-\ *n pl* [modif. of MexSp *chaparreras,* fr. *chaparro*] (1887) **:** CHAPS

chap·ar·ral \ˌsha-pə-ˈral, -ˈrel\ *n* [Sp, fr. *chaparro* dwarf evergreen oak, fr. Basque *txapar*] (1845) **1 :** a thicket of dwarf evergreen oaks; *broadly* **:** a dense impenetrable thicket of shrubs or dwarf trees **2 :** an ecological community composed of shrubby plants adapted to dry summers and moist winters that occurs esp. in southern California

chaparral cock *n* (1853) **:** ROADRUNNER — called also *chaparral bird*

cha·pa·ti *also* **chap·pa·ti** \chə-ˈpä-tē\ *n, pl* **chapatis** *also* **chappatis** [Hindi *capātī* & Urdu *chapātī*] (1810) **:** a round flat unleavened bread of India that is usu. made of whole wheat flour and cooked on a griddle

chap·book \ˈchap-ˌbu̇k\ *n* [*chap*man + *book*] (1798) **:** a small book containing ballads, poems, tales, or tracts

chape \ˈchāp, ˈchap\ *n* [ME, scabbard, fr. AF, cape, fr. LL *cappa*] (14c) **:** the metal mounting or trimming of a scabbard or sheath

cha·peau \sha-ˈpō, shə-\ *n, pl* **cha·peaus** \-ˈpōz\ *or* **cha·peaux** \-ˈpō(z)\ [MF, fr. OF *chapel* — more at CHAPLET] (1523) **:** HAT

chap·el \ˈcha-pəl\ *n* [ME, fr. AF *chapele,* fr. ML *cappella,* fr. dim. of LL *cappa* cloak; fr. the cloak of St. Martin of Tours preserved as a sacred relic in a chapel built for that purpose] (13c) **1 :** a subordinate or private place of worship: as **a :** a place of worship serving a residence or institution **b :** a small house of worship usu. associated with a main church **c :** a room or recess in a church for meditation and prayer or small religious services **2 :** a place of worship used by a Christian group other than an established church ⟨a nonconformist ~⟩ **3 :** a choir of singers belonging to a chapel **4 :** a chapel service or assembly at a school or college **5 :** an association of the employees in a printing office **6 a :** FUNERAL HOME **b :** a room for funeral services in a funeral home

chapel of ease (1538) **:** a chapel or dependent church built to accommodate an expanding parish

[1]**chap·er·one** *or* **chap·er·on** \ˈsha-pə-ˌrōn\ *n* [F *chaperon,* lit., hood, fr. MF, head covering, fr. *chape*] (1720) **1 :** a person (as a matron) who for propriety accompanies one or more young unmarried women in public or in mixed company **2 :** an older person who accompanies young people at a social gathering to ensure proper behavior; *broadly* **:** one delegated to ensure proper behavior **3 :** any of a class of proteins that facilitate the proper folding of proteins by binding to and stabilizing unfolded or partially folded proteins — called also *molecular chaperone*

[2]**chaperone** *or* **chaperon** *vb* **-oned; -on·ing** *vt* (1796) **1 :** ESCORT **2 :** to act as chaperone to or for ⟨~ a dance⟩ ⟨*chaperoning* teenagers⟩ ~ *vi* **:** to act as a chaperone — **chap·er·on·age** \-ˌrō-nij\ *n*

chap·fall·en \ˈchap-ˌfȯ-lən, ˈchäp-\ *also* **chop·fall·en** \ˈchäp-\ *adj* (1598) **1 :** having the lower jaw hanging loosely **2 :** cast down in spirit **:** DEPRESSED

chap·i·ter \ˈcha-pə-tər\ *n* [ME *chapitre,* modif. of AF *chapitral,* prob. blend of *capital* capital and *chapitre* chapter] (15c) **:** the capital of a column

chap·lain \ˈcha-plən\ *n* [ME *chapelein,* fr. AF, fr. ML *cappellanus,* fr. *cappella*] (14c) **1 :** a clergyman in charge of a chapel **2 :** a clergyman officially attached to a branch of the military, to an institution, or to a family or court **3 :** a person chosen to conduct religious exercises (as at a meeting of a club or society) **4 :** a clergyman appointed to assist a bishop (as at a liturgical function) — **chap·lain·cy** \-sē\ *n*

chap·let \ˈchap-lət\ *n* [ME *chapelet,* fr. AF, dim. of *chapel* hat, garland, fr. ML *cappellus* head covering, fr. LL *cappa*] (14c) **1 :** a wreath to be worn on the head **2 a :** a string of beads **b :** a part of a rosary comprising five decades **3 :** a small molding carved with small decorative forms — **chap·let·ed** \-lə-təd\ *adj*

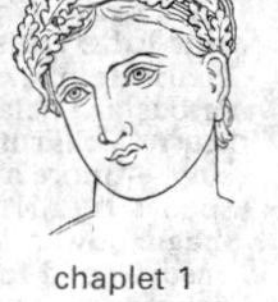

chaplet 1

chap·man \ˈchap-mən\ *n* [ME, fr. OE *cēapman,* fr. *cēap* trade + *man* — more at CHEAP] (bef. 12c) **1** *archaic* **:** MERCHANT, TRADER **2** *Brit* **:** PEDDLER

chap·pie \ˈcha-pē\ *n* (1821) *Brit* **:** FELLOW 4c

chaps \ˈshaps, ˈchaps\ *n pl* [modif. of MexSp *chaparreras*] (1844) **:** leather leggings joined by a belt or lacing, often having flared outer flaps, and worn over the trousers (as by western ranch hands)

chap·ter \ˈchap-tər\ *n* [ME *chapitre,* fr. AF *chapitre, chapitle,* fr. LL *capitulum* division of a book & ML, meeting place of canons, fr. L, dim. of *capit-, caput* head — more at HEAD] (13c) **1 a :** a main division of a book **b :** something resembling a chapter in being a significant specified unit ⟨a new ~ in my life⟩ **2 a :** a regular meeting of the canons of a cathedral or collegiate church or of the members of a religious house **b :** the body of canons of a cathedral or collegiate church **3 :** a local branch of an organization

chapter and verse *n* (1628) **1 :** the exact reference or source of information or justification for an assertion ⟨clinched their arguments by citing *chapter and verse* —J. M. Burns⟩ **2 :** full precise information or detail ⟨can give *chapter and verse* on the effects of diverting defense spending —Horace Sutton⟩ — **chapter and verse** *adv*

Chapter 11 *n* (1970) **:** bankruptcy as provided under Chapter 11 of the Bankruptcy Code which governs corporate reorganization ⟨filed for *Chapter 11*⟩

[1]**char** *also* **charr** \ˈchär\ *n, pl* **char** *or* **chars** *also* **charr** *or* **charrs** [origin unknown] (1662) **:** any of a genus (*Salvelinus*) of small-scaled trouts with light-colored spots

[2]**char** *vb* **charred; char·ring** [*charcoal*] *vt* (1679) **1 :** to convert to charcoal or carbon usu. by heat **:** BURN **2 :** to burn slightly or partly **:** SCORCH ⟨the fire *charred* the beams⟩ ~ *vi* **:** to become charred

[3]**char** *n* (1879) **:** a charred substance **:** CHARCOAL; *specif* **:** a combustible residue remaining after the destructive distillation of coal

[4]**char** *vi* **charred; char·ring** [*charwoman*] (1732) **:** to work as a cleaning woman

[5]**char** *n* [by shortening] (1906) *Brit* **:** CHARWOMAN

char·a·banc \ˈshar-ə-ˌbaŋ, -ˌbäŋ\ *n* [F *char à bancs,* lit., wagon with benches] (1914) *Brit* **:** a sight-seeing motor coach

char·a·cin \ˈker-ə-sən, ˈka-rə-\ *n* [ultim. fr. Gk *charak-, charax* pointed stake, a fish] (1882) **:** any of a family (Characidae) of usu. small brightly colored tropical freshwater fishes that includes many aquarium fishes — **characin** *adj*

[1]**char·ac·ter** \ˈker-ik-tər, ˈka-rik-\ *n* [ME *caracter,* fr. L *character* mark, distinctive quality, fr. Gk *charaktēr,* fr. *charassein* to scratch, engrave; perh. akin to Lith *žerti* to scratch] (14c) **1 a :** a conventionalized graphic device placed on an object as an indication of ownership, origin, or relationship **b :** a graphic symbol (as a hieroglyph or alphabet letter) used in writing or printing **c :** a magical or astrological emblem **d :** ALPHABET **e** (1) **:** WRITING, PRINTING (2) **:** style of writing or printing (3) **:** CIPHER **f :** a symbol (as a letter or number) that represents information; *also* **:** a representation of such a character that may be accepted by a computer **2 a :** one of the attributes or features that make up and distinguish an individual **b** (1) **:** a feature used to separate distinguishable things into categories; *also* **:** a group or kind so separated ⟨advertising of a very primitive ~⟩ (2) **:** the detectable expression of the action of a gene or group of genes (3) **:** the aggregate of distinctive qualities characteristic of a breed, strain, or type ⟨a wine of great ~⟩ **c :** the complex of mental and ethical traits marking and often individualizing a person, group, or nation ⟨the ~ of the American people⟩ **d :** main or essential nature esp. as strongly marked and serving to distinguish ⟨excess sewage gradually changed the ~ of the lake⟩ **3 :** POSITION, CAPACITY ⟨his ~ as a town official⟩ **4 :** REFERENCE 4b **5 :** REPUTATION ⟨the scandal has damaged his ~ and image⟩ **6 :** moral excellence and firmness ⟨a man of sound ~⟩ **7 a :** a person marked by notable or conspicuous traits ⟨quite a ~⟩ **b :** one of the persons of a drama or novel **c :** the personality or part which an actor recreates ⟨an actress who can create a ~ convincingly⟩ **d :** characterization esp. in drama or fiction **e :** PERSON, INDIVIDUAL ⟨a suspicious ~⟩ **8 :** a short literary sketch of the qualities of a social type ***syn*** see DISPOSITION, QUALITY, TYPE — **char·ac·ter·less** \-ləs\ *adj* — **in character :** in accord with a person's usual qualities or traits ⟨behaving *in character*⟩ — **out of character :** not in accord with a person's usual qualities or traits ⟨his rudeness was completely *out of character*⟩

[2]**character** *vt* (1591) **1** *archaic* **:** ENGRAVE, INSCRIBE **2 a** *archaic* **:** REPRESENT, PORTRAY **b :** CHARACTERIZE

[3]**character** *adj* (1883) **1 :** capable of portraying an unusual or eccentric personality often markedly different from the player ⟨a ~ actor⟩ **2 :** requiring the qualities of a character actor ⟨a ~ role⟩

character assassination *n* (1944) **:** the slandering of a person usu. with the intention of destroying public confidence in that person

char·ac·ter·ful \ˈker-ik-tər-fəl, ˈka-rik-\ *adj* (1901) **1 :** markedly expressive of character ⟨a ~ face⟩ **2 :** marked by character ⟨a ~ decision⟩

char·ac·ter·i·sa·tion, char·ac·ter·ise *Brit var of* CHARACTERIZATION, CHARACTERIZE

[1]**char·ac·ter·is·tic** \ˌker-ik-tə-ˈris-tik, ˌka-rik-\ *n* (1664) **1 :** a distinguishing trait, quality, or property **2 :** the integral part of a common logarithm **3 :** the smallest positive integer *n* which for an operation in a ring or field yields 0 when any element is used *n* times with the operation

[2]**characteristic** *adj* (1665) **:** revealing, distinguishing, or typical of an individual character — **char·ac·ter·is·ti·cal·ly** \-ti-k(ə-)lē\ *adv*

syn CHARACTERISTIC, INDIVIDUAL, PECULIAR, DISTINCTIVE mean indicating a special quality or identity. CHARACTERISTIC applies to something that distinguishes or identifies a person or thing or class ⟨responded with her *characteristic* wit⟩. INDIVIDUAL stresses qualities that distinguish one from all other members of the same kind or class ⟨a highly *individual* writing style⟩. PECULIAR applies to qualities possessed only by a particular individual or class or kind and stresses rarity or uniqueness ⟨an eccentricity that is *peculiar* to the British⟩. DISTINCTIVE indicates qualities distinguishing and uncommon and often superior or praiseworthy ⟨a *distinctive* aura of grace and elegance⟩.

characteristic equation *n* (ca. 1925) **:** an equation in which the characteristic polynomial of a matrix is set equal to 0

characteristic polynomial *n* (ca. 1957) **:** the determinant of a square matrix in which an arbitrary variable (as *x*) is subtracted from each of the elements along the principal diagonal

characteristic root *n* (ca. 1957) **:** EIGENVALUE

characteristic value *n* (1942) **:** EIGENVALUE

characteristic vector *n* (1957) **:** EIGENVECTOR

char·ac·ter·i·za·tion \ˌker-ik-t(ə-)rə-ˈzā-shən, ˌka-rik-\ *n* (1814) **:** the act of characterizing; *esp* **:** the artistic representation (as in fiction or drama) of human character or motives

char·ac·ter·ize \ˈker-ik-tə-ˌrīz, ˈka-rik-\ *vt* **-ized; -iz·ing** (1633) **1 :** to describe the character or quality of ⟨~*s* him as ambitious⟩ **2 :** to be a characteristic of **:** DISTINGUISH ⟨an era *characterized* by greed⟩

char·ac·ter·olog·i·cal \ˌker-ik-t(ə-)rə-ˈlä-ji-kəl, ˌka-rik-\ *adj* [*characterology* study of character] (1916) **:** of, relating to, or based on character or the study of character including its development and its differences in different individuals — **char·ac·ter·olog·i·cal·ly** \-ˈlä-ji-k(ə-)lē\ *adv*

character witness *n* (1952) **:** a person who gives evidence in a legal action concerning the reputation, conduct, and moral nature of a party

char·ac·tery \ˈker-ik-t(ə-)rē, ˈka-rik-, kə-ˈrak-\ *n, pl* **-ter·ies** (1598) **:** a system of written letters or symbols used in the expression of thought

cha·rade \shə-ˈrād, -ˈräd\ *n* [F, fr. Occitan *charrado* chat, fr. *charrâ* to chat, chatter] (1776) **1 :** a word represented in riddling verse or by picture, tableau, or dramatic action **2** *pl* **:** a game in which some of the players try to guess a word or phrase from the actions of another

\ə\ **abut** \ᵊ\ kitten, F table \ər\ **fur**ther \a\ **ash** \ā\ **ace** \ä\ mop, mar \au̇\ **out** \ch\ **chin** \e\ bet \ē\ **easy** \g\ **go** \i\ **hit** \ī\ **ice** \j\ **job** \ŋ\ **sing** \ō\ **go** \ȯ\ **law** \ȯi\ **boy** \th\ **thin** \t͟h\ **the** \ü\ **loot** \u̇\ **foot** \y\ yet \zh\ **vision**, beige \k̲, ⁿ, œ, ue, ʸ\ *see* Guide to Pronunciation

player who may not speak **3 :** an empty or deceptive act or pretense ‹his concern was a ~›

cha·ras \ˈchär-əs\ *n* [Hindi *caras* & Urdu *charas*] (1845) **:** HASHISH

char·broil \ˈchär-ˌbrȯi(-ə)l\ *vt* (1968) **:** to broil on a rack over hot charcoal ‹~*ed* steak› — **char·broil·er** \-ˌbrȯi-lər\ *n*

[1]**char·coal** \ˈchär-ˌkōl\ *n* [ME *charcole*] (14c) **1 :** a dark or black porous carbon prepared from vegetable or animal substances (as from wood by charring in a kiln from which air is excluded) **2 a :** a piece or pencil of fine charcoal used in drawing **b :** a charcoal drawing **3 :** a dark gray

[2]**charcoal** *vt* (1965) **:** CHARBROIL

char·cu·te·rie \(ˌ)shär-ˌkü-tə-ˈrē\ *n* [F, lit., pork-butcher's shop, fr. MF *chaircuiterie,* fr. *chaircutier* pork butcher, fr. *chair cuite* cooked meat] (ca. 1858) **:** a delicatessen specializing in dressed meats and meat dishes; *also* **:** the products sold in such a shop

[1]**chard** \ˈchärd\ *n* [modif. of F *carde,* fr. Occitan *cardo,* fr. VL **carda,* alter. of L *carduus* thistle, cardoon] (1658) **:** SWISS CHARD

[2]**chard** \ˈshärd\ *n* (1987) **:** CHARDONNAY

char·don·nay \ˌshär-dᵊn-ˈā\ *n, often cap* [F] (ca. 1911) **:** a dry white table wine typically made from a single white grape variety orig. grown in France; *also* **:** the grape

chare \ˈcher\ *or* **char** \ˈchär\ *n* [ME *char* turn, piece of work, fr. OE *cierr;* akin to OE *cierran* to turn] (bef. 12c) **:** CHORE

[1]**charge** \ˈchärj\ *n* [ME, fr. AF, fr. *charger*] (13c) **1 a** *obs* **:** a material load or weight **b :** a figure borne on a heraldic field **2 a :** the quantity that an apparatus is intended to receive and fitted to hold **b :** the quantity of explosive used in a single discharge **c :** a store or accumulation of impelling force ‹the deeply emotional ~ of the drama› **d :** a definite quantity of electricity; *esp* **:** an excess or deficiency of electrons in a body **e :** THRILL, KICK ‹got a ~ out of the game› **3 a :** OBLIGATION, REQUIREMENT **b :** MANAGEMENT, SUPERVISION ‹has ~ of the home office› **c :** the ecclesiastical jurisdiction (as a parish) committed to a clergyman **d :** a person or thing committed to the care of another **4 a :** INSTRUCTION, COMMAND **b :** instruction in points of law given by a court to a jury **5 a :** EXPENSE, COST ‹gave the banquet at his own ~› **b :** the price demanded for something ‹no admission ~› **c :** a debit to an account ‹the purchase was a ~› **d :** the record of a loan (as of a book from a library) **e** *Brit* **:** an interest in property granted as security for a loan **6 a :** a formal assertion of illegality ‹a ~ of murder› **b :** a statement of complaint or hostile criticism ‹denied the ~*s* of nepotism that were leveled against him› **7 a** (1) **:** a violent rush forward (as to attack) ‹the ~ of the brigade› (2) **:** the signal for attack ‹sound the ~› **b :** a usu. illegal rush into an opponent in various sports (as basketball) — **in charge :** having control or custody of something ‹he is *in charge* of the training program›

[2]**charge** *vb* **charged; charg·ing** [ME, fr. AF *charger,* fr. LL *carricare,* fr. L *carrus* wheeled vehicle — more at CAR] *vt* (14c) **1 a** *archaic* **:** to lay or put a load on or in **:** LOAD **b** (1) **:** to place a charge (as of powder) in (2) **:** to load or fill to capacity **c** (1) **:** to restore the active materials in (a storage battery) by the passage of a direct current through in the opposite direction to that of discharge (2) **:** to give an electric charge to ‹~ a capacitor› **d** (1) **:** to assume as a heraldic bearing (2) **:** to place a heraldic bearing on **e :** to fill or furnish fully ‹the music is *charged* with excitement› **f :** ELECTRIFY 2 ‹the crowd was *charged* by her performance› **2 a :** to impose a task or responsibility on ‹~ him with the job of finding a new meeting place› **b :** to command, instruct, or exhort with authority ‹I ~ you not to go› **c** *of a judge* **:** to give a charge to (a jury) **3 a :** to make an assertion against esp. by ascribing guilt or blame ‹~*s* him with armed robbery› ‹they were *charged* as being instigators› **b :** to place the guilt or blame for ‹~ her failure to negligence› **c :** to assert as an accusation ‹~*s* that he distorted the data› **4 a :** to bring (a weapon) into position for attack **:** LEVEL ‹~ a lance› **b :** to rush against **:** ATTACK; *also* **:** to rush into (an opponent) usu. illegally in various sports **5 a** (1) **:** to impose a financial burden on ‹~ his estate with debts incurred› (2) **:** to impose or record as financial obligation ‹~ debts to an estate› **b** (1) **:** to fix or ask as fee or payment ‹~*s* $50 for an office visit› (2) **:** to ask payment of (a person) ‹~ a client for expenses› **c :** to record (an item) as an expense, debt, obligation, or liability ‹*charged* a new sofa› ~ *vi* **1 :** to rush forward in or as if in assault **:** ATTACK; *also* **:** to charge an opponent in sports **2 :** to ask or set a price ‹do you ~ for this service?› **3 :** to charge an item to an account ‹~ now, pay later› ***syn*** see COMMAND

charge·able \ˈchär-jə-bəl\ *adj* (14c) **1** *archaic* **:** financially burdensome **:** EXPENSIVE **2 :** liable to be charged: as **a :** liable to be accused or held responsible **b :** suitable to be charged to a particular account **c :** qualified to be made a charge on the county or parish

charge account *n* (1903) **:** a customer's account with a creditor (as a merchant) to which the purchase of goods is charged

charge card *n* (1950) **:** CREDIT CARD

charge–coup·led device \ˈchärj-ˌkə-pəld-\ *n* (1971) **:** a semiconductor device that is used esp. as an optical sensor and that stores charge and transfers it sequentially to an amplifier and detector — called also *CCD, charged coupled device*

charged \ˈchärjd\ *adj* (1934) **1 :** possessing or showing strong emotion ‹attacked the author in a highly ~ review› **2 :** capable of arousing strong emotion ‹a politically ~ subject›; *also* **:** EXCITING ‹a highly ~ palette of bold colors›

char·gé d'af·faires \(ˌ)shär-ˌzhā-də-ˈfer\ *n, pl* **chargés d'affaires** \-ˌzhā-də-, -ˌzhāz-də-\ [F, lit., one charged with affairs] (1767) **1 :** a subordinate diplomat who substitutes for an absent ambassador or minister **2 :** a diplomat inferior in rank to an ambassador or minister who heads a mission when no ambassador or minister is assigned

charge·hand \ˈchärj-ˌhand\ *n* (1916) *Brit* **:** FOREMAN

charge off *vt* (1892) **:** to treat as a loss or expense — **charge–off** \ˈchärj-ˌȯf\ *n*

charge of quarters (ca. 1918) **:** an enlisted man designated to handle administrative matters in a unit esp. after duty hours — abbr. *CQ*

[1]**char·ger** \ˈchär-jər\ *n* [ME *chargeour,* fr. AF, fr. *charger*] (14c) **:** a large flat dish or platter

[2]**charg·er** *n* (1539) **1 :** one that charges: as **a :** an appliance for holding or inserting a charge of powder or shot in a gun **b :** a cartridge clip **c :** a device for charging storage batteries **2 :** a horse for battle or parade

char·i·ness \ˈcher-ē-nəs\ *n* (1571) **1 :** the quality or state of being chary **:** CAUTION **2 :** carefully preserved state **:** INTEGRITY

[1]**char·i·ot** \ˈcher-ē-ət, ˈcha-rē-\ *n* [ME, fr. MF, fr. OF, fr. *charrier* to transport, fr. *char* vehicle, fr. L *carrus* — more at CAR] (14c) **1 :** a light four-wheeled pleasure or state carriage **2 :** a two-wheeled horse-drawn battle car of ancient times used also in processions and races

[2]**chariot** *vi* (1550) **:** to drive or ride in or as if in a chariot ~ *vt* **:** to carry in or as if in a chariot

char·i·ot·eer \ˌcher-ē-ə-ˈtir, ˌchar-rē-\ *n* (14c) **1 :** one who drives a chariot **2** *cap* **:** AURIGA

char·ism \ˈker-ˌi-zəm, ˈka-ˌri-\ *n, pl* **cha·ris·ma·ta** \kə-ˈriz-mə-tə; ˌker-iz-ˈmä-tə, ˌka-riz-\ *or* **charisms** [Gk *charisma*] (ca. 1641) **:** an extraordinary power (as of healing) given a Christian by the Holy Spirit for the good of the church

cha·ris·ma \kə-ˈriz-mə\ *n* [Gk, favor, gift, fr. *charizesthai* to favor, fr. *charis* grace; akin to Gk *chairein* to rejoice — more at YEARN] (1930) **1 :** a personal magic of leadership arousing special popular loyalty or enthusiasm for a public figure (as a political leader) **2 :** a special magnetic charm or appeal ‹the ~ of a popular actor›

[1]**char·is·mat·ic** \ˌker-əz-ˈma-tik, ˌka-rəz-\ *adj* [*charisma*] (ca. 1868) **1 :** of, relating to, or constituting charisma or charism ‹~ gifts› **2 :** having, exhibiting, or based on charisma or charism ‹~ sects› ‹a ~ leader›

[2]**charismatic** *n* (1951) **:** a member of a religious group or movement that stresses the seeking of direct divine inspiration and charisms (as glossolalia or healing)

char·i·ta·ble \ˈcher-ə-tə-bəl, ˈcha-rə-\ *adj* (14c) **1 :** full of love for and goodwill toward others **:** BENEVOLENT **2 a :** liberal in benefactions to the needy **:** GENEROUS **b :** of or relating to charity ‹~ institutions› **3 :** merciful or kind in judging others **:** LENIENT — **char·i·ta·ble·ness** *n* — **char·i·ta·bly** \-blē\ *adv*

char·i·ty \ˈcher-ə-tē, ˈcha-rə-\ *n, pl* **-ties** [ME *charite,* fr. AF *charité,* fr. LL *caritat-, caritas* Christian love, fr. L, dearness, fr. *carus* dear; akin to OIr *carae* friend, Skt *kāma* love] (13c) **1 :** benevolent goodwill toward or love of humanity **2 a :** generosity and helpfulness esp. toward the needy or suffering; *also* **:** aid given to those in need **b :** an institution engaged in relief of the poor **c :** public provision for the relief of the needy **3 a :** a gift for public benevolent purposes **b :** an institution (as a hospital) founded by such a gift **4 :** lenient judgment of others ***syn*** see MERCY

cha·ri·va·ri \ˌshi-və-ˈrē, ˈshi-və-ˌ\ *n* [F, perh. fr. LL *caribaria* headache, fr. Gk *karēbaria,* fr. *kara, karē* head + *barys* heavy — more at CEREBRAL, GRIEVE] (ca. 1681) **:** SHIVAREE

char·la·tan \ˈshär-lə-tən\ *n* [It *ciarlatano,* alter. of *cerretano,* lit., inhabitant of Cerreto, fr. *Cerreto,* Italy] (1618) **1 :** QUACK 2 **2 :** one making usu. showy pretenses to knowledge or ability **:** FRAUD, FAKER — **char·la·tan·ism** \-tə-ˌni-zəm\ *n* — **char·la·tan·ry** \-rē\ *n*

Charles's Wain \ˈchärlz-ˈwān, ˌchärl-zəz-\ *n* [*Charlemagne*] (bef. 12c) **:** BIG DIPPER

Charles·ton \ˈchärl-stən\ *n* [*Charleston,* S. C.] (1925) **:** a lively ballroom dance in which the knees are twisted in and out and the heels are swung sharply outward on each step

char·ley horse \ˈchär-lē-ˌhȯrs\ *n* [fr. *Charley,* nickname for *Charles*] (1888) **:** a muscular pain, cramping, or stiffness esp. of the quadriceps that results from a strain or bruise

char·lie *also* **char·ley** \ˈchär-lē\ *n, often cap* [fr. the name *Charlie*] (ca. 1946) *Brit* **:** FOOL

[1]**Char·lie** \ˈchär-lē\ [fr. the name *Charlie*] (1946) — a communications code word for the letter *c*

[2]**Charlie** *n* [short for *Victor Charlie,* fr. the communications code words for *VC* (Vietcong)] (1965) — used as a collective name for the Vietcong during the war in Vietnam

char·lock \ˈchär-ˌläk, -lək\ *n* [ME *cherlok,* fr. OE *cerlic*] (bef. 12c) **:** an Old World mustard (*Brassica kaber* syn. *Sinapis arvensis*) that is a common weed in grain fields — called also *wild mustard*

char·lotte \ˈshär-lət\ *n* [F] (1796) **:** a dessert consisting of a filling (as of fruit, whipped cream, or custard) layered with or placed in a mold lined with strips of bread, ladyfingers, or biscuits

char·lotte russe \ˈshär-lət-ˈrüs\ *n* [F, lit., Russian charlotte] (1839) **:** a charlotte made with sponge cake or ladyfingers and a whipped-cream or custard-gelatin filling

[1]**charm** \ˈchärm\ *n* [ME *charme,* fr. AF, fr. L *carmen* song, fr. *canere* to sing — more at CHANT] (14c) **1 a :** the chanting or reciting of a magic spell **:** INCANTATION **b :** a practice or expression believed to have magic power **2 :** something worn about the person to ward off evil or ensure good fortune **:** AMULET **3 a :** a trait that fascinates, allures, or delights **b :** a physical grace or attraction — used in pl. ‹her feminine ~*s*› **c :** compelling attractiveness ‹the island possessed great ~› **4 :** a small ornament worn on a bracelet or chain **5 :** a fundamental quark that has an electric charge of +⅔ and a measured energy of approximately 1.5 GeV; *also* **:** the flavor characterizing this particle — **charm·less** \-ləs\ *adj*

[2]**charm** *vt* (14c) **1 a :** to affect by or as if by magic **:** COMPEL **b :** to please, soothe, or delight by compelling attraction ‹~*s* customers with his suave manner› **2 :** to endow with or as if with supernatural powers by means of charms; *also* **:** to protect by or as if by spells, charms, or supernatural influences **3 :** to control (an animal) typically by charms (as the playing of music) ‹~ a snake› ~ *vi* **1 :** to practice magic and enchantment **2 :** to have the effect of a charm **:** FASCINATE ***syn*** see ATTRACT — **charm·er** \ˈchär-mər\ *n*

charmed \ˈchärmd\ *adj* (1605) **1 :** extremely lucky or prosperous ‹living a ~ life› **2 :** of, relating to, or being a charm quark

charmed circle *n* (1898) **:** a group marked by exclusiveness

char·meuse \(ˌ)shär-ˈmüz, -ˈmüs, -ˈmyüz, -ˈmə(r)z\ *n* [F, fem. of *charmeur* charmer, fr. *charmer* to charm] (1907) **:** a fine semilustrous crepe in satin weave

charm·ing \ˈchär-miŋ\ *adj* (1634) **:** extremely pleasing or delightful **:** ENTRANCING ‹a ~ restaurant› — **charm·ing·ly** \-miŋ-lē\ *adv*

char·nel \ˈchär-nᵊl\ *n* [ME, fr. AF *carnel, charnel,* prob. alter. of *charner,* fr. ML *carnarium,* fr. L *carn-, caro* flesh — more at CARNAL] (14c) **:** a building or chamber in which bodies or bones are deposited — called also *charnel house* — **charnel** *adj*

Cha·ro·lais \ˌsha-rə-ˈlā\ *n* [*Charolais,* district in eastern France] (1893) **:** any of a breed of large white cattle developed in France and used primarily for beef and crossbreeding

Char·on \ˈker-ən, -än\ *n* [L, fr. Gk *Charōn*] (1513) **:** a son of Erebus who in Greek mythology ferries the souls of the dead over the Styx

char·poy \ˈchär-ˌpȯi\ *n, pl* **charpoys** [Hindi *cārpāī* & Urdu *chārpāī*] (1845) **:** a bed used esp. in India consisting of a frame strung with tapes or light rope

charr *var of* 1CHAR

1**chart** \ˈchärt\ *n* [MF *charte,* fr. L *charta* piece of papyrus, document — more at CARD] (1571) **1 :** MAP: as **a :** an outline map exhibiting something (as climatic or magnetic variations) in its geographical aspects **b :** a map for the use of navigators **2 a :** a sheet giving information in tabular form **b :** GRAPH **c :** DIAGRAM **d :** a sheet of paper ruled and graduated for use in a recording instrument **e :** a record of medical information about a patient **f :** a listing by rank (as of sales) — usu. used in pl. ⟨number one on the ~*s* —Tim Cahill⟩ **3 :** a musical arrangement; *also* **:** a part in such an arrangement

2**chart** *vt* (1842) **1 :** to lay out a plan for ⟨~ a course⟩ **2 :** to make a map or chart of ⟨~ the coastline⟩ **3 :** CHRONICLE ⟨the book ~*s* the last years of his life⟩ ~ *vi* **:** to be ranked on a chart ⟨the song ~*ed* for three months⟩

1**char·ter** \ˈchär-tər\ *n* [ME *chartre,* fr. AF, fr. ML *chartula,* fr. L, dim. of *charta*] (13c) **1 :** a written instrument or contract (as a deed) executed in due form **2 a :** a grant or guarantee of rights, franchises, or privileges from the sovereign power of a state or country **b :** a written instrument that creates and defines the franchises of a city, educational institution, or corporation **c :** CONSTITUTION **3 :** a written instrument from the authorities of a society creating a lodge or branch **4 :** a special privilege, immunity, or exemption **5 :** a mercantile lease of a ship or some principal part of it **6 :** a charter travel arrangement

2**charter** *vt* (15c) **1 a :** to establish, enable, or convey by charter **b** *Brit* **:** CERTIFY ⟨a ~*ed* mechanical engineer⟩ **2 :** to hire, rent, or lease for usu. exclusive and temporary use ⟨~*ed* a boat for deep-sea fishing⟩ ***syn*** see HIRE — **char·ter·er** \-tər-ər\ *n*

3**charter** *adj* (1922) **:** of, relating to, or being a travel arrangement in which transportation (as a bus or plane) is hired by and for one specific group of people ⟨a ~ flight⟩

chartered accountant *n* (1855) *Brit* **:** a member of a chartered institute of accountants

charter member *n* (ca. 1909) **:** an original member of a group (as a society or corporation) — **charter membership** *n*

charter school *n* (1992) **:** a tax-supported school established by a charter between a granting body (as a school board) and an outside group (as of teachers and parents) which operates the school without most local and state educational regulations so as to achieve set goals

Char·tism \ˈchär-ˌti-zəm\ *n* [ML *charta* charter, fr. L, document] (1839) **:** the principles and practices of a body of 19th century English political reformers advocating better social and industrial conditions for the working classes — **Char·tist** \ˈchär-tist\ *n or adj*

chart·ist \ˈchär-tist\ *n* (1919) **1 :** an analyst of market action whose predictions of market courses are based on study of graphic presentations of past market performance **2 :** CARTOGRAPHER

char·treuse \shär-ˈtrüz, -ˈtrüs\ *n* [*Chartreuse*] (1884) **:** a variable color averaging a brilliant yellow green

Chartreuse *trademark* — used for a usu. green or yellow liqueur

char·tu·lary \ˈkär-chə-ˌler-ē\ *n, pl* **-lar·ies** [ML *chartularium*] (1571) **:** CARTULARY

char·wom·an \ˈchär-ˌwu̇-mən\ *n* [*chare* + *woman*] (1596) **:** a cleaning woman esp. in a large building

chary \ˈcher-ē\ *adj* **chari·er; -est** [ME, sorrowful, dear, fr. OE *cearig* sorrowful, fr. *caru* sorrow — more at CARE] (15c) **1** *archaic* **:** DEAR, TREASURED **2 :** discreetly cautious: as **a :** hesitant and vigilant about dangers and risks **b :** slow to grant, accept, or expend ⟨a person very ~ of compliments⟩ ***syn*** see CAUTIOUS — **chari·ly** \ˈcher-ə-lē\ *adv*

Cha·ryb·dis \kə-ˈrib-dəs *also* shə- *or* chə-\ *n* [L, fr. Gk] (1511) **:** a whirlpool off the coast of Sicily personified in Greek mythology as a female monster — compare SCYLLA

1**chase** \ˈchās\ *n* [ME, fr. AF *chace,* fr. *chacer*] (13c) **1 a :** the hunting of wild animals — used with *the* **b :** the act of chasing **:** PURSUIT **c :** an earnest or frenzied seeking after something desired **2 :** something pursued **:** QUARRY **3 :** a tract of unenclosed land used as a game preserve **4 :** STEEPLECHASE 1 **5 :** a sequence (as in a movie) in which the characters pursue one another

2**chase** *vb* **chased; chas·ing** [ME, fr. AF *chacer,* fr. VL **captiare* — more at CATCH] *vt* (14c) **1 a :** to follow rapidly **:** PURSUE **b :** HUNT **c :** to follow regularly or persistently with the intention of attracting or alluring **2** *obs* **:** HARASS **3 :** to seek out — often used with *down* ⟨detectives *chasing* down clues⟩ **4 :** to cause to depart or flee **:** DRIVE ⟨~ the dog out of the garden⟩ **5 :** to cause the removal of (a baseball pitcher) by a batting rally **6 :** to swing at (a baseball pitched out of the strike zone) ~ *vi* **1 :** to chase an animal, person, or thing ⟨~ after material possessions⟩ **2 :** RUSH, HASTEN ⟨*chased* all over town looking for a place to stay⟩

syn CHASE, PURSUE, FOLLOW, TRAIL mean to go after or on the track of something or someone. CHASE implies going swiftly after and trying to overtake something fleeing or running ⟨a dog *chasing* a cat⟩. PURSUE suggests a continuing effort to overtake, reach, or attain ⟨*pursued* the criminal through narrow streets⟩. FOLLOW puts less emphasis upon speed or intent to overtake ⟨friends *followed* me home in their car⟩. TRAIL may stress a following of tracks or traces rather than a visible object ⟨*trail* deer⟩ ⟨*trailed* a suspect across the country⟩.

3**chase** *vt* **chased; chas·ing** [ME, modif. of AF *enchaser* to set] (15c) **1 a :** to ornament (metal) by indenting with a hammer and tools without a cutting edge **b :** to make by such indentation **c :** to set with gems **2 a :** GROOVE, INDENT **b :** to cut (a thread) with a chaser

4**chase** *n* [F *chas* eye of a needle, fr. LL *capsus* enclosed space, alter. of L *capsa* box — more at CASE] (1611) **1 :** GROOVE, FURROW **2 :** the bore of a cannon **3 a :** TRENCH **b :** a channel (as in a wall) for something to lie in or pass through

5**chase** *n* [prob. fr. F *châsse* frame, reliquary, fr. MF *chasse,* fr. L *capsa*] (1612) **:** a rectangular steel or iron frame in which letterpress matter is locked (as for printing)

1**chas·er** \ˈchā-sər\ *n* (13c) **1 :** one that chases **2 :** a mild drink (as beer) taken after hard liquor

2**chaser** *n* (1707) **1 :** a skilled worker who produces ornamental chasing **2 :** a tool for cutting screw threads

Chasid *or* **Chassid** *n, pl* **Chasidim** *or* **Chassidim** *var of* HASID

chasm \ˈka-zᵊm\ *n* [L *chasma,* fr. Gk; akin to L *hiare* to yawn — more at YAWN] (1596) **1 :** a deep cleft in the surface of a planet (as the earth) **:** GORGE **2 :** a marked division, separation, or difference

1**chas·sé** \sha-ˈsā\ *vi* **chas·séd; chas·sé·ing** (1803) **1 :** to make a chassé **2 :** SASHAY

2**chassé** *n* [F, fr. pp. of *chasser* to chase] (1828) **:** a sliding dance step resembling the galop

chasse·pot \ˈshas-ˌpō, ˈsha-sə-\ *n* [F, fr. Antoine A. *Chassepot* †1905 Fr. inventor] (1869) **:** a bolt-action rifle firing a paper cartridge

chas·seur \sha-ˈsər\ *n* [F, fr. OF *chaceur,* fr. *chacier* to hunt, chase, fr. VL **captiare* — more at CATCH] (1795) **1 :** HUNTER, HUNTSMAN **2 :** one of a body of light cavalry or infantry trained for rapid maneuvering **3 :** a liveried attendant **:** FOOTMAN

chas·sis \ˈcha-sē, ˈsha-sē *also* ˈcha-səs\ *n, pl* **chas·sis** \-sēz\ [F *châssis,* fr. MF *chaciz,* fr. *chasse*] (ca. 1864) **:** the supporting frame of a structure (as an automobile or television); *also* **:** the frame and working parts (as of an automobile or electronic device) exclusive of the body or housing

chaste \ˈchāst\ *adj* **chast·er; chast·est** [ME, fr. AF, fr. L *castus* pure] (13c) **1 :** innocent of unlawful sexual intercourse **2 :** CELIBATE **3 :** pure in thought and act **:** MODEST **4 a :** severely simple in design or execution **:** AUSTERE ⟨~ classicism⟩ **b :** CLEAN, SPOTLESS — **chaste·ly** *adv* — **chaste·ness** \ˈchās(t)-nəs\ *n*

syn CHASTE, PURE, MODEST, DECENT mean free from all taint of what is lewd or salacious. CHASTE primarily implies a refraining from acts or even thoughts or desires that are not virginal or not sanctioned by marriage vows ⟨they maintained *chaste* relations⟩. PURE differs from CHASTE in implying innocence and absence of temptation rather than control of one's impulses and actions ⟨the *pure* of heart⟩. MODEST and DECENT apply esp. to deportment and dress as outward signs of inward chastity or purity ⟨preferred more *modest* swimsuits⟩ ⟨*decent* people didn't go to such movies⟩.

chas·ten \ˈchā-sᵊn\ *vt* **chas·tened; chas·ten·ing** \ˈchās-niŋ, ˈchā-sᵊn-iŋ\ [alter. of obs. E *chaste* to chasten, fr. ME, fr. AF *chastier,* fr. L *castigare,* fr. *castus* + *-igare* (fr. *agere* to drive) — more at ACT] (13c) **1 :** to correct by punishment or suffering **:** DISCIPLINE; *also* **:** PURIFY **2 a :** to prune (as a work or style of art) of excess, pretense, or falsity **:** REFINE **b :** to cause to be more humble or restrained **:** SUBDUE ***syn*** see PUNISH — **chas·ten·er** \ˈchās-nər, ˈchā-sᵊn-ər\ *n*

chas·tise \(ˌ)chas-ˈtīz\ *vt* **chas·tised; chas·tis·ing** [ME *chastisen,* alter. of *chasten*] (14c) **1 :** to inflict punishment on (as by whipping) **2 :** to censure severely **:** CASTIGATE **3** *archaic* **:** CHASTEN 2 ***syn*** see PUNISH — **chas·tise·ment** \(ˌ)chas-ˈtīz-mənt *also* ˈchas-təz-\ *n* — **chas·tis·er** \(ˌ)chas-ˈtī-zər\ *n*

chas·ti·ty \ˈchas-tə-tē\ *n* (13c) **1 :** the quality or state of being chaste: as **a :** abstention from unlawful sexual intercourse **b :** abstention from all sexual intercourse **c :** purity in conduct and intention **d :** restraint and simplicity in design or expression **2 :** personal integrity

chastity belt *n* (1931) **:** a belt device (as of medieval times) designed to prevent sexual intercourse on the part of the woman wearing it

cha·su·ble \ˈcha-zə-bəl, -zhə-, -sə-\ *n* [ME *chesible,* fr. AF *chesible, chasuble,* fr. LL *casubla* hooded garment] (14c) **:** a sleeveless outer vestment worn by the officiating priest at mass

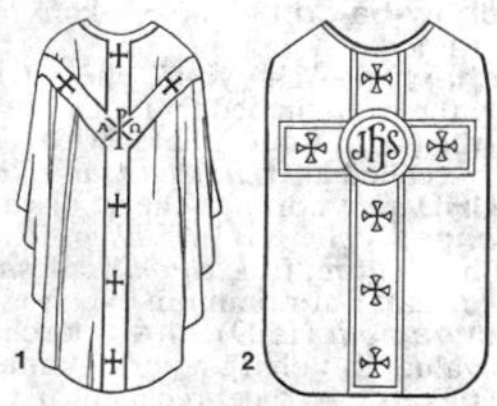

chasuble: *1* Gothic, *2* fiddleback

1**chat** \ˈchat\ *vb* **chat·ted; chat·ting** [ME *chatten,* short for *chatteren*] *vi* (15c) **1 :** CHATTER, PRATTLE **2 a :** to talk in an informal or familiar manner **b :** to take part in an online discussion in a chat room ~ *vt, chiefly Brit* **:** to talk to; *esp* **:** to talk lightly, glibly, or flirtatiously with — often used with *up*

2**chat** *n* (1530) **1 :** idle small talk **:** CHATTER **2 :** light informal or familiar talk; *esp* **:** CONVERSATION **3** [imit.] **:** any of several songbirds (as of the genera *Cercomela, Granatellus,* or *Icteria*) **4 :** online discussion in a chat room; *also* **:** an instance of such discussion ⟨participate in computer ~*s*⟩

châ·teau \sha-ˈtō\ *n, pl* **châ·teaus** \-ˈtōz\ *or* **châ·teaux** \-ˈtō(z)\ [F, fr. OF *chastel,* L *castellum* fortress] (1720) **1 :** a feudal castle or fortress in France **2 :** a large country house **:** MANSION **3 :** a French vineyard estate

cha·teau·bri·and \(ˌ)sha-ˌtō-brē-ˈäⁿ\ *n, often cap* [François René de *Chateaubriand*] (1877) **:** a large tenderloin steak usu. grilled or broiled and served with a sauce (as béarnaise)

chat·e·lain \ˈsha-tə-ˌlān\ *n* [ME *chateleyn,* fr. MF *chatelaine,* fr. OF *chastelein, castelain*] (15c) **:** CASTELLAN

chat·e·laine \ˈsha-tə-ˌlān\ *n* [F *châtelaine,* fem. of *châtelain*] (1845) **1 a :** the wife of a castellan **:** the mistress of a château **b :** the mistress of a household or of a large establishment **2 :** a clasp or hook for a watch, purse, or bunch of keys

cha·toy·ance \shə-ˈtȯi-ən(t)s\ *n* (1910) **:** CHATOYANCY

cha·toy·an·cy \-ən(t)-sē\ *n* (1894) **:** the quality or state of being chatoyant

1**cha·toy·ant** \shə-ˈtȯi-ənt\ *adj* [F, fr. prp. of *chatoyer* to shine like a cat's eyes] (1816) **:** having a changeable luster or color with an undulating narrow band of white light ⟨a ~ gem⟩

2**chatoyant** *n* (ca. 1828) **:** a chatoyant gem

chat room *n* (1986) **:** a real-time online interactive discussion group

chat show *n* (1969) *chiefly Brit* **:** TALK SHOW

\ə\ **abut** \ᵊ\ **kitten**, F table \ər\ **further** \a\ **ash** \ā\ **ace** \ä\ **mop, mar**
\au̇\ **out** \ch\ **chin** \e\ **bet** \ē\ **easy** \g\ **go** \i\ **hit** \ī\ **ice** \j\ **job**
\ŋ\ **sing** \ō\ **go** \ȯ\ **law** \ȯi\ **boy** \th\ **thin** \t͟h\ **the** \ü\ **loot** \u̇\ **foot**
\y\ **yet** \zh\ **vision, beige** \ḵ, ⁿ, œ, ue, ʸ\ *see* Guide to Pronunciation

chat·tel \ˈcha-tᵊl\ *n* [ME *chatel* property, fr. AF — more at CATTLE] (14c) **1 :** an item of tangible movable or immovable property except real estate and things (as buildings) connected with real property **2 :** SLAVE, BONDMAN

[1]**chat·ter** \ˈcha-tər\ *vb* [ME *chatteren,* of imit. origin] *vi* (13c) **1 :** to utter rapid short sounds suggestive of language but inarticulate and indistinct ⟨squirrels ~*ed* angrily⟩ **2 :** to talk idly, incessantly, or fast **3 a :** to click repeatedly or uncontrollably ⟨teeth ~*ing* with cold⟩ **b :** to vibrate rapidly in cutting ⟨a ~*ing* tool⟩ **c :** to vibrate esp. audibly as a consequence of repeated sticking and slipping ⟨~*ing* brakes⟩ ~ *vt* **:** to utter rapidly, idly, or indistinctly — **chat·ter·er** *n* — **chat·tery** \-tə-rē\ *adj*

[2]**chatter** *n* (13c) **1 :** the action or sound of chattering **2 :** idle talk **:** PRATTLE **3 :** electronic and esp. radio communication between individuals engaged in a common or related form of activity; *also* **:** such chatter regarding future hostile activities

chat·ter·box \ˈcha-tər-ˌbäks\ *n* (1774) **:** one who engages in much idle talk

chatter mark *n* (1888) **1 :** a fine undulation formed on the surface of work by a chattering tool **2 :** one of a series of short curved cracks on a glaciated rock surface transverse to the glacial striae

chat·ty \ˈcha-tē\ *adj* **chat·ti·er; -est** (1756) **1 :** fond of chatting **:** TALKATIVE ⟨a ~ neighbor⟩ **2 :** having the style and manner of light familiar conversation ⟨a ~ letter⟩ — **chat·ti·ly** \ˈcha-tə-lē\ *adv* — **chat·ti·ness** \ˈcha-tē-nəs\ *n*

[1]**chauf·feur** \ˈshō-fər, shō-ˈ\ *n* [F, lit., stoker, fr. *chauffer* to heat, fr. OF *chaufer* — more at CHAFE] (1899) **:** a person employed to drive a motor vehicle

[2]**chauffeur** *vb* **chauf·feured; chauf·feur·ing** \ˈshō-f(ə-)riŋ, shō-ˈfər-iŋ\ *vi* (1917) **:** to do the work of a chauffeur ~ *vt* **1 :** to transport in the manner of a chauffeur ⟨~*s* the children to school⟩ **2 :** to operate (as an automobile) as chauffeur

chaul·moo·gra \chȯl-ˈmü-grə\ *n* [Beng *cālmugrā*] (ca. 1815) **:** any of several East Indian trees (family Flacourtiaceae) that yield an acrid oil used esp. formerly in treating leprosy and skin diseases

chaunt, chaunt·er *archaic var of* CHANT, CHANTER

chaus·sure \shō-ˈsu̇r\ *n, pl* **chaussures** *same*\ [ME *chaucer,* fr. AF *chausure,* fr. OF *chaucier* to put on footwear, fr. L *calceare,* fr. *calceus* shoe — more at CALZONE] (14c) **1 :** FOOTGEAR **2** *pl* **:** SHOES

chau·tau·qua \shə-ˈtȯ-kwə\ *n, often cap* [*Chautauqua* Lake] (1873) **:** any of various traveling shows and local assemblies that flourished in the U.S. in the late 19th and early 20th centuries, that provided popular education combined with entertainment in the form of lectures, concerts, and plays, and that were modeled after activities at the Chautauqua Institution of western New York

chau·vin·ism \ˈshō-və-ˌni-zəm\ *n* [F *chauvinisme,* fr. Nicolas *Chauvin,* character noted for his excessive patriotism and devotion to Napoleon in Théodore and Hippolyte Cogniard's play *La Cocarde tricolore* (1831)] (1851) **1 :** excessive or blind patriotism — compare JINGOISM **2 :** undue partiality or attachment to a group or place to which one belongs or has belonged **3 :** an attitude of superiority toward members of the opposite sex; *also* **:** behavior expressive of such an attitude — **chau·vin·ist** \-və-nist\ *n or adj* — **chau·vin·is·tic** \ˌshō-və-ˈnis-tik\ *adj* — **chau·vin·is·ti·cal·ly** \-ti-k(ə-)lē\ *adv*

[1]**chaw** \ˈchȯ\ *vb* [by alter.] (1506) **:** CHEW 1

[2]**chaw** *n* (1709) **:** a chew esp. of tobacco

chaw·ba·con \ˈchȯ-ˌbā-kən\ *n* [[1]*chaw* + *bacon*] (1537) **:** BUMPKIN, HICK

cha·yo·te \chī-ˈyō-tē, chē-, -(ˌ)tā\ *n* [Sp, fr. Nahuatl *chayohtli*] (1887) **:** the pear-shaped fruit of a West Indian annual vine (*Sechium edule*) of the gourd family that is widely cultivated as a vegetable; *also* **:** the plant — called also *chayote squash, christophene, mirliton*

CHD *abbr* coronary heart disease

[1]**cheap** \ˈchēp\ *n* [ME *chep,* fr. OE *cēap* trade; akin to OHG *kouf* trade; both ultim. fr. L *caupo* tradesman] (bef. 12c) *obs* **:** BARGAIN — **on the cheap :** at minimum expense **:** CHEAPLY ⟨did the job *on the cheap*⟩

[2]**cheap** *adj* (1509) **1 a :** purchasable below the going price or the real value **b :** charging or obtainable at a low price ⟨a good ~ hotel⟩ ⟨~ tickets⟩ **c :** depreciated in value (as by currency inflation) ⟨~ dollars⟩ **2 :** gained or done with little effort ⟨a ~ victory⟩ ⟨talk is ~⟩ **3 a :** of inferior quality or worth **:** TAWDRY, SLEAZY ⟨~ workmanship⟩ **b :** contemptible because of lack of any fine, lofty, or redeeming qualities ⟨feeling ~⟩ **c :** STINGY ⟨my ~ uncle⟩ **4** *of money* **:** obtainable at a low rate of interest — **cheap** *adv* — **cheap·ish** \ˈchē-pish\ *adj* — **cheap·ish·ly** *adv* — **cheap·ly** \ˈchē-plē\ *adv* — **cheap·ness** *n*

cheap·en \ˈchē-pən\ *vb* **cheap·ened; cheap·en·ing** \ˈchēp-niŋ, ˈchē-pə-\ *vt* (1562) **1** [obs. E *cheap* to price, bid for] *archaic* **a :** to ask the price of **b :** to bid or bargain for **2 a :** to make cheap in price or value **b :** to lower in general esteem **c :** to make tawdry, vulgar, or inferior ~ *vi* **:** to become cheap

cheap·ie \ˈchē-pē\ *n* (ca. 1898) **:** one that is cheap; *esp* **:** an inexpensively produced motion picture — **cheapie** *adj*

[1]**cheap·jack** \ˈchēp-ˌjak\ *n* [*cheap* + the name *Jack*] (1851) **1 :** a haggling huckster **2 :** a dealer in cheap merchandise

[2]**cheapjack** *adj* (1865) **1 :** being inferior, cheap, or worthless ⟨~ movie companies⟩ **2 :** unscrupulously opportunistic ⟨~ speculators⟩

cheapo \ˈchē-(ˌ)pō\ *adj* (1967) **:** CHEAP

cheap shot *n* (1971) **1 :** an act of deliberate roughness against a defenseless opponent esp. in a contact sport ⟨taking *cheap shots* at the quarterback⟩ **2 :** a critical statement that takes unfair advantage of a known weakness of the target — **cheap–shot** *vt*

cheap·skate \ˈchēp-ˌskāt\ *n* (1896) **:** a miserly or stingy person; *esp* **:** one who tries to avoid paying a fair share of costs or expenses

[1]**cheat** \ˈchēt\ *vt* [[2]*cheat*] (1590) **1 :** to deprive of something valuable by the use of deceit or fraud **2 :** to influence or lead by deceit, trick, or artifice **3 :** to elude or thwart by or as if by outwitting ⟨~ death⟩ ~ *vi* **1 a :** to practice fraud or trickery **b :** to violate rules dishonestly ⟨~ at cards⟩ ⟨~*ing* on a test⟩ **2 :** to be sexually unfaithful — usu. used with *on* ⟨was ~*ing* on his wife⟩ **3 :** to position oneself defensively near a particular area in anticipation of a play in that area ⟨the shortstop was ~*ing* toward second base⟩ — **cheat·er** *n*

syn CHEAT, COZEN, DEFRAUD, SWINDLE mean to get something by dishonesty or deception. CHEAT suggests using trickery that escapes observation ⟨*cheated* me out of a dollar⟩. COZEN implies artful persuading or flattering to attain a thing or a purpose ⟨always able to *cozen* her grandfather out of a few dollars⟩. DEFRAUD stresses depriving one of his or her rights and usu. connotes deliberate perversion of the truth ⟨*defrauded* of her inheritance by an unscrupulous lawyer⟩. SWINDLE implies large-scale cheating by misrepresentation or abuse of confidence ⟨*swindled* of their savings by con artists⟩.

[2]**cheat** *n* [earlier *cheat* forfeited property, fr. ME *chet* escheat, short for *eschete* — more at ESCHEAT] (1615) **1 :** the act or an instance of fraudulently deceiving **:** DECEPTION, FRAUD **2 :** one that cheats **:** PRETENDER, DECEIVER **3** [prob. fr. a deceptive resemblance to grain] **a :** CHESS 1 **b :** CHEATGRASS **4 :** the obtaining of property from another by an intentional active distortion of the truth

cheat·grass \ˈchēt-ˌgras\ *n* (1866) **:** an annual weedy Eurasian bromegrass (*Bromus tectorum*) naturalized in No. America

cheat sheet *n* (ca. 1935) **1 :** a sheet containing information (as test answers) used secretly for cheating **2 :** a written or graphic aid (as a sheet of notes) that can be referred to for help in understanding or remembering something complex

[1]**check** \ˈchek\ *n* [ME *chek,* fr. AF *eschec,* fr. Ar *shāh,* fr. Pers, lit., king; akin to Gk *ktasthai* to acquire, Skt *kṣatra* dominion] (15c) **1 :** exposure of a chess king to an attack from which he must be protected or moved to safety **2 a :** a sudden stoppage of a forward course or progress **:** ARREST **b :** a checking of an opposing player (as in ice hockey) **3 :** a sudden pause or break in a progression **4** *archaic* **:** REPRIMAND, REBUKE **5 :** one that arrests, limits, or restrains **:** RESTRAINT ⟨against all ~*s,* rebukes, and manners, I must advance —Shak.⟩ **6 a :** a standard for testing and evaluation **:** CRITERION **b :** EXAMINATION ⟨a quick ~ of the engine⟩ **c :** INSPECTION, INVESTIGATION ⟨a loyalty ~ on government employees⟩ **d :** the act of testing or verifying; *also* **:** the sample or unit used for testing or verifying **7 :** a written order directing a bank to pay money as instructed **:** DRAFT **8 a :** a ticket or token showing ownership or identity or indicating payment made ⟨a baggage ~⟩ **b :** a counter in various games **c :** a slip indicating the amount due **:** BILL **9** [ME *chek,* short for *cheker* checker] **a :** a pattern in squares that resembles a checkerboard **b :** a fabric woven or printed with such a design **10 :** a mark typically ✓ placed beside an item to show it has been noted, examined, or verified **11 :** CRACK, BREAK — **check·less** \ˈche-kləs\ *adj* — **in check :** under restraint or control ⟨trying to keep his emotions *in check*⟩

[2]**check** *vt* (14c) **1 :** to put (a chess king) in check **2** *chiefly dial* **:** REBUKE, REPRIMAND **3 a :** to slow or bring to a stop **:** BRAKE ⟨hastily ~*ed* the impulse⟩ **b :** to block the progress of (as a hockey player) **4 a :** to restrain or diminish the action or force of **:** CONTROL **b :** to slack or ease off and then belay again (as a rope) **5 a :** to compare with a source, original, or authority **:** VERIFY ⟨needs to ~ her facts⟩ **b :** to inspect, examine, or look at appraisingly — usu. used with *out* or *over* ⟨~*ing* out new cars⟩ **c :** to mark with a check as examined, verified, or satisfactory — often used with *off* ⟨~*ed* off each item⟩ **6 a :** to consign (as luggage) to a common carrier from which one has purchased a passenger ticket ⟨~*ed* our bags before boarding⟩ **b :** to ship or accept for shipment under such a consignment **7 :** to mark into squares **:** CHECKER **8 :** to leave or accept for safekeeping in a checkroom ⟨~ a coat⟩ **9 :** to make checks or chinks **:** cause to crack ⟨the sun ~*s* timber⟩ ~ *vi* **1 a** *of a dog* **:** to stop in a chase esp. when scent is lost **b :** to halt through caution, uncertainty, or fear **:** STOP **2 a :** to investigate conditions ⟨~*ed* on the passengers' safety⟩ **b :** to prove to be consistent or truthful ⟨the description ~*s* with the photograph⟩ — often used with *out* ⟨the story ~*ed* out⟩ **3 :** to draw a check on a bank **4 :** to waive the right to initiate the betting in a round of poker **5 :** CRACK, SPLIT ***syn*** see RESTRAIN — **check into 1 :** to check in at ⟨*check into* a hotel⟩ **2 :** INVESTIGATE ⟨the police are *checking into* his alibi⟩ — **check up on :** INVESTIGATE ⟨*check up on* a possible investment⟩

[3]**check** *inter* — used to express assent or agreement

check·able *adj* (1877) **1 :** capable of being checked ⟨a ~ story⟩ **2 :** held in or being a bank account on which checks can be drawn ⟨~ deposits⟩

check·book \ˈchek-ˌbu̇k\ *n* (ca. 1846) **:** a book containing blank checks to be drawn on a bank

checkbook journalism *n* (1963) **:** the practice of paying someone for a news story and esp. for granting an interview

[1]**check·er** \ˈche-kər\ *n* [ME *cheker,* fr. AF *checker, escheker,* fr. *eschec* — more at CHECK] (14c) **1** *archaic* **:** CHESSBOARD **2 :** a square or spot resembling the markings of a checkerboard **3** [sing. of *checkers*] **:** a piece in checkers

[2]**checker** *vt* **check·ered; check·er·ing** \ˈche-k(ə-)riŋ\ (15c) **1 a :** to variegate with different colors or shades **b :** to vary with contrasting elements or situations **2 :** to mark into squares

[3]**checker** *n* (1535) **1 :** one that checks ⟨a fact ~⟩ **2 :** an employee who checks out purchases in a self-service store

check·er·ber·ry \ˈche-kər-ˌber-ē, -ˌbe-rē\ *n* [*checker* wild service tree + *berry*] (1776) **1 :** the spicy red berrylike fruit of a No. American wintergreen (*Gaultheria procumbens*) **2 :** a plant producing checkerberries

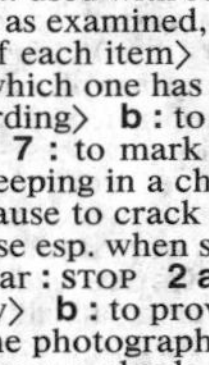

checkerberry

check·er·board \-ˌbȯrd\ *n* (1775) **1 :** a board used in various games (as checkers) with usu. 64 squares in 2 alternating colors **2 :** something that has a pattern or arrangement like a checkerboard

check·ered \ˈche-kərd\ *adj* (1656) **:** marked by alternation or contrast of fortune ⟨the best album of his ~ career —Mark Coleman⟩; *esp* **:** marked by many problems or failures ⟨trying to prevent discovery of his ~ past⟩

check·ers \ˈche-kərz\ *n pl but sing in constr* (1712) **:** a checkerboard game for 2 players each with 12 pieces

check–in \ˈchek-ˌin\ *n* (1927) **:** an act or instance of checking in

check in *vi* (1918) **1 :** to register at a hotel **2 :** to report one's presence or arrival ⟨*check in* at a convention⟩ ~ *vt* **:** to satisfy all requirements in returning ⟨*check in* the equipment after using⟩

checking account *n* (ca. 1909) **:** a bank account against which the depositor can draw checks

check·list \ˈchek-ˌlist\ *n* (1853) **:** a list of things to be checked or done ⟨a pilot's ~ before takeoff⟩; *also* **:** a comprehensive list

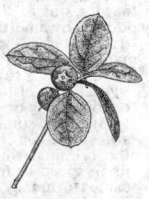

check mark *n* (1917) : CHECK 10 — **check·mark** *vt*

[1]**check·mate** \ˈchek-ˌmāt\ *vt* [ME *chekmaten,* fr. *chekmate,* interj. used to announce checkmate, fr. AF *eschec mat,* fr. Ar *shāh māt,* fr. Pers, lit., the king is left unable to escape] (14c) **1 :** to arrest, thwart, or counter completely **2 :** to check (a chess opponent's king) so that escape is impossible

[2]**checkmate** *n* (15c) **1 a :** the act of checkmating **b :** the situation of a checkmated king **2 :** a complete check

check·off \ˈchek-ˌȯf\ *n* (1911) **1 a :** the deduction of union dues from a worker's paycheck by the employer **b :** designation on an income tax return of a small amount of money to be applied to a special fund (as for financing political campaigns) **2 :** AUDIBLE

check off *vt* (1884) **1 :** to eliminate from further consideration **2 :** to deduct (union dues) from a worker's paycheck ~ *vi* **:** to change a play at the line of scrimmage in football by calling an audible

check·out \ˈchek-ˌau̇t\ *n* (1933) **1 :** the action or an instance of checking out **2 :** the time at which a lodger must vacate a room (as in a hotel) or be charged for retaining it **3 :** a counter or area in a store where goods are checked out **4 a :** the action of examining and testing something for performance, suitability, or readiness **b :** the action of familiarizing oneself with the operation of a mechanical thing (as an airplane)

check out *vi* (1921) **1 :** to vacate and pay for one's lodging (as at a hotel) **2 :** DIE ~ *vt* **1 :** to satisfy all requirements in taking away ⟨*checked out* a library book⟩ **2 a :** to itemize and total the cost of and receive payment for (outgoing merchandise) esp. in a self-service store **b :** to have the cost totaled and pay for (purchases) at a checkout

check·point \ˈchek-ˌpȯint\ *n* (1926) **:** a point at which a check is performed ⟨vehicles were inspected at various ~*s*⟩

check·rein \-ˌrān\ *n* (1786) **1 :** a short rein looped over a hook on the saddle of a harness to prevent a horse from lowering its head **2 :** a branch rein connecting the driving rein of one horse of a pair with the bit of the other

check·room \-ˌrüm, -ˌru̇m\ *n* (1900) **:** a room at which baggage, parcels, or clothing can be left for safekeeping

checks and balances *n pl* (1787) **:** a system that allows each branch of a government to amend or veto acts of another branch so as to prevent any one branch from exerting too much power

check·sum \ˈchek-ˌsəm\ *n* (1940) **:** a sum derived from the bits of a segment of computer data that is calculated before and after transmission or storage to assure that the data is free from errors or tampering

check·up \ˈchek-ˌəp\ *n* (1921) **:** EXAMINATION; *esp* **:** a general physical examination

check valve *n* (ca. 1877) **:** a valve that permits flow in one direction only

ched·dar \ˈche-dər\ *n, often cap* [*Cheddar,* village in Somersetshire, England] (1646) **:** a hard white, yellow, or orange smooth-textured cheese with a flavor that ranges from mild to strong as the cheese matures — called also *cheddar cheese*

cheder *var of* HEDER

chee·cha·ko \chē-ˈchä-(ˌ)kō, -ˈchȯ- *also* -ˈcha-\ *n, pl* **-kos** [Chinook Jargon, fr. *chee* new (fr. Lower Chinook *čxi* right away) + *chako* come, fr. Nootka *čokʷa·* come, imper.] (1897) **:** TENDERFOOT 1 — used chiefly in Alaska

[1]**cheek** \ˈchēk\ *n* [ME *cheke,* fr. OE *cēace;* akin to MLG *kāke* jawbone] (bef. 12c) **1 :** the fleshy side of the face below the eye and above and to the side of the mouth; *broadly* **:** the lateral aspect of the head **2 :** something suggestive of the human cheek in position or form; *esp* **:** one of two laterally paired parts **3 :** insolent boldness and self-assurance **4 :** BUTTOCK 1 ***syn*** see TEMERITY — **cheek·ful** \-ˌfu̇l\ *n*

[2]**cheek** *vt* (1840) *chiefly Brit* **:** to speak rudely or impudently to

cheek·bone \ˈchēk-ˌbōn\ *n* (15c) **:** the prominence below the eye that is formed by the zygomatic bone; *also* **:** ZYGOMATIC BONE

cheek by jowl *adv* (1577) **:** SIDE BY SIDE

cheeked \ˈchēkt\ *adj* (1580) **:** having cheeks of a specified nature — used in combination ⟨rosy-*cheeked*⟩

cheek tooth *n* (14c) **:** any of the molar or premolar teeth

cheeky \ˈchē-kē\ *adj* **cheek·i·er; -est** (1846) **:** insolently bold **:** IMPUDENT — **cheek·i·ly** \-kə-lē\ *adv* — **cheek·i·ness** \-kē-nəs\ *n*

cheep \ˈchēp\ *vi* [imit.] (1513) **1 :** to utter faint shrill sounds **:** PEEP **2 :** to utter a single word or sound — **cheep** *n*

[1]**cheer** \ˈchir\ *n* [ME *chere* face, cheer, fr. AF, face, fr. ML *cara,* prob. fr. Gk *kara* head, face — more at CEREBRAL] (13c) **1 a** *obs* **:** FACE **b** *archaic* **:** facial expression **2 :** state of mind or heart **:** SPIRIT ⟨be of good ~ —Mt 9:2(AV)⟩ **3 :** lightness of mind and feeling **:** ANIMATION, GAIETY **4 :** hospitable entertainment **:** WELCOME **5 :** food and drink for a feast **:** FARE **6 :** something that gladdens ⟨words of ~⟩ **7 :** a shout of applause or encouragement

[2]**cheer** *vt* (14c) **1 a :** to instill with hope or courage **:** COMFORT — usu. used with *up* **b :** to make glad or happy — usu. used with *up* **2 :** to urge on or encourage esp. by shouts ⟨~*ed* the team on⟩ **3 :** to applaud with shouts ~ *vi* **1** *obs* **:** to be mentally or emotionally disposed **2 :** to grow or be cheerful **:** REJOICE — usu. used with *up* **3 :** to utter a shout of applause or triumph — **cheer·er** *n*

cheer·ful \ˈchir-fəl\ *adj* (15c) **1 a :** full of good spirits **:** MERRY ⟨a ~ host⟩ **b :** UNGRUDGING ⟨~ obedience⟩ **2 :** conducive to cheer **:** likely to dispel gloom or worry ⟨sunny ~ room⟩ — **cheer·ful·ly** \-f(ə-)lē\ *adv* — **cheer·ful·ness** \-fəl-nəs\ *n*

cheer·io \ˌchir-ē-ˈō\ *interj* [*cheery* + *-o*] (1910) *chiefly Brit* — usu. used as a farewell and sometimes as a greeting or toast

cheer·lead·er \ˈchir-ˌlē-dər\ *n* (1903) **:** one that calls for and directs organized cheering (as at a football game) — **cheer·lead** \-ˌlēd\ *vt* — **cheer·lead·ing** \-ˌlē-diŋ\ *n*

cheer·less \-ləs\ *adj* (1579) **:** lacking qualities that cheer **:** BLEAK, JOYLESS ⟨a ~ room⟩ ***syn*** see DISMAL — **cheer·less·ly** *adv* — **cheer·less·ness** *n*

cheer·ly \ˈchir-lē\ *adv* (1558) **:** in a cheerful manner ⟨lusty, young, and ~ drawing breath —Shak.⟩

cheers \ˈchirz\ *interj* (1919) — used as a toast

cheery \ˈchir-ē\ *adj* **cheer·i·er; -est** (15c) **1 :** marked by cheerfulness or good spirits **2 :** causing or suggesting cheerfulness ⟨~ music⟩ — **cheer·i·ly** \ˈchir-ə-lē\ *adv* — **cheer·i·ness** \ˈchir-ē-nəs\ *n*

[1]**cheese** \ˈchēz\ *n, often attrib* [ME *chese,* fr. OE *cēse,* fr. L *caseus* cheese] (bef. 12c) **1 a :** a food consisting of the coagulated, compressed, and usu. ripened curd of milk separated from the whey **b :** an often cylindrical cake of this food **2 :** something resembling cheese in shape or consistency **3 :** something cheap or shabby **:** cheesy material ⟨cinematic ~⟩

[2]**cheese** *vt* **cheesed; chees·ing** [origin unknown] (ca. 1811) **:** to put an end to **:** STOP — **cheese it** — used in the imperative as a warning of danger ⟨*cheese it,* the cops⟩

[3]**cheese** *n* [perh. fr. Hindi *cīz* & Urdu *chīz* thing, fr. Pers *chīz*] (1920) *slang* **:** someone important

cheese·burg·er \ˈchēz-ˌbər-gər\ *n* [*cheese* + ham*burger*] (1928) **:** a hamburger topped with a slice of cheese

cheese·cake \-ˌkāk\ *n* (15c) **1 :** a dessert consisting of a creamy filling usu. containing cheese baked in a pastry or pressed-crumb shell **2 :** a photographic display of shapely and scantily clothed female figures — often used attributively; compare BEEFCAKE

cheese·cloth \-ˌklȯth\ *n* [fr. its use in the making of cheese] (14c) **:** a very lightweight unsized cotton gauze

cheesed off *adj* [origin unknown] (1942) *chiefly Brit* **:** ANGRY, IRRITATED

cheese·par·ing \-ˌper-iŋ\ *n* (1597) **1 :** something worthless or insignificant **2 :** miserly economizing — **cheeseparing** *adj*

cheese·steak \-ˌstāk\ *n* (1977) **:** a sandwich consisting of thinly sliced beef topped with melted cheese and condiments (as fried onions or peppers)

cheesy \ˈchē-zē\ *adj* **chees·i·er; -est** (14c) **1 a :** resembling or suggesting cheese esp. in consistency or odor **b :** containing cheese **2 :** SHABBY 3c, CHEAP ⟨a ~ movie⟩ ⟨~ motels⟩ — **chees·i·ness** *n*

chee·tah \ˈchē-tə\ *n, pl* **cheetahs** *also* **cheetah** [Hindi *cītā* & Urdu *chītā* leopard, fr. Skt *citraka,* fr. *citra* bright, variegated; akin to OHG *heitar* bright — more at -HOOD] (1610) **:** a long-legged spotted swift-moving African and formerly Asian cat (*Acinonyx jubatus*) about the size of a small leopard that has blunt nonretractile claws

chef \ˈshef\ *n* [F, short for *chef de cuisine* head of the kitchen] (1840) **1 :** a skilled cook who manages the kitchen (as of a restaurant) **2 :** COOK — **chef** *vi* — **chef·dom** \-dəm\ *n*

chef d'oeu·vre \shā-dœvrᵊ, (ˌ)shā-ˈdə(r)v\ *n, pl* **chefs d'oeuvre** \-dœvrᵊ, -ˈdə(r)v(z)\ [F *chef-d'oeuvre,* lit., leading work] (1619) **:** a masterpiece esp. in art or literature

che·la \ˈkē-lə\ *n, pl* **che·lae** \-(ˌ)lē\ [NL, fr. Gk *chēlē* claw] (1635) **:** a pincerlike organ or claw borne by a limb of a crustacean or arachnid

[1]**che·late** \ˈkē-ˌlāt *also* ˈchē-\ *adj* (1826) **1 :** resembling or having chelae **2** [fr. the pincerlike way in which the metal ion is held] **:** of, relating to, or being a chelate

[2]**chelate** *vb* **che·lat·ed; che·lat·ing** *vt* (1922) **:** to combine with (a metal) so as to form a chelate ring ~ *vi* **:** to react so as to form a chelate ring — **che·lat·able** \-ˌlā-tə-bəl\ *adj*

[3]**chelate** *n* (1943) **:** a compound having a ring structure that usu. contains a metal ion held by coordinate bonds

che·la·tion \kē-ˈlā-shən *also* chē-\ *n* (1932) **1 :** the process of chelating or the quality or state of being chelated **2 :** CHELATION THERAPY

chelation therapy *n* (1976) **:** the use of a chelator (as EDTA) to bind with a metal (as lead or iron) in the body to form a chelate so that the metal loses its chemical effect (as toxicity or physiological activity)

che·la·tor \kē-ˈlā-tər *also* chē-\ *n* (1957) **:** one that chelates; *esp* **:** a binding agent that suppresses chemical activity by forming chelates

che·lic·era \ki-ˈli-sə-rə\ *n, pl* **-er·ae** \-ˌrē\ [NL, fr. F *chélicère,* fr. Gk *chēlē* + *keras* horn — more at HORN] (1835) **:** one of the anterior pair of appendages of an arachnid often specialized as fangs — **che·lic·er·al** \-sə-rəl\ *adj*

che·li·ped \ˈkē-lə-ˌped\ *n* [Gk *chēlē* claw + E *-i-* + *-ped*] (1869) **:** one of the pair of legs that bears the large chelae in decapod crustaceans

Chel·le·an *or* **Chel·li·an** \ˈshe-lē-ən\ *adj* [F *chelléen,* fr. *Chelles,* France] (1893) **:** ABBEVILLIAN

che·lo·ni·an \ki-ˈlō-nē-ən\ *n* [Gk *chelōnē* tortoise] (1828) **:** TURTLE — **chelonian** *adj*

chem *abbr* chemical; chemist; chemistry

chem- *or* **chemo-** *also* **chemi-** *comb form* [NL, fr. LGk *chēmeia* alchemy — more at ALCHEMY] **1 :** chemical **:** chemistry ⟨*chemo*taxis⟩ **2 :** chemically ⟨*chemi*sorb⟩

chem·ic \ˈke-mik\ *adj* [NL *chimicus* alchemist, fr. ML *alchimicus,* fr. *alchymia* alchemy] (1576) **1** *archaic* **:** ALCHEMIC **2 :** CHEMICAL

[1]**chem·i·cal** \ˈke-mi-kəl\ *adj* (1576) **1 :** of, relating to, used in, or produced by chemistry or the phenomena of chemistry ⟨~ reactions⟩ **2 a :** acting or operated or produced by chemicals ⟨a ~ fire extinguisher⟩ **b :** detectable by chemical means — **chem·i·cal·ly** \-mi-k(ə-)lē\ *adv*

[2]**chemical** *n* (1739) **1 :** a substance obtained by a chemical process or producing a chemical effect **2 :** DRUG 3

chemical engineering *n* (1869) **:** engineering dealing with the industrial application of chemistry — **chemical engineer** *n*

chemical peel *n* (1978) **:** a cosmetic procedure for the removal of facial blemishes and wrinkles involving the application of a caustic chemical and esp. an acid (as trichloroacetic acid) to the skin

chemical warfare *n* (1917) **:** tactical warfare using incendiary mixtures, smokes, or irritant, burning, poisonous, or asphyxiating gases

chemical weapon *n* (1920) **:** a weapon used in chemical warfare

chemi·lu·mi·nes·cence \ˌke-mē-ˌlü-mə-ˈne-sᵊn(t)s, ˌkē-\ *n* [ISV] (1889) **:** luminescence (as bioluminescence) due to chemical reaction — **chemi·lu·mi·nes·cent** \-ˈne-sᵊnt\ *adj*

che·min de fer \shə-ˌman-də-ˈfer\ *n, pl* **che·mins de fer** *same*\ [F, lit., railroad] (1891) **:** a card game in which two hands are dealt, any number of players may bet against the dealer, and the winning hand is the one that comes closer to but does not exceed a count of nine on two or three cards

chemi·os·mot·ic \ˌke-mē-äz-ˈmä-tik, ˌkē-\ *adj* (1957) **:** relating to or being a theory that seeks to explain the mechanism of ATP formation in oxidative phosphorylation by mitochondria and chloroplasts without recourse to the formation of high-energy intermediates by postulating the formation of an energy gradient of hydrogen ions across the organelle membranes that results in the reversible movement of hydrogen ions to the outside and is generated by electron transport or the activity of electron carriers

che·mise \shə-ˈmēz, *sometimes* -ˈmēs\ *n* [ME, shirt, fr. AF, fr. LL *camisia*] (13c) **1 :** a woman's one-piece undergarment **2 :** a loose straight-hanging dress

chem·i·sette \ˌshe-mi-ˈzet\ *n* [F, dim. of *chemise*] (1796) **:** a woman's garment; *esp* **:** one (as of lace) to fill the open front of a dress

chem·i·sorb \ˈke-mi-ˌsȯrb, ˈkē-, -ˌzȯrb\ *vt* [*chem-* + *-sorb* (as in *adsorb*)] (1935) **:** to take up and hold usu. irreversibly by chemical forces — **chem·i·sorp·tion** \ˌke-mi-ˈsȯrp-shən, ˌkē-, -ˈzȯrp-\ *n*

chem·ist \ˈke-mist\ *n* [NL *chimista,* short for ML *alchimista*] (1562) **1 a** *obs* **:** ALCHEMIST **b :** one trained in chemistry **2** *Brit* **:** PHARMACIST

chem·is·try \ˈke-mə-strē\ *n, pl* **-tries** (1646) **1 :** a science that deals with the composition, structure, and properties of substances and with the transformations that they undergo **2 a :** the composition and chemical properties of a substance ⟨the ~ of iron⟩ **b :** chemical processes and phenomena (as of an organism) ⟨blood ~⟩ **3 a :** a strong mutual attraction, attachment, or sympathy ⟨they have a special ~⟩ **b :** interaction between people working together; *specif* **:** such interaction when harmonious or effective ⟨a team lacking ~⟩

che·mo \ˈkē-(ˌ)mō\ *n* (1977) **:** CHEMOTHERAPY

che·mo·au·to·tro·phic \ˌkē-mō-ˌȯ-tə-ˈtrō-fik *also* ˌke-\ *adj* (1941) **:** being autotrophic and oxidizing an inorganic compound as a source of energy ⟨~ bacteria⟩ — **che·mo·au·tot·ro·phy** \-ȯ-ˈtä-trə-fē\ *n*

chemo brain *n* (1991) **:** impaired cognition (as memory loss or lack of concentration) that has been observed in patients who have received chemotherapy

che·mo·kine \-ˈkīn\ *n* [*chem-* + *-kine* (as in *cytokine*)] (1992) **:** any of a group of cytokines produced by various cells (as at sites of inflammation) that stimulate chemotaxis in white blood cells (as neutrophils and T cells)

che·mo·pre·ven·tion \-pri-ˈven(t)-shən\ *n* (1980) **:** the use of chemical agents to prevent or slow the development of cancer — **che·mo·pre·ven·tive** \-ˈven-tiv\ *adj*

che·mo·pro·phy·lax·is \-ˌprō-fə-ˈlak-səs *also* -ˌprä-fə-\ *n* (1936) **:** the prevention of infectious disease by the use of chemical agents — **che·mo·pro·phy·lac·tic** \-ˈlak-tik\ *adj*

che·mo·re·cep·tion \-ri-ˈsep-shən\ *n* [ISV] (1919) **:** the physiological reception of chemical stimuli — **che·mo·re·cep·tive** \-ˈsep-tiv\ *adj*

che·mo·re·cep·tor \-ri-ˈsep-tər\ *n* [ISV] (1906) **:** a sense organ (as a taste bud) responding to chemical stimuli

che·mo·sur·gery \ˌkē-mō-ˈsərj-rē, -ˈsər-jə-rē\ *n* (ca. 1944) **:** chemical removal of diseased or unwanted tissue — **che·mo·sur·gi·cal** \-ˈsər-ji-kəl\ *adj*

che·mo·syn·the·sis \-ˈsin(t)-thə-səs\ *n* [NL] (1901) **:** synthesis of organic compounds (as in living cells) by energy derived from inorganic chemical reactions — **che·mo·syn·thet·ic** \-sin-ˈthe-tik\ *adj*

che·mo·tac·tic \-ˈtak-tik\ *adj* (1893) **:** involving, inducing, or exhibiting chemotaxis — **che·mo·tac·ti·cal·ly** \-ti-k(ə-)lē\ *adv*

che·mo·tax·is \-ˈtak-səs\ *n* [NL] (ca. 1887) **:** orientation or movement of an organism or cell in relation to chemical agents

che·mo·tax·on·o·my \-(ˌ)tak-ˈsä-nə-mē\ *n* (1963) **:** the classification of plants and animals based on similarities and differences in biochemical composition — **che·mo·tax·o·nom·ic** \-ˌtak-sə-ˈnä-mik\ *adj* — **che·mo·tax·on·o·mist** \-(ˌ)tak-ˈsä-nə-mist\ *n*

che·mo·ther·a·peu·tic \-ˌther-ə-ˈpyü-tik\ *adj* (1907) **:** of, relating to, or used in chemotherapy — **chemotherapeutic** *n* — **che·mo·ther·a·peu·ti·cal·ly** \-ti-k(ə-)lē\ *adv*

che·mo·ther·a·py \-ˈther-ə-pē\ *n* [ISV] (1910) **:** the use of chemical agents in the treatment or control of disease (as cancer) or mental illness — **che·mo·ther·a·pist** \-pist\ *n*

che·mot·ro·pism \ki-ˈmä-trə-ˌpi-zəm, ke-\ *n* [ISV] (1895) **:** orientation of cells or organisms in relation to chemical stimuli

che·nille \shə-ˈnēl\ *n* [F, lit., caterpillar, fr. L *canicula,* dim. of *canis* dog; fr. its hairy appearance — more at HOUND] (ca. 1739) **1 :** a wool, cotton, silk, or rayon yarn with protruding pile; *also* **:** a pile-face fabric with a filling of this yarn **2 :** an imitation of chenille yarn or fabric

che·nin blanc \ˈshe-nən-ˈbläŋk, shə-na^{n}-ˈblä^{n}\ *n, often cap C&B* [F, lit., white Chenin (a grape variety)] (1913) **:** any of various white wines ranging from dry to sweet made from a grape orig. grown in the Loire valley

che·no·pod \ˈkē-nə-ˌpäd, ˈke-\ *n* [ultim. fr. Gk *chēn* goose + *podion,* dim. of *pod-, pous* foot — more at GOOSE, FOOT] (1555) **:** any plant of the goosefoot family

cheong·sam \ˈchȯŋ-ˌsäm\ *n* [Chin (Guangdong) *chèuhng-sāam,* lit., long gown] (1952) **:** a dress of southern Chinese origin with a slit skirt and a mandarin collar

cheque *chiefly Brit var of* [1]CHECK 7

che·quer *chiefly Brit var of* CHECKER

cher·i·moya \ˌcher-ə-ˈmȯi-ə\ *also* **chir·i·moya** \ˌchir-\ *n* [Sp *chirimoya*] (1736) **:** a round, oblong, or heart-shaped fruit with a pitted pale green rind that is borne by a widely cultivated tropical American tree (*Annona cherimola*) of the custard-apple family; *also* **:** this tree

cher·ish \ˈcher-ish, ˈche-rish\ *vt* [ME *cherisshen,* fr. AF *cheriss-,* stem of *cherir* to cherish, fr. *cher* dear, fr. L *carus* — more at CHARITY] (14c) **1 a :** to hold dear **:** feel or show affection for ⟨~*ed* her friends⟩ **b :** to keep or cultivate with care and affection **:** NURTURE ⟨~*es* his marriage⟩ **2 :** to entertain or harbor in the mind deeply and resolutely ⟨still ~*es* that memory⟩ ***syn*** see APPRECIATE — **cher·ish·able** \-i-shə-bəl\ *adj* — **cher·ish·er** \-i-shər\ *n*

cher·no·zem \ˌcher-nə-ˈzyȯm, -ˈzem\ *n* [Russ, fr. *chërnyĭ* black + *zemlya* earth] (1841) **:** any of a group of dark-colored zonal soils with a deep rich humus horizon found in regions (as the grasslands of central No. America) of temperate to cool climate — **cher·no·zem·ic** \-ˈzyō-mik, -ˈze-\ *adj*

Cher·o·kee \ˈcher-ə-(ˌ)kē, ˈche-rə-\ *n, pl* **Cherokee** *or* **Cherokees** [prob. ultim. fr. Creek *calá·kki*] (1674) **1 :** a member of an American Indian people orig. of Tennessee and No. Carolina **2 :** the language of the Cherokee people

Cherokee rose *n* (1823) **:** a Chinese climbing rose (*Rosa laevigata*) with a fragrant white blossom

che·root \shə-ˈrüt, chə-\ *n* [Tamil *curuṭṭu,* lit., roll] (ca. 1679) **:** a cigar cut square at both ends

cher·ry \ˈcher-ē, ˈche-rē\ *n, pl* **cherries** [ME *chery,* fr. AF *cherise, cirice* (taken as a plural), fr. LL *ceresia,* fr. L *cerasus* cherry tree, fr. Gk *kerasos*] (14c) **1 a :** any of numerous trees and shrubs (genus *Prunus*) of the rose family that bear pale yellow to deep red or blackish smooth-skinned drupes enclosing a smooth seed and that include some cultivated for their fruits or ornamental flowers — compare SOUR CHERRY, SWEET CHERRY **b :** the fruit of a cherry **c :** the reddish-brown wood of a cherry; *esp* **:** BLACK CHERRY 2 **2 :** a variable color averaging a moderate red **3 a :** HYMEN **b :** VIRGINITY — **cher·ry·like** \-ˌlīk\ *adj*

cherry bomb *n* (1953) **:** a powerful globular red firecracker

cher·ry–pick \ˈcher-ē-ˌpik\ *vi* (1965) **:** to select the best or most desirable ~ *vt* **:** to select as being the best or most desirable; *also* **:** to select the best or most desirable from ⟨~*ed* the art collection⟩

cherry picker *n* (ca. 1944) **1 :** a traveling crane equipped for holding a passenger at the end of the boom **2 :** one who cherry-picks

cher·ry·stone \ˈcher-ē-ˌstōn\ *n* (1872) **:** a small quahog

cherry tomato *n* (1847) **:** a small globose red or orange tomato borne in long dense clusters; *also* **:** a tropical American plant (*Lycopersicon esculentum cerasiforme*) bearing cherry tomatoes

cher·ry·wood \-ˌwu̇d\ *n* (1821) **:** CHERRY 1c

chert \ˈchərt, ˈchat\ *n* [origin unknown] (1679) **:** a rock resembling flint and consisting essentially of a large amount of fibrous chalcedony with smaller amounts of cryptocrystalline quartz and amorphous silica — **cherty** \ˈchər-tē, ˈcha-\ *adj*

cher·ub \ˈcher-əb, ˈche-rəb\ *n, pl usu* **cher·u·bim** \ˈcher-ə-ˌbim, ˈker- *also* ˈcher-yə-\ [L, fr. Gk *cheroub,* fr. Heb *kĕrūbh*] (13c) **1** *pl* **:** an order of angels — see CELESTIAL HIERARCHY **2** *pl usu* **cherubs a :** a beautiful usu. winged child in painting and sculpture **b :** an innocent-looking usu. chubby and rosy person — **che·ru·bic** \chə-ˈrü-bik *also* ˈcher-ə-\ *adj* — **che·ru·bi·cal·ly** \-bi-k(ə-)lē\ *adv* — **cher·ub·like** \ˈcher-əb-ˌlīk\ *adj*

cher·vil \ˈchər-vəl\ *n* [ME *cherville,* fr. OE *cerfille,* fr. L *caerefolium,* modif. of Gk **chairephyllon,* fr. *chairein* to rejoice + *phyllon* leaf — more at YEARN, BLADE] (bef. 12c) **:** an aromatic herb (*Anthriscus cerefolium*) of the carrot family with divided leaves that are often used in soups and salads; *also* **:** any of several related plants

Ches·a·peake Bay retriever \ˈche-sə-ˌpēk-ˈbā-\ *n* (1891) **:** any of a breed of powerful brown sporting dogs developed in Maryland and having a dense oily water-shedding coat

Chesh·ire cat \ˈche-shər-\ *n* [*Cheshire,* England] (1866) **:** a broadly grinning cat in Lewis Carroll's *Alice's Adventures in Wonderland*

Cheshire cheese *n* (1597) **:** a cheese similar to cheddar made chiefly in Cheshire, England

[1]chess \ˈches\ *n* [ME *ches,* fr. AF *esches, eschés,* pl. of *eschec* check at chess — more at CHECK] (14c) **:** a game for 2 players each of whom moves 16 pieces according to fixed rules across a checkerboard and tries to checkmate the opponent's king

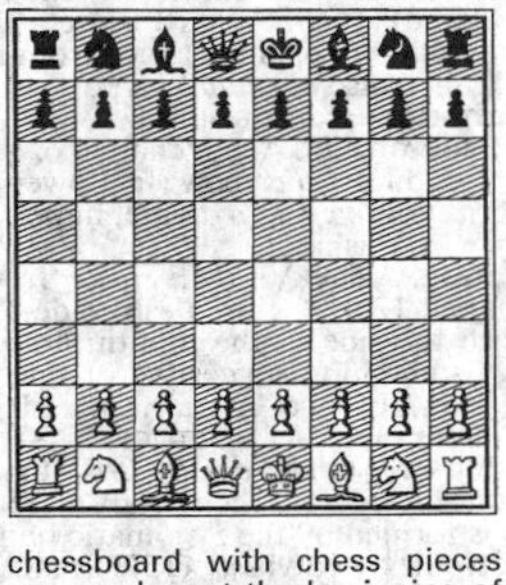

chessboard with chess pieces arranged as at the beginning of a game

[2]chess *n* [origin unknown] (1736) **1 :** a weedy annual European bromegrass (*Bromus secalinus*) widely naturalized in No. America as a weed esp. in grain **2 :** any of several weedy bromegrasses related to chess

chess·board \ˈches-ˌbȯrd\ *n* (15c) **:** a checkerboard used in the game of chess

chess·man \-ˌman, -mən\ *n* (15c) **:** any of the pieces used in chess

chess pie *n* [perh. alter. of *chest*] (1932) **:** a pie or tart with a filling made esp. of eggs, butter, and sugar

chest \ˈchest\ *n* [ME, fr. OE *cest, cist* chest, box, fr. L *cista,* fr. Gk *kistē* basket, hamper] (bef. 12c) **1 a :** a container for storage or shipping; *esp* **:** a box with a lid used esp. for the safekeeping of belongings **b :** a cupboard used esp. for the storing of medicines or first-aid supplies **2 :** the place where money of a public institution is kept **:** TREASURY; *also* **:** the fund so kept **3 a :** THORAX 1; *esp* **:** the part of the human body enclosed by the ribs and sternum **b :** BREAST 2a ⟨a hairy ~⟩ — **chest·ful** \-ˌfu̇l\ *n*

chest·ed \ˈches-təd\ *adj* (1662) **:** having a chest of a specified kind — used in combination ⟨flat-*chested*⟩

ches·ter·field \ˈches-tər-ˌfēld\ *n* [fr. a 19th cent. Earl of *Chesterfield*] (1852) **1 :** a single-breasted or double-breasted semifitted overcoat with velvet collar **2 :** a davenport usu. with upright armrests

Ches·ter White \ˈches-tər-\ *n* [*Chester* County, Pa.] (1856) **:** any of a breed of large white swine

[1]chest·nut \ˈches(t)-(ˌ)nət\ *n* [ME *chasteine, chesten* chestnut tree, fr. AF *chastein, chastain,* fr. L *castanea,* fr. Gk *kastanea*] (14c) **1 a :** any of a genus (*Castanea*) of trees or shrubs of the beech family; *esp* **:** an American tree (*C. dentata*) that was formerly a dominant or codominant member of many deciduous forests of the eastern U.S. but has now been largely eliminated by the chestnut blight and seldom grows beyond the shrub or sapling stage **b :** the edible nut of a chestnut **c :** the wood of a chestnut **2 :** a grayish to reddish brown **3 :** HORSE CHESTNUT **4 :** a chestnut-colored animal; *specif* **:** a horse having a body color of any shade of pure or reddish brown with mane, tail, and points of the same or a lighter shade — compare [2]BAY 1, [1]SORREL 1 **5 :** a callosity on the inner side of the leg of the horse — see HORSE illustration **6 a :** an old joke or story **b :** something (as a musical piece or a saying) repeated to the point of staleness

[2]chestnut *adj* (1555) **1 :** of the color chestnut **2 :** of, relating to, or resembling a chestnut

chestnut blight *n* (ca. 1909) **:** a destructive disease of the American chestnut marked by cankers of the bark and cambium and caused by an imported fungus (*Endothia parasitica* syn. *Cryphonectria parasitica*)

chestnut oak *n* (1703) **:** any of several oaks having oblong to lanceolate leaves with crenate or serrate edges: as **a :** CHINQUAPIN OAK **b :** a medium-sized oak (*Quercus prinus*) of eastern No. America with large acorns and leaves that are yellow-green above and paler below

chest of drawers (1649) : a piece of furniture designed to contain a set of drawers (as for holding clothing)
chest–thump·ing \'ches(t)-ˌthəm-piŋ\ *n* (1948) : conduct or expression marked by pompous or arrogant self-assertion ⟨political ~⟩
chesty \'ches-tē\ *adj* **chest·i·er; -est** (1899) **1** : proudly or arrogantly self-assertive **2** : marked by a large or well-developed chest
Chet·nik \chet-'nēk, 'chet-nik\ *n* [Serbian *četnik,* fr. *četa* band, troop] (1909) **1** : an irregular Slav soldier in the Balkans; *esp* : a member of various irregular Serbian military forces that in periods of disorder (as during World War II and following the breakup of Yugoslavia in 1991) pursued ultranationalist aims **2** : an ultranationalist Serb
chet·rum \'chē-trəm, 'che-\ *n, pl* **chetrums** *or* **chetrum** [Tibetan] (1973) — see *ngultrum* at MONEY table
che·val–de–frise \shə-ˌval-də-'frēz\ *n, pl* **che·vaux–de–frise** \shə-ˌvō-\ [F, lit., horse from Friesland] (1668) **1** : a defense consisting typically of a timber or an iron barrel covered with projecting spikes and often strung with barbed wire **2** : a protecting line (as of spikes) on top of a wall — usu. used in pl.
che·val glass \shə-'val-\ *n* [F *cheval* horse, support] (1828) : a full-length mirror in a frame in which it may be tilted
che·va·lier \ˌshe-və-'lir, *esp for 1b & 2 also* shə-'val-ˌyā\ *n* [ME, fr. AF, fr. LL *caballarius* horseman — more at CAVALIER] (14c) **1 a** : CAVALIER 2 **b** : a member of any of various orders of knighthood or of merit (as the Legion of Honor) **2 a** : a member of the lowest rank of French nobility **b** : a cadet of the French nobility **3** : a chivalrous man
che·ve·lure \shəv-lu̇r\ *n* [F, fr. OF *chevelëure,* fr. LL *capillatura,* fr. L *capillatus* having long hair, fr. *capillus* hair] (15c) : a head of hair
chev·i·ot \'she-vē-ət, *esp Brit* 'che-\ *n, often cap* (1815) **1** : any of a breed of hardy hornless relatively small sheep that are a source of quality mutton and have their origin in the Cheviot hills **2 a** : a fabric of cheviot wool **b** : a heavy rough napped plain or twill fabric of coarse wool or worsted **c** : a sturdy soft-finished plain or twill cotton shirting
chèvre \'shev(rᵊ), 'shev-rə\ *n* [F, lit., goat, fr. OF *chievre,* fr. L *capra* she-goat, fr. *caper* he-goat — more at CAPRIOLE] (1950) : GOAT CHEESE
chev·ron \'shev-rən\ *n* [ME *cheveron,* fr. AF, rafter, chevron, fr. VL **caprion-, *caprio* rafter; akin to L *caper* goat] (14c) : a figure, pattern, or object having the shape of a V or an inverted V: as **a** : a heraldic charge consisting of two diagonal stripes meeting at an angle usu. with the point up **b** : a sleeve badge that usu. consists of one or more chevron-shaped stripes that indicates the wearer's rank and service (as in the armed forces)
[1]**chew** \'chü\ *vb* [ME, fr. OE *cēowan;* akin to OHG *kiuwan* to chew, Russ *zhevat'*] *vt* (bef. 12c) **1** : to crush, grind, or gnaw (as food) with or as if with the teeth : MASTICATE **2** : to injure, destroy, or consume as if by chewing — usu. used with *up* ⟨~*ing* up profits⟩ ~ *vi* : to chew something; *specif* : to chew tobacco — **chew·able** \-ə-bəl\ *adj* — **chew·er** *n* — **chewy** \'chü-ē\ *adj* — **chew on** : to think about : PONDER ⟨*chewing on* the new developments⟩ — **chew the fat** *also* **chew the rag** : to make friendly familiar conversation : CHAT
[2]**chew** *n* (13c) **1** : the act of chewing **2** : something for chewing
chewing gum *n* (1850) : a sweetened and flavored insoluble plastic material (as a preparation of chicle) used for chewing
che·wink \chi-'wiŋk\ *n* [imit.] (1793) : TOWHEE 1
chew out *vt* (1943) : REPRIMAND, BAWL OUT
chew over *vt* (1939) : to meditate on : think about reflectively
Chey·enne \shī-'an, -'en\ *n, pl* **Cheyenne** *or* **Cheyennes** [AmerF, fr. Dakota *šahíyena*] (1778) **1** : a member of an American Indian people of the western plains of the U.S. **2** : the Algonquian language of the Cheyenne people
chez \'shā\ *prep* [F, fr. L *casa* cottage] (1740) : at or in the home or business place of
CHF *abbr* congestive heart failure
ChFC *abbr* chartered financial consultant
chg *abbr* **1** change **2** charge
[1]**chi** \'kī, 'kē\ *n* [Gk *chei, chi*] (15c) : the 22d letter of the Greek alphabet — see ALPHABET table
[2]**chi** *or* **ch'i** *also* **qi** \'chē\ *n, often cap* [Ch (Beijing) *qì,* lit., air, breath] (1850) : vital energy that is held to animate the body internally and is of central importance in some Eastern systems of medical treatment (as acupuncture) and of exercise or self-defense (as tai chi)
Chi·a·ni·na \ˌkē-ə-'nē-nə\ *n, pl* **Chianina** *or* **Chianinas** [It, fr. fem. of *chianino* of the *Chiani* River valley, Italy] (1914) : any of a breed of tall white cattle of Italian origin noted esp. for producing lean meat
Chi·an·ti \kē-'än-tē, -'an-\ *n* [It, fr. the *Chianti* region, Italy] (1833) : a dry usu. red wine from the Tuscany region of Italy; *also* : a similar wine made elsewhere
chiar·oscu·rist \kē-ˌär-ə-'skyu̇r-ist, kē-ˌer-, kē-ˌa-rə-, -'sku̇r-\ *n* (ca. 1798) : an artist who specializes in chiaroscuro
chiar·oscu·ro \-'skyu̇r-(ˌ)ō, -'sku̇r-\ *n, pl* **-ros** [It, fr. *chiaro* clear, light + *oscuro* obscure, dark] (1686) **1** : pictorial representation in terms of light and shade without regard to color **2 a** : the arrangement or treatment of light and dark parts in a pictorial work of art **b** : the interplay or contrast of dissimilar qualities (as of mood or character) **3** : a 16th century woodcut technique involving the use of several blocks to print different tones of the same color; *also* : a print made by this technique **4** : the interplay of light and shadow on or as if on a surface **5** : the quality of being veiled or partly in shadow
chi·asm \'kī-ˌa-zᵊm, 'kē-\ *n* [NL *chiasma*] (1870) : CHIASMA 1
chi·as·ma \kī-'az-mə, kē-\ *n, pl* **-ma·ta** \-mə-tə\ [NL, X-shaped configuration, fr. Gk, crosspiece, fr. *chiazein* to mark with a chi, fr. *chi* (x)] (1839) **1** : an anatomical intersection or decussation — compare OPTIC CHIASMA **2** : a cross-shaped configuration of paired chromatids visible in the diplotene stage of meiotic prophase and considered the cytological equivalent of genetic crossing-over — **chi·as·mat·ic** \ˌkī-əz-'ma-tik, ˌkē-\ *adj*
chi·as·mus \kī-'az-məs, kē-\ *n* [NL, fr. Gk *chiasmos,* fr. *chiazein* to mark with a chi] (1871) : an inverted relationship between the syntactic elements of parallel phrases (as in Goldsmith's *to stop too fearful, and too faint to go*)
chiaus \'chau̇s, 'chau̇sh\ *n* [Turk *çavuş*] (1595) : a Turkish messenger or sergeant

Chib·cha \'chib-(ˌ)chä\ *n, pl* **Chibcha** *or* **Chibchas** [Sp] (1814) **1** : a member of an Indian people of central Colombia **2** : the extinct language of the Chibcha people
Chib·chan \-chən\ *adj* (1902) : of, relating to, or constituting a language family of Colombia and Central America
chi·bouk *or* **chi·bouque** \chə-'bük, shə-\ *n* [F *chibouque,* fr. Turk *çubuk*] (1811) : a long-stemmed Turkish tobacco pipe with a clay bowl
[1]**chic** \'shēk\ *n* [F] (1856) **1** : smart elegance and sophistication esp. of dress or manner : STYLE ⟨wears her clothes with superb ~⟩ **2** : a distinctive mode of dress or manner associated with a fashionable lifestyle, ideology, or pursuit ⟨wearing the latest in urban ~⟩ **3** : a faddishly popular quality or appeal; *also* : something (as a practice or interest) having such appeal ⟨the transient tides of academic ~ —Irving Kristol⟩
[2]**chic** *adj* **chic·er; chic·est** (1865) **1** : cleverly stylish : SMART ⟨the woman who is ~ adapts fashion to her own personality —Elizabeth L. Post⟩ **2** : currently fashionable ⟨a ~ restaurant⟩ — **chic·ly** *adv* — **chic·ness** *n*
Chi·ca·na \chi-'kä-nə *also* shi-\ *n* [MexSp, fem. of *chicano*] (1967) : an American woman or girl of Mexican descent — **Chicana** *adj*
[1]**chi·cane** \shi-'kān, chi-\ *vb* **chi·caned; chi·can·ing** [F *chicaner,* fr. MF, to quibble, prevent justice] *vi* (ca. 1672) : to use chicanery ⟨a wretch he had taught to lie and ~ —George Meredith⟩ ~ *vt* : TRICK, CHEAT
[2]**chicane** *n* (1686) **1** : CHICANERY **2 a** : an obstacle on a racecourse **b** : a series of tight turns in opposite directions in an otherwise straight stretch of a road-racing course **3** : the absence of trumps in a hand of cards
chi·ca·nery \-'kān-rē, -'kā-nə-\ *n, pl* **-ner·ies** (1609) **1** : deception by artful subterfuge or sophistry : TRICKERY **2** : a piece of sharp practice (as at law) : TRICK
Chi·ca·no \chi-'kä-(ˌ)nō *also* shi-\ *n, pl* **-nos** [MexSp, alter. of Sp *mexicano* Mexican] (1947) : an American and esp. a man or boy of Mexican descent — **Chicano** *adj*
[1]**chi·chi** \'shē-(ˌ)shē *also* 'chē-(ˌ)chē\ *n* [F] (1908) **1** : frilly or elaborate ornamentation **2** : AFFECTATION, PRECIOSITY **3** : CHIC
[2]**chichi** *adj* (1926) **1** : elaborately ornamented : SHOWY, FRILLY ⟨a ~ dress⟩ **2** : ARTY, PRECIOUS ⟨~ poetry⟩ **3** : CHIC, FASHIONABLE ⟨a ~ nightclub⟩
chick \'chik\ *n* [ME *chyke,* alter. of *chiken*] (15c) **1 a** : a domestic chicken; *esp* : one newly hatched **b** : the young of any bird **2** : CHILD **3** *slang* : GIRL, WOMAN
chick·a·dee \'chi-kə-(ˌ)dē\ *n* [imit.] (1838) : any of several small No. American oscine birds (genus *Poecile* of the family Paridae) that are related to the titmice, usu. have the crown of the head distinctly darker than the body, and have sometimes been placed esp. formerly in a related genus (*Parus*)
chick·a·ree \'chi-kə-ˌrē\ *n* [imit.] (1829) : RED SQUIRREL; *also* : a related squirrel (*Tamiasciurus douglasii*) of forests from southwestern British Columbia to central California
Chick·a·saw \'chi-kə-ˌsȯ\ *n, pl* **Chickasaw** *or* **Chickasaws** [Chickasaw *čikašša*] (1674) **1** : a member of an American Indian people of Mississippi and Alabama **2** : the Muskogean language of the Chickasaw
[1]**chick·en** \'chi-kᵊn, *sometimes* -kᵊŋ\ *n* [ME *chiken,* fr. OE *cicen* young chicken; akin to OE *cocc* cock] (14c) **1 a** : the common domestic fowl (*Gallus gallus*) esp. when young; *also* : its flesh used as food — compare JUNGLE FOWL **b** : any of various birds or their young **2** : a young woman **3 a** : COWARD **b** : any of various contests in which the participants risk personal safety in order to see which one will give up first **4** [short for *chickenshit*] *slang* : petty details **5** *slang* : a young male homosexual
[2]**chicken** *adj* (1941) **1 a** : SCARED **b** : TIMID, COWARDLY **2** *slang* **a** : insistent on petty details of duty or discipline **b** : PETTY, UNIMPORTANT
[3]**chicken** *vi* **chick·ened; chick·en·ing** \'chi-kᵊn-iŋ, 'chik-niŋ\ (1943) : to lose one's nerve — usu. used with *out* ⟨seemed to exhibit courage, manliness, and conviction when others ~*ed* out —J. R. Seeley⟩
chicken–and–egg *adj* [fr. the proverbial question "which came first, the chicken or the egg?"] (1959) : of, relating to, or being a cause-and-effect dilemma
chicken colonel *n* [fr. the eagle serving as insignia of the rank] (1918) *slang* : COLONEL 1a
chicken feed *n* (1836) *slang* : a paltry sum (as in profits or wages)
chick·en–fried steak \'chi-kᵊn-'frīd-\ *n* (1952) : steak coated with batter, fried, and served with gravy
chicken hawk *n* (1827) **1** : a hawk that preys or is believed to prey on chickens **2** *slang* : a man who pursues boys or young men for sexual purposes
chick·en·heart·ed \'chi-kən-ˌhär-təd\ *adj* (1653) : TIMID, COWARDLY ⟨too . . . ~ to accompany me in this perilous undertaking —Washington Irving⟩
Chicken Little *n* [fr. the fable in which a chick attempts to warn other barnyard animals that the sky is falling after she is struck on the head by a chance falling object] (1895) : one who warns of or predicts calamity esp. without justification
chick·en–liv·ered \-ˌli-vərd\ *adj* (1849) : FAINTHEARTED, COWARDLY
chicken pox *n* (1619) : an acute contagious disease esp. of children marked by low-grade fever and formation of vesicles and caused by a herpesvirus (species *Human herpesvirus 3* of the genus *Varicellovirus*) — compare SHINGLES
[1]**chick·en·shit** \'chi-kᵊn-ˌshit\ *adj* (1945) **1** *usu vulgar* : PETTY, INSIGNIFICANT **2** *usu vulgar* : lacking courage, manliness, or effectiveness
[2]**chickenshit** *n* (1947) **1** *usu vulgar* : the petty details of a duty or discipline **2** *usu vulgar* : COWARD, CHICKEN
chicken snake *n* (1709) : RAT SNAKE

chicken wire *n* [fr. its use for making enclosures for chickens] (ca. 1904) **:** a light galvanized wire netting of hexagonal mesh
chick flick *n* (1988) *sometimes disparaging* **:** a motion picture intended to appeal esp. to women
chick·pea \ˈchik-ˌpē\ *n* [alter. of *chich pea,* fr. ME *chiche,* fr. AF, fr. L *cicer*] (ca. 1722) **:** an Asian herb (*Cicer arietinum*) of the legume family cultivated for its short pods with one or two seeds; *also* **:** its seed
chick·weed \-ˌwēd\ *n* (14c) **:** any of various low-growing small-leaved weedy plants of the pink family (esp. genera *Cerastium* and *Stellaria*); *esp* **:** a cosmopolitan weed (*Stelleria media*) naturalized in the U.S. from Eurasia

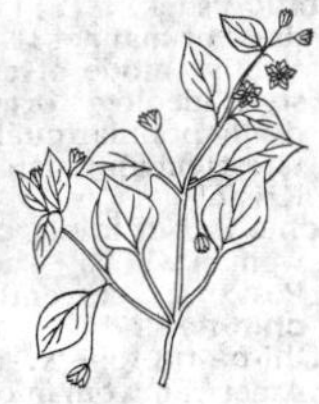
chickweed

chi·cle \ˈchi-kəl, ˈchi-klē\ *n* [AmerSp, fr. Nahautl *tzictli*] (1884) **:** a gum from the latex of the sapodilla used as the chief ingredient of chewing gum
chic·o·ry *also* **chick·o·ry** \ˈchi-k(ə-)rē\ *n, pl* **-ries** [alter. of ME *cicoree,* fr. AF, fr. L *cichoreum,* fr. Gk *kichoreia*] (15c) **1 :** a thick-rooted usu. blue-flowered European perennial composite herb (*Cichorium intybus*) widely grown for its roots and as a salad plant — compare BELGIAN ENDIVE, RADICCHIO **2 :** the dried ground roasted root of chicory used to flavor or adulterate coffee
chide \ˈchīd\ *vb* **chid** \ˈchid\ *or* **chid·ed** \ˈchī-dəd\; **chid** *or* **chid·den** \ˈchi-dᵊn\ *or* **chided; chid·ing** \ˈchī-diŋ\ [ME, fr. OE *cīdan* to quarrel, chide, fr. *cīd* strife] *vi* (bef. 12c) **:** to speak out in angry or displeased rebuke ~ *vt* **:** to voice disapproval to **:** reproach in a usu. mild and constructive manner **:** SCOLD ***syn*** see REPROVE
[1]**chief** \ˈchēf\ *adj* (14c) **1 :** accorded highest rank or office ⟨~ librarian⟩ **2 :** of greatest importance or influence ⟨the ~ reasons⟩
[2]**chief** *adv* (14c) *archaic* **:** CHIEFLY
[3]**chief** *n* [ME, fr. AF *chief, chef* head, chief, fr. L *caput* head — more at HEAD] (15c) **1 :** the upper part of a heraldic field **2 :** the head of a body of persons or an organization **:** LEADER ⟨~ of police⟩ **3 :** the principal or most valuable part ⟨would never rest till she had read the ~ of the letter to him —Jane Austen⟩ — **chief·dom** \-dəm\ *n* — **chief·ship** \-ˌship\ *n* — **in chief :** in the chief position or place — often used in titles ⟨commander *in chief*⟩
chief executive *n* (1793) **:** a principal executive: as **a :** the president of a republic **b :** the governor of a state **c :** CEO
chief justice *n* (1534) **:** the presiding or principal judge of a court of justice
[1]**chief·ly** \ˈchē-flē\ *adv* (14c) **1 :** most importantly **:** PRINCIPALLY, ESPECIALLY **2 :** for the most part **:** MOSTLY, MAINLY
[2]**chiefly** *adj* (1870) **:** of or relating to a chief ⟨~ duties⟩
chief master sergeant *n* (1959) **:** a noncommissioned officer in the air force ranking above a senior master sergeant
chief master sergeant of the air force (ca. 1961) **:** the ranking noncommissioned officer in the air force serving as adviser to the chief of staff
chief of naval operations (1915) **:** the ranking officer of the navy and a member of the Joint Chiefs of Staff
chief of staff (1862) **1 :** the ranking officer of a staff in the armed forces serving as principal adviser to a commander **2 :** the ranking officer of the army or air force and a member of the Joint Chiefs of Staff
chief of state (1948) **:** the formal head of a national state as distinguished from the head of the government
chief petty officer *n* (1865) **:** an enlisted man in the navy or coast guard ranking above a petty officer first class and below a senior chief petty officer
chief·tain \ˈchēf-tən\ *n* [ME *chieftaine,* fr. AF *chevetain,* fr. LL *capitaneus* chief — more at CAPTAIN] (14c) **:** a chief esp. of a band, tribe, or clan — **chief·tain·ship** \-ˌship\ *n*
chief·tain·cy \-sē\ *n, pl* **-cies** (1788) **1 :** the rank, dignity, office, or rule of a chieftain **2 :** a region or a people ruled by a chief
chief warrant officer *n* (1917) **:** a warrant officer of senior rank in the armed forces; *also* **:** a commissioned officer in the navy or coast guard ranking below an ensign
chiel \ˈchēl\ *or* **chield** \ˈchēld\ *n* [ME (Sc) *cheld,* alter. of ME *child* child] (1507) *chiefly Scot* **:** FELLOW, LAD
chiff·chaff \ˈchif-ˌchaf\ *n* [imit.] (1780) **:** a small grayish European warbler (*Phylloscopus collybita*)
[1]**chif·fon** \shi-ˈfän, ˈshi-ˌ\ *n* [F, lit., rag, fr. *chiffe* old rag, alter. of MF *chipe,* fr. ME *chip* chip] (1765) **1 :** an ornamental addition (as a knot of ribbons) to a woman's dress **2 :** a sheer fabric esp. of silk
[2]**chiffon** *adj* (1903) **1 :** resembling chiffon in sheerness or softness **2 :** having a light delicate texture achieved usu. by adding whipped egg whites or whipped gelatin ⟨lemon ~ pie⟩
chif·fo·nade \ˌshi-fə-ˈnäd, -ˈnäd\ *n* [F *chiffonnade,* fr. *chiffonner* to crumple, fr. *chiffon*] (1877) **:** shredded or finely cut vegetables or herbs used esp. as a garnish
chif·fo·nier \ˌshi-fə-ˈnir\ *n* [F *chiffonnier,* fr. *chiffon*] (1765) **:** a high narrow chest of drawers
chif·fo·robe \ˈshi-fə-ˌrōb\ *n* [*chiffonier* + ward*robe*] (1908) **:** a combination of wardrobe and chest of drawers
chig·ger \ˈchi-gər, ˈji-\ *n* (1756) **1 :** CHIGOE 1 **2** [alter. of [2]*jigger*] **:** a six-legged usu. red or orange mite larva (family Trombiculidae) that feeds on skin cells and causes intensely itchy reddish welts; *also* **:** the adult mite of this larva
chi·gnon \ˈshēn-ˌyän *also* -ˌyȯn\ *n* [F, fr. MF *chaignon* chain, collar, nape] (1783) **:** a knot of hair that is worn at the back of the head and esp. at the nape of the neck
chi·goe \ˈchi-(ˌ)gō, ˈchē-\ *n* [Carib *chico*] (1691) **1 :** a tropical flea (*Tunga penetrans*) of which the fertile female causes great discomfort by burrowing under the skin **2 :** CHIGGER 2
Chi·hua·hua \chə-ˈwä-(ˌ)wä, shə-, -wə\ *n* [MexSp, fr. *Chihuahua,* Mexico] (1858) **:** any of a breed of very small roundheaded dogs that occur in short-coated and long-coated varieties
chil·blain \ˈchil-ˌblān\ *n* [[1]*chill*] (1547) **:** an inflammatory swelling or sore caused by exposure (as of the feet or hands) to cold
child \ˈchī(-ə)ld\ *n, pl* **chil·dren** \ˈchil-drən, -dərn\ *often attrib* [ME, fr. OE *cild;* akin to Goth *kilthei* womb, and perh. to Skt *jaṭhara* belly] (bef. 12c) **1 a :** an unborn or recently born person **b** *dial* **:** a female infant **2 a :** a young person esp. between infancy and youth **b :** a childlike or childish person **c :** a person not yet of age **3** *usu* **childe** \ˈchī(-ə)ld\ *archaic* **:** a youth of noble birth **4 a :** a son or daughter of human parents **b :** DESCENDANT **5 :** one strongly influenced by another or by a place or state of affairs **6 :** PRODUCT, RESULT ⟨barbed wire . . . is truly a ~ of the plains —W. P. Webb⟩ — **child·less** \ˈchī(-ə)l(d)-ləs\ *adj* — **child·less·ness** *n* — **with child :** PREGNANT
child·bear·ing \ˈchī(-ə)l(d)-ˌber-iŋ\ *adj* (14c) **:** of or relating to the process of conceiving, being pregnant with, and giving birth to children ⟨women of ~ age⟩ — **childbearing** *n*
child·bed \-ˌbed\ *n* (13c) **:** the condition of a woman in childbirth
childbed fever *n* (1823) **:** PUERPERAL FEVER
child·birth \-ˌbərth\ *n* (15c) **:** PARTURITION
child·hood \ˈchī(-ə)ld-ˌhu̇d\ *n* (bef. 12c) **1 :** the state or period of being a child **2 :** the early period in the development of something
child·ish \ˈchī(-ə)l-dish\ *adj* (bef. 12c) **1 :** of, relating to, or befitting a child or childhood **2 a :** marked by or suggestive of immaturity and lack of poise ⟨a ~ spiteful remark⟩ **b :** lacking complexity **:** SIMPLE ⟨it's a ~ device, but it works⟩ **c :** deteriorated with age esp. in mind **:** SENILE — **child·ish·ly** *adv* — **child·ish·ness** *n*
child·like \ˈchī(-ə)l(d)-ˌlīk\ *adj* (1586) **:** resembling, suggesting, or appropriate to a child or childhood; *esp* **:** marked by innocence, trust, and ingenuousness ⟨~ delight⟩ — **child·like·ness** *n*
child·ly \ˈchī(-ə)l(d)-lē\ *adj* (bef. 12c) **:** CHILDLIKE
[1]**child·proof** \ˈchīl(d)-ˌprüf\ *adj* (1956) **1 :** designed to prevent tampering or opening by children ⟨~ pill bottles⟩ **2 :** made safe for children (as by safe storage of dangerous materials) ⟨a ~ home⟩
[2]**childproof** *vt* (1971) **:** to make childproof ⟨~ a house⟩
child's play *n* (14c) **1 :** an extremely simple task or act **2 :** something that is insignificant ⟨figuring out the password was *child's play*⟩
child support *n* (1901) **:** payment for the support of the children of divorced or separated parents while the children are minors or as otherwise legally required — compare ALIMONY
chile re·lle·no \-rā-ˈyā-(ˌ)nō\ *n, pl* **chiles re·lle·nos** *also* **chile rellenos** [Sp, stuffed chili pepper] (1929) **:** a stuffed chili pepper that usu. contains cheese or meat and is fried or grilled
Chile saltpeter \ˈchi-lē-, ˈchē-(ˌ)lā-\ *n* [*Chile,* So. America] (1869) **:** sodium nitrate esp. occurring naturally (as in caliche)
chili *also* **chile** *or* **chil·li** \ˈchi-lē\ *n, pl* **chil·ies** *also* **chil·es** *or* **chilis** *or* **chil·lies** [Sp *chile,* fr. Nahuatl *chīlli*] (1604) **1 a** *usu chile, pl* **chil·es :** a hot pepper of any of a group of cultivars (*Capsicum annuum annuum* group *longum*) noted for their pungency — called also *chili pepper* **b** *usu chilli, pl* **chillies** *also* **chil·lis** *chiefly Brit* **:** a pepper whether hot or sweet **2 a :** a thick sauce of meat and chiles **b :** CHILI CON CARNE; *also* **:** a similar dish made without meat ⟨vegetarian ~⟩
chil·i·ad \ˈki-lē-ˌad, -əd\ *n* [LL *chiliad-, chilias,* fr. Gk, fr. *chilioi* thousand] (1598) **1 :** a group of 1000 **2 :** MILLENNIUM 2a
chil·i·asm \ˈki-lē-ˌa-zəm\ *n* [NL *chiliasmus,* fr. LL *chiliastes* one that believes in chiliasm, fr. *chilias*] (1610) **:** MILLENARIANISM — **chil·i·ast** \-lē-ˌast, -lē-əst\ *n* — **chil·i·as·tic** \ˌki-lē-ˈas-tik\ *adj*
chili con car·ne \ˌchi-lē-ˌkän-ˈkär-nē, -kən-\ *n* [AmerSp *chile con carne* chili with meat] (1857) **:** a spiced stew of ground beef and minced chiles or chili powder usu. with beans
chili dog *n* (1956) **:** a hot dog topped with chili
chili powder *n* (1908) **:** a spice mixture made with ground chiles
chili sauce *n* (1880) **:** a spiced tomato sauce usu. made with red and green peppers
[1]**chill** \ˈchil\ *n* [ME *chile* chill, frost, fr. OE *ciele;* akin to OE *ceald* cold] (bef. 12c) **1 a :** a sensation of cold accompanied by shivering **b :** a disagreeable sensation of coldness **2 :** a moderate but disagreeable degree of cold **3 :** a check to enthusiasm or warmth of feeling
[2]**chill** *adj* (14c) **1 a :** moderately cold **b :** COLD, RAW **2 :** affected by cold ⟨~ travelers⟩ **3 :** DISTANT, FORMAL ⟨a ~ reception⟩ **4 :** DEPRESSING, DISPIRITING ⟨~ penury —Thomas Gray⟩ — **chill·ness** *n*
[3]**chill** *vi* (14c) **1 a :** to become cold **b :** to shiver or quake with or as if with cold **2 :** to become taken with a chill **3 a :** CHILL OUT **b :** HANG 12 ~ *vt* **1 a :** to make cold or chilly ⟨~*ed* by a cold wind⟩ **b :** to make cool esp. without freezing ⟨~ the wine⟩ **2 :** to affect as if with cold **:** DISPIRIT — **chill·ing·ly** \ˈchi-liŋ-lē\ *adv*
chil·lax \chi-ˈlaks\ *vi* [blend of *chill* and *relax*] (1999) *slang* **:** to calm down **:** RELAX
chill·er \ˈchi-lər\ *n* (1798) **1 :** one that chills **2 :** an eerie or frightening story of murder, violence, or the supernatural
chill factor *n* (1965) **:** WINDCHILL
chill·ing \ˈchi-liŋ\ *adj* (1814) **:** gravely disturbing or frightening ⟨a ~ case of abuse⟩ — **chil·ling·ly** *adv*
chill out *vi* (1980) *slang* **:** to calm down **:** go easy **:** RELAX — often used in the imperative
chil·lum \ˈchi-ləm\ *n* [Hindi *cilam* & Urdu *chilam,* fr. Pers *chilam*] (1781) **1 :** the part of a water pipe that contains the substance (as tobacco or hashish) which is smoked; *also* **:** a quantity of a substance thus smoked **2 :** a funnel-shaped clay pipe for smoking
chilly \ˈchi-lē\ *adj* **chill·i·er; -est** (1570) **1 :** noticeably cold **:** CHILLING ⟨a ~ day⟩ **2 :** unpleasantly affected by cold ⟨~ spectators⟩ **3 :** lacking warmth of feeling **:** UNFRIENDLY ⟨a ~ reception⟩ **4 :** tending to arouse fear or apprehension ⟨~ suspicions⟩ — **chill·i·ly** \ˈchi-lə-lē\ *adv* — **chill·i·ness** \ˈchi-lē-nəs\ *n*
chil·te·pin *also* **chil·te·pine** \ˈchil-tə-ˌpēn\ *n* [MexSp *chiltepín,* fr. Nahuatl *chīltecpin,* fr. *chīlli* chili pepper + *tecpin, tecpintli* flea] (1985) **:** a small red oblong wild chili pepper of marked pungency that is produced by a capsicum (*Capsicum annuum glabriusculum* syn. *C. annuum aviculare*) occurring from northern So. America to northern Mexico and the southwestern U.S.; *also* **:** this plant
[1]**chi·mae·ra** \kī-ˈmir-ə, kə-\ *chiefly Brit var of* CHIMERA
[2]**chimaera** *n* [NL, genus name, fr. L, chimera] (1804) **:** any of a family (Chimaeridae) of marine cartilaginous fishes with a tapering or threadlike tail and usu. no anal fin
chi·mae·ric, chi·mae·rism *chiefly Brit var of* CHIMERIC, CHIMERISM
[1]**chime** \ˈchīm\ *n* [ME *chimbe,* fr. OE *cimb-;* akin to MD *kimme* edge of a cask] (14c) **:** the edge or rim of a cask or drum
[2]**chime** *vb* **chimed; chim·ing** *vi* (14c) **1 a :** to make a musical and esp. a harmonious sound **b :** to make the sounds of a chime **2 :** to be or act in accord ⟨the music and the mood *chimed* well together⟩ ~ *vt* **1 :** to cause to sound musically by striking **2 :** to produce by chiming

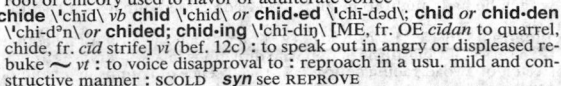

3 : to call or indicate by chiming ⟨the clock *chimed* midnight⟩ 4 : to utter repetitively : DIN 2 — **chim·er** *n*

[3]chime *n* [ME, cymbal, prob. fr. AF *chimbe, cime,* fr. L *cymbalum* cymbal] (15c) 1 : an apparatus for chiming a bell or set of bells 2 a : a musically tuned set of bells b : one of a set of objects giving a bell-like sound when struck 3 a : the sound of a set of bells — usu. used in pl. b : a musical sound suggesting that of bells 4 : ACCORD, HARMONY ⟨such happy ~ of fact and theory —Henry Maudsley⟩

chime in *vi* (1681) 1 : to combine harmoniously ⟨the artist's illustrations *chime in* perfectly with the text —*Book Production*⟩ 2 : to break into a conversation or discussion esp. to express an opinion ~ *vt* : to remark while chiming in

chi·me·ra \kī-ˈmir-ə, kə-\ *n* [L *chimaera,* fr. Gk *chimaira* she-goat, chimera; akin to ON *gymbr* yearling ewe, Gk *cheimōn* winter — more at HIBERNATE] 1 a *cap* : a fire-breathing she-monster in Greek mythology having a lion's head, a goat's body, and a serpent's tail b : an imaginary monster compounded of incongruous parts 2 : an illusion or fabrication of the mind; *esp* : an unrealizable dream ⟨a fancy, a ~ in my brain, troubles me in my prayer —John Donne⟩ 3 : an individual, organ, or part consisting of tissues of diverse genetic constitution

chi·mere \shə-ˈmir, chə-\ *n* [ME *chimmer, chemeyr*] (14c) : a loose sleeveless robe worn by Anglican bishops over the rochet

chi·me·ric \kī-ˈmir-ik, kə-, -ˈmer-, -ˈme-rik\ *adj* (1963) : relating to, derived from, or being a genetic chimera or its genetic material ⟨a ~ cat⟩

chi·me·ri·cal \kī-ˈmer-i-kəl, kə-, -ˈmir-\ *also* **chi·me·ric** \-ik\ *adj* [*chimera*] (1638) 1 : existing only as the product of unchecked imagination : fantastically visionary or improbable 2 : given to fantastic schemes *syn* see IMAGINARY — **chi·me·ri·cal·ly** \-i-k(ə-)lē\ *adv*

chi·me·rism \kī-ˈmir-ˌi-zəm, kə-; ˈkī-mə-ˌri-\ *n* (1961) : the state of being a genetic chimera

chi·mi·chan·ga \ˌchi-mē-ˈchäŋ-gə\ *n* [MexSp, trinket] (1970) : a tortilla wrapped around a filling (as of meat) and deep-fried

chim·ney \ˈchim-nē\ *n, pl* **chimneys** [ME, fr. AF *chiminee,* fr. LL *caminata,* fr. L *caminus* furnace, fireplace, fr. Gk *kaminos;* perh. akin to Gk *kamara* vault] (14c) 1 *dial* : FIREPLACE, HEARTH 2 : a vertical structure incorporated into a building and enclosing a flue or flues that carry off smoke; *esp* : the part of such a structure extending above a roof 3 : SMOKESTACK 4 : a tube usu. of glass placed around a flame (as of a lamp) 5 : something resembling a chimney: as a : a narrow cleft or passage in rock b : a tall column of rock on the ocean floor that is formed by the precipitation of minerals from superheated water issuing from a hydrothermal vent and rising through the column of rock — **chim·ney·like** \-ˌlīk\ *adj*

chim·ney·piece \ˈchim-nē-ˌpēs\ *n* (1664) : an ornamental construction over and around a fireplace that includes the mantel

chimney pot *n* (ca. 1806) : a usu. earthenware pipe placed at the top of a chimney

chimney sweep *n* (1727) : a person whose occupation is cleaning soot from chimney flues — called also *chimney sweeper*

chimney swift *n* (1849) : a small sooty-gray swift (*Chaetura pelagica*) with long narrow wings that often builds its nest inside an unused chimney — called also *chimney swallow*

chimp \ˈchimp *sometimes* ˈshimp\ *n* (1877) : CHIMPANZEE

chim·pan·zee \(ˌ)chim-ˌpan-ˈzē, -pən-ˈzē, -ˈpan-zē *sometimes* (ˌ)shim-\ *n* [Kongo dial. *chimpenzi*] (1738) : an anthropoid ape (*Pan troglodytes*) of equatorial Africa that is smaller and more arboreal than the gorilla — compare BONOBO

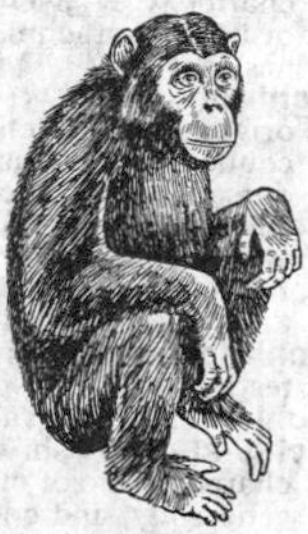

chimpanzee

[1]chin \ˈchin\ *n* [ME, fr. OE *cinn;* akin to OHG *kinni* chin, L *gena* cheek, Gk *genys* jaw, cheek] (bef. 12c) 1 : the lower portion of the face lying below the lower lip and including the prominence of the lower jaw 2 : the surface beneath or between the branches of the lower jaw — **chin·less** \-ləs\ *adj*

[2]chin *vb* **chinned; chin·ning** *vt* (1869) 1 : to bring to or hold with the chin ⟨~ a violin⟩ 2 : to raise (oneself) while hanging by the hands until the chin is level with the support ~ *vi, slang* : to talk idly

chi·na \ˈchī-nə\ *n* [Pers *chīnī* Chinese porcelain] (1579) 1 : PORCELAIN; *also* : vitreous porcelain wares (as dishes, vases, or ornaments) for domestic use 2 : earthenware or porcelain tableware

China aster *n* (1736) : a common annual garden aster (*Callistephus chinensis*) native to northern China that occurs in many showy forms

chi·na·ber·ry \ˈchī-nə-ˌber-ē, *Southern also* ˈchā-nē-ˌber-ē\ *n* (1890) : a small Asian tree (*Melia azedarach*) of the mahogany family naturalized in the southern U.S. where it is widely planted for shade or ornament

china clay *n* (1840) : KAOLIN

china closet *n* (1771) : a cabinet or cupboard for the storage or display of household china

Chi·na·man \ˈchī-nə-mən\ *n* (1789) *often offensive* : a native of China : CHINESE

China rose *n* (ca. 1731) : any of numerous garden roses derived from a shrubby Chinese rose (*Rosa chinensis*)

China Syndrome *n* [fr. the notion that the molten reactor contents could hypothetically sink through the earth to reach China] (1970) : MELTDOWN 1

Chi·na·town \ˈchī-nə-ˌtau̇n\ *n* (1857) : the Chinese quarter of a city

China tree *n* (1819) : CHINABERRY

chi·na·ware \ˈchī-nə-ˌwer\ *n* (1634) : tableware made of china

chin·bone \ˈchin-ˌbōn\ *n* (bef. 12c) : MANDIBLE; *esp* : the median anterior part of the human mandible

chinch \ˈchinch\ *n* [Sp *chinche,* fr. L *cimic-, cimex*] (1616) : BEDBUG

chinch bug *n* (1785) : a small black-and-white bug (*Blissus leucopterus*) that is very destructive to cereal grasses

chin·che·rin·chee \ˌchin-chə-ri(n)-ˈchē, ˌchiŋ-kə-\ *n, pl* **chincherinchee** *or* **chincherinchees** [Afrik *tjienkerientjee*] (1904) : a southern African perennial bulbous herb (*Ornithogalum thyrsoides*) of the lily family with spikes of white to golden-yellow blossoms

chin·chil·la \chin-ˈchi-lə\ *n* [Sp] (1604) 1 : either of two small So. American rodents (*Chinchilla laniger* and *C. brevicaudata* of the family Chinchillidae) of the high Andes that are the size of large squirrels, have very soft pearly-gray fur, and are extensively bred in captivity; *also* : the fur of a chinchilla 2 : a heavy twilled woolen coating

[1]chine \ˈchīn\ *n* [ME, fr. AF *eschine,* of Gmc origin; akin to OHG *scina* shinbone, needle — more at SHIN] (14c) 1 : BACKBONE, SPINE; *also* : a cut of meat including all or part of the backbone 2 : the intersection of the bottom and the sides of a flat or V-bottomed boat

[2]chine *vt* **chined; chin·ing** (15c) : to cut through the backbone of (as in butchering)

Chi·nese \chī-ˈnēz, -ˈnēs\ *n, pl* **Chinese** (1606) 1 a : a native or inhabitant of China b : a person of Chinese descent 2 : a group of related languages used by the people of China that are often mutually unintelligible in their spoken form but share a single system of writing and that constitute a branch of the Sino-Tibetan language family; *esp* : MANDARIN — **Chinese** *adj*

Chinese boxes *n pl* (1829) 1 : a set of boxes graduated in size so that each fits into the next larger one 2 : something that resembles a set of Chinese boxes esp. in complexity

Chinese cabbage *n* (1842) : either of two Asian brassicas now grown in the U.S. and widely used as greens: a : BOK CHOY b : one (*Brassica rapa pekinensis*) that forms elongate more or less solid cylindrical heads and has pale green or cream-colored leaves

Chinese checkers *n pl but sing or pl in constr* (1936) : a game in which each player seeks to be the first to transfer a set of marbles from a home point to the opposite point of a pitted 6-pointed star by single moves or jumps

Chinese chestnut *n* (ca. 1909) : an Asian chestnut (*Castanea mollissima*) that is resistant to chestnut blight

Chinese chive *n* (1968) : GARLIC CHIVE — usu. used in pl.

Chinese copy *n* (1920) : an exact imitation or duplicate that includes defects as well as desired qualities

Chinese crested *n* (1976) : any of a breed of hairless or coated dogs with a plumed tail and a crest of hair on the head

Chinese gooseberry *n* (1925) : a subtropical vine (*Actinidia deliciosa* syn. *A. chinensis* of the family Actinidiaceae) that bears kiwifruit; *also* : KIWIFRUIT

Chinese lantern *n* (1825) : a collapsible translucent covering for a light

Chinese parsley *n* (ca. 1953) : CILANTRO

Chinese puzzle *n* (ca. 1815) 1 : an intricate or ingenious puzzle 2 : something intricate and obscure

Chinese restaurant syndrome *n* (1968) : a group of symptoms (as numbness of the neck, arms, and back with headache, dizziness, and palpitations) that is held to affect susceptible persons eating food and esp. Chinese food heavily seasoned with monosodium glutamate

Chinese shar–pei *n* (1975) : SHAR-PEI

Chinese wall *n* [*Chinese Wall,* a defensive wall built in the 3d cent. B.C. between China and Mongolia] (1900) : a strong barrier; *esp* : a serious obstacle to understanding

Chinese white *n* (ca. 1884) : ZINC WHITE

Ching *or* **Ch'ing** \ˈchiŋ\ *n* [Chin (Beijing) *Qīng*] (1795) : a Manchu dynasty in China dated 1644–1912 and the last imperial dynasty

[1]chink \ˈchiŋk\ *n* [prob. alter. of ME *chine* crack, fissure] (1535) 1 : a small cleft, slit, or fissure ⟨a ~ in the fence⟩ 2 : a weak spot that may leave one vulnerable ⟨his lawyers found a ~ in the law⟩ 3 : a narrow beam of light shining through a chink

[2]chink *vt* (1609) : to fill the chinks of (as by caulking) ⟨~ a log cabin⟩

[3]chink *n* [imit.] (1573) 1 *archaic* : COIN, MONEY 2 : a short sharp sound

[4]chink *vi* (1589) : to make a slight sharp metallic sound ~ *vt* : to cause to make a chink

Chink \ˈchiŋk\ *n or adj* [perh. alter. of *Chinese*] (1887) *usu offensive* : CHINESE

chin music *n* (1826) 1 : idle talk 2 : a usu. high inside pitch in baseball intended to intimidate the batter

chi·no \ˈchē-(ˌ)nō, ˈshē-\ *n, pl* **chinos** [origin unknown] (1943) 1 : a usu. khaki cotton or synthetic-fiber twill of the type used for military uniforms 2 *pl* : an article of clothing made of chino

chi·noi·se·rie \shēn-ˈwäz-rē, -ˈwä-zə-; ˌshēn-ˌwäz-ˈrē, -ˌwä-zə-\ *n* [F, fr. *chinois* Chinese, fr. *Chine* China] (1883) : a style in art (as in decoration) reflecting Chinese qualities or motifs; *also* : an object or decoration in this style

Chi·nook \shə-ˈnu̇k, chə-, -ˈnük\ *n, pl* **Chinook** *or* **Chinooks** [Lower Chehalis (Salishan language of western Washington) *činúk,* name of a Chinook village] (1795) 1 : a member of an American Indian people of the north shore of the Columbia River at its mouth 2 : a Chinookan language of the Chinook and other nearby peoples 3 *often not cap* a : a warm moist southwest wind of the coast from Oregon northward b : a warm dry wind that descends the eastern slopes of the Rocky Mountains 4 *not cap* : CHINOOK SALMON

Chi·nook·an \-ˈnu̇-kən, -ˈnü-\ *n* (ca. 1890) : an American Indian language family of Washington and Oregon — **Chinookan** *adj*

Chinook jargon *n, often cap J* (1840) : a pidgin language based on Chinook and other Indian languages, French, and English and formerly used as a lingua franca in the northwestern U.S. and on the Pacific coast of Canada and Alaska

Chinook salmon *n* (1851) : a large commercially important Pacific salmon (*Oncorhynchus tshawytscha*) with red flesh that occurs in the northern Pacific Ocean — called also *king salmon*

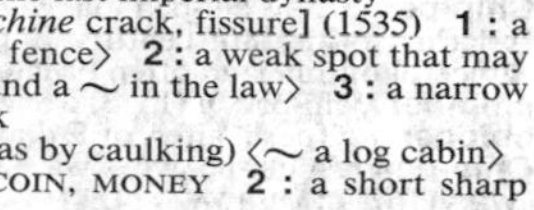

Chinook salmon

chin·qua·pin *or* **chin·ka·pin** \ˈchiŋ-ki-ˌpin\ *n* [prob. modif. of Virginia Algonquian *chechinquamin* chinquapin nut] (1612) 1 : the edible nut of a chinquapin 2 : any of several trees (genera *Castanea* and *Castanopsis*); *esp* : a dwarf chestnut (*Castanea pumila*) of the U.S.

\ə\ **abut** \ᵊ\ kitten, F table \ər\ **further** \a\ **ash** \ā\ **ace** \ä\ **mop, mar**
\au̇\ **out** \ch\ **chin** \e\ **bet** \ē\ **easy** \g\ **go** \i\ **hit** \ī\ **ice** \j\ **job**
\ŋ\ **sing** \ō\ **go** \ȯ\ **law** \ȯi\ **boy** \th\ **thin** \t͟h\ **the** \ü\ **loot** \u̇\ **foot**
\y\ **yet** \zh\ **vision, beige** \k͟, ⁿ, œ, ue, ʸ\ *see* Guide to Pronunciation

chinquapin oak *n* (1785) : either of two chestnut oaks (*Quercus muhlenbergii* and *Q. prinoides*) of the eastern U.S.

chin·strap penguin \'chin-ˌstrap-\ *n* (1936) : a penguin (*Pygoscelis antarctica*) with a narrow band of black feathers from ear to ear under its chin that breeds on the Antarctic Peninsula and nearby islands — called also *chinstrap*

chintz \'chin(t)s\ *n* [earlier *chints*, pl. of *chint*, fr. Hindi *chīṭ* & Urdu *chīnṭ*] (1614) **1** : a printed calico from India **2** : a usu. glazed printed cotton fabric

chintzy \'chin(t)-sē\ *adj* **chintz·i·er; -est** (1851) **1** : decorated with or as if with chintz **2 a** : GAUDY, CHEAP ⟨~ toys⟩ **b** : STINGY — **chintz·i·ness** *n*

chin–up \'chin-(ˌ)əp\ *n* (1954) : the act or an instance of chinning oneself performed esp. as a conditioning exercise

chin–wag \'chin-ˌwag\ *n* (1879) *slang* : CONVERSATION, CHAT

chi·o·no·doxa \ˌkī-ə-nō-'däk-sə, kī-ˌä-nə-\ *n* [NL, genus name, fr. Gk *chion-*, *chiōn* snow (akin to Gk *cheimōn* winter) + *doxa* glory — more at HIBERNATE, DOXOLOGY] (1879) : GLORY-OF-THE-SNOW

[1]**chip** \'chip\ *n* [ME; akin to OE *-cippian*] (14c) **1 a** : a small usu. thin and flat piece (as of wood or stone) cut, struck, or flaked off **b** : a small piece of food: as (1) : a small thin slice of food; *esp* : POTATO CHIP (2) : FRENCH FRY (3) : a small cone-shaped bit of food often used for baking ⟨chocolate ~*s*⟩ **2** : something small, worthless, or trivial **3 a** : one of the counters used as a token for money in poker and other games **b** *pl* : MONEY — used esp. in the phrase *in the chips* **c** : something valuable that can be used for advantage in negotiation or trade ⟨a bargaining ~⟩ **4** : a piece of dried dung — usu. used in combination ⟨cow ~⟩ **5** : a flaw left after a chip has been broken off **6 a** : INTEGRATED CIRCUIT **b** : a small wafer of semiconductor material that forms the base for an integrated circuit **7** : CHIP SHOT 1 **8** : MICROARRAY ⟨DNA ~*s*⟩ — **chip off the old block** : a child that resembles his or her parent — **chip on one's shoulder** : a challenging or belligerent attitude

[2]**chip** *vb* **chipped; chip·ping** [ME *chippen*, fr. OE *-cippian* (as in *forcippian* to cut off); akin to OE *cipp* beam, OHG *chipfa* stave] *vt* (15c) **1 a** : to cut or hew with an edged tool **b** (1) : to cut or break (a small piece) from something (2) : to cut or break a fragment from ⟨~ a tooth⟩ (3) : to cut into chips ⟨~ a tree stump⟩ **2** *Brit* : CHAFF, BANTER **3** : to hit (a return in tennis) with backspin ~ *vi* **1** : to break off in small pieces **2** : to play a chip shot

chip·board \'chip-ˌbȯrd\ *n* (1919) : a cardboard usu. made entirely from wastepaper

chip in *vi* (1861) **1** : CONTRIBUTE ⟨everyone *chipped in* for the gift⟩ **2** *chiefly Brit* : CHIME IN 2 ~ *vt* : CONTRIBUTE ⟨*chip in* five dollars⟩

chip·munk \'chip-ˌməŋk\ *n* [alter. of earlier *chitmunk*, prob. fr. Ojibwa *ačitamoˑnʔ* red squirrel] (1832) : any of a genus (*Tamias*) of small striped No. American and Asian rodents of the squirrel family

chi·pot·le \chə-'pōt-lā, chē-, -'pȯt-, -lē\ *n* [MexSp *chipotle*, *chilpotle*, fr. Nahuatl **chīlpōctli*, fr. *chīlli* chili pepper + *pōctli* smoke, something smoked] (1950) : a smoked and usu. dried jalapeño pepper

chipped beef \'chip(t)-\ *n* (1833) : smoked dried beef sliced thin

Chip·pen·dale \'chi-pən-ˌdāl\ *adj* [Thomas *Chippendale*] (1876) : of or relating to an 18th century English furniture style characterized by graceful outline and often ornate rococo ornamentation

[1]**chip·per** \'chi-pər\ *n* (1513) : one that chips ⟨a wood ~⟩

[2]**chipper** *adj* [perh. alter. of E dial. *kipper* lively] (1822) : SPRIGHTLY 1

Chip·pe·wa \'chi-pə-ˌwȯ, -ˌwä, -ˌwā, -wə\ *n, pl* **Chippewa** *or* **Chippewas** (1671) : OJIBWA

chip·pie *also* **chip·py** \'chi-pē\ *n, pl* **chippies** [origin unknown] (1886) : TRAMP, PROSTITUTE

chip·ping sparrow \'chi-piŋ-\ *n* [*chip* to cheep] (1791) : a small gray-breasted No. American sparrow (*Spizella passerina*) with a black line through the eye, a white line above it, and in breeding plumage a reddish patch on the top of the head

chip·py \'chi-pē\ *adj* **chip·pi·er; -est** [*chip* on one's shoulder] (1898) : aggressively belligerent ⟨a ~ hockey player⟩; *also* : marked by much fighting ⟨a ~ game⟩

chip shot *n* (1909) **1** : a short usu. low approach shot in golf that lofts the ball to the green and allows it to roll **2** : a short and easy field goal in football

chir- *or* **chiro-** *comb form* [L, fr. Gk *cheir-*, *cheiro-*, fr. *cheir*; akin to Hitt *keššar* hand] : hand ⟨*chiro*practic⟩

chi·ral \'kī-rəl\ *adj* [*chir-* + [1]*-al*] (1894) : of or relating to a molecule that is not superimposable on its mirror image — **chi·ral·i·ty** \kī-'ra-lə-tē, kə-\ *n*

chiral center *n* (1970) : an atom esp. in an organic molecule that has four unique atoms or groups attached to it

Chi–Rho \'kī-'rō, 'kē-\ *n, pl* **Chi–Rhos** [*chi* + *rho*] (1868) : a Christian monogram and symbol formed from the first two letters X and P of the Greek word for *Christ* — called also *Christogram*

Chir·i·ca·hua \ˌchir-ə-'kä-wə\ *n, pl* **Chiricahua** *or* **Chiricahuas** [*Chiricahua* Mountains, southeast Arizona] (1885) : a member of an Apache people of Arizona

chirimoya *var of* CHERIMOYA

chirk \'chərk\ *vt* [ME *charken*, *chirken* to creak, chirp, fr. OE *cearcian* to creak; akin to OE *cracian* to crack] (1843) : CHEER ⟨play with her and ~ her up a little —Harriet B. Stowe⟩

chi·rog·ra·phy \kī-'rä-grə-fē\ *n* (1631) **1** : HANDWRITING, PENMANSHIP **2** : CALLIGRAPHY 1 — **chi·rog·ra·pher** \-fər\ *n* — **chi·ro·graph·ic** \ˌkī-rə-'gra-fik\ *or* **chi·ro·graph·i·cal** \-fi-kəl\ *adj*

chi·ro·man·cy \'kī-rə-ˌman(t)-sē\ *n* [prob. fr. MF *chiromancie*, fr. ML *chiromantia*, fr. Gk *cheir-* chir- + *-manteia* -mancy] (ca. 1528) : PALMISTRY — **chi·ro·man·cer** \-ˌman(t)-sər\ *n*

chi·ron·o·mid \kī-'rä-nə-məd\ *n* [ultim. fr. Gk *cheironomos* one who gestures with his hands] (1915) : any of a family (Chironomidae) of midges that lack piercing mouthparts — **chironomid** *adj*

chi·rop·o·dy \kə-'rä-pə-dē, shə- *also* kī-\ *n* [*chir-* + *pod-*; fr. its original concern with both hands and feet] (1886) : PODIATRY — **chi·rop·o·dist** \-dist\ *n*

chi·ro·prac·tic \'kī-rə-ˌprak-tik, ˌkī-rə-'\ *n* [*chir-* + Gk *praktikos* practical, operative — more at PRACTICAL] (1898) : a system of therapy which holds that disease results from a lack of normal nerve function and which employs manipulation and specific adjustment of body structures (as the spinal column) ⟨holds a current license to practice ~ in this state⟩ — **chiropractic** *adj* — **chi·ro·prac·tor** \-tər\ *n*

chi·rop·ter·an \kī-'räp-tə-rən\ *n* [ultim. fr. Gk *cheir* hand + *pteron* wing — more at FEATHER] (1835) : [3]BAT

[1]**chirp** \'chərp\ *vb* [imit.] *vi* (1557) : to make a chirp or a sound resembling a chirp ~ *vt* : to utter with a cheerful liveliness ⟨she ~*ed* "good morning"⟩

[2]**chirp** *n* (ca. 1586) : the characteristic short sharp sound esp. of a small bird or insect

chirpy \'chər-pē\ *adj* **chirp·i·er; -est** (1837) **1** : cheerfully lively ⟨a ~ manner⟩ **2 a** : making chirps **b** : suggestive of chirping ⟨a ~ voice⟩ — **chirp·i·ly** \-pə-lē\ *adv* — **chirp·i·ness** \-pē-nəs\ *n*

chirr \'chər\ *n* [imit.] (ca. 1600) : the short vibrant or trilled sound characteristic of an insect (as a grasshopper or cicada) — **chirr** *vi*

chir·rup \'chər-əp, 'chir-\ *n* [imit.] (1722) : CHIRP — **chirrup** *vi*

chir·rupy \'chər-ə-pē, 'chir-\ *adj* (1808) : CHIRPY

chiru \'chir-(ˌ)ü\ *n* [prob. of Tibeto-Burman origin] (1825) : an antelope (*Pantholops hodgsoni*) chiefly of the Tibetan plateau having a pinkish-fawn wooly coat and in the male long nearly straight horns

chi·rur·geon \kī-'rər-jən\ *n* [ME *cirurgian*, fr. AF *cirurgien*, fr. *cirurgie* surgery] (13c) *archaic* : SURGEON

[1]**chis·el** \'chi-zəl\ *n* [ME, fr. AF **chisel*, *cisel*, fr. VL **cisellum*, alter. of *caesellum*, fr. L *caesus*, pp. of *caedere* to cut] (14c) : a metal tool with a sharpened edge at one end used to chip, carve, or cut into a solid material (as wood, stone, or metal)

[2]**chisel** *vb* **-eled** *or* **-elled; -el·ing** *or* **-el·ling** \'chi-zə-liŋ, 'chiz-liŋ\ *vt* (1509) **1** : to cut or work with or as if with a chisel **2** : to employ shrewd or unfair practices on in order to obtain one's end; *also* : to obtain by such practices ⟨~ a job⟩ ~ *vi* **1** : to work with or as if with a chisel **2 a** : to employ shrewd or unfair practices **b** : to thrust oneself : INTRUDE ⟨~ in on a racket⟩ — **chis·el·er** *or* **chis·el·ler** \'chi-zə-lər, 'chiz-lər\ *n*

chis·eled *or* **chis·elled** \'chi-zəld\ *adj* (1781) : formed or crafted as if with a chisel ⟨~ good looks⟩ ⟨a ~ essay⟩ ⟨a ~ physique⟩

chi–square \'kī-'skwer\ *n, often attrib* (1900) : a statistic that is a sum of terms each of which is a quotient obtained by dividing the square of the difference between the observed and theoretical values of a quantity by the theoretical value

chi–square distribution *n* (ca. 1956) : a probability density function that gives the distribution of the sum of the squares of a number of independent random variables each with a normal distribution with zero mean and unit variance, that has the property that the sum of two or more random variables with such a distribution also has one, and that is widely used in testing statistical hypotheses esp. about the theoretical and observed values of a quantity and about population variances and standard deviations

[1]**chit** \'chit\ *n* [ME *chitte* kitten, cub] (1578) **1** *archaic* : CHILD **2** : a pert young woman

[2]**chit** *n* [Hindi *ciṭṭhī* & Urdu *chitthī*] (1757) **1** : a short letter or note; *esp* : a signed voucher of a small debt (as for food) **2** : a small slip of paper with writing on it

chit·chat \'chit-ˌchat\ *n* [redupl. of *chat*] (1605) : SMALL TALK, GOSSIP — **chitchat** *vi*

chi·tin \'kī-tən\ *n* [F *chitine*, fr. Gk *chitōn*] (ca. 1839) : a horny polysaccharide $(C_8H_{13}NO_5)_n$ that forms part of the hard outer integument esp. of insects, arachnids, and crustaceans — **chi·tin·ous** \'kī-tən-əs, 'kīt-nəs\ *adj*

chi·ton \'kī-tən, 'kī-ˌtän\ *n* [NL, genus name, fr. Gk *chitōn* tunic, of Sem origin; akin to Heb *kuttōneth* tunic] (1816) **1** : any of a class (Polyplacophora) of elongated bilaterally symmetrical marine mollusks with a dorsal shell of calcareous plates **2** [Gk *chitōn*] : the basic garment of ancient Greece worn usu. knee-length by men and full-length by women

chit·ter \'chi-tər\ *vi* [ME *chiteren*, prob. of imit. origin] (13c) : TWITTER, CHIRP; *also* : CHATTER

chit·ter·lings *or* **chit·lins** \'chit-lənz\ *n pl* [ME *chiterling*] (13c) : the intestines of hogs esp. when prepared as food

chi·val·ric \shə-'val-rik\ *adj* (1794) : relating to chivalry : CHIVALROUS

chiv·al·rous \'shi-vəl-rəs\ *adj* (14c) **1** : VALIANT **2** : of, relating to, or characteristic of chivalry and knight-errantry **3 a** : marked by honor, generosity, and courtesy **b** : marked by gracious courtesy and high-minded consideration esp. to women ***syn*** see CIVIL — **chiv·al·rous·ly** *adv* — **chiv·al·rous·ness** *n*

chiv·al·ry \'shi-vəl-rē\ *n, pl* **-ries** [ME *chivalrie*, fr. AF *chevalerie*, fr. *chevaler* knight — more at CHEVALIER] (14c) **1** : mounted men-at-arms **2** *archaic* **a** : martial valor **b** : knightly skill **3** : gallant or distinguished gentlemen **4** : the system, spirit, or customs of medieval knighthood **5** : the qualities of the ideal knight : chivalrous conduct

chive \'chīv\ *n* [ME, fr. AF, fr. L *cepa* onion] (14c) : a perennial plant (*Allium schoenoprasum*) related to the onion and having slender leaves used as a seasoning; *also* : its leaves — usu. used in pl.; compare GARLIC CHIVE

chivy *or* **chiv·vy** \'chi-vē\ *vt* **chiv·ied** *or* **chiv·vied; chivy·ing** *or* **chiv·vy·ing** [*chivy*, n., chase, hunt, prob. fr. E dial. *Chevy Chase* chase, confusion, fr. the name of a ballad describing the battle of Otterburn (1388)] (1918) **1** : to tease or annoy with persistent petty attacks **2** : to move or obtain by small maneuvers ⟨~ an olive out of a bottle⟩ ***syn*** see BAIT

chla·myd·ia \klə-'mi-dē-ə\ *n, pl* **-i·ae** \-dē-ˌē\ [NL, fr. Gk *chlamyd-*, *chlamys*] (1966) **1** : any of a genus (*Chlamydia*, family Chlamydiaceae) of spherical gram-negative intracellular bacteria; *esp* : one (*C. trachomatis*) that causes or is associated with various diseases of the eye and urogenital tract including trachoma, lymphogranuloma venereum, cervicitis, and some forms of urethritis **2** : a disease or infection caused by chlamydiae — **chla·myd·i·al** \-dē-əl\ *adj*

chla·mydo·spore \klə-'mi-də-ˌspȯr\ *n* [L *chlamyd-*, *chlamys* + ISV *spore*] (1884) : a thick-walled usu. resting fungal spore

chla·mys \'kla-məs, 'klā-\ *n, pl* **chla·mys·es** *or* **chla·my·des** \-mə-ˌdēz\ [L *chlamyd-*, *chlamys*, fr. Gk] (1699) : a short oblong mantle worn by young men of ancient Greece

Chloe \'klō-ē\ *n* [L, fr. Gk *Chloē*] (1587) : a lover of Daphnis in a Greek pastoral romance

chlor- *or* **chloro-** *comb form* [NL, fr. Gk, fr. *chlōros* greenish yellow — more at YELLOW] **1** : green ⟨*chlor*ine⟩ ⟨*chlor*osis⟩ **2** : chlorine : containing chlorine ⟨*chloro*prene⟩

chlor·ac·ne \klȯ-ˈrak-nē\ *n* (ca. 1928) **:** a skin eruption resembling acne and resulting from exposure to chlorine or its compounds

chlo·ral \ˈklȯr-əl\ *n* [F, fr. *chlor-* + *al*cool alcohol] (1838) **1 :** a pungent colorless oily aldehyde CCl_3CHO used in making DDT and chloral hydrate **2 :** CHLORAL HYDRATE

chloral hydrate *n* (1874) **:** a bitter white crystalline drug $C_2H_3Cl_3O_2$ used as a hypnotic and sedative or in knockout drops

chlo·ral·ose \ˈklȯr-ə-ˌlōs, -ˌlōz\ *n* (1893) **:** a bitter crystalline compound $C_8H_{11}Cl_3O_6$ used esp. to anesthetize animals

chlo·ra·mine \ˈklȯr-ə-ˌmēn\ *n* [ISV] (1893) **:** any of various compounds containing nitrogen and chlorine

chlor·am·phen·i·col \ˌklȯr-ˌam-ˈfe-ni-ˌkȯl, -ˌkōl\ *n* [*chlor-* + *am*ide + *phen-* + *ni*tr- + gly*col*] (1949) **:** a broad-spectrum antibiotic $C_{11}H_{12}Cl_2N_2O_5$ isolated from cultures of a soil actinomycete (*Streptomyces venezuelae*) or prepared synthetically

chlo·rate \ˈklȯr-ˌāt\ *n* (1823) **:** a salt containing the anion ClO_3^- ⟨~ of potassium⟩

chlor·dane \ˈklȯr-ˌdān\ *n* [*chlor-* + in*dane* (C_9H_{10})] (1947) **:** a viscous volatile toxic liquid insecticide $C_{10}H_6Cl_8$ formerly used in the U.S.

chlor·di·az·epox·ide \ˌklȯr-dī-ˌa-zə-ˈpäk-ˌsīd\ *n* [*chlor-* + benzo*diazepine* + *oxide*] (1960) **:** a benzodiazepine $C_{16}H_{14}ClN_3O$ related to diazepam and used in the form of its hydrochloride esp. as a tranquilizer and to treat the withdrawal symptoms of alcoholism

chlo·rel·la \klə-ˈre-lə\ *n* [NL, genus name, fr. Gk *chlōros*] (1904) **:** any of a genus (*Chlorella*) of unicellular green algae

chlor·en·chy·ma \klȯr-ˈeŋ-kə-mə\ *n* (1894) **:** chlorophyll-containing parenchyma of plants

chlor·hex·i·dine \klȯr-ˈhek-sə-ˌdīn, -ˌdēn\ *n* [ISV *chlor-* + *hex-* + *-idine*] (1957) **:** an antibacterial compound $C_{22}H_{30}Cl_2N_{10}$ used as a local antiseptic (as in mouthwash) and disinfectant esp. in the form of its hydrochloride or gluconate

chlo·ride \ˈklȯr-ˌīd\ *n* [G *Chlorid,* fr. *chlor-* + *-id* -ide] (1812) **1 :** a compound of chlorine with another element or group; *esp* **:** a salt or ester of hydrochloric acid **2 :** a monovalent anion consisting of one atom of chlorine

chloride of lime (1826) **:** BLEACHING POWDER

chlo·ri·nate \ˈklȯr-ə-ˌnāt\ *vt* **-nat·ed; -nat·ing** (1855) **:** to treat or combine with chlorine or a chlorine compound — **chlo·ri·na·tion** \ˌklȯr-ə-ˈnā-shən\ *n* — **chlo·ri·na·tor** \ˈklȯr-ə-ˌnā-tər\ *n*

chlorinated lime *n* (1876) **:** BLEACHING POWDER

chlo·rine \ˈklȯr-ˌēn, -ən\ *n* (1810) **:** a halogen element that is isolated as a heavy greenish-yellow diatomic gas of pungent odor and is used esp. as a bleach, oxidizing agent, and disinfectant in water purification — see ELEMENT table

chlorine dioxide *n* (ca. 1925) **:** a heavy reddish-yellow gas ClO_2 used esp. as a bleach and disinfectant

chlorine monoxide *n* (1965) **:** a reactive monovalent radical ClO that plays a major role in stratospheric ozone depletion

chlo·rin·i·ty \klȯ-ˈri-nə-tē\ *n* (ca. 1931) **:** a measure of the concentration of halides in one kilogram of seawater

[1]**chlo·rite** \ˈklȯr-ˌīt\ *n* [G *Chlorit,* fr. L *chloritis,* a green stone, fr. Gk *chlōritis,* fr. *chlōros*] (1794) **:** any of a group of usu. green silicate minerals associated with and resembling the micas — **chlo·rit·ic** \klȯ-ˈri-tik\ *adj*

[2]**chlorite** *n* [prob. fr. F, fr. *chlor-*] (1853) **:** a salt containing the anion ClO_2^- ⟨~ of sodium⟩

chloro- — see CHLOR-

chlo·ro·ben·zene \ˌklȯr-ō-ˈben-ˌzēn, -ben-ˈ\ *n* [ISV] (ca. 1889) **:** a colorless flammable volatile toxic liquid C_6H_5Cl used in organic synthesis (as of DDT) and as a solvent

chlo·ro·fluo·ro·car·bon \ˌklȯr-ō-ˌflȯr-ō-ˈkär-bən, -ˌflu̇r-\ *n* (1949) **:** any of several simple gaseous compounds that contain carbon, chlorine, fluorine, and sometimes hydrogen, that are used as refrigerants, cleaning solvents, and aerosol propellants and in the manufacture of plastic foams, and that are believed to be a major cause of stratospheric ozone depletion — abbr. *CFC*

chlo·ro·fluo·ro·meth·ane \-ˈme-ˌthān, *Brit usu* -ˈmē-\ *n* (1965) **:** a chlorofluorocarbon derived from methane

[1]**chlo·ro·form** \ˈklȯr-ə-ˌfȯrm\ *n* [F *chloroforme,* fr. *chlor-* + *formyle* formyl; fr. its having been regarded as a trichloride of this group] (1838) **:** a colorless volatile heavy toxic liquid $CHCl_3$ with an ether odor used esp. as a solvent

[2]**chloroform** *vt* (1848) **:** to treat with or as if with chloroform esp. so as to produce anesthesia, insensibility, or death

chlo·ro·gen·ic acid \ˌklȯr-ə-ˈje-nik-\ *n* (ca. 1889) **:** a crystalline acid $C_{16}H_{18}O_9$ occurring in various plant parts (as coffee beans)

chlo·ro·hy·drin \ˌklȯr-ə-ˈhī-drən\ *n* [ISV *chlor-* + *hydr-* + [1]*-in*] (ca. 1890) **:** any of various organic compounds derived from diols or polyhydroxy alcohols by substitution of chlorine for part of the hydroxyl groups

chlo·ro·phyll \ˈklȯr-ə-ˌfil, -fəl\ *n* [F *chlorophylle,* fr. *chlor-* + Gk *phyllon* leaf — more at BLADE] (1819) **1 :** the green photosynthetic pigment found chiefly in the chloroplasts of plants and occurring esp. as a blue-black ester $C_{55}H_{72}MgN_4O_5$ or a dark green ester $C_{55}H_{70}MgN_4O_6$ — called also respectively *chlorophyll a, chlorophyll b* **2 :** a waxy green chlorophyll-containing substance extracted from green plants and used as a coloring agent or deodorant — **chlo·ro·phyl·lous** \ˌklȯr-ə-ˈfi-ləs\ *adj*

chlo·ro·pic·rin \ˌklȯr-ə-ˈpi-krən\ *n* [G *Chlorpikrin,* fr. *chlor-* + Gk *pikros* sharp — more at PAINT] (ca. 1889) **:** a colorless liquid CCl_3NO_2 that causes tears and vomiting and is used esp. as a soil fumigant

chlo·ro·plast \ˈklȯr-ə-ˌplast\ *n* [ISV] (1887) **:** a plastid that contains chlorophyll and is the site of photosynthesis — see CELL illustration — **chlo·ro·plas·tic** \ˌklȯr-ə-ˈplas-tik\ *adj*

chlo·ro·prene \-ˌprēn\ *n* [*chlor-* + iso*prene*] (1931) **:** a colorless liquid C_4H_5Cl used esp. in making neoprene by polymerization

chlo·ro·quine \ˈklȯr-ə-ˌkwēn\ *n* [*chlor-* + *quin*ol*ine*] (1946) **:** an antimalarial drug $C_{18}H_{26}ClN_3$ administered in the form of its bitter crystalline diphosphate

chlo·ro·sis \klə-ˈrō-səs\ *n* (1678) **1 :** an iron-deficiency anemia esp. of adolescent girls that may impart a greenish tint to the skin — called also *greensickness* **2 :** a diseased condition in green plants marked by yellowing or blanching — **chlo·rot·ic** \-ˈrä-tik\ *adj*

chlo·ro·thi·a·zide \ˌklȯr-ə-ˈthī-ə-ˌzīd, -zəd\ *n* (1957) **:** a thiazide diuretic $C_7H_6ClN_3O_4S_2$ used esp. in the treatment of edema and hypertension

chlor·phen·ir·amine \ˌklȯr-(ˈ)fen-ˈir-ə-ˌmēn, -mən\ *n* [*chlor-* + *phen-* + *-ir-* (prob. alter. of p*yr*idine) + *amine*] (1964) **:** an antihistamine $C_{16}H_{19}ClN_2$ that is usu. administered in the form of its maleate

chlor·prom·a·zine \klȯr-ˈprä-mə-ˌzēn\ *n* [*chlor-* + *pro*pyl + *m*ethyl + *azine*] (1952) **:** a phenothiazine $C_{17}H_{19}ClN_2S$ used chiefly as a tranquilizer esp. in the form of its hydrochloride to control the symptoms of psychotic disorders (as schizophrenia)

chlor·prop·amide \-ˈprä-pə-ˌmīd, -ˈprō-\ *n* [*chlor-* + *prop*ane + *amide*] (1960) **:** a sulfonylurea drug $C_{10}H_{13}ClN_2O_3S$ used orally to reduce blood sugar in the treatment of mild diabetes

chlor·pyr·i·fos \-ˈpir-ə-fäs, -ˈpī-rə-\ *n* [*chlor-* + *pyri*dine + *-fos* (alter. of *phos*phorus)] (1970) **:** a toxic crystalline organophosphate pesticide $C_9H_{11}Cl_3NO_3PS$ that inhibits acetylcholinesterase and is used to control insect pests and ticks

chlor·tet·ra·cy·cline \ˌklȯr-ˌte-trə-ˈsī-ˌklēn\ *n* (1953) **:** a yellow crystalline broad-spectrum antibiotic $C_{22}H_{23}ClN_2O_8$ that is produced by a soil actinomycete (*Streptomyces aureofaciens*) and is sometimes used in animal feeds to stimulate growth

chm *abbr* **1** chairman **2** checkmate

Chmn *abbr* chairman

cho·ano·cyte \kō-ˈa-nə-ˌsīt\ *n* [ISV *choan-* funnel-shaped (fr. Gk *choanē* funnel) + *-cyte*] (1888) **:** COLLAR CELL

[1]**chock** \ˈchäk\ *n* [origin unknown] (1769) **1 :** a wedge or block for steadying a body (as a cask) and holding it motionless, for filling in an unwanted space, or for blocking the movement of a wheel **2 :** a heavy metal casting (as on the bow or stern of a ship) with two short horn-shaped arms curving inward between which ropes or hawsers may pass for mooring or towing

[2]**chock** *adv* (1834) **:** as close or as completely as possible

[3]**chock** *vt* (ca. 1841) **:** to stop or make fast with or as if with chocks

[1]**chock·a·block** \ˈchä-kə-ˌbläk\ *adv* (1840) **:** CHOCK ⟨~ full⟩

[2]**chockablock** *adj* (1850) **1 :** brought close together **2 :** very full ⟨shelves ~ with books⟩

chock–full *or* **chock·ful** \ˈchək-ˈfu̇l, ˈchäk-, -ˌfu̇l\ *adj* [ME *chokkefull,* prob. fr. *choken* to choke + *full*] (15c) **:** full to the limit ⟨hotels ~ of tourists⟩

choc·o·hol·ic *also* **choc·a·hol·ic** \ˌchä-kə-ˈhȯ-lik, ˌchȯ-, -ˈhä-\ *n* [*choc*olate + *-aholic*] (1968) **:** a person who craves or compulsively consumes chocolate

choc·o·late \ˈchä-k(ə-)lət, ˈchȯ-\ *n* [Sp, fr. Nahuatl *chocolātl,* prob. alter. of eastern Nahuatl dial. *chikolātl,* fr. *chikolli* hook (prob. used to refer to the beater used to mix chocolate with water) + *ātl* water, liquid] (1604) **1 :** a beverage made by mixing chocolate with water or milk **2 :** a food prepared from ground roasted cacao beans **3 :** a small candy with a center (as a fondant) and a chocolate coating **4 :** a brownish gray — **chocolate** *adj*

chocolate–box *adj* [fr. the pictures formerly commonly seen on boxes of chocolates] (1901) **:** superficially pretty or sentimental

choc·o·la·tier \ˌchä-k(ə-)lə-ˈtir, ˌchȯ-\ *n* [F, fr. *chocolat* chocolate] (1888) **:** a maker or seller of chocolate candy

choc·o·laty *or* **choc·o·lat·ey** \ˈchä-k(ə-)lə-tē, ˈchȯ-\ *adj* (1926) **:** made of or like chocolate; *also* **:** having a rich chocolate flavor

Choc·taw \ˈchäk-(ˌ)tȯ\ *n, pl* **Choctaw** *or* **Choctaws** [Choctaw *čahta*] (1722) **1 :** a member of an American Indian people of Mississippi, Alabama, and Louisiana **2 :** the language of the Choctaw people

[1]**choice** \ˈchȯis\ *n* [ME *chois,* fr. AF, fr. *choisir* to choose, of Gmc origin; akin to OHG *kiosan* to choose — more at CHOOSE] (13c) **1 :** the act of choosing **:** SELECTION ⟨finding it hard to make a ~⟩ **2 :** power of choosing **:** OPTION ⟨you have no ~⟩ **3 a :** the best part **:** CREAM **b :** a person or thing chosen ⟨she was their first ~⟩ **4 :** a number and variety to choose among ⟨a plan with a wide ~ of options⟩ **5 :** care in selecting **6 :** a grade of meat between prime and good — **of choice :** to be preferred

syn CHOICE, OPTION, ALTERNATIVE, PREFERENCE, SELECTION, ELECTION mean the act or opportunity of choosing or the thing chosen. CHOICE suggests the opportunity or privilege of choosing freely ⟨freedom of *choice*⟩. OPTION implies a power to choose that is specifically granted or guaranteed ⟨the *option* of paying now or later⟩. ALTERNATIVE implies a need to choose one and reject another possibility ⟨equally attractive *alternatives*⟩. PREFERENCE suggests a choice guided by one's judgment or predilections ⟨a *preference* for cool weather⟩. SELECTION implies a range of choice ⟨a varied *selection* of furniture⟩. ELECTION implies an end or purpose which requires exercise of judgment ⟨doing a tax return forces certain *elections* on you⟩.

[2]**choice** *adj* **choic·er; choic·est** (14c) **1 :** worthy of being chosen **2 :** selected with care **3 a :** of high quality **b :** of a grade between prime and good ⟨~ meat⟩ — **choice·ly** *adv* — **choice·ness** *n*

syn CHOICE, EXQUISITE, ELEGANT, RARE, DELICATE, DAINTY mean having qualities that appeal to a cultivated taste. CHOICE stresses preeminence in quality or kind ⟨*choice* fabric⟩. EXQUISITE implies a perfection in workmanship or design that appeals only to very sensitive taste ⟨an *exquisite* gold bracelet⟩. ELEGANT applies to what is rich and luxurious but restrained by good taste ⟨a sumptuous but *elegant* dining room⟩. RARE suggests an uncommon excellence ⟨*rare* beauty⟩. DELICATE implies exquisiteness, subtlety, and fragility ⟨*delicate* craftsmanship⟩. DAINTY sometimes carries an additional suggestion of smallness and of appeal to the eye or palate ⟨*dainty* sandwiches⟩.

[1]**choir** \ˈkwī(-ə)r\ *n* [ME *quer,* fr. AF *queor,* fr. ML *chorus,* fr. L, chorus — more at CHORUS] (14c) **1 :** an organized company of singers (as in a church service) **2 :** a group of instruments of the same class ⟨a brass ~⟩ **3 :** an organized group of persons or things **4 :** a division of angels **5 :** the part of a church occupied by the singers or by the clergy; *also* **:** the part of a church where the services are performed **6 :** a group organized for ensemble speaking

[2]**choir** *vi* (1596) **:** to sing or sound in chorus or concert

choir·boy \ˈkwī(-ə)r-ˌbȯi\ *n* (1837) **:** a boy member of a choir

choir loft *n* (1929) **:** a gallery occupied by a church choir

\ə\ **abut** \ᵊ\ **kitten,** F **table** \ər\ **further** \a\ **ash** \ā\ **ace** \ä\ **mop, mar**
\au̇\ **out** \ch\ **chin** \e\ **bet** \ē\ **easy** \g\ **go** \i\ **hit** \ī\ **ice** \j\ **job**
\ŋ\ **sing** \ō\ **go** \ȯ\ **law** \ȯi\ **boy** \th\ **thin** \t͟h\ **the** \ü\ **loot** \u̇\ **foot**
\y\ **yet** \zh\ **vision, beige** \k̲, ⁿ, œ, ue, ʸ\ *see* Guide to Pronunciation

choir·mas·ter \-ˌmas-tər\ *n* (1840) : the director of a choir

[1]**choke** \ˈchōk\ *vb* **choked; chok·ing** [ME, alter. of *achoken,* fr. OE *ācēocian,* fr. *ā-,* perfective prefix + *cēoce, cēace* jaw, cheek — more at ABIDE, CHEEK] *vt* (14c) **1 :** to check or block normal breathing of by compressing or obstructing the trachea or by poisoning or adulterating available air **2 a :** to check or hinder the growth, development, or activity of ⟨the flowers were *choked* by the weeds⟩ **b :** to obstruct by filling up or clogging ⟨leaves *choked* the drain⟩ **c :** to fill completely **:** JAM ⟨roads *choked* with traffic⟩ **3 :** to enrich the fuel mixture of (a motor) by partially shutting off the air intake of the carburetor **4 :** to grip (as a baseball bat) some distance from the end of the handle — usu. used with *up* ~ *vi* **1 :** to become choked in breathing ⟨he *choked* on a bone⟩ **2 a :** to become obstructed or checked **b :** to become or feel constricted in the throat (as from strong emotion) — usu. used with *up* ⟨*choked* up and couldn't finish the speech⟩ **3 :** to shorten one's grip esp. on the handle of a bat — usu. used with *up* **4 :** to lose one's composure and fail to perform effectively in a critical situation ⟨had a chance to win the game but he *choked*⟩

[2]**choke** *n* (1736) **1** [by folk etymology fr. arti*choke*] **:** the filamentous inedible center of an artichoke flower head; *broadly* **:** an artichoke flower head **2 :** something that obstructs passage or flow: as **a :** a valve for choking a gasoline engine **b :** a constriction in an outlet (as of an oil well) that restricts flow **c :** REACTOR 2 **d :** a constriction (as a narrowing of the barrel or an attachment) at the muzzle of a shotgun that serves to limit the spread of shot **3 :** the act of choking

choke·ber·ry \-ˌber-ē\ *n* (1778) **:** a small berrylike astringent fruit; *also* **:** any of a genus (*Aronia*) of No. American shrubs of the rose family bearing chokeberries

choke chain *n* (1955) **:** a collar that may be tightened as a noose and that is used esp. in training and controlling powerful or stubborn dogs — called also *choke collar*

choke·cher·ry \ˈchōk-ˌcher-ē\ *n* (1784) **:** a wild cherry (*Prunus virginiana*) of the U.S. and Canada having bitter or astringent red to black edible fruit; *also* **:** this fruit

choke coil *n* (ca. 1896) **:** REACTOR 2

choke hold *n* (1964) **1 :** a hold that involves strong choking pressure applied to the neck of another **2 :** absolute dominance or control ⟨had a *choke hold* on the city's finances⟩

choke off *vt* (1818) **:** to bring to a stop or to an end as if by choking

choke point *n* (1944) **:** a strategic narrow route providing passage through or to another region

chok·er \ˈchō-kər\ *n* (ca. 1552) **1 :** one that chokes **2 :** something (as a collar or necklace) worn closely about the throat or neck

chok·ing \ˈchō-kiŋ\ *adj* (1556) **1 :** producing the feeling of strangulation ⟨a ~ cloud of smog⟩ **2 :** indistinct in utterance — used esp. of a person's voice ⟨a low ~ laugh⟩ — **chok·ing·ly** \-kiŋ-lē\ *adv*

choky \ˈchō-kē\ *adj* (1579) **:** tending to cause choking or to become choked

chol- *or* **chole-** *or* **cholo-** *comb form* [Gk *chol-, cholē-, cholo-,* fr. *cholē, cholos* — more at GALL] **:** bile **:** gall ⟨*chol*ate⟩

chol·an·gi·og·ra·phy \kə-ˌlan-jē-ˈä-grə-fē, (ˌ)kō-\ *n* (1936) **:** radiographic visualization of the bile ducts after injection of a radiopaque substance — **chol·an·gio·graph·ic** \-jē-ə-ˈgra-fik\ *adj* — **chol·an·gio·gram** \-ˈlan-jē-ə-ˌgram\ *n*

cho·late \ˈkō-ˌlāt\ *n* (ca. 1846) **:** a salt or ester of cholic acid

cho·le·cal·cif·er·ol \ˌkō-lə-(ˌ)kal-ˈsi-fə-ˌrȯl, -ˌrōl\ *n* [ISV] (1955) **:** a sterol $C_{27}H_{43}OH$ that is a natural form of vitamin D found esp. in fish, egg yolks, and fish-liver oils and is formed in the skin on exposure to sunlight or ultraviolet rays — called also *vitamin D_3*

cho·le·cys·tec·to·my \-(ˌ)sis-ˈtek-tə-mē\ *n, pl* **-mies** [NL *cholecystis* gallbladder (fr. *chol-* + Gk *kystis* bladder) + ISV *-ectomy* — more at CYST] (1885) **:** surgical excision of the gallbladder — **cho·le·cys·tec·to·mized** \-ˌmīzd\ *adj*

cho·le·cys·ti·tis \-(ˌ)sis-ˈtī-təs\ *n* [NL, fr. *cholecystis*] (1866) **:** inflammation of the gallbladder

cho·le·cys·to·ki·nin \-ˌsis-tə-ˈkī-nən\ *n* [NL *cholecystis* + E *-o-* + *kinin*] (ca. 1929) **:** a hormone secreted esp. by the duodenal mucosa that regulates the emptying of the gallbladder and secretion of enzymes by the pancreas and that has been found in the brain — called also *cholecystokinin-pancreozymin, pancreozymin*

cho·le·li·thi·a·sis \ˌkō-lə-li-ˈthī-ə-səs\ *n* [NL] (ca. 1860) **:** production of gallstones; *also* **:** the resulting abnormal condition

cho·ler \ˈkä-lər, ˈkō-\ *n* [ME *coler,* fr. AF *colre, colere,* fr. L *cholera* cholera, fr. Gk] (14c) **1 a** *archaic* **:** YELLOW BILE **b** *obs* **:** BILE 1a **2** *obs* **:** the quality or state of being bilious **3 :** ready disposition to irritation **:** IRASCIBILITY; *also* **:** ANGER

chol·era \ˈkä-lə-rə\ *n* [L] (1601) **:** any of several diseases of humans and domestic animals usu. marked by severe gastrointestinal symptoms; *esp* **:** an acute diarrheal disease caused by an enterotoxin produced by a comma-shaped gram-negative bacillus (*Vibrio cholerae* syn. *V. comma*) when it is present in large numbers in the proximal part of the human small intestine

chol·era mor·bus \-ˈmȯr-bəs, *dial* -ˈmä(r)-; *dial* ˈkä-lē-\ *n* [NL, lit., the disease cholera] (1673) **:** gastrointestinal illness characterized by cramps, diarrhea, and sometimes vomiting — not used technically

cho·ler·ic \ˈkä-lə-rik, kə-ˈler-ik\ *adj* (1566) **1 :** easily moved to often unreasonable or excessive anger **:** hot-tempered **2 :** ANGRY, IRATE — **cho·ler·i·cal·ly** \-ri-k(ə-)lē, -i-k(ə-)lē\ *adv*

cho·le·sta·sis \ˌkō-lə-ˈstā-səs\ *n, pl* **-sta·ses** \-ˌsēz\ [NL] (ca. 1935) **:** a checking or failure of bile flow — **cho·le·stat·ic** \-ˈsta-tik\ *adj*

cho·le·ster·ic \ˌkō-lə-ˈster-ik, kə-ˈles-tə-rik\ *adj* [*cholesteric* relating to cholesterol, fr. F *cholesterique*] (1942) **:** of, relating to, or being the phase of a liquid crystal characterized by arrangement of molecules in layers with the long molecular axes parallel to one another in the plane of each layer and incrementally displaced in successive layers to give helical stacking — compare NEMATIC, SMECTIC

cho·les·ter·ol \kə-ˈles-tə-ˌrōl, -ˌrȯl\ *n* [ISV, fr. *chol-* + Gk *stereos* solid] (1894) **:** a steroid alcohol $C_{27}H_{45}OH$ that is present in animal cells and body fluids, regulates membrane fluidity, and functions as a precursor molecule in various metabolic pathways and as a constituent of LDL may cause atherosclerosis — compare BAD CHOLESTEROL, GOOD CHOLESTEROL

cho·le·styr·amine \(ˌ)kō-ˌles-tə-ˈra-ˌmēn, kə-; ˌkō-lə-ˈstir-ə-ˌmēn\ *n* [*chol-* + *styrene* + *amine*] (ca. 1962) **:** a strongly basic synthetic resin that forms insoluble complexes with bile acids and has been used to lower cholesterol levels in hypercholesterolemic patients

cho·lic acid \ˈkō-lik-\ *n* [Gk *cholikos* bilious, fr. *cholē*] (1846) **:** a crystalline bile acid $C_{24}H_{40}O_5$

cho·line \ˈkō-ˌlēn\ *n* [ISV] (ca. 1871) **:** a basic compound $C_5H_{15}NO_2$ that is found in various foods (as egg yolks and legumes) or is synthesized in the liver and that is a component of lecithin, is a precursor of acetylcholine, and is essential to liver function

cho·lin·er·gic \ˌkō-lə-ˈnər-jik\ *adj* [ISV] (1934) **1 :** liberating, activated by, or involving acetylcholine ⟨~ nerve fiber⟩ ⟨~ functions⟩ **2 :** resembling acetylcholine esp. in physiologic action ⟨a ~ drug⟩ — **cho·lin·er·gi·cal·ly** \-ji-k(ə-)lē\ *adv*

cho·lin·es·ter·ase \ˌkō-lə-ˈnes-tə-ˌrās, -ˌrāz\ *n* (1932) **1 :** ACETYLCHOLINESTERASE **2 :** an enzyme that hydrolyzes choline esters and that is found esp. in blood plasma — called also *pseudocholinesterase*

chol·la \ˈchȯi-yə\ *n* [MexSp, fr. Sp, head] (1846) **:** any of numerous shrubby opuntias chiefly of the southwestern U.S. and Mexico that have needlelike spines partly enclosed in a papery sheath and cylindrical joints — called also *cholla cactus*

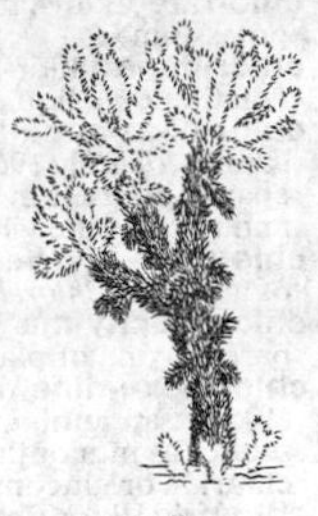
cholla

cho·lo \ˈchō-(ˌ)lō\ *n, pl* **cholos** [AmerSp, Europeanized Indian, mestizo] (1851) **1** *often disparaging* **:** a man or boy of Mexican descent **2 :** a Mexican-American youth who belongs to a street gang

chomp \ˈchämp, ˈchȯmp\ *vb* [alter. of *champ*] *vi* (1581) **1 :** to chew or bite on something **2 :** CHAMP 2 — usu. used in the phrase *chomping at the bit* ~ *vt* **:** to chew or bite on — **chomp** *n*

chon \ˈchän\ *n, pl* **chon** [Korean *chŏn*] — see *won* at MONEY table

chon·drio·some \ˈkän-drē-ə-ˌsōm\ *n* [Gk *chondrion,* dim. of *chondros* grain + ISV *-some*] (1910) **:** MITOCHONDRION

chon·drite \ˈkän-ˌdrīt\ *n* [ISV, fr. Gk *chondros*] (1883) **:** a meteoric stone characterized by the presence of chondrules — **chon·drit·ic** \kän-ˈdri-tik\ *adj*

chon·dro·cra·ni·um \ˌkän-drō-ˈkrā-nē-əm\ *n* [Gk *chondros* grain, cartilage] (1875) **:** the cartilaginous parts of an embryonic cranium; *also* **:** the part of the adult skull derived therefrom

chon·dro·cyte \ˈkän-drə-ˌsīt\ *n* [Gk *chondros* cartilage] (1903) **:** a cartilage cell

chon·droi·tin \kän-ˈdrȯi-tᵊn, -ˈdrō-ə-tən\ *n* [ISV *chondroitic* acid, an acid found in cartilage + [1]*-in*] (1895) **:** any of several glycosaminoglycans occurring in sulfated form in various animal tissues (as cartilage)

chon·drule \ˈkän-(ˌ)drül\ *n* [Gk *chondros* grain] (ca. 1889) **:** a rounded granule of cosmic origin often found embedded in meteoric stones and sometimes free in marine sediments

chook \ˈchu̇k\ *n* [imit.] (1880) *Austral & NewZeal* **:** CHICKEN 1

choose \ˈchüz\ *vb* **chose** \ˈchōz\; **cho·sen** \ˈchō-zᵊn\; **choos·ing** \ˈchü-ziŋ\ [ME *chosen,* fr. OE *cēosan;* akin to OHG *kiosan* to choose, L *gustare* to taste] *vt* (bef. 12c) **1 a :** to select freely and after consideration ⟨~ a career⟩ **b :** to decide on esp. by vote **:** ELECT **2 a :** to have a preference for **b :** DECIDE ⟨*chose* to go by train⟩ ~ *vi* **1 :** to make a selection ⟨finding it hard to ~⟩ **2 :** to take an alternative — used after *cannot* and usu. followed by *but* ⟨when earth is so kind, men cannot ~ but be happy —J. A. Froude⟩ — **choos·er** \ˈchü-zər\ *n*

choose up *vt* (1850) **:** to form (sides) esp. for a game by having opposing captains choose their players ~ *vi* **:** to form sides for a game

choosy *also* **choos·ey** \ˈchü-zē\ *adj* **choos·i·er; -est** (1862) **:** fastidiously selective **:** PARTICULAR ⟨~ shoppers⟩

[1]**chop** \ˈchäp\ *vb* **chopped; chop·ping** [ME *chappen, choppen* — more at CHAP] *vt* (14c) **1 a :** to cut into or sever usu. by repeated blows of a sharp instrument **b :** to cut into pieces — often used with *up* ⟨~ up an onion⟩ **c :** to weed and thin out (young cotton) **d :** to cut as if by chopping ⟨~ prices⟩ ⟨a bridge ~*s* the lake in two⟩ **2 :** to strike (as a ball) with a short quick downward stroke **3 :** to subject to the action of a chopper ⟨~ a beam of light⟩ ~ *vi* **1 :** to make a quick stroke or repeated strokes with or as if with a sharp instrument (as an ax) **2** *archaic* **:** to move or act suddenly or violently

[2]**chop** *n* (14c) **1 a :** a forceful usu. slanting blow with or as if with an ax or cleaver **b :** a sharp downward blow or stroke **2 :** a small cut of meat often including part of a rib — see LAMB illustration **3 :** a mark made by or as if by chopping **4 :** material that has been chopped up **5 a :** a short abrupt motion (as of a wave) **b :** a stretch of choppy sea **6 :** CHOPPER 6 **7** *chiefly Brit* **:** AX 3 ⟨it is the very top men who have got the ~ —*Daily Mirror*⟩

[3]**chop** *vi* **chopped; chop·ping** [ME *chappen, choppen* to barter] (1540) **1 :** to change direction **2 :** to veer with or as if with wind — **chop logic :** to argue with sophistical reasoning and minute distinctions

[4]**chop** *n* [Hindi *chāp* & Urdu *chhāp* stamp] (1614) **1 a :** a seal or official stamp or its impression **b :** a license validated by a seal **2 a :** a mark on goods or coins to indicate nature or quality **b :** a kind, brand, or lot of goods bearing the same chop **c :** QUALITY, GRADE ⟨of the first ~⟩

chop–chop \ˌchäp-ˈchäp, ˈchäp-ˈ\ *adv* [Chin Pidgin E, redupl. of *chop* fast] (1834) **:** without delay **:** QUICKLY

chopfallen *var of* CHAPFALLEN

chop·house \ˈchäp-ˌhau̇s\ *n* (ca. 1690) **:** RESTAURANT

cho·pine \shä-ˈpēn, chä-\ *n* [MF *chapin,* fr. OSp] (1577) **:** a woman's shoe of the 16th and 17th centuries with a very high sole designed to increase stature and protect the feet from mud and dirt

chop·log·ic \ˈchäp-ˌlä-jik\ *n* [obs. *chop* to exchange, trade, fr. ME *choppen* to barter] (1533) **:** involved and often specious argumentation — **choplogic** *adj*

chop mark *n* (1949) **:** an indentation made on a coin to attest weight, silver content, or legality — **chop–marked** \ˈchäp-ˌmärkt\ *adj*

chopped liver *n* (1947) *slang* **:** one that is insignificant or not worth considering

[1]**chop·per** \ˈchä-pər\ *n* (1552) **1 :** one that chops **2** *pl, slang* **:** TEETH **3 :** a device that interrupts an electric current or a beam of radiation (as light) at short regular intervals **4 :** MACHINE GUN **5 :** HELICOPTER **6 :** a high-bouncing batted baseball **7 :** a customized motorcycle

[2]**chopper** *vb* (1955) **:** HELICOPTER

chop·pi·ness \ˈchä-pē-nəs\ *n* (1881) **:** the quality or state of being choppy

chopping block *n* (1600) **1 :** a wooden block on which material (as meat, wood, or vegetables) is cut, split, or diced **2 :** a situation in which someone or something is threatened with elimination ⟨government programs on the *chopping block*⟩

[1]**chop·py** \ˈchä-pē\ *adj* **chop·pi·er; -est** [[2]*chop*] (1605) **1 :** being roughened **:** CHAPPED **2 :** rough with small waves **3 a :** interrupted by ups and downs ⟨~ terrain⟩ ⟨a ~ career⟩ **b :** JERKY ⟨short ~ strides⟩ **c :** DISCONNECTED ⟨~ writing⟩ — **chop·pi·ly** \ˈchä-pə-lē\ *adv*

[2]**choppy** *adj* **chop·pi·er; -est** [[3]*chop*] (1865) **:** CHANGEABLE, VARIABLE ⟨a ~ wind⟩

chops \ˈchäps\ *n pl* [alter. of [3]*chap*] (1589) **1 :** JAW **2 a :** MOUTH **b :** the fleshy covering of the jaws ⟨a dog licking its ~⟩ **3 :** EMBOUCHURE; *broadly* **:** the technical facility of a musical performer **4 :** expertise in a particular field or activity ⟨acting ~⟩

chop shop *n* (1977) **:** a place where stolen automobiles are stripped of salable parts

chop–socky \ˈchäp-ˈsä-kē\ *n, often attrib* (1978) **:** a genre of motion pictures featuring martial arts violence ⟨a ~ star⟩

chop·stick \ˈchäp-ˌstik\ *n* [Chin Pidgin E *chop* fast + E *stick*] (1699) **:** one of a pair of slender sticks held between thumb and fingers and used chiefly in Asian countries to lift food to the mouth

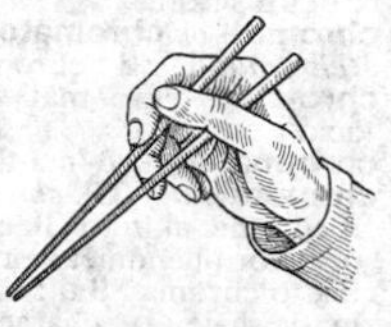

chopstick

chop su·ey \ˌchäp-ˈsü-ē\ *n, pl* **chop sueys** [Chin (Guangdong) *jaahp-seui* odds and ends, fr. *jaahp* miscellaneous + *seui* bits] (1888) **:** a dish prepared chiefly from bean sprouts, bamboo shoots, water chestnuts, onions, mushrooms, and meat or fish and served with rice and soy sauce

cho·ra·gus \kə-ˈrā-gəs\ *or* **cho·re·gus** \-ˈrē-, -ˈrā-\ *n* [L & Gk; L *choragus,* fr. Gk *choragos, chorēgos,* fr. *choros* chorus + *agein* to lead — more at AGENT] (1625) **1 :** the leader of a chorus or choir; *broadly* **:** the leader of any group or movement **2 :** a leader of a dramatic chorus in ancient Greece — **cho·rag·ic** \-ˈra-jik\ *adj*

cho·ral \ˈkȯr-əl\ *adj* [F or ML; F *choral,* fr. ML *choralis,* fr. L *chorus*] (1587) **1 :** of or relating to a chorus or choir ⟨a ~ group⟩ **2 :** sung or designed for singing by a choir ⟨a ~ arrangement⟩ — **cho·ral·ly** \-ə-lē\ *adv*

cho·rale \kə-ˈral, -ˈräl\ *n* [G *Choral,* short for *Choralgesang* choral song] (1841) **1 :** a hymn or psalm sung to a traditional or composed melody in church; *also* **:** a harmonization of a chorale melody ⟨a Bach ~⟩ **2 :** CHORUS, CHOIR

chorale prelude *n* (ca. 1924) **:** a composition usu. for organ based on a chorale

[1]**chord** \ˈkȯrd\ *n* [alter. of ME *cord,* short for *accord*] (1608) **:** three or more musical tones sounded simultaneously

[2]**chord** *vi* (14c) **1 :** ACCORD **2 :** to play chords esp. on a stringed instrument ~ *vt* **1 :** to make chords on **2 :** HARMONIZE

[3]**chord** *n* [alter. of [1]*cord*] (1543) **1 :** CORD 3a **2 :** a straight line segment joining and included between two points on a circle; *broadly* **:** a straight line joining two points on a curve **3 :** an individual emotion or disposition ⟨struck a responsive ~⟩ **4 :** either of the two outside members of a truss connected and braced by the web members **5 :** the straight line distance joining the leading and trailing edges of an airfoil

chord·al \ˈkȯr-dᵊl\ *adj* (1848) **1 :** of, relating to, or suggesting a chord **2 :** relating to music characterized more by harmony than by counterpoint

chor·da·meso·derm \ˌkȯr-də-ˈme-zə-ˌdərm *also* -ˈme-sə-\ *n* [NL *chorda* cord + E *mesoderm*] (1939) **:** the portion of the embryonic mesoderm that forms the notochord and related structures and induces the formation of neural structures — **chor·da·meso·der·mal** \-ˌme-zə-ˈdər-məl, -ˌme-sə-\ *adj*

chor·date \ˈkȯr-ˌdāt, -dət\ *n* [ultim. fr. L *chorda* cord] (1897) **:** any of a phylum (Chordata) of animals having at least at some stage of development a notochord, dorsally situated central nervous system, and gill clefts and including the vertebrates, lancelets, and tunicates — **chordate** *adj*

chore \ˈchȯr\ *n* [alter. of *chare*] (1746) **1** *pl* **:** the regular or daily light work of a household or farm **2 :** a routine task or job **3 :** a difficult or disagreeable task ⟨doing taxes can be a real ~⟩ ***syn*** see TASK

cho·rea \kə-ˈrē-ə\ *n* [NL, fr. L, dance, fr. Gk *choreia,* fr. *choros* chorus] (1804) **:** any of various nervous disorders (as of humans or dogs) marked by spasmodic movements of limbs and facial muscles and by incoordination — compare HUNTINGTON'S DISEASE — **cho·re·ic** \-ˈrē-ik\ *adj*

cho·re·i·form \kə-ˈrē-ə-ˌfȯrm\ *adj* [ISV] (ca. 1899) **:** resembling or characteristic of chorea ⟨~ movements⟩

cho·reo·graph \ˈkȯr-ē-ə-ˌgraf\ *vt* (1943) **1 :** to compose the choreography of ⟨~ a ballet⟩ **2 :** to arrange or direct the movements, progress, or details of ⟨a carefully ~*ed* meeting⟩ ~ *vi* **:** to engage in choreography — **cho·re·og·ra·pher** \ˌkȯr-ē-ˈä-grə-fər\ *n*

cho·re·og·ra·phy \ˌkȯr-ē-ˈä-grə-fē\ *n, pl* **-phies** [F *chorégraphie,* fr. Gk *choreia* + F *-graphie* -graphy] (ca. 1789) **1 :** the art of symbolically representing dancing **2 a :** the composition and arrangement of dances esp. for ballet **b :** a composition created by this art **3 :** something resembling choreography ⟨a snail-paced ~ of delicate high diplomacy —Wolfgang Saxon⟩ — **cho·reo·graph·ic** \ˌkȯr-ē-ə-ˈgra-fik\ *adj* — **cho·reo·graph·i·cal·ly** \-fi-k(ə-)lē\ *adv*

cho·ric \ˈkȯr-ik, ˈkär-\ *adj* (1830) **:** of, relating to, or being in the style of a chorus and esp. a Greek chorus

cho·rine \ˈkȯr-ˌēn\ *n* [*chorus* + *-ine,* fem. n. suffix (as in *Pauline*)] (1922) **:** CHORUS GIRL

cho·rio·al·lan·to·is \ˌkȯr-ē-(ˌ)ō-ə-ˈlan-tə-wəs\ *n* [NL, fr. Gk *chorion* + NL *allantois*] (1933) **:** a vascular fetal membrane composed of the fused chorion and adjacent wall of the allantois that in the hen's egg is used as a living culture medium for viruses and for tissues — called also *chorioallantoic membrane* — **cho·rio·al·lan·to·ic** \-ˌa-lən-ˈtō-ik\ *adj*

cho·rio·car·ci·no·ma \-ˌkär-sə-ˈnō-mə\ *n* [NL, fr. *chorion* + *carcinoma*] (1901) **:** a malignant tumor typically developing in the uterus from the trophoblast

cho·ri·on \ˈkȯr-ē-ˌän\ *n* [NL, fr. Gk, afterbirth] (1545) **:** the highly vascular outer embryonic membrane of reptiles, birds, and mammals that in placental mammals is associated with the allantois in the formation of the placenta

cho·ri·on·ic \ˌkȯr-ē-ˈä-nik\ *adj* (1892) **1 :** of, relating to, or being part of the chorion ⟨~ villi⟩ **2 :** secreted or produced by chorionic or related tissue (as in the placenta or a choriocarcinoma)

chorionic villus sampling *n* (1983) **:** biopsy of a villus of the chorion at usu. 10 to 12 weeks of gestation to obtain fetal cells for the prenatal diagnosis of chromosomal abnormalities — abbr. *CVS;* called also *chorionic villi sampling*

cho·ris·ter \ˈkȯr-ə-stər, ˈkär-\ *n* [ME *querister,* fr. AF *cueristre,* fr. ML *chorista,* fr. L *chorus*] (14c) **1 :** a singer in a choir; *specif* **:** CHOIRBOY **2 :** the leader of a church choir

cho·ri·zo \chə-ˈrē-(ˌ)zō, -(ˌ)sō\ *n, pl* **-zos** [Sp] (1802) **:** a pork sausage highly seasoned esp. with chili powder and garlic

C horizon *n* (1935) **:** the soil layer lying beneath the B horizon and consisting essentially of more or less weathered parent rock

cho·rog·ra·phy \kə-ˈrä-grə-fē\ *n* [L *chorographia,* fr. Gk *chōrographia,* fr. *chōros* place + *-graphia* -graphy] (1559) **1 :** the art of describing or mapping a region or district **2 :** a description or map of a region; *also* **:** the physical conformation and features of such a region — **cho·rog·ra·pher** \-grə-fər\ *n* — **cho·ro·graph·ic** \ˌkȯr-ə-ˈgra-fik, ˌkär-\ *adj*

cho·roid \ˈkȯr-ˌȯid\ *also* **cho·ri·oid** \ˈkȯr-ē-ˌȯid\ *n* [NL *choroides* resembling the chorion, fr. Gk *chorioeidēs,* fr. *chorion* chorion] (1683) **:** a vascular membrane containing large branched pigmented cells that lies between the retina and the sclera of the vertebrate eye — called also *choroid coat;* see EYE illustration — **choroid** *or* **cho·roi·dal** \kə-ˈrȯi-dᵊl\ *adj*

chor·ten \ˈchȯr-ˌten\ *n* [Tibetan *mchod rten,* lit., offering holder] (1891) **:** a Lamaist shrine or monument

chor·tle \ˈchȯr-tᵊl\ *vb* **chor·tled; chor·tling** \ˈchȯrt-liŋ, ˈchȯr-tᵊl-iŋ\ [prob. blend of *chuckle* and *snort*] *vi* (1872) **1 :** to sing or chant exultantly ⟨he *chortled* in his joy —Lewis Carroll⟩ **2 :** to laugh or chuckle esp. in satisfaction or exultation ~ *vt* **:** to say or sing with a chortling intonation — **chortle** *n* — **chor·tler** \ˈchȯrt-lər, ˈchȯr-tᵊl-ər\ *n*

[1]**cho·rus** \ˈkȯr-əs\ *n* [L, ring dance, chorus, fr. Gk *choros*] (1567) **1 a :** a company of singers and dancers in Athenian drama participating in or commenting on the action; *also* **:** a similar company in later plays **b :** a character in Elizabethan drama who speaks the prologue and epilogue and comments on the action **c :** an organized company of singers who sing in concert **:** CHOIR; *esp* **:** a body of singers who sing the choral parts of a work (as in opera) **d :** a group of dancers and singers supporting the featured players in a musical comedy or revue **2 a :** a part of a song or hymn recurring at intervals **b :** the part of a drama sung or spoken by the chorus **c :** a composition to be sung by a number of voices in concert **d :** the main part of a popular song; *also* **:** a jazz variation on a melodic theme **3 a :** something performed, sung, or uttered simultaneously or unanimously by a number of persons or animals ⟨a ~ of boos⟩ ⟨that eternal ~ of: "Are we there yet?" from the back seat —Sheila More⟩ **b :** sounds so uttered ⟨visitors are taken to the woods by car to hear the mournful ~*es* of howling wolves —Bob Gaines⟩ — **in chorus :** in unison ⟨answering *in chorus*⟩

[2]**chorus** *vt* (1826) **:** to sing or utter in chorus

chorus boy *n* (1943) **:** a young man who sings or dances in the chorus of a theatrical production (as a musical or revue)

chorus girl *n* (1894) **:** a young woman who sings or dances in the chorus of a theatrical production (as a musical or revue)

[1]**chose** *past of* CHOOSE

[2]**chose** \ˈshōz\ *n* [F, fr. L *causa* cause, reason] (1670) **:** a piece of personal property **:** THING

[1]**cho·sen** \ˈchō-zᵊn\ *n, pl* **chosen** (13c) **:** one who is the object of choice or of divine favor **:** an elect person

[2]**chosen** *adj* [ME, fr. pp. of *chosen* to choose] (14c) **1 :** ELECT **2 :** selected or marked for favor or special privilege ⟨a ~ few⟩

Chou \ˈjō\ *n* [Chin (Beijing) *Zhōu*] (1771) **:** a Chinese dynasty traditionally dated 1122 to about 256 B.C. and marked by the development of the philosophical schools of Confucius, Mencius, Lao-tzu, and Mo Ti

chou·croute \shü-ˈkrüt\ *n* [F, modif. of G *Sauerkraut*] (1849) **1 :** SAUERKRAUT **2 :** sauerkraut cooked and served with meat — called also *choucroute gar·nie* \-gär-ˈnē\

chough \ˈchəf\ *n* [ME] (13c) **:** either of two Old World birds (*Pyrrhocorax pyrrhocorax* and *P. graculus*) that are related to the crows and have red legs and glossy blue-black plumage

[1]**chouse** \ˈchau̇s\ *vt* **choused; chous·ing** [perh. fr. Turk *çavuş* doorkeeper, messenger] (ca. 1659) **:** CHEAT, TRICK

[2]**chouse** *vt* **choused; chous·ing** [origin unknown] (1904) *West* **:** to drive or herd roughly

[1]**chow** \ˈchau̇\ *n* [short for *chowchow*] (1856) **:** FOOD, VICTUALS

[2]**chow** *vi* (1917) **:** EAT — often used with *down* ⟨~*ing* down on pizza⟩

[3]**chow** *n* [by shortening] (1889) **:** CHOW CHOW

chow·chow \ˈchau̇-ˌchau̇\ *n* [Chin Pidgin E *chowchow* food] (1850) **1 :** a Chinese preserve of ginger, fruits, and peels in heavy syrup **2 :** a relish of chopped mixed pickles in mustard sauce

chow chow \ˈchau̇-ˌchau̇\ *n, often cap both Cs* [perh. fr. *chow-chow* Chinese person, fr. Chin Pidgin E *chowchow* food] (1886) **:** any of a breed of heavy-coated sturdy muscular dogs of Chinese origin having a broad head and muzzle, a distinctive blue-black tongue and black-lined mouth, and either a long dense coat with a full ruff or a short smooth coat — called also *chow*

[1]**chow·der** \ˈchau̇-dər\ *vt* (1732) **:** to make chowder of

[2]**chowder** *n* [F *chaudière* kettle, contents of a kettle, fr. LL *caldaria* — more at CAULDRON] (1751) **:** a soup or stew of seafood (as clams or

fish) usu. made with milk or tomatoes, salt pork, onions, and other vegetables (as potatoes); *also* : a soup resembling chowder ⟨corn ~⟩
chow·der·head \-ˌhed\ *n* [alter. of dial. *jolterhead* blockhead] (1833) : DOLT, BLOCKHEAD — **chow·der·head·ed** \ˈchau̇-dər-ˌhe-dəd\ *adj*
chow·hound \ˈchau̇-ˌhau̇nd\ *n* (1917) : one fond of eating
chow line *n* (1917) : a line of people waiting to be served food
chow mein \ˈchau̇-ˈmān\ *n* [Chin (Guangdong) *cháau-mihn* fried noodles] (1898) : a seasoned stew of shredded or diced meat, mushrooms, and vegetables that is usu. served with fried noodles
chres·tom·a·thy \kre-ˈstä-mə-thē\ *n, pl* **-thies** [NL *chrestomathia,* fr. Gk *chrēstomatheia,* fr. *chrēstos* useful + *manthanein* to learn — more at MATHEMATICAL] (1832) **1 :** a selection of passages used to help learn a language **2 :** a volume of selected passages or stories of an author
chrism \ˈkri-zəm\ *n* [ME *crisme,* fr. OE *crisma,* fr. LL *chrisma,* fr. Gk, ointment, fr. *chriein* to anoint] (bef. 12c) : consecrated oil used in Greek and Latin churches esp. in baptism, chrismation, confirmation, and ordination
chris·ma·tion \kriz-ˈmā-shən\ *n* [ML *chrismation-, chrismatio* anointment with chrism, fr. LL *chrismare* to anoint with chrism, fr. *chrisma*] (1642) : a confirmatory sacrament of the Eastern Orthodox Church in which a baptized member is anointed with chrism
chris·mon \ˈkriz-ˌmän\ *n, pl* **chris·ma** \-mə\ *or* **chrismons** [ML, fr. L *Chris*tus Christ + LL *mon*ogramma monogram] (1872) : CHI-RHO
chris·om \ˈkri-zəm\ *n* [ME *crisom,* short for *crisom cloth,* fr. *crisom* chrism + *cloth*] (13c) : a white cloth or robe put on a person at baptism as a symbol of innocence
chrisom child *n* (1593) : a child that dies in its first month
Christ \ˈkrīst\ *n* [ME *Crist,* fr. OE, fr. L *Christus,* fr. Gk *Christos,* lit., anointed, fr. *chriein*] (bef. 12c) **1 :** MESSIAH **2 :** JESUS **3 :** an ideal type of humanity **4** *Christian Science* : the ideal truth that comes as a divine manifestation of God to destroy incarnate error — **Christ·like** \-ˌlīk\ *adj* — **Christ·ly** \-lē\ *adj*
chris·ten \ˈkri-sᵊn\ *vt* **chris·tened; chris·ten·ing** \ˈkris-niŋ, ˈkri-sə-niŋ\ [ME *cristnen,* fr. OE *cristnian,* fr. *cristen* Christian, fr. L *christianus*] (bef. 12c) **1 a :** BAPTIZE 1 **b :** to name at baptism **2 :** to name or dedicate (as a ship) by a ceremony suggestive of baptism **3 :** NAME 1 **4 :** to use for the first time
Chris·ten·dom \ˈkri-sᵊn-dəm\ *n* [ME *cristendom,* fr. OE *cristendōm,* fr. *cristen*] (bef. 12c) **1 :** CHRISTIANITY 1 **2 :** the part of the world in which Christianity prevails
chris·ten·ing *n* (14c) : the ceremony of baptizing and naming a child
1**Chris·tian** \ˈkris-chən, ˈkrish-\ *n* [L *christianus,* adj. & n., fr. Gk *christianos,* fr. *Christos*] (1526) **1 a :** one who professes belief in the teachings of Jesus Christ **b** (1) : DISCIPLE 2 (2) : a member of one of the Churches of Christ separating from the Disciples of Christ in 1906 (3) : a member of the Christian denomination having part in the union of the United Church of Christ concluded in 1961 **2 :** the hero in Bunyan's *Pilgrim's Progress*
2**Christian** *adj* (1547) **1 a :** of or relating to Christianity ⟨~ scriptures⟩ **b :** based on or conforming with Christianity ⟨~ ethics⟩ **2 a :** of, relating to, or being a Christian ⟨~ responsibilities⟩ **b :** professing Christianity ⟨a ~ affirmation⟩ ⟨a ~ country⟩ **3 :** commendably decent or generous ⟨has a very ~ concern for others⟩ — **Chris·tian·ly** *adj or adv*
Christian Brother *n* (1883) : a member of the Roman Catholic institute of Brothers of the Christian Schools founded by St. John Baptist de la Salle in France in 1684 and dedicated to education
Christian era *n* (1657) : the period dating from the birth of Christ
chris·ti·ania \ˌkris-chē-ˈa-nē-ə, ˌkrish-, ˌkris-tē-, -ˈä-nē-ə\ *n* [*Christiania,* former name of Oslo, Norway] (1905) : CHRISTIE
Chris·tian·i·ty \ˌkris-chē-ˈa-nə-tē, ˌkrish-, -ˈcha-nə-, ˌkris-tē-ˈa-\ *n* (14c) **1 :** the religion derived from Jesus Christ, based on the Bible as sacred scripture, and professed by Eastern, Roman Catholic, and Protestant bodies **2 :** conformity to the Christian religion **3 :** the practice of Christianity
Chris·tian·ize \ˈkris-chə-ˌnīz, ˈkrish-\ *vt* **-ized; -iz·ing** (1593) : to make Christian — **Chris·tian·i·za·tion** \ˌkris-chə-nə-ˈzā-shən, ˌkrish-\ *n*
Christian name *n* (1549) : GIVEN NAME
Christian Science *n* (ca. 1867) : a religion founded by Mary Baker Eddy in 1866 that was organized under the official name of the Church of Christ, Scientist, that derives its teachings from the Scriptures as understood by its adherents, and that includes a practice of spiritual healing — **Christian Scientist** *n*
chris·tie *or* **chris·ty** \ˈkris-tē\ *n, pl* **christies** [by shortening & alter. fr. *christiania*] (1925) : a skiing turn used for altering the direction of hill descent or for stopping and executed usu. at high speed by shifting the body weight forward and skidding into a turn with parallel skis
Christ·mas \ˈkris-məs\ *n, often attrib* [ME *Christemasse,* fr. OE *Cristes mæsse,* lit., Christ's mass] (bef. 12c) **1 :** a Christian feast on December 25 or among some Eastern Orthodox Christians on January 7 that commemorates the birth of Christ and is usu. observed as a legal holiday **2 :** CHRISTMASTIDE — **Christ·mas·sy** *or* **Christ·masy** \-mə-sē\ *adj*
Christmas cactus *n* [fr. its annual blooming around Christmastime] (ca. 1900) : a branching Brazilian cactus (*Schlumbergera bridgesii* syn. *S. buckleyi*) having flat jointed stems with scalloped margins and showy usu. red, pink, white, violet, or yellow flowers; *also* : a related cactus (*Schlumbergera truncata* syn. *Zygocactus truncatus*) or a hybrid of this and the Christmas cactus
Christmas card *n* (1883) : a greeting card sent at Christmas
Christmas club *n* (ca. 1925) : a savings account in which regular deposits are made year-round to provide money for Christmas shopping
Christmas fern *n* (1878) : a No. American evergreen fern (*Polystichum acrostichoides*)
Christmas pudding *n* (1797) : PLUM PUDDING
Christmas rose *n* (1688) : a European evergreen herb (*Helleborus niger*) of the buttercup family that has usu. white flowers produced in winter
Christ·mas·tide \ˈkris-məs-ˌtīd\ *n* (1626) : the festival season from Christmas Eve till after New Year's Day or esp. in England till Epiphany
Christ·mas·time \-ˌtīm\ *n* (1607) : the Christmas season
Christmas tree *n* (1835) **1 :** a usu. evergreen tree decorated at Christmas **2 :** an oil-well control device consisting of an assembly of fittings placed at the top of the well
Chris·to·cen·tric \ˌkris-tə-ˈsen-trik, ˌkrīs-\ *adj* [Gk *Christos* Christ + E *-centric*] (1873) : centering theologically on Christ
Chris·to·gram \ˈkris-tə-ˌgram, ˈkrīs-\ *n* [Gk *Christos* + E *-gram*] (1900) : a graphic symbol of Christ; *esp* : CHI-RHO
Chris·tol·o·gy \kris-ˈtä-lə-jē, krīs-\ *n, pl* **-gies** [Gk *Christos* + E *-logy*] (1673) : theological interpretation of the person and work of Christ — **Chris·to·log·i·cal** \ˌkris-tə-ˈlä-ji-kəl, ˈkrīs-\ *adj*
chris·to·phene *or* **chris·to·phine** \ˈkris-tə-ˌfēn\ *n* [AmerF] (1887) : CHAYOTE
Christ's–thorn \ˈkrīs(ts)-ˈthȯrn\ *or* **Christ–thorn** \ˈkrīs(t)-\ *n* (1562) : any of several prickly or thorny shrubs (as the shrub *Paliurus spina-christi* or the jujube *Ziziphus spina-christi*)
chrom- *or* **chromo-** *comb form* [ISV, fr. Gk *chrōma* color] **1 :** chromium ⟨*chrom*ize⟩ **2 a :** color : colored ⟨*chromo*lithograph⟩ **b :** pigment ⟨*chromo*gen⟩
chro·ma \ˈkrō-mə\ *n* [Gk *chrōma*] (ca. 1889) **1 :** SATURATION 4a **2 :** a quality of color combining hue and saturation
chro·maf·fin \ˈkrō-mə-fən\ *adj* [ISV *chrom-* + L *affinis* bordering on, related — more at AFFINITY] (1903) : staining deeply with chromium salts ⟨~ cells of the adrenal medulla⟩
chro·ma–key \ˈkrō-mə-ˌkē\ *n* (1974) : a photographic compositing technique based on the separation of colors in the original images; *esp* : BLUE SCREEN
chromat- *or* **chromato-** *comb form* [Gk *chrōmat-, chrōma*] **1 :** color ⟨*chromat*id⟩ **2 :** chromatin ⟨*chromato*lysis⟩
chro·mate \ˈkrō-ˌmāt\ *n* [F, fr. Gk *chrōma*] (1815) : a salt of chromic acid
1**chro·mat·ic** \krō-ˈma-tik\ *n* (1708) : ACCIDENTAL 2
2**chromatic** *adj* [Gk *chrōmatikos,* fr. *chrōmat-, chrōma* skin, color, modified tone; akin to Gk *chrōs* color] (1630) **1 a :** of or relating to color or color phenomena or sensations **b :** highly colored **2 :** of or relating to chroma **3 a :** of, relating to, or giving all the tones of the chromatic scale **b :** characterized by frequent use of accidentals — **chro·mat·i·cal·ly** \-ti-k(ə-)lē\ *adv* — **chro·mat·i·cism** \-ˈma-tə-ˌsi-zəm\ *n*
chromatic aberration *n* (1831) : aberration caused by the differences in refraction of the colored rays of the spectrum
chro·ma·tic·i·ty \ˌkrō-mə-ˈti-sə-tē\ *n* (1922) : the quality of color characterized by its dominant or complementary wavelength and purity taken together
chro·mat·ics \krō-ˈma-tiks\ *n pl but sing in constr* (ca. 1790) : the branch of colorimetry that deals with hue and saturation
chromatic scale *n* (ca. 1789) : a musical scale consisting entirely of half steps
chro·ma·tid \ˈkrō-mə-təd\ *n* (1900) : one of the usu. paired and parallel strands of a duplicated chromosome joined by a single centromere
chro·ma·tin \ˈkrō-mə-tən\ *n* (1882) : a complex of nucleic acid and basic proteins (as histone) in eukaryotic cells that is usu. dispersed in the interphase nucleus and condensed into chromosomes in mitosis and meiosis — see CELL illustration; compare EUCHROMATIN, HETEROCHROMATIN — **chro·ma·tin·ic** \ˌkrō-mə-ˈti-nik\ *adj*
chro·mato·gram \krō-ˈma-tə-ˌgram, krə-\ *n* (1922) **1 :** the pattern formed on an adsorbent medium by the layers of components separated by chromatography **2 :** a time-based graphic record (as of concentration of eluted materials) of a chromatographic separation
chro·mato·graph \krō-ˈma-tə-ˌgraf, krə-\ *n* (1946) : an instrument for performing chromatographic separations and producing chromatograms — **chromatograph** *vb* — **chro·ma·tog·ra·pher** \ˌkrō-mə-ˈtä-grə-fər\ *n*
chro·ma·tog·ra·phy \ˌkrō-mə-ˈtä-grə-fē\ *n* (1936) : a process in which a chemical mixture carried by a liquid or gas is separated into components as a result of differential distribution of the solutes as they flow around or over a stationary liquid or solid phase — **chro·mato·graph·ic** \krō-ˌma-tə-ˈgra-fik, krə-\ *adj* — **chro·mato·graph·i·cal·ly** \-fi-k(ə-)lē\ *adv*
chro·ma·tol·y·sis \ˌkrō-mə-ˈtä-lə-səs\ *n* [NL] (1901) : the dissolution and breaking up of chromophil material (as chromatin) of a cell and esp. a nerve cell — **chro·mato·lyt·ic** \krō-ˌma-tə-ˈli-tik, krə-\ *adj*
chro·mato·phore \krō-ˈma-tə-ˌfȯr, krə-\ *n* [ISV] (ca. 1859) **1 :** a pigment-bearing cell; *esp* : one of the cells of an animal integument capable of causing integumentary color changes by expanding or contracting **2 :** the organelle of photosynthesis in photosynthetic bacteria (as the cyanobacteria); *broadly* : CHROMOPLAST, CHLOROPLAST
1**chrome** \ˈkrōm\ *n* [F, fr. Gk *chrōma*] (1800) **1 a :** CHROMIUM **b :** a chromium pigment **2 :** something plated with an alloy of chromium
2**chrome** *vt* **chromed; chrom·ing** (1876) **1 :** to treat with a compound of chromium (as in dyeing) **2 :** CHROMIZE
-chrome \ˌkrōm\ *n comb form or adj comb form* [ML *-chromat-, -chroma* colored thing, fr. Gk *chrōmat-, chrōma*] **1 :** colored thing ⟨helio*chrome*⟩ **2 :** coloring matter ⟨uro*chrome*⟩
chrome green *n* (ca. 1859) : any of various brilliant green pigments containing or consisting of chromium compounds
chrome yellow *n* (1819) : a yellow pigment consisting essentially of neutral lead chromate $PbCrO_4$
chro·mic \ˈkrō-mik\ *adj* (1800) : of, relating to, or derived from chromium esp. with a valence of three
chromic acid *n* (1800) : an acid H_2CrO_4 analogous to sulfuric acid but known only in solution and esp. in the form of its salts
chro·mi·nance \ˈkrō-mə-nən(t)s\ *n* [*chrom-* + lumi*nance*] (1952) : the difference between a color and a chosen reference color of the same luminous intensity in color television
chro·mite \ˈkrō-ˌmīt\ *n* [G *Chromit,* fr. *chrom-*] (1799) **1 :** a black mineral that consists of an oxide of iron and chromium and is the only chromium ore **2 :** an oxide of divalent chromium
chro·mi·um \ˈkrō-mē-əm\ *n* [NL, fr. F *chrome*] (1807) : a blue-white metallic element found naturally only in combination and used esp. in alloys and in electroplating — see ELEMENT table
chromium pi·co·li·nate \-pi-ˈkä-lə-ˌnāt, -ˈpi-k(ə)li-\ *n* (1989) : a biologically active chromium salt $C_{18}H_{12}CrN_3O_6$ used as a dietary supplement
chro·mize \ˈkrō-ˌmīz\ *vt* **chro·mized; chro·miz·ing** (1939) : to treat (metal) with chromium in order to form a protective surface alloy
chro·mo \ˈkrō-(ˌ)mō\ *n, pl* **chromos** (1868) : CHROMOLITHOGRAPH
chro·mo·cen·ter \ˈkrō-mə-ˌsen-tər\ *n* (1926) : a densely staining aggregation of heterochromatic regions in the nucleus of some cells

chro·mo·dy·nam·ics \ˌkrō-mə-dī-ˈna-miks\ *n pl but sing in constr* (1976) : QUANTUM CHROMODYNAMICS
chro·mo·gen \ˈkrō-mə-jən\ *n* [ISV] (1858) **1** : a precursor of a biochemical pigment **2** : a pigment-producing microorganism
chro·mo·gen·ic \ˌkrō-mə-ˈje-nik\ *adj* (1859) **1** : of or relating to a chromogen **2** : being a process of photographic film development in which silver halides activate precursors of chemical dyes that form the final image while the silver is removed; *also* : being a film developed by this process
chro·mo·litho·graph \ˌkrō-mə-ˈli-thə-ˌgraf\ *n* (1850) : a picture printed in colors from a series of lithographic stones or plates — **chromolithograph** *vt* — **chro·mo·litho·graph·ic** \-ˌli-thə-ˈgra-fik\ *adj* — **chro·mo·li·thog·raph·er** \-li-ˈthä-grə-fər\ *n* — **chro·mo·li·thog·ra·phy** \-grə-fē\ *n*
chro·mo·mere \ˈkrō-mə-ˌmir\ *n* [ISV] (1896) : one of the small bead-shaped and heavily staining masses of coiled chromatin that are linearly arranged along the chromosome — **chro·mo·mer·ic** \ˌkrō-mə-ˈmer-ik, -ˈmir-\ *adj*
chro·mo·ne·ma \ˌkrō-mə-ˈnē-mə\ *n, pl* **-ne·ma·ta** \-ˈnē-mə-tə\ [NL, fr. *chrom-* + Gk *nēmat-, nēma* thread — more at NEMAT-] (ca. 1925) : the coiled filamentous core of a chromatid — **chro·mo·ne·mat·ic** \-ni-ˈma-tik\ *adj*
chro·mo·phil \ˈkrō-mə-ˌfil\ *adj* [ISV] (1899) : staining readily with dyes
chro·mo·phobe \-ˌfōb\ *adj* (ca. 1909) : resisting staining with dyes
chro·mo·phore \ˈkrō-mə-ˌfȯr\ *n* [ISV] (1879) : a chemical group (as an azo group) that absorbs light at a specific frequency and so imparts color to a molecule; *also* : a colored chemical compound — **chro·mo·phor·ic** \ˌkrō-mə-ˈfȯr-ik, -ˈfär-\ *adj*
chro·mo·plast \ˈkrō-mə-ˌplast\ *n* [ISV] (1885) : a colored plastid usu. containing red or yellow pigment (as carotene)
chro·mo·pro·tein \ˌkrō-mə-ˈprō-ˌtēn, -ˈprō-tē-ən\ *n* (1924) : any of various proteins (as hemoglobins, carotenoids, or flavoproteins) having a pigment as a prosthetic group
chro·mo·some \ˈkrō-mə-ˌsōm, -ˌzōm\ *n* [ISV] (1889) : any of the rod-shaped or threadlike DNA-containing structures of cellular organisms that are located in the nucleus of eukaryotes, are usu. ring-shaped in prokaryotes (as bacteria), and contain all or most of the genes of the organism; *also* : the genetic material of a virus — compare CHROMATIN — **chro·mo·som·al** \ˌkrō-mə-ˈsō-məl, -ˈzō-\ *adj* — **chro·mo·som·al·ly** \-mə-lē\ *adv*
chromosome number *n* (1910) : the usu. constant number of chromosomes characteristic of a particular kind of animal or plant
chro·mo·sphere \ˈkrō-mə-ˌsfir\ *n* (1868) : the region of the atmosphere of a star (as the sun) between the star's photosphere and its corona — **chro·mo·spher·ic** \ˌkrō-mə-ˈsfir-ik, -ˈsfer-\ *adj*
chro·mous \ˈkrō-məs\ *adj* (1830) : of, relating to, or derived from chromium esp. with a valence of two
chron *abbr* **1** chronicle **2** chronological; chronology
Chron *abbr* Chronicles
chron- *or* **chrono-** *comb form* [Gk, fr. *chronos*] : time ⟨*chrono*gram⟩
chron·ax·ie *also* **chron·axy** \ˈkrō-ˌnak-sē, ˈkrä-\ *n* [F *chronaxie,* fr. *chron-* + Gk *axia* value, fr. *axios* worthy — more at AXIOM] (1922) : the minimum time required for excitation of a structure (as a neuron) by a constant electric current of twice the threshold voltage
chron·ic \ˈkrä-nik\ *adj* [F *chronique,* fr. Gk *chronikos* of time, fr. *chronos*] (1601) **1 a** : marked by long duration or frequent recurrence : not acute ⟨~ indigestion⟩ ⟨~ experiments⟩ **b** : suffering from a chronic disease ⟨the special needs of ~ patients⟩ **2 a** : always present or encountered; *esp* : constantly vexing, weakening, or troubling ⟨~ petty warfare⟩ **b** : being such habitually ⟨a ~ grumbler⟩ ***syn*** see INVETERATE — **chronic** *n* — **chron·i·cal·ly** \-ni-k(ə-)lē\ *adv* — **chro·nic·i·ty** \krä-ˈni-sə-tē, krō-\ *n*
chronic fatigue syndrome *n* (1947) : a disorder of unknown cause that is characterized by persistent profound fatigue usu. accompanied by other symptoms (as headache and tender lymph nodes) unrelated to any preexisting medical condition — abbr. *CFS*
1**chron·i·cle** \ˈkrä-ni-kəl\ *n* [ME *cronicle,* fr. AF, alter. of *chronike,* fr. L *chronica,* fr. Gk *chronika,* fr. neut. pl. of *chronikos*] (14c) **1** : a historical account of events arranged in order of time usu. without analysis or interpretation ⟨a ~ of the Civil War⟩ **2** : NARRATIVE 1
2**chronicle** *vt* **-cled; -cling** \-k(ə-)liŋ\ (15c) : to present a record of in or as if in a chronicle ⟨~ Victorian society⟩ ⟨~ the doings of the rich and famous⟩ — **chron·i·cler** \-k(ə-)lər\ *n*
chronicle play *n* (1863) : a play with a theme from history consisting usu. of rather loosely connected episodes chronologically arranged
Chron·i·cles \ˈkrä-ni-kəlz\ *n pl but sing in constr* (1535) : either of two historical books of canonical Jewish and Christian Scripture — called also *Paralipomenon*; see BIBLE table
chronic obstructive pulmonary disease *n* (1967) : pulmonary disease (as emphysema or chronic bronchitis) that is characterized by chronic typically irreversible airway obstruction resulting in a slowed rate of exhalation — abbr. *COPD*
chro·no·bi·ol·o·gy \ˌkrä-nō-bī-ˈä-lə-jē, ˌkrō-\ *n* (1969) : the study of biological rhythms — **chro·no·bi·o·log·ic** \-bī-ə-ˈlä-jik\ *or* **chro·no·bi·o·log·i·cal** \-ji-kəl\ *adj* — **chro·no·bi·ol·o·gist** \-bī-ˈä-lə-jist\ *n*
chro·no·gram \ˈkrä-nə-ˌgram, ˈkrō-\ *n* (1621) : an inscription, sentence, or phrase in which certain letters express a date or epoch
chro·no·graph \ˈkrä-nə-ˌgraf, ˈkrō-\ *n* (1851) : an instrument for measuring and recording time intervals: as **a** : an instrument having a revolving drum on which a stylus makes marks **b** : STOPWATCH; *also* : a watch incorporating the functions of a stopwatch **c** : an instrument for measuring the time of flight of projectiles — **chro·no·graph·ic** \ˌkrä-nə-ˈgra-fik, ˌkrō-\ *adj* — **chro·nog·ra·phy** \krə-ˈnä-grə-fē\ *n*
chro·nol·o·ger \krə-ˈnä-lə-jər\ *n* (ca. 1572) : CHRONOLOGIST
chro·no·log·i·cal \ˌkrä-nə-ˈlä-ji-kəl, ˌkrō-\ *also* **chro·no·log·ic** \-jik\ *adj* (1614) : of, relating to, or arranged in or according to the order of time ⟨~ tables of American history⟩; *also* : reckoned in units of time ⟨~ age⟩ — **chro·no·log·i·cal·ly** \-ji-k(ə-)lē\ *adv*
chro·nol·o·gist \krə-ˈnä-lə-jist\ *n* (1611) : an expert in chronology
chro·nol·o·gy \-jē\ *n, pl* **-gies** [NL *chronologia,* fr. *chron-* + *-logia* -logy] (1585) **1** : the science that deals with measuring time by regular divisions and that assigns to events their proper dates **2** : a chronological table, list, or account **3** : an arrangement (as of events) in order of occurrence ⟨reconstruct the ~ of the trip⟩
chro·nom·e·ter \krə-ˈnä-mə-tər\ *n* (ca. 1735) : TIMEPIECE; *esp* : one designed to keep time with great accuracy
chro·no·met·ric \ˌkrä-nə-ˈme-trik, ˌkrō-\ *also* **chro·no·met·ri·cal** \-tri-kəl\ *adj* (1830) : of or relating to a chronometer or chronometry — **chro·no·met·ri·cal·ly** \-tri-k(ə-)lē\ *adv*
chro·nom·e·try \krə-ˈnä-mə-trē\ *n* (1833) : the measuring of time
chro·no·ther·a·py \ˌkrä-nō-ˈther-ə-pē, ˌkrō-\ *n* (1973) : treatment of a sleep disorder (as insomnia) by changing sleeping and waking times in an attempt to reset the patient's biological clock
chrys- *or* **chryso-** *comb form* [Gk, fr. *chrysos*] : gold : yellow ⟨*chrysa*robin⟩
chrys·a·lid \ˈkri-sə-ləd\ *n* (1777) : CHRYSALIS — **chrysalid** *adj*
chrys·a·lis \ˈkri-sə-ləs\ *n, pl* **chry·sal·i·des** \kri-ˈsa-lə-ˌdēz\ *or* **chrys·a·lis·es** [L *chrysallid-, chrysallis* gold-colored pupa of butterflies, fr. Gk, fr. *chrysos* gold, of Sem origin; akin to Heb *ḥārūṣ* gold] (1601) **1 a** : a pupa of a butterfly; *broadly* : an insect pupa **b** : the hardened outer protective layer of a pupa **2** : a protecting covering : a sheltered state or stage of being or growth ⟨a budding writer could not emerge from his ~ too soon —William Du Bois⟩

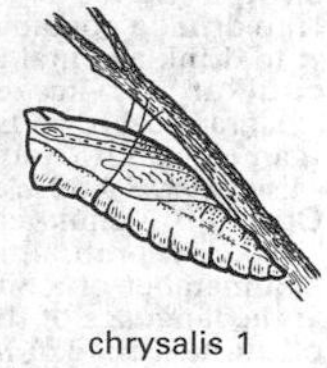
chrysalis 1

chry·san·the·mum \kri-ˈsan(t)-thə-məm *also* -ˈzan(t)-\ *n* [L, fr. Gk *chrysanthemon,* fr. *chrys-* + *anthemon* flower; akin to Gk *anthos* flower] (1548) **1** : any of various composite plants (genus *Chrysanthemum*) including weeds, ornamentals grown for their brightly colored often double flower heads, and others important as sources of medicinals and insecticides **2** : a flower head of an ornamental chrysanthemum
chrys·a·ro·bin \ˌkri-sə-ˈrō-bən\ *n* [*chrys-* + araroba, powder found in the wood of a Brazilian tree (*Andira araroba*) + 1*-in*] (1887) : a powder derived from the wood of a tropical tree used to treat skin diseases
Chry·se·is \krī-ˈsē-əs\ *n* [L, fr. Gk *Chryseïs*] (1567) : a daughter of a priest of Apollo in the *Iliad* narrative taken at Troy by Agamemnon but later restored to her father
chryso·ber·yl \ˈkri-sə-ˌber-əl\ *n* [L *chrysoberyllus,* fr. Gk *chrysobēryllos,* fr. *chrys-* + *bēryllos* beryl] (1661) **1** *obs* : a yellowish beryl **2** : a hard usu. yellow or green mineral consisting of beryllium aluminum oxide and sometimes used as a gem
chrys·o·lite \ˈkri-sə-ˌlīt\ *n* [ME *crisolite,* fr. AF, fr. L *chrysolithos,* fr. Gk, fr. *chrys-* + *-lithos* -lite] (13c) : OLIVINE
chrys·o·me·lid \ˌkri-sə-ˈme-ləd, -ˈmē-\ *n* [ultim. fr. Gk *chrysomēlolonthē* golden cockchafer] (ca. 1904) : any of a large family (Chrysomelidae) of small, usu. oval and smooth, shining, and brightly colored beetles (as the Colorado potato beetle) — **chrysomelid** *adj*
chryso·phyte \ˈkri-sə-ˌfīt\ *n* [ultim. fr. Gk *chrysos* + *phyton* plant — more at PHYT-] (1959) : GOLDEN-BROWN ALGA
chrys·o·prase \ˈkri-sə-ˌprāz\ *n* [alter. of ME *crisopace,* fr. AF, fr. L *chrysoprasus,* fr. Gk *chrysoprasos,* fr. *chrys-* + *prason* leek; akin to L *porrum* leek] (15c) : an apple-green chalcedony valued as a gem
chrys·o·tile \-ˌtī(-ə)l\ *n* [G *Chrysotil,* fr. *chrys-* + *-til* fiber, fr. Gk *tillein* to pluck] (1850) : a mineral consisting of a fibrous silky variety of serpentine and constituting a common form and principal source of asbestos
chthon·ic \ˈthä-nik\ *also* **chtho·ni·an** \ˈthō-nē-ən\ *adj* [Gk *chthon-, chthōn* earth — more at HUMBLE] (1882) : of or relating to the underworld : INFERNAL ⟨~ deities⟩
chub \ˈchəb\ *n, pl* **chub** *or* **chubs** [ME *chubbe*] (15c) **1** : any of numerous freshwater cyprinid fishes (as of the genera *Gila* and *Nocomis*) **2** : any of several marine or freshwater fishes that are not cyprinids
chub·bi·ly \ˈchə-bə-lē\ *adv* (1909) : in the manner of one that is chubby
chub·by \ˈchə-bē\ *adj* **chub·bi·er; -est** [*chub*] (1722) : PLUMP ⟨a ~ boy⟩ — **chub·bi·ness** \ˈchə-bē-nəs\ *n*
1**chuck** \ˈchək\ *vb* [ME *chukken,* of imit. origin] (14c) : CLUCK
2**chuck** *n* [perh. fr. *chuck* chicken] (1595) — used as an endearment
3**chuck** *vt* [origin unknown] (15c) **1** : PAT, TAP **2 a** : TOSS, THROW **b** : DISCARD ⟨~*ed* his old shirt⟩ ⟨~ it out with the trash⟩ **c** : DISMISS, OUST — used esp. with *out* ⟨was ~*ed* out of office⟩ **3** : GIVE UP ⟨~*ed* his job⟩
4**chuck** *n* (1611) **1** : a pat or nudge under the chin **2** : an abrupt movement or toss
5**chuck** *n* [E dial. *chuck* lump] (1723) **1** : a cut of beef that includes most of the neck, the parts about the shoulder blade, and those about the first three ribs — see BEEF illustration **2** *chiefly West* : FOOD **3** : an attachment for holding a workpiece or tool in a machine (as a drill or lathe)
chuck·hole \ˈchək-ˌhōl\ *n* [perh. fr. 3*chuck* + *hole*] (1836) : a hole or rut in a road : POTHOLE
chuck·le \ˈchə-kəl\ *vi* **chuck·led; chuck·ling** [prob. freq. of 1*chuck*] (ca. 1770) **1** : to laugh inwardly or quietly **2** : to make a continuous gentle sound resembling suppressed mirth ⟨the clear bright water *chuckled* over gravel —B. A. Williams⟩ — **chuckle** *n* — **chuck·le·some** \-səm\ *adj* — **chuck·ling·ly** \-liŋ-lē\ *adv*
chuck·le·head \ˈchə-kəl-ˌhed\ *n* [*chuckle* lumpish + *head*] (1748) : BLOCKHEAD — **chuck·le·head·ed** \-ˌhe-dəd\ *adj*
chuck wagon *n* [5*chuck*] (1887) **1** : a wagon carrying supplies and provisions for cooking (as on a ranch) **2** *usu* **chuck·wag·on** \ˈchək-ˌwa-gən\, *chiefly West* : an informal buffet — often used attributively ⟨a ~ dinner⟩
chuck·wal·la \ˈchək-ˌwä-lə\ *or* **chuck·a·wal·la** \ˈchə-kə-ˌwä-lə\ *n* [AmerSp *chacahuala,* fr. Cahuilla (Uto-Aztecan language of southeast California) *čáxwal*] (1893) : a large herbivorous lizard (*Sauromalus obesus*) of the iguana family of desert regions of the southwestern U.S.
chuck–will's–wid·ow \ˌchək-ˌwilz-ˈwi-(ˌ)dō\ *n* [imit.] (1791) : a nightjar (*Caprimulgus carolinensis*) of the southeastern U.S.
1**chuff** \ˈchəf\ *n* [ME *chuffe*] (15c) : BOOR, CHURL

[2]**chuff** *vi* [imit.] (1914) **:** to produce noisy exhaust or exhalations **:** proceed or operate with chuffs ⟨the ~*ing* and snorting of switch engines —Paul Gallico⟩
[3]**chuff** *n* (1915) **:** the sound of noisy exhaust or exhalations
chuffed \ˈchəft\ *adj* [E dial. *chuff* pleased, puffed with fat] (1957) *Brit* **:** quite pleased **:** DELIGHTED
[1]**chug** \ˈchəg\ *n* [imit.] (1866) **:** a dull explosive sound made by or as if by a laboring engine
[2]**chug** *vi* **chugged; chug·ging** (1848) **:** to move or go with or as if with chugs ⟨a locomotive *chugging* along⟩ ⟨wearily ~ through the routine⟩ — **chug·ger** *n*
[3]**chug** *vt* **chugged; chug·ging** (1958) **:** CHUGALUG
chug·a·lug \ˈchə-gə-ˌləg\ *vb* **-lugged; -lug·ging** [imit.] *vt* (ca. 1936) **:** to drink a container of (as beer) without pause; *also* **:** GUZZLE 1 ~ *vi* **:** to drink a container (as of beer) without pause
chu·kar \ˈchə-kər *also* chə-ˈkär\ *n* [Hindi *cakor* & Urdu *chakor*] (1814) **:** a grayish-brown Eurasian partridge (*Alectoris chukar*) introduced as a game bird into arid mountainous regions of the western U.S. — called also *chukar partridge*
Chuk·chi \ˈchu̇k-ˌchē\ *n, pl* **Chukchi** *or* **Chukchis** [Russ *chukcha* (pl. *chukchi*), prob. ultim. fr. Chukchi *čavčəv* reindeer breeder] (1780) **1 :** a member of a Siberian people inhabiting the Chukchi Peninsula **2 :** the language of the Chukchi people
chuk·ka \ˈchə-kə\ *n* [*chukka*, alter. of *chukker;* fr. a similar polo player's boot] (1948) **:** a usu. ankle-high leather boot with two or three pairs of eyelets or a buckle and strap
chuk·ker \ˈchə-kər\ *also* **chuk·ka** \ˈchə-kə\ *n* [Hindi *cakkar* & Urdu *chakkar* circular course, fr. Skt *cakra* wheel, circle — more at WHEEL] (1898) **:** a playing period of a polo game
[1]**chum** \ˈchəm\ *n* [perh. by shortening & alter. fr. *chamber fellow* roommate] (1684) **:** a close friend **:** PAL — **chum·ship** \-ˌship\ *n*
[2]**chum** *vi* **chummed; chum·ming** (1730) **1 :** to room together **2 a :** to be a close friend **b :** to show affable friendliness
[3]**chum** *n* [origin unknown] (1857) **:** animal or vegetable matter (as chopped fish or corn) thrown overboard to attract fish
[4]**chum** *vb* **chummed; chum·ming** *vt* (1857) **:** to attract with chum ~ *vi* **:** to throw chum overboard to attract fish
[5]**chum** *n* [Chinook Jargon *cəm* spotted, striped, fr. Lower Chinook *čə́m* variegated] (1902) **:** CHUM SALMON
Chu·mash \ˈchü-ˌmash\ *n, pl* **Chumash** [fr. *Tcú-mac,* name in a coastal Chumash language for the inhabitants of Santa Rosa Island] (1891) **1 :** a member of an American Indian people of southwestern California **2 :** the family of languages spoken by the Chumash people
chum·my \ˈchə-mē\ *adj* **chum·mi·er; -est** (1884) **:** quite friendly — **chum·mi·ly** \ˈchə-mə-lē\ *adv* — **chum·mi·ness** \ˈchə-mē-nəs\ *n*
chump \ˈchəmp\ *n* [perh. blend of *chunk* and *lump*] (1876) **:** FOOL, DUPE
chump change *n* (1967) **:** a relatively small or insignificant amount of money
chum salmon *n* [[5]*chum*] (1907) **:** a salmon (*Oncorhynchus keta*) of the northern Pacific — called also *chum*
[1]**chunk** \ˈchəŋk\ *n* [perh. alter. of *chuck* short piece of wood] (1691) **1 :** a short thick piece or lump (as of wood or coal) **2 :** a large noteworthy quantity or part ⟨bet a sizable ~ of money on the race⟩ **3 :** a strong thickset horse usu. smaller than a draft horse
[2]**chunk** *vb* [imit.] *vi* (1890) **:** to make a dull plunging or explosive sound ⟨the rhythmic ~*ing* of thrown quoits —John Updike⟩ ~ *vt* **:** to mishit (a golf ball or shot) by striking the ground behind the ball
chunky \ˈchəŋ-kē\ *adj* **chunk·i·er; -est** (1733) **1 a :** heavy, solid, and thick or bulky ⟨a ~ sweater⟩ ⟨~ bracelets⟩; *esp* **:** STOCKY ⟨an athlete with a ~ build⟩ **b :** PLUMP, CHUBBY **2 :** filled with chunks ⟨~ peanut butter⟩ — **chunk·i·ly** \-kə-lē\ *adv*
chun·ter \ˈchən-tər\ *vi* [prob. of imit. origin] (1599) *Brit* **:** to talk in a low inarticulate way **:** MUTTER
chup·pah *or* **hup·pah** *also* **chup·pa** \ˈk̲u̇-pə, -(ˌ)pä\ *n* [Yiddish & Heb; Yiddish *khupe,* fr. Heb *ḥuppāh*] (1876) **:** a canopy under which the bride and groom stand during a Jewish wedding ceremony
[1]**church** \ˈchərch\ *n* [ME *chirche,* fr. OE *cirice,* ultim. fr. LGk *kyriakon,* fr. Gk, neut. of *kyriakos* of the lord, fr. *kyrios* lord, master; akin to Skt *śūra* hero, warrior] (bef. 12c) **1 :** a building for public and esp. Christian worship **2 :** the clergy or officialdom of a religious body **3** *often cap* **:** a body or organization of religious believers: as **a :** the whole body of Christians **b :** DENOMINATION ⟨the Presbyterian ~⟩ **c :** CONGREGATION **4 :** a public divine worship ⟨goes to ~ every Sunday⟩ **5 :** the clerical profession ⟨considered the ~ as a possible career⟩
[2]**church** *adj* (bef. 12c) **1 :** of or relating to a church ⟨~ government⟩ **2** *chiefly Brit* **:** of or relating to the established church
[3]**church** *vt* (14c) **:** to bring to church to receive one of its rites
churched \ˈchərcht\ *adj* (14c) **:** affiliated with a church
church father *n, often cap C&F* (1842) **:** FATHER 4
church·go·er \ˈchərch-ˌgō-ər\ *n* (1687) **:** one who habitually attends church — **church·go·ing** \-ˌgō-iŋ, -ˌgȯ(-)iŋ\ *adj or n*
church·i·an·i·ty \ˌchər-chē-ˈa-nə-tē\ *n* [*church* + *-ianity* (as in *Christianity*)] (1837) **:** a usu. excessive or narrowly sectarian attachment to the practices and interests of a particular church
church·ing *n* (15c) **:** the administration or reception of a rite of the church; *specif* **:** a ceremony in some churches by which women after childbirth are received in the church with prayers, blessings, and thanksgiving
church key *n* (ca. 1953) **:** an implement with a triangular pointed head at one end for piercing the tops of cans and often with a rounded head at the other end for opening bottles
church·less \ˈchərch-ləs\ *adj* (1641) **:** not affiliated with a church
church·ly \ˈchərch-lē\ *adj* (bef. 12c) **1 :** of or relating to a church ⟨~ authority⟩ **2 :** suitable to or suggestive of a church ⟨a ~ setting⟩ **3 :** adhering to a church ⟨a ~ community⟩ **4 :** CHURCHY 1 — **church·li·ness** *n*
church·man \ˈchərch-mən\ *n* (14c) **1 :** CLERGYMAN **2 :** a member of a church
church·man·ship \-mən-ˌship\ *n* (ca. 1680) **:** the attitude, belief, or practice of a churchman
church mode *n* (ca. 1864) **:** one of eight scales prevalent in medieval music each utilizing a different pattern of intervals and beginning on a different tone
Church of England (1534) **:** the established episcopal church of England
church register *n* (1606) **:** a parish register of baptisms, marriages, and deaths
church school *n* (1862) **1 :** a school providing a general education but supported by a particular church in contrast to a public school or a nondenominational private school **2 :** an organization of officers, teachers, and pupils for purposes of moral and religious education under the supervision of a local church
Church Slavonic *n* (1853) **:** any of several Slavic literary and liturgical languages that continue Old Church Slavonic but vary regionally under influence of vernacular languages — called also *Church Slavic*
church·war·den \ˈchərch-ˌwȯr-dᵊn\ *n* (15c) **1 :** one of two lay parish officers in Anglican churches with responsibility esp. for parish property and alms **2 :** a long-stemmed clay pipe
church·wom·an \-ˌwu̇-mən\ *n* (1681) **:** a woman who is a member of a church
churchy \ˈchər-chē\ *adj* (1843) **1 :** marked by strict conformity or zealous adherence to the forms or beliefs of a church **2 :** of or suggestive of a church or church services
church·yard \ˈchərch-ˌyärd\ *n* (12c) **:** a yard that belongs to a church and is often used as a burial ground
churl \ˈchər(-ə)l\ *n* [ME, fr. OE *ceorl* man, ceorl; akin to ON *karl* man, husband] (bef. 12c) **1 :** CEORL **2 :** a medieval peasant **3 :** RUSTIC, COUNTRYMAN **4 a :** a rude ill-bred person **b :** a stingy morose person
churl·ish \ˈchər-lish\ *adj* (bef. 12c) **1 :** of, resembling, or characteristic of a churl **:** VULGAR **2 :** marked by a lack of civility or graciousness **:** SURLY **3 :** difficult to work with or deal with **:** INTRACTABLE ⟨~ soil⟩ ***syn*** see BOORISH — **churl·ish·ly** *adv* — **churl·ish·ness** *n*
[1]**churn** \ˈchərn\ *n* [ME *chyrne,* fr. OE *cyrin;* akin to ON *kjarni* churn] (bef. 12c) **:** a vessel for making butter in which milk or cream is agitated in order to separate the oily globules from the watery medium
[2]**churn** *vt* (15c) **1 :** to agitate (milk or cream) in a churn in order to make butter **2 a :** to stir or agitate violently ⟨an old stern-wheeler ~*ing* the muddy river⟩ **b :** to make (as foam) by so doing **3 :** to make (the account of a client) excessively active by frequent purchases and sales primarily in order to generate commissions ~ *vi* **1 :** to work a churn **2 a :** to produce, proceed with, or experience violent motion or agitation ⟨her stomach was ~*ing*⟩ ⟨~*ing* legs⟩ **b :** to proceed by or as if by means of rotating members (as wheels or propellers) ⟨boats ~*ing* across the harbor⟩
churn out *vt* (1876) **:** to produce mechanically or copiously **:** GRIND OUT ⟨the usual pap which has been *churned out* about this superstar —W. S. Murphy⟩
churr \ˈchər\ *vi* [imit.] (1555) **:** to make a vibrant or whirring noise like that made by some insects (as the cockchafer) or some birds (as the partridge) — **churr** *n*
chur·ri·gue·resque \ˌchu̇r-i-gə-ˈresk\ *adj, often cap* [Sp *churrigueresco,* fr. José *Churriguera* †1725 Span. architect] (1845) **:** of or relating to a Spanish baroque architectural style characterized by elaborate surface decoration or its Latin-American adaptation
chur·ro \ˈchu̇r-ō, ˈchü-rō\ *n* [Sp] (1952) **:** a Spanish and Mexican pastry resembling a doughnut or cruller and made from deep-fried unsweetened dough and sprinkled with sugar
chuse *archaic var of* CHOOSE
[1]**chute** *also* **shute** \ˈshüt\ *n* [F, fr. OF, fr. *cheoir* to fall, fr. L *cadere* — more at CHANCE] (1805) **1 a :** FALL 6b **b :** a quick descent (as in a river) **:** RAPID **2 :** an inclined plane, sloping channel, or passage down or through which things may pass **:** SLIDE **3 :** PARACHUTE **4 :** SPINNAKER
[2]**chute** *vb* **chut·ed; chut·ing** *vt* (1884) **:** to convey by a chute ~ *vi* **1 :** to go in or as if in a chute **2 :** to utilize a chute (as by passing ore down it)
chut·ist \ˈshü-tist\ *n* (1920) **:** PARACHUTIST
chut·ney \ˈchət-nē\ *n, pl* **chutneys** [Hindi *caṭnī* & Urdu *chaṭnī*] (1813) **:** a thick sauce of Indian origin that contains fruits, vinegar, sugar, and spices and is used as a condiment
chutz·pah *also* **chutz·pa** *or* **hutz·pah** *or* **hutz·pa** \ˈhu̇t-spə, ˈk̲u̇t-, -(ˌ)spä\ *n* [Yiddish *khutspe,* fr. LHeb *ḥuṣpāh*] (1883) **:** supreme self-confidence **:** NERVE, GALL ***syn*** see TEMERITY
chyle \ˈkī(-ə)l\ *n* [LL *chylus,* fr. Gk *chylos* juice, chyle; akin to Gk *chein* to pour — more at FOUND] (1541) **:** lymph that is milky from emulsified fats, characteristically present in the lacteals, and most apparent during intestinal absorption of fats — **chy·lous** \ˈkī-ləs\ *adj*
chy·lo·mi·cron \ˌkī-lō-ˈmī-ˌkrän\ *n* [Gk *chylos* + *mikron,* neut. of *mikros* small — more at MICRO-] (1921) **:** a lipoprotein rich in triglyceride and common in the blood during fat digestion and assimilation
chyme \ˈkīm\ *n* [NL *chymus,* fr. LL, chyle, fr. Gk *chymos* juice; akin to Gk *chein*] (1607) **:** the semifluid mass of partly digested food expelled by the stomach into the duodenum
chy·mo·tryp·sin \ˌkī-mō-ˈtrip-sən\ *n* [*chyme* + *-o-* + *trypsin*] (1933) **:** a protease that hydrolyzes peptide bonds and is formed in the intestine from chymotrypsinogen — **chy·mo·tryp·tic** \-tik\ *adj*
chy·mo·tryp·sin·o·gen \-ˌtrip-ˈsi-nə-jən\ *n* (1933) **:** a zymogen that is secreted by the pancreas and is converted by trypsin to chymotrypsin
Ci *abbr* **1** cirrus **2** curie
CI *abbr* **1** cast iron **2** certificate of insurance **3** Channel Islands
cía *abbr* [S *compañía*] company
CIA *abbr* **1** Central Intelligence Agency **2** certified internal auditor
CIAA *abbr* Central Intercollegiate Athletic Association
cia·bat·ta \chə-ˈbä-tə\ *n* [It, lit., slipper] (1985) **:** a flat oblong bread having a moist interior and a crispy crust
ciao \ˈchau̇\ *interj* [It, fr. It dial., lit., (I am your) slave, fr. ML *sclavus* — more at SLAVE] (1929) — used conventionally as an utterance at meeting or parting
ci·bo·ri·um \sə-ˈbȯr-ē-əm\ *n, pl* **-ria** \-ē-ə\ [ML, fr. L, cup, fr. Gk *kibōrion*] (1651) **1 :** a goblet-shaped vessel for holding eucharistic bread **2 :** BALDACHIN; *specif* **:** a

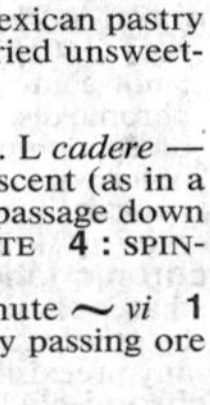

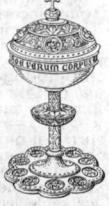

ciborium 1

freestanding vaulted canopy supported by four columns over a high altar
CIC *abbr* **1** combat information center **2** counterintelligence corps
ci·ca·da \sə-ˈkā-də, -ˈkä-; sī-ˈkā-\ *n, pl* **-das** *also* **-dae** \-ˈkā-(ˌ)dē, -ˈkä-\ [NL, genus name, fr. L, cicada] (14c) : any of a family (Cicadidae) of homopterous insects which have a stout body, wide blunt head, and large transparent wings and the males of which produce a loud buzzing noise usu. by stridulation
ci·ca·la \sə-ˈkä-lə\ *n* [It, fr. ML, alter. of L *cicada*] (1794) : CICADA
cic·a·tri·cial \ˌsi-kə-ˈtri-shəl\ *adj* (1881) : of or relating to a cicatrix
ci·ca·trix \ˈsi-kə-ˌtriks, sə-ˈkā-triks\ *n, pl* **ci·ca·tri·ces** \ˌsi-kə-ˈtrī-(ˌ)sēz, sə-ˈkā-trə-ˌsēz\ [L *cicatric-, cicatrix*] (1623) **1** : a scar resulting from formation and contraction of fibrous tissue in a wound **2** : a mark resembling a scar esp. when caused by the previous attachment of an organ or part (as a leaf)
cic·a·tri·za·tion \ˌsi-kə-trə-ˈzā-shən\ *n* (15c) : scar formation at the site of a healing wound — **cic·a·trize** \ˈsi-kə-ˌtrīz\ *vt*
ci·ce·ro·ne \ˌsi-sə-ˈrō-nē, ˌchē-chə-\ *n, pl* **-ni** \-(ˌ)nē\ [It, fr. *Cicerone* Cicero] (1726) **1** : a guide who conducts sightseers **2** : MENTOR, TUTOR
cich·lid \ˈsi-kləd\ *n* [ultim. fr. Gk *kichlē* thrush, a kind of wrasse; perh. akin to Gk *chelidōn* swallow] (1884) : any of a family (Cichlidae) of mostly tropical spiny-finned usu. freshwater fishes including several kept in tropical aquariums — **cichlid** *adj*
ci·cis·beo \ˌchē-chəz-ˈbā-(ˌ)ō\ *n, pl* **-bei** \-ˈbā-ˌē\ [It] (1718) : LOVER, GALLANT — **ci·cis·be·ism** \-ˈbā-ˌi-zəm\ *n*
cid *abbr* cubic inch displacement
CID *abbr* **1** civil investigative demand **2** Criminal Investigation Department
-cidal *adj comb form* [LL *-cidalis,* fr. L *-cida*] : killing : having power to kill ⟨insecti*cidal*⟩
-cide *n comb form* [MF, fr. L *-cida,* fr. *caedere* to cut, kill] **1** : killer ⟨insecti*cide*⟩ **2** [MF, fr. L *-cidium,* fr. *caedere*] : killing ⟨sui*cide*⟩
ci·der \ˈsī-dər\ *n* [ME *sidre,* fr. AF, fr. LL *sicera* strong drink, fr. Gk (Septuagint) *sikera,* fr. Heb *shēkhār*] (13c) **1** : fermented apple juice often made sparkling by carbonation or fermentation in a sealed container **2** : the expressed juice of fruit (as apples) used as a beverage or for making other products (as applejack)
cider vinegar *n* (1851) : vinegar made from fermented cider
ci–de·vant \ˌsē-də-ˈväⁿ\ *adj* [F, lit., formerly] (1790) : FORMER
cie *abbr* [F *compagnie*] company
CIF *abbr* **1** central information file **2** cost, insurance, and freight
cig \ˈsig\ *n* (1889) *slang* : CIGARETTE
ci·gar \si-ˈgär\ *n* [Sp *cigarro*] (1730) : a small roll of tobacco leaf for smoking
cig·a·rette *also* **cig·a·ret** \ˌsi-gə-ˈret, ˈsi-gə-ˌ\ *n* [F *cigarette,* dim. of *cigare* cigar, fr. Sp *cigarro*] (1835) : a slender roll of cut tobacco enclosed in paper and meant to be smoked; *also* : a similar roll of another substance (as marijuana)
cig·a·ril·lo \ˌsi-gə-ˈri-(ˌ)lō, -ˈrē-(ˌ)yō\ *n, pl* **-los** [Sp *cigarrillo* cigarette, dim. of *cigarro* cigar] (1832) **1** : a very small cigar **2** : a cigarette wrapped in tobacco leaf rather than paper
ci·gua·tera \ˌsē-gwə-ˈter-ə, ˌsi-\ *n* [AmerSp, fr. *ciguato* person ill with ciguatera, perh. fr. *cigua* sea snail] (1862) : poisoning caused by the ingestion of various normally edible tropical fish in whose flesh a toxic substance (as one produced by some dinoflagellates) has accumulated
ci·lan·tro \si-ˈlän-(ˌ)trō, -ˈlan-\ *n* [Sp, coriander, fr. ML *celiandrum,* alter. of L *coriandrum* — more at CORIANDER] (1903) : leaves of coriander used as a flavoring or garnish; *also* : CORIANDER 1
cil·i·ary \ˈsi-lē-ˌer-ē\ *adj* (1691) **1** : of, relating to, or being the annular suspension of the lens of the eye **2** : of or relating to cilia
cil·i·ate \ˈsi-lē-ət, -lē-ˌāt\ *n* (1916) : any of a phylum or subphylum (Ciliophora) of ciliated protozoans (as paramecia)
cil·i·at·ed \ˈsi-lē-ˌā-təd\ *or* **cil·i·ate** \-lē-ət, -lē-ˌāt\ *adj* (1753) : possessing cilia ⟨~ epithelial cells⟩ — **cil·i·a·tion** \ˌsi-lē-ˈā-shən\ *n*
cil·i·um \ˈsi-lē-əm\ *n, pl* **cil·ia** \-lē-ə\ [NL, fr. L, eyelid; akin to L *celare* to conceal — more at HELL] (1794) **1** : a minute short hairlike process often forming part of a fringe; *esp* : one on a cell that is capable of lashing movement and serves esp. in free unicellular organisms to produce locomotion or in higher forms a current of fluid **2** : EYELASH
ci·met·i·dine \sī-ˈme-tə-ˌdēn\ *n* [*ci-* (alter. of *cyan-*) + *meth*yl + *-idine*] (1975) : a histamine analog $C_{10}H_{16}N_6S$ that inhibits gastric acid secretion and is used esp. in the treatment of duodenal ulcers
¹**Cim·me·ri·an** \sə-ˈmir-ē-ən\ *adj* (1580) : very dark or gloomy ⟨under ebon shades . . . in dark ~ desert ever dwell —John Milton⟩
²**Cimmerian** *n* [L *Cimmerii,* a mythical people, fr. Gk *Kimmerioi*] (1584) : any of a mythical people described by Homer as dwelling in a remote realm of mist and gloom
C in C *abbr* commander in chief
¹**cinch** \ˈsinch\ *n* [Sp *cincha,* fr. L *cingula* girdle, girth, fr. *cingere* — more at CINCTURE] (1859) **1** : a girth for a pack or saddle **2** : a tight grip **3 a** : a thing done with ease **b** : a certainty to happen ⟨it's a ~ he'll break the record⟩
²**cinch** *vt* (1866) **1 a** : to put a cinch on **b** : to fasten (as a belt or strap) tightly **2** : to make certain : ASSURE ⟨the goal that ~*ed* the victory⟩ ~ *vi* : to tighten the cinch — often used with *up*
cin·cho·na \siŋ-ˈkō-nə, sin-ˈchō-\ *n* [NL, genus name, fr. the countess of *Chinchón* †1641 wife of the Peruvian viceroy] (1786) **1** : any of a genus (*Cinchona*) of So. American trees and shrubs of the madder family **2** : the dried bark of a cinchona (as *C. ledgeriana*) containing alkaloids (as quinine) and formerly used as a specific in malaria
cin·cho·nine \ˈsiŋ-kə-ˌnēn, ˈsin-chə-\ *n* (1825) : a bitter white crystalline alkaloid $C_{19}H_{22}N_2O$ found esp. in cinchona bark and used like quinine
cin·cho·nism \ˈsiŋ-kə-ˌni-zəm, ˈsin-chə-\ *n* (1857) : a disorder due to excessive or prolonged use of cinchona or its alkaloids and marked by temporary deafness, ringing in the ears, headache, dizziness, and rash
Cinco de Mayo \ˌsiŋ-kō-də-ˈmī-ō, ˌsēŋ-kō-t͟hā-ˈmä-yō\ *n* [Sp, fifth of May] (1931) : a Mexican and Mexican-American celebration held on May 5 in commemoration of the Mexican victory over the French at Puebla in 1862
cinc·ture \ˈsiŋ(k)-chər\ *n* [L *cinctura* girdle, fr. *cinctus,* pp. of *cingere* to gird; prob. akin to Skt *kāñcī* girdle] (1587) **1** : the act of encircling **2 a** : an encircling area **b** : GIRDLE, BELT; *esp* : a cord or sash of cloth worn around an ecclesiastical vestment or the habit of a religious
cin·der \ˈsin-dər\ *n* [ME *sinder,* fr. OE; akin to OHG *sintar* dross, slag, Serbian & Croatian *sedra* calcium carbonate] (bef. 12c) **1** : the slag from a metal furnace : DROSS **2 a** *pl* : ASHES **b** : a fragment of ash **3 a** : a partly burned combustible in which fire is extinct **b** : a hot coal without flame **c** : a partly burned coal capable of further burning without flame **4** : a fragment of lava from an erupting volcano — **cin·dery** \-d(ə-)rē\ *adj*
cinder block *n* (1926) : a hollow rectangular building block made of cement and coal cinders
cinder cone *n* (1849) : a conical hill formed by the accumulation of volcanic debris around a vent
Cin·der·el·la \ˌsin-də-ˈre-lə\ *n* [after *Cinderella,* fairy-tale heroine who is used as a drudge by her stepmother but ends up married to a prince] (1840) : one resembling the fairy-tale Cinderella: as **a** : one suffering undeserved neglect **b** : one suddenly lifted from obscurity to honor or significance — **Cinderella** *adj*
cine \ˈsi-nē\ *n* [prob. fr. F *ciné,* short for *cinéma* cinema] (1920) : MOTION PICTURE
cine·ast \ˈsi-nē-ˌast, -nē-əst\ *or* **cine·aste** \-ˌast\ *or* **ciné·aste** \-ˌast\ *n* [F *cinéaste,* fr. *ciné* + *-aste* (as in *enthousiaste* enthusiast)] (1926) : a devotee of motion pictures; *also* : MOVIEMAKER
cin·e·ma \ˈsi-nə-mə, *Brit also* -ˌmä\ *n* [short for *cinematograph*] (1909) **1 a** : MOTION PICTURE — usu. used attributively **b** : a motion-picture theater **2 a** : MOVIES; *esp* : the film industry **b** : the art or technique of making motion pictures
cin·e·ma·go·er \-ˌgō-ər\ *n* (1920) : MOVIEGOER
cin·e·ma·theque \ˌsi-nə-mə-ˈtek\ *n* [F *cinémathèque* film library, fr. *cinéma* + *-thèque* (as in *bibliothèque* library)] (1966) : a small movie house specializing in avant-garde films
cin·e·mat·ic \ˌsi-nə-ˈma-tik\ *adj* (1916) **1** : of, relating to, suggestive of, or suitable for motion pictures or the filming of motion pictures ⟨~ principles and techniques⟩ **2** : filmed and presented as a motion picture ⟨~ fantasies⟩ — **cin·e·mat·i·cal·ly** \-ˈma-ti-k(ə-)lē\ *adv*
cin·e·ma·tize \ˈsi-nə-mə-ˌtīz\ *vt* **-tized; -tiz·ing** (1916) : to make a motion picture of (as a novel) : adapt for motion pictures
cin·e·mat·o·graph \ˌsi-nə-ˈma-tə-ˌgraf\ *n* [F *cinématographe,* fr. Gk *kinēmat-, kinēma* movement (fr. *kinein* to move) + F *-o-* + *-graphe* -graph — more at -KINESIS] (1896) *chiefly Brit* : a motion-picture camera, projector, theater, or show
cin·e·ma·tog·ra·pher \ˌsi-nə-mə-ˈtä-grə-fər\ *n* (1897) : a specialist in cinematography
cin·e·ma·tog·ra·phy \ˌsi-nə-mə-ˈtä-grə-fē\ *n* (1897) : the art or science of motion-picture photography — **cin·e·mat·o·graph·ic** \-ˌma-tə-ˈgra-fik\ *adj* — **cin·e·mat·o·graph·i·cal·ly** \-fi-k(ə-)lē\ *adv*
ci·né·ma vé·ri·té \ˈsi-nə-mə-ˌver-i-ˈtā; si-nā-ˈmä-ve-rē-ˈtā\ *n* [F *cinéma-vérité,* lit., cinema-truth, trans. of Russ *kinopravda*] (1963) : the art or technique of filming a motion picture so as to convey candid realism
cin·e·ole \ˈsi-nē-ˌōl\ *n* [ISV, by transposition fr. NL *oleum cinae* wormseed oil] (1885) : EUCALYPTOL
cine·phile \ˈsi-nə-ˌfī(-ə)l\ *n* [F *cinéphile,* fr. *ciné* + *-phile*] (1968) : a devotee of motion pictures
Cine·plex \ˈsi-nə-ˌpleks\ *service mark* — used for a movie theater containing several auditoriums in one building
cin·er·ar·ia \ˌsi-nə-ˈrer-ē-ə\ *n* [NL, fr. L, fem. of *cinerarius* of ashes, fr. *ciner-, cinis* ashes — more at INCINERATE] (1597) : any of several garden or potted plants derived from a perennial senecio (*Senecio cruentus*) of the Canary Islands and having heart-shaped leaves and clusters of bright flower heads
cin·er·ar·i·um \-ē-əm\ *n, pl* **-ia** \-ē-ə\ [L, fr. *ciner-, cinis*] (1880) : a place to receive the ashes of the cremated dead — **cin·er·ary** \ˈsi-nə-ˌrer-ē\ *adj*
ci·ne·re·ous \sə-ˈnir-ē-əs\ *adj* [L *cinereus,* fr. *ciner-, cinis*] (1661) **1** : gray tinged with black **2** : resembling or consisting of ashes
cin·gu·lum \ˈsiŋ-gyə-ləm\ *n, pl* **-la** \-lə\ [NL, fr. L, girdle, fr. *cingere* to gird — more at CINCTURE] (1845) : an anatomical band or encircling ridge — **cin·gu·late** \-lət\ *adj*
cin·na·bar \ˈsi-nə-ˌbär\ *n* [ME *cynabare,* fr. AF & L; AF *sinopre,* fr. L *cinnabaris,* fr. Gk *kinnabari,* of non-IE origin; akin to Ar *zinjafr* cinnabar] (14c) **1** : artificial red mercuric sulfide used esp. as a pigment **2** : a red mineral consisting of native mercuric sulfide HgS that is the only important ore of mercury **3** : a deep vivid red — **cin·na·bar·ine** \-bə-ˌrīn, -ˌbär-in\ *adj*
cinnabar moth *n* (ca. 1893) : a European moth (*Tyria jacobaeae*) that has been introduced into the western U.S. in attempts to control the tansy ragwort on which its larvae feed — called also *cinnabar*
cin·nam·ic acid \sə-ˈna-mik-\ *n* [F *cinnamique* of cinnamon, fr. *cinname* cinnamon, fr. L *cinnamomum*] (ca. 1864) : a white crystalline odorless acid $C_9H_8O_2$ found esp. in cinnamon oil and storax
cin·na·mon \ˈsi-nə-mən\ *n, often attrib* [ME *cynamone,* fr. AF, fr. L *cinnamomum, cinnamon,* fr. Gk *kinnamōmon, kinnamon,* of non-IE origin; akin to Heb *qinnāmōn* cinnamon] (14c) **1 a** : any of several Asian trees (genus *Cinnamomum*) of the laurel family **b** : an aromatic spice prepared from the dried inner bark of a cinnamon (esp. *C. zeylanicum*); *also* : the bark **2** : a light yellowish brown — **cin·na·mony** \-mə-nē\ *adj*
cinnamon fern *n* (1818) : a large fern (*Osmunda cinnamomea*) with cinnamon-colored spore-bearing fronds shorter than and separate from the green foliage fronds
cinnamon stone *n* (1805) : ESSONITE
cin·quain \ˈsiŋ-ˌkān, ˈsaŋ-\ *n* [F, fr. *cinq* five, fr. OF, fr. L *quinque* — more at FIVE] (1882) : a 5-line stanza
cin·que·cen·tist \ˌchiŋ-kwi-ˈchen-tist\ *n* (1871) : an Italian of the cinquecento; *esp* : a poet or artist of this period
cin·que·cen·to \ˌchiŋ-kwi-ˈchen-(ˌ)tō\ *n* [It, lit., five hundred, fr. *cinque* five (fr. L *quinque*) + *cento* hundred, fr. L *centum* — more at HUNDRED] (1760) : the 16th century esp. in Italian art and literature

\ə\ **abut** \ᵊ\ kitten, F table \ər\ **further** \a\ **ash** \ā\ **ace** \ä\ **mop, mar** \au̇\ **out** \ch\ **chin** \e\ **bet** \ē\ **easy** \g\ **go** \i\ **hit** \ī\ **ice** \j\ **job** \ŋ\ **sing** \ō\ **go** \ȯ\ **law** \ȯi\ **boy** \th\ **thin** \t͟h\ **the** \ü\ **loot** \u̇\ **foot** \y\ **yet** \zh\ **vision, beige** \k, ⁿ, œ, ue, ʸ\ *see* Guide to Pronunciation

cinque·foil \ˈsiŋk-ˌfȯi(-ə)l, ˈsaŋk-\ *n* [ME *sink foil,* fr. AF *cincfoille,* fr. L *quinquefolium,* fr. *quinque* five + *folium* leaf — more at BLADE] (14c) **1 :** any of a genus (*Potentilla*) of herbs and shrubs of the rose family usu. having 5-lobed leaves and 5-petaled flowers — called also *potentilla* **2 :** a design enclosed by five joined foils

CIO *abbr* chief information officer

ciop·pi·no \chə-ˈpē-(ˌ)nō\ *n* [modif. of It dial. (Liguria) *ciuppin*] (1917) **:** a stew of fish and shellfish cooked usu. with tomatoes, wine, spices, and herbs

CIP *abbr* Cataloging in Publication

[1]**ci·pher** \ˈsī-fər\ *n, often attrib* [ME, fr. ML *cifra,* fr. Ar *ṣifr* empty, cipher, zero] (14c) **1 a :** ZERO 1a **b :** one that has no weight, worth, or influence **:** NONENTITY **2 a :** a method of transforming a text in order to conceal its meaning — compare CODE 3b **b :** a message in code **3 :** ARABIC NUMERAL **4 :** a combination of symbolic letters; *esp* **:** the interwoven initials of a name

[2]**cipher** *vb* **ci·phered; ci·pher·ing** \-f(ə-)riŋ\ *vi* (ca. 1530) **:** to use figures in a mathematical process ~ *vt* **1 :** ENCIPHER **2 :** to compute arithmetically

ci·pher·text \ˈsī-fər-ˌtekst\ *n* (1939) **:** the enciphered form of a text or of its elements — compare PLAINTEXT

cip·ro·flox·a·cin \ˌsi-prə-ˈfläk-sə-sən, -prō-\ *n* [prob. fr. ISV *ci-* (alter. of *cycl-*) + *propyl* + *fluor-* + *ox-* + *az-* + *-mycin*] (1983) **:** a synthetic broad-spectrum antibiotic $C_{17}H_{18}FN_3O_3$ that is a fluorinated derivative of quinolone and is often administered in the form of its hydrochloride

cir *abbr* **1** circle; circular **2** circuit **3** circumference

circ *abbr* **1** circular **2** circulation

cir·ca \ˈsər-kə\ *prep* [L, fr. *circum* around — more at CIRCUM-] (1861) **:** at, in, or of approximately — used esp. with dates ⟨born ~ 1600⟩

cir·ca·di·an \sər-ˈkā-dē-ən\ *adj* [L *circa* about + *dies* day + E [2]*-an* — more at DEITY] (1959) **:** being, having, characterized by, or occurring in approximately 24-hour periods or cycles (as of biological activity or function) ⟨~ rhythms in activity⟩

Cir·cas·sian \(ˌ)sər-ˈka-sh(ē-)ən\ *n* [*Circassia,* region of the Caucasus] (1555) **1 :** a member of a group of peoples of the northwestern Caucasus **2 :** the language of the Circassian peoples — **Circassian** *adj*

Circassian walnut *n* (1914) **:** the light brown irregularly black-veined wood of the English walnut much used for veneer and cabinetwork

Cir·ce \ˈsər-(ˌ)sē\ *n* [L, fr. Gk *Kirkē*] (14c) **:** a sorceress who changes Odysseus' men into swine but is forced by Odysseus to change them back

cir·ci·nate \ˈsər-sə-ˌnāt\ *adj* [L *circinatus,* pp. of *circinare* to round, fr. *circinus* pair of compasses, fr. *circus*] (1830) **:** ROUNDED, COILED; *esp* **:** rolled in the form of a flat coil with the apex as a center ⟨~ fern fronds unfolding⟩ — **cir·ci·nate·ly** *adv*

[1]**cir·cle** \ˈsər-kəl\ *n, often attrib* [ME *cercle,* fr. AF, fr. L *circulus,* dim. of *circus* circle, circus, fr. or akin to Gk *krikos, kirkos* ring; akin to OE *hring* ring — more at RING] (14c) **1 a :** RING, HALO **b :** a closed plane curve every point of which is equidistant from a fixed point within the curve **c :** the plane surface bounded by such a curve **2** *archaic* **:** the orbit of a celestial body **3 :** something in the form of a circle or section of a circle: as **a :** DIADEM **b :** an instrument of astronomical observation the graduated limb of which consists of an entire circle **c :** a balcony or tier of seats in a theater **d :** a circle formed on the surface of a sphere by the intersection of a plane that passes through it ⟨~ of latitude⟩ **e :** ROTARY 2 **4 :** an area of action or influence **:** REALM **5 a :** CYCLE, ROUND ⟨the wheel has come full ~⟩ **b :** fallacious reasoning in which something to be demonstrated is covertly assumed **6 :** a group of persons sharing a common interest or revolving about a common center ⟨the sewing ~ of her church⟩ ⟨family ~⟩ ⟨the gossip of court ~*s*⟩ **7 :** a territorial or administrative division or district **8 :** a curving side street

[2]**circle** *vb* **cir·cled; cir·cling** \-k(ə-)liŋ\ *vt* (14c) **1 :** to enclose in or as if in a circle **2 :** to move or revolve around ⟨satellites *circling* the earth⟩ ~ *vi* **1 a :** to move in or as if in a circle **b :** CIRCULATE **2 :** to describe or extend in a circle — **cir·cler** \-k(ə-)lər\ *n*

circle graph *n* (1928) **:** PIE CHART

cir·clet \ˈsər-klət\ *n* (15c) **:** a little circle; *esp* **:** a circular ornament

[1]**cir·cuit** \ˈsər-kət\ *n, often attrib* [ME, fr. MF & L; MF *circuite,* fr. L *circuitus,* fr. *circumire, circuire* to go around, fr. *circum-* + *ire* to go — more at ISSUE] (14c) **1 a :** a usu. circular line encompassing an area **b :** the space enclosed within such a line **2 a :** a course around a periphery **b :** a circuitous or indirect route **3 a :** a regular tour (as by a traveling judge or preacher) around an assigned district or territory **b :** the route traveled **c :** a group of church congregations ministered to by one pastor **4 a :** the complete path of an electric current including usu. the source of electric energy **b :** an assemblage of electronic elements **:** HOOKUP **c :** a two-way communication path between points (as in a computer) **d :** a neuronal pathway of the brain along which electrical and chemical signals travel **5 a :** an association of similar groups **:** LEAGUE **b :** a number or series of public outlets (as theaters, radio shows, or arenas) offering the same kind of presentation **c :** a number of similar social gatherings ⟨the cocktail ~⟩ — **cir·cuit·al** \-kə-tᵊl\ *adj*

[2]**circuit** *vt* (15c) **:** to make a circuit about ~ *vi* **:** to make a circuit

circuit board *n* (1948) **:** BOARD 9

circuit breaker *n* (1872) **:** a switch that automatically interrupts the current of an overloaded electric circuit

circuit court *n* (1708) **:** a court that sits at two or more places within one judicial district

circuit judge *n* (1801) **:** a judge who holds a circuit court

cir·cu·i·tous \(ˌ)sər-ˈkyü-ə-təs\ *adj* [perh. fr. ML *circuitosus,* fr. L *circuitus*] (1664) **1 :** having a circular or winding course ⟨a ~ route⟩ **2 :** not being forthright or direct in language or action ⟨a ~ explanation⟩ — **cir·cu·i·tous·ly** *adv* — **cir·cu·i·tous·ness** *n*

circuit rider *n* (1837) **:** a clergyman assigned to a circuit esp. in a rural area

cir·cuit·ry \ˈsər-kə-trē\ *n, pl* **-ries** (1946) **1 :** the detailed plan or arrangement of an electric circuit **2 :** the components of an electric circuit **3 :** the network of interconnected neurons in the nervous system and esp. the brain; *also* **:** CIRCUIT 4d

cir·cu·ity \(ˌ)sər-ˈkyü-ə-tē\ *n, pl* **-ities** [*circuitous*] (ca. 1626) **:** lack of straightforwardness **:** INDIRECTION

[1]**cir·cu·lar** \ˈsər-kyə-lər\ *adj* [ME *circuler,* fr. MF, fr. LL *circularis,* fr. L *circulus* circle] (15c) **1 a :** having the form of a circle **:** ROUND ⟨a ~ orbit⟩ **b :** moving in or describing a circle or spiral ⟨a ~ staircase⟩ **2 a :** of or relating to a circle or its mathematical properties ⟨a ~ arc⟩ **b :** having a circular base or bases ⟨a ~ cylinder⟩ **3 :** CIRCUITOUS, INDIRECT **4 :** marked by or moving in a cycle **5 :** being or involving reasoning that uses in the argument or proof a conclusion to be proved or one of its unproved consequences **6 :** intended for circulation ⟨a ~ letter⟩ — **cir·cu·lar·i·ty** \ˌsər-kyə-ˈler-ə-tē, -ˈla-rə-\ *n* — **cir·cu·lar·ly** \ˈsər-kyə-lər-lē\ *adv* — **cir·cu·lar·ness** *n*

[2]**circular** *n* (1789) **:** a paper (as a leaflet) intended for wide distribution

circular dichroism *n* (ca. 1961) **1 :** the property (as of an optically active medium) of unequal absorption of right and left plane-polarized light so that the emergent light is elliptically polarized **2 :** a spectroscopic technique that makes use of circular dichroism

circular file *n* (1967) **:** WASTEBASKET

circular function *n* (1884) **:** TRIGONOMETRIC FUNCTION

cir·cu·lar·ise *Brit var of* CIRCULARIZE

cir·cu·lar·ize \ˈsər-kyə-lə-ˌrīz\ *vt* **-ized; -iz·ing** (1848) **1 a :** to send circulars to **b :** to poll by questionnaire **2 :** PUBLICIZE **3 :** to make circular — **cir·cu·lar·i·za·tion** \ˌsər-kyə-lər-ə-ˈzā-shən\ *n*

circular saw *n* (1817) **:** a power saw with a circular cutting blade; *also* **:** the blade itself

cir·cu·late \ˈsər-kyə-ˌlāt\ *vb* **-lat·ed; -lat·ing** [L *circulatus,* pp. of *circulare,* fr. *circulus*] *vi* (1603) **1 :** to move in a circle, circuit, or orbit; *esp* **:** to follow a course that returns to the starting point ⟨blood ~*s* through the body⟩ **2 :** to pass from person to person or place to place: as **a :** to flow without obstruction **b :** to become well-known or widespread ⟨rumors *circulated* through the town⟩ **c :** to go from group to group at a social gathering **d :** to come into the hands of readers; *specif* **:** to become sold or distributed ~ *vt* **:** to cause to circulate — **cir·cu·lat·able** \-ˌlā-tə-bəl\ *adj* — **cir·cu·la·tive** \-ˌlā-tiv\ *adj* — **cir·cu·la·tor** \-ˌlā-tər\ *n*

circulating decimal *n* (1768) **:** REPEATING DECIMAL

cir·cu·la·tion \ˌsər-kyə-ˈlā-shən\ *n* (1535) **1 :** orderly movement through a circuit; *esp* **:** the movement of blood through the vessels of the body induced by the pumping action of the heart **2 :** FLOW **3 a :** passage or transmission from person to person or place to place; *esp* **:** the interchange of currency ⟨coins in ~⟩ **b :** the extent of dissemination: as **(1) :** the average number of copies of a publication sold over a given period **(2) :** the total number of items borrowed from a library

cir·cu·la·to·ry \ˈsər-kyə-lə-ˌtȯr-ē\ *adj* (1605) **:** of or relating to circulation or the circulatory system ⟨~ failure⟩

circulatory system *n* (1862) **:** the system of blood, blood vessels, lymphatics, and heart concerned with the circulation of the blood and lymph

circum- *prefix* [AF or L; AF, fr. L, fr. *circum,* fr. *circus* circle — more at CIRCLE] **:** around **:** about ⟨*circum*polar⟩

cir·cum·am·bi·ent \ˌsər-kᵊm-ˈam-bē-ənt\ *adj* [LL *circumambient-, circumambiens,* prp. of *circumambire* to surround in a circle, fr. L *circum-* + *ambire* to go around — more at AMBIENT] (1633) **:** being on all sides **:** ENCOMPASSING — **cir·cum·am·bi·ent·ly** *adv*

cir·cum·am·bu·late \-ˈam-byə-ˌlāt\ *vt* **-lat·ed; -lat·ing** [LL *circumambulatus,* pp. of *circumambulare,* fr. L *circum-* + *ambulare* to walk] (1606) **:** to circle on foot esp. ritualistically — **cir·cum·am·bu·la·tion** \-ˌam-byə-ˈlā-shən\ *n*

cir·cum·cen·ter \ˈsər-kᵊm-ˌsen-tər\ *n* (ca. 1889) **:** the point at which the perpendicular bisectors of the sides of a triangle intersect and which is equidistant from the three vertices

cir·cum·cir·cle \-ˌsər-kəl\ *n* (1885) **:** a circle which passes through all the vertices of a polygon (as a triangle)

cir·cum·cise \ˈsər-kᵊm-ˌsīz\ *vt* **-cised; -cis·ing** [ME, fr. L *circumcisus,* pp. of *circumcidere,* fr. *circum-* + *caedere* to cut] (13c) **1 :** to cut off the foreskin of (a male) or the prepuce of (a female) **2 :** to cut off all or part of the external genitalia and esp. the clitoris and labia minora of (a female) — **cir·cum·cis·er** *n*

cir·cum·ci·sion \ˌsər-kᵊm-ˈsi-zhən, ˈsər-kᵊm-ˌ\ *n* (12c) **1 a :** the act of circumcising; *esp* **:** a Jewish rite performed on male infants as a sign of inclusion in the Jewish religious community **b :** the condition of being circumcised **2** *cap* **:** January 1 observed as a festival in some churches in commemoration of the circumcision of Jesus

cir·cum·fer·ence \sə(r)-ˈkəm(p)-fərn(t)s, -f(ə-)rən(t)s\ *n* [ME, fr. MF & L; MF, fr. L *circumferentia,* fr. *circumferre* to carry around, fr. *circum-* + *ferre* to carry — more at BEAR] (14c) **1 :** the perimeter of a circle **2 :** the external boundary or surface of a figure or object **:** PERIPHERY — **cir·cum·fer·en·tial** \-ˌkəm(p)-fə-ˈren(t)-shəl\ *adj*

[1]**cir·cum·flex** \ˈsər-kᵊm-ˌfleks\ *adj* [L *circumflexus,* pp. of *circumflectere* to bend around, mark with a circumflex, fr. *circum-* + *flectere* to bend] (ca. 1577) **1 :** characterized by the pitch, quantity, or quality indicated by a circumflex **2 :** marked with a circumflex

[2]**circumflex** *n* (1609) **:** a mark ˆ, ˜, or ˉ orig. used in Greek over long vowels to indicate a rising-falling tone and in other languages to mark length, contraction, or a particular vowel quality

cir·cum·flu·ent \(ˌ)sər-ˈkəm-flü-ənt\ *adj* [fr. L *circumfluent-, circumfluens,* prp. of *circumfluere* to flow around, fr. *circum-* + *fluere* to flow — more at FLUID] (1577) **:** flowing round or surrounding in the manner of a fluid — **cir·cum·flu·ous** \(ˌ)sər-ˈkəm-flü-əs\ *adj*

cir·cum·fuse \ˌsər-kᵊm-ˈfyüz\ *vt* **-fused; -fus·ing** [L *circumfusus,* pp. of *circumfundere* to pour around, fr. *circum-* + *fundere* to pour — more at FOUND] (1605) **:** SURROUND 1 — **cir·cum·fu·sion** \-ˈfyü-zhən\ *n*

cir·cum·ja·cent \ˌsər-kᵊm-ˈjā-sᵊnt\ *adj* [L *circumjacent-, circumjacens,* prp. of *circumjacēre* to lie around, fr. *circum-* + *jacēre* to lie — more at ADJACENT] (15c) **:** lying adjacent on all sides **:** SURROUNDING

cir·cum·lo·cu·tion \ˌsər-kᵊm-lō-ˈkyü-shən\ *n* [ME *circumlocucyon,* fr. L *circumlocution-, circumlocutio,* fr. *circum-* + *locutio* speech, fr. *loqui* to speak] (15c) **1 :** the use of an unnecessarily large number of words to express an idea **2 :** evasion in speech — **cir·cum·loc·u·to·ry** \-ˈlä-kyə-ˌtȯr-ē\ *adj*

cir·cum·lu·nar \ˌsər-kəm-ˈlü-nər\ *adj* (ca. 1909) **:** revolving about or surrounding the moon ⟨a ~ orbit⟩

cir·cum·nav·i·gate \-ˈna-və-ˌgāt\ *vt* [L *circumnavigatus,* pp. of *circumnavigare* to sail around, fr. *circum-* + *navigare* to navigate] (1634) **:** to go completely around (as the earth) esp. by water; *also* **:** to go around instead of through : BYPASS ⟨~ a congested area⟩ — **cir·cum·nav·i·ga·tion** \-ˌna-və-ˈgā-shən\ *n* — **cir·cum·nav·i·ga·tor** \-ˈna-və-ˌgā-tər\ *n*

cir·cum·po·lar \ˌsər-kᵊm-ˈpō-lər\ *adj* (1686) **1 :** continually visible above the horizon ⟨a ~ star⟩ **2 :** surrounding or found in the vicinity of a terrestrial pole ⟨a ~ current⟩ ⟨~ species⟩

cir·cum·scis·sile \-ˈsi-səl, -ˌsī(-ə)l\ *adj* [L *circumscissus,* pp. of *circumscindere* to tear around, fr. *circum-* + *scindere* to cut, split — more at SHED] (1835) : dehiscing by fissure around the capsule of the fruit

cir·cum·scribe \ˈsər-kᵊm-ˌskrīb\ *vt* [ME *circumscriven,* fr. L *circumscribere,* fr. *circum-* + *scribere* to write, draw — more at SCRIBE] (14c) **1 a :** to constrict the range or activity of definitely and clearly ⟨his role was carefully *circumscribed*⟩ **b :** to define or mark off carefully ⟨a study of plant species in a *circumscribed* area⟩ **2 a :** to draw a line around **b :** to surround by or as if by a boundary ⟨fields *circumscribed* by tall trees⟩ **3 :** to construct or be constructed around (a geometrical figure) so as to touch as many points as possible ***syn*** see LIMIT

cir·cum·scrip·tion \ˌsər-kᵊm-ˈskrip-shən\ *n* [L *circumscription-, circumscriptio,* fr. *circumscribere*] (1531) **1 :** the act of circumscribing : the state of being circumscribed: as **a :** DEFINITION, DELIMITATION ⟨the ~ of her duties⟩ **b :** LIMITATION **2 :** something that circumscribes: as **a :** LIMIT, BOUNDARY **b :** RESTRICTION ⟨a ~ of his power to act⟩ **3 :** a circumscribed area or district

cir·cum·spect \ˈsər-kᵊm-ˌspekt\ *adj* [ME, fr. MF or L; MF *circonspect,* fr. L *circumspectus,* fr. pp. of *circumspicere* to look around, be cautious, fr. *circum-* + *specere* to look — more at SPY] (15c) : careful to consider all circumstances and possible consequences : PRUDENT ⟨diplomacy required a ~ response⟩ ***syn*** see CAUTIOUS — **cir·cum·spec·tion** \ˌsər-kᵊm-ˈspek-shən\ *n* — **cir·cum·spect·ly** \ˈsər-kᵊm-ˌspek(t)-lē\ *adv*

cir·cum·stance \ˈsər-kᵊm-ˌstan(t)s, -stən(t)s\ *n* [ME, fr. AF, fr. L *circumstantia,* fr. *circumstant-, circumstans,* prp. of *circumstare* to stand around, fr. *circum-* + *stare* to stand — more at STAND] (13c) **1 a :** a condition, fact, or event accompanying, conditioning, or determining another : an essential or inevitable concomitant ⟨the weather is a ~ to be taken into consideration⟩ **b :** a subordinate or accessory fact or detail ⟨cost is a minor ~ in this case⟩ **c :** a piece of evidence that indicates the probability or improbability of an event (as a crime) ⟨the ~ of the missing weapon told against him⟩ ⟨the ~*s* suggest murder⟩ **2 a :** the sum of essential and environmental factors (as of an event or situation) ⟨constant and rapid change in economic ~ —G. M. Trevelyan⟩ **b :** state of affairs : EVENTUALITY ⟨open rebellion was a rare ~⟩ — often used in pl. ⟨a victim of ~*s*⟩ **c** *pl* **:** situation with regard to wealth ⟨he was in easy ~*s*⟩ ⟨rose from difficult ~*s*⟩ **3 :** attendant formalities and ceremonial ⟨pride, pomp, and ~ of glorious war —Shak.⟩ **4 :** an event that constitutes a detail (as of a narrative or course of events) ⟨considering each ~ in turn⟩ ***syn*** see OCCURRENCE

cir·cum·stanced \-ˌstan(t)st, -stən(t)st\ *adj* (ca. 1611) : placed in particular circumstances esp. in regard to property or income

cir·cum·stan·tial \ˌsər-kᵊm-ˈstan(t)-shəl\ *adj* (1600) **1 :** belonging to, consisting in, or dependent on circumstances ⟨a ~ case⟩ ⟨~ factors⟩ **2 :** pertinent but not essential : INCIDENTAL **3 :** marked by careful attention to detail : abounding in factual details ⟨a ~ account of the fight⟩ **4 :** CEREMONIAL — **cir·cum·stan·ti·al·i·ty** \-ˌstan(t)-shē-ˈa-lə-tē\ *n* — **cir·cum·stan·tial·ly** \-ˈstan(t)-sh(ə-)lē\ *adv*

syn CIRCUMSTANTIAL, MINUTE, PARTICULAR, DETAILED mean dealing with a matter fully and usu. point by point. CIRCUMSTANTIAL implies fullness of detail that fixes something described in time and space ⟨a *circumstantial* account of our visit⟩. MINUTE implies close and searching attention to the smallest details ⟨a *minute* examination of a fossil⟩. PARTICULAR implies a precise attention to every detail ⟨a *particular* description of the scene of the crime⟩. DETAILED stresses abundance or completeness of detail ⟨a *detailed* analysis of the event⟩.

circumstantial evidence *n* (1736) : evidence that tends to prove a fact by proving other events or circumstances which afford a basis for a reasonable inference of the occurrence of the fact at issue

cir·cum·stan·ti·ate \ˌsər-kᵊm-ˈstan(t)-shē-ˌāt\ *vt* **-at·ed; -at·ing** (ca. 1652) : to supply with circumstantial evidence or support

cir·cum·stel·lar \ˌsər-kᵊm-ˈste-lər\ *adj* (1951) : surrounding or occurring in the vicinity of a star ⟨~ dust⟩

¹**cir·cum·val·late** \-ˈva-ˌlāt\ *vt* **-lat·ed; -lat·ing** [L *circumvallatus,* pp. of *circumvallare* to surround with siege works, fr. *circum-* + *vallum* rampart — more at WALL] (ca. 1798) : to surround by or as if by a rampart — **cir·cum·val·la·tion** \-ˌva-ˈlā-shən\ *n*

²**cir·cum·val·late** \-ˈva-ˌlāt, -ˈva-lət\ *adj* (ca. 1852) : being any of approximately 12 large papillae near the back of the tongue each of which is surrounded with a marginal sulcus and supplied with taste buds responsive esp. to bitter flavors

cir·cum·vent \ˌsər-kᵊm-ˈvent\ *vt* [L *circumventus,* pp. of *circumvenire,* fr. *circum-* + *venire* to come — more at COME] (1539) **1 a :** to hem in **b :** to make a circuit around **2 :** to manage to get around esp. by ingenuity or stratagem ⟨the setup ~*ed* the red tape —Lynne McTaggart⟩ — **cir·cum·ven·tion** \-ˈven(t)-shən\ *n*

cir·cum·vo·lu·tion \sər-ˌkəm-və-ˈlü-shən, ˌsər-kᵊm-vō-\ *n* [ME *circumvolucioun,* fr. ML *circumvolution-, circumvolutio,* fr. L *circumvolvere* to revolve, fr. *circum-* + *volvere* to roll — more at VOLUBLE] (15c) : an act or instance of turning around an axis

cir·cus \ˈsər-kəs\ *n, often attrib* [ME, fr. L, circle, circus — more at CIRCLE] (14c) **1 a :** a large arena enclosed by tiers of seats on three or all four sides and used esp. for sports or spectacles (as athletic contests, exhibitions of horsemanship, or in ancient times chariot racing) **b :** a public spectacle **2 a :** an arena often covered by a tent and used for variety shows usu. including feats of physical skill, wild animal acts, and performances by clowns **b :** a circus performance **c :** the physical plant, livestock, and personnel of such a circus **d :** something suggestive of a circus (as in frenzied activity, sensationalism, theatricality, or razzle-dazzle) ⟨a media ~⟩ **3 a** *obs* **:** CIRCLE, RING **b** *Brit* **:** a usu. circular area at an intersection of streets — **cir·cusy** \-kə-sē\ *adj*

circus catch *n* (1893) : a catch (as in baseball or football) requiring an extraordinary or spectacular effort

ci·ré *also* **ci·re** \sə-ˈrā, sē-\ *n* [F, fr. pp. of *cirer* to wax, fr. *cire* wax, fr. OF, fr. L *cera* — more at CERUMEN] (1921) **1 :** a highly glazed finish for fabrics usu. achieved by applying wax to the fabric **2 :** a fabric or garment with a ciré finish

cirque \ˈsərk\ *n* [F, fr. L *circus*] (1601) **1** *archaic* **:** CIRCUS **2 :** CIRCLE, CIRCLET **3 :** a deep steep-walled basin on a mountain usu. forming the blunt end of a valley

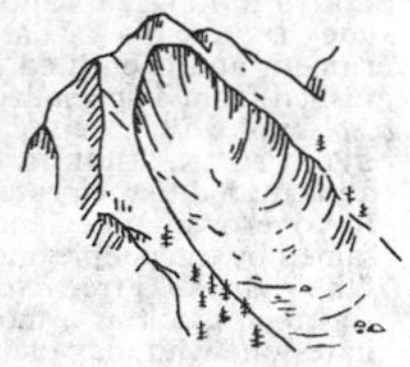

cirque 3

cir·rho·sis \sə-ˈrō-səs\ *n, pl* **-rho·ses** \-ˌsēz\ [NL, fr. Gk *kirrhos* orange-colored; akin to OE *hār* gray — more at HOAR] (ca. 1847) : widespread disruption of normal liver structure by fibrosis and the formation of regenerative nodules that is caused by any of various chronic progressive conditions affecting the liver (as long-term alcohol abuse or hepatitis) — **cir·rhot·ic** \-ˈrä-tik\ *adj or n*

cirro- *comb form* [NL *cirrus*] : cirrus ⟨*cirro*stratus⟩

cir·ro·cu·mu·lus \ˌsir-ō-ˈkyü-myə-ləs\ *n* [NL] (ca. 1803) : a high-altitude cloud form consisting of small white rounded masses usu. in regular groupings — see CLOUD illustration

cir·ro·stra·tus \ˌsir-ō-ˈstrā-təs, -ˈstra-\ *n* [NL] (ca. 1803) : a fairly uniform high thin cloud layer darker than cirrus and often covering the entire sky — see CLOUD illustration

cir·rus \ˈsir-əs\ *n, pl* **cir·ri** \ˈsir-ˌī\ [NL, fr. L, curl] (1708) **1 :** TENDRIL **2 :** a slender usu. flexible animal appendage or projection: as **a :** an arm of a barnacle **b :** a filament of a crinoid **c :** a fused group of cilia functioning like a limb on some protozoans **d :** the male copulatory organ of various invertebrate animals **3 :** a high wispy white cloud usu. of minute ice crystals formed at altitudes between about 20,000 and 40,000 feet (6,000 and 12,000 meters) — see CLOUD illustration

cis \ˈsis\ *adj* [L, lit., on this side] (1888) : characterized by having certain atoms or groups of atoms on the same side of the longitudinal axis of a double bond or of the plane of a ring in a molecule

CIS *abbr* Commonwealth of Independent States

cis- *prefix* [L, fr. *cis* — more at HE] **1 :** on this side ⟨*cis*lunar⟩ ⟨*cis*atlantic⟩ **2** *usu ital* **:** cis ⟨*cis*-dichloroethylene⟩ — compare TRANS- 2b

cis·al·pine \(ˌ)sis-ˈal-ˌpīn\ *adj* (1542) : situated on the south side of the Alps ⟨*Cisalpine* Gaul⟩ — compare TRANSALPINE

cis·at·lan·tic \-at-ˈlan-tik, -ət-\ *adj* (1785) : of, relating to, or characteristic of the side of the Atlantic Ocean regarded as the near side

cis·co \ˈsis-(ˌ)kō\ *n, pl* **ciscoes** [short for CanF *ciscoette*] (1848) : any of various whitefishes (genus *Coregonus*); *esp* **:** LAKE HERRING

cis·lu·nar \(ˌ)sis-ˈlü-nər\ *adj* (ca. 1877) : lying between the earth and the moon or the moon's orbit ⟨~ space⟩

cis·plat·in \(ˌ)sis-ˈpla-tᵊn\ *n* [*cis-* + *platinum*] (1977) : a platinum-containing antineoplastic drug $Cl_2H_6N_2Pt$ used esp. in the treatment of testicular and ovarian tumors and advanced bladder cancer

cis–plat·i·num \-ˈplat-nəm, -ˈpla-tᵊn-əm\ *n* (1977) : CISPLATIN

cis·sy *Brit var of* SISSY

cist \ˈsist, ˈkist\ *n* [W, chest, fr. L *cista*] (1804) : a neolithic or Bronze Age burial chamber typically lined with stone

Cis·ter·cian \sis-ˈtər-shən\ *n* [ML *Cistercium* Cîteaux] (1611) : a member of a monastic order founded by St. Robert of Molesme in 1098 at Cîteaux, France, under Benedictine rule — **Cistercian** *adj*

cis·tern \ˈsis-tərn\ *n* [ME, fr. AF, fr. L *cisterna,* fr. *cista* box, chest — more at CHEST] (13c) **1 :** an artificial reservoir (as an underground tank) for storing liquids and esp. water (as rainwater) **2 :** a large usu. silver vessel formerly used (as in cooling wine) at the dining table **3 :** a fluid-containing sac or cavity in an organism

cis·ter·na \sis-ˈtər-nə\ *n, pl* **-nae** \-ˌnē\ [NL, fr. L, reservoir] (ca. 1860) : CISTERN 3: as **a :** one of the large spaces under the arachnoid membrane **b :** one of the flattened vesicles comprising the Golgi apparatus and the part of the endoplasmic reticulum studded with ribosomes — **cis·ter·nal** \-nəl\ *adj*

cis·tron \ˈsis-ˌträn\ *n* [*cis-* + *trans-* + ²*-on*] (1957) : a segment of DNA that is equivalent to a gene and that specifies a single functional unit (as a protein or enzyme) — **cis·tron·ic** \sis-ˈträ-nik\ *adj*

cit *abbr* **1** citation; cited **2** citizen

cit·a·del \ˈsi-tə-dᵊl, -ˌdel\ *n* [MF *citadelle,* fr. OIt *cittadella,* dim. of *cittade* city, fr. ML *civitat-, civitas* — more at CITY] (1562) **1 :** a fortress that commands a city **2 :** STRONGHOLD ⟨the nation's ~ of health research —Constance Holden⟩ ⟨a ~ of higher education⟩

ci·ta·tion \sī-ˈtā-shən\ *n* (13c) **1 :** an official summons to appear (as before a court) **2 a :** an act of quoting; *esp* **:** the citing of a previously settled case at law **b :** EXCERPT, QUOTATION **3 :** MENTION: as **a :** a formal statement of the achievements of a person receiving an academic honor **b :** specific reference in a military dispatch to meritorious performance of duty ***syn*** see ENCOMIUM — **ci·ta·tion·al** \-shnəl, -shə-nᵊl\ *adj*

cite \ˈsīt\ *vt* **cit·ed; cit·ing** [ME, fr. AF *citer* to cite, summon, fr. L *citare* to put in motion, rouse, summon, fr. freq. of *ciēre* to stir, move — more at -KINESIS] (15c) **1 :** to call upon officially or authoritatively to appear (as before a court) **2 :** to quote by way of example, authority, or proof ⟨~*s* several noteworthy authors⟩ **3 a :** to refer to; *esp* **:** to mention formally in commendation or praise **b :** to name in a citation **4 :** to bring forward or call to another's attention esp. as an example, proof, or precedent ⟨~*d* the weather as a reason for canceling the picnic⟩ ***syn*** see SUMMON — **cit·able** \ˈsī-tə-bəl\ *adj*

cithara *var of* KITHARA

cith·er \ˈsi-t͟hər, -thər\ *n* [F *cithare,* fr. L *cithara* kithara, fr. Gk *kithara*] (1606) : CITTERN

cit·ied \ˈsi-tēd\ *adj* (1660) : occupied by cities

cit·i·fied \ˈsi-ti-ˌfīd\ *adj* (1828) : of, relating to, or characteristic of a sophisticated urban style of living ⟨~ tourists⟩ ⟨~ surroundings⟩

cit·i·fy \-ˌfī\ *vt* **-fied; -fy·ing** (1828) : URBANIZE — **cit·i·fi·ca·tion** \ˌsi-tə-fi-ˈkā-shən\ *n*

cit·i·zen \'si-tə-zən *also* -sən\ *n* [ME *citizein,* fr. AF *citezein,* alter. of *citeien,* fr. *cité* city] (14c) **1 :** an inhabitant of a city or town; *esp* **:** one entitled to the rights and privileges of a freeman **2 a :** a member of a state **b :** a native or naturalized person who owes allegiance to a government and is entitled to protection from it **3 :** a civilian as distinguished from a specialized servant of the state — **cit·i·zen·ly** \-zən-lē *also* -sən-\ *adj*

syn CITIZEN, SUBJECT, NATIONAL mean a person owing allegiance to and entitled to the protection of a sovereign state. CITIZEN is preferred for one owing allegiance to a state in which sovereign power is retained by the people and sharing in the political rights of those people ⟨the rights of a free *citizen*⟩. SUBJECT implies allegiance to a personal sovereign such as a monarch ⟨the king's *subjects*⟩. NATIONAL designates one who may claim the protection of a state and applies esp. to one living or traveling outside that state ⟨American *nationals* working in the Middle East⟩.

cit·i·zen·ess \-zə-nəs *also* -sə-\ *n* (1796) **:** a woman who is a citizen

cit·i·zen·ry \-zən-rē *also* -sən-\ *n, pl* **-ries** (1819) **:** a whole body of citizens

citizen's arrest *n* (1941) **:** an arrest made not by a law officer but by a citizen who derives authority from the fact of being a citizen

citizens band *n* (1948) **:** a range of radio-wave frequencies that in the U.S. is allocated officially for private radio communications

cit·i·zen·ship \'si-tə-zən-ˌship\ *n* (1611) **1 :** the status of being a citizen **2 a :** membership in a community (as a college) **b :** the quality of an individual's response to membership in a community

citr- *or* **citri-** *or* **citro-** *comb form* [NL, fr. *Citrus,* genus name] **1 :** citrus ⟨*citri*culture⟩ **2 :** citric acid ⟨*citr*ate⟩

cit·ral \'si-ˌtral\ *n* [ISV] (1891) **:** an unsaturated liquid isomeric aldehyde $C_{10}H_{16}O$ of many essential oils that has a strong lemon odor and is used esp. in perfumery and as a flavoring

cit·rate \'si-ˌtrāt\ *n* [ISV] (1794) **:** a salt or ester of citric acid

cit·ric acid \'si-trik-\ *n* [ISV] (1813) **:** a tricarboxylic acid $C_6H_8O_7$ occurring in cellular metabolism, obtained esp. from lemon and lime juices or by fermentation of sugars, and used chiefly as a flavoring

citric acid cycle *n* (1942) **:** KREBS CYCLE

cit·ri·cul·ture \'si-trə-ˌkəl-chər\ *n* (1916) **:** the cultivation of citrus fruits — **cit·ri·cul·tur·ist** \ˌsi-trə-'kəl-ch(ə-)rist\ *n*

[1]**cit·rine** \'si-ˌtrīn\ *adj* [ME, fr. AF *citrin,* fr. ML *citrinus,* fr. L *citrus* citron tree] (14c) **:** resembling a citron or lemon esp. in color

[2]**ci·trine** \si-'trēn\ *n* (1748) **:** a semiprecious yellow stone resembling topaz and formed by heating a black quartz in order to change its color

ci·tri·nin \si-'trī-nən\ *n* [NL *citrinum,* specific epithet of *Penicillium citrinum*] (1931) **:** a toxic antibiotic $C_{13}H_{14}O_5$ that is produced esp. by a penicillium (*Penicillium citrinum*) and an aspergillus (*Aspergillus niveus*) and is effective against some gram-positive bacteria

cit·ron \'si-trən\ *n* [MF, modif. of L *citrus*] (1530) **1 a :** a citrus fruit resembling a lemon but larger with little pulp and a very thick rind **b :** a small shrubby tree (*Citrus medica*) that produces citrons and is cultivated in tropical regions **c :** the preserved rind of the citron used esp. in cakes and puddings **2 :** a small hard-fleshed watermelon used esp. in pickles and preserves

cit·ro·nel·la \ˌsi-trə-'ne-lə\ *n* [NL, fr. F *citronnelle* lemon balm, fr. *citron*] (ca. 1858) **:** a lemon-scented grass (*Cymbopogon nardus*) of southern Asia that yields an oil used in perfumery and as an insect repellent; *also* **:** its oil

cit·ro·nel·lal \-'ne-ˌlal\ *n* [ISV, fr. NL *citronella*] (1893) **:** a lemon-odored aldehyde $C_{10}H_{18}O$ that is derived esp. from citronella oil and is used in perfumery and as an insect repellent

cit·ro·nel·lol \-'ne-ˌlȯl, -ˌlōl\ *n* [ISV, fr. NL *citronella*] (1872) **:** an unsaturated liquid alcohol $C_{10}H_{20}O$ with a roselike odor that is found in two optically active forms in many essential oils (as rose oil) and is used in perfumery and soaps

ci·trov·o·rum factor \sə-'trä-və-rəm-\ *n* [NL *citrovorum,* specific epithet of *Leuconostoc citrovorum,* bacterium that requires this form of folic acid] (1948) **:** a metabolically active form of folic acid that has been used in cancer therapy to protect normal cells against methotrexate

cit·rul·line \'si-trə-ˌlēn\ *n* [ISV, fr. NL *Citrullus,* genus name of the watermelon] (1930) **:** a crystalline amino acid $C_6H_{13}N_3O_3$ formed esp. as an intermediate in the conversion of ornithine to arginine

cit·rus \'si-trəs\ *n, pl* **citrus** *or* **cit·rus·es** *often attrib* [NL, genus name, fr. L] (1825) **:** any of a group of often thorny trees and shrubs (*Citrus* and related genera) of the rue family grown in warm regions for their edible fruit (as the orange or lemon) with firm usu. thick rind and pulpy flesh; *also* **:** the fruit — **cit·rusy** \'si-trə-sē\ *adj*

citrus canker *n* (1916) **:** a destructive disease of citrus caused by a bacterium (*Xanthomonas axonopodis citri* syn. *X. campestris citri*) that produces lesions on the leaves, twigs, and fruits

citrus red mite *n* (1945) **:** a relatively large mite (*Panonychus citri*) that is a destructive pest on the foliage of citrus

cit·tern \'si-tərn\ *also* **cith·ern** \'si-thərn, -thərn\ *or* **cith·ren** \'si-thrən\ *n* [blend of *cither* and *gittern*] (1566) **:** a Renaissance stringed instrument like a guitar with a flat pear-shaped body

city \'si-tē\ *n, pl* **cit·ies** *often attrib* [ME *citie* large or small town, fr. AF *cité,* fr. ML *civitat-, civitas,* fr. L, citizenship, state, city of Rome, fr. *civis* citizen — more at HIND] (13c) **1 a :** an inhabited place of greater size, population, or importance than a town or village **b :** an incorporated British town usu. of major size or importance having the status of an episcopal see **c** *cap* (1) **:** the financial district of London (2) **:** the influential financial interests of the British economy **d :** a usu. large or important municipality in the U.S. governed under a charter granted by the state **e :** an incorporated municipal unit of the highest class in Canada **2 :** CITY-STATE **3 :** the people of a city **4** *slang* **:** a thing, event, or situation that is strongly characterized by a specified quintessential feature or quality ⟨the movie was shoot-out ~⟩

city clerk *n* (1793) **:** a public officer charged with recording the official proceedings and vital statistics of a city

city council *n* (1789) **:** the legislative body of a city

city editor *n* (1834) **:** a newspaper editor usu. in charge of local news and staff assignments

city father *n* (1843) **:** a member (as an alderman or councilman) of the governing body of a city

city hall *n* (1675) **1 :** the chief administrative building of a city **2 a :** a municipal government **b :** city officialdom or bureaucracy ⟨you can't fight *city hall*⟩

city manager *n* (1913) **:** an official employed by an elected council to direct the administration of a city government

city planning *n* (1900) **:** the drawing up of an organized arrangement (as of streets, parks, and business and residential areas) of a city — **city planner** *n*

city room *n* (1895) **:** the department where local news is handled in a newspaper editorial office

city·scape \'si-tē-ˌskāp\ *n* (1856) **1 :** a city viewed as a scene **2 :** an artistic representation of a city **3 :** an urban environment ⟨a ~ cluttered with factories⟩

city slicker *n* (1924) **:** SLICKER 2b

city–state \'si-tē-ˌstāt *also* -'stāt\ *n* (1847) **:** an autonomous state consisting of a city and surrounding territory

city·wide \'si-tē-ˌwīd\ *adj* (1961) **:** including or involving all parts of a city ⟨a ~ blackout⟩

civ *abbr* civil; civilian; civilization

civ·et \'si-vət\ *n* [MF *civette,* fr. OIt *zibetto,* fr. Ar *zabād* civet perfume] (1532) **1 :** any of various Old World carnivorous viverrid mammals with long bodies, short legs, and a usu. long tail **2 :** a thick yellowish musky-odored substance found in a sac near the anus of the civet (esp. genera *Civettictis, Viverra,* and *Viverricula*) and used in perfume

civet cat *n* (1607) **1 :** CIVET 1 **2 :** RINGTAIL 2 **3 :** any of several small spotted skunks (genus *Spilogale*) of western No. America

civ·ic \'si-vik\ *adj* [L *civicus,* fr. *civis* citizen — more at CITY] (ca. 1656) **:** of or relating to a citizen, a city, citizenship, or community affairs ⟨~ duty⟩ ⟨~ pride⟩ — **civ·i·cal·ly** \'si-vi-k(ə-)lē\ *adv*

civ·ic–mind·ed \ˌsi-vik-'mīn-dəd\ *adj* (1947) **:** disposed to look after civic needs and interests — **civ·ic–mind·ed·ness** *n*

civ·ics \'si-viks\ *n pl but sing or pl in constr* (1886) **:** a social science dealing with the rights and duties of citizens

civ·il \'si-vəl\ *adj* [ME, fr. MF, fr. L *civilis,* fr. *civis*] (14c) **1 a :** of or relating to citizens **b :** of or relating to the state or its citizenry ⟨~ strife⟩ **2 a :** CIVILIZED ⟨~ society⟩ **b :** adequate in courtesy and politeness **:** MANNERLY ⟨a ~ question⟩ **3 a :** of, relating to, or based on civil law **b :** relating to private rights and to remedies sought by action or suit distinct from criminal proceedings **c :** established by law **4 :** of, relating to, or involving the general public, their activities, needs, or ways, or civic affairs as distinguished from special (as military or religious) affairs **5** *of time* **:** based on the mean sun and legally recognized for use in ordinary affairs

syn CIVIL, POLITE, COURTEOUS, GALLANT, CHIVALROUS mean observant of the forms required by good breeding. CIVIL often suggests little more than the avoidance of overt rudeness ⟨owed the questioner a *civil* reply⟩. POLITE commonly implies polish of speech and manners and sometimes suggests an absence of cordiality ⟨if you can't be pleasant, at least be *polite*⟩. COURTEOUS implies more actively considerate or dignified politeness ⟨clerks who were unfailingly *courteous* to customers⟩. GALLANT and CHIVALROUS imply courteous attentiveness esp. to women. GALLANT suggests spirited and dashing behavior and ornate expressions of courtesy ⟨a *gallant* suitor of the old school⟩. CHIVALROUS suggests high-minded and self-sacrificing behavior ⟨a *chivalrous* display of duty⟩.

civil death *n* (1719) **:** the status of a living person equivalent in its legal consequences to natural death; *specif* **:** deprivation of civil rights

civil defense *n* (1939) **:** the system of protective measures and emergency relief activities conducted by civilians in case of hostile attack, sabotage, or natural disaster

civil disobedience *n* (1866) **:** refusal to obey governmental demands or commands esp. as a nonviolent and usu. collective means of forcing concessions from the government

civil engineer *n* (ca. 1792) **:** an engineer whose training or occupation is in the design and construction esp. of public works (as roads or harbors) — **civil engineering** *n*

ci·vil·ian \sə-'vil-yən *also* -'vi-yən\ *n* (14c) **1 :** a specialist in Roman or modern civil law **2 a :** one not on active duty in the armed services or not on a police or firefighting force **b :** OUTSIDER 1 — **civilian** *adj*

ci·vil·ian·ize \-yə-ˌnīz\ *vt* **-ized; -iz·ing** (1870) **:** to convert from military to civilian status or control — **ci·vil·ian·i·za·tion** \-ˌvil-yə-nə-'zā-shən\ *n*

civ·i·li·sa·tion, civ·i·lise *chiefly Brit var of* CIVILIZATION, CIVILIZE

ci·vil·i·ty \sə-'vi-lə-tē\ *n, pl* **-ties** (1533) **1** *archaic* **:** training in the humanities **2 a :** civilized conduct; *esp* **:** COURTESY, POLITENESS **b :** a polite act or expression

civ·i·li·za·tion \ˌsi-və-lə-'zā-shən\ *n* (1772) **1 a :** a relatively high level of cultural and technological development; *specif* **:** the stage of cultural development at which writing and the keeping of written records is attained **b :** the culture characteristic of a particular time or place **2 :** the process of becoming civilized **3 a :** refinement of thought, manners, or taste **b :** a situation of urban comfort — **civ·i·li·za·tion·al** \-shnəl, -shə-nᵊl\ *adj*

civ·i·lize \'si-və-ˌlīz\ *vb* **-lized; -liz·ing** *vt* (1601) **1 :** to cause to develop out of a primitive state; *esp* **:** to bring to a technically advanced and rationally ordered stage of cultural development **2 a :** EDUCATE, REFINE **b :** SOCIALIZE 1 ~ *vi* **:** to acquire the customs and amenities of a civil community — **civ·i·liz·er** *n*

civilized *adj* (1611) **:** characteristic of a state of civilization ⟨~ society⟩; *esp* **:** characterized by taste, refinement, or restraint

civil law *n, often cap C&L* (14c) **1 :** Roman law esp. as set forth in the Justinian code **2 :** the body of private law developed from Roman law and used in Louisiana and in many countries outside the English-speaking world **3 :** the law established by a nation or state for its own jurisdiction **4 :** the law of civil or private rights

civil liberty *n* (1644) **:** freedom from arbitrary governmental interference (as with the right of free speech) specif. by denial of governmental power and in the U.S. esp. as guaranteed by the Bill of Rights — usu. used in pl. — **civil libertarian** *n or adj*

civ·il·ly \'si-və(l)-lē\ *adv* (15c) **1 :** in terms of civil rights, law, or matters ⟨~ dead⟩ **2 :** in a civil manner **:** POLITELY

civil marriage *n* (1820) **:** a marriage performed by a magistrate

civil rights *n pl* (1658) **:** the nonpolitical rights of a citizen; *esp* **:** the rights of personal liberty guaranteed to U.S. citizens by the 13th and 14th amendments to the Constitution and by acts of Congress

civil servant *n* (1800) **1 :** a member of a civil service **2 :** a member of the administrative staff of an international agency

civil service *n* (ca. 1770) **:** the administrative service of a government or international agency exclusive of the armed forces; *esp* **:** one in which appointments are determined by competitive examination

civil union *n* (1992) **:** the legal status that ensures to same-sex couples specified rights and responsibilities of married couples

civil war *n* (15c) **:** a war between opposing groups of citizens of the same country

Civ·i·tan \ˈsi-və-ˌtan\ *n* [*Civitan* (*Club*)] (1926) **:** a member of a major national and international service club

civ·vy *also* **civ·ie** \ˈsi-vē\ *n, pl* **civvies** *also* **civies** (ca. 1889) **1** *pl* **:** civilian clothes as distinguished from a particular uniform (as of the military) **2 :** CIVILIAN

civvy street *n, often cap C&S* (1943) *Brit* **:** civilian life

CIWS *abbr* close-in weapons system

CJ *abbr* chief justice

CJD *abbr* Creutzfeldt-Jakob disease

ck *abbr* **1** cask **2** check

cl *abbr* **1** centiliter **2** claiming **3** class **4** clause **5** close **6** closet **7** cloth

Cl *symbol* chlorine

CL *abbr* **1** carload **2** centerline **3** civil law **4** common law

clab·ber \ˈkla-bər\ *n* [short for *bonnyclabber*] (1634) *chiefly dial* **:** sour milk that has thickened or curdled

clab·bered \ˈkla-bərd\ *adj* (1873) *of milk or cream* **:** having thickened or curdled

clach·an \ˈkla-kən\ *n* [ME (Sc), fr. ScGael] (15c) *Scot & Irish* **:** HAMLET

[1]**clack** \ˈklak\ *vb* [ME, of imit. origin] *vi* (13c) **1 :** CHATTER, PRATTLE **2 :** to make an abrupt striking sound or series of sounds **3** *of fowl* **:** CACKLE, CLUCK ~ *vt* **1 :** to cause to make a clatter **2 :** to produce with a chattering sound; *specif* **:** BLAB — **clack·er** *n*

[2]**clack** *n* (15c) **1 a :** rapid continuous talk **:** CHATTER **b :** TONGUE **2** *archaic* **:** an object (as a valve) that produces clapping or rattling noises usu. in regular rapid sequence **3 :** a sound of clacking

Clac·to·ni·an \klak-ˈtō-nē-ən\ *adj* [*Clacton*-on-Sea, England] (1932) **:** of or relating to a Lower Paleolithic culture usu. characterized by stone flakes with a half cone at the point of striking

[1]**clad** *past and past part of* CLOTHE

[2]**clad** \ˈklad\ *adj* [ME, pp. of *clothen* to clothe] (14c) **1 :** being covered or clothed ⟨ivy-*clad* buildings⟩ **2** *of a coin* **:** consisting of outer layers of one metal bonded to a core of a different metal

[3]**clad** *vt* **clad** *or* **clad·ded; clad·ding** (1939) **:** SHEATHE, FACE; *specif* **:** to cover (a metal) with another metal by bonding

[4]**clad** *n* (1941) **1 a :** a composite material formed by cladding **b :** a clad coin **2 :** CLADDING; *specif* **:** the outer layer of a clad coin

clad- *or* **clado-** *comb form* [NL, fr. Gk *klad-, klado-,* fr. *klados* branch, shoot of a tree; akin to OE *holt* woods — more at HOLT] **:** slip **:** sprout ⟨*clado*phyll⟩

clad·dagh \ˈkla-də, ˈklä-\ *n* [*Claddagh,* former village across the river Corrib from Galway city, Ireland] (1922) **:** an Irish design (as on a ring) of two hands holding a crowned heart that symbolizes friendship, loyalty, and love

clad·ding \ˈkla-diŋ\ *n* (1936) **:** something that covers or overlays; *specif* **:** metal coating bonded to a metal core

clade \ˈklād\ *n* [Gk *klados*] (1911) **:** a group of biological taxa (as species) that includes all descendants of one common ancestor

cla·dis·tics \klə-ˈdis-tiks, kla-\ *n pl but sing in constr* (1965) **:** a system of biological taxonomy that defines taxa uniquely by shared characteristics not found in ancestral groups and uses inferred evolutionary relationships to arrange taxa in a branching hierarchy such that all members of a given taxon have the same ancestors — **cla·dist** \ˈkla-dist, ˈklā-\ *n* — **cla·dis·tic** \klə-ˈdis-tik, kla-\ *adj* — **cla·dis·ti·cal·ly** \-ti-k(ə-)lē\ *adv*

cla·doc·er·an \klə-ˈdä-sə-rən\ *n* [NL *Cladocera,* fr. *clad-* + Gk *keras* horn — more at HORN] (1909) **:** any of an order (Cladocera) of minute chiefly freshwater branchiopod crustaceans that includes the water fleas

clad·ode \ˈkla-ˌdōd\ *n* [NL *cladodium,* fr. Gk *klados*] (1870) **:** CLADOPHYLL — **cla·do·di·al** \kla-ˈdō-dē-əl\ *adj*

clad·o·gen·e·sis \ˌkla-də-ˈje-nə-səs\ *n* (1953) **:** evolutionary change characterized by treelike branching of taxa — compare ANAGENESIS — **clad·o·ge·net·ic** \ˌkla-dō-jə-ˈne-tik\ *adj* — **clad·o·ge·net·i·cal·ly** \-ti-k(ə-)lē\ *adv*

clad·o·gram \ˈkla-də-ˌgram\ *n* (1965) **:** a branching diagrammatic tree used in cladistic classification to illustrate phylogenetic relationships

clad·o·phyll \ˈkla-də-ˌfil\ *n* (1879) **:** a flattened photosynthetic branch assuming the form of and closely resembling an ordinary foliage leaf

cla·fou·ti *also* **cla·fou·tis** \ˌklä-fü-ˈtē\ *n* [F] (ca. 1968) **:** a dessert consisting of a layer of fruit (as cherries) topped with batter and baked

[1]**claim** \ˈklām\ *vt* [ME, fr. AF *claimer, clamer,* fr. L *clamare* to cry out, shout; akin to L *calare* to call — more at LOW] (14c) **1 a :** to ask for esp. as a right ⟨~*ed* the inheritance⟩ **b :** to call for **:** REQUIRE ⟨this matter ~*s* our attention⟩ **c :** TAKE 16b ⟨the accident ~*ed* her life⟩ **2 :** to take as the rightful owner **3 a :** to assert in the face of possible contradiction **:** MAINTAIN ⟨~*ed* that he'd been cheated⟩ **b :** to claim to have ⟨organization . . . which ~*s* 11,000 . . . members —*Rolling Stone*⟩ **c :** to assert to be rightfully one's own ⟨~*ed* responsibility for the attack⟩ ***syn*** see DEMAND — **claim·able** \ˈklā-mə-bəl\ *adj*

[2]**claim** *n* (14c) **1 :** a demand for something due or believed to be due ⟨an insurance ~⟩ **2 a :** a right to something; *specif* **:** a title to a debt, privilege, or other thing in the possession of another **b :** an assertion open to challenge ⟨a ~ of authenticity⟩ **3 :** something that is claimed; *esp* **:** a tract of land staked out

claim·ant \ˈklā-mənt\ *n* (15c) **:** one that asserts a right or title ⟨a ~ to an estate⟩; *also* **:** CLAIMER 1

claim·er \ˈklā-mər\ *n* (15c) **1 :** one that claims **2 a :** CLAIMING RACE **b :** a horse running in a claiming race

claiming race *n* (1935) **:** a horse race in which each entry is offered for sale for a specified price that must be deposited before the race

clair·au·di·ence \kler-ˈȯ-dē-ən(t)s, -ˈä-\ *n* [*clair-* (as in *clairvoyance*) + *audience* (act of hearing)] (1864) **:** the power or faculty of hearing something not present to the ear but regarded as having objective reality — **clair·au·di·ent** \-ənt\ *adj* — **clair·au·di·ent·ly** *adv*

clair·voy·ance \kler-ˈvȯi-ən(t)s\ *n* (1838) **1 :** the power or faculty of discerning objects not present to the senses **2 :** ability to perceive matters beyond the range of ordinary perception **:** PENETRATION

[1]**clair·voy·ant** \-ənt\ *adj* [F, fr. *clair* clear (fr. L *clarus*) + *voyant,* prp. of *voir* to see, fr. L *vidēre* — more at WIT] (1844) **1 :** having clairvoyance **:** able to see beyond the range of ordinary perception ⟨claims to be ~⟩ **2 :** of or relating to clairvoyance ⟨~ powers⟩ — **clair·voy·ant·ly** *adv*

[2]**clairvoyant** *n* (1846) **:** one having the power of clairvoyance

[1]**clam** \ˈklam\ *n* [ME, fr. OE *clamm* bond, fetter; akin to OHG *klamma* constriction and perh. to L *glomus* ball] (bef. 12c) **:** CLAMP, CLASP

[2]**clam** *n, often attrib* [[1]*clam;* fr. the clamping action of the shells] (ca. 1520) **1 a :** any of numerous edible marine bivalve mollusks living in sand or mud **b :** a freshwater mussel **2 :** a stolid or closemouthed person **3 :** CLAMSHELL **4 :** DOLLAR 3

[3]**clam** *vi* **clammed; clam·ming** (1636) **:** to gather clams esp. by digging — **clam·mer** \ˈkla-mər\ *n*

cla·mant \ˈklā-mənt, ˈkla-\ *adj* [L *clamant-, clamans,* prp. of *clamare* to cry out] (1639) **1 :** CLAMOROUS, BLATANT **2 :** demanding attention **:** URGENT — **cla·mant·ly** *adv*

clam·bake \ˈklam-ˌbāk\ *n* (1835) **1 a :** an outdoor party; *esp* **:** a seashore outing where food is usu. cooked on heated rocks covered by seaweed **b :** the food served at a clambake **2 :** a gathering characterized by noisy sociability; *esp* **:** a political rally

clam·ber \ˈklam-bər, ˈkla-mər\ *vi* **clam·bered; clam·ber·ing** \ˈklam-b(ə-)riŋ, ˈklam-riŋ, ˈkla-mər-iŋ\ [ME *clambren;* akin to OE *climban* to climb] (14c) **:** to climb awkwardly (as by scrambling) ⟨~*ed* over the rocks⟩ — **clam·ber·er** \-bər-ər, -mər-ər\ *n*

clam·my \ˈkla-mē\ *adj* **clam·mi·er; -est** [ME, prob. fr. *clammen* to smear, stick, fr. OE *clǣman;* akin to OE *clǣg* clay] (14c) **1 :** being damp, soft, sticky, and usu. cool ⟨cold ~ hands⟩ ⟨~ air⟩ **2 :** lacking normal human warmth ⟨the ~ atmosphere of an institution⟩ — **clam·mi·ly** \ˈkla-mə-lē\ *adv* — **clam·mi·ness** \ˈkla-mē-nəs\ *n*

[1]**clam·or** \ˈkla-mər\ *n* [ME, fr. AF *clamour,* fr. L *clamor,* fr. *clamare* to cry out — more at CLAIM] (14c) **1 a :** noisy shouting **b :** a loud continuous noise **2 :** insistent public expression (as of support or protest)

[2]**clamor** *vb* **clam·ored; clam·or·ing** \ˈklam-riŋ, ˈkla-mər-iŋ\ *vi* (14c) **1 :** to make a din **2 :** to become loudly insistent ⟨~*ed* for his impeachment⟩ ~ *vt* **1 :** to utter or proclaim insistently and noisily **2 :** to influence by means of clamor

[3]**clamor** *vt* [origin unknown] (1611) *obs* **:** SILENCE

clam·or·ous \ˈklam-rəs, ˈkla-mər-əs\ *adj* (15c) **1 :** marked by confused din or outcry **:** TUMULTUOUS **2 :** noisily insistent ***syn*** see VOCIFEROUS — **clam·or·ous·ly** *adv* — **clam·or·ous·ness** *n*

clam·our \ˈkla-mər\ *chiefly Brit var of* CLAMOR

[1]**clamp** \ˈklamp\ *n* [ME, prob. fr. MD **klampe;* akin to OE *clamm* bond, fetter — more at CLAM] (14c) **1 :** a device designed to bind or constrict or to press two or more parts together so as to hold them firmly **2 :** any of various instruments or appliances having parts brought together for holding or compressing something

[2]**clamp** *vt* (1683) **1 :** to fasten with or as if with a clamp ⟨~ two boards together⟩ **2 a :** to place by decree **:** IMPOSE — often used with *on* ⟨~*ed* on a curfew after the riots⟩ **b :** to hold tightly

clamp·down \ˈklamp-ˌdau̇n\ *n* (1940) **:** the act or action of making regulations and restrictions more stringent ⟨a ~ on charge accounts, bank loans, and other inflationary influences —*Time*⟩

clamp down *vi* (1938) **:** to impose restrictions **:** CRACK DOWN ⟨the police are *clamping down* on speeders⟩

clams casino *n pl but sing or pl in constr, often cap 2d C* (1908) **:** clams on the half shell usu. topped with green pepper and baked or broiled

clam·shell \ˈklam-ˌshel\ *n* (ca. 1520) **1 :** the shell of a clam **2 a :** a bucket or grapple (as on a dredge) having two hinged jaws **b :** an excavating machine having a clamshell **c :** either of a pair of doors (as in an airplane tail) that open out and away from each other **d :** a hinged container, case, or cover that opens like the shell of a clam

clam up *vi* (1916) **:** to become silent ⟨*clammed up* and refused to talk⟩

clam worm *n* (1885) **:** any of several large burrowing polychaete worms (as a nereid) often used as bait

clan \ˈklan\ *n* [ME, fr. ScGael *clann* offspring, clan, fr. OIr *cland* plant, offspring, fr. L *planta* plant] (15c) **1 a :** a Celtic group esp. in the Scottish Highlands comprising a number of households whose heads claim descent from a common ancestor **b :** a group of people tracing descent from a common ancestor **:** FAMILY **2 :** a group united by a common interest or common characteristics

clan·des·tine \klan-ˈdes-tən *also* -ˌtīn *or* -ˌtēn *or* ˈklan-dəs-\ *adj* [MF or L; MF *clandestin,* fr. L *clandestinus,* fr. *clam* secretly; akin to L *celare* to hide — more at HELL] (ca. 1528) **:** marked by, held in, or conducted with secrecy **:** SURREPTITIOUS ⟨a ~ love affair⟩ ***syn*** see SECRET — **clan·des·tine·ly** *adv* — **clan·des·tine·ness** *n* — **clan·des·tin·i·ty** \ˌklan-də-ˈsti-nə-tē, -des-ˈti-\ *n*

[1]**clang** \ˈklaŋ\ *vb* [L *clangere;* akin to Gk *klazein* to scream, bark, OE *hliehhan* to laugh] *vi* (1576) **1 a :** to make a loud metallic ringing sound ⟨anvils ~*ed*⟩ **b :** to go with a clang **2 :** to utter the characteristic harsh cry of a bird ~ *vt* **:** to cause to clang ⟨~ a bell⟩

[2]**clang** *n* (1557) **1 :** a loud ringing metallic sound ⟨the ~ of a fire alarm⟩ **2 :** a harsh cry of a bird (as a crane or goose)

clang·er \ˈklaŋ-ər\ *n* (1948) *Brit* **:** a conspicuous blunder — often used in the phrase *drop a clanger*

[1]**clan·gor** \ˈklaŋ-ər *also* -gər\ *n* [L *clangor,* fr. *clangere*] (1593) **:** a resounding clang or medley of clangs ⟨the ~ of hammers⟩ — **clan·gor·ous** \-(g)ə-rəs\ *adj* — **clan·gor·ous·ly** *adv*

[2]**clangor** *vi* (1837) **:** to make a clangor

clan·gour \ˈklaŋ-ər, -gər\ *chiefly Brit var of* CLANGOR

[1]**clank** \ˈklaŋk\ *vb* [prob. imit.] *vi* (1656) **1 :** to make a clank or series of clanks ⟨the radiator hissed and ~*ed*⟩ **2 :** to go with or as if with a clank ⟨tanks ~*ing* through the streets⟩ ~ *vt* **:** to cause to clank — **clank·ing·ly** \ˈklaŋ-kiŋ-lē\ *adv*

[2]**clank** *n* (1656) **:** a sharp brief metallic ringing sound

clan·nish \ˈkla-nish\ *adj* (1776) **1 :** of or relating to a clan ⟨~ traditions⟩ **2 :** tending to associate only with a select group of similar background or status ⟨a ~ community⟩ — **clan·nish·ly** *adv* — **clan·nish·ness** *n*

clans·man \ˈklanz-mən\ *n* (1810) **:** a member of a clan

[1]**clap** \ˈklap\ *vb* **clapped** *also* **clapt; clap·ping** [ME *clappen,* fr. OE *clæppan* to throb; akin to OHG *klaphōn* to beat] *vt* (14c) **1 :** to strike (as two flat hard surfaces) together so as to produce a sharp percussive noise **2 a :** to strike (the hands) together repeatedly usu. in applause **b :** APPLAUD **3 :** to strike with the flat of the hand in a friendly way ⟨*clapped* his friend on the shoulder⟩ **4 :** to place, put, or set esp. energetically ⟨~ him into jail⟩ ⟨since I first *clapped* eyes on it⟩ **5 :** to improvise or build hastily ⟨a hut *clapped* together from old plywood⟩ ~ *vi* **1 :** to produce a percussive sound; *esp* **:** SLAM **2 :** to go abruptly or briskly **3 :** APPLAUD

[2]**clap** *n* (13c) **1 :** a device that makes a clapping noise **2** *obs* **:** a sudden stroke of fortune and esp. ill fortune **3 :** a loud percussive noise; *specif* **:** a sudden crash of thunder **4 a :** a sudden blow **b :** a friendly slap ⟨a ~ on the back⟩ **5 :** the sound of clapping hands; *esp* **:** APPLAUSE

[3]**clap** *n* [MF *clapoir* bubo] (1587) **:** GONORRHEA — often used with *the*

clap·board \ˈkla-bərd; ˈkla(p)-ˌbȯrd\ *n* [part trans. of D *klaphout* stave wood] (ca. 1520) **1** *archaic* **:** a size of board for making staves and wainscoting **2 :** a narrow board usu. thicker at one edge than the other used for siding **3** \ˈklap-ˌbȯrd\ **:** a pair of hinged boards one of which has a slate with data identifying a piece of film and which are banged together in front of a motion-picture camera at the start of a take to facilitate editing — called also *clapper board* — **clapboard** *vt*

clapped–out \ˌklapt-ˈau̇t\ *adj* (1946) *chiefly Brit* **:** WORN-OUT; *also* **:** TIRED

clap·per \ˈkla-pər\ *n* (14c) **:** one that claps: as **a :** the tongue of a bell **b :** a mechanical device that makes noise esp. by the banging of one part against another **c :** a person who applauds

clap·per·claw \ˈkla-pər-ˌklȯ\ *vt* [perh. fr. *clapper* + *claw* (v.)] (1590) **1** *dial Eng* **:** to claw with the nails **2** *dial Eng* **:** SCOLD, REVILE

clapper rail *n* [fr. its rattle-like call] (1813) **:** a grayish-brown long-billed American rail (*Rallus longirostris*) that inhabits coastal marshes

[1]**clap·trap** \ˈklap-ˌtrap\ *n* [[2]*clap;* fr. its attempt to win applause] (1799) **:** pretentious nonsense **:** TRASH

[2]**claptrap** *adj* (1815) **:** characterized by or suggestive of claptrap; *esp* **:** of a cheap showy nature ⟨~ sentiment⟩

claque \ˈklak\ *n* [F, fr. *claquer* to clap, of imit. origin] (1848) **1 :** a group hired to applaud at a performance **2 :** a group of sycophants

cla·queur \kla-ˈkər\ *n* [F, fr. *claquer* to clap] (1837) **:** a member of a claque

clar·et \ˈkler-ət, ˈkla-rət\ *n* [ME, fr. AF (*vin*) *claret* clear wine, fr. *claret* clear, fr. *cler* clear] (1578) **1 :** a red Bordeaux wine; *also* **:** a similar wine produced elsewhere **2 :** a dark purplish red — **claret** *adj*

clar·i·fy \ˈkler-ə-ˌfī, ˈkla-rə-\ *vb* **-fied; -fy·ing** [ME *clarifien,* fr. AF *clarifier,* fr. LL *clarificare,* fr. L *clarus* clear — more at CLEAR] *vt* (14c) **1 :** to make (as a liquid) clear or pure usu. by freeing from suspended matter **2 :** to free of confusion ⟨needs time to ~ his thoughts⟩ **3 :** to make understandable ⟨~ a subject⟩ ~ *vi* **:** to become clear — **clar·i·fi·ca·tion** \ˌkler-ə-fə-ˈkā-shən, ˌkla-rə-\ *n* — **clar·i·fi·er** \ˈkler-ə-ˌfī(-ə)r, ˈkla-rə-\ *n*

clar·i·net \ˌkler-ə-ˈnet, ˌkla-rə-; ˈkler-ə-nət, ˈkla-rə-\ *n* [F *clarinette,* prob. ultim. fr. ML *clarion-, clario*] (1733) **:** a single-reed woodwind instrument having a cylindrical tube with a moderately flared bell and a usual range from D below middle C upward for 3½ octaves — **clar·i·net·ist** *or* **clar·i·net·tist** \ˌkler-ə-ˈne-tist, ˌkla-rə-\ *n*

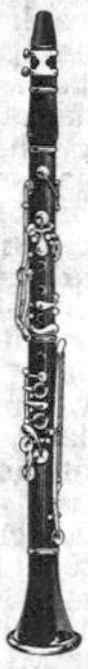

clarinet

[1]**clar·i·on** \ˈkler-ē-ən, ˈkla-rē-\ *n* [ME, fr. MF & ML; MF *clairon,* fr. ML *clarion-, clario,* fr. L *clarus*] (14c) **1 :** a medieval trumpet with clear shrill tones **2 :** the sound of or as if of a clarion

[2]**clarion** *adj* (1801) **:** brilliantly clear ⟨her ~ top notes⟩; *also* **:** loud and clear ⟨a ~ call to action⟩

clar·i·ty \ˈkler-ə-tē, ˈkla-rə-\ *n* [ME *clarite,* fr. L *claritat-, claritas,* fr. *clarus*] (1616) **:** the quality or state of being clear **:** LUCIDITY

clark·ia \ˈklär-kē-ə\ *n* [NL, fr. William *Clark*] (1827) **:** any of a genus (*Clarkia*) of showy annual herbs of the evening-primrose family that are native to western No. America and southwestern So. America

Clark's nutcracker \ˈklärks-\ *n* [William *Clark*] (1924) **:** a grayish-white bird (*Nucifraga columbiana*) of western No. America with black-and-white wings and tail

cla·ro \ˈklär-(ˌ)ō\ *n, pl* **claros** [Sp, fr. *claro* light, fr. L *clarus*] (1889) **:** a light-colored usu. mild cigar

clary sage \ˈkler-ē-\ *n* [ME *clarie,* fr. AF *sclaree,* fr. ML *sclareia*] (14c) **:** an aromatic mint (*Salvia sclarea*) of southern Europe that is widely cultivated esp. as an ornamental — called also *clary*

[1]**clash** \ˈklash\ *vb* [imit.] *vi* (ca. 1500) **1 :** to make a clash ⟨cymbals ~*ed*⟩ **2 :** to come into conflict ⟨where ignorant armies ~ by night —Matthew Arnold⟩; *also* **:** to be incompatible ⟨the colors ~*ed*⟩ ~ *vt* **:** to cause to clash — **clash·er** *n*

[2]**clash** *n* (1513) **1 :** a noisy usu. metallic sound of collision **2 a :** a hostile encounter **:** SKIRMISH **b :** a sharp conflict ⟨a ~ of opinions⟩

[1]**clasp** \ˈklasp\ *n* [ME *claspe*] (14c) **1 a :** a device (as a hook) for holding objects or parts together **b :** a device (as a bar) attached to a military medal to indicate an additional award of the medal or the action or service for which it was awarded **2 :** a holding or enveloping with or as if with the hands or arms

[2]**clasp** *vt* (14c) **1 :** to fasten with or as if with a clasp ⟨a robe ~*ed* with a brooch⟩ **2 :** to enclose and hold with the arms; *specif* **:** EMBRACE **3 :** to seize with or as if with the hand **:** GRASP

clasp·er \ˈklas-pər\ *n* (ca. 1847) **:** a male copulatory structure: **a :** one of a pair of external anal processes of an insect that are used to grasp a female **b :** one of a pair of organs that are extensions of the pelvic fins of cartilaginous fishes

clasp knife *n* (1734) **:** POCKETKNIFE; *esp* **:** a large one-bladed folding knife having a catch to hold the blade open

[1]**class** \ˈklas\ *n, often attrib* [F *classe,* fr. L *classis* group called to military service, fleet, class; perh. akin to L *calare* to call — more at LOW] (1602) **1 a :** a body of students meeting regularly to study the same subject **b :** the period during which such a body meets **c :** a course of instruction **d :** a body of students or alumni whose year of graduation is the same **2 a :** a group sharing the same economic or social status ⟨the working ~⟩ **b :** social rank; *esp* **:** high social rank **c :** high quality **:** ELEGANCE ⟨a hotel with ~⟩ **3 :** a group, set, or kind sharing common attributes: as **a :** a major category in biological taxonomy ranking above the order and below the phylum or division **b :** a collection of adjacent and discrete or continuous values of a random variable **c :** SET 21 **4 :** a division or rating based on grade or quality **5 :** the best of its kind ⟨the ~ of the league⟩ **6 :** a data type in object-oriented programming that consists of a group of objects with the same properties and behaviors and that is arranged in a hierarchy with other such data types — compare OBJECT

[2]**class** *vt* (1705) **:** CLASSIFY

class act *n* (1976) **:** an example of outstanding quality or prestige

class action *n* (1952) **:** a legal action undertaken by one or more plaintiffs on behalf of themselves and all other persons having an identical interest in the alleged wrong

class–conscious *adj* (1903) **1 :** actively aware of one's common status with others in a particular economic or social level of society **2 :** believing in class struggle — **class consciousness** *n*

[1]**clas·sic** \ˈkla-sik\ *adj* [F or L; F *classique,* fr. L *classicus* of the highest class of Roman citizens, of the first rank, fr. *classis*] (ca. 1604) **1 a :** serving as a standard of excellence **:** of recognized value ⟨~ literary works⟩ **b :** TRADITIONAL, ENDURING ⟨~ designs⟩ **c :** characterized by simple tailored lines in fashion year after year ⟨a ~ suit⟩ **2 :** of or relating to the ancient Greeks and Romans or their culture **:** CLASSICAL **3 a :** historically memorable ⟨a ~ battle⟩ **b :** noted because of special literary or historical associations ⟨Paris is the ~ refuge of expatriates⟩ **4 a :** AUTHENTIC, AUTHORITATIVE **b :** TYPICAL ⟨a ~ example of chicanery⟩ ⟨a ~ error⟩ **5** *cap* **:** of or relating to the period of highest development of Mesoamerican and esp. Mayan culture about A.D. 300–900

[2]**classic** *n* (1711) **1 :** a literary work of ancient Greece or Rome **2 a :** a work of enduring excellence; *also* **:** its author **b :** an authoritative source **3 :** a typical or perfect example **4 :** a traditional event ⟨a football ~⟩

clas·si·cal \ˈkla-si-kəl\ *adj* [L *classicus*] (1599) **1 :** STANDARD, CLASSIC **2 a :** of or relating to the ancient Greek and Roman world and esp. to its literature, art, architecture, or ideals ⟨~ civilization⟩ **b :** versed in the classics ⟨a ~ scholar⟩ **3 a :** of or relating to music of the late 18th and early 19th centuries characterized by an emphasis on balance, clarity, and moderation **b :** of, relating to, or being music in the educated European tradition that includes such forms as art song, chamber music, opera, and symphony as distinguished from folk or popular music or jazz **4 a :** AUTHORITATIVE, TRADITIONAL **b (1) :** of or relating to a form or system considered of first significance in earlier times ⟨~ Mendelian genetics⟩ **(2) :** not involving relativity, wave mechanics, or quantum theory ⟨~ physics⟩ **c :** conforming to a pattern of usage sanctioned by a body of literature rather than by everyday speech **5 :** concerned with or giving instruction in the humanities, the fine arts, and the broad aspects of science ⟨a ~ curriculum⟩

classical conditioning *n* (1949) **:** conditioning in which the conditioned stimulus (as the sound of a bell) is paired with and precedes the unconditioned stimulus (as the sight of food) until the conditioned stimulus alone is sufficient to elicit the response (as salivation in a dog) — compare OPERANT CONDITIONING

clas·si·cal·i·ty \ˌkla-sə-ˈka-lə-tē\ *n* (1819) **1 :** the quality or state of being classic **2 :** classical scholarship

clas·si·cal·ly \ˈkla-si-k(ə-)lē\ *adv* (1772) **1 :** in a classic or classical manner ⟨~ exact forms of the dance⟩ ⟨~ trained⟩ **2 a :** in classic or traditional circumstances **:** TYPICALLY ⟨~, the whole fish is stuffed⟩ **b :** as a classic example ⟨~ bad writing⟩

clas·si·cism \ˈkla-sə-ˌsi-zəm\ *n* (1830) **1 a :** the principles or style embodied in the literature, art, or architecture of ancient Greece and Rome **b :** classical scholarship **c :** a classical idiom or expression **2 :** adherence to traditional standards (as of simplicity, restraint, and proportion) that are universally and enduringly valid

clas·si·cist \-sist\ *n* (1830) **1 :** an advocate or follower of classicism **2 :** a classical scholar — **clas·si·cis·tic** \ˌkla-sə-ˈsis-tik\ *adj*

clas·si·cize \ˈkla-sə-ˌsīz\ *vb* **-cized; -ciz·ing** *vt* (1854) **:** to make classic or classical ~ *vi* **:** to follow classic style

clas·si·co \ˈkla-si-(ˌ)kō\ *adj* [It, fr. L *classicus*] (1968) **:** produced in a delimited area of Italy known for its standards of quality ⟨Chianti ~⟩

clas·si·fi·ca·tion \ˌkla-sə-fə-ˈkā-shən\ *n* (1790) **1 :** the act or process of classifying **2 a :** systematic arrangement in groups or categories according to established criteria; *specif* **:** TAXONOMY **b :** CLASS, CATEGORY — **clas·si·fi·ca·to·ry** \ˈkla-sə-fi-kə-ˌtȯr-ē, kla-ˈsi-fə-; ˈkla-sə-fə-ˌkā-tə-rē\ *adj*

[1]**clas·si·fied** \ˈkla-sə-ˌfīd\ *adj* (1889) **1 :** divided into classes or placed in a class ⟨~ ads⟩ **2 :** withheld from general circulation for reasons of national security ⟨~ information⟩

[2]**classified** *n* (1952) **:** an advertisement grouped with others according to subject — usu. used in pl.

clas·si·fi·er \ˈkla-sə-ˌfī(-ə)r\ *n* (1819) **1 :** one that classifies; *specif* **:** a machine for sorting out the constituents of a substance (as ore) **2 :** a word or morpheme used with numerals or with nouns designating countable or measurable objects

clas·si·fy \ˈkla-sə-ˌfī\ *vt* **-fied; -fy·ing** (1799) **1 :** to arrange in classes ⟨~*ing* books according to subject matter⟩ **2 :** to assign (as a document) to a category — **clas·si·fi·able** \ˌkla-sə-ˈfī-ə-bəl\ *adj*

class interval *n* (1929) **:** CLASS 3b; *also* **:** its numerical width

clas·sis \ˈkla-sis\ *n, pl* **clas·ses** \ˈkla-ˌsēz\ [NL, fr. L, class] (1593) **1 :** a governing body in some Reformed churches (as in the former Reformed Church in the U.S.) corresponding to a presbytery **2 :** the district governed by a classis

class·ism \ˈkla-ˌsi-zəm\ *n* (1842) **:** prejudice or discrimination based on class — **class·ist** \ˈkla-sist\ *adj*

class·less \ˈklas-ləs\ *adj* (1878) **1 :** belonging to no particular social class **2 :** free from distinctions of social class ⟨a ~ society⟩ **3 :** CRASS, BOORISH ⟨~ behavior⟩ — **class·less·ness** *n*

class·mate \-ˌmāt\ *n* (1713) **:** a member of the same class in a school or college

class·room \-ˌrüm, -ˌru̇m\ *n* (1811) **:** a place where classes meet

classy \ˈkla-sē\ *adj* **class·i·er; -est** (1891) **:** having or showing class: as **a :** ELEGANT, STYLISH ⟨a ~ clientele⟩ **b :** having or reflecting high standards of personal behavior ⟨a ~ guy⟩ ⟨a ~ gesture⟩ **c :** admirably skillful and graceful ⟨a ~ outfielder⟩ — **class·i·ness** *n*

clast \ˈklast\ *n* [Gk *klastos* broken, fr. *klan* to break; perh. akin to L *clades* disaster] (1952) **:** a fragment of rock

clas·tic \ˈklas-tik\ *adj* [ISV] (1877) **:** made up of fragments of preexisting rocks ⟨a ~ sediment⟩ — **clastic** *n*

clath·rate \ˈkla-ˌthrāt\ *adj* [L *clathratus,* furnished with a lattice, fr. *clathri* (pl.) lattice, fr. Gk *klēithron* bar, fr. *kleiein* to close — more at CLAVICLE] (1906) **:** relating to or being a compound formed by the inclusion of molecules of one kind in cavities of the crystal lattice of another — **clathrate** *n*

[1]**clat·ter** \ˈkla-tər\ *vb* [ME *clatren,* fr. OE **clatrian;* of imit. origin] *vi* (13c) **1 :** to make a rattling sound ⟨the dishes ~*ed* on the shelf⟩ **2 :** to talk noisily or rapidly **3 :** to move or go with a clatter ⟨~*ed* down the stairs⟩ ~ *vt* **:** to cause to clatter — **clat·ter·er** \-tər-ər\ *n* — **clat·ter·ing·ly** \ˈkla-tə-riŋ-lē\ *adv*

[2]**clatter** *n* (14c) **1 :** a rattling sound (as of hard bodies striking together) ⟨the ~ of pots and pans⟩ **2 :** COMMOTION ⟨the midday ~ of the business district⟩ **3 :** noisy chatter — **clat·tery** \ˈkla-tə-rē\ *adj*

clau·di·ca·tion \ˌklȯ-də-ˈkā-shən\ *n* [L *claudication-, claudicatio,* fr. *claudicare* to limp, fr. *claudus* lame] (15c) **:** the quality or state of being lame **:** LIMPING

claus·al \ˈklȯ-zəl\ *adj* (1904) **:** relating to or of the nature of a clause

clause \ˈklȯz\ *n* [ME, fr. AF, fr. ML *clausa* close of a rhetorical period, fr. L, fem. of *clausus,* pp. of *claudere* to close — more at CLOSE] (13c) **1 :** a group of words containing a subject and predicate and functioning as a member of a complex or compound sentence **2 :** a separate section of a discourse or writing; *specif* **:** a distinct article in a formal document

claus·tral \ˈklȯs-trəl\ *adj* [ME, fr. ML *claustralis,* fr. *claustrum* cloister, fr. L, bar, bolt, confining space, fr. *claudere*] (15c) **:** CLOISTRAL

claus·tro·pho·bia \ˌklȯs-trə-ˈfō-bē-ə\ *n* [NL, fr. L *claustrum* + NL *-phobia*] (1879) **:** abnormal dread of being in closed or narrow spaces — **claus·tro·phobe** \ˈklȯs-trə-ˌfōb\ *n*

claus·tro·pho·bic \ˌklȯs-trə-ˈfō-bik\ *adj* (ca. 1889) **1 :** affected with or inclined to claustrophobia **2 :** inducing or suggesting claustrophobia — **claus·tro·pho·bi·cal·ly** \-bi-k(ə-)lē\ *adv*

claus·trum \ˈklȯs-trəm, ˈklau̇s-\ *n, pl* **claus·tra** \-trə\ [NL, fr. L, bar] (1848) **:** the one of the four basal ganglia in each cerebral hemisphere that consists of a thin lamina of gray matter separated from the lenticular nucleus by a layer of white matter

cla·vate \ˈklā-ˌvāt\ *adj* [NL *clavatus,* fr. L *clava* club, fr. *clavus* nail, knot in wood] (1813) **:** thickened near the distal end **:** club-shaped

[1]**clave** *past of* CLEAVE

[2]**clave** \ˈklä-(ˌ)vā, ˈklāv\ *n* [AmerSp, fr. Sp, keystone, clef, fr. L *clavis*] (1928) **:** one of a pair of cylindrical hardwood sticks that are used as a percussion instrument

cla·ver \ˈklā-vər\ *vi* [origin unknown] (ca. 1605) *chiefly Scot* **:** PRATE, GOSSIP — **claver** *n, chiefly Scot*

clav·i·chord \ˈkla-və-ˌkȯrd\ *n* [ML *clavichordium,* fr. L *clavis* key + *chorda* string — more at CORD] (15c) **:** an early keyboard instrument having strings struck by tangents attached directly to the key ends — **clav·i·chord·ist** \-ˌkȯr-dist\ *n*

clav·i·cle \ˈkla-vi-kəl\ *n* [F *clavicule,* fr. NL *clavicula,* fr. L, dim. of L *clavis;* akin to Gk *kleid-, kleis* key, *kleiein* to close] (1615) **:** a bone of the vertebrate pectoral girdle typically serving to link the scapula and sternum — called also *collarbone* — **cla·vic·u·lar** \kla-ˈvi-kyə-lər, klə-\ *adj*

cla·vier \klə-ˈvir; ˈklā-vē-ər, ˈkla-\ *n* [F, fr. OF, key bearer, fr. L *clavis*] (1694) **1 :** the keyboard of a musical instrument **2** [G *Klavier,* fr. F *clavier*] **:** an early keyboard instrument — **cla·vier·ist** \klə-ˈvir-ist; ˈklā-vē-ə-rist, ˈkla-\ *n* — **cla·vier·is·tic** \klə-ˌvi-ˈris-tik; ˌklā-vē-ə-ˈris-tik, ˌkla-\ *adj*

[1]**claw** \ˈklȯ\ *n, often attrib* [ME *clawe,* fr. OE *clawu* hoof, claw; akin to ON *klō* claw, and prob. to OE *cliewen* ball — more at CLEW] (bef. 12c) **1 :** a sharp usu. slender and curved nail on the toe of an animal **2 :** any of various sharp curved processes esp. at the end of a limb (as of an insect); *also* **:** a limb ending in such a process **3 :** one of the pincerlike organs terminating some limbs of various arthropods (as a lobster or scorpion) **4 :** something that resembles a claw; *specif* **:** the forked end of a tool (as a hammer) — **clawed** \ˈklȯd\ *adj* — **claw·like** \-ˌlīk\ *adj*

[2]**claw** *vt* (bef. 12c) **:** to rake, seize, dig, or progress with or as if with claws ~ *vi* **:** to scrape, scratch, dig, or pull with or as if with claws

claw back *vt* (1953) *chiefly Brit* **:** to get back (as money) by strenuous or forceful means (as taxation) — **claw·back** \ˈklȯ-ˌbak\ *n*

claw–foot \ˈklȯ-ˌfu̇t\ *n* (1792) **:** a foot (as on a bathtub or piece of furniture) in the shape of a claw

claw·ham·mer \ˈklȯ-ˌha-mər\ *adj* (1964) **:** of, relating to, or being a style of banjo playing using the thumb and one or more fingers picking or strumming in a downward direction

claw hammer *n* (ca. 1769) **1 :** a hammer with one end of the head forked for pulling out nails **2 :** TAILCOAT

clay \ˈklā\ *n, often attrib* [ME, fr. OE *clǣg;* akin to OHG *klīwa* bran, L *gluten* glue, MGk *glia*] (bef. 12c) **1 a :** an earthy material that is plastic when moist but hard when fired, that is composed mainly of fine particles of hydrous aluminum silicates and other minerals, and that is used for brick, tile, and pottery; *specif* **:** soil composed chiefly of this material having particles less than a specified size **b :** EARTH, MUD **2 a :** a substance that resembles clay in plasticity and is used for modeling **b :** the human body as distinguished from the spirit **c :** fundamental nature or character ⟨the common ~⟩ **3 :** CLAY COURT — **clay·ey** \ˈklā-ē\ *adj* — **clay·ish** \ˈklā-ish\ *adj* — **clay·like** \-ˌlīk\ *adj*

clay·bank \ˈklā-ˌbaŋk\ *n* (1851) **:** a horse of yellowish color

clay court *n* (1885) **:** a tennis court with a clay surface or a synthetic surface that resembles clay

clay feet *n pl* (1862) **:** FEET OF CLAY

clay loam *n* (ca. 1889) **:** a loam containing from 20 to 30 percent clay

Clay·ma·tion \ˈklā-ˈmā-shən\ *service mark* — used for animation that features images of clay figures

clay mineral *n* (1937) **:** any of a group of hydrous silicates of aluminum and sometimes other metals formed chiefly in weathering processes and occurring esp. in clay and shale

clay·more \ˈklā-ˌmȯr\ *n* [ScGael *claidheamh mór,* lit., great sword] (1527) **:** a large 2-edged sword formerly used by Scottish Highlanders; *also* **:** their basket-hilted broadsword

claymore mine *n* [prob. fr. *claymore*] (1961) **:** a usu. electrically fired land mine containing steel fragments that are discharged in a predetermined direction

clay·pan \-ˌpan\ *n* (1837) **1 :** hardpan consisting mainly of clay **2** *Austral* **:** a shallow depression in which water collects after rain

clay pigeon *n* (1888) **:** a saucer-shaped target usu. made of baked clay or limestone and pitch and thrown from a trap in skeet and trapshooting

clay·ware \ˈklā-ˌwer\ *n* (1896) **:** articles made of fired clay

cld *abbr* called; cleared

[1]**clean** \ˈklēn\ *adj* [ME *clene,* fr. OE *clǣne;* akin to OHG *kleini* delicate, dainty] (bef. 12c) **1 a :** free from dirt or pollution ⟨changed to ~ clothes⟩ ⟨~ solar energy⟩ **b :** free from contamination or disease ⟨a ~ wound⟩ **c :** free or relatively free from radioactivity ⟨a ~ atomic explosion⟩ **2 a :** UNADULTERATED, PURE ⟨the ~ thrill of one's first flight⟩ **b** *of a precious stone* **:** having no interior flaws visible **c :** free from growth that hinders tillage ⟨~ farmland⟩ **3 a :** free from moral corruption or sinister connections of any kind ⟨a candidate with a ~ record⟩; *also* **:** free from violations ⟨a ~ driving record⟩ **b :** free from offensive treatment of sexual subjects and from the use of obscenity ⟨a ~ joke⟩ **c :** observing the rules **:** FAIR ⟨a ~ fight⟩ **4 :** ceremonially or spiritually pure ⟨and all who are ~ may eat flesh —Lev 7:19(RSV)⟩ **5 a :** THOROUGH, COMPLETE ⟨a ~ break with the past⟩ **b :** deftly executed **:** SKILLFUL ⟨~ ballet technique⟩ **c :** hit beyond the reach of an opponent ⟨a ~ single to center⟩ **6 a :** relatively free from error or blemish **:** CLEAR; *specif* **:** LEGIBLE ⟨~ copy⟩ **b :** UNENCUMBERED ⟨~ bill of sale⟩ **7 a :** characterized by clarity and precision **:** TRIM ⟨a ~ prose style⟩ ⟨architecture with ~ almost austere lines⟩ **b :** EVEN, SMOOTH ⟨a ~ edge⟩ ⟨a sharp blow causing a ~ break⟩ **c :** free from impedances to smooth flow (as of water or air) ⟨a ~ airplane⟩ ⟨a ship with a ~ bottom⟩ **8 a :** EMPTY ⟨the ship returned with a ~ hold⟩ **b :** free from drug addiction ⟨has been ~ for six months⟩ **c** *slang* **:** having no contraband (as weapons or drugs) in one's possession **9 :** habitually neat — **clean·ness** \ˈklēn-nəs\ *n*

[2]**clean** *adv* (bef. 12c) **1 a :** so as to clean ⟨a new broom sweeps ~⟩ **b :** in a clean manner ⟨play the game ~⟩ **2 :** all the way **:** COMPLETELY ⟨the bullet went ~ through his arm⟩

[3]**clean** *vt* (15c) **1 a :** to make clean: as (1) **:** to rid of dirt, impurities, or extraneous matter (2) **:** to rid of corruption ⟨vowing to ~ up city hall⟩ **b :** REMOVE, ERADICATE — usu. used with *up* or *off* ⟨~ up that mess⟩ **2 a :** STRIP, EMPTY ⟨a tree ~*ed* of fruit⟩ **b :** to remove the entrails from ⟨~ fish⟩ **c :** to deprive of money or possessions — often used with *out* ⟨they ~*ed* him out completely⟩ ~ *vi* **:** to undergo or perform a process of cleaning ⟨~ up before dinner⟩ — **clean·abil·i·ty** \ˌklē-nə-ˈbi-lə-tē\ *n* — **clean·able** \ˈklē-nə-bəl\ *adj* — **clean house 1 :** to clean a house and its furniture **2 :** to make sweeping reforms or changes (as of personnel) — **clean one's clock :** to beat one badly in a fight or competition — **clean up one's act :** to behave in a more acceptable manner

[4]**clean** *n* (ca. 1889) **:** an act of cleaning dirt esp. from the surface of something

clean and jerk *n* (1913) **:** a lift in weight lifting in which the weight is raised to shoulder height, held momentarily, and then quickly thrust overhead usu. with a lunge or a spring from the legs — compare PRESS, SNATCH — **clean–and–jerk** *vb*

clean–cut \ˈklēn-ˈkət\ *adj* (1843) **1 :** cut so that the surface or edge is smooth and even **2 :** sharply defined **3 :** of wholesome appearance

clean·er \ˈklē-nər\ *n* (1720) **1 a :** one whose work is cleaning **b :** DRY CLEANER; *also* **:** a dry-cleaning shop — usu. used in pl. **2 :** a preparation for cleaning **3 :** an implement or machine for cleaning

clean·hand·ed \ˈklēn-ˈhan-dəd\ *adj* (1728) **:** innocent of wrongdoing

clean–limbed \ˈklēn-ˈlimd\ *adj* (15c) **:** well proportioned **:** TRIM ⟨~ youths⟩

[1]**clean·ly** \ˈklēn-lē\ *adv* (13c) **:** in a clean manner

[2]**clean·ly** \ˈklen-lē\ *adj* **clean·li·er; -est** (ca. 1500) **1 :** careful to keep clean **:** FASTIDIOUS **2 :** habitually kept clean — **clean·li·ness** *n*

clean room \ˈklēn-ˌrüm, -ˌru̇m\ *n* (1963) **:** a room for the manufacture or assembly of objects (as precision parts) that is maintained at a high level of cleanliness by special means

cleanse \ˈklenz\ *vb* **cleansed; cleans·ing** [ME *clensen,* fr. OE *clǣnsian* to purify, fr. *clǣne* clean] (bef. 12c) **:** CLEAN; *esp* **:** to rid of impurities by or as if by washing

cleans·er \ˈklen-zər\ *n* (bef. 12c) **1 :** one that cleanses **2 :** a preparation (as a scouring powder or a skin cream) used for cleaning

[1]**clean·up** \ˈklēn-ˌəp\ *n* (1872) **1 :** an act or instance of cleaning **2 :** an exceptionally large profit **:** KILLING

[2]**cleanup** *adj* (1937) **:** being in the fourth position in the batting order of a baseball team ⟨a ~ hitter⟩ — **cleanup** *adv*

clean up *vi* (1920) **:** to make a spectacular profit in a business enterprise or a killing in speculation or gambling

[1]**clear** \ˈklir\ *adj* [ME *clere,* fr. AF *cler,* fr. L *clarus* clear, bright; akin to L *calare* to call — more at LOW] (13c) **1 a :** BRIGHT, LUMINOUS **b :** CLOUDLESS; *specif* **:** less than one-tenth covered ⟨a ~ sky⟩ **c :** free from mist, haze, or dust ⟨a ~ day⟩ **d :** UNTROUBLED, SERENE ⟨a ~ gaze⟩ **2 :** CLEAN, PURE: as **a :** free from blemishes ⟨~ skin⟩ **b :** easily seen through **:** TRANSPARENT ⟨~ glass⟩ **c :** free from abnormal sounds on auscultation **3 a :** easily heard ⟨a loud and ~ sound⟩ **b :** easily visible **:** PLAIN ⟨a ~ signal⟩ **c :** free from obscurity or ambiguity **:** easily understood **:** UNMISTAKABLE ⟨a ~ explanation⟩ **4 a :** capable of sharp discernment **:** KEEN ⟨a ~ thinker⟩ **b :** free from doubt **:** SURE ⟨not ~ on how to proceed⟩ **5 :** free from guile or guilt

\ə\ **abut** \ᵊ\ kitten, F table \ər\ **further** \a\ **ash** \ā\ **ace** \ä\ mop, mar \au̇\ **out** \ch\ **chin** \e\ **bet** \ē\ **easy** \g\ **go** \i\ **hit** \ī\ **ice** \j\ **job** \ŋ\ **sing** \ō\ **go** \ȯ\ **law** \ȯi\ **boy** \th\ **thin** \t͟h\ **the** \ü\ **loot** \u̇\ **foot** \y\ **yet** \zh\ **vision, beige** \k̲, ⁿ, œ, ue, ʸ\ *see* Guide to Pronunciation

: INNOCENT ⟨a ~ conscience⟩ **6** : unhampered by restriction or limitation: as **a** : unencumbered by debts or charges ⟨a ~ estate⟩ **b** : NET ⟨a ~ profit⟩ **c** : UNQUALIFIED, ABSOLUTE ⟨a ~ victory⟩ **d** : free from obstruction ⟨~ passage⟩ **e** : emptied of contents or cargo **f** : free from entanglement or contact ⟨staying ~ of controversy⟩ ⟨keep ~ of the boundary⟩ **g** : BARE, DENUDED ⟨~ ground⟩ — **clear•ness** *n*

syn CLEAR, TRANSPARENT, TRANSLUCENT, LIMPID mean capable of being seen through. CLEAR implies absence of cloudiness, haziness, or muddiness ⟨*clear* water⟩. TRANSPARENT implies being so clear that objects can be seen distinctly ⟨a *transparent* sheet of film⟩. TRANSLUCENT implies the passage of light but not a clear view of what lies beyond ⟨*translucent* frosted glass⟩. LIMPID suggests the soft clearness of pure water ⟨her eyes were *limpid* pools of blue⟩.

syn CLEAR, PERSPICUOUS, LUCID mean quickly and easily understood. CLEAR implies freedom from obscurity, ambiguity, or undue complexity ⟨*clear* instructions⟩. PERSPICUOUS applies to a style that is simple and elegant as well as clear ⟨a *perspicuous* style⟩. LUCID suggests a clear logical coherence and evident order of arrangement ⟨a *lucid* explanation⟩. ***syn*** see in addition EVIDENT

[2]**clear** *adv* (14c) **1** : in a clear manner ⟨to cry loud and ~⟩ **2** : all the way ⟨drove ~ across the state⟩

[3]**clear** *vt* (14c) **1 a** : to make clear or translucent **b** : to free from pollution or cloudiness **2** : to free from accusation or blame : EXONERATE, VINDICATE ⟨the opportunity to ~ himself⟩ **3 a** : to give insight to : ENLIGHTEN **b** : to make intelligible : EXPLAIN ⟨~ up the mystery⟩ **4 a** : to free from what obstructs or is unneeded: as (1) : OPEN 1b ⟨~ a path⟩ (2) : to remove unwanted growth or items from ⟨~ the land of timber⟩ (3) : to rid or make a rasping noise as if ridding (the throat) of phlegm (4) : to erase stored or displayed data from (as a computer or calculator) **b** : to empty of occupants ⟨~ the room⟩ **c** : DISENTANGLE ⟨~ a fishing line⟩ **d** : to remove from an area or place ⟨~ the dishes from the table⟩ **e** : TRANSMIT, DISPATCH **5 a** : to submit for approval ⟨~ it with me first⟩ **b** : AUTHORIZE, APPROVE ⟨~*ed* the article for publication⟩: as (1) : to certify as trustworthy ⟨~ a person for classified information⟩ (2) : to permit (an aircraft) to proceed usu. with a specified action ⟨the plane was ~*ed* to land⟩ **6 a** : to free from obligation or encumbrance **b** : SETTLE, DISCHARGE ⟨~ an account⟩ **c** (1) : to free (a ship or shipment) by payment of duties or harbor fees (2) : to pass through (customs) **d** : to gain without deduction : NET ⟨~ a profit⟩ **e** : to put through a clearinghouse **7 a** : to go over, under, or by without touching ⟨the ball just ~*ed* the uprights⟩ **b** : to move through successfully : PASS ⟨the bill ~*ed* the legislature⟩ ~ *vi* **1 a** : to become clear ⟨it ~*ed* up quickly after the rain⟩ **b** : to go away : VANISH ⟨the symptoms ~*ed* gradually⟩ **c** : SELL **2 a** : to obtain permission to discharge cargo **b** : to conform to regulations or pay requisite fees prior to leaving port **3** : to pass through a clearinghouse **4** : to go to an authority (as for approval) before becoming effective — **clear•able** \ˈklir-ə-bəl\ *adj* — **clear•er** \ˈklir-ər\ *n* — **clear the air** *also* **clear the atmosphere** : to remove elements of hostility, tension, confusion, or uncertainty ⟨had a long meeting to *clear the air*⟩ — **clear the decks** : to make sweeping preparations for action

[4]**clear** *n* (1674) **1** : a clear space or part **2** : a high arcing shot over an opponent's head in badminton — **in the clear** **1** : in inside measurement **2** : free from guilt or suspicion **3** : in plaintext : not in code or cipher ⟨a message sent *in the clear*⟩

clear–air turbulence \ˈklir-ˈer-\ *n* (1955) : sudden severe turbulence occurring in cloudless regions that causes violent jarring or buffeting of aircraft

clear•ance \ˈklir-ən(t)s\ *n* (1540) **1** : an act or process of clearing: as **a** : the removal of buildings from an area (as a city slum) **b** : the act of clearing a ship at the customhouse; *also* : the papers showing that a ship has cleared **c** : the offsetting of checks and other claims among banks through a clearinghouse **d** : certification as clear of objection : AUTHORIZATION ⟨security ~⟩ **e** : a sale to clear out stock **f** : authorization for an aircraft to proceed esp. with a specified action ⟨~ to land⟩ **2** : the distance by which one object clears another or the clear space between them **3** : the volume of blood or plasma that can be freed of a specified constituent in a specified time by its excretion into the urine through the kidneys ⟨a creatine ~ of 25 milliliters per minute⟩ — called also *renal clearance*

[1]**clear–cut** \ˈklir-ˈkət\ *adj* (1849) **1** : sharply outlined : DISTINCT **2** : free from ambiguity or uncertainty : UNAMBIGUOUS ⟨a ~ decision⟩

[2]**clear–cut** \-ˌkət\ *n* (ca. 1958) : an area of forest which has been clear-cut; *also* : CLEAR-CUTTING

clear–cut•ting \-ˌkə-tiŋ\ *n* (1922) : removal of all the trees in a stand of timber — **clear–cut** *vb*

clear–eyed \ˈklir-ˌīd\ *adj* (1530) : CLEAR-SIGHTED ⟨a ~ assessment⟩

clear–fell•ing \-ˌfe-liŋ\ *n* (1922) *chiefly Brit* : CLEAR-CUTTING — **clear–fell** \-ˌfel\ *vb*

clear•head•ed \-ˌhe-dəd\ *adj* (1709) **1** : having or showing a clear understanding : PERCEPTIVE ⟨~ comments⟩ **2** : able to think clearly ⟨stay calm and ~⟩ — **clear•head•ed•ly** *adv* — **clear•head•ed•ness** *n*

clear•ing \ˈklir-iŋ\ *n* (14c) **1** : the act or process of making or becoming clear **2** : a tract of land cleared of wood and brush **3** : the settlement of accounts or exchange of financial instruments esp. between banks

clear•ing•house \-ˌhau̇s\ *n* (1792) **1** : an establishment maintained by banks for settling mutual claims and accounts **2** : a central agency for the collection, classification, and distribution esp. of information; *broadly* : an informal channel for distributing information or assistance

clear•ly \ˈklir-lē\ *adv* (14c) **1** : in a clear manner ⟨speaking ~⟩ **2** : it is clear ⟨~, a new approach is needed⟩ ***usage*** see HOPEFULLY

clear off *vi* (1722) *chiefly Brit* : to go away : DEPART

clear out *vi* (1792) : DEPART ~ *vt* : to drive out or away usu. forcibly

clear–sight•ed \ˈklir-ˌsī-təd\ *adj* (1586) **1** : having clear vision **2** : DISCERNING ⟨a ~ appraisal⟩ — **clear–sight•ed•ly** *adv* — **clear–sight•ed•ness** *n*

clearstory *var of* CLERESTORY

clear•wing \-ˌwiŋ\ *n* (1867) : a moth (as of the families Aegeriidae or Sphingidae) having the wings largely transparent and devoid of scales

[1]**cleat** \ˈklēt\ *n* [ME *clete* wedge, fr. OE **clēat;* akin to MHG *klōz* lump — more at CLOUT] (14c) **1 a** : a wedge-shaped piece fastened to or projecting from something and serving as a support or check **b** : a wooden or metal fitting usu. with two projecting horns around which a rope may be made fast **2 a** : a strip fastened across something to give strength or hold in position **b** (1) : a projecting piece (as on the bottom of a shoe) that furnishes a grip (2) *pl* : shoes equipped with cleats

[2]**cleat** *vt* (1794) **1** : to secure to or by a cleat **2** : to provide with a cleat

cleav•able \ˈklē-və-bəl\ *adj* (ca. 1846) : capable of being split

cleav•age \ˈklē-vij\ *n* (1816) **1 a** : the quality of a crystallized substance or rock of splitting along definite planes; *also* : the occurrence of such splitting **b** : a fragment (as of a diamond) obtained by splitting **2** : the action of cleaving : the state of being cleft **3** : the series of synchronized mitotic cell divisions of a fertilized egg that results in the formation of the blastomeres and changes the single-celled zygote into a multicellular embryo; *also* : one of these cell divisions **4** : the splitting of a molecule into simpler molecules **5** : the depression between a woman's breasts esp. when made visible by a low-cut neckline

[1]**cleave** \ˈklēv\ *vi* **cleaved** \ˈklēvd\ *or* **clove** \ˈklōv\ *also* **clave** \ˈklāv\; **cleaved; cleav•ing** [ME *clevien,* fr. OE *clifian;* akin to OHG *kleben* to stick] (bef. 12c) : to adhere firmly and closely or loyally and unwaveringly ***syn*** see STICK

[2]**cleave** *vb* **cleaved** \ˈklēvd\ *also* **cleft** \ˈkleft\ *or* **clove** \ˈklōv\; **cleaved** *also* **cleft** *or* **clo•ven** \ˈklō-vən\; **cleav•ing** [ME *cleven,* fr. OE *clēofan;* akin to ON *kljūfa* to split, L *glubere* to peel, Gk *glyphein* to carve] *vt* (bef. 12c) **1** : to divide by or as if by a cutting blow : SPLIT **2** : to separate into distinct parts and esp. into groups having divergent views **3** : to subject to chemical cleavage ⟨a protein *cleaved* by an enzyme⟩ ~ *vi* **1** : to split esp. along the grain **2** : to penetrate or pass through something by or as if by cutting ***syn*** see TEAR

cleav•er \ˈklē-vər\ *n* (15c) **1** : one that cleaves; *esp* : a butcher's implement for cutting animal carcasses into joints or pieces **2** : a prehistoric stone tool having a sharp edge at one end

cleav•ers \ˈklē-vərz\ *n pl but sing or pl in constr* [ME *clivre,* alter. of OE *clife* burdock, cleavers; akin to OE *clifian*] (14c) : an annual bedstraw (*Galium aparine*) having many stalked white flowers and stems covered with curved prickles; *also* : any of several related plants

cleek \ˈklēk\ *n* [ME (northern) *cleke,* fr. *cleken* to clutch] (15c) *chiefly Scot* : a large hook (as for a pot over a fire)

clef \ˈklef\ *n* [F, lit., key, fr. OF, fr. L *clavis* — more at CLAVICLE] (ca. 1577) : a sign placed at the beginning of a musical staff to determine the pitch of the notes

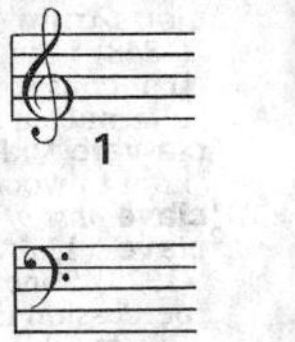

clef: *1* treble clef, *2* bass clef

[1]**cleft** \ˈkleft\ *n* [ME *clift,* fr. OE *geclyft;* akin to OE *clēofan* to cleave] (14c) **1** : a space or opening made by or as if by splitting : FISSURE **2** : a usu. V-shaped indented formation : a hollow between ridges or protuberances ⟨the anal ~ of the human body⟩

[2]**cleft** *adj* [ME, fr. pp. of *cleven*] (14c) : partially split or divided; *specif* : divided about halfway to the midrib ⟨a ~ leaf⟩

cleft lip *n* (ca. 1882) : a birth defect characterized by one or more clefts in the upper lip resulting from failure of the embryonic parts of the lip to unite

cleft palate *n* (1847) : congenital fissure of the roof of the mouth

clei•do•ic \klī-ˈdō-ik\ *adj* [Gk *kleidoun* to fasten, lock in, fr. *kleid-, kleis* key — more at CLAVICLE] (1931) *of an egg* : enclosed in a relatively impervious shell which reduces free exchange with the environment

cleis•tog•a•mous \klī-ˈstä-gə-məs\ *also* **cleis•to•gam•ic** \ˌklī-stə-ˈga-mik\ *adj* [Gk *kleistos* closed (fr. *kleiein* to close) + ISV *-gamous* — more at CLAVICLE] (1874) : characterized by or being small inconspicuous closed self-pollinating flowers additional to and often more fruitful than showier ones on the same plant ⟨violets are ~⟩ — **cleis•tog•a•mous•ly** \-ˈstä-gə-məs-lē\ *adv* — **cleis•tog•a•my** \-ˈstä-gə-mē\ *n*

cle•ma•tis \ˈkle-mə-təs; kli-ˈma-təs, -ˈmā-, -ˈmä-\ *n* [NL, genus name, fr. L, fr. Gk *klēmatis* brushwood, clematis, fr. *klēmat-, klēma* twig, fr. *klan* to break — more at CLAST] (1578) : any of a genus (*Clematis*) of vines or herbs of the buttercup family often having three leaflets on each leaf and usu. white, red, pink, or purple flowers

clem•en•cy \ˈkle-mən(t)-sē\ *n, pl* **-cies** (15c) **1 a** : disposition to be merciful and esp. to moderate the severity of punishment due **b** : an act or instance of leniency **2** : pleasant mildness of weather ***syn*** see MERCY

clem•ent \ˈkle-mənt\ *adj* [ME, fr. L *clement-, clemens*] (15c) **1** : inclined to be merciful : LENIENT ⟨a ~ judge⟩ **2** : MILD ⟨~ weather for this time of year⟩ — **clem•ent•ly** *adv*

clem•en•tine \ˈkle-mən-ˌtēn, -ˌtīn\ *n* [F *clémentine* prob. fr. *Clément* Rodier, Fr. priest who discovered the hybrid ca. 1902] (1943) : a small nearly seedless citrus fruit that is prob. a hybrid between a tangerine and an orange

clench \ˈklench\ *vt* [ME, fr. OE *-clencan;* akin to OE *clingan* to cling] (13c) **1** : CLINCH 2 **2** : to hold fast : CLUTCH ⟨~*ed* the arms of the chair⟩ **3** : to set or close tightly ⟨~ one's teeth⟩ ⟨~ one's fists⟩ — **clench** *n*

clepe \ˈklep\ *vt* **cleped** \ˈklept\; **yclept** \i-ˈklept\ *also* **cleped** *or* **ycleped** \i-ˈklept\; **clep•ing** \ˈkle-piŋ\ [ME, fr. OE *clipian* to speak, call; akin to OFris *kleppa* to ring] (bef. 12c) *archaic* : NAME, CALL

clep•sy•dra \ˈklep-sə-drə\ *n, pl* **-dras** *or* **-drae** \-ˌdrē, -ˌdrī\ [L, fr. Gk *klepsydra,* fr. *kleptein* to steal + *hydōr* water — more at KLEPT-, WATER] (1580) : WATER CLOCK

clere•sto•ry *also* **clear•story** \ˈklir-ˌstȯr-ē, -st(ə-)rē\ *n* [ME, fr. *clere* clear + *story*] (15c) **1** : an outside wall of a room or building that rises above an adjoining roof and contains windows **2** : GALLERY

cler•gy \ˈklər-jē\ *n, pl* **clergies** [ME *clergie,* fr. AF, fr. *clerc* clergyman] (13c) **1** : a group ordained to perform pastoral or sacerdotal functions in a Christian church **2** : the official or sacerdotal class of a non-Christian religion

cler•gy•man \-mən\ *n* (1577) : a member of the clergy

cler•gy•per•son \-ˌpər-sᵊn\ *n* (1976) : a member of the clergy

cler•gy•wom•an \-ˌwu̇-mən\ *n* (1673) : a woman who is a member of the clergy

cler•ic \ˈkler-ik, ˈkle-rik\ *n* [LL *clericus*] (1621) : a member of the clergy

[1]**cler•i•cal** \ˈkler-i-kəl, ˈkle-ri-\ *adj* (1592) **1** : of, relating to, or charac-

teristic of the clergy **2 :** of or relating to a clerk — **cler·i·cal·ly** \-i-k(ə-)lē\ *adv*

[2]**clerical** *n* (1605) **1 :** a member of the clergy **2 :** CLERICALIST **3 :** CLERK **4** *pl* **:** clerical garments

clerical collar *n* (1948) **:** a narrow stiffly upright white collar worn buttoned at the back of the neck by members of the clergy

cler·i·cal·ism \ˈkler-i-kə-ˌli-zəm, ˈkle-ri-\ *n* (1864) **:** a policy of maintaining or increasing the power of a religious hierarchy

cler·i·cal·ist \-list\ *n* (1881) **:** one who favors maintained or increased ecclesiastical power and influence

cler·i·hew \ˈkler-i-ˌhyü, ˈkle-ri-\ *n* [Edmund *Clerihew* Bentley †1956 Eng. writer] (1928) **:** a light verse quatrain rhyming *aabb* and usu. dealing with a person named in the initial rhyme

cler·i·sy \ˈkler-ə-sē, ˈkle-ri-\ *n* [G *Klerisei* clergy, fr. ML *clericia,* fr. LL *clericus* cleric] (1818) **:** INTELLIGENTSIA

[1]**clerk** \ˈklərk, *Brit usu* ˈklärk\ *n* [ME, fr. AF *clerk* & OE *cleric, clerc,* both fr. LL *clericus,* fr. LGk *klērikos,* fr. Gk *klēros* lot, inheritance (in allusion to Deut 18:2), stick of wood; akin to Gk *klan* to break — more at CLAST] (bef. 12c) **1 :** CLERIC **2** *archaic* **:** SCHOLAR **3 a :** an official responsible (as to a government agency) for correspondence, records, and accounts and vested with specified powers or authority (as to issue writs as ordered by a court) ⟨city ∼⟩ **b :** one employed to keep records or accounts or to perform general office work **c :** one who works at a sales or service counter — **clerk·ship** \-ˌship\ *n*

[2]**clerk** *vi* (1551) **:** to act or work as a clerk

clerk·ly \ˈklər-klē, *Brit usu* ˈklär-\ *adj* (15c) **1 :** of, relating to, or characteristic of a clerk ⟨∼ duties⟩ **2** *archaic* **:** SCHOLARLY — **clerkly** *adv*

Cleve·land bay \ˈklēv-lənd-\ *n* [*Cleveland,* former district in North Yorkshire, England] (1796) **:** any of a breed of large strong horses of English origin that are uniformly bay with black legs, mane, and tail

clev·er \ˈkle-vər\ *adj* [ME *cliver,* perh. of Scand origin; akin to Dan dial. *kløver* alert, skillful] (ca. 1595) **1 a :** skillful or adroit in using the hands or body **:** NIMBLE ⟨∼ fingers⟩ **b :** mentally quick and resourceful ⟨a ∼ young lawyer⟩ **2 :** marked by wit or ingenuity ⟨a ∼ solution⟩ ⟨a ∼ idea⟩ **3** *dial* **a :** GOOD **b :** easy to use or handle — **clev·er·ish** \-v(ə-)rish\ *adj* — **clev·er·ly** \-vər-lē\ *adv* — **clev·er·ness** \-vər-nəs\ *n*

syn CLEVER, ADROIT, CUNNING, INGENIOUS mean having or showing practical wit or skill in contriving. CLEVER stresses physical or mental quickness, deftness, or great aptitude ⟨a person *clever* with horses⟩. ADROIT often implies a skillful use of expedients to achieve one's purpose in spite of difficulties ⟨an *adroit* negotiator⟩. CUNNING implies great skill in constructing or creating ⟨a filmmaker *cunning* in his use of special effects⟩. INGENIOUS suggests the power of inventing or discovering a new way of accomplishing something ⟨an *ingenious* software engineer⟩. ***syn*** see in addition INTELLIGENT

clev·is \ˈkle-vəs\ *n* [earlier *clevi,* perh. of Scand origin; akin to ON *kljufa* to split — more at CLEAVE] (1592) **:** SHACKLE 3

[1]**clew** \ˈklü\ *n* [ME *clewe,* fr. OE *cliewen;* akin to OHG *kliuwa* ball, Skt *glauḥ* lump] (bef. 12c) **1 :** a ball of thread, yarn, or cord **2 :** CLUE 1 **3 a :** a lower corner or only the after corner of a sail **b :** a metal loop attached to the lower corner of a sail **c** *pl* **:** a combination of lines by which a hammock is suspended

[2]**clew** *vt* (15c) **1 :** to roll into a ball **2 :** CLUE **3 :** to haul (a sail) up or down by ropes through the clews

cli·ché *also* **cli·che** \klē-ˈshā, ˈklē-ˌ, kli-ˈ\ *n* [F, lit., printer's stereotype, fr. pp. of *clicher* to stereotype, of imit. origin] (1882) **1 :** a trite phrase or expression; *also* **:** the idea expressed by it **2 :** a hackneyed theme, characterization, or situation **3 :** something (as a menu item) that has become overly familiar or commonplace — **cliché** *adj*

cli·chéd \-ˈshād\ *adj* (1928) **1 :** marked by or abounding in clichés **2 :** HACKNEYED ⟨a ∼ phrase⟩

[1]**click** \ˈklik\ *vb* [prob. imit.] *vt* (1581) **1 :** to strike, move, or produce with a click ⟨∼*ed* his heels together⟩ **2 :** to select esp. in a computer interface by pressing a button on a control device (as a mouse) ∼ *vi* **1 :** to make a click **2 a :** to fit or agree exactly **b :** to fit together **:** hit it off ⟨they did not ∼ as friends⟩ **c :** to function smoothly **d :** SUCCEED ⟨a movie that ∼*s*⟩ **3 :** to select something by clicking — often used with *on* ⟨∼ on the icon⟩ — **click·able** \ˈkli-kə-bəl\ *adj*

[2]**click** *n* (1611) **1 a :** a slight sharp noise **b :** a speech sound in some languages made by enclosing air between two stop articulations of the tongue, enlarging the enclosure to rarefy the air, and suddenly opening the enclosure **2 :** DETENT **3 :** an instance of clicking ⟨a mouse ∼⟩

click beetle *n* (1835) **:** any of a family (Elateridae) of beetles able to right themselves with a click when inverted by flexing the articulation between the prothorax and mesothorax

click·er \ˈkli-kər\ *n* (1985) **:** REMOTE CONTROL 2

click stop *n* (1950) **:** a turnable control device (as for a camera diaphragm opening) that engages with a definite click at specific settings

click–through \ˈklik-ˌthrü\ *n* (1996) **:** an instance of clicking on a link on a Web page ⟨∼ rate⟩; *also* **:** the volume of click-throughs on a link

cli·ent \ˈklī-ənt\ *n* [ME, fr. AF & L; AF *client,* fr. L *client-, cliens;* perh. akin to L *clinare* to lean — more at LEAN] (14c) **1 :** one that is under the protection of another **:** DEPENDENT **2 a :** a person who engages the professional advice or services of another ⟨a lawyer's ∼*s*⟩ **b :** CUSTOMER ⟨hotel ∼*s*⟩ **c :** a person served by or utilizing the services of a social agency ⟨a welfare ∼⟩ **d :** a computer in a network that uses the services (as access to files or shared peripherals) provided by a server **3 :** CLIENT STATE — **cli·ent·age** \-ən-tij\ *n* — **cli·en·tal** \klī-ˈen-tᵊl, ˈklī-ən-\ *adj* — **cli·ent·less** \ˈklī-ənt-ləs\ *adj*

cli·en·tele \ˌklī-ən-ˈtel, ˌklē-ən- *also* ˌklē-ˌän-\ *n* [F *clientèle,* fr. L *clientela, fr. client-, cliens*] (ca. 1587) **:** a body of clients ⟨a shop that caters to an exclusive ∼⟩

client state *n* (1918) **:** a country that is economically, politically, or militarily dependent on another country

cliff \ˈklif\ *n* [ME *clif,* fr. OE; akin to OHG *klep* cliff, ON *klif*] (bef. 12c) **:** a very steep, vertical, or overhanging face of rock, earth, or ice **:** PRECIPICE — **cliffy** \ˈkli-fē\ *adj*

cliff dweller *n* (1881) **1** *often cap C&D* **a :** a member of a prehistoric American Indian people of the southwestern U.S. who built their homes on rock ledges or in the natural recesses of canyon walls and cliffs **b :** a member of any cliff-dwelling people **2 :** a resident of a large usu. metropolitan apartment building — **cliff dwelling** *n*

cliff–hang·er \ˈklif-ˌhaŋ-ər\ *n* (ca. 1931) **1 :** an adventure serial or melodrama; *esp* **:** one presented in installments each ending in suspense **2 :** a contest whose outcome is in doubt up to the very end; *broadly* **:** a suspenseful situation — **cliff–hang·ing** \-iŋ\ *adj*

cliff swallow *n* (1825) **:** a colonial swallow (*Petrochelidon pyrrhonota*) of the New World with a pale buff rump and dark throat patch that builds mud nests resembling jugs esp. under eaves and on cliffs

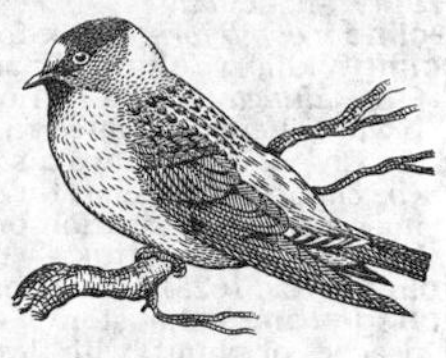

cliff swallow

[1]**cli·mac·ter·ic** \klī-ˈmak-t(ə-)rik; ˌklī-ˌmak-ˈter-ik, -ˈtir-\ *adj* [L *climactericus,* fr. Gk *klimaktērikos,* fr. *klimaktēr* critical point, lit., rung of a ladder, fr. *klimak-, klimax* ladder] (1582) **1 :** constituting or relating to a climacteric **2 :** CRITICAL, CRUCIAL

[2]**climacteric** *n* (ca. 1630) **1 :** a major turning point or critical stage **2 a :** MENOPAUSE 1 **b :** ANDROPAUSE **3 :** the marked and sudden rise in the respiratory rate of fruit just prior to full ripening

cli·mac·tic \klī-ˈmak-tik, klə-\ *adj* (1870) **:** of, relating to, or constituting a climax ⟨the film's ∼ scene⟩ — **cli·mac·ti·cal·ly** \-ti-k(ə-)lē\ *adv*

cli·mate \ˈklī-mət\ *n* [ME *climat,* fr. MF, fr. LL *climat-, clima,* fr. Gk *klimat-, klima* inclination, latitude, climate, fr. *klinein* to lean — more at LEAN] (14c) **1 :** a region of the earth having specified climatic conditions **2 a :** the average course or condition of the weather at a place usu. over a period of years as exhibited by temperature, wind velocity, and precipitation **b :** the prevailing set of conditions (as of temperature and humidity) indoors ⟨a *climate*-controlled office⟩ **3 :** the prevailing influence or environmental conditions characterizing a group or period **:** ATMOSPHERE ⟨a ∼ of fear⟩

cli·mat·ic \klī-ˈma-tik, klə-\ *adj* (ca. 1828) **1 :** of or relating to climate **2 :** resulting from or influenced by the climate rather than the soil — compare EDAPHIC 2 — **cli·mat·i·cal·ly** \-ti-k(ə-)lē\ *adv*

climatic climax *n* (1916) **:** the one of the ecological climaxes possible in a particular climatic area whose stability is directly due to the influence of climate — compare EDAPHIC CLIMAX

cli·ma·tol·o·gy \ˌklī-mə-ˈtä-lə-jē\ *n* (1842) **:** the science that deals with climates and their phenomena — **cli·ma·to·log·i·cal** \ˌklī-mə-tə-ˈlä-ji-kəl\ *adj* — **cli·ma·to·log·i·cal·ly** \-k(ə-)lē\ *adv* — **cli·ma·tol·o·gist** \-mə-ˈtä-lə-jist\ *n*

[1]**cli·max** \ˈklī-ˌmaks\ *n* [LL, fr. Gk *klimax,* lit., ladder, fr. *klinein* to lean] (ca. 1550) **1 :** a figure of speech in which a series of phrases or sentences is arranged in ascending order of rhetorical forcefulness **2 a :** the highest point **:** CULMINATION ⟨the ∼ of a distinguished career⟩ **b :** the point of highest dramatic tension or a major turning point in the action (as of a play) **c :** ORGASM **d :** MENOPAUSE **3 :** a relatively stable ecological stage or community esp. of plants that is achieved through successful adaptation to an environment; *esp* **:** the final stage in ecological succession ***syn*** see SUMMIT — **cli·max·less** *adj*

[2]**climax** *vt* (1835) **:** to bring to a climax ⟨∼*ed* his boxing career with a knockout⟩ ∼ *vi* **:** to come to a climax ⟨a riot ∼*ing* in the destruction of several houses⟩

[1]**climb** \ˈklīm\ *vb* [ME, fr. OE *climban;* prob. akin to OE *clifian* to adhere — more at CLEAVE] *vi* (bef. 12c) **1 a :** to go upward with gradual or continuous progress **:** RISE, ASCEND ⟨watching the smoke ∼⟩ **b :** to increase gradually ⟨prices are continuing to ∼⟩ **c :** to slope upward ⟨a ∼*ing* path⟩ **2 a :** to go upward or raise oneself esp. by grasping or clutching with the hands ⟨∼*ed* aboard the train⟩ **b** *of a plant* **:** to ascend in growth (as by twining) **3 :** to go about or down usu. by grasping or holding with the hands ⟨∼ down the ladder⟩ **4 :** to get into or out of clothing usu. with some haste or effort ⟨the firefighters ∼*ed* into their clothes⟩ ∼ *vt* **1 :** to go upward on or along, to the top of, or over ⟨∼ a hill⟩ **2 :** to draw or pull oneself up, over, or to the top of by using hands and feet ⟨children ∼*ing* the tree⟩ **3 :** to grow up or over ⟨ivy ∼*ing* the wall⟩ — **climb·able** \ˈklī-mə-bəl\ *adj*

[2]**climb** *n* (ca. 1587) **1 :** a place where climbing is necessary to progress **2 :** the act or an instance of climbing **:** RISE, ASCENT

climb down *vi* (1864) **:** BACK DOWN — **climb·down** \ˈklīm-ˌdau̇n\ *n*

climb·er \ˈklī-mər\ *n* (15c) **1 a :** one that climbs or helps in climbing **b :** a vine or twining plant (as a rose or sweet pea) that readily grows up a support or over other plants **2 :** one who attempts to gain a superior social or business position

climbing iron *n* (1857) **:** a steel framework with spikes attached that may be affixed to one's boots for climbing (as a pole or tree)

climbing wall *n* (1985) **:** a wall specially designed for climbing and often built to simulate a rocky surface

clime \ˈklīm\ *n* [LL *clima*] (14c) **:** CLIMATE ⟨traveled to warmer ∼*s*⟩

clin *abbr* clinical

-clinal *adj comb form* [ISV, fr. Gk *klinein* to lean — more at LEAN] **:** sloping ⟨*synclinal*⟩

[1]**clinch** \ˈklinch\ *vb* [prob. alter. of *clench*] *vt* (1542) **1 :** CLENCH 3 **2 a :** to turn over or flatten the protruding pointed end of (a driven nail); *also* **:** to treat (as a screw, bolt, or rivet) in a similar way **b :** to fasten in this way **3 a :** to make final or irrefutable **:** SETTLE ⟨that ∼*ed* the argument⟩ **b :** to assure the winning of ⟨scored a touchdown to ∼ the game⟩ ∼ *vi* **1 :** to hold an opponent (as in boxing) at close quarters with one or both arms **2 :** to hold fast or firmly — **clinch·ing·ly** \ˈklin-chiŋ-lē\ *adv*

[2]**clinch** *n* (1659) **1 :** a fastening by means of a clinched nail, rivet, or bolt; *also* **:** the clinched part of a nail, rivet, or bolt **2** *archaic* **:** PUN **3 :** an act or instance of clinching in boxing **4 :** EMBRACE

clinch·er \ˈklin-chər\ *n* (1703) **:** one that clinches: as **a :** a decisive fact, argument, act, or remark ⟨the expense was the ∼ that persuaded

\ə\ **abut** \ᵊ\ kitten, F table \ər\ **further** \a\ **ash** \ā\ **ace** \ä\ **mop, mar** \au̇\ **out** \ch\ **chin** \e\ **bet** \ē\ **easy** \g\ **go** \i\ **hit** \ī\ **ice** \j\ **job** \ŋ\ **sing** \ō\ **go** \ȯ\ **law** \ȯi\ **boy** \th\ **thin** \t͟h\ **the** \ü\ **loot** \u̇\ **foot** \y\ yet \zh\ vision, beige \k, ⁿ, œ, ue, ʸ\ *see* Guide to Pronunciation

us to give up the enterprise⟩ **b** : a tire with flanged beads fitting into the wheel rim

cline \ˈklīn\ *n* [Gk *klinein*] (1938) : a gradient of morphological or physiological change in a group of related organisms usu. along a line of environmental or geographic transition — **clin·al** \ˈklī-nᵊl\ *adj* — **clin·al·ly** \-nə-lē\ *adv*

-cline *n comb form* [back-formation fr. *-clinal*] : slope ⟨mono*cline*⟩

¹**cling** \ˈkliŋ\ *vi* **clung** \ˈkləŋ\; **cling·ing** [ME, fr. OE *clingan;* akin to OHG *klunga* tangled ball of thread] (bef. 12c) **1 a** : to hold together **b** : to adhere as if glued firmly **c** : to hold or hold on tightly or tenaciously **2 a** : to have a strong emotional attachment or dependence ⟨he *clung* to his friends for support⟩ **b** : to remain or linger as if resisting complete dissipation or dispersal ⟨the odor *clung* to the room for hours⟩ *syn* see STICK — **cling·er** \ˈkliŋ-ər\ *n* — **clingy** \ˈkliŋ-ē\ *adj*

²**cling** *n* (ca. 1625) : an act or instance of clinging : ADHERENCE

cling·stone \ˈkliŋ-ˌstōn\ *n* (1705) : any of various stone fruits (as some peaches or plums) with flesh that adheres strongly to the pit

clin·ic \ˈkli-nik\ *n* [F *clinique,* fr. Gk *klinikē* medical practice at the sickbed, fr. fem. of *klinikos* of a bed, fr. *klinē* bed, fr. *klinein* to lean, recline — more at LEAN] (1827) **1** : a class of medical instruction in which patients are examined and discussed **2** : a group meeting devoted to the analysis and solution of concrete problems or to the acquiring of specific skills or knowledge ⟨writing ∼*s*⟩ ⟨golf ∼*s*⟩ **3 a** : a facility (as of a hospital) for diagnosis and treatment of outpatients **b** : a group practice in which several physicians work cooperatively **4** : a facility that offers professional services or consultation usu. at discounted rates ⟨a legal ∼⟩ **5** : an exemplary display or performance ⟨put on a ∼ in the tournament⟩

-clinic *adj comb form* [ISV, fr. Gk *klinein*] **1** : inclining : dipping **2** : having (so many) oblique intersections of the axes ⟨tri*clinic*⟩

clin·i·cal \ˈkli-ni-kəl\ *adj* (ca. 1728) **1** : of, relating to, or conducted in or as if in a clinic: as **a** : involving direct observation of the patient **b** : based on or characterized by observable and diagnosable symptoms **2** : analytical or coolly dispassionate — **clin·i·cal·ly** \-k(ə-)lē\ *adv*

clinical thermometer *n* (1875) : a thermometer for measuring body temperature that has a constriction in the tube above the bulb preventing movement of the column of liquid downward once it has reached its maximum temperature so that it continues to indicate the maximum temperature until the liquid is shaken back down into the bulb

clinical trial *n* (1946) : a scientifically controlled study of the safety and effectiveness of a therapeutic agent (as a drug or vaccine) using consenting human subjects

cli·ni·cian \kli-ˈni-shən\ *n* (1875) **1** : a person qualified in the clinical practice of medicine, psychiatry, or psychology as distinguished from one specializing in laboratory or research techniques or in theory **2** : a person who conducts a clinic

clin·i·co·path·o·log·ic \ˌkli-ni-(ˌ)kō-ˌpa-thə-ˈlä-jik\ *or* **clin·i·co·path·o·log·i·cal** \-ˈlä-ji-kəl\ *adj* [*clinical*] (1898) : relating to or concerned both with the signs and symptoms directly observable by the physician and with the results of laboratory examination — **clin·i·co·path·o·log·i·cal·ly** \-ji-k(ə-)lē\ *adv*

¹**clink** \ˈkliŋk\ *vb* [ME, of imit. origin] *vi* (14c) : to give out a slight sharp short metallic sound ∼ *vt* : to cause to clink

²**clink** *n* (15c) : a clinking sound

³**clink** *n* [prob. fr. *Clink,* a prison in Southwark, London, England] (1515) **1** *slang* : a prison cell **2** *slang* : JAIL, PRISON

¹**clin·ker** \ˈkliŋ-kər\ *n* [alter. of earlier *klincard* a hard yellowish Dutch brick] (1641) **1** : a brick that has been burned too much in the kiln **2** : stony matter fused together : SLAG

²**clink·er** \ˈkliŋ-kər\ *n* [¹*clink*] (1733) **1** *Brit* : something first-rate **2 a** : a wrong note **b** : a serious mistake or error : BONER **c** : an utter failure : FLOP **d** : something of poor quality

clink·er–built \-ˌbilt\ *adj* [*clinker,* n., clinch] (1769) : having the external planks or plates overlapping like the clapboards on a house

clink·ety–clank \ˈkliŋ-kə-tē-ˈklaŋk\ *n* [imit.] (1901) : a repeated usu. rhythmic clanking sound ⟨the ∼ of a loose tire chain⟩

cli·nom·e·ter \klī-ˈnä-mə-tər\ *n* [Gk *klinein* to lean] (1811) : any of various instruments for measuring angles of elevation or inclination

-clinous *adj comb form* [prob. fr. NL *-clinus,* fr. Gk *klinē* bed — more at CLINIC] : having the androecium and gynoecium in a (single or different) flower or (two separate) flowers ⟨di*clinous*⟩

¹**clin·quant** \ˈkliŋ-kənt, klaⁿ-ˈkäⁿ\ *adj* [MF, fr. prp. of *clinquer* to glitter, lit., to clink, of imit. origin] (1591) : glittering with gold or tinsel

²**clinquant** *n* [F, fr. *clinquant,* adj.] (1682) : TINSEL

clin·to·nia \klin-ˈtō-nē-ə\ *n* [NL, genus name, fr. DeWitt *Clinton*] (1843) : any of a genus (*Clintonia*) of herbs of the lily family with yellow, white, or purplish flowers

Clio \ˈklī-(ˌ)ō, ˈklē-\ *n* [L, fr. Gk *Kleiō*] (1557) **1** : the Greek Muse of history **2** *pl* **Cli·os** : a statuette awarded annually by a professional organization for notable achievement in print and broadcast advertising

clio·met·rics \ˌklī-ə-ˈme-triks\ *n pl but sing in constr* [*Clio* + *-metrics* (as in *econometrics*)] (1960) : the application of methods developed in other fields (as economics, statistics, and data processing) to the study of history — **clio·met·ric** \-trik\ *adj* — **clio·met·ri·cian** \-me-ˈtri-shən\ *n*

¹**clip** \ˈklip\ *vt* **clipped; clip·ping** [ME *clippen,* fr. OE *clyppan;* akin to OHG *klāftra* fathom, Lith *globti* to embrace] (bef. 12c) **1** : ENCOMPASS **2 a** : to hold in a tight grip : CLUTCH **b** : to clasp, fasten, or secure with a clip

²**clip** *n* (15c) **1** : any of various devices that grip, clasp, or hook **2** : a device to hold cartridges for charging the magazines of some rifles; *also* : a magazine from which ammunition is fed into the chamber of a firearm **3** : a piece of jewelry held in position by a clip

³**clip** *vb* **clipped; clip·ping** [ME *clippen,* fr. ON *klippa*] *vt* (13c) **1 a** : to cut or cut off with or as if with shears ⟨∼ a dog's hair⟩ ⟨∼ an hour off traveling time⟩ **b** : to cut off the distal or outer part of **c** (1) : ³EXCISE (2) : to cut items out of (as a newspaper) **2 a** : CURTAIL, DIMINISH **b** : to abbreviate in speech or writing **3** : HIT, PUNCH; *esp* : to strike in passing ⟨the car skidded off the road and *clipped* a lamppost⟩ **4** : to illegally block (an opposing player) in football **5** : to take money from unfairly or dishonestly esp. by overcharging ⟨the nightclub *clipped* the tourist for $200⟩ ∼ *vi* **1** : to clip something **2** : to travel or pass rapidly **3** : to clip an opposing player in football

⁴**clip** *n* (15c) **1 a** *pl, Scot* : SHEARS **b** : a 2-bladed instrument for cutting esp. the nails **2** : something that is clipped: as **a** : the product of a single shearing (as of sheep) **b** : a crop of wool of a sheep, a flock, or a region **c** : a section of filmed, videotaped, or recorded material **d** : a clipping esp. from a newspaper **3** : an act of clipping **4** : a sharp blow **5** : RATE 4a ⟨continues at a brisk ∼⟩ **6** : a single instance or occasion : TIME ⟨he charged $10 a ∼⟩ — often used in the phrase *at a clip* ⟨trained 1000 workers at a ∼⟩

clip art *n* (1968) : ready-made usu. copyright-free illustrations sold in books or as part of a software package from which they may be cut and pasted or inserted as artwork

clip·board \ˈklip-ˌbȯrd\ *n* (1885) **1** : a small writing board with a clip at the top for holding papers **2** : a section of computer memory that temporarily stores data (as text or a graphics image) esp. to facilitate its movement or duplication

clip–clop \ˈklip-ˌkläp\ *n* [imit.] (1884) : the sound made by or as if by a horse walking on a hard surface — **clip–clop** *vi*

clip joint *n* (1932) **1** *slang* : a place of public entertainment (as a nightclub) that makes a practice of defrauding patrons (as by overcharging) **2** *slang* : a business that makes a practice of overcharging

clip–on \ˈklip-ˌȯn, -ˌän\ *adj* (1909) : attached with a clip ⟨a ∼ tie⟩ ⟨∼ earrings⟩ — **clip–on** *n*

clip·per \ˈkli-pər\ *n* (14c) **1** : one that clips something **2** : an implement for clipping esp. hair, fingernails, or toenails — usu. used in pl. **3 a** : one that moves swiftly **b** : a fast sailing ship; *esp* : one with long slender lines, an overhanging bow, tall masts, and a large sail area

clip·ping \ˈkli-piŋ\ *n* (15c) : something that is clipped off or out of something else ⟨grass ∼*s*⟩; *esp* : an item clipped from a publication

clip·sheet \ˈklip-ˌshēt\ *n* (1926) : a sheet of newspaper material issued by an organization for clipping and reprinting

clique \ˈklēk, ˈklik\ *n* [F] (1711) : a narrow exclusive circle or group of persons; *esp* : one held together by common interests, views, or purposes — **cliqu·ey** \ˈklē-kē, ˈkli-\ *adj* — **cliqu·ish** \ˈkli-kish\ *adj* — **cliqu·ish·ly** *adv* — **cliqu·ish·ness** *n*

cli·tel·lum \klī-ˈte-ləm\ *n, pl* **-la** \-lə\ [NL, alter. of L *clitellae* packsaddle] (1839) : a thickened glandular section of the body wall of some annelids that secretes a viscid sac in which the eggs are deposited

clit·ic \ˈkli-tik\ *n* [en*clitic* or pro*clitic*] (1946) : a word that is treated in pronunciation as forming a part of a neighboring word and that is often unaccented or contracted

clit·o·ri·dec·to·my \ˌkli-tə-ri-ˈdek-tə-mē\ *also* **clit·o·rec·to·my** \ˌkli-tə-ˈrek-tə-mē\ *n, pl* **-mies** (1866) : excision of all or part of the clitoris

cli·to·ris \ˈkli-tə-rəs, kli-ˈtȯr-əs\ *n, pl* **cli·to·ris·es** *also* **cli·to·ri·des** \kli-ˈtȯr-ə-ˌdēz\ [NL, fr. Gk *kleitoris*] (1615) : a small erectile female organ located within the anterior junction of the labia minora that develops from the same embryonic mass of tissue as the penis and is responsive to sexual stimulation — **cli·to·ral** \ˈkli-tə-rəl\ *also* **cli·tor·ic** \kli-ˈtȯr-ik, -ˈtär-\ *adj*

cli·via \ˈklī-vē-ə, ˈkli-\ *n* [NL, fr. Lady Charlotte *Clive* †1866 duchess of Northumberland] (1828) : any of a genus (*Clivia*) of perennial evergreen So. African herbs of the amaryllis family with fleshy roots and umbels of large funnel-shaped flowers

clk *abbr* clerk

clo *abbr* clothing

clo·a·ca \klō-ˈā-kə\ *n, pl* **-a·cae** \-ˌkē, -ˌsē\ [L; akin to Gk *klyzein* to wash — more at CLYSTER] (1599) **1** : ³SEWER **2** [NL, fr. L] : the common chamber into which the intestinal and urogenital tracts discharge esp. in monotreme mammals, birds, reptiles, amphibians, and elasmobranch fishes; *also* : a comparable chamber of an invertebrate **3** : CESSPOOL 2 — **clo·a·cal** \-ˈā-kəl\ *adj*

¹**cloak** \ˈklōk\ *n* [ME *cloke,* fr. AF *cloque* bell, cloak, fr. ML *clocca* bell; fr. its shape] (13c) **1** : a loose outer garment **2** : something likened to an outer garment: as **a** : something that envelops or conceals ⟨a ∼ of secrecy⟩ **b** : a distinctive character or role ⟨hung up his academic ∼ . . . to become a stay-at-home father —Charles Chamberlain⟩

²**cloak** *vt* (1509) : to cover or hide with or as if with a cloak *syn* see DISGUISE

cloak–and–dagger *adj* (1860) : dealing in or suggestive of melodramatic intrigue and action usu. involving secret agents and espionage ⟨a ∼ novel⟩ — **cloak–and–dagger** *n*

cloak·room \ˈklōk-ˌrüm, -ˌrum\ *n* (ca. 1852) **1 a** : a room in which outdoor clothing may be placed during one's stay **b** : CHECKROOM **2** : an anteroom of a legislative chamber where members may relax and confer with colleagues **3** *Brit* : LAVATORY 2

¹**clob·ber** \ˈklä-bər\ *n* [origin unknown] (1879) *slang Brit* : CLOTHES 1

²**clobber** *vt* **clob·bered; clob·ber·ing** \-b(ə-)riŋ\ [origin unknown] (ca. 1942) **1** : to pound mercilessly; *also* : to hit with force ⟨∼ a home run⟩ **2 a** : to defeat overwhelmingly **b** : to have a strongly negative impact on ⟨businesses ∼*ed* by the recession⟩ **c** : to criticize harshly

clo·chard \klō-ˈshär\ *n* [F, fr. *clocher* to limp, fr. VL **cloppicare,* fr. LL *cloppus* lame] (1937) : VAGRANT, TRAMP

cloche \ˈklōsh\ *n* [F, lit., bell, fr. ML *clocca*] (1882) **1** : a transparent plant cover used outdoors esp. for protection against cold **2** : a woman's close-fitting hat usu. with deep rounded crown and narrow brim

¹**clock** \ˈkläk\ *n, often attrib* [ME *clok,* fr. MD *clocke* bell, clock, fr. OF or ML; OF dial. (Picard) *cloque* bell, fr. ML *clocca,* of Celt origin; akin to MIr *clocc* bell] (14c) **1** : a device other than a watch for indicating or measuring time commonly by means of hands moving on a dial; *broadly* : any periodic system by which time is measured **2** : a registering device usu. with a dial; *specif* : ODOMETER **3** : TIME CLOCK **4** : a synchronizing device (as in a computer) that produces pulses at regular intervals **5** : BIOLOGICAL CLOCK — **against the clock** **1** : with or within a time constraint ⟨working *against the clock*⟩ **2** : with clocked speed rather than the order of finish as the criterion for placement ⟨trial races *against the clock*⟩ — **around the clock** *also* **round the clock** **1** : continuously for 24 hours : day and night without cessation **2** : without relaxation and heedless of time — **kill the clock** *or* **run out the clock** : to use up as much as possible of the playing time remaining in a game (as football) while retaining possession of the ball or puck esp. to protect a lead

²**clock** *vt* (1883) **1 a** : to time with a stopwatch or by an electric timing device **b** : to be timed at **2** : to register on a mechanical recording device ⟨wind velocities were ∼*ed* at 80 miles per hour⟩ **3** : to hit hard

4 *chiefly Brit* : ATTAIN, REALIZE — usu. used with *up* ⟨just ∼ed up a million . . . paperback sales —*Punch*⟩ **5 a** : to travel (a distance) over time ⟨∼s more than 15,000 miles a year on business⟩ **b** : PUT IN 3 ⟨∼ing long hours at the office⟩ ∼ *vi* **1** : to cause to clock or speed — used with *in* ⟨the movie ∼ed in at just under 3 hours⟩ ; *broadly* : to have a specified measure or value — used with *in* ⟨the meal ∼ed in at about $15⟩ **2** : to register on a time sheet or time clock : PUNCH — used with *in, out, on, off* ⟨he ∼ed in late⟩ — **clock·er** *n*

³**clock** *n* [perh. fr. ¹*clock*] (1530) : an ornamental figure on the ankle or side of a clock or sock

clock·like \ˈkläk-ˌlīk\ *adj* (1609) : unusually regular, undeviating, and precise ⟨does his job with ∼ efficiency⟩

clock radio *n* (1949) : a combination clock and radio device in which the clock can be set to turn on the radio at a designated time

clock-watch·er \-ˌwä-chər\ *n* (1911) : a person (as a worker or student) who keeps close watch on the passage of time — **clock-watching** \-chiŋ\ *n*

clock·wise \ˈkläk-ˌwīz\ *adv* (1888) : in the direction in which the hands of a clock rotate as viewed from in front or as if standing on a clock face — **clockwise** *adj*

clock·work \-ˌwərk\ *n* (1628) **1** : the inner workings of something **2** : the machinery (as springs and a train of gears) that run a clock; *also* : a similar mechanism running a mechanical device (as a toy) **3** : the precision, regularity, or absence of variation associated with a clock or clockwork ⟨a ∼ operation⟩ ⟨the planning went like ∼⟩

clod \ˈkläd\ *n* [ME *clodde*, fr. OE *clod-* (in *clodhamer* fieldfare)] (15c) **1 a** : a lump or mass esp. of earth or clay : SOIL, EARTH **2** : OAF, DOLT — **clod·dish** \ˈklä-dish\ *adj* — **clod·dish·ness** *n* — **clod·dy** \ˈklä-dē\ *adj*

clod·hop·per \ˈkläd-ˌhä-pər\ *n* (1709) **1** : a clumsy and uncouth rustic **2** : a large heavy work shoe or boot

clod·hop·ping \-ˌhä-piŋ\ *adj* (1787) : BOORISH, RUDE

clod·poll *or* **clod·pole** \ˈkläd-ˌpōl\ *n* (1601) : BLOCKHEAD

clo·fi·brate \klō-ˈfī-ˌbrāt, -ˈfi-\ *n* [perh. fr. *chlor-* + *fibr-* + ¹*-ate*] (1964) : a compound $C_{12}H_{15}ClO_3$ used esp. to lower abnormally high concentrations of fats and cholesterol in the blood

¹**clog** \ˈkläg, ˈklȯg\ *n* [ME *clogge* short thick piece of wood] (14c) **1 a** : a weight attached esp. to an animal to hinder motion **b** : something that shackles or impedes : ENCUMBRANCE **1 2** : a shoe, sandal, or overshoe having a thick typically wooden sole

²**clog** *vb* **clogged; clog·ging** *vt* (14c) **1 a** : to impede with a clog : HINDER **b** : to halt or retard the progress, operation, or growth of : ENCUMBER ⟨restraints that have been *clogging* the market —T. W. Arnold⟩ **2 a** : to fill beyond capacity : OVERLOAD ⟨cars *clogged* the main street⟩ — often used with *up* ⟨petty cases *clogging* up the courts⟩ **b** : to cause blockage in — often used with *up* ⟨arteries *clogged* up by cholesterol⟩ **c** : to become filled with extraneous matter — often used with *up* **2** : to unite in a mass : CLOT **3** : to dance a clog dance *syn* see HAMPER — **clog·ger** \ˈklä-gər, ˈklȯ-\ *n*

clog dance *n* (1869) : a dance in which the performer wears clogs and beats out a clattering rhythm on the floor — **clog dancer** *n* — **clog dancing** *n*

cloi·son·né *also* **cloi·son·ne** \ˌklȯi-zə-ˈnā, ˌklwä-\ *adj* [F, fr. pp. of *cloisonner* to partition] (1863) : of, relating to, or being a style of enamel decoration in which the enamel is applied and fired in raised cells (as of soldered wires) on a usu. metal background — compare CHAMPLEVÉ — **cloisonné** *n*

¹**clois·ter** \ˈklȯi-stər\ *n* [ME *cloistre*, fr. AF, fr. ML *claustrum*, fr. L, bar, bolt, fr. *claudere* to close — more at CLOSE] (13c) **1 a** : a monastic establishment **b** : an area within a monastery or convent to which the religious are normally restricted **c** : monastic life **d** : a place or state of seclusion **2** : a covered passage on the side of a court usu. having one side walled and the other an open arcade or colonnade

cloister 2

²**cloister** *vt* **clois·tered; clois·ter·ing** \-st(ə-)riŋ\ (1581) **1** : to seclude from the world in or as if in a cloister ⟨a scientist who ∼s herself in a laboratory⟩ **2** : to surround with a cloister ⟨∼ed gardens⟩

clois·tered \ˈklȯi-stərd\ *adj* (1581) **1** : being or living in or as if in a cloister **2** : providing shelter from contact with the outside world ⟨the ∼ atmosphere of a small college⟩

clois·tral \ˈklȯi-strəl\ *adj* (1605) : of, relating to, or suggestive of a cloister

clois·tress \ˈklȯi-strəs\ *n* (1601) *obs* : NUN

clo·mi·phene \ˈklō-mə-ˌfēn\ *n* [*chlor-* + *amine* + *-phene* (fr. *phenyl*)] (1963) : a synthetic drug $C_{26}H_{28}ClNO$ used in the form of its citrate to induce ovulation

clo·mip·ra·mine \klō-ˈmi-prə-ˌmēn\ *n* [*chlor-* + *imipramine*] (1975) : a tricyclic antidepressant $C_{19}H_{23}ClN_2$ used in the form of its hydrochloride to treat obsessive-compulsive disorder

clomp \ˈklämp, ˈklȯmp, ˈklomp\ *vi* [by alter.] (1829) : CLUMP 1

clo·naz·e·pam \klō-ˈna-zə-ˌpam\ *n* [*chlor-* + *phenyl* + *azepam* (as in *diazepam*)] (1970) : a benzodiazepine $C_{15}H_{10}ClN_3O_3$ used esp. as an anticonvulsant in the treatment of epilepsy

¹**clone** \ˈklōn\ *n* [Gk *klōn* twig, slip; akin to Gk *klan* to break — more at CLAST] (1903) **1 a** : the aggregate of genetically identical cells or organisms asexually produced by a single progenitor cell or organism **b** : an individual grown from a single somatic cell or cell nucleus and genetically identical to it **c** : a group of replicas of all or part of a macromolecule and esp. DNA ⟨∼s of identical recombinant DNA sequences⟩ **2** : one that appears to be a copy of an original form : DUPLICATE ⟨a ∼ of a personal computer⟩ — **clon·al** \ˈklō-nᵊl\ *adj* — **clon·al·ly** \-nᵊl-ē\ *adv*

²**clone** *vb* **cloned; clon·ing** *vt* (ca. 1948) **1** : to propagate a clone from **2** : to make a copy of ∼ *vi* : to produce a clone — **clon·er** *n*

clo·ni·dine \ˈklä-nə-ˌdēn, ˈklō-, -ˌdin\ *n* [*chlor-* + *aniline* + *imide* + ²*-ine*] (1970) : an antihypertensive drug $C_9H_9Cl_2N_3$ used esp. to treat essential

hypertension, to prevent migraine headache, and to diminish opioid and nicotine withdrawal symptoms

clonk \ˈkläŋk, ˈklȯŋk\ *vb* [imit.] *vi* (1930) : to make a dull hollow thumping sound ∼ *vt* : to cause to clonk — **clonk** *n*

clo·nus \ˈklō-nəs\ *n* [NL, fr. Gk *klonos* agitation — more at HOLD] (1817) : a rapid succession of alternating contractions and partial relaxations of a muscle occurring in some nervous diseases — **clon·ic** \ˈklä-nik\ *adj* — **clo·nic·i·ty** \klō-ˈni-sə-tē, klä-\ *n*

cloot \ˈklüt\ *n* [perh. akin to OE *clēat* — more at CLEAT] (1725) **1** *Scot* : a cloven hoof **2** *pl, cap, Scot* : CLOOTIE

Cloot·ie \ˈklü-tē\ *n* [dim. of *cloot*] (1785) *chiefly Scot* — used as a name of the devil

clop \ˈkläp\ *n* [imit.] (1841) : a sound made by or as if by a hoof or wooden shoe against the pavement — **clop** *vi*

clop-clop \ˈkläp-ˌkläp\ *n* (1841) : a sound of rhythmically repeated clops — **clop-clop** *vi*

clo·que *also* **clo·qué** \klō-ˈkā, ˈklō-ˌ\ *n* [F *cloqué*, fr. pp. of *cloquer* to become blistered, fr. F dial. (Picard) *cloque* bell, bubble, fr. ML *clocca* bell — more at CLOCK] (1936) **1** : a fabric with an embossed design **2** : a fabric esp. of piqué with small woven figures

¹**close** \ˈklōz\ *vb* **closed; clos·ing** [ME, fr. AF *clos-*, stem of *clore*, fr. L *claudere* to shut, close; perh. akin to Gk *kleiein* to close — more at CLAVICLE] *vt* (13c) **1 a** : to move so as to bar passage through something ⟨∼ the gate⟩ **b** : to block against entry or passage ⟨∼ a street⟩ **c** : to deny access to ⟨the city *closed* the beach⟩ **d** : SCREEN, EXCLUDE ⟨∼ a view⟩ — often used with *down* **2** *archaic* : ENCLOSE, CONTAIN **3 a** : to bring to an end or period ⟨∼ an account⟩ **b** : to conclude discussion or negotiation about ⟨the question is *closed*⟩ ; *also* : to consummate by performing something previously agreed ⟨∼ a transfer of real estate title⟩ **c** : to terminate access to ⟨a computer file or program⟩ **4 a** : to bring or bind together the parts or edges of ⟨a *closed* book⟩ **b** : to fill up (as an opening) **c** : to make complete by circling or enveloping or by making continuous ⟨∼ a circuit⟩ **d** : to reduce to nil ⟨*closed* the distance to the lead racer⟩ ∼ *vi* **1 a** : to contract, fold, swing, or slide so as to leave no opening ⟨the door *closed* quietly⟩ **b** : to cease operation ⟨the factory *closed* down⟩ ⟨the stores ∼ at 9 p.m.⟩ **2 a** : to draw near ⟨the ship was *closing* with the island⟩ **b** : to engage in a struggle at close quarters : GRAPPLE ⟨∼ with the enemy⟩ **3 a** : to come together : MEET **b** : to draw the free foot up to the supporting foot in dancing **4** : to enter into or complete an agreement ⟨∼ on a deal⟩ **5** : to come to an end or period ⟨the services *closed* with a short prayer⟩ **6** : to reduce a gap ⟨*closed* to within two points⟩ — **clos·able** *or* **close·able** \ˈklō-zə-bəl\ *adj* — **close one's doors 1** : to refuse admission ⟨the nation *closed its doors* to immigrants⟩ **2** : to go out of business — **close one's eyes to** : to ignore deliberately — **close ranks** : to unite in a concerted stand esp. to meet a challenge — **close the door** : to be uncompromisingly obstructive ⟨*closed the door* to further negotiation⟩

syn CLOSE, END, CONCLUDE, FINISH, COMPLETE, TERMINATE mean to bring or come to a stopping point or limit. CLOSE usu. implies that something has been in some way open as well as unfinished ⟨*close* a debate⟩. END conveys a strong sense of finality ⟨*ended* his life⟩. CONCLUDE may imply a formal closing (as of a meeting) ⟨the service *concluded* with a blessing⟩. FINISH may stress completion of a final step in a process ⟨after it is painted, the house will be *finished*⟩. COMPLETE implies the removal of all deficiencies or a successful finishing of what has been undertaken ⟨the resolving of this last issue *completes* the agreement⟩. TERMINATE implies the setting of a limit in time or space ⟨your employment *terminates* after three months⟩.

²**close** \ˈklōz\ *n* (14c) **1 a** : a coming or bringing to a conclusion ⟨at the ∼ of the party⟩ **b** : a conclusion or end in time or existence : CESSATION ⟨the decade drew to a ∼⟩ **c** : the concluding passage (as of a speech or play) **2** : the conclusion of a musical strain or period : CADENCE **3** *archaic* : a hostile encounter **4** : the movement of the free foot in dancing toward or into contact with the supporting foot

³**close** \ˈklōs, U.S. *also* ˈklōz\ *n* [ME *clos*, lit., enclosure, fr. AF *clos*, fr. L *clausum*, fr. neut. of *clausus*, pp.] (13c) **1 a** : an enclosed area **b** *chiefly Brit* : the precinct of a cathedral **2** *chiefly Brit* **a** : a narrow passage leading from a street to a court and the houses within or to the common stairway of tenements **b** : a road closed at one end

⁴**close** \ˈklōs\ *adj* **clos·er; clos·est** [ME *clos*, fr. AF, fr. L *clausus*, pp. of *claudere*] (14c) **1** : having no openings : CLOSED **2 a** : confined or carefully guarded ⟨∼ arrest⟩ **b** (1) *of a vowel* : HIGH 13 (2) : formed with the tongue in a higher position than for the other vowel of a pair **3** : restricted to a privileged class **4 a** : SECLUDED, SECRET **b** : SECRETIVE ⟨she could tell us something if she would . . . but she was as ∼ as wax —A. Conan Doyle⟩ **5** : STRICT, RIGOROUS ⟨keep ∼ watch⟩ **6** : hot and stuffy ⟨a room with an uncomfortably ∼ atmosphere⟩ **7** : not generous in giving or spending : TIGHT **8** : having little space between items or units ⟨a ∼ weave⟩ ⟨a ∼ grain⟩ **9 a** : fitting tightly or exactly ⟨a ∼ fit⟩ **b** : very short or near to the surface ⟨a ∼ haircut⟩ **10** : being near in time, space, effect, or degree ⟨at ∼ range⟩ ⟨∼ to my birthday⟩ ⟨∼ to the speed of sound⟩ **11** : INTIMATE, FAMILIAR ⟨∼ friends⟩ **12 a** : very precise and attentive to details ⟨a ∼ reading⟩ ⟨a ∼ study⟩ **b** : marked by fidelity to an original ⟨a ∼ copy of an old master⟩ **c** : TERSE, COMPACT **13** : decided or won by a narrow margin ⟨a ∼ baseball game⟩ **14** : difficult to obtain ⟨money is ∼⟩ **15** *of punctuation* : characterized by liberal use esp. of commas *syn* see STINGY — **close·ly** *adv* — **close·ness** *n* — **close to home** : within one's personal interests so that one is strongly affected ⟨the speaker's remarks hit *close to home*⟩ — **close to the bone** : within a sensitive or personal area ⟨the criticism cut *close to the bone*⟩ — **close to the vest** : in a reserved or cautious manner

⁵**close** \ˈklōs\ *adv* (15c) : in a close position or manner

close call \ˈklōs-\ *n* (1881) : a narrow escape

\ə\ abut \ᵊ\ kitten, F table \ər\ **further** \a\ ash \ā\ ace \ä\ mop, mar \au̇\ **out** \ch\ **chin** \e\ bet \ē\ **easy** \g\ go \i\ hit \ī\ ice \j\ **job** \ŋ\ **sing** \ō\ go \ȯ\ law \ȯi\ boy \th\ **thin** \t̲h̲\ the \ü\ loot \u̇\ foot \y\ yet \zh\ vision, beige \k, ⁿ, œ, ɶ, �826ᵉ\ see Guide to Pronunciation

close corporation \'klōs-\ *n* (ca. 1902) : a corporation whose stock is not publicly traded but held by a few persons (as those in management)
close–cropped \'klōs-ˌkräpt\ *adj* (1892) **1** : clipped short ⟨~ hair⟩ **2** : having the hair clipped short ⟨a ~ actor⟩
closed \'klōzd\ *adj* (13c) **1 a** : not open **b** : ENCLOSED **c** : composed entirely of closed tubes or vessels ⟨a ~ circulatory system⟩ **2 a** : forming a self-contained unit allowing no additions ⟨~ association⟩ **b** (1) : traced by a moving point that returns to an arbitrary starting point ⟨~ curve⟩; *also* : so formed that every plane section is a closed curve ⟨~ surface⟩ (2) : characterized by mathematical elements that when subjected to an operation produce only elements of the same set ⟨the set of whole numbers is ~ under addition and multiplication⟩ (3) : containing all the limit points of every possible subset ⟨a ~ interval contains its endpoints⟩ **c** : characterized by continuous return and reuse of the working substance ⟨a ~ cooling system⟩ **d** *of a racecourse* : having the same starting and finishing point **3 a** : confined to a few ⟨~ membership⟩ **b** : excluding participation of outsiders or witnesses : conducted in strict secrecy **c** : rigidly excluding outside influence ⟨a ~ mind⟩ **4** : ending in a consonant ⟨~ syllable⟩
closed book *n* (1913) : something beyond comprehension : ENIGMA
closed–cap·tioned \'klōz(d)-'kap-shənd\ *adj* (1979) *of a television program* : broadcast with captions that appear only on the screen of a receiver equipped with a decoder
closed–cap·tion·ing \-'kap-sh(ə-)niŋ\ *n* (1978) : a service that provides closed-captioned programming
closed–cell \-'scl\ *adj* (1976) : consisting of numerous small sealed cavities usu. filled with air ⟨~ foam⟩
closed–cir·cuit \-'sər-kət\ *adj* (1949) : used in, shown on, or being a television installation in which the signal is transmitted by wire to a limited number of receivers
closed corporation *n* (1924) : CLOSE CORPORATION
closed couplet *n* (1910) : a rhymed couplet in which the sense is complete
closed–door \'klōz(d)-'dȯr\ *adj* (1950) : barring public and press ⟨a ~ session of the investigating committee⟩
closed–end \'klōzd-'end\ *adj* (ca. 1938) : having a fixed capitalization of shares that are traded on the market at prices determined by the operation of the law of supply and demand ⟨a ~ investment company⟩ — compare OPEN-END
closed loop *n* (1951) : an automatic control system in which an operation, process, or mechanism is regulated by feedback
close·down \'klōz-ˌdau̇n\ *n* (1889) : an instance of suspending or stopping operations
closed shop *n* (1904) **1** : an establishment in which the employer by agreement hires only union members in good standing **2** : an exclusive group or establishment
closed stance *n* (ca. 1934) : a stance (as in golf) in which the forward foot is closer to the line of play than the back foot — compare OPEN STANCE
close·fist·ed \'klōs-ˌfis-təd\ *adj* (1608) : STINGY, TIGHTFISTED
close–grained \-ˌgrānd\ *adj* (1754) : having a compacted smooth texture; *esp* : having narrow annual rings or small wood elements
close–hauled \-'hȯld\ *adj* (1769) : having the sails set for sailing as nearly against the wind as the vessel will go
close–in \'klōs-'in\ *adj* (1945) **1** : near a center of activity and esp. a city ⟨~ suburbs⟩ **2** : occurring or designed for use within a narrowly limited area ⟨~ fighting⟩ ⟨~ weapons⟩
close in \'klōz-\ *vt* (14c) **1** : to encircle closely and isolate **2** : to enshroud to such an extent as to preclude entrance or exit ⟨the airport was *closed in* by the storm⟩ ~ *vi* **1** : to gather in close all around with an oppressing or isolating effect ⟨despair *closed in* on her⟩ **2** : to approach to close quarters esp. for an attack, raid, or arrest ⟨the police *closed in*⟩ **3** : to grow dark ⟨the short November day was already *closing in* —Ellen Glasgow⟩
close–knit \'klōs-'nit\ *adj* (1926) : bound together by intimate social or cultural ties or by close economic or political ties ⟨~ families⟩
closely held *adj* (1946) : having most stock shares and voting rights in the hands of a few ⟨a *closely held* business⟩
close·mouthed \'klōz-ˌmau̇tht, *also* 'klōs-ˌmau̇t͟hd\ *adj* (1881) : cautious in speaking : UNCOMMUNICATIVE; *also* : SECRETIVE
close order *n* (ca. 1797) : an arrangement of troops in a typical marching formation
close·out \'klōz-ˌau̇t\ *n* (1925) **1** : a clearing out by a sale usu. at reduced prices of the whole remaining stock (as of a business) **2** : an article offered or bought at a closeout
close out \'klōz-\ *vt* (14c) **1 a** : EXCLUDE **b** : PRECLUDE ⟨*close out* his chances⟩ **2 a** : to dispose of a whole stock of by sale **b** : to dispose of (a business) **c** : SELL ⟨*closed out* his share of the business⟩ **d** : to put (an account) in order for disposal or transfer **3 a** : to bring to an often rapid or abrupt conclusion ⟨*close out* a career⟩ **b** : to discontinue operation of ~ *vi* **1** : to sell out a business **2** : to buy or sell securities or commodities in order to terminate an account
close quarters \'klōs-\ *n pl* (1809) : immediate contact or close range ⟨fought at *close quarters*⟩
clos·er \'klō-zər\ *n* (1607) : one that closes; *esp* : a relief pitcher who specializes in finishing games
close shave \'klōs-, 'klōsh-\ *n* (1834) : a narrow escape
close·stool \'klōs-ˌstül\ *n* (15c) : a stool holding a chamber pot
[1]**clos·et** \'klä-zət, 'klȯ-\ *n* [ME, fr. AF *closett,* dim. of *clos* enclosure — more at CLOSE] (14c) **1 a** : an apartment or small room for privacy **b** : a monarch's or official's private chamber **2** : a cabinet or recess for esp. china, household utensils, or clothing **3** : a place of retreat or privacy **4** : WATER CLOSET **5** : a state or condition of secrecy, privacy, or obscurity ⟨came out of the ~⟩ — **clos·et·ful** \-ˌfu̇l\ *n*
[2]**closet** *vt* (1595) **1** : to shut up in or as if in a closet **2** : to take into a closet for a secret interview
[3]**closet** *adj* (ca. 1615) **1** : closely private **2** : working in or suited to the closet as the place of seclusion or study : THEORETICAL **3** : being so in private ⟨a ~ racist⟩
closet drama *n* (1922) : drama suited primarily for reading rather than production
clos·et·ed \'klä-zə-təd, 'klȯ-\ *adj* (1763) : CLOSET 3 ⟨a ~ homosexual⟩
closet queen *n* (1967) *often disparaging* : one who secretly engages in homosexual activities while leading an ostensibly heterosexual life
[1]**close–up** \'klōs-ˌəp\ *n* (1913) **1** : a photograph or movie shot taken at close range **2** : an intimate view or examination of something
[2]**close–up** \ˌklōs-'əp\ *adv or adj* (1926) : at close range
clos·ing \'klō-ziŋ\ *n* (1596) **1** : a concluding part (as of a speech) **2** : a closable gap (as in an article of clothing) **3** : a meeting of parties to a real-estate deal for formally transferring title
clos·trid·i·um \klä-'stri-dē-əm\ *n, pl* **-ia** \-dē-ə\ [NL, genus name, fr. Gk *klōstēr* spindle, fr. *klōthein* to spin] (1884) : any of a genus (*Clostridium*) of spore-forming mostly anaerobic soil or intestinal bacteria — compare BOTULISM, TETANUS — **clos·trid·i·al** \-dē-əl\ *adj*
clo·sure \'klō-zhər\ *n* [ME, fr. AF, fr. L *clausura,* fr. *clausus,* pp. of *claudere* to close — more at CLOSE] (14c) **1** *archaic* : means of enclosing : ENCLOSURE **2** : an act of closing : the condition of being closed ⟨~ of the eyelids⟩ ⟨business ~*s*⟩ **3** : something that closes ⟨pocket with zipper ~⟩ **4** [trans. of F *clôture*] : CLOTURE **5** : the property that a number system or a set has when it is mathematically closed under an operation **6** : a set that consists of a given set together with all the limit points of that set **7** : an often comforting or satisfying sense of finality ⟨victims needing ~⟩; *also* : something (as a satisfying ending) that provides such a sense
[1]**clot** \'klät\ *n* [ME, fr. OE *clott;* akin to MHG *klōz* lump, ball — more at CLOUT] (bef. 12c) **1** : a portion of a substance adhering together in a thick nondescript mass (as of clay or gum) **2 a** : a roundish viscous lump formed by coagulation of a portion of liquid or by melting **b** : a coagulated mass produced by clotting of blood **3** *Brit* : BLOCKHEAD **4** : CLUSTER, GROUP ⟨a ~ of spectators⟩
[2]**clot** *vb* **clot·ted; clot·ting** *vi* (15c) **1** : to become a clot : form clots **2** : to undergo a sequence of complex chemical and physical reactions that results in conversion of fluid blood into a coagulated mass : COAGULATE ~ *vt* **1** : to cause to form into or as if into a clot **2** : to fill with clots; *also* : CLOG ⟨*clotted* streets⟩
clot–bust·er \-ˌbəs-tər\ *n* (1984) : a drug (as streptokinase) used to dissolve blood clots — **clot–bust·ing** \-tiŋ\ *adj*
cloth \'klȯth\ *n, pl* **cloths** \'klȯt͟hz, 'klȯths\ *often attrib* [ME, fr. OE *clāth* cloth, garment; akin to MHG *kleit* garment] (bef. 12c) **1 a** : a pliable material made usu. by weaving, felting, or knitting natural or synthetic fibers and filaments **b** : a similar material (as of glass) **2** : a piece of cloth adapted for a particular purpose; *esp* : TABLECLOTH **3 a** : a distinctive dress of a profession or calling **b** : the dress of the clergy; *also* : CLERGY
cloth·bound \-ˌbau̇nd\ *adj* (1860) *of a book* : bound in stiff boards covered with cloth
clothe \'klōt͟h\ *vt* **clothed** *or* **clad** \'klad\; **cloth·ing** [ME, fr. OE *clāthian,* fr. *clāth*] (bef. 12c) **1 a** : to cover with or as if with cloth or clothing : DRESS **b** : to provide with clothes ⟨the cost of feeding and *clothing* a family⟩ **2** : to express or enhance by suitably significant language : COUCH ⟨treaties *clothed* in stately phraseology⟩ **3** : to endow esp. with power or a quality ⟨the nobility in which religion and history can ~ humanity —D.R. Wallace⟩
clothes \'klōz *also* 'klōt͟hz\ *n pl, often attrib* [ME, fr. OE *clāthas,* pl. of *clāth*] (bef. 12c) **1** : CLOTHING **2** : BEDCLOTHES **3** : all the cloth articles of personal and household use that can be washed
clothes·horse \-ˌhȯrs\ *n* (1775) **1** : a frame on which to hang clothes **2** : a conspicuously dressy person
[1]**clothes·line** \-ˌlīn\ *n* (1830) : a line (as of cord) on which clothes may be hung to dry
[2]**clothesline** *vt* (1964) : to knock down (as a football player) by catching by the neck with an outstretched arm
clothes moth *n* (1753) : any of several small yellowish or buff-colored moths (esp. *Tinea pellionella* and *Tineola bisselliella* of the family Tineidae) whose larvae eat wool, fur, or feathers
clothes–peg \'klōz-ˌpeg *also* 'klōt͟hz-\ *n* (1825) *Brit* : CLOTHESPIN
clothes·pin \-ˌpin\ *n* (1833) : a forked piece of wood or plastic or a small spring clamp used for fastening clothes on a clothesline
clothes·press \-ˌpres\ *n* (1713) : a receptacle for clothes
cloth·ier \'klōt͟h-yər, 'klō-t͟hē-ər\ *n* [ME, alter. of *clother,* fr. *cloth*] (14c) : one who makes or sells clothing
cloth·ing \'klō-t͟hiŋ\ *n* (13c) : garments in general; *also* : COVERING
cloth yard *n* (15c) : a yard esp. for measuring cloth; *specif* : a unit of 37 inches equal to the Scottish ell and used also as a length for arrows
clo·tri·ma·zole \klō-'trī-mə-ˌzōl, -ˌzȯl\ *n* [prob. fr. ISV *chlor-* + *tri-* + *imidazole*] (1970) : an antifungal agent $C_{22}H_{17}ClN_2$
clotted cream *n* (1542) : a thick cream made chiefly in England by slowly heating whole milk on which the cream has been allowed to rise and then skimming the cooled cream from the top — called also *Devonshire cream*
clotting factor *n* (1960) : any of several plasma components (as fibrinogen, prothrombin, and thromboplastin) that are involved in the clotting of blood — compare FACTOR VIII
clo·ture \'klō-chər\ *n* [F *clôture,* lit., closure, alter. of MF *closure*] (1871) : the closing or limitation of debate in a legislative body esp. by calling for a vote — **cloture** *vt*
[1]**cloud** \'klau̇d\ *n, often attrib* [ME, rock, cloud, fr. OE *clūd;* perh. akin to Gk *gloutos* buttock] (14c) **1** : a visible mass of particles of condensed vapor (as water or ice) suspended in the atmosphere of a planet (as the earth) or moon **2** : something resembling or suggesting a cloud: as **a** : a light filmy, puffy, or billowy mass seeming to float in the air ⟨a ~ of blond hair⟩ ⟨a ship under a ~ of sail⟩ **b** (1) : a usu. visible mass of minute particles suspended in the air or a gas (2) : an aggregation of usu. obscuring matter esp. in interstellar space (3) : an aggregate of charged particles (as electrons) **c** : a great crowd or multitude : SWARM ⟨~*s* of

1 2 3 4 5 6 7 8 9 10

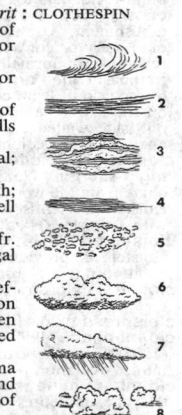

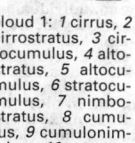

cloud 1: *1* cirrus, *2* cirrostratus, *3* cirrocumulus, *4* altostratus, *5* altocumulus, *6* stratocumulus, *7* nimbostratus, *8* cumulus, *9* cumulonimbus, *10* stratus

mosquitoes〉 **3 :** something that has a dark, lowering, or threatening aspect 〈~*s* of war〉 〈a ~ of suspicion〉 **4 :** something that obscures or blemishes 〈a ~ of ambiguity〉 **5 :** a dark or opaque vein or spot (as in marble or a precious stone) **6 :** the computers and connections that support cloud computing 〈storing files in the ~〉

[2]**cloud** *vi* (1562) **1 :** to grow cloudy — usu. used with *over* or *up* 〈~*ed* over before the storm〉 **2 a** *of facial features* **:** to become troubled, apprehensive, or distressed in appearance 〈her face ~*ed* with worry〉 **b :** to become blurry, dubious, or ominous — often used with *over* 〈the outlook is ~*ing* over〉 **3 :** to billow up in the form of a cloud ~ *vt* **1 a :** to envelop or hide with or as if with a cloud **b :** to make opaque esp. by condensation of moisture 〈steam ~*ed* the windows〉 **c :** to make murky esp. with smoke or mist 〈smoke ~*ed* the sky〉 **2 :** to make unclear or confused 〈~ the issue〉 **3 :** TAINT, SULLY 〈a ~*ed* reputation〉 **4 :** to cast gloom over 〈~ prospects for success〉

cloud·ber·ry \ˈklau̇d-ˌber-ē, -ˌbe-rē\ *n* (1597) **:** a creeping herbaceous raspberry (*Rubus chamaemorus*) of north temperate regions; *also* **:** its pale amber-colored edible fruit

cloud·burst \-ˌbərst\ *n* (1869) **1 :** a sudden copious rainfall **2 :** a sudden outpouring **:** DELUGE 〈a ~ of anger〉

cloud chamber *n* (1897) **:** a vessel containing air saturated with water vapor whose sudden expansion reveals the passage of an ionizing particle by a trail of visible droplets

cloud computing *n* (1996) **:** the practice of storing regularly used computer data on multiple servers that can be accessed through the Internet

cloud–cuck·oo–land \ˌklau̇d-ˈkü-(ˌ)kü-ˌland, -ˈku̇-\ *n* [trans. of Gk *nephelokokkygia*] (1899) **:** a realm of fantasy or of whimsical or foolish behavior

cloud ear *n* (1970) **:** WOOD EAR

cloud·ed leopard \ˈklau̇-dəd-\ *n* (1910) **:** a medium-sized often arboreal cat (*Neofelis nebulosa*) that occurs from Nepal to southeast China and Indonesia and is grayish to yellowish with darker irregular rings, ovals, and rosettes

cloud forest *n* (1922) **:** a wet tropical mountain forest at an altitude usu. between 3000 and 8000 feet (1000 and 2500 meters) that is characterized by a profusion of epiphytes and the presence of clouds even in the dry season

cloud·land \ˈklau̇d-ˌland\ *n* (1817) **1 :** the region of the clouds **2 :** the realm of visionary speculation or poetic imagination

cloud·less \-ləs\ *adj* (14c) **:** free from clouds **:** CLEAR — **cloud·less·ly** *adv* — **cloud·less·ness** *n*

cloud·let \ˈklau̇d-lət\ *n* (1788) **:** a small cloud

cloud nine *n* (1959) **:** a feeling of well-being or elation — usu. used with *on* 〈still on *cloud nine* weeks after winning the championship〉

cloud·scape \ˈklau̇d-ˌskāp\ *n* (1880) **:** a view or pictorial representation of a cloud formation

cloud street *n* (1943) **:** a row of cumulus clouds

cloudy \ˈklau̇-dē\ *adj* **cloud·i·er; -est** (14c) **1 :** of, relating to, or resembling cloud 〈~ smoke〉 **2 :** darkened by gloom or anxiety 〈a ~ mood〉 **3 a :** overcast with clouds 〈~ weather〉 **b :** having a cloudy sky 〈a ~ day〉 **4 :** obscure in meaning 〈~ issues〉; *also* **:** uncertain as to fact or outcome 〈a ~ future〉 **5 :** dimmed or dulled as if by clouds 〈a ~ mirror〉 **6 :** uneven in color or texture **7 :** having visible material in suspension **:** MURKY 〈a ~ liquid〉 — **cloud·i·ly** \ˈklau̇-də-lē\ *adv* — **cloud·i·ness** \ˈklau̇-dē-nəs\ *n*

[1]**clout** \ˈklau̇t\ *n* [ME, fr. OE *clūt;* akin to MHG *klōz* lump, Russ *gluda*] (bef. 12c) **1** *dial chiefly Brit* **:** a piece of cloth or leather **:** RAG **2 :** a blow esp. with the hand; *also* **:** a hard hit in baseball **3 :** a white cloth on a stake or frame used as a target in archery **4 :** PULL, INFLUENCE 〈political ~〉

[2]**clout** *vt* (14c) **1 :** to cover or patch with a clout **2 :** to hit forcefully

[1]**clove** \ˈklōv\ *n* [ME, fr. OE *clufu;* akin to OE *clēofan* to cleave] (bef. 12c) **:** one of the small bulbs (as in garlic) developed in the axils of the scales of a large bulb

[2]**clove** *past of* CLEAVE

[3]**clove** \ˈklōv\ *n* [alter. of ME *clowe,* fr. AF *clou* (*de girofle*), lit., nail of clove, fr. L *clavus* nail] (13c) **:** the dried flower bud of a tropical tree (*Syzygium aromaticum* syn. *Eugenia aromatica*) of the myrtle family that is used as a spice and is the source of an oil; *also* **:** this tree

clove hitch \ˈklōv-\ *n* [ME *cloven, clove* divided, fr. pp. of *clevien* to cleave] (ca. 1769) **:** a knot securing a rope temporarily to an object (as a post or spar) and consisting of a turn around the object, over the standing part, around the object again, and under the last turn — see KNOT illustration

cloven *past part of* CLEAVE

cloven foot *n* (13c) **:** CLOVEN HOOF — **clo·ven–foot·ed** \ˈklō-vən-ˌfu̇-təd\ *adj*

cloven hoof *n* (1611) **1 :** a foot (as of a sheep) divided into two parts at its distal extremity **2** [fr. the traditional representation of Satan as cloven-hoofed] **:** the sign of devilish character — **clo·ven–hoofed** \ˈklō-vən-ˌhu̇ft, -ˌhüft, -ˌhu̇vd, -ˌhüvd\ *adj*

clove pink *n* (1804) **:** CARNATION 2

clo·ver \ˈklō-vər\ *n* [ME, fr. OE *clāfre;* akin to OHG *klēo* clover] (bef. 12c) **1 :** any of a genus (*Trifolium*) of low leguminous herbs having trifoliolate leaves and flowers in dense heads and including many that are valuable for forage and attractive to bees **2 :** any of various related plants (as of the genera *Melilotus, Lespedeza,* or *Medicago*) of the legume family — **in clover** *also* **in the clover :** in prosperity or in pleasant circumstances

[1]**clo·ver·leaf** \-ˌlēf\ *adj* (1915) **:** resembling a clover leaf in shape

[2]**cloverleaf** *n, pl* **-leafs** \-ˌlēfs\ *or* **-leaves** \-ˌlēvz\ (1931) **:** an interchange between two major highways that allows traffic to change from one to the other without requiring any left turns or crossings and that from above resembles a 4-leaf clover

Clo·vis \ˈklō-vəs\ *adj* [*Clovis,* New Mexico] (1956) **:** of or relating to a widely distributed prehistoric culture of No. America characterized by leaf-shaped flint projectile points having fluted sides

[1]**clown** \ˈklau̇n\ *n* [prob. of LG origin; akin to Fris *klönne* clumsy fellow, OE *clyne* lump of metal] (1563) **1 :** FARMER, COUNTRYMAN **2 :** a rude ill-bred person **:** BOOR **3 a :** a fool, jester, or comedian in an entertainment (as a play); *specif* **:** a grotesquely dressed comedy performer in a circus **b :** a person who habitually jokes and plays the buffoon **c :** JOKER 1b

[2]**clown** *vi* (1599) **:** to act as or like a clown 〈always ~*ing* around〉

clown·ery \ˈklau̇-nə-rē\ *n, pl* **-er·ies** (1589) **:** clownish behavior or an instance of clownishness **:** BUFFOONERY

clown fish *n* (1957) **:** any of various small tropical fishes (genera *Amphiprion* and *Premnas*) of the Indian and Pacific oceans that are related to the damselfishes, are bright orange usu. with one or more vertical white stripes, and live symbiotically with sea anemones

clown·ish \ˈklau̇-nish\ *adj* (1563) **:** resembling or befitting a clown (as in ignorance and lack of sophistication) ***syn*** see BOORISH — **clown·ish·ly** *adv* — **clown·ish·ness** *n*

clox·a·cil·lin \ˌkläk-sə-ˈsi-lən\ *n* [*chlor-* + *oxacillin*] (1963) **:** a semisynthetic oral penicillin $C_{19}H_{17}ClN_3NaO_5S$ effective esp. against staphylococci which secrete beta-lactamase

cloy \ˈklȯi\ *vb* [ME, to hinder, lame, alter. of *acloyen* to harm, maim, modif. of AF *encloer* to nail, prick a horse with a nail in shoeing, fr. ML *inclavare,* fr. L *in* + *clavus* nail] *vt* (1528) **:** to surfeit with an excess usu. of something orig. pleasing ~ *vi* **:** to cause surfeit ***syn*** see SATIATE

cloy·ing \ˈklȯi-iŋ, ˈklȯiŋ\ *adj* (1594) **:** disgusting or distasteful by reason of excess 〈~ sweetness〉; *also* **:** excessively sweet or sentimental 〈a ~ romantic comedy〉 — **cloy·ing·ly** *adv*

clo·za·pine \ˈklō-zə-ˌpēn\ *n* [ISV *chlor-* + *-zapine,* alter. of *-azepine* (as in *benzodiazepine*)] (1970) **:** an antipsychotic drug $C_{18}H_{19}ClN_4$ used in the treatment of schizophrenia

cloze \ˈklōz\ *adj* [by shortening & alter. fr. *closure*] (1953) **:** of, relating to, or being a test of reading comprehension that involves having the person being tested supply words which have been systematically deleted from a text

clr *abbr* clear; clearance

CLU *abbr* chartered life underwriter

[1]**club** \ˈkləb\ *n, often attrib* [ME *clubbe,* fr. ON *klubba;* akin to OHG *kolbo* club] (13c) **1 a :** a heavy usu. tapering staff esp. of wood wielded as a weapon **b :** a stick or bat used to hit a ball in any of various games **c :** something resembling a club **2 a :** a playing card marked with a stylized figure of a black clover **b** *pl but sing or pl in constr* **:** the suit comprising cards marked with clubs **3 a :** an association of persons for some common object usu. jointly supported and meeting periodically; *also* **:** a group identified by some common characteristic 〈nations in the nuclear ~〉 **b :** the meeting place of a club 〈lunch at the ~〉 **c :** an association of persons participating in a plan by which they agree to make regular payments or purchases in order to secure some advantage **d :** NIGHTCLUB **e :** an athletic association or team **4 :** CLUB SANDWICH — **club·bish** \ˈklə-bish\ *adj*

[2]**club** *vb* **clubbed; club·bing** *vt* (1593) **1 a :** to beat or strike with or as if with a club **b :** to gather into a club-shaped mass 〈*clubbed* her hair〉 **2 a :** to unite or combine for a common cause **b :** to contribute to a common fund ~ *vi* **1 :** to form a club **:** COMBINE **2 :** to pay a share of a common expense **3 :** NIGHTCLUB

club·ba·ble *also* **club·able** \ˈklə-bə-bəl\ *adj* (1783) **:** SOCIABLE — **club·ba·bil·i·ty** \ˌklə-bə-ˈbi-lə-tē\ *n*

clubbed \ˈkləbd\ *adj* (14c) **:** shaped like a club 〈~ antennae〉

club·ber \ˈklə-bər\ *n* (1633) **:** a member or patron of a club

club·by \ˈklə-bē\ *adj* **club·bi·er; -est** (1859) **:** characteristic of a club or club members: as **a :** displaying friendliness esp. to other members of the same social group **:** SOCIABLE **b :** open only to qualified or approved persons **:** SELECT, ELITE — **club·bi·ness** *n*

club car *n* (1886) **:** a railroad passenger car with facilities for serving refreshments and drinks — called also *bar car, lounge car*

club chair *n* (1919) **:** a deep low thickly upholstered easy chair often with rather low back and heavy sides and arms

club cheese *n* (1916) **:** a process cheese made by grinding cheddar and other cheeses usu. with added condiments and seasoning

club·face \ˈkləb-ˌfās\ *n* (1878) **:** the forward striking surface of a clubhead

club·foot \ˈkləb-ˌfu̇t\ *n* (1538) **:** a congenitally misshapen foot twisted out of position; *also* **:** this deformity — **club·foot·ed** \-ˌfu̇-təd\ *adj*

club fungus *n* (1899) **:** any of various basidiomycetes (family Clavariaceae) with a simple or branched often club-shaped sporophore

club·head \ˈkləb-ˌhed\ *n* (1857) **:** the part of a golf club that strikes the ball

club·house \ˈkləb-ˌhau̇s\ *n* (1746) **1 :** a house occupied by a club or used for club activities **2 :** locker rooms used by an athletic team **3 :** a building at a golf course typically housing a locker room, pro shop, and restaurant

club·man \ˈkləb-mən, -ˌman\ *n* (1836) **:** a usu. wealthy man given to club life

club moss *n* (1597) **:** any of an order (Lycopodiales) of primitive vascular plants (as ground pine) often with the sporangia borne in club-shaped strobili

club·root \ˈkləb-ˌrüt, -ˌru̇t\ *n* (1846) **:** a disease of cruciferous plants (as cabbage) caused by a slime mold (*Plasmodiophora brassicae*) producing swellings or distortions of the root

club sandwich *n* (1889) **:** a sandwich of three slices of bread with two layers of meat (as turkey) and lettuce, tomato, and mayonnaise

club soda *n* (1877) **:** SODA WATER 2a

club steak *n* (1915) **:** a small steak cut from the end of the short loin — see BEEF illustration

[1]**cluck** \ˈklək\ *vb* [imit.] *vi* (15c) **1 :** to make a cluck **2 :** to make a clicking sound with the tongue **3 :** to express interest or concern 〈critics ~*ed* over the new developments〉 ~ *vt* **1 :** to call with a cluck **2 :** to express with interest or concern

[2]**cluck** *n* (1703) **1 :** the characteristic sound made by a hen esp. in calling her chicks **2 :** a stupid or naive person 〈a dumb ~〉

[1]**clue** \ˈklü\ *n* [alter. of *clew*] (1596) **1 :** something that guides through an intricate procedure or maze of difficulties; *specif* **:** a piece of evidence that leads one toward the solution of a problem **2 :** IDEA, NOTION 〈had no ~ what he meant〉

[2]**clue** *vt* **clued; clue·ing** *or* **clu·ing** (1934) **1 :** to provide with a clue

\ə\ **abut** \ᵊ\ **kitten,** F **table** \ər\ **further** \a\ **ash** \ā\ **ace** \ä\ **mop, mar**
\au̇\ **out** \ch\ **chin** \e\ **bet** \ē\ **easy** \g\ **go** \i\ **hit** \ī\ **ice** \j\ **job**
\ŋ\ **sing** \ō\ **go** \ȯ\ **law** \ȯi\ **boy** \th\ **thin** \t͟h\ **the** \ü\ **loot** \u̇\ **foot**
\y\ **yet** \zh\ **vision, beige** \ḵ, ⁿ, œ, ue, ʸ\ *see* Guide to Pronunciation

2 : to give reliable information to ⟨he *clued* me in on how it happened⟩
clue·less \ˈklü-ləs\ *adj* (1743) **1 :** having or providing no clue ⟨a ~ case for the police to solve⟩ **2 :** completely or hopelessly bewildered, unaware, ignorant, or foolish ⟨~ about what they want⟩
clum·ber spaniel \ˈkləm-bər-\ *n, often cap C* [*Clumber,* estate in Nottinghamshire, England] (1883) **:** any of a breed of large massive heavy-set spaniels with a dense silky largely white coat
[1]**clump** \ˈkləmp\ *n* [prob. fr. LG *klump*] (ca. 1586) **1 :** a group of things clustered together ⟨a ~ of bushes⟩ **2 :** a compact mass **3 :** a heavy tramping sound — **clumpy** \ˈkləm-pē\ *adj*
[2]**clump** *vi* (1665) **1 :** to walk or move clumsily and noisily **2 :** to form clumps ~ *vt* **:** to arrange in or cause to form clumps
clum·sy \ˈkləm-zē\ *adj* **clum·si·er; -est** [prob. fr. obs. E *clumse* benumbed with cold] (ca. 1598) **1 a :** lacking dexterity, nimbleness, or grace ⟨~ fingers⟩ **b :** lacking tact or subtlety ⟨a ~ joke⟩ **2 :** awkward or inefficient in use or construction **:** UNWIELDY ⟨a ~ contraption⟩ ***syn*** see AWKWARD — **clum·si·ly** \-zə-lē\ *adv* — **clum·si·ness** \-zē-nəs\ *n*
clung *past and past part of* CLING
[1]**clunk** \ˈkləŋk\ *vb* [imit.] *vi* (ca. 1796) **1 :** to make a clunk **2 :** to hit something with a clunk ~ *vt* **:** to strike or hit with a clunk
[2]**clunk** *n* (1823) **1 :** a blow or the sound of a blow **:** THUMP **2 :** a dull or stupid person
clunk·er \ˈkləŋ-kər\ *n* (1933) **1 :** an old or badly working piece of machinery; *esp* **:** a dilapidated automobile **2 :** someone or something notably unsuccessful ⟨told a joke that was a real ~⟩
clunky \ˈkləŋ-kē\ *adj* **clunk·i·er; -est** (1965) **:** clumsy in style, form, or execution ⟨a ~ thriller⟩ ⟨~ earrings⟩
clu·pe·id \ˈklü-pē-əd\ *n* [ultim. fr. L *clupea,* a small river fish] (1942) **:** HERRING 2
[1]**clus·ter** \ˈkləs-tər\ *n* [ME, fr. OE *clyster;* akin to OE *clott* clot] (bef. 12c) **:** a number of similar things that occur together: as **a :** two or more consecutive consonants or vowels in a segment of speech **b :** a group of buildings and esp. houses built close together on a sizable tract in order to preserve open spaces larger than the individual yard for common recreation **c :** an aggregation of stars or galaxies that appear close together in the sky and are gravitationally associated **d :** a larger than expected number of cases of disease (as leukemia) occurring in a particular locality, group of people, or period of time — **clus·tery** \-t(ə-)rē\ *adj*
[2]**cluster** *vb* **clus·tered; clus·ter·ing** \-t(ə-)riŋ\ *vt* (14c) **1 :** to collect into a cluster ⟨~ the tents together⟩ **2 :** to furnish with clusters ~ *vi* **:** to grow, assemble, or occur in a cluster ⟨they ~*ed* around the fire⟩
cluster analysis *n* (1948) **:** a statistical classification technique for discovering whether the individuals of a population fall into different groups by making quantitative comparisons of multiple characteristics
cluster bomb *n* (1967) **:** a canister of small individual bombs that is dropped from an aircraft
cluster headache *n* (1953) **:** a headache that is characterized by severe pain in the eye or temple and tends to recur in a series of attacks
[1]**clutch** \ˈkləch\ *vb* [ME *clucchen,* fr. OE *clyccan*] *vt* (bef. 12c) **1 :** to grasp or hold with or as if with the hand or claws usu. strongly, tightly, or suddenly **2** *obs* **:** CLENCH ~ *vi* **1 :** to seek to grasp and hold ⟨~*ed* at her hand⟩ **2 :** to operate an automobile clutch ***syn*** see TAKE
[2]**clutch** *n* (13c) **1 a :** the claws or a hand in the act of grasping or seizing firmly **b :** an often cruel or unrelenting control, power, or possession ⟨the fell ~ of circumstance —W. E. Henley⟩ **c :** the act of grasping, holding, or restraining **2 a :** a coupling used to connect and disconnect a driving and a driven part (as an engine and a transmission) of a mechanism **b :** a lever (as a pedal) operating such a clutch **3 :** a tight or critical situation **:** PINCH ⟨come through in the ~⟩ **4 :** CLUTCH BAG
[3]**clutch** *adj* (1929) **1 :** made or done in a crucial situation ⟨a ~ hit⟩ **2 :** successful in a crucial situation ⟨a ~ pitcher⟩
[4]**clutch** *n* [alter. of dial. E *cletch* hatching, brood] (1721) **1 :** a nest of eggs or a brood of chicks **2 :** GROUP, BUNCH
clutch bag *n* (1949) **:** a woman's small usu. strapless handbag
[1]**clut·ter** \ˈklə-tər\ *vb* [ME *clotteren* to clot, fr. *clot*] *vi* (1556) *chiefly dial* **:** to run in disorder ~ *vt* **:** to fill or cover with scattered or disordered things that impede movement or reduce effectiveness ⟨a room ~*ed* with toys⟩ — often used with *up*
[2]**clutter** *n* (1649) **1 a :** a crowded or confused mass or collection **b :** things that clutter a place **2 :** interfering radar echoes caused by reflection from objects (as on the ground) other than the target **3** *chiefly dial* **:** DISTURBANCE, HUBBUB
Clyde \ˈklīd\ *n* (1894) **:** CLYDESDALE
Clydes·dale \ˈklīdz-ˌdāl\ *n* (1786) **:** any of a breed of heavy draft horses orig. from Clydesdale, Scotland with long silky hair on the legs
clyp·e·us \ˈkli-pē-əs\ *n, pl* **clyp·ei** \-pē-ˌī, -pē-ˌē\ [NL, fr. L, round shield] (1834) **:** a plate on the anterior median aspect of an insect's head
clys·ter \ˈklis-tər\ *n* [ME, fr. MF or L; MF *clistere,* fr. L *clyster,* fr. Gk *klystēr,* fr. *klyzein* to wash out; akin to W *clir* pure, OE *hlūtor* clean] (14c) **:** ENEMA
Cly·tem·nes·tra \ˌklī-təm-ˈnes-trə\ *n* [L, fr. Gk *Klytaimnēstra*] (15c) **:** the wife and murderess of Agamemnon
cm *abbr* **1** centimeter **2** cumulative
Cm *symbol* curium
CM *abbr* **1** common meter **2** Congregation of the Mission
CMA *abbr* **1** calcium magnesium acetate **2** certified medical assistant
cmd *abbr* command
Cmdr *abbr* commander
CMG *abbr* Companion of the Order of St. Michael and St. George
CMOS *abbr* complementary metal-oxide semiconductor
CMSgt *abbr* chief master sergeant
CMV *abbr* cytomegalovirus
Cn *symbol* copernicium
CN *abbr* credit note
CNA *abbr* certified nurse aide; certified nurse assistant; certified nurse's aide; certified nurse's assistant
CNC *abbr* computer numerical control
CNG *abbr* compressed natural gas
cni·dar·i·an \nī-ˈder-ē-ən\ *n* [ultim. fr. NL *cnida* nematocyst, fr. Gk *knidē* nettle] (ca. 1909) **:** COELENTERATE — **cnidarian** *adj*
CNM *abbr* certified nurse-midwife
CNMI *abbr* Commonwealth of the Northern Mariana Islands
CNN *abbr* Cable News Network
CNO *abbr* chief of naval operations
C–note \ˈsē-ˌnōt\ *n* (1930) **:** a 100-dollar bill
CNS *abbr* central nervous system
co *abbr* **1** company **2** county
Co *symbol* cobalt
CO *abbr* **1** cash order **2** Colorado **3** commanding officer **4** conscientious objector **5** corrections officer
c/o *abbr* care of
co- *prefix* [ME, fr. L, fr. *com-;* akin to OE *ge-,* perfective and collective prefix, OIr *com-* with] **1 :** with **:** together **:** joint **:** jointly ⟨*co*exist⟩ ⟨*co*heir⟩ **2 :** in or to the same degree ⟨*co*extensive⟩ **3 a :** one that is associated in an action with another **:** fellow **:** partner ⟨*co*author⟩ ⟨*co*worker⟩ **b :** having a usu. lesser share in duty or responsibility **:** alternate **:** deputy ⟨*co*pilot⟩ **4 :** of, relating to, or constituting the complement of an angle ⟨*co*sine⟩

co·act
co·ac·tion
co·ac·tive
co·ac·tor
co·ad·min·is·tra·tion
co·an·chor
co·au·thor
co·au·thor·ship
co·cap·tain
co·cat·a·lyst
co·chair
co·chair·man
co·chair·per·son
co·chair·wom·an
co·cham·pi·on
co·com·pos·er
co·con·spir·a·tor
co·coun·sel
co·cre·ate
co·cre·ator
co·cul·ti·vate
co·cul·ti·va·tion
co·cul·ture
co·cu·ra·tor
co·de·fen·dant
co·de·sign
co·de·vel·op
co·de·vel·op·er
co·di·rect
co·di·rec·tion
co·di·rec·tor
co·dis·cov·er
co·dis·cov·er·er
co·drive
co·driv·er
co·ed·it
co·ed·i·tor
co·eter·nal
co·ex·ec·u·tor
co·fa·vor·ite
co·fea·ture
co·fi·nance
co·found
co·found·er
co·head
co·heir
co·heir·ess
co·hold·er
co·host
co·host·ess
co·in·vent
co·in·ven·tor
co·in·ves·ti·ga·tor
co·in·ves·tor
co·join
co·lead
co·lead·er
co·man·age
co·man·age·ment
co·man·ag·er
co·mem·ber
co·nom·i·nee
co–oc·cur
co–oc·cur·rence
co–oc·cur·rent
co–of·fi·cial
co–or·ga·niz·er
co–own
co–own·er
co–own·er·ship
co·part·ner
co·part·ner·ship
co·pre·sent
co·pres·i·dent
co·prince
co·prin·ci·pal
co·pris·on·er
co·pro·cess·ing
co·pro·duce
co·pro·duc·er
co·pro·duc·tion
co·pro·mot·er
co·pro·pri·etor
co·pros·per·i·ty
co·pub·lish
co·pub·lish·er
co·re·cip·i·ent
co·re·search·er
co·res·i·dent
co·res·i·den·tial
co·rul·er
co·sce·nar·ist
co·script
co·spon·sor
co·spon·sor·ship
co·star
co·sur·fac·tant
co·ten·ant
co·trans·duce
co·trans·duc·tion
co·trans·fer
co·trans·port
co·trust·ee
co·win·ner
co·work·er
co·write
co·writ·er

co·ac·er·vate \kō-ˈa-sər-ˌvāt\ *n* [L *coacervatus,* pp. of *coacervare* to heap up, fr. *co-* + *acervus* heap] (1929) **:** an aggregate of colloidal droplets held together by electrostatic attractive forces — **co·acer·vate** \ˌkō-ə-ˈsər-vət\ *adj* — **co·ac·er·va·tion** \(ˌ)kō-ˌa-sər-ˈvā-shən\ *n*
[1]**coach** \ˈkōch\ *n, often attrib* [ME *coche,* fr. MF, fr. G *Kutsche,* fr. Hung *kocsi* (*szekér*), lit., wagon from *Kocs,* Hungary] (1556) **1 a :** a large usu. closed four-wheeled horse-drawn carriage having doors in the sides and an elevated seat in front for the driver **b :** a railroad passenger car intended primarily for day travel **c :** BUS 1a **d :** TRAILER 3b **e :** a 2-door enclosed automobile **f :** a class of passenger air transportation at a lower fare than first class **2** [fr. the concept that the tutor conveys the student through examinations] **a :** a private tutor **b :** one who instructs or trains ⟨an acting ~⟩; *esp* **:** one who instructs players in the fundamentals of a sport and directs team strategy ⟨a football ~⟩

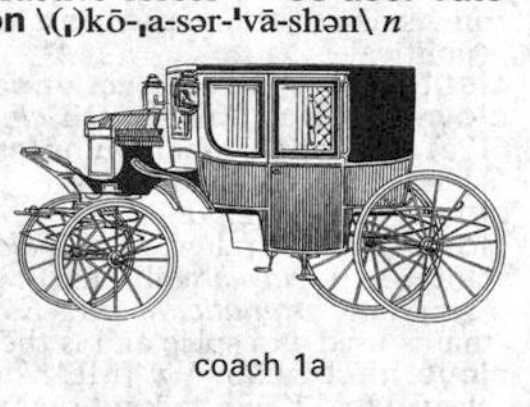
coach 1a

[2]**coach** *vi* (1630) **1 :** to go in a coach **2 :** to instruct, direct, or prompt as a coach ~ *vt* **1 :** to train intensively (as by instruction and demonstration) ⟨~ pupils⟩ **2 :** to act as coach of ⟨~ tennis⟩ ⟨~ a team⟩ — **coach·able** \ˈkō-chə-bəl\ *adj* — **coach·er** *n*
coach dog *n* (1764) **:** DALMATIAN
coach·man \ˈkōch-mən\ *n* (1579) **:** a man who drives a coach or carriage
coach·work \-ˌwərk\ *n* (1906) **:** an automobile body **:** BODYWORK
co·adapt·ed \ˌkō-ə-ˈdap-təd\ *adj* (1836) **:** mutually adapted esp. by natural selection — **co·ad·ap·ta·tion** \ˌkō-ˌa-ˌdap-ˈtā-shən, -dəp-ˈ\ *n*
co·ad·ju·tor \ˌkō-ə-ˈjü-tər, kō-ˈa-jə-tər\ *n* [ME *coadjutour,* fr. AF, fr. LL *coadjutor,* fr. L *co-* + *adjutor* helper, fr. *adjuvare* to help — more at AID] (15c) **1 :** one who works together with another **:** ASSISTANT **2 :** a bishop assisting a diocesan bishop and often having the right of succession — **coadjutor** *adj*
co·ad·ju·trix \ˌkō-ə-ˈjü-triks, kō-ˈa-jə-(ˌ)triks\ *n, pl* **co·ad·ju·tri·ces** \ˌkō-ə-ˈjü-trə-ˌsēz, (ˌ)kō-ˌa-jə-ˈtrī-(ˌ)sēz\ [NL, fem. of *coadjutor*] (1646) **:** a woman who is a coadjutor
co·ag·u·lant \kō-ˈa-gyə-lənt\ *n* (1770) **:** something that produces coagulation
co·ag·u·lase \kō-ˈa-gyə-ˌlās, -ˌlāz\ *n* (1914) **:** any of several enzymes that cause coagulation (as of blood)
[1]**co·ag·u·late** \-lət, -ˌlāt\ *adj* (14c) *archaic* **:** being clotted or congealed
[2]**co·ag·u·late** \kō-ˈa-gyə-ˌlāt\ *vb* **-lat·ed; -lat·ing** [L *coagulatus,* pp. of *coagulare* to curdle, fr. *coagulum* curdling agent, fr. *cogere* to drive together — more at COGENT] *vt* (15c) **1 :** to cause to become viscous or thickened into a coherent mass **:** CURDLE, CLOT **2 :** to gather together or form into a mass or group ~ *vi* **:** to become coagulated — **co·ag·u-**

la·bil·i·ty \kō-ˌa-gyə-lə-ˈbi-lə-tē\ *n* — **co·ag·u·la·ble** \-ˈa-gyə-lə-bəl\ *adj* — **co·ag·u·la·tion** \-ˈlā-shən\ *n*

co·ag·u·lum \kō-ˈa-gyə-ləm\ *n, pl* **-u·la** \-lə\ *or* **-ulums** [L] (1658) : a coagulated mass or substance : CLOT

[1]**coal** \ˈkōl\ *n, often attrib* [ME *col,* fr. OE; akin to OHG & ON *kol* burning ember, MIr *gúal* coal] (bef. 12c) **1** : a piece of glowing carbon or charred wood : EMBER **2** : CHARCOAL 1 **3 a** : a black or brownish-black solid combustible substance formed by the partial decomposition of vegetable matter without free access of air and under the influence of moisture and often increased pressure and temperature that is widely used as a natural fuel **b** *pl, Brit* : pieces or a quantity of the fuel broken up for burning

[2]**coal** *vt* (1602) **1** : to burn to charcoal : CHAR **2** : to supply with coal ~ *vi* : to take in coal

co·a·lesce \ˌkō-ə-ˈles\ *vb* **co·a·lesced; co·a·lesc·ing** [L *coalescere,* fr. *co-* + *alescere* to grow — more at OLD] *vi* (ca. 1656) **1** : to grow together **2 a** : to unite into a whole : FUSE ⟨separate townships have *coalesced* into a single, sprawling colony —Donald Gould⟩ **b** : to unite for a common end : join forces ⟨people with different points of view ~ into opposing factions —I. L. Horowitz⟩ **3** : to arise from the combination of distinct elements ⟨an organized and a popular resistance immediately *coalesced* —C. C. Menges⟩ ~ *vt* : to cause to unite ⟨sometimes a book ~*s* a public into a mass market —Walter Meade⟩ ***syn*** see MIX — **co·a·les·cence** \-ˈle-sᵊn(t)s\ *n* — **co·a·les·cent** \-sᵊnt\ *adj*

coal·field \ˈkōl-ˌfēld\ *n* (1805) : a region rich in coal deposits

coal·fish \-ˌfish\ *n* (1603) : any of several blackish or dark-backed fishes (as a pollack, cobia, or sablefish)

coal gas *n* (1809) : gas made from coal: as **a** : the mixture of gases thrown off by burning coal **b** : gas made by carbonizing bituminous coal in retorts and used for heating and lighting

coal·hole \ˈkōl-ˌhōl\ *n* (ca. 1662) *Brit* : a compartment for storing coal

coal·i·fi·ca·tion \ˌkō-lə-fə-ˈkā-shən\ *n* (1911) : a process in which vegetable matter becomes converted into coal of increasingly higher rank with anthracite as the final product — **coal·i·fy** \ˈkō-lə-ˌfī\ *vt*

co·a·li·tion \ˌkō-ə-ˈli-shən\ *n* [F, fr. L *coalescere*] (1604) **1 a** : the act of coalescing : UNION **b** : a body formed by the coalescing of orig. distinct elements : COMBINATION **2** : a temporary alliance of distinct parties, persons, or states for joint action — **co·a·li·tion·ist** \-ˈli-sh(ə-)nist\ *n*

coal measures *n pl* (1829) : beds of coal with the associated rocks

coal oil *n* (1851) **1** : petroleum or a refined oil prepared from it **2** : KEROSENE

coal seam *n* (1811) : a bed of coal usu. thick enough to be profitably mined

coal tar *n* (1785) : tar obtained by distillation of bituminous coal and used esp. as an industrial fuel, in making dyes, and in the topical treatment of skin disorders

coam·ing *also* **comb·ing** \ˈkō-miŋ\ *n* [prob. irreg. fr. *comb*] (1611) : a raised frame (as around a hatchway in the deck of a ship) to keep out water

co·apt \kō-ˈapt\ *vt* [LL *coaptare,* fr. L *co-* + *aptus* fastened, fit — more at APT] (1570) : to fit together and make fast — **co·ap·ta·tion** \(ˌ)kō-ˌap-ˈtā-shən\ *n*

co·arc·ta·tion \(ˌ)kō-ˌärk-ˈtā-shən\ *n* [L *coarctation-, coarctatio* tightening, fr. *coarctare, coartare* to constrict, fr. *co-* + *artare* to fix firmly, fr. *artus* close, tight; akin to L *artus* joint — more at ARTICLE] (1545) : a stricture or narrowing esp. of a canal or vessel (as the aorta)

coarse \ˈkōrs\ *adj* **coars·er; coars·est** [ME *cors,* perh. fr. *course,* n.] (14c) **1** : of ordinary or inferior quality or value : COMMON **2 a** (1) : composed of relatively large parts or particles ⟨~ sand⟩ (2) : loose or rough in texture ⟨~ cloth⟩ **b** : adjusted or designed for heavy, fast, or less delicate work ⟨a ~ saw with large teeth⟩ **c** : not precise or detailed with respect to adjustment or discrimination **3** : crude or unrefined in taste, manners, or language **4** : harsh, raucous, or rough in tone **5** *chiefly Brit* : of or relating to coarse fish ⟨~ fishing⟩ — **coarse·ly** *adv* — **coarse·ness** *n*

syn COARSE, VULGAR, GROSS, OBSCENE, RIBALD mean offensive to good taste or morals. COARSE implies roughness, rudeness, or crudeness of spirit, behavior, or language ⟨found the *coarse* humor of coworkers offensive⟩. VULGAR often implies boorishness or ill-breeding ⟨a loud *vulgar* belch⟩. GROSS implies extreme coarseness and insensitiveness ⟨*gross* eating habits⟩. OBSCENE applies to anything strongly repulsive to the sense of decency and propriety esp. in sexual matters ⟨*obscene* language not allowed on the air⟩. RIBALD applies to what is amusingly or picturesquely vulgar or irreverent or mildly indecent ⟨entertained the campers with *ribald* folk songs⟩.

coarse fish *n* (1857) **1** : ROUGH FISH **2** *chiefly Brit* : a freshwater fish other than a salmonid

coarse–grained \ˈkōrs-ˌgrānd\ *adj* (ca. 1774) **1** : having a coarse grain ⟨~ wood⟩ **2** : CRUDE ⟨~ humor⟩

coars·en \ˈkōr-sᵊn\ *vb* **coars·ened; coars·en·ing** *vt* (1805) : to make coarse ~ *vi* : to become coarse

[1]**coast** \ˈkōst\ *n* [ME *cost, coste,* fr. AF *coste,* fr. L *costa* rib, side; akin to OCS *kostĭ* bone] (14c) **1** : the land near a shore : SEASHORE **2** *obs* : BORDER, FRONTIER **3 a** : a hill or slope suited to coasting **b** : a slide down a slope (as on a sled) **4** *often cap* : the Pacific coast of the U.S. **5** : the immediate area of view — used in the phrase *the coast is clear* — **coast·al** \ˈkōs-tᵊl\ *adj* — **coast·wise** \ˈkōst-ˌwīz\ *adv or adj* — **from coast to coast** : across an entire nation or continent

[2]**coast** *vt* (14c) **1** *obs* : to move along or past the side of : SKIRT **2** : to sail along the shore of ~ *vi* **1 a** *archaic* : to travel on land along a coast or along or past the side of something **b** : to sail along the shore **2 a** : to slide, run, or glide downhill by the force of gravity **b** : to move along without or as if without further application of propulsive power (as by momentum or gravity) **c** : to proceed easily without special application of effort or concern ⟨~*ed* through school⟩ — often used with *on* ⟨a company ~*ing* on its good reputation⟩

coast·er \ˈkōs-tər\ *n* (1574) **1** : one that coasts: as **a** : a person engaged in coastal traffic or commerce **b** : a ship sailing along a coast or engaged in trade between ports of the same country **2** : a resident of a seacoast **3 a** : a tray or decanter stand usu. of silver and sometimes on wheels **b** : a shallow container or a plate or mat to protect a surface **4 a** : a small vehicle (as a sled or wagon) used in coasting **b** : ROLLER COASTER

coaster brake *n* (1899) : a brake in the hub of the rear wheel of a bicycle operated by reverse pressure on the pedals

coaster wagon *n* (1911) : a child's toy wagon often used for coasting

coast guard *n* (1833) **1** : a military or naval force employed in guarding a coast or responsible for the safety, order, and operation of maritime traffic in neighboring waters **2** *usu* **coast·guard,** *chiefly Brit* : COASTGUARDSMAN

coast·guards·man \ˈkōs(t)-ˌgärdz-mən\ *or* **coast·guard·man** \-ˌgärd-mən\ *n* (1848) : a member of a coast guard

coast·land \-ˌland\ *n* (1852) : land bordering the sea

coast·line \-ˌlīn\ *n* (1856) **1** : a line that forms the boundary between the land and the ocean or a lake **2** : the outline of a coast

coast redwood *n* (ca. 1897) : REDWOOD 3a

coast–to–coast \ˈkōs-tə-ˈkōst\ *adj* (1911) **1** : extending or airing across an entire nation or continent ⟨a ~ flight⟩ ⟨a ~ broadcast⟩ **2** : extending from one end of a playing surface (as a basketball court) to the other ⟨a ~ rush⟩; *also* : relating to or resulting from a coast-to-coast play ⟨a ~ layup⟩ — **coast–to–coast** *adv*

coast·ward \ˈkōst-wərd\ *or* **coast·wards** \-wərdz\ *adv* (1840) : toward the coast — **coastward** *adj*

[1]**coat** \ˈkōt\ *n, often attrib* [ME *cote,* fr. AF, of Gmc origin; akin to OHG *kozza* coarse wool mantle] (14c) **1 a** : an outer garment worn on the upper body and varying in length and style according to fashion and use **b** : something resembling a coat **2** : the external growth on an animal **3** : a layer of one substance covering another ⟨a ~ of paint⟩ — **coat·ed** \ˈkō-təd\ *adj* — **coat·less** *adj*

[2]**coat** *vt* (14c) **1** : to cover with a coat **2** : to cover or spread with a finishing, protecting, or enclosing layer — **coat·er** *n*

coat·dress \ˈkōt-ˌdres\ *n* (1854) : a dress styled like a coat usu. with a front buttoning from neckline to hemline

coat hanger *n* (1895) : a device which is shaped like the outline of a person's shoulders and over which garments may be hung

co·a·ti \kə-ˈwä-tē, kō-ˈä-, kwä-ˈtē\ *n* [Pg *quati, coati,* fr. Tupi *kwáti*] (1676) : either of two tropical American mammals (*Nasua nasua* and *N. narica*) related to the raccoon but with a longer body and tail and a long flexible snout

co·a·ti·mun·di \kə-ˌwä-tē-ˈmən-dē, kō-ˌä-, ˌkwä-, -ˈmu̇n-\ *n* [Pg *quatimundé,* fr. Tupi *kwatimúnde,* older male coati not with a band, fr. *kwáti* coati + *múnde* snare, trap] (1676) : COATI

coat·ing \ˈkō-tiŋ\ *n* (1768) **1** : cloth for coats **2** : COAT, COVERING

coat of arms [ME *cote of armes,* trans. of MF *cote d'armes*] (14c) **1** : a tabard or surcoat embroidered with armorial bearings **2 a** : heraldic bearings (as of a person) usu. depicted on an escutcheon often with accompanying adjuncts (as a crest, motto, and supporters) **b** : a similar symbolic emblem

coat of mail (15c) : a garment of metal scales or chain mail worn as armor

coat·rack \ˈkōt-ˌrak\ *n* (1915) : a stand or rack fitted with pegs, hooks, or hangers and used for the temporary storage of garments

coat·room \-ˌrüm, -ˌru̇m\ *n* (1870) : CLOAKROOM, CHECKROOM

coat·tail \ˈkōt-ˌtāl\ *n* (ca. 1600) **1** : the rear flap of a man's coat **2** *pl* : the skirts of a dress coat, cutaway, or frock coat **3** *pl* : the influence or pulling power of a popular movement or person (as a political candidate) ⟨congressmen riding into office on the president's ~*s*⟩

[1]**coax** \ˈkōks\ *vt* [earlier *cokes,* fr. *cokes* simpleton] (1581) **1** *obs* : FONDLE, PET **2** : to influence or gently urge by caressing or flattering : WHEEDLE ⟨~*ed* him into going⟩ **3** : to draw, gain, or persuade by means of gentle urging or flattery ⟨unable to ~ an answer out of him⟩ **4** : to manipulate with great perseverance and usu. with considerable effort toward a desired state or activity ⟨~ a fire to burn⟩ ***syn*** see CAJOLE

[2]**co·ax** \ˈkō-ˌaks\ *n* (1945) : COAXIAL CABLE

co·ax·i·al \(ˌ)kō-ˈak-sē-əl\ *adj* (1881) **1** : having coincident axes **2** : mounted on concentric shafts — **co·ax·i·al·ly** \-sē-ə-lē\ *adv*

coaxial cable *n* (1936) : a transmission line that consists of a tube of electrically conducting material surrounding a central conductor held in place by insulators and that is used to transmit telegraph, telephone, and television signals — called also *coax cable*

cob \ˈkäb\ *n* [ME *cobbe* leader of a group, head; prob. akin to *cub* (young animal), ME *kebbe* old cow or sheep, D dial. *kabbe, kebbe* piglet] (15c) **1** [perh. short for *cobswan* lead swan] : a male swan **2 a** *dial Eng* : a rounded mass, lump, or heap **b** : a mixture of unburnt clay and straw used esp. for constructing walls of small houses in England **3** : a crudely struck old Spanish coin of irregular shape **4** : CORNCOB 1 **5** : a stocky short-legged riding horse

co·bal·a·min \kō-ˈba-lə-mən\ *n* [*cobalt* + vit*amin*] (1956) : VITAMIN B_{12}

co·balt \ˈkō-ˌbōlt\ *n* [G *Kobalt,* alter. of *Kobold,* lit., goblin, fr. MHG *kobolt;* fr. its occurrence in silver ore, believed to be due to goblins] (1683) **1** : a tough lustrous silver-white magnetic metallic element that is related to and occurs with iron and nickel and is used esp. in alloys — see ELEMENT table **2** : COBALT BLUE 2

cobalt blue *n* (1835) **1** : a greenish-blue pigment consisting essentially of cobalt oxide and alumina **2** : a strong greenish blue

cobalt chloride *n* (1869) : a chloride of cobalt; *esp* : the dichloride $CoCl_2$ that is blue when dehydrated, turns red in the presence of moisture, and is used to indicate humidity

co·bal·tic \kō-ˈbōl-tik\ *adj* (1782) : of, relating to, or containing cobalt esp. with a valence of three

co·balt·ite \ˈkō-ˌbōl-ˌtīt, kō-ˈ\ *or* **co·balt·ine** \-ˌtēn\ *n* [*cobaltite,* alter. of *cobaltine,* fr. F, fr. *cobalt*] (1868) : a grayish to silver-white mineral consisting of a sulfur arsenide of cobalt also containing iron and sometimes nickel and used in making smalt

co·bal·tous \kō-ˈbōl-təs\ *adj* (1863) : of, relating to, or containing cobalt esp. with a valence of two

cobalt 60 *n* (1946) : a heavy radioactive isotope of cobalt of the mass number 60 produced in nuclear reactors and used as a source of gamma rays (as for radiotherapy)

\ə\ **abut** \ᵊ\ **kitten,** F **table** \ər\ **further** \a\ **ash** \ā\ **ace** \ä\ **mop, mar** \au̇\ **out** \ch\ **chin** \e\ **bet** \ē\ **easy** \g\ **go** \i\ **hit** \ī\ **ice** \j\ **job** \ŋ\ **sing** \ō\ **go** \ȯ\ **law** \ȯi\ **boy** \th\ **thin** \t͟h\ **the** \ü\ **loot** \u̇\ **foot** \y\ **yet** \zh\ **vision, beige** \k̲, ⁿ, œ, ue, ʸ\ *see* Guide to Pronunciation

cob·ber \ˈkȯ-bər\ *n* [perh. fr. Brit. dial (Suffolk) *cob* to take a liking to someone] (1893) *Austral & NewZeal* : BUDDY

[1]**cob·ble** \ˈkä-bəl\ *vt* **cob·bled; cob·bling** \-b(ə-)liŋ\ [ME *coblen*, perh. back-formation fr. *cobelere* cobbler] (15c) **1** *chiefly Brit* : to mend or patch coarsely **2** : REPAIR, MAKE ⟨~ shoes⟩ **3** : to make or put together roughly or hastily — often used with *together* or *up* ⟨~ together an agreement⟩ ⟨~ up a temporary solution⟩

[2]**cobble** *n* (1600) **1** : COBBLESTONE **2** *pl, chiefly Brit* : lump coal about the size of small cobblestones

cobbled *adj* (1853) : paved with cobblestones ⟨~ streets⟩

cob·bler \ˈkä-blər\ *n* [ME *cobelere*] (13c) **1** : a mender or maker of shoes and often of other leather goods **2** *archaic* : a clumsy workman **3** : a tall iced drink consisting usu. of wine, rum, or whiskey and sugar garnished with mint or a slice of lemon or orange **4** : a deep-dish fruit dessert with a thick top crust

cob·ble·stone \ˈkä-bəl-ˌstōn\ *n* [ME, fr. *cobble-* (prob. fr. *cob*) + *stone*] (15c) : a naturally rounded stone larger than a pebble and smaller than a boulder; *esp* : such a stone used in paving a street or in construction — **cob·ble·stoned** \-ˌstōnd\ *adj*

Cobb salad \ˈkäb-\ *n* [prob. fr. Robert H. *Cobb* †1970 Am. restaurateur] (1949) : a tossed salad made typically with chopped chicken or turkey, tomatoes, bacon, hard-boiled eggs, blue cheese, and lettuce and dressed with a vinaigrette

cob·by \ˈkä-bē\ *adj* **cob·bi·er; -est** (1845) : STOCKY ⟨a ~ horse⟩

co·bel·lig·er·ent \ˌkō-bə-ˈlij-rənt, -ˈli-jə-\ *n* (1813) : a country fighting with another power against a common enemy — **cobelligerent** *adj*

co·bia \ˈkō-bē-ə\ *n* [origin unknown] (ca. 1873) : a large bony fish (*Rachycentron canadum* of the family Rachycentridae) of warm seas that is a food and sport fish

co·ble \ˈkō-bəl\ *n* [ME] (14c) : a flat-bottomed boat propelled chiefly by oars and used in Scotland and northern England esp. for fishing

cob·nut \ˈkäb-ˌnət\ *n* (1580) : the fruit of a European hazel (*Corylus avellana grandis*); *also* : the plant bearing this fruit

CO·BOL *or* **Co·bol** \ˈkō-ˌbȯl\ *n* [*common business oriented language*] (1960) : a computer programming language designed for business applications

co·bra \ˈkō-brə\ *n* [Pg *cobra* (*de capello*), lit., hooded snake, fr. L *colubra* snake] (1802) : any of several venomous Asian and African elapid snakes (genera *Naja* and *Ophiophagus*) that when excited expand the skin of the neck into a hood by movement of the anterior ribs; *also* : any of several related African snakes

co–brand \ˈkō-ˌbrand\ *vt* (1982) : to market or issue (as a credit card) in conjunction with another company so that the product bears the name of both

cob·web \ˈkäb-ˌweb\ *n* [ME *coppeweb*, fr. *coppe* spider (fr. OE *ātorcoppe*) + *web*; akin to MD *coppe* spider] (14c) **1 a** : the network spread by a spider : SPIDERWEB **b** : tangles of the silken threads of a spiderweb usu. covered with accumulated dirt and dust **2** : something that entangles, obscures, or confuses ⟨a ~ of law and politics⟩ — **cobwebbed** \-ˌwebd\ *adj*

cob·web·by \-ˌwe-bē\ *adj* **cob·web·bi·er; -est** (1854) **1** : filled or covered with cobwebs ⟨a ~ barn⟩ **2** : GOSSAMER ⟨~ lace⟩ **3** : MUSTY, WELL-WORN ⟨a ~ plot device⟩ ⟨~ quaintness⟩

co·ca \ˈkō-kə\ *n* [Sp, fr. Quechua *kuka*] (1577) **1** : any of several So. American shrubs (genus *Erythroxylon*, family Erythroxylaceae); *esp* : one (*E. coca*) that is the primary source of cocaine **2** : dried leaves of a coca (esp. *Erythroxylon coca*) containing alkaloids including cocaine

co·caine \kō-ˈkān, ˈkō-ˌ\ *n* (1874) : a bitter crystalline alkaloid $C_{17}H_{21}NO_4$ obtained from coca leaves that is used esp. in the form of its hydrochloride medically as a topical anesthetic and illicitly for its euphoric effects and that may result in a compulsive psychological need

co·cain·ize \kō-ˈkā-ˌnīz\ *vt* **-ized; -iz·ing** (1887) : to treat or anesthetize with cocaine — **co·cain·i·za·tion** \-ˌkā-nə-ˈzā-shən\ *n*

co·car·box·yl·ase \ˌkō-kär-ˈbäk-sə-ˌlās, -ˌlāz\ *n* (1932) : a coenzyme $C_{12}H_{19}ClN_4O_7P_2S{\cdot}H_2O$ that is a pyrophosphate of thiamine and is important in metabolic reactions (as decarboxylation in the Krebs cycle)

co·car·cin·o·gen \ˌkō-kär-ˈsi-nə-jən, kō-ˈkär-sə-nə-ˌjen\ *n* (1938) : an agent that aggravates the carcinogenic effects of another substance — **co·car·cin·o·gen·ic** \ˌkō-ˌkär-sə-nō-ˈje-nik\ *adj*

coc·cid \ˈkäk-səd\ *n* [NL *Coccus*, genus of scales, fr. Gk *kokkos* grain, kermes] (ca. 1889) : SCALE INSECT

coc·cid·i·oi·do·my·co·sis \(ˌ)käk-ˌsi-dē-ˌȯi-dō-(ˌ)mī-ˈkō-səs\ *n* [NL, fr. *Coccidioides*, genus of fungi (fr. *coccidium*) + *mycosis*] (1937) : a disease esp. of humans and domestic animals caused by a fungus (*Coccidioides immitis*) and marked esp. by fever and pulmonary symptoms

coc·cid·i·o·sis \(ˌ)käk-ˌsi-dē-ˈō-səs\ *n, pl* **-o·ses** \-ˌsēz\ [NL] (1892) : infestation with or disease caused by coccidia

coc·cid·i·um \käk-ˈsi-dē-əm\ *n, pl* **-ia** \-dē-ə\ [NL, dim. of *coccus*] (ca. 1879) : any of an order (Coccidia) of protozoans usu. parasitic in the digestive epithelium of vertebrates

coc·coid \ˈkä-ˌkȯid\ *adj* (1893) : of, relating to, or resembling a coccus : GLOBULAR 1a(1) — **coccoid** *n*

coc·cus \ˈkä-kəs\ *n, pl* **coc·ci** \ˈkä-ˌkī, -ˌkē; ˈkäk-ˌsī, -ˌsē\ [NL, fr. Gk *kokkos*] (1888) : a spherical bacterium — **coc·cal** \ˈkä-kəl\ *adj*

-coccus *n comb form, pl* **-cocci** [NL] : berry-shaped microorganism ⟨micro*coccus*⟩

coc·cy·geal \käk-ˈsi-j(ē-)əl\ *adj* [ML *coccygeus* of the coccyx, fr. Gk *kokkyk-, kokkyx*] (1836) : of or relating to the coccyx

coc·cyx \ˈkäk-siks\ *n, pl* **coc·cy·ges** \ˈkäk-sə-ˌjēz\ *also* **coc·cyx·es** \ˈkäk-sik-səz\ [NL, fr. Gk *kokkyx* cuckoo, coccyx; fr. its resemblance to a cuckoo's beak] (1615) : a small bone that articulates with the sacrum and that usu. consists of four fused vertebrae which form the terminus of the spinal column in humans and tailless apes

Co·chin \ˈkō-chin\ *n* [*Cochin* China, part of French Indochina] (1853) : any of an Asian breed of large domestic chickens with thick plumage, small wings and tail, and densely feathered legs and feet — called also *Cochin China*

co·chi·neal \ˈkä-chə-ˌnēl, ˈkō-\ *n* [MF & Sp; MF *cochenille*, fr. OSp *cochinilla* cochineal insect] (1582) **1** : a red dye consisting of the dried bodies of female cochineal insects **2** : COCHINEAL INSECT

cochineal insect *n* (1801) : a small red cactus-feeding scale insect (*Dactylopius coccus*) the females of which are the source of cochineal

co·chlea \ˈkō-klē-ə, ˈkä-klē-\ *n, pl* **co·chle·as** *or* **co·chle·ae** \-klē-ˌē, -ˌī\ [NL, fr. L, snail, snail shell, fr. Gk *kochlias*, fr. *kochlos* snail; prob. akin to Gk *konchē* mussel] (1688) : a hollow tube in the inner ear of higher vertebrates that is usu. coiled like a snail shell and contains the sensory organ of hearing — see EAR illustration — **co·chle·ar** \ˈkō-klē-ər, ˈkä-\ *adj*

cochlear implant *n* (1980) : an electronic prosthetic device that enables individuals with sensorineural hearing loss to recognize some sounds and consists of an external microphone and speech processor and one or more electrodes implanted in the cochlea

[1]**cock** \ˈkäk\ *n* [ME *cok*, fr. OE *cocc*, of imit. origin] (bef. 12c) **1 a** : the adult male of the domestic chicken (*Gallus gallus*) **b** : the male of birds other than the domestic chicken **c** : WOODCOCK **d** *archaic* : the crowing of a cock; *also* : COCKCROW **e** : WEATHERCOCK **2** : a device (as a faucet or valve) for regulating the flow of a liquid **3 a** : a chief person : LEADER **b** : a person of spirit and often of a certain swagger or arrogance **4 a** : the hammer in the lock of a firearm **b** : the cocked position of the hammer **5** *usu vulgar* : PENIS — **cock of the walk** : one that dominates a group or situation esp. overbearingly

[2]**cock** *vi* (1575) **1** : STRUT, SWAGGER **2** : to turn, tip, or stick up **3** : to position the hammer of a firearm for firing ~ *vt* **1 a** : to draw the hammer of (a firearm) back and set for firing; *also* : to set (the trigger) for firing **b** : to draw or bend back in preparation for throwing or hitting ⟨a quarterback ~*ing* his arm⟩ ⟨~ a bat⟩ **c** : to set a mechanism (as a camera shutter) for tripping **2 a** : to set erect ⟨a dog with one ear ~*ed*⟩ **b** : to turn, tip, or tilt usu. to one side ⟨~ one's head⟩ **3** : to turn up (as a hat brim) — **cock a snook** *also* **cock snooks** : to thumb one's nose ⟨*cocking a snook* at the establishment⟩

[3]**cock** *n* (1717) : TILT, SLANT ⟨~ of the head⟩

[4]**cock** *n* [ME *cok*; akin to G dial. *Kocke* pile] (14c) : a small pile (as of hay)

[5]**cock** *vt* (14c) : to put (as hay) into cocks

cock·ade \kä-ˈkād\ *n* [modif. of F *cocarde*, fr. fem. of *cocard* vain, fr. *coq* cock, fr. OF *coc*, of imit. origin] (1709) : an ornament (as a rosette) usu. worn on a hat as a badge — **cock·ad·ed** \-ˈkā-dəd\ *adj*

cock–a–hoop \ˌkä-kə-ˈhüp, -ˈhu̇p\ *adj* [fr. the phrase *to set cock a hoop* to be festive] (1663) **1** : triumphantly boastful : EXULTING **2** : AWRY

Cock·aigne \kä-ˈkān\ *n* [ME *cokaygne*, fr. MF (*pais de*) *cocaigne* land of plenty] (13c) : an imaginary land of great luxury and ease

cock–a–leek·ie \ˌkä-ki-ˈlē-kē\ *n* [alter. of *cockie* (dim. of [1]*cock*) + *leekie*, dim. of *leek*] (1737) : a soup made of chicken and leeks

cock·a·lo·rum \ˌkä-kə-ˈlȯr-əm\ *n, pl* **-rums** [prob. modif. of obs. D dial. *kockeloeren* to crow, of imit. origin] (ca. 1715) **1** : a boastful and self-important person **2** : LEAPFROG **3** : boastful talk

cock·a·ma·my *or* **cock·a·ma·mie** \ˌkä-kə-ˈmā-mē\ *adj* [perh. alter. of *decalcomania*] (1960) : RIDICULOUS, INCREDIBLE ⟨of all the ~ excuses I ever heard —Leo Rosten⟩

cock–and–bull story \ˈkä-kən-ˈbu̇l-\ *n* (1778) : an incredible story told as true

cock·a·poo \ˈkä-kə-ˌpü\ *n* [alter. of *cocker* (*spaniel*) + *poodle*] (1970) : a dog that is a cross between a cocker spaniel and a poodle

cock·a·tiel \ˈkäk-ə-ˌtēl\ *n* [D *kaketielje*, fr. Pg *cacatilha*, fr. *cacatua* cockatoo] (1877) : a crested small gray Australian parrot (*Nymphicus hollandicus* of the family Cacatuidae) with a yellow head

cock·a·too \ˈkä-kə-ˌtü\ *n, pl* **-toos** [D *kaketoe*, fr. Malay *kakatua*] (1634) : any of various large noisy chiefly Australasian crested parrots (family Cacatuidae and esp. genus *Cacatua*)

cock·a·trice \ˈkä-kə-trəs, -ˌtrīs\ *n* [ME *cocatrice*, fr. MF *cocatris* ichneumon, cockatrice, fr. ML *cocatric-, cocatrix* ichneumon] (14c) : a legendary serpent that is hatched by a reptile from a cock's egg and that has a deadly glance

cock·cha·fer \ˈkäk-ˌchā-fər\ *n* [[1]*cock* + *chafer*] (1712) : a large European beetle (*Melolontha melolontha*) destructive to vegetation as an adult and to roots as a larva; *also* : any of various related beetles

cock·crow \ˈkäk-ˌkrō\ *n* (13c) : DAWN

cocked hat \ˈkäkt-\ *n* (1673) **1** : a hat with brim turned up to give a 3-cornered appearance **2** : a hat with brim turned up on two sides and worn either front to back or sideways

[1]**cock·er** \ˈkä-kər\ *vt* [ME *cokeren*] (15c) : INDULGE, PAMPER

[2]**cocker** *n* (1689) : a keeper or handler of fighting cocks

[3]**cocker** *n* (ca. 1811) : COCKER SPANIEL

cock·er·el \ˈkä-k(ə-)rəl\ *n* [ME *cokerelle*, fr. AF *cokerel*, dim. of *coc*] (15c) : a young male of the domestic chicken (*Gallus gallus*)

cock·er spaniel \ˈkä-kər-\ *n* [*cocking* woodcock hunting] (1840) **1** : ENGLISH COCKER SPANIEL **2** : any of a breed of spaniels developed in the U.S. from the English cocker spaniel that are smaller in size and have a shorter muzzle and longer thicker coat

cock·eye \ˈkäk-ˈī, -ˌī\ *n* (ca. 1825) : a squinting eye

cock·eyed \ˈkäk-ˌīd\ *adj* (1821) **1** : having a cockeye **2 a** : ASKEW, AWRY **b** : slightly crazy : TOPSY-TURVY ⟨a ~ scheme⟩ **c** : DRUNK 1a — **cock·eyed·ly** \ˈkäk-ˌī(-ə)d-lē\ *adv* — **cock·eyed·ness** \-ˌīd-nəs\ *n*

cock·fight \ˈkäk-ˌfīt\ *n* (ca. 1566) : a contest in which gamecocks usu. fitted with metal spurs are pitted against each other — **cock·fight·ing** \-ˌfī-tiŋ\ *adj or n*

cock·horse \ˈkäk-ˌhȯrs\ *n* [perh. fr. *cock*, adj., (male) + *horse*] (ca. 1541) : ROCKING HORSE

[1]**cock·le** \ˈkä-kəl\ *n* [ME, fr. OE *coccel*] (bef. 12c) : any of several weedy plants of the pink family; *esp* : CORN COCKLE

[2]**cockle** *n* [ME *cokille*, fr. MF *coquille* shell, modif. of L *conchylia*, pl. of *conchylium*, fr. Gk *konchylion*, fr. *konchē* conch] (14c) **1** : any of various chiefly marine bivalve mollusks (family Cardiidae) having a shell with convex radially ribbed valves; *esp* : a common edible European bivalve (*Cerastoderma edule* syn. *Cardium edule*) **2** : COCKLESHELL

[3]**cockle** *n* [ME *kokell*, ultim. fr. MF *coquillé* wavy or rounded like a shell, fr. *coquille*] (15c) : PUCKER, WRINKLE — **cockle** *vb*

cock·le·bur \ˈkä-kəl-ˌbər, ˈkə-\ *n* (1804) : any of a genus (*Xanthium*) of prickly-fruited composite plants; *also* : one of its stiff-spined fruits

cock·le·shell \ˈkä-kəl-ˌshel\ *n* (15c) **1 a** : the shell or one of the shell valves of a cockle **b** : a shell (as a scallop shell) suggesting a cockleshell **2** : a light flimsy boat

cockles of the heart [perh. fr. [2]*cockle*] (1671) : the core of one's being — usu. used in the phrase *warm the cockles of the heart*

cock·loft \ˈkäk-ˌlȯft\ *n* [prob. fr. [1]*cock*] (1589) : a small garret

cock·ney \ˈkäk-nē\ *n, pl* **cockneys** [ME *cokeney,* lit., cocks' egg, fr. *coken* (gen. pl. of *cok* cock) + *ey* egg, fr. OE *ǣg*] (14c) **1** *obs* **a :** a spoiled child **b :** a squeamish woman **2** *often cap* **a :** a native of London and esp. of the East End of London **b :** the dialect of London or of the East End of London — **cockney** *adj* — **cock·ney·fy** \ˈkäk-ni-ˌfī\ *vt* — **cock·ney·ish** \-nē-ish\ *adj* — **cock·ney·ism** \-ˌi-zəm\ *n*
cock·pit \ˈkäk-ˌpit\ *n* (1585) **1 a :** a pit or enclosure for cockfights **b :** a place noted for esp. bloody, violent, or long-continued conflict **2** *obs* **:** the pit of a theater **3 :** a compartment in a sailing warship used as quarters for junior officers and for treatment of the wounded in an engagement **4 :** a space or compartment in a usu. small vehicle (as a boat, airplane, or automobile) from which it is steered, piloted, or driven — see AIRPLANE illustration
cock·roach \ˈkäk-ˌrōch\ *n* [by folk etymology fr. Sp *cucaracha* cockroach] (1623) **:** any of an order or suborder (Blattodea syn. Blattaria) of chiefly nocturnal insects including some that are domestic pests — compare GERMAN COCKROACH
cocks·comb \ˈkäks-ˌkōm\ *n* (1534) **1 :** COXCOMB **2 :** a garden plant (*Celosia cristata*) of the amaranth family grown for its flowers
cocks·foot \-ˌfu̇t\ *n* (1697) **:** ORCHARD GRASS
cock·shut \ˈkäk-ˌshət\ *n* [fr. the time poultry are shut in to rest] (1592) *dial Eng* **:** evening twilight
cock·shy \-ˌshī\ *n, pl* **cockshies** [1*cock* + *shy,* n.] (1836) **1 a :** a throw at an object set up as a mark **b :** a mark or target so set up **2 :** an object or person taken as a butt (as of criticism)
cock·suck·er \-ˌsə-kər\ *n* (ca. 1891) *usu obscene* **:** one who performs fellatio — often used as a generalized term of abuse
cock·sure \ˈkäk-ˈshu̇r\ *adj* [prob. fr. 1*cock* + *sure*] (1608) **1 :** feeling perfect assurance sometimes on inadequate grounds **2 :** marked by overconfidence or presumptuousness **:** COCKY ***syn*** see SURE — **cock·sure·ly** *adv* — **cock·sure·ness** *n*
1**cock·tail** \ˈkäk-ˌtāl\ *n* [prob. fr. 1*cock* + *tail*] (1806) **1 a :** an iced drink of wine or distilled liquor mixed with flavoring ingredients **b :** something resembling or suggesting such a drink as being a mixture of often diverse elements or ingredients ⟨a ~ of remembered incidents and pure imagination —Charlotte Low⟩ ⟨a ~ of herbicides⟩ **c :** a mixture of agents usu. in solution that is taken or used together esp. for medical treatment or diagnosis **2 :** an appetizer served as a first course at a meal
2**cocktail** *adj* (1852) **1 :** of, relating to, or set aside for cocktails ⟨a ~ hour⟩ **2 :** designed for semiformal wear ⟨a ~ dress⟩
3**cocktail** *n* [1*cock* + *tail*] (1808) **:** a horse with its tail docked
cocktail glass *n* (1907) **:** a bell-shaped drinking glass usu. having a foot and stem and holding about three ounces (90 milliliters)
cocktail lounge *n* (1939) **:** a public room (as in a hotel, club, or restaurant) where cocktails and other drinks are served
cocktail party *n* (1928) **:** an informal or semiformal party or gathering at which cocktails are served
cocktail table *n* (1939) **:** COFFEE TABLE
cock–up \ˈkäk-ˌəp\ *n* (ca. 1948) *Brit* **:** MESS 3b
cocky \ˈkä-kē\ *adj* **cock·i·er; -est** (1768) **1 :** boldly or brashly self-confident ⟨a ~ young actor⟩ **2 :** JAUNTY — **cock·i·ly** \ˈkä-kə-lē\ *adv* — **cock·i·ness** \ˈkä-kē-nəs\ *n*
co·co \ˈkō-(ˌ)kō\ *n, pl* **cocos** [Sp *coco* & Pg *côco* bogeyman, grimace, coconut] (1555) **:** the coconut palm; *also* **:** its fruit
co·coa \ˈkō-(ˌ)kō\ *n* [modif. of Sp *cacao*] (1730) **1 a :** powdered ground roasted cacao beans from which a portion of the fat has been removed **b :** a beverage prepared by heating cocoa with water or milk **2 :** CACAO 2 **3 :** a medium brown color
cocoa bean *n* (1855) **:** CACAO 1
cocoa butter *also* **cacao butter** *n* (1868) **:** a pale vegetable fat with a low melting point obtained from cacao beans
co·co·nut \ˈkō-kə-(ˌ)nət\ *n* (1516) **1 :** the drupaceous fruit of the coconut palm whose outer fibrous husk yields coir and whose nut contains thick edible meat and coconut milk **2 :** the edible meat of the coconut
coconut crab *n* (ca. 1889) **:** a large edible coconut-eating burrowing land crab (*Birgus latro*) widely distributed about islands of the tropical Indian and Pacific Oceans
coconut oil *n* (1831) **:** a fatty oil or semisolid fat extracted from fresh coconuts and used esp. in making soaps and food products
coconut palm *n* (1852) **:** a tall pinnate-leaved coconut-bearing palm (*Cocos nucifera*) that grows along tropical coasts
1**co·coon** \kə-ˈkün\ *n* [F *cocon,* fr. Occitan *coucoun,* fr. *coco* shell, prob. ultim. fr. L *coccum* kermes (thought to be a gall or berry), fr. Gk *kokkos* berry, kermes] (1679) **1 a :** an envelope often largely of silk which an insect larva forms about itself and in which it passes the pupa stage **b :** any of various other protective coverings produced by animals **2 a :** something suggesting a cocoon esp. in providing protection or in producing isolation ⟨wrapped in a ~ of blankets⟩ ⟨an interest in the world beyond the everyday ~ most of us construct —Peter Mayle⟩ **b :** a protective covering placed or sprayed over military or naval equipment in storage
2**cocoon** *vt* (1881) **:** to wrap or envelop in or as if in a cocoon
co·coon·ing \-ˈkü-niŋ\ *n* (1986) **:** the practice of spending leisure time at home in preference to going out
co·cotte \kō-ˈkȯt\ *n, pl* **cocottes** \-ˈkȯt(s)\ [F] (1867) **1 :** PROSTITUTE **2 :** a shallow individual baking dish usu. with one or two handles
co·co·yam \ˈkō-(ˌ)kō-yam\ *n* [prob. *coco* + *yam*] (1922) **1 :** TARO **2 :** YAUTIA
co·cur·ric·u·lar \ˌkō-kə-ˈri-kyə-lər\ *adj* (1949) **:** being outside of but usu. complementing the regular curriculum ⟨~ activities⟩
cod \ˈkäd\ *n, pl* **cod** *also* **cods** [ME] (14c) **1 :** any of various bottom-dwelling fishes (family Gadidae, the cod family) that usu. occur in cold marine waters and often have barbels and three dorsal fins: as **a :** one (*Gadus morhua*) of the No. Atlantic that is an important food fish **b :** one (*Gadus macrocephalus*) of the Pacific Ocean **2 :** any of various bony fishes resembling the true cods
cod *abbr* codex
COD *abbr* cash on delivery; collect on delivery
co·da \ˈkō-də\ *n* [It, lit., tail, fr. L *cauda*] (ca. 1753) **1 a :** a concluding musical section that is formally distinct from the main structure **b :** a concluding part of a literary or dramatic work **2 :** something that serves to round out, conclude, or summarize and usu. has its own interest
cod·dle \ˈkä-dᵊl\ *vt* **cod·dled; cod·dling** \ˈkäd-liŋ, ˈkä-dᵊl-iŋ\ [perh. fr. *caudle*] (1598) **1 :** to cook (as eggs) in liquid slowly and gently just below the boiling point **2 :** to treat with extreme or excessive care or kindness **:** PAMPER ⟨accused the court of *coddling* criminals⟩ — **cod·dler** \ˈkäd-lər, ˈkä-dᵊl-ər\ *n*
1**code** \ˈkōd\ *n* [ME, fr. MF, fr. L *caudex, codex* trunk of a tree, document formed orig. from wooden tablets] (14c) **1 :** a systematic statement of a body of law; *esp* **:** one given statutory force **2 :** a system of principles or rules ⟨moral ~⟩ **3 a :** a system of signals or symbols for communication **b :** a system of symbols (as letters or numbers) used to represent assigned and often secret meanings **4 :** GENETIC CODE **5 :** a set of instructions for a computer — **code·less** \-ləs\ *adj*
2**code** *vb* **cod·ed; cod·ing** *vt* (1815) **:** to put in or into the form or symbols of a code ~ *vi* **:** to specify the genetic code ⟨a gene that ~s for a protein⟩ — **cod·able** \ˈkō-də-bəl\ *adj* — **cod·er** *n*
code·book *n* (1866) **:** a book containing an alphabetical list of words or expressions with their code equivalents
codec *abbr* compression/decompression
co·deine \ˈkō-ˌdēn\ *n* [F *codéine,* fr. Gk *kōdeia* poppyhead] (1850) **:** a morphine derivative $C_{18}H_{21}NO_3{\cdot}H_2O$ that is found in opium, is weaker in action than morphine, and is used esp. as an analgesic and antitussive
code name *n* (1919) **:** a designation having a coded and usu. secret meaning — **code–name** \ˈkōd-ˌnām\ *vt*
co·de·pen·dence \ˌkō-di-ˈpen-dən(t)s\ *n* (1985) **:** CODEPENDENCY
co·de·pen·den·cy \-dən(t)-sē\ *n* (1979) **:** a psychological condition or a relationship in which a person is controlled or manipulated by another who is affected with a pathological condition (as an addiction to alcohol or heroin); *broadly* **:** dependence on the needs of or control by another
co·de·pen·dent \-dənt\ *adj* (1982) **:** participating in or exhibiting codependency — **codependent** *n*
co·de·ter·mi·na·tion \ˌkō-di-ˌtər-mə-ˈnā-shən\ *n* (1949) **:** the participation of labor with management in determining business policy
code word *n* (1884) **1 :** CODE NAME **2 :** EUPHEMISM
co·dex \ˈkō-ˌdeks\ *n, pl* **co·di·ces** \ˈkō-də-ˌsēz, ˈkä-\ [L — more at CODE] (ca. 1665) **:** a manuscript book esp. of Scripture, classics, or ancient annals
cod·fish \ˈkäd-ˌfish\ *n* (14c) **:** COD; *also* **:** its flesh used as food
cod·ger \ˈkä-jər\ *n* [prob. alter. of *cadger*] (1756) **:** an often mildly eccentric and usu. elderly fellow ⟨old ~⟩
cod·i·cil \ˈkä-də-səl, -ˌsil\ *n* [ME *codicill,* fr. AF **codicille,* fr. L *codicillus,* dim. of *codic-, codex*] (15c) **1 :** a legal instrument made to modify an earlier will **2 :** APPENDIX, SUPPLEMENT — **cod·i·cil·la·ry** \ˌkä-də-ˈsi-lə-rē\ *adj*
co·di·col·o·gy \ˌkō-də-ˈkä-lə-jē, ˌkä-\ *n* [L *codic-, codex* + *-o-* + E *-logy*] (1953) **:** the study of manuscripts as cultural artifacts for historical purposes — **co·di·co·log·i·cal** \-kə-ˈlä-ji-kəl\ *adj*
cod·i·fy \ˈkä-də-ˌfī, ˈkō-\ *vt* **-fied; -fy·ing** (ca. 1800) **1 :** to reduce to a code **2 a :** SYSTEMATIZE **b :** CLASSIFY — **cod·i·fi·abil·i·ty** \ˌkä-də-ˌfī-ə-ˈbi-lə-tē, ˌkō-\ *n* — **cod·i·fi·ca·tion** \-fə-ˈkā-shən\ *n*
1**cod·ling** \ˈkäd-liŋ\ *n* (13c) **1 :** a young cod **2 :** any of several hakes (esp. genus *Urophycis*)
2**cod·ling** \ˈkäd-liŋ\ *or* **cod·lin** \-lən\ *n* [alter. of ME *querdlyng*] (15c) **:** a small immature apple; *also* **:** any of several elongated greenish English cooking apples
codling moth *n* (1747) **:** a small tortricid moth (*Cydia pomonella*) having larvae that live in apples, pears, quinces, and English walnuts
cod–liver oil *n* (1783) **:** an oil obtained from the liver of the cod and closely related fishes and used as a source of vitamins A and D
co·dom·i·nant \ˌkō-ˈdä-mə-nənt, -ˈdäm-nənt\ *adj* (ca. 1900) **1 a :** forming part of the main canopy of a forest ⟨~ trees⟩ **b :** sharing in the controlling influence of a biotic community **2 :** being fully expressed in the heterozygous condition ⟨~ alleles⟩ — **codominant** *n*
co·don \ˈkō-ˌdän\ *n* [1*code* + 2*-on*] (1963) **:** a specific sequence of three consecutive nucleotides that is part of the genetic code and that specifies a particular amino acid in a protein or starts or stops protein synthesis — called also *triplet*
cod·piece \ˈkäd-ˌpēs\ *n* [ME *codpese,* fr. *cod* bag, scrotum (fr. OE *codd*) + *pese* piece] (15c) **:** a flap or bag concealing an opening in the front of men's breeches esp. in the 15th and 16th centuries
cods·wal·lop \ˈkȯdz-ˌwä-ləp, ˈkädz-\ *n* [origin unknown] (1963) *Brit* **:** NONSENSE
1**co·ed** \ˈkō-(ˌ)ed\ *n* [short for *coeducational student*] (ca. 1878) **:** a female student in a coeducational institution
2**coed** *adj* (1889) **1 :** of or relating to a coed **2 :** of or relating to coeducation **3 :** open to or used by both men and women
co–edi·tion \ˌkō-ə-ˈdi-shən\ *n* (1964) **:** an edition of a book published simultaneously by more than one publisher usu. in different countries and in different languages
co·ed·u·ca·tion \(ˌ)kō-ˌe-jə-ˈkā-shən\ *n* (1852) **:** the education of students of both sexes at the same institution — **co·ed·u·ca·tion·al** \-shnəl, -shə-nᵊl\ *adj* — **co·ed·u·ca·tion·al·ly** *adv*
coeff *or* **coef** *abbr* coefficient
co·ef·fi·cient \ˌkō-ə-ˈfi-shənt\ *n* [NL *coefficient-, coefficiens,* fr. L *co-* + *efficient-, efficiens* efficient] (ca. 1715) **1 :** any of the factors of a product considered in relation to a specific factor; *esp* **:** a constant factor of a term as distinguished from a variable **2 a :** a number that serves as a measure of some property or characteristic (as of a substance, device, or process) ⟨~ of expansion of a metal⟩ **b :** MEASURE
coefficient of correlation (1892) **:** CORRELATION COEFFICIENT
coefficient of viscosity (1866) **:** VISCOSITY 3

\ə\ **abut** \ᵊ\ kitten, F table \ər\ **further** \a\ **ash** \ā\ **ace** \ä\ mop, mar \au̇\ **out** \ch\ **chin** \e\ **bet** \ē\ **easy** \g\ **go** \i\ **hit** \ī\ **ice** \j\ **job** \ŋ\ **sing** \ō\ **go** \ȯ\ **law** \ȯi\ **boy** \th\ **thin** \t͟h\ **the** \ü\ **loot** \u̇\ **foot** \y\ **yet** \zh\ **vision,** beige \k̲, ⁿ, œ, ue, ʸ\ *see* Guide to Pronunciation

coe·la·canth \ˈsē-lə-ˌkan(t)th\ *n* [ultim. fr. Gk *koilos* hollow + *akantha* spine — more at CAVE] (1857) : any of an order (Coelacanthiformes) of lobe-finned fishes known chiefly from Paleozoic and Mesozoic fossils

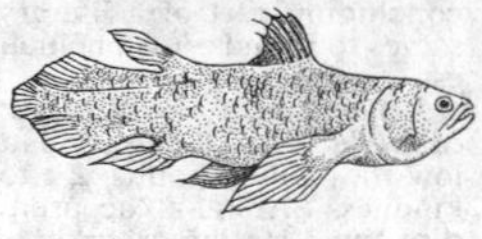
coelacanth

-coele *or* **-coel** *n comb form* [prob. fr. NL *-coela,* fr. neut. pl. of *-coelus* hollow, concave, fr. Gk *-koilos,* fr. *koilos*] : cavity : chamber : ventricle ⟨blasto*coel*⟩ ⟨entero*coele*⟩

coe·len·ter·ate \si-ˈlen-tə-ˌrāt, -rət\ *n* [ultim. fr. Gk *koilos* + *enteron* intestine — more at INTER-] (1872) : any of a phylum (Cnidaria syn. Coelenterata) of radially symmetrical invertebrate animals including the corals, sea anemones, jellyfishes, and hydroids — called also *cnidarian*

coe·len·ter·on \-ˌrän, -rən\ *n, pl* **-tera** \-rə\ [NL, fr. Gk *koilos* + *enteron*] (1885) : the internal cavity of a coelenterate

coeliac *var of* CELIAC

coe·lom \ˈsē-ləm\ *n, pl* **coeloms** *or* **coe·lo·ma·ta** \si-ˈlō-mə-tə\ [G, fr. Gk *koilōma* cavity, fr. *koilos*] (1875) : the usu. epithelium-lined space between the body wall and the digestive tract of metazoans above the lower worms — **coe·lo·mate** \ˈsē-lə-ˌmāt\ *adj or n* — **coe·lo·mic** \si-ˈlä-mik, -ˈlō-\ *adj*

coen- *or* **coeno-** *comb form* [NL, fr. Gk *koin-, koino-,* fr. *koinos*] : common : general ⟨*coeno*cyte⟩

coenobite *var of* CENOBITE

coe·no·cyte \ˈsē-nə-ˌsīt\ *n* [ISV] (1897) **1 a** : a multinucleate mass of protoplasm resulting from repeated nuclear division unaccompanied by cell fission **b** : an organism consisting of such a structure **2** : SYNCYTIUM 1 — **coe·no·cyt·ic** \ˌsē-nə-ˈsi-tik\ *adj*

co·en·zyme \(ˌ)kō-ˈen-ˌzīm\ *n* (1947) : a thermostable nonprotein compound that forms the active portion of an enzyme system after combination with an apoenzyme — **co·en·zy·mat·ic** \(ˌ)kō-ˌen-zə-ˈma-tik, -(ˌ)zī-\ *adj* — **co·en·zy·mat·i·cal·ly** \-ti-k(ə-)lē\ *adv*

coenzyme A *n* (1947) : a coenzyme $C_{21}H_{36}N_7O_{16}P_3S$ that occurs in all living cells and is essential to the metabolism of carbohydrates, fats, and some amino acids — compare ACETYL COENZYME A

coenzyme Q *n* (1958) : UBIQUINONE

co·equal \(ˌ)kō-ˈē-kwəl\ *adj* (14c) : equal with one another ⟨~ branches of government⟩ — **coequal** *n* — **co·equal·i·ty** \ˌkō-ē-ˈkwä-lə-tē\ *n* — **co·equal·ly** \(ˌ)kō-ˈē-kwə-lē\ *adv*

co·erce \kō-ˈərs\ *vt* **co·erced; co·erc·ing** [ME *cohercen,* fr. AF **cohercer* L *coercēre,* fr. *co-* + *arcēre* to shut up, enclose — more at ARK] (15c) **1** : to restrain or dominate by force ⟨religion in the past has tried to ~ the irreligious —W. R. Inge⟩ **2** : to compel to an act or choice ⟨was *coerced* into agreeing⟩ **3** : to achieve by force or threat ⟨~ compliance⟩ ***syn*** see FORCE — **co·erc·ible** \-ˈər-sə-bəl\ *adj*

co·er·cion \-ˈər-zhən, -shən\ *n* (15c) : the act, process, or power of coercing

co·er·cive \-ˈər-siv\ *adj* (ca. 1600) : serving or intended to coerce ⟨~ power⟩ ⟨~ measures⟩ — **co·er·cive·ly** *adv* — **co·er·cive·ness** *n*

coercive force *n* (1827) : the opposing magnetic intensity that must be applied to a magnetized material to remove the residual magnetism

co·er·civ·i·ty \ˌkō-ˌər-ˈsi-və-tē\ *n* (1898) : the property of a material determined by the value of the coercive force when the material has been magnetized to saturation

co·e·ta·ne·ous \ˌkō-ə-ˈtā-nē-əs\ *adj* [L *coaetaneus,* fr. *co-* + *aetas* age — more at AGE] (1608) : COEVAL

co·e·val \kō-ˈē-vəl\ *adj* [L *coaevus,* fr. *co-* + *aevum* age, lifetime — more at AYE] (1645) : of the same or equal age, antiquity, or duration ***syn*** see CONTEMPORARY — **coeval** *n* — **co·e·val·i·ty** \ˌkō-(ˌ)ē-ˈva-lə-tē\ *n*

co·evo·lu·tion \ˌkō-ˌe-və-ˈlü-shən *also* -ˌē-və-\ *n* (1964) : evolution involving successive changes in two or more ecologically interdependent species (as of a plant and its pollinators) that affect their interactions — **co·evo·lu·tion·ary** \-shə-ˌner-ē\ *adj* — **co·evolve** \ˌkō-i-ˈvälv, -ˈvȯlv\ *vi*

co·ex·ist \ˌkō-ig-ˈzist\ *vi* (1667) **1** : to exist together or at the same time **2** : to live in peace with each other esp. as a matter of policy — **co·ex·is·tence** \-ˈzis-tən(t)s\ *n* — **co·ex·is·tent** \-tənt\ *adj*

co·ex·ten·sive \ˌkō-ik-ˈsten(t)-siv\ *adj* (1679) : having the same spatial or temporal scope or boundaries — **co·ex·ten·sive·ly** *adv*

co·fac·tor \ˈkō-ˌfak-tər\ *n* (1885) **1** : the signed minor of an element of a square matrix or of a determinant with the sign positive if the sum of the column number and row number of the element is even and with the sign negative if it is odd **2** : a substance that acts with another substance to bring about certain effects; *esp* : COENZYME **3** : something (as diet or a virus) that acts with or aids another factor in causing disease

C of C *abbr* Chamber of Commerce

C of E *abbr, Brit* Church of England

cof·fee \ˈkȯ-fē, ˈkä-\ *n, often attrib* [It & Turk; It *caffè,* fr. Turk *kahve,* fr. Ar *qahwa*] (1598) **1 a** : a beverage made by percolation, infusion, or decoction from the roasted and ground seeds of a coffee plant **b** : any of several Old World tropical plants (genus *Coffea* and esp. *C. arabica* and *C. canephora*) of the madder family that are widely cultivated in warm regions for their seeds from which coffee is prepared **c** : coffee seeds esp. roasted and often ground — compare ARABICA, ROBUSTA **d** : a dehydrated product made from brewed coffee ⟨instant ~⟩; *also* : a beverage made from this **2** : a cup of coffee ⟨two ~*s*⟩ **3** : COFFEE HOUR

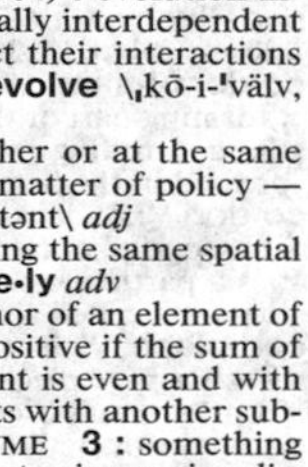
coffee 1b

coffee bar *n* (1886) : an establishment or counter where coffee and usu. light refreshments are served

coffee break *n* (1951) : a short period for rest and refreshments

coffee cake *n* (1865) : a sweet rich bread often with added fruit, nuts, and spices that is sometimes glazed after baking

coffee hour *n* (1867) **1** : a usu. fixed occasion of informal meeting and chatting at which refreshments are served **2** : COFFEE BREAK

cof·fee·house \-ˌhau̇s\ *n* (1612) : an establishment that sells coffee and usu. other refreshments and that commonly serves as an informal club for its regular customers

coffee klatch *also* **cof·fee–klatsch** \-ˌklach, -ˌkläch, -ˌkləch\ *n* [part trans. of G *Kaffeeklatsch*] (1895) : KAFFEEKLATSCH

cof·fee·mak·er \-ˌmā-kər\ *n* (1848) : a utensil or appliance in which coffee is brewed

coffee mill *n* (1691) : a mill for grinding coffee beans

cof·fee·pot \-ˌpät\ *n* (1704) : a pot for brewing and serving coffee

coffee ring *n* (1924) : coffee cake in the shape of a ring

coffee roll *n* (1945) : a sweet roll

coffee room *n* (1691) : a room where refreshments are served

coffee royal *n* (1733) : a drink of black coffee and a liquor

coffee shop *n* (1831) : a small restaurant

cof·fee–ta·ble \-ˌtā-bəl\ *adj* (1962) : of, relating to, or being an article (as a book or magazine) intended for display (as on a coffee table)

coffee table *n* (1877) : a low table customarily placed in front of a sofa — called also *cocktail table*

coffee tree *n* (1732) **1** : a tree (as arabica) that produces coffee **2** : KENTUCKY COFFEE TREE

[1]**cof·fer** \ˈkȯ-fər, ˈkä-\ *n* [ME *coffre,* fr. AF, ultim. fr. L *cophinus* basket, fr. Gk *kophinos*] (13c) **1** : CHEST; *esp* : STRONGBOX **2** : TREASURY, FUNDS — usu. used in pl. **3** : a recessed panel in a vault, ceiling, or soffit

[2]**coffer** *vt* (14c) **1** : to store or hoard up in a coffer **2** : to form (as a ceiling) with recessed panels

cof·fer·dam \-ˌdam\ *n* (1736) **1** : a watertight enclosure from which water is pumped to expose the bottom of a body of water and permit construction (as of a pier) **2** : a watertight structure for making repairs below the waterline of a ship

[1]**cof·fin** \ˈkȯ-fən\ *n* [ME, basket, receptacle, fr. AF, fr. L *cophinus*] (1525) : a box or chest for burying a corpse — compare CASKET

[2]**coffin** *vt* (1564) : to enclose in or as if in a coffin

coffin bone *n* (ca. 1720) : the principal bone enclosed within the hoof of a horse — called also *pedal bone*

coffin corner *n* (1940) : one of the corners formed by a goal line and a sideline on a football field into which a punt is often aimed so that it may go out of bounds close to the defender's goal line

coffin nail *n* (1888) *slang* : CIGARETTE

cof·fle \ˈkȯ-fəl, ˈkä-\ *n* [Ar *qāfila* caravan] (1799) : a train of slaves or animals fastened together

C of S *abbr* chief of staff

co·func·tion \ˈkō-ˌfəŋ(k)-shən\ *n* (1909) : a trigonometric function whose value for the complement of an angle is equal to the value of a given trigonometric function of the angle itself ⟨the sine is the ~ of the cosine⟩

[1]**cog** \ˈkäg\ *n* [ME *cogge,* of Scand origin; akin to Sw *kugge* cog] (13c) **1** : a tooth on the rim of a wheel or gear **2** : a subordinate but integral person or part — **cogged** \ˈkägd\ *adj*

[2]**cog** *vb* **cogged; cog·ging** [obs. *cog* a trick] *vi* (1532) **1** *obs* : to cheat in throwing dice **2** *obs* : DECEIVE **3** *obs* : to use venal flattery ~ *vt* **1** : to direct the fall of (dice) fraudulently **2** *obs* : WHEEDLE

[3]**cog** *vt* **cogged; cog·ging** [prob. alter. of *cock* to cog] (1823) : to connect (as timbers or joists) by means of mortises and tenons

[4]**cog** *n* (1830) : a tenon on a beam or timber

[5]**cog** *abbr* cognate

co·gen·cy \ˈkō-jən(t)-sē\ *n* (1667) : the quality or state of being cogent

co·gen·e·ra·tion \ˌkō-ˌje-nə-ˈrā-shən\ *n* (1976) : the production of electricity using waste heat (as in steam) from an industrial process or the use of steam from electric power generation as a source of heat — **co·gen·er·a·tor** \-ˈje-nə-ˌrā-tər\ *n*

co·gent \ˈkō-jənt\ *adj* [L *cogent-, cogens,* prp. of *cogere* to drive together, collect, fr. *co-* + *agere* to drive — more at AGENT] (1659) **1** : having power to compel or constrain ⟨~ forces⟩ **2 a** : appealing forcibly to the mind or reason : CONVINCING ⟨~ evidence⟩ **b** : PERTINENT, RELEVANT ⟨a ~ analysis⟩ ***syn*** see VALID — **co·gent·ly** *adv*

cog·i·ta·ble \ˈkä-jə-tə-bəl\ *adj* (15c) : CONCEIVABLE, THINKABLE

cog·i·tate \ˈkä-jə-ˌtāt\ *vb* **-tat·ed; -tat·ing** [L *cogitatus,* pp. of *cogitare* to think, think about, fr. *co-* + *agitare* to drive, agitate] *vt* (1582) : to ponder or meditate on usu. intently ~ *vi* : to meditate deeply or intently ⟨*cogitating* on her career plans⟩ ***syn*** see THINK

cog·i·ta·tion \ˌkä-jə-ˈtā-shən\ *n* (13c) **1 a** : the act of cogitating : MEDITATION **b** : the capacity to think or reflect **2** : a single thought

cog·i·ta·tive \ˈkä-jə-ˌtā-tiv\ *adj* (15c) **1** : of or relating to cogitation **2** : capable of or given to cogitation

co·gi·to \ˈkä-gi-ˌtō, ˈkō-, ˈkä-ji-\ *n* [NL *cogito, ergo sum,* lit., I think, therefore I am, principle stated by René Descartes] (1838) **1** : the philosophic principle that one's existence is demonstrated by the fact that one thinks **2** : the intellectual processes of the self or ego

co·gnac \ˈkōn-ˌyak *also* ˈkȯn- *or* ˈkän-\ *n, often cap* [F, fr. *Cognac,* France] (1751) : a brandy from the departments of Charente and Charente-Maritime distilled from white wine

[1]**cog·nate** \ˈkäg-ˌnāt\ *adj* [L *cognatus,* fr. *co-* + *gnatus, natus,* pp. of *nasci* to be born; akin to L *gignere* to beget — more at KIN] (ca. 1645) **1** : of the same or similar nature : generically alike **2** : related by blood; *also* : related on the mother's side **3 a** : related by descent from the same ancestral language **b** *of a word or morpheme* : related by derivation, borrowing, or descent **c** *of a substantive* : related to a verb usu. by derivation and serving as its object to reinforce the meaning — **cog·nate·ly** *adv*

[2]**cognate** *n* (1754) : one that is cognate with another

cog·na·tion \käg-ˈnā-shən\ *n* (14c) : cognate relationship

cog·ni·tion \käg-ˈni-shən\ *n* [ME *cognicion,* fr. AF, fr. L *cognition-, cognitio,* fr. *cognoscere* to become acquainted with, know, fr. *co-* + *gnoscere* to come to know — more at KNOW] (15c) : cognitive mental processes; *also* : a product of these processes — **cog·ni·tion·al** \-ˈnish-nəl, -ˈni-shə-nᵊl\ *adj*

cog·ni·tive \ˈkäg-nə-tiv\ *adj* (1586) **1** : of, relating to, being, or involving conscious intellectual activity (as thinking, reasoning, or remembering) ⟨~ impairment⟩ **2** : based on or capable of being reduced to empirical factual knowledge — **cog·ni·tive·ly** *adv*

cognitive dissonance *n* (1957) : psychological conflict resulting from incongruous beliefs and attitudes held simultaneously

cognitive science *n* (1975) : an interdisciplinary science that draws on many fields (as psychology, artificial intelligence, linguistics, and philosophy) in developing theories about human perception, thinking, and learning — **cognitive scientist** *n*

cognitive therapy *n* (1976) **:** psychotherapy esp. for depression that emphasizes the substitution of desirable patterns of thinking for maladaptive or faulty ones

cog·ni·za·ble \ˈkäg-nə-zə-bəl, käg-ˈnī-\ *adj* (ca. 1662) **1 :** capable of being judicially heard and determined ⟨a ~ claim⟩ **2 :** capable of being known ⟨~ events⟩ — **cog·ni·za·bly** \-blē\ *adv*

cog·ni·zance \ˈkäg-nə-zən(t)s\ *n* [ME *conisaunce,* fr. AF *conissance,* fr. *conoistre* to know, fr. L *cognoscere*] (14c) **1 :** a distinguishing mark or emblem (as a heraldic bearing) **2 a :** KNOWLEDGE, AWARENESS ⟨had no ~ of the situation⟩ **b :** NOTICE, ACKNOWLEDGMENT ⟨take ~ of their achievement⟩ **3 :** JURISDICTION, RESPONSIBILITY

cog·ni·zant \-zənt\ *adj* (1820) **:** knowledgeable of something esp. through personal experience; *also* **:** MINDFUL **syn** see AWARE

cog·nize \käg-ˈnīz, ˈkäg-ˌ\ *vt* **cog·nized; cog·niz·ing** [back-formation fr. *cognizance*] (ca. 1837) **:** KNOW, UNDERSTAND — **cog·niz·er** *n*

cog·no·men \käg-ˈnō-mən, ˈkäg-nə-\ *n, pl* **cognomens** *or* **cog·no·mi·na** \käg-ˈnä-mə-nə, -ˈnō-\ [L, irreg. fr. *co-* + *nomen* name — more at NAME] (1691) **1 :** SURNAME; *esp* **:** the third of usu. three names borne by a male citizen of ancient Rome — compare NOMEN, PRAENOMEN **2 :** NAME; *esp* **:** a distinguishing nickname or epithet — **cog·nom·i·nal** \käg-ˈnä-mə-nᵊl\ *adj*

co·gno·scen·te \ˌkän-yə-ˈshen-tē, ˌkäg-nə-, -ˈsen-\ *n, pl* **-scen·ti** \-tē\ [obs. It (now *conoscente*), fr. *cognoscente,* adj., wise, fr. L *cognoscent-, cognoscens,* prp. of *cognoscere*] (1776) **:** a person who has expert knowledge in a subject **:** CONNOISSEUR

cog·nos·ci·ble \käg-ˈnä-sə-bəl\ *adj* [LL *cognoscibilis,* fr. L *cognoscere*] (ca. 1644) **:** COGNIZABLE, KNOWABLE

co·gon \kō-ˈgōn\ *n* [Sp *cogón,* fr. Tag & Visayan *kugon*] (1898) **:** any of several tall grasses (genus *Imperata,* esp. *I. cylindrica*) of southeastern Asia used esp. for thatching, fodder, and erosion control

cog railway *n* (1896) **:** a steep mountain railroad that has a rail with cogs engaged by a cogwheel on the locomotive to ensure traction

cog·wheel \ˈkäg-ˌhwēl, -ˌwēl\ *n* (14c) **:** a wheel with cogs **:** GEAR 6a(2)

co·hab·it \(ˌ)kō-ˈha-bət\ *vi* [LL *cohabitare,* fr. L *co-* + *habitare* to inhabit, fr. freq. of *habēre* to have — more at GIVE] (ca. 1530) **1 :** to live together as or as if a married couple **2 a :** to live together or in company ⟨buffaloes *~ing* with crossbred cows —*Biol. Abstracts*⟩ **b :** to exist together ⟨two strains in his philosophy . . . ~ in each of his major works —Justus Buchler⟩ — **co·hab·i·tant** \-bə-tənt\ *n* — **co·hab·i·ta·tion** \(ˌ)kō-ˌha-bə-ˈtā-shən\ *n*

co·here \kō-ˈhir\ *vb* **co·hered; co·her·ing** [L *cohaerēre,* fr. *co-* + *haerēre* to stick] *vi* (1598) **1 a :** to hold together firmly as parts of the same mass; *broadly* **:** STICK, ADHERE **b :** to display cohesion of plant parts **2 :** to hold together as a mass of parts that cohere **3 a :** to become united in principles, relationships, or interests **b :** to be logically or aesthetically consistent ~ *vt* **:** to cause (parts or components) to cohere **syn** see STICK

co·her·ence \kō-ˈhir-ən(t)s, -ˈher-\ *n* (ca. 1580) **1 :** the quality or state of cohering: as **a :** systematic or logical connection or consistency **b :** integration of diverse elements, relationships, or values **2 :** the property of being coherent ⟨a plan that lacks ~⟩

co·her·en·cy \kō-ˈhir-ən(t)-sē, -ˈher-\ *n, pl* **-cies** (1603) **:** COHERENCE

co·her·ent \-ənt\ *adj* [MF or L; MF *cohérent,* fr. L *cohaerent-, cohaerens,* prp. of *cohaerēre*] (ca. 1555) **1 a :** logically or aesthetically ordered or integrated **:** CONSISTENT ⟨~ style⟩ ⟨a ~ argument⟩ **b :** having clarity or intelligibility **:** UNDERSTANDABLE ⟨a ~ person⟩ ⟨a ~ passage⟩ **2 :** having the quality of cohering; *esp* **:** COHESIVE, COORDINATED ⟨a ~ plan for action⟩ **3 a :** relating to or composed of waves having a constant difference in phase ⟨~ light⟩ **b :** producing coherent light ⟨a ~ source⟩ — **co·her·ent·ly** *adv*

co·her·er \kō-ˈhir-ər\ *n* (1894) **:** a radio detector in which an imperfectly conducting contact between pieces of conductive material loosely resting against each other is materially improved in conductance by the passage of high-frequency current

co·he·sion \kō-ˈhē-zhən\ *n* [L *cohaesus,* pp. of *cohaerēre*] (1660) **1 :** the act or state of sticking together tightly; *esp* **:** UNITY ⟨the lack of ~ in the Party —*Times Lit. Supp.*⟩ **2 :** union between similar plant parts or organs **3 :** molecular attraction by which the particles of a body are united throughout the mass — **co·he·sion·less** \-ləs\ *adj*

co·he·sive \kō-ˈhē-siv, -ziv\ *adj* (ca. 1731) **:** exhibiting or producing cohesion or coherence ⟨a ~ social unit⟩ ⟨~ soils⟩ — **co·he·sive·ly** *adv* — **co·he·sive·ness** *n*

co·ho \ˈkō-(ˌ)hō\ *n, pl* **cohos** *or* **coho** [Halkomelem (Salishan language of southwest British Columbia) kʷáxʷəθ] (1869) **:** a rather small Pacific salmon (*Oncorhynchus kisutch*) that has light-colored flesh and is native to both coasts of the No. Pacific and is stocked in the Great Lakes — called also *coho salmon, silver salmon*

co·ho·mol·o·gy \(ˌ)kō-hō-ˈmä-lə-jē\ *n* (ca. 1959) **:** a part of the theory of topology in which groups are used to study the properties of topological spaces and which is related in a complementary way to homology theory — called also *cohomology theory* — **co·ho·mo·log·i·cal** \-ˌhō-mə-ˈlä-ji-kəl, -ˌhä-\ *adj*

co·hort \ˈkō-ˌhȯrt\ *n* [ME, fr. L *cohort-, cohors* — more at COURT] (15c) **1 a :** one of 10 divisions of an ancient Roman legion **b :** a group of warriors or soldiers **c :** BAND, GROUP **d :** a group of individuals having a statistical factor (as age or class membership) in common in a demographic study ⟨a ~ of premedical students⟩ **2 :** COMPANION, COLLEAGUE ⟨a few of their . . . *~s* decided to form a company —Burt Hochberg⟩

co·hosh \ˈkō-ˌhäsh\ *n* [Eastern Abenaki *kkʷə̀has*] (1789) **:** any of several No. American medicinal or poisonous plants: as **a :** BLACK COHOSH **b :** BLUE COHOSH **c :** BANEBERRY

co·hous·ing \(ˌ)kō-ˈhau̇-ziŋ\ *n, often attrib* (1988) **:** semi-communal housing consisting of a cluster of private homes and a shared community space (as for cooking or laundry facilities)

[1]coif \ˈkȯif, *in sense 2 also* ˈkwäf\ *n* [ME *coife,* fr. AF, fr. LL *cofea*] (14c) **1 :** a close-fitting cap: as **a :** a hoodlike cap worn under a veil by nuns **b :** a protective usu. metal skullcap formerly worn under a hood of mail **c :** a white cap formerly worn by English lawyers and esp. by serjeants-at-law; *also* **:** the order or rank of a serjeant-at-law **2 :** COIFFURE

[2]coif \ˈkȯif, ˈkwäf\ *vt* **coiffed** *or* **coifed; coif·fing** *or* **coif·ing** (15c) **1 :** to cover or dress with or as if with a coif **2 :** to arrange (hair) by brushing, combing, or curling

coif·feur \kwä-ˈfər\ *n* [F, fr. *coiffer*] (1824) **:** a man who is a hairdresser

coif·feuse \kwä-ˈfə(r)z, -ˈfyüz, -ˈfüz\ *n* [F, fem. of *coiffeur*] (1864) **:** a woman who is a hairdresser

coif·fure \kwä-ˈfyu̇r\ *n* [F, fr. *coiffer* to cover with a coif, arrange (hair), fr. *coife,* fr. OF] (ca. 1631) **:** a style or manner of arranging the hair

coif·fured \-ˈfyu̇rd\ *adj* (1875) **1 :** being dressed ⟨beautifully ~ hair⟩ **2 :** having the hair brushed, combed, and curled ⟨stylishly ~ women⟩

coign of van·tage \ˌkȯi-nə-ˈvan-tij\ [*coign,* earlier spelling of [1]*coin* (corner)] (1605) **:** an advantageous position

[1]coil \ˈkȯi(-ə)l\ *n* [origin unknown] (1567) **1 :** TURMOIL **2 :** TROUBLE; *also* **:** everyday cares and worries ⟨when we have shuffled off this mortal ~ —Shak.⟩

[2]coil *vb* [F *coillir, cuillir* to gather — more at CULL] *vt* (1611) **1 :** to wind into rings or spirals ⟨~ a rope⟩ **2 :** to roll or twist into a shape resembling a coil ⟨*~ed* herself up on the couch⟩ ~ *vi* **1 :** to move in a circular or spiral course **2 :** to form or lie in a coil — **coil·abil·i·ty** \ˌkȯi-lə-ˈbi-lə-tē\ *n*

[3]coil *n* (1661) **1 a** (1) **:** a series of loops (2) **:** SPIRAL **b :** a single loop of such a coil **2 a :** a number of turns of wire wound around a core (as of iron) to create a magnetic field for an electromagnet or an induction coil **b :** INDUCTION COIL **3 :** a series of connected pipes in rows, layers, or windings **4 :** a roll of postage stamps; *also* **:** a stamp from such a roll

[1]coin \ˈkȯin\ *n* [ME, fr. AF *coing* wedge, corner, fr. L *cuneus* wedge] (14c) **1** *archaic* **a :** CORNER, CORNERSTONE, QUOIN **b :** WEDGE **2 a :** a usu. flat piece of metal issued by governmental authority as money **b :** metal money **c :** something resembling a coin esp. in shape **3 :** something used as if it were money (as in verbal or intellectual exchange) ⟨perhaps wisecracks . . . are respectable literary ~ in the U.S. —*Times Lit. Supp.*⟩ ⟨would repay him with the full ~ of his mind —Ian Fleming⟩ **4 :** something having two different and usu. opposing sides — usu. used in the phrase *the other side of the coin* **5 :** MONEY ⟨I'm in it for the ~ —Sinclair Lewis⟩

[2]coin *vt* (14c) **1 a :** to make (a coin) esp. by stamping **:** MINT **b :** to convert (metal) into coins **2 :** CREATE, INVENT ⟨~ a phrase⟩ — **coin·er** \ˈkȯi-nər\ *n* — **coin money :** to get rich quickly

[3]coin *adj* (ca. 1566) **1 :** of or relating to coins **2 :** operated by coins

coin·age \ˈkȯi-nij\ *n* (14c) **1 :** the act or process of coining **2 a :** COINS **b :** something (as a word) made up or invented

co·in·cide \ˌkō-ən-ˈsīd, ˈkō-ən-ˌ\ *vi* **-cid·ed; -cid·ing** [ML *coincidere,* fr. L *co-* + *incidere* to fall on, fr. *in-* + *cadere* to fall — more at CHANCE] (1719) **1 a :** to occupy the same place in space or time **b :** to occupy exactly corresponding or equivalent positions on a scale or in a series **2 :** to correspond in nature, character, or function **3 :** to be in accord or agreement **:** CONCUR **syn** see AGREE

co·in·ci·dence \kō-ˈin(t)-sə-dən(t)s, -sə-ˌden(t)s\ *n* (1605) **1 :** the act or condition of coinciding **:** CORRESPONDENCE **2 :** the occurrence of events that happen at the same time by accident but seem to have some connection; *also* **:** any of these occurrences

co·in·ci·dent \-sə-dənt, -ˌdent\ *adj* [F *coincident,* fr. ML *coincident-, coincidens,* prp. of *coincidere*] (ca. 1587) **1 :** of similar nature **:** HARMONIOUS ⟨a theory ~ with the facts⟩ **2 :** occupying the same space or time ⟨~ events⟩ **syn** see CONTEMPORARY — **co·in·ci·dent·ly** \-sə-dənt-lē, -ˌdent-; (ˌ)kō-ˌin(t)-sə-ˈdent-lē\ *adv*

co·in·ci·den·tal \(ˌ)kō-ˌin(t)-sə-ˈden-tᵊl\ *adj* (ca. 1800) **1 :** resulting from a coincidence ⟨a ~ resemblance⟩ **2 :** occurring or existing at the same time ⟨~ deaths⟩

co·in·ci·den·tal·ly \-ˈdent-lē, -ˈden-tə-lē\ *adv* (1837) **1 :** in a coincidental manner **:** by coincidence ⟨lonely singles who meet ~ and click —*People*⟩ **2 :** it is or seems coincidental that ⟨~, the dog died exactly one year after his owner did⟩

co·in·fec·tion \kō-in-ˈfek-shən\ *n* (1974) **:** concurrent infection of a cell or organism with two organisms — **co·in·fect** \-ˈfekt\ *vt*

coin of the realm (1816) **1 :** the legal money of a country **2 :** something valued or used as if it were money in a particular sphere ⟨information is the *coin of the realm* in the capital —Eloise Salholz *et al.*⟩

coin–op \ˈkȯin-ˌäp\ *n* (1961) **:** a self-service laundry where the machines are operated by coins

co·in·sur·ance \ˌkō-ən-ˈshu̇r-ən(t)s *also* -ˈin-ˌ\ *n* (ca. 1889) **1 :** joint assumption of risk (as by two underwriters) with another **2 :** insurance (as fire insurance) in which the insured is obligated to maintain coverage on a risk at a stipulated percentage of its total value or in the event of loss suffer a penalty in proportion to the deficiency

co·in·sure \ˌkō-ən-ˈshu̇r\ *vt* (1886) **:** to insure jointly — **co·in·sur·er** *n*

coir \ˈkȯi(-ə)r\ *n* [Tamil *kayiṟu* rope] (1582) **:** a stiff coarse fiber from the outer husk of a coconut

cois·trel \ˈkȯi-strəl\ *n* [MF *coustillier* soldier carrying a short sword, fr. *coustille* short sword, ultim. fr. L *cultellus* knife — more at CUTLASS] (1575) *archaic* **:** a mean fellow **:** VARLET

co·i·tion \kō-ˈi-shən\ *n* [LL, fr. L *coition-, coitio* a coming together, fr. *coire* to come together, fr. *co-* + *ire* to go — more at ISSUE] (1615) **:** COITUS — **co·i·tion·al** \-ˈish-nəl, -ˈi-shə-nᵊl\ *adj*

co·i·tus \ˈkō-ə-təs, kō-ˈē-, ˈkȯi-təs\ *n* [L, fr. *coire*] (1845) **:** physical union of male and female genitalia accompanied by rhythmic movements **:** SEXUAL INTERCOURSE 1 — compare ORGASM — **co·i·tal** \-tᵊl\ *adj* — **co·i·tal·ly** \-tə-lē\ *adv*

coitus in·ter·rup·tus \-ˌin-tə-ˈrəp-təs\ *n* [NL, interrupted coitus] (1900) **:** coitus in which the penis is withdrawn prior to ejaculation to prevent the deposit of sperm into the vagina

co·jo·nes \kə-ˈhō-ˌnās\ *n pl* [Sp, lit., testicles] (1932) **1** *slang* **:** NERVE 3 **2** *slang* **:** TESTES

[1]coke \ˈkōk\ *n* [perh. fr. dial. *coke, colk* core, fr. ME; akin to Sw *kälk* pith] (1669) **:** the residue of coal left after destructive distillation and used as fuel; *also* **:** a similar residue left by other materials (as petroleum) distilled to dryness

[2]coke *vb* **coked; cok·ing** *vt* (1763) **:** to change into coke ~ *vi* **:** to become coke or like coke

\ə\ **abut** \ᵊ\ **kitten,** F **table** \ər\ **further** \a\ **ash** \ā\ **ace** \ä\ **mop, mar**
\au̇\ **out** \ch\ **chin** \e\ **bet** \ē\ **easy** \g\ **go** \i\ **hit** \ī\ **ice** \j\ **job**
\ŋ\ **sing** \ō\ **go** \ȯ\ **law** \ȯi\ **boy** \th\ **thin** \t͟h\ **the** \ü\ **loot** \u̇\ **foot**
\y\ **yet** \zh\ **vision, beige** \k̲, ^{n}, œ, ue, ʸ\ *see* Guide to Pronunciation

[3]**coke** *n* [by shortening & alter.] (ca. 1903) : COCAINE
Coke \ˈkōk\ *trademark* — used for a cola drink
coke·head \ˈkō-ked, ˈkōk-ˌhed\ *n* (1922) : a person who uses cocaine compulsively
[1]**col** \ˈkäl\ *n* [F, fr. MF, neck, fr. L *collum*] (1853) : SADDLE 3
[2]**col** *abbr* **1** colonial **2** colony **3** color; colored **4** column **5** counsel
[3]**col** *or* **coll** *abbr* **1** collateral **2** collect; collected; collection **3** college; collegiate
Col *abbr* **1** colonel **2** Colorado **3** Colossians
COL *abbr* **1** colonel **2** cost of living
[1]**col-** — see COM-
[2]**col-** *or* **coli-** *or* **colo-** *comb form* [NL, fr. L *colon*] **1** : colon ⟨*col*itis⟩ ⟨*colo*stomy⟩ **2** [NL *Escherichia coli*, species of colon bacillus] : E. coli ⟨*coli*form⟩ ⟨*coli*phage⟩
[1]**cola** *pl of* COLON
[2]**co·la** \ˈkō-lə\ *n* [fr. *Coca-Cola*, a trademark] (1920) : a carbonated soft drink colored usu. with caramel and flavored usu. with extracts from kola nuts
COLA *abbr* **1** cost-of-living adjustment **2** cost-of-living allowance
col·an·der \ˈkä-lən-dər, ˈkə-\ *n* [ME *colyndore*, prob. modif. of Old Occitan *colador*, fr. ML *colatorium*, fr. L *colare* to sieve, fr. *colum* sieve] (14c) : a perforated utensil for washing or draining food
cola nut *var of* KOLA NUT
co·lat·i·tude \(ˌ)kō-ˈla-tə-ˌtüd, -ˌtyüd\ *n* (1790) : the complement of the latitude
cola tree *var of* KOLA TREE
Col·by \ˈkōl-bē\ *n* [*Colby*, Wis.] (1932) : a moist mild cheese similar to cheddar
col·can·non \käl-ˈka-nən\ *n* [Ir *cál ceannan*, lit., white-speckled cabbage] (ca. 1785) : potatoes and cabbage boiled and mashed together with butter and seasoning
col·chi·cine \ˈkäl-chə-ˌsēn, ˈkäl-kə-\ *n* (ca. 1847) : a poisonous alkaloid $C_{22}H_{25}NO_6$ that inhibits mitosis, is extracted from the corms or seeds of the autumn crocus (*Colchicum autumnale*), and is used esp. in the treatment of gout and to produce polyploidy in plants
col·chi·cum \ˈkäl-chi-kəm, ˈkäl-ki-\ *n* [NL, genus name, fr. L, a kind of plant with a poisonous root, fr. Gk *kolchikon*, lit., product of Colchis] (1597) **1** : any of a genus (*Colchicum*) of Old World corm-producing herbs of the lily family with flowers that resemble crocuses **2** : the dried corm or dried seeds of autumn crocus containing colchicine, possessing emetic, diuretic, and cathartic action, and used to treat gout
[1]**cold** \ˈkōld\ *adj* [ME, fr. OE *ceald*, *cald*; akin to OHG *kalt* cold, L *gelu* frost, *gelare* to freeze] (bef. 12c) **1 a** : having or being a temperature that is uncomfortably low for humans ⟨it is ~ outside today⟩ ⟨a ~ drafty attic⟩ **b** : having a relatively low temperature or one lower than normal or expected ⟨the bath water has gotten ~⟩ **c** : not heated: as (1) *of food* : served without heating esp. after initial cooking or processing ⟨~ cereal⟩ ⟨~ roast beef⟩ (2) : served chilled or with ice ⟨a ~ drink⟩ (3) : involving processing without the use of heat ⟨~ working of steel⟩ **2 a** : marked by a lack of the warmth of normal human emotion, friendliness, or compassion ⟨a ~ stare⟩ ⟨got a ~ reception⟩; *also* : not moved to enthusiasm ⟨the movie leaves me ~⟩ **b** : not colored or affected by personal feeling or bias : DETACHED, INDIFFERENT ⟨~ chronicles recorded by an outsider —Andrew Sarris⟩; *also* : IMPERSONAL, OBJECTIVE ⟨~ facts⟩ ⟨~ reality⟩ **c** : marked by sure familiarity : PAT ⟨had her lines ~ weeks before opening night⟩ **3** : conveying the impression of being cold: as **a** : DEPRESSING, GLOOMY ⟨~ gray skies⟩ **b** : COOL 6a **4 a** : marked by the loss of normal body heat ⟨~ hands⟩; *esp* : DEAD **b** : giving the appearance of being dead : UNCONSCIOUS ⟨passed out ~⟩ **5 a** : having lost freshness or vividness : STALE ⟨dogs trying to pick up a ~ scent⟩ **b** : far off the mark : not close to finding or solving — used esp. in children's games **c** : marked by poor or unlucky performance ⟨the team's shooting turned ~ in the second half⟩ **d** : not prepared or suitably warmed up — **cold·ish** \ˈkōl-dish\ *adj* — **cold·ly** \ˈkōl(d)-lē\ *adv* — **cold·ness** \ˈkōl(d)-nəs\ *n* — **in cold blood** : with premeditation : DELIBERATELY ⟨was killed *in cold blood*⟩
[2]**cold** *n* (13c) **1** : bodily sensation produced by loss or lack of heat ⟨they died of the ~⟩ **2** : a condition of low temperature ⟨extremes of heat and ~⟩; *esp* : cold weather **3** : a bodily disorder popularly associated with chilling; *specif* : COMMON COLD — **out in the cold** : deprived of benefits given others ⟨the plan benefits management but leaves labor *out in the cold*⟩
[3]**cold** *adv* (1889) **1** : with utter finality : ABSOLUTELY, COMPLETELY ⟨turned down ~⟩; *also* : ABRUPTLY ⟨stopped them ~⟩ **2 a** : without introduction or advance notice ⟨walked in ~ to apply for a job⟩ **b** : without preparation or warm-up ⟨was asked to perform the solo ~⟩
cold–blood·ed \ˈkōl(d)-ˈblə-dəd\ *adj* (1595) **1 a** : done or acting without consideration, compunction, or clemency ⟨~ murder⟩ **b** : MATTER-OF-FACT, EMOTIONLESS ⟨a ~ assessment⟩ **2** : having cold blood; *specif* : having a body temperature not internally regulated but approximating that of the environment **3** *or* **cold·blood** \-ˈbləd\ : of mixed or inferior breeding **4** : noticeably sensitive to cold — **cold–blood·ed·ly** *adv* — **cold–blood·ed·ness** *n*
cold call *n* (1966) : a telephone call soliciting business made directly to a potential customer without prior contact or without a lead — **cold–call** *vb*
cold cash *n* (1925) : money in hand
cold chisel *n* (1699) : a chisel made of tool steel of a strength, shape, and temper suitable for chipping or cutting cold metal
cold·cock \ˈkōl(d)-ˈkäk, ˌkōl(d)-\ *vt* [perh. [2]*cock*] (ca. 1918) : to knock unconscious
cold comfort *n* (14c) : quite limited sympathy, consolation, or encouragement
cold cream *n* (1693) : a soothing and cleansing cosmetic
cold cuts *n pl* (1859) : sliced assorted cold cooked meats
cold duck *n* [trans. of G *Kalte Ente*] (1969) : a beverage that consists of a blend of sparkling burgundy and champagne
cold–eyed \ˈkōld-ˈīd, -ˌīd\ *adj* (1819) : cold in manner or appearance; *esp* : coolly dispassionate ⟨~ analysis⟩
cold feet *n pl* (1893) : apprehension or doubt strong enough to prevent a planned course of action
cold fish *n* (1924) : a cold aloof person
cold frame *n* (1851) : a usu. glass- or plastic-covered frame without artificial heat used to protect plants and seedlings outdoors

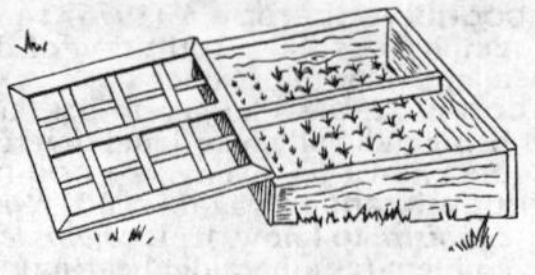
cold frame

cold front *n* (1921) : an advancing edge of a cold air mass
cold·heart·ed \ˈkōld-ˈhär-təd\ *adj* (1606) : marked by lack of sympathy, interest, or sensitivity ⟨~ criminals⟩ ⟨a ~ refusal⟩ — **cold·heart·ed·ly** *adv* — **cold·heart·ed·ness** *n*
cold–press \-ˌpres\ *vt* (1893) : to press (as olives) without applying heat from an external source; *also* : to extract (oil) by cold-pressing
cold shoulder *n* (1816) : intentionally cold or unsympathetic treatment ⟨got the *cold shoulder* from an old friend⟩ — **cold–shoulder** *vt*
cold sore *n* (1870) : a group of fluid-filled blisters appearing about or within the mouth that are caused by a herpes simplex virus and upon rupturing form crusts — called also *fever blister*; compare CANKER SORE
cold storage *n* (1877) **1** : storage (as of food) in a cold place for preservation **2** : a condition of being held or continued without being acted on : ABEYANCE
cold store *n* (1895) : a building for cold storage
cold sweat *n* (1582) : concurrent perspiration and chill usu. associated with fear, pain, or shock
[1]**cold turkey** *n* (1921) **1** : abrupt complete cessation of the use of an addictive drug; *also* : the symptoms experienced by a person undergoing withdrawal from a drug **2** : unrelieved blunt language or procedure **3** : a cold aloof person — **cold–turkey** *vt*
[2]**cold turkey** *adv* (1941) : all at once : ABRUPTLY: as **a** : without a period of gradual adjustment, adaptation, or withdrawal ⟨quit smoking *cold turkey*⟩ **b** : without preparation ⟨a new player who started the season *cold turkey*⟩
cold type *n* (1949) : composition or typesetting (as photocomposition) done without the casting of metal; *specif* : such composition produced directly on paper by a typewriter mechanism
cold war *n* (1945) **1** : a conflict over ideological differences carried on by methods short of sustained overt military action and usu. without breaking off diplomatic relations; *specif, often cap C&W* : the ideological conflict between the U.S. and the U.S.S.R. during the second half of the 20th century — compare HOT WAR **2** : a condition of rivalry, mistrust, and often open hostility short of violence esp. between power groups (as labor and management)
cold warrior *n* (1949) : one that supports or is engaged in a cold war
cold–water *adj* (1942) : having only running water without heat or utility services provided ⟨a ~ flat⟩
cold water *n* (1808) : depreciation of something as being ill-advised, unwarranted, or worthless ⟨threw *cold water* on our hopes⟩
cold wave *n* (1876) **1** : an unusually large and rapid drop in temperature over a short period of time (as 24 hours) **2** : a permanent wave set by a chemical preparation without the use of heat
cole \ˈkōl\ *n* [ME, fr. OE *cāl*, fr. L *caulis* stem, cabbage; akin to Gk *kaulos* stem, Latvian *kauls*] (bef. 12c) : any of several brassicas; *esp* : any of various crop plants (as broccoli, kale, brussels sprouts, cabbage, cauliflower, and kohlrabi) derived from the same wild cabbage (*Brassica oleracea*)
cole·man·ite \ˈkōl-mə-ˌnīt\ *n* [William T. *Coleman* †1893 Am. businessman and mine owner] (1884) : a colorless or white mineral consisting of a hydrous calcium borate occurring in monoclinic crystals
co·le·op·tera \ˌkō-lē-ˈäp-tə-rə\ *n pl* [NL, ultim. fr. Gk *koleon* sheath + *pteron* wing — more at FEATHER] (1771) : insects that are beetles — **co·le·op·ter·ist** \-tə-rist\ *n* — **co·le·op·ter·ous** \-tə-rəs\ *adj*
co·le·op·ter·an \-tə-rən\ *n* (ca. 1847) : [1]BEETLE 1 — **coleopteran** *adj*
co·le·op·tile \-ˈäp-tᵊl\ *n* [NL *coleoptilum*, fr. Gk *koleon* + *ptilon* down; akin to Gk *pteron*] (ca. 1866) : the first leaf of a monocotyledon forming a protective sheath about the plumule
co·le·o·rhi·za \ˌkō-lē-ə-ˈrī-zə\ *n, pl* **-zae** \-(ˌ)zē\ [NL, fr. Gk *koleon* + NL *-rhiza*] (ca. 1866) : the sheath investing the radicle in some monocotyledonous plants through which the roots emerge
cole·slaw \ˈkōl-ˌslȯ\ *n* [D *koolsla*, fr. *kool* cabbage + *sla* salad] (1794) : a salad made of raw sliced or chopped cabbage
co·le·us \ˈkō-lē-əs\ *n* [NL, genus name, fr. Gk *koleos*, *koleon* sheath] (1885) : any of a large genus (*Coleus*) of Old World herbs of the mint family including ones cultivated for their colorful foliage
cole·wort \ˈkōl-ˌwərt, -ˌwȯrt\ *n* (14c) : COLE; *esp* : one (as kale) that forms no head
coli- — see COL-
[1]**col·ic** \ˈkä-lik\ *n* [ME, fr. ML *colica (passio)* intestinal (suffering), fr. LL *colicus* of the colon, colicky, fr. Gk *kōlikos*, fr. *kōlon*, alter. of *kolon* colon] (15c) **1** : an attack of acute abdominal pain localized in a hollow organ and often caused by spasm, obstruction, or twisting **2** : a condition marked by recurrent episodes of prolonged and uncontrollable crying and irritability in an otherwise healthy infant that is of unknown cause and usu. subsides after three to four months of age
[2]**colic** *adj* (15c) : of or relating to colic : COLICKY ⟨~ crying⟩
[3]**co·lic** \ˈkō-lik, ˈkä-\ *adj* (1615) : of or relating to the colon ⟨~ lymph nodes⟩
co·li·cin \ˈkō-lə-sən\ *also* **co·li·cine** \-ˌsēn\ *n* [F *colicine*, fr. *col-* + *-cine* (as in *streptomycine* streptomycin)] (1946) : any of various antibacterial substances produced by strains of intestinal bacteria (as of E. coli)
col·icky \ˈkä-li-kē\ *adj* (1742) **1** : relating to or associated with colic ⟨~ pain⟩ **2** : suffering from colic ⟨~ babies⟩
col·ic·root \ˈkä-lik-ˌrüt, -ˌrüt\ *n* (1833) : any of several plants having roots used in folk medicine to treat colic; *esp* : either of two bitter herbs (*Aletris farinosa* and *A. aurea*) of the lily family
co·li·form \ˈkō-lə-ˌfȯrm, ˈkä-\ *adj* (1906) : of, relating to, or being gram-negative rod-shaped bacteria (as E. coli) normally present in the intestine ⟨monitored ~ levels in drinking water⟩ — **coliform** *n*
co·lin·ear \(ˌ)kō-ˈli-nē-ər\ *adj* (1927) **1** : COLLINEAR **2** : having corresponding parts arranged in the same linear order ⟨a gene and the protein it determines are ~⟩ — **co·lin·ear·i·ty** \(ˌ)kō-ˌli-nē-ˈer-ə-tē, -ˈa-rə-\ *n*

co·li·phage \ˈkō-lə-ˌfāj, -ˌfäzh\ *n* (1944) : any bacteriophage active against E. coli

col·i·se·um \ˌkä-lə-ˈsē-əm\ *n* [ML *Colosseum, Colisseum*] (ca. 1715) **1** *cap* : COLOSSEUM 1 **2** : a large sports stadium or building designed like the Colosseum for public entertainments

co·lis·tin \kə-ˈlis-tən, kō-\ *n* [NL *colistinus,* specific epithet of the bacterium producing it] (1951) : a polymyxin produced by a bacterium (*Bacillus polymyxa* var. *colistinus*) from Japanese soil

co·li·tis \kō-ˈlī-təs, kə-\ *n* (ca. 1860) : inflammation of the colon

coll- *or* **collo-** *comb form* [NL, fr. Gk *koll-, kollo-,* fr. *kolla* — more at PROTOCOL] **1** : glue ⟨*coll*enchyma⟩ **2** : colloid ⟨*collo*type⟩

col·lab·o·rate \kə-ˈla-bə-ˌrāt\ *vi* **-rat·ed; -rat·ing** [LL *collaboratus,* pp. of *collaborare* to labor together, fr. L *com-* + *laborare* to labor — more at LABOR] (1871) **1** : to work jointly with others or together esp. in an intellectual endeavor **2** : to cooperate with or willingly assist an enemy of one's country and esp. an occupying force **3** : to cooperate with an agency or instrumentality with which one is not immediately connected — **col·lab·o·ra·tion** \-ˌla-bə-ˈrā-shən\ *n* — **col·lab·o·ra·tive** \-ˈla-bə-ˌrā-tiv, -b(ə-)rə-\ *adj or n* — **col·lab·o·ra·tive·ly** \-lē\ *adv* — **col·lab·o·ra·tor** \-ˈla-bə-ˌrā-tər\ *n*

col·lab·o·ra·tion·ism \kə-ˌla-bə-ˈrā-shə-ˌni-zəm\ *n* (1923) : the advocacy or practice of collaboration with an enemy — **col·lab·o·ra·tion·ist** \-sh(ə-)nist\ *adj or n*

col·lage \kə-ˈläzh, kō-, kō-\ *n* [F, lit., gluing, fr. *coller* to glue, fr. *colle* glue, fr. VL **colla,* fr. Gk *kolla*] (1919) **1 a** : an artistic composition made of various materials (as paper, cloth, or wood) glued on a surface **b** : a creative work that resembles such a composition in incorporating various materials or elements ⟨the album is a ~ of several musical styles⟩ **2** : the art of making collages **3** : HODGEPODGE ⟨a ~ of ideas⟩ **4** : a work (as a film) having disparate scenes in rapid succession without transitions — **collage** *vt* — **col·lag·ist** \-ˈlä-zhist\ *n*

col·la·gen \ˈkä-lə-jən\ *n* [Gk *kolla* + ISV *-gen*] (ca. 1865) : any of a group of fibrous proteins that occur in vertebrates as the chief constituent of connective tissue fibrils and in bones and yield gelatin and glue upon boiling with water — **col·lag·e·nous** \kə-ˈla-jə-nəs\ *adj*

col·la·ge·nase \kə-ˈla-jə-ˌnās, ˈkä-lə-jə-, -ˌnāz\ *n* (1926) : any of a group of proteolytic enzymes that decompose collagen and gelatin

[1]**col·lapse** \kə-ˈlaps\ *vb* **col·lapsed; col·laps·ing** [L *collapsus,* pp. of *collabi,* fr. *com-* + *labi* to fall, slide — more at SLEEP] *vi* (1732) **1** : to fall or shrink together abruptly and completely : fall into a jumbled or flattened mass through the force of external pressure ⟨a blood vessel that *collapsed*⟩ **2** : to break down completely : DISINTEGRATE ⟨his case had *collapsed* in a mass of legal wreckage —Erle Stanley Gardner⟩ **3** : to cave or fall in or give way ⟨the bridge *collapsed*⟩ **4** : to suddenly lose force, significance, effectiveness, or worth ⟨fears that the currency may ~⟩ **5** : to break down in vital energy, stamina, or self-control through exhaustion or disease; *esp* : to fall helpless or unconscious **6** : to fold down into a more compact shape ⟨a chair that ~*s*⟩ ~ *vt* **1** : to cause to collapse ⟨buildings *collapsed* by an earthquake⟩ **2** : CONDENSE ⟨~ several stories into one⟩ — **col·laps·ibil·i·ty** \-ˌlap-sə-ˈbi-lə-tē\ *n* — **col·laps·ible** \-ˈlap-sə-bəl\ *adj*

[2]**collapse** *n* (1801) **1 a** : a breakdown in vital energy, strength, or stamina **b** : a state of extreme prostration and physical depression (as from circulatory failure or great loss of body fluids) **c** : an airless state of all or part of a lung originating spontaneously or induced surgically **2** : the act or action of collapsing ⟨the cutting of many tent ropes, the ~ of the canvas —Rudyard Kipling⟩ **3** : a sudden failure : BREAKDOWN, RUIN **4** : a sudden loss of force, value, or effect ⟨the ~ of respect for ancient law and custom —L. S. B. Leakey⟩

[1]**col·lar** \ˈkä-lər\ *n* [ME *coler,* fr. AF, fr. L *collare,* fr. *collum* neck; akin to OE *heals* neck, and prob. to OE *hwēol* wheel — more at WHEEL] (14c) **1** : a band, strip, or chain worn around the neck: as **a** : a band that serves to finish or decorate the neckline of a garment **b** : a short necklace **c** : a band placed about the neck of an animal **d** : a part of the harness of draft animals fitted over the shoulders and taking strain when a load is drawn **e** : an indication of control : a token of subservience **f** : a protective or supportive device (as a brace or cast) worn around the neck **g** : CLERICAL COLLAR **2** : something resembling a collar in shape or use (as a ring or round flange to restrain motion or hold something in place) **3** : any of various animal structures or markings similar to a collar **4** : an act of collaring : ARREST, CAPTURE — **col·lared** \-lərd\ *adj* — **col·lar·less** \-lər-ləs\ *adj*

[2]**collar** *vt* (1613) **1 a** : to seize by the collar or neck **b** : ARREST, GRAB **c** : to get control of : PREEMPT ⟨we can ~ nearly the whole of this market —Roald Dahl⟩ **d** : to stop and detain in unwilling conversation ⟨~ the guest of honor⟩ **2** : to put a collar on ⟨~ a dog⟩

col·lar·bone \ˈkä-lər-ˌbōn\ *n* (15c) : CLAVICLE

collar cell *n* (ca. 1889) : a flagellated endodermal cell that lines the cavity of a sponge and has a contractile protoplasmic cup surrounding the flagellum — called also *choanocyte*

col·lard \ˈkä-lərd\ *n* [alter. of *colewort*] (1755) : a cabbage (*Brassica oleracea acephala*) related to kale and having a loose head of stalked smooth leaves; *also* : its leaves cooked and eaten as a vegetable — usu. used in pl.; called also *collard greens*

collat *abbr* collateral

col·late \kə-ˈlāt, kä-, kō-; ˈkä-ˌ, ˈkō-ˌ\ *vt* **col·lat·ed; col·lat·ing** [back-formation fr. *collation*] (1612) **1 a** : to compare critically **b** : to collect, compare carefully in order to verify, and often to integrate or arrange in order **2** [L *collatus,* pp.] : to institute (a cleric) to a benefice **3 a** : to verify the order of (printed sheets) **b** : to assemble in proper order; *esp* : to assemble (as printed sheets) in order for binding ***syn*** see COMPARE — **col·la·tor** \-ˈlā-tər, -ˌlā-\ *n*

[1]**col·lat·er·al** \kə-ˈla-t(ə-)rəl\ *adj* [ME, fr. AF, fr. ML *collateralis,* fr. L *com-* + *lateralis* lateral] (14c) **1 a** : accompanying as secondary or subordinate : CONCOMITANT ⟨digress into ~ matters⟩ **b** : INDIRECT **c** : serving to support or reinforce : ANCILLARY **2** : belonging to the same ancestral stock but not in a direct line of descent — compare LINEAL 3a **3** : parallel, coordinate, or corresponding in position, order, time, or significance ⟨~ states like Athens and Sparta⟩ **4 a** : of, relating to, or being collateral used as security (as for payment of a debt or performance of a contract) **b** : secured by collateral — **col·lat·er·al·i·ty** \-ˌla-tə-ˈra-lə-tē\ *n* — **col·lat·er·al·ly** \-ˈla-t(ə-)rə-lē\ *adv*

[2]**collateral** *n* (1691) **1** : a collateral relative **2** : property (as securities) pledged by a borrower to protect the interests of the lender **3** : a branch of a bodily part (as a vein)

collateral damage *n* (1972) : injury inflicted on something other than an intended target; *specif* : civilian casualties of a military operation

col·lat·er·al·ize \kə-ˈla-t(ə-)rə-ˌlīz\ *vt* **-ized; -iz·ing** (1941) **1** : to make (a loan) secure with collateral **2** : to use (as securities) for collateral

col·la·tion \kə-ˈlā-shən, kä-, kō-\ *n* (14c) **1** [ME, fr. AF, fr. ML *collation-, collatio,* fr. LL, conference, fr. L, bringing together, comparison, fr. *conferre* (pp. *collatus*) to bring together — more at CONFER, TOLERATE] **a** : a light meal allowed on fast days in place of lunch or supper **b** : a light meal **2** [ME, fr. L *collation-, collatio*] : the act, process, or result of collating

col·league \ˈkä-(ˌ)lēg\ *n* [MF *collegue,* fr. L *collega,* fr. *com-* + *legare* to depute — more at LEGATE] (ca. 1533) : an associate in a profession or in a civil or ecclesiastical office — **col·league·ship** \-ˌship\ *n*

[1]**col·lect** \ˈkä-likt *also* -ˌlekt\ *n* [ME *collecte,* fr. AF, fr. ML *collecta* (short for *oratio ad collectam* prayer upon assembly), fr. LL, assembly, fr. L, assemblage, fr. fem. of *collectus*] (13c) **1** : a short prayer comprising an invocation, petition, and conclusion; *specif, often cap* : one preceding the eucharistic Epistle and varying with the day **2** : COLLECTION

[2]**col·lect** \kə-ˈlekt\ *vb* [L *collectus,* pp. of *colligere* to collect, fr. *com-* + *legere* to gather — more at LEGEND] *vt* (1563) **1 a** : to bring together into one body or place **b** : to gather or exact from a number of persons or sources ⟨~ taxes⟩ **c** : to gather an accumulation of (objects) esp. as a hobby ⟨~*s* stamps⟩ **2** : INFER, DEDUCE **3** : to gain or regain control of ⟨~ his thoughts⟩ **4** : to claim as due and receive payment for **5** : to get and bring with one; *specif* : PICK UP ⟨went to ~ her at the train station⟩ ~ *vi* **1** : to come together in a band, group, or mass : GATHER **2 a** : to collect objects **b** : to receive payment ⟨~*ing* on the insurance⟩ ***syn*** see GATHER

[3]**col·lect** \kə-ˈlekt\ *adv or adj* (1893) : to be paid for by the receiver

col·lec·ta·nea \ˌkä-ˌlek-ˈtā-nē-ə\ *n pl* [L, neut. pl. of *collectaneus* collected, fr. *collectus,* pp.] (1791) : collected writings; *also* : literary items forming a collection

col·lect·ed \kə-ˈlek-təd\ *adj* (ca. 1548) **1** : gathered together ⟨the ~ works of Scott⟩ **2** : possessed of calmness and composure often through concentrated effort **3** *of a horse's gait* : performed slowly and restrainedly with the animal's center of gravity toward the hindquarters — compare EXTENDED ***syn*** see COOL — **col·lect·ed·ly** *adv* — **col·lect·ed·ness** *n*

[1]**col·lect·ible** *or* **col·lect·able** \kə-ˈlek-tə-bəl\ *adj* (1660) **1** : suitable for being collected **2** : due for present payment : PAYABLE — **col·lect·ibil·i·ty** *or* **col·lect·abil·i·ty** \kə-ˌlek-tə-ˈbi-lə-tē\ *n*

[2]**collectible** *or* **collectable** *n* (1953) : an object that is collected by fanciers; *esp* : one other than such traditionally collectible items as art, stamps, coins, and antiques

col·lec·tion \kə-ˈlek-shən\ *n* (14c) **1** : the act or process of collecting **2 a** : something collected; *esp* : an accumulation of objects gathered for study, comparison, or exhibition or as a hobby **b** : GROUP, AGGREGATE **c** : a set of apparel designed for sale usu. in a particular season

[1]**col·lec·tive** \kə-ˈlek-tiv\ *adj* (15c) **1** : denoting a number of persons or things considered as one group or whole ⟨*flock* is a ~ word⟩ **2 a** : formed by collecting : AGGREGATED **b** *of a fruit* : MULTIPLE **3 a** : of, relating to, or being a group of individuals **b** : involving all members of a group as distinct from its individuals ⟨a ~ action⟩ **4** : marked by similarity among or with the members of a group **5** : collectivized or characterized by collectivism **6** : shared or assumed by all members of the group ⟨~ responsibility⟩ — **col·lec·tive·ly** *adv*

[2]**collective** *n* (1655) **1** : a collective body : GROUP **2** : a cooperative unit or organization; *specif* : COLLECTIVE FARM **3** : a helicopter control system governing lift

collective bargaining *n* (1891) : negotiation between an employer and a labor union usu. on wages, hours, and working conditions

collective farm *n* (1925) : a farm esp. in a Communist country formed from many small holdings collected into a single unit for joint operation under governmental supervision

collective mark *n* (1938) : a trademark or a service mark of a group (as a cooperative association)

collective security *n* (1934) : the maintenance by common action of the security of all members of an association of nations

collective unconscious *n* (1917) : the inherited part of the unconscious that esp. in the psychoanalytic theory of C. G. Jung occurs in and is shared by all the members of a people or race

col·lec·tiv·ise *chiefly Brit var of* COLLECTIVIZE

col·lec·tiv·ism \kə-ˈlek-ti-ˌvi-zəm\ *n* (1857) **1** : a political or economic theory advocating collective control esp. over production and distribution; *also* : a system marked by such control **2** : emphasis on collective rather than individual action or identity — **col·lec·tiv·ist** \-vist\ *adj or n* — **col·lec·tiv·is·tic** \-ˌlek-ti-ˈvis-tik\ *adj* — **col·lec·tiv·is·ti·cal·ly** \-ti-k(ə-)lē\ *adv*

col·lec·tiv·i·ty \kə-ˌlek-ˈti-və-tē, ˌkä-\ *n, pl* **-ties** (1862) **1** : the quality or state of being collective **2** : a collective whole; *esp* : the people as a body

col·lec·tiv·ize \kə-ˈlek-ti-ˌvīz\ *vt* **-ized; -iz·ing** (1893) : to organize by collectivism — **col·lec·tiv·i·za·tion** \kə-ˌlek-ti-və-ˈzā-shən\ *n*

col·lec·tor \kə-ˈlek-tər\ *n* (14c) : one that collects: as **a** : an official who collects funds or moneys **b** : a person who makes a collection ⟨stamp ~⟩ **c** : an object or device that collects ⟨the statuette was a dust ~⟩ **d** : SOLAR COLLECTOR — **col·lec·tor·ship** \-ˌship\ *n*

collector's item *n* (1932) : an item whose rarity or excellence makes it esp. worth collecting; *broadly* : COLLECTIBLE

col·leen \kä-ˈlēn, ˈkä-ˌ\ *n* [Ir *cailín*] (1828) : an Irish girl

col·lege \ˈkä-lij\ *n, often attrib* [ME, fr. AF, fr. L *collegium* society, fr. *collega* colleague — more at COLLEAGUE] (14c) **1** : a body of clergy living together and supported by a foundation **2 :** a building used for an educational or religious purpose **3 a :** a self-governing constituent body of a university offering living quarters and sometimes instruction but not granting degrees ⟨Balliol and Magdalen *Colleges* at Oxford⟩ — called also *residential college* **b :** a preparatory or high school **c :** an independent institution of higher learning offering a course of general studies leading to a bachelor's degree; *also* **:** a university division offering this **d :** a part of a university offering a specialized group of courses **e :** an institution offering instruction usu. in a professional, vocational, or technical field ⟨business ~⟩ **4 :** COMPANY, GROUP; *specif* **:** an organized body of persons engaged in a common pursuit or having common interests or duties **5 a :** a group of persons considered by law to be a unit **b :** a body of electors — compare ELECTORAL COLLEGE **6 :** the faculty, students, or administration of a college

College Board *service mark* — used for administration of tests of aptitude and achievement considered by some colleges in determining admission and placement of students

college try *n* [fr. the phrase "give it the old *college try*"] (1927) **:** a zealous all-out effort

col·le·gial \kə-ˈlē-j(ē-)əl, *esp for 2a also* -ˈlē-gē-əl\ *adj* (14c) **1 :** COLLEGIATE 2 **2 a :** marked by power or authority vested equally in each of a number of colleagues **b :** characterized by equal sharing of authority esp. by Roman Catholic bishops **3 :** marked by camaraderie among colleagues — **col·le·gial·ly** *adv*

col·le·gi·al·i·ty \-ˌlē-jē-ˈa-lə-tē, -ˌlē-gē-\ *n* (1887) **:** the cooperative relationship of colleagues; *specif* **:** the participation of bishops in the government of the Roman Catholic Church in collaboration with the pope

col·le·gian \kə-ˈlē-j(ē-)ən\ *n* (15c) **:** a student or recent graduate of a college

col·le·giate \kə-ˈlē-jət, -jē-ət\ *adj* [ME, fr. AF, fr. ML *collegiatus,* fr. L *collegium*] (15c) **1 :** of or relating to a collegiate church **2 :** of, relating to, or comprising a college **3 :** COLLEGIAL 2 **4 :** designed for or characteristic of college students — **col·le·giate·ly** *adv*

collegiate church *n* (15c) **1 :** a church other than a cathedral that has a chapter of canons **2 :** a church or corporate group of churches under the joint pastorate of two or more ministers

col·le·gi·um \kə-ˈle-gē-əm, -ˈlā-\ *n, pl* **-gia** \-gē-ə\ *or* **-giums** [modif. of Russ *kollegiya,* fr. L *collegium*] (1917) **:** a group in which each member has approximately equal power and authority

col·lem·bo·lan \kə-ˈlem-bə-lən\ *n* [ultim. fr. *coll-* + Gk *embolos* wedge, stopper — more at EMBOLUS] (1873) **:** SPRINGTAIL — **collembolan** *or* **col·lem·bo·lous** \-ləs\ *adj*

col·len·chy·ma \kə-ˈleŋ-kə-mə, kä-\ *n* [NL] (1857) **:** a plant tissue that consists of living usu. elongated cells with unevenly thickened walls and acts as support esp. in areas of primary growth — **col·len·chy·ma·tous** \ˌkä-lən-ˈki-mə-təs, -ˈkī-\ *adj*

col·let \ˈkä-lət\ *n* [MF, dim. of *col* collar, fr. L *collum* neck — more at COLLAR] (1528) **:** a metal band, collar, ferrule, or flange: as **a :** a casing or socket for holding a tool (as a drill bit) **b :** a circle or flange in which a gem is set

col·lide \kə-ˈlīd\ *vi* **col·lid·ed; col·lid·ing** [L *collidere,* fr. *com-* + *laedere* to injure by striking] (1700) **1 :** to come together with solid or direct impact ⟨the car *collided* with a tree⟩ **2 :** CLASH ⟨*colliding* cultures⟩

col·lid·er \kə-ˈlī-dər\ *n* (1979) **:** a particle accelerator in which two beams of particles moving in opposite directions are made to collide

col·lie \ˈkä-lē\ *n* [prob. fr. E dial. *colly* black] (ca. 1651) **:** any of a breed of large dogs developed in Scotland that occur in rough-coated and smooth-coated varieties and have erect ears and a long muzzle

col·lier \ˈkäl-yər\ *n* [ME *colier,* fr. *col* coal] (13c) **1 :** one that produces charcoal **2 :** a coal miner **3 :** a ship for transporting coal

col·liery \ˈkäl-yə-rē\ *n, pl* **-lier·ies** (1635) **:** a coal mine and its connected buildings

col·lie·shang·ie \ˈkä-lē-ˌshaŋ-ē, ˈkə-\ *n* [perh. fr. *collie* + *shang* kind of meal] (1737) *Scot* **:** SQUABBLE, BRAWL

col·li·gate \ˈkä-lə-ˌgāt\ *vb* **-gat·ed; -gat·ing** [L *colligatus,* pp. of *colligare,* fr. *com-* + *ligare* to tie — more at LIGATURE] *vt* (1545) **1 :** to bind, unite, or group together **2 :** to subsume (isolated facts) under a general concept ~ *vi* **:** to be or become a member of a group or unit — **col·li·ga·tion** \ˌkä-lə-ˈgā-shən\ *n*

col·li·ga·tive \ˈkä-lə-ˌgā-tiv, kə-ˈli-gə-\ *adj* (1901) **:** depending on the number of particles (as molecules) and not on the nature of the particles ⟨pressure is a ~ property⟩

col·li·mate \ˈkä-lə-ˌmāt\ *vt* **-mat·ed; -mat·ing** [L *collimatus,* pp. of *collimare,* MS var. of *collineare* to make straight, fr. *com-* + *linea* line] (1878) **:** to make (as light rays) parallel — **col·li·ma·tion** \ˌkä-lə-ˈmā-shən\ *n*

col·li·ma·tor \ˈkä-lə-ˌmā-tər\ *n* (1865) **1 :** a device for producing a beam of parallel rays (as of light) or for forming an infinitely distant virtual image that can be viewed without parallax **2 :** a device for obtaining a beam (as of particles) of limited cross section

col·lin·ear \kə-ˈli-nē-ər, kä-\ *adj* [ISV] (1863) **1 :** lying on or passing through the same straight line **2 :** having axes lying end to end in a straight line ⟨~ antenna elements⟩ — **col·lin·ear·i·ty** \-ˌli-nē-ˈer-ə-tē, -ˈa-rə-\ *n*

col·lins \ˈkä-lənz\ *n* [prob. fr. the name *Collins*] (ca. 1887) **:** a tall iced drink of soda water, sugar, lemon or lime juice, and liquor (as gin)

col·li·sion \kə-ˈli-zhən\ *n* [ME, fr. L *collision-, collisio,* fr. *collidere*] (15c) **1 :** an act or instance of colliding **:** CLASH **2 :** an encounter between particles (as atoms or molecules) resulting in exchange or transformation of energy ***syn*** see IMPACT — **col·li·sion·al** \-ˈlizh-nəl, -ˈli-zhə-nᵊl\ *adj* — **col·li·sion·al·ly** *adv*

collision course *n* (1944) **:** a course (as of moving bodies or antithetical philosophies) that will result in collision or conflict if continued unaltered

collo- — see COLL-

col·lo·cate \ˈkä-lə-ˌkāt\ *vb* **-cat·ed; -cat·ing** [L *collocatus,* pp. of *collocare,* fr. *com-* + *locare* to place, fr. *locus* place — more at STALL] *vt* (1513) **:** to set or arrange in a place or position; *esp* **:** to set side by side ~ *vi* **:** to occur in conjunction with something

col·lo·ca·tion \ˌkä-lə-ˈkā-shən\ *n* (1605) **:** the act or result of placing or arranging together; *specif* **:** a noticeable arrangement or conjoining of linguistic elements (as words) — **col·lo·ca·tion·al** \-shnəl, -shə-nᵊl\ *adj*

col·lo·di·on \kə-ˈlō-dē-ən\ *n* [modif. of NL *collodium,* fr. Gk *kollōdēs* glutinous, fr. *kolla* glue — more at PROTOCOL] (1851) **:** a viscous solution of pyroxylin used esp. as a coating for wounds or for photographic films

col·logue \kə-ˈlōg\ *vi* **col·logued; col·logu·ing** [origin unknown] (1646) **1** *dial* **:** INTRIGUE, CONSPIRE **2 :** to talk privately **:** CONFER

col·loid \ˈkä-ˌlȯid\ *n* [ISV *coll-* + *-oid*] (ca. 1852) **1 :** a gelatinous or mucinous substance found normally in the thyroid and also in diseased tissue **2 a :** a substance that consists of particles dispersed throughout another substance which are too small for resolution with an ordinary light microscope but are incapable of passing through a semipermeable membrane **b :** a mixture consisting of a colloid together with the medium in which it is dispersed ⟨smoke is a ~⟩ — **col·loi·dal** \kə-ˈlȯi-dᵊl, kä-\ *adj* — **col·loi·dal·ly** *adv*

col·lop \ˈkä-ləp\ *n* [ME] (14c) **1 :** a small piece or slice esp. of meat **2 :** a fold of fat flesh

colloq *abbr* colloquial

col·lo·qui·al \kə-ˈlō-kwē-əl\ *adj* (1751) **1 :** of or relating to conversation **:** CONVERSATIONAL **2 a :** used in or characteristic of familiar and informal conversation; *also* **:** unacceptably informal **b :** using conversational style — **colloquial** *n* — **col·lo·qui·al·i·ty** \-ˌlō-kwē-ˈa-lə-tē\ *n* — **col·lo·qui·al·ly** \-ˈlō-kwē-ə-lē\ *adv*

col·lo·qui·al·ism \-ˈlō-kwē-ə-ˌli-zəm\ *n* (1810) **1 a :** a colloquial expression **b :** a local or regional dialect expression **2 :** colloquial style

col·lo·quist \ˈkä-lə-kwist\ *n* (1792) **:** SPEAKER

col·lo·qui·um \kə-ˈlō-kwē-əm\ *n, pl* **-qui·ums** *or* **-quia** \-kwē-ə\ [L, colloquy] (1844) **:** a usu. academic meeting at which specialists deliver addresses on a topic or on related topics and then answer questions relating to them

col·lo·quy \ˈkä-lə-kwē\ *n, pl* **-quies** [L *colloquium,* fr. *colloqui* to converse, fr. *com-* + *loqui* to speak] (15c) **1 :** CONVERSATION, DIALOGUE **2 :** a high-level serious discussion **:** CONFERENCE

col·lo·type \ˈkä-lə-ˌtīp\ *n* [ISV] (1881) **1 :** a photomechanical process for making prints directly from a hardened film of gelatin or other colloid that has ink-receptive and ink-repellent parts **2 :** a print made by collotype

col·lude \kə-ˈlüd\ *vi* **col·lud·ed; col·lud·ing** [L *colludere,* fr. *com-* + *ludere* to play, fr. *ludus* game — more at LUDICROUS] (1525) **:** CONSPIRE, PLOT ⟨*colluded* to keep prices high⟩

col·lu·sion \kə-ˈlü-zhən\ *n* [ME, fr. AF, fr. L *collusion-, collusio,* fr. *colludere*] (14c) **:** secret agreement or cooperation esp. for an illegal or deceitful purpose — **col·lu·sive** \-ˈlü-siv, -ziv\ *adj* — **col·lu·sive·ly** *adv*

col·lu·vi·um \kə-ˈlü-vē-əm\ *n, pl* **-via** \-vē-ə\ *or* **-vi·ums** [NL, fr. ML, offscourings, alter. of L *colluvies,* fr. *colluere* to wash, fr. *com-* + *lavere* to wash — more at LYE] (ca. 1936) **:** rock detritus and soil accumulated at the foot of a slope — **col·lu·vi·al** \-vē-əl\ *adj*

col·ly \ˈkä-lē\ *vt* **col·lied; col·ly·ing** [alter. of ME *colwen,* fr. OE **colgian,* fr. OE *col* coal] (1590) *dial chiefly Brit* **:** to blacken with or as if with soot

col·lyr·i·um \kə-ˈlir-ē-əm\ *n, pl* **-ia** \-ē-ə\ *or* **-i·ums** [ME *collirium,* fr. L *collyrium,* fr. Gk *kollyrion* pessary, eye salve, fr. dim. of *kollyra* roll of bread] (14c) **:** EYEWASH 1

col·ly·wob·bles \ˈkä-lē-ˌwä-bəlz\ *n pl but sing or pl in constr* [perh. by folk etymology fr. NL *cholera morbus,* lit., the disease cholera] (ca. 1823) **:** BELLYACHE

Colo *abbr* Colorado

colo- — see COL-

col·o·bus monkey \ˈkä-lə-bəs-\ *n* [NL *colobus,* fr. Gk *kolobos* docked, mutilated, fr. *kolos* docked; prob. akin to Gk *klan* to break — more at CLAST] (1866) **:** any of various long-tailed African monkeys (genus *Colobus* and related genera) — called also *colobus*

co·lo·cate \(ˌ)kō-ˈlō-ˌkāt, -lō-ˈkāt\ *vt* (1965) **:** to locate together; *esp* **:** to place (two or more units) close together so as to share common facilities

col·o·cynth \ˈkä-lə-ˌsin(t)th\ *n* [L *colocynthis,* fr. Gk *kolokynthis*] (1543) **:** a Mediterranean and African herbaceous vine (*Citrullus colocynthis*) related to the watermelon; *also* **:** its spongy fruit from which a powerful cathartic is prepared

colog *abbr* cologarithm

co·log·a·rithm \(ˌ)kō-ˈlȯ-gə-ˌri-thəm, -ˈlä-\ *n* (1881) **:** the logarithm of the reciprocal of a number

co·logne \kə-ˈlōn\ *n* [*Cologne,* Germany] (1814) **1 :** a perfumed liquid composed of alcohol and fragrant oils **2 :** a cream or paste of cologne sometimes formed into a semisolid stick — **co·logned** \-ˈlōnd\ *adj*

[1]**co·lon** \ˈkō-lən\ *n, pl* **colons** *or* **co·la** \-lə\ [ME, fr. L, fr. Gk *kolon*] (14c) **:** the part of the large intestine that extends from the cecum to the rectum

[2]**colon** *n, pl* **colons** *or* **cola** [L, part of a poem, fr. Gk *kōlon* limb, part of a strophe] (ca. 1550) **1** *pl* **cola :** a rhythmical unit of an utterance; *specif, in Greek or Latin verse* **:** a system or series of from two to not more than six feet having a principal accent and forming part of a line **2** *pl* **colons a :** a punctuation mark **:** used chiefly to direct attention to matter (as a list, explanation, quotation, or amplification) that follows **b :** the sign **:** used between the parts of a numerical expression of time in hours and minutes (as in 1:15) or in hours, minutes, and seconds (as in 8:25:30), in a bibliographical reference (as in *Nation* 130:20), in a ratio where it is usu. read as "to" (as in 4:1 read "four to one"), or in a proportion where it is usu. read as "is to" or when doubled as "as" (as in 2:1::8:4 read "two is to one as eight is to four")

[3]**co·lon** \kō-ˈlō^{n}, kə-ˈlōn\ *n* [F, fr. L *colonus*] (1888) **:** a colonial farmer or plantation owner

co·lón *also* **co·lone** \kə-ˈlōn\ *n, pl* **co·lo·nes** \-ˈlō-ˌnās\ [Sp *colón,* fr. Cristóbal *Colón* Christopher Columbus] (1916) **1 :** the basic monetary unit of El Salvador until 2001 **2** — see MONEY table

colon bacillus *n* (1897) **:** E. COLI

col·o·nel \ˈkər-nᵊl\ *n* [alter. of *coronel,* fr. MF, modif. of OIt *colonnello* column of soldiers, colonel, dim. of *colonna* column, fr. L *columna*] (1567) **1 a :** a commissioned officer in the army, air force, or marine corps ranking above a lieutenant colonel and below a brigadier general **b :** LIEUTENANT COLONEL **2 :** a minor titular official of a state esp. in southern or midland U.S. — used as an honorific title — **col·o·nel·cy** \-nᵊl-sē\ *n*

Colonel Blimp \-ˈblimp\ *n* [*Colonel Blimp,* cartoon character created by David Low] (1937) **:** a pompous person with out-of-date or ultraconservative views; *broadly* : REACTIONARY — **Colonel Blimp·ism** \-ˈblim-ˌpi-zəm\ *n*

1co·lo·nial \kə-ˈlō-nē-əl, -nyəl\ *adj* (1768) **1** : of, relating to, or characteristic of a colony **2** *often cap* : of or relating to the original 13 colonies forming the United States: as **a** : made or prevailing in America during the colonial period ⟨~ architecture⟩ **b** : adapted from or reminiscent of an American colonial mode of design ⟨~ furniture⟩ **3** : forming or existing in a colony ⟨~ organisms⟩ **4** : possessing or composed of colonies ⟨a ~ empire⟩ — **co·lo·nial·ize** \-nē-ə-ˌlīz, -nyə-ˌlīz\ *vt* — **co·lo·nial·ly** *adv* — **co·lo·nial·ness** *n*

2colonial *n* (1798) **1** : a member or inhabitant of a colony **2 a** : a product (as a coin or stamp) made for use in a colony **b** : a product exhibiting colonial style; *esp, often cap* : a house built in the neoclassical style of the American colonial period

co·lo·nial·ism \kə-ˈlō-nē-ə-ˌli-zəm, -nyə-ˌli-\ *n* (1847) **1** : the quality or state of being colonial **2** : something characteristic of a colony **3 a** : control by one power over a dependent area or people **b** : a policy advocating or based on such control — **co·lo·nial·ist** \-list\ *n or adj* — **co·lo·nial·is·tic** \-ˌlō-nē-ə-ˈlis-tik, -nyə-ˈlis-\ *adj*

1co·lon·ic \kō-ˈlä-nik, kə-\ *adj* (1884) : of or relating to the colon of the intestine

2colonic *n* (1939) : irrigation of the colon : ENEMA

col·o·ni·sa·tion, col·o·nise *Brit var of* COLONIZATION, COLONIZE

col·o·nist \ˈkä-lə-nist\ *n* (1701) **1** : a member or inhabitant of a colony **2** : one that colonizes or settles in a new country

col·o·ni·za·tion \ˌkä-lə-nə-ˈzā-shən\ *n* (1766) : an act or instance of colonizing — **col·o·ni·za·tion·ist** \-sh(ə-)nist\ *n*

col·o·nize \ˈkä-lə-ˌnīz\ *vb* **-nized; -niz·ing** *vt* (1622) **1 a** : to establish a colony in or on or of ⟨~ an island⟩ **b** : to establish in a colony ⟨the rights of *colonized* people⟩ **2** : to send illegal or irregularly qualified voters into ⟨*colonizing* doubtful districts⟩ **3** : to infiltrate with usu. subversive militants for propaganda and strategy reasons ⟨~ industries⟩ ~ *vi* : to make or establish a colony : SETTLE — **col·o·niz·er** *n*

col·on·nade \ˌkä-lə-ˈnād\ *n* [F, fr. It *colonnato,* fr. *colonna* column] (1718) : a series of columns set at regular intervals and usu. supporting the base of a roof structure — **col·on·nad·ed** \-ˈnā-dəd\ *adj*

co·lo·nog·ra·phy \ˌkō-lə-ˈnä-grə-fē\ *n, pl* **-phies** (1975) : noninvasive visualization of the interior of the colon by means of computed tomography or magnetic resonance imaging esp. to screen for polyps or cancerous growths

co·lo·nos·co·py \ˌkō-lə-ˈnäs-kə-pē\ *n, pl* **-pies** (1926) : endoscopic examination of the colon — **co·lon·o·scope** \kō-ˈlä-nə-ˌskōp\ *n*

co·lo·nus \kə-ˈlō-nəs\ *n, pl* **-ni** \-ˌnī, -(ˌ)nē\ [L, lit., farmer] (1857) : a tenant farmer in the later Roman Empire who was bound to the land and obliged to pay a rent usu. in produce

col·o·ny \ˈkä-lə-nē\ *n, pl* **-nies** [ME *colonie,* fr. MF & L; MF, fr. L *colonia,* fr. *colonus* farmer, colonist, fr. *colere* to cultivate — more at WHEEL] (14c) **1 a** : a body of people living in a new territory but retaining ties with the parent state **b** : the territory inhabited by such a body **2** : a distinguishable localized population within a species ⟨a ~ of termites⟩ **3 a** : a circumscribed mass of microorganisms usu. growing in or on a solid medium **b** : the aggregation of zooids of a compound animal **4 a** : a group of individuals or things with common characteristics or interests situated in close association ⟨an artist ~⟩ **b** : the section occupied by such a group **5** : a group of persons institutionalized away from others ⟨a leper ~⟩ ⟨a penal ~⟩; *also* : the land or buildings occupied by such a group

colony–stimulating factor *n* (1969) : any of several glycoproteins that promote the differentiation of stem cells esp. into blood granulocytes and macrophages and that stimulate their proliferation into colonies in culture

col·o·phon \ˈkä-lə-fən, -ˌfän\ *n* [L, fr. Gk *kolophōn* summit, finishing touch; perh. akin to L *culmen* top — more at HILL] (1501) **1** : an inscription at the end of a book or manuscript usu. with facts about its production **2** : an identifying mark used by a printer or a publisher

co·lo·pho·ny \kə-ˈlä-fə-nē, ˈkä-lə-ˌfō-\ *n, pl* **-nies** [ME *colophonie,* ultim. fr. Gk *Kolophōn* Colophon, an Ionian city] (14c) : ROSIN

1col·or \ˈkə-lər\ *n, often attrib* [ME *colour,* fr. AF, fr. L *color;* akin to L *celare* to conceal — more at HELL] (13c) **1 a** : a phenomenon of light (as red, brown, pink, or gray) or visual perception that enables one to differentiate otherwise identical objects **b (1)** : the aspect of the appearance of objects and light sources that may be described in terms of hue, lightness, and saturation for objects and hue, brightness, and saturation for light sources ⟨the changing ~ of the sky⟩; *also* : a specific combination of hue, saturation, and lightness or brightness ⟨comes in six ~*s*⟩ **(2)** : a color other than and as contrasted with black, white, or gray **2 a** : an outward often deceptive show : APPEARANCE ⟨his story has the ~ of truth⟩ **b** : a legal claim to or appearance of a right, authority, or office **c** : a pretense offered as justification : PRETEXT ⟨she could have drawn from the Versailles treaty the ~ of legality for any action she chose —*Yale Rev.*⟩ **d** : an appearance of authenticity : PLAUSIBILITY ⟨lending ~ to this notion⟩ **3** : complexion tint: **a** : the tint characteristic of good health **b** : BLUSH **4 a** : vividness or variety of effects of language **b** : LOCAL COLOR **5 a** : an identifying badge, pennant, or flag — usu. used in pl. ⟨a ship sailing under Swedish ~*s*⟩ **b** : colored clothing distinguishing one as a member of a particular group or representative of a particular person or thing — usu. used in pl. ⟨a jockey wearing the ~*s* of the stable⟩ **6 a** *pl* : position as to a question or course of action : STAND ⟨the USSR changed neither its ~*s* nor its stripes during all of this —Norman Mailer⟩ **b** : CHARACTER, NATURE — usu. used in pl. ⟨showed himself in his true ~*s*⟩ **7 a** : the use or combination of colors **b** : two or more hues employed in a medium of presentation ⟨movies in ~⟩ **8** *pl* **a** : a naval or nautical salute to a flag being hoisted or lowered **b** : ARMED FORCES **9** : VITALITY, INTEREST ⟨the play had a good deal of ~ to it⟩ **10** : something used to give color : PIGMENT **11** : the quality of timbre in music ⟨the ~ and richness of the cello⟩ **12** : skin pigmentation esp. other than white characteristic of race ⟨a person of ~⟩ **13** : a small particle of gold in a gold miner's pan after washing **14** : analysis of game action or strategy, statistics and background information on participants, and often anecdotes provided by a sportscaster to give variety and interest to the broadcast of a game or contest ⟨a ~ commentator⟩ **15** : a hypothetical property of quarks that differentiates each type into three forms having a distinct role in binding quarks together

2color *vt* (14c) **1 a** : to give color to **b** : to change the color of (as by dyeing, staining, or painting) **2** : to change as if by dyeing or painting: as **a** : MISREPRESENT, DISTORT **b** : GLOSS, EXCUSE ⟨~ a lie⟩ **c** : INFLUENCE ⟨the lives of most of us have been ~*ed* by politics —Christine Weston⟩ **3** : CHARACTERIZE, LABEL ⟨call it progress; ~ it inevitable with shades of job security —C. E. Price⟩ ~ *vi* : to take on color; *specif* : BLUSH — **col·or·er** \ˈkə-lər-ər\ *n*

col·or·able \ˈkə-lə-rə-bəl, -lər-ə-, ˈkəl-rə-\ *adj* (14c) **1** : seemingly valid or genuine ⟨a ~ claim in law⟩ **2** : intended to deceive : COUNTERFEIT ⟨~ and false pretenses⟩ — **col·or·ably** \-blē\ *adv*

Col·o·ra·do blue spruce \ˌkä-lə-ˈra-dō-, -ˈrä-\ *n* [*Colorado,* state of the U.S.] (1897) : BLUE SPRUCE

Colorado potato beetle *n* (1874) : a black-and-yellow striped beetle (*Leptinotarsa decemlineata*) that feeds on the leaves of the potato — called also *potato beetle, potato bug*

col·or·ant \ˈkə-lə-rənt, -lər-ənt\ *n* (1884) : a substance used for coloring a material : DYE, PIGMENT

col·or·a·tion \ˌkə-lə-ˈrā-shən\ *n* (1617) **1 a** : the state of having color ⟨the dark ~ of his skin⟩ **b** : use or choice of colors (as by an artist) **c** : arrangement of colors ⟨the ~ of a butterfly's wing⟩ **2 a** : characteristic quality ⟨the newspapers . . . took on the former ~ of the magazine —L. B. Seltzer⟩ **b** : aspect suggesting an attitude ⟨the chameleon talent for taking on the intellectual ~ of whatever idea he happened to fasten onto —Budd Schulberg⟩ **3** : subtle variation of intensity or quality of tone ⟨a wide range of ~ from the orchestra⟩

col·or·a·tu·ra \ˌkə-lə-rə-ˈtu̇r-ə, -ˈtyu̇r-\ *n, often attrib* [obs. It, lit., coloring, fr. LL, fr. L *coloratus,* pp. of *colorare* to color, fr. *color*] (ca. 1740) **1** : elaborate embellishment in vocal music; *broadly* : music with ornate figuration **2** : a soprano with a light agile voice specializing in coloratura

color bar *n* (1913) : a barrier preventing persons of color from participating with whites in various activities — called also *color line*

col·or–bear·er \ˈkə-lər-ˌber-ər\ *n* (1800) : one who carries a color or standard esp. in a military parade or drill

col·or–blind \-ˌblīnd\ *adj* (1853) **1** : affected with partial or total inability to distinguish one or more chromatic colors **2** : INSENSITIVE, OBLIVIOUS **3** : not influenced by differences of race ⟨tried to get the welfare establishment . . . to abandon its ~ policy —D. P. Moynihan⟩; *esp* : free from racial prejudice ⟨a white man with an invisible black skin in a ~ community —James Farmer⟩ — **color blindness** *n*

col·or·bred \-ˌbred\ *adj* (1946) : selectively bred for the development of particular colors ⟨pure ~ dogs⟩

co·lo·rec·tal \ˌkō-lō-ˈrek-tᵊl\ *adj* (1959) : relating to or affecting the colon and rectum ⟨~ cancer⟩

1col·ored \ˈkə-lərd\ *adj* (14c) **1** : having color **2 a** : COLORFUL **b** : marked by exaggeration or bias **3 a** *sometimes offensive* : of a race other than the white; *esp* : BLACK 2b **b** *sometimes offensive* : of mixed race **4** *sometimes offensive* : of or relating to persons of races other than the white or of mixed race

2colored *n, pl* **colored** *or* **coloreds** *often cap* (1916) *often offensive* : a person of a race other than the white or of mixed race

col·or·fast \ˈkə-lər-ˌfast\ *adj* (1916) : having color that retains its original hue without fading or running — **col·or·fast·ness** \-ˌfas(t)-nəs\ *n*

col·or–field \-ˌfēld\ *n, often attrib* (1964) : abstract painting in which color is emphasized and form and surface are correspondingly de-emphasized

color filter *n* (1900) : FILTER 2b

col·or·ful \ˈkə-lər-fəl\ *adj* (1880) **1** : having striking colors ⟨~ scenery⟩ **2** : full of variety or interest ⟨a ~ description⟩ — **col·or·ful·ly** \-f(ə-)lē\ *adv* — **col·or·ful·ness** \-fəl-nəs\ *n*

color guard *n* (ca. 1823) : an honor guard for the colors of an organization

col·or·im·e·ter \ˌkə-lə-ˈri-mə-tər\ *n* [ISV] (ca. 1872) : an instrument or device for determining and specifying colors; *specif* : one used for chemical analysis by comparison of a liquid's color with standard colors — **col·or·i·met·ric** \ˌkə-lə-rə-ˈme-trik\ *adj* — **col·or·i·met·ri·cal·ly** \-tri-k(ə-)lē\ *adv* — **col·or·im·e·try** \ˌkə-lə-ˈri-mə-trē\ *n*

col·or·ing \ˈkə-lə-riŋ\ *n* (14c) **1 a** : the act of applying colors **b** : something that produces color or color effects **c (1)** : the effect produced by applying or combining colors **(2)** : natural color **(3)** : COMPLEXION, COLORATION **d** : change of appearance (as by adding color) **2** : INFLUENCE, BIAS **3** : COLOR 4 **4** : TIMBRE, QUALITY

coloring book *n* (1931) : a book of line drawings for coloring (as with crayons)

col·or·ist \ˈkə-lə-rist, -lər-ist\ *n* (1686) : one that colors or deals with color

col·or·is·tic \ˌkə-lə-ˈris-tik\ *adj* (1883) **1** : of or relating to color or coloring **2** : of or relating to timbre in music — **col·or·is·ti·cal·ly** \-ti-k(ə-)lē\ *adv*

col·or·ize \ˈkə-lə-ˌrīz, -lər-ˌīz\ *vt* **-ized; -iz·ing** (1979) : to add color to (a black-and-white film) by means of a computer — **col·or·i·za·tion** \ˌkə-lə-rə-ˈzā-shən, -lər-ə-\ *n*

col·or·less \ˈkə-lər-ləs\ *adj* (14c) : lacking color: as **a** : PALLID, BLANCHED ⟨a ~ complexion⟩ **b** : DULL, UNINTERESTING ⟨~ prose⟩ — **col·or·less·ly** *adv* — **col·or·less·ness** *n*

color phase *n* (1927) **1** : a seasonally variant pelage color **2 a** : a genetic variant manifested by the occurrence of a skin or pelage color unlike the wild type of the animal group in which it appears **b** : an individual marked by such a variant

col·or·point shorthair \ˈkə-lər-ˌpȯint-\ *n* (1974) : any of a breed of domestic cats of Siamese body type and coat pattern but occurring in different colors — called also *colorpoint*

color temperature *n* (1916) : the temperature at which a blackbody emits radiant energy competent to evoke a color the same as that evoked by radiant energy from a given source (as a lamp)

col·or·way \-ˌwā\ *n* (1952) : a color or arrangement of colors ⟨fabric sold in a variety of ~*s*⟩

color wheel *n* (ca. 1893) **:** a circular diagram of the spectrum used to show the relationships between the colors
co·los·sal \kə-ˈlä-səl\ *adj* (1712) **1 :** of, relating to, or resembling a colossus **2 :** of a bulk, extent, power, or effect approaching or suggesting the stupendous or incredible ⟨~ rock formations⟩ **3 :** of an exceptional or astonishing degree ⟨a ~ failure⟩ ***syn*** see ENORMOUS — **co·los·sal·ly** \-sə-lē\ *adv*
col·os·se·um \ˌkä-lə-ˈsē-əm\ *n* [ML, fr. L, neut. of *colosseus* colossal, fr. *colossus*] (ca. 1715) **1** *cap* **:** an amphitheater built in Rome in the first century A.D. **2 :** COLISEUM 2
Co·los·sians \kə-ˈlä-shənz *also* -shē-ənz, -sē-\ *n pl but sing in constr* **:** a letter written by St. Paul to the Christians of Colossae and included as a book in the New Testament — see BIBLE table
co·los·sus \kə-ˈlä-səs\ *n, pl* **co·los·si** \-ˈlä-ˌsī\ [L, fr. Gk *kolossos*] (14c) **1 :** a statue of gigantic size and proportions **2 :** a person or thing of immense size or power
co·los·to·my \kə-ˈläs-tə-mē\ *n, pl* **-mies** [ISV [2]*col-* + *-stomy*] (1888) **:** surgical formation of an artificial anus by connecting the colon to an opening in the abdominal wall
co·los·trum \kə-ˈläs-trəm\ *n* [L, beestings] (1577) **:** milk secreted for a few days after parturition and characterized by high protein and antibody content — **co·los·tral** \-trəl\ *adj*
col·our \ˈkə-lər\ *chiefly Brit var of* COLOR
-colous *adj comb form* [L *-cola* inhabitant; akin to L *colere* to inhabit — more at WHEEL] **:** living or growing in or on ⟨areni*colous*⟩
col·por·tage \ˈkäl-ˌpȯr-tij, ˌkäl-pȯr-ˈtäzh\ *n* (ca. 1846) **:** a colporteur's work
col·por·teur \ˈkäl-ˌpȯr-tər, ˌkäl-pȯr-ˈtər\ *n* [F, alter. of MF *comporteur,* fr. *comporter* to bear, peddle] (1796) **:** a peddler of religious books
col·po·scope \ˈkäl-pə-ˌskōp\ *n* [Gk *kolpos* hollow, bosom, vagina, womb + E *-scope* — more at GULF] (1937) **:** a magnifying instrument designed to facilitate visual inspection of the vagina and cervix — **col·pos·co·py** \käl-ˈpäs-kə-pē\ *n*
colt \ˈkōlt\ *n* [ME, fr. OE; akin to Sw dial. *kult* half-grown pig] (bef. 12c) **1 a :** FOAL; *esp* **:** a male foal **b :** a young male horse that is usu. not castrated and has not attained an arbitrarily designated age (as four years) **2 :** a young untried person
col·tan \ˈkōl-ˌtan\ *n* [ISV *co*lumbo-*tan*talite, fr. *columb*ite + *-o-* + *tantalite*] (1999) **:** a dull black ore that consists of a mixture of columbite and tantalite and is a minor source of tantalum
colt·ish \ˈkōl-tish\ *adj* (14c) **1 a :** not subjected to discipline **b :** FRISKY, PLAYFUL ⟨~ antics⟩ **2 :** of, relating to, or resembling a colt ⟨~ legs⟩ — **colt·ish·ly** *adv* — **colt·ish·ness** *n*
colts·foot \ˈkōlts-ˌfu̇t\ *n, pl* **coltsfoots** (14c) **:** any of various plants with large rounded leaves resembling the foot of a colt; *esp* **:** a perennial composite herb (*Tussilago farfara*) with yellow flower heads appearing before the leaves
col·u·brid \ˈkäl-yə-brəd, ˈkä-lə-\ *n* [ultim. fr. L *colubra* snake] (1887) **:** any of a large cosmopolitan family (Colubridae) of chiefly nonvenomous snakes — **colubrid** *adj*
col·u·brine \-ˌbrīn\ *adj* (ca. 1528) **1 :** of, relating to, or resembling a snake **2 :** of or relating to colubrids **:** COLUBRID
co·lu·go \kə-ˈlü-(ˌ)gō\ *n, pl* **-gos** [perh. fr. a language of the Philippines] (1702) **:** FLYING LEMUR
col·um·bar·i·um \ˌkä-ləm-ˈber-ē-əm\ *n, pl* **-ia** \-ē-ə\ [L, lit., dovecote, fr. *columba* dove] (1846) **1 :** a structure of vaults lined with recesses for cinerary urns **2 :** a recess in a columbarium
Co·lum·bia \kə-ˈləm-bē-ə\ *n* [NL, fr. Christopher *Columbus*] (1775) **:** the United States
Co·lum·bi·an \-bē-ən\ *adj* (1757) **:** of or relating to the United States or to Christopher Columbus
col·um·bine \ˈkä-ləm-ˌbīn\ *n* [ME, fr. AF, fr. ML *columbina,* fr. L, fem. of *columbinus* like a dove, fr. *columba* dove; akin to OHG *holuntar* elder tree, Gk *kolymbos* a small grebe, *kelainos* black] (14c) **:** any of a genus (*Aquilegia*) of plants of the buttercup family with irregular showy spurred flowers; as **a :** a red-flowered plant (*A. canadensis*) of eastern No. America **b :** a blue-flowered plant (*A. caerulea*) of the Rocky Mountains
Col·um·bine \-ˌbīn, -ˌbēn\ *n* [It *Colombina*] (1719) **:** the saucy sweetheart of Harlequin in comedy and pantomime
co·lum·bite \kə-ˈləm-ˌbīt, ˈkä-ləm-\ *n* [NL *columbium*] (1805) **:** a black mineral consisting mostly of iron and niobium
co·lum·bi·um \kə-ˈləm-bē-əm\ *n* [NL, fr. *Columbia*] (1801) **:** NIOBIUM
Co·lum·bus Day \kə-ˈləm-bəs-\ *n* (1892) **1 :** October 12 formerly observed as a legal holiday in many states of the U.S. in commemoration of the landing of Columbus in the Bahamas in 1492 **2 :** the second Monday in October observed as a legal holiday in many states of the U.S.
col·u·mel·la \ˌkäl-yə-ˈme-lə\ *n, pl* **-mel·lae** \-ˈme-(ˌ)lē, -ˌlī\ [NL, fr. L, dim. of *columna*] (ca. 1755) **1 :** the central column or axis of a spiral univalve shell **2 a :** the bony or partly cartilaginous rod connecting the tympanic membrane with the internal ear in birds and in many reptiles and amphibians **b :** the bony central axis of the cochlea — **col·u·mel·lar** \-ˈme-lər\ *adj*
col·umn \ˈkä-ləm *also* ˈkäl-yəm\ *n* [ME *columne,* fr. AF *columpne,* fr. L *columna,* fr. *columen* top; akin to L *collis* hill — more at HILL] (15c) **1 a :** a vertical arrangement of items printed or written on a page **b :** one of two or more vertical sections of a printed page separated by a rule or blank space **c :** an accumulation arranged vertically **:** STACK **d :** one in a usu. regular series of newspaper or magazine articles ⟨gossip ~⟩ **2 :** a supporting pillar; *esp* **:** one consisting of a usu. round shaft, a capital, and a base **3 a :** something resembling a column in form, position, or function ⟨a ~ of water⟩ **b :** a tube or cylinder in which a chromatographic separation takes place **4 :** a long row (as of soldiers) **5 :** one of the vertical lines of elements of a determinant or matrix **6 :** a statistical category or grouping ⟨put another game in the win ~⟩ — **col·umned** \-ləmd, -yəmd\ *adj*

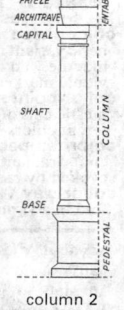

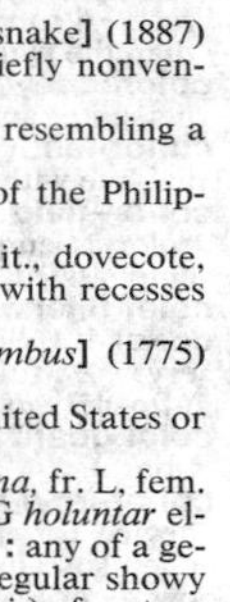
CORNICE
FRIEZE
ARCHITRAVE
ENTABLATURE
CAPITAL
SHAFT
COLUMN
BASE
PEDESTAL
column 2

co·lum·nar \kə-ˈləm-nər\ *adj* (1728) **1 :** of, relating to, resembling, or characterized by columns **2 :** of, relating to, being, or composed of tall narrow somewhat cylindrical or prismatic epithelial cells
co·lum·ni·a·tion \kə-ˌləm-nē-ˈā-shən\ *n* [prob. fr. *intercolumniation*] (1592) **:** the employment or the arrangement of columns in a structure
col·um·nist \ˈkä-ləm-nist, -lə-mist *also* ˈkäl-yəm-nist, -yə-mist\ *n* (1917) **:** one who writes a newspaper or magazine column — **col·um·nis·tic** \ˌkä-ləm-ˈnis-tik *also* ˌkäl-yəm-\ *adj*
col·za \ˈkäl-zə, ˈkōl-\ *n* [F, fr. D *koolzaad,* fr. MD *coolsaet,* fr. *coole* cabbage + *saet* seed] (1712) **1 :** [1]RAPE **2 :** RAPESEED
com *abbr* **1** comedy; comic **2** comma **3** commercial organization
com- *or* **col-** *or* **con-** *prefix* [ME, fr. AF, fr. L, with, together, thoroughly — more at CO-] **:** with **:** together **:** jointly — usu. *com-* before *b, p,* or *m* ⟨*com*mingle⟩, *col-* before *l* ⟨*col*linear⟩, and *con-* before other sounds ⟨*con*centrate⟩
[1]**co·ma** \ˈkō-mə\ *n* [NL, fr. Gk *kōma* deep sleep] (1646) **1 :** a state of profound unconsciousness caused by disease, injury, or poison **2 :** a state of mental or physical sluggishness **:** TORPOR
[2]**coma** *n, pl* **co·mae** \-ˌmē, -ˌmī\ [L, hair, fr. Gk *komē*] (1669) **1 :** a tufted bunch (as of branches, bracts, or seed hairs) **2 :** the head of a comet consisting of a cloud of gas and dust and usu. containing a nucleus **3 :** an optical aberration in which the image of a point source is a comet-shaped blur — **co·mat·ic** \kō-ˈma-tik\ *adj*
Co·ma Ber·e·ni·ces \ˈkō-mə-ˌber-ə-ˈnī-(ˌ)sēz\ *n* [L (gen. *Comae Berenices*), lit., Berenice's hair] (1616) **:** a constellation north of Virgo and between Boötes and Leo
co·mak·er \(ˌ)kō-ˈmā-kər\ *n* (ca. 1934) **:** one that participates in an agreement; *specif* **:** one who stands to meet a financial obligation in the event of the maker's default
Co·man·che \kə-ˈman-chē\ *n, pl* **Comanche** *or* **Comanches** [AmerSp, fr. Southern Paiute *kimmanciŋʷi* Shoshones, strangers] (1806) **1 :** a member of an American Indian people ranging from Wyoming and Nebraska south into New Mexico and northwestern Texas **2 :** the Uto-Aztecan language of the Comanche people
co·mate \(ˌ)kō-ˈmāt, ˈkō-ˌ\ *n* (1576) **:** COMPANION
co·ma·tose \ˈkō-mə-ˌtōs, ˈkä-\ *adj* [F *comateux,* fr. Gk *kōmat-, kōma*] (1755) **1 :** of, resembling, or affected with coma **2 :** characterized by lethargic inertness **:** TORPID ⟨a ~ economy⟩
[1]**comb** \ˈkōm\ *n* [ME, fr. OE *camb;* akin to OHG *kamb* comb, Gk *gomphos* tooth] (bef. 12c) **1 a :** a toothed instrument used esp. for adjusting, cleaning, or confining hair **b :** a structure resembling such a comb; *esp* **:** any of several toothed devices used in handling or ordering textile fibers **c :** CURRYCOMB **2 a :** a fleshy crest on the head of the domestic chicken and other domestic birds **b :** something (as the ridge of a roof) resembling the comb of a cock **3 :** HONEYCOMB — **combed** \ˈkōmd\ *adj* — **comb·like** \ˈkōm-ˌlīk\ *adj*
[2]**comb** *vt* (14c) **1 :** to draw a comb through for the purpose of arranging or cleaning **2 :** to pass across with a scraping or raking action **3 a :** to eliminate (as with a comb) by a thorough going-over **b :** to search or examine systematically ⟨police are ~*ing* the city⟩ **4 :** to use in a combing action ~ *vi* **1** *of a wave or its crest* **:** to roll over or break into foam **2 :** to make a thorough search ⟨~ through the classified ads⟩
[3]**comb** *abbr* **1** combination; combined; combining **2** combustion
[1]**com·bat** \ˈkäm-ˌbat\ *n* [AF, fr. *combatre* to attack, fight, fr. VL **combattere,* fr. L *com-* + *battuere* to beat] (1546) **1 :** a fight or contest between individuals or groups **2 :** CONFLICT, CONTROVERSY **3 :** active fighting in a war **:** ACTION ⟨casualties suffered in ~⟩
[2]**com·bat** \kəm-ˈbat, ˈkäm-ˌ\ *vb* **-bat·ed** *or* **-bat·ted; -bat·ing** *or* **-bat·ting** *vi* (1564) **:** to engage in combat **:** FIGHT ~ *vt* **1 :** to fight with **:** BATTLE **2 :** to struggle against; *esp* **:** to strive to reduce or eliminate ⟨~ pollution⟩ ***syn*** see OPPOSE
[3]**com·bat** \ˈkäm-ˌbat\ *adj* (1825) **1 :** relating to combat ⟨~ missions⟩ **2 :** designed or destined for combat ⟨~ boots⟩ ⟨~ troops⟩
com·bat·ant \kəm-ˈba-tᵊnt *also* ˈkäm-bə-tənt\ *n* (15c) **:** one that is engaged in or ready to engage in combat — **combatant** *adj*
combat fatigue *n* (1943) **:** post-traumatic stress disorder under wartime conditions (as combat) that cause intense stress — called also *battle fatigue, shell shock*
com·bat·ive \kəm-ˈba-tiv\ *adj* (1826) **:** marked by eagerness to fight or contend — **com·bat·ive·ly** *adv* — **com·bat·ive·ness** *n*
combe \ˈküm, ˈkōm\ *also* **coombe** *or* **coomb** \ˈküm\ *n* [ME *coumbe, cumbe,* fr. OE *cumb,* of Celt origin; akin to W *cwm* valley] (bef. 12c) **1** *Brit* **:** a deep narrow valley **2** *Brit* **:** a valley or basin on the flank of a hill
comb·er \ˈkō-mər\ *n* (1665) **1 :** one that combs **2 :** a long curling wave of the sea
com·bi·na·tion \ˌkäm-bə-ˈnā-shən\ *n, often attrib* (14c) **1 a :** a result or product of combining; *esp* **:** an alliance of individuals, corporations, or states united to achieve a social, political, or economic end **b :** two or more persons working as a team **2 :** an ordered sequence: as **a :** a sequence of letters or numbers chosen in setting a lock; *also* **:** the mechanism operating or moved by the sequence **b :** a rapid sequence of punches in boxing **c :** any subset of a set considered without regard to order within the subset **3 :** any of various one-piece undergarments for the upper and lower parts of the body — usu. used in pl. **4 :** an instrument designed to perform two or more tasks **5 a :** the act or process of combining; *esp* **:** that of uniting to form a chemical compound **b :** the quality or state of being combined — **com·bi·na·tion·al** \-shnəl, -shə-nᵊl\ *adj*
combination shot *n* (ca. 1909) **:** a shot in pool in which a ball is pocketed by an object ball
com·bi·na·tive \ˈkäm-bə-ˌnā-tiv, kəm-ˈbī-nə-\ *adj* (1855) **1 :** tending or able to combine **2 :** resulting from combination
com·bi·na·to·ri·al \ˌkäm-bə-nə-ˈtȯr-ē-əl, kəm-ˌbī-nə-, -(ˌ)bi-\ *adj* (1818) **1 :** of, relating to, or involving combinations **2 :** of or relating to the arrangement of, operation on, and selection of discrete mathematical elements belonging to finite sets or making up geometric configurations — **com·bi·na·to·ri·al·ly** \-ē-ə-lē\ *adv*
com·bi·na·tor·ics \-ˈtȯr-iks, -ˈtär-\ *n pl but sing in constr* (1941) **:** combinatorial mathematics
com·bi·na·to·ry \kəm-ˈbī-nə-ˌtȯr-ē\ *adj* (1647) **:** COMBINATIVE
[1]**com·bine** \kəm-ˈbīn\ *vb* **com·bined; com·bin·ing** [ME, fr. MF *combiner,* fr. LL *combinare,* fr. L *com-* + *bini* two by two — more at BIN-] *vt* (15c) **1 a :** to bring into such close relationship as to obscure individual characters **:** MERGE ⟨two companies *combining* forces⟩ **b :** to

cause to unite into a chemical compound **c :** to unite into a single number or expression ⟨~ fractions and simplify⟩ **2 :** INTERMIX, BLEND ⟨~ the sugar and flour⟩ **3 :** to possess in combination ⟨a writer whose works ~ imagination and scholarship⟩ ~ *vi* **1 a :** to become one **b :** to unite to form a chemical compound **2 :** to act together ⟨many factors *combined* to cause the recession⟩ ***syn*** see JOIN — **com·bin·able** \-ˈbī-nə-bəl\ *adj* — **com·bin·er** *n*

²**com·bine** \ˈkäm-ˌbīn\ *n* (1886) **1 :** a combination esp. of business or political interests **2 :** a harvesting machine that heads, threshes, and cleans grain while moving over a field

³**com·bine** \ˈkäm-ˌbīn\ *vb* **com·bined; com·bin·ing** *vt* (1926) **:** to harvest with a combine ~ *vi* **:** to combine a crop

com·bined \kəm-ˈbīnd\ *n* (1935) **:** a skiing competition combining two separate events (as downhill race and a slalom race)

combing *var of* COAMING

comb·ings \ˈkō-miŋz\ *n pl* (1614) **:** loose hair removed by a comb

combing wool *n* (1757) **:** long-staple strong-fibered wool found suitable for combing and used esp. in the manufacture of worsteds

combining form *n* (1884) **:** a linguistic form that occurs only in compounds or derivatives and can be distinguished descriptively from an affix by its ability to occur as one immediate constituent of a form whose only other immediate constituent is an affix (as *cephal-* in *cephalic*) or by its being derived from an independent word (as *electro-* representing *electric* in *electromagnet* or *para-* representing *parachute* in *paratrooper*) or can be distinguished historically from an affix by the fact that it is borrowed from another language in which it is descriptively a word or a combining form (as French *mal* giving English *mal-* in *malodorous*)

comb jelly *n* (ca. 1889) **:** CTENOPHORE

com·bo \ˈkäm-(ˌ)bō\ *n, pl* **combos** [*com*bination + ¹-*o*] (1921) **1 :** a usu. small jazz or dance band **2 :** COMBINATION

comb–over \ˈkōm-ˌō-vər\ *n* (1980) **:** an arrangement of hair on a balding man in which hair from the side of the head is combed over the bald spot

com·bust \kəm-ˈbəst\ *vb* [L *combustus,* pp. of *comburere* to burn up, irreg. fr. *com-* + *urere* to burn — more at EMBER] (15c) **:** BURN

com·bus·ti·ble \kəm-ˈbəs-tə-bəl\ *adj* (1529) **1 :** capable of combustion **2 :** easily excited ⟨a ~ temper⟩ — **com·bus·ti·bil·i·ty** \-ˌbəs-tə-ˈbi-lə-tē\ *n* — **combustible** *n* — **com·bus·ti·bly** \-ˈbəs-tə-blē\ *adv*

com·bus·tion \kəm-ˈbəs-chən\ *n* (15c) **1 :** an act or instance of burning **2 :** a usu. rapid chemical process (as oxidation) that produces heat and usu. light; *also* **:** a slower oxidation (as in the body) **3 :** violent agitation **:** TUMULT — **com·bus·tive** \-ˈbəs-tiv\ *adj*

com·bus·tor \-ˈbəs-tər\ *n* (1945) **:** a chamber (as in a gas turbine or a jet engine) in which combustion occurs — called also *combustion chamber*

comd *abbr* command

comdg *abbr* commanding

comdr *abbr* commander

comdt *abbr* commandant

¹**come** \ˈkəm\ *vb* **came** \ˈkām\; **come; com·ing** \ˈkə-miŋ\ [ME, fr. OE *cuman;* akin to OHG *queman* to come, L *venire,* Gk *bainein* to walk, go] *vi* (bef. 12c) **1 a :** to move toward something **:** APPROACH ⟨~ here⟩ **b :** to move or journey to a vicinity with a specified purpose ⟨~ see us⟩ ⟨~ and see what's going on⟩ **c** (1) **:** to reach a particular station in a series ⟨now we ~ to the section on health⟩ (2) **:** to arrive in due course ⟨the time has ~⟩ **d** (1) **:** to approach in kind or quality ⟨this ~*s* near perfection⟩ (2) **:** to reach a condition or conclusion ⟨*came* to regard him as a friend⟩ ⟨~ to think of it, you may be right⟩ **e** (1) **:** to advance toward accomplishment **:** COME ALONG ⟨the job is *coming* nicely⟩ (2) **:** to advance in a particular manner ⟨~ running when I call⟩ (3) **:** to advance, rise, or improve in rank or condition ⟨has ~ a long way⟩ **f :** EXTEND ⟨her dress *came* to her ankles⟩ **2 a** (1) **:** to arrive at a particular place, end, result, or conclusion ⟨*came* to his senses⟩ ⟨~ untied⟩ (2) **:** AMOUNT ⟨the taxes on it ~ to more than it's worth⟩ **b** (1) **:** to appear to the mind ⟨the answer *came* to them⟩ (2) **:** to appear on a scene **:** make an appearance ⟨children ~ equipped to learn any language⟩ **c** (1) **:** HAPPEN, OCCUR ⟨no harm will ~ to you⟩ (2) **:** to come to pass **:** take place — used in the subjunctive with inverted subject and verb to express the particular time or occasion ⟨~ spring the days will be longer⟩ **d :** ORIGINATE, ARISE ⟨wine ~*s* from grapes⟩ ⟨they ~ of sturdy stock⟩ **e :** to enter or assume a condition, position, or relation ⟨artillery *came* into action⟩ **f :** to fall within a field of view or a range of application ⟨this ~*s* within the terms of the treaty⟩ **g :** to issue forth ⟨a sob *came* from her throat⟩ **h :** to take form ⟨churn till the butter ~*s*⟩ **i :** to be available ⟨this model ~*s* in several sizes⟩ ⟨as good as they ~⟩ **j** *often vulgar* **:** to experience orgasm **3 :** to fall to a person in a division or inheritance of property **4** *obs* **:** to become moved favorably **:** RELENT **5 :** to turn out to be ⟨good clothes don't ~ cheap⟩ **6 :** BECOME ⟨a dream that *came* true⟩ ~ *vt* **1 :** to approach or be near (an age) ⟨a child *coming* eight years old⟩ **2 :** to take on the aspect of ⟨~ the stern parent⟩ — **come a cropper :** to fail completely ⟨the plan *came a cropper*⟩ — **come across :** to meet, find, or encounter esp. by chance ⟨researchers have *come across* important new evidence⟩ — **come again :** REPEAT; *also* **:** to speak further — used as an interrogative — **come clean :** to tell the whole story **:** CONFESS ⟨*came clean* about her crimes⟩ — **come into :** to acquire as a possession or achievement ⟨*come into* a fortune⟩ — **come into one's own :** to achieve one's potential; *also* **:** to gain recognition — **come of age :** to reach maturity — **come off it :** to cease foolish or pretentious talk or behavior — **come over :** to seize suddenly and strangely ⟨what's *come over* you⟩ — **come to :** to be a question of ⟨when it *comes to* pitching horseshoes, he's the champ⟩ — **come to grief :** to encounter misfortune (as calamity, defeat, or ruin) ⟨his campaign *came to grief*⟩ — **come to grips with :** to meet or deal with firmly, frankly, or straightforwardly ⟨*come to grips with* the unemployment problem⟩ — **come to oneself :** to get hold of oneself **:** regain self-control — **come to pass :** HAPPEN — **come to terms 1 :** to reach an agreement — often used with *with* ⟨the company has *come to terms* with the union⟩ **2 :** to become adjusted esp. emotionally or intellectually — usu. used with *with* ⟨*come to terms* with modern life⟩ — **come upon :** to meet or find by chance **:** come across ⟨*came upon* an old friend⟩ — **to come :** existing or arriving in the future ⟨in the days *to come*⟩ ⟨there will be more trouble *to come*⟩

²**come** *n* (1923) **1** *often vulgar* **:** SEMEN **2** *often vulgar* **:** ORGASM

come about *vi* (14c) **1 :** HAPPEN **2 :** to change direction ⟨the wind has *come about* into the north⟩ **3 :** to shift to a new tack

come across *vi* (1878) **1 :** to give over or furnish something demanded; *esp* **:** to pay over money **2 :** to produce an impression ⟨*comes across* as a good speaker⟩ **3 :** COME THROUGH 2

come–along \ˈkəm-ə-ˌlȯŋ\ *n* (1926) **:** a small portable winch usu. consisting of a cable attached to a hand-operated ratchet

come along *vi* (1559) **1 :** to accompany someone who leads the way ⟨asked me to *come along* on the trip⟩ **2 :** to make progress ⟨work is *coming along* well⟩ **3 :** to make an appearance ⟨won't just marry the first man that *comes along*⟩

come around *vi* (1807) **1 :** COME ROUND **2 :** MENSTRUATE

come·back \ˈkəm-ˌbak\ *n* (1889) **1 a :** a sharp or witty reply **:** RETORT **b :** a cause for complaint **2 :** a return to a former position or condition (as of success or prosperity) **:** RECOVERY, REVIVAL ⟨staging his ultimate ~ from self-imposed exile —Howard Mandel⟩

come back *vi* (1850) **1 :** to return to life or vitality **2 :** to return to memory ⟨it's all *coming back* to me now⟩ **3 :** REPLY, RETORT ⟨when questioned, he *came back* with a vehement denial⟩ **4 :** to regain a former favorable condition or position

come·back·er \ˈkəm-ˌba-kər\ *n* (1966) **:** a grounder in baseball hit directly to the pitcher

come by *vt* (14c) **:** to get possession of **:** ACQUIRE ⟨a good job is hard to *come by*⟩ ~ *vi* **:** to make a visit ⟨*came by* after dinner⟩

COMECON *abbr* Council for Mutual Economic Assistance

co·me·di·an \kə-ˈmē-dē-ən\ *n* (1581) **1** *archaic* **a :** a writer of comedies **b :** an actor who plays comic roles **2 :** a comical individual; *specif* **:** a professional entertainer who uses any of various physical or verbal means to be amusing

co·me·dic \-ˈmē-dik\ *adj* (1639) **1 :** of or relating to comedy **2 :** COMICAL 2 — **co·me·dic·al·ly** \-di-k(ə-)lē\ *adv*

co·me·di·enne \-ˌmē-dē-ˈen\ *n* [F *comédienne,* fem. of *comédien* comedian, fr. *comédie*] (ca. 1859) **:** a woman who is a comedian

com·e·do \ˈkä-mə-ˌdō\ *n, pl* **com·e·do·nes** \ˌkä-mə-ˈdō-(ˌ)nēz\ [NL, fr. L, glutton, fr. *comedere* to eat — more at COMESTIBLE] (1866) **:** BLACKHEAD 1

come·down \ˈkəm-ˌdau̇n\ *n* (1840) **:** a descent in rank or dignity

come down *vi* (14c) **1 :** to lose or fall in estate or condition ⟨has *come down* in the world⟩ **2 a :** to pass by tradition ⟨a story that has *come down* from medieval times⟩ **b :** to pass from a usu. high source ⟨word *came down* that the strike was over⟩ **3 :** to place oneself in opposition ⟨*came down* hard on gambling⟩ **4 a :** to deal with a subject directly ⟨when you *come down* to it, we all depend on others⟩ **b :** to reduce itself **:** AMOUNT ⟨it *comes down* to this⟩ **5 :** to become ill ⟨*came down* with measles⟩ **6 :** COME OUT 2 **7 :** GO ON, HAPPEN ⟨what's *coming down*⟩

com·e·dy \ˈkä-mə-dē\ *n, pl* **-dies** [ME, fr. ML *comoedia,* fr. L, drama with a happy ending, fr. Gk *kōmōidia,* fr. *kōmos* revel + *aeidein* to sing — more at ODE] (14c) **1 a :** a medieval narrative that ends happily ⟨Dante's *Divine Comedy*⟩ **b :** a literary work written in a comic style or treating a comic theme **2 a :** a drama of light and amusing character and typically with a happy ending **b :** the genre of dramatic literature dealing with the comic or with the serious in a light or satirical manner — compare TRAGEDY **3 :** a ludicrous or farcical event or series of events ⟨a ~ of errors⟩ **4 a :** the comic element ⟨the ~ of many life situations⟩ **b :** humorous entertainment ⟨nightclub ~⟩

comedy drama *n* (1870) **:** serious drama that has comic elements

comedy of manners (1822) **:** comedy that satirically portrays the manners and fashions of a particular class or set

come–hith·er \(ˌ)kəm-ˈhi-t͟hər, (ˌ)kə-ˈmi-\ *n, often attrib* (1925) **:** a tempting often sexual invitation ⟨that ~ look in your eyes⟩

come in *vi* (13c) **1 a :** to arrive on a scene ⟨new models *coming in*⟩ **b :** to become available ⟨data began *coming in*⟩ **2 :** to place among those finishing ⟨*came in* last⟩ **3 a :** to function in an indicated manner ⟨*come in* handy⟩ **b** *of a telecommunications signal* **:** to be received ⟨*came in* loud and clear⟩ **4 :** to assume a role or function ⟨that's where you *come in*⟩ **5 :** to attain maturity, fruitfulness, or production — **come in for :** to become subject to ⟨*came in for* harsh criticism⟩

come·ly \ˈkəm-lē *also* ˈkōm- *or* ˈkäm-\ *adj* **come·li·er; -est** [ME *comly,* alter. of OE *cȳmlic* glorious, fr. *cȳme* lively, fine; akin to OHG *kūmig* weak] (13c) **1 :** pleasurably conforming to notions of good appearance, suitability, or proportion **2 :** having a pleasing appearance **:** not homely or plain ***syn*** see BEAUTIFUL — **come·li·ness** *n*

come off *vi* (1596) **1 a :** to acquit oneself **:** FARE ⟨*came off* well in the contest⟩ **b :** APPEAR, SEEM **2 :** SUCCEED ⟨a television series that never *came off* —*TV Guide*⟩ **3 :** HAPPEN, OCCUR ~ *vt* **:** to have recently completed or recovered from ⟨*coming off* a good year⟩

come–on \ˈkəm-ˌȯn, -ˌän\ *n* (1902) **1 :** something (as an advertising promotion) intended to entice or allure **2 :** a usu. sexual advance

come on *vi* (15c) **1 a :** to advance by degrees ⟨darkness *came on*⟩ **b :** to begin by degrees ⟨rain *came on* toward noon⟩ **2 a :** PLEASE — used in cajoling or pleading **b** — used interjectionally to express astonishment, incredulity, or recognition of a put-on **3 :** to project an indicated personal image ⟨*comes on* as a conservative⟩ **4 :** to show sexual interest in someone; *also* **:** to make sexual advances — usu. used with *to* ⟨tried to *come on* to her⟩

come out *vi* (13c) **1 a :** to come into public view **:** make a public appearance ⟨a new magazine has *come out*⟩ **b :** to become evident ⟨his pride *came out* in his refusal to accept help⟩ **2 :** to declare oneself esp. in public utterance ⟨*came out* in favor of the proposal⟩ **3 :** to turn out in an outcome **:** end up ⟨everything *came out* all right⟩ **4 :** to make a debut **5 a :** to openly declare one's homosexuality **b :** to openly declare something about oneself previously kept hidden — often used with *as* ⟨blew his cover and *came out* as a CIA agent —William Prochnau⟩ — **com·ing–out** \ˌkə-miŋ-ˈau̇t\ *n or adj* — **come out with 1 :** to give expression to ⟨*came out with* a new proposal⟩ **2 :** PUBLISH

\ə\ **a**but \ᵊ\ **k**itten, F ta**ble** \ər\ **fur**ther \a\ **a**sh \ā\ **a**ce \ä\ **mo**p, **mar** \au̇\ **ou**t \ch\ **ch**in \e\ **be**t \ē\ **ea**sy \g\ **g**o \i\ **hi**t \ī\ **i**ce \j\ **j**ob \ŋ\ **si**ng \ō\ **go** \ȯ\ **law** \ȯi\ **boy** \th\ **th**in \t͟h\ **th**e \ü\ **loo**t \u̇\ **foo**t \y\ **y**et \zh\ **vi**sion, beige \k, ⁿ, œ, ue, ʸ\ *see* Guide to Pronunciation

come–out•er \(ˌ)kəm-ˈau̇-tər\ *n* (1840) **1 :** a person who withdraws from something established (as a religious body) **2 :** a person who advocates political reform

come over *vi* (1576) **1 a :** to change from one side (as of a controversy) to the other **b :** to visit casually : DROP IN ⟨*come over* whenever you like⟩ **2** *Brit* **:** BECOME

com•er \ˈkə-mər\ *n* (14c) **1 :** one that comes or arrives ⟨welcomed all ~*s*⟩ **2 :** one making rapid progress or showing promise

come round *vi* (1818) **1 :** to change direction **2 :** to return to a former condition; *esp* **:** COME TO 1 **3 :** to accede to a particular opinion or course of action ⟨you'll *come round* to our side eventually⟩

1**co•mes•ti•ble** \kə-ˈmes-tə-bəl\ *adj* [ML *comestibilis,* fr. L *comestus,* pp. of *comedere* to eat, fr. *com-* + *edere* to eat — more at EAT] (15c) **:** EDIBLE

2**comestible** *n* (1837) **:** FOOD — usu. used in pl.

com•et \ˈkä-mət\ *n* [ME *comete,* fr. OE *cometa,* fr. L, fr. Gk *komētēs,* lit., long-haired, fr. *koman* to wear long hair, fr. *komē* hair] (bef. 12c) **:** a celestial body that appears as a fuzzy head usu. surrounding a bright nucleus, that has a usu. highly eccentric orbit, that consists primarily of ice and dust, and that often develops one or more long tails when near the sun — **com•e•tary** \-mə-ˌter-ē\ *adj* — **co•met•ic** \kə-ˈme-tik, kä-\ *adj*

come through *vi* (1914) **1 :** to do what is needed or expected ⟨*came through* in the clutch⟩ **2 :** to become communicated ⟨the message *came through* loud and clear⟩

come to *vi* (ca. 1572) **1 :** to recover consciousness **2 a :** to bring a ship's head nearer the wind **:** LUFF **b :** to come to anchor or to a stop

come up *vi* (14c) **1 :** RISE 6 **2 :** to come near **:** make an approach ⟨*came up* and introduced himself⟩ **3 :** to rise in rank or status ⟨an officer who *came up* from the ranks⟩ **4 a :** to come to attention or consideration ⟨the question never *came up*⟩ **b :** to occur in the course of time ⟨any problem that may *come up*⟩ **5 :** to turn out to be ⟨the coin *came up* tails⟩ **6** *chiefly dial* **:** GROW UP — **come up empty :** to fail to achieve a desired result — **come up with :** to produce esp. in dealing with a problem or challenge ⟨*came up with* a solution⟩

come•up•pance \(ˌ)kəm-ˈə-pən(t)s\ *n* [*come up* + *-ance*] (1859) **:** a deserved rebuke or penalty **:** DESERTS

com•fit \ˈkəm(p)-fət, ˈkäm(p)-\ *n* [ME *confit,* fr. AF **confit,* fr. pp. of *confire, cumfire* to prepare, fr. L *conficere,* fr. *com-* + *facere* to make — more at DO] (14c) **:** a candy consisting of a piece of fruit, a root (as licorice), a nut, or a seed coated and preserved with sugar

1**com•fort** \ˈkəm(p)-fərt\ *vt* [ME, fr. AF *cunforter, comforter,* fr. LL *confortare* to strengthen greatly, fr. L *com-* + *fortis* strong] (13c) **1 :** to give strength and hope to **:** CHEER **2 :** to ease the grief or trouble of **:** CONSOLE — **com•fort•ing•ly** \-fər-tiŋ-lē\ *adv*

2**comfort** *n* (13c) **1 :** strengthening aid: **a :** ASSISTANCE, SUPPORT ⟨accused of giving aid and ~ to the enemy⟩ **b :** consolation in time of trouble or worry **:** SOLACE **2 a :** a feeling of relief or encouragement **b :** contented well-being ⟨a life of ease and ~⟩ **3 :** a satisfying or enjoyable experience **4 :** one that gives or brings comfort ⟨all the ~*s* of home⟩ — **com•fort•less** \-ləs\ *adj*

com•fort•able \ˈkəm(p)(f)-tə(r)-bəl, ˈkəm(p)-fə(r)-tə-bəl, ˈkəm-fə(r)-bəl\ *adj* (1769) **1 a :** affording or enjoying contentment and security ⟨a ~ income⟩ **b :** affording or enjoying physical comfort ⟨a ~ chair⟩ ⟨was too ~ to move⟩ **2 a :** free from vexation or doubt ⟨~ assumptions⟩ **b :** free from stress or tension ⟨a ~ routine⟩ — **com•fort•able•ness** *n* — **com•fort•ably** \-blē\ *adv*

syn COMFORTABLE, COZY, SNUG, EASY, RESTFUL mean enjoying or providing a position of contentment and security. COMFORTABLE applies to anything that encourages serenity, well-being, or complacency as well as physical ease ⟨started feeling *comfortable* in our new surroundings⟩. COZY suggests warmth, shelter, assured ease, and friendliness ⟨a *cozy* neighborhood coffee shop⟩. SNUG suggests having just enough space for comfort and safety but no more ⟨a *snug* little cottage⟩. EASY implies relief from or absence of anything likely to cause discomfort or constraint ⟨living in *easy* circumstances⟩. RESTFUL applies to whatever induces or contributes to rest or relaxation ⟨a quiet *restful* vacation⟩.

com•fort•er \ˈkəm(p)-fə(r)-tər\ *n* (14c) **1 a** *cap* **:** HOLY SPIRIT **b :** one that gives comfort **2 a :** a long narrow usu. knitted neck scarf **b :** a thick bed covering made of two layers of cloth containing a filling (as down)

comfort food *n* (1977) **:** food prepared in a traditional style having a usu. nostalgic or sentimental appeal

comfort station *n* (ca. 1913) **:** RESTROOM

comfort zone *n* (1923) **1 :** the temperature range within which one is comfortable **2 :** the level at which one functions with ease and familiarity

com•frey \ˈkəm(p)-frē\ *n, pl* **comfreys** [ME *cumfirie,* fr. AF *cunfirie,* fr. L *conferva* a water plant, fr. *confervēre* to grow together (of bones), fr. *com-* + *fervēre* to boil — more at BARM] (13c) **1 :** any of a genus (*Symphytum*) of perennial herbs of the borage family with coarse hairy entire leaves and flowers in one-sided racemes **2 :** an herbal preparation of the leaves or roots of comfrey that is toxic if taken internally

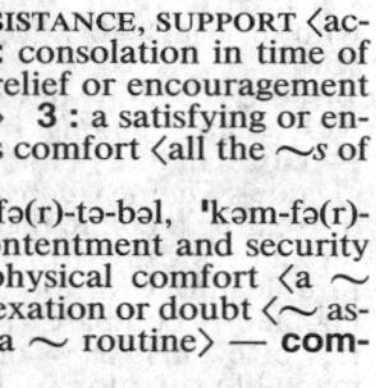

comfrey 1

com•fy \ˈkəm(p)-fē\ *adj* **com•fi•er; -est** [by shortening & alter.] (1829) **:** COMFORTABLE ⟨a ~ sofa⟩ ⟨a ~ routine⟩

1**com•ic** \ˈkä-mik\ *adj* [L *comicus,* fr. Gk *kōmikos,* fr. *kōmos* revel] (1576) **1 :** of, relating to, or marked by comedy ⟨a ~ actor⟩ **2 :** causing laughter or amusement **:** FUNNY ⟨a ~ monologue⟩ **3 :** of or relating to comic strips ⟨the newspaper's ~ section⟩ ***syn*** see LAUGHABLE

2**comic** *n* (1581) **1 :** COMEDIAN ⟨a stand-up ~⟩ **2 :** the comic element **3 a :** COMIC STRIP **b :** COMIC BOOK **c** *pl* **:** the part of a newspaper devoted to comic strips

com•i•cal \ˈkä-mi-kəl\ *adj* (15c) **1** *obs* **:** of or relating to comedy **2 :** causing laughter esp. because of a startlingly or unexpectedly humorous impact ⟨wearing a ~ expression⟩ ***syn*** see LAUGHABLE — **com•i•cal•i•ty** \ˌkä-mi-ˈka-lə-tē\ *n* — **com•i•cal•ly** \ˈkä-mi-k(ə-)lē\ *adv*

comic book *n* (1941) **:** a magazine containing sequences of comic strips — usu. hyphenated in attributive use

com•ic–op•era \ˈkä-mik-ˈä-p(ə-)rə\ *adj* (1906) **:** not to be taken seriously ⟨a ~ regime⟩

comic opera *n* (1762) **:** opera of a humorous character with a happy ending and usu. some spoken dialogue

comic relief *n* (1875) **:** a relief from the emotional tension esp. of a drama that is provided by the interposition of a comic episode or element

comic strip *n* (1920) **:** a group of cartoons in narrative sequence

1**com•ing** \ˈkə-miŋ\ *n* (13c) **:** an act or instance of arriving

2**coming** *adj* (15c) **1 :** immediately due in sequence or development ⟨in the ~ year⟩ **2 :** gaining importance ⟨the ~ trend⟩

co•min•gle \kə-ˈmiŋ-gəl\ *vt* (1602) **:** COMMINGLE

coming–of–age *n* (1916) **:** the attainment of prominence, respectability, recognition, or maturity

Com•in•tern \ˈkä-mən-ˌtərn\ *n* [Russ *Komintern,* fr. *Kom*munisticheskiĭ *Intern*atsional Communist International] (1923) **:** the Communist International established in 1919 and dissolved in 1943

co•mi•tia \kə-ˈmi-sh(ē-)ə\ *n, pl* **comitia** [L, pl. of *comitium,* fr. *com-* + *-it-* (akin to *ire* to go) — more at ISSUE] (1600) **:** any of several public assemblies of the people in ancient Rome for legislative, judicial, and electoral purposes — **co•mi•tial** \-ˈmi-shəl\ *adj*

co•mi•ty \ˈkä-mə-tē, ˈkō-\ *n, pl* **-ties** [L *comitat-, comitas,* fr. *comis* courteous, prob. fr. OL *cosmis,* fr. *com-* + *-smis* (akin to Skt *smayate* he smiles) — more at SMILE] (1543) **1 a :** friendly social atmosphere **:** social harmony ⟨group activities promoting ~⟩ **b :** a loose widespread community based on common social institutions ⟨the ~ of civilization⟩ **c :** COMITY OF NATIONS **d :** the informal and voluntary recognition by courts of one jurisdiction of the laws and judicial decisions of another **2 :** avoidance of proselytizing members of another religious denomination

comity of nations (1862) **1 :** the courtesy and friendship of nations marked esp. by mutual recognition of executive, legislative, and judicial acts **2 :** the group of nations practicing international comity

com•ix \ˈkä-miks\ *n pl* [alter. of *comics*] (1973) **:** comic books or comic strips

coml *abbr* commercial

comm *abbr* **1** command; commandant; commander; commanding **2** commentary **3** commerce; commercial **4** commission; commissioned; commissioner **5** committee **6** common; commoner **7** commonwealth **8** commune **9** communication **10** communist **11** community

com•ma \ˈkä-mə\ *n* [LL, fr. L, part of a sentence, fr. Gk *komma* segment, clause, fr. *koptein* to cut — more at CAPON] (1554) **1 :** a punctuation mark , used esp. as a mark of separation within the sentence **2 :** PAUSE, INTERVAL **3 :** any of several nymphalid butterflies (genus *Polygonia*) with a silvery comma-shaped mark on the underside of the hind wings

comma fault *n* (ca. 1934) **:** COMMA SPLICE

1**com•mand** \kə-ˈmand\ *vb* [ME *comanden,* fr. AF *cumander,* fr. VL **commandare,* alter. of L *commendare* to commit to one's charge — more at COMMEND] *vt* (14c) **1 :** to direct authoritatively **:** ORDER **2 :** to exercise a dominating influence over **:** have command of: as **a :** to have at one's immediate disposal ⟨~*s* many resources⟩ **b :** to demand or receive as one's due ⟨~*s* a high fee⟩ **c :** to overlook or dominate from or as if from a strategic position ⟨a hill that ~*s* the city⟩ **d :** to have military command of as senior officer ⟨~ a regiment⟩ **3** *obs* **:** to order or request to be given ~ *vi* **1 :** to have or exercise direct authority **:** GOVERN **2 :** to give orders **3 :** to be commander **4 :** to dominate as if from an elevated place — **com•mand•able** \-ˈman-də-bəl\ *adj*

syn COMMAND, ORDER, BID, ENJOIN, DIRECT, INSTRUCT, CHARGE mean to issue orders. COMMAND and ORDER imply authority and usu. some degree of formality and impersonality. COMMAND stresses official exercise of authority ⟨a general *commanding* troops⟩. ORDER may suggest peremptory or arbitrary exercise ⟨*ordered* his employees about like slaves⟩. BID suggests giving orders peremptorily (as to children or servants) ⟨she *bade* him be seated⟩. ENJOIN implies giving an order or direction authoritatively and urgently and often with admonition or solicitude ⟨a sign *enjoining* patrons to be quiet⟩. DIRECT and INSTRUCT both connote expectation of obedience and usu. concern specific points of procedure or method, INSTRUCT sometimes implying greater explicitness or formality ⟨*directed* her assistant to hold all calls⟩ ⟨the judge *instructed* the jury to ignore the remark⟩. CHARGE adds to ENJOIN an implication of imposing as a duty or responsibility ⟨*charged* by the President with a secret mission⟩.

2**command** *n* (15c) **1 a :** an order given **b :** a signal that actuates a device (as a control mechanism in a spacecraft or one step in a computer); *also* **:** the activation of a device by means of such a signal **2 a :** the ability to control **:** MASTERY **b :** the authority or right to command ⟨the officer in ~⟩ **c** (1) **:** the power to dominate (2) **:** scope of vision **d :** facility in use ⟨a good ~ of French⟩ **e :** CONTROL 1d ⟨a pitcher with good ~ of his curveball⟩ **3 :** the act of commanding **4 :** the personnel, area, or organization under a commander; *specif* **:** a unit of the U.S. Air Force higher than an air force **5 :** a position of highest usu. military authority ***syn*** see POWER

3**command** *adj* (1826) **:** done on command or request ⟨a ~ performance⟩

com•man•dant \ˈkä-mən-ˌdänt, -ˌdant\ *n* (1687) **:** COMMANDING OFFICER

command car *n* (1941) **:** an open armored car designed esp. for military reconnaissance and capable of traveling over rough terrain

command economy *n* (1942) **:** an economic system in which activity is controlled by a central authority and the means of production are publicly owned

com•man•deer \ˌkä-mən-ˈdir\ *vt* [Afrik *kommandeer,* fr. F *commander* to command, fr. OF *comander*] (1881) **1 a :** to compel to perform military service **b :** to seize for military purposes **2 :** to take arbitrary or forcible possession of

com•mand•er \kə-ˈman-dər\ *n* (14c) **1 :** one in an official position of command or control: as **a :** COMMANDING OFFICER **b :** the presiding officer of a society or organization **2 :** a commissioned officer in the navy or coast guard ranking above a lieutenant commander and below a captain — **com•mand•er•ship** \-ˌship\ *n*

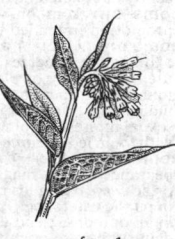

commander in chief (1654) : one who holds the supreme command of an armed force

com·mand·ery \kə-ˈman-d(ə-)rē\ *n, pl* **-er·ies** (15c) **1** : a district under the control of a commander of an order of knights **2** : an assembly or lodge in a secret order

com·mand·ing \kə-ˈman-diŋ\ *adj* (1591) **1** : drawing attention or priority ‹a ~ presence› **2** : difficult to overcome ‹a ~ lead› — **com·mand·ing·ly** \-diŋ-lē\ *adv*

commanding officer *n* (1720) : an officer in command; *esp* : an officer in the armed forces in command of an organization or installation

com·mand·ment \kə-ˈman(d)-mənt\ *n* (13c) **1** : the act or power of commanding **2** : something that is commanded; *esp* : one of the biblical Ten Commandments

command module *n* (1962) : a space vehicle module designed to carry the crew, the chief communication equipment, and the equipment for reentry

com·man·do \kə-ˈman-(ˌ)dō\ *n, pl* **-dos** *or* **-does** [Afrik *kommando,* fr. D *commando* command, fr. Sp *comando,* fr. *comandar* to command, fr. LL *commandare*] (1839) **1** *SoAfr* **a** : a military unit or command of the Boers **b** : a raiding expedition **2 a** : a military unit trained and organized as shock troops esp. for hit-and-run raids into enemy territory **b** : a member of such a unit — **go commando** *slang* : to wear no underwear

command post *n* (ca. 1918) : a post at which the commander of a unit in the field receives orders and exercises command

command sergeant major *n* (1967) : a noncommissioned officer in the army ranking above a first sergeant

comma splice *n* (1924) : the use of a comma between coordinate main clauses not connected by a conjunction (as in "nobody goes there anymore, it's boring")

com·me·dia del·l'ar·te \kə-ˌmā-dē-ə-(ˌ)del-ˈär-tē, kə-ˌme-\ *n* [It, lit., comedy of art] (1823) : Italian comedy of the 16th to 18th centuries improvised from standardized situations and stock characters

comme il faut \ˌkə-mē(l)-ˈfō\ *adj* [F, lit., as it should be] (1756) : conforming to accepted standards : PROPER

com·mem·o·rate \kə-ˈme-mə-ˌrāt\ *vt* **-rat·ed; -rat·ing** [L *commemoratus,* pp. of *commemorare,* fr. *com-* + *memorare* to remind of, fr. *memor* mindful — more at MEMORY] (1599) **1** : to call to remembrance **2** : to mark by some ceremony or observation : OBSERVE ‹~ an anniversary› **3** : to serve as a memorial of ‹a plaque that ~*s* the battle› ***syn*** see KEEP — **com·mem·o·ra·tor** \-ˌrā-tər\ *n*

com·mem·o·ra·tion \kə-ˌme-mə-ˈrā-shən\ *n* (14c) **1** : the act of commemorating **2** : something that commemorates

com·mem·o·ra·tive \kə-ˈmem-rə-tiv, -ˈme-mə-; -ˈme-mə-ˌrā-tiv\ *adj* (1612) : intended as a commemoration; *esp* : issued in limited quantities for a limited time to honor or feature someone or something ‹a ~ stamp› — **commemorative** *n* — **com·mem·o·ra·tive·ly** *adv*

com·mence \kə-ˈmen(t)s\ *vb* **com·menced; com·menc·ing** [ME *comencen,* fr. AF *comencer,* fr. VL **cominitiare,* fr. L *com-* + LL *initiare* to begin, fr. L, to initiate] *vt* (14c) : to enter upon : BEGIN ‹~ proceedings› ~ *vi* **1** : to have or make a beginning : START **2** *chiefly Brit* : to take a degree at a university ***syn*** see BEGIN — **com·menc·er** *n*

com·mence·ment \kə-ˈmen(t)s-mənt\ *n* (13c) **1** : an act, instance, or time of commencing **2 a** : the ceremonies or the day for conferring degrees or diplomas **b** : the period of activities at this time

com·mend \kə-ˈmend\ *vt* [ME, fr. AF *comander,* fr. L *commendare,* fr. *com-* + *mandare* to entrust — more at MANDATE] (14c) **1** : to entrust for care or preservation **2** : to recommend as worthy of confidence or notice **3** : to mention with approbation : PRAISE — **com·mend·able** \-ˈmen-də-bəl\ *adj* — **com·mend·ably** \-blē\ *adv* — **com·mend·er** *n*

com·men·da·tion \ˌkä-mən-ˈdā-shən, -ˌmen-\ *n* (14c) **1 a** : an act of commending **b** : something (as a formal citation) that commends **2** *archaic* : COMPLIMENT

com·men·da·to·ry \kə-ˈmen-də-ˌtȯr-ē\ *adj* (1544) : serving to commend ‹~ remarks›

com·men·sal \kə-ˈmen(t)-səl\ *adj* [ME, fr. ML *commensalis,* fr. L *com-* + LL *mensalis* of the table, fr. L *mensa* table] (1877) : of, relating to, or living in a state of commensalism ‹~ organisms› — **commensal** *n* — **com·men·sal·ly** \-sə-lē\ *adv*

com·men·sal·ism \-sə-ˌli-zəm\ *n* (1870) : a relation between two kinds of organisms in which one obtains food or other benefits from the other without damaging or benefiting it

com·men·su·ra·ble \kə-ˈmen(t)s-rə-bəl, -ˈmen(t)sh-; -ˈmen(t)-sə-, -shə-\ *adj* (1557) **1** : having a common measure; *specif* : divisible without remainder by a common unit **2** : COMMENSURATE 2 — **com·men·su·ra·bil·i·ty** \-ˌmen(t)s-rə-ˈbi-lə-tē, -ˌmen(t)sh-; -ˌmen(t)-sə-, -shə-\ *n* — **com·men·su·ra·bly** \-ˈmen(t)s-rə-blē, -ˈmen(t)sh-; -ˈmen(t)-sə-, -shə-\ *adv*

com·men·su·rate \kə-ˈmen(t)s-rət, -ˈmen(t)sh-; -ˈmen(t)-sə-, -shə-\ *adj* [LL *commensuratus,* fr. L *com-* + LL *mensuratus,* pp. of *mensurare* to measure, fr. L *mensura* measure — more at MEASURE] (1641) **1** : equal in measure or extent : COEXTENSIVE ‹lived a life ~ with the early years of the republic› **2** : corresponding in size, extent, amount, or degree : PROPORTIONATE ‹was given a job ~ with her abilities› **3** : COMMENSURABLE 1 — **com·men·su·rate·ly** *adv* — **com·men·su·ra·tion** \-ˌmen(t)-sə-ˈrā-shən, -shə-\ *n*

[1]**com·ment** \ˈkä-ˌment\ *n* [ME, fr. LL *commentum,* fr. L, invention, fr. neut. of *commentus,* pp. of *comminisci* to invent, fr. *com-* + *-minisci* (akin to *ment-, mens* mind) — more at MIND] (14c) **1** : COMMENTARY **2** : a note explaining, illustrating, or criticizing the meaning of a writing **3 a** : an observation or remark expressing an opinion or attitude ‹critical ~*s*› **b** : a judgment expressed indirectly ‹sees the film as a ~ on modern values›

[2]**comment** *vt* (15c) : to make a comment on ~ *vi* : to explain or interpret something by comment ‹~*ing* on recent developments›

com·men·tar·i·at \ˌkä-mən-ˈter-ē-at, -ē-ˌat\ *n* [*commentator* + *-ariat* (in *proletariat*)] (1993) : a group of powerful and influential commentators : PUNDITOCRACY

com·men·tary \ˈkä-mən-ˌter-ē, -ˌte-rē\ *n, pl* **-tar·ies** (15c) **1 a** : an explanatory treatise — usu. used in pl. **b** : a record of events usu. written by a participant — usu. used in pl. **2 a** : a systematic series of explanations or interpretations (as of a writing) **b** : COMMENT 2 **3 a** : something that serves for illustration or explanation ‹the dark, airless apartments and sunless factories . . . are a sad ~ upon our civilization —H. A. Overstreet› **b** : an expression of opinion

com·men·tate \ˈkä-mən-ˌtāt\ *vb* **-tat·ed; -tat·ing** [back-formation fr. *commentator*] *vt* (1794) : to give a commentary on ~ *vi* : to comment in a usu. expository or interpretive manner; *also* : to act as a commentator

com·men·ta·tor \-ˌtā-tər\ *n* (14c) : one who provides commentary: as **a** : one who reports and discusses news (as on television) **b** : a sportscaster who provides commentary during live events ‹a color ~›

[1]**com·merce** \ˈkä-(ˌ)mərs\ *n* [MF, fr. L *commercium,* fr. *com-* + *merc-, merx* merchandise] (1537) **1** : social intercourse : interchange of ideas, opinions, or sentiments **2** : the exchange or buying and selling of commodities on a large scale involving transportation from place to place **3** : SEXUAL INTERCOURSE ***syn*** see BUSINESS

[2]**com·merce** \ˈkä-(ˌ)mərs, kə-ˈmərs\ *vi* **com·merced; com·merc·ing** (1596) *archaic* : COMMUNE

[1]**com·mer·cial** \kə-ˈmər-shəl\ *adj* (1598) **1 a** (1) : occupied with or engaged in commerce or work intended for commerce ‹a ~ artist› (2) : of or relating to commerce ‹~ regulations› (3) : characteristic of commerce ‹~ weights› (4) : suitable, adequate, or prepared for commerce ‹found oil in ~ quantities› **b** (1) : being of an average or inferior quality ‹~ oxalic acid› ‹show-quality versus ~ cattle› (2) : producing artistic work of low standards for quick market success **2 a** : viewed with regard to profit ‹a ~ success› **b** : designed for a large market **3** : emphasizing skills and subjects useful in business ‹a ~ school› **4** : supported by advertisers ‹~ TV› — **com·mer·ci·al·i·ty** \kə-ˌmər-shē-ˈa-lə-tē\ *n* — **com·mer·cial·ly** \-ˈmər-sh(ə-)lē\ *adv*

[2]**commercial** *n* (1935) : an advertisement on radio or television

commercial bank *n* (1910) : a bank organized chiefly to handle the everyday financial transactions of businesses (as through demand deposit accounts and short-term commercial loans)

com·mer·cial·ise *Brit var of* COMMERCIALIZE

com·mer·cial·ism \kə-ˈmər-shə-ˌli-zəm\ *n* (1849) **1** : commercial spirit, institutions, or methods **2** : excessive emphasis on profit — **com·mer·cial·ist** \-ˈmər-sh(ə-)list\ *n* — **com·mer·cial·is·tic** \-ˌmər-shə-ˈlis-tik\ *adj*

com·mer·cial·ize \kə-ˈmər-shə-ˌlīz\ *vt* **-ized; -iz·ing** (1830) **1 a** : to manage on a business basis for profit **b** : to develop commerce in **2** : to exploit for profit ‹~ Christmas› **3** : to debase in quality for more profit — **com·mer·cial·i·za·tion** \-ˌmər-sh(ə-)lə-ˈzā-shən\ *n*

commercial paper *n* (1836) : short-term unsecured discounted paper usu. sold by one company to another for immediate cash needs

commercial traveler *n* (1807) : TRAVELING SALESMAN

com·mie \ˈkä-mē\ *n, often cap* [by shortening & alter.] (1940) : COMMUNIST

com·mi·na·tion \ˌkä-mə-ˈnā-shən\ *n* [ME, fr. MF or L; MF, fr. L *commination-, comminatio,* fr. *comminari* to threaten, fr. *com-* + *minari* to threaten — more at MOUNT] (15c) : DENUNCIATION — **com·mi·na·to·ry** \ˈkä-mə-nə-ˌtȯr-ē; kə-ˈmi-nə-, -ˈmī-\ *adj*

com·min·gle \kə-ˈmiŋ-gəl, kä-\ *vt* (1612) **1** : to blend thoroughly into a harmonious whole **2** : to combine (funds or properties) into a common fund or stock ~ *vi* : to become commingled ***syn*** see MIX

com·mi·nute \ˈkä-mə-ˌnüt, -ˌnyüt\ *vt* **-nut·ed; -nut·ing** [L *comminutus,* pp. of *comminuere,* fr. *com-* + *minuere* to lessen — more at MINOR] (1626) : to reduce to minute particles : PULVERIZE — **com·mi·nu·tion** \ˌkä-mə-ˈnü-shən, -ˈnyü-\ *n*

com·mis·er·ate \kə-ˈmi-zə-ˌrāt\ *vb* **-at·ed; -at·ing** [L *commiseratus,* pp. of *commiserari,* fr. *com-* + *miserari* to pity, fr. *miser* wretched] *vi* (1594) : to feel or express sympathy : CONDOLE ‹~*s* with them on their loss› ~ *vt* : to feel or express sorrow or compassion for — **com·mis·er·at·ing·ly** *adv* — **com·mis·er·a·tion** \-ˌmi-zə-ˈrā-shən\ *n* — **com·mis·er·a·tive** \-ˈmi-zə-ˌrā-tiv\ *adj*

com·mis·sar \ˈkä-mə-ˌsär\ *n* [Russ *komissar,* fr. G *Kommissar,* fr. ML *commissarius*] (1918) **1 a** : a Communist party official assigned to a military unit to teach party principles and policies and to ensure party loyalty **b** : one that attempts to control public opinion or its expression **2** : the head of a government department in the U.S.S.R. until 1946 — **com·mis·sar·i·al** \ˌkä-mə-ˈsär-ē-əl, -ˈser-\ *adj*

com·mis·sar·i·at \ˌkä-mə-ˈser-ē-ət, *esp for 3* -ˈsär-\ *n* [NL *commissariatus,* fr. ML *commissarius*] (1779) **1** : a system for supplying an army with food **2** : food supplies **3** [Russ *komissariat,* fr. G *Kommissariat,* fr. NL *commissariatus*] : a government department in the U.S.S.R. until 1946 **4** : a board of commissioners

com·mis·sary \ˈkä-mə-ˌser-ē, -ˌse-rē\ *n, pl* **-sar·ies** [ME *commissarie,* fr. AF, fr. ML *commissarius,* fr. L *commissus,* pp. of *committere*] (14c) **1** : one delegated by a superior to execute a duty or an office **2 a** : a store for equipment and provisions; *esp* : a supermarket for military personnel **b** : food supplies **c** : a lunchroom esp. in a motion-picture studio

[1]**com·mis·sion** \kə-ˈmi-shən\ *n* [ME, fr. AF, fr. L *commission-, commissio* act of bringing together, fr. *committere*] (14c) **1 a** : a formal written warrant granting the power to perform various acts or duties **b** : a certificate conferring military rank and authority; *also* : the rank and authority so conferred **2** : an authorization or command to act in a prescribed manner or to perform prescribed acts : CHARGE **3 a** : authority to act for, in behalf of, or in place of another **b** : a task or matter entrusted to one as an agent for another **4 a** : a group of persons directed to perform some duty **b** : a government agency having administrative, legislative, or judicial powers **c** : a city council having legislative and executive functions **5** : an act of committing something ‹~ of a crime› **6** : a fee paid to an agent or employee for transacting a piece of business or performing a service; *esp* : a percentage of the money received from a total paid to the agent responsible for the business **7** : an act of entrusting or giving authority — **in commission** *or* **into commission 1** : under the authority of commissioners **2** *of a ship* : ready for active service **3** : in use or in condition for use — **on commission** : with commission serving as partial or full pay

---

\ə\ **a**but \ᵊ\ kitten, F table \ər\ **fur**ther \a\ **a**sh \ā\ **a**ce \ä\ m**o**p, m**a**r \au̇\ **ou**t \ch\ **ch**in \e\ b**e**t \ē\ **ea**sy \g\ **g**o \i\ h**i**t \ī\ **i**ce \j\ **j**ob \ŋ\ si**ng** \ō\ g**o** \ȯ\ l**aw** \ȯi\ b**oy** \th\ **th**in \th\ **th**e \ü\ l**oo**t \u̇\ f**oo**t \y\ **y**et \zh\ vi**s**ion, beige \k, ⁿ, œ, ue, ʸ\ *see* Guide to Pronunciation

for work done — **out of commission** **1** : out of active service or use **2** : out of working order

[2]**commission** *vt* **-mis·sioned; -mis·sion·ing** \-ˈmi-sh(ə-)niŋ\ (ca. 1661) **1** : to furnish with a commission: as **a** : to confer a formal commission on ⟨was ~*ed* lieutenant⟩ **b** : to appoint or assign to a task or function ⟨was ~*ed* to do the biography⟩ **2** : to order to be made ⟨~*ed* a portrait⟩ **3** : to put (a ship) in commission

com·mis·sion·aire \kə-ˌmi-shə-ˈner\ *n* [F *commissionnaire,* fr. *commission*] (1641) *chiefly Brit* : a uniformed attendant

commissioned officer *n* (15c) : an officer of the armed forces holding by a commission a rank of second lieutenant or ensign or above

com·mis·sion·er \kə-ˈmi-sh(ə-)nər\ *n* (15c) : a person with a commission: as **a** : a member of a commission **b** : the representative of the governmental authority in a district, province, or other unit often having both judicial and administrative powers **c** : the officer in charge of a department or bureau of the public service **d** : the administrative head of a professional sport — **com·mis·sion·er·ship** \-ˌship\ *n*

commission merchant *n* (1796) : BROKER 1b

commission plan *n* (1919) : a method of municipal government under which a small elective commission exercises both executive and legislative powers and each commissioner directly administers one or more municipal departments

com·mis·sure \ˈkä-mə-ˌshu̇r\ *n* [ME, fr. MF or L; MF, fr. L *commissura* a joining, fr. *commissus,* pp.] (15c) **1** : a point or line of union or junction esp. between two anatomical parts (as adjacent heart valves) **2** : a connecting band of nerve tissue in the brain or spinal cord — **com·mis·sur·al** \ˌkä-mə-ˈshu̇r-əl\ *adj*

com·mit \kə-ˈmit\ *vb* **com·mit·ted; com·mit·ting** [ME *committen,* fr. AF *committer,* fr. L *committere* to connect, entrust, fr. *com-* + *mittere* to send] *vt* (14c) **1 a** : to put into charge or trust : ENTRUST **b** : to place in a prison or mental institution **c** : to consign or record for preservation ⟨~ it to memory⟩ **d** : to put into a place for disposal or safekeeping **e** : to refer (as a legislative bill) to a committee for consideration and report **2** : to carry into action deliberately : PERPETRATE ⟨~ a crime⟩ **3 a** : OBLIGATE, BIND ⟨a contract *committing* the company to complete the project on time⟩ **b** : to pledge or assign to some particular course or use ⟨~ all troops to the attack⟩ **c** : to reveal the views of ⟨refused to ~ himself on the issue⟩ ~ *vi* **1** *obs* : to perpetrate an offense **2** : to obligate or pledge oneself — **com·mit·ta·ble** \-ˈmi-tə-bəl\ *adj*

syn COMMIT, ENTRUST, CONFIDE, CONSIGN, RELEGATE mean to assign to a person or place for a definite purpose. COMMIT may express the general idea of delivering into another's charge or the special sense of transferring to a superior power or to a special place of custody ⟨*committed* the felon to prison⟩. ENTRUST implies committing with trust and confidence ⟨the president is *entrusted* with broad powers⟩. CONFIDE implies entrusting with great assurance or reliance ⟨*confided* complete control of my affairs to my attorney⟩. CONSIGN suggests removing from one's control with formality or finality ⟨*consigned* the damaging notes to the fire⟩. RELEGATE implies a consigning to a particular class or sphere often with a suggestion of getting rid of ⟨*relegated* to an obscure position in the company⟩.

com·mit·ment \kə-ˈmit-mənt\ *n* (1603) **1 a** : an act of committing to a charge or trust: as (1) : a consignment to a penal or mental institution (2) : an act of referring a matter to a legislative committee **b** : MITTIMUS **2 a** : an agreement or pledge to do something in the future; *esp* : an engagement to assume a financial obligation at a future date **b** : something pledged **c** : the state or an instance of being obligated or emotionally impelled ⟨a ~ to a cause⟩

com·mit·tal \kə-ˈmi-tᵊl\ *n* (1789) : COMMITMENT, CONSIGNMENT

com·mit·tee \kə-ˈmi-tē, *sense 1 also* ˌkä-mi-ˈtē\ *n* (15c) **1** *archaic* : a person to whom a charge or trust is committed **2 a** : a body of persons delegated to consider, investigate, take action on, or report on some matter; *esp* : a group of fellow legislators chosen by a legislative body to give consideration to legislative matters **b** : a self-constituted organization for the promotion of a common object

com·mit·tee·man \kə-ˈmi-tē-mən, -ˌman\ *n* (1654) **1** : a member of a committee **2** : a party leader of a ward or precinct

committee of the whole (1775) : the whole membership of a legislative house sitting as a committee and operating under informal rules

com·mit·tee·wom·an \-ˌwu̇-mən\ *n* (1853) **1** : a woman who is a member of a committee **2** : a woman who is a party leader of a ward or precinct

com·mix \kə-ˈmiks, kä-\ *vb* [back-formation fr. ME *comixt* blended, fr. L *commixtus,* pp. of *commiscēre* to mix together, fr. *com-* + *miscēre* to mix — more at MIX] *vt* (15c) : MINGLE, BLEND ~ *vi* : to become mingled or blended

com·mix·ture \-chər\ *n* [L *commixtura,* fr. *commixtus*] (1567) **1** : the act or process of mixing : the state of being mixed **2** : COMPOUND, MIXTURE

commo *abbr* commodore

com·mode \kə-ˈmōd\ *n* [F, fr. *commode,* adj., suitable, convenient, fr. L *commodus,* fr. *com-* + *modus* measure — more at METE] (ca. 1688) **1** : a woman's ornate cap popular in the late 17th and early 18th centuries **2 a** : a low chest of drawers **b** : a movable washstand with a cupboard underneath **c** : a boxlike structure holding a chamber pot under an open seat; *also* : CHAMBER POT **d** : TOILET 3b

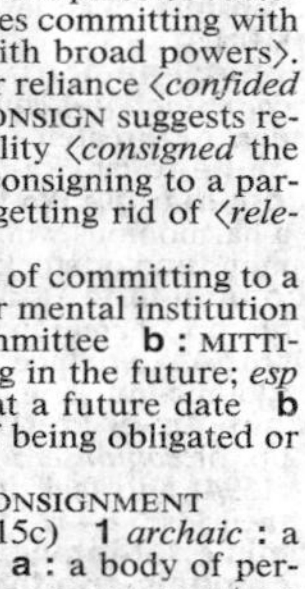
commode 1

com·mod·i·fy \kə-ˈmä-də-ˌfī\ *vt* **-fied; -fy·ing** (1982) : to turn (as an intrinsic value or a work of art) into a commodity — **com·mod·i·fi·ca·tion** \-ˌmä-də-fə-ˈkā-shən\ *n*

com·mo·di·ous \kə-ˈmō-dē-əs\ *adj* [ME, fertile, useful, modif. of ML *commodosus,* fr. L *commodum* convenience, fr. neut. of *commodus*] (15c) **1** : comfortably or conveniently spacious : ROOMY ⟨a ~ closet⟩ **2** *archaic* : HANDY, SERVICEABLE ***syn*** see SPACIOUS — **com·mo·di·ous·ly** *adv* — **com·mo·di·ous·ness** *n*

com·mod·i·tize \kə-ˈmä-də-ˌtīz\ *vt* **-tized; -tiz·ing** (1984) **1** : COMMODIFY; *specif* : to render (a good or service) widely available and interchangeable with one provided by another company **2** : to affect (as a brand or a market) by commoditizing goods or services ⟨fierce competition threatened to ~ prices⟩ — **com·mod·i·ti·za·tion** \kə-ˌmä-də-tə-ˈzā-shən\ *n*

com·mod·i·ty \kə-ˈmä-də-tē\ *n, pl* **-ties** [ME *commoditee,* fr. AF *commoditee,* fr. L *commoditat-, commoditas,* fr. *commodus*] (15c) **1** : an economic good: as **a** : a product of agriculture or mining **b** : an article of commerce esp. when delivered for shipment ⟨*commodities* futures⟩ **c** : a mass-produced unspecialized product ⟨~ chemicals⟩ ⟨~ memory chips⟩ **2 a** : something useful or valued ⟨that valuable ~ patience⟩; *also* : THING, ENTITY **b** : CONVENIENCE, ADVANTAGE **3** *obs* : QUANTITY, LOT **4** : a good or service whose wide availability typically leads to smaller profit margins and diminishes the importance of factors (as brand name) other than price **5** : one that is subject to ready exchange or exploitation within a market ⟨stars as individuals and as *commodities* of the film industry —*Film Quarterly*⟩

com·mo·dore \ˈkä-mə-ˌdȯr\ *n* [prob. modif. of D *commandeur* commander, fr. F, fr. OF *comandeor,* fr. *comander* to command] (1695) **1 a** : a captain in the navy in command of a squadron **b** : a commissioned officer in the navy formerly ranking above captain and below rear admiral and having an insignia of one star **2** : the ranking officer commanding a body of merchant ships **3** : the chief officer of a yacht club or boating association

[1]**com·mon** \ˈkä-mən\ *adj* [ME *commun,* fr. AF, fr. L *communis* — more at MEAN] (13c) **1 a** : of or relating to a community at large : PUBLIC ⟨work for the ~ good⟩ **b** : known to the community ⟨~ nuisances⟩ **2 a** : belonging to or shared by two or more individuals or things or by all members of a group ⟨a ~ friend⟩ ⟨buried in a ~ grave⟩ **b** : belonging equally to two or more mathematical entities ⟨triangles with a ~ base⟩ **c** : having two or more branches ⟨~ carotid artery⟩ **3 a** : occurring or appearing frequently : FAMILIAR ⟨a ~ sight⟩ **b** : of the best known or most frequently seen kind — used esp. of plants and animals ⟨the ~ housefly⟩ **c** : VERNACULAR 2 ⟨~ names⟩ **4 a** : WIDESPREAD, GENERAL ⟨~ knowledge⟩ **b** : characterized by a lack of privilege or special status ⟨~ people⟩ **c** : just satisfying accustomed criteria : ELEMENTARY ⟨~ decency⟩ **5 a** : falling below ordinary standards : SECOND-RATE **b** : lacking refinement : COARSE **6** : denoting nominal relations by a single linguistic form that in a more highly inflected language might be denoted by two or more different forms ⟨~ gender⟩ ⟨~ case⟩ **7** : of, relating to, or being common stock — **com·mon·ly** *adv* — **com·mon·ness** \-mən-nəs\ *n*

syn COMMON, ORDINARY, PLAIN, FAMILIAR, POPULAR, VULGAR mean generally met with and not in any way special, strange, or unusual. COMMON implies usual everyday quality or frequency of occurrence ⟨a *common* error⟩ ⟨lacked *common* honesty⟩ and may additionally suggest inferiority or coarseness ⟨*common* manners⟩. ORDINARY stresses conformance in quality or kind with the regular order of things ⟨an *ordinary* pleasant summer day⟩ ⟨a very *ordinary* sort of man⟩. PLAIN is likely to suggest homely simplicity ⟨*plain* hard-working people⟩. FAMILIAR stresses the fact of being generally known and easily recognized ⟨a *familiar* melody⟩. POPULAR applies to what is accepted by or prevalent among people in general sometimes in contrast to upper classes or special groups ⟨a writer of *popular* romances⟩. VULGAR, otherwise similar to POPULAR, is likely to carry derogatory connotations (as of inferiority or coarseness) ⟨souvenirs designed to appeal to the *vulgar* taste⟩.

[2]**common** *n* (14c) **1** *pl* : the common people **2** *pl but sing in constr* : a dining hall **3** *pl but sing or pl in constr, often cap* **a** : the political group or estate comprising the commoners **b** : the parliamentary representatives of the commoners **c** : HOUSE OF COMMONS **4** : the legal right of taking a profit in another's land in common with the owner or others **5** : a piece of land subject to common use: as **a** : undivided land used esp. for pasture **b** : a public open area in a municipality **6 a** : a religious service suitable for any of various festivals **b** : ORDINARY 2 **7** : COMMON STOCK — **in common** : shared together ⟨has a lot *in common* with his neighbors⟩

com·mon·age \ˈkä-mə-nij\ *n* (1649) **1** : community land **2** : COMMONALTY 1a(2)

com·mon·al·i·ty \ˌkä-mə-ˈna-lə-tē\ *n, pl* **-ties** [ME *communalite* commonwealth, alter. of *communalte*] (1543) **1** : the common people **2 a** : possession of common features or attributes : COMMONNESS **b** : a common feature or attribute

com·mon·al·ty \ˈkä-mə-nᵊl-tē\ *n, pl* **-ties** [ME *communalte,* fr. AF *comunalté,* fr. *comunal* communal] (14c) **1 a** (1) : the common people (2) : the political estate formed by the common people **b** : a usage or practice common to members of a group **2** : a general group or body

common carrier *n* (15c) : a business or agency that is available to the public for transportation of persons, goods, or messages

common cattle grub *n* (1947) : a cattle grub (*Hypoderma lineatum*) which is found throughout the U.S. and whose larva is particularly destructive to cattle

common cold *n* (1770) : an acute disease of the upper respiratory tract that is marked by inflammation of the mucous membranes of the nose, throat, eyes, and eustachian tubes and by a watery then purulent discharge and is caused by any of several viruses (as a rhinovirus or an adenovirus)

common denominator *n* (1594) **1** : a common multiple of the denominators of a number of fractions **2** : a common trait or theme

common difference *n* (ca. 1771) : the difference between two consecutive terms of an arithmetic progression

common divisor *n* (1674) : a number or expression that divides two or more numbers or expressions without remainder — called also *common factor*

com·mon·er \ˈkä-mə-nər\ *n* (14c) **1 a** : one of the common people **b** : one who is not of noble rank **2** : a student (as at Oxford) who pays for his own board

Common Era *n* (1846) : CHRISTIAN ERA

common fraction *n* (1823) : a fraction (as ½ or ¾) in which the numerator and denominator are both integers and are separated by a horizontal or slanted line — compare DECIMAL FRACTION

common ground *n* (1809) : a basis of mutual interest or agreement

com·mon–law \ˈkä-mən-ˌlȯ\ *adj* (1619) **1** : of, relating to, or based on the common law **2** : relating to or based on a common-law marriage

common law *n* (14c) : the body of law developed in England primarily from judicial decisions based on custom and precedent, unwritten in

statute or code, and constituting the basis of the English legal system and of the system in all of the U.S. except Louisiana
common–law marriage *n* (1888) **1** : a marriage recognized in some jurisdictions and based on the parties' agreement to consider themselves married and sometimes also on their cohabitation **2** : the cohabitation of a couple even when it does not constitute a legal marriage
common logarithm *n* (1849) : a logarithm whose base is 10
common market *n* (1893) : an economic association (as of nations) formed to remove trade barriers among its members
common measure *n* (1922) : a meter consisting chiefly of iambic lines of 7 accents each arranged in rhymed pairs usu. printed in 4-line stanzas — called also *common meter*
common multiple *n* (ca. 1823) : a multiple of each of two or more numbers or expressions ⟨90 is a *common multiple* of 6 and 10⟩
common noun *n* (1656) : a noun that may occur with limiting modifiers (as *a* or *an, some, every,* and *my*) and that designates any one of a class of beings or things
common or garden *adj* (ca. 1884) *chiefly Brit* : ORDINARY
[1]**com·mon·place** \ˈkä-mən-ˌplās\ *n* [trans. of L *locus communis* widely applicable argument, trans. of Gk *koinos topos*] (1561) **1** *archaic* : a striking passage entered in a commonplace book **2 a** : an obvious or trite comment : TRUISM **b** : something commonly found
[2]**commonplace** *adj* (1609) : commonly found or seen : ORDINARY, UNREMARKABLE ⟨a ~ occurrence⟩ ⟨the large mergers that had become ~⟩ — **com·mon·place·ness** *n*
commonplace book *n* (1578) : a book of memorabilia
common pleas *n pl* (15c) **1** *sing in constr* : COURT OF COMMON PLEAS **2 a** : actions over which the English crown did not exercise exclusive jurisdiction **b** : civil actions between English subjects
common ratio *n* (ca. 1771) : the ratio of each term of a geometric progression to the term preceding it
common room *n* (ca. 1670) **1** : a lounge available to all members of a residential community **2** : a room in a college for faculty use
common salt *n* (1585) : SALT 1a
common school *n* (1575) : a free public school
common sense *n* (1726) : sound and prudent judgment based on a simple perception of the situation or facts ***syn*** see SENSE — **com·mon·sense** \ˈkä-mən-ˈsen(t)s\ *adj* — **com·mon·sen·si·ble** \-ˈsen(t)-sə-bəl\ *adj* — **com·mon·sen·si·cal** \-ˈsen(t)-si-kəl\ *adj* — **com·mon·sen·si·cal·ly** \-si-k(ə-)lē\ *adv*
common situs picketing *n* (1965) : the picketing of an entire construction site by a trade union having a grievance with only a single subcontractor working there
common stock *n* (1784) : stock other than preferred stock
common time *n* (1662) : a musical meter marked by four beats per measure with the quarter note receiving a single beat
common touch *n* (1936) : the gift of appealing to or arousing the sympathetic interest of the common people
com·mon·weal \ˈkä-mən-ˌwēl\ *n* (14c) **1** *archaic* : COMMONWEALTH **2** : the general welfare
com·mon·wealth \-ˌwelth *also* -ˌweltth\ *n* (15c) **1** *archaic* : COMMONWEAL 2 **2** : a nation, state, or other political unit: as **a** : one founded on law and united by compact or tacit agreement of the people for the common good **b** : one in which supreme authority is vested in the people **c** : REPUBLIC **3** *cap* **a** : the English state from the death of Charles I in 1649 to the Restoration in 1660 **b** : PROTECTORATE 1b **4** : a state of the U.S. — used officially of Kentucky, Massachusetts, Pennsylvania, and Virginia **5** *cap* : a federal union of constituent states — used officially of Australia **6** *often cap* : an association of self-governing autonomous states more or less loosely associated in a common allegiance (as to the British crown) **7** *often cap* : a political unit having local autonomy but voluntarily united with the U.S. — used officially of Puerto Rico and of the Northern Mariana Islands
Commonwealth Day *n* (1958) : a holiday observed in parts of the Commonwealth of Nations formerly on May 24 as the anniversary of Queen Victoria's birthday and now on the second Monday in March
common year *n* (ca. 1751) : a calendar year containing no intercalary period
com·mo·tion \kə-ˈmō-shən\ *n* [ME, fr. AF *commocion,* fr. L *commotion-, commotio,* fr. *commovēre*] (15c) **1** : a condition of civil unrest or insurrection **2** : steady or recurrent motion **3** : mental excitement or confusion **4 a** : an agitated disturbance : TO-DO **b** : noisy confusion : AGITATION
com·move \kə-ˈmüv, kä-\ *vt* **com·moved; com·mov·ing** [ME *commoeven,* fr. AF *commoveir,* fr. L *commovēre,* fr. *com-* + *movēre* to move] (14c) **1** : to move violently : AGITATE **2** : to rouse intense feeling in : excite to passion
com·mu·nal \kə-ˈmyü-nᵊl, ˈkäm-yə-nᵊl\ *adj* [F, fr. LL *communalis,* fr. L *communis*] (1800) **1** : of or relating to one or more communes **2** : of or relating to a community **3 a** : characterized by collective ownership and use of property **b** : participated in, shared, or used in common by members of a group or community **4** : of, relating to, or based on racial or cultural groups — **com·mu·nal·ize** \kə-ˈmyü-nə-ˌlīz, ˈkäm-yə-\ *vt* — **com·mu·nal·ly** *adv*
com·mu·nal·ism \-nə-ˌli-zəm\ *n* (1871) **1** : social organization on a communal basis **2** : loyalty to a sociopolitical grouping based on religious or ethnic affiliation — **com·mu·nal·ist** \-nə-list\ *n or adj*
com·mu·nal·i·ty \ˌkäm-yu̇-ˈna-lə-tē\ *n, pl* **-ties** (1890) **1** : communal state or character **2** : a feeling of group solidarity
com·mu·nard \ˌkäm-yu̇-ˈnär(d)\ *n* [F] (1872) **1** *cap* : one who supported or participated in the Commune of Paris in 1871 **2** : a person who lives in a commune
[1]**com·mune** \kə-ˈmyün\ *vb* **com·muned; com·mun·ing** [ME, to share, receive Communion, fr. AF *communer, cummunier,* fr. LL *communicare,* fr. L] *vt* (15c) *obs* : TALK OVER, DISCUSS ⟨have more to ~ —Shak.⟩ ~ *vi* **1** : to receive Communion **2** : to communicate intimately ⟨~ with nature⟩
[2]**com·mune** \ˈkäm-ˌyün; kə-ˈmyün, kä-\ *n* [F, alter. of MF *comugne,* fr. ML *communia,* fr. L, neut. pl. of *communis*] (1673) **1** : the smallest administrative district of many countries esp. in Europe **2** : COMMONALTY 1a **3** : COMMUNITY: as **a** : a medieval usu. municipal corporation **b** (1) : MIR (2) : an often rural community organized on a communal basis

com·mu·ni·ca·ble \kə-ˈmyü-ni-kə-bəl\ *adj* (1534) **1** : capable of being communicated : TRANSMITTABLE ⟨~ diseases⟩ **2** : COMMUNICATIVE ⟨prove myself a gentleman, by being . . . virtuous and ~ —Izaac Walton⟩ — **com·mu·ni·ca·bil·i·ty** \-ˌmyü-ni-kə-ˈbi-lə-tē\ *n* — **com·mu·ni·ca·ble·ness** \-ˈmyü-ni-kə-bəl-nəs\ *n* — **com·mu·ni·ca·bly** \-blē\ *adv*
com·mu·ni·cant \-ˈmyü-ni-kənt\ *n* (1552) **1** : a church member entitled to receive Communion; *broadly* : a member of a fellowship **2** : one that communicates; *specif* : INFORMANT — **communicant** *adj*
com·mu·ni·cate \kə-ˈmyü-nə-ˌkāt\ *vb* **-cat·ed; -cat·ing** [L *communicatus,* pp. of *communicare* to impart, participate, fr. *communis* common — more at MEAN] *vt* (1526) **1** *archaic* : SHARE **2 a** : to convey knowledge of or information about : make known ⟨~ a story⟩ **b** : to reveal by clear signs ⟨his fear *communicated* itself to his friends⟩ **3** : to cause to pass from one to another ⟨some diseases are easily *communicated*⟩ ~ *vi* **1** : to receive Communion **2** : to transmit information, thought, or feeling so that it is satisfactorily received or understood ⟨two sides failing to ~ with each other⟩ **3** : to open into each other : CONNECT ⟨the rooms ~⟩ — **com·mu·ni·ca·tee** \-ˌmyü-ni-kə-ˈtē\ *n* — **com·mu·ni·ca·tor** \-ˈmyü-nə-ˌkā-tər\ *n*
com·mu·ni·ca·tion \kə-ˌmyü-nə-ˈkā-shən\ *n* (14c) **1** : an act or instance of transmitting **2 a** : information communicated **b** : a verbal or written message **3 a** : a process by which information is exchanged between individuals through a common system of symbols, signs, or behavior ⟨the function of pheromones in insect ~⟩; *also* : exchange of information **b** : personal rapport ⟨a lack of ~ between old and young persons⟩ **4** *pl* **a** : a system (as of telephones) for communicating **b** : a system of routes for moving troops, supplies, and vehicles **c** : personnel engaged in communicating **5** *pl but sing or pl in constr* **a** : a technique for expressing ideas effectively (as in speech) **b** : the technology of the transmission of information (as by print or telecommunication) — **com·mu·ni·ca·tion·al** \-shnəl, -shə-nᵊl\ *adj*
com·mu·ni·ca·tive \kə-ˈmyü-nə-ˌkā-tiv, -ni-kə-tiv\ *adj* (14c) **1** : tending to communicate : TALKATIVE **2** : of or relating to communication — **com·mu·ni·ca·tive·ly** *adv* — **com·mu·ni·ca·tive·ness** *n*
com·mu·ni·ca·to·ry \kə-ˈmyü-ni-kə-ˌtȯr-ē\ *adj* (1646) **1** : designed to communicate information ⟨~ letters⟩ **2** : COMMUNICATIVE 2
com·mu·nion \kə-ˈmyü-nyən\ *n* [ME, fr. L *communion-, communio* mutual participation, fr. *communis*] (14c) **1** : an act or instance of sharing **2 a** *cap* : a Christian sacrament in which consecrated bread and wine are consumed as memorials of Christ's death or as symbols for the realization of a spiritual union between Christ and communicant or as the body and blood of Christ **b** : the act of receiving Communion **c** *cap* : the part of a Communion service in which the sacrament is received **3** : intimate fellowship or rapport : COMMUNICATION **4** : a body of Christians having a common faith and discipline ⟨the Anglican ~⟩
com·mu·ni·qué \kə-ˈmyü-nə-ˌkā, -ˌmyü-nə-ˈ\ *n* [F, fr. pp. of *communiquer* to communicate, fr. L *communicare*] (1852) : BULLETIN 1
com·mu·nise *Brit var of* COMMUNIZE
com·mu·nism \ˈkäm-yə-ˌni-zəm, -yü-\ *n* [F *communisme,* fr. *commun* common] (1840) **1 a** : a theory advocating elimination of private property **b** : a system in which goods are owned in common and are available to all as needed **2** *cap* **a** : a doctrine based on revolutionary Marxian socialism and Marxism-Leninism that was the official ideology of the U.S.S.R. **b** : a totalitarian system of government in which a single authoritarian party controls state-owned means of production **c** : a final stage of society in Marxist theory in which the state has withered away and economic goods are distributed equitably **d** : communist systems collectively
com·mu·nist \-nist\ *n* (1840) **1** : an adherent or advocate of communism **2** *cap* : COMMUNARD **3 a** *cap* : a member of a Communist party or movement **b** *often cap* : an adherent or advocate of a Communist government, party, or movement **4** *often cap* : one held to engage in left-wing, subversive, or revolutionary activities — **communist** *adj, often cap* — **com·mu·nis·tic** \ˌkäm-yə-ˈnis-tik, -yü-\ *adj, often cap* — **com·mu·nis·ti·cal·ly** \-ti-k(ə-)lē\ *adv*
com·mu·ni·tar·i·an \kə-ˌmyü-nə-ˈter-ē-ən\ *adj* (ca. 1909) : of or relating to social organization in small cooperative partially collectivist communities — **communitarian** *n* — **com·mu·ni·tar·i·an·ism** \-ē-ə-ˌni-zəm\ *n*
com·mu·ni·ty \kə-ˈmyü-nə-tē\ *n, pl* **-ties** *often attrib* [ME *comunete,* fr. AF *communité,* fr. L *communitat-, communitas,* fr. *communis*] (14c) **1** : a unified body of individuals: as **a** : STATE, COMMONWEALTH **b** : the people with common interests living in a particular area; *broadly* : the area itself ⟨the problems of a large ~⟩ **c** : an interacting population of various kinds of individuals (as species) in a common location **d** : a group of people with a common characteristic or interest living together within a larger society ⟨a ~ of retired persons⟩ **e** : a group linked by a common policy **f** : a body of persons or nations having a common history or common social, economic, and political interests ⟨the international ~⟩ **g** : a body of persons of common and esp. professional interests scattered through a larger society ⟨the academic ~⟩ **2** : society at large **3 a** : joint ownership or participation ⟨~ of goods⟩ **b** : common character : LIKENESS ⟨~ of interests⟩ **c** : social activity : FELLOWSHIP **d** : a social state or condition
community antenna television *n* (1953) : CABLE TELEVISION
community center *n* (1915) : a building or group of buildings for a community's educational and recreational activities
community chest *n* (1919) : a general fund accumulated from individual subscriptions to defray demands on a community for charity and social welfare
community college *n* (1948) : a 2-year government-supported college that offers an associate degree
community property *n* (ca. 1925) : property held jointly by husband and wife

\ə\ **abut** \ᵊ\ kitten, F table \ər\ **further** \a\ **ash** \ā\ **ace** \ä\ **mop, mar** \au̇\ **out** \ch\ **chin** \e\ **bet** \ē\ **easy** \g\ **go** \i\ **hit** \ī\ **ice** \j\ **job** \ŋ\ **sing** \ō\ **go** \ȯ\ **law** \ȯi\ **boy** \th\ **thin** \t͟h\ **the** \ü\ **loot** \u̇\ **foot** \y\ **yet** \zh\ **vision, beige** \k̲, ⁿ, œ, ue, ʸ\ *see* Guide to Pronunciation

com·mu·nize \ˈkäm-yə-ˌnīz, -yü-\ *vt* **-nized; -niz·ing** [back-formation fr. *communization*] (1888) **1 a :** to make common **b :** to make into state-owned property **2 :** to subject to Communist principles of organization — **com·mu·ni·za·tion** \ˌkäm-yə-nə-ˈzā-shən, -yü-\ *n*
com·mu·tate \ˈkäm-yə-ˌtāt, -yü-\ *vt* **-tat·ed; -tat·ing** [back-formation fr. *commutation*] (1893) : to reverse every other half cycle of (an alternating current) so as to form a unidirectional current
com·mu·ta·tion \ˌkäm-yə-ˈtā-shən, -yü-\ *n* [ME *commutacion,* fr. AF, fr. L *commutation-, commutatio,* fr. *commutare*] (15c) **1 :** EXCHANGE, TRADE **2 :** REPLACEMENT; *specif* **:** a substitution of one form of payment or charge for another **3 :** a change of a legal penalty or punishment to a lesser one ⟨~ of a death sentence⟩ **4 :** an act or process of commuting **5 :** the action of commutating
commutation ticket *n* (1848) **:** a transportation ticket sold for a fixed number of trips over the same route during a limited period
com·mu·ta·tive \kə-ˈmyü-tə-tiv, ˈkäm-yə-ˌtā-tiv\ *adj* (1612) **1 :** of, relating to, or showing commutation **2 :** of, relating to, having, or being the property that a given mathematical operation and set have when the result obtained using any two elements of the set with the operation does not differ with the order in which the elements are used ⟨a ~ group⟩ ⟨addition of the positive integers is ~⟩
com·mu·ta·tiv·i·ty \kə-ˌmyü-tə-ˈti-və-tē, ˌkäm-yə-tə-\ *n* (1929) **:** the property of being commutative ⟨the ~ of a mathematical operation⟩
com·mu·ta·tor \ˈkäm-yə-ˌtā-tər, -yü-\ *n* (1880) **1 :** a series of bars or segments so connected to armature coils of a generator or motor that rotation of the armature will in conjunction with fixed brushes result in unidirectional current output in the case of a generator and in the reversal of the current into the coils in the case of a motor **2 :** an element of a mathematical group that when used to multiply the product of two given elements either on the right side or on the left side but not necessarily on both sides yields the product of the two given elements in reverse order
[1]**com·mute** \kə-ˈmyüt\ *vb* **com·mut·ed; com·mut·ing** [ME, fr. L *commutare* to change, exchange, fr. *com-* + *mutare* to change — more at MUTABLE] *vt* (15c) **1 a :** CHANGE, ALTER **b :** to give in exchange for another **:** EXCHANGE **2 :** to convert (as a payment) into another form **3 :** to change (a penalty) to another less severe ⟨~ a death sentence to life in prison⟩ **4 :** COMMUTATE ~ *vi* **1 :** MAKE UP, COMPENSATE **2 :** to pay in gross **3 :** to travel back and forth regularly (as between a suburb and a city) **4 :** to yield the same mathematical result regardless of order — used of two elements undergoing an operation or of two operations on elements — **com·mut·able** \-ˈmyü-tə-bəl\ *adj*
[2]**commute** *n* (1954) **1 :** an act or an instance of commuting **2 :** the distance covered in commuting ⟨a long ~⟩
com·mut·er \kə-ˈmyü-tər\ *n* (ca. 1859) **1 :** a person who commutes (as between a suburb and a city) **2 :** a small airline that carries passengers relatively short distances on a regular schedule
co·mo·no·mer \(ˌ)kō-ˈmä-nə-mər, -ˈmō-\ *n* [*co-* + *monomer*] (1945) **:** one of the constituents of a copolymer
co·mor·bid \(ˌ)kō-ˈmȯr-bəd\ *adj* [*co-* + *morbid*] (1981) **:** existing simultaneously with and usu. independently of another medical condition — **co·mor·bid·i·ty** \-ˌmȯr-ˈbi-də-tē\ *n*
[1]**comp** \ˈkämp\ *n* [short for *complimentary*] (1887) **:** a complimentary ticket; *broadly* **:** something provided free of charge
[2]**comp** \ˈkämp\ *vt* (1961) **:** to provide with something free ⟨a hotel ~*ing* celebrities for their rooms⟩; *also* **:** to provide free of charge ⟨their meals were ~*ed*⟩
[3]**comp** \ˈkəmp, ˈkämp\ *vi* [short for *accompany*] (1949) **:** to punctuate and support a jazz solo with irregularly spaced chords
[4]**comp** *abbr* **1** comparative; compare **2** compensation; compensatory **3** compiled; compiler **4** composition; compositor **5** compound **6** comprehensive **7** comptroller
[1]**com·pact** \kəm-ˈpakt, käm-ˈ, ˈkäm-ˌ\ *adj* [ME, firmly put together, fr. L *compactus,* fr. pp. of *compingere* to put together, fr. *com-* + *pangere* to fasten — more at PACT] (14c) **1 :** predominantly formed or filled **:** COMPOSED, MADE **2 a :** having a dense structure or parts or units closely packed or joined ⟨a ~ woolen⟩ ⟨~ bone⟩ **b :** not diffuse or verbose ⟨a ~ statement⟩ **c :** occupying a small volume by reason of efficient use of space ⟨a ~ camera⟩ ⟨a ~ formation of troops⟩ **d :** short-bodied, solid, and without excess flesh **3 :** being a topological space and esp. a metric space with the property that for any collection of open sets which contains it there is a subset of the collection with a finite number of elements which also contains it — **com·pact·ly** \-ˈpak(t)-lē, -ˌpak(t)-\ *adv* — **com·pact·ness** \-ˈpak(t)-nəs, -ˌpak(t)-\ *n*
[2]**compact** *vt* (15c) **1 :** to make up by connecting or combining **:** COMPOSE **2 a :** to knit or draw together **:** COMBINE **b :** to press together **:** COMPRESS ~ *vi* **:** to become compacted — **com·pact·ible** \-ˈpak-tə-bəl, -ˌpak-\ *adj* — **com·pac·tor** *also* **com·pact·er** \-ˈpak-tər, -ˌpak-\ *n*
[3]**com·pact** \ˈkäm-ˌpakt\ *n* (1601) **:** something that is compact or compacted: **a :** a small cosmetic case (as for compressed powder) **b :** an automobile smaller than an intermediate but larger than a subcompact
[4]**com·pact** \ˈkäm-ˌpakt\ *n* [L *compactum,* fr. neut. of *compactus,* pp. of *compacisci* to make an agreement, fr. *com-* + *pacisci* to contract — more at PACT] (1591) **:** an agreement or covenant between two or more parties
com·pact disc \ˈkäm-ˌpakt-\ *n* (1979) **:** CD
com·pac·tion \kəm-ˈpak-shən, käm-\ *n* (14c) **:** the act or process of compacting **:** the state of being compacted
com·pa·dre \kəm-ˈpä-drā, -drē\ *n* [Sp, lit., godfather, fr. ML *compater* — more at COMPEER] (1834) **:** a close friend **:** BUDDY
[1]**com·pan·ion** \kəm-ˈpan-yən\ *n, often attrib* [ME *compainoun,* fr. AF *cumpaing, cumpaignun,* fr. LL *companion-, companio,* fr. L *com-* + *panis* bread, food — more at FOOD] (13c) **1 :** one that accompanies another **:** COMRADE, ASSOCIATE; *also* **:** one that keeps company with another **2** *obs* **:** RASCAL **3 a :** one that is closely connected with something similar **b :** one employed to live with and serve another **4 :** a celestial body that appears close to another but that may or may not be associated with it in space
[2]**companion** *vt* (1622) **:** ACCOMPANY ~ *vi* **:** to keep company
[3]**companion** *n* [by folk etymology fr. D *kampanje* poop deck] (1762) **1 :** a hood covering at the top of a companionway **2 :** COMPANIONWAY
com·pan·ion·able \kəm-ˈpan-yə-nə-bəl\ *adj* (14c) **:** marked by, conducive to, or suggestive of companionship **:** SOCIABLE ⟨~ people⟩ ⟨~ laughter⟩ — **com·pan·ion·abil·i·ty** \-ˌpan-yə-nə-ˈbi-lə-tē\ *n* — **com·pan·ion·able·ness** *n* — **com·pan·ion·ably** \-ˈpan-yə-nə-blē\ *adv*
com·pan·ion·ate \kəm-ˈpan-yə-nət\ *adj* (1926) **:** relating to or having the manner of companions; *specif* **:** harmoniously or suitably accompanying
companion cell *n* (1887) **:** a living nucleated cell that is closely associated in origin, position, and prob. function with a cell making up part of a sieve tube of a vascular plant
companion piece *n* (1844) **:** a work (as of literature) that is associated with and complements another
com·pan·ion·ship \kəm-ˈpan-yən-ˌship\ *n* (1548) **:** the fellowship existing among companions **:** COMPANY
com·pan·ion·way \-yən-ˌwā\ *n* [[3]*companion*] (1822) **:** a ship's stairway from one deck to another
[1]**com·pa·ny** \ˈkəmp-nē, ˈkəm-pə-\ *n, pl* **-nies** *often attrib* [ME *companie,* fr. *cumpaignie,* fr. *cumpaing* companion — more at COMPANION] (13c) **1 a :** association with another **:** FELLOWSHIP ⟨enjoy a person's ~⟩ **b :** COMPANIONS, ASSOCIATES ⟨know a person by the ~ she keeps⟩ **c :** VISITORS, GUESTS ⟨having ~ for dinner⟩ **2 a :** a group of persons or things ⟨a ~ of horsemen⟩ **b :** a body of soldiers; *esp* **:** a unit (as of infantry) consisting usu. of a headquarters and two or more platoons **c :** an organization of performing artists **d :** the officers and crew of a ship **e :** a firefighting unit **3 a :** a chartered commercial organization or medieval trade guild **b :** an association of persons for carrying on a commercial or industrial enterprise **c :** those members of a partnership firm whose names do not appear in the firm name ⟨John Doe and *Company*⟩
[2]**company** *vb* **-nied; -ny·ing** *vt* (14c) **:** ACCOMPANY ⟨may . . . fair winds ~ your safe return —John Masefield⟩ ~ *vi* **:** ASSOCIATE
company man *n* (ca. 1921) **:** a worker who acquiesces in company policy without complaint
company officer *n* (1832) **:** a commissioned officer in the army, air force, or marine corps of the rank of captain, first lieutenant, or second lieutenant — called also *company grade officer*; compare FIELD OFFICER, GENERAL OFFICER
company town *n* (1927) **:** a community that is dependent on one firm for all or most of the necessary services or functions of town life (as employment, housing, and stores)
company union *n* (1917) **:** an unaffiliated labor union of the employees of a single firm; *esp* **:** one dominated by the employer
com·pa·ra·bil·i·ty \ˌkäm-p(ə-)rə-ˈbi-lə-tē *also* kəm-ˌpa-rə-, -ˌper-ə-\ *n* (1843) **:** the quality or state of being comparable
com·pa·ra·ble \ˈkäm-p(ə-)rə-bəl *also* kəm-ˈpa-rə-bəl, -ˈper-ə-\ *adj* (15c) **1 :** capable of or suitable for comparison **2 :** SIMILAR, LIKE ⟨fabrics of ~ quality⟩ — **com·pa·ra·ble·ness** *n* — **com·pa·ra·bly** \-blē\ *adv*
comparable worth *n* (1983) **:** the concept that women and men should receive equal pay for jobs calling for comparable skill and responsibility
com·par·a·tist \kəm-ˈper-ə-tist, -ˈpa-rə-\ *n* [*comparative* + *-ist*] (1933) **:** one that uses a comparative method (as in the study of literature)
[1]**com·par·a·tive** \-tiv\ *adj* (15c) **1 :** of, relating to, or constituting the degree of comparison in a language that denotes increase in the quality, quantity, or relation expressed by an adjective or adverb **2 :** considered as if in comparison to something else as a standard not quite attained **:** RELATIVE ⟨a ~ stranger⟩ **3 :** characterized by systematic comparison esp. of likenesses and dissimilarities ⟨~ anatomy⟩ — **com·par·a·tive·ly** *adv* — **com·par·a·tive·ness** *n*
[2]**comparative** *n* (15c) **1 a :** one that compares with another esp. on equal footing **:** RIVAL **b :** one that makes witty or mocking comparisons **2 :** the comparative degree or form in a language
com·par·a·tiv·ist \-ti-vist\ *n* (1887) **:** COMPARATIST
com·par·a·tor \-tər\ *n* (1883) **:** a device for comparing something with a similar thing or with a standard measure
[1]**com·pare** \kəm-ˈper\ *vb* **com·pared; com·par·ing** [ME, fr. AF *comparer,* fr. L *comparare* to couple, compare, fr. *compar* like, fr. *com-* + *par* equal] *vt* (14c) **1 :** to represent as similar **:** LIKEN ⟨shall I ~ thee to a summer's day? —Shak.⟩ **2 a :** to examine the character or qualities of esp. in order to discover resemblances or differences ⟨~ your responses with the answers⟩ **b :** to view in relation to ⟨tall *compared* to me⟩ ⟨easy *compared* with the last test⟩ **3 :** to inflect or modify (an adjective or adverb) according to the degrees of comparison ~ *vi* **1 :** to bear being compared ⟨the two don't even begin to ~⟩ **2 :** to make comparisons **3 :** to be equal or alike ⟨nothing ~*s* to you⟩
syn COMPARE, CONTRAST, COLLATE mean to set side by side in order to show differences and likenesses. COMPARE implies an aim of showing relative values or excellences by bringing out characteristic qualities whether similar or divergent ⟨*compared* the convention facilities of the two cities⟩. CONTRAST implies an emphasis on differences ⟨*contrasted* the computerized system with the old filing cards⟩. COLLATE implies minute and critical inspection in order to note points of agreement or divergence ⟨data from districts around the country will be *collated*⟩.
[2]**compare** *n* (1589) **:** the possibility of comparing ⟨beauty beyond ~⟩; *also* **:** something with which to be compared ⟨a city without ~⟩
com·par·i·son \kəm-ˈper-ə-sən, -ˈpa-rə-\ *n* [ME, fr. AF *comparison,* fr. L *comparation-, comparatio,* fr. *comparare*] (14c) **1 :** the act or process of comparing: as **a :** the representing of one thing or person as similar to or like another **b :** an examination of two or more items to establish similarities and dissimilarities ⟨his faults seem minor by ~⟩ **2 :** identity of features **:** SIMILARITY ⟨several points of ~ between the two⟩ **3 :** the modification of an adjective or adverb to denote different levels of quality, quantity, or relation
comparison shop *vi* (1970) **:** to compare prices (as of competing brands) in order to find the best value — **comparison shopper** *n*
[1]**com·part·ment** \kəm-ˈpärt-mənt\ *n* [MF *compartiment,* fr. It *compartimento,* fr. *compartire* to mark out in parts, fr. LL *compartiri* to share out, fr. L *com-* + *partiri* to share, fr. *part-, pars* part, share] (ca. 1578) **1 :** a separate division or section **2 :** one of the parts into which an enclosed space is divided — **com·part·men·tal** \kəm-ˌpärt-ˈmen-tᵊl, ˌkäm-\ *adj*
[2]**com·part·ment** \-ˌment, -mənt\ *vt* (1918) **:** COMPARTMENTALIZE
com·part·men·tal·ise *Brit var of* COMPARTMENTALIZE

com·part·men·tal·ize \kəm-ˌpärt-ˈmen-tə-ˌlīz, ˌkäm-\ *vt* **-ized; -iz·ing** (1925) **:** to separate into isolated compartments or categories — **com·part·men·tal·i·za·tion** \-ˌmen-tə-lə-ˈzā-shən\ *n*

com·part·men·ta·tion \kəm-ˌpärt-mən-ˈtā-shən, -ˌmen-\ *n* (1926) **:** division into separate sections or units

com·pas \kōm-ˈpä\ *n* [Haitian Creole *konpa,* lit., beat, rhythm, modif. of Sp *compás* beat, measure] (1985) **:** a popular music of Haiti that combines Cuban and African rhythms

[1]**com·pass** \ˈkəm-pəs *also* ˈkäm-\ *vt* [ME, fr. AF *cumpasser* to measure, fr. VL **compassare* to pace off, fr. L *com-* + *passus* pace] (14c) **1 :** to devise or contrive often with craft or skill **:** PLOT ⟨persons . . . who have ~*ed* my destruction —Charles Dickens⟩ **2 :** ENCOMPASS **3 a :** BRING ABOUT, ACHIEVE **b :** to get into one's possession or power **:** OBTAIN **4 :** COMPREHEND — **com·pass·able** \-pə-sə-bəl\ *adj*

[2]**compass** *n* (14c) **1 a :** BOUNDARY, CIRCUMFERENCE ⟨within the ~ of the city walls⟩ **b :** a circumscribed space ⟨within the narrow ~ of 21 pages —V. L. Parrington⟩ **c :** RANGE, SCOPE ⟨the ~ of my voice⟩ **2 :** a curved or roundabout course ⟨a ~ of seven days' journey —2 Kings 3:9(AV)⟩ **3 a :** a device for determining directions by means of a magnetic needle or group of needles turning freely on a pivot and pointing to the magnetic north **b :** any of various nonmagnetic devices that indicate direction **c :** an instrument for describing circles or transferring measurements that consists of two pointed branches joined at the top by a pivot — usu. used in pl.; called also *pair of compasses* **4 :** DIRECTION 6c ⟨his moral ~⟩ ***syn*** see RANGE

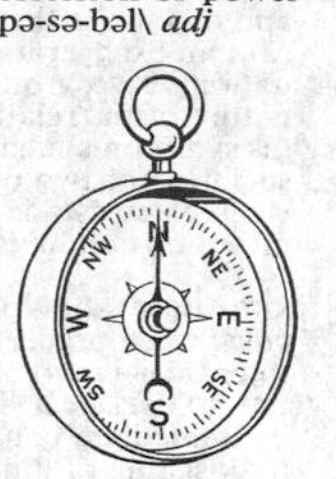

compass 3a

[3]**compass** *adj* (1523) **:** forming a curve **:** CURVED ⟨a ~ timber⟩

compass card *n* (1789) **:** the circular card attached to the needles of a mariner's compass on which are marked the 360° of the circle and 32 equidistant points

com·pas·sion \kəm-ˈpa-shən\ *n* [ME, fr. AF or LL; AF, fr. LL *compassion-, compassio,* fr. *compati* to sympathize, fr. L *com-* + *pati* to bear, suffer — more at PATIENT] (14c) **:** sympathetic consciousness of others' distress together with a desire to alleviate it ***syn*** see PITY — **com·pas·sion·less** \-ləs\ *adj*

[1]**com·pas·sion·ate** \kəm-ˈpa-sh(ə-)nət\ *adj* (1579) **1 :** having or showing compassion **:** SYMPATHETIC ⟨a ~ friend⟩ ⟨a ~ smile⟩ **2 :** granted because of unusual distressing circumstances affecting an individual — used of some military privileges (as leave) — **com·pas·sion·ate·ly** *adv* — **com·pas·sion·ate·ness** *n*

[2]**com·pas·sion·ate** \-ˈpa-shə-ˌnāt\ *vt* **-at·ed; -at·ing** (1592) **:** PITY

compass plant *n* (1848) **:** a yellow-flowered composite plant (*Silphium laciniatum*) that has large pinnatifid leaves in which the leaf edges typically align in a northerly and southerly direction and that occurs esp. in prairies and along roadsides of the central U.S.

compass rose *n* (ca. 1891) **:** a circle graduated to degrees or quarters and printed on a chart to show direction

com·pat·i·ble \kəm-ˈpa-tə-bəl\ *adj* [ME, fr. ML *compatibilis,* lit., sympathetic, fr. LL *compati*] (15c) **1 :** capable of existing together in harmony ⟨~ theories⟩ ⟨~ people⟩ **2 :** capable of cross-fertilizing freely or uniting vegetatively **3 :** capable of forming a homogeneous mixture that neither separates nor is altered by chemical interaction **4 :** capable of being used in transfusion or grafting without immunological reaction (as agglutination or tissue rejection) **5 :** designed to work with another device or system without modification; *esp* **:** being a computer designed to operate in the same manner and use the same software as another computer — **com·pat·i·bil·i·ty** \-ˌpa-tə-ˈbi-lə-tē\ *n* — **compatible** *n* — **com·pat·i·ble·ness** \-ˈpa-tə-bəl-nəs\ *n* — **com·pat·i·bly** \-blē\ *adv*

com·pa·tri·ot \kəm-ˈpā-trē-ət, käm-, -trē-ˌät, *chiefly Brit* -ˈpa-\ *n* [F *compatriote,* fr. LL *compatriota,* fr. L *com-* + LL *patriota* fellow countryman — more at PATRIOT] (1611) **1 :** a person born, residing, or holding citizenship in the same country as another **2 :** COMPANION, COLLEAGUE ⟨her ~*s* in academia⟩ — **com·pa·tri·ot·ic** \kəm-ˌpā-trē-ˈä-tik, ˌkäm-, *chiefly Brit* -ˌpa-\ *adj*

compd *abbr* compound

[1]**com·peer** \ˈkäm-ˌpir, käm-ˈ, kəm-ˈ\ *n* [ME, fr. AF *cumpere,* lit., godfather, fr. ML *compater,* fr. L *com-* + *pater* father — more at FATHER] (13c) **:** COMPANION

[2]**compeer** *n* [ME *comper,* fr. AF, fr. L *compar,* fr. *compar,* adj., like — more at COMPARE] (15c) **:** EQUAL, PEER — **compeer** *vt, obs*

com·pel \kəm-ˈpel\ *vt* **com·pelled; com·pel·ling** [ME *compellen,* fr. AF *compeller,* fr. L *compellere,* fr. *com-* + *pellere* to drive — more at FELT] (14c) **1 :** to drive or urge forcefully or irresistibly ⟨hunger *compelled* him to eat⟩ **2 :** to cause to do or occur by overwhelming pressure ⟨public opinion *compelled* her to sign the bill⟩ **3** *archaic* **:** to drive together ***syn*** see FORCE — **com·pel·la·ble** \-ˈpe-lə-bəl\ *adj*

com·pel·la·tion \ˌkäm-pə-ˈlā-shən, -ˌpe-\ *n* [L *compellation-, compellatio,* fr. *compellare* to address, fr. *com-* + *-pellare* (as in *appellare* to accost, appeal to)] (1603) **1 :** an act or action of addressing someone **2 :** APPELLATION 1

com·pel·ling \kəm-ˈpe-liŋ\ *adj* (1606) **:** that compels: as **a :** FORCEFUL ⟨a ~ personality⟩ **b :** demanding attention ⟨for ~ reasons⟩ **c :** CONVINCING ⟨no ~ evidence⟩ — **com·pel·ling·ly** *adv*

com·pend \ˈkäm-ˌpend\ *n* [ML *compendium*] (1596) **:** COMPENDIUM

com·pen·di·ous \kəm-ˈpen-dē-əs\ *adj* (14c) **:** marked by brief expression of a comprehensive matter **:** concise and comprehensive ⟨a ~ summary⟩; *also* **:** COMPREHENSIVE ⟨her ~ knowledge of the subject⟩ ***syn*** see CONCISE — **com·pen·di·ous·ly** *adv* — **com·pen·di·ous·ness** *n*

com·pen·di·um \kəm-ˈpen-dē-əm\ *n, pl* **-di·ums** *or* **-dia** \-dē-ə\ [ML, fr. L, saving, shortcut, fr. *compendere* to weigh together, fr. *com-* + *pendere* to weigh — more at PENDANT] (1589) **1 :** a brief summary of a larger work or of a field of knowledge **:** ABSTRACT **2 a :** a list of a number of items **b :** COLLECTION, COMPILATION

com·pen·sa·ble \kəm-ˈpen(t)-sə-bəl\ *adj* (1661) **:** that is to be or can be compensated ⟨a ~ job-related injury⟩ — **com·pen·sa·bil·i·ty** \kəm-ˌpen(t)-sə-ˈbi-lə-tē, ˌkäm-\ *n*

com·pen·sate \ˈkäm-pən-ˌsāt, -ˌpen-\ *vb* **-sat·ed; -sat·ing** [L *compensatus,* pp. of *compensare,* freq. of *compendere*] *vt* (1646) **1 :** to be equivalent to **:** COUNTERBALANCE **2 :** to make an appropriate and usu. counterbalancing payment to ⟨~ the victims for their loss⟩ **3 a :** to provide with means of counteracting variation **b :** to neutralize the effect of (variations) ~ *vi* **1 :** to supply an equivalent — used with *for* **2 :** to offset an error, defect, or undesired effect ⟨his enthusiasm ~*s* for his lack of skill⟩ **3 :** to undergo or engage in psychological or physiological compensation ***syn*** see PAY — **com·pen·sa·tive** \ˈkäm-pən-ˌsā-tiv, -ˌpen-; kəm-ˈpen(t)-sə-\ *adj* — **com·pen·sa·tor** \ˈkäm-pən-ˌsā-tər, -ˌpen-\ *n* — **com·pen·sa·to·ry** \kəm-ˈpen(t)-sə-ˌtȯr-ē\ *adj*

com·pen·sa·tion \ˌkäm-pən-ˈsā-shən, -ˌpen-\ *n* (14c) **1 a :** the act of compensating **:** the state of being compensated **b :** correction of an organic defect or loss by hypertrophy or by increased functioning of another organ or unimpaired parts of the same organ **c :** a psychological mechanism by which feelings of inferiority, frustration, or failure in one field are counterbalanced by achievement in another **2 a** (1) **:** something that constitutes an equivalent or recompense ⟨age has its ~*s*⟩ (2) **:** payment to unemployed or injured workers or their dependents **b :** PAYMENT, REMUNERATION ⟨working without ~⟩ — **com·pen·sa·tion·al** \-shnəl, -shə-nᵊl\ *adj*

compensatory education *n* (1965) **:** educational programs intended to make up for experiences (as cultural) lacked by disadvantaged children

[1]**com·pere** *or* **com·père** \ˈkäm-ˌper\ *n* [F *compère,* lit., godfather — more at COMPEER] (1914) *chiefly Brit* **:** the master of ceremonies of an entertainment (as a television program)

[2]**compere** *or* **compère** *vb* **com·pered** *or* **com·pèred; com·per·ing** *or* **com·pèr·ing** *vt* (1933) *chiefly Brit* **:** to act as compere for ~ *vi, chiefly Brit* **:** to act as a compere

com·pete \kəm-ˈpēt\ *vi* **com·pet·ed; com·pet·ing** [LL *competere* to seek together, fr. L, to come together, agree, be suitable, fr. *com-* + *petere* to go to, seek — more at FEATHER] (1620) **:** to strive consciously or unconsciously for an objective (as position, profit, or a prize) **:** be in a state of rivalry ⟨*competing* teams⟩ ⟨companies *competing* for customers⟩

com·pe·tence \ˈkäm-pə-tən(t)s\ *n* (1605) **1 :** a sufficiency of means for the necessities and conveniences of life ⟨provided his family with a comfortable ~ —Rex Ingamells⟩ **2 :** the quality or state of being competent: as **a :** the properties of an embryonic field that enable it to respond in a characteristic manner to an organizer **b :** readiness of bacteria to undergo genetic transformation **3 :** the knowledge that enables a person to speak and understand a language — compare PERFORMANCE 6

com·pe·ten·cy \-pə-tən(t)-sē\ *n, pl* **-cies** (1596) **:** COMPETENCE

com·pe·tent \ˈkäm-pə-tənt\ *adj* [ME, suitable, fr. AF & L; AF, fr. L *competent-, competens,* fr. prp. of *competere*] (15c) **1 :** proper or rightly pertinent **2 :** having requisite or adequate ability or qualities **:** FIT ⟨a ~ teacher⟩ ⟨a ~ piece of work⟩ **3 :** legally qualified or adequate ⟨a ~ witness⟩ **4 :** having the capacity to function or develop in a particular way; *specif* **:** having the capacity to respond (as by producing an antibody) to an antigenic determinant ⟨immunologically ~ cells⟩ ***syn*** see SUFFICIENT — **com·pe·tent·ly** *adv*

com·pe·ti·tion \ˌkäm-pə-ˈti-shən\ *n* [LL *competition-, competitio,* fr. L *competere*] (1579) **1 :** the act or process of competing **:** RIVALRY: as **a :** the effort of two or more parties acting independently to secure the business of a third party by offering the most favorable terms **b :** active demand by two or more organisms or kinds of organisms for some environmental resource in short supply **2 :** a contest between rivals; *also* **:** one's competitors ⟨faced tough ~⟩

com·pet·i·tive \kəm-ˈpe-tə-tiv\ *adj* (1829) **1 :** relating to, characterized by, or based on competition ⟨~ sports⟩ **2 :** inclined, desiring, or suited to compete ⟨a ~ personality⟩ ⟨salary benefits must be ~ —M. S. Eisenhower⟩ **3 :** depending for effectiveness on the relative concentration of two or more substances ⟨~ inhibition of an enzyme⟩ — **com·pet·i·tive·ly** *adv* — **com·pet·i·tive·ness** *n*

com·pet·i·tor \kəm-ˈpe-tə-tər\ *n* (1534) **:** one that competes: as **a :** RIVAL **b :** one selling or buying goods or services in the same market as another **c :** an organism that lives in competition with another

com·pi·la·tion \ˌkäm-pə-ˈlā-shən *also* -ˌpī-\ *n* (15c) **1 :** the act or process of compiling **2 :** something compiled ⟨a ~ of hit songs⟩

com·pile \kəm-ˈpī(-ə)l\ *vt* **com·piled; com·pil·ing** [ME, fr. AF *compiler,* fr. L *compilare* to plunder] (14c) **1 :** to compose out of materials from other documents **2 :** to collect and edit into a volume **3 :** to build up gradually ⟨*compiled* a record of four wins and two losses⟩ **4 :** to run (as a program) through a compiler

com·pil·er \kəm-ˈpī-lər\ *n* (14c) **1 :** one that compiles **2 :** a computer program that translates an entire set of instructions written in a higher-level symbolic language (as C) into machine language before the instructions can be executed

com·pla·cence \kəm-ˈplā-sᵊn(t)s\ *n* (15c) **1 :** calm or secure satisfaction with oneself or one's lot **:** SELF-SATISFACTION **2** *obs* **:** COMPLAISANCE **3 :** UNCONCERN

com·pla·cen·cy \-sᵊn(t)-sē\ *n, pl* **-cies** (1650) **1 :** self-satisfaction esp. when accompanied by unawareness of actual dangers or deficiencies **2 :** an instance of complacency

com·pla·cent \kəm-ˈplā-sᵊnt\ *adj* [L *complacent-, complacens,* prp. of *complacēre* to please greatly, fr. *com-* + *placēre* to please — more at PLEASE] (1760) **1 :** marked by complacency **:** SELF-SATISFIED ⟨a ~ smile⟩ **2 :** COMPLAISANT 1 **3 :** UNCONCERNED — **com·pla·cent·ly** *adv*

com·plain \kəm-ˈplān\ *vi* [ME *compleynen,* fr. AF *compleindre,* fr. VL **complangere,* fr. L *com-* + *plangere* to lament — more at PLAINT] (14c) **1 :** to express grief, pain, or discontent ⟨~*ing* about the weather⟩ **2 :** to make a formal accusation or charge — **com·plain·er** *n* — **com·plain·ing·ly** \-ˈplā-niŋ-lē\ *adv*

com·plain·ant \kəm-ˈplā-nənt\ *n* (15c) **1 :** the party who makes the complaint in a legal action or proceeding **2 :** one who complains

com·plaint \kəm-ˈplānt\ *n* [ME *compleynte,* fr. AF *compleint,* fr. *compleindre*] (14c) **1 :** expression of grief, pain, or dissatisfaction **2 a :** something that is the cause or subject of protest or outcry **b :** a bodily ailment or disease **3 :** a formal allegation against a party

com·plai·sance \kəm-ˈplā-sᵊn(t)s, -zᵊn(t)s; ˌkäm-plā-ˈzan(t)s, -plə-, -ˈzän(t)s\ *n* (1651) **:** disposition to please or comply **:** AFFABILITY

com·plai·sant \-sᵊnt, -zᵊnt, -ˈzant, -ˈzänt\ *adj* [F, fr. MF, fr. prp. of *complaire* to gratify, acquiesce, fr. L *complacēre*] (1638) **1 :** marked by an inclination to please or oblige **2 :** tending to consent to others' wishes ***syn*** see AMIABLE — **com·plai·sant·ly** *adv*

com·pleat \kəm-ˈplēt\ *adj* [archaic variant of *complete* in *The Compleat Angler* (1653) by Izaak Walton] (1526) **:** having all necessary or desired elements or skills **:** COMPLETE; *also* **:** CLASSIC, QUINTESSENTIAL

com·plect·ed \kəm-ˈplek-təd\ *adj* [irreg. fr. *complexion*] (1785) **:** having a specified facial complexion ⟨a tall, thin man, fairly dark ~ —E. J. Kahn⟩

usage Not an error, nor a dialectal term, nor nonstandard—all of which it has been labeled—*complected* still manages to raise hackles. It is an Americanism, apparently nonexistent in British English. Its currency in American English is attested as early as 1806 (by Meriwether Lewis) and it appears in the works of such notable American writers as Mark Twain, O. Henry, James Whitcomb Riley, and William Faulkner. The synonym *complexioned,* recommended by handbooks, appears now to be somewhat more common than *complected* in both literary and journalistic use.

[1]**com·ple·ment** \ˈkäm-plə-mənt\ *n* [ME, fr. L *complementum,* fr. *complēre* to fill up, complete, fr. *com-* + *plēre* to fill — more at FULL] (14c) **1 a :** something that fills up, completes, or makes perfect **b :** the quantity, number, or assortment required to make a thing complete ⟨the usual ~ of eyes and ears —Francis Parkman⟩; *esp* **:** the whole force or personnel of a ship **c :** one of two mutually completing parts **:** COUNTERPART **2 a :** the angle or arc that when added to a given angle or arc equals a right angle in measure **b :** the set of all elements that do not belong to a given set and are contained in a particular mathematical set containing the given set **c :** a number that when added to another number of the same sign yields zero if the significant digit farthest to the left is discarded — used esp. in assembly language programming **3 :** the musical interval required with a given interval to complete the octave **4 :** an added word or expression by which a predication is made complete (as *president* in "they elected him president" and *beautiful* in "he thought her beautiful") **5 :** the thermolabile group of proteins in normal blood serum and plasma that in combination with antibodies causes the destruction esp. of particulate antigens (as bacteria and foreign blood corpuscles)

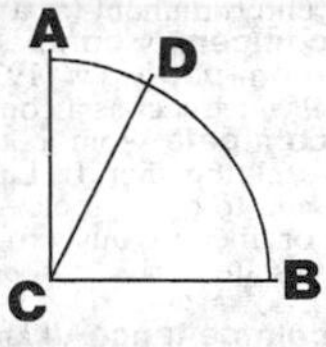

complement 2a: *ACB* right angle, *ACD* complement of *DCB* (and vice versa), *AD* complement of *DB* (and vice versa)

[2]**com·ple·ment** \-ˌment\ *vi* (1602) *obs* **:** to exchange formal courtesies ~ *vt* **1 :** to be complementary to ⟨the illustrations ~ the text⟩ **2** *obs* **:** COMPLIMENT

com·ple·men·tal \ˌkäm-plə-ˈmen-tᵊl\ *adj* (1597) **1 :** relating to or being a complement **2** *obs* **:** CEREMONIOUS, COMPLIMENTARY

com·ple·men·tar·i·ty \ˌkäm-plə-(ˌ)men-ˈter-ə-tē, -mən-, -ˈta-rə-\ *n* (1911) **1 :** the quality or state of being complementary **2 :** the complementary relationship of theories explaining the nature of light or other quantized radiation in terms of both electromagnetic waves and particles

com·ple·men·ta·ry \ˌkäm-plə-ˈmen-t(ə-)rē\ *adj* (1829) **1 :** relating to or constituting one of a pair of contrasting colors that produce a neutral color when combined in suitable proportions **2 :** serving to fill out or complete **3 :** mutually supplying each other's lack **4 :** being complements of each other ⟨~ acute angles⟩ **5 :** characterized by the capacity for precise pairing of purine and pyrimidine bases between strands of DNA and sometimes RNA such that the structure of one strand determines the other — **com·ple·men·ta·ri·ly** \-ˈmen-t(ə-)rə-lē, -(ˌ)men-ˈter-ə-lē, -ˈta-rə-\ *adv* — **com·ple·men·ta·ri·ness** \-ˈmen-t(ə-)rē-nəs\ *n* — **complementary** *n*

complementary medicine *n* (1982) **:** any of the practices (as acupuncture) of alternative medicine accepted and utilized by mainstream medical practitioners; *also* **:** ALTERNATIVE MEDICINE

com·ple·men·ta·tion \ˌkäm-plə-(ˌ)men-ˈtā-shən, -mən-\ *n* (1942) **1 :** the operation of determining the complement of a mathematical set **2 :** production of normal phenotype in an individual heterozygous for two closely related mutations with one on each homologous chromosome and at a slightly different position

complement fixation *n* (1906) **:** the process of binding serum complement to the product formed by the union of an antibody and the antigen for which it is specific that occurs when complement is added to a suitable mixture of such an antibody and antigen and that is the basis of some tests to detect the presence of specific antibodies or antigens

com·ple·men·ti·zer \ˈkäm-plə-mən-ˌtī-zər, -(ˌ)men-\ *n* (1965) **:** a function word or morpheme that combines with a clause or verbal phrase to form a subordinate clause

[1]**com·plete** \kəm-ˈplēt\ *adj* **com·plet·er; -est** [ME *complet,* fr. L *completus,* fr. pp. of *complēre*] (14c) **1 a :** having all necessary parts, elements, or steps ⟨a ~ diet⟩ **b :** having all four sets of floral organs **c** *of a subject or predicate* **:** including modifiers, complements, or objects **2 :** brought to an end **:** CONCLUDED ⟨a ~ period of time⟩ **3 :** highly proficient ⟨a ~ artist⟩ **4 a :** fully carried out **:** THOROUGH ⟨a ~ renovation⟩ **b :** TOTAL, ABSOLUTE ⟨~ silence⟩ **c** *of a football pass* **:** legally caught **5** *of insect metamorphosis* **:** characterized by the occurrence of a pupal stage between the motile immature stages and the adult — compare INCOMPLETE 1b **6** *of a metric space* **:** having the property that every Cauchy sequence of elements converges to a limit in the space ***syn*** see FULL — **com·plete·ly** *adv* — **com·plete·ness** *n* — **com·ple·tive** \-ˈplē-tiv\ *adj* — **complete with :** made complete by the inclusion of ⟨a birthday cake *complete with* candles⟩

[2]**complete** *vt* **com·plet·ed; com·plet·ing** (15c) **1 :** to bring to an end and esp. into a perfected state ⟨~ a painting⟩ **2 a :** to make whole or perfect ⟨its song ~*s* the charm of this bird⟩ **b :** to mark the end of ⟨a rousing chorus ~*s* the show⟩ **c :** EXECUTE, FULFILL ⟨~ a contract⟩ **3 :** to carry out (a forward pass) successfully ***syn*** see CLOSE

complete fertilizer *n* (1871) **:** a fertilizer that contains the three chief plant nutrients nitrogen, phosphoric acid, and potash

com·ple·tion \kəm-ˈplē-shən\ *n* (1657) **1 :** the act or process of completing **2 :** the quality or state of being complete **3 :** a completed forward pass in football

com·plet·ist \-tist\ *n* (1951) **:** one who wants to make something (as a collection) complete

[1]**com·plex** \ˈkäm-ˌpleks\ *n* [LL *complexus* totality, fr. L, embrace, fr. *complecti*] (1643) **1 :** a whole made up of complicated or interrelated parts ⟨a ~ of welfare programs⟩ ⟨the military-industrial ~⟩ **2 a :** a group of culture traits relating to a single activity (as hunting), process (as use of flint), or culture unit **b** (1) **:** a group of repressed desires and memories that exerts a dominating influence upon the personality (2) **:** an exaggerated reaction to or preoccupation with a subject or situation **c :** a group of obviously related units of which the degree and nature of the relationship is imperfectly known **d :** the sum of factors (as symptoms) characterizing a disease or condition **3 :** a chemical association of two or more species (as ions or molecules) joined usu. by weak electrostatic bonds rather than covalent bonds **4 :** a building or group of buildings housing related units ⟨an apartment ~⟩ ⟨a sports ~⟩

[2]**com·plex** \käm-ˈpleks, kəm-ˈ, ˈkäm-ˌ\ *adj* [L *complexus,* pp. of *complecti* to embrace, comprise (a multitude of objects), fr. *com-* + *plectere* to braid — more at PLY] (1645) **1 a :** composed of two or more parts **:** COMPOSITE **b** (1) *of a word* **:** having a bound form as one or more of its immediate constituents ⟨*unmanly* is a ~ word⟩ (2) *of a sentence* **:** consisting of a main clause and one or more subordinate clauses **2 :** hard to separate, analyze, or solve **3 :** of, concerned with, being, or containing complex numbers ⟨a ~ root⟩ ⟨~ analysis⟩ — **com·plex·ly** *adv* — **com·plex·ness** *n*

syn COMPLEX, COMPLICATED, INTRICATE, INVOLVED, KNOTTY mean having confusingly interrelated parts. COMPLEX suggests the unavoidable result of a necessary combining and does not imply a fault or failure ⟨a *complex* recipe⟩. COMPLICATED applies to what offers great difficulty in understanding, solving, or explaining ⟨*complicated* legal procedures⟩. INTRICATE suggests such interlacing of parts as to make it nearly impossible to follow or grasp them separately ⟨an *intricate* web of deceit⟩. INVOLVED implies extreme complication and often disorder ⟨a rambling, *involved* explanation⟩. KNOTTY suggests complication and entanglement that make solution or understanding improbable ⟨*knotty* ethical questions⟩.

[3]**com·plex** *same as* [2]\ *vt* (1658) **1 :** to make complex or into a complex **2 :** CHELATE — **com·plex·a·tion** \ˌkäm-ˌplek-ˈsā-shən, kəm-\ *n*

complex carbohydrate *n* (1938) **:** a polysaccharide (as starch or cellulose) consisting of usu. hundreds or thousands of monosaccharide units; *also* **:** a food (as rice or pasta) composed primarily of such polysaccharides

complex fraction *n* (1827) **:** a fraction with a fraction or mixed number in the numerator or denominator or both — compare SIMPLE FRACTION

com·plex·i·fy \käm-ˈplek-sə-ˌfī, kəm-\ *vb* **-fied; -fy·ing** *vt* (1830) **:** to make complex ~ *vi* **:** to become complex

com·plex·ion \kəm-ˈplek-shən\ *n* [ME, fr. AF, fr. ML *complexion-, complexio,* fr. L, combination, fr. *complecti*] (14c) **1 :** the combination of the hot, cold, moist, and dry qualities held in medieval physiology to determine the quality of a body **2 a :** an individual complex of ways of thinking or feeling **b :** a complex of attitudes and inclinations **3 :** the hue or appearance of the skin and esp. of the face ⟨a dark ~⟩ **4 :** overall aspect or character ⟨by changing the ~ of the legislative branch —Trevor Armbrister⟩ — **com·plex·ion·al** \-shnəl, -shə-nᵊl\ *adj* — **com·plex·ioned** \-shənd\ *adj*

com·plex·i·ty \kəm-ˈplek-sə-tē, käm-\ *n, pl* **-ties** (1661) **1 :** something complex **2 :** the quality or state of being complex

complex number *n* (1856) **:** a number of the form $a + b\sqrt{-1}$ where a and b are real numbers

complex plane *n* (ca. 1909) **:** a plane whose points are identified by means of complex numbers; *esp* **:** ARGAND DIAGRAM

com·pli·ance \kəm-ˈplī-ən(t)s\ *n* (ca. 1630) **1 a :** the act or process of complying to a desire, demand, proposal, or regimen or to coercion **b :** conformity in fulfilling official requirements **2 :** a disposition to yield to others **3 :** the ability of an object to yield elastically when a force is applied **:** FLEXIBILITY

com·pli·an·cy \-ən(t)-sē\ *n* (1643) **:** COMPLIANCE

com·pli·ant \-ənt\ *adj* (1642) **1 :** ready or disposed to comply **:** SUBMISSIVE ⟨a corrupt regime aided by a ~ press⟩ **2 :** conforming to requirements ⟨~ software⟩ — **com·pli·ant·ly** *adv*

com·pli·ca·cy \ˈkäm-pli-kə-sē\ *n, pl* **-cies** [[2]*complicate*] (ca. 1828) **1 :** the quality or state of being complicated **2 :** something that is complicated

[1]**com·pli·cate** \ˈkäm-pli-kət\ *adj* [L *complicatus,* pp. of *complicare* to fold together, fr. *com-* + *plicare* to fold — more at PLY] (1638) **1 :** COMPLEX, INTRICATE **2 :** CONDUPLICATE

[2]**com·pli·cate** \ˈkäm-plə-ˌkāt\ *vt* **-cat·ed; -cat·ing** (1672) **1 :** to combine esp. in an involved or inextricable manner **2 :** to make complex or difficult **3 :** INVOLVE; *esp* **:** to cause to be more complex or severe ⟨a virus disease *complicated* by bacterial infection⟩

com·pli·cat·ed \ˈkäm-plə-ˌkā-təd\ *adj* (1656) **1 :** consisting of parts intricately combined ⟨a ~ recipe⟩ **2 :** difficult to analyze, understand, or explain ⟨a ~ issue⟩ ***syn*** see COMPLEX — **com·pli·cat·ed·ly** *adv* — **com·pli·cat·ed·ness** *n*

com·pli·ca·tion \ˌkäm-plə-ˈkā-shən\ *n* (15c) **1 a :** COMPLEXITY, INTRICACY; *esp* **:** a situation or a detail of character complicating the main thread of a plot **b :** a making difficult, involved, or intricate **c :** a complex or intricate feature or element **d :** a difficult factor or issue often appearing unexpectedly and changing existing plans, methods, or attitudes **2 :** a secondary disease or condition developing in the course of a primary disease or condition

com·plice \ˈkäm-pləs, ˈkəm-\ *n* [ME, fr. MF, fr. LL *complic-, complex,* fr. L, closely connected, fr. *complicare*] (15c) *archaic* **:** ASSOCIATE

com·plic·it \kəm-ˈpli-sət\ *adj* (1928) **:** having complicity

com·plic·it·ous \-ˈpli-sə-təs\ *adj* (1860) **:** COMPLICIT

com·plic·i·ty \kəm-ˈpli-s(ə-)tē\ *n, pl* **-ties** (ca. 1656) **1 :** association or participation in or as if in a wrongful act **2 :** an instance of complicity

com·pli·er \-ˈplī(-ə)r\ *n* (1660) : one that complies

[1]**com·pli·ment** \ˈkäm-plə-mənt\ *n* [MF, fr. It *complimento,* fr. Sp *cumplimiento,* fr. *cumplir* to be courteous — more at COMPLY] (1598) **1 a** : an expression of esteem, respect, affection, or admiration; *esp* : an admiring remark **b** : formal and respectful recognition : HONOR **2** *pl* : best wishes : REGARDS ⟨accept my ~*s*⟩ ⟨~*s* of the season⟩

[2]**com·pli·ment** \-ˌment\ *vt* (1673) **1** : to pay a compliment to **2** : to present with a token of esteem

com·pli·men·ta·ry \ˌkäm-plə-ˈmen-t(ə-)rē\ *adj* (1714) **1 a** : expressing or containing a compliment ⟨a ~ remark⟩ **b** : FAVORABLE ⟨the novel received ~ reviews⟩ **2** : given free as a courtesy or favor ⟨~ tickets⟩ — **com·pli·men·ta·ri·ly** \-ˈmen-t(ə-)rə-lē, -(ˌ)men-ˈter-ə-lē\ *adv*

complimentary close *n* (1919) : the words (as *sincerely yours*) that conventionally come immediately before the signature of a letter and express the sender's regard for the receiver — called also *complimentary closing*

com·pline \ˈkäm-plən, -ˌplīn\ *n, often cap* [ME *compline, complie,* fr. AF *cumplie,* modif. of LL *completa,* fr. L, fem. of *completus* complete] (13c) : the seventh and last of the canonical hours

[1]**com·plot** \ˈkäm-ˌplät\ *n* [MF *complot* crowd, plot] (1577) *archaic* : PLOT, CONSPIRACY

[2]**com·plot** \kəm-ˈplät, käm-\ *vb* (1579) *archaic* : PLOT

com·ply \kəm-ˈplī\ *vi* **com·plied; com·ply·ing** [It *complire,* fr. Sp *cumplir* to complete, perform what is due, be courteous, modif. of L *complēre* to complete] (1602) **1** *obs* : to be ceremoniously courteous **2** : to conform, submit, or adapt (as to a regulation or to another's wishes) as required or requested ⟨~ with federal law⟩ ⟨the devices ~ with industry standards⟩

com·po \ˈkäm-(ˌ)pō\ *n, pl* **compos** [short for *composition*] (1823) : any of various composition materials

[1]**com·po·nent** \kəm-ˈpō-nənt, ˈkäm-ˌ, käm-ˈ\ *n* [L *component-, componens,* prp. of *componere* to put together — more at COMPOUND] (1645) **1** : a constituent part : INGREDIENT ⟨an important ~ of the program⟩ ⟨stereo ~*s*⟩ **2 a** : any one of the vector terms added to form a vector sum or resultant **b** : a coordinate of a vector; *also* : either member of an ordered pair of numbers ***syn*** see ELEMENT — **com·po·nen·tial** \ˌkäm-pə-ˈnen(t)-shəl\ *adj*

[2]**component** *adj* (1664) : serving or helping to constitute : CONSTITUENT ⟨~ parts⟩

[1]**com·port** \kəm-ˈpȯrt\ *vb* [MF *comporter* to bear, conduct, fr. L *comportare* to bring together, fr. *com-* + *portare* to carry — more at FARE] *vi* (1589) : to be fitting : ACCORD ⟨actions that ~ with policy⟩ ~ *vt* : BEHAVE; *esp* : to behave in a manner conformable to what is right, proper, or expected ⟨~*ed* himself well in the crisis⟩ ***syn*** see BEHAVE — **com·port·ment** \-mənt\ *n*

[2]**com·port** \ˈkäm-ˌpȯrt\ *n* (1771) : COMPOTE 2

com·pose \kəm-ˈpōz\ *vb* **com·posed; com·pos·ing** [ME, fr. AF *composer,* fr. L *componere* (perf. indic. *composui*) — more at COMPOUND] *vt* (15c) **1 a** : to form by putting together : FASHION ⟨a committee *composed* of three representatives —*Current Biog.*⟩ **b** : to form the substance of : CONSTITUTE ⟨*composed* of many ingredients⟩ **c** : to produce (as columns or pages of type) by composition **2 a** : to create by mental or artistic labor : PRODUCE ⟨~ a sonnet⟩ **b (1)** : to formulate and write (a piece of music) **(2)** : to compose music for **3** : to deal with or act on so as to reduce to a minimum ⟨~ their differences⟩ **4** : to arrange in proper or orderly form **5** : to free from agitation : CALM, SETTLE ⟨*composed* himself⟩ ~ *vi* : to practice composition

com·posed \-ˈpōzd\ *adj* (1607) : free from agitation : CALM; *esp* : SELF-POSSESSED ***syn*** see COOL — **com·pos·ed·ly** \-ˈpō-zəd-lē\ *adv* — **com·pos·ed·ness** \-ˈpō-zəd-nəs\ *n*

com·pos·er \kəm-ˈpō-zər\ *n* (1597) : one that composes; *esp* : a person who writes music

composing room *n* (1737) : the department in a printing office where typesetting and related operations are performed

composing stick *n* (1659) : a tray with an adjustable slide that a compositor holds in one hand and sets type into with the other

[1]**com·pos·ite** \käm-ˈpä-zət, kəm-ˈ, *esp Brit* ˈkäm-pə-zit\ *adj* [L *compositus,* pp. of *componere*] (1563) **1** : made up of distinct parts: as **a** *cap* : relating to or being a modification of the Corinthian order combining angular Ionic volutes with the acanthus-circled bell of the Corinthian **b** : of or relating to a very large family (Compositae syn. Asteraceae) of dicotyledonous herbs, shrubs, and trees often considered to be the most highly evolved plants and characterized by florets arranged in dense heads that resemble single flowers **c** : factorable into two or more prime factors other than 1 and itself ⟨8 is a positive ~ integer⟩ **2** : combining the typical or essential characteristics of individuals making up a group ⟨the ~ man called the Poet —Richard Poirier⟩ **3** *of a statistical hypothesis* : specifying a range of values for one or more statistical parameters — compare SIMPLE 10 — **com·pos·ite·ly** *adv*

[2]**composite** *n* (1656) **1** : something composite : COMPOUND ⟨a ~ of two images⟩ **2** : a composite plant **3** : COMPOSITE FUNCTION **4** : a solid material which is composed of two or more substances having different physical characteristics and in which each substance retains its identity while contributing desirable properties to the whole; *esp* : a structural material made of plastic within which a fibrous material (as silicon carbide) is embedded

[3]**composite** *vt* **-it·ed; -it·ing** (1923) : to make composite or into something composite ⟨*composited* four soil samples⟩ ⟨~ the images⟩

composite function *n* (1965) : a function whose values are found from two given functions by applying one function to an independent variable and then applying the second function to the result and whose domain consists of those values of the independent variable for which the result yielded by the first function lies in the domain of the second

com·po·si·tion \ˌkäm-pə-ˈzi-shən\ *n* [ME *composicioun,* fr. AF *composicion,* fr. L *composition-, compositio,* fr. *componere*] (14c) **1 a** : the act or process of composing; *specif* : arrangement into specific proportion or relation and esp. into artistic form **b (1)** : the arrangement of type for printing ⟨hand ~⟩ **(2)** : the production of type or typographic characters (as in photocomposition) arranged for printing **2 a** : the manner in which something is composed **b** : general makeup ⟨the changing ethnic ~ of the city —Leonard Buder⟩ **c** : the qualitative and quantitative makeup of a chemical compound **3** : mutual settlement or agreement **4** : a product of mixing or combining various elements or ingredients **5** : an intellectual creation: as **a** : a piece of writing; *esp* : a school exercise in the form of a brief essay **b** : a written piece of music esp. of considerable size and complexity **6** : the quality or state of being compound **7** : the operation of forming a composite function; *also* : COMPOSITE FUNCTION — **com·po·si·tion·al** \-ˈzish-nəl, -ˈzi-shə-nᵊl\ *adj* — **com·po·si·tion·al·ly** *adv*

com·po·si·tion·ist \-ˈzi-sh(ə-)nist\ *n* (1985) : a teacher of writing esp. in a college or university

com·pos·i·tor \kəm-ˈpä-zə-tər\ *n* (1569) : one who sets type

com·pos men·tis \ˈkäm-pəs-ˈmen-təs\ *adj* [L, lit., having mastery of one's mind] (1616) : of sound mind, memory, and understanding

[1]**com·post** \ˈkäm-ˌpōst, *esp Brit* -ˌpäst\ *n* [AF, fr. ML *compostum,* fr. L, neut. of *compositus, compostus,* pp. of *componere*] (1587) **1** : a mixture that consists largely of decayed organic matter and is used for fertilizing and conditioning land **2** : MIXTURE, COMPOUND

[2]**compost** *vt* (1829) : to convert (as plant debris) to compost — **compost·able** \ˈkäm-ˌpōs-tə-bəl\ *adj* — **com·post·er** \-tər\ *n*

com·po·sure \kəm-ˈpō-zhər\ *n* (1647) : a calmness or repose esp. of mind, bearing, or appearance : SELF-POSSESSION ***syn*** see EQUANIMITY

com·pote \ˈkäm-ˌpōt\ *n* [F, fr. OF *composte,* fr. L *composta,* fem. of *compostus,* pp.] (1693) **1** : a dessert of fruit cooked in syrup **2** : a bowl of glass, porcelain, or metal usu. with a base and stem from which compotes, fruits, nuts, or sweets are served

[1]**com·pound** \käm-ˈpau̇nd, kəm-ˈ, ˈkäm-ˌ\ *vb* [ME *compounen,* fr. AF **cumpundre,* fr. L *componere,* fr. *com-* + *ponere* to put — more at POSITION] *vt* (14c) **1** : to put together (parts) so as to form a whole : COMBINE ⟨~ ingredients⟩ **2** : to form by combining parts ⟨~ a medicine⟩ **3 a** : to settle amicably : adjust by agreement **b** : to agree for a consideration not to prosecute (an offense) ⟨~ a felony⟩ **4 a** : to pay (interest) on both the accrued interest and the principal **b** : to add to : AUGMENT ⟨we ~*ed* our error in later policy —Robert Lekachman⟩ ~ *vi* **1** : to become joined in a compound **2** : to come to terms of agreement — **com·pound·able** \-ˈpau̇n-də-bəl, -ˌpau̇n-\ *adj* — **com·pound·er** *n*

[2]**com·pound** \ˈkäm-ˌpau̇nd, käm-ˈ, kəm-ˈ\ *adj* [ME *compouned,* pp. of *compounen*] (14c) **1** : composed of or resulting from union of separate elements, ingredients, or parts: as **a** : composed of united similar elements esp. of a kind usu. independent ⟨a ~ plant ovary⟩ **b** : having the blade divided to the midrib and forming two or more leaflets on a common axis ⟨a ~ leaf⟩ **2** : involving or used in a combination **3 a** *of a word* : constituting a compound **b** *of a sentence* : having two or more main clauses

[3]**com·pound** \ˈkäm-ˌpau̇nd\ *n* (1530) **1 a** : a word consisting of components that are words (as *rowboat, high school, devil-may-care*) **b** : a word (as *anthropology, kilocycle, builder*) consisting of any of various combinations of words, combining forms, or affixes **2** : something formed by a union of elements or parts; *esp* : a distinct substance formed by chemical union of two or more ingredients in definite proportion by weight

[4]**com·pound** \ˈkäm-ˌpau̇nd\ *n* [by folk etymology fr. Malay *kampung* group of buildings, village] (1679) : a fenced or walled-in area containing a group of buildings and esp. residences

com·pound–com·plex \-ˈkäm-ˌpleks\ *adj* (1923) *of a sentence* : having two or more main clauses and one or more subordinate clauses

compound eye *n* (1836) : an eye (as of an insect) made up of many separate visual units

compound fracture *n* (1543) : a bone fracture resulting in an open wound through which bone fragments usu. protrude

compound interest *n* (1660) : interest computed on the sum of an original principal and accrued interest

compound microscope *n* (ca. 1859) : a microscope consisting of an objective and an eyepiece mounted in a drawtube

compound number *n* (15c) : a number (as 2 feet 5 inches) involving different denominations or more than one unit

com·pra·dor *or* **com·pra·dore** \ˌkäm-prə-ˈdȯr\ *n* [Pg *comprador,* lit., buyer] (1840) **1** : a Chinese agent engaged by a foreign establishment in China to have charge of its Chinese employees and to act as an intermediary in business affairs **2** : INTERMEDIARY

com·pre·hend \ˌkäm-pri-ˈhend, -prē-\ *vt* [ME, fr. AF *comprendre, comprehendre,* fr. L *comprehendere,* fr. *com-* + *prehendere* to grasp — more at GET] (14c) **1** : to grasp the nature, significance, or meaning of ⟨unable to ~ what has happened⟩ **2** : to contain or hold within a total scope, significance, or amount ⟨philosophy's scope ~*s* the truth of everything which man may understand —H. O. Taylor⟩ **3** : to include by construction or implication ⟨does not prudence ~ all the virtues? —Thomas B. Silver⟩ ***syn*** see UNDERSTAND, INCLUDE — **com·pre·hend·ible** \-ˈhen-də-bəl\ *adj*

com·pre·hen·si·ble \-ˈhen(t)-sə-bəl\ *adj* (1598) : capable of being comprehended : INTELLIGIBLE ⟨a ~ explanation⟩ — **com·pre·hen·si·bil·i·ty** \-ˌhen(t)-sə-ˈbi-lə-tē\ *n* — **com·pre·hen·si·ble·ness** \-ˈhen(t)-sə-bəl-nəs\ *n* — **com·pre·hen·si·bly** \-blē\ *adv*

com·pre·hen·sion \ˌkäm-pri-ˈhen(t)-shən, -prē-\ *n* [MF & L; MF, fr. L *comprehension-, comprehensio,* fr. *comprehendere* to understand, comprise] (15c) **1 a** : the act or action of grasping with the intellect : UNDERSTANDING **b** : knowledge gained by comprehending **c** : the capacity for understanding fully ⟨mysteries that are beyond our ~⟩ **2 a** : the act or process of comprising **b** : the faculty or capability of including : COMPREHENSIVENESS **3** : CONNOTATION 3

com·pre·hen·sive \-ˈhen(t)-siv\ *adj* (1614) **1** : covering completely or broadly : INCLUSIVE ⟨~ examinations⟩ ⟨~ insurance⟩ **2** : having or exhibiting wide mental grasp ⟨~ knowledge⟩ — **com·pre·hen·sive·ly** *adv* — **com·pre·hen·sive·ness** *n*

[1]**com·press** \kəm-ˈpres\ *vb* [ME, fr. LL *compressare* to press hard, freq. of L *comprimere* to compress, fr. *com-* + *premere* to press — more at PRESS] *vt* (14c) **1** : to press or squeeze together **2** : to reduce in size,

quantity, or volume as if by squeezing ⟨~ a computer file⟩ ~ *vi* : to undergo compression ***syn*** see CONTRACT

[2]**com·press** \ˈkäm-ˌpres\ *n* [MF *compresse,* fr. *compresser* to compress, fr. LL *compressare*] (1599) **1 :** a folded cloth or pad applied so as to press upon a body part **2 :** a machine for compressing

com·pressed \kəm-ˈprest *also* ˈkäm-ˌ\ *adj* (14c) **1 :** pressed together : reduced in size or volume (as by pressure) **2 :** flattened as though subjected to compression: **a :** flattened laterally ⟨petioles ~⟩ **b :** narrow from side to side and deep in a dorsoventral direction — **com·pressed·ly** \kəm-ˈprest-lē, -ˈpre-səd-lē\ *adv*

compressed air *n* (1669) : air under pressure greater than that of the atmosphere

com·press·ible \kəm-ˈpre-sə-bəl\ *adj* (ca. 1691) : capable of being compressed — **com·press·ibil·i·ty** \-ˌpre-sə-ˈbi-lə-tē\ *n*

com·pres·sion \kəm-ˈpre-shən\ *n* (15c) **1 a :** the act, process, or result of compressing **b :** the state of being compressed **2 :** the process of compressing the fuel mixture in a cylinder of an internal combustion engine (as in an automobile) **3 :** the compressed remains of a fossil plant **4 :** conversion (as of data, a data file, or a communications signal) in order to reduce the space occupied or bandwidth required — **com·pres·sion·al** \-ˈpresh-nəl, -ˈpre-shə-nᵊl\ *adj*

compressional wave *n* (1875) : a longitudinal wave (as a sound wave) propagated by the elastic compression of the medium — called also *compression wave*

com·pres·sive \kəm-ˈpre-siv\ *adj* (1572) **1 :** of or relating to compression **2 :** tending to compress — **com·pres·sive·ly** *adv*

com·pres·sor \-ˈpre-sər\ *n* (1839) : one that compresses: as **a :** a muscle that compresses a part **b :** a machine that compresses gases

com·prise \kəm-ˈprīz\ *vt* **com·prised; com·pris·ing** [ME, fr. AF *compris,* pp. of *comprendre,* fr. L *comprehendere*] (15c) **1 :** to include esp. within a particular scope ⟨civilization as Lenin used the term would then certainly have *comprised* the changes that are now associated in our minds with "developed" rather than "developing" states —*Times Lit. Supp.*⟩ **2 :** to be made up of ⟨a vast installation, *comprising* fifty buildings —Jane Jacobs⟩ **3 :** COMPOSE, CONSTITUTE ⟨a misconception as to what ~*s* a literary generation —William Styron⟩ ⟨about 8 percent of our military forces are *comprised* of women —Jimmy Carter⟩

usage Although it has been in use since the late 18th century, sense 3 is still attacked as wrong. Why it has been singled out is not clear, but until comparatively recent times it was found chiefly in scientific or technical writing rather than belles lettres. Our current evidence shows a slight shift in usage: sense 3 is somewhat more frequent in recent literary use than the earlier senses. You should be aware, however, that if you use sense 3 you may be subject to criticism for doing so, and you may want to choose a safer synonym such as *compose* or *make up.*

[1]**com·pro·mise** \ˈkäm-prə-ˌmīz\ *n* [ME, mutual promise to abide by an arbiter's decision, fr. AF *compromisse,* fr. L *compromissum,* fr. neut. of *compromissus,* pp. of *compromittere* to promise mutually, fr. *com-* + *promittere* to promise — more at PROMISE] (15c) **1 a :** settlement of differences by arbitration or by consent reached by mutual concessions **b :** something intermediate between or blending qualities of two different things **2 :** a concession to something derogatory or prejudicial ⟨a ~ of principles⟩

[2]**compromise** *vb* **-mised; -mis·ing** *vt* (1598) **1** *obs* **:** to bind by mutual agreement **2 :** to adjust or settle by mutual concessions **3 a :** to expose to suspicion, discredit, or mischief ⟨his reputation has been *compromised*⟩ **b :** to reveal or expose to an unauthorized person and esp. to an enemy ⟨confidential information was *compromised*⟩ **c :** to cause the impairment of ⟨a *compromised* immune system⟩ ⟨a seriously *compromised* patient⟩ ~ *vi* **1 a :** to come to agreement by mutual concession **b :** to find or follow a way between extremes **2 :** to make a shameful or disreputable concession ⟨wouldn't ~ with their principles⟩ — **com·pro·mis·er** *n*

compt \ˈkau̇nt, ˈkäm(p)t\ *archaic var of* COUNT

comp·trol·ler \kən-ˈtrō-lər, ˈkäm(p)-ˌ, käm(p)-ˈ\ *n* [ME, alter. of *countreroller* controller] (15c) **1 :** a royal-household official who examines and supervises expenditures **2 :** a public official who audits government accounts and sometimes certifies expenditures **3 :** CONTROLLER 1c — **comp·trol·ler·ship** \-ˌship\ *n*

com·pul·sion \kəm-ˈpəl-shən\ *n* [ME, fr. AF or LL; AF, fr. LL *compulsion-, compulsio,* fr. L *compellere* to compel] (15c) **1 a :** an act of compelling : the state of being compelled **b :** a force that compels **2 :** an irresistible persistent impulse to perform an act (as excessive hand washing); *also* **:** the act itself

com·pul·sive \-ˈpəl-siv\ *adj* (1588) **1 :** having power to compel **2 :** of, relating to, caused by, or suggestive of psychological compulsion or obsession ⟨~ actions⟩ ⟨a ~ gambler⟩ — **com·pul·sive·ly** *adv* — **com·pul·sive·ness** *n* — **com·pul·siv·i·ty** \kəm-ˌpəl-ˈsi-və-tē, ˌkäm-\ *n*

com·pul·so·ry \kəm-ˈpəls-rē, -ˈpəl-sə-\ *adj* (1581) **1 :** MANDATORY, ENFORCED ⟨~ retirement⟩ **2 :** COERCIVE, COMPELLING ⟨~ measures⟩ — **com·pul·so·ri·ly** \-rə-lē\ *adv*

com·punc·tion \kəm-ˈpəŋ(k)-shən\ *n* [ME *compunccioun,* fr. AF *compunction,* fr. LL *compunction-, compunctio,* fr. L *compungere* to prick hard, sting, fr. *com-* + *pungere* to prick — more at PUNGENT] (14c) **1 a :** anxiety arising from awareness of guilt ⟨~*s* of conscience⟩ **b :** distress of mind over an anticipated action or result ⟨showed no ~ in planning devilish engines of . . . destruction —Havelock Ellis⟩ **2 :** a twinge of misgiving : SCRUPLE ⟨cheated without ~⟩ ***syn*** see PENITENCE, QUALM — **com·punc·tious** \-shəs\ *adj*

com·pur·ga·tion \ˌkäm-(ˌ)pər-ˈgā-shən\ *n* [LL *compurgation-, compurgatio,* fr. L *compurgare* to clear completely, fr. *com-* + *purgare* to purge] (ca. 1658) : the clearing of an accused person by oaths of others who swear to the veracity or innocence of the accused

com·pur·ga·tor \ˈkäm-(ˌ)pər-ˌgā-tər\ *n* (1533) : one who under oath vouches for the character or conduct of an accused person

com·put·able \kəm-ˈpyü-tə-bəl\ *adj* (1646) : capable of being computed — **com·put·abil·i·ty** \-ˌpyü-tə-ˈbi-lə-tē\ *n*

com·pu·ta·tion \ˌkäm-pyu̇-ˈtā-shən, -pyü-\ *n* (15c) **1 a :** the act or action of computing : CALCULATION **b :** the use or operation of a computer **2 :** a system of reckoning **3 :** an amount computed — **com·pu·ta·tion·al** \-shnəl, -shə-nᵊl\ *adj* — **com·pu·ta·tion·al·ly** *adv*

com·pute \kəm-ˈpyüt\ *vb* **com·put·ed; com·put·ing** [L *computare* — more at COUNT] *vt* (1616) : to determine esp. by mathematical means; *also* **:** to determine or calculate by means of a computer ~ *vi* **1 :** to make calculation : RECKON **2 :** to use a computer

computed tomography *n* (1974) : radiography in which a three-dimensional image of a body structure is constructed by computer from a series of plane cross-sectional images made along an axis — called also *computed axial tomography, computerized axial tomography, computerized tomography*

com·put·er \kəm-ˈpyü-tər\ *n, often attrib* (1646) : one that computes; *specif* **:** a programmable usu. electronic device that can store, retrieve, and process data — **com·put·er·dom** \-dəm\ *n* — **com·put·er·less** \-ləs\ *adj* — **com·put·er·like** \-ˌlīk\ *adj*

com·put·er·ese \-ˌpyü-tə-ˈrēz, -ˈrēs\ *n* (ca. 1960) : jargon used by computer technologists

com·put·er·ise *chiefly Brit var of* COMPUTERIZE

com·put·er·ist \kəm-ˈpyü-tə-rist\ *n* (1973) : a person who uses or operates a computer

com·put·er·ize \kəm-ˈpyü-tə-ˌrīz, -tər-ˌīz\ *vt* **-ized; -iz·ing** (1957) **1 :** to carry out, control, or produce by means of a computer ⟨*computerized* music⟩ **2 :** to equip with computers ⟨~ public schools⟩ **3 a :** to store in a computer ⟨~ data⟩ **b :** to put in a form that a computer can use ⟨~ paperwork⟩ — **com·put·er·iz·able** \-ˌpyü-tə-ˈrī-zə-bəl\ *adj* — **com·put·er·i·za·tion** \-ˌpyü-tə-rə-ˈzā-shən\ *n*

com·put·er·nik \kəm-ˈpyü-tər-ˌnik\ *n* (1968) : a computer enthusiast or expert

com·put·er·phobe \-ˌfōb\ *n* (1976) : a person who experiences anxiety about computers and esp. about their use — **com·put·er·pho·bia** \-ˌpyü-tər-ˈfō-bē-ə\ *n* — **com·put·er·pho·bic** \-ˈfō-bik\ *adj*

computer science *n* (1961) : a branch of science that deals with the theory of computation or the design of computers

comr *abbr* commissioner

com·rade \ˈkäm-ˌrad, -rəd, *esp Brit* -ˌrād\ *n* [MF *camarade* group sleeping in one room, roommate, companion, fr. OSp *camarada,* fr. *cámara* room, fr. LL *camera, camara* — more at CHAMBER] (1544) **1 a :** an intimate friend or associate : COMPANION **b :** a fellow soldier **2** [fr. its use as a form of address by communists] **:** COMMUNIST — **com·rade·li·ness** \-lē-nəs\ *n* — **com·rade·ly** *adj* — **com·rade·ship** \-ˌship\ *n*

com·rad·ery \ˈkäm-ˌra-d(ə-)rē, -rə-drē, -ˌrā-d(ə-)rē\ *n* (1879) : CAMARADERIE

Comsat \ˈkäm-ˌsat\ *service mark* — used for communications services involving an artificial satellite

Com·stock·ery \ˈkäm-ˌstä-kə-rē *also* ˈkəm-\ *n* [Anthony *Comstock* + E *-ery*] (1905) **1 :** strict censorship of materials considered obscene **2 :** censorious opposition to alleged immorality (as in literature)

Com·stock·ian \käm-ˈstä-kē-ən *also* ˌkəm-\ *adj* (1921) : of or relating to Comstockery

com·symp \ˈkäm-ˌsimp\ *n* [*com*munist + *symp*athizer] (ca. 1961) *usu disparaging* **:** a person sympathetic to Communist causes

Comt·ian *or* **Comt·ean** \ˈkäm(p)-tē-ən, ˈkō^{n}(n)-tē-\ *adj* (1846) : of or relating to Auguste Comte or his doctrines — **Comt·ism** \ˈkäm(p)-ˌtizəm, ˈkō^{n}(n)-\ *n* — **Comt·ist** \ˈkäm(p)-tist, ˈkō^{n}(n)-\ *adj or n*

[1]**con** \ˈkän\ *vt* **conned; con·ning** [ME *connen* to know, learn, study, alter. of *cunnen* to know, infin. of *can* — more at CAN] (13c) **1 :** to commit to memory **2 :** to study or examine closely

[2]**con** *var of* CONN

[3]**con** *adv* [ME, short for *contra*] (15c) : on the negative side : in opposition ⟨so much has been written pro and ~⟩

[4]**con** *n* (1589) **1 :** an argument or evidence in opposition **2 :** the negative position or one holding it ⟨an appraisal of the pros and ~*s*⟩

[5]**con** *adj* [by shortening] (1889) : CONFIDENCE ⟨a ~ artist⟩ ⟨a ~ game⟩

[6]**con** *vt* **conned; con·ning** (1896) **1 :** SWINDLE ⟨accused of *conning* retirees out of their savings⟩ **2 :** MANIPULATE 2b **3 :** PERSUADE, CAJOLE

[7]**con** *n* (1901) : something (as a ruse) used deceptively to gain another's confidence; *also* **:** a confidence game : SWINDLE

[8]**con** *n* [by shortening] (1893) : CONVICT

[9]**con** *n* [short for *consumption*] (1915) *slang* **:** a destructive disease of the lungs; *esp* **:** TUBERCULOSIS

[10]**con** *abbr* **1** [L *conjunx*] consort **2** consolidated **3** consul **4** continued

con- — see COM-

con·al·bu·min \ˌkän-al-ˈbyü-mən\ *n* [*com-* + *albumin*] (1900) : a protein of the white of egg that binds with metal ions (as of iron and copper)

con amo·re \ˌkän-ə-ˈmȯr-ē, ˌkōn-ə-ˈmȯr-(ˌ)ā\ *adv* [It] (1739) **1 :** with love, devotion, or zest **2 :** in a tender manner — used as a direction in music

con ani·ma \kän-ˈa-nə-ˌmä, kōn-ˈä-ni-\ *adv* [It, lit., with spirit] (ca. 1906) : in a spirited manner — used as a direction in music

co·na·tion \kō-ˈnā-shən\ *n* [L *conation-, conatio* act of attempting, fr. *conari* to attempt — more at DEACON] (ca. 1837) : an inclination (as an instinct, a drive, a wish, or a craving) to act purposefully : IMPULSE 3 — **co·na·tive** \ˈkō-nə-tiv, ˈkä-, ˈkō-ˌnā-\ *adj*

con brio \kän-ˈbrē-(ˌ)ō, kōn-\ *adv* [It, lit., with vigor] (1798) : in a vigorous or brisk manner — often used as a direction in music

conc *abbr* **1** concentrate; concentrated; concentration **2** concrete

con·ca·nav·a·lin \ˌkän-kə-ˈna-və-lən\ *n* [*com-* + *canavalin,* a noncrystalline globulin found in the jack bean, fr. NL *Canavalia,* genus name of the jack bean] (1917) : a protein that occurs in the jack bean and is a mitogen and hemagglutinin

[1]**con·cat·e·nate** \kän-ˈka-tə-nət, kən-\ *adj* [ME, fr. LL *concatenatus,* pp. of *concatenare* to link together, fr. L *com-* + *catena* chain] (15c) : linked together

[2]**concatenate** \-ˌnāt\ *vt* **-nat·ed; -nat·ing** (1598) : to link together in a series or chain — **con·cat·e·na·tion** \(ˌ)kän-ˌka-tə-ˈnā-shən, kən-\ *n*

[1]**con·cave** \kän-ˈkāv, ˈkän-ˌ\ *adj* [ME, fr. L *concavus,* fr. *com-* + *cavus* hollow — more at CAVE] (15c) **1 :** hollowed or rounded inward like the inside of a bowl **2 :** arched in : curving in — used of the side of a curve or surface on which neighboring normals to the curve or surface converge and on which lies the chord joining two neighboring points of the curve or surface

[2]**con·cave** \ˈkän-ˌkāv\ *n* (1552) : a concave line or surface

con·cav·i·ty \kän-ˈka-və-tē\ *n, pl* **-ties** (15c) **1 :** a concave line, surface, or space : HOLLOW **2 :** the quality or state of being concave

con·ca·vo–con·vex \kän-ˈkā-vō-kän-ˈveks; ˈkän-, kən-ˈ\ *adj* (1676) **1 :** concave on one side and convex on the other **2 :** having the concave side curved more than the convex ⟨a ~ lens⟩

con·ceal \kən-ˈsēl\ *vt* [ME *concelen,* fr. AF *conceler,* fr. L *concelare,* fr. *com-* + *celare* to hide — more at HELL] (14c) **1 :** to prevent disclosure or recognition of ⟨~ the truth⟩ **2 :** to place out of sight ⟨~*ed* himself behind the door⟩ ***syn*** see HIDE — **con·ceal·able** \-ˈsē-lə-bəl\ *adj* — **con·ceal·ing·ly** \-ˈsē-liŋ-lē\ *adv* — **con·ceal·ment** \-ˈsēl-mənt\ *n*

con·ceal·er \-ˈsē-lər\ *n* (1514) **1 :** one that conceals ⟨a ~ of the truth⟩ **2 :** a cosmetic used to conceal blemishes or discoloration esp. under the eyes

con·cede \kən-ˈsēd\ *vb* **con·ced·ed; con·ced·ing** [F or L; F *concéder,* fr. L *concedere,* fr. *com-* + *cedere* to yield] *vt* (1626) **1 :** to grant as a right or privilege **2 a :** to accept as true, valid, or accurate ⟨the right of the state to tax is generally *conceded*⟩ **b (1) :** to acknowledge grudgingly or hesitantly ⟨*conceded* that it might be a good idea⟩ **(2) :** to relinquish grudgingly or hesitantly ⟨~ power⟩ ~ *vi* **:** to make concession : YIELD ***syn*** see GRANT — **con·ced·ed·ly** \-ˈsē-dəd-lē\ *adv* — **con·ced·er** *n*

[1]**con·ceit** \kən-ˈsēt\ *n* [ME, fr. AF, fr. *conceivre*] (14c) **1 a (1) :** a result of mental activity : THOUGHT **(2) :** individual opinion **b :** favorable opinion; *esp* **:** excessive appreciation of one's own worth or virtue **2 :** a fancy item or trifle **3 a :** a fanciful idea **b :** an elaborate or strained metaphor **c :** use or presence of such conceits in poetry **d :** an organizing theme or concept ⟨found his ~ for the film early —Peter Wilkinson⟩

[2]**conceit** *vt* (1557) **1** *obs* **:** CONCEIVE, UNDERSTAND **2** *chiefly dial* **:** IMAGINE **3** *dial Brit* **:** to take a fancy to

con·ceit·ed \-ˈsē-təd\ *adj* [[1]*conceit*] (1526) **1 :** ingeniously contrived : FANCIFUL **2 :** having or showing an excessively high opinion of oneself — **con·ceit·ed·ly** *adv* — **con·ceit·ed·ness** *n*

con·ceiv·able \kən-ˈsē-və-bəl\ *adj* (15c) **:** capable of being conceived : IMAGINABLE ⟨every ~ combination⟩ — **con·ceiv·abil·i·ty** \kən-ˌsē-və-ˈbi-lə-tē\ *n* — **con·ceiv·able·ness** \-ˈsē-və-bəl-nəs\ *n*

con·ceiv·ably \-blē\ *adv* (1625) **1 :** in a conceivable manner **2 :** it may be conceived : POSSIBLY ⟨we could ~ finish next week⟩

con·ceive \kən-ˈsēv\ *vb* **con·ceived; con·ceiv·ing** [ME, fr. AF *conceivre,* fr. L *concipere* to take in, conceive, fr. *com-* + *capere* to take — more at HEAVE] *vt* (14c) **1 a :** to become pregnant with (young) ⟨~ a child⟩ **b :** to cause to begin : ORIGINATE ⟨a project *conceived* by the company's founder⟩ **2 a :** to take into one's mind ⟨~ a prejudice⟩ **b :** to form a conception of : IMAGINE ⟨a badly *conceived* design⟩ **3 :** to apprehend by reason or imagination : UNDERSTAND ⟨unable to ~ his reasons⟩ **4 :** to have as an opinion ⟨I cannot ~ that he acted alone⟩ ~ *vi* **1 :** to become pregnant **2 :** to have a conception — usu. used with *of* ⟨~*s* of death as emptiness⟩ ***syn*** see THINK — **con·ceiv·er** *n*

con·cel·e·brant \kən-ˈse-lə-brənt, kän-\ *n* (ca. 1931) **:** one that concelebrates a Eucharist or Mass

con·cel·e·brate \kən-ˈse-lə-ˌbrāt, kän-\ *vb* [ML *concelebratus,* pp. of *concelebrare,* fr. L, to frequent, celebrate, fr. *com-* + *celebrare* to celebrate] *vt* (1879) **:** to participate in (a Eucharist) as a joint celebrant who recites the canon in unison with other celebrants ~ *vi* **:** to participate as a celebrant in a concelebrated Eucharist — **con·cel·e·bra·tion** \(ˌ)kän-ˌse-lə-ˈbrā-shən, kən-\ *n*

con·cent \kən-ˈsent\ *n* [L *concentus,* fr. *concinere* to sing together, fr. *com-* + *canere* to sing — more at CHANT] (1585) *archaic* **:** HARMONY

con·cen·ter \kən-ˈsen-tər, kän-\ *vb* [F *concentrer,* fr. *com-* + *centre* center] *vt* (1598) **:** to draw or direct to a common center : CONCENTRATE ~ *vi* **:** to come to a common center

[1]**con·cen·trate** \ˈkän(t)-sən-ˌtrāt, -ˌsen-\ *vb* **-trat·ed; -trat·ing** [*com-* + L *centrum* center] *vt* (1641) **1 a :** to bring or direct toward a common center or objective : FOCUS ⟨~ one's efforts⟩ **b :** to gather into one body, mass, or force ⟨power was *concentrated* in a few able hands⟩ **c :** to accumulate (a toxic substance) in bodily tissues ⟨fish ~ mercury⟩ **2 a :** to make less dilute ⟨~ syrup⟩ **b :** to express or exhibit in condensed form ~ *vi* **1 :** to draw toward or meet in a common center **2 :** GATHER, COLLECT **3 :** to focus one's powers, efforts, or attention ⟨~ on a problem⟩ — **con·cen·trat·ed·ly** \-ˌtrā-təd-lē; ˌkän(t)-sən-ˈtrā-\ *adv* — **con·cen·tra·tive** \-ˌtrā-tiv\ *adj*

[2]**concentrate** *n* (1883) **1 :** something concentrated: as **a :** a mineral-rich product obtained after an initial processing of ore **b :** a food reduced in bulk by elimination of fluid ⟨orange juice ~⟩ **2 :** a feedstuff (as grains) relatively rich in digestible nutrients — compare FIBER

con·cen·tra·tion \ˌkän(t)-sən-ˈtrā-shən, -ˌsen-\ *n* (1634) **1 a :** the act or process of concentrating : the state of being concentrated; *esp* **:** direction of attention to a single object **b :** an academic major or area of focus within a major **2 :** a concentrated mass or thing **3 :** the amount of a component in a given area or volume

concentration camp *n* (1901) **:** a camp where persons (as prisoners of war, political prisoners, or refugees) are detained or confined

con·cen·tra·tor \ˈkän(t)-sən-ˌtrā-tər\ *n* (1833) **:** one that concentrates: as **a :** an industrial plant that produces concentrates from ores **b :** a mirror or group of mirrors that focus sunlight for use as an energy source **c :** a device in a computer network that collects data from separate low-volume transmission channels and retransmits it over a single high-volume channel

con·cen·tric \kən-ˈsen-trik, ˌkän-\ *adj* [ME *consentrik,* fr. ML *concentricus,* fr. L *com-* + *centrum* center] (14c) **1 :** having a common center ⟨~ circles⟩ **2 :** having a common axis : COAXIAL — **con·cen·tri·cal·ly** \-tri-k(ə-)lē\ *adv* — **con·cen·tric·i·ty** \ˌkän-ˌsen-ˈtri-sə-tē\ *n*

[1]**con·cept** \ˈkän-ˌsept\ *n* [L *conceptum,* neut. of *conceptus,* pp. of *concipere* to conceive — more at CONCEIVE] (1556) **1 :** something conceived in the mind : THOUGHT, NOTION **2 :** an abstract or generic idea generalized from particular instances ***syn*** see IDEA

[2]**concept** *adj* (1896) **1 :** organized around a main idea or theme ⟨a ~ album⟩ **2 :** created to illustrate a concept ⟨a ~ car⟩

con·cep·ta·cle \kən-ˈsep-ti-kəl\ *n* [NL *conceptaculum,* fr. L, receptacle, fr. *conceptus,* pp. of *concipere* to take in] (1835) **:** an external cavity containing reproductive cells in algae (as of the genus *Fucus*)

con·cep·tion \kən-ˈsep-shən\ *n* [ME *concepcioun,* fr. AF *concepcion,* fr. L *conception-, conceptio,* fr. *concipere*] (14c) **1 a (1) :** the process of becoming pregnant involving fertilization or implantation or both **(2) :** EMBRYO, FETUS **b :** BEGINNING ⟨joy had the like ~ in our eyes —Shak.⟩ **2 a :** the capacity, function, or process of forming or understanding ideas or abstractions or their symbols **b :** a general idea : CONCEPT **c :** a complex product of abstract or reflective thinking **d :** the sum of a person's ideas and beliefs concerning something **3 :** the originating of something in the mind ***syn*** see IDEA — **con·cep·tion·al** \-shnəl, -shə-nᵊl\ *adj* — **con·cep·tive** \-ˈsep-tiv\ *adj*

con·cep·tu·al \kən-ˈsep-chə-wəl, -chü-əl, kän-, -chəl, -shwəl\ *adj* [ML *conceptualis* of thought, fr. LL *conceptus* act of conceiving, thought, fr. L *concipere*] (ca. 1834) **:** of, relating to, or consisting of concepts ⟨~ thinking⟩ — **con·cep·tu·al·i·ty** \-ˌsep-chə-ˈwa-lə-tē, -shə-; -chü-ˈa-, -shü-\ *n* — **con·cep·tu·al·ly** *adv*

conceptual art *n, often cap C* (ca. 1969) **:** an art form in which the artist's intent is to convey a concept rather than to create an art object — **conceptual artist** *n, often cap C*

con·cep·tu·al·ise *Brit var of* CONCEPTUALIZE

con·cep·tu·al·ism \-ˈsep-chə-wə-ˌli-zəm, -chü-ə-, -chə-ˌli-, -shwə-ˌli-\ *n* (ca. 1838) **1 :** a theory in philosophy intermediate between realism and nominalism that universals exist in the mind as concepts of discourse or as predicates which may be properly affirmed of reality **2** *often cap* **:** CONCEPTUAL ART — **con·cep·tu·al·is·tic** \-ˌsep-chə-wə-ˈlis-tik, -chü-ə-, -chə-ˈlis-, -shwə-ˈlis-\ *adj* — **con·cep·tu·al·is·ti·cal·ly** \-ti-k(ə-)lē\ *adv*

con·cep·tu·al·ist \-ˈsep-chə-wə-list, -chü-ə-, -chə-list, -shwə-list\ *n* (1785) **:** an adherent to the tenets of conceptualism or of conceptual art

con·cep·tu·al·ize \-ˌlīz\ *vt* **-ized; -iz·ing** (1878) **:** to form a concept of; *esp* **:** to interpret conceptually — **con·cep·tu·al·i·za·tion** \-ˌsep-chə-wə-lə-ˈzā-shən, -chü-ə-, -chə-lə-ˈ, -shwə-lə-ˈ\ *n* — **con·cep·tu·al·iz·er** \-ˈsep-chə-wə-ˌlī-zər, -chü-ə-, -chə-ˌlī-, -shwə-ˌlī-\ *n*

con·cep·tus \kən-ˈsep-təs\ *n, pl* **-tus·es** *also* **-ti** \-ˌtī\ [L, one conceived, fr. pp. of *concipere* to conceive] (1745) **:** a fertilized egg, embryo, or fetus

[1]**con·cern** \kən-ˈsərn\ *vb* [ME, fr. MF & ML; MF *concerner,* fr. ML *concernere,* fr. LL, to sift together, mingle, fr. L *com-* + *cernere* to sift — more at CERTAIN] *vt* (15c) **1 a :** to relate to : be about ⟨the novel ~*s* three soldiers⟩ **b :** to bear on **2 :** to have an influence on : INVOLVE; *also* **:** to be the business or affair of ⟨the problem ~*s* us all⟩ **3 :** to be a care, trouble, or distress to ⟨her ill health ~*s* me⟩ **4 :** ENGAGE, OCCUPY ⟨he ~*s* himself with trivia⟩ ~ *vi, obs* **:** to be of importance : MATTER

[2]**concern** *n* (1655) **1 a :** marked interest or regard usu. arising through a personal tie or relationship **b :** an uneasy state of blended interest, uncertainty, and apprehension **2 :** something that relates or belongs to one : AFFAIR ⟨it's no ~ of yours⟩ **3 :** matter for consideration **4 :** an organization or establishment for business or manufacture ⟨a banking ~⟩ **5 :** CONTRIVANCE, GADGET ***syn*** see CARE

concerned *adj* (1656) **1 a :** ANXIOUS, WORRIED ⟨~ for their safety⟩ **b :** INTERESTED ⟨~ to prove the point⟩ **2 a :** interestedly engaged ⟨~ with books and music⟩ **b :** culpably involved : IMPLICATED ⟨arrested all ~⟩

concerning *prep* (15c) **:** relating to : REGARDING

con·cern·ment \kən-ˈsərn-mənt\ *n* (1610) **1 :** something in which one is concerned **2 :** IMPORTANCE, CONSEQUENCE **3** *archaic* **:** INVOLVEMENT, PARTICIPATION **4 :** SOLICITUDE, ANXIETY

[1]**con·cert** \ˈkän(t)-sərt, ˈkän-ˌsərt\ *n* [F, fr. It *concerto,* fr. *concertare*] (1571) **1 :** agreement in design or plan : union formed by mutual communication of opinion and views **2** *obs* **:** musical harmony : CONCORD **3 :** a public performance (as of music or dancing) — **concert** *adj* — **in concert :** TOGETHER ⟨acting *in concert* with others⟩

[2]**con·cert** \kən-ˈsərt\ *vb* [MF *concerter,* fr. OIt *concertare,* perh. fr. *com-* + *certo* certain, decided, fr. L *certus* — more at CERTAIN] *vt* (1652) **1 :** to make a plan for ⟨~ measures for aiding the poor⟩ **2 :** to settle or adjust by conferring and reaching an agreement ⟨~*ed* their differences⟩ ~ *vi* **:** to act in harmony or conjunction

con·cert·ed \kən-ˈsər-təd\ *adj* (1706) **1 a :** mutually contrived or agreed on ⟨a ~ effort⟩ **b :** performed in unison ⟨~ artillery fire⟩ **2 :** arranged in parts for several voices or instruments — **con·cert·ed·ly** *adv* — **con·cert·ed·ness** *n*

con·cert·go·er \ˈkän(t)-sərt-ˌgō(-ə)r, ˈkän-ˌsərt-\ *n* (1853) **:** one who often attends concerts — **con·cert·go·ing** \-ˌgō-iŋ, -ˌgȯ(-)iŋ\ *n or adj*

concert grand *n* (1885) **:** a grand piano of the largest size adapted in volume, timbre, and brilliance of tone to concert use

con·cer·ti·na \ˌkän(t)-sər-ˈtē-nə\ *n* [prob. fr. [1]*concert* + It *-ina,* dim. suffix] (1837) **1 :** a musical instrument of the accordion family **2 :** CONCERTINA WIRE

concertina wire *n* (ca. 1917) **:** a coiled barbed wire used as an obstacle

con·cer·ti·no \ˌkän-chər-ˈtē-(ˌ)nō\ *n, pl* **-nos** [It, dim. of *concerto*] (ca. 1801) **1 :** the solo instruments in a concerto grosso **2 :** a short concerto

con·cert·ize \ˈkän(t)-sər-ˌtīz\ *vi* **-ized; -iz·ing** (1847) **:** to perform professionally in concerts

con·cert·mas·ter \ˈkän(t)-sərt-ˌmas-tər\ *or* **con·cert·meis·ter** \-ˌmī-stər\ *n* [G *Konzertmeister,* fr. *Konzert* concert + *Meister* master] (1853) **:** the leader of the first violins of an orchestra and by custom usu. the assistant to the conductor

con·cer·to \kən-ˈcher-(ˌ)tō *also* -ˈchər-\ *n, pl* **-ti** \-(ˌ)tē\ *or* **-tos** [It, fr. *concerto* concert] (1730) **:** a piece for one or more soloists and orchestra with three contrasting movements

concerto gros·so \-ˈgrō-(ˌ)sō, -ˈgrȯ-\ *n, pl* **concerti gros·si** \-(ˌ)sē\ [It, lit., big concerto] (1724) **:** a baroque orchestral composition featuring a small group of solo instruments contrasting with the full orchestra

concert pitch *n* (1767) **1 :** INTERNATIONAL PITCH **2 :** a high state of fitness, tension, or readiness

con·ces·sion \kən-ˈse-shən\ *n* [ME *concessyon,* fr. AF *concessioun,* fr. L *concession-, concessio,* fr. *concedere* to concede] (15c) **1 a :** the act or an instance of conceding **b :** the admitting of a point claimed in argument **2** : something conceded or granted: **a** : ACKNOWLEDGMENT, ADMISSION **b** : something done or agreed to usu. grudgingly in order to reach an agreement or improve a situation **c** (1) : a grant of land or property esp. by a government in return for services or for a particular use (2) : a right to undertake and profit by a specified activity (3) : a lease of a portion of premises for a particular purpose; *also* : the portion leased or the activities carried on — **con·ces·sion·al** \-ˈsesh-nəl, -ˈse-shə-nᵊl\ *adj* — **con·ces·sion·ary** \-ˈse-shə-ˌner-ē\ *adj*

con·ces·sion·aire \kən-ˌse-shə-ˈner\ *n* [F *concessionnaire,* fr. *concession*] (1862) : the owner or operator of a concession; *esp* : one that operates a refreshment stand at a recreational center

con·ces·sion·er \kən-ˈse-sh(ə-)nər\ *n* (ca. 1891) : CONCESSIONAIRE

con·ces·sive \kən-ˈse-siv\ *adj* (1711) **1** : denoting concession ⟨a ~ clause⟩ **2** : making for or being a concession — **con·ces·sive·ly** *adv*

conch \ˈkäŋk, ˈkänch, ˈkȯŋk\ *n, pl* **conchs** \ˈkäŋks, ˈkȯŋks\ *or* **conches** \ˈkän-chəz\ [ME, fr. L *concha* mussel, mussel shell, fr. Gk *konchē;* akin to Skt *śaṅkha* conch shell] (15c) **1** : any of various large spiral-shelled marine gastropod mollusks (as of the genus *Strombus*); *also* : its shell used esp. for cameos **2** *often cap* : a native or resident of the Florida Keys **3** : CONCHA 2

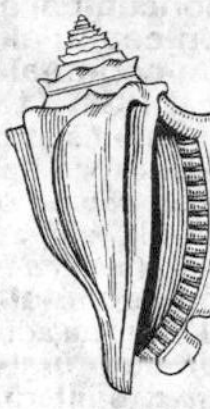

conch 1

[1]con·cha \ˈkäŋ-kə\ *n, pl* **con·chae** \-ˌkē, -ˌkī\ [It & L; It *conca* semidome, apse, fr. LL *concha,* fr. L, shell] (ca. 1639) **1 a** : the plain semidome of an apse **b** : APSE **2** : something shaped like a shell; *esp* : the largest and deepest concavity of the external ear — **con·chal** \-kəl\ *adj*

[2]con·cha \ˈkän-chə\ *also* **con·cho** \-(ˌ)chō\ *n* [AmerSp *concha,* fr. Sp, shell, fr. LL *conchula,* dim. of L *concha*] (1887) : an ornamental disk (as on clothing or tack) of American Indian origin featuring a shell or flower design

con·choi·dal \käŋ-ˈkȯi-dᵊl, kän-\ *adj* [Gk *konchoeidēs* like a mussel, fr. *konchē*] (1666) : having elevations or depressions shaped like the inside surface of a bivalve shell — **con·choi·dal·ly** \-dᵊl-ē\ *adv*

con·chol·o·gy \käŋ-ˈkä-lə-jē\ *n* [Gk *konchē*] (1776) : a branch of zoology that deals with shells — **con·cho·log·i·cal** \ˌkäŋ-kə-ˈlä-jə-kəl\ *adj* — **con·chol·o·gist** \käŋ-ˈkä-lə-jist\ *n*

con·cierge \kō^{n}-ˈsyerzh, ˌkän-sē-ˈerzh\ *n, pl* **con·cierges** \-ˈsyerzh, -ˈsyer-zhəz; -sē-ˈer-zhəz\ [F, fr. OF, prob. fr. VL **conservius,* alter. of L *conservus* fellow slave, fr. *com-* + *servus* slave] (ca. 1697) **1** : a resident in an apartment building esp. in France who serves as doorkeeper, landlord's representative, and janitor **2** : a usu. multilingual hotel staff member who handles luggage and mail, makes reservations, and arranges tours; *broadly* : a person employed (as by a business) to make arrangements or run errands

con·cil·i·ar \kən-ˈsi-lē-ər\ *adj* [L *concilium* council] (ca. 1677) : of, relating to, or issued by a council — **con·cil·i·ar·ly** *adv*

con·cil·i·ate \kən-ˈsi-lē-ˌāt\ *vb* **-at·ed; -at·ing** [L *conciliatus,* pp. of *conciliare* to assemble, unite, win over, fr. *concilium* assembly, council — more at COUNCIL] *vt* (1545) **1** : to gain (as goodwill) by pleasing acts **2** : to make compatible : RECONCILE **3** : APPEASE ~ *vi* : to become friendly or agreeable ***syn*** see PACIFY — **con·cil·i·a·tion** \-ˌsi-lē-ˈā-shən\ *n* — **con·cil·i·a·tive** \-ˈsi-lē-ˌā-tiv\ *adj* — **con·cil·i·a·tor** \-ˌā-tər\ *n* — **con·cil·ia·to·ry** \-ˈsil-yə-ˌtȯr-ē, -ˈsi-lē-ə-\ *adj*

con·cin·ni·ty \kən-ˈsi-nə-tē\ *n, pl* **-ties** [L *concinnitas,* fr. *concinnus* skillfully put together] (1531) : harmony or elegance of design esp. of literary style in adaptation of parts to a whole or to each other

con·cise \kən-ˈsīs\ *adj* [L *concisus,* fr. pp. of *concidere* to cut up, fr. *com-* + *caedere* to cut, strike] (ca. 1590) : marked by brevity of expression or statement : free from all elaboration and superfluous detail ⟨a ~ report⟩ ⟨a ~ definition⟩ — **con·cise·ly** *adv* — **con·cise·ness** *n*

syn CONCISE, TERSE, SUCCINCT, LACONIC, SUMMARY, PITHY, COMPENDIOUS mean very brief in statement or expression. CONCISE suggests the removal of all that is superfluous or elaborative ⟨a *concise* description⟩. TERSE implies pointed conciseness ⟨a *terse* reply⟩. SUCCINCT implies the greatest possible compression ⟨a *succinct* letter of resignation⟩. LACONIC implies brevity to the point of seeming rude, indifferent, or mysterious ⟨an aloof and *laconic* stranger⟩. SUMMARY suggests the statement of main points with no elaboration or explanation ⟨a *summary* listing of the year's main events⟩. PITHY adds to SUCCINCT or TERSE the implication of richness of meaning or substance ⟨a comedy sharpened by *pithy* one-liners⟩. COMPENDIOUS applies to what is at once full in scope and brief and concise in treatment ⟨a *compendious* dictionary⟩.

con·ci·sion \kən-ˈsi-zhən\ *n* [ME, fr. L *concision-, concisio,* fr. *concidere*] (14c) **1** *archaic* : a cutting up or off **2** : the quality or state of being concise

con·clave \ˈkän-ˌklāv\ *n* [ME, fr. MF or ML; MF, fr. ML, fr. L, room that can be locked up, fr. *com-* + *clavis* key — more at CLAVICLE] (1524) **1** : a private meeting or secret assembly; *esp* : a meeting of Roman Catholic cardinals secluded continuously while choosing a pope **2** : a gathering of a group or association

con·clude \kən-ˈklüd\ *vb* **con·clud·ed; con·clud·ing** [ME, fr. L *concludere* to shut up, end, infer, fr. *com-* + *claudere* to shut — more at CLOSE] *vt* (14c) **1** *obs* : to shut up : ENCLOSE **2** : to bring to an end esp. in a particular way or with a particular action ⟨~ a meeting with a prayer⟩ **3 a** : to reach as a logically necessary end by reasoning : infer on the basis of evidence ⟨*concluded* that her argument was sound⟩ **b** : to make a decision about : DECIDE ⟨*concluded* he would wait a little longer⟩ **c** : to come to an agreement on : EFFECT ⟨~ a sale⟩ **4** : to bring about as a result : COMPLETE ~ *vi* **1** : END **2 a** : to form a final judgment **b** : to reach a decision or agreement ***syn*** see CLOSE, INFER — **con·clud·er** *n*

con·clu·sion \kən-ˈklü-zhən\ *n* [ME, fr. AF, fr. L *conclusion-, conclusio,* fr. *concludere*] (14c) **1 a** : a reasoned judgment : INFERENCE **b** : the necessary consequence of two or more propositions taken as premises; *esp* : the inferred proposition of a syllogism **2** : the last part of something: as **a** : RESULT, OUTCOME **b** *pl* : trial of strength or skill — used in the phrase *try conclusions* **c** : a final summation **d** : the final decision in a law case **e** : the final part of a pleading in law **3** : an act or instance of concluding

con·clu·sion·ary \kən-ˈklü-zhə-ˌner-ē\ *adj* (1976) : CONCLUSORY

con·clu·sive \-ˈklü-siv, -ziv\ *adj* (1536) **1** : of, relating to, or being a conclusion **2** : putting an end to debate or question esp. by reason of irrefutability — **con·clu·sive·ly** *adv* — **con·clu·sive·ness** *n*

syn CONCLUSIVE, DECISIVE, DETERMINATIVE, DEFINITIVE mean bringing to an end. CONCLUSIVE applies to reasoning or logical proof that puts an end to debate or questioning ⟨*conclusive* evidence⟩. DECISIVE may apply to something that ends a controversy, a contest, or any uncertainty ⟨a *decisive* battle⟩. DETERMINATIVE adds an implication of giving a fixed character or direction ⟨the *determinative* factor in the court's decision⟩. DEFINITIVE applies to what is put forth as final and permanent ⟨the *definitive* biography⟩.

con·clu·so·ry \kən-ˈklüs-rē, -ˈklü-sə-\ *adj* (1923) : consisting of or relating to a conclusion or assertion for which no supporting evidence is offered ⟨~ allegations⟩

concn *abbr* concentration

con·coct \kən-ˈkäkt, kän-\ *vt* [L *concoctus,* pp. of *concoquere* to cook together, fr. *com-* + *coquere* to cook — more at COOK] (1594) **1** : to prepare by combining raw materials ⟨~ a recipe⟩ **2** : DEVISE, FABRICATE ⟨~ an explanation⟩ — **con·coct·er** *n* — **con·coc·tion** \-ˈkäk-shən\ *n* — **con·coc·tive** \-ˈkäk-tiv\ *adj*

con·com·i·tance \kən-ˈkä-mə-tən(t)s, kän-\ *n* (ca. 1535) : ACCOMPANIMENT; *esp* : a conjunction that is regular and is marked by correlative variation of accompanying elements

[1]con·com·i·tant \-mə-tənt\ *adj* [L *concomitant-, concomitans,* prp. of *concomitari* to accompany, fr. *com-* + *comitari* to accompany, fr. *comit-, comes* companion — more at COUNT] (1607) : accompanying esp. in a subordinate or incidental way — **con·com·i·tant·ly** *adv*

[2]concomitant *n* (1621) : something that accompanies or is collaterally connected with something else : ACCOMPANIMENT

con·cord \ˈkän-ˌkȯrd, ˈkäŋ-\ *n* [ME, fr. AF *concorde,* fr. L *concordia,* fr. *concord-, concors* agreeing, fr. *com-* + *cord-, cor* heart — more at HEART] (14c) **1 a** : a state of agreement : HARMONY **b** : a simultaneous occurrence of two or more musical tones that produces an impression of agreeableness or resolution on a listener — compare DISCORD **2** : agreement by stipulation, compact, or covenant **3** : grammatical agreement

con·cor·dance \kən-ˈkȯr-dᵊn(t)s, kän-\ *n* [ME, fr. AF, fr. ML *concordantia,* fr. L *concordant-, concordans,* prp. of *concordare* to agree, fr. *concord-, concors*] (14c) **1** : an alphabetical index of the principal words in a book or the works of an author with their immediate contexts **2** : CONCORD, AGREEMENT

con·cor·dant \-dᵊnt\ *adj* [ME, fr. AF, fr. L *concordant-, concordans*] (15c) : CONSONANT, AGREEING — **con·cor·dant·ly** *adv*

con·cor·dat \kən-ˈkȯr-ˌdat\ *n* [F, fr. ML *concordatum,* fr. L, neut. of *concordatus,* pp. of *concordare*] (1616) : COMPACT, COVENANT; *specif* : an agreement between a pope and a sovereign or government for the regulation of ecclesiastical matters

con·cours d'e·le·gance \(ˌ)kō^{n}-ˌku̇r-ˌdā-lā-ˈgä^{n}s\ *n, pl* **con·cours d'e·le·gance** *same or* -ˌku̇rz-ˌdā-\ [F *concours d'élégance,* lit., competition of elegance] (1950) : a show or contest of vehicles and accessories in which the entries are judged chiefly on excellence of appearance and turnout

con·course \ˈkän-ˌkȯrs, ˈkäŋ-\ *n* [ME, fr. MF & L; MF *concours,* fr. L *concursus,* fr. *concurrere* to run together — more at CONCUR] (14c) **1** : an act or process of coming together and merging **2** : a meeting produced by voluntary or spontaneous coming together **3 a** : an open space where roads or paths meet **b** : an open space or hall (as in a railroad terminal) where crowds gather

con·cres·cence \kən-ˈkre-sᵊn(t)s, kän-\ *n* [L *concrescentia,* fr. *concrescent-, concrescens,* prp. of *concrescere* to grow together, fr. *com-* + *crescere* to grow — more at CRESCENT] (1614) **1** : increase by the addition of particles **2** : a growing together : COALESCENCE — **con·cres·cent** \-sᵊnt\ *adj*

[1]con·crete \(ˌ)kän-ˈkrēt, ˈkän-ˌ, kən-ˈ\ *adj* [ME, fr. L *concretus,* fr. pp. of *concrescere*] (14c) **1** : naming a real thing or class of things ⟨the word *poem* is ~, *poetry* is abstract⟩ **2** : formed by coalition of particles into one solid mass **3 a** : characterized by or belonging to immediate experience of actual things or events **b** : SPECIFIC, PARTICULAR ⟨a ~ proposal⟩ **c** : REAL, TANGIBLE ⟨~ evidence⟩ **4** : relating to or made of concrete ⟨a ~ wall⟩ — **con·crete·ly** *adv* — **con·crete·ness** *n*

[2]con·crete \ˈkän-ˌkrēt, kän-ˈ\ *vb* **con·cret·ed; con·cret·ing** *vt* (1590) **1 a** : to form into a solid mass : SOLIDIFY **b** : COMBINE, BLEND **2** : to make actual or real : cause to take on the qualities of reality **3** : to cover with, form of, or set in concrete ~ *vi* : to become concreted

[3]con·crete \ˈkän-ˌkrēt, (ˌ)kän-ˈ\ *n* (1656) **1** : a mass formed by concretion or coalescence of separate particles of matter in one body **2** : a hard strong building material made by mixing a cementing material (as portland cement) and a mineral aggregate (as sand and gravel) with sufficient water to cause the cement to set and bind the entire mass **3** : a waxy essence of flowers prepared by extraction and evaporation and used in perfumery

concrete music *n* (1953) : MUSIQUE CONCRÈTE

concrete poetry *n* (1958) : poetry in which the poet's intent is conveyed by the graphic patterns of letters, words, or symbols rather than by the conventional arrangement of words

con·cre·tion \kän-ˈkrē-shən, kən-\ *n* (1541) **1** : something concreted: as **a** : a hard usu. inorganic mass (as a bezoar or tophus) formed in a living body **b** : a mass of mineral matter found generally in rock of a composition different from its own and produced by deposition from aqueous solution in the rock **2** : the act or process of concreting : the state of being concreted ⟨~ of ideas in a hypothesis⟩ — **con·cre·tion·ary** \-shə-ˌner-ē\ *adj*

con·cret·ism \kän-ˈkrē-ˌti-zəm, ˈkän-ˌ\ *n* (1865) : representation of abstract things as concrete; *esp* : the theory or practice of concrete poetry — **con·cret·ist** \-ˈkrē-tist, -ˌkrē-\ *n*

con·cret·ize \-ˌtīz\ *vb* **-ized; -iz·ing** *vt* (1884) : to make concrete, specific, or definite ⟨tried to ~ his ideas⟩ ~ *vi* : to become concrete — **con·cret·i·za·tion** \(ˌ)kän-ˌkrē-tə-ˈzā-shən\ *n*

con·cu·bi·nage \kän-ˈkyü-bə-nij, kən-\ *n* (14c) **1** : cohabitation of persons not legally married **2** : the state of being a concubine

con·cu·bine \ˈkäŋ-kyü-ˌbīn, ˈkän-, -kyü-\ *n* [ME, fr. AF, fr. L *concubina,* fr. *com-* + *cubare* to lie] (14c) : a woman with whom a man cohabits without being married: as **a** : one having a recognized social status in a household below that of a wife **b** : MISTRESS 4a

con·cu·pis·cence \kän-ˈkyü-pə-sən(t)s, kən-\ *n* [ME, fr. AF, fr. LL *concupiscentia,* fr. L *concupiscent-, concupiscens,* prp. of *concupiscere* to desire ardently, fr. *com-* + *cupere* to desire] (14c) : strong desire; *esp* : sexual desire — **con·cu·pis·cent** \-sənt\ *adj*

con·cu·pis·ci·ble \-ˈkyü-pə-sə-bəl\ *adj* [ME, fr. MF or LL; MF, fr. LL *concupiscibilis,* fr. L *concupiscere*] (14c) *archaic* : LUSTFUL, DESIROUS

con·cur \kən-ˈkər, kän-\ *vi* **con·curred; con·cur·ring** [ME *concurren,* fr. L *concurrere,* fr. *com-* + *currere* to run — more at CAR] (15c) **1** : to act together to a common end or single effect **2 a** : APPROVE ⟨~ in a statement⟩ **b** : to express agreement ⟨~ with an opinion⟩ **3** *obs* : to come together : MEET **4** : to happen together : COINCIDE ***syn*** see AGREE

con·cur·rence \-ˈkər-ən(t)s, -ˈkə-rən(t)s\ *n* (15c) **1 a** : the simultaneous occurrence of events or circumstances **b** : the meeting of concurrent lines in a point **2 a** : agreement or union in action : COOPERATION **b** (1) : agreement in opinion or design (2) : CONSENT **3** : a coincidence of equal powers in law

con·cur·ren·cy \-ən(t)-sē, -rən(t)-sē\ *n* (1597) : CONCURRENCE

con·cur·rent \-ˈkər-ənt, -ˈkə-rənt\ *adj* [ME, fr. L *concurrent-, concurrens,* prp. of *concurrere*] (14c) **1** : operating or occurring at the same time **2 a** : running parallel **b** : CONVERGENT; *specif* : meeting or intersecting in a point **3** : acting in conjunction **4** : exercised over the same matter or area by two different authorities ⟨~ jurisdiction⟩ — **concurrent** *n* — **con·cur·rent·ly** *adv*

concurrent resolution *n* (1778) : a resolution passed by both houses of a legislative body that lacks the force of law

con·cuss \kən-ˈkəs\ *vt* [L *concussus,* pp.] (1597) : to affect with or as if with concussion

con·cus·sion \kən-ˈkə-shən\ *n* [ME *concussioun,* fr. L *concussion-, concussio,* fr. *concutere* to shake violently, fr. *com-* + *quatere* to shake] (14c) **1 a** : a stunning, damaging, or shattering effect from a hard blow; *esp* : a jarring injury of the brain resulting in disturbance of cerebral function **b** : a hard blow or collision **2** : AGITATION, SHAKING ***syn*** see IMPACT — **con·cus·sive** \-ˈkə-siv\ *adj*

cond *abbr* **1** condition **2** conductivity

con·demn \kən-ˈdem\ *vt* [ME, fr. AF *condempner,* fr. L *condemnare,* fr. *com-* + *damnare* to condemn — more at DAMN] (14c) **1** : to declare to be reprehensible, wrong, or evil usu. after weighing evidence and without reservation ⟨a policy widely ~*ed* as racist⟩ **2 a** : to pronounce guilty : CONVICT **b** : SENTENCE, DOOM ⟨~ a prisoner to die⟩ **3** : to adjudge unfit for use or consumption ⟨~ an old apartment building⟩ **4** : to declare convertible to public use under the right of eminent domain ***syn*** see CRITICIZE — **con·dem·nable** \-ˈdem-nə-bəl, -ˈde-mə-\ *adj* — **con·dem·na·to·ry** \-ˈdem-nə-ˌtȯr-ē, -ˈde-mə-\ *adj* — **condemn·er** \-ˈde-mər\ *or* **con·dem·nor** \kən-ˈde-mər; kən-ˌdem-ˈnȯr, ˌkän-\ *n*

con·dem·na·tion \ˌkän-ˌdem-ˈnā-shən, -dəm-\ *n* (14c) **1** : CENSURE, BLAME **2** : the act of judicially condemning **3** : the state of being condemned **4** : a reason for condemning

con·den·sate \ˈkän-dən-ˌsāt, -ˌden-; kən-ˈden-\ *n* (1889) : a product of condensation; *esp* : a liquid obtained by condensation of a gas or vapor ⟨steam ~⟩

con·den·sa·tion \ˌkän-ˌden-ˈsā-shən, -dən-\ *n* (1594) **1** : the act or process of condensing: as **a** : a chemical reaction involving union between molecules often with elimination of a simple molecule (as water) to form a new more complex compound of often greater molecular weight **b** : the conversion of a substance (as water) from the vapor state to a denser liquid or solid state usu. initiated by a reduction in temperature of the vapor **c** : compression of a written or spoken work into more concise form **2** : the quality or state of being condensed **3** : a product of condensing — **con·den·sa·tion·al** \-shnəl, -shə-nᵊl\ *adj*

con·dense \kən-ˈden(t)s\ *vb* **con·densed; con·dens·ing** [ME, fr. L *condensare,* fr. *com-* + *densare* to make dense, fr. *densus* dense] *vt* (15c) : to make denser or more compact; *esp* : to subject to condensation ~ *vi* : to undergo condensation ***syn*** see CONTRACT — **con·dens·able** *also* **con·dens·ible** \-ˈden(t)-sə-bəl\ *adj*

condensed *adj* (15c) : reduced to a more compact or dense form; *also* : having a face narrower than that of a standard typeface

condensed milk *n* (1853) : evaporated milk with sugar added

con·dens·er \kən-ˈden(t)-sər\ *n* (1686) **1** : one that condenses: as **a** : a lens or mirror used to concentrate light on an object **b** : an apparatus in which gas or vapor is condensed **2** : CAPACITOR

con·de·scend \ˌkän-di-ˈsend\ *vi* [ME, fr. AF *condescendre,* fr. LL *condescendere,* fr. L *com-* + *descendere* to descend] (14c) **1 a** : to descend to a less formal or dignified level : UNBEND **b** : to waive the privileges of rank **2** : to assume an air of superiority

con·de·scen·dence \-ˈsen-dən(t)s\ *n* (1638) : CONDESCENSION

condescending *adj* (1660) : showing or characterized by condescension : PATRONIZING — **con·de·scend·ing·ly** \-ˈsen-diŋ-lē\ *adv*

con·de·scen·sion \ˌkän-di-ˈsen(t)-shən\ *n* [LL *condescension-, condescensio,* fr. *condescendere*] (1647) **1** : voluntary descent from one's rank or dignity in relations with an inferior **2** : patronizing attitude or behavior

con·dign \kən-ˈdīn, ˈkän-ˌ\ *adj* [ME *condigne,* fr. AF, fr. L *condignus,* fr. *com-* + *dignus* worthy — more at DECENT] (15c) : DESERVED, APPROPRIATE ⟨~ punishment⟩ — **con·dign·ly** *adv*

con·di·ment \ˈkän-də-mənt\ *n* [ME, fr. MF, fr. L *condimentum,* fr. *condire* to season] (15c) : something used to enhance the flavor of food; *esp* : a pungent seasoning — **con·di·men·tal** \ˌkän-də-ˈmen-tᵊl\ *adj*

[1]**con·di·tion** \kən-ˈdi-shən\ *n* [ME *condicion,* fr. AF, fr. L *condicion-, condicio* terms of agreement, condition, fr. *condicere* to agree, fr. *com-* + *dicere* to say, determine — more at DICTION] (14c) **1 a** : a premise upon which the fulfillment of an agreement depends : STIPULATION **b** *obs* : COVENANT **c** : a provision making the effect of a legal instrument contingent upon an uncertain event; *also* : the event itself **2** : something essential to the appearance or occurrence of something else : PREREQUISITE: as **a** : an environmental requirement ⟨available oxygen is an essential ~ for animal life⟩ **b** : the subordinate clause of a conditional sentence **3 a** : a restricting or modifying factor : QUALIFICATION **b** : an unsatisfactory academic grade that may be raised by doing additional work **4 a** : a state of being ⟨the human ~⟩ **b** : social status : RANK **c** : a usu. defective state of health ⟨a serious heart ~⟩ **d** : a state of physical fitness or readiness for use ⟨the car was in good ~⟩ ⟨exercising to get into ~⟩ **e** *pl* : attendant circumstances ⟨poor living ~*s*⟩ **5 a** *obs* : temper of mind **b** *obs* : TRAIT **c** *pl, archaic* : MANNERS, WAYS

[2]**condition** *vb* **con·di·tioned; con·di·tion·ing** \-ˈdi-sh(ə-)niŋ\ *vi* (15c) *archaic* : to make stipulations ~ *vt* **1** : to agree by stipulating **2** : to make conditional **3 a** : to put into a proper state for work or use **b** : AIR-CONDITION **4** : to give a grade of condition to **5 a** : to adapt, modify, or mold so as to conform to an environing culture ⟨traditional beliefs ~*ing* a child's attitude⟩ **b** : to modify so that an act or response previously associated with one stimulus becomes associated with another — **con·di·tion·able** \-sh(ə-)nə-bəl\ *adj*

[1]**con·di·tion·al** \kən-ˈdish-nəl, -ˈdi-shə-nᵊl\ *adj* (14c) **1** : subject to, implying, or dependent upon a condition ⟨a ~ promise⟩ **2** : expressing, containing, or implying a supposition ⟨the ~ clause *if he speaks*⟩ **3 a** : true only for certain values of the variables or symbols involved ⟨~ equations⟩ **b** : stating the case when one or more random variables are fixed or one or more events are known ⟨~ frequency distribution⟩ **4 a** : CONDITIONED 2 ⟨~ reflex⟩ ⟨~ response⟩ **b** : established by conditioning as the stimulus eliciting a conditional response — **con·di·tion·al·i·ty** \-ˌdi-shə-ˈna-lə-tē\ *n* — **con·di·tion·al·ly** \-ˈdish-nə-lē, -ˈdi-shə-nə-lē\ *adv*

[2]**conditional** *n* (1828) **1** : a conditional word, clause, verb form, or morpheme **2** : IMPLICATION 2b

conditional probability *n* (1937) : the probability that a given event will occur if it is certain that another event has taken place or will take place

conditioned *adj* (1537) **1** : brought or put into a specified state **2** : determined or established by conditioning

con·di·tion·er \-ˈdi-sh(ə-)nər\ *n* (1888) : something that conditions; *specif* : a preparation used to improve the condition of hair

con·di·tion·ing \-ˈdi-sh(ə-)niŋ\ *n* (1861) **1** : the process of training to become physically fit by a regimen of exercise, diet, and rest; *also* : the resulting state of physical fitness **2** : a simple form of learning involving the formation, strengthening, or weakening of an association between a stimulus and a response

con·do \ˈkän-(ˌ)dō\ *n, pl* **condos** (1964) : CONDOMINIUM 3

con·dole \kən-ˈdōl\ *vb* **con·doled; con·dol·ing** [LL *condolēre,* fr. L *com-* + *dolēre* to feel pain] *vi* (ca. 1586) **1** *obs* : GRIEVE **2** : to express sympathetic sorrow ~ *vt, archaic* : LAMENT, GRIEVE — **con·do·la·to·ry** \-ˈdō-le-ˌtȯr-ē\ *adj*

con·do·lence \kən-ˈdō-lən(t)s *also* ˈkän-də-\ *n* (1603) **1** : sympathy with another in sorrow **2** : an expression of sympathy ***syn*** see PITY

con·dom \ˈkän-dəm, ˈkən-, *dial* -drəm\ *n* [origin unknown] (ca. 1706) **1** : a sheath commonly of rubber worn over the penis (as to prevent conception or venereal infection during coitus) **2** : a device that is designed to be inserted into the vagina before coitus and that resembles in form and function the condom used by males

con·do·min·i·um \ˌkän-də-ˈmi-nē-əm\ *n, pl* **-iums** *also* **-ia** \-nē-ə\ [NL, fr. L *com-* + *dominium* domain] (ca. 1714) **1 a** : joint dominion; *esp* : joint sovereignty by two or more nations **b** : a government operating under joint rule **2** : a politically dependent territory under condominium **3 a** : individual ownership of a unit in a multiunit structure (as an apartment building) or on land owned in common (as a town house complex); *also* : a unit so owned **b** : a building containing condominiums

con·do·na·tion \ˌkän-də-ˈnā-shən, -dō-\ *n* (1625) : implied pardon of an offense by treating the offender as if it had not been committed

con·done \kən-ˈdōn\ *vt* **con·doned; con·don·ing** [L *condonare* to absolve, fr. *com-* + *donare* to give — more at DONATION] (1805) : to regard or treat (something bad or blameworthy) as acceptable, forgivable, or harmless ⟨a government accused of *condoning* racism⟩ ⟨~ corruption in politics⟩ ***syn*** see EXCUSE — **con·don·able** \-ˈdō-nə-bəl\ *adj* — **con·don·er** *n*

con·dor \ˈkän-dər, -ˌdȯr\ *n* [Sp *cóndor,* fr. Quechua *kuntur*] (1604) **1 a** : a very large American vulture (*Vultur gryphus*) of the high Andes having the head and neck bare and the plumage dull black with a downy white neck ruff and white patches on the wings — called also *Andean condor* **b** : CALIFORNIA CONDOR **2** *pl* **condors** *or* **con·do·res** \kən-ˈdȯr-ˌās\ : a coin (as the centesimo of Chile) bearing the picture of a condor

con·dot·tie·re \ˌkän-də-ˈtyer-ē, ˌkän-ˌdä-tē-ˈer-\ *n, pl* **-tie·ri** \-ē\ [It, fr. *condotta* troop of mercenaries, fr. fem. of *condotto,* pp. of *condurre* to conduct, hire, fr. L *conducere*] (1794) **1** : a leader of a band of mercenaries common in Europe between the 14th and 16th centuries; *also* : a member of such a band **2** : a mercenary soldier

con·duce \kən-ˈdüs, -ˈdyüs\ *vi* **con·duced; con·duc·ing** [ME, to conduct, fr. L *conducere* to conduct, conduce, fr. *com-* + *ducere* to lead — more at TOW] (1528) : to lead or tend to a particular and often desirable result : CONTRIBUTE

con·du·cive \-ˈdü-siv, -ˈdyü-\ *adj* (1646) : tending to promote or assist ⟨an atmosphere ~ to education⟩ — **con·du·cive·ness** *n*

[1]**con·duct** \ˈkän-(ˌ)dəkt\ *n* [ME, fr. ML *conductus,* fr. L *conducere*] (15c) **1** *obs* : ESCORT, GUIDE **2** : the act, manner, or process of carrying on : MANAGEMENT ⟨praised for his ~ of the campaign⟩ **3** : a mode or standard of personal behavior esp. as based on moral principles ⟨questionable ~⟩

[2]**con·duct** \kən-ˈdəkt *also* ˈkän-ˌdəkt\ *vt* (15c) **1** : to bring by or as if by leading : GUIDE ⟨~ tourists through a museum⟩ **2 a** : to lead from a position of command ⟨~ a siege⟩ ⟨~ a class⟩ **b** : to direct or take part in the operation or management of ⟨~ an experiment⟩ ⟨~ a business⟩ ⟨~ an investigation⟩ **c** : to direct the performance of ⟨~ an orchestra⟩ ⟨~ an opera⟩ **3 a** : to convey in a channel **b** : to act as a medium for conveying or transmitting **4** : to cause (oneself) to act or behave in a particular and esp. in a controlled manner ~ *vi* **1** *of a road or passage* : to show the way : LEAD **2 a** : to act as leader or director **b** : to have the quality of transmitting light, heat, sound, or

\ə\ **a**but \ᵊ\ kitten, F table \ər\ **fur**ther \a\ **a**sh \ā\ **a**ce \ä\ m**o**p, m**a**r
\au̇\ **ou**t \ch\ **ch**in \e\ b**e**t \ē\ **ea**sy \g\ **g**o \i\ h**i**t \ī\ **i**ce \j\ **j**ob
\ŋ\ si**ng** \ō\ g**o** \ȯ\ l**aw** \ȯi\ b**oy** \th\ **th**in \t͟h\ **th**e \ü\ l**oo**t \u̇\ f**oo**t
\y\ yet \zh\ vi**s**ion, beige \k, ⁿ, œ, ue, ʸ\ *see* Guide to Pronunciation

electricity — **con•duct•ibil•i•ty** \kən-ˌdək-tə-ˈbi-lə-tē\ *n* — **con•duct•ible** \-ˈdək-tə-bəl\ *adj*

syn CONDUCT, MANAGE, CONTROL, DIRECT mean to use one's powers to lead, guide, or dominate. CONDUCT implies taking responsibility for the acts and achievements of a group ⟨*conducted* negotiations⟩. MANAGE implies direct handling and manipulating or maneuvering toward a desired result ⟨*manages* a meat market⟩. CONTROL implies a regulating or restraining in order to keep within bounds or on a course ⟨*controlling* his appetite⟩. DIRECT implies constant guiding and regulating so as to achieve smooth operation ⟨*directs* the store's day-to-day business⟩. ***syn*** see in addition BEHAVE

con•duc•tance \kən-ˈdək-tən(t)s\ *n* (1885) **1 :** conducting power **2 :** the readiness with which a conductor transmits an electric current expressed as the reciprocal of electrical resistance

con•duc•tion \kən-ˈdək-shən\ *n* (1534) **1 :** the act of conducting or conveying **2 a :** transmission through or by means of a conductor; *also* **:** the transfer of heat through matter by communication of kinetic energy from particle to particle with no net displacement of the particles — compare CONVECTION, RADIATION **b :** CONDUCTIVITY **3 :** the transmission of excitation through living tissue and esp. nervous tissue

conduction band *n* (1939) **:** the range of permissible energy values which an electron in a solid material can have that allows the electron to dissociate from a particular atom and become a free charge carrier in the material — compare VALENCE BAND

con•duc•tive \kən-ˈdək-tiv\ *adj* (1840) **:** having conductivity **:** relating to conduction (as of electricity)

con•duc•tiv•i•ty \ˌkän-ˌdək-ˈti-və-tē, kən-\ *n, pl* **-ties** (1837) **:** the quality or power of conducting or transmitting: as **a :** the reciprocal of electrical resistivity **b :** the quality of living matter responsible for the transmission of and progressive reaction to stimuli

con•duc•to•met•ric *also* **con•duc•ti•met•ric** \kən-ˌdək-tə-ˈme-trik\ *adj* (ca. 1926) **1 :** of or relating to the measurement of conductivity **2 :** being or relating to titration based on determination of changes in the electrical conductivity of the solution

con•duc•tor \kən-ˈdək-tər\ *n* (15c) **:** one that conducts: as **a :** GUIDE **b :** a collector of fares in a public conveyance **c :** the leader of a musical ensemble **d** (1) **:** a material or object that permits an electric current to flow easily — compare INSULATOR, SEMICONDUCTOR (2) **:** a material capable of transmitting another form of energy (as heat or sound) — **con•duc•to•ri•al** \ˌkän-ˌdək-ˈtȯr-ē-əl, kən-\ *adj*

con•duc•tress \kən-ˈdək-trəs\ *n* (1624) **:** a woman who is a conductor

con•duit \ˈkän-ˌdü-ət, -ˌdyü- *also* -dwət, -dət\ *n* [ME, fr. AF *cunduit* pipe, passage, conduct, in part fr. *cunduit,* pp. of *cunduire* to lead, fr. L *conducere,* in part fr. ML *conductus* — more at CONDUCT] (14c) **1 :** a natural or artificial channel through which something (as a fluid) is conveyed **2** *archaic* **:** FOUNTAIN **3 :** a pipe, tube, or tile for protecting electric wires or cables **4 :** a means of transmitting or distributing ⟨a ~ for illicit payments⟩ ⟨a ~ of information⟩

con•du•pli•cate \(ˌ)kän-ˈdü-pli-kət, -ˈdyü-\ *adj* [L *conduplicatus,* pp. of *conduplicare* to double, fr. *com-* + *duplic-, duplex* double — more at DUPLEX] (1777) **:** folded lengthwise ⟨~ petals in the bud⟩

con•dy•lar \ˈkän-də-lər\ *adj* (1876) **:** of or relating to a condyle

con•dyle \ˈkän-ˌdī(-ə)l *also* -dᵊl\ *n* [F & L; F, fr. L *condylus* knuckle, fr. Gk *kondylos*] (1634) **:** an articular prominence of a bone; *esp* **:** one resembling a pair of knuckles — **con•dy•loid** \-də-ˌlȯid\ *adj*

con•dy•lo•ma \ˌkän-də-ˈlō-mə\ *n, pl* **-ma•ta** \-mə-tə\ *also* **-mas** [NL, fr. Gk *kondylōma,* fr. *kondylos*] (ca. 1526) **:** GENITAL WART — **con•dy•lo•ma•tous** \-mə-təs\ *adj*

[1]**cone** \ˈkōn\ *n* [MF or L; MF, fr. L *conus,* fr. Gk *kōnos*] (1545) **1 a :** a solid generated by rotating a right triangle about one of its legs — called also *right circular cone* **b :** a solid bounded by a circular or other closed plane base and the surface formed by line segments joining every point of the boundary of the base to a common vertex — see VOLUME table **c :** a surface traced by a moving straight line passing through a fixed vertex **2 a :** a mass of ovule-bearing or pollen-bearing scales or bracts in most conifers or in cycads that are arranged usu. on a somewhat elongated axis **b :** any of several flower or fruit clusters suggesting a cone **3 :** something that resembles a cone in shape: as **a :** any of the conical photosensitive receptor cells of the vertebrate retina that function in color vision — compare ROD 3 **b :** any of a family (Conidae) of tropical marine gastropod mollusks that inject their prey with a potent toxin **c :** the apex of a volcano **d :** a crisp usu. cone-shaped wafer for holding ice cream

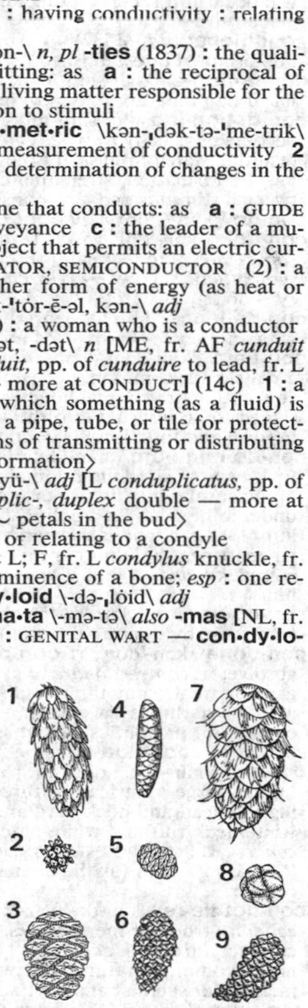

cone 2a: *1* Sitka spruce, *2* cryptomeria, *3* giant sequoia, *4* white spruce, *5* redwood, *6* lodgepole pine, *7* Douglas fir, *8* bald cypress, *9* jack pine

[2]**cone** *vt* **coned; con•ing** (1845) **1 :** to make cone-shaped **2 :** to bevel like the slanting surface of a cone ⟨~ a tire⟩

cone•flow•er \ˈkōn-ˌflau̇(-ə)r\ *n* (ca. 1818) **:** any of several composite plants (as of the genera *Echinacea* and *Ratibida*) having cone-shaped flower disks: as **a :** RUDBECKIA **b :** PURPLE CONEFLOWER

cone•nose \ˈkōn-ˌnōz\ *n* (ca. 1891) **:** KISSING BUG

con es•pres•sio•ne \ˌkän-ˌes-(ˌ)pre-sē-ˈō-nē, ˌkōn-, -ˈō-(ˌ)nā\ *adv* [It, lit., with expression] (1864) **:** with feeling — used as a direction in music

Con•es•to•ga wagon \ˌkä-nə-ˈstō-gə-\ *n* [*Conestoga,* Pa.] (1717) **:** a broad-wheeled covered wagon drawn usu. by six horses and used esp. for transporting freight across the prairies — called also *Conestoga*

co•ney *or* **co•ny** \ˈkō-nē, *1 also* ˈkə-nē\ *n, pl* **coneys** *or* **conies** [ME *conies,* pl., fr. AF *conis,* pl. of *conil,* fr. L *cuniculus*] (12c) **1 a :** rabbit fur **b** (1) **:** RABBIT; *esp* **:** the European rabbit (*Oryctolagus cuniculus*) (2) **:** PIKA **c :** HYRAX **2** *archaic* **:** DUPE **3 :** any of several fishes; *esp* **:** a dusky black-spotted reddish-finned grouper (*Epinephelus fulvus* syn. *Cephalopholis fulva*) of the tropical Atlantic

conf *abbr* **1** conference **2** confidential

con•fab \ˈkän-ˌfab, kən-ˈ\ *n* (1701) **1 :** CHAT 1 **2 :** DISCUSSION, CONFERENCE — **con•fab** \kən-ˈfab, ˈkän-ˌ\ *vi*

con•fab•u•late \kən-ˈfa-byə-ˌlāt\ *vi* **-lat•ed; -lat•ing** [L *confabulatus,* pp. of *confabulari,* fr. *com-* + *fabulari* to talk, fr. *fabula* story — more at FABLE] (ca. 1604) **1 :** to talk informally **:** CHAT **2 :** to hold a discussion **:** CONFER **3 :** to fill in gaps in memory by fabrication — **con•fab•u•la•tion** \kən-ˌfa-byə-ˈlā-shən\ *n* — **con•fab•u•la•tor** \kən-ˈfa-byə-ˌlā-tər\ *n* — **con•fab•u•la•to•ry** \-lə-ˌtȯr-ē\ *adj*

con•fect \kən-ˈfekt\ *vt* [ME, fr. L *confectus,* pp. of *conficere* to prepare — more at COMFIT] (14c) **1 :** to put together from varied material **2 a :** PREPARE **b :** PRESERVE — **con•fect** \ˈkän-ˌ\ *n*

con•fec•tion \kən-ˈfek-shən\ *n* (15c) **1 :** the act or process of confecting **2 :** something confected: as **a :** a fancy dish or sweetmeat; *also* **:** a sweet food **b :** a medicinal preparation usu. made with sugar, syrup, or honey **c :** a work of fine or elaborate craftsmanship **d :** a light but entertaining theatrical, cinematic, or literary work

con•fec•tion•ary \-shə-ˌner-ē\ *n, pl* **-ar•ies** (1599) **1 :** SWEETS **2** *archaic* **:** CONFECTIONER **3 :** CONFECTIONERY 3 — **confectionary** *adj*

con•fec•tion•er \-sh(ə-)nər\ *n* (1591) **:** a manufacturer of or dealer in confections

confectioners' sugar *n* (ca. 1889) **:** a refined finely powdered sugar

con•fec•tion•ery \-shə-ˌner-ē\ *n, pl* **-er•ies** (1751) **1 :** the confectioner's art or business **2 :** sweet foods (as candy or pastry) **3 :** a confectioner's shop

Confed *abbr* Confederate

con•fed•er•a•cy \kən-ˈfe-d(ə-)rə-sē\ *n, pl* **-cies** (14c) **1 :** a league or compact for mutual support or common action **:** ALLIANCE **2 :** a combination of persons for unlawful purposes **:** CONSPIRACY **3 :** the body formed by persons, states, or nations united by a league; *specif, cap* **:** the 11 southern states seceding from the U.S. in 1860 and 1861

con•fed•er•al \-d(ə-)rəl\ *adj* (1780) **:** of or relating to a confederation

[1]**con•fed•er•ate** \kən-ˈfe-d(ə-)rət\ *adj* [ME *confederat,* fr. LL *confoederatus,* pp. of *confoederare* to unite by a league, fr. L *com-* + *foeder-, foedus* compact — more at FEDERAL] (14c) **1 :** united in a league **:** ALLIED **2** *cap* **:** of or relating to the Confederate States of America

[2]**confederate** *n* (15c) **1 :** ALLY, ACCOMPLICE **2** *cap* **:** an adherent of the Confederate States of America or their cause

[3]**con•fed•er•ate** \-ˈfe-də-ˌrāt\ *vb* **-at•ed; -at•ing** *vt* (1531) **:** to unite in a confederacy ~ *vi* **:** to band together — **con•fed•er•a•tive** \-ˈfe-d(ə-)rə-tiv, -də-ˌrā-\ *adj*

Confederate Memorial Day *n* (1899) **:** any of several days appointed for the commemoration of servicemen of the Confederacy

con•fed•er•a•tion \kən-ˌfe-də-ˈrā-shən\ *n* (15c) **1 :** an act of confederating **:** a state of being confederated **:** ALLIANCE **2 :** LEAGUE

con•fer \kən-ˈfər\ *vb* **con•ferred; con•fer•ring** [L *conferre* to bring together, fr. *com-* + *ferre* to carry — more at BEAR] *vi* (ca. 1500) **:** to compare views or take counsel **:** CONSULT ~ *vt* **1 :** to bestow from or as if from a position of superiority ⟨*conferred* an honorary degree on her⟩ ⟨knowing how to read was a gift *conferred* with manhood —Murray Kempton⟩ **2 :** to give (as a property or characteristic) to someone or something ⟨a reputation for power will ~ power —John Spanier⟩ ***syn*** see GIVE — **con•fer•ment** \-ˈfər-mənt\ *n* — **con•fer•ra•ble** \-ˈfər-ə-bəl\ *adj* — **con•fer•ral** \-ˈfər-əl\ *n* — **con•fer•rer** \-ˈfər-ər\ *n*

con•fer•ee \ˌkän-fə-ˈrē\ *n* (1771) **:** one taking part in a conference

con•fer•ence \ˈkän-f(ə-)rən(t)s, -fərn(t)s, *for 2 usu* kən-ˈfər-ən(t)s\ *n* (1527) **1 a :** a meeting of two or more persons for discussing matters of common concern **b :** a usu. formal interchange of views **:** CONSULTATION **c :** a meeting of members of the two branches of a legislature to adjust differences **d :** CAUCUS **2** *also* **con•fer•rence** \kən-ˈfər-ən(t)s\ **:** BESTOWAL, CONFERMENT **3 a :** a representative assembly or administrative organization of a religious denomination **b :** a territorial division of a religious denomination **4 :** an association of athletic teams — **con•fer•en•tial** \ˌkän-fə-ˈren(t)-shəl\ *adj*

conference call *n* (1941) **:** a telephone call by which a caller can speak with several people at the same time

con•fer•enc•ing \ˈkän-f(ə-)rən(t)-siŋ, -fərn(t)-\ *n* (1865) **:** the holding of conferences esp. by means of an electronic communications system ⟨computer ~⟩

con•fess \kən-ˈfes\ *vb* [ME, fr. AF *confesser,* fr. *confés* having confessed, fr. L *confessus,* pp. of *confitēri* to confess, fr. *com-* + *fatēri* to confess; akin to L *fari* to speak — more at BAN] *vt* (14c) **1 :** to tell or make known (as something wrong or damaging to oneself) **:** ADMIT ⟨he ~*ed* his guilt⟩ **2 a :** to acknowledge (sin) to God or to a priest **b :** to receive the confession of (a penitent) **3 :** to declare faith in or adherence to **:** PROFESS **4 :** to give evidence of ~ *vi* **1 a :** to disclose one's faults; *specif* **:** to unburden one's sins or the state of one's conscience to God or to a priest **b :** to hear a confession **2 :** ADMIT, OWN ⟨~ to a crime⟩ ***syn*** see ACKNOWLEDGE — **con•fess•able** \-ˈfe-sə-bəl\ *adj*

con•fessed•ly \-ˈfe-səd-lē, -ˈfest-lē\ *adv* (1634) **:** by confession

con•fes•sion \kən-ˈfe-shən\ *n* (14c) **1 a :** an act of confessing; *esp* **:** a disclosure of one's sins in the sacrament of reconciliation **b :** a session for the confessing of sins ⟨go to ~⟩ **2 :** a statement of what is confessed: as **a :** a written or oral acknowledgment of guilt by a party accused of an offense **b :** a formal statement of religious beliefs **:** CREED **3 :** an organized religious body having a common creed

[1]**con•fes•sion•al** \-ˈfesh-nəl, -ˈfe-shə-nᵊl\ *n* (1727) **1 :** a place where a priest hears confessions **2 :** the practice of confessing to a priest

[2]**confessional** *adj* (1684) **1 :** of, relating to, or being a confession esp. of faith **2 :** of, relating to, or being intimately autobiographical ⟨~ fiction⟩ — **con•fes•sion•al•ism** \-nə-ˌli-zəm\ *n* — **con•fes•sion•al•ist** \-list\ *n* — **con•fes•sion•al•ly** \-nə-lē, -nᵊl-ē\ *adv*

con•fes•sor \kən-ˈfe-sər, *1 & 3 also* ˈkän-ˌfe-sər, *3 also* ˈkän-fə-ˌsȯr\ *n* (12c) **1 :** one who gives heroic evidence of faith but does not suffer martyrdom **2 :** one that confesses **3 a :** a priest who hears confessions **b :** a priest who is one's regular spiritual guide

con•fet•ti \kən-ˈfe-tē\ *n* [It, pl. of *confetto* sweetmeat, fr. ML *confectum,* fr. L, neut. of *confectus,* pp. of *conficere* to prepare — more at COMFIT] (1815) **:** small bits or streamers of brightly colored paper made for throwing (as at weddings)

con•fi•dant \ˈkän-fə-ˌdänt *also* -ˌdant, -dənt\ *n* [F *confident,* fr. It *confidente* confident, trustworthy, fr. L *confident-, confidens*] (1646) **:** one to whom secrets are entrusted; *esp* **:** INTIMATE

con•fi•dante *same as* CONFIDANT\ *n* [F *confidente,* fem. of *confident*] (1662) **:** CONFIDANT; *esp* **:** one who is a woman

con·fide \kən-ˈfīd\ *vb* **con·fid·ed; con·fid·ing** [ME (Sc), fr. L *confidere,* fr. *com-* + *fidere* to trust — more at BIDE] *vi* (15c) **1 :** to have confidence : TRUST **2 :** to show confidence by imparting secrets ⟨~ in a friend⟩ ~ *vt* **1 :** to tell confidentially **2 :** to give to the care or protection of another : ENTRUST ***syn*** see COMMIT — **con·fid·er** *n*

1**con·fi·dence** \ˈkän-fə-dən(t)s, -ˌden(t)s\ *n* (14c) **1 a :** a feeling or consciousness of one's powers or of reliance on one's circumstances ⟨had perfect ~ in her ability to succeed⟩ ⟨met the risk with brash ~⟩ **b :** faith or belief that one will act in a right, proper, or effective way ⟨have ~ in a leader⟩ **2 :** the quality or state of being certain : CERTITUDE ⟨they had every ~ of success⟩ **3 a :** a relation of trust or intimacy ⟨took his friend into his ~⟩ **b :** reliance on another's discretion ⟨their story was told in strictest ~⟩ **c :** support esp. in a legislative body ⟨vote of ~⟩ **4 :** a communication made in confidence : SECRET ⟨accused him of betraying a ~⟩

syn CONFIDENCE, ASSURANCE, SELF-POSSESSION, APLOMB mean a state of mind or a manner marked by easy coolness and freedom from uncertainty, diffidence, or embarrassment. CONFIDENCE stresses faith in oneself and one's powers without any suggestion of conceit or arrogance ⟨the *confidence* that comes from long experience⟩. ASSURANCE carries a stronger implication of certainty and may suggest arrogance or lack of objectivity in assessing one's own powers ⟨handled the cross-examination with complete *assurance*⟩. SELF-POSSESSION implies an ease or coolness under stress that reflects perfect self-control and command of one's powers ⟨answered the insolent question with complete *self-possession*⟩. APLOMB implies a manifest self-possession in trying or challenging situations ⟨handled the reporters with great *aplomb*⟩.

2**confidence** *adj* (1849) **:** of, relating to, or adept at swindling by false promises ⟨a ~ game⟩ ⟨a ~ man⟩

confidence interval *n* (1934) **:** a group of continuous or discrete adjacent values that is used to estimate a statistical parameter (as a mean or variance) and that tends to include the true value of the parameter a predetermined proportion of the time if the process of finding the group of values is repeated a number of times

confidence limits *n pl* (1939) **:** the end points of a confidence interval

con·fi·dent \ˈkän-fə-dənt, -ˌdent\ *adj* [L *confident-, confidens,* fr. prp. of *confidere*] (ca. 1567) **1 :** full of conviction : CERTAIN ⟨~ of success⟩ ⟨~ that conditions will improve⟩ **2 :** having or showing assurance and self-reliance ⟨a ~ young businessman⟩ ⟨a ~ manner⟩ **3** *obs* **:** TRUSTFUL, CONFIDING — **con·fi·dent·ly** *adv*

con·fi·den·tial \ˌkän-fə-ˈden(t)-shəl\ *adj* (1759) **1 :** marked by intimacy or willingness to confide ⟨a ~ tone⟩ **2 :** PRIVATE, SECRET ⟨~ information⟩ **3 :** entrusted with confidences ⟨a ~ clerk⟩ **4 :** containing information whose unauthorized disclosure could be prejudicial to the national interest — compare SECRET, TOP SECRET — **con·fi·den·ti·al·i·ty** \-ˌden(t)-shē-ˈa-lə-tē\ *n* — **con·fi·den·tial·ly** \-ˈden(t)-sh(ə-)lē\ *adv*

con·fid·ing \kən-ˈfī-diŋ\ *adj* (1797) **:** tending to confide : TRUSTFUL — **con·fid·ing·ly** \-diŋ-lē\ *adv* — **con·fid·ing·ness** *n*

con·fig·u·ra·tion \kən-ˌfi-gyə-ˈrā-shən, ˌkän-, -gə-ˈ\ *n* [LL *configuration-, configuratio* similar formation, fr. L *configurare* to form from or after, fr. *com-* + *figurare* to form, fr. *figura* figure] (1559) **1 a :** relative arrangement of parts or elements: as **(1) :** SHAPE **(2) :** contour of land ⟨~ of the mountains⟩ **(3) :** functional arrangement ⟨a small business computer system in its simplest ~⟩ **b :** something (as a figure, contour, pattern, or apparatus) that results from a particular arrangement of parts or components **c :** the stable structural makeup of a chemical compound esp. with reference to the space relations of the constituent atoms **2 :** GESTALT ⟨personality ~⟩ — **con·fig·u·ra·tion·al** \-shnəl, -shə-nᵊl\ *adj* — **con·fig·u·ra·tion·al·ly** *adv* — **con·fig·u·ra·tive** \-ˈfi-gyə-rə-tiv, -ˈfi-gə-\ *adj*

con·fig·ure \kən-ˈfi-gyər, *esp Brit* -ˈfi-gər\ *vt* **-ured; -ur·ing** (1677) **:** to set up for operation esp. in a particular way ⟨a fighter plane *configured* for the Malaysian air force⟩

1**con·fine** \ˈkän-ˌfīn *also* kən-ˈ\ *n* [ME, fr. AF or L; AF *confines,* pl., fr. L *confine* border, fr. neut. of *confinis* adjacent, fr. *com-* + *finis* end] (15c) **1** *pl* **a :** something (as borders or walls) that encloses ⟨outside the ~*s* of the office or hospital —W. A. Nolen⟩; *also* **:** something that restrains ⟨escape from the ~*s* of soot and clutter —E. S. Muskie⟩ **b :** SCOPE 3 ⟨work within the ~*s* of a small group —Frank Newman⟩ **2 a** *archaic* **:** RESTRICTION **b** *obs* **:** PRISON

2**con·fine** \kən-ˈfīn\ *vb* **con·fined; con·fin·ing** *vi* (1523) *archaic* **:** BORDER ~ *vt* **1 a :** to hold within a location **b :** IMPRISON **2 :** to keep within limits ⟨will ~ my remarks to one subject⟩ ***syn*** see LIMIT — **con·fin·er** *n*

con·fined \kən-ˈfīnd\ *adj* (1772) **:** undergoing childbirth

con·fine·ment \kən-ˈfīn-mənt\ *n* (1592) **:** an act of confining : the state of being confined ⟨solitary ~⟩; *esp* **:** LYING-IN

con·firm \kən-ˈfərm\ *vt* [ME, fr. AF *cunfermer,* fr. L *confirmare,* fr. *com-* + *firmare* to make firm, fr. *firmus* firm] (13c) **1 :** to give approval to : RATIFY ⟨~ a treaty⟩ **2 :** to make firm or firmer : STRENGTHEN ⟨~ one's resolve⟩ **3 :** to administer the rite of confirmation to **4 :** to give new assurance of the validity of : remove doubt about by authoritative act or indisputable fact ⟨~ a rumor⟩ ⟨~ an order⟩ — **con·firm·abil·i·ty** \-ˌfər-mə-ˈbi-lə-tē\ *n* — **con·firm·able** \-ˈfər-mə-bəl\ *adj*

syn CONFIRM, CORROBORATE, SUBSTANTIATE, VERIFY, AUTHENTICATE, VALIDATE mean to attest to the truth or validity of something. CONFIRM implies the removing of doubts by an authoritative statement or indisputable fact ⟨*confirmed* the reports⟩. CORROBORATE suggests the strengthening of what is already partly established ⟨witnesses *corroborated* his story⟩. SUBSTANTIATE implies the offering of evidence that sustains the contention ⟨the claims have yet to be *substantiated*⟩. VERIFY implies the establishing of correspondence of actual facts or details with those proposed or guessed at ⟨all statements of fact in the article have been *verified*⟩. AUTHENTICATE implies establishing genuineness by adducing legal or official documents or expert opinion ⟨handwriting experts *authenticated* the diaries⟩. VALIDATE implies establishing validity by authoritative affirmation or by factual proof ⟨*validated* the hypothesis by experiments⟩.

con·fir·mand \ˌkän-fər-ˈmand\ *n* [L *confirmandus,* gerundive of *confirmare*] (1884) **:** a candidate for religious confirmation

con·fir·ma·tion \ˌkän-fər-ˈmā-shən\ *n* (14c) **1 :** an act or process of confirming: as **a (1) :** a Christian rite conferring the gift of the Holy Spirit and among Protestants full church membership **(2) :** a ceremony esp. of Reform Judaism confirming youths in their faith **b :** the ratification of an executive act by a legislative body **2 a :** confirming proof : CORROBORATION **b :** the process of supporting a statement by evidence — **con·fir·ma·tion·al** \-shnəl, -shə-nᵊl\ *adj*

con·fir·ma·to·ry \kən-ˈfər-mə-ˌtȯr-ē\ *adj* (1636) **:** serving to confirm : CORROBORATIVE ⟨a ~ test⟩

con·firmed \kən-ˈfərmd\ *adj* (14c) **1 a :** marked by long continuance and likely to persist ⟨a ~ habit⟩ **b :** fixed in habit and unlikely to change ⟨a ~ do-gooder⟩ **2 :** having received the rite of confirmation ***syn*** see INVETERATE — **con·firm·ed·ly** \-ˈfər-məd-lē\ *adv* — **con·firmed·ness** \-ˈfər-məd-nəs, -ˈfərm(d)-nəs\ *n*

con·fis·ca·ble \kən-ˈfis-kə-bəl\ *adj* (ca. 1736) **:** liable to confiscation

con·fis·cat·able \ˈkän-fə-ˌskā-tə-bəl\ *adj* (1863) **:** CONFISCABLE

1**con·fis·cate** \ˈkän-fə-ˌskāt, kən-ˈfis-kət\ *adj* [L *confiscatus,* pp. of *confiscare* to confiscate, fr. *com-* + *fiscus* treasury] (ca. 1533) **1 :** appropriated by the government : FORFEITED **2 :** deprived of property by confiscation

2**con·fis·cate** \ˈkän-fə-ˌskāt\ *vt* **-cat·ed; -cat·ing** (1552) **1 :** to seize as forfeited to the public treasury **2 :** to seize by or as if by authority — **con·fis·ca·tion** \ˌkän-fə-ˈskā-shən\ *n* — **con·fis·ca·tor** \ˈkän-fə-ˌskā-tər\ *n* — **con·fis·ca·to·ry** \kən-ˈfis-kə-ˌtȯr-ē\ *adj*

con·fit \kōn-ˈfē, kȯn-, kän-\ *n* [F, fr. OF, preparation, preserves, fr. pp. of *confire* to prepare — more at COMFIT] (1951) **1 :** meat (as goose, duck, or pork) that has been cooked and preserved in its own fat **2 :** a garnish made usu. from fruit or vegetables that are cooked until tender in a seasoned liquid

con·fi·te·or \kən-ˈfē-tē-ˌȯr, -ər\ *n* [ME, fr. L, lit., I confess, fr. the opening words — more at CONFESS] (13c) **:** a liturgical form in which sinfulness is acknowledged and intercession for God's mercy requested

con·fi·ture \ˈkän-fə-ˌchu̇r, -ˌtyu̇r, -ˌtu̇r\ *n* [F, fr. MF, fr. *confit*] (1802) **:** preserved or candied fruit : JAM

con·fla·grant \kən-ˈflā-grənt\ *adj* [L *conflagrant-, conflagrans,* prp. of *conflagrare* to burn, fr. *com-* + *flagrare* to burn — more at BLACK] (ca. 1656) **:** BURNING, BLAZING

con·fla·gra·tion \ˌkän-flə-ˈgrā-shən\ *n* [L *conflagration-, conflagratio,* fr. *conflagrare*] (1600) **1 :** FIRE; *esp* **:** a large disastrous fire **2 :** CONFLICT, WAR

con·flate \kən-ˈflāt\ *vt* **con·flat·ed; con·flat·ing** [L *conflatus,* pp. of *conflare* to blow together, fuse, fr. *com-* + *flare* to blow — more at BLOW] (1610) **1 a :** to bring together : FUSE **b :** CONFUSE **2 :** to combine (as two readings of a text) into a composite whole

con·fla·tion \-ˈflā-shən\ *n* (15c) **:** BLEND, FUSION; *esp* **:** a composite reading or text

1**con·flict** \ˈkän-ˌflikt\ *n* [ME, fr. L *conflictus* act of striking together, fr. *confligere* to strike together, fr. *com-* + *fligere* to strike — more at PROFLIGATE] (15c) **1 :** FIGHT, BATTLE, WAR ⟨an armed ~⟩ **2 a :** competitive or opposing action of incompatibles : antagonistic state or action (as of divergent ideas, interests, or persons) **b :** mental struggle resulting from incompatible or opposing needs, drives, wishes, or external or internal demands **3 :** the opposition of persons or forces that gives rise to the dramatic action in a drama or fiction ***syn*** see DISCORD — **con·flict·ful** \ˈkän-ˌflikt-fəl\ *adj* — **con·flic·tu·al** \kän-ˈflik-chə-wəl, kən-, -chəl, -shwəl, -chü-əl\ *adj*

2**con·flict** \kən-ˈflikt, ˈkän-ˌ\ *vi* (15c) **1** *archaic* **:** to contend in warfare **2 :** to show antagonism or irreconcilability : fail to be in agreement or accord ⟨his statement ~*s* with the facts⟩ — **con·flic·tion** \kən-ˈflik-shən, kän-\ *n* — **con·flic·tive** \kən-ˈflik-tiv, ˈkän-ˌ\ *adj*

con·flict·ed \kən-ˈflik-təd\ *adj* (1914) **:** experiencing or marked by ambivalence or a conflict esp. of emotions ⟨this unhappy and ~ modern woman —John Updike⟩ ⟨~ feelings⟩

conflicting *adj* (1592) **:** being in conflict, collision, or opposition : INCOMPATIBLE ⟨~ theories⟩ — **con·flict·ing·ly** \-ˈflik-tiŋ-lē, -ˌflik-\ *adv*

conflict of interest (1843) **:** a conflict between the private interests and the official responsibilities of a person in a position of trust

con·flu·ence \ˈkän-ˌflü-ən(t)s, kən-ˈ\ *n* (15c) **1 :** a coming or flowing together, meeting, or gathering at one point ⟨a happy ~ of weather and scenery⟩ **2 a :** the flowing together of two or more streams **b :** the place of meeting of two streams **c :** the combined stream formed by conjunction

1**con·flu·ent** \-ənt\ *adj* [ME, fr. L *confluent-, confluens,* prp. of *confluere* to flow together, fr. *com-* + *fluere* to flow — more at FLUID] (15c) **1 :** flowing or coming together; *also* **:** run together ⟨~ pustules⟩ **2 :** characterized by confluent lesions ⟨~ smallpox⟩

2**confluent** *n* (1849) **:** a confluent stream; *broadly* **:** TRIBUTARY

con·flux \ˈkän-ˌfləks\ *n* [ML *confluxus,* fr. L *confluere*] (1606) **:** CONFLUENCE

con·fo·cal \(ˌ)kän-ˈfō-kəl\ *adj* (1867) **:** having the same foci ⟨~ ellipses⟩ ⟨~ lenses⟩ — **con·fo·cal·ly** \-kə-lē\ *adv*

con·form \kən-ˈfȯrm\ *vb* [ME, fr. AF *conformer,* fr. L *conformare,* fr. *com-* + *formare* to form, fr. *forma* form] *vt* (14c) **:** to give the same shape, outline, or contour to : bring into harmony or accord ⟨~ furrows to the slope of the land⟩ ~ *vi* **1 :** to be similar or identical; *also* **:** to be in agreement or harmony — used with *to* or *with* ⟨changes that ~ with our plans⟩ **2 a :** to be obedient or compliant — usu. used with *to* ⟨~ to another's wishes⟩ **b :** to act in accordance with prevailing standards or customs ⟨the pressure to ~⟩ ***syn*** see ADAPT — **con·form·er** *n* — **con·form·ism** \-ˈfȯr-ˌmi-zəm\ *n* — **con·form·ist** \-mist\ *n or adj*

con·form·able \kən-ˈfȯr-mə-bəl\ *adj* (15c) **1 :** corresponding or consistent in form or character ⟨conduct ~ to their principles⟩ **2 :** SUBMISSIVE, COMPLIANT ⟨be patient and ~ to my directions —Sir Walter Scott⟩ **3 :** following in unbroken sequence — used of geologic strata formed under uniform conditions — **con·form·ably** \-blē\ *adv*

con·for·mal \kən-ˈfȯr-məl, (ˌ)kän-\ *adj* [LL *conformalis* having the same shape, fr. L *com-* + *formalis* formal, fr. *forma*] (1893) **1 :** leaving the size of the angle between corresponding curves unchanged ⟨~

\ə\ **abut** \ᵊ\ **kitten, F table** \ər\ **further** \a\ **ash** \ā\ **ace** \ä\ **mop, mar**
\au̇\ **out** \ch\ **chin** \e\ **bet** \ē\ **easy** \g\ **go** \i\ **hit** \ī\ **ice** \j\ **job**
\ŋ\ **sing** \ō\ **go** \ȯ\ **law** \ȯi\ **boy** \th\ **thin** \t͟h\ **the** \ü\ **loot** \u̇\ **foot**
\y\ **yet** \zh\ **vision, beige** \k̲, ⁿ, œ, ue, ʸ\ *see* **Guide to Pronunciation**

transformation⟩ **2** *of a map* **:** representing small areas in their true shape
con·for·mance \kən-ˈfȯr-mən(t)s\ *n* (1606) **:** CONFORMITY
con·for·ma·tion \ˌkän-(ˌ)fȯr-ˈmā-shən, -fər-\ *n* (1511) **1 :** the act of conforming or producing conformity **:** ADAPTATION **2 :** formation of something by appropriate arrangement of parts or elements **:** an assembling into a whole ⟨the gradual ~ of the embryo⟩ **3 a :** correspondence esp. to a model or plan **b :** STRUCTURE **c :** the shape or proportionate dimensions esp. of an animal **d :** any of the spatial arrangements of a molecule that can be obtained by rotation of the atoms about a single bond — **con·for·ma·tion·al** \-shnəl, -shə-nᵊl\ *adj*
con·for·mi·ty \kən-ˈfȯr-mə-tē\ *n, pl* **-ties** (15c) **1 :** correspondence in form, manner, or character **:** AGREEMENT ⟨behaved in ~ with her beliefs⟩ **2 :** an act or instance of conforming **3 :** action in accordance with some specified standard or authority ⟨~ to social custom⟩
con·found \kən-ˈfau̇nd, kän-\ *vt* [ME, fr. AF *confundre,* fr. L *confundere* to pour together, confuse, fr. *com-* + *fundere* to pour — more at FOUND] (14c) **1 a** *archaic* **:** to bring to ruin **:** DESTROY **b :** BAFFLE, FRUSTRATE ⟨conferences . . . are not for accomplishment but to ~ knavish tricks —J. K. Galbraith⟩ **2** *obs* **:** CONSUME, WASTE **3 a :** to put to shame **:** DISCOMFIT ⟨a performance that ~*ed* the critics⟩ **b :** REFUTE ⟨sought to ~ his arguments⟩ **4 :** DAMN **5 :** to throw (a person) into confusion or perplexity **6 a :** to fail to discern differences between **:** mix up **b :** to increase the confusion of ***syn*** see PUZZLE — **con·found·er** \-ˈfau̇n-dər\ *n* — **con·found·ing·ly** \-diŋ-lē\ *adv*
con·found·ed \kən-ˈfau̇n-dəd, (ˌ)kän-ˈ, ˈkän-ˌ\ *adj* (14c) **1 :** CONFUSED, PERPLEXED **2 :** DAMNED — **con·found·ed·ly** *adv*
con·fra·ter·ni·ty \ˌkän-frə-ˈtər-nə-tē\ *n* [ME *confraternite,* fr. ML *confraternitat-, confraternitas,* fr. *confrater* fellow, brother, fr. L *com-* + *frater* brother — more at BROTHER] (15c) **1 :** a society devoted esp. to a religious or charitable cause **2 :** fraternal union
con·frere *also* **con·frère** \ˈkän-ˌfrer, kō^{n}-ˌ, kän-ˈ, kō^{n}-ˈ, kən-ˈ\ *n* [ME, fr. AF, trans. of ML *confrater*] (15c) **:** COLLEAGUE, COMRADE
con·front \kən-ˈfrənt\ *vt* [MF *confronter* to border on, confront, fr. ML *confrontare* to bound, fr. L *com-* + *front-, frons* forehead, front] (ca. 1568) **1 :** to face esp. in challenge **:** OPPOSE ⟨~ an enemy⟩ **2 a :** to cause to meet **:** bring face-to-face ⟨~ a reader with statistics⟩ **b :** to meet face-to-face **:** ENCOUNTER ⟨~*ed* the possibility of failure⟩ — **con·front·al** \-ˈfrən-tᵊl\ *n* — **con·front·er** *n*
con·fron·ta·tion \ˌkän-(ˌ)frən-ˈtā-shən\ *n* (1632) **:** the act of confronting **:** the state of being confronted: as **a :** a face-to-face meeting **b :** the clashing of forces or ideas **:** CONFLICT **c :** COMPARISON ⟨the flashbacks bring into meaningful ~ present and past, near and far —R. J. Clements⟩ — **con·fron·ta·tion·al** \-shnəl, -shə-nᵊl\ *adj* — **con·fron·ta·tion·al·ist** \-sh(ə-)nə-list\ *n* — **con·fron·ta·tion·ist** \-sh(ə-)nist\ *n or adj*
Con·fu·cian \kən-ˈfyü-shən\ *adj* (1837) **:** of or relating to the Chinese philosopher Confucius or his teachings or followers — **Confucian** *n* — **Con·fu·cian·ism** \-shə-ˌni-zəm\ *n* — **Con·fu·cian·ist** \-nist\ *n or adj*
con·fuse \kən-ˈfyüz\ *vt* **con·fused; con·fus·ing** [back-formation fr. ME *confused* frustrated, ruined, fr. AF *confus,* fr. L *confusus,* pp. of *confundere*] (14c) **1** *archaic* **:** to bring to ruin **2 a :** to make embarrassed **:** ABASH **b :** to disturb in mind or purpose **:** THROW OFF **3 a :** to make indistinct **:** BLUR ⟨stop *confusing* the issue⟩ **b :** to mix indiscriminately **:** JUMBLE **c :** to fail to differentiate from an often similar or related other ⟨~ money with comfort⟩ — **con·fus·ing·ly** \-ˈfyü-ziŋ-lē\ *adv*
con·fused \-ˈfyüzd\ *adj* (14c) **1 a :** being perplexed or disconcerted ⟨the ~ students⟩ **b :** disoriented with regard to one's sense of time, place, or identity ⟨the patient became ~⟩ **2 :** INDISTINGUISHABLE ⟨a zigzag, crisscross, ~ trail —Harry Hervey⟩ **3 :** being disordered or mixed up ⟨a contradictory and often ~ story⟩ — **con·fused·ly** \-ˈfyü-zəd-lē, -ˈfyüzd-\ *adv* — **con·fused·ness** \-ˈfyü-zəd-nəs, -ˈfyüz(d)-\ *n*
con·fu·sion \kən-ˈfyü-zhən\ *n* (14c) **1 :** an act or instance of confusing ⟨~ of the issue⟩ **2 a :** the quality or state of being confused ⟨try to relieve their ~⟩ **b :** a confused mass or mixture ⟨a ~ of voices⟩ — **con·fu·sion·al** \-ˈfyüzh-nəl, -ˈfyü-zhə-nᵊl\ *adj*
con·fu·ta·tion \ˌkän-fyü-ˈtā-shən, -fyü-\ *n* (15c) **1 :** the act or process of confuting **:** REFUTATION **2 :** something (as an argument or statement) that confutes — **con·fu·ta·tive** \kən-ˈfyü-tə-tiv\ *adj*
con·fute \kən-ˈfyüt\ *vt* **con·fut·ed; con·fut·ing** [L *confutare* to check, silence] (1529) **1 :** to overwhelm in argument **:** refute conclusively ⟨Elijah . . . *confuted* the prophets of Baal —G. B. Shaw⟩ **2** *obs* **:** CONFOUND — **con·fut·er** *n*
cong *abbr* congress; congressional
con·ga \ˈkäŋ-gə\ *n* [AmerSp, prob. fr. fem. of *congo* black person, fr. *Congo,* region in Africa] (1935) **1 :** a Cuban dance of African origin involving three steps followed by a kick and performed by a group usu. in single file **2 :** a tall barrel-shaped or tapering drum of Afro-Cuban origin that is played with the hands
conga line *n* (1946) **:** SNAKE DANCE 2
con·gé \kō^{n}-ˈzhā, ˈkän-ˌzhā\ *also* **con·gee** \ˈkän-(ˌ)jē, -(ˌ)zhē\ *n* [alter. of earlier *congee, congie,* fr. ME *conge,* fr. AF *cungé,* fr. L *commeatus* going back and forth, leave, fr. *commeare* to go back and forth, fr. *com-* + *meare* to go — more at PERMEATE] (14c) **1 a :** a formal permission to depart **b :** DISMISSAL **2 :** a ceremonious bow **3 :** FAREWELL **4 :** an architectural molding of concave profile — see MOLDING illustration
con·geal \kən-ˈjēl\ *vb* [ME *congelen,* fr. MF *congeler,* fr. L *congelare,* fr. *com-* + *gelare* to freeze — more at COLD] *vt* (14c) **1 :** to change from a fluid to a solid state by or as if by cold **2 :** to make viscid or curdled **:** COAGULATE **3 :** to make rigid, fixed, or immobile ~ *vi* **:** to become congealed **:** SOLIDIFY — **con·geal·ment** \-mənt\ *n*
con·gee \ˈkän-jē\ *n* [Tamil *kañci* water from cooked rice] (1930) **:** porridge made from rice
con·ge·la·tion \ˌkän-jə-ˈlā-shən\ *n* (15c) **:** the process or result of congealing
con·ge·ner \ˈkän-jə-nər, kən-ˈjē-\ *n* [L, of the same kind, fr. *com-* + *gener-, genus* kind — more at KIN] (ca. 1736) **1 :** a member of the same taxonomic genus as another plant or animal **2 :** a person, organism, or thing resembling another in nature or action ⟨the New England private schools and their ~*s* west of the Alleghenies —Oliver La Farge⟩ **3 :** a chemical substance related to another — **con·ge·ner·ic** \ˌkän-jə-ˈner-ik\ *adj* — **con·ge·ner·ous** \kən-ˈjē-nə-rəs, -ˈje-nə-, (ˌ)kän-\ *adj*
con·ge·nial \kən-ˈjē-nē-əl, -ˈjēn-yəl\ *adj* [*com-* + *genius*] (ca. 1625) **1 :** having the same nature, disposition, or tastes **:** KINDRED ⟨~ companions⟩ **2 a :** existing or associated together harmoniously **b :** PLEASANT; *esp* **:** agreeably suited to one's nature, tastes, or outlook ⟨a ~ atmosphere⟩ **c :** SOCIABLE, GENIAL ⟨a ~ host⟩ — **con·ge·nial·i·ty** \-ˌjē-nē-ˈa-lə-tē, -ˌjēn-ˈya-\ *n* — **con·ge·nial·ly** \-ˈjē-nē-ə-lē, -ˈjēn-yə-\ *adv*
con·gen·i·tal \kən-ˈje-nə-tᵊl, kän-\ *adj* [L *congenitus,* fr. *com-* + *genitus,* pp. of *gignere* to bring forth — more at KIN] (1796) **1 a :** existing at or dating from birth ⟨~ deafness⟩ **b :** constituting an essential characteristic **:** INHERENT ⟨~ fear of snakes⟩ **c :** acquired during development in the uterus and not through heredity ⟨~ syphilis⟩ **2 :** being such by nature ⟨a ~ liar⟩ ***syn*** see INNATE — **con·gen·i·tal·ly** \-tᵊl-ē\ *adv*
con·ger eel \ˈkäŋ-gər-\ *n* [ME *congre,* fr. AF, fr. L *congr-, conger,* prob. fr. Gk *gongros*] (1602) **:** a large strictly marine scaleless eel (*Conger oceanicus*) of the Atlantic; *broadly* **:** any of various related eels (family Congridae)

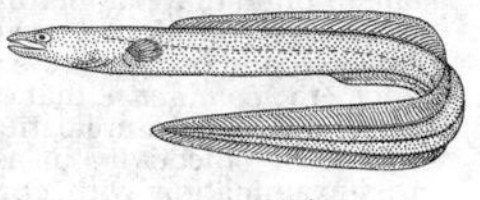
conger eel

con·ge·ries \ˈkän-jə-(ˌ)rēz\ *n, pl* **congeries** *same*\ [L, fr. *congerere*] (ca. 1619) **:** AGGREGATION, COLLECTION
con·gest \kən-ˈjest\ *vb* [L *congestus,* pp. of *congerere* to bring together, fr. *com-* + *gerere* to bear] *vt* (1599) **1 :** to concentrate in a small or narrow space **2 :** to cause an excessive accumulation esp. of blood or mucus in (as an organ or part) **3 :** CLOG ⟨traffic ~*ed* the highways⟩ ~ *vi* **:** to become congested — **con·ges·tion** \-ˈjes-chən, -ˈjesh-\ *n* — **con·ges·tive** \-ˈjes-tiv\ *adj*
congestive heart failure *n* (1930) **:** heart failure in which the heart is unable to maintain an adequate circulation of blood in the bodily tissues or to pump out the venous blood returned to it by the veins
con·glo·bate \kän-ˈglō-ˌbāt, kən-\ *vt* **-bat·ed; -bat·ing** [L *conglobatus,* pp. of *conglobare,* fr. *com-* + *globus* globe] (1635) **:** to form into a round compact mass — **con·glo·bate** \-bət, -ˌbāt\ *adj* — **con·glo·ba·tion** \ˌkän-(ˌ)glō-ˈbā-shən\ *n*
con·globe \kän-ˈglōb, kən-\ *vt* **con·globed; con·glob·ing** (1535) **:** CONGLOBATE
[1]**con·glom·er·ate** \kən-ˈgläm-rət, -ˈglä-mə-\ *adj* [L *conglomeratus,* pp. of *conglomerare* to roll together, fr. *com-* + *glomerare* to wind into a ball, fr. *glomer-, glomus* ball — more at CLAM] (1572) **:** made up of parts from various sources or of various kinds
[2]**con·glom·er·ate** \-ˈglä-mə-ˌrāt\ *vb* **-at·ed; -at·ing** *vi* (1642) **:** to gather into a mass or coherent whole ⟨numbers of dull people *conglomerated* round her —Virginia Woolf⟩ ~ *vt* **:** ACCUMULATE — **con·glom·er·a·tive** \-ˈgläm-rə-tiv, -ˈglä-mə-; -mə-ˌrā-\ *adj* — **con·glom·er·a·tor** \-ˈglä-mə-ˌrā-tər\ *n*
[3]**con·glom·er·ate** \-ˈgläm-rət, -ˈglä-mə-\ *n* (1818) **1 :** a composite mass or mixture; *esp* **:** rock composed of rounded fragments varying from small pebbles to large boulders in a cement (as of hardened clay) **2 :** a widely diversified corporation — **con·glom·er·at·ic** \kən-ˌglä-mə-ˈra-tik, ˌkän-\ *adj*
con·glom·er·a·teur \kən-ˌglä-mə-rə-ˈtər, -ˈtyu̇r, -ˈtu̇r\ *n* [[3]*conglomerate* + *-eur* (as in *entrepreneur*)] (1969) **:** a person who forms or heads a conglomerate **:** CONGLOMERATOR
con·glom·er·a·tion \kən-ˌglä-mə-ˈrā-shən, ˌkän-\ *n* (1626) **1 :** the act of conglomerating **:** the state of being conglomerated **2 :** something conglomerated **:** a mixed mass or collection
con·glu·ti·nate \kən-ˈglü-tᵊn-ˌāt, kän-\ *vb* **-nat·ed; -nat·ing** [L *conglutinatus,* pp. of *conglutinare* to glue together, fr. *com-* + *glutin-, gluten* glue — more at GLUTEN] *vt* (1546) **:** to unite by or as if by a glutinous substance ~ *vi* **:** to become conglutinated ⟨blood platelets ~ in blood clotting⟩ — **con·glu·ti·na·tion** \kən-ˌglü-tᵊn-ˈā-shən, kän-\ *n*
Con·go red \ˈkäŋ-(ˌ)gō-\ *n* [*Congo,* territory in Africa] (1885) **:** an azo dye $C_{32}H_{22}N_6Na_2O_6S_2$ that is red in alkaline and blue in acid solution and that is used esp. as an indicator and as a biological stain
con·gou \ˈkäŋ-(ˌ)gō, -(ˌ)gü\ *n* [prob. fr. Chin (Xiamen) *kong-hu* pains taken] (1725) **:** a black tea from China
con·grat·u·late \kən-ˈgra-chə-ˌlāt, -ˈgra-jə-\ *vt* **-lat·ed; -lat·ing** [L *congratulatus,* pp. of *congratulari* to wish joy, fr. *com-* + *gratulari* to wish joy, fr. *gratus* pleasing — more at GRACE] (1539) **1** *archaic* **:** to express sympathetic pleasure at (an event) **2 :** to express vicarious pleasure to (a person) on the occasion of success or good fortune ⟨graciously *congratulated* the winner⟩; *also* **:** to feel pleased with ⟨*congratulating* herself for a job well done⟩ **3** *obs* **:** SALUTE, GREET — **con·grat·u·la·tor** \-ˌlā-tər\ *n* — **con·grat·u·la·to·ry** \-lə-ˌtȯr-ē\ *adj*
con·grat·u·la·tion \kən-ˌgra-chə-ˈlā-shən, -ˌgra-jə-\ *n* (15c) **1 :** the act of congratulating **2 :** a congratulatory expression — usu. used in pl.
con·gre·gant \ˈkäŋ-gri-gənt\ *n* (1886) **:** one who congregates; *specif* **:** a member of a congregation
[1]**con·gre·gate** \-ˌgāt\ *vb* **-gat·ed; -gat·ing** [ME, fr. L *congregatus,* pp. of *congregare,* fr. *com-* + *greg-, grex* flock] *vt* (15c) **:** to collect into a group or crowd **:** ASSEMBLE ~ *vi* **:** to come together into a group, crowd, or assembly ***syn*** see GATHER — **con·gre·ga·tor** \-ˌgā-tər\ *n*
[2]**con·gre·gate** \-gət\ *adj* (1900) **:** providing or being group services or facilities designed esp. for elderly persons requiring supportive services ⟨~ housing⟩
con·gre·ga·tion \ˌkäŋ-gri-ˈgā-shən\ *n* (14c) **1 a :** an assembly of persons **:** GATHERING; *esp* **:** an assembly of persons met for worship and religious instruction **b :** a religious community: as **(1) :** an organized body of believers in a particular locality **(2) :** a Roman Catholic religious institute with only simple vows **(3) :** a group of monasteries forming an independent subdivision of an order **2 :** the act or an instance of congregating or bringing together **:** the state of being congregated **3 :** a body of cardinals and officials forming an administrative division of the papal curia
con·gre·ga·tion·al \-shnəl, -shə-nᵊl\ *adj* (1639) **1 :** of or relating to a congregation **2** *cap* **:** of or relating to a body of Protestant churches deriving from the English Independents of the 17th century and affirming the essential importance and the autonomy of the local congregation **3 :** of or relating to church government placing final authority in the assembly of the local congregation — **con·gre·ga·tion·al·ism**

\-shnə-ˌli-zəm, -shə-nə-ˌli-\ *n, often cap* — **con·gre·ga·tion·al·ist** \-shnə-list, -shə-nə-list\ *n or adj, often cap*
con·gress \ˈkäŋ-grəs *also* -rəs, *Brit usu* ˈkäŋ-ˌgres\ *n* [L *congressus,* fr. *congredi* to come together, fr. *com-* + *gradi* to go — more at GRADE] (1528) **1 a :** the act or action of coming together and meeting **b :** COITUS **2 :** a formal meeting of delegates for discussion and usu. action on some question **3 :** the supreme legislative body of a nation and esp. of a republic **4 :** an association usu. made up of delegates from constituent organizations **5 :** a single meeting or session of a group — **con·gres·sio·nal** \kən-ˈgresh-nəl, kän-, -ˈgre-shə-nᵊl\ *adj* — **con·gres·sio·nal·ly** *adv*
congressional district *n* (1812) **:** a territorial division of a state from which a member of the U.S. House of Representatives is elected
Congressional Medal *n* (1910) **:** MEDAL OF HONOR
con·gress·man \ˈkäŋ-(g)rəs-mən\ *n* (1780) **:** a member of a congress; *esp* **:** a member of the U.S. House of Representatives
con·gress·peo·ple \-(g)rəs-ˌpē-pəl\ *n pl* (1973) **:** congressmen or congresswomen
con·gress·per·son \-(g)rəs-ˌpər-sən\ *n* (1972) **:** a congressman or congresswoman
con·gress·wom·an \-(g)rəs-ˌwu̇-mən\ *n* (1917) **:** a woman who is a member of a congress; *esp* **:** a woman who is a member of the U.S. House of Representatives
con·gru·ence \kən-ˈgrü-ən(t)s, ˈkäŋ-grü-ən(t)s\ *n* (15c) **1 :** the quality or state of agreeing, coinciding, or being congruent **2 :** a statement that two numbers or geometric figures are congruent
con·gru·en·cy \-ən(t)-sē\ *n, pl* **-cies** (15c) **:** CONGRUENCE
con·gru·ent \kən-ˈgrü-ənt, ˈkäŋ-grü-ənt\ *adj* [ME, fr. L *congruent-, congruens,* prp. of *congruere*] (15c) **1 :** CONGRUOUS **2 :** superposable so as to be coincident throughout **3 :** having the difference divisible by a given modulus ⟨12 is ~ to 2 (modulo 5) since 12−2=2·5⟩ — **con·gru·ent·ly** *adv*
con·gru·i·ty \kən-ˈgrü-ə-tē, kän-\ *n, pl* **-ties** (14c) **1 :** the quality or state of being congruent or congruous **2 :** a point of agreement
con·gru·ous \ˈkäŋ-grü-əs\ *adj* [L *congruus,* fr. *congruere* to come together, agree] (1599) **1 a :** being in agreement, harmony, or correspondence **b :** conforming to the circumstances or requirements of a situation **:** APPROPRIATE ⟨a ~ room to work in —G. B. Shaw⟩ **2 :** marked or enhanced by harmonious agreement among constituent elements ⟨a ~ theme⟩ — **con·gru·ous·ly** *adv* — **con·gru·ous·ness** *n*
¹**con·ic** \ˈkä-nik\ *adj* (1570) **1 :** of or relating to a cone **2 :** CONICAL — **co·nic·i·ty** \kō-ˈni-sə-tē\ *n*
²**conic** *n* (1879) **:** CONIC SECTION
con·i·cal \ˈkä-ni-kəl\ *adj* (1570) **:** resembling a cone esp. in shape — **con·i·cal·ly** \-k(ə-)lē\ *adv*
conic section *n* (1664) **1 :** a plane curve, line, pair of intersecting lines, or point that is the intersection of or bounds the intersection of a plane and a cone with two nappes **2 :** a curve generated by a point which always moves so that the ratio of its distance from a fixed point to its distance from a fixed line is constant

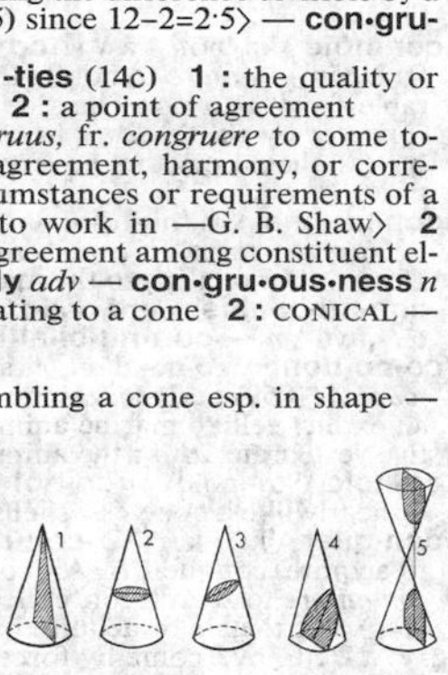

conic section 1: *1* straight lines, *2* circle, *3* ellipse, *4* parabola, *5* hyperbola

co·nid·i·o·phore \kə-ˈni-dē-ə-ˌfȯr\ *n* [NL *conidium* + ISV *-phore*] (1874) **:** a specialized hyphal branch of some fungi that produces conidia
co·nid·i·um \kə-ˈni-dē-əm\ *n, pl* **-ia** \-dē-ə\ [NL, fr. Gk *konis* dust — more at INCINERATE] (1856) **:** an asexual spore produced on a conidiophore of certain fungi — **co·nid·i·al** \-dē-əl\ *adj*
co·ni·fer \ˈkä-nə-fər *also* ˈkō-\ *n* [ultim. fr. L *conifer* cone-bearing, fr. *conus* cone + *-fer*] (ca. 1841) **:** any of an order (Coniferales) of mostly evergreen trees and shrubs having usu. needle-shaped or scalelike leaves and including forms (as pines) with true cones and others (as yews) with an arillate fruit — **co·nif·er·ous** \kō-ˈni-f(ə-)rəs, kə-\ *adj*
co·ni·ine \ˈkō-nē-ˌēn\ *n* [G *Koniin,* fr. LL *conium* hemlock, fr. Gk *kōneion*] (1831) **:** a poisonous alkaloid $C_8H_{17}N$ found in poison hemlock
conj *abbr* conjunction; conjunctive
con·jec·tur·al \kən-ˈjek-chə-rəl, -ˈjek-shrəl\ *adj* (1553) **1 :** of the nature of or involving or based on conjecture **2 :** given to conjectures — **con·jec·tur·al·ly** *adv*
¹**con·jec·ture** \kən-ˈjek-chər\ *n* [ME, fr. MF or L; MF, fr. L *conjectura,* fr. *conjectus,* pp. of *conicere,* lit., to throw together, fr. *com-* + *jacere* to throw — more at JET] (14c) **1** *obs* **a :** interpretation of omens **b :** SUPPOSITION **2 a :** inference from defective or presumptive evidence **b :** a conclusion deduced by surmise or guesswork **c :** a proposition (as in mathematics) before it has been proved or disproved
²**conjecture** *vb* **-tured; -tur·ing** \-ˈjek-chə-riŋ, -ˈjek-shriŋ\ *vt* (15c) **1 :** to arrive at or deduce by conjecture **:** GUESS ⟨scientists *conjecturing* that a disease is caused by a defective gene⟩ **2 :** to make conjectures as to ⟨~ the meaning of a statement⟩ ~ *vi* **:** to form conjectures — **con·jec·tur·er** \-ˈjek-chər-ər\ *n*
con·join \kən-ˈjȯin, kän-\ *vb* [ME, fr. AF *conjoindre,* fr. L *conjungere,* fr. *com-* + *jungere* to join — more at YOKE] *vt* (14c) **:** to join together (as separate entities) for a common purpose ~ *vi* **:** to join together for a common purpose
con·joined \-ˈjȯind\ *adj* (1570) **:** being, coming, or brought together so as to meet, touch, overlap, or unite ⟨~ heads on a coin⟩
con·joint \-ˈjȯint\ *adj* [ME, pp. of *conjoinen,* fr. AF, pp. of *conjoindre*] (1725) **1 :** UNITED, CONJOINED **2 :** related to, made up of, or carried on by two or more in combination **:** JOINT — **con·joint·ly** *adv*
con·ju·gal \ˈkän-ji-gəl *also* kən-ˈjü-\ *adj* [MF or L; MF, fr. L *conjugalis,* fr. *conjug-, conjux* husband, wife, fr. *conjungere* to join, unite in marriage] (1545) **:** of or relating to the married state or to married persons and their relations **:** CONNUBIAL ⟨~ happiness⟩ — **con·ju·gal·i·ty** \ˌkän-ji-ˈga-lə-tē, -jü-\ *n* — **con·ju·gal·ly** \ˈkän-ji-gə-lē *also* kən-ˈjü-\ *adv*
conjugal rights *n pl* (1768) **:** the sexual rights or privileges implied by and involved in the marriage relationship **:** the right of sexual intercourse between husband and wife
con·ju·gant \ˈkän-ji-gənt\ *n* (1910) **:** either of a pair of conjugating gametes or organisms
¹**con·ju·gate** \ˈkän-ji-gət, -jə-ˌgāt\ *adj* [ME *conjugat,* fr. L *conjugatus,* pp. of *conjugare* to unite, fr. *com-* + *jugare* to join, fr. *jugum* yoke — more at YOKE] (15c) **1 a :** joined together esp. in pairs **:** COUPLED **b :** acting or operating as if joined **2 a :** having features in common but opposite or inverse in some particular **b :** relating to or being conjugate complex numbers ⟨complex roots occurring in ~ pairs⟩ **3** *of an acid or base* **:** related by the difference of a proton ⟨the acid NH_4^+ and the base NH_3 are ~ to each other⟩ **4 :** having the same derivation and therefore usu. some likeness in meaning ⟨~ words⟩ **5** *of two leaves of a book* **:** forming a single piece — **con·ju·gate·ly** *adv* — **con·ju·gate·ness** *n*
²**con·ju·gate** \-jə-ˌgāt\ *vb* **-gat·ed; -gat·ing** *vt* (1530) **1 :** to give in prescribed order the various inflectional forms of — used esp. of a verb **2 :** to join together ~ *vi* **1 :** to become joined together **2 a :** to pair and fuse in conjugation **b :** to pair in synapsis
³**conjugate** *same as* ¹\ *n* (ca. 1586) **1 :** something conjugate **:** a product of conjugating **2 :** CONJUGATE COMPLEX NUMBER **3 :** an element of a mathematical group that is equal to a given element of the group multiplied on the right by another element and on the left by the inverse of the latter element
conjugate complex number *n* (ca. 1909) **:** one of two complex numbers differing only in the sign of the imaginary part
con·ju·gat·ed \-ˌgā-təd\ *adj* (1882) **1 :** formed by the union of two compounds or united with another compound ⟨~ bile acids⟩ **2 :** relating to, containing, or being a system of two double bonds separated by a single bond ⟨~ fatty acids⟩ ⟨~ double bonds⟩
conjugated protein *n* (ca. 1909) **:** a compound of a protein with a nonprotein ⟨hemoglobin is a *conjugated protein*⟩ — compare SIMPLE PROTEIN
con·ju·ga·tion \ˌkän-jə-ˈgā-shən\ *n* (15c) **1 a :** a schematic arrangement of the inflectional forms of a verb **b :** verb inflection **c :** a class of verbs having the same type of inflectional forms ⟨the weak ~⟩ **d :** a set of the simple or derivative inflectional forms of a verb esp. in Sanskrit or the Semitic languages ⟨the causative ~⟩ **2 :** the act of conjugating **:** the state of being conjugated **3 a :** fusion of usu. similar gametes with ultimate union of their nuclei and sexual reproduction that occurs in most fungi and in some algae (as green algae) **b :** temporary cytoplasmic union with exchange of nuclear material that is the usual sexual process in ciliated protozoans **c :** the one-way transfer of DNA between bacteria in cellular contact — **con·ju·ga·tion·al** \-shnəl, -shə-nᵊl\ *adj* — **con·ju·ga·tion·al·ly** *adv*
¹**con·junct** \kən-ˈjəŋ(k)t, kän-\ *adj* [ME, fr. L *conjunctus,* pp. of *conjungere*] (15c) **1 :** UNITED, JOINED **2 :** JOINT **3 :** relating to melodic progression by intervals of no more than a major second — compare DISJUNCT
²**con·junct** \ˈkän-ˌjəŋ(k)t\ *n* (1667) **1 :** something joined or associated with another; *specif* **:** one of the components of a conjunction **2 :** an adverb or adverbial (as *so, in addition, however, secondly*) that indicates the speaker's or writer's assessment of the connection between linguistic units (as clauses)
con·junc·tion \kən-ˈjəŋ(k)-shən\ *n* (14c) **1 :** the act or an instance of conjoining **:** the state of being conjoined **:** COMBINATION ⟨working in ~ with state and local authorities⟩ **2 :** occurrence together in time or space **:** CONCURRENCE **3 a :** the apparent meeting or passing of two or more celestial bodies in the same degree of the zodiac **b :** a configuration in which two celestial bodies have their least apparent separation **4 :** an uninflected linguistic form that joins together sentences, clauses, phrases, or words **5 :** a complex sentence in logic true if and only if each of its components is true — see TRUTH TABLE table — **con·junc·tion·al** \-shnəl, -shə-nᵊl\ *adj* — **con·junc·tion·al·ly** *adv*
con·junc·ti·va \ˌkän-ˌjəŋ(k)-ˈtī-və, kən-\ *n, pl* **-vas** *or* **-vae** \-(ˌ)vē\ [NL, fr. LL, fem. of *conjunctivus* conjoining, fr. L *conjunctus*] (14c) **:** the mucous membrane that lines the inner surface of the eyelids and is continued over the forepart of the eyeball — see EYE illustration — **con·junc·ti·val** \-vəl\ *adj*
con·junc·tive \kən-ˈjəŋ(k)-tiv\ *adj* (1581) **1 :** CONNECTIVE **2 :** CONJUNCT, CONJOINED **3 :** being or functioning like a conjunction **4 :** COPULATIVE 1a — **conjunctive** *n* — **con·junc·tive·ly** *adv*
con·junc·ti·vi·tis \kən-ˌjəŋ(k)-ti-ˈvī-təs\ *n* (1835) **:** inflammation of the conjunctiva
con·junc·ture \kən-ˈjəŋ(k)-chər\ *n* (1605) **1 :** CONJUNCTION, UNION **2 :** a combination of circumstances or events usu. producing a crisis **:** JUNCTURE
con·jun·to \kōn-ˈhün-tō\ *n* [AmerSp. lit., ensemble] (1982) **:** a kind of Mexican-American music that has been influenced by the music of German immigrants to Texas and that features the accordion in addition to Mexican elements
con·ju·ra·tion \ˌkän-jü-ˈrā-shən, ˌkən-, -jər-ˈā-\ *n* (14c) **1 :** the act or process of conjuring **:** INCANTATION **2 :** an expression or trick used in conjuring **3 :** a solemn appeal **:** ADJURATION
con·jure *vt 2 & vi senses* ˈkän-jər *also* ˈkən-; *vt 1* kən-ˈju̇r\ *vb* **con·jured; con·jur·ing** \ˈkänj-riŋ, ˈkän-jə-, ˈkənj-, ˈkən-jə-; kən-ˈju̇r-iŋ\ [ME, fr. AF *conjurer,* fr. L *conjurare* to join in taking an oath, fr. *com-* + *jurare* to swear — more at JURY] *vt* (13c) **1 :** to charge or entreat earnestly or solemnly **2 a :** to summon by or as if by invocation or incantation **b** (1) **:** to affect or effect by or as if by magic (2) **:** IMAGINE, CONTRIVE — often used with *up* ⟨we ~ up our own metaphors for our own needs —R. J. Kaufmann⟩ (3) **:** to bring to mind ⟨words that ~ pleasant images⟩ — often used with *up* ⟨~ up memories⟩ ~ *vi* **1 a :** to summon a devil or spirit by invocation or incantation **b :** to practice magical arts **2 :** to use a conjurer's tricks **:** JUGGLE — **conjure with** *chiefly Brit* **:** to treat or regard as important ⟨Victor Hugo is a name to *conjure with* —Peter France⟩
con·jur·er *or* **con·ju·ror** \ˈkän-jər-ər, ˈkən-\ *n* (14c) **1 :** one that practices magic arts **:** WIZARD **2 :** one that performs feats of sleight of hand and illusion **:** MAGICIAN, JUGGLER
¹**conk** \ˈkäŋk, ˈkȯŋk\ *n* [perh. fr. *conch*] (1812) *slang chiefly Brit* **:** NOSE

²conk *vt* [E slang *conk* head] (1821) : to hit esp. on the head : KNOCK OUT
³conk *n* [prob. alter. of *conch*] (1851) : the visible fruiting body of a bracket fungus; *also* : decay caused by such a fungus — **conky** \ˈkäŋ-kē, ˈkȯŋ-\ *adj*
⁴conk *vi* [prob. imit.] (1918) **1** : BREAK DOWN; *esp* : STALL — usu. used with *out* ⟨the motor suddenly ~*ed* out⟩ **2 a** : FAINT **b** : to go to sleep — usu. used with *off* or *out* ⟨~*ed* out for a while after lunch⟩ **c** : DIE ⟨I caught pneumonia. I almost ~*ed* —Truman Capote⟩
⁵conk *vt* [prob. by shortening & alter. fr. *congolene* preparation used for straightening hair] (1950) : to straighten out (hair) usu. by the use of chemicals
⁶conk *n* (1965) : a hairstyle in which the hair is straightened out and flattened down or lightly waved — called also *process*
conk·er \ˈkäŋ-kər\ *n* [*conch* + ²-*er*, fr. the original use of a snail shell on a string in the game] (ca. 1886) **1** : a horse chestnut esp. when used in conkers **2** *pl* : a game in which each player swings a horse chestnut on a string to try to break one held by the opponent
con mo·to \kän-ˈmō-(ˌ)tō, kōn-\ *adv* [It] (ca. 1854) : with movement : in a spirited manner — used as a direction in music
¹conn *also* **con** \ˈkän\ *vt* **conned; con·ning** [alter. of *cond*, prob. alter. of ME *condien, conduen* to conduct, fr. AF *cunduire* — more at CONDUIT] (1626) : to conduct or direct the steering of (as a ship)
²conn *also* **con** *n* (1825) : the control exercised by one who conns a ship
Conn *abbr* Connecticut
con·nate \kä-ˈnāt, ˈkä-ˌ\ *adj* [LL *connatus*, pp. of *connasci* to be born together, fr. L *com-* + *nasci* to be born — more at NATION] (1641) **1** : AKIN, CONGENIAL **2** : INNATE, INBORN **3** : born or originated together **4** : entrapped in sediments at the time of their deposition ⟨~ water⟩ — **con·nate·ly** *adv*
con·nat·u·ral \kä-ˈnach-rəl, kə-, -ˈna-chə-\ *adj* [ML *connaturalis*, fr. L *com-* + *naturalis* natural] (1592) **1** : connected by nature : INBORN **2** : of the same nature — **con·nat·u·ral·i·ty** \-ˌna-chə-ˈra-lə-tē\ *n* — **con·nat·u·ral·ly** \-ˈnach-rə-lē, -ˈna-chə-\ *adv*
con·nect \kə-ˈnekt\ *vb* [ME, fr. L *conectere, connectere*, fr. *com-* + *nectere* to bind] *vi* (15c) **1** : to become joined ⟨the two rooms ~ by a hallway⟩ ⟨ideas that ~ easily to form a theory⟩ **2 a** : to meet for the transference of passengers ⟨~*ing* flights⟩ **b** : to transfer (as from one airplane to another) as a step in traveling to a final destination ⟨passengers ~*ing* with international flights⟩ **3** : to make a successful hit, shot, or throw ⟨~*ed* for a home run⟩ ⟨~*ed* on 60 percent of his shots —*N.Y. Times*⟩ **4** : to have or establish a rapport ⟨tried to ~ with the younger generation⟩ **5** : to establish a communications connection ⟨~ to the Internet⟩ ~ *vt* **1** : to join or fasten together usu. by something intervening **2** : to place or establish in relationship ***syn*** see JOIN — **con·nect·able** *also* **con·nect·ible** \-ˈnek-tə-bəl\ *adj* — **con·nec·tor** *also* **con·nect·er** \-ˈnek-tər\ *n* — **connect the dots** : to link together logically related elements in order to draw a conclusion ⟨trying to *connect the dots* in the investigation⟩
connected *adj* (1712) **1** : joined or linked together **2** : having the parts or elements logically linked together ⟨presented a thoroughly ~ view of the problem⟩ **3** : related by blood or marriage **4** : having social, professional, or commercial relationships ⟨a well-*connected* lawyer⟩ **5** *of a set* : having the property that any two of its points can be joined by a line completely contained in the set; *also* : incapable of being separated into two or more closed disjoint subsets — **con·nect·ed·ly** *adv* — **con·nect·ed·ness** *n*
connecting rod *n* (1839) : a rod that transmits motion between a reciprocating part of a machine (as a piston) and a rotating part (as a crankshaft)
con·nec·tion \kə-ˈnek-shən\ *n* [L *connexion-, connexio*, fr. *conectere*] (14c) **1** : the act of connecting : the state of being connected: as **a** : causal or logical relation or sequence ⟨the ~ between two ideas⟩ **b** (1) : contextual relation or association ⟨in this ~ the word has a different meaning⟩ (2) : relationship in fact ⟨wanted in ~ with a robbery⟩ **c** : a relation of personal intimacy (as of family ties) **d** : COHERENCE, CONTINUITY **2 a** : something that connects : LINK ⟨a loose ~ in the wiring⟩ **b** : a means of communication or transport ⟨a telephone ~⟩ **3** : a person connected with another esp. by marriage, kinship, or common interest ⟨has powerful ~*s*⟩ **4** : a political, social, professional, or commercial relationship: as **a** : POSITION, JOB **b** : an arrangement to execute orders or advance interests of another ⟨a firm's foreign ~*s*⟩ **c** : a source of contraband (as illegal drugs) **5** : a set of persons associated together: as **a** : DENOMINATION **b** : CLAN — **con·nec·tion·al** \-shnəl, -shə-nᵊl\ *adj*
con·nec·tion·ism \-shə-ˌni-zəm\ *n* (1987) : a school of cognitive science that holds that human mental processes (as learning) can be explained by the computational modeling of neural nets which are thought to simulate the actions of interconnected neurons in the brain — **con·nec·tion·ist** \-sh(ə-)nist\ *n*
¹con·nec·tive \kə-ˈnek-tiv\ *adj* (ca. 1660) : serving to connect — **con·nec·tive·ly** *adv*
²connective *n* (1751) : something that connects: as **a** : a linguistic form that connects words or word groups **b** : a logical term (as *or, if-then, and, not*) or a symbol for it that relates propositions in such a way that the truth or falsity of the resulting statement is determined by the truth or falsity of the components
connective tissue *n* (1846) : a tissue of mesodermal origin that consists of various cells (as fibroblasts and macrophages) and interlacing protein fibers (as of collagen) embedded in a chiefly carbohydrate ground substance, that supports, ensheathes, and binds together other tissues, and that includes loose and dense forms (as adipose tissue, tendons, ligaments, and aponeuroses) and specialized forms (as cartilage and bone)
con·nec·tiv·i·ty \(ˌ)kä-ˌnek-ˈti-və-tē, kə-\ *n, pl* **-ties** (1893) : the quality, state, or capability of being connective or connected ⟨~ of a surface⟩; *esp* : the ability to connect to or communicate with another computer or computer system
connect–the–dots *adj* (1981) : done or proceeding in a series of simple and usu. predictable steps ⟨a movie with a ~ plot⟩
Con·ne·ma·ra \ˌkä-nə-ˈmär-ə, ˌkō-\ *n* [*Connemara*, Ireland] (ca. 1952) : any of a breed of hardy rugged ponies developed in Ireland
con·nex·ion \kə-ˈnek-shən\ *chiefly Brit var of* CONNECTION
con·ning tower \ˈkä-niŋ-\ *n* (1886) : a raised structure on the deck of a submarine used esp. formerly for navigation and attack direction
con·nip·tion \kə-ˈnip-shən\ *n* [origin unknown] (1833) : a fit of rage, hysteria, or alarm ⟨went into ~*s*⟩
con·niv·ance \kə-ˈnī-vən(t)s\ *n* (1593) : the act of conniving; *esp* : knowledge of and active or passive consent to wrongdoing
con·nive \kə-ˈnīv\ *vi* **con·nived; con·niv·ing** [F or L; F *conniver*, fr. L *conivēre, connivēre* to close the eyes, connive, fr. *com-* + *-nivēre* (akin to *nictare* to wink); akin to OE & OHG *hnīgan* to bow] (1601) **1** : to pretend ignorance of or fail to take action against something one ought to oppose ⟨the government *connived* in the rebels' military buildup⟩ **2 a** : to be indulgent or in secret sympathy : WINK **b** : to cooperate secretly or have a secret understanding **3** : CONSPIRE, INTRIGUE ⟨accused his opponents of *conniving* to defeat the proposal⟩ — **con·niv·er** *n*
con·nois·seur \ˌkä-nə-ˈsər *also* -ˈsu̇r\ *n* [obs. F (now *connaisseur*), fr. OF *connoisseor*, fr. *connoistre* to know, fr. L *cognoscere* — more at COGNITION] (1714) **1** : EXPERT; *esp* : one who understands the details, technique, or principles of an art and is competent to act as a critical judge **2** : one who enjoys with discrimination and appreciation of subtleties ⟨a ~ of fine wines⟩ — **con·nois·seur·ship** \-ˌship\ *n*
con·no·ta·tion \ˌkä-nə-ˈtā-shən\ *n* (1532) **1 a** : the suggesting of a meaning by a word apart from the thing it explicitly names or describes **b** : something suggested by a word or thing : IMPLICATION ⟨the ~*s* of comfort that surrounded that old chair⟩ **2** : the signification of something ⟨that abuse of logic which consists in moving counters about as if they were known entities with a fixed ~ —W. R. Inge⟩ **3** : an essential property or group of properties of a thing named by a term in logic — compare DENOTATION — **con·no·ta·tion·al** \-shnəl, -shə-nᵊl\ *adj*
con·no·ta·tive \ˈkä-nə-ˌtā-tiv, kə-ˈnō-tə-tiv\ *adj* (1614) **1** : connoting or tending to connote **2** : relating to connotation — **con·no·ta·tive·ly** *adv*
con·note \kə-ˈnōt, kä-\ *vt* **con·not·ed; con·not·ing** [ML *connotare*, fr. L *com-* + *notare* to note] (1665) **1** : to be associated with or inseparable from as a consequence or concomitant ⟨the remorse so often *connoted* by guilt⟩ **2 a** : to convey in addition to exact explicit meaning ⟨all the misery that poverty ~*s*⟩ **b** : to imply as a logical connotation
con·nu·bi·al \kə-ˈnü-bē-əl, -ˈnyü-\ *adj* [L *conubialis*, fr. *conubium, connubium* marriage, fr. *com-* + *nubere* to marry — more at NUPTIAL] (ca. 1656) : of or relating to the married state : CONJUGAL ⟨~ relations⟩ — **con·nu·bi·al·ism** \-bē-ə-ˌli-zəm\ *n* — **con·nu·bi·al·i·ty** \-ˌnü-bē-ˈa-lə-tē, -ˌnyü-\ *n* — **con·nu·bi·al·ly** \-ˈnü-bē-ə-lē, -ˈnyü-\ *adv*
co·no·dont \ˈkō-nə-ˌdänt, ˈkä-\ *n* [ISV *con-* (fr. Gk *kōnos* cone) + *-odont*] (1859) : a Paleozoic toothlike fossil that is prob. the remains of an extinct eellike marine animal that may be an invertebrate or primitive vertebrate; *also* : the animal from which conodonts are derived
co·noid \ˈkō-ˌnȯid\ *or* **co·noi·dal** \kō-ˈnȯi-dᵊl\ *adj* (1570) : shaped like or nearly like a cone ⟨~ shells⟩ ⟨~ pottery⟩ — **conoid** *n*
con·quer \ˈkäŋ-kər\ *vb* **con·quered; con·quer·ing** \-k(ə-)riŋ\ [ME, to acquire, conquer, fr. AF *conquerre*, fr. VL **conquaerere*, alter. of L *conquirere* to search for, collect, fr. *com-* + *quaerere* to ask, search] *vt* (14c) **1** : to gain or acquire by force of arms : SUBJUGATE ⟨~ territory⟩ **2** : to overcome by force of arms : VANQUISH ⟨~*ed* the enemy⟩ **3** : to gain mastery over or win by overcoming obstacles or opposition ⟨~*ed* the mountain⟩ **4** : to overcome by mental or moral power : SURMOUNT ⟨~*ed* her fear⟩ ~ *vi* : to be victorious — **con·quer·or** \-kər-ər\ *n*
syn CONQUER, VANQUISH, DEFEAT, SUBDUE, REDUCE, OVERCOME, OVERTHROW mean to get the better of by force or strategy. CONQUER implies gaining mastery of ⟨Caesar *conquered* Gaul⟩. VANQUISH implies a complete overpowering ⟨*vanquished* the enemy and ended the war⟩. DEFEAT does not imply the finality or completeness of VANQUISH which it otherwise equals ⟨the Confederates *defeated* the Union forces at Manassas⟩. SUBDUE implies a defeating and suppression ⟨*subdued* the native tribes after years of fighting⟩. REDUCE implies a forcing to capitulate or surrender ⟨the city was *reduced* after a month-long siege⟩. OVERCOME suggests getting the better of with difficulty or after hard struggle ⟨*overcame* a host of bureaucratic roadblocks⟩. OVERTHROW stresses the bringing down or destruction of existing power ⟨violently *overthrew* the old regime⟩.
con·quest \ˈkän-ˌkwest, ˈkäŋ-; ˈkäŋ-kwəst\ *n* [ME, fr. AF, fr. VL **conquaesitus*, alter. of L *conquisitus*, pp. of *conquirere*] (14c) **1** : the act or process of conquering **2 a** : something conquered; *esp* : territory appropriated in war **b** : a person whose favor or hand has been won
con·qui·an \ˈkäŋ-kē-ən\ *n* [MexSp *conquián* — more at COONCAN] (ca. 1911) : a card game for two played with 40 cards from which all games of rummy developed
con·quis·ta·dor \kän-ˈkēs-tə-ˌdȯr, kən- *also* -ˈkwis-, -ˈkis-\ *n, pl* **con·quis·ta·do·res** \(ˌ)kän-ˌkēs-tə-ˈdȯr-ēz, -ˈdȯr-ˌās, kən-; (ˌ)kän-ˌkwis-, -ˌkis-\ *or* **con·quis·ta·dors** [Sp, ultim. fr. L *conquirere*] (1830) : one that conquers; *specif* : a leader in the Spanish conquest of America and esp. of Mexico and Peru in the 16th century
cons *abbr* **1** consecrated **2** conservative **3** consigned; consignment **4** consolidated **5** consonant **6** constable **7** constitution **8** construction **9** consul **10** consulting
con·san·guine \kän-ˈsaŋ-gwən, kən-\ *adj* (1610) : CONSANGUINEOUS
con·san·guin·e·ous \ˌkän-ˌsan-ˈgwi-nē-əs, -ˌsaŋ-\ *adj* [L *consanguineus*, fr. *com-* + *sanguin-, sanguis* blood] (1601) : of the same blood or origin; *specif* : descended from the same ancestor — **con·san·guin·e·ous·ly** *adv*
con·san·guin·i·ty \-ˈgwi-nə-tē\ *n, pl* **-ties** (14c) **1** : the quality or state of being consanguineous **2** : a close relation or connection
con·science \ˈkän(t)-shən(t)s\ *n* [ME, fr. AF, fr. L *conscientia*, fr. *conscient-, consciens*, prp. of *conscire* to be conscious, be conscious of guilt, fr. *com-* + *scire* to know — more at SCIENCE] (13c) **1 a** : the sense or consciousness of the moral goodness or blameworthiness of one's own conduct, intentions, or character together with a feeling of obligation to do right or be good **b** : a faculty, power, or principle enjoining good acts **c** : the part of the superego in psychoanalysis that transmits commands and admonitions to the ego **2** *archaic* : CONSCIOUSNESS **3** : conformity to the dictates of conscience : CONSCIENTIOUSNESS **4** : sensitive regard for fairness or justice : SCRUPLE — **con·science·less** \-ləs\ *adj* — **in all conscience** *or* **in conscience** : in all fairness

conscience money *n* (1839) **:** money paid usu. anonymously to relieve the conscience by restoring what has been wrongfully acquired

con·sci·en·tious \ˌkän(t)-shē-ˈen(t)-shəs\ *adj* (1576) **1 :** governed by or conforming to the dictates of conscience **:** SCRUPULOUS ⟨a ~ public servant⟩ **2 :** METICULOUS, CAREFUL ⟨a ~ listener⟩ ***syn*** see UPRIGHT — **con·sci·en·tious·ly** *adv* — **con·sci·en·tious·ness** *n*

conscientious objection *n* (1775) **:** objection on moral or religious grounds (as to service in the armed forces or to bearing arms)

conscientious objector *n* (1899) **:** a person who refuses to serve in the armed forces or bear arms on moral or religious grounds

con·scio·na·ble \ˈkän(t)-sh(ə-)nə-bəl\ *adj* [irreg. fr. *conscience*] (1549) **:** CONSCIENTIOUS

[1]**con·scious** \ˈkän(t)-shəs\ *adj* [L *conscius,* fr. *com-* + *scire* to know] (1592) **1 :** perceiving, apprehending, or noticing with a degree of controlled thought or observation ⟨was ~ that someone was watching⟩ **2** *archaic* **:** sharing another's knowledge or awareness of an inward state or outward fact **3 :** personally felt ⟨~ guilt⟩ **4 :** capable of or marked by thought, will, design, or perception **5 :** SELF-CONSCIOUS **6 :** having mental faculties undulled by sleep, faintness, or stupor **:** AWAKE ⟨was ~ during the surgery⟩ **7 :** done or acting with critical awareness ⟨a ~ effort to do better⟩ **8 a :** likely to notice, consider, or appraise ⟨a bargain-*conscious* shopper⟩ **b :** being concerned or interested ⟨weight-*conscious* models⟩ **c :** marked by strong feelings or notions ⟨a race-*conscious* society⟩ ***syn*** see AWARE — **con·scious·ly** *adv*

[2]**conscious** *n* (1919) **:** CONSCIOUSNESS 5

con·scious·ness \-nəs\ *n* (1629) **1 a :** the quality or state of being aware esp. of something within oneself **b :** the state or fact of being conscious of an external object, state, or fact **c :** AWARENESS; *esp* **:** concern for some social or political cause **2 :** the state of being characterized by sensation, emotion, volition, and thought **:** MIND **3 :** the totality of conscious states of an individual **4 :** the normal state of conscious life ⟨regained ~⟩ **5 :** the upper level of mental life of which the person is aware as contrasted with unconscious processes

consciousness–raising *n* (1968) **:** an increasing of concerned awareness esp. of some social or political issue

con·scribe \kən-ˈskrīb\ *vt* **con·scribed; con·scrib·ing** [L *conscribere*] (1613) **1 :** LIMIT, CIRCUMSCRIBE ⟨ill-health . . . *conscribed* the force of his intentions —*Times Lit. Supp.*⟩ **2 :** CONSCRIPT

[1]**con·script** \ˈkän-ˌskript\ *n* [alter. of F *conscrit,* fr. L *conscriptus,* pp. of *conscribere* to enroll, enlist, fr. *com-* + *scribere* to write — more at SCRIBE] (1799) **:** a conscripted person (as a military recruit)

[2]**con·script** \ˈkän-ˌskript\ *adj* (1812) **1 :** enrolled into service by compulsion **:** DRAFTED **2 :** made up of conscripted persons

[3]**con·script** \kən-ˈskript\ *vt* (1813) **:** to enroll into service by compulsion **:** DRAFT ⟨was ~*ed* into the army⟩

con·scrip·tion \kən-ˈskrip-shən\ *n* (1800) **:** compulsory enrollment of persons esp. for military service **:** DRAFT

[1]**con·se·crate** \ˈkän(t)-sə-ˌkrāt\ *adj* (14c) **:** dedicated to a sacred purpose

[2]**consecrate** *vt* **-crat·ed; -crat·ing** [ME, fr. L *consecratus,* pp. of *consecrare,* fr. *com-* + *sacrare* to consecrate — more at SACRED] (14c) **1 :** to induct (a person) into a permanent office with a religious rite; *esp* **:** to ordain to the office of bishop **2 a :** to make or declare sacred; *esp* **:** to devote irrevocably to the worship of God by a solemn ceremony **b :** to effect the liturgical transubstantiation of (eucharistic bread and wine) **c :** to devote to a purpose with or as if with deep solemnity or dedication **3 :** to make inviolable or venerable ⟨principles *consecrated* by the weight of history⟩ ***syn*** see DEVOTE — **con·se·cra·tive** \-ˌkrā-tiv\ *adj* — **con·se·cra·tor** \-ˌkrā-tər\ *n* — **con·se·cra·to·ry** \ˈkän(t)-si-krə-ˌtȯr-ē, -ˌkrā-tə-rē\ *adj*

con·se·cra·tion \ˌkän(t)-sə-ˈkrā-shən\ *n* (14c) **1 :** the act or ceremony of consecrating **2 :** the state of being consecrated **3** *cap* **:** the part of a Communion rite in which the bread and wine are consecrated

con·se·cu·tion \ˌkän(t)-si-ˈkyü-shən\ *n* [L *consecution-, consecutio,* fr. *consequi* to follow along — more at CONSEQUENT] (1651) **:** SEQUENCE

con·sec·u·tive \kən-ˈse-kyə-tiv, -kə-tiv\ *adj* (1611) **:** following one after the other in order **:** SUCCESSIVE ⟨served four ~ terms in office⟩ — **con·sec·u·tive·ly** *adv* — **con·sec·u·tive·ness** *n*

con·sen·su·al \kən-ˈsen(t)-sh(ə-)wəl, -shəl, -shü-əl\ *adj* [L *consensus* + E *-al*] (1754) **1 :** existing or made by mutual consent without an act of writing ⟨a ~ contract⟩ **2 :** involving or based on mutual consent ⟨~ acts⟩ — **con·sen·su·al·ly** *adv*

con·sen·sus \kən-ˈsen(t)-səs\ *n, often attrib* [L, fr. *consentire*] (1843) **1 a :** general agreement **:** UNANIMITY ⟨the ~ of their opinion, based on reports . . . from the border —John Hersey⟩ **b :** the judgment arrived at by most of those concerned ⟨the ~ was to go ahead⟩ **2 :** group solidarity in sentiment and belief

usage The phrase *consensus of opinion,* which is not actually redundant (see sense 1a; the sense that takes the phrase is slightly older), has been so often claimed to be a redundancy that many writers avoid it. You are safe in using *consensus* alone when it is clear you mean consensus of opinion, and most writers in fact do so.

[1]**con·sent** \kən-ˈsent\ *vi* [ME, fr. AF *consentir,* fr. L *consentire,* fr. *com-* + *sentire* to feel — more at SENSE] (13c) **1 :** to give assent or approval **:** AGREE ⟨~ to being tested⟩ **2** *archaic* **:** to be in concord in opinion or sentiment ***syn*** see ASSENT — **con·sent·er** *n* — **con·sent·ing·ly** \-ˈsen-tiŋ-lē\ *adv*

[2]**consent** *n* (14c) **1 :** compliance in or approval of what is done or proposed by another **:** ACQUIESCENCE ⟨he shall have power, by and with the advice and ~ of the Senate, to make treaties —*U.S. Constitution*⟩ **2 :** agreement as to action or opinion; *specif* **:** voluntary agreement by a people to organize a civil society and give authority to the government

con·sen·ta·ne·ous \ˌkän(t)-sən-ˈtā-nē-əs, ˌkän-ˌsen-\ *adj* [L *consentaneus,* fr. *consentire* to agree] (1575) **1 :** expressing agreement **:** SUITED **2 :** done or made by the consent of all — **con·sen·ta·ne·ous·ly** *adv*

consent decree *n* (1904) **:** a judicial decree that sanctions a voluntary agreement between parties in dispute

con·se·quence \ˈkän(t)-sə-ˌkwen(t)s, -kwən(t)s\ *n* (14c) **1 :** a conclusion derived through logic **:** INFERENCE **2 :** something produced by a cause or necessarily following from a set of conditions ⟨the economic ~*s* of the war⟩ **3 a :** importance with respect to power to produce an effect ⟨a mistake of no ~⟩ **b :** social importance **4 :** the appearance of importance; *esp* **:** SELF-IMPORTANCE ***syn*** see IMPORTANCE — **in consequence :** as a result

[1]**con·se·quent** \-kwənt, -ˌkwent\ *n* [ME, fr. AF, fr. L *consequent-, consequens,* prp. of *consequi* to follow along, fr. *com-* + *sequi* to follow — more at SUE] (14c) **1 a :** DEDUCTION 2b **b :** the conclusion of a conditional sentence **2 :** the second term of a ratio

[2]**consequent** *adj* (15c) **1 :** following as a result or effect ⟨her new job and ~ relocation⟩ **2 :** observing logical sequence **:** RATIONAL

con·se·quen·tial \ˌkän(t)-sə-ˈkwen(t)-shəl\ *adj* (1626) **1 :** of the nature of a secondary result **:** INDIRECT **2 :** CONSEQUENT **3 :** having significant consequences **:** IMPORTANT ⟨a grave and ~ event⟩ **4 :** SELF-IMPORTANT — **con·se·quen·ti·al·i·ty** \-ˌkwen(t)-shē-ˈa-lə-tē\ *n* — **con·se·quen·tial·ly** \-ˈkwen(t)-sh(ə-)lē\ *adv* — **con·se·quen·tial·ness** \-ˈkwen(t)-shəl-nəs\ *n*

con·se·quen·tial·ism \-shə-ˌli-zəm\ *n* (1982) **:** the theory that the value and esp. the moral value of an act should be judged by the value of its consequences — **con·se·quen·tial·ist** \-ˌlist\ *adj or n*

con·se·quent·ly \ˈkän(t)-sə-ˌkwent-lē, -si-kwənt-\ *adv* (15c) **:** as a result **:** in view of the foregoing **:** ACCORDINGLY

con·ser·van·cy \kən-ˈsər-vən(t)-sē\ *n, pl* **-cies** [alter. of obs. *conservacy* conservation, fr. AF *conservacie,* fr. ML *conservatia,* fr. L *conservare*] (1667) **1** *Brit* **:** a board regulating fisheries and navigation in a river or port **2 a :** CONSERVATION **b :** an organization or area designated to conserve and protect natural resources

con·ser·va·tion \ˌkän(t)-sər-ˈvā-shən\ *n* [ME, fr. MF, fr. L *conservation-, conservatio,* fr. *conservare*] (14c) **1 :** a careful preservation and protection of something; *esp* **:** planned management of a natural resource to prevent exploitation, destruction, or neglect **2 :** the preservation of a physical quantity during transformations or reactions — **con·ser·va·tion·al** \-shnəl, -shə-nᵊl\ *adj*

con·ser·va·tion·ist \-sh(ə-)nist\ *n* (1870) **:** a person who advocates conservation esp. of natural resources

conservation of charge (1949) **:** a principle in physics: the total electric charge of an isolated system remains constant irrespective of whatever internal changes may take place

conservation of energy (1853) **:** a principle in physics: the total energy of an isolated system remains constant irrespective of whatever internal changes may take place with energy disappearing in one form reappearing in another

conservation of mass (1884) **:** a principle in classical physics: the total mass of any isolated material system is neither increased nor diminished by reactions between the parts — called also *conservation of matter*

con·ser·va·tism \kən-ˈsər-və-ˌti-zəm\ *n* (1832) **1** *cap* **a :** the principles and policies of a Conservative party **b :** the Conservative party **2 a :** disposition in politics to preserve what is established **b :** a political philosophy based on tradition and social stability, stressing established institutions, and preferring gradual development to abrupt change; *specif* **:** such a philosophy calling for lower taxes, limited government regulation of business and investing, a strong national defense, and individual financial responsibility for personal needs (as retirement income or health-care coverage) **3 :** the tendency to prefer an existing or traditional situation to change

[1]**con·ser·va·tive** \kən-ˈsər-və-tiv\ *adj* (14c) **1 :** PRESERVATIVE **2 a :** of or relating to a philosophy of conservatism **b** *cap* **:** of or constituting a political party professing the principles of conservatism: as (1) **:** of or constituting a party of the United Kingdom advocating support of established institutions (2) **:** PROGRESSIVE CONSERVATIVE **3 a :** tending or disposed to maintain existing views, conditions, or institutions **:** TRADITIONAL **b :** marked by moderation or caution ⟨a ~ estimate⟩ **c :** marked by or relating to traditional norms of taste, elegance, style, or manners **4 :** of, relating to, or practicing Conservative Judaism — **con·ser·va·tive·ly** *adv* — **con·ser·va·tive·ness** *n*

[2]**conservative** *n* (1831) **1 a :** an adherent or advocate of political conservatism **b** *cap* **:** a member or supporter of a conservative political party **2 a :** one who adheres to traditional methods or views **b :** a cautious or discreet person

Conservative Judaism *n* (1892) **:** Judaism as practiced esp. among some U.S. Jews with adherence to the Torah and Talmud but with allowance for some departures in keeping with differing times and circumstances — compare ORTHODOX JUDAISM, REFORM JUDAISM

con·ser·va·tize \-ˌtīz\ *vb* **-tized; -tiz·ing** *vi* (1849) **:** to grow conservative ~ *vt* **:** to make conservative

con·ser·va·toire \kən-ˈsər-və-ˌtwär\ *n* [F, fr. It *conservatorio*] (1832) **:** CONSERVATORY 2

con·ser·va·tor \kən-ˈsər-və-tər, -və-ˌtȯr; ˈkän(t)-sər-ˌvā-tər\ *n* (15c) **1 a :** one that preserves from injury or violation **:** PROTECTOR **b :** one that is responsible for the care, restoration, and repair of archival or museum articles **2 :** a person, official, or institution designated to take over and protect the interests of an incompetent **3 :** an official charged with the protection of something affecting public welfare and interests — **con·ser·va·to·ri·al** \kən-ˌsər-və-ˈtȯr-ē-əl, (ˌ)kän-\ *adj* — **con·ser·va·tor·ship** \kən-ˈsər-və-tər-ˌship, -və-ˌtȯr-; ˈkän(t)-sər-ˌvā-tər-\ *n*

con·ser·va·to·ry \kən-ˈsər-və-ˌtȯr-ē\ *n, pl* **-ries** (1664) **1 :** a greenhouse for growing or displaying plants **2** [It *conservatorio* home for foundlings, music school, fr. L *conservare*] **:** a school specializing in one of the fine arts ⟨a music ~⟩

[1]**con·serve** \kən-ˈsərv\ *vt* **con·served; con·serv·ing** [ME, fr. MF *conserver,* fr. L *conservare,* fr. *com-* + *servare* to keep, guard, observe; akin to Av *haurvaiti* he guards] (14c) **1 :** to keep in a safe or sound state ⟨he *conserved* his inheritance⟩; *esp* **:** to avoid wasteful or destructive use of ⟨~ natural resources⟩ **2 :** to preserve with sugar **3 :** to maintain (a quantity) constant during a process of chemical, physical, or evolutionary change ⟨*conserved* DNA sequences⟩ — **con·serv·er** *n*

[2]**con·serve** \ˈkän-ˌsərv\ *n* (15c) **1 :** SWEETMEAT; *esp* **:** a candied fruit **2 :** PRESERVE; *specif* **:** one prepared from a mixture of fruits

con·sid·er \kən-ˈsi-dər\ *vb* **con·sid·ered; con·sid·er·ing** \-d(ə-)riŋ\ [ME, fr. AF *considerer,* fr. L *considerare* to observe, think about, fr.

com- + *sider-, sidus* heavenly body] *vt* (14c) **1 :** to think about carefully: as **a :** to think of esp. with regard to taking some action ⟨is *~ing* you for the job⟩ ⟨*~ed* moving to the city⟩ **b :** to take into account ⟨defendant's age must be *~ed*⟩ **2 :** to regard or treat in an attentive or kindly way ⟨he *~ed* her every wish⟩ **3 :** to gaze on steadily or reflectively **4 :** to come to judge or classify ⟨~ thrift essential⟩ **5 :** REGARD ⟨his works are well *~ed* abroad⟩ **6 :** SUPPOSE **~** *vi* **:** REFLECT, DELIBERATE ⟨paused a moment to ~⟩

syn CONSIDER, STUDY, CONTEMPLATE, WEIGH mean to think about in order to arrive at a judgment or decision. CONSIDER may suggest giving thought to in order to reach a suitable conclusion, opinion, or decision ⟨refused even to *consider* my proposal⟩. STUDY implies sustained purposeful concentration and attention to details and minutiae ⟨*study* the plan closely⟩. CONTEMPLATE stresses focusing one's thoughts on something but does not imply coming to a conclusion or decision ⟨*contemplate* the consequences of refusing⟩. WEIGH implies attempting to reach the truth or arrive at a decision by balancing conflicting claims or evidence ⟨*weigh* the pros and cons of the case⟩.

[1]**con·sid·er·able** \-ˈsi-dər(-ə)-bəl, -ˈsi-drə-bəl\ *adj* (ca. 1619) **1 :** worth consideration **:** SIGNIFICANT ⟨a ~ artist⟩ **2 :** large in extent or degree ⟨a ~ number⟩ — **con·sid·er·ably** \-blē\ *adv*

[2]**considerable** *n* (1685) **:** a considerable amount, degree, or extent

con·sid·er·ate \kən-ˈsi-d(ə-)rət\ *adj* (1572) **1 :** marked by or given to careful consideration **:** CIRCUMSPECT **2 :** thoughtful of the rights and feelings of others — **con·sid·er·ate·ly** *adv* — **con·sid·er·ate·ness** *n*

con·sid·er·ation \kən-ˌsi-də-ˈrā-shən\ *n* (14c) **1 :** continuous and careful thought ⟨after long ~ he agreed to their requests⟩ **2 a :** a matter weighed or taken into account when formulating an opinion or plan ⟨economic *~s* forced her to leave college⟩ **b :** a taking into account **3 :** thoughtful and sympathetic regard **4 :** an opinion obtained by reflection **5 :** ESTEEM, REGARD ⟨the family built themselves a large, ugly villa . . . and became people of ~ —V. S. Pritchett⟩ **6 a :** RECOMPENSE, PAYMENT ⟨a ~ paid for legal services⟩ **b :** the inducement to a contract or other legal transaction; *specif* **:** an act or forbearance or the promise thereof done or given by one party in return for the act or promise of another — **in consideration of :** as payment or recompense for ⟨a small fee *in consideration of* many kind services⟩

con·sid·ered \kən-ˈsi-dərd\ *adj* (ca. 1677) **1 :** matured by extended deliberative thought ⟨a ~ opinion⟩ **2 :** viewed with respect or esteem

[1]**con·sid·er·ing** \-d(ə-)riŋ\ *prep* (14c) **:** in view of **:** taking into account ⟨he did well ~ his limitations⟩

[2]**considering** *conj* (15c) **:** INASMUCH AS ⟨~ he was new at the job, he did quite well⟩

con·sig·li·e·re \kōn-(ˌ)sil-ˈye-re, -ˈyer-ē; kän-(ˌ)si-glē-ˈye-rā, -rē, -ˈyer\ *n, pl* **-ri** \-rē\ *also* **-res** [It, fr. *consiglio* advice, counsel, fr. L *consilium* — more at COUNSEL] (1615) **:** COUNSELOR, ADVISER ⟨~ of a Mafia family⟩

con·sign \kən-ˈsīn\ *vb* [MF *consigner,* fr. L *consignare,* fr. *com-* + *signum* sign, mark, seal — more at SIGN] *vt* (1528) **1 :** to give over to another's care **2 :** to give, transfer, or deliver into the hands or control of another; *also* **:** to commit esp. to a final destination or fate ⟨a writer *~ed* to oblivion⟩ **3 :** to send or address to an agent to be cared for or sold **~** *vi, obs* **:** AGREE, SUBMIT ***syn*** see COMMIT — **con·sign·able** \-ˈsī-nə-bəl\ *adj* — **con·sig·na·tion** \ˌkän-ˌsī-ˈnā-shən, ˌkän(t)-sig-\ *n* — **con·sign·or** \ˌkän-ˌsī-ˈnȯr, kən-\ *n*

con·sign·ee \ˌkän(t)-sə-ˈnē, ˌkän-ˌsī-, kən-ˌsī-\ *n* (1773) **:** one to whom something is consigned or shipped

[1]**con·sign·ment** \kən-ˈsīn-mənt\ *n* (ca. 1668) **1 :** the act or process of consigning **2 :** something consigned esp. in a single shipment — **on consignment :** shipped to a dealer who pays only for what is sold and who may return what is unsold ⟨goods shipped *on consignment*⟩

[2]**consignment** *adj* (1913) **:** of, relating to, or received as goods on consignment ⟨a ~ sale⟩

con·sil·ience \kən-ˈsil-yən(t)s\ *n* [*com-* + *resilience*] (1840) **:** the linking together of principles from different disciplines esp. when forming a comprehensive theory

[1]**con·sist** \kən-ˈsist\ *vi* [MF & L; MF *consister,* fr. L *consistere,* lit., to stop, stand still, fr. *com-* + *sistere* to take a stand; akin to L *stare* to stand — more at STAND] (1526) **1 :** LIE, RESIDE — usu. used with *in* ⟨liberty *~s* in the absence of obstructions —A. E. Housman⟩ **2** *archaic* **a :** EXIST, BE **b :** to be capable of existing **3 :** to be composed or made up — usu. used with *of* ⟨breakfast *~ed* of cereal, milk, and fruit⟩ **4 :** to be consistent ⟨it *~s* with the facts⟩

[2]**con·sist** \ˈkän-ˌsist\ *n* (1898) **:** makeup or composition (as of coal sizes or a railroad train) by classes, types, or grades and arrangement

con·sis·tence \kən-ˈsis-tən(t)s\ *n* (1601) **:** CONSISTENCY

con·sis·ten·cy \kən-ˈsis-tən(t)-sē\ *n, pl* **-cies** (1594) **1 a** *archaic* **:** condition of adhering together **:** firmness of material substance **b :** firmness of constitution or character **:** PERSISTENCY **2 :** degree of firmness, density, viscosity, or resistance to movement or separation of constituent particles ⟨boil the juice to the ~ of a thick syrup⟩ **3 a :** agreement or harmony of parts or features to one another or a whole **:** CORRESPONDENCE; *specif* **:** ability to be asserted together without contradiction **b :** harmony of conduct or practice with profession ⟨followed her own advice with ~⟩

con·sis·tent \kən-ˈsis-tənt\ *adj* [L *consistent-, consistens,* prp. of *consistere*] (1638) **1** *archaic* **:** possessing firmness or coherence **2 a :** marked by harmony, regularity, or steady continuity **:** free from variation or contradiction ⟨a ~ style in painting⟩ **b :** marked by agreement **:** COMPATIBLE — usu. used with *with* ⟨statements not ~ with the truth⟩ **c :** showing steady conformity to character, profession, belief, or custom ⟨a ~ patriot⟩ **3 :** tending to be arbitrarily close to the true value of the parameter estimated as the sample becomes large ⟨a ~ statistical estimator⟩ — **con·sis·tent·ly** \-lē\ *adv*

con·sis·to·ry \kən-ˈsis-t(ə-)rē\ *n, pl* **-ries** [ME *consistorie,* fr. AF, fr. ML & LL; ML *consistorium* church tribunal, fr. LL, imperial council, fr. L *consistere*] (14c) **1 :** a solemn assembly **:** COUNCIL **2 :** a church tribunal or governing body: as **a :** a solemn meeting of Roman Catholic cardinals convoked and presided over by the pope **b :** a church session in some Reformed churches **3 :** the organization that confers the degrees of the Ancient and Accepted Scottish Rite of Freemasonry usu. from the 19th to the 32d inclusive; *also* **:** a meeting of such an organization — **con·sis·to·ri·al** \ˌkän-si-ˈstōr-ē-əl, -ˈstȯr-\ *adj*

con·so·ci·ate \kən-ˈsō-sē-ˌāt, -shē-ˌāt\ *vb* **-at·ed; -at·ing** [L *consociatus,* pp. of *consociare,* fr. *com-* + *socius* companion — more at SOCIAL] *vt* (1566) **:** to bring into association **~** *vi* **:** to associate esp. in fellowship or partnership

con·so·ci·a·tion \-ˌsō-sē-ˈā-shən, -shē-\ *n* (1593) **1 :** association in fellowship or alliance **2 :** an association of churches or religious societies **3 :** an ecological community with a single dominant species — **con·so·ci·a·tion·al** \-shnəl, -shə-nᵊl\ *adj*

consol *abbr* consolidated

con·so·la·tion \ˌkän(t)-sə-ˈlā-shən\ *n* (14c) **1 :** the act or an instance of consoling **:** the state of being consoled **:** COMFORT **2 :** something that consoles; *specif* **:** a contest held for those who have lost early in a tournament — **con·so·la·to·ry** \kən-ˈsō-lə-ˌtȯr-ē, -ˈsä-\ *adj*

consolation prize *n* (1886) **:** a prize given to a runner-up or a loser in a contest

[1]**con·sole** \ˈkän-ˌsōl\ *n* [F] (1664) **1 :** an architectural member projecting from a wall to form a bracket or from a keystone for ornament **2 :** CONSOLE TABLE **3 a :** an upright case that houses the keyboards and controlling mechanisms of an organ and from which the organ is played **b :** a combination of readouts or displays and an input device (as a keyboard or switches) by which an operator can monitor and interact with a system (as a computer or dubber) **4 a :** a cabinet (as for a radio or television set) designed to rest directly on the floor **b :** a small storage cabinet between bucket seats in an automobile **5 :** an electronic system that connects to a display (as a television set) and is used primarily to play video games

[2]**con·sole** \kən-ˈsōl\ *vt* **con·soled; con·sol·ing** [F *consoler,* fr. L *consolari,* fr. *com-* + *solari* to console] (1673) **:** to alleviate the grief, sense of loss, or trouble of **:** COMFORT ⟨~ a widow⟩ — **con·sol·ing·ly** \-ˈsō-liŋ-lē\ *adv*

console table *n* (1807) **:** a table fixed to a wall with its top supported by consoles or front legs; *broadly* **:** a table designed to fit against a wall

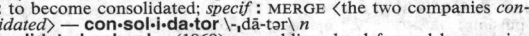

console table

con·sol·i·date \kən-ˈsä-lə-ˌdāt\ *vb* **-dat·ed; -dat·ing** [L *consolidatus,* pp. of *consolidare* to make solid, fr. *com-* + *solidus* solid] *vt* (ca. 1512) **1 :** to join together into one whole **:** UNITE ⟨~ several small school districts⟩ **2 :** to make firm or secure **:** STRENGTHEN ⟨~ their hold on first place⟩ **3 :** to form into a compact mass **~** *vi* **:** to become consolidated; *specif* **:** MERGE ⟨the two companies *consolidated*⟩ — **con·sol·i·da·tor** \-ˌdā-tər\ *n*

consolidated school *n* (1869) **:** a public school formed by merging other schools

con·sol·i·da·tion \kən-ˌsä-lə-ˈdā-shən\ *n* (15c) **1 :** the act or process of consolidating **:** the state of being consolidated **2 :** the process of uniting **:** the quality or state of being united; *specif* **:** the unification of two or more corporations by dissolution of existing ones and creation of a single new corporation **3 :** pathological alteration of lung tissue from an aerated condition to one of solid consistency

con·som·mé \ˌkän(t)-sə-ˈmā\ *n* [F, fr. pp. of *consommer* to complete, boil down, fr. L *consummare* to complete — more at CONSUMMATE] (1815) **:** clear soup made from well-seasoned stock

con·so·nance \ˈkän(t)-s(ə-)nən(t)s\ *n* (15c) **1 :** harmony or agreement among components **2 a :** correspondence or recurrence of sounds esp. in words; *specif* **:** recurrence or repetition of consonants esp. at the end of stressed syllables without the similar correspondence of vowels (as in the final sounds of "stroke" and "luck") **b :** CONCORD 1b **c :** SYMPATHETIC VIBRATION, RESONANCE

con·so·nan·cy \-s(ə-)nən(t)-sē\ *n, pl* **-cies** (14c) **:** CONSONANCE 1

[1]**con·so·nant** \ˈkän(t)-s(ə-)nənt\ *adj* [ME, fr. L *consonant-, consonans,* prp. of *consonare* to sound together, agree, fr. *com-* + *sonare* to sound — more at SOUND] (15c) **1 :** being in agreement or harmony **:** free from elements making for discord **2 :** marked by musical consonances **3 :** having similar sounds ⟨~ words⟩ **4 :** relating to or exhibiting consonance **:** RESONANT — **con·so·nant·ly** *adv*

[2]**consonant** *n* [ME, fr. AF, fr. L *consonant-, consonans,* fr. prp. of *consonare*] (14c) **:** one of a class of speech sounds (as \p\, \g\, \n\, \l\, \s\, \r\) characterized by constriction or closure at one or more points in the breath channel; *also* **:** a letter representing a consonant — usu. used in English of any letter except *a, e, i, o,* and *u*

con·so·nan·tal \ˌkän(t)-sə-ˈnan-tᵊl\ *adj* (1795) **:** relating to, being, or marked by a consonant or group of consonants

consonant shift *n* (1888) **:** a set of regular changes in consonant articulation in the history of a language or dialect: **a :** such a set affecting the Indo-European stops and distinguishing the Germanic languages from the other Indo-European languages — compare GRIMM'S LAW **b :** such a set affecting the Germanic stops and distinguishing High German from the other Germanic languages

[1]**con·sort** \ˈkän-ˌsȯrt\ *n* [ME, fr. MF, fr. L *consort-, consors* partner, sharer, fr. *com-* + *sort-, sors* lot, share — more at SERIES] (15c) **1 :** ASSOCIATE **2 :** a ship accompanying another **3 :** SPOUSE — compare PRINCE CONSORT, QUEEN CONSORT

[2]**consort** *n* [MF *consorte,* fr. *consort*] (1584) **1 :** CONJUNCTION, ASSOCIATION ⟨he ruled in ~ with his father⟩ **2 :** GROUP, ASSEMBLY ⟨a ~ of specialists⟩ **3 a :** a group of singers or instrumentalists performing together **b :** a set of musical instruments of the same family

[3]**con·sort** \kən-ˈsȯrt, kän-ˈ, ˈkän-ˌ\ *vt* (1588) **1 :** UNITE, ASSOCIATE **2** *obs* **:** ESCORT **~** *vi* **1 :** to keep company ⟨*~ing* with criminals⟩ **2** *obs* **:** to make harmony **:** PLAY **3 :** ACCORD, HARMONIZE ⟨the illustrations ~ admirably with the text —*Times Lit. Supp.*⟩

con·sor·tium \kən-ˈsȯr-sh(ē-)əm, -ˈsȯr-tē-əm\ *n, pl* **-sor·tia** \-ˈsȯr-sh(ē-)ə, -ˈsȯr-tē-ə\ *also* **-sortiums** [L, fellowship, fr. *consort-, consors*] (1829) **1 :** an agreement, combination, or group (as of companies) formed to undertake an enterprise beyond the resources of any one member **2 :** ASSOCIATION, SOCIETY **3 :** the legal right of one spouse to the company, affection, and assistance of and to sexual relations with the other

con·spe·cif·ic \ˌkän(t)-spi-ˈsi-fik\ *adj* (1859) **:** of the same species — **conspecific** *n*

con·spec·tus \kən-ˈspek-təs\ *n* [L, fr. *conspectus,* fr. *conspicere*] (1825) **1 :** a usu. brief survey or summary (as of an extensive subject) often providing an overall view **2 :** OUTLINE, SYNOPSIS

con·spi·cu·i·ty \ˌkän(t)-spə-ˈkyü-ə-tē\ *n* (1601) **:** the quality or state of being conspicuous **:** CONSPICUOUSNESS

con·spic·u·ous \kən-ˈspi-kyə-wəs, -kyü-əs\ *adj* [L *conspicuus,* fr. *conspicere* to get sight of, fr. *com-* + *specere* to look — more at SPY] (ca. 1534) **1 :** obvious to the eye or mind ⟨~ changes⟩ **2 :** attracting attention **:** STRIKING ⟨a ~ success⟩ **3 :** marked by a noticeable violation of good taste ***syn*** see NOTICEABLE — **con·spic·u·ous·ly** *adv* — **con·spic·u·ous·ness** \-nəs\ *n*

conspicuous consumption *n* (1899) **:** lavish or wasteful spending thought to enhance social prestige

con·spir·a·cist \kən-ˈspir-ə-sist\ *n* (1976) **:** one who believes or promotes a conspiracy theory

con·spir·a·cy \kən-ˈspir-ə-sē\ *n, pl* **-cies** [ME *conspiracie,* fr. L *conspirare*] (14c) **1 :** the act of conspiring together **2 a :** an agreement among conspirators **b :** a group of conspirators ***syn*** see PLOT

conspiracy of silence (1865) **:** a secret agreement to keep silent about an occurrence, situation, or subject esp. in order to promote or protect selfish interests

conspiracy theory *n* (1909) **:** a theory that explains an event or set of circumstances as the result of a secret plot by usu. powerful conspirators — **conspiracy theorist** *n*

con·spi·ra·tion \ˌkän(t)-spə-ˈrā-shən, ˌkän-(ˌ)spi-ˈrā-\ *n* (14c) **1 :** the act or action of plotting or secretly combining **2 :** a joint effort toward a particular end — **con·spi·ra·tion·al** \-shnəl, -shə-nᵊl\ *adj*

con·spir·a·tor \kən-ˈspir-ə-tər\ *n* (15c) **:** one who conspires **:** PLOTTER

con·spir·a·to·ri·al \kən-ˌspir-ə-ˈtȯr-ē-əl\ *adj* (1855) **:** of, relating to, or suggestive of a conspiracy — **con·spir·a·to·ri·al·ly** \-ē-ə-lē\ *adv*

con·spire \kən-ˈspī(-ə)r\ *vb* **con·spired; con·spir·ing** [ME, fr. AF *conspirer,* fr. L *conspirare* to be in harmony, conspire, fr. *com-* + *spirare* to breathe] *vt* (14c) **:** PLOT, CONTRIVE ~ *vi* **1 a :** to join in a secret agreement to do an unlawful or wrongful act or an act which becomes unlawful as a result of the secret agreement ⟨accused of *conspiring* to overthrow the government⟩ **b :** SCHEME **2 :** to act in harmony toward a common end ⟨circumstances *conspired* to defeat his efforts⟩

con spi·ri·to \kän-ˈspir-ə-ˌtō, kōn-\ *adv* [It] (1801) **:** with spirit or animation — used as a direction in music

const *abbr* **1** constant **2** constitution; constitutional **3** construction

con·sta·ble \ˈkän(t)-stə-bəl, ˈkən(t)-\ *n* [ME *conestable,* fr. AF, fr. LL *comes stabuli,* lit., officer of the stable] (13c) **1 :** a high officer of a royal court or noble household esp. in the Middle Ages **2 :** the warden or governor of a royal castle or a fortified town **3 a :** a public officer usu. of a town or township responsible for keeping the peace and for minor judicial duties **b** *chiefly Brit* **:** POLICE OFFICER; *esp* **:** one ranking below sergeant

¹**con·stab·u·lary** \kən-ˈsta-byə-ˌler-ē, -ˌle-rē\ *adj* (1824) **:** of or relating to a constable or constabulary

²**constabulary** *n, pl* **-lar·ies** (ca. 1715) **1 :** the organized body of constables of a particular district or country **2 :** an armed police force organized on military lines but distinct from the regular army

con·stan·cy \ˈkän(t)-stən(t)-sē\ *n, pl* **-cies** (15c) **1 a :** steadfastness of mind under duress **:** FORTITUDE **b :** FIDELITY, LOYALTY **2 :** a state of being constant or unchanging

¹**con·stant** \ˈkän(t)-stənt\ *adj* [ME, fr. MF, fr. L *constant-, constans,* fr. prp. of *constare* to stand firm, be consistent, fr. *com-* + *stare* to stand — more at STAND] (14c) **1 :** marked by firm steadfast resolution or faithfulness **:** exhibiting constancy of mind or attachment ⟨a ~ friend⟩ **2 :** INVARIABLE, UNIFORM ⟨a ~ flow⟩ **3 :** continually occurring or recurring **:** REGULAR ⟨a ~ annoyance⟩ ***syn*** see FAITHFUL, CONTINUAL — **con·stant·ly** *adv*

²**constant** *n* (1832) **:** something invariable or unchanging: as **a :** a number that has a fixed value in a given situation or universally or that is characteristic of some substance or instrument **b :** a number that is assumed not to change value in a given mathematical discussion **c :** a term in logic with a fixed designation

con·stan·tan \ˈkän(t)-stən-ˌtan\ *n* [fr. the fact that its resistance remains constant under change of temperature] (1903) **:** an alloy of copper and nickel used esp. for electrical resistors and in thermocouples

con·sta·tive \kən-ˈstā-tiv, ˈkän-stə-tiv\ *adj* [*constate* to assert positively, fr. F *constater,* fr. L *constat* it is certain, 3d sing. pres. indic. of *constare*] (1901) **1 :** of, relating to, or being a verbal form that expresses past completed action **2 :** being or relating to an utterance (as an assertion, question, or command) that is capable of being judged true or false — **constative** *n*

con·stel·late \ˈkän(t)-stə-ˌlāt\ *vb* **-lat·ed; -lat·ing** *vt* (1643) **1 :** to unite in a cluster **2 :** to set or adorn with or as if with constellations ~ *vi* **:** CLUSTER

con·stel·la·tion \ˌkän(t)-stə-ˈlā-shən\ *n* [ME *constellacioun,* fr. AF *constellation,* fr. LL *constellation-, constellatio,* fr. L *com-* + *stella* star — more at STAR] (14c) **1 :** the configuration of stars esp. at one's birth **2 :** any of 88 arbitrary configurations of stars or an area of the celestial sphere covering one of these configurations **3 :** an assemblage, collection, or group of usu. related persons, qualities, or things ⟨a ~ of . . . relatives, friends, and hangers-on —Brendan Gill⟩ ⟨a ~ of symptoms⟩ **4 :** PATTERN, ARRANGEMENT ⟨taking advantage of the shifting ~ of power throughout the known world —H. D. Lasswell⟩ — **con·stel·la·to·ry** \kən-ˈste-lə-ˌtȯr-ē\ *adj*

con·ster·nate \ˈkän(t)-stər-ˌnāt\ *vt* **-nat·ed; -nat·ing** (1651) **:** to fill with consternation

con·ster·na·tion \ˌkän(t)-stər-ˈnā-shən\ *n* [F or L; F, fr. L *consternation-, consternatio,* fr. *consternare* to throw into confusion, fr. *com-* + *-sternare,* prob. fr. *sternere* to spread, strike down — more at STREW] (1604) **:** amazement or dismay that hinders or throws into confusion ⟨the two . . . stared at each other in ~, and neither knew what to do —Pearl Buck⟩

con·sti·pate \ˈkän(t)-stə-ˌpāt\ *vt* **-pat·ed; -pat·ing** [ML *constipatus,* pp. of *constipare,* fr. L, to crowd together, fr. *com-* + *stipare* to pack tight — more at STIFF] (1533) **1 :** to cause constipation in **2 :** to make immobile, inactive, or dull **:** STULTIFY ⟨so much clutter . . . will tend to ~ the novel's working order —*Times Lit. Supp.*⟩

con·sti·pat·ed \-ˌpā-təd\ *adj* (1547) **1 :** affected with constipation **2 :** stilted or stodgy in appearance, expression, or action

con·sti·pa·tion \ˌkän(t)-stə-ˈpā-shən\ *n* (15c) **1 :** abnormally delayed or infrequent passage of usu. dry hardened feces **2 :** STULTIFICATION

con·stit·u·en·cy \kən-ˈstich-wən(t)-sē, -ˈsti-chə-, -ˈsti-chü-ən(t)-\ *n, pl* **-cies** (1831) **1 a :** a body of citizens entitled to elect a representative (as to a legislative or executive position) **b :** the residents in an electoral district **c :** an electoral district **2 a :** a group or body that patronizes, supports, or offers representation ⟨creating . . . a grass-roots ~ for continuing the project —Fred Reed⟩ **b :** the people involved in or served by an organization (as a business or institution) ⟨regards its corporate customers as its prime ~ —Andrew Hacker⟩

¹**con·stit·u·ent** \-wənt, -ənt\ *n* [F *constituant,* fr. MF, fr. prp. of *constituer* to constitute, fr. L *constituere*] (1622) **1 :** one who authorizes another to act as agent **:** PRINCIPAL **2 :** a member of a constituency **3 :** an essential part **:** COMPONENT, ELEMENT **4 :** a structural unit of a definable syntactic, semantic, or phonological category that consists of one or more linguistic elements (as words, morphemes, or features) and that can occur as a component of a larger construction ***syn*** see ELEMENT

²**constituent** *adj* [L *constituent-, constituens,* prp. of *constituere*] (1660) **1 :** serving to form, compose, or make up a unit or whole **:** COMPONENT ⟨~ parts⟩ **2 :** having the power to create a government or frame or amend a constitution ⟨a ~ assembly⟩ — **con·stit·u·ent·ly** *adv*

con·sti·tute \ˈkän(t)-stə-ˌtüt, -ˌtyüt\ *vt* **-tut·ed; -tut·ing** [ME, fr. L *constitutus,* pp. of *constituere* to set up, constitute, fr. *com-* + *statuere* to set — more at STATUTE] (15c) **1 :** to appoint to an office, function, or dignity **2 :** SET UP, ESTABLISH: as **a :** ENACT **b :** FOUND **c** (1) **:** to give due or lawful form to (2) **:** to legally process **3 :** MAKE UP, FORM, COMPOSE ⟨12 months ~ a year⟩ ⟨high school dropouts who ~ a major problem in large city slums —J. B. Conant⟩

con·sti·tu·tion \ˌkän(t)-stə-ˈtü-shən, -ˈtyü-\ *n* (14c) **1 :** an established law or custom **:** ORDINANCE **2 a :** the physical makeup of the individual esp. with respect to the health, strength, and appearance of the body ⟨a hearty ~⟩ **b :** the structure, composition, physical makeup, or nature of something ⟨the ~ of society⟩ **3 :** the act of establishing, making, or setting up **4 :** the mode in which a state or society is organized; *esp* **:** the manner in which sovereign power is distributed **5 a :** the basic principles and laws of a nation, state, or social group that determine the powers and duties of the government and guarantee certain rights to the people in it **b :** a written instrument embodying the rules of a political or social organization — **con·sti·tu·tion·less** \-ləs\ *adj*

¹**con·sti·tu·tion·al** \-shnəl, -shə-nᵊl\ *adj* (1682) **1 :** relating to, inherent in, or affecting the constitution of body or mind **2 :** of, relating to, or entering into the fundamental makeup of something **:** ESSENTIAL **3 :** being in accordance with or authorized by the constitution of a state or society ⟨a ~ government⟩ **4 :** regulated by or ruling according to a constitution ⟨a ~ monarchy⟩ **5 :** of or relating to a constitution ⟨a ~ crisis⟩ **6 :** loyal to or supporting an established constitution or form of government

²**constitutional** *n* (1829) **:** a walk taken for one's health

con·sti·tu·tion·al·ism \-sh(ə-)nə-ˌli-zəm\ *n* (1832) **:** adherence to or government according to constitutional principles; *also* **:** a constitutional system of government — **con·sti·tu·tion·al·ist** \-list\ *n*

con·sti·tu·tion·al·i·ty \-ˌtü-shə-ˈna-lə-tē, -ˌtyü-\ *n* (1787) **:** the quality or state of being constitutional; *esp* **:** accordance with the provisions of a constitution ⟨questioned the ~ of the law⟩

con·sti·tu·tion·al·ize \-ˈtü-shnə-ˌlīz, -shə-nə-ˌlīz\ *vt* **-ized; -iz·ing** (1831) **:** to provide with a constitution **:** organize along constitutional principles — **con·sti·tu·tion·al·i·za·tion** \-ˌtü-shnə-lə-ˈzā-shən, -shə-nə-lə-\ *n*

con·sti·tu·tion·al·ly \-ˈtü-shnə-lē, -ˈtyü-, -shə-nə-lē\ *adv* (1742) **1 a :** in accordance with one's constitution ⟨~ unable to grasp subtleties⟩ **b :** in structure, composition, or constitution ⟨despite repeated heatings the material remained ~ the same⟩ **2 :** in accordance with a political constitution ⟨was not ~ eligible to fill the office⟩

con·sti·tu·tive \ˈkän(t)-stə-ˌtü-tiv, -ˌtyü-; kən-ˈsti-chə-tiv\ *adj* (1592) **1 :** having the power to enact or establish **:** CONSTRUCTIVE **2 :** CONSTITUENT, ESSENTIAL **3 :** relating to or dependent on constitution ⟨a ~ property of all electrolytes⟩ — **con·sti·tu·tive·ly** *adv*

con·strain \kən-ˈstrān\ *vt* [ME, fr. AF *constraindre,* fr. L *constringere* to constrict, constrain, fr. *com-* + *stringere* to draw tight — more at STRAIN] (14c) **1 a :** to force by imposed stricture, restriction, or limitation **b :** to restrict the motion of (a mechanical body) to a particular mode **2 :** COMPRESS; *also* **:** to clasp tightly **3 :** to secure by or as if by bonds **:** CONFINE; *broadly* **:** LIMIT **4 :** to force or produce in an unnatural or strained manner ⟨a ~*ed* smile⟩ **5 :** to hold back by or as if by force ⟨~*ing* my mind not to wander from the task —Charles Dickens⟩ ***syn*** see FORCE — **con·strained·ly** \-ˈstrā-nəd-lē, -ˈstrānd-lē\ *adv*

con·straint \kən-ˈstrānt\ *n* [ME, fr. MF *constrainte,* fr. *constraindre*] (15c) **1 a :** the act of constraining **b :** the state of being checked, restricted, or compelled to avoid or perform some action ⟨the ~ and monotony of a monastic life —Matthew Arnold⟩ **c :** a constraining condition, agency, or force **:** CHECK ⟨put legal ~*s* on the board's activities⟩ **2 a :** repression of one's own feelings, behavior, or actions **b :** a sense of being constrained **:** EMBARRASSMENT

con·strict \kən-ˈstrikt\ *vb* [L *constrictus,* pp. of *constringere*] *vt* (1732) **1 a :** to make narrow or draw together **b :** COMPRESS, SQUEEZE ⟨~ a nerve⟩ **2 :** to stultify, stop, or cause to falter **:** INHIBIT ~ *vi* **:** to become constricted ***syn*** see CONTRACT — **con·stric·tive** \-ˈstrik-tiv\ *adj*

con·stric·tion \-ˈstrik-shən\ *n* (15c) **1 :** an act or product of constricting **2 :** the quality or state of being constricted **3 :** something that constricts

con·stric·tor \-ˈstrik-tər\ *n* (1735) **1 :** a muscle that contracts a cavity or orifice or compresses an organ **2 :** a snake (as a boa constrictor) that coils around and compresses prey **3 :** one that constricts

con·stringe \kən-ˈstrinj\ *vt* **con·stringed; con·string·ing** [L *constringere*] (1604) **1 :** to cause to shrink ⟨cold ~*s* the pores⟩ **2 :** CONSTRICT — **con·strin·gent** \-ˈstrin-jənt\ *adj*

con·stru·al \kən-ˈstrü-əl\ *n* (1948) **:** INTERPRETATION 1 ⟨political ~*s* of reality —R. J. Neuhaus⟩

1**con·struct** \kən-ˈstrəkt\ *vt* [L *constructus,* pp. of *construere,* fr. *com-* + *struere* to build — more at STRUCTURE] (1663) **1 :** to make or form by combining or arranging parts or elements **:** BUILD; *also* **:** CONTRIVE, DEVISE **2 :** to draw (a geometrical figure) with suitable instruments and under specified conditions **3 :** to set in logical order — **con·struct·abil·i·ty** *also* **con·struct·ibil·i·ty** \-ˌstrək-tə-ˈbi-lə-tē\ *n* — **con·struct·able** *or* **con·struct·ible** \-ˈstrək-tə-bəl\ *adj* — **con·struc·tor** \-tər\ *n*

2**con·struct** \ˈkän-ˌstrəkt\ *n* (1933) **1 :** something constructed by the mind: as **a :** a theoretical entity ⟨the deductive study of abstract ~*s* —D. J. Boorstin⟩ **b :** a working hypothesis or concept ⟨the unconscious was a ~ that came from the daily effort to understand patients⟩ **2 :** a product of ideology, history, or social circumstances ⟨privacy is more than a social ~ or an idea; it is a condition of the body —Sallie Tisdale⟩

con·struc·tion \kən-ˈstrək-shən\ *n* (14c) **1 :** the act or result of construing, interpreting, or explaining **2 a :** the process, art, or manner of constructing something; *also* **:** a thing constructed **b :** the construction industry ⟨working in ~⟩ **3 :** the arrangement and connection of words or groups of words in a sentence **:** syntactical arrangement **4 :** a sculpture that is put together out of separate pieces of often disparate materials — **con·struc·tion·al** \-shnəl, -shə-nᵊl\ *adj* — **con·struc·tion·al·ly** *adv*

con·struc·tion·ist \-sh(ə-)nist\ *n* (1838) **:** one who construes a legal document (as the U.S. Constitution) in a specific way ⟨a strict ~⟩

construction paper *n* (ca. 1924) **:** a thick groundwood paper available in many colors and used esp. for school artwork

con·struc·tive \kən-ˈstrək-tiv\ *adj* (ca. 1680) **1 :** declared such by judicial construction or interpretation ⟨~ fraud⟩ **2 :** of or relating to construction or creation **3 :** promoting improvement or development ⟨~ criticism⟩ — **con·struc·tive·ly** *adv* — **con·struc·tive·ness** *n*

con·struc·tiv·ism \kən-ˈstrək-ti-ˌvi-zəm\ *n, often cap* (1925) **:** a nonobjective art movement originating in Russia and concerned with formal organization of planes and expression of volume in terms of modern industrial materials (as glass and plastic) — **con·struc·tiv·ist** \-vist\ *adj or n, often cap*

1**con·strue** \kən-ˈstrü\ *vb* **con·strued; con·stru·ing** [ME, fr. LL *construere,* fr. L, to construct] *vt* (14c) **1 :** to analyze the arrangement and connection of words in (a sentence or sentence part) **2 :** to understand or explain the sense or intention of usu. in a particular way or with respect to a given set of circumstances ⟨*construed* my actions as hostile⟩ ~ *vi* **:** to construe a sentence or sentence part esp. in connection with translating — **con·stru·able** \-ˈstrü-ə-bəl\ *adj*

2**con·strue** \ˈkän-ˌstrü\ *n* (1844) **:** an act or the result of construing esp. by piecemeal translation

con·sub·stan·tial \ˌkän(t)-səb-ˈstan(t)-shəl\ *adj* [LL *consubstantialis,* fr. L *com-* + *substantia* substance] (14c) **:** of the same substance

con·sub·stan·ti·a·tion \ˌkän(t)-səb-ˌstan(t)-shē-ˈā-shən\ *n* (1597) **:** the actual substantial presence and combination of the body and blood of Christ with the eucharistic bread and wine according to a teaching associated with Martin Luther — compare TRANSUBSTANTIATION

con·sue·tude \ˈkän(t)-swi-ˌtüd, kən-ˈsü-ə-, -ˌtyüd\ *n* [ME, fr. L *consuetudo* — more at CUSTOM] (14c) **:** social usage **:** CUSTOM — **con·sue·tu·di·nary** \ˌkän(t)-swi-ˈtü-də-ˌner-ē, kən-ˌsü-ə-, -ˈtyü-\ *adj*

con·sul \ˈkän(t)-səl\ *n* [ME, fr. L; perh. akin to L *consulere* to consult] (14c) **1 a :** either of two annually elected chief magistrates of the Roman republic **b :** one of three chief magistrates of the French republic from 1799 to 1804 **2 :** an official appointed by a government to reside in a foreign country to represent the commercial interests of citizens of the appointing country — **con·sul·ar** \-s(ə-)lər\ *adj* — **con·sul·ship** \-səl-ˌship\ *n*

con·sul·ate \-s(ə-)lət\ *n* (14c) **1 :** a government by consuls **2 :** the office, term of office, or jurisdiction of a consul **3 :** the residence or official premises of a consul

consulate general *n, pl* **consulates general** (1865) **:** the residence, office, or jurisdiction of a consul general

consul general *n, pl* **consuls general** (1753) **:** a consul of the first rank stationed in an important place or having jurisdiction in several places or over several consuls

1**con·sult** \kən-ˈsəlt\ *vb* [MF or L; MF *consulter,* fr. L *consultare,* freq. of *consulere* to deliberate, counsel, consult] *vt* (1527) **1 :** to have regard to **:** CONSIDER **2 a :** to ask the advice or opinion of ⟨~ a doctor⟩ **b :** to refer to ⟨~ a dictionary⟩ ~ *vi* **1 :** to consult an individual **2 :** to deliberate together **:** CONFER **3 :** to serve as a consultant — **con·sult·er** *n*

2**con·sult** \kən-ˈsəlt, ˈkän-ˌ\ *n* (1560) **:** CONSULTATION

con·sul·tan·cy \kən-ˈsəl-tᵊn(t)-sē\ *n, pl* **-cies** (1955) **1 :** CONSULTATION **2 :** an agency that provides consulting services **3 :** the position of a consultant

con·sul·tant \kən-ˈsəl-tᵊnt\ *n* (1697) **1 :** one who consults another **2 :** one who gives professional advice or services **:** EXPERT — **con·sul·tant·ship** \-ˌship\ *n*

con·sul·ta·tion \ˌkän(t)-səl-ˈtā-shən\ *n* (15c) **1 :** COUNCIL, CONFERENCE; *specif* **:** a deliberation between physicians on a case or its treatment **2 :** the act of consulting or conferring

con·sul·ta·tive \kən-ˈsəl-tə-tiv, ˈkän(t)-səl-ˌtā-tiv\ *adj* (1583) **:** of, relating to, or intended for consultation **:** ADVISORY ⟨a ~ committee⟩ ⟨a ~ document⟩

con·sult·ing \kən-ˈsəl-tiŋ\ *adj* (1801) **1 :** providing professional or expert advice ⟨a ~ architect⟩ **2 :** of or relating to consultation or a consultant ⟨the ~ room of a psychiatrist⟩

con·sul·tive \kən-ˈsəl-tiv\ *adj* (1616) **:** CONSULTATIVE

con·sul·tor \kən-ˈsəl-tər\ *n* (1520) **:** one who consults or advises; *esp* **:** an adviser to a Roman Catholic bishop, provincial, or sacred congregation

1**con·sum·able** \kən-ˈsü-mə-bəl\ *adj* (1641) **:** capable of being consumed ⟨~ goods⟩

2**consumable** *n* (1802) **:** something (as food or fuel) that is consumable — usu. used in pl.

con·sume \kən-ˈsüm\ *vb* **con·sumed; con·sum·ing** [ME, fr. MF or L; MF *consumer,* fr. L *consumere,* fr. *com-* + *sumere* to take up, take, fr. *sub-* up + *emere* to take — more at SUB-, REDEEM] *vt* (14c) **1 :** to do away with completely **:** DESTROY ⟨fire *consumed* several buildings⟩ **2 a :** to spend wastefully **:** SQUANDER **b :** USE UP ⟨writing *consumed* much of his time⟩ **3 a :** to eat or drink esp. in great quantity ⟨*consumed* several bags of pretzels⟩ **b :** to enjoy avidly **:** DEVOUR ⟨mysteries, which she ~*s* for fun —E. R. Lipson⟩ **4 :** to engage fully **:** ENGROSS ⟨*consumed* with curiosity⟩ **5 :** to utilize as a customer ⟨~ goods and services⟩ ~ *vi* **1 :** to waste or burn away **:** PERISH **2 :** to utilize economic goods

con·sum·ed·ly \-ˈsü-məd-lē\ *adv* (1707) **:** as if consumed **:** EXCESSIVELY ⟨a baby granddaughter . . . in whom to be ~ interested —A. N. Wilson⟩

con·sum·er \kən-ˈsü-mər\ *n, often attrib* (15c) **:** one that consumes: as **a :** one that utilizes economic goods **b :** an organism requiring complex organic compounds for food which it obtains by preying on other organisms or by eating particles of organic matter — compare PRODUCER 3 — **con·sum·er·ship** \-ˌship\ *n*

consumer credit *n* (1927) **:** credit granted to an individual esp. to finance the purchase of consumer goods or to defray personal expenses

consumer goods *n pl* (1890) **:** goods that directly satisfy human wants

con·sum·er·ism \kən-ˈsü-mə-ˌri-zəm, -mər-ˌi-\ *n* (1944) **1 :** the promotion of the consumer's interests **2 :** the theory that an increasing consumption of goods is economically desirable; *also* **:** a preoccupation with and an inclination toward the buying of consumer goods — **con·sum·er·ist** \-rist, -ist\ *n or adj* — **con·sum·er·is·tic** \kən-ˌsü-mə-ˈris-tik, -mər-ˈis-\ *adj*

consumer price index *n* (1948) **:** an index measuring the change in the cost of typical wage-earner purchases of goods and services expressed as a percentage of the cost of these same goods and services in some base period — called also *cost-of-living index*

con·sum·ing \kən-ˈsü-miŋ\ *adj* (1905) **:** deeply felt **:** ARDENT ⟨a ~ interest⟩; *also* **:** ENGROSSING

1**con·sum·mate** \ˈkän(t)-sə-mət, kən-ˈsə-mət\ *adj* [ME *consummat* fulfilled, fr. L *consummatus,* pp. of *consummare* to sum up, finish, fr. *com-* + *summa* sum] (1527) **1 :** complete in every detail **:** PERFECT **2 :** extremely skilled and accomplished ⟨a ~ liar⟩ ⟨a ~ professional⟩ **3 :** of the highest degree ⟨~ skill⟩ ⟨~ cruelty⟩ — **con·sum·mate·ly** *adv*

2**con·sum·mate** \ˈkän(t)-sə-ˌmāt\ *vb* **-mat·ed; -mat·ing** *vt* (1530) **1 a :** FINISH, COMPLETE ⟨~ a business deal⟩ **b :** to make perfect **c :** ACHIEVE **2 :** to make (marital union) complete by sexual intercourse ⟨~ a marriage⟩ ~ *vi* **:** to become perfected — **con·sum·ma·tive** \ˈkän(t)-sə-ˌmā-tiv, kən-ˈsə-mə-tiv\ *adj* — **con·sum·ma·tor** \ˈkän(t)-sə-ˌmāt-ər\ *n*

con·sum·ma·tion \ˌkän-sə-ˈmā-shən\ *n* (14c) **1 :** the act of consummating ⟨the ~ of a contract by mutual signature⟩; *specif* **:** the consummating of a marriage **2 :** the ultimate end **:** FINISH

con·sum·ma·to·ry \kən-ˈsə-mə-ˌtȯr-ē\ *adj* (1648) **1 :** of or relating to consummation **:** CONCLUDING **2 :** of, relating to, or being a response or act (as eating or copulating) that terminates a period of usu. goal-directed behavior

con·sump·tion \kən-ˈsəm(p)-shən\ *n* [ME *consumpcioun,* fr. L *consumption-, consumptio,* fr. *consumere*] (14c) **1 a :** a progressive wasting away of the body esp. from pulmonary tuberculosis **b :** TUBERCULOSIS **2 a :** the act or process of consuming ⟨~ of food⟩ ⟨~ of resources⟩ **b :** use by or exposure to a particular group or audience ⟨the document was not intended for public ~⟩ **3 :** the utilization of economic goods in the satisfaction of wants or in the process of production resulting chiefly in their destruction, deterioration, or transformation

1**con·sump·tive** \-ˈsəm(p)-tiv\ *adj* (1647) **1 :** tending to consume **2 :** of, relating to, or affected with consumption — **con·sump·tive·ly** *adv*

2**consumptive** *n* (1666) **:** a person affected with consumption

cont *abbr* **1** containing **2** contents **3** continent **4** continental **5** continued **6** control

1**con·tact** \ˈkän-ˌtakt\ *n* [F or L; F, fr. L *contactus,* fr. *contingere* to have contact with — more at CONTINGENT] (1626) **1 a :** union or junction of surfaces **b :** the apparent touching or mutual tangency of the limbs of two celestial bodies or of the disk of one body with the shadow of another during an eclipse, transit, or occultation **c (1) :** the junction of two electrical conductors through which a current passes **(2) :** a special part made for such a junction **2 a :** ASSOCIATION, RELATIONSHIP **b :** CONNECTION, COMMUNICATION **c :** an establishing of communication with someone or an observing or receiving of a significant signal from a person or object ⟨radar ~ with Mars⟩ **3 :** a person serving as a go-between, messenger, connection, or source of special information ⟨business ~*s*⟩ **4 :** CONTACT LENS

2**con·tact** \ˈkän-ˌtakt, kən-ˈ\ *vi* (1834) **:** to make contact ~ *vt* **1 :** to bring into contact **2 a :** to enter or be in contact with **:** JOIN **b :** to get in communication with ⟨~ your local dealer⟩

usage The use of *contact* as a verb, esp. in sense 2b, is accepted as standard by almost all commentators except those who write college handbooks.

3**con·tact** \ˈkän-ˌtakt\ *adj* (1859) **:** maintaining, involving, or activated or caused by contact ⟨~ poisons⟩ ⟨~ sports⟩ ⟨~ dermatitis⟩

contact binary *n* (1952) **:** a binary star system in which the two stars are close enough together for material to pass between them

contact hitter *n* (1982) **:** a hitter in baseball who seldom strikes out

contact inhibition *n* (1965) **:** cessation of cellular movement, growth, and division upon contact with other cells

contact language *n* (1950) **:** PIDGIN

contact lens *n* (1888) **:** a thin lens designed to fit over the cornea and usu. worn to correct defects in vision

contact print *n* (1890) **:** a photographic print made with the negative in contact with the sensitized paper, plate, or film

con·ta·gion \kən-ˈtā-jən\ *n* [ME, fr. L *contagion-, contagio,* fr. *contingere* to have contact with, pollute — more at CONTINGENT] (14c) **1 a :** a contagious disease **b :** the transmission of a disease by direct or indirect contact **c :** a disease-producing agent (as a virus) **2 a :** POISON **b :** contagious influence, quality, or nature **c :** corrupting influence or contact **3 a :** rapid communication of an influence (as a doctrine or emotional state) **b :** an influence that spreads rapidly

con·ta·gious \-jəs\ *adj* (14c) **1 :** communicable by contact : CATCHING ⟨∼ diseases⟩ **2 :** bearing contagion ⟨∼ people⟩ **3 :** used for contagious diseases ⟨a ∼ ward⟩ **4 :** exciting similar emotions or conduct in others ⟨∼ enthusiasm⟩ — **con·ta·gious·ly** *adv* — **con·ta·gious·ness** *n*

contagious abortion *n* (1910) **:** a contagious or infectious disease (as a brucellosis) of domestic animals characterized by abortion

con·ta·gium \kən-ˈtā-j(ē-)əm\ *n, pl* **-gia** \-j(ē-)ə\ [L, contagion, fr. *contingere*] (1870) **:** an agent capable of causing a communicable disease

con·tain \kən-ˈtān\ *vb* [ME *conteinen,* fr. AF *cunteign-, cuntyen-,* stem of *cuntenir,* fr. L *continēre* to hold together, hold in, contain, fr. *com-* + *tenēre* to hold — more at THIN] *vt* (14c) **1 :** to keep within limits: as **a :** RESTRAIN, CONTROL ⟨could hardly ∼ her enthusiasm⟩ **b :** CHECK, HALT ⟨∼ the spread of a deadly disease⟩ **c :** to follow successfully a policy of containment toward ⟨efforts to ∼ Communism⟩ **d :** to prevent (as an enemy or opponent) from advancing or from making a successful attack **2 a :** to have within : HOLD **b :** COMPRISE, INCLUDE ⟨the bill ∼*s* several new clauses⟩ **3 a :** to be divisible by usu. without a remainder **b :** ENCLOSE, BOUND ∼ *vi* **:** to restrain oneself — **con·tain·able** \-ˈtā-nə-bəl\ *adj*

syn CONTAIN, HOLD, ACCOMMODATE mean to have or be capable of having within. CONTAIN implies the actual presence of a specified substance or quantity within something ⟨the can *contains* a quart of oil⟩. HOLD implies the capacity of containing or the usual or permanent function of containing or keeping ⟨the bookcase will *hold* all my textbooks⟩. ACCOMMODATE stresses holding without crowding or inconvenience ⟨the hall can *accommodate* 500 people⟩.

contained *adj* (1653) **:** RESTRAINED; *also* **:** CALM

con·tain·er \kən-ˈtā-nər\ *n* (15c) **:** one that contains: as **a :** a receptacle (as a box or jar) for holding goods **b :** a portable compartment in which freight is placed (as on a train or ship) for convenience of movement — **con·tain·er·less** \-ləs\ *adj*

con·tain·er·board \-ˌbȯrd\ *n* (ca. 1924) **:** corrugated or solid cardboard used for making containers

con·tain·er·i·sa·tion, con·tain·er·ise *Brit var of* CONTAINERIZATION, CONTAINERIZE

con·tain·er·i·za·tion \kən-ˌtā-nə-rə-ˈzā-shən, -nər-ə-\ *n* (1956) **:** a shipping method in which a large amount of material (as merchandise) is packaged into large standardized containers

con·tain·er·ize \kən-ˈtā-nə-ˌrīz, -nər-ˌīz\ *vt* **-ized; -iz·ing** (1956) **1 :** to ship by containerization **2 :** to pack in containers

con·tain·er·port \-nər-ˌpȯrt\ *n* (1970) **:** a shipping port specially equipped to handle containerized cargo

con·tain·er·ship \-nər-ˌship\ *n* (1966) **:** a ship specially designed or equipped for carrying containerized cargo

con·tain·ment \kən-ˈtān-mənt\ *n* (1655) **1 :** the act, process, or means of containing **2 :** the policy, process, or result of preventing the expansion of a hostile power or ideology

con·tam·i·nant \kən-ˈta-mə-nənt\ *n* (1922) **:** something that contaminates

con·tam·i·nate \kən-ˈta-mə-ˌnāt\ *vt* **-nat·ed; -nat·ing** [ME, fr. L *contaminatus,* pp. of *contaminare;* akin to L *contingere* to have contact with — more at CONTINGENT] (15c) **1 a :** to soil, stain, corrupt, or infect by contact or association ⟨bacteria *contaminated* the wound⟩ **b :** to make inferior or impure by admixture ⟨iron *contaminated* with phosphorus⟩ **2 :** to make unfit for use by the introduction of unwholesome or undesirable elements — **con·tam·i·na·tive** \-ˌnā-tiv\ *adj* — **con·tam·i·na·tor** \-ˌnā-tər\ *n*

syn CONTAMINATE, TAINT, POLLUTE, DEFILE mean to make impure or unclean. CONTAMINATE implies intrusion of or contact with dirt or foulness from an outside source ⟨water *contaminated* by industrial wastes⟩. TAINT stresses the loss of purity or cleanliness that follows contamination ⟨*tainted* meat⟩ ⟨a politician's *tainted* reputation⟩. POLLUTE, sometimes interchangeable with *contaminate,* distinctively may imply that the process which begins with contamination is complete and that what was pure or clean has been made foul, poisoned, or filthy ⟨the *polluted* waters of the river⟩. DEFILE implies befouling of what could or should have been kept clean and pure or held sacred and commonly suggests violation or desecration ⟨*defile* a hero's memory with slanderous innuendo⟩.

con·tam·i·na·tion \kən-ˌta-mə-ˈnā-shən\ *n* (15c) **1 :** a process of contaminating **:** a state of being contaminated **2 :** CONTAMINANT

contd *abbr* continued

conte \ˈkō^{n}(n)t\ *n* [F] (1843) **:** a usu. short tale of adventure

con·temn \kən-ˈtem\ *vt* [ME *contempnen,* fr. MF *contempner,* fr. L *contemnere,* fr. *com-* + *temnere* to despise] (15c) **:** to view or treat with contempt : SCORN ***syn*** see DESPISE — **con·tem·ner** *also* **con·tem·nor** \-ˈtem-nər, -ˈte-mər\ *n*

con·tem·plate \ˈkän-təm-ˌplāt, -ˌtem-\ *vb* **-plat·ed; -plat·ing** [L *contemplatus,* pp. of *contemplari,* fr. *com-* + *templum* space marked out for observation of auguries — more at TEMPLE] *vt* (ca. 1533) **1 :** to view or consider with continued attention : meditate on ⟨∼ the vastness of the universe⟩ **2 :** to view as contingent or probable or as an end or intention ⟨∼ marriage⟩ ∼ *vi* **:** PONDER, MEDITATE ***syn*** see CONSIDER — **con·tem·pla·tor** \-ˌplā-tər\ *n*

con·tem·pla·tion \ˌkän-təm-ˈplā-shən, -ˌtem-\ *n* (13c) **1 a :** concentration on spiritual things as a form of private devotion **b :** a state of mystical awareness of God's being **2 :** an act of considering with attention : STUDY **3 :** the act of regarding steadily **4 :** INTENTION, EXPECTATION

[1]**con·tem·pla·tive** \kən-ˈtem-plə-tiv; ˈkän-təm-ˌplā-, -ˌtem-\ *adj* (14c) **:** marked by or given to contemplation; *specif* **:** of or relating to a religious order devoted to prayer and penance — **con·tem·pla·tive·ly** *adv* — **con·tem·pla·tive·ness** *n*

[2]**contemplative** *n* (14c) **:** a person who practices contemplation

con·tem·po \kən-ˈtem-pō\ *adj* (1972) **:** CONTEMPORARY, PRESENT-DAY ⟨∼ music⟩

con·tem·po·ra·ne·i·ty \kən-ˌtem-p(ə-)rə-ˈnē-ə-tē, -ˈnā-\ *n* (1772) **:** the quality or state of being contemporaneous or contemporary

con·tem·po·ra·ne·ous \kən-ˌtem-pə-ˈrā-nē-əs\ *adj* [L *contemporaneus,* fr. *com-* + *tempor-, tempus* time] (ca. 1656) **:** existing, occurring, or originating during the same time ***syn*** see CONTEMPORARY — **con·tem·po·ra·ne·ous·ly** *adv* — **con·tem·po·ra·ne·ous·ness** *n*

[1]**con·tem·po·rary** \kən-ˈtem-pə-ˌrer-ē, -ˌre-rē\ *adj* [*com-* + L *tempor-, tempus*] (1631) **1 :** happening, existing, living, or coming into being during the same period of time **2 a :** SIMULTANEOUS **b :** marked by characteristics of the present period : MODERN, CURRENT — **con·tem·po·rar·i·ly** \-ˌtem-pə-ˈrer-ə-lē\ *adv*

syn CONTEMPORARY, CONTEMPORANEOUS, COEVAL, SYNCHRONOUS, SIMULTANEOUS, COINCIDENT mean existing or occurring at the same time. CONTEMPORARY is likely to apply to people and what relates to them ⟨Abraham Lincoln was *contemporary* with Charles Darwin⟩. CONTEMPORANEOUS is more often applied to events than to people ⟨*contemporaneous* accounts of the kidnapping⟩. COEVAL refers usu. to periods, ages, eras, eons ⟨two stars thought to be *coeval*⟩. SYNCHRONOUS implies exact correspondence in time and esp. in periodic intervals ⟨*synchronous* timepieces⟩. SIMULTANEOUS implies correspondence in a moment of time ⟨the two shots were *simultaneous*⟩. COINCIDENT is applied to events and may be used in order to avoid implication of causal relationship ⟨the end of World War II was *coincident* with a great vintage year⟩.

[2]**contemporary** *n, pl* **-rar·ies** (1638) **1 :** one that is contemporary with another **2 :** one of the same or nearly the same age as another

con·tem·po·rize \kən-ˈtem-pə-ˌrīz\ *vt* **-rized; -riz·ing** (1646) **:** to make contemporary ⟨∼ a magazine with the latest fashions⟩

con·tempt \kən-ˈtem(p)t\ *n* [ME, fr. AF, fr. L *contemptus,* fr. *contemnere*] (14c) **1 a :** the act of despising : the state of mind of one who despises : DISDAIN **b :** lack of respect or reverence for something **2 :** the state of being despised **3 :** willful disobedience to or open disrespect of a court, judge, or legislative body ⟨∼ of court⟩

con·tempt·ible \kən-ˈtem(p)-tə-bəl\ *adj* (14c) **1 :** worthy of contempt **2** *obs* **:** SCORNFUL, CONTEMPTUOUS — **con·tempt·i·bil·i·ty** \-ˌtem(p)-tə-ˈbi-lə-tē\ *n* — **con·tempt·ible·ness** *n* — **con·tempt·ibly** \-ˈtem(p)-tə-blē\ *adv*

syn CONTEMPTIBLE, DESPICABLE, PITIABLE, SORRY, SCURVY mean arousing or deserving scorn. CONTEMPTIBLE may imply any quality provoking scorn or a low standing in any scale of values ⟨a *contemptible* liar⟩. DESPICABLE may imply utter worthlessness and usu. suggests arousing an attitude of moral indignation ⟨a *despicable* crime⟩. PITIABLE applies to what inspires mixed contempt and pity ⟨a *pitiable* attempt at tragedy⟩. SORRY may stress pitiable inadequacy or may suggest wretchedness or sordidness ⟨this rattletrap is a *sorry* excuse for a car⟩. SCURVY adds to DESPICABLE an implication of arousing disgust ⟨a *scurvy* crew of hangers-on⟩.

con·temp·tu·ous \-ˈtem(p)-chə-wəs, -chəs, -shwəs, -chü-əs\ *adj* [L *contemptus*] (1574) **:** manifesting, feeling, or expressing contempt — **con·temp·tu·ous·ly** *adv* — **con·temp·tu·ous·ness** *n*

con·tend \kən-ˈtend\ *vb* [ME, fr. AF or L; AF *contendre,* fr. L *contendere,* fr. *com-* + *tendere* to stretch — more at THIN] *vi* (15c) **1 :** to strive or vie in contest or rivalry or against difficulties : STRUGGLE **2 :** to strive in debate : ARGUE ∼ *vt* **1 :** MAINTAIN, ASSERT ⟨∼*ed* that he was right⟩ **2 :** to struggle for : CONTEST

con·tend·er \-ˈten-dər\ *n* (1547) **:** one that contends; *esp* **:** a competitor for a championship or high honor ⟨a heavyweight title ∼⟩

[1]**con·tent** \kən-ˈtent\ *adj* [ME, fr. MF, fr. L *contentus,* fr. pp. of *continēre* to hold in, contain — more at CONTAIN] (15c) **:** CONTENTED, SATISFIED ⟨was ∼ with her life as it was⟩

[2]**content** *vt* (15c) **1 :** to appease the desires of **2 :** to limit (oneself) in requirements, desires, or actions

[3]**content** *n* (1579) **:** CONTENTMENT ⟨ate to his heart's ∼⟩

[4]**con·tent** \ˈkän-ˌtent\ *n* [ME, fr. L *contentus,* pp. of *continēre* to contain] (15c) **1 a :** something contained — usu. used in pl. ⟨the jar's ∼*s*⟩ ⟨the drawer's ∼*s*⟩ **b :** the topics or matter treated in a written work ⟨table of ∼*s*⟩ **c :** the principal substance (as written matter, illustrations, or music) offered by a World Wide Web site ⟨Internet users have evolved an ethos of free ∼ in the Internet —Ben Gerson⟩ **2 a :** SUBSTANCE, GIST **b :** MEANING, SIGNIFICANCE **c :** the events, physical detail, and information in a work of art — compare FORM 10b **3 a :** the matter dealt with in a field of study **b :** a part, element, or complex of parts **4 :** the amount of specified material contained : PROPORTION

content analysis *n* (1940) **:** analysis of the manifest and latent content of a body of communicated material (as a book or film) through a classification, tabulation, and evaluation of its key symbols and themes in order to ascertain its meaning and probable effect

con·tent·ed \kən-ˈten-təd\ *adj* (15c) **:** feeling or showing satisfaction with one's possessions, status, or situation ⟨a ∼ smile⟩ — **con·tent·ed·ly** *adv* — **con·tent·ed·ness** *n*

con·ten·tion \kən-ˈten(t)-shən\ *n* [ME *contencioun,* fr. AF *cuntencіun,* fr. L *contention-, contentio,* fr. *contendere*] (14c) **1 :** an act or instance of contending **2 :** a point advanced or maintained in a debate or argument **3 :** RIVALRY, COMPETITION ***syn*** see DISCORD

con·ten·tious \kən-ˈten(t)-shəs\ *adj* (15c) **1 :** likely to cause contention ⟨a ∼ argument⟩ **2 :** exhibiting an often perverse and wearisome tendency to quarrels and disputes ⟨a man of a most ∼ nature⟩ ***syn*** see BELLIGERENT — **con·ten·tious·ly** *adv* — **con·ten·tious·ness** *n*

con·tent·ment \kən-ˈtent-mənt\ *n* (15c) **1 :** the quality or state of being contented **2 :** something that contents

con·tent word \ˈkän-ˌtent-\ *n* (1940) **:** a word that primarily expresses lexical meaning — compare FUNCTION WORD

con·ter·mi·nous \kən-ˈtər-mə-nəs, kän-\ *adj* [L *conterminus,* fr. *com-* + *terminus* boundary — more at TERM] (1631) **1 :** having a common boundary ⟨∼ countries⟩ **2 :** COTERMINOUS **3 :** enclosed within one common boundary ⟨the 48 ∼ states⟩ — **con·ter·mi·nous·ly** *adv*

[1]**con·test** \kən-ˈtest, ˈkän-ˌ\ *vb* [MF *contester,* fr. L *contestari (litem)* to bring an action at law, fr. *contestari* to call to witness, fr. *com-* + *testis* witness — more at TESTAMENT] *vi* (1603) **:** STRIVE, VIE ∼ *vt* **:** to make the subject of dispute, contention, or litigation; *esp* **:** DISPUTE, CHALLENGE — **con·test·able** \-ˈtes-tə-bəl\ *adj* — **con·test·er** *n*

\ə\ **abut** \ᵊ\ **kitten**, F table \ər\ **further** \a\ **ash** \ā\ **ace** \ä\ **mop, mar** \au̇\ **out** \ch\ **chin** \e\ **bet** \ē\ **easy** \g\ **go** \i\ **hit** \ī\ **ice** \j\ **job** \ŋ\ **sing** \ō\ **go** \ȯ\ **law** \ȯi\ **boy** \th\ **thin** \t͟h\ **the** \ü\ **loot** \u̇\ **foot** \y\ **yet** \zh\ **vision, beige** \k, ^{n}, œ, ue, ^{y}\ *see* Guide to Pronunciation

[2]**con·test** \ˈkän-ˌtest\ *n* (1630) **1 :** a struggle for superiority or victory **:** COMPETITION **2 :** a competition in which each contestant performs without direct contact with or interference from competitors

con·tes·tant \kən-ˈtes-tənt *also* ˈkän-ˌ\ *n* (1665) **1 :** one that participates in a contest **2 :** one that contests an award or decision

con·tes·ta·tion \ˌkän-ˌtes-ˈtā-shən\ *n* (1580) **:** CONTROVERSY, DEBATE

con·text \ˈkän-ˌtekst\ *n* [ME, weaving together of words, fr. L *contextus* connection of words, coherence, fr. *contexere* to weave together, fr. *com-* + *texere* to weave — more at TECHNICAL] (ca. 1568) **1 :** the parts of a discourse that surround a word or passage and can throw light on its meaning **2 :** the interrelated conditions in which something exists or occurs **:** ENVIRONMENT, SETTING ⟨the historical ~ of the war⟩ — **con·text·less** \-ˌtekst-ləs\ *adj* — **con·tex·tu·al** \kän-ˈteks-chə-wəl, kən-, -chəl, -chü-əl\ *adj* — **con·tex·tu·al·ly** *adv*

con·text–free \ˈkän-ˌtekst-ˈfrē\ *adj* (1964) **:** of, relating to, or being a grammar or language based on rules that describe a change in a string without reference to elements not in the string; *also* **:** being such a rule

con·tex·tu·al·ize \kən-ˈteks-chə-wə-ˌlīz, -chə-ˌlīz, -chü-ə-\ *vt* **-ized; -iz·ing** (1934) **:** to place (as a word or activity) in a context — **con·tex·tu·al·i·za·tion** \-ˌteks-ch(ə-w)ə-lə-ˈzā-shən, -chü-ə-lə-\ *n*

con·tex·ture \kən-ˈteks-chər, ˈkän-ˌ, kän-ˈ\ *n* [F, fr. L *contextus,* pp. of *contexere*] (1603) **1 :** the act, process, or manner of weaving parts into a whole; *also* **:** a structure so formed ⟨a ~ of lies⟩ **2 :** CONTEXT

contg *abbr* containing

con·ti·gu·i·ty \ˌkän-tə-ˈgyü-ə-tē\ *n, pl* **-ties** (1612) **:** the quality or state of being contiguous **:** PROXIMITY

con·tig·u·ous \kən-ˈti-gyə-wəs, -gyü-əs\ *adj* [L *contiguus,* fr. *contingere* to have contact with — more at CONTINGENT] (ca. 1609) **1 :** being in actual contact **:** touching along a boundary or at a point **2** *of angles* **:** ADJACENT 2 **3 :** next or near in time or sequence **4 :** touching or connected throughout in an unbroken sequence ⟨~ row houses⟩ ***syn*** see ADJACENT — **con·tig·u·ous·ly** *adv* — **con·tig·u·ous·ness** *n*

con·ti·nence \ˈkän-tə-nən(t)s\ *n* (14c) **1 :** SELF-RESTRAINT; *esp* **:** a refraining from sexual intercourse **2 :** the ability to retain a bodily discharge voluntarily ⟨fecal ~⟩

[1]**con·ti·nent** \ˈkän-tə-nənt\ *adj* [ME, fr. MF, fr. L *continent-, continens,* fr. prp. of *continēre* to hold in — more at CONTAIN] (14c) **1 :** exercising continence **2** *obs* **:** RESTRICTIVE — **con·ti·nent·ly** *adv*

[2]**con·ti·nent** \ˈkän-tə-nənt, ˈkänt-nənt\ *n* [in senses 1 & 2, fr. L *continent-, continens,* prp. of *continēre,* to hold together, contain; in senses 3 & 4, fr. L *continent-, continens* continuous mass of land, mainland, fr. *continent-, continens,* prp.] (1541) **1** *archaic* **:** CONTAINER, CONFINES **2** *archaic* **:** EPITOME **3 :** MAINLAND **4 a :** one of the six or seven great divisions of land on the globe **b** *cap* **:** the continent of Europe — used with *the*

[1]**con·ti·nen·tal** \ˌkän-tə-ˈnen-tᵊl\ *adj* (1755) **1 a :** of, relating to, or characteristic of a continent ⟨~ waters⟩; *specif, often cap* **:** of or relating to the continent of Europe excluding the British Isles **b** *often cap* **:** of, relating to, or being a cuisine derived from the classic dishes of Europe and esp. France **2 a** *often cap* **:** of or relating to the colonies later forming the U.S. ⟨*Continental* Congress⟩ **b :** being the part of the U.S. on the No. American continent; *also* **:** being the part of the U.S. comprising the lower 48 states — **con·ti·nen·tal·ly** \-tə-lē\ *adv*

[2]**continental** *n* (1777) **1 a** *often cap* **:** an American soldier of the Revolution in the Continental army **b** (1) **:** a piece of Continental paper currency (2) **:** the least bit ⟨not worth a ~⟩ **2 :** an inhabitant of a continent and esp. the continent of Europe

continental breakfast *n, often cap C* (1896) **:** a light breakfast (as of rolls or toast and coffee)

continental drift *n* (1926) **:** a slow movement of the continents on a deep-seated viscous zone within the earth — compare PLATE TECTONICS

continental shelf *n* (1892) **:** a shallow submarine plain of varying width forming a border to a continent and typically ending in a comparatively steep slope to the deep ocean floor

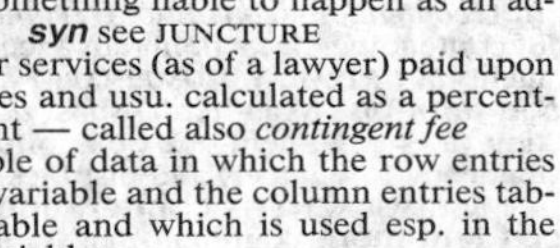

continental shelf: *1* seashore, *2* continental shelf, *3* continental slope, *4* abyssal plain, *5* seamount

continental slope *n* (1900) **:** the comparatively steep slope from a continental shelf to the ocean floor

con·tin·gence \kən-ˈtin-jən(t)s\ *n* (ca. 1530) **1 :** CONTINGENCY **2 :** TANGENCY

con·tin·gen·cy \kən-ˈtin-jən(t)-sē\ *n, pl* **-cies** (1561) **1 :** the quality or state of being contingent **2 :** a contingent event or condition: as **a :** an event (as an emergency) that may but is not certain to occur ⟨trying to provide for every ~⟩ **b :** something liable to happen as an adjunct to or result of something else ***syn*** see JUNCTURE

contingency fee *n* (1905) **:** a fee for services (as of a lawyer) paid upon successful completion of the services and usu. calculated as a percentage of the gain realized for the client — called also *contingent fee*

contingency table *n* (1904) **:** a table of data in which the row entries tabulate the data according to one variable and the column entries tabulate it according to another variable and which is used esp. in the study of the correlation between variables

[1]**con·tin·gent** \kən-ˈtin-jənt\ *adj* [ME, fr. MF, fr. L *contingent-, contingens,* prp. of *contingere* to have contact with, befall, fr. *com-* + *tangere* to touch — more at TANGENT] (14c) **1 :** likely but not certain to happen **:** POSSIBLE **2 :** not logically necessary; *esp* **:** EMPIRICAL **3 a :** happening by chance or unforeseen causes **b :** subject to chance or unseen effects **:** UNPREDICTABLE **c :** intended for use in circumstances not completely foreseen **4 :** dependent on or conditioned by something else ⟨payment is ~ on fulfillment of certain conditions⟩ **5 :** not necessitated **:** determined by free choice ***syn*** see ACCIDENTAL — **con·tin·gent·ly** *adv*

[2]**contingent** *n* (1548) **1 :** something contingent **:** CONTINGENCY **2 :** a representative group **:** DELEGATION, DETACHMENT ⟨a diplomatic ~⟩

con·tin·u·al \kən-ˈtin-yü-əl, -yəl\ *adj* [ME, fr. AF *continuel,* fr. L *continuus* continuous] (14c) **1 :** continuing indefinitely in time without interruption ⟨~ fear⟩ **2 :** recurring in steady usu. rapid succession ⟨a history of ~ invasions⟩ — **con·tin·u·al·ly** *adv*

syn CONTINUAL, CONTINUOUS, CONSTANT, INCESSANT, PERPETUAL, PERENNIAL mean characterized by continued occurrence or recurrence. CONTINUAL often implies a close prolonged succession or recurrence ⟨*continual* showers the whole weekend⟩. CONTINUOUS usu. implies an uninterrupted flow or spatial extension ⟨football's oldest *continuous* rivalry⟩. CONSTANT implies uniform or persistent occurrence or recurrence ⟨lived in *constant* pain⟩. INCESSANT implies ceaseless or uninterrupted activity ⟨annoyed by the *incessant* quarreling⟩. PERPETUAL suggests unfailing repetition or lasting duration ⟨a land of *perpetual* snowfall⟩. PERENNIAL implies enduring existence often through constant renewal ⟨a *perennial* source of controversy⟩.

con·tin·u·ance \kən-ˈtin-yü-ən(t)s\ *n* (14c) **1 :** CONTINUATION **2 :** the extent of continuing **:** DURATION **3 :** the quality of enduring **:** PERMANENCE **4 :** an adjournment of a court case to a future day

con·tin·u·ant \-yü-ənt\ *n* (1861) **1 :** something that continues or serves as a continuation **2 :** a speech sound (as a fricative or vowel) that is produced without a complete closure of the breath passage — compare STOP — **continuant** *adj*

con·tin·u·ate *adj* (1555) *obs* **:** CONTINUOUS, UNINTERRUPTED

con·tin·u·a·tion \kən-ˌtin-yə-ˈwā-shən, -yü-ˈā-\ *n* (14c) **1 :** the act or fact of continuing in or the prolongation of a state or activity **2 :** resumption after an interruption **3 :** something that continues, increases, or adds

con·tin·u·a·tive \kən-ˈtin-yə-ˌwā-tiv, -yü-ˌā-; -wə-tiv, -yü-ə-\ *adj* (1684) **:** expressing continuity or continuation (as of an idea or action)

con·tin·u·a·tor \-ˌwā-tər\ *n* (1646) **:** one that continues

con·tin·ue \kən-ˈtin-(ˌ)yü\ *vb* **-tin·ued; -tinu·ing** [ME, fr. AF *continuer,* fr. L *continuare,* fr. *continuus*] *vi* (14c) **1 :** to maintain without interruption a condition, course, or action ⟨the boat *continued* downstream⟩ **2 :** to remain in existence **:** ENDURE ⟨the tradition ~*s*⟩ **3 :** to remain in a place or condition **:** STAY ⟨cannot ~ here much longer⟩ **4 :** to resume an activity after interruption ⟨we'll ~ after lunch⟩ ~ *vt* **1 a :** KEEP UP, MAINTAIN ⟨~*s* walking⟩ **b :** to keep going or add to **:** PROLONG ⟨~ the battle⟩; *also* **:** to resume after intermission **2 :** to cause to continue ⟨chose not to ~ her subscription⟩ **3 :** to allow to remain in a place or condition **:** RETAIN ⟨the trustees were *continued*⟩ **4 :** to postpone (a legal proceeding) by a continuance — **con·tinu·er** \-yü-ər\ *n*

syn CONTINUE, LAST, ENDURE, ABIDE, PERSIST mean to exist over a period of time or indefinitely. CONTINUE applies to a process going on without ending ⟨the search for peace will *continue*⟩. LAST, esp. when unqualified, may stress existing beyond what is normal or expected ⟨buy shoes that will *last*⟩. ENDURE adds an implication of resisting destructive forces or agencies ⟨in spite of everything, her faith *endured*⟩. ABIDE implies stable and constant existing esp. as opposed to mutability ⟨a love that *abides* through 40 years of marriage⟩. PERSIST suggests outlasting the normal or appointed time and often connotes obstinacy or doggedness ⟨the sense of guilt *persisted*⟩.

continued *adj* (15c) **1 :** lasting or extending without interruption ⟨~ success⟩ **2 :** resumed after interruption ⟨a ~ story⟩

continued fraction *n* (1811) **:** a fraction whose numerator is an integer and whose denominator is an integer plus a fraction whose numerator is an integer and whose denominator is an integer plus a fraction and so on

continuing *adj* (14c) **1 :** CONTINUOUS, CONSTANT ⟨~ poverty⟩ **2 :** needing no renewal **:** ENDURING ⟨~ fame⟩ — **con·tin·u·ing·ly** *adv*

continuing education *n* (1954) **:** formal courses of study for adult part-time students

con·ti·nu·i·ty \ˌkän-tə-ˈnü-ə-tē, -ˈnyü-\ *n, pl* **-ties** (15c) **1 a :** uninterrupted connection, succession, or union **b :** uninterrupted duration or continuation esp. without essential change **2 :** something that has, exhibits, or provides continuity: as **a :** a script or scenario in the performing arts **b :** transitional spoken or musical matter esp. for a radio or television program **c :** the story and dialogue of a comic strip **3 :** the property of being mathematically continuous

con·tin·uo \kən-ˈtin-yə-ˌwō, -ˈti-nə-\ *n, pl* **-u·os** [It, fr. *continuo* continuous, fr. L *continuus*] (ca. 1724) **:** a bass part (as for a keyboard or stringed instrument) used esp. in baroque ensemble music and consisting of a succession of bass notes with figures that indicate the required chords — called also *figured bass, thoroughbass*

con·tin·u·ous \kən-ˈtin-yü-əs\ *adj* [L *continuus,* fr. *continēre* to hold together — more at CONTAIN] (1673) **1 :** marked by uninterrupted extension in space, time, or sequence **2** *of a function* **:** having the property that the absolute value of the numerical difference between the value at a given point and the value at any point in a neighborhood of the given point can be made as close to zero as desired by choosing the neighborhood small enough ***syn*** see CONTINUAL — **con·tin·u·ous·ly** *adv* — **con·tin·u·ous·ness** *n*

continuous positive airway pressure *n* (1975) **:** a technique for relieving breathing problems (as those associated with sleep apnea or congestive heart failure) by pumping a steady flow of air through the nose to prevent the narrowing or collapse of air passages or to help the lungs to expand — abbr. *CPAP*

con·tin·u·um \kən-ˈtin-yü-əm\ *n, pl* **con·tin·ua** \-yü-ə\ *also* **con·tin·u·ums** [L, neut. of *continuus*] (1646) **1 :** a coherent whole characterized as a collection, sequence, or progression of values or elements varying by minute degrees ⟨"good" and "bad" . . . stand at opposite ends of a ~ instead of describing the two halves of a line —Wayne Shumaker⟩ **2 :** the set of real numbers including both the rationals and the irrationals; *broadly* **:** a compact set which cannot be separated into two sets neither of which contains a limit point of the other

con·tort \kən-ˈtȯrt\ *vb* [ME, fr. L *contortus,* pp. of *contorquēre,* fr. *com-* + *torquēre* to twist — more at TORTURE] *vt* (15c) **:** to twist in a violent manner ⟨features ~*ed* with fury⟩ ~ *vi* **:** to twist into or as if into a strained shape or expression ***syn*** see DEFORM — **con·tor·tion** \-ˈtȯr-shən\ *n* — **con·tor·tive** \-ˈtȯr-tiv\ *adj*

con·tor·tion·ist \kən-ˈtȯr-sh(ə-)nist\ *n* (1844) **:** one who contorts; *specif* **:** an acrobat able to twist the body into unusual postures — **con·tor·tion·is·tic** \-ˌtȯr-shə-ˈnis-tik\ *adj*

[1]**con·tour** \ˈkän-ˌtu̇r\ *n* [F, fr. It *contorno,* fr. *contornare* to round off, fr. ML, to turn around, fr. L *com-* + *tornare* to turn on a lathe — more at TURN] (1662) **1 :** an outline esp. of a curving or irregular figure **:** SHAPE; *also* **:** the line representing this outline **2 :** the general form or structure of something **:** CHARACTERISTIC — often used in pl. ⟨~*s* of a melody⟩ **3 :** a usu. meaningful change in intonation in speech ***syn*** see OUTLINE

[2]**contour** *adj* (1844) **1 :** following contour lines or forming furrows or ridges along them ⟨~ flooding⟩ ⟨~ farming⟩ **2 :** made to fit the contour of something ⟨a ~ couch⟩ ⟨~ sheets⟩

[3]**contour** *vt* (1871) **1 a :** to shape the contour of **b :** to shape so as to fit contours **2 :** to construct (as a road) in conformity to a contour

contour feather *n* (1867) **:** one of the medium-sized feathers that form the general covering of a bird and determine the external contour

contour line *n* (1844) **:** a line (as on a map) connecting the points on a land surface that have the same elevation

contour map *n* (1862) **:** a map having contour lines

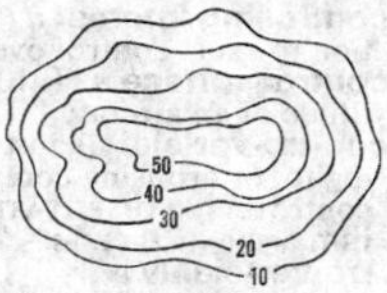

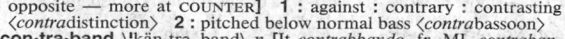

contour map

contr *abbr* **1** contract; contraction **2** contralto **3** contrary **4** control; controller

[1]**con·tra** \ˈkän-trə\ *prep* [ME, fr. L] (15c) **1 :** AGAINST — used chiefly in the phrase *pro and contra* **2 :** in opposition or contrast to

[2]**con·tra** \ˈkän-trə, ˈkōn-, -ˌträ\ *n* [AmerSp, short for *contrarrevolucionario* counterrevolutionary] (1981) **:** a member of a guerrilla group opposed to the Sandinista government in Nicaragua in the 1980s

contra- *prefix* [ME, fr. L, fr. *contra* against, opposite — more at COUNTER] **1 :** against **:** contrary **:** contrasting ⟨*contra*distinction⟩ **2 :** pitched below normal bass ⟨*contra*bassoon⟩

con·tra·band \ˈkän-trə-ˌband\ *n* [It *contrabbando,* fr. ML *contrabannum,* fr. *contra-* + *bannus, bannum* decree, of Gmc origin; akin to OHG *bannan* to command — more at BAN] (ca. 1529) **1 :** illegal or prohibited traffic in goods **:** SMUGGLING **2 :** goods or merchandise whose importation, exportation, or possession is forbidden; *also* **:** smuggled goods **3 :** a slave who during the American Civil War escaped to or was brought within the Union lines — **contraband** *adj*

con·tra·band·ist \-ˌban-dist\ *n* (ca. 1818) **:** SMUGGLER

[1]**con·tra·bass** \ˈkän-trə-ˌbās\ *n* [It *contrabbasso,* fr. *contra-* + *basso* bass] (1813) **:** DOUBLE BASS — **con·tra·bass·ist** \-ˌbā-sist\ *n*

[2]**contrabass** *adj* **:** pitched lower than a bass instrument of the same type ⟨a ~ clarinet⟩

con·tra·bas·soon \ˌkän-trə-bə-ˈsün, -ba-\ *n* (1877) **:** a double-reed woodwind instrument having a range an octave lower than that of the bassoon — called also *double bassoon*

con·tra·cep·tion \ˌkän-trə-ˈsep-shən\ *n* [*contra-* + *conception*] (1886) **:** deliberate prevention of conception or impregnation — **con·tra·cep·tive** \-ˈsep-tiv\ *adj or n*

[1]**con·tract** \ˈkän-ˌtrakt\ *n* [ME, fr. AF, fr. L *contractus,* fr. *contrahere* to draw together, make a contract, reduce in size, fr. *com-* + *trahere* to draw] (14c) **1 a :** a binding agreement between two or more persons or parties; *esp* **:** one legally enforceable **b :** a business arrangement for the supply of goods or services at a fixed price ⟨make parts on ~⟩ **c :** the act of marriage or an agreement to marry **2 :** a document describing the terms of a contract **3 :** the final bid to win a specified number of tricks in bridge **4 :** an order or arrangement for a hired assassin to kill someone ⟨his enemies put out a ~ on him⟩

[2]**con·tract** *vt 2a & vi 1 usu* ˈkän-ˌtrakt, *others usu* kən-ˈ\ *vb* [ME, fr. MF or L; MF *contracter* to agree upon, fr. L *contractus*] *vt* (14c) **1 a :** to bring on oneself esp. inadvertently **:** INCUR ⟨~*ing* debts⟩ **b :** to become affected with ⟨~ pneumonia⟩ **2 a :** to establish or undertake by contract ⟨~ a job⟩ **b :** BETROTH; *also* **:** to establish (a marriage) formally **c** (1) **:** to hire by contract ⟨~ a lawyer⟩ (2) **:** to purchase (as goods or services) on a contract basis — often used with *out* **3 a :** LIMIT, RESTRICT ⟨~ the scope of their activities⟩ **b :** KNIT, WRINKLE ⟨frown ~*ed* his brow⟩ **c :** to draw together **:** CONCENTRATE **4 :** to reduce to smaller size by or as if by squeezing or forcing together ⟨~ a muscle⟩ **5 :** to shorten (as a word) by omitting one or more sounds or letters ~ *vi* **1 :** to make a contract **2 :** to draw together so as to become diminished in size ⟨metal ~*s* on cooling⟩; *also* **:** to become less in compass, duration, or length ⟨muscle ~*s* in tetanus⟩ — **con·tract·ibil·i·ty** \kən-ˌtrak-tə-ˈbi-lə-tē, ˌkän-\ *n* — **con·tract·ible** \kən-ˈtrak-tə-bəl, ˈkän-ˌ\ *adj*

syn CONTRACT, SHRINK, CONDENSE, COMPRESS, CONSTRICT, DEFLATE mean to decrease in bulk or volume. CONTRACT applies to a drawing together of surfaces or particles or a reduction of area or length ⟨caused her muscles to *contract*⟩. SHRINK implies a contracting or a loss of material and stresses a falling short of original dimensions ⟨the sweater will *shrink* when washed⟩. CONDENSE implies a reducing of something homogeneous to greater compactness without significant loss of content ⟨*condense* the essay into a paragraph⟩. COMPRESS implies a pressing into a small compass and definite shape usu. against resistance ⟨*compressed* cotton into bales⟩. CONSTRICT implies a tightening that reduces diameter ⟨the throat is *constricted* by a tight collar⟩. DEFLATE implies a contracting by reducing the internal pressure of contained air or gas ⟨*deflate* the balloon⟩.

[3]**contract** *adj* (1936) **:** hired to execute a contract ⟨a ~ worker⟩ ⟨a ~ killer⟩

contract bridge \ˈkän-ˌtrakt-\ *n* (1924) **:** a bridge game distinguished by the fact that overtricks do not count toward game or slam bonuses

con·trac·tile \kən-ˈtrak-t^{ə}l, -ˌtī(-ə)l\ *adj* (ca. 1706) **:** having or concerned with the power or property of contracting ⟨~ proteins of muscle fibrils⟩ — **con·trac·til·i·ty** \ˌkän-ˌtrak-ˈti-lə-tē\ *n*

contractile vacuole *n* (1876) **:** a vacuole in a unicellular organism that contracts regularly to discharge fluid from the body

con·trac·tion \kən-ˈtrak-shən\ *n* (15c) **1 a :** the action or process of contracting **:** the state of being contracted **b :** the shortening and thickening of a functioning muscle or muscle fiber **c :** a reduction in business activity or growth **2 :** a shortening of a word, syllable, or word group by omission of a sound or letter; *also* **:** a form produced by such shortening — **con·trac·tion·al** \-shnəl, -shə-n^{ə}l\ *adj* — **con·trac·tive** \kən-ˈtrak-tiv, ˈkän-ˌ\ *adj* — **con·trac·tion·ary** \kən-ˈtrak-shə-ˌner-ē\ *adj*

con·trac·tor *1 usu* ˈkän-ˌtrak-tər, *2 usu* kən-ˈ\ *n* (1548) **1 :** one that contracts or is party to a contract: as **a :** one that contracts to perform work or provide supplies **b :** one that contracts to erect buildings **2 :** something (as a muscle) that contracts or shortens

con·trac·tu·al \kən-ˈtrak-chə-wəl, -chəl, -shwəl, -chü-əl\ *adj* (1861) **:** of, relating to, or constituting a contract — **con·trac·tu·al·ly** *adv*

con·trac·ture \kən-ˈtrak-chər\ *n* (1658) **:** a permanent shortening (as of muscle, tendon, or scar tissue) producing deformity or distortion

contra dance \ˈkän-trə-ˌdan(t)s\ *or* **con·tre·danse** *also* kō^{n}-trə-ˈdä^{n}s\ *n* [F *contredanse,* by folk etymology fr. E *country-dance*] (1803) **1 :** a folk dance in which couples face each other in two lines or a square **2 :** a piece of music for a contra dance

con·tra·dict \ˌkän-trə-ˈdikt\ *vt* [L *contradictus,* pp. of *contradicere,* fr. *contra-* + *dicere* to say, speak — more at DICTION] (1582) **1 :** to assert the contrary of **:** take issue with ⟨~ a rumor⟩ **2 :** to imply the opposite or a denial of ⟨your actions ~ your words⟩ ***syn*** see DENY — **con·tra·dict·able** \-ˈdik-tə-bəl\ *adj* — **con·tra·dic·tor** \-ˈdik-tər\ *n*

con·tra·dic·tion \ˌkän-trə-ˈdik-shən\ *n* (14c) **1 :** act or an instance of contradicting **2 a :** a proposition, statement, or phrase that asserts or implies both the truth and falsity of something **b :** a statement or phrase whose parts contradict each other ⟨a round square is a ~ in terms⟩ **3 a :** logical incongruity **b :** a situation in which inherent factors, actions, or propositions are inconsistent or contrary to one another

con·tra·dic·tious \-shəs\ *adj* (1604) **1 :** CONTRADICTORY, OPPOSITE **2 :** given to or marked by contradiction **:** CONTRARY

[1]**con·tra·dic·to·ry** \ˌkän-trə-ˈdik-t(ə-)rē\ *n, pl* **-ries** (14c) **:** a proposition so related to another that if either of the two is true the other is false and if either is false the other must be true

[2]**contradictory** *adj* (1656) **:** involving, causing, or constituting a contradiction ⟨~ statements⟩ ***syn*** see OPPOSITE — **con·tra·dic·to·ri·ly** \-t(ə-)rə-lē\ *adv* — **con·tra·dic·to·ri·ness** \-t(ə-)rē-nəs\ *n*

con·tra·dis·tinc·tion \ˌkän-trə-dis-ˈtiŋ(k)-shən\ *n* (1647) **:** distinction by means of contrast ⟨painting in ~ to sculpture⟩ — **con·tra·dis·tinc·tive** \-ˈtiŋ(k)-tiv\ *adj* — **con·tra·dis·tinc·tive·ly** *adv*

con·tra·dis·tin·guish \-ˈtiŋ-gwish\ *vt* (1622) **:** to distinguish by contrasting qualities

con·trail \ˈkän-ˌtrāl\ *n* [*con*densation *trail*] (1943) **:** streaks of condensed water vapor created in the air by an airplane or rocket at high altitudes

con·tra·in·di·cate \ˌkän-trə-ˈin-də-ˌkāt\ *vt* (1666) **:** to make (a treatment or procedure) inadvisable

con·tra·in·di·ca·tion \-ˌin-də-ˈkā-shən\ *n* (1623) **:** something (as a symptom or condition) that makes a particular treatment or procedure inadvisable

con·tra·lat·er·al \-ˈla-t(ə-)rəl\ *adj* [ISV] (1882) **:** occurring on or acting in conjunction with a part on the opposite side of the body

con·tral·to \kən-ˈtral-(ˌ)tō\ *n, pl* **-tos** [It, fr. *contra-* + *alto*] (1740) **1 a :** a singing voice having a range between tenor and mezzo-soprano **b :** a person having this voice **2 :** the part sung by a contralto

con·tra·po·si·tion \-pə-ˈzi-shən\ *n* [LL *contraposition-, contrapositio,* fr. L *contraponere* to place opposite, fr. *contra-* + *ponere* to place — more at POSITION] (1551) **:** the relationship between two propositions when the subject and predicate of one are respectively the negation of the predicate and the negation of the subject of the other

con·tra·pos·i·tive \-ˈpä-zə-tiv, -ˈpäz-tiv\ *n* (1870) **:** a proposition or theorem formed by contradicting both the subject and predicate or both the hypothesis and conclusion of a given proposition or theorem and interchanging them ⟨"if not-*B* then not-*A* " is the ~ of "if *A* then *B* "⟩

con·trap·tion \kən-ˈtrap-shən\ *n* [perh. blend of *contrivance, trap,* and *invention*] (ca. 1825) **:** DEVICE, GADGET

con·tra·pun·tal \ˌkän-trə-ˈpən-t^{ə}l\ *adj* [It *contrappunto* counterpoint, fr. ML *contrapunctus* — more at COUNTERPOINT] (1845) **1 :** POLYPHONIC **2 :** of, relating to, or marked by counterpoint — **con·tra·pun·tal·ly** \-t^{ə}l-ē\ *adv*

con·tra·pun·tist \-ˈpən-tist\ *n* (1776) **:** one who writes counterpoint

con·trar·i·an \kən-ˈtrer-ē-ən, kän-\ *n* (1657) **:** a person who takes a contrary position or attitude; *specif* **:** an investor who buys shares of stock when most others are selling and sells when others are buying — **contrarian** *adj* — **con·trar·i·an·ism** \-ə-ˌniz-əm\ *n*

con·tra·ri·ety \ˌkän-trə-ˈrī-ə-tē\ *n, pl* **-eties** [ME *contrariete,* fr. AF *contrarieté,* fr. LL *contrarietat-, contrarietas,* fr. L *contrarius* contrary] (14c) **1 :** the quality or state of being contrary **2 :** something contrary

con·trar·i·ous \kən-ˈtrer-ē-əs, kän-\ *adj* (13c) **:** PERVERSE, ANTAGONISTIC

con·trari·wise \ˈkän-ˌtrer-ē-ˌwīz, kən-ˈ\ *adv* (14c) **1 :** on the contrary **2 :** VICE VERSA **3 :** in a contrary manner

[1]**con·trary** \ˈkän-ˌtrer-ē, -ˌtre-rē\ *n, pl* **-trar·ies** [ME *contrarie,* fr. AF *contraire, contrairie,* fr. ML *contrarius,* fr. L, adj., opposite, adverse, fr. *contra* opposite] (13c) **1 :** a fact or condition incompatible with another **:** OPPOSITE — usu. used with *the* **2 :** one of a pair of opposites **3 a :** a proposition so related to another that though both may be false they cannot both be true — compare SUBCONTRARY **b :** either of two terms (as *good* and *evil*) that cannot both be affirmed of the same subject — **by contraries** *obs* **:** in a manner opposite to what is logical or expected — **on the contrary :** just the opposite — **to the contrary 1 :** on the contrary **2 :** NOTWITHSTANDING

[2]**con·trary** \ˈkän-ˌtrer-ē, -ˌtre-rē, *4 often* kən-ˈtrer-ē\ *adj* (14c) **1 :** being so different as to be at opposite extremes **:** OPPOSITE ⟨come to the ~ conclusion⟩ ⟨went off in ~ directions⟩; *also* **:** being opposite to or in conflict with each other ⟨~ viewpoints⟩ **2 :** being not in conformity with what is usual or expected ⟨actions ~ to company policy⟩ ⟨~ evidence⟩ **3 :** UNFAVORABLE — used of wind or weather **4 :** temperamentally unwilling to accept control or advice — **con·trari·ly** \-ˌtrer-ə-lē, -ˈtrer-\ *adv* — **con·trari·ness** \-ˌtrer-ē-nəs, -ˈtrer-\ *n*

syn CONTRARY, PERVERSE, RESTIVE, BALKY, WAYWARD mean inclined to resist authority or control. CONTRARY implies a temperamental unwillingness to accept orders or advice ⟨a *contrary* child⟩. PERVERSE may imply wrongheaded, determined, or cranky opposition to what is reasonable or normal ⟨a *perverse,* intractable critic⟩. RESTIVE suggests unwillingness or inability to submit to discipline or follow orders ⟨tired soldiers growing *restive*⟩. BALKY suggests a refusing to proceed in a desired direction or course of action ⟨a *balky* witness⟩. WAYWARD suggests strong-willed capriciousness and irregularity in behavior ⟨a school for *wayward* youths⟩. ***syn*** see in addition OPPOSITE

[3]**contrary** *same as* [2]\ *adv* (15c) : CONTRARIWISE, CONTRARILY

contrary to *prep* (14c) : in conflict with : DESPITE ⟨*contrary to* orders, he set out alone⟩

[1]**con·trast** \kən-ˈtrast, ˈkän-ˌ\ *vb* [F *contraster,* fr. MF, to oppose, resist, alter. of *contrester,* fr. VL **contrastare,* fr. L *contra-* + *stare* to stand — more at STAND] *vt* (1646) : to set off in contrast : compare or appraise in respect to differences ⟨~ European and American manners⟩ — often used with *to* or *with* ⟨~*ing* her with other women —Victoria Sackville-West⟩ ~ *vi* : to form a contrast ***syn*** see COMPARE — **con·trast·able** \-ˈtras-tə-bəl, -ˌtras-\ *adj* — **con·trast·ing·ly** \-tiŋ-lē\ *adv*

[2]**con·trast** \ˈkän-ˌtrast\ *n* (1711) **1 a :** juxtaposition of dissimilar elements (as color, tone, or emotion) in a work of art **b :** degree of difference between the lightest and darkest parts of a picture **2 a :** the difference or degree of difference between things having similar or comparable natures ⟨the ~ between the two forms of government⟩ **b :** comparison of similar objects to set off their dissimilar qualities : the state of being so compared ⟨the enforced simplicity in this diary . . . is in ~ to the intensity of his former life —*Times Lit. Supp.*⟩ **3 :** a person or thing that exhibits differences when compared with another

con·tras·tive \kən-ˈtras-tiv, ˈkän-ˌ\ *adj* (1841) : forming or consisting of a contrast — **con·tras·tive·ly** *adv*

contrasty \ˈkän-ˌtras-tē\ *adj* (1891) : having or producing in photography great contrast between highlights and shadows ⟨a ~ image⟩

con·tra·vene \ˌkän-trə-ˈvēn\ *vt* **-vened; -ven·ing** [MF or LL; MF *contrevenir,* fr. LL *contravenire,* fr. L *contra-* + *venire* to come — more at COME] (1567) **1 :** to go or act contrary to : VIOLATE ⟨~ a law⟩ **2 :** to oppose in argument : CONTRADICT ⟨~ a proposition⟩ ***syn*** see DENY — **con·tra·ven·er** *n*

con·tra·ven·tion \ˌkän-trə-ˈven(t)-shən\ *n* [MF, fr. LL *contravenire*] (1579) : the act of contravening : VIOLATION

contredanse *var of* CONTRA DANCE

con·tre·temps \ˈkän-trə-ˌtä^{n}, kō^{n}-trə-tä^{n}\ *n, pl* **con·tre·temps** \-(ˌ)tä^{n}(z)\ [F, fr. *contre-* counter- + *temps* time, fr. L *tempus*] (1769) **1 :** an inopportune or embarrassing occurrence or situation **2 :** DISPUTE, ARGUMENT

contrib *abbr* contribution; contributor

con·trib·ute \kən-ˈtri-byət, -(ˌ)byüt *also & esp before -ed or -ing* -ˈtri-bət; *chiefly Brit also* ˈkän-trə-ˌbyüt\ *vb* **-ut·ed; -ut·ing** [L *contributus,* pp. of *contribuere,* fr. *com-* + *tribuere* to grant — more at TRIBUTE] *vt* (1530) **1 :** to give or supply in common with others ⟨~ money to a cause⟩ **2 :** to supply (as an article) for a publication ~ *vi* **1 a :** to give a part to a common fund or store ⟨~ to a fund-raising campaign⟩ **b :** to play a significant part in bringing about an end or result ⟨many players have *contributed* to the team's success⟩ **2 :** to submit articles to a publication — **con·trib·u·tor** \-byə-tər, -bə-, -ˌbyü-\ *n*

con·tri·bu·tion \ˌkän-trə-ˈbyü-shən\ *n* (14c) **1 :** a payment (as a levy or tax) imposed by military, civil, or ecclesiastical authorities usu. for a special or extraordinary purpose **2 :** the act of contributing; *also* : the thing contributed — **con·trib·u·tive** \kən-ˈtri-byə-tiv\ *adj* — **con·trib·u·tive·ly** *adv*

con·trib·u·to·ry \kən-ˈtri-byə-ˌtȯr-ē\ *adj* (15c) **1 a :** subject to a levy of supplies, money, or men **b :** contributing to a common fund or enterprise **2 :** of, relating to, or forming a contribution

con·trite \ˈkän-ˌtrīt, kən-ˈ\ *adj* [ME *contrit,* fr. AF, fr. ML *contritus,* fr. L, pp. of *conterere* to grind, bruise, fr. *com-* + *terere* to rub — more at THROW] (14c) : feeling or showing sorrow and remorse for a sin or shortcoming ⟨a ~ criminal⟩ ⟨a ~ apology⟩ ⟨~ sighs⟩ — **con·trite·ly** *adv* — **con·trite·ness** *n*

con·tri·tion \kən-ˈtri-shən\ *n* (14c) : the state of being contrite : REPENTANCE ***syn*** see PENITENCE

con·triv·ance \kən-ˈtrī-vən(t)s\ *n* (ca. 1628) **1 a :** a thing contrived; *esp* : a mechanical device **b :** an artificial arrangement or development **2 :** the act or faculty of contriving : the state of being contrived

con·trive \kən-ˈtrīv\ *vb* **con·trived; con·triv·ing** [ME *controven, contreven,* fr. AF *controver, contrever,* fr. ML *contropare* to compare, fr. L *com-* + VL **tropare* to compose, find — more at TROUBADOUR] *vt* (14c) **1 a :** DEVISE, PLAN ⟨~ ways of handling the situation⟩ **b :** to form or create in an artistic or ingenious manner ⟨*contrived* household utensils from stone⟩ **2 :** to bring about by stratagem or with difficulty : MANAGE ⟨he *contrived* to win their support⟩ ~ *vi* : to make schemes — **con·triv·er** *n*

contrived *adj* (15c) : ARTIFICIAL, LABORED ⟨a ~ plot⟩

[1]**con·trol** \kən-ˈtrōl\ *vb* **con·trolled; con·trol·ling** [ME *countrollen,* fr. AF *contrerouler,* fr. *contreroule* copy of an account, audit, fr. ML *contrarotulus,* fr. L *contra-* + ML *rotulus* roll — more at ROLL] *vt* (15c) **1 a** *archaic* : to check, test, or verify by evidence or experiments **b :** to incorporate suitable controls in ⟨a *controlled* experiment⟩ **2 a :** to exercise restraining or directing influence over : REGULATE **b :** to have power over : RULE **c :** to reduce the incidence or severity of esp. to innocuous levels ⟨~ an insect population⟩ ⟨~ a disease⟩ ~ *vi* : to incorporate controls in an experiment or study — used with *for* ⟨*control* for socioeconomic differences⟩ ***syn*** see CONDUCT — **con·trol·la·bil·i·ty** \-ˌtrō-lə-ˈbi-lə-tē\ *n* — **con·trol·la·ble** \-ˈtrō-lə-bəl\ *adj* — **con·trol·ment** \-ˈtrōl-mənt\ *n*

[2]**control** *n, often attrib* (1590) **1 a :** an act or instance of controlling; *also* : power or authority to guide or manage **b :** skill in the use of a tool, instrument, technique, or artistic medium **c :** the regulation of economic activity esp. by government directive — usu. used in pl. ⟨price ~*s*⟩ **d :** the ability of a baseball pitcher to control the location of a pitch within the strike zone **2 :** RESTRAINT, RESERVE **3 :** one that controls: as **a** (1) : an experiment in which the subjects are treated as in a parallel experiment except for omission of the procedure or agent under test and which is used as a standard of comparison in judging experimental effects — called also *control experiment* (2) : one (as an organism, culture, or group) that is part of a control **b :** a device or mechanism used to regulate or guide the operation of a machine, apparatus, or system **c :** an organization that directs a spaceflight ⟨mission ~⟩ **d :** a personality or spirit believed to actuate the utterances or performances of a spiritualist medium ***syn*** see POWER

control freak *n* (1971) : a person whose behavior indicates a powerful need to control people or circumstances in everyday matters

con·trolled \kən-ˈtrōld\ *adj* (1586) **1 :** RESTRAINED **2 :** regulated by law with regard to possession and use ⟨~ drugs⟩

con·trol·ler \kən-ˈtrō-lər, ˈkän-ˌ\ *n* [ME *countreroller,* fr. AF *contreroulur,* fr. *contreroule*] (15c) **1 a :** COMPTROLLER 1 **b :** COMPTROLLER 2 **c :** the chief accounting officer of a business enterprise or an institution (as a college) **2 a :** one that controls or has power or authority to control ⟨air traffic ~⟩ **b :** CONTROL 3b — **con·trol·ler·ship** \-ˌship\ *n*

controlling *adj* (1974) : inclined to control others' behavior : DOMINEERING

controlling interest *n* (1867) : sufficient stock ownership in a corporation to exert control over policy

control surface *n* (1910) : a movable airfoil designed to change the attitude of an aircraft

con·tro·ver·sial \ˌkän-trə-ˈvər-shəl, -ˈvər-sē-əl\ *adj* (1583) **1 :** of, relating to, or arousing controversy ⟨a ~ policy⟩ ⟨a ~ film⟩ **2 :** given to controversy : DISPUTATIOUS ⟨a ~ temperament⟩ — **con·tro·ver·sial·ism** \-shə-ˌli-zəm, -sē-ə-ˌ\ *n* — **con·tro·ver·sial·ist** \-list\ *n* — **con·tro·ver·sial·ly** *adv*

con·tro·ver·sy \ˈkän-trə-ˌvər-sē, *Brit also* kən-ˈträ-vər-sē\ *n, pl* **-sies** [ME *controversie,* fr. AF, fr. L *controversia,* fr. *controversus* disputable, lit., turned against, fr. *contro-* (akin to *contra-*) + *versus,* pp. of *vertere* to turn — more at WORTH] (14c) **1 :** a discussion marked esp. by the expression of opposing views : DISPUTE **2 :** QUARREL, STRIFE

con·tro·vert \ˈkän-trə-ˌvərt, ˌkän-trə-ˈ\ *vb* [*controversy*] *vt* (1584) : to dispute or oppose by reasoning ⟨~ a point in a discussion⟩ ~ *vi* : to engage in controversy — **con·tro·vert·er** \-ˌvər-tər, -ˈvər-\ *n* — **con·tro·vert·ible** \-tə-bəl\ *adj*

con·tu·ma·cious \ˌkän-tü-ˈmā-shəs, -tyü-ˈ, -chə-ˈ\ *adj* (1583) : stubbornly disobedient : REBELLIOUS — **con·tu·ma·cious·ly** *adv*

con·tu·ma·cy \kən-ˈtü-mə-sē, -ˈtyü-; ˈkän-tü-, -tyü-, -chə-\ *n* [ME *contumacie,* fr. AF, fr. L *contumacia,* fr. *contumac-, contumax* rebellious] (13c) : stubborn resistance to authority; *specif* : willful contempt of court

con·tu·me·li·ous \ˌkän-tü-ˈmē-lē-əs, -tyü-ˈ, -chə-ˈ\ *adj* (15c) : insolently abusive and humiliating — **con·tu·me·li·ous·ly** *adv*

con·tume·ly \kän-ˈtü-mə-lē, kən-, -ˈtyü-; ˈkän-tü-ˌmē-lē, -tyü-ˌ, -chə-ˌ; *in "Hamlet"* ˈkän-(ˌ)tyüm-lē *or* ˈkän-chəm-\ *n, pl* **-lies** [ME *contumelie,* fr. MF, fr. L *contumelia*] (14c) : harsh language or treatment arising from haughtiness and contempt; *also* : an instance of such language or treatment

con·tu·sion \kən-ˈtü-zhən, -ˈtyü-\ *n* [ME *conteschown,* fr. L *contusion-, contusio,* fr. *contundere* to pound, bruise, fr. *com-* + *tundere* to beat; akin to Goth *stautan* to strike, Skt *tudati* he pushes] (15c) : injury to tissue usu. without laceration : BRUISE 1a — **con·tuse** \-ˈtüz, -ˈtyüz\ *vt*

co·nun·drum \kə-ˈnən-drəm\ *n* [origin unknown] (1645) **1 :** a riddle whose answer is or involves a pun **2 a :** a question or problem having only a conjectural answer **b :** an intricate and difficult problem

con·ur·ba·tion \ˌkä-(ˌ)nər-ˈbā-shən\ *n* [*com-* + L *urb-, urbs* city] (1915) : an aggregation or continuous network of urban communities

co·nus ar·te·ri·o·sus \ˈkō-nəs-är-ˌtir-ē-ˈō-səs\ *n, pl* **co·ni ar·te·ri·o·si** \-ˌnī-är-ˌtir-ē-ˈō-ˌsī\ [NL, lit., arterial cone] (ca. 1860) **1 :** a conical prolongation of the right ventricle in mammals from which the pulmonary arteries emerge — called also *conus* **2 :** a prolongation of the ventricle of amphibians and some fishes that has a spiral valve separating venous blood going to the respiratory arteries from blood going to the aorta and systemic arteries

conv *abbr* **1** convention; conventional **2** convertible **3** convocation

con·va·lesce \ˌkän-və-ˈles\ *vi* **-lesced; -lesc·ing** [L *convalescere,* fr. *com-* + *valescere* to grow strong, fr. *valēre* to be strong, be well — more at WIELD] (15c) : to recover health and strength gradually after sickness or weakness — **con·va·les·cence** \-ˈle-s^{ə}n(t)s\ *n* — **con·va·les·cent** \-s^{ə}nt\ *adj or n*

con·vect \kən-ˈvekt\ *vb* [back-formation fr. *convection*] *vi* (1881) : to transfer heat by convection ~ *vt* : to circulate (as air) by convection — **con·vec·tive** \-ˈvek-tiv\ *adj*

con·vec·tion \kən-ˈvek-shən\ *n* [LL *convection-, convectio,* fr. L *convehere* to bring together, fr. *com-* + *vehere* to carry — more at WAY] (ca. 1623) **1 :** the action or process of conveying **2 a :** the circulatory motion that occurs in a fluid at a nonuniform temperature owing to the variation of its density and the action of gravity **b :** the transfer of heat by convection — compare CONDUCTION, RADIATION — **con·vec·tion·al** \-shnəl, -shə-n^{ə}l\ *adj*

convection oven *n* (1946) : an oven having a fan that circulates hot air uniformly and continuously around food

con·vec·tor \-ˈvek-tər\ *n* (1907) : a heating unit in which air heated by contact with a heating device (as a radiator or a tube with fins) in a casing circulates by convection

con·vene \kən-ˈvēn\ *vb* **con·vened; con·ven·ing** [ME, fr. ML *convenire,* fr. L, to assemble — more at CONVENIENT] *vi* (15c) : to come together in a body ~ *vt* **1 :** to summon before a tribunal **2 :** to cause to assemble ***syn*** see SUMMON — **con·ven·er** *or* **con·ve·nor** \-ˈvē-nər\ *n*

[1]**con·ve·nience** \kən-ˈvēn-yən(t)s\ *n* (14c) **1 :** fitness or suitability for performing an action or fulfilling a requirement **2 a :** something (as an appliance, device, or service) conducive to comfort or ease **b** *chiefly Brit* : TOILET 3 **3 :** a suitable or convenient time ⟨at your ~⟩ **4 :** freedom from discomfort : EASE

[2]**convenience** *adj* (1917) : designed for quick and easy preparation or use ⟨~ foods⟩

convenience store *n* (1965) : a small often franchised market that is open long hours

con·ve·nien·cy \-yən(t)-sē\ *n* (1601) *archaic* : CONVENIENCE

con·ve·nient \kən-ˈvēn-yənt\ *adj* [ME, fr. L *convenient-, conveniens,* fr. prp. of *convenire* to assemble, come together, be suitable, fr. *com-* + *venire* to come — more at COME] (14c) **1** *obs* : SUITABLE, PROPER **2 a :** suited to personal comfort or to easy performance ⟨meeting at a ~ time⟩ **b :** suited to a particular situation ⟨a ~ excuse⟩ **c :** affording accommodation or advantage ⟨found it ~ to deal with both problems at the same time⟩ **3 :** being near at hand : CLOSE ⟨a location ~ to the train station⟩ — **con·ve·nient·ly** *adv*

[1]**con·vent** \ˈkän-vənt, -ˌvent\ *n* [ME *covent,* fr. AF, fr. ML *conventus,* fr. L, assembly, fr. *convenire*] (13c) : a local community or house of a religious order or congregation; *esp* : an establishment of nuns

2con·vent \kən-ˈvent\ *vb* [L *conventus,* pp. of *convenire*] (1514) *obs* **:** CONVENE

con·ven·ti·cle \kən-ˈven-ti-kəl\ *n* [ME, fr. L *conventiculum,* dim. of *conventus* assembly] (14c) **1 :** ASSEMBLY, MEETING **2 :** an assembly of an irregular or unlawful character **3 :** an assembly for religious worship; *esp* **:** a secret meeting for worship not sanctioned by law **4 :** MEETINGHOUSE — **con·ven·ti·cler** \-k(ə-)lər\ *n*

con·ven·tion \kən-ˈven(t)-shən\ *n* [ME, fr. MF or L; MF, fr. L *convention-, conventio,* fr. *convenire*] (15c) **1 a :** AGREEMENT, CONTRACT **b :** an agreement between states for regulation of matters affecting all of them **c :** a compact between opposing commanders esp. concerning prisoner exchange or armistice **d :** a general agreement about basic principles or procedures; *also* **:** a principle or procedure accepted as true or correct by convention **2 a :** the summoning or convening of an assembly **b :** an assembly of persons met for a common purpose; *esp* **:** a meeting of the delegates of a political party for the purpose of formulating a platform and selecting candidates for office **c :** the usu. state or national organization of a religious denomination **3 a :** usage or custom esp. in social matters **b :** a rule of conduct or behavior **c :** a practice in bidding or playing that conveys information between partners in a card game (as bridge) **d :** an established technique, practice, or device (as in the theater)

con·ven·tion·al \kən-ˈvench-nəl, -ˈven(t)-shə-nᵊl\ *adj* (15c) **1 :** formed by agreement or compact **2 a :** according with, sanctioned by, or based on convention **b :** lacking originality or individuality **:** TRITE **c** (1) **:** ORDINARY, COMMONPLACE (2) **:** NONNUCLEAR 1 ⟨~ warfare⟩ **3 a :** according with a mode of artistic representation that simplifies or provides symbols or substitutes for natural forms **b :** of traditional design **4 :** of, resembling, or relating to a convention, assembly, or public meeting ***syn*** see CEREMONIAL — **con·ven·tion·al·ism** \-nə-ˌli-zəm\ *n* — **con·ven·tion·al·ist** \-list\ *n or adj* — **con·ven·tion·al·i·za·tion** \-ˌvench-nə-lə-ˈzā-shən, -ˌven(t)-shə-nə-\ *n* — **con·ven·tion·al·ize** \-ˈvench-nə-ˌlīz, -ˈven(t)-shə-nə-\ *vt* — **con·ven·tion·al·ly** *adv*

con·ven·tion·al·i·ty \-ˌven(t)-shə-ˈna-lə-tē\ *n, pl* **-ties** (ca. 1834) **1 :** a conventional usage, practice, or thing **2 :** the quality or state of being conventional; *esp* **:** adherence to conventions

conventional wisdom *n* (1850) **:** the generally accepted belief, opinion, judgment, or prediction about a particular matter

con·ven·tion·eer \kən-ˌven(t)-shə-ˈnir\ *n* (1926) **:** a person attending a convention

1con·ven·tu·al \kən-ˈven-chə-wəl, -chü-əl, kän-, -ˈvench-wəl\ *adj* [ME, fr. AF or ML; AF *conventuel,* fr. ML *conventualis,* fr. *conventus* convent] (15c) **1 :** of, relating to, or befitting a convent or monastic life **:** MONASTIC **2** *cap* **:** of or relating to the Conventuals — **con·ven·tu·al·ly** *adv*

2conventual *n* (1533) **1** *cap* **:** a member of the Order of Friars Minor Conventual forming a branch of the first order of St. Francis of Assisi under a mitigated rule **2 :** a member of a conventual community

con·verge \kən-ˈvərj\ *vb* **con·verged; con·verg·ing** [LL *convergere,* fr. L *com-* + *vergere* to bend, incline — more at WRENCH] *vi* (1691) **1 :** to tend or move toward one point or one another **:** come together **:** MEET ⟨*converging* paths⟩ **2 :** to come together and unite in a common interest or focus **3 :** to approach a limit as the number of terms increases without limit ⟨the series ~*s*⟩ ~ *vt* **:** to cause to converge

con·ver·gence \kən-ˈvər-jən(t)s\ *n* (1713) **1 :** the act of converging and esp. moving toward union or uniformity; *esp* **:** coordinated movement of the two eyes so that the image of a single point is formed on corresponding retinal areas **2 :** the state or property of being convergent **3 :** independent development of similar characters (as of bodily structure of unrelated organisms or cultural traits) often associated with similarity of habits or environment **4 :** the merging of distinct technologies, industries, or devices into a unified whole

con·ver·gen·cy \-jən(t)-sē\ *n* (1709) **:** CONVERGENCE

con·ver·gent \-jənt\ *adj* (ca. 1751) **1 :** tending to move toward one point or to approach each other **:** CONVERGING ⟨~ lines⟩ **2 :** exhibiting convergence in form, function, or development ⟨~ evolution⟩ **3 a** *of an improper integral* **:** having a value that is a real number **b :** characterized by having the *n*th term or the sum of the first *n* terms approach a finite limit ⟨a ~ sequence⟩ ⟨a ~ series⟩

converging lens *n* (1860) **:** a lens that causes parallel rays (as of light) to come to a focus

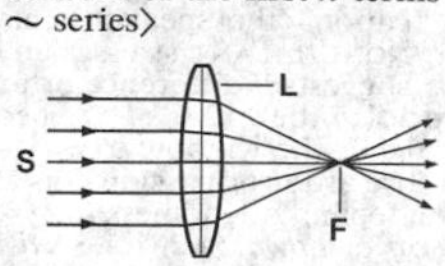

converging lens: *S* light source, *L* lens, *F* focal point

con·vers·able \kən-ˈvər-sə-bəl\ *adj* (ca. 1631) **1** *archaic* **:** relating to or suitable for social interaction **2 :** pleasant and easy to converse with

con·ver·sance \kən-ˈvər-sᵊn(t)s *also* ˈkän-vər-sən(t)s\ *n* (1609) **:** the quality or state of being conversant

con·ver·san·cy \-sᵊn(t)-sē, -sən(t)-\ *n* (1798) **:** CONVERSANCE

con·ver·sant \kən-ˈvər-sᵊnt *also* ˈkän-vər-sənt\ *adj* (14c) **1** *archaic* **:** having frequent or familiar association **2** *archaic* **:** CONCERNED, OCCUPIED **3 :** having knowledge or experience — used with *with*

con·ver·sate \ˈkän-vər-ˌsāt\ *vi* **-sat·ed; -sat·ing** [back-formation fr. *conversation*] (1973) *nonstand* **:** CONVERSE 2a

con·ver·sa·tion \ˌkän-vər-ˈsā-shən\ *n* [ME *conversacioun,* fr. AF *conversacion,* fr. L *conversation-, conversatio,* fr. *conversari* to associate with, freq. of *convertere* to turn around] (14c) **1** *obs* **:** CONDUCT, BEHAVIOR **2 a** (1) **:** oral exchange of sentiments, observations, opinions, or ideas (2) **:** an instance of such exchange **:** TALK ⟨a quiet ~⟩ **b :** an informal discussion of an issue by representatives of governments, institutions, or groups **c :** an exchange similar to conversation — **con·ver·sa·tion·al** \-shnəl, -shə-nᵊl\ *adj* — **con·ver·sa·tion·al·ly** *adv*

con·ver·sa·tion·al·ist \-shnə-list, -shə-nᵊl-ist\ *n* (1819) **:** one who converses a great deal or who excels in conversation

conversation piece *n* (1712) **1 :** a painting of a group of persons in their customary surroundings **2 :** something (as a novel or unusual object) that stimulates conversation

con·ver·sa·zi·o·ne \ˌkän-vər-ˌsät-sē-ˈō-nē, ˌkōn-\ *n, pl* **-o·nes** *or* **-o·ni** \-ˈō-(ˌ)nē\ [It, lit., conversation, fr. L *conversation-, conversatio*] (1739) **:** a meeting for conversation esp. about art, literature, or science

1con·verse \ˈkän-ˌvərs\ *n* [ME *convers,* fr. AF *converse,* fr. *converser*] (15c) **1** *archaic* **:** social interaction **2 :** CONVERSATION

2con·verse \kən-ˈvərs\ *vi* **con·versed; con·vers·ing** [ME, to live (with), fr. AF *converser,* fr. L *conversari*] (1520) **1** *archaic* **a :** to have acquaintance or familiarity **b :** to become occupied or engaged **2 a :** to exchange thoughts and opinions in speech **:** TALK **b :** to carry on an exchange similar to a conversation (as with a computer) — **con·vers·er** \-ˈvər-sər\ *n*

3con·verse \ˈkän-ˌvərs\ *n* [L *conversus,* pp. of *convertere*] (1570) **:** something reversed in order, relation, or action: as **a :** a theorem formed by interchanging the hypothesis and conclusion of a given theorem **b :** a proposition obtained by interchange of the subject and predicate of a given proposition ⟨"no *P* is *S* " is the ~ of "no *S* is *P* "⟩

4con·verse \kən-ˈvərs, ˈkän-ˌ\ *adj* (1794) **1 :** reversed in order, relation, or action **2 :** being a logical or mathematical converse ⟨the ~ theorem⟩ — **con·verse·ly** *adv*

con·ver·sion \kən-ˈvər-zhən, -shən\ *n* [ME, fr. AF, fr. L *conversion-, conversio,* fr. *convertere*] (14c) **1 :** the act of converting **:** the process of being converted **2 :** an experience associated with the definite and decisive adoption of a religion **3 a :** the operation of finding a converse in logic or mathematics **b :** reduction of a mathematical expression by clearing of fractions **4 :** a successful attempt for a point or points esp. after a touchdown or for a first down ⟨a 2-point ~⟩ ⟨a third-down ~⟩ **5 :** something converted from one use to another **6 :** GENE CONVERSION — **con·ver·sion·al** \-ˈvərzh-nəl; -ˈvər-zhə-, -ˈvər-shnəl, -shə-nᵊl\ *adj*

conversion disorder *n* (1980) **:** a psychoneurosis in which bodily symptoms (as paralysis of the limbs) appear without physical basis — called also *conversion hysteria, conversion reaction*

con·ver·so \kən-ˈver-(ˌ)sō, kōn-\ *n, pl* **-sos** [Sp, lit., convert] (1889) **:** a Jew who publicly recanted the Jewish faith and adopted Christianity under the pressure of the Spanish Inquisition

1con·vert \kən-ˈvərt\ *vb* [ME, fr. AF *convertir,* fr. L *convertere* to turn around, transform, convert, fr. *com-* + *vertere* to turn — more at WORTH] *vt* (14c) **1 a :** to bring over from one belief, view, or party to another **b :** to bring about a religious conversion in **2 a :** to alter the physical or chemical nature or properties of esp. in manufacturing **b** (1) **:** to change from one form or function to another (2) **:** to alter for more effective utilization (3) **:** to appropriate without right **c :** to exchange for an equivalent ⟨~ foreign currency into dollars⟩ ⟨~ a bond⟩ **3** *obs* **:** TURN **4 :** to subject to logical conversion **5 a :** to make a goal after receiving (a pass) from a teammate **b :** to score on (as a try for point or free throw) **c :** to make (a spare) in bowling ~ *vi* **1 :** to undergo conversion **2 :** to succeed in an attempt for a point, field goal, or free throw ***syn*** see TRANSFORM

2con·vert \ˈkän-ˌvərt\ *n* (1561) **:** one that is converted

con·vert·er \kən-ˈvər-tər\ *n* (1533) **:** one that converts: as **a :** the furnace used in the Bessemer process **b** *or* **con·ver·tor** \-ˈvər-tər\ **:** a device employing mechanical rotation for changing electrical energy from one form to another (as from direct current to alternating current or vice versa); *also* **:** a radio device for converting one frequency to another **c :** a device for adapting a television or radio receiver to receive channels or frequencies for which it was not orig. designed ⟨a cable ~⟩ ⟨FM ~⟩ **d :** a device that accepts data in one form and converts it to another ⟨analog-digital ~⟩ **e :** CATALYTIC CONVERTER

1con·vert·ible \kən-ˈvər-tə-bəl\ *adj* (14c) **1 :** capable of being converted ⟨a bond ~ to 12 shares of common stock⟩ **2 :** having a top that may be lowered or removed ⟨~ coupe⟩ — **con·vert·ibil·i·ty** \-ˌvər-tə-ˈbi-lə-tē\ *n* — **con·vert·ible·ness** \-ˈvər-tə-bəl-nəs\ *n* — **con·vert·ibly** \-blē\ *adv*

2convertible *n* (1615) **:** something convertible; *esp* **:** a convertible automobile

con·verti·plane *also* **con·verta·plane** \kən-ˈvər-tə-ˌplān\ *n* (1949) **:** an aircraft that takes off and lands like a helicopter and is convertible to a fixed-wing configuration for forward flight

con·vex \kän-ˈveks; ˈkän-ˌ, kən-ˈ\ *adj* [MF or L; MF *convexe,* fr. L *convexus* vaulted, concave, convex, fr. *com-* + *-vexus;* perh. akin to L *vehere* to carry — more at WAY] (1571) **1 a :** curved or rounded outward like the exterior of a sphere or circle **b :** being a continuous function or part of a continuous function with the property that a line joining any two points on its graph lies on or above the graph **2 a** *of a set of points* **:** containing all points in a line joining any two constituent points **b** *of a geometric figure* **:** comprising a convex set when combined with its interior ⟨a ~ polygon⟩

con·vex·i·ty \kən-ˈvek-sət-ē, kän-\ *n, pl* **-ties** (1599) **1 :** the quality or state of being convex **2 :** a convex surface or part

con·vexo–con·cave \kən-ˌvek-(ˌ)sō-kän-ˈkāv, kän-ˌvek-, -ˈkän-ˌkāv\ *adj* (1693) **1 :** CONCAVO-CONVEX **2 :** having the convex side of greater curvature than the concave

con·vey \kən-ˈvā\ *vt* **con·veyed; con·vey·ing** [ME, fr. AF *conveer* to accompany, escort, fr. VL **conviare,* fr. L *com-* + *via* way — more at WAY] (14c) **1** *obs* **:** LEAD, CONDUCT **2 a :** to bear from one place to another; *esp* **:** to move in a continuous stream or mass **b :** to impart or communicate by statement, suggestion, gesture, or appearance ⟨struggling to ~ his feelings⟩ **c** (1) *archaic* **:** STEAL (2) *obs* **:** to carry away secretly **d :** to transfer or deliver (as property) to another esp. by a sealed writing **e :** to cause to pass from one place or person to another ⟨~ a message⟩

con·vey·ance \kən-ˈvā-ən(t)s\ *n* (15c) **1 :** the action of conveying **2 :** a means or way of conveying: as **a :** an instrument by which title to property is conveyed **b :** a means of transport **:** VEHICLE

con·vey·anc·er \-ən(t)-sər\ *n* (1650) **:** one whose business is conveyancing

con·vey·anc·ing \-ən(t)-siŋ\ *n* (1690) **:** the act or business of drawing deeds, leases, or other writings for transferring the title to property

con·vey·or *also* **con·vey·er** \kən-ˈvā-ər\ *n* (ca. 1514) **:** one that conveys: as **a :** a person who transfers property **b** *usu conveyor* **:** a mechanical apparatus for moving articles or bulk material from place to place (as by an endless moving belt or a chain of receptacles)

\ə\ **abut** \ᵊ\ kitten, F table \ər\ **further** \a\ **ash** \ā\ **ace** \ä\ **mop, mar**
\au̇\ **out** \ch\ **chin** \e\ **bet** \ē\ **easy** \g\ **go** \i\ **hit** \ī\ **ice** \j\ **job**
\ŋ\ **sing** \ō\ **go** \ȯ\ **law** \ȯi\ **boy** \th\ **thin** \t͟h\ **the** \ü\ **loot** \u̇\ **foot**
\y\ **yet** \zh\ **vision, beige** \k, ⁿ, œ, ue, ʸ\ *see* Guide to Pronunciation

con·vey·or·ise *Brit var of* CONVEYORIZE
con·vey·or·ize \-ə-ˌrīz\ *vt* **-ized; -iz·ing** (1941) : to equip with a conveyor — **con·vey·or·i·za·tion** \-ˌvā-ə-rə-ˈzā-shən\ *n*
[1]**con·vict** \kən-ˈvikt\ *adj* (14c) *archaic* : having been convicted
[2]**con·vict** \kən-ˈvikt\ *vb* [ME, fr. AF *convicter,* fr. L *convictus,* pp. of *convincere* to refute, convict] *vt* (14c) **1** : to find or prove to be guilty **2** : to convince of error or sinfulness ~ *vi* : to find a defendant guilty
[3]**con·vict** \ˈkän-ˌvikt\ *n* (15c) **1** : a person convicted of and under sentence for a crime **2** : a person serving a usu. long prison sentence
con·vic·tion \kən-ˈvik-shən\ *n* (15c) **1** : the act or process of convicting of a crime esp. in a court of law **2 a** : the act of convincing a person of error or of compelling the admission of a truth **b** : the state of being convinced of error or compelled to admit the truth **3 a** : a strong persuasion or belief **b** : the state of being convinced ***syn*** see CERTAINTY, OPINION
con·vince \kən-ˈvin(t)s\ *vt* **con·vinced; con·vinc·ing** [L *convincere* to refute, convict, prove, fr. *com-* + *vincere* to conquer — more at VICTOR] (1530) **1** *obs* **a** : to overcome by argument **b** : OVERPOWER, OVERCOME **2** *obs* : DEMONSTRATE, PROVE **3** : to bring (as by argument) to belief, consent, or a course of action : PERSUADE ⟨*convinced* himself that she was all right —William Faulkner⟩ ⟨something I could never ~ him to read —John Lahr⟩ — **con·vinc·er** *n*
con·vinc·ing \kən-ˈvin(t)-siŋ\ *adj* (1624) **1** : satisfying or assuring by argument or proof ⟨a ~ test of a new product⟩ **2** : having power to convince of the truth, rightness, or reality of something : PLAUSIBLE ⟨told a ~ story⟩ ***syn*** see VALID — **con·vinc·ing·ly** \-siŋ-lē\ *adv* — **con·vinc·ing·ness** *n*
con·viv·ial \kən-ˈviv-yəl, -ˈvi-vē-əl\ *adj* [LL *convivialis,* fr. L *convivium* banquet, fr. *com-* + *vivere* to live — more at QUICK] (ca. 1668) : relating to, occupied with, or fond of feasting, drinking, and good company ⟨a ~ host⟩ ⟨a ~ gathering⟩ — **con·viv·i·al·i·ty** \-ˌvi-vē-ˈa-lə-tē\ *n* — **con·viv·ial·ly** \-ˈviv-yə-lē, -ˈvi-vē-ə-lē\ *adv*
con·vo·ca·tion \ˌkän-və-ˈkā-shən\ *n* [ME, fr. MF & L; MF, fr. L *convocation-, convocatio,* fr. *convocare*] (14c) **1 a** : an assembly of persons convoked **b (1)** : an assembly of bishops and representative clergy of the Church of England **(2)** : a consultative assembly of clergy and lay delegates from one part of an Episcopal diocese; *also* : a territorial division of an Episcopal diocese **c** : a ceremonial assembly of members of a college or university **2** : the act or process of convoking — **con·vo·ca·tion·al** \-shnəl, -shə-nᵊl\ *adj*
con·voke \kən-ˈvōk\ *vt* **con·voked; con·vok·ing** [MF *convoquer,* fr. L *convocare,* fr. *com-* + *vocare* to call, fr. *voc-, vox* voice — more at VOICE] (1598) : to call together to a meeting ***syn*** see SUMMON
con·vo·lute \ˈkän-və-ˌlüt\ *vb* **-lut·ed; -lut·ing** [L *convolutus,* pp. of *convolvere*] (1698) : TWIST, COIL
con·vo·lut·ed \-ˌlü-təd\ *adj* (1766) **1** : having convolutions **2** : INVOLVED, INTRICATE ⟨a ~ argument⟩
convoluted tubule *n* (1923) : all or part of the coiled sections of a nephron: **a** : PROXIMAL CONVOLUTED TUBULE **b** : DISTAL CONVOLUTED TUBULE
con·vo·lu·tion \ˌkän-və-ˈlü-shən\ *n* (1545) **1** : a form or shape that is folded in curved or tortuous windings **2** : one of the irregular ridges on the surface of the brain and esp. of the cerebrum of higher mammals **3** : a complication or intricacy of form, design, or structure
con·volve \kən-ˈvälv, -ˈvȯlv *also* -ˈväv *or* -ˈvȯv\ *vb* **con·volved; con·volv·ing** [L *convolvere,* fr. *com-* + *volvere* to roll — more at VOLUBLE] *vt* (1616) : to roll together : WRITHE ~ *vi* : to roll together or circulate involvedly
con·vol·vu·lus \kən-ˈväl-vyə-ləs, -ˈvȯl- *also* -ˈväv-yə- *or* -ˈvȯv-yə-\ *n, pl* **-lus·es** *or* **-li** \-ˌlī, -ˌlē\ [NL, fr. L *convolvere*] (1548) : any of a genus (*Convolvulus*) of erect, trailing, or twining herbs and shrubs of the morning-glory family
[1]**con·voy** \ˈkän-ˌvȯi, kən-ˈ\ *vt* [ME, fr. MF *convoier,* fr. OF *conveier,* fr. VL **conviare* — more at CONVEY] (14c) : ACCOMPANY; *esp* : to escort for protection
[2]**con·voy** \ˈkän-ˌvȯi\ *n* (1523) **1** : one that convoys; *esp* : a protective escort (as for ships) **2** : the act of convoying **3** : a group convoyed or organized for convenience or protection in moving
con·vul·sant \kən-ˈvəl-sənt\ *adj* (1875) : causing convulsions : CONVULSIVE 1a — **convulsant** *n*
con·vulse \kən-ˈvəls\ *vb* **con·vulsed; con·vuls·ing** [L *convulsus,* pp. of *convellere* to pluck up, convulse, fr. *com-* + *vellere* to pluck — more at VULNERABLE] *vt* (1614) : to shake or agitate violently; *esp* : to shake with or as if with irregular spasms ⟨was *convulsed* with laughter⟩ ~ *vi* : to become affected with convulsions ***syn*** see SHAKE
con·vul·sion \kən-ˈvəl-shən\ *n* (1547) **1** : an abnormal violent and involuntary contraction or series of contractions of the muscles **2 a** : a violent disturbance **b** : an uncontrolled fit : PAROXYSM — **con·vul·sion·ary** \-shə-ˌner-ē\ *adj*
con·vul·sive \kən-ˈvəl-siv\ *adj* (1615) **1 a** : constituting or producing a convulsion **b** : caused by or affected with convulsions **2** : resembling a convulsion in being violent, sudden, frantic, or spasmodic ⟨~ laughter⟩ ***syn*** see FITFUL — **con·vul·sive·ly** *adv* — **con·vul·sive·ness** *n*
cony *var of* CONEY
coo \ˈkü\ *vi* [imit.] (1577) **1** : to make the low soft cry of a dove or pigeon or a similar sound **2** : to talk fondly, amorously, or appreciatively ⟨the family ~*ed* over the baby pictures⟩ — **coo** *n*
COO *abbr* chief operating officer
[1]**cook** \ˈku̇k\ *n* [ME, fr. OE *cōc,* fr. L *coquus,* fr. *coquere* to cook; akin to OE *āfigen* fried, Gk *pessein* to cook] (bef. 12c) **1** : a person who prepares food for eating **2** : a technical or industrial process comparable to cooking food; *also* : a substance so processed
[2]**cook** *vi* (14c) **1** : to prepare food for eating esp. by means of heat ⟨French ~*ing*⟩ **2** : to undergo the action of being cooked ⟨the rice is ~*ing* now⟩ **3** : OCCUR, HAPPEN ⟨find out what was ~*ing* in the committee⟩ **4** : to perform, do, or proceed well ⟨the jazz quartet was ~*ing* along⟩ ⟨the party ~*ed* right through the night⟩ ~ *vt* **1** : CONCOCT, FABRICATE — usu. used with *up* ⟨~*ed up* a scheme⟩ **2** : to prepare for eating by a heating process **3** : FALSIFY, DOCTOR ⟨~*ed* the books with phony spending cuts and accounting gimmickry —Colleen O'Connor⟩ **4** : to subject to the action of heat or fire — **cook·able** \ˈku̇-kə-bəl\ *adj* — **cook one's goose** : to make one's failure or ruin certain
[1]**cook·book** \-ˌbu̇k\ *n* (1809) : a book of cooking directions and recipes; *broadly* : a book of detailed instructions
[2]**cookbook** *adj* (1944) : involving or using step-by-step procedures whose rationale is usu. not explained ⟨a ~ approach⟩
cook cheese *n* (1941) : an unripened cheese made from curd that has been cooked to a soft consistency — called also *cooked cheese*
cook·er \ˈku̇-kər\ *n* (1884) : one that cooks: as **a** : a utensil, device, or apparatus for cooking **b** : a person who tends a cooking process : COOK **c** *Brit* : STOVE
cook·ery \ˈku̇-k(ə-)rē\ *n, pl* **-er·ies** (14c) **1** : the art or practice of cooking **2** : an establishment for cooking
cookery book *n* (1639) *chiefly Brit* : COOKBOOK
cook·house \ˈku̇k-ˌhau̇s\ *n* (1789) : a building for cooking
cook·ie *or* **cooky** \ˈku̇-kē\ *n, pl* **cook·ies** [D *koekje,* dim. of *koek* cake] (1703) **1** : a small flat or slightly raised cake **2 a** : an attractive woman ⟨a buxom French ~ who haunts the . . . colony's one night spot —*Newsweek*⟩ **b** : PERSON, GUY ⟨a tough ~⟩ **3** *cookie* : a small file or part of a file stored on a World Wide Web user's computer, created and subsequently read by a Web site server, and containing personal information (as a user identification code, customized preferences, or a record of pages visited)
cookie–cutter *adj* (1963) : marked by lack of originality or distinction ⟨~ shopping malls⟩
cookie cutter *n* (1903) : a device used to cut rolled cookie dough into shapes before baking
cookie sheet *n* (1926) : a flat rectangle of metal with at least one rolled edge used esp. for the baking of cookies or biscuits
cooking *adj* (ca. 1813) : suitable for or used in cooking ⟨~ apples⟩
cooking spray *n* (1971) : an aerosol that contains vegetable oil for spraying on cookware to prevent food from sticking
cook–off \ˈku̇k-ˌȯf, -ˌäf\ *n* (1936) : a cooking competition
cook off *vi* (1945) *of a cartridge* : to fire as a result of overheating
cook·out \ˈku̇k-ˌau̇t\ *n* (1947) : an outing at which a meal is cooked and served in the open; *also* : the meal cooked
cook·shack \-ˌshak\ *n* (1909) : a shack used for cooking
cook·shop \-ˌshäp\ *n* (ca. 1552) : a shop providing cooked food
Cook's tour \ˈku̇ks-\ *n* [Thomas *Cook* & Son, Eng. travel agency] (ca. 1909) : a rapid or cursory survey or review
cook·stove \ˈku̇k-ˌstōv\ *n* (1824) : a stove for cooking
cook·top \ˈku̇k-ˌtäp\ *n* (1948) **1** : the flat top of a range **2** : a built-in cabinet-top cooking apparatus containing usu. four heating units
cook·ware \ˈku̇k-ˌwer\ *n* (1922) : utensils used in cooking
[1]**cool** \ˈkül\ *adj* [ME *col,* fr. OE *cōl;* akin to OHG *kuoli* cool, OE *ceald* cold — more at COLD] (bef. 12c) **1** : moderately cold : lacking in warmth **2 a** : marked by steady dispassionate calmness and self-control ⟨a ~ and calculating administrator —*Current Biog.*⟩ **b** : lacking ardor or friendliness ⟨a ~ impersonal manner⟩ **c** *of jazz* : marked by restrained emotion and the frequent use of counterpoint **d** : free from tensions or violence ⟨we used to fight, but we're ~ now⟩ **3** — used as an intensive ⟨a ~ million dollars⟩ **4** : marked by deliberate effrontery or lack of due respect or discretion ⟨a ~ reply⟩ **5** : facilitating or suggesting relief from heat ⟨a ~ dress⟩ **6 a** *of a color* : producing an impression of being cool; *specif* : of a hue in the range violet through blue to green **b** *of a musical tone* : relatively lacking in timbre or resonance **7** *slang* **a** : very good : EXCELLENT; *also* : ALL RIGHT **b** : FASHIONABLE, HIP ⟨not happy with the new shoes . . . because they were not ~ —Celestine Sibley⟩ — **cool·ish** \ˈkü-lish\ *adj* — **cool·ly** *also* **cooly** \ˈkü(l)-lē\ *adv* — **cool·ness** \ˈkül-nəs\ *n*

syn COOL, COMPOSED, COLLECTED, UNRUFFLED, IMPERTURBABLE, NONCHALANT mean free from agitation or excitement. COOL may imply calmness, deliberateness, or dispassionateness ⟨kept a *cool* head⟩. COMPOSED implies freedom from agitation as a result of self-discipline or a sedate disposition ⟨the *composed* pianist gave a flawless concert⟩. COLLECTED implies a concentration of mind that eliminates distractions esp. in moments of crisis ⟨the nurse stayed calm and *collected*⟩. UNRUFFLED suggests apparent serenity and poise in the face of setbacks or in the midst of excitement ⟨harried but *unruffled*⟩. IMPERTURBABLE implies coolness or assurance even under severe provocation ⟨the speaker remained *imperturbable* despite the heckling⟩. NONCHALANT stresses an easy coolness of manner or casualness that suggests indifference or unconcern ⟨a *nonchalant* driver⟩.

[2]**cool** *vi* (bef. 12c) **1** : to become cool : lose heat or warmth ⟨placed the pie in the window to ~⟩ — sometimes used with *off* or *down* **2** : to lose ardor or passion ⟨his anger ~*ed*⟩ ~ *vt* **1** : to make cool : impart a feeling of coolness to ⟨~*ed* the room with a fan⟩ — often used with *off* or *down* ⟨a swim ~*ed* us off a little⟩ **2 a** : to moderate the heat, excitement, or force of : CALM ⟨~*ed* her growing anger⟩ **b** : to slow or lessen the growth or activity of — usu. used with *off* or *down* ⟨wants to ~ off the economy without freezing it —*Newsweek*⟩ — **cool it** : to calm down : go easy ⟨the word went out to the young to *cool it* —W. M. Young⟩ — **cool one's heels** : to wait or be kept waiting for a long time esp. from or as if from disdain or discourtesy
[3]**cool** *n* (15c) **1** : a cool time, place, or situation ⟨the ~ of the evening⟩ **2 a** : absence of excitement or emotional involvement : DETACHMENT ⟨must surrender his fine ~ and enter the closed crazy world of suicide —Wilfrid Sheed⟩ **b** : POISE, COMPOSURE ⟨press questions . . . seemed to rattle him and he lost his ~ —*New Republic*⟩ **3** : HIPNESS
[4]**cool** *adv* (1841) : in a casual and nonchalant manner ⟨play it ~⟩
cool·ant \ˈkü-lənt\ *n* (1926) : a usu. fluid cooling agent
cool·down \ˈkül-ˌdau̇n\ *n* (1978) : the act or an instance of allowing physiological activity to return to normal gradually after strenuous exercise by engaging in less strenuous exercise
cool·er \ˈkü-lər\ *n* (1575) **1** : one that cools: as **a** : a container for cooling liquids **b** : REFRIGERATOR **2** : LOCKUP, JAIL; *esp* : a cell for violent or unmanageable prisoners **3** : an iced drink usu. with an alcoholic beverage as a base
Coo·ley's anemia \ˈkü-lēz-\ *n* [Thomas B. *Cooley* †1945 Am. pediatrician] (ca. 1935) : a severe thalassemic anemia that is associated with the presence of microcytes, enlargement of the liver and spleen, increase in the erythroid bone marrow, and jaundice and that occurs esp. in children of Mediterranean parents
cool·head·ed \ˈkül-ˌhe-dəd\ *adj* (1777) : not easily excited
coo·lie \ˈkü-lē\ *n* [Hindi & Urdu *qulī*] (1638) : an unskilled laborer or porter usu. in or from the Far East hired for low or subsistence wages

coolie hat *n* (1924) **:** a conical-shaped usu. straw hat worn esp. to protect the head from the heat of the sun

cool·ing–off \ˈkü-liŋ-ˈȯf\ *adj* (1926) **:** designed to allow passions to cool or to permit negotiation between parties ⟨a ~ period⟩

cooling tower *n* (1901) **:** a structure over which circulated water is trickled to reduce its temperature by partial evaporation

coombe *or* **coomb** *var of* COMBE

coon \ˈkün\ *n* (1742) **1 :** RACCOON **2** *usu offensive* **:** BLACK 4

coon·can \ˈkün-ˌkan\ *n* [by folk etymology fr. MexSp *conquián* conquian, fr. Sp *¿con quién?* with whom?] (1889) **:** a game of rummy played with two packs including two jokers

coon cat *n* (1901) **:** MAINE COON

coon cheese \ˈkün-\ *n* [Edward W. *Coon,* patenter in 1926 of a method for curing cheddar at a high temperature] (1946) **:** a sharp cheddar cheese that has been cured at higher than usual temperature and humidity and that is usu. coated with black wax

coon·hound \ˈkün-ˌhau̇nd\ *n* (1919) **:** a sporting dog trained to hunt raccoons; *esp* **:** BLACK-AND-TAN COONHOUND

coon's age *n* (1843) **:** a long while ⟨haven't seen him in a *coon's age*⟩

coon·skin \ˈkün-ˌskin\ *n* (1818) **1 :** the skin or pelt of the raccoon **2 :** an article (as a cap or coat) made of coonskin

coon·tie \ˈkün-tē\ *n* [Creek (Florida dial.) *kontí·*] (1791) **:** any of several tropical American woody cycads (genus *Zamia*) whose roots and stems yield a starchy foodstuff — called also *arrowroot*

[1]**coop** \ˈküp, ˈku̇p\ *n* [ME *cupe;* akin to OE *cȳpe* basket] (14c) **1 :** a cage or small enclosure (as for poultry); *also* **:** a small building for housing poultry **2 a :** a confined area **b :** JAIL

[2]**coop** *vt* (1583) **1 :** to confine in a restricted and often crowded area — usu. used with *up* ⟨children *~ed* up in the house all day⟩ **2 :** to place or keep in a coop **:** PEN — often used with *up*

co–op \ˈkō-ˌäp, kō-ˈ\ *n* (1861) **:** COOPERATIVE

[1]**coo·per** \ˈkü-pər, ˈku̇-\ *n* [ME *couper, cowper,* fr. MD *cūper* (fr. *cūpe* cask) or MLG *küper,* fr. *küpe* cask; MD *cūpe* & MLG *küpe,* fr. L *cupa;* akin to Gk *kypellon* cup — more at HIVE] (14c) **:** one that makes or repairs wooden casks or tubs

[2]**cooper** *vb* **coo·pered; coo·per·ing** \ˈkü-p(ə-)riŋ, ˈku̇-\ *vt* (1720) **:** to work as a cooper on ~ *vi* **:** to work at or do coopering

coo·per·age \ˈkü-p(ə-)rij, ˈku̇-\ *n* (1705) **1 :** a cooper's work or products **2 :** a cooper's place of business

co·op·er·ate \kō-ˈä-pə-ˌrāt\ *vi* [LL *cooperatus,* pp. of *cooperari,* fr. L *co-* + *operari* to work — more at OPERATE] (1582) **1 :** to act or work with another or others **:** act together or in compliance ⟨refused to ~ with the police⟩ **2 :** to associate with another or others for mutual benefit ⟨nations *cooperating* to fight terrorism⟩ — **co·op·er·a·tor** \-ˌrā-tər\ *n*

co·op·er·a·tion \(ˌ)kō-ˌä-pə-ˈrā-shən\ *n* (14c) **1 :** the action of cooperating **:** common effort **2 :** association of persons for common benefit — **co·op·er·a·tion·ist** \-sh(ə-)nist\ *n*

[1]**co·op·er·a·tive** \kō-ˈä-p(ə-)rə-tiv, -ˈä-pə-ˌrā-\ *adj* (1603) **1 a :** marked by cooperation ⟨~ efforts⟩ **b :** marked by a willingness and ability to work with others ⟨~ neighbors⟩ **2 :** of, relating to, or organized as a cooperative ⟨a ~ store⟩ **3 :** relating to or comprising a program of combined liberal arts and technical studies at different schools — **co·op·er·a·tive·ly** *adv* — **co·op·er·a·tive·ness** *n*

[2]**cooperative** *n* (1883) **:** an enterprise or organization owned by and operated for the benefit of those using its services

Coo·per's hawk \ˈkü-pərz-, ˈku̇-\ *n* [William *Cooper* †1864 Am. naturalist] (1828) **:** an American hawk (*Accipiter cooperii*) that is larger than the similarly colored sharp-shinned hawk and has a more rounded tail

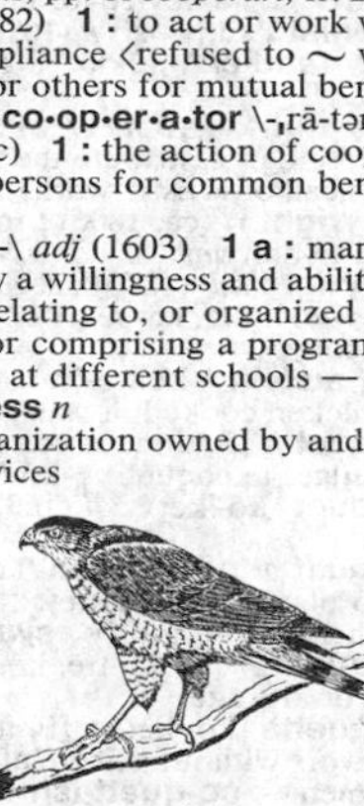
Cooper's hawk

co–opt \kō-ˈäpt\ *vt* [L *cooptare,* fr. *co-* + *optare* to choose] (1651) **1 a :** to choose or elect as a member **b :** to appoint as a colleague or assistant **2 a :** to take into a group (as a faction, movement, or culture) **:** ABSORB, ASSIMILATE ⟨the students are *~ed* by a system they serve even in their struggle against it —A. C. Danto⟩ **b :** TAKE OVER, APPROPRIATE ⟨a style *~ed* by advertisers⟩ — **co–op·ta·tion** \ˌkō-ˌäp-ˈtā-shən\ *n* — **co–op·ta·tive** \kō-ˈäp-tə-tiv\ *adj* — **co–op·tion** \-ˈäp-shən\ *n* — **co–op·tive** \-ˈäp-tiv\ *adj*

[1]**co·or·di·nate** \kō-ˈȯrd-nət; -ˈȯr-də-nət, -də-ˌnāt\ *adj* [prob. back-formation fr. *coordination*] (1641) **1 a :** equal in rank, quality, or significance **b :** being of equal rank in a sentence ⟨~ clauses⟩ **2 :** relating to or marked by coordination **3 a :** being a university that awards degrees to men and women taught usu. by the same faculty but attending separate classes often on separate campuses **b :** being one of the colleges and esp. the women's branch of a coordinate university **4 :** of, relating to, or being a system of indexing by two or more terms so that documents may be retrieved through the intersection of index terms — **co·or·di·nate·ly** *adv* — **co·or·di·nate·ness** *n*

[2]**co·or·di·nate** \kō-ˈȯr-də-ˌnāt\ *vb* **-nat·ed; -nat·ing** *vt* (1665) **1 :** to put in the same order or rank **2 :** to bring into a common action, movement, or condition **:** HARMONIZE ⟨~ schedules⟩ **3 :** to attach so as to form a coordination complex ~ *vi* **1 :** to be or become coordinate esp. so as to act or work together well **2 :** to combine by means of a coordinate bond — **co·or·di·na·tive** \kō-ˈȯrd-nə-tiv; -ˈȯr-də-nə-tiv, -də-ˌnā-\ *adj* — **co·or·di·na·tor** \-ˈȯr-də-ˌnā-tər\ *n*

[3]**co·or·di·nate** *\same as* [1]\ *n* (1806) **1 a :** any of a set of numbers used in specifying the location of a point on a line, on a surface, or in space **b :** any one of a set of variables used in specifying the state of a substance or the motion of a particle or momentum **2 :** one who is of equal rank, authority, or importance with another **3** *pl* **:** articles (as of clothing) designed to be used together and to attain their effect through pleasing contrast (as of color, material, or texture)

coordinate bond *n* (1947) **:** a covalent bond that consists of a pair of electrons supplied by only one of the two atoms it joins

co·or·di·nat·ed \-ˈȯr-də-ˌnā-təd\ *adj* (1885) **:** able to use more than one set of muscle movements to a single end ⟨a well-*coordinated* athlete⟩

Coordinated Universal Time *n* (1969) **:** the international standard of time that is kept by atomic clocks around the world — abbr. *UTC;* compare GREENWICH MEAN TIME, UNIVERSAL TIME

coordinate geometry *n* (ca. 1844) **:** ANALYTIC GEOMETRY

coordinating conjunction *n* (1916) **:** a conjunction (as *and* or *or*) that joins together words or word groups of equal grammatical rank

co·or·di·na·tion \(ˌ)kō-ˌȯr-də-ˈnā-shən\ *n* [LL *coordination-, coordinatio,* fr. L *co-* + *ordination-, ordinatio* arrangement, fr. *ordinare* to arrange — more at ORDAIN] (ca. 1643) **1 :** the act or action of coordinating **2 :** the harmonious functioning of parts for effective results

coordination complex *n* (1951) **:** a compound or ion with a central usu. metallic atom or ion combined by coordinate bonds with a definite number of surrounding ions, groups, or molecules — called also *coordination compound*

coordination number *n* (1908) **1 :** the number of attachments to the central atom in a coordination complex **2 :** a number used in specifying the spatial arrangement of the constituent groups of crystals

coot \ˈküt\ *n* [ME *coote;* akin to D *koet* coot] (15c) **1 :** any of various slaty-black birds (genus *Fulica*) of the rail family that somewhat resemble ducks and have lobed toes and the upper mandible prolonged on the forehead as a horny frontal shield **2 :** any of several No. American scoters **3 :** a harmless simple person; *broadly* **:** FELLOW 4c

coo·ter \ˈkü-tər *also* ˈku̇-tə\ *n* [of African origin; akin to Bambara & Malinke *kuta* turtle] (1832) *chiefly Southern* **:** any of several freshwater turtles (genus *Pseudemys* syn. *Chrysemys,* esp. *P. concinna*) esp. of the southern and eastern U.S.

coo·tie \ˈkü-tē\ *n* [perh. modif. of Malay *kutu*] (1917) **:** BODY LOUSE

[1]**cop** \ˈkäp\ *n* [ME, fr. OE *copp*] (bef. 12c) **1** *dial chiefly Eng* **:** TOP, CREST **2 :** a cylindrical or conical mass of thread, yarn, or roving wound on a quill or tube; *also* **:** a quill or tube upon which it is wound

[2]**cop** *vb* **copped; cop·ping** [perh. fr. D *kapen* to steal, fr. Fris *kāpia* to buy; akin to OHG *kouf* trade — more at CHEAP] *vt* (1704) **1** *slang* **:** to get hold of **:** CATCH, CAPTURE; *also* **:** PURCHASE **2** *slang* **:** STEAL, SWIPE **3 :** ADOPT 2 ⟨~ an attitude⟩ ~ *vi, slang* **:** ADMIT 2b — used with *to* ⟨these small-timers would . . . ~ to the smallest offense their attorney could negotiate —Tom Clancy⟩ — **cop a plea :** to plead guilty to a lesser charge in order to avoid standing trial for a more serious one; *broadly* **:** to admit fault and plead for mercy

[3]**cop** *n* [short for [3]*copper*] (1859) **:** POLICE OFFICER

[4]**cop** *abbr* **1** copper **2** copulative **3** copy **4** copyright

co·pa·cet·ic *also* **co·pa·set·ic** *or* **co·pe·set·ic** \ˌkō-pə-ˈse-tik\ *adj* [origin unknown] (1919) **:** very satisfactory

co·pai·ba \kō-ˈpī-bə, -ˈpā-\ *n* [Sp & Pg; Sp, fr. Pg *copaíba,* fr. Tupi *kopaʔíβa*] (1712) **:** a stimulant oleoresin obtained from several pinnate-leaved So. American trees (genus *Copaifera*) of the legume family; *also* **:** one of these trees

co·pal \ˈkō-pəl, -ˌpal; kō-ˈpal\ *n* [Sp, fr. Nahuatl *copalli* resin] (1577) **:** a recent or fossil resin from various tropical trees

co·par·ce·nary \kō-ˈpär-sə-ˌner-ē\ *n, pl* **-nar·ies** (ca. 1504) **1 :** joint heirship **2 :** joint ownership

co·par·ce·ner \-ˈpärs-nər, -ˈpär-sə-nər\ *n* (15c) **:** a joint heir

co–pay \ˈkō-ˈpā\ *n* (1959) **:** CO-PAYMENT

co–pay·ment \ˈkō-ˌpā-mənt, ˌkō-ˈ\ *n* (1966) **:** a small fixed fee that a health insurer (as an HMO) requires the patient to pay for certain covered medical expenses (as office visits or prescription drugs)

COPD *abbr* chronic obstructive pulmonary disease

[1]**cope** \ˈkōp\ *n* [ME, fr. OE *-cāp,* fr. LL *cappa* head covering] (13c) **1 :** a long enveloping ecclesiastical vestment **2 a :** something resembling a cope (as by concealing or covering) ⟨the dark sky's starry ~ —P. B. Shelley⟩ **b :** COPING

[2]**cope** *vt* **coped; cop·ing** (14c) **:** to cover or furnish with a cope

[3]**cope** *vb* **coped; cop·ing** [ME *copen, coupen,* fr. AF *couper* to strike, cut, fr. *cop, colp* blow, fr. LL *colpus,* alter. of L *colaphus,* fr. Gk *kolaphos* buffet] *vi* (14c) **1** *obs* **:** STRIKE, FIGHT **2 a :** to maintain a contest or combat usu. on even terms or with success — used with *with* **b :** to deal with and attempt to overcome problems and difficulties — often used with *with* ⟨learning to ~ with the demands of her schedule⟩ **3** *archaic* **:** MEET, ENCOUNTER ~ *vt* **1** *obs* **:** to meet in combat **2** *obs* **:** to come in contact with **3** *obs* **:** MATCH

[4]**cope** *vt* **coped; cop·ing** [prob. fr. F *couper* to cut] (ca. 1901) **1 :** to shape (a structural member) to fit a coping or conform to the shape of another member **2 :** NOTCH

copeck *var of* KOPECK

co·pe·pod \ˈkō-pə-ˌpäd\ *n* [ultim. fr. Gk *kōpē* oar, handle + *pod-, pous* foot; prob. akin to L *capere* to take — more at HEAVE, FOOT] (1836) **:** any of a large subclass (Copepoda) of usu. minute freshwater and marine crustaceans — **copepod** *adj*

cop·er \ˈkō-pər\ *n* [E dial. *cope* to trade] (1825) *Brit* **:** a horse dealer; *esp* **:** a dishonest one

Co·per·ni·can \kə-ˈpər-ni-kən, kō-\ *adj* [Nicolaus *Copernicus*] (1667) **1 :** of or relating to Copernicus or the belief that the earth rotates daily on its axis and the planets revolve in orbits around the sun **2 :** of radical or major importance or degree ⟨effected a ~ revolution in philosophy —*Times Lit. Supp.*⟩ — **Copernican** *n* — **Co·per·ni·can·ism** \-kə-ˌni-zəm\ *n*

co·per·nic·i·um \ˌkō-pər-ˈni-sē-əm\ *n* [NL, fr. *Copernicus*] (2009) **:** a short-lived artificially produced radioactive element that has 112 protons — see ELEMENT table

cope·stone \ˈkōp-ˌstōn\ *n* (1567) **1 :** a stone forming a coping **2 :** a finishing touch **:** CROWN

copi·er \ˈkä-pē-ər\ *n* (1597) **:** one that copies; *specif* **:** a machine for making copies of graphic matter (as printing, drawings, or pictures)

co·pi·lot \ˈkō-ˌpī-lət\ *n* (1927) **:** a qualified pilot who assists or relieves the pilot but is not in command

cop·ing \ˈkō-piŋ\ *n* (1601) **:** the covering course of a wall usu. with a sloping top

cop·ing saw \ˈkō-piŋ-\ *n* [fr. prp. of [4]*cope*] (1925) **:** a handsaw with a very narrow blade held under tension in a U-shaped frame and used esp. for cutting curves in wood

cop·ing·stone \ˈkō-piŋ-ˌstōn\ *n* (1778) *chiefly Brit* **:** COPESTONE

co·pi·ous \ˈkō-pē-əs\ *adj* [ME, fr. L *copiosus,* fr. *copia* abundance, fr. *co-* + *ops* wealth — more at OPULENT] (14c) **1 a :** yielding something abundantly ⟨a ~ harvest⟩ ⟨~ springs⟩ **b :** plentiful in number ⟨~ references to other writers⟩ **2 a :** full of thought, information, or matter **b :** profuse or exuberant in words, expression, or style ⟨a ~ talker⟩ **3 :** present in large quantity : taking place on a large scale ⟨~ weeping⟩ ⟨~ food and drink⟩ ***syn*** see PLENTIFUL — **co·pi·ous·ly** *adv* — **co·pi·ous·ness** *n*

co·pla·nar \(ˌ)kō-ˈplā-nər, -ˌnär\ *adj* (1853) **:** lying or acting in the same plane — **co·pla·nar·i·ty** \ˌkō-plā-ˈner-ə-tē, -ˈna-rə-\ *n*

co·pol·y·mer \(ˌ)kō-ˈpä-lə-mər\ *n* (1936) **:** a product of copolymerization — **co·pol·y·mer·ic** \ˌkō-ˌpä-lə-ˈmer-ik\ *adj*

co·po·ly·mer·i·za·tion \ˌkō-pə-ˌli-mə-rə-ˈzā-shən, ˌkō-ˌpä-lə-mə-\ *n* (1936) **:** the polymerization of two substances (as different monomers) together — **co·po·ly·mer·ize** \ˌkō-pə-ˈli-mə-ˌrīz, ˌkō-ˈpä-lə-mə-\ *vb*

cop–out \ˈkäp-ˌau̇t\ *n* (ca. 1942) **1 :** the act or an instance of copping out **2 :** an excuse or means for copping out **:** PRETEXT **3 :** a person who cops out

cop out *vi* (1952) **1 :** to back out (as of an unwanted responsibility) ⟨*cop out* on jury duty⟩ **2 :** to avoid or neglect problems, responsibilities, or commitments ⟨accused the mayor of *copping out* on the issue⟩

[1]**cop·per** \ˈkä-pər\ *n, often attrib* [ME *coper,* fr. OE, fr. LL *cuprum* copper, fr. L *(aes) Cyprium,* lit., Cyprian metal] (bef. 12c) **1 :** a common reddish metallic element that is ductile and malleable and is one of the best conductors of heat and electricity — see ELEMENT table **2 :** a coin or token made of copper or bronze **3** *chiefly Brit* **:** a large boiler (as for cooking) **4 :** any of a subfamily (Lycaeninae of the family Lycaenidae) of small butterflies with usu. copper-colored wings

[2]**copper** *vt* **cop·pered; cop·per·ing** \ˈkä-p(ə-)riŋ\ (1530) **:** to coat or sheathe with or as if with copper

[3]**copper** *n* [[2]*cop*] (1846) **:** POLICE OFFICER

cop·per·as \ˈkä-p(ə-)rəs\ *n* [ME *coperas,* fr. AF *coperose,* fr. ML *cuprosa,* prob. fr. *aqua cuprosa,* lit., copper water, fr. LL *cuprum*] (14c) **:** FERROUS SULFATE

copper beech *n* (1846) **:** a beech with shining coppery-red leaves that is a widely planted cultivar of a beech (*Fagus sylvatica*) native to Europe

cop·per·head \ˈkä-pər-ˌhed\ *n* (1775) **1 :** a common pit viper (*Agkistrodon contortrix*) of the eastern and central U.S. usu. having a copper-colored head and often a reddish-brown hourglass pattern on the body **2 :** a person in the northern states who sympathized with the South during the American Civil War

cop·per·plate \ˈkä-pər-ˌplāt\ *n* (1663) **1 :** an engraved or etched copper printing plate; *also* **:** a print made from such a plate **2 :** a neat script handwriting based on engraved models

copper pyrites *n* (1757) **:** CHALCOPYRITE

cop·per·smith \ˈkä-pər-ˌsmith\ *n* (14c) **:** a worker in copper

copper sulfate *n* (1869) **:** a sulfate of copper; *esp* **:** the normal sulfate that is white in the anhydrous form but blue in the crystalline hydrous form $CuSO_4 \cdot 5H_2O$ and that is often used as an algicide and fungicide

cop·pery \ˈkä-p(ə-)rē\ *adj* (ca. 1775) **:** resembling or suggesting copper; *esp* **:** having the reddish to brownish-orange color of copper

[1]**cop·pice** \ˈkä-pəs\ *n* [ME *copies* cutover area overgrown with brush, fr. MF *copeis,* fr. OF, fr. VL **colpaticium,* fr. **colpare* to cut, fr. LL *colpus* blow — more at COPE] (1534) **1 :** a thicket, grove, or growth of small trees **2 :** forest originating mainly from shoots or root suckers rather than seed

[2]**coppice** *vb* **cop·piced; cop·pic·ing** *vt* (1538) **:** to cut back so as to regrow in the form of a coppice ~ *vi* **:** to form a coppice; *specif, of a tree* **:** to sprout freely from the base

copr- *or* **copro-** *comb form* [NL, fr. Gk *kopr-, kopro-,* fr. *kopros* akin to Skt *śakṛt* dung] **:** dung **:** feces ⟨*copro*lite⟩

co·pra \ˈkō-prə *also* ˈkä-\ *n* [Pg, fr. Malayalam *koppara*] (1584) **:** dried coconut meat yielding coconut oil

co·pro·ces·sor \(ˌ)kō-ˈprä-se-sər, -ˈprō-\ *n* (1980) **:** an extra processor in a computer that is designed to perform specialized tasks (as mathematical calculations)

co·prod·uct \(ˌ)kō-ˈprä-(ˌ)dəkt\ *n* (1942) **:** BY-PRODUCT 1

cop·ro·la·lia \ˌkä-prə-ˈlā-lē-ə\ *n* [NL] (1886) **:** obsessive or uncontrollable use of obscene language

cop·ro·lite \ˈkä-prə-ˌlīt\ *n* (1829) **:** fossilized excrement — **cop·ro·lit·ic** \ˌkä-prə-ˈli-tik\ *adj*

co·proph·a·gous \kə-ˈprä-fə-gəs\ *adj* [Gk *koprophagos,* fr. *kopr-* + *-phagos* -phagous] (1826) **:** feeding on dung — **co·proph·a·gy** \-fə-jē\ *n*

cop·ro·phil·ia \ˌkä-prə-ˈfi-lē-ə\ *n* [NL] (1923) **:** marked interest in excrement; *esp* **:** the use of feces or filth for sexual excitement — **cop·ro·phil·i·ac** \-lē-ˌak\ *n*

co·proph·i·lous \kə-ˈprä-fə-ləs\ *adj* (ca. 1900) **:** growing or living on dung ⟨~ fungi⟩

copse \ˈkäps\ *n* [by alter.] (1578) **:** COPPICE 1

Copt \ˈkäpt\ *n* [Ar *qubṭ* Copts, fr. Coptic *kyptios, gyptios* Egyptian, fr. Gk *Aigyptios*] (ca. 1520) **1 :** a member of the traditional Monophysite Christian church originating and centering in Egypt **2 :** a member of a people descended from the ancient Egyptians

cop·ter \ˈkäp-tər\ *n* (1943) **:** HELICOPTER

[1]**Cop·tic** \ˈkäp-tik\ *n* (1668) **:** an Afro-Asiatic language descended from ancient Egyptian and used as the liturgical language of the Coptic church

[2]**Coptic** *adj* (1677) **:** of or relating to the Copts, their liturgical language, or their church

cop·u·la \ˈkä-pyə-lə\ *n* [L, bond — more at COUPLE] (1619) **:** something that connects: as **a :** the connecting link between subject and predicate of a proposition **b :** LINKING VERB

cop·u·late \ˈkä-pyə-ˌlāt\ *vi* **-lat·ed; -lat·ing** [L *copulatus,* pp. of *copulare* to join, fr. *copula*] (1630) **:** to engage in sexual intercourse — **cop·u·la·tion** \ˌkä-pyə-ˈlā-shən\ *n* — **cop·u·la·to·ry** \ˈkä-pyə-lə-ˌtȯr-ē\ *adj*

[1]**cop·u·la·tive** \ˈkä-pyə-lə-tiv, -ˌlā-\ *adj* (14c) **1 a :** joining together coordinate words or word groups and expressing addition of their meanings ⟨a ~ conjunction⟩ **b :** functioning as a copula **2 :** relating to or serving for copulation

[2]**copulative** *n* (1530) **:** a copulative word

[1]**copy** \ˈkä-pē\ *n, pl* **cop·ies** [ME *copie,* fr. AF, fr. ML *copia,* fr. L, abundance — more at COPIOUS] (14c) **1 :** an imitation, transcript, or reproduction of an original work (as a letter, a painting, a table, or a dress) **2 :** one of a series of esp. mechanical reproductions of an original impression; *also* **:** an individual example of such a reproduction **3** *archaic* **:** something to be imitated **:** MODEL **4 a :** matter to be set esp. for printing **b :** something considered printable or newsworthy — used without an article ⟨remarks that make good ~ —Norman Cousins⟩ **c :** text esp. of an advertisement **5 :** DUPLICATE 1a ⟨a ~ of a computer file⟩ ⟨a ~ of a gene⟩ ***syn*** see REPRODUCTION

[2]**copy** *vb* **cop·ied; copy·ing** *vt* (14c) **1 :** to make a copy or duplicate of ⟨~ a document⟩ ⟨~ a computer file⟩ **2 :** to model oneself on ~ *vi* **1 :** to make a copy **2 :** to undergo copying ⟨the map did not ~ well⟩

syn COPY, IMITATE, MIMIC, APE, MOCK mean to make something so that it resembles an existing thing. COPY suggests duplicating an original as nearly as possible ⟨*copied* the painting and sold the fake as an original⟩. IMITATE suggests following a model or a pattern but may allow for some variation ⟨*imitate* a poet's style⟩. MIMIC implies a close copying (as of voice or mannerism) often for fun, ridicule, or lifelike imitation ⟨pupils *mimicking* their teacher⟩. APE may suggest presumptuous, slavish, or inept imitating of a superior original ⟨American fashion designers *aped* their European colleagues⟩. MOCK usu. implies imitation with derision ⟨*mocking* a vain man's pompous manner⟩.

copy·book \ˈkä-pē-ˌbu̇k\ *n* (1588) **:** a book formerly used in teaching penmanship and containing models for imitation

copy·boy \-ˌbȯi\ *n* (1888) **:** one who carries copy and runs errands (as in a newspaper office)

[1]**copy·cat** \-ˌkat\ *n, often attrib* (1896) **1 :** one who imitates or adopts the behavior or practices of another **2 :** an imitative act or product ⟨~ board games⟩

[2]**copycat** *vb* **copy·cat·ted; copy·cat·ting** *vi* (1926) **:** to act as a copycat ~ *vt* **:** IMITATE

copy·desk \-ˌdesk\ *n* (1921) **:** the desk at which newspaper copy is edited

copy editor *n* (1899) **1 :** an editor who prepares copy for the typesetter **2 :** one who edits and headlines newspaper copy — **copy·ed·it** \ˈkä-pē-ˌe-dət\ *vt*

copy·hold \ˈkä-pē-ˌhōld\ *n* (15c) **1 :** a former tenure of land in England and Ireland by right of being recorded in the court of the manor **2 :** an estate held by copyhold

copy·hold·er \-ˌhōl-dər\ *n* (1847) **1 :** one who reads copy for a proofreader **2 :** a device for holding copy esp. for a typesetter

copy·ist \ˈkä-pē-ist\ *n* (1696) **1 :** one who makes copies **2 :** IMITATOR

copy·read·er \-ˌrē-dər\ *n* (1892) **:** COPY EDITOR — **copy·read** \-ˌrēd\ *vt*

[1]**copy·right** \-ˌrīt\ *n* (1735) **:** the exclusive legal right to reproduce, publish, sell, or distribute the matter and form of something (as a literary, musical, or artistic work)

[2]**copyright** *vt* (ca. 1806) **:** to secure a copyright on — **copy·right·able** \-ˌrī-tə-bəl\ *adj*

[3]**copyright** *adj* (1870) **:** secured by copyright

copy·writ·er \ˈkä-pē-ˌrī-tər\ *n* (1911) **:** a writer of advertising or publicity copy

coq au vin \ˌkȯk-ō-ˈvaⁿ, ˌkäk-ō-\ *n* [F, cock with wine] (ca. 1938) **:** chicken cooked in usu. red wine

[1]**co·quet** *n* [F, dim. of *coq* cock] (1691) **1** \kō-ˈket, -ˈkā\ **:** a man who indulges in coquetry **2** \-ˈket\ **:** COQUETTE

[2]**co·quet** \kō-ˈket\ *adj* (1697) **:** characteristic of a coquette **:** COQUETTISH

[3]**co·quet** *or* **co·quette** \-ˈket\ *vi* **co·quet·ted; co·quet·ting** (1701) **1 :** to play the coquette **:** FLIRT **2 :** to deal with something playfully rather than seriously ***syn*** see TRIFLE

co·que·try \ˈkō-kə-trē, kō-ˈke-trē\ *n, pl* **-tries** (ca. 1656) **:** a flirtatious act or attitude

co·quette \kō-ˈket\ *n* [F, fem. of *coquet*] (ca. 1611) **:** a woman who endeavors without sincere affection to gain the attention and admiration of men — **co·quett·ish** \-ˈke-tish\ *adj* — **co·quett·ish·ly** *adv* — **co·quett·ish·ness** *n*

co·qui \kō-ˈkē\ *n* [AmerSp *coquí*] (ca. 1903) **:** a small chiefly nocturnal arboreal frog (*Eleutherodactylus coqui*) native to Puerto Rico that has a high-pitched call and has been introduced into Hawaii and southern Florida

co·qui·na \kō-ˈkē-nə\ *n* [Sp, prob. dim. of *coca* head, alter. of *coco* bogeyman, coconut] (1837) **1 :** a soft whitish limestone formed of broken shells and corals cemented together and used for building **2 :** a small wedge-shaped clam (*Donax variabilis*) used for broth or chowder and occurring in the intertidal zone of sandy Atlantic beaches from Delaware to the Gulf of Mexico

[1]**cor** *also* **kor** \ˈkȯr\ *n* [ME, fr. LL *corus,* fr. Heb *kōr*] (14c) **:** an ancient Hebrew and Phoenician unit of measure of capacity

[2]**cor** *abbr* **1** corner **2** coroner **3** corpus **4** corresponding

Cor *abbr* Corinthians

cor·a·cle \ˈkȯr-ə-kəl, ˈkär-\ *n* [W *corwgl*] (ca. 1547) **:** a small boat used in Britain from ancient times and made of a frame (as of wicker) covered usu. with hide or tarpaulin

cor·a·coid \ˈkȯr-ə-ˌkȯid, ˈkär-\ *adj* [NL *coracoides,* fr. Gk *korakoeidēs,* lit., like a raven, fr. *korak-, korax* raven — more at RAVEN] (1741) **:** of, relating to, or being a process of the scapula in most mammals or a well-developed cartilage bone of many lower vertebrates that extends from the scapula to or toward the sternum — **coracoid** *n*

cor·al \ˈkȯr-əl, ˈkär-\ *n* [ME, fr. AF, fr. L *corallium,* fr. Gk *korallion*] (14c) **1 a :** the calcareous or horny skeletal deposit produced by anthozoan or rarely hydrozoan polyps; *esp* **:** a richly red precious coral secreted by a gorgonian (genus *Corallium*) **b :** a polyp or polyp colony together with its membranes and skeleton **2 :** a piece of coral and esp. of red coral **3 a :** a bright reddish ovary (as of a lobster or scallop) **b :** a deep pink — **coral** *adj* — **cor·al·loid** \-ə-ˌlȯid\ *adj*

cor·al·bells \ˈkȯr-əl-ˌbelz, ˈkär-\ *n pl but sing or pl in constr* (ca. 1900) **:** a perennial alumroot (*Heuchera sanguinea*) widely cultivated for its feathery spikes of tiny usu. reddish bell-shaped flowers

cor·al·ber·ry \-ˌber-ē, -ˌbe-rē\ *n* (ca. 1859) **:** a No. American dwarf shrub (*Symphoricarpos orbiculatus*) that bears clusters of small flowers succeeded by red or white berries

[1]**cor·al·line** \ˈkȯr-ə-ˌlīn, ˈkär-\ *n* (1543) **1 :** a coralline red alga **2 :** a bryozoan or hydroid that resembles a coral

[2]**coralline** *adj* [F, fr. fem. of *corallin* coral-like, fr. MF, fr. LL *corallinus,* fr. L *corallium*] (ca. 1633) **1 :** of, relating to, or resembling coral **2 :** of, relating to, or being any of a family (Corallinaceae) of calcareous red algae

coral snake *n* (ca. 1772) **1 :** any of several venomous chiefly tropical New World elapid snakes (genus *Micrurus*) brilliantly banded in red, black, and yellow or white that include two (*M. fulvius* and *M. euryxanthus*) ranging northward into the southern U.S. **2 :** any of several harmless snakes resembling the coral snakes

co·ran·to \kə-ˈran-(ˌ)tō\ *n, pl* **-tos** *or* **-toes** [modif. of F *courante*] (1564) **:** COURANTE

cor·ban \ˈkȯr-ˌban\ *n* [Heb *qorbān* offering] (14c) **:** a sacrifice or offering to God among the ancient Hebrews

cor·beil *or* **cor·beille** \ˈkȯr-bəl, kȯr-ˈbā\ *n* [F *corbeille,* lit., basket, fr. OF, fr. LL *corbicula*] (ca. 1734) **:** a sculptured basket of flowers or fruit as an architectural decoration

[1]**cor·bel** \ˈkȯr-bəl\ *n* [ME, fr. MF, fr. dim. of *corp* raven, fr. L *corvus* — more at RAVEN] (15c) **:** an architectural member that projects from within a wall and supports a weight; *esp* **:** one that is stepped upward and outward from a vertical surface

corbel

[2]**corbel** *vt* **-beled** *or* **-belled; -bel·ing** *or* **-bel·ling** (1843) **:** to furnish with or make into a corbel

corbeling *n* (1548) **1 :** corbel work **2 :** the construction of a corbel

cor·bic·u·la \kȯr-ˈbi-kyə-lə\ *n, pl* **-lae** \-(ˌ)lē, -ˌlī\ [LL, dim. of L *corbis* basket] (1816) **:** POLLEN BASKET

cor·bie \ˈkȯr-bē\ *n* [ME, modif. of AF *corbin,* fr. L *corvinus* of a raven — more at CORVINE] (15c) *chiefly Scot* **:** CARRION CROW; *also* **:** RAVEN

cor·bi·na \kȯr-ˈbē-nə\ *n* [MexSp, fr. Sp *corvina,* a marine fish (*Argyrosomus regius*), fr. fem. of *corvino* of a raven, fr. L *corvinus*] (1901) **:** a coastal marine croaker (*Menticirrhus undulatus*) favored by surf casters along the California coast

[1]**cord** \ˈkȯrd\ *n* [ME, fr. AF *corde,* fr. L *chorda* string, fr. Gk *chordē* — more at YARN] (14c) **1 a :** a long slender flexible material usu. consisting of several strands (as of thread or yarn) woven or twisted together **b :** the hangman's rope **2 :** a moral, spiritual, or emotional bond **3 a :** an anatomical structure (as a nerve or tendon) resembling a cord; *esp* **:** UMBILICAL CORD 1a **b :** a small flexible insulated electrical cable having a plug at one or both ends used to connect a lamp or other appliance with a receptacle **4 :** a unit of wood cut for fuel equal to a stack 4 x 4 x 8 feet or 128 cubic feet **5 a :** a rib like a cord on a textile **b (1) :** a fabric made with such ribs or a garment made of such a fabric **(2)** *pl* **:** trousers made of such a fabric

[2]**cord** *vt* (15c) **1 :** to furnish, bind, or connect with a cord **2 :** to pile up (wood) in cords — **cord·er** *n*

cord·age \ˈkȯr-dij\ *n* (1582) **1 :** ropes or cords; *esp* **:** the ropes in the rigging of a ship **2 :** the number of cords (as of wood) on a given area

cor·date \ˈkȯr-ˌdāt\ *adj* [NL *cordatus,* fr. L *cord-, cor*] (1769) **:** shaped like a heart ⟨a ~ leaf⟩ — see LEAF illustration — **cor·date·ly** *adv*

cord·ed \ˈkȯr-dəd\ *adj* (14c) **1 a :** made of or provided with cords or ridges; *specif* **:** muscled in ridges **b** *of a muscle* **:** TENSE, TAUT **2 :** bound, fastened, or wound about with cords **3 :** striped or ribbed with or as if with cord **:** TWILLED ⟨~ fabric⟩ **4 :** equipped with an electrical cord ⟨a ~ phone⟩

cord·grass \ˈkȯrd-ˌgras\ *n* (1857) **:** any of a genus (*Spartina*) of chiefly salt-marsh grasses of coastal regions of Europe, northern Africa, and the New World that have stiff culms and panicled spikelets

[1]**cor·dial** \ˈkȯr-jəl\ *adj* [ME, fr. ML *cordialis,* fr. L *cord-, cor* heart — more at HEART] (14c) **1** *obs* **:** of or relating to the heart **:** VITAL **2 :** tending to revive, cheer, or invigorate ⟨bottles full of excellent ~ waters —Daniel Defoe⟩ **3 a :** sincerely or deeply felt ⟨a ~ dislike for each other⟩ **b :** warmly and genially affable ⟨~ relations⟩ ***syn*** see GRACIOUS — **cor·dial·ly** \ˈkȯrj-lē, ˈkȯr-jə-\ *adv* — **cor·dial·ness** \ˈkȯr-jəl-nəs\ *n*

[2]**cordial** *n* (14c) **1 :** a stimulating medicine or drink **2 :** LIQUEUR

cor·dial·i·ty \ˌkȯr-jē-ˈa-lə-tē, kȯr-ˈja- *also* kȯr-ˈdya-\ *n* (1611) **:** sincere affection and kindness **:** cordial regard

cordia pulmonalia *pl of* COR PULMONALE

cor·di·er·ite \ˈkȯr-dē-ə-ˌrīt\ *n* [F, fr. Pierre L. A. *Cordier* †1861 Fr. geologist] (ca. 1814) **:** a blue mineral of vitreous luster and strong dichroism that consists of a silicate of aluminum, iron, and magnesium

cor·di·form \ˈkȯr-də-ˌfȯrm\ *adj* [F *cordiforme,* fr. L *cord-, cor* + F *-iforme* -iform] (1828) **:** shaped like a heart ⟨a ~ sea-urchin shell⟩

cor·dil·le·ra \ˌkȯr-dᵊl-ˈyer-ə, -də-ˈler- *also* kȯr-ˈdi-lə-rə\ *n* [Sp] (1704) **:** a system of mountain ranges often consisting of a number of more or less parallel chains — **cor·dil·le·ran** \-ˈyer-ən, -ˈler-, -ˈdi-lə-rən\ *adj*

cord·ite \ˈkȯr-ˌdīt\ *n* (1889) **:** a smokeless powder composed of nitroglycerin, guncotton, and a petroleum substance usu. gelatinized by addition of acetone and pressed into cords resembling brown twine

cord·less \ˈkȯrd-ləs\ *adj* (1906) **:** having no cord; *esp* **:** powered by a battery ⟨a ~ telephone⟩ — **cordless** *n*

cór·do·ba \ˈkȯr-də-bə, -və\ *n* [Sp *córdoba,* fr. Francisco Fernández de *Córdoba* †1526 Span. explorer] (1913) — see MONEY table

[1]**cor·don** \ˈkȯr-dᵊn, -ˌdän\ *n* [F, dim. of *corde* cord] (15c) **1 a :** an ornamental cord or ribbon **b :** STRINGCOURSE **2 a :** a line of troops or of military posts enclosing an area to prevent passage **b :** a line of persons or objects around a person or place ⟨a ~ of police⟩ **3 :** an espalier esp. of a fruit tree trained as a single horizontal shoot or two diverging horizontal shoots in a single line

[2]**cordon** *vt* (1561) **:** to form a protective or restrictive cordon around — usu. used with *off* ⟨police ~*ed* off the area around the crime scene⟩

cor·don sa·ni·taire \kȯr-ˌdōⁿ-sä-nē-ˈter\ *n* [F, lit., sanitary cordon (quarantine line)] (1920) **:** a protective barrier (as of buffer states) against a potentially aggressive nation or a dangerous influence (as an ideology)

[1]**cor·do·van** \ˈkȯr-də-vən\ *adj* [OSp *cordovano,* fr. *Córdova* (now *Córdoba*), Spain] (1591) **1** *cap* **:** of or relating to Córdoba and esp. Córdoba, Spain **2 :** made of cordovan leather

[2]**cordovan** *n* (ca. 1625) **1 :** a soft fine-grained colored leather **2 :** dense nonporous leather tanned from the inner layer of horsehide

[1]**cor·du·roy** \ˈkȯr-də-ˌrȯi\ *n, pl* **-roys** [origin unknown] (ca. 1791) **1 a** *pl* **:** trousers of corduroy fabric **b :** a durable usu. cotton pile fabric with vertical ribs or wales **2 :** logs laid side by side transversely to make a road surface

[2]**corduroy** *vt* **-royed; -roy·ing** (1854) **:** to build (a road) of logs laid side by side transversely; *also* **:** to build a corduroy road across

cord·wain \ˈkȯrd-ˌwān\ *n* [ME *cordwane,* fr. AF *cordewan,* fr. OSp *cordovano, cordován*] (14c) *archaic* **:** cordovan leather

cord·wain·er \-ˌwā-nər\ *n* (14c) **1** *archaic* **:** a worker in cordovan leather **2 :** SHOEMAKER — **cord·wain·ery** \-ˌwā-nə-rē\ *n*

cord·wood \ˈkȯrd-ˌwu̇d\ *n* (ca. 1639) **:** wood piled or sold in cords

[1]**core** \ˈkȯr\ *n, often attrib* [ME] (14c) **1 :** a central and often foundational part usu. distinct from the enveloping part by a difference in nature ⟨the ~ of the city⟩: as **a :** the usu. inedible central part of some fruits (as a pineapple); *esp* **:** the papery or leathery carpels composing the ripened ovary in a pome fruit (as an apple) **b :** the portion of a foundry mold that shapes the interior of a hollow casting **c :** a vertical space (as for elevator shafts, stairways, or plumbing apparatus) in a multistory building **d (1) :** a mass of iron serving to concentrate and intensify the magnetic field resulting from a current in a surrounding coil **(2) :** a tiny doughnut-shaped piece of magnetic material (as ferrite) used in computer memories **(3) :** a computer memory consisting of an array of cores strung on fine wires; *broadly* **:** the internal memory of a computer **e :** the central part of a celestial body (as the earth or sun) usu. having different physical properties from the surrounding parts **f :** a nodule of stone (as flint or obsidian) from which flakes have been struck for making implements **g :** the conducting wire with its insulation in an electric cable **h :** an arrangement of a course of studies that combines under basic topics material from subjects conventionally separated and aims to provide a common background for all students ⟨~ curriculum⟩ **i :** the place in a nuclear reactor where fission occurs **2 a :** a basic, essential, or enduring part (as of an individual, a class, or an entity) ⟨the staff had a ~ of experts⟩ ⟨the ~ of her beliefs⟩ **b :** the essential meaning **:** GIST ⟨the ~ of the argument⟩ **c :** the inmost or most intimate part ⟨honest to the ~⟩ **3 :** a part (as a thin cylinder of material) removed from the interior of a mass esp. to determine composition

[2]**core** *vt* **cored; cor·ing** (15c) **:** to remove a core from ⟨~ an apple⟩ — **cor·er** *n*

[3]**core** *n* [perh. alter. of ME *chore* chorus, company, perh. fr. L *chorus*] (1622) *chiefly Scot* **:** a group of people

CORE *abbr* Congress of Racial Equality

core city *n* (1965) **:** INNER CITY

cored \ˈkȯrd\ *adj* (1945) **:** having a core of a specified kind — usu. used in combination ⟨a balsa-*cored* deck⟩

co·re·li·gion·ist \ˌkō-ri-ˈlij-nist, -ˈli-jə-\ *n* (1826) **:** a person of the same religion

co·re·op·sis \ˌkȯr-ē-ˈäp-səs\ *n, pl* **coreopsis** [NL, genus name, fr. Gk *koris* bedbug + NL *-opsis;* akin to Gk *keirein* to cut — more at SHEAR] (ca. 1753) **:** any of a genus (*Coreopsis*) of widely cultivated composite herbs with showy often yellow flower heads and pinnately lobed or dissected leaves

co·re·pres·sor \ˌkō-ri-ˈpre-sər\ *n* (1963) **:** a small molecule that activates a particular genetic repressor by combining with it

co·req·ui·site \kō-ˈre-kwə-zət\ *n* (ca. 1948) **:** a formal course of study required to be taken simultaneously with another

co·re·spon·dent \ˌkō-ri-ˈspän-dənt\ *n* (1857) **:** a person named as guilty of adultery with the defendant in a divorce suit

corf \ˈkȯrf\ *n, pl* **corves** \ˈkȯrvz\ [ME, basket, fr. MD *corf* or MLG *korf,* fr. L *corbis* basket] (1653) *Brit* **:** a basket, tub, or truck used in a mine

cor·gi \ˈkȯr-gē\ *n, pl* **corgis** [W, fr. *cor* dwarf + *ci* dog] (1926) **:** WELSH CORGI

co·ri·a·ceous \ˌkȯr-ē-ˈā-shəs\ *adj* [LL *coriaceus* — more at CUIRASS] (1674) **:** resembling leather ⟨~ foliage⟩

co·ri·an·der \ˈkȯr-ē-ˌan-dər, ˌkȯr-ē-ˈ\ *n* [ME *coriandre,* fr. AF, fr. L *coriandrum,* fr. Gk *koriandron, koriannon*] (14c) **1 :** an Old World annual herb (*Coriandrum sativum*) of the carrot family with aromatic fruits **2 :** the ripened dried fruit of coriander used as a flavoring — called also *coriander seed*

[1]**Co·rin·thi·an** \kə-ˈrin(t)-thē-ən\ *n* (1520) **1 :** a native or resident of Corinth, Greece **2 :** a merry profligate man

[2]**Corinthian** *adj* (1594) **1 :** of, relating to, or characteristic of Corinth or Corinthians **2 :** of or relating to the lightest and most ornate of the three ancient Greek architectural orders distinguished esp. by its large capitals decorated with carved acanthus leaves — see ORDER illustration

Co·rin·thi·ans \-thē-ənz\ *n pl but sing in constr* (1520) **:** either of two letters written by St. Paul to the Christians of Corinth and included as books in the New Testament — see BIBLE table

Co·ri·o·lis effect \ˌkȯr-ē-ˈō-ləs-\ *n* (ca. 1946) **:** the apparent deflection of a moving object that is the result of the Coriolis force

Coriolis force *n* [Gaspard G. *Coriolis* †1843 Fr. civil engineer] (1923) **:** an apparent force that as a result of the earth's rotation deflects moving objects (as projectiles or air currents) to the right in the northern hemisphere and to the left in the southern hemisphere

co·ri·um \ˈkȯr-ē-əm\ *n, pl* **co·ria** \-ē-ə\ [NL, fr. L, leather — more at CUIRASS] (1836) **:** DERMIS

[1]**cork** \ˈkȯrk\ *n* [ME, cork, bark, prob. fr. MD *kurk or MLG *korck,* fr. OSp *alcorque,* ultim. fr. dial. Ar *qurq,* fr. L *quercus* oak — more at FIR] (14c) **1 a :** the elastic tough outer tissue of the cork oak that is used esp. for stoppers and insulation **b :** PHELLEM **2 :** a usu. cork stopper for a bottle or jug **3 :** a fishing float

[2]**cork** *vt* (1535) **1 :** to furnish or fit with cork or a cork **2 :** to stop up with a cork ⟨~ a bottle⟩ **3 :** to blacken with burnt cork ⟨~*ed* faces⟩

cork·age \ˈkȯr-kij\ *n* (1838) **:** a charge (as by a restaurant) for opening a bottle of wine bought elsewhere

cork·board \ˈkȯrk-ˌbȯrd\ *n* (ca. 1893) : a heat-insulating material made of compressed granulated cork; *also* : a bulletin board made with this material

cork cambium *n* (1878) : PHELLOGEN

corked \ˈkȯrkt\ *adj* (1828) : CORKY 2

cork·er \ˈkȯr-kər\ *n* (1881) **1** : one that corks containers (as bottles) **2** : one that is excellent or remarkable

cork·ing \ˈkȯr-kiŋ\ *adj or adv* (1895) : extremely fine — often used as an intensive esp. before *good* ⟨had a ~ good time⟩

cork oak *n* (1873) : an oak (*Quercus suber*) of southern Europe and northern Africa that is the source of the cork of commerce

[1]**cork·screw** \ˈkȯrk-ˌskrü\ *n* (1698) : a device for drawing corks from bottles that has a pointed spiral piece of metal turned by a handle

[2]**corkscrew** *adj* (1790) : resembling a corkscrew : SPIRAL

[3]**corkscrew** *vt* (1837) **1** : WIND **2** : to draw out with difficulty **3** : to twist into a spiral ~ *vi* : to move in a winding course

cork·wood \ˈkȯrk-ˌwu̇d\ *n* (1756) : any of several trees having light or corky wood; *esp* : a small or shrubby tree (*Leitneria floridana*) of the southeastern U.S. that has extremely light soft wood

corky \ˈkȯr-kē\ *adj* **cork·i·er; -est** (1756) **1** : resembling cork **2** : having an unpleasant odor and taste (as from a tainted cork) ⟨~ wine⟩ — **cork·i·ness** \-kē-nəs\ *n*

corm \ˈkȯrm\ *n* [NL *cormus*, fr. Gk *kormos* tree trunk, fr. *keirein* to cut — more at SHEAR] (1830) : a rounded thick modified underground stem base bearing membranous or scaly leaves and buds and acting as a vegetative reproductive structure — compare BULB, TUBER

corm·el \ˈkȯr-məl, kȯr-ˈmel\ *n* [dim. of *corm*] (ca. 1900) : a small or secondary corm produced by a larger corm

cor·mo·rant \ˈkȯrm-rənt, ˈkȯr-mə-, ˈkȯr-mə-ˌrant\ *n* [ME *cormeraunt*, fr. MF *cormorant*, fr. OF *cormareng*, fr. *corp* raven + *marenc* of the sea, fr. L *marinus* — more at CORBEL, MARINE] (14c) **1** : any of various dark-colored web-footed waterbirds (family Phalacrocoracidae, esp. genus *Phalacrocorax*) that have a long neck, hooked bill, and distensible throat pouch **2** : a gluttonous, greedy, or rapacious person

[1]**corn** \ˈkȯrn\ *n, often attrib* [ME, fr. OE; akin to OHG & ON *korn* grain, L *granum*] (bef. 12c) **1** *chiefly dial* : a small hard particle : GRAIN **2** : a small hard seed — usu. used in combination ⟨pepper*corn*⟩ ⟨barley*corn*⟩ **3** *Brit* : the grain of a cereal grass that is the primary crop of a region (as wheat in Britain and oats in Scotland and Ireland); *also* : a plant that produces corn **4 a** : a tall annual cereal grass (*Zea mays*) orig. domesticated in Mexico and widely grown for its large elongated ears of starchy seeds — called also *Indian corn, maize* **b** : the typically yellow or whitish seeds of corn used esp. as food for humans and livestock **c** : an ear of corn with or without its leafy outer covering **5** : CORN WHISKEY **6 a** : something (as writing, music, or acting) that is corny **b** : the quality or state of being corny : CORNINESS **7** : CORN SNOW

[2]**corn** *vt* (1560) **1** : to form into grains : GRANULATE **2 a** : to preserve or season with salt in grains **b** : to cure or preserve in brine containing preservatives and often seasonings ⟨~*ed* beef⟩ **3** : to feed with corn

[3]**corn** *n* [ME *corne*, fr. AF, horn, fr. L *cornu* horn, point — more at HORN] (15c) : a local hardening and thickening of epidermis (as on a toe)

[1]**corn·ball** \ˈkȯrn-ˌbȯl\ *n* (ca. 1949) : an unsophisticated person; *also* : something corny

[2]**cornball** *adj* (1951) : CORNY ⟨~ humor⟩

corn borer *n* (1861) : any of several insects that bore in corn: as **a** : EUROPEAN CORN BORER **b** : SOUTHWESTERN CORN BORER

corn bread *n* (1719) : bread made with cornmeal

corn chip *n* (1917) : a piece of a dry crisp snack food prepared from a seasoned cornmeal batter

corn·cob \ˈkȯrn-ˌkäb\ *n* (1792) **1** : the core on which the kernels of corn are arranged **2** : an ear of corn

corncob pipe *n* (1832) : a tobacco pipe with a bowl made of a corncob

corn cockle *n* (1713) : an annual hairy weed (*Agrostemma githago*) of the pink family with purplish-red flowers that is found in grain fields

corn·crake \ˈkȯrn-ˌkrāk\ *n* (15c) : a Eurasian short-billed rail (*Crex crex*) that frequents grain fields

corn·crib \-ˌkrib\ *n* (1681) : a crib for storing ears of corn

corn dodger *n* (1834) *chiefly Southern & Midland* : a cake of corn bread that is fried, baked, or boiled as a dumpling

corn dog *n* (1967) : a frankfurter dipped in cornmeal batter, fried, and served on a stick

cor·nea \ˈkȯr-nē-ə\ *n* [ME, fr. ML, fr. L, fem. of *corneus* horny, fr. *cornu*] (14c) : the transparent part of the coat of the eyeball that covers the iris and pupil and admits light to the interior — see EYE illustration — **cor·ne·al** \-əl\ *adj*

corn ear·worm \-ˈir-ˌwərm\ *n* (1802) : a noctuid moth (*Helicoverpa zea* syn. *Heliothis zea*) whose large striped yellow-headed larva is esp. destructive to corn, tomatoes, tobacco, and cotton bolls

cor·nel \ˈkȯr-nᵊl, -ˌnel\ *n* [ultim. fr. L *cornus* cornel cherry tree; akin to Gk *kranon* cornel cherry tree] (1551) : any of various shrubs or trees (genus *Cornus*) of the dogwood family; *specif* : DOGWOOD

cor·ne·lian \kȯr-ˈnēl-yən\ *n* (15c) : CARNELIAN

cor·ne·ous \ˈkȯr-nē-əs\ *adj* [L *corneus*] (1646) : of a horny texture

[1]**cor·ner** \ˈkȯr-nər\ *n* [ME, fr. AF *cornere*, fr. *corne* horn] (13c) **1 a** : the point where converging lines, edges, or sides meet : ANGLE **b** : the place of intersection of two streets or roads **c** : a piece designed to form, mark, or protect a corner **2** : the angular part or space between meeting lines, edges, or borders near the vertex of the angle ⟨the southwest ~ of the state⟩ ⟨the ~*s* of the tablecloth⟩: as **a** : the area of a playing field or court near the intersection of the sideline and the goal line or baseline **b (1)** : either of the four angles of a boxing ring; *esp* : the area in which a boxer rests or is worked on by his seconds during periods between rounds **(2)** : a group of supporters, well-wishers, or adherents associated esp. with a contestant **c** : the side of home plate nearest to or farthest from a batter **d** : CORNER KICK **e (1)** : the outside of a football formation **(2)** : CORNERBACK **3 a** : a private, secret, or remote place ⟨a quiet ~ of New England⟩ ⟨to every ~ of the earth⟩ **b** : a difficult or embarrassing situation : a position from which escape or retreat is difficult or impossible ⟨was backed into a ~⟩ **4** : control or ownership of enough of the available supply of a commodity or security esp. to permit manipulation of the price **5** : a point at which significant change occurs — often used in the phrase *turn the corner* — **cor·nered** \-nərd\ *adj* — **around the corner** : at hand : IMMINENT ⟨good times are just *around the corner*⟩

[2]**corner** *adj* (13c) **1** : situated at a corner ⟨the ~ drugstore⟩ **2** : used or fitted for use in or on a corner ⟨a ~ table⟩

[3]**corner** *vt* (1824) **1 a** : to drive into a corner ⟨the animal is dangerous when ~*ed*⟩ **b** : to catch and hold the attention of esp. to force an interview **2** : to get a corner on ⟨~ the market⟩ ~ *vi* **1** : to meet or converge at a corner or angle **2** : to turn a corner ⟨the car ~*s* well⟩

cor·ner·back \ˈkȯr-nər-ˌbak\ *n* (1955) : a defensive halfback in football who defends the flank

corner kick *n* (1882) : a free kick from a corner of a soccer field awarded to an attacker when a defender plays the ball out-of-bounds over the end line

cor·ner·man \ˈkȯr-nər-ˌman\ *n* (1957) **1** : one who plays in or near the corner: as **a** : CORNERBACK **b** : a basketball forward **2** : a boxer's second

cor·ner·stone \-ˌstōn\ *n* (13c) **1** : a stone forming a part of a corner or angle in a wall; *specif* : such a stone laid at a formal ceremony **2** : a basic element : FOUNDATION ⟨a ~ of foreign policy⟩

cor·ner·ways \-ˌwāz\ *adv* (1845) : DIAGONALLY

cor·ner·wise \-ˌwīz\ *adv* (15c) : DIAGONALLY

[1]**cor·net** \kȯr-ˈnet, *Brit usu* ˈkȯr-nit\ *n* [ME, fr. MF, fr. dim. of *corn* horn, fr. L *cornu*] (14c) **1** : a valved brass instrument resembling a trumpet in design and range but having a shorter partly conical tube and less brilliant tone **2** : something shaped like a cone: as **a** : a piece of paper twisted for use as a container **b** : a cone-shaped pastry shell that is often filled with whipped cream **c** *Brit* : an ice-cream cone — **cor·net·ist** *or* **cor·net·tist** \kȯr-ˈne-tist, ˈkȯr-ni-\ *n*

[2]**cornet** *n* [MF *cornette* woman's headdress with a lappet, pennon, standard, fr. dim. of *corn*] (1579) **1** : the standard of a cavalry troop **2 a** : the onetime fifth grade of commissioned officer in a British cavalry troop who carried the standard **b** : the onetime lowest commissioned rank in the U.S. cavalry

corn–fed \ˈkȯrn-ˌfed\ *adj* (14c) **1** : fed or fattened on grain (as corn) ⟨~ hogs⟩ **2** : looking well-fed : PLUMP **3** : rustically wholesome or corny ⟨~ humor⟩

corn·field \-ˌfēld\ *n* (14c) : a field in which corn is grown

corn·flakes \-ˌflāks\ *n pl* (1907) : toasted flakes made from the coarse meal of hulled corn for use as a breakfast cereal

corn flour *n* (1791) *Brit* : CORNSTARCH

corn·flow·er \ˈkȯrn-ˌflau̇(-ə)r\ *n* (1841) **1** : CORN COCKLE **2** : BACHELOR'S BUTTON

cornflower blue *n* (1907) : a moderate purplish blue

Corn·husk·er \ˈkȯrn-ˌhəs-kər\ *n* (ca. 1948) : a native or resident of Nebraska — used as a nickname

corn·husk·ing \-ˌhəs-kiŋ\ *n* (1692) : a social gathering esp. of farm families to husk corn

[1]**cor·nice** \ˈkȯr-nəs, -nish\ *n* [MF, fr. It, frame, cornice, fr. L *cornic-*, *cornix* crow; akin to Gk *korax* raven — more at RAVEN] (1563) **1 a** : the molded and projecting horizontal member that crowns an architectural composition — see COLUMN illustration **b** : a top course that crowns a wall **2** : a decorative band of metal or wood used to conceal curtain fixtures **3** : an overhanging mass of windblown snow or ice usu. on a ridge

[2]**cornice** *vt* **cor·niced; cor·nic·ing** (1744) : to furnish or crown with a cornice

cor·niche \kȯr-ˈnēsh\ *n* [F *cornice, corniche*, lit., cornice, fr. It *cornice*] (1835) : a road built along a coast and esp. along the face of a cliff

cor·ni·chon \kȯr-nē-ˈshōⁿ\ *n* [F, gherkin, lit., little horn, dim. of *corne* horn] (1928) : a sour gherkin usu. flavored with tarragon

cor·nic·u·late cartilage \kȯr-ˈni-kyə-lət-\ *n* [L *corniculatus* horned, fr. *corniculum*, dim. of *cornu* horn] (ca. 1909) : a small nodule of yellow elastic cartilage articulating with the apex of the arytenoid

cor·ni·fi·ca·tion \ˌkȯr-nə-fə-ˈkā-shən\ *n* [L *cornu* horn] (ca. 1843) : conversion into horn or a horny or keratinous substance or tissue

[1]**Cor·nish** \ˈkȯr-nish\ *adj* [ME *Cornysshe*, fr. *Cornwaile* Cornwall, England] (14c) : of, relating to, or characteristic of Cornwall, Cornishmen, or Cornish

[2]**Cornish** *n* (1547) **1** : the Celtic language of Cornwall **2** : any of an English breed of domestic chickens much used in crossbreeding for meat production — compare ROCK CORNISH HEN

Cor·nish·man \-mən\ *n* (15c) : a native or resident of Cornwall, England

Cornish pasty *n* (1871) : a filled pastry containing cooked meat and vegetables

Cornish rex *n, often cap R* (1972) : any of a breed of cats with a very short soft wavy coat free of guard hairs and a small head with large ears

Corn Law *n* (1766) : one of a series of laws in force in Great Britain before 1846 prohibiting or discouraging the importation of grain

corn leaf aphid *n* (ca. 1939) : a dusky greenish or brownish aphid (*Rhopalosiphum maidis*) that feeds on the flowers and foliage of various commercially important grasses (as corn)

corn·meal \ˈkȯrn-ˌmēl\ *n* (1749) : meal ground from corn

corn oil *n* (1879) : a yellow fatty oil obtained from the germ of corn kernels and used chiefly as salad oil, in soft soap, and in margarine

corn·pone \ˈkȯrn-ˌpōn\ *adj* (1972) : DOWN-HOME, COUNTRIFIED

corn pone *n* (1859) *Southern & Midland* : corn bread often made without milk or eggs and baked or fried

corn poppy *n* (ca. 1859) : an annual red-flowered Eurasian poppy (*Papaver rhoeas*) common in fields and cultivated in several varieties

corn rootworm *n* (1892) : any of several chrysomelid beetles (genus *Diabrotica*) whose root-eating larvae are pests esp. of corn

corn·row \ˈkȯrn-ˌrō\ *n* (1946) **1** : a section of hair which is braided usu. flat to the scalp **2** : a hairstyle in which the hair is divided into cornrow sections arranged in rows — **cornrow** *vb*

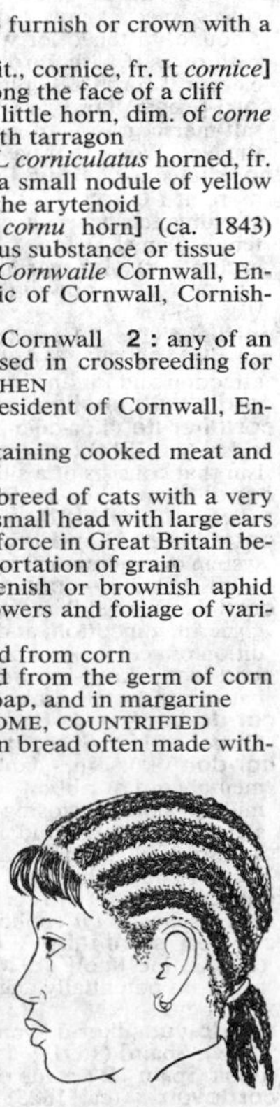

cornrow 2

corn salad *n* [fr. its occurrence as a weed in fields of grain] (1597) : any of several herbs (genus *Valerianella*) of the valerian family;

esp : a low European herb (*V. locusta* syn. *V. olitoria*) that is widely cultivated for its leaves used in salads and as a potherb — called also *lamb's lettuce, mâche*

corn silk *n* (1846) : the silky styles on an ear of Indian corn

corn snow *n* (1935) : granular snow formed by alternate thawing and freezing

corn•stalk \ˈkȯrn-ˌstȯk\ *n* (1645) : a stalk of Indian corn

corn•starch \-ˌstärch\ *n* (1853) : starch made from corn and used in foods as a thickening agent, in making corn syrup and sugars, and in the manufacture of adhesives and sizes for paper and textiles

corn sugar *n* (1850) : DEXTROSE

corn syrup *n* (1903) : a syrup containing dextrins, maltose, and dextrose that is obtained by partial hydrolysis of cornstarch

cor•nu \ˈkȯr-(ˌ)nü, -(ˌ)nyü\ *n, pl* **cor•nua** \-nü-ə, -nyü-\ [L] (1691) : a horn-shaped anatomical part (as of the uterus) — **cor•nu•al** \-nü-əl, -nyü-\ *adj*

cor•nu•co•pia \ˌkȯr-nə-ˈkō-pē-ə, -nyə-\ *n* [LL, fr. L *cornu copiae* horn of plenty] (1508) **1** : a curved goat's horn overflowing with fruit and ears of grain that is used as a decorative motif emblematic of abundance **2** : an inexhaustible store : ABUNDANCE **3** : a receptacle shaped like a horn or cone — **cor•nu•co•pi•an** \-pē-ən\ *adj*

cor•nu•to \kȯr-ˈnü-(ˌ)tō, -ˈnyü-\ *n, pl* **-tos** [It, fr. L *cornutus* having horns, fr. *cornu*] (1598) : CUCKOLD

corn whiskey *n* (1780) : whiskey distilled from a mash made up of not less than 80 percent corn — compare BOURBON

¹**corny** \ˈkȯr-nē\ *adj* **corn•i•er; -est** (14c) **1** *archaic* : tasting strongly of malt **2** : of or relating to corn **3** : mawkishly old-fashioned : tiresomely simple and sentimental ⟨told ~ jokes⟩ — **corn•i•ly** \ˈkȯr-nə-lē\ *adv* — **corn•i•ness** \ˈkȯr-nē-nəs\ *n*

²**corny** *adj* **corn•i•er; -est** (1689) : relating to or having corns on the feet

cor•o•dy *or* **cor•ro•dy** \ˈkȯr-ə-dē, ˈkär-\ *n, pl* **-dies** [ME *corrodie,* fr. AF, fr. ML *corrodium*] (15c) : an allowance of provisions for maintenance dispensed as a charity

co•rol•la \kə-ˈrä-lə, -ˈrō-\ *n* [NL, fr. L, dim. of *corona*] (ca. 1753) : the part of a flower that consists of the separate or fused petals and constitutes the inner whorl of the perianth — **co•rol•late** \kə-ˈrä-lət; ˈkȯr-ə-ˌlāt, ˈkär-\ *adj*

cor•ol•lary \ˈkȯr-ə-ˌler-ē, ˈkär-, -le-rē, *Brit* kə-ˈrä-lə-rē\ *n, pl* **-lar•ies** [ME *corolarie,* fr. LL *corollarium,* fr. L, money paid for a garland, gratuity, fr. *corolla*] (14c) **1** : a proposition inferred immediately from a proved proposition with little or no additional proof **2 a** : something that naturally follows : RESULT **b** : something that incidentally or naturally accompanies or parallels — **corollary** *adj*

cor•o•man•del \ˌkȯr-ə-ˈman-dᵊl, ˌkär-\ *n* [*Coromandel* coast region, India] (1843) : CALAMANDER

coromandel screen *n, often cap C* (1926) : a Chinese lacquered folding screen

co•ro•na \kə-ˈrō-nə\ *n* [L, garland, crown, cornice — more at CROWN] (1548) **1** : the projecting part of a classic cornice **2 a** : a usu. colored circle often seen around and close to a luminous body (as the sun or moon) caused by diffraction produced by suspended droplets or occas. particles of dust **b** : the tenuous outermost part of the atmosphere of a star (as the sun) **c** : a circle of light made by the apparent convergence of the streamers of the aurora borealis **d** : the upper portion of a bodily part (as a tooth or the skull) **e** : an appendage or series of united appendages on the inner side of the corolla in some flowers (as the daffodil, jonquil, or milkweed) **f** : a faint glow adjacent to the surface of an electrical conductor at high voltage **3** [fr. *La Corona,* a trademark] : a long cigar having the sides straight to the end to be lit and being roundly blunt at the other end

Corona Aus•tra•lis \-ȯ-ˈstrā-ləs, -ä-\ *n* [NL (gen. *Coronae Australis*), lit., southern crown] (1594) : a southern constellation adjoining Sagittarius on the south

Corona Bo•re•al•is \-ˌbȯr-ē-ˈa-ləs\ *n* [NL (gen. *Coronae Borealis*), lit., northern crown] (1615) : a northern constellation between Hercules and Boötes

cor•o•nach \ˈkȯr-ə-nək, ˈkär-\ *n* [ScGael *corranach* & Ir *corânach*] (1530) : a funeral dirge sung or played on the bagpipes in Scotland and Ireland

co•ro•na•graph *also* **co•ro•no•graph** \kə-ˈrō-nə-ˌgraf\ *n* (1885) : a telescope for observation of the sun's corona

¹**cor•o•nal** *also* **cor•o•nel** \ˈkȯr-ə-nᵊl, ˈkär-\ *n* [ME *coronal,* fr. AF, fr. L *coronalis* of a crown, fr. *corona*] (14c) : a circlet for the head usu. implying rank or dignity

²**co•ro•nal** \ˈkȯr-ə-nᵊl, ˈkär-; kə-ˈrō-\ *adj* (14c) **1 a** : lying in the direction of the coronal suture **b** : of or relating to the frontal plane that passes through the long axis of the body **2** : of or relating to a corona or crown

coronal suture *n* (1615) : a suture extending across the skull between the parietal and frontal bones

co•ro•na ra•di•a•ta \kə-ˈrō-nə-ˌrā-dē-ˈä-tə, -ˈā-tə\ *n, pl* **co•ro•nae ra•di•a•tae** \-(ˌ)nē-ˌrā-dē-ˈä-(ˌ)tē, -ˈā-(ˌ)tē\ [NL, lit., crown with rays] (1892) : the zone of small follicular cells immediately surrounding the ovum in the graafian follicle and accompanying the ovum on its discharge from the follicle

¹**cor•o•nary** \ˈkȯr-ə-ˌner-ē, ˈkär-, -ˌne-rē\ *adj* (1610) **1** : of, relating to, resembling, or being a crown or coronal **2** : of, relating to, or being the coronary arteries or veins of the heart; *broadly* : of or relating to the heart

²**coronary** *n, pl* **-nar•ies** (1893) **1 a** : CORONARY ARTERY **b** : CORONARY VEIN **2** : CORONARY THROMBOSIS; *broadly* : HEART ATTACK

coronary artery *n* (1741) : either of two arteries that arise one from the left and one from the right side of the aorta immediately above the semilunar valves and supply the tissues of the heart itself

coronary heart disease *n* (1949) : a condition and esp. one caused by atherosclerosis that reduces blood flow through the coronary arteries to the heart and typically results in chest pain or heart damage — called also *coronary artery disease*

coronary occlusion *n* (1940) : the partial or complete blocking (as by a thrombus, by spasm, or by sclerosis) of a coronary artery

coronary sinus *n* (1831) : a venous channel that is derived from the sinus venosus, is continuous with the largest of the cardiac veins, receives most of the blood from the walls of the heart, and empties into the right atrium

coronary thrombosis *n* (1912) : the blocking of a coronary artery of the heart by a thrombus

coronary vein *n* (1686) : any of several veins that drain the tissues of the heart and empty into the coronary sinus

cor•o•nate \ˈkȯr-ə-ˌnāt, ˈkär-\ *vt* **-nat•ed; -nat•ing** [L *coronatus,* pp. of *coronare* to crown, fr. *corona*] (ca. 1623) : CROWN 1a

cor•o•na•tion \ˌkȯr-ə-ˈnā-shən, ˌkär-\ *n* [ME *coronacion,* fr. AF, fr. *coroner* to crown] (14c) : the act or occasion of crowning; *also* : accession to the highest office

co•ro•na•vi•rus \kə-ˈrō-nə-ˌvī-rəs\ *n* [NL, fr. *corona* + *virus*] (1968) : any of a family (*Coronaviridae* and esp. genus *Coronavirus*) of single-stranded RNA viruses that have a lipid envelope studded with club-shaped projections, infect birds and many mammals including humans, and include the causative agent of SARS

cor•o•ner \ˈkȯr-ə-nər, ˈkär-\ *n* [ME, an officer of the crown, fr. AF, fr. *corone* crown, fr. L *corona*] (15c) : a usu. elected public officer whose principal duty is to inquire by an inquest into the cause of any death which there is reason to suppose is not due to natural causes — compare MEDICAL EXAMINER

cor•o•net \ˌkȯr-ə-ˈnet, ˌkär-\ *n* [MF *coronette,* fr. OF *coronete,* fr. *corone*] (15c) **1** : a small or lesser crown usu. signifying a rank below that of a sovereign **2** : a wreath or band for the head usu. for wear by women on formal occasions **3** : the lower part of a horse's pastern where the horn terminates in skin — see HORSE illustration

co•ro•tate \(ˌ)kō-ˈrō-ˌtāt\ *vi* (1962) : to rotate in conjunction with or at the same rate as another rotating body — **co•ro•ta•tion** \ˌkō-rō-ˈtā-shən\ *n*

corp *abbr* **1** corporal **2** corporation

corpora *pl of* CORPUS

¹**cor•po•ral** \ˈkȯr-p(ə-)rəl\ *n* [ME, fr. AF, fr. ML *corporale,* fr. L, neut. of *corporalis;* fr. the doctrine that the bread of the Eucharist becomes or represents the body of Christ] (14c) : a linen cloth on which the eucharistic elements are placed

²**corporal** *adj* [ME, fr. AF, fr. L *corporalis,* fr. *corpor-, corpus* body — more at MIDRIFF] (14c) **1** *obs* : CORPOREAL, PHYSICAL **2** : of, relating to, or affecting the body ⟨~ punishment⟩ — **cor•po•ral•ly** \-p(ə-)rə-lē\ *adv*

³**corporal** *n* [MF, lowest noncommissioned officer, alter. of *caporal,* fr. OIt *caporale,* fr. *capo* head, fr. L *caput* — more at HEAD] (1579) : a noncommissioned officer ranking in the army above a private first class and below a sergeant and in the marine corps above a lance corporal and below a sergeant

cor•po•ral•i•ty \ˌkȯr-pə-ˈra-lə-tē\ *n, pl* **-ties** (14c) : the quality or state of being or having a body or a material or physical existence

corporal's guard *n* (1832) **1** : the small detachment commanded by a corporal **2** : a small group

cor•po•rate \ˈkȯr-p(ə-)rət\ *adj* [L *corporatus,* pp. of *corporare* to make into a body, fr. *corpor-, corpus*] (1512) **1 a** : formed into an association and endowed by law with the rights and liabilities of an individual : INCORPORATED **b** : of or relating to a corporation ⟨a plan to reorganize the ~ structure⟩ **c** : of, relating to, or being the large corporations of a country or region considered as a unit ⟨the latest trend in ~ America⟩ **d** : having qualities (as commercialism or lack of originality) associated with large corporations or attributed to their influence or control ⟨~ rock music⟩ ⟨~ art⟩ **2** : of, relating to, or formed into a unified body of individuals ⟨human law arises by the ~ action of a people —G. H. Sabine⟩ **3** : CORPORATIVE 2 — **cor•po•rate•ly** *adv*

cor•po•rate–wide \-ˌwīd\ *adj* (1974) : extending throughout or involving an entire corporation

cor•po•ra•tion \ˌkȯr-pə-ˈrā-shən\ *n* (15c) **1 a** : a group of merchants or traders united in a trade guild **b** : the municipal authorities of a town or city **2** : a body formed and authorized by law to act as a single person although constituted by one or more persons and legally endowed with various rights and duties including the capacity of succession **3** : an association of employers and employees in a basic industry or of members of a profession organized as an organ of political representation in a corporative state **4** : POTBELLY 1

cor•po•rat•ism \ˈkȯr-p(ə-)rə-ˌti-zəm\ *n* (1890) : the organization of a society into industrial and professional corporations serving as organs of political representation and exercising control over persons and activities within their jurisdiction — **cor•po•rat•ist** \-p(ə-)rə-tist\ *adj*

cor•po•ra•tive \ˈkȯr-pə-ˌrā-tiv, -p(ə-)rə-\ *adj* (1833) **1** : of or relating to a corporation **2** : of or relating to corporatism ⟨a ~ state⟩

cor•po•ra•tiv•ism \ˈkȯr-pə-ˌrā-ti-ˌvi-zəm, -p(ə-)rə-\ *n* (1930) : CORPORATISM

cor•po•rat•ize \ˈkȯr-p(ə-)rə-ˌtīz\ *vt* **-ized; -iz•ing** (1974) : to subject to corporate ownership or control ⟨afraid that medicine was becoming *corporatized*⟩ — **cor•po•rat•i•za•tion** \ˌkȯr-p(ə-)rə-tə-ˈzā-shən\ *n*

cor•po•ra•tor \ˈkȯr-pə-ˌrā-tər\ *n* (1784) : a corporation organizer, member, or stockholder

cor•po•re•al \kȯr-ˈpȯr-ē-əl\ *adj* [ME, fr. L *corporeus* of the body, fr. *corpor-, corpus*] (15c) **1** : having, consisting of, or relating to a physical material body: as **a** : not spiritual **b** : not immaterial or intangible : SUBSTANTIAL **2** *archaic* : CORPORAL ***syn*** see MATERIAL — **cor•po•re•al•ly** \-ē-ə-lē\ *adv* — **cor•po•re•al•ness** *n*

cor•po•re•al•i•ty \(ˌ)kȯr-ˌpȯr-ē-ˈa-lə-tē\ *n, pl* **-ties** (1651) : corporeal existence

cor•po•re•i•ty \ˌkȯr-pə-ˈrē-ə-tē, -ˈrā-\ *n, pl* **-ties** (1610) : the quality or state of having or being a body : MATERIALITY

cor•po•sant \ˈkȯr-pə-ˌsant, -ˌzant\ *n* [Pg *corpo-santo,* lit., holy body] (ca. 1595) : SAINT ELMO'S FIRE

corps \ˈkȯr\ *n, pl* **corps** \ˈkȯrz\ [F, fr. OF *cors,* fr. L *corpus* body] (1707) **1 a** : an organized subdivision of the military establishment ⟨Marine *Corps*⟩ ⟨Signal *Corps*⟩ **b** : a tactical unit usu. consisting of two or more divisions and auxiliary arms and services **2** : a group of

\ə\ **abut** \ᵊ\ kitten, F table \ər\ **further** \a\ **ash** \ā\ **ace** \ä\ mop, mar \au̇\ **out** \ch\ **chin** \e\ bet \ē\ **easy** \g\ **go** \i\ **hit** \ī\ **ice** \j\ **job** \ŋ\ **sing** \ō\ **go** \ȯ\ **law** \ȯi\ **boy** \th\ **thin** \t͟h\ **the** \ü\ **loot** \u̇\ **foot** \y\ **yet** \zh\ vision, beige \k̲, ⁿ, œ, ue, ʸ\ *see* Guide to Pronunciation

persons associated together or acting under common direction; *esp* : a body of persons having a common activity or occupation ⟨the press ~⟩ **3 :** CORPS DE BALLET

corps de bal·let \ˌkȯr-də-(ˌ)ba-ˈlā\ *n, pl* **corps de ballet** *same or* ˌkȯrz-də-\ [F] (1818) : the ensemble of a ballet company

corps d'elite \ˌkȯr-dā-ˈlēt\ *n, pl* **corps d'elite** *same or* ˌkȯrz-dā-\ [F *corps d'élite*] (1832) **1 :** a body of picked troops **2 :** a group of the best people in a category

corpse \ˈkȯrps\ *n* [ME *corps,* fr. AF *cors, corps,* fr. L *corpus*] (13c) **1** *archaic* : a human or animal body whether living or dead **2 a :** a dead body esp. of a human being **b :** the remains of something discarded or defunct ⟨the ~*s* of rusting cars⟩

corps·man \ˈkȯr(z)-mən\ *n* (1901) **1 :** an enlisted man trained to give first aid and minor medical treatment **2 :** a member of a government-sponsored service corps

cor·pu·lence \ˈkȯr-pyə-lən(t)s\ *n* (1547) : the state of being corpulent

cor·pu·len·cy \-lən(t)-sē\ *n, pl* **-cies** (1577) : CORPULENCE

cor·pu·lent \-lənt\ *adj* [ME, fr. L *corpulentus,* fr. *corpus*] (14c) : having a large bulky body : OBESE — **cor·pu·lent·ly** *adv*

cor pul·mo·na·le \ˌkȯr-ˌpu̇l-mə-ˈnä-lē, -ˌpəl-, -ˈna-\ *n, pl* **cor·dia pul·mo·na·lia** \ˈkȯr-dē-ə-ˌpu̇l-mə-ˈnä-lē-ə, -ˌpəl-, -ˈna-\ [NL, lit., pulmonary heart] (1857) : disease of the heart characterized by hypertrophy and dilatation of the right ventricle and secondary to disease of the lungs or their blood vessels

cor·pus \ˈkȯr-pəs\ *n, pl* **cor·po·ra** \-p(ə-)rə\ [ME, fr. L] (15c) **1 :** the body of a human or animal esp. when dead **2 a :** the main part or body of a bodily structure or organ ⟨the ~ of the uterus⟩ **b :** the main body or corporeal substance of a thing; *specif* : the principal of a fund or estate as distinct from income or interest **3 a :** all the writings or works of a particular kind or on a particular subject; *esp* : the complete works of an author **b :** a collection or body of knowledge or evidence; *esp* : a collection of recorded utterances used as a basis for the descriptive analysis of a language

corpus al·la·tum \-ə-ˈlā-təm, -ˈlä-\ *n, pl* **corpora al·la·ta** \-ˈlā-tə, -ˈlä-tə\ [NL, lit., applied body] (1947) : one of a pair of separate or fused bodies in many insects that are sometimes closely associated with the corpora cardiaca and that secrete hormones (as juvenile hormone)

corpus cal·lo·sum \-ka-ˈlō-səm\ *n, pl* **corpora cal·lo·sa** \-sə\ [NL, lit., callous body] (1677) : the great band of commissural fibers uniting the cerebral hemispheres of higher mammals including humans — see BRAIN illustration

corpus car·di·a·cum \-kär-ˈdī-ə-kəm\ *n, pl* **corpora car·di·a·ca** \-ə-kə\ [NL, lit., cardiac body] (1960) : one of a pair of separate or fused bodies of nervous tissue in many insects that lie posterior to the brain and function in the storage and secretion of brain hormone

Cor·pus Chris·ti \ˈkȯr-pəs-ˈkris-tē\ *n* [ME, fr. ML, lit., body of Christ] (14c) : the Thursday after Trinity observed as a Roman Catholic festival in honor of the Eucharist

cor·pus·cle \ˈkȯr-(ˌ)pə-səl\ *n* [L *corpusculum,* dim. of *corpus*] (1660) **1 :** a minute particle **2 a :** a living cell; *esp* : one (as a red or white blood cell or a cell in cartilage or bone) not aggregated into continuous tissues **b :** any of various small circumscribed multicellular bodies — **cor·pus·cu·lar** \kȯr-ˈpəs-kyə-lər\ *adj*

cor·pus de·lic·ti \ˈkȯr-pəs-di-ˈlik-ˌtī, -(ˌ)tē\ *n, pl* **corpora delicti** [NL, lit., body of the crime] (1818) **1 :** the substantial and fundamental fact necessary to prove the commission of a crime **2 :** the material substance (as the body of the victim of a murder) upon which a crime has been committed

corpus lu·te·um \-ˈlü-tē-əm\ *n, pl* **corpora lu·tea** \-tē-ə\ [NL, lit., yellowish body] (1788) : a yellowish mass of progesterone-secreting endocrine tissue that forms immediately after ovulation from the ruptured graafian follicle in the mammalian ovary

corpus striatum *n, pl* **corpora striata** [NL, lit., striated body] (1851) : either of a pair of masses of nervous tissue within the brain that contain two large nuclei of gray matter separated by sheets of white matter

corr *abbr* **1** correct; corrected; correction **2** correspondence; correspondent; corresponding **3** corrupt; corruption

cor·rade \kə-ˈrād\ *vb* **cor·rad·ed; cor·rad·ing** [L *corradere* to scrape together, fr. *com-* + *radere* to scrape — more at RODENT] *vt* (1646) : to wear away by abrasion ~ *vi* : to crumble away through abrasion — **cor·ra·sion** \-ˈrā-zhən\ *n* — **cor·ra·sive** \-ˈrā-siv, -ziv\ *adj*

[1]**cor·ral** \kə-ˈral, -ˈrel\ *n* [Sp, fr. VL **currale* enclosure for vehicles, fr. L *currus* cart, fr. *currere* to run — more at CAR] (1582) **1 :** a pen or enclosure for confining or capturing livestock **2 :** an enclosure made with wagons for defense of an encampment

[2]**corral** *vt* **cor·ralled; cor·ral·ling** (1847) **1 :** to enclose in a corral **2 :** to arrange (wagons) so as to form a corral **3 :** COLLECT, GATHER ⟨*corralling* votes for the upcoming election⟩

[1]**cor·rect** \kə-ˈrekt\ *vt* [ME, fr. L *correctus,* pp. of *corrigere,* fr. *com-* + *regere* to lead straight — more at RIGHT] (14c) **1 a :** to make or set right : AMEND ⟨~ an error⟩ **b :** COUNTERACT, NEUTRALIZE ⟨~ a harmful tendency⟩ **c :** to alter or adjust so as to bring to some standard or required condition ⟨~ a lens for spherical aberration⟩ **2 a :** to punish (as a child) with a view to reforming or improving **b :** to point out usu. for amendment the errors or faults of ⟨spent the day ~*ing* tests⟩ — **cor·rect·able** \-ˈrek-tə-bəl\ *adj* — **cor·rec·tor** \-ˈrek-tər\ *n*

syn CORRECT, RECTIFY, EMEND, REMEDY, REDRESS, AMEND, REFORM, REVISE mean to make right what is wrong. CORRECT implies taking action to remove errors, faults, deviations, defects ⟨*correct* your spelling⟩. RECTIFY implies a more essential changing to make something right, just, or properly controlled or directed ⟨*rectify* a misguided policy⟩. EMEND specif. implies correction of a text or manuscript ⟨*emend* a text⟩. REMEDY implies removing or making harmless a cause of trouble, harm, or evil ⟨set out to *remedy* the evils of the world⟩. REDRESS implies making compensation or reparation for an unfairness, injustice, or imbalance ⟨*redress* past social injustices⟩. AMEND, REFORM, REVISE imply an improving by making corrective changes, AMEND usu. suggesting slight changes ⟨*amend* a law⟩, REFORM implying drastic change ⟨plans to *reform* the court system⟩, and REVISE suggesting a careful examination of something and the making of necessary changes ⟨*revise* the schedule⟩. ***syn*** see in addition PUNISH

[2]**correct** *adj* [ME, corrected, fr. L *correctus,* fr. pp. of *corrigere*] (1668) **1 :** conforming to an approved or conventional standard ⟨~ behavior⟩ **2 :** conforming to or agreeing with fact, logic, or known truth ⟨a ~ response⟩ **3 :** conforming to a set figure ⟨enclosed the ~ return postage⟩ **4 :** conforming to the strict requirements of a specific ideology or set of beliefs or values ⟨environmentally ~⟩ ⟨spiritually ~⟩ — **cor·rect·ly** \kə-ˈrek(t)-lē\ *adv* — **cor·rect·ness** \-ˈrek(t)-nəs\ *n*

syn CORRECT, ACCURATE, EXACT, PRECISE, NICE, RIGHT mean conforming to fact, standard, or truth. CORRECT usu. implies freedom from fault or error ⟨*correct* answers⟩ ⟨socially *correct* dress⟩. ACCURATE implies fidelity to fact or truth attained by exercise of care ⟨an *accurate* description⟩. EXACT stresses a very strict agreement with fact, standard, or truth ⟨*exact* measurements⟩. PRECISE adds to EXACT an emphasis on sharpness of definition or delimitation ⟨*precise* calibration⟩. NICE stresses great precision and delicacy of adjustment or discrimination ⟨makes *nice* distinctions⟩. RIGHT is close to CORRECT but has a stronger positive emphasis on conformity to fact or truth rather than mere absence of error or fault ⟨the *right* thing to do⟩.

corrected time *n* (ca. 1891) : a boat's elapsed time less its time allowance in yacht racing

cor·rec·tion \kə-ˈrek-shən\ *n* (14c) **1 :** the action or an instance of correcting: as **a :** AMENDMENT, RECTIFICATION **b :** REBUKE, PUNISHMENT **c :** a bringing into conformity with a standard **d :** NEUTRALIZATION, COUNTERACTION ⟨~ of acidity⟩ **2 :** a decline in market price or business activity following and counteracting a rise **3 a :** something substituted in place of what is wrong ⟨marking ~*s* on the students' papers⟩ **b :** a quantity applied by way of correcting (as for adjustment of an instrument) **4 :** the treatment and rehabilitation of offenders through a program involving penal custody, parole, and probation; *also* : the administration of such treatment as a matter of public policy — usu. used in pl. — **cor·rec·tion·al** \-shnəl, -shə-nᵊl\ *adj*

correction fluid *n* (1968) : a liquid used to paint over typing or writing errors

cor·rec·ti·tude \kə-ˈrek-tə-ˌtüd, -ˌtyüd\ *n* [blend of *correct* and *rectitude*] (1893) : correctness or propriety of conduct

cor·rec·tive \kə-ˈrek-tiv\ *adj* (1531) : intended to correct ⟨~ lenses⟩ ⟨~ punishment⟩ — **corrective** *n* — **cor·rec·tive·ly** *adv*

[1]**cor·re·late** \ˈkȯr-ə-lət, ˈkär-, -ˌlāt\ *n* [back-formation fr. *correlation*] (1643) **1 :** either of two things so related that one directly implies or is complementary to the other (as husband and wife) **2 :** a phenomenon that accompanies another phenomenon, is usu. parallel to it, and is related in some way to it ⟨precise electrical ~*s* of conscious thinking in the human brain —Bayard Webster⟩ — **correlate** *adj*

[2]**cor·re·late** \-ˌlāt\ *vb* **-lat·ed; -lat·ing** *vi* (ca. 1742) : to bear reciprocal or mutual relations : CORRESPOND ~ *vt* **1 a :** to establish a mutual or reciprocal relation between ⟨~ activities in the lab and the field⟩ **b :** to show correlation or a causal relationship between **2 :** to present or set forth so as to show relationship ⟨he ~*s* the findings of the scientists, the psychologists, and the mystics —Eugene Exman⟩ — **cor·re·lat·able** \-ˌlā-tə-bəl\ *adj* — **cor·re·lat·or** \-ˌlā-tər\ *n*

cor·re·la·tion \ˌkȯr-ə-ˈlā-shən, ˌkär-\ *n* [ML *correlation-, correlatio,* fr. L *com-* + *relation-, relatio* relation] (1561) **1 :** the state or relation of being correlated; *specif* : a relation existing between phenomena or things or between mathematical or statistical variables which tend to vary, be associated, or occur together in a way not expected on the basis of chance alone ⟨the obviously high positive ~ between scholastic aptitude and college entrance —J. B. Conant⟩ **2 :** the act of correlating — **cor·re·la·tion·al** \-shnəl, -shə-nᵊl\ *adj*

correlation coefficient *n* (1895) : a number or function that indicates the degree of correlation between two sets of data or between two random variables and that is equal to their covariance divided by the product of their standard deviations

cor·rel·a·tive \kə-ˈre-lə-tiv\ *adj* (1530) **1 :** naturally related : CORRESPONDING **2 :** reciprocally related **3 :** regularly used together but typically not adjacent ⟨the ~ conjunctions *either . . . or*⟩ — **correlative** *n* — **cor·rel·a·tive·ly** *adv*

cor·re·spond \ˌkȯr-ə-ˈspänd, ˌkär-\ *vi* [MF or ML; MF *correspondre,* fr. ML *correspondēre,* fr. L *com-* + *respondēre* to respond] (1529) **1 a :** to be in conformity or agreement ⟨the ideal failed . . . to ~ with the reality —J. R. Sutherland⟩ **b :** to compare closely : MATCH — usu. used with *to* or *with* **c :** to be equivalent or parallel **2 :** to communicate with a person by exchange of letters

cor·re·spon·dence \-ˈspän-dən(t)s\ *n* (15c) **1 a :** the agreement of things with one another **b :** a particular similarity **c :** a relation between sets in which each member of one set is associated with one or more members of the other — compare FUNCTION 5a **2 a :** communication by letters; *also* : the letters exchanged **b :** the news, information, or opinion contributed by a correspondent to a newspaper or periodical

correspondence course *n* (1902) : a course offered by a correspondence school

correspondence school *n* (1889) : a school that teaches nonresident students by mailing them lessons and exercises which upon completion are returned to the school for grading

cor·re·spon·den·cy \ˌkȯr-ə-ˈspän-dən(t)-sē, ˌkär-\ *n, pl* **-cies** (1589) : CORRESPONDENCE

[1]**cor·re·spon·dent** \ˌkȯr-ə-ˈspän-dənt, ˌkär-\ *adj* [ME, fr. MF or ML; MF, fr. ML *correspondent-, correspondens,* prp. of *correspondēre*] (15c) **1 :** CORRESPONDING **2 :** FITTING, CONFORMING — used with *with* or *to* ⟨the outcome was entirely ~ with my wishes⟩

[2]**correspondent** *n* (ca. 1630) **1 a :** one who communicates with another by letter **b :** one who has regular commercial relations with another **c :** one who contributes news or commentary to a publication (as a newspaper) or a radio or television network often from a distant place ⟨a war ~⟩ **2 :** something that corresponds

corresponding *adj* (1579) **1 a :** having or participating in the same relationship (as kind, degree, position, correspondence, or function) esp. with regard to the same or like wholes (as geometric figures or sets) ⟨~ parts of similar triangles⟩ **b :** RELATED, ACCOMPANYING ⟨all rights carry with them ~ responsibilities —W. P. Paepcke⟩ **2 a :** charged with the duty of writing letters ⟨~ secretary⟩ **b :** participating or serving at a distance and by mail ⟨a ~ member of the society⟩ — **cor·re·spond·ing·ly** \-ˈspän-diŋ-lē\ *adv*

corresponding angles *n pl* (1784) : any pair of angles each of which is on the same side of one of two lines cut by a transversal and on the same side of the transversal

cor·re·spon·sive \ˌkȯr-ə-ˈspän(t)-siv, ˌkär-\ *adj* (1606) : mutually responsive

cor·ri·da \kō-ˈrē-thə\ *n* [Sp, lit., act of running] (1802) : BULLFIGHT

cor·ri·dor \ˈkȯr-ə-dər, ˈkär-, -ˌdȯr\ *n* [MF, fr. It dial. (N Italy) *corridore,* fr. *correre* to run, fr. L *currere* — more at CAR] (1719) **1 a :** a passageway (as in a hotel or office building) into which compartments or rooms open **b :** a place or position in which esp. political power is wielded through discussion and deal-making ⟨was excluded from the ~*s* of power after losing the election⟩ **2 :** a usu. narrow passageway or route: as **a :** a narrow strip of land through foreign-held territory **b :** a restricted lane for air traffic **c :** a land path used by migrating animals **3 a :** a densely populated strip of land including two or more major cities ⟨the Northeast ~ stretching from Washington into New England —S. D. Browne⟩ **b :** an area or stretch of land identified by a specific common characteristic or purpose ⟨a ~ of liberalism⟩ ⟨the city's industrial ~⟩

cor·rie \ˈkȯr-ē, ˈkär-ē\ *n* [ScGael *coire,* lit., kettle] (1795) : CIRQUE 3

Cor·rie·dale \-ˌdāl\ *n* [*Corriedale,* ranch in New Zealand] (1902) : any of a breed of rather large usu. hornless sheep developed in New Zealand and raised for mutton and wool

cor·ri·gen·dum \ˌkȯr-ə-ˈjen-dəm, ˌkär-\ *n, pl* **-da** \-də\ [L, neut. of *corrigendus,* gerundive of *corrigere* to correct] (1823) : an error in a printed work discovered after printing and shown with its correction on a separate sheet

cor·ri·gi·ble \ˈkȯr-ə-jə-bəl, ˈkär-\ *adj* [ME, fr. MF, fr. ML *corrigibilis,* fr. L *corrigere*] (15c) : capable of being set right : REPARABLE ⟨a ~ defect⟩ — **cor·ri·gi·bil·i·ty** \ˌkȯr-ə-jə-ˈbi-lə-tē, ˌkär-\ *n*

cor·ri·val \kə-ˈrī-vəl, kȯ-, kō-\ *n* [MF, fr. L *corrivalis,* fr. *com-* + *rivalis* rival] (1579) : RIVAL, COMPETITOR — **corrival** *adj*

cor·rob·o·rant \kə-ˈrä-bə-rənt\ *adj* (1626) *archaic* : having an invigorating effect — used of a medicine

cor·rob·o·rate \kə-ˈrä-bə-ˌrāt\ *vt* **-rat·ed; -rat·ing** [L *corroboratus,* pp. of *corroborare,* fr. *com-* + *robor-, robur* strength] (1529) : to support with evidence or authority : make more certain ***syn*** see CONFIRM — **cor·rob·o·ra·tion** \-ˌrä-bə-ˈrā-shən\ *n* — **cor·rob·o·ra·tive** \-ˈrä-bə-ˌrā-tiv, -ˈrä-b(ə-)rə-\ *adj* — **cor·rob·o·ra·tor** \-ˈrä-bə-ˌrā-tər\ *n* — **cor·rob·o·ra·to·ry** \-ˈrä-b(ə-)rə-ˌtȯr-ē\ *adj*

cor·rob·o·ree \kə-ˈrȯ-bə-rē, -ˈrä-\ *n* [Dharuk (Australian aboriginal language of the Port Jackson area) *garaabara*] (1811) **1 :** a nocturnal festivity with songs and symbolic dances by which the Australian aborigines celebrate events of importance **2** *Austral* **a :** a noisy festivity **b :** TUMULT

cor·rode \kə-ˈrōd\ *vb* **cor·rod·ed; cor·rod·ing** [ME, fr. L *corrodere* to gnaw to pieces, fr. *com-* + *rodere* to gnaw — more at RODENT] *vt* (14c) **1 :** to eat away by degrees as if by gnawing; *esp* : to wear away gradually usu. by chemical action ⟨the metal was *corroded* beyond repair⟩ **2 :** to weaken or destroy gradually : UNDERMINE ⟨manners and miserliness that ~ the human spirit —Bernard De Voto⟩ ~ *vi* : to undergo corrosion — **cor·rod·ible** \-ˈrō-də-bəl\ *adj*

corrody *var of* CORODY

cor·ro·sion \kə-ˈrō-zhən\ *n* [ME, fr. LL *corrosion-, corrosio* act of gnawing, fr. L *corrodere*] (14c) **1 :** the action, process, or effect of corroding **2 :** a product of corroding

cor·ro·sive \-ˈrō-siv, -ziv\ *adj* (14c) **1 :** tending or having the power to corrode ⟨~ acids⟩ ⟨~ action⟩ ⟨the ~ effects of alcoholism⟩ **2 :** bitingly sarcastic ⟨~ satire⟩ — **corrosive** *n* — **cor·ro·sive·ly** *adv* — **cor·ro·sive·ness** *n*

corrosive sublimate *n* (ca. 1747) : MERCURIC CHLORIDE

cor·ru·gate \ˈkȯr-ə-ˌgāt, ˈkär-\ *vb* **-gat·ed; -gat·ing** [L *corrugatus,* pp. of *corrugare,* fr. *com-* + *ruga* wrinkle; prob. akin to Lith *raukas* wrinkle — more at ROUGH] *vt* (1620) : to form or shape into wrinkles or folds or into alternating ridges and grooves : FURROW ~ *vi* : to become corrugated

corrugated *adj* (1590) : having corrugations ⟨~ paper⟩; *also* : made of corrugated material (as cardboard) ⟨~ boxes⟩

cor·ru·ga·tion \ˌkȯr-ə-ˈgā-shən, ˌkär-\ *n* (1528) **1 :** the act of corrugating **2 :** a ridge or groove of a surface that has been corrugated

[1]**cor·rupt** \kə-ˈrəpt\ *vb* [ME, fr. L *corruptus,* pp. of *corrumpere,* fr. *com-* + *rumpere* to break — more at REAVE] *vt* (14c) **1 a :** to change from good to bad in morals, manners, or actions; *also* : BRIBE **b :** to degrade with unsound principles or moral values **2 :** ROT, SPOIL **3 :** to subject (a person) to corruption of blood **4 :** to alter from the original or correct form or version ⟨the file was ~*ed*⟩ ~ *vi* **1 a :** to become tainted or rotten **b :** to become morally debased **2 :** to cause disintegration or ruin ***syn*** see DEBASE — **cor·rupt·er** *also* **cor·rup·tor** \-ˈrəp-tər\ *n* — **cor·rupt·ibil·i·ty** \-ˌrəp-tə-ˈbi-lə-tē\ *n* — **cor·rupt·ible** \-ˈrəp-tə-bəl\ *adj* — **cor·rupt·ibly** \-blē\ *adv*

[2]**corrupt** *adj* [ME, fr. AF or L; AF, fr. L *corruptus*] (14c) **1 a :** morally degenerate and perverted : DEPRAVED **b :** characterized by improper conduct (as bribery or the selling of favors) ⟨~ judges⟩ **2 :** PUTRID, TAINTED **3 :** adulterated or debased by change from an original or correct condition ⟨a ~ version of the text⟩ ***syn*** see VICIOUS — **cor·rupt·ly** \-ˈrəp(t)-lē\ *adv* — **cor·rupt·ness** \-ˈrəp(t)-nəs\ *n*

cor·rup·tion \kə-ˈrəp-shən\ *n* (14c) **1 a :** impairment of integrity, virtue, or moral principle : DEPRAVITY **b :** DECAY, DECOMPOSITION **c :** inducement to wrong by improper or unlawful means (as bribery) **d :** a departure from the original or from what is pure or correct **2** *archaic* : an agency or influence that corrupts **3** *chiefly dial* : PUS

cor·rup·tion·ist \-sh(ə-)nist\ *n* (1810) : one who practices or defends corruption esp. in politics

corruption of blood (1563) : the effect of an attainder which bars a person from inheriting, retaining, or transmitting any estate, rank, or title

cor·rup·tive \kə-ˈrəp-tiv\ *adj* (15c) : producing or tending to produce corruption — **cor·rup·tive·ly** *adv*

cor·sage \kȯr-ˈsäzh, -ˈsäj, ˈkȯr-ˌ\ *n* [F, bust, bodice, fr. OF, bust, fr. *cors* body, fr. L *corpus*] (1830) **1 :** the waist or bodice of a dress **2 :** an arrangement of flowers worn as a fashion accessory

cor·sair \ˈkȯr-ˌser; kȯr-ˈ\ *n* [MF & OIt; MF *corsaire* pirate, fr. Old Occitan *corsari,* fr. OIt *corsaro,* fr. ML *cursarius,* fr. L *cursus* course — more at COURSE] (1549) : PIRATE; *esp* : a privateer of the Barbary Coast

corse \ˈkȯrs\ *n* [ME *cors,* fr. AF] (13c) *archaic* : CORPSE

corse·let *for 1* ˈkȯr-slət, *for 2* ˌkȯr-sə-ˈlet\ *n* (1563) **1** *or* **cors·let** [MF, dim. of *cors* body, bodice] : a piece of armor covering the trunk **2** *or* **cor·se·lette** [fr. *Corselette,* a trademark] : an undergarment combining girdle and brassiere

[1]**cor·set** \ˈkȯr-sət\ *n* [ME, fr. AF, dim. of *cors*] (13c) **1 :** a usu. close-fitting and often laced medieval jacket **2 :** a woman's close-fitting boned supporting undergarment that is often hooked and laced and that extends from above or beneath the bust or from the waist to below the hips and has garters attached

[2]**corset** *vt* (1845) **1 :** to dress in or fit with a corset **2 :** to restrict closely : control rigidly

cor·se·tiere \ˌkȯr-sə-ˈtir, -ˈtyer\ *n* [F *corsetière,* fem. of *corsetier,* fr. *corset*] (1848) : one who makes, fits, or sells corsets, girdles, or brassieres

cor·set·ry \ˈkȯr-sə-trē\ *n* (1904) : underwear (as corsets, girdles, and brassieres) meant to shape a woman's body

cor·tege *also* **cor·tège** \kȯr-ˈtezh, ˈkȯr-ˌ\ *n* [F *cortège,* fr. It *corteggio,* fr. *corteggiare* to court, fr. *corte* court, fr. L *cohort-, cohors* enclosure — more at COURT] (1648) **1 :** a train of attendants : RETINUE **2 :** PROCESSION; *esp* : a funeral procession

cor·tex \ˈkȯr-ˌteks\ *n, pl* **cor·ti·ces** \ˈkȯr-tə-ˌsēz\ *or* **cor·tex·es** [L *cortic-, cortex* bark — more at CUIRASS] (1677) **1 a** (1) **:** the outer or superficial part of an organ or bodily structure (as the kidney, adrenal gland, or cerebellum or a bone); *esp* : CEREBRAL CORTEX (2) **:** the proteinaceous usu. pigmented layer of a hair below the cuticle **b :** the outer part of some organisms (as paramecia) **2 :** a plant bark or rind (as cinchona) used medicinally **3 a :** the typically parenchymatous layer of tissue external to the vascular tissue and internal to the corky or epidermal tissues of a green plant; *broadly* : all tissues external to the xylem **b :** an outer or investing layer of various algae, lichens, or fungi

cor·ti·cal \ˈkȯr-ti-kəl\ *adj* (1671) **1 :** of, relating to, or consisting of cortex **2 :** involving or resulting from the action or condition of the cerebral cortex — **cor·ti·cal·ly** \-k(ə-)lē\ *adv*

cortico- *comb form* : cortex ⟨*cortico*tropin⟩

cor·ti·coid \ˈkȯr-ti-ˌkȯid\ *n* (1941) : CORTICOSTEROID — **corticoid** *adj*

cor·ti·co·ste·roid \ˌkȯr-ti-kō-ˈstir-ˌȯid *also* -ˈster-\ *n* (1944) : any of various adrenal-cortex steroids (as corticosterone, cortisone, and aldosterone) used medically esp. as anti-inflammatory agents — compare GLUCOCORTICOID, MINERALOCORTICOID

cor·ti·co·ste·rone \ˌkȯr-tə-ˈkäs-tə-ˌrōn, -ti-kō-stə-ˈ; ˌkȯr-ti-kō-ˈstir-ˌōn, -ˈster-\ *n* (1937) : a colorless crystalline corticosteroid $C_{21}H_{30}O_4$ that is important in protein and carbohydrate metabolism

cor·ti·co·tro·pin \ˌkȯr-ti-kō-ˈtrō-pən\ *also* **cor·ti·co·tro·phin** \-fən\ *n* (1946) : ACTH; *also* : a preparation of ACTH that is used esp. in the treatment of rheumatoid arthritis and rheumatic fever

cor·ti·sol \ˈkȯr-tə-ˌsȯl, -ˌzȯl, -ˌsōl, -ˌzōl\ *n* [*cortisone* + [1]*-ol*] (1951) : a glucocorticoid $C_{21}H_{30}O_5$ produced by the adrenal cortex upon stimulation by ACTH that mediates various metabolic processes (as gluconeogenesis), has anti-inflammatory and immunosuppressive properties, and whose levels in the blood may become elevated in response to physical or psychological stress — called also *hydrocortisone*

cor·ti·sone \-ˌsōn, -ˌzōn\ *n* [alter. of *corticosterone*] (1949) : a glucocorticoid $C_{21}H_{28}O_5$ of the adrenal cortex used in synthetic form esp. as an anti-inflammatory agent (as for rheumatoid arthritis)

Cort·land \ˈkȯrt-lənd\ *n* [prob. fr. *Cortland* Co., New York] (1935) : a juicy apple having red skin and crisp mildly tart white flesh

co·run·dum \kə-ˈrən-dəm\ *n* [Tamil *kuruntam;* akin to Skt *kuruvinda* ruby] (1804) : a very hard mineral that consists of aluminum oxide occurring in massive and crystalline forms, that can be synthesized, and that is used for gemstones (as ruby and sapphire) and as an abrasive

co·rus·cant \kə-ˈrəs-kənt\ *adj* (15c) : SHINING, GLITTERING

cor·us·cate \ˈkȯr-ə-ˌskāt, ˈkär-\ *vi* **-cat·ed; -cat·ing** [L *coruscatus,* pp. of *coruscare* to flash] (1705) **1 :** to give off or reflect light in bright beams or flashes : SPARKLE **2 :** to be brilliant or showy in technique or style

cor·us·ca·tion \ˌkȯr-ə-ˈskā-shən, ˌkär-\ *n* (15c) **1 :** GLITTER, SPARKLE **2 :** a flash of wit

cor·vée \ˈkȯr-ˌvā, kȯr-ˈ\ *n* [F, fr. ML *corrogata,* fr. L, fem. of *corrogatus,* pp. of *corrogare* to collect, requisition, fr. *com-* + *rogare* to ask — more at RIGHT] (14c) **1 :** unpaid labor (as toward constructing roads) due from a feudal vassal to his lord **2 :** labor exacted in lieu of taxes by public authorities esp. for highway construction or repair

corves *pl of* CORF

cor·vette \kȯr-ˈvet\ *n* [F, fr. MF, prob. fr. MD *corf,* a kind of ship, lit., basket — more at CORF] (1636) **1 :** a warship ranking in the old sailing navies next below a frigate **2 :** a highly maneuverable armed escort ship that is smaller than a destroyer

cor·vid \ˈkȯr-vəd\ *n* [NL *Corvidae,* fr. *Corvus,* genus name, fr. L, raven] (ca. 1909) : any of a family (Corvidae) of stout-billed passerine birds including the crows, jays, magpies, and the raven

cor·vi·na \kȯr-ˈvē-nə\ *n* [AmerSp, fr. Sp — more at CORBINA] (1787) : any of several marine bony fishes (genus *Cynoscion* of the family Sciaenidae) of the Pacific coast of No. America

cor·vine \ˈkȯr-ˌvīn\ *adj* [L *corvinus,* fr. *corvus* raven — more at RAVEN] (ca. 1656) : of or relating to the crows : resembling a crow

Cor·vus \ˈkȯr-vəs\ *n* [L (gen. *Corvi*), lit., raven] (1658) : a small constellation adjoining Virgo on the south

Cor·y·bant \ˈkȯr-ə-ˌbant, ˈkär-\ *n, pl* **Cor·y·bants** \-ˌban(t)s\ *or* **Cor·y·ban·tes** \ˌkȯr-ə-ˈban-tēz, ˌkär-\ [MF *Corybante,* fr. L *Corybas,* fr. Gk *Korybas*] (14c) : one of the attendants or priests of Cybele noted for wildly emotional processions and rites

cor·y·ban·tic \ˌkȯr-ē-ˈban-tik, ˌkär-\ *adj* (1642) : being in the spirit or manner of a Corybant; *esp* : WILD, FRENZIED ⟨~ dancing⟩

co·ryd·a·lis \kə-ˈri-də-ləs\ *n* [NL, genus name, fr. Gk *korydallis* crested lark (*Galerida cristata*), fr. *korydos* crested lark] (1818) : any of a large

genus (*Corydalis*) of chiefly temperate herbs of the fumitory family with racemose irregular flowers and dissected leaves
cor·ymb \ˈkȯr-ˌim(b), ˈkär-, -əm(b)\ *n, pl* **corymbs** \-ˌimz, -əmz\ [F *corymbe,* fr. L *corymbus* cluster of fruit or flowers, fr. Gk *korymbos*] (1794) **:** a flat-topped inflorescence; *specif* **:** one in which the flower stalks arise at different levels on the main axis and reach about the same height and in which the outer flowers open first — see INFLORESCENCE illustration — **cor·ym·bose** \-əm-ˌbōs\ *adj*
co·ry·ne·bac·te·ri·um \ˌkȯr-ə-(ˌ)nē-bak-ˈtir-ē-əm, kə-ˌri-nə-\ *n* [NL, fr. Gk *korynē* club] (1909) **:** any of a large genus (*Corynebacterium*) of usu. gram-positive nonmotile bacteria that occur as irregular or branching rods and include numerous important animal and plant pathogens — **co·ry·ne·bac·te·ri·al** \-ē-əl\ *adj*
co·ryn·e·form \kə-ˈri-nə-ˌfȯrm\ *adj* (1952) **:** being or resembling corynebacteria
cor·y·phae·us \ˌkȯr-ə-ˈfē-əs, ˌkär-\ *n, pl* **-phaei** \-ˈfē-ˌī\ [L, leader, fr. Gk *koryphaios,* fr. *koryphē* summit] (1655) **1 :** the leader of a party or school of thought **2 :** the leader of a chorus
co·ry·phée \ˌkȯr-i-ˈfā\ *n* [F, fr. L *coryphaeus*] (1828) **:** a ballet dancer who dances in a small group instead of in the corps de ballet or as a soloist
co·ry·za \kə-ˈrī-zə\ *n* [LL, fr. Gk *koryza* nasal mucus; akin to OE *hrot* nasal mucus, Skt *kardama* mud] (1634) **:** an acute inflammatory contagious disease involving the upper respiratory tract; *esp* **:** COMMON COLD — **co·ry·zal** \-zəl\ *adj*
cos *abbr* **1** companies **2** consul; consulship **3** cosine **4** counties
COS *abbr* **1** cash on shipment **2** chief of staff
cosec *abbr* cosecant
co·se·cant \(ˌ)kō-ˈsē-ˌkant, -kənt\ *n* [NL *cosecant-, cosecans,* fr. *co-* + *secant-, secans* secant] (ca. 1706) **1 :** a trigonometric function that for an acute angle is the ratio between the hypotenuse of a right triangle of which the angle is considered part and the leg opposite the angle **2 :** a trigonometric function csc θ that is the reciprocal of the sine for all real numbers θ for which the sine is not zero and that is exactly equal to the cosecant of an angle of measure θ in radians
co·set \ˈkō-ˌset\ *n* (1910) **:** a subset of a mathematical group that consists of all the products obtained by multiplying either on the right or the left a fixed element of the group by each of the elements of a given subgroup
[1]**cosh** \ˈkäsh\ *n* [perh. fr. Romany *kaš, kašt* stick, piece of wood] (1869) *chiefly Brit* **:** a weighted weapon similar to a blackjack
[2]**cosh** *vt* (1896) *chiefly Brit* **:** to strike or assault with or as if with a cosh
co·sig·na·to·ry \(ˌ)kō-ˈsig-nə-ˌtȯr-ē\ *n* (1865) **:** a joint signer
co·sign·er \ˈkō-ˌsī-nər\ *n* (ca. 1903) **:** COSIGNATORY; *esp* **:** a joint signer of a promissory note — **co·sign** \ˈkō-ˌsīn\ *vb*
co·sine \ˈkō-ˌsīn\ *n* [NL *cosinus,* fr. *co-* + ML *sinus* sine] (1635) **1 :** a trigonometric function that for an acute angle is the ratio between the leg adjacent to the angle when it is considered part of a right triangle and the hypotenuse **2 :** a trigonometric function cos θ that for all real numbers θ is given by the sum of the alternating series

$$\cos\theta = 1 - \frac{\theta^2}{2!} + \frac{\theta^4}{4!} - \frac{\theta^6}{6!} + \frac{\theta^8}{8!} - \dots$$

and that is exactly equal to the cosine of an angle of measure θ in radians
cos lettuce \ˈkäs-, ˈkōs-\ *n* [*Kos, Cos,* Greek island] (1699) **:** ROMAINE
cos·me·ceu·ti·cal \ˌkäz-mə-ˈsü-ti-kəl\ *n* [*cosme*tic + pharma*ceutical*] (1985) **:** a cosmetic preparation that has pharmaceutical properties
[1]**cos·met·ic** \käz-ˈme-tik\ *adj* [Gk *kosmētikos* skilled in adornment, fr. *kosmein* to arrange, adorn, fr. *kosmos* order] (1638) **1 :** of, relating to, or making for beauty esp. of the complexion **:** BEAUTIFYING ⟨~ salves⟩ **2 :** done or made for the sake of appearance: as **a :** correcting defects esp. of the face ⟨~ surgery⟩ **b :** DECORATIVE, ORNAMENTAL **c :** not substantive **:** SUPERFICIAL ⟨~ changes⟩ **3 :** visually appealing — **cos·met·i·cal·ly** \-ti-k(ə-)lē\ *adv*
[2]**cosmetic** *n* (1650) **:** something that is cosmetic: as **a :** a cosmetic preparation for external use **b** *pl* **:** superficial features ⟨a poem without rhetorical ~*s* —Guy Davenport⟩
cosmetic case *n* (1948) **:** a small piece of luggage esp. for cosmetics
cos·me·ti·cian \ˌkäz-mə-ˈti-shən\ *n* (1924) **:** a person who is professionally trained in the use of cosmetics
cos·met·i·cize \käz-ˈme-tə-ˌsīz\ *vt* **-cized; -ciz·ing** (1824) **:** to make (something unpleasant or ugly) superficially attractive
cos·me·tol·o·gist \ˌkäz-mə-ˈtä-lə-jist\ *n* (1926) **:** a person who gives beauty treatments (as to skin and hair) — called also *beautician*
cos·me·tol·o·gy \-jē\ *n* [F *cosmétologie,* fr. *cosmétique* cosmetic (fr. E *cosmetic*) + *-logie* -logy] (1926) **:** the cosmetic treatment of the skin, hair, and nails
cos·mic \ˈkäz-mik\ *also* **cos·mi·cal** \-mi-kəl\ *adj* [Gk *kosmikos,* fr. *kosmos* order, universe] (1685) **1 a :** of or relating to the cosmos, the extraterrestrial vastness, or the universe in contrast to the earth alone **b :** of, relating to, or concerned with abstract spiritual or metaphysical ideas **2 :** characterized by greatness esp. in extent, intensity, or comprehensiveness ⟨a ~ thinker⟩ — **cos·mi·cal·ly** \-mi-k(ə-)lē\ *adv*
cosmic background radiation *n* (ca. 1976) **:** BACKGROUND RADIATION
cosmic dust *n* (1881) **:** very fine particles of solid matter found in any part of the universe
cosmic microwave background *n* (1981) **:** BACKGROUND RADIATION
cosmic noise *n* (1947) **:** unidentified celestial radio-frequency radiation; *esp* **:** such radiation originating from outside the Milky Way
cosmic ray *n* (1925) **:** a stream of atomic nuclei of extremely penetrating character that enter the earth's atmosphere from outer space at speeds approaching that of light
cosmic string *n* (1983) **:** any of a class of hypothetical supermassive astronomical objects that are extremely thin but are millions of light years long and that are postulated to have formed very early in the history of the universe
cos·mo·chem·is·try \ˌkäz-mō-ˈke-mə-strē\ *n* [Gk *kosmos* universe] (1940) **:** a branch of chemistry that deals with the chemical composition of and changes in the universe — **cos·mo·chem·i·cal** \-ˈke-mi-kəl\ *adj* — **cos·mo·chem·ist** \-mist\ *n*
cos·mo·gen·ic \ˌkäz-mə-ˈje-nik\ *adj* [*cosm*ic ray + *-o-* + *-genic*] (1962) **:** produced by the action of cosmic rays ⟨~ carbon 14⟩
cos·mog·o·ny \käz-ˈmä-gə-nē\ *n, pl* **-nies** [NL *cosmogonia,* fr. Gk *kosmogonia,* fr. *kosmos* + *gonos* offspring; akin to Gk *genos* race — more at KIN] (1696) **1 :** a theory of the origin of the universe **2 :** the creation or origin of the world or universe — **cos·mo·gon·ic** \ˌkäz-mə-ˈgä-nik\ *or* **cos·mo·gon·i·cal** \-ni-kəl\ *adj* — **cos·mog·o·nist** \käz-ˈmä-gə-nist\ *n*
cos·mog·ra·phy \käz-ˈmä-grə-fē\ *n, pl* **-phies** [ME *cosmographie,* fr. LL *cosmographia,* fr. Gk *kosmographia,* fr. *kosmos* + *-graphia* -graphy] (14c) **1 :** a general description of the world or of the universe **2 :** the science that deals with the constitution of the whole order of nature — **cos·mog·ra·pher** \-fər\ *n* — **cos·mo·graph·ic** \ˌkäz-mə-ˈgra-fik\ *or* **cos·mo·graph·i·cal** \-fi-kəl\ *adj*
Cos·mo·line \ˈkäz-mə-ˌlēn\ *trademark* — used for corrosion-preventing petroleum jelly
cosmological constant *n* (1928) **:** a constant term used in the relativistic equations for gravity to represent a repulsive force which may account in part for the rate of expansion of the universe
cos·mol·o·gy \käz-ˈmä-lə-jē\ *n, pl* **-gies** [NL *cosmologia,* fr. Gk *kosmos* + NL *-logia* -logy] (ca. 1656) **1 a :** a branch of metaphysics that deals with the nature of the universe **b :** a theory or doctrine describing the natural order of the universe **2 :** a branch of astronomy that deals with the origin, structure, and space-time relationships of the universe; *also* **:** a theory dealing with these matters — **cos·mo·log·i·cal** \ˌkäz-mə-ˈlä-ji-kəl\ *adj* — **cos·mo·log·i·cal·ly** \-ji-k(ə-)lē\ *adv* — **cos·mol·o·gist** \käz-ˈmä-lə-jist\ *n*
cos·mo·naut \ˈkäz-mə-ˌnȯt, -ˌnät\ *n* [Russ *kosmonavt,* fr. Gk *kosmos* + Russ *-navt* (as in *aeronavt* aeronaut)] (1955) **:** an astronaut of the Soviet or Russian space program
cos·mop·o·lis \käz-ˈmä-pə-ləs\ *n* [NL, back-formation fr. *cosmopolites*] (1849) **:** a cosmopolitan city
[1]**cos·mo·pol·i·tan** \ˌkäz-mə-ˈpä-lə-tən\ *n* (ca. 1645) **1 :** COSMOPOLITE **2 :** a cocktail made of vodka, orange-flavored liqueur, lime juice, and cranberry juice — called also *cos·mo* \ˈkäz-(ˌ)mō\
[2]**cosmopolitan** *adj* (1798) **1 :** having worldwide rather than limited or provincial scope or bearing **2 :** having wide international sophistication **:** WORLDLY **3 :** composed of persons, constituents, or elements from all or many parts of the world **4 :** found in most parts of the world and under varied ecological conditions ⟨a ~ herb⟩ — **cos·mo·pol·i·tan·ism** \-tə-ˌni-zəm\ *n*
cos·mop·o·lite \käz-ˈmä-pə-ˌlīt\ *n* [NL *cosmopolites,* fr. Gk *kosmopolitēs,* fr. *kosmos* + *politēs* citizen] (ca. 1618) **:** a cosmopolitan person or organism — **cos·mo·po·li·tism** \käz-ˈmä-pə-ˌlī-ˌti-zəm, -lə-ˌti-; ˌkäz-mə-ˈpä-lə-ˌti-\ *n*
cos·mos \ˈkäz-məs, *1 & 2 also* -ˌmōs, -ˌmäs\ *n* [Gk *kosmos*] (1596) **1 a :** UNIVERSE 1 **b (1) :** an orderly harmonious systematic universe — compare CHAOS **(2) :** ORDER, HARMONY **2 :** a complex orderly self-inclusive system **3** *pl* **cosmos** \-məs, -məz\ *also* **cos·mos·es** \-mə-səz\ [NL, genus name, fr. Gk *kosmos*] **:** any of a genus (*Cosmos*) of tropical American composite herbs; *esp* **:** a widely cultivated tall annual (*C. bipinnatus*) with yellow or red disks and showy ray flowers

cosmos 3

Cos·sack \ˈkä-ˌsak, -sək\ *n* [Pol & Ukrainian *kozak,* of Turkic origin; akin to Volga Tatar *kazak* free person] (1589) **1 :** a member of any of a number of autonomous communities drawn from various ethnic and linguistic groups (as Slavs, Tatars, and Circassians) that formed in Ukraine, southern Russia, the Caucasus Mountains, and Siberia after about 1400 and that were completely incorporated into czarist Russia during the 18th and 19th centuries **2 :** a mounted soldier serving in a unit drafted from Cossack communities
[1]**cos·set** \ˈkä-sət\ *n* [origin unknown] (1579) **:** a pet lamb; *broadly* **:** PET
[2]**cosset** *vt* (1640) **:** to treat as a pet **:** PAMPER
[1]**cost** \ˈkȯst\ *n* (13c) **1 a :** the amount or equivalent paid or charged for something **:** PRICE **b :** the outlay or expenditure (as of effort or sacrifice) made to achieve an object **2 :** loss or penalty incurred esp. in gaining something **3** *pl* **:** expenses incurred in litigation; *esp* **:** those given by the law or the court to the prevailing party against the losing party — **cost·less** \-ləs\ *adj* — **cost·less·ly** *adv* — **at all costs :** regardless of the cost or consequences ⟨was determined to win *at all costs*⟩ — **at cost :** for the price of production ⟨buys clothes *at cost* directly from the manufacturer⟩
[2]**cost** *vb* **cost; cost·ing** [ME, fr. AF *custer, couster,* fr. L *constare* to stand firm, cost — more at CONSTANT] *vi* (14c) **1 :** to require expenditure or payment ⟨the best goods ~ more⟩ **2 :** to require effort, suffering, or loss ~ *vt* **1 :** to have a price of **2 :** to cause to pay, suffer, or lose something ⟨frequent absences ~ him his job⟩ **3** *past* **cost·ed :** to estimate or set the cost of — often used with *out*
cos·ta \ˈkäs-tə\ *n, pl* **cos·tae** \-(ˌ)tē, -ˌtī\ [L — more at COAST] (ca. 1771) **1 :** [1]RIB 1a **2 :** a part (as the midrib of a leaf or the anterior vein of an insect wing) that resembles a rib — **cos·tal** \-tᵊl\ *adj*
cost accountant *n* (1918) **:** a specialist in cost accounting
cost accounting *n* (1913) **:** the systematic recording and analysis of the costs of material, labor, and overhead incident to production
cos·tard \ˈkäs-tərd\ *n* [ME] (13c) **1 :** any of several large English cooking apples **2** *archaic* **:** NODDLE, PATE
cost–ben·e·fit \ˈkȯs(t)-ˈbe-nə-ˌfit\ *adj* (1963) **:** of, relating to, or being economic analysis that assigns a numerical value to the cost-effectiveness of an operation, procedure, or program
cost–ef·fec·tive \ˈkȯst-ə-ˈfek-tiv, -ˌfek-\ *adj* (1967) **:** economical in terms of tangible benefits produced by money spent ⟨~ measures to combat poverty⟩ — **cost–ef·fec·tive·ness** *n*
cost–ef·fi·cient \-i-ˈfi-shənt, -ˌfi-\ *adj* (1970) **:** COST-EFFECTIVE
cos·ter \ˈkäs-tər\ *n* (1851) *Brit* **:** COSTERMONGER
cos·ter·mon·ger \-ˌməŋ-gər, -ˌmäŋ-\ *n* [*costard* + *monger*] (1514) *Brit* **:** a hawker of fruit or vegetables
cos·tive \ˈkäs-tiv, ˈkȯs-\ *adj* [ME, fr. AF *costivé,* pp. of *costiver* to constipate, fr. L *constipare*] (14c) **1 a :** affected with constipation **b :** causing constipation **2 :** slow in action or expression **3 :** not generous **:** STINGY — **cos·tive·ly** *adv* — **cos·tive·ness** *n*

cost·ly \ˈkȯs(t)-lē\ *adj* **cost·li·er; -est** (14c) **1 a :** commanding a high price esp. because of intrinsic worth ⟨~ gems⟩ **b :** RICH, SPLENDID **2 :** made or done at heavy expense or sacrifice ⟨a ~ mistake⟩ — **cost·li·ness** *n*

cost·mary \ˈkȯst-ˌmer-ē, ˈkäst-\ *n, pl* **-mar·ies** [ME *costmarie,* fr. *coste* costmary (fr. OE *cost,* fr. L *costum,* fr. Gk *kostos,* a fragrant root) + *Marie* the Virgin Mary] (14c) **:** an aromatic composite Eurasian herb (*Chrysanthemum balsamita* syn. *Tanacetum balsamita*) having leaves used as a potherb and in flavoring

cost of living (1826) **:** the cost of purchasing those goods and services which are included in an accepted standard level of consumption

cost–of–living index *n* (1913) **:** CONSUMER PRICE INDEX

cost–plus \ˈkȯs(t)-ˈpləs\ *adj* (1918) **1 :** paid on the basis of a fixed fee or a percentage added to actual cost ⟨a ~ contract⟩ **2 :** of or relating to a cost-plus contract

cost–push \ˈkȯs(t)-ˌpu̇sh\ *n* (1951) **:** an increase or upward trend in production costs (as wages) that tends to result in increased consumer prices irrespective of the level of demand — compare DEMAND-PULL — **cost–push** *adj*

cos·trel \ˈkäs-trəl\ *n* [ME, fr. ML & AF; ML *costrellus,* fr. AF **costrel,* fr. *costere* side, fr. *coste* rib, side — more at COAST] (14c) **:** a flat usu. earthenware container for liquids with loops through which a belt or cord may be passed for easy carrying — called also *pilgrim bottle*

[1]**cos·tume** \ˈkäs-ˌtüm, -ˌtyüm *also* -təm *or* -ˌchüm\ *n* [F, fr. It, custom, dress, fr. L *consuetudin-, consuetudo* custom — more at CUSTOM] (1799) **1 :** the prevailing fashion in coiffure, jewelry, and apparel of a period, country, or class **2 :** an outfit worn to create the appearance characteristic of a particular period, person, place, or thing ⟨Halloween ~*s*⟩ **3 :** a person's ensemble of outer garments; *esp* **:** a woman's ensemble of dress with coat or jacket — **cos·tum·ey** *adj*

[2]**cos·tume** \käs-ˈtüm, -ˈtyüm *also* -ˈchüm; *or* ˈkäs-ˌ *or* -təm\ *vt* **cos·tumed; cos·tum·ing** (1823) **1 :** to provide with a costume **2 :** to design costumes for ⟨~ a play⟩

[3]**costume** *same as* [1]\ *adj* (1847) **1 :** characterized by the use of costumes ⟨a ~ ball⟩ ⟨a ~ drama⟩ **2 :** suitable for or enhancing the effect of a particular costume ⟨a ~ handbag⟩

costume jewelry *n* (1927) **:** jewelry designed for wear with current fashions and usu. made of inexpensive materials

cos·tum·er \ˈkäs-ˌtü-mər, -ˌtyü- *also* -ˌchü-; käs-ˈ\ *n* (1840) **1 :** one that deals in or makes costumes **2 :** an upright stand with hooks or pegs on which to hang clothes

cos·tum·ery \-mə-rē\ *n* (1838) **1 :** articles of costume **2 :** the art of costuming

cos·tu·mi·er \käs-ˈtü-mē-ˌā, -ˈtyü-, -mē-ər\ *n* [F] (1831) *chiefly Brit* **:** COSTUMER 1

co·sy \ˈkō-zē\ *chiefly Brit, var of* COZY

[1]**cot** \ˈkät\ *n* [ME, fr. OE; akin to ON *kot* small hut] (bef. 12c) **1 :** a small house **2 :** COVER, SHEATH; *esp* **:** STALL 4

[2]**cot** *n* [Hindi & Urdu *khāṭ* bedstead, fr. Skt *khaṭvā,* perh. of Dravidian origin; akin to Tamil *kaṭṭil* bedstead] (1634) **1 :** a small usu. collapsible bed often of fabric stretched on a frame **2** *Brit* **:** CRIB 2b

[3]**cot** *abbr* cotangent

co·tan·gent \(ˌ)kō-ˈtan-jənt, ˈkō-ˌ\ *n* [NL *cotangent-, cotangens,* fr. *co-* + *tangent-, tangens* tangent] (1635) **1 :** a trigonometric function that for an acute angle is the ratio between the leg adjacent to the angle when it is considered part of a right triangle and the leg opposite **2 :** a trigonometric function cot θ that is equal to the cosine divided by the sine for all real numbers θ for which the sine is not equal to zero and is exactly equal to the cotangent of an angle of measure θ in radians

[1]**cote** \ˈkōt, ˈkät\ *n* [ME, fr. OE] (bef. 12c) **1** *dial Eng* **:** [1]COT 1 **2 :** a shed or coop for small domestic animals and esp. pigeons

[2]**cote** \ˈkōt\ *vt* [prob. fr. MF *cotoyer*] (1555) *obs* **:** to pass by

co·te·rie \ˈkō-tə-(ˌ)rē, ˌkō-tə-ˈ\ *n* [F, fr. MF, tenants, fr. OF *cotier* cotter, of Gmc origin; akin to OE *cot* hut] (1738) **:** an intimate and often exclusive group of persons with a unifying common interest or purpose

co·ter·mi·nous \(ˌ)kō-ˈtər-mə-nəs\ *adj* [alter. of *conterminous*] (1799) **1 :** having the same or coincident boundaries ⟨a voting district ~ with the city⟩ **2 :** coextensive in scope or duration ⟨an experience of life ~ with the years of his father —Elizabeth Hardwick⟩ — **co·ter·mi·nous·ly** *adv*

co·thur·nus \kō-ˈthər-nəs\ *n, pl* **-ni** \-ˌnī, -(ˌ)nē\ [L, fr. Gk *kothornos*] (1606) **1 :** a high thick-soled laced boot worn by actors in Greek and Roman tragic drama — called also *co·thurn* \ˈkō-ˌthərn, kō-ˈ\ **2 :** the dignified somewhat stilted style of ancient tragedy

co·tid·al \(ˌ)kō-ˈtī-dᵊl\ *adj* (1833) **:** indicating equality in the tides or a coincidence in the time of high or low tide

co·til·lion \kō-ˈtil-yən, kə-\ *also* **co·til·lon** \kō-ˈtil-yən, kə-, kȯ-tē-(y)ōⁿ\ *n* [F *cotillon,* lit., petticoat, fr. OF, fr. *cote* coat] (1728) **1 :** a ballroom dance for couples that resembles the quadrille **2 :** an elaborate dance with frequent changing of partners carried out under the leadership of one couple at formal balls **3 :** a formal ball

co·tin·ine \ˈkō-tə-ˌnēn, -ˌnīn\ *n* [prob. anagram of *nicotine*] (1893) **:** an alkaloid $C_{10}H_{12}N_2O$ that is the principal metabolite of nicotine

co·to·ne·as·ter \kə-ˈtō-nē-ˌas-tər, ˈkä-tᵊn-ˌēs-\ *n* [NL, genus name, fr. L *cotoneum* quince + NL *-aster*] (1796) **:** any of a genus (*Cotoneaster*) of Old World flowering shrubs of the rose family

cot·quean \ˈkät-ˌkwēn\ *n* [[1]*cot* + *quean*] (1547) **1** *archaic* **:** a coarse masculine woman **2** *archaic* **:** a man who busies himself with women's work or affairs

Cots·wold \ˈkät-ˌswōld, -swəld\ *n* [*Cotswold* Hills, England] (ca. 1658) **:** any of an English breed of large long-wooled sheep

cot·ta \ˈkä-tə\ *n* [ML, of Gmc origin; akin to OHG *kozza* coarse mantle — more at COAT] (1848) **:** a waist-length surplice

cot·tage \ˈkä-tij\ *n* [ME *cotage,* fr. AF, fr. ME *cot* — more at COT] (14c) **1 :** the dwelling of a farm laborer or small farmer **2 :** a usu. small frame one-family house **3 :** a small detached dwelling unit at an institution **4 :** a usu. small house for vacation use — **cot·tag·ey** \-ti-jē\ *adj*

cottage cheese *n* (1848) **:** a bland soft white cheese made from the curds of skim milk — called also *Dutch cheese, pot cheese, smearcase*

cottage curtains *n pl* (1943) **:** a double set of upper and lower straight-hanging window curtains

cottage industry *n* (1921) **1 :** an industry whose labor force consists of family units or individuals working at home with their own equipment **2 :** a small and often informally organized industry **3 :** a limited but enthusiastically pursued activity or subject ⟨this debate about sex and law became a *cottage industry* for feminist academics —Wendy Kaminer⟩

cottage pie *n* (1791) **:** a shepherd's pie made esp. with beef

cottage pudding *n* (ca. 1854) **:** plain cake covered with a hot sweet sauce

cot·tag·er \ˈkä-ti-jər\ *n* (1550) **:** a person who lives in a cottage

cottage tulip *n* (1928) **:** any of various tall late-flowering tulips

cot·tar *or* **cot·ter** \ˈkä-tər\ *n* [ME *cottar,* fr. ML *cotarius,* fr. ME *cot*] (14c) **:** a peasant or farm laborer who occupies a cottage and sometimes a small holding of land usu. in return for services

cot·ter \ˈkä-tər\ *n* [origin unknown] (14c) **1 :** a wedge-shaped or tapered piece used to fasten together parts of a structure **2 :** COTTER PIN — **cot·tered** \-tərd\ *adj* — **cot·ter·less** \-tər-ləs\ *adj*

cotter pin *n* (1881) **:** a half-round metal strip bent into a pin whose ends can be flared after insertion through a slot or hole

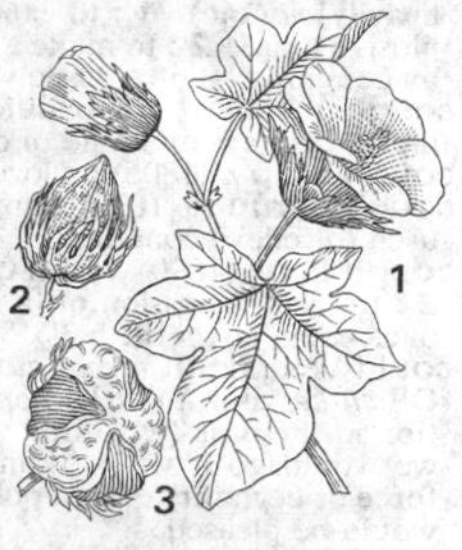

cotton: *1* flowering branch; *2* fruit, unopened; *3* fruit, partly opened

[1]**cot·ton** \ˈkä-tᵊn\ *n, often attrib* [ME *coton,* fr. AF *cotun,* fr. OIt *cotone,* fr. Ar *quṭun, quṭn*] (14c) **1 a :** a soft usu. white fibrous substance composed of the hairs surrounding the seeds of various erect freely branching tropical plants (genus *Gossypium*) of the mallow family **b :** a plant producing cotton; *esp* **:** one grown for its cotton **c :** a crop of cotton **2 a :** fabric made of cotton **b :** yarn spun from cotton **3 :** a downy cottony substance produced by various plants (as the cottonwood)

[2]**cotton** *vi* **cot·toned; cot·ton·ing** \ˈkät-niŋ, ˈkä-tᵊn-iŋ\ (1605) **1 :** to take a liking — used with *to* ⟨~*s* to people easily⟩ **2 :** to come to understand — used with *to* or *on to* ⟨~*ed* on to the fact that our children work furiously —H. M. McLuhan⟩

cotton bollworm *n* (1870) **:** CORN EARWORM

cotton candy *n* (1926) **1 :** a candy made of spun sugar **2 :** something attractive but insubstantial

cotton gin *n* (1796) **:** a machine that separates the seeds, hulls, and foreign material from cotton

cotton grass *n* (1597) **:** any of a genus (*Eriophorum*) of sedges with tufted spikes

cot·ton·mouth \ˈkä-tᵊn-ˌmau̇th\ *n* [fr. the white interior of its mouth] (1832) **:** WATER MOCCASIN

cottonmouth moccasin *n* (1879) **:** WATER MOCCASIN

cot·ton–pick·ing \ˈkä-tᵊn-ˌpi-kiŋ, -ˌpi-kən\ *adj* (ca. 1952) **1 :** DAMNED — used as a generalized expression of disapproval ⟨a ~ hypocrite⟩ **2 :** DAMNED — used as an intensive ⟨out of his ~ mind —Irving Kristol⟩

cot·ton·seed \ˈkä-tᵊn-ˌsēd\ *n* (1774) **:** the seed of the cotton plant

cottonseed oil *n* (1833) **:** a pale yellow semidrying fatty oil that is obtained from the cottonseed and is used chiefly in salad and cooking oils and after hydrogenation in shortenings and margarine

cotton stainer *n* (1856) **:** any of several bugs (genus *Dysdercus*) that damage and stain the lint of developing cotton; *esp* **:** a red and brown bug (*D. suturellus*) that attacks cotton in the southern U.S.

cot·ton·tail \ˈkä-tᵊn-ˌtāl\ *n* (1835) **:** any of several rather small No. American rabbits (genus *Sylvilagus*) sandy to grayish brown in color with a white-tufted underside of the tail

cot·ton·weed \-ˌwēd\ *n* (1562) **:** any of various weedy plants (as cudweed) with whitish pubescence or cottony seeds

cot·ton·wood \-ˌwu̇d\ *n* (1802) **:** any of several poplars having seeds with cottony hairs; *esp* **:** one (*Populus deltoides*) of the eastern and central U.S. often cultivated for its rapid growth and luxuriant foliage

cotton wool *n* (14c) **:** raw cotton; *esp* **:** cotton batting

cot·tony \ˈkät-nē, ˈkä-tᵊn-ē\ *adj* (1578) **:** resembling cotton in appearance or character: as **a :** covered with hairs or pubescence **b :** SOFT

cot·tony–cush·ion scale \-ˈku̇-shən-\ *n* (1886) **:** a scale insect (*Icerya purchasi*) introduced into the U.S. from Australia that infests citrus and other plants

-cotyl *n comb form* [*cotyledon*] **:** cotyledon ⟨hypo*cotyl*⟩

cot·y·le·don \ˌkä-tə-ˈlē-dᵊn\ *n* [NL, fr. Gk *kotylēdōn* cup-shaped hollow, fr. *kotylē* cup, anything hollow] (1540) **1 :** a lobule of the mammalian placenta **2 :** the first leaf or one of the first pair or whorl of leaves developed by the embryo of a seed plant or of some lower plants (as ferns) — **cot·y·le·don·ary** \-ˈlē-də-ˌner-ē\ *adj*

co·ty·lo·saur \ˈkä-tə-lō-ˌsȯr, kə-ˈti-lə-\ *n* [ultim. fr. Gk *kotylē* + *sauros* lizard] (1895) **:** any of an order (Cotylosauria) of extinct primitive reptiles of the Carboniferous to Triassic with short legs and massive bodies that were prob. the earliest truly terrestrial vertebrate animals

[1]**couch** \ˈkau̇ch\ *vb* [ME, fr. AF *cucher,* fr. L *collocare* to set in place — more at COLLOCATE] *vt* (14c) **1 :** to lay (oneself) down for rest or sleep **2 :** to embroider (a design) by laying down a thread and fastening it with small stitches at regular intervals **3 :** to place or hold level and pointed forward ready for use **4 :** to phrase or express in a specified manner ⟨the comments were ~*ed* in strong terms⟩ ~ *vi* **1 :** to lie down or recline for sleep or rest **2 :** to lie in ambush

[2]**couch** *n* [ME *couche* bed, fr. AF *kuche,* fr. *cucher*] (14c) **1 a :** an article of furniture for sitting or reclining **b :** a couch on which a patient reclines when undergoing psychoanalysis **2 :** the den of an animal (as an otter) — **on the couch :** receiving psychiatric treatment

couch·ant \ˈkau̇-chənt\ *adj* [ME, fr. AF *cuchant,* fr. prp. of *coucher*] (15c) **:** lying down esp. with the head up ⟨a heraldic lion ~⟩

couch grass \ˈkau̇ch-, ˈkŭch-\ *n* [alter. of *quitch*] (1578) **1 :** QUACK GRASS **2 :** any of several grasses that resemble quack grass in spreading by creeping rhizomes

couch potato *n* (1982) : a lazy and inactive person; *esp* : one who spends a great deal of time watching television

cou·dé \kü-ˈdā\ *adj* [F *coudé* bent like an elbow, fr. *coude* elbow, fr. L *cubitum*] (ca. 1889) : of, relating to, or being a telescope constructed so that the light is reflected along the polar axis to come to a focus at a point where the holder for a photographic plate or a spectrograph may be mounted

cou·gar \ˈkü-gər *also* -ˌgär\ *n, pl* **cougars** *also* **cougar** [F *couguar,* modif. of NL *cuguacuarana,* fr. Tupi *siwasuarána,* fr. *siwásu* deer + *-ran* resembling] (1774) **1 :** a large powerful tawny-brown cat (*Felis concolor*) formerly widespread in the Americas but now reduced in number or extinct in many areas — called also *catamount, mountain lion, panther, puma* **2** *slang* **:** a middle-aged woman seeking a romantic relationship with a younger man

[1]**cough** \ˈkȯf\ *vb* [ME, fr. OE **cohhian;* akin to MHG *kūchen* to breathe heavily] *vi* (14c) **1 :** to expel air from the lungs suddenly with an explosive noise **2 :** to make a noise like that of coughing ~ *vt* **:** to expel by coughing — often used with *up* ⟨~ up mucus⟩

[2]**cough** *n* (14c) **1 :** a condition marked by repeated or frequent coughing **2 :** an act or sound of coughing

cough drop *n* (1806) : a lozenge or troche used to relieve coughing

cough syrup *n* (1836) : any of various sweet usu. medicated liquids used to relieve coughing

cough up *vt* (1890) **1 :** HAND OVER, DELIVER ⟨*cough up* the money⟩ **2 :** to lose possession of (a ball or puck) during a game ⟨the quarterback *coughed up* the ball⟩

could \kəd, ˈku̇d\ *verbal auxiliary, past of* CAN [ME *couthe, coude,* fr. OE *cūthe;* akin to OHG *konda* could] (13c) — used in auxiliary function in the past ⟨we found we ~ go⟩, in the past conditional ⟨we said we would go if we ~⟩, and as an alternative to *can* suggesting less force or certainty or as a polite form in the present ⟨if you ~ come we would be pleased⟩

could·est \ˈku̇-dəst\ *archaic past 2d sing of* CAN

couldn't \ˈku̇-dᵊnt, -dᵊn, *dial also* ˈku̇-tᵊn(t) *or* ˈku̇nt\ (1646) : could not

couldst \kədst, ˈku̇dst, kətst, ˈku̇tst\ *archaic past 2d sing of* CAN

cou·lee \ˈkü-lē\ *n* [CanF *coulée,* fr. F, flowing, flow of lava, fr. *couler* to flow, fr. OF, fr. L *colare* to strain, fr. *colum* sieve] (1807) **1 a :** a small stream **b :** a dry streambed **c :** a usu. small or shallow ravine : GULLY **2 :** a thick sheet or stream of lava

cou·lis \kü-ˈlē\ *n* [F, fr. OF *coleïs,* fr. *coleïs, coleïz* flowing] (1978) : a thick sauce made with pureed vegetable or fruit and often used as a garnish

cou·lisse \kü-ˈlēs, -ˈlis\ *n* [F, fr. OF *coulice* portcullis, fr. fem. of *coleïz* flowing, sliding, fr. *couler*] (1786) **1 a :** a side scene of a stage; *also* **:** the space between the side scenes **b :** a backstage area **c :** HALLWAY **2 :** a piece of timber having a groove in which something glides

cou·loir \kül-ˈwär\ *n* [F, lit., passage, fr. *couler*] (1822) : a steep mountainside gorge

[1]**cou·lomb** \ˈkü-ˌläm, -ˌlōm\ *n* [Charles A. de *Coulomb*] (1881) : the practical meter-kilogram-second unit of electric charge equal to the quantity of electricity transferred by a current of one ampere in one second

[2]**coulomb** *or* **cou·lom·bic** \kü-ˈläm-bik, -ˈlōm-, -ˈlä-mik, -ˈlō-\ *adj* (1930) : of, relating to, or being the electrostatic force of attraction or repulsion between charged particles

Cou·lomb's law \ˈkü-ˌlämz-, -ˌlōmz-\ *n* (1854) : a statement in physics: the force of attraction or repulsion acting along a straight line between two electric charges is directly proportional to the product of the charges and inversely to the square of the distance between them

cou·lo·me·ter \kü-ˈlä-mə-tər, ˈkü-lə-ˌmē-tər\ *n* [alter. of *coulombmeter,* fr. *coulomb* + *-meter*] (ca. 1889) : an instrument of chemical analysis that determines the amount of a substance released in electrolysis by measurement of the quantity of electricity used — **cou·lo·met·ric** \ˌkü-lə-ˈme-trik\ *adj* — **cou·lo·met·ri·cal·ly** \-tri-k(ə-)lē\ *adv* — **cou·lom·e·try** \kü-ˈlä-mə-trē\ *n*

coul·ter \ˈkōl-tər\ *n* [ME *colter,* fr. OE *culter* & OF *coltre,* both fr. L *culter* plowshare; akin to Gk *skallein* to hoe — more at SHELL] (bef. 12c) : a cutting tool (as a knife or sharp disc) that is attached to the beam of a plow, makes a vertical cut in the surface, and permits clean separation and effective covering of the soil and materials being turned under

cou·ma·rin \ˈkü-mə-rən\ *n* [F *coumarine,* fr. *coumarou* tonka bean tree, fr. Sp or Pg; Sp *cumarú,* fr. Pg, fr. Tupi **kumarú,* **kumbarú*] (1830) : a toxic white crystalline lactone $C_9H_6O_2$ with an odor of new-mown hay found in plants or made synthetically and used esp. in perfumery and as a parent compound in anticoagulant agents; *also* : a derivative of this compound

[1]**coun·cil** \ˈkau̇n(t)-səl\ *n* [ME *counceil,* fr. AF *cunseil, cuncile,* fr. L *concilium,* fr. *com-* + *calare* to call — more at LOW] (12c) **1 :** an assembly or meeting for consultation, advice, or discussion **2 :** a group elected or appointed as an advisory or legislative body **3 a :** a usu. administrative body **b :** an executive body whose members are equal in power and authority **c :** a governing body of delegates from local units of a federation **4 :** deliberation in a council **5 a :** a federation of or a central body uniting a group of organizations **b :** a local chapter of an organization **c :** CLUB, SOCIETY

[2]**council** *adj* (14c) **1 :** used for councils esp. by or with No. American Indians ⟨a ~ ground⟩ **2** *Brit* **:** built, maintained, or operated by a local governing agency ⟨~ housing⟩ ⟨~ flats⟩

coun·cil·lor *or* **coun·cil·or** \ˈkau̇n(t)-s(ə-)lər\ *n* (15c) : a member of a council — **coun·cil·lor·ship** \-ˌship\ *n*

coun·cil·man \ˈkau̇n(t)-səl-mən\ *n* (ca. 1637) : a member of a council (as of a town or city) — **coun·cil·man·ic** \ˌkau̇n(t)-səl-ˈma-nik\ *adj*

council of ministers *often cap C&M* (1848) : CABINET 3b

coun·cil·wom·an \ˈkau̇n(t)-səl-ˌwu̇-mən\ *n* (ca. 1928) : a woman who is a member of a council

[1]**coun·sel** \ˈkau̇n(t)-səl\ *n* [ME *conseil,* fr. AF *cunseil,* fr. L *consilium,* fr. *consulere* to consult] (13c) **1 a :** advice given esp. as a result of consultation **b :** a policy or plan of action or behavior **2 :** DELIBERATION, CONSULTATION **3 a** *archaic* **:** PURPOSE **b :** guarded thoughts or intentions **4 a** *pl* **counsel** (1) : a lawyer engaged in the trial or management of a case in court (2) : a lawyer appointed to advise and represent in legal matters an individual client or a corporate and esp. a public body **b :** CONSULTANT 2

[2]**counsel** *vb* **-seled** *or* **-selled; -sel·ing** *or* **-sel·ling** \-s(ə-)liŋ\ *vt* (14c) : ADVISE ⟨~*ed* them to avoid rash actions —George Orwell⟩ ~ *vi* : CONSULT ⟨~*ed* with her husband⟩

coun·sel·ee \ˌkau̇n(t)-sə-ˈlē\ *n* (1923) : one who is being counseled

counseling *or* **counselling** *n* (1927) : professional guidance of the individual by utilizing psychological methods esp. in collecting case history data, using various techniques of the personal interview, and testing interests and aptitudes

coun·sel·or *or* **coun·sel·lor** \ˈkau̇n(t)-s(ə-)lər\ *n* (13c) **1 :** a person who gives advice or counseling ⟨marriage ~⟩ **2 :** LAWYER; *specif* : one that gives advice in law and manages cases for clients in court **3 :** one who has supervisory duties at a summer camp — **coun·sel·or·ship** \-ˌship\ *n*

counselor–at–law *n, pl* **counselors–at–law** (1617) : COUNSELOR 2

[1]**count** \ˈkau̇nt, *dial* ˈkyau̇nt\ *vb* [ME, fr. AF *cunter, counter,* fr. L *computare,* fr. *com-* + *putare* to consider] *vt* (14c) **1 a :** to indicate or name by units or groups so as to find the total number of units involved : NUMBER **b :** to name the numbers in order up to and including ⟨~ ten⟩ **c :** to include in a tallying and reckoning ⟨about 100 present, ~*ing* children⟩ **d :** to call aloud (beats or time units) ⟨~ cadence⟩ ⟨~ eighth notes⟩ **2 a :** CONSIDER, ACCOUNT ⟨~ oneself lucky⟩ **b :** to record as of an opinion or persuasion ⟨~ me as uncommitted⟩ **3 :** to include or exclude by or as if by counting ⟨~ me in⟩ ~ *vi* **1 a :** to recite or indicate the numbers in order by units or groups ⟨~ by fives⟩ **b :** to count the units in a group **2 :** to rely or depend on someone or something — used with *on* ⟨~*ed* on his parents to help with the expenses⟩ **3 :** ADD, TOTAL ⟨it ~*s* up to a sizable amount⟩ **4 a :** to have value or significance ⟨these are the people who really ~⟩ ⟨his opinions don't ~ for much⟩ **b :** to deserve to be regarded or considered ⟨a job so easy it hardly ~*s* as work⟩ — **and counting :** with more to come ⟨in business for 50 years *and counting*⟩ — **count heads** *or* **count noses :** to count the number present — **count on :** to look forward to as certain : ANTICIPATE ⟨*counted on* winning⟩

[2]**count** *n* (14c) **1 a :** the action or process of counting **b :** a total obtained by counting : TALLY **2** *archaic* **a :** RECKONING, ACCOUNT **b :** CONSIDERATION, ESTIMATION **3 a :** ALLEGATION, CHARGE; *specif* : one separately stating the cause of action or prosecution in a legal declaration or indictment ⟨guilty on all ~*s*⟩ **b :** a specific point under consideration : ISSUE **4 :** the total number of individual things in a given unit or sample obtained by counting all or a subsample of them ⟨bacteria ~⟩ **5 a :** the calling off of the seconds from one to ten when a boxer has been knocked down **b :** the number of balls and strikes charged to a baseball batter during one turn ⟨the ~ stood at 3 and 2⟩ **c :** SCORE ⟨tied the ~ with a minute to play⟩ **6 a :** a measurement of the thickness or fineness of yarn by determining the number of hanks or yards per pound it produces **b :** the number of threads per square inch in a cloth

[3]**count** *n* [ME, fr. AF *cunte,* fr. LL *comit-, comes,* fr. L, companion, one of the imperial court, fr. *com-* + *ire* to go — more at ISSUE] (15c) : a European nobleman whose rank corresponds to that of a British earl

count·able \ˈkau̇n-tə-bəl\ *adj* (1581) : capable of being counted; *esp* : capable of being put into one-to-one correspondence with the positive integers ⟨a ~ set⟩ — **count·abil·i·ty** \ˌkau̇n-tə-ˈbi-lə-tē\ *n* — **count·ably** \ˈkau̇n-tə-blē\ *adv*

count·down \ˈkau̇nt-ˌdau̇n\ *n* (ca. 1952) : an audible backward counting in fixed units (as seconds) from an arbitrary starting number to mark the time remaining before an event; *also* : preparations carried on during such a count — **count down** \-ˈdau̇n\ *vi*

[1]**coun·te·nance** \ˈkau̇n-tᵊn-ən(t)s, ˈkau̇nt-nən(t)s\ *n* [ME *contenance,* fr. AF *cuntenance, contenance,* fr. ML *continentia,* fr. L, restraint, fr. *continent-, continens,* prp. of *continēre* to hold together — more at CONTAIN] (13c) **1** *obs* **:** BEARING, DEMEANOR **2 a :** calm expression **b :** mental composure **c :** LOOK, EXPRESSION **3** *archaic* **a :** ASPECT, SEMBLANCE **b :** PRETENSE **4 :** FACE, VISAGE; *esp* : the face as an indication of mood, emotion, or character **5 :** bearing or expression that offers approval or sanction : moral support

[2]**countenance** *vt* **-nanced; -nanc·ing** (1568) : to extend approval or toleration to : SANCTION ⟨refused to ~ any changes in the policy⟩ — **coun·te·nanc·er** *n*

[1]**count·er** \ˈkau̇n-tər\ *n* [ME *countour,* fr. AF, fr. ML *computatorium* computing place, fr. L *computare*] (14c) **1 :** a piece (as of metal or plastic) used in reckoning or in games **2 :** something of value in bargaining : ASSET **3 :** a level surface (as a table, shelf or display case) over which transactions are conducted or food is served or on which goods are displayed or work is conducted ⟨jewelry ~⟩ ⟨a lunch ~⟩ — **over the counter 1 :** in or through a broker's office rather than through a stock exchange ⟨stock bought *over the counter*⟩ **2 :** without a prescription ⟨drugs available *over the counter*⟩ — **under the counter :** by surreptitious means : in an illicit and private manner ⟨workers being paid *under the counter*⟩

[2]**count·er** \ˈkau̇n-tər\ *n* [ME, fr. AF *cuntur,* fr. *cunter* to count] (14c) : one that counts; *esp* : a device for indicating a number or amount

[3]**coun·ter** *vb* **coun·tered; coun·ter·ing** \ˈkau̇n-t(ə-)riŋ\ [ME *countren,* fr. AF *cuntre* against, opposite, fr. L *contra;* akin to L *com-* with, together — more at CO-] *vt* (14c) **1 a :** to act in opposition to : OPPOSE **b :** OFFSET, NULLIFY ⟨tried to ~ the trend toward depersonalization⟩ **2 :** to assert in answer ⟨we ~*ed* that our warnings had been ignored⟩ ~ *vi* : to meet attacks or arguments with defensive or retaliatory steps

[4]**coun·ter** *adv* [ME *contre,* fr. AF *cuntre*] (15c) **1 :** in an opposite or wrong direction **2 :** to or toward a different or opposite direction, result, or effect ⟨values that run ~ to those of society⟩

[5]**coun·ter** *n* (15c) **1 :** CONTRARY, OPPOSITE **2 :** the after portion of a boat from the waterline to the extreme outward swell or stern overhang **3 a :** the act of making an attack while parrying one (as in boxing); *also* : a blow thus given in boxing **b :** an agency or force that offsets : CHECK **4 :** a stiffener to give permanent form to a boot or shoe upper around the heel **5 :** an area within the face of a letter wholly or partly enclosed by strokes **6 :** a football play in which the ballcarrier goes in a direction opposite to the movement of the play

[6]**coun·ter** *adj* (1582) **1 :** marked by or tending toward or in an opposite direction or effect **2 :** given to or marked by opposition, hostility, or

antipathy **3 :** situated or lying opposite ⟨the ~ side⟩ **4 :** recalling or ordering back by a superseding contrary order : COUNTERMANDING ⟨~ orders from the colonel⟩

counter- *prefix* [ME *contre-,* fr. AF, fr. *cuntre*] **1 a :** contrary : opposite ⟨*counter*clockwise⟩ ⟨*counter*march⟩ **b :** opposing : retaliatory ⟨*counter*force⟩ ⟨*counter*offensive⟩ **2 :** complementary : corresponding ⟨*counter*weight⟩ ⟨*counter*part⟩ **3 :** duplicate : substitute ⟨*counter*foil⟩

coun·ter·ac·cu·sa·tion
coun·ter·ad·ap·ta·tion
coun·ter·ad·ver·tis·ing
coun·ter·agent
coun·ter·ag·gres·sion
coun·ter·ar·gue
coun·ter·ar·gu·ment
coun·ter·as·sault
coun·ter·at·tack
coun·ter·at·tack·er
coun·ter·bid
coun·ter·blast
coun·ter·block·ade
coun·ter·blow
coun·ter·cam·paign
coun·ter·charge
coun·ter·com·mer·cial
coun·ter·com·plaint
coun·ter·con·spir·a·cy
coun·ter·con·ven·tion
coun·ter·coun·ter·mea·sure
coun·ter·coup
coun·ter·crit·i·cism
coun·ter·cry
coun·ter·de·mand
coun·ter·dem·on·strate
coun·ter·dem·on·stra·tion
coun·ter·dem·on·stra·tor
coun·ter·de·ploy·ment
coun·ter·ed·u·ca·tion·al
coun·ter·ef·fort
coun·ter·ev·i·dence
coun·ter·fire
coun·ter·force
coun·ter·gov·ern·ment
coun·ter·hy·poth·e·sis
coun·ter·im·age
coun·ter·in·cen·tive
coun·ter·in·fla·tion
coun·ter·in·fla·tion·ary
coun·ter·in·flu·ence
coun·ter·in·stance
coun·ter·in·sti·tu·tion
coun·ter·in·ter·pre·ta·tion
coun·ter·in·va·sion
coun·ter·memo
coun·ter·mo·bi·li·za·tion
coun·ter·move
coun·ter·move·ment
coun·ter·myth
coun·ter·or·der
coun·ter·pe·ti·tion
coun·ter·pick·et
coun·ter·play
coun·ter·ploy
coun·ter·pow·er
coun·ter·pres·sure
coun·ter·pro·ject
coun·ter·pro·pa·ganda
coun·ter·pro·test
coun·ter·pro·test·er
coun·ter·ques·tion
coun·ter·raid
coun·ter·ral·ly
coun·ter·re·ac·tion
coun·ter·re·form
coun·ter·re·form·er
coun·ter·re·sponse
coun·ter·re·tal·i·a·tion
coun·ter·shot
coun·ter·snip·er
coun·ter·spell
coun·ter·state
coun·ter·state·ment
coun·ter·step
coun·ter·strat·e·gist
coun·ter·strat·e·gy
coun·ter·stream
coun·ter·strike
coun·ter·stroke
coun·ter·style
coun·ter·sue
coun·ter·sug·ges·tion
coun·ter·suit
coun·ter·sur·veil·lance
coun·ter·tac·tics
coun·ter·ten·den·cy
coun·ter·ter·ror
coun·ter·ter·ror·ism
coun·ter·ter·ror·ist
coun·ter·threat
coun·ter·thrust
coun·ter·tra·di·tion
coun·ter·trend
coun·ter·vi·o·lence
coun·ter·world

coun·ter·act \ˌkau̇n-tər-ˈakt\ *vt* (1655) **:** to make ineffective or restrain or neutralize the usu. ill effects of by means of an opposite force, action, or influence ⟨a drug used to ~ fatigue⟩ — **coun·ter·ac·tion** \-ˈak-shən\ *n* — **coun·ter·ac·tive** \-ˈak-tiv\ *adj*

¹**coun·ter·bal·ance** \ˈkau̇n-tər-ˌba-lən(t)s, ˌkau̇n-tər-ˈ\ *n* (ca. 1611) **1 :** a weight that balances another **2 :** a force or influence that offsets or checks an opposing force

²**counterbalance** \ˌkau̇n-tər-ˈ, ˈkau̇n-tər-ˌ\ *vt* (ca. 1611) **1 :** to oppose or balance with an equal weight or force **2 :** to equip with counterbalances

coun·ter·change \ˈkau̇n-tər-ˌchānj\ *vt* (ca. 1604) **1 :** INTERCHANGE, TRANSPOSE **2 :** CHECKER 1a

¹**coun·ter·check** \-ˌchek\ *n* (1584) **:** a check or restraint often operating against something that is itself a check

²**countercheck** *vt* (1579) **1 :** CHECK, COUNTERACT **2 :** to check a second time for verification

counter check *n* (1856) **:** a check obtainable at a bank usu. to be cashed only at the bank by the drawer

¹**coun·ter·claim** \ˈkau̇n-tər-ˌklām\ *n* (1784) **:** an opposing claim; *esp* **:** a claim brought by a defendant against a plaintiff in a legal action

²**counterclaim** *vi* (1857) **:** to enter or plead a counterclaim ~ *vt* **:** to ask in a counterclaim

coun·ter·clock·wise \ˌkau̇n-tər-ˈkläk-ˌwīz\ *adv* (1888) **:** in a direction opposite to that in which the hands of a clock rotate as viewed from in front — **counterclockwise** *adj*

coun·ter·con·di·tion·ing \-kən-ˈdi-sh(ə-)niŋ\ *n* (1962) **:** conditioning in order to replace an undesirable response (as fear) to a stimulus (as an engagement in public speaking) by a favorable one

coun·ter·cul·ture \ˈkau̇n-tər-ˌkəl-chər\ *n* (1968) **:** a culture with values and mores that run counter to those of established society — **coun·ter·cul·tur·al** \ˌkau̇n-tər-ˈkəlch-rəl, -ˈkəl-chə-\ *adj* — **coun·ter·cul·tur·al·ism** \-rə-ˌli-zəm\ *n* — **coun·ter·cul·tur·ist** \-rist\ *n*

¹**coun·ter·cur·rent** \ˈkau̇n-tər-ˌkər-ənt, -ˌkə-rənt\ *n* (1684) **:** a current flowing in a direction opposite that of another current

²**countercurrent** \ˌkau̇n-tər-ˈ\ *adj* (1799) **1 :** flowing in an opposite direction **2 :** involving flow of materials in opposite directions ⟨~ dialysis⟩ — **coun·ter·cur·rent·ly** *adv*

coun·ter·cy·cli·cal \-ˈsī-kli-kəl, -ˈsi-\ *adj* (1944) **:** calculated to check excessive developments in a business cycle : COMPENSATORY ⟨~ budget policies⟩ — **coun·ter·cy·cli·cal·ly** \-k(ə-)lē\ *adv*

coun·ter·es·pi·o·nage \ˌkau̇n-tər-ˈes-pē-ə-ˌnäzh, -ˌnäj, -nij, *Canad also* -ˌnazh; -ˌes-pē-ə-ˈnäzh; -ə-ˈspē-ə-nij\ *n* (1899) **:** the activity concerned with detecting and thwarting enemy espionage

coun·ter·ex·am·ple \ˈkau̇n-tər-ig-ˌzam-pəl\ *n* (1852) **:** an example that refutes or disproves a proposition or theory

coun·ter·fac·tu·al \ˌkau̇n-tər-ˈfak-chə-wəl, -chəl, -shwəl, -chü-əl\ *adj* (1946) **:** contrary to fact ⟨~ assumptions⟩

¹**coun·ter·feit** \ˈkau̇nt-ər-ˌfit\ *adj* [ME *countrefet,* fr. AF *cuntrefeit,* fr. pp. of *cuntrefere, contrefaire* to imitate, fr. *cuntre-* + *faire* to make, fr. L *facere* — more at DO] (14c) **1 :** made in imitation of something else with intent to deceive : FORGED ⟨~ money⟩ **2 a :** INSINCERE, FEIGNED ⟨~ sympathy⟩ **b :** IMITATION ⟨~ Georgian houses⟩

²**counterfeit** *vt* (14c) **:** to imitate or feign esp. with intent to deceive; *also* **:** to make a fraudulent replica of ⟨~*ing* $20 bills⟩ ~ *vi* **1 :** to try to deceive by pretense or dissembling **2 :** to engage in counterfeiting something of value ***syn*** see ASSUME — **coun·ter·feit·er** *n*

³**counterfeit** *n* (15c) **1 :** something counterfeit : FORGERY **2 :** something likely to be mistaken for something of higher value ⟨pity was a ~ of love —Harry Hervey⟩ ***syn*** see IMPOSTURE

coun·ter·flow \ˈkau̇n-tər-ˌflō\ *n* (1870) **:** the flow of a fluid in opposite directions (as in an apparatus)

coun·ter·foil \-ˌfȯi(-ə)l\ *n* (1706) **:** a detachable stub (as on a check or ticket) usu. serving as a record or receipt

coun·ter·guer·ril·la *also* **coun·ter·gue·ril·la** \ˌkau̇n-tər-gə-ˈri-lə, -gi-, -gyi-, -ge-\ *n* (1901) **:** a guerrilla who is trained to thwart enemy guerrilla operations

coun·ter·in·sur·gen·cy \ˌkau̇n-tər-in-ˈsər-jən(t)-sē\ *n* (1962) **:** organized military activity designed to combat insurgency — **coun·ter·in·sur·gent** \-jənt\ *n*

coun·ter·in·tel·li·gence \ˌkau̇n-tər-in-ˈte-lə-jən(t)s\ *n* (1940) **:** organized activity of an intelligence service designed to block an enemy's sources of information, to deceive the enemy, to prevent sabotage, and to gather political and military information

coun·ter·in·tu·i·tive \-in-ˈtü-ə-tiv, -ˈtyü-\ *adj* (1955) **:** contrary to what one would intuitively expect — **coun·ter·in·tu·i·tive·ly** \-lē\ *adv*

coun·ter·ion \ˈkau̇n-tər-ˌī-ən, -ˌän\ *n* (1940) **:** an ion having a charge opposite to that of the substance with which it is associated

coun·ter·ir·ri·tant \ˌkau̇n-tər-ˈir-ə-tənt\ *n* (1844) **1 :** an agent applied locally to produce superficial inflammation with the object of reducing inflammation in deeper adjacent structures **2 :** an irritation or discomfort that diverts attention from another — **counterirritant** *adj*

count·er·man \ˈkau̇n-tər-ˌman, -mən\ *n* (1849) **:** one who tends a counter

¹**coun·ter·mand** \ˈkau̇n-tər-ˌmand, ˌkau̇n-tər-ˈ\ *vt* [ME *countermaunden,* fr. AF *cuntremander,* fr. *cuntre-* counter- + *mander* to command, fr. L *mandare* — more at MANDATE] (15c) **1 :** to revoke (a command) by a contrary order **2 :** to recall or order back by a superseding contrary order ⟨~ reinforcements⟩

²**coun·ter·mand** \ˈkau̇n-tər-ˌmand\ *n* (1548) **1 :** a contrary order **2 :** the revocation of an order or command

coun·ter·march \ˈkau̇n-tər-ˌmärch\ *n* (1598) **1 :** a marching back; *specif* **:** a movement in marching by which a unit of troops reverses direction while marching but keeps the same order **2 :** a march (as of political demonstrators) designed to counter the effect of another march — **countermarch** *vi*

coun·ter·mea·sure \-ˌme-zhər, -ˌmā-\ *n* (1923) **:** an action or device designed to negate or offset another; *esp* **:** a military system or device intended to thwart a sensing mechanism (as radar) ⟨electronic ~*s*⟩

coun·ter·mel·o·dy \-ˌme-lə-dē\ *n* (1926) **:** a secondary melody that is sounded simultaneously with the principal one

coun·ter·mine \-ˌmīn\ *n* (1548) **:** a tunnel for intercepting an enemy mine

coun·ter·of·fen·sive \ˈkau̇n-tər-ə-ˌfen(t)-siv\ *n* (1909) **:** a large-scale military offensive undertaken by a force previously on the defensive

coun·ter·of·fer \-ˌȯ-fər, -ˌä-fər\ *n* (1788) **:** a return offer made by one who has rejected an offer

coun·ter·pane \ˈkau̇n-tər-ˌpān\ *n* [alter. of ME *countrepointe,* modif. of MF *coute pointe,* lit., embroidered quilt] (15c) **:** BEDSPREAD

coun·ter·part \-ˌpärt\ *n* (15c) **1 :** one of two corresponding copies of a legal instrument : DUPLICATE **2 a :** a thing that fits another perfectly **b :** something that completes : COMPLEMENT **3 a :** one remarkably similar to another **b :** one having the same function or characteristics as another ⟨college presidents and their ~*s* in business⟩

coun·ter·par·ty \-ˌpär-tē\ *n* (1980) **:** a party to a financial transaction

coun·ter·plan \ˈkau̇n-tər-ˌplan\ *n* (1788) **1 :** a plan designed to counter another plan **2 :** an alternate or substitute plan

coun·ter·plea \-ˌplē\ *n* (1523) **:** a replication to a legal plea

¹**coun·ter·plot** \-ˌplät\ *n* (ca. 1611) **:** a plot designed to thwart an opponent's plot

²**counterplot** *vt* (1662) **:** to intrigue against : foil with a plot

¹**coun·ter·point** \ˈkau̇n-tər-ˌpȯint\ *n* [ME, fr. MF *contrepoint,* fr. ML *contrapunctus,* fr. L *contra-* counter- + ML *punctus* musical note, melody, fr. L, act of pricking, fr. *pungere* to prick — more at PUNGENT] (15c) **1 a :** one or more independent melodies added above or below a given melody **b :** the combination of two or more independent melodies into a single harmonic texture in which each retains its linear character : POLYPHONY **2 a :** a complementing or contrasting item : OPPOSITE **b :** use of contrast or interplay of elements in a work of art (as a drama)

²**counterpoint** *vt* (1875) **1 :** to compose or arrange in counterpoint **2 :** to set off or emphasize by juxtaposition : set in contrast ⟨~*s* the public and the private man —Tom Bishop⟩

¹**coun·ter·poise** \-ˌpȯiz\ *vt* [ME *countrepesen,* fr. AF *contrepeser,* fr. *cuntre-* + *peser* to weigh — more at POISE] (14c) **:** COUNTERBALANCE

²**counterpoise** *n* (15c) **1 :** COUNTERBALANCE **2 :** an equivalent power or force acting in opposition **3 :** a state of balance

coun·ter·pose \ˌkau̇n-tər-ˈpōz\ *vt* [*counter-* + *-pose* (as in *compose*)] (1594) **:** to place in opposition, contrast, or equilibrium ⟨~ a positive view to the negative assessment⟩

coun·ter·pro·duc·tive \-prə-ˈdək-tiv\ *adj* (1959) **:** tending to hinder the attainment of a desired goal ⟨violence as a means to achieve an end is ~ —W. E. Brock *b*1930⟩

coun·ter·pro·gram·ming \ˌkau̇n-tər-ˈprō-ˌgra-miŋ, -grə-\ *n* (ca. 1966) **:** the scheduling of programs by television networks so as to attract audiences away from simultaneously telecast programs of competitors

coun·ter·pro·pos·al \ˈkau̇n-tər-prə-ˌpō-zəl\ *n* (1885) **:** a return proposal made by one who has rejected a proposal

coun·ter·punch \ˈkau̇n-tər-ˌpənch\ *n* (1942) **:** a counter in boxing; *also* **:** a countering blow or attack — **counterpunch** *vi* — **coun·ter·punch·er** \-ˌpən-chər\ *n*

coun·ter·ref·or·ma·tion \ˌkau̇n-tə(r)-ˌre-fər-ˈmā-shən\ *n* (1840) **1** *usu* **Counter–Reformation :** the reform movement in the Roman Catholic Church following the Reformation **2 :** a reformation designed to counter the effects of a previous reformation

coun·ter·rev·o·lu·tion \-ˌre-və-ˈlü-shən\ *n* (1793) **1 :** a revolution directed toward overthrowing a government or social system established

\ə\ **abut** \ᵊ\ kitten, F table \ər\ **further** \a\ **ash** \ā\ **ace** \ä\ **mop, mar** \au̇\ **out** \ch\ **chin** \e\ **bet** \ē\ **easy** \g\ **go** \i\ **hit** \ī\ **ice** \j\ **job** \ŋ\ **sing** \ō\ **go** \ȯ\ **law** \ȯi\ **boy** \th\ **thin** \t͟h\ **the** \ü\ **loot** \u̇\ **foot** \y\ **yet** \zh\ **vision, beige** \k̲, ⁿ, œ, ue, ʸ\ *see* Guide to Pronunciation

by a previous revolution **2 :** a movement to counteract revolutionary trends — **coun·ter·rev·o·lu·tion·ary** \-shə-ˌner-ē\ *adj or n*

coun·ter·shad·ing \ˈkau̇n-tər-ˌshā-diŋ\ *n* (1896) **:** cryptic coloration of an animal with parts normally in shadow being light and parts normally illuminated being dark thereby reducing shadows and contours

coun·ter·sign \-ˌsīn\ *n* (1591) **1 :** a signature attesting the authenticity of a document already signed by another **2 :** a sign given in reply to another; *specif* **:** a military secret signal that must be given by one wishing to pass a guard — **countersign** *vt* — **coun·ter·sig·na·ture** \ˌkau̇n-tər-ˈsig-nə-ˌchu̇r, -chər, -ˌtyu̇r, -ˌtu̇r\ *n*

[1]**coun·ter·sink** \ˈkau̇n-tər-ˌsiŋk\ *vt* **-sunk** \-ˌsəŋk\; **-sink·ing** (1816) **1 :** to make a countersink on (a hole) **2 :** to set the head of (as a screw) at or below the surface

[2]**countersink** *n* (1816) **1 :** a bit or drill for making a funnel-shaped enlargement at the outer end of a drilled hole **2 :** the enlargement made by a countersink

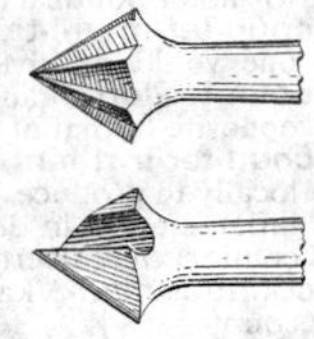

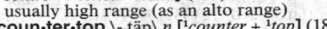

countersink 1

coun·ter·spy \ˈkau̇n-tər-ˌspī\ *n* (1939) **:** a spy engaged in counterespionage

coun·ter·stain \-ˌstān\ *vt* (1895) **:** to stain (as a microscopy specimen) so as to color parts (as the cytoplasm of cells) not colored by another stain (as a nuclear stain) — **counterstain** *n*

coun·ter·ten·or \-ˌte-nər\ *n* [ME *countretenour* part balancing the tenor, fr. MF *contreteneur,* fr. *contre-* + *teneur* tenor] (15c) **:** a tenor with an unusually high range (as an alto range)

coun·ter·top \-ˌtäp\ *n* [[1]*counter* + [1]*top*] (1897) **:** the flat working surface on top of waist-level kitchen cabinets

coun·ter·trade \-ˌtrād\ *n* (1976) **:** a form of international trade in which purchases made by an importing nation are linked to offsetting purchases made by the exporting nation

coun·ter·trans·fer·ence \ˌkau̇n-tər-(ˌ)tran(t)s-ˈfər-ən(t)s, -ˈtran(t)s-(ˌ)\ *n* (1920) **1 :** psychological transference esp. by a psychotherapist during the course of treatment; *esp* **:** the psychotherapist's reactions to the patient's transference **2 :** the complex of feelings of a psychotherapist toward the patient

coun·ter·vail \ˌkau̇n-tər-ˈvāl\ *vb* [ME *countrevailen,* fr. AF *cuntrevaloir,* fr. *cuntre-* counter- + *valoir* to be worth, fr. L *valēre* — more at WIELD] *vt* (14c) **1 :** to compensate for **2** *archaic* **:** EQUAL, MATCH **3 :** to exert force against **:** COUNTERACT ~ *vi* **:** to exert force against an opposing and often bad or harmful force or influence

coun·ter·view \ˈkau̇n-tər-ˌvyü\ *n* (1590) **1** *archaic* **:** CONFRONTATION **2 :** an opposite point of view

coun·ter·weight \-ˌwāt\ *n* (1693) **:** an equivalent weight or force **:** COUNTERBALANCE — **counterweight** *vt*

count·ess \ˈkau̇n-təs\ *n* (12c) **1 :** the wife or widow of an earl or count **2 :** a woman who holds in her own right the rank of earl or count

coun·ti·an \ˈkau̇n-tē-ən\ *n* (15c) **:** a native or resident of a usu. specified county

count·ing·house \ˈkau̇n-tiŋ-ˌhau̇s\ *n* (15c) **:** a building, room, or office used for keeping books and transacting business

counting number *n* (ca. 1965) **:** NATURAL NUMBER

counting room *n* (1712) **:** COUNTINGHOUSE

count·less \ˈkau̇nt-ləs\ *adj* (1588) **:** too numerous to be counted **:** MYRIAD, MANY — **count·less·ly** *adv*

count noun *n* (1952) **:** a noun (as *bean* or *sheet*) that forms a plural and is used with a numeral, with words such as *many* or *few,* or with the indefinite article *a* or *an* — compare MASS NOUN

count palatine *n* (1539) **1 a :** a count of the Holy Roman Empire having imperial powers in his own domain **b :** a high judicial official in the Holy Roman Empire **2 :** the proprietor of a county palatine in England or Ireland

coun·tri·fied *also* **coun·try·fied** \ˈkən-tri-ˌfīd\ *adj* [*country* + *-fied* (as in *glorified*)] (1653) **1 :** RURAL, RUSTIC **2 :** UNSOPHISTICATED **3 :** played or sung in the manner of country music ⟨~ rock⟩

[1]**coun·try** \ˈkən-trē\ *n, pl* **countries** [ME *contree,* fr. AF *cuntree, contré,* fr. ML *contrata,* fr. L *contra* against, on the opposite side] (13c) **1 :** an indefinite usu. extended expanse of land **:** REGION ⟨miles of open ~⟩ **2 a :** the land of a person's birth, residence, or citizenship **b :** a political state or nation or its territory **3 a :** the people of a state or district **:** POPULACE **b :** JURY **c :** ELECTORATE 2 **4 :** rural as distinguished from urban areas ⟨prefers the ~ to the city⟩ **5 :** COUNTRY MUSIC — **coun·try·ish** \-trē-ish\ *adj*

[2]**country** *adj* (14c) **1 :** of, relating to, or characteristic of the country **2 a :** of or relating to a decorative style associated with life in the country ⟨an English ~ look⟩; *also* **:** possessing a style of rustic simplicity ⟨~ furniture⟩ **b :** prepared or processed with farm supplies and procedures ⟨~ ham⟩ **3 :** of, relating to, suitable for, or featuring country music ⟨~ singers⟩

country and western *n* (1960) **:** COUNTRY MUSIC — usu. hyphenated in attributive use

country–club *adj* (1894) **1 :** typical, characteristic, or suggestive of a country club ⟨a ~ atmosphere⟩ ⟨a ~ prison⟩ **2 :** having qualities (as affluence) associated with the members of a country club ⟨a ~ conservative⟩

country club *n* (1867) **:** a suburban club for social life and recreation; *esp* **:** one having a golf course

coun·try–dance \ˈkən-trē-ˌdan(t)s\ *n* (1579) **:** any of various native English dances in which partners face each other esp. in rows

country gentleman *n* (1632) **1 :** a well-to-do country resident **:** an owner of a country estate **2 :** one of the English landed gentry

country house *n* (14c) **:** a house and esp. a mansion in the country

coun·try·man \ˈkən-trē-mən, *3 often* -ˌman\ *n* (14c) **1 :** an inhabitant or native of a specified country **2 :** COMPATRIOT **3 :** one living in the country or marked by country ways **:** RUSTIC

country mile *n* (1950) **:** a long distance

country music *n* (1952) **:** music derived from or imitating the folk style of the Southern U.S. or of the Western cowboy

country rock *n* (1968) **:** rock music containing elements of country music

coun·try·seat \ˌkən-trē-ˈsēt\ *n* (1583) **:** a house or estate in the country

coun·try·side \ˈkən-trē-ˌsīd\ *n* (1727) **1 :** a rural area **2 :** the inhabitants of a countryside

coun·try·wide \ˈkən-trē-ˈwīd\ *adj* (1915) **:** extending throughout a country

coun·try·wom·an \ˈkən-trē-ˌwu̇-mən\ *n* (15c) **1 :** a woman who is a compatriot **2 :** a woman who is a resident of the country

[1]**coun·ty** \ˈkau̇n-tē\ *n, pl* **counties** [ME *counte,* fr. AF *cunté, counté,* fr. ML *comitatus,* fr. LL, office of a count, fr. *comit-, comes* count — more at COUNT] (14c) **1 :** the domain of a count **2 a :** one of the territorial divisions of England and Wales and formerly also of Scotland and Northern Ireland constituting the chief units for administrative, judicial, and political purposes **b (1) :** the people of a county **(2)** *Brit* **:** the gentry of a county **3 :** the largest territorial division for local government within a state of the U.S. **4 :** the largest local administrative unit in various countries — **county** *adj*

[2]**county** *n, pl* **counties** [modif. of MF *comte*] (1550) *archaic* **:** [3]COUNT

county agent *n* (1705) **:** a consultant employed jointly by federal and state governments to provide information about agriculture and home economics

county court *n* (1639) **:** a court in some states that has a designated jurisdiction usu. both civil and criminal within the limits of a county

county fair *n* (1856) **:** a fair usu. held annually at a set location in a county esp. to exhibit local agricultural products and livestock

county palatine *n* (15c) **:** the territory of a count palatine

county seat *n* (1803) **:** a town that is the seat of county administration

county town *n* (1670) *chiefly Brit* **:** COUNTY SEAT

[1]**coup** \ˈkōp\ *vb* [ME, to strike, fr. AF *couper* — more at COPE] (ca. 1572) *chiefly Scot* **:** OVERTURN, UPSET

[2]**coup** \ˈkü\ *n, pl* **coups** \ˈküz\ [F, blow, stroke — more at COPE] (1791) **1 :** a brilliant, sudden, and usu. highly successful stroke or act **2 :** COUP D'ÉTAT

coup de grâce *or* **coup de grace** \ˌkü-də-ˈgräs\ *n, pl* **coups de grâce** *or* **coups de grace** \ˌkü-də-\ [F *coup de grâce,* lit., stroke of mercy] (1699) **1 :** a deathblow or death shot administered to end the suffering of one mortally wounded **2 :** a decisive finishing blow, act, or event

coup de main \-ˈmaⁿ\ *n, pl* **coups de main** \ˌkü-də-\ [F, lit., hand stroke] (1758) **:** a sudden attack in force

coup d'état *or* **coup d'etat** \ˌkü-(ˌ)dā-ˈtä, ˈkü-(ˌ)dā-ˌ, -də-\ *n, pl* **coups d'état** *or* **coups d'etat** \-ˈtä(z), -ˌtä(z)\ [F, lit., stroke of state] (1646) **:** a sudden decisive exercise of force in politics; *esp* **:** the violent overthrow or alteration of an existing government by a small group

coup de thé·âtre *or* **coup de the·atre** \ˌkü-də-tā-ˈätrᵊ\ *n, pl* **coups de théâtre** *or* **coups de theatre** \ˌkü-də-\ [F *coup de théâtre,* lit., stroke of theater] (1747) **1 :** a sudden sensational turn in a play; *also* **:** a sudden dramatic effect or turn of events **2 :** a theatrical success

coup d'oeil \kü-ˈdə(r), -ˈdə-ē, -ˈdœ-yə\ *n, pl* **coups d'oeil** *same*\ [F, lit., stroke of the eye] (1739) **:** a brief survey **:** GLANCE

cou·pé *or* **coupe** \kü-ˈpā, *2 often* ˈküp\ *n* [F *coupé,* fr. pp. of *couper* to cut, strike] (1825) **1 :** a four-wheeled closed horse-drawn carriage for two persons inside with an outside seat for the driver in front **2** *usu* *coupe* **:** a 2-door automobile often seating only two persons; *also* **:** one with a tight-spaced rear seat — compare SEDAN

[1]**cou·ple** \ˈkə-pəl; *"couple of" is often* ˌkə-plə(v)\ *n* [ME, pair, bond, fr. AF *cuple,* fr. L *copula* bond, fr. *co-* + *apere* to fasten — more at APT] (13c) **1 a :** two persons married, engaged, or otherwise romantically paired **b :** two persons paired together **2 :** PAIR, BRACE **3 :** something that joins or links two things together: as **a :** two equal and opposite forces that act along parallel lines **b :** a pair of substances that in contact with an electrolyte participate in a transfer of electrons which causes an electric current to flow **4 :** an indefinite small number **:** FEW ⟨a ~ of days ago⟩ — **cou·ple·dom** \-dəm\ *n*

[2]**cou·ple** \ˈkə-pəl\ *vb* **cou·pled; cou·pling** \-p(ə-)liŋ\ *vt* (13c) **1 a :** to connect for consideration together **b :** to join for combined effect **2 a :** to fasten together **:** LINK **b :** to bring (two electric circuits) into such close proximity as to permit mutual influence **3 :** to join in marriage or sexual union ~ *vi* **1 :** to unite in sexual union **2 :** JOIN **3 :** to unite chemically

[3]**couple** *adj* (1924) **:** TWO; *also* **:** FEW — used with *a* ⟨a ~ drinks⟩

usage The adjective use of *a couple,* without *of,* has been called nonstandard, but it is not. In both British and American English it is standard before a word (as *more* or *less*) indicating degree ⟨a *couple* more examples of Middle English writing —Charles Barber⟩. Its use before an ordinary plural noun is an Americanism, common in speech and in writing that is not meant to be formal or elevated ⟨the first *couple* chapters are pretty good —E. B. White (letter)⟩ ⟨still operated a *couple* wagons for hire —Garrison Keillor⟩. It is most frequently used with periods of time ⟨a *couple* weeks⟩ and numbers ⟨a *couple* hundred⟩ ⟨a *couple* dozen⟩.

cou·ple·ment \ˈkə-pəl-mənt\ *n* [MF, fr. OF *cupler* to join, fr. L *copulare,* fr. *copula*] (1548) *archaic* **:** the act or result of coupling

cou·pler \ˈkə-p(ə-)lər\ *n* (1552) **1 :** one that couples **2 :** a contrivance on a keyboard instrument by which keyboards or keys are connected to play together

cou·plet \ˈkə-plət\ *n* [MF, dim. of OF *cuple, couple*] (1580) **1 :** two successive lines of verse forming a unit marked usu. by rhythmic correspondence, rhyme, or the inclusion of a self-contained utterance **:** DISTICH **2 :** COUPLE

cou·pling \ˈkə-pliŋ (*usual for 2*), -pə-liŋ\ *n* (14c) **1 :** the act of bringing or coming together **:** PAIRING; *specif* **:** sexual union **2 :** a device that serves to connect the ends of adjacent parts or objects **3 :** the joining of or the part of the body that joins the hindquarters to the forequarters of a quadruped **4 :** a means of electric connection of two electric circuits by having a part common to both

cou·pon \ˈkü-ˌpän, ˈkyü-\ *n* [F, fr. OF, piece, fr. *couper* to cut — more at COPE] (1822) **1 :** a statement of due interest to be cut from a bearer bond when payable and presented for payment; *also* **:** the interest rate of a coupon **2 :** a form surrendered in order to obtain an article, service, or accommodation: as **a :** one of a series of attached tickets or certificates often to be detached and presented as needed **b :** a ticket or form authorizing purchases of rationed commodities **c :** a certificate or similar evidence of a purchase redeemable in premiums **d :** a part of a printed advertisement to be cut off to use as an order blank or inquiry form or to obtain a discount on merchandise or services

cou·pon·ing \ˈkü-ˌpä-niŋ, ˈkyü-\ *n* (1954) **:** the distribution or redemption of coupons

cour·age \ˈkər-ij, ˈkə-rij\ *n* [ME *corage,* fr. AF *curage,* fr. *quer, coer* heart, fr. L *cor* — more at HEART] (14c) **:** mental or moral strength to venture, persevere, and withstand danger, fear, or difficulty

syn COURAGE, METTLE, SPIRIT, RESOLUTION, TENACITY mean mental or moral strength to resist opposition, danger, or hardship. COURAGE implies firmness of mind and will in the face of danger or extreme difficulty ⟨the *courage* to support unpopular causes⟩. METTLE suggests an ingrained capacity for meeting strain or difficulty with fortitude and resilience ⟨a challenge that will test your *mettle*⟩. SPIRIT also suggests a quality of temperament enabling one to hold one's own or keep up one's morale when opposed or threatened ⟨her *spirit* was unbroken by failure⟩. RESOLUTION stresses firm determination to achieve one's ends ⟨the *resolution* of pioneer women⟩. TENACITY adds to RESOLUTION implications of stubborn persistence and unwillingness to admit defeat ⟨held to their beliefs with great *tenacity*⟩.

cou·ra·geous \kə-ˈrā-jəs\ *adj* (14c) **:** having or characterized by courage **:** BRAVE ⟨a ~ soldier⟩ ⟨a ~ decision⟩ — **cou·ra·geous·ly** *adv* — **cou·ra·geous·ness** *n*

cou·rante \kü-ˈränt, -ˈrant\ *n* [MF, fr. *courir* to run, fr. L *currere*] (1586) **1 :** a dance of Italian origin marked by quick running steps **2 :** music in quick triple time or in a mixture of 3/2 and 6/4 time

cou·reur de bois \kü-ˌrər-də-ˈbwä\ *n, pl* **coureurs de bois** *same*\ [CanF, lit., woods runner] (1700) **:** a French or métis trapper of No. America and esp. of Canada

cour·gette \kür-ˈzhet\ *n* [F, dim. of *courge* gourd, fr. MF, fr. L *cucurbita*] (1931) *chiefly Brit* **:** ZUCCHINI

cou·ri·er \ˈkür-ē-ər, ˈkər-ē-, ˈkə-rē-\ *n* [MF *courrier,* fr. OIt *corriere,* fr. *correre* to run, fr. L *currere*] (1579) **1 :** MESSENGER: as **a :** a member of a diplomatic service entrusted with bearing messages **b (1) :** an espionage agent transferring secret information **(2) :** a runner of contraband **c :** a member of the armed services whose duties include carrying mail, information, or supplies **2 :** a traveler's paid attendant; *esp* **:** a tourists' guide employed by a travel agency

[1]**course** \ˈkōrs\ *n* [ME, fr. AF *curs, course,* fr. L *cursus,* fr. *currere* to run — more at CAR] (14c) **1 :** the act or action of moving in a path from point to point **2 :** the path over which something moves or extends: as **a :** RACECOURSE **b (1) :** the direction of travel of a vehicle (as a ship or airplane) usu. measured as a clockwise angle from north; *also* **:** the projected path of travel **(2) :** a point of the compass **c :** WATERCOURSE **d :** GOLF COURSE **3 a :** accustomed procedure or normal action ⟨the law taking its ~⟩ **b :** a chosen manner of conducting oneself **:** way of acting ⟨our wisest ~ is to retreat⟩ **c (1) :** progression through a development or period or a series of acts or events **(2) :** LIFE HISTORY, CAREER **4 :** an ordered process or succession: as **a :** a number of lectures or other matter dealing with a subject; *also* **:** a series of such courses constituting a curriculum ⟨a premed ~⟩ **b :** a series of doses or medications administered over a designated period **5 a :** a part of a meal served at one time ⟨the main ~⟩ **b :** LAYER; *esp* **:** a continuous level range of brick or masonry throughout a wall **c :** the lowest sail on a square-rigged mast — **in due course :** after a normal passage of time **:** in the expected or allotted time ⟨his discoveries led *in due course* to new forms of treatment⟩ — **of course 1 :** following the ordinary way or procedure ⟨will be done as a matter *of course*⟩ **2 :** as might be expected ⟨*of course* we will go⟩

[2]**course** *vb* **coursed; cours·ing** *vt* (15c) **1 :** to follow close upon **:** PURSUE **2 a :** to hunt or pursue (game) with hounds **b :** to cause (dogs) to run (as after game) **3 :** to run or move swiftly through or over **:** TRAVERSE ⟨jets *coursed* the area daily⟩ ~ *vi* **:** to run or pass rapidly along or as if along an indicated path ⟨blood *coursing* through the veins⟩

course of study (1647) **1 :** CURRICULUM **2 :** COURSE 4a

[1]**cours·er** \ˈkōr-sər\ *n* [ME, fr. AF *cursier, corser,* fr. *curs* course, run] (14c) **:** a swift or spirited horse **:** CHARGER

[2]**courser** *n* (1600) **1 :** a dog for coursing **2 :** one that courses **:** HUNTSMAN **3 :** any of various Old World birds (subfamily Cursoriinae of the family Glareolidae) noted for their speed in running

course·ware \ˈkōrs-ˌwer\ *n* (1972) **:** educational software

coursing *n* (1538) **1 :** the pursuit of running game with dogs that follow by sight instead of by scent **2 :** the act of one that courses

[1]**court** \ˈkōrt\ *n, often attrib* [ME, fr. AF *curt, court,* fr. L *cohort-, cohors* enclosure, group, retinue, cohort, fr. *co-* + *-hort-, -hors* (akin to *hortus* garden) — more at YARD] (12c) **1 a :** the residence or establishment of a sovereign or similar dignitary **b :** a sovereign's formal assembly of councillors and officers **c :** the sovereign and officers and advisers who are the governing power **d :** the family and retinue of a sovereign **e :** a reception held by a sovereign **2 a (1) :** a manor house or large building surrounded by usu. enclosed grounds **(2) :** MOTEL **b :** an open space enclosed wholly or partly by buildings or circumscribed by a single building **c :** a quadrangular space walled or marked off for playing one of various games with a ball (as lawn tennis, handball, or basketball); *also* **:** a division of such a court **d :** a wide alley with only one opening onto a street **3 a :** an official assembly for the transaction of judicial business **b :** a session of such a court ⟨~ is now adjourned⟩ **c :** a place (as a chamber) for the administration of justice **d :** a judge or judges in session; *also* **:** a faculty or agency of judgment or evaluation ⟨rest our case in the ~ of world opinion —L. H. Marks⟩ **4 a :** an assembly or board with legislative or administrative powers **b :** PARLIAMENT, LEGISLATURE **5 :** conduct or attention intended to win favor or dispel hostility **:** HOMAGE ⟨pay ~ to the king⟩

[2]**court** *vt* (1567) **1 a :** to seek to gain or achieve ⟨~ power⟩ **b (1) :** ALLURE, TEMPT **(2) :** to act so as to invite or provoke ⟨~*s* disaster⟩ **2 a :** to seek the affections of; *esp* **:** to seek to win a pledge of marriage from **b** *of an animal* **:** to perform actions in order to attract for mating ⟨a male bird ~*ing* a female⟩ **3 a :** to seek to attract (as by solicitous attention or offers of advantages) ⟨college teams ~*ing* high school basketball stars⟩ **b :** to seek an alliance with ~ *vi* **1 :** to engage in social activities leading to engagement and marriage **2** *of an animal* **:** to engage in activity leading to mating

court bouil·lon \ˈkür-(ˌ)bü-ˈyōⁿ, -(ˌ)bwē-, ˈkōr-\ *n* [F *court-bouillon,* lit., short bouillon] (1723) **:** a liquid made usu. with water, white wine, vegetables, and seasonings and used to poach fish

cour·te·ous \ˈkər-tē-əs, *Brit also* ˈkōr-\ *adj* [ME *corteis,* fr. AF *curteis,* fr. *curt*] (13c) **1 :** marked by polished manners, gallantry, or ceremonial usage of a court **2 :** marked by respect for and consideration of others *syn* see CIVIL — **cour·te·ous·ly** *adv* — **cour·te·ous·ness** *n*

cour·te·san \ˈkōr-tə-zən, -ˌzan *also* ˈkər-, -ˌzän; *esp Brit* ˌkōr-tə-ˈzan\ *n* [MF *courtisane,* fr. northern It dial. form of It *cortigiana* woman courtier, fem. of *cortigiano* courtier, fr. *corte* court, fr. L *cohort-, cohors*] (1533) **:** a prostitute with a courtly, wealthy, or upper-class clientele

[1]**cour·te·sy** \ˈkər-tə-sē, *Brit also* ˈkōr-\ *n, pl* **-sies** [ME *corteisie,* fr. AF *curteisie,* fr. *curteis*] (13c) **1 a :** courteous behavior **b :** a courteous act or expression **2 a :** general allowance despite facts **:** INDULGENCE ⟨hills called mountains by ~ only⟩ **b :** consideration, cooperation, and generosity in providing something (as a gift or privilege); *also* **:** AGENCY, MEANS — used chiefly in the phrases *through the courtesy of* or *by courtesy of* or sometimes simply *courtesy of*

[2]**courtesy** *adj* (1613) **:** granted, provided, or performed as a courtesy or by way of courtesy ⟨made a ~ call on the ambassador⟩

courtesy card *n* (1934) **:** a card entitling its holder to some special privilege

courtesy title *n* (1865) **1 :** a title (as "Lord" added to the Christian name of a peer's younger son) used in addressing certain lineal relatives of British peers **2 :** a title (as "Professor" for any teacher) taken by the user and commonly accepted without consideration of official right

court·house \ˈkōrt-ˌhau̇s\ *n* (15c) **1 a :** a building in which courts of law are regularly held **b :** the principal building in which county offices are housed **2 :** COUNTY SEAT

cour·tier \ˈkōr-tē-ər, ˈkōrt-yər, ˈkōr-chər\ *n* (14c) **1 :** one in attendance at a royal court **2 :** one who practices flattery

[1]**court·ly** \ˈkōrt-lē\ *adj* **court·li·er; -est** (15c) **1 a :** of a quality befitting the court **:** ELEGANT **b :** insincerely flattering **2 :** favoring the policy or party of the court — **court·li·ness** *n*

[2]**courtly** *adv* (ca. 1592) **:** in a courtly manner **:** POLITELY

courtly love *n* (1702) **:** a late medieval conventionalized code prescribing conduct and emotions of ladies and their lovers

[1]**court–mar·tial** \ˈkōrt-ˌmär-shəl, -ˈmär-\ *n, pl* **courts–martial** *also* **court–martials** (1651) **1 :** a court consisting of commissioned officers and in some instances enlisted personnel for the trial of members of the armed forces or others within its jurisdiction **2 :** a trial by court-martial

[2]**court–martial** *vt* **–mar·tialed** *also* **–mar·tialled; –mar·tial·ing** *also* **–mar·tial·ling** \-ˌmär-sh(ə-)liŋ, -ˈmär-\ (1833) **:** to subject to trial by court-martial

court of appeals *often cap C&A* (1768) **:** a court hearing appeals from the decisions of lower courts — called also *court of appeal*

court of claims (1691) **:** a court that has jurisdiction over claims (as against a government)

court of common pleas (1606) **1 :** a former English superior court having civil jurisdiction **2 :** an intermediate court in some American states that usu. has civil and criminal jurisdiction

court of domestic relations (1926) **:** a court that has jurisdiction and often special advisory powers over family disputes involving the rights and duties of husband, wife, parent, or child esp. in matters affecting the support, custody, and welfare of children

court of honor (1593) **:** a tribunal (as a military court) for investigating questions of personal honor

court of inquiry (1757) **:** a military court that inquires into and reports on some military matter (as an officer's questionable conduct)

court of law (14c) **:** a court that hears cases and decides them on the basis of statutes or the common law

court of record (15c) **:** a court whose acts and proceedings are kept on permanent record

Court of St. James's \-sənt-ˈjāmz, -ˈjām-zəz, -ˌsānt-\ [fr. *St. James's* Palace, London, former seat of the British court] (1797) **:** the British royal court

court of sessions (1843) **:** any of various state criminal courts of record

court order *n* (1650) **:** an order issuing from a competent court that requires a party to do or abstain from doing a specified act

court plaster *n* [fr. its use for beauty spots by ladies at royal courts] (1772) **:** an adhesive plaster esp. of silk coated with isinglass and glycerin

court reporter *n* (1894) **:** a stenographer who records and transcribes a verbatim report of all proceedings in a court of law

court·room \ˈkōrt-ˌrüm, -ˌru̇m\ *n* (1677) **:** a room in which a court of law is held

court·ship \-ˌship\ *n* (1596) **:** the act, process, or period of courting

court·side \-ˌsīd\ *n* (1969) **:** the area at the edge of a court (as for tennis or basketball)

court tennis *n* (ca. 1890) **:** a game played with a ball and racket in an enclosed court divided by a net

court·yard \ˈkōrt-ˌyärd\ *n* (1552) **:** a court or enclosure adjacent to a building (as a house or palace)

cous·cous \ˈküs-ˌküs\ *n* [F *couscous, couscoussou,* fr. Ar *kuskus, kuskusū*] (1738) **:** a No. African dish of steamed semolina usu. served with meat or vegetables; *also* **:** the semolina itself

cous·in \ˈkə-zən\ *n* [ME *cosin,* fr. AF *cusin, cosin,* fr. L *consobrinus,* fr. *com-* + *sobrinus* second cousin, fr. *soror* sister — more at SISTER] (13c) **1 a :** a child of one's uncle or aunt **b :** a relative descended from one's grandparent or more remote ancestor by two or more steps and in a different line **c :** KINSMAN, RELATIVE ⟨a distant ~⟩ **2 :** one associated with or related to another **:** COUNTERPART **3 —** used as a title by a sovereign in addressing a nobleman **4 :** a person of a race or people ethnically or culturally related ⟨our English ~*s*⟩ — **cous·in·hood** \-ˌhu̇d\ *n* — **cous·in·ly** *adj* — **cous·in·ship** \-ˌship\ *n*

cous·in·age \ˈkə-zə-nij\ *n* (14c) **1 :** relationship of cousins **:** KINSHIP **2 :** a collection of cousins **:** KINFOLK

\ə\ **abut** \ᵊ\ kitten, F table \ər\ **fur**ther \a\ **a**sh \ā\ **a**ce \ä\ m**o**p, m**a**r \au̇\ **ou**t \ch\ **ch**in \e\ b**e**t \ē\ **ea**sy \g\ **g**o \i\ h**i**t \ī\ **i**ce \j\ **j**ob \ŋ\ si**ng** \ō\ g**o** \ȯ\ l**aw** \ȯi\ b**oy** \th\ **th**in \t͟h\ **th**e \ü\ l**oo**t \u̇\ f**oo**t \y\ **y**et \zh\ vi**s**ion, beige \k, ⁿ, œ, ue, ʸ\ *see* Guide to Pronunciation

cous·in–ger·man \ˌkə-zən-ˈjər-mən\ *n, pl* **cous·ins–ger·man** \-zənz-\ [ME *cosin germain,* fr. MF, fr. OF, fr. *cosin* + *germain* german] (14c) : COUSIN 1a
Cousin Jack \ˌkə-zən-ˈjak\ *n* (1890) : CORNISHMAN; *esp* : a Cornish miner
¹**couth** \ˈküth\ *adj* [back-formation fr. *uncouth*] (1896) : SOPHISTICATED, POLISHED
²**couth** *n* (1947) : POLISH, REFINEMENT ⟨I expected kindness and gentility . . . but there is such a thing as too much ~ —S. J. Perelman⟩
couth·ie \ˈkü-thē\ *adj* [ME *couth* familiar, fr. OE *cūth* — more at UNCOUTH] (1719) *chiefly Scot* : PLEASANT, KINDLY
cou·ture \kü-ˈtu̇r, -ˈtœr\ *n* [F, fr. OF *cousture* sewing, fr. VL **consutura,* fr. L *consutus,* pp. of *consuere* to sew together, fr. *com-* + *suere* to sew — more at SEW] (1908) **1** : the business of designing, making, and selling fashionable custom-made women's clothing **2** : the designers and establishments engaged in couture **3** : the clothes created by couture
cou·tu·ri·er \kü-ˈtu̇r-ē-ər, -ē-ˌā\ *n* [F, dressmaker, fr. OF *cousturier* tailor's assistant, fr. *cousture*] (1899) : an establishment engaged in couture; *also* : the proprietor of or designer for such an establishment
cou·tu·ri·ere \kü-ˈtu̇r-ē-ər, -ē-ˌer\ *n* [F *couturière,* fr. OF *cousturiere,* fem. of *cousturier*] (1818) : a woman who is a couturier
cou·vade \kü-ˈväd\ *n* [F, fr. MF, cowardly inactivity, fr. *cover* to sit on, brood over — more at COVEY] (1865) : a custom in some cultures in which when a child is born the father takes to bed as if bearing the child and submits himself to fasting, purification, or taboos
co·va·lence \ˌkō-ˈvā-lən(t)s, ˈkō-ˌ\ *n* (1919) : valence characterized by the sharing of electrons
co·va·len·cy \-lən(t)-sē\ *n* (1919) : COVALENCE
co·va·lent \ˌkō-ˈvā-lənt, ˈkō-ˌ\ *adj* (ca. 1926) : of, relating to, or characterized by covalent bonds — **co·va·lent·ly** \-lē\ *adv*
covalent bond *n* (1939) : a chemical bond formed between atoms by the sharing of electrons
co·vari·ance \ˌkō-ˈver-ē-ən(t)s, ˈkō-ˌ\ *n* (1931) **1** : the expected value of the product of the deviations of two random variables from their respective means **2** : the arithmetic mean of the products of the deviations of corresponding values of two quantitative variables from their respective means
co·var·i·ant \-ənt\ *adj* [ISV] (1893) : varying with something else so as to preserve certain mathematical interrelations
co·var·i·ate \-ˌāt, -ət\ *n* (1965) : any of two or more random variables exhibiting correlated variation
co·vari·a·tion \ˌkō-ˌver-ē-ˈā-shən\ *n* (1906) : correlated variation of two or more variables
co·vary \-ˈver-ē\ *vi* **-var·ied; -vary·ing** (1950) : to exhibit covariation
¹**cove** \ˈkōv\ *n* [ME, den, fr. OE *cofa;* akin to OHG *chubisi* hut] (bef. 12c) **1** : a recessed place : CONCAVITY: as **a** : an architectural member with a concave cross section **b** : a trough for concealed lighting at the upper part of a wall **2** : a small sheltered inlet or bay **3 a** : a deep recess or small valley in the side of a mountain **b** : a level area sheltered by hills or mountains
²**cove** *vt* **coved; cov·ing** (1756) : to make in a hollow concave form
³**cove** *n* [Romany *kova* thing, person] (1567) *Brit* : MAN, FELLOW
co·vel·lite \kō-ˈve-ˌlīt, ˈkō-və-ˌ\ *also* **co·vel·line** \-ˌlēn\ *n* [F *covelline,* fr. Niccolò *Covelli* †1829 Ital. chemist] (1850) : a usu. blue mineral consisting of a sulfide of copper
co·ven \ˈkə-vən *also* ˈkō-\ *n* [ME *covin* agreement, confederacy, fr. AF *covine,* fr. ML *convenium* agreement, fr. L *convenire* to agree — more at CONVENIENT] (ca. 1520) **1** : a collection of individuals with similar interests or activities ⟨a ~ of intellectuals⟩ **2** : an assembly or band of usu. 13 witches
¹**cov·e·nant** \ˈkəv-nənt, ˈkə-və-\ *n* [ME, fr. AF, fr. prp. of *covenir* to be fitting, fr. L *convenire*] (14c) **1** : a usu. formal, solemn, and binding agreement : COMPACT **2 a** : a written agreement or promise usu. under seal between two or more parties esp. for the performance of some action **b** : the common-law action to recover damages for breach of such a contract — **cov·e·nan·tal** \ˌkə-və-ˈnan-tᵊl\ *adj*
²**cov·e·nant** \-nənt, -ˌnant\ *vt* (14c) : to promise by a covenant : PLEDGE ~ *vi* : to enter into a covenant : CONTRACT
cov·e·nan·tee \ˌkə-və-ˌnan-ˈtē, -nən-\ *n* (1649) : the person to whom a promise in the form of a covenant is made
cov·e·nant·er \ˈkə-və-ˌnan-tər, *1 also* ˌkə-və-ˈ\ *n* (1638) **1** *cap* : a signer or adherent of the Scottish National Covenant of 1638 **2** : one that makes a covenant
cov·e·nan·tor \ˈkə-və-ˌnan-tər; ˌkə-və-ˌnan-ˈtȯr, -nən-\ *n* (1649) : a party bound by a covenant
Cov·en·try \ˈkə-vən-trē *also* ˈkä-\ *n* [*Coventry,* England] (1765) : a state of ostracism or exclusion ⟨sent to ~⟩
¹**cov·er** \ˈkə-vər\ *vb* **cov·ered; cov·er·ing** \ˈkəv-riŋ, ˈkə-və-\ [ME, fr. AF *coverir, covrir,* fr. L *cooperire* to close, cover, fr. *co-* + *operire* to close, cover] *vt* (13c) **1 a** : to guard from attack **b** (1) : to have within the range of one's guns : COMMAND (2) : to hold within range of an aimed firearm **c** (1) : to afford protection or security to : INSURE (2) : to afford protection against or compensation for ⟨a policy *~ing* loss by fire⟩ **d** (1) : to guard (an opponent) in order to obstruct a play ⟨a linebacker assigned to ~ the tight end⟩ (2) : to be in position to receive a throw to (a base in baseball) ⟨the shortstop was *~ing* second⟩ **e** (1) : to make provision for (a demand or charge) by means of a reserve or deposit ⟨your balance is insufficient to ~ the check⟩ (2) : to maintain a check on esp. by patrolling (3) : to protect by contrivance or expedient **2 a** : to hide from sight or knowledge : CONCEAL ⟨~ up a scandal⟩ **b** : to lie over : ENVELOP ⟨a blanket *~ing* her legs⟩ **3** : to lay or spread something over : OVERLAY ⟨~ the seed bed with straw⟩ **4 a** : to spread over ⟨snow *~ed* the hills⟩ **b** : to appear here and there on the surface of ⟨a region *~ed* with lakes⟩ **5** : to place or set a cover or covering over ⟨~ the pot⟩ **6 a** : to copulate with (a female animal) ⟨a horse *~s* a mare⟩ **b** : to sit on and incubate (eggs) **7** : to invest with a large or excessive amount of something ⟨*~ed* herself with glory⟩ **8** : to play a higher-ranking card on (a previously played card) **9** : to have sufficient scope to include or take into account ⟨an examination *~ing* a full year's work⟩ **10** : to deal with : TREAT ⟨material *~ed* in the first chapter⟩ **11 a** : to have as one's territory or field of activity ⟨one sales rep *~s* the whole state⟩ **b** : to report news about ⟨reporters *~ing* the campaign⟩ **12** : to pass over : TRAVERSE ⟨the hikers *~ed* 12 miles that day⟩ **13** : to defray the cost of ⟨~ expenses⟩ **14** : to place one's stake in equal jeopardy with in a bet **15** : to buy securities or commodities for delivery against (an earlier short sale) **16** : to record or perform a cover of (a song) ~ *vi* **1** : to conceal something illicit, blameworthy, or embarrassing from notice — usu. used with *up* **2** : to act as a substitute or replacement during an absence — **cov·er·able** \ˈkəv-rə-bəl, ˈkə-və-\ *adj* — **co·ver·er** \ˈkə-vər-ər\ *n* — **cover one's tracks** : to conceal traces in order to elude pursuers or escape detection — **cover the ground** *or* **cover ground** : to deal with a subject or assignment in a particular manner ⟨the new book *covers* a lot of *ground*⟩
²**cover** *n, often attrib* (14c) **1** : something that protects, shelters, or guards: as **a** : natural shelter for an animal; *also* : the factors that provide such shelter **b** (1) : a position or situation affording protection from enemy fire (2) : the protection offered by airplanes in tactical support of a military operation **c** *Brit* : COVERAGE 1a, b, 2a **2** : something that is placed over or about another thing: **a** : LID, TOP **b** : a binding or case for a book or the analogous part of a magazine; *also* : the front or back of such a binding **c** : an overlay or outer layer esp. for protection ⟨a mattress ~⟩ **d** : a tablecloth and the other table accessories **e** : COVER CHARGE **f** : ROOF **g** : a cloth used on a bed for warmth or for decoration — usu. used in pl. ⟨lying under the *~s*⟩ **h** : something (as vegetation or snow) that covers the ground **i** : the extent to which clouds obscure the sky **3 a** : something that conceals or obscures ⟨under ~ of darkness⟩ **b** : a masking device : PRETEXT ⟨the project was a ~ for intelligence operations⟩ **4** : an envelope or wrapper for mail **5** : one who substitutes for another during an absence **6** : a recording or performance of a song previously recorded by another performer — **cov·er·less** \ˈkə-vər-ləs\ *adj* — **under cover 1** : in an envelope or wrapper **2** : under concealment : in secret
cov·er·age \ˈkəv-rij, ˈkə-və-\ *n* (1912) **1** : something that covers: as **a** : inclusion within the scope of an insurance policy or protective plan : INSURANCE **b** : the amount available to meet liabilities **c** : inclusion within the scope of discussion or reporting ⟨the news ~ of the trial⟩ **2** : the total group covered : SCOPE: as **a** : all the risks covered by the terms of an insurance contract **b** : the number or percentage of persons reached by a communications medium **3** : the act or fact of covering
cov·er·all \ˈkə-vər-ˌȯl\ *n* (1824) : a one-piece outer garment worn to protect other garments — usu. used in pl. — **cov·er·alled** \-ˌȯld\ *adj*
cov·er–all \ˈkə-vər-ˌȯl\ *adj* (1895) : COMPREHENSIVE ⟨~ provisions⟩
cover charge *n* (1921) : a charge made by a restaurant or nightclub in addition to the charge for food and drink
cover crop *n* (1899) : a crop planted to prevent soil erosion and to provide humus
covered bridge *n* (1809) : a bridge that has its roadway protected by a roof and enclosing sides
covered smut *n* (1900) : a smut disease of grains in which the spore masses are held together by the persistent grain membrane and glumes
covered wagon *n* (1719) : a wagon with a canvas top supported by bowed strips of wood or metal
cover girl *n* (1915) : an attractive young woman whose picture appears on a magazine cover
cover glass *n* (1881) : a piece of very thin glass or plastic used to cover material on a microscope slide
¹**cov·er·ing** \ˈkəv-riŋ, ˈkə-və-\ *n* (14c) : something that covers or conceals
²**covering** *adj* (1887) : containing explanation of or additional information about an accompanying communication ⟨a ~ letter⟩
cov·er·let \ˈkə-vər-lət, -(ˌ)lid\ *n* [ME, alter. of *coverlite,* fr. AF *coverlit,* fr. *covre* (it) covers + *lit* bed, fr. L *lectus* — more at LIE] (14c) : BEDSPREAD
cov·er·slip \ˈkə-vər-ˌslip\ *n* (1875) : COVER GLASS
cover story *n* (1948) : a story accompanying a magazine-cover illustration
¹**co·vert** \ˈkō-(ˌ)vərt, kō-ˈ; ˈkə-vərt\ *adj* [ME, fr. AF, pp. of *coverir* to cover] (14c) **1** : not openly shown, engaged in, or avowed : VEILED ⟨a ~ alliance⟩ **2** : covered over : SHELTERED ***syn*** see SECRET — **co·vert·ly** *adv* — **co·vert·ness** *n*
²**co·vert** \ˈkə-vərt, ˈkō-vərt *also* ˈkə-vər\ *n* (14c) **1 a** : hiding place : SHELTER **b** : a thicket affording cover for game **c** : a masking or concealing device **2** : a feather covering the bases of the quills of the wings and tail of a bird — see WING illustration **3** : a firm durable twilled sometimes waterproofed cloth usu. of mixed-color yarns
cov·er·ture \ˈkə-vər-ˌchu̇r, -chər, -ˌtyu̇r, -ˌtu̇r\ *n* (13c) **1 a** : COVERING **b** : SHELTER **2** : the status a woman acquires upon marriage under common law
cov·er–up \ˈkə-vər-ˌəp\ *n* (1927) **1 a** : a device or stratagem for masking or concealing ⟨his garrulousness is a ~ for insecurity⟩ **b** : a usu. concerted effort to keep an illegal or unethical act or situation from being made public **2** : a loose outer garment
cov·et \ˈkə-vət\ *vb* [ME *coveiten,* fr. AF *coveiter,* fr. VL **cupidietare,* fr. L *cupiditat-, cupiditas* desire, fr. *cupidus* desirous, fr. *cupere* to desire] *vt* (14c) **1** : to wish for earnestly ⟨~ an award⟩ **2** : to desire (what belongs to another) inordinately or culpably ~ *vi* : to feel inordinate desire for what belongs to another ***syn*** see DESIRE — **cov·et·able** \-və-tə-bəl\ *adj* — **cov·et·er** \-tər\ *n* — **cov·et·ing·ly** \-tiŋ-lē\ *adv*
cov·et·ous \ˈkə-və-təs\ *adj* (13c) **1** : marked by inordinate desire for wealth or possessions or for another's possessions **2** : having a craving for possession ⟨~ of power⟩ — **cov·et·ous·ly** *adv* — **cov·et·ous·ness** *n*

syn COVETOUS, GREEDY, ACQUISITIVE, GRASPING, AVARICIOUS mean having or showing a strong desire for esp. material possessions. COVETOUS implies inordinate desire often for another's possessions ⟨*covetous* of his brother's country estate⟩. GREEDY stresses lack of restraint and often of discrimination in desire ⟨*greedy* for status symbols⟩. ACQUISITIVE implies both eagerness to possess and ability to acquire and keep ⟨an eagerly *acquisitive* mind⟩. GRASPING adds to COVETOUS and GREEDY an implication of selfishness and often suggests unfair or ruthless means ⟨a hard *grasping* trader who cheated the natives⟩. AVARICIOUS implies obsessive acquisitiveness esp. of money and strongly suggests stinginess ⟨an *avaricious* miser⟩.

cov·ey \ˈkə-vē\ *n, pl* **coveys** [ME, fr. AF *covee* sitting (of hen), fr. *cover* to sit on, brood over, fr. L *cubare* to lie] (14c) **1** : a mature bird or pair of birds with a brood of young; *also* : a small flock   **2** : COMPANY, GROUP ⟨a ~ of schoolchildren⟩

¹cow \'kaù\ *n* [ME *cou*, fr. OE *cū*; akin to OHG *kuo* cow, L *bos* head of cattle, Gk *bous*, Skt *go*] (bef. 12c)   **1 a** : the mature female of cattle (genus *Bos*)   **b** : the mature female of various usu. large animals (as an elephant, whale, or moose)   **2** : a domestic bovine animal regardless of sex or age — **cowy** \-ē\ *adj*

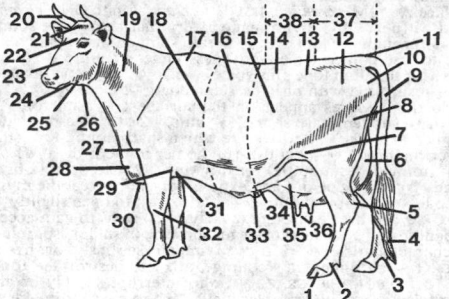

cow 1a: *1* hoof, *2* pastern, *3* dewclaw, *4* switch, *5* hock, *6* rear udder, *7* flank, *8* thigh, *9* tail, *10* pinbone, *11* tail head, *12* thurl, *13* hip, *14* barrel, *15* ribs, *16* crops, *17* withers, *18* heart girth, *19* neck, *20* horn, *21* poll, *22* forehead, *23* bridge of nose, *24* muzzle, *25* jaw, *26* throat, *27* point of shoulder, *28* dewlap, *29* point of elbow, *30* brisket, *31* chest floor, *32* knee, *33* milk well, *34* milk vein, *35* fore udder, *36* teats, *37* rump, *38* loin

²cow *vt* [prob. of Scand origin; akin to Dan *kue* to subdue] (1581) : to destroy the resolve or courage of; *also* : to bring to a state or an action by intimidation — used with *into* ⟨like too many Asian armies, adept at ~*ing* a population into feeding them —Edward Lansdale⟩   *syn* see INTIMIDATE — **cowed·ly** \'kaù(-ə)d-lē\ *adv*

cow·ard \'kaù(-ə)rd\ *n* [ME, fr. AF *cuard*, fr. *cue, coe* tail, fr. L *cauda*] (13c) : one who shows disgraceful fear or timidity — **coward** *adj*

cow·ard·ice \'kaù(-ə)r-dəs, *dial* -(,)dīs\ *n* [ME *cowardise*, fr. AF *coardise*, fr. *cuard*] (14c) : lack of courage or resolution

¹cow·ard·ly \-lē\ *adv* (14c) : in a cowardly manner

²cowardly *adj* (1551) : being, resembling, or befitting a coward ⟨a ~ retreat⟩ — **cow·ard·li·ness** *n*

syn COWARDLY, PUSILLANIMOUS, CRAVEN, DASTARDLY mean having or showing a lack of courage. COWARDLY implies a weak or ignoble lack of courage ⟨a *cowardly* failure to stand up for principle⟩. PUSILLANIMOUS suggests a contemptible lack of courage ⟨the *pusillanimous* fear of a future full of possibility⟩. CRAVEN suggests extreme defeatism and complete lack of resistance ⟨secretly despised her own *craven* yes-men⟩. DASTARDLY often implies behavior that is both cowardly and treacherous or skulking or outrageous ⟨a *dastardly* attack on unarmed civilians⟩.

cow·bane \'kaù-,bān\ *n* (1776) : any of several poisonous plants (as a water hemlock) of the carrot family

cow·bell \-,bel\ *n* (1625) : a bell hung around the neck of a cow to make a sound by which the cow can be located

cow·ber·ry \-,ber-ē\ *n* (1800) : MOUNTAIN CRANBERRY; *also* : its fruit

cow·bird \-,bərd\ *n* (1810) : any of a genus (*Molothrus* of the family Icteridae) of New World blackbirds that lay their eggs in the nests of other birds; *esp* : one (*M. ater*) widespread in the U.S. and southern Canada in which the male is black with a brown head and the female is gray

¹cow·boy \-,bòi\ *n* (1623)   **1** : one who tends cattle or horses; *esp* : a usu. mounted cattle-ranch hand   **2** : a rodeo performer   **3** : one having qualities (as recklessness, aggressiveness, or independence) popularly associated with cowboys: as   **a** : a reckless driver   **b** : a business or businessperson operating in an uncontrolled or unregulated manner

²cowboy *vi* (1948) : to work as a cowboy ⟨~*ed* in Texas and Oklahoma⟩

cowboy boot *n* (1895) : a boot made with a high arch, a high Cuban heel, and usu. fancy stitching

cowboy hat *n* (1895) : a wide-brimmed hat with a large soft crown — called also *ten-gallon hat*

cow·catch·er \'kaù-,ka-chər, -,ke-\ *n* (1838) : an inclined frame on the front of a railroad locomotive used for throwing obstacles off the track

cow college *n* (ca. 1915)   **1** : a college that specializes in agriculture   **2** : a provincial college or university that lacks culture, sophistication, and tradition

cow·er \'kaù(-ə)r\ *vi* [ME *couren*, prob. fr. MLG *kūren*] (14c) : to shrink away or crouch esp. for shelter from something that menaces, domineers, or dismays   *syn* see FAWN

cow·fish \'kaù-,fish\ *n* (1870) : any of various small bright-colored bony fishes (family Ostraciidae) with hornlike projections over the eyes

cow·girl \-,gərl\ *n* (1884)   **1** : a girl or woman who tends cattle or horses   **2** : a girl or woman who is a rodeo performer

cow·hage *also* **cow·age** \'kaù-ij\ *n* [Hindi *kavāc, kevāc*] (1640) : a tropical woody vine (*Mucuna pruriens*) of the legume family with crooked pods covered with barbed hairs that cause severe itching; *also* : these hairs formerly used as a vermifuge

cow·hand \'kaù-,hand\ *n* (1852) : COWBOY 1

cow·herd \-,hərd\ *n* (14c) : one who tends cows

¹cow·hide \-,hīd\ *n* (14c)   **1** : the hide of a cow; *also* : leather made from this hide   **2** : a coarse whip of rawhide or braided leather

²cowhide *vt* **cow·hid·ed; cow·hid·ing** (1794) : to flog with a cowhide whip

cow horse *n* (1853) : COW PONY

¹cowl \'kaù(-ə)l\ *n* [ME *cowle*, fr. OE *cugele*, fr. LL *cuculla* monk's hood, fr. L *cucullus* hood] (bef. 12c)   **1 a** : a hood or long hooded cloak esp. of a monk   **b** : a draped neckline on a woman's garment   **2 a** : a chimney covering designed to improve the draft   **b** : the top portion of the front part of an automobile body forward of the two front doors to

which are attached the windshield and instrument board   **c** : COWLING

²cowl *vt* (1536) : to cover with or as if with a cowl

cow·lick \'kaù-,lik\ *n* (1598) : a lock or tuft of hair growing in a different direction from the rest of the hair

cowl·ing \'kaù-liŋ\ *n* (1917) : a removable metal covering that houses the engine and sometimes a part of the fuselage or nacelle of an airplane; *also* : a metal cover for an engine

cowl–neck \'kaù(-ə)l-,nek\ *n* (1978) : a high loose-fitting turnover collar used esp. for sweaters — **cowl–necked** \-,nekt\ *adj*

cowl–staff \'kōl-,staf, 'kaù(-ə)l-, 'kül-\ *n* [ME *cuvelstaff*, fr. *cuvel* vessel (fr. OE *cūfel*, ultim. fr. LL *cupella*, dim. of L *cūpa* tub) + *¹staff* — more at HIVE] (13c) *archaic* : a staff from which a vessel is suspended and carried between two persons

cow·man \'kaù-mən, -,man\ *n* (1677)   **1** : COWHERD, COWBOY   **2** : a cattle owner or rancher

cow parsnip *n* (1548) : a tall perennial No. American plant (*Heracleum lanatum*) of the carrot family with large compound leaves and broad umbels of white or purplish flowers; *also* : a related Eurasian plant (*H. sphondylium*) naturalized in the U.S.

cow–pat \'kaù-,pat\ *n* (1937) *chiefly Brit* : COW PIE

cow·pea \'kaù-,pē\ *n* (1776) : a sprawling herb (*Vigna unguiculata* syn. *V. sinensis*) of the legume family related to the bean and widely cultivated in the southern U.S. esp. for forage and green manure; *also* : its edible seed — called also *black-eyed pea, field pea*

Cow·per's gland \'kaù-pərz-, 'kü-, 'kü-\ *n* [William *Cowper* †1709 Eng. surgeon] (1738) : either of two small glands lying on either side of the male urethra below the prostate gland and discharging a secretion into the semen — called also *bulbourethral gland*; compare BARTHOLIN'S GLAND

cow pie *n* (1951) : a dropping of cow dung

cow·poke \'kaù-,pōk\ *n* (ca. 1881) : COWBOY 1

cow pony *n* (1874) : an agile saddle horse trained for herding cattle

cow·pox \'kaù-,päks\ *n* (1798) : a mild eruptive disease of the cow that is caused by a poxvirus (species *Cowpox virus* of the genus *Orthopoxvirus*) and that when communicated to humans protects against smallpox

cow·punch·er \-,pən-chər\ *n* (1878) : COWBOY 1

cow·rie *also* **cow·ry** \'kaù-rē\ *n, pl* **cowries** [Hindi & Urdu *kaurī*] (1662) : any of various marine gastropods (family Cypraeidae) that are widely distributed in warm seas and have glossy and often brightly colored shells; *also* : the shell of a cowrie

cow·shed \'kaù-,shed\ *n* (1763) : a shed for the housing of cows

cow·slip \'kaù-,slip\ *n* [ME *cowslyppe*, fr. OE *cūslyppe*, lit., cow dung, fr. *cū* cow + *slypa, slyppe* paste] (bef. 12c)   **1** : a common European primrose (*Primula veris*) with fragrant yellow flowers   **2** : MARSH MARIGOLD

cow town *n* (1885)   **1** : a town or city that serves as a market center or shipping point for cattle   **2** : a usu. small unsophisticated town within a cattle-raising area

¹cox \'käks\ *n* (1869) : COXSWAIN — **coxed** \'käkst\ *adj* — **cox·less** \'käks-ləs\ *adj*

²cox *vb* (1881) : COXSWAIN

COX \'käks\ *n* [by shortening & alter.] (1990) : CYCLOOXYGENASE — often used with the number 1 or 2 to indicate one of the two variants of the enzyme

coxa \'käk-sə\ *n, pl* **cox·ae** \-,sē, -,sī\ [L, hip; akin to OHG *hāhsina* hock, Skt *kakṣa* armpit] (1826) : the basal segment of a limb of various arthropods (as an insect) — **cox·al** \-səl\ *adj*

cox·comb \'käks-,kōm\ *n* [ME *cokkes comb*, lit., cock's comb] (1573)   **1 a** : a jester's cap adorned with a strip of red   **b** *archaic* : PATE, HEAD   **2 a** *obs* : FOOL   **b** : a conceited foolish person : FOP — **cox·comb·i·cal** \käks-'kō-mi-kəl, -'kä-\ *adj*

cox·comb·ry \'käks-kəm-rē, -,kōm-\ *n, pl* **-ries** (1770) : behavior that is characteristic of a coxcomb : FOPPERY

Cox·sack·ie virus \(,)käk-'sa-kē-, \ *n* [*Coxsackie*, N.Y.] (1949) : any of numerous serotypes of three enteroviruses (species *Human enterovirus A, Human enterovirus B,* and *Human enterovirus C*) that are associated with or cause human disease (as hand, foot and mouth disease and some forms of meningitis)

¹cox·swain \'käk-sən, -,swān\ *n* [ME *cokswayne*, fr. *cok* cockboat (a small boat) + *swain* servant] (15c)   **1** : a sailor who has charge of a ship's boat and its crew and who usu. steers   **2** : a steersman of a racing shell who usu. directs the rowers

²coxswain *vt* (1928) : to direct as coxswain ~ *vi* : to act as coxswain

COX–2 inhibitor \'käks-'tü-\ *n* (1994) : any of a class of drugs used to treat the pain and inflammation of arthritis by selectively blocking the variant of cyclooxygenase causing these symptoms

¹coy \'kòi\ *adj* [ME, quiet, shy, fr. AF *quoi, quei, koi* quiet, fr. L *quietus*] (14c)   **1 a** : shrinking from contact or familiarity ⟨'tis but a kiss I beg, Why art thou ~? —Shak.⟩   **b** : marked by cute, coquettish, or artful playfulness   **2** : showing reluctance to make a definite commitment ⟨a ~ response⟩   *syn* see SHY — **coy·ly** *adv* — **coy·ness** *n*

²coy *vt* (14c) *obs* : CARESS ~ *vi, archaic* : to act coyly

coy·dog \'kòi-,dòg\ *n* [*coyote* + *dog*] (1950) : a hybrid between a coyote and a feral dog

coy·ote \kī-'ō-tē, *chiefly Western* 'kī-,ōt\ *n, pl* **coyotes** *or* **coyote** [MexSp, fr. Nahuatl *coyotl*] (1759)   **1** : a buff-gray to reddish-gray No. American canid (*Canis latrans*) closely related to but smaller than the wolf   **2** : one who smuggles immigrants into the U.S.

coy·o·til·lo \,kī-ə-'ti-(,)lō, ,kòi-ə-, -'tē-(,)yō\ *n* [MexSp, dim. of *coyote*] (ca. 1892) : a shrub (*Karwinskia humboldtiana*) of the buckthorn

coyote 1

family of the southwestern U.S. and Mexico having poisonous berries
coy•pu \'kȯi-(ˌ)pü, kȯi-'\ *n* [AmerSp *coipú,* fr. Mapuche *coipu*] (1793) : NUTRIA
coz \'kəz\ *n* [by shortening & alter.] (1559) : COUSIN
coz•en \'kə-zən\ *vt* **coz•ened; coz•en•ing** \'kəz-niŋ, 'kə-zə-\ [perh. fr. obs. It *cozzonare,* fr. It *cozzone* horse trader, fr. L *cocion-, cocio* trader] (1573) **1 :** to deceive, win over, or induce to do something by artful coaxing and wheedling or shrewd trickery **2 :** to gain by cozening someone ⟨~*ed* his supper out of the old couple⟩ ***syn*** see CHEAT — **coz•en•er** \'kəz-nər, 'kə-zə-\ *n*
coz•en•age \'kəz-nij, 'kə-zə-\ *n* (1583) **1 :** the art or practice of cozening : FRAUD **2 :** an act or an instance of cozening
[1]**co•zy** \'kō-zē\ *adj* **co•zi•er; -est** [perh. of Scand origin; akin to Norw *koselig* cozy] (1709) **1 a :** enjoying or affording warmth and ease : SNUG ⟨a ~ lakeside cabin⟩ **b :** marked by or providing contentment or comfort ⟨won by a ~ margin⟩ **2 a :** marked by the intimacy of the family or a close group **b :** marked by or suggesting close association or connivance ⟨a ~ agreement⟩ **3 :** marked by a discreet and cautious attitude or procedure ***syn*** see COMFORTABLE — **co•zi•ly** \-zə-lē\ *adv* — **co•zi•ness** \-zē-nəs\ *n*
[2]**cozy** *n, pl* **co•zies** (1863) **1 :** a padded covering esp. for a teapot to keep the contents hot **2 :** a light detective story that usu. features a well-educated protagonist and little explicit violence
[3]**cozy** *adv* (1946) **:** in a cautious manner ⟨play it ~ and wait for the other team to make a mistake —Bobby Dodd⟩
cozy up *vi* (1965) **:** to attain or try to attain familiarity, friendship, or intimacy : ingratiate oneself ⟨*cozying up* to the boss⟩
cp *abbr* **1** compare **2** coupon
CP *abbr* **1** candlepower **2** center of pressure **3** cerebral palsy **4** charter party **5** chemically pure **6** command post **7** Communist party **8** Congregation of the Passion **9** custom of port
CPA *abbr* certified public accountant
CPAP *abbr* continuous positive airway pressure
CPB *abbr* Corporation for Public Broadcasting
CPCU *abbr* chartered property casualty underwriter
cpd *abbr* compound
CPFF *abbr* cost plus fixed fee
cpi *abbr* characters per inch
CPI *abbr* consumer price index
cpl *abbr* **1** complete **2** compline
Cpl *abbr* corporal
CPM *abbr* [L *mille* thousand] cost per thousand
CPO *abbr* chief petty officer
CPR *abbr* cardiopulmonary resuscitation
CPS *abbr* **1** cards per second **2** certified professional secretary **3** characters per second **4** cycles per second
CPSC *abbr* Consumer Product Safety Commission
CPT *abbr* captain
cpu \ˌsē-(ˌ)pē-'yü\ *n, often cap C&P&U* [central processing unit] (1962) **:** the component of a computer system that performs the basic operations (as processing data) of the system, that exchanges data with the system's memory or peripherals, and that manages the system's other components — called also *processor*
[1]**CQ** \'sē-'kyü\ [call to quarters] (1924) — communications code letters used at the beginning of messages of general information or safety notices or by shortwave amateurs as an invitation to talk to other shortwave amateurs
[2]**CQ** *abbr* **1** charge of quarters **2** commercial quality
cr *abbr* **1** center **2** circular **3** commander **4** cream **5** creased **6** credit; creditor **7** creek **8** crescendo
Cr *symbol* chromium
CR *abbr* **1** carrier's risk **2** cathode ray **3** conditioned reflex; conditioned response **4** consciousness-raising **5** current rate
[1]**crab** \'krab\ *n, often attrib* [ME *crabbe,* fr. OE *crabba;* akin to OHG *krebiz* crab and perh. to OE *ceorfan* to carve — more at CARVE] (bef. 12c) **1** *pl* **crabs** *also* **crab :** any of numerous chiefly marine broadly built decapod crustaceans: **a :** any of an infraorder (Brachyura) with a short broad usu. flattened carapace, a small abdomen that curls forward beneath the body, short antennae, and the anterior pair of limbs modified as grasping pincers **b :** any of various crustaceans of an infraorder (Anomura) resembling true crabs in the more or less reduced condition of the abdomen **2** *cap* **:** CANCER 1 **3** *pl* **:** infestation with crab lice **4 :** the angular difference between an aircraft's course and the heading necessary to make that course in the presence of a crosswind
[2]**crab** *vb* **crabbed; crab•bing** *vi* (1657) **1 :** to fish for crabs **2 a** (1) **:** to move sideways indirectly or diagonally (2) **:** to crab an airplane **b :** to scuttle or scurry sideways ~ *vt* **1 :** to cause to move sideways or in an indirect or diagonal manner; *specif* **:** to head (an airplane) into a crosswind to counteract drift **2 :** to subject to crabbing — **crab•ber** *n*
[3]**crab** *n* [ME *crabbe,* perh. fr. *crabbe* [1]crab] (14c) **:** CRAB APPLE
[4]**crab** *n* (1580) **:** an ill-tempered person : GROUCH
[5]**crab** *vb* **crabbed; crab•bing** [ME *crabben,* prob. back-formation fr. *crabbed*] *vt* (1662) **1 :** to make sullen : SOUR ⟨old age has *crabbed* his nature⟩ **2 :** to complain about peevishly **3 :** SPOIL, RUIN ~ *vi* **:** CARP, GROUSE ⟨always ~*s* about the weather⟩ — **crab•ber** *n*
crab apple *n* [[3]*crab*] (1680) **:** any of various wild or cultivated trees (genus *Malus*) that are cultivars or relatives of the cultivated apple and that produce small sour fruit; *also* **:** the fruit
crab•bed \'kra-bəd\ *adj* [ME, partly fr. *crabbe* crustacean, partly fr. *crabbe* crab apple] (14c) **1 :** marked by a forbidding moroseness ⟨a ~ view of human nature⟩ **2 :** difficult to read or understand ⟨~ handwriting⟩ ***syn*** see SULLEN — **crab•bed•ness** *n*
crab•by \'kra-bē\ *adj* **crab•bi•er; -est** [[4]*crab*] (1599) **:** CROSS, ILL-NATURED ⟨a ~ recluse⟩
crab•eat•er seal \'krab-ˌē-tər-\ *n* (1913) **:** an Antarctic hair seal (*Lobodon carcinophaga*) that feeds on krill and lives and breeds on pack ice — called also *crabeater*
crab•grass \'krab-ˌgras\ *n* (1743) **:** a grass (esp. *Digitaria sanguinalis*) that has creeping or decumbent stems which root freely at the nodes and that is often a pest in turf or cultivated lands
crab louse *n* (1547) **:** a sucking louse (*Phthirus pubis*) infesting the pubic region of the human body
crab•meat \'krab-ˌmēt\ *n* (1876) **:** the edible part of a crab
crab spider *n* (1861) **:** any of a family (Thomisidae) of spiders that resemble crabs in shape and in being able to walk forward, backward, and sideways
crab•stick \-ˌstik\ *n* (1636) **1 :** a stick, cane, or cudgel of crab apple tree wood **2 :** a crabbed ill-natured person
crab•wise \-ˌwīz\ *adv* (1863) **1 :** SIDEWAYS **2 :** in a sidling or cautiously indirect manner
[1]**crack** \'krak\ *vb* [ME *crakken,* fr. OE *cracian;* akin to OHG *chrahhōn* to resound] *vi* (bef. 12c) **1 :** to make a very sharp explosive sound ⟨the whip ~*s* through the air⟩ **2 :** to break, split, or snap apart **3 :** FAIL: as **a :** to lose control or effectiveness under pressure — often used with *up* **b :** to fail in tone ⟨his voice ~*ed*⟩ **4 :** to go or travel at good speed — usu. used with *on* ⟨the steamboat ~*ed* on⟩ ~ *vt* **1 a :** to break so that fissures appear on the surface ⟨~ a mirror⟩ **b :** to break with a sudden sharp sound ⟨~ nuts⟩ **2 :** to tell esp. suddenly or strikingly ⟨~ a joke⟩ **3 :** to strike with a sharp noise : RAP ⟨then ~*s* him over the head⟩ ⟨~*ed* a two-run homer in the fifth —*N.Y. Times*⟩ **4 a** (1) **:** to open (as a bottle) for drinking (2) **:** to open (a book) for studying **b :** to puzzle out and expose, solve, or reveal the mystery of ⟨~ a code⟩ **c :** to break into ⟨~ a safe⟩ **d :** to open slightly ⟨~ the throttle⟩ **e :** to break through (as a barrier) so as to gain acceptance or recognition **f :** to show or begin showing (a smile) esp. reluctantly or uncharacteristically **5 a :** to impair seriously or irreparably : WRECK ⟨~ an opponent's courage⟩ **b :** to destroy the tone of (a voice) **c :** DISORDER, CRAZE **d :** to interrupt sharply or abruptly ⟨the criticism ~*ed* our complacency⟩ **6 :** to cause to make a sharp noise ⟨~*s* his knuckles⟩ **7 a** (1) **:** to subject (hydrocarbons) to cracking (2) **:** to produce by cracking ⟨~*ed* gasoline⟩ **b :** to break up (chemical compounds) into simpler compounds by means of heat — **crack the whip :** to adopt or apply an authoritative, tyrannical, or threatening approach or policy (as in demanding harder work from employees) — **crack wise :** to make a wisecrack
[2]**crack** *n* (14c) **1 a :** a loud roll or peal ⟨a ~ of thunder⟩ **b :** a sudden sharp noise ⟨the ~ of rifle fire⟩ **2 :** a sharp witty remark : QUIP **3 a :** a narrow break : FISSURE ⟨a ~ in the ice⟩ **b :** a narrow opening ⟨leave the door open a ~⟩ ⟨~*s* between floorboards⟩ — used figuratively in phrases like *fall through the cracks* to describe one that has been improperly or inadvertently ignored or left out ⟨a player who fell through the ~*s* in the college draft⟩ ⟨children slipping through the ~*s* of available youth services⟩ **4 a :** a weakness or flaw caused by decay, age, or deficiency : UNSOUNDNESS **b :** a broken tone of the voice **c :** CRACKPOT **5 :** MOMENT, INSTANT ⟨the ~ of dawn⟩ **6 :** HOUSE-BREAKING, BURGLARY **7 :** a sharp resounding blow ⟨gave him a ~ on the head⟩ **8 :** an attempt or opportunity to do something ⟨her first ~ at writing a novel⟩ ⟨got first ~ at the job opening⟩ **9 :** a potent form of cocaine that is obtained by treating the hydrochloride of cocaine with sodium bicarbonate to create small chips used illicitly for smoking — called also *crack cocaine*
[3]**crack** *adj* (1793) **:** of superior excellence or ability ⟨a ~ marksman⟩
crack baby *n* (1986) **:** an infant subjected to prolonged exposure to crack cocaine in the mother's womb
crack•back \'krak-ˌbak\ *n* (1967) **:** a blind-side block on a defensive back in football by a pass receiver who starts downfield and then cuts back to the middle of the line
crack•brain \-ˌbrān\ *n* (ca. 1570) **:** an erratic person : CRACKPOT — **crack•brained** \-'brānd\ *adj*
crack•down \-ˌdau̇n\ *n* (1935) **:** an act or instance of cracking down
crack down *vi* (1939) **:** to take positive regulatory or disciplinary action
cracked \'krakt\ *adj* (1503) **1 a :** broken (as by a sharp blow) so that the surface is fissured ⟨~ china⟩ **b :** broken into coarse particles ⟨~ wheat⟩ **c :** marked by harshness, dissonance, or failure to sustain a tone ⟨a ~ voice⟩ **2 :** mentally disturbed : CRAZY
crack•er \'kra-kər\ *n* (15c) **1** *chiefly dial* **:** a bragging liar : BOASTER **2 :** something that makes a cracking or snapping noise: as **a :** FIRE-CRACKER **b :** the snapping end of a whiplash : SNAPPER **c :** a paper holder for a party favor that pops when the ends are pulled sharply **3** *pl* **:** NUTCRACKER **4 :** a dry thin crispy baked bread product that may be leavened or unleavened **5 a** *usu disparaging* **:** a poor usu. Southern white **b** *cap* **:** a native or resident of Florida or Georgia — used as a nickname **6 :** the equipment in which cracking (as of petroleum) is carried out **7 :** HACKER 4
crack•er–bar•rel \-ˌba-rəl\ *adj* [fr. the cracker barrel in country stores around which customers lounged for informal conversation] (1916) **:** suggestive of the friendly homespun character of a country store ⟨a ~ philosopher⟩
crack•er•jack \'kra-kər-ˌjak\ *also* **crack•a•jack** \-kə-ˌjak\ *n* [prob. alter. of [3]*crack* + *jack* (man)] (1893) **:** a person or thing of marked excellence — **crackerjack** *adj*
Cracker Jack *trademark* — used for a candied popcorn confection
crack•ers \'kra-kərz\ *adj* [prob. fr. *cracked* + *-ers* (as in *starkers*)] (1928) **:** CRAZY
crack•head \'krak-ˌhed\ *n* (1986) **:** one who smokes crack
crack house *n* (1985) **:** a house or apartment where crack is made, sold, or used
[1]**crack•ing** \'kra-kiŋ\ *adj* (1830) **:** very impressive or effective : GREAT
[2]**cracking** *adv* (1903) **:** VERY, EXTREMELY ⟨a ~ good book⟩
[3]**cracking** *n* (1868) **:** a process in which relatively heavy hydrocarbons are broken up by heat into lighter products (as gasoline)
[1]**crack•le** \'kra-kəl\ *vb* **crack•led; crack•ling** \-k(ə-)liŋ\ [freq. of [1]*crack*] *vi* (ca. 1560) **1 a :** to make small sharp sudden repeated noises ⟨the fire ~*s* on the hearth⟩ **b :** to show animation : SPARKLE ⟨the essays ~ with wit⟩ **2 :** CRAZE 3 ~ *vt* **:** to crush or crack with snapping noises — **crack•ling•ly** *adv*
[2]**crackle** *n* (1833) **1 a :** the noise of repeated small cracks or reports **b :** SPARKLE, EFFERVESCENCE **2 :** a network of fine cracks on an otherwise smooth surface
crack•le•ware \'kra-kəl-ˌwer\ *n* (1881) **:** ceramic ware with a decorative crazed glaze
crack•ling *n* (1599) **1** \'kra-k(ə-)liŋ\ **:** a series of small sharp cracks or reports ⟨the ~ of frozen snow as we walk⟩ **2** \'kra-klən, -kliŋ\ **:** the crisp residue left after the rendering of lard from fat or the frying or roasting of the skin (as of pork) — usu. used in pl.

crack·ly \ˈkra-k(ə-)lē\ *adj* (1732) : inclined to crackle : CRISP

crack·nel \ˈkrak-nᵊl\ *n* [ME *krakenelle*] (14c) **1 :** a hard brittle biscuit **2 :** CRACKLING 2 — usu. used in pl.

crack·pot \ˈkrak-ˌpät\ *n* (1883) : one given to eccentric or lunatic notions — **crackpot** *adj*

cracks·man \ˈkraks-mən\ *n* (ca. 1812) : BURGLAR; *also* : SAFECRACKER

crack–up \ˈkrak-ˌəp\ *n* (ca. 1926) **1 :** CRASH, WRECK ⟨an automobile ~⟩ **2 a :** a mental collapse : NERVOUS BREAKDOWN ⟨his wife's death brought on his ~⟩ **b :** COLLAPSE, BREAKDOWN

crack up *vt* (1829) **1 :** PRAISE, TOUT 4 ⟨wasn't all that it was *cracked up* to be⟩ **2 :** to damage or destroy (a vehicle) by crashing ⟨*crack up* a car⟩ **3 :** to cause to laugh out loud ⟨that joke really *cracks* him *up*⟩ ~ *vi* **1 :** to damage or destroy a vehicle (as by losing control) ⟨*cracked up* on a curve⟩ **2 :** to laugh out loud

-cracy *n comb form* [MF & LL; MF *-cratie,* fr. LL *-cratia,* fr. Gk *-kratia,* fr. *kratos* strength, power — more at HARD] **1 :** form of government; *also* : state having such a form ⟨mono*cracy*⟩ **2 :** social or political class (as of powerful persons) ⟨mob*ocracy*⟩ **3 :** theory of social organization ⟨techno*cracy*⟩

1**cra·dle** \ˈkrā-dᵊl\ *n* [ME *cradel,* fr. OE *cradol;* perh. akin to OHG *kratto* basket, Skt *grantha* knot] (bef. 12c) **1 a :** a bed or cot for a baby usu. on rockers or pivots **b :** a framework or support suggestive of a baby's cradle: as **(1) :** a framework of bars and rods **(2) :** the support for a telephone receiver or handset **c :** an implement with rods like fingers attached to a scythe and used formerly for harvesting grain **d :** a frame to keep the bedclothes from contact with an injured part of the body **2 a :** the earliest period of life : INFANCY ⟨from the ~ to the grave⟩ **b :** a place of origin ⟨the ~ of civilization⟩ **3 :** a rocking device used in panning for gold

2**cradle** *vb* **cra·dled; cra·dling** \ˈkrād-liŋ, ˈkrā-dᵊl-iŋ\ *vt* (15c) **1 a :** to place or keep in or as if in a cradle **b :** SHELTER, REAR **c :** to support protectively or intimately ⟨*cradling* the injured man's head in her arms⟩ **2 :** to cut (grain) with a cradle scythe **3 :** to place, raise, support, or transport on a cradle ~ *vi, obs* : to rest in or as if in a cradle

cradle cap *n* (ca. 1890) : a seborrheic condition in infants that usu. affects the scalp and is characterized by greasy gray or dark brown adherent scaly crusts

cra·dle·song \ˈkrā-dᵊl-ˌsȯŋ\ *n* (14c) : LULLABY

1**craft** \ˈkraft\ *n* [ME, strength, skill, fr. OE *cræft;* akin to OHG *kraft* strength] (bef. 12c) **1 :** skill in planning, making, or executing : DEXTERITY **2 a :** an occupation or trade requiring manual dexterity or artistic skill ⟨the carpenter's ~⟩ ⟨the ~ of writing plays⟩ ⟨~*s* such as pottery, carpentry, and sewing⟩ **b** *pl* **:** articles made by craftspeople ⟨a store selling ~*s*⟩ ⟨a ~*s* fair⟩ **3 :** skill in deceiving to gain an end ⟨used ~ and guile to close the deal⟩ **4 :** the members of a trade or trade association **5** *pl usu* **craft a :** a boat esp. of small size **b :** AIRCRAFT **c :** SPACECRAFT ***syn*** see ART

2**craft** *vt* (15c) : to make or produce with care, skill, or ingenuity ⟨is ~*ing* a new sculpture⟩ ⟨a carefully ~*ed* story⟩ — **craft·er** \ˈkraf-tər\ *n*

craft beer *n* (1986) : a specialty beer produced in limited quantities : MICROBREW

crafts·man \ˈkraf(t)s-mən\ *n* (13c) **1 :** a worker who practices a trade or handicraft **2 :** one who creates or performs with skill or dexterity esp. in the manual arts ⟨jewelry made by European *craftsmen*⟩ — **crafts·man·like** \-ˌlīk\ *adj* — **crafts·man·ly** \-lē\ *adj* — **crafts·man·ship** \-ˌship\ *n*

crafts·peo·ple \-ˌpē-pəl\ *n pl* (1953) : workers who practice a trade or craft

crafts·per·son \-ˌpər-sᵊn\ *n* (1920) : a craftsman or craftswoman

crafts·wom·an \ˈkraf(t)s-ˌwu̇-mən\ *n* (1886) **1 :** a woman who is an artisan **2 :** a woman who is skilled in a craft

craft union *n* (1922) : a labor union with membership limited to workers of the same craft — compare INDUSTRIAL UNION

crafty \ˈkraf-tē\ *adj* **craft·i·er; -est** (bef. 12c) **1 :** SKILLFUL, CLEVER **2 a :** adept in the use of subtlety and cunning **b :** marked by subtlety and guile ⟨a ~ scheme⟩ ***syn*** see SLY — **craft·i·ly** \ˈkraf-tə-lē\ *adv* — **craft·i·ness** \-tē-nəs\ *n*

1**crag** \ˈkrag\ *n* [ME, of Celt origin; akin to W *craig* rock] (14c) **1 :** a steep rugged rock or cliff **2** *archaic* **:** a sharp detached fragment of rock — **crag·ged** \ˈkra-gəd\ *adj*

2**crag** *n* [ME, fr. MD *crāghe;* akin to OE *cræga* throat — more at CRAW] (14c) *chiefly Scot* : NECK, THROAT

crag·gy \ˈkra-gē\ *adj* **crag·gi·er; -est** (15c) **1 :** full of crags ⟨~ slopes⟩ **2 :** ROUGH, RUGGED ⟨a ~ face⟩ ⟨a ~ voice⟩ — **crag·gi·ly** \ˈkra-gə-lē\ *adv* — **crag·gi·ness** \ˈkra-gē-nəs\ *n*

crags·man \ˈkragz-mən\ *n* (1816) : one who is expert in climbing crags or cliffs

crake \ˈkrāk\ *n* [ME, prob. fr. ON *krāka* crow or *krākr* raven; akin to OE *crāwan* to crow] (14c) **1 :** any of various rails; *esp* : a short-billed rail (as the corncrake) **2 :** the corncrake's cry

1**cram** \ˈkram\ *vb* **crammed; cram·ming** [ME *crammen,* fr. OE *crammian;* akin to ON *kremja* to squeeze] *vt* (bef. 12c) **1 :** to pack tight : JAM ⟨~ a suitcase with clothes⟩ ⟨a novel *crammed* with surprises⟩ **2 a :** to fill with food to satiety : STUFF **b :** to eat voraciously : BOLT ⟨the child ~*s* her food⟩ **3 :** to thrust in or as if in a rough or forceful manner ⟨*crammed* the letters into his pocket⟩ **4 :** to prepare hastily for an examination ⟨~ the students for the test⟩ ~ *vi* **1 :** to eat greedily or to satiety : STUFF **2 :** to study a subject intensively esp. for an imminent examination — **cram·mer** *n*

2**cram** *n* (1810) **1 :** a compressed multitude or crowd : CRUSH **2 :** last-minute study esp. for an examination

cram·bo \ˈkram-(ˌ)bō\ *n, pl* **cramboes** [alter. of earlier *crambe,* fr. L, cabbage, fr. Gk *krambē*] (1660) : a game in which one player gives a word or line of verse to be matched in rhyme by other players

1**cramp** \ˈkramp\ *n* [ME *crampe,* fr. AF, of Gmc origin; akin to MD *crampe;* akin to OHG *krampf* bent] (14c) **1 :** a painful involuntary spasmodic contraction of a muscle **2 :** a temporary paralysis of muscles from overuse — compare WRITER'S CRAMP **3 a :** sharp abdominal pain — usu. used in pl. **b :** persistent and often intense though dull lower abdominal pain associated with dysmenorrhea — usu. used in pl. — **crampy** \ˈkram-pē\ *adj*

2**cramp** *n* [ME *crampe,* fr. MD] (15c) **1 a :** a usu. iron device bent at the ends and used to hold timbers or blocks of stone together **b :** CLAMP **2 a :** something that confines : SHACKLE **b :** the state of being confined

3**cramp** *vt* (15c) **1 :** to affect with or as if with a cramp or cramps **2 a :** CONFINE, RESTRAIN ⟨was ~*ed* in the tiny apartment⟩ **b :** to restrain from free expression — used esp. in the phrase *cramp one's style* **3 :** to fasten or hold with a cramp ~ *vi* : to be affected with cramps

4**cramp** *adj* (1674) **1 :** hard to understand or figure out ⟨~ law terms⟩ ⟨~ handwriting⟩ **2 :** being cramped ⟨a ~ corner⟩

cram·pon \ˈkram-ˌpän\ *n* [ME, fr. MF *crampon,* of Gmc origin; akin to MD *crampe*] (15c) **1 :** a hooked clutch or dog for raising heavy objects — usu. used in pl. **2 :** a climbing iron used esp. on ice and snow in mountaineering — usu. used in pl.

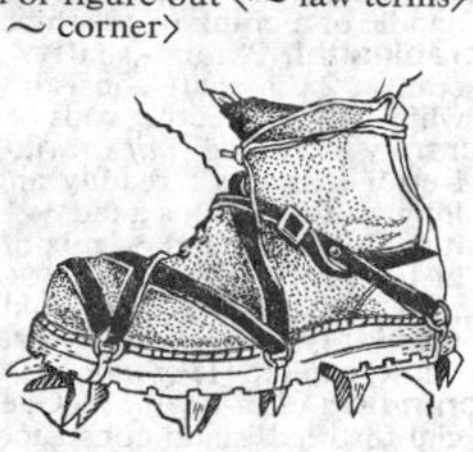

crampon 2

cran·ber·ry \ˈkran-ˌber-ē, -ˌbe-rē, -b(ə-)rē\ *n* [part trans. of LG *kraanbere,* fr. *kraan* crane + *bere* berry] (1647) **1 :** the red acid berry produced by some plants (as *Vaccinium oxycoccos* and *V. macrocarpon*) of the heath family; *also* : a plant producing these **2 :** any of various plants with a fruit that resembles a cranberry **3 :** a dark red

cranberry bush *n* (1778) : HIGHBUSH CRANBERRY

1**crane** \ˈkrān\ *n* [ME *cran,* fr. OE; akin to OHG *krano* crane, Gk *geranos,* L *grus*] (bef. 12c) **1 :** any of a family (Gruidae of the order Gruiformes) of tall wading birds superficially resembling the herons but structurally more nearly related to the rails **2 :** any of several herons **3 :** an often horizontal projection swinging about a vertical axis: as **a :** a machine for raising, shifting, and lowering heavy weights by means of a projecting swinging arm or with the hoisting apparatus supported on an overhead track **b :** an iron arm in a fireplace for supporting kettles **c :** a boom for holding a motion-picture or television camera

2**crane** *vb* **craned; cran·ing** *vt* (1570) **1 :** to raise or lift by or as if by a crane **2 :** to stretch (as the neck) toward an object of attention ⟨*craning* her neck to get a better view⟩ ~ *vi* **1 :** to stretch one's neck toward an object of attention ⟨I *craned* out of the window of my compartment —Webb Waldron⟩ **2 :** HESITATE

crane fly *n* (1658) : any of a family (Tipulidae) of long-legged slender dipteran flies that resemble large mosquitoes but do not bite

cranes·bill \ˈkrānz-ˌbil\ *n* (1548) : GERANIUM 1

crani- *or* **cranio-** *comb form* [ML *cranium*] : cranium ⟨*crani*ate⟩ : cranial and ⟨*cranio*sacral⟩

cra·ni·al \ˈkrā-nē-əl\ *adj* (1800) **1 :** of or relating to the skull or cranium **2 :** CEPHALIC — **cra·ni·al·ly** \-ə-lē\ *adv*

cranial index *n* (1868) : the ratio multiplied by 100 of the maximum breadth of the bare skull to its maximum length from front to back

cranial nerve *n* (1840) : any of the nerves that arise in pairs from the lower surface of the brain one on each side and pass through openings in the skull to the periphery of the body and that comprise 12 pairs in reptiles, birds, and mammals and usu. 10 in fishes and amphibians

cra·ni·ate \ˈkrā-nē-ət, -ˌāt\ *adj* (1879) : having a cranium — **craniate** *n*

cra·nio·ce·re·bral \ˌkrā-nē-ō-sə-ˈrē-brəl, -ˈser-ə-\ *adj* (1876) : involving both cranium and brain ⟨~ injury⟩

cra·nio·fa·cial \-ˈfā-shəl\ *adj* (ca. 1859) : of, relating to, or involving both the cranium and the face ⟨a ~ deformity⟩

cra·ni·ol·o·gy \ˌkrā-nē-ˈä-lə-jē\ *n* [prob. fr. G *Kraniologie,* fr. *kranio-* crani- + *-logie* -logy] (1851) : a science dealing with variations in size, shape, and proportions of skulls among human races

cra·ni·om·e·try \-ˈä-mə-trē\ *n* [ISV] (ca. 1828) : a science dealing with cranial measurement — compare CEPHALOMETRY

cra·nio·sa·cral \ˌkrā-nē-ō-ˈsa-krəl, -ˈsā-\ *adj* (ca. 1923) : PARASYMPATHETIC

craniosacral therapy *n* (1986) : a system of gentle touch designed to enhance the functioning of the membranes, tissues, fluids, and bones surrounding or associated with the brain and spinal cord

cra·nio·syn·os·to·sis \-ˌsi-ˌnäs-ˈtō-səs\ *n* [NL] (1951) : premature fusion of the sutures of the skull

cra·ni·ot·o·my \ˌkrā-nē-ˈä-tə-mē\ *n, pl* **-mies** [ISV] (1855) : surgical opening of the skull

cra·ni·um \ˈkrā-nē-əm\ *n, pl* **-ni·ums** *or* **-nia** \-nē-ə\ [ML, fr. Gk *kranion;* akin to Gk *kara* head — more at CEREBRAL] (15c) : SKULL; *specif* : the part that encloses the brain : BRAINCASE

1**crank** \ˈkraŋk\ *n* [ME *cranke,* fr. OE *cranc-* (as in *crancstæf,* a weaving instrument); prob. akin to MHG *krank* weak, sick — more at CRINGE] (13c) **1 :** a bent part of an axle or shaft or an arm keyed at right angles to the end of a shaft by which circular motion is imparted to or received from the shaft or by which reciprocating motion is changed into circular motion or vice versa **2 a** *archaic* **:** BEND **b :** a twist or turn of speech : CONCEIT — used esp. in the phrase *quips and cranks* **c (1) :** CAPRICE, CROTCHET **(2) :** an annoyingly eccentric person; *also* : one who is overly enthusiastic about a particular subject or activity **d :** a bad-tempered person : GROUCH **3 :** CRYSTAL 7 — **crank·ish** \ˈkraŋ-kish\ *adj*

2**crank** *vi* (1592) **1 :** to move with a winding course : ZIGZAG **2 a :** to turn a crank **b :** to get started by or as if by the turning of a crank **c :** to gain speed, momentum, or intensity — usu. used with *up* ⟨the campaign is ~*ing* up⟩ ~ *vt* **1 :** to move or operate by or as if by a crank ⟨~ the window down⟩ **2 a :** to cause to start (as an automobile) **b :** to rotate the shaft (as a crankshaft) of esp. with a starter ⟨~ over an engine⟩ **c :** to use in trying to start an engine ⟨~ the starter⟩ **3 a :** to start as if by use of a crank — usu. used with *up* ⟨she ~*ed* up the air conditioner⟩ **b :** TURN UP 2 — usu. used with *up* ⟨~ up the volume⟩

3**crank** *adj* (1924) : of, relating to, or being a cranky or eccentric person; *also* : made or sent by such a person ⟨~ calls⟩ ⟨a ~ letter⟩

[4]**crank** *adj* [ME *cranke*] (15c) **1** *chiefly dial* : MERRY, HIGH-SPIRITED **2** *chiefly dial* : COCKY, CONFIDENT

[5]**crank** *adj* [short for *crank-sided* easily tipped] (ca. 1649) *of a boat* : easily tipped : TENDER 7d

crank·case \ˈkraŋk-ˌkās\ *n* (ca. 1878) : the housing of a crankshaft

crank out *vt* (1956) : to produce esp. in a mechanical manner ⟨*crank out* a manuscript⟩

crank·pin \ˈkraŋk-ˌpin\ *n* (1839) : the cylindrical piece which forms the handle of a crank or to which a connecting rod is attached

crank·shaft \ˈkraŋk-ˌshaft\ *n* (1854) **1** : a shaft driven by or driving a crank **2** : a shaft consisting of a series of cranks and crankpins to which the connecting rods of an engine are attached

[1]**cranky** \ˈkraŋ-kē\ *adj* **crank·i·er; -est** [[1]*crank*] (1821) **1 a** : given to fretful fussiness : readily angered when opposed : CROTCHETY ⟨our long wait . . . left us a tad ~ —*Connecticut*⟩ **b** : marked by eccentricity ⟨his bizarre and ~ mix of ideas and beliefs —R. J. Evans⟩ **2** : full of twists and turns : TORTUOUS ⟨a ~ road⟩ **3** : working erratically : UNPREDICTABLE ⟨a ~ old tractor⟩ **4** *dial* : CRAZY, IMBECILE — **crank·i·ly** \-kə-lē\ *adv* — **crank·i·ness** \-kē-nəs\ *n*

[2]**cranky** *adj* (1841) *of a boat* : [5]CRANK

cran·nog \ˈkra-nəg\ *n* [ScGael *crannag* & Ir *crannóg*] (1608) : an artificial fortified island constructed in a lake or marsh orig. in prehistoric Ireland and Scotland

cran·ny \ˈkra-nē\ *n, pl* **crannies** [ME *crany,* fr. MF *cren, cran* notch] (15c) **1** : a small break or slit : CREVICE **2** : an obscure nook or corner — **cran·nied** \-nēd\ *adj*

cran·reuch \ˈkran-ˌrük\ *n* [prob. modif. of ScGael *crannreotha*] (1682) *Scot* : HOARFROST, RIME

[1]**crap** \ˈkrap\ *vi* **crapped; crap·ping** (1846) *usu vulgar* : DEFECATE

[2]**crap** *n* [Brit. dial. *crap, craps* residue from rendered fat, fr. ME *crappe,* perh. fr. OF *crappe* chaff, residue, fr. ML *crappa*] (ca. 1897) **1 a** *usu vulgar* : FECES **b** *usu vulgar* : the act of defecating **2** *sometimes vulgar* : NONSENSE, RUBBISH; *also* : STUFF 4b

[3]**crap** *n* [sing. of *craps*] (1885) **1** — used as an attributive form of *craps* ⟨~ game⟩ ⟨~ table⟩ **2** : a throw of 2, 3, or 12 in the game of craps losing the shooter his bet unless he has a point — called also *craps*; compare NATURAL

[4]**crap** *vi* **crapped; crap·ping** (ca. 1930) **1** : to throw a crap **2** : to throw a seven while trying to make a point — usu. used with *out*

[1]**crape** \ˈkrāp\ *n* [alter. of F *crêpe,* fr. MF *crespe,* fr. *crespe* curly, fr. L *crispus* — more at CRISP] (1633) **1** : CREPE **2** : a band of crepe worn on a hat or sleeve as a sign of mourning

[2]**crape** *vt* **craped; crap·ing** (1815) : to cover or shroud with or as if with crape

[3]**crape** *vt* **craped; crap·ing** [F *crêper,* fr. MF *cresper,* fr. *crespe*] (1774) : to make (the hair) curly

crape myrtle *n* (1850) : an Asian shrub (*Lagerstroemia indica*) of the loosestrife family widely grown in warm regions for its flowers

crap·o·la \ˌkrap-ˈō-lə\ *n* [[2]*crap* + *-ola,* suffix forming jocular variants of words] (1941) *slang* : NONSENSE, RUBBISH; *also* : STUFF 4b

crap·per \ˈkra-pər\ *n* [[1]*crap*] (ca. 1932) *usu vulgar* : TOILET

crap·pie \ˈkrä-pē\ *n* [CanF *crapet*] (ca. 1827) **1** : BLACK CRAPPIE **2** : WHITE CRAPPIE

crap·py \ˈkra-pē\ *adj* **crap·pi·er; -est** (1846) *slang* : markedly inferior in quality : LOUSY

craps \ˈkraps\ *n pl but sing or pl in constr* [LaF, fr. F *crabs, craps,* fr. E *crabs* lowest throw at hazard, fr. pl. of [1]*crab*] (1842) **1** : a gambling game played with two dice **2** : [3]CRAP 2

crap·shoot \ˈkrap-ˌshüt\ *n* (1971) : something (as a business venture) that has an unpredictable outcome

crap·shoot·er \ˈkrap-ˌshü-tər\ *n* (1895) : one who plays craps

crap·u·lous \ˈkra-pyə-ləs\ *adj* [LL *crapulosus,* fr. L *crapula* intoxication, fr. Gk *kraipalē*] (1536) **1** : marked by intemperance esp. in eating or drinking **2** : sick from excessive indulgence in liquor

[1]**crash** \ˈkrash\ *vb* [ME *crasschen*] *vt* (15c) **1 a** : to break violently and noisily : SMASH **b** : to damage (an airplane) in landing **2 a** : to cause to make a loud noise ⟨~ the cymbals together⟩ **b** : to force (as one's way) through with loud crashing noises **3** : to enter or attend without invitation or without paying ⟨~ the party⟩ **4** : to move toward aggressively (as in fighting for a rebound) ⟨basketball players ~*ing* the boards⟩ **5** : to cause (a computer system, component, or program) to crash ~ *vi* **1 a** : to break or go to pieces with or as if with violence and noise **b** : to fall, land, or hit with destructive force **c** : to decline suddenly and steeply **d** *of a computer system, component, or program* : to suffer a sudden major failure usu. with attendant loss of data **2** : to make a smashing noise ⟨thunder ~*ing* overhead⟩ **3** : to move or force one's way with or as if with a crash ⟨~*es* into the room⟩ **4** *slang* : to experience the aftereffects (as lethargy or depression) of a usu. prolonged episode of drug use (as of amphetamines) **5** *slang* : to go to bed or fall asleep; *also* : to reside temporarily : STAY ⟨~*ing* with friends for a few days⟩ — **crash·er** *n*

[2]**crash** *n* (ca. 1580) **1** : a loud sound (as of things smashing) ⟨a ~ of thunder⟩ **2 a** : a breaking to pieces by or as if by collision **b** : an instance of crashing ⟨a plane ~⟩ ⟨a system ~⟩ **3** : a sudden decline (as of a population) or failure (as of a business) ⟨a stock market ~⟩ **4** *slang* : the process of crashing after drug intoxication

[3]**crash** *adj* (1945) : marked by a concerted effort and effected in the shortest possible time esp. to meet emergency conditions ⟨a ~ renovation program⟩

[4]**crash** *n* [prob. fr. Russ *krashenina* colored linen] (1812) : a coarse fabric used for draperies, toweling, and clothing and for strengthening joints of cased-in books

crash cart *n* (1976) : a cart stocked with emergency medical equipment, supplies, and drugs for use by medical personnel esp. during efforts to resuscitate a patient experiencing cardiac arrest

crash course *n* (1966) : a rapid and intense course of study; *also* : an experience that resembles such a course ⟨has been given a *crash course* in diplomacy in his first weeks in office⟩

crash dive *n* (1918) : a dive made by a submarine in the least possible time — **crash–dive** *vi*

crash helmet *n* (ca. 1918) : a helmet that is worn (as by motorcyclists) as protection for the head in the event of an accident

crash·ing \ˈkra-shiŋ\ *adj* (1924) **1** : UTTER, ABSOLUTE ⟨a ~ bore⟩ **2** : SUPERLATIVE ⟨a ~ effect⟩ — **crash·ing·ly** \-lē\ *adv*

crash–land \ˈkrash-ˈland\ *vt* (1941) : to land (an airplane or spacecraft) under emergency conditions usu. with damage to the craft ~ *vi* : to crash-land an airplane or spacecraft — **crash landing** *n*

crash pad *n* (1939) **1** : protective padding (as on the inside of an automobile or a tank) **2** : a place to stay temporarily

crash·wor·thy \ˈkrash-ˌwər-t͟hē\ *adj* (1966) : resistant to the effects of collision ⟨~ cars⟩ — **crash·wor·thi·ness** *n*

crass \ˈkras\ *adj* [L *crassus* thick, gross] (ca. 1625) **1 a** : GROSS 6a; *esp* : having or indicating such grossness of mind as precludes delicacy and discrimination **b** : being beneath one's dignity ⟨~ concerns of daily life⟩ **c** — used as a pejorative intensifier ⟨~ flattery⟩ ⟨~ propaganda⟩ **2** : guided by or indicative of base or materialistic values ⟨~ commercialism⟩ ⟨~ measures of success⟩ ***syn*** see STUPID — **crass·ly** *adv* — **crass·ness** *n*

cras·si·tude \ˈkra-sə-ˌtüd, -ˌtyüd\ *n* (1679) : the quality or state of being crass : GROSSNESS; *also* : an instance of grossness

-crat *n comb form* [F *-crate,* back-formation fr. *-cratie* -cracy] **1** : advocate or partisan of a (specified) theory of government ⟨theo*crat*⟩ **2** : member of a (specified) dominant class ⟨pluto*crat*⟩ — **-cratic** *adj comb form*

cratch \ˈkrach\ *n* [ME *cracche,* fr. AF *creche* manger — more at CRÈCHE] (13c) **1** *archaic* : MANGER **2** : a crib or rack esp. for fodder; *also* : FRAME

[1]**crate** \ˈkrāt\ *n* [ME, fr. L *cratis*] (15c) **1** : an open box of wooden slats or a usu. wooden protective case or framework for shipping **2** : JALOPY

[2]**crate** *vt* **crat·ed; crat·ing** (1871) : to pack in a crate

[1]**cra·ter** \ˈkrā-tər\ *n* [L, mixing bowl, crater, fr. Gk *kratēr,* fr. *kerannynai* to mix; akin to Skt *śrīṇāti* he mixes] (1613) **1 a** : the bowl-shaped depression around the orifice of a volcano **b** : a depression formed by an impact (as of a meteorite) **c** : a hole in the ground made by the explosion of a bomb or shell **2** : an eroded lesion **3** : a dimple in a painted surface — **cra·ter·like** \ˈkrā-tər-ˌlīk\ *adj*

[2]**crater** *vi* (1884) **1** : to exhibit or form craters **2** : to fail or fall suddenly and dramatically : COLLAPSE, CRASH ⟨the deal ~*ed*⟩ ⟨~*ing* stock prices⟩ ~ *vt* : to form craters in

[3]**crater** *var of* KRATER

cra·ter·let \ˈkrā-tər-lət\ *n* (1881) : a small crater

C ration *n* (1942) : a canned field ration of the U.S. Army

cra·ton \ˈkrā-ˌtän, ˈkra-\ *n* [G *Kraton,* modif. of Gk *kratos* strength — more at HARD] (1944) : a stable relatively immobile area of the earth's crust that forms the nuclear mass of a continent or the central basin of an ocean — **cra·ton·ic** \krə-ˈtä-nik, krā-, kra-\ *adj*

craunch \ˈkrȯnch, ˈkränch\ *vb* [prob. imit.] (1631) : CRUNCH — **craunch** *n*

cra·vat \krə-ˈvat\ *n* [F *cravate,* fr. *Crabate, Cravate* Croatian] (ca. 1656) **1** : a band or scarf worn around the neck **2** : NECKTIE

crave \ˈkrāv\ *vb* **craved; crav·ing** [ME, fr. OE *crafian;* akin to ON *krefja* to crave, demand] *vt* (bef. 12c) **1** : to ask for earnestly : BEG, DEMAND ⟨~ a pardon for neglect⟩ **2 a** : to want greatly : NEED ⟨~*s* drugs⟩ **b** : to yearn for ⟨~ a vanished youth⟩ ~ *vi* : to have a strong or inward desire ⟨~*s* after affection⟩ ***syn*** see DESIRE — **crav·er** *n*

cra·ven \ˈkrā-vən\ *adj* [ME *cravant*] (13c) **1** *archaic* : DEFEATED, VANQUISHED **2** : lacking the least bit of courage : contemptibly fainthearted ***syn*** see COWARDLY — **craven** *n* — **cra·ven·ly** *adv* — **cra·ven·ness** \-vən-nəs\ *n*

crav·ing \ˈkrā-viŋ\ *n* (1633) : an intense, urgent, or abnormal desire or longing

craw \ˈkrȯ\ *n* [ME *crawe,* fr. OE **cræga;* perh. akin to L *vorare* to devour — more at VORACIOUS] (14c) **1** : the crop of a bird or insect **2** : the stomach esp. of a lower animal

craw·dad \ˈkrȯ-ˌdad\ *n* [alter. of *crawfish*] (ca. 1905) : CRAYFISH 1 — used chiefly west of the Appalachians

[1]**craw·fish** \ˈkrȯ-ˌfish\ *n* [by folk etymology fr. ME *crevis, kraveys*] (1624) **1** : CRAYFISH 1 **2** : SPINY LOBSTER

[2]**crawfish** *vi* (1842) : to retreat from a position : back out ⟨I ~*ed* as fast as I could —Mark Twain⟩

[1]**crawl** \ˈkrȯl\ *vb* [ME, fr. ON *krafla*] *vi* (14c) **1** : to move slowly in a prone position without or as if without the use of limbs ⟨the snake ~*ed* into its hole⟩ **2** : to move or progress slowly or laboriously ⟨traffic ~*s* along at 10 miles an hour⟩ **3** : to advance by guile or servility ⟨~*ing* into favor by toadying to his boss⟩ **4** : to spread by extending stems or tendrils ⟨a ~*ing* vine⟩ **5 a** : to be alive or swarming with or as if with creeping things ⟨a kitchen ~*ing* with ants⟩ **b** : to have the sensation of insects creeping over one ⟨the story made her flesh ~⟩ **6** : to fail to stay evenly spread — used of paint, varnish, or glaze ~ *vt* **1** : to move upon in or as if in a creeping manner ⟨all the creatures that ~ the earth⟩ **2** : to reprove harshly ⟨they got no good right to ~ me for what I wrote —Marjorie K. Rawlings⟩

[2]**crawl** *n* (1818) **1 a** : the act or action of crawling **b** : slow or laborious progress **c** *chiefly Brit* : a going from one pub to another **2** : a fast swimming stroke executed in a prone position with alternating overarm strokes and a flutter kick **3** : lettering that moves vertically or horizontally across a television or motion-picture screen to give information (as performer credits or news bulletins)

crawl·er \ˈkrȯ-lər\ *n* (1607) **1** : one that crawls **2** : a vehicle (as a crane) that travels on endless chain belts

crawl space *n* (1946) : a shallow unfinished space beneath the first floor or under the roof of a building esp. for access to plumbing or wiring

crawl·way \ˈkrȯl-ˌwā\ *n* (1843) : a low passageway (as in a cave) that can be traversed only by crawling

crawly \ˈkrȯ-lē\ *adj* **crawl·i·er; -est** (1857) **1** : CREEPY 1 **2** : marked by crawling or slow motion ⟨~ creatures⟩

cray·fish \ˈkrā-ˌfish\ *n* [by folk etymology fr. ME *crevis,* fr. AF *creveis, escreveice,* of Gmc origin; akin to OHG *krebiz* crab — more at CRAB] (14c) **1** : any of numerous freshwater decapod crustaceans (esp. families Astacidea, Cambaridae, and Parastacidae) resembling the lobster but usu. much smaller **2** : SPINY LOBSTER

[1]**cray·on** \ˈkrā-ˌän, -ən *also* ˈkran\ *n* [F, crayon, pencil, fr. dim. of *craie* chalk, fr. L *creta*] (1644) **1** : a stick of white or colored chalk or of colored wax used for writing or drawing **2** : a crayon drawing

[2]**crayon** *vt* (1662) : to draw with a crayon — **cray·on·ist** \ˈkrā-ə-nist\ *n*

1craze \ˈkrāz\ *vb* **crazed; craz·ing** [ME *crasen* to crush, craze, of Scand origin; akin to OSw *krasa* to crush] *vt* (14c) **1** *obs* **:** BREAK, SHATTER **2 :** to produce minute cracks on the surface or glaze of ⟨*crazed* glass⟩ **3 :** to make insane or as if insane ⟨*crazed* by pain and fear⟩ ~ *vi* **1** *archaic* **:** SHATTER, BREAK **2 :** to become insane **3 :** to develop a mesh of fine cracks

2craze *n* (1812) **1 :** an exaggerated and often transient enthusiasm **:** MANIA ⟨the latest ~ in music⟩ **2 :** a crack in a surface or coating (as of glaze or enamel) ***syn*** see FASHION

1cra·zy \ˈkrā-zē\ *adj* **cra·zi·er; -est** (1566) **1 a :** full of cracks or flaws **:** UNSOUND ⟨they were very ~, wretched cabins —Charles Dickens⟩ **b :** CROOKED, ASKEW **2 a :** MAD, INSANE ⟨yelling like a ~ man⟩ **b** (1) **:** IMPRACTICAL ⟨a ~ plan⟩ (2) **:** ERRATIC ⟨~ drivers⟩ **c :** being out of the ordinary **:** UNUSUAL ⟨a taste for ~ hats⟩ **3 a :** distracted with desire or excitement ⟨a thrill-*crazy* mob⟩ **b :** absurdly fond **:** INFATUATED ⟨he's ~ about the girl⟩ **c :** passionately preoccupied **:** OBSESSED ⟨~ about boats⟩ — **cra·zi·ly** \-zə-lē\ *adv* — **cra·zi·ness** \-zē-nəs\ *n* — **like crazy :** to an extreme degree ⟨everyone dancing *like crazy*⟩

2crazy *n, pl* **cra·zies** (1867) **:** one who is or acts crazy; *esp* **:** such a one associated with a radical or extremist political cause

3crazy *adv* (1887) **:** EXTREMELY, WILDLY ⟨~ good⟩

crazy bone *n* (1876) **:** FUNNY BONE

crazy quilt *n* (1886) **1 :** a patchwork quilt without a design **2 :** JUMBLE, HODGEPODGE ⟨a *crazy quilt* of regulations⟩

crazy–quilt *adj* (1888) **:** resembling a crazy quilt **:** HAPHAZARD ⟨a ~ system⟩

cra·zy·weed \ˈkrā-zē-ˌwēd\ *n* (ca. 1889) **:** LOCOWEED

CRC *abbr* Civil Rights Commission

C–re·ac·tive protein \ˈsē-rē-ˈak-tiv-\ *n* [*C-polysaccharide,* a polysaccharide found in the cell wall of pneumococci and precipitated by this protein, fr. *carbohydrate*] (1955) **:** a protein present in blood serum in various abnormal states (as inflammation or neoplasia)

1creak \ˈkrēk\ *vi* [ME *creken* to croak, of imit. origin] (1583) **:** to make a prolonged grating or squeaking sound often as a result of being worn-out; *also* **:** to proceed slowly with or as if with creaking wheels ⟨the story ~*s* along to a dull conclusion⟩

2creak *n* (1604) **:** a rasping or grating noise

creaky \ˈkrē-kē\ *adj* **creak·i·er; -est** (1834) **1 :** marked by creaking **:** SQUEAKY ⟨~ shoes⟩ **2 :** showing signs of deterioration or decrepitude ⟨a ~ old house⟩ ⟨a ~ economy⟩ — **creak·i·ly** \-kə-lē\ *adv* — **creak·i·ness** \-nəs\ *n*

1cream \ˈkrēm\ *n, often attrib* [ME *creime, creme,* fr. AF *creme, cresme,* fr. LL *cramum,* of Celt origin; akin to W *cramen* scab, crust] (14c) **1 :** the yellowish part of milk containing from 18 to about 40 percent butterfat **2 a :** a food prepared with cream **b :** something having the consistency of cream; *esp* **:** a usu. emulsified medicinal or cosmetic preparation **3 :** the choicest part **:** BEST ⟨the ~ of the crop⟩ **4 :** CREAMER 1 **5 a :** a pale yellow **b :** a cream-colored animal

2cream *vi* (1596) **1 :** to form cream or a surface layer like the cream on standing milk **2 :** to break into or cause something to break into a creamy froth; *also* **:** to move like froth ~ *vt* **1 a :** SKIM 1c **b :** to remove (something choice) from an aggregate ⟨she has ~*ed* off her favorite stories from her earlier books —*Times Lit. Supp.*⟩ **2 :** to furnish, prepare, or treat with cream; *also* **:** to dress with a cream sauce **3 a :** to beat into a creamy froth **b :** to work or blend to the consistency of cream ⟨~ butter and sugar together⟩ **c :** to cause to form a surface layer of or like cream **4 a :** to defeat decisively ⟨was ~*ed* in the first round⟩ **b :** WRECK ⟨~*ed* the car on the turnpike⟩ **c :** to hit with force **:** SMASH ⟨the quarterback got ~*ed* by the pass rush⟩

cream cheese *n* (1583) **:** a mild soft unripened cheese made from whole sweet milk enriched with cream

cream·cups \ˈkrēm-ˌkəps\ *n pl but sing or pl in constr* (1888) **:** a California annual (*Platystemon californicus*) of the poppy family

cream·er \ˈkrē-mər\ *n* (1858) **1 :** a small vessel for serving cream **2 :** a nondairy product used as a substitute for cream (as in coffee)

cream·ery \ˈkrēm-rē, ˈkre-mə-\ *n, pl* **-er·ies** (1872) **:** an establishment where butter and cheese are made or where milk and cream are prepared or sold

cream of tartar (1662) **:** a white crystalline salt $C_4H_5KO_6$ used esp. in baking powder and in certain treatments of metals

cream puff *n* (1880) **1 :** a round shell of light pastry filled with whipped cream or a cream filling **2 :** an ineffectual person **3 :** something trifling, inconsiderable, or easily dealt with **4 :** a usu. used motor vehicle that is in especially good condition

cream soda *n* (1854) **:** a carbonated soft drink flavored with vanilla

cream·ware \ˈkrēm-ˌwer\ *n* (1780) **:** earthenware having a cream-colored glaze

creamy \ˈkrē-mē\ *adj* **cream·i·er; -est** (1618) **1 :** containing cream **2 :** resembling cream (as in color, texture, or taste) ⟨a ~ consistency⟩ ⟨~ skin⟩ ⟨a ~ voice⟩ — **cream·i·ly** \ˈkrē-mə-lē\ *adv* — **cream·i·ness** \-mē-nəs\ *n*

1crease \ˈkrēs\ *n* [prob. alter. of earlier *creaste,* fr. ME *creste* crest] (1578) **1 :** a line, mark, or ridge made by or as if by folding a pliable substance **2 :** a specially marked area in various sports; *esp* **:** an area surrounding or in front of a goal (as in lacrosse or hockey) — **crease·less** \-ləs\ *adj*

2crease *vb* **creased; creas·ing** *vt* (1588) **1 :** to make a crease in or on **:** WRINKLE ⟨a smile *creased* her face⟩ **2 :** to wound slightly esp. by grazing ⟨*creased* by a bullet⟩ ~ *vi* **:** to become creased — **creas·er** *n*

1cre·ate \krē-ˈāt, ˈkrē-ˌ\ *vb* **cre·at·ed; cre·at·ing** [ME, fr. L *creatus,* pp. of *creare;* akin to L *crescere* to grow — more at CRESCENT] *vt* (14c) **1 :** to bring into existence ⟨God *created* the heaven and the earth —Gen 1:1(AV)⟩ **2 a :** to invest with a new form, office, or rank ⟨was *created* a lieutenant⟩ **b :** to produce or bring about by a course of action or behavior ⟨her arrival *created* a terrible fuss⟩ ⟨~ new jobs⟩ **3 :** CAUSE, OCCASION ⟨famine ~*s* high food prices⟩ **4 a :** to produce through imaginative skill ⟨~ a painting⟩ **b :** DESIGN ⟨~*s* dresses⟩ ~ *vi* **1 :** to make or bring into existence something new **2 :** to set up a scoring opportunity in basketball ⟨~ off the dribble⟩

2create *adj* (15c) *archaic* **:** CREATED

cre·a·tine \ˈkrē-ə-ˌtēn, -tᵊn\ *n* [F *créatine,* fr. Gk *kreat-, kreas* flesh — more at RAW] (1840) **:** a white crystalline nitrogenous substance $C_4H_9N_3O_2$ found esp. in the muscles of vertebrates either free or as phosphocreatine; *also* **:** a synthetic usu. hydrated form of creatine taken esp. as a dietary supplement

creatine kinase *n* (1964) **:** any of three isoenzymes found esp. in vertebrate skeletal and myocardial muscle that catalyze the transfer of a high-energy phosphate group from phosphocreatine to ADP with the formation of ATP and creatine

creatine phosphate *n* (1945) **:** PHOSPHOCREATINE

cre·at·i·nine \krē-ˈa-tə-ˌnēn, -nən\ *n* [G *Kreatinin,* fr. *Kreatin* creatine] (1851) **:** a white crystalline strongly basic compound $C_4H_7N_3O$ formed from creatine and found esp. in muscle, blood, and urine

cre·a·tion \krē-ˈā-shən\ *n* (14c) **1 :** the act of creating; *esp* **:** the act of bringing the world into ordered existence **2 :** the act of making, inventing, or producing: as **a :** the act of investing with a new rank or office **b :** the first representation of a dramatic role **3 :** something that is created: as **a :** WORLD **b :** creatures singly or in aggregate **c :** an original work of art **d :** a new usu. striking article of clothing

cre·a·tion·ism \-shə-ˌni-zəm\ *n* (1880) **:** a doctrine or theory holding that matter, the various forms of life, and the world were created by God out of nothing and usu. in the way described in Genesis — compare EVOLUTION 4b — **cre·a·tion·ist** \-shə-nist\ *n or adj*

creation science *n* (1979) **:** CREATIONISM; *also* **:** scientific evidence or arguments put forth in support of creationism

1cre·a·tive \krē-ˈā-tiv, ˈkrē-ˌ\ *adj* (1678) **1 :** marked by the ability or power to create **:** given to creating ⟨the ~ impulse⟩ **2 :** having the quality of something created rather than imitated **:** IMAGINATIVE ⟨the ~ arts⟩ **3 :** managed so as to get around legal or conventional limits ⟨~ financing⟩; *also* **:** deceptively arranged so as to conceal or defraud ⟨~ accounting⟩ — **cre·a·tive·ly** *adv* — **cre·a·tive·ness** *n*

2creative *n* (1962) **1 :** one who is creative; *esp* **:** one involved in the creation of advertisements **2 :** creative activity or the material produced by it esp. in advertising

creative evolution *n* (1909) **:** evolution that is a creative product of a vital force rather than a spontaneous process explicable in terms of scientific laws — compare EMERGENT EVOLUTION

cre·a·tiv·i·ty \ˌkrē-(ˌ)ā-ˈti-və-tē, ˌkrē-ə-\ *n* (1875) **1 :** the quality of being creative **2 :** the ability to create

cre·a·tor \krē-ˈā-tər\ *n* (13c) **:** one that creates usu. by bringing something new or original into being; *esp, cap* **:** GOD 1

crea·ture \ˈkrē-chər\ *n* [ME, fr. AF, fr. LL *creatura,* fr. L *creatus,* pp. of *creare*] (14c) **1 :** something created either animate or inanimate: as **a :** a lower animal; *esp* **:** a farm animal **b :** a human being **c :** a being of anomalous or uncertain aspect or nature ⟨~*s* of fantasy⟩ **2 :** one that is the servile dependent or tool of another **:** INSTRUMENT — **crea·tur·al** \ˈkrē-chə-rəl\ *adj* — **crea·ture·hood** \ˈkrē-chər-ˌhu̇d\ *n* — **crea·ture·li·ness** \-lē-nəs\ *n* — **crea·ture·ly** \-lē\ *adj*

creature comfort *n* (1652) **:** something (as food, warmth, or special accommodations) that gives bodily comfort

crèche \ˈkresh, ˈkrāsh\ *n* [F, fr. OF *creche* manger, crib, of Gmc origin; akin to OHG *krippa* manger — more at CRIB] (1792) **1 :** a representation of the Nativity scene **2 :** DAY NURSERY **3 :** a foundling hospital **4 :** a group of young animals (as penguins or bats) gathered in one place for care and protection usu. by one or more adults

cred \ˈkred\ *n* (1981) **:** CREDIBILITY; *specif* **:** the ability to gain acceptance as a member of a particular group or class ⟨used . . . his new street ~ to develop contacts —Dale Keiger⟩

cre·dence \ˈkrē-dᵊn(t)s\ *n* [ME, fr. AF or ML; AF, fr. ML *credentia,* fr. L *credent-, credens,* prp. of *credere* to believe, trust — more at CREED] (14c) **1 a :** mental acceptance as true or real ⟨give ~ to gossip⟩ **b :** CREDIBILITY 1 ⟨lends ~ to the theory⟩ **2 :** CREDENTIALS — used in the phrase *letters of credence* **3** [MF, fr. OIt *credenza*] **:** a Renaissance sideboard used chiefly for valuable plate **4 :** a small table where the bread and wine rest before consecration ***syn*** see BELIEF

cre·dent \ˈkrē-dᵊnt\ *adj* [L *credent-, credens,* prp.] (1602) **1** *archaic* **:** giving credence **:** CONFIDING **2** *obs* **:** CREDIBLE

1cre·den·tial \kri-ˈden(t)-shəl\ *adj* (15c) **:** warranting credit or confidence — used chiefly in the phrase *credential letters*

2credential *n* (1655) **1 :** something that gives a title to credit or confidence; *also* **:** QUALIFICATION 3a **2** *pl* **:** testimonials or certified documents showing that a person is entitled to credit or has a right to exercise official power **3 :** CERTIFICATE, DIPLOMA

3credential *vt* **-tialed** *also* **-tialled; -tial·ing** *also* **-tial·ling** (1888) **:** to furnish with credentials ⟨to ~ adequate academic performance —K. Patricia Cross⟩

cre·den·tial·ism \-shə-ˌli-zəm\ *n* (1967) **:** undue emphasis on credentials (as college degrees) as prerequisites to employment

cre·den·za \kri-ˈden-zə\ *n* [It, lit., belief, confidence, fr. ML *credentia*] (1880) **1 :** CREDENCE 3 **2 :** a sideboard, buffet, or bookcase patterned after a Renaissance credence; *esp* **:** one without legs

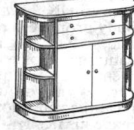

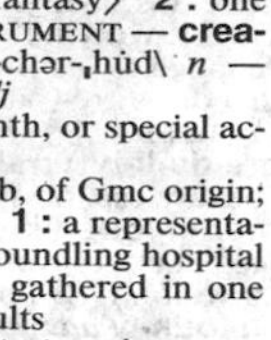
credenza 2

cred·i·bil·i·ty \ˌkre-də-ˈbi-lə-tē\ *n* (1594) **1 :** the quality or power of inspiring belief ⟨an account lacking in ~⟩ **2 :** capacity for belief ⟨strains her reader's ~ —*Times Lit. Supp.*⟩

credibility gap *n* (1966) **1 a :** lack of trust ⟨a *credibility gap* between generations⟩ **b :** lack of believability ⟨a *credibility gap* created by contradictory official statements —Samuel Ellenport⟩ **2 :** DISCREPANCY ⟨the *credibility gap* between the professed ideals . . . and their actual practices —Jeanne L. Noble⟩

cred·i·ble \ˈkre-də-bəl\ *adj* [ME, fr. L *credibilis,* fr. *credere*] (14c) **1 :** offering reasonable grounds for being believed ⟨a ~ account of an accident⟩ ⟨~ witnesses⟩ **2 :** of sufficient capability to be militarily effective ⟨a ~ deterrent⟩ ⟨~ forces⟩ — **cred·i·bly** \ˈkre-də-blē\ *adv*

1cred·it \ˈkre-dit\ *n* [MF, fr. OIt *credito,* fr. L *creditum* something entrusted to another, loan, fr. neut. of *creditus,* pp. of *credere* to believe, entrust — more at CREED] (1537) **1 :** reliance on the truth or reality of something ⟨gave ~ to everything he said⟩ **2 a :** the balance in a

\ə\ **abut** \ᵊ\ **kitten,** F **table** \ər\ **further** \a\ **ash** \ā\ **ace** \ä\ **mop, mar** \au̇\ **out** \ch\ **chin** \e\ **bet** \ē\ **easy** \g\ **go** \i\ **hit** \ī\ **ice** \j\ **job** \ŋ\ **sing** \ō\ **go** \ȯ\ **law** \ȯi\ **boy** \th\ **thin** \t͟h\ **the** \ü\ **loot** \u̇\ **foot** \y\ **yet** \zh\ **vision, beige** \k, ⁿ, œ, ue, ʸ\ *see* Guide to Pronunciation

person's favor in an account **b** : an amount or sum placed at a person's disposal by a bank **c** : the provision of money, goods, or services with the expectation of future payment ⟨long-term ~⟩; *also* : money, goods, or services so provided ⟨exhausted their ~⟩ **d** (1) : an entry on the right-hand side of an account constituting an addition to a revenue, net worth, or liability account (2) : a deduction from an expense or asset account **e** : any one of or the sum of the items entered on the right-hand side of an account **f** : a deduction from an amount otherwise due **3 a** : influence or power derived from enjoying the confidence of another or others **b** : good name : ESTEEM; *also* : financial or commercial trustworthiness **4** *archaic* : CREDIBILITY **5** : a source of honor ⟨a ~ to the school⟩ **6 a** : something that gains or adds to reputation or esteem : HONOR ⟨took no ~ for his kindly act⟩ **b** : RECOGNITION, ACKNOWLEDGMENT ⟨quite willing to accept undeserved ~⟩ **7** : recognition by name of a person contributing to a performance (as a film or telecast) ⟨the opening ~*s*⟩ **8 a** : recognition by a school or college that a student has fulfilled a requirement leading to a degree **b** : CREDIT HOUR ***syn*** see BELIEF, INFLUENCE

[2]**credit** *vt* [partly fr. [1]*credit;* partly fr. L *creditus,* pp.] (ca. 1530) **1** : to trust in the truth of : BELIEVE ⟨find his story hard to ~⟩ **2** : to supply goods on credit to **3** *archaic* : to bring credit or honor upon **4 a** : to enter upon the credit side of an account **b** : to place an amount to the credit of ⟨~ his account with ten dollars⟩ **5 a** : to consider usu. favorably as the source, agent, or performer of an action or the possessor of a trait ⟨~*s* him with an excellent sense of humor⟩ **b** : to attribute to some person ⟨they ~ the invention to him⟩ ***syn*** see ASCRIBE

cred·it·able \ˈkre-di-tə-bəl\ *adj* (1526) **1** : worthy of belief ⟨a ~ report⟩ **2** : sufficiently good to bring esteem or praise ⟨a ~ performance⟩ **3** : worthy of commercial credit **4** : capable of being assigned — **cred·it·abil·i·ty** \ˌkre-di-tə-ˈbi-lə-tē\ *n* — **cred·it·able·ness** \ˈkre-di-tə-bəl-nəs\ *n* — **cred·it·ably** \-blē\ *adv*

credit card *n* (1888) : a card authorizing purchases on credit

credit hour *n* (ca. 1927) : the unit of measuring educational credit usu. based on the number of classroom hours per week throughout a term

credit line *n* (1899) **1** : LINE OF CREDIT **2** : a line, note, or name that acknowledges the source of an item (as a news dispatch or television program)

cred·i·tor \ˈkre-di-tər, -ˌtȯr\ *n* (15c) : one to whom a debt is owed; *esp* : a person to whom money or goods are due

credit union *n* (1881) : a cooperative association that makes small loans to its members at low interest rates and offers other banking services (as savings and checking accounts)

cred·it·wor·thy \ˈkre-dit-ˌwər-t͟hē\ *adj* (1924) : financially sound enough to justify the extension of credit — **cred·it·wor·thi·ness** *n*

cre·do \ˈkrē-(ˌ)dō, ˈkrā-\ *n, pl* **credos** [ME, fr. L, I believe] (12c) : CREED

cre·du·li·ty \kri-ˈdü-lə-tē, -ˈdyü-\ *n* (15c) : readiness or willingness to believe esp. on slight or uncertain evidence

cred·u·lous \ˈkre-jə-ləs\ *adj* [L *credulus,* fr. *credere*] (1576) **1** : ready to believe esp. on slight or uncertain evidence ⟨accused of swindling ~ investors⟩ **2** : proceeding from credulity ⟨~ superstitions⟩ — **cred·u·lous·ly** *adv* — **cred·u·lous·ness** *n*

Cree \ˈkrē\ *n, pl* **Cree** *or* **Crees** [CanF *Cris,* pl., short for *Cristinaux,* fr. Ojibwa dial. *kirištino·,* sing., member of a band living south of James Bay] (1744) **1** : a member of an American Indian people of Quebec, Ontario, Manitoba, and Saskatchewan **2** : the Algonquian language of the Cree people

creed \ˈkrēd\ *n* [ME *crede,* fr. OE *crēda,* fr. L *credo* (first word of the Apostles' and Nicene Creeds), fr. *credere* to believe, trust, entrust; akin to OIr *cretid* he believes, Skt *śrad-dadhāti*] (bef. 12c) **1** : a brief authoritative formula of religious belief **2** : a set of fundamental beliefs; *also* : a guiding principle — **creed·al** *or* **cre·dal** \ˈkrē-dᵊl\ *adj*

creek \ˈkrēk, ˈkrik\ *n* [ME *crike, creke,* fr. ON *-kriki* bend] (13c) **1** *chiefly Brit* : a small inlet or bay narrower and extending farther inland than a cove **2** : a natural stream of water normally smaller than and often tributary to a river **3** *archaic* : a narrow or winding passage — **up the creek** : in a difficult or perplexing situation

Creek \ˈkrēk\ *n* (1725) **1** : an American Indian confederacy of peoples chiefly of Muskogean stock of Alabama, Georgia, and Florida **2** : a member of any of the Creek peoples **3** : the Muskogean language of the Creek Indians

[1]**creel** \ˈkrēl\ *n* [ME *creille, crele*] (14c) **1** : a wicker basket (as for carrying newly caught fish) **2** : a bar with skewers for holding bobbins in a spinning machine

[2]**creel** *vt* (1844) : to put (caught fish) in a creel

[1]**creep** \ˈkrēp\ *vi* **crept** \ˈkrept\; **creep·ing** [ME *crepen,* fr. OE *crēopan;* akin to ON *krjūpa* to creep] (bef. 12c) **1 a** : to move along with the body prone and close to the ground **b** : to move slowly on hands and knees **2 a** : to go very slowly ⟨the hours *crept* by⟩ **b** : to go timidly or cautiously so as to escape notice ⟨she *crept* away from the festive scene⟩ **c** : to enter or advance gradually so as to be almost unnoticed ⟨age ~*s* up on us⟩ ⟨a note of irritation *crept* into her voice⟩ **3** : to have the sensation of being covered with creeping things ⟨the thought made his flesh ~⟩ **4** *of a plant* : to spread or grow over a surface rooting at intervals or clinging with tendrils, stems, or aerial roots **5 a** : to slip or gradually shift position **b** : to change shape permanently from prolonged stress or exposure to high temperatures

[2]**creep** *n* (1818) **1** : a movement of or like creeping ⟨traffic moving at a ~⟩ **2** : a distressing sensation like that caused by the creeping of insects over one's flesh; *esp* : a feeling of apprehension or horror — usu. used in pl. with *the* ⟨that gives me the *creeps*⟩ **3** : a feed trough accessible only by young animals and used esp. to supply special or supplementary feed — called also *creep feeder* **4** : the slow change of dimensions of an object from prolonged exposure to high temperature or stress **5** : an unpleasant or obnoxious person **6** : a slow but persistent increase or elevation ⟨this political inertia . . . makes budget ~ inevitable —*Wall Street Jour.*⟩

creep·age \ˈkrē-pij\ *n* (1903) : gradual movement : CREEP

creep·er \ˈkrē-pər\ *n* (bef. 12c) **1** : one that creeps: as **a** : a creeping plant **b** : a bird (as of the family Certhiidae) that creeps about on trees or bushes searching for insects **c** : a creeping insect or reptile **2** : any of various devices used for creeping: as **a** : a fixture with iron points worn on the shoe to prevent slipping **b** : a low wheeled platform for supporting the body when working under an automobile **3** : a usu. one-piece garment for a child at the crawling age

creep·ing \ˈkrē-piŋ\ *adj* (14c) : developing or advancing by slow imperceptible degrees ⟨a period of ~ inflation⟩

creeping eruption *n* (1926) : a skin disorder marked by a spreading red line of eruption and caused esp. by larvae (as of hookworms not normally parasitic in humans) burrowing beneath the human skin

creepy \ˈkrē-pē\ *adj* **creep·i·er; -est** (1836) **1** : producing a nervous shivery apprehension ⟨a ~ horror story⟩; *also* : EERIE **2** : of, relating to, or being a creep : annoyingly unpleasant — **creep·i·ly** \-pə-lē\ *adv* — **creep·i·ness** \-pē-nəs\ *n*

cre·mains \kri-ˈmānz\ *n pl* [blend of *cremated* and *remains*] (1947) : the ashes of a cremated human body

cre·mate \ˈkrē-ˌmāt, kri-ˈ\ *vt* **cre·mat·ed; cre·mat·ing** [L *crematus,* pp. of *cremare* to burn up, cremate] (1874) : to reduce (as a dead body) to ashes by burning — **cre·ma·tion** \kri-ˈmā-shən\ *n*

cre·ma·to·ri·um \ˌkrē-mə-ˈtȯr-ē-əm, ˌkre-\ *n, pl* **-ri·ums** *or* **-ria** \-ē-ə\ (1880) : CREMATORY

cre·ma·to·ry \ˈkrē-mə-ˌtȯr-ē, ˈkre-\ *n, pl* **-ries** (1876) : a furnace for cremating; *also* : an establishment containing such a furnace — **crematory** *adj*

crème *or* **creme** \ˈkrem *also* ˈkrēm *or* ˈkrām\ *n, pl* **crèmes** *or* **cremes** \ˈkrem(z), ˈkrēmz\ [F, fr. OF *cresme* — more at CREAM] (ca. 1821) **1** : a sweet liqueur **2** : cream or a preparation made with or resembling cream used in cooking **3** : CREAM 2b

crème an·glaise \-äŋ-ˈglāz, -aŋ-, -äⁿ-ˈglez\ *n* [F, lit., English cream] (1975) : a vanilla-flavored custard sauce usu. served with desserts

crème brû·lée \-brue-ˈlā, -brü-\ *n* [F, lit., scorched cream] (1886) : a rich custard topped with caramelized sugar

crème car·a·mel \-kä-rə-ˈmel, *or see* CARAMEL\ *n* [F, lit., caramel cream] (1906) : a custard that has been baked with caramel sauce

crème de ca·cao \ˈkrēm-də-ˈkō-(ˌ)kō; ˌkrem-də-kə-ˈkau̇, -kə-ˈkā-(ˌ)ō\ *n* [F, lit., cream of cacao] (ca. 1878) : a sweet brown or colorless liqueur flavored with cacao beans and vanilla

crème de cas·sis \ˌkrem-də-kə-ˈsēs\ *n* [F, lit., cream of black currants] (1899) : a liqueur made from black currants

crème de la crème \ˈkrem-də-lä-ˈkrem, -lə-\ *n* [F, lit., cream of the cream] (1848) : the very best

crème de menthe \ˈkrem-də-ˈmen(t)th, ˈkrēm-, -ˈmint, ˈkrem-də-ˈmänt\ *n* [F, lit., cream of mint] (ca. 1878) : a sweet green or colorless mint-flavored liqueur

crème fraîche *or* **crème fraiche** \ˈkrem-ˈfresh *also* ˈkrēm- *or* ˈkrām-\ *n* [F, lit., fresh cream] (1950) : heavy cream thickened and slightly soured with buttermilk and often served on fruit

cre·mi·ni *or* **cri·mi·ni** \kri-ˈmē-nē\ *n, pl* **-ni** *also* **-nis** [It, pl. of *cremino,* fr. *crema* cream, fr. MF *cresme;* prob. fr. their color — more at CREAM] (1984) : a meaty cultivated brown or tan mushroom that is of the same variety of button mushroom as the larger and more mature portobello

cre·nate \ˈkrē-ˌnāt\ *or* **cre·nat·ed** \-ˌnā-təd\ *adj* [NL *crenatus,* fr. ML *crena* notch] (1688) : having the margin or surface cut into rounded scallops ⟨a ~ leaf⟩

cre·na·tion \kri-ˈnā-shən\ *n* (1846) **1 a** : a crenate formation; *esp* : one of the rounded projections on an edge (as of a coin) **b** : the quality or state of being crenate **2** : shrinkage of red blood cells resulting in crenate margins

cren·el·lat·ed *or* **cren·el·at·ed** \ˈkre-nə-ˌlā-təd\ *adj* [F *créneler* to furnish with embrasures, fr. OF *querneler,* fr. *kernel, crenel* embrasure, dim of *cren* notch, fr. *crener* to notch; akin to ML *crena*] (ca. 1823) : having crenellations ⟨a ~ wall⟩

cren·el·la·tion *also* **cren·el·a·tion** \ˌkre-nə-ˈlā-shən\ *n* (1849) **1** : BATTLEMENT **2** : any of the embrasures alternating with merlons in a battlement — see BATTLEMENT illustration

cren·shaw \ˈkren-ˌshȯ\ *n, often cap* [prob. fr. the name *Crenshaw* or *Cranshaw*] (1955) : a winter melon having smooth green and gold skin and sweet salmon-colored flesh

cren·u·lat·ed \ˈkren-yə-ˌlā-təd\ *or* **cren·u·late** \-lət, -ˌlāt\ *adj* [NL *crenulatus,* fr. *crenula,* dim. of ML *crena*] (1777) : having an irregularly wavy or serrate outline ⟨a ~ shoreline⟩ — **cren·u·la·tion** \ˌkren-yə-ˈlā-shən\ *n*

cre·ole \ˈkrē-ˌōl\ *adj* (1737) **1** *often cap* : of or relating to Creoles or their language **2** *often cap* : relating to or being highly seasoned food typically prepared with rice, okra, tomatoes, and peppers ⟨shrimp ~⟩

Cre·ole \ˈkrē-ˌōl\ *n* [F *créole,* fr. Sp *criollo,* fr. Pg *crioulo* white person born in the colonies] (1737) **1** : a person of European descent born esp. in the West Indies or Spanish America **2** : a white person descended from early French or Spanish settlers of the U.S. Gulf states and preserving their speech and culture **3** : a person of mixed French or Spanish and black descent speaking a dialect of French or Spanish **4 a** : a language evolved from pidginized French that is spoken by blacks in southern Louisiana **b** : HAITIAN **c** *not cap* : a language that has evolved from a pidgin but serves as the native language of a speech community

cre·ol·ise *Brit var of* CREOLIZE

cre·ol·ize \ˈkrē-ə-ˌlīz, ˈkrē-ˌō-\ *vt* **-ized; -iz·ing** (ca. 1932) : to cause (a pidginized language) to become a creole in a speech community — **cre·ol·i·za·tion** \ˌkrē-ə-lə-ˈzā-shən, ˌkrē-(ˌ)ō-\ *n*

[1]**cre·o·sote** \ˈkrē-ə-ˌsōt\ *n* [G *Kreosot,* fr. Gk *kreas* flesh + *sōtēr* preserver, fr. *sōzein* to preserve, fr. *sōs* safe (prob. akin to Skt *tavīti* he is strong); fr. its antiseptic properties — more at RAW] (1835) **1** : a clear or yellowish flammable oily liquid mixture of phenolic compounds obtained by the distillation of tar derived from wood and esp. from beech wood **2** : a brownish oily liquid consisting chiefly of aromatic hydrocarbons obtained by distillation of coal tar and used esp. as a wood preservative **3** : a dark brown or black flammable tar deposited from esp. wood smoke on the walls of a chimney **4** : CREOSOTE BUSH

[2]**creosote** *vt* **-sot·ed; -sot·ing** (1836) : to treat with creosote

creosote bush *n* (1846) : a resinous desert shrub (*Larrea tridentata*) of the caltrop family found in the southwestern U.S. and Mexico

crepe *or* **crêpe** \ˈkrāp\ *n* [F *crêpe* — more at CRAPE] (1750) **1** : a light crinkled fabric woven of any of various fibers **2** : CRAPE 2 **3** : crude rubber in the form of nearly white to brown crinkled sheets used esp. for shoe soles ⟨*crepe*-soled shoes⟩ **4** : a small very thin pancake — **crepe** *adj* — **crep·ey** *or* **crepy** \ˈkrā-pē\ *adj*

crepe de chine *or* **crêpe de chine** \ˌkrāp-də-ˈshēn\ *n, often cap 2d C* [F *crêpe de Chine,* lit., China crepe] (1869) : a soft fine or sheer clothing crepe esp. of silk

crepe myrtle *or* **crêpe myrtle** *n* (1916) : CRAPE MYRTLE

crepe paper *n* (1896) : paper with a crinkled or puckered texture

crêpe su·zette \ˌkrāp-sü-ˈzet\ *n, pl* **crêpes suzette** \ˌkrāp(s)-sü-ˈzet\ *or* **crêpe suzettes** \ˌkrāp-sü-ˈzets\ *often cap S* [F *crêpe Suzette,* prob. fr. *Suzette,* nickname of Suzanne Reichenberg †1924 Fr. actress] (1922) : a thin folded or rolled pancake in a hot orange-butter sauce that is sprinkled with a liqueur (as cognac or curaçao) and set ablaze for serving

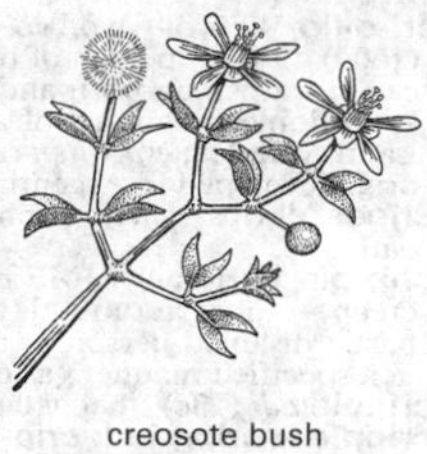
creosote bush

crep·i·tant \ˈkre-pə-tənt\ *adj* (1851) : having or making a crackling sound ⟨~ sounds in breathing⟩

crep·i·tate \ˈkre-pə-ˌtāt\ *vi* **-tat·ed; -tat·ing** [L *crepitatus,* pp. of *crepitare* to crackle, freq. of *crepare* to rattle, crack] (ca. 1828) : to make a crackling sound : CRACKLE — **crep·i·ta·tion** \ˌkre-pə-ˈtā-shən\ *n*

cre·pon \ˈkrā-ˌpän\ *n* [F, fr. *crêpe*] (1836) : a heavy crepe fabric with lengthwise crinkles

crept *past and past part of* CREEP

cre·pus·cu·lar \kri-ˈpəs-kyə-lər\ *adj* (1668) **1** : of, relating to, or resembling twilight : DIM ⟨~ light⟩ **2** : occurring or active during twilight ⟨~ insects⟩ ⟨~ activity⟩

cre·pus·cule \kri-ˈpəs-(ˌ)kyül\ *or* **cre·pus·cle** \-ˈpə-səl\ *n* [L *crepusculum,* fr. *creper* dusky] (14c) : TWILIGHT

cresc *abbr* crescendo

[1]cre·scen·do \krə-ˈshen-(ˌ)dō\ *n, pl* **-dos** *also* **-does** *or* **-di** \-dē\ [It, fr. *crescendo,* adj., increasing, gerund of *crescere* to grow, increase, fr. L] (1775) **1 a** : a gradual increase; *specif* : a gradual increase in volume of a musical passage **b** : the peak of a gradual increase : CLIMAX ⟨complaints about stifling smog conditions reach a ~ —*Down Beat*⟩ **2** : a crescendo musical passage — **crescendo** *vi*

[2]crescendo *adv or adj* (1807) : with an increase in volume — used as a direction in music

[1]cres·cent \ˈkre-sᵊnt\ *n* [ME *cressant,* fr. AF, fr. prp. of *crestre* to grow, increase, fr. L *crescere;* akin to OHG *hirsi* millet, Lith *šerti* to feed, Gk *koros* boy] (15c) **1 a** : the moon at any stage between new moon and first quarter and between last quarter and the succeeding new moon when less than half of the illuminated hemisphere is visible **b** : the figure of the moon at such a stage defined by a convex and a concave edge **2** : something shaped like a crescent — **cres·cen·tic** \kre-ˈsen-tik, krə-\ *adj*

[2]crescent *adj* [L *crescent-, crescens,* prp. of *crescere*] (1574) : marked by an increase : INCREASING ⟨my powers are ~ —Shak.⟩

Cres·cent \ˈkre-sᵊnt\ *trademark* — used for an adjustable open-end wrench

cres·cive \ˈkre-siv\ *adj* [L *crescere* to grow] (1566) : marked by gradual spontaneous development — **cres·cive·ly** *adv*

cre·sol \ˈkrē-ˌsȯl, -ˌsōl\ *n* [ISV, irreg. fr. *creosote*] (ca. 1869) : any of three poisonous colorless crystalline or liquid isomeric phenols C_7H_8O

cress \ˈkres\ *n* [ME *cresse,* fr. OE *cærse, cressa;* akin to OHG *kressa* cress] (bef. 12c) : any of various crucifers with moderately pungent leaves used esp. in salads: as **a** : a watercress (*Nasturtium officinale*) **b** : GARDEN CRESS

cres·set \ˈkre-sət\ *n* [ME, fr. AF, fr. *creisse, gresse* grease — more at GREASE] (14c) : an iron vessel or basket used for holding an illuminant (as oil) and mounted as a torch or suspended as a lantern

Cres·si·da \ˈkre-sə-də\ *n* (14c) : a Trojan woman of medieval legend who pledges herself to Troilus but while a captive of the Greeks gives herself to Diomedes

[1]crest \ˈkrest\ *n* [ME *creste,* fr. AF, fr. L *crista;* prob. akin to L *crinis* hair] (14c) **1 a** : a showy tuft or process on the head of an animal and esp. a bird — see BIRD illustration **b** : the plume or identifying emblem worn on a knight's helmet; *also* : the top of a helmet **c** (1) : a heraldic representation of the crest (2) : a heraldic device depicted above the escutcheon but not upon a helmet (3) : COAT OF ARMS 2a **d** : a ridge or prominence on a part of an animal body **2** : something suggesting a crest esp. in being an upper prominence, edge, or limit: as **a** : PEAK; *esp* : the top line of a mountain or hill **b** : the ridge of a roof **c** : the top of a wave **3 a** : a high point of an action or process and esp. of one that is rhythmic **b** : CLIMAX, CULMINATION ⟨at the ~ of his fame⟩ — **crest·al** \ˈkres-tᵊl\ *adj* — **crest·less** \-ləs\ *adj*

[2]crest *vt* (15c) **1** : to furnish with a crest; *also* : CROWN **2** : to reach the crest of ⟨~*ed* the hill and looked around⟩ ~ *vi* : to rise to a crest ⟨waves ~*ing* in the storm⟩

crest·ed \ˈkres-təd\ *adj* (14c) : having a crest ⟨a ~ bird⟩

crested wheatgrass *n* (1923) : either of two Eurasian grasses (*Agropyron cristatum* or *A. desertorum* syn. *A. sibiricum*) that are grown in the U.S. for forage and for erosion control

crest·fall·en \ˈkrest-ˌfȯ-lən\ *adj* (1589) **1** : having a drooping crest or hanging head **2** : feeling shame or humiliation : DEJECTED — **crest·fall·en·ly** *adv* — **crest·fall·en·ness** \-lən-nəs\ *n*

crest·ing \ˈkres-tiŋ\ *n* (1862) : a decorative edging or railing (as on pottery or furniture)

Cre·ta·ceous \kri-ˈtā-shəs\ *adj* [L *cretaceus* resembling chalk, fr. *creta* chalk] (1832) : of, relating to, or being the last period of the Mesozoic era characterized by continued dominance of reptiles, emergent dominance of angiosperms, diversification of mammals, and the extinction of many types of organisms at the close of the period; *also* : of, relating to, or being the corresponding system of rocks — see GEOLOGIC TIME table — **Cretaceous** *n*

cre·tin \ˈkrē-tᵊn\ *n* [F *crétin,* fr. F dial. *cretin,* lit., wretch, innocent victim, fr. L *christianus* Christian] (1779) **1** *often offensive* : one afflicted with cretinism **2** : a stupid, vulgar, or insensitive person : CLOD, LOUT — **cre·tin·ous** \-tᵊn-əs\ *adj*

cre·tin·ism \-tᵊn-ˌi-zəm\ *n* (1801) : a usu. congenital abnormal condition marked by physical stunting and mental retardation and caused by severe hypothyroidism

cre·tonne \ˈkrē-ˌtän, kri-ˈ\ *n* [F, fr. *Creton,* Normandy] (1863) : a strong cotton or linen cloth used esp. for curtains and upholstery

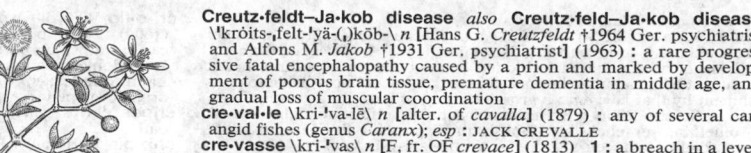

Creutz·feldt–Ja·kob disease *also* **Creutz·feld–Ja·kob disease** \ˈkrȯits-ˌfelt-ˈyä-(ˌ)kōb-\ *n* [Hans G. *Creutzfeldt* †1964 Ger. psychiatrist and Alfons M. *Jakob* †1931 Ger. psychiatrist] (1963) : a rare progressive fatal encephalopathy caused by a prion and marked by development of porous brain tissue, premature dementia in middle age, and gradual loss of muscular coordination

cre·val·le \kri-ˈva-lē\ *n* [alter. of *cavalla*] (1879) : any of several carangid fishes (genus *Caranx*); *esp* : JACK CREVALLE

cre·vasse \kri-ˈvas\ *n* [F, fr. OF *crevace*] (1813) **1** : a breach in a levee **2** : a deep crevice or fissure (as in a glacier or the earth)

crev·ice \ˈkre-vəs\ *n* [ME, fr. AF *crevace,* fr. *crever* to break, fr. L *crepare* to crack] (14c) : a narrow opening resulting from a split or crack (as in a cliff) : FISSURE

[1]crew \ˈkrü\ *chiefly Brit past of* CROW

[2]crew \ˈkrü\ *n* [ME *crue,* fr. MF, reinforcement, lit., increase, fr. *crue,* fem. pp. of *croistre* to grow, fr. L *crescere* — more at CRESCENT] (15c) **1** *archaic* : a band or force of armed men **2 a** : a group of people associated together in a common activity or by common traits or interests **b** : GANG 1b(2) **3 a** : a company of people working on one job or under one foreman or operating a machine **b** : the whole company belonging to a ship sometimes including the officers and master; *also* : one who assists the skipper of a sailboat **c** : the persons who have duties on an aircraft in flight **d** : the rowers and coxswain of a racing shell; *also* : ROWING — **crew·less** \-ləs\ *adj*

[3]crew *vi* (1935) : to act as a member of a crew ~ *vt* : to serve as a crew member on (as a ship or aircraft)

crew chief *n* (1926) : one who is in charge of a crew of workers; *esp* : a noncommissioned officer (as in the air force) who supervises an airplane's ground crew

crew cut *n* (1942) : a very short haircut usu. for men or boys in which the hair resembles the bristle surface of a brush

crew·el \ˈkrü-əl\ *n* [ME *crule*] (15c) **1** : slackly twisted worsted yarn used for embroidery **2** : CREWELWORK

crew·el·work \-ˌwərk\ *n* (1863) : embroidery work with crewel

crew·man \ˈkrü-mən\ *n* (ca. 1927) : a member of a crew

crew·mate \-ˌmāt\ *n* (1938) : a fellow crewman

crew neck *n* [fr. the sweaters with this neckline worn by oarsmen] (1939) **1** : a round collarless neckline **2** *usu* **crew·neck** \ˈkrü-ˌnek\ : a sweater with a crew neck

crew sock *n* (1948) : a short bulky usu. ribbed sock

[1]crib \ˈkrib\ *n* [ME, fr. OE *cribb;* akin to OHG *krippa* manger, and perh. to Gk *griphos* reed basket] (bef. 12c) **1** : a manger for feeding animals **2** : an enclosure esp. of framework: as **a** : a stall for a stabled animal **b** : a small child's bedstead with high enclosing usu. slatted sides **c** : any of various devices resembling a crate or framework in structure **d** : a building for storage : BIN **3 a** : a small narrow room or dwelling : HUT, SHACK **b** : a room or shack used for prostitution **4** : the cards discarded in cribbage for the dealer to use in scoring **5 a** : a small theft **b** : PLAGIARISM **c** : a literal translation; *esp* : PONY 3 **d** : a summary and key to understanding a literary work **e** : something used for cheating in an examination **6** : CRÈCHE 1

[2]crib *vb* **cribbed; crib·bing** *vt* (1605) **1** : CONFINE, CRAMP **2** : to provide with or put into a crib; *esp* : to line or support with a framework of timber **3** : PILFER, STEAL; *esp* : PLAGIARIZE ~ *vi* **1 a** : STEAL, PLAGIARIZE **b** : to use a crib : CHEAT **2** : to have the vice of cribbing — **crib·ber** *n*

crib·bage \ˈkri-bij\ *n* [[1]*crib*] (1630) : a card game for two players in which each player tries to form various counting combinations of cards

crib·bing \ˈkri-biŋ\ *n* (1841) **1** : material for use in making a crib **2** : a vice of horses in which they grasp a solid object (as a stall door) with their teeth and gulp air

crib biting *n* (1831) : CRIBBING 2

crib death *n* (1965) : SUDDEN INFANT DEATH SYNDROME

crib·ri·form \ˈkri-brə-ˌfȯrm\ *adj* [L *cribrum* sieve; akin to L *cernere* to sift — more at CERTAIN] (1741) : pierced with small holes

crib sheet *n* (1960) : CHEAT SHEET

cri·ce·tid \krī-ˈsē-təd, -ˈse-\ *n* [ultim. fr. NL *Cricetus,* genus name, of Slav origin; akin to Czech *křeček* hamster] (1960) : any of a family (Cricetidae) of small rodents including the hamsters, voles, lemmings, gerbils, and New World rats and mice that are often grouped with the murids — **cricetid** *adj*

[1]crick \ˈkrik\ *n* [ME *cryk*] (15c) : a painful spasmodic condition of muscles (as of the neck or back)

[2]crick *vt* (1884) **1** : to cause a crick in (as the neck) **2** : to turn or twist (as the head) esp. into a strained position

[1]crick·et \ˈkri-kət\ *n* [ME *criket,* fr. AF, of imit. origin] (14c) **1** : any of a family (Gryllidae) of leaping orthopteran insects noted for the chirping notes produced by the male by rubbing together specially modified parts of the forewings **2** : a low wooden footstool **3** : a small metal toy or signaling device that makes a sharp click or snap when pressed

[2]cricket *n* [MF *criquet* goal stake in a bowling game] (1598) **1** : a game played with a ball and bat by two sides of usu. 11 players each on a large field centering upon two wickets each defended by a batsman **2** : fair and honorable behavior ⟨it wasn't ~ for her to break her contract —Gerry Nadel⟩

[3]cricket *vi* (ca. 1809) : to play the game of cricket — **crick·et·er** *n*

cri·coid \ˈkrī-ˌkȯid\ *adj* [NL *cricoides,* fr. Gk *krikoeidēs* ring-shaped, fr. *krikos* ring — more at CIRCLE] (1746) : of, relating to, or being a cartilage of the larynx with which arytenoid cartilages articulate

cri de coeur \ˌkrē-də-ˈkər\ *n, pl* **cris de coeur** *same*\ [F, lit., cry from the heart] (1904) : a passionate outcry (as of appeal or protest)

cri·er \ˈkrī(-ə)r\ *n* (14c) : one that cries: **a** : an officer who proclaims the orders of a court **b** : TOWN CRIER

cri·key \ˈkrī-kē\ *also* **crick·ey** \ˈkri-kē\ *interj* [euphemism for *Christ*] (1838) — used as a mild oath

crim *abbr* criminal

\ə\ **a**but \ᵊ\ kitten, F table \ər\ **fur**ther \a\ **a**sh \ā\ **a**ce \ä\ m**o**p, m**a**r
\au̇\ **ou**t \ch\ **ch**in \e\ b**e**t \ē\ **ea**sy \g\ **g**o \i\ h**i**t \ī\ **i**ce \j\ **j**ob
\ŋ\ si**ng** \ō\ g**o** \ȯ\ l**aw** \ȯi\ b**oy** \th\ **th**in \th\ **th**e \ü\ l**oo**t \u̇\ f**oo**t
\y\ **y**et \zh\ vi**si**on, bei**ge** \k, ⁿ, œ, ue, ʸ\ *see* Guide to Pronunciation

crim con *abbr* criminal conversation
crime \ˈkrīm\ *n* [ME, fr. AF, fr. L *crimen* accusation, reproach, crime; prob. akin to L *cernere* to sift, determine] (14c) **1 :** an act or the commission of an act that is forbidden or the omission of a duty that is commanded by a public law and that makes the offender liable to punishment by that law; *esp* **:** a gross violation of law **2 :** a grave offense esp. against morality **3 :** criminal activity ⟨efforts to fight ~⟩ **4 :** something reprehensible, foolish, or disgraceful ⟨it's a ~ to waste good food⟩ ***syn*** see OFFENSE — **crime·less** \-ləs\ *adj*
crime against humanity (1945) **:** atrocity (as extermination or enslavement) that is directed esp. against an entire population or part of a population on specious grounds and without regard to individual guilt or responsibility even on such grounds
crime against nature (1796) **:** SODOMY
[1]**crim·i·nal** \ˈkri-mə-nᵊl, ˈkrim-nəl\ *adj* [ME, fr. AF or LL; AF *criminal,* fr. LL *criminalis,* fr. L *crimin-, crimen* crime] (15c) **1 :** relating to, involving, or being a crime ⟨~ neglect⟩ **2 :** relating to crime or to the prosecution of suspects in a crime ⟨~ statistics⟩ ⟨brought ~ action⟩ **3 :** guilty of crime; *also* **:** of or befitting a criminal ⟨a ~ mind⟩ **4 :** DISGRACEFUL — **crim·i·nal·ly** *adv*
[2]**criminal** *n* (ca. 1626) **1 :** one who has committed a crime **2 :** a person who has been convicted of a crime
criminal conversation *n* (1732) **:** adultery considered as a tort
criminal court *n* (1678) **:** a court that has jurisdiction to try and punish offenders against criminal law
crim·i·nal·ist \ˈkri-mə-nᵊl-ist\ *n* (1951) **:** a specialist in criminalistics
crim·i·nal·is·tics \ˌkri-mə-nᵊl-ˈis-tiks, ˌkrim-nə-ˈlis-\ *n pl but sing in constr* (1943) **:** application of scientific techniques in collecting and analyzing physical evidence in criminal cases
crim·i·nal·i·ty \ˌkri-mə-ˈna-lə-tē\ *n* (1611) **1 :** the quality or state of being criminal **2 :** criminal activity ⟨urban ~⟩
crim·i·nal·ize \ˈkri-mə-nᵊl-ˌīz, ˈkrim-nə-ˌlīz\ *vt* **-ized; -iz·ing** (ca. 1956) **:** to make illegal; *also* **:** to turn into a criminal or treat as criminal — **crim·i·nal·i·za·tion** \ˌkri-mə-nᵊl-ə-ˈzā-shən, ˌkrim-nə-lə-ˈzā-\ *n*
criminal law *n* (1769) **:** the law of crimes and their punishments
criminal lawyer *n* (1869) **:** a lawyer who specializes in criminal law; *esp* **:** a lawyer who represents defendants in criminal cases
crim·i·nate \ˈkri-mə-ˌnāt\ *vt* **-nat·ed; -nat·ing** [L *criminatus,* pp. of *criminari,* fr. *crimin-, crimen* accusation] (1645) **:** INCRIMINATE — **crim·i·na·tion** \ˌkri-mə-ˈnā-shən\ *n*
crimini *var of* CREMINI
crim·i·nol·o·gy \ˌkri-mə-ˈnä-lə-jē\ *n* [It *criminologia,* fr. L *crimin-, crimen* + It *-o-* + *-logia* -logy] (1872) **:** the scientific study of crime as a social phenomenon, of criminals, and of penal treatment — **crim·i·no·log·i·cal** \-mə-nᵊl-ˈä-ji-kəl\ *adj* — **crim·i·no·log·i·cal·ly** \-k(ə-)lē\ *adv* — **crim·i·nol·o·gist** \ˌkri-mə-ˈnä-lə-jist\ *n*
crim·i·nous \ˈkri-mə-nəs\ *adj* (15c) **:** CRIMINAL
crim·i·ny \ˈkri-mə-nē, ˈkrī-\ *interj* [perh. alter. of *jiminy, gemini,* mild oath, prob. euphemism for LL *Jesu domine* Jesus Lord!] (1681) — used as a mild oath or to express surprise
[1]**crimp** \ˈkrimp\ *vt* [D or LG *krimpen* to shrivel; akin to MD *crampe* hook, cramp] (1712) **1 :** to cause to become wavy, bent, or pinched: as **a :** to form (leather) into a desired shape **b :** to give (synthetic fibers) a curl or wave like that of natural fibers **c :** to pinch or press together (as the margins of a pie crust) in order to seal **2 :** to be an inhibiting or restraining influence on **:** CRAMP ⟨sales had been *~ed* by credit controls —*Time*⟩ — **crimp·er** \ˈkrim-pər\ *n*
[2]**crimp** *n* (1863) **1 :** something produced by or as if by crimping: as **a :** a section of hair artificially waved or curled **b :** a succession of waves (as in wool fiber) **c :** a bend or crease formed in something **2 :** something that cramps or inhibits **:** RESTRAINT, CURB
[3]**crimp** *n* [perh. fr. [1]*crimp*] (1758) **:** a person who entraps or forces men into shipping as sailors or into enlisting in an army or navy
[4]**crimp** *vt* (1812) **:** to trap into military or sea service **:** IMPRESS
crimpy \ˈkrim-pē\ *adj* **crimp·i·er; -est** (1888) **:** FRIZZY
[1]**crim·son** \ˈkrim-zən\ *n* [ME *crimisin,* fr. OSp *cremesín,* fr. Ar *qirmizī,* fr. *qirmiz* kermes] (15c) **:** any of several deep purplish reds
[2]**crimson** *adj* (15c) **:** of the color crimson
[3]**crimson** *vt* (1601) **:** to make crimson ~ *vi* **:** to become crimson; *esp* **:** BLUSH
crimson clover *n* (1839) **:** an annual European clover (*Trifolium incarnatum*) that has cylindrical heads of crimson flowers and is cultivated in the U.S. esp. as a cover crop
[1]**cringe** \ˈkrinj\ *vi* **cringed; cring·ing** [ME *crengen;* akin to OE *cringan* to yield, MHG *krank* weak] (13c) **1 :** to draw in or contract one's muscles involuntarily (as from cold or pain) **2 :** to shrink in fear or servility **3 :** to behave in an excessively humble or servile way **4 :** to recoil in distaste ⟨Americans *cringed* . . . at the use of a term now regarded as a slur —William Safire⟩ ***syn*** see FAWN — **cring·er** *n*
[2]**cringe** *n* (1597) **:** a cringing act; *specif* **:** a servile bow
cringe·wor·thy \ˈkrinj-ˌwər-t͟hē\ *adj* (1977) **:** so embarrassing, awkward, or upsetting as to cause one to cringe ⟨a ~ performance⟩
crin·gle \ˈkriŋ-gəl\ *n* [LG *kringel,* dim. of *kring* ring] (1627) **:** a loop or grommet at the corner of a sail to which a line is attached
[1]**crin·kle** \ˈkriŋ-kəl\ *vb* **crin·kled; crin·kling** \-k(ə-)liŋ\ [ME *crynkelen;* akin to OE *cringan* to yield] *vi* (14c) **1 a :** to form many short bends or ripples **b :** WRINKLE **2 :** to give forth a thin crackling sound **:** RUSTLE ⟨*crinkling* silks⟩ ~ *vt* **:** to cause to crinkle **:** make crinkles in
[2]**crinkle** *n* (1596) **1 :** WRINKLE, CORRUGATION, PUCKER **2 :** any of several virus diseases of plants marked by crinkling of leaves — **crin·kly** \-k(ə-)lē\ *adj*
cri·noid \ˈkrī-ˌnȯid\ *n* [ultim. fr. Gk *krinon* lily] (1847) **:** any of a large class (Crinoidea) of echinoderms usu. having a somewhat cup-shaped body with five or more feathery arms — compare FEATHER STAR, SEA LILY — **crinoid** *adj*

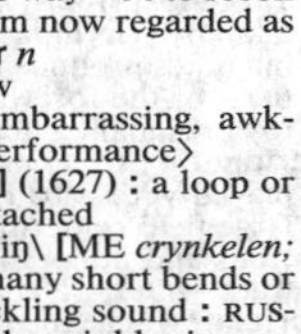
crinoid

crin·o·line \ˈkri-nə-lən\ *n* [F, fr. It *crinolino,* fr. *crino* horsehair (fr. L *crinis* hair) + *lino* flax, linen, fr. L *linum* — more at CREST] (1830) **1 :** an open-weave fabric of horsehair or cotton that is usu. stiffened and used esp. for interlinings and millinery **2 :** a full stiff skirt or underskirt made of crinoline; *also* **:** HOOPSKIRT — **crinoline** *or* **crin·o·lined** \-lənd\ *adj*
cri·o·llo \krē-ˈōl-(ˌ)yō, -ˈō-(ˌ)yō\ *n, pl* **-llos** [Sp — more at CREOLE] (1604) **1 a :** a person of pure Spanish descent born in Spanish America **b :** a person born and usu. raised in a Spanish-American country **2 :** a domestic animal of a breed or strain (as of cattle) developed in Latin America; *esp, often cap* **:** any of a breed of hardy muscular ponies orig. developed in Argentina — **criollo** *adj*
cripes \ˈkrīps\ *interj* [euphemism for *Christ*] (1910) — used as a mild oath
[1]**crip·ple** \ˈkri-pəl\ *n* [ME *cripel,* fr. OE *crypel;* akin to OE *crēopan* to creep — more at CREEP] (bef. 12c) **1 a** *sometimes offensive* **:** a lame or partly disabled person or animal **b :** one that is disabled or deficient in a specified manner ⟨a social ~⟩ **2 :** something flawed or imperfect
[2]**cripple** *adj* (13c) **:** being lame, flawed, or imperfect
[3]**cripple** *vt* **crip·pled; crip·pling** \-p(ə-)liŋ\ (14c) **1 :** to deprive of the use of a limb and esp. a leg ⟨the accident left him *crippled*⟩ **2 :** to deprive of capability for service or of strength, efficiency, or wholeness ⟨an economy *crippled* by inflation⟩ ***syn*** see MAIM, WEAKEN — **crip·pler** \-p(ə-)lər\ *n* — **crip·pling·ly** \-p(ə-)liŋ-lē\ *adv*
cri·sis \ˈkrī-səs\ *n, pl* **cri·ses** \ˈkrī-ˌsēz\ [ME, fr. L, fr. Gk *krisis,* lit., decision, fr. *krinein* to decide — more at CERTAIN] (15c) **1 a :** the turning point for better or worse in an acute disease or fever **b :** a paroxysmal attack of pain, distress, or disordered function **c :** an emotionally significant event or radical change of status in a person's life ⟨a midlife ~⟩ **2 :** the decisive moment (as in a literary plot) **3 a :** an unstable or crucial time or state of affairs in which a decisive change is impending; *esp* **:** one with the distinct possibility of a highly undesirable outcome ⟨a financial ~⟩ **b :** a situation that has reached a critical phase ⟨the environmental ~⟩ ***syn*** see JUNCTURE
[1]**crisp** \ˈkrisp\ *adj* [ME, fr. OE, fr. L *crispus;* akin to W *crych* curly] (bef. 12c) **1 :** CURLY, WAVY; *also* **:** having close stiff or wiry curls or waves **2 a :** easily crumbled **:** BRITTLE ⟨a ~ cracker⟩ **b :** desirably firm and crunchy ⟨~ lettuce⟩ **3 a :** notably sharp, clean-cut, and clear ⟨a ~ illustration⟩; *also* **:** concise and to the point ⟨a ~ reply⟩ **b :** noticeably neat ⟨~ new clothes⟩ **c :** BRISK, LIVELY ⟨a ~ tale of intrigue⟩ ⟨~ musical tempi⟩ **d :** briskly cold ⟨~ winter weather⟩; *also* **:** FRESH, INVIGORATING ⟨~ autumn air⟩ ⟨a ~ white wine⟩ **e :** deftly and powerfully executed ⟨a ~ tennis serve⟩ ***syn*** see FRAGILE — **crisp·ly** *adv* — **crisp·ness** *n*
[2]**crisp** *vt* (14c) **1 :** CURL, CRIMP **2 :** to cause to ripple **:** WRINKLE **3 :** to make or keep crisp ~ *vi* **1 :** CURL **2 :** RIPPLE **3 :** to become crisp
[3]**crisp** *n* (14c) **1 a :** something crisp or brittle ⟨burned to a ~⟩ ⟨rye *~s*⟩ **b** *chiefly Brit* **:** POTATO CHIP — usu. used in pl. **2 :** a baked dessert of fruit with crumb topping ⟨apple ~⟩
crisp·bread \ˈkrisp-ˌbred\ *n* (ca. 1927) **:** a plain dry unsweetened cracker made from crushed grain (as wheat or rye)
crisp·en \ˈkris-pən\ *vt* (1931) **:** to make crisp ~ *vi* **:** to become crisp
crisp·er \ˈkris-pər\ *n* (1835) **:** one that crisps; *specif* **:** a closed container in a refrigerator intended to prevent loss of moisture from fresh produce
crisp·head \ˈkrisp-ˌhed\ *n* (1966) **:** ICEBERG LETTUCE
crispy \ˈkris-pē\ *adj* **crisp·i·er; -est** (14c) **1 :** CRISP 1 ⟨~ hair⟩ **2 :** appealingly crunchy **:** CRISP ⟨~ fried chicken⟩ — **crisp·i·ness** *n*
[1]**criss·cross** \ˈkris-ˌkrȯs\ *vb* [obs. *christcross, crisscross* mark of a cross] *vt* (1818) **1 :** to mark with intersecting lines **2 :** to pass back and forth through or over ~ *vi* **1 :** to go or pass back and forth **2 :** OVERLAP, INTERSECT
[2]**crisscross** *adj* (1840) **:** marked or characterized by crisscrossing — **crisscross** *adv*
[3]**crisscross** *n* (1833) **1 :** a crisscross pattern **:** NETWORK **2 :** the state of being at cross-purposes; *also* **:** a confused state
cris·ta \ˈkris-tə\ *n, pl* **cris·tae** \-ˌtē, -ˌtī\ [NL, fr. L, crest — more at CREST] (1959) **:** any of the inwardly projecting folds of the inner membrane of a mitochondrion
crit *abbr* critical; criticism; criticized
cri·te·ri·on \krī-ˈtir-ē-ən *also* krə-\ *n, pl* **-ria** \-ē-ə\ *also* **-ri·ons** [Gk *kritērion,* fr. *krinein* to judge, decide — more at CERTAIN] (1622) **1 :** a standard on which a judgment or decision may be based **2 :** a characterizing mark or trait ***syn*** see STANDARD
usage The plural *criteria* has been used as a singular for over half a century ⟨let me now return to the third *criteria* —R. M. Nixon⟩ ⟨that really is the *criteria* —Bert Lance⟩. Many of our examples, like the two foregoing, are taken from speech. But singular *criteria* is not uncommon in edited prose, and its use both in speech and writing seems to be increasing. Only time will tell whether it will reach the unquestioned acceptability of *agenda.*
cri·te·ri·um \krī-ˈtir-ē-əm, krē-ter-ˈyōm\ *n* [F *critérium* competition, lit., criterion, fr. LL *criterium,* fr. Gk *kritērion*] (1970) **:** a bicycle race of a specified number of laps on a closed course over public roads closed to normal traffic
[1]**crit·ic** \ˈkri-tik\ *n* [L *criticus,* fr. Gk *kritikos,* fr. *kritikos* able to discern or judge, fr. *krinein*] (1588) **1 a :** one who expresses a reasoned opinion on any matter esp. involving a judgment of its value, truth, righteousness, beauty, or technique **b :** one who engages often professionally in the analysis, evaluation, or appreciation of works of art or artistic performances **2 :** one given to harsh or captious judgment
[2]**critic** *n* [Gk *kritikē* art of the critic, fr. fem. of *kritikos*] (1651) **1** *archaic* **:** CRITICISM **2** *archaic* **:** CRITIQUE
crit·i·cal \ˈkri-ti-kəl\ *adj* (1547) **1 a :** of, relating to, or being a turning point or specially important juncture ⟨a ~ phase⟩: as (1) **:** relating to or being the stage of a disease at which an abrupt change for better or worse may be expected; *also* **:** being or relating to an illness or condition involving danger of death ⟨~ care⟩ ⟨a patient listed in ~ condition⟩ (2) **:** relating to or being a state in which or a measurement or point at which some quality, property, or phenomenon suffers a definite change ⟨~ temperature⟩ **b :** CRUCIAL, DECISIVE ⟨a ~ test⟩ **c :** INDISPENSABLE, VITAL ⟨a ~ waterfowl habitat⟩ ⟨a component ~ to the operation of a machine⟩ **d :** being in or approaching a state of crisis ⟨a ~ shortage⟩ ⟨a ~ situation⟩ **2 a :** inclined to criticize severely and unfavorably **b :** consisting of or involving criticism ⟨~ writings⟩; *also* **:** of or relating to the judgment of critics ⟨the play was a ~ success⟩ **c :** exercising or involving careful judgment or judicious evaluation ⟨~ thinking⟩ **d :** including variant readings and scholarly emendations ⟨a ~ edition⟩ **3 a :** of sufficient size to sustain a chain

reaction — used of a mass of fissionable material ⟨a ~ mass⟩ **b :** sustaining a nuclear chain reaction ⟨the reactor went ~⟩ — **crit·i·cal·i·ty** \ˌkri-tə-ˈka-lə-tē\ *n* — **crit·i·cal·ly** \ˈkri-ti-k(ə-)lē\ *adv* — **crit·i·cal·ness** \-kəl-nəs\ *n*

syn CRITICAL, HYPERCRITICAL, FAULTFINDING, CAPTIOUS, CARPING, CENSORIOUS mean inclined to look for and point out faults and defects. CRITICAL may also imply an effort to see a thing clearly and truly in order to judge it fairly ⟨a *critical* essay⟩. HYPERCRITICAL suggests a tendency to judge by unreasonably strict standards ⟨*hypercritical* disparagement of other people's work⟩. FAULTFINDING implies a querulous or exacting temperament ⟨a *faultfinding* reviewer⟩. CAPTIOUS suggests a readiness to detect trivial faults or raise objections on trivial grounds ⟨a *captious* critic⟩. CARPING implies an ill-natured or perverse picking of flaws ⟨a *carping* editorial⟩. CENSORIOUS implies a disposition to be severely critical and condemnatory ⟨the *censorious* tone of the review⟩. ***syn*** see in addition ACUTE

critical angle *n* (1873) **:** the least angle of incidence at which total reflection takes place

critical mass *n* (1919) **:** a size, number, or amount large enough to produce a particular result ⟨the *critical mass* of activity needed for a retail store⟩

critical point *n* (ca. 1912) **:** a point on the graph of a function where the derivative is zero or infinite

critical region *n* (1951) **:** the set of outcomes of a statistical test for which the null hypothesis is to be rejected

critical value *n* (ca. 1909) **:** the value of an independent variable corresponding to a critical point of a function

crit·ic·as·ter \ˈkri-ti-ˌkas-tər\ *n* (1684) **:** an inferior or petty critic

crit·i·cise *Brit var of* CRITICIZE

crit·i·cism \ˈkri-tə-ˌsi-zəm\ *n* (1607) **1 a :** the act of criticizing usu. unfavorably ⟨seeking encouragement rather than ~⟩ **b :** a critical observation or remark ⟨an unfair ~⟩ **c :** CRITIQUE **2 :** the art of evaluating or analyzing works of art or literature; *also* **:** writings expressing such evaluation or analysis ⟨an anthology of literary ~⟩ **3 :** the scientific investigation of literary documents (as the Bible) in regard to such matters as origin, text, composition, or history

crit·i·cize \ˈkri-tə-ˌsīz\ *vb* **-cized; -ciz·ing** *vi* (1643) **:** to act as a critic ~ *vt* **1 :** to consider the merits and demerits of and judge accordingly **:** EVALUATE **2 :** to find fault with **:** point out the faults of — **crit·i·ciz·able** \-ˌsī-zə-bəl\ *adj* — **crit·i·ciz·er** *n*

syn CRITICIZE, REPREHEND, CENSURE, REPROBATE, CONDEMN, DENOUNCE mean to find fault with openly. CRITICIZE implies finding fault esp. with methods or policies or intentions ⟨*criticized* the police for using violence⟩. REPREHEND implies both criticism and severe rebuking ⟨*reprehends* the self-centeredness of today's students⟩. CENSURE carries a strong suggestion of authority and of reprimanding ⟨a Senator formally *censured* by his peers⟩. REPROBATE implies strong disapproval or firm refusal to sanction ⟨*reprobated* his son's unconventional lifestyle⟩. CONDEMN usu. suggests an unqualified and final unfavorable judgment ⟨*condemned* the government's racial policies⟩. DENOUNCE adds to CONDEMN the implication of a public declaration ⟨a pastoral letter *denouncing* abortion⟩.

[1]**cri·tique** \krə-ˈtēk, kri-\ *n* [alter. of [2]*critic*] (1710) **:** an act of criticizing; *esp* **:** a critical estimate or discussion ⟨a ~ of the poet's work⟩

[2]**critique** *vt* **cri·tiqued; cri·tiqu·ing** (1751) **:** to examine critically **:** REVIEW ⟨~ the plan⟩

crit·ter \ˈkri-tər\ *n* [by alter.] (1815) **:** CREATURE 1

CRNA *abbr* certified registered nurse anesthetist

[1]**croak** \ˈkrōk\ *vb* [ME *croken,* of imit. origin] *vi* (15c) **1 a :** to make a deep harsh sound **b :** to speak in a hoarse throaty voice **2 :** GRUMBLE 1 **3** *slang* **:** DIE ~ *vt* **1 :** to utter in a hoarse raucous voice **2** *slang* **:** KILL

[2]**croak** *n* (1561) **:** a hoarse harsh cry or sound — **croaky** \ˈkrō-kē\ *adj*

croak·er \ˈkrō-kər\ *n* (1648) **1 :** an animal (as a frog) that croaks **2 :** any of various fishes and esp. the drums that produce croaking, drumming, or grunting noises **3** *slang* **:** DOCTOR

Croat \ˈkrō-ˌat *also* ˈkrō(-ə)t\ *n* [NL *Croata,* fr. Croatian & Serbian *Hrvat*] (1657) **:** CROATIAN — **Croat** *adj*

Cro·a·tian \krō-ˈā-shən\ *n* (1555) **1 :** a native or inhabitant of Croatia **2 :** a south Slavic language spoken by the Croatian people — **Croatian** *adj*

croc \ˈkräk\ *n* (1884) **:** CROCODILE

[1]**cro·chet** \krō-ˈshā\ *n* [F, hook, crochet, fr. MF, dim. of *croche* hook, of Scand origin; akin to ON *krōkr* hook] (1844) **:** needlework consisting of the interlocking of looped stitches formed with a single thread and a hooked needle

[2]**crochet** *vt* (1854) **:** to make of crochet ⟨~*ed* a doily⟩ ~ *vi* **:** to work with crochet — **cro·chet·er** \-ˈshā-ər\ *n*

cro·cid·o·lite \krō-ˈsi-də-ˌlīt\ *n* [G *Krokydolith,* fr. Gk *krokyd-, krokys* nap on cloth (akin to Gk *krekein* to weave) + G *-lith* -lite — more at REEL] (1835) **:** a lavender-blue or light green mineral of the amphibole group that occurs in silky fibers and in massive form and is a type of asbestos — compare TIGEREYE

[1]**crock** \ˈkräk\ *n* [ME, fr. OE *crocc;* akin to OE *crūce* pot, pitcher, MHG *krūche*] (bef. 12c) **1 :** a thick earthenware pot or jar **2** [fr. its formation on cooking pots] *dial* **:** SOOT, SMUT **3 :** coloring matter that rubs off from cloth or dyed leather **4 :** BUNKUM — usu. used with *a* ⟨the story in the paper is a ~⟩

[2]**crock** *vt* (1594) **1 :** to put or preserve in a crock **2** *dial* **:** to soil with crock **:** SMUDGE ~ *vi* **:** to transfer color (as when rubbed or washed) ⟨a suede that will not ~⟩

[3]**crock** *n* [ME *crok;* akin to LG *krakke* broken-down horse] (1528) **1 :** one that is broken-down, disabled, or impaired ⟨so many old . . . ~*s* with one foot in the grave —Angus Wilson⟩ **2** *slang* **:** a complaining medical patient whose illness is largely imaginary or psychosomatic

[4]**crock** *vt* (1839) **:** to cause to become disabled ~ *vi* **:** BREAK DOWN

crocked \ˈkräkt\ *adj* (ca. 1927) **:** DRUNK 1a

crock·ery \ˈkrä-k(ə-)rē\ *n* (1715) **:** EARTHENWARE

crock·et \ˈkrä-kət\ *n* [ME *croket,* fr. AF, crook, dim. of *croc* hook, of Scand origin; akin to ON *krōkr* hook] (1673) **:** an ornament usu. in the form of curved and bent foliage used on the edge of a gable or spire — **crock·et·ed** \-kə-təd\ *adj*

Crock–Pot \ˈkräk-ˌpät\ *trademark* — used for an electric cooking pot

croc·o·dile \ˈkrä-kə-ˌdī(-ə)l\ *n* [ME & L; ME *cocodrille,* fr. AF, fr. ML *cocodrillus,* alter. of L *crocodilus,* fr. Gk *krokodilos* lizard, crocodile, fr. *krokē* shingle, pebble + *drilos* worm; akin to Skt *śarkara* pebble] (1555) **1 a :** any of several large carnivorous thick-skinned long-bodied aquatic reptiles (family Crocodylidae) of tropical and subtropical waters; *broadly* **:** CROCODILIAN **b :** the skin or hide of a crocodile **2** *chiefly Brit* **:** a line of people (as schoolchildren) usu. walking in pairs

crocodile bird *n* (1868) **:** an African bird (*Pluvianus aegyptius*) that is related to the pratincoles and lights on the crocodile and eats its insect parasites

crocodile tears *n pl* (1563) **:** false or affected tears; *also* **:** hypocritical sorrow

croc·o·dil·ian \ˌkrä-kə-ˈdi-lē-ən, -ˈdil-yən\ *n* (1837) **:** any of an order (Crocodylia) of reptiles including the crocodiles, alligators, caimans, gharials, and related extinct forms — **crocodilian** *adj*

cro·cus \ˈkrō-kəs\ *n, pl* **cro·cus·es** [ME, the saffron plant, fr. L, fr. Gk *krokos,* of Sem origin; akin to Akkadian *kurkānū* saffron] (14c) **1 a** *pl also* **crocus** *or* **cro·ci** \-ˌkē, -ˌkī, -ˌsī\ **:** any of a genus (*Crocus*) of herbs of the iris family developing from corms and having solitary long-tubed flowers and slender linear leaves **b :** SAFFRON 1a **2 :** a dark red ferric oxide used for polishing metals

Croe·sus \ˈkrē-səs\ *n* [*Croesus,* king of Lydia, famed for his wealth] (1621) **:** a very rich man

croft \ˈkrȯft\ *n* [ME, fr. OE; akin to MD *krocht* hill] (bef. 12c) **1** *chiefly Brit* **:** a small enclosed field usu. adjoining a house **2** *chiefly Brit* **:** a small farm worked by a tenant — **croft·er** \ˈkrȯf-tər\ *n, chiefly Brit*

Crohn's disease \ˈkrōnz-\ *n* [Burrill B. *Crohn* †1983 Am. physician] (1935) **:** a chronic inflammatory disease of the gastrointestinal tract that typically involves the distal portion of the ileum and is characterized by cramping and diarrhea

crois·sant \krȯ-ˈsänt, krə-; krwä-ˈsäⁿ\ *n, pl* **croissants** \-ˈsänt(s), -ˈsäⁿ(z)\ [F, lit., crescent, fr. MF, fr. prp. of *croistre* to grow, fr. L *crescere* — more at CRESCENT] (1875) **:** a flaky rich crescent-shaped roll

Croix de Guerre \ˌkrwä-di-ˈger\ *n* [F, lit., war cross] (1915) **:** a French military decoration awarded for gallant action in war

cro·ker sack \ˈkrō-kər-\ *n* [alter. of *crocus sack, crocus bag,* of unknown origin] (1895) *chiefly Southern* **:** a sack of a coarse material (as burlap)

Cro–Ma·gnon \krō-ˈmag-nən, -ˈman-yən\ *n* [*Cro-Magnon,* a cave near Les Eyzies, France] (1869) **:** a hominid of a tall erect race of the Upper Paleolithic known from skeletal remains found chiefly in southern France and classified as the same species (*Homo sapiens*) as present-day humans

crom·lech \ˈkräm-ˌlek\ *n* [W, lit., bent stone] (1695) **1 :** DOLMEN **2 :** a circle of monoliths usu. enclosing a dolmen or mound

crone \ˈkrōn\ *n* [ME, a term of abuse, fr. AF *caroine, charoine* dead flesh — more at CARRION] (14c) **:** a withered old woman

Cro·nus \ˈkrō-nəs, ˈkrä-\ *n* [L, fr. Gk *Kronos*] (1664) **:** a Titan dethroned by his son Zeus

cro·ny \ˈkrō-nē\ *n, pl* **cronies** [perh. fr. Gk *chronios* long-lasting, fr. *chronos* time] (1656) **:** a close friend esp. of long standing **:** PAL

cro·ny·ism \-nē-ˌi-zəm\ *n* (1840) **:** partiality to cronies esp. as evidenced in the appointment of political hangers-on to office without regard to their qualifications

[1]**crook** \ˈkru̇k\ *vt* (12c) **:** BEND ~ *vi* **:** CURVE, WIND

[2]**crook** *n* [ME *crok,* fr. ON *krōkr* hook] (13c) **1 :** an implement having a bent or hooked form: as **a :** POTHOOK **b** (1) **:** a shepherd's staff (2) **:** CROSIER 1 **2 :** a part of something that is hook-shaped, curved, or bent ⟨the ~ of an umbrella handle⟩ **3 :** BEND, CURVE **4 :** a person who engages in fraudulent or criminal practices

[3]**crook** *adj* [prob. short for *crooked*] (1898) *Austral & NewZeal* **:** not right: **a :** UNSATISFACTORY **b :** DISHONEST, CROOKED **c :** IRRITABLE, ANGRY — used esp. in the phrase *go crook* **d :** ILL, UNWELL

crook·back \ˈkru̇k-ˌbak\ *n* (1508) **1** *obs* **:** a crooked back **2** *obs* **:** HUNCHBACK — **crook·backed** \-ˈbakt\ *adj*

crook·ed \ˈkru̇-kəd\ *adj* (13c) **1 :** not straight ⟨a ~ road⟩ ⟨your tie is ~⟩ **2 :** DISHONEST ⟨a ~ election⟩ ⟨~ politicians⟩ — **crook·ed·ly** *adv* — **crook·ed·ness** *n*

crook·ery \ˈkru̇-kə-rē\ *n* (1927) **:** crooked dealings or practices

crook·neck \ˈkru̇k-ˌnek\ *n* (1784) **:** a squash with a long recurved neck

croon \ˈkrün\ *vb* [ME *croynen,* fr. MD *cronen;* akin to OHG *crōnen* to chatter] *vi* (15c) **1** *chiefly Scot* **:** BELLOW, BOOM **2 :** to sing or speak in a gentle murmuring manner; *esp* **:** to sing in a soft intimate manner adapted to amplifying systems ~ *vt* **:** to sing (as a popular song or a lullaby) in a crooning manner — **croon** *n*

croon·er \ˈkrü-nər\ *n* (1888) **:** one that croons; *esp* **:** a singer of popular songs

[1]**crop** \ˈkräp\ *n* [ME, craw, head of a plant, yield of a field, fr. OE *cropp* craw, head of a plant; akin to OHG *kropf* goiter, craw] (bef. 12c) **1 :** a pouched enlargement of the gullet of many birds that serves as a receptacle for food and for its preliminary maceration; *also* **:** an enlargement of the gullet of another animal (as an insect) **2 a** (1) **:** a plant or animal or plant or animal product that can be grown and harvested extensively for profit or subsistence ⟨an apple ~⟩ ⟨a ~ of wool⟩ (2) **:** the total yearly production from a specified area **b :** the product or yield of something formed together ⟨the ice ~⟩ **c :** a batch or lot of something produced during a particular cycle ⟨the current ~ of films⟩ **d :** COLLECTION ⟨a ~ of lies⟩ **3 :** the stock or handle of a whip; *also* **:** a riding whip with a short straight stock and a loop **4** [[2]*crop*] **a :** the part of the chine of a quadruped (as a domestic cow) lying immediately behind the withers — usu. used in pl.; see COW illustration **b :** an earmark on an animal; *esp* **:** one made by a straight cut squarely removing the upper part of the ear **c :** a close cut of the hair

[2]**crop** *vb* **cropped; crop·ping** *vt* (13c) **1 a :** to remove the upper or outer parts of ⟨~ a hedge⟩ ⟨~ a dog's ears⟩ **b :** HARVEST ⟨~ trout⟩ **c :** to cut off short **:** TRIM ⟨~ a photograph⟩ **2 :** to cause (land) to

\ə\ **abut** \ᵊ\ **kitten,** F **table** \ər\ **further** \a\ **ash** \ā\ **ace** \ä\ **mop, mar** \au̇\ **out** \ch\ **chin** \e\ **bet** \ē\ **easy** \g\ **go** \i\ **hit** \ī\ **ice** \j\ **job** \ŋ\ **sing** \ō\ **go** \ȯ\ **law** \ȯi\ **boy** \th\ **thin** \t͟h\ **the** \ü\ **loot** \u̇\ **foot** \y\ **yet** \zh\ **vision, beige** \k̲, ⁿ, œ, ue, ʸ\ *see* Guide to Pronunciation

bear a crop ⟨planned to ~ another 40 acres⟩; *also* : to grow as a crop ~ *vi* **1** : to feed by cropping something **2** : to yield or make a crop **3** : to appear unexpectedly or casually ⟨problems ~ up daily⟩

crop circle *n* (1988) : a geometric and esp. a circular pattern of flattened stalks in a field of grain now usu. attributed to natural phenomena or to the work of hoaxers trying to create the impression of a visit by extraterrestrial beings

crop duster *n* (1939) : a person who sprays crops with fungicidal or insecticidal dusts from an airplane; *also* : the airplane thus used

crop–eared \ˈkräp-ˌird\ *adj* (1530) : having the ears cropped

crop·land \-ˌland\ *n* (1846) : land that is suited to or used for crops

[1]**crop·per** \ˈkrä-pər\ *n* (15c) **1** : one that crops **2** : one that raises crops; *specif* : SHARECROPPER

[2]**cropper** *n* [prob. fr. E dial. *crop* neck, fr. [1]*crop*] (1850) **1** : a severe fall **2** : a sudden or violent failure or collapse

crop rotation *n* (1909) : the practice of growing different crops in succession on the same land chiefly to preserve the productive capacity of the soil

crop top *n* (1971) : a short upper body garment for women that does not cover the midriff

croque mon·sieur \ˌkrȯk-məs-ˈyə(r), ˌkräk-, ˌkrōk-, -məsh-\ *n* [F, lit., (one) bites with a crunch (the) gentleman] (1915) : a ham and cheese sandwich that is usu. dipped in batter and grilled

cro·quet \krō-ˈkā\ *n* [prob. ultim. fr. obs. F, sharp blow, fr. *croquer*] (1855) **1** : a game in which players using mallets drive wooden balls through a series of wickets set out on a lawn **2** : the act of driving away an opponent's croquet ball by striking one's own ball placed against it — **croquet** *vt*

cro·quette \krō-ˈket\ *n* [F, fr. *croquer* to crunch, fr. MF, to strike, break, cause to crack, of imit. origin] (1706) : a small often rounded mass consisting usu. of minced meat, fish, or vegetable coated with egg and bread crumbs and deep-fried

cro·qui·gnole \ˈkrō-kə-ˌnōl *also* -kən-ˌyōl\ *n* [F, light blow, fillip] (1932) : a method used in waving the hair by winding it on curlers from the ends of the hair toward the scalp

cro·quis \krō-ˈkē\ *n, pl* **cro·quis** \-ˈkē(z)\ [F, fr. *croquer* to sketch, rough out, lit., to crunch] (1805) : a rough draft : SKETCH

crore \ˈkrȯr\ *n, pl* **crores** *also* **crore** [Hindi & Urdu *karoṛ*] (1609) : a unit of value equal to ten million rupees or 100 lakhs

cro·sier *or* **cro·zier** \ˈkrō-zhər\ *n* [ME *crocer* crosier bearer, fr. AF *crosser*, fr. *croce, crosse* crosier, of Gmc origin; akin to OE *crycc* crutch — more at CRUTCH] (15c) **1** : a staff resembling a shepherd's crook carried by bishops and abbots as a symbol of office **2** : a plant structure with a coiled end

[1]**cross** \ˈkrȯs\ *n* [ME, fr. OE, fr. ON or OIr; ON *kross*, fr. OIr *cros*, fr. L *cruc-, crux*] (bef. 12c) **1 a** : a structure consisting of an upright with a transverse beam used esp. by the ancient Romans for execution **b** *often cap* : the cross on which Jesus was crucified **2 a** : CRUCIFIXION **b** : an affliction that tries one's virtue, steadfastness, or patience **3** : a cruciform sign made to invoke the blessing of Christ esp. by touching the forehead, breast, and shoulders **4 a** : a device composed of an upright bar traversed by a horizontal one; *specif* : one used as a Christian symbol **b** *cap* : the Christian religion **5** : a structure (as a monument) shaped like or surmounted by a cross **6** : a figure or mark formed by two intersecting lines crossing at their midpoints; *specif* : such a mark used as a signature **7** : a cruciform badge, emblem, or decoration **8** : the intersection of two ways or lines : CROSSING **9** : ANNOYANCE, THWARTING ⟨a ~ in love⟩ **10 a** : an act of crossing dissimilar individuals **b** : a crossbred individual or kind **c** : one that combines characteristics of two different types or individuals **11 a** : a fraudulent or dishonest contest **b** : dishonest or illegal practices — used esp. in the phrase *on the cross* **12** : a movement from one part of a theater stage to another **13 a** : a punch thrown over the opponent's lead in boxing **b** : an attacking pass in soccer played across the field from one side to the other or to the middle **14** : a security transaction in which a broker acts for both buyer and seller (as in the placing of a large lot of common stock) — called also *cross-trade*

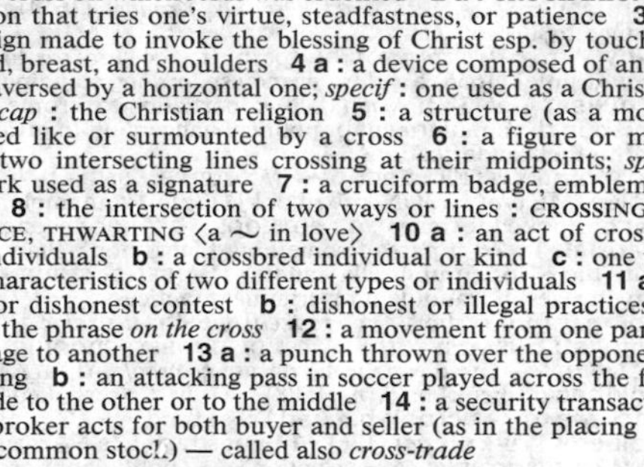

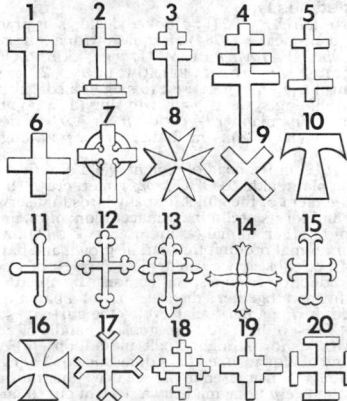

cross 4a: *1* Latin, *2* Calvary, *3* patriarchal *or* cross of Lorraine, *4* papal, *5* cross of Lorraine, *6* Greek, *7* Celtic, *8* Maltese, *9* Saint Andrew's, *10* tau, *11* pommée, *12* botonée, *13* fleury, *14* avellan, *15* moline, *16* formée, *17* fourchée, *18* crosslet, *19* quadrate, *20* potent

[2]**cross** *vt* (14c) **1 a** : to lie or be situated across **b** : INTERSECT **2** : to make the sign of the cross upon or over **3** : to cancel by marking a cross on or drawing a line through : strike out ⟨~ names off a list⟩ **4** : to place or fold crosswise one over the other ⟨~ the arms⟩ **5 a** (1) : to run counter to : OPPOSE (2) : to deny the validity of : CONTRADICT **b** : to confront in a troublesome manner : OBSTRUCT **c** (1) : to spoil completely : DISRUPT — used with *up* ⟨his failure to appear ~*ed* up the whole program⟩ (2) : to turn against : BETRAY ⟨~*ed* me up on the deal⟩ **6 a** : to extend across or over : TRAVERSE ⟨a highway ~*ing* the entire state⟩ **b** : REACH, ATTAIN ⟨only two ~*ed* the finish line⟩ **c** : to go from one side of to the other ⟨~ a street⟩ ⟨~*es* racial barriers⟩ **7 a** : to draw a line across **b** : to mark or figure with lines : STREAK **8** : to cause (an animal or plant) to interbreed with one of a different kind : HYBRIDIZE **9** : to meet and pass on the way ⟨our letters must have ~*ed* each other⟩ **10** : to occur to ⟨it never ~*ed* my mind⟩ **11** : to carry or take across something ⟨~*ed* the children at the intersection⟩ ~ *vi* **1 a** : to move, pass, or extend across something ⟨~*ed* through France⟩ ⟨~*ed* over to the other side of the river⟩ **b** : to move or pass from one character, condition, or allegiance to another — used with *over* ⟨~*ing* over to vote for another party's candidate⟩ **2** : to lie or be athwart each other **3** : to meet in passing esp. from opposite directions **4** : INTERBREED, HYBRIDIZE — **cross·er** *n* — **cross paths** : to meet esp. by chance ⟨*crossed paths* with an old friend on a business trip⟩ — **cross swords** : to engage in a dispute

[3]**cross** *adj* (14c) **1 a** : lying across or athwart **b** : moving across ⟨~ traffic⟩ **2 a** : running counter : OPPOSITE **b** : mutually opposed ⟨~ purposes⟩ **3** : involving mutual interchange : RECIPROCAL **4** : marked by typically transitory bad temper **5** : extending over or treating several groups, conditions, or classes ⟨a ~ sample from 25 colleges⟩ **6** : CROSSBRED, HYBRID — **cross·ly** *adv* — **cross·ness** *n*

[4]**cross** *prep* (1551) : ACROSS

cross·abil·i·ty \ˌkrȯ-sə-ˈbi-lə-tē\ *n* (1916) : the ability of different species or varieties to cross with each other

cross·able \ˈkrȯ-sə-bəl\ *adj* (1865) : capable of being crossed

cross action *n* (ca. 1859) : a legal action in which the defendant in an existing action files a suit against the plaintiff on the same subject matter : COUNTERSUIT

cross·band·ing \ˈkrȯs-ˌban-diŋ\ *n* (1904) : a veneer border (as on furniture) with its grain at right angles to the grain of the adjacent wood — **cross·band·ed** \-ˌban-dəd\ *adj*

cross·bar \ˈkrȯs-ˌbär\ *n* (1562) : a transverse bar or stripe

cross·beam \-ˌbēm\ *n* (1594) : a transverse beam

cross·bear·er \ˈkrȯs-ˌber-ər\ *n* (1568) : CRUCIFER 1

cross·bill \-ˌbil\ *n* (ca. 1672) : any of a genus (*Loxia* of the family Fringillidae) of finches with curved mandibles that cross each other

cross·bones \-ˌbōnz\ *n pl* (1686) : two leg or arm bones placed or depicted crosswise — compare SKULL AND CROSSBONES

cross·bow \-ˌbō\ *n* (15c) : a weapon for shooting quarrels and stones that consists chiefly of a short bow mounted crosswise near the end of a stock

cross·bred \ˈkrȯs-ˈbred\ *adj* (1856) : produced by crossbreeding : HYBRID — **cross·bred** \-ˌbred\ *n*

[1]**cross·breed** \ˈkrȯs-ˌbrēd, -ˈbrēd\ *vb* **-bred** \-ˌbred, -ˈbred\; **-breed·ing** *vt* (1675) : HYBRIDIZE, CROSS; *esp* : to cross (two varieties or breeds) within the same species ~ *vi* : to engage in or undergo hybridization

[2]**cross·breed** \-ˌbrēd\ *n* (1774) : HYBRID

[1]**cross–check** \-ˌchek\ *vt* (ca. 1930) **1** : to obstruct in ice hockey or lacrosse by thrusting one's stick held in both hands across an opponent's face or body **2** : to check (as data or reports) from various angles or sources to determine validity or accuracy

[2]**cross–check** *n* (1937) : an act or instance of cross-checking

cross–claim \-ˌklām\ *n* (1952) : a claim against a party on the same side of a legal action

[1]**cross–coun·try** \ˈkrȯs-ˈkən-trē, -ˌkən-\ *adj* (1767) **1** : extending or moving across a country ⟨a ~ concert tour⟩ **2** : proceeding over countryside (as across fields and through woods) and not by roads **3** : of or relating to racing or skiing over the countryside instead of over a track or run — **cross–country** *adv*

[2]**cross–country** *n* (1918) : cross-country racing or skiing

cross·court \ˈkrȯs-ˈkȯrt\ *adv or adj* (1915) : to or toward the opposite side of a court (as in tennis or basketball)

cross–cul·tur·al \ˈkrȯs-ˈkəlch-rəl, -ˈkəl-chə-\ *adj* (ca. 1942) : dealing with or offering comparison between two or more different cultures or cultural areas — **cross–cul·tur·al·ly** \-rə-lē\ *adv*

cross·cur·rent \ˈkrȯs-ˌkər-ənt, -ˌkə-rənt\ *n* (1598) **1** : a current running counter to the general forward direction **2** : a conflicting tendency — usu. used in pl. ⟨political ~*s*⟩

[1]**cross·cut** \ˈkrȯs-ˌkət, -ˈkət\ *vt* (1590) **1** : to cut, go, or move across or through **2** : to cut with a crosscut saw **3** : to subject (as movie scenes) to crosscutting

[2]**crosscut** *adj* (1645) **1** : made or used for cutting transversely ⟨a saw with ~ teeth⟩ **2** : cut across or transversely ⟨a ~ incision⟩

[3]**cross·cut** \ˈkrȯs-ˌkət\ *n* (1789) **1** : something that cuts across or through; *specif* : a mine working driven horizontally and at right angles to an adit, drift, or level **2** : CROSS SECTION **3** : CROSSCUT SAW **4** : an instance of crosscutting (as in a movie)

crosscut saw *n* (1645) : a saw designed chiefly to cut across the grain of wood — compare RIPSAW

cross·cut·ting \ˈkrȯs-ˌkə-tiŋ\ *n* (1930) : a technique esp. in filmmaking of interweaving bits of two or more separate scenes

cross–dress·ing \ˈkrȯs-ˌdre-siŋ\ *n* (1911) : the wearing of clothes designed for the opposite sex — **cross–dress** *vi* — **cross–dress·er** *n*

crosse \ˈkrȯs\ *n* [F, lit., crosier — more at CROSIER] (1867) : a stick with a small net at one end that is used in lacrosse

cross–ex·am·i·na·tion \ˈkrȯs-ig-ˌza-mə-ˈnā-shən\ *n* (ca. 1707) : the examination of a witness who has already testified in order to check or discredit the witness's testimony, knowledge, or credibility — compare DIRECT EXAMINATION — **cross–ex·am·ine** \-ig-ˈza-mən\ *vb* — **cross–ex·am·in·er** \-ˈzam-nər, -ˈza-mə-\ *n*

cross–eye \ˈkrȯs-ˌī\ *n* (1826) **1** : strabismus in which the eye turns inward toward the nose **2** *pl* : eyes affected with cross-eye — **cross–eyed** \-ˌīd\ *adj*

cross–fer·tile \ˈkrȯs-ˈfər-tᵊl, -ˌfər-\ *adj* (1929) : fertile in a cross or capable of cross-fertilization

cross–fer·til·i·za·tion \-ˌfər-tə-lə-ˈzā-shən\ *n* (1870) **1 a** : fertilization in which the gametes are produced by separate individuals or sometimes by individuals of different kinds **b** : CROSS-POLLINATION 1 **2** : interchange or interaction (as between different ideas, cultures, or categories) esp. of a broadening or productive nature

cross–fer·til·ize \-ˈfər-tə-ˌlīz\ *vt* (1876) : to accomplish cross-fertilization of ~ *vi* : to undergo cross-fertilization
cross–file \-ˈfī(-ə)l\ *vi* (1949) : to register as a candidate in the primary elections of more than one political party ~ *vt* : to register (a person) as a candidate for more than one party
cross fire *n* (1799) **1 a** : firing (as in combat) from two or more points so that the lines of fire cross **b** : a situation wherein the forces of opposing factions meet, cross, or clash ⟨caught in a political *cross fire*⟩ **2** : rapid or heated exchange of words
cross–grained \ˈkrȯs-ˌgrānd\ *adj* (1647) **1** : difficult to deal with ⟨her husband's self-absorbed and ~ nature —Lance Morrow⟩ **2** : having the grain or fibers running diagonally, transversely, or irregularly
cross·hair \-ˌher\ *n* (ca. 1884) : a fine wire or thread in the focus of the eyepiece of an optical instrument used as a reference line in the field or for marking the instrumental axis — used figuratively to describe someone or something being targeted as if through an aiming device having crosshairs ⟨. . . is in the ~*s* this political season —J. H. Alter⟩
cross·hatch \ˈkrȯs-ˌhach\ *vt* (1662) : to mark with two series of parallel lines that intersect — **crosshatch** *n* — **cross–hatch·ing** *n*
cross·head \-ˌhed\ *n* (1827) **1** : a metal block to which one end of a piston rod is secured **2** : a heading centered usu. between portions of text
cross–in·dex \ˈkrȯs-ˈin-ˌdeks\ *vt* (1892) **1** : to index (an item) under a second or under more than one heading **2** : to supply (as a book) with a cross-referenced index — **cross–index** *n*
cross·ing \ˈkrȯ-siŋ\ *n* (1575) **1** : the act or action of crossing: as **a** : a traversing or traveling across **b** : an opposing, blocking, or thwarting esp. in an unfair or dishonest manner **2 a** : a place or structure (as on a street or over a river) where pedestrians or vehicles cross; *esp* : CROSSWALK **b** : the place in a cruciform church where the transept crosses the nave **c** : a place where a railroad track crosses a street
cross·ing–over \ˌkrȯ-siŋ-ˈō-vər\ *n* (1912) : an interchange of genes or segments between homologous chromosomes
cross–legged \ˈkrȯs-ˌle-gəd, -ˌlā-; -ˌlegd, -ˌlāgd\ *adv or adj* (ca. 1530) **1** : with legs crossed and knees spread wide apart **2** : with one leg placed over and across the other
cross·let \ˈkrȯs-lət\ *n* (15c) : a small cross usu. with crossed arms; *esp* : one used as a heraldic bearing — see CROSS illustration
cross·lin·guis·tic \-liŋ-ˈgwis-tik\ *adj* (1954) : of or relating to languages of different families and types; *esp* : relating to the comparison of different languages — **cross·lin·guis·ti·cal·ly** \-ti-k(ə-)lē\ *adv*
cross–link \ˈkrȯs-ˌliŋk\ *n* (1936) : a crosswise connecting part (as an atom or group) that connects parallel chains in a complex chemical molecule (as a polymer) — **cross–link** *vb*
cross–link·age \ˈkrȯs-ˈliŋ-kij\ *n* (1937) : the process of forming cross-links; *also* : CROSS-LINK
cross multiply *vi* (1951) : to clear an equation of fractions when each side consists of a fraction with a single denominator by multiplying the numerator of each side by the denominator of the other side and equating the two products obtained — **cross multiplication** *n*
cross–na·tion·al \ˈkrȯs-ˈnash-nəl, -ˈna-shə-nᵊl\ *adj* (1965) : of or relating to two or more nations
cross of Lor·raine \-lə-ˈrān, -lȯ-\ [*Lorraine*, France] (ca. 1889) : a cross with two crossbars the lower one of which is longer than the upper one and intersects the upright below its center; *also* : PATRIARCHAL CROSS — see CROSS illustration
cros·sop·ter·yg·ian \ˌkrȯ-ˌsäp-tə-ˈri-j(ē-)ən\ *n* [NL *Crossopterygii*, subclass name, fr. Gk *krossoi* fringe + *pterygion*, dim. of *pteryg-*, *pteryx* wing, fin; akin to Gk *pteron* wing — more at FEATHER] (1861) : any of a subclass (Crossopterygii) of bony fishes (as a coelacanth) that have paired fins suggesting limbs, that may be ancestral to the terrestrial vertebrates, and that are mostly extinct — called also *lobe-fin* — **crossopterygian** *adj*
¹**cross·over** \ˈkrȯs-ˌō-vər\ *n* (1884) **1** : CROSSING 2a **2** : an instance or product of genetic crossing-over **3** : a voter registered as a member of one political party who votes in the primary of the other party **4** : a broadening of the popular appeal of an artist (as a musician) that is often the result of a change of the artist's medium or style; *also* : an artist or artistic work that has achieved a crossover **5** : an instance of breaking into another category **6** : a basketball maneuver in which a player dribbles the ball quickly from one hand to the other
²**crossover** *adj* (1893) **1** : having two pieces that cross esp. one over the other ⟨a ~ vest⟩ **2** : CRITICAL 1 ⟨the ~ point⟩
cross over *vi* (1973) : to reach a broader audience by a change of medium or style ⟨a country singer *crossing over* to the pop charts⟩
cross–own·er·ship \-ˈō-nər-ˌship\ *n* (1969) : single ownership of two or more related businesses (as a newspaper and a television station) that allows the owner to control competition
cross·patch \ˈkrȯs-ˌpach\ *n* [³*cross* + ³*patch*] (ca. 1700) : GROUCH 2
cross·piece \ˈkrȯs-ˌpēs\ *n* (1706) : a horizontal member (as of a structure)
cross–pol·li·nate \ˈkrȯs-ˈpä-lə-ˌnāt\ *vt* (ca. 1900) : to subject to cross-pollination
cross–pol·li·na·tion \ˌkrȯs-ˌpä-lə-ˈnā-shən\ *n* (1882) **1** : the transfer of pollen from one flower to the stigma of another **2** : CROSS-FERTILIZATION 2 ⟨~ of fantasy and realism⟩
cross product *n* (1929) **1** : VECTOR PRODUCT **2** : either of the two products obtained by multiplying the two means or the two extremes of a proportion
cross–pur·pose \ˈkrȯs-ˈpər-pəs\ *n* (1668) : a purpose usu. unintentionally contrary to another purpose of oneself or of someone or something else — usu. used in pl. ⟨the two were always working at ~*s*⟩
cross–ques·tion \ˈkrȯs-ˈkwes-chən, -ˈkwesh-\ *n* (ca. 1694) : a question asked in cross-examination — **cross–question** *vt*
cross–re·ac·tion \ˌkrȯs-rē-ˈak-shən\ *n* (1946) : reaction of one antigen with antibodies developed against another antigen — **cross–re·act** \-rē-ˈakt\ *vi* — **cross–re·ac·tive** \-ˈak-tiv\ *adj* — **cross–re·ac·tiv·i·ty** \-(ˌ)rē-ˌak-ˈti-və-tē\ *n*
cross–re·fer \ˌkrȯs-ri-ˈfər\ *vt* (1879) : to refer (a reader) by a notation or direction from one place to another (as in a book, list, or catalog) ~ *vi* : to make a cross-reference
¹**cross–ref·er·ence** \ˈkrȯs-ˈre-fərn(t)s, -ˈre-f(ə-)rən(t)s\ *n* (1834) : a notation or direction at one place (as in a book or filing system) to pertinent information at another place
²**cross–reference** *vt* (1902) **1** : to supply with cross-references ⟨~ a book⟩ **2** : to research, verify, or organize by means of cross-references ⟨~ information⟩
cross–re·sis·tance \ˌkrȯs-ri-ˈzis-tən(t)s\ *n* (1946) : tolerance (as of a virus) to a usu. toxic substance (as an antibiotic) that is acquired not as a result of direct exposure but by exposure to a related substance
cross·road \ˈkrȯs-ˌrōd *also* -ˈrōd\ *n* (1686) **1** : a road that crosses a main road or runs cross-country between main roads **2** *usu pl but sing or pl in constr* **a** : the place of intersection of two or more roads **b** (1) : a small community located at such a crossroads (2) : a central meeting place **c** : a crucial point esp. where a decision must be made
cross·ruff \ˈkrȯs-ˌrəf, -ˈrəf\ *n* (1862) : a series of plays in a card game (as bridge) in which partners alternately trump different suits and lead to each other for that purpose — **crossruff** *vb*
cross section *n* (1835) **1 a** : a cutting or piece of something cut off at right angles to an axis; *also* : a representation of such a cutting **b** : SECTION 3b **2** : a measure of the probability of an encounter between particles such as will result in a specified effect (as scattering or capture) **3** : a composite representation typifying the constituents of a thing in their relations — **cross–section** *vt* — **cross–sec·tion·al** \ˈkrȯs-ˈsek-shnəl, -shə-nᵊl\ *adj*
cross–staff \-ˌstaf\ *n* (1582) : an instrument formerly used at sea for taking the altitude of a celestial body
cross–stitch \ˈkrȯ(s)-ˌstich\ *n* (1640) **1** : a needlework stitch that forms an X **2** : work having cross-stitch — **cross–stitch** *vb*
cross talk *n* (1887) **1** : unwanted signals in a communication channel (as in a telephone, radio, or computer) caused by transference of energy from another circuit (as by leakage or coupling) **2 a** : conversation that does not relate to the main topic being discussed **b** : conversation or repartee engaged in for an audience
cross–tol·er·ance \ˈkrȯs-ˈtäl-rən(t)s, -ˈtä-lə-\ *n* (ca. 1923) : tolerance or resistance to a drug that develops through continued use of another drug with similar pharmacological action
cross·town \ˈkrȯs-ˈtau̇n\ *adj* (1886) **1** : situated at opposite points of a town ⟨~ schools⟩ **2** : extending or running across a town ⟨a ~ street⟩ ⟨a ~ bus⟩
cross–trade \ˈkrȯs-ˌtrād\ *n* (ca. 1923) : CROSS 14
cross–train \-ˌtrān\ *vi* (1903) : to engage in various sports or exercises esp. for well-rounded health and muscular development ~ *vt* : to train (an employee) to do more than one specific job — **cross–training** *n*
cross–train·er \-ˌtrā-nər\ *n* (1987) : a sport shoe designed for cross-training
cross·trees \-(ˌ)trēz\ *n pl* (1626) : two horizontal crosspieces of timber or metal that spread the upper shrouds of a ship in order to support the mast
cross vault *n* (1850) : a vault formed by the intersection of two or more simple vaults — called also *cross vaulting*
cross·walk \ˈkrȯs-ˌwȯk\ *n* (1671) : a specially paved or marked path for pedestrians crossing a street or road
cross·way \-ˌwā\ *n* (14c) : CROSSROAD — often used in pl.
cross·ways \-ˌwāz\ *adv* (1564) : CROSSWISE, DIAGONALLY
cross·wind \-ˌwind\ *n* (ca. 1641) : a wind blowing in a direction not parallel to a course (as of an airplane)
¹**cross·wise** \-ˌwīz\ *adv* (14c) **1** *archaic* : in the form of a cross **2** : so as to cross something : ACROSS ⟨carrot sticks cut ~⟩
²**crosswise** *adj* (1883) **1** : TRANSVERSE, CROSSING **2** : involved in conflict or disagreement ⟨got ~ with his teacher⟩
cross·word \ˈkrȯs-ˌwərd\ *n* (1914) : a puzzle in which words are filled into a pattern of numbered squares in answer to correspondingly numbered clues and in such a way that the words read across and down
cros·ti·ni \krȯ-ˈstē-nē\ *n pl* [It, pl. of *crostino*, fr. *crosta* crust, rind, fr. L *crusta* shell, crust — more at CRUST] (1945) : small slices of usu. toasted bread topped with a spread or other food
crotch \ˈkräch\ *n* [prob. alter. of ¹*crutch*] (1563) **1** : a pole with a forked end used esp. as a prop **2** : an angle formed by the parting of two legs, branches, or members — **crotched** \ˈkrächt\ *adj*
crotch·et \ˈkrä-chət\ *n* [ME *crochet*, fr. AF *crochet*, *croket* — more at CROCKET] (14c) **1** *obs* **a** : a small hook or hooked instrument **b** : BROOCH **2 a** : a highly individual and usu. eccentric opinion or preference **b** : a peculiar trick or device **3** : QUARTER NOTE ***syn*** see CAPRICE
crotch·ety \ˈkrä-chə-tē\ *adj* (1825) **1** : given to crotchets : subject to whims, crankiness, or ill temper ⟨a ~ old man⟩ **2** : full of or arising from crotchets ⟨a ~ style⟩ — **crotch·et·i·ness** \-tē-nəs\ *n*
cro·ton \ˈkrō-tᵊn\ *n* [NL, genus name, fr. Gk *krotōn* castor-oil plant] (1751) **1** : any of a genus (*Croton*) of herbs, shrubs, and trees of the spurge family: as **a** : one (*C. eluteria*) of the Bahamas yielding cascarilla bark **b** : an Asian plant (*C. tiglium*) yielding croton oil **2** : any of a genus (*Codiaeum*) of shrubs and trees related to the crotons
Cro·ton bug \ˈkrō-tᵊn-\ *n* [*Croton* River, N.Y., used as a water supply for New York City] (1877) : GERMAN COCKROACH
croton oil *n* (1827) : a viscid acrid fixed oil obtained from seeds of an Asian croton (*Croton tiglium*) formerly used as a powerful purgative but now used esp. in pharmacological experiments as an irritant
crouch \ˈkrau̇ch\ *vb* [ME] *vi* (14c) **1 a** : to lower the body stance esp. by bending the legs ⟨a sprinter ~*ed* ready to go⟩ **b** : to lie close to the ground with the legs bent ⟨a pair of cats, ~*ing* on the brink of a fight —Aldous Huxley⟩ **2** : to bend or bow servilely : CRINGE **3** : to stand at a low height ⟨cottages ~*ed* along the river⟩ ~ *vt* : to bow esp. in humility or fear : BEND — **crouch** *n*
¹**croup** \ˈkrüp\ *n* [ME *croupe*, fr. OF, of Gmc origin; akin to OHG *kropf* craw — more at CROP] (14c) : the rump of a quadruped
²**croup** *n* [E dial. *croup* to cry hoarsely, cough, prob. of imit. origin] (1765) : inflammation, edema, and subsequent obstruction of the larynx, trachea, and bronchi esp. of infants and young children that is typically caused by a virus and is marked by episodes of difficult breathing and hoarse metallic cough — **croupy** \-pē\ *adj*

\ə\ abut \ᵊ\ kitten, F table \ər\ further \a\ ash \ā\ ace \ä\ mop, mar \au̇\ out \ch\ chin \e\ bet \ē\ easy \g\ go \i\ hit \ī\ ice \j\ job \ŋ\ sing \ō\ go \ȯ\ law \ȯi\ boy \th\ thin \t͟h\ the \ü\ loot \u̇\ foot \y\ yet \zh\ vision, beige \k, ⁿ, œ, ue, ʸ\ *see* Guide to Pronunciation

crou·pi·er \'krü-pē-ər, -pē-ˌā\ *n* [F, lit., rider on the croup of a horse, fr. *croupe* croup] (1709) : an employee of a gambling casino who collects and pays bets and assists at the gaming tables

crouse \'krüs\ *adj* [ME] (15c) *chiefly Scot* : BRISK, LIVELY

crous·tade \krü-'städ\ *n* [F, prob. fr. It *crostata* tart, fr. *crosta* pastry shell, crust, fr. L *crusta* — more at CRUST] (ca. 1845) : a crisp shell (as of toast or puff pastry) in which to serve food

crou·ton \'krü-ˌtän, krü-'\ *n* [F *croûton,* dim. of *croûte* crust, fr. MF *crouste,* fr. OF, fr. L *crusta*] (1806) : a small cube of toasted or crisply fried bread

[1]**crow** \'krō\ *n* [ME *crowe,* fr. OE *crāwe;* akin to OHG *krāwa* crow, OE *crāwan* to crow] (bef. 12c) **1 :** any of various large usu. entirely glossy black passerine birds (family Corvidae and esp. genus *Corvus*) **2** *cap* **a :** a member of an American Indian people of the region between the Platte and Yellowstone rivers **b :** the language of the Crow people **3** *cap* : CORVUS **4 :** HUMBLE PIE ⟨the braggart was forced to eat ~⟩ — **as the crow flies :** in a straight line

[2]**crow** *vb* **crowed** \'krōd\ *also in sense 1 chiefly Brit* **crew** \'krü\; **crow·ing** [ME, fr. OE *crāwan*] *vi* (bef. 12c) **1 :** to make the loud shrill sound characteristic of a cock **2 :** to utter a sound expressive of pleasure **3 a :** to exult gloatingly esp. over the distress of another **b :** to brag exultantly or blatantly ~ *vt* **:** to say with self-satisfaction ***syn*** see BOAST

[3]**crow** *n* (13c) **1 :** the cry of the cock **2 :** a triumphant cry

crow·bar \'krō-ˌbär\ *n* (1748) : an iron or steel bar that is usu. wedge-shaped at the working end for use as a pry or lever — **crowbar** *vt*

[1]**crowd** \'krau̇d\ *vb* [ME *crouden,* fr. OE *crūdan;* akin to MHG *kroten* to crowd, OE *crod* multitude, MIr *gruth* curds] *vi* (bef. 12c) **1 a :** to press on : HURRY **b :** to press close ⟨the players *~ed* around the coach⟩ **2 :** to collect in numbers ~ *vt* **1 a :** to fill by pressing or thronging together ⟨a room *~ed* with children⟩ **b :** to press, force, or thrust into a small space **2 :** PUSH, FORCE — often used with *off* or *out* ⟨~ a person off the sidewalk⟩ **3 a :** to urge on **b :** to put on (sail) in excess of the usual for greater speed **4 :** to put pressure on ⟨don't ~ me, I'll pay⟩ **5 :** THRONG, JOSTLE **6 :** to press or stand close to ⟨the batter was *~ing* the plate⟩

[2]**crowd** *n* (1565) **1 :** a large number of persons esp. when collected together : THRONG **2 a :** the great body of the people : POPULACE **b :** most of one's peers ⟨follow the ~⟩ **3 :** a large number of things close together ⟨I saw a ~ . . . of golden daffodils —William Wordsworth⟩ **4 :** a group of people having something (as a habit, interest, or occupation) in common ⟨in with the wrong ~⟩ ⟨the Hollywood ~⟩
syn CROWD, THRONG, HORDE, CRUSH, MOB mean an assembled multitude. CROWD implies a close gathering and pressing together ⟨a *crowd* gathered⟩. THRONG and HORDE suggest movement and pushing ⟨a *throng* of reporters⟩ ⟨a *horde* of shoppers⟩. CRUSH emphasizes the compactness of the group, the difficulty of individual movement, and the attendant discomfort ⟨a *crush* of fans⟩. MOB implies a disorderly crowd with the potential for violence ⟨an angry *mob*⟩.

[3]**crowd** \'krau̇d, 'krüd\ *n* [ME *crowde,* fr. MW *crwth*] (14c) **1 :** an ancient Celtic stringed instrument that is plucked or bowed — called also *crwth* **2** *dial Eng* : VIOLIN

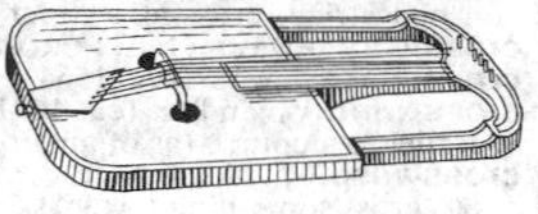

[3]crowd 1

crowd·ed·ness \'krau̇-dəd-nəs\ *n* (1823) : the quality or state of being crowded

crowd·fund·ing \'krau̇d-ˌfən-diŋ\ *n* (2006) : the practice of soliciting financial contributions from a large number of people esp. from the online community

crow·die \'krau̇-dē\ *n* [alter. of *crud* curd] (1820) : a Scottish cottage cheese that is partially cooked

crowd–pleas·er \'krau̇d-ˌplē-zər\ *n* (1943) : one (as a performer or product) that is notably or reliably popular or appealing ⟨a flamboyant ~ given to mad feats of daring —Tony Hendra⟩ — **crowd–pleas·ing** \-ziŋ\ *adj*

crowd·sourc·ing \'krau̇d-ˌsȯr-siŋ\ *n* [[2]*crowd* + out*sourcing*] (2006) : the practice of obtaining needed services, ideas, or content by soliciting contributions from a large group of people and esp. from the online community rather than from traditional employees or suppliers

crow·foot \'krō-ˌfu̇t\ *n, pl* **crow·feet** \-ˌfēt\ (14c) **1** *pl usu* **crow·foots :** any of numerous plants having leaves with cleft lobes; *esp* : BUTTERCUP **2 :** CROW'S-FOOT 1 — usu. used in pl.

[1]**crown** \'krau̇n\ *n, often attrib* [ME *coroune, crowne,* fr. AF *corone,* fr. L *corona* wreath, crown, fr. Gk *korōnē* culmination, something curved like a crow's beak, lit., crow; akin to L *cornix* crow, Gk *korax* raven — more at RAVEN] (12c) **1 :** a reward of victory or mark of honor; *esp* **:** the title representing the championship in a sport **2 :** a royal or imperial headdress or cap of sovereignty : DIADEM **3 :** the highest part: as **a :** the topmost part of the skull or head **b :** the summit of a mountain **c :** the head of foliage of a tree or shrub **d :** the part of a hat or other headgear covering the crown of the head **e :** the part of a tooth external to the gum or an artificial substitute for this — see TOOTH illustration **4 :** a wreath, band, or circular ornament for the head **5 a :** something resembling a wreath or crown **b :** the knurled cap on top of a watch stem **6** *often cap* **a** (1) : imperial or regal power : SOVEREIGNTY (2) : the government under a constitutional monarchy **b :** MONARCH **7 :** something that imparts splendor, honor, or finish : CULMINATION **8 a :** any of several old gold coins with a crown as part of the device **b :** an old usu. silver British coin worth five shillings **9 a :** KORUNA **b :** KRONA **c :** KRONE **d :** KROON **10 a :** the region of a seed plant at which stem and root merge **b :** the arching end of the shank of an anchor where the arms join it — see ANCHOR illustration — **crowned** \'krau̇nd\ *adj* — **crown·less** \-ləs\ *adj*

[2]**crown** *vb* [ME *corounen,* fr. AF *coroner,* fr. L *coronare,* fr. *corona*] *vt* (12c) **1 a :** to place a crown or wreath on the head of; *specif* : to invest with regal dignity and power **b :** to recognize officially as ⟨they *~ed* her athlete of the year⟩ **c :** to award a championship to ⟨~ a new champion⟩ **2 :** to bestow something on as a mark of honor or recompense : ADORN **3 :** SURMOUNT, TOP; *esp* : to top (a checker) with a checker to make a king **4 :** to bring to a successful conclusion : CLIMAX ⟨the role that *~ed* her career⟩ **5 :** to provide with something like a crown: as **a :** to fill so that the surface forms a crown **b :** to put an artificial crown on (a tooth) **6 :** to hit on the head ~ *vi* **1** *of a forest fire* : to burn rapidly through the tops of trees **2** *in childbirth* : to appear and begin to emerge headfirst or crown first at the vaginal opening ⟨the baby's head *~ed*⟩

crown colony *n, often cap both Cs* (1828) : a British colony over which the Crown retains some control

crown court *n* (1827) : a court in England and Wales that exercises jurisdiction over matters formerly heard by the quarter sessions and criminal matters formerly heard by the courts of assize

crow·ner \'krü-nər, 'krau̇-\ *n* [ME, alter. of *coroner*] (14c) *dial chiefly Eng* : CORONER

crown·et \'krau̇-nət\ *n* (15c) *archaic* : CORONET

crown gall *n* (1900) : a disease that affects many species of plants and is caused by a bacterium (*Agrobacterium tumefaciens*) which forms tumorous enlargements usu. just below the ground on the stem

crown glass *n* (1706) **1 :** a glass blown and whirled into the form of a disk with a center lump left by the worker's rod **2 :** alkali-lime silicate optical glass having relatively low refractive index and low dispersion value

crown jewel *n* (1649) **1** *pl* : the jewels (as crown and scepter) belonging to a sovereign's regalia **2 :** the most attractive or valuable one of a collection or group

crown land *n* (1613) **1 :** land belonging to the crown and yielding revenues that the reigning sovereign is entitled to **2 :** public land in some British dominions or colonies

crown molding *n* (1946) : molding that crowns a surface or structure; *esp* : molding that runs between the top of an internal wall and a ceiling

crown of thorns (1964) : a starfish (*Acanthaster planci*) of the Pacific region that is covered with long spines and feeds on coral polyps sometimes causing destruction of coral reefs — called also *crown-of-thorns starfish*

crown prince *n* (1791) **1 :** a male heir apparent to a crown or throne **2 :** one prepared or favored to fill a prospective position

crown princess *n* (1863) **1 :** the wife of a crown prince **2 :** a female heir apparent or heir presumptive to a crown or throne

crown roast *n* (ca. 1909) : a fancy roast of lamb, veal, or pork made from the rib portions of two loins skewered together at the ends to form a circle

crown rust *n* (ca. 1899) : a leaf rust of oats and other grasses that is caused by a fungus (*Puccinia coronata*) and is characterized by rounded light-orange uredinia and buried telia

crown vetch *n* (ca. 1900) : a Eurasian herb (*Coronilla varia*) of the legume family that is naturalized in the eastern U.S. and has umbels of pink-and-white flowers and sharp-angled pods

crow's–foot \'krōz-ˌfu̇t\ *n, pl* **crow's–feet** \-ˌfēt\ (14c) **1 :** a wrinkle extending from the outer corner of the eye — usu. used in pl. **2 :** CROWFOOT 1

crow's nest *n* (1818) : a partly enclosed platform high on a ship's mast for use as a lookout; *also* : a similar lookout (as for traffic control)

crow·step \'krō-ˌstep\ *n* (1822) : any of a series of steps at the top of a gable wall — **crow·stepped** \-ˌstept\ *adj*

crozier *var of* CROSIER

CRP *abbr* C-reactive protein

[1]**CRT** \ˌsē-(ˌ)är-'tē\ *n, pl* **CRTs** *or* **CRT's** (1941) : CATHODE-RAY TUBE; *also* : a display device incorporating a cathode-ray tube

[2]**CRT** *abbr* carrier route

cruces *pl of* CRUX

cru·cial \'krü-shəl\ *adj* [F, fr. L *cruc-, crux* cross] (1706) **1** *archaic* : CRUCIFORM **2 a :** important or essential as resolving a crisis : DECISIVE **b :** marked by final determination of a doubtful issue ⟨the ~ game of a series⟩ **c :** IMPORTANT, SIGNIFICANT ⟨what use we make of them will be the ~ question —Stanley Kubrick⟩ ***syn*** see ACUTE

cru·cial·ly \'krü-sh(ə-)lē\ *adv* (1879) **1 :** in a crucial manner **2 :** very importantly

cru·cian carp \'krü-shən-\ *n* [modif. of LG *karuse,* fr. MLG *karusse,* perh. of Baltic origin; akin to Lith *karušis* carp] (1836) : a European cyprinid fish (*Carassius carassius*) — called also *crucian*

cru·ci·ate \'krü-shē-ˌāt\ *adj* [NL *cruciatus,* fr. L *cruc-, crux*] (1826) : cross-shaped : CRUCIFORM

cruciate ligament *n* (ca. 1934) : either of two ligaments in the knee joint which cross each other from femur to tibia; *esp* : ANTERIOR CRUCIATE LIGAMENT

cru·ci·ble \'krü-sə-bəl\ *n* [ME *corusible,* fr. ML *crucibulum* earthen pot for melting metals] (15c) **1 :** a vessel of a very refractory material (as porcelain) used for melting and calcining a substance that requires a high degree of heat **2 :** a severe test **3 :** a place or situation in which concentrated forces interact to cause or influence change or development ⟨conditioned by having grown up within the ~ of Chinatown —Tom Wolfe⟩

crucible steel *n* (1868) : hard cast steel made in pots that are lifted from the furnace before the metal is poured into molds

cru·ci·fer \'krü-sə-fər\ *n* [LL, fr. L *cruc-, crux* + *-fer*] (1574) **1 :** one who carries a cross esp. at the head of an ecclesiastical procession **2 :** any of a family (Cruciferae syn. Brassicaceae) of plants including the cabbage, turnip, and mustard — **cru·cif·er·ous** \krü-'si-f(ə-)rəs\ *adj*

cru·ci·fix \'krü-sə-ˌfiks\ *n* [ME, fr. LL *crucifixus* the crucified Christ, fr. *crucifixus,* pp. of *crucifigere* to crucify, fr. L *cruc-, crux* + *figere* to fasten — more at FIX] (13c) : a representation of Christ on the cross

cru·ci·fix·ion \ˌkrü-sə-'fik-shən\ *n* (15c) **1 a** *cap* : the crucifying of Christ **b :** the act of crucifying **2 :** extreme and painful punishment, affliction, or suffering

cru·ci·form \'krü-sə-ˌfȯrm\ *adj* [L *cruc-, crux* + E *-form*] (1661) : forming or arranged in a cross — **cruciform** *n*

cru·ci·fy \'krü-sə-ˌfī\ *vt* **-fied; -fy·ing** [ME *crucifien,* fr. AF *crucifier,* fr. LL *crucifigere*] (14c) **1 :** to put to death by nailing or binding the wrists or hands and feet to a cross **2 :** to destroy the power of : MORTIFY ⟨~ the flesh⟩ **3 a :** to treat cruelly : TORMENT **b :** PILLORY 2 ⟨*crucified* in the press⟩ — **cru·ci·fi·er** \-ˌfī-ər\ *n*

cruck \'krək\ *n* [prob. fr. dial. form of [2]*crook* (curved timber)] (1898) : one of a pair of curved timbers forming a principal support of a roof in primitive English house construction

[1]**crud** \'krəd\ *n* [ME *curd, crudd*] (14c) **1** *dial* : CURD **2 a :** a deposit or incrustation of filth, grease, or refuse **b :** something disgusting : RUBBISH **c** *slang* : a contemptible person **3 :** a usu. ill-defined or imperfectly identified bodily disorder — **crud·dy** \'krə-dē\ *adj*

[2]**crud** *vb* **crud•ded; crud•ding** (14c) *dial* : [2]CURD

[1]**crude** \ˈkrüd\ *adj* **crud•er; crud•est** [ME, fr. L *crudus* raw, crude, undigested — more at RAW] (14c) **1 :** existing in a natural state and unaltered by cooking or processing ⟨~ oil⟩ **2** *archaic* **:** UNRIPE, IMMATURE **3 :** marked by the primitive, gross, or elemental or by uncultivated simplicity or vulgarity ⟨a ~ stereotype⟩ **4 :** rough or inexpert in plan or execution ⟨a ~ shelter⟩ **5 :** lacking a covering, glossing, or concealing element **:** OBVIOUS ⟨~ facts⟩ **6 :** tabulated without being broken down into classes ⟨the ~ death rate⟩ ***syn*** see RUDE — **crude•ly** *adv* — **crude•ness** *n*

[2]**crude** *n* (ca. 1904) **:** a substance in its natural unprocessed state; *esp* **:** unrefined petroleum

cru•di•tés \krue-dē-tā, ˌkrü-di-ˈtā\ *n pl* [F, fr. pl. of *crudité* rawness, fr. L *cruditas* indigestion, fr. *crudus*] (1960) **:** pieces of raw vegetables (as celery or carrot sticks) served as an hors d'oeuvre often with a dip

cru•di•ty \ˈkrü-də-tē\ *n, pl* **-ties** (1547) **1 :** the quality or state of being crude **2 :** something that is crude

cru•do \ˈkrü-(ˌ)dō\ *n, pl* **cru•dos** [It, raw, fr. L *crudus*] (2000) **:** a dish of sliced, seasoned, uncooked seafood often served with a sauce

cru•el \ˈkrü(-ə)l\ *adj* **cru•el•er** *or* **cru•el•ler; cru•el•est** *or* **cru•el•lest** [ME, fr. AF, fr. L *crudelis,* fr. *crudus*] (14c) **1 :** disposed to inflict pain or suffering **:** devoid of humane feelings ⟨a ~ tyrant⟩ **2 a :** causing or conducive to injury, grief, or pain ⟨a ~ joke⟩ **b :** unrelieved by leniency ⟨~ punishment⟩ ***syn*** see FIERCE — **cru•el•ly** \ˈkrü-(ə-)lē\ *adv* — **cru•el•ness** *n*

cru•el•ty \ˈkrü(-ə)l-tē\ *n, pl* **-ties** [ME *cruelte,* fr. AF *crualté,* fr. L *crudelitat-, crudelitas,* fr. *crudelis*] (13c) **1 :** the quality or state of being cruel **2 a :** a cruel action **b :** inhuman treatment **3 :** marital conduct held (as in a divorce action) to endanger life or health or to cause mental suffering or fear

cru•el•ty–free \-ˈfrē\ *adj* (1983) **:** developed or produced without inhumane testing on animals ⟨~ cosmetics⟩

cru•et \ˈkrü-ət\ *n* [ME, fr. AF, dim. of OF *crue,* of Gmc origin; akin to MHG *krūche* pitcher — more at CROCK] (14c) **1 :** a vessel to hold wine or water for the Eucharist **2 :** a usu. glass bottle used to hold a condiment (as oil or vinegar) for use at the table

[1]**cruise** \ˈkrüz\ *vb* **cruised; cruis•ing** [D *kruisen* to make a cross, cruise, fr. MD *crucen,* fr. *crūce* cross, fr. L *cruc-, crux*] *vi* (1651) **1 :** to sail about touching at a series of ports **2 :** to move or proceed speedily, smoothly, or effortlessly ⟨I'll ~ over to her house to see if she's home⟩ **3 :** to travel without destination or purpose **4 a :** to go about the streets at random but on the lookout for possible developments ⟨the cabdriver *cruised* for an hour before being hailed⟩ **b :** to search (as in public places) for a sexual partner **5 a** *of an airplane* **:** to fly at the most efficient operating speed **b** *of an automobile* **:** to travel at a speed suitable for being maintained for a long distance ~ *vt* **1 :** to cruise over or about **2 :** to inspect (as land) with reference to possible lumber yield **3 a :** to search in (a public place) for a sexual partner **b :** to approach and suggest sexual relations to **4 :** to explore or search the offerings of; *esp* **:** SURF ⟨~ the Internet⟩

[2]**cruise** *n* (1696) **:** an act or an instance of cruising; *esp* **:** a tour by ship

cruise control *n* (1960) **1 :** an electronic device in a vehicle that controls the throttle so as to maintain a constant speed **2 :** a relaxed and seemingly automatic pace that is easily maintained

cruise missile *n* (1959) **:** a guided missile that has a terrain-following radar system and that flies at moderate speed and low altitude

cruis•er \ˈkrü-zər\ *n* (1695) **1 :** a vehicle that cruises: as **a :** SQUAD CAR **b :** a powerboat with facilities (as a cabin and plumbing) necessary for living aboard — called also *cabin cruiser* **2 :** a large fast moderately armored and gunned warship **3 :** a person who cruises

cruis•er•weight \-ˌwāt\ *n* (1920) **:** a boxer in a weight division having a maximum limit of 190 pounds

crul•ler \ˈkrə-lər\ *n* [D *krulle,* a twisted cake, fr. *krul* curly, fr. MD *crul* — more at CURL] (1801) **1 :** a small sweet cake in the form of a twisted strip fried in deep fat **2** *Northern & Midland* **:** an unraised doughnut

[1]**crumb** \ˈkrəm\ *n* [ME *crumme,* fr. OE *cruma;* akin to MHG *krume* crumb] (bef. 12c) **1 a :** a small fragment esp. of something baked (as bread) **b :** a porous aggregate of soil particles **2 :** BIT ⟨a ~ of good news⟩ **3 :** the soft part of bread **4** *slang* **:** a worthless person

[2]**crumb** *vt* (14c) **1 :** to break into crumbs **2 :** to cover or thicken with crumbs **3 :** to remove crumbs from ⟨~ a table⟩

[1]**crum•ble** \ˈkrəm-bəl\ *vb* **crum•bled; crum•bling** \-b(ə-)liŋ\ [alter. of ME *kremelen,* freq. of OE *gecrymian* to crumble, fr. *cruma*] *vt* (1547) **:** to break into small pieces ~ *vi* **1 :** to fall into small pieces **:** DISINTEGRATE **2 :** to break down completely **:** COLLAPSE ⟨marriages ~⟩

[2]**crumble** *n* (1860) **1 :** something crumbled **:** fine debris **2 :** CRISP 2

crum•blings \ˈkrəm-b(ə-)liŋz\ *n pl* (1660) **:** crumbled particles

crum•bly \-b(ə-)lē\ *adj* **crum•bli•er; -est** (1523) **:** easily crumbled **:** FRIABLE ⟨~ soil⟩ — **crum•bli•ness** *n*

crumb structure *n* (ca. 1906) **:** a soil condition suitable for farming in which the soil particles are aggregated into crumbs

crum•mie *or* **crum•my** \ˈkrə-mē\ *n, pl* **crummies** [Sc *crumb* crooked, fr. ME, fr. OE] (1724) *chiefly Scot* **:** COW; *esp* **:** one with crooked horns

crum•my *also* **crumby** \ˈkrə-mē\ *adj* **crum•mi•er** *also* **crumb•i•er; -est** [ME *crumme*] (1567) **1** *obs* **:** CRUMBLY **2 :** very poor or inferior **:** LOUSY ⟨~ weather⟩ ⟨has a ~ job⟩ — **crum•mi•ness** *n*

[1]**crump** \ˈkrəmp\ *vi* [imit.] (1646) **1 :** CRUNCH **2 :** to explode heavily

[2]**crump** *n* (1914) **1 :** a crunching sound **2 :** SHELL, BOMB

[3]**crump** *adj* [perh. alter. of *crimp* friable] (ca. 1706) *chiefly Scot* **:** BRITTLE

crum•pet \ˈkrəm-pət\ *n* [perh. fr. ME *crompid* (*cake*) wafer, lit., curled-up cake, fr. *crumped,* pp. of *crumpen* to curl up, fr. *crump, crumb* crooked, fr. OE *crumb;* akin to OHG *krump* crooked] (1638) **:** a small round unsweetened bread cooked on a griddle and usu. split and toasted before serving

[1]**crum•ple** \ˈkrəm-pəl\ *vb* **crum•pled; crum•pling** \-p(ə-)liŋ\ [ME *crumplen,* freq. of ME *crumpen*] *vt* (14c) **1 :** to press, bend, or crush out of shape **:** RUMPLE **2 :** to cause to collapse ~ *vi* **1 :** to become crumpled **2 :** COLLAPSE

[2]**crumple** *n* (15c) **:** a wrinkle or crease made by crumpling — **crum•ply** \ˈkrəm-p(ə-)lē\ *adj*

crumple zone *n* (1973) **:** a section of an automobile body designed to absorb the force of an impact in order to protect the passengers

[1]**crunch** \ˈkrənch\ *vb* [alter. of *craunch*] *vi* (1706) **1 :** to chew or press with a crushing noise **2 :** to make one's way with a crushing noise ~ *vt* **1 :** to chew, press, or grind with a crunching sound **2 :** PROCESS; *esp* **:** to perform mathematical computations on ⟨~ numbers⟩ — **crunch•able** \ˈkrən-chə-bəl\ *adj*

[2]**crunch** *n* (1832) **1 :** an act of crunching **2 :** a sound made by crunching **3 :** a tight or critical situation: as **a :** a critical point in the build-up of pressure between opposing elements **:** SHOWDOWN **b :** a severe economic squeeze (as on credit) **c :** SHORTAGE ⟨an energy ~⟩ **4 :** a conditioning exercise performed from a supine position by raising and lowering the upper torso without reaching a sitting position

crunch•er \ˈkrən-chər\ *n* (1946) **1 :** one that crunches **2 :** a finishing blow

crunch time *n* (1976) **:** a critical moment or period (as near the end of a game) when decisive action is needed

crunchy \ˈkrən-chē\ *adj* **crunch•i•er; -est** (1913) **:** making a crunching sound when chewed or pressed ⟨~ lettuce⟩ — **crunch•i•ly** \-chə-lē\ *adv* — **crunch•i•ness** \-chē-nəs\ *n*

crunk \ˈkrəŋk\ *n* [*crunk,* word of fluctuating meaning used during the 1990s in lyrics of the rap groups OutKast and Lil Jon & The East Side Boyz] (2000) **:** a style of Southern rap music featuring repetitive chants and rapid dance rhythms

crup•per \ˈkrə-pər, ˈkrü-\ *n* [ME *cruper,* fr. AF *crupere,* fr. *crupe, croupe* hindquarters — more at CROUP] (14c) **1 :** a leather loop passing under a horse's tail and buckled to the saddle **2 :** [1]CROUP; *broadly* **:** BUTTOCKS

cru•ral \ˈkrůr-əl\ *adj* [L *crur-, crus* leg] (1599) **:** of or relating to the thigh or leg; *specif* **:** FEMORAL ⟨~ artery⟩

crus \ˈkrüs, ˈkrəs\ *n, pl* **cru•ra** \ˈkrůr-ə\ [L *crur-, crus*] (ca. 1751) **:** any of various anatomical parts that resemble a leg or a pair of legs

[1]**cru•sade** \krü-ˈsād\ *n* [blend of MF *croisade* & Sp *cruzada;* both ultim. fr. L *cruc-, crux* cross] (ca. 1708) **1** *cap* **:** any of the military expeditions undertaken by Christian powers in the 11th, 12th, and 13th centuries to win the Holy Land from the Muslims **2 :** a remedial enterprise undertaken with zeal and enthusiasm

[2]**crusade** *vi* **cru•sad•ed; cru•sad•ing** (1732) **:** to engage in a crusade — **cru•sad•er** *n*

cru•sa•do \krü-ˈsä-(ˌ)dō\ *also* **cru•za•do** \-ˈzä-(ˌ)dō, -(ˌ)dü\ *n, pl* **-does** *or* **-dos** [Pg *cruzado,* lit., marked with a cross] (1542) **:** an old gold or silver coin of Portugal having a cross on the reverse

cruse \ˈkrüz, ˈkrüs\ *n* [ME; akin to OE *crūse* pitcher] (13c) **:** a small vessel (as a jar or pot) for holding a liquid (as water or oil)

[1]**crush** \ˈkrəsh\ *vb* [ME *crusshen,* fr. AF *croissir, croistre,* of Gmc origin; akin to MLG *krossen* to crush] *vt* (15c) **1 a :** to squeeze or force by pressure so as to alter or destroy structure ⟨~ grapes⟩ **b :** to squeeze together into a mass **2 :** HUG, EMBRACE **3 :** to reduce to particles by pounding or grinding ⟨~ rock⟩ **4 a :** to suppress or overwhelm as if by pressure or weight **b :** to oppress or burden grievously ⟨~*ed* by debt⟩ **c :** to subdue completely **5 :** CROWD, PUSH ⟨were ~*ed* into the elevator⟩ **6** *archaic* **:** DRINK ~ *vi* **1** *obs* **:** CRASH **2 :** to become crushed **3 :** to advance with or as if with crushing — **crush•able** \ˈkrə-shə-bəl\ *adj* — **crush•er** *n* — **crush•ing•ly** *adv*

[2]**crush** *n* (1599) **1 :** an act of crushing **2 :** the quantity of material crushed **3 a :** a crowding together (as of people) **b :** CROWD, MOB; *esp* **:** a crowd of people pressing against one another **4 :** an intense and usu. passing infatuation ⟨have a ~ on someone⟩; *also* **:** the object of infatuation ***syn*** see CROWD — **crush•proof** \-ˌprüf\ *adj*

crust \ˈkrəst\ *n* [ME, fr. L *crusta;* akin to OE *hrūse* earth, Gk *kryos* icy cold, *krystallos* ice, crystal] (14c) **1 a :** the hardened exterior or surface part of bread **b :** a piece of this or of bread grown dry or hard **2 :** the pastry cover of a pie **3 :** a hard or brittle external coat or covering: as **a :** a hard surface layer (as of soil or snow) **b :** the outer part of a planet, moon, or asteroid composed essentially of crystalline rocks **c :** a deposit built up on the interior surface of a wine bottle during long aging **d :** an encrusting deposit (as of the eye) of dried secretions or exudate; *also* **:** SCAB **4 :** GALL, NERVE — **crust** *vb* — **crust•al** \ˈkrəs-tᵊl\ *adj* — **crust•less** \ˈkrəs(t)-ləs\ *adj*

crus•ta•cea \ˌkrəs-ˈtā-sh(ē-)ə\ *n pl* [NL, group name, fr. neut. pl. of *crustaceus*] (1814) **:** arthropods that are crustaceans

crus•ta•cean \ˌkrəs-ˈtā-shən\ *n* (1835) **:** any of a large class (Crustacea) of mostly aquatic mandibulate arthropods that have a chitinous or calcareous and chitinous exoskeleton, a pair of often much modified appendages on each segment, and two pairs of antennae and that include the lobsters, shrimps, crabs, wood lice, water fleas, and barnacles — **crustacean** *adj*

crus•ta•ceous \-shəs\ *adj* [NL *crustaceus,* fr. L *crusta* crust, shell] (ca. 1646) **:** of, relating to, having, or forming a crust or shell

crus•tose \ˈkrəs-ˌtōs\ *adj* [L *crustosus* crusted, fr. *crusta*] (ca. 1879) **:** having a thin thallus adhering closely to a substrate (as of rock, bark, or soil) ⟨~ lichens⟩ — compare FOLIOSE, FRUTICOSE

crusty \ˈkrəs-tē\ *adj* **crust•i•er; -est** (14c) **1 :** having or being a crust **2 :** giving an effect of surly incivility in address or disposition ***syn*** see BLUFF — **crust•i•ly** \-tə-lē\ *adv* — **crust•i•ness** \-tē-nəs\ *n*

[1]**crutch** \ˈkrəch\ *n* [ME *crucche,* fr. OE *crycc;* akin to OHG *krucka* crutch] (bef. 12c) **1 a :** a support typically fitting under the armpit for use by the disabled in walking **b :** PROP, STAY **2 :** a forked leg rest constituting the pommel of a sidesaddle **3 :** the crotch of a human being or an animal **4 :** a forked support

[2]**crutch** *vt* (1609) **:** to support on crutches **:** prop up

crux \ˈkrəks, ˈkrüks\ *n, pl* **crux•es** *also* **cru•ces** \ˈkrü-ˌsēz\ [L *cruc-, crux* cross, torture] (1718) **1 :** a puzzling or difficult problem **:** an unsolved question **2 :** an essential point requiring resolution or resolving an outcome **3 :** a main or central feature (as of an argument)

cru•za•do \krü-ˈzä-(ˌ)dō, -(ˌ)dü\ *n, pl* **-dos** [Pg] (1986) **:** the basic monetary unit of Brazil from 1986 to 1990

Cru•zan \krü-ˈzan\ *n* [AmerSp *cruzano, fr. *Santa Cruz* St. Croix] (1958) **:** a native or inhabitant of St. Croix — **Cruzan** *adj*

\ə\ **abut** \ᵊ\ **kitten,** F table \ər\ **further** \a\ **ash** \ā\ **ace** \ä\ **mop, mar**
\aů\ **out** \ch\ **chin** \e\ **bet** \ē\ **easy** \g\ **go** \i\ **hit** \ī\ **ice** \j\ **job**
\ŋ\ **sing** \ō\ **go** \ȯ\ **law** \ȯi\ **boy** \th\ **thin** \t͟h\ **the** \ü\ **loot** \ů\ **foot**
\y\ **yet** \zh\ **vision, beige** \k, ⁿ, œ, ue, ʸ\ *see* Guide to Pronunciation

cru·zei·ro \krü-ˈzer-(ˌ)ō, -(ˌ)ü\ *n, pl* **-ros** [Pg] (1927) : the basic monetary unit of Brazil from 1942 to 1985 and from 1991 to 1993

crwth \ˈkrüth\ *n* [W] (1793) : 3CROWD 1

1**cry** \ˈkrī\ *vb* **cried; cry·ing** [ME *crien,* fr. AF *crier,* fr. L *quiritare* to make a public outcry, perh. fr. *Quirit-, Quiris,* Roman citizen] *vt* (13c) **1** : to utter loudly : SHOUT **2** *archaic* : BEG, BESEECH **3** : to proclaim publicly : ADVERTISE ⟨~ their wares⟩ ~ *vi* **1** : to call loudly : SHOUT **2** : to shed tears often noisily : WEEP, SOB **3** : to utter a characteristic sound or call **4** : to require or suggest strongly a remedy or disposition ⟨a hundred things which ~ out for planning —Roger Burlingame⟩ — **cry havoc** : to sound an alarm — **cry over spilled milk** : to express vain regrets for what cannot be recovered or undone — **cry wolf** : to give alarm unnecessarily

2**cry** *n, pl* **cries** (13c) **1** : an instance of crying: as **a** : an inarticulate utterance of distress, rage, or pain **b** *obs* : OUTCRY, CLAMOR **2 a** *obs* : PROCLAMATION **b** *pl, Scot* : BANNS **3** : ENTREATY, APPEAL ⟨a ~ for help⟩ **4** : a loud shout **5** : WATCHWORD, SLOGAN **6 a** : common report **b** : a general opinion **7** : the public voice raised in protest or approval **8** : a fit of weeping **9** : the characteristic sound or call of an animal **10 a** : a pack of hounds **b** (1) : PURSUIT — used in the phrase *in full cry* ⟨hounds in full ~⟩ (2) : a peak of activity or excitement — used in the phrase *in full cry* ⟨a campaign in full ~⟩

cry- *or* **cryo-** *comb form* [G *kryo-,* fr. Gk, fr. *kryos* — more at CRUST] : cold : freezing ⟨*cryo*nics⟩ ⟨*cryo*gen⟩

cry·ba·by \ˈkrī-ˌbā-bē\ *n* (1851) : one who cries or complains easily or often

cry down *vt* (1598) : DISPARAGE, DEPRECIATE

cry·ing \ˈkrī-iŋ\ *adj* (ca. 1605) **1** : calling for notice ⟨a ~ need⟩ **2** : NOTORIOUS, HEINOUS ⟨a ~ shame⟩

cryo·bi·ol·o·gy \ˌkrī-ō-bī-ˈä-lə-jē\ *n* (1960) : the study of the effects of extremely low temperature on living organisms and cells — **cryo·bi·o·log·i·cal** \-ˌbī-ə-ˈlä-ji-kəl\ *adj* — **cryo·bi·ol·o·gist** \-bī-ˈä-lə-jist\ *n*

cry off *vi* (1775) *chiefly Brit* : to beg off ~ *vt* : to call off (as a bargain)

cryo·gen \ˈkrī-ə-jən\ *n* (1875) : a substance for obtaining low temperatures : REFRIGERANT — called also *cryogenic*

cryo·gen·ic \ˌkrī-ə-ˈje-nik\ *adj* (1896) **1 a** : of or relating to the production of very low temperatures **b** : being or relating to very low temperatures **2 a** : requiring or involving the use of a cryogenic temperature **b** : requiring cryogenic storage **c** : suitable for storage of a cryogenic substance — **cryo·gen·i·cal·ly** \-ni-k(ə-)lē\ *adv*

cryo·gen·ics \-niks\ *n pl but sing in constr* (ca. 1934) : a branch of physics that deals with the production and effects of very low temperatures

cryo·lite \ˈkrī-ə-ˌlīt\ *n* (1801) : a mineral consisting of a fluoride of sodium and aluminum found esp. in Greenland usu. in white cleavable masses and formerly used as a source of aluminum

cry·on·ics \krī-ˈä-niks\ *n pl but usu sing in constr* [*cry-* + *-onics* (as in *electronics*)] (1967) : the practice of freezing a person who has died of a disease in hopes of restoring life at some future time when a cure for the disease has been developed — **cry·on·ic** \-nik\ *adj*

cryo·phil·ic \ˌkrī-ə-ˈfi-lik\ *adj* (1942) : thriving at low temperatures

cryo·pres·er·va·tion \ˌkrī-ō-ˌpre-zər-ˈvā-shən\ *n* (1968) : preservation (as of cells) by subjection to extremely low temperatures — **cryo·pre·serve** \ˌkrī-ō-pri-ˈzərv, ˈkrī-ō-pri-ˌ\ *vt*

cryo·probe \ˈkrī-ə-ˌprōb\ *n* (1965) : a blunt chilled instrument used to freeze tissues in cryosurgery

cryo·pro·tec·tive \ˌkrī-ō-prə-ˈtek-tiv\ *adj* (1967) : serving to protect against the deleterious effects of freezing ⟨an intracellular ~ agent⟩ — **cryo·pro·tec·tant** \-ˈtek-tənt\ *n or adj*

cryo·scope \ˈkrī-ə-ˌskōp\ *n* (1920) : an instrument for determining freezing points

cry·os·co·py \krī-ˈäs-kə-pē\ *n* [ISV] (ca. 1900) : the determination of the lowered freezing points produced in liquid by dissolved substances in order to determine molecular weights of solutes and various properties of solutions — **cryo·scop·ic** \ˌkrī-ə-ˈskä-pik\ *adj*

cryo·stat \ˈkrī-ə-ˌstat\ *n* [ISV] (1913) : an apparatus for maintaining a constant low temperature esp. below 0°C — **cryo·stat·ic** \ˌkrī-ə-ˈsta-tik\ *adj*

cryo·sur·gery \ˌkrī-ō-ˈsərj-rē, -ˈsər-jə-\ *n* (1962) : surgery in which usu. diseased or abnormal tissue (as of a tumor or wart) is destroyed or removed by freezing (as by liquid nitrogen) — **cryo·sur·geon** \-ˈsər-jən\ *n* — **cryo·sur·gi·cal** \-ji-kəl\ *adj*

cryo·ther·a·py \-ˈther-ə-pē\ *n* (1926) : the therapeutic use of cold; *esp* : CRYOSURGERY

crypt \ˈkript\ *n* [L *crypta,* fr. Gk *kryptē,* fr. fem. of *kryptos* hidden, fr. *kryptein* to hide; perh. akin to Lith *krauti* to pile up] (1789) **1 a** : a chamber (as a vault) wholly or partly underground; *esp* : a vault under the main floor of a church **b** : a chamber in a mausoleum **2 a** : an anatomical pit or depression **b** : a simple tubular gland

crypt- *or* **crypto-** *comb form* [NL, fr. Gk *kryptos*] **1** : hidden : covered ⟨*crypto*genic⟩ **2** : CRYPTOGRAPHIC ⟨*crypt*analysis⟩

crypt·anal·y·sis \ˌkrip-tə-ˈna-lə-səs\ *n* (1923) **1** : the solving of cryptograms or cryptographic systems **2** : the theory of solving cryptograms or cryptographic systems : the art of devising methods for cryptanalysis — **crypt·an·a·lyt·ic** \ˌkrip-ˌta-nə-ˈli-tik\ *also* **crypt·an·a·lyt·i·cal** \-ti-kəl\ *adj*

crypt·an·a·lyst \krip-ˈta-nə-list\ *n* (1921) : a specialist in cryptanalysis

cryp·ta·rithm \ˈkrip-tə-ˌri-thəm\ *n* [*crypt-* + *-arithm* (as in *logarithm*)] (1943) : an arithmetic problem in which letters have been substituted for numbers and which is solved by finding all possible pairings of digits with letters that produce a numerically correct answer

cryp·tic \ˈkrip-tik\ *adj* [LL *crypticus,* fr. Gk *kryptikos,* fr. *kryptos*] (ca. 1638) **1** : SECRET, OCCULT **2 a** : having or seeming to have a hidden or ambiguous meaning : MYSTERIOUS ⟨~ messages⟩ **b** : marked by an often perplexing brevity ⟨~ marginal notes⟩ **3** : serving to conceal ⟨~ coloration in animals⟩; *also* : exhibiting cryptic coloration ⟨~ animals⟩ **4** : not recognized ⟨a ~ infection⟩ **5** : employing cipher or code ***syn*** see OBSCURE — **cryp·ti·cal·ly** \-ti-k(ə-)lē\ *adv*

1**cryp·to** \ˈkrip-(ˌ)tō\ *n, pl* **cryptos** [*crypt-*] (1946) **1** : a person who adheres or belongs secretly to a party, sect, or other group **2** : CRYPTOGRAPHY 2

2**crypto** *adj* (1681) **1** : not openly avowed or declared — often used in combination ⟨*crypto*-fascist⟩ **2** : CRYPTOGRAPHIC

cryp·to·coc·co·sis \ˌkrip-tə-(ˌ)kä-ˈkō-səs\ *n, pl* **-co·ses** \-(ˌ)sēz\ [NL] (1938) : an infectious disease that is caused by a fungus (*Cryptococcus neoformans*) and is characterized by the production of lesions in subcutaneous tissues, joints, and esp. the lungs, brain, and meninges and often by pneumonia or meningitis

cryp·to·coc·cus \-ˈkä-kəs\ *n, pl* **-coc·ci** \-ˈkäk-ˌsī, -ˌsē, -ˈkä-ˌkī, -ˌkē\ [NL] (ca. 1902) : any of a genus (*Cryptococcus*) of budding imperfect fungi that resemble yeasts and include a number of saprophytes and a few serious pathogens — **cryp·to·coc·cal** \-ˈkä-kəl\ *adj*

cryp·to·crys·tal·line \ˌkrip-tō-ˈkris-tə-lən\ *adj* [ISV] (1862) : having a crystalline structure so fine that no distinct particles are recognizable under a microscope ⟨~ quartz⟩

cryp·to·gam \ˈkrip-tə-ˌgam\ *n* [ultim. fr. Gk *kryptos* + *-gamia* -gamy] (1847) : a plant or plantlike organism (as a fern, moss, alga, or fungus) reproducing by spores and not producing flowers or seed — **cryp·to·gam·ic** \ˌkrip-tə-ˈga-mik\ *also* **cryp·tog·a·mous** \krip-ˈtä-gə-məs\ *adj*

cryp·to·gen·ic \ˌkrip-tə-ˈje-nik\ *adj* (1908) : of obscure or unknown origin ⟨a ~ disease⟩

cryp·to·gram \ˈkrip-tə-ˌgram\ *n* [F *cryptogramme,* fr. *crypt-* + *-gramme* -gram] (1878) **1** : a communication in cipher or code **2** : a figure or representation having a hidden significance

cryp·to·graph \ˈkrip-tə-ˌgraf\ *n* (1845) : CRYPTOGRAM

cryp·tog·ra·pher \krip-ˈtä-grə-fər\ *n* (1641) : a specialist in cryptography: as **a** : a clerk who enciphers and deciphers messages **b** : one who devises cryptographic methods or systems **c** : CRYPTANALYST

cryp·to·graph·ic \ˌkrip-tə-ˈgra-fik\ *adj* (1824) : of, relating to, or using cryptography — **cryp·to·graph·i·cal·ly** \-fi-k(ə-)lē\ *adv*

cryp·tog·ra·phy \krip-ˈtä-grə-fē\ *n* [NL *cryptographia,* fr. *crypt-* + *-graphia* -graphy] (1658) **1** : secret writing **2** : the enciphering and deciphering of messages in secret code or cipher; *also* : the computerized encoding and decoding of information **3** : CRYPTANALYSIS

cryp·tol·o·gy \krip-ˈtä-lə-jē\ *n* (1935) : the scientific study of cryptography and cryptanalysis — **cryp·to·log·i·cal** \ˌkrip-tə-ˈlä-ji-kəl\ *or* **cryp·to·log·ic** \-jik\ *adj* — **cryp·tol·o·gist** \krip-ˈtä-lə-jist\ *n*

cryp·to·me·ria \ˌkrip-tə-ˈmir-ē-ə\ *n* [NL, genus name, fr. *crypt-* + Gk *meros* part — more at MERIT] (1841) : an evergreen tree (*Cryptomeria japonica*) of the bald cypress family that is a valuable timber tree of Japan — see CONE illustration

cryp·to·nym \ˈkrip-tə-ˌnim\ *n* (1876) : a secret name

crypt·or·chid \krip-ˈtȯr-kəd\ *n* [NL *cryptorchid-, cryptorchis,* fr. *crypt-* + *orchid-, orchis* testicle, fr. Gk *orchis* — more at ORCHIS] (1874) : one affected with cryptorchidism — **cryptorchid** *adj*

crypt·or·chi·dism \-kə-ˌdi-zəm\ *also* **crypt·or·chism** \-ˌki-zəm\ *n* (ca. 1882) : a condition in which one or both testes fail to descend normally

cryp·to·spo·rid·i·o·sis \ˌkrip-tō-spȯr-ˌi-dē-ˈō-səs\ *n, pl* **-o·ses** \-ˌsēz\ [NL] (1982) : infection with or disease caused by cryptosporidia

cryp·to·spo·rid·i·um \ˌkrip-tō-spȯr-ˈi-dē-əm\ *n, pl* **-rid·ia** \-ē-ə\ [NL, fr. *crypt-* + *spora* spore + *-idium*] (1982) : any of a genus (*Cryptosporidium* of the order Coccidia) of protozoans parasitic in the gut of vertebrates including humans and sometimes causing diarrhea

cryp·to·sys·tem \-ˈsis-təm\ *n* (1955) : a method for encoding and decoding messages

cryp·to·zo·ol·o·gy \ˌkrip-tə-zō-ˈä-lə-jē, -zə-ˈwä-\ *n* (1969) : the study of and search for animals and esp. legendary animals (as Sasquatch) usu. in order to evaluate the possibility of their existence — **cryp·to·zoo·log·i·cal** \-ˌzō-ə-ˈlä-ji-kəl\ *adj* — **cryp·to·zo·ol·o·gist** \-ˈä-lə-jist, -ˈwä-\ *n*

cryst *abbr* crystalline; crystallized

1**crys·tal** \ˈkris-tᵊl\ *n* [ME *cristal,* fr. AF, fr. L *crystallum,* fr. Gk *krystallos* — more at CRUST] (13c) **1** : quartz that is transparent or nearly so and that is either colorless or only slightly tinged **2** : something resembling crystal in transparency and colorlessness **3** : a body that is formed by the solidification of a chemical element, a compound, or a mixture and has a regularly repeating internal arrangement of its atoms and often external plane faces **4** : a clear colorless glass of superior quality; *also* : objects or ware of such glass **5** : the glass or transparent plastic cover over a watch or clock dial **6** : a crystalline material used in electronics as a frequency-determining element or for rectification **7** : ICE 7; *broadly* : methamphetamine in any form when used illicitly

2**crystal** *adj* (14c) **1** : consisting of or resembling crystal : CLEAR, LUCID **2** : relating to or using a crystal ⟨a ~ radio receiver⟩

crystal ball *n* (1848) **1** : a sphere esp. of quartz crystal traditionally used by fortune-tellers **2** : a means or method of predicting future events

crystal clear *adj* (1815) : perfectly or transparently clear ⟨*crystal clear* water⟩ ⟨her directions were *crystal clear*⟩

crystal gazing *n* (1889) **1** : the art or practice of concentrating on a glass or crystal globe with the aim of inducing a psychic state in which divination can be performed **2** : the attempt to predict future events or make difficult judgments esp. without adequate data — **crystal gazer** *n*

crystall- *or* **crystallo-** *comb form* [Gk *krystallos*] : crystal ⟨*crystallo*graphy⟩

crys·tal·line \ˈkris-tə-lən *also* -ˌlīn, -ˌlēn\ *adj* [ME *cristallin,* fr. AF & L; AF, fr. L *crystallinus,* fr. Gk *krystallinos,* fr. *krystallos*] (15c) **1** : resembling crystal: as **a** : strikingly clear or sparkling ⟨~ air⟩ ⟨a ~ lake⟩ **b** : CLEAR-CUT **2** : made of crystal : composed of crystals **3** : constituting or relating to a crystal — **crys·tal·lin·i·ty** \ˌkris-tə-ˈli-nə-tē\ *n*

crystalline lens *n* (1794) : the lens of the eye in vertebrates

crys·tal·lise *Brit var of* CRYSTALLIZE

crys·tal·lite \ˈkris-tə-ˌlīt\ *n* [G *Kristallit,* fr. Gk *krystallos*] (1805) **1 a** : a minute mineral form (as in glassy volcanic rocks) that marks the beginning of crystallization **b** : a single grain in a polycrystalline substance **2** : MICELLE

crys·tal·lize *also* **crys·tal·ize** \ˈkris-tə-ˌlīz\ *vb* **-lized; -liz·ing** *vt* (1598) **1** : to cause to form crystals or assume crystalline form **2** : to cause to take a definite form ⟨tried to ~ his thoughts⟩ **3** : to coat with crystals esp. of sugar ⟨~ grapes⟩ ~ *vi* : to become crystallized — **crys·tal·liz·able** \-ˌlī-zə-bəl, ˌkris-tə-ˈ\ *adj* — **crys·tal·li·za·tion** \ˌkris-tə-li-ˈzā-shən\ *n* — **crys·tal·liz·er** *n*

crys·tal·lo·graph·ic \ˌkris-tə-lə-ˈgra-fik\ *adj* (1804) : of or relating to crystals or crystallography — **crys·tal·lo·graph·i·cal·ly** \-fi-k(ə-)lē\ *adv*

crys·tal·log·ra·phy \ˌkris-tə-ˈlä-grə-fē\ n (1802) : a science that deals with the forms and structures of crystals — **crys·tal·log·ra·pher** \-fər\ n

crys·tal·loid \ˈkris-tə-ˌlȯid\ n (1861) : a substance that forms a true solution and is capable of being crystallized — **crystalloid** or **crys·tal·loi·dal** \ˌkris-tə-ˈlȯi-dᵊl\ adj

crystal meth n [meth short for methamphetamine] (1984) : CRYSTAL 7

crystal pleat n (1976) : any of a series of narrow sharply pressed pleats all turned in one direction — **crystal pleated** adj

crystal violet n (ca. 1893) : a triphenylmethane dye found in gentian violet

cry up vt (1593) : to praise publicly in order to enhance in value or repute ⟨cried up his skills as a writer⟩

cs abbr 1 case; cases 2 census 3 consciousness 4 consul
¹**Cs** abbr cirrostratus
²**Cs** symbol cesium
¹**CS** \ˌsē-ˈes\ n [Ben B. Corson †1987 and Roger W. Staughton †1957 Am. chemists] (1960) : a potent tear gas $C_{10}H_5ClN_2$ used esp. for riot control
²**CS** abbr 1 capital stock 2 cesarean section 3 chief of staff 4 Christian Science 5 civil service 6 conditioned stimulus 7 county seat
CSA abbr Confederate States of America
csc abbr cosecant
CSC abbr Civil Service Commission
C–sec·tion \ˈsē-ˌsek-shən\ n (1973) : CESAREAN SECTION
CSF abbr cerebrospinal fluid
CSM abbr command sergeant major
C–Span abbr cable-satellite public affairs network
CST abbr central standard time
ct abbr 1 carat 2 cent 3 count 4 county 5 court
CT abbr 1 central time 2 certificated teacher; certified teacher 3 computed tomography; computerized tomography 4 Connecticut
cte·noid \ˈte-ˌnȯid, ˈtē-\ adj [ISV, fr. Gk ktenoeidēs, fr. kten-, kteis comb — more at PECTINATE] (1872) : having the margin toothed ⟨~ scale⟩; also : having or consisting of ctenoid scales ⟨~ fishes⟩
cteno·phore \ˈte-nə-ˌfȯr, ˈtē-\ n [ultim. fr. Gk kten-, kteis + pherein to carry — more at BEAR] (ca. 1882) : any of a phylum (Ctenophora) of marine animals superficially resembling jellyfishes but having biradial symmetry and swimming by means of eight bands of transverse ciliated plates — called also comb jelly — **cte·noph·o·ran** \tə-ˈnä-fə-rən\ n or adj
ctf abbr certificate
ctn abbr 1 carton 2 cotangent
c to c abbr center to center
ctr abbr 1 center 2 counter
CT scan \ˌsē-ˈtē-\ n [computerized tomography] (1974) : CAT SCAN — **CT scanner** n
cu abbr 1 cubic 2 cumulative
¹**Cu** abbr cumulus
²**Cu** symbol [L cuprum] copper
CU abbr close-up
cua·dri·lla \kwä-ˈdrē-yə, -ˈdrēl-\ n [Sp, dim. of cuadra square, fr. L quadra] (1893) : the team assisting the matador in the bullring
cub \ˈkəb\ n [prob. akin to ME cobbe leader of a group, head — more at COB] (1530) **1 a** : a young carnivorous mammal (as a bear, fox, or lion) **b** : a young shark **2** : a young person **3** : APPRENTICE; esp : an inexperienced newspaper reporter
cub·age \ˈkyü-bij\ n (1840) : cubic content, volume, or displacement
Cu·ba li·bre \ˌkyü-bə-ˈlē-brə\ n [Sp, lit., free Cuba] (1937) : a cocktail made with rum, lime juice, and cola
Cu·ban heel \ˈkyü-bən-\ n [Cuba, West Indies] (1908) : a broad medium-high heel with a moderately curved back
Cuban sandwich n (1950) : a usu. grilled and pressed sandwich in Cuban-American cuisine served on a long split roll and typically containing roasted meats, cheese, and pickles; broadly : SUBMARINE 2
cub·by \ˈkə-bē\ n, pl **cubbies** [obs. E cub pen, fr. D kub fish basket; akin to OE cofa den] (ca. 1859) : CUBBYHOLE
cub·by·hole \ˈkə-bē-ˌhōl\ n (ca. 1842) : a small snug place (as for hiding or storage); also : a cramped space
¹**cube** \ˈkyüb\ n [L cubus, fr. Gk kybos die, cube] (1551) **1 a** : the regular solid of six equal square sides — see VOLUME table **b** : something shaped like a cube ⟨an ice ~⟩ **c** : CUBICLE 2 ⟨an office ~⟩ **2** : the product of a number multiplied by itself twice
²**cube** adj (1570) : raised to the third power
³**cube** vt **cubed; cub·ing** (1588) **1** : to raise to the third power **2** : to form into a cube **3** : to cut partly through (a steak) in a checkered pattern to increase tenderness by breaking the fibers — **cub·er** n
⁴**cu·be** or **cu·bé** \ˈkyü-ˌbā, kyü-ˈ\ n [AmerSp cubé] (1924) : any of several tropical American plants (genus Lonchocarpus) furnishing rotenone
cu·beb \ˈkyü-ˌbeb\ n [ME quibibe, cubebe, fr. AF quibibe, cubibe, fr. ML cubeba, fr. dial. Ar kubāba] (14c) : the dried unripe berry of a tropical shrub (Piper cubeba) of the pepper family that is used as a spice
cube farm n (1997) slang : an office in which employees work in cubicles
cube root n (1679) : a number whose cube is a given number
cube steak n (1930) : a thin slice of beef that has been cubed
¹**cu·bic** \ˈkyü-bik\ adj (15c) **1** : having the form of a cube : CUBICAL **2 a** : relating to the cube considered as a crystal form **b** : ISOMETRIC 1 **3 a** : THREE-DIMENSIONAL **b** : being the volume of a cube whose edge is a specified unit ⟨~ inch⟩ **4** : of third degree, order, or power ⟨a ~ polynomial⟩
²**cubic** n (1799) : a cubic curve, equation, or polynomial
cu·bi·cal \ˈkyü-bi-kəl\ adj (15c) **1** : CUBIC; esp : shaped like a cube **2** : relating to volume — **cu·bi·cal·ly** \-k(ə-)lē\ adv
cubic equation n (ca. 1751) : a polynomial equation in which the highest sum of exponents of variables in any term is three
cu·bi·cle \ˈkyü-bi-kəl\ n [L cubiculum, fr. cubare to lie, recline] (15c) **1** : a sleeping compartment partitioned off from a large room **2 a** : a small partitioned space; esp : one with a desk used for work in a business office **b** : CARREL
cubic measure n (1660) : a unit (as cubic inch or cubic centimeter) for measuring volume — see METRIC SYSTEM table, WEIGHT table
cubic zirconia also **cubic zirconium** n (1979) : a synthetic gemstone of zirconia resembling a diamond

cub·ism \ˈkyü-ˌbi-zəm\ n, often cap (1911) : a style of art that stresses abstract structure at the expense of other pictorial elements esp. by displaying several aspects of the same object simultaneously and by fragmenting the form of depicted objects — **cub·ist** \-bist\ n or adj, often cap — **cu·bis·tic** \kyü-ˈbis-tik\ adj
cu·bit \ˈkyü-bət\ n [ME, fr. L cubitum elbow, cubit] (14c) : any of various ancient units of length based on the length of the forearm from the elbow to the tip of the middle finger and usu. equal to about 18 inches (46 centimeters)
¹**cu·boid** \ˈkyü-ˌbȯid\ adj (ca. 1828) **1** : approximately cubical in shape **2** : relating to or being the cuboid
²**cuboid** n (1839) : the outermost bone in the distal row of tarsal bones of many higher vertebrates
cu·boi·dal \kyü-ˈbȯi-dᵊl\ adj (1803) **1** : somewhat cubical **2** : composed of nearly cubical elements ⟨~ epithelium⟩
Cub Scout n (ca. 1935) : a member of the scouting program of the Boy Scouts for boys in the first through fifth grades in school
cuck·ing stool \ˈkə-kiŋ-\ n [ME cucking stol, lit., defecating chair] (12c) : a chair formerly used for punishing offenders (as dishonest tradesmen) by public exposure or ducking in water
cuck·old \ˈkə-kəld, -(ˌ)kōld\ n [ME cokewold] (13c) : a man whose wife is unfaithful — **cuckold** vt
cuck·old·ry \-ˌkəl-drē\ n (1529) **1** : the practice of making cuckolds **2** : the state of being a cuckold
¹**cuck·oo** \ˈkü-(ˌ)kü, ˈkù-\ n, pl **cuckoos** [ME cuccu, of imit. origin] (13c) **1** : a largely grayish-brown European bird (Cuculus canorus) that is a parasite given to laying its eggs in the nests of other birds which hatch them and rear the offspring; broadly : any of a large family (Cuculidae of the order Cuculiformes) to which this bird belongs **2** : the call of the cuckoo **3** : a silly or slightly crackbrained person
²**cuckoo** vt (1648) : to repeat monotonously as a cuckoo does its call
³**cuckoo** adj (1627) **1** : of, relating to, or resembling the cuckoo **2** : deficient in sense or intelligence : SILLY
cuckoo clock n (1789) : a wall or shelf clock that announces the hours by sounds resembling a cuckoo's call
cuck·oo·flow·er \ˈkü-(ˌ)kü-ˌflaù(-ə)r, ˈkù-\ n (1578) **1** : a bitter cress (Cardamine pratensis) of Eurasia and No. America **2** : RAGGED ROBIN
cuck·oo·pint \-ˌpint\ n [ME cuccupintel, fr. cuccu + pintel pintle] (1551) : a European arum (Arum maculatum) with erect spathe and short purple spadix
cuckoo spit n (1592) **1** : a frothy secretion exuded on plants by the nymphs of spittle insects **2** : SPITTLEBUG
cu·cul·late \ˈkyü-kə-ˌlāt, kyü-ˈkə-lət\ adj [ML cucullatus, fr. L cucullus hood] (1794) : having the shape of a hood ⟨a ~ leaf⟩
cu·cum·ber \ˈkyü-(ˌ)kəm-bər\ n [ME, fr. AF cucumbre, fr. L cucumer-, cucumis] (14c) : the fruit of a vine (Cucumis sativus) of the gourd family cultivated as a garden vegetable; also : this vine

cucumber

cucumber mosaic n (1916) : a plant disease esp. of cucumbers that is caused by a single-stranded RNA virus (species Cucumber mosaic virus of the genus Cucumovirus, family Bromoviridae) and is transmitted chiefly by an aphid and produces mottled foliage and often pale warty fruits
cucumber tree n (ca. 1782) : a magnolia (Magnolia acuminata) of the eastern U.S. having fruit resembling a small cucumber
cu·cur·bit \kyü-ˈkər-bət\ n [ME cucurbite, fr. AF, fr. L cucurbita gourd] (14c) **1** : a vessel or flask for distillation used with or forming part of an alembic **2** : a plant of the gourd family
cud \ˈkəd, chiefly Southern ˈkùd or ˈküd\ n [ME cudde, fr. OE cwudu; akin to OHG kuti glue, Skt jatu gum] (bef. 12c) **1** : food brought up into the mouth by a ruminating animal from its first stomach to be chewed again **2** : ²QUID
cud·bear \ˈkəd-ˌber\ n [irreg. fr. Dr. Cuthbert Gordon, 18th cent. Scot. chemist] (1764) : a reddish coloring matter from lichens
¹**cud·dle** \ˈkə-dᵊl\ vb **cud·dled; cud·dling** \ˈkəd-liŋ, ˈkə-dᵊl-iŋ\ [origin unknown] vt (1520) : to hold close for warmth or comfort or in affection — vi : to lie close or snug : NESTLE, SNUGGLE — **cud·dler** \ˈkəd-lər, ˈkə-dᵊl-ər\ n
²**cuddle** n (1825) : a close embrace
cud·dle·some \ˈkə-dᵊl-səm\ adj (1876) : CUDDLY
cud·dly \ˈkəd-lē, ˈkə-dᵊl-ē\ adj **cud·dli·er; -est** (1863) : fit for or inviting cuddling ⟨a ~ kitten⟩
cud·dy \ˈkə-dē\ n, pl **cuddies** [origin unknown] (1660) **1** : a usu. small cabin or shelter (as on a sailboat) **2** : a small room or cupboard
²**cud·dy** or **cud·die** \ˈkə-dē\ n, pl **cuddies** [perh. fr. Cuddy, nickname for Cuthbert] (ca. 1715) **1** dial Brit : DONKEY **2** dial Brit : BLOCKHEAD
cud·gel \ˈkə-jəl\ n [ME kuggel, fr. OE cycgel; perh. akin to MHG kugele ball] (bef. 12c) : a short heavy club
²**cudgel** vt **-geled** or **-gelled; -gel·ing** or **-gel·ling** \ˈkəj-liŋ, ˈkə-jə-\ (1596) : to beat with or as if with a cudgel — **cudgel one's brains** : to think hard (as for a solution to a problem)
cud·weed \ˈkəd-ˌwēd, chiefly Southern ˈkùd- or ˈküd-\ n (1548) : any of several composite plants (as of the genus Gnaphalium) with silky or woolly foliage
¹**cue** \ˈkyü\ n [ME cu half a farthing (spelled form of q, abbr. for L quadrans quarter of an as)] (ca. 1755) : the letter q
²**cue** n [prob. fr. qu, abbr. (used as a direction in actors' copies of plays) of L quando when] (1553) **1 a** : a signal (as a word, phrase, or bit of stage business) to a performer to begin a specific speech or action **b** : something serving a comparable purpose : HINT **2** : a feature indicating the nature of something perceived **3** archaic : the part one has to perform in or as if in a play **4** archaic : MOOD, HUMOR

[3]**cue** *vt* **cued; cu·ing** *or* **cue·ing** (1922) **1 :** to give a cue to **:** PROMPT **2 :** to insert into a continuous performance ⟨~ in sound effects⟩

[4]**cue** *n* [F *queue,* lit., tail, fr. OF *cue, coe, queue,* fr. L *cauda*] (ca. 1749) **1 a :** a leather-tipped tapering rod for striking the cue ball (as in billiards and pool) **b :** a long-handled instrument with a concave head for shoving disks in shuffleboard **2 :** QUEUE 2

[5]**cue** *vb* **cued; cu·ing** *or* **cue·ing** *vt* (ca. 1784) **1 :** QUEUE **2 :** to strike with a cue ~ *vi* **1 :** QUEUE **2 :** to use a cue

cue ball *n* (1881) **:** the ball a player strikes with the cue in billiards and pool

cues·ta \ˈkwes-tə\ *n* [Sp, fr. L *costa* side, rib — more at COAST] (1818) **:** a hill or ridge with a steep face on one side and a gentle slope on the other

[1]**cuff** \ˈkəf\ *n* [ME *coffe, cuffe* mitten] (1522) **1 :** something (as a part of a sleeve or glove) encircling the wrist **2 :** the turned-back hem of a trouser leg **3 a :** HANDCUFF — usu. used in pl. **b :** a usu. wide metal band worn as a bracelet **4 :** an inflatable band that is wrapped around an extremity to control the flow of blood through the part when recording blood pressure with a sphygmomanometer — **cuff·less** \ˈkəf-ləs\ *adj* — **off the cuff :** without preparation **:** AD LIB ⟨speaking *off the cuff*⟩ — **on the cuff :** on credit ⟨transacting business *on the cuff*⟩

[2]**cuff** *vt* (1693) **1 :** to furnish with a cuff **2 :** HANDCUFF

[3]**cuff** *vb* [perh. fr. obs. E, glove, fr. ME] *vt* (1530) **:** to strike esp. with or as if with the palm of the hand **:** BUFFET ~ *vi* **:** FIGHT, SCUFFLE

[4]**cuff** *n* (1570) **:** a blow with the hand esp. when open **:** SLAP

cuff link *n* (1897) **:** a usu. ornamental device consisting of two parts joined by a shank, chain, or bar for passing through buttonholes to fasten shirt cuffs — usu. used in pl.

cui bo·no \ˈkwē-ˈbō-(ˌ)nō\ *n* [L, to whose advantage?] (1604) **1 :** a principle that probable responsibility for an act or event lies with one having something to gain **2 :** usefulness or utility as a principle in estimating the value of an act or policy

cui·rass \kwi-ˈras, kyu̇-\ *n* [ME *curas,* fr. MF *cuirasse,* prob. fr. Old Occitan *coirassa,* fr. LL *coreacea,* fem. of *coreaceus* leathern, fr. L *corium* skin, leather; akin to OE *heortha* deerskin, L *cortex* bark, Gk *keirein* to cut — more at SHEAR] (15c) **1 :** a piece of armor covering the body from neck to waist; *also* **:** the breastplate of such a piece **2 :** something (as bony plates covering an animal) resembling a cuirass — **cuirassed** *adj*

cui·ras·sier \ˌkwir-ə-ˈsir, ˌkyu̇r-\ *n* (1625) **:** a mounted soldier wearing a cuirass

Cui·se·naire rod \ˌkwē-zə-ˈner-\ *n* [fr. *Cuisenaire,* a trademark] (1954) **:** any of a set of colored rods usu. of 1 centimeter cross section and of 10 lengths from 1 to 10 centimeters that are used for teaching number concepts and the basic operations of arithmetic

cui·sine \kwi-ˈzēn, kwē-\ *n* [F, lit., kitchen, fr. OF, fr. LL *coquina* — more at KITCHEN] (1786) **:** manner of preparing food **:** style of cooking; *also* **:** the food prepared

cuisse \ˈkwis\ *also* **cuish** \ˈkwish\ *n* [ME *cusseis,* pl., fr. AF *quisez,* pl. of *quissel,* fr. *quisse* thigh, fr. L *coxa* hip — more at COXA] (15c) **:** a piece of plate armor for the front of the thigh — see ARMOR illustration

cuke \ˈkyük\ *n* (1903) **:** CUCUMBER

cul–de–sac \ˈkəl-di-ˌsak, ˈku̇l-; ˌkəl-di-ˈ, ˌku̇l-\ *n, pl* **culs–de–sac** \ˈkəl(z)-, ˈku̇l(z)-, ˌkəl(z)-, ˌku̇l(z)-\ *also* **cul–de–sacs** \-ˌsaks, -ˈsaks\ [F, lit., bottom of the bag] (1738) **1 :** a blind diverticulum or pouch **2 :** a street or passage closed at one end **3 :** BLIND ALLEY

cu·let \ˈkyü-lət, ˈkə-lət\ *n* [F, fr. dim. of *cul* backside, fr. L *culus;* akin to OIr *cúl* back] (1678) **1 :** the small flat facet at the bottom of a brilliant parallel to the table — see BRILLIANT illustration **2 :** plate armor covering the buttocks

cu·lex \ˈkyü-ˌleks\ *n* [NL, fr. L, gnat; akin to OIr *cuil* fly] (15c) **:** any of a large cosmopolitan genus (*Culex*) of mosquitoes that includes the common house mosquito (*C. pipiens*) of Europe and No. America and vectors of the viruses causing Saint Louis encephalitis and West Nile fever

cu·li·nar·i·an \ˌkə-lə-ˈner-ē-ən, ˌkyü-, ˌkü-\ *n* (1949) **:** COOK, CHEF

cu·li·nary \ˈkə-lə-ˌner-ē, ˈkyü-, ˈkü-\ *adj* [L *culinarius,* fr. *culina* kitchen — more at KILN] (1638) **:** of or relating to the kitchen or cookery — **cu·li·nar·i·ly** \ˌkə-lə-ˈner-ə-lē, ˌkyü-, ˌkü-\ *adv*

[1]**cull** \ˈkəl\ *vt* [ME, fr. AF *culier, coillir,* fr. L *colligere* to bind together — more at COLLECT] (13c) **1 :** to select from a group **:** CHOOSE ⟨~*ed* the best passages from the poet's work⟩ **2 :** to reduce or control the size of (as a herd) by removal (as by hunting) of esp. weaker animals; *also* **:** to hunt or kill (animals) as a means of population control — **cull·er** *n*

[2]**cull** *n* (1809) **:** something rejected esp. as being inferior or worthless ⟨how to separate good-looking pecans from ~*s* —*Washington Post*⟩

cul·len·der \ˈkə-lən-dər\ *archaic var of* COLANDER

cul·let \ˈkə-lət\ *n* [perh. fr. F *cueillette* act of gathering, fr. L *collecta,* fr. fem. of *collectus,* pp. of *colligere*] (1817) **:** broken or refuse glass usu. added to new material to facilitate melting in making glass

cul·lion \ˈkəl-yən\ *n* [ME *coillon* testicle, fr. AF, fr. VL **coleon-, coleo,* fr. L *coleus* scrotum] (1575) *archaic* **:** a mean or base fellow

[1]**cul·ly** \ˈkə-lē\ *n, pl* **cullies** [perh. alter. of *cullion*] (1664) **:** one easily tricked or imposed on **:** DUPE

[2]**cully** *vt* **cul·lied; cul·ly·ing** (1676) *archaic* **:** CHEAT, DECEIVE

[1]**culm** \ˈkəlm\ *n* [ME] (14c) **:** refuse coal screenings **:** SLACK

[2]**culm** *n* [L *culmus* stalk — more at HAULM] (ca. 1657) **:** a monocotyledonous stem (as of a grass or sedge)

cul·mi·nant \ˈkəl-mə-nənt\ *adj* (1605) **1 :** being at greatest altitude or on the meridian **2 :** fully developed

cul·mi·nate \ˈkəl-mə-ˌnāt\ *vb* **-nat·ed; -nat·ing** [ML *culminatus,* pp. of *culminare,* fr. LL, to crown, fr. L *culmin-, culmen* top — more at HILL] *vi* (1647) **1** *of a celestial body* **:** to reach its highest altitude; *also* **:** to be directly overhead **2 a :** to rise to or form a summit **b :** to reach the highest or a climactic or decisive point ~ *vt* **:** to bring to a head or to the highest point

cul·mi·na·tion \ˌkəl-mə-ˈnā-shən\ *n* (1633) **1 :** the action of culminating **2 :** culminating position **:** CLIMAX ***syn*** see SUMMIT

cu·lotte \ˈkü-ˌlät, ˈkyü-; kü-ˈlät, kyü-\ *n* [F, breeches, fr. dim. of *cul* backside — more at CULET] (1911) **:** a divided skirt; *also* **:** a garment having a divided skirt — often used in pl.

cul·pa·ble \ˈkəl-pə-bəl\ *adj* [ME *coupable,* fr. AF *cupable, culpable,* fr. L *culpabilis,* fr. *culpare* to blame, fr. *culpa* guilt] (14c) **1** *archaic* **:** GUILTY, CRIMINAL **2 :** meriting condemnation or blame esp. as wrong or harmful ⟨~ negligence⟩ ***syn*** see BLAMEWORTHY — **cul·pa·bil·i·ty** \ˌkəl-pə-ˈbi-lə-tē\ *n* — **cul·pa·ble·ness** \ˈkəl-pə-bəl-nəs\ *n* — **cul·pa·bly** \-blē\ *adv*

cul·prit \ˈkəl-prət, -ˌprit\ *n* [AF *cul.* (abbr. of *culpable* guilty) + *prest, prit* ready (i.e., to prove it), fr. L *praestus* — more at PRESTO] (1678) **1 :** one accused of or charged with a crime **2 :** one guilty of a crime or a fault **3 :** the source or cause of a problem

cult \ˈkəlt\ *n, often attrib* [F & L; F *culte,* fr. L *cultus* care, adoration, fr. *colere* to cultivate — more at WHEEL] (1617) **1 :** formal religious veneration **:** WORSHIP **2 :** a system of religious beliefs and ritual; *also* **:** its body of adherents **3 :** a religion regarded as unorthodox or spurious; *also* **:** its body of adherents **4 :** a system for the cure of disease based on dogma set forth by its promulgator ⟨health ~*s*⟩ **5 a :** great devotion to a person, idea, object, movement, or work (as a film or book); *esp* **:** such devotion regarded as a literary or intellectual fad **b :** the object of such devotion **c :** a usu. small group of people characterized by such devotion — **cul·tic** \ˈkəl-tik\ *adj* — **cult·ish** \-tish\ *adj* — **cult·ish·ly** \-lē\ *adv* — **cult·ish·ness** \-nəs\ *n* — **cult·ism** \ˈkəl-ˌti-zəm\ *n* — **cult·ist** \ˈkəl-tist\ *n* — **cult·like** \-ˌlīk\ *adj*

cultch *also* **culch** \ˈkəlch\ *n* [perh. fr. a F dial. form of F *couche* couch] (1667) **1 :** material (as oyster shells) laid down on oyster grounds to furnish points of attachment for the spat **2** *chiefly NewEng* **:** CLUTTER, TRASH

cul·ti·gen \ˈkəl-tə-jən\ *n* [*cultivated* + *-gen*] (1924) **:** a cultivated or domestic organism (as the kidney bean *Phaseolus vulgaris,* the dog *Canis familiaris,* or corn *Zea mays*) which has diverged enough while in domestication or cultivation from its ancestors or closest wild relatives to be classified as a species, subspecies, or major variety

cul·ti·va·ble \ˈkəl-tə-və-bəl\ *adj* (1682) **:** capable of being cultivated ⟨~ land⟩ — **cul·ti·va·bil·i·ty** \ˌkəl-tə-və-ˈbi-lə-tē\ *n*

cul·ti·var \ˈkəl-tə-ˌvär, -ˌver\ *n* [*cultivated* + *variety*] (1923) **:** an organism and esp. one of an agricultural or horticultural variety or strain originating and persistent under cultivation

cul·ti·vate \ˈkəl-tə-ˌvāt\ *vt* **-vat·ed; -vat·ing** [ML *cultivatus,* pp. of *cultivare,* fr. *cultivus* cultivable, fr. L *cultus,* pp. of *colere*] (ca. 1655) **1 :** to prepare or prepare and use for the raising of crops; *also* **:** to loosen or break up the soil about (growing plants) **2 a :** to foster the growth of ⟨~ vegetables⟩ **b :** CULTURE 2a **c :** to improve by labor, care, or study **:** REFINE ⟨~ the mind⟩ **3 :** FURTHER, ENCOURAGE ⟨~ the arts⟩ **4 :** to seek the society of **:** make friends with — **cul·ti·vat·able** \-ˌvā-tə-bəl\ *adj*

cultivated *adj* (1665) **:** REFINED, EDUCATED ⟨~ speech⟩ ⟨~ tastes⟩

cul·ti·va·tion \ˌkəl-tə-ˈvā-shən\ *n* (ca. 1716) **1 :** CULTURE, REFINEMENT **2 :** the act or art of cultivating or tilling

cul·ti·va·tor \ˈkəl-tə-ˌvā-tər\ *n* (1665) **:** one that cultivates; *esp* **:** an implement for loosening the soil while crops are growing

cul·tur·al \ˈkəlch-rəl, ˈkəl-chə-\ *adj* (ca. 1864) **1 :** of or relating to culture or culturing **2 :** concerned with the fostering of plant or animal growth — **cul·tur·al·ly** \-rə-lē\ *adv*

cultural anthropology *n* (1933) **:** anthropology that deals with human culture esp. with respect to social structure, language, law, politics, religion, magic, art, and technology — compare PHYSICAL ANTHROPOLOGY — **cultural anthropologist** *n*

cul·tur·a·ti \ˌkəl-chə-ˈrä-(ˌ)tē\ *n pl* [[1]*culture* + *-ati* (as in *literati*)] (1964) **:** people intensely interested in cultural affairs

[1]**cul·ture** \ˈkəl-chər\ *n* [ME, cultivated land, cultivation, fr. AF, fr. L *cultura,* fr. *cultus,* pp.] (15c) **1 :** CULTIVATION, TILLAGE **2 :** the act of developing the intellectual and moral faculties esp. by education **3 :** expert care and training ⟨beauty ~⟩ **4 a :** enlightenment and excellence of taste acquired by intellectual and aesthetic training **b :** acquaintance with and taste in fine arts, humanities, and broad aspects of science as distinguished from vocational and technical skills **5 a :** the integrated pattern of human knowledge, belief, and behavior that depends upon the capacity for learning and transmitting knowledge to succeeding generations **b :** the customary beliefs, social forms, and material traits of a racial, religious, or social group; *also* **:** the characteristic features of everyday existence (as diversions or a way of life) shared by people in a place or time ⟨popular ~⟩ ⟨southern ~⟩ **c :** the set of shared attitudes, values, goals, and practices that characterizes an institution or organization ⟨a corporate ~ focused on the bottom line⟩ **d :** the set of values, conventions, or social practices associated with a particular field, activity, or societal characteristic ⟨studying the effect of computers on print ~⟩ ⟨changing the ~ of materialism will take time —Peggy O'Mara⟩ **6 :** the act or process of cultivating living material (as bacteria or viruses) in prepared nutrient media; *also* **:** a product of such cultivation

[2]**culture** *vt* **cul·tured; cul·tur·ing** \ˈkəlch-riŋ, ˈkəl-chə-\ (1510) **1 :** CULTIVATE **2 a :** to grow in a prepared medium **b :** to start a culture from

cultured *adj* (ca. 1746) **1 :** CULTIVATED **2 :** produced under artificial conditions ⟨~ viruses⟩ ⟨~ pearls⟩

culture shock *n* (1940) **:** a sense of confusion and uncertainty sometimes with feelings of anxiety that may affect people exposed to an alien culture or environment without adequate preparation

cul·tus \ˈkəl-təs\ *n* [L, adoration] (1640) **:** CULT

cul·ver \ˈkəl-vər, ˈku̇l-\ *n* [ME, fr. OE *culfer,* fr. VL **columbra,* fr. L *columbula,* dim. of L *columba* dove — more at COLUMBINE] (bef. 12c) **:** PIGEON

cul·ver·in \ˈkəl-və-rən\ *n* [ME, fr. MF *couleuvrine,* fr. *couleuvre* snake, fr. L *colubra*] (15c) **:** an early firearm: **a :** a rude musket **b :** a long cannon (as an 18-pounder) of the 16th and 17th centuries

cul·vert \ˈkəl-vərt\ *n* [origin unknown] (1773) **1 :** a transverse drain **2 :** a conduit for a culvert **3 :** a bridge over a culvert

[1]**cum** \ˈku̇m, ˈkəm\ *conj* [L, with; akin to L *com-* — more at CO-] (ca. 1869) **:** along with being **:** AND — used to form usu. hyphenated phrases ⟨a credible mining camp elder-*cum*-publican —G. B. Shaw⟩ ⟨Christian and Christian-*cum*-voodoo churches —David Binder⟩

[2]**cum** *abbr* cumulative

Cumb *abbr* Cumbria

[1]**cum·ber** \ˈkəm-bər\ *vt* **cum·bered; cum·ber·ing** \-b(ə-)riŋ\ [ME *combren,* short for *acombren,* fr. AF *acumbrer, encumbrer* — more at

ENCUMBER] (14c) **1** *archaic* : TROUBLE, HARASS **2 a** : to hinder or encumber by being in the way ⟨~*ed* with heavy clothing⟩ **b** : to clutter up ⟨rocks ~*ing* the yard⟩

[2]**cumber** *n* (14c) : something that cumbers; *esp* : HINDRANCE

cum·ber·some \ˈkəm-bər-səm\ *adj* (1535) **1** *dial* : BURDENSOME, TROUBLESOME **2** : unwieldy because of heaviness and bulk **3** : slow-moving : PONDEROUS ***syn*** see HEAVY — **cum·ber·some·ly** *adv* — **cum·ber·some·ness** *n*

cum·brous \ˈkəm-b(ə-)rəs\ *adj* (15c) : CUMBERSOME ***syn*** see HEAVY — **cum·brous·ly** *adv* — **cum·brous·ness** *n*

cum·in \ˈkə-mən, ˈkyü-, ˈkü-\ *n* [ME, fr. OE *cymen,* fr. L *cuminum,* fr. Gk *kyminon,* of Sem origin; akin to Akkadian *kamūnu* cumin] (bef. 12c) : a small annual herb (*Cuminum cyminum*) of the carrot family cultivated for its aromatic fruits; *also* : the seedlike fruit of cumin used as a spice

cum lau·de \ku̇m-ˈlau̇-də, -dē; ˌkəm-ˈlȯ-dē\ *adv or adj* [NL, with praise] (1893) : with distinction ⟨graduated *cum laude*⟩ — compare MAGNA CUM LAUDE, SUMMA CUM LAUDE

cum·mer·bund \ˈkə-mər-ˌbənd, ˈkəm-bər-\ *also* **cum·ber·bund** \ˈkəm-bər-\ *n* [Hindi & Urdu *kamarband,* fr. Pers, fr. *kamar* waist + *band* band] (1616) : a broad waistband usu. worn in place of a vest with men's dress clothes and adapted in various styles of women's clothes

cum·shaw \ˈkəm-ˌshȯ\ *n* [Chin (Xiamen) *kam siā* grateful thanks] (1839) : PRESENT, GRATUITY; *also* : BRIBE, PAYOFF

cumul- *or* **cumuli-** *or* **cumulo-** *comb form* [NL, fr. L *cumulus*] : cumulus and ⟨*cumulo*nimbus⟩

cu·mu·late \ˈkyü-myə-ˌlāt\ *vb* **-lat·ed; -lat·ing** [L *cumulatus,* pp. of *cumulare,* fr. *cumulus* mass] *vt* (1534) **1** : to gather or pile in a heap **2** : to combine into one **3** : to build up by addition of new material ~ *vi* : to become massed — **cu·mu·late** \-lət, -ˌlāt\ *adj* — **cu·mu·la·tion** \ˌkyü-myə-ˈlā-shən\ *n*

cu·mu·la·tive \ˈkyü-myə-lə-tiv, -ˌlā-\ *adj* (1605) **1 a** : made up of accumulated parts **b** : increasing by successive additions **2** : tending to prove the same point ⟨~ evidence⟩ **3 a** : taking effect upon completion of another penal sentence ⟨a ~ sentence⟩ **b** : increasing in severity with repetition of the offense ⟨~ penalty⟩ **4** : formed by the addition of new material of the same kind ⟨a ~ book index⟩ **5** : summing or integrating overall data or values of a random variable less than or less than or equal to a specified value ⟨~ normal distribution⟩ ⟨~ frequency distribution⟩ — **cu·mu·la·tive·ly** *adv* — **cu·mu·la·tive·ness** *n*

cumulative distribution function *n* (1950) : a function that gives the probability that a random variable is less than or equal to the independent variable of the function

cu·mu·li·form \ˈkyü-myə-lə-ˌfȯrm\ *adj* (1885) : of the form of a cumulus ⟨~ clouds⟩

cu·mu·lo·nim·bus \-ˈnim-bəs\ *n* [NL] (1887) : cumulus cloud having a low base and often spread out in the shape of an anvil extending to great heights — see CLOUD illustration

cu·mu·lous \ˈkyü-myə-ləs\ *adj* (1815) : resembling cumulus

cu·mu·lus \-ləs\ *n, pl* **-li** \-ˌlī, -ˌlē\ [L] (1659) **1** : HEAP, ACCUMULATION **2** [NL, fr. L] : a dense puffy cloud form having a flat base and rounded outlines often piled up like a mountain — see CLOUD illustration

cunc·ta·tion \ˌkəŋ(k)-ˈtā-shən\ *n* [L *cunctation-, cunctatio,* fr. *cunctari* to hesitate; akin to Skt *śaṅkate* he wavers, OE *hangian* to hang] (1585) : DELAY — **cunc·ta·tive** \ˈkəŋ(k)-ˌtā-tiv, -tə-tiv\ *adj*

cu·ne·ate \ˈkyü-nē-ˌāt, -ət\ *adj* [L *cuneatus,* fr. *cuneus* wedge] (1658) : narrowly triangular with the acute angle toward the base — see LEAF illustration

[1]**cu·ne·i·form** \kyü-ˈnē-ə-ˌfȯrm, ˈkyü-n(ē-)ə-\ *adj* [prob. fr. F *cunéiforme,* fr. MF, fr. L *cuneus* + MF *-iforme* -iform] (1677) **1** : having the shape of a wedge **2** : composed of or written in wedge-shaped characters ⟨~ syllabary⟩

[2]**cuneiform** *n* (1808) **1** : a cuneiform part; *specif* : a cuneiform bone or cartilage **2** : cuneiform writing

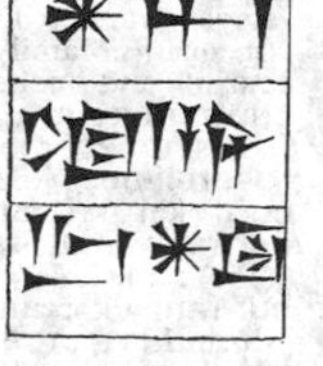

cuneiform 2

cun·ner \ˈkə-nər\ *n* [origin unknown] (1602) : either of two wrasses: **a** : a European wrasse (*Crenilabrus melops*) **b** : a wrasse (*Tautogolabrus adspersus*) common along the northeastern U.S. and adjacent Canadian coast

cun·ni·lin·gus \ˌkə-ni-ˈliŋ-gəs\ *also* **cun·ni·linc·tus** \-ˈliŋ(k)-təs\ *n* [*cunnilingus,* NL, fr. L, one who licks the vulva, fr. *cunnus* vulva + *lingere* to lick; *cunnilinctus,* NL, fr. L *cunnus* + *linctus,* act of licking, fr. *lingere* — more at LICK] (1887) : oral stimulation of the vulva or clitoris

[1]**cun·ning** \ˈkə-niŋ\ *adj* [ME, fr. prp. of *can* know] (14c) **1** : dexterous or crafty in the use of special resources (as skill or knowledge) or in attaining an end ⟨a ~ plotter⟩ **2** : displaying keen insight ⟨a ~ observation⟩ **3** : characterized by wiliness and trickery ⟨~ schemes⟩ **4** : prettily appealing : CUTE ⟨a ~ little kitten⟩ ***syn*** see CLEVER, SLY — **cun·ning·ly** \-niŋ-lē\ *adv* — **cun·ning·ness** *n*

[2]**cunning** *n* (14c) **1** *obs* **a** : KNOWLEDGE, LEARNING **b** : magic art **2** : dexterous skill and subtlety (as in inventing, devising, or executing) ⟨high-ribbed vault . . . with perfect ~ framed —William Wordsworth⟩ **3** : CRAFT, SLYNESS ***syn*** see ART

cunt \ˈkənt\ *n* [ME *cunte;* akin to MLG *kunte* female pudenda] (14c) **1** *usu obscene* : the female genital organs; *also* : sexual intercourse with a woman **2** *usu disparaging & obscene* : WOMAN 1a

[1]**cup** \ˈkəp\ *n* [ME *cuppe,* fr. OE, fr. LL *cuppa* cup, alter. of L *cupa* tub — more at HIVE] (bef. 12c) **1** : an open usu. bowl-shaped drinking vessel **2 a** : a drinking vessel and its contents **b** : the consecrated wine of the Communion **3** : something that falls to one's lot **4** : an ornamental cup offered as a prize (as in a championship) **5** : something resembling a cup: as **a** : a cup-shaped plant organ **b** : an athletic supporter reinforced usu. with plastic to provide extra protection to the wearer **c** : either of two parts of a brassiere that are shaped like and fit over the breasts **d** : the metal case inside a hole in golf; *also* : the hole itself **6** : a usu. iced beverage resembling punch but served from a pitcher rather than a bowl **7** : a half pint : eight fluid ounces **8** : a food served in a cup-shaped usu. footed vessel ⟨a fruit ~⟩ **9** : the symbol ∪ indicating the union of two sets — compare CAP 7 — **cup·like** \-ˌlīk\ *adj* — **in one's cups** : DRUNK

[2]**cup** *vt* **cupped; cup·ping** (14c) **1** : to treat by cupping **2 a** : to curve into the shape of a cup ⟨*cupped* his hands around his mouth⟩ **b** : to place in or as if in a cup

cup·bear·er \ˈkəp-ˌber-ər\ *n* (15c) : one who has the duty of filling and handing around the cups in which wine is served

cup·board \ˈkə-bərd\ *n* (1530) : a closet with shelves where dishes, utensils, or food is kept; *also* : a small closet

cup·cake \ˈkəp-ˌkāk\ *n* (1828) : a small cake baked in a cuplike mold

[1]**cu·pel** \kyü-ˈpel, ˈkyü-pəl\ *n* [F *coupelle,* dim. of *coupe* cup, fr. LL *cuppa*] (1605) : a small shallow porous cup esp. of bone ash used in assaying to separate precious metals from lead

[2]**cupel** *vt* **-pelled** *or* **-peled; -pel·ling** *or* **-pel·ing** (1644) : to refine by means of a cupel — **cu·pel·ler** *n*

cu·pel·la·tion \ˌkyü-pə-ˈlā-shən, -ˌpe-\ *n* (ca. 1691) : refinement (as of gold or silver) in a cupel by exposure to high temperature in a blast of air by which the unwanted metals are oxidized

cup·ful \ˈkəp-ˌfu̇l\ *n, pl* **cup·fuls** \-ˌfu̇lz\ *also* **cups·ful** \ˈkəps-ˌfu̇l\ (12c) **1** : as much as a cup will hold **2** : CUP 7

cup fungus *n* (ca. 1905) : any of an order (Pezizales) of mostly saprophytic ascomycetous fungi with a fleshy or horny apothecium that is often colored and typically shaped like a cup, saucer, or disk

Cu·pid \ˈkyü-pəd\ *n* [L *Cupido*] (14c) **1** : the Roman god of erotic love — compare EROS **2** *not cap* : a figure that represents Cupid as a naked usu. winged boy often holding a bow and arrow

cu·pid·i·ty \kyu̇-ˈpi-də-tē\ *n, pl* **-ties** [ME *cupidite,* fr. AF *cupidité,* fr. L *cupiditat-, cupiditas* — more at COVET] (15c) **1** : inordinate desire for wealth : AVARICE, GREED **2** : strong desire : LUST

Cupid's bow *n* (1567) : a bow that consists of two convex curves usu. with recurved ends

cup of tea (1932) **1** : something one likes or excels in ⟨I see already that storytelling isn't my *cup of tea* —John Barth⟩; *also* : a person suited to one's taste **2** : a thing to be reckoned with : MATTER ⟨poltergeists are a different *cup of tea* —D. B. W. Lewis⟩

cu·po·la \ˈkyü-pə-lə, ÷-ˌlō\ *n* [It, fr. L *cupula,* dim. of *cupa* tub] (1549) **1 a** : a rounded vault resting on a usu. circular base and forming a roof or a ceiling **b** : a small structure built on top of a roof **2** : a vertical cylindrical furnace for melting iron in the foundry that has tuyeres and tapping spouts near the bottom **3** : a raised observation post in the roof of a railroad caboose — **cu·po·laed** \-ləd, ÷-ˌlōd\ *adj*

cup·pa \ˈkə-pə\ *n* [short for *cuppa tea,* pronunciation spelling of *cup of tea*] (1934) *chiefly Brit* : a cup of tea

cup·ping *n* (14c) : an operation of drawing blood to the surface of the body by use of a glass vessel evacuated by heat

cup·py \ˈkə-pē\ *adj* **cup·pi·er; -est** (1882) **1** : resembling a cup **2** : full of small depressions ⟨a ~ racetrack⟩

cupr- *or* **cupri-** *or* **cupro-** *comb form* [LL *cuprum* — more at COPPER] **1** : copper ⟨*cupri*ferous⟩ **2** : copper and ⟨*cupro*nickel⟩

cu·pric \ˈkyü-prik, ˈkü-\ *adj* (1799) : of, relating to, or containing copper with a valence of two

cu·prif·er·ous \kyü-ˈpri-f(ə-)rəs, kü-\ *adj* (1784) : containing copper

cu·prite \ˈkyü-ˌprīt, ˈkü-\ *n* [G *Kuprit,* fr. LL *cuprum*] (ca. 1850) : a red mineral consisting of copper oxide that is a minor ore of copper

cu·pro·nick·el \ˌkyü-prō-ˈni-kəl, ˌkü-\ *n* (1900) : an alloy of copper and nickel; *esp* : one containing about 70 percent copper and 30 percent nickel

cu·prous \ˈkyü-prəs, ˈkü-\ *adj* (1669) : of, relating to, or containing copper with a valence of one

cu·pu·late \ˈkyü-pyə-ˌlāt, -lət\ *adj* (1835) : shaped like, having, or bearing a cupule

cu·pule \ˈkyü-(ˌ)pyül\ *n* [NL *cupula,* fr. LL, dim. of L *cupa* tub — more at HIVE] (1826) : a cup-shaped anatomical structure: as **a** : an involucre characteristic of the oak in which the bracts are indurated and coherent **b** : an outer integument partially enclosing the seed of some seed ferns

[1]**cur** \ˈkər\ *n* [ME, short for *curdogge,* fr. ME **curren* to growl (perh. fr. ON *kurra* to grumble) + ME *dogge* dog] (13c) **1** : a mongrel or inferior dog **2** : a surly or cowardly fellow

[2]**cur** *abbr* **1** currency **2** current

cur·able \ˈkyu̇r-ə-bəl\ *adj* (14c) : capable of being cured ⟨a ~ illness⟩ — **cur·abil·i·ty** \ˌkyu̇r-ə-ˈbi-lə-tē\ *n* — **cur·able·ness** \ˈkyu̇r-ə-bəl-nəs\ *n* — **cur·ably** \-blē\ *adv*

cu·ra·çao \ˈkyu̇r-ə-ˌsō, -ˌsau̇, ˈku̇r-; ˌk(y)u̇r-ə-ˈ\ *also* **cu·ra·çoa** *same, or* ˌkyu̇r-ə-ˈsō-ə\ *n* [D *curaçao,* fr. *Curaçao,* Netherlands Antilles] (1813) : a liqueur flavored with the dried peel of the sour orange

cu·ra·cy \ˈkyu̇r-ə-sē\ *n, pl* **-cies** (1682) : the office or term of office of a curate

cu·ra·re *also* **cu·ra·ri** \kyu̇-ˈrär-ē, ku̇-\ *n* [Pg & Sp *curare,* fr. Carib *kurari*] (1777) : a dried aqueous extract esp. of a vine (as *Strychnos toxifera* of the family Loganiaceae or *Chondodendron tomentosum* of the family Menispermaceae) used by So. American Indians to poison arrow tips and in medicine to produce muscular relaxation

cu·ra·rize \-ˈrär-ˌīz\ *vt* **-rized; -riz·ing** (1875) : to treat with curare — **cu·ra·ri·za·tion** \-ˌrär-ə-ˈzā-shən\ *n*

cu·ras·sow \ˈkyu̇r-ə-ˌsō, ˈku̇r-\ *n* [alter. of *Curaçao*] (1685) : any of several large arboreal gallinaceous game birds (family Cracidae, esp. genus *Crax*) of So. and Central America

[1]**cu·rate** \ˈkyu̇r-ət *also* ˈkyu̇r-ˌāt\ *n* [ME, fr. ML *curatus,* fr. *cura* cure of souls, fr. L, care] (14c) **1** : a clergyman in charge of a parish **2** : a clergyman serving as assistant (as to a rector) in a parish

[2]**cu·rate** \ˈkyu̇r-ˌāt, kyu̇-ˈrāt\ *vt* **cu·rat·ed; cu·rat·ing** (1909) : to act as curator of ⟨~ a museum⟩ ⟨an exhibit *curated* by the museum's director⟩

curate's egg *n* [fr. the story of a curate who was given a stale egg by his bishop and declared that parts of it were excellent] (1905) *chiefly Brit* : something with both good and bad parts or qualities

\ə\ **abut** \ᵊ\ kitten, F table \ər\ **fur**ther \a\ **a**sh \ā\ **a**ce \ä\ m**o**p, m**a**r
\au̇\ **ou**t \ch\ **ch**in \e\ b**e**t \ē\ **ea**sy \g\ **g**o \i\ h**i**t \ī\ **i**ce \j\ **j**ob
\ŋ\ si**ng** \ō\ g**o** \ȯ\ l**aw** \ȯi\ b**oy** \th\ **th**in \t͟h\ **th**e \ü\ l**oo**t \u̇\ f**oo**t
\y\ **y**et \zh\ vi**si**on, bei**ge** \k, ⁿ, œ, ue, ʸ\ *see* Guide to Pronunciation

cu·ra·tive \ˈkyu̇r-ə-tiv\ *adj* (15c) : relating to or used in the cure of diseases : tending to cure — **curative** *n* — **cu·ra·tive·ly** *adv*
cu·ra·tor \ˈkyu̇r-ˌā-tər, kyu̇-ˈrā-, ˈkyu̇r-ə-\ *n* [L, fr. *curare* to care, fr. *cura* care] (1561) : one who has the care and superintendence of something; *esp* : one in charge of a museum, zoo, or other place of exhibit — **cu·ra·to·ri·al** \ˌkyu̇r-ə-ˈtȯr-ē-əl\ *adj* — **cu·ra·tor·ship** \ˈkyu̇r-ˌā-tər-ˌship, kyu̇-ˈrā-, ˈkyu̇r-ə-\ *n*
[1]**curb** \ˈkərb\ *n* [MF *courbe* curve, curved piece of wood or iron, fr. *courbe* curved, fr. L *curvus*] (15c) **1** : a bit that exerts severe pressure on a horse's jaws; *also* : the chain or strap attached to it — see BIT illustration **2** : an enclosing frame, border, or edging **3** : CHECK, RESTRAINT ⟨a price ∼⟩ **4** : a raised edge or margin to strengthen or confine **5** : an edging (as of concrete) built along a street to form part of a gutter **6** [fr. the fact that it orig. transacted its business on the street] : a market for trading in securities not listed on a stock exchange
[2]**curb** *vt* (1530) **1** : to furnish with a curb **2** : to check or control with or as if with a curb ⟨trying to ∼ her curiosity⟩ **3** : to lead (a dog) to a suitable place (as a gutter) for defecation ***syn*** see RESTRAIN
curb appeal *n* (1975) : the visual attractiveness of a house as seen from the street
curb·ing \ˈkər-biŋ\ *n* (1838) **1** : the material for a curb **2** : CURB
curb service *n* (1925) : service extended (as by a restaurant) to persons sitting in parked automobiles
curb·side \ˈkərb-ˌsīd\ *n, often attrib* (1946) **1** : the side of a pavement bordered by a curb **2** : SIDEWALK
[1]**curb·stone** \-ˌstōn\ *n* (1791) : a stone or edging of concrete forming a curb
[2]**curbstone** *adj* (1848) **1** : operating on the street without maintaining an office ⟨a ∼ broker⟩ **2** : not having the benefit of training or experience ⟨a ∼ critic⟩
curb weight *n* (1949) : the weight of an automobile with standard equipment and fuel, oil, and coolant
curch \ˈkərch\ *n* [ME] (14c) *Scot* : KERCHIEF 1
cur·cu·lio \(ˌ)kər-ˈkyü-lē-ˌō\ *n, pl* **-li·os** [L, grain weevil] (1756) : any of various weevils; *esp* : one that injures fruit
cur·cu·min \ˈkər-kyə-mən\ *n* [F *curcumine*, fr. *curcum-* (fr. NL *Curcuma*, the turmeric plant, fr. Ar *kurkum*) + *-ine* [1]-in] (1850) : an orange-yellow crystalline compound $C_{21}H_{20}O_6$ that constitutes the chief coloring principle of turmeric
[1]**curd** \ˈkərd\ *n* [ME *crud;* prob. akin to OE *crūdan* to press — more at CROWD] (15c) **1** : the thick casein-rich part of coagulated milk **2** : something suggesting the curd of milk — **curdy** \ˈkər-dē\ *adj*
[2]**curd** *vb* (15c) : COAGULATE, CURDLE
cur·dle \ˈkər-dᵊl\ *vb* **cur·dled; cur·dling** \ˈkərd-liŋ, ˈkər-dᵊl-iŋ\ [freq. of [2]*curd*] *vi* (1590) **1** : to form curds; *also* : to congeal as if by forming curds ⟨a scream *curdled* in her throat⟩ **2** : to go bad or wrong : SPOIL ∼ *vt* **1** : to cause curds to form in ⟨*curdled* milk⟩ **2** : SPOIL, SOUR
[1]**cure** \ˈkyu̇r\ *n* [ME, fr. AF, fr. ML & L; ML *cura,* cure of souls, fr. L, care] (14c) **1 a** : spiritual charge : CARE **b** : pastoral charge of a parish **2 a** : recovery or relief from a disease **b** : something (as a drug or treatment) that cures a disease **c** : a course or period of treatment ⟨take the ∼ for alcoholism⟩ **d** : SPA 1 **3** : a complete or permanent solution or remedy ⟨seeking a ∼ for unemployment⟩ **4** : a process or method of curing — **cure·less** \-ləs\ *adj*
[2]**cure** *vb* **cured; cur·ing** *vt* (14c) **1 a** : to restore to health, soundness, or normality **b** : to bring about recovery from ⟨∼ a disease⟩ **2 a** : to deal with in a way that eliminates or rectifies ⟨his small size, which time would ∼ for him —William Faulkner⟩ **b** : to free from something objectionable or harmful ⟨trying to ∼ him of a bad habit⟩ **3** : to prepare or alter esp. by chemical or physical processing for keeping or use ⟨fish *cured* with salt⟩ ∼ *vi* **1 a** : to undergo a curing process **b** : SET 11 **2** : to effect a cure — **cur·er** *n*
cu·ré \kyu̇-ˈrā, ˈkyu̇r-ˌā\ *n* [F, fr. OF, fr. ML *curatus* — more at CURATE] (1655) : a parish priest
cure–all \ˈkyu̇r-ˌȯl\ *n* (1801) : a remedy for all ills : PANACEA
cu·ret·tage \ˌkyu̇r-ə-ˈtäzh\ *n* (1897) : a surgical scraping or cleaning by means of a curette
[1]**cu·rette** *also* **cu·ret** \kyu̇-ˈret\ *n* [F *curette,* fr. *curer* to cure, fr. L *curare,* fr. *cura*] (1753) : a surgical instrument that has a scoop, ring, or loop at the tip and is used in performing curettage
[2]**curette** *also* **curet** *vt* **cu·rett·ed; cu·rett·ing** (1888) : to perform curettage on — **cu·rette·ment** \kyu̇-ˈret-mənt\ *n*
cur·few \ˈkər-(ˌ)fyü\ *n* [ME, fr. AF *coverfeu,* signal given to bank the hearth fire, curfew, fr. *coverir* to cover + *fu, feu* fire, fr. L *focus* hearth] (14c) **1** : the sounding of a bell at evening **2 a** : a regulation enjoining the withdrawal of usu. specified persons (as juveniles or military personnel) from the streets or the closing of business establishments or places of assembly at a stated hour **b** : a signal to announce the beginning of a curfew **c** : the hour at which a curfew becomes effective **d** : the period during which a curfew is in effect
cu·ria \ˈkyu̇r-ē-ə, ˈku̇r-\ *n, pl* **cu·ri·ae** \ˈkyu̇r-ē-ˌē, ˈku̇r-ē-ˌī\ [L, perh. fr. *co-* + *vir* man — more at VIRILE] (1600) **1 a** : a division of the ancient Roman people comprising several gentes of a tribe **b** : the place of assembly of one of these divisions **2 a** : the court of a medieval king **b** : a court of justice **3** *often cap* : the body of congregations, tribunals, and offices through which the pope governs the Roman Catholic Church — **cu·ri·al** \ˈkyu̇r-ē-əl, ˈku̇r-\ *adj*
cu·rie \ˈkyu̇r-(ˌ)ē, kyu̇-ˈrē\ *n* [Marie & Pierre *Curie*] (1910) **1** : a unit quantity of any radioactive nuclide in which 3.7×10^{10} disintegrations occur per second **2** : a unit of radioactivity equal to 3.7×10^{10} disintegrations per second
Curie point *n* (1911) **1** : the temperature at which there is a transition between the ferromagnetic and paramagnetic phases **2** : a temperature at which the anomalies that characterize a ferroelectric substance disappear — called also *Curie temperature*
cu·rio \ˈkyu̇r-ē-ˌō\ *n, pl* **cu·ri·os** [short for *curiosity*] (1849) : something (as a decorative object) considered novel, rare, or bizarre : CURIOSITY; *also* : an unusual or bizarre person
cu·ri·o·sa \ˌkyu̇r-ē-ˈō-sə, -ˈō-zə\ *n pl* [NL, fr. L, neut. pl. of *curiosus*] (1883) : CURIOSITIES, RARITIES; *esp* : unusual or erotic books
cu·ri·os·i·ty \ˌkyu̇r-ē-ˈä-s(ə-)tē\ *n, pl* **-ties** (14c) **1** : desire to know: **a** : inquisitive interest in others' concerns : NOSINESS **b** : interest leading to inquiry ⟨intellectual ∼⟩ **2** *archaic* : undue nicety or fastidiousness **3 a** : one that arouses interest esp. for uncommon or exotic characteristics **b** : an unusual knickknack : CURIO **c** : a curious trait or aspect
cu·ri·ous \ˈkyu̇r-ē-əs\ *adj* [ME, fr. AF *curios,* fr. L *curiosus* careful, inquisitive, fr. *cura* cure] (14c) **1 a** *archaic* : made carefully **b** *obs* : ABSTRUSE **c** *archaic* : precisely accurate **2 a** : marked by desire to investigate and learn **b** : marked by inquisitive interest in others' concerns : NOSY **3** : exciting attention as strange, novel, or unexpected : ODD ⟨a ∼ coincidence⟩ — **cu·ri·ous·ness** *n*
syn CURIOUS, INQUISITIVE, PRYING mean interested in what is not one's personal or proper concern. CURIOUS, a neutral term, basically connotes an active desire to learn or to know ⟨children are *curious* about everything⟩. INQUISITIVE suggests impertinent and habitual curiosity and persistent quizzing ⟨dreaded the visits of their *inquisitive* relatives⟩. PRYING implies busy meddling and officiousness ⟨*prying* neighbors who refuse to mind their own business⟩.
cu·ri·ous·ly \-lē\ *adv* (14c) **1** : in a curious manner ⟨seemed ∼ calm⟩ **2** : as is curious ⟨∼, he continues to win reelection⟩
cu·ri·um \ˈkyu̇r-ē-əm\ *n* [NL, fr. Marie & Pierre *Curie*] (1946) : a metallic radioactive element produced artificially — see ELEMENT table
[1]**curl** \ˈkər(-ə)l\ *vb* [ME, fr. *crul* curly, prob. fr. MD; akin to OHG *krol* curly] *vt* (14c) **1** : to form (as the hair) into coils or ringlets **2** : to form into a curved shape : TWIST ⟨∼*ed* his lip in a sneer⟩ **3** : to furnish with curls ∼ *vi* **1 a** : to grow in coils or spirals **b** : to form ripples or crinkles ⟨bacon ∼*ing* in a pan⟩ **2** : to move or progress in curves or spirals : WIND ⟨the path ∼*ed* along the mountainside⟩ **3** : TWIST, CONTORT **4** : to play the game of curling
[2]**curl** *n* (1578) **1** : a lock of hair that coils : RINGLET **2** : something having a spiral or winding form : COIL **3** : the action of curling : the state of being curled **4** : a curved or spiral marking in the grain of wood **5** : a hollow arch of water formed when the crest of a breaking wave spills forward **6** : a usu. short pass pattern in football in which a receiver runs downfield and then curves back toward the line of scrimmage **7** : a body-building exercise in which a weight held with the palms facing up is raised and lowered by flexing only the wrists or elbows
curl·er \ˈkər-lər\ *n* (1638) **1** : a player of curling **2** : one that curls; *esp* : a device on which hair is wound for curling
cur·lew \ˈkər-(ˌ)lü, ˈkərl-(ˌ)yü\ *n, pl* **curlews** *or* **curlew** [ME, fr. AF *curleu,* of imit. origin] (14c) : any of various largely brownish chiefly migratory birds (esp. genus *Numenius*) having long legs and a long slender down-curved bill and related to the sandpipers and snipes
[1]**cur·li·cue** *also* **cur·ly·cue** \ˈkər-lē-ˌkyü, -li-\ *n* [*curly* + *cue* a braid of hair] (1843) : a fancifully curved or spiral figure : FLOURISH
[2]**curlicue** *vb* **-cued; -cu·ing** *vi* (1844) : to form curlicues ∼ *vt* : to embellish with curlicues
curl·ing \ˈkər-liŋ\ *n* (1620) : a game in which two teams of four players each slide curling stones over a stretch of ice toward a target circle
curling iron *n* (1616) : a rod-shaped usu. metal instrument which is heated and around which a lock of hair to be curled or waved is wound
curling stone *n* (1620) : an ellipsoid stone or occas. piece of iron with a gooseneck handle used in the game of curling
curl·pa·per \ˈkər(-ə)l-ˌpā-pər\ *n* (ca. 1817) : a strip or piece of paper around which a lock of hair is wound for curling
curl up *vi* (1840) : to arrange oneself in or as if in a ball or curl ⟨*curl up* by the fire⟩ ⟨*curl up* with a good book⟩

curling stone

curly \ˈkər-lē\ *adj* **curl·i·er; -est** (1598) **1** : tending to curl; *also* : having curls ⟨∼ hair⟩ **2** : having the grain composed of fibers that undulate without crossing and that often form alternating light and dark lines ⟨∼ maple⟩ — **curl·i·ness** *n*
curly–coat·ed retriever \ˈkər-lē-ˈkō-təd-\ *n* (1885) : any of a breed of sporting dogs with a short curly black or liver-colored coat
curly endive *n* (1978) : FRISÉE
curly top *n* (1901) : a destructive plant disease of beets caused by a single-stranded DNA virus (species *Beet curly top virus* of the genus *Curtovirus,* family *Geminiviridae*) that kills young plants and causes curling and puckering of the leaves in older plants
cur·mud·geon \(ˌ)kər-ˈmə-jən\ *n* [origin unknown] (1568) **1** *archaic* : MISER **2** : a crusty, ill-tempered, and usu. old man — **cur·mud·geon·li·ness** \-lē-nəs\ *n* — **cur·mud·geon·ly** \-lē\ *adj*
curr \ˈkər\ *vi* [imit.] (1677) : to make a murmuring sound (as of doves)
cur·ragh *or* **cur·rach** \ˈkə-rə, -rək\ *n* [ME *currok,* fr. Ir *currach, curach*] (15c) : a usu. large coracle used esp. on the west coast of Ireland
cur·rant \ˈkər-ənt, ˈkə-rənt\ *n* [ME *raison of Coraunte,* lit., raisin of Corinth] (14c) **1** : a small seedless raisin grown chiefly in the Levant **2** : the acid edible fruit of various shrubs (genus *Ribes*) placed in either the saxifrage or gooseberry family; *also* : a plant bearing currants
cur·ren·cy \ˈkər-ən(t)-sē, ˈkə-rən(t)-\ *n, pl* **-cies** (1624) **1 a** : circulation as a medium of exchange **b** : general use, acceptance, or prevalence ⟨a story gaining ∼⟩ **c** : the quality or state of being current : CURRENTNESS **2 a** : something (as coins, treasury notes, and banknotes) that is in circulation as a medium of exchange **b** : paper money in circulation **c** : a common article for bartering **d** : a medium of verbal or intellectual expression
[1]**cur·rent** \ˈkər-ənt, ˈkə-rənt\ *adj* [ME *curraunt,* fr. AF *corant,* prp. of *cure, courre* to run, fr. L *currere* — more at CAR] (14c) **1 a** *archaic* : RUNNING, FLOWING **b (1)** : presently elapsing ⟨the ∼ year⟩ **(2)** : occurring in or existing at the present time ⟨the ∼ crisis⟩ **(3)** : most recent ⟨the magazine's ∼ issue⟩ **2** : used as a medium of exchange **3** : generally accepted, used, practiced, or prevalent at the moment ⟨∼ fashions⟩ — **cur·rent·ly** *adv* — **cur·rent·ness** *n*
[2]**current** *n* (14c) **1 a** : the part of a fluid body (as air or water) moving continuously in a certain direction **b** : the swiftest part of a stream **c** : a tidal or nontidal movement of lake or ocean water **d** : flow marked by force or strength **2 a** : a tendency or course of events that is usu. the result of an interplay of forces ⟨∼*s* of public opinion⟩ **b** : a prevailing mood : STRAIN **3** : a flow of electric charge; *also* : the rate of such flow ***syn*** see TENDENCY
current assets *n pl* (ca. 1909) : assets of a short-term nature that are readily convertible to cash
cur·ri·cle \ˈkər-i-kəl, ˈkə-ri-\ *n* [L *curriculum* running, chariot, fr. *currere*] (1752) : a 2-wheeled chaise usu. drawn by two horses

cur·ric·u·lar \kə-ˈri-kyə-lər\ *adj* (ca. 1909) **:** of or relating to a curriculum
cur·ric·u·lum \-ləm\ *n, pl* **-la** \-lə\ *also* **-lums** [NL, fr. L, running, course] (1824) **1 :** the courses offered by an educational institution **2 :** a set of courses constituting an area of specialization
cur·ric·u·lum vi·tae \kə-ˈri-kyə-ləm-ˈwē-ˌtī, -kə-ləm-, -ˈwē-ˌtī, -ˈvī-ˌtē\ *n, pl* **cur·ric·u·la vitae** \-lə-\ [L, course of (one's) life] (1902) **:** a short account of one's career and qualifications prepared typically by an applicant for a position
cur·ri·ery \ˈkər-ē-ə-rē, ˈkə-rē-\ *n, pl* **-er·ies** (ca. 1889) **1 :** the trade of a currier of leather **2 :** a place where currying is done
cur·rish \ˈkər-ish\ *adj* (15c) **1 :** IGNOBLE **2 :** resembling a cur **:** MONGREL — **cur·rish·ly** *adv*
[1]**cur·ry** \ˈkər-ē, ˈkə-rē\ *vt* **cur·ried; cur·ry·ing** [ME *currayen,* fr. AF *cunreier, correier* to prepare, curry, fr. VL **conredare,* fr. L *com-* + a base of Gmc origin; akin to Goth *garaiths* arrayed — more at READY] (13c) **1 :** to clean the coat of (as a horse) with a currycomb **2 :** to treat (tanned leather) esp. by incorporating oil or grease **3 :** BEAT, THRASH — **cur·ri·er** *n* — **curry favor** [ME *currayen favel* to curry a chestnut horse] **:** to seek to gain favor by flattery or attention
[2]**cur·ry** *also* **cur·rie** \ˈkər-ē, ˈkə-rē\ *n, pl* **curries** [Tamil *kaṟi* (or a cognate word in a Dravidian language)] (1681) **1 :** a food, dish, or sauce in Indian cuisine seasoned with a mixture of pungent spices; *also* **:** a food or dish seasoned with curry powder **2 :** CURRY POWDER
[3]**curry** *vt* **cur·ried; cur·ry·ing** (1839) **:** to flavor or cook with curry powder or a curry sauce
cur·ry·comb \-ˌkōm\ *n* (1573) **:** a comb made of rows of metallic teeth or serrated ridges and used esp. to curry horses — **currycomb** *vt*
curry powder *n* (1810) **:** a condiment consisting of several pungent ground spices (as cayenne pepper, fenugreek, and turmeric)
[1]**curse** \ˈkərs\ *n* [ME *curs,* fr. OE] (bef. 12c) **1 :** a prayer or invocation for harm or injury to come upon one **:** IMPRECATION **2 :** something that is cursed or accursed **3 :** evil or misfortune that comes as if in response to imprecation or as retribution **4 :** a cause of great harm or misfortune **:** TORMENT **5 :** MENSTRUATION — used with *the*
[2]**curse** *vb* **cursed; curs·ing** *vt* (bef. 12c) **1 :** to use profanely insolent language against **:** BLASPHEME ⟨∼ God and die —Job 2:9(REB)⟩ **2 a :** to call upon divine or supernatural power to send injury upon ⟨was *cursed* and fears he will die⟩ **b :** to execrate in fervent and often profane terms ⟨*cursed* by future generations unless we act now⟩ **3 :** to bring great evil upon **:** AFFLICT ⟨a land *cursed* with famine⟩ ∼ *vi* **:** to utter imprecations **:** SWEAR ⟨*cursing* loudly⟩
cursed \ˈkər-səd, ˈkərst\ *also* **curst** \ˈkərst\ *adj* (13c) **:** being under or deserving a curse — **cursed·ly** *adv* — **cursed·ness** *n*
[1]**cur·sive** \ˈkər-siv\ *adj* [F or ML; F *cursif,* fr. ML *cursivus,* lit., running, fr. L *cursus,* pp. of *currere* to run] (ca. 1784) **:** RUNNING, COURSING: as **a** *of writing* **:** flowing often with the strokes of successive characters joined and the angles rounded **b :** having a flowing, easy, impromptu character — **cur·sive·ly** *adv* — **cur·sive·ness** *n*
[2]**cursive** *n* (1838) **1 :** a manuscript written in cursive writing; *also* **:** cursive writing **2 :** a style of printed letter resembling handwriting
cur·sor \ˈkər-sər, -ˌsȯr\ *n* [L, runner, fr. *currere*] (1594) **:** a movable item used to mark a position: as **a :** a transparent slide with a line attached to a slide rule **b :** a visual cue (as a flashing rectangle) on a video display that indicates position (as for data entry)
cur·so·ri·al \ˌkər-ˈsȯr-ē-əl\ *adj* (1836) **:** adapted to or involving running
cur·so·ry \ˈkərs-rē, ˈkər-sə-\ *adj* [LL *cursorius* of running, fr. L *currere*] (1601) **:** rapidly and often superficially performed or produced **:** HASTY ⟨a ∼ glance⟩ ***syn*** see SUPERFICIAL — **cur·so·ri·ly** \-rə-lē\ *adv* — **cur·so·ri·ness** \-rē-nəs\ *n*
curt \ˈkərt\ *adj* [L *curtus* mutilated, curtailed — more at SHEAR] (1630) **1 a :** sparing of words **:** TERSE ⟨wrote ∼ precise sentences⟩ **b :** marked by rude or peremptory shortness **:** BRUSQUE ⟨a ∼ refusal⟩ **2 :** shortened in linear dimension ***syn*** see BLUFF — **curt·ly** *adv* — **curt·ness** *n*
cur·tail \(ˌ)kər-ˈtāl\ *vt* [by folk etymology fr. earlier *curtal* to dock an animal's tail, fr. *curtal,* n., animal with a docked tail, fr. MF *courtault* — more at CURTAL] (1580) **:** to make less by or as if by cutting off or away some part ⟨∼ the power of the executive branch⟩ ⟨∼ inflation⟩ ***syn*** see SHORTEN — **cur·tail·er** \-ˈtā-lər\ *n*
cur·tail·ment \-ˈtāl-mənt\ *n* (1794) **:** the act of curtailing **:** the state of being curtailed
[1]**cur·tain** \ˈkər-tᵊn\ *n* [ME *curtine,* fr. AF, fr. LL *cortina* (trans. of Gk *aulaia,* fr. *aulē* court), fr. L *cohort-, cohors* enclosure, court — more at COURT] (14c) **1 :** a hanging screen usu. capable of being drawn back or up; *esp* **:** window drapery **2 :** a device or agency that conceals or acts as a barrier — compare IRON CURTAIN **3 a :** the part of a bastioned front that connects two neighboring bastions **b** (1) **:** a similar stretch of plain wall (2) **:** a nonbearing exterior wall **4 a :** the movable screen separating the stage from the auditorium of a theater **b :** the ascent or opening (as at the beginning of a play) of a stage curtain; *also* **:** its descent or closing (as at the end of an act) **c :** the final situation, line, or scene of an act or play **d :** the time at which a theatrical performance begins **e** *pl* **:** END; *esp* **:** DEATH ⟨it will be ∼*s* for us if we're caught⟩ — **cur·tain·less** \-ləs\ *adj*
[2]**curtain** *vt* **cur·tained; cur·tain·ing** \ˈkərt-niŋ, -ˈkər-tᵊn-iŋ\ (14c) **1 :** to furnish with or as if with curtains **2 :** to veil or shut off with or as if with a curtain
curtain call *n* (1884) **:** an appearance by a performer (as after the final curtain of a play) in response to the applause of the audience
curtain lecture *n* [fr. its orig. being given behind the curtains of a bed] (1633) **:** a private lecture by a wife to her husband
cur·tain–rais·er \ˈkər-tᵊn-ˌrā-zər\ *n* (1886) **1 :** a short play usu. of one scene that is presented before the main full-length drama **2 :** a usu. short preliminary to a main event
curtain wall *n* (1853) **:** a nonbearing exterior wall between columns or piers
cur·tal \ˈkər-tᵊl\ *adj* [MF *courtault,* fr. *court* short, fr. L *curtus*] (1576) **1** *obs* **:** having a docked tail **2** *obs* **:** BRIEF, CURTAILED **3** *archaic* **:** wearing a short frock
cur·tal ax *or* **cur·tle ax** \ˈkər-tᵊl-\ *n* [modif. of MF *coutelas*] (ca. 1580) *archaic* **:** CUTLASS
cur·te·sy \ˈkər-tə-sē\ *n, pl* **-sies** [ME *corteisie* courtesy] (1523) **:** a husband's interest upon the death of his wife in the real property of an estate that she either solely owned or inherited provided they bore a child capable of inheriting the estate — compare DOWER
cur·ti·lage \ˈkər-tə-lij\ *n* [ME, fr. AF *curtillage,* fr. *curtil* garden, curtilage, fr. *curt* court] (14c) **:** a piece of ground (as a yard or courtyard) within the fence surrounding a house
[1]**curt·sy** *also* **curt·sey** *n, pl* **curtsies** *also* **curtseys** (1533) **:** an act of civility, respect, or reverence made mainly by women and consisting of a slight lowering of the body with bending of the knees
[2]**curtsy** *also* **curtsey** \ˈkərt-sē\ *vi* **curt·sied** *also* **curt·seyed; curt·sy·ing** *also* **curt·sey·ing** [alter. of *courtesy*] (ca. 1553) **:** to make a curtsy
cu·rule \ˈkyu̇r-ˌül\ *adj* [L *curulis,* perh. alter. of *currulis* of a chariot, fr. *currus* chariot, fr. *currere* to run] (1600) **1 :** relating to or being a high-ranking dignitary of ancient Rome entitled to occupy a special chair **2 :** of, relating to, or being a chair or seat reserved for Romans of high rank that resembles a backless stool with curved legs; *also* **:** of, relating to, or being a 19th century seat with legs of a similar style
cur·va·ceous *also* **cur·va·cious** \ˌkər-ˈvā-shəs\ *adj* (ca. 1935) **:** having or suggesting the curves of a well-proportioned feminine figure ⟨a ∼ actress⟩; *broadly* **:** having a smoothly curving shape ⟨a ∼ coastline⟩
cur·va·ture \ˈkər-və-ˌchu̇r, -chər, -ˌtyu̇r, -ˌtu̇r\ *n* (1603) **1 :** the act of curving **:** the state of being curved **2 :** a measure or amount of curving; *specif* **:** the rate of change of the angle through which the tangent to a curve turns in moving along the curve and which for a circle is equal to the reciprocal of the radius **3 a :** an abnormal curving (as of the spine) **b :** a curved surface of an organ
[1]**curve** \ˈkərv\ *adj* [ME, fr. L *curvus;* akin to Gk *kyrtos* convex, MIr *cruinn* round] (15c) *archaic* **:** bent or formed into a curve
[2]**curve** *vb* **curved; curv·ing** [L *curvare,* fr. *curvus*] *vi* (1594) **:** to have or take a turn, change, or deviation from a straight line or plane surface without sharp breaks or angularity ∼ *vt* **1 :** to cause to curve **2 :** to throw a curveball to (a batter) **3 :** to grade (as an examination) on a curve
[3]**curve** *n* (1666) **1 a :** a line esp. when curved: as (1) **:** the path of a moving point (2) **:** a line defined by an equation so that the coordinates of its points are functions of a single independent variable or parameter **b :** the graph of a variable **2 :** something curved: as **a :** a curving line of the human body **b** *pl* **:** PARENTHESIS **3 a :** CURVEBALL **b :** TRICK, DECEPTION **4 :** a distribution indicating the relative performance of individuals measured against each other that is used esp. in assigning good, medium, or poor grades to usu. predetermined proportions of students rather than in assigning grades based on predetermined standards of achievement **5 :** TREND ⟨a growth ∼ in advertising revenues⟩; *esp* **:** a prevalent trend or rate of progress — often used in the phrases *ahead of the curve* and *behind the curve* ⟨companies that are behind the ∼ in adopting new technologies⟩ — **curvy** \ˈkər-vē\ *adj*
curve·ball \ˈkərv-ˌbȯl\ *n* (1936) **:** a slow or moderately fast baseball pitch thrown with spin to make it swerve downward and usu. to the left when thrown from the right hand or to the right when thrown from the left hand — **curveball** *vb*
curve fitting *n* (1902) **:** the empirical determination of a curve or function that approximates a set of data
[1]**cur·vet** \(ˌ)kər-ˈvet\ *n* [It *corvetta,* fr. MF *courbette,* fr. *courber* to curve, fr. L *curvare*] (1575) **:** a prancing leap of a horse in which the hind legs are raised just before the forelegs touch the ground
[2]**curvet** *vi* **-vet·ted** *or* **-vet·ed; -vet·ting** *or* **-vet·ing** (1592) **:** to make a curvet; *also* **:** PRANCE, CAPER
cur·vi·lin·ear \ˌkər-və-ˈli-nē-ər\ *adj* [L *curvus* + *linea* line] (1696) **1 :** consisting of or bounded by curved lines **:** represented by a curved line **2 :** marked by flowing tracery ⟨∼ Gothic⟩ — **cur·vi·lin·ear·i·ty** \-ˌli-nē-ˈer-ə-tē, -ˈa-rə-\ *n*
cush·at \ˈkə-shət\ *n* [ME *cowschote,* fr. OE *cūscote*] (bef. 12c) *chiefly Scot* **:** WOOD PIGEON
cu·shaw \ku̇-ˈshȯ, ˈkü-ˌ\ *n* [origin unknown] (1698) **:** a squash of any of several cultivars of winter squash (*Cucurbita argyrosperma* syn. *C. mixta* and *C. moschata*)
Cush·ing's disease \ˈku̇-shiŋz-\ *n* [Harvey *Cushing*] (ca. 1935) **:** Cushing's syndrome esp. when caused by excessive production of ACTH by the pituitary gland
Cushing's syndrome *n* (1937) **:** an abnormal bodily condition that is caused by excess corticosteroids and esp. cortisol usu. from adrenal or pituitary hyperfunction and is characterized esp. by obesity, hypertension, muscular weakness, and easy bruising
[1]**cush·ion** \ˈku̇-shən\ *n* [ME *cusshin,* fr. AF *cussin, quissin,* fr. VL **coxinus,* fr. L *coxa* hip — more at COXA] (14c) **1 :** a soft pillow or pad usu. used for sitting, reclining, or kneeling **2 :** a bodily part resembling a pad **3 :** something resembling a cushion: as **a :** PILLOW 2 **b :** RAT 3 **c :** a pad of springy rubber along the inside of the rim of a billiard table **d :** a padded insert in a shoe **e :** an elastic body for reducing shock **f :** a mat laid under a large rug to ease the effect of wear **4 a :** something (as an economic factor or a medical procedure) serving to mitigate the effects of disturbances or disorders **b :** a reserve supply (as of money) **c :** a comfortable lead ⟨a 4–0 ∼ in the ninth inning⟩ — **cush·ion·less** \-ləs\ *adj* — **cush·iony** \-shə-nē\ *adj*
[2]**cushion** *vt* **cush·ioned; cush·ion·ing** \ˈku̇-sh(ə-)niŋ\ (ca. 1738) **1 :** to seat or place on a cushion **2 :** to suppress by ignoring **3 :** to furnish with a cushion ⟨a ∼*ed* seat⟩ **4 a :** to mitigate the effects of ⟨trying to ∼ the blow⟩ **b :** to protect against force or shock ⟨∼ the ride⟩ **5 :** to check gradually so as to minimize shock of moving parts
Cush·it·ic \kə-ˈshi-tik, ku̇-\ *n* [*Cush* (Kush), Africa] (ca. 1903) **:** a subfamily of the Afro-Asiatic language family comprising various languages spoken in eastern Africa and esp. in Ethiopia, Djibouti, Somalia, and Kenya — **Cushitic** *adj*
cushy \ˈku̇-shē\ *adj* **cush·i·er; cush·i·est** [Hindi *ḵẖuś* & Urdu *khush* fr. Pers *khūsh*] (1915) **:** entailing little hardship or difficulty ⟨a ∼ job with a high salary⟩ — **cush·i·ly** \ˈku̇-shə-lē\ *adv*

\ə\ **abut** \ᵊ\ **kitten,** F **table** \ər\ **further** \a\ **ash** \ā\ **ace** \ä\ **mop, mar**
\au̇\ **out** \ch\ **chin** \e\ **bet** \ē\ **easy** \g\ **go** \i\ **hit** \ī\ **ice** \j\ **job**
\ŋ\ **sing** \ō\ **go** \ȯ\ **law** \ȯi\ **boy** \th\ **thin** \t͟h\ **the** \ü\ **loot** \u̇\ **foot**
\y\ **yet** \zh\ **vision, beige** \ḵ, ⁿ, œ, ue, ʸ\ *see* Guide to Pronunciation

cusk \ˈkəsk\ *n, pl* **cusk** *or* **cusks** [prob. alter. of *tusk,* a kind of codfish] (1616) **1 :** a large edible No. Atlantic fish (*Brosme brosme*) of the cod family **2 :** BURBOT

cusp \ˈkəsp\ *n* [L *cuspis* point] (1585) **:** POINT, APEX: as **a :** a point of transition (as from one historical period to the next) **:** TURNING POINT; *also* **:** EDGE, VERGE ⟨on the ~ of stardom⟩ **b :** either horn of a crescent moon **c :** a fixed point on a mathematical curve at which a point tracing the curve would exactly reverse its direction of motion **d :** an ornamental pointed projection formed by or arising from the intersection of two arcs or foils **e** (1) **:** a point on the grinding surface of a tooth (2) **:** a fold or flap of a cardiac valve — **cus·pate** \ˈkəs-ˌpāt, -pət\ *adj* — **cusped** \ˈkəspt\ *adj*

cus·pid \ˈkəs-pəd\ *n* [*bicuspid*] (1841) **:** CANINE 1

cus·pi·date \ˈkəs-pə-ˌdāt\ *adj* [L *cuspidatus,* pp. of *cuspidare* to make pointed, fr. *cuspid-, cuspis* point] (1692) **:** having a cusp **:** terminating in a point ⟨a ~ leaf⟩ ⟨~ molars⟩

cus·pi·da·tion \ˌkəs-pə-ˈdā-shən\ *n* (1848) **:** decoration with cusps

cus·pi·dor \ˈkəs-pə-ˌdȯr\ *n* [Pg *cuspidouro* place for spitting, fr. *cuspir* to spit, fr. L *conspuere,* fr. *com-* + *spuere* to spit — more at SPEW] (1735) **:** SPITTOON

[1]**cuss** \ˈkəs\ *n* [alter. of *curse*] (1771) **1 a :** CURSE 1 **b :** CURSE 2 **2 :** FELLOW 4c

[2]**cuss** *vt* (1768) **:** CURSE — often used with *out* ⟨got ~*ed* out by his boss⟩ ~ *vi* **:** CURSE — **cuss·er** *n*

cuss·ed \ˈkə-səd\ *adj* (1834) **1 :** CURSED **2 :** OBSTINATE, CANTANKEROUS — **cuss·ed·ly** *adv* — **cuss·ed·ness** \-nəs\ *n*

cuss·word \ˈkəs-ˌwərd\ *n* (1872) **1 :** SWEARWORD **2 :** a term of abuse **:** a derogatory term

cus·tard \ˈkəs-tərd\ *n* [ME, a kind of pie, alter. of *crustarde, crustade,* prob. fr. AF **crustade,* fr. *cruste* crust, fr. L *crusta* — more at CRUST] (ca. 1706) **:** a pudding-like usu. sweetened mixture made with eggs and milk — **cus·tardy** \-tər-dē\ *adj*

custard apple *n* (1657) **1 a :** any of several chiefly tropical American soft-fleshed edible fruits **b :** any of a genus (*Annona* of the family Annonaceae, the custard-apple family) of trees or shrubs bearing this fruit; *esp* **:** a small West Indian tree (*A. reticulata*) **2 :** PAWPAW 2

cus·to·di·al \ˌkəs-ˈtō-dē-əl\ *adj* (1772) **1 a :** relating to guardianship **b :** relating to, providing, or being protective care or services for basic needs ⟨nursing and ~ care⟩ **2 :** having sole or primary custody of a child ⟨the ~ parent⟩

cus·to·di·an \ˌkəs-ˈtō-dē-ən\ *n* (1602) **:** one that guards and protects or maintains; *esp* **:** one entrusted with guarding and keeping property or records or with custody or guardianship of prisoners or inmates — **cus·to·di·an·ship** \-ˌship\ *n*

cus·to·dy \ˈkəs-tə-dē\ *n, pl* **-dies** [ME *custodie,* fr. L *custodia* guarding, fr. *custod-, custos* guardian] (15c) **:** immediate charge and control (as over a ward or a suspect) exercised by a person or an authority; *also* **:** SAFEKEEPING

[1]**cus·tom** \ˈkəs-təm\ *n* [ME *custume,* fr. AF, fr. L *consuetudin-, consuetudo,* fr. *consuescere* to accustom, fr. *com-* + *suescere* to accustom; akin to *suus* one's own — more at SUICIDE] (13c) **1 a :** a usage or practice common to many or to a particular place or class or habitual with an individual **b :** long-established practice considered as unwritten law **c :** repeated practice **d :** the whole body of usages, practices, or conventions that regulate social life **2** *pl* **a :** duties, tolls, or imposts imposed by the sovereign law of a country on imports or exports **b** *usu sing in constr* **:** the agency, establishment, or procedure for collecting such customs **3 a :** business patronage **b :** usu. habitual patrons **:** CUSTOMERS ***syn*** see HABIT

[2]**custom** *adj* (1830) **1 :** made or performed according to personal order **2 :** specializing in custom work or operation ⟨a ~ tailor⟩

cus·tom·ary \ˈkəs-tə-ˌmer-ē, -ˌme-rē\ *adj* (1535) **1 :** based on or established by custom **2 :** commonly practiced, used, or observed ***syn*** see USUAL — **cus·tom·ar·i·ly** \ˌkəs-tə-ˈmer-ə-lē, -ˈme-rə-\ *adv* — **cus·tom·ar·i·ness** \ˈkəs-tə-ˌmer-ē-nəs, -ˌme-rē-\ *n*

cus·tom–built \ˈkəs-təm-ˈbilt\ *adj* (1925) **:** built to individual specifications ⟨a ~ house⟩

cus·tom·er \ˈkəs-tə-mər\ *n* [ME *custumer,* fr. *custume*] (15c) **1 :** one that purchases a commodity or service **2 :** an individual usu. having some specified distinctive trait ⟨a real tough ~⟩

cus·tom·house \ˈkəs-təm-ˌhau̇s\ *also* **cus·toms·house** \-təmz-\ *n* (15c) **:** a building where customs and duties are paid or collected and where vessels are entered and cleared

cus·tom·ise *Brit var of* CUSTOMIZE

cus·tom·ize \ˈkəs-tə-ˌmīz\ *vt* **-ized; -iz·ing** (1923) **:** to build, fit, or alter according to individual specifications — **cus·tom·iz·able** \ˌkəs-tə-ˈmī-zə-bəl\ *adj* — **cus·tom·i·za·tion** \-mə-ˈzā-shən\ *n* — **cus·tom·iz·er** *n*

cus·tom–made \ˈkəs-tə(m)-ˈmād\ *adj* (1845) **:** made to individual specifications ⟨~ clothing⟩

cus·tom–tai·lor \-ˈtā-lər\ *vt* (1895) **:** to alter, plan, or build according to individual specifications or needs

[1]**cut** \ˈkət\ *vb* **cut; cut·ting** [ME *cutten*] *vt* (13c) **1 a :** to penetrate with or as if with an edged instrument **b :** to hurt the feelings of **c :** to strike sharply with a cutting effect **d :** to strike (a ball) with a glancing blow that imparts a reverse spin **e :** to experience the growth of (a tooth) through the gum **2 a :** TRIM, PARE ⟨~ one's nails⟩ **b :** to shorten by omissions ⟨~ the manuscript⟩ **c :** DILUTE, ADULTERATE ⟨~ the whiskey with water⟩ **d :** to reduce in amount ⟨~ costs⟩ **3 a :** MOW, REAP ⟨~ hay⟩ **b** (1) **:** to divide into parts with an edged tool ⟨~ bread⟩ (2) **:** FELL, HEW **c** (1) **:** to separate or discharge from an organization ⟨~ them from the team⟩ (2) **:** to single out and isolate ⟨~ a calf out from the herd⟩ **d :** to turn (as a steering wheel) sharply ⟨the driver ~ the wheel hard⟩ **e :** to go or pass around or about **:** BYPASS ⟨~ the checkout line⟩ **4 a :** to divide into segments ⟨~ the cake⟩ **b :** INTERSECT, CROSS ⟨one line *cutting* another⟩ **c :** BREAK, INTERRUPT ⟨~ our supply lines⟩ **d** (1) **:** to divide (a deck of cards) into two portions (2) **:** to draw (a card) from the deck **e :** to divide into shares **:** SPLIT **f :** ANALYZE, BREAK DOWN ⟨any way you ~ it, we won⟩ **5 a :** to make by or as if by cutting: as (1) **:** CARVE ⟨~ stone⟩ (2) **:** to shape by grinding ⟨~ a diamond⟩ (3) **:** ENGRAVE (4) **:** to shear or hollow out ⟨~ a groove⟩ **b** (1) **:** to sing, play, or act for the recording of ⟨~ an album⟩ ⟨~ a commercial⟩ (2) **:** to sing or play (as a song or a track) for a studio recording **c :** to type on a stencil **d :** EDIT 1b ⟨~ a motion picture⟩ **6 a :** STOP, CEASE ⟨~ the nonsense⟩ **b :** to refuse to recognize (an acquaintance) ⟨they ~ her dead at the party⟩ **c :** to absent oneself from (as a class) **d :** to stop (a motor) by opening a switch **e :** to stop the filming of (a motion-picture scene) **7 a :** to engage in (a frolicsome or mischievous action) ⟨on summer nights strange capers are ~ under the thin guise of a Christian festival —D. C. Peattie⟩ **b :** to give the appearance or impression of ⟨~ a fine figure⟩ **8 :** to be able to manage or handle — usu. used in negative constructions ⟨can't ~ that kind of work anymore⟩ **9 a :** to yield or accord to another **:** GIVE ⟨~ me some slack⟩ **b :** to fill out and sign (a check) ~ *vi* **1 a :** to function as or as if as an edged tool **b :** to undergo incision or severance ⟨cheese ~*s* easily⟩ **c :** to perform the operation of dividing, severing, incising, or intersecting **d :** to make a stroke with a whip, sword, or other weapon **e :** to wound feelings or sensibilities **f :** to cause constriction or chafing **g :** to be of effect, influence, or significance ⟨an analysis that ~*s* deep⟩ **2 a** (1) **:** to divide a pack of cards esp. in order to decide the deal or settle a bet (2) **:** to draw a card from the pack **b :** to divide spoils **:** SPLIT **3 a :** to proceed obliquely from a straight course ⟨~ across the yard⟩ **b :** to move swiftly ⟨a yacht *cutting* through the water⟩ **c :** to describe an oblique or diagonal line **d :** to change sharply in direction **:** SWERVE **e :** to make an abrupt transition from one sound or image to another in motion pictures, radio, or television **f :** to make a sudden transition or imaginative leap ⟨the story ~*s* to 1917⟩ **4 :** to stop photographing motion pictures **5 :** to advance by skipping or bypassing another ⟨~ to the front of the line⟩ — **cut a deal :** to negotiate an agreement — **cut both ways :** to have both favorable and unfavorable results or implications — **cut corners :** to perform some action in the quickest, easiest, or cheapest way — **cut ice :** to be of importance — usu. used in negative constructions ⟨his opinion *cuts* no *ice* with me⟩ — **cut it :** to cut the mustard — **cut loose 1 :** to free from control or restraint ⟨*cut* us *loose* from the contract⟩ **2 :** to act without restraint ⟨enjoyed *cutting loose* at nightclubs⟩ — **cut one's teeth :** to learn, do, or perform as a beginning or at the start of one's career ⟨an actress who *cut her teeth* on television⟩ — **cut the mustard :** to achieve the standard of performance necessary for success — **cut to the chase :** to get to the point

[2]**cut** *n* (1530) **1 :** a product of cutting: as **a** (1) **:** an opening made with an edged instrument (2) **:** a wound made by something sharp **:** GASH **b :** a creek, channel, or inlet made by excavation or worn by natural action **c :** a surface or outline left by cutting **d :** a passage cut as a roadway **e :** a grade or step esp. in a social scale ⟨a ~ above the ordinary⟩ **f :** a subset of a set such that when it is subtracted from the set the remainder is not connected **g :** a pictorial illustration **h :** TRACK 1e(2) **2 :** the act or an instance of cutting: as **a :** a gesture or expression that hurts the feelings ⟨made an unkind ~⟩ **b :** a straight passage or course **c :** a stroke or blow with the edge of a knife or other edged tool **d :** a lash with or as if with a whip **e :** the act of reducing or removing a part ⟨a ~ in pay⟩ **f :** an act or turn of cutting cards; *also* **:** the result of cutting **g :** the elimination of part of a large field from further participation, consideration, or competition (as in a golf tournament) — often used with *miss* or *make* to denote respectively being or not being among those eliminated ⟨played well and made the ~⟩ **3 :** something that is cut or cut off: as **a :** a length of cloth varying from 40 to 100 yards (36.6 to 91.4 meters) **b :** the yield of products cut esp. during one harvest **c :** a segment or section of a meat carcass or a part of one **d :** a group of animals selected from a herd **e :** SHARE ⟨took his ~ of the profits⟩ **4 :** a voluntary absence from a class **5 a :** a stroke that cuts a ball; *also* **:** the spin imparted by such a stroke **b :** a swing by a batter at a pitched baseball **c :** an exchange of captures in checkers **6 :** a result of editing: as **a :** an abrupt transition from one sound or image to another in motion pictures, radio, or television **b :** an edited version of a film **7 a :** the shape and style in which a thing is cut, formed, or made ⟨clothes of the latest ~⟩ **b :** PATTERN, TYPE **c :** HAIRCUT — **cut of one's jib :** APPEARANCE, STYLE

[3]**cut** *adj* **:** marked by a well-developed and highly defined musculature ⟨~ abs⟩

cut·abil·i·ty \ˌkə-tə-ˈbi-lə-tē\ *n* (1965) **:** the proportion of lean salable meat yielded by a carcass

cut–and–dried \ˌkət-ᵊn-ˈdrīd\ *also* **cut–and–dry** \-ˈdrī\ *adj* (1710) **:** being or done according to a plan, set procedure, or formula **:** ROUTINE ⟨a ~ presentation⟩

cut–and–paste \-ˈpāst\ *adj* (1953) **:** pieced together by excerpting and combining fragments from multiple sources ⟨the book was a ~ job⟩

cut–and–try \-ˈtrī\ *adj* (1903) **:** marked by trial and error ⟨~ methods⟩ ⟨~ testing⟩

cu·ta·ne·ous \kyü-ˈtā-nē-əs\ *adj* [NL *cutaneus,* fr. L *cutis* skin — more at HIDE] (1578) **:** of, relating to, or affecting the skin ⟨a ~ nerve⟩ ⟨~ anthrax⟩ — **cu·ta·ne·ous·ly** *adv*

[1]**cut·away** \ˈkət-ə-ˌwā\ *adj* (1841) **:** having or showing parts cut away ⟨a ~ drawing⟩

[2]**cutaway** *n* (1849) **1 :** a coat with skirts tapering from the front waistline to form tails at the back **2 a :** a cutaway picture or representation **b :** a shot that interrupts the main action of a film or television program to take up a related subject or to depict action supposed to be going on at the same time as the main action **3 :** a back dive in which the head is lowered toward the board after the takeoff

cut·back \ˈkət-ˌbak\ *n* (1897) **1 :** something cut back **2 :** REDUCTION ⟨a ~ in funding⟩

cut back *vt* (1871) **:** to shorten by cutting **:** PRUNE ~ *vi* **1 :** to interrupt the sequence of a plot (as of a movie) by introducing events prior to those last presented **2 :** CUT DOWN ⟨*cut back* on sugar⟩

cutch \ˈkəch\ *n* [modif. of Malay *kachu*] (1759) **:** CATECHU a

cut down *vt* (1571) **1 a :** to strike down and kill or incapacitate **b :** KNOCK DOWN **2 a :** to remodel by removing extras or unwanted furnishings and fittings **b :** to remake in a smaller size ~ *vi* **:** to reduce or curtail volume or activity ⟨*cut down* on smoking⟩ — **cut down to size :** to reduce from an inflated or exaggerated importance to true or suitable stature

[1]**cute** \ˈkyüt\ *adj* **cut·er; cut·est** [short for *acute*] (ca. 1731) **1 a :** clever or shrewd often in an underhanded manner **b :** IMPERTINENT, SMART-ALECKY ⟨don't get ~ with me⟩ **2 :** attractive or pretty esp. in

a childish, youthful, or delicate way **3 :** obviously straining for effect — **cute·ly** *adv* — **cute·ness** *n*

[2]**cute** *n* (1965) **:** the quality or state of being cute or cutesy; *also* **:** an instance of cuteness or cutesiness — usu. used in pl. ⟨a movie suffering from a case of the ~*s*⟩

cute·sy \ˈkyüt-sē\ *adj* **cute·si·er; -est** [*cute* + *-sy* (as in *folksy*)] (1914) **:** self-consciously or excessively cute — **cute·si·ness** *n*

cut glass *n* (1761) **:** glass ornamented with patterns cut into its surface by an abrasive wheel and polished

cut–grass \ˈkət-ˌgras\ *n* (ca. 1818) **:** a grass (esp. genus *Leersia*) with minute hooked bristles along the edges of the leaf blade

cu·ti·cle \ˈkyü-ti-kəl\ *n* [L *cuticula,* dim. of *cutis* skin — more at HIDE] (1615) **1 :** an outer covering layer: as **a :** an external envelope (as of an insect) secreted usu. by epidermal cells **b :** the outermost layer of animal integument composed of epidermis **c :** a thin continuous fatty or waxy film on the external surface of many higher plants that consists chiefly of cutin **d :** the outermost membranous layer of a hair consisting of overlapping scales of epithelial cells **2 :** dead or horny epidermis — **cu·tic·u·lar** \kyu̇-ˈti-kyə-lər\ *adj*

cut·ie *or* **cut·ey** \ˈkyü-tē\ *n, pl* **cuties** *or* **cuteys** [*cute* + *-ie*] (1908) **:** an attractive person; *esp* **:** a pretty girl

cutie–pie \-ˌpī\ *n* (1956) **:** a cute person **:** SWEETHEART

cu·tin \ˈkyü-tᵊn\ *n* [ISV, fr. L *cutis*] (ca. 1872) **:** an insoluble mixture containing waxes, fatty acids, soaps, and resinous material that forms a continuous layer on the outer epidermal wall of a plant

cut–in \ˈkət-ˌin\ *n* (1883) **:** something cut in — **cut–in** *adj*

cut in *vi* (1612) **1 :** to thrust oneself into a position between others or belonging to another **2 :** to join in something suddenly ⟨*cut in* on the conversation⟩ **3 :** to interrupt a dancing couple and take one as one's partner **4 :** to become automatically connected or started in operation ⟨waiting for the auxiliary motor to *cut in*⟩ ~ *vt* **1 :** to mix with cutting motions ⟨after sifting the flour into a mixing bowl, *cut* the lard *in*⟩ **2 :** to introduce into a number, group, or sequence **3 :** to connect into an electrical circuit to a mechanical apparatus so as to permit operation **4 :** to include esp. among those benefiting or favored ⟨*cut* them *in* on the profits⟩

cu·tin·ized \ˈkyü-tᵊn-ˌīzd\ *adj* (1901) **:** infiltrated with cutin

cu·tis \ˈkyü-təs\ *n, pl* **cu·tes** \ˈkyü-ˌtēz\ *or* **cu·tis·es** [L] (1603) **:** DERMIS

cut·lass \ˈkət-ləs\ *n* [MF *coutelas,* aug. of *coutel* knife, fr. L *cultellus,* dim. of *culter* knife, plowshare] (1584) **1 :** a short curving sword formerly used by sailors on warships **2 :** MACHETE

cut·ler \ˈkət-lər\ *n* [ME, fr. AF *cuteler,* fr. LL *cultellarius,* fr. L *cultellus*] (14c) **:** one who makes, deals in, or repairs cutlery

cut·lery \ˈkət-lə-rē\ *n* (15c) **1 :** the business of a cutler **2 :** edged or cutting tools; *specif* **:** implements for cutting and eating food

cut·let \ˈkət-lət\ *n* [F *côtelette,* fr. OF *costelette,* dim. of *coste* rib, side, fr. L *costa* — more at COAST] (1682) **1 :** a small slice of meat ⟨a veal ~⟩ **2 :** a flat croquette of chopped meat or fish

cut·line \ˈkət-ˌlīn\ *n* (1943) **:** CAPTION, LEGEND

cut·off \ˈkət-ˌȯf\ *n* (1741) **1 :** the act or action of cutting off **2 a :** the new and relatively short channel formed when a stream cuts through the neck of an oxbow **b :** SHORTCUT 1 **c :** a channel made to straighten a stream **3 :** a device for cutting off **4 a :** something cut off **b** *pl* **:** shorts orig. made from jeans with the legs cut off at the knees or higher **5 :** the point, date, or period for a cutoff — **cutoff** *adj*

cut off *vt* (14c) **1 :** to bring to an untimely end **2 :** to stop the passage of ⟨*cut off* communications⟩ **3 :** SHUT OFF, BAR ⟨the river *cut off* their retreat⟩ **4 :** DISCONTINUE, TERMINATE ⟨*cut off* a subscription⟩ **5 :** SEPARATE, ISOLATE ⟨*cut* herself *off* from her family⟩ **6 :** DISINHERIT ⟨threatened to *cut* him *off* without a penny⟩ **7 a :** to stop the operation of **:** TURN OFF ⟨*cut off* the engine⟩ **b :** to stop or interrupt while in communication ⟨the operator *cut* me *off*⟩ ~ *vi* **:** to cease operating

cutoff man *n* (1967) **:** a player in baseball who relays a ball from an outfielder to the infield

cut·out \ˈkət-ˌau̇t\ *n* (1851) **1 :** something cut out or off from something else; *also* **:** the space or hole left after cutting **2 :** one that cuts out **3 :** an intermediary in a clandestine operation **4 :** a record album no longer in production that is sold at a discount — **cutout** *adj*

[1]**cut out** *vt* (15c) **1 :** to form by erosion **2 :** to determine or assign through necessity ⟨you've got your work *cut out* for you⟩ **3 :** to take the place of **:** SUPPLANT **4 :** to put an end to **:** desist from ⟨*cut out* wasteful spending⟩ **5 :** DEPRIVE, DEFRAUD ⟨*cut* him *out* of his share⟩ **6 a :** to remove from a series or circuit **:** DISCONNECT ⟨*cut out* a car from a train⟩ **b :** to make inoperative ~ *vi* **1 :** to depart in haste **2 :** to cease operating **3 :** to swerve out of a traffic line

[2]**cut out** *adj* (1645) **:** naturally fitted or suited ⟨not *cut out* to be a vet⟩

cut·over \ˈkət-ˈō-vər\ *adj* (1899) **:** having most of the salable timber cut down

cut–price \-ˈprīs\ *adj* (1910) *chiefly Brit* **:** CUT-RATE

cut·purse \ˈkət-ˌpərs\ *n* (14c) **:** PICKPOCKET

cut–rate \ˈkət-ˈrāt\ *adj* (1904) **1 :** marked by, offering, or making use of a reduced rate or price ⟨~ stores⟩ **2 :** SECOND-RATE, CHEAP

cut·ta·ble \ˈkə-tə-bəl\ *adj* (15c) **:** capable of being cut **:** ready for cutting ⟨~ timber⟩

cut·ter \ˈkə-tər\ *n* (15c) **1 :** one that cuts: **a :** one whose work is cutting or involves cutting **b** (1) **:** an instrument, machine, machine part, or tool that cuts (2) **:** a device for vibrating a cutting stylus in disc recording; *also* **:** the stylus or its point **2 a :** a ship's boat for carrying stores or passengers **b :** a single-masted fore-and-aft rigged sailing vessel **c :** a small armed vessel in government service **3 :** a light sleigh

[1]**cut·throat** \ˈkət-ˌthrōt\ *n* (1535) **1 :** KILLER, MURDERER **2 :** a cruel unprincipled person

[2]**cutthroat** *adj* (1565) **1 :** MURDEROUS, CRUEL **2 :** marked by unprincipled practices **:** RUTHLESS ⟨~ competition⟩ **3 :** characterized by each player playing independently rather than having a permanent partner — used esp. of partnership games adapted for three players ⟨~ bridge⟩

cutthroat contract *n* (ca. 1944) **:** contract bridge in which partnerships are determined by the bidding

cutthroat trout *n* (ca. 1891) **:** a large spotted trout (*Oncorhynchus clarki* syn. *Salmo clarki*) chiefly of northwestern No. America that has reddish streaks on the integument of the lower jaw — called also *cutthroat*

cut time *n* (1951) **:** duple or quadruple time with the beat represented by a half note

[1]**cut·ting** \ˈkə-tiŋ\ *n* (14c) **1 :** something cut or cut off or out: as **a :** a plant section originating from stem, leaf, or root and capable of developing into a new plant **b :** HARVEST **2 :** something made by cutting; *esp* **:** RECORD 4

[2]**cutting** *adj* (15c) **1 :** given to or designed for cutting; *esp* **:** SHARP, EDGED **2 :** marked by sharp piercing cold ⟨~ winds⟩ **3 :** inclined or likely to wound the feelings of others esp. because of a ruthless incisiveness ⟨a ~ remark⟩ **4 :** INTENSE, PIERCING ⟨a ~ pain⟩ — **cut·ting·ly** \-tiŋ-lē\ *adv*

cutting board *n* (1639) **:** a board on which something (as food or cloth) is placed for cutting

cutting edge *n* (1804) **1 :** a sharp effect or quality **2 :** the foremost part or place **:** VANGUARD — **cutting–edge** *adj*

cutting horse *n* (1881) **:** an agile saddle horse trained to separate individual animals from a cattle herd

cutting room *n* (1918) **:** a room where film or videotape is edited — often used attributively in *cutting-room floor* to describe something removed or discarded in or as if in editing a film

cut·tle·bone \ˈkə-tᵊl-ˌbōn\ *n* [ME *cotul* cuttlefish (fr. OE *cudele*) + E *bone*] (1547) **:** the shell of a cuttlefish that is sometimes used for polishing powder or for supplying cage birds with lime and salts

cut·tle·fish \-ˌfish\ *n* [ME *cotul* + E *fish*] (ca. 1828) **:** any of various marine cephalopod mollusks (order Sepioidea, esp. genus *Sepia*) having eight short arms and two usu. longer tentacles and differing from the related squid in having a calcified internal shell

cuttlefish

cut·ty sark \ˈkə-tē-ˈsärk\ *n* [E dial. *cutty* short + *sark*] (1779) *chiefly Scot* **:** a short garment; *esp* **:** a woman's short undergarment

cutty stool *n* (1820) **1** *chiefly Scot* **:** a low stool **2 :** a seat in a Scottish church where offenders formerly sat for public rebuke

cut·up \ˈkət-ˌəp\ *n* (1843) **:** a person who clowns or acts boisterously

cut up *vt* (1580) **1 a :** to cut into parts or pieces **b :** to injure or damage by or as if by cutting **:** GASH, SLASH **2 :** to subject to hostile criticism **:** CENSURE ~ *vi* **1 :** to undergo being cut up **2 :** to behave in a comic, boisterous, or unruly manner **:** CLOWN

cut·wa·ter \ˈkət-ˌwȯ-tər, -ˌwä-\ *n* (1644) **:** the forepart of a ship's stem

cut·work \-ˌwərk\ *n* (15c) **:** embroidery usu. on linen in which a design is outlined in buttonhole stitch and the enclosed material cut away

cut·worm \-ˌwərm\ *n* (1816) **:** any of various smooth-bodied chiefly nocturnal noctuid moth caterpillars which often feed on young plant stems near ground level

cu·vée *also* **cu·vee** \kü-ˈvā, kyü-; kœ-vā\ *n* [F, fr. *cuve*] (1833) **1 :** bulk wine; *esp* **:** wine in casks or vats so blended as to ensure uniformity and marketability **2 :** a blend of still wines used in the production of champagne

cu·vette \kyü-ˈvet\ *n* [F, dim. of *cuve* tub, fr. L *cupa* — more at HIVE] (ca. 1909) **:** a small often transparent laboratory vessel (as a tube)

cv *abbr* **1** convertible **2** cultivar

CV *abbr* **1** cardiovascular **2** curriculum vitae

CVA *abbr* **1** cerebrovascular accident **2** Columbia Valley Authority

CVS *abbr* chorionic villus sampling

cw *abbr* clockwise

CW *abbr* **1** chemical warfare; chemical weapon **2** chief warrant officer

cwm \ˈküm\ *n* [W, valley] (1853) *chiefly Brit* **:** CIRQUE 3

CWO *abbr* **1** cash with order **2** chief warrant officer

cwt *abbr* hundredweight

CY *abbr* calendar year

-cy *n suffix* [ME *-cie,* fr. AF, fr. L *-tia,* partly fr. *-t-* (final stem consonant) + *-ia* -y, partly fr. Gk *-tia, -teia,* fr. *-t-* (final stem consonant) + *-ia, -eia* -y] **1 :** action **:** practice ⟨mendican*cy*⟩ **2 :** rank **:** office ⟨chaplain*cy*⟩ **3 :** body **:** class ⟨magistra*cy*⟩ **4 :** state **:** quality ⟨bankrupt*cy*⟩ — often replacing a final *-t* or *-te* of the base word ⟨accura*cy*⟩

cy·an \ˈsī-ˌan, -ən\ *n* [Gk *kyanos*] (ca. 1889) **:** a greenish-blue color — used in photography and color printing of one of the primary colors

cyan- *or* **cyano-** *comb form* [G, fr. Gk *kyan-, kyano-,* fr. *kyanos* dark blue enamel] **1 :** dark blue **:** blue ⟨*cyano*bacterium⟩ **2 :** cyanogen ⟨*cyan*ide⟩ **3 :** cyanide ⟨*cyano*genetic⟩

cy·an·a·mide \sī-ˈa-nə-məd\ *n* [ISV] (1838) **1 :** a caustic acidic compound CH_2N_2 **2 :** CALCIUM CYANAMIDE

cy·a·nate \ˈsī-ə-ˌnāt, -nət\ *n* [ISV] (1825) **:** a salt (as ammonium cyanate) or ester of cyanic acid

cy·an·ic acid \sī-ˈa-nik-\ *n* (1825) **:** a strong acid HOCN used to prepare cyanates

cy·a·nide \ˈsī-ə-ˌnīd, -nəd\ *n* [ISV] (1826) **1 :** a compound of cyanogen with a more electropositive element or group: as **a :** POTASSIUM CYANIDE **b :** SODIUM CYANIDE **2 :** CYANOGEN 1

cy·a·nine \ˈsī-ə-ˌnēn, -nən\ *n* [ISV] (ca. 1872) **:** any of various dyes used esp. to sensitize photographic film to light from the green, yellow, red, and infrared regions of the spectrum

cy·a·no \ˈsī-ə-(ˌ)nō, sī-ˈa-(ˌ)nō\ *adj* [*cyan-*] (1929) **:** relating to or containing the cyanogen group

cy·a·no·ac·ry·late \ˌsī-ə-nō-ˈa-krə-ˌlāt, sī-ˌa-nō-\ *n* (1963) **:** any of several liquid acrylate monomers that readily polymerize as anions and are used as adhesives in industry and in closing wounds in surgery

cy·a·no·bac·te·ri·um \-bak-ˈtir-ē-əm\ *n* [NL] (1974) **:** any of a major group (Cyanobacteria) of photosynthetic bacteria that have two photosystems, produce molecular oxygen, and use water as an electron-donating substrate in photosynthesis — called also *blue-green alga*

\ə\ **abut** \ᵊ\ **kitten,** F **table** \ər\ **further** \a\ **ash** \ā\ **ace** \ä\ **mop, mar**
\au̇\ **out** \ch\ **chin** \e\ **bet** \ē\ **easy** \g\ **go** \i\ **hit** \ī\ **ice** \j\ **job**
\ŋ\ **sing** \ō\ **go** \ȯ\ **law** \ȯi\ **boy** \th\ **thin** \t͟h\ **the** \ü\ **loot** \u̇\ **foot**
\y\ **yet** \zh\ **vision, beige** \k͟, ⁿ, œ, ue, ʸ\ *see* **Guide to Pronunciation**

cy·a·no·co·bal·a·min \-kō-ˈba-lə-mən\ *also* **cy·a·no·co·bal·a·mine** \-ˌmēn\ *n* [*cyan-* + *cobal*t + vit*amin*] (1950) : VITAMIN B_{12} 1

cy·an·o·gen \sī-ˈa-nə-jən\ *n* [F *cyanogène,* fr. *cyan-* + *gène* -gen] (1816) **1** : a monovalent group –CN present in cyanides **2** : a colorless flammable poisonous gas $(CN)_2$

cy·a·no·ge·net·ic \ˌsī-ə-nō-jə-ˈne-tik, sī-ˌa-nō-\ *or* **cy·a·no·gen·ic** \-ˈje-nik\ *adj* (1902) : capable of producing cyanide (as hydrogen cyanide) ⟨a ~ glucoside⟩ — **cy·a·no·gen·e·sis** \-ˈje-nə-səs\ *n*

cy·a·no·hy·drin \-ˈhī-drən\ *n* [ISV, fr. *cyan-* + *hydr-* + [1]*-in*] (1925) : any of various compounds containing both cyano and hydroxyl groups

cy·a·no·sis \ˌsī-ə-ˈnō-səs\ *n* [NL, fr. Gk *kyanōsis* dark blue color, fr. *kyanos*] (1834) : a bluish or purplish discoloration (as of skin) due to deficient oxygenation of the blood — **cy·a·not·ic** \-ˈnä-tik\ *adj*

cy·an·uric acid \ˌsī-ə-ˈnu̇r-ik-, -ˈnyu̇r-\ *n* [*cyan-* + *urea*] (1838) : a crystalline weak acid $C_3N_3(OH)_3$ that yields cyanic acid when heated

Cyb·e·le \ˈsi-bə-(ˌ)lē\ *n* [L, fr. Gk *Kybelē*] (1576) : a nature goddess of the ancient peoples of Asia Minor

cy·ber \ˈsī-bər\ *adj* [*cyber-*] (1991) : of, relating to, or involving computers or computer networks (as the Internet) ⟨the ~ marketplace⟩

cyber- *comb form* [*cybernetic*] : computer : computer network ⟨*cyber*space⟩

cy·ber·bul·ly·ing \ˈsī-bər-ˌbu̇-lē-iŋ, -ˈbə-\ *n* (2000) : the electronic posting of mean-spirited messages about a person (as a student) often done anonymously — **cy·ber·bul·ly** \-ˌbu̇-lē, -ˌbə-\ *n or vb*

cy·ber·ca·fe \ˈsī-bər-ka-ˈfā\ *n* (1994) : a café or coffee shop providing computers for access to the Internet

cy·ber·cit·i·zen \-ˈsi-tə-zən\ *n* (1994) : NETIZEN

cy·ber·na·tion \ˌsī-bər-ˈnā-shən\ *n* [*cyber*netics + *-ation*] (1962) : the automatic control of a process or operation (as in manufacturing) by means of computers — **cy·ber·nat·ed** \ˈsī-bər-ˌnā-təd\ *adj*

cy·ber·naut \ˈsī-bər-ˌnȯt, -ˌnät\ *n* [*cyber-* + *-naut* (as in *astronaut*)] (1989) : NETIZEN

cy·ber·ne·ti·cian \ˌsī-(ˌ)bər-nə-ˈti-shən\ *n* (1951) : a specialist in cybernetics

cy·ber·net·i·cist \ˌsī-bər-ˈne-tə-sist\ *n* (1948) : CYBERNETICIAN

cy·ber·net·ics \ˌsī-bər-ˈne-tiks\ *n pl but sing in constr* [Gk *kybernētēs* pilot, governor (fr. *kybernan* to steer, govern) + E *-ics*] (1948) : the science of communication and control theory that is concerned esp. with the comparative study of automatic control systems (as the nervous system and brain and mechanical-electrical communication systems) — **cy·ber·net·ic** \-tik\ *also* **cy·ber·net·i·cal** \-ti-kəl\ *adj* — **cy·ber·net·i·cal·ly** \-ti-k(ə-)lē\ *adv*

cy·ber·porn \ˈsī-bər-ˌpȯrn\ *n* (1992) : pornography accessible online esp. via the Internet

cy·ber·punk \ˈsī-bər-ˌpəŋk\ *n* (1983) **1** : science fiction dealing with future urban societies dominated by computer technology **2** : an opportunistic computer hacker

cy·ber·se·cu·ri·ty \-si-ˌkyu̇r-ə-tē\ *n* (1994) measures taken to protect a computer or computer system (as on the Internet) against unauthorized access or attack

cy·ber·sex \-ˌseks\ *n* (1991) **1** : online sex-oriented conversations and exchanges **2** : sex-oriented material available on a computer

cy·ber·space \-ˌspās\ *n* (1982) : the online world of computer networks and esp. the Internet

cy·ber·speak \-ˌspēk\ *n* (1991) : jargon relating to or used in online communications

cy·ber·surf·er \-ˌsər-fər\ *n* (1993) : one who surfs the Internet

cy·ber·ter·ror·ism \-ˌter-ər-ˌi-zəm\ *n* (1994) : terrorist activities intended to damage or disrupt vital computer systems

cy·borg \ˈsī-ˌbȯrg\ *n* [*cyb*ernetic + *org*anism] (1960) : a bionic human

cy·brar·ian \sī-ˈbrer-ē-ən, -ˈbre-rē-\ *n* [blend of *cyber-* and *librarian*] (1992) : a person whose job is to find, collect, and manage information that is available on the World Wide Web

cy·cad \ˈsī-kəd\ *n* [NL *Cycad-, Cycas,* genus name, fr. Gk *kykas,* MS var. of *koïkas,* acc. pl. of *koïx,* a kind of palm] (1845) : any of an order (Cycadales) of dioecious cycadophytes that flourished esp. during the Jurassic and are represented by four surviving families of palmlike tropical plants

cy·cad·e·oid \sī-ˈka-dē-ˌȯid\ *n* [NL *Cycadeoidales,* group name, ultim. fr. *Cycad-, Cycas*] (1860) : any of a division (Cycadeoidophyta syn. Bennettitophyta) of extinct Jurassic to Cretaceous gymnosperms that differ from the cycadophytes chiefly in having the reproductive organs on the trunk embedded in a thick covering of bracts and scales

cy·cad·o·phyte \sī-ˈka-də-ˌfīt\ *n* [ultim. fr. NL *Cycad-, Cycas* + Gk *phyton* plant — more at -PHYTE] (1911) : any of a division (Cycadophyta) of usu. unbranched mostly extinct gymnosperms with pinnate leaves, large pith, little xylem, and a thick cortex that includes the cycads, cycadeoids, and seed ferns

cy·ca·sin \ˈsī-kə-sən\ *n* [NL *Cycas* cycad + ISV [1]*-in*] (ca. 1965) : a glucoside $C_8H_{16}N_2O_7$ that occurs in cycads and results in toxic and carcinogenic effects when introduced into mammals

cycl- *or* **cyclo-** *comb form* [NL, fr. Gk *kykl-, kyklo-,* fr. *kyklos*] **1** : circle ⟨*cyclo*meter⟩ **2** : cyclic ⟨*cyclo*hexane⟩

cy·cla·mate \ˈsī-klə-ˌmāt, -mət\ *n* [*cyclo*hexyl-sulf*amate*] (1954) : an artificially prepared salt of sodium or calcium used esp. formerly as a sweetener

cy·cla·men \ˈsī-klə-mən, ˈsi-\ *n* [NL, genus name, fr. Gk *kyklaminos*] (ca. 1550) : any of a genus (*Cyclamen*) of Old World plants of the primrose family having showy nodding flowers

cy·clase \ˈsī-ˌklās, -ˌklāz\ *n* [*cycl-* + *-ase*] (1946) : an enzyme (as adenylate cyclase) that catalyzes cyclization of a compound

cy·claz·o·cine \sī-ˈkla-zə-ˌsēn, -sən\ *n* [*cycl-* + *azocine* (C_7H_7N), prob. fr. *az-* + *oc*ta- + [2]*-ine*] (1966) : an analgesic drug $C_{18}H_{25}NO$ that inhibits the effect of morphine and related addictive drugs and is used in the treatment of drug addiction

[1]**cy·cle** \ˈsī-kəl\ *n* [ME *cicle,* fr. LL *cyclus,* fr. Gk *kyklos* circle, wheel, cycle — more at WHEEL] (14c) **1** : an interval of time during which a sequence of a recurring succession of events or phenomena is completed ⟨a 4-year ~ of growth and development⟩ **2 a** : a course or series of events or operations that recur regularly and usu. lead back to the starting point **b** : one complete performance of a vibration, electric oscillation, current alternation, or other periodic process **c** : a permutation of a set of ordered elements in which each element takes the place of the next and the last becomes first **d** : a takeoff and landing of an airplane **3** : a circular or spiral arrangement: as **a** : an imaginary circle or orbit in the heavens **b** : RING 10 **4** : a long period of time : AGE **5 a** : a group of creative works (as poems, plays, or songs) treating the same theme **b** : a series of narratives dealing typically with the exploits of a legendary hero **6 a** : BICYCLE **b** : TRICYCLE **c** : MOTORCYCLE **7** : the series of a single, double, triple, and home run hit in any order by one player during one baseball game

[2]**cycle** *vb* **cy·cled; cy·cling** \ˈsī-k(ə-)liŋ\ *vi* (1842) **1 a** : to pass through a cycle **b** : to recur in cycles **2** : to ride a cycle; *specif* : BICYCLE ~ *vt* : to cause to go through a cycle — **cy·cler** \ˈsī-k(ə-)lər\ *n*

cy·cle·way \-ˌwā\ *n* (1899) *Brit* : BIKEWAY

cy·clic \ˈsī-klik *also* ˈsi-\ *or* **cy·cli·cal** \ˈsī-kli-kəl, ˈsi-\ *adj* (1794) **1 a** : of, relating to, or being a cycle **b** : moving in cycles ⟨~ time⟩ **c** : of, relating to, or being a chemical compound containing a ring of atoms **2** *cyclic* : being a mathematical group that has an element such that every element of the group can be expressed as one of its powers — **cy·cli·cal·ly** \-k(ə-)lē\ *also* **cy·clic·ly** \ˈsī-kli-klē, ˈsi-\ *adv*

cyclic AMP *n* (1966) : a cyclic mononucleotide of adenosine that is formed from ATP and is responsible for the intracellular mediation of hormonal effects on various cellular processes — called also *adenosine 3′,5′-monophosphate*

cyclic GMP \-ˌjē-(ˌ)em-ˈpē\ *n* [*g*uanosine + *m*on- + *p*hosphate] (1969) : a cyclic mononucleotide of guanosine that acts similarly to cyclic AMP as a secondary messenger in response to hormones

cy·clic·i·ty \sī-ˈkli-sə-tē, si-\ *n* (1944) : the quality or state of being cyclic ⟨estrous ~⟩ — called also *cy·cli·cal·i·ty* \ˌsī-klə-ˈka-lə-tē, ˌsi-\

cy·clin \ˈsī-klən, ˈsi-\ *n* (1983) : any of a group of proteins active in controlling the cell cycle and in initiating DNA synthesis

cy·clist \ˈsī-k(ə-)ləst\ *n* (1882) : one who rides a cycle

cy·cli·tol \ˈsī-klə-ˌtȯl, ˈsi-, -ˌtōl\ *n* [*cycl-* + *-itol* (as in *inositol*)] (1943) : an alicyclic polyhydroxy compound (as inositol)

cy·cli·za·tion \ˌsī-k(ə-)lə-ˈzā-shən, ˌsi-\ *n* (1909) : formation of a ring in a chemical compound — **cy·clize** \ˈsī-kə-ˌlīz, ˈsi-, -ˌklīz\ *vb*

cy·clo \ˈsē-(ˌ)klō, ˈsi-\ *n, pl* **cyclos** [F, bicycle, moped, fr. *cyclo-* (as in *cyclomoteur* moped), fr. *cycle* 2- or 3-wheeled vehicle] (1964) : a 3-wheeled often motor-driven taxi

cy·clo·ad·di·tion \ˌsī-(ˌ)klō-ə-ˈdi-shən\ *n* (1963) : a chemical reaction leading to ring formation in a compound

cy·clo·al·i·phat·ic \ˌsī-klō-ˌa-lə-ˈfa-tik\ *adj* (1936) : ALICYCLIC

cy·clo–cross \ˈsī-klə-ˌkrȯs, -klō-\ *n* [F, fr. *cyclo* + *cross*-country (fr. E)] (1953) : the sport of racing bicycles over rough terrain that usu. requires carrying the bicycle over obstacles

cy·clo·dex·trin \-ˈdek-strən\ *n* (1960) : any of a class of complex cyclic sugars that are products of the enzymatic decomposition of starch and that can catalyze reactions between simpler molecules which come together within the cylindrical body of the sugar

cy·clo·di·ene \-ˈdī-ˌēn, -dī-ˈ\ *n* (1942) : an organic insecticide (as dieldrin or chlordane) with a chlorinated methylene group forming a bridge across a 6-membered carbon ring

cy·clo·gen·e·sis \-ˈje-nə-səs\ *n* [*cyclo*ne + *genesis*] (ca. 1938) : the development or intensification of a cyclone

cy·clo·hex·ane \ˌsī-klō-ˈhek-ˌsān\ *n* [ISV] (ca. 1909) : a pungent saturated cyclic hydrocarbon C_6H_{12} found in petroleum or made synthetically and used chiefly as a solvent and in organic synthesis

cy·clo·hex·a·none \-ˈhek-sə-ˌnōn\ *n* (ca. 1909) : a liquid ketone $C_6H_{10}O$ used esp. as a solvent and in organic synthesis

cy·clo·hex·i·mide \-ˈhek-sə-ˌmīd, -məd\ *n* [*cyclohex*ane + *imide*] (1950) : an agricultural fungicide $C_{15}H_{23}NO_4$ that inhibits protein synthesis and is obtained from a soil bacterium (*Streptomyces griseus*)

cy·clo·hex·yl·amine \-hek-ˈsi-lə-ˌmēn\ *n* [*cyclohex*ane + *-yl* + *amine*] (1943) : a colorless liquid amine $C_6H_{11}NH_2$ that is used in organic synthesis and to prevent corrosion in boilers and that is believed to be harmful as a metabolic breakdown product of cyclamate

[1]**cy·cloid** \ˈsī-ˌklȯid\ *n* [F *cycloïde,* fr. Gk *kykloeidēs* circular, fr. *kyklos*] (1661) : a curve that is generated by a point on the circumference of a circle as it rolls along a straight line — **cy·cloi·dal** \sī-ˈklȯi-dᵊl\ *adj*

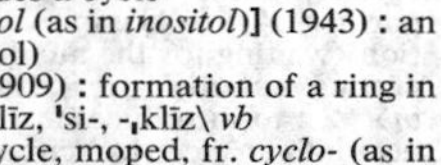

cycloid

[2]**cycloid** *adj* (1847) **1** : smooth with concentric lines of growth ⟨~ scales⟩; *also* : having or consisting of cycloid scales **2** : characterized by alternating high and low moods ⟨a ~ personality⟩

cy·clom·e·ter \sī-ˈklä-mə-tər\ *n* (1880) : a device made for recording the revolutions of a wheel and often used for registering distance traversed by a wheeled vehicle

cy·clone \ˈsī-ˌklōn\ *n* [modif. of Gk *kyklōma* wheel, coil, fr. *kykloun* to go around, fr. *kyklos* circle] (1848) **1 a** : a storm or system of winds that rotates about a center of low atmospheric pressure, advances at a speed of 20 to 30 miles (about 30 to 50 kilometers) an hour, and often brings heavy rain **b** : TORNADO **c** : [4]LOW 1b **2** : any of various centrifugal devices for separating materials (as solid particles from gases) — **cy·clon·ic** \sī-ˈklä-nik\ *adj* — **cy·clon·i·cal·ly** \-ni-k(ə-)lē\ *adv*

Cy·clone \ˈsī-ˌklōn\ *trademark* — used for a chain-link fence

cyclone cellar *n* (1887) : STORM CELLAR

cy·clo·ole·fin \ˌsī-klō-ˈō-lə-fən\ *n* [ISV] (ca. 1929) : a hydrocarbon containing a ring having one or more double bonds — **cy·clo·ole·fin·ic** \-ˌō-lə-ˈfi-nik\ *adj*

cy·clo·oxy·gen·ase \-ˈäk-si-jə-ˌnās\ *n* [*cycl-* + *oxygenase,* an enzyme, fr. *oxygen* + *-ase*] (1975) : an enzyme that catalyzes the conversion of arachidonic acid to prostaglandins and that has two isoforms of which one is involved in the creation of prostaglandins which mediate inflammation and pain

cy·clo·par·af·fin \-ˈper-ə-fən, -ˈpa-rə-\ *n* (1900) : a saturated cyclic hydrocarbon of the formula C_nH_{2n}

cy·clo·pe·an \ˌsī-klə-ˈpē-ən, sī-ˈklō-pē-\ *adj* (1582) **1** *often cap* : of, relating to, or characteristic of a Cyclops **2** : HUGE, MASSIVE **3** : of or relating to a style of stone construction marked typically by the use of large irregular blocks without mortar

cy·clo·pe·dia *also* **cy·clo·pae·dia** \ˌsī-klə-ˈpē-dē-ə\ *n* (1728) : ENCYCLOPEDIA — **cy·clo·pe·dic** \-ˈpē-dik\ *adj*

cy·clo·phos·pha·mide \ˌsī-klō-ˈfäs-fə-ˌmīd\ *n* (1960) : an immunosuppressive and antineoplastic agent $C_7H_{15}Cl_2N_2O_2P$ used esp. in the treatment of lymphomas and some leukemias

cy·clo·pro·pane \ˌsī-klə-ˈprō-ˌpān\ *n* [ISV] (1894) : a flammable gaseous saturated cyclic hydrocarbon C_3H_6 sometimes used as a general anesthetic

cy·clops \ˈsī-ˌkläps\ *n* [L, fr. Gk *Kyklōps,* fr. *kykl-* cycl- + *ōps* eye] (1513) **1** *pl* **cy·clo·pes** \sī-ˈklō-(ˌ)pēz\ *cap* : any of a race of giants in Greek mythology with a single eye in the middle of the forehead **2** *pl* **cyclops** [NL, genus name, fr. L] : any of a genus (*Cyclops*) of freshwater predatory copepods having a single median eye

cy·clo·ra·ma \ˌsī-klə-ˈra-mə, -ˈrä-\ *n* [*cycl-* + *-orama* (as in *panorama*)] (1840) **1** : a large pictorial representation encircling the spectator and often having real objects as a foreground **2** : a curved curtain or wall used as a background of a stage set to suggest unlimited space — **cy·clo·ram·ic** \-ˈra-mik\ *adj*

cy·clo·ser·ine \ˌsī-klō-ˈser-ˌēn\ *n* (1952) : a broad-spectrum antibiotic $C_3H_6N_2O_2$ produced by an actinomycete (*Streptomyces orchidaceus*) and used esp. in the treatment of tuberculosis

cy·clo·sis \sī-ˈklō-səs\ *n* [NL, fr. Gk *kyklōsis* encirclement, fr. *kykloun* to go around] (1835) : the streaming of protoplasm within a cell

cy·clo·spo·ra \ˌsī-klō-ˈspȯr-ə\ *n* [NL, fr. *cycl-* + *spora* spore] (1993) : any of a genus (*Cyclospora* of the order Coccidia) of sporozoans including one (*C. cayetanensis*) causing diarrhea in humans

cy·clo·spor·ine \ˌsī-klə-ˈspȯr-ᵊn, -ˌēn\ *also* **cy·clo·spor·in** \-ˈspȯr-ᵊn\ *n* [ISV *cycl-* + *spor-* + ²*-ine*] (1976) : an immunosuppressive polypeptide drug $C_{62}H_{111}N_{11}O_{12}$ obtained from various imperfect fungi and used esp. to prevent rejection of organ transplants

cy·clo·stome \ˈsī-klə-ˌstōm\ *n* [ultim. fr. Gk *kykl-* + *stoma* mouth — more at STOMACH] (1835) : any of a class (Cyclostomata) of jawless fishes having a large sucking mouth and comprising the hagfishes and lampreys

cy·clo·style \-ˌstī(-ə)l\ *n* [fr. *Cyclostyle,* a trademark] (1883) : a machine for making multiple copies that utilizes a stencil cut by a graver whose tip is a small rowel — **cyclostyle** *vt*

cy·clo·thy·mic \ˌsī-klə-ˈthī-mik\ *adj* [NL *cyclothymia* (fr. G *Zyklothymie,* fr. *zykl-* cycl- + *-thymie* -thymia) + E *-ic*] (1923) : relating to or being a mood disorder characterized by alternating episodes of depression and elation in a form less severe than that of bipolar disorder — **cy·clo·thy·mia** \-ˈthī-mē-ə\ *n*

cy·clo·tom·ic \-ˈtä-mik\ *adj* [*cyclotomy* mathematical theory of the division of the circle into equal parts, fr. *cycl-* + *-tomy*] (1879) : relating to, being, or containing a polynomial of the form $x^{p-1} + x^{p-2} + \ldots + x + 1$ where p is a prime number

cy·clo·tron \ˈsī-klə-ˌträn\ *n* [*cycl-* + *-tron;* fr. the circular movement of the particles] (1935) : an accelerator in which charged particles (as protons, deuterons, or ions) are propelled by an alternating electric field in a constant magnetic field

cy·der *Brit var of* CIDER

cyg·net \ˈsig-nət\ *n* [ME *sygnett,* fr. AF *cignet,* fr. *cigne* swan, fr. L *cycnus, cygnus,* fr. Gk *kyknos*] (15c) : a young swan

Cyg·nus \ˈsig-nəs\ *n* [L (gen. *Cygni*), lit., swan] (1551) : a northern constellation between Lyra and Pegasus in the Milky Way

cyl *abbr* cylinder

cyl·in·der \ˈsi-lən-dər\ *n* [MF or L; MF *cylindre,* fr. L *cylindrus,* fr. Gk *kylindros,* fr. *kylindein* to roll; perh. akin to Gk *kyklos* wheel — more at WHEEL] (1570) **1 a** : the surface traced by a straight line moving parallel to a fixed straight line and intersecting a fixed planar closed curve **b** : a solid or surface bounded by a cylinder and two parallel planes cutting all its elements; *esp* : RIGHT CIRCULAR CYLINDER — see VOLUME table **2** : a cylindrical body or space: as **a** : the turning chambered breech of a revolver **b** (1) : the piston chamber in an engine (2) : a chamber in a pump from which the piston expels the fluid **c** : any of various rotating members in a press (as a printing press); *esp* : one that impresses paper on an inked form **d** : a cylindrical clay object inscribed with cuneiform inscriptions — **cyl·in·dered** \-dərd\ *adj* — **on all cylinders** : with maximum effort or intensity : at full capacity or speed ⟨the economy is running *on all cylinders*⟩

cylinder head *n* (1884) : the closed end of an engine or pump cylinder

cylinder seal *n* (1887) : a cylinder (as of stone) engraved in intaglio and used esp. in ancient Mesopotamia to roll an impression on wet clay

cy·lin·dri·cal \sə-ˈlin-dri-kəl\ *also* **cy·lin·dric** \-drik\ *adj* (1646) : relating to or having the form or properties of a cylinder — **cy·lin·dri·cal·ly** \-dri-k(ə-)lē\ *adv*

cylindrical coordinate *n* (ca. 1934) : any of the coordinates in space obtained by constructing in a plane a polar coordinate system and on a line perpendicular to the plane a linear coordinate system

cy·ma \ˈsī-mə\ *n* [Gk *kyma,* lit., wave] (1563) **1** : a projecting molding whose profile is an S-shaped curve **2** : an S-shaped curve formed by the union of a concave line and a convex line

cy·ma·tium \sī-ˈmā-sh(ē-)əm\ *n, pl* **-tia** \-sh(ē-)ə\ [L, fr. Gk *kymation,* dim. of *kymat-, kyma*] (1563) : a crowning molding in classic architecture; *esp* : CYMA

cym·bal \ˈsim-bəl\ *n* [ME, fr. OE *cymbal* & AF *cymbele,* fr. L *cymbalum,* fr. Gk *kymbalon,* fr. *kymbē* bowl, boat] (bef. 12c) : a concave brass plate that produces a brilliant clashing tone and that is struck with a drumstick or is used in pairs struck glancingly together — **cym·bal·ist** \-bə-list\ *n*

cym·bid·i·um \sim-ˈbi-dē-əm\ *n* [NL, genus name, fr. L *cymba* boat, fr. Gk *kymbē*] (1815) : any of a genus (*Cymbidium*) of tropical Old World epiphytic orchids with showy flowers

cyme \ˈsīm\ *n* [NL *cyma,* fr. L, cabbage sprout, fr. Gk *kyma* swell, wave, cabbage sprout, fr. *kyein* to be pregnant; akin to Skt *śvayati* it swells, grows] (1794) : an inflorescence in which each floral axis terminates in a single flower; *esp* : a determinate inflorescence of this type containing several flowers with the first-opening central flower terminating the main axis and subsequent flowers developing from lateral buds — see INFLORESCENCE illustration

cym·ling \ˈsim-lən, -liŋ\ *n* [prob. alter. of *simnel*] (1779) : PATTYPAN

cy·mo·phane \ˈsī-mə-ˌfān\ *n* [F, fr. Gk *kyma* wave + F *-phane* -phane] (ca. 1804) : CHRYSOBERYL; *esp* : an opalescent chrysoberyl

cy·mose \ˈsī-ˌmōs\ *adj* (1807) : of, relating to, being, or bearing a cyme

¹**Cym·ric** *also* **Kym·ric** \ˈkəm-rik, ˈkim-\ *adj* (1838) : of, relating to, or characteristic of the non-Gaelic Celtic people of Britain or their language; *specif* : WELSH

²**Cymric** *also* **Kymric** *n* (1875) : BRYTHONIC; *specif* : the Welsh language

Cym·ry \-rē\ *n* [W, pl. of *Cymro* Welshman] (1833) : WELSH 2

cyn·ic \ˈsi-nik\ *n* [MF or L, MF *cynique,* fr. L *cynicus,* fr. Gk *kynikos,* lit., like a dog, fr. *kyn-, kyōn* dog — more at HOUND] (1542) **1** *cap* : an adherent of an ancient Greek school of philosophers who held the view that virtue is the only good and that its essence lies in self-control and independence **2** : a faultfinding captious critic; *esp* : one who believes that human conduct is motivated wholly by self-interest — **cynic** *adj*

cyn·i·cal \ˈsi-ni-kəl\ *adj* (1542) **1** : CAPTIOUS, PEEVISH **2** : having or showing the attitude or temper of a cynic: as **a** : contemptuously distrustful of human nature and motives ⟨those ~ men who say that democracy cannot be honest and efficient —F. D. Roosevelt⟩ **b** : based on or reflecting a belief that human conduct is motivated primarily by self-interest ⟨a ~ ploy to win votes⟩ — **cyn·i·cal·ly** \-k(ə-)lē\ *adv*

syn CYNICAL, MISANTHROPIC, PESSIMISTIC mean deeply distrustful. CYNICAL implies having a sneering disbelief in sincerity or integrity ⟨*cynical* about politicians' motives⟩. MISANTHROPIC suggests a rooted distrust and dislike of human beings and their society ⟨a solitary and *misanthropic* artist⟩. PESSIMISTIC implies having a gloomy, distrustful view of life ⟨*pessimistic* about the future⟩.

cyn·i·cism \ˈsi-nə-ˌsi-zəm\ *n* (1663) **1** *cap* : the doctrine of the Cynics **2** : cynical attitude or quality; *also* : a cynical comment or act

cy·no·mol·gus monkey \ˌsī-nə-ˈmäl-gəs-\ *n* [NL, alter. of *cynamolgus,* fr. L, member of an ancient tribe in Africa, fr. Gk *Kynamolgoi,* lit., dog milkers] (1936) : a macaque (*Macaca fascicularis*) of southeastern Asia, Borneo, and the Philippines that sometimes feeds on marine crustaceans and shellfish and is often used in medical research

cy·no·sure \ˈsī-nə-ˌshu̇r, ˈsi-\ *n* [MF & L; MF, Ursa Minor, guide, fr. L *cynosura* Ursa Minor, fr. Gk *kynosoura,* fr. *kynos oura,* lit., dog's tail] (1565) **1** *cap* : the northern constellation Ursa Minor; *also* : NORTH STAR **2** : one that serves to direct or guide **3** : a center of attraction or attention ⟨turned an eyesore into a ~ —Catherine Reynolds⟩

Cyn·thia \ˈsin(t)-thē-ə\ *n* [L, fr. fem. of *Cynthius* of Cynthus, fr. *Cynthus,* mountain on Delos where she was born, fr. Gk *Kynthos*] (14c) **1** : ARTEMIS **2** : the moon personified as a goddess

CYO *abbr* Catholic Youth Organization

cy·pher *chiefly Brit var of* CIPHER

¹**cy pres** \ˌsī-ˈprā, ˌsē-\ *n* [AF, so near, as near (as may be)] (1802) : a rule providing for the interpretation of instruments in equity as nearly as possible in conformity to the intention of the testator when literal construction is illegal, impracticable, or impossible — called also *cy pres doctrine*

²**cy pres** *adv* (1885) : in accordance with the rule of cy pres

¹**cy·press** \ˈsī-prəs\ *n* [ME *cipres,* fr. AF *ciprès,* fr. L *cyparissus,* fr. Gk *kyparissos*] (14c) **1 a** (1) : any of a genus (*Cupressus* of the family Cupressaceae, the cypress family) of evergreen trees and shrubs with small overlapping leaves resembling scales (2) : any of several coniferous trees of the cypress family or the bald cypress family; *esp* : BALD CYPRESS 1 **b** : the wood of a cypress tree **2** : branches of cypress used as a symbol of mourning

²**cypress** *n* [ME *ciprus, cipres,* fr. *Cyprus,* Mediterranean island] (15c) : a silk or cotton usu. black gauze formerly used for mourning

cypress vine *n* (1819) : a tropical American annual vine (*Ipomoea quamoclit* syn. *Quamoclit pennata*) of the morning-glory family with usu. red or white tubular flowers and finely dissected leaves

cypress vine

cyp·ri·an \ˈsi-prē-ən\ *n, often cap* [L *cyprius* of Cyprus, fr. Gk *kyprios,* fr. *Kypros* Cyprus, birthplace of Aphrodite] (1819) : PROSTITUTE

cyp·ri·nid \ˈsi-prə-nəd\ *n* [ultim. fr. L *cyprinus* carp, fr. Gk *kyprinos*] (1861) : any of a family (Cyprinidae) of soft-finned freshwater fishes including the carps and minnows — **cyprinid** *adj*

cyp·ri·pe·di·um \ˌsi-prə-ˈpē-dē-əm\ *n* [NL, genus name, fr. LL *Cypris,* a name for Venus + *-pedium* (modif. of Gk *pedilon* sandal)] (1807) **1** : any of a genus (*Cypripedium*) of Eurasian and No. American terrestrial orchids having large usu. showy drooping flowers with the lip inflated or pouched — compare LADY'S SLIPPER **2** : any of a genus (*Paphiopedalum*) of widely cultivated Asian orchids

cy·pro·hep·ta·dine \ˌsī-prō-ˈhep-tə-ˌdēn\ *n* [*cyclic* + *propyl* + *hepta-* + *piperidine*] (1971) : a histamine and serotonin antagonist $C_{21}H_{21}N$ used esp. in the form of its hydrochloride to treat allergy symptoms and hives

cy·prot·er·one \sī-ˈprä-tə-ˌrōn\ *n* [prob. fr. cycl- + *progesterone*] (1966) : a synthetic steroid $C_{22}H_{27}ClO_3$ that inhibits the action and secretion of testosterone by blocking the activity of androgen receptors

Cy·re·na·ic \ˌsir-ə-ˈnā-ik, ˌsī-rə-\ *n* [L *cyrenaicus,* fr. Gk *kyrēnaikos,* fr. *Kyrēnē* Cyrene, Africa, home of Aristippus, author of the doctrine] (1586) : an adherent of the doctrine that pleasure is the chief end of life — **Cyrenaic** *adj* — **Cy·re·na·icism** \-ˈnā-ə-ˌsi-zəm\ *n*

Cy·ril·lic \sə-ˈri-lik\ *adj* [St. *Cyril,* reputed inventor of the Cyrillic alphabet] (1813) : of, relating to, or constituting an alphabet used for writing Old Church Slavic and for Russian and a number of other languages of eastern Europe and Asia

cyst \ˈsist\ *n* [NL *cystis,* fr. Gk *kystis* bladder, pouch; akin to Skt *śvasiti* he blows, snorts — more at WHEEZE] (ca. 1720) **1** : a closed sac having a distinct membrane and developing abnormally in a cavity or structure of the body **2** : a body resembling a cyst: as **a** : a resting spore of many algae **b** : a gas-filled vesicle (as of a rockweed or bladderwort) **c** : a capsule formed about a minute organism going into a resting or spore stage; *also* : this capsule with its contents **d** : a resistant cover about a parasite produced by the parasite or the host

cyst- *or* **cysti-** *or* **cysto-** *comb form* [F, fr. Gk *kyst-, kysto-,* fr. *kystis*] : bladder ⟨*cyst*itis⟩ : sac ⟨*cysto*carp⟩

-cyst *n comb form* [NL *-cystis,* fr. Gk *kystis*] : bladder : sac ⟨blasto*cyst*⟩

cys·te·amine \sis-ˈtē-ə-mən\ *n* [*cysteine* + *amine*] (1943) : a cysteine derivative C_2H_7NS used esp. to treat cystinuria

cys·te·ine \'sis-tə-ˌēn\ n [ISV, fr. *cystine* + *-ein*] (1884) : a crystalline sulfur-containing amino acid $C_3H_7NO_2S$ readily oxidizable to cystine

cys·tic \'sis-tik\ adj (1713) **1** : of or relating to the urinary bladder or the gallbladder **2** : relating to, composed of, or containing cysts **3** : enclosed in a cyst

cys·ti·cer·coid \ˌsis-tə-'sər-ˌkoid\ n (ca. 1858) : a tapeworm larva having an invaginated scolex and solid tailpiece

cys·ti·cer·co·sis \ˌsis-tə-(ˌ)sər-'kō-səs\ n, pl **-co·ses** \-'kō-ˌsēz\ [NL] (1905) : infestation with or disease caused by cysticerci

cys·ti·cer·cus \-'sər-kəs\ n, pl **-cer·ci** \-'sər-ˌsī, -ˌkī\ [NL, fr. *cyst-* + Gk *kerkos* tail] (ca. 1871) : a tapeworm larva that consists of a fluid-filled sac containing an invaginated scolex and is situated in the tissues of an intermediate host

cystic fibrosis n (1938) : a hereditary disease esp. among whites that appears usu. in early childhood, is inherited as an autosomal recessive trait, involves functional disorder of the exocrine glands, and is marked esp. by faulty digestion due to a deficiency of pancreatic enzymes, by difficulty in breathing due to mucus accumulation in airways, and by excessive loss of salt in the sweat

cys·tine \'sis-ˌtēn\ n [fr. its discovery in bladder stones] (1843) : a crystalline amino acid $C_6H_{12}N_2O_4S_2$ that is widespread in proteins (as keratins) and is a major metabolic sulfur source

cys·tin·uria \ˌsis-tə-'nur-ē-ə, -'nyur-\ n [NL] (1853) : a metabolic defect characterized by excretion of excessive amounts of cystine in the urine and inherited as an autosomal recessive trait

cys·ti·tis \sis-'tī-təs\ n [NL] (ca. 1783) : inflammation of the urinary bladder

cys·to·lith \'sis-tə-ˌlith\ n [G *Zystolith*, fr. *zyst-* cyst- + *-lith*] (1857) : a calcium carbonate concretion arising from the cellulose wall of cells of higher plants

cys·to·scope \'sis-tə-ˌskōp\ n [ISV] (1889) : a rigid endoscope for inspecting and passing instruments into the urethra and bladder — **cys·to·scop·ic** \ˌsis-tə-'skä-pik\ adj — **cys·tos·co·py** \sis-'täs-kə-pē\ n

cyt- or **cyto-** comb form [G *zyt-*, *zyto-*, fr. Gk *kytos* hollow vessel — more at HIDE] **1** : cell ⟨*cytology*⟩ **2** : cytoplasm ⟨*cytokinesis*⟩

-cyte n comb form [NL *-cyta*, fr. Gk *kytos* hollow vessel] : cell ⟨*leukocyte*⟩

Cyth·er·ea \ˌsi-thə-'rē-ə\ n [L, fr. Gk *Kythereia*, fr. *Kythēra* Cythera, island associated with Aphrodite] (15c) : APHRODITE

Cyth·er·e·an \-'rē-ən\ adj (1885) : of or relating to the planet Venus

cy·ti·dine \'si-tə-ˌdēn, 'sī-\ n [*cytosine* + *-idine*] (1911) : a nucleoside containing cytosine

cy·to·cha·la·sin \ˌsī-tō-kə-'lā-sən\ n [*cyt-* + Gk *chalasis* slackening + E ^{1}-*in*] (1966) : any of a group of metabolites isolated from fungi (esp. *Helminthosporium dematioideum*) that inhibit various cell processes

cy·to·chem·is·try \-'ke-mə-strē\ n (ca. 1905) **1** : microscopic biochemistry **2** : the chemistry of cells — **cy·to·chem·i·cal** \-'ke-mi-kəl\ adj

cy·to·chrome \'sī-tə-ˌkrōm\ n (1925) : any of several intracellular hemoprotein respiratory pigments that are enzymes functioning in electron transport as carriers of electrons

cytochrome c n, often ital 2d c (1940) : the most abundant and stable of the cytochromes

cytochrome oxidase n (1942) : an iron-porphyrin enzyme important in cell respiration due to its ability to catalyze the oxidation of reduced cytochrome c in the presence of oxygen

cy·to·dif·fer·en·ti·a·tion \ˌsī-tō-ˌdi-fə-ˌren(t)-shē-'ā-shən\ n (1959) : the development of specialized cells (as muscle, blood, or nerve cells) from undifferentiated precursors

cy·to·ge·net·ics \ˌsī-tō-jə-'ne-tiks\ n pl but sing or pl in constr [ISV] (1931) : a branch of biology that deals with the study of heredity and variation by the methods of both cytology and genetics — **cy·to·ge·net·ic** \-jə-'ne-tik\ or **cy·to·ge·net·i·cal** \-ti-kəl\ adj — **cy·to·ge·net·i·cal·ly** \-ti-k(ə-)lē\ adv — **cy·to·ge·net·i·cist** \-'ne-tə-sist\ n

cy·to·kine \'sī-tə-ˌkīn\ n [*cyt-* + *-kine* (as in *lymphokine*)] (1979) : any of a class of immunoregulatory proteins (as interleukin or interferon) that are secreted by cells esp. of the immune system

cy·to·ki·ne·sis \ˌsī-tō-kə-'nē-səs, -kī-\ n [NL] (1919) **1** : the cytoplasmic changes accompanying mitosis **2** : cleavage of the cytoplasm into daughter cells following nuclear division — **cy·to·ki·net·ic** \-'ne-tik\ adj

cy·to·ki·nin \ˌsī-tə-'kī-nən\ n [*cyt-* + *kinin*] (1965) : any of various plant growth substances (as kinetin) that are usu. derivatives of adenine

cy·tol abbr cytological; cytology

cy·tol·o·gy \sī-'tä-lə-jē\ n [ISV] (1889) **1** : a branch of biology dealing with the structure, function, multiplication, pathology, and life history of cells **2** : the cytological aspects of a process or structure — **cy·to·log·i·cal** \ˌsī-tə-'lä-ji-kəl\ or **cy·to·log·ic** \-'lä-jik\ adj — **cy·to·log·i·cal·ly** \-ji-k(ə-)lē\ adv — **cy·tol·o·gist** \sī-'tä-lə-jist\ n

cy·to·ly·sin \ˌsī-tə-'lī-sᵊn\ n [ISV] (ca. 1903) : a substance (as an antibody that lyses bacteria) producing cytolysis

cy·tol·y·sis \sī-'tä-lə-səs\ n [NL] (1907) : the usu. pathologic dissolution or disintegration of cells — **cy·to·lyt·ic** \ˌsī-tə-'li-tik\ adj

cy·to·me·gal·ic \ˌsī-tō-mi-'ga-lik\ adj [NL *cytomegalia* condition of having enlarged cells, fr. *cyt-* + *megal-* + *-ia*] (1950) : characterized by or causing the formation of enlarged cells

cy·to·meg·a·lo·vi·rus \ˌsī-tə-ˌme-gə-lō-'vī-rəs\ n [NL, fr. *cytomegalia* + *-o-* + *virus*] (1963) : a herpesvirus (species *Human herpesvirus 5* of the genus *Cytomegalovirus*) that causes cellular enlargement and formation of eosinophilic inclusion bodies esp. in the nucleus and acts as an opportunistic infectious agent in immunosuppressed conditions (as AIDS)

cy·to·mem·brane \ˌsī-tō-'mem-ˌbrān\ n (1962) : one of the cellular membranes including those of the plasma membrane, endoplasmic reticulum, nuclear envelope, and Golgi apparatus; specif : UNIT MEMBRANE

cy·to·path·ic \ˌsī-tə-'pa-thik\ adj (1952) : of, relating to, characterized by, or producing pathological changes in cells

cy·to·path·o·gen·ic \-ˌpa-thə-'je-nik\ adj (1952) : pathologic for or destructive to cells — **cy·to·path·o·ge·nic·i·ty** \-jə-'ni-sə-tē\ n

cy·to·pa·thol·o·gy \-pə-'thä-lə-jē, -pa-\ n (1936) : a branch of pathology that deals with manifestations of disease at the cellular level — **cy·to·pa·thol·o·gist** \-jəst\ n

cy·to·phil·ic \ˌsī-tə-'fi-lik\ adj (ca. 1909) : having an affinity for cells

cy·to·pho·tom·e·try \-ˌfō-'tä-mə-trē\ n (1952) : photometry applied to the study of the cell or its constituents — **cy·to·pho·to·met·ric** \-ˌfō-tə-'me-trik\ adj

cy·to·plasm \'sī-tə-ˌpla-zəm\ n [ISV] (1874) : the organized complex of inorganic and organic substances external to the nuclear membrane of a cell and including the cytosol and membrane-bound organelles (as mitochondria or chloroplasts) — see CELL illustration — **cy·to·plas·mic** \ˌsī-tə-'plaz-mik\ adj — **cy·to·plas·mi·cal·ly** \-mi-k(ə-)lē\ adv

cy·to·sine \'sī-tə-ˌsēn\ n [ISV *cyt-* + *-ose* + ^{2}-*ine*] (1894) : a pyrimidine base $C_4H_5N_3O$ that codes genetic information in the polynucleotide chain of DNA or RNA — compare ADENINE, GUANINE, THYMINE, URACIL

cy·to·skel·e·ton \ˌsī-tə-'ske-lə-tən\ n (1940) : the network of protein filaments and microtubules in the cytoplasm that controls cell shape, maintains intracellular organization, and is involved in cell movement — **cy·to·skel·e·tal** \-t³l\ adj

cy·to·sol \'sī-tə-ˌsäl, -ˌsȯl\ n (1970) : the fluid portion of the cytoplasm exclusive of organelles and membranes — called also *ground substance* — **cy·to·sol·ic** \ˌsī-tə-'sä-lik, -'sȯl-\ adj

cy·to·stat·ic \ˌsī-tə-'sta-tik\ adj (1949) : tending to retard cellular activity and multiplication ⟨~ treatment of tumor cells⟩ — **cytostatic** n

cy·to·tax·on·o·my \ˌsī-tō-(ˌ)tak-'sä-nə-mē\ n (1930) **1** : study of the relationships and classification of organisms using both classical systematic techniques and comparative studies of chromosomes **2** : the nuclear cytologic makeup of a kind of organism — **cy·to·tax·o·nom·ic** \-ˌtak-sə-'nä-mik\ adj — **cy·to·tax·o·nom·i·cal·ly** \-mi-k(ə-)lē\ adv

cy·to·tech·nol·o·gist \ˌsī-tə-tek-'nä-lə-jist\ n (1961) : a medical technician trained in the identification of cells and cellular abnormalities (as in cancer) — **cy·to·tech·nol·o·gy** \-'nä-lə-jē\ n

cy·to·tox·ic \ˌsī-tə-'täk-sik\ adj (1904) **1** : of or relating to a cytotoxin **2** : toxic to cells ⟨~ drugs⟩ — **cy·to·tox·ic·i·ty** \-(ˌ)täk-'si-sə-tē\ n

cytotoxic T cell n (1972) : KILLER T CELL

cy·to·tox·in \-'täk-sən\ n (1902) : a substance (as a toxin or antibody) having a toxic effect on cells

CZ abbr Canal Zone

czar also **tsar** or **tzar** \'zär, '(t)sär\ n [NL *czar*, fr. Russ *tsar'*, fr. ORuss *tsĭsarĭ*, fr. Goth *kaisar*, fr. Gk or L; Gk, fr. L *Caesar* — more at CAESAR] (1555) **1** : EMPEROR; specif : the ruler of Russia until the 1917 revolution **2** : one having great power or authority ⟨a banking ~⟩ — **czar·dom** also **tsar·dom** or **tzar·dom** \'zär-dəm, '(t)sär-\ n

czar·das \'chär-ˌdash, -ˌdäsh\ n, pl **czardas** [Hung *csárdás*] (1860) : a Hungarian dance to music in duple time in which the dancers start slowly and finish with a rapid whirl

czar·e·vitch also **tsar·e·vitch** or **tzar·e·vitch** \'zär-ə-ˌvich, '(t)sär-\ n [Russ *tsarevich*, fr. *tsar'* + *-evich*, patronymic suffix] (1710) : an heir apparent of a Russian czar

cza·ri·na also **tsa·ri·na** or **tza·ri·na** \zä-'rē-nə, (t)sä-\ n [prob. modif. of G *Zarin*, fr. *Zar* czar, fr. Russ *tsar'*] (1717) : the wife of a czar

czar·ism also **tsar·ism** or **tzar·ism** \'zär-ˌi-zəm, '(t)sär-\ n (1855) **1** : the government of Russia under the czars **2** : autocratic rule — **czar·ist** also **tsar·ist** or **tzar·ist** \'zär-ist, '(t)sär-\ n or adj

Czech \'chek\ n [Czech *Čech*] (1841) **1** : a native or inhabitant of western Czechoslovakia including Bohemia and Moravia **2** : the Slavic language of the Czechs **3** : a native or inhabitant of Czechoslovakia or the Czech Republic — **Czech** adj — **Czech·ish** \'che-kish\ adj

D

[1]**d** \ˈdē\ *n, pl* **d's** *or* **ds** \ˈdēz\ *often cap, often attrib* (bef. 12c) **1 a :** the 4th letter of the English alphabet **b :** a graphic representation of this letter **c :** a speech counterpart of orthographic *d* **2 :** five hundred — see NUMBER table **3 :** the second tone of a C-major scale **4 :** a graphic device for reproducing the letter *d* **5 :** one designated *d* esp. as the fourth in order or class **6 a :** a grade rating a student's work as poor in quality **b :** one graded or rated with a D **7 :** something shaped like the letter D; *specif* **:** a semicircle on a pool table about 23 inches in diameter for use esp. in snooker **8** *cap* **a :** DEFENSE 2b ⟨play tough *D*⟩ **b :** DEFENSE 4b

[2]**d** *abbr* **1** date **2** daughter **3** day **4** dead; deceased **5** deci- **6** degree **7** [L *denarius, denarii*] penny; pence **8** depart; departure **9** diameter **10** differential **11** dimensional **12** distance **13** dorsal **14** drive; driving

[1]**D** *abbr* **1** Democrat **2** derivative **3** Dutch

[2]**D** *symbol* deuterium

d- \ˌdē, ˈdē\ *prefix* [ISV, fr. *dextr-*] **1 :** dextrorotatory ⟨*d*-tartaric acid⟩ **2 :** having a similar configuration at a selected carbon atom to the configuration of dextrorotatory glyceraldehyde — usu. printed as a small capital ⟨D-fructose⟩

-d *symbol* — used after the figure 2 or 3 to indicate the ordinal number second or third ⟨*2d*⟩ ⟨*53d*⟩

'd \d, əd, id\ *vb* (1712) **1 :** HAD **2 :** WOULD **3 :** DID

da *abbr* deka-

[1]**DA** \ˌdē-ˈā\ *n* [*d*uck's *a*ss; fr. its resemblance to the tail of a duck] (1951) **:** DUCKTAIL

[2]**DA** *abbr* **1** days after acceptance **2** delayed action **3** deposit account **4** Dictionary of Americanisms **5** district attorney **6** documents against acceptance; documents for acceptance **7** don't answer

D/A *abbr* digital to analog

[1]**dab** \ˈdab\ *n* [ME *dabbe*] (14c) **1 :** a sudden blow or thrust **:** POKE **2 :** a small amount **3 :** a gentle touch or stroke **:** PAT **4 :** DAUB

[2]**dab** *vb* **dabbed; dab·bing** *vt* (1562) **1 :** to strike or touch lightly **:** PAT ⟨*dabbing* her eyes with a handkerchief⟩ **2 :** to apply lightly or irregularly **:** DAUB ⟨~ paint⟩ ~ *vi* **:** to make a dab — **dab·ber** *n*

[3]**dab** *n* [AF *dabbe*] (15c) **:** FLATFISH; *esp* **:** any of several flounders (genus *Limanda,* esp. *L. limanda*) — compare SAND DAB

[4]**dab** *n* [origin unknown] (1691) *chiefly Brit* **:** a skillful person

DAB *abbr* Dictionary of American Biography

dab·ble \ˈda-bəl\ *vb* **dab·bled; dab·bling** \-b(ə-)liŋ\ [perh. freq. of [2]*dab*] *vt* (1557) **:** to wet by splashing or by little dips or strokes **:** SPATTER ~ *vi* **1 a :** to paddle, splash, or play in or as if in water **b :** to reach with the bill to the bottom of shallow water in order to obtain food **2 :** to work or involve oneself superficially or intermittently esp. in a secondary activity or interest ⟨~*s* in art⟩

dab·bler \-b(ə-)lər\ *n* (1611) **:** one that dabbles: as **a :** one not deeply engaged in or concerned with something **b :** a duck (as a mallard or shoveler) that feeds by dabbling — called also *dabbling duck, puddle duck, river duck* ***syn*** see AMATEUR

dab·bling \-b(ə-)liŋ\ *n* (ca. 1847) **:** a superficial or intermittent interest, investigation, or experiment ⟨his ~*s* in philosophy and art⟩

dab·chick \ˈdab-ˌchik\ *n* [prob. irreg. fr. obs. E *dop* to dive + E *chick*] (ca. 1550) **:** any of several small grebes

dab hand *n* [[4]*dab*] (ca. 1828) *chiefly Brit* **:** EXPERT

da ca·po \dä-ˈkä-(ˌ)pō, də-\ *adv or adj* [It] (ca. 1724) **:** from the beginning — used as a direction in music to repeat

dace \ˈdās\ *n, pl* **dace** [ME *dace, darce,* fr. AF *dars,* fr. ML *darsus*] (15c) **1 :** a small freshwater European cyprinid fish (*Leuciscus leuciscus*) **2 :** any of various small No. American freshwater cyprinid fishes

da·cha \ˈdä-chə *also* ˈda-\ *n* [Russ, fr. ORuss, land allotted by a prince; akin to L *dos* dowry — more at DATE] (1896) **:** a Russian country cottage used esp. in the summer

dachs·hund \ˈdäks-ˌhu̇nt, -ˌhu̇nd; ˈdäk-sənt; *esp Brit* ˈdak-sənd\ *n* [G, fr. *Dachs* badger + *Hund* dog] (1882) **:** any of a breed of long-bodied, short-legged dogs of German origin that occur in short-haired, long-haired, and wirehaired varieties

dachshund

Da·cron \ˈdā-ˌkrän, ˈda-\ *trademark* — used for a synthetic polyester textile fiber

dac·tyl \ˈdak-tᵊl, -ˌtil\ *n* [ME *dactile,* fr. L *dactylus,* fr. Gk *daktylos,* lit., finger; fr. the fact that the first of three syllables is the longest, like the joints of the finger] (14c) **:** a metrical foot consisting of one long and two short syllables or of one stressed and two unstressed syllables (as in *tenderly*) — **dac·tyl·ic** \dak-ˈti-lik\ *adj or n*

dactyl- *or* **dactylo-** *comb form* [Gk *daktyl-, daktylo-,* fr. *daktylos*] **:** finger **:** toe **:** digit ⟨*dactylo*logy⟩

dac·ty·lol·o·gy \ˌdak-tə-ˈlä-lə-jē\ *n* (ca. 1656) **:** FINGER SPELLING

dad \ˈdad\ *n* [prob. baby talk] (15c) **:** FATHER 1a

Da·da \ˈdä-(ˌ)dä\ *n* [F] (1919) **:** a movement in art and literature based on deliberate irrationality and negation of traditional artistic values; *also* **:** the art and literature produced by this movement

da·da·ism \-ˌi-zəm\ *n, often cap* [F *dadaïsme*] (1919) **:** DADA — **da·da·ist** \-ˌist\ *n or adj, often cap* — **da·da·is·tic** \ˌdä-dä-ˈis-tik\ *adj, often cap*

dad·dy \ˈda-dē\ *n, pl* **daddies** (15c) **1 :** FATHER 1a **2 :** GRANDDADDY 2

dad·dy long·legs \ˌda-dē-ˈlȯŋ-ˌlegz, -ˌlāgz\ *n, pl* **daddy longlegs** (ca. 1814) **1** *chiefly Brit* **:** CRANE FLY **2 :** any of an order (Opiliones) of arachnids that have slender usu. long legs and that resemble spiders but have an oval body lacking a constriction — called also *harvestman*

[1]**da·do** \ˈdā-(ˌ)dō\ *n, pl* **da·does** [It, die, plinth] (1664) **1 a :** the part of a pedestal of a column above the base **b :** the lower part of an interior wall when specially decorated or faced; *also* **:** the decoration adorning this part of a wall **2 :** a rectangular groove cut to make a joint in woodworking; *specif* **:** one cut across the grain

[2]**dado** *vt* **da·doed; da·do·ing** (1881) **1 :** to provide with a dado **2 a :** to set into a groove **b :** to cut a dado in (as a plank)

DAE *abbr* Dictionary of American English

dae·dal \ˈdē-dᵊl\ *adj* [L *daedalus,* fr. Gk *daidalos*] (1590) **1 a :** SKILLFUL, ARTISTIC **b :** INTRICATE ⟨the computer's ~ circuitry⟩ **2 :** adorned with many things ⟨visions of cloud and light and ~ earth are the airman's daily scene —Laurence Binyon⟩

Dae·da·lus \ˈde-də-ləs, ˈdē-\ *n* [L, fr. Gk *Daidalos*] (1546) **:** the legendary builder of the Cretan labyrinth who makes wings to enable himself and his son Icarus to escape imprisonment — **Dae·da·lian** *or* **Dae·da·lean** \di-ˈdāl-yən\ *adj*

daemon *var of* DEMON

daff \ˈdaf\ *vt* [alter. of *doff*] (1596) **1** *archaic* **:** to thrust aside **2** *obs* **:** to put off (as with an excuse)

daf·fo·dil \ˈda-fə-ˌdil\ *n* [perh. fr. D *de affodil* the asphodel] (1548) **:** any of various perennial bulbous herbs (genus *Narcissus*) of the amaryllis family; *esp* **:** one whose flowers have a large corona elongated into a trumpet — compare JONQUIL, NARCISSUS

daf·fy \ˈda-fē\ *adj* **daf·fi·er; -est** [obs. E *daff,* n., fool] (ca. 1884) **:** CRAZY, FOOLISH — **daf·fi·ly** \ˈda-fə-lē\ *adv*

daft \ˈdaft *also* ˈdäft\ *adj* [ME *dafte* gentle, stupid; akin to OE *gedæfte* mild, gentle, ME *defte* deft, OCS po*dobati* to be fitting] (14c) **1 a :** SILLY, FOOLISH **b :** MAD, INSANE **2** *Scot* **:** frivolously merry — **daft·ly** *adv* — **daft·ness** \ˈdaf(t)-nəs\ *n*

[1]**dag** \ˈdag\ *n* [ME *dagge*] (14c) **1 :** a hanging end or shred **2 :** matted or manure-coated wool

[2]**dag** *abbr* dekagram

dag·ger \ˈda-gər\ *n* [ME] (14c) **1 :** a sharp pointed knife for stabbing **2 a :** something that resembles a dagger **b :** a character † used as a reference mark or to indicate a death date — **dag·ger·like** \-ˌlīk\ *adj* — **at daggers drawn :** in a state of open hostility or conflict — **look daggers** *or* **stare daggers :** to stare angrily ⟨they *looked daggers* at each other across the table⟩

dag·ger·board \ˈda-gər-ˌbȯrd\ *n* (ca. 1930) **:** a removable narrow centerboard in some small boats that is raised and lowered by sliding up and down

da·go \ˈdā-(ˌ)gō\ *n, pl* **dagos** *or* **dagoes** [alter. of earlier *diego,* fr. *Diego,* a common Sp given name] (1832) *usu offensive* **:** a person of Italian or Spanish birth or descent

da·guerre·o·type \də-ˈger-rō-ˌtīp, -rə-; -ˈger-ō-, -ə- *also* də-ˈge-rē-ō-ˌtīp, -ˈger-ē-\ *n* [F *daguerréotype,* fr. L. J. M. *Daguerre* + F *-o-* + *type*] (1839) **:** an early photograph produced on a silver or a silver-covered copper plate; *also* **:** the process of producing such photographs — **daguerreotype** *vt* — **da·guerre·o·typ·ist** \-ˌtī-pist\ *n* — **da·guerre·o·typy** \-ˌtī-pē\ *n*

dah \ˈdä\ *n* [imit.] (1940) **:** DASH 7

DAH *abbr* Dictionary of American History

dahl·ia \ˈdal-yə, ˈdäl-, *U.S. also & Brit usu* ˈdāl-\ *n* [NL, genus name, fr. Anders *Dahl* †1789 Swed. botanist] (1835) **:** any of a genus (*Dahlia*) of American tuberous-rooted composite herbs having opposite pinnate leaves and rayed flower heads and including many that are cultivated as ornamentals

daid·zein \ˈdād-ˌzīn, -ˌzēn\ *n* [ISV, alter. of *daidzin,* substance from which daidzein is derived, fr. *daidz-* (fr. Jp *daizu* soybean) + [1]*-in*] (1945) **:** an isoflavone $C_{15}H_{10}O_4$ found chiefly in legumes and esp. soybeans

dai·kon \ˈdī-kən\ *n* [Jp, fr. *dai* big + *kon* root] (1876) **:** a large long hard white radish used esp. in Asian cuisine; *also* **:** a plant (*Raphanus sativus longipinnatus*) whose root is a daikon

dai·li·ness \ˈdā-lē-nəs, -li-\ *n* (1596) **:** daily or routine quality **:** ORDINARINESS ⟨the ~ of family life⟩

[1]**dai·ly** \ˈdā-lē\ *adj* (15c) **1 a :** occurring, made, or acted upon every day ⟨~ needs⟩ **b :** issued every day or every weekday ⟨a ~ newspaper⟩ **c :** of or providing for every day ⟨a ~ schedule⟩ **2 a :** reckoned by the day ⟨average ~ wage⟩ **b :** covering the period of or based on a day ⟨~ statistics⟩

[2]**daily** *adv* (15c) **1 :** every day **2 :** every weekday

[3]**daily** *n, pl* **dai·lies** (1832) **1 :** a newspaper published every weekday **2** *Brit* **:** a servant who works on a daily basis **3** *pl* **:** RUSH 6

daily double *n* (1932) **:** a system of betting (as on horse races) in which the bettor must pick the winners of two stipulated races in order to win

daily dozen *n* (1919) **1 :** a series of physical exercises to be performed daily **:** WORKOUT **2 :** a set of routine duties or tasks

dai·mon \ˈdī-ˌmōn\ *n, pl* **dai·mo·nes** \ˈdī-mə-ˌnēz\ *or* **daimons** [Gk *daimōn*] (1769) **1 :** DEMON 2 **2 :** DEMON 3 — **dai·mon·ic** \dī-ˈmä-nik\ *adj*

dai·myo *also* **dai·mio** \ˈdī-mē-ˌō, -(ˌ)myō\ *n, pl* **-myo** *or* **-myos** *also* **-mio** *or* **-mios** [Jp *daimyō*] (1727) **:** a Japanese feudal baron

[1]**dain·ty** \ˈdān-tē\ *n, pl* **dain·ties** [ME *deinte* high esteem, delight, fr. AF *deinté,* fr. L *dignitat-, dignitas* dignity, worth] (14c) **1 a :** something delicious to the taste **b :** something choice or pleasing **2** *obs* **:** FASTIDIOUSNESS

[2]**dainty** *adj* **dain·ti·er; -est** (14c) **1 a :** tasting good **:** TASTY **b :** attractively prepared and served **2 :** marked by delicate or diminutive beauty, form, or grace ⟨~ teacups⟩ **3** *obs* **:** CHARY, RELUCTANT **4 a :** marked by fastidious discrimination or finicky taste **b :** showing avoidance of anything rough ***syn*** see CHOICE — **dain·ti·ly** \ˈdān-tə-lē\ *adv* — **dain·ti·ness** \ˈdān-tē-nəs\ *n*

dai·qui·ri \ˈda-kə-rē, ˈdī-\ *n* [*Daiquirí,* Cuba] (1920) **:** a cocktail made usu. of rum, lime juice, and sugar

dairy \ˈder-ē\ *n, pl* **dair·ies** *often attrib* [ME *deyerie,* fr. *deye* dairymaid, fr. OE *dǣge* kneader of bread; akin to OE *dāg* dough — more at DOUGH] (14c) **1 :** a room, building, or establishment where milk is kept and butter or cheese is made **2 a :** the department of farming or of a farm that is concerned with the production of milk, butter, and cheese **b :** a farm devoted to such production **3 :** an establishment for the sale or distribution chiefly of milk and milk products

dairy cattle *n pl* (1895) **:** cattle kept for milk production

dairy•ing \ˈder-ē-iŋ\ *n* (1649) **:** the business of operating a dairy
dairy•maid \-ˌmād\ *n* (1599) **:** a woman employed in a dairy
dairy•man \-mən, -ˌman\ *n* (ca. 1617) **:** one who operates a dairy farm or works in a dairy
da•is \ˈdā-əs, ÷ˈdī-\ *n* [ME *deis,* fr. AF, fr. LL *discus* high table, fr. L, dish, quoit — more at DISH] (13c) **:** a raised platform (as in a hall or large room)
daishiki *var of* DASHIKI
dai•sy \ˈdā-zē\ *n, pl* **daisies** [ME *dayeseye,* fr. OE *dægesēage,* fr. *dæg* day + *ēage* eye] (bef. 12c) **1 :** a composite plant (as of the genera *Bellis* or *Chrysanthemum*) having a flower head with well-developed ray flowers usu. arranged in one or a few whorls: as **a :** a low European herb (*Bellis perennis*) with white or pink ray flowers — called also *English daisy* **b :** a leafy-stemmed perennial herb (*Chrysanthemum leucanthemum*) with long white ray flowers and a yellow disk that was introduced into the U.S. from Europe — called also *oxeye daisy* **2 :** the flower head of a daisy **3 :** a first-rate person or thing **4** *cap* **:** a member of a program of the Girl Scouts for girls in kindergarten and first grade
daisy–chain *vt* (1955) **:** to link (as computer components) together in series
daisy chain *n* (1841) **1 :** a string of daisies with stems linked to form a chain **2 :** an interlinked series ‹a *daisy chain* of computer peripherals› ‹a *daisy chain* of toddlers›
daisy ham *n* (ca. 1933) **:** a boned and smoked piece of pork from the shoulder
daisy wheel *n* [fr. its resemblance to the flower] (ca. 1977) **:** a disk with spokes bearing type that serves as the printing element of an electric typewriter or printer; *also* **:** a printer that uses such a disk
Da•ko•ta \də-ˈkō-tə\ *n, pl* **Dakotas** *also* **Dakota** [Dakota (Yankton-Yanktonai and Santee dialects) *dakʰóta,* perh. lit., friendly, allied] (1804) **1 :** a member of an American Indian people of the northern Mississippi River valley **2 :** the Siouan language of the Dakota people
[1]**dal** *also* **dahl** \ˈdäl\ *n* [Hindi & Urdu *dāl*] (1673) **:** a dried legume (as lentils, beans, or peas); *also* **:** an Indian dish made of simmered and usu. pureed and spiced legumes
[2]**dal** *also* **daL** *abbr* dekaliter
Da•lai La•ma \ˌdä-lī-ˈlä-mə, ˌdä-lā-, ˌda-\ *n* [Mongolian *dalai* ocean] (1698) **:** the spiritual head of Tibetan Buddhism
da•la•si \dä-ˈlä-sē\ *n, pl* **dalasi** *or* **dalasis** [Wolof, prob. ultim. fr. West African F *dala* 5-franc coin, fr. E dollar] (1966) — see MONEY table
dale \ˈdāl\ *n* [ME, fr. OE *dæl;* akin to OHG *tal* valley, W *dôl*] (bef. 12c) **:** VALLEY, VALE ‹went riding over hill and ~›
dales•man \ˈdālz-mən\ *n* (1769) *Brit* **:** one living or born in a dale
da•leth \ˈdä-ˌleth, -ˌlet *also* -ləd\ *n* [Heb *dāleth,* fr. *deleth* door] (1567) **:** the 4th letter of the Hebrew alphabet — see ALPHABET table
dal•li•ance \ˈda-lē-ən(t)s\ *n* (14c) **:** an act of dallying: as **a :** PLAY; *esp* **:** amorous play **b :** frivolous action **:** TRIFLING
Dal•lis grass \ˈda-ləs-\ *n* [A. T. *Dallis,* 19th cent. Am. farmer] (1907) **:** a tall tufted tropical So. American perennial grass (*Paspalum dilatatum*) introduced as a pasture and forage grass in the southern U.S.
Dall sheep \ˈdȯl-\ *n* [William H. *Dall* †1927 Am. naturalist] (1887) **:** a large white wild sheep (*Ovis dalli*) of Alaska and northern British Columbia — called also *Dall's sheep* \ˈdȯlz-\
Dall's por•poise *n* [W. H. *Dall*] (1951) **:** a black-and-white porpoise (*Phocoenoides dalli*) of temperate and arctic waters of the rim of the No. Pacific Ocean — called also *Dall porpoise*
dal•ly \ˈda-lē\ *vi* **dal•lied; dal•ly•ing** [ME *dalyen,* fr. AF *dalier*] (15c) **1 a :** to act playfully; *esp* **:** to play amorously **b :** to deal lightly **:** TOY ‹accused him of *~ing* with a serious problem› **2 a :** to waste time **b :** LINGER, DAWDLE ***syn*** see TRIFLE, DELAY — **dal•li•er** *n*
dal•ma•tian \dal-ˈmā-shən\ *n, often cap* [fr. the supposed origin of the breed in Dalmatia] (1824) **:** any of a breed of medium-sized dogs having a white short-haired coat with many black or brown spots
dal•mat•ic \dal-ˈma-tik\ *n* [ME *dalmatyk,* fr. OE *dalmatice,* fr. LL *dalmatica,* fr. L, fem. of *dalmaticus* Dalmatian, fr. *Dalmatia*] (bef. 12c) **1 :** a wide-sleeved overgarment with slit sides worn by a deacon or prelate **2 :** a robe worn by a British sovereign at his or her coronation
dal se•gno \däl-ˈsā-(ˌ)nyō\ *adv* [It, from the sign] (ca. 1854) — used as a direction in music to return to the sign that marks the beginning of a repeat
dal•ton \ˈdȯl-tᵊn\ *n* [John *Dalton* †1844 Eng. chemist] (ca. 1928) **:** ATOMIC MASS UNIT — used chiefly in biochemistry
[1]**dam** \ˈdam\ *n* [ME *dam, dame* lady, dam — more at DAME] (13c) **:** the female parent of an animal and esp. of a domestic animal
[2]**dam** *n* [ME, prob. fr. MD; akin to OE *fordemman* to stop up] (14c) **1 :** a body of water confined by a barrier **2 a :** a barrier preventing the flow of water or of loose solid materials (as soil or snow); *esp* **:** a barrier built across a watercourse for impounding water **b :** a barrier to check the flow of liquid, gas, or air
[3]**dam** *vt* **dammed; dam•ming** (15c) **1 :** to provide or restrain with a dam ‹~ a river› **2 :** to stop up **:** BLOCK ‹*damming* up their emotions›
[4]**dam** *abbr* dekameter
[1]**dam•age** \ˈda-mij\ *n* [ME, fr. AF, fr. *dan* damage, fr. L *damnum*] (14c) **1 :** loss or harm resulting from injury to person, property, or reputation **2** *pl* **:** compensation in money imposed by law for loss or injury **3 :** EXPENSE, COST ‹"What's the ~?" he asked the waiter›
[2]**damage** *vt* **dam•aged; dam•ag•ing** (14c) **:** to cause damage to ‹don't ~ the furniture› ‹returning soldiers *damaged* by war› ***syn*** see INJURE — **dam•age•abil•i•ty** \ˌda-mi-jə-ˈbi-lə-tē\ *n* — **dam•ag•er** *n*
damage control *n* (1943) **:** measures taken to offset or minimize damage to reputation, credibility, or public image caused by a controversial act, remark, or revelation
damaged goods *n pl* (1807) **:** a person considered to be flawed or spoiled in character, efficiency, or worth
dam•ag•ing *adj* (ca. 1828) **:** causing or able to cause damage **:** INJURIOUS ‹has a ~ effect on wildlife› — **dam•ag•ing•ly** \ˈda-mi-jiŋ-lē\ *adv*
dam•ar *or* **dam•mar** \ˈda-mər\ *n* [Malay] (1698) **:** any of various resins used in varnishes and inks and obtained chiefly in Malaya and Indonesia from several timber trees (families Dipterocarpaceae and Burseraceae)
[1]**dam•a•scene** \ˈda-mə-ˌsēn, ˌda-mə-ˈ\ *n* (14c) **1** *cap* **:** a native or inhabitant of Damascus **2 :** the characteristic markings of Damascus steel
[2]**damascene** *adj* (14c) **1** *cap* **:** of, relating to, or characteristic of Damascus or the Damascenes **2 :** of or relating to damask or the art of damascening
[3]**damascene** *vt* **-scened; -scen•ing** [MF *damasquiner,* fr. *damasquin* of Damascus] (1585) **:** to ornament (as iron or steel) with wavy patterns like those of watered silk or with inlaid work of precious metals
Da•mas•cus steel \də-ˈmas-kəs-\ *n* (ca. 1727) **:** hard elastic steel ornamented with wavy patterns and used esp. for sword blades
[1]**dam•ask** \ˈda-məsk\ *n* [ME *damaske,* fr. ML *damascus,* fr. *Damascus*] (14c) **1 :** a firm lustrous fabric (as of linen, cotton, silk, or rayon) made with flat patterns in a satin weave on a plain-woven ground on jacquard looms **2 :** DAMASCUS STEEL; *also* **:** the characteristic markings of this steel **3 :** a grayish red
[2]**damask** *adj* (15c) **1 :** made of or resembling damask **2 :** of the color damask
damask rose *n* [obs. *Damask* of Damascus, fr. obs. *Damask* Damascus] (1540) **:** a hardy rose (*Rosa damascena*) widely introduced from Asia Minor and having large fragrant pink or white flowers that are the major source of attar of roses
dame \ˈdām\ *n* [ME, fr. AF, fr. L *domina,* fem. of *dominus* master; akin to L *domus* house — more at DOME] (13c) **1 :** a woman of rank, station, or authority: as **a** *archaic* **:** the mistress of a household **b :** the wife or daughter of a lord **c :** a female member of an order of knighthood — used as a title prefixed to the given name **2 a :** an elderly woman **b :** WOMAN
dame school *n* (1810) **:** a school in which the rudiments of reading and writing were taught by a woman in her own home
dame's rocket *n* (ca. 1900) **:** a Eurasian perennial plant (*Hesperis matronalis*) of the mustard family cultivated for its spikes of showy fragrant white or purplish flowers — called also *dame's violet, rocket*
dam•i•ana \ˌda-mē-ˈa-nə\ *n* [AmerSp] (1868) **1 :** the dried leaf of a tropical American shrub (*Turnera diffusa* syn. *T. aphrodisiaca*) used esp. formerly as an aphrodisiac and tonic; *also* **:** a preparation containing damiana **2 :** the plant from which damiana is obtained
[1]**damn** \ˈdam\ *vb* **damned; damn•ing** \ˈda-miŋ\ [ME *dampnen,* fr. AF *dampner,* fr. L *damnare,* fr. *damnum* damage, loss, fine] *vt* (13c) **1 :** to condemn to a punishment or fate; *esp* **:** to condemn to hell **2 a :** to condemn vigorously and often irascibly for some real or fancied fault or defect ‹*~ed* the storm for their delay› **b :** to condemn as a failure by public criticism **3 :** to bring ruin on **4 :** to swear at **:** CURSE — often used to express annoyance, disgust, or surprise ‹~ him, he should have been careful› ‹I'll be *~ed*› ~ *vi* **:** CURSE, SWEAR
[2]**damn** *n* (1619) **1 :** the utterance of the word *damn* as a curse **2 :** a minimum amount or degree (as of care or consideration) **:** the least bit ‹don't give a ~›
[3]**damn** *adj or adv* (1775) **:** DAMNED ‹a ~ nuisance› ‹ran ~ fast› — **damn well :** beyond doubt or question **:** CERTAINLY ‹knew *damn well* what would happen›
dam•na•ble \ˈdam-nə-bəl\ *adj* (14c) **1 :** liable to or deserving condemnation **2 :** very bad **:** DETESTABLE ‹~ weather› — **dam•na•ble•ness** *n* — **dam•na•bly** \-blē\ *adv*
dam•na•tion \dam-ˈnā-shən\ *n* (14c) **:** the act of damning **:** the state of being damned
dam•na•to•ry \ˈdam-nə-ˌtȯr-ē\ *adj* (1682) **:** expressing, imposing, or causing condemnation **:** CONDEMNATORY
[1]**damned** \ˈdam(d)\ *adj* **damned•er** \ˈdam-dər\; **damned•est** *or* **damnd•est** \-dəst\ (1596) **1 :** DAMNABLE ‹this ~ smog› **2 :** COMPLETE, UTTER — often used as an intensive ‹a ~ shame› **3 :** EXTRAORDINARY — used in the superlative ‹the *~est* contraption you ever saw›
[2]**damned** \ˈdam(d)\ *adv* (1757) **:** EXTREMELY, VERY ‹a ~ good job›
damned•est *or* **damnd•est** \ˈdam-dəst\ *n* (1682) **:** UTMOST, BEST — used chiefly in the phrase *do one's damnedest* ‹doing my ~ to win›
dam•ni•fy \ˈdam-nə-ˌfī\ *vt* **-fied; -fy•ing** [MF *damnifier,* fr. OF, fr. LL *damnificare,* fr. L *damnificus* injurious, fr. *damnum* damage] (1512) **:** to cause loss or damage to
damn•ing \ˈda-miŋ\ *adj* (1595) **1 :** bringing damnation ‹a ~ sin› **2 :** causing or leading to condemnation or ruin ‹presented some ~ testimony› — **damn•ing•ly** \-miŋ-lē\ *adv*
Dam•o•cles \ˈda-mə-ˌklēz\ *n* [L, fr. Gk *Damoklēs*] (1578) **:** a courtier of ancient Syracuse held to have been seated at a banquet beneath a sword hung by a single hair — **Dam•o•cle•an** \ˌda-mə-ˈklē-ən\ *adj*
Da•mon \ˈdā-mən\ *n* [L, fr. Gk *Damōn*] (1557) **:** a legendary Sicilian who pledges his life for his condemned friend Pythias
[1]**damp** \ˈdamp\ *n* [ME, black damp, fr. MD or MLG, vapor; akin to OHG *damph* vapor] (14c) **1 :** a noxious gas — compare BLACK DAMP, FIREDAMP **2 :** MOISTURE: **a :** HUMIDITY, DAMPNESS **b** *archaic* **:** FOG, MIST **3 a :** DISCOURAGEMENT, CHECK **b** *archaic* **:** DEPRESSION, DEJECTION
[2]**damp** *vt* (14c) **1 a :** to affect with or as if with a noxious gas **:** CHOKE **b :** to diminish the activity or intensity of ‹*~ing* down the causes of inflation› ‹liquid *~s* out compass oscillations› **c :** to check the vibration or oscillation of (as a string or voltage) **2 :** DAMPEN ~ *vi* **:** to diminish progressively in vibration or oscillation
[3]**damp** *adj* (1590) **1 a** *archaic* **:** being confused, bewildered, or shocked **:** STUPEFIED **b :** DEPRESSED, DULL **2 :** slightly or moderately wet **:** MOIST ‹a ~ towel›; *also* **:** HUMID ‹~ weather› ***syn*** see WET — **damp•ish** \ˈdam-pish\ *adj* — **damp•ly** *adv* — **damp•ness** *n*
damp•en \ˈdam-pən\ *vb* **damp•ened; damp•en•ing** \ˈdamp-niŋ, ˈdam-pə-\ *vt* (1547) **1 :** to check or diminish the activity or vigor of **:** DEADEN ‹the heat *~ed* our spirits› **2 :** to make damp ‹the shower barely *~ed* the ground› **3 :** DAMP 1c ~ *vi* **1 :** to become damp **2 :** to become deadened or depressed — **damp•en•er** \-nər\ *n*
damp•er \ˈdam-pər\ *n* (1707) **1 :** a dulling or deadening influence ‹put a ~ on the celebration› **2 :** a device that damps: as **a :** a valve or plate (as in the flue of a furnace) for regulating the draft **b :** a small felted block to stop the vibration of a piano string **c** *chiefly Brit* **:** SHOCK ABSORBER **3** *Austral* **:** a simple usu. unleavened bread of a kind made originally in the Australian bush
damp•ing–off \ˌdam-piŋ-ˈȯf\ *n* (1890) **:** a diseased condition of seedlings or cuttings caused by fungi and marked by wilting or rotting
dam•sel \ˈdam-zəl\ *also* **dam•o•sel** *or* **dam•o•zel** \ˈda-mə-ˌzel\ *n* [ME *damesel,* fr. AF *dameisele,* fr. VL **domnicella* young noblewoman, dim.

of L *domina* lady] (13c) **:** a young woman: **a** *archaic* **:** a young unmarried woman of noble birth **b :** GIRL
dam·sel·fish \ˈdam-zəl-ˌfish\ *n* (1904) **:** any of numerous often brilliantly colored marine fishes (family Pomacentridae) living esp. along coral reefs — called also *demoiselle*
dam·sel·fly \-ˌflī\ *n* (1815) **:** any of numerous odonate insects (suborder Zygoptera) distinguished from dragonflies by laterally projecting eyes and usu. stalked wings folded above the body when at rest
dam·son \ˈdam-zən\ *n* [ME, fr. L (*prunum*) *damascenum,* lit., plum of Damascus] (14c) **:** the small tart fruit of a widely cultivated Asian plum tree (*Prunus insititia*); *also* **:** this tree
[1]**Dan** \ˈdan\ *n* [Heb *Dān*] (bef. 12c) **:** a son of Jacob and the traditional eponymous ancestor of one of the tribes of Israel
[2]**Dan** \ˈdan\ *n* [ME, title of members of religious orders, fr. AF, fr. L *dominus* master] (13c) *archaic* **:** MASTER, SIR
[3]**Dan** *abbr* **1** Daniel **2** Danish
Dan·aë \ˈda-nə-ˌē\ *n* [L, fr. Gk *Danaē*] (1562) **:** a princess of Argos visited by Zeus in the form of a shower of gold and by him the mother of Perseus
da·na·zol \ˈdä-nə-ˌzōl, ˈda-, -ˌzȯl\ *n* [*dan-* (perh. anagram of *and*rogenic) + isox*azole*, the compound C_3H_3NO] (1974) **:** a synthetic androgen $C_{22}H_{27}NO_2$ that inhibits the release of gonadotropins by the pituitary gland and is used esp. to treat endometriosis
[1]**dance** \ˈdan(t)s, ˈdän(t)s\ *vb* **danced; danc·ing** [ME *dauncen,* fr. AF *dancer*] *vi* (14c) **1 :** to engage in or perform a dance **2 :** to move or seem to move up and down or about in a quick or lively manner ~ *vt* **1 :** to perform or take part in as a dancer **2 :** to cause to dance **3 :** to bring into a specified condition by dancing — **dance·able** \ˈdan(t)-sə-bəl\ *adj* — **danc·er** *n* — **dance attendance :** to attend in an eager and servile manner ⟨a celebrity used to having people *dance attendance* on him⟩
[2]**dance** *n, often attrib* (14c) **1 :** an act or instance of dancing **2 :** a series of rhythmic and patterned bodily movements usu. performed to music **3 :** a social gathering for dancing **4 :** a piece of music by which dancing may be guided **5 :** the art of dancing
dance card *n* (1895) **1 :** a card listing partners for scheduled dances **2 :** a calendar of engagements
D & C *abbr* dilation and curettage
dan·de·li·on \ˈdan-də-ˌlī-ən, -dē-\ *n* [ME *dendelyoun,* fr. AF *dent de lion,* lit., lion's tooth] (14c) **:** any of a genus (*Taraxacum*) of yellow-flowered composite herbs with milky sap; *esp* **:** one (*T. officinale*) sometimes grown as a potherb and nearly cosmopolitan as a weed

dandelion

dan·der \ˈdan-dər\ *n* [alter. of *dandruff*] (1786) **1 :** DANDRUFF; *specif* **:** minute scales from hair, feathers, or skin that may be allergenic **2 :** ANGER, TEMPER ⟨now don't get your ~ up⟩
dan·di·a·cal \dan-ˈdī-ə-kəl\ *adj* [ˈ*dandy* + *-acal* (as in *demoniacal*)] (1831) **:** of, relating to, or suggestive of a dandy
Dan·die Din·mont terrier \ˈdan-dē-ˈdin-ˌmänt-\ *n* [*Dandie Dinmont,* character owning six such dogs in the novel *Guy Mannering* by Sir Walter Scott] (1875) **:** any of a breed of terriers characterized by short legs, a long body, pendulous ears, a rough coat, and a full silky topknot
dan·di·fy \ˈdan-di-ˌfī\ *vt* **-fied; -fy·ing** (1823) **:** to cause to resemble a dandy — **dan·di·fi·ca·tion** \ˌdan-di-fə-ˈkā-shən\ *n*
dan·dle \ˈdan-dᵊl\ *vt* **dan·dled; dan·dling** \-(d)liŋ, -dᵊl-iŋ\ [origin unknown] (1530) **1 :** to move (as a baby) up and down in one's arms or on one's knee in affectionate play **2 :** PAMPER, PET
dan·druff \ˈdan-drəf\ *n* [prob. fr. *dand-* (origin unknown) + *-ruff,* fr. ME *rove* scabby condition, fr. ON *hrūfa* scab; akin to OHG *hruf* scurf, Lith *kraupus* rough] (1545) **:** scaly white or grayish flakes of dead skin cells esp. of the scalp; *also* **:** the condition marked by excessive shedding of such flakes and usu. accompanied by itching — **dan·druffy** \-drə-fē\ *adj*
[1]**dan·dy** \ˈdan-dē\ *n, pl* **dandies** [prob. short for *jack-a-dandy,* fr. ˈ*jack* + *a* (of) + *dandy* (origin unknown)] (ca. 1780) **1 :** a man who gives exaggerated attention to personal appearance **2 :** something excellent in its class — **dan·dy·ish** \-dē-ish\ *adj* — **dan·dy·ish·ly** *adv*
[2]**dandy** *adj* **dan·di·er; -est** (1792) **1 :** of, relating to, or suggestive of a dandy **:** FOPPISH **2 :** very good **:** FIRST-RATE ⟨a ~ place to stay⟩
dan·dy·ism \ˈdan-dē-ˌi-zəm\ *n* (1819) **1 :** the style or conduct of a dandy **2 :** a literary and artistic style of the latter part of the 19th century marked by artificiality and excessive refinement
Dane \ˈdān\ *n* [ME *Dan,* fr. ON *Danr*] (14c) **1 :** a native or inhabitant of Denmark **2 :** a person of Danish descent **3 :** GREAT DANE
dane·geld \ˈdān-ˌgeld\ *n, often cap* (bef. 12c) **:** an annual tax believed to have been imposed orig. to buy off Danish invaders in England or to maintain forces to oppose them but continued as a land tax
Dane·law \ˈdān-ˌlȯ\ *n* (bef. 12c) **1 :** the law in force in the part of England held by the Danes before the Norman Conquest **2 :** the part of England under the Danelaw
[1]**dang** \ˈdaŋ\ *vt* [euphemism] (ca. 1797) **:** DAMN 4
[2]**dang** *adj or adv* (1914) **:** DAMNED
[1]**dan·ger** \ˈdān-jər\ *n* [ME *daunger,* fr. AF *dangier, dongier,* fr. VL **dominiarium,* fr. L *dominium* ownership] (13c) **1 a** *archaic* **:** JURISDICTION **b** *obs* **:** REACH, RANGE **2** *obs* **:** HARM, DAMAGE **3 :** exposure or liability to injury, pain, harm, or loss ⟨a place where children could play without ~⟩ **4 :** a case or cause of danger ⟨the ~*s* of mining⟩
[2]**danger** *vt* (14c) *archaic* **:** ENDANGER
dan·ger·ous \ˈdān-jə-rəs; ˈdān-jərs, -zhrəs\ *adj* (15c) **1 :** exposing to or involving danger ⟨a ~ job⟩ **2 :** able or likely to inflict injury or harm ⟨a ~ man⟩ — **dan·ger·ous·ly** *adv* — **dan·ger·ous·ness** *n*
syn DANGEROUS, HAZARDOUS, PRECARIOUS, PERILOUS, RISKY mean bringing or involving the chance of loss or injury. DANGEROUS applies to something that may cause harm or loss unless dealt with carefully ⟨soldiers on a *dangerous* mission⟩. HAZARDOUS implies great and continuous risk of harm or failure ⟨claims that smoking is *hazardous* to your health⟩. PRECARIOUS suggests both insecurity and uncertainty ⟨earned a *precarious* living by gambling⟩. PERILOUS strongly implies the immediacy of danger ⟨*perilous* mountain roads⟩. RISKY often applies to a known and accepted danger ⟨shied away from *risky* investments⟩.
[1]**dan·gle** \ˈdaŋ-gəl\ *vb* **dan·gled; dan·gling** \-g(ə-)liŋ\ [prob. of Scand origin; akin to Dan *dangle* to dangle] *vi* (1565) **1 :** to hang loosely and usu. so as to be able to swing freely **2 :** to be a hanger-on or a dependent **3 :** to occur in a sentence without having a normally expected syntactic relation to the rest of the sentence (as *climbing* in "Climbing the mountain the cabin came into view") ⟨a *dangling* participle⟩ ⟨a *dangling* modifier⟩ ~ *vt* **1 :** to cause to dangle **:** SWING ⟨*dangled* her feet in the water⟩ **2 a :** to keep hanging uncertainly **b :** to hold out as an inducement — **dan·gler** \-g(ə-)lər\ *n*
[2]**dangle** *n* (1756) **1 :** the action of dangling **2 :** something that dangles
Dan·iel \ˈdan-yəl *also* ˈda-nᵊl\ *n* [Heb *Dānīʼēl*] (bef. 12c) **1 :** the Jewish hero of the Book of Daniel who as an exile in Babylon interprets dreams, gives accounts of apocalyptic visions, and is divinely delivered from a den of lions **2 :** a book of narratives, visions, and prophecies in canonical Jewish and Christian Scripture — see BIBLE table
da·nio \ˈdā-nē-ˌō\ *n, pl* **da·ni·os** [NL, genus name] (ca. 1889) **:** any of various small brightly colored Asian cyprinid fishes (genera *Danio* and *Brachydanio*) — compare ZEBRA FISH
[1]**Dan·ish** \ˈdā-nish\ *adj* (14c) **:** of, relating to, or characteristic of Denmark, the Danes, or the Danish language
[2]**Danish** *n* (15c) **1 :** the Germanic language of the Danes **2** *pl* **Danish :** a piece of Danish pastry
Danish pastry *n* (1921) **:** a pastry made of a rich raised dough
dank \ˈdaŋk\ *adj* [ME *danke*] (1573) **:** unpleasantly moist or wet ⟨a ~ basement⟩ ***syn*** see WET — **dank·ly** *adv* — **dank·ness** *n*
dan·seur \däⁿ-ˈsər, dän-\ *n* [F, fr. *danser* to dance] (1776) **:** a male ballet dancer
dan·seuse \däⁿ-sœz; däⁿ-ˈsə(r)z, dän-ˈsüz\ *n* [F, fem. of *danseur*] (1776) **:** a female ballet dancer
Dan·te·an \ˈdan-tē-ən, ˈdän-\ *adj* (1785) **:** of, relating to, or suggestive of Dante or his writings; *esp* **:** having a hellish or bizarre quality ⟨refugees lived a ~ existence —A. E. Cowdrey⟩
Daoism *var of* TAOISM
daph·ne \ˈdaf-nē\ *n* [NL, genus name, fr. L, laurel, fr. Gk *daphnē*] (ca. 1841) **:** any of a genus (*Daphne*) of Eurasian shrubs of the mezereon family with apetalous flowers whose colored calyx resembles a corolla
Daph·ne \ˈdaf-nē\ *n* [L, fr. Gk *Daphnē*] (15c) **:** a nymph in Greek mythology who is transformed into a laurel tree to escape the pursuing Apollo
daph·nia \ˈdaf-nē-ə\ *n* [NL, genus name] (1847) **:** any of a genus (*Daphnia*) of minute freshwater branchiopod crustaceans with biramous antennae used as locomotor organs — compare WATER FLEA
Daph·nis \ˈdaf-nəs\ *n* [L, fr. Gk] (1563) **:** a Sicilian shepherd renowned in Greek mythology as the inventor of pastoral poetry
dap·per \ˈda-pər\ *adj* [ME *dapyr,* fr. MD *dapper* quick, strong; akin to OHG *tapfar* heavy, OCS *debelŭ* thick] (15c) **1 a :** neat and trim in appearance **b :** very spruce and stylish **2 :** alert and lively in movement and manners — **dap·per·ly** *adv* — **dap·per·ness** *n*
[1]**dap·ple** \ˈda-pəl\ *n* [ME *dappel-gray,* adj., gray marked with spots of another color] (1580) **1 :** any of numerous usu. cloudy and rounded spots or patches of a color or shade different from their background **2 :** the quality or state of being dappled **3 :** a dappled animal
[2]**dapple** *vb* **dap·pled; dap·pling** \-p(ə-)liŋ\ *vt* (1599) **:** to mark with dapples ~ *vi* **:** to produce a dappled pattern ⟨sun *dappling* through trees⟩
dap·pled *also* **dap·ple** *adj* (15c) **:** marked with small spots or patches contrasting with the background ⟨a ~ fawn⟩
dap·sone \ˈdap-ˌsōn\ *n* [*di*amine + *p*henyl + *sulfone*] (1952) **:** an antimicrobial agent $C_{12}H_{12}N_2O_2S$ used esp. to treat leprosy and a chronic form of dermatitis
DAR *abbr* Daughters of the American Revolution
Dar·by and Joan \ˌdär-bē-ən-ˈjōn\ *n* [prob. fr. *Darby & Joan,* couple in an 18th cent. song] (1760) **:** a happily married usu. elderly couple
Dard \ˈdärd\ *n* (1902) **:** DARDIC
Dar·dan \ˈdär-dᵊn\ *adj or n* [L *Dardanus,* fr. Gk *Dardanos*] (1513) *archaic* **:** TROJAN
Dar·da·ni·an \där-ˈdā-nē-ən\ *adj* (1581) **:** TROJAN
Dar·dic \ˈdär-dik\ *n* (1910) **:** a complex of Indo-Aryan languages spoken in the upper valley of the Indus
[1]**dare** \ˈder\ *vb* **dared; dar·ing; dares** *or (auxiliary)* **dare** [ME *dar* (1st & 3d sing. pres. indic.), fr. OE *dear;* akin to OHG *gitar* (1st & 3d sing. pres. indic.) dare, Gk *tharsos* courage] *verbal auxiliary* (bef. 12c) **:** to be sufficiently courageous to ⟨no one *dared* say a word⟩ ⟨she ~ not let herself love —G. B. Shaw⟩ ~ *vi* **:** to have sufficient courage ⟨try it if you ~⟩ ~ *vt* **1 a :** to challenge to perform an action esp. as a proof of courage ⟨*dared* him to jump⟩ **b :** to confront boldly **:** DEFY ⟨*dared* the anger of his family⟩ **2 :** to have the courage to contend against, venture, or try ⟨the actress *dared* a new interpretation of this classic role⟩ — **dar·er** \ˈder-ər\ *n*
[2]**dare** *n* (1594) **1 :** an act or instance of daring **:** CHALLENGE ⟨foolishly took a ~⟩ **2 :** imaginative or vivacious boldness **:** DARING
DARE *abbr* Dictionary of American Regional English
[1]**dare·dev·il** \ˈder-ˌde-vᵊl\ *adj* (1727) **:** recklessly and often ostentatiously daring ***syn*** see ADVENTUROUS
[2]**daredevil** *n* (1794) **:** a recklessly bold person — **dare·dev·il·ry** \-vᵊl-rē\ *n* — **dare·dev·il·try** \-vᵊl-trē\ *n*
dareful *adj* (1580) *obs* **:** DARING
daren't \ˈder-ənt\ **:** dare not **:** dared not
dare·say \ˌder-ˈsā\ *vt* (13c) **:** venture to say **:** think probable — used in pres. 1st sing. ~ *vi* **:** AGREE, SUPPOSE — used in pres. 1st sing.
[1]**dar·ing** *adj* (1575) **:** venturesomely bold in action or thought ***syn*** see ADVENTUROUS — **dar·ing·ly** \-iŋ-lē\ *adv* — **dar·ing·ness** *n*
[2]**daring** *n* (1584) **:** venturesome boldness
Dar·jee·ling \där-ˈjē-liŋ\ *n* [*Darjeeling,* India] (1895) **:** a tea of high quality grown esp. in the mountainous districts of northern India

\ə\ **abut** \ᵊ\ kitten, F table \ər\ **fur**ther \a\ **a**sh \ā\ **a**ce \ä\ m**o**p, m**a**r
\au̇\ **ou**t \ch\ **ch**in \e\ b**e**t \ē\ **ea**sy \g\ **g**o \i\ h**i**t \ī\ **i**ce \j\ **j**ob
\ŋ\ si**ng** \ō\ g**o** \ȯ\ l**aw** \ȯi\ b**oy** \th\ **th**in \th\ **th**e \ü\ l**oo**t \u̇\ f**oo**t
\y\ **y**et \zh\ vi**s**ion, beige \k, ⁿ, œ, ue, ʸ\ *see* Guide to Pronunciation

[1]**dark** \ˈdärk\ *adj* [ME *derk,* fr. OE *deorc;* akin to OHG *tarchannen* to hide] (bef. 12c) **1 a :** devoid or partially devoid of light : not receiving, reflecting, transmitting, or radiating light ⟨a ~ room⟩ **b :** transmitting only a portion of light ⟨~ glasses⟩ **2 a :** wholly or partially black ⟨~ clothing⟩ **b** *of a color* **:** of low or very low lightness **c :** being less light in color than other substances of the same kind ⟨~ rum⟩ **3 a :** arising from or showing evil traits or desires : EVIL ⟨the ~ powers that lead to war⟩ **b :** DISMAL, GLOOMY ⟨had a ~ view of the future⟩ **c :** lacking knowledge or culture : UNENLIGHTENED ⟨a ~ period in history⟩ **d :** relating to grim or depressing circumstances ⟨~ humor⟩ **4 a :** not clear to the understanding **b :** not known or explored because of remoteness ⟨the ~*est* reaches of the continent⟩ **5 :** not fair in complexion : SWARTHY **6 :** SECRET ⟨kept his plans ~⟩ **7 :** possessing depth and richness ⟨a ~ voice⟩ **8 :** closed to the public ⟨the theater is ~ in the summer⟩ ***syn*** see OBSCURE — **dark·ish** \ˈdär-kish\ *adj* — **dark·ly** *adv* — **dark·ness** *n*

[2]**dark** *n* (13c) **1 a :** a place or time of little or no light : NIGHT, NIGHTFALL **b :** absence of light : DARKNESS **2 :** a dark or deep color — **in the dark 1 :** in secrecy ⟨most of his dealings were done *in the dark*⟩ **2 :** in ignorance ⟨kept the public *in the dark* about the agreement⟩

[3]**dark** *vi* (14c) *obs* **:** to grow dark ~ *vt* **:** to make dark

dark adaptation *n* (1900) **:** the process including dilation of the pupil, increase in sensitivity of the retinal rods, and regeneration of rhodopsin by which the eye adapts to conditions of reduced illumination — **dark–adapt·ed** \ˌdärk-ə-ˈdap-təd\ *adj*

dark age *n* (1640) **1 :** a time during which a civilization undergoes a decline: as **a** *pl, cap D&A* **:** the European historical period from about A.D. 476 to about 1000; *broadly* **:** MIDDLE AGES **b** *often pl, often cap D&A* **:** the Greek historical period of three to four centuries from about 1100 B.C. **2 a** *often pl, often cap D&A* **:** the primitive period in the development of something ⟨in the *dark ages* of medicine⟩ **b** *often pl, often cap D&A* **:** a state of stagnation or decline

dark continent *n* (1829) **1** *often cap D&C* **:** the continent of Africa **2 :** something unknown or unexplored

dark·en \ˈdär-kən\ *vb* **dark·ened; dark·en·ing** \ˈdär-kə-niŋ\ *vi* (14c) **1 :** to grow dark : become obscured ⟨the skies were ~*ing*⟩ **2 :** to become gloomy ⟨his mood ~*ed*⟩ ~ *vt* **1 :** to make dark **2 :** to make less clear : OBSCURE ⟨the financial crisis ~*ed* the future of the company⟩ **3 :** TAINT, TARNISH ⟨~*ed* his reputation⟩ **4 :** to cast a gloom over **5 :** to make of darker color — **dark·en·er** \-kə-nər\ *n*

dark energy *n* (1998) **:** a hypothetical form of energy that produces a force that opposes gravity and is thought to be the cause of the accelerating expansion of the universe

dark–eyed junco *n* (1974) **:** a common No. American junco (*Junco hyemalis*)

dark field *n* (1865) **:** the dark area that serves as the background for objects viewed in an ultramicroscope

dark–field microscope *n* (1926) **:** ULTRAMICROSCOPE

dark horse *n* (1831) **1 a :** a usu. little known contender (as a racehorse) that makes an unexpectedly good showing **b :** an entrant in a contest that is judged unlikely to succeed **2 :** a political candidate unexpectedly nominated usu. as a compromise between factions

dark lantern *n* (1640) **:** a lantern that can be closed to conceal the light

dar·kle \ˈdär-kəl\ *vi* **dar·kled; dar·kling** \-k(ə-)liŋ\ [back-formation fr. *darkling*] (1800) **1 a :** to become clouded or gloomy **b :** to grow dark **2 :** to become concealed in the dark

[1]**dark·ling** \ˈdär-kliŋ\ *adv* [ME *derkelyng,* fr. *derk* dark + *-lyng* -ling] (15c) **:** in the dark

[2]**dark·ling** *adj* (1718) **1 :** DARK **2 :** done or taking place in the dark

darkling beetle *n* (1816) **:** any of a family (Tenebrionidae) of firm-bodied mostly dark-colored vegetable-feeding nocturnal beetles which often have vestigial and functionless wings and whose larvae are usu. hard cylindrical worms (as a mealworm) — called also *tenebrionid*

dark matter *n* (1982) **:** nonluminous matter not yet directly detected by astronomers that is hypothesized to exist to account for various observed gravitational effects

dark reaction *n* (1927) **:** any of a series of chemical reactions in photosynthesis not requiring the presence of light and involving the reduction of carbon dioxide to form carbohydrate; *esp* **:** CALVIN CYCLE

dark·room \ˈdärk-ˌrüm, -ˌru̇m\ *n* (1841) **:** a room with no light or with a safelight for developing light-sensitive photographic materials

dark·some \ˈdärk-səm\ *adj* (ca. 1530) **:** gloomily somber : DARK

darky *or* **dark·ie** \ˈdär-kē\ *n, pl* **darkies** (1775) *usu offensive* **:** a black person

[1]**dar·ling** \ˈdär-liŋ\ *n* [ME *derling,* fr. OE *dēorling,* fr. *dēore* dear] (bef. 12c) **1 :** a dearly loved person **2 :** FAVORITE ⟨a director who is the ~ of the critics⟩

[2]**darling** *adj* (15c) **1 :** dearly loved : FAVORITE **2 :** very pleasing : CHARMING — **dar·ling·ly** \-liŋ-lē\ *adv* — **dar·ling·ness** *n*

darm·stadt·i·um \ˌdärm-ˈsta-tē-əm\ *n* [NL, fr. *Darmstadt,* Germany] (2003) **:** a short-lived radioactive element produced artificially — see ELEMENT table

[1]**darn** \ˈdärn\ *vb* [perh. fr. F dial. *darner*] *vt* (ca. 1600) **1 :** to mend with interlacing stitches **2 :** to embroider by filling in with long running or interlacing stitches ~ *vi* **:** to do darning — **darn·er** *n*

[2]**darn** *n* (1720) **:** a place that has been darned ⟨a sweater full of ~*s*⟩

[3]**darn** \ˈdärn\ *also* **durn** \ˈdərn\ *adj or adv* [euphemism] (1781) **:** DAMNED

[4]**darn** *also* **durn** *vb* (1781) **:** DAMN — **darned** \ˈdärn(d)\ *also* **durned** \ˈdərn(d)\ *adj or adv*

[5]**darn** *also* **durn** *n* (1840) **:** DAMN

dar·nel \ˈdär-nᵊl\ *n* [ME] (14c) **:** any of several usu. weedy ryegrasses (genus *Lolium*)

darning needle *n* (1742) **1 :** a long needle with a large eye for use in darning **2 :** DRAGONFLY, DAMSELFLY

DARPA *abbr* Defense Advanced Research Projects Agency

[1]**dart** \ˈdärt\ *n* [ME, fr. AF, of Gmc origin; akin to OHG *tart* dart, OE *daroth*] (14c) **1 a** *archaic* **:** a light spear **b (1) :** a small missile usu. with a pointed shaft at one end and feathers at the other **(2)** *pl but sing in constr* **:** a game in which darts are thrown at a target **2 a :** something projected with sudden speed; *esp* **:** a sharp glance **b :** something causing sudden pain or distress ⟨~*s* of sarcasm⟩ **3 :** something with a slender pointed shaft or outline; *specif* **:** a stitched tapering fold in a garment **4 :** a quick movement ⟨made a ~ for the door⟩

[2]**dart** *vt* (1573) **1 :** to throw with a sudden movement **2 :** to thrust or move with sudden speed **3 :** to shoot with a dart containing a usu. tranquilizing drug ~ *vi* **:** to move suddenly or rapidly ⟨~*ed* across the street⟩

dart·board \ˈdärt-ˌbȯrd\ *n* (1901) **:** a usu. circular board (as of compressed bristles) used as a target in the game of darts

dart·er \ˈdär-tər\ *n* (1796) **1 :** ANHINGA **2 :** any of numerous small No. American freshwater bony fishes (esp. genera *Ammocrypta, Etheostoma,* and *Percina* of the family Percidae)

Dar·win·i·an \där-ˈwi-nē-ən\ *adj* (1860) **1 :** of or relating to Charles Darwin, his theories esp. of evolution, or his followers **2 :** of, relating to, or being a competitive environment or situation in which only the fittest persons or organizations prosper — **Darwinian** *n*

Dar·win·ism \ˈdär-wə-ˌni-zəm\ *n* (1864) **1 :** a theory of the origin and perpetuation of new species of animals and plants that offspring of a given organism vary, that natural selection favors the survival of some of these variations over others, that new species have arisen and may continue to arise by these processes, and that widely divergent groups of plants and animals have arisen from the same ancestors — compare EVOLUTION 4, NEO-DARWINISM **2 :** a theory that inherent dynamic forces allow only the fittest persons or organizations to prosper in a competitive environment or situation ⟨economic ~⟩ — compare SOCIAL DARWINISM — **Dar·win·ist** \-wə-nist\ *n or adj*

Dar·win's finches \ˌdär-wənz-\ *n pl* [Charles *Darwin*] (1947) **:** finches of a subfamily (Geospizinae) having great variation in bill shape and confined mostly to the Galápagos Islands

Dar·win tulip \ˌdär-wən-\ *n* (1889) **:** a tall late-flowering tulip with the flowers single and of one color

[1]**dash** \ˈdash\ *vb* [ME *dasshen,* prob. fr. MF *dachier* to impel forward] *vt* (14c) **1 :** to break by striking or knocking **2 :** to knock, hurl, or thrust violently **3 :** SPLASH, SPATTER **4 a :** RUIN, DESTROY ⟨the news ~*ed* his hopes⟩ **b :** DEPRESS, SADDEN **c :** to make ashamed **5 :** to affect by mixing in something different ⟨his delight was ~*ed* with bitterness⟩ **6 :** to complete, execute, or finish off hastily — used with *down* or *off* ⟨~*ed* down a drink⟩ ⟨~ off a letter⟩ **7** [euphemism] **:** [1]DAMN 4 ~ *vi* **1 :** to move with sudden speed **2 :** SMASH

[2]**dash** *n* (14c) **1 a** *archaic* **:** BLOW **b (1) :** a sudden burst or splash **(2) :** the sound produced by such a burst **2 a :** a stroke of a pen **b :** a punctuation mark — that is used esp. to indicate a break in the thought or structure of a sentence **3 :** a small usu. distinctive addition ⟨a ~ of salt⟩ ⟨a ~ of humor⟩ **4 :** flashy display **5 :** animation in style and action **6 a :** a sudden onset, rush, or attempt **b :** a short fast race **7 :** a long click or buzz forming a letter or part of a letter (as in Morse code) **8 :** DASHBOARD 2

dash·board \ˈdash-ˌbȯrd\ *n* (1842) **1 :** a screen on the front of a usu. horse-drawn vehicle to intercept water, mud, or snow **2 :** a panel extending across the interior of a vehicle (as an automobile) below the windshield and usu. containing instruments and controls

dashed \ˈdasht\ *adj* (ca. 1889) **:** made up of a series of dashes

da·sheen \da-ˈshēn, də-\ *n* [origin unknown] (ca. 1899) **:** TARO

dash·er \ˈda-shər\ *n* (1790) **1 :** a dashing person **2 :** one that dashes **3 :** a device having blades for agitating a liquid or semisolid

dashi \ˈdä-(ˌ)shē\ *n* [Jp, broth] (1955) **:** a fish broth made from dried bonito

da·shi·ki \də-ˈshē-kē, dä-, da-\ *also* **dai·shi·ki** \dī-\ *n* [modif. of Yoruba *dàńṣíkí*] (ca. 1968) **:** a usu. brightly colored loose-fitting pullover garment

dashiki

dash·ing *adj* (ca. 1697) **1 :** marked by vigorous action **:** SPIRITED ⟨a ~ young horse⟩ **2 :** marked by smartness esp. in dress and manners — **dash·ing·ly** \-iŋ-lē\ *adv*

dash·pot \ˈdash-ˌpät\ *n* (1861) **:** a device for cushioning or damping a movement (as of a mechanical part) to avoid shock

das·sie \ˈda-sē\ *n* [Afrik] (1814) **:** HYRAX

das·tard \ˈdas-tərd\ *n* [ME] (15c) **1 :** COWARD **2 :** a person who acts treacherously or underhandedly

das·tard·ly \-lē\ *adj* (1542) **1 :** COWARDLY **2 :** characterized by underhandedness or treachery ⟨a ~ attack⟩ ⟨a ~ villain⟩ ***syn*** see COWARDLY — **das·tard·li·ness** *n*

dat *abbr* dative

DAT *abbr* **1** differential aptitude test **2** digital audiotape

da·ta \ˈdā-tə, ˈda- *also* ˈdä-\ *n pl but sing or pl in constr, often attrib* [L, pl. of *datum*] (1646) **1 :** factual information (as measurements or statistics) used as a basis for reasoning, discussion, or calculation ⟨the ~ is plentiful and easily available —H. A. Gleason, Jr.⟩ ⟨comprehensive ~ on economic growth have been published —N. H. Jacoby⟩ **2 :** information output by a sensing device or organ that includes both useful and irrelevant or redundant information and must be processed to be meaningful **3 :** information in numerical form that can be digitally transmitted or processed

usage *Data* leads a life of its own quite independent of *datum,* of which it was originally the plural. It occurs in two constructions: as a plural noun (like *earnings*), taking a plural verb and plural modifiers (as *these, many, a few*) but not cardinal numbers, and serving as a referent for plural pronouns; and as an abstract mass noun (like *information*), taking a singular verb and singular modifiers (as *this, much, little*), and being referred to by a singular pronoun. Both constructions are standard. The plural construction is more common in print, perhaps because the house style of some publishers mandates it.

data bank *n* (1966) **:** DATABASE

da·ta·base \ˈdā-tə-ˌbās, ˈda- *also* ˈdä-\ *n* (ca. 1962) **:** a usu. large collection of data organized esp. for rapid search and retrieval (as by a computer) — **database** *vt*

data mining *n* (1988) **:** the practice of searching through large amounts of computerized data to find useful patterns or trends

data processing *n* (1954) **:** the converting of raw data to machine-readable form and its subsequent processing (as storing, updating, rearranging, or printing out) by a computer — **data processor** *n*

data structure *n* (1963) **:** any of various methods or formats (as an array, file, or record) for organizing data in a computer

[1]**date** \ˈdāt\ *n* [ME, fr. AF, ultim. fr. L *dactylus* — more at DACTYL] (14c) **1 :** the oblong edible fruit of a palm (*Phoenix dactylifera*) **2 :** the tall palm with pinnate leaves that yields the date

[2]**date** *n* [ME, fr. AF, fr. LL *data,* fr. *data* (as in *data Romae* given at Rome), fem. of L *datus,* pp. of *dare* to give; akin to L *dos* gift, dowry, Gk *didonai* to give] (14c) **1 a :** the time at which an event occurs ⟨the ~ of his birth⟩ **b :** a statement of the time of execution or making ⟨the ~ on the letter⟩ **2 :** DURATION **3 :** the period of time to which something belongs **4 a :** an appointment to meet at a specified time; *esp* **:** a social engagement between two persons that often has a romantic character **b :** a person with whom one has a usu. romantic date **5 :** an engagement for a professional performance (as of a dance band) — **to date :** up to the present moment

[3]**date** *vb* **dat·ed; dat·ing** *vt* (15c) **1 :** to determine the date of ⟨~ an antique⟩ **2 :** to record the date of **:** mark with the date **3 a :** to mark with characteristics typical of a particular period **b :** to show up plainly the age of **4 :** to make or have a date with ~ *vi* **1 :** to reckon chronologically **2 :** ORIGINATE ⟨a friendship *dating* from college days⟩ **3 :** to become dated **4 :** to go out on usu. romantic dates — **dat·able** *also* **date·able** \ˈdā-tə-bəl\ *adj* — **dat·er** \ˈdā-tər\ *n*

dat·ed *adj* (1578) **1 :** provided with a date ⟨a ~ document⟩ **2 :** OUTMODED, OLD-FASHIONED ⟨~ formalities⟩ — **dat·ed·ly** *adv* — **dat·ed·ness** *n*

date·less \ˈdāt-ləs\ *adj* (1593) **1 :** ENDLESS **2 :** having no date **3 :** too ancient to be dated **4 :** TIMELESS ⟨the play's ~ theme⟩

date·line \ˈdāt-ˌlīn\ *n* (1888) **1 :** a line in a written document or a printed publication giving the date and place of composition or issue **2** *usu* **date line :** INTERNATIONAL DATE LINE — **dateline** *vt*

date–rape *vt* (1984) **:** to commit date rape on — **date rapist** *n*

date rape *n* (1975) **:** rape committed by the victim's date; *broadly* **:** ACQUAINTANCE RAPE

date rape drug *n* (1995) **:** a drug (as GHB) administered surreptitiously (as in a drink) to induce an unconscious or sedated state in a potential date rape victim

[1]**da·tive** \ˈdā-tiv\ *adj* [ME *datif,* fr. L *dativus,* fr. *datus*] (15c) **:** of, relating to, or being the grammatical case that marks typically the indirect object of a verb, the object of some prepositions, or a possessor

[2]**dative** *n* (15c) **:** a dative case or form

dative bond *n* [fr. the donation of electrons by one of the atoms] (ca. 1929) **:** COORDINATE BOND

da·tum \ˈdā-təm, ˈda-, ˈdä-\ *n* [L, fr. neut. of *datus*] (1646) **1** *pl* **da·ta** \-ə\ **:** something given or admitted esp. as a basis for reasoning or inference **2** *pl* **datums :** something used as a basis for calculating or measuring ***usage*** see DATA

da·tu·ra \də-ˈt(y)u̇r-ə\ *n* [ultim. fr. Hindi *dhatūrā* jimsonweed (or a cognate descendant of Skt *dhattūraḥ*)] (1598) **:** any of a genus (*Datura*) of widely distributed strong-scented herbs, shrubs, or trees of the nightshade family including some used as sources of medicinal alkaloids (as stramonium) or in folk rites or illicitly for their poisonous, narcotic, or hallucinogenic properties — compare JIMSONWEED

dau *abbr* daughter

[1]**daub** \ˈdȯb, ˈdäb\ *vb* [ME, fr. AF *dauber*] *vt* (14c) **1 :** to cover or coat with soft adhesive matter **:** PLASTER **2 :** to coat with a dirty substance **3 a :** to apply coloring material crudely to **b :** to apply (as paint) crudely ~ *vi* **1** *archaic* **:** to put on a false exterior **2 :** to apply colors crudely — **daub·er** *n*

[2]**daub** *n* (15c) **1 :** material used to daub walls **2 :** an act or instance of daubing **3 :** something daubed on **:** SMEAR **4 :** a crude picture

daube \ˈdōb\ *n* [F] (1723) **:** a stew of braised meat, vegetables, herbs, and spices

[1]**daugh·ter** \ˈdȯ-tər, ˈdä-\ *n* [ME, *doughter,* fr. OE *dohtor;* akin to OHG *tohter* daughter, Gk *thygatēr*] (bef. 12c) **1 a :** a female offspring esp. of human parents **b :** a female adopted child **c :** a human female descendant **2 :** something considered as a daughter ⟨the United States is a ~ of Great Britain⟩ **3 :** an atomic species that is the product of the radioactive decay of a given element — **daugh·ter·less** \-ləs\ *adj*

[2]**daughter** *adj* (1614) **1 :** having the characteristics or relationship of a daughter **2 :** belonging to the first generation of offspring, organelles, or molecules produced by reproduction, division, or replication ⟨~ cell⟩ ⟨~ DNA molecules⟩

daugh·ter–in–law \ˈdȯ-tər-in-ˌlȯ, ˈdȯ-tərn-\ *n, pl* **daugh·ters–in–law** \-tər-zin-\ (14c) **:** the wife of one's son

dau·no·my·cin \ˌdȯ-nə-ˈmī-sᵊn, ˌdau̇-\ *n* [ISV *dauno-* (fr. L *Daunus* Apulian) + *-mycin*] (1963) **:** DAUNORUBICIN

dau·no·ru·bi·cin \-ˈrü-bə-sᵊn\ *n* [*dauno-* (as in *daunomycin*) + *rubidomycin,* a substance found to be identical with daunomycin (fr. ISV *rubido-* —fr. L *rubidus* red— + *-mycin*)] (ca. 1968) **:** an antibiotic $C_{27}H_{29}NO_{10}$ that is a nitrogenous glycoside and is used esp. in the treatment of leukemia

daunt \ˈdȯnt, ˈdänt\ *vt* [ME, fr. AF *danter, daunter,* fr. L *domitare* to tame, freq. of *domare* — more at TAME] (14c) **:** to lessen the courage of **:** COW, SUBDUE ***syn*** see DISMAY

daunt·ing \ˈdȯn-tiŋ\ *adj* (13c) **:** tending to overwhelm or intimidate ⟨a ~ task⟩ — **daunt·ing·ly** \-tiŋ-lē\ *adv*

daunt·less \-ləs\ *adj* (1588) **:** FEARLESS, UNDAUNTED ⟨a ~ hero⟩ — **daunt·less·ly** *adv* — **daunt·less·ness** *n*

dau·phin \ˈdȯ-fən, ˈdō-; ˌdō-ˈfaⁿ\ *n, often cap* [ME *dolphin,* fr. AF *dolphyn,* fr. OF *dalfin,* title of lords of the Dauphiné, fr. *Dalfin,* a surname] (15c) **:** the eldest son of a king of France

dau·phine \dȯ-ˈfēn, dō-\ *n, often cap* [F] (1824) **:** the wife of the dauphin

DAV *abbr* Disabled American Veterans

da·ven *also* **do·ven** \ˈdä-vən, ˈdȯ-\ *vi* [Yiddish *davnen*] (ca. 1930) **:** to recite the prescribed prayers in a Jewish liturgy

dav·en·port \ˈda-vᵊn-ˌpȯrt, ˈda-vᵊm-\ *n* [prob. fr. the name *Davenport*] (1853) **1 :** a small compact writing desk **2 :** a large upholstered sofa often convertible into a bed

Da·vid \ˈdā-vəd\ *n* [Heb *Dāwīdh*] (bef. 12c) **1 :** a Hebrew shepherd who became the second king of Israel in succession to Saul according to biblical accounts **2 :** UNDERDOG 1 — **Da·vid·ic** \də-ˈvi-dik, dā-\ *adj*

da·vit \ˈdā-vət, ˈda-\ *n* [ME *daviot,* fr. AF, fr. MF *daviet* joiner's cramp, dim. of *david* cramp, prob. fr. the name *David*] (15c) **:** a crane that projects over the side of a ship or a hatchway and is used esp. for boats, anchors, or cargo

Da·vy Jones \ˌdā-vē-ˈjōnz\ *n* (1751) **:** the bottom of the sea personified

Da·vy Jones's locker \ˌdā-vē-ˌjōnz(-əz)-\ *n* (ca. 1777) **:** the bottom of the ocean

[1]**daw** \ˈdȯ, ˈdä\ *vi* [ME, fr. OE *dagian;* akin to OHG *tagēn* to dawn, OE *dæg* day] (13c) *chiefly Scot* **:** DAWN

[2]**daw** \ˈdȯ\ *n* [ME *dawe;* akin to OHG *taha* jackdaw] (15c) **:** JACKDAW

daw·dle \ˈdȯ-dᵊl\ *vb* **daw·dled; daw·dling** \ˈdȯ-dliŋ, -dᵊl-iŋ\ [origin unknown] *vi* (ca. 1656) **1 :** to spend time idly **2 :** to move lackadaisically ~ *vt* **:** to spend fruitlessly or lackadaisically ⟨*dawdled* the day away⟩ ***syn*** see DELAY — **daw·dler** \ˈdȯ-dlər, -dᵊl-ər\ *n*

[1]**dawn** \ˈdȯn, ˈdän\ *vi* [ME, prob. back-formation fr. *dawning* daybreak, alter. of *dawing,* fr. OE *dagung,* fr. *dagian*] (15c) **1 :** to begin to grow light as the sun rises **2 :** to begin to appear or develop **3 :** to begin to be perceived or understood ⟨the truth finally ~*ed* on us⟩

[2]**dawn** *n* (15c) **1 :** the first appearance of light in the morning followed by sunrise **2 :** BEGINNING ⟨the ~ of the space age⟩

dawn horse *n* (1930) **:** EOHIPPUS

dawn redwood *n* (1948) **:** a metasequoia (*Metasequoia glyptostroboides*) of China resembling the coast redwood but having deciduous foliage

day \ˈdā\ *n* [ME, fr. OE *dæg;* akin to OHG *tag* day] (bef. 12c) **1 a :** the time of light between one night and the next **b :** DAYLIGHT 1 **c :** DAYTIME **2 :** the period of rotation of a planet (as earth) or a moon on its axis **3 :** the mean solar day of 24 hours beginning at mean midnight **4 :** a specified day or date **5 :** a specified time or period **:** AGE ⟨in grandfather's ~⟩ — often used in pl. ⟨the old ~*s*⟩ ⟨the ~*s* of sailing ships⟩ **6 :** the conflict or contention of the day ⟨played hard and won the ~⟩ **7 :** the time established by usage or law for work, school, or business — **day after day :** for an indefinite or seemingly endless number of days — **day in, day out :** for an indefinite number of successive days

Day·ak *also* **Dy·ak** \ˈdī-ˌak\ *n, pl* **Dayaks** *or* **Dayak** *also* **Dyaks** *or* **Dyak** [Malay, lit., up-country] (1836) **:** a member of any of several Indonesian peoples of the interior of Borneo

day·bed \ˈdā-ˌbed\ *n* (1679) **1 :** a chaise longue of a type made 1680–1780 **2 :** a couch that can be converted into a bed

day·book \-ˌbu̇k\ *n* (1580) **:** DIARY, JOURNAL

day·break \-ˌbrāk\ *n* (1530) **:** DAWN

day care *n* (1945) **1 :** supervision of and care for children or disabled adults that is provided during the day by a person or organization **2 :** a program, facility, or organization offering day care

[1]**day·dream** \ˈdā-ˌdrēm\ *n* (1685) **:** a pleasant visionary usu. wishful creation of the imagination — **day·dream·like** \-ˌlīk\ *adj*

[2]**daydream** *vi* (1820) **:** to have a daydream — **day·dream·er** *n*

day·flow·er \ˈdā-ˌflau̇(-ə)r\ *n* (ca. 1688) **:** any of a genus (*Commelina*) of herbs of the spiderwort family having one petal smaller than the other two; *esp* **:** a blue-flowered Asian herb (*C. communis*) with the smaller petal white that has become naturalized as a weed in the U.S.

Day–Glo \ˈdā-ˌglō\ *trademark* — used for fluorescent materials or colors

day·glow \ˈdā-ˌglō\ *n* (ca. 1960) **:** airglow seen during the day

day job *n* (1977) **:** one's regular employment as contrasted with an occasional, secondary, or coveted job

day laborer *n* (1548) **:** one who works for daily wages esp. as an unskilled laborer

day letter *n* (ca. 1913) **:** a telegram sent during the day that has a lower priority than a regular telegram

day·light \ˈdā-ˌlīt\ *n* (13c) **1 :** the light of day **2 :** DAYTIME **3 :** DAWN **4 a :** knowledge or understanding of something that has been obscure ⟨began to see ~ on the problem⟩ **b :** the quality or state of being open **:** OPENNESS **5** *pl* **a :** CONSCIOUSNESS **b :** mental soundness or stability **:** WITS ⟨scared the ~*s* out of him⟩ **6 :** a perceptible space, gap, or difference ⟨denied there was any ~ between the two governments' positions⟩

day·light·ing \ˈdā-ˌlī-tiŋ\ *n* (1929) **:** illumination of indoor spaces by natural light

daylight saving time *n* (1919) **:** time usu. one hour ahead of standard time — called also *daylight saving, daylight savings, daylight savings time, daylight time*

day·lily \ˈdā-ˌli-lē\ *n* (1597) **:** any of various Eurasian perennial herbs (genus *Hemerocallis*) of the lily family that have short-lived flowers resembling lilies and are widespread in cultivation and as escapes

day·long \ˈdā-ˌlȯŋ\ *adj* (1855) **:** lasting all day ⟨a ~ tour⟩

day·mare \ˈdā-ˌmer\ *n* [*day* + *-mare* (as in *nightmare*)] (1737) **:** a nightmarish fantasy experienced while awake

day–neutral *adj* (1941) **:** developing and maturing regardless of relative length of alternating exposures to light and dark periods — used esp. of a plant; compare LONG-DAY, SHORT-DAY

day nursery *n* (1844) **:** a public center for the care and training of young children; *specif* **:** NURSERY SCHOOL

Day of Atonement (1611) **:** YOM KIPPUR

day one *n, often cap D&O* (1971) **:** the first day or very beginning of something

day·room \ˈdā-ˌrüm, -ˌru̇m\ *n* (1823) **:** a room (as in a hospital) equipped for relaxation and recreation

days \ˈdāz\ *adv* (bef. 12c) **:** in the daytime repeatedly **:** on any day

day school *n* (1831) **:** an elementary or secondary school held on weekdays; *specif* **:** a private school without boarding facilities

day·side \ˈdā-ˌsīd\ *n* (1963) **:** the side of a planet in sunlight

day·star \ˈdā-ˌstär\ *n* (bef. 12c) **1 :** MORNING STAR **2 :** SUN 1a

day student *n* (1883) **:** a student who attends regular classes at a college or preparatory school but does not live at the institution

day·time \ˈdā-ˌtīm\ *n, often attrib* (1535) **:** the time during which there is daylight

day·times \ˈdā-ˌtīmz\ *adv* (1854) **:** DAYS ⟨has a housekeeper ~⟩

\ə\ **abut** \ᵊ\ kitten, F table \ər\ **further** \a\ **ash** \ā\ **ace** \ä\ **mop, mar** \au̇\ **out** \ch\ **chin** \e\ **bet** \ē\ **easy** \g\ **go** \i\ **hit** \ī\ **ice** \j\ **job** \ŋ\ **sing** \ō\ **go** \ȯ\ **law** \ȯi\ **boy** \th\ **thin** \t͟h\ **the** \ü\ **loot** \u̇\ **foot** \y\ **yet** \zh\ **vision, beige** \k̲, ⁿ, œ, ue, ʸ\ *see* Guide to Pronunciation

day–to–day \ˈdā-tə-ˌdā\ *adj* (1862) **1 :** taking place, made, or done in the course of days ⟨in charge of ~ operations⟩; *also* **:** EVERYDAY ⟨~ life⟩ **2 :** providing for a day at a time with little thought for the future ⟨an aimless ~ existence⟩
day trader *n* (1953) **:** a speculator who seeks profit from the intraday fluctuation in the price of a security or commodity by completing double trades of buying and selling or selling and covering during a single session of the market — **day–trade** \ˈdā-ˌtrād\ *n or vb*
day–trip·per \ˈdā-ˌtri-pər\ *n* (1897) **:** one who takes a trip that does not last overnight
daze \ˈdāz\ *vt* **dazed; daz·ing** [ME *dasen,* fr. ON **dasa;* akin to ON *dasask* to become exhausted] (14c) **1 :** to stupefy esp. by a blow **:** STUN **2 :** to dazzle with light — **daze** *n* — **da·zed·ly** \ˈdā-zəd-lē\ *adv* — **dazed·ness** \ˈdā-zəd-nəs, ˈdāzd-\ *n*
daz·zle \ˈda-zəl\ *vb* **daz·zled; daz·zling** \-z(ə-)liŋ\ [freq. of *daze*] *vi* (15c) **1 :** to lose clear vision esp. from looking at bright light **2 a :** to shine brilliantly **b :** to arouse admiration by an impressive display ~ *vt* **1 :** to overpower with light **2 :** to impress deeply, overpower, or confound with brilliance ⟨*dazzled* us with her wit⟩ — **dazzle** *n* — **dazzler** \-z(ə-)lər\ *n* — **daz·zling·ly** \-z(ə-)liŋ-lē\ *adv*
dB *abbr* decibel
Db *symbol* dubnium
DB *abbr* daybook
d/b/a *abbr* doing business as
DBA *abbr* doctor of business administration
DBCP \ˌdē-(ˌ)bē-(ˌ)sē-ˈpē\ *n* [*di-* + *b*rom- + *c*hlor- + *p*ropane] (1967) **:** a compound $C_3H_5Br_2Cl$ used esp. formerly as an agricultural pesticide that is a suspected carcinogen and cause of sterility in human males
DBE *abbr* Dame Commander of the Order of the British Empire
DBH *abbr* diameter at breast height
dbl *or* **dble** *abbr* double
DBMS *abbr* database management system
DBS *abbr* direct broadcast satellite
DC *abbr* **1** [It *da capo*] from the beginning **2** decimal classification **3** direct current **4** District of Columbia **5** doctor of chiropractic **6** double crochet
DChE *abbr* doctor of chemical engineering
DCL *abbr* **1** doctor of canon law **2** doctor of civil law
dd *abbr* **1** dated **2** delivered
DD *abbr* **1** days after date **2** demand draft **3** dishonorable discharge **4** doctor of divinity **5** due date
D–day *n* [*D,* abbr. for *day*] (1918) **:** a day set for launching an operation; *specif* **:** June 6, 1944, on which Allied forces began the invasion of France in World War II
ddC \ˌdē-(ˌ)dē-ˈsē\ *n, often all cap* [*d*i- + *d*eoxy + *c*ytidine] (1986) **:** a synthetic nucleoside $C_9H_{13}N_3O_3$ that inhibits replication of retroviruses and is used in the treatment of advanced HIV infection — called also *zalcitabine*
DDC *abbr* Dewey Decimal Classification
DDD \ˌdē-(ˌ)dē-ˈdē\ *n* [*d*ichlor- + *d*iphenyl + *d*ichlor-] (1946) **:** an insecticide $C_{14}H_{10}Cl_4$ closely related chemically and similar in properties to DDT
DDE \ˌdē-(ˌ)dē-ˈē\ *n* [*d*ichlor- + *d*iphenyl + *e*thylene] (1949) **:** a persistent organochlorine $C_{15}H_8Cl_4$ that is produced by the metabolic breakdown of DDT
ddI \ˌdē-(ˌ)dē-ˈī\ *n, often all cap* [*di-* + *d*eoxy + *i*nosine, a nucleoside] (1988) **:** a synthetic nucleoside $C_{10}H_{12}N_4O_3$ having properties and uses similar to those of ddC — called also *didanosine*
DDS *abbr* doctor of dental surgery
DDT \ˌdē-(ˌ)dē-ˈtē\ *n* [*d*ichlor- + *d*iphenyl + *t*richlor- (fr. *tri-* + *chlor-*)] (1943) **:** a colorless odorless water-insoluble insecticide $C_{14}H_9Cl_5$ that is an aromatic organochlorine banned in the U.S. that tends to accumulate and persist in ecosystems and has toxic effects on many vertebrates
DDVP \ˌdē-(ˌ)dē-ˌvē-ˈpē\ *n* [*d*imethyl + *d*ichlor- + *v*inyl + *p*hosphate] (1954) **:** DICHLORVOS
DE *abbr* **1** defensive end **2** Delaware **3** diatomaceous earth **4** doctor of engineering
de- *prefix* [ME, fr. AF *de-, des-,* partly fr. L *de-* from, down, away (fr. *de,* prep.) and partly fr. L *dis-;* L *de* akin to OIr *di* from, OE *tō* to — more at TO, DIS-] **1 a :** do the opposite of ⟨*de*activate⟩ **b :** reverse of ⟨*de*emphasis⟩ **2 a :** remove (a specified thing) from ⟨*de*louse⟩ **b :** remove from (a specified thing) ⟨*de*throne⟩ **3 :** reduce ⟨*de*value⟩ **4 :** something derived from (a specified thing) ⟨*de*compound⟩ **:** derived from something (of a specified nature) ⟨*de*nominative⟩ **5 :** get off of (a specified thing) ⟨*de*train⟩ **6 :** having a molecule characterized by the removal of one or more atoms (of a specified element) ⟨*de*oxy-⟩
DEA *abbr* Drug Enforcement Administration
de·ac·ces·sion \ˌdē-ik-ˈse-shən, -ak-\ *vt* (1972) **:** to sell or otherwise dispose of (an item in a collection) ⟨the museum ~*ed* several paintings⟩ — **deaccession** *n*
de·acid·i·fy \ˌdē-ə-ˈsi-də-ˌfī\ *vt* (1786) **:** to remove acid from **:** reduce the acidity of (as by neutralization) — **de·acid·i·fi·ca·tion** \-ˌsi-də-fə-ˈkā-shən\ *n*
dea·con \ˈdē-kən\ *n* [ME *dekene,* fr. OE *dēacon,* fr. LL *diaconus,* fr. Gk *diakonos,* lit., servant, fr. *dia-* + *-konos* (akin to en*konein* to be active); perh. akin to L *conari* to attempt] (bef. 12c) **:** a subordinate officer in a Christian church: as **a :** a Roman Catholic, Anglican, or Eastern Orthodox cleric ranking next below a priest **b :** one of the laymen elected by a church with congregational polity to serve in worship, in pastoral care, and on administrative committees **c :** a Mormon in the lowest grade of the Aaronic priesthood
dea·con·ess \ˈdē-kə-nəs\ *n* (15c) **:** a woman chosen to assist in the church ministry; *specif* **:** one in a Protestant order
deacon's bench *n* (1922) **:** a bench with usu. spindled arms and back
de·ac·ti·vate \(ˌ)dē-ˈak-tə-ˌvāt\ *vt* (1926) **:** to make inactive or ineffective ⟨~ a bomb⟩ ⟨~ a chemical compound⟩ — **de·ac·ti·va·tion** \(ˌ)dē-ˌak-tə-ˈvā-shən\ *n* — **de·ac·ti·va·tor** \(ˌ)dē-ˈak-tə-ˌvā-tər\ *n*

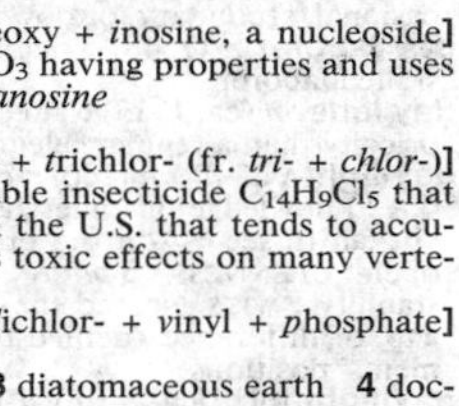
deacon's bench

[1]**dead** \ˈded\ *adj* [ME *deed,* fr. OE *dēad;* akin to ON *dauthr* dead, *deyja* to die, OHG *tōt* dead — more at DIE] (bef. 12c) **1 :** deprived of life **:** no longer alive **2 a** (1) **:** having the appearance of death **:** DEATHLY ⟨in a ~ faint⟩ (2) **:** lacking power to move, feel, or respond **:** NUMB **b :** very tired **c** (1) **:** incapable of being stirred emotionally or intellectually **:** UNRESPONSIVE ⟨~ to pity⟩ (2) **:** grown cold **:** EXTINGUISHED ⟨~ coals⟩ **3 a :** INANIMATE, INERT ⟨~ matter⟩ **b :** BARREN, INFERTILE ⟨~ soil⟩ **c :** no longer producing or functioning **:** EXHAUSTED ⟨a ~ battery⟩ **4 a** (1) **:** lacking power or effect ⟨a ~ law⟩ (2) **:** no longer having interest, relevance, or significance ⟨a ~ issue⟩ **b :** no longer in use **:** OBSOLETE ⟨a ~ language⟩ **c :** no longer active **:** EXTINCT ⟨a ~ volcano⟩ **d :** lacking in gaiety or animation ⟨a ~ party⟩ **e** (1) **:** lacking in commercial activity **:** QUIET (2) **:** commercially idle or unproductive ⟨~ capital⟩ **f :** lacking elasticity ⟨a ~ tennis ball⟩ **g :** being out of action or out of use ⟨the phone went ~⟩; *specif* **:** free from any connection to a source of voltage and free from electric charges **h** (1) **:** being out of play ⟨a ~ ball⟩ (2) **:** temporarily forbidden to play or to make a certain play in croquet **5 a :** not running or circulating **:** STAGNANT ⟨~ water⟩ **b :** not turning ⟨the ~ center of a lathe⟩ **c :** not imparting motion or power although otherwise functioning ⟨a ~ rear axle⟩ **d :** lacking warmth, vigor, or taste **6 a :** absolutely uniform ⟨a ~ level⟩ **b** (1) **:** UNERRING (2) **:** EXACT ⟨~ center of the target⟩ (3) **:** certain to be doomed ⟨he's ~ if he's late for curfew⟩ (4) **:** IRREVOCABLE ⟨a ~ loss⟩ **c :** ABRUPT ⟨brought to a ~ stop⟩ **d** (1) **:** COMPLETE, ABSOLUTE ⟨a ~ silence⟩ (2) **:** ALL-OUT ⟨caught it on the ~ run⟩ **7 :** devoid of former occupants ⟨~ villages⟩ — **dead·ness** *n* — **dead in the water** **1 :** incapable of being effective **:** STALLED ⟨peace talks were *dead in the water*⟩ **2 :** as good as dead **:** DOOMED ⟨most books are *dead in the water* long before their publication —Phillip Lopate⟩ — **dead to rights :** with no chance of escape or excuse **:** RED-HANDED ⟨had him *dead to rights* for the robbery⟩ — **over one's dead body :** only by overcoming one's utter and determined resistance ⟨vows that they'll raise his taxes *over his dead body*⟩
syn DEAD, DEFUNCT, DECEASED, DEPARTED, LATE mean devoid of life. DEAD applies literally to what is deprived of vital force but is used figuratively of anything that has lost any attribute (as energy, activity, radiance) suggesting life ⟨a *dead,* listless performance⟩. DEFUNCT stresses cessation of active existence or operation ⟨a *defunct* television series⟩. DECEASED, DEPARTED, and LATE apply to persons who have died recently. DECEASED is the preferred term in legal use ⟨the estate of the *deceased*⟩. DEPARTED is used usu. as a euphemism ⟨our *departed* sister⟩. LATE is used esp. with reference to a person in a specific relation or status ⟨the company's *late* president⟩.
[2]**dead** *n, pl* **dead** (bef. 12c) **1 :** one that is dead — usu. used collectively **2 :** the state of being dead ⟨raised him from the ~ —Col 2:12(RSV)⟩ **3 :** the time of greatest quiet ⟨the ~ of night⟩
[3]**dead** *adv* (14c) **1 :** ABSOLUTELY, UTTERLY ⟨~ certain⟩ ⟨finished ~ last⟩ **2 :** suddenly and completely ⟨stopped ~⟩ **3 :** DIRECTLY ⟨~ ahead⟩
dead air *n* (ca. 1943) **:** a period of silence esp. during a broadcast
dead–air space \ˈded-ˈer-\ *n* (1902) **:** an unventilated air space
[1]**dead·beat** \ˈded-ˌbēt\ *n* (1863) **1 :** LOAFER **2 :** one who persistently fails to pay personal debts or expenses
[2]**deadbeat** *adj* (ca. 1864) **:** having a pointer that gives a reading with little or no oscillation
dead bolt *n* (ca. 1902) **:** a lock bolt that is moved by turning a knob or key without action of a spring
dead–cat bounce *n* [fr. the facetious notion that even a dead cat would bounce slightly if dropped from a sufficient height] (1985) **:** a brief and insignificant recovery (as of stock prices) after a steep decline
dead duck *n* (1943) **:** one that is doomed
dead·en \ˈde-dᵊn\ *vb* **dead·ened; dead·en·ing** \ˈded-niŋ, ˈde-dᵊn-iŋ\ *vt* (1613) **1 :** to impair in vigor or sensation **:** BLUNT ⟨~*ed* his enthusiasm⟩ ⟨~*ed* the pain⟩ **2 a :** to deprive of brilliance **b :** to make vapid or spiritless ⟨oxygen ~*s* wine⟩ **c :** to make (as a wall) impervious to sound **3 :** to deprive of life **:** KILL ~ *vi* **:** to become dead **:** lose life or vigor — **dead·en·er** \ˈded-nər, -dᵊn-ər\ *n* — **dead·en·ing·ly** \-niŋ-lē, -dᵊn-iŋ-\ *adv*
[1]**dead–end** \ˈded-ˌend\ *adj* (1919) **1 a :** lacking opportunities esp. for advancement ⟨a ~ job⟩ **b :** lacking an exit ⟨a ~ street⟩ **2 :** UNRULY ⟨~ kids⟩ — **dead–end·ed·ness** \ˌded-ˈen-dəd-nəs\ *n*
[2]**dead–end** \ˈded-ˈend\ *vi* (1944) **:** to come to a dead end **:** TERMINATE ⟨the road ~*s* at the lake⟩ ⟨the investigation ~*ed*⟩
dead end \ˈded-ˈend\ *n* (1886) **1 :** an end (as of a street) without an exit **2 :** a position, situation, or course of action that leads to nothing further
dead·en·ing *n* (ca. 1874) **:** material used to soundproof walls or floors
dead·eye \ˈded-ˌī\ *n* (1748) **1 :** a rounded wood block encircled by a rope or an iron band and having holes to receive the lanyard that is used esp. to set up shrouds and stays **2 :** an unerring marksman
dead·fall \-ˌfôl\ *n* (1598) **1 :** a trap so constructed that a weight (as a heavy log) falls on an animal and kills or disables it **2 :** a tangled mass of fallen trees and branches
dead hand *n* (14c) **1 :** MORTMAIN 1 **2 :** the oppressive influence of the past
[1]**dead·head** \ˈded-ˌhed\ *n* (1841) **1 :** one who has not paid for a ticket **2 :** a dull or stupid person **3 :** a partially submerged log
[2]**deadhead** *vi* (1911) **1 :** to make esp. a return trip without a load **2 :** to deadhead a plant ~ *vt* **:** to remove the faded flowers of (a plant) esp. to keep a neat appearance and to promote reblooming by preventing seed production
dead heat *n* (1796) **:** a tie with no single winner of a race; *broadly* **:** TIE
dead horse *n* (1830) **:** an exhausted or profitless topic or issue — usu. used in the phrases *beat a dead horse* and *flog a dead horse*

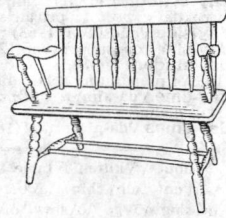

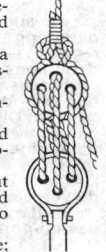

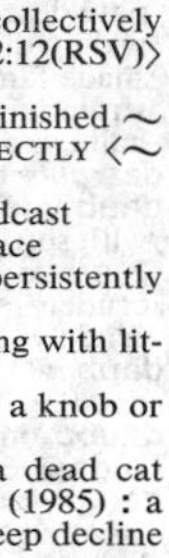
deadeye

dead letter *n* (1627) **1 :** something that has lost its force or authority without being formally abolished **2 :** a letter that is undeliverable and unreturnable by the post office

dead lift *n* (1963) **:** a lift in weight lifting in which the weight is lifted from the floor to hip level — **dead•lift** \ˈded-ˌlift\ *vt*
dead•light \ˈded-ˌlīt\ *n* (1726) **:** a metal cover or shutter fitted to a port to keep out light and water
dead•line \-ˌlīn\ *n* (1864) **1 :** a line drawn within or around a prison that a prisoner passes at the risk of being shot **2 a :** a date or time before which something must be done **b :** the time after which copy is not accepted for a particular issue of a publication — **on deadline** *or* **under deadline :** with the requirement of meeting a deadline ⟨working *on deadline*⟩
dead load *n* (ca. 1888) **:** a constant load in a structure (as a bridge, building, or machine) that is due to the weight of the members, the supported structure, and permanent attachments or accessories
dead•lock \ˈded-ˌläk\ *n* (1779) **1 :** a state of inaction or neutralization resulting from the opposition of equally powerful uncompromising persons or factions **:** STANDSTILL ⟨the ~ was broken with a key compromise⟩ **2 :** a tie score — **deadlock** *vb*
[1]**dead•ly** \ˈded-lē\ *adj* **dead•li•er; -est** (bef. 12c) **1 :** likely to cause or capable of producing death ⟨~ poison⟩ **2 a :** aiming to kill or destroy **:** IMPLACABLE ⟨a ~ enemy⟩ **b :** highly effective ⟨a ~ exposé⟩ **c :** UNERRING ⟨a ~ marksman⟩ **d :** marked by determination or extreme seriousness **3 a :** tending to deprive of force or vitality ⟨a ~ habit⟩ **b :** suggestive of death esp. in dullness or lack of animation ⟨~ bores⟩ ⟨a ~ conversation⟩ **4 :** very great **:** EXTREME — **dead•li•ness** *n*
syn DEADLY, MORTAL, FATAL, LETHAL mean causing or capable of causing death. DEADLY applies to an established or very likely cause of death ⟨a *deadly* disease⟩. MORTAL implies that death has occurred or is inevitable ⟨a *mortal* wound⟩. FATAL stresses the inevitability of what has in fact resulted in death or destruction ⟨*fatal* consequences⟩. LETHAL applies to something that is bound to cause death or exists for the destruction of life ⟨*lethal* gas⟩.
[2]**deadly** *adv* (bef. 12c) **1** *archaic* **:** in a manner to cause death **:** MORTALLY **2 :** suggesting death **3 :** EXTREMELY ⟨~ serious⟩
deadly nightshade *n* (1578) **:** BELLADONNA 1
deadly sin *n* (13c) **:** one of seven sins of pride, covetousness, lust, anger, gluttony, envy, and sloth held to be fatal to spiritual progress
dead•man \ˈded-ˌman\ *n* (1965) **:** an anchor (as a metal plate) buried in snow and used (as in mountain climbing) to secure a rope
dead man's float *n* (ca. 1946) **:** a prone floating position with the arms extended forward
dead march *n* (1591) **:** a solemn march for a funeral
dead meat *n* (1849) **:** one that is doomed ⟨he's *dead meat* if they catch him⟩
dead metaphor *n* (1922) **:** a word or phrase (as *time is running out*) that has lost its metaphoric force through common usage
dead–on \ˈded-ˈȯn, -ˈän\ *adj* (ca. 1889) **:** exactly correct or accurate ⟨a ~ analysis⟩ ⟨his impersonations were ~⟩
[1]**dead•pan** \ˈded-ˌpan\ *adj* (ca. 1928) **:** marked by an impassive matter-of-fact manner, style, or expression ⟨a ~ comedy⟩ — **deadpan** *adv*
[2]**deadpan** *n* (ca. 1930) **1 :** a completely expressionless face **2 :** a deadpan manner of behavior or presentation
[3]**deadpan** *vt* (ca. 1942) **:** to express in a deadpan manner — **dead•pan•ner** *n*
dead presidents *n pl* (1944) *slang* **:** U.S. money in the form of bills; *specif* **:** DOLLARS
dead reckoning *n* (1613) **1 :** the determination without the aid of celestial observations of the position of a ship or aircraft from the record of the courses sailed or flown, the distance made, and the known or estimated drift **2 :** GUESSWORK — **dead reckon** *vb*
dead space *n* (ca. 1923) **:** the portion of the respiratory system which is external to the bronchioles and through which air must pass to reach the bronchioles and alveoli
dead–stick landing \ˈded-ˌstik-\ *n* (ca. 1917) **:** a landing of an airplane or spacecraft made without power
dead–tree \ˈded-ˈtrē\ *adj* (1993) **:** being the print version of a work available in both print and electronic formats ⟨reads the ~ edition⟩
dead•weight \ˈded-ˈwāt\ *n* (1659) **1 :** the unrelieved weight of an inert mass **2 :** DEAD LOAD **3 :** a ship's load including the total weight of cargo, fuel, stores, crew, and passengers
deadweight ton *n* (ca. 1917) **:** a long ton used in indicating a ship's gross capacity — abbr. *dwt*
dead•wood \-ˌwu̇d\ *n* (15c) **1 :** wood dead on the tree **2 :** useless personnel or material **3 :** solid timbers built in at the extreme bow and stern of a ship when too narrow to permit framing **4 :** bowling pins that have been knocked down but remain on the alley
de•aer•ate \ˌdē-ˈer-ˌāt\ *vt* (1791) **:** to remove air or gas from — **de•aer•a•tion** \ˌdē-ˌer-ˈā-shən\ *n* — **de•aer•a•tor** \-ˈer-ˌā-tər\ *n*
deaf \ˈdef, *dial* ˈdēf\ *adj* [ME *deef,* fr. OE *dēaf;* akin to Gk *typhlos* blind, *typhein* to smoke, L *fumus* smoke — more at FUME] (bef. 12c) **1 :** lacking or deficient in the sense of hearing **2 :** unwilling to hear or listen **:** not to be persuaded ⟨was overwrought and ~ to reason⟩ — **deaf•ish** \ˈde-fish\ *adj* — **deaf•ly** *adv* — **deaf•ness** *n*
deaf–aid \ˈdef-ˌād\ *n* (1934) *Brit* **:** HEARING AID
deaf•en \ˈde-fən\ *vt* **deaf•ened; deaf•en•ing** \-fə-niŋ, ˈdef-niŋ\ (1597) **:** to make deaf ⟨was ~*ed* by the explosion⟩
deaf•en•ing *adj* (1597) **1 :** that deafens **2 :** very loud **:** EARSPLITTING ⟨fell with a ~ clap⟩ **3 :** very noticeable ⟨their silence on the issue was ~⟩ — **deaf•en•ing•ly** *adv*
deaf–mute \ˈdef-ˈmyüt\ *n* (ca. 1837) *often offensive* **:** a deaf person who cannot speak — **deaf–mute** *adj, often offensive*
[1]**deal** \ˈdēl\ *n* [ME *deel,* fr. OE *dǣl;* akin to OE *dāl* division, portion, OHG *teil* part] (bef. 12c) **1** *obs* **:** PART, PORTION **2 :** a usu. large or indefinite quantity or degree ⟨a great ~ of support⟩ ⟨a good ~ faster⟩ **3 a :** the act or right of distributing cards to players in a card game **b :** HAND 9b
[2]**deal** *vb* **dealt** \ˈdelt\; **deal•ing** \ˈdē-liŋ\ *vt* (bef. 12c) **1 a :** to give as one's portion **:** APPORTION ⟨tried to ~ justice to all⟩ ⟨*dealt* out three sandwiches apiece⟩ **b :** to distribute (playing cards) to players in a game **2 :** ADMINISTER, DELIVER ⟨*dealt* him a blow⟩ **3 a :** SELL ⟨~*s* drugs⟩ **b :** TRADE ⟨~ a player to another team⟩ ~ *vi* **1 :** to distribute the cards in a card game **2 :** to concern oneself or itself ⟨the book ~*s* with education⟩ **3 a :** to engage in bargaining **:** TRADE **b :** to sell or distribute something as a business ⟨~ in insurance⟩ **4 a :** to take action with regard to someone or something ⟨~ with an offender⟩ **b :** to reach or try to reach a state of acceptance or reconcilement ⟨trying to ~ with her son's death⟩ ***syn*** see DISTRIBUTE — **deal•er** \ˈdē-lər\ *n*
[3]**deal** *n* (15c) **1 a :** an act of dealing **:** TRANSACTION **b :** BARGAIN **c :** CONTRACT 1a ⟨signed a 2-year ~⟩ **2 :** PACKAGE DEAL **3 :** treatment received ⟨a dirty ~⟩ **4 :** an arrangement for mutual advantage **5 :** AFFAIR 2 ⟨dinner was an informal ~⟩ **6 :** SITUATION, STORY ⟨what is the ~ with that guy?⟩ **7 :** MCCOY — used in the phrase *the real deal*
[4]**deal** *n* [ME *dele,* fr. MD or MLG, plank; akin to OHG *dili* plank — more at THILL] (14c) **1** *Brit* **:** a board of fir or pine **2 :** pine or fir wood — **deal** *adj*
de•alat•ed \(ˌ)dē-ˈā-ˌlā-təd\ *adj* (1904) **:** divested of the wings — used of postnuptial adults of insects (as ants) that drop their wings after a nuptial flight — **de•ala•tion** \ˌdē-(ˌ)ā-ˈlā-shən\ *n*
deal•er•ship \ˈdē-lər-ˌship\ *n* (1916) **:** an authorized sales agency ⟨an automobile ~⟩
deal•fish \ˈdēl-ˌfish\ *n* [[4]*deal*] (1845) **:** any of several silvery ribbonfishes (genus *Trachipterus,* esp. *T. arcticus*) inhabiting deep seas
deal•ing *n* (15c) **1 :** method of business **:** manner of conduct **2** *pl* **:** friendly or business interactions
dealing box *n* (1897) **:** a case that holds a deck of playing cards so that they may be dealt one by one
de•am•i•nase \(ˌ)dē-ˈa-mi-ˌnās, -ˌnāz\ *n* [*de-* + *amino* + *-ase*] (1920) **:** an enzyme that hydrolyzes amino compounds (as amino acids) with removal of the amino group
de•am•i•nate \-ˌnāt\ *vt* **-nat•ed; -nat•ing** (1926) **:** to remove the amino group from (a compound) — **de•am•i•na•tion** \(ˌ)dē-ˌa-mi-ˈnā-shən\ *n*
dean \ˈdēn\ *n* [ME *deen,* fr. AF *deen, deien,* fr. LL *decanus* chief of ten, fr. Gk *dekanos,* fr. *deka* ten — more at TEN] (13c) **1 a :** the head of the chapter of a collegiate or cathedral church **b :** a Roman Catholic priest who supervises one district of a diocese **2 a :** the head of a division, faculty, college, or school of a university **b :** a college or secondary school administrator in charge of counseling and disciplining students **3 :** DOYEN 1 — **dean** *vi* — **dean•ship** \-ˌship\ *n*
dean•ery \ˈdēn-rē, ˈdē-nə-rē\ *n, pl* **-er•ies** (15c) **:** the office, jurisdiction, or official residence of a clerical dean
dean's list *n* (ca. 1926) **:** a list of students receiving special recognition from the dean of a college because of superior scholarship
[1]**dear** \ˈdir\ *adj* [ME *dere,* fr. OE *dēor*] (bef. 12c) **:** SEVERE, SORE ⟨in our ~ peril —Shak.⟩
[2]**dear** *adj* [ME *dere,* fr. OE *dēore;* akin to OHG *tiuri* distinguished, costly] (bef. 12c) **1** *obs* **:** NOBLE **2 :** highly valued **:** PRECIOUS ⟨a ~ friend⟩ — often used in a salutation ⟨~ Sir⟩ **3 :** AFFECTIONATE, FOND **4 :** high or exorbitant in price **:** EXPENSIVE ⟨eggs are very ~ just now⟩ **5 :** HEARTFELT ⟨our ~*est* prayers⟩ — **dear•ness** *n*
[3]**dear** *adv* (bef. 12c) **1 :** DEARLY 3 ⟨the effort cost them ~⟩ **2 :** DEARLY 1 ⟨so ~ I loved the man —Shak.⟩
[4]**dear** *n* (13c) **1 :** a loved one **:** SWEETHEART **2 :** a lovable person
[5]**dear** *interj* (1694) — used esp. to express annoyance or dismay
Dear John \-ˈjän\ *n* (1945) **:** a letter (as to a soldier) in which a wife asks for a divorce or a girlfriend breaks off an engagement or a friendship
dear•ly *adv* (13c) **1 :** with affection **:** FONDLY **2 :** HEARTILY, EARNESTLY ⟨prayed so ~ for peace⟩ **3 :** at a high rate or price ⟨paid ~ for the error⟩
dearth \ˈdərth\ *n* [ME *derthe,* fr. OE **dierth,* fr. *dēore* dear] (13c) **1 :** scarcity that makes dear; *specif* **:** FAMINE **2 :** an inadequate supply **:** LACK ⟨a ~ of evidence⟩
dea•sil \ˈdē-zəl\ *adv* [ScGael *deiseil,* fr. MIr *dessel,* fr. OIr *dess* right, south + *sel* turn; akin to L *dexter* right hand — more at DEXTER] (1771) **:** CLOCKWISE — compare WIDDERSHINS
death \ˈdeth\ *n* [ME *deeth,* fr. OE *dēath;* akin to ON *dauthi* death, *deyja* to die — more at DIE] (bef. 12c) **1 a :** a permanent cessation of all vital functions **:** the end of life — compare BRAIN DEATH **b :** an instance of dying ⟨a disease causing many ~*s*⟩ **2 a :** the cause or occasion of loss of life ⟨drinking was the ~ of him⟩ **b :** a cause of ruin ⟨the slander that was ~ to my character —Wilkie Collins⟩ **3** *cap* **:** the destroyer of life represented usu. as a skeleton with a scythe **4 :** the state of being dead **5 a :** the passing or destruction of something inanimate ⟨the ~ of vaudeville⟩ **b :** EXTINCTION **6 :** CIVIL DEATH **7 :** SLAUGHTER **8** *Christian Science* **:** the lie of life in matter **:** that which is unreal and untrue — **at death's door :** close to death **:** critically ill — **to death :** beyond endurance **:** EXCESSIVELY ⟨bored *to death*⟩
death•bed \ˈdeth-ˌbed\ *n* (bef. 12c) **1 :** the bed in which a person dies **2 :** the last hours of life — **on one's deathbed :** near the point of death
death benefit *n* (1921) **:** money payable to the beneficiary of a deceased
death•blow \ˈdeth-ˌblō\ *n* (1795) **:** a destructive or killing stroke or event
death camas *n* (ca. 1889) **:** any of several plants (genus *Zigadenus*) of the lily family that cause poisoning of livestock in the western U.S.
death camp *n* (1944) **:** a concentration camp in which large numbers of prisoners are systematically killed
death cap *n* (1925) **:** a very poisonous mushroom (*Amanita phalloides*) of deciduous woods of No. America and Europe that varies in color from pure white to olive or yellow and has a prominent volva at the base — called also *death cup*
death•care \ˈdeth-ˌker\ *adj* (1987) **:** of, relating to, or providing products or services for the burial or cremation of the dead ⟨the ~ industry⟩
death duty *n* (1881) *chiefly Brit* **:** DEATH TAX
death grip *n* (1829) **1 :** an extremely tight grip caused esp. by fear **2 :** HOLD 3b ⟨maintained their *death grip* on overseas markets⟩
death instinct *n* (1922) **:** an innate and unconscious tendency toward self-destruction postulated in psychoanalytic theory to explain aggres-

sive and destructive behavior not satisfactorily explained by the pleasure principle — called also *Thanatos;* compare EROS 2
death·less \ˈdeth-ləs\ *adj* (1589) : IMMORTAL, IMPERISHABLE ⟨~ fame⟩ — **death·less·ly** *adv* — **death·less·ness** *n*
death·ly \ˈdeth-lē\ *adj* (bef. 12c) **1** : FATAL **2** : of, relating to, or suggestive of death ⟨a ~ pallor⟩ — **deathly** *adv*
death mask *n* (1877) : a cast taken from the face of a dead person
death metal *n* (1987) : a type of heavy metal music that is characterized by the use of dark, violent, or gory imagery
death rate *n* (1852) : the ratio between deaths and individuals in a specified population and time
death rattle *n* (1822) : a rattling or gurgling sound produced by air passing through mucus in the lungs and air passages of a dying person
death ray *n* (1919) : a weapon that generates an intense beam of particles or radiation by which it destroys its target
death row *n* (1950) : a prison area housing inmates sentenced to death — usu. used with *on* ⟨prisoners waiting on *death row*⟩
death sentence *n* (1799) **1** : a sentence condemning a convicted defendant to death **2** : an affliction or a situation that is considered to be fatal; *also* : a prognosis of death
death's–head \ˈdeths-ˌhed\ *n* (1596) : a human skull or a depiction of a human skull symbolizing death
death's–head hawk moth *n* (1879) : a large dark hawk moth (*Acherontia atropos*) esp. of Mediterranean regions with markings resembling a human skull on the back of the thorax — called also *death's-head moth*
deaths·man \ˈdeths-mən\ *n* (1589) *archaic* : EXECUTIONER
death squad *n* (1969) : any of various extremist groups whose members kill suspected political adversaries and criminals
death tax *n* (1937) : a tax arising on the transmission of property after the owner's death; *esp* : ESTATE TAX
death trap *n* (1835) : a structure or situation that is potentially very dangerous to life
death warrant *n* (1692) **1** : a warrant for the execution of a death sentence **2** : DEATHBLOW
[1]**death·watch** \ˈdeth-ˌwäch\ *n* [*death* + *watch* (timepiece); fr. the superstition that its ticking presages death] (1646) : a small insect that makes a ticking sound; *esp* : DEATHWATCH BEETLE
[2]**deathwatch** *n* [*death* + *watch* (vigil)] (ca. 1890) **1** : a vigil kept over the dead or dying **2** : the guard set over a criminal to be executed
deathwatch beetle *n* (1877) : any of various small beetles (family Anobiidae, esp. *Xestobium rufovillosum*) that bore in seasoned or dead wood (as of old buildings) and make a tapping noise as a mating call
death wish *n* (1913) : the conscious or unconscious desire for the death of oneself or of another
[1]**deb** \ˈdeb\ *n* (1920) : DEBUTANTE
[2]**deb** *abbr* debenture
de·ba·cle \dē-ˈbä-kəl, di-, -ˈba-; ÷ˈde-bə-kəl\ *also* **dé·bâ·cle** *also* dā-ˈbäk(lᵊ)\ *n* [F *débâcle,* fr. *débâcler* to clear, fr. MF *desbacler,* fr. *des-* de- + *bacler* to block, perh. fr. VL *bacculare, fr. L *baculum* staff] (1802) **1** : a tumultuous breakup of ice in a river **2** : a violent disruption (as of an army) : ROUT **3 a** : a great disaster **b** : a complete failure : FIASCO
de·bar \di-ˈbär, dē-\ *vt* [ME *debarren,* fr. AF *debarrer,* fr. *de-* + *barrer* to bar] (15c) : to bar from having or doing something : PRECLUDE — **de·bar·ment** \-mənt\ *n*
[1]**de·bark** \di-ˈbärk, dē-\ *vb* [F *debarquer,* fr. *de-* + *barque* bark (ship)] (1654) : DISEMBARK — **de·bar·ka·tion** \ˌdē-ˌbär-ˈkā-shən\ *n*
[2]**de·bark** \(ˌ)dē-ˈbärk\ *vt* (1742) : to remove bark from — **de·bark·er** \-ˈbär-kər\ *n*
de·base \di-ˈbās, dē-\ *vt* (1565) **1** : to lower in status, esteem, quality, or character **2 a** : to reduce the intrinsic value of (a coin) by increasing the base-metal content **b** : to reduce the exchange value of (a monetary unit) — **de·base·ment** \-ˈbās-mənt\ *n* — **de·bas·er** \-ˈbā-sər\ *n*
syn DEBASE, VITIATE, DEPRAVE, CORRUPT, DEBAUCH, PERVERT mean to cause deterioration or lowering in quality or character. DEBASE implies a loss of position, worth, value, or dignity ⟨commercialism has *debased* the holiday⟩. VITIATE implies a destruction of purity, validity, or effectiveness by allowing entrance of a fault or defect ⟨a foreign policy *vitiated* by partisanship⟩. DEPRAVE implies moral deterioration by evil thoughts or influences ⟨the claim that society is *depraved* by pornography⟩. CORRUPT implies loss of soundness, purity, or integrity ⟨the belief that bureaucratese *corrupts* the language⟩. DEBAUCH implies a debasing through sensual indulgence ⟨the long stay on a tropical isle had *debauched* the ship's crew⟩. PERVERT implies a twisting or distorting from what is natural or normal ⟨*perverted* the original goals of the institute⟩.
de·bat·able \di-ˈbā-tə-bəl, dē-\ *adj* (1536) **1** : claimed by more than one country ⟨~ border territory⟩ **2 a** : open to dispute : QUESTIONABLE ⟨the ~ wisdom of his advice⟩ **b** : open to debate **3** : capable of being debated — **de·bat·ably** \-blē\ *adv*
[1]**de·bate** \di-ˈbāt, dē-\ *n* (13c) : a contention by words or arguments: as **a** : the formal discussion of a motion before a deliberative body according to the rules of parliamentary procedure **b** : a regulated discussion of a proposition between two matched sides
[2]**debate** *vb* **de·bat·ed; de·bat·ing** [ME, fr. AF *debatre,* fr. *de-* + *batre* to beat, fr. L *battuere*] *vi* (14c) **1** *obs* : FIGHT, CONTEND **2 a** : to contend in words **b** : to discuss a question by considering opposed arguments **3** : to participate in a debate ~ *vt* **1 a** : to argue about ⟨the subject was hotly *debated*⟩ **b** : to engage (an opponent) in debate **2** : to turn over in one's mind ⟨he's still *debating* what to do⟩ ***syn*** see DISCUSS — **de·bate·ment** \-ˈbāt-mənt\ *n* — **de·bat·er** *n*
[1]**de·bauch** \di-ˈbȯch, -ˈbäch, dē-\ *vt* [MF *debaucher,* fr. OF *desbauchier* to scatter, disperse, fr. *des-* de- + *bauch* beam, of Gmc origin; akin to OHG *balko* beam — more at BALK] (1595) **1 a** *archaic* : to make disloyal **b** : to seduce from chastity **2 a** : to lead away from virtue or excellence **b** : to corrupt by intemperance or sensuality ***syn*** see DEBASE — **de·bauch·er** *n*
[2]**debauch** *n* (1603) **1** : an act or occasion of debauchery **2** : ORGY
de·bauch·ee \di-ˌbȯ-ˈchē, -ˌbä-; ˌde-bə-ˈshē, -ˈshā\ *n* [F *débauché,* fr. pp. of *débaucher*] (1661) : one given to debauchery
de·bauch·ery \di-ˈbȯ-chə-rē, -chrē, -ˈbä-\ *n, pl* **-er·ies** (1642) **1 a** : extreme indulgence in sensuality **b** *pl* : ORGIES **2** *archaic* : seduction from virtue or duty
de·beak \(ˌ)dē-ˈbēk\ *vt* (1937) : to remove the tip of the upper mandible of (as a chicken) to prevent cannibalism and fighting
de·beard \-ˈbird\ *vt* (1980) : to remove the byssus from (a mussel)
de·ben·ture \di-ˈben-chər\ *n* [ME *debentur,* fr. L, they are due, 3d pl. pres. pass. of *debēre* to owe — more at DEBT] (15c) **1** *Brit* : a corporate security other than an equity security : BOND **2** : a bond backed by the general credit of the issuer rather than a specific lien on particular assets
de·bil·i·tate \di-ˈbi-lə-ˌtāt, dē-\ *vt* **-tat·ed; -tat·ing** [L *debilitatus,* pp. of *debilitare* to weaken, fr. *debilis* weak] (1533) : to impair the strength of : ENFEEBLE ***syn*** see WEAKEN — **de·bil·i·ta·tion** \-ˌbi-lə-ˈtā-shən\ *n*
de·bil·i·ty \di-ˈbi-lə-tē, dē-\ *n, pl* **-ties** [ME *debilite,* fr. MF *debilité,* fr. L *debilitat-, debilitas,* fr. *debilis,* fr. *de-* de- + *-bilis;* akin to Skt *bala* strength] (15c) : WEAKNESS, INFIRMITY
[1]**deb·it** \ˈde-bət\ *vt* (1682) : to enter upon the debit side of an account : charge with a debit
[2]**debit** *n* [L *debitum* debt] (1746) **1 a** : a record of an indebtedness; *specif* : an entry on the left-hand side of an account constituting an addition to an expense or asset account or a deduction from a revenue, net worth, or liability account **b** : the sum of the items entered as debits **2** : a charge against a bank deposit account **3** : DRAWBACK, SHORTCOMING
debit card *n* (1975) : a card like a credit card by which money may be withdrawn or the cost of purchases paid directly from the holder's bank account without the payment of interest
deb·o·nair \ˌde-bə-ˈner\ *adj* [ME *debonere,* fr. AF *deboneire,* fr. *de bon aire* of good family or nature] (13c) **1** *archaic* : GENTLE, COURTEOUS **2 a** : SUAVE, URBANE ⟨a ~ performer⟩ **b** : LIGHTHEARTED, NONCHALANT — **deb·o·nair·ly** *adv* — **deb·o·nair·ness** *n*
de·bone \(ˌ)dē-ˈbōn\ *vt* (1944) : BONE ⟨~ a roast⟩ — **de·bon·er** *n*
Deb·o·rah \ˈde-b(ə-)rə\ *n* [Heb *Dĕbhōrāh*] (14c) : a Hebrew prophetess who rallied the Israelites in their struggles against the Canaanites
de·bouch \di-ˈbau̇ch, -ˈbüsh, dē-\ *vb* [F *déboucher,* fr. *dé-* de- + *bouche* mouth, fr. OF *boche,* fr. L *bucca* cheek] *vt* (1745) : to cause to emerge : DISCHARGE ~ *vi* **1** : to march out into open ground ⟨troops ~*ing* from the town⟩ **2** : EMERGE, ISSUE ⟨rivers ~*ing* into the sea⟩ — **de·bouch·ment** \-mənt\ *n*
de·bride·ment \di-ˈbrēd-mənt, dā-, -ˌmänt, dā-brēd-ˈmä^{n}\ *n* [F *débridement,* fr. *débrider* to remove adhesions, lit., to unbridle, fr. MF *desbrider,* fr. *des-* de- + *bride* bridle, fr. MHG *brīdel* — more at BRIDLE] (ca. 1842) : the usu. surgical removal of lacerated, devitalized, or contaminated tissue — **de·bride** \di-ˈbrēd, dā-\ *vt*
de·brief \(ˌ)dē-ˈbrēf\ *vt* (1945) **1** : to interrogate (as a pilot) usu. upon return (as from a mission) in order to obtain useful information **2** : to carefully review upon completion ⟨~ the flight⟩
de·bris \də-ˈbrē, dā-ˈ, ˈdā-ˌ, *Brit usu* ˈde-(ˌ)brē\ *n, pl* **de·bris** \-ˈbrēz, -ˌbrēz\ [F *débris,* fr. MF, fr. *debriser* to break to pieces, fr. OF *debrisier,* fr. *de-* + *brisier* to break, of Celtic origin; akin to OIr *brisid* he breaks; perh. akin to L *fricare* to rub — more at FRICTION] (1708) **1** : the remains of something broken down or destroyed **2** : an accumulation of fragments of rock **3** : something discarded : RUBBISH
debt \ˈdet\ *n* [ME *dette, debte,* fr. AF *dette* something owed, fr. VL *debita, fr. L, pl. of *debitum* debt, fr. neut. of *debitus,* pp. of *debēre* to owe, fr. *de-* + *habēre* to have — more at GIVE] (13c) **1** : SIN, TRESPASS **2** : something owed : OBLIGATION ⟨unable to pay off his ~*s*⟩ **3** : a state of owing ⟨deeply in ~⟩ **4** : the common-law action for the recovery of money held to be due — **debt·less** \-ləs\ *adj*
debt·or \ˈde-tər\ *n* (13c) **1** : one guilty of neglect or violation of duty **2** : one who owes a debt
debt service *n* (1929) : the amount of interest and sinking fund payments due annually on long-term debt
de·bug \(ˌ)dē-ˈbəg\ *vt* (1944) **1** : to remove insects from **2** : to eliminate errors in or malfunctions of ⟨~ a computer program⟩ **3** : to remove a concealed microphone or wiretapping device from — **de·bug·ger** *n*
de·bunk \(ˌ)dē-ˈbəŋk\ *vt* (1923) : to expose the sham or falseness of ⟨~ a legend⟩ — **de·bunk·er** *n*
[1]**de·but** *also* **dé·but** \ˈdā-ˌbyü, dā-ˈ\ *n* [F *début,* fr. *débuter* to begin, fr. MF *desbuter* to play first, fr. *des-* de- + *but* starting point, goal — more at BUTT] (1751) **1** : a first appearance ⟨made her singing ~⟩ **2** : a formal entrance into society
[2]**debut** *vi* (1830) : to make a debut ~ *vt* : to present to the public for the first time : INTRODUCE ⟨~ a new product⟩
deb·u·tant \ˈde-byu̇-ˌtänt\ *n* [F *débutant,* prp. of *débuter*] (ca. 1822) : one making a debut
deb·u·tante \ˈde-byu̇-ˌtänt\ *n* [F *débutante,* fem. of *débutant*] (1801) : DEBUTANT; *esp* : a young woman making her formal entrance into society
dec *abbr* **1** deceased **2** declaration; declared **3** declination **4** decorated; decorative **5** decrease **6** decrescendo
Dec *abbr* December
deca- *or* **dec-** *or* **deka-** *or* **dek-** *comb form* [ME, fr. L, fr. Gk *deka-, dek-,* fr. *deka* — more at TEN] : ten ⟨*deca*syllabic⟩ ⟨*deka*meter⟩
de·cade \ˈde-ˌkād, de-ˈkād; *esp sense 1b* ˈde-kəd\ *n* [ME, fr. MF *décade,* fr. LL *decad-, decas,* fr. Gk *dekad-, dekas,* fr. *deka*] (15c) **1** : a group or set of 10: as **a** : a period of 10 years **b** : a division of the rosary that consists primarily of 10 Hail Marys **2** : a ratio of 10 to 1 : ORDER OF MAGNITUDE — **de·cad·al** \ˈde-kə-dᵊl\ *adj*
de·cade·long \ˈde-ˌkād-ˌlȯŋ\ *adj* (1974) : lasting a decade
dec·a·dence \ˈde-kə-dən(t)s *also* di-ˈkā-\ *n* [MF, fr. ML *decadentia,* fr. LL *decadent-, decadens,* prp. of *decadere* to fall, sink — more at DECAY] (1530) **1** : the process of becoming decadent : the quality or state of being decadent **2** : a period of decline ***syn*** see DETERIORATION
dec·a·den·cy \-dᵊn-sē\ *n* (1632) : DECADENCE 1
[1]**dec·a·dent** \ˈde-kə-dənt *also* di-ˈkā-\ *adj* [back-formation fr. *decadence*] (1837) **1** : marked by decay or decline **2** : of, relating to, or having the characteristics of the decadents **3** : characterized by or appealing to self-indulgence ⟨~ pleasures⟩ — **dec·a·dent·ly** *adv*

[2]decadent *n* (1886) **1 :** one of a group of late 19th century French and English writers tending toward artificial and unconventional subjects and subtilized style **2 :** one that is decadent

de·caf \ˈdē-ˌkaf\ *n* [short for *decaffeinated*] (1961) **:** decaffeinated coffee

de·caf·fein·at·ed \(ˌ)dē-ˈka-fə-nā-təd, -fē-ə-\ *adj* (1921) **:** having the caffeine removed ⟨~ coffee⟩ ⟨~ tea⟩

deca·gon \ˈde-kə-ˌgän\ *n* [NL *decagonum,* fr. Gk *dekagōnon,* fr. *deka-* deca- + *-gōnon* -gon] (ca. 1639) **:** a plane polygon of 10 angles and 10 sides

deca·gram \-ˌgram\ *n* [F *décagramme,* fr. *déca-* deca- + *gramme* gram] (1810) **:** DEKAGRAM

deca·he·dron \ˌde-kə-ˈhē-drən\ *n, pl* **-drons** *or* **-dra** \-drə\ [ISV] (ca. 1828) **:** a polyhedron of 10 faces

de·cal \ˈdē-ˌkal, di-ˈkal; *Canad usu* ˈde-kəl\ *n* [short for *decalcomania*] (1937) **:** a picture, design, or label made to be transferred (as to glass) from specially prepared paper

de·cal·ci·fi·ca·tion \(ˌ)dē-ˌkal-sə-fə-ˈkā-shən\ *n* (1859) **:** the removal or loss of calcium or calcium compounds (as from bones or soil) — **de·cal·ci·fy** \(ˌ)dē-ˈkal-sə-ˌfī\ *vt*

de·cal·co·ma·nia \di-ˌkal-kə-ˈmā-nē-ə\ *n* [F *décalcomanie,* fr. *décalquer* to copy by tracing (fr. *dé-* de- + *calquer* to trace, fr. It *calcare,* lit., to tread, fr. L) + *manie* mania, fr. LL *mania* — more at CAULK] (1864) **1 :** the art or process of transferring pictures and designs from specially prepared paper (as to glass) **2 :** DECAL

deca·li·ter \ˈde-kə-ˌlē-tər\ *n* [F *décalitre,* fr. *déca-* + *litre* liter] (1810) **:** DEKALITER

deca·logue \ˈde-kə-ˌlȯg, -ˌläg\ *n* [ME *decaloge,* fr. LL *decalogus,* fr. Gk *dekalogos,* fr. *deka-* + *logos* word — more at LEGEND] (14c) **1** *cap* **:** TEN COMMANDMENTS **2 :** a basic set of rules carrying binding authority

[1]deca·me·ter \ˈde-kə-ˌmē-tər\ *n* [F *décamètre,* fr. *déca-* + *mètre* meter] (1810) **:** DEKAMETER

[2]de·cam·e·ter \de-ˈka-mə-tər, də-\ *n* [Gk *dekametron,* fr. *deka-* + *metron* measure, meter] (1821) **:** a line of verse consisting of 10 metrical feet

deca·me·tho·ni·um \ˌde-kə-mə-ˈthō-nē-əm\ *n* [*deca-* + *meth*ylene + *-onium*] (ca. 1949) **:** a synthetic ion used in the form of either its bromide or iodide salts ($C_{16}H_{38}Br_2N_2$ or $C_{16}H_{38}I_2N_2$) as a skeletal muscle relaxant; *also* **:** either of these salts

deca·met·ric \ˌde-kə-ˈme-trik\ *adj* [*decameter* + *-ic;* fr. the wavelength range being between 1 and 10 dekameters] (1950) **:** of, relating to, or being a radio wave of high frequency

de·camp \di-ˈkamp, dē-\ *vi* [F *décamper,* fr. MF *descamper,* fr. *des-* de- + *camper* to camp] (1676) **1 :** to break up a camp **2 :** to depart suddenly **:** ABSCOND — **de·camp·ment** \-mənt\ *n*

dec·ane \ˈde-ˌkān\ *n* [ISV *deca-*] (ca. 1875) **:** any of several isomeric liquid alkanes $C_{10}H_{22}$

de·cant \di-ˈkant, dē-\ *vt* [NL *decantare,* fr. L *de-* + ML *cantus* edge, fr. L, iron ring round a wheel — more at CANT] (1633) **1 :** to draw off (a liquid) without disturbing the sediment or the lower liquid layers **2 :** to pour from one vessel into another **3 :** to pour out, transfer, or unload as if by pouring — **de·can·ta·tion** \ˌdē-ˌkan-ˈtā-shən\ *n*

de·cant·er \di-ˈkan-tər, dē-\ *n* (1708) **:** a vessel used to decant or to receive decanted liquids; *esp* **:** an ornamental glass bottle used for serving wine

de·cap·i·tate \di-ˈka-pə-ˌtāt, dē-\ *vt* **-tat·ed; -tat·ing** [LL *decapitatus,* pp. of *decapitare,* fr. L *de-* + *capit-, caput* head — more at HEAD] (ca. 1611) **:** to cut off the head of **:** BEHEAD — **de·cap·i·ta·tion** \-ˌka-pə-ˈtā-shən\ *n* — **de·cap·i·ta·tor** \-ˈka-pə-ˌtā-tər\ *n*

deca·pod \ˈde-kə-ˌpäd\ *n* [NL *Decapoda,* fr. *deca-* + *-poda* -pod] (1826) **1 :** any of an order (Decapoda) of crustaceans (as shrimps, lobsters, and crabs) with five pairs of thoracic appendages one or more of which are modified into pincers, with stalked eyes, and with the head and thorax fused into a cephalothorax and covered by a carapace **2 :** any of the cephalopod mollusks (orders Sepioidea and Teuthoidea) with 10 arms including cuttlefishes, squids, and related forms — **decapod** *adj* — **de·cap·o·dan** \di-ˈka-pə-dən\ *adj or n* — **de·cap·o·dous** \-ə-dəs\ *adj*

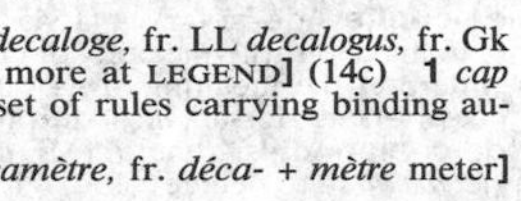

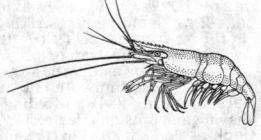

decapod 1

de·car·bon·ate \(ˌ)dē-ˈkär-bə-ˌnāt\ *vt* (1831) **:** to remove carbon dioxide or carbonic acid from — **de·car·bon·ation** \-ˌkär-bə-ˈnā-shən\ *n*

de·car·bon·ize \(ˌ)dē-ˈkär-bə-ˌnīz\ *vt* [ISV] (1825) **:** to remove carbon from — **de·car·bon·iz·er** *n*

de·car·box·yl·ase \ˌdē-kär-ˈbäk-sə-ˌlās, -ˌlāz\ *n* (1940) **:** any of a group of enzymes that accelerate decarboxylation esp. of amino acids

de·car·box·yl·ation \-ˌbäk-sə-ˈlā-shən\ *n* (1922) **:** the removal or elimination of carboxyl from a molecule — **de·car·box·yl·ate** \-ˈbäk-sə-ˌlāt\ *vt*

de·car·bu·rize \(ˌ)dē-ˈkär-b(y)ə-ˌrīz\ *vt* (1856) **:** DECARBONIZE — **de·car·bu·ri·za·tion** \-ˌkär-b(y)ə-rə-ˈzā-shən\ *n*

dec·are \ˈde-ˌker, -ˌkär\ *n* [F *décare,* fr. *déca-* deca- + *are*] (1810) **:** a metric unit of area equal to 10 ares or 0.2471 acre

de·ca·su·al·iza·tion \(ˌ)dē-ˌka-zh(ə-)wə-lə-ˈzā-shən, -ˌka-zhə-lə, -ˌka-zhü-ə-lə-\ *n* (1892) **:** the process of eliminating the employment of casual workers in order to stabilize the workforce

deca·syl·lab·ic \ˌde-kə-sə-ˈla-bik\ *adj* [prob. fr. F *décasyllabique,* fr. Gk *dekasyllabos,* fr. *deka-* deca- + *syllabē* syllable] (1771) **:** consisting of 10 syllables or composed of verses of 10 syllables — **decasyllabic** *n* — **deca·syl·la·ble** \ˈde-kə-ˌsi-lə-bəl, ˌde-kə-ˈ\ *n*

de·cath·lete \di-ˈkath-ˌlēt\ *n* [blend of *decathlon* and *athlete*] (1968) **:** an athlete who competes in the decathlon

de·cath·lon \di-ˈkath-lən, -ˌlän, -ˈka-thə-\ *n* [F *décathlon,* fr. *déca-* deca- + *-athlon* (as in *pentathlon*)] (1912) **:** a 10-event athletic contest; *specif* **:** a composite contest that consists of the 100-meter, 400-meter, and 1500-meter runs, the 110-meter high hurdles, the javelin and discus throws, shot put, pole vault, high jump, and long jump

[1]de·cay \di-ˈkā\ *vb* [ME, fr. AF *decaïr,* fr. LL *decadere* to fall, sink, fr. L *de-* + *cadere* to fall — more at CHANCE] *vi* (15c) **1 :** to decline from a sound or prosperous condition **2 :** to decrease usu. gradually in size, quantity, activity, or force **3 :** to fall into ruin **4 :** to decline in health, strength, or vigor **5 :** to undergo decomposition ⟨~*ing* fruit⟩ ~ *vt* **1** *obs* **:** to cause to decay **:** IMPAIR ⟨infirmity that ~*s* the wise —Shak.⟩ **2 :** to destroy by decomposition — **de·cay·er** *n*

syn DECAY, DECOMPOSE, ROT, PUTREFY, SPOIL mean to undergo destructive dissolution. DECAY implies a slow change from a state of soundness or perfection ⟨a *decaying* mansion⟩. DECOMPOSE stresses a breaking down by chemical change and when applied to organic matter a corruption ⟨the strong odor of *decomposing* vegetation⟩. ROT is a close synonym of DECOMPOSE and often connotes foulness ⟨fruit was left to *rot* in warehouses⟩. PUTREFY implies the rotting of animal matter and offensiveness to sight and smell ⟨corpses *putrefying* on the battlefield⟩. SPOIL applies chiefly to the decomposition of foods ⟨keep the ham from *spoiling*⟩.

[2]decay *n* (15c) **1 :** gradual decline in strength, soundness, or prosperity or in degree of excellence or perfection **2 :** a wasting or wearing away **:** RUIN **3** *obs* **:** DESTRUCTION, DEATH **4 a :** ROT; *specif* **:** aerobic decomposition of proteins chiefly by bacteria **b :** the product of decay **5 :** a decline in health or vigor **6 :** decrease in quantity, activity, or force: as **a :** spontaneous decrease in the number of radioactive atoms in radioactive material **b :** spontaneous disintegration (as of an atom or a particle)

Dec·ca \ˈde-kə\ *n* [*Decca* Co., British firm which developed it] (1946) **:** a system of long-range navigation used chiefly in Europe that utilizes the phase differences of continuous-wave signals from synchronized ground transmitters to establish position

decd *abbr* deceased

de·cease \di-ˈsēs\ *n* [ME *deces,* fr. AF, fr. L *decessus* departure, death, fr. *decedere* to depart, die, fr. *de-* + *cedere* to go] (14c) **:** departure from life **:** DEATH — **decease** *vi*

[1]de·ceased \-ˈsēst\ *adj* (15c) **:** no longer living; *esp* **:** recently dead — used of persons ***syn*** see DEAD

[2]deceased *n, pl* **deceased** (1548) **:** a dead person ⟨the will of the ~⟩

de·ce·dent \di-ˈsē-dᵊnt\ *n* [L *decedent-, decedens,* prp. of *decedere*] (1599) **:** a deceased person — used chiefly in law

de·ceit \di-ˈsēt\ *n* [ME *deceite,* fr. AF, fr. L *decepta,* fem. of *deceptus,* pp. of *decipere*] (14c) **1 :** the act or practice of deceiving **:** DECEPTION **2 :** an attempt or device to deceive **:** TRICK **3 :** the quality of being deceitful **:** DECEITFULNESS

de·ceit·ful \-fəl\ *adj* (15c) **:** having a tendency or disposition to deceive: **a :** not honest ⟨a ~ child⟩ **b :** DECEPTIVE, MISLEADING ⟨~ advertising⟩ ***syn*** see DISHONEST — **de·ceit·ful·ly** \-fə-lē\ *adv* — **de·ceit·ful·ness** *n*

de·ceiv·able \di-ˈsē-və-bəl\ *adj* (14c) **1** *archaic* **:** DECEITFUL, DECEPTIVE **2** *archaic* **:** capable of being deceived

de·ceive \di-ˈsēv\ *vb* **de·ceived; de·ceiv·ing** [ME, fr. AF *deceivre,* fr. L *decipere,* fr. *de-* + *capere* to take — more at HEAVE] *vt* (13c) **1** *archaic* **:** ENSNARE **2 a** *obs* **:** to be false to **b** *archaic* **:** to fail to fulfill **3** *obs* **:** CHEAT **4 :** to cause to accept as true or valid what is false or invalid **5** *archaic* **:** to while away ~ *vi* **:** to practice deceit; *also* **:** to give a false impression ⟨appearances can ~⟩ — **de·ceiv·er** *n* — **de·ceiv·ing·ly** \-ˈsē-viŋ-lē\ *adv*

syn DECEIVE, MISLEAD, DELUDE, BEGUILE mean to lead astray or frustrate usu. by underhandedness. DECEIVE implies imposing a false idea or belief that causes ignorance, bewilderment, or helplessness ⟨tried to *deceive* me about the cost⟩. MISLEAD implies a leading astray that may or may not be intentional ⟨I was *misled* by the confusing sign⟩. DELUDE implies deceiving so thoroughly as to obscure the truth ⟨we were *deluded* into thinking we were safe⟩. BEGUILE stresses the use of charm and persuasion in deceiving ⟨was *beguiled* by false promises⟩.

de·cel·er·ate \(ˌ)dē-ˈse-lə-ˌrāt\ *vb* **-at·ed; -at·ing** [*de-* + *accelerate*] *vt* (1899) **1 :** to reduce the speed of **:** slow down ⟨~ a car⟩ **2 :** to decrease the rate of progress of ⟨~ growth⟩ ⟨~ soil erosion⟩ ~ *vi* **:** to move at decreasing speed — **de·cel·er·a·tion** \(ˌ)dē-ˌse-lə-ˈrā-shən\ *n* — **de·cel·er·a·tor** \(ˌ)dē-ˈse-lə-rā-tər\ *n*

De·cem·ber \di-ˈsem-bər, dē-\ *n* [ME *Decembre,* fr. OE or AF, both fr. L *December* (tenth month), fr. *decem* ten — more at TEN] (bef. 12c) **:** the 12th month of the Gregorian calendar

De·cem·brist \-brist\ *n* (1877) **:** one taking part in the unsuccessful uprising against the Russian emperor Nicholas I in December 1825

de·cem·vir \di-ˈsem-vər\ *n* [ME, fr. L, back-formation fr. *decemviri,* pl., fr. *decem* + *viri,* pl. of *vir* man — more at VIRILE] (15c) **:** one of a ruling body of 10; *specif* **:** one of a body of 10 magistrates in ancient Rome — **de·cem·vi·ral** \-vər-əl\ *adj* — **de·cem·vi·rate** \-vər-ət\ *n*

de·cen·cy \ˈdē-sᵊn-sē\ *n, pl* **-cies** (1567) **1** *archaic* **a :** FITNESS **b :** ORDERLINESS **2 a :** the quality or state of being decent **:** PROPRIETY **b :** conformity to standards of taste, propriety, or quality **3 :** standard of propriety — usu. used in pl. **4** *pl* **:** conditions or services considered essential for a proper standard of living **5 :** literary decorum

de·cen·ni·al \di-ˈse-nē-əl\ *adj* (ca. 1656) **1 :** consisting of or lasting for 10 years **2 :** occurring or being done every 10 years ⟨the ~ census⟩ — **decennial** *n* — **de·cen·ni·al·ly** \-nē-ə-lē\ *adv*

de·cen·ni·um \-nē-əm\ *n, pl* **-ni·ums** *or* **-nia** \-nē-ə\ [L, fr. *decem* + *annus* year — more at ANNUAL] (1685) **:** a period of 10 years **:** DECADE

de·cent \ˈdē-sᵊnt\ *adj* [MF or L; MF, fr. L *decent-, decens,* prp. of *decēre* to be fitting; akin to L *decus* honor, *dignus* worthy, Gk *dokein* to seem, seem good] (1539) **1** *archaic* **a :** APPROPRIATE **b :** well-formed **:** HANDSOME **2 a :** conforming to standards of propriety, good taste, or morality ⟨~ behavior⟩ **b :** modestly clothed **3 :** free from immodesty or obscenity ⟨~ language⟩ **4 :** fairly good **:** ADEQUATE, SATISFACTORY ⟨~ wages⟩ **5 :** marked by moral integrity, kindness, and goodwill ⟨hard-working and ~ folks⟩ ⟨it's very ~ of them to help⟩ ***syn*** see CHASTE — **de·cent·ly** *adv*

de·cen·ter \(ˌ)dē-ˈsen-tər, -ˈse-nər\ *vt* (1870) **:** to cause to lose or shift from an established center or focus; *esp* **:** to disconnect from practical

\ə\ **abut** \ᵊ\ **kitten**, F table \ər\ **further** \a\ **ash** \ā\ **ace** \ä\ **mop, mar** \au̇\ **out** \ch\ **chin** \e\ **bet** \ē\ **easy** \g\ **go** \i\ **hit** \ī\ **ice** \j\ **job** \ŋ\ **sing** \ō\ **go** \ȯ\ **law** \ȯi\ **boy** \th\ **thin** \t͟h\ **the** \ü\ **loot** \u̇\ **foot** \y\ **yet** \zh\ **vision, beige** \k̲, ⁿ, œ, ue, ʸ\ *see* Guide to Pronunciation

or theoretical assumptions of origin, priority, or essence ⟨~ Western conceptions of history —Ernest Larsen⟩
de·cen·tral·i·sa·tion *Brit var of* DECENTRALIZATION
de·cen·tral·i·za·tion \(ˌ)dē-ˌsen-trə-lə-ˈzā-shən\ *n* (1846) **1 :** the dispersion or distribution of functions and powers; *specif* **:** the delegation of power from a central authority to regional and local authorities **2 :** the redistribution of population and industry from urban centers to outlying areas — **de·cen·tral·ize** \(ˌ)dē-ˈsen-trə-ˌlīz\ *vb*
de·cep·tion \di-ˈsep-shən\ *n* [ME *decepcioun,* fr. AF *deception,* fr. LL *deception-, deceptio,* fr. L *decipere* to deceive] (15c) **1 a :** the act of deceiving **b :** the fact or condition of being deceived **2 :** something that deceives **:** TRICK ⟨a clever ~⟩ — **de·cep·tion·al** \-shə-nəl\ *adj*
syn DECEPTION, FRAUD, DOUBLE-DEALING, SUBTERFUGE, TRICKERY mean the acts or practices of one who deliberately deceives. DECEPTION may or may not imply blameworthiness, since it may suggest cheating or merely tactical resource ⟨magicians are masters of *deception*⟩. FRAUD always implies guilt and often criminality in act or practice ⟨indicted for *fraud*⟩. DOUBLE-DEALING suggests treachery or at least action contrary to a professed attitude ⟨a go-between suspected of *double-dealing*⟩. SUBTERFUGE suggests the adoption of a stratagem or the telling of a lie in order to escape guilt or to gain an end ⟨obtained the papers by *subterfuge*⟩. TRICKERY implies ingenious acts intended to dupe or cheat ⟨resorted to *trickery* to gain their ends⟩.
de·cep·tive \di-ˈsep-tiv\ *adj* (ca. 1611) **:** tending or having power to deceive **:** MISLEADING ⟨a ~ appearance⟩ — **de·cep·tive·ly** *adv* — **de·cep·tive·ness** *n*
¹**de·cer·e·brate** \(ˌ)dē-ˈser-ə-brət, -ˌbrāt\ *adj* (1897) **1 :** characteristic of decerebration ⟨~ rigidity⟩ **2 :** having the cerebrum removed or made inactive
²**de·cer·e·brate** \(ˌ)dē-ˈser-ə-ˌbrāt\ *vt* (ca. 1900) **:** to remove the cerebrum from; *also* **:** to make incapable of cerebral activity — **de·cer·e·bra·tion** \(ˌ)dē-ˌser-ə-ˈbrā-shən\ *n*
de·cer·ti·fy \(ˌ)dē-ˈsər-tə-ˌfī\ *vt* (1918) **:** to withdraw or revoke the certification of — **de·cer·ti·fi·ca·tion** \(ˌ)dē-ˌsər-tə-fə-ˈkā-shən\ *n*
de·chlo·ri·nate \(ˌ)dē-ˈklōr-ə-ˌnāt\ *vt* (1941) **:** to remove chlorine from ⟨~ water⟩ — **de·chlo·ri·na·tion** \(ˌ)dē-ˌklōr-ə-ˈnā-shən\ *n*
deci- *comb form* [F *déci-,* fr. L *decimus* tenth, fr. *decem* ten — more at TEN] **:** one tenth part of ⟨*decimeter*⟩
deci·bel \ˈde-sə-ˌbel, -bəl\ *n* [ISV *deci-* + *bel*] (1928) **1 a :** a unit for expressing the ratio of two amounts of electric or acoustic signal power equal to 10 times the common logarithm of this ratio **b :** a unit for expressing the ratio of the magnitudes of two electric voltages or currents or analogous acoustic quantities equal to 20 times the common logarithm of the voltage or current ratio **2 :** a unit for expressing the relative intensity of sounds on a scale from zero for the average least perceptible sound to about 130 for the average pain level **3 :** degree of loudness; *also* **:** extremely loud sound — usu. used in pl.
de·cide \di-ˈsīd, dē-\ *vb* **de·cid·ed; de·cid·ing** [ME, fr. L *decidere,* lit., to cut off, fr. *de-* + *caedere* to cut] *vt* (14c) **1 a :** to make a final choice or judgment about ⟨~ what to do⟩ **b :** to select as a course of action — used with an infinitive ⟨*decided* to go⟩ **c :** to infer on the basis of evidence **:** CONCLUDE ⟨they *decided* that he was right⟩ **2 :** to bring to a definitive end ⟨one blow *decided* the fight⟩ **3 :** to induce to come to a choice ⟨her pleas *decided* him to help⟩ ~ *vi* **:** to make a choice or judgment ⟨~ on where to go⟩ — **de·cid·abil·i·ty** \di-ˌsī-də-ˈbi-lə-tē\ *n* — **de·cid·able** \di-ˈsī-də-bəl\ *adj* — **de·cid·er** *n*
syn DECIDE, DETERMINE, SETTLE, RULE, RESOLVE mean to come or cause to come to a conclusion. DECIDE implies previous consideration of a matter causing doubt, wavering, debate, or controversy ⟨she *decided* to sell her house⟩. DETERMINE implies fixing the identity, character, scope, or direction of something ⟨*determined* the cause of the problem⟩. SETTLE implies a decision reached by someone with power to end all dispute or uncertainty ⟨the dean's decision *settled* the campus alcohol policy⟩. RULE implies a determination by judicial or administrative authority ⟨the judge *ruled* that the evidence was inadmissible⟩. RESOLVE implies an expressed or clear decision or determination to do or refrain from doing something ⟨he *resolved* to quit smoking⟩.
de·cid·ed *adj* (1790) **1 :** UNQUESTIONABLE ⟨a ~ advantage⟩ **2 :** free from doubt or wavering ⟨has ~ ideas on politics⟩ — **de·cid·ed·ly** *adv* — **de·cid·ed·ness** *n*
de·cid·ing *adj* (1611) **:** that decides **:** DECISIVE ⟨drove in the ~ run⟩
de·cid·ua \di-ˈsi-jə-wə, -jü-ə\ *n, pl* **-u·ae** \-jə-ˌwē, -jü-ˌē\ [NL, fr. L, fem. of *deciduus*] (1785) **1 :** the part of the endometrium that in higher placental mammals undergoes special modifications in preparation for and during pregnancy and is cast off at parturition **2 :** the part of the endometrium cast off in the process of menstruation — **de·cid·u·al** \-wəl, -əl\ *adj*
de·cid·u·ous \di-ˈsi-jə-wəs, -jü-əs\ *adj* [L *deciduus,* fr. *decidere* to fall off, fr. *de-* + *cadere* to fall — more at CHANCE] (1688) **1 :** falling off or shed seasonally or at a certain stage of development in the life cycle ⟨~ leaves⟩ ⟨~ scales⟩ **2 a :** having deciduous parts ⟨maples, birches, and other ~ trees⟩ **b :** having the dominant plants deciduous ⟨a ~ forest⟩ **3 :** EPHEMERAL — **de·cid·u·ous·ness** *n*
deciduous tooth *n* (1856) **:** MILK TOOTH
deci·gram \ˈde-sə-ˌgram\ *n* [F *décigramme,* fr. *déci-* + *gramme* gram] (1810) — see METRIC SYSTEM table
dec·ile \ˈde-ˌsī(-ə)l, -səl\ *n* [L *decem* ten — more at TEN] (1882) **:** any one of nine numbers that divide a frequency distribution into 10 classes such that each contains the same number of individuals; *also* **:** any one of these 10 classes — **decile** *adj*
deci·li·ter \ˈde-sə-ˌlē-tər\ *n* [F *décilitre,* fr. *déci-* + *litre* liter] (1801) — see METRIC SYSTEM table
de·cil·lion \di-ˈsil-yən\ *n, often attrib* [L decem + E *-illion* (as in *million*)] (1847) — see NUMBER table
¹**dec·i·mal** \ˈde-sə-məl, ˈdes-məl\ *adj* [F *décimal,* fr. ML *decimalis* of a tithe, fr. L *decima* tithe — more at DIME] (1608) **:** numbered or proceeding by tens: **a :** based on the number 10; *esp* **:** expressed in or utilizing a decimal system esp. with a decimal point **b :** subdivided into 10th or 100th units ⟨~ coinage⟩ — **dec·i·mal·ly** \-mə-lē\ *adv*
²**decimal** *n* (1651) **:** any real number expressed in base 10; *esp* **:** DECIMAL FRACTION
decimal fraction *n* (1660) **:** a fraction (as .25 = ²⁵⁄₁₀₀ or .025 = ²⁵⁄₁₀₀₀) or mixed number (as 3.025 = 3²⁵⁄₁₀₀₀) in which the denominator is a power of 10 usu. expressed by use of the decimal point
dec·i·mal·i·sa·tion *Brit var of* DECIMALIZATION
dec·i·mal·i·za·tion \ˌde-sə-mə-lə-ˈzā-shən\ *n* (1855) **:** conversion (as of a currency) to a decimal system — **dec·i·mal·ize** \ˈde-sə-mə-ˌlīz\ *vt*
decimal place *n* (1706) **:** the position of a digit as counted to the right of the decimal point in a decimal
decimal point *n* (ca. 1771) **:** a period, centered dot, or in some countries a comma at the left of a proper decimal fraction (as .678) or between the parts of a mixed number (as 3.678) expressed by a whole number and a decimal fraction
decimal system *n* (1811) **1 :** a number system that uses a notation in which each number is expressed in base 10 by using one of the first nine integers or 0 in each place and letting each place value be a power of 10 **2 :** a system of measurement or currency in which the basic units increase by powers of 10
dec·i·mate \ˈde-sə-ˌmāt\ *vt* **-mat·ed; -mat·ing** [L *decimatus,* pp. of *decimare,* fr. *decimus* tenth, fr. *decem* ten] (1660) **1 :** to select by lot and kill every tenth man of **2 :** to exact a tax of 10 percent from ⟨poor as a *decimated* Cavalier —John Dryden⟩ **3 a :** to reduce drastically esp. in number ⟨cholera *decimated* the population⟩ **b :** to cause great destruction or harm to ⟨firebombs *decimated* the city⟩ ⟨an industry *decimated* by recession⟩ — **dec·i·ma·tion** \ˌde-sə-ˈmā-shən\ *n*
deci·me·ter \ˈde-sə-ˌmē-tər\ *n* [F *décimètre,* fr. *déci-* deci- + *mètre* meter] (1809) — see METRIC SYSTEM table
de·ci·pher \dē-ˈsī-fər\ *vt* (1545) **1 :** DECODE 1a **2** *obs* **:** DEPICT **3 a :** to make out the meaning of despite indistinctness or obscurity **b :** to interpret the meaning of — **de·ci·pher·able** \-f(ə-)rə-bəl\ *adj* — **de·ci·pher·er** \-fər-ər\ *n* — **de·ci·pher·ment** \-fər-mənt\ *n*
¹**de·ci·sion** \di-ˈsi-zhən\ *n* [ME *decisioun,* fr. MF, fr. L *decision-, decisio,* fr. *decidere* to decide] (15c) **1 a :** the act or process of deciding **b :** a determination arrived at after consideration **:** CONCLUSION ⟨make a ~⟩ **2 :** a report of a conclusion ⟨a 5-page ~⟩ **3 :** promptness and firmness in deciding **:** DETERMINATION ⟨acting with ~⟩ **4 a :** WIN; *specif* **:** a victory in boxing decided on points ⟨a unanimous ~⟩ **b :** a win or loss officially credited to a pitcher in baseball ⟨has five wins in eight ~*s*⟩ — **de·ci·sion·al** \-ˈsi-zhnəl, -ˈsi-zhə-nᵊl\ *adj*
²**decision** *vt* (1943) **:** to win a decision over (a boxing opponent)
decision theory *n* (1961) **:** a branch of statistical theory concerned with quantifying the process of making choices between alternatives
decision tree *n* (1964) **:** a tree diagram which is used for making decisions in business or computer programming and in which the branches represent choices with associated risks, costs, results, or probabilities
de·ci·sive \di-ˈsī-siv\ *adj* (1611) **1 :** having the power or quality of deciding ⟨a ~ battle⟩ **2 :** RESOLUTE, DETERMINED ⟨a ~ manner⟩ **3 :** UNMISTAKABLE, UNQUESTIONABLE ⟨a ~ superiority⟩ ***syn*** see CONCLUSIVE — **de·ci·sive·ly** *adv* — **de·ci·sive·ness** *n*
¹**deck** \ˈdek\ *n* [ME *dekke* covering of a ship, fr. MD **dec* covering, prob. fr. MLG *vordeck,* fr. *vordecken* to cover, fr. *vor-* for- + *decken* to cover; akin to OHG *decchen* to cover — more at THATCH] (1509) **1 :** a platform in a ship serving usu. as a structural element and forming the floor for its compartments **2 :** something resembling the deck of a ship: as **a :** a story or tier of a building (as a sports stadium) ⟨the upper ~⟩ **b :** the roadway of a bridge **c :** a flat floored roofless area adjoining a house **d :** the lid of the compartment at the rear of the body of an automobile; *also* **:** the compartment **e :** a layer of clouds **3 a :** a pack of playing cards **b :** a packet of narcotics **4 :** TAPE DECK — **on deck 1 :** ready for duty **2 :** next in line **:** next in turn
²**deck** *vt* [D *dekken* to cover; akin to OHG *decchen*] (1513) **1** *obs* **:** COVER **2 a :** to clothe in a striking or elegant manner **:** ARRAY ⟨~*ed* out in furs⟩ **b :** DECORATE ⟨~ the halls with boughs of holly —*English carol*⟩ **c :** to portray or present with embellishments **3** [¹*deck*] **:** to furnish with or as if with a deck **4** [¹*deck*] **:** to knock down forcibly **:** FLOOR ⟨~*ed* him with one punch⟩ ***syn*** see ADORN
deck chair *n* (1884) **:** a folding chair often having an adjustable leg rest

deck chair

deck·er \ˈde-kər\ *n* (1762) **:** something having a specified number of decks, levels, floors, or layers — used in combination ⟨many of the city's buses are double-*deckers*⟩
deck·hand \ˈdek-ˌhand\ *n* (1844) **:** a sailor who performs manual duties
deck·house \-ˌhau̇s\ *n* (1856) **:** a superstructure on a ship's upper deck
deck·ing \ˈde-kiŋ\ *n* (1580) **:** DECK; *also* **:** material for a deck
deck·le \ˈde-kəl\ *n* [G *Deckel,* lit., cover, fr. *decken* to cover, fr. OHG *decchen*] (1816) **:** a frame around the edges of a mold used in making paper by hand; *also* **:** either of the bands around the edge of the wire of a papermaking machine that determine the width of the web
deckle edge *n* (ca. 1874) **:** the rough untrimmed edge of paper left by a deckle or produced artificially — **deck·le–edged** \-ˈejd\ *adj*
deck shoe *n* (1911) **:** a low shoe having a nonslip sole and a lace that is threaded through a channel around the back of the shoe
deck tennis *n* [fr. its being played on the decks of ocean liners] (1927) **:** a game in which players toss a ring or quoit back and forth over a net
de·claim \di-ˈklām, dē-\ *vb* [ME *declamen,* fr. L *declamare,* fr. *de-* + *clamare* to cry out; akin to L *calare* to call — more at LOW] *vi* (14c) **1 :** to speak rhetorically; *specif* **:** to recite something as an exercise in elocution **2 :** to speak pompously or bombastically **:** HARANGUE ~ *vt* **:** to deliver rhetorically ⟨an actor ~*ing* his lines⟩; *specif* **:** to recite in elocution — **de·claim·er** *n* — **dec·la·ma·tion** \ˌde-klə-ˈmā-shən\ *n*
de·clam·a·to·ry \di-ˈkla-mə-ˌtōr-ē\ *adj* (1581) **:** of, relating to, or marked by declamation or rhetorical display ⟨~ speeches⟩
de·clar·ant \di-ˈkler-ənt\ *n* (1681) **:** a person who makes a statement or declaration esp. in connection with a legal proceeding
dec·la·ra·tion \ˌde-klə-ˈrā-shən\ *n* (15c) **1 :** the act of declaring **:** ANNOUNCEMENT **2 a :** the first pleading in a common-law action **b :** a statement made by a party to a legal transaction usu. not under oath **3**

a : something that is declared ⟨a ∼ of love⟩ **b :** a document containing such a declaration

de·clar·a·tive \di-ˈkler-ə-tiv\ *adj* (1628) **:** making a declaration **:** DECLARATORY ⟨a ∼ sentence⟩ — **de·clar·a·tive·ly** *adv*

de·clar·a·to·ry \-ə-ˌtȯr-ē\ *adj* (15c) **1 :** serving to declare, set forth, or explain **2 a :** declaring what is the existing law ⟨∼ statute⟩ **b :** declaring a legal right or interpretation ⟨a ∼ judgment⟩

de·clare \di-ˈkler\ *vb* **de·clared; de·clar·ing** [ME, fr. AF & L; AF *declarer,* fr. L *declarare,* fr. *de-* + *clarare* to make visible, fr. *clarus* clear — more at CLEAR] *vt* (14c) **1 :** to make known formally, officially, or explicitly **2** *obs* **:** to make clear **3 :** to make evident **:** SHOW **4 :** to state emphatically **:** AFFIRM ⟨∼*s* his innocence⟩ **5 :** to make a full statement of (one's taxable or dutiable property) **6 a :** to announce (as a trump suit) in a card game **b :** MELD **7 :** to make payable ⟨∼ a dividend⟩ ∼ *vi* **1 :** to make a declaration **2 :** to avow one's opinion or support **3 :** to announce one's intentions (as to run for political office) ⟨*declared* for mayor⟩ — **de·clar·able** \-ˈkler-ə-bəl\ *adj*

syn DECLARE, ANNOUNCE, PROCLAIM, PROMULGATE mean to make known publicly. DECLARE implies explicitness and usu. formality in making known ⟨the referee *declared* the contest a draw⟩. ANNOUNCE implies the declaration of something for the first time ⟨*announced* their engagement at a party⟩. PROCLAIM implies declaring clearly, forcefully, and authoritatively ⟨the president *proclaimed* a national day of mourning⟩. PROMULGATE implies the proclaiming of a dogma, doctrine, or law ⟨*promulgated* an edict of religious toleration⟩. ***syn*** see in addition ASSERT

de·clar·er \di-ˈkler-ər\ *n* (14c) **:** one that declares; *specif* **:** the bridge player who names the trump and plays both his or her own hand and that of the dummy

de·class \(ˌ)dē-ˈklas\ *vt* (1888) **:** to remove from a class; *esp* **:** to assign to a lower social status

dé·clas·sé \ˌdā-ˌkla-ˈsā, -ˌklä-\ *adj* [F, fr. pp. of *déclasser* to declass] (1887) **1 :** fallen or lowered in class, rank, or social position **2 :** of inferior status

de·clas·si·fy \(ˌ)dē-ˈkla-sə-ˌfī\ *vt* (1945) **:** to remove or reduce the security classification of ⟨∼ a secret document⟩ — **de·clas·si·fi·ca·tion** \(ˌ)dē-ˌkla-sə-fə-ˈkā-shən\ *n*

de·claw \-ˈklȯ\ *vt* (1953) **:** to remove the claws of (as a cat) surgically

de·clen·sion \di-ˈklen(t)-shən\ *n* [ME *declenson,* modif. of MF *declinaison,* fr. L *declination-, declinatio* grammatical inflection, turning aside, fr. *declinare* to inflect, turn aside] (15c) **1 a :** noun, adjective, or pronoun inflection esp. in some prescribed order of the forms **b :** a class of nouns or adjectives having the same type of inflectional forms **2 :** a falling off or away **:** DETERIORATION **3 :** DESCENT, SLOPE — **de·clen·sion·al** \-ˈklen(t)-shə-nᵊl\ *adj*

dec·li·na·tion \ˌde-klə-ˈnā-shən\ *n* [ME *declinacioun,* fr. MF *declination,* fr. L *declination-, declinatio* angle of the heavens, turning aside] (14c) **1 :** angular distance north or south from the celestial equator measured along a great circle passing through the celestial poles **2 :** a turning aside or swerving **3 :** DETERIORATION ⟨moral ∼⟩ **4 :** a bending downward **:** INCLINATION **5 :** a formal refusal **6 :** the angle formed between a magnetic needle and the geographical meridian — **dec·li·na·tion·al** \-shnəl, -shə-nᵊl\ *adj*

1**de·cline** \di-ˈklīn, dē-\ *vb* **de·clined; de·clin·ing** [ME, fr. AF *decliner,* fr. L *declinare* to turn aside, inflect, fr. *de-* + *clinare* to incline — more at LEAN] *vi* (14c) **1** *archaic* **:** to turn from a straight course **:** STRAY **2 a :** to slope downward **:** DESCEND **b :** to bend down **:** DROOP **c :** to stoop to what is unworthy **3 a** *of a celestial body* **:** to sink toward setting **b :** to draw toward a close **:** WANE ⟨the day *declined*⟩ **4 :** to tend toward an inferior state or weaker condition ⟨his health *declined*⟩ ⟨morale *declined*⟩ **5 :** to withhold consent **6 :** to become less in amount ⟨prices *declined*⟩ ∼ *vt* **1 :** to give in prescribed order the grammatical forms of (a noun, pronoun, or adjective) **2** *obs* **a :** AVERT **b :** AVOID **3 :** to cause to bend or bow downward **4 a :** to refuse to undertake, undergo, engage in, or comply with ⟨∼ battle⟩ **b :** to refuse esp. courteously ⟨∼ an invitation⟩ — **de·clin·able** \-ˈklī-nə-bəl\ *adj* — **de·clin·er** \-ˈklī-nər\ *n*

syn DECLINE, REFUSE, REJECT, REPUDIATE, SPURN mean to turn away by not accepting, receiving, or considering. DECLINE often implies courteous refusal esp. of offers or invitations ⟨*declined* his party's nomination⟩. REFUSE suggests more positiveness or ungraciousness and often implies the denial of something asked for ⟨*refused* to lend them the money⟩. REJECT implies a peremptory refusal by sending away or discarding ⟨*rejected* the manuscript as unpublishable⟩. REPUDIATE implies a casting off or disowning as untrue, unauthorized, or unworthy of acceptance ⟨teenagers who *repudiate* the values of their parents⟩. SPURN stresses contempt or disdain in rejection or repudiation ⟨*spurned* his overtures of friendship⟩.

2**decline** *also* ˈdē-ˌklīn\ *n* (14c) **1 :** the process of declining: **a :** a gradual physical or mental sinking and wasting away **b :** a change to a lower state or level ⟨the ∼ of the aristocracy⟩ **2 :** the period during which something is deteriorating or approaching its end ⟨an empire in ∼⟩ **3 :** a downward slope **4 :** a wasting disease; *esp* **:** pulmonary tuberculosis ***syn*** see DETERIORATION

de·clin·ing \-niŋ\ *adj* (1593) **:** of or relating to the period during which something is deteriorating or nearing its end ⟨her ∼ years⟩

de·clin·ist \di-ˈklī-nist\ *n* (1988) **:** one who theorizes that a nation or society is in or is headed for a state of economic, political, or social decline

de·cliv·i·tous \di-ˈkli-və-təs\ *adj* (1799) **:** moderately steep

de·cliv·i·ty \-tē\ *n, pl* **-ties** [L *declivitat-, declivitas,* fr. *declivis* sloping down, fr. *de-* + *clivus* slope, hill; akin to L *clinare*] (1612) **1 :** downward inclination **2 :** a descending slope

de·co \ˈde-(ˌ)kō, dā-ˈkō, ˈdā-ˌ\ *n, often cap, often attrib* (1969) **:** ART DECO

de·coct \di-ˈkäkt\ *vt* [ME, fr. L *decoctus,* pp. of *decoquere,* fr. *de-* + *coquere* to cook — more at COOK] (15c) **1 :** to extract the flavor of by boiling **2 :** BOIL DOWN, CONCENTRATE

de·coc·tion \di-ˈkäk-shən\ *n* (15c) **1 :** an extract obtained by decocting **2 :** the act or process of decocting

de·code \(ˌ)dē-ˈkōd\ *vt* (1896) **1 a :** to convert (as a coded message) into intelligible form **b :** to recognize and interpret (an electronic signal) **2 a :** DECIPHER 3a **b :** to discover the underlying meaning of ⟨∼ the play's imagery⟩

de·cod·er \-ˈkō-dər\ *n* (1920) **:** one that decodes; *esp* **:** an electronic device that converts signals from one form to another (as for unscrambling a television transmission)

de·col·late \dē-ˈkä-ˌlāt\ *vt* **-lat·ed; -lat·ing** [L *decollatus,* pp. of *decollare,* fr. *de-* + *collum* neck — more at COLLAR] (15c) **:** BEHEAD — **de·col·la·tion** \ˌdē-kä-ˈlā-shən\ *n*

dé·col·le·tage \(ˌ)dā-ˌkä-lə-ˈtäzh, (ˌ)dā-ˌkȯl-ˈtäzh, ˌde-klə-\ *n* [F, action of cutting or wearing a low neckline, fr. *décolleter*] (1894) **1 :** the low-cut neckline of a dress **2 :** a décolleté dress **3 :** 1BUST 2

1**dé·col·le·té** \(ˌ)dā-ˌkäl-ˈtā, -ˌkȯl-, -lə-ˈtā; *also* dā-ˈkȯl-tā\ *adj* [F, fr. pp. of *décolleter* to give a low neckline to, fr. *dé-* de- + *collet* collar, fr. OF *colet,* fr. *col* collar, neck, fr. L *collum* neck] (1831) **1 :** wearing a strapless or low-necked dress **2 :** having a low-cut neckline

2**décolleté** *also* **de·col·le·te** *n* (1894) **:** DÉCOLLETAGE

de·col·o·nize \(ˌ)dē-ˈkä-lə-ˌnīz\ *vt* (1963) **:** to free from colonial status — **de·col·o·ni·za·tion** \(ˌ)dē-ˌkä-lə-nə-ˈzā-shən\ *n*

de·col·or·ize \(ˌ)dē-ˈkə-lə-ˌrīz\ *vt* **-ized; -iz·ing** (1830) **:** to remove color from ⟨∼ vinegar by adsorption of impurities on activated charcoal⟩ — **de·col·or·i·za·tion** \(ˌ)dē-ˌkə-lə-rə-ˈzā-shən\ *n* — **de·col·or·iz·er** \(ˈ)dē-ˈkə-lə-ˌrī-zər\ *n*

de·com·mis·sion \ˌdē-kə-ˈmi-shən\ *vt* (1922) **:** to remove (as a ship or nuclear power plant) from service

de·com·pen·sa·tion \(ˌ)dē-ˌkäm-pən-ˈsā-shən, -ˌpen-\ *n* [ISV] (ca. 1903) **:** loss of physiological or psychological compensation; *esp* **:** inability of the heart to maintain adequate circulation — **de·com·pen·sate** \(ˌ)dē-ˈkäm-pən-ˌsāt, -ˌpen-\ *vb*

de·com·pose \ˌdē-kəm-ˈpōz\ *vb* [F *décomposer,* fr. *dé-* de + *composer* to compose] *vt* (1718) **1 :** to separate into constituent parts or elements or into simpler compounds ⟨∼ water by electrolysis⟩ ⟨∼ a word into its base and affixes⟩ **2 :** ROT ∼ *vi* **:** to break up into constituent parts by or as if by a chemical process **:** DECAY, ROT ⟨fruit ∼*s*⟩ ***syn*** see DECAY — **de·com·pos·abil·i·ty** \-ˌpō-zə-ˈbi-lə-tē\ *n* — **de·com·pos·able** \-ˈpō-zə-bəl\ *adj* — **de·com·po·si·tion** \(ˌ)dē-ˌkäm-pə-ˈzi-shən\ *n*

de·com·pos·er \ˌdē-kəm-ˈpō-zər\ *n* (1959) **:** any of various organisms (as many bacteria and fungi) that return constituents of organic substances to ecological cycles by feeding on and breaking down dead protoplasm — compare CONSUMER, PRODUCER 4

de·com·pound \ˌdē-ˈkäm-ˌpau̇nd, ˌdē-kəm-ˈ\ *adj* (ca. 1793) *of a leaf* **:** having divisions that are themselves compound

de·com·press \ˌdē-kəm-ˈpres\ *vt* (1905) **1 :** to release from pressure or compression **2 :** to convert (as a compressed file or signal) to an expanded or original size ∼ *vi* **:** to undergo release from pressure; *esp* **:** RELAX ⟨need a week off to ∼⟩ — **de·com·pres·sion** \-ˈpre-shən\ *n*

decompression sickness *n* (1941) **:** a sometimes fatal disorder that is marked by neuralgic pains and paralysis, distress in breathing, and often collapse and that is caused by the release of gas bubbles (as of nitrogen) in tissue upon too rapid decrease in air pressure after a stay in a compressed atmosphere — called also *bends, caisson disease;* compare AEROEMBOLISM

de·con·cen·trate \(ˌ)dē-ˈkän(t)-sən-ˌtrāt\ *vt* (ca. 1889) **:** to reduce or abolish the concentration of **:** DECENTRALIZE — **de·con·cen·tra·tion** \(ˌ)dē-ˌkän(t)-sən-ˈtrā-shən\ *n*

de·con·di·tion \ˌdē-kən-ˈdi-shən\ *vt* (1941) **1 :** to cause extinction of (a conditioned response) **2 :** to cause to lose physical fitness

de·con·ges·tant \ˌdē-kən-ˈjes-tənt\ *n* (1947) **:** an agent that relieves congestion (as of mucous membranes) — **decongestant** *adj*

de·con·ges·tion \ˌdē-kən-ˈjes(h)-chən\ *n* (1908) **:** the process of relieving congestion — **de·con·gest** \-ˈjest\ *vt* — **de·con·ges·tive** \-ˈjes-tiv\ *adj*

de·con·se·crate \(ˌ)dē-ˈkän(t)-sə-ˌkrāt\ *vt* (1876) **:** to remove the sacred character of ⟨∼ a church⟩ — **de·con·se·cra·tion** \(ˌ)dē-ˌkän(t)-sə-ˈkrā-shən\ *n*

de·con·struct \ˌdē-kən-ˈstrəkt\ *vt* (1973) **1 :** to examine (as a work of literature) using the methods of deconstruction **2 :** to take apart or examine in order to reveal the basis or composition of often with the intention of exposing biases, flaws, or inconsistencies ⟨∼ the myths of both the left and the right —Wayne Karlin⟩ **3 :** to adapt or separate the elements of for use in an ironic or radically new way ⟨uses his masterly tailoring skills to ∼ the classics —*Vogue*⟩ **4 :** DESTROY, DEMOLISH ⟨nations that are ∼*ing* themselves —Jim Hoagland⟩ — **de·con·struc·tive** \-tiv\ *adj* — **de·con·struc·tor** \-tər\ *n*

de·con·struc·tion \ˌdē-kən-ˈstrək-shən\ *n* [F *déconstruction,* fr. *dé-* de- + *construction*] (1973) **1 :** a philosophical or critical method which asserts that meanings, metaphysical constructs, and hierarchical oppositions (as between key terms in a philosophical or literary work) are always rendered unstable by their dependence on ultimately arbitrary signifiers; *also* **:** an instance of the use of this method ⟨a ∼ of the nature–culture opposition in Rousseau's work⟩ **2 :** the analytic examination of something (as a theory) often in order to reveal its inadequacy

de·con·struc·tion·ism \-shə-ˌni-zəm\ *n* (1977) **:** DECONSTRUCTION 1 — **de·con·struc·tion·ist** \-shə-nist\ *adj or n*

de·con·struc·tiv·ism \-ˈstrək-ti-ˌvi-zəm\ *n, often cap* (1988) **:** an architectural movement or style influenced by deconstruction that encourages radical freedom of form and the open manifestation of complexity in a building rather than strict attention to functional concerns and conventional design elements (as right angles or grids) — **de·con·struc·ti·vist** \-vist\ *adj or n, often cap*

de·con·tam·i·nate \ˌdē-kən-ˈta-mə-ˌnāt\ *vt* (1936) **:** to rid of contamination (as radioactive material) — **de·con·tam·i·na·tion** \-ˌta-mə-ˈnā-shən\ *n* — **de·con·tam·i·na·tor** \-ˈta-mə-ˌnā-tər\ *n*

de·con·tex·tu·al·ize \ˌdē-kən-ˈteks-chə-wə-ˌlīz, -chə-ˌlīz, -chü-ə-ˌlīz\ *vt* (1977) **:** to remove from a context

de·con·trol \ˌdē-kən-ˈtrōl\ *vt* (1919) **:** to end control of — **decontrol** *n*

\ə\ **abut** \ᵊ\ **kitten, F table** \ər\ **further** \a\ **ash** \ā\ **ace** \ä\ **mop, mar** \au̇\ **out** \ch\ **chin** \e\ **bet** \ē\ **easy** \g\ **go** \i\ **hit** \ī\ **ice** \j\ **job** \ŋ\ **sing** \ō\ **go** \ȯ\ **law** \ȯi\ **boy** \th\ **thin** \t͟h\ **the** \ü\ **loot** \u̇\ **foot** \y\ **yet** \zh\ **vision, beige** \k, n, œ, ue, y\ *see* Guide to Pronunciation

de·cor *or* **dé·cor** \dā-ˈkȯr, di-ˈ; ˈde-ˌkȯr, ˈdā-ˌ\ *n* [F *décor,* fr. *décorer* to decorate, fr. L *decorare*] (1897) **1 :** a stage setting **2 a :** DECORATION 2 **b :** the style and layout of interior furnishings

dec·o·rate \ˈde-kə-ˌrāt\ *vt* **-rat·ed; -rat·ing** [L *decoratus,* pp. of *decorare,* fr. *decor-, decus* ornament, honor — more at DECENT] (1530) **1 :** to add honor to **2 :** to furnish with something ornamental ⟨~ a room⟩ **3 :** to award a mark of honor to ⟨a soldier *decorated* for valor⟩ ***syn*** see ADORN

dec·o·ra·tion \ˌde-kə-ˈrā-shən\ *n* (1585) **1 :** the act or process of decorating **2 :** something that adorns, enriches, or beautifies : ORNAMENT **3 :** a badge of honor (as a U.S. military award)

Decoration Day *n* [fr. the custom of decorating graves on this day] (1871) : MEMORIAL DAY

dec·o·ra·tive \ˈde-k(ə-)rə-tiv, ˈde-kə-ˌrā-\ *adj* (1791) : serving to decorate; *esp* : purely ornamental — **dec·o·ra·tive·ly** *adv* — **dec·o·ra·tive·ness** *n*

decorative art *n* (1853) **1 :** art that is concerned primarily with the creation of useful items (as furniture, ceramics, or textiles) — usu. used in pl. **2 :** objects of decorative art

1**dec·o·ra·tor** \ˈde-kə-ˌrā-tər\ *n* (ca. 1755) : one that decorates; *esp* : one that designs or executes interiors and their furnishings

2**decorator** *adj* (1950) : suitable for interior decoration ⟨~ fabrics⟩

dec·o·rous \ˈde-kər-əs *also* di-ˈkȯr-əs\ *adj* [L *decorus,* fr. *decor* beauty, grace; akin to L *decēre* to be fitting — more at DECENT] (1653) : marked by propriety and good taste : CORRECT ⟨~ conduct⟩ — **dec·o·rous·ly** *adv* — **dec·o·rous·ness** *n*

de·cor·ti·ca·tion \(ˌ)dē-ˌkȯr-tə-ˈkā-shən\ *n* [L *decortication-, decorticatio,* fr. *decorticare* to remove the bark from, fr. *de-* + *cortic-, cortex* bark — more at CUIRASS] (ca. 1623) **1 :** the act or process of removing the outer coverings (as bark or husks) from something (as fiber or seed) **2 :** the surgical removal of the outer layer or covering of an organ or structure (as the brain or a kidney) — **de·cor·ti·cate** \(ˌ)dē-ˈkȯr-tə-ˌkāt\ *vt* — **de·cor·ti·cat·or** \-ˌkā-tər\ *n*

de·co·rum \di-ˈkȯr-əm\ *n* [L, fr. neut. of *decorus*] (1568) **1 :** literary and dramatic propriety : FITNESS **2 :** propriety and good taste in conduct or appearance **3 :** ORDERLINESS **4** *pl* **:** the conventions of polite behavior

de·cou·page *or* **dé·cou·page** \ˌdā-(ˌ)kü-ˈpäzh\ *n* [F *découpage,* lit., act of cutting out, fr. MF, fr. *decouper* to cut out, fr. *de-* + *couper* to cut — more at COPE] (1946) **1 :** the art of decorating surfaces by applying cutouts (as of paper) and then coating with usu. several layers of finish (as lacquer or varnish) **2 :** work produced by decoupage — **decoupage** *or* **découpage** *vt*

de·cou·ple \(ˌ)dē-ˈkə-pəl\ *vt* (1938) : to eliminate the interrelationship of : SEPARATE

1**de·coy** \ˈdē-ˌkȯi, di-ˈ\ *n* [prob. fr. D *de kooi,* lit., the cage] (1630) **1 :** a pond into which wildfowl are lured for capture **2 :** someone or something used to lure or lead another into a trap; *esp* : an artificial bird used to attract live birds within shot **3 :** someone or something used to draw attention away from another

2**de·coy** \di-ˈkȯi, ˈdē-ˌ\ *vt* (1648) : to lure by or as if by a decoy : ENTICE ***syn*** see LURE

1**de·crease** \di-ˈkrēs, ˈdē-ˌ\ *vb* **de·creased; de·creas·ing** [ME *decreessen,* fr. AF *decrestre,* fr. L *decrescere,* fr. *de-* + *crescere* to grow — more at CRESCENT] *vi* (14c) : to grow progressively less (as in size, amount, number, or intensity) ~ *vt* : to cause to decrease — **de·creas·ing·ly** \di-ˈkrē-siŋ-lē, dē-\ *adv*

syn DECREASE, LESSEN, DIMINISH, REDUCE, ABATE, DWINDLE mean to grow or make less. DECREASE suggests a progressive decline in size, amount, numbers, or intensity ⟨slowly *decreased* the amount of pressure⟩. LESSEN suggests a decline in amount rather than in number ⟨has been unable to *lessen* her debt⟩. DIMINISH emphasizes a perceptible loss and implies its subtraction from a total ⟨his visual acuity has *diminished*⟩. REDUCE implies a bringing down or lowering ⟨you must *reduce* your caloric intake⟩. ABATE implies a reducing of something excessive or oppressive in force or amount ⟨the storm *abated*⟩. DWINDLE implies progressive lessening and is applied to things growing visibly smaller ⟨their provisions *dwindled* slowly⟩.

2**de·crease** \ˈdē-ˌkrēs, di-ˈ\ *n* (14c) **1 :** the process of decreasing **2 :** an amount of diminution : REDUCTION

1**de·cree** \di-ˈkrē\ *n* [ME, fr. AF *decré,* fr. L *decretum,* fr. neut. of *decretus,* pp. of *decernere* to decide, fr. *de-* + *cernere* to sift, decide — more at CERTAIN] (14c) **1 :** an order usu. having the force of law **2 a :** a religious ordinance enacted by council or titular head **b :** a foreordaining will **3 a :** a judicial decision of the Roman emperor **b :** a judicial decision esp. in an equity or probate court

2**decree** *vb* **de·creed; de·cree·ing** *vt* (14c) **1 :** to command or enjoin by or as if by decree ⟨~ an amnesty⟩ **2 :** to determine or order judicially ⟨~ a punishment⟩ ~ *vi* : ORDAIN — **de·cre·er** \-ˈkrē-ər\ *n*

de·cree–law \di-ˈkrē-ˌlȯ\ *n* (1926) : a decree of a ruler or ministry having the force of a law enacted by the legislature

dec·re·ment \ˈde-krə-mənt\ *n* [L *decrementum,* fr. *decrescere*] (1610) **1 :** a gradual decrease in quality or quantity **2 a :** the quantity lost by diminution or waste **b :** the amount of decrease (as of a variable) — **dec·re·men·tal** \ˌde-krə-ˈmen-tᵊl\ *adj*

de·crep·it \di-ˈkre-pət\ *adj* [ME, fr. L *decrepitus*] (15c) **1 :** wasted and weakened by or as if by the infirmities of old age **2 a :** impaired by use or wear : WORN-OUT **b :** fallen into ruin or disrepair **3 :** DILAPIDATED, RUN-DOWN ***syn*** see WEAK — **de·crep·it·ly** *adv*

de·crep·i·tate \di-ˈkre-pə-ˌtāt\ *vb* [prob. fr. NL **decrepitatus,* pp. of **decrepitare,* fr. L *de-* + *crepitare* to crackle — more at CREPITATE] *vt* (1646) : to roast or calcine (as salt) so as to cause crackling or until crackling stops ~ *vi* : to become decrepitated — **de·crep·i·ta·tion** \-ˌkre-pə-ˈtā-shən\ *n*

de·crep·i·tude \di-ˈkre-pə-ˌtüd, -ˌtyüd\ *n* (1603) : the quality or state of being decrepit

1**de·cre·scen·do** \ˌdā-krə-ˈshen-(ˌ)dō\ *n, pl* **-dos** [It, lit., decreasing, fr. L *decrescendum,* gerund of *decrescere*] (1877) **1 :** a gradual decrease in volume of a musical passage **2 :** a decrescendo musical passage

2**decrescendo** *adv or adj* (1877) : with a decrease in volume — used as a direction in music

de·cres·cent \di-ˈkre-sᵊnt\ *adj* [alter. of earlier *decressant,* fr. AF, prp. of AF *decrestre* to decrease] (1610) : becoming less by gradual diminution : DECREASING, WANING

de·cre·tal \di-ˈkrē-tᵊl, ˈde-kri-tᵊl\ *n* [ME, fr. AF, fr. LL *decretalis* of a decree, fr. L *decretum* decree] (14c) : DECREE; *esp* : a papal letter giving an authoritative decision on a point of canon law

de·cre·tive \-ˈkrē-tiv\ *adj* (1609) : having the force of a decree : DECRETORY

de·cre·to·ry \ˈde-krə-ˌtȯr-ē, di-ˈkrē-tər-ē\ *adj* (ca. 1631) : relating to or fixed by a decree or decision

de·crim·i·nal·ize \(ˌ)dē-ˈkri-mə-nə-ˌlīz, -ˈkrim-nəl-\ *vt* (1969) : to remove or reduce the criminal classification or status of; *esp* : to repeal a strict ban on while keeping under some form of regulation ⟨~ the possession of marijuana⟩ — **de·crim·i·nal·iza·tion** \(ˌ)dē-ˌkri-mə-nə-lə-ˈzā-shən, -ˌkrim-nəl-\ *n*

de·cry \di-ˈkrī, dē-\ *vt* [F *décrier,* fr. OF *decrier,* fr. *de-* + *crier* to cry] (1614) **1 :** to depreciate (as a coin) officially or publicly **2 :** to express strong disapproval of ⟨~ the emphasis on sex⟩ — **de·cri·er** \-ˈkrī(-ə)r\ *n*

syn DECRY, DEPRECIATE, DISPARAGE, BELITTLE mean to express a low opinion of. DECRY implies open condemnation with intent to discredit ⟨*decried* their defeatist attitude⟩. DEPRECIATE implies a representing as being of less value than commonly believed ⟨critics *depreciate* his plays for being unabashedly sentimental⟩. DISPARAGE implies depreciation by indirect means such as slighting or invidious comparison ⟨*disparaged* polo as a game for the rich⟩. BELITTLE usu. suggests a contemptuous or envious attitude ⟨*belittled* the achievements of others⟩.

de·crypt \(ˌ)dē-ˈkript\ *vt* [ISV *de-* + *crypto*gram, *crypto*graph] (1935) : DECODE 1a — **de·cryp·tion** \-ˈkrip-shən\ *n*

de·cu·bi·tus ulcer \di-ˈkyü-bə-təs-\ *n* [NL *decubitus* position assumed in lying down, fr. L *decumbere*] (1946) : BEDSORE

de·cum·bent \di-ˈkəm-bənt, dē-\ *adj* [L *decumbent-, decumbens,* prp. of *decumbere* to lie down, fr. *de-* + *-cumbere* to lie down; akin to L *cubare* to lie] (1656) **1 :** lying down **2** *of a plant* **:** reclining on the ground but with ascending apex or extremity

dec·u·ple \ˈde-kyə-pəl\ *adj* [F *décuple,* fr. MF, fr. LL *decuplus,* fr. L *decem* ten + *-uplus* (as in *quadruplus* quadruple)] (1613) **1 :** TENFOLD **2 :** taken in groups of 10

de·cu·ri·on \di-ˈkyu̇r-ē-ən\ *n* [ME *decurioun,* fr. L *decurion-, decurio,* fr. *decuria* division of ten, fr. *decem*] (14c) **1 :** a Roman cavalry officer in command of 10 men **2 :** a member of a Roman senate

de·cur·rent \di-ˈkər-ənt, -ˈkə-rənt\ *adj* [L *decurrent-, decurrens,* prp. of *decurrere* to run down, fr. *de-* + *currere* to run — more at CAR] (ca. 1753) : running or extending downward along the stem ⟨~ leaves⟩

de·curved \(ˌ)dē-ˈkərvd\ *adj* [part trans. of LL *decurvatus,* fr. L *de-* + *curvatus* curved] (1835) : curved downward : bent down ⟨a ~ bill⟩

1**de·cus·sate** \ˈde-kə-ˌsāt, di-ˈkə-ˌsāt\ *vb* **-sat·ed; -sat·ing** [L *decussatus,* pp. of *decussare* to arrange crosswise, fr. *decussis* the number ten, numeral X, intersection, fr. *decem* + *ass-, as* unit — more at ACE] (1658) : INTERSECT, CROSS

2**de·cus·sate** \ˈde-kə-ˌsāt, di-ˈkə-sət\ *adj* (ca. 1823) : arranged in pairs each at right angles to the next pair above or below ⟨~ leaves⟩

de·cus·sa·tion \ˌde-kə-ˈsā-shən, ˌdē-ˌkə-\ *n* (ca. 1656) **1 :** the action of crossing (as of nerve fibers) esp. in the form of an X **2 :** a crossed tract of nerve fibers passing between centers on opposite sides of the nervous system

1**ded·i·cate** \ˈde-di-kət\ *adj* [ME, fr. L *dedicatus,* pp. of *dedicare* to dedicate, fr. *de-* + *dicare* to proclaim, dedicate — more at DICTION] (14c) : DEDICATED 1

2**ded·i·cate** \ˈde-di-ˌkāt *also* ˈde-ˌdē-\ *vt* **-cat·ed; -cat·ing** (15c) **1 :** to devote to the worship of a divine being; *specif* : to set apart (a church) to sacred uses with solemn rites **2 a :** to set apart to a definite use ⟨money *dedicated* to their vacation fund⟩ **b :** to commit to a goal or way of life ⟨ready to ~ his life to public service⟩ **3 :** to inscribe or address by way of compliment ⟨~ a book to a friend⟩ **4 :** to open to public use ***syn*** see DEVOTE — **ded·i·ca·tor** \-ˌkā-tər\ *n*

ded·i·cat·ed *adj* (ca. 1600) **1 :** devoted to a cause, ideal, or purpose : ZEALOUS ⟨a ~ scholar⟩ **2 :** given over to a particular purpose ⟨a ~ Web server⟩ — **ded·i·cat·ed·ly** *adv*

ded·i·ca·tee \ˌde-di-kə-ˈtē\ *n* (ca. 1770) : one to whom a thing is dedicated

ded·i·ca·tion \ˌde-di-ˈkā-shən\ *n* (14c) **1 :** an act or rite of dedicating to a divine being or to a sacred use **2 :** a devoting or setting aside for a particular purpose **3 :** a name and often a message prefixed to a literary, musical, or artistic production in tribute to a person or cause **4 :** self-sacrificing devotion ⟨her ~ to the cause⟩ **5 :** a ceremony to mark the official completion or opening of something (as a building) — **ded·i·ca·to·ry** \ˈde-di-kə-ˌtȯr-ē\ *adj*

de·dif·fer·en·ti·a·tion \(ˌ)dē-ˌdi-fə-ˌren-chē-ˈā-shən\ *n* (1915) : reversion of specialized structures (as cells) to a more generalized or primitive condition often as a preliminary to major physiological or structural change — **de·dif·fer·en·ti·ate** \-ˈren-chē-ˌāt\ *vi*

de·duce \di-ˈdüs, dē-; *chiefly Brit* -ˈdyüs\ *vt* **de·duced; de·duc·ing** [ME, fr. L *deducere,* lit., to lead away, fr. *de-* + *ducere* to lead — more at TOW] (15c) **1 :** to determine by deduction; *specif* : to infer from a general principle **2 :** to trace the course of ***syn*** see INFER — **de·duc·ible** \-ˈd(y)ü-sə-bəl\ *adj*

de·duct \di-ˈdəkt, dē-\ *vt* [L *deductus,* pp. of *deducere*] (15c) **1 :** to take away (an amount) from a total : SUBTRACT **2 :** DEDUCE, INFER

1**de·duct·ible** \di-ˈdək-tə-bəl, dē-\ *adj* (1856) : allowable as a deduction ⟨expenses that are ~ from taxable income⟩ — **de·duct·ibil·i·ty** \-ˌdək-tə-ˈbi-lə-tē\ *n*

2**deductible** *n* (1929) : a clause in an insurance policy that relieves the insurer of responsibility for an initial specified loss of the kind insured against; *also* : the amount of the loss specified in such a clause

de·duc·tion \di-ˈdək-shən, dē-\ *n* (15c) **1 a :** an act of taking away ⟨~ of legitimate business expenses⟩ **b :** something that is or may be subtracted ⟨~*s* from his taxable income⟩ **2 a :** the deriving of a conclusion by reasoning; *specif* : inference in which the conclusion about particulars follows necessarily from general or universal premises — compare INDUCTION **b :** a conclusion reached by logical deduction

de·duc·tive \di-ˈdək-tiv, dē-\ *adj* (1665) **1 :** of, relating to, or provable by deduction **2 :** employing deduction in reasoning — **de·duc·tive·ly** *adv*

dee \ˈdē\ *n* (13c) **1 :** the letter *d* **2 :** something shaped like the letter D

[1]**deed** \ˈdēd\ *n* [ME *dede,* fr. OE *dǣd;* akin to OE *dōn* to do] (bef. 12c) **1 :** something that is done ⟨evil ~*s*⟩ **2 :** a usu. illustrious act or action **:** FEAT, EXPLOIT ⟨a hero's daring ~*s*⟩ **3 :** the act of performing **:** ACTION ⟨righteous in word and in ~⟩ **4 :** a signed and usu. sealed instrument containing some legal transfer, bargain, or contract — **deed·less** \-ləs\ *adj*

[2]**deed** *vt* (1758) **:** to convey or transfer by deed

deed poll \-ˈpōl\ *n, pl* **deeds poll** [[1]*deed* + *poll,* adj., having the edges cut even rather than indented, fr. [2]*poll*] (1574) *Brit* **:** a deed (as to change one's name) made and executed by only one party

deedy \ˈdē-dē\ *adj* **deed·i·er; -est** (1615) *dial chiefly Eng* **:** INDUSTRIOUS

dee·jay \ˈdē-ˌjā\ *n* [*d*isc *j*ockey] (ca. 1948) **:** DISC JOCKEY — **deejay** *vb*

deem \ˈdēm\ *vb* [ME *demen,* fr. OE *dēman;* akin to OHG *tuomen* to judge, OE *dōm* doom] *vt* (bef. 12c) **:** to come to think or judge **:** CONSIDER ⟨~*ed* it wise to go slow⟩ ~ *vi* **:** to have an opinion **:** BELIEVE

de–em·pha·size \(ˌ)dē-ˈem(p)-fə-ˌsīz\ *vt* (1938) **:** to reduce in relative importance; *also* **:** PLAY DOWN — **de–em·pha·sis** \-fə-səs\ *n*

de–en·er·gize \ˌdē-ˈe-nər-ˌjīz\ *vt* (1886) **:** to disconnect from a source of electricity **:** shut off the power to

[1]**deep** \ˈdēp\ *adj* [ME *dep,* fr. OE *dēop;* akin to OHG *tiof* deep, OE *dyppan* to dip — more at DIP] (bef. 12c) **1 :** extending far from some surface or area: as **a :** extending far downward ⟨a ~ well⟩ **b** (1) **:** extending well inward from an outer surface ⟨a ~ gash⟩ ⟨a *deep*-chested animal⟩ (2) **:** not located superficially within the body ⟨~ pressure receptors in muscles⟩ **c :** extending well back from a surface accepted as front ⟨a ~ closet⟩ **d :** extending far laterally from the center ⟨~ borders of lace⟩ **e :** occurring or located near the outer limits of the playing area ⟨hit to ~ right field⟩ **f :** thrown deep ⟨a ~ pass⟩ **2 :** having a specified extension in an implied direction usu. downward or backward ⟨a shelf 20 inches ~⟩ ⟨cars parked three-*deep*⟩ **3 a :** difficult to penetrate or comprehend **:** RECONDITE ⟨~ mathematical problems⟩ **b :** MYSTERIOUS, OBSCURE ⟨a ~ dark secret⟩ **c :** grave in nature or effect ⟨in ~*est* disgrace⟩ **d :** of penetrating intellect **:** WISE ⟨a ~ thinker⟩ **e :** intensely engrossed or immersed ⟨she was ~ in her book⟩ **f :** characterized by profundity of feeling or quality ⟨a ~ sleep⟩; *also* **:** DEEP-SEATED ⟨~ religious beliefs⟩ **4 a** *of color* **:** high in saturation and low in lightness **b :** having a low musical pitch or pitch range ⟨a ~ voice⟩ **5 a :** situated well within the boundaries ⟨a house ~ in the woods⟩ **b :** remote in time or space **c :** being below the level of consciousness ⟨~ neuroses⟩ **d :** covered, enclosed, or filled to a specified degree — usu. used in combination ⟨ankle-*deep* in mud⟩ **6 :** LARGE ⟨~ discounts⟩ **7 :** having many good players ⟨a ~ bull pen⟩ ***syn*** see BROAD — **deep·ly** *adv* — **deep·ness** *n* — **in deep water :** in difficulty or distress

[2]**deep** *adv* (bef. 12c) **1 :** to a great depth **:** DEEPLY ⟨still waters run ~⟩ **2 :** far on **:** LATE ⟨danced ~ into the night⟩ **3 a :** near the outer limits of the playing area ⟨the shortstop was playing ~⟩ **b :** LONG 6

[3]**deep** *n* (bef. 12c) **1 a :** a vast or immeasurable extent **:** ABYSS **b** (1) **:** the extent of surrounding space or time (2) **:** OCEAN **2 :** any of the deep portions of a body of water; *specif* **:** a generally long and narrow area in the ocean where the depth exceeds 3000 fathoms (5500 meters) **3 :** the middle or most intense part ⟨the ~ of winter⟩ **4 :** any of the fathom points on a sounding line other than the marks

deep–dish \-ˌdish\ *adj* (1918) **:** baked in a deep dish ⟨a ~ pizza⟩; *esp* **:** baked in a deep dish with usu. a fruit filling and no bottom crust

deep ecology *n* (1984) **:** a movement or a body of concepts that considers humans no more important than other species and that advocates a corresponding radical readjustment of the relationships between humans and nature — **deep ecologist** *n*

deep·en \ˈdē-pən\ *vb* **deep·ened; deep·en·ing** \ˈdē-pə-niŋ, ˈdēp-niŋ\ *vt* (1598) **:** to make deep or deeper ~ *vi* **:** to become deeper or more profound

deep fat *n* (1908) **:** hot fat or oil deep enough in a cooking utensil to cover the food to be fried

deep focus *n* (1948) **:** a photographic effect or technique (as in filmmaking) characterized by great depth of field

Deep·freeze \ˈdēp-ˌfrēz\ *trademark* — used for a freezer for food storage

deep–freeze \ˈdēp-ˈfrēz\ *vt* **-froze** \-ˈfrōz\; **-fro·zen** \-ˈfrō-zᵊn\ (1943) **1 :** QUICK-FREEZE **2 :** to store in a frozen state

deep freeze \ˈdēp-ˌfrēz\ *n* (1948) **1 :** COLD STORAGE 2 ⟨a bill . . . in *deep freeze* awaiting a new congress —*Newsweek*⟩ **2 :** intense cold

deep–fry \ˈdēp-ˈfrī\ *vt* (1922) **:** to cook in deep fat

deep fryer *n* (1950) **:** a utensil suitable for deep-fat frying

deep pocket *n* (1975) **1 :** a person or an organization having substantial financial resources **2** *pl* **:** substantial financial resources ⟨a corporation with *deep pockets*⟩ — **deep–pock·et·ed** \ˈdēp-ˈpä-kə-təd\ *adj*

deep–root·ed \ˈdēp-ˈrü-təd, -ˈrù-\ *adj* (15c) **:** deeply implanted or established ⟨a ~ loyalty⟩

deep–sea \ˈdēp-ˈsē\ *adj* (1626) **:** of, relating to, or occurring in the deeper parts of the sea ⟨~ fishing⟩

deep–seat·ed \ˈdēp-ˈsē-təd\ *adj* (1741) **1 :** situated far below the surface ⟨a ~ inflammation⟩ **2 :** firmly established ⟨a ~ tradition⟩

deep–six \ˈdēp-ˈsiks\ *vt* (1952) **1 :** to get rid of **:** DISCARD, ELIMINATE ⟨legislators voting to ~ a government program⟩ **2** *slang* **:** to throw overboard

deep six *n* [fr. the leadsman's call *by the deep six* for a depth corresponding to the sixth deep on a sounding line] (1929) *slang* **:** a place of disposal or abandonment — used esp. in the phrase *give it the deep six*

deep–sky \ˈdēp-ˌskī\ *adj* (1968) **:** relating to or existing in space outside the solar system ⟨~ objects⟩

deep space *n* (ca. 1952) **:** space well outside the earth's atmosphere and esp. that part lying beyond the earth-moon system

deep structure *n* (1964) **:** a formal representation of the underlying semantic content of a sentence; *also* **:** the structure which such a representation specifies

deep throat *n, often cap D&T* [fr. the nickname given to such an informant in the Watergate scandal by Bob Woodward *b*1943 U.S. journalist, fr. the title of a pornographic film (1972)] (1973) **:** an informant who divulges damaging information under cover of anonymity

deep·wa·ter \ˈdēp-ˌwò-tər, -ˌwä-\ *adj* (1795) **:** of, relating to, or characterized by water of considerable depth ⟨~ sailors⟩; *esp* **:** able to accommodate oceangoing vessels ⟨~ ports⟩

deer \ˈdir\ *n, pl* **deer** *also* **deers** [ME, deer, animal, fr. OE *dēor* beast; akin to OHG *tior* wild animal, Lith *dvasia* breath, spirit] (bef. 12c) **1** *archaic* **:** ANIMAL; *esp* **:** a small mammal **2 :** any of numerous slender-legged ruminant mammals (family Cervidae, the deer family) having usu. brownish fur and antlers borne by the males of nearly all and by the females of a few forms — **deer·like** \-ˌlīk\ *adj*

deer·ber·ry \-ˌber-ē, -ˌbe-rē\ *n* (1814) **1 :** either of two shrubs (*Vaccinium stamineum* or *V. caesium*) of the heath family that are found in dry woods and scrub of the eastern U.S. **2 :** the edible fruit of a deerberry

deer·fly \ˈdir-ˌflī\ *n* (1853) **:** any of numerous small horseflies (as of the genus *Chrysops*) that include important vectors of tularemia

deer·hound \-ˌhau̇nd\ *n* (1816) **:** SCOTTISH DEERHOUND

deer mouse *n* [fr. its agility] (1833) **:** any of various mice (genus *Peromyscus*) of No. and Central America; *esp* **:** one (*P. maniculatus*) widely distributed in forests and grasslands of No. America

deer·skin \ˈdir-ˌskin\ *n* (14c) **:** leather made from the skin of a deer; *also* **:** a garment of this leather

deer·stalk·er \-ˌstò-kər\ *n* (1870) **:** a close-fitting hat with a visor at the front and the back and with earflaps that may be worn up or down — called also *deerstalker cap, deerstalker hat*

deer tick *n* (1982) **:** an ixodid tick (*Ixodes scapularis* syn. *I. dammini*) of the eastern U.S. and Canada that transmits the bacterium causing Lyme disease — called also *black-legged tick*

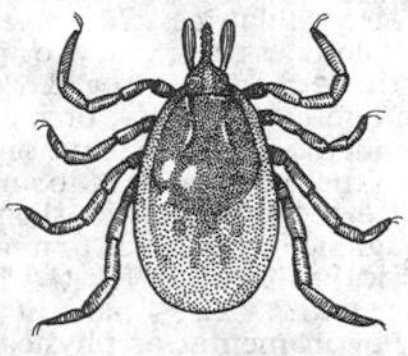
deer tick

deer·yard \ˈdir-ˌyärd\ *n* (1849) **:** a place where deer herd in winter

de–es·ca·late \(ˌ)dē-ˈes-kə-ˌlāt, ÷-kyə-\ *vt* (1964) **:** LIMIT 2b ~ *vi* **:** to decrease in extent, volume, or scope — **de–es·ca·la·tion** \(ˌ)dē-ˌes-kə-ˈlā-shən, ÷-kyə-\ *n* — **de–es·ca·la·to·ry** \(ˌ)dē-ˈes-kə-lə-ˌtòr-ē, ÷-kyə-\ *adj*

deet \ˈdēt\ *n, often all cap* [prob. fr. *d. e. t.,* fr. *di*- + *e*thyl + *t*oluamide (C_8H_9NO)] (1962) **:** a colorless oily liquid insect and tick repellent $C_{12}H_{17}NO$

[1]**def** \ˈdef\ *adj* **def·er; def·fest** [prob. alter. of *death* (fr. the phrase *to death* excessively)] (1979) *slang* **:** COOL 7

[2]**def** *abbr* **1** defendant; defense **2** deferred **3** defined; definition **4** definite

de·face \di-ˈfās, dē-\ *vt* [ME, fr. AF **desfacer,* **deffacer,* fr. *des*- de- + *face* front, face] (14c) **1 :** to mar the appearance of **:** injure by effacing significant details ⟨~ an inscription⟩ **2 :** IMPAIR **3** *obs* **:** DESTROY — **de·face·ment** \-ˈfās-mənt\ *n* — **de·fac·er** *n*

[1]**de fac·to** \di-ˈfak-(ˌ)tō, dā-, dē-\ *adv* [ML, lit., from the fact] (1601) **:** in reality **:** ACTUALLY

[2]**de facto** *adj* (ca. 1689) **1 :** ACTUAL; *esp* **:** being such in effect though not formally recognized ⟨a *de facto* state of war⟩ **2 :** exercising power as if legally constituted ⟨a *de facto* government⟩ **3 :** resulting from economic or social factors rather than from laws or actions of the state ⟨*de facto* segregation⟩

de·fal·cate \di-ˈfal-ˌkāt, -ˈfòl-, dē-; ˈde-fəl-\ *vb* **-cat·ed; -cat·ing** [ML *defalcatus,* pp. of *defalcare,* fr. L *de*- + *falc*-, *falx* sickle] *vt* (1541) *archaic* **:** DEDUCT, CURTAIL ~ *vi* **:** to engage in embezzlement — **de·fal·ca·tor** \-ˌkā-tər\ *n*

de·fal·ca·tion \ˌdē-ˌfal-ˈkā-shən, ˌdē-ˌfòl-, di-; ˌde-fəl-\ *n* (15c) **1** *archaic* **:** DEDUCTION **2 :** the act or an instance of embezzling **3 :** a failure to meet a promise or an expectation

def·a·ma·tion \ˌde-fə-ˈmā-shən\ *n* (14c) **:** the act of defaming another **:** CALUMNY — **de·fam·a·to·ry** \di-ˈfa-mə-ˌtòr-ē, dē-\ *adj*

de·fame \di-ˈfām, dē-\ *vt* **de·famed; de·fam·ing** [ME, fr. AF & ML; AF *deffamer, diffamer,* fr. ML *defamare,* alter. of L *diffamare,* fr. *dis*- + *fama* reputation, fame] (14c) **1** *archaic* **:** DISGRACE **2 :** to harm the reputation of by libel or slander **3** *archaic* **:** ACCUSE ***syn*** see MALIGN — **de·fam·er** *n*

de·fa·mil·iar·ize \(ˌ)dē-fə-ˈmil-yə-ˌrīz\ *vt* (1971) **:** to present or render in an unfamiliar artistic form usu. to stimulate fresh perception — **de·fa·mil·iar·i·za·tion** \-ˌmil-yə-rə-ˈzā-shən\ *n*

de·fang \(ˌ)dē-ˈfaŋ\ *vt* (1953) **:** to make harmless or less powerful

de·fat \(ˌ)dē-ˈfat\ *vt* (1919) **:** to remove fat from

[1]**de·fault** \di-ˈfòlt, dē-; ˈdē-ˌfòlt\ *n* [ME *defaute, defaulte,* fr. AF, fr. *defaillir* to be lacking, fail, fr. *de*- + *faillir* to fail] (13c) **1 :** failure to do something required by duty or law **:** NEGLECT **2** *archaic* **:** FAULT **3 :** a failure to pay financial debts **4 a :** failure to appear at the required time in a legal proceeding **b :** failure to compete in or to finish an appointed contest ⟨lost the game by ~⟩ **5 a :** a selection made usu. automatically or without active consideration due to lack of a viable alternative ⟨remained the club's president by ~⟩ **b :** a selection automatically used by a computer program in the absence of a choice made by the user — **in default of :** in the absence of

[2]**default** *vi* (15c) **1 :** to fail to fulfill a contract, agreement, or duty: as **a :** to fail to meet a financial obligation ⟨~ on a loan⟩ **b :** to fail to appear in court **c :** to fail to compete in or to finish an appointed contest; *also* **:** to forfeit a contest by such failure **2 :** to make a default selection ⟨the program ~*s* to a standard font⟩ ~ *vt* **1 :** to fail to perform, pay, or make good **2 a :** FORFEIT **b :** to exclude (a player or a team) from a contest by default — **de·fault·er** *n*

DEF·CON \ˈdef-ˌkän\ *n* [*def*ense *con*dition] (1962) **:** any of five levels of U.S. military defense readiness ranked according to the perceived threat to national security

de·fea·sance \di-ˈfē-zən(t)s\ *n* [ME *defesance,* fr. AF, fr. *defesaunt,* prp. of *defaire*] (15c) **1 a** (1) **:** the termination of a property interest in accordance with stipulated conditions (as in a deed) (2) **:** an instrument stating such conditions of limitation **b :** a rendering null or void **2 :** DEFEAT, OVERTHROW

\ə\ **abut** \ᵊ\ kitten, F table \ər\ **further** \a\ **ash** \ā\ **ace** \ä\ **mop, mar**
\au̇\ **out** \ch\ **chin** \e\ **bet** \ē\ **easy** \g\ **go** \i\ **hit** \ī\ **ice** \j\ **job**
\ŋ\ **sing** \ō\ **go** \ò\ **law** \ȯi\ **boy** \th\ **thin** \t͟h\ **the** \ü\ **loot** \u̇\ **foot**
\y\ **yet** \zh\ **vision, beige** \k̟, ⁿ, œ, ue, ʸ\ *see* Guide to Pronunciation

de·fea·si·ble \di-ˈfē-zə-bəl\ *adj* (15c) : capable of being annulled or made void ⟨a ~ claim⟩ — **de·fea·si·bil·i·ty** \-ˌfē-zə-ˈbi-lə-tē\ *n*

1**de·feat** \di-ˈfēt, dē-\ *vt* [ME *deffeten,* fr. AF *defait,* pp. of *defaire, desfaire* to destroy, fr. ML *disfacere,* fr. L *dis-* + *facere* to do — more at DO] (14c) **1** *obs* : DESTROY **2 a** : NULLIFY ⟨~ an estate⟩ **b** : FRUSTRATE 2a(1) ⟨~ a hope⟩ **3** : to win victory over : BEAT ⟨~ the opposing team⟩ ***syn*** see CONQUER — **de·feat·able** \-ˈfē-tə-bəl\ *adj*

2**defeat** *n* (1590) **1** : frustration by nullification or by prevention of success ⟨the bill suffered ~ in the Senate⟩ **2** *obs* : DESTRUCTION **3 a** : an overthrow esp. of an army in battle **b** : the loss of a contest

de·feat·ism \di-ˈfē-ˌti-zəm, dē-\ *n* (1918) : an attitude of accepting, expecting, or being resigned to defeat — **de·feat·ist** \-tist\ *n or adj*

de·fea·ture \di-ˈfē-chər, dē-\ *n* [prob. fr. *de-* + *feature*] (1590) **1** *archaic* : DISFIGUREMENT **2** *archaic* : DEFEAT

def·e·cate \ˈde-fi-ˌkāt\ *vb* **-cat·ed; -cat·ing** [L *defaecatus,* pp. of *defaecare,* fr. *de-* + *faec-, faex* dregs, lees] *vt* (1575) **1** : to free from impurity or corruption **2** : to discharge from the anus ~ *vi* : to discharge feces from the bowels — **def·e·ca·tion** \ˌde-fi-ˈkā-shən\ *n*

1**de·fect** \ˈdē-ˌfekt, di-ˈ\ *n* [ME, fr. L *defectus* lack, fr. *deficere* to desert, fail, fr. *de-* + *facere* to do — more at DO] (15c) **1 a** : an imperfection that impairs worth or utility : SHORTCOMING ⟨the grave ~*s* in our foreign policy⟩ **b** : an imperfection (as a vacancy or an unlike atom) in a crystal lattice **2** [L *defectus*] : a lack of something necessary for completeness, adequacy, or perfection : DEFICIENCY ⟨a hearing ~⟩

2**de·fect** \di-ˈfekt\ *vi* [L *defectus,* pp. of *deficere*] (1596) **1** : to forsake one cause, party, or nation for another often because of a change in ideology **2** : to leave one situation (as a job) often to go over to a rival ⟨the reporter ~*ed* to another network⟩ — **de·fec·tor** \-ˈfek-tər\ *n*

de·fec·tion \di-ˈfek-shən\ *n* (1546) : conscious abandonment of allegiance or duty (as to a person, cause, or doctrine) : DESERTION

1**de·fec·tive** \di-ˈfek-tiv\ *adj* (14c) **1 a** : imperfect in form or function : FAULTY ⟨a ~ pane of glass⟩ **b** : falling below the norm in structure or in mental or physical function ⟨~ eyesight⟩ **2** : lacking one or more of the usual forms of grammatical inflection ⟨*must* is a ~ verb⟩ — **de·fec·tive·ly** *adv* — **de·fec·tive·ness** *n*

2**defective** *n* (1592) : a person who is subnormal physically or mentally

de·fem·i·nize \(ˌ)dē-ˈfe-mə-ˌnīz\ *vt* (1907) : to divest of feminine qualities or characteristics : MASCULINIZE — **de·fem·i·ni·za·tion** \(ˌ)dē-ˌfe-mə-nə-ˈzā-shən\ *n*

de·fence, de·fence·man *chiefly Brit var of* DEFENSE, DEFENSEMAN

de·fend \di-ˈfend\ *vb* [ME, fr. AF *defendre,* fr. L *defendere,* fr. *de-* + *-fendere* to strike; akin to OE *gūth* battle, war, Gk *theinein* to strike] *vt* (14c) **1 a** : to drive danger or attack away from ⟨~ our shores⟩ **b** (1) : to maintain or support in the face of argument or hostile criticism ⟨~ a theory⟩ (2) : to prove (as a doctoral thesis) valid by answering questions in an oral exam **c** : to attempt to prevent an opponent from scoring at ⟨elects to ~ the south goal⟩ **2** *archaic* : PREVENT, FORBID **3** : to act as attorney for **4** : to deny or oppose the right of a plaintiff in regard to (a suit or a wrong charged) : CONTEST **5** : to retain or seek to retain (as a title or position) against a challenge in a contest ⟨they successfully ~*ed* their championship⟩ ~ *vi* **1** : to take action against attack or challenge **2** : to play or be on defense ⟨playing deep to ~ against a pass⟩ **3** : to play against the high bidder in a card game — **de·fend·able** \-ˈfen-də-bəl\ *adj*

syn DEFEND, PROTECT, SHIELD, GUARD, SAFEGUARD mean to keep secure from danger or against attack. DEFEND denotes warding off actual or threatened attack ⟨*defend* the country⟩. PROTECT implies the use of something (as a covering) as a bar to the admission or impact of what may attack or injure ⟨a hard hat to *protect* your head⟩. SHIELD suggests protective intervention in imminent danger or actual attack ⟨*shielded* her eyes from the sun with her hand⟩. GUARD implies protecting with vigilance and force against expected danger ⟨White House entrances are well *guarded*⟩. SAFEGUARD implies taking precautionary protective measures against merely possible danger ⟨our civil liberties must be *safeguarded*⟩. ***syn*** see in addition MAINTAIN

1**de·fen·dant** \di-ˈfen-dənt, *in legal circles often* -ˌdant\ *n* (14c) : a person required to make answer in a legal action or suit — compare PLAINTIFF

2**defendant** *adj* (15c) : being on the defensive : DEFENDING

de·fend·er \di-ˈfen-dər\ *n* (14c) **1** : one that defends **2** : a player in a sport (as football) assigned to a defensive position

de·fen·es·tra·tion \(ˌ)dē-ˌfe-nə-ˈstrā-shən\ *n* [*de-* + L *fenestra* window] (1620) **1** : a throwing of a person or thing out of a window **2** : a usu. swift dismissal or expulsion (as from a political party or office) — **de·fen·es·trate** \(ˌ)dē-ˈfe-nə-ˌstrāt\ *vt*

1**de·fense** \di-ˈfen(t)s; *as antonym of "offense," often* ˈdē-ˌ\ *n* [ME, fr. AF, fr. LL *defensa* vengeance, fr. L, fem. of *defensus,* pp. of *defendere*] (14c) **1 a** : the act or action of defending ⟨the ~ of our country⟩ ⟨speak out in ~ of justice⟩ **b** : a defendant's denial, answer, or plea **2 a** : capability of resisting attack **b** : defensive play or ability ⟨a player known for good ~⟩ **3 a** : means or method of defending or protecting oneself, one's team, or another; *also* : a defensive structure **b** : an argument in support or justification **c** : the collected facts and method adopted by a defendant to protect and defend against a plaintiff's action **d** : a sequence of moves available in chess to the second player in the opening **4 a** : a defending party or group (as in a court of law) ⟨the ~ rests⟩ **b** : a defensive team **5** : the military and industrial aggregate that authorizes and supervises arms production ⟨appropriations for ~⟩ ⟨~ contract⟩ — **de·fense·less** \-ləs\ *adj* — **de·fense·less·ly** *adv* — **de·fense·less·ness** *n*

2**defense** *vt* **de·fensed; de·fens·ing** (1950) : to take specific defensive action against (an opposing team or player or an offensive play)

de·fense·man \-mən, -ˌman\ *n* (1895) : a player in a sport (as hockey) who is assigned to a defensive zone or position

defense mechanism *n* (1913) **1** : an often unconscious mental process (as repression) that makes possible compromise solutions to personal problems **2** : a defensive reaction by an organism

de·fen·si·ble \di-ˈfen(t)-sə-bəl\ *adj* (14c) : capable of being defended ⟨~ theories⟩ ⟨a ~ hill⟩ — **de·fen·si·bil·i·ty** \di-ˌfen(t)-sə-ˈbi-lə-tē, ˌdē-\ *n* — **de·fen·si·bly** \-blē\ *adv*

1**de·fen·sive** \di-ˈfen(t)-siv, ˈdē-ˌ\ *adj* (14c) **1** : serving to defend or protect ⟨~ fortifications⟩ **2 a** : devoted to resisting or preventing aggression or attack ⟨~ behavior⟩ **b** : of or relating to the attempt to keep an opponent from scoring in a game or contest ⟨a player with good ~ skills⟩ **3 a** : valuable in defensive play ⟨a ~ card in bridge⟩ **b** : designed to keep an opponent from being the highest bidder ⟨a ~ bid⟩ — **de·fen·sive·ly** *adv* — **de·fen·sive·ness** *n*

2**defensive** *n* (1601) : a defensive position — **on the defensive** : in the state or condition of being prepared or required to defend against attack or criticism ⟨keeping his political rivals *on the defensive*⟩

defensive medicine *n* (1973) : the practice of ordering medical tests, procedures, or consultations of doubtful clinical value in order to protect the prescribing physician from malpractice suits

1**de·fer** \di-ˈfər\ *vt* **de·ferred; de·fer·ring** [ME *deferren, differren,* fr. MF *differer,* fr. L *differre* to postpone, be different — more at DIFFER] (14c) **1** : PUT OFF, DELAY **2** : to postpone induction of (a person) into military service — **de·fer·rer** *n*

syn DEFER, POSTPONE, SUSPEND, STAY mean to delay an action or proceeding. DEFER implies a deliberate putting off to a later time ⟨*deferred* buying a car until spring⟩. POSTPONE implies an intentional deferring usu. to a definite time ⟨the game is *postponed* until Saturday⟩. SUSPEND implies temporary stoppage with an added suggestion of waiting until some condition is satisfied ⟨business will be *suspended* while repairs are under way⟩. STAY often suggests the stopping or checking by an intervening agency or authority ⟨the governor *stayed* the execution⟩.

2**defer** *vb* **deferred; deferring** [ME *deferren, differren,* fr. MF *deferer, defferer,* fr. LL *deferre,* fr. L, to bring down, bring, fr. *de-* + *ferre* to carry — more at BEAR] *vt* (15c) : to delegate to another ⟨he could ~ his job to no one —J. A. Michener⟩ ~ *vi* : to submit to another's wishes, opinion, or governance usu. through deference or respect ⟨*deferred* to her father's wishes⟩ ***syn*** see YIELD

def·er·ence \ˈde-fə-rən(t)s, ˈdef-rən(t)s\ *n* (1660) : respect and esteem due a superior or an elder; *also* : affected or ingratiating regard for another's wishes ***syn*** see HONOR — **in deference to** : in consideration of ⟨returned early *in deference to* her parents' wishes⟩

def·er·ent \ˈde-fə-rənt, ˈdef-rənt\ *adj* [back-formation fr. *deference*] (1822) : DEFERENTIAL

def·er·en·tial \ˌde-fə-ˈren-chəl\ *adj* (1822) : showing or expressing deference ⟨~ attention⟩ — **def·er·en·tial·ly** \-ˈren-chə-lē\ *adv*

de·fer·ment \di-ˈfər-mənt\ *n* (1607) : the act of delaying or postponing; *specif* : official postponement of military service

de·fer·ra·ble \di-ˈfər-ə-bəl\ *adj* (1943) : capable of or suitable or eligible for being deferred — **deferrable** *n*

de·fer·ral \di-ˈfər-əl\ *n* (1865) : the act of delaying : POSTPONEMENT

de·ferred *adj* (1651) **1** : withheld for or until a stated time ⟨a ~ payment⟩ **2** : charged in cases of delayed handling ⟨a ~ rate⟩

de·fer·ves·cence \ˌdē-(ˌ)fər-ˈve-sᵊn(t)s, ˌde-fər-ˈ\ *n* [G *Deferveszenz,* fr. L *defervescent-, defervescens,* prp. of *defervescere* to stop boiling, fr. *de-* + *fervescere* to begin to boil — more at EFFERVESCE] (1866) : the subsidence of a fever

deffer *comparative of* DEF

deffest *superlative of* DEF

de·fi·ance \di-ˈfī-ən(t)s, dē-\ *n* (15c) **1** : the act or an instance of defying : CHALLENGE **2** : disposition to resist : willingness to contend or fight — **in defiance of** : contrary to : DESPITE ⟨seemingly *in defiance of* the laws of physics⟩

de·fi·ant \-ənt\ *adj* [MF, fr. OF, prp. of *defier* to defy] (1583) : full of or showing defiance : BOLD, IMPUDENT ⟨~ rebels⟩ ⟨a ~ refusal⟩ — **de·fi·ant·ly** *adv*

de·fi·bril·la·tor \(ˌ)dē-ˈfi-brə-ˌlā-tər\ *n* (1952) : an electronic device that applies an electric shock to restore the rhythm of a fibrillating heart — **de·fi·bril·late** \-ˌlāt\ *vt* — **de·fi·bril·la·tion** \-ˌfi-brə-ˈlā-shən\ *n*

de·fi·brin·ate \(ˌ)dē-ˈfi-brə-ˌnāt, -ˈfī-\ *vt* **-at·ed; -at·ing** (1845) : to remove fibrin from (blood) — **de·fi·brin·ation** \(ˌ)dē-ˌfi-brə-ˈnā-shən, -ˌfī-\ *n*

de·fi·cien·cy \di-ˈfi-shən-sē\ *n, pl* **-cies** (1603) **1** : the quality or state of being deficient : INADEQUACY **2** : an amount that is lacking or inadequate : SHORTAGE: as **a** : a shortage of substances necessary to health **b** : DELETION 2b(1)

deficiency disease *n* (1912) : a disease (as scurvy) caused by a lack of essential dietary elements and esp. a vitamin or mineral

1**de·fi·cient** \di-ˈfi-shənt\ *adj* [L *deficient-, deficiens,* prp. of *deficere* to be wanting — more at DEFECT] (1581) **1** : lacking in some necessary quality or element ⟨~ in judgment⟩ **2** : not up to a normal standard or complement : DEFECTIVE ⟨~ strength⟩ — **de·fi·cient·ly** *adv*

2**deficient** *n* (1906) : one that is deficient ⟨a mental ~⟩

def·i·cit \ˈde-fə-sət, *Brit also* di-ˈfis-ət *or* ˈdē-fə-sət\ *n* [F *déficit,* fr. L *deficit* it is wanting, 3d sing. pres. indic. of *deficere*] (1782) **1 a** (1) : deficiency in amount or quality ⟨a ~ in rainfall⟩ (2) : a lack or impairment in a functional capacity ⟨cognitive ~*s*⟩ ⟨a hearing ~⟩ **b** : DISADVANTAGE ⟨scored two runs to overcome a 2–1 ~⟩ **2 a** : an excess of expenditure over revenue **b** : a loss in business operations

deficit spending *n* (1938) : the spending of public funds raised by borrowing rather than by taxation

de·fi·er \di-ˈfī(-ə)r\ *n* (1584) : one that defies ⟨a ~ of convention⟩

def·i·lade \ˈde-fə-ˌlād, -ˌläd\ *vt* **-lad·ed; -lad·ing** [prob. fr. *de-* + *-filade* (as in *enfilade*)] (1828) : to arrange (fortifications) so as to protect the lines from frontal or enfilading fire and the interior from fire from above or behind — **defilade** *n*

1**de·file** \di-ˈfī(-ə)l, dē-\ *vt* **de·filed; de·fil·ing** [ME, alter. (influenced by *filen* to defile, fr. OE *fȳlan*) of *defoilen* to trample, defile, fr. AF *defoiller, defuler,* to trample, fr. *de-* + *fuller, foller* to trample, lit., to full — more at FULL] (14c) : to make unclean or impure: as **a** : to corrupt the purity or perfection of : DEBASE ⟨the countryside *defiled* by billboards⟩ **b** : to violate the chastity of : DEFLOWER **c** : to make physically unclean esp. with something unpleasant or contaminating ⟨boots *defiled* with blood⟩ **d** : to violate the sanctity of : DESECRATE ⟨~ a sanctuary⟩ **e** : SULLY, DISHONOR ***syn*** see CONTAMINATE — **de·file·ment** \-ˈfī(-ə)l-mənt\ *n* — **de·fil·er** \-ˈfī-lər\ *n*

2**de·file** \di-ˈfī(-ə)l, ˈdē-ˌfī(-ə)l\ *n* [F *défilé,* fr. pp. of *défiler*] (1685) : a narrow passage or gorge

3**de·file** \di-ˈfī(-ə)l, ˈdē-ˌfī(-ə)l\ *vi* **de·filed; de·fil·ing** [F *défiler,* fr. *dé-* de- + *filer* to move in a column — more at FILE] (1705) : to march off in a line

de·fin·able \di-ˈfī-nə-bəl\ *adj* (1610) **1** : able to be defined **2** : able to be specified to have a particular function or operation ⟨~ keys⟩ — **de·fin·ably** \-ˈfī-nə-blē\ *adv*

de·fine \di-ˈfīn\ *vb* **de·fined; de·fin·ing** [ME, fr. L *definire,* fr. *de-* + *finire* to limit, end, fr. *finis* boundary, end] *vt* (14c) **1 a :** to determine or identify the essential qualities or meaning of ⟨whatever ~*s* us as human⟩ **b :** to discover and set forth the meaning of (as a word) **c :** to create on a computer ⟨~ a window⟩ ⟨~ a procedure⟩ **2 a :** to fix or mark the limits of : DEMARCATE ⟨rigidly *defined* property lines⟩ **b :** to make distinct, clear, or detailed esp. in outline ⟨the issues aren't too well *defined*⟩ **3 :** CHARACTERIZE, DISTINGUISH ⟨you ~ yourself by the choices you make —*Denison Univ. Bull.*⟩ ~ *vi* **:** to make a definition — **de·fine·ment** \-ˈfīn-mənt\ *n* — **de·fin·er** \-ˈfī-nər\ *n*

de·fin·i·en·dum \di-ˌfi-nē-ˈen-dəm\ *n, pl* **-da** \-də\ [L, something to be defined, neut. of *definiendus,* gerundive of *definire*] (1871) **:** an expression that is being defined

de·fin·i·ens \di-ˈfi-nē-ˌenz\ *n, pl* **de·fin·i·en·tia** \di-ˌfi-nē-ˈen(t)-shē-ə\ [L, prp. of *definire*] (1838) **:** an expression that defines : DEFINITION

def·i·nite \ˈde-fə-nit, ˈdef-nət\ *adj* [L *definitus,* pp. of *definire*] (1553) **1 :** having distinct or certain limits ⟨set ~ standards for pupils to meet⟩ **2 a :** free of all ambiguity, uncertainty, or obscurity ⟨demanded a ~ answer⟩ **b :** UNQUESTIONABLE, DECIDED ⟨the quarterback was a ~ hero today⟩ **3 :** typically designating an identified or immediately identifiable person or thing ⟨the ~ article *the*⟩ **4 a** *of floral organs* **:** being constant in number, usu. less than 20, and occurring in multiples of the petal number ⟨stamens ~⟩ **b :** CYMOSE ⟨a ~ inflorescence⟩ ***syn*** see EXPLICIT — **def·i·nite·ly** *adv* — **def·i·nite·ness** *n*

definite integral *n* (1834) **:** the difference between the values of the integral of a given function *f*(*x*) for an upper value *b* and a lower value *a* of the independent variable *x*

def·i·ni·tion \ˌde-fə-ˈni-shən\ *n* [ME *diffinicioun,* fr. AF, fr. L *definition-, definitio,* fr. *definire*] (14c) **1 :** an act of determining; *specif* **:** the formal proclamation of a Roman Catholic dogma **2 a :** a statement expressing the essential nature of something **b :** a statement of the meaning of a word or word group or a sign or symbol ⟨dictionary ~*s*⟩ **c :** a product of defining **3 :** the action or process of defining **4 a :** the action or the power of describing, explaining, or making definite and clear ⟨the ~ of a telescope⟩ ⟨her comic genius is beyond ~⟩ **b** (1) **:** clarity of visual presentation : distinctness of outline or detail ⟨improve the ~ of an image⟩ (2) **:** clarity esp. of musical sound in reproduction **c :** sharp demarcation of outlines or limits ⟨a jacket with distinct waist ~⟩ — **def·i·ni·tion·al** \-ˈni-shə-nᵊl\ *adj*

1**de·fin·i·tive** \di-ˈfi-nə-tiv\ *adj* [ME *diffinityf,* fr. AF *diffinitive,* fr. L *definitivus,* fr. *definitus*] (14c) **1 :** serving to provide a final solution or to end a situation ⟨a ~ victory⟩ **2 :** authoritative and apparently exhaustive ⟨a ~ edition⟩ **3 a :** serving to define or specify precisely ⟨~ laws⟩ **b :** serving as a perfect example : QUINTESSENTIAL ⟨a ~ bourgeois⟩ **4 :** fully differentiated or developed ⟨a ~ organ⟩ **5** *of a postage stamp* **:** issued as a regular stamp for the country or territory in which it is to be used ***syn*** see CONCLUSIVE — **de·fin·i·tive·ly** *adv* — **de·fin·i·tive·ness** *n*

2**definitive** *n* (1951) **:** a definitive postage stamp — compare PROVISIONAL

definitive host *n* (1901) **:** the host in which the sexual reproduction of a parasite takes place — compare INTERMEDIATE HOST 1

de·fi·ni·tize \ˈde-fə-nə-ˌtīz, di-ˈfi-\ *vt* **-tized; -tiz·ing** (1876) **:** to make definite

de·fi·ni·tude \di-ˈfi-nə-ˌtüd, -ˌtyüd\ *n* [irreg. fr. *definite*] (1836) **:** PRECISION, DEFINITENESS

def·la·grate \ˈdef-lə-ˌgrāt\ *vb* **-grat·ed; -grat·ing** [L *deflagratus,* pp. of *deflagrare* to burn down, fr. *de-* + *flagrare* to burn — more at BLACK] *vt* (ca. 1727) **:** to cause to deflagrate — compare DETONATE 1 ~ *vi* **:** to burn rapidly with intense heat and sparks being given off — **def·la·gra·tion** \ˌdef-lə-ˈgrā-shən\ *n*

de·flate \di-ˈflāt, ˌdē-\ *vb* **de·flat·ed; de·flat·ing** [*de-* + *-flate* (as in *inflate*)] *vt* (1891) **1 :** to release air or gas from ⟨~ a tire⟩ **2 :** to reduce in size, importance, or effectiveness ⟨~ his ego with cutting remarks⟩ **3 :** to reduce (a price level) or cause (a volume of credit) to contract ~ *vi* **:** to lose firmness through or as if through the escape of contained gas ***syn*** see CONTRACT — **de·fla·tor** *also* **de·fla·ter** \-ˈflā-tər\ *n*

de·fla·tion \di-ˈflā-shən, ˌdē-\ *n* (1891) **1 :** an act or instance of deflating : the state of being deflated **2 :** a contraction in the volume of available money or credit that results in a general decline in prices **3 :** the erosion of soil by the wind — **de·fla·tion·ary** \-shə-ˌner-ē\ *adj*

de·flect \di-ˈflekt, dē-\ *vb* [L *deflectere* to bend down, turn aside, fr. *de-* + *flectere* to bend] *vt* (ca. 1555) **:** to turn aside esp. from a straight course or fixed direction ~ *vi* **:** to turn aside : DEVIATE — **de·flect·able** \-ˈflek-tə-bəl\ *adj* — **de·flec·tive** \-tiv\ *adj* — **de·flec·tor** \-tər\ *n*

de·flec·tion \di-ˈflek-shən, dē-\ *n* (1605) **1 :** a turning aside or off course : DEVIATION **2 :** the departure of an indicator or pointer from the zero reading on the scale of an instrument

de·flexed \ˈdē-ˌflekst, di-ˈ\ *adj* [L *deflexus,* pp. of *deflectere*] (1826) **:** turned abruptly downward ⟨a ~ leaf⟩

de·flo·ra·tion \ˌdef-lə-ˈrā-shən, ˌdē-flō-\ *n* [ME *defloracioun,* fr. MF & LL; MF *defloracion,* fr. LL *defloration-, defloratio,* fr. *deflorare*] (15c) **:** rupture of the hymen

de·flow·er \(ˌ)dē-ˈflau̇(-ə)r\ *vt* [ME *deflouren,* fr. MF or LL; OF *desflorer,* fr. LL *deflorare,* fr. L *de-* + *flor-, flos* flower — more at BLOW] (14c) **1 :** to deprive of virginity **2 :** to take away the prime beauty of — **de·flow·er·er** *n*

de·fog \(ˌ)dē-ˈfȯg, -ˈfäg\ *vt* (1904) **:** to remove fog or condensed moisture from ⟨~ a windshield⟩ — **de·fog·ger** *n*

de·fo·li·ant \(ˌ)dē-ˈfō-lē-ənt\ *n* (1943) **:** a chemical spray or dust applied to plants in order to cause the leaves to drop off prematurely

de·fo·li·ate \-lē-ˌāt\ *vt* [LL *defoliatus,* pp. of *defoliare,* fr. L *de-* + *folium* leaf — more at BLADE] (1791) **:** to deprive of leaves esp. prematurely — **de·fo·li·a·tion** \(ˌ)dē-ˌfō-lē-ˈā-shən\ *n* — **de·fo·li·a·tor** \(ˌ)dē-ˈfō-lē-ˌā-tər\ *n*

de·force \(ˌ)dē-ˈfȯrs\ *vt* [ME, fr. AF *deforcer,* fr. *de-* + *forcer* to force] (15c) **1 :** to keep (as lands) by force from the rightful owner **2 :** to eject (a person) from possession by force — **de·force·ment** \-ˈfȯrs-mənt\ *n*

de·for·es·ta·tion \(ˌ)dē-ˌfȯr-ə-ˈstā-shən, -ˌfär-\ *n* (1874) **:** the action or process of clearing of forests; *also* **:** the state of having been cleared of forests — **de·for·est** \(ˈ)dē-ˈfȯr-əst, -ˈfär-\ *vt*

de·form \di-ˈfȯrm, dē-\ *vb* [ME, fr. AF or L; AF *desfurmer,* fr. L *deformare,* fr. *de-* + *formare* to form, fr. *forma* form] *vt* (15c) **1 :** to spoil the form of **2 a :** to spoil the looks of : DISFIGURE ⟨a face ~*ed* by bitterness⟩ **b :** to mar the character of ⟨a marriage ~*ed* by jealousy⟩ **3 :** to alter the shape of by stress ~ *vi* **:** to become misshapen or changed in shape — **de·form·able** \-mə-bəl\ *adj*

syn DEFORM, DISTORT, CONTORT, WARP means to mar or spoil by or as if by twisting. DEFORM may imply a change of shape through stress, injury, or accident of growth ⟨a face *deformed* by hatred⟩. DISTORT and CONTORT both imply a wrenching from the natural or normal, but CONTORT suggests a more involved twisting and a more grotesque and painful result ⟨the odd camera angle *distorts* the figure⟩ ⟨disease had *contorted* her body⟩. WARP indicates an uneven shrinking that bends or twists out of a flat plane ⟨*warped* floorboards⟩.

de·for·mal·ize \(ˌ)dē-ˈfȯr-mə-ˌlīz\ *vt* (1880) **:** to make less formal

de·for·ma·tion \ˌdē-ˌfȯr-ˈmā-shən, ˌde-fər-\ *n* (15c) **1 :** alteration of form or shape; *also* **:** the product of such alteration **2 :** the action of deforming : the state of being deformed **3 :** change for the worse — **de·for·ma·tion·al** \-shə-nᵊl\ *adj*

de·for·ma·tive \di-ˈfȯr-mə-tiv, dē-\ *adj* (1641) **:** tending to deform

de·formed *adj* (15c) **:** distorted or unshapely in form : MISSHAPEN

de·for·mi·ty \di-ˈfȯr-mə-tē, dē-\ *n, pl* **-ties** [ME *deformite,* fr. MF *defformeteit,* fr. L *deformitat-, deformitas,* fr. *deformis* deformed, fr. *de-* + *forma*] (15c) **1 :** the state of being deformed **2 :** IMPERFECTION, BLEMISH: as **a :** a physical blemish or distortion : DISFIGUREMENT **b :** a moral or aesthetic flaw or defect

de·frag \dē-ˈfrag\ *vt* **defragged; defragging** (1988) **:** DEFRAGMENT

de·frag·ment \(ˌ)dē-ˈfrag-mənt\ *vt* (1983) **:** to reorganize separated fragments of related data on (a computer disk) into a contiguous arrangement — **de·frag·men·ta·tion** \-ˌfrag-mən-ˈtā-shən, -ˌmen-\ *n*

de·frag·ment·er \-ˈfrag-ˌmen-tər, -mən-\ *n* (1986) **:** software that defragments a computer disk

de·fraud \di-ˈfrȯd, dē-\ *vt* [ME, fr. AF *defrauder,* fr. L *defraudare,* fr. *de-* + *fraudare* to cheat, fr. *fraud-, fraus* fraud] (14c) **:** to deprive of something by deception or fraud ***syn*** see CHEAT — **de·fraud·er** \di-ˈfrȯ-dər\ *n*

de·fray \di-ˈfrā, dē-\ *vt* [MF *deffroyer,* fr. *des-* de- + *frayer* to expend, fr. OF, fr. *frais,* pl. of *fret, frait* expenditure, lit., damage by breaking, fr. L *fractum,* neut. of *fractus,* pp. of *frangere* to break — more at BREAK] (1536) **1 :** to provide for the payment of : PAY **2** *archaic* **:** to bear the expenses of — **de·fray·able** \-ə-bəl\ *adj* — **de·fray·al** \-ˈfrā(-ə)l\ *n*

de·friend \(ˌ)dē-ˈfrend\ *vt* (2004) **:** UNFRIEND

de·frock \(ˌ)dē-ˈfräk\ *vt* (1581) **1 :** to deprive (as a priest) of the right to exercise the functions of office **2 :** to remove from a position of honor or privilege

de·frost \di-ˈfrȯst, ˈdē-ˌ\ *vt* (1895) **1 :** to release from a frozen state ⟨~ meat⟩ **2 :** to free from ice ⟨~ the refrigerator⟩; *also* **:** DEFOG ~ *vi* **:** to thaw out esp. from a deep-frozen state — **de·frost·er** *n*

deft \ˈdeft\ *adj* [ME *defte* gentle — more at DAFT] (15c) **:** characterized by facility and skill ***syn*** see DEXTEROUS — **deft·ly** *adv* — **deft·ness** \ˈdef(t)-nəs\ *n*

de·funct \di-ˈfəŋkt, dē-\ *adj* [L *defunctus,* fr. pp. of *defungi* to finish, die, fr. *de-* + *fungi* to perform — more at FUNCTION] (1599) **:** no longer living, existing, or functioning ⟨that firm is now ~⟩ ***syn*** see DEAD

de·fund \(ˌ)dē-ˈfənd\ *vt* (1948) **:** to withdraw funding from

de·fuse \(ˌ)dē-ˈfyüz\ *vt* (1943) **1 :** to remove the fuse from (as a mine or bomb) **2 :** to make less harmful, potent, or tense ⟨~ the crisis⟩

1**de·fy** \di-ˈfī, dē-\ *vt* **de·fied; de·fy·ing** [ME, to renounce faith in, challenge, fr. AF *desfier, defier,* fr. *des-* de- + *fier* to entrust, fr. VL **fidare,* alter. of L *fidere* to trust — more at BIDE] (14c) **1** *archaic* **:** to challenge to combat **2 :** to challenge to do something considered impossible : DARE **3 :** to confront with assured power of resistance : DISREGARD ⟨~ public opinion⟩ **4 :** to resist attempts at : WITHSTAND ⟨the paintings ~ classification⟩

2**de·fy** \di-ˈfī, ˈdē-ˌ\ *n, pl* **defies** (1580) **:** CHALLENGE, DEFIANCE

deg *abbr* degree

dé·ga·gé \ˌdā-ˌgä-ˈzhā\ *adj* [F, fr. pp. of *dégager* to put at ease, fr. OF *desgagier* to redeem a pledge, free, fr. *des-* de- + *gage* pledge — more at GAGE] (1696) **1 :** free of constraint : NONCHALANT **2 :** being free and easy ⟨clothes with a ~ look⟩ **3 :** extended with toe pointed in preparation for a ballet step

de·gas \(ˌ)dē-ˈgas\ *vt* (1928) **:** to remove gas from ⟨~ an electron tube⟩

de Gaull·ism \di-ˈgō-ˌli-zəm, -ˈgȯ-\ *n* (1943) **:** GAULLISM — **de Gaull·ist** \-ləst\ *n*

de·gauss \(ˌ)dē-ˈgau̇s\ *vt* [*de-* + *gauss,* after Karl F. *Gauss*] (ca. 1940) **:** to remove or neutralize the magnetic field of ⟨~ a ship⟩ ⟨~ a magnetic tape⟩ — **de·gauss·er** *n*

de·gen·der·ize \dē-ˈjen-də-ˌrīz\ *vt* **-ized; -iz·ing** (1987) **:** to eliminate any reference to a specific gender in (as a word, text, or act)

de·gen·er·a·cy \di-ˈjen-rə-sē, -ˈje-nə-, dē-\ *n, pl* **-cies** (1664) **1 :** the state of being degenerate **2 :** the process of becoming degenerate **3 :** sexual perversion **4 :** the coding of an amino acid by more than one codon

1**de·gen·er·ate** \di-ˈjen-rət, -ˈje-nə-, dē-\ *adj* [ME *degenerat,* fr. L *degeneratus,* pp. of *degenerare* to degenerate, fr. *de-* + *gener-, genus* race, kind — more at KIN] (15c) **1 a :** having declined or become less specialized (as in nature, character, structure, or function) from an ancestral or former state **b :** having sunk to a condition below that which is normal to a type; *esp* **:** having sunk to a lower and usu. corrupt and vicious state **c :** DEGRADED 2 **2 :** being mathematically simpler (as by having a factor or constant equal to zero) than the typical case ⟨a ~ hyperbola⟩ **3 :** characterized by atoms stripped of their electrons and by very great density ⟨~ matter⟩; *also* **:** consisting of degenerate matter ⟨a ~ star⟩ **4 :** having two or more states or subdivisions ⟨~ energy level⟩ **5 :** having more than one codon representing an amino acid; *also* **:** being such a codon ***syn*** see VICIOUS — **de·gen·er·ate·ly** *adv* — **de·gen·er·ate·ness** *n*

2**de·gen·er·ate** \di-ˈje-nə-ˌrāt, dē-\ *vi* (1545) **1 :** to pass from a higher to a lower type or condition : DETERIORATE **2 :** to sink into a low intel-

\ə\ abut \ᵊ\ kitten, F table \ər\ further \a\ ash \ā\ ace \ä\ mop, mar \au̇\ out \ch\ chin \e\ bet \ē\ easy \g\ go \i\ hit \ī\ ice \j\ job \ŋ\ sing \ō\ go \ȯ\ law \ȯi\ boy \th\ thin \t͟h\ the \ü\ loot \u̇\ foot \y\ yet \zh\ vision, beige \k, ⁿ, œ, ue, ʸ\ *see* Guide to Pronunciation

lectual or moral state **3 :** to decline in quality ⟨the poetry gradually ∼*s* into jingles⟩ **4 :** to decline from a condition or from the standards of a species, race, or breed **5 :** to evolve or develop into a less autonomous or less functionally active form ⟨*degenerated* into dependent parasites⟩ ∼ *vt* **:** to cause to degenerate

[3]**de·gen·er·ate** \di-ˈjen-rət, -ˈje-nə-, dē-\ *n* (1555) **:** one that is degenerate: as **a :** one degraded from the normal moral standard **b :** a sexual pervert **c :** one showing signs of reversion to an earlier culture stage

de·gen·er·a·tion \di-ˌje-nə-ˈrā-shən, ˌdē-\ *n* (15c) **1 :** degenerate condition **2 :** a lowering of effective power, vitality, or essential quality to an enfeebled and worsened kind or state **3 :** intellectual, moral, or artistic decline **4 a :** progressive deterioration of physical characters from a level representing the norm of earlier generations or forms **b :** deterioration of a tissue or an organ in which its function is diminished or its structure is impaired ***syn*** see DETERIORATION

de·gen·er·a·tive \di-ˈje-nə-rə-tiv, -ˈjen-rə-; -ˈje-nə-ˌrā-; dē-\ *adj* (ca. 1846) **:** of, relating to, involving, or causing degeneration ⟨a ∼ disease⟩

de·gla·ci·a·tion \(ˌ)dē-ˌglā-s(h)ē-ˈā-shən\ *n* (1895) **:** the melting of ice; *specif* **:** the retreat of a glacier or ice sheet — **de·gla·ci·at·ed** \-ˈglā-s(h)ē-ˌā-təd\ *adj*

de·glam·or·ize \(ˌ)dē-ˈgla-mə-ˌrīz\ *vt* (1938) **:** to remove the glamour from ⟨a book that ∼*s* Hollywood⟩ — **de·glam·or·iza·tion** \(ˌ)dē-ˌgla-mə-rə-ˈzā-shən\ *n*

[1]**de·glaze** \(ˌ)dē-ˈglāz\ *vt* (ca. 1889) **:** to remove the glaze from ⟨∼ pottery⟩

[2]**deglaze** *vt* [modif. of F *déglacer,* lit., to melt the ice from, fr. *dé-* + *glacer* to freeze — more at GLACÉ] (1968) **:** to dissolve the small particles of sautéed meat remaining in (a pan) by adding a liquid and heating

de·glu·ti·tion \ˌdē-glü-ˈti-shən, ˌde-glü-\ *n* [F *déglutition,* fr. L *deglutire* to swallow down, fr. *de-* + *glutire, gluttire* to swallow — more at GLUTTON] (1650) **:** the act or process of swallowing

de·grad·able \di-ˈgrā-də-bəl, dē-\ *adj* (ca. 1962) **:** capable of being chemically degraded ⟨∼ detergents⟩ — compare BIODEGRADABLE — **de·grad·abil·i·ty** \-ˌgrā-də-ˈbi-lə-tē\ *n*

deg·ra·da·tion \ˌde-grə-ˈdā-shən\ *n* (ca. 1535) **1 :** the act or process of degrading **2 a :** decline to a low, destitute, or demoralized state **b :** moral or intellectual decadence **:** DEGENERATION — **deg·ra·da·tive** \ˈde-grə-ˌdā-tiv\ *adj*

de·grade \di-ˈgrād, dē-\ *vb* [ME, fr. AF *degrader,* fr. LL *degradare,* fr. L *de-* + *gradus* step, grade — more at GRADE] *vt* (14c) **1 a :** to lower in grade, rank, or status **:** DEMOTE **b :** to strip of rank or honors **c :** to lower to an inferior or less effective level ⟨∼ the image quality⟩ **d :** to scale down in desirability or salability **2 a :** to bring to low esteem or into disrepute ⟨his actions have *degraded* his profession⟩ **b :** to drag down in moral or intellectual character **:** CORRUPT **3 :** to impair in respect to some physical property ⟨material *degraded* by exposure to sunlight⟩ **4 :** to wear down by erosion **5 :** to reduce the complexity of (a chemical compound) **:** DECOMPOSE ∼ *vi* **1 :** to pass from a higher grade or class to a lower **2** *of a chemical compound* **:** to become reduced in complexity — **de·grad·er** *n* — **de·grad·ing·ly** \-ˈgrā-diŋ-lē\ *adv*

de·grad·ed \-ˈgrā-dəd\ *adj* (1643) **1 :** reduced far below ordinary standards of civilized life and conduct **2 :** characterized by degeneration of structure or function — **de·grad·ed·ly** *adv*

de·gran·u·la·tion \(ˌ)dē-ˌgra-nyə-ˈlā-shən\ *n* (ca. 1941) **:** the process of losing granules; *specif* **:** the process by which cytoplasmic granules (as of mast cells) release their contents

de·grease \(ˌ)dē-ˈgrēs, -ˈgrēz\ *vt* (ca. 1889) **:** to remove grease from — **de·greas·er** \-ˈgrē-sər, -zər\ *n*

de·gree \di-ˈgrē\ *n* [ME, fr. AF *degré,* fr. VL **degradus,* fr. L *de-* + *gradus*] (13c) **1 :** a step or stage in a process, course, or order of classification ⟨advanced by ∼*s*⟩ **2 a :** a rank or grade of official, ecclesiastical, or social position ⟨people of low ∼⟩ **b** *archaic* **:** a particular standing esp. as to dignity or worth **c :** the civil condition or status of a person **3 :** a step in a direct line of descent or in the line of ascent to a common ancestor **4 a** *obs* **:** STEP, STAIR **b** *archaic* **:** a member of a series arranged in steps **5 :** a measure of damage to tissue caused by injury or disease — compare FIRST-DEGREE BURN, SECOND-DEGREE BURN, THIRD-DEGREE BURN **6 a :** the extent, measure, or scope of an action, condition, or relation ⟨different in ∼ but not in kind⟩ **b :** relative intensity ⟨a high ∼ of stress⟩ **c :** one of the forms or sets of forms used in the comparison of an adjective or adverb **d :** a legal measure of guilt or negligence ⟨found guilty of robbery in the first ∼⟩ **7 a :** a title conferred on students by a college, university, or professional school on completion of a program of study **b :** a grade of membership attained in a ritualistic order or society **c :** an academic title conferred to honor distinguished achievement or service **d :** the formal ceremonies observed in the conferral of such a distinction **8 :** a unit of measure for angles equal to an angle with its vertex at the center of a circle and its sides cutting off ¹⁄₃₆₀ of the circumference; *also* **:** a unit of measure for arcs of a circle equal to the amount of arc that subtends a central angle of one degree **9** *archaic* **:** a position or space on the earth or in the heavens as measured by degrees of latitude **10 a :** a step, note, or tone of a musical scale **b :** a line or space of the musical staff **11 :** one of the divisions or intervals marked on a scale of a measuring instrument; *specif* **:** any of various units for measuring temperature **12 a :** the sum of the exponents of the variables in the term of highest degree in a polynomial, polynomial function, or polynomial equation **b :** the sum of the exponents of the variable factors of a monomial **c :** the greatest power of the derivative of highest order in a differential equation after the equation has been rationalized and cleared of fractions with respect to the derivative — **de·greed** \-ˈgrēd\ *adj* — **to a degree 1 :** to a remarkable extent **:** EXCEEDINGLY ⟨I felt desolate *to a degree* —Charlotte Brontë⟩ **2 :** in a small way ⟨*to a degree* he succeeded⟩

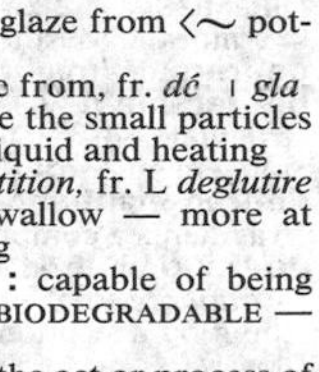

degree 8

de·gree–day \di-ˈgrē-ˌdā\ *n* (1832) **:** a unit that represents one degree of difference from a given point (as 65°) in the mean daily outdoor temperature and that is used esp. to measure heat requirements

degree of freedom (1867) **1 :** any of a limited number of ways in which a body may move or in which a dynamic system may change **2 :** one of the capabilities of a statistic for variation of which there are as many as the number of unrestricted and independent variables determining its value

de·gres·sive \di-ˈgre-siv, ˈdē-\ *adj* [*de-* + *-gressive* (as in *progressive*)] (1886) **:** tending to descend or decrease — **de·gres·sive·ly** *adv*

dé·grin·go·lade \ˌdā-ˌgra^{n}(ŋ)-gə-ˈläd\ *n* [F, fr. *dégringoler* to tumble down, fr. MF *desgringueler,* fr. *des-* de- + *gringueler* to tumble, fr. MD *crinkelen* to make curl, fr. *crinc, cring* ring, circle] (1873) **:** a rapid decline or deterioration (as in strength, position, or condition) **:** DOWNFALL

de·gum \(ˌ)dē-ˈgəm\ *vt* (ca. 1884) **:** to free from gum, a gummy substance, or sericin

de·gus·ta·tion \ˌdē-ˌgəs-ˈtā-shən\ *n* [F *dégustation,* fr. L *degustation-, degustatio,* fr. *degustare* to taste, fr. *de-* + *gustare* to taste — more at CHOOSE] (ca. 1656) **:** the action or an instance of tasting esp. in a series of small portions — **de·gust** \di-ˈgəst, dē-\ *vt*

de haut en bas \də-ō-tä^{n}-bä\ *adj or adv* [F, lit., from top to bottom] (1696) **:** of superiority **:** of or with condescension

de·hisce \di-ˈhis\ *vi* **de·hisced; de·hisc·ing** [L *dehiscere* to split open, fr. *de-* + *hiscere* to gape; akin to L *hiare* to yawn — more at YAWN] (1657) **:** to split along a natural line; *also* **:** to discharge contents by so splitting ⟨seedpods *dehiscing* at maturity⟩

de·his·cence \di-ˈhi-s^{ə}n(t)s\ *n* [NL *dehiscentia,* fr. L *dehiscent-, dehiscens,* prp. of *dehiscere*] (1819) **:** an act or instance of dehiscing ⟨pollen freed by ∼ of the anther⟩ — **de·his·cent** \-s^{ə}nt\ *adj*

de·horn \(ˌ)dē-ˈhȯrn\ *vt* (1888) **1 :** to deprive of horns **2 :** to prevent the growth of the horns of — **de·horn·er** *n*

de·hu·man·ize \(ˌ)dē-ˈhyü-mə-ˌnīz, (ˌ)dē-ˈyü-\ *vt* (1818) **:** to deprive of human qualities, personality, or spirit — **de·hu·man·i·za·tion** \(ˌ)dē-ˌhyü-mə-nə-ˈzā-shən, (ˌ)dē-ˌyü-\ *n*

de·hu·mid·i·fy \ˌdē-hyü-ˈmi-də-ˌfī, ˌdē-yü-\ *vt* (1927) **:** to remove moisture from (as air) — **de·hu·mid·i·fi·ca·tion** \-ˌmi-də-fə-ˈkā-shən\ *n* — **de·hu·mid·i·fi·er** \-ˈmi-də-ˌfī(-ə)r\ *n*

de·hy·drate \(ˌ)dē-ˈhī-ˌdrāt\ *vt* (1876) **1 a :** to remove bound water or hydrogen and oxygen from (a chemical compound) in the proportion in which they form water **b :** to remove water from (as foods) **2 :** to deprive of vitality or savor ∼ *vi* **:** to lose water or body fluids — **de·hy·dra·tor** \-ˌdrā-tər\ *n*

de·hy·dra·tion \ˌdē-ˌhī-ˈdrā-shən\ *n* (1854) **:** the process of dehydrating; *esp* **:** an abnormal depletion of body fluids

de·hy·dro·chlo·ri·na·tion \(ˌ)dē-ˌhī-drə-ˌklȯr-ə-ˈnā-shən\ *n* (1936) **:** the process of removing hydrogen and chlorine or hydrogen chloride from a compound — **de·hy·dro·chlo·ri·nate** \-ˈklȯr-ə-ˌnāt\ *vt*

de·hy·dro·epi·an·dros·ter·one \(ˌ)dē-ˌhī-drō-ˌe-pē-an-ˈdräs-tə-ˌrōn\ *n* [ISV *de-* + *hydr-* + *epi-* + *androsterone*] (1961) **:** a weakly androgenic ketosteroid $C_{19}H_{28}O_2$ secreted by the adrenal glands that is an intermediate in the biosynthesis of testosterone and estrogens (as estradiol); *also* **:** a synthetic derivative of this compound — abbr *DHEA*

de·hy·dro·ge·nase \ˌdē-(ˌ)hī-ˈdrä-jə-ˌnās, (ˌ)dē-ˈhī-drə-jə-, -ˌnāz\ *n* [ISV] (1923) **:** an enzyme that accelerates the removal of hydrogen from metabolites and its transfer to other substances — compare SUCCINATE DEHYDROGENASE

de·hy·dro·ge·na·tion \ˌdē-(ˌ)hī-ˌdrä-jə-ˈnā-shən, (ˌ)dē-ˌhī-drə-jə-\ *n* (1866) **:** the removal of hydrogen from a chemical compound — **de·hy·dro·ge·nate** \ˌdē-(ˌ)hī-ˈdrä-jə-ˌnāt, (ˌ)dē-ˈhī-drə-jə-\ *vt*

de·ice \(ˌ)dē-ˈīs\ *vt* (1934) **:** to rid or keep free of ice ⟨∼ an airplane's wings⟩ — **de·ic·er** *n*

de·i·cide \ˈdē-ə-ˌsīd, ˈdā-ə-\ *n* [ultim. fr. L *deus* god + *-cidium, -cida* -cide — more at DEITY] (1577) **1 :** the act of killing a divine being or a symbolic substitute of such a being **2 :** the killer or destroyer of a god

deic·tic \ˈdīk-tik *also* ˈdāk-\ *adj* [Gk *deiktikos* able to show, fr. *deiktos,* verbal of *deiknynai* to show — more at DICTION] (1876) **:** showing or pointing out directly ⟨the words *this, that,* and *those* have a ∼ function⟩

de·i·fi·ca·tion \ˌdē-ə-fə-ˈkā-shən, ˌdā-\ *n* (14c) **:** the act or an instance of deifying

de·i·fy \ˈdē-ə-ˌfī, ˈdā-\ *vt* **-fied; -fy·ing** [ME, fr. MF *deifier,* fr. LL *deificare,* fr. L *deus* god + *-ficare* -fy] (14c) **1 a :** to make a god of **b :** to take as an object of worship **2 :** to glorify as of supreme worth

deign \ˈdān\ *vb* [ME, fr. AF *deigner,* fr. L *dignare, dignari,* fr. *dignus* worthy — more at DECENT] *vi* (14c) **:** to condescend reluctantly and with a strong sense of the affront to one's superiority that is involved **:** STOOP ⟨would not even ∼ to talk to him⟩ ∼ *vt* **:** to condescend to give or offer

deil \ˈdēl\ *n* [ME *devel, del*] (15c) *Scot* **:** DEVIL

de·in·dus·tri·al·i·za·tion \(ˌ)dē-in-ˌdəs-trē-ə-lə-ˈzā-shən\ *n* (1940) **:** the reduction or destruction of a nation's or region's industrial capacity — **de·in·dus·tri·al·ize** \(ˌ)dē-in-ˈdəs-trē-ə-ˌlīz\ *vb*

dei·non·y·chus \(ˌ)dī-ˈnä-ni-kəs\ *n* [NL, fr. Gk *deinos* terrifying + *-onychos* -clawed (fr. *onych-, onyx* claw, nail) — more at DIRE, NAIL] (1969) **:** any of a genus (*Deinonychus*) of small bipedal carnivorous theropod dinosaurs from the Cretaceous having a very large sharp claw on the second digit of both hind feet

de·in·sti·tu·tion·al·i·za·tion \(ˌ)dē-ˌin(t)-stə-ˌtü-shə-nə-lə-ˈzā-shən, -ˌtyü-\ *n* (1955) **1 :** the release of institutionalized individuals from institutional care (as in a psychiatric hospital) to care in the community **2 :** the reform or modification of an institution to remove or disguise its institutional character — **de·in·sti·tu·tion·al·ize** \-ˈtü-shə-nə-ˌlīz, -ˈtyü-\ *vt*

de·ion·ize \(ˌ)dē-ˈī-ə-ˌnīz\ *vt* (1906) **:** to remove ions from ⟨∼ water by ion exchange⟩ — **de·ion·i·za·tion** \(ˌ)dē-ˌī-ə-nə-ˈzā-shən\ *n* — **de·ion·iz·er** \-ˌnī-zər\ *n*

de·ism \ˈdē-ˌi-zəm, ˈdā-\ *n, often cap* (1682) **:** a movement or system of thought advocating natural religion, emphasizing morality, and in the 18th century denying the interference of the Creator with the laws of the universe — **de·ist** \ˈdē-ist, ˈdā-\ *n, often cap* — **de·is·tic** \dē-ˈis-tik, dā-\ *adj* — **de·is·ti·cal** \-ti-kəl\ *adj* — **de·is·ti·cal·ly** \-ti-k(ə-)lē\ *adv*

de·i·ty \ˈdē-ə-tē, ˈdā-\ *n, pl* **-ties** [ME *deitee,* fr. AF *deité,* fr. LL *deitat-, deitas,* fr. L *deus* god; akin to OE *Tīw,* god of war, L *divus* god, *dies* day, Gk *dios* heavenly, Skt *deva* heavenly, god] (14c) **1 a :** the rank or essential nature of a god **:** DIVINITY **b** *cap* **:** GOD 1, SUPREME BEING **2 :** a god or goddess ⟨the *deities* of ancient Greece⟩ **3 :** one exalted or revered as supremely good or powerful

deix·is \ˈdīk-sis *also* ˈdāk-\ *n* [Gk, lit., display, fr. *deiknynai* to show — more at DICTION] (1946) **:** the pointing or specifying function of some

words (as definite articles and demonstrative pronouns) whose denotation changes from one discourse to another

dé·jà vu \ˌdā-ˌzhä-ˈvü, -ˈvœ\ *n* [F, adj., lit., already seen] (1903) **1 a** : the illusion of remembering scenes and events when experienced for the first time **b** : a feeling that one has seen or heard something before **2** : something overly or unpleasantly familiar

[1]**de·ject** \di-ˈjekt, dē-\ *adj* (15c) *archaic* : DEJECTED

[2]**deject** *vt* [ME, to throw down, fr. L *dejectus,* pp. of *deicere,* fr. *de-* + *jacere* to throw — more at JET] (1581) : to make gloomy

de·jec·ta \di-ˈjek-tə, dē-\ *n pl* [NL, fr. L, neut. pl. of *dejectus*] (ca. 1829) : FECES, EXCREMENT

de·ject·ed \di-ˈjek-təd, dē-\ *adj* (1581) **1** : cast down in spirits : DEPRESSED **2 a** *obs, of the eyes* : DOWNCAST **b** *archaic* : thrown down **3** *obs* : lowered in rank or condition — **de·ject·ed·ly** *adv* — **de·ject·ed·ness** *n*

de·jec·tion \di-ˈjek-shən, dē-\ *n* (15c) : lowness of spirits

de ju·re \(ˌ)dē-ˈju̇r-ē, (ˌ)dā-ˈyu̇r-\ *adv or adj* [ML] (1611) **1** : by right : of right **2** : based on laws or actions of the state ⟨*de jure* segregation⟩

deka- *or* **dek-** — see DECA-

deka·gram \ˈde-kə-ˌgram\ *n* (1810) — see METRIC SYSTEM table

deka·li·ter \-ˌlē-tər\ *n* (ca. 1879) — see METRIC SYSTEM table

deka·me·ter \-ˌmē-tər\ *n* (ca. 1879) — see METRIC SYSTEM table

deka·met·ric \ˌde-kə-ˈme-trik\ *adj* (1968) : DECAMETRIC

deke \ˈdēk\ *vb* **deked; deke·ing** [short for [2]*decoy*] *vt* (1961) : to fake (an opponent) out of position (as in ice hockey) ~ *vi* : to deke an opponent — **deke** *n*

del *abbr* **1** delegate; delegation **2** delete

Del *abbr* Delaware

de·lam·i·na·tion \(ˌ)dē-ˌla-mə-ˈnā-shən\ *n* (1877) : separation into constituent layers — **de·lam·i·nate** \(ˌ)dē-ˈla-mə-ˌnāt\ *vi*

de·late \di-ˈlāt, dē-\ *vt* **de·lat·ed; de·lat·ing** [L *delatus* (pp. of *deferre* to bring down, report, accuse), fr. *de-* + *latus,* pp. of *ferre* to bear — more at TOLERATE] (15c) **1** : ACCUSE, DENOUNCE **2** : REPORT, RELATE — **de·la·tion** \-ˈlā-shən\ *n* — **de·la·tor** \-ˈlā-tər\ *n*

Del·a·ware \ˈde-lə-ˌwer, -wər\ *n, pl* **Delaware** *or* **Delawares** [*Delaware* River] (1721) **1** : a member of an American Indian people orig. of the Delaware valley **2** : the Algonquian language of the Delaware

[1]**de·lay** \di-ˈlā, dē-\ *n* (13c) **1 a** : the act of delaying : the state of being delayed ⟨get started without ~⟩ **b** : an instance of being delayed **2** : the time during which something is delayed ⟨a ~ of 30 minutes⟩

[2]**delay** *vb* [ME, fr. AF *delaier,* fr. *de-* + *laier* to leave, fr. *lai-,* pres. and fut. stem of *lesser, laisser* to leave, fr. L *laxare* to slacken, fr. *laxus* loose — more at SLACK] *vt* (14c) **1** : PUT OFF, POSTPONE ⟨~ a departure⟩ **2** : to stop, detain, or hinder for a time ⟨the mails were ~*ed* by heavy snows⟩ **3** : to cause to be slower or to occur more slowly than normal ⟨~ a child's development⟩ ~ *vi* : to move or act slowly; *also* : to cause delay — **de·lay·er** *n*

syn DELAY, RETARD, SLOW, SLACKEN, DETAIN mean to cause to be late or behind in movement or progress. DELAY implies a holding back, usu. by interference, from completion or arrival ⟨bad weather *delayed* our arrival⟩. RETARD suggests reduction of speed without actual stopping ⟨language barriers *retarded* their progress⟩. SLOW and SLACKEN also imply a reduction of speed, SLOW often suggesting deliberate intention ⟨medication *slowed* the patient's heart rate⟩, SLACKEN an easing up or relaxing of power or effort ⟨on hot days runners *slacken* their pace⟩. DETAIN implies a holding back beyond a reasonable or appointed time ⟨unexpected business had *detained* her⟩.

syn DELAY, PROCRASTINATE, LAG, LOITER, DAWDLE, DALLY mean to move or act slowly so as to fall behind. DELAY usu. implies a putting off (as a beginning or departure) ⟨we cannot *delay* any longer⟩. PROCRASTINATE implies blameworthy delay esp. through laziness or apathy ⟨*procrastinates* about making decisions⟩. LAG implies failure to maintain a speed set by others ⟨*lagging* behind in technology⟩. LOITER and DAWDLE imply delay while in progress, esp. in walking, but DAWDLE more clearly suggests an aimless wasting of time ⟨*loitered* at several store windows⟩ ⟨children *dawdling* on their way home from school⟩. DALLY suggests delay through trifling or vacillation when promptness is necessary ⟨stop *dallying* and get to work⟩.

[1]**de·le** \ˈdē-(ˌ)lē\ *vt* **de·led; de·le·ing** [L, imper. sing. of *delēre*] (1705) : to delete esp. from typeset matter

[2]**dele** *n* (ca. 1751) : a mark indicating that something is to be deled

[1]**de·lec·ta·ble** \di-ˈlek-tə-bəl\ *adj* [ME, fr. MF, fr. L *delectabilis,* fr. *delectare* to delight — more at DELIGHT] (15c) **1** : highly pleasing : DELIGHTFUL ⟨a ~ melody⟩ **2** : DELICIOUS ⟨a ~ meal⟩ — **de·lec·ta·bil·i·ty** \-ˌlek-tə-ˈbi-lə-tē\ *n* — **de·lec·ta·bly** \-blē\ *adv*

[2]**delectable** *n* (1921) : something that is delectable; *esp* : a delicious food item

de·lec·ta·tion \ˌdē-ˌlek-ˈtā-shən, di-; ˌde-lək-\ *n* (14c) : DELIGHT, ENJOYMENT

del·e·ga·ble \ˈde-li-gə-bəl\ *adj* (1660) : capable of being delegated

del·e·ga·cy \-gə-sē\ *n, pl* **-cies** (15c) **1** : a body of delegates : BOARD **2 a** : the act of delegating **b** : appointment as delegate

[1]**del·e·gate** \ˈde-li-gət, -ˌgāt\ *n* [ME *delegat,* fr. ML *delegatus,* fr. L, pp. of *delegare* to delegate, fr. *de-* + *legare* to send — more at LEGATE] (15c) : a person acting for another: as **a** : a representative to a convention or conference **b** : a representative of a U.S. territory in the House of Representatives **c** : a member of the lower house of the legislature of Maryland, Virginia, or West Virginia

[2]**del·e·gate** \-ˌgāt\ *vb* **-gat·ed; -gat·ing** *vt* (1530) **1** : to entrust to another ⟨~ authority⟩ **2** : to appoint as one's representative ~ *vi* : to assign responsibility or authority ⟨a good manager knows how to ~⟩ — **del·e·ga·tee** \ˌde-li-gə-ˈtē\ *n* — **del·e·ga·tor** \ˈde-li-ˌgā-tər\ *n*

del·e·ga·tion \ˌde-li-ˈgā-shən\ *n* (1612) **1** : the act of empowering to act for another **2** : a group of persons chosen to represent others

de·le·git·i·mate \ˌdē-lə-ˈji-tə-ˌmāt\ *vt* (1972) : DELEGITIMIZE — **de·le·git·i·ma·tion** \ˌdē-lə-ˌji-tə-ˈmā-shən\ *n*

de·le·git·i·mize \-ˈji-tə-ˌmīz\ *vt* (1968) : to diminish or destroy the legitimacy, prestige, or authority of ⟨~ a government⟩ — **de·le·git·i·mi·za·tion** \-ˌji-tə-mə-ˈzā-shən\ *n*

de·lete \di-ˈlēt, dē-\ *vt* **de·let·ed; de·let·ing** [L *deletus,* pp. of *delēre* to wipe out, destroy] (ca. 1605) : to eliminate esp. by blotting out, cutting out, or erasing ⟨~ a passage in a manuscript⟩ ⟨~ a computer file⟩

del·e·te·ri·ous \ˌde-lə-ˈtir-ē-əs\ *adj* [Gk *dēlētērios,* fr. *dēleisthai* to hurt] (1643) : harmful often in a subtle or unexpected way ⟨~ effects⟩ ⟨~ to health⟩ ***syn*** see PERNICIOUS — **del·e·te·ri·ous·ly** *adv* — **del·e·te·ri·ous·ness** *n*

de·le·tion \di-ˈlē-shən, dē-\ *n* [L *deletion-, deletio* destruction, fr. *delēre*] (1590) **1** : the act of deleting **2 a** : something deleted **b** (1) : the absence of a section of genetic material from a gene or chromosome (2) : the mutational process that results in a deletion

delft \ˈdelft\ *n, often attrib* [*Delft,* Netherlands] (1723) **1** : tin-glazed Dutch earthenware with blue and white or polychrome decoration **2** : ceramic ware (as tiles) resembling or imitative of Dutch delft

delft·ware \ˈdelft-ˌwer\ *n* (1714) : DELFT

Del·hi belly \ˈde-lē-\ *n* [*Delhi,* India] (1943) : diarrhea contracted in India esp. by tourists; *broadly* : TRAVELER'S DIARRHEA

deli \ˈde-lē\ *n, pl* **del·is** (ca. 1954) : DELICATESSEN

[1]**de·lib·er·ate** \di-ˈli-bə-ˌrāt\ *vb* **-at·ed; -at·ing** *vi* (14c) : to think about or discuss issues and decisions carefully ~ *vt* : to think about deliberately and often with formal discussion before reaching a decision ***syn*** see THINK

[2]**de·lib·er·ate** \di-ˈli-bə-rət, -ˈlib-rət\ *adj* [ME, fr. L *deliberatus,* pp. of *deliberare* to consider carefully, perh. alter. of **delibrare,* fr. *de-* + *libra* scale, pound] (15c) **1** : characterized by or resulting from careful and thorough consideration ⟨a ~ decision⟩ **2** : characterized by awareness of the consequences ⟨~ falsehood⟩ **3** : slow, unhurried, and steady as though allowing time for decision on each individual action involved ⟨a ~ pace⟩ ***syn*** see VOLUNTARY — **de·lib·er·ate·ly** *adv* — **de·lib·er·ate·ness** *n*

de·lib·er·a·tion \di-ˌli-bə-ˈrā-shən\ *n* (14c) **1 a** : the act of deliberating **b** : a discussion and consideration by a group of persons (as a jury or legislature) of the reasons for and against a measure **2** : the quality or state of being deliberate — **de·lib·er·a·tive** \-ˈli-bə-ˌrā-tiv, -ˈli-b(ə-)rə-\ *adj* — **de·lib·er·a·tive·ly** *adv* — **de·lib·er·a·tive·ness** *n*

del·i·ca·cy \ˈde-li-kə-sē\ *n, pl* **-cies** (14c) **1** *obs* **a** : the quality or state of being luxurious **b** : INDULGENCE **2** : something pleasing to eat that is considered rare or luxurious ⟨considered caviar a ~⟩ **3 a** : the quality or state of being dainty : FINENESS ⟨lace of great ~⟩ **b** : FRAILTY 1 ⟨the ~ of his health⟩ **4** : fineness or subtle expressiveness of touch (as in painting or music) **5 a** : precise and refined perception and discrimination **b** : extreme sensitivity : PRECISION ⟨an electronic instrument of great ~⟩ **6 a** : refined sensibility in feeling or conduct **b** : the quality or state of being squeamish **7** : the quality or state of requiring delicate handling

[1]**del·i·cate** \ˈde-li-kət\ *adj* [ME *delicat,* fr. L *delicatus* given to self-indulgence, fastidious, subtly pleasing, not robust; akin to L *delicere* to allure] (14c) **1** : pleasing to the senses: **a** : generally pleasant ⟨the climate's ~, the air most sweet —Shak.⟩ **b** : pleasing to the sense of taste or smell esp. in a mild or subtle way ⟨a ~ aroma⟩ ⟨a robust wine will dominate ~ dishes⟩ **c** : marked by daintiness or charm of color, lines, or proportions ⟨a ~ floral print⟩ ⟨an ample tear trilled down her ~ cheek —Shak.⟩ **d** : marked by fineness of structure, workmanship, or texture ⟨a ~ tracery⟩ ⟨a ~ lace⟩ **2 a** : marked by keen sensitivity or fine discrimination ⟨~ insights⟩ ⟨a more ~ syntactic analysis —R. H. Robins⟩ **b** : FASTIDIOUS, SQUEAMISH ⟨a person of ~ tastes⟩ **3 a** : not robust in health or constitution : WEAK, SICKLY ⟨had been considered a ~ child⟩ **b** : easily torn or damaged : FRAGILE ⟨the ~ chain of life⟩ **4 a** : requiring careful handling: (1) : easily unsettled or upset ⟨a ~ balance⟩ ⟨the ~ relationships defined by the Constitution —*New Yorker*⟩ (2) : requiring skill or tact ⟨in a ~ position⟩ ⟨~ negotiations⟩ ⟨a ~ operation⟩ (3) : involving matters of a deeply personal nature : SENSITIVE ⟨this is a ~ matter. Could I possibly speak to you alone —Daphne Du Maurier⟩ **b** : marked by care, skill, or tact ⟨~ handling of a difficult situation⟩ **5** : marked by great precision or sensitivity ⟨a ~ instrument⟩ ***syn*** see CHOICE — **del·i·cate·ly** *adv*

[2]**delicate** *n* (15c) : something delicate

del·i·ca·tes·sen \ˌde-li-kə-ˈte-sᵊn\ *n pl* [obs. G (now *Delikatessen*), pl. of *Delicatesse* delicacy, fr. F *délicatesse,* prob. fr. OIt *delicatezza,* fr. *delicato* delicate, fr. L *delicatus*] (1885) **1** : ready-to-eat food products (as cooked meats and prepared salads) **2** *sing, pl* **delicatessens** [*delicatessen* (*store*)] : a store where delicatessen are sold

de·li·cious \di-ˈli-shəs\ *adj* [ME, fr. MF, fr. LL *deliciosus,* fr. L *deliciae* delights, fr. *delicere* to allure] (14c) **1** : affording great pleasure : DELIGHTFUL ⟨~ anecdotes⟩ **2** : appealing to one of the bodily senses esp. of taste or smell — **de·li·cious·ly** *adv* — **de·li·cious·ness** *n*

Delicious *n, pl* **De·li·cious·es** *or* **Delicious** (ca. 1903) : a sweet red or yellow eating apple of U.S. origin that has a crown of five rounded prominences on the end opposite the stem

de·lict \di-ˈlikt, dē-\ *n* [L *delictum* fault, fr. neut. of *delictus,* pp. of *delinquere*] (1523) : an offense against the law

[1]**de·light** \di-ˈlīt, dē-\ *n* (13c) **1** : a high degree of gratification : JOY; *also* : extreme satisfaction **2** : something that gives great pleasure ⟨her performance was a ~⟩ **3** *archaic* : the power of affording pleasure

[2]**delight** *vb* [ME *deliten,* fr. AF *deliter,* fr. L *delectare,* freq. of *delicere* to allure, fr. *de-* + *lacere* to allure] *vi* (13c) **1** : to take great pleasure ⟨~*ed* in playing the guitar⟩ **2** : to give keen enjoyment ⟨a book certain to ~⟩ ~ *vt* : to give joy or satisfaction to — **de·light·er** *n*

de·light·ed *adj* (1601) **1** *obs* : DELIGHTFUL **2** : highly pleased — **de·light·ed·ly** *adv* — **de·light·ed·ness** *n*

de·light·ful \di-ˈlīt-fəl, dē-\ *adj* (ca. 1530) : highly pleasing ⟨a ~ surprise⟩ — **de·light·ful·ly** \-fə-lē\ *adv* — **de·light·ful·ness** *n*

de·light·some \-ˈlīt-səm\ *adj* (ca. 1520) : very pleasing : DELIGHTFUL

De·li·lah \di-ˈlī-lə\ *n* [Heb *Dĕlīlāh*] (1573) : the mistress and betrayer of Samson in the book of Judges

de·lim·it \di-ˈli-mət, dē-\ *vt* [F *délimiter,* fr. L *delimitare,* fr. *de-* + *limitare* to limit, fr. *limit-, limes* boundary, limit] (1852) : to fix or define the limits of — **de·lim·i·ta·tion** \di-ˌli-mə-ˈtā-shən, ˌdē-\ *n*

\ə\ **abut** \ᵊ\ kitten, F table \ər\ **further** \a\ **ash** \ā\ **ace** \ä\ **mop, mar** \au̇\ **out** \ch\ **chin** \e\ **bet** \ē\ **easy** \g\ **go** \i\ **hit** \ī\ **ice** \j\ **job** \ŋ\ **sing** \ō\ **go** \ȯ\ **law** \ȯi\ **boy** \th\ **thin** \t͟h\ **the** \ü\ **loot** \u̇\ **foot** \y\ **yet** \zh\ **vision, beige** \k̲, ⁿ, œ, ue, ʸ\ *see* Guide to Pronunciation

de·lim·it·er \di-ˈli-mə-tər, dē-\ *n* (1958) **:** a character that marks the beginning or end of a unit of data

de·lin·eate \di-ˈli-nē-ˌāt, dē-\ *vt* **-eat·ed; -eat·ing** [L *delineatus,* pp. of *delineare,* fr. *de-* + *linea* line] (1559) **1 a :** to indicate or represent by drawn or painted lines **b :** to mark the outline of ⟨lights *delineating* the narrow streets⟩ **2 :** to describe, portray, or set forth with accuracy or in detail ⟨~ a character in the story⟩ ⟨~ the steps to be taken by the government⟩ — **de·lin·ea·tor** \-ē-ˌā-tər\ *n*

de·lin·ea·tion \-ˌli-nē-ˈā-shən\ *n* (1570) **1 :** the act of delineating **2 :** something made by delineating — **de·lin·ea·tive** \-ˈli-nē-ˌā-tiv\ *adj*

de·lin·quen·cy \di-ˈliŋ-kwən-sē, -ˈlin-\ *n, pl* **-cies** (1625) **1 a :** a delinquent act **b :** conduct that is out of accord with accepted behavior or the law; *esp* **:** JUVENILE DELINQUENCY **2 :** a debt on which payment is overdue

[1]**de·lin·quent** \-kwənt\ *n* (15c) **:** a delinquent person

[2]**delinquent** *adj* [L *delinquent-, delinquens,* prp. of *delinquere* to fail, offend, fr. *de-* + *linquere* to leave — more at LOAN] (1603) **1 :** offending by neglect or violation of duty or of law **2 :** being overdue in payment ⟨a ~ charge account⟩ **3 :** of, relating to, or characteristic of delinquents **:** marked by delinquency ⟨~ behavior⟩ — **de·lin·quent·ly** *adv*

del·i·quesce \ˌde-li-ˈkwes\ *vi* **-quesced; -quesc·ing** [L *deliquescere,* fr. *de-* + *liquescere,* incho. of *liquēre* to be fluid — more at LIQUID] (1756) **1 :** to dissolve or melt away **2 :** to become soft or liquid with age or maturity — used of some fungal structures (as gills)

del·i·ques·cent \-ˈkwe-sᵊnt\ *adj* [L *deliquescent-, deliquescens,* prp. of *deliquescere*] (1771) **1 :** tending to melt or dissolve; *esp* **:** tending to undergo gradual dissolution and liquefaction by the attraction and absorption of moisture from the air **2 :** having repeated division into branches ⟨elms are ~ trees⟩ — compare EXCURRENT 2a — **del·i·ques·cence** \-sᵊn(t)s\ *n*

de·lir·i·ous \di-ˈlir-ē-əs\ *adj* (1599) **1 :** of, relating to, or characteristic of delirium ⟨~ mutterings⟩ **2 :** affected with or marked by delirium ⟨~ with fever⟩ ⟨~ fans⟩ — **de·lir·i·ous·ly** *adv* — **de·lir·i·ous·ness** *n*

de·lir·i·um \di-ˈlir-ē-əm\ *n* [L, fr. *delirare* to be crazy, lit., to leave the furrow (in plowing), fr. *de-* + *lira* furrow — more at LEARN] (ca. 1563) **1 :** an acute mental disturbance characterized by confused thinking and disrupted attention usu. accompanied by disordered speech and hallucinations **2 :** frenzied excitement ⟨he would stride about his room in a ~ of joy —Thomas Wolfe⟩

delirium tre·mens \-ˈtrē-mənz, -ˈtre-\ *n* [NL, lit., trembling delirium] (1827) **:** a violent delirium with tremors that is induced by excessive and prolonged use of alcoholic liquors — called also *d.t.'s*

de·lish \di-ˈlish\ *adj* [by shortening & alter.] (1920) **:** DELICIOUS

de·list \(ˌ)dē-ˈlist\ *vt* (1933) **:** to remove from a list; *esp* **:** to remove (a security) from the list of securities that may be dealt in on a particular exchange

de·liv·er \di-ˈli-vər, dē-\ *vb* **de·liv·ered; de·liv·er·ing** \-v(ə-)riŋ\ [ME, fr. AF *deliverer, delivrer,* fr. LL *deliberare,* fr. L *de-* + *liberare* to liberate] *vt* (13c) **1 :** to set free ⟨and lead us not into temptation, but ~ us from evil —Mt 6:13(AV)⟩ **2 a :** to take and hand over to or leave for another **:** CONVEY ⟨~ a package⟩ **b :** HAND OVER, SURRENDER ⟨~*ed* the prisoners to the sheriff⟩ ⟨~*ed* themselves over to God⟩ **3 a** (1) **:** to assist in giving birth (2) **:** to aid in the birth of **b :** to give birth to **c :** to cause (oneself) to produce as if by giving birth ⟨has ~*ed* himself of half an autobiography —H. C. Schonberg⟩ **4 :** SPEAK, SING, UTTER ⟨~*ed* their lines with style⟩ ⟨~ a song⟩ ⟨~ a speech⟩ **5 :** to send (something aimed or guided) to an intended target or destination ⟨ability to ~ nuclear warheads⟩ ⟨~*ed* a fastball⟩ **6 a :** to bring (as votes) to the support of a candidate or cause **b :** to come through with **:** PRODUCE ⟨can ~ the best results⟩ ⟨the new car ~*s* high gas mileage⟩ ~ *vi* **:** to produce the promised, desired, or expected results **:** COME THROUGH ⟨can't ~ on all these promises⟩ ***syn*** see RESCUE — **de·liv·er·abil·i·ty** \-ˌli-v(ə-)rə-ˈbi-lə-tē\ *n* — **de·liv·er·able** \-ˈli-v(ə-)rə-bəl\ *adj* — **de·liv·er·er** \-ˈli-vər-ər\ *n* — **deliver the goods :** to give results that are promised, expected, or desired

de·liv·er·ance \di-ˈli-v(ə-)rən(t)s, dē-\ *n* (14c) **1 :** the act of delivering someone or something **:** the state of being delivered; *esp* **:** LIBERATION, RESCUE **2 :** something delivered; *esp* **:** an opinion or decision (as the verdict of a jury) expressed publicly

de·liv·ery \di-ˈli-v(ə-)rē, dē-\ *n, pl* **-er·ies** (15c) **:** the act or manner of delivering something; *also* **:** something delivered

delivery boy *n* (1918) **:** a person employed by a retail store to deliver small orders to customers on call

de·liv·ery·man \-v(ə-)rē-mən, -ˌman\ *n* (1889) **:** a person who delivers wholesale or retail goods to customers usu. over a regular local route

dell \ˈdel\ *n* [ME *delle;* akin to MHG *telle* ravine, OE *dæl* valley — more at DALE] (13c) **:** a secluded hollow or small valley usu. covered with trees or turf

Del·mon·i·co steak \del-ˈmä-ni-(ˌ)kō-\ *n* [fr. the *Delmonico* restaurants, New York City, after Lorenzo Delmonico †1881 Am. restaurateur] (1925) **:** CLUB STEAK — called also *Delmonico*

de·lo·cal·ize \(ˌ)dē-ˈlō-kə-ˌlīz\ *vt* (1855) **:** to free from the limitations of locality; *specif* **:** to remove (a charge or charge carrier) from a particular position — **de·lo·cal·i·za·tion** \(ˌ)dē-ˌlō-kə-lə-ˈzā-shən\ *n*

de·louse \(ˌ)dē-ˈlau̇s, -ˈlau̇z\ *vt* (ca. 1919) **:** to remove lice from

Del·phi·an \ˈdel-fē-ən\ *adj* (1567) **:** DELPHIC

Del·phic \ˈdel-fik\ *adj* (1567) **1 :** of or relating to ancient Delphi or its oracle **2** *often not cap* **:** AMBIGUOUS, OBSCURE ⟨~ utterances⟩ — **del·phi·cal·ly** \-fi-k(ə-)lē\ *adv*

del·phin·i·um \del-ˈfi-nē-əm\ *n* [NL, genus name, fr. Gk *delphinion* larkspur, dim. of *delphin-, delphis* dolphin; prob. fr. the shape of the nectary] (1664) **:** any of a large genus (*Delphinium*) of the buttercup family that comprises chiefly perennial erect branching herbs with palmately divided leaves and irregular flowers in showy spikes and includes several that are poisonous — compare LARKSPUR

Del·phi·nus \del-ˈfī-nəs, -ˈfē-\ *n* [L (gen. *Delphini*), lit., dolphin, fr. Gk *delphin-, delphis*] (1854) **:** a northern constellation nearly west of Pegasus

delt \ˈdelt\ *n* (1980) **:** DELTOID — usu. used in pl.

[1]**del·ta** \ˈdel-tə\ *n* [ME *deltha,* fr. Gk *delta,* of Sem origin; akin to Heb *dāleth* daleth] (13c) **1 :** the 4th letter of the Greek alphabet — see ALPHABET table **2 :** something shaped like a capital Greek delta; *esp* **:** the alluvial deposit at the mouth of a river **3 :** an increment of a variable — symbol Δ **4 :** DELTA WAVE — **del·ta·ic** \del-ˈtā-ik\ *adj*

[2]**delta** *adj* (ca. 1929) **:** fourth in position in the structure of an organic molecule from a particular group or atom — symbol δ

Delta (1952) — a communications code word for the letter *d*

delta ray *n* (1908) **:** an electron ejected by an ionizing particle in its passage through matter

delta wave *n* (1936) **:** a high amplitude electrical rhythm of the brain with a frequency of less than four cycles per second that occurs esp. in slow-wave sleep, in infancy, and in many diseased conditions of the brain — called also *delta, delta rhythm*

delta wing *n* [[1]*delta;* fr. its shape] (1946) **:** a triangular swept-back airplane wing with a usu. straight trailing edge

[1]**del·toid** \ˈdel-ˌtȯid\ *n* [NL *deltoides,* fr. Gk *deltoeidēs* shaped like a delta, fr. *delta*] (ca. 1681) **:** a large triangular muscle that covers the shoulder joint and serves to raise the arm laterally

[2]**deltoid** *adj* (ca. 1753) **1 :** having a triangular shape ⟨a ~ leaf⟩ — see LEAF illustration **2 :** relating to, associated with, or supplying the deltoid

del·toi·de·us \del-ˈtȯi-dē-əs\ *n, pl* **del·toi·dei** \-ē-ˌī\ [NL, alter. of *deltoides*] (ca. 1860) **:** DELTOID

de·lude \di-ˈlüd, dē-\ *vt* **de·lud·ed; de·lud·ing** [ME, fr. L *deludere,* fr. *de-* + *ludere* to play — more at LUDICROUS] (15c) **1 :** to mislead the mind or judgment of **:** DECEIVE, TRICK **2** *obs* **a :** FRUSTRATE, DISAPPOINT **b :** EVADE, ELUDE ***syn*** see DECEIVE — **de·lud·er** *n*

[1]**del·uge** \ˈdel-ˌyüj, -ˌyüzh; ÷də-ˈlüj, ˈdā-ˌlüj\ *n* [ME, fr. AF *deluje,* fr. L *diluvium,* fr. *diluere* to wash away, fr. *dis-* + *lavere* to wash — more at LYE] (14c) **1 a :** an overflowing of the land by water **b :** a drenching rain **2 :** an overwhelming amount or number ⟨received a ~ of offers⟩

[2]**deluge** *vt* **del·uged; del·ug·ing** (1593) **1 :** to overflow with water **:** INUNDATE **2 :** OVERWHELM, SWAMP

de·lu·sion \di-ˈlü-zhən, dē-\ *n* [ME, fr. LL *delusion-, delusio,* fr. *deludere*] (15c) **1 :** the act of deluding **:** the state of being deluded **2 a :** something that is falsely or delusively believed or propagated **b :** a persistent false psychotic belief regarding the self or persons or objects outside the self that is maintained despite indisputable evidence to the contrary; *also* **:** the abnormal state marked by such beliefs — **de·lu·sion·al** \-ˈlüzh-nəl, -ˈlü-zhə-nᵊl\ *adj* — **de·lu·sion·ary** \-zhə-ˌner-ē\ *adj*

syn DELUSION, ILLUSION, HALLUCINATION, MIRAGE mean something that is believed to be true or real but that is actually false or unreal. DELUSION implies an inability to distinguish between what is real and what only seems to be real, often as the result of a disordered state of mind ⟨*delusions* of persecution⟩. ILLUSION implies a false ascribing of reality based on what one sees or imagines ⟨an *illusion* of safety⟩. HALLUCINATION implies impressions that are the product of disordered senses, as because of mental illness or drugs ⟨suffered from terrifying *hallucinations*⟩. MIRAGE in its extended sense applies to an illusory vision, dream, hope, or aim ⟨claimed a balanced budget is a *mirage*⟩.

de·lu·sive \-ˈlü-siv, -ˈlü-ziv\ *adj* (1605) **1 :** likely to delude ⟨~ promises⟩ **2 :** constituting a delusion ⟨~ beliefs⟩ — **de·lu·sive·ly** *adv* — **de·lu·sive·ness** *n*

de·lu·so·ry \-sə-rē, -zə-\ *adj* (15c) **:** DECEPTIVE, DELUSIVE

de·lus·ter \(ˌ)dē-ˈləs-tər\ *vt* (1926) **:** to reduce the sheen of (as yarn or fabric)

de·luxe \di-ˈləks, dē- *also* -ˈlu̇ks, -ˈlüks\ *adj* [F *de luxe,* lit., of luxury] (1819) **:** notably luxurious, elegant, or expensive ⟨a ~ edition⟩ ⟨~ hotels⟩

[1]**delve** \ˈdelv\ *vb* **delved; delv·ing** [ME, fr. OE *delfan;* akin to OHG *telban* to dig] *vt* (bef. 12c) *archaic* **:** EXCAVATE ~ *vi* **1 :** to dig or labor with or as if with a spade **2 a :** to make a careful or detailed search for information ⟨*delved* into the past⟩ **b :** to examine a subject in detail ⟨the book ~*s* into the latest research⟩ — **delv·er** *n*

[2]**delve** *n* (14c) *archaic* **:** CAVE, HOLLOW

dely *abbr* delivery

dem *abbr* demonstrative

Dem \ˈdem\ *n* (1875) **:** DEMOCRAT 2

de·mag·ne·tize \(ˌ)dē-ˈmag-nə-ˌtīz\ *vt* (1839) **:** to deprive of magnetic properties — **de·mag·ne·ti·za·tion** \(ˌ)dē-ˌmag-nə-tə-ˈzā-shən\ *n* — **de·mag·ne·tiz·er** \(ˌ)dē-ˈmag-nə-ˌtī-zər\ *n*

dem·a·gog·ic \ˌde-mə-ˈgä-gik *also* -ˈgä-jik *or* -ˈgō-jik\ *adj* (1831) **:** of, relating to, or characteristic of a demagogue **:** employing demagoguery — **dem·a·gog·i·cal·ly** \-gi-k(ə-)lē, -ji-\ *adv*

[1]**dem·a·gogue** *also* **dem·a·gog** \ˈde-mə-ˌgäg\ *n* [Gk *dēmagōgos,* fr. *dēmos* people (perh. akin to Gk *daiesthai* to divide) + *agōgos* leading, fr. *agein* to lead — more at TIDE, AGENT] (1648) **1 :** a leader who makes use of popular prejudices and false claims and promises in order to gain power **2 :** a leader championing the cause of the common people in ancient times — **dem·a·gogu·ery** \-ˌgä-g(ə-)rē\ *n* — **dem·a·gogy** \-ˌgä-gē, -ˌgä-jē, -ˌgō-jē\ *n*

[2]**demagogue** *also* **demagog** *vb* **-gogued** *also* **-goged; -gogu·ing** *also* **-gog·ing** *vi* (1656) **:** to behave like a demagogue ~ *vt* **:** to treat (as an issue) in a demagogic manner

[1]**de·mand** \di-ˈmand, -ˈmänd, dē-\ *n* (13c) **1 a :** an act of demanding or asking esp. with authority ⟨a ~ for obedience⟩ **b :** something claimed as due ⟨a list of ~*s*⟩ **2** *archaic* **:** QUESTION **3 a :** willingness and ability to purchase a commodity or service ⟨the ~ for quality day care⟩ **b :** the quantity of a commodity or service wanted at a specified price and time ⟨supply and ~⟩ **4 a :** a seeking or state of being sought after ⟨in great ~ as an entertainer⟩ **b :** urgent need **5 :** the requirement of work or of the expenditure of a resource ⟨equal to the ~*s* of the office⟩ ⟨~*s* on one's time⟩ ⟨oxygen ~ for waste oxidation⟩ — **on demand :** upon presentation and request for payment; *also* **:** when requested or needed ⟨video *on demand*⟩

[2]**demand** *vb* [ME *demaunden,* fr. AF *demander,* fr. ML *demandare,* fr. L, to entrust, charge, fr. *de-* + *mandare* to enjoin — more at MANDATE] *vi* (14c) **:** to make a demand **:** ASK ~ *vt* **1 :** to ask or call for with authority **:** claim as due or just ⟨~*ed* to see a lawyer⟩ **2 :** to call for urgently, peremptorily, or insistently ⟨~*ed* that the rioters disperse⟩ **3 a :** to ask authoritatively or earnestly to be informed of ⟨~ the reason for the dismissal⟩ **b :** to require to come **:** SUMMON **4 :** to call for as

useful or necessary ⟨etiquette ~*s* a handwritten thank-you⟩ — **de·mand·able** \-ˈman-də-bəl\ *adj* — **de·mand·er** *n*

syn DEMAND, CLAIM, REQUIRE, EXACT mean to ask or call for something as due or as necessary. DEMAND implies peremptoriness and insistence and often the right to make requests that are to be regarded as commands ⟨*demanded* payment of the debt⟩. CLAIM implies a demand for the delivery or concession of something due as one's own or one's right ⟨*claimed* the right to manage his own affairs⟩. REQUIRE suggests the imperativeness that arises from inner necessity, compulsion of law or regulation, or the exigencies of the situation ⟨the patient *requires* constant attention⟩. EXACT implies not only demanding but getting what one demands ⟨*exacts* absolute loyalty⟩.

de·man·dant \di-ˈman-dənt\ *n* (15c) **1** *archaic* **:** the plaintiff in a real action **2** *archaic* **:** one who makes a demand or claim

demand deposit *n* (1923) **:** a bank deposit that can be withdrawn without advance notice

de·mand·ing *adj* (1926) **:** requiring much time, effort, or attention **:** EXACTING ⟨a ~ job⟩ ⟨~ customers⟩ — **de·mand·ing·ly** \-ˈman-diŋ-lē\ *adv* — **de·mand·ing·ness** *n*

demand loan *n* (1913) **:** CALL LOAN

demand note *n* (1844) **:** a note payable on demand

de·mand–pull \di-ˈman(d)-ˌpu̇l\ *n* (1952) **:** an increase or upward trend in spendable money that tends to result in increased competition for available goods and services and a corresponding increase in consumer prices — compare COST-PUSH — **demand–pull** *adj*

de·mand–side \di-ˈmand-ˌsīd\ *adj* (1980) **:** of, relating to, or being an economic theory that advocates use of government spending and growth in the money supply to stimulate the demand for goods and services and therefore expand economic activity — compare SUPPLY-SIDE

dem·an·toid \ˈde-mən-ˌtȯid\ *n* [G, fr. obs. G *Demant* diamond, fr. MHG *diemant,* fr. OF *diamant* — more at DIAMOND] (ca. 1890) **:** a green variety of garnet used as a gem

de·mar·cate \di-ˈmär-ˌkāt, ˈdē-ˌ\ *vt* **-cat·ed; -cat·ing** [back-formation fr. *demarcation,* fr. Sp *demarcación,* fr. *demarcar* to delimit, fr. *de-* + *marcar* to mark, prob. fr. It *marcare,* of Gmc origin; akin to OHG *marha* boundary — more at MARK] (1816) **1 :** DELIMIT **2 :** to set apart **:** DISTINGUISH ⟨~ teachers as mentor, master and model teachers based on their level of education —Shanay Cadette⟩ — **de·mar·ca·tion** \ˌdē-ˌmär-ˈkā-shən\ *n*

dé·marche *or* **de·marche** \dā-ˈmärsh, di-ˈ, ˈdā-ˌ\ *n* [F *démarche,* lit., gait, fr. MF, fr. *demarcher* to march, fr. OF *demarchier,* fr. *de-* + *marchier* to march] (1658) **1 a :** a course of action **:** MANEUVER **b :** a diplomatic or political initiative or maneuver **2 :** a petition or protest presented through diplomatic channels

de·mark \di-ˈmärk\ *vt* (1834) **:** DEMARCATE

de·ma·te·ri·al·ize \ˌdē-mə-ˈtir-ē-ə-ˌlīz\ *vt* (ca. 1864) **:** to cause to become or appear immaterial ~ *vi* **:** to lose or appear to lose materiality — **de·ma·te·ri·al·i·za·tion** \-ˌtir-ē-ə-lə-ˈzā-shən\ *n*

deme \ˈdēm\ *n* [Gk *dēmos* people, deme] (1833) **1 :** a unit of local government in ancient Attica **2 :** a local population of closely related interbreeding organisms

[1]**de·mean** \di-ˈmēn\ *vt* **de·meaned; de·mean·ing** [ME *demenen,* fr. AF *demener* to conduct, fr. *de-* + *mener* to lead, fr. L *minare* to drive, fr. *minari* to threaten — more at MOUNT] (14c) **:** to conduct or behave (oneself) usu. in a proper manner

[2]**demean** *vt* **de·meaned; de·mean·ing** [*de-* + [1]*mean*] (1601) **:** to lower in character, status, or reputation

de·mean·or \di-ˈmē-nər\ *n* [[1]*demean*] (15c) **:** behavior toward others **:** outward manner ***syn*** see BEARING

de·mean·our *Brit var of* DEMEANOR

de·ment·ed \di-ˈmen-təd\ *adj* (1632) **1 :** MAD, INSANE **2 :** suffering from or exhibiting cognitive dementia — **de·ment·ed·ly** *adv* — **de·ment·ed·ness** *n*

de·men·tia \di-ˈmen(t)-shə, -shē-ə\ *n* [L, fr. *dement-, demens* mad, fr. *de-* + *ment-, mens* mind — more at MIND] (1806) **1 :** a usu. progressive condition (as Alzheimer's disease) marked by deteriorated cognitive functioning often with emotional apathy **2 :** MADNESS, INSANITY ⟨a fanaticism bordering on ~⟩ — **de·men·tial** \-shəl\ *adj*

dementia prae·cox \-ˈprē-ˌkäks\ *n* [NL, lit., premature dementia] (1899) **:** SCHIZOPHRENIA

dem·e·rara sugar \ˌde-mə-ˈrär-ə-, -ˈrer-\ *n* [*Demerara,* river and region in Guyana] (1848) **:** a coarse light-brown raw sugar

de·mer·it \di-ˈmer-ət, dē-, -ˈme-rət\ *n* [ME, fr. AF & ML; AF *demerite,* fr. ML *demeritum,* fr. neut. of *demeritus,* pp. of *demerēre* to be undeserving of, fr. L, to earn, fr. *de-* + *merēre* to merit] (15c) **1** *obs* **:** OFFENSE **2 a :** a quality that deserves blame or lacks merit **:** FAULT, DEFECT **b :** lack of merit **3 :** a mark usu. entailing a loss of privilege given to an offender

De·mer·ol \ˈde-mə-ˌrȯl, -ˌrōl\ *trademark* — used for meperidine

de·mer·sal \di-ˈmər-səl\ *adj* [L *demersus* (pp. of *demergere* to sink, fr. *de-* + *mergere* to dip, sink) + E [1]*-al* — more at MERGE] (1889) **:** living near, deposited on, or sinking to the bottom of the sea ⟨~ fish eggs⟩

de·mesne \di-ˈmān, -ˈmēn\ *n* [ME, fr. AF *demesne, demeine* — more at DOMAIN] (14c) **1 :** legal possession of land as one's own **2 :** manorial land actually possessed by the lord and not held by tenants **3 a :** the land attached to a mansion **b :** landed property **:** ESTATE **c :** REGION 2, TERRITORY **4 :** REALM 2, DOMAIN

De·me·ter \di-ˈmē-tər\ *n* [L, fr. Gk *Dēmētēr*] (1835) **:** the Greek goddess of agriculture — compare CERES

de·meth·yl·ate \(ˈ)dē-ˈme-thə-ˌlāt\ *vt* (1926) **:** to remove a methyl group from (a chemical compound) — **de·meth·yl·a·tion** \(ˌ)dē-ˌme-thə-ˈlā-shən\ *n*

demi- *prefix* [ME, fr. *demi,* fr. AF, fr. VL **dimedius,* modif. of L *dimidius,* fr. *dis-* + *medius* mid — more at MID] **1 :** half ⟨*demi*semiquaver⟩ **2 :** one that partly belongs to (a specified type or class) ⟨*demi*god⟩

demi–glace \ˈde-mē-ˌglas\ *n* [F, half cooking stock, lit., half-ice] (1900) **:** a highly concentrated reduced brown sauce often used as a base for other sauces

demi·god \ˈde-mē-ˌgäd\ *n* (1530) **1 :** a mythological being with more power than a mortal but less than a god **2 :** a person so outstanding as to seem to approach the divine ⟨the ~*s* of jazz⟩

demi·god·dess \ˈde-mē-ˌgä-dəs\ *n* (1603) **:** a female demigod

demi·john \ˈde-mē-ˌjän\ *n* [by folk etymology fr. F *dame-jeanne,* lit., Lady Jane] (1769) **:** a large narrow-necked bottle usu. enclosed in wickerwork

demijohn

de·mil·i·ta·rize \(ˌ)dē-ˈmi-lə-tə-ˌrīz, di-\ *vt* (1883) **1 a :** to do away with the military organization or potential of **b :** to prohibit (as a zone or frontier area) from being used for military purposes **2 :** to rid of military characteristics or uses — **de·mil·i·tar·i·za·tion** \(ˌ)dē-ˌmi-lə-t(ə-)rə-ˈzā-shən, di-\ *n*

demi·mon·daine \ˌde-mi-ˌmän-ˈdān, -ˈmän-ˌ, -mē-\ *n* [F *demi-mondaine,* fr. fem. of *demi-mondain,* fr. *demi-monde*] (1894) **:** a woman supported by a wealthy lover **:** a woman of the demimonde

demi·monde \ˈde-mi-ˌmänd, -mē-\ *n* [F *demi-monde,* fr. *demi-* + *monde* world, fr. L *mundus*] (1855) **1 a :** a class of women on the fringes of respectable society supported by wealthy lovers; *also* **:** their world **b :** the world of prostitution **2 :** a distinct circle or world that is often an isolated part of a larger world ⟨a night in the disco ~⟩; *esp* **:** one having low reputation or prestige

de·min·er·al·i·za·tion \(ˌ)dē-ˌmi-nə-rə-lə-ˈzā-shən, di-\ *n* (1903) **1 :** loss of bodily minerals (as calcium salts) esp. in disease **2 :** the process of removing mineral matter or salts (as from water) — **de·min·er·al·ize** \(ˌ)dē-ˈmi-nə-rə-ˌlīz\ *vt* — **de·min·er·al·iz·er** \-ˌlī-zər\ *n*

de min·i·mis \dē-ˈmi-nə-məs, dā-ˈmē-ni-mis\ *adj* [NL, concerning trifles] (1948) **:** lacking significance or importance **:** so minor as to merit disregard ⟨*de minimis* fringe benefits⟩

demi·rep \ˈde-mi-ˌrep, -mē-\ *n* [*demi-* + *rep* (reprobate)] (1749) **:** DEMIMONDAINE

[1]**de·mise** \di-ˈmīz\ *vb* **de·mised; de·mis·ing** *vt* (15c) **1 :** to convey (as an estate) by will or lease **2** *obs* **:** CONVEY, GIVE **3 :** to transmit by succession or inheritance ~ *vi* **1 :** DIE, DECEASE **2 :** to pass by descent or bequest ⟨the property has *demised* to the king's heirs⟩

[2]**demise** *n* [ME *dimise,* fr. AF *demise,* fem. of *demis,* pp. of *demettre* to dismiss, fr. L *demittere* to send down, fr. *de-* + *mittere* to send] (15c) **1 :** the conveyance of an estate **2 :** transfer of the sovereignty to a successor **3 a :** DEATH **b :** a cessation of existence or activity **c :** a loss of position or status

demi–sec \ˌde-mi-ˈsek, -mē-\ *adj* [F] (1926) *of champagne* **:** moderately sweet

demi·semi·qua·ver \ˌde-mē-ˈse-mē-ˌkwā-vər\ *n* (ca. 1706) **:** THIRTY-SECOND NOTE

de·mis·sion \di-ˈmi-shən\ *n* [ME *dimission* relinquishment, conveyance, fr. AF *dimissioun,* fr. L *demission-, demissio* lowering, fr. *demittere*] (15c) **:** RESIGNATION, ABDICATION

de·mit \di-ˈmit\ *vb* **de·mit·ted; de·mit·ting** [ME *dimitten,* fr. AF *demettre*] *vt* (15c) **1** *archaic* **:** DISMISS **2 :** RESIGN 2 ~ *vi* **:** to withdraw from office or membership

demi·tasse \ˈde-mi-ˌtas, -ˌtäs, -mē-\ *n* [F *demi-tasse,* fr. *demi-* + *tasse* cup, fr. MF, fr. Ar *ṭass* — more at TAZZA] (1842) **:** a small cup of black coffee; *also* **:** the cup used to serve it

demi·urge \ˈde-mē-ˌərj\ *n* [LL *demiurgus,* fr. Gk *dēmiourgos,* lit., artisan, one with special skill, fr. *dēmios* of the people (fr. *dēmos* people) + *-ourgos* worker (fr. *ergon* work) — more at DEMAGOGUE, WORK] (1840) **1** *cap* **a :** a Platonic subordinate deity who fashions the sensible world in the light of eternal ideas **b :** a Gnostic subordinate deity who is the creator of the material world **2 :** one that is an autonomous creative force or decisive power — **demi·ur·gic** \-ji-jik\ *also* **demi·ur·gi·cal** \-ji-kəl\ *adj*

demi·world \ˈde-mē-ˌwərld\ *n* (1862) **:** DEMIMONDE 2 ⟨the ~ of drugs⟩

demo \ˈde-(ˌ)mō\ *n, pl* **dem·os** (1793) **1** *cap* **:** DEMOCRAT 2 **2 a :** DEMONSTRATION 1b **b** *Brit* **:** DEMONSTRATION 4 **3 a :** DEMONSTRATOR a **b :** a recording intended to show off a song or performer to a record producer **c :** an example of a product that is not yet ready to be sold ⟨a ~ version of the software⟩ **4 :** DEMOGRAPHIC 2

[1]**de·mob** \(ˌ)dē-ˈmäb, di-\ *vt* (1919) *chiefly Brit* **:** DEMOBILIZE

[2]**demob** *n* (1945) *chiefly Brit* **:** the act or process of demobilizing

de·mo·bi·lize \di-ˈmō-bə-ˌlīz, ˌdē-\ *vt* (1882) **1 :** DISBAND **2 :** to discharge from military service — **de·mo·bi·li·za·tion** \di-ˌmō-bə-lə-ˈzā-shən, ˌdē-\ *n*

de·moc·ra·cy \di-ˈmä-krə-sē\ *n, pl* **-cies** [MF *democratie,* fr. LL *democratia,* fr. Gk *dēmokratia,* fr. *dēmos* + *-kratia* -cracy] (1576) **1 a :** government by the people; *esp* **:** rule of the majority **b :** a government in which the supreme power is vested in the people and exercised by them directly or indirectly through a system of representation usu. involving periodically held free elections **2 :** a political unit that has a democratic government **3** *cap* **:** the principles and policies of the Democratic party in the U.S. ⟨from emancipation Republicanism to New Deal *Democracy* —C. M. Roberts⟩ **4 :** the common people esp. when constituting the source of political authority **5 :** the absence of hereditary or arbitrary class distinctions or privileges

dem·o·crat \ˈde-mə-ˌkrat\ *n* (1789) **1 a :** an adherent of democracy **b :** one who practices social equality **2** *cap* **:** a member of the Democratic party of the U.S.

dem·o·crat·ic \ˌde-mə-ˈkra-tik\ *adj* (1602) **1 :** of, relating to, or favoring democracy **2** *often cap* **:** of or relating to one of the two major political parties in the U.S. evolving in the early 19th century from the anti-federalists and the Democratic-Republican party and associated in modern times with policies of broad social reform and internationalism **3 :** relating to, appealing to, or available to the broad masses of the people ⟨~ art⟩ **4 :** favoring social equality **:** not snobbish — **dem·o·crat·i·cal·ly** \-ti-k(ə-)lē\ *adv*

democratic centralism *n* (1926) **:** a principle of Communist party organization by which members take part in policy discussions and elections at all levels but must follow decisions made at higher levels

Democratic–Republican *adj* (1818) **:** of or relating to a major American political party of the early 19th century favoring a strict interpretation of the Constitution to restrict the powers of the federal government and emphasizing states' rights

\ə\ **abut** \ᵊ\ kitten, F table \ər\ **further** \a\ **ash** \ā\ **ace** \ä\ **mop, mar** \au̇\ **out** \ch\ **chin** \e\ **bet** \ē\ **easy** \g\ **go** \i\ **hit** \ī\ **ice** \j\ **job** \ŋ\ **sing** \ō\ **go** \ȯ\ **law** \ȯi\ **boy** \th\ **thin** \t͟h\ **the** \ü\ **loot** \u̇\ **foot** \y\ **yet** \zh\ **vision, beige** \k̲, ⁿ, œ, ue, ʸ\ *see* Guide to Pronunciation

de·moc·ra·tize \di-ˈmä-krə-ˌtīz\ *vt* **-tized; -tiz·ing** (1798) **:** to make democratic — **de·moc·ra·ti·za·tion** \-ˌmä-krə-tə-ˈzā-shən\ *n* — **de·moc·ra·tiz·er** \-ˈmä-krə-ˌtī-zər\ *n*
dé·mo·dé \ˌdā-mō-ˈdā\ *adj* [F, fr. *dé-* de- + *mode*] (1873) **:** no longer fashionable **:** OUT-OF-DATE
de·mod·ed \(ˌ)dē-ˈmō-dəd\ *adj* (1887) **:** DÉMODÉ
de·mod·u·late \(ˌ)dē-ˈmä-jə-ˌlāt\ *vt* (1927) **:** to extract the information from (a modulated signal) — **de·mod·u·la·tion** \(ˌ)dē-ˌmä-jə-ˈlā-shən\ *n* — **de·mod·u·la·tor** \(ˈ)dē-ˈmä-jə-ˌlā-tər\ *n*
De·mo·gor·gon \ˌdē-mə-ˈgȯr-gən, ˈdē-mə-ˌ\ *n* [LL] (1590) **:** a mysterious spirit or deity often explained as a primeval creator god who antedates the gods of Greek mythology
1**de·mo·graph·ic** \ˌde-mə-ˈgra-fik, ˌdē-mə-\ *also* **de·mo·graph·i·cal** \-fi-kəl\ *adj* (1882) **1 :** of or relating to demography or demographics **2 :** relating to the dynamic balance of a population esp. with regard to density and capacity for expansion or decline — **de·mo·graph·i·cal·ly** \-fi-k(ə-)lē\ *adv*
2**demographic** *n* (ca. 1966) **1** *pl* **:** the statistical characteristics of human populations (as age or income) used esp. to identify markets **2 :** a market or segment of the population identified by demographics
de·mog·ra·phy \di-ˈmä-grə-fē\ *n* [F *démographie,* fr. Gk *dēmos* people + F *-graphie* -graphy] (1880) **:** the statistical study of human populations esp. with reference to size and density, distribution, and vital statistics — **de·mog·ra·pher** \-fər\ *n*
dem·oi·selle \ˌdem-wə-ˈzel\ *n* [F, fr. OF *dameisele* — more at DAMSEL] (1520) **1 :** a young lady **2 :** DAMSELFISH
De·Moi·vre's theorem \di-ˈmȯi-vərz-, -ˈmwäv(-rə)z-\ *n* [Abraham *De Moivre* †1754 Fr. mathematician] (1840) **:** a theorem of complex numbers: the *n*th power of a complex number has for its absolute value and its argument respectively the *n*th power of the absolute value and *n* times the argument of the complex number
de·mol·ish \di-ˈmä-lish\ *vt* [MF *demoliss-,* stem of *demolir,* fr. L *demoliri,* fr. *de-* + *moliri* to construct, fr. *moles* mass — more at MOLE] (1570) **1 a :** TEAR DOWN, RAZE **b :** to break to pieces **:** SMASH **2 a :** to do away with **:** DESTROY **b :** to strip of any pretense of merit or credence — **de·mol·ish·er** *n* — **de·mol·ish·ment** \-lish-mənt\ *n*
de·mo·li·tion \ˌde-mə-ˈli-shən, ˌdē-mə-\ *n* (1549) **1 :** the act of demolishing; *esp* **:** destruction in war by means of explosives **2** *pl* **:** explosives for destruction in war — **de·mo·li·tion·ist** \-ˈli-sh(ə-)nəst\ *n*
demolition derby *n* (ca. 1953) **1 :** a contest in which skilled drivers ram old cars into one another until only one car remains running **2 :** something that resembles a demolition derby in destructiveness
de·mon *or* **dae·mon** \ˈdē-mən\ *n* [ME *demon,* fr. LL & L; LL *daemon* evil spirit, fr. L, divinity, spirit, fr. Gk *daimōn,* prob. fr. *daiesthai* to distribute — more at TIDE] (13c) **1 a :** an evil spirit **b :** a source or agent of evil, harm, distress, or ruin **2** *usu daemon* **:** an attendant power or spirit **:** GENIUS **3** *usu daemon* **:** a supernatural being of Greek mythology intermediate between gods and men **4 :** one that has exceptional enthusiasm, drive, or effectiveness ⟨a ~ for work⟩ — **de·mo·ni·an** \di-ˈmō-nē-ən\ *adj* — **de·mon·i·za·tion** \ˌdē-mə-nə-ˈzā-shən\ *n* — **de·mon·ize** \ˈdē-mə-ˌnīz\ *vt*
de·mon·e·tize \(ˌ)dē-ˈmä-nə-ˌtīz, -ˈmə-\ *vt* [F *démonétiser,* fr. *dé-* de- + L *moneta* coin — more at MINT] (1852) **1 :** to stop using (a metal) as a monetary standard **2 :** to deprive of value for official payment — **de·mon·e·ti·za·tion** \(ˌ)dē-ˌmä-nə-tə-ˈzā-shən, -ˌmə-\ *n*
1**de·mo·ni·ac** \di-ˈmō-nē-ˌak\ *also* **de·mo·ni·a·cal** \ˌdē-mə-ˈnī-ə-kəl\ *adj* [ME *demoniak,* fr. LL *daemoniacus,* fr. Gk *daimoniakos,* fr. *daimon-, daimōn*] (14c) **1 :** possessed or influenced by a demon **2 :** DEMONIC ⟨~ rage⟩ — **de·mo·ni·a·cal·ly** \ˌdē-mə-ˈnī-ə-k(ə-)lē\ *adv*
2**demoniac** *n* (14c) **:** one possessed by a demon
de·mon·ic \di-ˈmä-nik, dē-\ *also* **de·mon·i·cal** \-ni-kəl\ *adj* (1662) **:** of, relating to, or suggestive of a demon **:** FIENDISH ⟨~ cruelty⟩ ⟨~ laughter⟩ — **de·mon·i·cal·ly** \-ni-k(ə-)lē\ *adv*
de·mon·ol·o·gy \ˌdē-mə-ˈnä-lə-jē\ *n* (1597) **1 :** the study of demons or evil spirits **2 :** belief in demons **:** a doctrine of evil spirits **3 :** a catalog of enemies ⟨the liberal creed at that time put Big Business in a central place in its ~ —Carl Kaysen⟩ — **de·mon·olog·i·cal** \ˌdē-mə-nə-ˈlä-ji-kəl\ *adj* — **de·mon·ol·o·gist** \-ˈnä-lə-jist\ *n*
de·mon·stra·ble \di-ˈmän(t)-strə-bəl\ *adj* (15c) **1 :** capable of being demonstrated **2 :** APPARENT, EVIDENT — **de·mon·stra·bil·i·ty** \-ˌmän(t)-strə-ˈbi-lə-tē\ *n* — **de·mon·stra·bly** \-blē\ *adv*
dem·on·strate \ˈde-mən-ˌstrāt\ *vb* **-strat·ed; -strat·ing** [L *demonstratus,* pp. of *demonstrare,* fr. *de-* + *monstrare* to show — more at MUSTER] *vt* (1548) **1 :** to show clearly ⟨~ a willingness to cooperate⟩ **2 a :** to prove or make clear by reasoning or evidence **b :** to illustrate and explain esp. with many examples ⟨~ a procedure⟩ **3 :** to show or prove the value or efficiency of to a prospective buyer ⟨~ a new product⟩ ~ *vi* **:** to make a demonstration ⟨crowds *demonstrating* for the right to vote⟩ ***syn*** see SHOW
dem·on·stra·tion \ˌde-mən-ˈstrā-shən\ *n* (14c) **1 :** an act, process, or means of demonstrating to the intelligence: as **a (1) :** conclusive evidence **:** PROOF **(2) :** DERIVATION 5 **b :** a showing of the merits of a product or service to a prospective consumer **2 :** an outward expression or display **3 :** a show of armed force **4 :** a public display of group feelings toward a person or cause — **dem·on·stra·tion·al** \-shnəl, -shə-nᵊl\ *adj*
1**de·mon·stra·tive** \di-ˈmän(t)-strə-tiv\ *adj* (14c) **1 a :** demonstrating as real or true **b :** characterized or established by demonstration **2 :** pointing out the one referred to and distinguishing it from others of the same class ⟨~ pronouns⟩ **3 a :** marked by display of feeling **b :** inclined to display feelings openly — **de·mon·stra·tive·ly** *adv* — **de·mon·stra·tive·ness** *n*
2**demonstrative** *n* (15c) **:** a demonstrative word or morpheme
dem·on·stra·tor \ˈde-mən-ˌstrā-tər\ *n* (1611) **:** one that demonstrates: **a :** a product (as an automobile) used to demonstrate performance or merits to prospective buyers **b :** a person who engages in a public demonstration
de·mor·al·ize \di-ˈmȯr-ə-ˌlīz, ˌdē-, -ˈmär-\ *vt* (ca. 1793) **1 :** to corrupt the morals of **2 a :** to weaken the morale of **:** DISCOURAGE, DISPIRIT **b :** to upset or destroy the normal functioning of **c :** to throw into disorder — **de·mor·al·i·za·tion** \di-ˌmȯr-ə-lə-ˈzā-shən, ˌdē-, -ˌmär-\ *n* — **de·mor·al·iz·er** \di-ˈmȯr-ə-ˌlī-zər, ˌdē-, -ˈmär-\ *n* — **de·mor·al·iz·ing·ly** \-ziŋ-lē\ *adv*
de·mos \ˈdē-ˌmäs\ *n* [Gk *dēmos* — more at DEMAGOGUE] (1806) **1 :** POPULACE **2 :** the common people of an ancient Greek state
de·mote \di-ˈmōt, ˌdē-\ *vt* **de·mot·ed; de·mot·ing** [*de-* + *-mote* (as in *promote*)] (ca. 1891) **1 :** to reduce to a lower grade or rank **2 :** to relegate to a less important position — **de·mo·tion** \-ˈmō-shən\ *n*
de·mot·ic \di-ˈmä-tik\ *adj* [Gk *dēmotikos,* fr. *dēmotēs* commoner, fr. *dēmos*] (1822) **1 :** of, relating to, or written in a simplified form of the ancient Egyptian hieratic writing **2 :** POPULAR, COMMON ⟨~ idiom⟩ **3 :** of or relating to the form of Modern Greek that is based on everyday speech
de·mount \(ˌ)dē-ˈmau̇nt\ *vt* (ca. 1930) **1 :** to remove from a mounted position **2 :** DISASSEMBLE — **de·mount·able** \-tə-bəl\ *adj*
1**de·mul·cent** \di-ˈməl-sənt\ *adj* [L *demulcent-, demulcens,* prp. of *demulcēre* to soothe, fr. *de-* + *mulcēre* to soothe] (1732) **:** SOOTHING
2**demulcent** *n* (1732) **:** a usu. mucilaginous or oily substance (as tragacanth) that can soothe or protect an abraded mucous membrane
de·mul·ti·plex·er \(ˌ)dē-ˈməl-tə-ˌplek-sər\ *n* (1963) **:** an electronic device that separates a multiplex signal into its component parts
1**de·mur** \di-ˈmər\ *vi* **de·murred; de·mur·ring** [ME *demuren, demeren* to linger, fr. AF *demurer, demoerer,* fr. L *demorari,* fr. *de-* + *morari* to linger, fr. *mora* delay — more at MORA] (13c) **1** *archaic* **:** DELAY, HESITATE **2 :** to file a demurrer **3 :** to take exception **:** OBJECT — often used with *to* or *at*
2**demur** *n* (13c) **1 :** hesitation (as in doing or accepting) usu. based on doubt of the acceptability of something offered or proposed **2 :** the act or an instance of objecting **:** PROTEST ***syn*** see QUALM
de·mure \di-ˈmyu̇r\ *adj* [ME] (14c) **1 :** RESERVED, MODEST **2 :** affectedly modest, reserved, or serious **:** COY — **de·mure·ly** *adv* — **de·mure·ness** *n*
de·mur·rage \di-ˈmər-ij, -ˈmə-rij\ *n* (1641) **1 :** the detention of a ship by the freighter beyond the time allowed for loading, unloading, or sailing **2 :** a charge for detaining a ship, freight car, or truck
de·mur·ral \di-ˈmər-əl, -ˈmə-rəl\ *n* (1810) **:** the act or an instance of demurring
1**de·mur·rer** \di-ˈmər-ər, -ˈmə-rər\ *n* [AF *demourer,* v.] (ca. 1521) **1 :** a response in a court proceeding in which the defendant does not dispute the truth of the allegation but claims it is not sufficient grounds to justify legal action **2 :** OBJECTION
2**de·mur·rer** \-ˈmər-ər\ *n* [1*demur*] (1711) **:** one that demurs
de·my·e·lin·at·ing \(ˌ)dē-ˈmī-ə-lə-ˌnā-tiŋ\ *adj* (1939) **:** causing or characterized by the loss or destruction of myelin ⟨~ diseases⟩ ⟨a ~ agent⟩ — **de·my·e·lin·ation** \(ˌ)dē-ˌmī-ə-lə-ˈnā-shən\ *n*
de·mys·ti·fy \(ˌ)dē-ˈmis-tə-ˌfī\ *vt* (1963) **:** to eliminate the mystifying features of — **de·mys·ti·fi·ca·tion** \(ˌ)dē-ˌmis-tə-fə-ˈkā-shən\ *n*
de·my·thol·o·gize \ˌdē-mi-ˈthä-lə-ˌjīz\ *vt* (1950) **1 :** to divest of mythological forms in order to uncover the meaning underlying them ⟨~ the Gospels⟩ **2 :** to divest of mythical elements or associations — **de·my·thol·o·gi·za·tion** \-ˌthä-lə-jə-ˈzā-shən\ *n* — **de·my·thol·o·giz·er** \-ˈthä-lə-ˌjī-zər\ *n*
1**den** \ˈden\ *n* [ME, fr. OE *denn;* akin to OE *denu* valley, OHG *tenni* threshing floor] (bef. 12c) **1 :** the lair of a wild usu. predatory animal **2 a (1) :** a hollow or cavern used esp. as a hideout **(2) :** a center of secret activity **b :** a small usu. squalid dwelling **3 :** a comfortable usu. secluded room **4 :** a subdivision of a Cub Scout pack made up of two or more boys
2**den** *vb* **denned; den·ning** *vi* (13c) **:** to live in or retire to a den ⟨polar bears ~ in ice caves or snowdrifts⟩ ~ *vt* **:** to drive into a den
Den *abbr* Denmark
de·nar \ˈde-ˌnär, ˈdā-\ *n, pl* **de·nars** \-ˌnärz\ *also* **denar** *or* **de·na·ri** \ˈde-nä-ˌrē, ˈdā-\ [Macedonian, alter. of *dinar* dinar, ultim. fr. Ar *dīnār* — more at DINAR] (15c) — see MONEY table
de·nar·i·us \di-ˈner-ē-əs\ *n, pl* **de·nar·ii** \-ē-ˌī, -ē-ˌē\ [ME, fr. L — more at DENIER] (14c) **1 :** a small silver coin of ancient Rome **2 :** a gold coin of the Roman Empire equivalent to 25 denarii

denarius of Julius Caesar, 44 B.C.

de·na·tion·al·ize \(ˈ)dē-ˈnash-nə-ˌlīz, -ˈna-shə-nə-ˌlīz\ *vt* (1807) **1 :** to divest of national character or rights **2 :** to remove from ownership or control by the national government — **de·na·tion·al·i·za·tion** \(ˌ)dē-ˌnash-nə-lə-ˈzā-shən, -ˌna-shə-nə-lə-ˈzā-\ *n*
de·nat·u·ral·ize \(ˌ)dē-ˈna-ch(ə-)rə-ˌlīz\ *vt* (1800) **1 :** to make unnatural **2 :** to deprive of the rights and duties of a citizen — **de·nat·u·ral·i·za·tion** \(ˌ)dē-ˌna-ch(ə-)rə-lə-ˈzā-shən\ *n*
de·na·ture \(ˌ)dē-ˈnā-chər\ *vb* **de·na·tured; de·na·tur·ing** \-ˈnā-ch(ə-)riŋ\ *vt* (1685) **1 :** DEHUMANIZE **2 :** to deprive of natural qualities **:** change the nature of: as **a :** to make (alcohol) unfit for drinking (as by adding an obnoxious substance) without impairing usefulness for other purposes **b :** to modify the molecular structure of (as a protein or DNA) esp. by heat, acid, alkali, or ultraviolet radiation so as to destroy or diminish some of the original properties and esp. the specific biological activity ~ *vi* **:** to become denatured — **de·na·tur·ant** \(ˌ)dē-ˈnā-chər-ənt\ *n* — **de·na·tur·ation** \(ˌ)dē-ˌnā-chə-ˈrā-shən\ *n*
de·na·zi·fy \(ˌ)dē-ˈnät-si-ˌfī, -ˈnat-\ *vt* **-fied; -fy·ing** (1940) **:** to rid of Nazism and its influence — **de·na·zi·fi·ca·tion** \(ˌ)dē-ˌnät-si-fə-ˈkā-shən, -ˌnat-\ *n*
dendr- *or* **dendro-** *comb form* [Gk, fr. *dendron;* akin to Gk *drys* tree — more at TREE] **:** tree ⟨*dendr*ology⟩ **:** resembling a tree ⟨*dendr*ite⟩
den·dri·form \ˈden-drə-ˌfȯrm\ *adj* (ca. 1847) **:** treelike in form
den·drite \ˈden-ˌdrīt\ *n* (1751) **1 :** a branching treelike figure produced on or in a mineral by a foreign mineral; *also* **:** the mineral so marked **2 :** a crystallized arborescent form **3 :** any of the usu. branching protoplasmic processes that conduct impulses toward the body of a neuron — see NEURON illustration
den·drit·ic \(ˌ)den-ˈdri-tik\ *adj* (1816) **:** resembling or having dendrites **:** branching like a tree ⟨a ~ drainage system⟩ ⟨~ cells⟩
dendritic cell *n* (1934) **:** any of various antigen-presenting cells with long irregular processes

den·dro·chro·nol·o·gy \ˌden-(ˌ)drō-krə-ˈnä-lə-jē\ *n* (ca. 1928) : the science of dating events and variations in environment in former periods by comparative study of growth rings in trees and aged wood — **den·dro·chro·no·log·i·cal** \-ˌkrä-nə-ˈlä-ji-kəl, -ˌkrō-\ *adj* — **den·dro·chro·no·log·i·cal·ly** \-ji-k(ə-)lē\ *adv* — **den·dro·chro·nol·o·gist** \-krə-ˈnä-lə-jist\ *n*

den·dro·gram \ˈden-drə-ˌgram\ *n* (ca. 1953) : a branching diagram representing a hierarchy of categories based on degree of similarity or number of shared characteristics esp. in biological taxonomy

den·droid \ˈden-ˌdrȯid\ *adj* [Gk *dendroeidēs,* fr. *dendron*] (ca. 1828) : resembling a tree in form : ARBORESCENT

den·drol·o·gy \den-ˈdrä-lə-jē\ *n* (ca. 1708) : the study of trees — **den·dro·log·i·cal** \ˌden-drə-ˈlä-ji-kəl\ *adj* — **den·drol·o·gist** \den-ˈdrä-lə-jist\ *n*

dene \ˈdēn\ *n* [ME, fr. OE *denu*] (bef. 12c) *Brit* : VALLEY

Dé·né \de-ˈnā, dā-\ *n, pl* **Déné** *or* **Dé·nés** \-āz\ [CanF, of Athabascan origin; akin to Chipewyan & Slave (Athabascan languages of Canada) *dene* person] (1891) : a member of any of the Athabascan-speaking peoples of the interior of Alaska and northwestern Canada; *also* : the languages of these peoples

Den·eb \ˈde-ˌneb, -nəb\ *n* [Ar *dhanab al-dajāja,* lit., the tail of the hen] (ca. 1867) : a star of the first magnitude in Cygnus

den·e·ga·tion \ˌde-ni-ˈgā-shən\ *n* [MF or L; MF *denegation,* fr. L *denegation-, denegatio,* fr. *denegare* to deny — more at DENY] (15c) : DENIAL

de·ner·vate \ˈdē-(ˌ)nər-ˌvāt\ *vt* **-vat·ed; -vat·ing** (1905) : to deprive of a nerve supply — **de·ner·va·tion** \ˌdē-(ˌ)nər-ˈvā-shən\ *n*

den·gue \ˈdeŋ-gē, -ˌgā\ *n* [AmerSp] (1828) : an acute infectious disease caused by a flavivirus (species *Dengue virus* of the genus *Flavivirus*), transmitted by aedes mosquitoes, and characterized by headache, severe joint pain, and a rash — called also *breakbone fever, dengue fever*

de·ni \ˈde-nē, ˈdā-\ *n pl* [Macedonian, prob. alter. of *denari,* pl. of *denar* denar] (1992) — see *denar* at MONEY table

de·ni·abil·i·ty \dē-ˌnī-ə-ˈbi-lə-tē\ *n* (1973) : the ability to deny something esp. on the basis of being officially uninformed

de·ni·able \di-ˈnī-ə-bəl, dē-\ *adj* (1548) : capable of being denied

de·ni·al \di-ˈnī(-ə)l, dē-\ *n* (1528) **1** : refusal to satisfy a request or desire **2 a** (1) : refusal to admit the truth or reality (as of a statement or charge) (2) : assertion that an allegation is false **b** : refusal to acknowledge a person or a thing : DISAVOWAL **3** : the opposing by the defendant of an allegation of the opposite party in a lawsuit **4** : SELF-DENIAL **5** : negation in logic **6** : a psychological defense mechanism in which confrontation with a personal problem or with reality is avoided by denying the existence of the problem or reality — **in denial** : refusing to admit the truth or reality of something unpleasant ⟨a patient *in denial* about his health problems⟩

[1]**de·ni·er** \di-ˈnī(-ə)r, dē-\ *n* (15c) : one who denies ⟨~*s* of the truth⟩

[2]**de·nier** *n* [ME *denere,* fr. AF *dener, denier,* fr. L *denarius,* coin worth ten asses, fr. *denarius* containing ten, fr. *deni* ten each, fr. *decem* ten — more at TEN] (15c) **1** \də-ˈnir, də-ˈnyā\ : a small orig. silver coin formerly used in western Europe **2** \ˈde-nyər\ : a unit of fineness for yarn equal to the fineness of a yarn weighing one gram for each 9000 meters ⟨100-*denier* yarn is finer than 150-*denier* yarn⟩

den·i·grate \ˈde-ni-ˌgrāt\ *vt* **-grat·ed; -grat·ing** [L *denigratus,* pp. of *denigrare,* fr. *de-* + *nigrare* to blacken, fr. *nigr-, niger* black] (1526) **1** : to attack the reputation of : DEFAME ⟨~ one's opponents⟩ **2** : to deny the importance or validity of : BELITTLE ⟨~ their achievements⟩ — **den·i·gra·tion** \ˌde-ni-ˈgrā-shən\ *n* — **den·i·gra·tive** \ˈde-ni-ˌgrā-tiv\ *adj* — **den·i·gra·tor** \-ˌgrā-tər\ *n* — **den·i·gra·to·ry** \ˈde-ni-grə-ˌtȯr-ē\ *adj*

den·im \ˈde-nəm\ *n* [F *(serge) de Nîmes* serge of Nîmes, France] (1695) **1 a** : a firm durable twilled usu. cotton fabric woven with colored warp and white filling threads **b** : a similar fabric woven in colored stripes **2** *pl* : overalls or trousers usu. of blue denim — **den·imed** \-nəmd\ *adj*

de·ni·tri·fi·ca·tion \(ˌ)dē-ˌnī-trə-fə-ˈkā-shən\ *n* (1883) : the loss or removal of nitrogen or nitrogen compounds; *specif* : reduction of nitrates or nitrites commonly by bacteria (as in soil) that usu. results in the escape of nitrogen into the air — **de·ni·tri·fi·er** \-ˈnī-trə-ˌfī-ər\ *n* — **de·ni·tri·fy** \-ˈnī-trə-ˌfī\ *vt*

den·i·zen \ˈde-nə-zən\ *n* [ME *denizeine,* fr. AF *denisein, denzein* inhabitant, inner part, inner, fr. *denz* within, fr. LL *deintus,* fr. L *de-* + *intus* within — more at ENT-] (15c) **1** : INHABITANT ⟨~*s* of the forest⟩ **2** : a person admitted to residence in a foreign country; *esp* : an alien admitted to rights of citizenship **3** : one that frequents a place ⟨nightclub ~*s*⟩

den mother *n* (1936) : a female adult leader of a Cub Scout den; *also* : a person seen in the role of leader or protector of a group

de·nom·i·nal \dē-ˈnä-mə-nᵊl\ *adj* (1959) : derived from a noun

de·nom·i·nate \di-ˈnä-mə-ˌnāt, dē-\ *vt* [L *denominatus,* pp. of *denominare,* fr. *de-* + *nominare* to name — more at NOMINATE] (ca. 1552) **1** : to give a name to : DESIGNATE **2** : to express or designate in some denomination ⟨will ~ prices in U.S. dollars⟩

de·nom·i·nate number \di-ˌnä-mə-nət-\ *n* [L *denominatus*] (1579) : a number (as 7 in *7 feet*) that specifies a quantity in terms of a unit of measurement

de·nom·i·na·tion \di-ˌnä-mə-ˈnā-shən\ *n* (15c) **1** : an act of denominating **2** : a value or size of a series of values or sizes (as of money) **3** : NAME, DESIGNATION; *esp* : a general name for a category **4** : a religious organization whose congregations are united in their adherence to its beliefs and practices — **de·nom·i·na·tion·al** \-shnəl, -shə-nᵊl\ *adj* — **de·nom·i·na·tion·al·ly** *adv*

de·nom·i·na·tion·al·ism \-shə-nə-ˌli-zəm\ *n* (ca. 1855) **1** : devotion to denominational principles or interests **2** : the emphasizing of denominational differences to the point of being narrowly exclusive : SECTARIANISM

de·nom·i·na·tive \di-ˈnä-mə-nə-tiv\ *adj* [L *de* from + *nomin-, nomen* name] (ca. 1783) : derived from a noun or adjective — **denominative** *n*

de·nom·i·na·tor \di-ˈnä-mə-ˌnā-tər\ *n* (ca. 1542) **1** : the part of a fraction that is below the line and that functions as the divisor of the numerator **2 a** : a shared trait ⟨a common ~⟩ **b** : the average level (as of taste or opinion) : STANDARD

de·no·ta·tion \ˌdē-nō-ˈtā-shən\ *n* (ca. 1532) **1** : an act or process of denoting **2** : MEANING; *esp* : a direct specific meaning as distinct from an implied or associated idea **3 a** : a denoting term : NAME **b** : SIGN, INDICATION ⟨visible ~*s* of divine wrath⟩ **4** : the totality of things to which a term is applicable esp. in logic — compare CONNOTATION

de·no·ta·tive \ˈdē-nō-ˌtā-tiv, di-ˈnō-tə-tiv\ *adj* (ca. 1611) **1** : denoting or tending to denote **2** : relating to denotation

de·note \di-ˈnōt, dē-\ *vt* [MF *denoter,* fr. L *denotare,* fr. *de-* + *notare* to note] (1562) **1** : to serve as an indication of : BETOKEN ⟨the swollen bellies that ~ starvation⟩ **2** : to serve as an arbitrary mark for ⟨red flares *denoting* danger⟩ **3** : to make known : ANNOUNCE ⟨his crestfallen look *denoted* his distress⟩ **4 a** : to serve as a linguistic expression of the notion of : MEAN **b** : to stand for : DESIGNATE — **de·note·ment** \-ˈnōt-mənt\ *n*

de·noue·ment *also* **dé·noue·ment** \ˌdā-ˌnü-ˈmäⁿ, dā-ˈnü-ˌ\ *n* [F *dénouement,* lit., untying, fr. MF *desnouement,* fr. *desnouer* to untie, fr. OF *desnoer,* fr. *des-* de- + *noer* to tie, fr. L *nodare,* fr. *nodus* knot — more at NODE] (1705) **1** : the final outcome of the main dramatic complication in a literary work **2** : the outcome of a complex sequence of events

de·nounce \di-ˈnau̇n(t)s, dē-\ *vt* **de·nounced; de·nounc·ing** [ME, fr. AF *denuncier* to proclaim, fr. L *denuntiare,* fr. *de-* + *nuntiare* to report — more at ANNOUNCE] (13c) **1** : to pronounce esp. publicly to be blameworthy or evil ⟨they *denounced* him as a bigot⟩ **2** *archaic* **a** : PROCLAIM **b** : to announce threateningly **3** : to inform against : ACCUSE **4** *obs* : PORTEND **5** : to announce formally the termination of (as a treaty) ***syn*** see CRITICIZE — **de·nounce·ment** \-ˈnau̇n(t)-smənt\ *n* — **de·nounc·er** *n*

de no·vo \di-ˈnō-(ˌ)vō, dā-, dē-\ *adv or adj* [L] (1536) : over again : ANEW ⟨a case tried *de novo*⟩

dense \ˈden(t)s\ *adj* **dens·er; dens·est** [L *densus;* akin to Gk *dasys* thick with hair or leaves] (15c) **1 a** : marked by compactness or crowding together of parts ⟨~ vegetation⟩ ⟨~ traffic⟩ **b** : having a high mass per unit volume ⟨carbon dioxide is a ~ gas⟩ **2 a** : slow to understand : STUPID, THICKHEADED ⟨was too ~ to get the joke⟩ **b** : EXTREME ⟨~ ignorance⟩ **3** : having between any two elements at least one element ⟨the set of rational numbers is ~⟩ **4** : demanding concentration to follow or comprehend ⟨~ prose⟩ **5** : having high or relatively high opacity ⟨a ~ fog⟩ ⟨a ~ photographic negative⟩ ***syn*** see STUPID — **dense·ly** *adv* — **dense·ness** \ˈden(t)-snəs\ *n*

den·si·fy \ˈden(t)-sə-ˌfī\ *vt* **-fied; -fy·ing** (1820) : to make denser : COMPRESS — **den·si·fi·ca·tion** \ˌden(t)-sə-fə-ˈkā-shən\ *n*

den·si·tom·e·ter \ˌden(t)-sə-ˈtä-mə-tər\ *n* (1901) : an instrument for determining optical, photographic, or mass density ⟨diagnose osteoporosis using an X-ray bone ~⟩ — **den·si·to·met·ric** \ˌden(t)-sə-tə-ˈme-trik\ *adj* — **den·si·tom·e·try** \ˌden(t)-sə-ˈtä-mə-trē\ *n*

den·si·ty \ˈden(t)-sə-tē\ *n, pl* **-ties** (1598) **1** : the quality or state of being dense **2** : the quantity per unit volume, unit area, or unit length: as **a** : the mass of a substance per unit volume **b** : the distribution of a quantity (as mass, electricity, or energy) per unit usu. of space (as length, area, or volume) **c** : the average number of individuals or units per space unit ⟨a population ~ of 500 per square mile⟩ ⟨a housing ~ of 10 houses per acre⟩ **3 a** : the degree of opacity of a translucent medium **b** : the common logarithm of the opacity

density function *n* (ca. 1960) : PROBABILITY DENSITY FUNCTION

[1]**dent** \ˈdent\ *vb* [ME, short for *indenten* to make dents in, indent] *vt* (14c) **1** : to make a dent in ⟨~ a car⟩ **2** : to have a weakening effect on ~ *vi* : to form a dent by sinking inward : become dented

[2]**dent** *n* (1565) **1** : a depression or hollow made by a blow or by pressure **2** : an appreciable impression or effect often made against resistance ⟨hasn't made a ~ in the problem⟩; *specif* : a weakening or lessening effect ⟨costs that have made a ~ in the budget⟩

[3]**dent** *n* [F, lit., tooth, fr. L *dent-, dens*] (1703) : TOOTH 3a

[4]**dent** *abbr* dental; dentist; dentistry

dent- *or* **denti-** *or* **dento-** *comb form* [ME *denti-,* fr. L, fr. *dent-, dens* tooth — more at TOOTH] : tooth : teeth ⟨*denti*form⟩

[1]**den·tal** \ˈden-tᵊl\ *adj* [L *dentalis,* fr. *dent-, dens*] (1594) **1** : of or relating to the teeth or dentistry **2** : articulated with the tip or blade of the tongue against or near the upper front teeth — **den·tal·ly** \-ē\ *adv*

[2]**dental** *n* (ca. 1727) : a dental consonant

dental floss *n* (1910) : a thread used to clean between the teeth

dental hygienist *n* (1916) : a licensed dental professional who cleans and examines teeth

den·ta·li·um \den-ˈtā-lē-əm\ *n, pl* **-lia** \-lē-ə\ [NL, genus name, fr. L *dentalis*] (1847) : any of a genus (*Dentalium*) of widely distributed tooth shells; *broadly* : TOOTH SHELL

dental technician *n* (1946) : one who makes dental appliances

den·tate \ˈden-ˌtāt\ *adj* [L *dentatus,* fr. *dent-, dens*] (1760) : having teeth or pointed conical projections ⟨a ~ margin of a leaf⟩

dent corn *n* (1852) : corn of a variety (*Zea mays indentata*) having kernels that become indented at the top during ripening

den·ti·cle \ˈden-ti-kəl\ *n* [ME, fr. L *denticulus,* dim. of *dent-, dens*] (14c) : a conical pointed projection (as a small tooth)

den·tic·u·late \den-ˈti-kyə-lət\ *or* **den·tic·u·lat·ed** \-ˌlā-təd\ *adj* (1661) **1** : finely dentate or serrate ⟨a ~ shell⟩ ⟨a ~ margin of a leaf⟩ **2** : cut into dentils — **den·tic·u·la·tion** \(ˌ)den-ˌti-kyə-ˈlā-shən\ *n*

den·ti·form \ˈden-tə-ˌfȯrm\ *adj* (1708) : shaped like a tooth

den·ti·frice \ˈden-tə-frəs\ *n* [ME *dentifricie,* fr. L *dentifricium,* fr. *denti-* + *fricare* to rub — more at FRICTION] (15c) : a powder, paste, or liquid for cleaning the teeth

den·til \ˈden-tᵊl, -ˌtil\ *n* [obs. F *dentille,* fr. MF, dim. of *dent*] (1663) : one of a series of small projecting rectangular blocks forming a molding esp. under a cornice — **den·tiled** \-tᵊld, -ˌtild\ *adj*

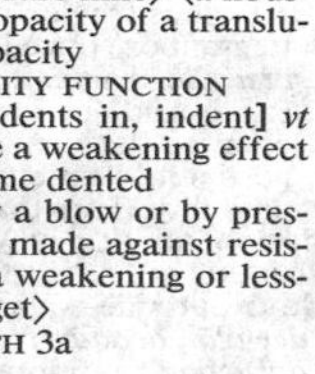

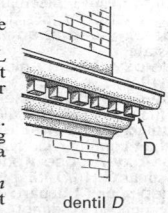

dentil *D*

den·tin \ˈden-tᵊn\ *or* **den·tine** \ˈden-ˌtēn, den-ˈ\ *n* (ca. 1845) : a calcareous material similar to but

\ə\ **abut** \ᵊ\ **kitten, F table** \ər\ **further** \a\ **ash** \ā\ **ace** \ä\ **mop, mar** \au̇\ **out** \ch\ **chin** \e\ **bet** \ē\ **easy** \g\ **go** \i\ **hit** \ī\ **ice** \j\ **job** \ŋ\ **sing** \ō\ **go** \ȯ\ **law** \ȯi\ **boy** \th\ **thin** \t͟h\ **the** \ü\ **loot** \u̇\ **foot** \y\ **yet** \zh\ **vision, beige** \k̲, ⁿ, œ, ue, ʸ\ *see* Guide to Pronunciation

harder and denser than bone that composes the principal mass of a tooth — see TOOTH illustration — **den·tin·al** \den-ˈtē-nᵊl, ˈden-tə-nəl\ *adj*

den·tist \ˈden-təst\ *n* [F *dentiste,* fr. *dent*] (1752) : one who is skilled in and licensed to practice the prevention, diagnosis, and treatment of diseases, injuries, and malformations of the teeth, jaws, and mouth and who makes and inserts false teeth

den·tist·ry \ˈden-tə-strē\ *n* (1838) : the art or profession of a dentist

den·ti·tion \den-ˈti-shən\ *n* [L *dentition-, dentitio,* fr. *dentire* to cut teeth, fr. *dent-, dens*] (1615) **1** : the development and cutting of teeth **2** : the character of a set of teeth esp. with regard to their number, kind, and arrangement — see TOOTH illustration **3** : TEETH

den·tu·lous \ˈden-chə-ləs\ *adj* [back-formation fr. *edentulous*] (1926) : having teeth

den·ture \ˈden-chər\ *n* [F, fr. MF, fr. *dent*] (1842) **1** : a set of teeth **2** : an artificial replacement for one or more teeth; *esp* : a set of false teeth

den·tur·ist \ˈden-chə-rist\ *n* (1964) : a dental technician who makes, fits, and repairs dentures directly for the public

de·nu·cle·ar·ize \(ˌ)dē-ˈn(y)ü-klē-ə-ˌrīz, ÷-kyə-lə-ˌrīz\ *vt* **-ized; -iz·ing** (1958) : to remove nuclear arms from : prohibit the use of nuclear arms in — **de·nu·cle·ar·i·za·tion** \(ˌ)dē-ˌn(y)ü-klē-ə-rə-ˈzā-shən, ÷-kyə-lə-rə-\ *n*

de·nude \di-ˈn(y)üd, dē-\ *vt* **de·nud·ed; de·nud·ing** [ME, fr. L *denudare,* fr. *de-* + *nudus* bare — more at NAKED] (15c) **1** : to deprive of something important **2 a** : to strip of all covering or surface layers **b** : to lay bare by erosion **c** : to strip (land) of forests — **de·nu·da·tion** \ˌdē-(ˌ)n(y)ü-ˈdā-shən, ˌden-yü-\ *n* — **de·nude·ment** \di-ˈn(y)üd-mənt\ *n*

de·nu·mer·a·ble \di-ˈn(y)ü-mə-rə-bəl\ *adj* (1902) : COUNTABLE — **de·nu·mer·a·bil·i·ty** \-ˌn(y)ü-mə-rə-ˈbi-lə-tē\ *n* — **de·nu·mer·a·bly** \-ˈn(y)ü-mə-rə-blē\ *adv*

de·nun·ci·a·tion \di-ˌnən(t)-sē-ˈā-shən\ *n* (1548) : an act of denouncing; *esp* : a public condemnation — **de·nun·ci·a·tive** \-ˈnən(t)-sē-ˌā-tiv\ *adj* — **de·nun·ci·a·to·ry** \-sē-ə-ˌtȯr-ē\ *adj*

Den·ver boot \ˈden-vər-\ *n* [*Denver,* Colo.] (1968) : a metal clamp that is locked onto one of the wheels of an automobile to immobilize it esp. until its owner pays accumulated parking fines

Denver omelet *n* (1954) : WESTERN OMELET

Denver sandwich *n* (1925) : WESTERN SANDWICH

de·ny \di-ˈnī, dē-\ *vt* **de·nied; de·ny·ing** [ME, fr. AF *deneier, denier,* fr. L *denegare,* fr. *de-* + *negare* to deny — more at NEGATE] (14c) **1** : to declare untrue ⟨~ an allegation⟩ **2** : to refuse to admit or acknowledge : DISAVOW ⟨~ responsibility⟩ **3 a** : to give a negative answer to ⟨~*ing* the petitioners⟩ **b** : to refuse to grant ⟨~ a request⟩ **c** : to restrain (oneself) from gratification of desires **4** *archaic* : DECLINE **5** : to refuse to accept the existence, truth, or validity of — **de·ny·ing·ly** \-ˈnī-iŋ-lē\ *adv*

syn DENY, GAINSAY, CONTRADICT, CONTRAVENE mean to refuse to accept as true or valid. DENY implies a firm refusal to accept as true, to grant or concede, or to acknowledge the existence or claims of ⟨*denied* the charges⟩. GAINSAY implies disputing the truth of what another has said ⟨no one can *gainsay* her claims⟩. CONTRADICT implies an open or flat denial ⟨her account *contradicts* his⟩. CONTRAVENE implies not so much an intentional opposition as some inherent incompatibility ⟨laws that *contravene* tradition⟩.

deoch an dor·is \ˌd(y)ȯk-ᵊn-ˈdȯr-əs\ *Scot & Irish var of* DOCH-AN-DORRIS

de·o·dar \ˈdē-ə-ˌdär\ *also* **de·o·da·ra** \ˌdē-ə-ˈdär-ə\ *n* [Hindi & Urdu *devadār, deodār,* fr. Skt *devadāru,* lit., timber of the gods, fr. *deva* god + *dāru* wood — more at DEITY, TREE] (1842) : an East Indian cedar (*Cedrus deodara*)

de·odor·ant \dē-ˈō-də-rənt\ *n* (1869) : a preparation that destroys or masks unpleasant odors — **deodorant** *adj*

de·odor·ize \dē-ˈō-də-ˌrīz\ *vt* (1856) **1** : to eliminate or prevent the offensive odor of **2** : to make (something unpleasant or reprehensible) more acceptable ⟨the movie ~*s* his scandalous career⟩ — **de·odor·i·za·tion** \-ˌō-də-rə-ˈzā-shən\ *n* — **de·odor·iz·er** *n*

de·on·tic \(ˌ)dē-ˈän-tik\ *adj* [Gk *deont-, deon* that which is obligatory, fr. neut. of prp. of *dein* to lack, be needful — more at DEUTER-] (1951) : of or relating to moral obligation : DEONTOLOGICAL

de·on·tol·o·gy \ˌdē-ˌän-ˈtä-lə-jē\ *n* (1826) : the theory or study of moral obligation — **de·on·to·log·i·cal** \ˌdē-ˌän-tə-ˈlä-ji-kəl\ *adj* — **de·on·tol·o·gist** \ˌdē-ˌän-ˈtä-lə-jist\ *n*

Deo vo·len·te \ˌdā-(ˌ)ō-vō-ˈlen-tē, ˌdē-\ [L] (1763) : God being willing

de·ox·i·dize \(ˌ)dē-ˈäk-sə-ˌdīz\ *vt* (1794) : to remove esp. elemental oxygen from ⟨~ the compound⟩ — **de·ox·i·da·tion** \(ˌ)dē-ˌäk-sə-ˈdā-shən\ *n* — **de·ox·i·diz·er** \(ˌ)dē-ˈäk-sə-ˌdī-zər\ *n*

de·oxy \(ˌ)dē-ˈäk-sē\ *also* **des·oxy** \(ˌ)de-ˈzäk-sē, -ˈsäk-\ *adj* [ISV] (1931) : containing less oxygen in the molecule than the compound from which it is derived ⟨~ sugars⟩ — usu. used in combination ⟨*deoxy*ribonucleic acid⟩

de·ox·y·gen·ate \(ˌ)dē-ˈäk-si-jə-ˌnāt, ˌdē-äk-ˈsi-jə-\ *vt* (1799) : to remove esp. molecular oxygen from ⟨~*s* the lake water⟩ — **de·ox·y·gen·ation** \(ˌ)dē-ˌäk-si-jə-ˈnā-shən, ˌdē-äk-ˌsi-jə-\ *n*

de·oxy·gen·at·ed *adj* (1799) : having the hemoglobin in the reduced state

de·oxy·ri·bo·nu·cle·ase \(ˌ)dē-ˈäk-si-ˌrī-bō-ˈn(y)ü-klē-ˌās, -ˌāz\ *n* (1946) : DNASE

de·oxy·ri·bo·nu·cle·ic acid \(ˌ)dē-ˈäk-si-ˌrī-bō-n(y)ú-ˌklē-ik-, -ˌklā-\ *n* [*deoxyribose* + *nucleic acid*] (1938) : DNA

de·oxy·ri·bo·nu·cle·o·tide \-ˈn(y)ü-klē-ə-ˌtīd\ *n* (1958) : a nucleotide that contains deoxyribose and is a constituent of DNA

de·oxy·ri·bose \(ˌ)dē-ˌäk-si-ˈrī-ˌbōs, -ˌbōz\ *n* [ISV] (1938) : a pentose sugar $C_5H_{10}O_4$ that is a structural element of DNA

dep *abbr* **1** depart; departure **2** department **3** deponent **4** deposed **5** deposit **6** depot **7** deputy

de·part \di-ˈpärt, dē-\ *vb* [ME, to divide, part company, fr. AF *departir,* fr. *de-* + *partir* to divide, fr. L *partire,* fr. *part-, pars* part] *vi* (13c) **1 a** : to go away : LEAVE **b** : DIE **2** : to turn aside : DEVIATE ~ *vt* : to go away from : LEAVE ***syn*** see SWERVE

de·part·ed *adj* (14c) **1** : BYGONE ⟨~ days⟩ **2** : having died esp. recently ⟨mourning our ~ friend⟩ ***syn*** see DEAD

de·part·ee \-pär-ˈtē\ *n* (1943) : a person who is departing or who has departed

de·part·ment \di-ˈpärt-mənt\ *n* [F *département,* fr. OF, act of dividing, fr. *departir*] (1735) **1 a** : a distinct sphere : PROVINCE ⟨that's not my ~⟩ **b** : a category consisting esp. of a measurable activity or attribute ⟨lacking in the trustworthiness ~ —Garrison Keillor⟩ **2** : a functional or territorial division: as **a** : a major administrative division of a government **b** : a major territorial administrative subdivision **c** : a division of a college or school giving instruction in a particular subject **d** : a major division of a business **e** : a section of a department store handling a particular kind of merchandise **f** : a territorial subdivision made for the administration and training of military units — **de·part·men·tal** \di-ˌpärt-ˈmen-tᵊl, ˌdē-\ *adj* — **de·part·men·tal·ly** \-tə-lē\ *adv*

de·part·men·tal·ize \di-ˌpärt-ˈmen-tə-ˌlīz, ˌdē-\ *vt* **-ized; -iz·ing** (ca. 1895) : to divide into departments — **de·part·men·tal·i·za·tion** \-ˌmen-tə-lə-ˈzā-shən\ *n*

department store *n* (1887) : a store having separate sections for a wide variety of goods

de·par·ture \di-ˈpär-chər\ *n* (15c) **1 a** (1) : the act or an instance of departing (2) *archaic* : DEATH **b** : a setting out (as on a new course) **2** : DIVERGENCE 2 ⟨a ~ from tradition⟩

de·pau·per·ate \di-ˈpȯ-pə-rət\ *adj* [ME *depauperat,* fr. ML *depauperatus,* pp. of *depauperare* to impoverish, fr. L *de-* + *pauperare* to impoverish, fr. *pauper* poor — more at POOR] (15c) **1** : falling short of natural development or size **2** : IMPOVERISHED ⟨a ~ fauna⟩

de·pend \di-ˈpend\ *vi* [ME, fr. AF *dependre,* modif. of L *dependēre,* fr. *de-* + *pendēre* to hang — more at PENDANT] (15c) **1** : to be determined, based, or contingent ⟨life ~*s* on food⟩ ⟨the value of *Y* ~*s* on *X*⟩ **2** : to be pending or undecided **3 a** : to place reliance or trust ⟨you can ~ on me⟩ **b** : to be dependent esp. for financial support **4** : to hang down

de·pend·able \di-ˈpen-də-bəl\ *adj* (1735) : capable of being depended on : RELIABLE ⟨a ~ source of income⟩ — **de·pend·abil·i·ty** \-ˌpen-də-ˈbi-lə-tē\ *n* — **de·pend·able·ness** *n* — **de·pend·ably** \-blē\ *adv*

de·pen·dence *also* **de·pen·dance** \di-ˈpen-dən(t)s\ *n* (15c) **1** : the quality or state of being dependent; *esp* : the quality or state of being influenced or determined by or subject to another **2** : RELIANCE, TRUST **3** : one that is relied on **4 a** : drug addiction ⟨developed a ~ on painkillers⟩ **b** : HABITUATION 2b

de·pen·den·cy \-dən(t)-sē\ *n, pl* **-cies** (1594) **1** : DEPENDENCE 1 **2** : something that is dependent on something else; *esp* : a territorial unit under the jurisdiction of a nation but not formally annexed by it **3** : a building (as a stable) that is an adjunct to a main dwelling

[1]**de·pen·dent** \di-ˈpen-dənt\ *adj* [ME *dependant,* fr. AF, prp. of *dependre*] (14c) **1** : hanging down **2 a** : determined or conditioned by another : CONTINGENT ⟨plans that are ~ on the weather⟩ **b** (1) : relying on another for support ⟨~ children⟩ (2) : affected with a drug dependence **c** : subject to another's jurisdiction ⟨a ~ territory⟩ **d** : SUBORDINATE 3a ⟨~ clauses⟩ **3 a** : not mathematically or statistically independent ⟨a ~ set of vectors⟩ ⟨~ events⟩ **b** : EQUIVALENT 6a ⟨~ equations⟩ — **de·pen·dent·ly** *adv*

[2]**dependent** *also* **de·pen·dant** \-dənt\ *n* (1523) **1** *archaic* : DEPENDENCY **2** : one that is dependent; *esp* : a person who relies on another for support

dependent variable *n* (ca. 1852) : a mathematical variable whose value is determined by that of one or more other variables in a function

de·per·son·al·i·za·tion \(ˌ)dē-ˌpər-snə-lə-ˈzā-shən, -ˌpər-sə-nə-lə-\ *n* (1906) **1 a** : an act or process of depersonalizing **b** : the quality or state of being depersonalized **2** : a psychopathological syndrome characterized by loss of identity and feelings of unreality and strangeness about one's own behavior

de·per·son·al·ize \(ˈ)dē-ˈpər-snə-ˌlīz, -ˈpər-sə-nə-\ *vt* (1866) **1** : to deprive of the sense of personal identity ⟨schools that ~ students⟩ **2** : to make impersonal ⟨*depersonalizing* medical care⟩

de·phos·phor·y·la·tion \(ˌ)dē-ˌfäs-fȯr-ə-ˈlā-shən\ *n* (1931) : the process of removing phosphate groups from an organic compound (as ATP) by hydrolysis; *also* : the resulting state — **de·phos·phor·y·late** \(ˌ)dē-fäs-ˈfȯr-ə-ˌlāt\ *vt*

de·pict \di-ˈpikt, dē-\ *vt* [L *depictus,* pp. of *depingere,* fr. *de-* + *pingere* to paint — more at PAINT] (15c) **1** : to represent by or as if by a picture ⟨a mural ~*ing* a famous battle⟩ **2** : DESCRIBE 1 — **de·pic·ter** \-ˈpik-tər\ *n* — **de·pic·tion** \-ˈpik-shən\ *n*

de·pig·men·ta·tion \(ˌ)dē-ˌpig-mən-ˈtā-shən, -ˌmen-\ *n* (1889) : loss of normal pigmentation

dep·i·la·tion \ˌde-pə-ˈlā-shən\ *n* [MF or ML; MF, fr. ML *depilation-, depilatio,* fr. L *depilare,* fr. *de-* + *pilus* hair — more at PILE] (1547) : the removal of hair, wool, or bristles by chemical or mechanical methods — **dep·i·late** \ˈde-pə-ˌlāt\ *vt*

de·pil·a·to·ry \di-ˈpi-lə-ˌtȯr-ē\ *n, pl* **-ries** (1606) : an agent for removing hair, wool, or bristles — **depilatory** *adj*

de·plane \(ˌ)dē-ˈplān\ *vi* (1923) : to disembark from an airplane

de·plete \di-ˈplēt\ *vt* **de·plet·ed; de·plet·ing** [L *depletus,* pp. of *deplēre,* fr. *de-* + *plēre* to fill — more at FULL] (1807) **1** : to empty of a principal substance **2** : to lessen markedly in quantity, content, power, or value — **de·plet·able** \-ˈplē-tə-bəl\ *adj* — **de·plet·er** \-ˈplē-tər\ *n* — **de·ple·tion** \-ˈplē-shən\ *n* — **de·ple·tive** \-ˈplē-tiv\ *adj*

syn DEPLETE, DRAIN, EXHAUST, IMPOVERISH, BANKRUPT mean to deprive of something essential to existence or potency. DEPLETE implies a reduction in number or quantity so as to endanger the ability to function ⟨*depleting* our natural resources⟩. DRAIN implies a gradual withdrawal and ultimate deprivation of what is necessary to an existence ⟨personal tragedy had *drained* him of all spirit⟩. EXHAUST stresses a complete emptying ⟨her lecture *exhausted* the subject⟩. IMPOVERISH suggests a deprivation of something essential to richness or productiveness ⟨*impoverished* soil⟩. BANKRUPT suggests impoverishment to the point of imminent collapse ⟨war had *bankrupted* the nation of resources⟩.

de·plor·able \di-ˈplȯr-ə-bəl\ *adj* (1612) **1** : LAMENTABLE ⟨a ~ death⟩ **2** : deserving censure or contempt : WRETCHED ⟨~ living conditions⟩ — **de·plor·able·ness** *n* — **de·plor·ably** \-blē\ *adv*

de·plore \di-ˈplȯr\ *vt* **de·plored; de·plor·ing** [MF or L; MF *deplorer,* fr. L *deplorare,* fr. *de-* + *plorare* to wail] (1559) **1 a** : to feel or express grief for **b** : to regret strongly **2** : to consider unfortunate or deserving of deprecation ⟨many critics ~ his methods⟩ — **de·plor·er** \-ˈplȯr-ər\ *n* — **de·plor·ing·ly** \-iŋ-lē\ *adv*

syn DEPLORE, LAMENT, BEWAIL, BEMOAN mean to express grief or sorrow for something. DEPLORE implies regret for the loss or impairment of something of value ⟨*deplores* the breakdown in family values⟩. LAMENT implies a profound or demonstrative expression of sorrow ⟨*lamenting* the loss of their only child⟩. BEWAIL and BEMOAN imply sorrow, disappointment, or protest finding outlet in words or cries, BEWAIL commonly suggesting loudness, and BEMOAN lugubriousness ⟨fans *bewailed* the defeat⟩ ⟨purists *bemoaning* the corruption of the language⟩.

de·ploy \di-ˈplȯi\ *vb* [F *déployer,* lit., to unfold, fr. OF *desploier,* fr. *des-* dis- + *ploier, plier* to fold — more at PLY] *vt* (1616) **1 a :** to extend (a military unit) esp. in width **b :** to place in battle formation or appropriate positions **2 :** to spread out, utilize, or arrange for a deliberate purpose ⟨~ a sales force⟩ ⟨~ a parachute⟩ ~ *vi* **:** to move, spread out, or function while being deployed ⟨the troops ~*ed* along the front⟩ ⟨the parachute failed to ~⟩ — **de·ploy·able** \-ə-bəl\ *adj* — **de·ploy·ment** \-mənt\ *n*

de·po·lar·ize \(ˌ)dē-ˈpō-lə-ˌrīz\ *vt* (1818) **1 :** to cause to become partially or wholly unpolarized **2 :** to prevent or remove polarization of (as a dry cell or cell membrane) — **de·po·lar·i·za·tion** \(ˌ)dē-ˌpō-lə-rə-ˈzā-shən\ *n* — **de·po·lar·iz·er** \(ˌ)dē-ˈpō-lə-ˌrī-zər\ *n*

de·po·lit·i·cize \ˌdē-pə-ˈli-tə-ˌsīz\ *vt* (1937) **:** to remove the political character of **:** take out of the realm of politics ⟨~ foreign aid⟩ — **de·po·lit·i·ci·za·tion** \ˌdē-pə-ˌli-tə-sə-ˈzā-shən\ *n*

de·po·ly·mer·ize \(ˌ)dē-pə-ˈli-mə-ˌrīz, -ˈpä-lə-mə-\ *vt* (ca. 1909) **:** to decompose (macromolecules) into simpler compounds (as monomers) ~ *vi* **:** to undergo decomposition into simpler compounds — **de·po·ly·mer·i·za·tion** \ˌdē-pə-ˌli-mə-rə-ˈzā-shən, (ˌ)dē-ˌpä-lə-mə-rə-\ *n*

de·pone \di-ˈpōn\ *vb* **de·poned; de·pon·ing** [ME, fr. ML *deponere,* fr. L, to put down, fr. *de-* + *ponere* to put — more at POSITION] (15c) **:** TESTIFY

¹de·po·nent \di-ˈpō-nənt\ *adj* [LL *deponent-, deponens,* fr. L, prp. of *deponere*] (15c) **:** occurring with passive or middle voice forms but with active voice meaning ⟨the ~ verbs in Latin and Greek⟩

²deponent *n* (1530) **1 :** a deponent verb **2 :** one who gives evidence

de·pop·u·late \(ˌ)dē-ˈpä-pyə-ˌlāt\ *vt* [L *depopulatus,* pp. of *depopulari,* fr. *de-* + *populari* to ravage] (1548) **1** *obs* **:** RAVAGE **2 :** to reduce greatly the population of — **de·pop·u·la·tion** \(ˌ)dē-ˌpä-pyə-ˈlā-shən\ *n*

de·port \di-ˈpȯrt, dē-\ *vt* [MF *deporter,* fr. L *deportare* to carry away, fr. *de-* + *portare* to carry — more at FARE] (1598) **1 :** to behave or comport (oneself) esp. in accord with a code **2** [L *deportare*] **a :** to carry away **b :** to send out of the country by legal deportation ***syn*** see BANISH, BEHAVE

de·port·able \di-ˈpȯr-tə-bəl, dē-\ *adj* (1891) **1 :** punishable by deportation ⟨~ offenses⟩ **2 :** subject to deportation ⟨~ aliens⟩

de·por·ta·tion \ˌdē-ˌpȯr-ˈtā-shən, -pər-\ *n* (1595) **1 :** an act or instance of deporting **2 :** the removal from a country of an alien whose presence is unlawful or prejudicial

de·por·tee \ˌdē-ˌpȯr-ˈtē, di-\ *n* (1865) **:** one who has been deported or is under sentence of deportation

de·port·ment \di-ˈpȯrt-mənt, dē-\ *n* (1601) **:** the manner in which one conducts oneself **:** BEHAVIOR ***syn*** see BEARING

de·pos·al \di-ˈpō-zəl, dē-\ *n* (14c) **:** an act of deposing from office

de·pose \di-ˈpōz, dē-\ *vb* **de·posed; de·pos·ing** [ME, fr. AF *deposer,* fr. LL *deponere* (perf. indic. *deposui*), fr. L, to put down] *vt* (14c) **1 :** to remove from a throne or other high position **2 :** to put down **:** DEPOSIT **3** [ME, fr. ML *deponere,* fr. LL] **a :** to testify to under oath or by affidavit **b :** AFFIRM, ASSERT **c :** to take a deposition of ⟨~ a witness⟩ ~ *vi* **:** to bear witness

¹de·pos·it \di-ˈpä-zət\ *vb* **de·pos·it·ed** \-ˈpä-zə-təd, -ˈpäz-təd\; **de·pos·it·ing** \-ˈpä-zə-tiŋ, -ˈpäz-tiŋ\ [L *depositus,* pp. of *deponere*] *vt* (1624) **1 :** to place esp. for safekeeping or as a pledge; *esp* **:** to put in a bank **2 a :** to lay down **:** PLACE **b :** to let fall (as sediment) ~ *vi* **:** to become deposited — **de·pos·i·tor** \-ˈpä-zə-tər, -ˈpäz-tər\ *n*

²deposit *n* (1621) **1 :** the state of being deposited **2 :** something placed for safekeeping: as **a :** money deposited in a bank **b :** money given as a pledge or down payment **3 :** a place of deposit **:** DEPOSITORY **4 :** an act of depositing **5 a :** something laid down; *esp* **:** matter deposited by a natural process **b :** a natural accumulation (as of iron ore, coal, or gas)

de·pos·i·tary \di-ˈpä-zə-ˌter-ē\ *n, pl* **-tar·ies** (1605) **1 :** a person to whom something is entrusted **2 :** DEPOSITORY 2

de·po·si·tion \ˌde-pə-ˈzi-shən, ˌdē-pə-\ *n* (14c) **1 :** an act of removing from a position of authority **2 a :** a testifying esp. before a court **b :** DECLARATION; *specif* **:** testimony taken down in writing under oath **c :** out-of-court testimony made under oath and recorded by an authorized officer for later use in court; *also* **:** a meeting at which such testimony is taken **3 :** an act or process of depositing **4 :** something deposited **:** DEPOSIT — **de·po·si·tion·al** \-ˈzish-nəl, -shə-nᵊl\ *adj*

de·pos·i·to·ry \di-ˈpä-zə-ˌtȯr-ē\ *n, pl* **-ries** (1656) **1 :** DEPOSITARY 1 **2 :** a place where something is deposited esp. for safekeeping

depository library *n* (ca. 1930) **:** a library designated to receive U.S. government publications

de·pot *1 & 2 are* ˈde-(ˌ)pō *also* ˈdē-, *3 is* ˈdē- *sometimes* ˈde-\ *n* [F *dépôt,* fr. MF *depost,* fr. ML *depositum,* fr. L, neut. of *depositus*] (1795) **1 a :** a place for storing goods or motor vehicles **b :** STORE, CACHE ⟨a fat ~ in the body⟩ **2 a :** a place for the storage of military supplies **b :** a place for the reception and forwarding of military replacements **3 :** a building for railroad or bus passengers or freight

depr *abbr* **1** depreciation **2** depression

de·prave \di-ˈprāv\ *vt* **de·praved; de·prav·ing** [ME, fr. AF *depraver,* fr. L *depravare* to pervert, fr. *de-* + *pravus* crooked, bad] (14c) **1** *archaic* **:** to speak ill of **:** MALIGN **2 :** to make bad **:** CORRUPT; *esp* **:** to corrupt morally ***syn*** see DEBASE — **de·pra·va·tion** \ˌde-prə-ˈvā-shən, ˌdē-ˌprā-\ *n* — **de·prave·ment** \di-ˈprāv-mənt\ *n* — **de·prav·er** \di-ˈprā-vər\ *n*

de·praved \di-ˈprāvd\ *adj* (14c) **:** marked by corruption or evil; *esp* **:** PERVERTED — **de·praved·ly** \-ˈprā-vəd-lē, -ˈprāvd-lē\ *adv* — **de·praved·ness** \-ˈprā-vəd-nəs, -ˈprāvd-nəs\ *n*

de·prav·i·ty \di-ˈpra-və-tē *also* -ˈprā-\ *n, pl* **-ties** (1641) **1 :** a corrupt act or practice **2 :** the quality or state of being depraved

dep·re·cate \ˈde-pri-ˌkāt\ *vt* **-cat·ed; -cat·ing** [L *deprecatus,* pp. of *deprecari* to avert by prayer, fr. *de-* + *precari* to pray — more at PRAY] (1628) **1 a** *archaic* **:** to pray against (as an evil) **b :** to seek to avert ⟨~ the wrath . . . of the Roman people —Tobias Smollett⟩ **2 :** to express disapproval of **3 a :** PLAY DOWN **:** make little of ⟨speaks five languages . . . but ~*s* this facility —*Time*⟩ **b :** BELITTLE, DISPARAGE ⟨the most reluctantly admired and least easily *deprecated* of . . . novelists —*New Yorker*⟩ — **dep·re·cat·ing·ly** \-ˌkā-tiŋ-lē\ *adv* — **dep·re·ca·tion** \ˌde-pri-ˈkā-shən\ *n*

dep·re·ca·to·ry \ˈde-pri-kə-ˌtȯr-ē, ˈde-prə-ˌkā-tə-rē\ *adj* (1586) **1 :** seeking to avert disapproval **:** APOLOGETIC **2 :** serving to deprecate **:** DISAPPROVING — **dep·re·ca·to·ri·ly** \ˌde-pri-kə-ˈtȯr-ə-lē\ *adv*

de·pre·ci·ate \di-ˈprē-shē-ˌāt\ *vb* **-at·ed; -at·ing** [ME, fr. LL *depretiatus,* pp. of *depretiare,* fr. L *de-* + *pretium* price — more at PRICE] *vt* (15c) **1 :** to lower in estimation or esteem **2 a :** to lower the price or estimated value of ⟨~ property⟩ **b :** to deduct from taxable income a portion of the original cost of (a business asset) over several years as the value of the asset decreases ~ *vi* **:** to fall in value ***syn*** see DECRY — **de·pre·cia·ble** \-shə-bəl\ *adj* — **de·pre·ci·at·ing·ly** \-shē-ˌā-tiŋ-lē\ *adv* — **de·pre·ci·a·tion** \-ˌprē-shē-ˈā-shən\ *n* — **de·pre·ci·a·tive** \-ˈprē-shə-tiv, -shē-ˌā-tiv\ *adj* — **de·pre·ci·a·tor** \-shē-ˌā-tər\ *n* — **de·pre·cia·to·ry** \-shə-ˌtȯr-ē\ *adj*

dep·re·date \ˈde-prə-ˌdāt\ *vb* **-dat·ed; -dat·ing** [LL *depraedatus,* pp. of *depraedari,* fr. L *de-* + *praedari* to plunder — more at PREY] *vt* (1626) **:** to lay waste **:** PLUNDER, RAVAGE ~ *vi* **:** to engage in plunder — **dep·re·da·tion** \ˌde-prə-ˈdā-shən\ *n* — **dep·re·da·tor** \ˈde-prə-ˌdā-tər, di-ˈpre-də-\ *n* — **dep·re·da·to·ry** \di-ˈpre-də-ˌtȯr-ē, ˈde-pri-də-\ *adj*

dep·re·nyl \ˈde-prə-ˌnil\ *n* [perh. fr. ISV *d*imethyl + *pr*opionic acid + ph*enyl* + eth*yl*] (1975) **:** a monoamine oxidase inhibitor $C_{13}H_{17}N$ used esp. to treat Parkinson's disease

de·press \di-ˈpres, dē-\ *vt* [ME, fr. MF *depresser,* fr. L *depressus,* pp. of *deprimere* to press down, fr. *de-* + *premere* to press — more at PRESS] (14c) **1** *obs* **:** REPRESS, SUBJUGATE **2 a :** to press down ⟨~ a typewriter key⟩ **b :** to cause to sink to a lower position **3 :** to lessen the activity or strength of ⟨drugs that may ~ the appetite⟩ **4 :** SADDEN, DISCOURAGE ⟨don't let the news ~ you⟩ **5 :** to decrease the market value or marketability of — **de·press·ible** \-ˈpre-sə-bəl\ *adj*

de·pres·sant \di-ˈpre-sᵊnt, dē-\ *n* (1876) **:** one that depresses; *specif* **:** an agent that reduces a bodily functional activity or an instinctive desire (as appetite) — **depressant** *adj*

de·pressed *adj* (1598) **1 :** low in spirits **:** SAD; *esp* **:** affected by psychological depression **2 a :** vertically flattened ⟨a ~ cactus⟩ **b :** having the central part lower than the margin **c :** lying flat or prostrate **d :** dorsoventrally flattened **3 :** suffering from economic depression; *esp* **:** UNDERPRIVILEGED **4 :** being below the standard

de·press·ing *adj* (1629) **:** that depresses; *esp* **:** causing emotional depression ⟨a ~ story⟩ — **de·press·ing·ly** \-siŋ-lē\ *adv*

de·pres·sion \di-ˈpre-shən, dē-\ *n* (14c) **1 a :** the angular distance of a celestial object below the horizon **b :** the size of an angle of depression **2 :** an act of depressing or a state of being depressed: as **a :** a pressing down **:** LOWERING **b** (1) **:** a state of feeling sad **:** DEJECTION (2) **:** a psychoneurotic or psychotic disorder marked esp. by sadness, inactivity, difficulty in thinking and concentration, a significant increase or decrease in appetite and time spent sleeping, feelings of dejection and hopelessness, and sometimes suicidal tendencies **c** (1) **:** a reduction in activity, amount, quality, or force (2) **:** a lowering of vitality or functional activity **3 :** a depressed place or part **:** HOLLOW **4 :** LOW 1b **5 :** a period of low general economic activity marked esp. by rising levels of unemployment

Depression glass *n* [Great *Depression* of 1929 to ca. 1939] (1971) **:** tinted glassware machine-produced during the 1930s

¹de·pres·sive \di-ˈpre-siv, dē-\ *adj* (1620) **1 :** tending to depress **2 :** of, relating to, marked by, or affected by psychological depression ⟨~ symptoms⟩ ⟨a ~ patient⟩ — **de·pres·sive·ly** *adv*

²depressive *n* (1937) **:** one who is affected with or prone to psychological depression

de·pres·sor \di-ˈpre-sər, dē-\ *n* [LL, fr. L *deprimere*] (1611) **:** one that depresses: as **a :** a muscle that draws down a part — compare LEVATOR **b :** a device for pressing down or aside **c :** a nerve or nerve fiber that decreases the activity or the tone of the organ or the part it innervates

de·pres·sur·ize \(ˌ)dē-ˈpre-shə-ˌrīz\ *vt* (1944) **:** to release pressure from — **de·pres·sur·i·za·tion** \(ˌ)dē-ˌpre-shə-rə-ˈzā-shən\ *n*

dep·ri·va·tion \ˌde-prə-ˈvā-shən *also* ˌdē-ˌprī-\ *n* (15c) **1 :** the state of being deprived **:** PRIVATION; *esp* **:** removal from an office, dignity, or benefice **2 :** an act or instance of depriving **:** LOSS

de·prive \di-ˈprīv\ *vt* **de·prived; de·priv·ing** [ME *depriven,* fr. AF *depriver,* fr. ML *deprivare,* fr. L *de-* + *privare* to deprive — more at PRIVATE] (14c) **1** *obs* **:** REMOVE **2 :** to take something away from ⟨*deprived* him of his professorship —J. M. Phalen⟩ **3 :** to remove from office **4 :** to withhold something from ⟨*deprived* a citizen of her rights⟩

de·prived *adj* (ca. 1552) **:** marked by deprivation esp. of the necessities of life or of healthful environmental influences ⟨culturally ~ children⟩

de·pro·gram \(ˌ)dē-ˈprō-ˌgram, -grəm\ *vt* (1973) **:** to dissuade or try to dissuade from strongly held convictions (as religious beliefs) or a firmly established or innate behavior ⟨the necessity of countering propaganda and *deprogramming* the indoctrinated —Toni Cade Bambara⟩ — **de·pro·gram·mer** \-mər\ *n*

dept *abbr* department

depth \ˈdepth\ *n, pl* **depths** \ˈdepths, ˈdep(t)s\ [ME, fr. *dep* deep] (14c) **1 a** (1) **:** a deep place in a body of water ⟨fish living at great ~*s*⟩ (2) **:** a part that is far from the outside or surface ⟨the ~*s* of the woods⟩ (3) **:** ABYSS 2 **b** (1) **:** a profound or intense state (as of thought or feeling) ⟨the ~*s* of misery⟩; *also* **:** a reprehensibly low condition ⟨hadn't realized that standards had fallen to such ~*s*⟩ (2) **:** the middle of a

\ə\ **abut** \ᵊ\ kitten, F table \ər\ **further** \a\ ash \ā\ ace \ä\ mop, mar
\au̇\ **out** \ch\ **chin** \e\ bet \ē\ **easy** \g\ go \i\ **hit** \ī\ ice \j\ job
\ŋ\ sing \ō\ go \ȯ\ **law** \ȯi\ **boy** \th\ **thin** \t͟h\ **the** \ü\ **loot** \u̇\ **foot**
\y\ yet \zh\ vision, beige \k̲, ⁿ, œ, ue, ʸ\ *see* Guide to Pronunciation

time (as winter) (3) : the worst part **2 a** : the perpendicular measurement downward from a surface **b** : the direct linear measurement from front to back **3** : the quality of being deep **4** : the degree of intensity ⟨~ of a color⟩; *also* : the quality of being profound (as in insight) or full (as of knowledge) **5** : the quality or state of being complete or thorough ⟨a study will be made in ~⟩ **6** : a large number of good players ⟨a team that lacks ~⟩ — **depth·less** \ˈdepth-ləs\ *adj* — **beyond one's depth** *or* **out of one's depth** : beyond the limits of one's capabilities ⟨an actor who is *out of his depth* in serious drama⟩

depth charge *n* (1917) : an antisubmarine weapon that consists essentially of a drum filled with explosives which is dropped near a target and descends to a predetermined depth where it explodes — called also *depth bomb*

depth of field (1911) : the range of distances of the object in front of an image-forming device (as a camera lens) measured along the axis of the device throughout which the image has acceptable sharpness

depth perception *n* (ca. 1911) : the ability to judge the distance of objects and the spatial relationship of objects at different distances

depth psychology *n* (1924) : PSYCHOANALYSIS; *also* : psychology concerned esp. with the unconscious mind

dep·u·ta·tion \ˌde-pyə-ˈtā-shən\ *n* (14c) **1** : the act of appointing a deputy **2** : a group of people appointed to represent others

de·pute \di-ˈpyüt\ *vt* **de·put·ed; de·put·ing** [ME, to appoint, fr. AF *deputer,* fr. LL *deputare* to assign, fr. L, to consider (as), fr. *de-* + *putare* to consider] (14c) : DELEGATE

dep·u·tize \ˈde-pyə-ˌtīz\ *vb* **-tized; -tiz·ing** *vt* (ca. 1736) : to appoint as deputy ~ *vi* : to act as deputy — **dep·u·ti·za·tion** \ˌde-pyə-tə-ˈzā-shən\ *n*

dep·u·ty \ˈde-pyə-tē\ *n, pl* **-ties** *often attrib* [ME, fr. AF *deputé,* pp. of *deputer*] (15c) **1 a** : a person appointed as a substitute with power to act **b** : a second in command or assistant who usu. takes charge when his or her superior is absent **2** : a member of the lower house of some legislative assemblies

der *or* **deriv** *abbr* derivation; derivative

de·rac·i·nate \(ˌ)dē-ˈra-sə-ˌnāt\ *vt* **-nat·ed; -nat·ing** [MF *desraciner,* fr. *des-* de- + *racine* root, fr. LL *radicina,* fr. L *radic-, radix* — more at ROOT] (1599) **1** : UPROOT **2** : to remove or separate from a native environment or culture; *esp* : to remove the racial or ethnic characteristics or influences from — **de·rac·i·na·tion** \(ˌ)dē-ˌra-sə-ˈnā-shən\ *n*

de·rail \di-ˈrāl, dē-\ *vb* [F *dérailler* to throw off the track, fr. *dé-* de- + *rail,* fr. E] *vt* (1850) **1** : to cause to run off the rails **2 a** : to obstruct the progress of : FRUSTRATE ⟨security problems ~*ed* the tour⟩ **b** : to upset the stability or composure of ⟨divorce . . . can seriously ~ an employee —Joanne Gordon⟩ ~ *vi* : to leave the rails — **de·rail·ment** \-mənt\ *n*

de·rail·leur \di-ˈrā-lər\ *n* [F *dérailleur,* fr. *dérailler*] (1930) : a mechanism for shifting gears on a bicycle that operates by moving the chain from one set of exposed gears to another

de·range \di-ˈrānj\ *vt* **de·ranged; de·rang·ing** [F *déranger,* fr. OF *desrengier,* fr. *des-* de- + *reng* line, row — more at RANK] (1769) **1** : to disturb the operation or functions of **2** : DISARRANGE ⟨hatless, with tie *deranged* —G. W. Stonier⟩ **3** : to make insane — **de·range·ment** \-mənt\ *n*

de·rate \(ˌ)dē-ˈrāt\ *vt* (1947) : to lower the rated capability of (as electrical or mechanical apparatus) because of deterioration or inadequacy

der·by \ˈdər-bē, *esp Brit* ˈdär-\ *n, pl* **derbies** [Edward Stanley †1834, 12th earl of *Derby*] (1796) **1** : any of several horse races held annually and usu. restricted to three-year-olds **2** : a race or contest open to all comers or to a specified category of contestants ⟨bicycle ~⟩ **3** : a man's stiff felt hat with dome-shaped crown and narrow brim

Derbys *abbr* Derbyshire

de·re·al·i·za·tion \(ˌ)dē-ˌrē-ə-lə-ˈzā-shən\ *n* (1942) : a feeling of altered reality (as that occurring in schizophrenia or in some drug reactions) in which one's surroundings appear unreal or unfamiliar

de·re·cho \də-ˈrā-(ˌ)chō\ *n, pl* **-chos** [Sp, straight (contrasted with *tornado,* taken to mean "turned"), fr. L *directus* — more at [1]DIRECT] (1889) : a large fast-moving complex of thunderstorms with powerful straight-line winds that cause widespread destruction

de·reg·u·la·tion \(ˌ)dē-ˌre-gyə-ˈlā-shən\ *n* (1963) : the act or process of removing restrictions and regulations — **de·reg·u·late** \(ˌ)dē-ˈre-gyə-ˌlāt\ *vt*

[1]**der·e·lict** \ˈder-ə-ˌlikt, ˈde-rə-\ *adj* [L *derelictus,* pp. of *derelinquere* to abandon, fr. *de-* + *relinquere* to leave — more at RELINQUISH] (1649) **1** : abandoned esp. by the owner or occupant; *also* : RUN-DOWN **2** : lacking a sense of duty : NEGLIGENT

[2]**derelict** *n* (1670) **1 a** : something voluntarily abandoned; *esp* : a ship abandoned on the high seas **b** : a tract of land left dry by receding water **2** : a destitute homeless social misfit : VAGRANT, BUM

der·e·lic·tion \ˌder-ə-ˈlik-shən, ˌde-rə-\ *n* (1597) **1 a** : an intentional abandonment **b** : the state of being abandoned **2** : a recession of water leaving permanently dry land **3 a** : intentional or conscious neglect : DELINQUENCY ⟨~ of duty⟩ **b** : FAULT, SHORTCOMING

de·re·press \ˌdē-ri-ˈpres\ *vt* (1960) : to activate (a gene or enzyme) by releasing from a blocked state — **de·re·pres·sion** \-ˈpre-shən\ *n*

de·ride \di-ˈrīd, dē-\ *vt* **de·rid·ed; de·rid·ing** [L *deridēre,* fr. *de-* + *ridēre* to laugh] (ca. 1526) **1** : to laugh at contemptuously **2** : to subject to usu. bitter or contemptuous ridicule ***syn*** see RIDICULE — **de·rid·er** *n* — **de·rid·ing·ly** \-ˈrī-diŋ-lē\ *adv*

de ri·gueur \də-(ˌ)rē-ˈgər\ *adj* [F] (1833) : prescribed or required by fashion, etiquette, or custom : PROPER

de·ri·sion \di-ˈri-zhən\ *n* [ME, fr. MF, fr. LL *derision-, derisio,* fr. L *deridēre*] (14c) **1 a** : the use of ridicule or scorn to show contempt **b** : a state of being derided **2** : an object of ridicule or scorn

de·ri·sive \di-ˈrī-siv, -ziv; -ˈri-ziv, -ˈri-siv\ *adj* (ca. 1662) : expressing or causing derision — **de·ri·sive·ly** *adv* — **de·ri·sive·ness** *n*

de·ri·so·ry \di-ˈrī-sə-rē, -zə-\ *adj* (1618) **1** : expressing derision : DERISIVE **2** : worthy of derision; *esp* : laughably small ⟨land could be bought for a ~ sum⟩

de·riv·able \di-ˈrī-və-bəl\ *adj* (1653) : capable of being derived

der·i·vate \ˈder-ə-ˌvāt, ˈde-rə-\ *n* (1660) : DERIVATIVE

der·i·va·tion \ˌder-ə-ˈvā-shən, ˌde-rə-\ *n* (15c) **1 a** (1) : the formation of a word from another word or base (as by the addition of a usu. noninflectional affix) (2) : an act of ascertaining or stating the derivation of a word (3) : ETYMOLOGY 1 **b** : the relation of a word to its base **2 a** : SOURCE, ORIGIN **b** : DESCENT, ORIGINATION **3** : something derived : DERIVATIVE **4** : an act or process of deriving **5** : a sequence of statements (as in logic or mathematics) showing that a result is a necessary consequence of previously accepted statements — **der·i·va·tion·al** \-shnəl, -shə-nᵊl\ *adj*

[1]**de·riv·a·tive** \di-ˈri-və-tiv\ *n* (15c) **1** : a word formed by derivation **2** : something derived **3** : the limit of the ratio of the change in a function to the corresponding change in its independent variable as the latter change approaches zero **4 a** : a chemical substance related structurally to another substance and theoretically derivable from it **b** : a substance that can be made from another substance **5** : a contract or security that derives its value from that of an underlying asset (as another security) or from the value of a rate (as of interest or currency exchange) or index of asset value (as a stock index)

[2]**derivative** *adj* (ca. 1530) **1** : formed by derivation ⟨a ~ word⟩ **2** : made up of or marked by derived elements **3** : lacking originality : BANAL — **de·riv·a·tive·ly** *adv* — **de·riv·a·tive·ness** *n*

de·riv·a·ti·za·tion \də-ˌri-və-tə-ˈzā-shən\ *n* (1967) : the conversion of a chemical compound into a derivative (as for identification) — **de·riv·a·tize** \də-ˈri-və-ˌtīz\ *vt*

de·rive \di-ˈrīv, dē-\ *vb* **de·rived; de·riv·ing** [ME, fr. AF *deriver,* fr. L *derivare,* lit., to draw off (water), fr. *de-* + *rivus* stream — more at RUN] *vt* (14c) **1 a** : to take, receive, or obtain esp. from a specified source **b** : to obtain (a chemical substance) actually or theoretically from a parent substance **2** : INFER, DEDUCE **3** *archaic* : BRING **4** : to trace the derivation of ~ *vi* : to have or take origin : come as a derivative ***syn*** see SPRING — **de·riv·er** *n*

derived *adj* (1969) : being, possessing, or marked by a character (as the large brain in humans) not present in the ancestral form ⟨~ features⟩

derm *abbr* dermatologist; dermatology

derm- *or* **derma-** *or* **dermo-** *comb form* [NL, fr. Gk *derm-, dermo-,* fr. *derma,* fr. *derein* to skin — more at TEAR] : skin ⟨*derm*al⟩

-derm *n comb form* [prob. fr. F *-derme,* fr. Gk *derma*] : skin : covering ⟨ecto*derm*⟩

-derma *n comb form, pl* **-dermas** *or* **-dermata** [NL, fr. Gk *dermat-, derma* skin] : skin or skin ailment of a (specified) type ⟨sclero*derma*⟩

derm·abra·sion \ˌdər-mə-ˈbrā-zhən\ *n* (ca. 1954) : surgical removal of skin blemishes or imperfections (as scars or tattoos) by abrasion (as with sandpaper or wire brushes)

der·mal \ˈdər-məl\ *adj* (ca. 1803) **1** : of or relating to skin and esp. to the dermis : CUTANEOUS **2** : EPIDERMAL

dermat- *or* **dermato-** *comb form* [Gk, fr. *dermat-, derma*] : skin ⟨*dermat*itis⟩ ⟨*dermato*logy⟩

der·ma·ti·tis \ˌdər-mə-ˈtī-təs\ *n, pl* **der·ma·tit·i·des** \-ˈti-tə-ˌdēz\ *or* **der·ma·ti·tis·es** (1876) : inflammation of the skin

der·ma·to·glyph·ics \ˌdər-mə-tə-ˈgli-fiks\ *n pl but sing or pl in constr* [*dermat-* + Gk *glyphein* to carve + E *-ics* — more at CLEAVE] (1926) **1** : skin patterns; *esp* : patterns of the specialized skin of the inferior surfaces of the hands and feet **2** : the science of the study of skin patterns — **der·ma·to·glyph·ic** \-fik\ *adj*

der·ma·tol·o·gy \ˌdər-mə-ˈtä-lə-jē\ *n* (1819) : a branch of medicine dealing with the skin, its structure, functions, and diseases — **der·ma·to·log·ic** \-mə-tə-ˈlä-jik\ *or* **der·ma·to·log·i·cal** \-ji-kəl\ *adj* — **der·ma·tol·o·gist** \-mə-ˈtä-lə-jist\ *n*

der·ma·tome \ˈdər-mə-ˌtōm\ *n* [ISV *dermat-* + *-ome*] (1910) : the lateral wall of a somite from which the dermis is produced — **der·ma·to·mal** \ˌdər-mə-ˈtō-məl\ *adj*

der·ma·to·my·o·si·tis \ˌdər-mə-tō-ˌmī-ə-ˈsī-təs, (ˌ)dər-ˌma-\ *n* [NL] (ca. 1899) : an inflammatory disease of skin and muscle marked esp. by muscular weakness and skin rash

der·ma·to·phyte \(ˌ)dər-ˈma-tə-ˌfīt, ˈdər-mə-\ *n* [ISV] (1882) : a fungus parasitic on the skin or skin derivatives (as hair or nails)

der·ma·to·sis \ˌdər-mə-ˈtō-səs\ *n, pl* **-to·ses** \-ˌsēz\ (1864) : a disease of the skin

-dermatous *adj comb form* [Gk *dermat-, derma* skin] : having a (specified) type of skin ⟨pachy*dermatous*⟩

der·mes·tid \(ˌ)dər-ˈmes-təd\ *n* [ultim. fr. Gk *dermēstēs,* a leather-eating worm, lit., skin eater, fr. *derm-* + *edmenai* to eat — more at EAT] (ca. 1888) : any of a family (Dermestidae) of beetles with clubbed antennae that are very destructive to organic material of animal origin (as dried meat, wool, or museum specimens) — **dermestid** *adj*

der·mis \ˈdər-məs\ *n* [NL, fr. LL *-dermis*] (ca. 1830) : the sensitive vascular inner mesodermic layer of the skin — called also *corium, cutis;* see HAIR illustration

-dermis *n comb form* [LL, fr. Gk, fr. *derma*] : layer of skin or tissue ⟨endo*dermis*⟩

der·moid cyst \ˈdər-ˌmȯid-\ *n* (1872) : a cystic tumor often of the ovary that contains skin and skin derivatives (as hair or teeth) — called also *dermoid*

der·nier cri \ˌdern-ˌyā-ˈkrē\ *n* [F, lit., last cry] (1896) : the newest fashion

der·o·gate \ˈder-ə-ˌgāt, ˈde-rə-\ *vb* **-gat·ed; -gat·ing** [ME, fr. LL *derogatus,* pp. of *derogare,* fr. L, to annul (a law), detract, fr. *de-* + *rogare* to ask, propose (a law) — more at RIGHT] *vt* (15c) : to cause to seem inferior : DISPARAGE ~ *vi* **1** : to take away a part so as to impair : DETRACT **2** : to act beneath one's position or character — **der·o·ga·tion** \ˌder-ə-ˈgā-shən, ˌde-rə-\ *n* — **de·rog·a·tive** \di-ˈrä-gə-tiv\ *adj*

de·rog·a·to·ry \di-ˈrä-gə-ˌtȯr-ē\ *adj* (ca. 1503) **1** : detracting from the character or standing of something — often used with *to, towards,* or *of* **2** : expressive of a low opinion : DISPARAGING ⟨~ remarks⟩ — **de·rog·a·to·ri·ly** \-ˌrä-gə-ˈtȯr-ə-lē\ *adv*

der·rick \ˈder-ik, ˈde-rik\ *n* [obs. *derrick* hangman, gallows, fr. *Derick,* name of 17th cent. Eng. hangman] (ca. 1752) **1** : a hoisting apparatus employing a tackle rigged at the end of a beam **2** : a framework or tower over a deep drill hole (as of an oil well) for supporting boring tackle or for hoisting and lowering

der·ri·ere *or* **der·ri·ère** \ˌder-ē-ˈer, ˌde-rē-\ *n* [F *derrière,* fr. OF *derrier* back part, rear, fr. *derier,* adv., behind, fr. LL *deretro,* fr. L *de* from + *retro* back] (1774) : BUTTOCKS

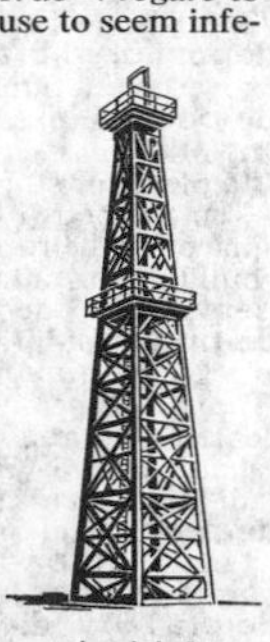
derrick 2

der·ring–do \ˌder-iŋ-ˈdü, ˌde-riŋ-\ *n* [ME *dorring don* daring to do, fr. *dorring* (gerund of *dorren* to dare) + *don* to do] (1579) **:** daring action **:** DARING ⟨deeds of ~⟩

der·rin·ger \ˈder-ən-jər, ˈde-rən-\ *n* [Henry *Deringer* †1869 Am. inventor] (1853) **:** a short-barreled pocket pistol

der·ris \ˈder-əs, ˈde-rəs\ *n* [NL, genus name, fr. Gk, skin, fr. *derein* to skin — more at TEAR] (1919) **1 :** a preparation chiefly of ground derris roots used as an insecticide **2 :** any of a large genus (*Derris*) of tropical Eurasian shrubs and woody vines of the legume family including sources of poisons and esp. commercial sources of rotenone

der·vish \ˈdər-vish\ *n* [Turk *derviş,* lit., beggar, fr. Pers *darvīsh*] (1585) **1 :** a member of a Muslim religious order noted for devotional exercises (as bodily movements leading to a trance) **2 :** one that whirls or dances with or as if with the abandonment of a dervish

des- *prefix* [F *dés-,* fr. OF *des-* — more at DE-] **:** DE- 6 — esp. before vowels ⟨*des*oxy⟩

DES \ˌdē-(ˌ)ē-ˈes\ *n* (1970) **:** DIETHYLSTILBESTROL

de·sa·cral·ize \(ˌ)dē-ˈsā-krə-ˌlīz, -ˈsa-\ *vt* **-ized; -iz·ing** (1911) **:** to divest of sacred qualities or status — **de·sa·cral·i·za·tion** \(ˌ)dē-ˌsā-krə-lī-ˈzā-shən, -ˌsa-\ *n*

de·sa·li·nate \(ˌ)dē-ˈsa-lə-ˌnāt *also* -ˈsā-\ *vt* **-nat·ed; -nat·ing** (1949) **:** DESALT — **de·sa·li·na·tion** \(ˌ)dē-ˌsa-lə-ˈnā-shən *also* -ˌsā-\ *n* — **de·sa·li·na·tor** \(ˌ)dē-ˈsa-lə-ˌnā-tər *also* -ˈsā-\ *n*

de·sa·li·nize \(ˌ)dē-ˈsa-lə-ˌnīz *also* -ˈsā-\ *vt* **-nized; -niz·ing** (1934) **:** DESALT — **de·sa·li·ni·za·tion** \(ˌ)dē-ˌsa-lə-nə-ˈzā-shən *also* -ˌsā-\ *n*

de·salt \(ˌ)dē-ˈsȯlt\ *vt* (ca. 1904) **:** to remove salt from — **de·salt·er** *n*

de·sanc·ti·fy \(ˌ)dē-ˈsaŋ(k)-tə-ˌfī\ *vt* (1956) **:** DESACRALIZE — **de·sanc·ti·fi·ca·tion** \-ˌsaŋ(k)-tə-fə-ˈkā-shən\ *n*

[1]**des·cant** \ˈdes-ˌkant\ *also* **dis·cant** \ˈdis-\ *n* [ME *dyscant,* fr. AF & ML; AF *descaunt,* fr. ML *discantus,* fr. L *dis-* + *cantus* song — more at CHANT] (14c) **1 a :** a melody or counterpoint sung above the plainsong of the tenor **b :** the art of composing or improvising contrapuntal part music; *also* **:** the music so composed or improvised **c :** SOPRANO, TREBLE **d :** a superimposed counterpoint to a simple melody sung typically by some or all of the sopranos **2 :** discourse or comment on a theme

[2]**des·cant** \ˈdes-ˌkant, des-ˈ, dis-ˈ\ *vi* (15c) **1 :** to sing or play a descant; *broadly* **:** SING **2 :** COMMENT, DISCOURSE

de·scend \di-ˈsend, dē-\ *vb* [ME, fr. AF *descendre,* fr. L *descendere,* fr. *de-* + *scandere* to climb — more at SCAN] *vi* (13c) **1 :** to pass from a higher place or level to a lower one ⟨~*ed* from the platform⟩ **2 :** to pass in discussion from what is logically prior or more comprehensive **3 a :** to originate or come from an ancestral stock or source **:** DERIVE ⟨~*s* from an old merchant family⟩ **b :** to pass by inheritance ⟨a desk that has ~*ed* in the family⟩ **c :** to pass by transmission ⟨songs ~*ed* from old ballads⟩ **4 :** to incline, lead, or extend downward ⟨the road ~*s* to the river⟩ **5 a :** to swoop or pounce down (as in a sudden attack) **b :** to appear suddenly and often disconcertingly as if from above ⟨reporters ~*ed* on the candidate⟩ **6 :** to proceed in a sequence or gradation from higher to lower or from more remote to nearer or more recent **7 a :** to lower oneself in status or dignity **:** STOOP **b :** to worsen and sink in condition or estimation ~ *vt* **1 :** to pass, move, or climb down or down along **2 :** to extend down along — **de·scend·ible** \-ˈsen-də-bəl\ *adj*

[1]**de·scen·dant** *also* **de·scen·dent** \di-ˈsen-dənt\ *adj* [ME *dessendaunte,* fr. AF *descendant,* fr. L *descendent-, descendens,* prp. of *descendere*] (ca. 1555) **1 :** moving or directed downward **2 :** proceeding from an ancestor or source

[2]**descendant** *also* **descendent** *n* [F & L; F *descendant,* fr. LL *descendent-, descendens,* fr. L] (1600) **1 :** one descended from another or from a common stock **2 :** one deriving directly from a precursor or prototype

de·scend·er \di-ˈsen-dər, ˈdē-ˌ\ *n* (1802) **:** the part of a lowercase letter (as p) that descends below the main body of the letter; *also* **:** a letter that has such a part

de·scen·sion \di-ˈsen-chən\ *n* (15c) *archaic* **:** DESCENT 2

de·scent \di-ˈsent\ *n* [ME, fr. AF *descente,* fr. AF *descendre*] (14c) **1 a :** derivation from an ancestor **:** BIRTH, LINEAGE ⟨of French ~⟩ **b :** transmission or devolution of an estate by inheritance usu. in the descending line **c :** the fact or process of originating from an ancestral stock **d :** the shaping or development in nature and character by transmission from a source **:** DERIVATION **2 :** the act or process of descending **3 :** a step downward in a scale of gradation; *specif* **:** one generation in an ancestral line or genealogical scale **4 a :** an inclination downward **:** SLOPE **b :** a descending way (as a downgrade or stairway) **c** *obs* **:** the lowest part **5 a :** ATTACK, INVASION **b :** a sudden disconcerting appearance (as for a visit) **6 :** a downward step (as in station or value) **:** DECLINE ⟨~ of the family to actual poverty⟩

de·scram·ble \(ˌ)dē-ˈskram-bəl\ *vt* (1957) **:** UNSCRAMBLE 2 — **de·scram·bler** \-b(ə-)lər\ *n*

de·scribe \di-ˈskrīb\ *vt* **de·scribed; de·scrib·ing** [ME, fr. L *describere,* fr. *de-* + *scribere* to write — more at SCRIBE] (15c) **1 :** to represent or give an account of in words ⟨~ a picture⟩ **2 :** to represent by a figure, model, or picture **:** DELINEATE **3** *obs* **:** DISTRIBUTE **4 :** to trace or traverse the outline of ⟨~ a circle⟩ **5** *archaic* **:** OBSERVE, PERCEIVE — **de·scrib·able** \-ˈskrī-bə-bəl\ *adj* — **de·scrib·er** *n*

de·scrip·tion \di-ˈskrip-shən\ *n* [ME *descripcioun,* fr. AF & L; AF, fr. L *description-, descriptio,* fr. *describere*] (14c) **1 a :** an act of describing; *specif* **:** discourse intended to give a mental image of something experienced **b :** a descriptive statement or account **2 :** kind or character esp. as determined by salient features ⟨opposed to any tax of so radical a ~⟩ *syn* see TYPE

de·scrip·tive \di-ˈskrip-tiv\ *adj* (1723) **1 :** serving to describe ⟨a ~ account⟩ **2 a :** referring to, constituting, or grounded in matters of observation or experience ⟨the ~ basis of science⟩ **b :** factually grounded or informative rather than normative, prescriptive, or emotive ⟨~ cultural studies⟩ **3** *of a modifier* **a :** expressing the quality, kind, or condition of what is denoted by the modified term ⟨*hot* in "hot water" is a ~ adjective⟩ **b :** NONRESTRICTIVE **4 :** of, relating to, or dealing with the structure of a language at a particular time usu. with exclusion of historical and comparative data ⟨~ linguistics⟩ — **de·scrip·tive·ly** *adv* — **de·scrip·tive·ness** *n*

de·scrip·tor \di-ˈskrip-tər\ *n* (1933) **:** something (as a word or characteristic feature) that serves to describe or identify; *esp* **:** a word or phrase (as an index term) used to identify an item (as a subject or document) in an information retrieval system

[1]**de·scry** \di-ˈskrī\ *vt* **de·scried; de·scry·ing** [ME *descrien* to proclaim, reveal, fr. AF **descrier,* alter. of OF *decrier* — more at DECRY] (14c) **1 a :** to catch sight of ⟨I *descried* a sail —Jonathan Swift⟩ **b :** FIND OUT, DISCOVER **2** *obs* **:** to make known **:** REVEAL

[2]**descry** *n* (1605) *obs* **:** discovery or view from afar

Des·de·mo·na \ˌdez-də-ˈmō-nə\ *n* (ca. 1605) **:** the wife of Othello in Shakespeare's *Othello*

des·e·crate \ˈde-si-ˌkrāt\ *vt* **-crat·ed; -crat·ing** [*de-* + *-secrate* (as in *consecrate*)] (1675) **1 :** to violate the sanctity of **:** PROFANE ⟨~ a shrine⟩ **2 :** to treat disrespectfully, irreverently, or outrageously ⟨the kind of shore development . . . that has *desecrated* so many waterfronts —John Fischer⟩ — **des·e·crat·er** *or* **des·e·cra·tor** \-ˌkrā-tər\ *n*

des·e·cra·tion \ˌde-si-ˈkrā-shən\ *n* (ca. 1717) **:** an act or instance of desecrating **:** the state of being desecrated

de·seg·re·gate \(ˌ)dē-ˈse-gri-ˌgāt\ *vt* (1944) **:** to eliminate segregation in; *specif* **:** to free of any law, provision, or practice requiring isolation of the members of a particular race in separate units ~ *vi* **:** to become desegregated

de·seg·re·ga·tion \(ˌ)dē-ˌse-gri-ˈgā-shən\ *n* (1935) **1 :** the state of being desegregated **2 :** the action or an instance of desegregating

de·se·lect \ˌdē-sə-ˈlekt\ *vt* (1965) **1 :** DISMISS, REJECT **2 :** to cause (something previously selected) to no longer be selected in a software interface ⟨~ the songs you don't want to hear⟩

de·sen·si·tize \(ˌ)dē-ˈsen(t)-sə-ˌtīz\ *vt* (1898) **1 :** to make (a sensitized or hypersensitive individual) insensitive or nonreactive to a sensitizing agent **2 :** to make emotionally insensitive or callous; *specif* **:** to extinguish an emotional response (as of fear, anxiety, or guilt) to stimuli that formerly induced it — **de·sen·si·ti·za·tion** \(ˌ)dē-ˌsen(t)-sə-tə-ˈzā-shən\ *n* — **de·sen·si·tiz·er** \(ˌ)dē-ˈsen-sə-ˌtī-zər\ *n*

[1]**des·ert** \ˈde-zərt\ *n* [ME, fr. AF, fr. LL *desertum,* fr. L, neut. of *desertus,* pp. of *deserere* to desert, fr. *de-* + *serere* to join together — more at SERIES] (13c) **1 a :** arid land with usu. sparse vegetation; *esp* **:** such land having a very warm climate and receiving less than 25 centimeters (10 inches) of sporadic rainfall annually **b :** an area of water apparently devoid of life **2** *archaic* **:** a wild uninhabited and uncultivated tract **3 :** a desolate or forbidding area ⟨lost in a ~ of doubt⟩ — **de·ser·tic** \de-ˈzər-tik\ *adj* — **des·ert·like** \-ˌlīk\ *adj*

[2]**des·ert** \ˈde-zərt\ *adj* (13c) **1 :** desolate and sparsely occupied or unoccupied ⟨a ~ island⟩ **2 :** of or relating to a desert **3** *archaic* **:** FORSAKEN

[3]**de·sert** \di-ˈzərt\ *n* [ME *deserte,* fr. AF, fr. fem. of *desert,* pp. of *deservir* to deserve] (13c) **1 :** the quality or fact of deserving reward or punishment **2 :** deserved reward or punishment — usu. used in plural ⟨got their just ~*s*⟩ **3 :** EXCELLENCE, WORTH

[4]**de·sert** \di-ˈzərt\ *vb* [F *déserter,* fr. LL *desertare,* freq. of L *deserere*] *vt* (1603) **1 :** to withdraw from or leave usu. without intent to return ⟨~ a town⟩ **2 a :** to leave in the lurch ⟨~ a friend in trouble⟩ **b :** to abandon (military service) without leave ~ *vi* **:** to quit one's post, allegiance, or service without leave or justification; *esp* **:** to abandon military duty without leave and without intent to return *syn* see ABANDON — **de·sert·er** *n*

de·sert·i·fi·ca·tion \di-ˌzər-tə-fə-ˈkā-shən\ *n* (1974) **:** the process of becoming desert (as from land mismanagement or climate change) — **de·sert·i·fy** \-ˈzər-tə-ˌfī\ *vt*

de·ser·tion \di-ˈzər-shən\ *n* (1591) **1 :** an act of deserting; *esp* **:** the abandonment without consent or legal justification of a person, post, or relationship and the associated duties and obligations ⟨sued for divorce on grounds of ~⟩ **2 :** a state of being deserted or forsaken

desert locust *n* (1944) **:** a destructive migratory locust (*Schistocerca gregaria*) of southwestern Asia and parts of northern Africa

desert soil *n* (ca. 1938) **:** a soil that develops under sparse shrub vegetation in warm to cool arid climates with a light-colored surface soil usu. underlain by calcareous material and a hardpan layer

desert tortoise *n* (1933) **:** a large burrowing land tortoise (*Gopherus agassizii*) of arid regions of the southwestern U.S. and adjacent Mexico

desert varnish *n* (ca. 1898) **:** a dark coating which is found on rocks after long exposure in desert regions and whose color is due to iron and manganese oxides

de·serve \di-ˈzərv\ *vb* **de·served; de·serv·ing** [ME, fr. AF *deservir,* fr. L *deservire* to devote oneself to, fr. *de-* + *servire* to serve] *vt* (13c) **:** to be worthy of **:** MERIT ⟨~*s* another chance⟩ ~ *vi* **:** to be worthy, fit, or suitable for some reward or requital ⟨have become recognized as they ~ —T. S. Eliot⟩ — **de·serv·er** *n*

de·served \-ˈzərvd\ *adj* (ca. 1552) **:** of, relating to, or being that which one deserves ⟨a ~ reputation⟩ — **de·served·ly** \-ˈzər-vəd-lē, -ˈzərvd-lē\ *adv* — **de·served·ness** \-ˈzər-vəd-nəs, -ˈzərvd-nəs\ *n*

[1]**de·serv·ing** \-ˈzər-viŋ\ *n* (14c) **:** DESERT, MERIT ⟨reward the proud according to their ~*s* —Charles Kingsley⟩

[2]**deserving** *adj* (1549) **:** MERITORIOUS, WORTHY; *esp* **:** meriting financial aid ⟨scholarships for ~ students⟩

de·sex \(ˌ)dē-ˈseks\ *vt* (1911) **1 :** CASTRATE, SPAY **2 :** to eliminate perceived sexism from ⟨~ the language of church Bible study programs —R. M. Harley⟩ **3 :** DESEXUALIZE 2

de·sex·u·al·ize \(ˌ)dē-ˈsek-sh(ə-)wə-ˌlīz, -ˈsek-shə-ˌlīz, -ˈsek-shü-ə-\ *vt* (1894) **1 :** to deprive of sexual characters or power **2 :** to divest of sexual quality — **de·sex·u·al·i·za·tion** \(ˌ)dē-ˌsek-sh(ə-)wə-lə-ˈzā-shən, -ˌsek-shə-lə-, -ˌsek-shü-ə-\ *n*

deshabille *var of* DISHABILLE

des·ic·cant \ˈde-si-kənt\ *n* (1676) **:** a drying agent (as calcium chloride)

des·ic·cate \ˈde-si-ˌkāt\ *vb* **-cat·ed; -cat·ing** [L *desiccatus,* pp. of *desiccare* to dry up, fr. *de-* + *siccare* to dry, fr. *siccus* dry — more at SACK] *vt* (1575) **1 :** to dry up **2 :** to preserve (a food) by drying **:** DEHYDRATE **3 :** to drain of emotional or intellectual vitality ~ *vi* **:** to become dried up — **des·ic·ca·tion** \ˌde-si-ˈkā-shən\ *n* — **de·sic·ca·tive** \ˈde-si-ˌkā-tiv\ *adj* — **des·ic·ca·tor** \ˈde-si-ˌkā-tər\ *n*

de·sid·er·ate \di-ˈsi-də-ˌrāt, -ˈzi-\ *vt* **-at·ed; -at·ing** [L *desideratus,* pp. of *desiderare* to desire — more at DESIRE] (1645) **:** to entertain or express a wish to have or attain — **de·sid·er·a·tion** \-ˌsi-də-ˈrā-shən, -ˌzi-\ *n* — **de·sid·er·a·tive** \-ˈsi-də-ˌrā-tiv, -ˈsi-d(ə-)rət-, -ˈzi-\ *adj*

de·sid·er·a·tum \di-ˌsi-də-ˈrä-təm, -ˌzi-, -ˈrā-\ *n, pl* **-ta** \-tə\ [L, neut. of *desideratus*] (1652) **:** something desired as essential

[1]**de·sign** \di-ˈzīn\ *vb* [ME, to outline, indicate, mean, fr. AF & ML; AF *designer* to designate, fr. ML *designare,* fr. L, to mark out, fr. *de-* + *signare* to mark — more at SIGN] *vt* (14c) **1 :** to create, fashion, execute, or construct according to plan **:** DEVISE, CONTRIVE **2 a :** to conceive and plan out in the mind ⟨he *~ed* the perfect crime⟩ **b :** to have as a purpose **:** INTEND ⟨she *~ed* to excel in her studies⟩ **c :** to devise for a specific function or end ⟨a book *~ed* primarily as a college textbook⟩ **3** *archaic* **:** to indicate with a distinctive mark, sign, or name **4 a :** to make a drawing, pattern, or sketch of **b :** to draw the plans for ⟨~ a building⟩ ~ *vi* **1 :** to conceive or execute a plan **2 :** to draw, lay out, or prepare a design — **de·sign·ed·ly** \-ˈzī-nəd-lē\ *adv*

[2]**design** *n* (1569) **1 a :** a particular purpose held in view by an individual or group ⟨he has ambitious *~s* for his son⟩ **b :** deliberate purposive planning ⟨more by accident than ~⟩ **2 :** a mental project or scheme in which means to an end are laid down **3 a :** a deliberate undercover project or scheme **:** PLOT **b** *pl* **:** aggressive or evil intent — used with *on* or *against* ⟨he has *~s* on the money⟩ **4 :** a preliminary sketch or outline showing the main features of something to be executed ⟨the ~ for the new stadium⟩ **5 a :** an underlying scheme that governs functioning, developing, or unfolding **:** PATTERN, MOTIF ⟨the general ~ of the epic⟩ **b :** a plan or protocol for carrying out or accomplishing something (as a scientific experiment); *also* **:** the process of preparing this **6 :** the arrangement of elements or details in a product or work of art **7 :** a decorative pattern ⟨a floral ~⟩ **8 :** the creative art of executing aesthetic or functional designs ***syn*** see INTENTION, PLAN

[1]**des·ig·nate** \ˈde-zig-ˌnāt, -nət\ *adj* [L *designatus,* pp. of *designare*] (1629) **:** chosen but not yet installed ⟨ambassador ~⟩

[2]**des·ig·nate** \-ˌnāt\ *vt* **-nat·ed; -nat·ing** (1639) **1 :** to indicate and set apart for a specific purpose, office, or duty ⟨~ a group to prepare a plan⟩ **2 a :** to point out the location of ⟨a marker *designating* the battle⟩ **b :** to distinguish as to class ⟨the area we ~ as that of spiritual values —J. B. Conant⟩ **c :** SPECIFY, STIPULATE ⟨to be sent by a *designated* shipper⟩ **3 :** DENOTE ⟨associate names with the people they ~⟩ **4 :** to call by a distinctive title, term, or expression ⟨a particle *designated* the neutron⟩ — **des·ig·na·tive** \-ˌnā-tiv\ *adj* — **des·ig·na·tor** \-ˌnā-tər\ *n* — **des·ig·na·to·ry** \-nə-ˌtȯr-ē\ *adj*

designated driver *n* (1982) **:** a person chosen to abstain from intoxicants (as alcohol) so as to transport others safely who are not abstaining

designated hitter *n* (1973) **1 :** a baseball player designated at the start of the game to bat in place of the pitcher without causing the pitcher to be removed from the game **2 :** REPRESENTATIVE, SUBSTITUTE

des·ig·na·tion \ˌde-zig-ˈnā-shən\ *n* (14c) **1 :** the act of indicating or identifying **2 :** appointment to or selection for an office, post, or service **3 :** a distinguishing name, sign, or title **4 :** the relation between a sign and the thing signified

des·ig·nee \ˌde-zig-ˈnē\ *n* (1925) **:** one that is designated

[1]**de·sign·er** \di-ˈzī-nər\ *n* (1662) **:** one that designs: as **a :** one who creates and often executes plans for a project or structure ⟨urban *~s*⟩ ⟨a theater set ~⟩ **b :** one that creates and manufactures a new product style or design; *esp* **:** one who designs and manufactures high-fashion clothing ⟨the *~'s* new fall line⟩

[2]**designer** *adj* (1966) **1 :** of, relating to, or produced by a designer ⟨~ wallpaper⟩ ⟨wearing a ~ original⟩; *also* **:** displaying the name, signature, or logo of a designer or manufacturer ⟨~ jeans⟩ **2 :** intended to reflect the latest in sophisticated taste or fashion ⟨~ ice cream⟩ ⟨a ~ haircut⟩ **3 :** modified artificially (as by genetic engineering) to fulfill individual specifications or meet a need ⟨~ foods⟩ ⟨~ estrogens⟩

designer drug *n* (1983) **:** a synthetic version of a controlled substance (as heroin) that is produced with a slightly altered molecular structure to avoid having it classified as an illicit drug

de·sign·ing \di-ˈzī-niŋ\ *adj* (1653) **1 :** practicing forethought **2 :** CRAFTY, SCHEMING ⟨falling into the snares of a ~ enemy —Charles Dickens⟩

de·sign·ment \di-ˈzīn-mənt\ *n* (1583) *obs* **:** PLAN, PURPOSE

de·sip·ra·mine \də-ˈzi-prə-ˌmēn\ *n* [*des*methyl (fr. *des-* + *methyl*) + *imipramine*] (1965) **:** a tricyclic antidepressant $C_{18}H_{22}N_2$

de·sir·abil·i·ty \di-ˌzī-rə-ˈbi-lə-tē\ *n, pl* **-ties** (1824) **1** *pl* **:** desirable conditions ⟨had understood and studied certain *desirabilities* —D. D. Eisenhower⟩ **2 :** the quality, fact, or degree of being desirable

[1]**de·sir·able** \di-ˈzī-rə-bəl\ *adj* (14c) **1 :** having pleasing qualities or properties **:** ATTRACTIVE ⟨a ~ woman⟩ **2 :** worth seeking or doing as advantageous, beneficial, or wise **:** ADVISABLE ⟨~ legislation⟩ — **de·sir·able·ness** *n* — **de·sir·ably** \-blē\ *adv*

[2]**desirable** *n* (1645) **:** one that is desirable

[1]**de·sire** \di-ˈzī(-ə)r, dē-\ *vb* **de·sired; de·sir·ing** [ME, fr. AF *desirer,* fr. L *desiderare,* fr. *de-* + *sider-, sidus* heavenly body] *vt* (13c) **1 :** to long or hope for **:** exhibit or feel desire for ⟨~ success⟩ **2 a :** to express a wish for **:** REQUEST ⟨they ~ an immediate answer⟩ **b** *archaic* **:** to express a wish to **:** ASK **3** *obs* **:** INVITE **4** *archaic* **:** to feel the loss of ~ *vi* **:** to have or feel desire

syn DESIRE, WISH, WANT, CRAVE, COVET mean to have a longing for. DESIRE stresses the strength of feeling and often implies strong intention or aim ⟨*desires* to start a new life⟩. WISH sometimes implies a general or transient longing esp. for the unattainable ⟨*wishes* for permanent world peace⟩. WANT specif. suggests a felt need or lack ⟨*wants* to have a family⟩. CRAVE stresses the force of physical appetite or emotional need ⟨*craves* sweets⟩. COVET implies strong envious desire ⟨*covets* his rise to fame⟩.

[2]**desire** *n* (14c) **1 :** conscious impulse toward something that promises enjoyment or satisfaction in its attainment **2 a :** LONGING, CRAVING **b :** sexual urge or appetite **3 :** a usu. formal request or petition for some action **4 :** something desired

de·sir·ous \di-ˈzī(-ə)r-əs\ *adj* (14c) **:** impelled or governed by desire ⟨~ of fame⟩ — **de·sir·ous·ly** *adv* — **de·sir·ous·ness** *n*

de·sist \di-ˈsist, -ˈzist, dē-\ *vi* [ME, fr. AF *desister,* fr. L *desistere,* fr. *de-* + *sistere* to stand, stop; akin to L *stare* to stand — more at STAND] (15c) **:** to cease to proceed or act ***syn*** see STOP — **de·sis·tance** \-ˈsis-tən(t)s, -ˈzis-\ *n*

desk \ˈdesk\ *n* [ME *deske,* fr. ML *desca,* modif. of OIt *desco* table, fr. L *discus* dish, disc — more at DISH] (14c) **1 a :** a table, frame, or case with a sloping or horizontal surface esp. for writing and reading and often with drawers, compartments, and pigeonholes **b :** a reading table or lectern from which a liturgical service is read **c :** a table, counter, stand, or booth at which a person works **2 a :** a division of an organization specializing in a particular phase of activity ⟨the Russian ~ in the Department of State⟩ **b :** a seating position according to rank in an orchestra ⟨a first-*desk* violinist⟩

desk·bound \ˈdesk-ˌbau̇nd\ *adj* (1944) **:** restricted to work at a desk

de–skill \ˌdē-ˈskil\ *vt* (1941) **1 :** to reduce the level of skill needed for (a job) **2 :** to reduce the level of skill needed for a job by (a worker)

desk jockey *n* (1980) **:** a person whose job involves working at a desk

desk·man \ˈdesk-ˌman, -mən\ *n* (1913) **:** a person who works at a desk; *specif* **:** a newspaperman who processes news and prepares copy

[1]**desk·top** \ˈdesk-ˌtäp\ *n* (1925) **1 :** the top of a desk; *also* **:** an area or window on a computer screen in which icons are arranged in a manner analogous to objects on top of a desk **2 :** a desktop computer

[2]**desktop** *adj* (1958) **:** of a size that can be conveniently used on a desk or table ⟨~ computers⟩ — compare LAPTOP

desktop publishing *n* (1984) **:** the production of printed matter by means of a desktop computer having a layout program that integrates text and graphics

desm- *or* **desmo-** *comb form* [NL, fr. Gk, fr. *desmos,* fr. *dein* to bind — more at DIADEM] **:** bond **:** ligament ⟨*desmo*some⟩

des·mid \ˈdez-məd\ *n* [ultim. fr. Gk *desmos*] (1862) **:** any of numerous unicellular or colonial green algae (order Zygnematales, esp. family Desmidiaceae)

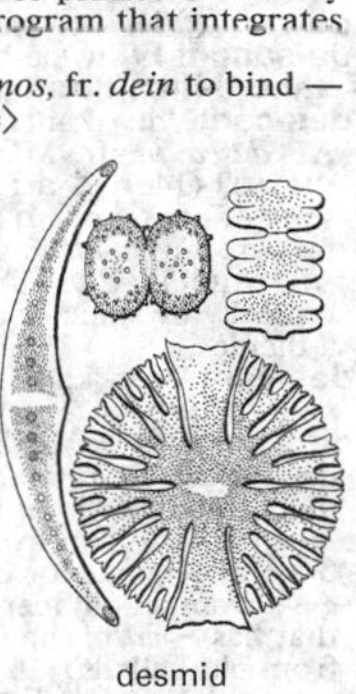
desmid

des·mo·some \ˈdez-mə-ˌsōm\ *n* (ca. 1932) **:** a specialized structure of the cell membrane esp. of an epithelial cell that serves as a zone of adhesion to anchor contiguous cells together — **des·mo·som·al** \-ˌsō-məl\ *adj*

[1]**des·o·late** \ˈde-sə-lət, ˈde-zə-\ *adj* [ME *desolat,* fr. L *desolatus,* pp. of *desolare* to abandon, fr. *de-* + *solus* alone] (14c) **1 :** devoid of inhabitants and visitors **:** DESERTED **2 :** joyless, disconsolate, and sorrowful through or as if through separation from a loved one ⟨a ~ widow⟩ **3 a :** showing the effects of abandonment and neglect **:** DILAPIDATED ⟨a ~ old house⟩ **b :** BARREN, LIFELESS ⟨a ~ landscape⟩ **c :** devoid of warmth, comfort, or hope **:** GLOOMY ⟨~ memories⟩ ***syn*** see ALONE, DISMAL — **des·o·late·ly** *adv* — **des·o·late·ness** *n*

[2]**des·o·late** \-ˌlāt\ *vt* **-lat·ed; -lat·ing** (14c) **:** to make desolate: **a :** to deprive of inhabitants **b :** to lay waste **c :** FORSAKE **d :** to make wretched — **des·o·lat·er** *or* **des·o·la·tor** \-ˌlā-tər\ *n* — **des·o·lat·ing·ly** \-ˌlā-tiŋ-lē\ *adv*

des·o·la·tion \ˌde-sə-ˈlā-shən, ˌde-zə-\ *n* (14c) **1 :** the action of desolating **2 a :** GRIEF, SADNESS **b :** LONELINESS **3 :** DEVASTATION, RUIN ⟨a scene of utter ~⟩ **4 :** barren wasteland

de·sorb \(ˌ)dē-ˈsȯrb, -ˈzȯrb\ *vt* (1924) **:** to remove (a sorbed substance) by the reverse of adsorption or absorption

de·sorp·tion \-ˈsȯrp-shən, -ˈzȯrp-\ *n* (1924) **:** the process of desorbing

desoxy- — see DEOXY-

des·oxy·ri·bo·nu·cle·ic acid \de-ˌzäk-sē-ˈrī-bō-n(y)u̇-ˌklē-ik-, -ˌklā-\ *n* (1931) **:** DNA

[1]**de·spair** \di-ˈsper\ *vb* [ME *despeiren,* fr. AF *desperer,* fr. L *desperare,* fr. *de-* + *sperare* to hope; akin to L *spes* hope — more at SPEED] *vi* (14c) **:** to lose all hope or confidence ⟨~ of winning⟩ ~ *vt, obs* **:** to lose hope for — **de·spair·er** *n*

[2]**despair** *n* (14c) **1 :** utter loss of hope ⟨a cry of ~⟩ ⟨gave up in ~⟩ **2 :** a cause of hopelessness ⟨an incorrigible child is the ~ of his parents⟩

de·spair·ing *adj* (1589) **:** given to, arising from, or marked by despair **:** devoid of hope ***syn*** see DESPONDENT — **de·spair·ing·ly** \-iŋ-lē\ *adv*

des·patch *chiefly Brit var of* DISPATCH

des·per·a·do \ˌdes-pə-ˈrä-(ˌ)dō, -ˈrā-\ *n, pl* **-does** *or* **-dos** [prob. alter. of obs. *desperate* desperado, fr. *desperate,* adj.] (1647) **:** a bold or violent criminal; *esp* **:** a bandit of the western U.S. in the 19th century

des·per·ate \ˈdes-p(ə-)rət, -pərt\ *adj* [L *desperatus,* pp. of *desperare*] (15c) **1 a :** having lost hope ⟨a ~ spirit crying for relief⟩ **b :** giving no ground for hope ⟨the outlook was ~⟩ **2 a :** moved by despair ⟨victims made ~ by abuse⟩ **b :** involving or employing extreme measures in an attempt to escape defeat or frustration ⟨made a ~ leap for the rope⟩ **3 :** suffering extreme need or anxiety ⟨~ for money⟩ **4 :** involving extreme danger or possible disaster ⟨a ~ situation⟩ **5 :** of extreme intensity **6 :** SHOCKING, OUTRAGEOUS ***syn*** see DESPONDENT — **des·per·ate·ness** *n*

des·per·ate·ly \ˈdes-p(ə-)rət-lē, -pərt-\ *adv* (ca. 1547) **1 :** in a desperate manner ⟨struggling ~⟩ **2 :** EXTREMELY, TERRIBLY ⟨~ tired⟩ ⟨~ important⟩

des·per·a·tion \ˌdes-pə-ˈrā-shən\ *n* (14c) **1 :** loss of hope and surrender to despair **2 :** a state of hopelessness leading to rashness

de·spi·ca·ble \di-ˈspi-kə-bəl, ˈdes-(ˌ)pi-\ *adj* [LL *despicabilis,* fr. L *despicari* to despise] (1553) **:** deserving to be despised **:** so worthless or obnoxious as to rouse moral indignation ⟨~ behavior⟩ ***syn*** see CONTEMPTIBLE — **de·spi·ca·ble·ness** *n* — **de·spi·ca·bly** \-blē\ *adv*

de·spir·i·tu·al·ize \(ˌ)dē-ˈspi-ri-ch(ə-)wə-ˌlīz, -chə-ˌlīz, -chü-ə-\ *vt* (1840) **:** to deprive of spiritual character or influence

de·spise \di-ˈspīz\ *vt* **de·spised; de·spis·ing** [ME, fr. AF *despis-,* stem of *despire,* fr. L *despicere,* fr. *de-* + *specere* to look — more at SPY] (14c) **1 :** to look down on with contempt or aversion ⟨*despised* the weak⟩ **2 :** to regard as negligible, worthless, or distasteful — **de·spise·ment** \-ˈspīz-mənt\ *n* — **de·spis·er** \-ˈspī-zər\ *n*

syn DESPISE, CONTEMN, SCORN, DISDAIN mean to regard as unworthy of one's notice or consideration. DESPISE may suggest an emotional response ranging from strong dislike to loathing ⟨*despises* cowards⟩.

CONTEMN implies a vehement condemnation of a person or thing as low, vile, feeble, or ignominious ⟨*contemns* the image of women promoted by advertisers⟩. SCORN implies a ready or indignant contempt ⟨*scorns* the very thought of retirement⟩. DISDAIN implies an arrogant or supercilious aversion to what is regarded as unworthy ⟨*disdained* popular music⟩.

[1]**de·spite** \di-ˈspīt\ *n* [ME, fr. AF *despit,* fr. L *despectus,* fr. *despicere*] (13c) **1 :** the feeling or attitude of despising : CONTEMPT **2 :** MALICE, SPITE **3 a :** an act showing contempt or defiance **b :** DETRIMENT, DISADVANTAGE ⟨I know of no government which stands to its obligations, even in its own ~, more solidly —Sir Winston Churchill⟩ — **in despite of :** in spite of

[2]**despite** *vt* **de·spit·ed; de·spit·ing** (14c) **1** *archaic* **:** to treat with contempt **2** *obs* **:** to provoke to anger : VEX

[3]**despite** *prep* (15c) **:** in spite of ⟨played ~ an injury⟩

de·spite·ful \di-ˈspīt-fəl\ *adj* (15c) **:** expressing malice or hate — **de·spite·ful·ly** \-fə-lē\ *adv* — **de·spite·ful·ness** *n*

de·spit·eous \di-ˈspi-tē-əs\ *adj* (14c) *archaic* **:** feeling or showing despite : MALICIOUS — **de·spit·eous·ly** *adv, archaic*

de·spoil \di-ˈspȯi(-ə)l\ *vt* [ME *despoylen,* fr. AF *despoiller,* fr. L *despoliare,* fr. *de-* + *spoliare* to strip, rob — more at SPOIL] (14c) **:** to strip of belongings, possessions, or value : PILLAGE ***syn*** see RAVAGE — **despoil·er** *n* — **de·spoil·ment** \-mənt\ *n*

de·spo·li·a·tion \di-ˌspō-lē-ˈā-shən\ *n* [LL *despoliation-, despoliatio,* fr. *despoliare*] (ca. 1657) **:** the action or process of despoiling : SPOLIATION

[1]**de·spond** \di-ˈspänd\ *vi* [L *despondēre,* fr. *de-* + *spondēre* to promise solemnly — more at SPOUSE] (1655) **:** to become despondent

[2]**despond** *n* (1678) **:** DESPONDENCY

de·spon·dence \di-ˈspän-dən(t)s\ *n* (1657) **:** DESPONDENCY

de·spon·den·cy \-dən-sē\ *n* (1653) **:** the state of being despondent : DEJECTION, HOPELESSNESS

de·spon·dent \-dənt\ *adj* [L *despondent-, despondens,* prp. of *despondēre*] (ca. 1699) **:** feeling or showing extreme discouragement, dejection, or depression ⟨~ about his health⟩ — **de·spon·dent·ly** *adv*

syn DESPONDENT, DESPAIRING, DESPERATE, HOPELESS mean having lost all or nearly all hope. DESPONDENT implies a deep dejection arising from a conviction of the uselessness of further effort ⟨*despondent* about yet another rejection⟩. DESPAIRING suggests the slipping away of all hope and often despondency ⟨*despairing* appeals for the return of the kidnapped child⟩. DESPERATE implies despair that prompts reckless action or violence in the face of defeat or frustration ⟨one last *desperate* attempt to turn the tide of battle⟩. HOPELESS suggests despair and the cessation of effort or resistance and often implies acceptance or resignation ⟨the situation of the trapped miners is *hopeless*⟩.

des·pot \ˈdes-pət, -ˌpät\ *n* [MF *despote,* fr. Gk *despotēs* master, lord, autocrat, fr. *des-* (akin to *domos* house) + *-potēs* (akin to *posis* husband); akin to Skt *dampati* lord of the house — more at DOME, POTENT] (1585) **1 a :** a Byzantine emperor or prince **b :** a bishop or patriarch of the Eastern Orthodox Church **c :** an Italian hereditary prince or military leader during the Renaissance **2 a :** a ruler with absolute power and authority **b :** a person exercising power tyrannically

des·pot·ic \des-ˈpä-tik, dis-\ *adj* (1604) **:** of, relating to, or characteristic of a despot — **des·pot·i·cal·ly** \-ti-k(ə-)lē\ *adv*

des·po·tism \ˈdes-pə-ˌti-zəm\ *n* (ca. 1727) **1 a :** rule by a despot **b :** despotic exercise of power **2 a :** a system of government in which the ruler has unlimited power : ABSOLUTISM **b :** a despotic state

des·qua·mate \ˈdes-kwə-ˌmāt\ *vi* **-mat·ed; -mat·ing** [L *desquamatus,* pp. of *desquamare* to scale, fr. *de-* + *squama* scale] (1828) **:** to peel off in scales — **des·qua·ma·tion** \ˌdes-kwə-ˈmā-shən\ *n*

des·sert \di-ˈzərt\ *n* [MF, fr. *desservir* to clear the table, fr. *des-* de- + *servir* to serve, fr. L *servire*] (1600) **1 :** a usu. sweet course or dish (as of pastry or ice cream) usu. served at the end of a meal **2** *Brit* **:** a fresh fruit served after a sweet course

des·sert·spoon \-ˌspün\ *n* (1754) **1 :** a spoon intermediate in size between a teaspoon and a tablespoon for use in eating dessert **2 :** DESSERTSPOONFUL

des·sert·spoon·ful \di-ˈzərt-ˌspün-ˌfu̇l\ *n* (1839) **1 :** as much as a dessertspoon will hold **2** *chiefly Brit* **:** a unit of measure equal to about 2½ fluid drams

dessert wine *n* (1773) **:** a usu. sweet wine typically served with dessert or afterward

de·sta·bi·lize \(ˌ)dē-ˈstā-bə-ˌlīz\ *vt* (1924) **1 :** to make unstable **2 :** to cause (as a government) to be incapable of functioning or surviving — **de·sta·bi·li·za·tion** \(ˌ)dē-ˌstā-bə-lə-ˈzā-shən\ *n*

de·stain \(ˌ)dē-ˈstān\ *vt* (1927) **:** to selectively remove stain from (a specimen for microscopic study)

de–Sta·lin·i·za·tion \(ˌ)dē-ˌstä-lə-nə-ˈzā-shən, -ˌsta-\ *n* (1951) **:** the discrediting of Stalin and his policies

de·stig·ma·tize \(ˌ)dē-ˈstig-mə-ˌtīz\ *vt* (1973) **:** to remove associations of shame or disgrace from ⟨~ mental illness⟩

de Stijl \də-ˈstī(-ə)l, -ˈstāl\ *n* [D *De Stijl,* lit., the style, magazine published by members of the school] (1917) **:** a school of art founded in Holland in 1917 typically using rectangular forms and the primary colors plus black and white and asymmetric balance

des·ti·na·tion \ˌdes-tə-ˈnā-shən\ *n* (14c) **1 :** the purpose for which something is destined **2 :** an act of appointing, setting aside for a purpose, or predetermining **3 :** a place to which one is journeying or to which something is sent ⟨kept their ~ secret⟩ **4 :** a place worthy of travel or an extended visit — often used attributively ⟨a ~ restaurant⟩ ⟨a ~ resort⟩

des·tine \ˈdes-tən\ *vt* **des·tined; des·tin·ing** [ME, fr. AF *destiner,* fr. L *destinare,* fr. *de-* + *-stinare* (akin to L *stare* to stand) — more at STAND] (14c) **1 :** to decree beforehand : PREDETERMINE **2 a :** to designate, assign, or dedicate in advance ⟨the younger son was *destined* for the priesthood⟩ ⟨a trait that ~*s* them to failure⟩ **b :** to direct, devise, or set apart for a specific purpose or place ⟨freight *destined* for European ports⟩

des·ti·ny \ˈdes-tə-nē\ *n, pl* **-nies** [ME *destineé,* fr. AF, fr. fem. of *destiné,* pp. of *destiner*] (14c) **1 :** something to which a person or thing is destined : FORTUNE ⟨wants to control his own ~⟩ **2 :** a predetermined course of events often held to be an irresistible power or agency ***syn*** see FATE

des·ti·tute \ˈdes-tə-ˌtüt, -ˌt(y)üt\ *adj* [ME, fr. L *destitutus,* pp. of *destituere* to abandon, deprive, fr. *de-* + *statuere* to set up — more at STATUTE] (14c) **1 :** lacking something needed or desirable ⟨a lake ~ of fish⟩ **2 :** lacking possessions and resources; *esp* **:** suffering extreme poverty ⟨a ~ old man⟩ — **des·ti·tute·ness** *n*

des·ti·tu·tion \ˌdes-tə-ˈtü-shən, -ˈtyü-\ *n* (15c) **:** the state of being destitute; *esp* **:** such extreme want as threatens life unless relieved ***syn*** see POVERTY

de–stress \ˈdē-ˈstres\ *vi* (1979) **:** to release bodily or mental tension : UNWIND

des·trier \ˈdes-trē-ər, də-ˈstrir\ *n* [ME, fr. AF *destrer, destrier,* fr. *destre* right hand, fr. L *dextra,* fr. fem. of *dexter*] (14c) *archaic* **:** WARHORSE; *also* **:** a charger used esp. in medieval tournaments

de·stroy \di-ˈstrȯi, dē-\ *vb* [ME, fr. AF *destroy-, destrui-,* stem of *destrure,* fr. VL **destrugere,* alter. of L *destruere,* fr. *de-* + *struere* to build — more at STRUCTURE] *vt* (13c) **1 :** to ruin the structure, organic existence, or condition of ⟨~*ed* the files⟩; *also* **:** to ruin as if by tearing to shreds ⟨their reputation was ~*ed*⟩ **2 a :** to put out of existence : KILL ⟨~ an injured horse⟩ **b :** NEUTRALIZE ⟨the moon ~*s* the light of the stars⟩ **c :** ANNIHILATE, VANQUISH ⟨armies had been crippled but not ~*ed* —W. L. Shirer⟩ ~ *vi* **:** to cause destruction

de·stroy·er \di-ˈstrȯi(-ə)r, dē-\ *n* (14c) **1 :** one that destroys **2 :** a small fast warship used esp. to support larger vessels and usu. armed with guns, depth charges, torpedoes, and often guided missiles

destroyer escort *n* (1924) **:** a warship similar to but smaller than a destroyer

destroying angel *n* (ca. 1900) **:** any of several very poisonous pure white amanita mushrooms (as *Amanita verna* or *A. virosa*) : DEATH CAP

de·struc·ti·ble \di-ˈstrək-tə-bəl\ *adj* (ca. 1755) **:** capable of being destroyed — **de·struc·ti·bil·i·ty** \di-ˌstrək-tə-ˈbi-lə-tē\ *n*

de·struc·tion \di-ˈstrək-shən\ *n* [ME *destruccioun,* fr. AF *destruction,* fr. L *destruction-, destructio,* fr. *destruere*] (14c) **1 :** the state or fact of being destroyed : RUIN **2 :** the action or process of destroying something **3 :** a destroying agency

de·struc·tion·ist \-sh(ə-)nəst\ *n* (1833) **:** one who delights in or advocates destruction

de·struc·tive \di-ˈstrək-tiv\ *adj* (15c) **1 :** causing destruction : RUINOUS ⟨~ storm⟩ **2 :** designed or tending to hurt or destroy ⟨~ criticism⟩ — **de·struc·tive·ly** *adv* — **de·struc·tive·ness** *n*

destructive distillation *n* (ca. 1831) **:** decomposition of a substance (as wood, coal, or oil) by heat in a closed container and collection of the volatile products produced

de·struc·tiv·i·ty \di-ˌstrək-ˈti-və-tē, ˌdē-\ *n* (1902) **:** capacity for destruction

de·sue·tude \ˈde-swi-ˌtüd, -ˌtyüd, di-ˈsü-ə-, -ˈsyü-\ *n* [ME *dissuetude,* fr. L *desuetudo,* fr. *desuescere* to become unaccustomed, fr. *de-* + *suescere* to become accustomed; akin to L *sodalis* comrade — more at SIB] (15c) **:** discontinuance from use or exercise : DISUSE

de·sul·fur·i·za·tion \(ˌ)dē-ˌsəl-fər-ə-ˈzā-shən\ *n* (1854) **:** the removal of sulfur or sulfur compounds (as from coal or flue gas) — **de·sul·fur·ize** \(ˌ)dē-ˈsəl-fər-ˌīz\ *vt*

des·ul·to·ry \ˈde-səl-ˌtȯr-ē *also* -zəl-\ *adj* [L *desultorius,* lit., of a circus rider who leaps from horse to horse, fr. *desilire* to leap down, fr. *de-* + *salire* to leap — more at SALLY] (1581) **1 :** marked by lack of definite plan, regularity, or purpose ⟨a dragged-out ordeal of . . . ~ shopping —Herman Wouk⟩ **2 :** not connected with the main subject **3 :** disappointing in progress, performance, or quality ⟨a ~ fifth place finish⟩ ⟨a ~ wine⟩ — **des·ul·to·ri·ly** \ˌde-səl-ˈtȯr-ə-lē\ *adv* — **des·ul·to·ri·ness** \ˈde-səl-ˌtȯr-ē-nəs\ *n*

det *abbr* **1** detached; detachment **2** detail **3** determine

de·tach \di-ˈtach, dē-\ *vt* [F *détacher,* fr. OF *destachier,* fr. *des-* de- + *-tachier* (as in *atachier* to attach)] (1686) **1 :** to separate esp. from a larger mass and usu. without violence or damage **2 :** DISENGAGE, WITHDRAW — **de·tach·abil·i·ty** \-ˌta-chə-ˈbi-lə-tē\ *n* — **de·tach·able** \-ˈta-chə-bəl\ *adj* — **de·tach·ably** \-blē\ *adv*

de·tached \di-ˈtacht, dē-\ *adj* (ca. 1706) **1 :** standing by itself : SEPARATE, UNCONNECTED; *esp* **:** not sharing any wall with another building ⟨a ~ house⟩ **2 :** exhibiting an aloof objectivity usu. free from prejudice or self-interest ⟨a ~ observer⟩ ***syn*** see INDIFFERENT — **de·tached·ly** \-ˈta-chəd-lē, -ˈtacht-lē\ *adv* — **de·tached·ness** \-ˈta-chəd-nəs, -ˈtacht-nəs\ *n*

detached service *n* (1835) **:** military service away from one's assigned organization

de·tach·ment \di-ˈtach-mənt, dē-\ *n* (1669) **1 :** the action or process of detaching : SEPARATION **2 a :** the dispatch of a body of troops or part of a fleet from the main body for a special mission or service **b :** the part so dispatched **c :** a permanently organized separate unit usu. smaller than a platoon and of special composition **3 a :** indifference to worldly concerns : ALOOFNESS **b :** freedom from bias or prejudice

[1]**de·tail** \di-ˈtāl, ˈdē-ˌtāl\ *n* [F *détail,* fr. OF *detail* slice, piece, fr. *detaillier* to cut in pieces, fr. *de-* + *taillier* to cut — more at TAILOR] (1603) **1 :** extended treatment of or attention to particular items **2 :** a part of a whole: as **a :** a small and subordinate part : PARTICULAR; *also* **:** a reproduction of such a part of a work of art **b :** a part considered or requiring to be considered separately from the whole **c :** the small elements that collectively constitute a work of art **d :** the small elements of a photographic image corresponding to those of the subject **3 a :** selection of a person or group for a particular task (as in military service) **b (1) :** the person or group selected **(2) :** the task to be performed ***syn*** see ITEM — **in detail :** with all the particulars ⟨explained the job *in detail*⟩

[2]**detail** *vt* (1650) **1 :** to report minutely and distinctly : SPECIFY ⟨~*ed* their grievances⟩ **2 :** to assign to a particular task **3 :** to furnish with the smaller elements of design and finish ⟨trimmings that ~ slips and petticoats⟩ **4 :** to clean and refurbish (a vehicle) very thoroughly and meticulously ⟨~ a car⟩ ~ *vi* **:** to make detail drawings — **de·tail·er** *n*

\ə\ **abut** \ᵊ\ **kitten, F table** \ər\ **further** \a\ **ash** \ā\ **ace** \ä\ **mop, mar** \au̇\ **out** \ch\ **chin** \e\ **bet** \ē\ **easy** \g\ **go** \i\ **hit** \ī\ **ice** \j\ **job** \ŋ\ **sing** \ō\ **go** \ȯ\ **law** \ȯi\ **boy** \th\ **thin** \t͟h\ **the** \ü\ **loot** \u̇\ **foot** \y\ **yet** \zh\ **vision, beige** \k̲, ⁿ, œ, ue, ʸ\ *see* Guide to Pronunciation

de·tailed \di-ˈtāld, ˈdē-ˌtāld\ *adj* (1740) : marked by abundant detail or by thoroughness in treating small items or parts ⟨the ~ study of history⟩ ***syn*** see CIRCUMSTANTIAL — **de·tailed·ly** \di-ˈtāld-lē, -ˈtā-ləd-, ˈdē-ˌ\ *adv* — **de·tailed·ness** \di-ˈtā-ləd-nəs, -ˈtāld-, ˈdē-ˌ\ *n*

de·tail·ing \ˈdē-ˌtāl-iŋ\ *n* (1970) : the act or process of meticulously cleaning and refurbishing an automobile

detail man *n* (1928) : a sales representative of a drug manufacturer who introduces new drugs esp. to physicians and pharmacists

de·tain \di-ˈtān, dē-\ *vt* [ME *deteynen,* fr. AF *deteign-,* stem of *detenir,* modif. of L *detinēre,* fr. *de-* + *tenēre* to hold — more at THIN] (15c) **1** : to hold or keep in or as if in custody ⟨~*ed* by the police for questioning⟩ **2** *obs* : to keep back (as something due) : WITHHOLD **3** : to restrain esp. from proceeding ⟨was ~*ed* by a flat tire⟩ ***syn*** see KEEP, DELAY — **de·tain·ment** \-mənt\ *n*

de·tain·ee \di-ˌtā-ˈnē, ˌdē-\ *n* (ca. 1928) : a person held in custody esp. for political reasons

de·tain·er \di-ˈtā-nər\ *n* [AF *detenour,* alter. of *detenir*] (1619) **1** : the act of keeping something in one's possession; *specif* : the withholding from the rightful owner of something that has lawfully come into the possession of the holder **2** : detention in custody **3** : a writ authorizing the keeper of a prison to continue to hold a person in custody

detd *abbr* determined

de·tect \di-ˈtekt, dē-\ *vb* [ME, fr. L *detectus,* pp. of *detegere* to uncover, detect, fr. *de-* + *tegere* to cover — more at THATCH] *vt* (1574) **1** : to discover the true character of **2** : to discover or determine the existence, presence, or fact of ⟨~ alcohol in the blood⟩ **3** : DEMODULATE ~ *vi* : to work as a detective — **de·tect·abil·i·ty** \-ˌtek-tə-ˈbi-lə-tē\ *n* — **de·tect·able** \-ˈtek-tə-bəl\ *adj*

de·tec·tion \di-ˈtek-shən\ *n* (15c) **1** : the act of detecting : the state or fact of being detected **2** : the process of demodulating

[1]**de·tec·tive** \di-ˈtek-tiv\ *adj* (1732) **1** : fitted for or used in detecting something ⟨had perfected his ~ sensibilities⟩ **2** : of or relating to detectives or their work ⟨a ~ novel⟩ — **de·tec·tive·like** \-ˌlīk\ *adj*

[2]**detective** *n* (1849) : one employed or engaged in detecting lawbreakers or in getting information that is not readily or publicly accessible

de·tec·tor \di-ˈtek-tər\ *n* (1541) : one that detects: as **a** : a device for detecting the presence of electromagnetic waves or of radioactivity **b** : a rectifier of high-frequency current used esp. for extracting the intelligence from a radio signal

de·tent \ˈdē-ˌtent, di-ˈ\ *n* [F *détente,* fr. MF *destente,* fr. *destendre* to slacken, fr. OF, fr. *des-* de- + *tendre* to stretch, fr. L *tendere* — more at THIN] (1688) : a device (as a catch, dog, or spring-operated ball) for positioning and holding one mechanical part in relation to another in a manner such that the device can be released by force applied to one of the parts

dé·tente *or* **de·tente** \dā-ˈtänt\ *n* [F] (1908) **1** : the relaxation of strained relations or tensions (as between nations); *also* : a policy promoting this **2** : a period of détente

de·ten·tion \di-ˈten-chən\ *n* [ME *detencion,* fr. AF or L; AF, fr. L *detention-, detentio,* fr. *detinēre* to detain] (15c) **1** : the act or fact of detaining or holding back; *esp* : a holding in custody **2** : the state of being detained; *esp* : a period of temporary custody prior to disposition by a court

detention home *n* (ca. 1930) : a house of detention for juvenile delinquents usu. under the supervision of a juvenile court

de·ter \di-ˈtər, dē-\ *vt* **de·terred; de·ter·ring** [L *deterrēre,* fr. *de-* + *terrēre* to frighten — more at TERROR] (ca. 1547) **1** : to turn aside, discourage, or prevent from acting ⟨she would not be *deterred* by threats⟩ **2** : INHIBIT ⟨painting to ~ rust⟩ — **de·ter·ment** \-ˈtər-mənt\ *n* — **de·ter·ra·bil·i·ty** \-ˌtər-ə-ˈbi-lə-tē\ *n* — **de·ter·ra·ble** \-ˈtər-ə-bəl\ *adj*

de·terge \di-ˈtərj\ *vt* **de·terged; de·terg·ing** [F or L; F *déterger,* fr. L *detergēre,* fr. *de-* + *tergēre* to wipe] (ca. 1623) : to wash off : CLEANSE — **de·terg·er** *n*

de·ter·gen·cy \di-ˈtər-jən(t)-sē\ *n* (1710) : cleansing quality or power

[1]**de·ter·gent** \-jənt\ *adj* (1616) : that cleanses : CLEANSING ⟨a ~ oil⟩

[2]**detergent** *n* (1676) : a cleansing agent: as **a** : SOAP **b** : any of numerous synthetic water-soluble or liquid organic preparations that are chemically different from soaps but are able to emulsify oils, hold dirt in suspension, and act as wetting agents **c** : an oil-soluble substance that holds insoluble foreign matter in suspension and is used in lubricating oils and dry-cleaning solvents

de·te·ri·o·rate \di-ˈtir-ē-ə-ˌrāt, dē-\ *vb* **-rat·ed; -rat·ing** [LL *deterioratus,* pp. of *deteriorare,* fr. L *deterior* worse, fr. *de-* + *-ter* (suffix as in L *uter* which of two) + *-ior* (compar. suffix) — more at WHETHER, -ER] *vt* (1572) **1** : to make inferior in quality or value : IMPAIR **2** : DISINTEGRATE ~ *vi* : to become impaired in quality, functioning, or condition : DEGENERATE ⟨allowed a tradition of academic excellence to ~⟩ ⟨his health *deteriorated*⟩ — **de·te·ri·o·ra·tive** \-ˌrā-tiv\ *adj*

de·te·ri·o·ra·tion \di-ˌtir-ē-ə-ˈrā-shən, dē-\ *n* (ca. 1658) : the action or process of deteriorating : the state of having deteriorated

syn DETERIORATION, DEGENERATION, DECADENCE, DECLINE mean the falling from a higher to a lower level in quality, character, or vitality. DETERIORATION implies generally the impairment of value or usefulness ⟨the *deterioration* of the house through neglect⟩. DEGENERATION stresses physical, intellectual, or esp. moral retrogression ⟨the *degeneration* of their youthful idealism into cynicism⟩. DECADENCE presupposes a reaching and passing the peak of development and implies a turn downward with a consequent loss in vitality or energy ⟨cited love of luxury as a sign of cultural *decadence*⟩. DECLINE differs from DECADENCE in suggesting a more markedly downward direction and greater momentum as well as more obvious evidence of deterioration ⟨the meteoric *decline* of his career after the scandal⟩.

de·ter·min·able \-ˈtər-mə-nə-bəl\ *adj* (15c) **1** : capable of being determined, definitely ascertained, or decided upon ⟨a ~ cause⟩ **2** : liable to be terminated : TERMINABLE ⟨a ~ estate⟩ — **de·ter·min·able·ness** *n* — **de·ter·min·ably** \-blē\ *adv*

de·ter·mi·na·cy \di-ˈtər-mə-nə-sē\ *n, pl* **-cies** (1873) **1** : the quality or state of being determinate **2 a** : the state of being definitely and unequivocally characterized : EXACTNESS **b** : the state of being determined or necessitated

de·ter·mi·nant \di-ˈtər-mə-nənt\ *n* (1686) **1** : an element that identifies or determines the nature of something or that fixes or conditions an outcome **2** : a square array of numbers bordered on the left and right by a vertical line and having a value equal to the algebraic sum of all possible products where the number of factors in each product is the same as the number of rows or columns, each factor in a given product is taken from a different row and column, and the sign of a product is positive or negative depending upon whether the number of permutations necessary to place the indices representing each factor's position in its row or column in the order of the natural numbers is odd or even **3** : GENE **4** : EPITOPE — **de·ter·mi·nan·tal** \-ˌtər-mə-ˈnan-tᵊl\ *adj*

de·ter·mi·nate \di-ˈtər-mə-nət\ *adj* [ME, fr. L *determinatus,* pp. of *determinare*] (14c) **1** : having defined limits ⟨a ~ period of time⟩ **2** : definitely settled ⟨a ~ order of precedence⟩ **3** : conclusively determined : DEFINITIVE ⟨a ~ answer⟩ **4** : characterized by sequential flowering from the central or uppermost bud to the lateral or basal buds; *also* : characterized by growth in which the main stem ends in an inflorescence and stops growing with only branches from the main stem having further and similarly restricted growth ⟨~ tomato plants⟩ — compare INDETERMINATE 4 **5** : relating to, being, or undergoing egg cleavage in which each division irreversibly separates portions of the zygote with specific potencies for further development — **de·ter·mi·nate·ly** *adv* — **de·ter·mi·nate·ness** *n*

de·ter·mi·na·tion \di-ˌtər-mə-ˈnā-shən\ *n* (14c) **1 a** : a judicial decision settling and ending a controversy **b** : the resolving of a question by argument or reasoning **2** *archaic* : TERMINATION **3 a** : the act of deciding definitely and firmly; *also* : the result of such an act of decision **b** : firm or fixed intention to achieve a desired end ⟨a woman of great courage and ~⟩ **4** : a fixing or finding of the position, magnitude, value, or character of something: as **a** : the act, process, or result of an accurate measurement **b** : an identification of the taxonomic position of a plant or animal **5 a** : the definition of a concept in logic by its essential constituents **b** : the addition of a differentia to a concept to limit its denotation **6** : direction or tendency to a certain end : IMPULSION **7** : the fixation of the destiny of undifferentiated embryonic tissue

de·ter·mi·na·tive \-ˈtər-mə-ˌnā-tiv, -ˈtər-mə-nə-\ *adj* (1655) : having power or tendency to determine : tending to fix, settle, or define something ⟨regard experiments as ~ of the principles from which deductions could be made —S. F. Mason⟩ ***syn*** see CONCLUSIVE — **determinative** *n*

de·ter·mi·na·tor \di-ˈtər-mə-ˌnā-tər\ *n* (1556) : DETERMINER

de·ter·mine \di-ˈtər-mən, dē-\ *vb* **de·ter·mined; de·ter·min·ing** [ME, fr. AF *determiner,* fr. L *determinare,* fr. *de-* + *terminare* to limit, fr. *terminus* boundary, limit — more at TERM] *vt* (14c) **1 a** : to fix conclusively or authoritatively ⟨~ national policy⟩ **b** : to decide by judicial sentence ⟨~ a plea⟩ **c** : to settle or decide by choice of alternatives or possibilities ⟨trying to ~ the best time to go⟩ **d** : RESOLVE ⟨she ~*ed* to do better⟩ **2 a** : to fix the form, position, or character of beforehand : ORDAIN ⟨two points ~ a straight line⟩ **b** : to bring about as a result : REGULATE ⟨demand ~*s* the price⟩ **3 a** : to fix the boundaries of **b** : to limit in extent or scope **c** : to put or set an end to : TERMINATE ⟨~ an estate⟩ **4** : to find out or come to a decision about by investigation, reasoning, or calculation ⟨~ the answer to the problem⟩ ⟨~ a position at sea⟩ **5** : to bring about the determination of ⟨~ the fate of a cell⟩ ~ *vi* **1** : to come to a decision **2** : to come to an end or become void ***syn*** see DECIDE, DISCOVER

de·ter·mined \-ˈtər-mənd\ *adj* (1513) **1** : having reached a decision : firmly resolved ⟨~ to be a pilot⟩ **2 a** : showing determination ⟨a ~ effort⟩ **b** : characterized by determination ⟨will deter all but the most ~ thief —*Security World*⟩ — **de·ter·mined·ly** \-mənd-lē, -mə-nəd-lē\ *adv* — **de·ter·mined·ness** \-mənd-nəs\ *n*

de·ter·min·er \-ˈtər-mə-nər\ *n* (ca. 1530) : one that determines: as **a** : GENE **b** : a word (as an article, possessive, demonstrative, or quantifier) that makes specific the denotation of a noun phrase

de·ter·min·ism \di-ˈtər-mə-ˌni-zəm, dē-\ *n* (1846) **1 a** : a theory or doctrine that acts of the will, occurrences in nature, or social or psychological phenomena are causally determined by preceding events or natural laws **b** : a belief in predestination **2** : the quality or state of being determined — **de·ter·min·ist** \-nəst\ *n or adj* — **de·ter·min·is·tic** \-ˌtər-mə-ˈnis-tik\ *adj* — **de·ter·min·is·ti·cal·ly** \-ti-k(ə-)lē\ *adv*

de·ter·rence \di-ˈtər-ən(t)s, -ˈter-; -ˈtə-rən(t)s, -ˈte-; dē-\ *n* (1861) : the act or process of deterring: as **a** : the inhibition of criminal behavior by fear esp. of punishment **b** : the maintenance of military power for the purpose of discouraging attack

de·ter·rent \-ənt, -rənt\ *adj* [L *deterrent-, deterrens,* prp. of *deterrēre* to deter] (1829) **1** : serving to deter ⟨a ~ effect⟩ **2** : relating to deterrence ⟨a ~ view of punishment⟩ — **deterrent** *n* — **de·ter·rent·ly** *adv*

de·ter·sive \di-ˈtər-siv, -ziv\ *adj* [MF *detersif,* fr. L *detersus,* pp. of *detergēre* to deterge] (1586) : DETERGENT — **detersive** *n*

de·test \di-ˈtest, dē-\ *vt* [MF *detester* or L *detestari;* MF *detester,* fr. L *detestari,* lit., to curse while calling a deity to witness, fr. *de-* + *testari* to call to witness — more at TESTAMENT] (ca. 1535) **1** : to feel intense and often violent antipathy toward : LOATHE **2** *obs* : CURSE, DENOUNCE ***syn*** see HATE — **de·test·er** *n*

de·test·able \di-ˈtes-tə-bəl, dē-\ *adj* (15c) : arousing or meriting intense dislike : ABOMINABLE — **de·test·able·ness** *n* — **de·test·ably** \-blē\ *adv*

de·tes·ta·tion \ˌdē-ˌtes-ˈtā-shən, di-\ *n* (15c) **1** : extreme hatred or dislike : ABHORRENCE, LOATHING **2** : an object of hatred or contempt

de·throne \di-ˈthrōn, dē-\ *vt* (1609) : to remove from a throne or place of power or prominence ⟨~ a king⟩ ⟨trying to ~ the champion⟩ — **de·throne·ment** \-mənt\ *n* — **de·thron·er** *n*

de·tick \(ˌ)dē-ˈtik\ *vt* (1925) : to remove ticks from — **de·tick·er** *n*

det·i·nue \ˈde-tᵊn-ˌ(y)ü\ *n* [ME *detenewe,* fr. AF *detenue* detention, fr. fem. of *detenu,* pp. of *detenir* to detain] (15c) **1** : a common-law action for the recovery of a personal chattel wrongfully detained or of its value **2** : detention of something due; *esp* : the unlawful detention of a personal chattel from another

detn *abbr* **1** detention **2** determination

det·o·na·ble \ˈde-tᵊn-ə-bəl, -tə-nə-\ *adj* (1884) : capable of being detonated — **det·o·na·bil·i·ty** \ˌde-tᵊn-ə-ˈbil-ət-ē, ˌde-tə-nə-\ *n*

det·o·nate \ˈde-tᵊn-ˌāt, ˈde-tə-ˌnāt\ *vb* **-nat·ed; -nat·ing** [F *détoner* to explode, fr. L *detonare* to expend thunder, fr. *de-* + *tonare* to thunder — more at THUNDER] *vi* (1729) : to explode with sudden violence ~ *vt* **1** : to cause to detonate ⟨~ a bomb⟩ — compare DEFLAGRATE **2** : to set off in a burst of activity : SPARK ⟨programs that *detonated* controversies⟩ — **det·o·nat·able** \ˈ-ˌā-tə-bəl, -ˌnā-\ *adj* — **det·o·na·tive** \ˈde-tᵊn-ˌā-tiv, ˈde-tə-ˌnā-\ *adj*

det·o·na·tion \ˌde-tᵊn-ˈā-shən, ˌde-tə-ˈnā-\ *n* (1686) **1 :** the action or process of detonating **2 :** rapid combustion in an internal combustion engine that results in knocking

det·o·na·tor \ˈde-tᵊn-ˌā-tər, -tə-ˌnā-\ *n* (1822) **:** a device or small quantity of explosive used for detonating a high explosive

[1]**de·tour** \ˈdē-ˌtu̇r *also* di-ˈtu̇r\ *n* [F *détour,* fr. OF *destor,* fr. *destorner* to divert, fr. *des-* de- + *torner* to turn — more at TURN] (1738) **:** a deviation from a direct course or the usual procedure; *esp* **:** a roundabout way temporarily replacing part of a route

[2]**detour** *vi* (1836) **:** to proceed by a detour ⟨~ around road construction⟩ ~ *vt* **1 :** to send by a circuitous route ⟨~ traffic around an accident⟩ **2 :** to avoid by going around **:** BYPASS ⟨~ an accident site⟩

de·tox \ˈdē-ˌtäks, di-ˈtäks\ *n, often attrib* (1973) **1 :** detoxification from an intoxicating or addictive substance ⟨a ~ clinic⟩ **2 :** a detox program or facility ⟨spent one week in ~⟩ — **detox** *vb*

de·tox·i·cate \(ˌ)dē-ˈtäk-sə-ˌkāt\ *vt* **-cat·ed; -cat·ing** [*de-* + [2]*intoxicate*] (1867) **1 :** DETOXIFY 1 **2 :** DETOXIFY 2 — **de·tox·i·cant** \-si-kənt\ *n* — **de·tox·i·ca·tion** \(ˌ)dē-ˌtäk-sə-ˈkā-shən\ *n*

de·tox·i·fy \(ˌ)dē-ˈtäk-sə-ˌfī\ *vt* **-fied; -fy·ing** (ca. 1905) **1 a :** to remove a harmful substance (as a poison or toxin) or the effect of such from **b :** to render (a harmful substance) harmless **2 :** to free (as a drug user or an alcoholic) from an intoxicating or an addictive substance in the body or from dependence on or addiction to such a substance **3 :** NEUTRALIZE 2 — **de·tox·i·fi·ca·tion** \(ˌ)dē-ˌtäk-sə-fə-ˈkā-shən\ *n*

de·tract \di-ˈtrakt, dē-\ *vb* [ME, fr. L *detractus,* pp. of *detrahere* to pull down, disparage, fr. *de-* + *trahere* to draw] *vt* (15c) **1** *archaic* **:** to speak ill of **2** *archaic* **:** to take away **3 :** DIVERT ⟨~ attention⟩ ~ *vi* **:** to diminish the importance, value, or effectiveness of something — often used with *from* ⟨small errors that do not seriously ~ from the book⟩ — **de·trac·tor** \-ˈtrak-tər\ *n*

de·trac·tion \di-ˈtrak-shən, dē-\ *n* (14c) **1 :** a lessening of reputation or esteem esp. by envious, malicious, or petty criticism **:** BELITTLING, DISPARAGEMENT **2 :** a taking away ⟨it is no ~ from its dignity or prestige —J. F. Golay⟩ — **de·trac·tive** \-ˈtrak-tiv\ *adj* — **de·trac·tive·ly** *adv*

de·train \(ˌ)dē-ˈtrān\ *vi* (1881) **:** to get off a railroad train ~ *vt* **:** to remove from a railroad train — **de·train·ment** \-mənt\ *n*

de·trib·al·ize \(ˌ)dē-ˈtrī-bə-ˌlīz\ *vt* **-ized; -iz·ing** (1920) **:** to cause to lose tribal identity **:** ACCULTURATE — **de·trib·al·i·za·tion** \(ˌ)dē-ˌtrī-bə-lə-ˈzā-shən\ *n*

det·ri·ment \ˈde-trə-mənt\ *n* [ME, fr. MF or L; MF, fr. L *detrimentum,* fr. *deterere* to wear away, impair, fr. *de-* + *terere* to rub — more at THROW] (15c) **1 :** INJURY, DAMAGE ⟨did hard work without ~ to his health⟩ **2 :** a cause of injury or damage ⟨a ~ to progress⟩

[1]**det·ri·men·tal** \ˌde-trə-ˈmen-tᵊl\ *adj* (1590) **:** obviously harmful **:** DAMAGING ⟨the ~ effects of pollution⟩ ***syn*** see PERNICIOUS — **det·ri·men·tal·ly** \-tᵊl-ē\ *adv*

[2]**detrimental** *n* (1831) **:** an undesirable or harmful person or thing

de·tri·tion \di-ˈtri-shən\ *n* (1674) **:** a wearing off or away

de·tri·ti·vore \di-ˈtrī-tə-ˌvȯr\ *n* [ISV *detritus* + *-i-* + *-vore* (fr. L *-vorus* -vorous)] (1959) **:** an organism (as an earthworm or a fungus) that feeds on dead and decomposing organic matter

de·tri·tus \di-ˈtrī-təs\ *n, pl* **de·tri·tus** \-ˈtrī-təs, -ˈtrī-ˌtüs\ [F *détritus,* fr. L *detritus,* pp. of *deterere*] (1802) **1 :** loose material (as rock fragments or organic particles) that results directly from disintegration **2 a :** a product of disintegration, destruction, or wearing away **:** DEBRIS **b :** miscellaneous remnants **:** ODDS AND ENDS ⟨sifting through the ~ of his childhood —Michael Tomasky⟩ — **de·tri·tal** \-ˈtrī-tᵊl\ *adj*

de trop \də-ˈtrō\ *adj* [F] (1752) **:** too much or too many **:** SUPERFLUOUS, EXCESSIVE

de·tu·mes·cence \ˌdē-t(y)ü-ˈme-sᵊn(t)s\ *n* [L *detumescere* to become less swollen, fr. *de-* + *tumescere* to swell — more at TUMESCENT] (1678) **:** subsidence or diminution of swelling or erection — **de·tu·mes·cent** \-sᵊnt\ *adj*

Deu·ca·lion \d(y)ü-ˈkāl-yən\ *n* [L, fr. Gk *Deukaliōn*] (1565) **:** a survivor with his wife Pyrrha of a great flood by which Zeus destroys the rest of the human race

[1]**deuce** \ˈdüs *also* ˈdyüs\ *n* [ME *dewes,* fr. AF *deus* two, fr. L *duos,* acc. masc. of *duo* two — more at TWO] (15c) **1 a (1) :** the face of a die that bears two spots **(2) :** a playing card bearing an index number two **b :** a throw of the dice yielding two points **2 :** a tie in tennis after each side has scored 40 requiring two consecutive points by one side to win **3** [obs. E *deuce* bad luck] **a :** DEVIL, DICKENS — used chiefly as a mild oath ⟨what the ~ is he up to now⟩ **b :** something notable of its kind ⟨a ~ of a mess⟩

[2]**deuce** *vt* **deuced; deuc·ing** (1919) **:** to bring the score of (a tennis game or set) to deuce

deuc·ed \ˈdü-səd *also* ˈdyü-\ *adj* (1782) **:** DAMNED, CONFOUNDED ⟨in a ~ fix⟩ — **deuc·ed** *or* **deuc·ed·ly** *adv*

deuces wild *n* (1927) **:** a card game (as poker) in which each deuce may represent any card designated by its holder

de·us ex ma·chi·na \ˈdā-əs-ˌeks-ˈmä-ki-nə, -ˈma-, -ˌnä; -mə-ˈshē-nə\ *n* [NL, a god from a machine, trans. of Gk *theos ek mēchanēs*] (1697) **1 :** a god introduced by means of a crane in ancient Greek and Roman drama to decide the final outcome **2 :** a person or thing (as in fiction or drama) that appears or is introduced suddenly and unexpectedly and provides a contrived solution to an apparently insoluble difficulty

Deut *abbr* Deuteronomy

deuter- *or* **deutero-** *comb form* [Gk *deuter-, deutero-,* fr. *deuteros;* prob. akin to Gk *dein* to lack, Skt *doṣa* fault, lack] **:** second **:** secondary ⟨*deuteranopia*⟩

deu·ter·ag·o·nist \ˌdü-tə-ˈra-gə-nist *also* ˌdyü-\ *n* [Gk *deuteragōnistēs,* fr. *deuter-* + *agōnistēs* combatant, actor — more at PROTAGONIST] (1855) **1 :** the actor taking the part of second importance in a classical Greek drama **2 :** a person who serves as a foil to another

deu·ter·anom·a·lous \ˌdü-tə-rə-ˈnä-mə-ləs *also* ˌdyü-\ *adj* [NL *deuteranomal*ia (fr. *deuter-* + L *anomalia* anomaly) abnormal trichromatism + E *-ous*] (1911) **:** exhibiting partial loss of green color vision so that an increased intensity of green is required in a mixture of red and green to match a given yellow — **deu·ter·anom·a·ly** \-ˈnä-mə-lē\ *n*

deu·ter·an·ope \ˈdü-tə-rə-ˌnōp *also* ˈdyü-\ *n* (1902) **:** an individual affected with deuteranopia

deu·ter·an·opia \ˌdü-tə-rə-ˈnō-pē-ə *also* ˌdyü-\ *n* [NL, fr. *deuter-* + [2]*a-* + *-opia;* fr. the blindness to green, regarded as the second primary color] (ca. 1901) **:** color blindness marked by usu. complete loss of ability to distinguish colors — **deu·ter·an·opic** \-ˈnō-pik, -ˈnä-pik\ *adj*

deu·ter·ate \ˈdü-tə-ˌrāt *also* ˈdyü-\ *vt* **-at·ed; -at·ing** (1947) **:** to introduce deuterium into (a compound) — **deu·ter·a·tion** \ˌdyü-tə-ˈrā-shən\ *n*

deu·te·ri·um \dü-ˈtir-ē-əm *also* dyü-\ *n* [NL, fr. Gk *deuteros* second] (1933) **:** an isotope of hydrogen that has one proton and one neutron in its nucleus and that has twice the mass of ordinary hydrogen — symbol *D;* called also *heavy hydrogen*

deuterium oxide *n* (1934) **:** HEAVY WATER 1

deu·tero·ca·non·i·cal \ˌdü-tə-rō-kə-ˈnä-ni-kəl *also* ˌdyü-\ *adj* [NL *deuterocanonicus,* fr. *deuter-* + LL *canonicus* canonical] (1684) **:** of, relating to, or constituting the books of Scripture contained in the Septuagint but not in the Hebrew canon

deu·ter·on \ˈdü-tə-ˌrän *also* ˈdyü-\ *n* (1933) **:** a deuterium nucleus

Deu·ter·o·nom·ic \ˌdü-tə-rə-ˈnä-mik *also* ˌdyü-\ *adj* (1857) **:** of or relating to the book of Deuteronomy, its style, or its contents

Deu·ter·on·o·mist \ˌdü-tə-ˈrä-nə-mist *also* ˌdyü-\ *n* (1862) **:** any of the writers or editors of a Deuteronomic body of source material often distinguished in the earlier books of the Old Testament — **Deu·ter·on·o·mis·tic** \-ˌrä-nə-ˈmis-tik\ *adj*

Deu·ter·on·o·my \ˌdü-tə-ˈrä-nə-mē *also* ˌdyü-\ *n* [ME *Deutronomie,* fr. LL *Deuteronomium,* fr. Gk *Deuteronomion,* fr. *deuter-* + *nomos* law — more at NIMBLE] **:** the fifth book of canonical Jewish and Christian Scripture containing narrative and Mosaic laws — see BIBLE table

deu·tero·stome \ˈdü-tə-rō-ˌstōm *also* ˈdyü-\ *n* [NL *Deuterostomia,* group name, fr. *deuter-* + Gk *stoma* mouth — more at STOMACH] (1950) **:** any of a major division (Deuterostomia) of the animal kingdom that includes the bilaterally symmetrical animals (as the chordates) with indeterminate cleavage and a mouth that does not arise from the blastopore

deut·sche mark \ˈdȯich-ˌmärk, ˈdȯi-chə-ˌ\ *also* **deutsch·mark** \ˈdȯich-\ *n* [G, German mark] (1948) **:** the basic monetary unit of West Germany from 1948 to 1990 and of reunited Germany from 1990 to 2001

deut·zia \ˈdüt-sē-ə *also* ˈdyüt-\ *n* [NL, fr. Jean *Deutz* †1784? Du. patron of botanical research] (1837) **:** any of a genus (*Deutzia*) of the saxifrage family of ornamental shrubs with usu. white or pink flowers

dev *abbr* deviation

de·val·u·ate \(ˌ)dē-ˈval-yə-ˌwāt, -yü-ˌāt\ *vb* (1898) **:** DEVALUE

de·val·u·a·tion \(ˌ)dē-ˌval-yə-ˈwā-shən, -yü-ˈā-\ *n* (1914) **1 :** an official reduction in the exchange value of a currency by a lowering of its gold equivalency or its value relative to another currency **2 :** a lessening esp. of status or stature **:** DECLINE

de·val·ue \(ˌ)dē-ˈval-(ˌ)yü\ *vt* (1918) **1 :** to institute the devaluation of (money) **2 :** to lessen the value of ~ *vi* **:** to institute devaluation

De·va·na·ga·ri \ˌdā-və-ˈnä-gə-rē\ *n* [Skt *devanāgarī,* fr. *deva* divine + *nāgarī* (writing) of the city — more at DEITY] (1781) **:** an alphabet usu. employed for Sanskrit and also used as a literary hand for various modern languages of India — see ALPHABET table

dev·as·tate \ˈde-və-ˌstāt\ *vt* **-tat·ed; -tat·ing** [L *devastatus,* pp. of *devastare,* fr. *de-* + *vastare* to lay waste — more at WASTE] (1638) **1 :** to bring to ruin or desolation by violent action ⟨a country *devastated* by war⟩ **2 :** to reduce to chaos, disorder, or helplessness **:** OVERWHELM ⟨*devastated* by grief⟩ ⟨her wisecrack *devastated* the class⟩ ***syn*** see RAVAGE — **dev·as·tat·ing·ly** \-ˌstā-tiŋ-lē\ *adv* — **dev·as·ta·tion** \ˌde-və-ˈstā-shən\ *n* — **dev·as·ta·tive** \ˈde-və-ˌstā-tiv\ *adj* — **dev·as·ta·tor** \-ˌstā-tər\ *n*

de·vein \(ˌ)dē-ˈvān\ *vt* (1953) **:** to remove the dark dorsal vein from (shrimp)

de·vel·op \di-ˈvel-əp, dē-\ *vb* [F *développer,* fr. OF *desveloper, desvoluper* to unwrap, expose, fr. *des-* de- + *envoloper* to enclose — more at ENVELOP] *vt* (1750) **1 a :** to set forth or make clear by degrees or in detail **:** EXPOUND ⟨~ a thesis⟩ **b :** to make visible or manifest **c :** to treat (as in dyeing) with an agent to cause the appearance of color **d :** to subject (exposed photograph material) esp. to chemicals in order to produce a visible image ⟨~ film⟩; *also* **:** to make visible by such a method ⟨~ pictures⟩ **e :** to elaborate (a musical idea) by the working out of rhythmic and harmonic changes in the theme **2 a :** to work out the possibilities of ⟨~ an idea⟩ **b :** to create or produce esp. by deliberate effort over time ⟨~ new ways of doing business⟩ ⟨~ software⟩ **3 a :** to make active or promote the growth of ⟨~*ed* his muscles⟩ **b (1) :** to make available or usable ⟨~ natural resources⟩ **(2) :** to make suitable for commercial or residential purposes ⟨~ land⟩ **c :** to move (as a chess piece) from the original position to one providing more opportunity for effective use **4 a :** to cause to unfold gradually ⟨~*ed* his argument⟩ **b :** to expand by a process of growth ⟨working to ~ the company further⟩ **c :** to cause to grow and differentiate along lines natural to its kind ⟨rain and sun ~ the grain⟩ **d :** to become infected or affected by ⟨~*ed* pneumonia⟩ **5 :** to acquire gradually ⟨~ an appreciation for ballet⟩ ~ *vi* **1 a :** to go through a process of natural growth, differentiation, or evolution by successive changes ⟨a blossom ~*s* from a bud⟩ **b :** to acquire secondary sex characteristics **2 :** to become gradually manifest **3 :** to come into being gradually ⟨the situation ~*ing* in eastern Europe⟩; *also* **:** TURN OUT 2a ⟨it ~*ed* that no one had paid the bill⟩ — **de·vel·op·able** \-ˈve-lə-pə-bəl\ *adj*

de·vel·oped \di-ˈve-ləpt\ *adj* (1940) **:** having a relatively high level of industrialization and standard of living ⟨a ~ country⟩

de·vel·op·er \-lə-pər\ *n* (1796) **:** one that develops: as **a :** a chemical used to develop exposed photographic materials **b :** a person who develops real estate **c :** a person or company that develops computer software

de·vel·op·ing \-lə-piŋ\ *adj* (1963) **:** UNDERDEVELOPED 2 ⟨~ nations⟩

\ə\ **abut** \ᵊ\ **kitten,** F **table** \ər\ **further** \a\ **ash** \ā\ **ace** \ä\ **mop, mar** \au̇\ **out** \ch\ **chin** \e\ **bet** \ē\ **easy** \g\ **go** \i\ **hit** \ī\ **ice** \j\ **job** \ŋ\ **sing** \ō\ **go** \ȯ\ **law** \ȯi\ **boy** \th\ **thin** \th̲\ **the** \ü\ **loot** \u̇\ **foot** \y\ **yet** \zh\ **vision, beige** \k̲, ⁿ, œ, ue, ʸ\ *see* Guide to Pronunciation

de·vel·op·ment \di-ˈve-ləp-mənt, dē-\ *n* (1756) **1 :** the act, process, or result of developing ⟨~ of new ideas⟩ ⟨an interesting ~⟩ **2 :** the state of being developed ⟨a project in ~⟩ **3 :** a developed tract of land; *esp* **:** one with houses built on it

de·vel·op·men·tal \dē-ˌve-ləp-ˈmen-tᵊl\ *adj* (1849) **1 a :** of, relating to, or being development ⟨~ processes⟩ ⟨~ biology⟩; *broadly* **:** EXPERIMENTAL 2 ⟨~ aircraft⟩ **b :** serving economic development ⟨~ highways⟩ **2 :** designed to assist growth or bring about improvement (as of a skill) ⟨~ toys⟩ — **de·vel·op·men·tal·ly** \-tᵊl-ē\ *adv*

developmentally disabled *adj* (1975) **:** having a physical or mental disability that becomes apparent in childhood and prevents, impedes, or limits normal development

de·verb·al \(ˌ)dē-ˈvər-bəl\ *adj* (1943) **:** DEVERBATIVE

de·verb·a·tive \(ˌ)dē-ˈvər-bə-tiv\ *adj* (1930) **1 :** derived from a verb ⟨the ~ noun *developer* is derived from *develop*⟩ **2 :** used in derivation from a verb ⟨the ~ suffix *-er* in *developer*⟩ — **deverbative** *n*

de·vest \di-ˈvest\ *vt* [MF *desvestir,* fr. ML *disvestire,* fr. L *dis-* + *vestire* to clothe — more at VEST] (1563) **:** DIVEST

de·vi·ance \ˈdē-vē-ən(t)s\ *n* (1944) **:** deviant quality, state, or behavior

de·vi·an·cy \-ən-sē\ *n, pl* **-cies** (1947) **:** DEVIANCE

de·vi·ant \-ənt\ *adj* (15c) **:** deviating esp. from an accepted norm ⟨~ behavior⟩ — **deviant** *n*

[1]**de·vi·ate** \ˈdē-vē-ˌāt\ *vb* **-at·ed; -at·ing** [LL *deviatus,* pp. of *deviare,* fr. L *de-* + *via* way — more at WAY] *vi* (ca. 1633) **1 :** to stray esp. from a standard, principle, or topic **2 :** to depart from an established course or norm ⟨a flight forced by weather to ~ south⟩ ~ *vt* **:** to cause to turn out of a previous course ***syn*** see SWERVE — **de·vi·a·tor** \-ˌā-tər\ *n* — **de·vi·a·to·ry** \-ə-ˌtȯr-ē\ *adj*

[2]**de·vi·ate** \-vē-ət, -vē-ˌāt\ *n* (1912) **1 :** one that deviates from a norm; *esp* **:** a person who differs markedly from a group norm **2 :** a statistical variable that gives the deviation of another variable from a fixed value (as the mean)

[3]**de·vi·ate** \-vē-ət, -vē-ˌāt\ *adj* (1929) **:** departing significantly from the behavioral norms of a particular society ⟨~ behavior⟩

de·vi·a·tion \ˌdē-vē-ˈā-shən\ *n* (15c) **:** an act or instance of deviating: as **a :** deflection of the needle of a compass caused by local magnetic influences (as in a ship) **b :** the difference between a value in a frequency distribution and a fixed number (as the mean) **c :** departure from an established ideology or party line **d :** noticeable or marked departure from accepted norms of behavior — **de·vi·a·tion·ism** \-shə-ˌni-zəm\ *n* — **de·vi·a·tion·ist** \-sh(ə-)nist\ *n or adj*

de·vice \di-ˈvīs\ *n* [ME *devis, devise,* fr. AF, division, plan, fr. *deviser* to divide, regulate, tell — more at DEVISE] (14c) **1 :** something devised or contrived: as **a (1) :** PLAN, PROCEDURE, TECHNIQUE **(2) :** a scheme to deceive **:** STRATAGEM, TRICK **b :** something fanciful, elaborate, or intricate in design **c :** something (as a figure of speech) in a literary work designed to achieve a particular artistic effect **d** *archaic* **:** MASQUE, SPECTACLE **e :** a conventional stage practice or means (as a stage whisper) used to achieve a particular dramatic effect **f :** a piece of equipment or a mechanism designed to serve a special purpose or perform a special function ⟨an electronic ~⟩ **2 :** DESIRE, INCLINATION ⟨left to my own ~*s*⟩ **3 :** an emblematic design used esp. as a heraldic bearing

[1]**dev·il** \ˈde-vᵊl *dial* ˈdi-\ *n* [ME *devel,* fr. OE *dēofol,* fr. LL *diabolus,* fr. Gk *diabolos,* lit., slanderer, fr. *diaballein* to throw across, slander, fr. *dia-* + *ballein* to throw; prob. akin to Skt *gurate* he lifts up] (bef. 12c) **1** *often cap* **:** the personal supreme spirit of evil often represented in Jewish and Christian belief as the tempter of humankind, the leader of all apostate angels, and the ruler of hell — usu. used with *the*; often used as an interjection, an intensive, or a generalized term of abuse ⟨what the ~ is this?⟩ ⟨the ~ you say!⟩ **2 :** an evil spirit **:** DEMON **3 a :** an extremely wicked person **:** FIEND **b** *archaic* **:** a great evil **4 :** a person of notable energy, recklessness, and dashing spirit; *also* **:** one who is mischievous ⟨those kids are little ~*s* today⟩ **5 :** FELLOW — usu. used in the phrases *poor devil, lucky devil* **6 a :** something very trying or provoking ⟨having a ~ of a time with this problem⟩ **b :** severe criticism or rebuke **:** HELL — used with *the* ⟨I'll probably catch the ~ for this⟩ **c :** the difficult, deceptive, or problematic part of something ⟨the ~ is in the details⟩ **7 :** DUST DEVIL **8** *Christian Science* **:** the opposite of Truth **:** a belief in sin, sickness, and death **:** EVIL, ERROR — **between the devil and the deep blue sea :** faced with two equally objectionable alternatives — **devil to pay :** severe consequences — used with *the* ⟨there'll be the *devil to pay* if we're late⟩

[2]**devil** *vt* **-iled** *or* **-illed; -il·ing** *or* **-il·ling** \ˈde-və-liŋ, ˈdev-liŋ\ (1800) **1 :** to season highly ⟨~*ed* eggs⟩ **2 :** TEASE, ANNOY

dev·il·fish \ˈde-vᵊl-ˌfish\ *n* (1709) **1 :** MANTA RAY **2 :** OCTOPUS; *broadly* **:** any large cephalopod

dev·il·ish \ˈde-vᵊl-ish, ˈdev-lish\ *adj* (15c) **1 :** resembling or befitting a devil: as **a :** EVIL, SINISTER **b :** MISCHIEVOUS, ROGUISH ⟨a ~ grin⟩ **2 :** EXTREME ⟨in a ~ hurry⟩ — **devilish** *adv* — **dev·il·ish·ly** *adv* — **dev·il·ish·ness** *n*

dev·il–may–care \ˌde-vᵊl-(ˌ)mā-ˈker\ *adj* (1837) **:** EASYGOING, CAREFREE ⟨a ~ attitude⟩

dev·il·ment \ˈde-vᵊl-mənt, -ˌment\ *n* (1771) **:** MISCHIEF

dev·il·ry \ˈde-vᵊl-rē\ *or* **dev·il·try** \-vᵊl-trē\ *n, pl* **-ries** *or* **-tries** (14c) **1 a :** action performed with the help of the devil **:** WITCHCRAFT **b :** WICKEDNESS **c :** MISCHIEF **2 :** an act of devilry

devil's advocate *n* [trans. of NL *advocatus diaboli*] (1760) **1 :** a Roman Catholic official whose duty is to examine critically the evidence on which a demand for beatification or canonization rests **2 :** a person who champions the less accepted cause for the sake of argument

devil's claw *n* (ca. 1900) **:** any of several herbs (genus *Proboscidea* syn. *Martynia* of the family Martyniaceae) of the southwestern U.S. and Mexico that have edible pods yielding a black sewing material used in basket making

devil's club *n* (ca. 1889) **:** a spiny western No. American shrub (*Oplopanax horridus*) of the ginseng family having large lobed leaves and stems covered with dense sharp prickles

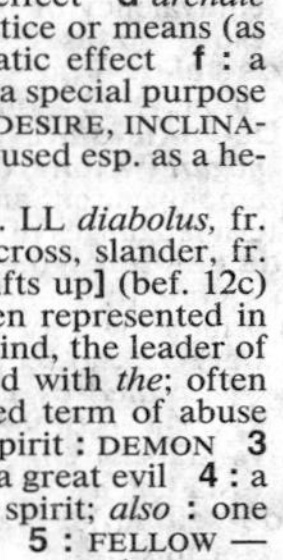

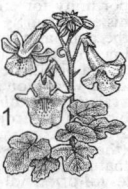

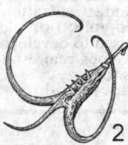

devil's claw: *1* flower and leaf, *2* dried seed pod

devil's darning needle *n* (1809) **1 :** DRAGONFLY **2 :** DAMSELFLY

devil's food cake *n* (1905) **:** a rich chocolate cake

devil's paintbrush *n* (1900) **:** ORANGE HAWKWEED; *broadly* **:** any of various hawkweeds that are naturalized weeds in the eastern U.S.

devil theory *n* (1937) **:** a theory of history: political and social crises arise from the deliberate actions of evil or misguided leaders rather than as a natural result of conditions

dev·il·wood \ˈde-vᵊl-ˌwu̇d\ *n* (1818) **:** a small tree (*Osmanthus americanus*) of the olive family that is native to the southern U.S.

de·vi·ous \ˈdē-vē-əs, -vyəs\ *adj* [L *devius,* fr. *de* from + *via* way — more at DE-, WAY] (1599) **1 a :** WANDERING, ROUNDABOUT ⟨a ~ path⟩ **b :** moving without a fixed course **:** ERRANT ⟨~ breezes⟩ **2 :** OUT-OF-THE-WAY, REMOTE **3 a :** deviating from a right, accepted, or common course ⟨~ conduct⟩ **b :** not straightforward **:** CUNNING ⟨a ~ politician⟩; *also* **:** DECEPTIVE ⟨a ~ trick⟩ — **de·vi·ous·ly** *adv* — **de·vi·ous·ness** *n*

[1]**de·vise** \di-ˈvīz\ *vt* **de·vised; de·vis·ing** [ME, fr. AF *deviser, diviser,* to divide, distinguish, invent, fr. VL **divisare,* freq. of L *dividere* to divide] (13c) **1 a :** to form in the mind by new combinations or applications of ideas or principles **:** INVENT ⟨~ a new strategy⟩ **b** *archaic* **:** CONCEIVE, IMAGINE **c :** to plan to obtain or bring about **:** PLOT ⟨~ one's death⟩ **2 :** to give (real estate) by will — compare BEQUEATH — **de·vis·able** \-ˈvī-zə-bəl\ *adj* — **de·vis·er** *n*

[2]**devise** *n* (15c) **1 :** the act of giving or disposing of real property by will **2 :** a will or clause of a will disposing of real property **3 :** property devised by will

de·vi·see \ˌde-və-ˈzē, di-ˌvī-ˈzē\ *n* (1543) **:** one to whom a devise of property is made

de·vi·sor \ˌde-və-ˈzȯr; di-ˈvī-zər, -ˌvī-ˈzȯr\ *n* (1543) **:** one who devises property in a will

de·vi·tal·ize \(ˌ)dē-ˈvī-tə-ˌlīz\ *vt* (1849) **:** to deprive of life, vigor, or effectiveness — **de·vi·tal·i·za·tion** \-ˌvī-tə-lə-ˈzā-shən\ *n*

de·vit·ri·fy \(ˌ)dē-ˈvi-trə-ˌfī\ *vt* [F *dévitrifier,* fr. *dé-* de- + *vitrifier* to vitrify] (1832) **:** to deprive of glassy luster and transparency; *esp* **:** to change (as a glass) from a vitreous to a crystalline condition — **de·vit·ri·fi·ca·tion** \(ˌ)dē-ˌvi-trə-fə-ˈkā-shən\ *n*

de·vo·cal·ize \(ˌ)dē-ˈvō-kə-ˌlīz\ *vt* (1877) **:** DEVOICE

de·voice \(ˌ)dē-ˈvȯis\ *vt* (1932) **:** to pronounce (as a sometimes or formerly voiced sound) without vibration of the vocal cords

de·void \di-ˈvȯid\ *adj* [ME, pp. of *devoiden* to dispel, fr. AF **desvoider,* fr. *des-* dis- + *voider* to empty — more at VOID] (15c) **:** being without a usual, typical, or expected attribute or accompaniment — used with *of* ⟨an argument ~ of sense⟩ ⟨a landscape ~ of life⟩

de·voir \də-ˈvwär, ˈde-ˌ\ *n* [alter. of ME *dever, devoir,* fr. AF, fr. *deveir, devoer* to owe, be obliged, fr. L *debēre* — more at DEBT] (14c) **1 :** DUTY, RESPONSIBILITY **2 :** a usu. formal act of civility or respect

de·vo·lu·tion \ˌde-və-ˈlü-shən *also* ˌdē-və-\ *n* [ML *devolution-, devolutio,* fr. L *devolvere*] (1545) **1 :** transference (as of rights, powers, property, or responsibility) to another; *esp* **:** the surrender of powers to local authorities by a central government **2 :** retrograde evolution **:** DEGENERATION — **de·vo·lu·tion·ary** \-shə-ˌner-ē\ *adj* — **de·vo·lu·tion·ist** \-sh(ə-)nist\ *n*

de·volve \di-ˈvälv, -ˈvȯlv, dē-\ *vb* **de·volved; de·volv·ing** [ME, fr. L *devolvere,* fr. *de-* + *volvere* to roll — more at VOLUBLE] *vt* (15c) **:** to pass on (as responsibility, rights, or powers) from one person or entity to another ⟨*devolving* to western Europe full responsibility for its own defense —Christopher Lane⟩ ~ *vi* **1 a :** to pass by transmission or succession ⟨the estate *devolved* on a distant cousin⟩ **b :** to fall or be passed usu. as a responsibility or obligation ⟨the responsibility for breadwinning has *devolved* increasingly upon women —Barbara Ehrenreich⟩ **2 :** to come by or as if by flowing down ⟨his allegedly subversive campaigns . . . ~ from his belief in basic American rights —Frank Deford⟩ **3 :** to degenerate through a gradual change or evolution ⟨where order ~*s* into chaos —*Johns Hopkins Mag.*⟩

dev·on \ˈde-vən\ *n, often cap* [*Devon,* England] (1834) **:** any of an English breed of vigorous red cattle used for meat and milk

Devon *abbr* Devonshire

De·vo·ni·an \di-ˈvō-nē-ən\ *adj* [*Devon,* England] (1612) **1 :** of or relating to Devonshire, England **2 :** of, relating to, or being the period of the Paleozoic era between the Silurian and the Mississippian or the corresponding system of rocks — see GEOLOGIC TIME table — **Devonian** *n*

Devon rex *n* [*Devon,* England] (1972) **:** any of a breed of large-eared cats having a very short wavy or curly coat with sparse guard hairs

Dev·on·shire cream \ˌde-vən-ˌshir-, -shər-\ *n* (1791) **:** CLOTTED CREAM

de·vote \di-ˈvōt, dē-\ *vt* **de·vot·ed; de·vot·ing** [L *devotus,* pp. of *devovēre,* fr. *de-* + *vovēre* to vow] (1586) **1 :** to commit by a solemn act ⟨*devoted* herself to serving God⟩ **2 :** to give over or direct (as time, money, or effort) to a cause, enterprise, or activity — **de·vote·ment** \-ˈvōt-mənt\ *n*

syn DEVOTE, DEDICATE, CONSECRATE, HALLOW mean to set apart for a special and often higher end. DEVOTE is likely to imply compelling motives and often attachment to an objective ⟨*devoted* his evenings to study⟩. DEDICATE implies solemn and exclusive devotion to a sacred or serious use or purpose ⟨*dedicated* her life to medical research⟩. CONSECRATE stresses investment with a solemn or sacred quality ⟨*consecrate* a church to the worship of God⟩. HALLOW, often differing little from *dedicate* or *consecrate,* may distinctively imply an attribution of intrinsic sanctity ⟨battlegrounds *hallowed* by the blood of patriots⟩.

devoted *adj* (1586) **:** characterized by loyalty and devotion ⟨a ~ fan⟩ ⟨he is ~ to her⟩ — **de·vot·ed·ly** *adv* — **de·vot·ed·ness** *n*

dev·o·tee \ˌde-ˌvō-ˈtē, ˌde-, ˌdā-, də-, -ˈtā\ *n* (1645) **:** an ardent follower, supporter, or enthusiast (as of a religion, art form, or sport)

de·vo·tion \di-ˈvō-shən, dē-\ *n* (13c) **1 a :** religious fervor **:** PIETY **b :** an act of prayer or private worship — usu. used in pl. **c :** a religious exercise or practice other than the regular corporate worship of a congregation **2 a :** the act of devoting ⟨~ of time and energy⟩ **b :** the fact or state of being ardently dedicated and loyal ⟨her ~ to the cause⟩ ⟨filial ~⟩ **3** *obs* **:** the object of one's devotion ***syn*** see FIDELITY

[1]**de·vo·tion·al** \-shnəl, -shə-nᵊl\ *adj* (1648) **:** of, relating to, or characterized by devotion ⟨~ literature⟩ — **de·vo·tion·al·ly** \-ē\ *adv*

[2]**devotional** *n* (1659) **:** a short worship service

de·vour \di-ˈvau̇(-ə)r, dē-\ *vt* [ME, fr. AF *devour-,* stem of *devorer,* fr. L *devorare,* fr. *de-* + *vorare* to devour — more at VORACIOUS] (14c) **1** : to eat up greedily or ravenously **2** : to use up or destroy as if by eating ⟨we are ~*ing* the world's resources⟩ **3** : to prey upon ⟨~*ed* by guilt⟩ **4** : to enjoy avidly ⟨~*s* books⟩ — **de·vour·er** *n*

de·vout \di-ˈvau̇t\ *adj* [ME, fr. AF, fr. LL *devotus,* fr. L, pp. of *devovēre*] (13c) **1** : devoted to religion or to religious duties or exercises **2** : expressing devotion or piety ⟨a ~ attitude⟩ **3 a** : devoted to a pursuit, belief, or mode of behavior : SERIOUS, EARNEST ⟨a ~ baseball fan⟩ ⟨born a ~ coward —G. B. Shaw⟩ **b** : warmly sincere ⟨a ~ wish for peace⟩ — **de·vout·ly** *adv* — **de·vout·ness** *n*

dew \ˈdü *also* ˈdyü\ *n* [ME, fr. OE *dēaw;* akin to OHG *tou* dew, Gk *thein* to run] (bef. 12c) **1** : moisture condensed upon the surfaces of cool bodies esp. at night **2** : something resembling dew in purity, freshness, or power to refresh **3** : moisture esp. when appearing in minute droplets: as **a** : TEARS **b** : SWEAT **c** : droplets of water produced by a plant in transpiration — **dew** *vt* — **dew·less** \-ləs\ *adj*

DEW *abbr* distant early warning

dew·ar \ˈdü-ər *also* ˈdyü-\ *n, often cap* [Sir James *Dewar*] (1939) : a glass or metal container made like a vacuum bottle that is used esp. for storing liquefied gases — called also *Dewar flask*

de·wa·ter \(ˌ)dē-ˈwȯt-ər, -ˈwät-\ *vt* (ca. 1909) : to remove water from — **de·wa·ter·er** *n*

dew·ber·ry \ˈdü-ˌber-ē *also* ˈdyü-\ *n* (ca. 1578) **1** : any of several sweet edible berries related to and resembling blackberries **2** : a trailing or decumbent bramble (genus *Rubus*) that bears dewberries

dew·claw \ˈdü-ˌklȯ *also* ˈdyü-\ *n* (1576) : a vestigial digit not reaching to the ground on the foot of a mammal; *also* : a claw or hoof terminating such a digit — see COW illustration

dew·drop \ˈdü-ˌdräp *also* ˈdyü-\ *n* (13c) : a drop of dew

Dew·ey decimal classification \ˈdü-ē- *also* ˈdyü-\ *n* [Melvil *Dewey*] (1924) : a system of classifying books and other publications whereby main classes are designated by a 3-digit number and subdivisions are shown by numbers after a decimal point — called also *Dewey decimal system*

dew·fall \ˈdü-ˌfȯl *also* ˈdyü-\ *n* (1622) : formation of dew; *also* : the time when dew begins to deposit

dew·lap \ˈdü-ˌlap *also* ˈdyü-\ *n* (14c) **1** : loose skin hanging under the neck of an animal — see COW illustration **2** : loose flesh on the human throat — **dew·lapped** \-ˌlapt\ *adj*

de·worm \(ˌ)dē-ˈwərm\ *vt* (1926) : to rid (as a dog) of worms : WORM 4 — **de·worm·er** \(ˌ)dē-ˈwər-mər\ *n*

dew point *n* (1826) : the temperature at which a vapor (as water) begins or would begin to condense

dew worm *n* (1599) : NIGHT CRAWLER

dewy \ˈdü-ē *also* ˈdyü-\ *adj* **dew·i·er; -est** (bef. 12c) **1** : moist with, affected by, or suggestive of dew ⟨~ grass⟩ **2** : INNOCENT, UNSOPHISTICATED ⟨from a ~ bride to an ill-mannered, murderous courtesan —Melvin Gussow⟩ — **dew·i·ly** \ˈdü-ə-lē, ˈdyü-\ *adv* — **dew·i·ness** \ˈdü-ē-nəs, ˈdyü-\ *n*

dewy–eyed \ˈdü-ē-ˌīd *also* ˈdyü-\ *adj* (1938) : naively innocent and trusting ⟨a ~ optimist⟩

dex \ˈdeks\ *n* (1961) : the sulfate of dextroamphetamine

DEXA *abbr* dual-energy X-ray absorptiometry

dexa·meth·a·sone \ˌdek-sə-ˈme-thə-ˌsōn, -ˌzōn\ *n* [*dexa-* (blend of *deca-* and *hexa-*) + *meth*yl + *-a-* (perh. fr. *pregnane,* a parent compound of corticoid hormones) + *-sone* (as in *cortisone*)] (1958) : a synthetic glucocorticoid $C_{22}H_{29}FO_5$ used esp. as an anti-inflammatory agent

Dex·e·drine \ˈdek-sə-ˌdrēn, -drən\ *trademark* — used for a preparation of the sulfate of dextroamphetamine

dex·fen·flur·a·mine \ˌdeks-ˈfen-flu̇r-ə-ˌmēn\ *n* [*dex*trorotatory] (1987) : the dextrorotatory form of fenfluramine formerly used to treat obesity but withdrawn due to its association with heart valve disease — compare FEN-PHEN

dex·ies \ˈdek-sēz\ *n pl* [*Dex*edrine + *-ie* + [1]*-s*] (1956) *slang* : tablets or capsules of the sulfate of dextroamphetamine

dex·ter \ˈdek-stər\ *adj* [L; akin to OHG *zeso* situated on the right, Gk *dexios*] (1562) **1** : relating to or situated on the right **2** : being or relating to the side of a heraldic shield at the right of the person bearing it — **dexter** *adv*

dex·ter·i·ty \dek-ˈster-ə-tē, -ˈste-rə-\ *n, pl* **-ties** [MF or L; MF *dexterité,* fr. L *dexteritat-, dexteritas,* fr. *dexter*] (1518) **1** : mental skill or quickness : ADROITNESS **2** : readiness and grace in physical activity; *esp* : skill and ease in using the hands ⟨manual ~⟩

dex·ter·ous *also* **dex·trous** \ˈdek-st(ə-)rəs\ *adj* [L *dextr-, dexter* on the right side, skillful] (1609) **1** : mentally adroit and skillful : CLEVER ⟨her ~ handling of the crisis⟩ **2** : done with dexterity : ARTFUL ⟨a ~ maneuver⟩ **3** : skillful and competent with the hands ⟨a ~ surgeon⟩ — **dex·ter·ous·ly** *adv* — **dex·ter·ous·ness** *n*

syn DEXTEROUS, ADROIT, DEFT mean ready and skilled in physical movement. DEXTEROUS implies expertness with consequent facility and quickness in manipulation ⟨unrolled the sleeping bag with a *dexterous* toss⟩. ADROIT implies dexterity but usu. also stresses resourcefulness or artfulness or inventiveness ⟨the magician's *adroit* response to the failure of her prop won applause⟩. DEFT emphasizes lightness, neatness, and sureness of touch or handling ⟨a surgeon's *deft* manipulation of the scalpel⟩.

dextr- *or* **dextro-** *comb form* [L *dextr-, dexter*] **1** : right : on or toward the right ⟨*dextro*rotatory⟩ **2** *usu* **dextro-** : dextrorotatory ⟨*dextro*amphetamine⟩

dex·tral \ˈdek-strəl\ *adj* (1646) : of or relating to the right : inclined to the right: as **a** : RIGHT-HANDED 3 **b** *of a gastropod shell* : having the whorls coiling clockwise down the spire when viewed with the apex toward the observer and having the aperture situated on the right of the axis when held with the spire uppermost and with the aperture opening toward the observer — compare SINISTRAL

dex·tran \ˈdek-stran, -strən\ *n* [ISV] (1879) : any of numerous glucose biopolymers of variable molecular weight that are produced esp. by the fermentation of sucrose by bacteria (as genus *Leuconostoc*), are found in dental plaque, and are used esp. in blood plasma substitutes

dex·tran·ase \-strə-ˌnās, -ˌnāz\ *n* (ca. 1949) : a hydrolase that prevents tooth decay by breaking down dextran and eliminating dental plaque

dex·trin \ˈdek-strən\ *also* **dex·trine** \-ˌstrēn, -strən\ *n* [F *dextrine,* fr. *dextr-*] (1838) : any of various water-soluble gummy polysaccharides $(C_6H_{10}O_5)_n$ obtained from starch by the action of heat, acids, or enzymes and used as adhesives, as sizes for paper and textiles, as thickening agents (as in syrups), and in beer

dex·tro \ˈdek-(ˌ)strō\ *adj* [*dextr-*] (1889) : DEXTROROTATORY

dex·tro·am·phet·amine \ˈdek-(ˌ)strō-am-ˈfe-tə-ˌmēn, -mən\ *n* (1943) : the dextrorotatory sulfate of amphetamine

dex·tro·me·thor·phan \ˌdek-strō-mi-ˈthȯr-ˌfan\ *n* [*dextr-* + *meth*yl + *morph*inan parent substance of morphine alkaloids, fr. *morphine* + [3]*-an*] (1967) : a cough suppressant $C_{18}H_{25}NO$ that is widely used esp. in the form of a hydrated hydrogen bromide complex

dex·tro·ro·ta·to·ry \-ˈrō-tə-ˌtȯr-ē\ *adj* (ca. 1872) : turning clockwise or toward the right; *specif* : rotating the plane of polarization of light toward the right ⟨~ crystals⟩ — compare LEVOROTATORY

dex·trose \ˈdek-ˌstrōs, -ˌstrōz\ *n* (ca. 1869) : dextrorotatory glucose

dey \ˈdā\ *n* [F, fr. Turk *dayı,* lit., maternal uncle] (1659) : a ruling official of the Ottoman Empire in northern Africa

DF *abbr* **1** damage free **2** direction finder; direction finding

DFA *abbr* doctor of fine arts

DFC *abbr* Distinguished Flying Cross

d4T \ˌdē-(ˌ)fȯr-ˈtē\ *n* [*d*ideoxy-*4*-*t*hymidine] (1988) : a synthetic antiretroviral nucleoside $C_{10}H_{12}N_2O_4$ that is an analog of thymidine and is administered orally in the treatment of HIV infection — called also *stavudine*

dft *abbr* **1** defendant **2** draft

dg *abbr* decigram

DG *abbr* **1** [LL *Dei gratia*] by the grace of God **2** director general

[1]**DH** \ˌdē-ˈāch\ *n, pl* **DHs** (1973) : DESIGNATED HITTER 1

[2]**DH** \ˌdē-ˈāch, ˈdē-ˌāch\ *vi* **DHed; DHing** (1975) : to play as a designated hitter in a baseball game

[3]**DH** *abbr* doctor of humanities

DHA *abbr* docosahexaenoic acid

dhar·ma \ˈdər-mə, ˈdär-\ *n* [Skt; akin to L *firmus* firm] (1796) **1** *Hinduism* : an individual's duty fulfilled by observance of custom or law **2** *Hinduism & Buddhism* **a** : the basic principles of cosmic or individual existence : divine law **b** : conformity to one's duty and nature — **dhar·mic** \-mik\ *adj*

dhar·na \ˈdər-nə, ˈdär-\ *n* [Hindi & Urdu *dharnā,* fr. Skt *dharaṇam* support, prop; akin to L *firmus* firm] (1747) : a fast held at the door of an offender in India as an appeal for justice

DHEA *abbr* dehydroepiandrosterone

DHL *abbr* doctor of Hebrew letters; doctor of Hebrew literature

dhole \ˈdōl\ *n* [perh. fr. Kannada *tōḷa* wolf] (ca. 1827) : a wild dog (*Cuon alpinus*) occurring from India to southern Siberia

dho·ti \ˈdō-tē\ *n, pl* **dhotis** [Hindi & Urdu *dhotī*] (1612) : a loincloth worn by men in some parts of India

dhow \ˈdau̇\ *n* [Ar *dāwa*] (1785) : an Arab lateen-rigged boat usu. having a long overhang forward, a high poop, and a low waist

DHS *abbr* Department of Homeland Security

Dhu'l–Hij·ja \ˌdül-ˈhi-(ˌ)jä, ˌt͟hül-\ *n* [Ar *Dhū-al-ḥijja,* lit., the one of the pilgrimage] (ca. 1771) : the 12th month of the Islamic year — see MONTH table

Dhu'l–Qa·dah \-ˈkä-(ˌ)dä\ *n* [Ar *Dhū-al-qaʿda,* lit., the one of the sitting] (ca. 1771) : the 11th month of the Islamic year — see MONTH table

dhur·rie \ˈdə-rē, ˈdər-ē\ *n* [Hindi & Urdu *darī*] (1880) : a thick flat-woven cotton or wool cloth or rug made in India

DI *abbr* drill instructor

di- *comb form* [L, fr. Gk; akin to OE *twi-*] **1** : twice : twofold : double ⟨*di*chromatic⟩ **2** : containing two atoms, radicals, or groups ⟨*di*oxide⟩

dia *abbr* diameter

DIA *abbr* Defense Intelligence Agency

dia- *also* **di-** *prefix* [L, fr. Gk, through, apart, fr. *dia;* akin to L *dis-*] : through ⟨*dia*positive⟩ : across ⟨*dia*dromous⟩

di·a·base \ˈdī-ə-ˌbās\ *n* [F, prob. fr. Gk *diabasis* act of crossing over, fr. *diabainein* to cross over, fr. *dia-* + *bainein* to go — more at COME] (ca. 1816) **1** *archaic* : DIORITE **2** *chiefly Brit* : an altered basalt **3** : a fine-grained rock of the composition of gabbro but with an ophitic texture — **di·a·ba·sic** \ˌdī-ə-ˈbā-sik\ *adj*

di·a·be·tes \ˌdī-ə-ˈbē-tēz, -ˈbē-təs\ *n* [L, fr. Gk *diabētēs* diabetes insipidus, fr. *diabainein* to walk with the legs apart, cross over] (15c) : any of various abnormal conditions characterized by the secretion and excretion of excessive amounts of urine; *esp* : DIABETES MELLITUS

diabetes in·sip·i·dus \-in-ˈsi-pə-dəs\ *n* [NL, lit., bland diabetes] (ca. 1846) : a disorder of the pituitary gland characterized by intense thirst and by the excretion of large amounts of urine

diabetes mel·li·tus \-ˈme-lə-təs\ *n* [NL, lit., honey-sweet diabetes] (1830) : a variable disorder of carbohydrate metabolism caused by a combination of hereditary and environmental factors and usu. characterized by inadequate secretion or utilization of insulin, by excessive urine production, by excessive amounts of sugar in the blood and urine, and by thirst, hunger, and loss of weight — compare TYPE 1 DIABETES, TYPE 2 DIABETES

[1]**di·a·bet·ic** \ˌdī-ə-ˈbe-tik\ *adj* (1799) **1** : of or relating to diabetes or diabetics **2** : affected with diabetes **3** : occurring in or caused by diabetes ⟨~ coma⟩ **4** : suitable for diabetics ⟨~ food⟩

[2]**diabetic** *n* (1840) : a person affected with diabetes

di·a·be·to·gen·ic \ˌdī-ə-ˌbe-tə-ˈje-nik, -ˌbē-\ *adj* (ca. 1903) : producing diabetes

di·a·be·tol·og·ist \ˌdī-ə-(ˌ)be-ˈtä-lə-jist, -ˌbē-\ *n* (1970) : a specialist in diabetes

di·a·ble·rie \dē-ˈä-blə-(ˌ)rē, -ˈa-blə-\ *n* [F, fr. OF, fr. *diable* devil, fr. LL *diabolus* — more at DEVIL] (1751) **1** : black magic : SORCERY **2 a** : a representation in words or pictures of black magic or of dealings with the devil **b** : demon lore **3** : mischievous conduct or manner

di·a·bol·i·cal \ˌdī-ə-ˈbä-li-kəl\ *or* **di·a·bol·ic** \-ˈbä-lik\ *adj* [ME *deabolik,* fr. MF *diabolique,* fr. LL *diabolicus,* fr. *diabolus*] (14c) : of, relating

\ə\ **abut** \ᵊ\ **kitten,** F **table** \ər\ **further** \a\ **ash** \ā\ **ace** \ä\ **mop, mar**
\au̇\ **out** \ch\ **chin** \e\ **bet** \ē\ **easy** \g\ **go** \i\ **hit** \ī\ **ice** \j\ **job**
\ŋ\ **sing** \ō\ **go** \ȯ\ **law** \ȯi\ **boy** \th\ **thin** \t͟h\ **the** \ü\ **loot** \u̇\ **foot**
\y\ **yet** \zh\ **vision, beige** \k, ⁿ, œ, ue, ʸ\ *see* Guide to Pronunciation

to, or characteristic of the devil : DEVILISH ⟨a ~ plot⟩ — **di·a·bol·i·cal·ly** \-li-k(ə-)lē\ *adv* — **di·a·bol·i·cal·ness** \-li-kəl-nəs\ *n*

di·ab·o·lism \dī-ˈa-bə-ˌli-zəm\ *n* (1614) **1 :** dealings with or possession by the devil **2 :** belief in or worship of devils **3 :** evil character or conduct — **di·ab·o·list** \-list\ *n*

di·ab·o·lize \-ˌlīz\ *vt* **-lized; -liz·ing** (1702) : to represent as or make diabolical

dia·chron·ic \ˌdī-ə-ˈkrä-nik\ *adj* (1922) : of, relating to, or dealing with phenomena (as of language or culture) as they occur or change over a period of time — **dia·chron·i·cal·ly** \-ˈkrä-ni-k(ə-)lē\ *adv*

di·ach·ro·ny \dī-ˈa-krə-nē\ *n* [ISV *dia-* + *-chrony* (as in *synchrony*)] (ca. 1939) **1 :** diachronic analysis **2 :** change extending through time

[1]**di·ac·id** \(ˌ)dī-ˈa-səd\ *or* **di·acid·ic** \ˌdī-ə-ˈsi-dik\ *adj* (1866) : able to react with two molecules of a monobasic acid or one of a dibasic acid to form a salt or ester — used esp. of bases

[2]**diacid** *n* [ISV] (ca. 1929) : an acid with two acid hydrogen atoms

di·ac·o·nal \dī-ˈa-kə-nᵊl, dē-\ *adj* [LL *diaconalis,* fr. *diaconus* deacon — more at DEACON] (ca. 1611) : of or relating to a deacon or deaconess

di·ac·o·nate \-ˈa-kə-nət, -ˌnāt\ *n* (ca. 1751) **1 :** the office or period of office of a deacon or deaconess **2 :** an official body of deacons

di·a·crit·ic \ˌdī-ə-ˈkri-tik\ *n* (1866) : a mark near or through an orthographic or phonetic character or combination of characters indicating a phonetic value different from that given the unmarked or otherwise marked element

DIACRITICS

´	(é)	acute accent	˘	(ŭ)	breve
`	(è)	grave accent	ˇ	(č)	haček
ˆ	(ô)	circumflex	¨	(naïve)	diaeresis
˜	(ñ)	tilde	¨	(glögg)	umlaut
¯	(ō)	macron	¸	(ç)	cedilla

di·a·crit·i·cal \ˌdī-ə-ˈkri-ti-kəl\ *also* **di·a·crit·ic** \-ˈkri-tik\ *adj* [Gk *diakritikos* separative, fr. *diakrinein* to distinguish, fr. *dia-* + *krinein* to separate — more at CERTAIN] (1749) **1 :** serving as a diacritic **2 a :** DISTINCTIVE ⟨the ~ elements in culture —S. F. Nadel⟩ **b :** capable of distinguishing ⟨students of superior ~ powers⟩

di·adel·phous \ˌdī-ə-ˈdel-fəs\ *adj* [*di-* + *-adelphous*] (1807) : united by filaments into two fascicles — used of stamens

di·a·dem \ˈdī-ə-ˌdem, -dəm\ *n* [ME *diademe,* fr. AF, fr. L *diadema,* fr. Gk *diadēma,* fr. *diadein* to bind around, fr. *dia-* + *dein* to bind; akin to Skt *dāman* rope] (13c) **1 a :** CROWN 2; *specif* : a royal headband **b :** CROWN 6a(1) **2 :** something that adorns like a crown

di·ad·ro·mous \dī-ˈa-drə-məs\ *adj* (ca. 1949) *of a fish* : migratory between salt and fresh waters

di·aer·e·sis *or* **di·er·e·sis** \dī-ˈer-ə-səs, *Brit also* -ˈir-\ *n, pl* **-e·ses** \-ˌsēz\ [LL *diaeresis,* fr. Gk *diairesis,* lit., division, fr. *diairein* to divide, fr. *dia-* + *hairein* to take] (ca. 1611) **1 :** a mark ¨ placed over a vowel to indicate that the vowel is pronounced in a separate syllable (as in *naïve* or *Brontë*) — compare UMLAUT **2 :** the break in a verse caused by the coincidence of the end of a foot with the end of a word — **di·ae·ret·ic** \ˌdī-ə-ˈre-tik\ *adj*

diag *abbr* **1** diagonal **2** diagram

dia·gen·e·sis \ˌdī-ə-ˈje-nə-səs\ *n* [NL] (ca. 1886) **1 :** recombination or rearrangement of constituents (as of a chemical or mineral) resulting in a new product **2 :** the conversion (as by compaction or chemical reaction) of sediment into rock — **dia·ge·net·ic** \ˌdī-ə-jə-ˈne-tik\ *adj* — **dia·ge·net·i·cal·ly** \-ˈne-ti-k(ə-)lē\ *adv*

dia·geo·tro·pic \ˌdī-ə-ˌjē-ə-ˈtrō-pik, -ˈträ-pik\ *adj* (1880) : tending to grow at right angles to the line of gravity ⟨~ branches and roots⟩

di·ag·nose \ˈdī-ig-ˌnōs, -ˌnōz, ˌdī-ig-ˈ, -əg-\ *vb* **-nosed; -nos·ing** [back-formation fr. *diagnosis*] *vt* (ca. 1859) **1 a :** to recognize (as a disease) by signs and symptoms **b :** to diagnose a disease or condition in ⟨*diagnosed* the patient⟩ **2 :** to analyze the cause or nature of ⟨~ the problem⟩ ~ *vi* : to make a diagnosis — **di·ag·nos·able** *or* **di·ag·nose·able** \ˌdī-ig-ˈnō-sə-bəl, -əg-, -zə-\ *adj*

di·ag·no·sis \ˌdī-ig-ˈnō-səs, -əg-\ *n, pl* **-no·ses** \-ˌsēz\ [NL, fr. Gk *diagnōsis,* fr. *diagignōskein* to distinguish, fr. *dia-* + *gignōskein* to know — more at KNOW] (1655) **1 a :** the art or act of identifying a disease from its signs and symptoms **b :** the decision reached by diagnosis **2 :** a concise technical description of a taxon **3 a :** investigation or analysis of the cause or nature of a condition, situation, or problem ⟨~ of engine trouble⟩ **b :** a statement or conclusion from such an analysis

diagnosis related group *n* (1977) : DRG

[1]**di·ag·nos·tic** \-ˈnäs-tik\ *also* **di·ag·nos·ti·cal** \-ti-kəl\ *adj* (1625) **1 a :** of, relating to, or used in diagnosis ⟨a ~ tool⟩ **b :** using the methods of or yielding a diagnosis ⟨~ tests⟩ **2 :** serving to distinguish or identify ⟨a ~ feature⟩ — **di·ag·nos·ti·cal·ly** \-ti-k(ə-)lē\ *adv*

[2]**diagnostic** *n* (1625) **1 :** the art or practice of diagnosis — often used in pl. **2 :** a distinguishing mark — **di·ag·nos·ti·cian** \-(ˌ)näs-ˈti-shən\ *n*

[1]**di·ag·o·nal** \dī-ˈa-gə-nᵊl, -ˈag-nəl\ *adj* [L *diagonalis,* fr. Gk *diagōnios* from angle to angle, fr. *dia-* + *gōnia* angle; akin to Gk *gony* knee — more at KNEE] (1563) **1 a :** joining two vertices of a rectilinear figure that are nonadjacent or two vertices of a polyhedral figure that are not in the same face **b :** passing through two nonadjacent edges of a polyhedron ⟨a ~ plane⟩ **2 a :** inclined obliquely from a reference line (as the vertical) ⟨wood with a ~ grain⟩ **b :** having diagonal markings or parts ⟨a ~ weave⟩

[2]**diagonal** *n* (1571) **1 :** a diagonal straight line or plane **2 a** (1) **:** a diagonal direction (2) **:** a diagonal row, arrangement, or pattern **b :** something oriented in diagonal position **3 :** SLASH 4 — **on the diagonal :** in an oblique direction : DIAGONALLY

di·ag·o·nal·ize \-nə-ˌlīz\ *vt* **-ized; -iz·ing** (1942) : to put (a matrix) in a form with all the nonzero elements along the diagonal from upper left to lower right — **di·ag·o·nal·iz·able** \-ˌlī-zə-bəl\ *adj* — **di·ag·o·nal·i·za·tion** \-ˌa-gə-nə-lə-ˈzā-shən, -ˌag-nə-lə-ˈzā-\ *n*

di·ag·o·nal·ly \dī-ˈa-gə-nə-lē, -ˈag-nə-lē\ *adv* (1541) : in a diagonal manner

diagonal matrix *n* (1927) : a diagonalized matrix

[1]**di·a·gram** \ˈdī-ə-ˌgram\ *n* [Gk *diagramma,* fr. *diagraphein* to mark out by lines, fr. *dia-* + *graphein* to write — more at CARVE] (1619) **1 :** a graphic design that explains rather than represents; *esp* : a drawing that shows arrangement and relations (as of parts) **2 :** a line drawing made for mathematical or scientific purposes — **di·a·gram·ma·ble** \-ˌgra-mə-bəl\ *adj* — **di·a·gram·mat·ic** \ˌdī-ə-grə-ˈma-tik\ *also* **di·a·gram·mat·i·cal** \-ˈma-ti-kəl\ *adj* — **di·a·gram·mat·i·cal·ly** \-ti-k(ə-)lē\ *adv*

[2]**diagram** *vt* **-grammed** *or* **-gramed** \-ˌgramd\; **-gram·ming** *or* **-gram·ing** \-ˌgra-miŋ\ (1785) : to represent by or put into the form of a diagram ⟨~ a sentence⟩ ⟨~ a football play⟩

dia·ki·ne·sis \ˌdī-ə-kə-ˈnē-səs, -(ˌ)kī-\ *n, pl* **-ne·ses** \-ˌsēz\ [NL] (ca. 1902) : the final stage of the meiotic prophase marked by contraction of the bivalents

[1]**di·al** \ˈdī(-ə)l\ *n* [ME *dyal,* fr. ML *dialis* clock wheel revolving daily, fr. L *dies* day — more at DEITY] (15c) **1 :** the face of a sundial **2** *obs* **:** TIMEPIECE **3 :** the graduated face of a timepiece **4 a :** a face upon which some measurement is registered usu. by means of graduations and a pointer ⟨the thermometer ~ reads 70°F⟩ **b :** a device that may be operated to make electrical connections or to regulate the operation of a machine ⟨a radio ~⟩ ⟨a telephone ~⟩

[2]**dial** *vb* **di·aled** *or* **di·alled; di·al·ing** *or* **di·al·ling** *vt* (1653) **1 :** to measure with a dial **2 a :** to manipulate a device (as a dial) so as to operate, regulate, or select ⟨~ your favorite program⟩ ⟨~*ed* the wrong number⟩ **b :** CALL 1m(1) ⟨~*ed* the office⟩ ~ *vi* **1 :** to manipulate a dial **2 :** to make a telephone call or connection — **di·al·er** *n*

[3]**dial** *abbr* **1** dialect **2** dialectical

di·a·lect \ˈdī-ə-ˌlekt\ *n, often attrib* [MF *dialecte,* fr. L *dialectus,* fr. Gk *dialektos* conversation, dialect, fr. *dialegesthai* to converse — more at DIALOGUE] (1577) **1 a :** a regional variety of language distinguished by features of vocabulary, grammar, and pronunciation from other regional varieties and constituting together with them a single language ⟨the Doric ~ of ancient Greek⟩ **b :** one of two or more cognate languages ⟨French and Italian are Romance ~*s*⟩ **c :** a variety of a language used by the members of a group ⟨such ~*s* as politics and advertising —Philip Howard⟩ **d :** a variety of language whose identity is fixed by a factor other than geography (as social class) ⟨spoke a rough peasant ~⟩ **e :** REGISTER 4c **f :** a version of a computer programming language **2 :** manner or means of expressing oneself : PHRASEOLOGY — **di·a·lec·tal** \ˌdī-ə-ˈlek-tᵊl\ *adj* — **di·a·lec·tal·ly** \-tə-lē\ *adv*

dialect atlas *n* (1925) : LINGUISTIC ATLAS

dialect geography *n* (1926) : LINGUISTIC GEOGRAPHY

di·a·lec·tic \ˌdī-ə-ˈlek-tik\ *n* [ME *dialetik,* fr. AF *dialetiqe,* fr. L *dialectica,* fr. Gk *dialektikē,* fr. fem. of *dialektikos* of conversation, fr. *dialektos*] (14c) **1 :** LOGIC 1a(1) **2 a :** discussion and reasoning by dialogue as a method of intellectual investigation; *specif* : the Socratic techniques of exposing false beliefs and eliciting truth **b :** the Platonic investigation of the eternal ideas **3 :** the logic of fallacy **4 a :** the Hegelian process of change in which a concept or its realization passes over into and is preserved and fulfilled by its opposite; *also* : the critical investigation of this process **b** (1) *usu pl but sing or pl in constr* : development through the stages of thesis, antithesis, and synthesis in accordance with the laws of dialectical materialism (2) **:** the investigation of this process (3) **:** the theoretical application of this process esp. in the social sciences **5** *usu pl but sing or pl in constr* **a :** any systematic reasoning, exposition, or argument that juxtaposes opposed or contradictory ideas and usu. seeks to resolve their conflict **b :** an intellectual exchange of ideas **6 :** the dialectical tension or opposition between two interacting forces or elements

di·a·lec·ti·cal \ˌdī-ə-ˈlek-ti-kəl\ *also* **di·a·lec·tic** \-tik\ *adj* (1548) **1 a :** of, relating to, or in accordance with dialectic ⟨~ method⟩ **b :** practicing, devoted to, or employing dialectic ⟨a ~ philosopher⟩ **2 :** of, relating to, or characteristic of a dialect — **di·a·lec·ti·cal·ly** \-ti-k(ə-)lē\ *adv*

dialectical materialism *n* (1927) : the Marxist theory that maintains the material basis of a reality constantly changing in a dialectical process and the priority of matter over mind — compare HISTORICAL MATERIALISM

di·a·lec·ti·cian \ˌdī-ə-ˌlek-ˈti-shən\ *n* (ca. 1693) **1 :** one who is skilled in or practices dialectic **2 :** a student of dialects

di·a·lec·tol·o·gist \-ˈtä-lə-jist\ *n* (ca. 1874) : a specialist in dialectology

di·a·lec·tol·o·gy \-jē\ *n* [ISV] (ca. 1864) **1 :** the systematic study of dialect **2 :** the body of data available for study of a dialect — **di·a·lec·to·log·i·cal** \-ˌlek-tə-ˈlä-ji-kəl\ *adj* — **di·a·lec·to·log·i·cal·ly** \-k(ə-)lē\ *adv*

di·al·lel \ˈdī-ə-ˌlel\ *adj* [Gk *diallēlos* reciprocating, fr. *dia* through + *allēlōn* one another — more at ALLELO-] (1920) : relating to or being the crossing of each of several individuals with two or more others in order to determine the relative genetic contribution of each parent to specific characters in the offspring

dialog box *n* (1984) : a window on a computer screen for choosing options or inputting information

di·a·log·ic \ˌdī-ə-ˈlä-jik\ *or* **di·a·log·i·cal** \-ji-kəl\ *adj* (1833) : of, relating to, or characterized by dialogue ⟨~ writing⟩ — **di·a·log·i·cal·ly** \-ji-k(ə-)lē\ *adv*

di·a·lo·gist \dī-ˈa-lə-jist; ˈdī-ə-ˌlȯ-gist, -ˌlä-\ *n* (1651) **1 :** a writer of dialogues **2 :** one who participates in a dialogue — **di·a·lo·gis·tic** \(ˌ)dī-ˌa-lə-ˈjis-tik; ˌdī-ə-ˌlȯ-ˈgis-, -ˌlä-ˈgis-\ *adj*

[1]**di·a·logue** *also* **di·a·log** \ˈdī-ə-ˌlȯg, -ˌläg\ *n* [ME *dialoge,* fr. AF *dialogue,* fr. L *dialogus,* fr. Gk *dialogos,* fr. *dialegesthai* to converse, fr. *dia-* + *legein* to speak — more at LEGEND] (13c) **1 :** a written composition in which two or more characters are represented as conversing **2 a :** a conversation between two or more persons; *also* : a similar exchange between a person and something else (as a computer) **b :** an exchange of ideas and opinions ⟨organized a series of ~*s* on human rights⟩ **c :** a discussion between representatives of parties to a conflict that is aimed at resolution ⟨a constructive ~ between loggers and environmentalists⟩ **3 :** the conversational element of literary or dramatic composition ⟨very little ~ in this film⟩ **4 :** a musical composition for two or more parts suggestive of a conversation

[2]**dialogue** *vb* **-logued; -logu·ing** *vt* (1566) : to express in dialogue ~ *vi* : to take part in a dialogue ⟨managers *dialoguing* with employees⟩

dial tone *n* (1923) : a tone emitted by a telephone as a signal that the system is ready for dialing

dial–up \ˈdī(-ə)l-ˌəp\ *adj* (1961) : relating to or being a standard telephone line used for computer communications; *also* : accessible via a standard telephone line ⟨a ~ Internet provider⟩

di·al·y·sate \dī-ˈa-lə-ˌzāt, -ˌsāt\ *also* **di·al·y·zate** \-ˌzāt\ *n* (ca. 1867) : the material that passes through the membrane in dialysis

di·a·lyse, di·a·lys·er *chiefly Brit var of* DIALYZE, DIALYZER

di·al·y·sis \dī-ˈa-lə-səs\ *n, pl* **-y·ses** \-ˌsēz\ [NL, fr. Gk, separation, fr. *dialyein* to dissolve, fr. *dia-* + *lyein* to loosen — more at LOSE] (1861) **1** : the separation of substances in solution by means of their unequal diffusion through semipermeable membranes; *esp* : such a separation of colloids from soluble substances **2** : the process of removing blood from an artery (as of a kidney patient), purifying it by dialysis, adding vital substances, and returning it to a vein — called also *hemodialysis* — **di·a·lyt·ic** \ˌdī-ə-ˈli-tik\ *adj*

di·a·lyze \ˈdī-ə-ˌlīz\ *vb* **-lyzed; -lyz·ing** *vt* (1861) : to subject to dialysis ~ *vi* : to undergo dialysis — **di·a·lyz·able** \-ˌlī-zə-bəl\ *adj*

di·a·lyz·er \-ˌlī-zər\ *n* (1861) : an apparatus in which dialysis is carried out

diam *abbr* diameter

dia·mag·net·ic \ˌdī-ə-mag-ˈne-tik\ *adj* (1846) : having a magnetic permeability less than that of a vacuum : slightly repelled by a magnet — **dia·mag·ne·tism** \-ˈmag-nə-ˌti-zəm\ *n*

di·a·man·té \ˌdē-ə-ˌmän-ˈtā\ *n* [F, adj., like a diamond, fr. *diamant* diamond, fr. MF] (1904) : a sparkling decoration (as of sequins) or material decorated with this ⟨a gown trimmed with ~⟩

di·am·e·ter \dī-ˈa-mə-tər\ *n* [ME *diametre,* fr. MF, fr. L *diametros,* fr. Gk, fr. *dia-* + *metron* measure — more at MEASURE] (14c) **1** : a chord passing through the center of a figure or body **2** : the length of a straight line through the center of an object **3** : a unit of enlargement used with a number to indicate magnification by a lens or optical system ⟨an object one millimeter wide magnified 40 ~*s* appears 40 millimeters wide⟩ — **di·am·e·tral** \-ˈa-mə-trəl\ *adj*

di·a·met·ric \ˌdī-ə-ˈme-trik\ *or* **di·a·met·ri·cal** \-tri-kəl\ *adj* (1553) **1** : of, relating to, or constituting a diameter : located at the diameter **2** : completely opposed : being at opposite extremes ⟨in ~ contradiction to his claims⟩ — **di·a·met·ri·cal·ly** \-tri-k(ə-)lē\ *adv*

di·amide \ˈdī-ə-ˌmīd, dī-ˈa-məd\ *n* (1866) : a compound containing two amido groups

di·amine \ˈdī-ə-ˌmēn, dī-ˈa-mən\ *n* [ISV] (1866) : a compound containing two amino groups

di·am·mo·ni·um phosphate \ˌdī-ə-ˈmō-nē-əm-\ *n* (ca. 1929) : a white crystalline compound $(NH_4)_2HPO_4$ used esp. as a fertilizer and as a fire retardant

[1]**di·a·mond** \ˈdī-(ə-)mənd\ *n, often attrib* [ME *diamaunde,* fr. MF *diamand,* fr. LL *diamant-, diamas,* alter. of L *adamant-, adamas* hardest metal, diamond, fr. Gk] (14c) **1 a** : native crystalline carbon that is the hardest known mineral, that is usu. nearly colorless, that when transparent and free from flaws is highly valued as a precious stone, and that is used industrially esp. as an abrasive; *also* : a piece of this substance **b** : crystallized carbon produced artificially **2** : something that resembles a diamond (as in brilliance, value, or fine quality) **3** : a square or rhombus-shaped figure usu. oriented with the long diagonal vertical **4 a** : a playing card marked with a stylized figure of a red diamond **b** *pl but sing or pl in constr* : the suit comprising cards marked with diamonds **5** : a baseball infield; *also* : the entire playing field

[2]**diamond** *vt* (1751) : to adorn with or as if with diamonds

[3]**diamond** *adj* (1872) : of, relating to, or being a 60th or 75th anniversary or its celebration ⟨~ jubilee⟩

di·a·mond·back \ˈdī-(ə-)mən(d)-ˌbak\ *adj* (1887) : having marks like diamonds or lozenges on the back

diamondback moth *n* (1891) : a nearly cosmopolitan moth (*Plutella xylostella* of the family Plutellidae) whose larva is a pest on cruciferous plants

diamondback rattlesnake *n* (1894) : either of two large and deadly rattlesnakes (*Crotalus adamanteus* of the southeastern U.S. and *C. atrox* of the south central and southwestern U.S. and Mexico) — called also *diamondback, diamondback rattler*

diamondback terrapin *n* (1887) : any of several terrapins (genus *Malaclemys*) formerly widely distributed in salt marshes along the Atlantic and Gulf coasts but now much restricted

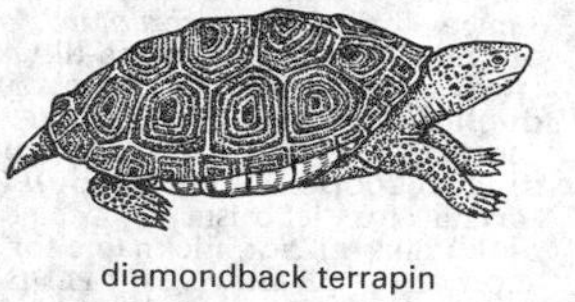

diamondback terrapin

di·a·mond·if·er·ous \ˌdī-(ə-)mən-ˈdi-fə-rəs\ *adj* (1870) : containing diamonds ⟨~ earth⟩

diamond in the rough (1785) : one having exceptional qualities or potential but lacking refinement or polish

Di·ana \dī-ˈa-nə\ *n* [L] (13c) : an ancient Italian goddess of the forest and of childbirth who was identified with Artemis by the Romans

di·an·thus \dī-ˈan(t)-thəs\ *n* [NL, genus name, fr. Gk *dios* heavenly + *anthos* flower — more at DEITY, ANTHOLOGY] (ca. 1766) : [2]PINK 1

di·a·pa·son \ˌdī-ə-ˈpā-zᵊn, -sᵊn\ *n* [ME, fr. L, fr. Gk (*hē*) *dia pasōn* (*chordōn symphōnia*), lit., the concord through all the notes, fr. *dia* through + *pasōn,* gen. fem. pl. of *pas* all — more at DIA-, PAN-] (ca. 1501) **1 a** : a burst of sound ⟨~*s* of laughter⟩ **b** : the principal foundation stop in the organ extending through the complete range of the instrument **c (1)** : the entire compass of musical tones **(2)** : RANGE, SCOPE ⟨registers the full ~ of her responses —Mindy Aloff⟩ **2 a** : TUNING FORK **b** : a standard of pitch

dia·pause \ˈdī-ə-ˌpȯz\ *n* [Gk *diapausis* pause, fr. *diapauein* to pause, fr. *dia-* + *pauein* to stop] (1893) : a period of physiologically enforced dormancy between periods of activity

dia·paus·ing \-ˌpȯ-ziŋ\ *adj* (1944) : undergoing diapause

di·a·pe·de·sis \ˌdī-ə-pə-ˈdē-səs\ *n, pl* **-de·ses** \-ˌsēz\ [NL, fr. Gk *diapēdēsis,* lit., act of leaping through, fr. *diapēdan* to leap through, fr. *dia-* + *pēdan* to leap] (1625) : the passage of blood cells through capillary walls into the tissues

[1]**di·a·per** \ˈdī-pər *also* ˈdī-ə-\ *n* [ME *diapre,* fr. AF *diaspre,* fr. ML *diasprum*] (14c) **1** : a fabric with a distinctive pattern: **a** : a rich silk fabric **b** : a soft usu. white linen or cotton fabric used for tablecloths or towels **2** : an allover pattern consisting of one or more small repeated units of design (as geometric figures) connecting with one another or growing out of one another with continuously flowing or straight lines **3** : a basic garment for infants consisting of a folded cloth or other absorbent material drawn up between the legs and fastened about the waist; *also* : a similar garment esp. for incontinent adults

[2]**diaper** *vt* **di·a·pered; di·a·per·ing** \-p(ə-)riŋ\ (14c) **1** : to ornament with diaper designs **2** : to put on or change the diaper of (an infant)

diaper rash *n* (1945) : skin irritation of the diaper-covered area of an infant esp. from exposure to feces and urinary ammonia

di·a·pha·ne·ity \(ˌ)dī-ˌa-fə-ˈnē-ə-tē, ˌdī-ə-fə-, -ˈnā-\ *n* (15c) : the quality or state of being diaphanous

di·aph·a·nous \dī-ˈa-fə-nəs\ *adj* [ML *diaphanus,* fr. Gk *diaphanēs,* fr. *diaphainein* to show through, fr. *dia-* + *phainein* to show — more at FANCY] (1614) **1** : characterized by such fineness of texture as to permit seeing through ⟨~ fabrics⟩ **2** : characterized by extreme delicacy of form : ETHEREAL ⟨painted ~ landscapes⟩ **3** : INSUBSTANTIAL, VAGUE ⟨had only a ~ hope of success⟩ — **di·aph·a·nous·ly** *adv* — **di·aph·a·nous·ness** *n*

dia·phone \ˈdī-ə-ˌfōn\ *n* (1906) : a fog signal similar to a siren but producing a blast of two tones

di·aph·o·rase \dī-ˈa-fə-ˌrās, -ˌrāz\ *n* [ISV *diaphor-* (fr. Gk *diaphoros* different, fr. *diapherein* to differ, fr. *dia-* + *pherein* to carry) + *-ase* — more at BEAR] (1938) : a flavoprotein enzyme capable of oxidizing the reduced form of NAD

di·a·pho·re·sis \ˌdī-ə-fə-ˈrē-səs, (ˌ)dī-ˌa-fə-\ *n, pl* **-re·ses** \-ˌsēz\ [LL, fr. Gk *diaphorēsis,* fr. *diaphorein* to dissipate by perspiration, fr. *dia-* + *phorein,* freq. of *pherein* to carry] (ca. 1681) : PERSPIRATION; *esp* : profuse perspiration artificially induced

di·a·pho·ret·ic \-ˈre-tik\ *adj* (15c) **1** : having the power to increase perspiration **2** : perspiring profusely — **diaphoretic** *n*

di·a·phragm \ˈdī-ə-ˌfram\ *n* [ME *diafragma,* fr. LL *diaphragma,* fr. Gk, fr. *diaphrassein* to barricade, fr. *dia-* + *phrassein* to enclose] (14c) **1** : a body partition of muscle and connective tissue; *specif* : the partition separating the chest and abdominal cavities in mammals **2** : a dividing membrane or thin partition esp. in a tube **3 a** : a more or less rigid partition in the body or shell of an invertebrate **b** : a transverse septum in a plant stem **4** : a device that limits the aperture of a lens or optical system — compare IRIS DIAPHRAGM **5** : a thin flexible disk (as in a microphone or loudspeaker) that vibrates when struck by sound waves or that vibrates to generate sound waves **6** : a molded cap usu. of thin rubber fitted over the uterine cervix to act as a mechanical contraceptive barrier — **di·a·phrag·mat·ic** \ˌdī-ə-frə(g)-ˈma-tik, -ˌfrag-\ *adj* — **di·a·phrag·mat·i·cal·ly** \-ˈma-ti-k(ə-)lē\ *adv*

di·aph·y·sis \dī-ˈa-fə-səs\ *n, pl* **-y·ses** \-ˌsēz\ [NL, fr. Gk, spinous process of the tibia, fr. *diaphyesthai* to grow between, fr. *dia-* + *phyein* to bring forth — more at BE] (1831) : the shaft of a long bone — **di·aph·y·se·al** \(ˌ)dī-ˌa-fə-ˈsē-əl\ *or* **di·a·phys·i·al** \ˌdī-ə-ˈfi-zē-əl\ *adj*

di·a·pir \ˈdī-ə-ˌpir\ *n* [F, prob. fr. Gk *diapeirein* to drive through, fr. *dia-* + *peirein* to pierce; akin to Gk *poros* passage — more at FARE] (1918) : an anticlinal fold in which a mobile core has broken through brittle overlying rocks — **di·a·pir·ic** \ˌdī-ə-ˈpir-ik\ *adj*

dia·pos·i·tive \ˌdī-ə-ˈpä-zə-tiv, -ˈpäz-tiv\ *n* (1893) : a positive photographic image on transparent material (as glass or film)

di·ap·sid \dī-ˈap-səd\ *adj* [ultim. fr. Gk *di-* + *hapsid-, hapsis* loop, arch — more at APSIS] (ca. 1909) : of, relating to, or including reptiles (as the crocodiles) with two pairs of temporal openings in the skull

diarchy *var of* DYARCHY

di·a·rist \ˈdī-ə-rəst\ *n* (ca. 1818) : one who keeps a diary

di·a·ris·tic \ˌdī-ə-ˈris-tik\ *adj* (1884) : of, relating to, or characteristic of a diary ⟨her ~ tone⟩

di·ar·rhea \ˌdī-ə-ˈrē-ə\ *n* [ME *diaria,* fr. LL *diarrhoea,* fr. Gk *diarrhoia,* fr. *diarrhein* to flow through, fr. *dia-* + *rhein* to flow — more at STREAM] (14c) **1** : abnormally frequent intestinal evacuations with more or less fluid stools **2** : excessive flow ⟨verbal ~⟩ — **di·ar·rhe·al** \-ˈrē-əl\ *adj* — **di·ar·rhe·ic** \-ˈrē-ik\ *adj* — **di·ar·rhet·ic** \-ˈre-tik\ *adj*

di·ar·rhoea *chiefly Brit var of* DIARRHEA

di·ar·thro·sis \ˌdī-är-ˈthrō-səs\ *n, pl* **-thro·ses** \-ˌsēz\ [NL, fr. Gk *diarthrōsis,* fr. *diarthroun* to joint, fr. *dia-* + *arthroun* to fasten by a joint, fr. *arthron* joint — more at ARTHR-] (1578) **1** : articulation that permits free movement **2** : a freely movable joint

di·a·ry \ˈdī-(ə-)rē\ *n, pl* **-ries** [L *diarium,* fr. *dies* day — more at DEITY] (1581) **1** : a record of events, transactions, or observations kept daily or at frequent intervals : JOURNAL; *esp* : a daily record of personal activities, reflections, or feelings **2** : a book intended or used for a diary

di·as·po·ra \dī-ˈas-p(ə-)rə, dē-\ *n* [Gk, dispersion, fr. *diaspeirein* to scatter, fr. *dia-* + *speirein* to sow] (1881) **1** *cap* **a** : the settling of scattered colonies of Jews outside Palestine after the Babylonian exile **b** : the area outside Palestine settled by Jews **c** : the Jews living outside Palestine or modern Israel **2 a** : the movement, migration, or scattering of a people away from an established or ancestral homeland ⟨the black ~ to northern cities⟩ **b** : people settled far from their ancestral homelands ⟨African ~⟩ **c** : the place where these people live — **di·a·spor·ic** \ˌdī-ə-ˈspȯr-ik\ *adj*

di·a·spore \ˈdī-ə-ˌspȯr\ *n* [F, fr. Gk *diaspora*] (1805) : a mineral consisting of aluminum hydrogen oxide

di·a·stase \ˈdī-ə-ˌstās, -ˌstāz\ *n* [F, fr. Gk *diastasis* separation, interval, fr. *diistanai* to separate, fr. *dia-* + *histanai* to cause to stand — more at STAND] (1838) **1** : AMYLASE; *esp* : a mixture of amylases from malt **2** : ENZYME

di·a·stat·ic \ˌdī-ə-ˈsta-tik\ *adj* (1881) : relating to or having the properties of diastase; *esp* : converting starch into sugar

di·a·ste·ma \ˌdī-ə-ˈstē-mə\ *n, pl* **-mas** *or* **-ma·ta** \-mə-tə\ [NL, fr. LL, interval, fr. Gk *diastēma,* fr. *diistanai*] (1854) : a space between teeth in a jaw

\ə\ **abut** \ᵊ\ kitten, F table \ər\ **further** \a\ **ash** \ā\ **ace** \ä\ **mop, mar**
\au̇\ **out** \ch\ **chin** \e\ **bet**, \ē\ **easy** \g\ **go** \i\ **hit** \ī\ **ice** \j\ **job**
\ŋ\ **sing** \ō\ **go** \ȯ\ **law** \ȯi\ **boy** \th\ **thin** \t͟h\ **the** \ü\ **loot** \u̇\ **foot**
\y\ **yet** \zh\ **vision, beige** \k͟, ⁿ, œ, ue, ʸ\ *see* Guide to Pronunciation

di·a·ste·reo·mer \ˌdī-ə-ˈster-ē-ō-(ˌ)mər, -ˈstir-\ *or* **di·a·ste·reo·iso·mer** \-ˌster-ē-ō-ˈī-sə-mər, -ˌstir-\ *n* (1936) : a stereoisomer of a compound having two or more chiral centers that is not a mirror image of another stereoisomer of the same compound — compare ENANTIOMER — **di·a·ste·reo·mer·ic** \-ˌster-ē-ō-ˈmer-ik, -ˌstir-\ *or* **di·a·ste·reo·iso·mer·ic** \-ˌī-sə-ˈmer-ik\ *adj* — **di·a·ste·reo·isom·er·ism** \-ī-ˈsä-mə-ˌri-zəm\ *n*

di·as·to·le \dī-ˈas-tə-(ˌ)lē\ *n* [Gk *diastolē* dilatation, fr. *diastellein* to expand, fr. *dia-* + *stellein* to prepare, send] (ca. 1578) : a rhythmically recurrent expansion; *esp* : the dilatation of the cavities of the heart during which they fill with blood — **di·a·stol·ic** \ˌdī-ə-ˈstä-lik\ *adj*

di·as·tro·phism \dī-ˈas-trə-ˌfi-zəm\ *n* [Gk *diastrophē* twisting, fr. *diastrephein* to distort, fr. *dia-* + *strephein* to twist] (1890) : TECTONISM — **di·a·stroph·ic** \ˌdī-ə-ˈsträ-fik\ *adj* — **di·a·stroph·i·cal·ly** \-fi-k(ə-)lē\ *adv*

di·a·tes·sa·ron \ˌdī-ə-ˈte-sə-rən\ *n* [Gk (*Euangelion*) *dia tessarōn,* lit., Gospel out of four, fr. *dia* through, out of + *tessarōn,* gen. of *tessares* four — more at DIA-, FOUR] (1803) : a harmony of the four Gospels edited and arranged into a single connected narrative

dia·ther·my \ˈdī-ə-ˌthər-mē\ *n* [ISV] (1909) : the generation of heat in tissue by electric currents for medical or surgical purposes — **dia·ther·mic** \ˌdī-ə-ˈthər-mik\ *adj*

di·ath·e·sis \dī-ˈa-thə-səs\ *n, pl* **-e·ses** \-ˌsēz\ [NL, fr. Gk, lit., arrangement, fr. *diatithenai* to arrange, fr. *dia-* + *tithenai* to set — more at DO] (1651) : a constitutional predisposition toward a particular state or condition and esp. one that is abnormal or diseased — **di·a·thet·ic** \ˌdī-ə-ˈthe-tik\ *adj*

di·a·tom \ˈdī-ə-ˌtäm\ *n* [ultim. fr. Gk *diatomos* cut in half, fr. *diatemnein* to cut through, fr. *dia-* + *temnein* to cut — more at TOME] (1845) : any of a class (Bacillariophyceae) of minute planktonic unicellular or colonial algae with silicified skeletons that form diatomaceous earth

di·a·to·ma·ceous \ˌdī-ə-tə-ˈmā-shəs, (ˌ)dī-ˌa-tə-\ *adj* (1847) : consisting of or abounding in diatoms or their siliceous remains ⟨~ silica⟩

diatomaceous earth *n* (1883) : a light friable siliceous material derived chiefly from diatom remains and used esp. as a filter

di·atom·ic \ˌdī-ə-ˈtä-mik\ *adj* [ISV] (ca. 1859) : consisting of two atoms : having two atoms in the molecule

di·at·o·mite \dī-ˈa-tə-ˌmīt\ *n* (1887) : DIATOMACEOUS EARTH

dia·ton·ic \ˌdī-ə-ˈtä-nik\ *adj* [LL *diatonicus,* fr. Gk *diatonikos,* fr. *diatonos* stretching, fr. *diateinein* to stretch out, fr. *dia-* + *teinein* to stretch — more at THIN] (1694) : of, relating to, or being a musical scale (as a major or minor scale) comprising intervals of five whole steps and two half steps — **dia·ton·i·cal·ly** \-ˈtä-ni-k(ə-)lē\ *adv*

di·a·tribe \ˈdī-ə-ˌtrīb\ *n* [L *diatriba,* fr. Gk *diatribē* pastime, discourse, fr. *diatribein* to spend (time), wear away, fr. *dia-* + *tribein* to rub — more at THROW] (1581) **1** *archaic* : a prolonged discourse **2** : a bitter and abusive speech or writing **3** : ironic or satirical criticism

di·az·e·pam \dī-ˈa-zə-ˌpam\ *n* [benzo*diazepine* + *-am* (of unknown origin)] (ca. 1961) : a tranquilizer $C_{16}H_{13}ClN_2O$ used esp. to relieve anxiety and tension and as a muscle relaxant

di·az·i·non \dī-ˈa-zi-ˌnän\ *n* [fr. *Diazinon,* a trademark] (1957) : a cholinesterase-inhibiting organophosphate insecticide $C_{12}H_{21}N_2O_3PS$

di·azo \dī-ˈa-(ˌ)zō, -ˈā-\ *adj* [ISV *diaz-, diazo-,* fr. *di-* + *az-*] (1878) **1 a** : relating to or containing the group N_2 composed of two nitrogen atoms united to a single carbon atom of an organic radical — often used in combination **b** : relating to or containing diazonium — often used in combination **2** : of or relating to a photograph or photocopy whose production involves the use of a coating of a diazo compound that is decomposed by exposure to light

di·a·zo·ni·um \ˌdī-ə-ˈzō-nē-əm\ *n* [ISV *di-* + *az-* + *-onium*] (1895) : the monovalent cation N_2^+ that is composed of two nitrogen atoms united to carbon in an organic radical and that usu. exists in salts used in the manufacture of azo dyes

di·az·o·tize \dī-ˈa-zə-ˌtīz\ *vt* **-tized; -tiz·ing** [ISV *di-* + *azote* nitrogen + *-ize* — more at AZ-] (ca. 1889) : to convert (a compound) into a diazo compound (as a diazonium salt) — **di·az·o·ti·za·tion** \-ˌa-zə-tə-ˈzā-shən\ *n*

di·ba·sic \(ˌ)dī-ˈbā-sik\ *adj* (1857) : having two replaceable hydrogen atoms — used of acids

dib·ber \ˈdi-bər\ *n* (1658) : DIBBLE

¹**dib·ble** \ˈdi-bəl\ *n* [ME *debylle*] (15c) : a small hand implement used to make holes in the ground for plants, seeds, or bulbs

²**dibble** *vt* **dib·bled; dib·bling** \ˈdi-b(ə-)liŋ\ (1583) **1** : to plant with a dibble **2** : to make holes in (soil) with or as if with a dibble

di·ben·zo·fu·ran \ˌdī-ˌben-zō-ˈfyu̇-ˌran, -fyə-ˈran\ *n* (1940) : a highly toxic chemical compound $C_{12}H_8O$ that is used in chemical synthesis and as an insecticide and is a hazardous pollutant when chlorinated

dibs \ˈdibz\ *n pl* [short for *dibstones* jacks, fr. obs. *dib* to dab] (1812) **1** *slang* : money esp. in small amounts **2** : CLAIM, RIGHTS ⟨I have ~ on that piece of cake⟩

di·bu·tyl phthal·ate \ˌdī-ˌbyü-tᵊl-ˈtha-ˌlāt\ *n* [*phthal*ic acid + ¹*-ate*] (1925) : a colorless oily ester $C_{16}H_{22}O_4$ used chiefly as a solvent, plasticizer, pesticide, and repellent (as for chiggers and mites)

di·cal·ci·um silicate \(ˌ)dī-ˈkal-sē-əm-\ *n* (1925) : a calcium silicate $2CaO{\cdot}SiO_2$ that is an essential ingredient of portland cement

di·cam·ba \ˌdī-ˈkam-bə\ *n* [perh. fr. *di*chlor- + *Cam*bilene + *Ba*nlene (two commercial preparations containing dicamba)] (1965) : a systemic herbicide $C_8H_6Cl_2O_3$

di·car·box·yl·ic \ˌdī-ˌkär-ˌbäk-ˈsi-lik\ *adj* (ca. 1890) : containing two carboxyl groups in the molecule ⟨~ acids⟩

di·cast \ˈdī-ˌkast, ˈdi-\ *n* [Gk *dikastēs,* fr. *dikazein* to judge, fr. *dikē* judgment — more at DICTION] (1820) : an ancient Athenian performing the functions of both judge and juror at a trial

¹**dice** \ˈdīs\ *n, pl* **dice** [ME *dyce,* fr. *dees, dyce,* pl. of *dee* die — more at DIE] (14c) **1 a** : DIE 1 **b** : a gambling game played with dice **2** *pl also* **dic·es** : a small cubical piece (as of food) **3** : a close contest between two racing-car drivers for position during a race — **no dice 1** : of no avail : no use : FUTILE **2** : ¹NO 3 ⟨said *no dice* to my request⟩

²**dice** *vb* **diced; dic·ing** [ME *dycen,* fr. *dyce*] *vt* (14c) **1 a** : to cut into small cubes ⟨*diced* onions⟩ **b** : to ornament with square markings ⟨*diced* leather⟩ **2 a** : to bring by playing dice ⟨~ himself into debt⟩ **b** : to lose by dicing ⟨~ her money away⟩ ~ *vi* **1** : to play games with dice ⟨~ for drinks in the bar —Malcolm Lowry⟩ **2** : to take a chance ⟨the temptation to ~ with death —*Newsweek*⟩ — **dic·er** *n*

di·cen·tric \(ˌ)dī-ˈsen-trik\ *adj* (1937) : having two centromeres ⟨a ~ chromosome⟩ — **dicentric** *n*

dic·ey \ˈdī-sē\ *adj* **dic·i·er; -est** [ˈ*dice* + *-y*] (1950) : RISKY, UNPREDICTABLE ⟨a ~ proposition⟩ ⟨~ weather⟩

dich- *or* **dicho-** *comb form* [LL, fr. Gk, fr. *dicha;* akin to Gk *di-*] : in two : apart ⟨*dicho*gamous⟩

di·cha·sium \dī-ˈkā-z(h)ē-əm, -zhəm\ *n, pl* **-sia** \-z(h)ē-ə, -zhə\ [NL, fr. Gk *dichasis* halving, fr. *dichazein* to halve, fr. *dicha*] (1875) : a cymose inflorescence that produces two main axes

dichlor- *or* **dichloro-** *comb form* : containing two atoms of chlorine ⟨*dichloro*ethane⟩

di·chlo·ro·ben·zene \(ˌ)dī-ˌklȯr-ə-ˈben-ˌzēn, -(ˌ)ben-ˈ\ *n* (1873) : any of three isomeric compounds $C_6H_4Cl_2$; *esp* : PARADICHLOROBENZENE

di·chlo·ro·di·flu·o·ro·meth·ane \-ˌdī-ˌflu̇r-ə-ˈme-ˌthān\ *n* (1936) : a chlorofluoromethane CCl_2F_2

di·chlo·ro·eth·ane \(ˌ)dī-ˌklȯ-rō-ˈe-ˌthān\ *n* (1936) : a colorless toxic liquid compound $C_2H_4Cl_2$ that is used chiefly as a solvent

di·chlor·vos \(ˈ)dī-ˈklȯr-ˌväs, -vəs\ *n* [*dichlor-* + *v*inyl + ph*os*phate] (1957) : an organophosphorus insecticide and anthelmintic $C_4H_7Cl_2O_4P$ used esp. in veterinary medicine — called also *DDVP*

di·chog·a·my \dī-ˈkä-gə-mē\ *n, pl* **-mies** [G *Dichogamie,* fr. *dich-* + *-gamie* -gamy] (1862) : the production of male and female reproductive elements at different times by a hermaphroditic organism in order to ensure cross-fertilization — **di·chog·a·mous** \-gə-məs\ *adj*

di·chon·dra \dī-ˈkän-drə\ *n* [NL, genus name, fr. *di-* + Gk *chondros* grain — more at GRIND] (1947) : any of a genus (*Dichondra*) of chiefly tropical perennial herbs of the morning glory family that includes some (esp. *D. repens* or its varieties) used as a ground cover and a substitute for lawn grasses in warmer parts of the U.S.

dich·otic \(ˌ)dī-ˈkō-tik\ *adj* [*dich-* + ²*-otic*] (ca. 1911) : relating to or involving the presentation of a stimulus to one ear that differs in some respect (as pitch, loudness, frequency, or energy) from a stimulus presented to the other ear ⟨~ listening⟩ — **dich·oti·cal·ly** \-ti-k(ə-)lē\ *adv*

di·chot·o·mist \dī-ˈkä-tə-məst *also* də-\ *n* (ca. 1592) : one that dichotomizes

di·chot·o·mize \-ˌmīz\ *vb* **-mized; -miz·ing** [LL *dichotomos*] *vt* (1606) : to divide into two parts, classes, or groups ~ *vi* : to exhibit dichotomy — **di·chot·o·mi·za·tion** \-ˌkä-tə-mə-ˈzā-shən\ *n*

di·chot·o·mous \dī-ˈkä-tə-məs *also* də-\ *adj* [LL *dichotomos,* fr. Gk, fr. *dich-* + *temnein* to cut — more at TOME] (1752) **1** : dividing into two parts **2** : relating to, involving, or proceeding from dichotomy — **di·chot·o·mous·ly** *adv* — **di·chot·o·mous·ness** *n*

dichotomous key *n* (ca. 1889) : a key for the identification of organisms based on a series of choices between alternative characters

di·chot·o·my \dī-ˈkä-tə-mē *also* də-\ *n, pl* **-mies** [Gk *dichotomia,* fr. *dichotomos*] (1610) **1** : a division into two esp. mutually exclusive or contradictory groups or entities ⟨the ~ between theory and practice⟩; *also* : the process or practice of making such a division ⟨~ of the population into two opposed classes⟩ **2** : the phase of the moon or an inferior planet in which half its disk appears illuminated **3 a** : BIFURCATION; *esp* : repeated bifurcation (as of a plant's stem) **b** : a system of branching in which the main axis forks repeatedly into two branches **c** : branching of an ancestral line into two equal diverging branches **4** : something with seemingly contradictory qualities ⟨it's a ~, this opulent Ritz-style luxury in a place that fronts on a boat harbor —Jean T. Barrett⟩

di·chro·ic \dī-ˈkrō-ik\ *adj* [Gk *dichroos* two-colored, fr. *di-* + *chrōs* color, lit., skin] (ca. 1859) **1** : having the property of dichroism ⟨a ~ crystal⟩ ⟨a ~ mirror⟩ **2** : DICHROMATIC

di·chro·ism \ˈdī-(ˌ)krō-ˌi-zəm\ *n* (1819) : the property of some crystals and solutions of absorbing one of two plane-polarized components of transmitted light more strongly than the other; *also* : the property of exhibiting different colors by reflected or transmitted light — compare CIRCULAR DICHROISM

di·chro·mat \ˈdī-krō-ˌmat, (ˌ)dī-ˈ\ *n* [back-formation fr. *dichromatic*] (ca. 1909) : one affected with dichromatism

di·chro·mate \(ˌ)dī-ˈkrō-ˌmāt, ˈdī-krō-\ *n* [ISV] (ca. 1864) : a usu. orange to red chromium salt containing the anion $Cr_2O_7^{2-}$ ⟨~ of potassium⟩ — called also *bichromate*

di·chro·mat·ic \ˌdī-krō-ˈma-tik\ *adj* (ca. 1847) **1** : having or exhibiting two colors **2** : of, relating to, or exhibiting dichromatism

di·chro·ma·tism \dī-ˈkrō-mə-ˌti-zəm\ *n* (ca. 1901) : partial color blindness in which only two colors are perceptible

di·chro·scope \ˈdī-krə-ˌskōp\ *n* (1857) : an instrument for examining crystals for dichroism

dick \ˈdik\ *n* [*Dick,* nickname for *Richard*] (1553) **1** *chiefly Brit* : FELLOW, CHAP **2** *usu vulgar* : PENIS **3** [by shortening & alter.] : DETECTIVE

dick·cis·sel \dik-ˈsi-səl, ˈdik-ˌ\ *n* [imit.] (1886) : a common migratory black-throated finch (*Spiza americana* of the family Cardinalidae) of the central U.S.

dick·ens \ˈdi-kənz\ *n* [euphemism] (1598) : DEVIL, DEUCE

¹**dick·er** \ˈdi-kər\ *n* [ME *dyker,* fr. L *decuria* quantity of ten, fr. *decem* ten — more at TEN] (14c) : the number or quantity of 10 esp. of hides or skins

²**dicker** *vi* **dick·ered; dick·er·ing** \ˈdi-k(ə-)riŋ\ [origin unknown] (1797) : BARGAIN ⟨~*ed* over the price⟩

³**dicker** *n* (1797) **1** : BARTER **2** : an act or session of bargaining

dick·ey *or* **dicky** *also* **dick·ie** \ˈdi-kē\ *n, pl* **dickeys** *or* **dick·ies** [*Dicky,* nickname for *Richard*] (1807) **1** : any of various articles of clothing: as **a** : a man's separate or detachable shirtfront **b** : a small fabric insert worn to fill in the neckline **2** *chiefly Brit* **a** : the driver's seat in a carriage **b** : a seat at the back of a carriage or automobile

dickey bird *or* **dicky bird** *n* (1781) : a small bird

dick·head \ˈdik-ˌhed\ *n* [*dick* (penis) + *head*] (1964) *usu vulgar* : a stupid or contemptible person

Dick test \ˈdik-\ *n* [George F. *Dick* and Gladys H. *Dick*] (1925) : a test to determine susceptibility or immunity to scarlet fever by an injection of scarlet fever toxin

di·cli·nous \(ˌ)dī-ˈklī-nəs\ *adj* (1828) : having the stamens and pistils in separate flowers

di·cot \ˈdī-ˌkät\ *n* (1877) : DICOTYLEDON

di·cot·y·le·don \ˌdī-ˌkä-tə-ˈlē-dᵊn\ *n* [NL] (ca. 1727) **:** any of a class or subclass (Magnoliopsida or Dicotyledoneae) of angiospermous plants that produce an embryo with two cotyledons and usu. have floral organs arranged in cycles of four or five and leaves with reticulate venation — compare MONOCOTYLEDON — **di·cot·y·le·don·ous** \-də-nəs\ *adj*

di·cou·ma·rin \(ˌ)dī-ˈkü-mə-rən\ *n* (1886) **:** DICUMAROL

di·crot·ic \dī-ˈkrä-tik\ *adj* [Gk *dikrotos,* fr. *di-* + *krotos* rattling noise, beat] (ca. 1811) **1** *of the pulse* **:** having a double beat **2 :** being or relating to the second part of the arterial pulse occurring during diastole of the heart or of an arterial pressure recording made during the same period — **di·cro·tism** \ˈdī-krə-ˌti-zəm\ *n*

dict *abbr* dictionary

Dic·ta·phone \ˈdik-tə-ˌfōn\ *trademark* — used for a dictating machine

[1]**dic·tate** \ˈdik-ˌtāt, dik-ˈ\ *vb* **dic·tat·ed; dic·tat·ing** [L *dictatus,* pp. of *dictare* to assert, dictate, freq. of *dicere* to say — more at DICTION] *vi* (1581) **1 :** to give dictation **2 :** to speak or act domineeringly **:** PRESCRIBE ~ *vt* **1 :** to speak or read for a person to transcribe or for a machine to record **2 a :** to issue as an order **b :** to impose, pronounce, or specify authoritatively **c :** to require or determine necessarily ⟨injuries *dictated* the choice of players⟩

[2]**dic·tate** \ˈdik-ˌtāt\ *n* (1594) **1 a :** an authoritative rule, prescription, or injunction **b :** a ruling principle ⟨according to the ~*s* of your conscience⟩ **2 :** a command by one in authority

dictating machine *n* (1907) **:** a machine used esp. for the recording of human speech for transcription

dic·ta·tion \dik-ˈtā-shən\ *n* (1651) **1 a :** PRESCRIPTION **b :** arbitrary command **2 a (1) :** the act or manner of uttering words to be transcribed **(2) :** material that is dictated or transcribed **b (1) :** the performing of music to be reproduced by a student **(2) :** music so reproduced

dic·ta·tor \ˈdik-ˌtā-tər, dik-ˈ\ *n* [L, fr. *dictare*] (14c) **1 a :** a person granted absolute emergency power; *esp* **:** one appointed by the senate of ancient Rome **b :** one holding complete autocratic control **c :** one ruling absolutely and often oppressively **2 :** one that dictates

dic·ta·to·ri·al \ˌdik-tə-ˈtȯr-ē-əl\ *adj* (1701) **1 a :** of, relating to, or befitting a dictator ⟨~ power⟩ **b :** ruled by a dictator **2 :** oppressive to or arrogantly overbearing toward others — **dic·ta·to·ri·al·ly** \-ē-ə-lē\ *adv* — **dic·ta·to·ri·al·ness** *n*

syn DICTATORIAL, MAGISTERIAL, DOGMATIC, DOCTRINAIRE, ORACULAR mean imposing one's will or opinions on others. DICTATORIAL stresses autocratic, high-handed methods and a domineering manner ⟨exercised *dictatorial* control over the office⟩. MAGISTERIAL stresses assumption or use of prerogatives appropriate to a magistrate or schoolmaster in forcing acceptance of one's opinions ⟨the *magisterial* tone of his pronouncements⟩. DOGMATIC implies being unduly and offensively positive in laying down principles and expressing opinions ⟨*dogmatic* about what is art and what is not⟩. DOCTRINAIRE implies a disposition to follow abstract theories in framing laws or policies affecting people ⟨a *doctrinaire* approach to improving the economy⟩. ORACULAR implies the manner of one who delivers opinions in cryptic phrases or with pompous dogmatism ⟨a designer who is the *oracular* voice of fashion⟩.

dic·ta·tor·ship \dik-ˈtā-tər-ˌship, ˈdik-ˌ\ *n* (1542) **1 :** the office of dictator **2 :** autocratic rule, control, or leadership **3 a :** a form of government in which absolute power is concentrated in a dictator or a small clique **b :** a government organization or group in which absolute power is so concentrated **c :** a despotic state

dic·tion \ˈdik-shən\ *n* [L *diction-, dictio* speaking, style, fr. *dicere* to say; akin to OE *tēon* to accuse, L *dicare* to proclaim, dedicate, Gk *deiknynai* to show, *dikē* judgment, right] (1581) **1** *obs* **:** verbal description **2 :** choice of words esp. with regard to correctness, clearness, or effectiveness **3 a :** vocal expression **:** ENUNCIATION **b :** pronunciation and enunciation of words in singing — **dic·tion·al** \-shnəl, -shə-nᵊl\ *adj* — **dic·tion·al·ly** \-ē\ *adv*

dic·tio·nary \ˈdik-shə-ˌner-ē, -ˌne-rē\ *n, pl* **-nar·ies** [ML *dictionarium,* fr. LL *diction-, dictio* word, fr. L, speaking] (1526) **1 :** a reference source in print or electronic form containing words usu. alphabetically arranged along with information about their forms, pronunciations, functions, etymologies, meanings, and syntactical and idiomatic uses **2 :** a reference book listing alphabetically terms or names important to a particular subject or activity along with discussion of their meanings and applications **3 :** a reference book giving for words of one language equivalents in another **4 :** a computerized list (as of items of data or words) used for reference (as for information retrieval or word processing)

dic·tum \ˈdik-təm\ *n, pl* **dic·ta** \-tə\ *also* **dictums** [L, fr. neut. of *dictus,* pp. of *dicere*] (1599) **1 :** a noteworthy statement: as **a :** a formal pronouncement of a principle, proposition, or opinion **b :** an observation intended or regarded as authoritative **2 :** a judge's expression of opinion on a point other than the precise issue involved in determining a case

dicty- *or* **dictyo-** *comb form* [NL, fr. Gk *dikty-, diktyo-,* fr. *diktyon,* fr. *dikein* to throw] **:** net ⟨*dictyo*stele⟩ ⟨*dictyo*some⟩

dic·tyo·some \ˈdik-tē-ə-ˌsōm\ *n* (1893) **:** any of the membranous or vesicular structures making up the Golgi apparatus

dic·tyo·stele \ˈdik-tē-ə-ˌstēl, ˌdik-tē-ə-ˈstē-lē\ *n* (ca. 1902) **:** a stele in which the vascular cylinder is broken up into a longitudinal series or network of vascular strands around a central pith (as in many ferns)

di·cu·ma·rol *also* **di·cou·ma·rol** \dī-ˈk(y)ü-mə-ˌrȯl, -ˌrōl\ *n* [*di-* + *coumarin* + [1]*-ol*] (1942) **:** a crystalline compound $C_{19}H_{12}O_6$ orig. obtained from spoiled sweet clover hay and used to delay clotting of blood esp. in preventing and treating thromboembolic disease

di·cyn·o·dont \(ˌ)dī-ˈsi-nō-ˌdänt, -ˈsī-\ *n* [ultim. fr. Gk *di-* + *kyn-, kyōn* dog + *odont-, odous* tooth — more at HOUND, TOOTH] (1854) **:** any of a suborder (Dicynodontia) of small herbivorous therapsid reptiles with reduced dentition — **dicynodont** *adj*

did *past of* DO

di·dact \ˈdī-ˌdakt\ *n* [back-formation fr. *didactic*] (1954) **:** a didactic person

di·dac·tic \dī-ˈdak-tik, də-\ *adj* [Gk *didaktikos,* fr. *didaskein* to teach] (1658) **1 a :** designed or intended to teach **b :** intended to convey instruction and information as well as pleasure and entertainment ⟨~ poetry⟩ **2 :** making moral observations — **di·dac·ti·cal** \-ti-kəl\ *adj* — **di·dac·ti·cal·ly** \-ti-k(ə-)lē\ *adv* — **di·dac·ti·cism** \-tə-ˌsi-zəm\ *n*

di·dac·tics \-tiks\ *n pl but sing or pl in constr* (1800) **:** systematic instruction **:** PEDAGOGY

di·dan·o·sine \dī-ˈda-nə-ˌsēn\ *n* [alter. of *dideoxyinosine,* an alternate name, fr. *di-* + *deoxy* + *inosine,* a nucleoside] (1990) **:** DDI

did·dle \ˈdi-dᵊl\ *vb* **did·dled; did·dling** \ˈdid-liŋ, -dᵊl-iŋ\ [origin unknown] *vt* (1786) **1** *chiefly dial* **:** to move with short rapid motions **2 :** to waste (as time) in trifling **3 :** HOAX, SWINDLE **4** *often vulgar* **:** to copulate with ~ *vi* **1 :** DAWDLE, FOOL **2 :** FIDDLE, TOY — usu. used with *with* ⟨*diddled* with the machine until it broke⟩ — **did·dler** \ˈdid-lər, -dᵊl-ər\ *n*

did·dly \ˈdi-dᵊl-ē, ˈdid-lē\ *n* (1964) *slang* **:** DIDDLY-SQUAT

did·dly–squat \-ˌskwät\ *n* [prob. alter. of *doodly-squat*] (1963) *slang* **:** the least amount **:** anything at all ⟨didn't know ~ about sports —Sam Toperoff⟩

did·ger·i·doo *also* **did·jer·i·doo** \ˌdi-jə-rē-ˈdü, ˌdi-jə-rē-ˌ\ *n* [prob. of imit. origin] (1919) **:** a large bamboo or wooden trumpet of the Australian aborigines

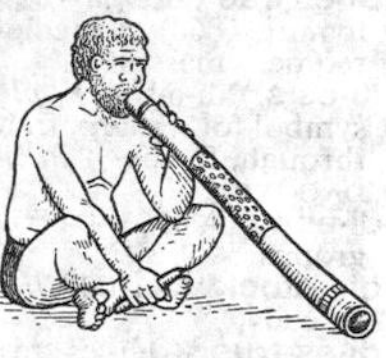

didgeridoo

didn't \ˈdi-dᵊnt, -dᵊn, *dial also* ˈdit-ᵊn(t) *or* ˈdint\ (1675) **:** did not

di·do \ˈdī-(ˌ)dō\ *n, pl* **didoes** *or* **didos** [origin unknown] (1807) **1 :** a mischievous or capricious act **:** PRANK, ANTIC — often used in the phrase *cut didoes* **2 :** something that is frivolous or showy

Di·do \ˈdī-(ˌ)dō\ *n* [L, fr. Gk *Didō*] (14c) **:** a legendary queen of Carthage in Virgil's *Aeneid* who kills herself when Aeneas leaves her

didst \ˈdidst, ˈditst\ *archaic past 2d sing of* DO

di·dym·i·um \dī-ˈdi-mē-əm\ *n* [NL, fr. Gk *didymos* twin, fr. *dyo* two — more at TWO] (1842) **:** a mixture of rare-earth elements made up chiefly of neodymium and praseodymium and used esp. for coloring glass for optical filters

[1]**die** \ˈdī\ *vi* **died; dy·ing** \ˈdī-iŋ\ [ME *dien,* fr. or akin to ON *deyja* to die; akin to OHG *touwen* to die] (12c) **1 :** to pass from physical life **:** EXPIRE **2 a :** to pass out of existence **:** CEASE ⟨their anger *died* at these words⟩ **b :** to disappear or subside gradually — often used with *away, down,* or *out* ⟨the storm *died* down⟩ **3 a :** SINK, LANGUISH ⟨*dying* from fatigue⟩ **b :** to long keenly or desperately ⟨*dying* to go⟩ **c :** to be overwhelmed by emotion ⟨~ of embarrassment⟩ **4 a :** to cease functioning **:** STOP ⟨the motor *died*⟩ **b :** to end in failure ⟨the bill *died* in committee⟩ **5 :** to become indifferent ⟨~ to worldly things⟩ — **die hard 1 :** to be long in dying ⟨such rumors *die hard*⟩ **2 :** to continue resistance against hopeless odds ⟨that kind of determination *dies hard*⟩ — **die on the vine :** to fail esp. at an early stage through lack of support or enthusiasm ⟨let the proposal *die on the vine*⟩ — **to die for :** extremely desirable or appealing ⟨the dessert was *to die for*⟩

[2]**die** \ˈdī\ *n, pl* **dice** \ˈdīs\ *or* **dies** \ˈdīz\ [ME *dee,* fr. AF *dé*] (14c) **1** *pl* *dice* **:** a small cube marked on each face with from one to six spots and used usu. in pairs in various games and in gambling by being shaken and thrown to come to rest at random on a flat surface — often used figuratively in expressions concerning chance or the irrevocability of a course of action ⟨the ~ was cast⟩ **2** *pl dies* **:** DADO 1a **3** *pl dies* **:** any of various tools or devices for imparting a desired shape, form, or finish to a material or for impressing an object or material: as **a (1) :** the larger of a pair of cutting or shaping tools that when moved toward each other produce a desired form in or impress a desired device on an object by pressure or by a blow **(2) :** a device composed of a pair of such tools **b :** a hollow internally threaded screw-cutting tool used for forming screw threads **c :** a mold into which molten metal or other material is forced **d :** a perforated block through which metal or plastic is drawn or extruded for shaping

die·back \ˈdī-ˌbak\ *n* (ca. 1886) **:** a condition in woody plants in which peripheral parts are killed (as by parasites)

dief·fen·bach·ia \ˌdē-fən-ˈba-kē-ə, ˌdi-, -ˈbä-\ *n* [NL, fr. Ernst *Dieffenbach* †1855 Ger. naturalist] (ca. 1900) **:** any of a genus (*Dieffenbachia*) of erect poisonous tropical American plants of the arum family having usu. variegated leaves and often grown as houseplants

die–hard \ˈdī-ˌhärd\ *adj* (1922) **:** strongly or fanatically determined or devoted ⟨~ fans⟩; *esp* **:** strongly resisting change ⟨a ~ conservative⟩ — **die·hard** *n* — **die–hard·ism** \-ˌiz-əm\ *n*

di·el \ˈdī-əl, -ˌel\ *adj* [irreg. fr. L *dies* day + E *-al*] (ca. 1935) **:** involving a 24-hour period that usu. includes a day and the adjoining night ⟨~ fluctuations in temperature⟩

diel·drin \ˈdēl-drən\ *n* [*Diels-Alder* reaction (an addition reaction forming a 6-membered ring), after Otto *Diels* & Kurt *Alder*] (ca. 1949) **:** a white crystalline persistent toxic chlorinated compound $C_{12}H_8Cl_6O$ used esp. formerly as an insecticide

di·elec·tric \ˌdī-ə-ˈlek-trik\ *n* [*dia-* + *electric*] (1837) **:** a nonconductor of direct electric current — **dielectric** *adj*

dielectric constant *n* (1875) **:** PERMITTIVITY

dielectric heating *n* (1944) **:** the rapid and uniform heating throughout a nonconducting material by means of a high-frequency electromagnetic field

di·en·ceph·a·lon \ˌdī-ən-ˈse-fə-ˌlän, ˌdī-(ˌ)en-, -lən\ *n* [NL, fr. *dia-* + *encephalon*] (ca. 1883) **:** the posterior subdivision of the forebrain — **di·en·ce·phal·ic** \-sə-ˈfa-lik\ *adj*

di·ene \ˈdī-ˌēn\ *n* [*di-* + *-ene*] (1917) **:** a compound containing two double bonds between carbon atoms

die–off \ˈdī-ˌȯf\ *n* (1936) **:** a sudden sharp decline of a population of animals or plants that is not caused directly by human activity

die off \ˈdī-ˈȯf\ *vi* (1697) **:** to die sequentially either singly or in numbers so that the total number is greatly diminished

\ə\ **abut** \ᵊ\ **kitten,** F **table** \ər\ **further** \a\ **ash** \ā\ **ace** \ä\ **mop, mar** \au̇\ **out** \ch\ **chin** \e\ **bet** \ē\ **easy** \g\ **go** \i\ **hit** \ī\ **ice** \j\ **job** \ŋ\ **sing** \ō\ **go** \ȯ\ **law** \ȯi\ **boy** \th\ **thin** \t͟h\ **the** \ü\ **loot** \u̇\ **foot** \y\ **yet** \zh\ **vision, beige** \k, ⁿ, œ, ue, ʸ\ *see* Guide to Pronunciation

die out *vi* (1853) : to become extinct
dieresis *var of* DIAERESIS
die·sel \ˈdē-zəl, -səl\ *n* [Rudolf *Diesel*] (1894) **1** : DIESEL ENGINE **2** : a vehicle driven by a diesel engine **3** : DIESEL FUEL
diesel–electric *adj* (1914) : of, relating to, or employing a diesel engine for driving an electric generator or for charging batteries ⟨a ~ locomotive⟩ ⟨~ submarines⟩
diesel engine *n* (1894) : an internal combustion engine in which air is compressed to a temperature sufficiently high to ignite fuel injected into the cylinder where the combustion and expansion actuate a piston
diesel fuel *n* (1949) : a heavy mineral oil used as fuel in diesel engines
die·sel·ing \ˈdē-zə-liŋ, -sə-\ *n* (ca. 1955) : the continued operation of an internal combustion engine after the ignition is turned off
die·sel·ize \ˈdē-zə-ˌlīz, -sə-\ *vt* **-ized; -iz·ing** (1925) : to equip with a diesel engine or with diesel-electric locomotives — **die·sel·i·za·tion** \ˌdē-zə-lə-ˈzā-shən, -sə-\ *n*
Di·es Irae \ˌdē-(ˌ)ās-ˈē-ˌrā\ *n* [ML, day of wrath; fr. the first words of the hymn] (1860) : a medieval Latin hymn on the Day of Judgment sung in requiem masses
di·esis \ˈdī-ə-səs\ *n, pl* **di·eses** \-ˌsēz\ [prob. fr. It, sharp (in music), symbol for a sharp, fr. ML, quarter tone, fr. L, fr. Gk, fr. *diienai* to send through, fr. *dia-* + *hienai* to send — more at JET] (ca. 1706) : DOUBLE DAGGER
di·es·ter \ˈdī-ˌes-tər\ *n* (1935) : a compound containing two ester groups
die·stock \ˈdī-ˌstäk\ *n* (ca. 1859) : a stock to hold dies used for cutting threads
di·es·trus \(ˌ)dī-ˈes-trəs\ *n* [NL, fr. *dia-* + *estrus*] (1942) : a period of sexual quiescence that intervenes between two periods of estrus — **di·es·trous** \-trəs\ *adj*
1**di·et** \ˈdī-ət\ *n* [ME *diete,* fr. AF, fr. L *diaeta,* fr. Gk *diaita,* lit., manner of living, fr. *diaitasthai* to lead one's life] (13c) **1 a** : food and drink regularly provided or consumed **b** : habitual nourishment **c** : the kind and amount of food prescribed for a person or animal for a special reason **d** : a regimen of eating and drinking sparingly so as to reduce one's weight ⟨going on a ~⟩ **2** : something provided or experienced repeatedly ⟨a ~ of Broadway shows and nightclubs —Frederick Wyatt⟩
2**diet** *vt* (14c) **1** : to cause to take food : FEED **2** : to cause to eat and drink sparingly or according to prescribed rules ~ *vi* : to eat sparingly or according to prescribed rules — **di·et·er** *n*
3**diet** *adj* (1963) **1** : reduced in calories ⟨a ~ soft drink⟩ **2** : promoting weight loss (as by depressing appetite) ⟨~ pills⟩
4**diet** *n* [ME *diete* day's journey, day set for a meeting, fr. ML *dieta,* lit., daily regimen, diet (taken as a derivative of L *dies* day), fr. L *diaeta*] (1565) **1** : a formal deliberative assembly of princes or estates **2** : any of various national or provincial legislatures
1**di·e·tary** \ˈdī-ə-ˌter-ē, -ˌte-rē\ *n, pl* **di·e·tar·ies** (1838) : the kinds and amounts of food available to or eaten by an individual, group, or population
2**dietary** *adj* (1614) : of or relating to a diet or to the rules of a diet ⟨~ guidelines⟩ — **di·e·tar·i·ly** \ˌdī-ə-ˈter-ə-lē, -ˈte-rə-\ *adv*
dietary law *n* (1907) : any of the laws observed by Orthodox Jews that permit or prohibit certain foods
dietary supplement *n* (1967) : a product taken orally that contains one or more ingredients (as vitamins or amino acids) that are intended to supplement one's diet and are not considered food
di·e·tet·ic \ˌdī-ə-ˈte-tik\ *adj* (1579) **1** : of or relating to diet **2** : adapted for use in special diets — **di·e·tet·i·cal·ly** \-ti-k(ə-)lē\ *adv*
di·e·tet·ics \-ˈte-tiks\ *n pl but sing or pl in constr* (1799) : the science or art of applying the principles of nutrition to the diet
di·ether \(ˌ)dī-ˈē-thər\ *n* (1950) : a compound containing two atoms of oxygen with ether linkages
di·eth·yl·car·bam·a·zine \ˌdī-ˌe-thəl-kär-ˈba-mə-ˌzēn, -zən\ *n* [*di-* + *ethyl* + *carboxy-* + *amide* + *azine*] (1948) : an anthelmintic administered in the form of its crystalline citrate $C_{10}H_{21}N_3O{\cdot}C_6H_8O_7$ esp. to control human filariasis and large nematodes (as heartworms) in dogs and cats
di·eth·yl ether \(ˌ)dī-ˌe-thəl-\ *n* (ca. 1930) : ETHER 3a
di·eth·yl·stil·bes·trol \-stil-ˈbes-ˌtrȯl, -ˌtrōl\ *n* [ISV] (1938) : a colorless crystalline synthetic compound $C_{18}H_{20}O_2$ used as a potent estrogen but contraindicated in pregnancy for its tendency to cause cancer or birth defects in offspring — called also *DES, stilbestrol*
di·eth·yl zinc *n* (1952) : a volatile pyrophoric liquid compound $C_4H_{10}Zn$ used esp. to catalyze polymerization and to deacidify paper
di·e·ti·tian *or* **di·e·ti·cian** \ˌdī-ə-ˈti-shən\ *n* [*dietitian* irreg. fr. 1*diet* + *-ician*] (ca. 1846) : a specialist in dietetics
diff \ˈdif\ *n* (1896) *slang* : DIFFERENCE
dif·fer \ˈdi-fər\ *vi* **dif·fered; dif·fer·ing** \-f(ə-)riŋ\ [ME, fr. MF or L; MF *differer* to postpone, be different, fr. L *differre,* fr. *dis-* + *ferre* to carry — more at BEAR] (14c) **1 a** : to be unlike or distinct in nature, form, or characteristics ⟨the law of one state ~*s* from that of another⟩ **b** : to change from time to time or from one instance to another : VARY ⟨the number of cookies in a box may ~⟩ **2** : to be of unlike or opposite opinion : DISAGREE ⟨they ~ on religious matters⟩
1**dif·fer·ence** \ˈdi-fərn(t)s, ˈdi-f(ə-)rən(t)s\ *n* (14c) **1 a** : the quality or state of being different ⟨the ~ between right and wrong⟩ **b** : an instance of differing in nature, form, or quality ⟨noted the ~*s* in color and texture⟩ **c** *archaic* : a characteristic that distinguishes one from another or from the average **d** : the element or factor that separates or distinguishes contrasting situations **2** : distinction or discrimination in preference ⟨timing is often the ~ between success and failure⟩ **3 a** : disagreement in opinion : DISSENSION **b** : an instance or cause of disagreement ⟨unable to settle their ~*s*⟩ **4** : the degree or amount by which things differ in quantity or measure; *specif* : REMAINDER 2b(1) **5** : a significant change in or effect on a situation ⟨it makes no ~ to me⟩
2**difference** *vt* **-enced; -enc·ing** (1576) : DIFFERENTIATE, DISTINGUISH
1**dif·fer·ent** \ˈdi-fərnt, ˈdi-f(ə-)rənt\ *adj* [ME, fr. L *different-, differens,* prp. of *differre*] (14c) **1** : partly or totally unlike in nature, form, or quality : DISSIMILAR ⟨could hardly be more ~⟩ — often followed by *from, than,* or chiefly Brit. to ⟨small, neat hand, very ~ from the captain's tottery characters —R. L. Stevenson⟩ ⟨vastly ~ in size than it was twenty-five years ago —N. M. Pusey⟩ ⟨a very ~ situation to the . . . one under which we live —Sir Winston Churchill⟩ **2** : not the same: as **a** : DISTINCT ⟨~ age groups⟩ **b** : VARIOUS ⟨~ members of the class⟩ **c** : ANOTHER ⟨switched to a ~ TV program⟩ **3** : UNUSUAL, SPECIAL ⟨she was ~ and superior⟩ — **dif·fer·ent·ness** *n*
syn DIFFERENT, DIVERSE, DIVERGENT, DISPARATE, VARIOUS mean unlike in kind or character. DIFFERENT may imply little more than separateness but it may also imply contrast or contrariness ⟨*different* foods⟩. DIVERSE implies both distinctness and marked contrast ⟨such *diverse* interests as dancing and football⟩. DIVERGENT implies movement away from each other and unlikelihood of ultimate meeting or reconciliation ⟨went on to pursue *divergent* careers⟩. DISPARATE emphasizes incongruity or incompatibility ⟨*disparate* notions of freedom⟩. VARIOUS stresses the number of sorts or kinds ⟨tried *various* methods⟩.
usage Numerous commentators have condemned *different than* in spite of its use since the 17th century by many of the best-known names in English literature. It is nevertheless standard and is even recommended in many handbooks when followed by a clause, because insisting on *from* in such instances often produces clumsy or wordy formulations. *Different from,* the generally safe choice, is more common esp. when it is followed by a noun or pronoun.
2**different** *adv* (1744) : DIFFERENTLY
dif·fer·en·tia \ˌdi-fə-ˈren(t)-sh(ē-)ə\ *n, pl* **-ti·ae** \-shē-ˌē, -shē-ˌī\ [L, difference, fr. *different-, differens*] (1551) : an element, feature, or factor that distinguishes one entity, state, or class from another; *esp* : a characteristic trait distinguishing a species from other species of the same genus
1**dif·fer·en·tial** \ˌdi-fə-ˈren(t)-shəl\ *adj* (1647) **1 a** : of, relating to, or constituting a difference : DISTINGUISHING **b** : making a distinction between individuals or classes **c** : based on or resulting from a differential **d** : functioning or proceeding differently or at a different rate **2** : being, relating to, or involving a differential or differentiation **3 a** : relating to quantitative differences **b** : producing effects by reason of quantitative differences — **dif·fer·en·tial·ly** \-ˈren(t)-shə-lē\ *adv*
2**differential** *n* (1704) **1 a** : the product of the derivative of a function of one variable by the increment of the independent variable **b** : a sum of products in which each product consists of a partial derivative of a given function of several variables multiplied by the corresponding increment and which contains as many products as there are independent variables in the function **2** : a difference between comparable individuals or classes ⟨a price ~⟩; *also* : the amount of such a difference **3 a** : a drivetrain gear assembly connecting two collinear shafts or axles (as those of the rear wheels of an automobile) and permitting one shaft to revolve faster than the other **b** : a case covering such an assembly
differential calculus *n* (1702) : a branch of mathematics concerned chiefly with the study of the rate of change of functions with respect to their variables esp. through the use of derivatives and differentials
differential diagnosis *n* (ca. 1860) : the distinguishing of a disease or condition from others presenting with similar signs and symptoms
differential equation *n* (1763) : an equation containing differentials or derivatives of functions — compare PARTIAL DIFFERENTIAL EQUATION
differential gear *n* (ca. 1859) : DIFFERENTIAL 3a
differential geometry *n* (ca. 1909) : a branch of mathematics using calculus to study the geometric properties of curves and surfaces
dif·fer·en·ti·ate \ˌdif-ə-ˈren(t)-shē-ˌāt\ *vb* **-at·ed; -at·ing** *vt* (1816) **1** : to obtain the mathematical derivative of **2** : to mark or show a difference in : constitute a difference that distinguishes **3** : to develop differential characteristics in **4** : to cause differentiation of in the course of development **5** : to express the specific distinguishing quality of : DISCRIMINATE ~ *vi* **1** : to recognize or give expression to a difference **2** : to become distinct or different in character **3** : to undergo differentiation — **dif·fer·en·tia·bil·i·ty** \-ˌren(t)-sh(ē-)ə-ˈbi-lə-tē\ *n* — **dif·fer·en·tia·ble** \-ˈren(t)-sh(ē-)ə-bəl\ *adj*
dif·fer·en·ti·a·tion \-ˌren(t)-shē-ˈā-shən\ *n* (1802) **1** : the act or process of differentiating **2** : development from the one to the many, the simple to the complex, or the homogeneous to the heterogeneous **3 a** : modification of body parts for performance of particular functions **b** : the sum of the processes whereby apparently indifferent or unspecialized cells, tissues, and structures attain their adult form and function **4** : the processes by which various rock types are produced from a common magma
dif·fer·ent·ly \ˈdi-fərnt-lē, ˈdi-f(ə-)rənt-\ *adv* (14c) **1** : in a different manner **2** : OTHERWISE
differently abled *adj* (1981) : DISABLED, CHALLENGED — compare ABLED
dif·fi·cile \ˌdē-fi-ˈsēl\ *adj* [F, lit., difficult] (1536) : STUBBORN, UNREASONABLE
dif·fi·cult \ˈdi-fi-(ˌ)kəlt\ *adj* [ME, back-formation fr. *difficulty*] (14c) **1** : hard to do, make, or carry out : ARDUOUS ⟨a ~ climb⟩ **2 a** : hard to deal with, manage, or overcome ⟨a ~ child⟩ **b** : hard to understand : PUZZLING ⟨~ reading⟩ ***syn*** see HARD — **dif·fi·cult·ly** *adv*
dif·fi·cul·ty \-(ˌ)kəl-tē\ *n, pl* **-ties** [ME *difficulte,* fr. AF & L; AF *difficulté,* fr. L *difficultas,* fr. *difficilis* not easy, fr. *dis-* + *facilis* easy — more at FACILE] (14c) **1** : the quality or state of being difficult **2** : CONTROVERSY, DISAGREEMENT **3** : OBJECTION **4** : something difficult : IMPEDIMENT **5** : EMBARRASSMENT, TROUBLE — usu. used in pl.
dif·fi·dence \ˈdi-fə-dən(t)s, -fə-ˌden(t)s\ *n* (14c) : the quality or state of being diffident
dif·fi·dent \-dənt, -ˌdent\ *adj* [ME, fr. L *diffident-, diffidens,* prp. of *diffidere* to distrust, fr. *dis-* + *fidere* to trust — more at BIDE] (15c) **1** : hesitant in acting or speaking through lack of self-confidence **2** *archaic* : DISTRUSTFUL **3** : RESERVED, UNASSERTIVE ***syn*** see SHY — **dif·fi·dent·ly** *adv*
dif·fract \di-ˈfrakt\ *vt* [back-formation fr. *diffraction*] (1803) : to cause to undergo diffraction
dif·frac·tion \di-ˈfrak-shən\ *n* [NL *diffraction-, diffractio,* fr. L *diffringere* to break apart, fr. *dis-* + *frangere* to break — more at BREAK] (1671) : a modification which light undergoes esp. in passing by the edges of opaque bodies or through narrow openings and in which the rays appear to be deflected; *also* : a similar modification of other waves (as sound waves) or of moving particles (as electrons)
diffraction grating *n* (1867) : GRATING 3

dif·frac·tom·e·ter \di-ˌfrak-ˈtä-mə-tər\ *n* (ca. 1909) **:** an instrument for analyzing the structure of a usu. crystalline substance from the scattering pattern produced when a beam of radiation or particles (as X-rays or neutrons) strikes it — **dif·frac·to·met·ric** \di-ˌfrak-tə-ˈme-trik\ *adj* — **dif·frac·tom·e·try** \di-ˌfrak-ˈtä-mə-trē\ *n*

[1]**dif·fuse** \di-ˈfyüs\ *adj* [ME, fr. L *diffusus,* pp. of *diffundere* to spread out, fr. *dis-* + *fundere* to pour — more at FOUND] (15c) **1 :** being at once verbose and ill-organized ⟨a ~ report from the scene of the earthquake⟩ **2 :** not concentrated or localized ⟨~ lighting⟩ ⟨~ sclerosis⟩ ***syn*** see WORDY — **dif·fuse·ly** *adv* — **dif·fuse·ness** *n*

[2]**dif·fuse** \di-ˈfyüz\ *vb* **dif·fused; dif·fus·ing** [ME *diffused,* pp., fr. L *diffusus,* pp.] *vt* (14c) **1 a :** to pour out and permit or cause to spread freely **b :** EXTEND, SCATTER **c :** to spread thinly or wastefully **2 :** to subject to diffusion; *esp* **:** to break up and distribute (incident light) by reflection ~ *vi* **1 :** to spread out or become transmitted esp. by contact **2 :** to undergo diffusion — **dif·fus·ible** \di-ˈfyü-zə-bəl\ *adj*

dif·fuse–po·rous \di-ˌfyüs-ˈpȯr-əs\ *adj* [[1]*diffuse*] (ca. 1902) **:** having vessels more or less evenly distributed throughout an annual ring and not varying greatly in size — compare RING-POROUS

dif·fus·er \di-ˈfyü-zər\ *n* (ca. 1679) **1 :** one that diffuses: as **a :** a device (as a reflector) for distributing the light of a lamp evenly **b :** a screen (as of cloth or frosted glass) for softening lighting (as in photography) **c :** a device (as slats at different angles) for deflecting air from an outlet in various directions **2 :** a device for reducing the velocity and increasing the static pressure of a fluid passing through a system

dif·fu·sion \di-ˈfyü-zhən\ *n* (14c) **1 :** the action of diffusing **:** the state of being diffused **2 :** PROLIXITY, DIFFUSENESS **3 a :** the process whereby particles of liquids, gases, or solids intermingle as the result of their spontaneous movement caused by thermal agitation and in dissolved substances move from a region of higher to one of lower concentration **b (1) :** reflection of light by a rough reflecting surface **(2) :** transmission of light through a translucent material **:** SCATTERING **4 :** the spread of cultural elements from one area or group of people to others by contact **5 :** the softening of sharp outlines in a photographic image — **dif·fu·sion·al** \-ˈfyü-zhə-nᵊl\ *adj*

dif·fu·sion·ist \-ˈfyü-zhə-nəst\ *n* (1893) **:** an anthropologist who emphasizes the role of diffusion in the history of culture rather than independent invention or discovery — **dif·fu·sion·ism** \-ˈfyü-zhə-ˌni-zəm\ *n* — **diffusionist** *adj*

dif·fu·sive \di-ˈfyü-siv, -ziv\ *adj* (1614) **:** tending to diffuse **:** characterized by diffusion ⟨~ motion of atoms⟩ — **dif·fu·sive·ly** *adv* — **dif·fu·sive·ness** *n* — **dif·fu·siv·i·ty** \di-ˌfyü-ˈsi-və-tē, -ˈzi-\ *n*

di·func·tion·al \(ˌ)dī-ˈfəŋ(k)-shnəl, -shə-nᵊl\ *adj* (1943) **:** of, relating to, or being a compound with two highly reactive sites in each molecule

[1]**dig** \ˈdig\ *vb* **dug** \ˈdəg\; **dig·ging** [ME *diggen*] *vt* (13c) **1 a :** to break up, turn, or loosen (as earth) with an implement **b :** to prepare the soil of ⟨~ a garden⟩ **2 a :** to bring to the surface by digging **:** UNEARTH ⟨~ potatoes⟩ **b :** to bring to light or out of hiding ⟨~ up facts⟩ **3 :** to hollow out or form by removing earth **:** EXCAVATE ⟨~ a hole⟩ **4 :** to drive down so as to penetrate **:** THRUST **5 :** POKE, PROD **6** *slang* **a :** to pay attention to **:** NOTICE ⟨~ that fancy hat⟩ **b :** UNDERSTAND ⟨couldn't ~ the medical jargon⟩ **c :** LIKE, ADMIRE ⟨high school students ~ short poetry —David Burmester⟩ ~ *vi* **1 :** to turn up, loosen, or remove earth **2 :** to work hard or laboriously **3 :** to advance by or as if by removing or pushing aside material

[2]**dig** *n* (1797) **1 a :** THRUST, POKE **b :** a cutting remark **2** *pl* **a :** accommodations for living or working **b** *chiefly Brit* **:** LODGING 2b **3 :** an archaeological excavation site; *also* **:** the excavation itself

[3]*dig abbr* digest

dig·a·my \ˈdi-gə-mē\ *n, pl* **-mies** [LL *digamia,* fr. LGk, fr. Gk *digamos* married to two people, fr. *di-* + *-gamos* -gamous] (1635) **:** a second marriage after the termination of the first

di·gas·tric \(ˌ)dī-ˈgas-trik\ *adj* [NL *digastricus,* fr. *di-* + *gastricus* gastric] (ca. 1721) **:** of, relating to, or being either of a pair of muscles that depress the lower jaw and raise the hyoid bone during swallowing

di·ge·net·ic \ˌdī-jə-ˈne-tik\ *adj* [NL *Digenetica,* subclass name (syn. of *Digenea*), fr. *di-* + *genetica,* neut. pl. of *geneticus* genetic] (ca. 1883) **:** of or relating to a subclass (Digenea) of trematode worms in which sexual reproduction as an internal parasite of a vertebrate alternates with asexual reproduction in a mollusk

di·ge·ra·ti \ˌdi-jə-ˈrä-(ˌ)tē\ *n pl* [*digital* + *-erati* (as in *literati*)] (1992) **:** persons well versed in computer use and technology

[1]**di·gest** \ˈdī-ˌjest\ *n* [ME, systematic arrangement of laws, fr. L *digesta,* fr. neut. pl. of *digestus,* pp. of *digerere* to arrange, distribute, digest, fr. *dis-* + *gerere* to carry] (14c) **1 :** a summation or condensation of a body of information: as **a :** a systematic compilation of legal rules, statutes, or decisions **b :** a periodical devoted to condensed versions of previously published articles **2 :** a product of digestion

[2]**di·gest** \dī-ˈjest, də-\ *vb* [ME, fr. L *digestus*] *vt* (14c) **1 :** to distribute or arrange systematically **:** CLASSIFY **2 :** to convert (food) into absorbable form **3 :** to take into the mind or memory; *esp* **:** to assimilate mentally **4 a :** to soften, decompose, or break down by heat and moisture or chemical action ⟨DNA ~*ed* by restriction enzymes⟩ **b :** to extract soluble ingredients from by warming with a liquid **5 :** to compress into a short summary **6 :** ABSORB 1 ⟨the capacity of the U.S. to ~ immigrants⟩ ~ *vi* **1 :** to digest food **2 :** to become digested

di·gest·er \-ˈjes-tər\ *n* (1614) **1 :** one that digests or makes a digest **2 :** a vessel for digesting esp. plant or animal materials

di·gest·ibil·i·ty \-ˌjes-tə-ˈbi-lə-tē\ *n, pl* **-ties** (1740) **1 :** the fitness of something for digestion **2 :** the percentage of a foodstuff taken into the digestive tract that is absorbed into the body

di·gest·ible \-ˈjes-tə-bəl\ *adj* (14c) **:** capable of being digested

di·ges·tif \ˌdē-zhes-ˈtēf\ *n* [F, lit., digestive] (1934) **:** an alcoholic drink (as brandy or a liqueur) usu. taken after a meal

di·ges·tion \dī-ˈjes-chən, də-, -ˈjesh-\ *n* (14c) **:** the action, process, or power of digesting: as **a :** the process of making food absorbable by dissolving it and breaking it down into simpler chemical compounds that occurs in the living body chiefly through the action of enzymes secreted into the alimentary canal **b :** the process in sewage treatment by which organic matter in sludge is decomposed by anaerobic bacteria with the release of a burnable mixture of gases

[1]**di·ges·tive** \-ˈjes-tiv\ *n* (14c) **:** an aid to digestion esp. of food

[2]**digestive** *adj* (15c) **1 :** relating to or functioning in digestion ⟨the ~ system⟩ ⟨~ disorders⟩ ⟨~ organs⟩ **2 :** having the power to cause or promote digestion ⟨~ enzymes⟩ — **di·ges·tive·ly** *adv*

digestive gland *n* (1940) **:** a gland secreting digestive enzymes

dig·ger \ˈdi-gər\ *n* (15c) **1 a :** one that digs **b :** a tool or machine for digging **2** *cap, usu disparaging, esp formerly* **:** a No. American Indian (as a Paiute) who dug roots for food **3** *often cap, chiefly Austral & New-Zeal* **:** an Australian or New Zealand soldier

digger wasp *n* (1880) **:** a burrowing wasp; *esp* **:** any of numerous usu. solitary wasps (superfamily Sphecoidea) that dig nest burrows in the soil and provision them with insects or spiders paralyzed by stinging

dig·gings \ˈdi-giŋz\ *n pl* (1538) **1 :** a place of excavating esp. for ore, metals, or precious stones **2 :** material dug out **3 a :** QUARTERS, PREMISES **b** *chiefly Brit* **:** lodgings for a student

dight \ˈdīt\ *vt* **dight·ed** *or* **dight; dight·ing** [ME, fr. OE *dihtan* to arrange, compose, fr. L *dictare* to dictate, compose] (13c) *archaic* **:** DRESS, ADORN

dig in *vt* (1827) **1 :** to cover or incorporate by burying ⟨*dig in* compost⟩ **2 :** to establish in a dug defensive position ⟨the platoon was well *dug in*⟩ ~ *vi* **1 :** to establish a defensive position esp. by digging trenches **2 a :** to go resolutely to work **b :** to begin eating **3 :** to hold stubbornly to a position **4 :** to scuff the ground for better footing while batting (as in baseball) — **dig in one's heels :** to take or persist in an uncompromising position or attitude despite opposition

dig·it \ˈdi-jət\ *n* [ME, fr. L *digitus* finger, toe; perh. akin to Gk *deiknynai* to show — more at DICTION] (14c) **1 a :** any of the Arabic numerals 1 to 9 and usu. the symbol 0 **b :** one of the elements that combine to form numbers in a system other than the decimal system **2 :** a unit of length based on the breadth of a finger and equal in English measure to ¾ inch **3 :** any of the divisions in which the limbs of most vertebrates terminate, which are typically five in number but may be reduced (as in the horse), and which typically have a series of phalanges bearing a nail, claw, or hoof at the tip — compare FINGER 1, TOE 1a

dig·i·tal \ˈdi-jə-tᵊl\ *adj* [L *digitalis*] (ca. 1656) **1 :** of or relating to the fingers or toes ⟨~ dexterity⟩ **2 :** done with a finger ⟨a ~ rectal examination⟩ **3 :** of, relating to, or using calculation by numerical methods or by discrete units **4 :** of, relating to, or being data in the form of esp. binary digits ⟨~ images⟩ ⟨a ~ readout⟩; *esp* **:** of, relating to, or employing digital communications signals ⟨a ~ broadcast⟩ — compare ANALOG 2 **5 :** providing a readout in numerical digits ⟨a ~ voltmeter⟩ **6 :** relating to an audio recording method in which sound waves are represented digitally (as on magnetic tape) so that in the recording wow and flutter are eliminated and background noise is reduced **7 :** ELECTRONIC ⟨~ devices⟩; *also* **:** characterized by electronic and esp. computerized technology — **dig·i·tal·ly** \-tᵊl-ē\ *adv*

digital camera *n* (1976) **:** a camera that records images as digital data instead of on film

digital computer *n* (1947) **:** a computer that operates with numbers expressed directly as digits — compare ANALOG COMPUTER, HYBRID COMPUTER

digital divide *n* (1996) **:** the economic, educational, and social inequalities between those who have computers and online access and those who do not

dig·i·tal·in \ˌdi-jə-ˈta-lən *also* -ˈtā-\ *n* [NL *Digitalis*] (1837) **1 :** a white crystalline steroid glycoside $C_{36}H_{56}O_{14}$ obtained from seeds esp. of the common foxglove **2 :** a mixture of the glycosides of digitalis

dig·i·tal·is \-ˈta-ləs *also* -ˈtā-\ *n* [NL, genus name, fr. L, of a finger, fr. *digitus;* fr. its finger-shaped corolla] (1664) **1 :** FOXGLOVE **2 :** the dried powdered leaf of the common foxglove that contains glycosides which act on the heart and that is a powerful cardiotonic serving esp. to increase the force of myocardial contraction; *broadly* **:** any of various cardiac glycosides (as digitalin or digoxin) that are constituents of digitalis or are derived from a related foxglove (*Digitalis lanata*)

dig·i·ta·li·za·tion \ˌdi-jə-tə-lə-ˈzā-shən\ *n* [*digitalis*] (ca. 1882) **:** the administration of digitalis until the desired physiological adjustment is attained; *also* **:** the bodily state so produced

[1]**dig·i·ta·lize** \ˈdi-jə-tə-ˌlīz\ *vt* **-lized; -liz·ing** [*digitalis*] (1927) **:** to subject to digitalization

[2]**dig·i·tal·ize** \ˈdi-jə-tə-ˌlīz\ *vt* **-ized; -iz·ing** [*digital*] (1962) **:** DIGITIZE

digital subscriber line *n* (1984) **:** a high-speed communications connection used for accessing the Internet and carrying short-range transmissions over ordinary telephone lines

digital video disc *n* (1993) **:** DVD

dig·i·tate \ˈdi-jə-ˌtāt\ *adj* (1661) **:** having divisions arranged like those of a bird's foot ⟨~ leaves⟩ — **dig·i·tate·ly** *adv*

digiti- *comb form* [F, fr. L *digitus*] **:** digit **:** finger ⟨*digiti*grade⟩

dig·i·ti·grade \ˈdi-jə-tə-ˌgrād\ *adj* [F, fr. *digiti-* + *-grade*] (1824) **:** walking on the digits with the posterior of the foot more or less raised

dig·i·tize \ˈdi-jə-ˌtīz\ *vt* **-tized; -tiz·ing** (1953) **:** to convert (as data or an image) to digital form — **dig·i·ti·za·tion** \ˌdi-jə-tə-ˈzā-shən\ *n* — **dig·i·tiz·er** \ˈdi-jə-ˌtī-zər\ *n*

digitizing tablet *n* (1980) **:** GRAPHICS TABLET

dig·i·to·nin \ˌdi-jə-ˈtō-nən\ *n* [ISV *digit-* (fr. NL *Digitalis*) + *saponin*] (1875) **:** a steroid saponin $C_{56}H_{92}O_{29}$ occurring in the leaves and seeds of the common foxglove

digi·toxi·gen·in \ˌdi-jə-ˌtäk-sə-ˈje-nən\ *n* [ISV, blend of *digitoxin* and *-gen*] (ca. 1909) **:** a steroid lactone $C_{23}H_{34}O_4$ obtained esp. by hydrolysis of digitoxin

digi·tox·in \ˌdi-jə-ˈtäk-sən\ *n* [ISV, blend of NL *Digitalis* and ISV *toxin*] (ca. 1883) **:** a poisonous cardiotonic glycoside $C_{41}H_{64}O_{13}$ that is the most active constituent of digitalis; *also* **:** a mixture of digitalis glycosides consisting chiefly of digitoxin

di·glyc·er·ide \ˌdī-ˈgli-sə-ˌrīd\ *n* (1918) **:** an ester formed from glycerol by reacting two of its hydroxyl groups with fatty acids

dig·ni·fied \ˈdig-nə-ˌfīd\ *adj* (1584) **:** showing or expressing dignity

dig·ni·fy \ˈdig-nə-ˌfī\ *vt* **-fied; -fy·ing** [ME *dignifien,* fr. MF *dignifier,* fr. LL *dignificare,* fr. L *dignus* worthy — more at DECENT] (15c) **1 :** to give distinction to **:** ENNOBLE **2 :** to confer dignity upon; *also* **:** to give undue attention or status to ⟨won't ~ that remark with a reply⟩

dig·ni·tary \ˈdig-nə-ˌter-ē, -ˌte-rē\ *n, pl* **-tar·ies** (1603) **:** one who possesses exalted rank or holds a position of dignity or honor — **dignitary** *adj*

dig·ni·ty \ˈdig-nə-tē\ *n, pl* **-ties** [ME *dignete,* fr. AF *digneté,* fr. L *dignitat-, dignitas,* fr. *dignus*] (13c) **1 :** the quality or state of being worthy, honored, or esteemed **2 a :** high rank, office, or position **b :** a legal title of nobility or honor **3** *archaic* **:** DIGNITARY **4 :** formal reserve or seriousness of manner, appearance, or language

dig out *vt* (14c) **1 :** FIND, UNEARTH **2 :** to make hollow by digging ~ *vi* **:** TAKE OFF 2a

di·gox·in \di-ˈjäk-sən, -ˈgäk-\ *n* [ISV *dig-* (fr. NL *Digitalis*) + *toxin*] (ca. 1930) **:** a poisonous cardiotonic steroid $C_{41}H_{64}O_{14}$ obtained from a foxglove (*Digitalis lanata*) and used esp. to treat atrial fibrillation

di·graph \ˈdī-ˌgraf\ *n* (1780) **1 :** a group of two successive letters whose phonetic value is a single sound (as *ea* in *bread* or *ng* in *sing*) or whose value is not the sum of a value borne by each in other occurrences (as *ch* in *chin* where the value is \t\ + \sh\) **2 :** a group of two successive letters **3 :** LIGATURE 4 — **di·graph·ic** \dī-ˈgra-fik\ *adj* — **di·graph·i·cal·ly** \-fi-k(ə-)lē\ *adv*

di·gress \dī-ˈgres, də-\ *vi* [L *digressus,* pp. of *digredi,* fr. *dis-* + *gradi* to step — more at GRADE] (1529) **:** to turn aside esp. from the main subject of attention or course of argument ***syn*** see SWERVE

di·gres·sion \-ˈgre-shən\ *n* (14c) **1 :** the act or an instance of digressing in a discourse or other usu. organized literary work **2** *archaic* **:** a going aside — **di·gres·sion·al** \-ˈgresh-nəl, -ə-n^{ə}l\ *adj* — **di·gres·sion·ary** \-ˈgre-shə-ˌner-ē\ *adj*

di·gres·sive \-ˈgre-siv\ *adj* (ca. 1611) **:** characterized by digressions ⟨a ~ talk⟩ — **di·gres·sive·ly** *adv* — **di·gres·sive·ness** *n*

dig up *vt* (14c) **:** FIND, UNEARTH

di·he·dral \(ˌ)dī-ˈhē-drəl\ *n* (ca. 1911) **1 :** DIHEDRAL ANGLE **2 :** the angle between an aircraft supporting surface (as a wing) and a horizontal transverse line

dihedral angle *n* [*di-* + *-hedral*] (1826) **:** a figure formed by two intersecting planes

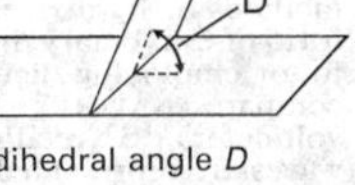

dihedral angle *D*

di·hy·brid \(ˌ)dī-ˈhī-brəd\ *adj* [ISV] (1907) **:** of, relating to, involving, or being an individual or strain that is heterozygous at two genetic loci — **dihybrid** *n*

dihydr- *or* **dihydro-** *comb form* **:** combined with two atoms of hydrogen ⟨*dihydro*ergotamine⟩

di·hy·dro·er·got·a·mine \(ˌ)dī-ˌhī-drō-ˌər-ˈgä-tə-ˌmēn\ *n* (1945) **:** a hydrogenated derivative $C_{33}H_{37}N_5O_5$ of ergotamine that is used in the treatment of migraine

di·hy·dro·tes·tos·ter·one \(ˌ)dī-ˌhī-drō-te-ˈstäs-tə-ˌrōn\ *n* (1965) **:** a biologically active metabolite $C_{19}H_{30}O_2$ of testosterone having similar androgenic activity

dihydroxy- *comb form* **:** containing two hydroxyl groups ⟨*dihydroxy*acetone⟩

di·hy·droxy·ac·e·tone \ˌdī-hī-ˌdräk-sē-ˈa-sə-ˌtōn\ *n* (1895) **:** a glyceraldehyde isomer $C_3H_6O_3$ used esp. to stain the skin to simulate a tan

Di·jon mustard \ˈdē-ˌzhän-, di-ˈzhän-, dē-ˈzhō^{n}-\ *n* [*Dijon,* France] (1938) **:** a prepared mustard made from dark mustard seeds, white wine, and spices

dik–dik \ˈdik-ˌdik\ *n, pl* **dik–diks** *or* **dik–dik** [origin unknown] (1883) **:** any of a genus (*Madoqua*) of small antelopes of eastern and southern Africa having an elongated snout

[1]**dike** \ˈdīk\ *n* [ME, prob. fr. ON *dīk* ditch and MLG *dīk* dam; akin to OE *dīc* ditch — more at DITCH] (13c) **1 :** an artificial watercourse **:** DITCH **2 a :** a bank usu. of earth constructed to control or confine water **:** LEVEE **b :** a barrier preventing passage esp. of something undesirable **3 a :** a raised causeway **b :** a tabular body of igneous rock that has been injected while molten into a fissure

[2]**dike** *vt* **diked; dik·ing** (14c) **1 :** to surround or protect with a dike **2 :** to drain by a dike — **dik·er** *n*

[3]**dike** *var of* DYKE

dik·tat \dik-ˈtät\ *n* [G, lit., something dictated, fr. NL *dictatum,* fr. L, neut. of *dictatus,* pp. of *dictare* to dictate] (1933) **1 :** a harsh settlement unilaterally imposed (as on a defeated nation) **2 :** DECREE, ORDER

dil *abbr* dilute

Di·lan·tin \dī-ˈlan-t^{ə}n, də-\ *trademark* — used for phenytoin

di·lap·i·date \də-ˈla-pə-ˌdāt\ *vb* **-dat·ed; -dat·ing** [L *dilapidatus,* pp. of *dilapidare* to squander, destroy, fr. *dis-* + *lapidare* to pelt with stones, fr. *lapid-, lapis* stone] *vt* (1565) **1 :** to bring into a condition of decay or partial ruin ⟨furniture is *dilapidated* by use —Janet Flanner⟩ **2** *archaic* **:** SQUANDER ~ *vi* **:** to become dilapidated — **di·lap·i·da·tion** \-ˌla-pə-ˈdā-shən\ *n*

di·lap·i·dat·ed *adj* (1565) **:** decayed, deteriorated, or fallen into partial ruin esp. through neglect or misuse ⟨a ~ old house⟩

di·lat·an·cy \dī-ˈlā-t^{ə}n(t)-sē\ *n* (1565) **:** the property of being dilatant

di·lat·ant \-t^{ə}nt\ *adj* (1885) **:** increasing in viscosity and setting to a solid as a result of deformation by expansion, pressure, or agitation

di·la·ta·tion \ˌdi-lə-ˈtā-shən, ˌdī-\ *n* (14c) **1 :** amplification in writing or speech **2 a :** the condition of being stretched beyond normal dimensions esp. as a result of overwork, disease, or abnormal relaxation ⟨~ of the heart⟩ ⟨~ of the stomach⟩ **b :** DILATION 2 **3 :** the action of expanding **:** the state of being expanded **4 :** a dilated part or formation — **di·la·ta·tion·al** \-shnəl, -shə-n^{ə}l\ *adj*

di·late \ˈdī-ˌlāt, dī-ˈ\ *vb* **di·lat·ed; di·lat·ing** [ME, fr. MF *dilater,* fr. L *dilatare,* lit., to spread wide, fr. *dis-* + *latus* wide — more at LATITUDE] *vt* (14c) **1** *archaic* **:** to describe or set forth at length or in detail **2 :** to enlarge or expand in bulk or extent **:** DISTEND, WIDEN ~ *vi* **1 :** to comment at length **:** DISCOURSE — usu. used with *on* or *upon* **2 :** to become wide **:** SWELL ⟨the pupil of the eye ~*s* and contracts⟩ ***syn*** see EXPAND — **di·lat·abil·i·ty** \(ˌ)dī-ˌlā-tə-ˈbi-lə-tē\ *n* — **di·lat·able** \dī-ˈlā-tə-bəl, ˈdī-ˌ\ *adj* — **di·la·tor** \dī-ˈlā-tər, ˈdī-ˌ\ *n*

di·lat·ed *adj* (15c) **1 :** expanded laterally; *esp* **:** being flat and widened ⟨~ leaves⟩ **2 :** expanded normally or abnormally in all dimensions

di·la·tion \dī-ˈlā-shən\ *n* (15c) **1 :** the act or action of dilating **:** the state of being dilated **:** EXPANSION, DILATATION **2 :** the action of stretching or enlarging an organ or part of the body

di·la·tive \dī-ˈlā-tiv, ˈdī-ˌ\ *adj* (1634) **:** causing dilation **:** tending to dilate

di·la·tom·e·ter \ˌdi-lə-ˈtä-mə-tər, ˌdī-\ *n* [ISV] (ca. 1883) **:** an instrument for measuring expansion — **di·la·to·met·ric** \-tō-ˈme-trik\ *adj* — **di·la·tom·e·try** \-ˈtä-mə-trē\ *n*

dil·a·to·ry \ˈdi-lə-ˌtȯr-ē\ *adj* [ME, fr. AF *dilatorie,* LL *dilatorius,* fr. L *differre* (pp. *dilatus*) to postpone, differ — more at DIFFER, TOLERATE] (15c) **1 :** tending or intended to cause delay ⟨~ tactics⟩ **2 :** characterized by procrastination **:** TARDY ⟨~ in paying bills⟩ — **dil·a·to·ri·ly** \ˌdi-lə-ˈtȯr-ə-lē\ *adv* — **dil·a·to·ri·ness** \ˈdi-lə-ˌtȯr-ē-nəs\ *n*

dil·do \ˈdil-(ˌ)dō\ *n, pl* **dildos** *also* **dildoes** [origin unknown] (1598) **:** an object resembling a penis used for sexual stimulation

di·lem·ma \də-ˈle-mə *also* dī-\ *n* [LL, fr. LGk *dilēmmat-, dilēmma,* prob. back-formation fr. Gk *dilēmmatos* involving two assumptions, fr. *di-* + *lēmmat-, lēmma* assumption — more at LEMMA] (1523) **1 :** an argument presenting two or more equally conclusive alternatives against an opponent **2 a :** a usu. undesirable or unpleasant choice ⟨faces this ~: raise interest rates and slow the economy or lower them and risk serious inflation⟩ **b :** a situation involving such a choice ⟨here am I brought to a very pretty ~; I must commit murder or commit matrimony —George Farquhar⟩; *broadly* **:** PREDICAMENT ⟨lords and bailiffs were in a terrible ~ —G. M. Trevelyan⟩ **3 a :** a problem involving a difficult choice ⟨the ~ of "liberty versus order" —J. M. Burns⟩ **b :** a difficult or persistent problem ⟨unemployment . . . the great central ~ of our advancing technology —August Heckscher⟩ — **dil·em·mat·ic** \ˌdi-lə-ˈma-tik *also* -ˌdī-\ *adj*

usage Although some commentators insist that *dilemma* be restricted to instances in which the alternatives to be chosen are equally unsatisfactory, their concern is misplaced; the unsatisfactoriness of the options is usu. a matter of how the author presents them. What is distressing or painful about a dilemma is having to make a choice one does not want to make. The use of such adjectives as *terrible, painful,* and *irreconcilable* suggests that *dilemma* is losing some of its unpleasant force. There also seems to be a tendency esp. in sense 3b toward applying the word to less weighty problems ⟨solved their goaltending ~ —Pat Calabria⟩.

dil·et·tante \ˈdi-lə-ˌtänt, -ˌtant; ˌdi-lə-ˈ\ *n, pl* **-tantes** *or* **-tan·ti** \-ˈtän-tē, -ˈtan-tē\ [It, fr. prp. of *dilettare* to delight, fr. L *dilectare* — more at DELIGHT] (1748) **1 :** an admirer or lover of the arts **2 :** a person having a superficial interest in an art or a branch of knowledge **:** DABBLER ***syn*** see AMATEUR — **dilettante** *adj* — **dil·et·tant·ish** \-ˌtän-tish, -ˌtan-, ˌdi-lə-ˈ\ *adj* — **dil·et·tan·tism** \-ˌtän-ˌti-zəm, -ˌtan-, ˌdi-lə-ˈ\ *n*

[1]**dil·i·gence** \ˈdi-lə-jən(t)s\ *n* [ME, fr. AF, fr. L *diligentia,* fr. *diligent-, diligens*] (14c) **1 a :** persevering application **:** ASSIDUITY **b** *obs* **:** SPEED, HASTE **2 :** the attention and care legally expected or required of a person (as a party to a contract)

[2]**di·li·gence** \ˈdi-lə-ˌzhän^{n}s, ˈdi-lə-jən(t)s\ *n* [F, lit., haste, fr. MF, persevering application] (1742) **:** STAGECOACH

dil·i·gent \ˈdi-lə-jənt\ *adj* [ME, fr. AF, fr. L *diligent-, diligens,* fr. prp. of *diligere* to esteem, love, fr. *di-* (fr. *dis-* apart) + *legere* to select — more at LEGEND] (14c) **:** characterized by steady, earnest, and energetic effort **:** PAINSTAKING ⟨a ~ worker⟩ ***syn*** see BUSY — **dil·i·gent·ly** *adv*

dill \ˈdil\ *n* [ME *dile,* fr. OE; akin to OHG *tilli* dill] (bef. 12c) **1 a :** any of several plants of the carrot family; *esp* **:** a European herb (*Anethum graveolens*) with aromatic foliage and seeds both of which are used in flavoring foods and esp. pickles **b :** the foliage of dill **2 :** DILL PICKLE — **dilled** *adj*

dill pickle *n* (1904) **:** a pickle seasoned with fresh dill

dill weed *n* (1933) **:** DILL 1

dil·ly \ˈdi-lē\ *n, pl* **dillies** [obs. *dilly,* adj., delightful, perh. by shortening & alter. fr. *delightful*] (1935) **:** one that is remarkable or outstanding ⟨had a ~ of a storm⟩ ⟨for a practical joke, that was a ~⟩

dil·ly bag \ˈdi-lē-\ *n* [Yagara (Australian aboriginal language of Queensland) *dili* coarse grass, fiber bag] (1867) **:** an Australian mesh bag made of native fibers

dil·ly·dal·ly \ˈdi-lē-ˌda-lē\ *vi* [redupl. of *dally*] (1741) **:** to waste time by loitering or delaying **:** DAWDLE

dil·ti·a·zem \dil-ˈtī-ə-(ˌ)zem\ *n* [prob. fr. ISV *dilator* + benzo*thiazepin,* tricyclic compound structurally similar to benzodiazepine + *-m* (as in *diazepam*)] (1975) **:** a calcium channel blocker $C_{22}H_{26}N_2O_4S$ used esp. in the form of its hydrochloride as a coronary vasodilator

dil·u·ent \ˈdil-yə-wənt, -yü-ənt\ *n* [L *diluent-, diluens,* prp. of *diluere*] (ca. 1721) **:** a diluting agent (as the vehicle in a medicinal preparation)

[1]**di·lute** \dī-ˈlüt, də-\ *vt* **di·lut·ed; di·lut·ing** [L *dilutus,* pp. of *diluere* to wash away, dilute, fr. *di-* + *lavere* to wash — more at LYE] (ca. 1555) **1 :** ATTENUATE **2 :** to make thinner or more liquid by admixture ⟨*diluted* wine⟩ **3 :** to diminish the strength, flavor, or brilliance of by admixture ⟨~ a color⟩ **4 :** to decrease the per share value of (common stock) by increasing the total number of shares — **di·lut·er** *or* **di·lu·tor** \-ˈlü-tər\ *n* — **di·lu·tive** \-ˈlü-tiv\ *adj*

[2]**dilute** *adj* (1605) **:** WEAK, DILUTED — **di·lute·ness** *n*

di·lu·tion \dī-ˈlü-shən, də-\ *n* (1646) **1 :** the action of diluting **:** the state of being diluted **2 :** something (as a solution) that is diluted **3 :** a lessening of real value (as of equity) by a decrease in relative worth; *specif* **:** a decrease of per share value of common stock by an increase in the total number of shares

di·lu·vi·al \də-ˈlü-vē-əl, dī-\ *or* **di·lu·vi·an** \-vē-ən\ *adj* [LL *diluvialis,* fr. L *diluvium* deluge — more at DELUGE] (ca. 1656) **:** of, relating to, or brought about by a flood

[1]**dim** \ˈdim\ *adj* **dim·mer; dim·mest** [ME, fr. OE *dimm;* akin to OHG *timber* dark] (bef. 12c) **1 a :** emitting or having a limited or insufficient amount of light ⟨~ stars⟩ ⟨a ~ lamp⟩ ⟨a ~ hallway⟩ **b :** DULL, LUSTERLESS ⟨~ colors⟩ **c :** lacking pronounced, clear-cut, or vigorous quality or character ⟨a ~ echo of the past⟩ **2 a :** seen indistinctly ⟨a ~ outline⟩ **b :** perceived by the senses or mind indistinctly or weakly **:** FAINT ⟨had only a ~ notion of what was going on⟩ **c :** having little prospect of favorable result or outcome ⟨a ~ future⟩ **d :** characterized by an unfavorable, skeptical, or pessimistic attitude — usu. used in the phrase *take a dim view of* **3 :** not perceiving clearly and distinctly ⟨~ eyes⟩ **4 :** DIM-WITTED — **dim·ly** *adv* — **dim·ma·ble** \ˈdi-mə-bəl\ *adj* — **dim·ness** *n*

[2]**dim** *vb* **dimmed; dim·ming** *vt* (bef. 12c) **1 :** to make dim or lusterless **2 :** to reduce the light from ~ *vi* **:** to become dim

[3]**dim** *n* (14c) **1** *archaic* **:** DUSK, DIMNESS **2 :** LOW BEAM

[4]**dim** *abbr* **1** dimension **2** diminished **3** diminuendo **4** diminutive

dim bulb *n* (1927) *slang* : DIMWIT

dime \ˈdīm\ *n* [ME, tenth part, tithe, fr. AF *disme, dime,* fr. L *decima,* fr. fem. of *decimus* tenth, fr. *decem* ten — more at TEN] (1786) **1 a** : a coin of the U.S. worth ¹⁄₁₀ dollar **b** : a petty sum of money **2** : a Canadian 10-cent piece **3** *slang* : a packet containing 10 dollars worth of an illicit drug (as marijuana) — called also *dime bag* — **a dime a dozen** : so plentiful or commonplace as to be of little esteem or slight value — **on a dime 1** : in a very small area ⟨these cars can turn *on a dime*⟩ **2** : INSTANTLY

di·men·hy·dri·nate \ˌdī-ˌmen-ˈhī-drə-ˌnāt\ *n* [*dime*thyl + amin*e* + *hydr-* + amin*e* + ¹*-ate*] (ca. 1950) : a crystalline antihistamine $C_{24}H_{28}ClN_5O_3$ used esp. to prevent nausea (as in motion sickness)

dime novel *n* (1864) : a usu. paperback melodramatic novel; *esp* : one popular in the U.S. from about the mid-19th century to the early 20th often featuring a Western theme

¹**di·men·sion** \də-ˈmen(t)-shən *also* dī-\ *n* [ME, fr. AF, fr. L *dimension-, dimensio,* fr. *dimetiri* to measure out, fr. *dis-* + *metiri* to measure — more at MEASURE] (14c) **1 a** (1) : measure in one direction; *specif* : one of three coordinates determining a position in space or four coordinates determining a position in space and time (2) : one of a group of properties whose number is necessary and sufficient to determine uniquely each element of a system of usu. mathematical entities (as an aggregate of points in real or abstract space) ⟨the surface of a sphere has two ∼*s*⟩; *also* : a parameter or coordinate variable assigned to such a property ⟨the three ∼*s* of momentum⟩ (3) : the number of elements in a basis of a vector space **b** : the quality of spatial extension : MAGNITUDE, SIZE **c** : a lifelike or realistic quality **d** : the range over which or the degree to which something extends : SCOPE — usu. used in pl. **e** : one of the elements or factors making up a complete personality or entity : ASPECT **2** *obs* : bodily form or proportions **3** : any of the fundamental units (as of mass, length, or time) on which a derived unit is based; *also* : the power of such a unit **4** : wood or stone cut to pieces of specified size **5** : a level of existence or consciousness — **di·men·sion·al** \-ˈmench-nəl, -ˈmen(t)-shə-nᵊl\ *adj* — **di·men·sion·al·i·ty** \-ˌmen(t)-shə-ˈna-lə-tē\ *n* — **di·men·sion·al·ly** \-ˈmench-nə-lē, -ˈmen(t)-shə-nᵊl-ē\ *adv* — **di·men·sion·less** \-ˈmen(t)-shən-ləs\ *adj*

²**dimension** *vt* **di·men·sioned; di·men·sion·ing** \-ˈmen(t)-shə-niŋ\ (1754) **1** : to form to the required dimensions **2** : to indicate the dimensions of (as on a drawing)

di·mer \ˈdī-mər\ *n* [ISV] (ca. 1926) : a compound formed by the union of two radicals or two molecules of a simpler compound; *specif* : a polymer formed from two molecules of a monomer — **di·mer·ic** \(ˌ)dī-ˈmer-ik\ *adj* — **di·mer·iza·tion** \ˌdī-mə-rə-ˈzā-shən\ *n* — **di·mer·ize** \ˈdī-mə-ˌrīz\ *vt*

di·mer·cap·rol \ˌdī-mər-ˈka-ˌprȯl, -ˌprōl\ *n* [*di-* + *mercap*tan + *pro*pane + ¹*-ol*] (1947) : a compound $C_3H_8OS_2$ developed as an antidote against lewisite and used to treat arsenic, mercury, and gold poisoning — called also *BAL*

dime–store \ˈdīm-ˌstȯr\ *adj* (1938) **1** : INEXPENSIVE ⟨∼ perfume⟩ **2** : TAWDRY, SECOND-RATE ⟨∼ philosophy⟩

dime store *n* (ca. 1928) : FIVE-AND-TEN

dim·e·ter \ˈdi-mə-tər\ *n* [LL, fr. Gk *dimetros,* adj., being a dimeter, fr. *di-* + *metron* measure — more at MEASURE] (1589) : a line of verse consisting of two metrical feet or of two dipodies

di·meth·o·ate \dī-ˈme-thə-ˌwāt, -thō-ˌāt\ *n* [*di*meth*yl* + *thio* acid + ¹*-ate*] (1960) : an organophosphorous insecticide and miticide $C_5H_{12}NO_3PS_2$ used esp. on crops and ornamental plants

di·meth·yl \ˌdī-ˈme-thəl\ *adj* : containing two methyl groups in the molecule — often used in combination

di·meth·yl·hy·dra·zine \ˌdī-ˌme-thəl-ˈhī-drə-ˌzēn\ *n* (1961) : either of two flammable corrosive isomeric liquids $C_2H_8N_2$ which are methylated derivatives of hydrazine and of which one is used as a rocket fuel

di·meth·yl·ni·tros·a·mine \-nī-ˈtrō-sə-ˌmēn\ *n* (1965) : a carcinogenic nitrosamine $C_2H_6N_2O$ that occurs esp. in tobacco smoke

dimethyl sulfoxide *n* (1964) : a compound C_2H_6SO obtained as a by-product in wood-pulp manufacture and used as a solvent and in medicine as an anti-inflammatory agent — called also *DMSO*

di·meth·yl·tryp·ta·mine \-ˈtrip-tə-ˌmēn\ *n* (1966) : a naturally occurring or easily synthesized hallucinogenic drug $C_{12}H_{16}N_2$ that is chemically similar to but shorter acting than psilocybin — called also *DMT*

dimin *abbr* diminuendo

di·min·ish \də-ˈmi-nish\ *vb* [ME *deminishen,* alter. of *diminuen,* fr. AF *diminuer,* fr. LL *diminuere,* alter. of L *deminuere,* fr. *de-* + *minuere* to lessen — more at MINOR] *vt* (15c) **1** : to make less or cause to appear less ⟨∼ an army's strength⟩ **2** : to lessen the authority, dignity, or reputation of : BELITTLE ⟨∼ a rival's accomplishments⟩ **3** : to cause to taper ∼ *vi* **1** : to become gradually less (as in size or importance) : DWINDLE **2** : TAPER *syn* see DECREASE — **di·min·ish·able** \-ni-shə-bəl\ *adj* — **di·min·ish·ment** \-mənt\ *n*

di·min·ished *adj* (ca. 1751) *of a musical interval* : made one half step less than perfect or minor ⟨a ∼ fifth⟩

diminishing returns *n pl* (1815) **1** : a rate of yield that beyond a certain point fails to increase in proportion to additional investments of labor or capital **2** : benefits that beyond a certain point fail to increase in proportion to extended efforts

di·min·u·en·do \də-ˌmin-yə-ˈwen-(ˌ)dō, -yü-ˈen- *also* -ˌmi-nə-ˈ\ *adv or adj* [It, lit., diminishing, fr. LL *diminuendum,* gerund of *diminuere*] (1775) : DECRESCENDO — **diminuendo** *n*

dim·i·nu·tion \ˌdi-mə-ˈnü-shən *also* -ˈnyü-\ *n* [ME *diminucioun,* fr. AF *diminutiun,* fr. ML *diminution-, diminutio,* alter. of L *deminution-, deminutio,* fr. *deminuere*] (14c) : the act, process, or an instance of diminishing : DECREASE

¹**di·min·u·tive** \də-ˈmi-nyə-tiv\ *n* [ME *diminutif,* fr. ML *diminutivum,* alter. of LL *deminutivum,* fr. neut. of *deminutivus,* adj., fr. *deminutus,* pp. of *deminuere*] (14c) **1** : a diminutive word, affix, or name **2** : a diminutive individual

²**diminutive** *adj* (14c) **1** : indicating small size and sometimes the state or quality of being familiarly known, lovable, pitiable, or contemptible — used of affixes (as *-ette, -kin, -ling*) and of words formed with them (as *kitchenette, manikin, duckling*), of clipped forms (as *Jim*), and of altered forms (as *Peggy*); compare AUGMENTATIVE **2** : exceptionally or notably small : TINY ⟨a ∼ performer⟩ *syn* see SMALL — **di·min·u·tive·ly** *adv* — **di·min·u·tive·ness** *n*

dim·i·ty \ˈdi-mə-tē\ *n, pl* **-ties** [alter. of ME *demyt,* fr. ML *dimitum,* fr. MGk *dimitos* of double thread, fr. Gk *di-* + *mitos* warp thread] (1570) : a sheer usu. corded cotton fabric of plain weave in checks or stripes

DIMM *abbr* dual in-line memory module

dim·mer \ˈdi-mər\ *n* (ca. 1896) **1** : a device for regulating the intensity of an electric lighting unit **2** : LOW BEAM

di·mor·phic \(ˌ)dī-ˈmȯr-fik\ *adj* (1859) **1 a** : DIMORPHOUS 1 **b** : occurring in two distinct forms ⟨∼ leaves⟩ ⟨sexually ∼ coloration in birds⟩ **2** : combining qualities of two kinds of individuals in one

di·mor·phism \-ˌfi-zəm\ *n* (1832) : the condition or property of being dimorphic or dimorphous: as **a** : the existence of two different forms (as of color or size) of a species esp. in the same population ⟨sexual ∼⟩ **b** : the existence of a part (as leaves of a plant) in two different forms

di·mor·phous \(ˌ)dī-ˈmȯr-fəs\ *adj* [Gk *dimorphos* having two forms, fr. *di-* + *-morphos* -morphous] (1832) **1** : crystallizing in two different forms **2** : DIMORPHIC 1b

dim·out \ˈdim-ˌau̇t\ *n* (1942) : a restriction limiting the use or showing of lights at night esp. during the threat of an air raid; *also* : a condition of partial darkness produced by this restriction

¹**dim·ple** \ˈdim-pəl\ *n* [ME *dympull;* akin to OHG *tumphilo* whirlpool, OE *dyppan* to dip — more at DIP] (15c) **1** : a slight natural indentation in the surface of some part of the human body **2** : a depression or indentation on a surface (as of a golf ball) — **dim·ply** \-p(ə-)lē\ *adj*

²**dimple** *vb* **dim·pled; dim·pling** \-p(ə-)liŋ\ *vt* (1602) : to mark with dimples ∼ *vi* : to exhibit or form dimples

dim sum \ˈdim-ˈsəm\ *n, pl* **dim sums** *also* **dim sum** [Chin (Guangdong) *dímsām,* fr. *dím* dot, speck + *sām* heart] (1948) : traditional Chinese food consisting of a variety of items (as steamed or fried dumplings, pieces of cooked chicken, and rice balls) served in small portions

dim·wit \ˈdim-ˌwit\ *n* (1921) : a stupid or mentally slow person

dim–wit·ted \-ˈwi-təd\ *adj* (1934) : not mentally bright : STUPID — **dim–wit·ted·ly** *adv* — **dim–wit·ted·ness** *n*

¹**din** \ˈdin\ *n* [ME, fr. OE *dyne;* akin to ON *dynr* din, Skt *dhvanati* it roars] (bef. 12c) **1** : a loud continued noise; *esp* : a welter of discordant sounds **2** : a situation or condition resembling a din

²**din** *vb* **dinned; din·ning** *vi* (bef. 12c) : to make a loud noise ∼ *vt* **1** : to assail with loud continued noise **2** : to impress by insistent repetition — often used with *into* ⟨lessons *dinned* into us as children⟩

³**din** *abbr* dinar

DIN *abbr* [G *Deutsche Industrie-Normen*] German Industrial Standards

di·nar \di-ˈnär, ˈdē-ˌ\ *n* [Ar *dīnār,* fr. LGk *dēnarion* denarius, fr. L *denarius* — more at DENIER] (1634) **1** : a gold coin formerly used in countries of southwest Asia and north Africa **2 a** — see MONEY table **b** — see *rial* at MONEY table

¹**dine** \ˈdīn\ *vb* **dined; din·ing** [ME, fr. AF *disner, diner* to eat, have a meal, fr. VL **disjejunare* to break one's fast, fr. L *dis-* + LL *jejunare* to fast, fr. L *jejunus* fasting] *vi* (13c) : to take dinner — often used with *on* ⟨∼ on pasta⟩ ∼ *vt* : to give a dinner to ⟨wined her and *dined* her⟩

²**dine** *n* (15c) *Scot* : DINNER

dine out *vi* (1736) : to eat a meal away from home — **dine out on** : to use as a subject for dining table conversation

din·er \ˈdī-nər\ *n* (1815) **1** : a person who dines (as in a restaurant) **2 a** : DINING CAR **b** : a restaurant usu. resembling a dining car in shape

din·er–out \ˌdī-nər-ˈau̇t\ *n, pl* **di·ners–out** \-nərz-ˈau̇t\ (1808) : a person who dines out

di·nette \dī-ˈnet\ *n* (1925) : a small space usu. off a kitchen used for informal dining; *also* : furniture for such a space

¹**ding** \ˈdiŋ\ *vb* [prob. imit.] *vt* (1582) : to dwell on with tiresome repetition ⟨keeps ∼*ing* it into him that the less he smokes the better —Samuel Butler †1902⟩ ∼ *vi* **1** : to make a ringing sound : CLANG **2** : to speak with tiresome reiteration

²**ding** *n* [*ding* to strike, fr. ME *dingen*] (ca. 1945) : an instance of minor surface damage (as a dent)

³**ding** *vt* (1968) : to cause minor surface damage to ⟨∼ a car door⟩

ding–a–ling \ˈdiŋ-ə-ˌliŋ\ *n* [redupl. of ¹*ding*] (ca. 1935) : NITWIT, KOOK

ding·bat \ˈdiŋ-ˌbat\ *n* [origin unknown] (1904) **1** : a typographical symbol or ornament (as •, ¶, or ✠) **2** : NITWIT, KOOK

¹**ding–dong** \ˈdiŋ-ˌdȯŋ, -ˌdäŋ\ *n* [imit.] (1611) **1** : the ringing sound produced by repeated strokes esp. on a bell **2** : NITWIT, KOOK

²**ding–dong** *vi* (1659) **1** : to make a ding-dong sound **2** : to repeat a sound or action tediously or insistently

³**ding–dong** *adj* (1869) *chiefly Brit* : marked by a rapid exchange or alternation (as of blows) ⟨a ∼ battle⟩

dinge \ˈdinj\ *n* [back-formation fr. *dingy*] (1846) : the condition of being dingy

ding·er \ˈdiŋ-ər\ *n* [perh. fr. *ding* to strike + ²*-er*] (1974) : HOME RUN 1

din·ghy \ˈdiŋ-ē, -gē\ *n, pl* **dinghies** [Bengali *ḍiṅgi,* Urdu *ḍiṅgī* & Hindi *ḍieṅgī*] (1810) **1** : an East Indian rowboat or sailboat **2 a** : a small boat carried on or towed behind a larger boat as a tender or a lifeboat **b** : a small sailboat **3** : a rubber life raft

din·gle \ˈdiŋ-gəl\ *n* [ME, deep hollow] (13c) : a small wooded valley : DELL

din·go \ˈdiŋ-(ˌ)gō\ *n, pl* **dingoes** [Dharuk (Australian aboriginal language of the Port Jackson area) *diŋgu*] (1789) : a wild dog (*Canis dingo*) of Australia having a tan or reddish coat that is often considered a subspecies (*C. familiaris dingo*) of the domestic dog

din·gus \ˈdiŋ-(g)əs\ *n* [D or G; D *dinges,* prob. fr. G *Dings,* fr. gen. of *Ding* thing, fr. OHG — more at THING] (1876) : DOODAD 2

din·gy \ˈdin-jē\ *adj* **din·gi·er; -est** [origin unknown] (1691) **1** : DIRTY, UNCLEAN **2** : SHABBY, SQUALID — **din·gi·ly** \-jə-lē\ *adv* — **din·gi·ness** \-jē-nəs\ *n*

dining car *n* (1838) : a railroad car in which meals are served

dining room *n* (1601) : a room used for eating meals

di·ni·tro \(ˌ)dī-ˈnī-trō\ *adj* : containing two nitro groups — often used in combination

di·ni·tro·ben·zene \(ˌ)dī-ˌnī-trō-ˈben-ˌzēn, -(ˌ)ben-ˈ\ *n* [ISV] (1873) : any of three isomeric toxic compounds $C_6H_4(NO_2)_2$

\ə\ **abut** \ᵊ\ **kitten**, F **table** \ər\ **further** \a\ **ash** \ā\ **ace** \ä\ **mop, mar** \au̇\ **out** \ch\ **chin** \e\ **bet** \ē\ **easy** \g\ **go** \i\ **hit** \ī\ **ice** \j\ **job** \ŋ\ **sing** \ō\ **go** \ȯ\ **law** \ȯi\ **boy** \th\ **thin** \t͟h\ **the** \ü\ **loot** \u̇\ **foot** \y\ **yet** \zh\ **vision, beige** \k̟, ⁿ, œ, ue, ʸ\ *see* Guide to Pronunciation

di·ni·tro·phe·nol \-ˈfē-ˌnōl, -fi-ˈ\ *n* (1873) **:** any of six isomeric crystalline compounds $C_6H_4N_2O_5$ some of whose derivatives are pesticides

[1]**dink** \ˈdiŋk\ *n* [by shortening & alter.] (1903) **:** DINGHY

[2]**dink** *n* [*dink* to hit with a drop shot, prob. of imit. origin] (1939) **:** DROP SHOT

[3]**dink** *n* [perh. fr. *dink,* disparaging name for a Vietnamese] (1974) *slang* **:** NITWIT, JERK, NERD

[4]**dink** *n, often all cap* [*d*ouble *i*ncome, *n*o *k*ids] (1986) **:** a couple with two incomes and no children; *also* **:** a member of such a couple

Din·ka \ˈdiŋ-kə\ *n, pl* **Dinkas** *also* **Dinka** [prob. ultim. fr. Dinka *jieŋ,* a self-designation] (1861) **1 :** a member of a pastoral people of the Nile Valley in south central Sudan **2 :** the Nilotic language of the Dinkas

din·key *or* **din·ky** \ˈdiŋ-kē\ *n, pl* **dinkeys** *or* **dinkies** [prob. fr. *dinky*] (1874) **:** a small locomotive

[1]**din·kum** \ˈdiŋ-kəm\ *adj* [E dial. *dinkum,* n., work, share of work] (1905) *Austral & NewZeal* **:** AUTHENTIC, GENUINE — often used with *fair* ⟨I was fair ~ about my interest in their culture —Percy Trezise⟩

[2]**dinkum** *adv* (1915) *Austral & NewZeal* **:** TRULY, HONESTLY — often used with *fair;* often used interjectionally

din·ky \ˈdiŋ-kē\ *adj* **din·ki·er; -est** [Sc *dink* neat] (1880) **:** overly or unattractively small ⟨drives a ~ little car⟩; *also, Brit* **:** attractively small **:** CUTE

din·ner \ˈdi-nər\ *n, often attrib* [ME *diner,* fr. AF *disner, diner* meal, fr. *disner* to dine] (13c) **1 a :** the principal meal of the day **b :** a formal feast or banquet **2 :** TABLE D'HÔTE 2 **3 :** the food prepared for a dinner ⟨eat your ~⟩ **4 :** a packaged meal usu. for quick preparation ⟨warmed up a frozen ~⟩ — **din·ner·less** \-ləs\ *adj*

dinner jacket *n* (1891) **:** a jacket for formal evening wear — **din·ner–jac·ket·ed** \-ˈja-kə-təd\ *adj*

dinner theater *n* (1960) **:** a restaurant in which a play is presented after the meal is over

din·ner·time \ˈdi-nər-ˌtīm\ *n* (14c) **:** the customary time for dinner

din·ner·ware \-ˌwer\ *n* (1895) **:** tableware other than flatware

di·no \ˈdī-(ˌ)nō\ *n, pl* **dinos** (1936) **1 :** DINOSAUR 1 **2 :** DINOSAUR 2

di·no·fla·gel·late \ˌdī-nō-ˈfla-jə-lət, -ˌlāt; -flə-ˈje-lət\ *n* [ultim. fr. Gk *dinos* rotation, eddy + NL *flagellum*] (1889) **:** any of an order (Dinoflagellata) of chiefly marine planktonic usu. solitary unicellular phytoflagellates that include luminescent forms, forms important in marine food chains, and forms causing red tide

di·no·saur \ˈdī-nə-ˌsȯr\ *n* [NL *Dinosaurus,* genus name, fr. Gk *deinos* terrifying + *sauros* lizard — more at DIRE] (1841) **1 :** any of a group (Dinosauria) of extinct often very large chiefly terrestrial carnivorous or herbivorous reptiles of the Mesozoic era **2 :** any of various large extinct reptiles (as ichthyosaurs) other than the true dinosaurs **3 :** one that is impractically large, out-of-date, or obsolete — **di·no·sau·ri·an** \ˌdī-nə-ˈsȯr-ē-ən\ *adj* — **di·no·sau·ric** \-ˈsȯr-ik\ *adj*

[1]**dint** \ˈdint\ *n* [ME, fr. OE *dynt;* akin to ON *dyntr* noise] (bef. 12c) **1** *archaic* **:** BLOW, STROKE **2 :** FORCE, POWER **3 :** [2]DENT — **by dint of :** by force of **:** BECAUSE OF ⟨succeeded *by dint of* hard work⟩

[2]**dint** *vt* (1597) **1 :** to make a dent in **2 :** to impress or drive in with force

di·nu·cle·o·tide \(ˌ)dī-ˈn(y)ü-klē-ə-ˌtīd\ *n* (ca. 1927) **:** a nucleotide consisting of two units each composed of a phosphate, a pentose, and a nitrogen base

di·oc·e·san \dī-ˈä-sə-sən *also* ˈdī-ə-ˌsē-sᵊn\ *n* (15c) **:** a bishop having jurisdiction over a diocese

di·o·cese \ˈdī-ə-səs, -ˌsēs, -ˌsēz\ *n, pl* **-ces·es** \ˈdī-ə-sə-səz, -ˌsē-zəz, ÷ˈdī-ə-ˌsēz\ [ME *diocise,* fr. AF, fr. LL *diocesis,* alter. of *dioecesis,* fr. L, administrative division, fr. Gk *dioikēsis* administration, administrative division, fr. *dioikein* to keep house, govern, fr. *dia-* + *oikein* to dwell, manage, fr. *oikos* house — more at VICINITY] (14c) **:** the territorial jurisdiction of a bishop — **di·oc·e·san** \dī-ˈä-sə-sən *also* ˈdī-ə-ˌsē-sᵊn\ *adj*

di·ode \ˈdī-ˌōd\ *n* [ISV] (1919) **:** an electronic device that has two electrodes or terminals and is used esp. as a rectifier

di·oe·cious \(ˌ)dī-ˈē-shəs\ *adj* [ultim. fr. Gk *di-* + *oikos*] (1752) **1 :** having male reproductive organs in one individual and female in another **2 :** having staminate and pistillate flowers borne on different individuals — **di·oe·cism** \-ˈē-ˌsi-zəm\ *n* — **di·oe·cy** \ˈdī-ˌē-sē\ *n*

di·ol \ˈdī-ˌōl, -ˌȯl\ *n* [ISV] (1920) **:** a compound containing two hydroxyl groups

di·ole·fin \dī-ˈō-lə-fən\ *n* [ISV] (ca. 1909) **:** DIENE

Di·o·me·des \ˌdī-ə-ˈmē-dēz\ *n* [L, fr. Gk *Diomēdēs*] (14c) **:** one of the Greek heroes of the Trojan War

Di·o·ny·sia \ˌdī-ə-ˈni-zhē-ə, -ˈnē-, -shē-, -zē-, -sē-\ *n pl* [L, fr. Gk, fr. neut. pl. of *dionysios* of Dionysus, fr. *Dionysos*] (1812) **:** ancient Greek seasonal observances held in seasonal cycles in honor of Dionysus; *esp* **:** such observances marked by dramatic performances

Di·o·ny·si·ac \-ˈni-zhē-ˌak, -ˈnē-, -shē-, -zē-, -sē-\ *adj* [L *dionysiacus,* fr. Gk *dionysiakos,* fr. *Dionysos*] (1844) **:** DIONYSIAN 2 — **Dionysiac** *n*

Di·o·ny·sian \-ˈni-zhē-ən, -ˈnē-, -shē-, -zē-, -sē-; -zhən, -shən\ *adj* (1607) **1 a :** of or relating to Dionysius **b :** of or relating to the theological writings once mistakenly attributed to Dionysius the Areopagite **2 a :** devoted to the worship of Dionysus **b :** characteristic of Dionysus or the cult of worship of Dionysus; *esp* **:** being of a frenzied or orgiastic character — compare APOLLONIAN

Di·o·ny·sus \ˌdī-ə-ˈnī-səs, -ˈnē-\ *n* [L, fr. Gk *Dionysos*] (1812) **:** BACCHUS

Di·o·phan·tine equation \ˌdī-ə-ˈfan-ˌtīn-, -ˈfan-tᵊn-\ *n* [*Diophantus,* 3d cent. A.D. Gk. mathematician] (ca. 1928) **:** an indeterminate polynomial equation which has integral coefficients and for which it is required to find all integral solutions

di·op·side \dī-ˈäp-ˌsīd\ *n* [F, fr. *di-* + Gk *opsis* appearance — more at OPTIC] (ca. 1808) **:** a green to white mineral that consists of pyroxene containing little or no aluminum — **di·op·sid·ic** \ˌdī-ˌäp-ˈsi-dik\ *adj*

di·op·ter \dī-ˈäp-tər, ˈdī-ˌäp-\ *n* [*diopter* (an optical instrument), fr. MF *dioptre,* fr. L *dioptra,* fr. Gk, fr. *dia-* + *opsesthai* to be going to see — more at OPTIC] (ca. 1864) **:** a unit of measurement of the refractive power of lenses equal to the reciprocal of the focal length in meters

di·op·tric \dī-ˈäp-trik\ *adj* [Gk *dioptrikos* of a diopter (instrument), fr. *dioptra*] (1653) **:** REFRACTIVE; *specif* **:** assisting vision by refracting and focusing light

di·ora·ma \ˌdī-ə-ˈra-mə, -ˈrä-\ *n* [F, fr. *dia-* + *-orama* (as in *panorama,* fr. E)] (1823) **1 :** a scenic representation in which a partly translucent painting is seen from a distance through an opening **2 a :** a scenic representation in which sculptured figures and lifelike details are displayed usu. in miniature so as to blend indistinguishably with a realistic painted background **b :** a life-size exhibit (as of a wildlife specimen or scene) with realistic natural surroundings and a painted background — **di·oram·ic** \-ˈra-mik\ *adj*

di·o·rite \ˈdī-ə-ˌrīt\ *n* [F, irreg. fr. Gk *diorizein* to distinguish, fr. *dia-* + *horizein* to define — more at HORIZON] (1826) **:** a granular crystalline igneous rock commonly of acid plagioclase and hornblende, pyroxene, or biotite — **di·o·rit·ic** \ˌdī-ə-ˈri-tik\ *adj*

Di·os·cu·ri \ˌdī-əs-ˈkyu̇r-ˌī, dī-ˈäs-kyə-ˌrī\ *n pl* [NL, fr. Gk *Dioskouroi,* lit., sons of Zeus, fr. *Dios* (gen. of *Zeus;* akin to L *divus* divine) + *kouroi,* pl. of *kouros, koros* boy — more at DEITY, CRESCENT] (1640) **:** the twins Castor and Pollux reunited as stars in the sky by Zeus after Castor's death and regarded as patrons of athletes and sailors

di·ox·ane \dī-ˈäk-ˌsān\ *also* **di·ox·an** \-ˌsan, -sən\ *n* [ISV] (1912) **:** a flammable toxic liquid diether $C_4H_8O_2$ used esp. as a solvent

di·ox·ide \(ˌ)dī-ˈäk-ˌsīd\ *n* [ISV] (ca. 1847) **:** an oxide (as carbon dioxide) containing two atoms of oxygen in the molecule

di·ox·in \(ˌ)dī-ˈäk-sən\ *n* (ca. 1919) **:** any of several persistent toxic heterocyclic hydrocarbons that occur esp. as by-products of various industrial processes (as pesticide manufacture and paper making) and waste incineration; *esp* **:** TCDD

[1]**dip** \ˈdip\ *vb* **dipped; dip·ping** [ME *dippen,* fr. OE *dyppan;* akin to OHG *tupfen* to wash, Lith *dubus* deep] *vt* (bef. 12c) **1 a :** to plunge or immerse momentarily or partially under the surface (as of a liquid) so as to moisten, cool, or coat ⟨~ candles⟩ **b :** to thrust in a way to suggest immersion **c :** to immerse (as a sheep or dog) in an antiseptic or parasiticidal solution **2 a :** to lift a portion of by reaching below the surface with something shaped to hold liquid **:** LADLE **b :** to take a portion of (snuff) **3 a** *archaic* **:** INVOLVE **b :** MORTGAGE **4 a :** to lower and then raise again ⟨~ a flag in salute⟩ **b** *chiefly Brit* **:** DIM 2 ~ *vi* **1 a :** to plunge into a liquid and quickly emerge **b :** to immerse something into a processing liquid or finishing material **2 a :** to suddenly drop down or out of sight **b** *of an airplane* **:** to drop suddenly before climbing **c :** to decline or decrease moderately and usu. temporarily ⟨prices *dipped*⟩ **d :** to lower the body momentarily esp. as part of an athletic or dancing motion **3 a :** to withdraw a part of the contents of something by or as if by reaching down inside it — used with *into* ⟨*dipped* into his pocket for change⟩ ⟨*dipped* into the family's savings⟩ **4 :** to examine or read something casually or superficially — used with *into* ⟨~ into a book⟩ **5 :** to incline downward from the plane of the horizon — **dip·pa·ble** \ˈdi-pə-bəl\ *adj*

[2]**dip** *n* (1599) **1 :** an act of dipping; *esp* **:** a brief plunge into the water for sport or exercise ⟨a quick ~ in the pool⟩ **2 :** inclination downward: **a :** PITCH **b :** a sharp downward course **:** DROP ⟨a ~ in popularity⟩ **c :** the angle that a stratum or similar geological feature makes with a horizontal plane **3 :** the angle formed with the horizon by a magnetic needle free to rotate in the vertical plane **4 :** HOLLOW, DEPRESSION ⟨a ~ in the road⟩ **5 :** something obtained by or used in dipping ⟨a ~ of ice cream⟩ ⟨a ~ of snuff⟩ **6 a :** a sauce or soft mixture into which food may be dipped ⟨bean ~⟩ **b :** a liquid preparation for the dipping of something; *esp* **:** an insecticide or parasiticide for the dipping of animals ⟨a sheep ~⟩ **7** *slang* **:** PICKPOCKET

[3]**dip** *n* [back-formation fr. *dippy*] (1932) **:** a stupid or unsophisticated person

[4]**dip** *abbr* diploma

DIP *abbr* dual in-line package; dual in-line packaging

di·pep·ti·dase \dī-ˈpep-tə-ˌdās, -ˌdāz\ *n* (1927) **:** any of various enzymes that hydrolyze dipeptides but not polypeptides

di·pep·tide \(ˌ)dī-ˈpep-ˌtīd\ *n* (1903) **:** a peptide that yields two molecules of amino acid on hydrolysis

di·pha·sic \(ˌ)dī-ˈfā-zik\ *adj* (1881) **:** having two phases

di·phen·hy·dra·mine \ˌdī-ˌfen-ˈhī-drə-ˌmēn\ *n* (1948) **:** an antihistamine $C_{17}H_{21}NO$ used esp. in the form of its hydrochloride

di·phe·nyl·amine \(ˌ)dī-ˌfe-nᵊl-ə-ˈmēn, -ˌfē-, -nᵊl-ˈa-mən\ *n* [ISV] (1872) **:** a crystalline pleasant-smelling compound $(C_6H_5)_2NH$ used chiefly in the manufacture of dyes and as an indicator

di·phe·nyl·hy·dan·to·in \-hī-ˈdan-tə-wən\ *n* [*di-* + *phenyl* + *hyd*rogen + *all*antoin] (1937) **:** PHENYTOIN

di·phos·gene \(ˌ)dī-ˈfäz-ˌjēn\ *n* [ISV] (1918) **:** a liquid compound $C_2Cl_4O_2$ used as a poison gas in World War I

di·phos·phate \(ˌ)dī-ˈfäs-ˌfāt\ *n* (1826) **:** a phosphate containing two phosphate groups

di·phos·pho·gly·cer·ic acid \(ˌ)dī-ˈfäs-fō-gli-ˌser-ik-\ *n* (1959) **:** a diphosphate of glyceric acid that is an important intermediate in photosynthesis and in glycolysis and fermentation

di·phos·pho·pyr·i·dine nucleotide \-ˌpir-ə-ˌdēn-\ *n* (1938) **:** NAD

diph·the·ria \dif-ˈthir-ē-ə, ÷dip-\ *n* [NL, fr. F *diphthérie,* fr. Gk *diphthera* leather; fr. the toughness of the false membrane] (ca. 1851) **:** an acute febrile contagious disease typically marked by the formation of a false membrane esp. in the throat and caused by a gram-positive bacterium (*Corynebacterium diphtheriae*) that produces a toxin causing inflammation of the heart and nervous system — **diph·the·ri·al** \-ē-əl\ *adj* — **diph·the·rit·ic** \ˌdif-thə-ˈri-tik, ÷ˌdip-\ *adj*

[1]**diph·the·roid** \ˈdif-thə-ˌrȯid\ *adj* (1861) **:** resembling diphtheria

[2]**diphtheroid** *n* (1908) **:** a bacterium (esp. genus *Corynebacterium*) that resembles the bacterium of diphtheria but does not produce diphtheria toxin

diph·thong \ˈdif-ˌthȯŋ, ˈdip-\ *n* [ME *diptonge,* fr. MF *diptongue,* fr. LL *dipthongus,* fr. Gk *diphthongos,* fr. *di-* + *phthongos* voice, sound] (15c) **1 :** a gliding monosyllabic speech sound (as the vowel combination at the end of *toy*) that starts at or near the articulatory position for one vowel and moves to or toward the position of another **2 :** DIGRAPH **3 :** the ligature æ or œ — **diph·thon·gal** \dif-ˈthȯŋ-(g)əl, dip-\ *adj*

diph·thong·ize \ˈdif-ˌthȯŋ-ˌīz, ˈdip-\ *vb* **-ized; -iz·ing** *vi* (1867) *of a simple vowel* **:** to change into a diphthong ~ *vt* **:** to pronounce as a diphthong — **diph·thong·i·za·tion** \(ˌ)dif-ˌthȯŋ-ə-ˈzā-shən, (ˌ)dip-\ *n*

diphy- *or* **diphyo-** *comb form* [NL, fr. Gk *diphy-,* fr. *diphyēs,* fr. *di-* + *phyein* to bring forth — more at BE] **:** double **:** bipartite ⟨*diphyodont*⟩

di·phy·let·ic \ˌdī-fī-ˈle-tik\ *adj* (1902) **:** derived from two lines of evolutionary descent ⟨~ hadrosaurs⟩

di·phy·odont \(ˌ)dī-ˈfī-ə-ˌdänt\ *adj* [ISV] (1854) **:** marked by the successive development of deciduous and permanent sets of teeth

dipl- *or* **diplo-** *comb form* [Gk, fr. *diploos* — more at DOUBLE] **1 :** double : twofold ⟨*diplo*pia⟩ **2 :** diploid ⟨*diplo*phase⟩
di·ple·gia \dī-ˈplē-j(ē-)ə\ *n* [NL] (ca. 1881) **:** paralysis of corresponding parts on both sides of the body
dip·lo·blas·tic \ˌdip-lō-ˈblas-tik\ *adj* (ca. 1885) **:** having two germ layers — used of an embryo or lower invertebrate lacking a true mesoderm
dip·lo·coc·cus \-ˈkä-kəs\ *n, pl* **-coc·ci** \-ˈkäk-ˌsī, -ˌsē, -ˈkä-ˌkī, -ˌkē\ [NL, genus name] (ca. 1881) **:** any of various encapsulated bacteria (as *Streptococcus pneumoniae,* a common cause of pneumonia) that usu. occur in pairs and that were formerly grouped in a single taxon (genus *Diplococcus*) but are now all assigned to other genera
di·plod·o·cus \də-ˈplä-də-kəs, dī-\ *n* [NL, genus name, fr. *dipl-* + Gk *dokos* beam, fr. *dekesthai, dechesthai* to receive; akin to L *decēre* to be fitting — more at DECENT] (1884) **:** any of a genus (*Diplodocus*) of large herbivorous sauropod dinosaurs of the Late Jurassic known from remains found in Colorado, Wyoming, Montana, and Utah
dip·loe \ˈdi-plə-ˌwē, -plō-ˌē\ *n* [NL, fr. Gk *diploē,* fr. *diploos* double] (1597) **:** cancellous bony tissue between the external and internal layers of the skull — **di·plo·ic** \də-ˈplō-ik, dī-\ *adj*
[1]**dip·loid** \ˈdi-ˌplȯid\ *adj* [ISV] (1908) **:** having two haploid sets of homologous chromosomes ⟨~ somatic cells⟩ — **dip·loi·dy** \-ˌplȯi-dē\ *n*
[2]**diploid** *n* (1908) **:** a single cell, individual, or generation characterized by the diploid chromosome number
di·plo·ma \də-ˈplō-mə\ *n, pl* **diplomas** [L, passport, diploma, fr. Gk *diplōma* folded paper, passport, fr. *diploun* to double, fr. *diploos*] (1622) **1** *pl also* **di·plo·ma·ta** \-mə-tə\ **:** an official or state document **:** CHARTER **2 :** a writing usu. under seal conferring some honor or privilege **3 :** a document bearing record of graduation from or of a degree conferred by an educational institution
di·plo·ma·cy \də-ˈplō-mə-sē\ *n* (1796) **1 :** the art and practice of conducting negotiations between nations **2 :** skill in handling affairs without arousing hostility **:** TACT
diploma mill *n* (1914) **:** a usu. unregulated institution of higher education granting degrees with few or no academic requirements
dip·lo·mat \ˈdi-plə-ˌmat\ *n* [F *diplomate,* back-formation fr. *diplomatique*] (1813) **:** one employed or skilled in diplomacy
dip·lo·mate \ˈdi-plə-ˌmāt\ *n* (1879) **:** a person who holds a diploma; *esp* **:** a physician qualified to practice in a medical specialty by advanced training and experience in the specialty followed by passing an intensive examination by a national board of senior specialists
dip·lo·mat·ic \ˌdi-plə-ˈma-tik\ *adj* [in sense 1, fr. NL *diplomaticus,* fr. L *diplomat-, diploma;* in other senses, fr. F *diplomatique* connected with documents regulating international relations, fr. NL *diplomaticus*] (1711) **1 a :** PALEOGRAPHIC **b :** exactly reproducing the original ⟨a ~ edition⟩ **2 :** of, relating to, or concerned with diplomacy or diplomats ⟨~ relations⟩ **3 :** employing tact and conciliation esp. in situations of stress ***syn*** see SUAVE — **dip·lo·mat·i·cal·ly** \-ti-k(ə-)lē\ *adv*
di·plo·ma·tist \də-ˈplō-mə-tist\ *n* (1768) **:** DIPLOMAT
dip·lo·phase \ˈdi-plə-ˌfāz\ *n* (ca. 1925) **:** a diploid phase in a life cycle
dip·lo·pia \di-ˈplō-pē-ə\ *n* [NL] (ca. 1811) **:** a disorder of vision in which two images of a single object are seen (as from unequal action of the eye muscles) — called also *double vision* — **dip·lo·pic** \-ˈplō-pik, -ˈplä-pik\ *adj*
dip·lo·pod \ˈdi-plə-ˌpäd\ *n* [ultim. fr. Gk *dipl-* + *pod-, pous* foot — more at FOOT] (ca. 1864) **:** MILLIPEDE
dip·lo·tene \ˈdi-plə-ˌtēn\ *n* [ISV] (1925) **:** a stage of meiotic prophase which follows the pachytene and during which the paired homologous chromosomes begin to separate and chiasmata become visible — **diplotene** *adj*
dip net *n* (1820) **:** a bag net with a handle that is used esp. to scoop fish from the water — **dip·net** \ˈdip-ˌnet\ *vt*
dip·no·an \ˈdip-nə-wən, -nō-ən\ *n* [ultim. fr. Gk *dipnoos* having two breathing apertures, fr. *di-* + *pnoē* breath, fr. *pnein* to breathe — more at SNEEZE] (1883) **:** LUNGFISH
dip·o·dy \ˈdi-pə-dē\ *n, pl* **-dies** [LL *dipodia,* fr. Gk, fr. *dipod-, dipous* having two feet, fr. *di-* + *pod-, pous*] (ca. 1844) **:** a prosodic unit or measure of two feet — **di·pod·ic** \dī-ˈpä-dik\ *adj*
di·pole \ˈdī-ˌpōl\ *n* [ISV] (1912) **1 a :** a pair of equal and opposite electric charges or magnetic poles of opposite sign separated esp. by a small distance **b :** a body or system (as a molecule) having such charges or poles **2 :** a radio antenna consisting of two horizontal rods in line with each other with their ends slightly separated — **di·po·lar** \ˈdī-ˌpō-lər, ˌdī-ˈpō-\ *adj*
dipole moment *n* (1926) **:** the moment produced by a magnetic or electric dipole; *esp* **:** the product of the distance between the two poles and the magnitude of either pole
dip·per \ˈdi-pər\ *n* (1611) **1 :** one that dips: as **a :** a worker who dips articles **b :** something (as a long-handled cup) used for dipping **c** *slang* **:** PICKPOCKET **2 :** any of a genus (*Cinclus* and esp. *C. cinclus* of the Old World and *C. mexicanus* of No. America) of birds that comprise an oscine family (Cinclidae) and include individuals that wade and dive into swift mountain streams in search of food — called also *water ouzel* **3** *cap* **:** a group of stars that resembles a dipper: as **a :** BIG DIPPER **b :** LITTLE DIPPER — **dip·per·ful** \-ˌfu̇l\ *n*
dip·py \ˈdi-pē\ *adj* **dip·pi·er; -est** [origin unknown] (1899) **:** FOOLISH — **dip·pi·ness** *n*
dip·shit \ˈdip-ˌshit\ *n* (1962) *usu vulgar* **:** a stupid or incompetent person
dip·so \ˈdip-(ˌ)sō\ *n, pl* **dipsos** [by shortening] (1880) **:** one affected with dipsomania
dip·so·ma·nia \ˌdip-sə-ˈmā-nē-ə, -nyə\ *n* [NL, fr. Gk *dipsa* thirst + LL *mania*] (ca. 1844) **:** an uncontrollable craving for alcoholic liquors — **dip·so·ma·ni·ac** \-nē-ˌak\ *n* — **dip·so·ma·ni·a·cal** \ˌdip-sō-mə-ˈnī-ə-kəl\ *adj*
dip·stick \ˈdip-ˌstik\ *n* (1927) **1 :** a graduated rod for indicating depth (as of oil in a crankcase) **2** [euphemism for *dipshit*] **:** NITWIT **3 :** a chemically sensitive strip of paper used to identify one or more constituents (as glucose or protein) of urine by immersion
dip·ter·an \ˈdip-tə-rən\ *adj* [ultim. fr. Gk *dipteros* two-winged, fr. *di-* + *pteron* wing — more at FEATHER] (ca. 1842) **:** of, relating to, or being a fly (sense 2a) — **dipteran** *n* — **dip·ter·ous** \ˈdip-t(ə-)rəs\ *adj*
dip·tero·carp \ˈdip-tə-rō-ˌkärp\ *n* [ultim. fr. Gk *dipteros* + *-karpos* -carpous] (ca. 1876) **:** any of a family (Dipterocarpaceae) of tall hardwood tropical trees chiefly of southeastern Asia that have a 2-winged fruit and are the source of valuable timber, aromatic oils, and resins; *esp* **:** a tree of the type genus (*Dipterocarpus*)
dip·tych \ˈdip-(ˌ)tik\ *n* [LL *diptycha,* pl., fr. Gk, fr. neut. pl. of *diptychos* folded in two, fr. *di-* + *ptychē* fold] (1622) **1 :** a 2-leaved hinged tablet folding together to protect writing on its waxed surfaces **2 :** a picture or series of pictures (as an altarpiece) painted or carved on two hinged tablets **3 :** a work made up of two matching parts

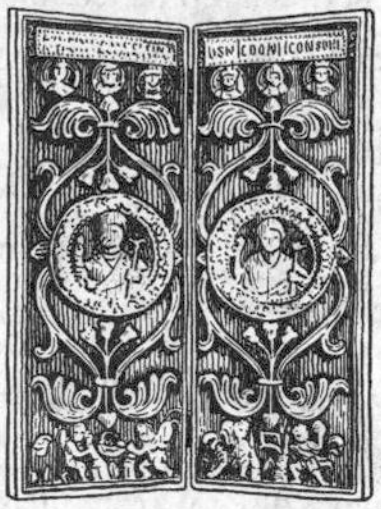

diptych 2

di·quat \ˈdī-ˌkwät\ *n* [*di-* + *quat*ernary] (1960) **:** a powerful herbicide and plant desiccant $C_{12}H_{12}Br_2N_2$ used esp. to control aquatic weeds and to desiccate aerial plant parts (as of potatoes) before harvesting
dir *abbr* **1** direction **2** director
di·ram \di-ˈram\ *n* [Tajik, fr. Pers *dirham* coin, money, fr. Ar — more at DIRHAM] (1991) — see *somoni* at MONEY table
dir·dum \ˈdir-dəm, ˈdər-\ *n* [ME (northern dial.) *durdan, durdum* uproar, of Celt origin; akin to W *dwrdd* noise, clamor, MIr *dordán* humming, droning] (ca. 1693) *Scot* **:** BLAME
dire \ˈdī(-ə)r\ *adj* **dir·er; dir·est** [L *dirus;* akin to Gk *deinos* terrifying, Skt *dveṣṭi* he hates] (1565) **1 a :** exciting horror ⟨~ suffering⟩ **b :** DISMAL, OPPRESSIVE ⟨~ days⟩ **2 :** warning of disaster ⟨a ~ forecast⟩ **3 a :** desperately urgent ⟨~ need⟩ **b :** EXTREME ⟨~ poverty⟩ — **dire·ly** *adv* — **dire·ness** *n*
[1]**di·rect** \də-ˈrekt, dī-\ *vb* [ME, fr. AF *directer,* fr. L *directus* straight, fr. pp. of *dirigere* to direct — more at DRESS] *vt* (14c) **1 a** *obs* **:** to write (a letter) to a person **b :** to mark with the name and address of the intended recipient **c :** to impart orally **d :** to adapt in expression so as to have particular applicability ⟨arguments ~*ed* at the emotions⟩ **2 a :** to regulate the activities or course of **b :** to carry out the organizing, energizing, and supervising of ⟨~ a project⟩ **c :** to dominate and determine the course of **d :** to train and lead performances of ⟨~ a movie⟩ **3 :** to cause to turn, move, or point undeviatingly or to follow a straight course ⟨X-rays ~*ed* through the body⟩ **4 :** to point, extend, or project in a specified line or course ⟨~ the nozzle down⟩ **5 :** to request or enjoin with authority ⟨the judge ~*ed* the jury to acquit⟩ **6 :** to show or point out the way for ⟨signs ~*ing* us to the entrance⟩ ~ *vi* **1 :** to point out, prescribe, or determine a course or procedure **2 :** to act as director ***syn*** see COMMAND, CONDUCT
[2]**direct** *adj* [ME, fr. L *directus*] (15c) **1 :** having or being motion in the general planetary direction from west to east **:** not retrograde **2 a :** stemming immediately from a source ⟨~ result⟩ **b :** being or passing in a straight line of descent from parent to offspring **:** LINEAL ⟨~ ancestor⟩ **c :** having no compromising or impairing element ⟨a ~ insult⟩ **3 a :** proceeding from one point to another in time or space without deviation or interruption **:** STRAIGHT ⟨a ~ line⟩ **b :** proceeding by the shortest way ⟨the ~ route⟩ **4 :** NATURAL, STRAIGHTFORWARD ⟨a ~ manner⟩ **5 a :** marked by absence of an intervening agency, instrumentality, or influence ⟨making ~ observations of nature⟩ **b :** effected by the action of the people or the electorate and not by representatives ⟨~ democracy⟩ **c :** consisting of or reproducing the exact words of a speaker or writer ⟨a ~ quotation⟩ **6 :** characterized by close logical, causal, or consequential relationship ⟨~ evidence⟩ **7 :** capable of dyeing without the aid of a mordant
[3]**direct** *adv* (14c) **:** in a direct way: as **a :** from point to point without deviation **:** by the shortest way ⟨flew ~ to Miami⟩ **b :** from the source without interruption or diversion ⟨the writer must take his material ~ from life —Douglas Stewart⟩ **c :** without an intervening agency or step ⟨buy ~ from the manufacturer⟩
direct action *n* (1912) **:** action that seeks to achieve an end directly and by the most immediately effective means (as boycott or strike)
direct broadcast satellite *n* (1975) **:** a television broadcasting system in which satellite transmissions are received by a dish antenna at the viewing location (as a home) — called also *satellite, satellite television*
direct current *n* (1849) **:** an electric current flowing in one direction only and substantially constant in value — abbr. *DC*
direct deposit *n* (1974) **:** a method of payment in which money is transferred to the payee's account without the use of checks or cash
di·rect·ed \də-ˈrek-təd, dī-\ *adj* (1891) **1 :** subject to supervision or regulation ⟨a ~ reading program for students⟩ **2 :** having a positive or negative sense ⟨~ line segment⟩ — **di·rect·ed·ness** *n*
direct examination *n* (ca. 1859) **:** the first examination of a witness by the party calling the witness — compare CROSS-EXAMINATION
di·rec·tion \də-ˈrek-shən, dī-\ *n* (15c) **1 :** guidance or supervision of action or conduct **:** MANAGEMENT **2** *archaic* **:** SUPERSCRIPTION **3 a :** an explicit instruction **:** ORDER **b :** assistance in pointing out the proper route — usu. used in pl. ⟨asked for ~*s* to the beach⟩ **4 :** the line or course on which something is moving or is aimed to move or along which something is pointing or facing **5** *archaic* **:** DIRECTORATE 1 **6 a :** a channel or direct course of thought or action **b :** TENDENCY, TREND **c :** a guiding, governing, or motivating purpose **7 a :** the art and technique of directing an orchestra, band, or a show (as for stage or screen) **b :** a word, phrase, or sign indicating the appropriate tempo, mood, or intensity of a passage or movement in music — **di·rec·tion·less** \-ləs\ *adj* — **di·rec·tion·less·ness** *n*
di·rec·tion·al \-shnəl, -shə-nᵊl\ *adj* (1842) **1 :** of, relating to, or indicating direction in space: as **a :** suitable for detecting the direction from which radio signals come or for sending out radio signals in one direction only ⟨a ~ antenna⟩ **b :** operating most effectively in a particular direction ⟨a ~ microphone⟩ **2 :** relating to direction or guidance esp. of thought or effort — **di·rec·tion·al·i·ty** \-ˌrek-shə-ˈna-lə-tē\ *n*
direction angle *n* (1882) **:** an angle made by a given line with an axis of reference; *specif* **:** such an angle made by a straight line with the three axes of a rectangular Cartesian coordinate system — usu. used in pl.

\ə\ **abut** \ᵊ\ **kitten, F table** \ər\ **further** \a\ **ash** \ā\ **ace** \ä\ **mop, mar** \au̇\ **out** \ch\ **chin** \e\ **bet** \ē\ **easy** \g\ **go** \i\ **hit** \ī\ **ice** \j\ **job** \ŋ\ **sing** \ō\ **go** \ȯ\ **law** \ȯi\ **boy** \th\ **thin** \t͟h\ **the** \ü\ **loot** \u̇\ **foot** \y\ **yet** \zh\ **vision, beige** \k̲, ⁿ, œ, ue, ʸ\ *see* Guide to Pronunciation

direction cosine *n* (ca. 1889) : any of the cosines of the three angles between a directed line in space and the positive direction of the axes of a rectangular Cartesian coordinate system — usu. used in pl.

direction finder *n* (1913) : a radio receiving device for determining the direction of incoming radio waves that typically consists of a coil antenna rotating freely on a vertical axis

[1]**di·rec·tive** \də-ˈrek-tiv, dī-\ *adj* (15c) **1 :** serving or intended to guide, govern, or influence **2 :** serving to point direction; *specif* : DIRECTIONAL 1b **3 :** of or relating to psychotherapy or counseling in which the counselor introduces information, content, or attitudes not previously expressed by the client

[2]**directive** *n* (1902) : something that serves to direct, guide, and usu. impel toward an action or goal; *esp* : an authoritative instrument issued by a high-level body or official

di·rec·tiv·i·ty \də-ˌrek-ˈti-və-tē, (ˌ)dī-\ *n* (1928) : the property of being directional

direct lighting *n* (1928) : lighting in which the greater part of the light goes directly from the source to the area lit

[1]**di·rect·ly** \də-ˈrek(t)-lē, dī-, *in sense 2 esp* də-ˈrek-lē *or* ˈdrek-lē\ *adv* (15c) **1 a :** in a direct manner ⟨~ relevant⟩ ⟨the road runs ~ east and west⟩ **b :** in immediate physical contact **c :** in the manner of direct variation **2 a :** without delay : IMMEDIATELY ⟨the second game followed ~ after the first⟩ **b :** in a little while : SHORTLY ⟨we'll be leaving ~⟩

[2]**di·rect·ly** \də-ˈrek(t)-lē, dī-; ˈdrek-lē\ *conj* (1795) *chiefly Brit* : immediately after : AS SOON AS ⟨~ I received it I rang up the shipping company —F. W. Crofts⟩

directly proportional *adj* (1796) : related by direct variation — compare INVERSELY PROPORTIONAL

direct mail *n* (ca. 1923) : printed matter (as circulars) prepared for soliciting business or contributions and mailed directly to individuals

direct marketing *n* (1961) : marketing by means of direct communication with consumers (as through catalogs and telemarketing)

di·rect·ness \də-ˈrek(t)-nəs, dī-\ *n* (1598) **1 :** the character of being accurate in course or aim **2 :** strict pertinence : STRAIGHTFORWARDNESS ⟨her ~ was disarming —Robin Cook⟩

direct object *n* (1879) : a word or phrase denoting the goal or the result of the action of a verb

Di·rec·toire \dē-(ˌ)rek-ˈtwär(r), -ˈrek-ˌ\ *adj* [F, fr. *Directoire,* the group of five officials who governed France from 1795–99, fr. *directeur* director] (1864) : of, relating to, or imitative of the style of clothing, furniture, or decoration prevalent in France during the period of the Directory

di·rec·tor \də-ˈrek-tər, dī-\ *n* (15c) : one who directs: as **a :** the head of an organized group or administrative unit (as a bureau or school) **b :** one of a group of persons entrusted with the overall direction of a corporate enterprise **c :** a person who supervises the production of a show (as for stage or screen) usu. with responsibility for action, lighting, music, and rehearsals **d :** CONDUCTOR c — **di·rec·tor·ship** \-ˌship\ *n*

di·rec·tor·ate \də-ˈrek-t(ə-)rət, dī-\ *n* (1837) **1 :** the office of director **2 a :** a board of directors (as of a corporation) **b :** membership on a board of directors **3 :** an executive staff (as of a department)

di·rec·to·ri·al \də-ˌrek-ˈtȯr-ē-əl, (ˌ)dī-\ *adj* (1770) **1 :** serving to direct **2 :** of or relating to a director or to theatrical or motion-picture direction **3 :** of, relating to, or administered by a directory

director's chair *n* [fr. its use by motion-picture directors on the set] (1953) : a lightweight folding armchair with a back and seat usu. of cotton duck

director's cut *n* (1980) : a version of a motion picture that is edited according to the director's wishes and that usu. includes scenes cut from the version created for general distribution

[1]**di·rec·to·ry** \də-ˈrek-t(ə-)rē, dī-\ *adj* (15c) : serving to direct; *specif* : providing advisory but not compulsory guidance

[2]**directory** *n, pl* **-ries** [ME *directorie* guide, fr. ML *directorium,* fr. neut. of LL *directorius* directorial, fr. L *dirigere*] (1543) **1 a :** a book or collection of directions, rules, or ordinances **b :** an alphabetical or classified list (as of names and addresses) **2 :** a body of directors **3 :** FOLDER 3b

direct primary *n* (1900) : a primary in which nominations of candidates for office are made by direct vote

direct product *n* (ca. 1925) : CARTESIAN PRODUCT; *esp* : a group that is the Cartesian product of two other groups

di·rect–re·sponse \də-ˈrekt-ri-ˈspän(t)s, dī-\ *adj* (1976) : of or relating to direct marketing ⟨~ advertising⟩

di·rec·tress \də-ˈrek-trəs, dī-\ *n* (1580) : a woman who is a director

di·rec·trice \də-ˌrek-ˈtrēs\ *n* [F, fr. ML *directric-, directrix*] (1631) : DIRECTRESS

di·rec·trix \-ˈrek-triks\ *n, pl* **-trix·es** \-trik-səz\ *also* **-tri·ces** \-trə-ˌsēz\ [ML, fem. of LL *director,* fr. L *dirigere*] (1622) **1** *archaic* : DIRECTRESS **2 :** a fixed curve with which a generatrix maintains a given relationship in generating a geometric figure; *specif* : a straight line the distance to which from any point of a conic section is in fixed ratio to the distance from the same point to a focus

direct sum *n* (ca. 1928) : CARTESIAN PRODUCT — compare DIRECT PRODUCT

direct tax *n* (1770) : a tax exacted directly from the taxpayer

direct variation *n* (ca. 1949) **1 :** mathematical relationship between two variables that can be expressed by an equation in which one variable is equal to a constant times the other **2 :** an equation or function expressing direct variation — compare INVERSE VARIATION

dire·ful \ˈdī(-ə)r-fəl\ *adj* (1565) **1 :** DREADFUL ⟨~ war began again —Charles Dickens⟩ **2 :** OMINOUS — **dire·ful·ly** \-fə-lē\ *adv*

dire wolf *n* (1925) : a large extinct wolflike mammal (*Canis dirus*) known from Pleistocene deposits of No. America

dirge \ˈdərj\ *n* [ME *dirige,* the Office of the Dead, fr. the first word of a LL antiphon, fr. L, imper. of *dirigere* to direct — more at DRESS] (13c) **1 :** a song or hymn of grief or lamentation; *esp* : one intended to accompany funeral or memorial rites **2 :** a slow, solemn, and mournful piece of music **3 :** something (as a poem) that has the qualities of a dirge — **dirge·like** \-ˌlīk\ *adj*

dir·ham \ˈdir-həm\ *n* [Ar, fr. L *drachma* drachma] (1788) **1 —** see MONEY table **2 —** see *dinar, riyal* at MONEY table

[1]**di·ri·gi·ble** \ˈdir-ə-jə-bəl, də-ˈri-jə-\ *adj* [L *dirigere*] (1581) : capable of being steered

[2]**dirigible** *n* [*dirigible (balloon)*] (1885) : AIRSHIP

di·ri·gisme \di-ri-ˈzhi-zᵊm, dē-rē-ˈzhēs-mᵊ\ *n* [F, fr. *diriger* to direct (fr. L *dirigere*) + *-isme* -ism] (1947) : economic planning and control by the state — **di·ri·giste** \di-ri-ˈzhēst, dē-rē-\ *adj*

[1]**dirk** \ˈdərk\ *n* [Sc *durk*] (1557) : a long straight-bladed dagger

[2]**dirk** *vt* (1599) : to stab with a dirk

dirl \ˈdir(-ə)l, ˈdərl\ *vi* [perh. alter. of *thirl*] (1513) *Scot* : TREMBLE, QUIVER

dirndl \ˈdərn-dᵊl\ *n* [short for G *Dirndlkleid,* fr. G dial. *Dirndl* girl + G *Kleid* dress] (1937) **1 :** a dress style with tight bodice, short sleeves, low neck, and gathered skirt **2 :** a full skirt with a tight waistband

dirt \ˈdərt\ *n* [ME *drit,* fr. ON; akin to OE *drītan* to defecate] (13c) **1 a :** EXCREMENT **b :** a filthy or soiling substance (as mud, dust, or grime) **c** *archaic* : something worthless **d :** a contemptible person ⟨treated me like ~⟩ **2 :** loose or packed soil or sand : EARTH ⟨a mound of ~⟩ ⟨a ~ road⟩ **3 a :** an abject or filthy state : SQUALOR ⟨living in ~⟩ **b :** CORRUPTION, CHICANERY ⟨vowed to clean up the ~ in the city government⟩ **c :** licentiousness of language or theme **d :** scandalous or malicious gossip ⟨spreading ~ about his ex-wife⟩ **e :** embarrassing or incriminating information ⟨trying to dig up ~ on her political rivals⟩

dirt·bag \ˈdərt-ˌbag\ *n* (ca. 1967) *slang* : a dirty, unkempt, or contemptible person

dirt bike *n* (1970) : a usu. lightweight motorcycle designed for operation on unpaved surfaces

dirt cheap *adj or adv* (1819) : exceedingly cheap

dirt farmer *n* (1920) : a farmer who earns a living by farming the land esp. without the help of hired hands or tenants

dirt–poor \ˈdərt-ˈpu̇r\ *adj* (1937) : suffering extreme poverty

[1]**dirty** \ˈdər-tē\ *adj* **dirt·i·er; -est** (14c) **1 a :** not clean or pure ⟨~ clothes⟩ **b :** likely to befoul or defile with dirt ⟨~ jobs⟩ **c :** contaminated with infecting organisms ⟨~ wounds⟩ **d :** containing impurities ⟨~ coal⟩ **2 a :** morally unclean or corrupt: as (1) : INDECENT, VULGAR ⟨~ jokes⟩ ⟨a ~ movie⟩ (2) : DISHONORABLE, BASE ⟨a ~ trick⟩ (3) : UNSPORTSMANLIKE ⟨~ players⟩ **b :** acquired by disreputable or illegal means : ILL-GOTTEN ⟨~ money⟩ **c :** disagreeable, distasteful, or objectionable but usu. necessary (as in achieving a desired result) ⟨hired a thug to do their ~ work⟩ **3 a :** ABOMINABLE, HATEFUL ⟨war is a ~ business⟩ **b :** highly regrettable ⟨a ~ shame⟩ **c :** likely to cause disgrace or scandal ⟨~ little secrets⟩ **4 :** FOGGY, STORMY ⟨~ weather⟩ **5 a** *of color* : not clear and bright : DULLISH ⟨~ blond⟩ **b :** characterized by a husky, rasping, or raw tonal quality ⟨~ trumpet tones⟩ **6 :** conveying ill-natured resentment ⟨gave him a ~ look⟩ — **dirt·i·ly** \ˈdər-tə-lē\ *adv* — **dirt·i·ness** \ˈdər-tē-nəs\ *n*

syn DIRTY, FILTHY, FOUL, NASTY, SQUALID mean conspicuously unclean or impure. DIRTY emphasizes the presence of dirt more than an emotional reaction to it ⟨a *dirty* littered street⟩. FILTHY carries a strong suggestion of offensiveness and typically of gradually accumulated dirt that begrimes and besmears ⟨a stained greasy floor, utterly *filthy*⟩. FOUL implies extreme offensiveness and an accumulation of what is rotten or stinking ⟨a *foul*-smelling open sewer⟩. NASTY applies to what is actually foul or is repugnant to one expecting freshness, cleanliness, or sweetness ⟨it's a *nasty* job to clean up after a sick cat⟩. In practice, *nasty* is often weakened to the point of being no more than a synonym of *unpleasant* or *disagreeable* ⟨had a *nasty* fall⟩ ⟨his answer gave her a *nasty* shock⟩. SQUALID adds to the idea of dirtiness and filth that of slovenly neglect ⟨*squalid* slums⟩. All these terms are also applicable to moral uncleanness or baseness or obscenity. DIRTY then stresses meanness or despicableness ⟨don't ask me to do your *dirty* work⟩, while FILTHY and FOUL describe disgusting obscenity or loathsome behavior ⟨*filthy* street language⟩ ⟨a *foul* story of lust and greed⟩, and NASTY implies a peculiarly offensive unpleasantness ⟨a stand-up comedian known for *nasty* humor⟩. Distinctively, SQUALID implies sordidness as well as baseness and dirtiness ⟨engaged in a series of *squalid* affairs⟩.

[2]**dirty** *adv* **dirt·i·er; -est** (ca. 1931) : in a dirty manner: as **a :** DECEPTIVELY, UNDERHANDEDLY ⟨fight ~⟩ **b :** INDECENTLY ⟨talk ~⟩

[3]**dirty** *vb* **dirt·ied; dirty·ing** *vt* (1591) **1 :** to make dirty **2 a :** to stain with dishonor : SULLY **b :** to debase by distorting the real nature of ~ *vi* : to become soiled

dirty bomb *n* (1956) : a bomb designed to release radioactive material

dirty laundry *n* (1967) : private matters whose public exposure brings distress and embarrassment — called also *dirty linen*

dirty old man *n* (1932) : a lecherous older man

dirty pool *n* (1918) : underhanded or unsportsmanlike conduct

dirty rice *n* (1954) : a Cajun dish of white rice cooked with chopped or ground giblets

dirty tricks *n pl* (1963) : underhanded stratagems for obtaining secret information about or sabotaging an enemy or for discrediting an opponent (as in politics) — **dirty trickster** *n*

dirty word *n* (ca. 1774) : a word, expression, or idea that is disagreeable or unpopular in a particular frame of reference

[1]**dis** \ˈdis\ *also* **diss** *vt* **dissed; dis·sing** [short for *disrespect*] (1980) **1** *slang* : to treat with disrespect or contempt : INSULT **2** *slang* : to find fault with : CRITICIZE

[2]**dis** *also* **diss** *n* (1986) **1** *slang* : a disparaging remark or act : INSULT ⟨was meant as a tribute, not a ~ —*Vibe*⟩ **2** *slang* : DISRESPECT

[3]**dis** *abbr* **1** discharge **2** discount **3** distance

Dis \ˈdis\ *n* [L] (1567) : the Roman god of the underworld — compare PLUTO

dis- *prefix* [ME *dis-, des-,* fr. AF & L; AF *des-, dis-,* fr. L *dis-,* lit., apart; akin to OE *te-* apart, L *duo* two — more at TWO] **1 a :** do the opposite of ⟨*dis*establish⟩ **b :** deprive of (a specified quality, rank, or object) ⟨*dis*franchise⟩ **c :** exclude or expel from ⟨*dis*bar⟩ **2 :** opposite or absence of ⟨*dis*union⟩ ⟨*dis*affection⟩ **3 :** not ⟨*dis*agreeable⟩ **4 :** completely ⟨*dis*annul⟩ **5** [by folk etymology] : DYS- ⟨*dis*function⟩

dis·abil·i·ty \ˌdis-ə-ˈbi-lə-tē\ *n* (1557) **1 a :** the condition of being disabled **b :** limitation in the ability to pursue an occupation because of a physical or mental impairment; *also* : a program providing financial support to one affected by disability ⟨went on ~ after the injury⟩ **2 :** lack of legal qualification to do something **3 :** a disqualification, restriction, or disadvantage

dis·able \dis-ˈā-bəl, diz-ˈā-\ *vt* **dis·abled; dis·abling** \-b(ə-)liŋ\ (15c) **1 :** to deprive of legal right, qualification, or capacity **2 :** to make in-

capable or ineffective; *esp* : to deprive of physical, moral, or intellectual strength ***syn*** see WEAKEN — **dis·able·ment** \-bəl-mənt\ *n*
disabled *adj* (1633) : incapacitated by illness or injury; *also* : physically or mentally impaired in a way that substantially limits activity esp. in relation to employment or education
dis·abuse \ˌdis-ə-ˈbyüz\ *vt* [F *désabuser,* fr. *dés-* dis- + *abuser* to abuse] (ca. 1611) : to free from error, fallacy, or misconception
di·sac·cha·ri·dase \(ˌ)dī-ˈsa-kə-rə-ˌdās, -ˌdāz\ *n* (1961) : an enzyme (as maltase or lactase) that hydrolyzes disaccharides
di·sac·cha·ride \(ˌ)dī-ˈsa-kə-ˌrīd\ *n* (1889) : any of a class of sugars (as sucrose) that yields on hydrolysis two monosaccharide molecules
dis·ac·cord \ˌdis-ə-ˈkȯrd\ *vi* [ME *disacorden,* fr. AF *desacorder,* fr. *desacord* disagreement, fr. *des-* dis- + *acord* accord] (15c) : CLASH, DISAGREE — **disaccord** *n*
dis·ac·cus·tom \ˌdis-ə-ˈkəs-təm\ *vt* [MF *desaccoustumer,* fr. OF *desacostumer,* fr. *des-* dis- + *acostomer* to accustom] (1530) : to free from a habit
[1]**dis·ad·van·tage** \ˌdis-əd-ˈvan-tij\ *n* [ME *disavauntage,* fr. AF *desavantage,* fr. *des-* dis- + *avantage* advantage] (14c) **1** : loss or damage esp. to reputation, credit, or finances : DETRIMENT ⟨the deal worked to their ~⟩ **2 a** : an unfavorable, inferior, or prejudicial condition ⟨we were at a ~⟩ **b** : a quality or circumstance that makes achievement unusually difficult : HANDICAP ⟨his lack of formal schooling was a serious ~⟩
[2]**disadvantage** *vt* (ca. 1534) : to place at a disadvantage : HARM
dis·ad·van·taged \-tijd\ *adj* (1879) : lacking in the basic resources or conditions (as standard housing, medical and educational facilities, and civil rights) believed to be necessary for an equal position in society — **dis·ad·van·taged·ness** \-tijd-nəs\ *n*
dis·ad·van·ta·geous \(ˌ)dis-ˌad-ˌvan-ˈtā-jəs, -vən-\ *adj* (1603) **1** : constituting a disadvantage **2** : DEROGATORY, DISPARAGING — **dis·ad·van·ta·geous·ly** *adv* — **dis·ad·van·ta·geous·ness** *n*
dis·af·fect \ˌdis-ə-ˈfekt\ *vt* (1635) : to alienate the affection or loyalty of; *also* : to fill with discontent and unrest ***syn*** see ESTRANGE — **dis·af·fec·tion** \-ˈfek-shən\ *n*
dis·af·fect·ed *adj* (1632) : discontented and resentful esp. against authority : REBELLIOUS ⟨~ youth⟩
dis·af·fil·i·ate \ˌdis-ə-ˈfi-lē-ˌāt\ *vt* (ca. 1870) : DISASSOCIATE ~ *vi* : to terminate an affiliation — **dis·af·fil·i·a·tion** \-ˌfil-ē-ˈā-shən\ *n*
dis·af·firm \ˌdis-ə-ˈfərm\ *vt* (1531) **1** : to refuse to confirm : ANNUL, REPUDIATE **2** : CONTRADICT — **dis·af·fir·mance** \-ˈfər-mən(t)s\ *n*
dis·ag·gre·gate \(ˌ)dis-ˈa-gri-ˌgāt\ *vt* (ca. 1828) : to separate into component parts ⟨~ sandstone⟩ ⟨~ demographic data⟩ ~ *vi* : to break up or apart ⟨the molecules of a gel ~ to form a sol⟩ — **dis·ag·gre·ga·tion** \(ˌ)dis-ˌa-gri-ˈgā-shən\ *n* — **dis·ag·gre·ga·tive** \(ˌ)dis-ˈa-gri-ˌgā-tiv\ *adj*
dis·agree \ˌdis-ə-ˈgrē\ *vi* [ME, to refuse assent, fr. AF *desagreer,* fr. *des-* dis- + *agreer* to agree] (15c) **1** : to fail to agree ⟨the two accounts ~⟩ **2** : to differ in opinion ⟨he *disagreed* with me on every topic⟩ **3** : to cause discomfort or distress ⟨fried foods ~ with me⟩
dis·agree·able \-ə-bəl\ *adj* (15c) **1** : causing discomfort : UNPLEASANT, OFFENSIVE ⟨a ~ odor⟩ **2** : marked by ill temper : PEEVISH ⟨a ~ person⟩ — **dis·agree·able·ness** *n* — **dis·agree·ably** \-blē\ *adv*
dis·agree·ment \ˌdis-ə-ˈgrē-mənt\ *n* (15c) **1** : the act of disagreeing **2 a** : the state of being at variance : DISPARITY **b** : QUARREL
dis·al·low \ˌdis-ə-ˈlau̇\ *vt* (14c) **1** : to deny the force, truth, or validity of **2** : to refuse to allow — **dis·al·low·ance** \-ən(t)s\ *n*
dis·am·big·u·ate \ˌdis-am-ˈbi-gyə-ˌwāt, -gyü-ˌāt\ *vt* **-at·ed; -at·ing** (1963) : to establish a single semantic or grammatical interpretation for — **dis·am·big·u·a·tion** \-ˌbi-gyə-ˈwā-shən, -gyü-ˈā-\ *n*
dis·an·nul \ˌdis-ə-ˈnəl\ *vt* (15c) : ANNUL, CANCEL
dis·ap·pear \ˌdis-ə-ˈpir\ *vi* (15c) **1** : to pass from view **2** : to cease to be : pass out of existence or notice ~ *vt* : to cause the disappearance of — **dis·ap·pear·ance** \-ˈpir-ən(t)s\ *n*
dis·ap·point \ˌdis-ə-ˈpȯint\ *vb* [ME *disapointen* to dispossess, fr. MF *desapointer,* fr. *des-* dis- + *appointer* to arrange — more at APPOINT] *vt* (15c) : to fail to meet the expectation or hope of : FRUSTRATE ⟨the team ~*ed* its fans⟩ ~ *vi* : to cause disappointment ⟨where the show ~*s* most is in the work of the younger generation —John Ashbery⟩
dis·ap·point·ed \-ˈpȯin-təd\ *adj* (1537) **1** : defeated in expectation or hope **2** *obs* : not adequately equipped — **dis·ap·point·ed·ly** *adv*
dis·ap·point·ing \-ˈpȯin-tiŋ\ *adj* (1530) : failing to meet expectations ⟨a ~ meal⟩ — **dis·ap·point·ing·ly** \-ˈpȯin-tiŋ-lē\ *adv*
dis·ap·point·ment \ˌdis-ə-ˈpȯint-mənt\ *n* (1604) **1** : the act or an instance of disappointing : the state or emotion of being disappointed **2** : one that disappoints ⟨he's a ~ to his parents⟩
dis·ap·pro·ba·tion \(ˌ)dis-ˌa-prə-ˈbā-shən\ *n* (1647) : the act or state of disapproving : the state of being disapproved : CONDEMNATION
dis·ap·prov·al \ˌdis-ə-ˈprü-vəl\ *n* (1662) : DISAPPROBATION, CENSURE
dis·ap·prove \-ˈprüv\ *vt* (1614) **1** : to pass unfavorable judgment on **2** : to refuse approval to : REJECT ~ *vi* : to feel or express disapproval — **dis·ap·prov·er** *n* — **dis·ap·prov·ing·ly** \-ˈprü-viŋ-lē\ *adv*
dis·arm \dis-ˈärm, diz-, ˈdis-ˌärm\ *vb* [ME *desarmen,* lit., to divest of arms, fr. AF *desarmer,* fr. *des-* dis- + *armer* to arm] *vt* (14c) **1 a** : to deprive of means, reason, or disposition to be hostile ⟨~*ed* criticism by admitting her errors⟩ **b** : to win over **2 a** : to divest of arms ⟨~ captured troops⟩ **b** : to deprive of a means of attack or defense ⟨~ a ship⟩ **c** : to make harmless ⟨~ a bomb⟩ ~ *vi* **1** : to lay aside arms **2** : to give up or reduce armed forces — **dis·ar·ma·ment** \-ˈär-mə-mənt\ *n* — **dis·arm·er** *n*
dis·arm·ing *adj* (1839) : allaying criticism or hostility : INGRATIATING ⟨a ~ smile⟩ — **dis·arm·ing·ly** \-ˈär-miŋ-lē\ *adv*
dis·ar·range \ˌdis-ə-ˈrānj\ *vt* (1744) : to disturb the arrangement or order of ⟨hair *disarranged* by the wind⟩ — **dis·ar·range·ment** \-mənt\ *n*
[1]**dis·ar·ray** \ˌdis-ə-ˈrā\ *n* (15c) **1** : a lack of order or sequence : CONFUSION, DISORDER ⟨the room was in ~⟩ **2** : disorderly dress : DISHABILLE
[2]**disarray** *vt* [ME *disarayen,* fr. AF *desaraier,* fr. *des-* dis- + *arraier* to array] (14c) **1** : to throw into disorder **2** : UNDRESS
dis·ar·tic·u·late \ˌdis-är-ˈti-kyə-ˌlāt\ *vi* (1830) : to become disjointed ~ *vt* : DISJOINT — **dis·ar·tic·u·la·tion** \-ˌti-kyə-ˈlā-shən\ *n*
dis·as·sem·ble \ˌdis-ə-ˈsem-bəl\ *vt* (1903) : to take apart ⟨~ a watch⟩ ~ *vi* **1** : to come apart ⟨the frame ~*s* into sections⟩ **2** : DISPERSE, SCATTER ⟨the crowd began to ~⟩ — **dis·as·sem·bly** \-blē\ *n*
dis·as·so·ci·ate \ˌdis-ə-ˈsō-sē-ˌāt, -shē-\ *vt* (1603) : to detach from association : DISSOCIATE — **dis·as·so·ci·a·tion** \-ˌsō-sē-ˈā-shən, -shē-\ *n*
di·sas·ter \di-ˈzas-tər, -ˈsas-\ *n* [MF & OIt; MF *desastre,* fr. OIt *disastro,* fr. *dis-* (fr. L) + *astro* star, fr. L *astrum* — more at ASTRAL] (1568) **1** *obs* : an unfavorable aspect of a planet or star **2** : a sudden calamitous event bringing great damage, loss, or destruction; *broadly* : a sudden or great misfortune or failure ⟨the party was a ~⟩
disaster area *n* (1953) : an area officially declared to be the scene of an emergency created by a disaster and therefore qualified to receive certain types of governmental aid (as emergency loans and relief supplies)
di·sas·trous \di-ˈzas-trəs *also* -ˈsas-\ *adj* (1594) **1** : attended by or causing suffering or disaster : CALAMITOUS ⟨a ~ flood⟩ **2** : TERRIBLE, HORRENDOUS ⟨a ~ score⟩ — **di·sas·trous·ly** *adv*
dis·avow \ˌdis-ə-ˈvau̇\ *vt* [ME *desavowen,* fr. AF *desavouer,* fr. *des-* dis- + *avouer* to avow] (14c) **1** : to deny responsibility for : REPUDIATE **2** : to refuse to acknowledge or accept : DISCLAIM ⟨party leaders ~*ed* him⟩ — **dis·avow·able** \-ə-bəl\ *adj* — **dis·avow·al** \-ˈvau̇(-ə)l\ *n*
dis·band \dis-ˈband\ *vb* [MF *desbander,* fr. *des-* dis- + *bande* band] *vt* (1591) : to break up the organization of : DISSOLVE ~ *vi* : to break up as an organization : DISPERSE — **dis·band·ment** \-ˈban(d)-mənt\ *n*
dis·bar \dis-ˈbär\ *vt* (1633) : to expel from the bar or the legal profession : deprive (an attorney) of legal status and privileges — **dis·bar·ment** \-mənt\ *n*
dis·be·lief \ˌdis-bə-ˈlēf\ *n* (1672) : the act of disbelieving : mental rejection of something as untrue
dis·be·lieve \-ˈlēv\ *vt* (ca. 1644) : to hold not worthy of belief : not believe ~ *vi* : to withhold or reject belief — **dis·be·liev·er** *n*
dis·ben·e·fit \(ˌ)dis-ˈbe-nə-fit\ *n* (1968) : something disadvantageous or objectionable : DRAWBACK
dis·bud \(ˌ)dis-ˈbəd\ *vt* (1727) **1** : to thin out flower buds in order to improve the quality of bloom of **2** : to dehorn (cattle) by destroying the undeveloped horn bud
dis·bur·den \(ˌ)dis-ˈbər-dᵊn\ *vt* (1532) **1 a** : to rid of a burden ⟨~ a pack animal⟩ **b** : UNBURDEN ⟨~ your conscience⟩ **2** : UNLOAD ⟨~*ed* their merchandise in the town square⟩ ~ *vi* : DISCHARGE ⟨the vessels ~*ed* at the dock⟩ — **dis·bur·den·ment** \-mənt\ *n*
dis·burse \dis-ˈbərs\ *vt* **dis·bursed; dis·burs·ing** [MF *desbourser,* fr. OF *desborser,* fr. *des-* dis- + *borse* purse, fr. ML *bursa*] (1530) **1 a** : to pay out : expend esp. from a fund ⟨~ money⟩ **b** : to make a payment in settlement of ⟨~ a bill⟩ **2** : DISTRIBUTE — **dis·burs·er** *n*
dis·burse·ment \-ˈbərs-mənt\ *n* (1596) : the act of disbursing; *also* : funds paid out
[1]**disc** *var of* DISK
[2]**disc** *abbr* discount
disc- *or* **disci-** *or* **disco-** *comb form* [L, fr. Gk *disk-, disko-,* fr. *diskos*] **1** : disk ⟨*disc*oid⟩ **2** : phonograph record ⟨*disco*phile⟩
dis·calced \(ˌ)dis-ˈkalst\ *adj* [part trans. of L *discalceatus,* fr. *dis-* + *calceatus,* pp. of *calceare* to put on shoes, fr. *calceus* shoe, fr. *calc-, calx* heel] (1631) : UNSHOD, BAREFOOT ⟨~ friars⟩
discant *var of* DESCANT
[1]**dis·card** \dis-ˈkärd, ˈdis-ˌ\ *vt* (ca. 1586) **1** : to get rid of esp. as useless or unwanted ⟨a pile of ~*ed* tires⟩ **2 a** : to remove (a playing card) from one's hand **b** : to play (any card except a trump) from a suit different from the one led ~ *vi* : to discard a playing card — **dis·card·able** \-də-bəl\ *adj* — **dis·card·er** *n*
syn DISCARD, CAST, SHED, SLOUGH, SCRAP, JUNK mean to get rid of. DISCARD implies the letting go or throwing away of something that has become useless or superfluous though often not intrinsically valueless ⟨*discard* old clothes⟩. CAST, esp. when used with *off, away,* or *out,* implies a forceful rejection or repudiation ⟨*cast* off her friends⟩. SHED and SLOUGH imply a throwing off of something both useless and encumbering and often suggest a consequent renewal of vitality or luster ⟨*shed* a bad habit⟩ ⟨finally *sloughed* off the depression⟩. SCRAP and JUNK imply throwing away or breaking up as worthless in existent form ⟨*scrap* all the old ways⟩ ⟨would *junk* our educational system⟩.
[2]**dis·card** \ˈdis-ˌkärd\ *n* (1744) **1 a** : the act of discarding in a card game **b** : a card discarded **2** : one that is cast off or rejected
dis·car·nate \dis-ˈkär-nət, -ˌnāt\ *adj* [*dis-* + *-carnate* (as in *incarnate*)] (1895) : having no physical body : INCORPOREAL
disc brake *n* (1904) : a brake that operates by the action of a frictional material pressed against the sides of a rotating disc by a caliper

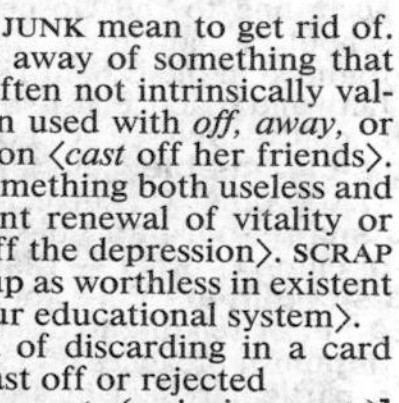

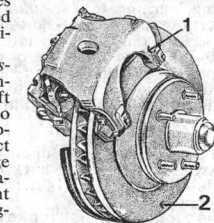

disc brake: *1* caliper, *2* disc

dis·cern \di-ˈsərn, -ˈzərn\ *vb* [ME, fr. MF *discerner,* fr. L *discernere* to separate, distinguish between, fr. *dis-* apart + *cernere* to sift — more at DIS-, CERTAIN] *vt* (14c) **1 a** : to detect with the eyes ⟨~*ed* a figure approaching through the fog⟩ **b** : to detect with senses other than vision ⟨~*ed* a strange odor⟩ **2** : to recognize or identify as separate and distinct : DISCRIMINATE ⟨~ right from wrong⟩ **3** : to come to know or recognize mentally ⟨unable to ~ his motives⟩ ~ *vi* : to see or understand the difference — **dis·cern·er** *n* — **dis·cern·ible** *also* **dis·cern·able** \-ˈsər-nə-bəl, -ˈzər-\ *adj* — **dis·cern·ibly** \-blē\ *adv*
dis·cern·ing *adj* (1589) : showing insight and understanding : DISCRIMINATING ⟨a ~ critic⟩ — **dis·cern·ing·ly** \-ˈsər-niŋ-lē, -ˈzər-\ *adv*
dis·cern·ment \di-ˈsərn-mənt, -ˈzərn-\ *n* (1586) **1** : the quality of being able to grasp and comprehend what is obscure : skill in discerning **2** : an act of discerning
syn DISCERNMENT, DISCRIMINATION, PERCEPTION, PENETRATION, INSIGHT, ACUMEN mean a power to see what is not evident to the average mind. DISCERNMENT stresses accuracy (as in reading character or motives or appreciating art) ⟨the *discernment* to know true

friends⟩. DISCRIMINATION stresses the power to distinguish and select what is true or appropriate or excellent ⟨the *discrimination* that develops through listening to a lot of great music⟩. PERCEPTION implies quick and often sympathetic discernment (as of shades of feeling) ⟨a novelist of keen *perception* into human motives⟩. PENETRATION implies a searching mind that goes beyond what is obvious or superficial ⟨lacks the *penetration* to see the scorn beneath their friendly smiles⟩. INSIGHT suggests depth of discernment coupled with understanding sympathy ⟨a documentary providing *insight* into the plight of the homeless⟩. ACUMEN implies characteristic penetration combined with keen practical judgment ⟨a director of reliable box-office *acumen*⟩.

[1]**dis·charge** \dis-ˈchärj, ˈdis-ˌ\ *vb* [ME, fr. AF *descharger,* fr. LL *discarricare,* fr. L *dis-* + LL *carricare* to load — more at CHARGE] *vt* (14c) **1** : to relieve of a charge, load, or burden: **a** : UNLOAD ⟨~ a cargo ship⟩ **b** : to release from an obligation **c** : to release electrical energy from (as a battery or capacitor) by a discharge **2 a** : to let or put off ⟨~ passengers⟩ ⟨~ cargo⟩ **b** : SHOOT ⟨~ an arrow⟩ **c** : to release from confinement, custody, or care ⟨~ a prisoner⟩ ⟨~ a patient⟩ **d** : to give outlet or vent to : EMIT ⟨~ emotions⟩ **3 a** (1) : to dismiss from employment (2) : to release from service or duty ⟨~ a soldier⟩ **b** : to get rid of (as a debt or obligation) by performing an appropriate action (as payment) **c** : to set aside : ANNUL **d** : to order (a legislative committee) to end consideration of a bill in order to bring it before the house for action **4** : to bear and distribute (as the weight of a wall above an opening) **5** : to bleach out or remove (color or dye) in dyeing and printing textiles **6** : to cancel the record of the loan of (a library book) upon return ~ *vi* **1 a** : to throw off or deliver a load, charge, or burden **b** : to release electrical energy by a discharge **2 a** : GO OFF, FIRE — used of a gun **b** : SPREAD, RUN ⟨some dyes ~⟩ **c** : to pour forth fluid or other contents ***syn*** see PERFORM — **dis·charge·able** \-jə-bəl\ *adj* — **dis·charg·ee** \(ˌ)dis-ˌchär-ˈjē\ *n* — **dis·charg·er** \dis-ˈchär-jər, ˈdis-ˌ\ *n*

[2]**dis·charge** \ˈdis-ˌchärj, dis-ˈ\ *n* (14c) **1 a** : the act of relieving of something that oppresses : RELEASE **b** : something that discharges or releases; *esp* : a certification of release or payment **2** : the state of being discharged or relieved **3** : the act of discharging or unloading **4** : legal release from confinement **5** : a firing off **6 a** : a flowing or issuing out ⟨a ~ of spores⟩; *also* : a rate of flow **b** : something that is emitted ⟨a purulent ~⟩ **7** : the act of removing an obligation or liability **8 a** : release or dismissal esp. from an office or employment **b** : complete separation from military service **9 a** : the equalization of a difference of electric potential between two points **b** : the conversion of the chemical energy of a battery into electrical energy

discharge lamp *n* (1933) : an electric lamp in which an enclosed gas or vapor glows or causes a phosphor coating on the lamp's inner surface to glow

discharge tube *n* (1898) : an electron tube which contains gas or vapor at low pressure and through which conduction takes place when a high voltage is applied

disci- — see DISC-

dis·ci·form \ˈdi-sə-ˌfȯrm\ *adj* (1830) : round or oval in shape

dis·ci·ple \di-ˈsī-pəl\ *n* [ME, fr. OE *discipul* & AF *disciple,* fr. LL and L; LL *discipulus* follower of Jesus Christ in his lifetime, fr. L, pupil] (bef. 12c) **1** : one who accepts and assists in spreading the doctrines of another: as **a** : one of the twelve in the inner circle of Christ's followers according to the Gospel accounts **b** : a convinced adherent of a school or individual **2** *cap* : a member of the Disciples of Christ founded in the U.S. in 1809 that holds the Bible alone to be the rule of faith and practice, usu. baptizes by immersion, and has a congregational polity ***syn*** see FOLLOWER — **dis·ci·ple·ship** \-ˌship\ *n*

dis·ci·plin·able \ˌdi-sə-ˈpli-nə-bəl; ˈdi-sə-pli-\ *adj* (15c) **1** : DOCILE, TEACHABLE **2** : subject to or deserving discipline ⟨a ~ offense⟩

dis·ci·pli·nar·i·an \ˌdi-sə-plə-ˈner-ē-ən\ *n* (1639) : one who disciplines or enforces order — **disciplinarian** *adj*

dis·ci·plin·ary \ˈdi-sə-plə-ˌner-ē, *esp Brit* ˌdi-sə-ˈpli-nə-rē\ *adj* (1598) **1 a** : of or relating to discipline ⟨~ problems⟩ **b** : designed to correct or punish breaches of discipline ⟨took ~ action⟩ **2** : of or relating to a particular field of study ⟨~ specialization⟩ — **dis·ci·plin·ar·i·ly** \ˌdi-sə-plə-ˈner-ə-lē\ *adv* — **dis·ci·plin·ar·i·ty** \-ˈnar-ə-tē\ *n*

[1]**dis·ci·pline** \ˈdi-sə-plən\ *n* [ME, fr. AF & L; AF, fr. L *disciplina* teaching, learning, fr. *discipulus* pupil] (13c) **1** : PUNISHMENT **2** *obs* : INSTRUCTION **3** : a field of study **4** : training that corrects, molds, or perfects the mental faculties or moral character **5 a** : control gained by enforcing obedience or order **b** : orderly or prescribed conduct or pattern of behavior **c** : SELF-CONTROL **6** : a rule or system of rules governing conduct or activity — **dis·ci·plin·al** \-plə-nᵊl\ *adj*

[2]**discipline** *vt* **-plined; -plin·ing** (14c) **1** : to punish or penalize for the sake of discipline **2** : to train or develop by instruction and exercise esp. in self-control **3 a** : to bring (a group) under control ⟨~ troops⟩ **b** : to impose order upon ⟨serious writers ~ and refine their writing styles⟩ ***syn*** see PUNISH, TEACH — **dis·ci·plin·er** *n*

dis·ci·plined *adj* (14c) : marked by or possessing discipline ⟨a ~ mind⟩

disc jockey *or* **disk jockey** *n* (1941) : an announcer of a radio show of popular recorded music; *also* : one who plays recorded music for dancing at a nightclub or party

dis·claim \dis-ˈklām\ *vb* [ME, fr. AF *disclaimer,* fr. *dis-* + *claimer* to claim] *vi* (15c) **1** : to make a disclaimer **2 a** *obs* : to disavow all part or share **b** : to utter denial ~ *vt* **1** : to renounce a legal claim to **2** : DENY, DISAVOW ⟨~*ed* any knowledge of the contents of the letter⟩

dis·claim·er \-ˈklā-mər\ *n* (15c) **1 a** : a denial or disavowal of legal claim : relinquishment of or formal refusal to accept an interest or estate **b** : a writing that embodies a legal disclaimer **2 a** : DENIAL, DISAVOWAL **b** : REPUDIATION

dis·cla·ma·tion \ˌdis-klə-ˈmā-shən\ *n* (1592) : RENUNCIATION, DISAVOWAL

dis·cli·max \(ˌ)dis-ˈklī-ˌmaks\ *n* (1935) : a relatively stable ecological community often including kinds of organisms foreign to the region and displacing the climax because of disturbance esp. by humans

[1]**dis·close** \dis-ˈklōz\ *vt* [ME, fr. AF *desclos-,* stem of *desclore* to open, unlock, reveal, fr. ML *disclaudere,* fr. L *dis-* + *claudere* to close — more at CLOSE] (14c) **1** *obs* : to open up **2 a** : to expose to view **b** *archaic* : HATCH **c** : to make known or public ⟨demands that politicians ~ the sources of their income⟩ ***syn*** see REVEAL — **dis·clos·er** *n*

[2]**disclose** *n* (1548) *obs* : DISCLOSURE

dis·clos·ing \-ˈklō-ziŋ\ *adj* (1965) : being or using an agent (as a tablet or liquid) that contains a usu. red dye that stains dental plaque

dis·clo·sure \dis-ˈklō-zhər\ *n* (1567) **1** : the act or an instance of disclosing : EXPOSURE **2** : something disclosed : REVELATION

[1]**dis·co** \ˈdis-(ˌ)kō\ *n, pl* **discos** [short for *discotheque*] (1964) **1** : a nightclub for dancing to live and recorded music **2** : popular dance music characterized by hypnotic rhythm, repetitive lyrics, and electronically produced sounds

[2]**disco** *vi* (1979) : to dance to disco music

disco- — see DISC-

dis·cog·ra·pher \dis-ˈkä-grə-fər\ *n* (1941) : a person who compiles discographies

dis·cog·ra·phy \-fē\ *n, pl* **-phies** [F *discographie,* fr. *disc-* + *-graphie* -graphy] (1933) **1** : a descriptive list of recordings by category, composer, performer, or date of release **2** : the history of recorded music — **dis·co·graph·i·cal** \ˌdis-kə-ˈgra-fi-kəl\ *also* **dis·co·graph·ic** \-fik\ *adj* — **dis·co·graph·i·cal·ly** \-fi-k(ə-)lē\ *adv*

dis·coid \ˈdis-ˌkȯid\ *adj* [LL *discoides* quoit-shaped, fr. Gk *diskoeidēs,* fr. *diskos* disk] (1794) **1** : relating to or having a disk: as **a** : situated in the floral disk ⟨~ florets⟩ **b** : having only disk flowers ⟨a ~ flower head⟩ **2** : flat and circular like a disc

dis·coi·dal \dis-ˈkȯi-dᵊl\ *adj* (ca. 1706) : of, resembling, or producing a disk

discoidal cleavage *n* (ca. 1909) : meroblastic cleavage in which a disk of cells is produced at the animal pole of the zygote (as in bird eggs)

dis·col·or \(ˌ)dis-ˈkə-lər\ *vb* [ME *discolouren,* fr. AF *desculurer,* fr. LL *discolorari,* fr. L *discolor* of another color, fr. *dis-* + *color* color] *vt* (14c) : to alter or change the hue or color of ~ *vi* : to change color esp. for the worse

dis·col·or·ation \(ˌ)dis-ˌkə-lə-ˈrā-shən\ *n* (1642) **1** : the act of discoloring : the state of being discolored **2** : a discolored spot or formation : STAIN

dis·com·bob·u·late \ˌdis-kəm-ˈbä-b(y)ə-ˌlāt\ *vt* **-lat·ed; -lat·ing** [prob. alter. of *discompose*] (ca. 1916) : UPSET, CONFUSE ⟨inventing cool new ways to ~ the old order —Kurt Andersen⟩ — **dis·com·bob·u·la·tion** \-ˌbä-b(y)ə-ˈlā-shən\ *n*

[1]**dis·com·fit** \dis-ˈkəm(p)-fət, *esp Southern* ˌdis-kəm-ˈfit\ *vt* [ME, fr. AF *descumfit,* pp. of *descumfire,* fr. *des-* dis- + *cumfire* to prepare — more at COMFIT] (13c) **1 a** *archaic* : to defeat in battle **b** : to frustrate the plans of : THWART **2** : to put into a state of perplexity and embarrassment : DISCONCERT ***syn*** see EMBARRASS — **dis·com·fit·ing·ly** \dis-ˈkəm(p)-fə-tiŋ-lē, ˌdīs-kəm-ˈfi-\ *adv*

[2]**discomfit** *n* (15c) : DISCOMFITURE

dis·com·fi·ture \dis-ˈkəm(p)-fə-ˌchu̇r, -chər, *esp Southern* -ˌt(y)u̇r\ *n* (14c) : the act of discomfiting : the state of being discomfited

[1]**dis·com·fort** \dis-ˈkəm(p)-fərt\ *vt* [ME, fr. AF *descomforter,* fr. *des-* dis- + *comforter* to comfort] (14c) **1** *archaic* : DISMAY **2** : to make uncomfortable or uneasy — **dis·com·fort·able** \-ˈkəm(p)-fər-tə-bəl, -ˈkəm(p)f-tər-bəl\ *adj*

[2]**discomfort** *n* (14c) **1** *archaic* : DISTRESS, GRIEF **2** : mental or physical uneasiness : ANNOYANCE

dis·com·mend \ˌdis-kə-ˈmend\ *vt* [ME *dyscommenden*] (15c) **1** : DISAPPROVE, DISPARAGE **2** : to cause to be viewed unfavorably

dis·com·mode \ˌdis-kə-ˈmōd\ *vt* **-mod·ed; -mod·ing** [F *discommoder,* fr. *dis-* + *commode* convenient — more at COMMODE] (1678) : to cause inconvenience to : TROUBLE

dis·com·pose \ˌdis-kəm-ˈpōz\ *vt* [ME] (15c) **1** : to destroy the composure of **2** : to disturb the order of — **dis·com·po·sure** \-ˈpō-zhər\ *n*

syn DISCOMPOSE, DISQUIET, DISTURB, PERTURB, AGITATE, UPSET, FLUSTER mean to destroy capacity for collected thought or decisive action. DISCOMPOSE implies some degree of loss of self-control or self-confidence esp. through emotional stress ⟨*discomposed* by the loss of his beloved wife⟩. DISQUIET suggests loss of sense of security or peace of mind ⟨the *disquieting* news of factories closing⟩. DISTURB implies interference with one's mental processes caused by worry, perplexity, or interruption ⟨the discrepancy in accounts *disturbed* me⟩. PERTURB implies deep disturbance of mind and emotions ⟨*perturbed* by her husband's strange behavior⟩. AGITATE suggests obvious external signs of nervous or emotional excitement ⟨in his *agitated* state we could see he was unable to work⟩. UPSET implies the disturbance of normal or habitual functioning by disappointment, distress, or grief ⟨the family's constant bickering *upsets* the youngest child⟩. FLUSTER suggests bewildered agitation ⟨his declaration of love completely *flustered* her⟩.

dis·con·cert \ˌdis-kən-ˈsərt\ *vt* [obs. F *disconcerter,* alter. of MF *desconcerter,* fr. *des-* dis- + *concerter* to concert] (1687) **1** : to throw into confusion **2** : to disturb the composure of ***syn*** see EMBARRASS — **dis·con·cert·ing** *adj* — **dis·con·cert·ing·ly** \-tiŋ-lē\ *adv* — **dis·con·cert·ment** \-mənt\ *n*

dis·con·firm \ˌdis-kən-ˈfərm\ *vt* (1936) : to deny or refute the validity of — **dis·con·fir·ma·tion** \-ˌkän-fər-ˈmā-shən\ *n*

dis·con·for·mi·ty \ˌdis-kən-ˈfȯr-mə-tē\ *n* (1587) **1** : NONCONFORMITY **2** : a break in a sequence of sedimentary rocks all of which have approximately the same dip

[1]**dis·con·nect** \ˌdis-kə-ˈnekt\ *vt* (1770) **1** : to sever the connection of or between **2** : DISSOCIATE 1 ⟨are ~*ed* from meaningful relationships⟩ ~ *vi* **1** : to terminate a connection **2** : to become detached or withdrawn ⟨~*s* into dark moods⟩ — **dis·con·nec·tion** \-ˈnek-shən\ *n*

[2]**disconnect** *n* (1976) : a lack of or a break in connection, consistency, or agreement ⟨a huge ~ . . . between the nation's capital and the rest of the country —R. J. Samuelson⟩

dis·con·nect·ed *adj* (1783) : not connected : SEPARATE; *also* : INCOHERENT ⟨a ~ narrative⟩ — **dis·con·nect·ed·ly** *adv* — **dis·con·nect·ed·ness** *n*

dis·con·so·late \dis-ˈkän(t)-sə-lət\ *adj* [ME, fr. ML *disconsolatus,* fr. L *dis-* + *consolatus,* pp. of *consolari* to console] (14c) **1** : CHEERLESS ⟨a clutch of ~ houses —D. H. Lawrence⟩ **2** : DEJECTED, DOWNCAST ⟨the team returned ~ from three losses⟩ — **dis·con·so·late·ly** *adv* — **dis·con·so·late·ness** *n* — **dis·con·so·la·tion** \(ˌ)dis-ˌkän(t)-sə-ˈlā-shən\ *n*

[1]**dis·con·tent** \ˌdis-kən-ˈtent\ *adj* (15c) : DISCONTENTED

[2]**discontent** *n* (1534) : lack of contentment: **a** : a sense of grievance : DISSATISFACTION ⟨the winter of our ~ —Shak.⟩ **b** : restless aspiration for improvement

[3]**discontent** *vt* (1549) : to make discontented — **dis·con·tent·ment** \-mənt\ *n*

[4]**discontent** *n* (1596) : one who is discontented : MALCONTENT

dis·con·tent·ed \ˌdis-kən-ˈten-təd\ *adj* (1525) : DISSATISFIED, MALCONTENT — **dis·con·tent·ed·ly** *adv* — **dis·con·tent·ed·ness** *n*

dis·con·tinu·ance \ˌdis-kən-ˈtin-yə-wən(t)s, -yü-ən(t)s\ *n* (14c) **1 :** the act or an instance of discontinuing **2 :** the interruption or termination of a legal action by the plaintiff's not continuing it

dis·con·tin·ue \ˌdis-kən-ˈtin-(ˌ)yü\ *vb* [ME, fr. AF *discontinuer,* fr. ML *discontinuare,* fr. L *dis-* + *continuare* to continue] *vt* (14c) **1 :** to break the continuity of : cease to operate, administer, use, produce, or take **2 :** to abandon or terminate by a legal discontinuance ~ *vi* : to come to an end ***syn*** see STOP — **dis·con·tin·u·a·tion** \-kən-ˌtin-yə-ˈwā-shən, -yü-ˈā-\ *n*

dis·con·ti·nu·ity \(ˌ)dis-ˌkän-tə-ˈnü-ə-tē, -ˈnyü-\ *n* (1570) **1 :** lack of continuity or cohesion **2 :** GAP 5 **3 a :** the property of being not mathematically continuous ⟨a point of ~⟩ **b :** an instance of being not mathematically continuous; *esp* : a value of an independent variable at which a function is not continuous

dis·con·tin·u·ous \ˌdis-kən-ˈtin-yə-wəs, -yü-əs\ *adj* (1718) **1 a (1)** : not continuous ⟨a ~ series of events⟩ **(2)** : not continued : DISCRETE ⟨~ features of terrain⟩ **b :** lacking sequence or coherence **2** : having one or more mathematical discontinuities — used of a variable or a function — **dis·con·tin·u·ous·ly** *adv*

dis·co·phile \ˈdis-kə-ˌfī(-ə)l\ *n* (1940) : one who studies and collects phonograph records or CDs

[1]**dis·cord** \ˈdis-ˌkȯrd\ *n* [ME *descorde, discord,* fr. AF *descorde,* fr. L *discordia,* fr. *discord-, discors*] (13c) **1 a :** lack of agreement or harmony (as between persons, things, or ideas) **b :** active quarreling or conflict resulting from discord among persons or factions : STRIFE **2 a (1) :** a combination of musical sounds that strikes the ear harshly **(2) :** DISSONANCE **b :** a harsh or unpleasant sound

syn DISCORD, STRIFE, CONFLICT, CONTENTION, DISSENSION, VARIANCE mean a state or condition marked by a lack of agreement or harmony. DISCORD implies an intrinsic or essential lack of harmony producing quarreling, factiousness, or antagonism ⟨a political party long racked by *discord*⟩. STRIFE emphasizes a struggle for superiority rather than the incongruity or incompatibility of the persons or things involved ⟨during his brief reign the empire was never free of civil *strife*⟩. CONFLICT usu. stresses the action of forces in opposition but in static applications implies an irreconcilability as of duties or desires ⟨the *conflict* of freedom and responsibility⟩. CONTENTION applies to strife or competition that shows itself in quarreling, disputing, or controversy ⟨several points of *contention* about the new zoning law⟩. DISSENSION implies strife or discord and stresses a division into factions ⟨religious *dissension* threatened to split the colony⟩. VARIANCE implies a clash between persons or things owing to a difference in nature, opinion, or interest ⟨cultural *variances* that work against a national identity⟩.

[2]**dis·cord** \ˈdis-ˌkȯrd, dis-ˈ\ *vi* [ME, fr. AF *descorder,* fr. L *discordare,* fr. *discord-, discors* discordant, fr. *dis-* + *cord-, cor* heart — more at HEART] (14c) : DISAGREE, CLASH

dis·cor·dance \dis-ˈkȯr-dᵊn(t)s\ *n* (14c) **1 :** the state or an instance of being discordant **2 :** DISSONANCE

dis·cor·dan·cy \-dᵊn-sē\ *n, pl* **-cies** (1607) : DISCORDANCE

dis·cor·dant \-dᵊnt\ *adj* (14c) **1 a :** being at variance : DISAGREEING ⟨~ opinions⟩ **b :** QUARRELSOME ⟨a ~ family⟩ **2 :** relating to a discord ⟨a ~ tone⟩ — **dis·cor·dant·ly** *adv*

dis·co·theque *or* **discothèque** \ˈdis-kə-ˌtek, ˌdis-kə-ˈ\ *n* [F *discothèque,* fr. *disque* disk, record + *-o-* + *-thèque* (as in *bibliothèque* library)] (1954) : DISCO 1

[1]**dis·count** \ˈdis-ˌkau̇nt\ *n* (1622) **1 :** a reduction made from the gross amount or value of something: as **a (1) :** a reduction made from a regular or list price **(2) :** a proportionate deduction from a debt account usu. made for cash or prompt payment **b :** a deduction made for interest in advancing money upon or purchasing a bill or note not due **2** : the act or practice of discounting **3 :** a deduction taken or allowance made

[2]**dis·count** \ˈdis-ˌkau̇nt, dis-ˈ\ *vb* [modif. of F *décompter,* fr. OF *desconter,* fr. ML *discomputare,* fr. L *dis-* + *computare* to count — more at COUNT] *vt* (1629) **1 a :** to make a deduction from usu. for cash or prompt payment ⟨a ~*ed* price⟩ **b :** to sell or offer for sale at a discount ⟨~*ing* last year's model⟩ **2 :** to lend money on after deducting the discount **3 a :** to leave out of account : DISREGARD **b :** to minimize the importance of ⟨shouldn't ~ his contributions⟩ **c (1) :** to make allowance for bias or exaggeration in **(2) :** to view with doubt ⟨~ a rumor⟩ **d :** to take into account (as a future event) in present calculations ~ *vi* : to give or make discounts — **dis·count·er** \-ˌkau̇n-tər, -ˈkau̇n-\ *n*

[3]**dis·count** \ˈdis-ˌkau̇nt\ *adj* (1863) **1 a :** selling goods or services at a discount ⟨~ stores⟩ ⟨a ~ broker⟩ ⟨~ airlines⟩ **b :** offered or sold at a discount ⟨~ tickets⟩ **2 :** reflecting a discount ⟨~ prices⟩

dis·count·able \dis-ˈkau̇n-tə-bəl, ˈdis-ˌ\ *adj* (1800) **1 :** set apart for discounting ⟨within the ~ period⟩ **2 :** subject to being discounted ⟨a ~ note⟩

[1]**dis·coun·te·nance** \dis-ˈkau̇n-tə-nən(t)s, -ˈkau̇nt-nən(t)s\ *vt* (1580) **1** : ABASH, DISCONCERT **2 :** to look with disfavor on : discourage by evidence of disapproval ⟨*discountenanced* all bellicose statements⟩

[2]**discountenance** *n* (1580) : DISAPPROBATION, DISFAVOR

discount rate *n* (ca. 1927) **1 :** the interest on an annual basis deducted in advance on a loan **2 :** the charge levied by a central bank for advances and rediscounts

dis·cour·age \dis-ˈkər-ij, -ˈkə-rij\ *vt* **-aged; -ag·ing** [ME *discoragen,* fr. MF *descorager,* fr. OF *descoragier,* fr. *des-* dis- + *corage* courage] (15c) **1 :** to deprive of courage or confidence : DISHEARTEN ⟨was *discouraged* by repeated failure⟩ **2 a :** to hinder by disfavoring ⟨trying to ~ absenteeism⟩ **b :** to dissuade or attempt to dissuade from doing something ⟨tried to ~ her from going⟩ — **dis·cour·age·able** \-jə-bəl\ *adj* — **dis·cour·ag·er** *n* — **dis·cour·ag·ing·ly** \-jiŋ-lē\ *adv*

dis·cour·age·ment \-mənt\ *n* (1561) **1 :** the act of discouraging : the state of being discouraged **2 :** something that discourages

[1]**dis·course** \ˈdis-ˌkȯrs, dis-ˈ\ *n* [ME *discours,* fr. ML & LL *discursus;* ML, argument, fr. LL, conversation, fr. L, act of running about, fr. *discurrere* to run about, fr. *dis-* + *currere* to run — more at CAR] (14c) **1** *archaic* : the capacity of orderly thought or procedure : RATIONALITY **2 :** verbal interchange of ideas; *esp* : CONVERSATION **3 a :** formal and orderly and usu. extended expression of thought on a subject **b :** connected speech or writing **c :** a linguistic unit (as a conversation or a story) larger than a sentence **4** *obs* : social familiarity **5 :** a mode of organizing knowledge, ideas, or experience that is rooted in language and its concrete contexts (as history or institutions) ⟨critical ~⟩

[2]**dis·course** \dis-ˈkȯrs, ˈdis-ˌ\ *vb* **dis·coursed; dis·cours·ing** *vi* (1559) **1 :** to express oneself esp. in oral discourse **2 :** TALK, CONVERSE ~ *vt,* *archaic* : to give forth : UTTER — **dis·cours·er** *n*

discourse analysis *n* (1952) : the study of linguistic relations and structures in discourse

dis·cour·te·ous \(ˌ)dis-ˈkər-tē-əs\ *adj* (1578) : lacking courtesy : RUDE — **dis·cour·te·ous·ly** *adv* — **dis·cour·te·ous·ness** *n*

dis·cour·te·sy \-ˈkər-tə-sē\ *n* (1555) **1 :** RUDENESS **2 :** a rude act

dis·cov·er \dis-ˈkə-vər\ *vb* **dis·cov·ered; dis·cov·er·ing** \-ˈkə-v(ə-)riŋ\ [ME, fr. AF *descoverir, descovrir,* fr. LL *discooperire,* fr. L *dis-* + *cooperire* to cover — more at COVER] *vt* (14c) **1 a :** to make known or visible : EXPOSE **b** *archaic* : DISPLAY **2 a :** to obtain sight or knowledge of for the first time : FIND ⟨~ the solution⟩ **b :** FIND OUT ⟨~*ed* he was out of gas⟩ ~ *vi* : to make a discovery — **dis·cov·er·able** \-ˈkə-v(ə-)rə-bəl\ *adj* — **dis·cov·er·er** \-ər-ər\ *n*

syn DISCOVER, ASCERTAIN, DETERMINE, UNEARTH, LEARN mean to find out what one did not previously know. DISCOVER may apply to something requiring exploration or investigation or to a chance encounter ⟨*discovered* the source of the river⟩. ASCERTAIN implies effort to find the facts or the truth proceeding from awareness of ignorance or uncertainty ⟨attempts to *ascertain* the population of the region⟩. DETERMINE emphasizes the intent to establish the facts definitely or precisely ⟨unable to *determine* the origin of the word⟩. UNEARTH implies bringing to light something forgotten or hidden ⟨*unearth* old records⟩. LEARN may imply acquiring knowledge with little effort or conscious intention (as by simply being told) or it may imply study and practice ⟨I *learned* her name only today⟩ ⟨*learning* Greek⟩.

Discoverers' Day *n* (1974) : COLUMBUS DAY

dis·cov·ery \dis-ˈkə-v(ə-)rē\ *n, pl* **-er·ies** (1529) **1 a :** the act or process of discovering **b (1)** *archaic* : DISCLOSURE **(2)** *obs* : DISPLAY **c** *obs* : EXPLORATION **2 :** something discovered **3 :** the usu. pretrial disclosure of pertinent facts or documents by one or both parties to a legal action or proceeding

Discovery Day *n* (ca. 1913) : COLUMBUS DAY

[1]**dis·cred·it** \(ˌ)dis-ˈkre-dət\ *vt* (1559) **1 :** to refuse to accept as true or accurate : DISBELIEVE ⟨~ a rumor⟩ **2 :** to cause disbelief in the accuracy or authority of ⟨a ~*ed* theory⟩ **3 :** to deprive of good repute : DISGRACE ⟨personal attacks meant to ~ his opponent⟩

[2]**discredit** *n* (1565) **1 :** loss of credit or reputation ⟨I knew stories to the ~ of England —W. B. Yeats⟩ **2 :** lack or loss of belief or confidence : DOUBT ⟨contradictions cast ~ on his testimony⟩

dis·cred·it·able \-tə-bəl\ *adj* (1640) : injurious to reputation : DISGRACEFUL ⟨~ conduct⟩ — **dis·cred·it·ably** \-blē\ *adv*

dis·creet \di-ˈskrēt\ *adj* [ME, fr. AF *discret,* fr. ML *discretus,* fr. L, pp. of *discernere* to separate, distinguish between — more at DISCERN] (14c) **1 :** having or showing discernment or good judgment in conduct and esp. in speech : PRUDENT; *esp* : capable of preserving prudent silence **2 :** UNPRETENTIOUS, MODEST ⟨the warmth and ~ elegance of a civilized home —Joseph Wechsberg⟩ **3 :** UNOBTRUSIVE, UNNOTICEABLE ⟨followed at a ~ distance⟩ — **dis·creet·ly** *adv* — **dis·creet·ness** *n*

dis·crep·an·cy \dis-ˈkre-pən-sē\ *n, pl* **-cies** (ca. 1623) **1 :** the quality or state of being discrepant **2 :** an instance of being discrepant

dis·crep·ant \-pənt\ *adj* [ME *discrepaunt,* fr. L *discrepant-, discrepans,* prp. of *discrepare* to sound discordantly, fr. *dis-* + *crepare* to rattle, creak — more at RAVEN] (15c) : being at variance : DISAGREEING ⟨widely ~ conclusions⟩ — **dis·crep·ant·ly** *adv*

dis·crete \dis-ˈkrēt, ˈdis-ˌ\ *adj* [ME, fr. L *discretus*] (14c) **1 :** constituting a separate entity : individually distinct ⟨several ~ sections⟩ **2 a** : consisting of distinct or unconnected elements : NONCONTINUOUS **b** : taking on or having a finite or countably infinite number of values ⟨~ probabilities⟩ ⟨a ~ random variable⟩ ***syn*** see DISTINCT — **discrete·ly** *adv* — **dis·crete·ness** *n*

dis·cre·tion \dis-ˈkre-shən\ *n* (14c) **1 :** the quality of being discreet : CIRCUMSPECTION; *esp* : cautious reserve in speech **2 :** ability to make responsible decisions **3 a :** individual choice or judgment ⟨left the decision to his ~⟩ **b :** power of free decision or latitude of choice within certain legal bounds ⟨reached the age of ~⟩ **4 :** the result of separating or distinguishing

dis·cre·tion·ary \-ˈkre-shə-ˌner-ē\ *adj* (1698) **1 :** left to discretion : exercised at one's own discretion **2 :** available for discretionary use ⟨~ purchasing power⟩

discretionary account *n* (ca. 1920) : a security or commodity market account in which an agent (as a broker) is given power of attorney so as to be able to make independent decisions and buy and sell for the principal's account

dis·crim·i·na·bil·i·ty \-ˌkri-mə-nə-ˈbi-lə-tē\ *n, pl* **-ties** (ca. 1901) **1** : the quality of being discriminable **2 :** the ability to discriminate

dis·crim·i·na·ble \dis-ˈkri-mə-nə-bəl\ *adj* (1736) : capable of being discriminated — **dis·crim·i·na·bly** \-blē\ *adv*

dis·crim·i·nant \-ˈkri-mə-nənt\ *n* (ca. 1948) : a mathematical expression providing a criterion for the behavior of another more complicated expression, relation, or set of relations

discriminant function *n* (ca. 1936) : a function of a set of variables that is evaluated for samples of events or objects and used as an aid in discriminating between or classifying them

dis·crim·i·nate \dis-ˈkri-mə-ˌnāt\ *vb* **-nat·ed; -nat·ing** [L *discriminatus,* pp. of *discriminare,* fr. *discrimin-, discrimen* distinction, fr. *discernere* to distinguish between — more at DISCERN] *vt* (1628) **1 a :** to mark or perceive the distinguishing or peculiar features of **b :** DISTIN-

GUISH, DIFFERENTIATE ⟨~ hundreds of colors⟩ **2 :** to distinguish by discerning or exposing differences; *esp* **:** to distinguish from another like object ~ *vi* **1 a :** to make a distinction ⟨~ among historical sources⟩ **b :** to use good judgment **2 :** to make a difference in treatment or favor on a basis other than individual merit ⟨~ in favor of your friends⟩ ⟨~ against a certain nationality⟩

dis·crim·i·nat·ing *adj* (1647) **1 :** making a distinction **:** DISTINGUISHING ⟨a ~ mark⟩ **2 :** marked by discrimination: **a :** DISCERNING, JUDICIOUS ⟨~ buyers⟩ **b :** DISCRIMINATORY ⟨accused of ~ practices⟩ — **dis·crim·i·nat·ing·ly** \-ˌnā-tiŋ-lē\ *adv*

dis·crim·i·na·tion \dis-ˌkri-mə-ˈnā-shən\ *n* (1648) **1 a :** the act of discriminating **b :** the process by which two stimuli differing in some aspect are responded to differently **2 :** the quality or power of finely distinguishing **3 a :** the act, practice, or an instance of discriminating categorically rather than individually **b :** prejudiced or prejudicial outlook, action, or treatment ⟨racial ~⟩ ***syn*** see DISCERNMENT — **dis·crim·i·na·tion·al** \-shnəl, -shə-nᵊl\ *adj*

dis·crim·i·na·tive \dis-ˈkri-mə-ˌnā-tiv, -ˈkri-mə-nət-\ *adj* (1677) **1 :** making distinctions **2 :** DISCRIMINATORY 2

dis·crim·i·na·tor \dis-ˈkri-mə-ˌnā-tər\ *n* (1828) **:** one that discriminates; *esp* **:** a circuit that can be adjusted to accept or reject signals of different characteristics (as amplitude or frequency)

dis·crim·i·na·to·ry \dis-ˈkri-mə-nə-ˌtōr-ē, -ˈkrim-nə-\ *adj* (1828) **1 :** DISCRIMINATIVE 1 **2 :** applying or favoring discrimination in treatment — **dis·crim·i·na·to·ri·ly** \-ˌkri-mə-nə-ˈtōr-ə-lē, -ˌkrim-nə-\ *adv*

dis·cur·sive \dis-ˈkər-siv\ *adj* [ML *discursivus,* fr. L *discursus,* pp. of *discurrere* to run about — more at DISCOURSE] (1598) **1 a :** moving from topic to topic without order **:** RAMBLING **b :** proceeding coherently from topic to topic **2 :** marked by analytical reasoning **3 :** of or relating to discourse ⟨~ practices⟩ — **dis·cur·sive·ly** *adv* — **dis·cur·sive·ness** *n*

dis·cus \ˈdis-kəs\ *n, pl* **dis·cus·es** [L — more at DISH] (1656) **:** a heavy disk (as of wood or plastic) that is thicker in the center than at the perimeter and that is hurled for distance as a track-and-field event; *also* **:** the event

discus

dis·cuss \di-ˈskəs\ *vt* [ME, fr. AF *discusser,* L *discussus,* pp. of *discutere* to disperse, fr. *dis-* apart + *quatere* to shake — more at DIS-, QUASH] (14c) **1** *obs* **:** DISPEL **2 a :** to investigate by reasoning or argument **b :** to present in detail for examination or consideration ⟨~*ed* plans for the party⟩ **c :** to talk about **3** *obs* **:** DECLARE — **dis·cuss·able** *or* **dis·cuss·ible** \-ˈskə-sə-bəl\ *adj* — **dis·cuss·er** *n*

syn DISCUSS, ARGUE, DEBATE mean to discourse about in order to reach conclusions or to convince. DISCUSS implies a sifting of possibilities esp. by presenting considerations pro and con ⟨*discussed* the need for a new highway⟩. ARGUE implies the offering of reasons or evidence in support of convictions already held ⟨*argued* that the project would be too costly⟩. DEBATE suggests formal or public argument between opposing parties ⟨*debated* the merits of the amendment⟩; it may also apply to deliberation with oneself ⟨I'm *debating* whether I should go⟩.

dis·cus·sant \di-ˈskə-sᵊnt\ *n* (1926) **:** one who takes part in a formal discussion or symposium

dis·cus·sion \di-ˈskə-shən\ *n* (14c) **1 :** consideration of a question in open and usu. informal debate **2 :** a formal treatment of a topic in speech or writing

¹dis·dain \dis-ˈdān\ *n* [ME *desdeyne,* fr. AF *desdaign,* fr. *desdeigner*] (14c) **:** a feeling of contempt for someone or something regarded as unworthy or inferior **:** SCORN

²disdain *vt* [ME *desdeynen,* fr. AF *desdeigner, dedeigner,* fr. VL **dis-dignare,* fr. L *dis-* + *dignare* to deign — more at DEIGN] (14c) **1 :** to look on with scorn ⟨~*ed* him as a coward⟩ **2 :** to refuse or abstain from because of disdain ⟨~*ed* to answer their questions⟩ **3 :** to treat as beneath one's notice or dignity ***syn*** see DESPISE

dis·dain·ful \-fəl\ *adj* (ca. 1542) **:** full of or expressing disdain ***syn*** see PROUD — **dis·dain·ful·ly** \-fə-lē\ *adv* — **dis·dain·ful·ness** *n*

dis·ease \di-ˈzēz\ *n* [ME *disese,* fr. AF *disese, desaise,* fr. *des-* dis- + *eise* ease] (14c) **1** *obs* **:** TROUBLE **2 :** a condition of the living animal or plant body or of one of its parts that impairs normal functioning and is typically manifested by distinguishing signs and symptoms **:** SICKNESS, MALADY **3 :** a harmful development (as in a social institution) — **dis·eased** \-ˈzēzd\ *adj*

dis·econ·o·my \ˌdis-i-ˈkä-nə-mē\ *n* (1937) **1 :** a lack of economy **2 :** a factor responsible for an increase in cost

dis·em·bark \ˌdis-əm-ˈbärk\ *vb* [MF *desembarquer,* fr. *des-* dis- + *embarquer* to embark] *vt* (1582) **:** to remove to shore from a ship ~ *vi* **1 :** to go ashore out of a ship **2 :** to get out of a vehicle or craft — **dis·em·bar·ka·tion** \(ˌ)dis-ˌem-ˌbär-ˈkā-shən, -bər-\ *n*

dis·em·bar·rass \ˌdis-əm-ˈbar-əs\ *vt* (1726) **:** to free (as oneself) from something troublesome or superfluous ***syn*** see EXTRICATE

dis·em·body \ˌdis-əm-ˈbä-dē\ *vt* (1714) **:** to divest of a body, of corporeal existence, or of reality

dis·em·bogue \ˌdis-im-ˈbōg\ *vb* **-bogued; -bogu·ing** [modif. of Sp *desembocar,* fr. *des-* dis- (fr. L *dis-*) + *embocar* to put into the mouth, fr. *en* in (fr. L *in*) + *boca* mouth, fr. L *bucca*] *vi* (1595) **:** to flow or come forth from or as if from a channel ~ *vt, archaic* **:** to pour out from or as if from a container

dis·em·bow·el \ˌdis-əm-ˈbau̇(-ə)l\ *vt* (1618) **1 :** to take out the bowels of **:** EVISCERATE **2 :** to remove the substance of ⟨a program ~*ed* by spending cuts⟩ — **dis·em·bow·el·ment** \-mənt\ *n*

dis·em·pow·er \ˌdis-im-ˈpau̇(-ə)r\ *vt* (1813) **:** to deprive of power, authority, or influence **:** make weak, ineffectual, or unimportant — **dis·em·pow·er·ment** \-mənt\ *n*

dis·en·chant \ˌdis-in-ˈchant\ *vt* [MF *desenchanter,* fr. *des-* dis- + *enchanter* to enchant] (ca. 1586) **:** to free from illusion — **dis·en·chant·er** *n* — **dis·en·chant·ing** *adj* — **dis·en·chant·ing·ly** \-ˈchan-tiŋ-lē\ *adv* — **dis·en·chant·ment** \-mənt\ *n*

dis·en·chant·ed \-ˈchan-təd\ *adj* (1832) **:** DISAPPOINTED, DISSATISFIED

dis·en·cum·ber \ˌdis-ᵊn-ˈkəm-bər\ *vt* [MF *desencombrer,* fr. *des-* dis- + *encombrer* to encumber] (1598) **:** to free from encumbrance **:** DISBURDEN ***syn*** see EXTRICATE

dis·en·dow \ˌdis-in-ˈdau̇\ *vt* (1861) **:** to strip of endowment — **dis·en·dow·er** \-ˈdau̇(-ə)r\ *n* — **dis·en·dow·ment** \-ˈdau̇-mənt\ *n*

dis·en·fran·chise \ˌdis-in-ˈfran-ˌchīz\ *vt* (1664) **:** to deprive of a franchise, of a legal right, or of some privilege or immunity; *esp* **:** to deprive of the right to vote — **dis·en·fran·chise·ment** \-ˌchīz-mənt, -chəz-\ *n*

dis·en·gage \ˌdis-ᵊn-ˈgāj\ *vb* [F *désengager,* fr. MF, fr. *des-* dis- + *engager* to engage] *vt* (1611) **:** to release from something that engages or involves ~ *vi* **:** to release or detach oneself **:** WITHDRAW — **dis·en·gage·ment** \-mənt\ *n*

dis·en·gaged \-ˈgājd\ *adj* (1651) **:** DETACHED 2 ⟨a ~ observer⟩

dis·en·tail \ˌdis-in-ˈtāl\ *vt* (1641) **:** to free from entail

dis·en·tan·gle \ˌdis-in-ˈtaŋ-gəl\ *vt* (1598) **:** to free from entanglement **:** UNRAVEL ~ *vi* **:** to become disentangled ***syn*** see EXTRICATE — **dis·en·tan·gle·ment** \-mənt\ *n*

dis·en·thrall *also* **dis·en·thral** \ˌdis-in-ˈthrȯl\ *vt* (1643) **:** to free from bondage **:** LIBERATE

dis·en·ti·tle \ˌdis-in-ˈtī-tᵊl\ *vt* (1654) **:** to deprive of title, claim, or right

dis·equil·i·brate \ˌdis-i-ˈkwi-lə-ˌbrāt\ *vt* (1891) **:** to put out of balance — **dis·equil·i·bra·tion** \-ˌkwi-lə-ˈbrā-shən\ *n*

dis·equi·lib·ri·um \(ˌ)dis-ˌē-kwə-ˈli-brē-əm, -ˌe-kwə-\ *n* (1840) **:** loss or lack of equilibrium

dis·es·tab·lish \ˌdis-ə-ˈstab-lish\ *vt* (1598) **:** to deprive of an established status; *esp* **:** to deprive of the status and privileges of an established church — **dis·es·tab·lish·ment** \-mənt\ *n*

dis·es·tab·lish·men·tar·i·an \-ˌstab-lish-ˌmen-ˈter-ē-ən, -mən-\ *n, often cap* [*disestablishment*] (1885) **:** one who opposes an established order — **disestablishmentarian** *adj, often cap*

¹dis·es·teem \ˌdis-ə-ˈstēm\ *vt* (1594) **:** to regard with disfavor

²disesteem *n* (1603) **:** DISFAVOR, DISREPUTE

di·seuse \dē-ˈzüz, -ˈzœz\ *n, pl* **di·seuses** *same*\ [F, fem. of *diseur,* fr. OF, fr. *dire* to say, fr. L *dicere* — more at DICTION] (1896) **:** a woman who is a skilled and usu. professional reciter

¹dis·fa·vor \(ˌ)dis-ˈfā-vər\ *n* [prob. fr. MF *desfaveur,* fr. *des-* dis- + *faveur* favor, fr. OF *favor*] (ca. 1533) **1 :** DISAPPROVAL, DISLIKE ⟨practices looked upon with ~⟩ **2 :** the state or fact of being no longer favored ⟨fell into ~⟩ **3 :** DISADVANTAGE

²disfavor *vt* (1570) **:** to withhold or withdraw favor from

dis·fig·ure \dis-ˈfi-gyər, *esp Brit* -ˈfi-gər\ *vt* [ME, fr. AF *desfigurer,* fr. *des-* dis- + *figure* figure] (14c) **1 :** to impair (as in beauty) by deep and persistent injuries ⟨a face *disfigured* by smallpox⟩ **2** *obs* **:** DISGUISE — **dis·fig·ure·ment** \-mənt\ *n*

dis·fran·chise \(ˌ)dis-ˈfran-ˌchīz\ *vt* (15c) **:** DISENFRANCHISE — **dis·fran·chise·ment** \-ˌchīz-mənt, -chəz-\ *n*

dis·frock \(ˌ)dis-ˈfräk\ *vt* (1837) **:** DEFROCK

disfunction *var of* DYSFUNCTION

dis·fur·nish \(ˌ)dis-ˈfər-nish\ *vt* [MF *desfourniss-,* stem of *desfournir,* fr. *des-* dis- + *fournir* to furnish] (1531) **:** to make destitute of possessions **:** DIVEST — **dis·fur·nish·ment** \-mənt\ *n*

dis·gorge \(ˌ)dis-ˈgȯrj\ *vb* [MF *desgorger,* fr. *des-* dis- + *gorge* gorge] *vt* (15c) **1 a :** to discharge by the throat and mouth **:** VOMIT **b :** to discharge or let go of rapidly or forcefully ⟨the train *disgorged* its passengers⟩ **c :** to give up on request or under pressure ⟨refused to ~ his ill-gotten gains⟩ **2 :** to discharge the contents of (as the stomach) ~ *vi* **:** to discharge contents ⟨where the river ~*s* into the sea⟩

¹dis·grace \di-ˈskrās, dis-ˈgrās\ *vt* (1580) **1** *archaic* **:** to humiliate by a superior showing **2 :** to be a source of shame to ⟨your actions *disgraced* the family⟩ **3 :** to cause to lose favor or standing ⟨was *disgraced* by the hint of scandal⟩ — **dis·grac·er** *n*

²disgrace *n* [MF, fr. OIt *disgrazia,* fr. *dis-* (fr. L) + *grazia* grace, fr. L *gratia* — more at GRACE] (1586) **1 a :** the condition of one fallen from grace or honor **b :** loss of grace, favor, or honor **2 :** a source of shame ⟨your manners are a ~⟩ ⟨he's a ~ to the profession⟩

syn DISGRACE, DISHONOR, DISREPUTE, INFAMY, IGNOMINY mean the state or condition of suffering loss of esteem and of enduring reproach. DISGRACE often implies humiliation and sometimes ostracism ⟨sent home in *disgrace*⟩. DISHONOR emphasizes the loss of honor that one has enjoyed or the loss of self-esteem ⟨preferred death to life with *dishonor*⟩. DISREPUTE stresses loss of one's good name or the acquiring of a bad reputation ⟨a once proud name fallen into *disrepute*⟩. INFAMY usu. implies notoriety as well as exceeding shame ⟨a day that lives in *infamy*⟩. IGNOMINY stresses humiliation ⟨the *ignominy* of being arrested⟩.

dis·grace·ful \-fəl\ *adj* (1597) **:** bringing or involving disgrace ⟨~ conduct⟩ — **dis·grace·ful·ly** \-fə-lē\ *adv* — **dis·grace·ful·ness** *n*

dis·grun·tle \dis-ˈgrən-tᵊl\ *vt* **dis·grun·tled; dis·grun·tling** \-ˈgrənt-liŋ, -ˈgrən-tᵊl-iŋ\ [*dis-* + *gruntle* to grumble, fr. ME *gruntlen,* freq. of *grunten* to grunt] (1682) **:** to make ill-humored or discontented — usu. used as a participial adjective ⟨they were a very *disgruntled* crew —Flannery O'Connor⟩ — **dis·grun·tle·ment** \-tᵊl-mənt\ *n*

¹dis·guise \də-ˈskīz, dis-ˈgīz *also* diz-\ *vt* **dis·guised; dis·guis·ing** [ME *disgisen,* fr. AF *desguiser, deguiser,* fr. *des-* dis- + *guise* guise] (14c) **1 a :** to change the customary dress or appearance of **b :** to furnish with a false appearance or an assumed identity **2** *obs* **:** DISFIGURE **3 :** to obscure the existence or true state or character of **:** CONCEAL ⟨unable to ~ his true feelings⟩ — **dis·guised·ly** \-ˈgīz(-ə)d-lē, -ˈkīz(-ə)d-\ *adv* — **dis·guise·ment** \-ˈgīz-mənt, -ˈkīz-\ *n* — **dis·guis·er** *n*

syn DISGUISE, CLOAK, MASK mean to alter the dress or appearance of so as to conceal the identity or true nature. DISGUISE implies a change in appearance or behavior that misleads by presenting a different apparent identity ⟨*disguised* herself as a peasant⟩. CLOAK suggests a means of hiding a movement or an intention ⟨*cloaked* their maneuvers in secrecy⟩. MASK suggests some often obvious means of hiding or disguising something ⟨smiling to *mask* his discontent⟩.

²disguise *n* (14c) **1 :** apparel assumed to conceal one's identity or counterfeit another's **2 :** the act of disguising **3 a :** form misrepresenting the true nature of something ⟨blessings in ~⟩ **b :** an artificial manner **:** PRETENSE ⟨threw off all ~⟩

¹dis·gust \di-ˈskəst, dis-ˈgəst *also* diz-\ *n* (1598) **:** marked aversion aroused by something highly distasteful **:** REPUGNANCE

²disgust *vb* [MF *desgouster,* fr. *des-* dis- + *goust* taste, fr. L *gustus;* akin to L *gustare* to taste — more at CHOOSE] *vt* (1616) **1 :** to provoke to loathing, repugnance, or aversion : be offensive to **2** : to cause (one) to lose an interest or intention ~ *vi* : to cause disgust — **dis·gust·ed** *adj* — **dis·gust·ed·ly** *adv*

dis·gust·ful \-fəl\ *adj* (ca. 1616) **1** : provoking disgust **2** : full of or accompanied by disgust — **dis·gust·ful·ly** \-fə-lē\ *adv*

dis·gust·ing *adj* (1754) : causing disgust — **dis·gust·ing·ly** \di-ˈskəs-tiŋ-lē, dis-ˈgəs- *also* diz-\ *adv*

[1]**dish** \ˈdish\ *n* [ME, fr. OE *disc* plate, fr. L *discus* quoit, disk, dish, fr. Gk *diskos,* fr. *dikein* to throw] (bef. 12c) **1 a** : a more or less concave vessel from which food is served **b** : the contents of a dish ⟨a ~ of strawberries⟩ **2 a** : food prepared in a particular way **b** : something one particularly enjoys : CUP OF TEA **3 a** (1) : any of various shallow concave vessels; *broadly* : anything shallowly concave (2) : a directional receiver having a concave usu. parabolic reflector; *esp* : one used as a microwave or radar antenna **b** : the state of being concave or the degree of concavity **4 a** : something that is favored ⟨entertainment that is just his ~⟩ **b** : an attractive or sexy person **5** : GOSSIP 2a ⟨the latest ~⟩

[2]**dish** *vt* (14c) **1** : to put (as food for serving) into a dish — often used with *up* **2** : PRESENT — usu. used with *up* **3** : to make concave like a dish **4** : to disclose or discuss esp. publicly ⟨~ the dirt⟩ **5** : to pass (a basketball) to a teammate — often used with *off* ~ *vi* **1** : GOSSIP; *also* : to disclose private or personal information **2** : to pass a basketball to a teammate — often used with *off*

dis·ha·bille \ˌdis-ə-ˈbēl, -ˈbil\ *or* **des·ha·bille** \ˌde-sə-ˈbēl, -ˈbil, -ˈbē\ *n* [F *déshabillé,* fr. pp. of *déshabiller* to undress, fr. *dés-* dis- + *habiller* to dress — more at HABILIMENT] (1673) **1 a** *archaic* : NEGLIGEE **b** : the state of being dressed in a casual or careless style **2** : a deliberately careless or casual manner

dis·har·mo·ni·ous \ˌdis-(ˌ)här-ˈmō-nē-əs\ *adj* (1659) : lacking in harmony

dis·har·mo·nize \(ˌ)dis-ˈhär-mə-ˌnīz\ *vt* (1801) : to make disharmonious

dis·har·mo·ny \-nē\ *n* (ca. 1602) : lack of harmony : DISCORD — **dis·har·mon·ic** \-här-ˈmä-nik\ *adj*

dish·cloth \ˈdish-ˌklȯth\ *n* (ca. 1828) : a cloth for washing dishes

dish·clout \ˈdish-ˌklau̇t\ *n* (ca. 1530) *Brit* : DISHCLOTH

dish·dasha \ˌdish-ˈdä-shə\ *n* [Ar *dishdāsha*] (1938) : a long usu. white robe traditionally worn by men in the Middle East

dis·heart·en \(ˌ)dis-ˈhär-tᵊn\ *vt* (1590) : to cause to lose spirit or morale — **dis·heart·en·ing·ly** \-ˈhärt-niŋ-lē, -ˈhär-tᵊn-iŋ-\ *adv* — **dis·heart·en·ment** \-ˈhär-tᵊn-mənt\ *n*

dished \ˈdisht\ *adj* (1737) : curved in : CONCAVE

di·shev·el \di-ˈshev-əl\ *vt* **di·shev·eled** *or* **di·shev·elled; di·shev·el·ing** *or* **di·shev·el·ling** \-ˈshe-v(ə-)liŋ\ [back-formation fr. *disheveled*] (1598) : to throw into disorder or disarray — **di·shev·el·ment** \-ˈshev-əl-mənt\ *n*

di·shev·eled *or* **di·shev·elled** *adj* [ME *discheveled* bareheaded, with disordered hair, part trans. of AF *deschevelé,* fr. *des-* dis- + *chevoil* hair, fr. L *capillus*] (1583) : marked by disorder or disarray ⟨~ hair⟩

dis·hon·est \(ˌ)dis-ˈä-nəst *also* (ˌ)diz-\ *adj* [ME, fr. AF *deshoneste,* fr. *des-* dis- + *honeste* honest] (14c) **1** *obs* : SHAMEFUL, UNCHASTE **2** : characterized by lack of truth, honesty, or trustworthiness : UNFAIR, DECEPTIVE — **dis·hon·est·ly** *adv*

syn DISHONEST, DECEITFUL, MENDACIOUS, UNTRUTHFUL mean unworthy of trust or belief. DISHONEST implies a willful perversion of truth in order to deceive, cheat, or defraud ⟨a swindle usually involves two *dishonest* people⟩. DECEITFUL usu. implies an intent to mislead and commonly suggests a false appearance or double-dealing ⟨the secret affairs of a *deceitful* spouse⟩. MENDACIOUS may suggest bland or even harmlessly mischievous deceit and when used of people often suggests a habit of telling untruths ⟨*mendacious* tales of adventure⟩. UNTRUTHFUL stresses a discrepancy between what is said and fact or reality ⟨an *untruthful* account of their actions⟩.

dis·hon·es·ty \-nə-stē\ *n* (1599) **1** : lack of honesty or integrity : disposition to defraud or deceive **2** : a dishonest act : FRAUD

[1]**dis·hon·or** \(ˌ)dis-ˈä-nər *also* (ˌ)diz-\ *n* [ME *dishonour,* fr. AF *deshonur,* fr. *des-* dis- + *honur* honor] (13c) **1** : lack or loss of honor or reputation **2** : the state of one who has lost honor or prestige : SHAME ⟨has brought ~ on his family⟩ **3** : a cause of disgrace **4** : the nonpayment or nonacceptance of commercial paper by the party on whom it is drawn ***syn*** see DISGRACE — **dis·hon·or·er** \-ˈän-ər-ər\ *n*

[2]**dishonor** *vt* (13c) **1 a** : to treat in a degrading manner **b** : to bring shame on **2** : to refuse to accept or pay (as a bill or check)

dis·hon·or·able \(ˌ)dis-ˈä-nə-rə-bəl, -ˈä-nər-bəl\ *adj* (1534) **1** : lacking honor : SHAMEFUL ⟨~ conduct⟩ **2** *archaic* : not honored — **dis·hon·or·able·ness** *n* — **dis·hon·or·ably** \-blē\ *adv*

dish out *vt* (1641) : to give or dispense freely ⟨*dish out* gifts⟩ ⟨*dish out* advice⟩ ⟨*dish out* punishment⟩

dish·pan \ˈdish-ˌpan\ *n* (1872) : a large flat-bottomed pan used for washing dishes

dishpan hands *n pl but sing or pl in constr* (1944) : a condition of dryness, redness, and scaling of the hands that results typically from repeated exposure to, sensitivity to, or overuse of cleaning materials (as detergents) used esp. in housework

dish·rag \ˈdish-ˌrag\ *n* (1839) : DISHCLOTH

dish·ware \ˈdish-ˌwer\ *n* (1946) : tableware (as of china) used in serving food

dish·wash·er \-ˌwȯ-shər, -ˌwä-\ *n* (15c) **1** : a worker employed to wash dishes **2** : a machine for washing dishes

dish·wa·ter \-ˌwȯ-tər, -ˌwä-\ *n* (15c) : water in which dishes have been or are to be washed

dishy \ˈdi-shē\ *adj* **dish·i·er; -est** (1961) **1** : ATTRACTIVE, GOOD-LOOKING **2** : characterized by, full of, or given to gossip or disclosure ⟨a ~ biography⟩

[1]**dis·il·lu·sion** \ˌdis-ə-ˈlü-zhən\ *n* (1591) : the condition of being disenchanted

[2]**disillusion** *vt* **dis·il·lu·sioned; dis·il·lu·sion·ing** \-ˈlü-zhə-niŋ\ (1855) : to free from illusion; *also* : to cause to lose naive faith and trust — **dis·il·lu·sion·ment** \-ˈlü-zhən-mənt\ *n*

disillusioned *adj* (1871) : DISAPPOINTED, DISSATISFIED

dis·in·cen·tive \ˌdis-in-ˈsen-tiv\ *n* (1946) : DETERRENT

dis·in·cli·na·tion \(ˌ)dis-ˌin-klə-ˈnā-shən, -ˌsiŋ-\ *n* (1647) : a preference for avoiding something : slight aversion

dis·in·cline \ˌdis-in-ˈklīn\ *vt* (1647) : to make unwilling

dis·in·clined *adj* (1647) : unwilling because of mild dislike or disapproval

syn DISINCLINED, HESITANT, RELUCTANT, LOATH, AVERSE mean lacking the will or desire to do something indicated. DISINCLINED implies lack of taste for or inclination ⟨*disinclined* to move again⟩ ⟨*disinclined* for reading⟩. HESITANT implies a holding back esp. through fear or uncertainty ⟨*hesitant* about asking for a date⟩. RELUCTANT implies a holding back through unwillingness ⟨a *reluctant* witness⟩. LOATH implies hesitancy because of conflict with one's opinions, predilections, or liking ⟨seems *loath* to trust anyone⟩. AVERSE implies a holding back from or avoiding because of distaste or repugnance ⟨*averse* to hard work⟩ ⟨not *averse* to an occasional drink⟩.

dis·in·fect \ˌdis-in-ˈfekt\ *vt* [MF *desinfecter,* fr. *des-* dis- + *infecter* to infect] (1598) : to free from infection esp. by destroying harmful microorganisms; *broadly* : CLEANSE — **dis·in·fec·tion** \-ˈfek-shən\ *n*

dis·in·fec·tant \-ˈfek-tənt\ *n* (1837) : an agent that frees from infection; *esp* : a chemical that destroys vegetative forms of harmful microorganisms (as bacteria and fungi) esp. on inanimate objects but that may be less effective in destroying spores

dis·in·fest \ˌdis-in-ˈfest\ *vt* (ca. 1920) : to rid of small animal pests (as insects or rodents) — **dis·in·fes·ta·tion** \(ˌ)dis-ˌin-ˌfes-ˈtā-shən\ *n*

dis·in·fla·tion \ˌdis-in-ˈflā-shən\ *n* (1880) : a reversal of inflationary pressures — **dis·in·fla·tion·ary** \-shə-ˌner-ē\ *adj*

dis·in·for·ma·tion \(ˌ)dis-ˌin-fər-ˈmā-shən\ *n* (1939) : false information deliberately and often covertly spread (as by the planting of rumors) in order to influence public opinion or obscure the truth

dis·in·gen·u·ous \ˌdis-in-ˈjen-yə-wəs, -yü-əs-\ *adj* (1655) : lacking in candor; *also* : giving a false appearance of simple frankness : CALCULATING — **dis·in·gen·u·ous·ly** *adv* — **dis·in·gen·u·ous·ness** *n*

dis·in·her·it \ˌdis-in-ˈher-ət, -ˈhe-rət\ *vt* [ME] (15c) **1** : to prevent deliberately from inheriting something (as by making a will) **2** : to deprive of natural or human rights or of previously held special privileges — **dis·in·her·i·tance** \-ˈher-ə-tən(t)s, -ˈhe-rə-\ *n*

dis·in·hi·bi·tion \(ˌ)dis-ˌin-(h)ə-ˈbi-shən\ *n* (ca. 1927) : loss or reduction of an inhibition (as by the action of interfering stimuli or events) ⟨~ of a reflex⟩ ⟨~ of violent tendencies⟩ — **dis·in·hib·it** \(ˌ)dis-in-ˈhi-bət\ *vt* — **dis·in·hib·i·tor** \-in-ˈhi-bə-tər\ *n*

dis·in·te·grate \(ˌ)dis-ˈin-tə-ˌgrāt\ *vt* (1796) **1** : to break or decompose into constituent elements, parts, or small particles **2** : to destroy the unity or integrity of ~ *vi* **1** : to break or separate into constituent elements or parts **2** : to lose unity or integrity by or as if by breaking into parts **3** : to undergo a change in composition ⟨an atomic nucleus that ~s because of radioactivity⟩ — **dis·in·te·gra·tion** \(ˌ)dis-ˌin-tə-ˈgrā-shən\ *n* — **dis·in·te·gra·tive** \(ˌ)dis-ˈin-tə-ˌgrā-tiv\ *adj* — **dis·in·te·gra·tor** \-ˌgrā-tər\ *n*

dis·in·ter \ˌdis-in-ˈtər\ *vt* (1611) **1** : to take out of the grave or tomb **2** : to bring back into awareness or prominence; *also* : to bring to light : UNEARTH — **dis·in·ter·ment** \-mənt\ *n*

[1]**dis·in·ter·est** \(ˌ)dis-ˈin-trəst; -ˈin-tə-ˌrest, -tə-rəst, -tərst; -ˈin-ˌtrest\ *vt* (1612) : to cause to regard something with no interest or concern

[2]**disinterest** *n* (1658) **1** : DISINTERESTEDNESS **2** : lack of interest : INDIFFERENCE

dis·in·ter·est·ed \-təd\ *adj* (ca. 1612) **1 a** : not having the mind or feelings engaged : not interested ⟨telling them in a ~ voice —Tom Wicker⟩ ⟨~ in women —J. A. Brussel⟩ **b** : no longer interested ⟨husband and wife become ~ in each other —T. I. Rubin⟩ **2** : free from selfish motive or interest : UNBIASED ⟨a ~ decision⟩ ⟨~ intellectual curiosity is the lifeblood of real civilization —G. M. Trevelyan⟩ ***syn*** see INDIFFERENT — **dis·in·ter·est·ed·ly** *adv*

usage *Disinterested* and *uninterested* have a tangled history. *Uninterested* orig. meant impartial, but this sense fell into disuse during the 18th century. About the same time the original sense of *disinterested* also disappeared, with *uninterested* developing a new sense—the present meaning—to take its place. The original sense of *uninterested* is still out of use, but the original sense of *disinterested* revived in the early 20th century. The revival has since been under frequent attack as an illiteracy and a blurring or loss of a useful distinction. Actual usage shows otherwise. Sense 2 of *disinterested* is still its most frequent sense, esp. in edited prose; it shows no sign of vanishing. A careful writer may choose sense 1a of *disinterested* in preference to *uninterested* for emphasis ⟨teaching the letters of the alphabet to her wiggling and supremely *disinterested* little daughter —C. L. Sulzberger⟩. Further, *disinterested* has developed a sense (1b), perhaps influenced by sense 1 of the prefix *dis-*, that contrasts with *uninterested* ⟨when I grow tired or *disinterested* in anything, I experience a disgust —Jack London (letter, 1914)⟩. Still, use of senses 1a and 1b will incur the disapproval of some who may not fully appreciate the history of this word or the subtleties of its present use.

dis·in·ter·est·ed·ness \-təd-nəs\ *n* (ca. 1682) : the quality or state of being objective or impartial

dis·in·ter·me·di·a·tion \ˌdis-ˌin-tər-ˌmē-dē-ˈā-shən\ *n* (1967) **1** : the diversion of savings from accounts with low fixed interest rates to direct investment in high-yielding instruments **2** : the elimination of an intermediary in a transaction between two parties — **dis·in·ter·me·di·ate** \-ˈmē-dē-ˌāt\ *vb*

dis·in·tox·i·cate \ˌdis-in-ˈtäk-sə-ˌkāt\ *vt* (1685) : DETOXIFY 2 — **dis·in·tox·i·ca·tion** \-ˌtäk-sə-ˈkā-shən\ *n*

dis·in·vest \(ˌ)dis-in-ˈvest\ *vi* (1945) : to reduce or eliminate capital investment (as in an industry or area)

dis·in·vest·ment \ˌdis-in-ˈves(t)-mənt\ *n* (1936) : consumption of capital; *also* : the withdrawing of investment

dis·in·vite \(ˌ)dis-in-ˈvīt\ *vt* (1580) : to withdraw an invitation to

dis·join \(ˌ)dis-ˈjȯin\ *vb* [ME *disjoynen,* fr. AF *desjoindre,* fr. L *disjungere,* fr. *dis-* + *jungere* to join — more at YOKE] *vt* (15c) : to end the joining of ~ *vi* : to become detached

\ə\ **abut** \ᵊ\ kitten, F table \ər\ **fur**ther \a\ **a**sh \ā\ **a**ce \ä\ m**o**p, m**a**r
\au̇\ **ou**t \ch\ **ch**in \e\ b**e**t \ē\ **ea**sy \g\ **g**o \i\ h**i**t \ī\ **i**ce \j\ **j**ob
\ŋ\ si**ng** \ō\ g**o** \ȯ\ l**aw** \ȯi\ b**oy** \th\ **th**in \t͟h\ **th**e \ü\ l**oo**t \u̇\ f**oo**t
\y\ **y**et \zh\ vi**si**on, bei**ge** \k̟, ⁿ, œ, ue, ʸ\ *see* Guide to Pronunciation

[1]**dis·joint** \-ˈjȯint\ *adj* [ME *disjoynt,* fr. AF *desjoint,* pp. of *desjoindre*] (15c) **1** *obs* : DISJOINTED 1a **2 :** having no elements in common ⟨~ mathematical sets⟩

[2]**disjoint** *vt* (15c) **1 :** to disturb the orderly structure or arrangement of **2 :** to take apart at the joints ~ *vi* **:** to come apart at the joints

dis·joint·ed \-ˈjȯin-təd\ *adj* (ca. 1586) **1 a :** being thrown out of orderly function ⟨a ~ society⟩ **b :** lacking coherence or orderly sequence ⟨an incomplete and ~ history⟩ **2 :** separated at or as if at the joint — **dis·joint·ed·ly** *adv* — **dis·joint·ed·ness** *n*

[1]**dis·junct** \dis-ˈjəŋ(k)t\ *adj* [ME, fr. L *disjunctus,* pp. of *disjungere* to disjoin] (15c) **:** marked by separation of or from usu. contiguous parts or individuals: as **a :** DISCONTINUOUS **b :** relating to melodic progression by intervals larger than a major second — compare CONJUNCT

[2]**dis·junct** \ˈdis-ˌjəŋ(k)t, dis-ˈ\ *n* (1921) **1 :** any of the alternatives that make up a logical disjunction **2 :** an adverb or adverbial (as *luckily* in "Luckily we had an extra set" or *in short* in "In short, there is nothing we can do") that is loosely connected to a sentence and conveys the speaker's or writer's comment on its content, truth, or manner — compare ADJUNCT 2b

dis·junc·tion \dis-ˈjəŋ(k)-shən\ *n* (14c) **1 :** a sharp cleavage **:** DISUNION, SEPARATION ⟨the ~ between theory and practice⟩ **2 :** a compound sentence in logic formed by joining two simple statements by *or:* **a :** INCLUSIVE DISJUNCTION **b :** EXCLUSIVE DISJUNCTION

[1]**dis·junc·tive** \-ˈjəŋ(k)-tiv\ *adj* (15c) **1 a :** relating to, being, or forming a logical disjunction **b :** expressing an alternative or opposition between the meanings of the words connected ⟨the ~ conjunction *or*⟩ **c :** expressed by mutually exclusive alternatives joined by *or* ⟨~ pleading⟩ **2 :** marked by breaks or disunity ⟨a ~ narrative sequence⟩ **3** *of a pronoun form* **:** stressed and not attached to the verb as an enclitic or proclitic — **dis·junc·tive·ly** *adv*

[2]**disjunctive** *n* (1530) **:** a disjunctive conjunction

dis·junc·ture \-ˈjəŋ(k)-chər\ *n* [ME, modif. (influenced by L *disjunctus*) of AF *desjointure,* fr. *desjoint* disjoint] (14c) **:** DISJUNCTION 1

[1]**disk** *or* **disc** \ˈdisk\ *n, often attrib* [L *discus* — more at DISH] (1664) **1 a :** the seemingly flat figure of a celestial body ⟨the solar ~⟩ **b** *archaic* **:** DISCUS **2 :** any of various rounded and flattened animal anatomical structures; *esp* **:** INTERVERTEBRAL DISK — compare SLIPPED DISK **3 :** the central part of the flower head of a typical composite made up of closely packed tubular flowers **4 :** a thin circular object: as **a** *usu disc* **:** a phonograph record **b :** a round flat plate coated with a magnetic substance on which data for a computer is stored **c** *usu disc* **:** OPTICAL DISK: as **(1) :** VIDEODISC **(2) :** CD **5** *usu disc* **:** one of the concave circular steel tools with sharpened edge making up the working part of a disc harrow or plow; *also* **:** an implement employing such tools — **disk·like** \-ˌlīk\ *adj*

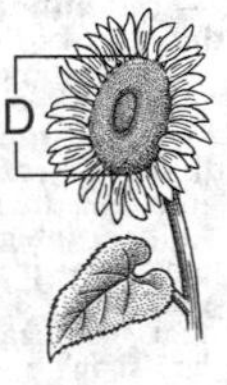

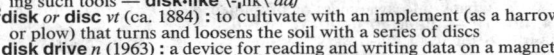

disk 3 *D*

[2]**disk** *or* **disc** *vt* (ca. 1884) **:** to cultivate with an implement (as a harrow or plow) that turns and loosens the soil with a series of discs

disk drive *n* (1963) **:** a device for reading and writing data on a magnetic disk

dis·kette \ˌdis-ˈket\ *n* (1973) **:** FLOPPY DISK

disk flower *n* (1870) **:** one of the tubular flowers in the disk of a composite plant — called also *disk floret*

disk jockey *var of* DISC JOCKEY

dis·lik·able *also* **dis·like·able** \(ˌ)dis-ˈlī-kə-bəl\ *adj* (1843) **:** easy to dislike

[1]**dis·like** \(ˌ)dis-ˈlīk, ˈdis-ˌ\ *n* (1567) **1 :** a feeling of aversion or disapproval **2** *obs* **:** DISCORD

[2]**dislike** *vt* (1567) **1 :** to regard with dislike **:** DISAPPROVE **2** *archaic* **:** DISPLEASE **3** *obs* **:** to show aversion to — **dis·lik·er** *n*

dis·limn \(ˌ)dis-ˈlim\ *vb* (1606) **:** DIM

dis·lo·cate \ˈdis-lō-ˌkāt, -lə-; (ˌ)dis-ˈlō-\ *vt* [ML *dislocatus,* pp. of *dislocare,* fr. L *dis-* + *locare* to locate] (1601) **1 :** to put out of place; *specif* **:** to displace (a bone) from normal connections with another bone **2 :** to force a change in the usual status, relationship, or order of **:** DISRUPT

dis·lo·ca·tion \ˌdis-(ˌ)lō-ˈkā-shən, -lə-\ *n* (14c) **:** the act of dislocating **:** the state of being dislocated: as **a :** displacement of one or more bones at a joint **:** LUXATION **b :** a discontinuity in the otherwise normal lattice structure of a crystal **c :** disruption of an established order

dis·lodge \(ˌ)dis-ˈläj\ *vb* [ME *disloggen,* fr. AF **desloger,* fr. *des-* dis- + *loger* to find lodging for, encamp, fr. *loge* shelter — more at LODGE] *vt* (15c) **1 :** to drive from a position of hiding, defense, or advantage **2 :** to force out of a secure or settled position ⟨*dislodged* the rock with a shovel⟩ ~ *vi* **:** to leave a place previously occupied — **dis·lodg·ment** *or* **dis·lodge·ment** *n*

dis·loy·al \(ˌ)dis-ˈlȯi(-ə)l\ *adj* [ME, fr. AF *desleial, desloial,* fr. *des-* dis- + *leal* loyal] (15c) **:** lacking in loyalty; *also* **:** showing an absence of allegiance, devotion, obligation, faith, or support ⟨his ~ refusal to help his friend⟩ ***syn*** see FAITHLESS — **dis·loy·al·ly** \-ˈlȯi-ə-lē\ *adv*

dis·loy·al·ty \-ˈlȯi(-ə)l-tē\ *n* (15c) **:** lack of loyalty

dis·mal \ˈdiz-məl\ *adj* [ME, fr. *dismal,* n., days marked as unlucky in medieval calendars, fr. AF, fr. ML *dies mali,* lit., evil days] (15c) **1** *obs* **:** DISASTROUS, DREADFUL **2 :** showing or causing gloom or depression **3 :** lacking merit **:** particularly bad ⟨a ~ performance⟩ — **dis·mal·ly** \-mə-lē\ *adv* — **dis·mal·ness** *n*

syn DISMAL, DREARY, BLEAK, GLOOMY, CHEERLESS, DESOLATE mean devoid of cheer or comfort. DISMAL indicates extreme and utterly depressing gloominess ⟨*dismal* weather⟩. DREARY, often interchangeable with *dismal,* emphasizes discouragement resulting from sustained dullness or futility ⟨a *dreary* job⟩. BLEAK suggests chill, dull, and barren characteristics that utterly dishearten ⟨the *bleak* years of the depression⟩. GLOOMY often suggests lack of hope or promise ⟨*gloomy* war news⟩. CHEERLESS stresses absence of anything cheering ⟨a drab and *cheerless* office⟩. DESOLATE adds an element of utter remoteness or lack of human contact to any already disheartening aspect ⟨a *desolate* outpost⟩.

dis·man·tle \(ˌ)dis-ˈman-tᵊl\ *vt* **dis·man·tled; dis·man·tling** \-ˈmant-liŋ, -ˈman-tᵊl-\ [MF *desmanteler,* fr. *des-* dis- + *mantel* mantle] (1579) **1 :** to take to pieces; *also* **:** to destroy the integrity or functioning of **2 :** to strip of dress or covering **:** DIVEST **3 :** to strip of furniture and equipment — **dis·man·tle·ment** \-ˈman-tᵊl-mənt\ *n*

dis·mast \(ˌ)dis-ˈmast\ *vt* (1747) **:** to remove or break off the mast of

[1]**dis·may** \dis-ˈmā, diz-\ *vt* **dis·mayed; dis·may·ing** [ME, fr. AF *desmaier,* fr. *des-* dis- + *-maier,* fr. VL **-magare,* of Gmc origin; akin to OHG *magan* to be able — more at MAY] (13c) **1 :** to cause to lose courage or resolution (as because of alarm or fear) ⟨must not let ourselves be ~*ed* by the task before us⟩ **2 :** UPSET, PERTURB ⟨were ~*ed* by the condition of the building⟩ — **dis·may·ing·ly** \-iŋ-lē\ *adv*

syn DISMAY, APPALL, HORRIFY, DAUNT mean to unnerve or deter by arousing fear, apprehension, or aversion. DISMAY implies that one is disconcerted and at a loss as to how to deal with something ⟨*dismayed* at the size of the job⟩. APPALL implies that one is faced with that which perturbs, confounds, or shocks ⟨I am *appalled* by your behavior⟩. HORRIFY stresses a reaction of horror or revulsion ⟨was *horrified* by such wanton cruelty⟩. DAUNT suggests a cowing, disheartening, or frightening in a venture requiring courage ⟨a cliff that would *daunt* the most intrepid climber⟩.

[2]**dismay** *n* (14c) **1 :** sudden loss of courage or resolution from alarm or fear **2 a :** sudden disappointment **b :** PERTURBATION 1

disme \ˈdīm\ *n* [obs. E, tenth, fr. obs. F, fr. OF *disme, dime* — more at DIME] (1792) **:** a U.S. 10-cent coin struck in 1792

dis·mem·ber \(ˌ)dis-ˈmem-bər\ *vt* **-bered; -ber·ing** \-b(ə-)riŋ\ [ME *dismembren,* fr. AF *desmembrer,* fr. *des-* dis- + *membre* member] (14c) **1 :** to cut off or disjoin the limbs, members, or parts of **2 :** to break up or tear into pieces — **dis·mem·ber·ment** \-bər-mənt\ *n*

dis·miss \dis-ˈmis\ *vt* [ME, modif. of L *dimissus,* pp. of *dimittere,* fr. *dis-* + *mittere* to send] (15c) **1 :** to permit or cause to leave ⟨~*ed* the visitors⟩ **2 :** to remove from position or service **:** DISCHARGE ⟨~*ed* the thievish servant⟩ **3 a :** to reject serious consideration of ⟨~*ed* the thought⟩ **b :** to put out of judicial consideration ⟨~*ed* all charges⟩ — **dis·mis·sion** \-ˈmi-shən\ *n* — **dis·mis·sive** \-ˈmi-siv\ *adj* — **dis·mis·sive·ly** *adv*

dis·miss·al \-ˈmi-səl\ *n* (1778) **:** the act of dismissing **:** the fact or state of being dismissed

[1]**dis·mount** \(ˌ)dis-ˈmau̇nt\ *vb* [prob. modif. of MF *desmonter,* fr. *des-* dis- + *monter* to mount] *vt* (1566) **1 :** to throw down or remove from a mount or an elevated position; *esp* **:** UNHORSE **2 :** DISASSEMBLE ~ *vi* **1** *obs* **:** DESCEND **2 :** to alight from an elevated position (as on a horse); *also* **:** to get out of an enclosed craft or vehicle

[2]**dismount** *n* (1654) **:** the act of dismounting

Dis·ney·esque \ˌdiz-nē-ˈesk\ *or* **Dis·ney·ish** \ˈdiz-nē-ish\ *adj* (1939) **:** resembling or suggestive of the films, television productions, or amusement parks made by Walt Disney or his organization

Dis·ney·fi·ca·tion \ˌdiz-nē-fə-ˈkā-shən\ *n* [Walt *Disney* + *-fication*] (1982) **:** the transformation (as of something real or unsettling) into carefully controlled and safe entertainment or an environment with similar qualities ⟨the ~ of a downtown⟩

dis·obe·di·ence \ˌdis-ə-ˈbē-dē-ən(t)s, -ō-ˈbē-\ *n* (15c) **:** refusal or neglect to obey

dis·obe·di·ent \-ənt\ *adj* (15c) **:** refusing or neglecting to obey — **dis·obe·di·ent·ly** *adv*

dis·obey \ˌdis-ə-ˈbā, -ō-\ *vb* [ME, fr. AF *desobeir,* fr. *des-* dis- + *obeir* to obey] *vi* (14c) **:** to be disobedient ~ *vt* **:** to fail to obey — **dis·obey·er** *n*

dis·oblige \ˌdis-ə-ˈblīj\ *vt* [F *désobliger,* fr. MF, fr. *des-* dis- + *obliger* to oblige] (1632) **1 :** to go counter to the wishes of **2 :** INCONVENIENCE

di·so·di·um phosphate \(ˌ)dī-ˈsō-dē-əm-\ *n* (ca. 1928) **:** a sodium phosphate Na_2HPO_4

di·so·mic \(ˌ)dī-ˈsō-mik\ *adj* [*di-* + *-somic*] (1922) **:** having one or more chromosomes present in two copies ⟨the ~ state is normal in humans⟩

[1]**dis·or·der** \(ˌ)dis-ˈȯr-dər, (ˌ)diz-\ *vt* (15c) **1 :** to disturb the order of **2 :** to disturb the regular or normal functions of

[2]**disorder** *n* (1523) **1 :** lack of order ⟨clothes in ~⟩ **2 :** breach of the peace or public order ⟨troubled times marked by social ~*s*⟩ **3 :** an abnormal physical or mental condition ⟨a liver ~⟩ ⟨a personality ~⟩

dis·or·dered *adj* (1505) **1** *obs* **a :** morally reprehensible **b :** UNRULY **2 a :** marked by disorder ⟨a ~ room⟩ **b :** not functioning in a normal orderly healthy way ⟨a ~ mind⟩ — **dis·or·dered·ly** *adv* — **dis·or·dered·ness** *n*

[1]**dis·or·der·ly** \-ˈȯrd-ər-lē\ *adv* (1560) *archaic* **:** in a disorderly manner

[2]**disorderly** *adj* (1555) **1 :** engaged in conduct offensive to public order ⟨charged with being drunk and ~⟩ **2 :** characterized by disorder ⟨a ~ pile of clothes⟩ — **dis·or·der·li·ness** *n*

disorderly conduct *n* (1786) **:** a petty offense chiefly against public order and decency that falls short of an indictable misdemeanor

disorderly house *n* [euphemism] (1749) **:** BORDELLO

dis·or·ga·nize \(ˌ)dis-ˈȯr-gə-ˌnīz\ *vt* [F *désorganiser,* fr. *dés-* dis- + *organiser* to organize] (1793) **:** to destroy or interrupt the orderly structure or function of — **dis·or·ga·ni·za·tion** \(ˌ)dis-ˌȯr-gə-nə-ˈzā-shən\ *n*

dis·or·ga·nized \-ˌnīzd\ *adj* (1801) **:** lacking coherence, system, or central guiding agency **:** not organized ⟨~ work habits⟩

dis·ori·ent \(ˌ)dis-ˈȯr-ē-ˌent\ *vt* [F *désorienter,* fr. *dés-* dis- + *orienter* to orient] (1655) **1 a :** to cause to lose bearings **:** displace from normal position or relationship **b :** to cause to lose the sense of time, place, or identity **2 :** CONFUSE

dis·ori·en·tate \-ē-ən-ˌtāt, -ē-ˌen-\ *vt* (ca. 1704) **:** DISORIENT — **dis·ori·en·ta·tion** \(ˌ)dis-ˌȯr-ē-ən-ˈtā-shən, -ē-ˌen-\ *n*

dis·own \(ˌ)dis-ˈōn\ *vt* (1630) **1 :** to refuse to acknowledge as one's own **2 a :** to repudiate any connection or identification with **b :** to deny the validity or authority of — **dis·own·ment** \-mənt\ *n*

disp *abbr* dispensary

dis·par·age \di-ˈsper-ij, -ˈspa-rij\ *vt* **-aged; -ag·ing** [ME, to degrade by marriage below one's class, disparage, fr. AF *desparager* to marry below one's class, fr. *des-* dis- + *parage* equality, lineage, fr. *per* peer] (14c) **1 :** to lower in rank or reputation **:** DEGRADE **2 :** to depreciate by indirect means (as invidious comparison) **:** speak slightingly about ***syn*** see DECRY — **dis·par·age·ment** \-ij-mənt\ *n* — **dis·par·ag·er** *n* — **dis·par·ag·ing** *adj* — **dis·par·ag·ing·ly** \-ij-iŋ-lē\ *adv*

dis·pa·rate \ˈdis-p(ə-)rət, di-ˈsper-ət, -ˈspa-rət\ *adj* [ME *desparat,* fr. L *disparatus,* pp. of *disparare* to separate, fr. *dis-* + *parare* to prepare — more at PARE] (15c) **1 :** containing or made up of fundamentally different and often incongruous elements **2 :** markedly distinct in quality or character ***syn*** see DIFFERENT — **dis·pa·rate·ly** *adv* — **dis·pa·rate·ness** *n* — **dis·par·i·ty** \di-ˈsper-ə-tē, -ˈspa-rə-\ *n*

dis·part \(ˌ)dis-ˈpärt\ *vb* [It & L; It *dispartire,* fr. L, fr. *dis-* + *partire* to divide — more at PART] (1590) *archaic* **:** SEPARATE, DIVIDE

dis·pas·sion \(ˌ)dis-ˈpa-shən\ *n* (1692) **:** absence of passion **:** COOLNESS

dis·pas·sion·ate \-sh(ə-)nət\ *adj* (1594) **:** not influenced by strong feeling; *esp* **:** not affected by personal or emotional involvement ⟨a ~ critic⟩ ⟨a ~ approach to an issue⟩ ***syn*** see FAIR — **dis·pas·sion·ate·ly** *adv* — **dis·pas·sion·ate·ness** *n*

[1]**dis·patch** \di-ˈspach\ *vb* [Sp *despachar* or It *dispacciare,* fr. Occitan *despachar* to get rid of, fr. MF *despechier* to set free, fr. OF, fr. *des-* dis- + *-pechier* (as in *enpechier* to ensnare) — more at IMPEACH] *vt* (1517) **1 :** to send off or away with promptness or speed; *esp* **:** to send off on official business **2 a :** to kill with quick efficiency **b** *obs* **:** DEPRIVE **3 :** to dispose of (as a task) rapidly or efficiently **4 :** DEFEAT 3 ~ *vi, archaic* **:** to make haste **:** HURRY ***syn*** see KILL — **dis·patch·er** *n*

[2]**dis·patch** \di-ˈspach, ˈdis-ˌpach\ *n* (1537) **1 a :** a message sent with speed; *esp* **:** an important official message sent by a diplomatic, military, or naval officer **b :** a news item filed by a correspondent **2 :** the act of dispatching: as **a** *obs* **:** DISMISSAL **b :** the act of killing **c** (1) **:** prompt settlement (as of an item of business) (2) **:** quick riddance **d :** a sending off **:** SHIPMENT **3 :** promptness and efficiency in performance or transmission ⟨done with ~⟩ ***syn*** see HASTE

dispatch case *n* (ca. 1918) **:** a case for carrying papers

dis·pel \di-ˈspel\ *vt* **dis·pelled; dis·pel·ling** [ME, fr. L *dispellere,* fr. *dis-* + *pellere* to drive, beat — more at FELT] (15c) **:** to drive away by or as if by scattering **:** DISSIPATE ⟨~ a rumor⟩ ***syn*** see SCATTER

dis·pens·able \di-ˈspen(t)-sə-bəl\ *adj* (1649) **:** capable of being dispensed with — **dis·pens·abil·i·ty** \-ˌspen(t)-sə-ˈbi-lə-tē\ *n*

dis·pen·sa·ry \di-ˈspen(t)s-(ə-)rē\ *n, pl* **-ries** (1699) **:** a place where medicine or medical or dental treatment is dispensed

dis·pen·sa·tion \ˌdis-pən-ˈsā-shən, -ˌpen-\ *n* (14c) **1 a :** a general state or ordering of things; *specif* **:** a system of revealed commands and promises regulating human affairs **b :** a particular arrangement or provision esp. of providence or nature **2 a :** an exemption from a law or from an impediment, vow, or oath **b :** a formal authorization **3 a :** the act of dispensing **b :** something dispensed or distributed — **dis·pen·sa·tion·al** \-shnəl, -shə-nᵊl\ *adj*

dis·pen·sa·to·ry \di-ˈspen(t)-sə-ˌtȯr-ē\ *n, pl* **-ries** (1566) **:** a medicinal formulary

dis·pense \di-ˈspen(t)s\ *vb* **dis·pensed; dis·pens·ing** [ME, fr. ML & L; ML *dispensare* to exempt, fr. L, to distribute, fr. *dis-* + *pensare* to weigh, freq. of *pendere* to weigh, pay out — more at SPIN] *vt* (14c) **1 a :** to deal out in portions **b :** ADMINISTER ⟨~ justice⟩ **2 :** to give dispensation to **:** EXEMPT **3 :** to prepare and distribute (medication) ~ *vi, archaic* **:** to grant dispensation ***syn*** see DISTRIBUTE — **dispense with 1 :** to set aside **:** DISCARD ⟨*dispensing with* the usual introduction⟩ **2 :** to do without ⟨could *dispense with* such a large staff⟩

dis·pens·er \-ˈspen(t)-sər\ *n* (14c) **:** one that dispenses: as **a :** a container that extrudes, sprays, or feeds out in convenient units **b :** a usu. mechanical device for vending merchandise

dis·peo·ple \(ˌ)dis-ˈpē-pəl\ *vt* (15c) **:** DEPOPULATE

dis·pers·al \di-ˈspər-səl\ *n* (1821) **:** the act or result of dispersing; *esp* **:** the process or result of the spreading of organisms from one place to another

dis·per·sant \di-ˈspər-sənt\ *n* (1941) **:** a dispersing agent; *esp* **:** a substance for promoting the formation and stabilization of a dispersion of one substance in another — **dispersant** *adj*

dis·perse \di-ˈspərs\ *vb* **dis·persed; dis·pers·ing** [ME, fr. L *dispersus,* pp. of *dispergere* to scatter, fr. *dis-* + *spargere* to scatter — more at SPARK] *vt* (14c) **1 a :** to cause to break up ⟨police *dispersed* the crowd⟩ **b :** to cause to become spread widely **c :** to cause to evaporate or vanish ⟨sunlight *dispersing* the mist⟩ **2 :** to spread or distribute from a fixed or constant source: as **a** *archaic* **:** DISSEMINATE **b :** to subject (as light) to dispersion **c :** to distribute (as fine particles) more or less evenly throughout a medium ~ *vi* **1 :** to break up in random fashion ⟨the crowd *dispersed* on request⟩ **2 a :** to become dispersed **b :** DISSIPATE, VANISH ⟨the fog *dispersed* toward morning⟩ ***syn*** see SCATTER — **dis·persed·ly** \-ˈspər-səd-lē, -ˈspərst-lē\ *adv* — **dis·pers·er** *n* — **dis·pers·ible** \-ˈspər-sə-bəl\ *adj*

dis·per·sion \di-ˈspər-zhən, -shən\ *n* (14c) **1** *cap* **:** DIASPORA 1a **2 :** the act or process of dispersing **:** the state of being dispersed **3 :** the scattering of the values of a frequency distribution from an average **4 :** the separation of light into colors by refraction or diffraction with formation of a spectrum; *also* **:** the separation of radiation into components in accordance with some varying characteristic (as energy) **5 a :** a dispersed substance **b :** a system consisting of a dispersed substance and the medium in which it is dispersed **:** COLLOID 2b

dis·per·sive \-ˈspər-siv, -ziv\ *adj* (1677) **1 :** of or relating to dispersion ⟨a ~ medium⟩ ⟨the ~ power of a lens⟩ **2 :** tending to disperse — **dis·per·sive·ly** *adv* — **dis·per·sive·ness** *n*

dis·per·soid \-ˈspər-ˌsȯid\ *n* (1911) **:** finely divided particles of one substance dispersed in another

dis·pir·it \(ˌ)dis-ˈpir-ət, -ˈpi-rət\ *vt* [*dis-* + *spirit*] (1647) **:** to deprive of morale or enthusiasm — **dis·pir·it·ed** *adj* — **dis·pir·it·ed·ly** *adv* — **dis·pir·it·ed·ness** *n*

dis·pit·eous \di-ˈspi-tē-əs\ *adj* [alter. of *despiteous*] (1803) *archaic* **:** CRUEL

dis·place \(ˌ)dis-ˈplās, di-ˈsplās\ *vt* [prob. fr. MF *desplacer,* fr. *des-* dis- + *place* place] (1549) **1 a :** to remove from the usual or proper place; *specif* **:** to expel or force to flee from home or homeland ⟨*displaced* persons⟩ **b :** to remove from an office, status, or job **c** *obs* **:** to drive out **:** BANISH **2 a :** to move physically out of position ⟨a floating object ~*s* water⟩ **b :** to take the place of (as in a chemical reaction) **:** SUPPLANT ***syn*** see REPLACE — **dis·place·able** \-ˈplā-sə-bəl\ *adj*

dis·place·ment \(ˌ)dis-ˈplā-smənt, di-ˈsplā-\ *n* (1611) **1 :** the act or process of displacing **:** the state of being displaced **2 a :** the volume or weight of a fluid (as water) displaced by a floating body (as a ship) of equal weight **b :** the difference between the initial position of something (as a body or geometric figure) and any later position **c :** the volume displaced by a piston (as in a pump or an engine) in a single stroke; *also* **:** the total volume so displaced by all the pistons in an internal combustion engine (as in an automobile) **3 a :** the redirection of an emotion or impulse from its original object (as an idea or person) to another **b :** the substitution of another form of behavior for what is usual or expected esp. when the usual response is nonadaptive — called also *displacement activity, displacement behavior*

dis·plant \dis-ˈplant\ *vt* [MF *desplanter,* fr. *des-* dis- + *planter* to plant, fr. LL *plantare*] (15c) **1 :** DISPLACE, REMOVE **2 :** SUPPLANT

[1]**dis·play** \di-ˈsplā\ *vb* [ME, fr. AF *desplaier, desploier,* lit., to unfold — more at DEPLOY] *vt* (14c) **1 a :** to put or spread before the view ⟨~ the flag⟩ **b :** to make evident ⟨~*ed* great skill⟩ **c :** to exhibit ostentatiously ⟨liked to ~ his erudition⟩ **2** *obs* **:** DESCRY ~ *vi* **1** *obs* **:** SHOW OFF **2 :** to make a breeding display ⟨penguins ~*ed* and copulated⟩ ***syn*** see SHOW — **dis·play·able** \-ˈsplā-ə-bəl\ *adj*

[2]**display** *n, often attrib* (1665) **1 a** (1) **:** a setting or presentation of something in open view ⟨a fireworks ~⟩ (2) **:** a clear sign or evidence **:** EXHIBITION ⟨a ~ of courage⟩ **b :** ostentatious show **c :** type, composition, or printing designed to catch the eye **d :** an eye-catching arrangement by which something is exhibited ⟨a ~ of artifacts⟩ — often used with *on* ⟨her early paintings are currently on ~⟩ **e :** an electronic device (as a cathode-ray tube) that presents information in visual form; *also* **:** the visual information **2 :** a pattern of behavior exhibited esp. by male birds in the breeding season

dis·please \(ˌ)dis-ˈplēz\ *vb* [ME *displesen,* fr. AF *despleisir, desplere,* fr. *des-* dis- + *pleisir* to please — more at PLEASE] *vt* (14c) **1 :** to incur the disapproval or dislike of esp. by annoying ⟨their gossip ~*s* her⟩ **2 :** to be offensive to ⟨abstract art ~*s* him⟩ ~ *vi* **:** to give displeasure ⟨behavior calculated to ~⟩

dis·plea·sure \(ˌ)dis-ˈple-zhər, -ˈplā-\ *n* (15c) **1 :** the feeling of one that is displeased **:** DISFAVOR **2 :** DISCOMFORT, UNHAPPINESS **3** *archaic* **:** OFFENSE, INJURY

dis·plode \di-ˈsplōd\ *vb* **dis·plod·ed; dis·plod·ing** [L *displodere,* fr. *dis-* + *plaudere* to clap, applaud] (1667) *archaic* **:** EXPLODE — **dis·plo·sion** \-ˈsplō-zhən\ *n*

[1]**dis·port** \di-ˈspȯrt\ *n* (14c) *archaic* **:** SPORT, PASTIME

[2]**disport** *vb* [ME, fr. AF *desporter,* to carry away, comfort, entertain, fr. *des-* dis- + *porter* to carry, fr. L *portare* — more at FARE] *vt* (14c) **1 :** DIVERT, AMUSE **2 :** DISPLAY ~ *vi* **:** to amuse oneself in light or lively fashion **:** FROLIC — **dis·port·ment** \-mənt\ *n*

[1]**dis·pos·able** \di-ˈspō-zə-bəl\ *adj* (1643) **1 :** subject to or available for disposal; *specif* **:** remaining to an individual after deduction of taxes and necessary living expenses ⟨~ income⟩ **2 :** designed to be used once and then thrown away ⟨~ diapers⟩ — **dis·pos·abil·i·ty** \-ˌspō-zə-ˈbi-lə-tē\ *n*

[2]**disposable** *n* (1963) **:** something that is disposable

dis·pos·al \di-ˈspō-zəl\ *n* (1630) **1 :** the power or authority to dispose or make use of as one chooses ⟨the car was at my ~⟩ **2 :** the act or process of disposing: as **a :** orderly placement or distribution **b :** REGULATION, ADMINISTRATION **c :** the act or action of presenting or bestowing something ⟨~ of favors⟩ **d :** systematic destruction; *esp* **:** destruction or transformation of garbage **3** [*garbage disposal unit*] **:** a device used to reduce waste matter (as by grinding)

[1]**dis·pose** \di-ˈspōz\ *vb* **dis·posed; dis·pos·ing** [ME, fr. AF *desposer,* fr. L *disponere* to arrange (perf. indic. *disposui*), fr. *dis-* + *ponere* to put — more at POSITION] *vt* (14c) **1 :** to give a tendency to **:** INCLINE ⟨faulty diet ~*s* one to sickness⟩ **2 a :** to put in place **:** set in readiness **:** ARRANGE ⟨*disposing* troops for withdrawal⟩ **b** *obs* **:** REGULATE **c :** BESTOW ~ *vi* **1 :** to settle a matter finally **2** *obs* **:** to come to terms ***syn*** see INCLINE — **dis·pos·er** *n* — **dispose of 1 :** to place, distribute, or arrange esp. in an orderly way **2 a :** to transfer to the control of another ⟨*disposing of* personal property to a total stranger⟩ **b** (1) **:** to get rid of ⟨how to *dispose of* toxic waste⟩ (2) **:** to deal with conclusively ⟨*disposed of* the matter efficiently⟩

[2]**dispose** *n* (1590) **1** *obs* **:** DISPOSAL **2** *obs* **a :** DISPOSITION **b :** DEMEANOR

dis·po·si·tion \ˌdis-pə-ˈzi-shən\ *n* [ME, fr. AF, fr. L *disposition-, dispositio,* fr. *disponere*] (14c) **1 :** the act or the power of disposing or the state of being disposed: as **a :** ADMINISTRATION, CONTROL **b :** final arrangement **:** SETTLEMENT ⟨the ~ of the case⟩ **c** (1) **:** transfer to the care or possession of another (2) **:** the power of such transferal **d :** orderly arrangement **2 a :** prevailing tendency, mood, or inclination **b :** temperamental makeup **c :** the tendency of something to act in a certain manner under given circumstances — **dis·po·si·tion·al** \-ˈzish-nəl, -ˈzi-shə-nᵊl\ *adj*

syn DISPOSITION, TEMPERAMENT, TEMPER, CHARACTER, PERSONALITY mean the dominant quality or qualities distinguishing a person or group. DISPOSITION implies customary moods and attitude toward the life around one ⟨a cheerful *disposition*⟩. TEMPERAMENT implies a pattern of innate characteristics associated with one's specific physical and nervous organization ⟨an artistic *temperament*⟩. TEMPER implies the qualities acquired through experience that determine how a person or group meets difficulties or handles situations ⟨a resilient *temper*⟩. CHARACTER applies to the aggregate of moral qualities by which a person is judged apart from intelligence, competence, or special talents ⟨strength of *character*⟩. PERSONALITY applies to an aggregate of qualities that distinguish one as a person ⟨a somber *personality*⟩.

dis·pos·i·tive \di-ˈspä-zə-tiv\ *adj* (ca. 1618) **:** directed toward or effecting disposition (as of a case) ⟨~ evidence⟩

dis·pos·sess \ˌdis-pə-ˈzes *also* -ˈses\ *vt* [MF *despossesser,* fr. *des-* dis- + *possesser* to possess] (15c) **:** to put out of possession or occupancy ⟨~*ed* the nobles of their land⟩ — **dis·pos·ses·sion** \-ˈze-shən *also* -ˈse-\ *n* — **dis·pos·ses·sor** \-ˈze-sər *also* -ˈse-\ *n*

dis·pos·sessed \-ˈzest *also* -ˈsest\ *adj* (15c) **:** deprived of homes, possessions, and security

dis·po·sure \di-ˈspō-zhər\ *n* (1569) *archaic* **:** DISPOSAL, DISPOSITION

dis·praise \(ˌ)dis-ˈprāz\ *vt* [ME *dispraisen,* fr. AF *despreiser, despriser,* fr. *des-* dis- + *preiser* to praise] (13c) **:** to comment on with disapproval or censure — **dispraise** *n* — **dis·prais·er** *n* — **dis·prais·ing·ly** \-ˈprā-ziŋ-lē\ *adv*

dispread \di-ˈspred\ *vt* (1590) **:** to spread abroad or out

dis·prize \(ˌ)dis-ˈprīz\ *vt* [ME *disprisen,* fr. AF *despriser*] (15c) *archaic* : UNDERVALUE, SCORN

dis·proof \(ˌ)dis-ˈprüf\ *n* (15c) **1** : the action of disproving **2** : evidence that disproves

[1]**dis·pro·por·tion** \ˌdis-prə-ˈpȯr-shən\ *n* (1555) : lack of proportion, symmetry, or proper relation : DISPARITY; *also* : an instance of such disparity — **dis·pro·por·tion·al** \-shnəl, -shə-nᵊl\ *adj*

[2]**disproportion** *vt* (1593) : to make out of proportion : MISMATCH

dis·pro·por·tion·ate \-sh(ə-)nət\ *adj* (1555) : being out of proportion ⟨a ~ share⟩ — **dis·pro·por·tion·ate·ly** *adv*

dis·pro·por·tion·ation \-ˌpȯr-shə-ˈnā-shən\ *n* (ca. 1929) : the transformation of a substance into two or more dissimilar substances usu. by simultaneous oxidation and reduction — **dis·pro·por·tion·ate** \-ˈpȯr-shə-ˌnāt\ *vi*

dis·prove \(ˌ)dis-ˈprüv\ *vt* [ME, fr. AF *desprover,* fr. *des-* dis- + *prover* to prove] (14c) : to prove to be false or wrong : REFUTE ⟨~ a theory⟩ — **dis·prov·able** \-ˈprü-və-bəl\ *adj*

dis·pu·tant \di-ˈspyü-tᵊnt, ˈdis-pyə-tənt\ *n* (1593) : one that is engaged in a dispute

dis·pu·ta·tion \ˌdis-pyə-ˈtā-shən\ *n* (14c) **1** : the action of disputing : verbal controversy ⟨continuous ~ between them⟩ ⟨ideological ~*s*⟩ **2** : an academic exercise in oral defense of a thesis by formal logic

dis·pu·ta·tious \-shəs\ *adj* (1660) **1 a** : inclined to dispute **b** : marked by disputation **2** : provoking debate : CONTROVERSIAL — **dis·pu·ta·tious·ly** *adv* — **dis·pu·ta·tious·ness** *n*

[1]**dis·pute** \di-ˈspyüt\ *vb* **dis·put·ed; dis·put·ing** [ME, fr. AF *desputer,* fr. L *disputare* to discuss, fr. *dis-* + *putare* to think] *vi* (13c) : to engage in argument : DEBATE; *esp* : to argue irritably or with irritating persistence ~ *vt* **1 a** : to make the subject of disputation ⟨legislators hotly *disputed* the bill⟩ **b** : to call into question ⟨her honesty was never *disputed*⟩ **2 a** : to struggle against : OPPOSE ⟨*disputed* the advance of the invaders⟩ **b** : to contend over ⟨both sides *disputed* the bridgehead⟩ — **dis·put·able** \di-ˈspyü-tə-bəl, ˈdis-pyə-\ *adj* — **dis·put·ably** \-blē\ *adv* — **dis·put·er** *n*

[2]**dis·pute** \di-ˈspyüt, ˈdis-ˌpyüt\ *n* (1555) **1 a** : verbal controversy : DEBATE **b** : QUARREL **2** *obs* : physical combat

dis·qual·i·fi·ca·tion \(ˌ)dis-ˌkwä-lə-fə-ˈkā-shən\ *n* (ca. 1714) **1** : something that disqualifies or incapacitates **2** : the act of disqualifying : the state of being disqualified ⟨~ from office⟩

dis·qual·i·fy \(ˌ)dis-ˈkwä-lə-ˌfī\ *vt* (1712) **1** : to deprive of the required qualities, properties, or conditions : make unfit **2** : to deprive of a power, right, or privilege **3** : to make ineligible for a prize or for further competition because of violations of the rules

dis·quan·ti·ty \(ˌ)dis-ˈkwän-(t)ə-tē\ *vt* (1605) *obs* : DIMINISH, LESSEN

[1]**dis·qui·et** \(ˌ)dis-ˈkwī-ət\ *vt* (ca. 1530) : to take away the peace or tranquillity of : DISTURB, ALARM *syn* see DISCOMPOSE — **dis·qui·et·ing** *adj* — **dis·qui·et·ing·ly** \-ˈkwī-ə-tiŋ-lē\ *adv*

[2]**disquiet** *n* (1581) : lack of peace or tranquillity : ANXIETY

[3]**disquiet** *adj* (1582) *archaic* : UNEASY, DISQUIETED — **dis·qui·et·ly** *adv*

dis·qui·etude \(ˌ)dis-ˈkwī-ə-ˌt(y)üd\ *n* (1682) : ANXIETY, AGITATION

dis·qui·si·tion \ˌdis-kwə-ˈzi-shən\ *n* [L *disquisition-, disquisitio,* fr. *disquirere* to investigate, fr. *dis-* + *quaerere* to seek] (1640) : a formal inquiry into or discussion of a subject : DISCOURSE

dis·rate \(ˌ)dis-ˈrāt\ *vt* (1751) : to reduce in rank : DEMOTE

[1]**dis·re·gard** \ˌdis-ri-ˈgärd\ *vt* (1613) : to pay no attention to : treat as unworthy of regard or notice *syn* see NEGLECT

[2]**disregard** *n* (1659) : the act of disregarding : the state of being disregarded : NEGLECT — **dis·re·gard·ful** \-fəl\ *adj*

dis·re·lat·ed \ˌdis-ri-ˈlā-təd\ *adj* (1894) : not related

dis·re·la·tion \-ˈlā-shən\ *n* (1893) : lack of a fitting or proportionate connection or relationship

[1]**dis·rel·ish** \(ˌ)dis-ˈre-lish\ *vt* (1604) : to find unpalatable or distasteful

[2]**disrelish** *n* (ca. 1625) : lack of relish : DISTASTE, DISLIKE

dis·re·mem·ber \ˌdis-ri-ˈmem-bər\ *vt* (1805) : FORGET

dis·re·pair \ˌdis-ri-ˈper\ *n* (1798) : the state of being in need of repair ⟨a building fallen into ~⟩

dis·rep·u·ta·ble \(ˌ)dis-ˈre-pyə-tə-bəl\ *adj* (ca. 1726) : not reputable — **dis·rep·u·ta·bil·i·ty** \(ˌ)dis-ˌre-pyə-tə-ˈbi-lə-tē\ *n* — **dis·rep·u·ta·ble·ness** \(ˌ)dis-ˈre-pyə-tə-bəl-nəs\ *n* — **dis·rep·u·ta·bly** \-blē\ *adv*

dis·re·pute \ˌdis-ri-ˈpyüt\ *n* (1637) : lack or decline of good reputation : a state of being held in low esteem *syn* see DISGRACE

[1]**dis·re·spect** \ˌdis-ri-ˈspekt\ *vt* (1614) **1** : to have disrespect for **2** : to show or express disrespect or contempt for : INSULT, DIS ⟨~*ed* the officer⟩

[2]**disrespect** *n* (1621) : lack of respect — **dis·re·spect·ful** \-fəl\ *adj* — **dis·re·spect·ful·ly** \-fə-lē\ *adv* — **dis·re·spect·ful·ness** *n*

dis·re·spect·able \ˌdis-ri-ˈspek-tə-bəl\ *adj* (1798) : not respectable — **dis·re·spect·abil·i·ty** \-ˌspek-tə-ˈbi-lə-tē\ *n*

dis·robe \(ˌ)dis-ˈrōb\ *vb* [MF *desrober,* fr. *des-* dis- + *robe* garment, fr. OF] *vi* (1581) : to take off one's clothing ~ *vt* : to strip of clothing or covering

dis·rupt \dis-ˈrəpt\ *vt* [L *disruptus,* pp. of *disrumpere,* fr. *dis-* + *rumpere* to break — more at REAVE] (1793) **1 a** : to break apart : RUPTURE **b** : to throw into disorder ⟨agitators trying to ~ the meeting⟩ **2** : to interrupt the normal course or unity of — **dis·rupt·er** *n* — **dis·rup·tion** \-ˈrəp-shən\ *n* — **dis·rup·tive** \-ˈrəp-tiv\ *adj* — **dis·rup·tive·ly** *adv* — **dis·rup·tive·ness** *n*

[1]**diss** *var of* DIS

[2]**diss** *abbr* dissertation

dis·sat·is·fac·tion \(ˌ)di(s)-ˌsa-təs-ˈfak-shən\ *n* (ca. 1610) : the quality or state of being dissatisfied : DISCONTENT

dis·sat·is·fac·to·ry \-ˈfak-t(ə-)rē\ *adj* (ca. 1610) : causing dissatisfaction

dis·sat·is·fied \(ˌ)di(s)-ˈsa-təs-ˌfīd\ *adj* (ca. 1630) : expressing or showing lack of satisfaction : not pleased or satisfied ⟨~ customers⟩ ⟨~ with his response⟩

dis·sat·is·fy \-ˌfī\ *vt* (1666) : to fail to satisfy : DISPLEASE

dis·save \(ˌ)dis-ˈsāv\ *vi* (1936) : to use savings for current expenses

dis·seat \(ˌ)di(s)-ˈsēt\ *vt* (1612) *archaic* : UNSEAT

dis·sect \dī-ˈsekt *also* di-, ˈdī-ˌ\ *vb* [L *dissectus,* pp. of *dissecare* to cut apart, fr. *dis-* + *secare* to cut — more at SAW] *vt* (1598) **1** : to separate into pieces : expose the several parts of (as an animal) for scientific examination **2** : to analyze and interpret minutely ⟨~ a problem⟩ ~ *vi* : to make a dissection *syn* see ANALYZE — **dis·sec·tor** \-ˈsek-tər\ *n*

dis·sect·ed \-ˈsek-təd\ *adj* (1652) **1** : cut deeply into fine lobes ⟨a ~ leaf⟩ **2** : divided into hills and ridges (as by gorges) ⟨a ~ plateau⟩

dis·sect·ing microscope \-tiŋ-\ *n* (ca. 1897) : a low-magnification stereomicroscope used esp. in examining or dissecting biological specimens

dis·sec·tion \dī-ˈsek-shən *also* di-, ˈdī-ˌ\ *n* (1578) **1** : the act or process of dissecting : the state of being dissected **2** : an anatomical specimen prepared by dissecting

dis·seise *or* **dis·seize** \(ˌ)di(s)-ˈsēz\ *vt* **dis·seised** *or* **dis·seized; dis·seis·ing** *or* **dis·seiz·ing** [ME *disseisen,* fr. AF *disseisir, dis-* + *seisir* to put in possession of — more at SEIZE] (14c) : to deprive esp. wrongfully of seisin : DISPOSSESS — **dis·sei·sor** \-ˈsē-zər\ *n*

dis·sei·sin *or* **dis·sei·zin** \-ˈsē-zᵊn\ *n* [ME *dysseysyne,* fr. AF *disseisine,* fr. *disseisir*] (14c) : the act of disseising : the state of being disseised

dis·sem·ble \di-ˈsem-bəl\ *vb* **dis·sem·bled; dis·sem·bling** \-b(ə-)liŋ\ [ME *dissymblen,* alter. of *dissimulen,* fr. MF *dissimuler,* fr. L *dissimulare* — more at DISSIMULATE] *vt* (15c) **1** : to hide under a false appearance **2** : to put on the appearance of : SIMULATE ~ *vi* : to put on a false appearance : conceal facts, intentions, or feelings under some pretense — **dis·sem·bler** \-b(ə-)lər\ *n*

dis·sem·i·nate \di-ˈse-mə-ˌnāt\ *vt* **-nat·ed; -nat·ing** [L *disseminatus,* pp. of *disseminare,* fr. *dis-* + *seminare* to sow, fr. *semin-, semen* seed — more at SEMEN] (1566) **1** : to spread abroad as though sowing seed ⟨~ ideas⟩ **2** : to disperse throughout — **dis·sem·i·na·tion** \-ˌse-mə-ˈnā-shən\ *n* — **dis·sem·i·na·tor** \-ˈse-mə-ˌnā-tər\ *n*

disseminated *adj* (1876) : widely dispersed in a tissue, organ, or the entire body ⟨~ gonococcal disease⟩

dis·sem·i·nule \di-ˈsem-ə-ˌnyül\ *n* (1904) : a part or organ (as a seed or spore) of a plant that ensures propagation

dis·sen·sion *also* **dis·sen·tion** \di-ˈsen(t)-shən\ *n* [ME, fr. AF *discension,* fr. L *dissension-, dissensio,* fr. *dissentire*] (14c) : DISAGREEMENT; *esp* : partisan and contentious quarreling *syn* see DISCORD

dis·sen·sus \(ˌ)di(s)-ˈsen(t)-səs\ *n* [*dis-* + *consensus*] (1962) : difference of opinion

[1]**dis·sent** \di-ˈsent\ *vi* [ME, fr. L *dissentire,* fr. *dis-* + *sentire* to feel — more at SENSE] (15c) **1** : to withhold assent **2** : to differ in opinion

[2]**dissent** *n* (1585) : difference of opinion ⟨heard voices of ~ at the meeting⟩: as **a** : religious nonconformity **b** : a justice's nonconcurrence with a decision of the majority — called also *dissenting opinion* **c** : political opposition to a government or its policies ⟨attempts to suppress domestic ~⟩

dis·sent·er \di-ˈsen-tər\ *n* (1639) **1** : one that dissents **2** *cap* : an English Nonconformist

dis·sen·tient \di-ˈsen(t)-sh(ē-)ənt\ *adj* [L *dissentient-, dissentiens,* prp. of *dissentire*] (1651) : expressing dissent — **dissentient** *n*

dis·sent·ing \di-ˈsen-tiŋ\ *adj, often cap* (1644) : of or relating to the English Nonconformists ⟨a ~ church⟩ ⟨~ merchants⟩

dis·sen·tious \di-ˈsen(t)-shəs\ *adj* (1560) : characterized by dissension or dissent

dis·sep·i·ment \di-ˈse-pə-mənt\ *n* [L *dissaepimentum* partition, fr. *dissaepire* to divide, fr. *dis-* + *saepire* to fence in — more at SEPTUM] (ca. 1727) : a dividing tissue : SEPTUM

dis·sert \di-ˈsərt\ *vi* [L *dissertus,* pp. of *disserere,* fr. *dis-* + *serere* to join, arrange — more at SERIES] (1657) : to speak or write at length

dis·ser·tate \ˈdi-sər-ˌtāt\ *vi* **-tat·ed; -tat·ing** [L *dissertatus,* pp. of *dissertare,* fr. *dissertus*] (1766) : DISSERT; *also* : to write a dissertation — **dis·ser·ta·tor** \-ˌtā-tər\ *n*

dis·ser·ta·tion \ˌdi-sər-ˈtā-shən\ *n* (1651) : an extended usu. written treatment of a subject; *specif* : one submitted for a doctorate — **dis·ser·ta·tion·al** \-ˈtāsh-nəl, -ˈtā-shə-nᵊl\ *adj*

dis·serve \(ˌ)di(s)-ˈsərv\ *vt* (ca. 1629) : to serve badly or falsely : HARM

dis·ser·vice \(ˌ)di(s)-ˈsər-vəs\ *n* (1599) : ill service : HARM; *also* : an unhelpful, unkind, or harmful act ⟨misinformation that does a ~ to readers⟩

dis·ser·vice·able \di(s)-ˈsər-və-sə-bəl\ *adj* (1635) : COUNTERPRODUCTIVE

dis·sev·er \di-ˈse-vər\ *vb* [ME, fr. AF *deseivr-,* stem of *desevrer,* fr. LL *disseparare,* fr. L *dis-* + *separare* to separate] *vt* (13c) : SEVER, SEPARATE ~ *vi* : to come apart : DISUNITE — **dis·sev·er·ance** \-ˈse-v(ə-)rən(t)s\ *n* — **dis·sev·er·ment** \-ˈse-vər-mənt\ *n*

dis·si·dence \ˈdi-sə-dən(t)s\ *n* (ca. 1656) : DISSENT, DISAGREEMENT ⟨political ~⟩

dis·si·dent \-dənt\ *adj* [L *dissident-, dissidens,* prp. of *dissidēre* to sit apart, disagree, fr. *dis-* + *sedēre* to sit — more at SIT] (1769) : disagreeing esp. with an established religious or political system, organization, or belief — **dissident** *n*

dis·sim·i·lar \(ˌ)di(s)-ˈsi-mə-lər, -ˈsim-lər\ *adj* (1599) : UNLIKE ⟨people with ~ backgrounds⟩ — **dis·sim·i·lar·i·ty** \(ˌ)di(s)-ˌsi-mə-ˈlar-ə-tē\ *n* — **dis·sim·i·lar·ly** \(ˈ)di(s)-ˈsi-mə-lər-lē, -ˈsim-lər-\ *adv*

dis·sim·i·late \(ˌ)di-ˈsi-mə-ˌlāt\ *vi* **-lat·ed; -lat·ing** [*dis-* + *-similate* (as in *assimilate*)] (1841) : to undergo dissimilation — **dis·sim·i·la·to·ry** \-mə-lə-ˌtȯr-ē\ *adj*

dis·sim·i·la·tion \(ˌ)di-ˌsi-mə-ˈlā-shən\ *n* (ca. 1874) : the change or omission of one of two identical or closely related sounds in a word

dis·si·mil·i·tude \ˌdi(s)-sə-ˈmi-lə-ˌtüd, -ˌtyüd\ *n* [ME, fr. L *dissimilitudo,* fr. *dissimilis* unlike, fr. *dis-* + *similis* like — more at SAME] (15c) : lack of resemblance

dis·sim·u·late \(ˌ)di-ˈsim-yə-ˌlāt\ *vb* **-lat·ed; -lat·ing** [ME, fr. L *dissimulatus,* pp. of *dissimulare,* fr. *dis-* + *simulare* to simulate] *vt* (15c) : to hide under a false appearance ⟨smiled to ~ her urgency —Alice Glenday⟩ ~ *vi* : DISSEMBLE — **dis·sim·u·la·tion** \(ˌ)di-ˌsim-yə-ˈlā-shən\ *n* — **dis·sim·u·la·tor** \(ˈ)di-ˈsim-yə-ˌlā-tər\ *n*

dis·si·pate \ˈdi-sə-ˌpāt\ *vb* **-pat·ed; -pat·ing** [L *dissipatus,* pp. of *dissipare, dissupare,* fr. *dis-* + *supare* to throw] *vt* (15c) **1 a** : to break up and drive off (as a crowd) **b** : to cause to spread thin or scatter and gradually vanish ⟨one's sympathy is eventually *dissipated* —Andrew Feinberg⟩ **c** : to lose (as heat or electricity) irrecoverably **2** : to spend or use up wastefully or foolishly ⟨*dissipated* the family fortune in reckless business ventures⟩ ~ *vi* **1** : to break up and scatter or vanish ⟨the clouds soon *dissipated*⟩ ⟨the team's early momentum has *dissipated*⟩ **2** : to be extravagant or dissolute in the pursuit of pleasure; *esp* : to drink to excess *syn* see SCATTER — **dis·si·pat·er** *n*

dissipated *adj* (1744) : given to or marked by dissipation : DISSOLUTE — **dis·si·pat·ed·ly** *adv* — **dis·si·pat·ed·ness** *n*
dis·si·pa·tion \ˌdi-sə-ˈpā-shən\ *n* (15c) **1** : the action or process of dissipating : the state of being dissipated: **a** : DISPERSION, DIFFUSION **b** *archaic* : DISSOLUTION, DISINTEGRATION **c** : wasteful expenditure **d** : intemperate living; *esp* : excessive drinking **2** : an act of self-indulgence; *esp* : one that is not harmful : AMUSEMENT
dis·si·pa·tive \ˈdi-sə-ˌpā-tiv\ *adj* (1665) : relating to dissipation esp. of heat
dis·so·cia·ble \(ˌ)di-ˈsō-sh(ē-)ə-bəl, -sē-ə-\ *adj* (1833) : SEPARABLE — **dis·so·cia·bil·i·ty** \(ˌ)di-ˌsō-sh(ē-)ə-ˈbi-lə-tē, -sē-ə-\ *n*
dis·so·cial \(ˌ)di(s)-ˈsō-shəl\ *adj* (1762) : UNSOCIAL, SELFISH
dis·so·ci·ate \(ˌ)di-ˈsō-shē-ˌāt, -sē-\ *vb* **-at·ed; -at·ing** [L *dissociatus,* pp. of *dissociare,* fr. *dis-* + *sociare* to join, fr. *socius* companion — more at SOCIAL] *vt* (1582) **1** : to separate from association or union with another ⟨attempts to ~ herself from her past⟩ **2** : DISUNITE; *specif* : to subject to chemical dissociation ~ *vi* **1** : to undergo dissociation **2** : to mutate esp. reversibly
dis·so·ci·a·tion \(ˌ)di-ˌsō-sē-ˈā-shən, -shē-\ *n* (1611) **1** : the act or process of dissociating : the state of being dissociated: as **a** : the process by which a chemical combination breaks up into simpler constituents; *esp* : one that results from the action of energy (as heat) on a gas or of a solvent on a dissolved substance **b** : the separation of whole segments of the personality (as in multiple personality disorder) or of discrete mental processes (as in the schizophrenias) from the mainstream of consciousness or of behavior **2** : the property inherent in some biological stocks (as of certain bacteria) of differentiating into two or more distinct and relatively permanent strains; *also* : such a strain — **dis·so·cia·tive** \(ˌ)di-ˈsō-shē-ˌā-tiv, -sē-, -shə-tiv\ *adj*
dissociative identity disorder *n* (1993) : MULTIPLE PERSONALITY DISORDER
dis·sol·u·ble \di-ˈsäl-yə-bəl\ *adj* [L *dissolubilis,* fr. *dissolvere* to dissolve] (1534) : capable of being dissolved or disintegrated
dis·so·lute \ˈdi-sə-ˌlüt, -lət\ *adj* [ME, fr. L *dissolutus,* fr. pp. of *dissolvere* to loosen, dissolve] (14c) : lacking restraint; *esp* : marked by indulgence in things (as drink or promiscuous sex) deemed vices ⟨the ~ and degrading aspects of human nature —Wallace Fowlie⟩ — **dis·so·lute·ly** *adv* — **dis·so·lute·ness** *n*
dis·so·lu·tion \ˌdi-sə-ˈlü-shən\ *n* (14c) **1** : the act or process of dissolving: as **a** : separation into component parts **b (1)** : DECAY, DISINTEGRATION **(2)** : DEATH **c** : termination or destruction by breaking down, disrupting, or dispersing ⟨the ~ of the republic⟩ **d** : the dissolving of an assembly or organization **e** : LIQUEFACTION **2** : a dissolute act or practice
[1]**dis·solve** \di-ˈzälv, -ˈzȯlv *also* -ˈzäv *or* -ˈzȯv\ *vb* [ME, fr. L *dissolvere,* fr. *dis-* + *solvere* to loosen — more at SOLVE] *vt* (14c) **1 a** : to cause to disperse or disappear : DESTROY ⟨do not ~ and deface the laws of charity —Francis Bacon⟩ **b** : to separate into component parts : DISINTEGRATE **c** : to bring to an end : TERMINATE ⟨~ parliament⟩ **d** : ANNUL ⟨~ an injunction⟩ **2 a** : to cause to pass into solution ⟨~ sugar in water⟩ **b** : MELT, LIQUEFY **c** : to cause to be emotionally moved **d** : to cause to fade in or out in a dissolve **3** *archaic* : DETACH, LOOSEN **4** : to clear up ⟨~ a problem⟩ ~ *vi* **1 a** : to become dissipated or decomposed **b** : BREAK UP, DISPERSE **c** : to fade away **2 a** : to become fluid : MELT **b** : to pass into solution **c** : to be overcome emotionally ⟨*dissolved* into tears⟩ **d** : to resolve itself as if by dissolution ⟨hate *dissolved* into fear⟩ **e** : to change by a dissolve ⟨the scene ~*s* to a Victorian parlor⟩ — **dis·solv·able** \-ˈzäl-və-bəl, -ˈzȯl-\ *adj* — **dis·sol·vent** \-ˈzäl-vənt, -ˈzȯl-\ *n or adj* — **dis·solv·er** *n*
[2]**dissolve** *n* (1916) : a gradual superimposing of one motion-picture or television shot upon another on a screen
dis·so·nance \ˈdi-sə-nən(t)s\ *n* (15c) **1 a** : lack of agreement; *esp* : inconsistency between the beliefs one holds or between one's actions and one's beliefs — compare COGNITIVE DISSONANCE **b** : an instance of such inconsistency or disagreement **2** : a mingling of discordant sounds; *esp* : a clashing or unresolved musical interval or chord
dis·so·nant \-nənt\ *adj* [ME *dissonaunte,* fr. L *dissonant-, dissonans,* prp. of *dissonare* to be discordant, fr. *dis-* + *sonare* to sound — more at SOUND] (15c) **1** : marked by dissonance : DISCORDANT **2** : INCONGRUOUS **3** : harmonically unresolved — **dis·so·nant·ly** *adv*
dis·suade \di-ˈswād\ *vt* **dis·suad·ed; dis·suad·ing** [MF or L; MF *dissuader,* fr. L *dissuadēre,* fr. *dis-* + *suadēre* to urge — more at SWEET] (15c) **1 a** : to advise (a person) against something **b** *archaic* : to advise against (an action) **2** : to turn from something by persuasion ⟨unable to ~ him from going⟩ — **dis·suad·er** *n*
dis·sua·sion \di-ˈswā-zhən\ *n* [ME *dissuasioun,* fr. MF or L; MF, fr. L *dissuasion-, dissuasio,* fr. *dissuadēre*] (15c) : the action of dissuading
dis·sua·sive \di-ˈswā-siv, -ziv\ *adj* (1609) : tending to dissuade ⟨a ~ effect⟩ — **dis·sua·sive·ly** *adv* — **dis·sua·sive·ness** *n*
dissyllable *var of* DISYLLABLE
dis·sym·me·try \(ˌ)di(s)-ˈsi-mə-trē\ *n* (1845) : the absence of or the lack of symmetry — **dis·sym·met·ric** \(ˌ)di(s)-sə-ˈme-trik\ *adj*
dist *abbr* **1** distance **2** district
[1]**dis·taff** \ˈdis-ˌtaf\ *n, pl* **distaffs** \-ˌtafs, -ˌtavz\ [ME *distaf,* fr. OE *distæf,* fr. *dis-* (akin to MLG *dise* bunch of flax) + *stæf* staff] (bef. 12c) **1 a** : a staff for holding the flax, tow, or wool in spinning **b** : woman's work or domain **2** : the female branch or side of a family
[2]**distaff** *adj* (ca. 1633) **1** : MATERNAL 2 ⟨the ~ side of the family⟩ — compare SPEAR **2** : FEMALE 1 ⟨~ executives⟩
dis·tain \dis-ˈtān\ *vt* [ME *disteynen,* fr. AF *desteindre* to take away the color of, fr. *de-* + *teindre* to dye, fr. L *tingere* to wet, dye — more at TINGE] (14c) **1** *archaic* : STAIN **2** *archaic* : DISHONOR
dis·tal \ˈdis-tᵊl\ *adj* [*distant* + *-al*] (1803) **1** : situated away from the point of attachment or origin or a central point esp. of the body — compare PROXIMAL **2** : of, relating to, or being the surface of a tooth that is next to the tooth behind it or that is farthest from the middle of the front of the jaw — compare MESIAL 2 — **dis·tal·ly** \-tᵊl-ē\ *adv*

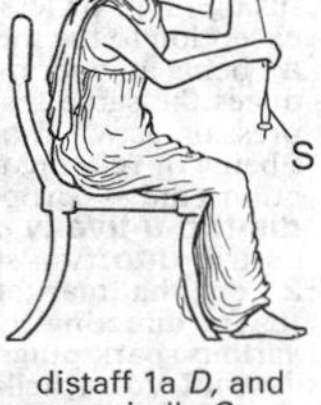

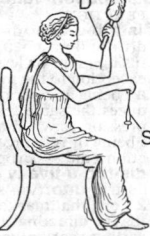

distaff 1a *D*, and spindle *S*

distal convoluted tubule *n* (ca. 1901) : the convoluted portion of the vertebrate nephron that lies between the loop of Henle and the nonsecretory part of the nephron and that is concerned esp. with the concentration of urine
[1]**dis·tance** \ˈdis-tən(t)s\ *n* (14c) **1** *obs* : DISCORD **2 a** : separation in time **b** : the degree or amount of separation between two points, lines, surfaces, or objects **c (1)** : an extent of area or an advance along a route measured linearly **(2)** : an extent of space measured other than linearly ⟨within walking ~⟩ **d** : an extent of advance from a beginning **e** : EXPANSE **f (1)** : length of a race or contest ⟨won at all ~*s*⟩ **(2)** : the full length (as of a prizefight or ball game) **(3)** : a long race ⟨~ training⟩ **3** : the quality or state of being distant: as **a** : spatial remoteness **b** : personal and esp. emotional separation; *also* : RESERVE, COLDNESS **c** : DIFFERENCE, DISPARITY **4** : a distant point or region **5 a** : AESTHETIC DISTANCE **b** : capacity to observe dispassionately — **go the distance** *also* **last the distance** : to complete a course of action
[2]**distance** *vt* **dis·tanced; dis·tanc·ing** (1578) **1** : to place or keep at a distance ⟨able to ~ themselves from the tragedy⟩ ⟨~*s* herself from her coworkers⟩ **2** : to leave far behind : OUTSTRIP ⟨easily *distanced* the other candidates in the race⟩
[3]**distance** *adj* (1972) : taking place via electronic media linking instructors and students who are not together in a classroom ⟨~ learning⟩ ⟨~ education⟩
dis·tant \ˈdis-tənt\ *adj* [ME, fr. MF, fr. L *distant-, distans,* prp. of *distare* to stand apart, be distant, fr. *dis-* + *stare* to stand — more at STAND] (14c) **1 a** : separated in space : AWAY ⟨a mile ~⟩ **b** : situated at a great distance : FAR-OFF ⟨a ~ galaxy⟩ **c** : separated by a great distance from each other : far apart **d** : far behind ⟨finished a ~ third⟩ **2** : separated in a relationship other than spatial ⟨a ~ cousin⟩ ⟨the ~ past⟩ **3** : different in kind ⟨from two very ~ backgrounds⟩ **4** : reserved or aloof in personal relationship : COLD ⟨was ~ and distracted⟩ **5 a** : going a long distance ⟨~ voyages⟩ **b** : concerned with remote things ⟨~ thoughts⟩ — **dis·tant·ly** *adv* — **dis·tant·ness** *n*
[1]**dis·taste** \(ˌ)dis-ˈtāst\ *vt* (1592) **1** *archaic* : to feel aversion to **2** *archaic* : OFFEND, DISPLEASE ~ *vi, obs* : to have an offensive taste
[2]**distaste** *n* (1584) **1 a** *archaic* : dislike of food or drink **b** : AVERSION, DISINCLINATION ⟨a ~ for opera⟩ **2** *obs* : ANNOYANCE, DISCOMFORT
dis·taste·ful \(ˌ)dis-ˈtāst-fəl\ *adj* (1607) **1 a** : objectionable because offensive to one's personal taste : UNPLEASANT, DISAGREEABLE ⟨found the job ~⟩ ⟨a shady, ~ character⟩ **b** : objectionable because in poor taste, inappropriate, or unethical ⟨a harmless stroking . . . but it seems oddly ~ in retrospect —Richard Sandza *et al.*⟩ **2** : unpleasant to the taste ⟨~ unripe fruit⟩ — **dis·taste·ful·ly** \-fə-lē\ *adv* — **dis·taste·ful·ness** *n*
dis·tel·fink \ˈdish-tᵊl-ˌfiŋk, ˈdis-\ *n* [PaG *dischdelfink,* lit., goldfinch, fr. *dischdel* thistle + *fink* finch] (1939) : a traditional Pennsylvania Dutch design motif in the form of a stylized bird
[1]**dis·tem·per** \dis-ˈtem-pər\ *vt* [ME *distempren,* fr. LL *distemperare* to temper badly, fr. L *dis-* + *temperare* to temper] (14c) **1** : to throw out of order **2** *archaic* : DERANGE, UNSETTLE
[2]**distemper** *n* (1546) **1** : bad humor or temper **2** : a disordered or abnormal bodily state esp. of quadruped mammals: as **a** : a highly contagious virus disease of canines and esp. of dogs that is caused by a morbillivirus (species *Canine distemper virus*) and is marked by fever, leukopenia, and respiratory, gastrointestinal, and neurological symptoms — called also *canine distemper* **b** : STRANGLES **c** : PANLEUKOPENIA **3** : AILMENT, DISORDER ⟨vice and folly are situated not in human nature . . . but in ~*s* of intellect —George Stade⟩ — **dis·tem·per·ate** \-p(ə-)rət\ *adj*
[3]**distemper** *n* [obs. *distemper,* v., to dilute, mix to produce distemper, fr. ME, fr. AF *destemprer,* fr. L *dis-* + *temperare*] (1632) **1** : a process of painting in which the pigments are mixed with an emulsion of egg yolk, with size, or with white of egg as a vehicle and which is used for painting scenery and murals **2 a** : the paint or the prepared ground used in the distemper process **b** : a painting done in distemper **3** : any of various water-based paints
[4]**distemper** *vt* (ca. 1873) : to paint in or with distemper
dis·tem·per·a·ture \di-ˈstem-p(ə-)rə-ˌchu̇r, -pə(r)-, -chər, *chiefly Southern* -ˌt(y)u̇(ə)r\ *n* (1531) : a disordered condition
dis·tend \di-ˈstend\ *vb* [ME, fr. L *distendere,* fr. *dis-* + *tendere* to stretch — more at THIN] *vt* (15c) **1** : EXTEND **2** : to enlarge from internal pressure : SWELL ~ *vi* : to become expanded ***syn*** see EXPAND
dis·ten·si·ble \-ˈsten(t)-sə-bəl\ *adj* [*distens-* (fr. L *distensus,* pp. of *distendere*) + *-ible*] (ca. 1828) : capable of being distended — **dis·ten·si·bil·i·ty** \-ˌsten(t)-sə-ˈbi-lə-tē\ *n*
dis·ten·sion *or* **dis·ten·tion** \di-ˈsten(t)-shən\ *n* [ME *distensioun,* fr. L *distention-, distentio,* fr. *distendere*] (15c) : the act of distending or the state of being distended esp. unduly or abnormally
dis·tich \ˈdis-(ˌ)tik\ *n* [L *distichon,* fr. Gk, fr. neut. of *distichos* having two rows, fr. *di-* + *stichos* row, verse; akin to Gk *steichein* to go — more at STAIR] (1553) : a strophic unit of two lines
dis·ti·chous \ˈdis-ti-kəs\ *adj* [LL *distichus,* fr. Gk *distichos*] (ca. 1753) : disposed in two vertical rows ⟨~ leaves⟩
dis·till *also* **dis·til** \di-ˈstil\ *vb* **dis·tilled; dis·till·ing** [ME *distillen,* fr. AF *distiller,* fr. LL *distillare,* alter. of L *destillare,* fr. *de-* + *stillare* to drip, fr. *stilla* drop] *vt* (14c) **1** : to let fall, exude, or precipitate in drops or in a wet mist **2 a** : to subject to or transform by distillation ⟨~ molasses into rum⟩ **b** : to obtain by or as if by distillation ⟨~ whiskey⟩ ⟨able to ~ humor from personal loss⟩ **c** : to extract the essence of : CONCENTRATE ~ *vi* **1 a** : to fall or materialize in drops or in a fine moisture **b** : to appear slowly or in small quantities at a time **2 a** : to undergo distillation **b** : to perform distillation
dis·til·late \ˈdis-tə-ˌlāt, -lət; di-ˈsti-lət\ *n* (1839) **1** : a liquid product condensed from vapor during distillation **2** : something concentrated or extracted as if by distilling

dis·til·la·tion \ˌdis-tə-ˈlā-shən\ *n* (14c) **1 a :** the process of purifying a liquid by successive evaporation and condensation **b :** a process like distillation ⟨gradual ~ of the truth⟩; *also* **:** an instance of such distilling **2 :** something distilled **:** DISTILLATE 2

dis·till·er \di-ˈsti-lər\ *n* (1562) **:** one that distills esp. alcoholic liquors

dis·till·ery \di-ˈsti-lə-rē, -ˈstil-rē\ *n, pl* **-er·ies** (1758) **:** the works where distilling (as of alcoholic liquors) is done

dis·tinct \di-ˈstiŋ(k)t\ *adj* [ME, fr. L *distinctus,* fr. pp. of *distinguere*] (14c) **1 :** distinguishable to the eye or mind as discrete **:** SEPARATE ⟨a ~ cultural group⟩ ⟨teaching as ~ from research⟩ **2 :** presenting a clear unmistakable impression ⟨a neat ~ handwriting⟩ **3** *archaic* **:** notably decorated **4 a :** NOTABLE ⟨a ~ contribution to scholarship⟩ **b :** readily and unmistakably apprehended ⟨a ~ possibility of snow⟩ ⟨a ~ British accent⟩ — **dis·tinct·ly** \-ˈstiŋ(k)-tlē, -ˈstiŋ-klē\ *adv* — **dis·tinct·ness** \-ˈstiŋ(k)t-nəs, -ˈstiŋk-nəs\ *n*

syn DISTINCT, SEPARATE, DISCRETE mean not being each and every one the same. DISTINCT indicates that something is distinguished by the mind or eye as being apart or different from others ⟨two *distinct* versions⟩. SEPARATE often stresses lack of connection or a difference in identity between two things ⟨*separate* rooms⟩. DISCRETE strongly emphasizes individuality and lack of connection ⟨broke the job down into *discrete* stages⟩. ***syn*** see in addition EVIDENT

dis·tinc·tion \di-ˈstiŋ(k)-shən\ *n* (13c) **1 a** *archaic* **:** DIVISION **b :** CLASS 4 **2 :** the distinguishing of a difference ⟨without ~ as to race, sex, or religion⟩; *also* **:** the difference distinguished ⟨the ~ between *imply* and *infer*⟩ **3 :** something that distinguishes ⟨regional ~*s*⟩ **4 :** the quality or state of being distinguishable ⟨no ~ of facial features in the twins⟩ **5 a :** the quality or state of being distinguished or worthy ⟨a politician of some ~⟩ **b :** special honor or recognition ⟨took a law degree with ~⟩ ⟨won many ~*s*⟩ **c :** an accomplishment that sets one apart ⟨the ~ of being the oldest to win the title⟩

dis·tinc·tive \di-ˈstiŋ(k)-tiv\ *adj* (15c) **1 a :** serving to distinguish ⟨the ~ flight of the crane⟩ **b :** having or giving style or distinction ⟨a ~ table setting⟩ **2 :** capable of making a segment of utterance different in meaning as well as in sound from an otherwise identical utterance ***syn*** see CHARACTERISTIC — **dis·tinc·tive·ly** *adv* — **dis·tinc·tive·ness** *n*

dis·tin·gué \ˌdēs-ˌtaŋ-ˈgā, (ˌ)dis-; di-ˈstaŋ-ˌ\ *adj* [F, fr. pp. of *distinguer*] (1813) **:** distinguished esp. in manner or bearing

dis·tin·guish \di-ˈstiŋ-(g)wish\ *vb* [alter. of ME *distinguen,* fr. AF *distinguer,* fr. L *distinguere,* lit., to separate by pricking, fr. *dis-* + *-stinguere* (akin to L *instigare* to urge on) — more at STICK] *vt* (15c) **1 :** to perceive a difference in **:** mentally separate ⟨so alike they could not be ~*ed*⟩ **2 a :** to mark as separate or different ⟨a policy that ~*es* him from other candidates⟩ **b :** to separate into kinds, classes, or categories ⟨~ words by their part of speech⟩ **c :** to give prominence or distinction to ⟨~*ed* themselves in music⟩ **d :** CHARACTERIZE ⟨recipes ~*ed* by simplicity⟩ **3 a :** DISCERN ⟨~*ed* a light in the distance⟩ **b :** to single out **:** take special notice of ~ *vi* **:** to perceive a difference ⟨~ between right and wrong⟩ — **dis·tin·guish·abil·i·ty** \-ˌstiŋ-(g)wi-shə-ˈbi-lə-tē\ *n* — **dis·tin·guish·able** \-ˈstiŋ-(g)wi-shə-bəl\ *adj* — **dis·tin·guish·ably** \-blē\ *adv*

dis·tin·guished \-(g)wisht\ *adj* (1714) **1 :** marked by eminence, distinction, or excellence ⟨~ leadership⟩ **2 :** befitting an eminent person ⟨a ~ setting⟩ ***syn*** see FAMOUS

Distinguished Conduct Medal *n* (1862) **:** a British military decoration awarded for distinguished conduct in the field

Distinguished Flying Cross *n* (1918) **1 :** a British military decoration awarded for acts of gallantry when flying in operations against an enemy **2 :** a U.S. military decoration awarded for heroism or extraordinary achievement while participating in an aerial flight

Distinguished Service Cross *n* (1914) **1 :** a British military decoration awarded for distinguished service against the enemy **2 :** a U.S. Army decoration awarded for extraordinary heroism during operations against an armed enemy

Distinguished Service Medal *n* (1914) **1 :** a British military decoration awarded for distinguished conduct in war **2 :** a U.S. military decoration awarded for exceptionally meritorious service to the government in a wartime duty of great responsibility

Distinguished Service Order *n* (1886) **:** a British military decoration awarded for special services in action

dis·tort \di-ˈstȯrt\ *vb* [L *distortus,* pp. of *distorquēre,* fr. *dis-* + *torquēre* to twist — more at TORTURE] *vt* (1567) **1 :** to twist out of the true meaning or proportion ⟨~*ed* the facts⟩ **2 :** to twist out of a natural, normal, or original shape or condition ⟨a face ~*ed* by pain⟩; *also* **:** to cause to be perceived unnaturally ⟨the new lights ~*ed* colors⟩ **3 :** PERVERT ⟨~ justice⟩ ~ *vi* **:** to become distorted; *also* **:** to cause a twisting from the true, natural, or normal ***syn*** see DEFORM — **dis·tort·er** *n*

dis·tor·tion \di-ˈstȯr-shən\ *n* (1581) **1 :** the act of distorting **2 :** the quality or state of being distorted **:** a product of distorting: as **a :** a lack of proportionality in an image resulting from defects in the optical system **b :** falsified reproduction of an audio or video signal caused by change in the wave form of the original signal — **dis·tor·tion·al** \-shnəl, -shə-nᵊl\ *adj*

distr *abbr* distribute; distribution

[1]**dis·tract** \di-ˈstrakt, ˈdis-ˌtrakt\ *adj* (14c) *archaic* **:** INSANE, MAD

[2]**dis·tract** \di-ˈstrakt\ *vt* [ME, fr. L *distractus,* pp. of *distrahere,* lit., to draw apart, fr. *dis-* + *trahere* to draw] (14c) **1 a :** to turn aside **:** DIVERT ⟨refused to be ~*ed* from her purpose⟩ **b :** to draw or direct (as one's attention) to a different object or in different directions at the same time ⟨was ~*ed* by a sudden noise⟩ **2 :** to stir up or confuse with conflicting emotions or motives ***syn*** see PUZZLE — **dis·tract·i·bil·i·ty** \-ˌstrak-tə-ˈbi-lə-tē\ *n* — **dis·tract·ible** *also* **dis·tract·able** \-ˈstrak-tə-bəl\ *adj* — **dis·tract·ing·ly** \-tiŋ-lē\ *adv*

dis·tract·ed *adj* (1576) **1 :** mentally confused, troubled, or remote **2 :** maddened or deranged esp. by grief or anxiety ***syn*** see ABSTRACTED — **dis·tract·ed·ly** *adv*

dis·trac·tion \di-ˈstrak-shən\ *n* (15c) **1 :** the act of distracting or the state of being distracted; *esp* **:** mental confusion ⟨driven to ~⟩ **2 :** something that distracts; *esp* **:** AMUSEMENT ⟨a harmless ~⟩ — **dis·trac·tive** \-ˈstrak-tiv\ *adj*

dis·train \di-ˈstrān\ *vb* [ME *distreynen,* fr. AF *destreindre,* fr. ML *distringere,* fr. L, to draw apart, detain, fr. *dis-* + *stringere* to bind tight — more at STRAIN] *vt* (14c) **1 :** to force or compel to satisfy an obligation by means of a distress **2 :** to seize by distress ~ *vi* **:** to levy a distress — **dis·train·able** \-ˈstrā-nə-bəl\ *adj* — **dis·train·er** \-ˈstrā-nər\ *also* **dis·train·or** \-ˈstrā-nər, -ˌstrā-ˈnȯr\ *n*

dis·traint \di-ˈstrānt\ *n* [*distrain* + *-t* (as in *constraint*)] (ca. 1736) **:** the act or action of distraining

dis·trait \di-ˈstrā\ *adj* [ME, fr. AF *destreit,* fr. L *distractus*] (15c) **:** apprehensively divided or withdrawn in attention **:** DISTRACTED

dis·traite \di-ˈstrāt\ *adj* (15c) **:** DISTRAIT — used esp. of women

dis·traught \di-ˈstrȯt\ *adj* [ME, modif. of L *distractus*] (14c) **1 :** agitated with doubt or mental conflict or pain ⟨~ mourners⟩ **2 :** mentally deranged **:** CRAZED ⟨as if thou wert ~ and mad with terror —Shak.⟩ — **dis·traught·ly** *adv*

[1]**dis·tress** \di-ˈstres\ *n* [ME *destresse,* fr. AF *destresce,* fr. VL **districtia,* fr. L *districtus,* pp. of *distringere*] (13c) **1 a :** seizure and detention of the goods of another as pledge or to obtain satisfaction of a claim by the sale of the goods seized **b :** something that is distrained **2 a :** pain or suffering affecting the body, a bodily part, or the mind **:** TROUBLE ⟨gastric ~⟩ **b :** a painful situation **:** MISFORTUNE **3 :** a state of danger or desperate need ⟨a ship in ~⟩

syn DISTRESS, SUFFERING, MISERY, AGONY mean the state of being in great trouble. DISTRESS implies an external and usu. temporary cause of great physical or mental strain and stress ⟨the hurricane put everyone in great *distress*⟩. SUFFERING implies conscious endurance of pain or distress ⟨the *suffering* of famine victims⟩. MISERY stresses the unhappiness attending esp. sickness, poverty, or loss ⟨the homeless live with *misery* every day⟩. AGONY suggests pain too intense to be borne ⟨in *agony* over the death of their child⟩.

[2]**distress** *vt* (14c) **1 :** to subject to great strain or difficulties ⟨homes ~*ed* by poverty⟩ **2** *archaic* **:** to force or overcome by inflicting pain **3 :** to cause to worry or be troubled **:** UPSET ⟨don't let the news ~ you⟩ **4 :** to mar (as clothing or wood) deliberately to give an effect of age ⟨a ~*ed* table⟩ — **dis·tress·ing·ly** \-ˈstre-siŋ-lē\ *adv*

[3]**distress** *adj* (1926) **1 :** offered for sale at a loss ⟨~ merchandise⟩ **2 :** involving distress goods ⟨a ~ sale⟩

dis·tress·ed \-ˈstrest\ *adj* (1613) **:** of, relating to, or experiencing economic decline or difficulty ⟨federal grants for ~ cities⟩

dis·tress·ful \di-ˈstres-fəl\ *adj* (1591) **:** causing distress **:** full of distress — **dis·tress·ful·ly** \-fə-lē\ *adv* — **dis·tress·ful·ness** *n*

dis·trib·u·tary \di-ˈstri-byə-ˌter-ē, -ˌte-rē\ *n, pl* **-tar·ies** (1863) **:** a river branch flowing away from the main stream

dis·trib·ute \di-ˈstri-byüt *also* -byət *Brit also* ˈdis-tri-ˌbyüt\ *vb* **-ut·ed; -ut·ing** [ME, fr. L *distributus,* pp. of *distribuere,* fr. *dis-* + *tribuere* to allot — more at TRIBUTE] *vt* (15c) **1 :** to divide among several or many **:** APPORTION ⟨~ expenses⟩ **2 a :** to spread out so as to cover something **:** SCATTER **b :** to give out or deliver esp. to members of a group ⟨~ newspapers⟩ ⟨~ leaflets⟩ **c :** to place or position so as to be properly apportioned over or throughout an area ⟨200 pounds *distributed* on a 6-foot frame⟩ **d :** to use (a term) so as to convey information about every member of the class named ⟨the proposition "all men are mortal" ~*s* "man" but not "mortal"⟩ **3 a :** to divide or separate esp. into kinds **b :** to return the units of (as typeset matter) to storage **4 :** to use in or as an operation so as to be mathematically distributive ~ *vi* **:** to be mathematically distributive ⟨multiplication ~*s* over addition⟩ — **dis·trib·u·tee** \dis-ˌtri-byü-ˈtē\ *n*

syn DISTRIBUTE, DISPENSE, DIVIDE, DEAL, DOLE OUT mean to give out, usu. in shares, to each member of a group. DISTRIBUTE implies an apportioning by separation of something into parts, units, or amounts ⟨*distributed* food to the needy⟩. DISPENSE suggests the giving of a carefully weighed or measured portion to each of a group according to due or need ⟨*dispensed* wisdom to the students⟩. DIVIDE stresses the separation of a whole into parts and implies that the parts are equal ⟨three charitable groups *divided* the proceeds⟩. DEAL emphasizes the allotment of something piece by piece ⟨*deal* out equipment and supplies⟩. DOLE OUT implies a carefully measured portion of something that is often in short supply ⟨*doled out* what little food there was⟩.

distributed *adj* (1968) **1 :** characterized by a statistical distribution of a particular kind ⟨a normally ~ random variable⟩ **2 :** of, relating to, or being a computer network in which at least some of the processing is done by the individual workstations and information is shared by and often stored at the workstations

dis·tri·bu·tion \ˌdis-trə-ˈbyü-shən\ *n* (14c) **1 a :** the act or process of distributing **b :** the apportionment by a court of the personal property of an intestate **2 a :** the position, arrangement, or frequency of occurrence (as of the members of a group) over an area or throughout a space or unit of time **b :** the natural geographic range of an organism **3 a :** something distributed: as **(1) :** a sum of money withdrawn from a fund (as a retirement fund) and given to the beneficiary or holder of the fund **(2) :** DIVIDEND 1a **b (1) :** FREQUENCY DISTRIBUTION **(2) :** PROBABILITY FUNCTION **(3) :** PROBABILITY DENSITY FUNCTION 2 **4 :** the pattern of branching and termination of a ramifying structure (as a nerve) **5 :** the marketing or merchandising of commodities — **dis·tri·bu·tion·al** \-shnəl, -shə-nᵊl\ *adj*

distribution function *n* (ca. 1909) **:** CUMULATIVE DISTRIBUTION FUNCTION

dis·trib·u·tive \di-ˈstri-byü-tiv, -byə-\ *adj* (15c) **1 :** of or relating to distribution: as **a :** dealing a proper share to each of a group **b :** diffusing more or less evenly **2** *of a word* **:** referring singly and without exception to the members of a group ⟨*each, either,* and *none* are ~⟩ **3 a :** being an operation (as multiplication in $a(b + c) = ab + ac$) that produces the same result when operating on the whole mathematical expression as when operating on each part and collecting the results **b :** being or relating to a rule or property concerning a distributive operation ⟨the ~ property of multiplication with respect to addition⟩ — **dis·trib·u·tive·ly** *adv* — **dis·trib·u·tiv·i·ty** \-ˌstri-byü-ˈti-və-tē\ *n*

dis·trib·u·tor \di-ˈstri-byü-tər, -byə-\ *n* (1526) **1 :** one that distributes **2 :** one that markets a commodity; *esp* **:** WHOLESALER **3 :** an apparatus for directing the secondary current from the induction coil to the various spark plugs of an engine in their proper firing order

[1]**dis·trict** \ˈdis-(ˌ)trikt\ *n, often attrib* [F, fr. ML *districtus* jurisdiction, district, fr. *distringere* to distrain — more at DISTRAIN] (1611) **1 a :** a territorial division (as for administrative or electoral purposes) **b :** the basic administrative unit for local government in Northern Ireland **2**

: an area, region, or section with a distinguishing character ⟨a shopping ~⟩

[2]**district** *vt* (1792) : to divide or organize into districts

district attorney *n* (1789) : the prosecuting officer of a judicial district

district court *n* (1789) : a trial court that has jurisdiction over certain cases within a specific judicial district

[1]**dis·trust** \(ˌ)dis-ˈtrəst\ *n* (1513) : the lack or absence of trust

[2]**distrust** *vt* (1548) : to have no trust or confidence in

dis·trust·ful \-ˈtrəs(t)-fəl\ *adj* (1589) : having or showing distrust — **dis·trust·ful·ly** \-fə-lē\ *adv* — **dis·trust·ful·ness** *n*

dis·turb \di-ˈstərb\ *vb* [ME *disturben, destourben,* fr. AF & L; AF *destorber,* fr. L *disturbare,* fr. *dis-* + *turbare* to throw into disorder, fr. *turba* disorder — more at TURBID] *vt* (14c) **1 a :** to interfere with : INTERRUPT ⟨~*ing* the flow of traffic⟩ **b :** to alter the position or arrangement of ⟨the items on her desk had been ~*ed*⟩ **c :** to upset the natural and esp. the ecological balance or relations of ⟨wetlands ~*ed* by development⟩ **2 a :** to destroy the tranquillity or composure of ⟨the noisy lawnmower ~*ed* their sleep⟩ **b :** to throw into disorder **c :** ALARM **d :** to put to inconvenience ⟨sorry to ~ you at such a late hour⟩ ~ *vi* **:** to cause disturbance ***syn*** see DISCOMPOSE — **dis·turb·er** *n* — **dis·turb·ing·ly** \-ˈstər-biŋ-lē\ *adv*

dis·tur·bance \di-ˈstər-bən(t)s\ *n* (13c) **1 :** the act of disturbing : the state of being disturbed **2 :** a local variation from the average or normal wind conditions

dis·turbed *adj* (1904) : showing symptoms of emotional illness ⟨~ children⟩ ⟨~ behavior⟩

di·sub·sti·tut·ed \(ˌ)dī-ˈsəb-stə-ˌtü-təd, -ˌtyü-\ *adj* (ca. 1909) : having two substituent atoms or groups in a molecule

di·sul·fide \(ˌ)dī-ˈsəl-ˌfīd\ *n* (1869) **1 :** a compound containing two atoms of sulfur combined with an element or radical **2 :** an organic compound containing the divalent group SS composed of two sulfur atoms

di·sul·fi·ram \dī-ˈsəl-fə-ˌram\ *n* [*disulf*ide + *thi*ourea + *am*yl] (1952) : a compound $C_{10}H_{20}N_2S_4$ that causes a severe physiological reaction to alcohol and is used esp. in the treatment of alcoholism

di·sul·fo·ton \dī-ˈsəl-fə-ˌtän\ *n* [*di-* + *sulfo-* + *-ton* (prob. fr. *thion-*)] (1965) : a toxic organophosphorus systemic insecticide $C_8H_{19}O_2PS_3$

dis·union \(ˌ)dis-ˈyü-nyən, dish-\ *n* (15c) **1 :** the termination of union : SEPARATION **2 :** DISUNITY — **dis·union·ist** \-nyə-nist\ *n*

dis·unite \(ˌ)dis-yü-ˈnīt, -yə-, dish-\ *vt* (1598) : DIVIDE, SEPARATE

dis·uni·ty \(ˌ)dis-ˈyü-nə-tē, dish-\ *n* (1632) : lack of unity; *esp* : DISSENSION

[1]**dis·use** \(ˌ)dis-ˈyüz, dish-\ *vt* (15c) : to discontinue the use or practice of

[2]**dis·use** \-ˈyüs\ *n* (15c) : cessation of use or practice

dis·used \-ˈyüzd\ *adj* (1611) : no longer used or occupied : ABANDONED ⟨~ buildings⟩

dis·util·i·ty \(ˌ)dis-yü-ˈti-lə-tē, -yə-, dish-\ *n* (1879) : the state or fact of being counterproductive

[1]**dis·val·ue** \(ˌ)dis-ˈval-(ˌ)yü\ *vt* (1603) **1** *archaic* : UNDERVALUE, DEPRECIATE **2 :** to consider of little value

[2]**disvalue** *n* (1603) **1** *obs* : DISREGARD, DISESTEEM **2 :** a negative value

di·syl·la·ble *also* **dis·syl·la·ble** \ˈdī-ˌsi-lə-bəl, (ˌ)dī-ˈsil-; ˈdi-ˌsil-, (ˌ)di(s)-ˈsil-\ *n* [part trans. of MF *dissilabe,* fr. L *disyllabus* having two syllables, fr. Gk *disyllabos,* fr. *di-* + *syllabē* syllable] (1589) : a linguistic form consisting of two syllables — **di·syl·lab·ic** \ˌdī-sə-ˈla-bik, ˌdi(s)-sə-\ *adj*

dit \ˈdit\ *n* [imit.] (1940) : a dot in radio or telegraphic code

[1]**ditch** \ˈdich\ *n* [ME *dich,* fr. OE *dīc* dike, ditch; akin to MHG *tīch* pond, dike] (bef. 12c) : a long narrow excavation dug in the earth (as for drainage)

[2]**ditch** *vt* (14c) **1 a :** to enclose with a ditch **b :** to dig a ditch in **2 :** to make a forced landing of (an airplane) on water **3 a :** to get rid of : DISCARD ⟨~ an old car⟩ **b :** to end association with : LEAVE ⟨~*ed* school⟩ ⟨his girlfriend ~*ed* him⟩ ~ *vi* **1 :** to dig a ditch **2 :** to crash-land at sea

ditch·dig·ger \-ˌdi-gər\ *n* (1843) **1 :** one that digs ditches **2 :** one employed at menial and usu. hard physical labor

dite \ˈdīt\ *n* [var. of *doit*] (ca. 1877) *dial* : MITE, BIT

[1]**dith·er** \ˈdi-thər\ *vi* **dith·ered; dith·er·ing** \-th(ə-)riŋ\ [ME *didderen*] (15c) **1 :** SHIVER, TREMBLE **2 :** to act nervously or indecisively : VACILLATE — **dith·er·er** \-thər-ər\ *n*

[2]**dither** *n* (1819) : a highly nervous, excited, or agitated state : EXCITEMENT, CONFUSION — **dith·ery** \ˈdi-thə-rē\ *adj*

di·thio·car·ba·mate \ˌdī-ˌthī-ō-ˈkär-bə-ˌmāt\ *n* (1929) : any of several sulfur analogs of the carbamates including some used as fungicides

dith·y·ramb \ˈdi-thi-ˌram(b)\ *n, pl* **-rambs** \-ˌramz\ [Gk *dithyrambos*] (ca. 1647) **1 :** a usu. short poem in an inspired wild irregular strain **2 :** a statement or writing in an exalted or enthusiastic vein — **dith·y·ram·bic** \ˌdi-thi-ˈram-bik\ *adj* — **dith·y·ram·bi·cal·ly** \-bi-k(ə-)lē\ *adv*

di·tran·si·tive \ˌdī-ˈtran(t)-sə-tiv, -ˈtran-zə-\ *adj* (1972) : able to take both a direct and an indirect object ⟨a ~ verb⟩ — **ditransitive** *n*

dit·ta·ny \ˈdi-tə-nē\ *n, pl* **-nies** [ME *ditoyne,* detony fr. AF *ditayne,* fr. L *dictamnum,* fr. Gk *diktamnon*] (12c) **1 :** a pink-flowered mint (*Origanum dictamnus*) that is native to Crete **2 :** a No. American mint (*Cunila origanoides*) having purplish or white flowers

[1]**dit·to** \ˈdi-(ˌ)tō\ *n, pl* **dittos** [It *ditto, detto,* pp. of *dire* to say, fr. L *dicere* — more at DICTION] (ca. 1639) **1 :** a thing mentioned previously or above — used to avoid repeating a word; often symbolized by inverted commas or apostrophes **2 :** a ditto mark

[2]**ditto** *adj* (1776) : having the same characteristics : SIMILAR

[3]**ditto** *adv* (1706) : as before or aforesaid : in the same manner

[4]**ditto** *vt* (1725) **1 :** to repeat the action or statement of **2** [fr. *Ditto,* a trademark] : to copy (as printed matter) on a duplicator

dit·ty \ˈdi-tē\ *n, pl* **ditties** [ME *ditee,* fr. AF *dité* story, song, fr. pp. of *diter* to compose, fr. L *dictare* to dictate, compose] (14c) : an esp. simple and unaffected song

ditty bag *n* [origin unknown] (ca. 1860) : a bag used esp. by sailors to hold small articles (as needles and thread)

ditty box *n* (ca. 1880) : a box used for the same purpose as a ditty bag

ditz \ˈdits\ *n* (1982) : a ditzy person

dit·zy *or* **dit·sy** \ˈdit-sē\ *adj* **ditz·i·er** *or* **dits·i·er; -est** [origin unknown] (1973) : eccentrically silly, giddy, or inane : DIZZY — **dit·zi·ness** *or* **dit·si·ness** \-nəs\ *n*

di·ure·sis \ˌdī-yə-ˈrē-səs\ *n, pl* **-ure·ses** \-ˌsēz\ [NL] (ca. 1681) : an increased excretion of urine

di·uret·ic \ˌdī-yə-ˈre-tik\ *adj* [ME *duretik, diuretic,* fr. LL *diureticus,* fr. Gk *diourētikos,* fr. *diourein* to urinate, fr. *dia-* + *ourein* to urinate — more at URINE] (14c) : tending to increase the excretion of urine ⟨~ drugs⟩ — **diuretic** *n* — **di·uret·i·cal·ly** \-ti-k(ə-)lē\ *adv*

[1]**di·ur·nal** \dī-ˈər-nᵊl\ *adj* [ME, fr. L *diurnalis* — more at JOURNAL] (14c) **1 a :** recurring every day ⟨~ tasks⟩ **b :** having a daily cycle ⟨~ tides⟩ **2 a :** of, relating to, or occurring in the daytime ⟨the city's ~ noises⟩ **b :** active chiefly in the daytime ⟨~ animals⟩ **c :** opening during the day and closing at night ⟨~ flowers⟩ — **di·ur·nal·ly** \-nᵊl-ē\ *adv*

[2]**diurnal** *n* (1600) **1** *archaic* : DIARY, DAYBOOK **2 :** JOURNAL 2a

di·u·ron \ˈdī-yə-ˌrän\ *n* [*di*chlor- + *ur*ea + *-on* (as in *parathion*)] (1957) : a persistent herbicide $C_9H_{10}Cl_2N_2O$ used esp. to control annual weeds

div *abbr* **1** divided **2** dividend **3** division **4** divorced

di·va \ˈdē-və\ *n, pl* **divas** *or* **di·ve** \-(ˌ)vā\ [It, lit., goddess, fr. L, fem. of *divus* divine, god — more at DEITY] (1883) **1 a :** PRIMA DONNA 1 **b :** PRIMA DONNA 2 **2 :** a usu. glamorous and successful female performer or personality ⟨a fashion ~⟩; *esp* : a popular female singer ⟨pop ~*s*⟩

di·va·gate \ˈdī-və-ˌgāt, ˈdi-\ *vi* **-gat·ed; -gat·ing** [LL *divagatus,* pp. of *divagari,* fr. L *dis-* + *vagari* to wander — more at VAGARY] (1599) : to wander or stray from a course or subject : DIVERGE, DIGRESS — **di·va·ga·tion** \ˌdī-və-ˈgā-shən, ˌdi-\ *n*

di·va·lent \(ˌ)dī-ˈvā-lənt\ *adj* (1868) : having a chemical valence of two; *also* : bonded to two other atoms or groups

di·van \di-ˈvan, ˈdī-ˌvan, *esp in senses 1, 2, & 4 also* di-ˈvän, dī-ˈvan\ *n* [Turk, fr. Pers *dīvān* account book] (1586) **1 a :** the privy council of the Ottoman Empire **b :** COUNCIL **2 :** a council chamber **3 :** a large couch usu. without back or arms often designed for use as a bed **4 :** a collection of poems in Persian or Arabic usu. by one author

di·var·i·cate \dī-ˈver-ə-ˌkāt, də-, -ˈva-rə-\ *vt* **-cat·ed; -cat·ing** [L *divaricatus,* pp. of *divaricare,* fr. *dis-* + *varicare* to straddle — more at PREVARICATE] (1673) : to spread apart : branch off : DIVERGE

di·var·i·ca·tion \(ˌ)dī-ˌver-ə-ˈkā-shən, də-, -ˌva-rə-\ *n* (1578) **1 :** the action, process, or fact of divaricating **2 :** a divergence of opinion

[1]**dive** \ˈdīv\ *vb* **dived** \ˈdīvd\ *or* **dove** \ˈdōv\; **dived** *also* **dove; div·ing** [ME *diven, duven,* fr. OE *dȳfan* to dip & *dūfan* to dive; akin to OE *dyppan* to dip — more at DIP] *vi* (bef. 12c) **1 a :** to plunge into water intentionally and esp. headfirst; *also* : to execute a dive **b :** SUBMERGE ⟨the submarine *dived*⟩ **2 a :** to come or drop down precipitously : PLUNGE ⟨the temperature is *diving*⟩ **b :** to plunge one's hand into something **c** *of an airplane* : to descend in a dive **3 a :** to plunge into some matter or activity ⟨she *dove* into her studies⟩ **b :** to plunge or dash for some place ⟨*diving* for cover⟩; *also* : to lunge esp. in order to seize something ⟨*dove* for the ball⟩ ~ *vt* **1 :** to thrust into something **2 :** to cause to dive ⟨~ a submarine⟩

usage *Dive,* which was orig. a weak verb, developed a past tense *dove,* prob. by analogy with verbs like *drive, drove. Dove* exists in some British dialects and has become the standard past tense esp. in speech in some parts of Canada. In the U.S. *dived* and *dove* are both widespread in speech as past tense and past participle, with *dove* less common than *dived* in the south Midland area, and *dived* less common than *dove* in the Northern and north Midland areas. In writing, the past tense *dived* is usual in British English and somewhat more common in American English. *Dove* seems relatively rare as a past participle in writing.

[2]**dive** *n* (1700) **1 :** the act or an instance of diving: as **a** (1) : a plunge into water executed in a prescribed manner (2) : a submerging of a submarine (3) : a steep descent of an airplane at greater than the maximum horizontal speed **b :** a sharp decline **2 :** a shabby and disreputable establishment (as a bar or nightclub) **3 :** a faked knockout — usu. used in the phrase *take a dive* **4 :** an offensive play in football in which the ballcarrier plunges into the line for short yardage

dive–bomb \ˈdīv-ˌbäm\ *vt* (1935) : to bomb from an airplane by making a steep dive toward the target before releasing the bomb — **dive–bomb·er** *n*

div·er \ˈdī-vər\ *n* (1506) **1 :** one that dives **2 a :** a person who stays underwater for long periods by having air supplied from the surface or by carrying a supply of compressed air **b :** any of various birds that obtain food by diving in water; *esp* : LOON

di·verge \də-ˈvərj, dī-\ *vb* **di·verged; di·verg·ing** [ML *divergere,* fr. L *dis-* + *vergere* to incline — more at WRENCH] *vi* (1665) **1 a :** to move or extend in different directions from a common point : draw apart ⟨*diverging* roads⟩ **b :** to become or be different in character or form : differ in opinion **2 :** to turn aside from a path or course : DEVIATE **3 :** to be mathematically divergent ~ *vt* : DEFLECT ***syn*** see SWERVE

di·ver·gence \-ˈvər-jən(t)s\ *n* (1656) **1 a :** a drawing apart (as of lines extending from a common center) **b :** DIFFERENCE, DISAGREEMENT **c :** the acquisition of dissimilar characters by related organisms in unlike environments **2 :** a deviation from a course or standard **3 :** the condition of being mathematically divergent

di·ver·gen·cy \-jən(t)-sē\ *n, pl* **-cies** (1709) : DIVERGENCE

di·ver·gent \-jənt\ *adj* [L *divergent-, divergens,* prp. of *divergere*] (1696) **1 a :** diverging from each other ⟨~ paths⟩ **b :** differing from each other or from a standard ⟨the ~ interests of capital and labor⟩ **2 :** relating to or being an infinite sequence that does not have a limit or an infinite series whose partial sums do not have a limit **3 :** causing divergence of rays ⟨a ~ lens⟩ ***syn*** see DIFFERENT — **di·ver·gent·ly** *adv*

[1]**di·vers** \ˈdī-vərz\ *adj* [ME *divers, diverse*] (14c) : VARIOUS

[2]**divers** *pron, pl in constr* (1528) : an indefinite number more than one ⟨with ~ of the leaves torn and stitched across —Charles Dickens⟩

di·verse \dī-ˈvərs, də-ˈ, ˈdī-ˌ\ *adj* [ME *divers, diverse,* fr. AF & L; AF *divers,* fr. L *diversus,* fr. pp. of *divertere*] (14c) **1 :** differing from one another : UNLIKE ⟨people with ~ interests⟩ **2 :** composed of distinct or unlike elements or qualities ⟨a ~ population⟩ ***syn*** see DIFFERENT — **di·verse·ly** *adv* — **di·verse·ness** *n*

di·ver·si·fy \də-ˈvər-sə-ˌfī, dī-\ *vb* **-fied; -fy·ing** *vt* (15c) **1 :** to make diverse : give variety to ⟨~ a course of study⟩ **2 :** to balance (as an investment portfolio) defensively by dividing funds among securities of different industries or of different classes **3 :** to increase the variety of the products of ⟨~ a business⟩ ~ *vi* **1 :** to produce variety **2 :** to engage in varied operations — **di·ver·si·fi·ca·tion** \-ˌvər-sə-fə-ˈkā-shən\ *n* — **di·ver·si·fi·er** \-ˈvər-sə-ˌfī(-ə)r\ *n*

di·ver·sion \də-ˈvər-zhən, dī-, -shən\ *n* (1600) **1 :** the act or an instance of diverting from a course, activity, or use : DEVIATION ⟨bad weather forced the ~ of several flights⟩ **2 :** something that diverts or amuses : PASTIME **3 :** an attack or feint that draws the attention and force of an enemy from the point of the principal operation **4** *Brit* **:** a temporary traffic detour

di·ver·sion·ary \də-ˈvər-zhə-ˌner-ē, dī-, -shə-\ *adj* (1846) **:** tending to draw attention away from the principal concern : being a diversion

di·ver·sion·ist \-zhə-nəst, -shə-\ *n* (1937) **1 :** one engaged in diversionary activities **2 :** one characterized by political deviation

di·ver·si·ty \də-ˈvər-sə-tē, dī-\ *n, pl* **-ties** (14c) **1 :** the condition of being diverse : VARIETY; *esp* **:** the inclusion of diverse people (as people of different races or cultures) in a group or organization ⟨programs intended to promote ~ in schools⟩ **2 :** an instance of being diverse ⟨a ~ of opinion⟩

di·vert \də-ˈvərt, dī-\ *vb* [ME, fr. MF & L; MF *divertir,* fr. L *divertere* to turn in opposite directions, fr. *dis-* + *vertere* to turn — more at WORTH] *vi* (15c) **:** to turn aside : DEVIATE ⟨studied law but ~*ed* to diplomacy⟩ ~ *vt* **1 a :** to turn from one course or use to another : DEFLECT ⟨~ traffic to a side street⟩ **b :** DISTRACT ⟨trying to ~ her attention⟩ **2 :** to give pleasure to esp. by distracting the attention from what burdens or distresses ***syn*** see AMUSE

di·ver·tic·u·li·tis \ˌdī-vər-ˌti-kyə-ˈlī-təs\ *n* [NL] (ca. 1900) **:** inflammation of a diverticulum

di·ver·tic·u·lo·sis \ˌdī-vər-ˌti-kyə-ˈlō-səs\ *n* [NL] (1917) **:** an intestinal disorder characterized by the presence of many diverticula

di·ver·tic·u·lum \ˌdī-vər-ˈti-kyə-ləm\ *n, pl* **-la** \-lə\ [NL, fr. L, bypath, prob. alter. of *deverticulum,* fr. *devertere* to turn aside, fr. *de-* + *vertere*] (ca. 1819) **1 :** an abnormal pouch or sac opening from a hollow organ (as the intestine or bladder) **2 :** a pocket or closed branch opening off a main passage — **di·ver·tic·u·lar** \-kyə-lər\ *adj*

di·ver·ti·men·to \di-ˌvər-tə-ˈmen-(ˌ)tō, -ˌver-\ *n, pl* **-men·ti** \-ˈmen-(ˌ)tē\ *or* **-mentos** [It, lit., diversion, fr. *divertire* to divert, amuse, fr. L *divertere*] (1823) **1 :** an instrumental chamber work in several movements usu. light in character **2 :** DIVERTISSEMENT 1

di·vert·ing \də-ˈvər-tiŋ, dī-\ *adj* (1655) **:** providing amusement or entertainment ⟨a ~ evening⟩ — **di·vert·ing·ly** *adv*

di·ver·tisse·ment \di-ˈvər-təs-mənt, -təz-, *F* dē-ver-tē-smäⁿ\ *n, pl* **divertissements** \-mən(t)s, -smäⁿ(z)\ [F, lit., diversion, fr. *divertiss-* (stem of *divertir*)] (ca. 1728) **1 :** a dance sequence or short ballet usu. used as an interlude **2 :** DIVERTIMENTO 1 **3 :** DIVERSION, ENTERTAINMENT

Di·ves \ˈdī-(ˌ)vēz\ *n* [ME, fr. L, rich, rich man; misunderstood as a proper name in Lk 16:19] (14c) **:** a rich man

di·vest \dī-ˈvest, də-\ *vt* [alter. of *devest*] (1623) **1 a :** to deprive or dispossess esp. of property, authority, or title **b :** to undress or strip esp. of clothing, ornament, or equipment **c :** RID, FREE **2 :** to take away from a person — **di·vest·ment** \-ˈves(t)-mənt\ *n*

di·ves·ti·ture \dī-ˈves-tə-ˌchu̇r, -chər, də-, *chiefly Southern* -t(y)u̇(ə)r\ *n* [*divest* + *-iture* (as in *investiture*)] (1601) **1 :** the act of divesting **2 :** the compulsory transfer of title or disposal of interests (as stock in a corporation) upon government order

¹**di·vide** \də-ˈvīd\ *vb* **di·vid·ed; di·vid·ing** [ME, fr. L *dividere,* fr. *dis-* + *-videre* to separate — more at WIDOW] *vt* (14c) **1 a :** to separate into two or more parts, areas, or groups ⟨~ the city into wards⟩ **b :** to separate into classes, categories, or divisions ⟨~ history into epochs⟩ **c :** CLEAVE, PART ⟨a ship *dividing* the waves⟩ **2 a :** to separate into portions and give out in shares : DISTRIBUTE ⟨~ profits⟩ **b :** to possess, enjoy, or make use of in common ⟨~ the blame⟩ **c :** APPORTION ⟨~*s* her time between the office and home⟩ **3 a :** to cause to be separate, distinct, or apart from one another ⟨fields *divided* by stone walls⟩ **b :** to separate into opposing sides or parties ⟨the issues that ~ us⟩ **c :** to cause (a parliamentary body) to vote by division **4 a :** to subject (a number or quantity) to the operation of finding how many times it contains another number or quantity ⟨~ 42 by 14⟩ **b :** to be used as a divisor with respect to (a dividend) ⟨4 ~*s* 16 evenly⟩ **c :** to use as a divisor — used with *into* ⟨~ 14 into 42⟩ ~ *vi* **1 :** to perform mathematical division **2 a (1) :** to undergo replication, multiplication, fission, or separation into parts **(2) :** to branch out **b :** to become separated or disunited esp. in opinion or interest ***syn*** see SEPARATE, DISTRIBUTE — **di·vid·able** \-ˈvī-də-bəl\ *adj*

²**divide** *n* (1642) **1 :** an act of dividing **2 a :** a dividing ridge between drainage areas **b :** a point or line of division or disagreement

divided *adj* (14c) **1 a :** separated into parts or pieces **b** *of a leaf* **:** cut into distinct parts by incisions extending to the base or to the midrib **c :** having a barrier (as a guardrail) to separate lanes of traffic going in opposite directions ⟨a ~ highway⟩ **2 a :** disagreeing with each other : DISUNITED **b :** directed or moved toward conflicting interests, states, or objects ⟨~ loyalties⟩ **3 :** separated by distance ⟨familiar objects from which she had never dreamed of being ~ —James Joyce⟩ — **di·vid·ed·ly** \də-ˈvī-dəd-lē\ *adv* — **di·vid·ed·ness** \-nəs\ *n*

div·i·dend \ˈdi-və-ˌdend, -dənd\ *n* [ME *divident,* fr. L *dividendus,* gerundive of *dividere*] (15c) **1 :** an individual share of something distributed: as **a :** a share in a pro rata distribution (as of profits) to stockholders **b :** a share of surplus allocated to a policyholder in a participating insurance policy **2 a :** a resultant return or reward ⟨our efforts are finally paying ~*s*⟩ **b :** BONUS **3 a :** a number to be divided **b :** a sum or fund to be divided and distributed — **div·i·dend·less** \-ləs\ *adj*

di·vid·er \də-ˈvī-dər\ *n* (1534) **1 :** one that divides **2** *pl* **:** an instrument for measuring or marking (as in dividing lines) **3 :** something serving as a partition between separate spaces or areas ⟨a highway ~⟩

di·vi–di·vi \ˌdē-vē-ˈdē-vē, ˌdi-vē-ˈdi-vē\ *n* [AmerSp *dividivi,* prob. fr. Cumaná (extinct Cariban language of northern Venezuela) or a cognate Cariban word] (ca. 1837) **:** a small tropical American tree (*Caesalpinia coriaria*) of the legume family with twisted astringent pods that contain a large proportion of tannin

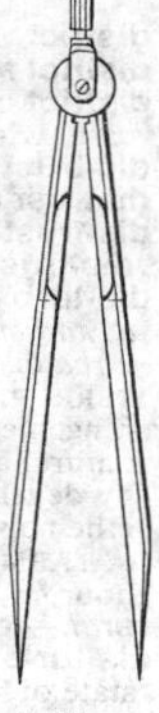

dividers

div·i·na·tion \ˌdi-və-ˈnā-shən\ *n* [ME *divinacioun,* fr. L *divination-, divinatio,* fr. *divinare*] (14c) **1 :** the art or practice that seeks to foresee or foretell future events or discover hidden knowledge usu. by the interpretation of omens or by the aid of supernatural powers **2 :** unusual insight : intuitive perception — **di·vi·na·to·ry** \də-ˈvi-nə-ˌtȯr-ē, də-ˈvī-nə-, ˈdi-və-nə-\ *adj*

¹**di·vine** \də-ˈvīn\ *adj* **di·vin·er; -est** [ME *divin,* fr. AF, fr. L *divinus,* fr. *divus* god — more at DEITY] (14c) **1 a :** of, relating to, or proceeding directly from God or a god ⟨~ love⟩ **b :** being a deity ⟨the ~ Savior⟩ **c :** directed to a deity ⟨~ worship⟩ **2 a :** supremely good : SUPERB ⟨the pie was ~⟩ **b :** HEAVENLY, GODLIKE — **di·vine·ly** *adv*

²**divine** *n* [ME, fr. ML *divinus,* fr. L, soothsayer, fr. *divinus,* adj.] (14c) **1 :** CLERGYMAN **2 :** THEOLOGIAN

³**divine** *vb* **di·vined; di·vin·ing** [ME, fr. AF & L; AF *deviner,* fr. L *divinare,* fr. *divinus,* n.] *vt* (14c) **1 :** to discover by intuition or insight : INFER ⟨~ the truth⟩ **2 :** to discover or locate (as water or minerals underground) usu. by means of a divining rod ~ *vi* **1 :** to practice divination : PROPHESY **2 :** to perceive intuitively ***syn*** see FORESEE

Divine Liturgy *n* (1640) **:** the eucharistic rite of Eastern churches

Divine Office *n* (15c) **:** the office for the canonical hours of prayer that priests and religious say daily

di·vin·er \də-ˈvī-nər\ *n* (14c) **1 :** a person who practices divination : SOOTHSAYER **2 :** a person who divines the location of water or minerals

divine right *n* (ca. 1600) **:** the right of a sovereign to rule as set forth by the theory of government that holds that a monarch receives the right to rule directly from God and not from the people

divine service *n* (14c) **:** a service of Christian worship; *specif* **:** such a service that is not sacramental in character

diving beetle *n* (ca. 1889) **:** any of various predatory aquatic beetles (family Dytiscidae) that breathe while submerged using air trapped under their elytra

diving bell *n* (1661) **:** a diving apparatus consisting of a container open only at the bottom and supplied with compressed air by a hose

diving board *n* (1891) **:** SPRINGBOARD 1

diving duck *n* (1813) **:** any of various ducks (as a bufflehead) that frequent deep waters and obtain their food by diving

diving suit *n* (1908) **:** a waterproof suit with a removable helmet that is worn by a diver who is supplied with air pumped through a tube

divining rod *n* (1751) **:** a forked rod believed to indicate the presence of water or minerals esp. by dipping downward when held over a vein

di·vin·i·ty \də-ˈvi-nə-tē\ *n, pl* **-ties** (14c) **1 :** THEOLOGY **2 :** the quality or state of being divine **3** *often cap* **:** a divine being: as **a :** GOD 1 **b (1) :** GOD 2 **(2) :** GODDESS **4 :** fudge made of whipped egg whites, sugar, and nuts

divinity school *n* (ca. 1555) **:** a professional school having a religious curriculum esp. for ministerial candidates

di·vis·i·ble \də-ˈvi-zə-bəl\ *adj* (15c) **:** capable of being divided ⟨a number ~ by 3⟩ — **di·vis·i·bil·i·ty** \də-ˌvi-zə-ˈbi-lə-tē\ *n*

di·vi·sion \də-ˈvi-zhən\ *n* [ME, fr. AF *devision,* fr. L *division-, divisio,* fr. *dividere* to divide] (14c) **1 a :** the act or process of dividing : the state of being divided **b :** the act, process, or an instance of distributing among a number : DISTRIBUTION **c** *obs* **:** a method of arranging or disposing (as troops) **2 :** one of the parts or groupings into which a whole is divided or is divisible **3 :** the condition or an instance of being divided in opinion or interest : DISAGREEMENT, DISUNITY ⟨exploited the ~*s* between the two countries⟩ **4 a :** something that divides, separates, or marks off **b :** the act, process, or an instance of separating or keeping apart : SEPARATION **5 :** the mathematical operation of dividing something **6 a :** a self-contained major military unit capable of independent action **b :** a tactical military unit composed of headquarters and usu. three to five brigades **c (1) :** the basic naval administrative unit **(2) :** a tactical subdivision of a squadron of ships **d :** a unit of the U.S. Air Force higher than a wing and lower than an air force **7 a :** a portion of a territorial unit marked off for a particular purpose (as administrative or judicial functions) **b :** an administrative or operating unit of a governmental, business, or educational organization **8 :** the physical separation into different lobbies of the members of a parliamentary body voting for and against a question **9 :** plant propagation by dividing parts and planting segments capable of producing roots and shoots **10 :** a group of organisms forming part of a larger group; *specif* **:** a primary category of the plant kingdom in biological taxonomy that is typically equivalent to a phylum **11 :** a competitive class or category (as in boxing or wrestling) ***syn*** see PART — **di·vi·sion·al** \-ˈvizh-nəl, -ˈvi-zhə-nᵊl\ *adj*

di·vi·sion·ism \-ˈvi-zhə-ˌni-zəm\ *n, often cap* (1901) **:** POINTILLISM — **di·vi·sion·ist** \-ˈvi-zhə-nəst\ *n or adj*

division of labor (1776) **:** the breakdown of labor into its components and their distribution among different persons, groups, or machines to increase productive efficiency

division sign *n* (ca. 1934) **1 :** the symbol ÷ used to indicate division **2 :** the slash / used to indicate a fraction

di·vi·sive \də-ˈvī-siv *also* -ˈvi- *or* -ziv\ *adj* (1642) **:** creating disunity or dissension ⟨a ~ issue⟩ — **di·vi·sive·ly** *adv* — **di·vi·sive·ness** *n*

di·vi·sor \də-ˈvī-zər\ *n* (15c) **:** the number by which a dividend is divided

¹**di·vorce** \də-ˈvȯrs *also* dī-\ *n* [ME *divorse,* fr. AF, fr. L *divortium,* fr. *divertere, divortere* to divert, to leave one's husband] (14c) **1 :** the action or an instance of legally dissolving a marriage **2 :** SEPARATION, SEVERANCE ⟨~ of the secular and the spiritual⟩

²**divorce** *vb* **di·vorced; di·vorc·ing** *vt* (15c) **1 a :** to end marriage with (one's spouse) by divorce ⟨she *divorced* her husband⟩ **b :** to dissolve the marriage contract between ⟨they were *divorced* last year⟩ **2 :** to make or keep separate : SEPARATE ⟨~ church from state⟩ ~ *vi* **:** to obtain a divorce ***syn*** see SEPARATE — **di·vorce·ment** \-ˈvȯr-smənt\ *n*

di·vor·cé \də-ˌvȯr-ˈsā, -ˈsē, -ˈvȯr-ˌ\ n (1877) : a divorced man
di·vor·cée \də-ˌvȯr-ˈsā, -ˈsē, -ˈvȯr-ˌ\ n [F, fr. fem. of *divorcé*, pp. of *divorcer* to divorce, fr. MF *divorse*] (1813) : a divorced woman
div·ot \ˈdi-vət\ n [alter. of earlier Sc *devat*, fr. ME (Sc) *duvat*] (1586) **1** *Scot* : a square of turf or sod **2** : a loose piece of turf (as one dug from a golf fairway in making a shot)
di·vulge \də-ˈvəlj, dī-\ vt **di·vulged; di·vulg·ing** [ME, fr. L *divulgare*, fr. *dis-* + *vulgare* to make known, fr. *vulgus* mob] (15c) **1** *archaic* : to make public : PROCLAIM **2** : to make known (as a confidence or secret) **syn** see REVEAL — **di·vul·gence** \-ˈvəl-jən(t)s\ n
div·vy \ˈdi-vē\ vt **div·vied; div·vy·ing** [by shortening & alter. fr. *divide*] (1877) : DIVIDE, SHARE — usu. used with *up*
Dix·ie \ˈdik-sē\ *trademark* — used for a paper cup
Dix·ie·crat \-ˌkrat\ n (1948) : a dissident Southern Democrat; *specif* : a supporter of a 1948 presidential ticket opposing the civil rights stand of the Democrats — **Dix·ie·crat·ic** \ˌdik-sē-ˈkra-tik\ *adj*
Dix·ie·land \-ˌland\ n [prob. fr. the *Original Dixieland Jazz Band*] (1927) : jazz music in duple time usu. played by a small band and characterized by ensemble and solo improvisation
DIY \ˌdē-(ˌ)ī-ˈwī\ n, *often attrib* (1955) : DO-IT-YOURSELF
di·zen \ˈdī-zᵊn, ˈdi-\ vt [earlier *disen* to dress a distaff with flax, fr. MD] (1619) *archaic* : BEDIZEN
di·zy·got·ic \ˌdī-(ˌ)zī-ˈgä-tik\ *also* **di·zy·gous** \(ˌ)dī-ˈzī-gəs\ *adj* (1916) *of twins* : FRATERNAL 2
[1]diz·zy \ˈdi-zē\ *adj* **diz·zi·er; -est** [ME *disy*, fr. OE *dysig* stupid; akin to OHG *tusig* stupid] (bef. 12c) **1** : FOOLISH, SILLY **2 a** : having a whirling sensation in the head with a tendency to fall **b** : mentally confused **3 a** : causing giddiness or mental confusion ⟨~ heights⟩ **b** : caused by or marked by giddiness **c** : extremely rapid ⟨prices climbing at a ~ rate⟩ — **diz·zi·ly** \ˈdi-zə-lē\ *adv* — **diz·zi·ness** \-zē-nəs\ n
[2]dizzy vt **diz·zied; diz·zy·ing** (1501) **1** : to make dizzy or giddy **2** : BEWILDER ⟨disasters that ~ the mind⟩ — **diz·zy·ing·ly** \-zē-iŋ-lē\ *adv*
[1]DJ \ˈdē-ˌjā\ n, *often not cap* (1950) : DISC JOCKEY
[2]DJ *abbr* **1** district judge **2** doctor of jurisprudence **3** dust jacket
djel·la·ba *also* **djel·la·bah** \jə-ˈlä-bə\ n [F, fr. Ar *jallāba, jallābīya*] (1919) : a long loose garment with full sleeves and a hood
DJIA *abbr* Dow Jones Industrial Average
djinni *or* **djinn** \ˈjin\ *var of* JINNI
dk *abbr* **1** dark **2** deck **3** dock
dl *abbr* deciliter
DL *abbr* disabled list
dl- \(ˌ)dē-ˈel, ˈdē-ˌ\ *prefix* **1** *also* **d,l-** : consisting of equal amounts of the dextrorotatory and levorotatory forms of a specified compound ⟨*dl*-tartaric acid⟩ **2** : consisting of equal amounts of the D- and L-forms of a specified compound ⟨DL-fructose⟩
D layer n (ca. 1934) : a layer within the D region of the ionosphere; *also* : D REGION
DLitt *or* **DLit** *abbr* [NL *doctor litterarum*] doctor of letters; doctor of literature
DLO *abbr* dead letter office
DLS *abbr* doctor of library science
dm *abbr* decimeter
DM *abbr* deutsche mark
DMA *abbr* doctor of musical arts
D–mark \ˈdȯich-ˌmärk, ˈdoi-chə-ˌ\ n (1948) : DEUTSCHE MARK
DMD *abbr* [NL *dentariae medicinae doctor*] doctor of dental medicine
DME \ˌdē-(ˌ)em-ˈē\ n [*distance measuring equipment*] (1947) : an electronic device that informs the pilot of an airplane of its distance from a particular ground station
DMin *abbr* doctor of ministry
DMSO \ˌdē-ˌem-ˌes-ˈō\ n (1964) : DIMETHYL SULFOXIDE
DMT \ˌdē-(ˌ)em-ˈtē\ n (ca. 1966) : DIMETHYLTRYPTAMINE
DMV *abbr* Department of Motor Vehicles
DMZ *abbr* demilitarized zone
dn *abbr* down
DNA \ˌdē-ˌen-ˈā\ n [*deoxyribonucleic acid*] (1944) : any of various nucleic acids that are usu. the molecular basis of heredity, are constructed of a double helix held together by hydrogen bonds between purine and pyrimidine bases which project inward from two chains containing alternate links of deoxyribose and phosphate, and that in eukaryotes are localized chiefly in cell nuclei — compare RECOMBINANT DNA

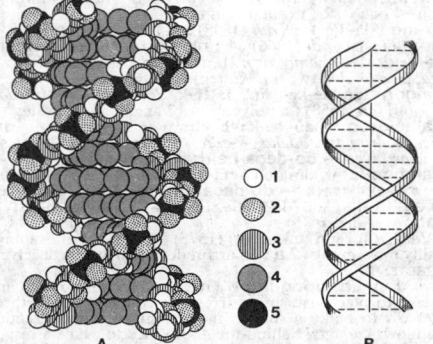

DNA: *A* molecular model: *1* hydrogen, *2* oxygen, *3* carbon in the helical phosphate ester chains, *4* carbon and nitrogen in the crosslinked purine and pyrimidine bases, *5* phosphorus; *B* double helix

DNA fingerprinting n (1984) : a technique used esp. for identification (as for forensic purposes) by extracting and identifying the base-pair pattern in an individual's DNA — called also *DNA typing* — **DNA fingerprint** n

DNA polymerase n (ca. 1962) : any of several polymerases that promote replication or repair of DNA usu. using single-stranded DNA as a template
DN·ase \(ˌ)dē-ˈen-ˌās, -ˌāz\ *also* **DNA·ase** \(ˌ)dē-ˌen-ˈā-ˌās, -ˌāz\ n (ca. 1956) : an enzyme that hydrolyzes DNA to nucleotides — called also *deoxyribonuclease*
DNA virus n (1963) : a virus whose genome consists of DNA
DNB *abbr* Dictionary of National Biography
DNF *abbr* did not finish
DNP *abbr* did not play
DNR *abbr* do not resuscitate
[1]do \ˈdü\ vb **did** \ˈdid, dəd\; **done** \ˈdən\; **do·ing** \ˈdü-iŋ\; **does** \ˈdəz\ [ME *don*, fr. OE *dōn*; akin to OHG *tuon* to do, L *-dere* to put, *facere* to make, do, Gk *tithenai* to place, set] vt (bef. 12c) **1** : to bring to pass : CARRY OUT ⟨~ another's wishes⟩ **2** : PUT — used chiefly in *do to death* **3 a** : PERFORM, EXECUTE ⟨~ some work⟩ ⟨*did* his duty⟩ **b** : COMMIT ⟨crimes *done* deliberately⟩ **4 a** : BRING ABOUT, EFFECT ⟨trying to ~ good⟩ ⟨~ violence⟩ **b** : to give freely : PAY ⟨~ honor to her memory⟩ **5** : to bring to an end : FINISH — used in the past participle ⟨the job is finally *done*⟩ **6** : to put forth : EXERT ⟨*did* her best to win the race⟩ **7 a** : to wear out esp. by physical exertion : EXHAUST ⟨at the end of the race they were pretty well *done*⟩ **b** : to attack physically : BEAT; *also* : KILL **8** : to bring into existence : PRODUCE ⟨~ a biography on the general⟩ **9** — used as a substitute verb esp. to avoid repetition ⟨if you must make such a racket, ~ it somewhere else⟩ **10 a** : to play the role or character of ~ MIMIC; *also* : to behave like ⟨~ a Houdini and disappear⟩ **c** : to perform in or serve as producer of ⟨~ a play⟩ **11** : to treat unfairly; *esp* : CHEAT ⟨*did* him out of his inheritance⟩ **12** : to treat or deal with in any way typically with the sense of preparation or with that of care or attention: **a** (1) : to put in order : CLEAN ⟨was ~*ing* the kitchen⟩ (2) : WASH ⟨*did* the dishes after supper⟩ **b** : to prepare for use or consumption; *esp* : COOK ⟨like my steak *done* rare⟩ **c** : SET, ARRANGE ⟨had her hair *done*⟩ **d** : to apply cosmetics to ⟨wanted to ~ her face before the party⟩ **e** : DECORATE, FURNISH ⟨*did* the living room in Early American⟩ ⟨~ over the kitchen⟩ **13** : to be engaged in the study or practice of ⟨~ science⟩; *esp* : to work at as a vocation ⟨what to ~ after college⟩ **14 a** : to pass over (as distance) : TRAVERSE ⟨~ 20 miles yesterday⟩ **b** : to travel at a speed of ⟨~*ing* 55 on the turnpike⟩ **15** : TOUR ⟨~*ing* 12 countries in 30 days⟩ **16 a** : to spend (time) in prison ⟨has been ~*ing* time in a federal penitentiary⟩ **b** : to serve out (a period of imprisonment) ⟨*did* ten years for armed robbery⟩ **17** : to serve the needs of : SUIT, SUFFICE ⟨worms will ~ us for bait⟩ **18** : to approve esp. by custom, opinion, or propriety ⟨you oughtn't to say a thing like that . . . it's not *done* —Dorothy Sayers⟩ **19** : to treat with respect to physical comforts ⟨*did* themselves well⟩ **20** : USE 3 ⟨doesn't ~ drugs⟩ **21** : to have sexual intercourse with **22** : to partake of ⟨let's ~ lunch⟩ ~ vi **1** : ACT, BEHAVE ⟨~ as I say⟩ **2 a** : GET ALONG, FARE ⟨~ well in school⟩ **b** : to carry on business or affairs : MANAGE ⟨we can ~ without your help⟩ **3** : to take place : HAPPEN ⟨what's ~*ing* across the street⟩ **4** : to come to or make an end : FINISH — used in the past participle **5** : to be active or busy ⟨let us then be up and ~*ing* —H. W. Longfellow⟩ **6** : to be adequate or sufficient : SERVE ⟨half of that will ~⟩ **7** : to be fitting : conform to custom or propriety ⟨won't ~ to be late⟩ **8** — used as a substitute verb to avoid repetition ⟨wanted to run and play as children ~⟩; used esp. in British English following a modal auxiliary or perfective *have* ⟨a great many people had died, or would ~ —Bruce Chatwin⟩ **9** — used in the imperative after an imperative to add emphasis ⟨be quiet ~⟩ ~ *verbal auxiliary* **1 a** — used with the infinitive without *to* to form present and past tenses in legal and parliamentary language ⟨~ hereby bequeath⟩ and in poetry ⟨give what she *did* crave —Shak.⟩ **b** — used with the infinitive without *to* to form present and past tenses in declarative sentences with inverted word order ⟨fervently ~ we pray —Abraham Lincoln⟩, in interrogatory sentences ⟨*did* you hear that?⟩, and in negative sentences ⟨we *don't* know⟩ ⟨*don't* go⟩ **2** — used with the infinitive without *to* to form present and past tenses expressing emphasis ⟨I ~ say⟩ ⟨~ be careful⟩ — **do·able** \ˈdü-ə-bəl\ *adj* — **do a number on** : to defeat or confound thoroughly esp. by indirect or deceptive means — **do away with 1** : to put an end to : ABOLISH **2** : to put to death — **do by** : to deal with : TREAT — **do for** *chiefly Brit* **1** : to attend to the wants and needs of : take care of **2** : to bring about the death or ruin of — **do it** : to have sexual intercourse — **do justice 1** : to act justly **b** : to treat fairly or adequately **c** : to show due appreciation for **2** : to acquit in a way worthy of one's abilities — **do proud** : to give cause for pride or gratification ⟨she *did* herself *proud*⟩ — **do the trick** : to produce a desired result — **do with** : to make good use of : benefit by ⟨could *do with* a cup of coffee⟩ — **to do** : necessary to be done ⟨I've done my best and all's *to do* again —A. E. Housman⟩
[2]do \ˈdü\ n, pl **dos** *or* **do's** \ˈdüz\ (1599) **1** *chiefly dial* : FUSS, ADO **2** *archaic* : DEED, DUTY **3 a** : a festive get-together : AFFAIR, PARTY **b** *chiefly Brit* : BATTLE **4** : a command or entreaty to do something ⟨a list of ~*s* and don'ts⟩ **5** *Brit* : CHEAT, SWINDLE **6** : HAIRDO
[3]do \ˈdō\ n [It] (ca. 1754) : the first tone of the diatonic scale in solmization
[4]do *abbr* **1** ditto **2** double occupancy
DO *abbr* **1** defense order **2** doctor of osteopathy
DOA *abbr* dead on arrival
DOB *abbr* date of birth
dob·bin \ˈdä-bᵊn\ n [*Dobbin*, nickname for *Robert*] (1596) **1** : a farm horse **2** : a quiet plodding horse
dob·by \ˈdä-bē\ n, pl **dobbies** [perh. fr. *Dobby*, nickname for *Robert*] (1878) **1** : a loom attachment for weaving small figures **2** : a fabric or figured weave made with a dobby
Dobe \ˈdōb\ n (1946) : DOBERMAN PINSCHER

Do·ber·man pin·scher \ˌdō-bər-mən-ˈpin-chər\ *n* [G *Dobermann-pinscher,* fr. Friedrich Ludwig *Dobermann* †1894 Ger. dog breeder + G *Pinscher,* a breed of hunting dog] (1917) : any of a breed of short-haired medium-sized dogs of German origin — called also *Doberman*
do·bra \ˈdō-brə, ˈdȯ-\ *n* [Pg, fr. fem. of obs. *dobro* double, fr. L *duplus* — more at DOUBLE] (1978) — see MONEY table
Do·bro \ˈdō-(ˌ)brō\ *trademark* — used for an acoustic guitar having a metal resonator
dob·son·fly \ˈdäb-sən-ˌflī\ *n* [origin unknown] (ca. 1904) : a winged insect (family Corydalidae) that has very long slender mandibles in the male and a large carnivorous aquatic larva and that is now usu. considered a neuropteran — compare HELLGRAMMITE
[1]**doc** \ˈdäk\ *n* (1756) : DOCTOR
[2]**doc** *abbr* document
do·cent \ˈdō-sᵊnt, dō(t)-ˈsent\ *n* [obs. G (now *Dozent*), fr. L *docent-, docens,* prp. of *docēre*] (1880) **1** : a college or university teacher or lecturer **2** : a person who leads guided tours esp. through a museum or art gallery
do·ce·tic \dō-ˈsē-tik, -ˈse-\ *adj, often cap* [LGk *Dokētai* Docetists, fr. Gk *dokein* to seem — more at DECENT] (1846) : of or relating to Docetism or the Docetists
Do·ce·tism \dō-ˈsē-ˌti-zəm, ˈdō-sə-\ *n* (1846) : a belief opposed as heresy in early Christianity that Christ only seemed to have a human body and to suffer and die on the cross — **Do·ce·tist** \-ˈsē-tist, -sə-\ *n*
doch–an–dor·ris *or* **doch–an–dor·is** \ˌdäk-ən-ˈdȯr-əs\ *n* [ScGael *deoch an doruis* & Ir *deoch an dorais,* lit., drink of the door] (1691) *Scot & Irish* : a parting drink : STIRRUP CUP
doc·ile \ˈdä-səl *also* -ˌsī(-ə)l, *esp Brit* ˈdō-ˌsī(-ə)l\ *adj* [L *docilis,* fr. *docēre* to teach; akin to L *decēre* to be fitting — more at DECENT] (15c) **1** : easily taught **2** : easily led or managed ***syn*** see OBEDIENT — **doc·ile·ly** \ˈdä-sə(l)-lē\ *adv* — **do·cil·i·ty** \dä-ˈsi-lə-tē, dō-\ *n*
[1]**dock** \ˈdäk\ *n* [ME, fr. OE *docce;* akin to MD *docke* dock] (bef. 12c) **1** : any of a genus (*Rumex*) of coarse weedy plants of the buckwheat family having long taproots and sometimes used as potherbs **2** : any of several usu. broad-leaved weedy plants (as of the genus *Silphium*)
[2]**dock** *n* [ME *dok,* perh. fr. OE *-docca* (as in *fingirdocca* finger muscle); akin to OHG *tocka* doll, ON *dokka* bundle] (14c) **1** : the solid part of an animal's tail as distinguished from the hair **2** : the part of an animal's tail left after it has been shortened
[3]**dock** *vt* (14c) **1 a** : to cut off the end of a body part of; *specif* : to remove part of the tail of **b** : to cut (as ears or a tail) short **2 a** : to take away a part of : ABRIDGE **b** : to subject (as wages) to a deduction **c** : to penalize by depriving of a benefit ordinarily due; *esp* : to fine by a deduction of wages ⟨~*ed* him for tardiness⟩
[4]**dock** *n* [ME *dokke,* prob. fr. MD *docke*] (15c) **1** : a usu. artificial basin or enclosure for the reception of ships that is equipped with means for controlling the water height **2** : [2]SLIP 1b **3 a** : a place (as a wharf or platform) for the loading or unloading of materials **b** : a usu. wooden pier used as a landing place or moorage for boats
[5]**dock** *vt* (1600) **1** : to haul or guide into or alongside a dock **2** : to join (as two spacecraft) mechanically while in space ~ *vi* **1** : to come into or alongside a dock **2** : to become docked
[6]**dock** *n* [D dial. (Flanders) *docke* cage] (1586) : the place in a criminal court where a prisoner stands or sits during trial — **in the dock** : on trial
dock·age \ˈdä-kij\ *n* (1648) **1** : a charge for the use of a dock **2** : the docking of ships **3** : docking facilities
[1]**dock·er** \ˈdä-kər\ *n* (1765) : one that docks the tails of animals
[2]**docker** *n* (1887) *chiefly Brit* : one connected with docks; *esp* : LONGSHOREMAN
[1]**dock·et** \ˈdä-kət\ *n* [ME *doggette*] (15c) **1** : a brief written summary of a document : ABSTRACT **2 a** (1) : a formal abridged record of the proceedings in a legal action (2) : a register of such records **b** (1) : a list of legal causes to be tried; *also* : the caseload of a court or judge (2) : a calendar of business matters to be acted on : AGENDA **3** : an identifying statement about a document placed on its outer surface or cover
[2]**docket** *vt* (1615) **1** : to place on the docket for legal action **2** : to make a brief abstract of (as a legal matter) and inscribe it in a list **3** : to inscribe (as a document) with an identifying statement
dock·hand \ˈdäk-ˌhand\ *n* (1920) : LONGSHOREMAN
dock·land \-ˌland\ *n* (1904) *Brit* : the part of a port occupied by docks; *also* : a residential section adjacent to docks
dock·mas·ter \ˈdäk-ˌmas-tər\ *n* (1736) : a person in charge of a dock or marina or of the docking of ships
dock·side \-ˌsīd\ *n, often attrib* (1887) : the shore or area adjacent to a dock
dock·work·er \-ˌwər-kər\ *n* (1913) : LONGSHOREMAN
dock·yard \-ˌyärd\ *n* (1704) **1** : SHIPYARD **2** *Brit* : NAVY YARD
do·co·sa·hex·a·e·no·ic acid \ˌdō-kō-sə-ˌhek-sə-ˌē-ˈnō-ik-\ *n* [ISV *docosanoic* acid (a crystalline fatty acid) + *hexa-* + *-ene* + *-oic*] : an omega-3 fatty acid $C_{22}H_{32}O_2$ found esp. in fish of cold waters
[1]**doc·tor** \ˈdäk-tər\ *n* [ME *doctour* teacher, doctor, fr. AF & ML; AF, fr. ML *doctor,* fr. L, teacher, fr. *docēre* to teach — more at DOCILE] (14c) **1 a** : an eminent theologian declared a sound expounder of doctrine by the Roman Catholic Church — called also *doctor of the church* **b** : a learned or authoritative teacher **c** : a person who has earned one of the highest academic degrees (as a PhD) conferred by a university **d** : a person awarded an honorary doctorate (as an LLD or Litt D) by a college or university **2 a** : a person skilled or specializing in healing arts; *esp* : one (as a physician, dentist, or veterinarian) who holds an advanced degree and is licensed to practice **b** : MEDICINE MAN **3 a** : material added (as to food) to produce a desired effect **b** : a blade (as of metal) for spreading a coating or scraping a surface **4** : a person who restores, repairs, or fine-tunes things — **doc·tor·al** \-t(ə-)rəl\ *adj* — **doc·tor·less** \-tər-ləs\ *adj* — **doc·tor·ship** \-ˌship\ *n*
[2]**doctor** *vb* **doc·tored; doc·tor·ing** \-t(ə-)riŋ\ *vt* (1712) **1 a** : to give medical treatment to **b** : to restore to good condition : REPAIR ⟨~ an old clock⟩ **2 a** : to adapt or modify for a desired end by alteration or special treatment ⟨~*ed* the play to suit the audience⟩ ⟨the drink was ~*ed*⟩ **b** : to alter deceptively ⟨accused of ~*ing* the election returns⟩ ~ *vi* **1** : to practice medicine **2** *dial* : to take medicine
doc·tor·ate \ˈdäk-t(ə-)rət\ *n* (1570) : the degree, title, or rank of a doctor
[1]**doc·tri·naire** \ˌdäk-trə-ˈner\ *n* [F, fr. *doctrine*] (1831) : one who attempts to put into effect an abstract doctrine or theory with little or no regard for practical difficulties
[2]**doctrinaire** *adj* (1834) : of, relating to, or characteristic of a doctrinaire : DOGMATIC ***syn*** see DICTATORIAL — **doc·tri·nair·ism** \-ˈner-ˌi-zəm\ *n*
doc·trin·al \ˈdäk-trə-nᵊl, *esp Brit* däk-ˈtrī-\ *adj* (15c) : of, relating to, or preoccupied with doctrine — **doc·trin·al·ly** \-nᵊl-ē\ *adv*
doc·trine \ˈdäk-trən\ *n* [ME, fr. AF & L; AF, fr. L *doctrina,* fr. *doctor*] (14c) **1** *archaic* : TEACHING, INSTRUCTION **2 a** : something that is taught **b** : a principle or position or the body of principles in a branch of knowledge or system of belief : DOGMA **c** : a principle of law established through past decisions **d** : a statement of fundamental government policy esp. in international relations **e** : a military principle or set of strategies
docu·dra·ma \ˈdä-kyə-ˌdrä-mə, -ˌdra-, -kyü-\ *n* [*docu*mentary + *drama*] (ca. 1961) : a drama (as for television) dealing freely with historical events esp. of a recent and controversial nature
[1]**doc·u·ment** \ˈdä-kyə-mənt, -kyü-\ *n* [ME, precept, teaching, fr. AF, fr. LL & L; LL *documentum* official paper, fr. L, lesson, proof, fr. *docēre* to teach — more at DOCILE] (15c) **1 a** *archaic* : PROOF, EVIDENCE **b** : an original or official paper relied on as the basis, proof, or support of something **c** : something (as a photograph or a recording) that serves as evidence or proof **2 a** : a writing conveying information **b** : a material substance (as a coin or stone) having on it a representation of thoughts by means of some conventional mark or symbol **c** : DOCUMENTARY **3** : a computer file containing information input by a computer user and usu. created with an application (as a word processor) — **doc·u·men·tal** \ˌdä-kyə-ˈmen-tᵊl, -kyü-\ *adj*
[2]**doc·u·ment** \ˈdä-kyə-ˌment\ *vt* (1711) **1** : to furnish documentary evidence of **2** : to furnish with documents **3 a** : to provide with factual or substantial support for statements made or a hypothesis proposed; *esp* : to equip with exact references to authoritative supporting information **b** (1) : to construct or produce (as a movie or novel) with authentic situations or events (2) : to portray realistically **4** : to furnish (a ship) with ship's papers — **doc·u·ment·able** \-ˌmen-tə-bəl, ˌdä-kyə-ˈ, -kyü-\ *adj* — **doc·u·ment·er** \ˈdä-kyə-ˌmen-tər\ *n*
doc·u·men·tal·ist \ˌdä-kyə-ˈmen-tᵊl-ist, -kyü-\ *n* (1939) : a specialist in documentation
doc·u·men·tar·i·an \-mən-ˈter-ē-ən, -ˌmen-\ *n* [[2]*documentary*] (1943) : one who makes a documentary
doc·u·men·ta·rist \-ˈmen-tə-rist\ *n* [[2]*documentary*] (1949) : DOCUMENTARIAN
[1]**doc·u·men·ta·ry** \-ˈmen-tə-rē, -ˈmen-trē\ *adj* (1802) **1** : being or consisting of documents : contained or certified in writing ⟨~ evidence⟩ **2** : of, relating to, or employing documentation in literature or art; *broadly* : FACTUAL, OBJECTIVE ⟨a ~ film of the war⟩ — **doc·u·men·tar·i·ly** \-mən-ˈter-ə-lē, -ˌmen-\ *adv*
[2]**documentary** *n, pl* **-ries** (1935) : a documentary presentation (as a film or novel)
doc·u·men·ta·tion \-mən-ˈtā-shən, -ˌmen-\ *n* (1884) **1** : the act or an instance of furnishing or authenticating with documents **2 a** : the provision of documents in substantiation; *also* : documentary evidence **b** (1) : the use of historical documents (2) : conformity to historical or objective facts (3) : the provision of footnotes, appendices, or addenda referring to or containing documentary evidence **3** : INFORMATION SCIENCE **4** : the usu. printed instructions, comments, and information for using a particular piece or system of computer software or hardware — **doc·u·men·ta·tion·al** \-shnəl, -shə-nᵊl\ *adj*
doc·u·se·ries \ˈdä-kyə-ˌsir-(ˌ)ēz, -kyü-\ *n* [*docu*mentary + *series*] (1988) : a documentary that is telecast in a series of programs
doc·u·soap \ˈdä-kyə-ˌsōp\ *n* [*docu*mentary + [1]*soap*] (1991) : a TV series in which the real-life activities of a group of people are presented in soap-opera style
DOD *abbr* Department of Defense
[1]**dod·der** \ˈdä-dər\ *n* [ME *doder;* akin to MHG *toter* dodder, egg yolk] (13c) : any of a genus (*Cuscuta*) of wiry twining vines of the morning-glory family that are highly deficient in chlorophyll, are parasitic on other plants, and have tiny scales instead of leaves
[2]**dodder** *vi* **dod·dered; dod·der·ing** \ˈdä-d(ə-)riŋ\ [ME *dadiren*] (14c) **1** : to tremble or shake from weakness or age **2** : to progress feebly and unsteadily ⟨was ~*ing* down the walk⟩ — **dod·der·er** \-dər-ər\ *n*
dod·dered \ˈdä-dərd\ *adj* [prob. alter. of *dodded,* fr. pp. of E dial. *dod* to lop, fr. ME *dodden*] (1697) **1** : deprived of branches through age or decay ⟨a ~ oak⟩ **2** : INFIRM, ENFEEBLED
dod·der·ing \ˈdä-d(ə-)riŋ\ *adj* (1898) : FEEBLE, SENILE
dod·dery \-d(ə-)rē\ *adj* (1866) **1** : DODDERED 2 **2** : DODDERING
dodeca- *or* **dodec-** *comb form* [L, fr. Gk *dōdeka-, dōdek-,* fr. *dōdeka, dyōdeka,* fr. *dyō, dyo* two + *deka* ten] : twelve ⟨*dodeca*phonic⟩
do·deca·gon \dō-ˈde-kə-ˌgän\ *n* [Gk *dōdekagōnon,* fr. *dōdeka-* + *-gōnon* -gon] (ca. 1658) : a polygon of 12 angles and 12 sides
do·deca·he·dron \(ˌ)dō-ˌde-kə-ˈhē-drən\ *n, pl* **-drons** *or* **-dra** \-drə\ [Gk *dōdekaedron,* fr. *dōdeka-* + *-edron* -hedron] (ca. 1570) : a solid having 12 plane faces — **do·deca·he·dral** \-drəl\ *adj*
do·deca·phon·ic \(ˌ)dō-ˌde-kə-ˈfä-nik\ *adj* [*dodeca-* + *phon-* + *-ic*] (1949) : TWELVE-TONE — **do·deca·phon·i·cal·ly** \-ni-k(ə-)lē\ *adv* — **do·deca·pho·nist** \dō-ˈde-kə-fə-nist, -ˌfō-; ˌdō-di-ˈka-fə-nist\ *n* — **do·deca·pho·ny** \-nē\ *n*
[1]**dodge** \ˈdäj\ *n* [origin unknown] (1575) **1** : an act of evading by sudden bodily movement **2 a** : an artful device to evade, deceive, or trick **b** : EXPEDIENT
[2]**dodge** *vb* **dodged; dodg·ing** *vi* (1680) **1 a** : to move to and fro or from place to place usu. in an irregular course ⟨*dodged* through the crowd⟩ **b** : to make a sudden movement in a new direction (as to evade a blow) ⟨*dodged* behind the door⟩ **2** : to evade a responsibility or duty esp. by trickery or deceit ~ *vt* **1 a** : to evade by a sudden or repeated shift of position ⟨~ tacklers⟩ **b** : to avoid an encounter with ⟨celebrities *dodging* the media⟩ **2** : to evade (as a duty) usu. indirectly or by trickery ⟨*dodged* the draft by leaving the country⟩ ⟨*dodged* questions⟩ — **dodge a bullet** *also* **dodge the bullet** : to narrowly avoid an unwelcome, harmful, or disastrous outcome or occurrence ⟨coastal towns *dodged a bullet* when the hurricane veered out to sea⟩
dodge·ball \ˈdäj-ˌbȯl\ *n* (1903) : a game in which players stand in a circle and try to hit opponents within the circle with a large inflated ball

dodg·em \'dä-jəm\ n (1945) chiefly Brit : BUMPER CAR — called also *dodgem car*

dodg·er \'dä-jər\ n (1568) **1 :** one that dodges; esp : one who uses tricky devices **2 :** a small leaflet : CIRCULAR **3 :** CORN DODGER **4 :** a usu. canvas screen on a boat or ship that provides protection from spray

dodg·ery \'dä-jə-rē\ n, pl **-er·ies** (1670) : EVASION, TRICKERY

dodgy \'dä-jē\ adj (1861) **1** chiefly Brit : EVASIVE, TRICKY **2** chiefly Brit **a :** not sound, good, or reliable **b :** QUESTIONABLE, SUSPICIOUS **3** chiefly Brit : requiring skill or care in handling or coping with — **dodg·i·ness** \-nəs\ n

do·do \'dō-(ˌ)dō\ n, pl **dodoes** or **dodos** [Pg doudo, fr. doudo silly, stupid] (1628) **1 a :** an extinct heavy flightless bird (Raphus cucullatus syn. Didus ineptus of the family Raphidae) of the island of Mauritius that was larger than a turkey and was related to the pigeon **b :** an extinct flightless bird (Raphus solitarius) of the island of Réunion similar to and closely related to the dodo **2 a :** one hopelessly behind the times **b :** a stupid person

do down vt (14c) Brit : to get the better of (as by trickery)

doe \'dō\ n, pl **does** or **doe** [ME do, fr. OE dā; akin to G dial. tē doe] (bef. 12c) : the adult female of various mammals (as a deer, rabbit, or kangaroo) of which the male is called buck

DOE abbr **1** Department of Energy **2** depends on experience

doe–eyed \'dō-ˌīd\ adj (1933) : having large innocent-looking eyes

do·er \'dü-ər\ n (14c) : one that takes an active part ⟨a thinker or a ∼⟩

does pres 3d sing of DO, pl of DOE

doe·skin \'dō-ˌskin\ n (15c) **1 :** the skin of does or leather made of it; also : soft leather from sheep- or lambskins **2 :** a compact coating and sportswear fabric napped and felted for a smooth surface

doesn't \'də-zənt\ (1739) : does not

do·est \'dü-əst\ archaic pres 2d sing of DO

do·eth \'dü-əth\ archaic pres 3d sing of DO

doff \'däf, 'dȯf\ vt [ME, fr. don to do + of off] (14c) **1 a :** to remove (an article of wear) from the body **b :** to take off (the hat) in greeting or as a sign of respect **2 :** to rid oneself of : put aside — **doff one's hat to** or **doff one's cap to** : to show respect to : SALUTE

¹dog \'dȯg, 'däg\ n, often attrib [ME, fr. OE docga] (bef. 12c) **1 a :** CANID; esp : a highly variable domestic mammal (Canis familiaris) closely related to the gray wolf **b :** a male dog; also : a male usu. carnivorous mammal **2 a :** a worthless or contemptible person **b :** FELLOW, CHAP ⟨a lazy ∼⟩ ⟨you lucky ∼⟩ **3 a :** any of various usu. simple mechanical devices for holding, gripping, or fastening that consist of a spike, bar, or hook **b :** ANDIRON **4 :** uncharacteristic or affected stylishness or dignity ⟨put on the ∼⟩ **5** cap : either of the constellations Canis Major or Canis Minor **6** pl : FEET **7** pl : RUIN ⟨going to the ∼s⟩ **8 :** one inferior of its kind ⟨the movie was a ∼⟩; also : an investment not worth its price ⟨an undesirable piece of merchandise⟩ **9 :** an unattractive person; esp : an unattractive girl or woman **10 :** HOT DOG 1 — **dog·like** \'dȯg-ˌlīk\ adj

dog 1a: *1* pastern, *2* chest, *3* flews, *4* muzzle, *5* stop, *6* occiput, *7* leather, *8* crest, *9* withers, *10* loin, *11* point of rump, *12* hock or tarsus, *13* knee or stifle, *14* brisket, *15* elbow, *16* feathering

²dog adj (14c) **1 :** CANINE **2 :** SPURIOUS; esp : unlike that used by native speakers or writers ⟨∼ Latin⟩ ⟨∼ French⟩

³dog vt **dogged; dog·ging** (1519) **1 a :** to hunt, track, or follow like a hound ⟨dogged her every move⟩ **b :** to worry as if by pursuit with dogs : PLAGUE ⟨dogged by his past failures⟩ **c :** to bother or pester persistently ⟨dogged him about his grades⟩ **2 :** to fasten with a dog — **dog it :** to fail to do one's best : GOLDBRICK

⁴dog adv (1526) : EXTREMELY, UTTERLY ⟨dog-tired⟩

dog and pony show n (1970) : an often elaborate public relations or sales presentation; also : an elaborate or overblown affair or event

dog·bane \'dȯg-ˌbān\ n (1597) : any of a genus (Apocynum of the family Apocynaceae, the dogbane family) of often poisonous plants chiefly of temperate-zone regions with milky juice and fibrous bark

dog biscuit n (ca. 1858) : a hard dry cracker for dogs

dog·cart \'dȯg-ˌkärt\ n (1668) **1 :** a cart drawn by a dog **2 :** a light two-wheeled carriage with two transverse seats set back to back

dog·catch·er \-ˌka-chər, -ˌke-\ n (1835) : a community official assigned to catch and dispose of stray dogs

dog collar n (1501) **1 :** a collar for a dog **2** slang : CLERICAL COLLAR **3 :** a wide flexible snug-fitting necklace

dog days n pl [fr. their being reckoned from the heliacal rising of the Dog Star (Sirius)] (1538) **1 :** the period between early July and early September when the hot sultry weather of summer usu. occurs in the northern hemisphere **2 :** a period of stagnation or inactivity

dog·dom \'dȯg-dəm\ n (1854) : the world of dogs or of dog fanciers

doge \'dōj\ n [It dial., fr. L duc-, dux leader — more at DUKE] (1549) : the chief magistrate in the republics of Venice and Genoa

dog–ear \'dȯg-ˌir\ n (1856) : the turned-down corner of a page esp. of a book — **dog–ear** vt

dog–eared \-ˌird\ adj (ca. 1800) **1 :** having dog-ears ⟨a ∼ book⟩ **2 :** SHABBY, TIMEWORN ⟨a ∼ resort⟩ ⟨∼ myths⟩

dog–eat–dog \ˌdȯg-ˌē(t)-'dȯg\ adj (1834) : marked by ruthless self-interest ⟨∼ competition⟩

dog–face \'dȯg-ˌfās\ n (1932) : SOLDIER; esp : INFANTRYMAN

dog fennel n (14c) **1 :** an ill-scented Eurasian chamomile (Anthemis cotula) naturalized as a weed in the U.S. **2 :** a usu. annual composite weed (Eupatorium capillifolium) chiefly of the southern U.S.

dog·fight \'dȯg-ˌfīt\ n (1656) **1 :** a fight between dogs; broadly : a fiercely disputed contest **2 :** a fight between two or more fighter planes usu. at close quarters — **dogfight** vi — **dog-fight·er** \-ˌfī-tər\ n

dog·fish \-ˌfish\ n (15c) : any of various usu. small bottom-dwelling sharks (as of the families Squalidae, Carcharhinidae, and Scyliorhinidae) that often appear in schools near shore, prey chiefly on fish and invertebrates, and are a valuable food source

dog·ged \'dȯ-gəd\ adj (1653) : marked by stubborn determination ⟨a ∼ competitor⟩ ⟨∼ devotion⟩ **syn** see OBSTINATE — **dog·ged·ly** adv — **dog·ged·ness** n

¹dog·ger·el \'dȯ-g(ə-)rəl, 'dä-\ adj [ME dogerel, prob. dim. of dogge dog] (14c) : loosely styled and irregular in measure esp. for burlesque or comic effect; also : marked by triviality or inferiority

²doggerel n (1630) : doggerel verse

dog·gery \'dȯ-gə-rē\ n, pl **-ger·ies** (1830) : a cheap saloon : DIVE

dog·gie bag or **doggy bag** \'dȯ-gē-\ n ['doggy; fr. the presumption that such leftovers are intended for a pet dog] (1963) : a container for leftover food to be carried home from a meal eaten at a restaurant

dog·gish \'dȯ-gish\ adj (15c) **1 :** CANINE **2 :** stylish in a showy way — **dog·gish·ly** adv — **dog·gish·ness** n

dog·go \'dȯ-(ˌ)gō\ adv [prob. fr. 'dog] (1893) : in hiding — used chiefly in the phrase to lie doggo

¹dog·gone \'dȯg-ˌgän, 'dȯg-ˌgȯn\ vb **dog·goned; dog·gon·ing** [euphemism for God damn] (1851) : DAMN

²dog·gone or **dog·goned** \ˌdȯg-ˌgän(d), ˌdȯg-ˌgȯn(d)\ adj or adv (1851) : DAMNED

³doggone n (1928) : DAMN

¹dog·gy or **dog·gie** \'dȯ-gē\ n, pl **doggies** (1788) : a usu. small dog

²dog·gy \'dȯ-gē\ adj **dog·gi·er; -est** (1859) **1 :** concerned with or fond of dogs **2 :** resembling or suggestive of a dog ⟨∼ odor⟩ **3 :** STYLISH, SHOWY **4 :** not worthy or profitable : INFERIOR ⟨∼ stocks⟩

dog·house \'dȯg-ˌhaůs\ n (1594) **1 :** a shelter for a dog **2 :** a state of disfavor — often used in the phrase in the doghouse

do·gie \'dō-gē\ n [origin unknown] (1888) chiefly West : a motherless calf in a range herd

dog in the manger [fr. the fable of the dog who prevented an ox from eating hay which he did not want himself] (1573) : a person who selfishly withholds from others something useless to himself

¹dog·leg \'dȯg-ˌleg, -ˌläg\ adj (1808) : crooked or bent like a dog's hind leg ⟨a sharp ∼ bend in the fairway⟩

²dogleg n (ca. 1909) **1 :** something having an abrupt angle **b :** a sharp bend (as in a road) **2 :** a golf hole having an angled fairway

³dogleg vi (1944) : to proceed along a dogleg course ⟨the single narrow street that ∼s through town —Russ Leadabrand⟩

dog·ma \'dȯg-mə, 'däg-\ n, pl **dogmas** also **dog·ma·ta** \-mə-tə\ [L dogmat-, dogma, fr. Gk, fr. dokein to seem — more at DECENT] (1638) **1 a :** something held as an established opinion; esp : a definite authoritative tenet **b :** a code of such tenets ⟨pedagogical ∼⟩ **c :** a point of view or tenet put forth as authoritative without adequate grounds **2 :** a doctrine or body of doctrines concerning faith or morals formally stated and authoritatively proclaimed by a church

dog·mat·ic \dȯg-'ma-tik, däg-\ also **dog·mat·i·cal** \-ti-kəl\ adj (1660) **1 :** characterized by or given to the expression of opinions very strongly or positively as if they were facts ⟨a ∼ critic⟩ **2 :** of or relating to dogma **syn** see DICTATORIAL — **dog·mat·i·cal·ly** \-ti-k(ə-)lē\ adv — **dog·mat·i·cal·ness** \-ti-kəl-nəs\ n

dog·mat·ics \-tiks\ n pl but sing or pl in constr (1845) : a branch of theology that seeks to interpret the dogmas of a religious faith

dogmatic theology n (ca. 1766) : DOGMATICS

dog·ma·tism \'dȯg-mə-ˌti-zəm, 'däg-\ n (1603) **1 :** positiveness in assertion of opinion esp. when unwarranted or arrogant **2 :** a viewpoint or system of ideas based on insufficiently examined premises

dog·ma·tist \-mə-tist\ n (1606) : one who dogmatizes

dog·ma·tize \'dȯg-mə-ˌtīz, 'däg-\ vb **-tized; -tiz·ing** [F dogmatiser, fr. LL dogmatizare, fr. Gk dogmatizein, fr. dogmat-, dogma] vi (1611) : to speak or write dogmatically ∼ vt : to state as a dogma or in a dogmatic manner — **dog·ma·ti·za·tion** \ˌdȯg-mə-tə-'zā-shən, ˌdäg-\ n — **dog·ma·tiz·er** n

dog·nap \'dȯg-ˌnap\ vt **-napped** or **-napt** \-ˌnapt\; **-nap·ping** or **-nap·ing** \ˌna-pin\ ['dog + -nap (as in kidnap)] (ca. 1942) : to steal (a dog) esp. to obtain a reward for its return or to sell to a scientific laboratory — **dog·nap·per** or **dog·nap·er** n

Do·gon \'dō-ˌgän\ n, pl **Dogon** or **Dogons** [Dogon dogõ, a self-designation] (ca. 1931) **1 :** a member of a people of Mali noted for their sculpture **2 :** the language of the Dogon

do–good \'dü-ˌgůd\ adj (1952) : designed or disposed sometimes impracticably and too zealously toward bettering the conditions under which others live — **do–good·ism** \-ˌi-zəm\ n

do–good·er \-ˌgů-dər\ n (1926) : an earnest often naive humanitarian or reformer — **do–good·ing** \-diŋ\ n or adj

dog paddle n (1904) : an elementary swimming stroke in which the arms paddle in the water and the legs maintain a kicking motion — **dog–pad·dle** vi

dog rose n (1713) : a chiefly European wild rose (Rosa canina)

dogs·body \'dȯgz-ˌbä-dē\ n [Brit naval slang dogsbody pudding made of peas, junior officer] (1922) chiefly Brit : DRUDGE 1

dog's breakfast n (ca. 1934) chiefly Brit : a confused mess or mixture

---

dog's chance *n* (1902) : a bare chance in one's favor
dog·sled \'dȯg-ˌsled\ *n* (1810) : a sled drawn by dogs — **dogsled** *vi* — **dog·sled·der** \-ˌsle-dər\ *n*
Dog Star *n* (1567) : SIRIUS
dog tag *n* (1918) : an identification tag (as for military personnel or pets)
dog tick *n* (ca. 1552) : AMERICAN DOG TICK
dog·tooth \'dȯg-ˌtüth\ *n* (1552) **1** : CANINE 1, EYETOOTH **2** : an architectural ornament common in early English Gothic consisting usu. of four leaves radiating from a raised point at the center **3** *chiefly Brit* : HOUNDSTOOTH
dogtooth violet *n* (1629) : any of a genus (*Erythronium*) of small spring-flowering bulbous herbs of the lily family
[1]**dog·trot** \'dȯg-ˌträt\ *n* (15c) **1** : a quick easy gait suggesting that of a dog **2** *chiefly Southern & Midland* : a roofed passage similar to a breezeway; *esp* : one connecting two parts of a cabin
[2]**dogtrot** *vi* (ca. 1900) : to move or progress at a dogtrot
dog·watch \'dȯg-ˌwäch\ *n* (1700) **1** : either of two watches of two hours on shipboard that extend from 4 to 6 and 6 to 8 p.m. **2** : any of various night shifts; *esp* : the last shift
dog·wood \'dȯg-ˌwu̇d\ *n* (1617) : any of various trees and shrubs (genus *Cornus* of the family Cornaceae, the dogwood family) with clusters of small flowers and often large white, pink, or red involucral bracts
d'oh *or* **doh** \'dō\ *interj* (1993) — used to express sudden recognition of a foolish blunder or an ironic turn of events
doi·ly \'dȯi-lē\ *n, pl* **doilies** [*Doily* or *Doyley* *fl*1711 London draper] (1711) **1** : a small napkin **2** : a small often decorative mat
do in *vt* (1905) **1 a** : to bring about the defeat or destruction of ⟨a businessman *done in* by greed⟩; *also* : KILL **b** : EXHAUST, WEAR OUT **2** : CHEAT
do·ing \'dü-iŋ\ *n* (14c) **1** : the act of performing or executing : ACTION ⟨that will take a great deal of ~⟩ **2** *pl* **a** : things that are done or that occur : GOINGS-ON ⟨everyday ~*s*⟩ **b** : social activities
doit \'dȯit\ *also* **duit** \'dȯit, 'dīt\ *n* [D *duit;* akin to ON *thveiti* small coin, *thveita* to hew] (1592) **1** : an old Dutch coin equal to about ⅛ stiver **2** : TRIFLE 1
do–it–yourself *n, often attrib* (1952) : the activity of doing or making something (as in woodworking or home repair) without professional training or assistance; *broadly* : an activity in which one does something oneself or on one's own initiative — **do–it–your·self·er** *n*
do·jo \'dō-(ˌ)jō\ *n, pl* **dojos** [Jp *dōjō,* fr. *dō* way, art + *-jō* ground] (1942) : a school for training in various arts of self-defense (as judo or karate)
Dol·by \'dȯl-bē, 'dōl-\ *trademark* — used for an electronic device that eliminates noise from recorded or broadcast sound
dol·ce \'dōl-(ˌ)chā\ *adj or adv* [It, lit., sweet, fr. L *dulcis* — more at DULCET] (ca. 1847) : SOFT, SMOOTH — used as a direction in music
dol·ce far nien·te \'dōl-chē-ˌfär-nē-'en-tē\ *n* [It, lit., sweet doing nothing] (1814) : pleasant relaxation in carefree idleness
dol·cet·to \dōl-'che-tō\ *n, often cap* [It, a grape variety, wine made from the grape, fr. *dolcetto* somewhat sweet, fr. *dolce*] (1979) : a light fruity red wine from the Piedmont region of Italy
dol·ce vi·ta \ˌdōl-chā-'vē-(ˌ)tä\ *n* [It, lit., sweet life] (1961) : a life of indolence and self-indulgence — called also *la dolce vita*
dol·drums \'dōl-drəmz, 'däl-, 'dȯl-\ *n pl* [prob. akin to OE *dol* foolish] (1811) **1** : a spell of listlessness or despondency **2** *often cap* : a part of the ocean near the equator abounding in calms, squalls, and light shifting winds **3** : a state or period of inactivity, stagnation, or slump
[1]**dole** \'dōl\ *n* [ME, fr. OE *dāl* portion — more at DEAL] (bef. 12c) **1** *archaic* : one's allotted share, portion, or destiny **2 a** (1) : a giving or distribution of food, money, or clothing to the needy (2) : a grant of government funds to the unemployed **b** : something distributed at intervals to the needy; *also* : HANDOUT 1 **c** : something portioned out bit by bit
[2]**dole** *vt* **doled; dol·ing** (15c) : to give or distribute as a charity — usu. used with *out*
[3]**dole** *n* [ME *dol,* fr. AF *duel, dol,* fr. LL *dolus,* alter. of L *dolor*] (13c) *archaic* : GRIEF, SORROW
dole·ful \'dōl-fəl\ *adj* (13c) **1** : causing grief or affliction ⟨a ~ loss⟩ **2** : full of grief : CHEERLESS ⟨a ~ face⟩ **3** : expressing grief : SAD ⟨a ~ melody⟩ — **dole·ful·ly** \-fə-lē\ *adv* — **dole·ful·ness** *n*
dole out *vt* (1749) **1** : to give or deliver in small portions **2** : DISH OUT *syn* see DISTRIBUTE
dol·er·ite \'dä-lə-ˌrīt\ *n* [F *dolérite,* fr. Gk *doleros* deceitful, fr. *dolos* deceit; fr. its being easily mistaken for diorite] (1838) **1** : any of various coarse basalts **2** *chiefly Brit* : DIABASE 3 — **dol·er·it·ic** \ˌdä-lə-'ri-tik\ *adj*
dole·some \'dōl-səm\ *adj* (1533) : DOLEFUL
dol·i·cho·ce·phal·ic \ˌdä-li-kō-sə-'fa-lik\ *adj* [NL *dolichocephalus* long-headed, fr. Gk *dolichos* long + *-kephalos,* fr. *kephalē* head — more at CEPHALIC] (1852) : having a relatively long head with cephalic index of less than 75 — **dol·i·cho·ceph·a·ly** \-'se-fə-lē\ *n*
doll \'däl, 'dȯl\ *n* [prob. fr. *Doll,* nickname for *Dorothy*] (ca. 1700) **1** : a small-scale figure of a human being used esp. as a child's plaything **2 a** (1) : a pretty but often empty-headed young woman (2) : WOMAN **b** : DARLING, SWEETHEART **c** : an attractive person — **doll·ish** \'dä-lish, 'dȯ-\ *adj* — **doll·ish·ly** *adv* — **doll·ish·ness** *n*
dol·lar \'dä-lər\ *n, often attrib* [D or LG *daler,* fr. G *Taler,* short for *Joachimstaler,* fr. Sankt *Joachimsthal,* Bohemia, where talers were first made] (1553) **1** : TALER **2** : any of numerous coins patterned after the taler (as a Spanish peso) **3 a** : any of various basic monetary units (as in the U.S. and Canada) — see MONEY table **b** : a coin, note, or token representing one dollar **4** : RINGGIT **5** : money obtained from a specific source ⟨the tourism ~⟩
dollar–a–year *adj* (1918) : compensated by a token salary usu. for government service ⟨a ~ man⟩
dollar cost averaging *n* (ca. 1957) : investment in a security at regular intervals of a uniform sum regardless of the price level in order to obtain an overall reduction in cost per unit — called also *dollar averaging*
dollar day *n* (1949) : a day on which special low prices are offered
dollar diplomacy *n* (1910) **1** : diplomacy used by a country to promote its financial or commercial interests abroad **2** : diplomacy that seeks to strengthen the power of a country or effect its purposes in foreign relations by the use of its financial resources
dol·lar·i·za·tion \ˌdä-lə-rə-'zā-shən\ *n* (1982) : the adoption of the U.S. dollar as a country's official national currency — **dol·lar·ize** \'dä-lə-ˌrīz\ *vb*
dollars–and–cents *adj* (1899) : dealing with or expressed in terms of money, sales, or profits
dollar sign *n* (1881) : a mark $ placed before a number to indicate that it stands for dollars — called also *dollar mark*
doll·house \'däl-ˌhau̇s, 'dȯl-\ *also* **doll's house** *or* **dolls' house** *n* (1783) **1** : a child's small-scale toy house **2** : a dwelling so small as to suggest a house for dolls
[1]**dol·lop** \'dä-ləp\ *n* [origin unknown] (ca. 1812) **1** *chiefly Brit* : an indefinite often large quantity esp. of something liquid **2** : a lump or glob of something soft or mushy ⟨top it with a ~ of jam⟩ **3** : an amount given, spooned, or ladled out : PORTION ⟨hold out their mess tins for a ~ of gruel —Robert Craft⟩ **4** : a small lump, portion, or amount ⟨want just a ~ of ketchup⟩ **5** : something added or served as if in dollops ⟨a delicious ~ of gossip —Leon Harris⟩
[2]**dollop** *vt* (ca. 1860) : to serve or dispense in dollops
doll up *vt* (1906) **1** : to dress elegantly or extravagantly **2** : to make more attractive (as by decorating) ~ *vi* : to get dolled up
[1]**dol·ly** \'dä-lē, 'dȯ-lē\ *n, pl* **dollies** (1790) **1** : DOLL **2** : a wooden-pronged instrument for beating and stirring clothes in the process of washing them in a tub **3** : a compact narrow-gauge railroad locomotive for moving construction trains and for switching **4 a** : a platform on a roller or on wheels or casters for moving heavy objects **b** : a wheeled platform for a television or motion-picture camera
[2]**dolly** *vb* **dol·lied; dol·ly·ing** *vt* (1878) **1** : to treat with a dolly **2** : to move or convey on a dolly ~ *vi* : to move a motion-picture or television camera about on a dolly while shooting a scene; *also, of a camera* : to be moved on a dolly
dol·ly bird \'dä-lē-ˌbərd, 'dȯ-lē-\ *n* (1964) *Brit* : a pretty young woman
dolly shot *n* (1933) : TRACKING SHOT
Dol·ly Var·den \ˌdä-lē-'vär-dᵊn-\ *n* [*Dolly Varden,* gaily dressed coquette in *Barnaby Rudge* (1841), novel by Charles Dickens] (ca. 1876) : a large anadromous or freshwater char (*Salvelinus malma*) widespread in streams of northwestern No. America and eastern Asia — called also *Dolly Varden trout*
dol·ma \ˌdōl-'mä, 'dōl-mə, 'däl-\ *n, pl* **dolmas** *or* **dol·ma·des** \dōl-'mä-(ˌ)thēz, dȯl-, däl-\ [Turk, lit., something stuffed] (ca. 1889) : a stuffed grape leaf or vegetable shell
dol·man sleeve \'dōl-mən-, 'dȯl-, 'däl-\ *n* [F *dolman* coat with dolman sleeves, fr. G *Dolman* or Hung *dolmány,* fr. Turk *dolama,* a Turkish robe] (1934) : a sleeve very wide at the armhole and tight at the wrist often cut in one piece with the bodice
dol·men \ˌdōl-mən, 'dȯl-, 'däl-\ *n* [F, prob. modif. of Cornish *tolmen,* fr. *tol* hole + *men* stone] (1859) : a prehistoric monument of two or more upright stones supporting a horizontal stone slab found esp. in Britain and France and thought to be a tomb
do·lo·mite \'dō-lə-ˌmīt, 'dä-\ *n* [F, fr. Déodat de *Dolomieu* †1801 Fr. geologist] (1794) **1** : a mineral $CaMg(CO_3)_2$ consisting of a calcium magnesium carbonate found in crystals and in extensive beds as a compact limestone **2** : a limestone or marble rich in magnesium carbonate — **do·lo·mit·ic** \ˌdō-lə-'mi-tik, ˌdä-\ *adj*
do·lo·mi·ti·za·tion \ˌdō-lə-mə-tə-'zā-shən, ˌdä-, -ˌmī-\ *n* (1862) : the process of converting into dolomite — **do·lo·mi·tize** \'dō-lə-mə-ˌtīz, 'dä-\ *vt*
do·lor \'dō-lər *also* 'dä-\ *n* [ME *dolour,* fr. AF, fr. L *dolor* pain, grief, fr. *dolēre* to feel pain, grieve] (14c) : mental suffering or anguish : GRIEF
do·lor·ous \'dō-lə-rəs *also* 'dä-\ *adj* (15c) : causing, marked by, or expressing misery or grief — **do·lor·ous·ly** *adv* — **do·lor·ous·ness** *n*
do·lour *chiefly Brit var of* DOLOR
dol·phin \'däl-fən, 'dȯl-\ *n* [ME *delphyn, dolphyn,* fr. AF *delphin,* alter. of OF *dalfin,* fr. ML *dalfinus,* alter. of L *delphinus,* fr. Gk *delphin-, delphis;* akin to Gk *delphys* womb, Skt *garbha*] (14c) **1 a** (1) : any of various small marine toothed whales (family Delphinidae) with the snout more or less elongated into a beak and the neck vertebrae partially fused (2) : any of several related chiefly freshwater toothed whales (as of the family Platanistidae) **b** : PORPOISE 1 **2** : DOLPHINFISH **3** *cap* : DELPHINUS **4** : a spar or buoy for mooring boats; *also* : a cluster of closely driven piles used as a fender for a dock or as a mooring or guide for boats

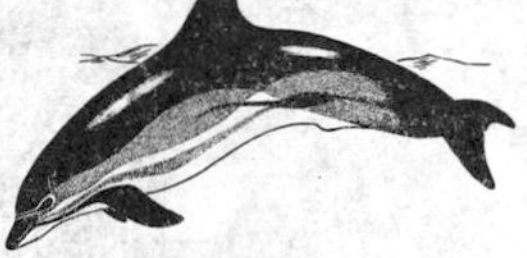

dolphin 1a

dol·phin·fish \'däl-fən-ˌfish, 'dȯl-\ *n* (1840) : either of two active pelagic bony food fishes (*Coryphaena equiselis* and *C. hippurus* of the family Coryphaenidae) of tropical and temperate seas — called also *dolphin*
dolphin striker *n* (1833) : a vertical spar under the end of the bowsprit of a sailboat to extend and support the martingale
dolt \'dōlt\ *n* [prob. akin to OE *dol* foolish] (1553) : a stupid person — **dolt·ish** \'dōl-tish\ *adj* — **dolt·ish·ly** *adv* — **dolt·ish·ness** *n*
Dom [L *dominus* master] (1716) **1** \'däm\ — used as a title for some monks and canons regular **2** \'dōⁿ\ — used as a title prefixed to the Christian name of a Portuguese or Brazilian man of rank
dom *abbr* **1** domestic **2** dominant **3** dominion
-dom *n suffix* [ME, fr. OE *-dōm;* akin to OHG *-tuom* -dom, OE *dōm* judgment — more at DOOM] **1 a** : dignity : office ⟨duke*dom*⟩ **b** : realm : jurisdiction ⟨king*dom*⟩ **2** : state or fact of being ⟨free*dom*⟩ **3** : those having a (specified) office, occupation, interest, or character ⟨official*dom*⟩
do·main \dō-'mān, də-\ *n* [alter. of ME *demayne,* fr. AF *demeine,* fr. L *dominium,* fr. *dominus*] (15c) **1 a** : complete and absolute ownership of land — compare EMINENT DOMAIN **b** : land so owned **2** : a territory over which dominion is exercised **3** : a region distinctively marked by some physical feature ⟨the ~ of rushing streams, tall trees, and lakes⟩ **4** : a sphere of knowledge, influence, or activity ⟨the ~ of art⟩ **5** : the set of elements to which a mathematical or logical variable is limited; *specif* : the set on which a function is defined **6** : any of the small randomly oriented regions of uniform magnetization in a ferromagnetic substance **7** : INTEGRAL DOMAIN **8** : the highest taxonomic category in biological classification ranking above the kingdom **9** : any of the three-dimensional subunits of a protein that are formed

by the folding of its linear peptide chain and that together make up its tertiary structure **10** : a subdivision of the Internet consisting of computers or sites usu. with a common purpose (as providing commercial information) and denoted in Internet addresses by a unique abbreviation (as *com* or *gov*); *also* : DOMAIN NAME

do·maine \dō-ˈmān, -ˈmen\ *n* [F (short for *domaine vinicole* or *viticole*), lit., property, domain] (1956) : a vineyard esp. in Burgundy that makes and bottles wine from its own grapes

domain name *n* (1982) : a sequence of usu. alphanumeric characters (as Merriam-Webster.com) that specifies a group of online resources (as of a particular company or person) and that forms part of the corresponding Internet addresses

[1]**dome** \ˈdōm\ *n* [F, It, & L; F *dôme* dome, cathedral, fr. It *duomo* cathedral, fr. ML *domus* church, fr. L, house; akin to Gk *domos* house, Skt *dam*] (1513) **1** *archaic* : a stately building : MANSION **2** : a large hemispherical roof or ceiling **3** : a natural formation or structure that resembles the dome or cupola of a building **4** : a form of crystal composed of planes parallel to a lateral axis that meet above in a horizontal edge like a roof **5** : an upward fold in rock whose sides dip uniformly in all directions **6** : a roofed sports stadium **7** : a person's head — **dom·al** \ˈdō-məl\ *adj*

[2]**dome** *vb* **domed; dom·ing** *vt* (1876) **1** : to cover with a dome **2** : to form into a dome ~ *vi* : to swell upward or outward like a dome

Domes·day Book \ˈdümz-ˌdā-, ˈdōmz-\ *n* [ME, fr. *domesday* doomsday] (1591) : a record of a survey of English lands and landholdings made by order of William the Conqueror about 1086

[1]**do·mes·tic** \də-ˈmes-tik\ *adj* [ME, fr. MF *domestique*, fr. L *domesticus*, fr. *domus*] (15c) **1 a** : living near or about human habitations **b** : TAME, DOMESTICATED ⟨the ~ cat⟩ **2** : of, relating to, or originating within a country and esp. one's own country ⟨~ politics⟩ ⟨~ wines⟩ **3** : of or relating to the household or the family ⟨~ chores⟩ ⟨~ happiness⟩ **4** : devoted to home duties and pleasures ⟨leading a quietly ~ life⟩ **5** : INDIGENOUS — **do·mes·ti·cal·ly** \-ti-k(ə-)lē\ *adv*

[2]**domestic** *n* (1613) **1** : a household servant **2** : an article of domestic manufacture — usu. used in pl.

domestic animal *n* (1743) : any of various animals (as the horse or sheep) domesticated so as to live and breed in a tame condition

[1]**do·mes·ti·cate** \də-ˈmes-ti-ˌkāt\ *vt* **-cat·ed; -cat·ing** (ca. 1639) **1** : to bring into domestic use : ADOPT **2** : to adapt (an animal or plant) to life in intimate association with and to the advantage of humans **3** : to make domestic : fit for domestic life **4** : to bring to the level of ordinary people — **do·mes·ti·ca·tion** \-ˌmes-ti-ˈkā-shən\ *n*

[2]**do·mes·ti·cate** \-kət, -ˌkāt\ *n* (1951) : a domesticated animal or plant

do·mes·tic·i·ty \ˌdō-ˌmes-ˈti-sə-tē, -məs-; ˌdä-\ *n, pl* **-ties** (1721) **1** : the quality or state of being domestic or domesticated **2** : domestic activities or life **3** *pl* : domestic affairs

domestic partner *n* (1975) **1** : a company esp. in a developing country that joins in a commercial venture with an international company **2** : either one of an unmarried heterosexual or homosexual cohabiting couple esp. when considered as to eligibility for spousal benefits — **domestic partnership** *n*

domestic prelate *n* (1929) : a priest having permanent honorary membership in the papal household

domestic relations court *n* (ca. 1939) : COURT OF DOMESTIC RELATIONS

domestic science *n* (1869) : HOME ECONOMICS

domestic shorthair *n* (1935) : AMERICAN SHORTHAIR; *broadly* : a short-haired domestic cat esp. of unknown pedigree

domestic violence *n* (1891) : the inflicting of physical injury by one family or household member on another; *also* : a repeated or habitual pattern of such behavior

dom·i·cal \ˈdō-mi-kəl, ˈdä-\ *adj* (1846) : relating to, shaped like, or having a dome

[1]**do·mi·cile** \ˈdä-mə-ˌsī(-ə)l, ˈdō-; ˈdä-mə-sil\ *also* **dom·i·cil** \ˈdäm-ə-səl\ *n* [ME, fr. MF, fr. L *domicilium*, fr. *domus*] (15c) **1** : a dwelling place : place of residence : HOME **2 a** : a person's fixed, permanent, and principal home for legal purposes **b** : RESIDENCE 2b

[2]**domicile** *vt* **-ciled; -cil·ing** (1809) : to establish in or provide with a domicile

do·mi·cil·i·ary \ˌdä-mə-ˈsi-lē-ˌer-ē, ˌdō-\ *adj* (1790) : of, relating to, or constituting a domicile: as **a** : provided or taking place in the home **b** : providing care and living space (as for disabled veterans)

do·mi·cil·i·ate \ˌdä-mə-ˈsi-lē-ˌāt, ˌdō-\ *vb* **-at·ed; -at·ing** [L *domicilium*] *vt* (1778) : DOMICILE ~ *vi* : RESIDE — **do·mi·cil·i·a·tion** \-ˌsi-lē-ˈā-shən\ *n*

dom·i·nance \ˈdä-mə-nən(t)s, ˈdäm-nən(t)s\ *n* (1819) **1** : the fact or state of being dominant: as **a** : dominant position esp. in a social hierarchy **b** : the property of one of a pair of alleles or traits that suppresses expression of the other in the heterozygous condition **c** : the influence or control over ecological communities exerted by a dominant **2** : functional asymmetry between a pair of bodily structures (as the right and left hands)

[1]**dom·i·nant** \-nənt\ *adj* [MF or L; MF, fr. L *dominant-, dominans*, prp. of *dominari*] (ca. 1532) **1 a** : commanding, controlling, or prevailing over all others ⟨the ~ culture⟩ **b** : very important, powerful, or successful ⟨a ~ theme⟩ ⟨a ~ industry⟩ **2** : overlooking and commanding from a superior position ⟨a ~ hill⟩ **3** : of, relating to, or exerting ecological or genetic dominance **4** : being the one of a pair of bodily structures that is the more effective or predominant in action ⟨~ eye⟩ — **dom·i·nant·ly** *adv*

syn DOMINANT, PREDOMINANT, PARAMOUNT, PREPONDERANT mean superior to all others in influence or importance. DOMINANT applies to something that is uppermost because ruling or controlling ⟨a *dominant* social class⟩. PREDOMINANT applies to something that exerts, often temporarily, the most marked influence ⟨a *predominant* emotion⟩. PARAMOUNT implies supremacy in importance, rank, or jurisdiction ⟨unemployment was the *paramount* issue in the campaign⟩. PREPONDERANT applies to an element or factor that outweighs all others in influence or effect ⟨*preponderant* evidence in her favor⟩.

[2]**dominant** *n* (1819) **1** : the fifth tone of a major or minor scale **2 a** : a dominant genetic character or factor **b** : any of one or more kinds of organism (as a species) in an ecological community that exerts a controlling influence on the environment and thereby largely determines what other kinds of organisms are present **c** : a dominant individual in a social hierarchy

dom·i·nate \ˈdä-mə-ˌnāt\ *vb* **-nat·ed; -nat·ing** [L *dominatus*, pp. of *dominari*, fr. *dominus* master; akin to L *domus* house — more at DOME] *vt* (1611) **1** : RULE, CONTROL ⟨an empire that *dominated* the world⟩ **2** : to exert the supreme determining or guiding influence on ⟨the ambition that has *dominated* his life⟩ **3** : to overlook from a superior elevation or command because of superior height or position ⟨a hill that ~*s* the town⟩ **4 a** : to be predominant in ⟨sugar maples ~ the forest⟩ **b** : to have a commanding or preeminent place or position in ⟨name brands ~ the market⟩ ~ *vi* **1** : to have or exert mastery, control, or preeminence **2** : to occupy a more elevated or superior position — **dom·i·na·tive** \-ˌnā-tiv\ *adj* — **dom·i·na·tor** \-ˌnā-tər\ *n*

dom·i·na·tion \ˌdä-mə-ˈnā-shən\ *n* (14c) **1** : supremacy or preeminence over another **2** : exercise of mastery or ruling power **3** : exercise of preponderant, governing, or controlling influence **4** *pl* : DOMINION 3

do·mi·na·trix \ˌdä-mi-ˈnā-triks\ *n, pl* **-tri·ces** \-ˈnā-trə-ˌsēz, -nə-ˈtrī-sēz\ [L, fem. of *dominator*] (1971) : a woman who physically or psychologically dominates her partner in a sadomasochistic encounter; *broadly* : a dominating woman

dom·i·neer \ˌdä-mə-ˈnir\ *vb* [D *domineren*, fr. F *dominer*, fr. L *dominari*] *vi* (1591) : to exercise arbitrary or overbearing control ~ *vt* : to tyrannize over

dom·i·neer·ing \-ˈnir-iŋ\ *adj* (1588) : inclined to exercise arbitrary and overbearing control over others ***syn*** see MASTERFUL — **dom·i·neer·ing·ly** *adv* — **dom·i·neer·ing·ness** *n*

do·min·i·cal \də-ˈmi-ni-kəl\ *adj* [ME, fr. LL *dominicalis*, fr. *dominicus* (*dies*) the Lord's day, fr. L *dominicus* of a lord, fr. *dominus* lord, master] (15c) **1** : of or relating to Jesus Christ as Lord **2** : of or relating to the Lord's day

Do·min·i·can \də-ˈmi-ni-kən\ *n* [St. *Dominic*] (1534) : a member of a mendicant order of friars founded by St. Dominic in 1215 and dedicated esp. to preaching — **Dominican** *adj*

dom·i·nick·er \ˈdä-mə-ˌne-kər, -ˌni-\ *also* **dom·i·nick** \-(ˌ)nik, -nek\ *n, often cap* (1806) : DOMINIQUE

do·mi·nie *1 usu* ˈdä-mə-nē, *2 usu* ˈdō-\ *n* [L *domine*, voc. of *dominus*] (1612) **1** *chiefly Scot* : SCHOOLMASTER **2** : CLERGYMAN

do·min·ion \də-ˈmi-nyən\ *n* [ME *dominioun*, fr. MF *dominion*, modif. of L *dominium*, fr. *dominus*] (14c) **1** : DOMAIN **2** : supreme authority : SOVEREIGNTY **3** *pl* : an order of angels — see CELESTIAL HIERARCHY **4** *often cap* : a self-governing nation of the Commonwealth of Nations other than the United Kingdom that acknowledges the British monarch as chief of state **5** : absolute ownership ***syn*** see POWER

Dominion Day *n* (1867) : CANADA DAY

dom·i·nique \ˈdä-mə-ˌnēk\ *n* [*Dominique* (Dominica), one of the Windward islands, West Indies] (1849) : any of a U.S. breed of domestic chickens with a rose comb, yellow legs, and barred plumage

dom·i·no \ˈdä-mə-ˌnō\ *n, pl* **-noes** *or* **-nos** [F, prob. fr. L (in the ritual formula *benedicamus Domino* let us bless the Lord)] (ca. 1694) **1 a** (1) : a long loose hooded cloak usu. worn with a half mask as a masquerade costume (2) : a half mask worn over the eyes with a masquerade costume **b** : a person wearing a domino **2 a** : a flat rectangular block (as of wood or plastic) whose face is divided into two equal parts that are blank or bear usu. from one to six dots arranged as on dice faces **b** *pl but usu sing in constr* : any of several games played with a set of usu. 28 dominoes **3** : a member of a group (as of nations) expected to behave in accordance with the domino theory

domino effect *n* (1966) : a cumulative effect produced when one event initiates a succession of similar events — compare RIPPLE EFFECT

domino theory *n* [fr. the fact that if dominoes are stood on end one slightly behind the other, a slight push on the first will topple the others] (1965) **1** : a theory that if one nation becomes Communist-controlled the neighboring nations will also become Communist-controlled **2** : the theory that if one act or event is allowed to take place a series of similar acts or events will follow

do·mo·ic acid \də-ˈmō-ik-\ *n* [Jp *dōmoi*, the alga *Chondria armata*] (1982) : a neurotoxin $C_{15}H_{21}NO_6$ that is produced by some diatoms (esp. genus *Pseudo-nitzschia*) and has caused poisoning in vertebrates (as sea lions, birds, and humans) that have consumed diatom-contaminated fish or shellfish

[1]**don** \ˈdän\ *vt* **donned; don·ning** [ME, contr. of *do on*] (14c) **1** : to put on (an article of clothing) **2** : to wrap oneself in : TAKE ON 3a

[2]**don** \ˈdän\ *n* [Sp, fr. L *dominus* master — more at DAME] (1523) **1** : a Spanish nobleman or gentleman — used as a title prefixed to the Christian name **2** *archaic* : a person of consequence : GRANDEE **3** : a head, tutor, or fellow in a college of Oxford or Cambridge University; *broadly* : a college or university professor **4** [It, title of respect, fr. *donno*, lit., lord, fr. L *dominus*] : a powerful Mafia leader

DON *abbr* director of nursing

do·na \ˈdō-nə\ *n* [Pg, fr. L *domina* lady — more at DAME] (ca. 1897) : a Portuguese or Brazilian woman of rank — used as a title prefixed to the Christian name

do·ña \ˈdō-nyə\ *n* [Sp, fr. L *domina*] (1606) : a Spanish woman of rank — used as a title prefixed to the Christian name

do·nate \ˈdō-ˌnāt, dō-ˈ\ *vb* **do·nat·ed; do·nat·ing** [back-formation fr. *donation*] *vt* (1785) **1** : to make a gift of; *esp* : to contribute to a public or charitable cause **2** : to transfer (as electrons) to another atom or molecule ~ *vi* : to make a donation ***syn*** see GIVE

do·na·tion \dō-ˈnā-shən\ *n* [ME *donatyowne*, fr. L *donation-, donatio*, fr. *donare* to present, fr. *donum* gift; akin to L *dare* to give — more at DATE] (15c) : the act or an instance of donating: as **a** : the making of a gift esp. to a charity or public institution **b** : a free contribution : GIFT

Do·na·tism \ˈdō-nə-ˌti-zəm, ˈdä-\ *n* [*Donatus*, 4th cent. bishop of Carthage] (1588) : the doctrines of a Christian sect arising in No. Africa in 311 and holding that sanctity is essential for the administration of sacraments and church membership — **Do·na·tist** \-tist\ *n*

\ə\ **abut** \ᵊ\ **kitten**, F table \ər\ **further** \a\ **ash** \ā\ **ace** \ä\ **mop, mar**
\au̇\ **out** \ch\ **chin** \e\ **bet** \ē\ **easy** \g\ **go** \i\ **hit** \ī\ **ice** \j\ **job**
\ŋ\ **sing** \ō\ **go** \ȯ\ **law** \ȯi\ **boy** \th\ **thin** \t͟h\ **the** \ü\ **loot** \u̇\ **foot**
\y\ **yet** \zh\ **vision, beige** \k̲, ⁿ, œ, ue, ʸ\ *see* Guide to Pronunciation

[1]**do·na·tive** \ˈdō-nə-tiv, ˈdä-\ *n* (15c) : a special gift or donation
[2]**do·na·tive** *same or* ˈdō-ˌnā-, dō-ˈ\ *adj* [L *donativus,* fr. *donatus*] (1559) : of or relating to donation
do·na·tor \ˈdō-ˌnā-tər, dō-ˈ\ *n* (15c) : DONOR
[1]**done** \ˈdən\ *past part of* DO
[2]**done** *adj* (14c) **1 :** arrived at or brought to an end ⟨one more question and we're ~⟩ **2 :** doomed to failure, defeat, or death **3 :** gone by : OVER ⟨the day of the circus big top is ~⟩ **4 :** physically exhausted **5 :** cooked sufficiently ⟨check to see if the meat is ~⟩ **6 :** conformable to social convention ⟨not the ~ thing⟩
done deal *n* (1979) : FAIT ACCOMPLI ⟨thought the trade was a *done deal*⟩
do·nee \ˌdō-ˈnē\ *n* [*donor*] (1523) : a recipient of a gift
done for \ˈdən-ˌfȯr\ *adj* (1803) **1 :** sunk in defeat : BEATEN **2 :** mortally stricken : DOOMED
done·ness \ˈdən-nəs\ *n* (1927) : the condition of being cooked to the desired degree
[1]**dong** \ˈdȯŋ, ˈdäŋ\ *n* [origin unknown] (ca. 1930) *usu vulgar* : PENIS
[2]**dong** *n, pl* **dong** [Vietnamese *đồng*] (1824) — see MONEY table
don·gle \ˈdäŋ-gəl, ˈdȯŋ-\ *n* [perh. alter. of *dangle*] (1981) : a small device that plugs into a computer and serves as an adapter or as a security measure to enable the use of certain software
dong quai \ˈdäŋ-ˈkwī, ˈdȯŋ-\ *n* [Chin (southern Fujian) *dōngguī* (or a cognate form in another Chin dialect)] (1988) : the root of an Asian angelica (*Angelica sinensis*) used esp. in traditional Chinese medicine as a tonic, analgesic, antispasmodic, and laxative; *also* : an extract or preparation of dong quai
don·jon \ˈdän-jən, ˈdən-\ *n* [ME — more at DUNGEON] (14c) : a massive inner tower in a medieval castle — see CASTLE illustration
Don Juan \ˈdän-ˈ(h)wän, *chiefly Brit & in poetry* dän-ˈjü-ən\ *n* [Sp] (1679) **1 :** a legendary Spaniard proverbial for his seduction of women **2 :** a captivating man known as a great lover or seducer of women — **Don Juan·ism** \-ˈ(h)wän-ˌi-zəm, -ˈjü-ə-ˌni-\ *n*
don·key \ˈdäŋ-kē, ˈdəŋ-, ˈdȯŋ-\ *n, pl* **donkeys** [origin unknown] (ca. 1785) **1 :** the domestic ass (*Equus asinus*) **2 :** a stupid or obstinate person
donkey engine *n* (1858) **1 :** a small usu. portable auxiliary engine **2 :** a small locomotive used in switching
donkey jacket *n* (1929) *Brit* : a jacket of heavy material worn esp. by laborers
donkey's years *n pl* (1927) *chiefly Brit* : a very long time
don·key·work \ˈdäŋ-kē-ˌwərk, ˈdəŋ-, ˈdȯŋ-\ *n* (1920) : monotonous and routine work : DRUDGERY
don·na \ˌdä-nə, ˌdȯ-\ *n, pl* **don·ne** \-(ˌ)nā\ [It, fr. L *domina*] (1738) : an Italian woman esp. of rank — used as a title prefixed to the given name
don·née \dȯ-ˈnā, (ˌ)də-\ *n, pl* **données** \-ˈnā(z)\ [F, fr. fem. of *donné,* pp. of *donner* to give, fr. L *donare* to donate — more at DONATION] (1876) : the set of assumptions on which a work of fiction or drama proceeds
don·nick·er *or* **don·ni·ker** \ˈdä-ni-kər\ *n* [alter. of E dial. *dunnekin* toilet, cesspool] (ca. 1931) : TOILET 3a
don·nish \ˈdä-nish\ *adj* (1848) : of, relating to, or characteristic of a university don — **don·nish·ly** *adv* — **don·nish·ness** *n*
don·ny·brook \ˈdä-nē-ˌbru̇k\ *n, often cap* [*Donnybrook* Fair, annual Irish event known for its brawls] (1852) **1 :** FREE-FOR-ALL, BRAWL **2 :** a usu. public quarrel or dispute
do·nor \ˈdō-nər, -ˌnȯr\ *n* [ME *donoure,* fr. AF *doneur,* fr. L *donator,* fr. *donare*] (15c) **1 :** one that gives, donates, or presents something **2 :** one used as a source of biological material (as blood or an organ) **3 a :** a compound capable of giving up a part (as an atom, chemical group, or subatomic particle) for combination with an acceptor **b :** an impurity added to a semiconductor to increase the number of mobile electrons
[1]**do–noth·ing** \ˈdü-ˌnə-thiŋ\ *n* (1579) : a shiftless or lazy person
[2]**do–nothing** *adj* (1832) : marked by inactivity or failure to make positive progress — **do–noth·ing·ism** \-ˌi-zəm\ *n*
Don Qui·xote \ˌdän-kē-ˈ(h)ō-tē, ˌdäŋ-; *chiefly Brit* dän-ˈkwik-sət\ *n* [Sp, hero of Cervantes' *Don Quixote*] (1630) : an impractical idealist
don·sie *or* **don·sy** \ˈdän(t)-sē\ *adj* [ScGael *donas* evil, harm + E *-ie*] (1720) **1** *dial Brit* : UNLUCKY **2** *Scot* **a :** RESTIVE **b :** SAUCY **3** *chiefly northern Midland* : slightly ill
[1]**don't** \ˈdōnt\ (1639) **1 :** do not **2 :** does not
usage Don't is the earliest attested contraction of *does not* and until about 1900 was the standard spoken form in the U.S. (it survived as spoken standard longer in British English). Dialect surveys find it more common in the speech of the less educated than in that of the educated; in those places (as the Midland and southern Atlantic seaboard regions) where it has lasted in educated speech, it is most common with older informants. Surveys of attitudes toward usage show it more widely disapproved in 1971 than it had been 40 years earlier. Its chief use in edited prose is in fiction for purposes of characterization. It is sometimes used consciously, like *ain't,* to gain an informal effect.
[2]**don't** \ˈdōnt\ *n* (1894) : a command or entreaty not to do something ⟨a list of dos and ~*s*⟩
donut *var of* DOUGHNUT
doo·bie \ˈdü-bē\ *n* [origin unknown] (1967) *slang* : a marijuana cigarette : JOINT
doo·dad \ˈdü-ˌdad\ *n* [origin unknown] (1888) **1 :** an ornamental attachment or decoration **2 :** an often small article whose common name is unknown or forgotten : GADGET
[1]**doo·dle** \ˈdü-dᵊl\ *vb* **doo·dled; doo·dling** \ˈdüd-liŋ, ˈdü-dᵊl-iŋ\ [perh. fr. *doodle* to ridicule] *vi* (1935) **1 :** to make a doodle **2 :** DAWDLE, TRIFLE ~ *vt* : to produce by doodling — **doo·dler** \ˈdüd-lər, ˈdü-dᵊl-ər\ *n*
[2]**doodle** *n* (1937) : an aimless or casual scribble, design, or sketch; *also* : a minor work
doo·dle·bug \ˈdü-dᵊl-ˌbəg\ *n* [prob. fr. *doodle* fool + *bug*] (ca. 1866) **1 :** the larva of an ant lion; *also* : any of several other insects **2 :** a device (as a divining rod) used in attempting to locate underground gas, water, oil, or ores **3 :** BUZZ BOMB
doodley–squat *or* **doodly–squat** \ˈdü-dᵊl-ē-ˌskwät\ *n* [*doodley* (perh. alter. of *do one's do* to defecate) + *squat*] (1934) : DIDDLY-SQUAT
doo–doo \ˈdü-(ˌ)dü\ *n* [baby talk] (1948) : FECES — **in deep doo–doo :** in trouble

doo·fus \ˈdü-fəs, -fis\ *n, pl* **doo·fus·es** \-fə-siz\ [perh. alter. of [1]*goof*] (1960) *slang* : a stupid, incompetent, or foolish person
doo·hick·ey \ˈdü-ˌhi-kē\ *n, pl* **-hickeys** *also* **-hickies** [prob. fr. *doodad* + *hickey*] (1914) : DOODAD 2
[1]**doom** \ˈdüm\ *n* [ME, fr. OE *dōm;* akin to OHG *tuom* condition, state, OE *dōn* to do] (bef. 12c) **1 :** a law or ordinance esp. in Anglo-Saxon England **2 a :** JUDGMENT, DECISION; *esp* : a judicial condemnation or sentence **b (1) :** JUDGMENT 3a **(2) :** JUDGMENT DAY 1 **3 a :** DESTINY; *esp* : unhappy destiny **b :** DEATH, RUIN *syn* see FATE
[2]**doom** *vt* (15c) **1 :** to give judgment against : CONDEMN **2 a :** to fix the fate of : DESTINE ⟨felt he was ~*ed* to a life of loneliness⟩ **b :** to make certain the failure or destruction of ⟨the scandal ~*ed* her chances for election⟩
doom·ful \ˈdüm-fəl\ *adj* (1586) : presaging doom : OMINOUS ⟨~ predictions⟩ — **doom·ful·ly** \-fə-lē\ *adv*
doom·say·er \ˈdüm-ˌsā-ər\ *n* (1953) : one given to forebodings and predictions of impending calamity — **doom·say·ing** \-ˌsā-iŋ\ *n*
dooms·day \ˈdümz-ˌdā\ *n, often attrib* (bef. 12c) **1 :** a day of final judgment **2 :** a time of catastrophic destruction and death
dooms·day·er \-ˌdā-ər, -ˌder\ *n* (1972) : DOOMSAYER
doom·ster \ˈdüm(p)-stər\ *n* (15c) **1 :** JUDGE **2 :** DOOMSAYER
doomy \ˈdü-mē\ *adj* **doom·i·er; -est** (1971) : suggestive of doom : DOOMFUL — **doom·i·ly** \ˈdü-mi-lē\ *adv*
door \ˈdȯr\ *n, often attrib* [ME *dure, dor,* fr. OE *duru* door & *dor* gate; akin to OHG *turi* door, L *fores,* Gk *thyra*] (bef. 12c) **1 :** a usu. swinging or sliding barrier by which an entry is closed and opened; *also* : a similar part of a piece of furniture **2 :** DOORWAY **3 :** a means of access or participation : OPPORTUNITY ⟨opens new ~*s*⟩ ⟨~ to success⟩ — **door·less** \-ləs\ *adj* — **at one's door :** as a charge against one as being responsible ⟨laid the blame *at our door*⟩
door·bell \ˈdȯr-ˌbel\ *n* (1807) : a bell or set of chimes to be rung usu. by a push button at an outer door
do–or–die \ˈdü-ər-ˈdī, -ȯr-\ *adj* (1873) **1 :** doggedly determined to reach one's objective : INDOMITABLE **2 :** presenting as the only alternatives complete success or complete ruin ⟨a ~ situation⟩
door·jamb \ˈdȯr-ˌjam\ *n* (1727) : an upright piece forming the side of a door opening
door·keep·er \-ˌkē-pər\ *n* (1535) : a person who tends a door
door·knob \-ˌnäb\ *n* (1835) : a knob that releases a door latch
door·man \-ˌman, -mən\ *n* (ca. 1897) : a usu. uniformed attendant at the door of a building (as a hotel or apartment building)
door·mat \-ˌmat\ *n* (1665) **1 :** a mat placed before or inside a door for wiping dirt from the shoes **2 :** one that submits without protest to abuse or indignities **3 :** a team that regularly finishes last
door·nail \-ˌnāl, -ˈnāl\ *n* (14c) : a large-headed nail — used chiefly in the phrase *dead as a doornail*
door·plate \-ˌplāt\ *n* (1822) : a nameplate on a door
door·post \-ˌpōst\ *n* (1535) : DOORJAMB
door prize *n* (1951) : a prize awarded to the holder of a winning ticket passed out at the entrance to an entertainment or function
door·sill \ˈdȯr-ˌsil\ *n* (ca. 1587) : SILL 1b
door·step \-ˌstep\ *n* (1767) : a step before an outer door — **on one's doorstep :** close at hand; *esp* : too close to be overlooked
door·stop \-ˌstäp\ *n* (1878) **1 :** a usu. rubber-tipped device attached to a wall or floor to prevent damaging contact between an opened door and the wall **2 :** a device (as a wedge or weight) for holding a door open
door–to–door \ˌdȯr-tə-ˈdȯr\ *adj* (1902) : going or made by going to each house in a neighborhood ⟨~ salespeople⟩ ⟨a ~ canvass⟩ — **door–to–door** *adv*
door·way \ˈdȯr-ˌwā\ *n* (1666) **1 :** the opening that a door closes; *esp* : an entrance into a building or room **2 :** DOOR 3
door·yard \-ˌyärd\ *n* (ca. 1764) : a yard next to the door of a house
doo–wop \ˈdü-ˌwäp\ *n* [fr. nonsense syllables typical of the style] (1969) : a vocal style of rock and roll characterized by the a cappella singing of nonsense syllables in rhythmical support of the melody
doo·zy *or* **doo·zie** \ˈdü-zē\ *also* **doo·zer** \-zər\ *n, pl* **doozies** *or* **doozers** [perh. alter. of *daisy*] (1916) : an extraordinary one of its kind
do·pa \ˈdō-pə, -(ˌ)pä\ *n* [ISV *d*ihydr*o*xy- + *p*henyl*a*lanine] (1917) : a phenolic amino acid $C_9H_{11}NO_4$ occurring naturally (as in broad beans) or prepared synthetically (as from tyrosine) — compare L-DOPA
do·pa·mine \ˈdō-pə-ˌmēn\ *n* [*dopa* + *amine*] (1959) : a monoamine $C_8H_{11}NO_2$ that is a decarboxylated form of dopa and that occurs esp. as a neurotransmitter in the brain
do·pa·mi·ner·gic \ˌdō-pə-ˌmē-ˈnər-jik\ *adj* (1966) : liberating, activated by, or involving dopamine or related substances
dop·ant \ˈdō-pənt\ *n* [[2]*dope*] (1962) : an impurity added usu. in minute amounts to a pure substance to alter its properties (as conductivity)
[1]**dope** \ˈdōp\ *n* [D *doop* sauce, fr. *dopen* to dip; akin to OE *dyppan* to dip] (1786) **1 a :** a thick liquid or pasty preparation **b :** a preparation for giving a desired quality to a substance or surface **2 :** absorbent or adsorbent material used in various manufacturing processes (as the making of dynamite) **3 a (1) :** an illicit, habit-forming, or narcotic drug; *esp* : MARIJUANA **(2) :** a preparation given to a racehorse to help or hinder its performance **b** *chiefly Southern* : a cola drink **c :** a stupid person **4 :** information esp. from a reliable source ⟨the inside ~⟩
[2]**dope** *vb* **doped; dop·ing** *vt* (1889) **1 :** to treat or affect with dope; *esp* : to give a narcotic to **2 :** FIGURE OUT — usu. used with *out* **3 :** to treat with a dopant ~ *vi* : to take dope — **dop·er** *n*
[3]**dope** *adj* (1981) *slang* : EXCELLENT — used as a generalized term of approval
dope·head \ˈdōp-ˌhed\ *n* (1903) : a drug addict
dope·ster \ˈdōp-stər\ *n* (1907) : a forecaster of the outcome of future events (as sports contests or elections)
dop·ey *also* **dopy** \ˈdō-pē\ *adj* **dop·i·er; -est** (1896) **1 a :** dulled by alcohol or a narcotic **b :** SLUGGISH, STUPEFIED **2 :** STUPID, FATUOUS ⟨~ sitcoms⟩ — **dop·i·ly** \-pə-lē\ *adv* — **dop·i·ness** *n*
doping *n* (1900) : the use of a substance (as an anabolic steroid or erythropoietin) or technique (as blood doping) to illegally improve athletic performance
dop·pel·gäng·er *or* **dop·pel·gang·er** \ˈdä-pəl-ˌgaŋ-ər, -ˌgeŋ-, ˌdä-pəl-ˈ\ *n* [G *Doppelgänger,* fr. *doppel-* double + *-gänger* goer] (1851) **1 :** a ghostly counterpart of a living person **2 a :** DOUBLE 2a **b :** ALTER EGO b **c :** a person who has the same name as another

Dopp·ler \ˈdä-plər\ *adj* (1905) **:** of, relating to, being, or utilizing a shift in frequency in accordance with the Doppler effect; *also* **:** of or relating to Doppler radar

Doppler effect *n* [Christian J. *Doppler*] (1905) **:** a change in the frequency with which waves (as of sound or light) from a given source reach an observer when the source and the observer are in motion with respect to each other so that the frequency increases or decreases according to the speed at which the distance is decreasing or increasing

Doppler radar *n* (1954) **:** a radar system that utilizes the Doppler effect for measuring velocity

do·ra·do \də-ˈrä-(ˌ)dō\ *n* [Sp, fr. pp. of *dorar* to gild, fr. L *deaurare,* fr. *de-* + *aurum* gold — more at AUREUS] (1604) **:** MAHIMAHI

do–rag \ˈdü-ˌrag\ *n* [[2]*do* (hairdo)] (1984) **:** a kerchief worn esp. to cover the hair

Dor·cas \ˈdȯr-kəs\ *n* [Gk *Dorkas*] (1553) **:** a Christian woman of New Testament times who made clothing for the poor

Do·ri·an \ˈdȯr-ē-ən\ *n* [L *Dorius* of Doris, fr. Gk *dōrios,* fr. *Dōris,* region of ancient Greece] (1662) **:** a member of an ancient Hellenic race that completed the overthrow of Mycenaean civilization and settled esp. in the Peloponnisos and Crete — **Dorian** *adj*

[1]**Dor·ic** \ˈdȯr-ik, ˈdär-\ *adj* (1569) **1 :** of, relating to, or characteristic of the Dorians **2 :** belonging to the oldest and simplest Greek architectural order — see ORDER illustration **3 :** of, relating to, or constituting Doric

[2]**Doric** *n* (1602) **:** a dialect of ancient Greek spoken esp. in the Peloponnisos, Crete, Sicily, and southern Italy

dork \ˈdȯrk\ *n* [perh. alter. of *dick*] (1967) *slang* **:** NERD; *also* **:** JERK 4a

dorky \ˈdȯr-kē\ *adj* **dork·i·er; -est** (ca. 1970) *slang* **:** foolishly stupid **:** CLUELESS — **dork·i·ness** *n*

dorm \ˈdȯrm\ *n* (1900) **:** DORMITORY

dor·man·cy \ˈdȯr-mən(t)-sē\ *n* (1789) **:** the quality or state of being dormant

dor·mant \ˈdȯr-mənt\ *adj* [ME, fixed, stationary, fr. AF, fr. prp. of *dormir* to sleep, fr. L *dormire;* akin to Skt *drāti* he sleeps] (ca. 1500) **1 :** represented on a coat of arms in a lying position with the head on the forepaws **2 :** marked by a suspension of activity: as **a :** temporarily devoid of external activity ⟨a ~ volcano⟩ **b :** temporarily in abeyance yet capable of being activated **3 a :** ASLEEP, INACTIVE **b :** having the faculties suspended **:** SLUGGISH **c :** having biological activity suspended: as **(1) :** being in a state of suspended animation **(2) :** not actively growing but protected (as by bud scales) from the environment — used of plant parts **4 :** associated with, carried out, or applied during a period of dormancy ⟨~ grafting⟩ ***syn*** see LATENT

dor·mer \ˈdȯr-mər\ *n* [MF *dormeor* dormitory, fr. L *dormitorium*] (1592) **:** a window set vertically in a structure projecting through a sloping roof; *also* **:** the roofed structure containing such a window — **dor·mered** \-mərd\ *adj*

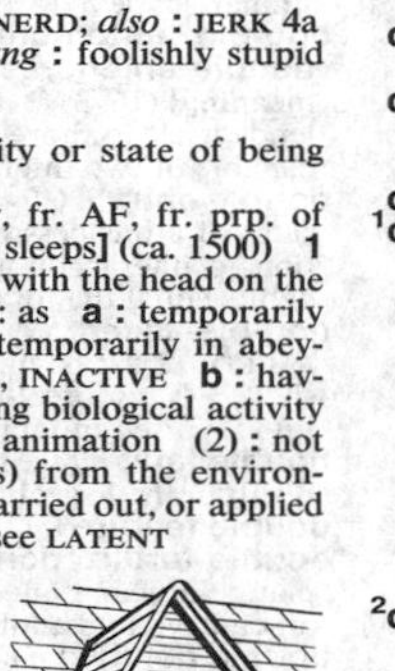

dormer

dor·mie *or* **dor·my** \ˈdȯr-mē\ *adj* [origin unknown] (1847) **:** being ahead by as many holes in golf as remain to be played in match play

dor·mi·to·ry \ˈdȯr-mə-ˌtȯr-ē\ *n, pl* **-ries** [ME, fr. L *dormitorium,* fr. *dormire*] (15c) **1 :** a room for sleeping; *esp* **:** a large room containing numerous beds **2 :** a residence hall providing rooms for individuals or for groups usu. without private baths **3** *chiefly Brit* **:** a residential community inhabited chiefly by commuters

dor·mouse \ˈdȯr-ˌmau̇s\ *n, pl* **dor·mice** \-ˌmīs\ [ME *dormowse,* perh. fr. AF *dormir* + ME *mous* mouse] (15c) **:** any of numerous small Old World rodents (esp. family Myoxidae) that are intermediate in form and behavior between mice and squirrels

dor·nick \ˈdȯr-nik, ˈdä-nik\ *n* [prob. fr. Ir *dornóg*] (1840) **:** a stone small enough to throw; *also* **:** a large piece of rock

do·ron·i·cum \də-ˈrä-ni-kəm\ *n* [NL, genus name, fr. Ar *darūnaj,* a plant of this genus] (1753) **:** any of a genus (*Doronicum*) of Eurasian perennial composite herbs including several cultivated for their showy yellow flower heads

dorp \ˈdȯrp\ *n* [D, fr. MD; akin to OHG *dorf* village — more at THORP] (ca. 1576) **:** VILLAGE

dors- *or* **dorsi-** *or* **dorso-** *comb form* [LL *dors-,* fr. L *dorsum*] **1 :** back ⟨*dors*ad⟩ **2 :** dorsal and ⟨*dorso*lateral⟩

dor·sad \ˈdȯr-ˌsad\ *adv* (ca. 1803) **:** toward the back **:** DORSALLY

[1]**dorsal** *var of* DOSSAL

[2]**dor·sal** \ˈdȯr-səl\ *adj* [LL *dorsalis,* fr. L *dorsum* back] (1727) **1 :** relating to or situated near or on the back esp. of an animal or of one of its parts **2 :** ABAXIAL — **dor·sal·ly** \-sə-lē\ *adv*

[3]**dorsal** *n* (1834) **:** a dorsally located part; *esp* **:** a thoracic vertebra

dorsal lip *n* (1924) **:** the margin of the fold of blastula wall that delineates the dorsal limit of the blastopore, constitutes the primary organizer, and forms the point of origin of chordamesoderm

dorsal root *n* (1922) **:** the one of the two roots of a spinal nerve that passes dorsally to the spinal cord and consists of sensory fibers

Dor·set \ˈdȯr-sət\ *n* (1891) **:** any of a breed of domestic white-faced sheep orig. developed in Dorset, England

dor·si·ven·tral \ˌdȯr-si-ˈven-trəl\ *adj* (ca. 1882) **1 :** having distinct dorsal and ventral surfaces **2 :** DORSOVENTRAL 1 — **dor·si·ven·tral·i·ty** \-ven-ˈtra-lə-tē\ *n* — **dor·si·ven·tral·ly** \-ˈven-trə-lē\ *adv*

dor·so·lat·er·al \ˌdȯr-sō-ˈla-tə-rəl, -ˈla-trəl\ *adj* (1835) **:** of, relating to, or involving both the back and the sides

dor·so·ven·tral \-ˈven-trəl\ *adj* [ISV] (1870) **1 :** relating to, involving, or extending along the axis joining the dorsal and ventral sides **2 :** DORSIVENTRAL 1 — **dor·so·ven·tral·i·ty** \-ven-ˈtra-lə-tē\ *n* — **dor·so·ven·tral·ly** \-trə-lē\ *adv*

dor·sum \ˈdȯr-səm\ *n, pl* **dor·sa** \-sə\ [L] (1615) **1 :** the upper surface of an appendage or part **2 :** BACK; *esp* **:** the entire dorsal surface of an animal

do·ry \ˈdȯr-ē\ *n, pl* **dories** [Miskito *dóri* dugout] (1709) **:** a flat-bottomed boat with high flaring sides, sharp bow, and deep V-shaped transom

dos *or* **do's** *pl of* [2]DO

DOS *abbr* disk operating system

dos·age \ˈdō-sij\ *n* (ca. 1867) **1 a :** the addition of an ingredient or the application of an agent in a measured dose **b :** the presence and relative representation or strength of a factor or agent **2 a :** DOSE 2 **b (1) :** the giving of a dose **(2) :** regulation or determination of doses **3 :** an exposure to some experience in or as if in measured portions

[1]**dose** \ˈdōs\ *n* [ME, fr. MF, fr. LL *dosis,* fr. Gk, lit., act of giving, fr. *didonai* to give — more at DATE] (15c) **1 a :** the measured quantity of a therapeutic agent to be taken at one time **b :** the quantity of radiation administered or absorbed **2 :** a portion of a substance added during a process **3 :** an amount of something likened to a prescribed or measured quantity of medicine ⟨a daily ~ of hard work⟩ ⟨a ~ of scandal⟩ **4 :** a gonorrheal infection

[2]**dose** *vt* **dosed; dos·ing** (1654) **1 :** to give a dose to; *esp* **:** to give medicine to **2 :** to divide (as a medicine) into doses **3 :** to treat with an application or agent

do–si–do \ˌdō-(ˌ)sē-ˈdō\ *n, pl* **do–si–dos** [F *dos-à-dos* back to back] (1926) **:** a square-dance figure: **a :** a figure in which the dancers pass each other right shoulder to right shoulder and circle each other back to back **b :** a figure in which the woman moves in a figure circling first her partner and then the man on her right

do·sim·e·ter \dō-ˈsi-mə-tər\ *n* [LL *dosis* + ISV *-meter*] (1906) **:** a device for measuring doses of radiations (as X-rays) — **do·si·met·ric** \ˌdō-sə-ˈme-trik\ *adj* — **do·sim·e·try** \dō-ˈsi-mə-trē\ *n*

[1]**doss** \ˈdȯs, ˈdäs\ *vi* [origin unknown] (ca. 1785) *chiefly Brit* **:** to sleep or bed down in a convenient place — usu. used with *down*

[2]**doss** *n* (ca. 1789) *chiefly Brit* **:** a crude or makeshift bed

dos·sal \ˈdä-səl\ *or* **dor·sal** \ˈdȯr-səl\ *or* **dos·sel** \ˈdä-səl\ *n* [ML *dossale, dorsale,* fr. neut. of LL *dorsalis* dorsal] (1851) **:** an ornamental cloth hung behind and above an altar

doss–house \ˈdȯs-ˌhau̇s, ˈdäs-\ *n* (1888) *chiefly Brit* **:** a cheap rooming house or hotel

dos·sier \ˈdȯs-ˌyā, ˈdäs-; ˈdȯ-sē-ˌā, ˈdä-\ *n* [F, bundle of documents labeled on the back, dossier, fr. *dos* back, fr. L *dorsum*] (1880) **:** a file containing detailed records on a particular person or subject

dost \ˈdəst\ *archaic pres 2d sing of* DO

[1]**dot** \ˈdät\ *n* [ME **dot,* fr. OE *dott* head of a boil; akin to OHG *tutta* nipple] (1674) **1 :** a small spot **:** SPECK **2 :** a small round mark: as **a (1) :** a small point made with a pointed instrument ⟨a ~ on the chart marked the ship's position⟩ **(2) :** a small round mark used in orthography or punctuation ⟨put a ~ over the *i*⟩ **b :** a centered point used as a multiplication sign (as in 6 · 5 = 30) **c (1) :** a point after a note or rest in music indicating augmentation of the time value by one half **(2) :** a point over or under a note indicating that it is to be played staccato **3 :** a precise point esp. in time ⟨arrived at six on the ~⟩ **4 :** a short click or buzz forming a letter or part of a letter (as in the Morse code) **5 :** a point used to separate components of an address on the Internet

[2]**dot** *vb* **dot·ted; dot·ting** *vt* (ca. 1740) **1 :** to mark with a dot **2 :** to intersperse with dots or objects scattered at random ⟨boats *dotting* the lake⟩ ~ *vi* **:** to make a dot — **dot·ter** *n*

[3]**dot** \ˈdȯt\ *n* [F, fr. L *dot-, dos* dowry] (1855) **:** DOWRY 2

DOT *abbr* Department of Transportation

dot·age \ˈdō-tij\ *n* [ME, fr. *doten* to dote] (14c) **:** a state or period of senile decay marked by decline of mental poise and alertness

do·tal \ˈdō-tᵊl\ *adj* [L *dotalis,* fr. *dot-, dos*] (1513) **:** of or relating to a woman's marriage dowry

dot·ard \ˈdō-tərd\ *n* (14c) **:** a person in his or her dotage

dot–com \ˈdät-ˌkäm\ *n, often attrib* [fr. the use of *.com* in the URLs of such companies] (1994) **:** a company that markets its products or services usu. exclusively online via a Web site

dot–com·mer \-ˌkä-mər\ *n* (1997) **:** a person who owns or works for a dot-com

dote \ˈdōt\ *vi* **dot·ed; dot·ing** [ME; akin to MLG *dotten* to be foolish] (13c) **1 :** to exhibit mental decline of or like that of old age **:** be in one's dotage **2 :** to be lavish or excessive in one's attention, fondness, or affection — usu. used with *on* ⟨*doted* on her only grandchild⟩ — **dot·er** *n* — **dot·ing·ly** \ˈdō-tiŋ-lē\ *adv*

doth \ˈdəth\ *archaic pres 3d sing of* DO

dot matrix *n* (1963) **:** a pattern of dots in a grid from which alphanumeric characters can be formed ⟨a *dot matrix* printer⟩

dot product *n* [[1]*dot;* fr. its being commonly written *A* · *B*] (1901) **:** SCALAR PRODUCT

dotted swiss *n* (1886) **:** a sheer light muslin ornamented with evenly spaced raised dots

dot·ter·el \ˈdä-tə-rəl, ˈdä-trəl\ *n* [ME *dotrelle,* irreg. fr. *doten* to dote] (15c) **:** a Eurasian plover (*Eudromias morinellus*) formerly common in England; *also* **:** any of various related plovers chiefly of eastern Asia, Australia, and So. America

dot·tle \ˈdä-tᵊl, ˈdȯ-\ *n* [ME *dottel* plug, fr. ME **dot*] (ca. 1825) **:** unburned and partially burned tobacco in the bowl of a pipe

[1]**dot·ty** \ˈdä-tē\ *adj* **dot·ti·er; -est** [alter. of Sc *dottle* fool, fr. ME *dotel,* fr. *doten*] (15c) **1 a :** mentally unbalanced **:** CRAZY **b :** amiably eccentric ⟨a ~ old relative⟩ **2 :** being obsessed or infatuated ⟨~ fans⟩ **3 :** amusingly absurd **:** RIDICULOUS ⟨~ traditions⟩ — **dot·ti·ly** \ˈdä-tᵊl-ē\ *adv* — **dot·ti·ness** \ˈdä-tē-nəs\ *n*

[2]**dotty** *adj* (1812) **:** composed of or marked by dots

Dou·ay Version \dü-ˈā-\ *n* [*Douay,* France] (1837) **:** an English translation of the Vulgate used by Roman Catholics

[1]**dou·ble** \ˈdə-bəl\ *adj* [ME, fr. AF *duble, double,* fr. L *duplus* (akin to Gk *diploos*), fr. *duo* two + *-plus* multiplied by; akin to OE *-feald* -fold — more at TWO, -FOLD] (13c) **1 :** having a twofold relation or character **:** DUAL **2 :** consisting of two usu. combined members or parts ⟨an egg with a ~ yolk⟩ **3 a :** being twice as great or as many ⟨~ the number of expected applicants⟩ **b** *of a coin* **:** worth two of the specified amount ⟨a ~ eagle⟩ ⟨a ~ crown⟩ **4 :** marked by duplicity **:** DECEITFUL **5 :** folded in two **6 :** of extra size, strength, or value ⟨a ~ martini⟩ **7 :** having more than the normal number of floral leaves often at the expense of the sporophylls **8** *of rhyme* **:** involving correspondence of two syllables (as in *exciting* and *inviting*) **9 :** designed for the use of two persons ⟨a ~ room⟩ ⟨a ~ bed⟩ — **dou·ble·ness** *n*

\ə\ **abut** \ᵊ\ **kitten, F table** \ər\ **further** \a\ **ash** \ā\ **ace** \ä\ **mop, mar** \au̇\ **out** \ch\ **chin** \e\ **bet** \ē\ **easy** \g\ **go** \i\ **hit** \ī\ **ice** \j\ **job** \ŋ\ **sing** \ō\ **go** \ȯ\ **law** \ȯi\ **boy** \th\ **thin** \t͟h\ **the** \ü\ **loot** \u̇\ **foot** \y\ **yet** \zh\ **vision, beige** \ḵ, ⁿ, œ, ue, ʸ\ *see* Guide to Pronunciation

[2]**double** *vb* **dou·bled; dou·bling** \'də-b(ə-)liŋ\ *vt* (13c) **1** : to make twice as great or as many: as **a** : to increase by adding an equal amount **b** : to amount to twice the number of **c** : to make a call in bridge that increases the value of odd tricks or undertricks at (an opponent's bid) **2 a** : to bend or fold (as a sheet of paper) usu. in the middle so that one part lies directly against the other part **b** : CLENCH ⟨*doubled* his fist⟩ **c** : to cause to stoop **3** : to avoid by doubling : ELUDE **4 a** : to replace in a dramatic role **b** : to play (dramatic roles) by doubling **5 a (1)** : to advance or score (a base runner) by a double **(2)** : to bring about the scoring of (a run) by a double **b** : to put out (a base runner) in completing a double play ~ *vi* **1 a** : to become twice as much or as many **b** : to double a bid (as in bridge) **2 a** : to turn sharply and suddenly; *esp* : to turn back on one's course ⟨the rabbit *doubled* back on its tracks⟩ **b** : to follow a circuitous course **3** : to become bent or folded usu. in the middle — usu. used with *up* ⟨she *doubled* up in pain⟩ **4 a** : to serve an additional purpose or perform an additional duty **b** : to play a dramatic role as a double **5** : to make a double in baseball — **dou·bler** \-b(ə-)lər\ *n*

[3]**double** *adv* (14c) **1** : to twice the extent or amount **2** : two together ⟨the children had to sleep ~⟩ **3** : downward and forward from the usual position ⟨he was bent ~ with pain⟩

[4]**double** *n* (14c) **1** : something twice the usual size, strength, speed, quantity, or value: as **a** : a double amount **b** : a base hit that enables the batter to reach second base **2** : one that is the counterpart of another : DUPLICATE: as **a** : a living person that closely resembles another living person **b** : WRAITH **c (1)** : UNDERSTUDY **(2)** : one who resembles an actor and takes his or her place esp. in scenes calling for special skills **(3)** : an actor who plays more than one role in a production **3 a** : a sharp turn (as in running) : REVERSAL **b** : an evasive shift **4** : something consisting of two paired members: as **a** : FOLD **b** : a combined bet placed on two different contests **c** : two consecutive strikes in bowling **5** *pl* : a game between two pairs of players **6** : an act of doubling in a card game **7** : a room (as in a hotel) for two guests — compare SINGLE 4 — **on the double** : very quickly : RIGHT AWAY

double agent *n* (1935) : a spy pretending to serve one government while actually serving another

double bar *n* (1662) : two adjacent vertical lines or a heavy single line separating principal sections of a musical composition

dou·ble–bar·rel \ˌdə-bəl-'ba-rəl\ *n* (1811) : a double-barreled gun

dou·ble–bar·reled \-rəld\ *adj* (1709) **1** *of a firearm* : having two barrels mounted side by side or one beneath the other **2** : TWOFOLD; *esp* : having a double purpose ⟨asked a ~ question⟩

double bass *n* (1752) : the largest and lowest-pitched of the stringed instruments tuned in fourths — **double bass·ist** \-'bā-sist\ *n*

double bassoon *n* (ca. 1876) : CONTRABASSOON

double bill *n* (1917) : a bill (as at a theater) offering two features

double bind *n* (1956) : a psychological predicament in which a person receives from a single source conflicting messages that allow no appropriate response to be made; *broadly* : DILEMMA 2

dou·ble–blind \ˌdə-bəl-'blīnd\ *adj* (1950) : of, relating to, or being an experimental procedure in which neither the subjects nor the experimenters know which subjects are in the test and control groups during the actual course of the experiments — compare OPEN-LABEL, SINGLE-BLIND

double bogey *n* (1954) : a golf score of two strokes over par on a hole — **double–bogey** *vt*

double boiler *n* (1864) : a cooking utensil consisting of two saucepans fitting together so that the contents of the upper can be cooked or heated by boiling water in the lower

double bond *n* (1889) : a chemical bond in which two pairs of electrons are shared by two atoms in a molecule — compare SINGLE BOND, TRIPLE BOND

dou·ble–breast·ed \ˌdə-bəl-'bres-təd\ *adj* (1701) **1** : having one half of the front lapped over the other and usu. a double row of buttons and a single row of buttonholes ⟨a ~ coat⟩ **2** : having a double-breasted coat ⟨a ~ suit⟩

double–check \ˌdə-bəl-'chek, 'də-bəl-ˌ\ *vt* (1944) : to subject to a double check ⟨data ~*ed* for accuracy⟩ ~ *vi* : to make a double check

double check *n* (1953) : a careful checking to determine accuracy, condition, or progress esp. of something already checked

dou·ble–clutch \ˌdə-bəl-'kləch\ *vi* (1928) : to shift gears in an automotive vehicle by shifting into neutral and pumping the clutch before shifting to another gear

dou·ble–crest·ed cormorant \-'kres-təd-\ *n* (1835) : a No. American cormorant (*Phalacrocorax auritus*) of which the breeding adults have a tuft of feathers on each side of the head

dou·ble–crop \ˌdə-bəl-'kräp\ *vi* (1918) : to grow two or more crops on the same land in the same season or at the same time ~ *vt* : to grow (a crop) by double-cropping ⟨~ soybeans with wheat⟩

dou·ble–cross \ˌdə-bəl-'krȯs\ *vt* (1903) : to deceive by double-dealing : BETRAY — **dou·ble–cross·er** *n*

double cross *n* (1834) **1 a** : an act of winning or trying to win a fight or match after agreeing to lose it **b** : an act of betraying or cheating an associate **2** : a cross between first-generation hybrids of four separate inbred lines (as in the production of hybrid seed corn)

double dagger *n* (1706) : the character ‡ used as a reference mark — called also *diesis*

double date *n* (ca. 1931) : a date participated in by two couples — **dou·ble–date** *vi*

[1]**dou·ble–deal·ing** \ˌdə-bəl-'dē-liŋ\ *n* (1529) : action contradictory to a professed attitude : DUPLICITY ***syn*** see DECEPTION — **dou·ble–deal·er** \-'dē-lər\ *n*

[2]**double–dealing** *adj* (1587) : given to or marked by duplicity

dou·ble–deck \ˌdə-bəl-ˌdek\ *or* **dou·ble–decked** \-'dekt\ *adj* (1850) : having two decks, levels, or layers ⟨a ~ bus⟩ ⟨a ~ sandwich⟩

dou·ble–deck·er \-'de-kər\ *n, often attrib* (1835) : something that is double-deck ⟨a ~ bus⟩

dou·ble–dig·it \ˌdə-bəl-'di-jət\ *adj* (1959) : amounting to 10 percent or more ⟨~ inflation⟩ ⟨~ price increases⟩

dou·ble–dip·per \-'di-pər\ *n* (ca. 1974) : a person who collects both a government pension and a government salary — **dou·ble–dip·ping** \-piŋ\ *n*

dou·ble–dome \'də-bəl-ˌdōm\ *n* (1938) : INTELLECTUAL

double door *n* (1840) : an opening with two vertical doors that meet in the middle of the opening when closed — compare DUTCH DOOR

dou·ble–dou·ble \-'də-bəl\ *n* (1985) : an instance of a player's accumulating a total of 10 or more in two statistical categories (as points and rebounds) in one basketball game

double down *vi* (1949) **1** : to double the original bid in blackjack in exchange for only one more card **2** : to become more tenacious, zealous, or resolute in a position or undertaking ⟨the administration needs to *double down* on the call for political reform —*Washington Post*⟩

double dribble *n* (ca. 1949) : an illegal action in basketball made when a player dribbles the ball with two hands simultaneously or continues to dribble after allowing the ball to come to rest in one or both hands

double Dutch *n* (1876) **1** : unintelligible language **2** : the jumping of two jump ropes rotating in opposite directions simultaneously

double eagle *n* (1925) : a golf score of three strokes less than par on a hole — **double–eagle** *vt*

dou·ble–edged \ˌdə-bəl-'ejd\ *adj* (15c) **1** : having two cutting edges ⟨a ~ knife⟩ **2 a** : having two components or aspects ⟨a spy with a ~ mission⟩ **b** : capable of being taken in two ways ⟨a ~ remark⟩

double–edged sword *n* (15c) : something that has or can have both favorable and unfavorable consequences ⟨freedom of expression . . . can be a *double-edged sword* —Linda Connors⟩

dou·ble–end·ed \ˌdə-bəl-'en-dəd\ *adj* (ca. 1874) : similar at both ends ⟨a ~ bolt⟩

dou·ble–end·er \-dər\ *n* (1864) : a ship or boat with bow and stern of similar shape

dou·ble en·ten·dre \'düb-ᵊl-äⁿ-'täⁿd(-rᵊ); 'də-bəl-än-'tänd(-rə)\ *n, pl* **double entendres** *same also* -'täⁿz; -'tän-drəz\ [obs. F, lit., double meaning] (1673) **1** : ambiguity of meaning arising from language that lends itself to more than one interpretation **2** : a word or expression capable of two interpretations with one usu. risqué

double entry *n* (1741) : a method of bookkeeping that recognizes both sides of a business transaction by debiting the amount of the transaction to one account and crediting it to another account so the total debits equal the total credits

dou·ble–faced \ˌdə-bəl-'fāst\ *adj* (1577) **1** : HYPOCRITICAL, TWO-FACED **2 a** : having two faces or sides designed for use ⟨a ~ bookshelf⟩ **b** *also* **dou·ble–face** \-'fās\ : finished on both sides : REVERSIBLE — used of fabric

double fault *n* (ca. 1909) : two consecutive serving faults in tennis that result in the loss of a point — **dou·ble–fault** \ˌdə-bəl-'fȯlt\ *vi*

double feature *n* (1928) : a movie program with two main films

double fertilization *n* (ca. 1909) : fertilization characteristic of seed plants in which one sperm nucleus fuses with the egg nucleus to form an embryo and another fuses with polar nuclei to form endosperm

double genitive *n* (1824) : a syntactic construction in English in which possession is marked both by the preposition *of* and a noun or pronoun in the possessive case (as in "A friend of Bob's is a friend of mine") — called also *double possessive*

double glazing *n* (1943) : two layers of glass set in a window to reduce heat flow in either direction

Double Glouces·ter \-'gläs-tər, -ˌglȯs-\ *n* [*Gloucester,* England] (1816) : a firm mild orange-colored English cheese similar to cheddar

dou·ble·hand·ed \'də-bəl-'han-dəd\ *adj* (1979) : having, requiring, or suitable for two sailors ⟨a ~ dinghy⟩; *also* : involving boats each manned by two sailors ⟨a ~ race⟩

dou·ble·head·er \ˌdə-bəl-'he-dər\ *n* (1878) **1** : a train pulled by two locomotives **2** : two games, contests, or events held consecutively on the same program

double helix *n* (1954) : a helix or spiral consisting of two strands in the surface of a cylinder that coil around its axis; *esp* : the structural arrangement of DNA in space that consists of paired polynucleotide strands stabilized by cross-links between purine and pyrimidine bases — compare ALPHA-HELIX, WATSON-CRICK MODEL — **dou·ble–he·li·cal** \-'he-li-kəl, -'hē-\ *adj*

double–hung \ˌdə-bəl-'həŋ\ *adj* (1823) *of a window* : having an upper and a lower sash that can slide vertically past each other

double hyphen *n* (1893) : a punctuation mark ⸗ used in place of a hyphen at the end of a line to indicate that the word so divided is normally hyphenated

double indemnity *n* (1924) : a provision in a life-insurance or accident policy whereby the company agrees to pay twice the face of the contract in case of accidental death

double jeopardy *n* (1862) **1** : the putting of a person on trial for an offense for which he or she has previously been put on trial under a valid charge : two adjudications for one offense **2** : considerable danger or trouble from two sources

dou·ble–joint·ed \ˌdə-bəl-'jȯin-təd\ *adj* (ca. 1820) : having a joint that permits an exceptional degree of freedom of motion of the parts joined

double knit *n* (1895) : a knitted fabric (as wool) made with a double set of needles to produce a double thickness of fabric with each thickness joined by interlocking stitches; *also* : an article of clothing made of such fabric

double negative *n* (1827) : a now nonstandard syntactic construction containing two negatives and having a negative meaning ⟨"I didn't hear nothing" is a *double negative*⟩

dou·ble–park \ˌdə-bəl-'pärk\ *vt* (1927) : to park (a vehicle) beside a row of vehicles already parked parallel to the curb ~ *vi* : to double-park a vehicle

double play *n* (1867) : a play in baseball by which two players are put out

double pneumonia *n* (1892) : pneumonia affecting both lungs

double prime *n* (1904) : the symbol ″ used to distinguish arbitrary characters (as *a, a′,* and *a″*), to indicate a specific unit (as inches), or to indicate the second derivative of a function (as *p″* or *f″(x)*) — compare PRIME 7

dou·ble–quick \'də-bəl-ˌkwik\ *n* (1834) : DOUBLE TIME 1; *broadly* : a rapid pace — **double–quick** *adj or adv*

double reed *n* (ca. 1876) : two reeds bound together with a slight separation between them so that air passing through them causes them to beat against one another and that are used as a sound-producing device in certain woodwind instruments (as members of the oboe family)

double refraction *n* (1831) : BIREFRINGENCE

dou·ble–ring \'də-bəl-ˌriŋ\ *adj* (ca. 1959) : of or relating to a wedding ceremony in which each partner ceremonially gives the other a wedding ring while reciting vows
double salt *n* (ca. 1849) : a salt (as an alum) yielding on hydrolysis two different cations or anions
dou·ble–space \ˌdə-bəl-'spās\ *vt* (ca. 1937) : to type (text) leaving alternate lines blank ~ *vi* : to type on every other line
dou·ble·speak \'də-bəl-ˌspēk\ *n* (1952) : language used to deceive usu. through concealment or misrepresentation of truth; *also* : GOBBLEDYGOOK — **dou·ble·speak·er** \-ˌspē-kər\ *n*
double standard *n* (1894) **1** : BIMETALLISM **2** : a set of principles that applies differently and usu. more rigorously to one group of people or circumstances than to another; *esp* : a code of morals that applies more severe standards of sexual behavior to women than to men
double star *n* (1781) **1** : BINARY STAR **2** : two stars in very nearly the same line of sight but actually physically separate
dou·ble–stop \ˌdə-bəl-'stäp\ *vt* (ca. 1889) : to produce two or more tones simultaneously on (as a violin) — **double–stop** *n*
double sugar *n* (1956) : DISACCHARIDE
dou·blet \'dəb-lət\ *n* [ME, fr. AF *dublet,* fr. *duble*] (14c) **1** : a man's close-fitting jacket worn in Europe esp. during the Renaissance **2** : something consisting of two identical or similar parts: as **a** : a lens consisting of two components; *esp* : a handheld magnifier consisting of two lenses in a metal cylinder **b** : a spectrum line having two close components **c** : a domino with the same number of spots on each end **3** : a set of two identical or similar things: as **a** : two thrown dice with the same number of spots on the upper face **b** : one of nine pairs of microtubules found in cilia and flagella **4** : one of a pair; *specif* : one of two or more words (as *guard* and *ward*) in the same language derived by different routes of transmission from the same source
dou·ble take \'də-bəl-ˌtāk\ *n* (1930) : a delayed reaction to a surprising or significant situation after an initial failure to notice anything unusual — usu. used in the phrase *do a double take*
dou·ble–talk \-ˌtȯk\ *n* (1936) **1** : language that appears to be earnest and meaningful but in fact is a mixture of sense and nonsense **2** : inflated, involved, and often deliberately ambiguous language — **double–talk** *vi* — **dou·ble–talk·er** *n*
dou·ble–team \-ˌtēm\ *vt* (1860) : to block or guard (an opponent) with two players at one time — **double–team** *n*
Double Ten *n* [trans. of Chin (Beijing) *shuāngshí;* fr. its being the tenth day of the tenth month] (1940) : October 10 observed by the Republic of China in commemoration of the revolution of 1911
dou·ble·think \'də-bəl-ˌthiŋk\ *n* (1949) : a simultaneous belief in two contradictory ideas
dou·ble–time \'də-bəl-ˌtīm\ *vi* (1943) : to move at double time
double time *n* (1853) **1** : a marching cadence of 180 30-inch steps per minute **2** : payment of a worker at twice the regular wage rate
dou·ble·ton \'də-bəl-tən\ *n* [*double* + *-ton* (as in *singleton*)] (ca. 1894) : two cards that are the only ones of their suit orig. dealt to a player — compare SINGLETON 1, VOID 4
dou·ble–tongue \ˌdə-bəl-'təŋ\ *vi* (ca. 1900) : to cause the tongue to alternate rapidly between the positions for *t* and *k* so as to produce a fast succession of detached notes on a wind instrument
dou·ble–u *as at* W\ *n* (1840) : the letter *w*
double up *vi* (1789) : to share accommodations designed for one
double vision *n* (ca. 1860) : DIPLOPIA
double whammy *n* (1951) : a combination of two usu. adverse forces, circumstances, or effects
double–wide \ˌdə-bəl-'wīd\ *n* (1970) : a mobile home consisting of two units that have been fastened together along their length
dou·bloon \ˌdə-'blün\ *n* [Sp *doblón,* aug. of *dobla,* an old Spanish coin, fr. L *dupla,* fem. of *duplus* double — more at DOUBLE] (1622) : an old gold coin of Spain and Spanish America
dou·bly \'də-b(ə-)lē\ *adv* (15c) **1** : in a twofold manner **2** : to twice the degree ⟨~ glad⟩ ⟨~ frustrating⟩
[1]**doubt** \'dau̇t\ *vb* [ME *douten,* fr. AF *duter, douter,* fr. L *dubitare* to be in doubt; akin to L *dubius* dubious] *vt* (13c) **1** *archaic* **a** : FEAR **b** : SUSPECT **2** : to be in doubt about ⟨he ~*s* everyone's word⟩ **3 a** : to lack confidence in : DISTRUST ⟨find myself ~*ing* him even when I know that he is honest —H. L. Mencken⟩ **b** : to consider unlikely ⟨I ~ if I can go⟩ ~ *vi* : to be uncertain — **doubt·able** \'dau̇-tə-bəl\ *adj* — **doubt·er** *n* — **doubt·ing·ly** \-tiŋ-lē\ *adv*
[2]**doubt** *n* (13c) **1 a** : uncertainty of belief or opinion that often interferes with decision-making **b** : a deliberate suspension of judgment **2** : a state of affairs giving rise to uncertainty, hesitation, or suspense ⟨the outcome is still in ~⟩ **3 a** : a lack of confidence : DISTRUST ⟨has ~*s* about his abilities⟩ **b** : an inclination not to believe or accept ⟨a claim met with ~⟩ ***syn*** see UNCERTAINTY — **no doubt** : [1]DOUBTLESS
doubt·ful \'dau̇t-fəl\ *adj* (14c) **1** : giving rise to doubt : open to question ⟨it is ~ that they ever knew what happened⟩ **2 a** : lacking a definite opinion, conviction, or determination ⟨they were ~ about the advantages of the new system⟩ **b** : uncertain in outcome : UNDECIDED ⟨the outcome of the election remains ~⟩ **3** : marked by qualities that raise doubts about worth, honesty, or validity ⟨of ~ repute⟩ — **doubt·ful·ly** \-fə-lē\ *adv* — **doubt·ful·ness** *n*
syn DOUBTFUL, DUBIOUS, PROBLEMATIC, QUESTIONABLE mean not affording assurance of the worth, soundness, or certainty of something. DOUBTFUL implies little more than a lack of conviction or certainty ⟨*doubtful* about whether I said the right thing⟩. DUBIOUS stresses suspicion, mistrust, or hesitation ⟨*dubious* about the practicality of the scheme⟩. PROBLEMATIC applies esp. to things whose existence, meaning, fulfillment, or realization is highly uncertain ⟨whether the project will ever be finished is *problematic*⟩. QUESTIONABLE may imply no more than the existence of doubt but usu. suggests that the suspicions are well-grounded ⟨a man of *questionable* honesty⟩.
doubting Thom·as \-'tä-məs\ *n* [St. *Thomas,* apostle who doubted Jesus' resurrection until he had proof of it (Jn 20:24–29)] (1883) : an incredulous or habitually doubtful person
[1]**doubt·less** \'dau̇t-ləs\ *adv* (14c) **1** : without doubt **2** : PROBABLY
[2]**doubtless** *adj* (14c) : free from doubt : CERTAIN — **doubt·less·ly** *adv* — **doubt·less·ness** *n*
douce \'düs\ *adj* [ME, sweet, pleasant, fr. AF, fr. fem. of *duz, douz,* fr. L *dulcis* sweet — more at DULCET] (1721) *chiefly Scot* : SOBER, SEDATE ⟨the ~ faces of the mourners —L. J. A. Bell⟩ — **douce·ly** *adv, chiefly Scot*
dou·ceur \dü-'sər\ *n* [F, pleasantness, fr. LL *dulcor* sweetness, fr. L *dulcis*] (1763) : a conciliatory gift
douche \'düsh\ *n* [F, fr. It *doccia,* fr. *docciare* to douche, fr. *doccia* water pipe, prob. back-formation fr. *doccione* conduit, fr. L *duction-, ductio* means of conveying water, fr. *ducere* to lead — more at TOW] (1766) **1 a** : a jet or current of liquid (as a cleansing solution) directed against or into a bodily part or cavity (as the vagina) **b** : an act of cleansing with a douche **2** : a device for giving douches **3** *Brit* : an abrupt often chastening shock to the nerves, emotions, or awareness ⟨the icy ~ (what he said about my work) —John Fowles⟩ — **douche** *vb*
douche bag *n* (ca. 1963) *slang* : an unattractive or offensive person
dough \'dō\ *n* [ME *dogh,* fr. OE *dāg;* akin to OHG *teic* dough, L *fingere* to shape, Gk *teichos* wall] (bef. 12c) **1** : a mixture that consists essentially of flour or meal and a liquid (as milk or water) and is stiff enough to knead or roll **2** : something resembling dough esp. in consistency **3** : MONEY **4** : DOUGHBOY — **dough·like** \-ˌlīk\ *adj*
dough box *n* (ca. 1944) : a rectangular wooden box mounted on legs that is used as a worktable and storage space
dough·boy \-ˌbȯi\ *n* (ca. 1847) : an American infantryman esp. in World War I
dough·face \-ˌfās\ *n* (1830) : a Northern congressman not opposed to slavery in the South before or during the American Civil War; *also* : a Northerner sympathetic to the South during the same period — **dough–faced** \-'fāst\ *adj*
dough·nut *also* **do·nut** \-(ˌ)nət\ *n* (ca. 1809) **1** : a small usu. ring-shaped cake fried in fat **2** : something (as a mathematical torus) that resembles a doughnut esp. in shape — **dough·nut·like** \-ˌlīk\ *adj*
dough·ty \'dau̇-tē\ *adj* **dough·ti·er; -est** [ME, fr. OE *dohtig;* akin to OHG *toug* is useful, Gk *teuchein* to make] (bef. 12c) : marked by fearless resolution : VALIANT ⟨a ~ warrior⟩ — **dough·ti·ly** \'dau̇-t^{ə}l-ē\ *adv* — **dough·ti·ness** \'dau̇-tē-nəs\ *n*
doughy \'dō-ē\ *adj* **dough·i·er; -est** (1601) : resembling dough: as **a** : not thoroughly baked ⟨~ bread⟩ **b** : unhealthily pale : PASTY ⟨a ~ face⟩
Doug·las fir \ˌdə-gləs-\ *n* [David *Douglas* †1834 Scot. botanist] (1873) : any of a genus (*Pseudotsuga*) of tall evergreen timber trees of the pine family having thick bark, pitchy wood, and pendulous cones; *esp* : one (*P. menziesii* syn. *P. taxifolia*) chiefly of the western U.S. — see CONE illustration
Dou·kho·bor *also* **Du·kho·bor** \'dü-kə-ˌbȯr\ *n* [Russ *dukhobor, dukhoborets,* fr. *dukh* spirit + *borets* wrestler] (1876) : a member of a Christian sect of 18th century Russian origin emphasizing the duty of obeying the inner light and rejecting church or civil authority
dou·la \'dü-lə\ *n* [Mod Gk, female helper, maidservant, fr. Gk *doulē* female slave] (1981) : a woman experienced in childbirth who provides advice, information, emotional support, and physical comfort to a mother before, during, and just after childbirth
do up *vt* (1666) **1** : to prepare (as by cleaning or repairing) for wear or use ⟨*do up* a shirt⟩ **2 a** : to wrap up ⟨*do up* a package⟩ **b** : PUT UP, CAN **3 a** : to deck out : CLOTHE **b** : to furnish with something ornamental : DECORATE **4** : EXHAUST, WEAR OUT **5** : FASTEN
dour \'du̇r, 'dau̇(-ə)r\ *adj* [ME, fr. L *durus* hard — more at DURING] (14c) **1** : STERN, HARSH **2** : OBSTINATE, UNYIELDING **3** : GLOOMY, SULLEN — **dour·ly** *adv* — **dour·ness** *n*
dou·rou·cou·li \ˌdu̇r-ə-'kü-lē\ *n* [F, fr. an unidentified American Indian language of Venezuela] (1842) : OWL MONKEY
[1]**douse** *also* **dowse** \'dau̇s *also* 'dau̇z\ *vb* **doused** *also* **dowsed; dous·ing** *also* **dows·ing** [perh. fr. obs. E *douse* to smite] *vt* (1600) **1** : to plunge into water **2 a** : to throw a liquid on : DRENCH **b** : SLOSH **3** : EXTINGUISH ⟨~ the lights⟩ ~ *vi* : to fall or become plunged into water — **dous·er** *also* **dows·er** *n*
[2]**douse** \'dau̇s *also* 'dau̇z\ *n* (1881) : a heavy drenching
[3]**douse** \'düs, 'dau̇s\ *n* [origin unknown] (ca. 1625) *Brit* : BLOW, STROKE
[4]**douse** \'dau̇s\ *vt* **doused; dous·ing** (1627) **1 a** : to take in : LOWER, STRIKE ⟨~ a sail⟩ **b** : SLACKEN ⟨~ a rope⟩ **2** : TAKE OFF, DOFF
doux \'dü\ *adj* [F, lit., sweet, fr. OF *douz* — more at DOUCE] (ca. 1943) *of champagne* : very sweet
[1]**dove** \'dəv\ *n* [ME, fr. OE **dūfe;* akin to OHG *tūba* dove] (13c) **1** : any of numerous pigeons; *esp* : a small wild pigeon **2** : a gentle woman or child **3** : one who takes a conciliatory attitude and advocates negotiations and compromise; *esp* : an opponent of war — compare HAWK — **dov·ish** \'də-vish\ *adj* — **dov·ish·ness** *n*
[2]**dove** \'dōv\ *past of* DIVE
dove·cote \'dəv-ˌkōt, -ˌkät\ *also* **dove·cot** \-ˌkät\ *n* (15c) **1** : a small compartmented raised house or box for domestic pigeons **2** : a settled or harmonious group or organization
dove·kie \'dəv-kē\ *n* [dim. of *dove*] (1821) : a small short-billed auk (*Alle alle*) breeding on arctic coasts and ranging south in winter
doven *var of* DAVEN
Dover sole *n* [prob. fr. *Dover,* England] (ca. 1911) **1** : a common European sole (*Solea solea*) esteemed as a food fish **2** : a flatfish (*Microstomus pacificus* of the family Pleuronectidae) of the Pacific coast of No. America that is a commercially important food fish

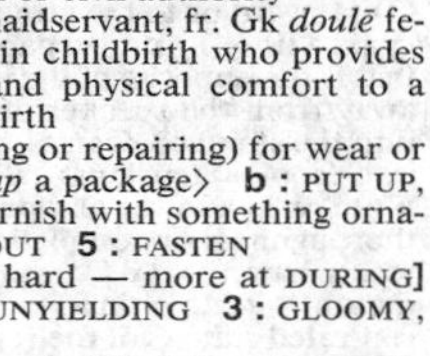

dovetail: *1* mortises, *2* tenons, *3* joint

Do·ver's powder \ˌdō-vərz-\ *n* [Thomas *Dover* †1742 Eng. physician] (1801) : a powder of ipecac and opium formerly used as a pain reliever and diaphoretic
[1]**dove·tail** \'dəv-ˌtāl\ *n* (1573) : something resembling a dove's tail; *esp* : a flaring tenon and a mortise into which it fits tightly making an interlocking joint between two pieces (as of wood)
[2]**dovetail** *vt* (ca. 1656) **1 a** : to join by

means of dovetails **b :** to cut to a dovetail **2 a :** to fit skillfully to form a whole **b :** to fit together with ~ *vi* **:** to fit together into a whole

dow \'dau̇\ *vi* **dought** \'dau̇t\ *or* **dowed** \'dau̇d\; **dow·ing** [ME *dow, deih* have worth, am able, fr. OE *dēah, dēag;* akin to OHG *toug* is worthy, is useful — more at DOUGHTY] (bef. 12c) *chiefly Scot* **:** to be able or capable

Dow \'dau̇\ *n* (1949) **:** DOW JONES AVERAGE

dow·a·ger \'dau̇-i-jər\ *n* [MF *douagiere*, fr. *douage* dower, fr. *douer* to endow — more at ENDOW] (1530) **1 :** a widow holding property or a title from her deceased husband **2 :** a dignified elderly woman

dowager's hump *n* (1948) **:** an abnormal outward curvature of the upper back with round shoulders and stooped posture caused esp. by bone loss and anterior compression of the vertebrae in osteoporosis

[1]**dowdy** \'dau̇-dē\ *n, pl* **dowd·ies** [dim. of *dowd* dowdy, fr. ME *doude*] (1581) *archaic* **:** a dowdy woman

[2]**dowdy** *adj* **dowd·i·er; -est** (1676) **1 :** not neat or becoming in appearance **:** SHABBY ⟨a ~ old hat⟩ **2 a :** lacking smartness or taste ⟨a ~ room⟩ **b :** OLD-FASHIONED ⟨a ~ institution⟩ — **dowd·i·ly** \'dau̇-də-lē\ *adv* — **dowd·i·ness** \'dau̇-dē-nəs\ *n* — **dowdy·ish** \-ish\ *adj*

[3]**dowdy** *n* [origin unknown] (1936) **:** PANDOWDY

[1]**dow·el** \'dau̇(-ə)l\ *n* [ME *dowle;* akin to OHG *tubili* plug, LGk *typhos* wedge] (14c) **1 :** a pin fitting into a hole in an abutting piece to prevent motion or slipping; *also* **:** a round rod or stick used esp. for cutting up into dowels **2 :** a piece of wood driven into a wall so that other pieces can be nailed to it

[2]**dowel** *vt* **-elled** *also* **-eled; -elling** *also* **-eling** (1713) **:** to fasten by or furnish with dowels

[1]**dow·er** \'dau̇(-ə)r\ *n* [ME *dowere*, fr. AF *dower, douaire*, fr. ML *dotarium*, fr. L *dot-, dos* gift, marriage portion — more at DATE] (14c) **1 :** the part of or interest in the real estate of a deceased husband given by law to his widow during her life — compare CURTESY **2 a :** DOWRY 2 **b :** DOWRY 3

[2]**dower** *vt* (1605) **:** to supply with a dower or dowry **:** ENDOW

dow·itch·er \'dau̇-i-chər\ *n, pl* **dowitchers** *also* **dowitcher** [prob. of Iroquoian origin; akin to Oneida *tawístawis* dowitcher] (1841) **:** any of several long-billed wading birds (esp. *Limnodromus griseus* and *L. scolopaceus* of the family Scolopacidae) related to the sandpipers

Dow Jones average \ˌdau̇-'jōnz-\ *n* [Charles H. *Dow* †1902 & Edward D. *Jones* †1920 Am. financial statisticians] (1922) **:** an index of the relative price of securities

[1]**down** \'dau̇n\ *adv* [ME *doun*, fr. OE *dūne*, short for *adūne, of dūne*, fr. *a-* (fr. *of*), *of* off, from + *dūne*, dat. of *dūn* hill] (bef. 12c) **1 a** (1) **:** toward or in a lower physical position (2) **:** to a lying or sitting position (3) **:** toward or to the ground, floor, or bottom **b :** as a down payment ⟨paid $10 ~⟩ **c :** on paper ⟨put ~ what he says⟩ **2 :** in a direction that is the opposite of up: as **a :** SOUTHWARD **b :** to or toward a point away from the speaker or the speaker's point of reference **c :** in or into the stomach ⟨can't keep food ~⟩ **3 :** to a lesser degree, level, or rate ⟨cool ~ tensions⟩ **4 :** to or toward a lower position in a series **5 a :** to or in a lower or worse condition or status **b** — used to indicate thoroughness or completion ⟨dusted ~ the house⟩ ⟨described him ~ to his haircut⟩ **6 :** from a past time ⟨stories passed ~ by word of mouth⟩ **7 :** to or in a state of less activity or prominence **8 :** to a concentrated state ⟨got the report ~ to three pages⟩ **9 :** into defeat ⟨voted the motion ~⟩ — **down to the ground :** PERFECTLY, COMPLETELY ⟨that suits me *down to the ground*⟩

[2]**down** *prep* (14c) **:** down along, around, through, toward, in, into, or on ⟨fell ~ the stairs⟩ ⟨~ the years⟩

[3]**down** *vt* (1562) **1 :** to cause to go or come down: as **a :** BRING DOWN 1 ⟨~*ed* the enemy helicopter⟩ **b :** CONSUME 3 ⟨~*ing* slices of pizza⟩ **2 :** to cause (a football) to be out of play **3 :** DEFEAT ⟨~ a proposal⟩ ~ *vi* **:** to go down

[4]**down** *adj* (ca. 1565) **1 a** (1) **:** occupying a low position; *specif* **:** lying on the ground ⟨~ timber⟩ (2) **:** directed or going downward ⟨attendance is ~⟩ **b :** lower in price **c :** not being in play in football because of wholly stopped progress or because the officials stop the play ⟨the ball was ~⟩ **d :** defeated or trailing an opponent (as in points scored) ⟨~ by two runs⟩ **e** *baseball* **:** OUT ⟨two ~ in the top of the third inning⟩ **2 a :** reduced or low in activity, frequency, or intensity ⟨a ~ economy⟩ **b :** not operating or able to function ⟨the computer is ~⟩ **c :** DEPRESSED, DEJECTED ⟨feeling a bit ~⟩; *also* **:** DEPRESSING ⟨a ~ movie⟩ **d :** SICK ⟨~ with flu⟩ **3 :** DONE, FINISHED ⟨eight ~ and two to go⟩ **4 :** completely mastered ⟨had her lines ~⟩ — often used with *pat* ⟨got the answers ~ pat⟩ **5 a** *slang* **:** COOL 7 **b** *slang* **:** understanding or supportive of something or someone — usu. used with *with* ⟨trying to prove that they were ~ with hip-hop culture —J. E. White⟩ **6 :** being on record ⟨you're ~ for two tickets⟩ — **down on :** having a low opinion of or dislike for — **down on one's luck :** experiencing misfortune and esp. financial distress

[5]**down** *n* (1710) **1 :** DESCENT, DEPRESSION **2 :** an instance of putting down **3 a :** a complete play to advance the ball in football **b :** one of a series of four attempts in American football or three attempts in Canadian football to advance the ball 10 yards **4** *chiefly Brit* **:** DISLIKE, GRUDGE **5 :** DOWNER **6 :** a fundamental quark that has an electric charge of -⅓ and that is one of the constituents of a nucleon

[6]**down** *n* [ME *doun* hill, fr. OE *dūn*] (14c) **1 :** an undulating usu. treeless upland with sparse soil — usu. used in pl. **2** *often cap* **:** a sheep of any breed originating in the downs of southern England

[7]**down** *n* [ME *doun*, fr. ON *dūnn*] (14c) **1 :** a covering of soft fluffy feathers; *also* **:** these feathers **2 :** something soft and fluffy like down

Down *n* (1994) **:** DOWN SYNDROME — usu. used attributively ⟨a ~ baby⟩

down and dirty *adj or adv* (1967) **1 :** UNVARNISHED ⟨the *down and dirty* truth⟩ **2 :** made or done hastily **:** not revised or polished ⟨a *down and dirty* solution⟩ **3 :** marked by or given to fierce often unscrupulous competition ⟨*down and dirty* campaigning⟩ **4 :** BAWDY ⟨*down and dirty* sexuality⟩ **5 :** SEEDY ⟨a *down and dirty* neighborhood⟩ **6 :** relating to or involved with what is crudely basic and practical ⟨*down and dirty* details⟩

down–and–out *adj* (1901) **1 :** DESTITUTE, IMPOVERISHED **2 :** physically weakened or incapacitated — **down–and–out** *or* **down–and–outer** *n*

down–at–the–heels *or* **down–at–heel** *also* **down–at–the–heel** *or* **down–at–heels** *adj* (1732) **:** SHABBY

[1]**down·beat** \'dau̇n-ˌbēt\ *n* (1869) **1 :** the downward stroke of a conductor indicating the principally accented note of a measure of music; *also* **:** the first beat of a measure **2 :** a decline in activity or prosperity

[2]**downbeat** *adj* (1950) **:** PESSIMISTIC, GLOOMY ⟨a ~ assessment⟩

down–bow \'dau̇n-ˌbō\ *n* (1883) **:** a stroke in playing a bowed instrument (as a violin) in which the bow is drawn across the strings from the frog to the tip

down·burst \-ˌbərst\ *n* (1978) **:** a powerful downdraft usu. associated with a thunderstorm that strikes the ground and deflects in all directions; *also* **:** MICROBURST

down·cast \'dau̇n-ˌkast\ *adj* (14c) **1 :** low in spirit **:** DEJECTED **2 :** directed downward ⟨with ~ eyes⟩

down·court \-'kȯrt\ *adv or adj* (1952) **:** in or into the opposite end of the court (as in basketball)

down·draft \-ˌdraft\ *n* (1849) **1 :** a downward current of gas (as air during a thunderstorm) **2 :** DECLINE 1 ⟨an economic ~⟩

down east *adv, often cap D&E* (1825) **:** in or into the northeast coastal section of the U.S. and parts of the Maritime Provinces of Canada; *specif* **:** in or into coastal Maine — **down east** *adj, often cap D&E*

down–east·er \dau̇n-'ē-stər\ *n, often cap D&E* (1827) **:** one born or living down east

down·er \'dau̇-nər\ *n* (1913) **1 :** a weak, sick, or crippled animal in shipment that is down and cannot get up — often used attributively ⟨a ~ cow⟩ **2 :** a depressant drug; *esp* **:** BARBITURATE **3 :** someone or something depressing, disagreeable, or unsatisfactory

down·fall \'dau̇n-ˌfȯl\ *n* (13c) **1 a :** a sudden fall (as from power) **b :** a fall (as of snow or rain) esp. when sudden or heavy **2 :** something that causes a downfall (as of a person) ⟨gambling was his ~⟩ — **down·fall·en** \-ˌfȯ-lən\ *adj*

down·field \-'fēld\ *adv or adj* (1922) **:** in or into the part of the field toward which the offensive team is headed

down·force \-ˌfȯrs\ *n* (1973) **:** a downward aerodynamic force generated esp. by an airfoil (as a spoiler on a race car)

[1]**down·grade** \'dau̇n-ˌgrād\ *n* (1857) **1 :** a downward grade (as of a road) **2 :** a descent toward an inferior state ⟨a career on the ~⟩

[2]**downgrade** *vt* (1930) **1 :** to lower in quality, value, status, or extent **2 :** MINIMIZE, DEPRECIATE

down·haul \'dau̇n-ˌhȯl\ *n* (1669) **:** a rope or line for hauling down or holding down a sail or spar

down·heart·ed \-'här-təd\ *adj* (ca. 1774) **:** DOWNCAST, DEJECTED — **down·heart·ed·ly** *adv* — **down·heart·ed·ness** *n*

[1]**down·hill** \ˌdau̇n-'hil\ *adv* (14c) **1 :** toward the bottom of a hill **2 :** toward a worsened or inferior state or level — used esp. in the phrase *go downhill*

[2]**down·hill** \'dau̇n-ˌhil\ *n* (1548) **1 :** a descending slope **2 a :** the sport of skiing on downhill trails — often used attributively **b :** a skiing race against time down a trail ⟨finished second in the ~⟩

[3]**down·hill** \-ˌhil\ *adj* (1622) **1 :** not difficult **:** EASY ⟨after that problem the rest was ~⟩ **2 :** sloping downhill **3 :** closer to the bottom of an incline ⟨your ~ ski⟩ **4 :** progressively worse

down·hill·er \-hi-lər\ *n* (1967) **:** a downhill skier

down–home \'dau̇n-ˌhōm\ *adj* (1938) **:** of, relating to, or having qualities (as informality and simplicity) associated with rural or small-town people esp. of the Southern U.S. ⟨~ country cooking⟩; *broadly* **:** SIMPLE, UNPRETENTIOUS

down in the mouth *adj* (1649) **:** DEJECTED 1

down·land \'dau̇n-ˌland\ *n* (bef. 12c) **:** [6]DOWN 1

down·light \-ˌlīt\ *n* (1949) **:** a small spotlight set in a ceiling and directed downward

[1]**down·link** \'dau̇n-ˌliŋk\ *n* (ca. 1969) **:** a communications channel for receiving transmissions from a spacecraft; *also* **:** such transmissions

[2]**downlink** *vt* (1977) **:** to transmit (as data) from a spacecraft or satellite to a receiver on earth

[1]**down·load** \'dau̇n-ˌlōd\ *n* (1977) **:** an act or instance of downloading something; *also* **:** the item downloaded

[2]**download** *vt* (1979) **:** to transfer (as data or files) from a usu. large computer to the memory of another device (as a smaller computer) — **down·load·able** \-ˌlō-də-bəl\ *adj*

down–market \'dau̇n-ˌmär-kət\ *adj* (1970) **:** relating or appealing to lower-income consumers ⟨a ~ tabloid⟩

down payment *n* (1926) **:** a part of the full price paid at the time of purchase or delivery with the balance to be paid later; *broadly* **:** the first step in a process

down·pipe \'dau̇n-ˌpīp\ *n* (ca. 1852) *Brit* **:** DOWNSPOUT

down·play \'dau̇n-ˌplā\ *vt* (1954) **:** PLAY DOWN, DE-EMPHASIZE

down·pour \-ˌpȯr\ *n* (1801) **:** a pouring or streaming downward; *esp* **:** a heavy rain

down·range \-'rānj\ *adv* (1952) **:** away from a launching site

[1]**down·right** \-ˌrīt\ *adv* (13c) **1** *archaic* **:** straight down **2 :** ABSOLUTELY 1 ⟨~ handsome⟩ ⟨~ mean⟩ **3** *obs* **:** FORTHRIGHT

[2]**downright** *adj* (1530) **1** *archaic* **:** directed vertically downward **2 :** OUTRIGHT, THOROUGH ⟨a ~ lie⟩ **3 :** PLAIN, BLUNT ⟨stories he had heard of her ~ tongue —Angus Wilson⟩ — **down·right·ly** *adv* — **down·right·ness** *n*

down·riv·er \'dau̇n-'ri-vər\ *adv or adj* (1760) **:** toward or at a point nearer the mouth of a river

Down's \'dau̇nz\ *n, often attrib* (1971) **:** DOWN SYNDROME ⟨a ~ patient⟩

[1]**down·scale** \'dau̇n-ˌskāl\ *vt* **down·scaled; down·scal·ing** (1945) **:** to cut back in size or scope ⟨the recession forced us to ~ vacation plans⟩

[2]**downscale** *adj* (ca. 1966) **:** lower in class, income, or quality

down·shift \-ˌshift\ *vi* (1955) **1 :** to shift an automotive vehicle into a lower gear **2 :** to move or shift to a lower level (as of speed, activity, or intensity) — **downshift** *n*

down·side \'dau̇n-ˌsīd\ *n* (1930) **1 :** a downward trend (as of prices) **2 :** a negative aspect ⟨the ~ of fame⟩

down·size \'dau̇n-ˌsīz\ *vt* (1975) **1 :** to reduce in size; *esp* **:** to design or produce in smaller size **2 :** to fire (employees) for the purpose of downsizing a business ~ *vi* **:** to undergo a reduction in size

down·slide \'dau̇n-ˌslīd\ *n* (1926) **:** a downward movement

down·slope \'dau̇n-ˌslōp\ *adj or adv* (1928) **:** toward the bottom of a slope

down·spout \ˈdau̇n-ˌspau̇t\ *n* (ca. 1896) : a vertical pipe used to drain rainwater from a roof

1**down·stage** \ˈdau̇n-ˈstāj\ *adv or adj* (1793) **1** : toward or at the front of a theatrical stage **2** : toward a motion-picture or television camera

2**down·stage** \-ˌstāj\ *n* (ca. 1931) : the part of a stage that is nearest the audience or camera

1**down·stairs** \ˈdau̇n-ˈsterz\ *adv* (1596) : down the stairs : on or to a lower floor

2**down·stairs** \ˈdau̇n-ˌsterz\ *adj* (1819) : situated on the main, lower, or ground floor of a building

3**down·stairs** \ˈdau̇n-ˈ, ˈdau̇n-ˌ\ *n pl but sing or pl in constr* (1843) : the lower floor of a building

down·state \-ˌstāt\ *n* (1909) : the chiefly southerly sections of a state; *also* : the chiefly rural part of a state when the major metropolitan area is to the north — **down·state** \-ˈstāt\ *adj or adv* — **down·stat·er** \-ˈstā-tər\ *n*

down·stream \ˈdau̇n-ˈstrēm\ *adv or adj* (1706) **1** : in the direction of or nearer to the mouth of a stream **2** : in or toward the latter stages of a usu. industrial process or the stages (as marketing) after manufacture

down·stroke \-ˌstrōk\ *n* (1852) : a downward stroke

down·swing \-ˌswiŋ\ *n* (1899) **1** : a downward swing **2** : DOWNTURN

Down syndrome *n* [J. L. H. *Down* †1896 Eng. physician] (1961) : a congenital condition characterized by moderate to severe mental retardation, slanting eyes, a broad short skull, broad hands with short fingers, and trisomy of the human chromosome numbered 21 — called also *Down's syndrome*

down–the–line *adj* (1940) : COMPLETE ⟨a ~ union supporter⟩

down·time \ˈdau̇n-ˌtīm\ *n* (1928) **1** : time during which production is stopped esp. during setup for an operation or when making repairs **2** : inactive time (as between periods of work) ⟨napping during our ~⟩ ⟨an injured athlete facing months of ~⟩

down–to–earth *adj* (1932) **1** : PRACTICAL ⟨~ traveling tips⟩ **2** : UNPRETENTIOUS ⟨surprised to find the movie star so ~⟩ — **down–to–earthness** *n*

down–to–the–wire *adj* (1952) : full of suspense; *esp* : unsettled until the very end

1**down·town** \ˌdau̇n-ˈtau̇n\ *adj* (1836) **1** : of, relating to, or located in the lower part or business center of a city **2** : HIP, TRENDY ⟨~ music⟩ — **downtown** *adv*

2**down·town** \ˌdau̇n-ˈtau̇n, ˈdau̇n-ˌ\ *n* (1845) : the lower part of a city; *esp* : the main business district — **down·town·er** \-ˈtau̇-nər\ *n*

down·trend \ˈdau̇n-ˌtrend\ *n* (1926) : DOWNTURN

down·trod·den \ˈdau̇n-ˈträ-dᵊn\ *adj* (1595) : suffering oppression

down·turn \-ˌtərn\ *n* (1926) : a downward turn esp. toward a decline in business and economic activity

down under *adv or adj, often cap D&U* (1886) : to or in Australia or New Zealand

1**down·ward** \ˈdau̇n-wərd\ *or* **down·wards** \-wərdz\ *adv* (13c) **1 a** : from a higher to a lower place **b** : toward a direction that is the opposite of up **2** : from a higher to a lower condition **3 a** : from an earlier time **b** : from an ancestor or predecessor

2**downward** *adj* (ca. 1552) **1** : moving or extending downward **2** : descending from a head, origin, or source — **down·ward·ly** *adv* — **down·ward·ness** *n*

down·wash \ˈdau̇n-ˌwȯsh, -ˌwäsh\ *n* (1915) : an airstream directed downward (as by an airfoil)

down·wind \ˈdau̇n-ˈwind\ *adv or adj* (1826) : in the direction that the wind is blowing

downy \ˈdau̇-nē\ *adj* **down·i·er; -est** (1578) **1** : resembling a bird's down **2** : covered with down **3** : made of down **4** : SOFT, SOOTHING

downy mildew *n* (1886) **1** : any of various parasitic lower fungi (family Peronosporaceae) that produce whitish masses of sporangiophores or conidiophores on the undersurface of the leaves of the host **2** : a plant disease caused by a downy mildew

downy woodpecker *n* (1808) : a small black-and-white woodpecker (*Picoides pubescens*) of No. America that has a white back and is smaller than the hairy woodpecker

down·zone \ˈdau̇n-ˌzōn\ *vt* (1954) : to reduce or limit development or the number of buildings permitted on ⟨the county *downzoned* rural land to allow only one home per ten acres⟩

dow·ry \ˈdau̇(-ə)-rē\ *n, pl* **dowries** [ME *dowarie,* fr. AF, alter. of *dower, douaire* — more at DOWER] (14c) **1** *archaic* : DOWER 1 **2** : the money, goods, or estate that a woman brings to her husband in marriage **3** : a gift of money or property by a man to or for his bride **4** : a natural talent

dowsabel *n* [*Dowsabel,* fem. name] (ca. 1652) *obs* : SWEETHEART

1**dowse** *var of* DOUSE

2**dowse** \ˈdau̇z\ *vb* **dowsed; dows·ing** [origin unknown] *vi* (1691) : to use a divining rod ~ *vt* : to find (as water) by dowsing

dows·er \ˈdau̇-zər\ *n* (1838) : DIVINING ROD; *also* : a person who uses it

dowsing rod *n* (1691) : DIVINING ROD

dox·ol·o·gy \däk-ˈsä-lə-jē\ *n, pl* **-gies** [ML *doxologia,* fr. LGk, fr. Gk *doxa* opinion, glory (fr. *dokein* to seem, seem good) + *-logia* -logy — more at DECENT] (ca. 1645) : a usu. liturgical expression of praise to God

doxo·ru·bi·cin \ˌdäk-sə-ˈrü-bə-sən\ *n* [*deoxy-* + *-orubicin* (as in *daunorubicin*)] (1971) : an antibiotic with broad antineoplastic activity that is obtained from a bacterium (*Streptomyces peucetius*) and is administered in the form of its hydrochloride $C_{27}H_{29}NO_{11}·HCl$

doxy *also* **dox·ie** \ˈdäk-sē\ *n, pl* **dox·ies** [perh. modif. of obs. D *docke* doll, fr. MD] (1515) **1** : FLOOZY, PROSTITUTE **2** : MISTRESS 4a

doxy·cy·cline \ˌdäk-sə-ˈsī-ˌklēn\ *n* [*deoxy-* + tetra*cycline*] (1966) : a broad-spectrum tetracycline antibiotic $C_{22}H_{24}N_2O_8$ with potent antibacterial activity that is often taken by travelers to prevent diarrhea

doy·en \ˈdȯi-ən, -ˌ(y)en; ˈdwä-ˌyaⁿ(n)\ *n* [F, fr. OF *deien,* fr. LL *decanus* dean — more at DEAN] (1670) **1 a** : the senior member of a body or group **b** : a person considered to be knowledgeable or uniquely skilled as a result of long experience in some field of endeavor **2** : the oldest example of a category

doy·enne \dȯi-ˈ(y)en, dwä-ˈyen\ *n* [F, fem. of *doyen*] (ca. 1897) : a woman who is a doyen

doy·ley *chiefly Brit var of* DOILY

doz *abbr* dozen

1**doze** \ˈdōz\ *vb* **dozed; doz·ing** [perh. of Scand origin; akin to ON *dūsa* to doze] *vi* (1677) **1 a** : to sleep lightly **b** : to fall into a light sleep — usu. used with *off* **2** : to be in a dull or stupefied condition ~ *vt* : to pass (as time) drowsily — **doze** *n* — **doz·er** *n*

2**doze** *vt* **dozed; doz·ing** [prob. back-formation fr. *dozer* (bulldozer)] (1945) : BULLDOZE 2 — **doz·er** *n*

doz·en \ˈdə-zᵊn\ *n, pl* **dozens** *or* **dozen** [ME *dozeine,* fr. AF *duzeine, dozeyne,* fr. *duze* twelve, fr. L *duodecim,* fr. *duo* two + *decem* ten — more at TWO, TEN] (13c) **1** : a group of 12 **2** : an indefinitely large number ⟨~*s* of times⟩ **3** *pl but sing in constr* : a ritualized word game that consists of exchanging insults usu. about the members of the opponent's family — used with *the* — **dozen** *adj* — **doz·enth** \-zᵊn(t)th\ *adj*

doz·er \ˈdō-zər\ *n* (1942) : BULLDOZER 2

dozy \ˈdō-zē\ *adj* **doz·i·er; -est** (1693) : DROWSY, SLEEPY — **doz·i·ly** \ˈdō-zə-lē\ *adv* — **doz·i·ness** *n*

1**DP** \ˌdē-ˈpē\ *n, pl* **DP's** *or* **DPs** (ca. 1944) **1** : a displaced person **2** : DOUBLE PLAY

2**DP** *abbr* **1** data processing **2** degree of polymerization **3** dew point **4** director of photography **5** doctor of podiatry

DPE *abbr* doctor of physical education

DPH *abbr* **1** department of public health **2** doctor of public health

dpi *abbr* dots per inch

DPM *abbr* doctor of podiatric medicine

DPN \ˌdē-ˌpē-ˈen\ *n* [*d*iphospho*p*yridine *n*ucleotide] (1938) : NAD

dpt *abbr* **1** department **2** deponent

DPT *abbr* diphtheria, pertussis, tetanus

DQ *abbr* disqualification; disqualify

dr *abbr* **1** debtor **2** drachma **3** dram **4** drive **5** drum

Dr *abbr* doctor

DR *abbr* **1** dead reckoning **2** dining room

1**drab** \ˈdrab\ *n* [origin unknown] (ca. 1515) **1** : SLATTERN **2** : PROSTITUTE

2**drab** *vi* **drabbed; drab·bing** (1599) : to associate with prostitutes

3**drab** *n* [MF *drap* cloth, fr. LL *drappus*] (1541) **1** : any of various cloths of a dull brown or gray color **2 a** : a light olive brown **b** : a dull, lifeless, or faded appearance or quality

4**drab** *adj* **drab·ber; drab·best** (1686) **1 a** : of the dull brown color of drab **b** : of the color drab **2** : characterized by dullness and monotony : CHEERLESS ⟨a ~ life⟩ — **drab·ly** *adv* — **drab·ness** *n*

5**drab** *n* [prob. alter. of *drib*] (1809) : a small amount — usu. used in the phrase *dribs and drabs* ⟨receiving donations in dribs and ~*s*⟩

dra·cae·na \drə-ˈsē-nə\ *n* [NL, fr. LL, she-serpent, fr. Gk *drakaina,* fem. of *drakōn* serpent — more at DRAGON] (ca. 1823) : any of two genera (*Dracaena* and *Cordyline*) of chiefly Old World tropical shrubs or trees of the agave family that have naked branches ending in tufts of sword-shaped leaves and include some used as houseplants

drachm \ˈdram\ *n* [alter. of ME *dragme* — more at DRAM] (14c) **1** : DRACHMA **2** *chiefly Brit* : 1DRAM

drach·ma \ˈdrak-mə\ *n, pl* **drachmas** *or* **drach·mai** \-ˌmī\ *or* **drach·mae** \-(ˌ)mē, -ˌmī\ [L, fr. Gk *drachmē* — more at DRAM] (1525) **1 a** : any of various ancient Greek units of weight **b** : any of various modern units of weight; *esp* : 1DRAM 1 **2 a** : an ancient Greek silver coin equivalent to six obols **b** : the basic monetary unit of Greece from circa 1831 to 2001

Dra·co \ˈdrā-(ˌ)kō\ *n* [L (gen. *Draconis*), lit., dragon — more at DRAGON] (1621) : a northern circumpolar constellation within which is the north pole of the ecliptic

dra·co·ni·an \drā-ˈkō-nē-ən, drə-\ *adj, often cap* [L *Dracon-, Draco,* fr. Gk *Drakōn* Draco (Athenian lawgiver)] (1775) **1** : of, relating to, or characteristic of Draco or the severe code of laws held to have been framed by him **2** : CRUEL; *also* : SEVERE ⟨~ littering fines⟩

1**dra·con·ic** \drə-ˈkä-nik\ *adj* [L *dracon-, draco*] (1680) : of or relating to a dragon

2**dra·con·ic** \drā-ˈkä-nik, drə-\ *adj* (1708) : DRACONIAN

dra·cun·cu·li·a·sis \drə-ˌkəŋ-kyə-ˈlī-ə-səs\ *n* [NL, fr. *Dracunculus,* the guinea worm genus, fr. L, dim. of *dracon-, draco* serpent, dragon — more at DRAGON] (1942) : a disease that is caused by infestation with the guinea worm and that has been eradicated in most regions except Africa — called also *guinea worm disease*

1**draft** \ˈdraft, ˈdräft\ *n* [ME *draght;* akin to OE *dragan* to draw — more at DRAW] (13c) **1 a** : the act of drawing a net **b** : HAUL 2b **2 a** : the act or an instance of drinking or inhaling; *also* : the portion drunk or inhaled in one such act **b** : a portion poured out or mixed for drinking : DOSE **3 a** : the force required to pull an implement **b** : load or load-pulling capacity **4 a** : the act of moving loads by drawing or pulling : PULL **b** : a team of animals together with what they draw **5 a** : DELINEATION, REPRESENTATION **b** : SCHEME, DESIGN **c** : a preliminary sketch, outline, or version ⟨the author's first ~⟩ ⟨a ~ treaty⟩ **6** : the act, result, or plan of drawing out or stretching **7 a** : the act of drawing (as from a cask) **b** : a portion of liquid so drawn ⟨a ~ of ale⟩ **c** : draft beer ⟨a glass of ~⟩ **8** : the depth of water a ship draws esp. when loaded **9 a (1)** : a system for or act of selecting individuals from a group (as for compulsory military service) **(2)** : an act or process of selecting an individual (as for political candidacy) without the individual's expressed consent **b** : a group of individuals selected esp. by military draft **c** : a system whereby exclusive rights to selected new players are apportioned among professional teams **10 a** : an order for the payment of money drawn by one person or bank on another **b** : the act or an instance of drawing from or making demands upon something : DEMAND **11 a** : a current of air in a closed-in space ⟨felt a ~⟩ **b** : a device for regulating the flow of air (as in a fireplace) **12** : ANGLE, TAPER; *specif* : the taper given to a pattern or die so that the work can be easily withdrawn **13** : a pocket of reduced air pressure behind a moving object; *also* : the use of such a draft to save energy — **on draft** : ready to be drawn from a receptacle ⟨beer *on draft*⟩

\ə\ **abut** \ᵊ\ kitten, F table \ər\ **further** \a\ **ash** \ā\ **ace** \ä\ **mop, mar**
\au̇\ **out** \ch\ **chin** \e\ **bet** \ē\ **easy** \g\ **go** \i\ **hit** \ī\ **ice** \j\ **job**
\ŋ\ **sing** \ō\ **go** \ȯ\ **law** \ȯi\ **boy** \th\ **thin** \th\ **the** \ü\ **loot** \u̇\ **foot**
\y\ **yet** \zh\ **vision, beige** \k, ⁿ, œ, ue, ʸ\ *see* Guide to Pronunciation

[2]**draft** *adj* (15c) **1 :** used or adapted for drawing loads ⟨~ horses⟩ **2 :** being or having been on draft ⟨drinking ~ beer⟩

[3]**draft** *vt* (1714) **1 :** to select for some purpose: as **a :** to conscript for military service **b :** to select (a professional athlete) by draft **2 a :** to draw the preliminary sketch, version, or plan of ⟨~ legislation⟩ **b :** COMPOSE, PREPARE ⟨~ a memo⟩ **3 :** to draw off or away ⟨water ~*ed* by pumps⟩ **4 :** to stay close behind (another racer) so as to take advantage of the reduced air pressure created by the leading racer ~ *vi* **1 :** to practice draftsmanship **2 :** to draft another racer (as in car or bike racing) — **draft·able** \ˈdraf-tə-bəl, ˈdräf-\ *adj* — **draft·ee** \ˌdraf-ˈtē, ˌdräf-\ *n* — **draft·er** \ˈdraf-tər, ˈdräf-\ *n*

draft board *n* (1941) **:** a civilian board that registers, classifies, and selects men for compulsory military service

drafts·man \ˈdraf(t)-smən, ˈdräf(t)-\ *n* (1663) **1 :** a person who draws plans and sketches (as of machinery or structures) **2 :** a person who draws legal documents or other writings **3 :** an artist who excels in drawing — **drafts·man·ly** \-lē\ *adj* — **drafts·man·ship** \-ˌship\ *n*

drafts·person \ˈdraf(t)s-ˌpər-sᵊn\ *n* (1975) **:** DRAFTSMAN 1

drafty \ˈdraf-tē, ˈdräf-\ *adj* **draft·i·er; -est** (1846) **:** exposed to or abounding in drafts of air ⟨a ~ room⟩ — **draft·i·ly** \-tə-lē\ *adv* — **draft·i·ness** \-tē-nəs\ *n*

[1]**drag** \ˈdrag\ *n* [ME *dragge,* prob. fr. MLG *draggen* grapnel; akin to OE *dragan* to draw — more at DRAW] (14c) **1 :** something used to drag with; *esp* **:** a device for dragging under water to detect or obtain objects **2 :** something that is dragged, pulled, or drawn along or over a surface: as **a :** HARROW **b :** a sledge for conveying heavy bodies **c :** CONVEYANCE **3 a :** the act or an instance of dragging or drawing: as (1) **:** a drawing along or over a surface with effort or pressure (2) **:** motion effected with slowness or difficulty; *also* **:** the condition of having or seeming to have such motion (3) **:** a draw on a pipe, cigarette, or cigar; *also* **:** a draft of liquid **b :** a movement, inclination, or retardation caused by or as if by dragging **c** *slang* **:** influence securing special favor **:** PULL **4 a :** something that retards motion, action, or advancement **b** (1) **:** the retarding force acting on a body (as an airplane) moving through a fluid (as air) parallel and opposite to the direction of motion (2) **:** friction between engine parts; *also* **:** retardation due to friction **c :** BURDEN, ENCUMBRANCE ⟨the ~ of population growth on living standards⟩ **d :** one that is boring or gets in the way of enjoyment ⟨thinks studying is a ~⟩ ⟨this sickly kid is going to be a social ~ —Edmund Morris⟩ **5 a :** an object drawn over the ground to leave a scented trail **b :** a clog fastened to a trap to prevent the escape of a trapped animal **6 :** STREET, ROAD ⟨the main ~⟩ **7 a :** COSTUME, OUTFIT ⟨in Victorian ~⟩ **b :** clothing typical of one sex worn by a person of the opposite sex — often used in the phrase *in drag* **8 :** DRAG RACE

[2]**drag** *vb* **dragged; drag·ging** *vt* (15c) **1 a** (1) **:** to draw slowly or heavily **:** HAUL (2) **:** to cause (as oneself) to move with slowness or difficulty ⟨*dragged* myself up the stairs⟩ (3) **:** to cause to trail along a surface ⟨wandered off *dragging* the leash⟩ **b** (1) **:** to bring by or as if by force or compulsion ⟨had to ~ her husband to the opera⟩ (2) **:** to extract by or as if by pulling **c :** PROTRACT ⟨~ a story out⟩ **2 a :** to pass a drag over ⟨~ a field⟩ **b :** to explore with a drag ⟨~ a pond⟩ **c :** to catch with a dragnet **3 :** to hit (a drag bunt) while moving toward first base **4 :** to move (items on a computer screen) esp. by means of a mouse ~ *vi* **1 :** to hang or lag behind **2 :** to fish or search with a drag **3 :** to trail along on the ground **4 a :** to move slowly because of fatigue ⟨was *dragging* after the long trip⟩ **b :** to proceed or continue laboriously or tediously ⟨the lawsuit *dragged* on for years⟩ **5 :** DRAW 4a ⟨~ on a cigarette⟩ **6 :** to make a plucking or pulling movement **7 :** to participate in a drag race — **drag·ging·ly** \ˈdra-giŋ-lē\ *adv* — **drag one's feet** *also* **drag one's heels :** to act in a deliberately slow or dilatory manner

[3]**drag** *adj* (1887) **:** of, being, involving, or intended for a person in drag ⟨a ~ ball⟩

drag–and–drop *adj* (1985) **:** of, relating to, or allowing movement of items on a computer screen by dragging them and fixing their new locations by releasing the mouse button ⟨a ~ interface⟩

drag bunt *n* (ca. 1949) **:** a bunt in baseball made by a left-handed batter by trailing the bat while moving toward first base; *broadly* **:** a bunt made with the object of getting on base safely rather than sacrificing

drag coefficient *n* (1937) **:** a factor representing the drag acting on a body (as an automobile or airfoil)

dra·gée \dra-ˈzhā\ *n* [F, fr. MF *dragie* — more at DREDGE] (1682) **1 :** a sugar-coated nut **2 :** a small silver-colored ball used as a decoration (as on a cake)

drag·ger \ˈdra-gər\ *n* (ca. 1500) **:** one that drags; *specif* **:** a fishing boat operating a trawl or dragnet

drag·gle \ˈdra-gəl\ *vb* **drag·gled; drag·gling** \-g(ə-)liŋ\ [freq. of *drag*] *vt* (1513) **:** to make wet and dirty by dragging ~ *vi* **1 :** to trail on the ground **2 :** STRAGGLE

drag·gle–tail \ˈdra-gəl-ˌtāl\ *n* (1596) **:** SLATTERN

drag·gy \ˈdra-gē\ *adj* **drag·gi·er; -est** (15c) **:** SLUGGISH, DULL

drag·line \ˈdrag-ˌlīn\ *n* (1874) **1 :** a line used in or for dragging **2 :** an excavating machine in which the bucket is attached by cables and operates by being drawn toward the machine **3 :** a strong stiff strand of silk produced by a spider esp. to form the framework of its web and as a means of lowering itself from and returning to a height

drag·net \ˈdrag-ˌnet\ *n* (ca. 1541) **1 a :** a net drawn along the bottom of a body of water **b :** a net used on the ground (as to capture small game) **2 :** a network of measures for apprehension (as of criminals)

drag·o·man \ˈdra-gə-mən\ *n, pl* **-mans** *or* **-men** \-mən\ [ME *drugeman,* fr. AF, fr. OIt *dragomanno,* fr. MGk *dragomanos,* fr. Ar *tarjumān,* fr. Aram *tūrgĕmānā*] (14c) **:** an interpreter chiefly of Arabic, Turkish, or Persian employed esp. in the Near East

drag·on \ˈdra-gən\ *n* [ME, fr. AF *dragun,* fr. L *dracon-, draco* serpent, dragon, fr. Gk *drakōn* serpent; akin to OE *torht* bright, Gk *derkesthai* to see, look at] (13c) **1** *archaic* **:** a huge serpent **2 :** a mythical animal usu. represented as a monstrous winged and scaly serpent or saurian with a crested head and enormous claws **3 :** a violent, combative, or very strict person **4** *cap* **:** DRACO **5 :** something or someone formidable or baneful — **drag·on·ish** \-gə-nish\ *adj*

drag·on·et \ˌdra-gə-ˈnet, ˈdra-gə-nət\ *n* (14c) **1 :** a little dragon **2 :** any of a family (Callionymidae) of small often brightly colored scaleless marine fishes that have sharp spines on the gill covers; *esp* **:** a European fish (*Callionymus lyra*) that is sometimes used as food

drag·on·fly \ˈdra-gən-ˌflī\ *n* (1626) **:** any of a suborder (Anisoptera) of odonate insects that are larger and stouter than damselflies, hold the wings horizontal in repose, and have rectal gills during the naiad stage; *broadly* **:** ODONATE

drag·on·head \-ˌhed\ *n* (1753) **:** any of several mints (genus *Dracocephalum*) often grown for their showy flower heads; *esp* **:** a No. American plant (*D. parviflorum*) with dense spikes of blue or violet flowers

dragon lady *n* [character in the comic strip "Terry and the Pirates" by Milton Caniff] (1949) **:** an overbearing or tyrannical woman; *also* **:** a glamorous often mysterious woman

dragon's blood *n* (ca. 1598) **:** any of several resinous mostly dark-red plant products; *specif* **:** a resin from the fruit of a palm (genus *Daemonorops*) used for coloring varnish and in photoengraving

dragon's teeth *n pl* [fr. the dragon's teeth sown by Cadmus which sprang up as armed warriors who killed one another off] (1853) **1 :** seeds of strife **2 :** wedge-shaped concrete antitank barriers laid in multiple rows

[1]**dra·goon** \drə-ˈgün, dra-\ *n* [F *dragon* dragon, dragoon, fr. MF] (1604) **1 :** a member of a European military unit formerly composed of heavily armed mounted troops **2 :** CAVALRYMAN

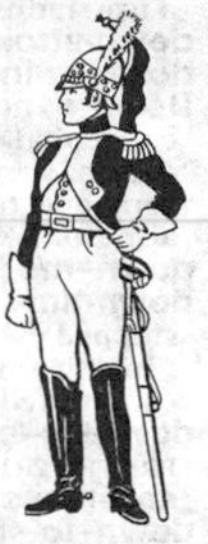
dragoon 1

[2]**dragoon** *vt* (1689) **1 :** to subjugate or persecute by harsh use of troops **2 :** to force into submission or compliance esp. by violent measures

drag queen *n* (ca. 1941) **:** a male homosexual who dresses as a woman esp. for comic or theatrical effect

drag race *n* (1948) **:** an acceleration contest between vehicles — **drag racer** *n* — **drag racing** *n*

drag·ster \ˈdrag-stər\ *n* (ca. 1954) **1 :** a vehicle built or modified for use in a drag race **2 :** one who participates in a drag race

drag strip *n* (1952) **:** the site of a drag race; *specif* **:** a strip of pavement with a racing area at least ¼ mile long

[1]**drain** \ˈdrān\ *vb* [ME *draynen,* fr. OE *drēahnian* — more at DRY] *vt* (bef. 12c) **1** *obs* **:** FILTER **2 a :** to draw off (liquid) gradually or completely ⟨~*ed* all the water out⟩ **b :** to cause the gradual disappearance of ⟨~ the region's wealth⟩ **c :** to exhaust physically or emotionally ⟨feeling ~*ed* at the end of a long workday⟩ **3 a :** to make gradually dry ⟨~ a swamp⟩ **b :** to carry away the surface water of ⟨the river that ~*s* the valley⟩ **c :** to deplete or empty by or as if by drawing off by degrees or in increments ⟨~*ed* the country of its resources⟩ **d :** to empty by drinking the contents of ⟨~ a mug of beer⟩ **4 :** DROP 7c, SINK ⟨~*ed* the putt⟩ ~ *vi* **1 a :** to flow off gradually **b :** to disappear gradually **:** DWINDLE **2 :** to become emptied or freed of liquid by its flowing or dropping ⟨waiting for the tub to ~⟩ **3 :** to discharge surface or surplus water ***syn*** see DEPLETE — **drain·er** *n*

[2]**drain** *n* (1552) **1 :** a means (as a pipe) by which usu. liquid matter is drained **2 a :** the act of draining **b :** a gradual outflow or withdrawal **:** DEPLETION **3 :** something that causes depletion **:** BURDEN **4 :** an electrode in a field-effect transistor toward which charge carriers move — compare GATE, SOURCE — **down the drain :** to a state of being wasted or irretrievably lost

drain·age \ˈdrā-nij\ *n* (1652) **1 :** the act, process, or mode of draining; *also* **:** something drained off **2 :** a device for draining **:** DRAIN; *also* **:** a system of drains **3 :** an area or district drained

drain·pipe \ˈdrān-ˌpīp\ *n* (1857) **:** a pipe for drainage

Draize test \ˈdrāz-\ *n* [John H. *Draize* †1992 Am. pharmacologist] (1980) **:** a test for harmfulness of chemicals to the human eye that involves dropping the test substance into one eye of a rabbit without anesthesia using the other eye as a control — called also *Draize eye test*

drake \ˈdrāk\ *n* [ME; akin to OHG an*trahho* drake] (14c) **:** a male duck

[1]**dram** \ˈdram\ *n* [ME *dragme,* fr. AF & LL; AF, dram, drachma, fr. LL *dragma,* fr. L *drachma,* fr. Gk *drachmē,* lit., handful, fr. *drassesthai* to grasp] (14c) **1 a —** see WEIGHT table **b :** FLUID DRAM **2 a :** a small portion of something to drink **b :** a small amount

[2]**dram** \ˈdräm\ *n* [Arm, lit., coin, money, ultim. fr. Gk *drachmē* drachma] (1993) — see MONEY table

[3]**dram** *abbr* dramatic; dramatist

DRAM \ˈdram *also* ˈdē-ˌram\ *n* [*d*ynamic + *RAM* (*r*andom-*a*ccess *m*emory)] (1980) **:** a type of RAM that must be continuously supplied with power and periodically rewritten in order to retain data — compare SRAM

dra·ma \ˈdrä-mə, ˈdra-\ *n* [LL *dramat-, drama,* fr. Gk, deed, drama, fr. *dran* to do, act] (1515) **1 a :** a composition in verse or prose intended to portray life or character or to tell a story usu. involving conflicts and emotions through action and dialogue and typically designed for theatrical performance **:** PLAY — compare CLOSET DRAMA **b :** a movie or television production with characteristics (as conflict) of a serious play; *broadly* **:** a play, movie, or television production with a serious tone or subject ⟨a police ~⟩ **2 :** dramatic art, literature, or affairs **3 a :** a state, situation, or series of events involving interesting or intense conflict of forces **b :** dramatic state, effect, or quality ⟨the ~ of the courtroom proceedings⟩

Dram·a·mine \ˈdra-mə-ˌmēn\ *trademark* — used for dimenhydrinate

drama queen *n* (1979) **:** a person given to often excessively emotional performances or reactions

dra·mat·ic \drə-ˈma-tik\ *adj* (1589) **1 :** of or relating to the drama ⟨a ~ actor⟩ **2 a :** suitable to or characteristic of the drama ⟨a ~ attempt to escape⟩ **b :** striking in appearance or effect ⟨a ~ pause⟩ **3** *of an opera singer* **:** having a powerful voice and a declamatory style — compare LYRIC — **dra·mat·i·cal·ly** \-ti-k(ə-)lē\ *adv*

syn DRAMATIC, THEATRICAL, HISTRIONIC, MELODRAMATIC mean having a character or an effect like that of acted plays. DRAMATIC applies to situations in life and literature that stir the imagination and emotions deeply ⟨a *dramatic* meeting of world leaders⟩. THEATRICAL implies a crude appeal through artificiality or exaggeration in gesture or vocal expression ⟨a *theatrical* oration⟩. HISTRIONIC applies to tones, gestures, and motions and suggests a deliberate affectation or staginess ⟨a *histrionic* show of grief⟩. MELODRAMATIC suggests an exaggerated emotionalism or an inappropriate theatricalism ⟨made a *melodramatic* plea⟩.

dramatic irony *n* (ca. 1907) **:** IRONY 3b

dramatic monologue *n* (ca. 1935) **:** a literary work (as a poem) in which a speaker's character is revealed in a monologue usu. addressed to a second person

dra·mat·ics \drə-ˈma-tiks\ *n pl but sing or pl in constr* (1796) **1 :** the study or practice of theatrical arts (as acting and stagecraft) **2 :** dramatic behavior or expression

dramatic unities *n pl* (ca. 1922) **:** the unities of time, place, and action that are observed in classical drama

dra·ma·ti·sa·tion, dra·ma·tise *Brit var of* DRAMATIZATION, DRAMATIZE

dra·ma·tis per·so·nae \ˌdra-mə-təs-pər-ˈsō-(ˌ)nē, ˌdrä-, -ˌnī\ *n pl* [NL] (1730) **1 :** the characters or actors in a drama **2** *sing in constr* **:** a list of the characters or actors in a drama **3 :** people who figure prominently in something (as an event)

dra·ma·tist \ˈdra-mə-tist, ˈdrä-\ *n* (1678) **:** PLAYWRIGHT

dra·ma·ti·za·tion \ˌdra-mə-tə-ˈzā-shən, ˌdrä-\ *n* (1796) **1 :** the action of dramatizing **2 :** a dramatized version (as of a novel)

dra·ma·tize \ˈdra-mə-ˌtīz, ˈdrä-\ *vb* **-tized; -tiz·ing** *vt* (1783) **1 :** to adapt (as a novel) for theatrical presentation **2 :** to present or represent in a dramatic manner ~ *vi* **1 :** to be suitable for dramatization **2 :** to behave dramatically — **dra·ma·tiz·able** \-ˌtī-zə-bəl\ *adj*

dra·ma·turge *or* **dra·ma·turg** \ˈdra-mə-ˌtərj, ˈdrä-\ *n* (1870) **:** a specialist in dramaturgy

dra·ma·tur·gy \ˈdra-mə-ˌtər-jē, ˈdrä-\ *n* [G *Dramaturgie,* fr. Gk *dramatourgia* dramatic composition, fr. *dramat-, drama* + *-ourgia* -urgy] (1801) **:** the art or technique of dramatic composition and theatrical representation — **dra·ma·tur·gic** \ˌdra-mə-ˈtər-jik, ˌdrä-\ *or* **dra·ma·tur·gi·cal** \-ji-kəl\ *adj* — **dra·ma·tur·gi·cal·ly** \-ji-k(ə-)lē\ *adv*

dra·me·dy \ˈdrä-mə-dē, ˈdra-\ *n* [blend of *drama* and *comedy*] (1978) **:** a comedy (as a film or television show) having dramatic moments

dram·mock \ˈdra-mək\ *n* [ScGael *dramag*] (1562) *chiefly Scot* **:** raw oatmeal mixed with cold water

dram·shop \ˈdram-ˌshäp\ *n* (1725) **:** BARROOM

drank *past and past part of* DRINK

[1]**drape** \ˈdrāp\ *vb* **draped; drap·ing** [prob. back-formation fr. *drapery*] *vt* (1847) **1 :** to cover or adorn with or as if with folds of cloth **2 :** to cause to hang or stretch out loosely or carelessly **3 :** to arrange in flowing lines or folds ~ *vi* **:** to become arranged in folds ⟨this silk ~*s* beautifully⟩ — **drap·abil·i·ty** *also* **drape·abil·i·ty** \ˌdrā-pə-ˈbi-lə-tē\ *n* — **drap·able** *also* **drape·able** \ˈdrā-pə-bəl\ *adj*

[2]**drape** *n* (1889) **1 :** arrangement in or of folds **2 a :** a drapery esp. for a window **:** CURTAIN **b :** a sterile covering used in an operating room — usu. used in pl. **3 :** the cut or hang of clothing — **drap·ey** \ˈdrā-pē\ *adj*

drap·er \ˈdrā-pər\ *n* [ME, weaver, clothier, fr. AF *draper,* fr. *drap* cloth — more at DRAB] (14c) *chiefly Brit* **:** a dealer in cloth and sometimes also in clothing and dry goods

drap·ery \ˈdrā-p(ə-)rē\ *n, pl* **-er·ies** (14c) **1** *Brit* **:** DRY GOODS **2 a :** a decorative piece of material usu. hung in loose folds and arranged in a graceful design **b :** hangings of heavy fabric for use as a curtain **3 :** the draping or arranging of materials

dras·tic \ˈdras-tik\ *adj* [Gk *drastikos,* fr. *dran* to do] (ca. 1691) **1 :** acting rapidly or violently ⟨a ~ purgative⟩ **2 :** extreme in effect or action **:** SEVERE ⟨~ measures⟩ — **dras·ti·cal·ly** \-ti-k(ə-)lē\ *adv*

drat \ˈdrat\ *vb* **drat·ted; drat·ting** [prob. euphemistic alter. of *God rot*] (1815) **:** DAMN — used as a mild oath

draught \ˈdräft\, **draughty** \ˈdräf-tē\ *chiefly Brit var of* DRAFT, DRAFTY

draughts \ˈdräf(t)s\ *n pl but sing or pl in constr* [ME *draghtes,* fr. pl. of *draght* draft, move in chess] (15c) *Brit* **:** CHECKERS

draughts·man *chiefly Brit var of* DRAFTSMAN

Dra·vid·i·an \drə-ˈvi-dē-ən\ *n* [Skt *Drāviḍa*] (1856) **1 :** a member of an ancient dark-skinned people of southern India **2 :** DRAVIDIAN LANGUAGES — **Dravidian** *adj*

Dravidian languages *n pl* (1871) **:** a language family of India, Sri Lanka, and Pakistan that includes Tamil, Telugu, Kannada, and Malayalam

[1]**draw** \ˈdrȯ\ *vb* **drew** \ˈdrü\; **drawn** \ˈdrȯn, ˈdrän\; **draw·ing** [ME *drawen, dragen,* fr. OE *dragan;* akin to ON *draga* to draw, drag] *vt* (bef. 12c) **1 :** to cause to move continuously toward or after a force applied in advance **:** PULL ⟨~ your chair up by the fire⟩: as **a :** to move (as a covering) over or to one side ⟨~ the drapes⟩ **b :** to pull up or out of a receptacle or place where seated or carried ⟨~ water from the well⟩ ⟨*drew* a gun⟩; *also* **:** to cause to come out of a container or source ⟨~ water for a bath⟩ ⟨the nurse *drew* a blood sample⟩ ⟨the wound *drew* blood⟩ **2 :** to cause to go in a certain direction (as by leading) ⟨*drew* him aside⟩ **3 a :** to bring by inducement or allure **:** ATTRACT ⟨honey ~*s* flies⟩ **b :** to bring in or gather from a specified group or area ⟨a college that ~*s* its students from many states⟩ **c :** BRING ON, PROVOKE ⟨*drew* enemy fire⟩ **d :** to bring out by way of response **:** ELICIT ⟨*drew* cheers from the audience⟩ **e :** to receive in the course of play ⟨the batter *drew* a walk⟩ ⟨~ a foul⟩ **4 :** INHALE ⟨*drew* a deep breath⟩ **5 a :** to extract the essence from ⟨~ tea⟩ **b :** EVISCERATE ⟨plucking and ~*ing* a goose before cooking⟩ **c :** to derive to one's benefit ⟨*drew* inspiration from the old masters⟩ **6 :** to require (a specified depth) to float in ⟨a ship that ~*s* 12 feet of water⟩ **7 a :** ACCUMULATE, GAIN ⟨~*ing* interest⟩ **b :** to take (money) from a place of deposit **c :** to use in making a cash demand ⟨~*ing* a check against his account⟩ **d :** to receive regularly or in due course ⟨~ a salary⟩ **8 a :** to take (cards) from a stack or from the dealer **b :** to receive or take at random ⟨*drew* a winning number⟩ **9 :** to bend (a bow) by pulling back the string **10 :** to cause to shrink, contract, or tighten **11 a :** to strike (a ball) so as to impart a backward spin **b :** to strike (a golf ball) so that a slight to moderate hook results **12 :** to leave (a contest) undecided **:** TIE **13 a** (1) **:** to produce a likeness or representation of by making lines on a surface ⟨~ a picture⟩ ⟨~ a graph with chalk⟩ (2) **:** to give a portrayal of **:** DELINEATE ⟨a writer who ~*s* characters well⟩ **b :** to write out in due form ⟨~ a will⟩ **c :** to design or describe in detail **:** FORMULATE ⟨~ comparisons⟩ **14 :** to infer from evidence or premises ⟨~ a conclusion⟩ **15 :** to spread or elongate (metal) by hammering or by pulling through dies; *also* **:** to shape (as plastic) by stretching or by pulling through dies ~ *vi* **1 :** to come or go steadily or gradually ⟨night ~*s* near⟩ **2 a :** to move something by pulling ⟨~*ing* at the well⟩ **b :** to exert an attractive force ⟨the play is ~*ing* well⟩ **3 a :** to pull back a bowstring **b :** to bring out a weapon ⟨*drew,* aimed, and fired⟩ **4 a :** to produce a draft ⟨the chimney ~*s* well⟩ ⟨~ on a cigar⟩ **b :** to swell out in a wind ⟨all sails ~*ing*⟩ **5 a :** to wrinkle or tighten up **:** SHRINK **b :** to change shape by pulling or stretching **6 :** to cause blood or pus to localize at one point **7 :** to create a likeness or a picture in outlines **:** SKETCH **8 :** to come out even in a contest **9 a :** to make a written demand for payment of money on deposit **b :** to obtain resources (as of information) ⟨~*ing* from a common fund of knowledge⟩ — **draw·able** \-ə-bəl\ *adj* — **draw a bead on :** to take aim at — **draw a blank :** to fail to gain a desired object (as information sought); *also* **:** to be unable to think of something — **draw on** *or* **draw upon :** to use as a source of supply ⟨*drawing on* the whole community for support⟩ — **draw straws :** to decide or assign something by lottery in which straws of unequal length are used — **draw the line** *or* **draw a line 1 :** to fix an arbitrary boundary between things that tend to intermingle **2 :** to fix a boundary excluding what one will not tolerate or engage in

[2]**draw** *n* (1663) **1 :** the act or process of drawing: as **a :** a sucking pull on something held with the lips **b :** a removal of a handgun from its holster ⟨quick on the ~⟩ **c :** backward spin given to a ball by striking it below center — compare FOLLOW **2 :** something that is drawn: as **a :** a card drawn to replace a discard in poker **b :** a lot or chance drawn at random **c :** the movable part of a drawbridge **3 :** a contest left undecided or deadlocked **:** TIE **4 :** one that draws attention or patronage **:** ATTRACTION **5 a :** the distance from the string to the back of a drawn bow **b :** the force required to draw a bow fully **6 :** a gully shallower than a ravine **7 :** the deal in draw poker to improve the players' hands after discarding **8 :** a football play that simulates a pass play so a runner can go straight up the middle past the pass rushers **9 :** a slight to moderate and usu. intentional hook in golf

draw away *vi* (1670) **:** to move ahead (as of an opponent in a race)

draw·back \ˈdrȯ-ˌbak\ *n* (1697) **1 :** a refund of duties esp. on an imported product subsequently exported or used to produce a product for export **2 :** an objectionable feature **:** DISADVANTAGE

draw back \drȯ-ˈbak\ *vi* (14c) **:** to avoid an issue or commitment

draw·bar \ˈdrȯ-ˌbär\ *n* (1839) **1 :** a railroad coupler **2 :** a beam across the rear of a vehicle (as a tractor) to which implements are hitched

draw·bridge \-ˌbrij\ *n* (14c) **:** a bridge made to be raised up, let down, or drawn aside so as to permit or hinder passage — see CASTLE illustration

draw·down \-ˌdau̇n\ *n* (1918) **1 :** a lowering of a water level (as in a reservoir) **2 a :** the process of depleting **b :** REDUCTION

draw down \ˌdrȯ-ˈdau̇n\ *vt* (1949) **:** to deplete by using or spending

draw·ee \drȯ-ˈē\ *n* (1766) **:** the party on which an order or bill of exchange is drawn

draw·er \ˈdrȯ(-ə)r\ *n* (14c) **1 :** one that draws: as **a :** a person who draws liquor **b :** DRAFTSMAN **c :** one that draws a bill of exchange or order for payment or makes a promissory note **2** *dial also* ˈdrȯ\ **:** a sliding box or receptacle opened by pulling out and closed by pushing in **3** *dial also* ˈdrȯ\ *pl* **:** an article of clothing (as underwear) for the lower body — **drawer·ful** \-ˌfu̇l\ *n*

draw in *vt* (1558) **1 :** to cause or entice to enter or participate **2 :** to sketch roughly ~ *vi* **1 a :** to draw to an end ⟨the day *drew in*⟩ **b :** to shorten seasonally ⟨the evenings are already *drawing in*⟩ **2 :** to become more cautious or economical

draw·ing \ˈdrȯ(-)iŋ\ *n* (14c) **1 :** an act or instance of drawing; *esp* **:** the process of deciding something by drawing lots **2 :** the art or technique of representing an object or outlining a figure, plan, or sketch by means of lines **3 :** something drawn or subject to drawing: as **a :** an amount drawn from a fund **b :** a representation formed by drawing **:** SKETCH

drawing account *n* (1885) **:** an account showing payments made to an employee in advance of actual earnings or for traveling expenses

drawing board *n* (1725) **1 :** a board used as a base for drafting on paper **2 :** a planning stage ⟨a project still on the *drawing board*⟩

drawing card *n* (1886) **:** one that attracts attention or patronage

drawing pin *n* (1859) *Brit* **:** THUMBTACK

drawing room *n* [short for *withdrawing room*] (1642) **1 a :** a formal reception room **b :** a private room on a railroad passenger car with three berths and an enclosed toilet **2 :** a formal reception

drawing table *n* (1706) **:** a table with a surface adjustable for elevation and angle of incline

draw·knife \ˈdrȯ-ˌnīf\ *n* (1677) **:** a woodworker's tool consisting of a blade with a handle at each end for use in shaving off surfaces

[1]**drawl** \ˈdrȯl\ *vb* [prob. freq. of *draw*] *vi* (1598) **:** to speak slowly with vowels greatly prolonged ~ *vt* **:** to utter in a slow lengthened tone — **drawl·er** *n* — **drawl·ing·ly** \ˈdrȯ-liŋ-lē\ *adv*

[2]**drawl** *n* (ca. 1742) **:** a drawling manner of speaking — **drawly** \ˈdrȯ-lē\ *adj*

[1]**drawn** *past part of* DRAW

[2]**drawn** \ˈdrȯn, ˈdrän\ *adj* (1613) **:** showing the effects of tension, pain, or illness **:** HAGGARD ⟨a face ~ with pain⟩

drawn butter *n* (ca. 1740) **:** melted clarified butter

drawn·work \ˈdrȯn-ˌwərk\ *n* (1594) **:** decoration on cloth made by drawing out threads according to a pattern

draw off *vt* (13c) **:** REMOVE, WITHDRAW ~ *vi* **:** to move apart or ahead

draw on *vi* (15c) **:** APPROACH ⟨night *draws on*⟩ ~ *vt* **:** BRING ON, CAUSE

draw out *vt* (14c) **1 :** REMOVE, EXTRACT **2 :** to extend beyond a minimum in time **:** PROTRACT **2 3 :** to cause to speak freely ⟨a reporter's ability to *draw* a person *out*⟩

draw·plate \ˈdrȯ-ˌplāt\ *n* (1793) **:** a die with holes through which wires are drawn

draw play *n* (1952) **:** DRAW 8

draw poker *n* (1849) **:** poker in which each player is dealt five cards face down and after betting may get replacements for discards

draw·shave \ˈdrȯ-ˌshāv\ *n* (1828) **:** DRAWKNIFE

draw shot *n* (1897) **:** a shot in billiards or pool made by hitting the cue ball with draw so it moves back after striking the object ball

\ə\ **abut** \ᵊ\ **kitten,** F **table** \ər\ **further** \a\ **ash** \ā\ **ace** \ä\ **mop, mar**
\au̇\ **out** \ch\ **chin** \e\ **bet** \ē\ **easy** \g\ **go** \i\ **hit** \ī\ **ice** \j\ **job**
\ŋ\ **sing** \ō\ **go** \ȯ\ **law** \ȯi\ **boy** \th\ **thin** \t͟h\ **the** \ü\ **loot** \u̇\ **foot**
\y\ **yet** \zh\ **vision, beige** \k̲, ⁿ, œ, ue, ʸ\ *see* Guide to Pronunciation

draw·string \ˈdrȯ-ˌstriŋ\ *n* (1845) **:** a string, cord, or tape inserted into hems or casings or laced through eyelets for use in closing a bag or controlling fullness in garments or curtains
draw·tube \-ˌtüb, -ˌtyüb\ *n* (1874) **:** a telescoping tube (as for the eyepiece of a microscope)
draw up *vt* (1605) **1 :** to bring (as troops) into array **2 :** to prepare a draft or version of ⟨*draw up* plans⟩ **3 :** to bring to a halt **4 :** to straighten (oneself) to an erect posture esp. as an assertion of dignity or resentment ~ *vi* **:** to come to a halt ⟨the car *drew up* at the door⟩
1**dray** \ˈdrā\ *n* [ME *draye,* a wheelless vehicle; akin to OE *dræge* dragnet, *dragan* to pull — more at DRAW] (14c) **:** a vehicle used to haul goods; *esp* **:** a strong cart or wagon without sides
2**dray** *vt* (1857) **:** to haul on a dray **:** CART
dray·age \ˈdrā-ij\ *n* (1791) **:** the work or cost of hauling by dray
dray horse *n* (1649) **:** a horse adapted for drawing heavy loads
dray·man \ˈdrā-mən\ *n* (1581) **:** one whose work is hauling by dray
1**dread** \ˈdred\ *vb* [ME *dreden,* fr. OE *drǣdan*] *vt* (bef. 12c) **1 a :** to fear greatly **b** *archaic* **:** to regard with awe **2 :** to feel extreme reluctance to meet or face ~ *vi* **:** to be apprehensive or fearful
2**dread** *n* (13c) **1 a :** great fear esp. in the face of impending evil **b :** extreme uneasiness in the face of a disagreeable prospect ⟨~ of a social blunder⟩ **c** *archaic* **:** AWE **2 :** one causing fear or awe **3 a :** DREADLOCK 1 **b** *pl* **:** DREADLOCK 2 ***syn*** see FEAR
3**dread** *adj* (15c) **1 :** causing great fear or anxiety **2 :** inspiring awe
1**dread·ful** \ˈdred-fəl\ *adj* (13c) **1 a :** inspiring dread **:** causing great and oppressive fear **b :** inspiring awe or reverence **2 :** extremely bad, distasteful, unpleasant, or shocking **3 :** EXTREME ⟨~ disorder⟩ — **dread·ful·ly** \-f(ə-)lē\ *adv* — **dread·ful·ness** \-fəl-nəs\ *n*
2**dreadful** *n* (ca. 1873) **:** a cheap and sensational story or periodical
dread·lock \ˈdred-ˌläk\ *n* (1960) **1 :** a narrow ropelike strand of hair formed by matting or braiding **2** *pl* **:** a hairstyle consisting of dreadlocks — **dread·locked** \-ˌläkt\ *adj*
dread·nought \ˈdred-ˌnȯt, -ˌnät\ *n* (1806) **1 :** a warm garment of thick cloth; *also* **:** the cloth **2** [*Dreadnought,* Brit. battleship] **a :** BATTLESHIP **b :** one that is among the largest or most powerful of its kind
1**dream** \ˈdrēm\ *n, often attrib* [ME *dreem,* fr. OE *drēam* noise, joy, and ON *draumr* dream; akin to OHG *troum* dream] (13c) **1 :** a series of thoughts, images, or emotions occurring during sleep — compare REM SLEEP **2 :** an experience of waking life having the characteristics of a dream: as **a :** a visionary creation of the imagination **:** DAYDREAM **b :** a state of mind marked by abstraction or release from reality **:** REVERIE **c :** an object seen in a dreamlike state **:** VISION **3 :** something notable for its beauty, excellence, or enjoyable quality ⟨the new car is a ~ to operate⟩ **4 a :** a strongly desired goal or purpose ⟨a ~ of becoming president⟩ **b :** something that fully satisfies a wish **:** IDEAL ⟨a meal that was a gourmet's ~⟩ — **dream·ful** \-fəl\ *adj* — **dream·ful·ly** \-fə-lē\ *adv* — **dream·ful·ness** *n* — **dream·less** *adj* — **dream·less·ly** *adv* — **dream·less·ness** *n* — **dream·like** \ˈdrēm-ˌlīk\ *adj*
2**dream** *vb* **dreamed** \ˈdrem(p)t, ˈdrēmd\ *or* **dreamt** \ˈdrem(p)t\; **dream·ing** \ˈdrē-miŋ\ *vi* (13c) **1 :** to have a dream **2 :** to indulge in daydreams or fantasies ⟨~*ing* of a better future⟩ **3 :** to appear tranquil or dreamy ⟨houses ~ in leafy shadows —Gladys Taber⟩ ~ *vt* **1 :** to have a dream of **2 :** to consider as a possibility **:** IMAGINE **3 :** to pass (time) in reverie or inaction ⟨~*ing* the hours away⟩ — **dream of :** to consider possible or fitting ⟨wouldn't *dream of* disturbing you⟩
dream·boat \ˈdrēm-ˌbōt\ *n* (ca. 1944) *slang* **:** one that is highly desirable; *esp* **:** a very attractive person
dream catcher *n* (1989) **:** a circular framed net with a hole in the center that is used by some American Indian peoples to help block bad dreams and catch good ones
dream·er \ˈdrē-mər\ *n* (14c) **1 :** one that dreams **2 a :** one who lives in a world of fancy and imagination **b :** one who has ideas or conceives projects regarded as impractical **:** VISIONARY
dream·land \ˈdrēm-ˌland\ *n* (1828) **:** an unreal delightful country existing only in imagination or in dreams **:** NEVER-NEVER LAND
dream·scape \ˈdrēm-ˌskāp\ *n* (1948) **:** a dreamlike usu. surrealistic scene; *also* **:** a painting of a dreamscape
dream team *n* (1977) **:** a team whose members are preeminent in a particular field ⟨a legal *dream team*⟩
dream·time \-ˌtīm\ *n, often cap* (1896) **:** the time of creation in the mythology of the Australian aborigines
dream up *vt* (1941) **:** to form in the mind **:** DEVISE, CONCOCT
dream vision *n* (1906) **:** a usu. medieval poem having a framework in which the poet pictures himself as falling asleep and envisioning in his dream a series of allegorical people and events
dream·world \ˈdrēm-ˌwərld\ *n* (1817) **:** a world of illusion or fantasy
dreamy \ˈdrē-mē\ *adj* **dream·i·er; -est** (1567) **1 a :** full of dreams ⟨a ~ night's sleep⟩ **b :** pleasantly abstracted from immediate reality **2 :** given to dreaming or fantasy **3 a :** suggestive of a dream or dreamlike state ⟨~ eyes⟩ ⟨~ silence⟩ **b :** quiet and soothing **c :** DELIGHTFUL, IDEAL — **dream·i·ly** \-mə-lē\ *adv* — **dream·i·ness** \-mē-nəs\ *n*
drear \ˈdrir\ *adj* (1629) **:** DREARY — **drear** *n*
drea·ry \ˈdrir-ē\ *adj* **drea·ri·er; -est** [ME *drery,* fr. OE *drēorig* sad, bloody, fr. *drēor* gore; akin to OHG *trūrēn* to be sad, Goth *driusan* to fall] (bef. 12c) **1 :** feeling, displaying, or reflecting listlessness or discouragement **2 :** having nothing likely to provide cheer, comfort, or interest **:** GLOOMY, DISMAL ***syn*** see DISMAL — **drea·ri·ly** \ˈdrir-ə-lē\ *adv* — **drea·ri·ness** \ˈdrir-ē-nəs\ *n*
dreck *also* **drek** \ˈdrek\ *n* [Yiddish *drek* & G *Dreck,* fr. MHG *drec;* akin to OE *threax* rubbish] (1922) **:** TRASH, RUBBISH
1**dredge** \ˈdrej\ *vb* **dredged; dredg·ing** *vt* (1508) **1 a :** to dig, gather, or pull out with or as if with a dredge — often used with *up* **b :** to deepen (as a waterway) with a dredging machine **2 :** to bring to light by deep searching — often used with *up* ⟨*dredging* up memories⟩ ~ *vi* **1 :** to use a dredge **2 :** to search deeply — **dredg·er** *n*
2**dredge** *n* [perh. fr. OE **drecge;* akin to OE *dræge* dragnet, *dragan* to draw] (1602) **1 :** an apparatus usu. in the form of an oblong iron frame with an attached bag net used esp. for gathering fish and shellfish **2 :** a machine for removing earth usu. by buckets on an endless chain or a suction tube **3 :** a barge used in dredging
3**dredge** *vt* **dredged; dredg·ing** [obs. *dredge,* n., sweetmeat, fr. ME *drage, drege,* fr. AF *dragee,* modif. of L *tragemata* sweetmeats, fr. Gk *tragēmata,* pl. of *tragēma* sweetmeat, fr. *trōgein* to gnaw] (1596) **:** to coat (food) by sprinkling (as with flour) — **dredg·er** *n*

dree \ˈdrē\ *vt* **dreed; dree·ing** [ME, fr. OE *drēogan;* akin to Goth *driugan* to perform military service] (bef. 12c) *chiefly Scot* **:** ENDURE, SUFFER
dreg \ˈdreg\ *n* [ME, fr. ON *dregg;* perh. akin to L *fraces* dregs of oil] (14c) **1 :** sediment contained in a liquid or precipitated from it **:** LEES — usu. used in pl. **2 :** the most undesirable part — usu. used in pl. ⟨the ~*s* of society⟩ **3 :** the last remaining part **:** VESTIGE — usu. used in pl. ⟨the last ~*s* of fuel⟩ — **dreg·gy** \ˈdre-gē\ *adj*
D region *n* (1930) **:** the lowest part of the ionosphere occurring approximately between 30 and 55 miles (50 and 90 kilometers) above the surface of the earth
dreich \ˈdrēk\ *adj* [ME, of Scand origin; akin to ON *drjūgr* lasting] (1813) *chiefly Scot* **:** DREARY
drei·del *also* **dreidl** \ˈdrā-dᵊl\ *n* [Yiddish *dreydl,* fr. *dreyen* to turn, fr. MHG *drǣjen,* fr. OHG *drāen* — more at THROW] (1916) **1 :** a 4-sided toy marked with Hebrew letters and spun like a top in a game of chance **2 :** a children's game of chance played esp. at Hanukkah with a dreidel

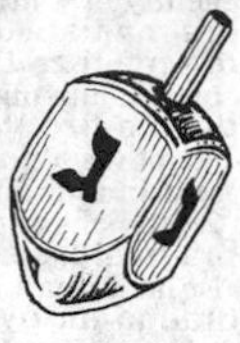
dreidel 1

1**drench** \ˈdrench\ *n* (bef. 12c) **1 :** a poisonous or medicinal drink; *specif* **:** a large dose of medicine mixed with liquid and put down the throat of an animal **2 a :** something that drenches **b :** a quantity sufficient to drench or saturate
2**drench** *vt* [ME, fr. OE *drencan;* akin to OE *drincan* to drink] (bef. 12c) **1 a** *archaic* **:** to force to drink **b :** to administer a drench to (an animal) **2 :** to wet thoroughly (as by soaking or immersing in liquid) **3 :** to soak or cover thoroughly with liquid that falls or is precipitated **4 :** to fill or cover completely as if by soaking or precipitation ⟨was ~*ed* in furs and diamonds —Richard Brautigan⟩ ***syn*** see SOAK — **drench·er** *n*
1**dress** \ˈdres\ *vb* [ME, fr. AF *drescer, dresser* to direct, put right, VL **directiare,* fr. L *directus* direct, pp. of *dirigere* to direct, fr. *dis-* + *regere* to lead straight — more at RIGHT] *vt* (14c) **1 a :** to make or set straight **b :** to arrange (as troops) in a straight line and at proper intervals **2 :** to prepare for use or service; *specif* **:** to prepare for cooking or for the table ⟨~ a salad⟩ **3 :** to add decorative details or accessories to **:** EMBELLISH **4 a :** to put clothes on ⟨~ a child⟩ **b :** to provide with clothing ⟨feed and ~ a growing family⟩ **5** *archaic* **:** DRESS DOWN **6 a :** to apply dressings or medicaments to ⟨~ a wound⟩ **b (1) :** to arrange (as the hair) by combing, brushing, or curling **(2) :** to groom and curry (an animal) **c :** to kill and prepare for market or for consumption — often used with *out* **d :** CULTIVATE, TEND; *esp* **:** to apply manure or fertilizer to ⟨~ a field⟩ **e :** to put through a finishing process; *esp* **:** to trim and smooth the surface of (as lumber or stone) ~ *vi* **1 a :** to put on clothing **b :** to put on or wear formal, elaborate, or fancy clothes ⟨~ for dinner⟩ **2** *of a food animal* **:** to weigh after being dressed — often used with *out* **3 :** to align oneself with the next soldier in a line to make the line straight — **dress ship :** to ornament a ship for a celebration by hoisting national ensigns at the mastheads and running a line of signal flags and pennants from bow to stern
2**dress** *n* (1606) **1 :** APPAREL, CLOTHING **2 :** an outer garment (as for a woman or girl) usu. consisting of a one-piece bodice and skirt **3 :** covering, adornment, or appearance appropriate or peculiar to a particular time **4 :** a particular form of presentation **:** GUISE
3**dress** *adj* (1767) **1 :** suitable for a formal occasion ⟨~ clothes⟩ ⟨~ shoes⟩ **2 :** requiring or permitting formal dress ⟨a ~ affair⟩ **3 :** relating to or used for a dress ⟨~ material⟩
dres·sage \drə-ˈsäzh, dre-\ *n, often attrib* [F, fr. *dresser* to train, drill, fr. MF] (1936) **:** the execution by a trained horse of precision movements in response to barely perceptible signals from its rider
dress circle *n* (1822) **:** the first or lowest curved tier of seats above the main floor in a theater or opera house
dress code *n* (1968) **:** formally or socially imposed standards of dress
dress down *vt* (1852) **:** to reprove severely ~ *vi* **:** to dress casually esp. for reasons of fashion
dress–down day *n* (1986) **:** a day during which employees are allowed to wear casual attire at work
1**dress·er** \ˈdre-sər\ *n* (15c) **1** *obs* **:** a table or sideboard for preparing and serving food **2 :** a cupboard to hold dishes and cooking utensils **3 :** a chest of drawers or bureau with a mirror
2**dresser** *n* (1520) **:** one that dresses ⟨a fashionable ~⟩
dresser set *n* (ca. 1934) **:** a set of toilet articles including hairbrush, comb, and mirror for use at a dresser or dressing table
dress·ing \ˈdre-siŋ\ *n* (15c) **1 a :** the act or process of one who dresses **b :** an instance of such act or process **2 a :** a sauce for adding to a dish (as a salad) **b :** a seasoned mixture usu. used as a stuffing (as for poultry) **3 a :** material (as ointment or gauze) applied to cover a lesion or wound **b :** fertilizing material (as manure or compost)
dres·sing–down \ˌdre-siŋ-ˈdau̇n\ *n* (1876) **:** a severe reprimand
dressing glass *n* (1703) **:** a small mirror set to swing in a standing frame and used at a dresser or dressing table
dressing gown *n* (1777) **:** a robe worn esp. while dressing or resting
dressing room *n* (1662) **:** a room used chiefly for dressing; *esp* **:** a room in a theater for changing costumes and makeup
dressing table *n* (1668) **:** a table often fitted with drawers and a mirror in front of which one sits while dressing and grooming oneself
1**dress·mak·er** \ˈdres-ˌmā-kər\ *n* (1803) **:** one that makes dresses — **dress·mak·ing** \-ˌmā-kiŋ\ *n*
2**dressmaker** *adj* (1904) *of women's clothes* **:** having softness, rounded lines, and intricate detailing ⟨a ~ suit⟩
dress rehearsal *n* (1828) **1 :** a full rehearsal (as of a play) in costume and with stage properties shortly before the first performance **2 :** a practice exercise for something to come **:** DRY RUN
dress shield *n* (1863) **:** a pad worn inside a part of the clothing liable to be soiled by perspiration (as at the underarm)
dress shirt *n* (1849) **:** a man's shirt esp. for wear with evening dress; *broadly* **:** a shirt suitable for wear with a necktie
dress uniform *n* (1814) **:** a uniform for formal wear
dress up *vt* (1635) **1 :** to make more attractive, glamorous, or fancy ⟨*dress up* a plain dessert with a rich chocolate sauce⟩ **2 a :** to attire in best or formal clothes **b :** to attire in clothes suited to a particular role **3 :** to present in the most attractive or impressive light ⟨a fiasco *dressed up* as a triumph⟩ ~ *vi* **:** to get dressed up

dressy \ˈdre-sē\ *adj* **dress·i·er; -est** (1768) **1 :** showy in dress **2 :** STYLISH, SMART ⟨~ clothes⟩ **3 :** requiring or characterized by fancy or formal dress ⟨a ~ affair⟩ — **dress·i·ness** *n*

drew *past of* DRAW

DRG \ˌdē-(ˌ)är-ˈjē\ *n* (1980) **:** any of the payment categories that are used to classify patients and esp. Medicare patients for the purpose of reimbursing hospitals for each case in a given category with a fixed fee regardless of the actual costs incurred — called also *diagnosis related group*

drib \ˈdrib\ *n* [prob. back-formation fr. *dribble & driblet*] (1709) **:** a small amount — usu. used in the phrase *dribs and drabs*

[1]**drib·ble** \ˈdri-bəl\ *vb* **drib·bled; drib·bling** \-(ə-)liŋ\ [freq. of *drib* to dribble] *vt* (ca. 1589) **1 :** to issue sporadically and in small bits **2 :** to let or cause to fall in drops little by little **3 a :** to propel by successive slight taps or bounces with hand, foot, or stick ⟨~ a basketball⟩ ⟨~ a puck⟩ **b :** to hit (as a baseball) so as to cause a slow bouncing ~ *vi* **1 :** to fall or flow in drops or in a thin intermittent stream **:** TRICKLE **2 :** to let saliva trickle from the corner of the mouth **:** DROOL **3 :** to come or issue in piecemeal or desultory fashion **4 a :** to dribble a ball or puck **b :** to proceed by dribbling **c** *of a ball* **:** to move with short bounces — **drib·bler** \-b(ə-)lər\ *n*

[2]**dribble** *n* (ca. 1680) **1 :** a tiny or insignificant bit or quantity **2 :** a small trickling stream or flow **3 :** an act, instance, or manner of dribbling a ball or puck — **drib·bly** \ˈdri-b(ə-)lē\ *adj*

drib·let \ˈdrib-lət\ *n* (1615) **1 :** a trifling or small sum or part **2 :** a drop of liquid

dried–up \ˈdrīd-ˌəp, ˌdrīd-ˈ\ *adj* (1821) **:** being wizened and shriveled

[1]**drier** *comparative of* DRY

[2]**dri·er** *or* **dry·er** \ˈdrī(-ə)r\ *n* (1528) **1 :** something that extracts or absorbs moisture **2 :** a substance that accelerates drying (as of oils, paints, and printing inks) **3** *usu dryer* **:** a device for drying

driest *superlative of* DRY

[1]**drift** \ˈdrift\ *n* [ME; akin to OE *drīfan* to drive — more at DRIVE] (14c) **1 a :** the act of driving something along **b :** the flow or the velocity of the current of a river or ocean stream **2 :** something driven, propelled, or urged along or drawn together in a clump by or as if by a natural agency: as **a :** wind-driven snow, rain, cloud, dust, or smoke usu. at or near the ground surface **b** (1) **:** a mass of matter (as sand) deposited together by or as if by wind or water (2) **:** a helter-skelter accumulation **c :** DROVE, FLOCK **d :** something (as driftwood) washed ashore **e :** rock debris deposited by natural agents; *specif* **:** a deposit of clay, sand, gravel, and boulders transported by a glacier or by running water from a glacier **3 a :** a general underlying design or tendency ⟨perceiving the ~ of the government's policies⟩ **b :** the underlying meaning, import, or purport of what is spoken or written ⟨the ~ of a conversation⟩ **4 :** something (as a tool) driven down upon or forced into a body **5 :** the motion or action of drifting esp. spatially and usu. under external influence: as **a :** the lateral motion of an aircraft due to air currents **b :** an easy moderate more or less steady flow or sweep along a spatial course **c :** a gradual shift in attitude, opinion, or position **d :** an aimless course; *esp* **:** a foregoing of any attempt at direction or control **e :** a deviation from a true reproduction, representation, or reading; *esp* **:** a gradual change in the zero reading of an instrument or in any quantitative characteristic that is supposed to remain constant **6 a :** a nearly horizontal mine passageway driven on or parallel to the course of a vein or rock stratum **b :** a small crosscut in a mine connecting two larger tunnels **7 a :** an assumed trend toward a general change in the structure of a language over a period of time **b :** GENETIC DRIFT **8 :** a grouping of similar flowers planted in an elongated mass ***syn*** see TENDENCY — **drifty** \ˈdrif-tē\ *adj*

[2]**drift** *vi* (ca. 1600) **1 a :** to become driven or carried along (as by a current of water, wind, or air) ⟨a balloon *~ing* in the wind⟩ **b :** to move or float smoothly and effortlessly **2 a :** to move along a line of least resistance **b :** to move in a random or casual way **c :** to become carried along subject to no guidance or control ⟨the talk *~ed* from topic to topic⟩ **3 a :** to accumulate in a mass or become piled up in heaps by wind or water ⟨*~ing* snow⟩ **b :** to become covered with a drift **4 :** to vary or deviate from a set course or adjustment ~ *vt* **1 a :** to cause to be driven in a current **b** *West* **:** to drive (livestock) slowly esp. to allow grazing **2 a :** to pile in heaps **b :** to cover with drifts — **drift·ing·ly** \ˈdrif-tiŋ-lē\ *adv*

drift·age \ˈdrif-tij\ *n* (1768) **:** drifted material

drift·er \ˈdrif-tər\ *n* (1897) **:** one that drifts; *esp* **:** one that travels or moves about aimlessly

drift fence *n* (1907) **:** a stretch of fence on rangeland esp. in the western U.S. for preventing cattle from drifting from their home range

drift net *n* (1662) **:** a fishing net often miles in extent arranged to drift with the tide or current and buoyed up by floats or attached to a boat

drift·wood \ˈdrift-ˌwu̇d\ *n* (1633) **1 :** wood drifted or floated by water **2 :** FLOTSAM 2

[1]**drill** \ˈdril\ *vb* [D *drillen*] *vt* (1619) **1 a :** to fix something in the mind or habit pattern of by repetitive instruction ⟨~ pupils in spelling⟩ **b :** to impart or communicate by repetition **c :** to train or exercise in military drill **2 a** (1) **:** to bore or drive a hole in (2) **:** to make by piercing action ⟨~ a hole⟩ **b :** to shoot with or as if with a gun **c** (1) **:** to propel (as a ball) with force or accuracy ⟨*~ed* a single to right field⟩ (2) **:** to hit with force ⟨*~ed* the batter with the first pitch⟩ ~ *vi* **1 :** to make a hole with a drill **2 :** to engage in an exercise — **drill·abil·i·ty** \ˌdri-lə-ˈbi-lə-tē\ *n* — **drill·able** \-lə-bəl\ *adj* — **drill·er** \ˈdri-lər\ *n*

[2]**drill** *n* (1611) **1 :** an instrument with an edged or pointed end for making holes in hard substances by revolving or by a succession of blows; *also* **:** a machine for operating such an instrument **2 :** the act or exercise of training soldiers in marching and in executing prescribed movements with a weapon **3 a :** a physical or mental exercise aimed at perfecting facility and skill esp. by regular practice **b :** a formal exercise by a team of marchers **c :** the approved, correct, or usual procedure for accomplishing something **:** ROUTINE **4 a :** a marine snail (*Urosalpinx cinerea*) destructive to oysters by boring through their shells and feeding on the soft parts **b :** any of several mollusks related to the drill **5 :** a drilling sound

[3]**drill** *n* [origin unknown] (1644) **:** a western African baboon (*Mandrillus leucophaeus* syn. *Papio leucophaeus*) having a black face and brown coat and closely related to the typical mandrills

[4]**drill** *n* [perh. fr. *drill* small stream, fr. obs. *drill* to trickle, drip] (1727) **1 a :** a shallow furrow or trench into which seed is sown **b :** a row of seed sown in such a furrow **2 :** a planting implement that makes holes or furrows, drops in the seed and sometimes fertilizer, and covers them with earth

[5]**drill** *vt* (ca. 1740) **1 :** to sow (seeds) by dropping along a shallow furrow **2 a :** to sow with seed or set with seedlings inserted in drills **b :** to distribute seed or fertilizer in by means of a drill

[6]**drill** *n* [short for *drilling*] (1743) **:** a durable cotton twilled fabric

dril·ling \ˈdri-liŋ\ *n* [modif. of G *Drillich,* fr. MHG *drilich* fabric woven with a threefold thread, fr. OHG *drilīh* made up of three threads, fr. L *trilic-, trilix,* fr. *tri-* + *licium* thread] (1640) **:** [6]DRILL

drill·mas·ter \ˈdril-ˌmas-tər\ *n* (1833) **1 :** an instructor in military drill **2 :** an instructor or director who maintains severe discipline and often stresses method and detail

drill press *n* (ca. 1864) **:** an upright drilling machine in which the drill is pressed to the work by a hand lever or by power

drill team *n* (1928) **:** an exhibition marching team that engages in precision drill

D ring \ˈdē-ˌriŋ\ *n* (ca. 1899) **:** a usu. metal ring having the shape of a capital D

[1]**drink** \ˈdriŋk\ *vb* **drank** \ˈdraŋk\; **drunk** \ˈdrəŋk\ *or* **drank; drink·ing** [ME, fr. OE *drincan;* akin to OHG *trinkan* to drink] *vt* (bef. 12c) **1 a :** SWALLOW, IMBIBE ⟨~ water⟩ **b :** to take in or suck up **:** ABSORB ⟨*~ing* air into his lungs⟩ **c :** to take in or receive avidly — usu. used with *in* ⟨*drank* in every word of the lecture⟩ **2 :** to join in a toast to ⟨I'll ~ your good health⟩ **3 :** to bring to a specified state by drinking alcoholic beverages ⟨*drank* himself into oblivion⟩ ~ *vi* **1 a :** to take liquid into the mouth for swallowing **b :** to receive into one's consciousness **2 :** to partake of alcoholic beverages ⟨has quit *~ing*⟩ **3 :** to make or join in a toast ⟨I'll ~ to that!⟩ — **drink the Kool–Aid** [after a 1978 mass suicide in Guyana brought about when members of the Peoples Temple cult were ordered to consume a flavored drink mixed with cyanide] **:** to comply unquestioningly with the demands or policies of a particular leader, ideology, or organization

[2]**drink** *n* (bef. 12c) **1 a :** a liquid suitable for swallowing **b :** alcoholic beverages **2 :** a draft or portion of liquid **3 :** excessive consumption of alcoholic beverages ⟨he took to ~ when his business failed⟩ **4 :** a sizable body of water — used with *the* ⟨landed in the ~⟩

[1]**drink·able** \ˈdriŋ-kə-bəl\ *adj* (1611) **:** suitable or safe for drinking — **drink·abil·i·ty** \ˌdriŋ-kə-ˈbi-lə-tē\ *n*

[2]**drinkable** *n* (1708) **:** a liquid suitable for drinking **:** BEVERAGE

drink–driv·ing \ˈdriŋk-ˈdrī-viŋ\ *n* (1964) *Brit* **:** driving a vehicle while drunk

drink·er \ˈdriŋ-kər\ *n* (bef. 12c) **1 a :** one that drinks **b :** a person who drinks alcoholic beverages esp. to a notable degree ⟨a heavy ~⟩ **2 :** WATERER b

drinking fountain *n* (1859) **:** a fixture with nozzle that delivers a stream of water for drinking

drinking song *n* (1597) **:** a song on a convivial theme appropriate for a group engaged in social drinking

[1]**drip** \ˈdrip\ *vb* **dripped; drip·ping** [ME *drippen,* fr. OE *dryppan;* akin to OE *dropa* drop] *vt* (bef. 12c) **1 :** to let fall in drops ⟨a brush *dripping* paint⟩ **2 :** to let out or seem to spill copiously ⟨her voice *dripping* sarcasm⟩ ⟨trees *dripping* Spanish moss⟩ ~ *vi* **1 a :** to let fall drops of moisture or liquid ⟨wet clothes *dripping* onto the floor⟩ **b :** to overflow with or as if with moisture ⟨stories *dripping* with pop-culture references⟩ ⟨toast *dripping* with butter⟩ **2 :** to fall in or as if in drops ⟨let the excess ~ off⟩ **3 :** to waft or pass gently — **drip·per** *n*

[2]**drip** *n* (1664) **1 :** a part of a cornice or other member that projects to throw off rainwater; *also* **:** an overlapping metal strip or an underneath groove for the same purpose **2 a :** a falling in drops **b :** liquid that falls, overflows, or is extruded in drops ⟨a pan to catch *~s*⟩ **3 :** the sound made by or as if by falling drops **4 :** a device for the administration of a fluid at a slow rate esp. into a vein; *also* **:** a material so administered **5 :** a dull or unattractive person

[3]**drip** *adj* (1895) **:** of, relating to, or being coffee made by letting boiling water drip slowly through finely ground coffee ⟨~ coffee⟩ ⟨a ~ pot⟩

DRIP *abbr* dividend reinvestment plan

[1]**drip–dry** \ˈdrip-ˌdrī\ *vi* (1953) **:** to dry with few or no wrinkles when hung wet ~ *vt* **:** to hang (as wet clothing) to drip-dry

[2]**drip–dry** *adj* (1957) **:** made of a washable fabric that drip-dries

drip·less \ˈdrip-ləs\ *adj* (1887) **:** designed not to drip ⟨~ candles⟩

drip·ping \ˈdri-piŋ\ *n* (15c) **:** fat and juices drawn from meat during cooking — often used in pl.

drip·py \ˈdri-pē\ *adj* **drip·pi·er; -est** (ca. 1718) **1 :** characterized by dripping; *esp* **:** RAINY, DRIZZLY **2 :** MAWKISH 2

drip·stone \ˈdrip-ˌstōn\ *n* (ca. 1816) **1 :** a stone drip (as over a window) **2 :** calcium carbonate in the form of stalactites or stalagmites

[1]**drive** \ˈdrīv\ *vb* **drove** \ˈdrōv\; **driv·en** \ˈdri-vən\; **driv·ing** \ˈdrī-viŋ\ [ME, fr. OE *drīfan;* akin to OHG *trīban* to drive] *vt* (bef. 12c) **1 a :** to frighten or prod (as game or cattle) into moving in a desired direction **b :** to go through (an area) driving game animals **2 :** to carry on or through energetically ⟨*~s* a hard bargain⟩ **3 a :** to impart a forward motion to by physical force ⟨waves *drove* the boat ashore⟩ **b :** to repulse, remove, or cause to go by force, authority, or influence ⟨~ the enemy back⟩ **c :** to set or keep in motion or operation ⟨~ machinery by electricity⟩ **d** *basketball* **:** to move quickly and forcefully down or along ⟨~ the lane⟩ ⟨~ the baseline⟩ **4 a :** to direct the motions and course of (a draft animal) **b :** to operate the mechanism and controls and direct the course of (as a vehicle) ⟨~ a car⟩ **c :** to convey in a vehicle ⟨his father *drove* me home⟩ **d :** to float (logs) down a stream **5 a :** to exert inescapable or coercive pressure on **:** FORCE ⟨*driven* by his passions⟩ **b :** to compel to undergo or suffer a change (as in situation or emotional state) ⟨*drove* him crazy⟩ ⟨*drove* her out of business⟩ **c :** to urge relentlessly to continuous exertion ⟨the sergeant *drove* his recruits⟩ **d :** to press or force into an activity, course, or direction ⟨the drug habit *~s* addicts to steal⟩ **e :** to project, inject, or impress inci-

sively ⟨*drove* her point home⟩ **6** : to force (a passage) by pressing or digging **7 a** : to propel (an object of play) swiftly or forcefully ⟨*drove* a long fly ball to the warning track⟩ **b** : to hit (a golf ball) from the tee esp. with a driver; *also* : to drive a golf ball onto (a green) **c** : to cause (a run or runner) to be scored in baseball — usu. used with *in* **8** : to give shape or impulse to ⟨factors that ~ the business cycle⟩ ⟨the ideas that have *driven* history⟩ ~ *vi* **1 a** : to dash, plunge, or surge ahead rapidly or violently **b** : to progress with strong momentum ⟨the rain was *driving* hard⟩ **c** : to make a quick and forceful move in basketball ⟨*driving* to the hoop⟩ **2 a** : to operate a vehicle **b** : to have oneself carried in a vehicle **3** : to drive a golf ball *syn* see MOVE — **driv·abil·i·ty** *also* **drive·abil·i·ty** \ˌdrī-və-ˈbi-lə-tē\ *n* — **driv·able** *also* **drive·able** \ˈdrī-və-bəl\ *adj* — **drive at** : to intend to express, convey, or accomplish ⟨couldn't understand what she was *driving* at⟩

²**drive** *n, often attrib* (1785) **1** : an act of driving: **a** : a trip in a carriage or automobile ⟨a short ~ to the coast⟩ **b** : a collection and driving together of animals; *also* : the animals gathered ⟨a driving of cattle or sheep overland⟩ **d** : a hunt or shoot in which the game is driven within the hunter's range **e** : the guiding of logs downstream to a mill; *also* : the floating logs amassed in a drive **f** (1) : the act or an instance of driving an object of play (as a golf ball) (2) : the flight of a ball ⟨a high ~ to left field⟩ **2 a** : a private road : DRIVEWAY **b** : a public road for driving (as in a park) **3** : the state of being hurried and under pressure **4 a** : a strong systematic group effort ⟨a fund-raising ~⟩ **b** : a sustained offensive effort ⟨the ~ ended in a touchdown⟩ **5 a** : the means for giving motion to a machine or machine part **b** : the means by which the propulsive power of an automobile is applied to the road ⟨front wheel ~⟩ **c** : the means by which the propulsion of an automotive vehicle is controlled and directed ⟨a left-hand ~⟩ **6 a** : an offensive, aggressive, or expansionist move; *esp* : a strong military attack against enemy-held terrain **b** : a quick and aggressive move toward the basket in basketball **7 a** : an urgent, basic, or instinctual need : a motivating physiological condition of an organism ⟨a sexual ~⟩ **b** : an impelling culturally acquired concern, interest, or longing ⟨the ~ to succeed⟩ **c** : dynamic quality **8** : a device for reading or writing on magnetic or optical media (as tapes or disks)

¹**drive–by** \ˈdrīv-ˌbī\ *adj* (1986) **1** : carried out from a moving vehicle ⟨a ~ shooting⟩ **2** : done or made in a quick or cursory manner ⟨a ~ analysis⟩

²**drive–by** \ˈdrīv-ˌbī\ *n, pl* **drive–bys** (1989) : a drive-by shooting

drive–in \ˈdrīv-ˌin\ *n* (1937) : an establishment (as a theater or restaurant) so laid out that patrons can be accommodated while remaining in their automobiles — **drive–in** *adj*

¹**driv·el** \ˈdri-vəl\ *vi* **-eled** *or* **-elled; -el·ing** *or* **-el·ling** \-v(ə-)liŋ\ [ME, fr. OE *dreflian;* perh. akin to ON *draf* malt dregs] (bef. 12c) **1** : to let saliva dribble from the mouth : SLAVER **2** : to talk stupidly and carelessly — **driv·el·er** \-v(ə-)lər\ *n*

²**drivel** *n* (14c) **1** *archaic* : DROOL 1 **2** : NONSENSE

drive·line \ˈdrīv-ˌlīn\ *n* (1949) : DRIVETRAIN

driven *adj* (1925) **1** : having a compulsive or urgent quality ⟨a ~ sense of obligation⟩ **2** : propelled or motivated by something — used in combination ⟨results-*driven*⟩ — **driv·en·ness** \ˈdri-vən-nəs\ *n*

driv·er \ˈdrī-vər\ *n* (14c) : one that drives: as **a** : COACHMAN **b** : the operator of a motor vehicle **c** : an implement (as a hammer) for driving **d** : a mechanical piece for imparting motion to another piece **e** : one that provides impulse or motivation ⟨a ~ in this economy⟩ **f** : a golf wood with a nearly straight face used in driving **g** : an electronic circuit that supplies input to another electronic circuit; *also* : LOUDSPEAKER **h** : a piece of computer software that controls input and output operations — **driv·er·less** \-ləs\ *adj*

driver ant *n* (1859) : ARMY ANT; *specif* : any of various African and Asian ants (*Dorylus* or related genera) that move in vast numbers

driver's license *n* (1926) : a license issued under governmental authority that permits the holder to operate a motor vehicle

driver's seat *n* (1923) : the position of top authority or dominance

drive·shaft \ˈdrīv-ˌshaft\ *n* (1895) : a shaft that transmits mechanical power

¹**drive–through** *also* **drive–thru** \ˈdrīv-ˌthrü\ *adj* (1949) : DRIVE-UP

²**drive–through** *also* **drive–thru** *n* (1949) : a drive-through establishment (as a restaurant or bank); *also* : the drive-through window at such an establishment

drive time *n* (1966) : a time during rush hour when radio audiences are swelled by commuters listening to car radios

drive·train \ˈdrīv-ˌtrān\ *n* (1954) : the parts (as the universal joint and the driveshaft) that connect the transmission with the driving axles of an automobile; *also* : POWER TRAIN ⟨the ~ warranty⟩

drive–up \ˈdrīv-ˌəp\ *adj* (1952) : designed to allow patrons or customers to be served while remaining in their automobiles ⟨a ~ window⟩

drive·way \-ˌwā\ *n* (1871) : a private road giving access from a public way to a building on abutting grounds

driving *adj* (14c) **1 a** : communicating force ⟨a ~ wheel⟩ **b** : exerting pressure ⟨a ~ influence⟩ **2 a** : having great force ⟨a ~ rain⟩ ⟨a ~ beat⟩ **b** : acting with vigor : ENERGETIC ⟨a hard-*driving* worker⟩

driving range *n* (ca. 1949) : an area equipped with distance markers, clubs, balls, and tees for practicing golf shots

¹**driz·zle** \ˈdri-zəl\ *n* (1554) **1** : a fine misty rain **2** : something that is drizzled ⟨a ~ of syrup⟩ — **driz·zly** \ˈdri-z(ə-)lē\ *adj*

²**drizzle** *vb* **driz·zled; driz·zling** \-z(ə-)liŋ\ [perh. alter. of ME *drysnen* to fall, fr. OE *-drysnian* to disappear; akin to Goth *driusan* to fall] *vt* (1584) **1** : to shed or let fall in minute drops or particles **2** : to make wet with minute drops : SPRINKLE ⟨vegetables *drizzled* with olive oil⟩ ~ *vi* : to rain in very small drops or very lightly : SPRINKLE — **driz·zling·ly** \-z(ə-)liŋ-lē\ *adv*

drogue \ˈdrōg\ *n* [prob. alter. of ¹*drag*] (1875) **1** : SEA ANCHOR **2 a** : a cylindrical or funnel-shaped device towed as a target by an airplane **b** : a small parachute for stabilizing or decelerating something (as an astronaut's capsule) or for pulling a larger parachute out of stowage **3** : a funnel-shaped device which is attached to the end of a long flexible hose suspended from a tanker airplane in flight and into which the probe of another airplane is fitted so as to receive fuel from the tanker

droid \ˈdrȯid\ *n* [by shortening] (1952) : ANDROID

droit \ˈdrȯit, ˈdrwä\ *n* [ME, fr. AF *dreit, droit,* fr. ML *directum,* fr. LL, neut. of *directus* just, fr. L, direct — more at DRESS] (15c) : a legal right

droit du sei·gneur \drwä-due-se-n�validʹœr\ *n* [F, right of the lord] (1825)

: a supposed legal or customary right of a feudal lord to have sexual relations with a vassal's bride on their wedding night

¹**droll** \ˈdrōl\ *adj* [F *drôle,* fr. *drôle* scamp, fr. MF *drolle,* fr. MD, imp] (1623) : having a humorous, whimsical, or odd quality ⟨his dignified presence decorated our ~ little quarters —Gwendolyn Brooks⟩ — **droll·ness** *n* — **drol·ly** \ˈdrō(l)-lē\ *adv*

²**droll** *n* (ca. 1645) : an amusing person : JESTER, COMEDIAN

³**droll** *vi* (1654) *archaic* : to make fun : JEST, SPORT

droll·ery \ˈdrōl-rē, ˈdrō-lə-\ *n, pl* **-er·ies** (1597) **1** : something that is droll; *esp* : a comic picture or drawing **2** : the act or an instance of jesting or burlesquing **3** : whimsical humor

-drome *n comb form* [*hippodrome*] **1** : racecourse ⟨motor*drome*⟩ **2** : large specially prepared place ⟨aero*drome*⟩

drom·e·dary \ˈdrä-mə-ˌder-ē *also* ˈdrə-, ˌdrȯ-, -ˌde-rē\ *n, pl* **-dar·ies** [ME *dromedarie,* fr. AF, fr. LL *dromedarius,* fr. L *dromad-, dromas,* fr. Gk, running; akin to Gk *dramein* to run, *dromos* racecourse, Skt *dramati* he runs about] (13c) : CAMEL 1a

-dromous *adj comb form* [NL *-dromus,* fr. Gk *-dromos* (akin to Gk *dramein*)] : running ⟨cata*dromous*⟩

¹**drone** \ˈdrōn\ *n* [ME, fr. OE *drān;* akin to OHG *treno* drone, Gk *thrēnos* dirge] (bef. 12c) **1** : a stingless male bee (as of the honeybee) that has the role of mating with the queen and does not gather nectar or pollen **2** : one that lives on the labors of others : PARASITE **3** : an unmanned aircraft or ship guided by remote control or onboard computers **4 a** : DRUDGE 1 **b** : DRUDGE 2

²**drone** *vb* **droned; dron·ing** *vi* (ca. 1520) **1 a** : to make a sustained deep murmuring, humming, or buzzing sound ⟨*droning* bees⟩ **b** : to talk in a persistently dull or monotonous tone ⟨*droning* on and on about his health⟩ **2** : to pass, proceed, or act in a dull, drowsy, or indifferent manner ⟨the afternoon *droned* on⟩ ~ *vt* **1** : to utter or pronounce with a drone **2** : to pass or spend in dull or monotonous activity or in idleness — **dron·er** *n* — **dron·ing·ly** \ˈdrō-niŋ-lē\ *adv*

³**drone** *n* (ca. 1520) **1** : a deep sustained or monotonous sound : HUM **2** : an instrument or part of an instrument (as one of the fixed-pitch pipes of a bagpipe) that sounds a continuous unvarying tone **3** : PEDAL POINT

dron·go \ˈdräŋ-(ˌ)gō\ *n, pl* **drongos** [Malagasy] (1841) : any of a family (Dicruridae) of insectivorous passerine birds native to Africa, Asia, and Australia that have glossy black plumage and long forked tails

¹**drool** \ˈdrül\ *vb* [perh. alter. of *drivel*] *vi* (1802) **1 a** : to secrete saliva in anticipation of food **b** : DRIVEL 1 **2** : to make an effusive show of pleasure or often envious or covetous appreciation **3** : to talk nonsense ~ *vt* : to express sentimentally or effusively

²**drool** *n* (1869) **1** : saliva trickling from the mouth **2** : NONSENSE

¹**droop** \ˈdrüp\ *vb* [ME *drupen,* fr. ON *drūpa;* akin to OE *dropa* drop] *vi* (13c) **1** : to hang or incline downward **2** : to sink gradually **3** : to become depressed or weakened : LANGUISH ~ *vt* : to let droop — **droop·ing·ly** \ˈdrü-piŋ-lē\ *adv*

²**droop** *n* (1647) : the condition or appearance of drooping

droopy \ˈdrü-pē\ *adj* **droop·i·er; -est** (13c) **1** : GLOOMY **2** : drooping or tending to droop

¹**drop** \ˈdräp\ *n, often attrib* [ME, fr. OE *dropa;* akin to OHG *tropfo* drop] (bef. 12c) **1 a** (1) : the quantity of fluid that falls in one spherical mass (2) *pl* : a dose of medicine measured by drops ⟨eye ~s for dilating the pupil of the eye⟩ **b** : a minute quantity or degree of something nonmaterial or intangible **c** : a small quantity of drink **d** : the smallest practical unit of liquid measure **2** : something that resembles a liquid drop: as **a** : a pendent ornament attached to a piece of jewelry; *also* : an earring with such a pendant **b** : a small globular cookie or candy **3** [²*drop*] **a** : the act or an instance of dropping : FALL **b** : a decline in quantity or quality **c** : a descent by parachute; *also* : the people or equipment dropped by parachute **d** : a place or central depository to which something (as mail, money, or stolen property) is brought for distribution or transmission; *also* : the act of depositing something at such a place ⟨made the ~⟩ **4 a** : the distance from a higher to a lower level or through which something drops **b** : a decrease in electric potential **5** : a slot into which something is to be dropped **6** [²*drop*] : something that drops, hangs, or falls: as **a** : a movable plate that covers the keyhole of a lock **b** : an unframed piece of cloth stage scenery; *also* : DROP CURTAIN **c** : a hinged platform on a gallows **d** : a fallen fruit **7** : the advantage of having an opponent covered with a firearm; *broadly* : ADVANTAGE, SUPERIORITY — usu. used in the phrase *get the drop on* **8** : a move back from the line of scrimmage (as in preparation for making a forward pass) ⟨a quick ~⟩ — **at the drop of a hat** : as soon as the slightest provocation is given : IMMEDIATELY — **drop in the bucket** : a part so small as to be negligible

²**drop** *vb* **dropped; drop·ping** *vi* (bef. 12c) **1** (1) : to fall in drops **a** (1) : to fall unexpectedly or suddenly (2) : to descend from one line or level to another **b** : to fall in a state of collapse or death **c** *of a ball* : to fall or roll into a hole or basket **3** : to enter or pass as if without conscious effort of will into some state, condition, or activity ⟨*dropped* into sleep⟩ **4 a** : to cease to be of concern : LAPSE ⟨let the matter ~⟩ **b** : to pass from view or notice : DISAPPEAR — often used with *out* ⟨~ out of sight⟩ **c** : to become less ⟨production *dropped*⟩ — often used with *off* **5** : to move with a favoring wind or current — usu. used with *down* ~ *vt* **1** : to let fall : cause to fall **2 a** : GIVE UP 2, ABANDON ⟨~ an idea⟩ ⟨~ the charges⟩ **b** : DISCONTINUE ⟨*dropped* what she was doing⟩ **c** : to break off an association or connection with : DISMISS ⟨~ a failing student⟩ **3 a** : to utter or mention in a casual way ⟨~ a suggestion⟩ ⟨~ names⟩ **b** : WRITE ⟨~ us a line soon⟩ **4 a** : to lower or cause to descend from one level or position to another **b** : to cause to lessen or decrease : REDUCE ⟨*dropped* his speed⟩ **5** *of an animal* : to give birth to **6 a** : LOSE ⟨*dropped* three games⟩ ⟨*dropped* $50 in a poker game⟩ **b** : SPEND ⟨~ $20 for lunch⟩ **c** : to get rid of ⟨*dropped* 20 pounds⟩ **7 a** : to bring down with a shot or a blow **b** : to cause (a high card) to fall **c** : to toss or roll into a hole or basket ⟨~ a putt⟩ **8 a** : to deposit or deliver during a usu. brief stop — usu. used with *off* ⟨~ the kids off at school⟩ **b** : AIRDROP **9** : to cause (the voice) to be less loud **10 a** : to leave (a letter representing a speech sound) unsounded ⟨~ the *g* in *running*⟩ **b** : to leave out in writing : OMIT **11** : to draw from an external point ⟨~ a perpendicular to the line⟩ **12** : to take (a drug) orally : SWALLOW ⟨~ acid⟩ — **drop·pa·ble** \ˈdrä-pə-bəl\ *adj* — **drop a dime** : to inform au-

thorities (as police) of another's wrongdoing — **drop behind** : to fail to keep up — **drop the ball** : to make a mistake esp. by failing to take timely, effective, or proper action

drop back *vi* (1927) **1** : RETREAT **2** : to move straight back from the line of scrimmage ⟨the quarterback *drops back* to pass⟩

drop by *vi* (ca. 1905) : to pay a brief casual visit ~ *vt* : to visit casually or unexpectedly ⟨*drop by* a friend's house⟩

drop cloth *n* (ca. 1928) : a protective sheet (as of cloth or plastic) used esp. by painters to cover floors and furniture

drop curtain *n* (1832) : a stage curtain that can be lowered and raised

drop–dead \ˈdräp-ˈded\ *adj* (1970) : sensationally striking, attractive, or impressive ⟨a ~ evening gown⟩ — **drop–dead** *adv*

drop–down \ˈdräp-ˌdau̇n\ *adj* (1951) : PULL-DOWN ⟨a ~ menu⟩

drop–forge \ˈdräp-ˈfȯrj\ *vt* (1886) : to forge between dies by means of a drop hammer or punch press — **drop forger** *n*

drop front *n* (1925) : a hinged cover on the front of a desk that may be lowered to provide a surface for writing

drop hammer *n* (ca. 1864) : a power hammer raised and then released to drop (as on metal resting on an anvil or die)

drop·head \ˈdräp-ˌhed\ *n, often attrib* (1932) *Brit* : a convertible automobile

drop–in \ˈdräp-ˌin\ *n* (1819) **1** : a casual visit or brief stop **2** : one who drops in : a casual visitor

drop in *vi* (ca. 1600) : to pay an unexpected or casual visit — often used with *on*

drop·kick \-ˌkik\ *n* (1857) : a kick made by dropping a ball to the ground and kicking it at the moment it starts to rebound

drop–kick \-ˌkik\ *vi* (1882) : to make a dropkick ~ *vt* : to kick by means of a dropkick ⟨~ a ball⟩ ⟨~ a field goal⟩ — **drop·kick·er** *n*

drop leaf *n* (1882) : a hinged leaf on the side or end of a table that can be folded down

drop·let \ˈdräp-lət\ *n* (1607) : a tiny drop (as of a liquid)

drop·light \ˈdräp-ˌlīt\ *n* (1890) : an electric light suspended by a cord or on a portable extension

drop–off \ˈdräp-ˌȯf\ *n* (1923) **1** : a very steep or perpendicular descent **2** : a marked dwindling or decline ⟨a ~ in attendance⟩ **3** : the act or an instance of making a usu. brief deposit or delivery ⟨~ points along the route⟩

drop off \ˌdräp-ˈȯf\ *vi* (1820) : to fall asleep

drop·out \ˈdräp-ˌau̇t\ *n* (1930) **1 a** : one who drops out of school **b** : one who drops out of conventional society **c** : one who abandons an attempt, activity, or chosen path ⟨a corporate ~⟩ **2** : a momentary defect on a magnetic tape or disk caused by a temporary loss of signal

drop out \ˌdräp-ˈau̇t\ *vi* (1875) : to withdraw from participation or membership : QUIT; *esp* : to withdraw from conventional society

drop pass *n* (1949) : a pass in ice hockey in which the passer skates past the puck leaving it for a teammate following close behind

dropped *adj* (1915) : designed to extend or begin lower than normal ⟨a dress with a ~ waist⟩ ⟨~ shoulders⟩

dropped egg *n* (1824) : a poached egg

drop·per \ˈdrä-pər\ *n* (ca. 1700) **1** : one that drops **2** : a short glass tube fitted with a rubber bulb and used to measure liquids by drops — called also *eyedropper, medicine dropper* — **drop·per·ful** \-ˌfu̇l\ *n*

dropping *n* (14c) **1** : something dropped **2** *pl* : DUNG

drop seat *n* (1926) **1** : a hinged seat (as in a taxi) that may be dropped down **2** : a seat (as in an undergarment) that can be unbuttoned

drop–ship \ˈdräp-ˌship\ *vt* (1999) : to ship (goods) from a manufacturer or wholesaler directly to a customer instead of to the retailer who took the order ~ *vi* : to ship goods from a supplier directly to a customer

drop shot *n* (1908) : a delicately hit shot (as in tennis or squash) that drops quickly after crossing the net or dies after hitting a wall

drop·si·cal \ˈdräp-si-kəl\ *adj* (1673) **1** : TURGID, SWOLLEN **2** : relating to or affected with dropsy

drop·sy \ˈdräp-sē\ *n* [ME *dropesie,* short for *ydropesie,* fr. AF, fr. L *hydropisis,* modif. of Gk *hydrōps,* fr. *hydōr* water — more at WATER] (13c) : EDEMA

drop tank *n* (1943) : an auxiliary fuel tank for airplanes that can be jettisoned (as when empty)

drop–top \ˈdräp-ˌtäp\ *n* (1986) : a convertible automobile

drop volley *n* (1907) : a drop shot made on a volley in tennis

drop zone *n* (ca. 1943) : the area in which troops, supplies, or equipment are to be air-dropped; *also* : the target on which a skydiver lands

drosh·ky \ˈdräsh-kē\ *also* **dros·ky** \ˈdräs-kē\ *n, pl* **droshkies** *also* **droskies** [Russ *drozhki,* fr. *droga* pole of a wagon] (1805) : any of various 2- or 4-wheeled carriages used esp. in Russia

dro·soph·i·la \drō-ˈsä-fə-lə\ *n* [NL, genus name, fr. Gk *drosos* dew + NL *-phila,* fem. of *-philus* -phil] (ca. 1829) : any of a genus (*Drosophila*) of fruit flies used in genetic research

dross \ˈdräs, ˈdrȯs\ *n* [ME *dros,* fr. OE *drōs* dregs] (bef. 12c) **1** : the scum that forms on the surface of molten metal **2** : waste or foreign matter : IMPURITY **3** : something that is base, trivial, or inferior — **drossy** \ˈdrä-sē, ˈdrȯ-\ *adj*

drought \ˈdrau̇t\ *also* **drouth** \ˈdrau̇th\ *n* [ME, fr. OE *drūgath,* fr. *drūgian* to dry up; akin to OE *drȳge* dry — more at DRY] (bef. 12c) **1** : a period of dryness esp. when prolonged; *specif* : one that causes extensive damage to crops or prevents their successful growth **2** : a prolonged or chronic shortage or lack of something expected or desired — **drought·i·ness** \ˈdrau̇-tē-nəs\ *n* — **droughty** \ˈdrau̇-tē\ *adj*

[1]**drove** \ˈdrōv\ *n* [ME, fr. OE *drāf,* fr. *drīfan* to drive — more at DRIVE] (bef. 12c) **1** : a group of animals driven or moving in a body **2** : a large number : CROWD — usu. used in pl. esp. with *in* ⟨came in ~*s*⟩

[2]**drove** *past of* DRIVE

drov·er \ˈdrō-vər\ *n* (15c) : one who drives cattle or sheep

drown \ˈdrau̇n\ *vb* **drowned** \ˈdrau̇nd\; **drown·ing** \ˈdrau̇-niŋ\ [ME *drounen*] *vi* (14c) : to become drowned ~ *vt* **1 a** : to suffocate by submersion esp. in water **b** : to submerge esp. by a rise in the water level ⟨villages ~*ed* by the flooding river⟩ **c** : to soak, drench, or cover with a liquid **2** : to engage (oneself) deeply and strenuously ⟨~*ed* himself in work⟩ **3** : to cause (a sound) not to be heard by making a loud noise — usu. used with *out* **4 a** : to drive out (as a sensation or an idea) ⟨~*ed* his sorrows in liquor⟩ **b** : OVERWHELM

drownd \ˈdrau̇nd\ *nonstand var of* DROWN

[1]**drowse** \ˈdrau̇z\ *vb* **drowsed; drows·ing** [prob. akin to Goth *driusan* to fall — more at DREARY] *vi* (1573) **1** : to be inactive **2** : to fall into a light slumber ~ *vt* **1** : to make drowsy or inactive **2** : to pass (time) drowsily or in drowsing

[2]**drowse** *n* (1796) : the act or an instance of drowsing : DOZE

drowsy \ˈdrau̇-zē\ *adj* **drows·i·er; -est** (1530) **1 a** : ready to fall asleep ⟨the pills made her ~⟩ **b** : inducing or tending to induce sleep ⟨~ music⟩ **c** : INDOLENT, LETHARGIC ⟨~ bureaucrats⟩ **2** : giving the appearance of peaceful inactivity ⟨a ~ village⟩ — **drows·i·ly** \-zə-lē\ *adv* — **drows·i·ness** \-zē-nəs\ *n*

drub \ˈdrəb\ *vb* **drubbed; drub·bing** [perh. fr. Ar *ḍaraba*] *vt* (1634) **1** : to beat severely **2** : to berate critically **3** : to defeat decisively ~ *vi* : DRUM, STAMP — **drub·ber** *n* — **drub·bing** *n*

[1]**drudge** \ˈdrəj\ *vb* **drudged; drudg·ing** [ME *druggen*] *vi* (14c) : to do hard, menial, or monotonous work ~ *vt* : to force to do hard, menial, or monotonous work — **drudg·er** *n*

[2]**drudge** *n* (15c) **1** : one who is obliged to do menial work **2** : one whose work is routine and boring **3** : menial or tedious labor

drudg·ery \ˈdrəj-rē, ˈdrə-jə-rē\ *n, pl* **-er·ies** (1550) : dull, irksome, and fatiguing work : uninspiring or menial labor ***syn*** see WORK

drudg·ing \ˈdrə-jiŋ\ *adj* (1548) : MONOTONOUS, TIRING — **drudg·ing·ly** \-jiŋ-lē\ *adv*

[1]**drug** \ˈdrəg\ *n* [ME *drogge*] (14c) **1 a** *obs* : a substance used in dyeing or chemical operations **b** : a substance used as a medication or in the preparation of medication **c** *according to the Food, Drug, and Cosmetic Act* (1) : a substance recognized in an official pharmacopoeia or formulary (2) : a substance intended for use in the diagnosis, cure, mitigation, treatment, or prevention of disease (3) : a substance other than food intended to affect the structure or function of the body (4) : a substance intended for use as a component of a medicine but not a device or a component, part, or accessory of a device **2** : a commodity that is not salable or for which there is no demand — used in the phrase *drug on the market* **3** : something and often an illegal substance that causes addiction, habituation, or a marked change in consciousness — **drug·gy** *also* **drug·gie** \ˈdrə-gē\ *adj*

[2]**drug** *vb* **drugged; drug·ging** *vt* (1605) **1** : to affect with a drug; *esp* : to stupefy by a narcotic drug **2** : to administer a drug to **3** : to lull or stupefy as if with a drug ~ *vi* : to take drugs for narcotic effect

[3]**drug** *dial past of* DRAG

drug·get \ˈdrə-gət\ *n* [MF *droguet,* dim. of *drogue* trash, drug] (1580) **1** : a wool or partly wool fabric formerly used for clothing **2** : a coarse durable cloth used chiefly as a floor covering **3** : a rug having a cotton warp and a wool filling

drug·gie *also* **drug·gy** \ˈdrə-gē\ *n, pl* **druggies** (1967) : a person who habitually uses drugs

drug·gist \ˈdrə-gist\ *n* (1611) : a person who sells or dispenses drugs and medicines: as **a** : PHARMACIST **b** : one who owns or manages a drugstore

drug·mak·er \ˈdrəg-ˌmā-kər\ *n* (1964) : a company that manufactures pharmaceuticals

drug·store \-ˌstȯr\ *n* (1810) : a retail store where medicines and miscellaneous articles are sold : PHARMACY

drugstore cowboy *n* (1923) **1** : one who wears cowboy clothes but has had no experience as a cowboy **2** : one who loafs on street corners and in drugstores

dru·id \ˈdrü-id\ *n, often cap* [L *druides, druidae,* pl., fr. Gaulish *druides;* akin to OIr *druí* druid, and perh. to OE *trēow* tree] (1563) : one of an ancient Celtic priesthood appearing in Irish and Welsh sagas and Christian legends as magicians and wizards — **dru·id·ic** \drü-ˈi-dik\ *or* **dru·id·i·cal** \-di-kəl\ *adj, often cap*

dru·id·ism \ˈdrü-ə-ˌdi-zəm\ *n, often cap* (1715) : the system of religion, philosophy, and instruction of the druids

[1]**drum** \ˈdrəm\ *n* [prob. fr. D *trom;* akin to MHG *trumme* drum] (1539) **1** : a percussion instrument consisting of a hollow shell or cylinder with a drumhead stretched over one or both ends that is beaten with the hands or with some implement (as a stick or wire brush) **2** : TYMPANIC MEMBRANE **3** : the sound of a drum; *also* : a sound similar to that of a drum **4** : any of various chiefly marine bony fishes (family Sciaenidae) that make a drumming or croaking noise using their air bladder and associated muscles **5** : something resembling a drum in shape: as **a** (1) : any of the cylindrical blocks that form the shaft of a column (2) : a round wall or structure that supports a dome **b** : a cylindrical machine or mechanical device or part **c** : a cylindrical container; *specif* : a large usu. metal container for liquids ⟨a 55-gallon ~⟩ **d** : a disk-shaped magazine for an automatic weapon — **drum·like** \-ˌlīk\ *adj*

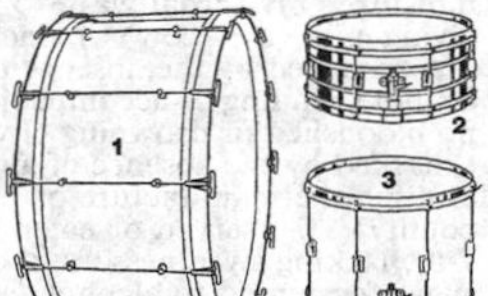

[1]drum 1: *1* bass, *2* snare (orchestra), *3* snare (parade)

[2]**drum** *vb* **drummed; drum·ming** *vi* (1583) **1** : to make a succession of strokes or vibrations that produce sounds like drumbeats **2** : to beat a drum **3** : to throb or sound rhythmically **4** : to stir up interest : SOLICIT ~ *vt* **1** : to summon or enlist by or as if by beating a drum ⟨were *drummed* into service⟩ **2** : to dismiss ignominiously : EXPEL — usu. used with *out* **3** : to drive or force by steady effort or reiteration ⟨*drummed* the speech into her head⟩ **4 a** : to strike or tap repeatedly **b** : to produce (rhythmic sounds) by such action

[3]**drum** *n* [ScGael *druim* back, ridge, fr. OIr *druimm*] (1725) **1** *chiefly Scot* : a long narrow hill or ridge **2** : DRUMLIN

drum·beat \ˈdrəm-ˌbēt\ *n* (1817) **1** : a stroke on a drum or its sound; *also* : a series of such strokes **2** : vociferous advocacy of a cause **3** : DRUMFIRE 2 — **drum·beat·er** \-ˌbē-tər\ *n* — **drum·beat·ing** \-tiŋ\ *n*

drum brake *n* (1950) : a brake that operates by the friction of usu. a pair of shoes pressing against the inner surface of the cylinder of a rotating drum — compare DISC BRAKE

\ə\ **abut** \ᵊ\ kitten, F table \ər\ **further** \a\ **ash** \ā\ **ace** \ä\ **mop, mar**
\au̇\ **out** \ch\ **chin** \e\ **bet** \ē\ **easy** \g\ **go** \i\ **hit** \ī\ **ice** \j\ **job**
\ŋ\ **sing** \ō\ **go** \ȯ\ **law** \ȯi\ **boy** \th\ **thin** \t͟h\ **the** \ü\ **loot** \u̇\ **foot**
\y\ **yet** \zh\ **vision, beige** \k, ⁿ, œ, ue, ʸ\ *see* Guide to Pronunciation

drum•fire \'drəm-ˌfī(-ə)r\ *n* (1916) **1 :** artillery firing so continuous as to sound like a drumroll **2 :** something suggestive of drumfire in intensity : BARRAGE ⟨a ~ of publicity⟩

drum•head \-ˌhed\ *n* (1622) **1 :** the material (as skin or plastic) stretched over one or both ends of a drum **2 :** the top of a capstan that is pierced with sockets for the levers used in turning it

drumhead court–martial *n* [fr. the use of a drumhead as a table] (1835) : a summary court-martial that tries offenses on the battlefield

drum•lin \'drəm-lən\ *n* [Ir *druim* back, ridge (fr. OIr *druimm*) + E *-lin* (alter. of *-ling*)] (ca. 1833) : an elongate or oval hill of glacial drift

drum machine *n* (1980) : an electronic device that simulates the sound of drums

drum major *n* (1807) : the leader of a marching band

drum majorette *n* (1938) **1 :** a girl or woman who leads a marching band **2 :** a baton twirler who accompanies a marching band

drum•mer \'drə-mər\ *n* (1580) **1 :** one that plays a drum — sometimes used figuratively in phrases denoting unconventional thought or action ⟨march to a different ~⟩ **2 :** TRAVELING SALESMAN

drum•roll \'drəm-ˌrōl\ *n* (1828) : a roll on a drum or its sound

drum•stick \-ˌstik\ *n* (1589) **1 :** a stick for beating a drum **2 :** the segment of a fowl's leg between the thigh and tarsus

drum up *vt* (1830) **1 :** to bring about by persistent effort ⟨*drum up* some business⟩ **2 :** INVENT, ORIGINATE ⟨*drum up* a new method⟩

[1]**drunk** *past part of* DRINK

[2]**drunk** \'drəŋk\ *adj* [ME *drunke,* alter. of *drunken*] (14c) **1 a :** having the faculties impaired by alcohol **b :** having a level of alcohol in the blood that exceeds a maximum prescribed by law ⟨legally ~⟩ **2 :** dominated by an intense feeling ⟨~ with rage⟩ **3 :** relating to, caused by, or characterized by intoxication : DRUNKEN ⟨~ driving⟩

[3]**drunk** *n* (1779) **1 :** a period of drinking to intoxication or of being intoxicated ⟨a 2-day ~⟩ **2 :** one who is drunk; *esp* : DRUNKARD

drunk•ard \'drəŋ-kərd\ *n* (15c) : one who is habitually drunk

drunk•en \'drəŋ-kən\ *adj* [ME, fr. OE *druncen,* fr. pp. of *drincan* to drink] (bef. 12c) **1 :** DRUNK 1 ⟨a ~ driver⟩ **2** *obs* **:** saturated with liquid **3 a :** given to habitual excessive use of alcohol **b :** of, relating to, or characterized by intoxication ⟨they come from . . . broken homes, ~ homes —P. B. Gilliam⟩ **c :** resulting from or as if from intoxication ⟨a ~ brawl⟩ **4 :** unsteady or lurching as if from alcoholic intoxication — **drunk•en•ly** *adv* — **drunk•en•ness** \-kən-nəs\ *n*

drunk tank *n* (1947) : a large detention cell for arrested drunks

dru•pa•ceous \drü-'pā-shəs\ *adj* (1822) **1 :** of or relating to a drupe **2 :** bearing drupes

drupe \'drüp\ *n* [NL *drupa,* fr. L, overripe olive, fr. Gk *dryppa* olive] (ca. 1753) : a one-seeded indehiscent fruit having a hard bony endocarp, a fleshy mesocarp, and a thin exocarp that is flexible (as in the cherry) or dry and almost leathery (as in the almond)

drupe•let \'drü-plət\ *n* (1880) : a small drupe; *specif* : one of the individual parts of an aggregate fruit (as the raspberry)

druth•ers \'drə-t͟hərz\ *n pl* [*druther,* alter. of *would rather*] (1870) *dial* : free choice : PREFERENCE — used esp. in the phrase *if one had one's druthers*

Druze *or* **Druse** \'drüz\ *n, pl* **Druze** *or* **Druzes** *or* **Druse** *or* **Druses** *often attrib* [Ar *Durūz,* pl., fr. Muḥammad ibn-Ismaʽīl al-*Darazī* †1019 Muslim religious leader] (1855) : a member of a religious sect originating among Muslims and centered in Lebanon and Syria

[1]**dry** \'drī\ *adj* **dri•er** *also* **dry•er** \'drī(-ə)r\; **dri•est** *also* **dry•est** \'drī-əst\ [ME, fr. OE *drȳge;* akin to OHG *truckan* dry, OE *drēahnian* to drain] (bef. 12c) **1 a :** free or relatively free from a liquid and esp. water **b :** not being in or under water **c :** lacking precipitation or humidity **2 a :** characterized by exhaustion of a supply of liquid ⟨a ~ well⟩ **b :** devoid of running water ⟨a ~ ravine⟩ **c :** devoid of natural moisture ⟨my throat was ~⟩ **d :** no longer sticky or damp **e :** not giving milk ⟨a ~ cow⟩ **f :** lacking freshness : STALE **g :** ANHYDROUS **3 a :** marked by the absence or scantiness of secretions ⟨a ~ cough⟩ **b :** not shedding or accompanied by tears ⟨a ~ sob⟩ **4** *obs* **:** involving no bloodshed or drowning ⟨I would fain die a ~ death —Shak.⟩ **5 a :** marked by the absence of alcoholic beverages ⟨a ~ party⟩ **b :** prohibiting the manufacture or distribution of alcoholic beverages ⟨a ~ county⟩ **6 :** served or eaten without butter or margarine ⟨~ toast⟩ **7 a :** lacking sweetness : SEC ⟨~ champagne⟩ **b :** having all or most sugar fermented to alcohol ⟨a ~ wine⟩ ⟨~ beer⟩ **8 a :** solid as opposed to liquid ⟨~ groceries⟩ **b :** reduced to powder or flakes : DEHYDRATED ⟨~ milk⟩ **9 :** functioning without lubrication ⟨a ~ clutch⟩ **10** *of natural gas* **:** containing no recoverable hydrocarbon (as gasoline) **11 :** requiring no liquid in preparation or operation ⟨a ~ photocopying process⟩ **12 a :** not showing or communicating warmth, enthusiasm, or tender feeling : SEVERE ⟨a ~ style of painting⟩ **b :** WEARISOME, UNINTERESTING ⟨~ passages of description⟩ **c :** lacking embellishment : PLAIN **13 a :** not yielding what is expected or desired : UNPRODUCTIVE ⟨a writer going through a ~ spell⟩ **b :** having no personal bias or emotional concern ⟨the ~ light of reason⟩ **c :** RESERVED, ALOOF **14 :** marked by matter-of-fact, ironic, or terse manner of expression ⟨a ~ wit⟩ **15 :** lacking smooth sound qualities ⟨a ~ rasping voice⟩ **16 :** being a dry run ⟨a ~ rehearsal⟩ — **dry•ish** \'drī-ish\ *adj* — **dri•ly** *or* **dry•ly** *adv* — **dry•ness** *n*

[2]**dry** *vb* **dried; dry•ing** *vt* (bef. 12c) : to make dry ~ *vi* : to become dry — **dry•able** \'drī-ə-bəl\ *adj*

[3]**dry** *n, pl* **drys** (13c) **1 :** the condition of being dry : DRYNESS **2 :** something dry; *esp* : a dry place **3 :** PROHIBITIONIST

dry•ad \'drī-əd, -ˌad\ *n* [L *dryad-, dryas,* fr. Gk, fr. *drys* tree — more at TREE] (14c) : WOOD NYMPH

dry•as•dust \'drī-əz-ˌdəst\ *adj* (ca. 1872) : BORING — **dryasdust** *n*

dry cell *n* (1893) : a voltaic cell whose contents are not spillable — called also *dry battery*

dry–clean \'drī-ˌklēn\ *vt* (1817) : to subject to dry cleaning ~ *vi* : to undergo dry cleaning — **dry–clean•able** \-'klē-nə-bəl\ *adj*

dry cleaner *n* (1897) : one whose business is dry cleaning

dry cleaning *n* (1855) **1 :** the cleansing of fabrics with substantially nonaqueous organic solvents **2 :** something that is dry-cleaned

dry–dock \'drī-ˌdäk\ *vt* (1854) : to place in a dry dock

dry dock *n* (1626) : a dock that can be kept dry for use during the construction or repairing of ships

dryer *var of* DRIER

dry–erase board *n* (1983) : WHITEBOARD

dry eye *n* (1970) : a condition associated with inadequate tear production and marked by redness, itching, and burning of the eye — called also *dry eye syndrome*

dry–eyed \'drī-ˌīd\ *adj* (1667) **1 :** not moved to tears or to empathy **2 :** marked by the absence of sentimentalism or romanticism

dry farming *n* (1878) : farming on nonirrigated land with little rainfall that relies on moisture-conserving tillage and drought-resistant crops — **dry–farm** *vt* — **dry farm** *n* — **dry farmer** *n*

dry fly *n* (1846) : an artificial angling fly designed to float

Dry•gas \'drī-ˌgas\ *trademark* — used for fuel-line antifreeze for motor vehicles

dry goods \'drī-ˌgu̇dz\ *n pl* (1657) : textiles, ready-to-wear clothing, and notions as distinguished esp. from hardware and groceries

dry heaves *n pl* (1950) : repeated involuntary retching unaccompanied by vomit

dry hole *n* (1883) : a well (as for gas or oil) that proves unproductive

dry ice *n* (1925) : solidified carbon dioxide

drying oil *n* (ca. 1760) : an oil (as linseed oil) that changes readily to a hard tough elastic substance when exposed in a thin film to air

dry•land \'drī-ˌland\ *adj* (1893) : of, relating to, or being a relatively arid region ⟨a ~ wheat state⟩; *also* : of, adapted to, practicing, or being agricultural methods (as dry farming) suited to such a region

dry•lot \'drī-ˌlät\ *n* (1924) : an enclosure of limited size usu. bare of vegetation and used for fattening livestock

dry measure *n* (1638) : a series of units of capacity for dry commodities — see METRIC SYSTEM table, WEIGHT table

dry mop *n* (1933) : a long-handled mop for dusting floors

dry–nurse *vt* (1581) **1 :** to act as dry nurse to **2 :** to give unnecessary supervision to

dry nurse *n* (1598) : a nurse who takes care of but does not breast-feed another woman's baby

dryo•pith•e•cine \ˌdrī-ō-'pi-thə-ˌsīn\ *n* [ultim. fr. Gk *drys* tree + *pithēkos* ape] (1939) : any of a subfamily (Dryopithecinae) of Miocene and Pliocene Old World anthropoid apes sometimes regarded as ancestors of both humans and modern anthropoids — **dryopithecine** *adj*

dry out *vi* (1892) : to undergo an extended period of withdrawal from alcohol or drug use esp. at a special clinic

dry•point \'drī-ˌpȯint\ *n* (1871) : an engraving made with a steel or jeweled point directly into the metal plate without the use of acid as in etching; *also* : a print made from such an engraving

dry–rot *vt* (1870) : to affect with dry rot ~ *vi* : to become affected with dry rot

dry rot *n* (1795) **1 a :** a decay of seasoned timber caused by fungi that consume the cellulose of wood leaving a soft skeleton which is readily reduced to powder **b :** a fungal rot of plant tissue in which the affected areas are dry and often firmer than normal or more or less mummified **2 :** a fungus causing dry rot **3 :** decay from within caused esp. by resistance to new forces

dry run *n* (ca. 1941) **1 :** a practice exercise : REHEARSAL, TRIAL **2 :** a practice firing without ammunition

dry•salt•er \'drī-ˌsȯl-tər\ *n* (1707) *Brit* : a dealer in crude dry chemicals and dyes — **dry•salt•ery** \-tə-rē\ *n, Brit*

dry–shod \'drī-ˌshäd\ *adj* (15c) : having dry shoes or feet

dry sink *n* (1946) : a cabinet with a tray top for holding a wash basin

dry•stone \'drī-ˌstōn\ *adj* (ca. 1702) *chiefly Brit* : constructed of stone without the use of mortar as an adhesive ⟨a ~ wall⟩

dry suit *n* (1955) : a close-fitting air-insulated waterproof suit for divers

dry up *vt* (14c) : to cut off the supply of ~ *vi* **1 :** to disappear as if by evaporation, draining, or cutting off of a source of supply **2 :** to wither or die through gradual loss of vitality **3 :** to stop talking

dry•wall \'drī-ˌwȯl\ *n* (1950) : a board made of several plies of fiberboard, paper, or felt bonded to a hardened gypsum plaster core and used esp. as wallboard

dry wash *n* (1872) *West* : WASH 1d

dry well *n* (ca. 1942) : a hole in the ground filled with gravel or rubble to receive drainage water and allow it to percolate away

Ds *symbol* darmstadtium

DS *abbr* **1** [It *dal segno*] from the sign **2** detached service **3** document signed

DSc *abbr* doctor of science

DSC *abbr* Distinguished Service Cross

DSL *abbr* digital subscriber line

DSM *abbr* Distinguished Service Medal

DSO *abbr* Distinguished Service Order

DSP *abbr* [L *decessit sine prole*] died without issue

DST *abbr* **1** daylight saving time **2** doctor of sacred theology

DSW *abbr* doctor of social welfare; doctor of social work

DT *abbr* **1** daylight time **2** doctor of theology **3** double time

DTh *abbr* doctor of theology

DTP *abbr* **1** desktop publishing **2** diphtheria, tetanus, pertussis

d.t.'s \ˌdē-'tēz\ *n pl, often cap D&T* (1857) : DELIRIUM TREMENS

[1]**du•al** \'dü(-ə)l *also* 'dyü-əl\ *adj* [L *dualis,* fr. *duo* two — more at TWO] (1597) **1** *of grammatical number* **:** denoting reference to two **2 a :** consisting of two parts or elements or having two like parts : DOUBLE **b :** having a double character or nature — **du•al•ly** \-ə(l)-lē\ *adv*

[2]**dual** *n* (1650) **1 :** the dual number of a language **2 :** a linguistic form in the dual

dual carriageway *n* (1933) *chiefly Brit* : a divided highway

dual citizenship *n* (ca. 1924) : the status of an individual who is a citizen of two or more nations

dual–energy X–ray absorptiometry *n* (1988) : absorptiometry in which the density or mass of a material (as bone) is measured by comparing the material's absorption of X rays of two different energies and which is used esp. for determining the mineral content of bone

du•al•ism \'dü-ə-ˌli-zəm *also* 'dyü-\ *n* (1794) **1 :** a theory that considers reality to consist of two irreducible elements or modes **2 :** the quality or state of being dual or of having a dual nature **3 a :** a doctrine that the universe is under the dominion of two opposing principles one of which is good and the other evil **b :** a view of human beings as constituted of two irreducible elements (as matter and spirit) — **du•al•ist** \-list\ *n* — **du•al•is•tic** \ˌdü-ə-'lis-tik, ˌdyü-\ *adj* — **du•al•is•ti•cal•ly** \-ti-k(ə-)lē\ *adv*

du•al•i•ty \dü-'a-lə-tē *also* dyü-\ *n, pl* **-ties** (15c) : DUALISM 2; *also* : DICHOTOMY

du·al·ize \ˈdü-ə-ˌlīz *also* ˈdyü-\ *vt* **-ized; -iz·ing** (1838) **:** to make dual

dual–purpose *adj* (1904) **:** having breed characteristics that serve two purposes ⟨~ cattle that supply milk and meat⟩

du·ath·lon \dü-ˈath-lən, -ˌlän *also* dyü-\ *n* [*duo-* + *-athlon* (as in *triathlon*)] (1988) **:** a three-part long-distance race typically having a running phase, a bicycling phase, and a final running phase — **du·ath·lete** \dü-ˈath-ˌlēt *also* dyü-\ *n*

¹dub \ˈdəb\ *vt* **dubbed; dub·bing** [ME *dubben,* fr. OE *dubbian;* akin to ON *dubba* to dub, OHG *tubili* plug] (bef. 12c) **1 a :** to confer knighthood on **b :** to call by a distinctive title, epithet, or nickname **2 :** to trim or remove the comb and wattles of **3 a :** to hit (a golf ball or shot) poorly **b :** to execute poorly ⟨a *dubbed* attempt⟩ — **dub·ber** *n*

²dub *n* (1884) **:** one who is inept or clumsy

³dub *n* [ME (Sc) *dubbe*] (15c) *chiefly Scot* **:** POOL, PUDDLE

⁴dub *vt* **dubbed; dub·bing** [by shortening & alter. fr. *double*] (1930) **1 :** to add (sound effects or new dialogue) to a film or to a radio or television production — usu. used with *in* **2 :** to provide (a motion-picture film) with a new sound track and esp. dialogue in a different language **3 :** to make a new recording of (sound or videotape already recorded); *also* **:** to mix (recorded sound or videotape from different sources) into a single recording — **dubber** *n*

⁵dub *n* (1974) **:** Jamaican music in which audio effects and spoken or chanted words are imposed on an instrumental reggae background

dub·bin \ˈdə-bən\ *also* **dub·bing** \-bən, -biŋ\ *n* [*dubbing,* gerund of *dub* to dress leather] (1781) **:** a dressing of oil and tallow for leather

du·bi·ety \dü-ˈbī-ət-ē *also* dyü-\ *n, pl* **-eties** [LL *dubietas,* fr. L *dubius*] (1750) **1 :** a usu. hesitant uncertainty or doubt that tends to cause vacillation **2 :** a matter of doubt ***syn*** see UNCERTAINTY

du·bi·ous \ˈdü-bē-əs *also* dyü-\ *adj* [L *dubius,* fr. *dubare* to vacillate; akin to L *duo* two — more at TWO] (1548) **1 :** giving rise to uncertainty: as **a :** of doubtful promise or outcome ⟨a ~ plan⟩ **b :** questionable or suspect as to true nature or quality ⟨the practice is of ~ legality⟩ **2 :** unsettled in opinion **:** DOUBTFUL ⟨I was ~ about the plan⟩ ***syn*** see DOUBTFUL — **du·bi·ous·ly** *adv* — **du·bi·ous·ness** *n*

du·bi·ta·ble \ˈdü-bə-tə-bəl *also* ˈdyü-\ *adj* [L *dubitabilis,* fr. *dubitare* to doubt — more at DOUBT] (ca. 1616) **:** open to doubt or question

du·bi·ta·tion \ˌd(y)ü-bə-ˈtā-shən\ *n* (15c) *archaic* **:** DOUBT

Dub·lin Bay prawn \ˈdə-blən-ˈbā-\ *n* (1949) **:** LANGOUSTINE

dub·ni·um \ˈdüb-nē-əm, ˈdəb-\ *n* [NL, fr. *Dubna,* city in Russia where a center for investigation of heavy elements is located] (1994) **:** a short-lived radioactive element produced artificially — see ELEMENT table

dub·step \ˈdəb-ˌstep\ *n* (2002) **:** a type of electronic dance music having prominent bass lines and syncopated drum patterns

du·cal \ˈdü-kəl *also* ˈdyü-\ *adj* [LL *ducalis* of a leader, fr. L *duc-, dux* leader — more at DUKE] (15c) **:** of or relating to a duke or dukedom — **du·cal·ly** \-kə-lē\ *adv*

duc·at \ˈdə-kət\ *n* [ME, fr. MF, fr. OIt *ducato* coin with the doge's portrait on it, fr. *duca* doge, fr. LGk *douk-, doux* leader, fr. L *duc-, dux*] (14c) **1 :** a former European usu. gold coin **2 :** TICKET 2

du·ce \ˈdü-(ˌ)chā\ *n* [It (*Il*) *Duce,* lit., the leader, title of Benito Mussolini, fr. L *duc-, dux*] (1923) **:** LEADER — used esp. for the leader of the Italian Fascist party

Du·chenne muscular dystrophy \dü-ˈshen-, də-\ *n* [Guillaume Armand *Duchenne* †1875 Fr. neurologist] (1971) **:** a severe progressive X-linked muscular dystrophy of males marked by early childhood onset and absence of the protein dystrophin — called also *Duchenne's muscular dystrophy;* compare BECKER MUSCULAR DYSTROPHY

duch·ess \ˈdə-chəs\ *n* [ME *duchesse,* fr. AF, fr. *duc* duke] (14c) **1 :** the wife or widow of a duke **2 :** a woman who holds the rank of duke in her own right

duchy \ˈdə-chē\ *n, pl* **duch·ies** [ME *duche,* fr. AF *duché,* fr. *duc*] (14c) **1 :** the territory of a duke or duchess **:** DUKEDOM **2 :** special domain

¹duck \ˈdək\ *n, pl* **ducks** *often attrib* [ME *duk, doke,* fr. OE *dūce*] (bef. 12c) **1** *or pl* **duck a :** any of various swimming birds (family Anatidae, the duck family) in which the neck and legs are short, the feet typically webbed, the bill often broad and flat, and the sexes usu. different from each other in plumage **b :** the flesh of any of these birds used as food **2 :** a female duck — compare DRAKE **3** *chiefly Brit* **:** DARLING — often used in pl. but sing. in constr. **4 :** PERSON, CREATURE

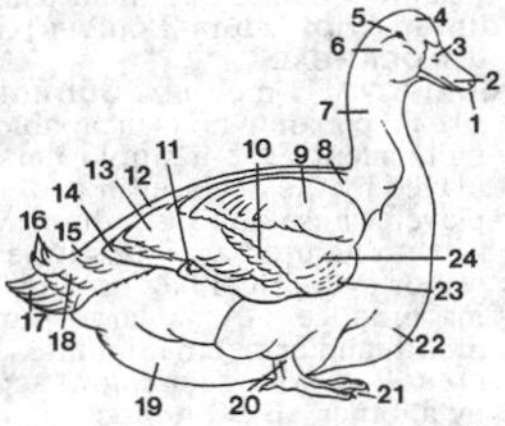

duck 1a (male): *1* bean, *2* bill, *3* nostril, *4* head, *5* eye, *6* auricular region, *7* neck, *8* cape, *9* shoulder, *10, 11* wing coverts, *12* saddle, *13* secondaries, *14* primaries, *15* rump, *16* drake feathers, *17* tail, *18* tail coverts, *19* down, *20* shank, *21* web, *22* breast, *23* wing front, *24* wing bow

²duck *vb* [ME *douken;* akin to OHG *tūhhan* to dive, OE *dūce* duck] *vt* (14c) **1 :** to thrust under water **2 :** to lower (as the head) quickly **:** BOW **3 :** AVOID, EVADE ⟨~ the issue⟩ ~ *vi* **1 a :** to plunge under the surface of water **b :** to descend suddenly **:** DIP **2 a :** to lower the head or body suddenly **:** DODGE **b :** BOW, BOB **3 a :** to move quickly **b :** to evade a duty, question, or responsibility — **duck·er** *n*

³duck *n* (1554) **:** an instance of ducking

⁴duck *n* [D *doek* cloth; akin to OHG *tuoh* cloth] (1640) **1 :** a durable closely woven usu. cotton fabric **2** *pl* **:** light clothes and esp. trousers made of duck

duck·bill \ˈdək-ˌbil\ *n* (1840) **1 :** PLATYPUS **2 :** HADROSAUR

duck–billed dinosaur *also* **duckbill dinosaur** *n* (1913) **:** HADROSAUR

duck–billed platypus *also* **duckbill platypus** *n* (1799) **:** PLATYPUS

duck·board \-ˌbȯrd\ *n* (1917) **:** a boardwalk or slatted flooring laid on a wet, muddy, or cold surface — usu. used in pl.

duck call *n* (1872) **:** a device for imitating the calls of ducks

duck hook *n* (1973) **:** a pronounced and unintended hook in golf — **duck–hook** *vt*

ducking stool *n* (1597) **:** a seat attached to a plank and formerly used to plunge culprits tied to it into water

duck·ling \ˈdək-liŋ, ˈdə-kliŋ\ *n* (15c) **:** a young duck

duck·pin \-ˌpin\ *n* (ca. 1911) **1 :** a small bowling pin shorter than a tenpin but proportionately wider at mid-diameter **2** *pl but sing in constr* **:** a bowling game using duckpins

ducks and drakes *or* **duck and drake** *n* (1583) **:** the pastime of skimming flat stones or shells along the surface of calm water — **play ducks and drakes with** *or* **make ducks and drakes of :** to use recklessly **:** SQUANDER ⟨*played ducks and drakes with* his money⟩

duck sauce *n* (1978) **:** a thick sauce in Chinese cuisine that contains fruits (as plums or apricots), vinegar, sweeteners, and seasonings

duck soup *n* (1912) **:** something easy to do

duck·tail \ˈdək-ˌtāl\ *n* [fr. its resemblance to the tail of a duck] (1948) **:** a hairstyle in which the hair on each side is slicked back to meet in a ridge at the back of the head

duck·walk \ˈdək-ˌwȯk\ *vi* (1950) **:** to walk while in a crouch or full squatting position

duck·weed \ˈdək-ˌwēd\ *n* (15c) **:** a small floating aquatic monocotyledonous plant (family Lemnaceae, the duckweed family)

ducky \ˈdə-kē\ *adj* **duck·i·er; -est** (1897) **1 :** DARLING, CUTE ⟨a ~ little tearoom⟩ **2 :** SATISFACTORY, FINE ⟨everything is just ~⟩

¹duct \ˈdəkt\ *n* [NL *ductus,* fr. ML, aqueduct, fr. L, act of leading, fr. *ducere* to lead — more at TOW] (1667) **1 :** a bodily tube or vessel esp. when carrying the secretion of a gland **2 a :** a pipe, tube, or channel that conveys a substance **b :** a pipe or tubular runway for carrying an electric power line, telephone cables, or other conductors **3 :** a tube or elongated cavity (as a xylem vessel) in plant tissue **4 :** a layer (as in the atmosphere or the ocean) which occurs under usu. abnormal conditions and in which radio or sound waves are confined to a restricted path — **duc·tal** \ˈdək-tᵊl\ *adj* — **duct·less** \ˈdək(t)-ləs\ *adj*

²duct *vt* (1936) **1 :** to enclose in a duct **2 :** to convey (as a gas) through a duct; *also* **:** to propagate (as radio waves) through a duct

duc·tile \ˈdək-tᵊl, -ˌtī(-ə)l\ *adj* [ME *ductil,* fr. L *ductilis,* fr. *ducere*] (14c) **1 :** capable of being drawn out into wire or thread ⟨~ iron⟩ **2 :** easily led or influenced **3 :** capable of being fashioned into a new form ***syn*** see PLASTIC — **duc·til·i·ty** \ˌdək-ˈti-lə-tē\ *n*

duct·ing \ˈdək-tiŋ\ *n* (1945) **:** a system of ducts; *also* **:** the material composing a duct

ductless gland *n* (ca. 1852) **:** ENDOCRINE GLAND

duct tape \ˈdək(t)-\ *n* (1973) **:** a wide cloth adhesive tape orig. designed for sealing joints in heating or air-conditioning ducts — **duct–tape** *vt*

duct·ule \ˈdək-(ˌ)chül\ *n* (1883) **:** a small duct

duc·tus ar·te·ri·o·sus \ˈdək-təs-är-ˌtir-ē-ˈō-səs\ *n* [NL, lit., arterial duct] (1811) **:** a short broad vessel in the fetus that connects the pulmonary artery with the aorta and conducts most of the blood directly from the right ventricle to the aorta bypassing the lungs

duct·work \ˈdəkt-ˌwərk\ *n* (1934) **:** DUCTING

¹dud \ˈdəd\ *n* [ME *dudde*] (1567) **1** *pl* **a :** CLOTHING **b :** personal belongings **2 a :** one that is ineffectual; *also* **:** FAILURE ⟨a box-office ~⟩ **b :** MISFIT **3 :** a bomb or missile that fails to explode

²dud *adj* (1903) **:** of little or no worth **:** VALUELESS ⟨~ checks⟩

¹dude \ˈdüd *also* ˈdyüd\ *n* [origin unknown] (1883) **1 :** a man extremely fastidious in dress and manner **:** DANDY **2 :** a city dweller unfamiliar with life on the range; *esp* **:** an Easterner in the West **3 :** FELLOW, GUY — sometimes used informally as a term of address ⟨hey, ~, what's up⟩ — **dud·ish** \ˈd(y)üd-ish\ *adj* — **dud·ish·ly** *adv*

²dude *vt* **dud·ed; dud·ing** (1899) **:** DRESS UP — usu. used with *up*

du·deen \dü-ˈdēn\ *n* [Ir *dúidín,* dim. of *dúd* pipe] (1841) **:** a short tobacco pipe made of clay

dude ranch *n* (1921) **:** a vacation resort offering activities (as horseback riding) typical of western ranches

¹dud·geon \ˈdə-jən\ *n* [ME *dogeon,* fr. AF *digeon, dogeon*] (15c) **1** *obs* **:** a wood used esp. for dagger hilts **2 a** *archaic* **:** a dagger with a handle of dudgeon **b** *obs* **:** a haft made of dudgeon

²dudgeon *n* [origin unknown] (1573) **:** a fit or state of indignation — often used in the phrase *in high dudgeon* ***syn*** see OFFENSE

¹due \ˈdü, ˈdyü\ *adj* [ME, fr. AF *deu,* pp. of *dever* to owe, fr. L *debēre* — more at DEBT] (14c) **1 :** owed or owing as a debt **2 a :** owed or owing as a natural or moral right ⟨everyone's right to dissent . . . is ~ the full protection of the Constitution —Nat Hentoff⟩ **b :** according to accepted notions or procedures **:** APPROPRIATE ⟨with all ~ respect⟩ **3 a :** satisfying or capable of satisfying a need, obligation, or duty **:** ADEQUATE ⟨giving the matter ~ attention⟩ **b :** REGULAR, LAWFUL ⟨~ proof of loss⟩ **4 :** capable of being attributed **:** ASCRIBABLE — used with *to* ⟨this advance is partly ~ to a few men of genius —A. N. Whitehead⟩ **5 :** having reached the date at which payment is required **:** PAYABLE ⟨the rent is ~⟩ **6 :** required or expected in the prescribed, normal, or logical course of events **:** SCHEDULED ⟨the train is ~ at noon⟩; *also* **:** expected to give birth — **due·ness** *n*

²due *n* (15c) **:** something due or owed: as **a :** something that rightfully belongs to one ⟨give him his ~⟩ **b :** a payment or obligation required by law or custom **:** DEBT **c** *pl* **:** FEES, CHARGES ⟨membership ~*s*⟩

³due *adv* (1582) **1 :** DIRECTLY, EXACTLY ⟨~ north⟩ **2** *obs* **:** DULY

due diligence *n* (1877) **1 :** the care that a reasonable person exercises to avoid harm to other persons or their property **2 :** research and analysis of a company or organization done in preparation for a business transaction (as a corporate merger or purchase of securities)

¹du·el \ˈdü-əl *also* ˈdyü-\ *n* [ME, fr. ML *duellum,* fr. OL, war] (15c) **1 :** a combat between two persons; *specif* **:** a formal combat with weapons fought between two persons in the presence of witnesses **2 :** a conflict between antagonistic persons, ideas, or forces; *also* **:** a hard-fought contest between two opponents

²duel *vb* **du·eled** *or* **du·elled; du·el·ing** *or* **du·el·ling** *vi* (ca. 1645) **:** to fight a duel ~ *vt* **:** to encounter (an opponent) in a duel — **du·el·er** *or* **du·el·ler** *n* — **du·el·ist** *or* **du·el·list** \ˈdü-ə-list\ *n*

du·el·lo \d(y)ü-ˈe-(ˌ)lō\ *n, pl* **-los** [It, fr. ML *duellum*] (1588) **1 :** the rules or practice of dueling **2 :** DUEL

du·en·de \dü-ˈen-(ˌ)dā\ *n* [Sp dial., charm, fr. Sp, ghost, goblin, prob. fr. *duen de casa,* fr. *dueño de casa* owner of a house] (1964) **:** the power to attract through personal magnetism and charm

---

\ə\ **abut** \ᵊ\ **kitten,** F table \ər\ **further** \a\ **ash** \ā\ **ace** \ä\ **mop, mar** \au̇\ **out** \ch\ **chin** \e\ **bet** \ē\ **easy** \g\ **go** \i\ **hit** \ī\ **ice** \j\ **job** \ŋ\ **sing** \ō\ **go** \ȯ\ **law** \ȯi\ **boy** \th\ **thin** \t͟h\ **the** \ü\ **loot** \u̇\ **foot** \y\ **yet** \zh\ **vision, beige** \ₖ, ⁿ, œ, ᵫ, ʸ\ *see* Guide to Pronunciation

du·en·na \dü-ˈe-nə, ˈdyü-\ *n* [Sp *dueña,* fr. L *domina* mistress — more at DAME] (1623) **1 :** an elderly woman serving as governess and companion to the younger ladies in a Spanish or a Portuguese family **2 :** CHAPERONE — **du·en·na·ship** \-ˌship\ *n*

due process *n* (15c) **1 :** a course of formal proceedings (as legal proceedings) carried out regularly and in accordance with established rules and principles — called also *procedural due process* **2 :** a judicial requirement that enacted laws may not contain provisions that result in the unfair, arbitrary, or unreasonable treatment of an individual — called also *substantive due process*

[1]**du·et** \dü-ˈet *also* dyü-\ *n* [It *duetto,* dim. of *duo* duo] (ca. 1740) **:** a composition for two performers

[2]**duet** *vi* **du·et·ted** *or* **du·et·ed; du·et·ting** *or* **du·et·ing** (1822) **:** to perform a duet

due to *prep* (1897) **:** as a result of **:** BECAUSE OF ‹*due to* the complaints of uptight parents . . . he lost his job —Herbert Gold›

usage The objection to *due to* as a preposition is only a continuation of disagreements that began in the 18th century over the proper uses of *owing* and *due. Due to* is as grammatically sound as *owing to,* which is frequently recommended in its place. It has been and is used by reputable writers and has been recognized as standard for decades. There is no solid reason to avoid *due to.*

[1]**duff** \ˈdəf\ *n* [E dial., alter. of *dough*] (1816) **1 :** a boiled or steamed pudding often containing dried fruit **2 :** the partly decayed organic matter on the forest floor **3 :** fine coal **:** SLACK

[2]**duff** *n* [origin unknown] (ca. 1837) **:** BUTTOCKS ‹get off your ~›

[3]**duff** *adj* [*duff,* n., something worthless, fr. [1]*duff*] (ca. 1889) *Brit* **:** INFERIOR, WORTHLESS

duf·fel *or* **duf·fle** \ˈdə-fəl\ *n* [D *duffel,* fr. *Duffel,* Belgium] (1677) **1 :** a coarse heavy woolen material with a thick nap **2 :** transportable personal belongings, equipment, and supplies **3 :** DUFFEL BAG **4 :** DUFFLE COAT

duffel bag *n* (1917) **:** a soft oblong bag for personal belongings

duf·fer \ˈdə-fər\ *n* [perh. fr. *duff,* n., something worthless] (1756) **1 a :** a peddler esp. of cheap flashy articles **b :** something counterfeit or worthless **2 :** an incompetent, ineffectual, or clumsy person; *esp* **:** a mediocre golfer **3** *Austral* **:** a cattle rustler

duffle coat \ˈdə-fəl-\ *or* **duffel coat** *n* (1684) **:** a heavy usu. woolen medium-length coat with toggle fasteners and a hood

dufus *var of* DOOFUS

[1]**dug** *past and past part of* DIG

[2]**dug** \ˈdəg\ *n* [perh. of Scand origin; akin to OSw *dæggia* to suckle; akin to OE *delu* nipple — more at FEMININE] (1530) **1 :** UDDER **2** *usu vulgar when used of a woman* **:** TEAT — usu. used of a suckling animal

du·gong \ˈdü-ˌgän, -ˌgȯŋ\ *n* [NL, genus name, prob. fr. *dugung* in Cebuano or a related Austronesian language of the central Philippines] (1800) **:** a sirenian mammal (*Dugong dugon* of the family Dugongidae) of a monotypic genus that has a bilobed tail and in the male upper incisors altered into short tusks and that inhabits warm coastal waters chiefly of southern Asia, Australia, and northeastern Africa

dug·out \ˈdəg-ˌau̇t\ *n* (1819) **1 :** a boat made by hollowing out a large log **2 a :** a shelter dug in a hillside; *also* **:** a shelter dug in the ground and roofed with sod **b :** an area in the side of a trench for quarters, storage, or protection **3 :** either of two low shelters on either side of and facing a baseball diamond that contain the players' benches

duh \ˈdə, *usu with prolonged* ə\ *interj* (1966) **1** — used to express actual or feigned ignorance or stupidity **2** — used derisively to indicate that something just stated is all too obvious or self-evident

DUI \ˌdē-(ˌ)yü-ˈī\ *n* [*d*riving *u*nder the *i*nfluence] (1969) **1 :** the act or crime of driving while affected by alcohol or drugs ‹was arrested for ~› **2 :** a person who is arrested for or convicted of driving under the influence **3 :** an arrest or conviction for driving under the influence

dui·ker \ˈdī-kər\ *n* [Afrik, lit., diver, fr. *duik* to dive, fr. MD *düken;* akin to OHG *tūhhan* to dive — more at DUCK] (1777) **:** any of several small African antelopes comprising two genera (*Cephalophus* and *Sylvicapra*)

duit *var of* DOIT

du jour \dü-ˈzhər, də-, -ˈzhu̇r, -ˈzhür\ *adj* [F, lit., of the day] (1786) **1 :** made for a particular day — used of an item not specified on the regular menu ‹soup *du jour*› **2 :** popular, fashionable, or prominent at a particular time ‹the buzzword *du jour*›

[1]**duke** \ˈdük *also* ˈdyük\ *n* [ME, fr. AF *duc,* fr. L *duc-, dux,* fr. *ducere* to lead — more at TOW] (12c) **1 :** a sovereign male ruler of a continental European duchy **2 :** a nobleman of the highest hereditary rank; *esp* **:** a member of the highest grade of the British peerage **3** [prob. fr. *dukes of York,* rhyming slang for *fork* (hand, fist)] *slang* **:** FIST, HAND — usu. used in pl. — **duke·dom** \-dəm\ *n*

[2]**duke** *vi* **duked; duk·ing** (ca. 1947) **:** FIGHT — **duke it out :** to engage in a fight and esp. a fistfight

Dukhobor *var of* DOUKHOBOR

dul·cet \ˈdəl-sət\ *adj* [ME *doucet,* fr. AF, fr. *duz, douz* sweet, fr. L *dulcis;* perh. akin to Gk *glykys* sweet] (14c) **1 :** sweet to the taste **2 :** pleasing to the ear ‹~ tones› **3 :** generally pleasing or agreeable ‹a ~ smile› — **dul·cet·ly** *adv*

dul·ci·fy \ˈdəl-sə-ˌfī\ *vt* **-fied; -fy·ing** [LL *dulcificare,* fr. L *dulcis*] (1599) **1 :** to make sweet **2 :** to make agreeable **:** MOLLIFY

dul·ci·mer \ˈdəl-sə-mər\ *n* [ME *dowcemere,* fr. MF *doulcemer,* fr. OIt *dolcimelo,* fr. *dolce* sweet, fr. L *dulcis*] (15c) **1 :** a stringed instrument of trapezoidal shape played with light hammers held in the hands **2** *or* **dul·ci·more** \-ˌmȯr\ **:** an American folk instrument with three or four strings stretched over an elongate fretted sound box that is held on the lap and played by plucking or strumming

dul·ci·nea \ˌdəl-sə-ˈnē-ə, -ˈsi-nē-ə\ *n* [Sp, fr. *Dulcinea* del Toboso, beloved of Don Quixote] (1748) **:** MISTRESS, SWEETHEART

[1]**dull** \ˈdəl\ *adj* [ME *dul;* akin to OE *dol* foolish, OIr *dall* blind] (13c) **1 :** mentally slow **:** STUPID **2 a :** slow in perception or sensibility **:** INSENSIBLE ‹somewhat ~ of hearing› **b :** lacking zest or vivacity **:** LISTLESS ‹a ~ performance› **3 :** slow in action **:** SLUGGISH **4 a :** lacking in force, intensity, or sharpness ‹a ~ ache› **b :** not resonant or ringing ‹a ~ booming sound› **5 :** lacking sharpness of edge or point ‹a ~ knife› **6 :** lacking brilliance or luster ‹a ~ finish› **7** *of a color* **:** low in saturation and low in lightness **8 :** CLOUDY ‹~ weather› **9 :** TEDIOUS, UNINTERESTING ‹~ lectures› — **dull·ness** *also* **dul·ness** \ˈdəl-nəs\ *n* — **dul·ly** \ˈdə(l)-lē\ *adv*

syn DULL, BLUNT, OBTUSE mean not sharp, keen, or acute. DULL suggests a lack or loss of keenness, zest, or pungency ‹a *dull* pain› ‹a *dull* mind›. BLUNT suggests an inherent lack of sharpness or quickness of feeling or perception ‹a person of *blunt* sensibility›. OBTUSE implies such bluntness as makes one insensitive in perception or imagination ‹too *obtuse* to take the hint›. ***syn*** see in addition STUPID

[2]**dull** *vt* (13c) **:** to make dull ‹~ a knife's edge› ~ *vi* **:** to become dull

dull·ard \ˈdə-lərd\ *n* (15c) **:** a stupid or unimaginative person

dull·ish \ˈdə-lish\ *adj* (14c) **:** somewhat dull — **dull·ish·ly** *adv*

dulls·ville \ˈdəlz-ˌvil\ *n* (ca. 1960) **:** something or some place that is dull or boring ‹the movie was ~›

dulse \ˈdəls\ *n* [modif. of ScGael *duileasg;* akin to W *delysg* dulse] (ca. 1698) **:** any of several coarse red seaweeds (esp. *Palmaria palmata*) found esp. in northern latitudes and used as a food condiment

du·ly \ˈdü-lē *also* ˈdyü-\ *adv* (14c) **:** in a due manner or time **:** PROPERLY ‹a ~ elected official› ‹~ noted›

du·ma \ˈdü-mə, -(ˌ)mä\ *n* [Russ, fr. ORuss, council, thought, prob. of Gmc origin; akin to OE *dōm* judgment — more at DOOM] (1870) **:** a representative council in Russia; *esp, often cap* **:** the principal legislative assembly in Russia from 1906 to 1917 and since 1993

[1]**dumb** \ˈdəm\ *adj* [ME, fr. OE; akin to OHG *tumb* mute] (bef. 12c) **1 a :** lacking the human power of speech ‹~ animals› **b** *of a person, often offensive* **:** lacking the ability to speak **2 :** temporarily unable to speak (as from shock or astonishment) ‹struck ~ with fear› **3 :** not expressed in uttered words ‹~ grief› **4 :** SILENT; *also* **:** TACITURN **5 :** lacking some usual attribute or accompaniment; *esp* **:** having no means of self-propulsion ‹a ~ barge› **6 a :** lacking intelligence **:** STUPID **b :** showing a lack of intelligence ‹asking ~ questions› **c :** requiring no intelligence ‹~ luck› **7 :** not having the capability to process data ‹a ~ terminal› — compare INTELLIGENT 3a ***syn*** see STUPID — **dumb·ly** \ˈdəm-lē\ *adv* — **dumb·ness** *n*

usage There is evidence that, when applied to persons who cannot speak, *dumb* has come to be considered offensive.

[2]**dumb** *vt* (1607) **:** to make silent **:** DEADEN ‹would lie around, ~*ed* by the drugs —Norman Mailer›

dumb·bell \ˈdəm-ˌbel\ *n* (1785) **1 :** a short bar with weights at each end that is used usu. in pairs for exercise **2 :** a stupid person **:** DUMMY

dumb cane *n* [fr. the fact that chewing it causes the tongue and throat to swell] (1696) **:** DIEFFENBACHIA

dumb down *vt* (1933) **:** to lower the level of difficulty and the intellectual content of (as a textbook); *also* **:** to lower the general level of intelligence in ‹the *dumbing down* of society›

dumb·found *also* **dum·found** \ˌdəm-ˈfau̇nd, ˈdəm-ˌ\ *vt* [*dumb* + *-found* (as in *confound*)] (1653) **:** to confound briefly and usu. with astonishment ***syn*** see PUZZLE — **dumb·found·ing·ly** \ˌdəm-ˈfau̇n-diŋ-lē, ˈdəm-ˌfau̇n-\ *adv*

dumb·head \ˈdəm-ˌhed\ *n* [prob. trans. of G *dummkopf*] (1887) *slang* **:** a stupid person **:** BLOCKHEAD

dumb show *n* (1561) **1 :** a part of a play presented in pantomime **2 :** signs and gestures without words **:** PANTOMIME

dumb·struck \ˈdəm-ˌstrək\ *adj* (1765) **:** made silent by astonishment

dumb·wait·er \ˈdəm-ˌwā-tər, ˌdəm-ˈ\ *n* (1737) **1 :** a portable serving table or stand **2 :** a small elevator used for conveying food and dishes from one story of a building to another

dum·dum \ˈdəm-ˌdəm\ *n* [*Dum Dum,* arsenal near Calcutta, India] (ca. 1889) **:** a bullet (as one with a hollow point) that expands more than usual upon hitting an object

dum–dum \ˈdəm-ˌdəm\ *n* [redupl. of [1]*dumb*] (1928) **:** a stupid person **:** DUMMY

dum·ka \ˈdu̇m-kə\ *n, pl* **dum·ky** \-kē\ [Czech, elegy, fr. Ukrainian, dim. of *duma* narrative folk poem, fr. ORuss] (1895) **:** an Eastern European folk ballad or lament usu. with alternating slow and fast sections

dumm·kopf \ˈdu̇m-ˌkȯpf\ *n* [G, fr. *dumm* stupid + *Kopf* head] (1809) **:** BLOCKHEAD

[1]**dum·my** \ˈdə-mē\ *n, pl* **dummies** [[1]*dumb* + [4]*-y*] (1598) **1 a** *usu offensive* **:** a person who is incapable of speaking **b :** a person who is habitually silent **c :** a stupid person **2 a :** the exposed hand in bridge played by the declarer in addition to his or her own hand **b :** a bridge player whose hand is a dummy **3 :** an imitation, copy, or likeness of something used as a substitute: as **a :** MANNEQUIN **b :** a stuffed figure or cylindrical bag used by football players for tackling and blocking practice **c :** a large puppet usu. having movable features (as mouth and arms) manipulated by a ventriloquist **d** *chiefly Brit* **:** PACIFIER 2 **4 :** one seeming to act independently but in reality controlled by another **5 a :** a mock-up of a proposed publication (as a book or magazine) **b :** a set of pages (as for a newspaper or magazine) with the position of text and artwork indicated for the printer

[2]**dummy** *adj* (1846) **1 a :** having the appearance of being real **:** ARTIFICIAL ‹~ foods in the display case› **b :** existing in name only **:** FICTITIOUS ‹~ corporations› **2 :** apparently acting for oneself while really acting for or at the direction of another ‹a ~ director›

[3]**dummy** *vt* **dum·mied; dum·my·ing** (ca. 1928) **:** to make a dummy of (as a publication) — often used with *up* ‹*dummied* up the front page›

dummy up *vi* (1926) **:** to say nothing **:** CLAM UP

dummy variable *n* (1957) **:** an arbitrary mathematical symbol or variable that can be replaced by another without affecting the value of the expression in which it occurs

du·mor·ti·er·ite \du̇-ˈmȯr-tē-ə-ˌrīt *also* dyu̇-\ *n* [F *dumortiérite,* fr. Eugène *Dumortier* †1876 Fr. paleontologist] (1881) **:** a bright esp. blue mineral consisting of a borosilicate of aluminum

[1]**dump** \ˈdəmp\ *vb* [perh. fr. MD *dompen* to immerse, topple; akin to ON *dumpa* to thump, fall suddenly] (1784) **1 a :** to let fall in or as if in a heap or mass ‹~*ed* his clothes on the bed› **b :** to get rid of unceremoniously or irresponsibly ‹got ~*ed* by his girlfriend› **c :** JETTISON ‹an airplane ~*ing* gasoline› **2** *slang* **:** to knock down **:** BEAT ‹the man rushed out and ~*ed* him —John Corry› **3 :** to sell in quantity at a very low price; *specif* **:** to sell abroad at less than the market price at home **4 :** to copy (data in a computer's internal storage) to an external storage or output device **5 a :** to hit or throw short and softly ‹~ a pass to a running back› ‹~ a bunt down the line› **b :** to hit (a puck) deep into the opponent's zone in ice hockey ~ *vi* **1 :** to fall abruptly **:** PLUNGE **2 :** to dump refuse — **dump on :** to treat disrespectfully; *esp* **:** BELITTLE, BAD-MOUTH

[2]**dump** *n* (1784) **1 a :** an accumulation of refuse and discarded materials **b :** a place where such materials are dumped **2 a :** a quantity of reserve materials accumulated at one place **b :** a place where such materials are stored ⟨ammunition ~⟩ **3 :** a disorderly, slovenly, or objectionable place **4 :** an instance of dumping data stored in a computer **5** *often vulgar* **:** an act of defecation — usu. used with *take*

dump·er \ˈdəm-pər\ *n* (1856) **1 :** one that dumps: as **a :** DUMP TRUCK **b :** a device used for unloading freight cars by tilting or dumping **2 :** a state of collapse, failure, or ruin ⟨the economy is in the ~⟩

dumper truck *n* (1972) *Brit* **:** DUMP TRUCK

dump·ing \ˈdəm-piŋ\ *n* (1857) **1 :** the act of one that dumps; *esp* **:** the selling of goods in quantity at below market price **2 :** the practice of refusing emergency medical care to poor or uninsured patients or of referring them to another hospital without that hospital's consent — called also *patient dumping*

dumping ground *n* (1857) **:** a place to which unwanted people or things are sent

dump·ish \ˈdəm-pish\ *adj* [*dumps*] (1519) **:** SAD, MELANCHOLY

dump·ling \ˈdəmp-liŋ\ *n* [perh. alter. of *lump*] (ca. 1600) **1 a :** a small mass of leavened dough cooked by boiling or steaming **b :** a usu. baked dessert of fruit wrapped in dough **2 :** something soft and rounded like a dumpling; *esp* **:** a short fat person or animal

dumps \ˈdəm(p)s\ *n pl* [prob. fr. D *domp* haze, fr. MD *damp* — more at DAMP] (1529) **:** a gloomy state of mind **:** DESPONDENCY ⟨in the ~⟩

Dump·ster \ˈdəm(p)-stər\ *trademark* — used for a large trash receptacle

dump truck *n* (ca. 1924) **:** an automotive truck for the transportation of bulk material that has a body which tilts to dump its contents

dumpy \ˈdəm-pē\ *adj* **dump·i·er; -est** [E dial. *dump* lump] (1750) **1 :** being short and thick in build **:** SQUAT **2 :** SHABBY, DINGY — **dump·i·ly** \-pə-lē\ *adv* — **dump·i·ness** \-pē-nəs\ *n*

dumpy level *n* (1838) **:** a surveyor's level with a short telescope rigidly fixed and rotating only in a horizontal plane

[1]**dun** \ˈdən\ *adj* [ME, fr. OE *dunn* — more at DUSK] (bef. 12c) **1 a :** having the color dun **b** *of a horse* **:** having a grayish-yellow coat with black mane and tail **2 :** marked by dullness and drabness — **dun·ness** \ˈdən-nəs\ *n*

[2]**dun** *n* (14c) **1 :** a dun horse **2 :** a variable color averaging a nearly neutral slightly brownish dark gray **3 :** a subadult mayfly; *also* **:** an artificial fly tied to imitate such an insect

[3]**dun** *vt* **dunned; dun·ning** [origin unknown] (ca. 1626) **1 :** to make persistent demands upon for payment **2 :** PLAGUE, PESTER

[4]**dun** *n* (1628) **1 :** a person who duns **2 :** an urgent request; *esp* **:** a demand for payment

Dun·can Phyfe \ˌdəŋ-kən-ˈfīf\ *adj* (1926) **:** of, relating to, or constituting furniture designed and built by or in the style of Duncan Phyfe

dunce \ˈdən(t)s\ *n* [John *Duns* Scotus, whose once accepted writings were ridiculed in the 16th cent.] (1570) **:** a slow-witted or stupid person

dunce cap *n* (1840) **:** a conical cap formerly used as a punishment for slow learners at school — called also *dunce's cap*

dun·der·head \ˈdən-dər-ˌhed\ *n* [perh. fr. D *donder* thunder + E *head;* akin to OHG *thonar* thunder — more at THUNDER] (ca. 1625) **:** DUNCE, BLOCKHEAD — **dun·der·head·ed** \ˌdən-dər-ˈhe-dəd\ *adj*

dun·drea·ries \ˌdən-ˈdrir-ēz\ *n pl, often cap* [Lord *Dundreary,* character in the play *Our American Cousin* (1858), by Tom Taylor] (ca. 1922) **:** long flowing sideburns

dune \ˈdün *also* ˈdyün\ *n* [F, fr. OF, fr. MD; akin to OE *dūn* down — more at DOWN] (1790) **:** a hill or ridge of sand piled up by the wind — **dune·like** \-ˌlīk\ *adj*

dune buggy *n* (1956) **:** an off-road motor vehicle with oversize tires for use esp. on sand

dune·land \ˈdün-ˌland\ *n* (1922) **:** an area having many dunes

[1]**dung** \ˈdəŋ\ *n* [ME, fr. OE; akin to ON *dyngja* manure pile] (bef. 12c) **1 :** the feces of an animal **:** MANURE **2 :** something repulsive — **dungy** \ˈdəŋ-ē\ *adj*

[2]**dung** *vt* (bef. 12c) **:** to fertilize or dress with manure ~ *vi* **:** DEFECATE

dun·ga·ree \ˌdəŋ-gə-ˈrē, ˈdəŋ-gə-ˌ\ *n* [Hindi *dũgrī* & Urdu *dungrī*] (1673) **1 :** a heavy coarse durable cotton twill woven from colored yarns; *specif* **:** blue denim **2** *pl* **:** clothes made usu. of blue denim — **dun·ga·reed** \-ˈrēd, -ˌrēd\ *adj*

dung beetle *n* (ca. 1634) **:** a beetle (as a tumblebug) that rolls balls of dung in which to lay eggs and on which the larvae feed

Dunge·ness crab \ˌdən-jə-ˌnes-\ *n* [*Dungeness,* village on the Strait of Juan de Fuca, Washington] (1925) **:** a large edible crab (*Cancer magister*) of the Pacific coast of No. America from Alaska to California

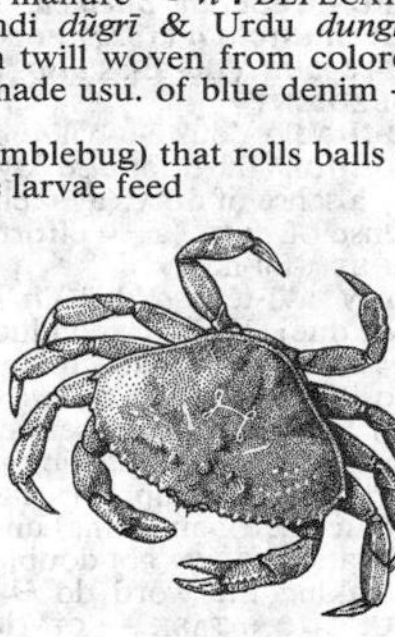

Dungeness crab

dun·geon \ˈdən-jən\ *n* [ME *dongeon, donjon,* fr. AF *donjun,* fr. VL **domnion-, domnio* keep, mastery, fr. L *dominus* lord — more at DOMINATE] (14c) **1 :** DONJON **2 :** a dark usu. underground prison or vault

dung·hill \ˈdəŋ-ˌhil\ *n* (14c) **1 :** a heap of dung **2 :** something (as a situation or condition) that is repulsive or degraded

du·nite \ˈdü-ˌnīt, ˈdə-\ *n* [Mt. *Dun,* New Zealand] (ca. 1868) **:** a granular igneous rock consisting chiefly of olivine — **du·nit·ic** \dü-ˈni-tik, ˌdə-\ *adj*

[1]**dunk** \ˈdəŋk\ *vb* [PaG *dunke,* fr. MHG *dunken,* fr. OHG *dunkōn* — more at TINGE] *vt* (1919) **1 :** to dip (as a piece of bread) into a beverage while eating **2 :** to dip or submerge temporarily in liquid **3 :** to throw (a basketball) into the basket from above the rim ~ *vi* **1 :** to submerge oneself in water **2 :** to make a dunk shot in basketball

[2]**dunk** *n* (ca. 1944) **:** the act or action of dunking; *esp* **:** DUNK SHOT

dunk·er \ˈdəŋ-kər\ *n* [[1]*dunk*] (1919) **:** one that dunks; *esp* **:** a basketball player who makes dunk shots

Dun·ker \ˈdəŋ-kər\ *or* **Dun·kard** \-kərd\ *n* [PaG *Dunker,* fr. *dunke*] (1744) **:** a member of the Church of the Brethren or any of several other orig. German Baptist denominations practicing trine immersion and love feasts and refusing to take oaths or to perform military service

Dun·kirk \ˈdən-ˌkərk, ˌdən-ˈ\ *n* [*Dunkirk* or *Dunkerque,* France, scene of the evacuation of Allied forces in 1940] (1941) **1 :** a retreat to avoid total defeat **2 :** a crisis situation that requires a desperate last effort to forestall certain failure ⟨a ~ for U.S. foreign policy —*Time*⟩

dunk shot *n* (ca. 1961) **:** a shot in basketball made by jumping high into the air and throwing the ball down through the basket

dun·lin \ˈdən-lən\ *n, pl* **dunlins** *or* **dunlin** [[1]*dun* + *-lin* (alter. of *-ling*)] (ca. 1532) **:** a small widely distributed sandpiper (*Calidris alpina*) largely cinnamon to rusty brown above and white below

Dun·lop \ˈdən-ˌläp, ˌdən-ˈ\ *n* [*Dunlop,* Ayrshire, Scotland] (ca. 1780) **:** a Scottish cheese similar to cheddar

dun·nage \ˈdə-nij\ *n* [origin unknown] (15c) **1 :** loose materials used to support and protect cargo in a ship's hold; *also* **:** padding in a shipping container **2 :** BAGGAGE

duo \ˈdü-(ˌ)ō *also* ˈdyü-\ *n, pl* **du·os** [It, fr. L, two — more at TWO] (1590) **1 :** DUET **2 :** PAIR 2

duo- *comb form* [L *duo*] **:** two ⟨*duo*logue⟩

duo·de·cil·lion \ˌdü-ō-di-ˈsil-yən, ˌdyü-\ *n, often attrib* [L *duodec*im twelve + E *-illion* (as in *million*)] (1875) — see NUMBER table

duo·dec·i·mal \ˌdü-ə-ˈde-sə-məl, ˌdyü-\ *adj* [L *duodecim* — more at DOZEN] (1663) **:** of, relating to, or proceeding by twelve or the scale of twelves — **duodecimal** *n*

duo·dec·i·mo \-ˌmō\ *n, pl* **-mos** [L, abl. of *duodecimus* twelfth, fr. *duodecim*] (1658) **:** TWELVEMO

du·o·de·num \ˌdü-ə-ˈdē-nəm, du̇-ˈä-də-nəm *also* (ˌ)dyü-\ *n, pl* **-de·na** \-ˈdē-nə, -də-nə\ *or* **-denums** [ME, fr. ML, fr. L *duodeni* twelve each, fr. *duodecim* twelve; fr. its length, about 12 fingers' breadth] (14c) **:** the first part of the small intestine extending from the pylorus to the jejunum — **du·o·de·nal** \-ˈdē-nᵊl, -də-nəl\ *adj*

duo·logue \ˈdü-ə-ˌlȯg, -ˌläg *also* ˈdyü-\ *n* (1864) **:** a dialogue between two persons

duo·mo \ˈdwȯ-(ˌ)mō\ *n, pl* **duomos** [It, fr. L *domus* house — more at DOME] (1549) **:** CATHEDRAL

du·op·o·ly \du̇-ˈä-pə-lē *also* dyu̇-\ *n, pl* **-lies** [*duo-* + *-poly* (as in *monopoly*)] (1920) **1 :** an oligopoly limited to two sellers **2 :** preponderant influence or control by two political powers — **du·op·o·lis·tic** \-ˌä-pə-ˈlis-tik\ *adj*

[1]**dup** \ˈdəp\ *vt* [contr. of *do up*] (1547) *archaic* **:** OPEN

[2]**dup** *abbr* **1** duplex **2** duplicate

[1]**dupe** \ˈdüp *also* ˈdyüp\ *n* [F, fr. MF *duppe,* prob. alter. of *huppe* hoopoe] (1681) **:** one that is easily deceived or cheated **:** FOOL

[2]**dupe** *vt* **duped; dup·ing** (1704) **:** to make a dupe of — **dup·er** *n*

[3]**dupe** *n* (ca. 1900) **:** DUPLICATE — **dupe** *vb*

dup·ery \ˈdü-pə-rē *also* ˈdyü-\ *n, pl* **-er·ies** (1759) **1 :** the condition of being duped **2 :** the act or practice of duping

du·ple \ˈdü-pəl *also* ˈdyü-\ *adj* [L *duplus* double — more at DOUBLE] (15c) **1 :** having two elements **2 a :** marked by two or a multiple of two beats per measure of music ⟨~ time⟩ **b** *of rhythm* **:** consisting of a meter based on disyllabic feet

[1]**du·plex** \ˈdü-ˌpleks *also* ˈdyü-\ *adj* [L, fr. *duo* two + *-plex* -fold — more at TWO, -FOLD] (1567) **1 a :** having two principal elements or parts **:** DOUBLE, TWOFOLD **b :** having two complementary polynucleotide strands of DNA or of DNA and RNA **2 :** allowing telecommunication in opposite directions simultaneously

[2]**duplex** *vt* (1833) **:** to make duplex

[3]**duplex** *n* (1922) **:** something duplex: as **a :** a 2-family house **b :** DUPLEX APARTMENT **c :** a duplex molecule of DNA or of RNA and DNA

duplex apartment *n* (ca. 1925) **:** an apartment having rooms on two floors

du·plex·er \ˈdü-ˌplek-sər *also* ˈdyü-\ *n* (ca. 1932) **:** a switching device that permits alternate transmission and reception with the same radio antenna

[1]**du·pli·cate** \ˈdü-pli-kət *also* ˈdyü-\ *adj* [ME, fr. L *duplicatus,* pp. of *duplicare* to double, fr. *duplic-, duplex*] (15c) **1 :** consisting of or existing in two corresponding or identical parts or examples ⟨~ invoices⟩ **2 :** being the same as another ⟨~ copies⟩

[2]**du·pli·cate** \ˈdü-pli-ˌkāt *also* ˈdyü-\ *vb* **-cat·ed; -cat·ing** *vt* (15c) **1 :** to make double or twofold **2 a :** to make a copy of ⟨a cell ~*s* itself when it divides⟩ **b :** to produce something equal to ⟨trying to ~ last year's success⟩ **c :** to do over or again often needlessly ⟨*duplicated* effort⟩ ~ *vi* **:** to become duplicated; *also* **:** REPEAT — **du·pli·ca·tive** \-ˌkā-tiv\ *adj*

[3]**du·pli·cate** \-kət\ *n* (1532) **1 a :** either of two things exactly alike and usu. produced at the same time or by the same process **b :** an additional copy of something (as a book or stamp) already in a collection **2 :** one that resembles or corresponds to another **:** COUNTERPART **3 :** two identical copies — used in the phrase *in duplicate* ***syn*** see REPRODUCTION

duplicate bridge *n* (1926) **:** a tournament form of contract bridge in which identical deals are played in order to compare individual scores

du·pli·ca·tion \ˌdü-pli-ˈkā-shən *also* ˌdyü-\ *n* (15c) **1 a :** the act or process of duplicating **b :** the quality or state of being duplicated **2 :** DUPLICATE, COUNTERPART **3 :** a part of a chromosome in which the genetic material is repeated; *also* **:** the process of forming a duplication

du·pli·ca·tor \ˈdü-pli-ˌkā-tər *also* ˈdyü-\ *n* (1893) **:** one that duplicates; *specif* **:** a machine for making copies of graphic matter

du·plic·i·tous \du̇-ˈpli-sə-təs *also* dyu̇-\ *adj* (1928) **:** marked by duplicity **:** deceptive in words or action — **du·plic·i·tous·ly** *adv*

du·plic·i·ty \du̇-ˈpli-sə-tē *also* dyu̇-\ *n, pl* **-ties** [ME *duplicite,* fr. MF, fr. LL *duplicitat-, duplicitas,* fr. L *duplex*] (15c) **1 :** contradictory doubleness of thought, speech, or action; *esp* **:** the belying of one's true intentions by deceptive words or action **2 :** the quality or state of being double or twofold **3 :** the technically incorrect use of two or more distinct items (as claims, charges, or defenses) in a single legal action

du·ra·ble \ˈdu̇r-ə-bəl *also* ˈdyu̇r-\ *adj* [ME, fr. AF, fr. L *durabilis,* fr. *durare* to last — more at DURING] (14c) **:** able to exist for a long time without significant deterioration; *also* **:** designed to be durable ⟨~ goods⟩ ***syn*** see LASTING — **du·ra·bil·i·ty** \ˌdu̇r-ə-ˈbi-lə-tē, ˌdyu̇r-\ *n* — **du·ra·ble·ness** \ˈdu̇r-ə-bəl-nəs, ˈdyu̇r-\ *n* — **du·ra·bly** \-blē\ *adv*

durable press *n* (1966) : PERMANENT PRESS
du·ra·bles \ˈdu̇r-ə-bəlz *also* ˈdyu̇r-\ *n pl* (1941) : consumer goods (as vehicles and household appliances) that are typically used repeatedly over a period of years — called also *durable goods*
du·ral·u·min \du̇-ˈral-yə-mən *also* dyu̇-\ *n* [fr. *Duralumin,* a trademark] (1910) : a light strong alloy of aluminum, copper, manganese, and magnesium
du·ra ma·ter \ˈdu̇r-ə-ˌmā-tər, ˈdyu̇r-, -ˌmä-\ *n* [ME, fr. ML, lit., hard mother] (14c) : the tough fibrous membrane that envelops the brain and spinal cord external to the arachnoid and pia mater
du·rance \ˈdu̇r-ən(t)s *also* ˈdyu̇r-\ *n* [ME, duration, fr. AF, fr. *durer* to last fr. L *durare*] (15c) **1** *archaic* : ENDURANCE **2** : restraint by or as if by physical force — usu. used in the phrase *durance vile*
du·ra·tion \du̇-ˈrā-shən *also* dyu̇-\ *n* (14c) **1** : continuance in time **2** : the time during which something exists or lasts
du·ra·tive \ˈdu̇r-ə-tiv, ˈdyu̇r-\ *adj* (1889) : CONTINUATIVE — **durative** *n*
dur·bar \ˈdər-ˌbär, ˌdər-ˈ\ *n* [Hindi & Urdu *darbār,* fr. Pers, fr. *dar* door + *bār* admission, audience] (1609) **1** : court held by an Indian prince **2** : a formal reception held by an Indian prince or an African ruler
du·ress \du̇-ˈres *also* dyu̇-\ *n* [ME *duresse,* fr. AF *duresce* hardness, severity, fr. L *duritia,* fr. *durus*] (15c) **1** : forcible restraint or restriction **2** : compulsion by threat; *specif* : unlawful constraint
Dur·ham \ˈdər-əm, ˈdə-rəm, ˈdu̇r-əm\ *n* [County *Durham,* England] (1810) : SHORTHORN
Durham Rule *n* [Monte *Durham,* 20th cent. Am. litigant] (1955) : a legal hypothesis under which a person is not judged responsible for a criminal act that is attributed to a mental disease or defect
du·ri·an \ˈdu̇r-ē-ən, -ē-ˌän *also* ˈdyu̇r-\ *n* [Malay] (1588) **1** : a large oval tasty but foul-smelling fruit with a prickly rind **2** : an East Indian tree (*Durio zibethinus*) of the silk-cotton family that bears durians
dur·ing \ˈdu̇r-iŋ *also* ˈdyu̇r-\ *prep* [ME, fr. prp. of *duren* to last, fr. AF *durer,* fr. L *durare* to harden, endure, last, fr. *durus* hard; perh. akin to Skt *dāru* wood — more at TREE] (14c) **1** : throughout the duration of ⟨swims every day ~ the summer⟩ **2** : at a point in the course of ⟨was offered a job ~ a visit to the capital⟩
dur·mast oak \ˈdər-ˌmast-\ *n* [perh. alter. of *dun mast,* fr. [1]*dun* + *mast*] (1791) : a European oak (*Quercus petraea*) valued esp. for its dark heavy tough elastic wood and for its tannin-rich bark
durn *var of* DARN
du·ro \ˈdu̇r-(ˌ)ō\ *n, pl* **duros** [Sp, short for *peso duro* hard peso] (1832) : a Spanish or Spanish American peso or silver dollar
du·roc \ˈdu̇r-ˌäk *also* ˈdyu̇r-\ *n, often cap* [*Duroc,* 19th cent. Am. stallion] (1883) : any of a breed of large vigorous red American hogs
du·rom·e·ter \du̇-ˈrä-mə-tər *also* dyu̇-\ *n* [L *durus* hard] (ca. 1879) : an instrument for measuring hardness
dur·ra *also* **du·ra** \ˈdu̇r-ə\ *n* [Ar *dhura*] (1798) : any of several grain sorghums widely grown in warm dry regions
durst \ˈdərst\ *archaic & dial past of* DARE
du·rum wheat \ˈdu̇r-əm-, ˈdyu̇r-, ˈdər-əm-, ˈdə-rəm-\ *n* [NL *durum,* fr. L, neut. of *durus* hard] (ca. 1903) : a wheat (*Triticum durum*) that yields a glutenous flour used esp. in pasta — called also *durum*
[1]**dusk** \ˈdəsk\ *adj* [ME *dosk,* alter. of OE *dox;* akin to L *fuscus* dark brown, OE *dunn* dun, *dūst* dust] (13c) : DUSKY
[2]**dusk** *vi* (13c) : to become dark ~ *vt* : to make dark or gloomy
[3]**dusk** *n* (1622) **1** : the darker part of twilight esp. at night **2** : darkness or semidarkness caused by the shutting out of light
dusky \ˈdəs-kē\ *adj* **dusk·i·er; -est** (1558) **1** : somewhat dark in color; *specif* : having dark skin **2** : marked by slight or deficient light : SHADOWY — **dusk·i·ly** \-kə-lē\ *adv* — **dusk·i·ness** \-kē-nəs\ *n*
[1]**dust** \ˈdəst\ *n* [ME, fr. OE *dūst;* akin to OHG *tunst* storm, and prob. to L *fumus* smoke — more at FUME] (bef. 12c) **1** : fine particles of matter (as of earth) **2** : the particles into which something disintegrates **3 a** : something worthless **b** : a state of humiliation **4 a** : the earth esp. as a place of burial **b** : the surface of the ground **5 a** : a cloud of dust **b** : CONFUSION, DISTURBANCE **6** *archaic* : a single particle (as of earth) **7** *Brit* : refuse ready for collection — **dust·less** \-ləs\ *adj* — **dust·like** \-ˌlīk\ *adj*
[2]**dust** *vt* (1530) **1** *archaic* : to make dusty **2** : to make free of dust ⟨~ the living room⟩ **3 a** : to sprinkle with fine particles ⟨a cake ~*ed* with sugar⟩ **b** : to sprinkle in the form of dust **4** : to throw a fastball close to (a batter) : BRUSH BACK — often used with *off* **5** : to defeat badly (as in a race) ~ *vi* **1** *of a bird* : to work dust into the feathers **2** : to remove dust **3** : to give off dust
dust·bin \ˈdəs(t)-ˌbin\ *n* (1848) **1** *Brit* : a can for trash or garbage **2** : DUSTHEAP 2
dust bowl *n* (1936) : a region that suffers from prolonged droughts and dust storms
dust bunny *n* (1966) : an aggregate of dust ⟨swept the *dust bunnies* from under the bed⟩
dust·cov·er \-ˌkə-vər\ *n* (1899) **1** : a cover (as of cloth or plastic) used to protect furniture or equipment from dust **2** : DUST JACKET
dust devil *n* (1888) : a small whirlwind containing sand or dust
dust·er \ˈdəs-tər\ *n* (1576) **1** : one that removes dust **2 a** (1) : a long lightweight overgarment to protect clothing from dust (2) : a long coat cut like a duster — called also *duster coat* **b** : a dress-length housecoat **3** : one that scatters fine particles; *specif* : a device for applying insecticidal or fungicidal dusts to crops **4** : DUST STORM
dust·heap \ˈdəst-ˌ(h)ēp\ *n* (1599) **1** : a pile of refuse **2** : a category of forgotten items ⟨the ~ of history —*New Republic*⟩
dust jacket *n* (1926) : a paper cover for a book
dust·man \ˈdəs(t)-mən\ *n* (1707) *Brit* : a collector of trash or garbage
dust mite *n* (1969) : any of various mites (esp. family Pyroglyphidae) commonly found in house dust — compare HOUSE-DUST MITE
dust mop *n* (1953) : DRY MOP
dust off *vt* (1940) : to bring out or back to use again ⟨*dusted off* his golf clubs when he retired⟩
dust·pan \ˈdəs(t)-ˌpan\ *n* (1783) : a shovel-shaped pan for sweepings
dust storm *n* (1879) **1** : a dust-laden whirlwind that moves across an arid region and is usu. associated with hot dry air and marked by high electrical tension **2** : strong winds bearing clouds of dust
dust-up \ˈdəst-ˌəp\ *n* (1897) : ROW, FIGHT
dust wrapper *n* (1932) : DUST JACKET
dusty \ˈdəs-tē\ *adj* **dust·i·er; -est** (13c) **1** : covered or abounding with dust **2** : consisting of dust : POWDERY **3** : resembling dust **4** : lacking vitality : DRY ⟨~ scholarship⟩ **5** *Brit* : UNSATISFACTORY — used esp. in the phrases *dusty answer* and *not so dusty* — **dust·i·ly** \ˈdəs-tə-lē\ *adv* — **dust·i·ness** \-tē-nəs\ *n*
dusty miller *n* (ca. 1825) : any of several plants having ashy-gray or white tomentose leaves; *esp* : an herbaceous artemisia (*Artemisia stelleriana*) with grayish foliage found esp. along the eastern coast of the U.S.
dutch \ˈdəch\ *adv, often cap* (1914) : with each person paying his or her own way ⟨went ~ to the movies⟩
[1]**Dutch** \ˈdəch\ *adj* [ME *Duch,* fr. MD *duutsch;* akin to OHG *diutisc* German, OE *thēod* nation, Goth *thiudisko* as a gentile, *thiuda* people, Oscan *touto* city] (14c) **1 a** *archaic* : of, relating to, or in any of the Germanic languages of Germany, Austria, Switzerland, and the Low Countries **b** : of, relating to, or in the Dutch of the Netherlands **2 a** *archaic* : of or relating to the Germanic peoples of Germany, Austria, Switzerland, and the Low Countries **b** : of or relating to the Netherlands or its inhabitants **c** : [2]GERMAN **3** : of or relating to the Pennsylvania Dutch or their language — **Dutch·ly** *adv*
[2]**Dutch** *n* (14c) **1 a** *archaic* (1) : any of the Germanic languages of Germany, Austria, Switzerland, and the Low Countries (2) : GERMAN 3 **b** : the Germanic language of the Netherlands and Belgium **2 Dutch** *pl* **a** *archaic* : the Germanic peoples of Germany, Austria, Switzerland, and the Low Countries **b** : GERMANS 2a, b **c** : the people of the Netherlands **3** : PENNSYLVANIA DUTCH **4** : DANDER ⟨her ~ is up⟩ **5** : DISFAVOR, TROUBLE ⟨in ~ with the boss⟩
Dutch cheese *n* (1828) *chiefly Northern* : COTTAGE CHEESE
Dutch clover *n* (1765) : WHITE CLOVER
Dutch Colonial *adj* (1922) : characterized by a gambrel roof with overhanging eaves
Dutch courage *n* (1807) : courage artificially stimulated esp. by drink; *also* : drink taken for courage
Dutch door *n* (ca. 1890) : a door divided horizontally so that the lower or upper part can be shut separately
Dutch elm disease *n* (1927) : a disease of elms caused by an ascomycetous fungus (*Ceratocystis ulmi*) and characterized by yellowing of the foliage, defoliation, and death
Dutch hoe *n* (ca. 1750) : SCUFFLE HOE
dutch·man \ˈdəch-mən\ *n* (14c) **1** *cap* **a** *archaic* : a member of any of the Germanic peoples of Germany, Austria, Switzerland, and the Low Countries **b** : a native or inhabitant of the Netherlands **c** : a person of Dutch descent **d** : GERMAN 2a, b **2** : a device for hiding or counteracting structural defects
Dutch·man's–breech·es \ˌdəch-mənz-ˈbri-chəz\ *n pl but sing or pl in constr* (1837) : a spring-flowering herb (*Dicentra cucullaria*) of the fumitory family occurring in the eastern U.S. and having finely divided leaves and cream-white double-spurred flowers
Dutchman's–pipe \-ˈpīp\ *n, pl* **Dutchman's–pipes** \-ˈpīps\ (1845) : a vine (*Aristolochia durior* syn. *A. macrophylla*) of the birthwort family with large leaves and early summer flowers having the tube of the calyx curved like the bowl of a pipe

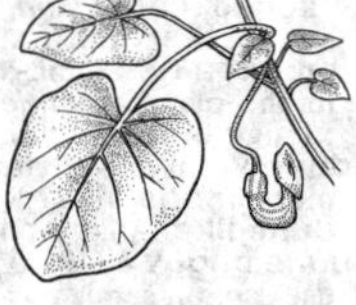

Dutchman's-pipe

Dutch oven *n* (1769) **1** : a metal shield for roasting before an open fire **2** : a brick oven in which cooking is done by the preheated walls **3 a** : a cast-iron kettle with a tight cover that is used for baking in an open fire **b** : a heavy pot with a tight-fitting domed cover
Dutch roll *n* (1916) : a combination of directional and lateral oscillation of an airplane
[1]**dutch treat** *n, often cap D* (1887) : a meal or other entertainment for which each person pays his or her own way
[2]**dutch treat** *adv, often cap D* (1942) : DUTCH ⟨go *dutch treat*⟩
Dutch uncle *n* (1837) : one who admonishes sternly and bluntly
du·te·ous \ˈdü-tē-əs *also* ˈdyü-\ *adj* [irreg. fr. *duty*] (1592) : DUTIFUL, OBEDIENT
du·ti·able \ˈdü-tē-ə-bəl *also* ˈdyü-\ *adj* (1770) : subject to a duty
du·ti·ful \ˈdü-ti-fəl *also* ˈdyü-\ *adj* (1552) **1** : filled with or motivated by a sense of duty ⟨a ~ child⟩ **2** : proceeding from or expressive of a sense of duty ⟨a ~ effort⟩ — **du·ti·ful·ly** \-f(ə-)lē\ *adv* — **du·ti·ful·ness** \-fəl-nəs\ *n*
[1]**du·ty** \ˈdü-tē *also* ˈdyü-\ *n, pl* **duties** [ME *duete,* fr. AF *deueté, dueté,* fr. *deu* due] (13c) **1** : conduct due to parents and superiors : RESPECT **2 a** : obligatory tasks, conduct, service, or functions that arise from one's position (as in life or in a group) **b** (1) : assigned service or business (2) : active military service (3) : a period of being on duty **3 a** : a moral or legal obligation **b** : the force of moral obligation **4** : TAX; *esp* : a tax on imports **5 a** : WORK 1a **b** (1) : the service required (as of an electric machine) under specified conditions (2) : functional application : USE ⟨got double ~ out of the trip⟩ (3) : use as a substitute ⟨making the word do ~ for the thing —Edward Sapir⟩ ***syn*** see FUNCTION, TASK — **off duty** : free from assignment or responsibility — **on duty** : engaged in or responsible for an assigned task or duty
[2]**duty** *adj* (1806) **1** : done as a duty **2** : being on duty : assigned to specified tasks or functions ⟨the ~ officer⟩
duty–free \ˌdü-tē-ˈfrē, ˌdyü-, ˈdü-tē-ˌ\ *adj or adv* (1689) **1** : without payment of customs duties : free from duties ⟨imported ~⟩ ⟨~ goods⟩ **2** : relating to or selling duty-free goods ⟨a ~ shop⟩
du·um·vir \du̇-ˈəm-vər *also* dyu̇-\ *n* [L, fr. *duum* (gen. of *duo* two) + *vir* man] (1600) **1** : one of two Roman officers or magistrates constituting a board or court **2** : one of two people jointly holding power — **du·um·vi·rate** \-və-rət\ *n*
du·vet \d(y)ü-ˈvā, ˈd(y)ü-ˌ\ *n* [F] (1758) : COMFORTER 2b
duve·tyn \ˈdü-və-ˌtēn, ˈdyü-, ˈdəv-ˌtēn\ *n* [F *duvetine,* fr. *duvet* down, fr. MF, alter. of **dumet,* dim. of OF *dun, dum* down, fr. ON *dūnn* — more at DOWN] (1913) : a smooth lustrous velvety fabric
dux·elles \ˌdük-ˈsel, (ˌ)dü-ˈsel\ *n* [Louis Chalon du Blé, Marquis *d'Uxelles* †1658 Fr. nobleman] (1877) : a garnish or stuffing made esp. of finely chopped sautéed mushrooms
DV *abbr* **1** [L *Deo volente*] God willing **2** Douay Version

DVD \ˌdē-(ˌ)vē-ˈdē\ *n* [*d*igital *v*ideo *d*isc] (1993) **:** a high-capacity optical disk format; *also* **:** an optical disk using such a format and containing esp. a video recording (as a movie) or computer data

DVM *abbr* doctor of veterinary medicine

Dvor·ak \də-ˈvȯr-ak\ *n, often attrib* [August *Dvorak* †1975 Am. educator] (1983) **:** a typing keyboard with frequently used letters placed centrally — compare QWERTY

DVR *abbr* digital video recorder

DW *abbr* **1** deadweight **2** delayed weather **3** distilled water **4** dust wrapper

[1]**dwarf** \ˈdwȯrf\ *n, pl* **dwarfs** \ˈdwȯrfs\ *also* **dwarves** \ˈdwȯrvz\ *often attrib* [ME *dwerg, dwerf,* fr. OE *dweorg, dweorh;* akin to OHG *twerg* dwarf] (bef. 12c) **1 a :** a person of unusually small stature; *esp* **:** one whose bodily proportions are abnormal **b :** an insignificant person ⟨a literary ∼⟩ **2 :** an animal or plant much below normal size **3 :** a small legendary manlike being who is usu. misshapen and ugly and skilled as a craftsman **4 :** a star (as the sun) of ordinary or low luminosity and relatively small mass and size — **dwarf·ish** \ˈdwȯr-fish\ *adj* — **dwarf·ish·ly** *adv* — **dwarf·ish·ness** *n* — **dwarf·like** \ˈdwȯrf-ˌlīk\ *adj* — **dwarf·ness** \ˈdwȯrf-nəs\ *n*

[2]**dwarf** *vt* (ca. 1626) **1 :** to restrict the growth of **:** STUNT **2 :** to cause to appear smaller or to seem inferior ⟨has ∼*ed* the achievements of her predecessors⟩ ∼ *vi* **:** to become smaller

[3]**dwarf** *adj* (1597) *of a plant* **:** low-growing in habit ⟨∼*er* forms of citrus⟩

dwarf·ism \ˈdwȯr-ˌfi-zəm\ *n* (1865) **:** the condition of stunted growth

dwarf planet *n* (1993) **:** a celestial body that orbits the sun and has a spherical shape but is too small to disturb other objects from its orbit

dweeb \ˈdwēb\ *n* [origin unknown] (1964) *slang* **:** an unattractive, insignificant, or inept person — **dweeb·ish** \ˈdwē-bish\ *adj, slang* — **dweeby** \-bē\ *adj, slang*

dwell \ˈdwel\ *vi* **dwelled** \ˈdweld, ˈdwelt\ *or* **dwelt** \ˈdwelt\; **dwelling** [ME, fr. OE *dwellan* to go astray, hinder; akin to OHG *twellen* to tarry] (13c) **1 :** to remain for a time **2 a :** to live as a resident **b :** EXIST, LIE **3 a :** to keep the attention directed — used with *on* or *upon* ⟨tried not to ∼ on my fears⟩ **b :** to speak or write insistently — used with *on* or *upon* ⟨reporters ∼*ing* on the recent scandal⟩ — **dwell·er** *n*

dwell·ing *n* (14c) **:** a shelter (as a house) in which people live

DWI \ˌdē-ˌdə-bəl-(ˌ)yü-ˈī\ *n* [*d*riving *w*hile *i*ntoxicated] (1969) **:** DUI

dwin·dle \ˈdwin-dᵊl\ *vb* **dwin·dled; dwin·dling** \-(d)liŋ, -dᵊl-iŋ\ [prob. freq. of *dwine* to waste away, fr. ME, fr. OE *dwīnan;* akin to ON *dvīna* to pine away, *deyja* to die — more at DIE] *vi* (1596) **:** to become steadily less **:** SHRINK ∼ *vt* **:** to make steadily less *syn* see DECREASE

dwt *abbr* **1** deadweight ton **2** pennyweight

DX \(ˌ)dē-ˈeks\ *n* (ca. 1924) **:** DISTANCE — used of long-distance radio transmission

DXA *abbr* dual-energy X-ray absorptiometry

dy *abbr* **1** delivery **2** deputy **3** duty

Dy *symbol* dysprosium

dy- *or* **dyo-** *comb form* [LL, fr. Gk, fr. *dyo* — more at TWO] **:** two ⟨*dy*archy⟩

dy·ad \ˈdī-ˌad, -əd\ *n* [LL *dyad-, dyas,* fr. Gk, fr. *dyo*] (1675) **1 :** PAIR; *specif* **:** two individuals (as husband and wife) maintaining a sociologically significant relationship **2 :** a meiotic chromosome after separation of the two homologous members of a tetrad **3 :** a mathematical operator indicated by writing the symbols of two vectors without a dot or cross between (as AB) — **dy·ad·ic** \dī-ˈa-dik\ *adj* — **dy·ad·i·cal·ly** \-di-k(ə-)lē\ *adv*

dy·ad·ic \dī-ˈa-dik\ *n* (1884) **:** a mathematical expression formed by addition or subtraction of dyads

Dyak *var of* DAYAK

dy·ar·chy *also* **di·ar·chy** \ˈdī-ˌär-kē\ *n, pl* **-chies** (1640) **:** a government in which power is vested in two rulers or authorities

dyb·buk \ˈdi-bək\ *n, pl* **dyb·bu·kim** \ˌdi-bu̇-ˈkēm\ *also* **dybbuks** [Yiddish *dibek,* fr. LHeb *dibbūq*] (ca. 1903) **:** a wandering soul believed in Jewish folklore to enter and control a living body until exorcised by a religious rite

[1]**dye** \ˈdī\ *n* [ME *dehe,* fr. OE *dēah, dēag*] (bef. 12c) **1 :** color from dyeing **2 :** a soluble or insoluble coloring matter

[2]**dye** *vb* **dyed; dye·ing** *vt* (bef. 12c) **1 :** to impart a new and often permanent color to esp. by impregnating with a dye **2 :** to impart (a color) by dyeing ∼ *vi* **:** to take up or impart color in dyeing — **dye·abil·i·ty** \ˌdī-ə-ˈbi-lə-tē\ *n* — **dye·able** \ˈdī-ə-bəl\ *adj* — **dy·er** \ˈdī(-ə)r\ *n*

dyed–in–the–wool \ˌdīd-ᵊn-t͟hə-ˈwu̇l\ *adj* (1580) **:** THOROUGHGOING, UNCOMPROMISING ⟨a ∼ conservative⟩

dye·stuff \ˈdī-ˌstəf\ *n* (1685) **:** DYE 2

dye·wood \-ˌwu̇d\ *n* (1699) **:** a wood (as logwood or fustic) from which coloring matter is extracted for dyeing

dying *pres part of* DIE

[1]**dyke** *chiefly Brit var of* DIKE

[2]**dyke** *also* **dike** \ˈdīk\ *n* [origin unknown] (1931) *often disparaging* **:** LESBIAN — **dykey** \ˈdī-kē\ *adj, often disparaging*

dynam *abbr* dynamics

[1]**dy·nam·ic** \dī-ˈna-mik\ *adj* [F *dynamique,* fr. Gk *dynamikos* powerful, fr. *dynamis* power, fr. *dynasthai* to be able] (1799) **1** *also* **dy·nam·i·cal** \-mi-kəl\ **a :** of or relating to physical force or energy **b :** of or relating to dynamics **2 a :** marked by usu. continuous and productive activity or change **b :** ENERGETIC, FORCEFUL ⟨a ∼ personality⟩ **3** *of random-access memory* **:** requiring periodic refreshment of charge in order to retain data — **dy·nam·i·cal·ly** \-mi-k(ə-)lē\ *adv*

[2]**dynamic** *n* (1868) **1 :** a dynamic force **2 :** DYNAMICS 2; *also* **:** an underlying cause of change or growth

dynamic range *n* (1917) **:** the ratio of the strongest to the weakest sound intensity that can be transmitted or reproduced by an audio or broadcasting system

dy·nam·ics \dī-ˈna-miks\ *n pl but sing or pl in constr* (ca. 1789) **1 :** a branch of mechanics that deals with forces and their relation primarily to the motion but sometimes also to the equilibrium of bodies **2 :** a pattern or process of change, growth, or activity ⟨population ∼⟩ **3 :** variation and contrast in force or intensity (as in music)

dy·na·mism \ˈdī-nə-ˌmi-zəm\ *n* (ca. 1857) **1 a :** a theory that all phenomena (as matter or motion) can be explained as manifestations of force — compare MECHANISM **b :** DYNAMICS 2 **2 :** a dynamic or expansionist quality — **dy·na·mist** \-mist\ *n* — **dy·na·mis·tic** \ˌdī-nə-ˈmis-tik\ *adj*

[1]**dy·na·mite** \ˈdī-nə-ˌmīt\ *n* [ISV *dynam-* (fr. Gk *dynamis* power) + [1]*-ite*] (1867) **1 :** an explosive that is made of nitroglycerin absorbed in a porous material and that often contains ammonium nitrate or cellulose nitrate; *also* **:** an explosive (as a mixture of ammonium nitrate and nitrocellulose) that contains no nitroglycerin **2 :** one that has a powerful effect ⟨an actress who's ∼ at the box office⟩; *also* **:** something that has great potential to cause trouble or conflict ⟨an issue regarded as political ∼⟩ — **dy·na·mit·ic** \ˌdī-nə-ˈmi-tik\ *adj*

[2]**dynamite** *vt* **-mit·ed; -mit·ing** (1881) **1 :** to blow up with dynamite **2 :** to cause the failure or destruction of — **dy·na·mit·er** *n*

[3]**dynamite** *adj* (1922) **:** TERRIFIC, WONDERFUL ⟨a ∼ performance⟩

dy·na·mo \ˈdī-nə-ˌmō\ *n, pl* **-mos** [short for *dynamoelectric machine*] (1882) **1 :** GENERATOR 1b **2 :** a forceful energetic individual

dy·na·mom·e·ter \ˌdī-nə-ˈmä-mə-tər\ *n* [F *dynamomètre,* fr. Gk *dynamis* power + F *-mètre* -meter] (1810) **1 :** an instrument for measuring mechanical force **2 :** an apparatus for measuring mechanical power (as of an engine) — **dy·na·mo·met·ric** \-mō-ˈme-trik\ *adj* — **dy·na·mom·e·try** \-ˈmä-mə-trē\ *n*

dy·na·mo·tor \ˈdī-nə-ˌmō-tər\ *n* [*dyna*mo + *motor*] (1899) **:** a motor generator combining the electric motor and generator

dy·nast \ˈdī-ˌnast, -nəst\ *n* [L *dynastes,* fr. Gk *dynastēs,* fr. *dynasthai* to be able, have power] (1606) **:** RULER 1

dy·nas·ty \ˈdī-nə-stē *also* -ˌnas-tē, *esp Brit* ˈdi-nə-stē\ *n, pl* **-ties** (14c) **1 :** a succession of rulers of the same line of descent **2 :** a powerful group or family that maintains its position for a considerable time — **dy·nas·tic** \dī-ˈnas-tik\ *adj* — **dy·nas·ti·cal·ly** \-ti-k(ə-)lē\ *adv*

dy·na·tron \ˈdī-nə-ˌträn\ *n* [Gk *dynamis* power] (1918) **:** a vacuum tube in which the secondary emission of electrons from the plate results in a decrease in the plate current as the plate voltage increases

dyne \ˈdīn\ *n* [F, fr. Gk *dynamis*] (ca. 1873) **:** the unit of force in the centimeter-gram-second system equal to the force that would give a free mass of one gram an acceleration of one centimeter per second per second

dy·nein \ˈdī-ˌnēn, -ˌnē-ən\ *n* [*dyne* (force) + *-in*] (1965) **:** an ATPase that is associated esp. with microtubules involved in the movement of cellular organelles and structures (as cilia, flagella, and chromosomes)

dy·node \ˈdī-ˌnōd\ *n* [Gk *dynamis*] (1939) **:** an electrode in an electron tube that functions to produce secondary emission of electrons

dys- *prefix* [L *dys-,* fr. Gk; akin to OE *tō-, te-* apart, Skt *dus-* bad, difficult] **1 :** abnormal ⟨*dys*plasia⟩ **2 :** difficult ⟨*dys*phagia⟩ — compare EU- **3 :** impaired ⟨*dys*function⟩ **4 :** bad ⟨*dys*logistic⟩ — compare EU-

dys·ar·thria \di-ˈsär-thrē-ə\ *n* [NL, fr. *dys-* + *arthr-* + *-ia*] (1878) **:** difficulty in articulating words due to disease of the central nervous system

dys·cra·sia \dis-ˈkrā-zh(ē-)ə\ *n* [NL, fr. ML, bad mixture of humors, fr. Gk *dyskrasia,* fr. *dys-* + *krasis* mixture, fr. *kerannynai* to mix — more at CRATER] (14c) **:** an abnormal condition of the body and esp. the blood

dys·en·ter·ic \ˌdi-sᵊn-ˈter-ik\ *adj* (1727) **:** of or relating to dysentery

dys·en·tery \ˈdi-sᵊn-ˌter-ē, -ˌte-rē\ *n, pl* **-ter·ies** [ME *dissenterie,* fr. L *dysenteria,* fr. Gk, fr. *dys-* + *enteron* intestine — more at INTER-] (14c) **1 :** a disease characterized by severe diarrhea with passage of mucus and blood and usu. caused by infection **2 :** DIARRHEA

dys·func·tion *also* **dis·func·tion** \(ˌ)dis-ˈfəŋ(k)-shən\ *n* (ca. 1916) **1 :** impaired or abnormal functioning ⟨gastrointestinal ∼⟩ **2 :** abnormal or unhealthy interpersonal behavior or interaction within a group ⟨family ∼⟩ — **dys·func·tion·al** \-shnəl, -shə-nᵊl\ *adj*

dys·gen·e·sis \(ˌ)dis-ˈje-nə-səs\ *n* [NL] (1962) **:** defective development esp. of the gonads (as in Klinefelter's syndrome)

dys·gen·ic \(ˌ)dis-ˈje-nik\ *adj* (1912) **1 :** tending to promote survival of or reproduction by less well-adapted individuals (as the weak or diseased) esp. at the expense of well-adapted individuals (as the strong or healthy) ⟨the ∼ effect of war⟩ **2 :** biologically defective or deficient

dys·ki·ne·sia \ˌdis-kə-ˈnē-zh(ē-)ə, -kī-\ *n* [NL, fr. Gk *dyskinēsia* difficulty in moving, fr. *dys-* + *-kinesia,* fr. *kinēsis* motion, fr. *kinein* to move — more at HIGHT] (ca. 1706) **:** impairment of voluntary movements resulting in fragmented or jerky motions (as in Parkinson's disease) — compare TARDIVE DYSKINESIA — **dys·ki·net·ic** \-ˈnet-ik\ *adj*

dys·lex·ia \dis-ˈlek-sē-ə\ *n* [NL, fr. *dys-* + Gk *lexis* word, speech, fr. *legein* to say — more at LEGEND] (ca. 1888) **:** a variable often familial learning disability involving difficulties in acquiring and processing language that is typically manifested by a lack of proficiency in reading, spelling, and writing — **dys·lex·ic** \-sik\ *adj or n*

dys·lo·gis·tic \ˌdis-lə-ˈjis-tik\ *adj* [*dys-* + *-logistic* (as in *eulogistic*)] (1812) **:** UNCOMPLIMENTARY — **dys·lo·gis·ti·cal·ly** \-ti-k(ə-)lē\ *adv*

dys·men·or·rhea \(ˌ)dis-ˌme-nə-ˈrē-ə\ *n* [NL] (ca. 1810) **:** painful menstruation — **dys·men·or·rhe·ic** \-ˈrē-ik\ *adj*

dys·men·or·rhoea *chiefly Brit var of* DYSMENORRHEA

dys·mor·phic \dis-ˈmȯr-fik\ *adj* (1954) **:** characterized by malformation ⟨mildly ∼ ears⟩ ⟨∼ cells⟩

dys·pep·sia \dis-ˈpep-shə, -sē-ə\ *n* [L, fr. Gk, fr. *dys-* + *pepsis* digestion, fr. *peptein, pessein* to cook, digest — more at COOK] (ca. 1706) **1 :** INDIGESTION **2 :** ill humor **:** DISGRUNTLEMENT — **dys·pep·tic** \-ˈpep-tik\ *adj or n* — **dys·pep·ti·cal·ly** \-ti-k(ə-)lē\ *adv*

dys·pha·gia \dis-ˈfā-j(ē-)ə\ *n* [NL] (1783) **:** difficulty in swallowing

dys·pha·sia \dis-ˈfā-zh(ē-)ə\ *n* [NL] (ca. 1883) **:** loss of or deficiency in the power to use or understand language as a result of injury to or disease of the brain — **dys·pha·sic** \-ˈfā-zik\ *n or adj*

dys·phe·mism \ˈdis-fə-ˌmi-zəm\ *n* [*dys-* + *-phemism* (as in *euphemism*)] (1884) **:** the substitution of a disagreeable, offensive, or disparaging expression for an agreeable or inoffensive one; *also* **:** an expression so substituted — **dys·phe·mis·tic** \ˌdis-fə-ˈmis-tik\ *adj*

dys·pho·nia \dis-ˈfō-nē-ə\ *n* [NL] (ca. 1706) **:** defective use of the voice

dys·pho·ria \dis-ˈfȯr-ē-ə\ *n* [NL, fr. Gk, fr. *dysphoros* hard to bear, fr. *dys-* + *pherein* to bear — more at BEAR] (ca. 1842) **:** a state of feeling unwell or unhappy — **dys·phor·ic** \-ˈfȯr-ik, -ˈfär-\ *adj*

dys·pla·sia \dis-ˈplā-zh(ē-)ə\ *n* [NL] (ca. 1923) **:** abnormal growth or development (as of organs or cells); *broadly* **:** abnormal anatomical structure due to such growth — **dys·plas·tic** \-ˈplas-tik\ *adj*

dys·pnea \'dis(p)-nē-ə\ *n* [L *dyspnoea*, fr. Gk *dyspnoia*, fr. *dyspnoos* short of breath, fr. *dys-* + *pnein* to breathe — more at SNEEZE] (ca. 1681) : difficult or labored respiration — **dys·pne·ic** \-nē-ik\ *adj*

dys·pnoea *chiefly Brit var of* DYSPNEA

dys·pro·si·um \dis-'prō-zē-əm, -zh(ē-)əm\ *n* [NL, fr. Gk *dysprositos* hard to get at, fr. *dys-* + *prositos* approachable, fr. *prosienai* to approach, fr. *pros-* + *ienai* to go — more at ISSUE] (1886) : an element of the rare-earth group that forms highly magnetic compounds — see ELEMENT table

dys·rhyth·mia \dis-'rith-mē-ə\ *n* [NL, fr. *dys-* + L *rhythmus* rhythm] (ca. 1909) : an abnormal rhythm; *esp* : a disordered rhythm exhibited in a record of electrical activity of the brain or heart — **dys·rhyth·mic** \-mik\ *adj*

dys·thy·mia \dis-'thī-mē-ə\ *n* [NL] (1844) : a mood disorder characterized by chronic mildly depressed or irritable mood often accompanied by other symptoms (as eating and sleeping disturbances, fatigue, and poor self-esteem) — called also *dysthymic disorder* — **dys·thy·mic** \-'thī-mik\ *adj or n*

dys·to·cia \dis-'tō-sh(ē-)ə\ *n* [NL, fr. Gk *dystokia*, fr. *dys-* + *tokos* childbirth; akin to Gk *tiktein* to give birth to — more at THANE] (ca. 1706) : slow or difficult labor or delivery

dys·to·nia \dis-'tō-nē-ə\ *n* [NL] (1860) : any of various conditions (as Parkinson's disease and torticollis) characterized by abnormalities of movement and muscle tone — **dys·ton·ic** \-'tä-nik\ *adj*

dys·to·pia \dis-'tō-pē-ə\ *n* [NL, fr. *dys-* + *-topia* (as in *utopia*)] (ca. 1950) **1** : an imaginary place where people lead dehumanized and often fearful lives   **2** : ANTI-UTOPIA 2 — **dys·to·pi·an** \-pē-ən\ *adj*

dys·tro·phic \dis-'trō-fik\ *adj* (1893) **1 a** : relating to or caused by faulty nutrition   **b** : relating to or affected with a dystrophy ⟨a ∼ patient⟩   **2** *of a lake* : brownish with much dissolved humic matter, a sparse bottom fauna, and a high oxygen consumption

dys·tro·phin \dis-trə-,fin\ *n* [*dystrophy* + *¹-in*] (1987) : a protein that is associated with a transmembrane complex of skeletal muscle cells and that is absent in Duchenne muscular dystrophy and deficient or defective in Becker muscular dystrophy

dys·tro·phy \'dis-trə-fē\ *n, pl* **-phies** [NL *dystrophia*, fr. *dys-* + *-trophia* -trophy] (1901) **1** : a condition produced by faulty nutrition   **2** : any myogenic atrophy; *esp* : MUSCULAR DYSTROPHY

dys·uria \dis-'yùr-ē-ə, dish-\ *n* [NL, fr. Gk *dysouria*, fr. *dys-* + *-ouria* -uria] (14c) : difficult or painful discharge of urine — compare STRANGURY

dz *abbr* dozen

DZ *abbr* drop zone

¹e \'ē\ *n, pl* **e's** *or* **es** \'ēz\ *often cap, often attrib* (bef. 12c) **1 a** : the 5th letter of the English alphabet   **b** : a graphic representation of this letter   **c** : a speech counterpart of orthographic *e*   **2** : the third tone of a C-major scale   **3** : a graphic device for reproducing the letter *e*   **4** : one designated *e* esp. as the fifth in order or class   **5 a** : a grade rating a student's work as poor and usu. constituting a conditional pass   **b** : a grade rating a student's work as failing   **c** : one graded or rated with an E   **6** : a transcendental number having a value to eight decimal places of 2.71828183 that is the base of natural logarithms   **7** : something shaped like the letter E   **8** *cap* : ECSTASY 4

²e *abbr* **1** earth   **2** east; easterly; eastern   **3** edge   **4** eldest   **5** ell   **6** empty   **7** end   **8** energy   **9** erg   **10** excellent

E *abbr* **1** electromotive force   **2** energy   **3** English   **4** error   **5** exponent

¹e- *prefix* [ME, fr. AF & L; AF, out, forth, away, fr. L, fr. *ex-*] **1** : missing : absent ⟨*e*dentulous⟩   **2** : away ⟨*e*luviation⟩

²e- *comb form* [*e-mail*] : electronic ⟨*e*-commerce⟩

ea *abbr* each

¹each \'ēch\ *adj* [ME *ech*, fr. OE *ǣlc*; akin to OHG *iogilīh* each; both fr. WGmc *aiw-* ever, always (whence OE *ā* always) + *galīkaz* having the same form, like (whence OE *gelīc* like) — more at AYE, LIKE] (bef. 12c) : being one of two or more distinct individuals having a similar relation and often constituting an aggregate

²each *pron* (bef. 12c) : each one ⟨to ∼ his own⟩

³each *adv* (bef. 12c) : to or for each : APIECE ⟨cost a dollar ∼⟩

each other *pron* (bef. 12c) : each of two or more in reciprocal action or relation ⟨looked at *each other* in surprise⟩

usage Some handbooks and textbooks recommend that *each other* be restricted to reference to two and *one another* to reference to three or more. The distinction, while neat, is not observed in actual usage. *Each other* and *one another* are used interchangeably by good writers and have been since at least the 16th century.

ea·ger \'ē-gər\ *adj* [ME *egre*, fr. AF *egre, aigre*, fr. L *acer* — more at EDGE] (14c) **1 a** *archaic* : SHARP   **b** *obs* : SOUR   **2** : marked by enthusiastic or impatient desire or interest — **ea·ger·ly** *adv* — **ea·ger·ness** *n*

syn EAGER, AVID, KEEN, ANXIOUS, ATHIRST mean moved by a strong and urgent desire or interest. EAGER implies ardor and enthusiasm and sometimes impatience at delay or restraint ⟨*eager* to get started⟩. AVID adds to EAGER the implication of insatiability or greed ⟨*avid* for new thrills⟩. KEEN suggests intensity of interest and quick responsiveness in action ⟨*keen* on the latest fashions⟩. ANXIOUS emphasizes fear of frustration or failure or disappointment ⟨*anxious* not to make a social blunder⟩. ATHIRST stresses yearning but not necessarily readiness for action ⟨*athirst* for adventure⟩.

eager beaver *n* (1943) : a person who is extremely zealous about performing duties and volunteering for more

¹ea·gle \'ē-gəl\ *n* [ME *egle*, fr. AF *egle, aigle*, fr. L *aquila*] (13c) **1** : any of various large diurnal birds of prey (family Accipitridae) noted for their strength, size, keenness of vision, and powers of flight   **2 a** : the eagle-bearing standard of the ancient Romans   **b** : one of a pair of eagle-bearing silver insignia of rank worn by a military colonel or a navy captain   **3** : a gold coin of the U.S. bearing an eagle on the reverse and usu. having a value of ten dollars   **4** : a golf score of two strokes less than par on a hole — compare BIRDIE   **5** *cap* [Fraternal Order of *Eagles*] : a member of a major fraternal order

²eagle *vt* **ea·gled; ea·gling** \-g(ə-)liŋ\ (1958) : to score an eagle on (a golf hole)

eagle eye *n* (1598) **1** : the ability to see or observe keenly   **2** : one that sees or observes keenly   **3** : close watch ⟨keeping an *eagle eye* on the prisoner⟩ — **eagle–eyed** \'ē-gəl-,īd\ *adj*

eagle ray *n* (ca. 1856) : any of several widely distributed large active marine stingrays (family Myliobatidae) with broad pectoral fins

Eagle Scout *n* (1913) **1** : a Boy Scout who has reached the highest level of achievement in scouting   **2** : a straight-arrow and self-reliant man

ea·glet \'ē-glət\ *n* (1572) : a young eagle

eal·dor·man \'al-dər-mən\ *n* [OE — more at ALDERMAN] (bef. 12c) : the chief officer in a district (as a shire) in Anglo-Saxon England

Eames \'ēmz, 'āmz\ *trademark* — used for chairs made from modern materials and designed to fit the contours of the body

EAN *abbr* European Article Number

-ean — see -AN

E and OE *abbr* errors and omissions excepted

¹ear \'ir\ *n* [ME *ere*, fr. OE *ēare*; akin to OHG *ōra* ear, L *auris*, Gk *ous*] (bef. 12c) **1 a** : the characteristic vertebrate organ of hearing and equilibrium consisting in the typical mammal of a sound-collecting outer ear separated by the tympanic membrane from a sound-transmitting middle ear that in turn is separated from a sensory inner ear by membranous fenestrae   **b** : any of various organs (as of a fish) capable of detecting vibratory motion   **2** : the external ear of humans and most mammals   **3 a** : the sense or act of hearing   **b** : acuity of hearing   **c** : sensitivity to musical tone and pitch; *also* : the ability to retain and reproduce music that has been heard   **d** : sensitivity to nuances of language esp. as revealed in the command of verbal melody and rhythm or in the ability to render a spoken idiom accurately   **4** : something resembling a mammalian ear in shape, position, or function: as   **a** : a projecting part (as a lug or handle)   **b** : either of a pair of tufts of lengthened feathers on the head of some birds   **5** : ATTENTION, AWARENESS ⟨lend an ∼⟩   **6** : a space in the upper corner of the front page of a periodical (as a newspaper) usu. containing advertising for the periodical itself or a weather forecast   **7** : a person who listens : LISTENER ⟨looking for a friendly ∼⟩ — **all ears** : eagerly listening ⟨if anybody spoke of that grisly matter, I was *all ears* . . . and alert to hear what might be said —Mark Twain⟩ — **by ear** : without reference to or memorization of written music ⟨plays *by ear*⟩ — **in one ear and out the other** : through one's mind without making an impression ⟨everything you say to him goes *in one ear and out the other*⟩ — **on one's ear** : in or into a state of irritation, shock, or discord ⟨set the racing world *on its ear* by breaking the record⟩ — **up to one's ears** : deeply involved : heavily implicated ⟨*up to his ears* in shady deals⟩

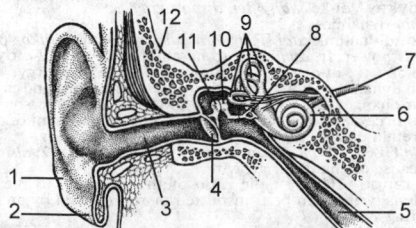

ear 1a: *1* pinna, *2* lobe, *3* auditory meatus, *4* tympanic membrane, *5* eustachian tube, *6* cochlea, *7* auditory nerve, *8* stapes, *9* semicircular canals, *10* incus, *11* malleus, *12* bones of skull

²ear *n* [ME *er*, fr. OE *ēar*; akin to OHG *ahir* ear, OE *ecg* edge — more at EDGE] (bef. 12c) : the fruiting spike of a cereal (as wheat or Indian corn) including both the seeds and protective structures

³ear *vi* (14c) : to form ears in growing ⟨the rye should be ∼ing up⟩

ear·ache \'ir-,āk\ *n* (1766) : an ache or pain in the ear

ear·bud \ˈir-ˌbəd\ *n* (1984) **:** a small earphone inserted into the ear
ear canal *n* (1930) **:** the tubular passage of the outer ear leading to the tympanic membrane
ear candy *n* (1977) **:** music that is pleasing to listen to but lacks depth
ear clip *n* (1945) **:** an earring with a clip fastener
ear·drop \-ˌdräp\ *n* (1720) **:** EARRING; *esp* **:** one with a pendant
ear·drum \-ˌdrəm\ *n* (1645) **:** TYMPANIC MEMBRANE
eared \ˈird\ *adj* (14c) **:** having ears esp. of a specified kind or number ‹a big-*eared* man› ‹golden-*eared* corn›
eared seal *n* (1880) **:** any of a family (Otariidae) of seals including the sea lions and fur seals and having independent mobile hind flippers and small well-developed external ears — compare HAIR SEAL
ear·flap \ˈir-ˌflap\ *n* (1839) **:** a warm covering for the ears; *esp* **:** an extension on the lower edge of a cap that may be folded up or down
ear·ful \ˈir-ˌfu̇l\ *n* (1911) **1 :** an outpouring of news or gossip **2 :** an outpouring of anger, abuse, or complaint
ear·ing \ˈir-iŋ\ *n* [perh. fr. [1]*ear*] (1626) **:** a line used to fasten a corner of a sail to the yard or gaff or to haul a reef cringle to the yard
earl \ˈər(-ə)l\ *n* [ME *erl,* fr. OE *eorl* warrior, nobleman; akin to ON *jarl* warrior, nobleman] (12c) **:** a member of the British peerage ranking below a marquess and above a viscount — **earl·dom** \-dəm\ *n*
Earl Grey *n* [Charles Grey, 2d *Earl Grey* †1845 Eng. statesman] (1958) **:** a black-tea blend flavored with bergamot oil
earl marshal *n* (13c) **:** an officer of state in England serving chiefly as a royal attendant on ceremonial occasions, as marshal of state processions, and as head of the College of Arms
ear·lobe \ˈir-ˌlōb\ *n* (1851) **:** the pendent part of the ear of humans or some domestic chickens
ear·lock \-ˌläk\ *n* (ca. 1775) **:** a curl of hair hanging in front of the ear
[1]**ear·ly** \ˈər-lē\ *adv* **ear·li·er; -est** [ME *erly,* fr. OE *ǣrlīce,* fr. *ǣr* early, soon — more at ERE] (bef. 12c) **1 a :** near the beginning of a period of time ‹awoke ~ in the morning› **b :** near the beginning of a course, process, or series ‹~ in his senatorial career› **2 a :** before the usual or expected time ‹the train arrived ~› **b** *archaic* **:** SOON **c :** sooner than related forms ‹these apples bear ~›
[2]**early** *adj* **ear·li·er; -est** (13c) **1 a :** of, relating to, or occurring near the beginning of a period of time, a development, or a series ‹in the ~ evening› ‹the ~ symptoms of the disease› **b (1) :** distant in past time **(2) :** PRIMITIVE ‹~ tools› **2 a :** occurring before the usual or expected time ‹an ~ arrival› **b :** occurring in the near future ‹at your *earliest* convenience› **c :** maturing or producing sooner than related forms ‹an ~ peach› — **ear·li·ness** *n*
Early American *n* (1895) **:** a style (as of furniture, architecture, or fabric) originating in or characteristic of colonial America
early bird *n* [fr. the proverb, "the early bird catches the worm"] (ca. 1917) **1 :** an early riser **2 :** one that arrives early and esp. before possible competitors
early on *adv* (1928) **:** at or during an early point or stage ‹the reasons were obvious *early on* in the experiment›
usage This adverb is sometimes objected to in American writing as an obtrusive Briticism. It is a relative newcomer to the language, having arisen in British English around 1928. It seems to have filled a need, however. It came into frequent use in American English in the late 1960s and is now well established on both sides of the Atlantic in both speech and writing.
ear·ly·wood \ˈər-lē-ˌwu̇d\ *n* (ca. 1914) **:** SPRINGWOOD
[1]**ear·mark** \ˈir-ˌmärk\ *n* (15c) **1 :** a mark of identification on the ear of an animal **2 :** a distinguishing mark ‹all the ~*s* of poverty› **3 :** a provision in Congressional legislation that allocates a specified amount of money for a specific project, program, or organization
[2]**earmark** *vt* (1591) **1 a :** to mark (livestock) with an earmark **b :** to mark in a distinguishing manner **2 :** to designate (as funds) for a specific use or owner ‹money ~*ed* for education›
ear·muff \ˈir-ˌməf\ *n* (1889) **:** one of a pair of ear coverings connected by a flexible band and worn as protection against cold or noises
[1]**earn** \ˈərn\ *vt* [ME *ernen,* fr. OE *earnian;* akin to OHG *arnōn* to reap, Czech *jeseň* autumn] (bef. 12c) **1 a :** to receive as return for effort and esp. for work done or services rendered **b :** to bring in by way of return ‹bonds ~*ing* 10 percent interest› **2 a :** to come to be duly worthy of or entitled or suited to ‹she ~*ed* a promotion› **b :** to make worthy of or obtain for ‹the suggestion ~*ed* him a promotion› — **earn·er** *n*
[2]**earn** *vi* [prob. alter. of *yearn*] (1599) *obs* **:** GRIEVE
earned run *n* (1880) **:** a run in baseball that scores without benefit of an error before the fielding team has had a chance to make the third putout of the inning
earned run average *n* (1947) **:** the average number of earned runs per game scored against a pitcher in baseball determined by dividing the total of earned runs scored against him by the total number of innings pitched and multiplying by nine
[1]**ear·nest** \ˈər-nəst\ *n* [ME *ernest,* fr. OE *eornost;* akin to OHG *ernust* earnest] (bef. 12c) **1 :** a serious and intent mental state ‹a proposal made in ~› **2 :** a considerable or impressive degree or amount ‹the sap started running in ~›
[2]**earnest** *adj* (bef. 12c) **1 :** characterized by or proceeding from an intense and serious state of mind **2 :** GRAVE, IMPORTANT ***syn*** see SERIOUS — **ear·nest·ly** *adv* — **ear·nest·ness** \-nəs(t)-nəs\ *n*
[3]**earnest** *n* [ME *ernes, ernest,* fr. AF *arres, erres,* pl. of *erre* earnest, fr. L *arra,* short for *arrabo,* fr. Gk *arrhabōn,* of Sem origin; akin to Heb *ʽērābhōn* pledge] (13c) **1 :** something of value given by a buyer to a seller to bind a bargain **2 :** a token of what is to come **:** PLEDGE
earn·ings \ˈər-niŋz\ *n pl* (1594) **1 :** something (as wages) earned **2 :** the balance of revenue after deduction of costs and expenses
ear·phone \ˈir-ˌfōn\ *n* (1924) **:** a device that converts electrical energy into sound waves and is worn over or inserted into the ear
ear pick *n* (14c) **:** a device often of precious metal for removing wax or foreign bodies from the ear
ear·piece \ˈir-ˌpēs\ *n* (1853) **1 :** a part of an instrument (as a telephone or stethoscope) that is placed against or inserted into the outer opening of the ear; *esp* **:** EARPHONE **2 :** one of the two sidepieces that support eyeglasses by passing over or behind the ears
ear·plug \-ˌpləg\ *n* (1904) **1 :** an ornament inserted in the lobe of the ear esp. to distend it **2 :** a device of pliable material for insertion into the outer opening of the ear (as to keep out water or deaden sound)
ear·ring \ˈir-(ˌ)iŋ, -ˌriŋ\ *n* (bef. 12c) **:** an ornament for the ear and esp. the earlobe
ear rot *n* (1926) **:** a condition of Indian corn that is characterized by molding and decay of the ears and that is caused by fungi (genera *Diplodia, Fusarium,* or *Gibberella*)
ear shell *n* (1752) **:** ABALONE
ear·shot \ˈir-ˌshät\ *n* (1607) **:** the range within which one may hear a person's unaided voice ‹waited until he was out of ~›
ear·split·ting \-ˌspli-tiŋ\ *adj* (1835) **:** distressingly loud or shrill ***syn*** see LOUD
[1]**earth** \ˈərth\ *n* [ME *erthe,* fr. OE *eorthe;* akin to OHG *erda* earth, Gk *era*] (bef. 12c) **1 :** the fragmental material composing part of the surface of the globe; *esp* **:** cultivable soil **2 :** the sphere of mortal life as distinguished from spheres of spirit life — compare HEAVEN, HELL **3 a :** areas of land as distinguished from sea and air **b :** the solid footing formed of soil **:** GROUND **4** *often cap* **:** the planet on which we live that is third in order from the sun — see PLANET table **5 a :** the people of the planet Earth **b :** the mortal human body **c :** the pursuits, interests, and pleasures of earthly life as distinguished from spiritual concerns **6 :** the lair of a burrowing animal **7 :** an excessive amount of money — used with *the* ‹real suede, which costs the ~ to clean —Joanne Winship› — **earth·like** \-ˌlīk\ *adj* — **on earth** — used as an intensive ‹to find out what *on earth* he was up to —Michael Holroyd›
[2]**earth** *vt* (1575) **1 :** to drive to hiding in the earth **2 :** to draw soil about (plants) — often used with *up* **3** *chiefly Brit* **:** GROUND 3 ~ *vi, of a hunted animal* **:** to hide in the ground
earth·born \ˈərth-ˌbȯrn\ *adj* (1621) **1 :** born on this earth **:** MORTAL **2 :** associated with earthly life ‹~ cares›
earth·bound \-ˌbau̇nd\ *adj* (1605) **1 a :** fast in or to the soil ‹~ roots› **b :** located on or restricted to land or to the surface of the earth **2 a :** bound by earthly interests **b :** PEDESTRIAN, UNIMAGINATIVE
earth color *n* (1931) **:** EARTH TONE
earth·en \ˈər-thən, -t͟hən\ *adj* (13c) **1 :** made of earth **2 :** EARTHLY
earth·en·ware \-ˌwer\ *n* (1646) **:** ceramic ware made of slightly porous opaque clay fired at low heat
earth·i·ly \ˈər-thə-lē, -t͟hə-\ *adv* (1953) **:** in an earthy manner
earth·light \ˈərth-ˌlīt\ *n* (1833) **:** EARTHSHINE
earth·ling \ˈərth-liŋ\ *n* (1593) **1 :** an inhabitant of the earth **2 :** WORLDLING
earth·ly \ˈərth-lē\ *adj* (bef. 12c) **1 a :** characteristic of or belonging to this earth **b :** relating to the human race's actual life on this earth **2 :** POSSIBLE ‹of what ~ use is it?› — **earth·li·ness** *n*
syn EARTHLY, WORLDLY, MUNDANE mean belonging to or characteristic of the earth. EARTHLY often implies a contrast with what is heavenly or spiritual ‹abandoned *earthly* concerns and entered a convent›. WORLDLY and MUNDANE both imply a relation to the immediate concerns and activities of human beings, WORLDLY suggesting tangible personal gain or gratification ‹*worldly* goods› and MUNDANE suggesting reference to the immediate and practical ‹a *mundane* discussion of finances›.
earth mother *n, often cap E&M* (1902) **1 :** the earth viewed (as in primitive theology) as the divine source of terrestrial life **2 :** an embodiment of the female principle of fertility **:** a nurturing maternal woman
earth·mov·er \ˈərth-ˌmü-vər\ *n* (1941) **:** a machine (as a bulldozer) for excavating, pushing, or transporting large quantities of earth (as in road building) — **earth·mov·ing** \-ˌmü-viŋ\ *n or adj*
earth·quake \ˈərth-ˌkwāk\ *n* (14c) **1 :** a shaking or trembling of the earth that is volcanic or tectonic in origin **2 :** UPHEAVAL 2
earth·rise \ˈərth-ˌrīz\ *n* (1968) **:** the rising of the earth above the horizon of the moon as seen from lunar orbit
earth science *n* (1939) **:** any of the sciences (as geology, meteorology, or oceanography) that deal with the earth or with one or more of its parts — compare GEOSCIENCE — **earth scientist** *n*
earth·shak·ing \ˈərth-ˌshā-kiŋ\ *adj* (1948) **:** of great importance **:** MOMENTOUS ‹an ~ announcement› — **earth·shak·ing·ly** *adv*
earth–shat·ter·ing \ˈərth-ˈsha-tə-riŋ\ *adj* (1970) **:** EARTHSHAKING
earth–shel·tered \ˈərth-ˌshel-tərd\ *adj* (1979) **:** built partly or mostly underground ‹an ~ house›
earth·shine \ˈərth-ˌshīn\ *n* (1834) **:** sunlight reflected by the earth that illuminates the dark part of the moon — called also *earthlight*
earth·star \-ˌstär\ *n* (1885) **:** any of a genus (*Geastrum*) of globose basidiomycetous fungi with an outer peridium that splits into the shape of a star
earth station *n* (1970) **:** DISH 3a(2); *esp* **:** one used primarily for receiving and transmitting television signals
earth tone *n* (1973) **:** any of various rich colors containing some brown — **earth–toned** *adj*
earth·ward \-wərd\ *also* **earth·wards** \-wərdz\ *adv* (14c) **:** toward the earth
earth·work \ˈərth-ˌwərk\ *n* (1633) **1 :** an embankment or other construction made of earth; *esp* **:** one used as a field fortification **2 :** the operations connected with excavations and embankments of earth **3 :** a work of art consisting of a portion of land modified by an artist
earth·worm \-ˌwərm\ *n* (14c) **:** a terrestrial annelid worm (class Oligochaeta); *esp* **:** any of a family (Lumbricidae) of numerous widely distributed hermaphroditic worms that move through the soil by means of setae and feed on decaying organic matter
earthy \ˈər-thē, -t͟hē\ *adj* **earth·i·er; -est** (14c) **1 a :** of, relating to, or consisting of earth ‹~ creatures like worms› **b :** suggestive of earth (as in texture, odor, or color) ‹an ~ yellow› **c :** rough, coarse, or plain in taste ‹~ flavors› **2 a** *archaic* **:** EARTHLY, WORLDLY **b :** characteristic of or associated with mortal life on the earth ‹prefers ~ to ethereal themes› **3 :** suggestive of plain or poor people or their ways: as **a :** PRACTICAL, DOWN-TO-EARTH ‹~ problems of daily life› **b :** CRUDE, GROSS ‹~ humor› **c :** plain and simple in style **:** UNSOPHISTICATED ‹~ peasant cookery› ‹~ decor› — **earth·i·ness** *n*

ear·wax \ˈir-ˌwaks\ *n* (14c) **:** the yellow waxy secretion from the glands of the external ear — called also *cerumen*

[1]**ear·wig** \-ˌwig\ *n* [ME *erwigge,* fr. OE *ēarwicga,* fr. *ēare* ear + *wicga* insect] (bef. 12c) **:** any of numerous insects (order Dermaptera) having slender many-jointed antennae and a pair of cerci resembling forceps at the end of the body

[2]**earwig** *vt* **ear·wigged; ear·wig·ging** (1837) **:** to annoy or attempt to influence by private talk

ear·wit·ness \ˈir-ˈwit-nəs\ *n* (1594) **:** one who overhears something; *esp* **:** one who gives a report on what has been heard

ear·worm \ˈir-ˌwərm\ *n* (1802) **1 :** CORN EARWORM **2 :** a song or melody that keeps repeating in one's mind

[1]**ease** \ˈēz\ *n* [ME *ese,* fr. AF *eise, aise* convenience, comfort, ultim. fr. L *adjacent-, adjacens* neighboring — more at ADJACENT] (13c) **1 :** the state of being comfortable: as **a :** freedom from pain or discomfort **b :** freedom from care **c :** freedom from labor or difficulty **d :** freedom from embarrassment or constraint **:** NATURALNESS ⟨known for his charm and ~ of manner⟩ **e :** an easy fit **2 :** relief from discomfort or obligation **3 :** FACILITY, EFFORTLESSNESS ⟨did it with ~⟩ **4 :** an act of easing or a state of being eased — **ease·ful** \-fəl\ *adj* — **ease·ful·ly** \-fə-lē\ *adv* — **at ease 1 :** free from pain or discomfort **2 a :** free from restraint or formality ⟨feels most *at ease* with old friends⟩ **b :** standing silently (as in a military formation) with the feet apart, the right foot in place, and one or both hands behind the body — often used as a command

[2]**ease** *vb* **eased; eas·ing** *vt* (14c) **1 :** to free from something that pains, disquiets, or burdens ⟨trying to ~ her of her worries⟩ **2 :** to make less painful **:** ALLEVIATE ⟨~ his suffering⟩ **3 a :** to lessen the pressure or tension of esp. by slackening, lifting, or shifting ⟨~ a spring⟩ **b :** to maneuver gently or carefully ⟨*eased* himself into the chair⟩ **c :** to moderate or reduce esp. in amount or intensity ⟨~ a flow⟩ **4 :** to make less difficult ⟨~ credit⟩ **5 a :** to put the helm of (a ship) alee **b :** to let (a helm or rudder) come back a little after having been put hard over ~ *vi* **1 :** to give freedom or relief **2 :** to move or pass slowly or easily — often used with a directional word (as *over* or *up*) ⟨the limo *eased* up in front of the house⟩ **3 a :** to become less intense, vigorous, or engaged **:** become moderate — usu. used with *up* or *off* ⟨told her staff to *ease* up a little⟩ ⟨expected the storm to *ease* off⟩ ⟨*ease* up on fatty foods⟩ **b :** to apply less pressure — usu. used with *up* or *off* ⟨*ease* up on the accelerator⟩ **c :** to act in a less harsh manner — usu. used with *up* or *off* ⟨decided to *ease* off on enforcement⟩

ea·sel \ˈē-zəl\ *n* [D *ezel,* lit., ass, fr. MD *esel;* akin to OE *esol* ass; both fr. a prehistoric EGmc-WGmc word borrowed fr. L *asinus* ass] (1596) **:** a frame for supporting something (as an artist's canvas)

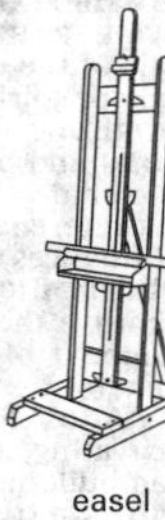
easel

ease·ment \ˈēz-mənt\ *n* (14c) **1 :** an act or means of easing or relieving (as from discomfort) **2 :** an interest in land owned by another that entitles its holder to a specific limited use or enjoyment; *also* **:** an area of land covered by an easement

eas·i·ly \ˈēz-lē, ˈē-zə-\ *adv* (13c) **1 :** in an easy manner **:** without difficulty ⟨won ~⟩ **2 a :** without question **:** by far ⟨was ~ the best meal I've ever had⟩ **b :** at the minimum **:** at least ⟨costs ~ twice as much⟩ **3 :** WELL 10b ⟨it could ~ have been me⟩

[1]**east** \ˈēst\ *adv* [ME *est,* fr. OE *ēast;* akin to OHG *ōstar* to the east, L *aurora* dawn, Gk *ēōs, heōs*] (bef. 12c) **:** to, toward, or in the east

[2]**east** *adj* (bef. 12c) **1 :** situated toward or at the east ⟨an ~ window⟩ **2 :** coming from the east ⟨an ~ wind⟩

[3]**east** *n* (bef. 12c) **1 a :** the general direction of sunrise **:** the direction toward the right of one facing north **b :** the compass point directly opposite to west **2** *cap* **a :** regions lying to the east of a specified or implied point of orientation **b :** regions having a culture derived from ancient non-European esp. Asian areas **3 :** the altar end of a church **4** *often cap* **a :** the one of four positions at 90-degree intervals that lies to the east or at the right of a diagram **b :** a person (as a bridge player) occupying this position in the course of a specified activity

east·bound \ˈēs(t)-ˌbau̇nd\ *adj* (1880) **:** traveling or heading east

east by north (1656) **:** a compass point that is one point north of due east **:** N78°45′E

east by south (14c) **:** a compass point that is one point south of due east **:** S78°45′E

East Caribbean dollar *n* (ca. 1974) **:** a basic monetary unit shared by a number of islands of the British West Indies

Eas·ter \ˈē-stər\ *n* [ME *estre,* fr. OE *ēastre;* akin to OHG *ōstarun* (pl.) Easter, OE *ēast* east] (bef. 12c) **:** a feast that commemorates Christ's resurrection and is observed with variations of date due to different calendars on the first Sunday after the paschal full moon

EASTER DATES[1]

YEAR	ASH WEDNESDAY	EASTER	YEAR	ASH WEDNESDAY	EASTER
2009	Feb. 25	Apr. 12	2016	Feb. 10	Mar. 27
2010	Feb. 17	Apr. 4	2017	Mar. 1	Apr. 16
2011	Mar. 9	Apr. 24	2018	Feb. 14	Apr. 1
2012	Feb. 22	Apr. 8	2019	Mar. 6	Apr. 21
2013	Feb. 13	Mar. 31	2020	Feb. 26	Apr. 12
2014	Mar. 5	Apr. 20	2021	Feb. 17	Apr. 4
2015	Feb. 18	Apr. 5	2022	Mar. 2	Apr. 17

[1]Western churches

Easter egg *n* (1737) **1 :** an egg that is dyed and sometimes decorated and that is associated with the celebration of Easter **2 :** a hidden feature in a commercially released product (as software or a DVD)

Easter lily *n* (1877) **:** any of several white cultivated lilies (esp. *Lilium longiflorum*) that bloom in early spring

[1]**east·er·ly** \ˈē-stər-lē\ *adj or adv* [obs. *easter* eastern] (1548) **1 :** situated toward or belonging to the east ⟨the ~ shore of the lake⟩ **2 :** coming from the east ⟨an ~ storm⟩

[2]**easterly** *n, pl* **-lies** (1901) **:** a wind from the east

Easter Monday *n* (14c) **:** the Monday after Easter observed as a legal holiday in parts of the Commonwealth of Nations and in No. Carolina

east·ern \ˈē-stərn\ *adj* [ME *estern,* fr. OE *ēasterne;* akin to OHG *ōstrōni* eastern, OE *ēast* east] (bef. 12c) **1** *cap* **:** of, relating to, or characteristic of a region conventionally designated East **2** *cap* **a :** of, relating to, or being the Christian churches originating in the church of the Eastern Roman Empire **b :** EASTERN ORTHODOX **3 a :** lying toward the east **b :** coming from the east ⟨an ~ wind⟩ — **east·ern·most** \-ˌmōst\ *adj*

eastern bluebird *n, often cap E* (1937) **:** a bluebird (*Sialia sialis*) chiefly of eastern No. America that has a reddish-brown throat and breast

East·ern·er \ˈē-stə(r)-nər\ *n* (1840) **:** a native or inhabitant of the East; *esp* **:** a native or resident of the eastern part of the U.S.

eastern hemisphere *n, often cap E&H* (1624) **:** the half of the earth east of the Atlantic Ocean including Europe, Asia, Australia, and Africa

Eastern Orthodox *adj* (1909) **:** of or consisting of the Eastern churches that form a loose federation according primacy of honor to the patriarch of Constantinople and adhering to the decisions of the first seven ecumenical councils and to the Byzantine rite

eastern time *n, often cap E* (1883) **:** the time of the fifth time zone west of Greenwich that includes the eastern U.S. — see TIME ZONE illustration

eastern white pine *n* (1925) **:** WHITE PINE 1a

Eas·ter·tide \ˈē-stər-ˌtīd\ *n* [ME *estertide,* fr. OE *ēastortīd,* fr. *ēastor* + *tīd* time — more at TIDE] (bef. 12c) **:** the period from Easter to Ascension Day, to Whitsunday, or to Trinity Sunday

East Germanic *n* (ca. 1901) **:** a subdivision of the Germanic languages that includes Gothic — see INDO-EUROPEAN LANGUAGES table

East Indiaman *n* (1709) **:** a large sailing ship formerly used for trading runs to the East Indies

east·ing \ˈēs-tiŋ\ *n* (1628) **1 :** easterly progress ⟨make as much ~ as possible —Kevin Patterson⟩ **2 :** difference in longitude to the east from the last preceding point of reckoning

east–northeast *n* (1613) **:** a compass point that is two points north of due east **:** N67°30′E

east–southeast *n* (1555) **:** a compass point that is two points south of due east **:** S67°30′E

[1]**east·ward** \ˈēst-wərd\ *adv or adj* (bef. 12c) **:** toward the east — **eastwards** \-wərdz\ *adv*

[2]**eastward** *n* (1582) **:** eastward direction or part ⟨sail to the ~⟩

[1]**easy** \ˈē-zē\ *adj* **eas·i·er; -est** [ME *esy,* fr. AF *eisé, aasié,* pp. of *eiser, aaisier* to ease, fr. *a-* ad- (fr. L *ad-*) + *eise* ease] (13c) **1 a :** causing or involving little difficulty or discomfort ⟨within ~ reach⟩ **b :** requiring or indicating little effort, thought, or reflection ⟨~ clichés⟩ **2 a :** not severe **:** LENIENT ⟨hopes they'll be ~ on him⟩ **b :** not steep or abrupt ⟨~ slopes⟩ **c :** not difficult to endure or undergo ⟨an ~ penalty⟩ **d :** readily taken advantage of ⟨an ~ target for takeovers⟩ ⟨an ~ mark for con men⟩ **e** (1) **:** readily available ⟨~ pickings⟩ (2) **:** plentiful in supply at low or declining interest rates ⟨~ money⟩ (3) **:** less in demand and usu. lower in price ⟨bonds were *easier*⟩ **f :** PLEASANT ⟨~ listening⟩ **g :** sexually promiscuous **3 a :** marked by peace and comfort ⟨the ~ life of a courtier⟩ **b :** not hurried or strenuous ⟨an ~ pace⟩ **4 a :** free from pain, annoyance, or anxiety ⟨did all she could to make him *easier*⟩ **b :** marked by social ease ⟨an air of ~ assurance⟩ **c :** EASYGOING ⟨an ~ disposition⟩ **5 a :** giving ease, comfort, or relaxation **b :** not burdensome or straitened ⟨bought on ~ terms⟩ **c :** fitting comfortably **:** allowing freedom of movement ⟨~ jackets⟩ **d :** marked by ready facility ⟨an ~ flowing style⟩ **e :** felt or attained to readily, naturally, and spontaneously ⟨an ~ smile⟩ — **eas·i·ness** *n*

syn EASY, FACILE, SIMPLE, LIGHT, EFFORTLESS, SMOOTH mean not demanding effort or involving difficulty. EASY is applicable either to persons or things imposing tasks or to activity required by such tasks ⟨an *easy* college course⟩. FACILE often adds to EASY the connotation of undue haste or shallowness ⟨*facile* answers to complex questions⟩. SIMPLE stresses ease in understanding or dealing with because complication is absent ⟨a *simple* problem in arithmetic⟩. LIGHT stresses freedom from what is burdensome ⟨a *light* teaching load⟩. EFFORTLESS stresses the appearance of ease and usu. implies the prior attainment of artistry or expertness ⟨moving with *effortless* grace⟩. SMOOTH stresses the absence or removal of all difficulties, hardships, or obstacles ⟨a *smooth* ride⟩. ***syn*** see in addition COMFORTABLE

[2]**easy** *adv* **eas·i·er; -est** (14c) **1 :** EASILY 1 ⟨promises come ~⟩ **2 :** without undue speed or excitement ⟨take it ~⟩ **3 a :** without worry or care ⟨rest ~⟩ **b :** without a severe penalty ⟨got off ~⟩ **c :** without violent movement ⟨the boat rode ~⟩ **4 :** EASILY 2 ⟨cost $500 ~⟩

easy chair *n* (1621) **:** a roomy upholstered chair

easy·go·ing \ˌē-zē-ˈgō-iŋ, -ˈgȯ(-)iŋ\ *adj* (1674) **1 a :** relaxed and casual in style or manner ⟨an ~ boss⟩ **b :** morally lax **2 :** UNHURRIED, COMFORTABLE ⟨an ~ pace⟩ — **easy·go·ing·ness** *n*

easy street *n* (1889) **:** a situation with no worries

easy virtue *n* (1785) **:** sexually promiscuous behavior or habits ⟨ladies of *easy virtue*⟩

[1]**eat** \ˈēt\ *vb* **ate** \ˈāt, *dial or Brit* ˈet\; **eat·en** \ˈē-tᵊn\; **eat·ing** [ME *eten,* fr. OE *etan;* akin to OHG *ezzan* to eat, L *edere,* Gk *edmenai*] *vt* (bef. 12c) **1 :** to take in through the mouth as food **:** ingest, chew, and swallow in turn **2 a :** to destroy, consume, or waste by or as if by eating ⟨expenses *ate* up the profits⟩ ⟨gadgets that ~ up too much space⟩ **b :** to bear the expense of **:** take a loss on ⟨the team was forced to ~ the rest of his contract⟩ **3 a :** to consume gradually **:** CORRODE ⟨cars *eaten* away by rust⟩ **b :** to consume with vexation **:** BOTHER ⟨what's ~*ing* you now⟩ **4 :** to enjoy eagerly or avidly **:** LAP — used with *up* ⟨it was an amazing performance and the crowd *ate* it up⟩ **5** *usu vulgar* **:** to perform fellatio or cunnilingus on — often used with *out* ~ *vi* **1 :** to take food or a meal **2 :** to affect something by gradual destruction or consumption — usu. used with *into, away,* or *at* ⟨the loss was really ~*ing* at her⟩ ⟨the controversy *ate* into his support⟩ — **eat·er** *n* — **eat alive :** to defeat, conquer, or overwhelm completely **:** CRUSH ⟨was *eaten alive* by the competition⟩ — **eat one out of house and home :** to consume more than one can easily provide or afford — **eat one's heart out 1 :** to grieve bitterly **2 :** to be jealous — **eat one's words :** to retract what one has said — **eat out of one's hand :** to

accept the domination of another — **eat someone's lunch** : to deprive of profit, dominance, or success

[2]**eat** *n* [ME *et,* fr. OE *ǣt;* akin to OHG *āz* food; derivative fr. the root of [1]*eat*] (bef. 12c) : something to eat : FOOD — usu. used in pl.

[1]**eat·able** \ˈē-tə-bəl\ *adj* (14c) : fit or able to be eaten

[2]**eatable** *n* (1672) **1** : something to eat **2** *pl* : FOOD

eat·ery \ˈē-tə-rē\ *n, pl* **-er·ies** (1901) : LUNCHEONETTE, RESTAURANT

eath \ˈēth\ *adv or adj* [ME *ethe,* fr. OE *ēathe;* akin to OHG *ōdi* easy] (bef. 12c) *Scot* : EASY

eating *adj* (15c) **1** : used for eating ⟨~ utensils⟩ **2** : suitable to eat ⟨the finest ~ fish⟩; *also* : suitable to eat raw ⟨an ~ apple⟩

eating disorder *n* (1984) : any of several psychological disorders (as anorexia nervosa or bulimia) characterized by serious disturbances of eating behavior

eau de co·logne \ˌō-də-kə-ˈlōn\ *n, pl* **eaux de cologne** \ˌō(z)-də-\ [F, lit., Cologne water, fr. *Cologne,* Germany] (1802) : COLOGNE

eau de par·fum \-ˌpär-ˈfa^{n}\ *n, pl* **eaux de parfum** *also* **eau de par·fums** \-ˌpär-ˈfa^{n}(z)\ *or* **eaux de parfums** [F, lit., perfume water] (1949) : a perfumed liquid containing a percentage of fragrant oils that is lower than that in perfume but greater than that in eau de toilette

eau de toi·lette \ˌō-də-twä-ˈlet\ *n, pl* **eaux de toilette** \ˌō(z)-\ *or* **eaux de toi·lettes** \ˌō(z)-də-twä-ˈlet(s)\ *or* **eau de toi·lettes** \ˌō-də-twä-ˈlet(s)\ [F, lit., water for washing and dressing] (1907) : a perfumed liquid containing a lower percentage of fragrant oils than is contained in ordinary perfume or eau de parfum — called also *toilet water*

eau–de–vie \ˌō-də-ˈvē\ *n, pl* **eaux–de–vie** \ˌō(z)-də-\ [F, lit., water of life, trans. of ML *aqua vitae*] (1683) : a clear brandy distilled from the fermented juice of fruit (as pears or raspberries)

eave \ˈēv\ *n* [ME *eves* (sing.), fr. OE *efes;* akin to OHG *obasa* portico, OE *ūp* up — more at UP] (bef. 12c) **1** : the lower border of a roof that overhangs the wall — usu. used in pl. **2** : a projecting edge (as of a hill) — usu. used in pl.

eaves·drop \ˈēvz-ˌdräp\ *vi* [prob. back-formation fr. *eavesdropper,* lit., one standing under the drip from the eaves] (1606) : to listen secretly to what is said in private — **eaves·drop·per** *n*

eaves trough *n* (1851) : GUTTER 1a

EB *abbr* eastbound

[1]**ebb** \ˈeb\ *n* [ME *ebbe,* fr. OE *ebba;* akin to MD *ebbe* ebb, OE *of* from — more at OF] (bef. 12c) **1** : the reflux of the tide toward the sea **2** : a point or condition of decline ⟨our spirits were at a low ~⟩

[2]**ebb** *vi* (bef. 12c) **1** : to recede from the flood **2** : to fall from a higher to a lower level or from a better to a worse state ⟨his popularity ~*ed*⟩ ***syn*** see ABATE

ebb tide *n* (1782) **1** : the tide while ebbing or at ebb **2** : a period or state of decline

EBC *abbr* Educational Broadcasting Corporation

EBCDIC \ˈep-sə-ˌdik, ˈeb-\ *n* [*e*xtended *b*inary *c*oded *d*ecimal *i*nter*c*hange code] (ca. 1966) : a code for representing alphanumeric information (as on magnetic tape)

EBITDA *also* **Ebitda** *abbr* earnings before interest, taxes, depreciation, and amortization

Ebo·la \ē-ˈbō-lə, i-, e-\ *n* (1977) **1** : EBOLA VIRUS **2** : the hemorrhagic fever caused by the Ebola virus — called also *Ebola Fever*

Ebola virus *n* [*Ebola* River, Democratic Republic of the Congo] (1976) : any of several filoviruses (genus *Ebolavirus* and esp. species *Zaire ebolavirus*) of African origin that cause an often fatal hemorrhagic fever

eb·on \ˈe-bən\ *adj* (15c) : EBONY

Ebon·ics \ē-ˈbä-niks, i-, e-\ *n pl but sing in constr* [blend of *ebony* and *phonics*] (1973) : BLACK ENGLISH

eb·o·nite \ˈe-bə-ˌnīt\ *n* (1861) : hard rubber esp. when black

eb·o·nize \-ˌnīz\ *vt* **-nized; -niz·ing** (ca. 1828) : to stain black in imitation of ebony

[1]**eb·o·ny** \ˈe-bə-nē\ *n, pl* **-nies** [prob. fr. LL *hebeninus* of ebony, fr. Gk *ebeninos,* fr. *ebenos* ebony, fr. Egypt *hbnj*] (1597) **1** : a hard heavy blackish wood yielded by various tropical chiefly southeast Asian trees (genus *Diospyros* of the family Ebenaceae, the ebony family) **2 a** : a tree yielding ebony **b** : any of several trees yielding wood like ebony

[2]**ebony** *adj* (1597) **1** : made of or resembling ebony **2** : BLACK, DARK

e–book \ˈē-ˌbu̇k\ *n* (1988) : a book composed in or converted to digital format for display on a computer screen or handheld device

ebul·lience \i-ˈbu̇l-yən(t)s, -ˈbəl-\ *n* (1749) : the quality of lively or enthusiastic expression of thoughts or feelings : EXUBERANCE

ebul·lien·cy \-yən(t)-sē\ *n* (1676) : EBULLIENCE

ebul·lient \-yənt\ *adj* [L *ebullient-, ebulliens,* prp. of *ebullire* to bubble out, fr. *e-* + *bullire* to bubble, boil — more at BOIL] (1599) **1** : BOILING, AGITATED **2** : characterized by ebullience : having or showing liveliness and enthusiasm ⟨~ performers⟩ — **ebul·lient·ly** *adv*

eb·ul·li·tion \ˌe-bə-ˈli-shən\ *n* (1534) **1** : a sudden violent outburst or display **2** : the act, process, or state of boiling or bubbling up

EBV *abbr* Epstein-Barr virus

EB virus \ˌē-ˈbē-\ *n* (1968) : EPSTEIN-BARR VIRUS

EC *abbr* European Community; European Communities

[1]**ec·cen·tric** \ik-ˈsen-trik, ek-\ *adj* [ME, fr. ML *eccentricus,* fr. Gk *ekkentros,* fr. *ex* out of + *kentron* center] (ca. 1630) **1 a** : deviating from an established or usual pattern or style ⟨~ products⟩ **b** : deviating from conventional or accepted usage or conduct esp. in odd or whimsical ways ⟨an ~ millionaire⟩ **2 a** : deviating from a circular path; *esp* : ELLIPTICAL 1 ⟨an ~ orbit⟩ **b** : located elsewhere than at the geometrical center; *also* : having the axis or support so located ⟨an ~ wheel⟩ ***syn*** see STRANGE — **ec·cen·tri·cal·ly** \-tri-k(ə-)lē\ *adv*

[2]**eccentric** *n* (1827) **1** : a mechanical device consisting of an eccentric disk communicating its motion to a rod so as to produce reciprocating motion **2** : an eccentric person

ec·cen·tric·i·ty \ˌek-(ˌ)sen-ˈtri-sə-tē\ *n, pl* **-ties** (1545) **1 a** : the quality or state of being eccentric **b** : deviation from an established pattern or norm; *esp* : odd or whimsical behavior **2 a** : a mathematical constant that for a given conic section is the ratio of the distances from any point of the conic section to a focus and the corresponding directrix **b** : the eccentricity of an astronomical orbit used as a measure of its deviation from circularity

ec·chy·mo·sis \ˌe-ki-ˈmō-səs\ *n, pl* **-mo·ses** \-ˌsēz\ [NL, fr. Gk *ekchymōsis,* fr. *ekchymousthai* to extravasate blood, fr. *ex-* + *chymos* juice — more at CHYME] (1541) : the escape of blood into the tissues from ruptured blood vessels — **ec·chy·mot·ic** \-ˈmä-tik\ *adj*

eccl *abbr* ecclesiastic; ecclesiastical

Eccles *abbr* Ecclesiastes

ecclesi- *or* **ecclesio-** *comb form* [LL *ecclesia,* fr. Gk *ekklēsia* assembly of citizens, church, fr. *ekkalein* to call forth, summon, fr. *ex-* + *kalein* to call — more at LOW] : church ⟨*ecclesio*logy⟩

ec·cle·si·al \i-ˈklē-zē-əl, e-ˈklē-\ *adj* (1641) : of or relating to a church

Ec·cle·si·as·tes \i-ˌklē-zē-ˈas-(ˌ)tēz, e-ˌklē-\ *n* [Gk *Ekklēsiastēs,* lit., preacher (trans. of Heb *qōheleth*), fr. *ekklēsiastēs* member of an assembly, fr. *ekklēsia*] (14c) : a book of wisdom literature in canonical Jewish and Christian Scripture — see BIBLE table

[1]**ec·cle·si·as·tic** \-ˈas-tik\ *adj* (15c) : ECCLESIASTICAL

[2]**ecclesiastic** *n* (1651) : CLERGYMAN

ec·cle·si·as·ti·cal \-ti-kəl\ *adj* [ME, fr. LL *ecclesiasticus,* fr. LGk *ekklēsiastikos,* fr. Gk, of an assembly of citizens, fr. *ekklēsiastēs*] (15c) **1** : of or relating to a church esp. as an established institution **2** : suitable for use in a church — **ec·cle·si·as·ti·cal·ly** \-ti-k(ə-)lē\ *adv*

ec·cle·si·as·ti·cism \-tə-ˌsi-zəm\ *n* (ca. 1859) : excessive attachment to ecclesiastical forms and practices

Ec·cle·si·as·ti·cus \-ti-kəs\ *n* [LL, fr. *ecclesiasticus*] (1533) : a didactic book included in the Protestant Apocrypha and as Sirach in the Roman Catholic canon of the Old Testament

ec·cle·si·ol·o·gy \i-ˌklē-zē-ˈä-lə-jē, e-ˌklē-\ *n, pl* **-gies** (ca. 1837) **1** : the study of church architecture and adornment **2** : theological doctrine relating to the church — **ec·cle·si·o·log·i·cal** \-zē-ə-ˈlä-ji-kəl\ *adj* — **ec·cle·si·ol·o·gist** \-zē-ˈä-lə-jist\ *n*

Ecclus *abbr* Ecclesiasticus

ec·crine gland \ˈe-krən-, -ˌkrīn-, -ˌkrēn-\ *n* [Gk *ekkrinein* to secrete, fr. *ek-, ex-* out + *krinein* to separate — more at CERTAIN] (ca. 1927) : any of the rather small sweat glands in the human skin that produce a fluid secretion without removing cytoplasm from the secretory cells — called also *eccrine sweat gland*

ec·dys·i·ast \ek-ˈdi-zē-ˌast, -zē-əst\ *n* [Gk *ekdysis*] (1940) : STRIPTEASER

ec·dy·sis \ˈek-də-səs\ *n, pl* **ec·dy·ses** \-də-ˌsēz\ [NL, fr. Gk *ekdysis* act of getting out, fr. *ekdyein* to strip, fr. *ex-* + *dyein* to enter, don] (ca. 1854) : the act of molting or shedding an outer cuticular layer

ec·dy·sone \ˈek-də-ˌsōn\ *also* **ec·dy·son** \-ˌsän\ *n* [ISV *ecdys*is + hor*mone*] (1956) : any of several arthropod hormones that in insects are produced by the prothoracic gland and that trigger molting and metamorphosis

ece·sis \i-ˈsē-səs, -ˈkē-\ *n* [NL, fr. Gk *oikēsis* inhabitation, fr. *oikein* to inhabit — more at ECUMENICAL] (ca. 1904) : the establishment of a plant or animal in a new habitat

ECG *abbr* electrocardiogram

echelle \ā-ˈshel\ *n* [F, lit., ladder, fr. OF *eschele*] (1949) : a diffraction grating made by ruling a plane metallic mirror with lines having a relatively wide spacing

[1]**ech·e·lon** \ˈe-shə-ˌlän\ *n* [F *échelon,* lit., rung of a ladder, fr. OF *eschelon,* fr. *eschele* ladder, fr. LL *scala*] (1796) **1 a (1)** : an arrangement of a body of troops with its units each somewhat to the left or right of the one in the rear like a series of steps **(2)** : a formation of units or individuals resembling such an echelon ⟨geese flying in ~⟩ **(3)** : a flight formation in which each airplane flies at a certain elevation above or below and at a certain distance behind and to the right or left of the airplane ahead **b** : any of several military units in echelon formation; *also* : any unit or group acting in a disciplined or organized manner ⟨served in a combat ~⟩ **2 a** : one of a series of levels or grades in an organization or field of activity ⟨involved employees at every ~⟩ **b** : a group of individuals at a particular level or grade in an organization ⟨the upper ~*s* of the bureaucracy⟩

[2]**echelon** *vt* (ca. 1860) : to form or arrange in an echelon ~ *vi* : to take position in an echelon

ech·e·ve·ria \ˌe-chə-və-ˈrē-ə\ *n* [NL, genus name, after Atanasio *Echevería fl*1771 Mex. botanical illustrator] (1883) : any of a large genus (*Echeveria*) of tropical American succulent plants of the orpine family that have showy rosettes of often plushy basal leaves and axillary clusters of flowers with erect petals

echid·na \i-ˈkid-nə\ *n* [NL, fr. L, viper, fr. Gk — more at OPHITIC] (1832) : a spiny-coated toothless burrowing nocturnal monotreme mammal (*Tachyglossus aculeatus*) of Australia, Tasmania, and New Guinea that has a long extensible tongue and long heavy claws and that feeds chiefly on ants; *also* : a related mammal (*Zaglossus bruijni*) of New Guinea having a longer snout and shorter spines

echin- *or* **echino-** *comb form* [L, fr. Gk, fr. *echinos* sea urchin] **1** : prickle ⟨*echino*derm⟩ **2** : sea urchin ⟨*echin*oid⟩

ech·i·na·cea \ˌe-ki-ˈnā-sē-ə, -sh(ē-)ə\ *n* [NL, genus name, fr. *echin-* + *-acea* (fem. of *-aceus* -aceous)] (ca. 1859) : the dried rhizome, roots, or other parts of any of three purple coneflowers that are used primarily in dietary supplements and herbal remedies for the stimulating effect they are held to have on the immune system; *also* : any of these herbs

echi·no·coc·co·sis \i-ˌkī-nə-kä-ˈkō-səs\ *n, pl* **-co·ses** \-ˌsēz\ [NL] (1900) : infestation with or disease caused by an echinococcus

echi·no·coc·cus \i-ˌkī-nə-ˈkä-kəs\ *n, pl* **-coc·ci** \-ˈkäk-ˌ(s)ī, -ˈkäk-(ˌ)(s)ē\ [NL, genus name] (1839) : any of a genus (*Echinococcus*) of tapeworms that alternate a minute adult living as a commensal in the intestine of carnivores with a hydatid larva invading tissues esp. of the liver of cattle, sheep, swine, and humans and acting as a dangerous pathogen

echi·no·derm \i-ˈkī-nə-ˌdərm\ *n* [NL *Echinodermata,* phylum name, fr. *echin-* + *-dermata* (ultim. fr. Gk *derma* skin)] (1835) : any of a phylum (Echinodermata) of radially symmetrical coelomate marine animals including the starfishes, sea urchins, and related forms — **echi·no·der·ma·tous** \-ˌkī-nə-ˈdər-mə-təs\ *adj*

echi·noid \i-ˈkī-ˌnȯid, ˈe-kə-ˌnȯid\ *n* (1864) : SEA URCHIN

echi·nus \i-ˈkī-nəs\ *n, pl* **-ni** \-ˌnī\ [ME, fr. L, fr. Gk *echinos* hedgehog, sea urchin — more at OPHITE] (14c) **1** : SEA URCHIN **2 a** : the rounded molding that lies directly beneath the abacus in the capital of a column in the Greek Doric order **b :** a similar member in other orders

echi·uroid \ˌe-ki-ˈyu̇r-ˌȯid\ *n* [NL *Echiuroidea* or *Echiura,* ultim. fr. Gk *echis* viper + *oura* tail] (ca. 1889) **:** any of a phylum (Echiura syn. Echiuroidea) of marine worms of uncertain taxonomic affinities that have a sensitive but nonretractile proboscis above the mouth

[1]**echo** \ˈe-(ˌ)kō\ *n, pl* **ech·oes** *also* **echos** [ME *ecco,* fr. MF & L; MF *echo,* fr. L, fr. Gk *ēchō;* akin to L *vagire* to wail, Gk *ēchē* sound] (14c) **1 a :** the repetition of a sound caused by reflection of sound waves **b :** the sound due to such reflection **2 a :** a repetition or imitation of another **:** REFLECTION **b :** REPERCUSSION, RESULT **c :** TRACE, VESTIGE **d :** RESPONSE **3 :** one who closely imitates or repeats another's words, ideas, or acts **4 :** a soft repetition of a musical phrase **5 a :** the repetition of a received radio signal due esp. to reflection of part of the wave from an ionized layer of the atmosphere **b** (1) **:** the reflection of transmitted radar signals by an object (2) **:** the visual indication of this reflection on a radarscope — **echo·ey** \ˈe-ˌkō-ē\ *adj*

[2]**echo** *vb* **ech·oed; echo·ing** \ˈe-(ˌ)kō-iŋ, ˈe-kə-wiŋ\ *vi* (1596) **1 :** to resound with echoes **2 :** to produce an echo ~ *vt* **1 a :** REPEAT, IMITATE ⟨children ~*ing* their teacher's words⟩ **b :** to restate in support or agreement ⟨his successor ~*ed* his opinion⟩ **c :** to be reminiscent of **:** EVOKE ⟨music that ~*es* an earlier time⟩ **2 :** to send back (a sound) by the reflection of sound waves

[1]**Echo** *n* [Gk *Ēchō*] (1595) **:** a nymph in Greek mythology who pines away for love of Narcissus until nothing is left of her but her voice

[2]**Echo** (1952) — a communications code word for the letter *e*

echo·car·dio·gram \ˌe-kō-ˈkär-dē-ə-ˌgram\ *n* (1967) **:** a visual record made by echocardiography; *also* **:** the procedure for producing such a record

echo·car·di·og·ra·phy \-ˌkär-dē-ˈä-grə-fē\ *n, pl* **-phies** (1965) **:** the use of ultrasound to examine the structure and functioning of the heart for abnormalities and disease — **echo·car·di·og·raph·er** \-grə-fər\ *n* — **echo·car·dio·graph·ic** \-dē-ə-ˈgra-fik\ *adj*

echo chamber *n* (ca. 1937) **:** a room with sound-reflecting walls used for producing hollow or echoing sound effects

echo·ic \ə-ˈkō-ik, e-\ *adj* (ca. 1880) **1 :** formed in imitation of some natural sound **:** ONOMATOPOEIC **2 :** of or relating to an echo

echo·la·lia \ˌe-kō-ˈlā-lē-ə\ *n* [NL] (ca. 1885) **:** the often pathological repetition of what is said by other people as if echoing them — **echo·lal·ic** \-ˈla-lik\ *adj*

echo·lo·ca·tion \ˌe-kō-lō-ˈkā-shən\ *n* (ca. 1944) **:** a physiological process for locating distant or invisible objects (as prey) by sound waves reflected back to the emitter (as a bat) from the objects

echo sounder *n* (1927) **:** an instrument for determining the depth of a body of water or of an object below the surface by sound waves

echo·vi·rus \ˈe-kō-ˌvī-rəs\ *n* [*e*nteric *c*ytopathogenic *h*uman *o*rphan + *virus*] (1955) **:** any of numerous serotypes of an enterovirus (species *Human enterovirus B*) found in the gastrointestinal tract that cause cytopathic changes in cells in tissue culture and are sometimes associated with respiratory ailments and meningitis

echt \ˈekt\ *adj* [G *echt* & Yiddish *ekht*] (1916) **:** TRUE, GENUINE ⟨an ~ New Yorker⟩

éclair \ē-ˈkler, ā-, e-, ə-; ˈē-ˌ, ˈā-ˌ, ˈe-ˌ\ *n* [F, lit., lightning] (1861) **:** a usu. chocolate-frosted oblong pastry filled with whipped cream or custard

éclair·cis·se·ment \ā-kler-sēs-(ə-)mä^{n}\ *n, pl* **-ments** \-mä^{n}(z)\ [F] (1667) **:** a clearing up of something obscure **:** ENLIGHTENMENT

eclamp·sia \i-ˈklam(p)-sē-ə\ *n* [NL, fr. Gk *eklampsis* sudden flashing, fr. *eklampein* to shine forth, fr. *ex-* out + *lampein* to shine] (ca. 1860) **:** a convulsive state; *esp* **:** an attack of convulsions during pregnancy or parturition — **eclamp·tic** \-ˈklam(p)-tik\ *adj*

éclat \ā-ˈklä, ˈā-ˌ\ *n* [F, splinter, burst, éclat] (1672) **1 :** ostentatious display **:** PUBLICITY **2 :** dazzling effect **:** BRILLIANCE **3 a :** brilliant or conspicuous success **b :** PRAISE, APPLAUSE

[1]**eclec·tic** \e-ˈklek-tik, i-\ *adj* [Gk *eklektikos,* fr. *eklegein* to select, fr. *ex-* out + *legein* to gather — more at LEGEND] (1683) **1 :** selecting what appears to be best in various doctrines, methods, or styles **2 :** composed of elements drawn from various sources; *also* **:** HETEROGENEOUS — **eclec·ti·cal·ly** \-ti-k(ə-)lē\ *adv*

[2]**eclectic** *n* (1817) **:** one who uses an eclectic method or approach

eclec·ti·cism \-ˈklek-tə-ˌsi-zəm\ *n* (1798) **:** the theory or practice of an eclectic method

[1]**eclipse** \i-ˈklips\ *n* [ME, fr. AF, fr. L *eclipsis,* fr. Gk *ekleipsis,* fr. *ekleipein* to omit, fail, suffer eclipse, fr. *ex-* + *leipein* to leave — more at LOAN] (13c) **1 a :** the total or partial obscuring of one celestial body by another **b :** the passing into the shadow of a celestial body — compare OCCULTATION, TRANSIT **2 :** a falling into obscurity or decline; *also* **:** the state of being eclipsed ⟨his reputation has fallen into ~⟩ **3 :** the state of being in eclipse plumage

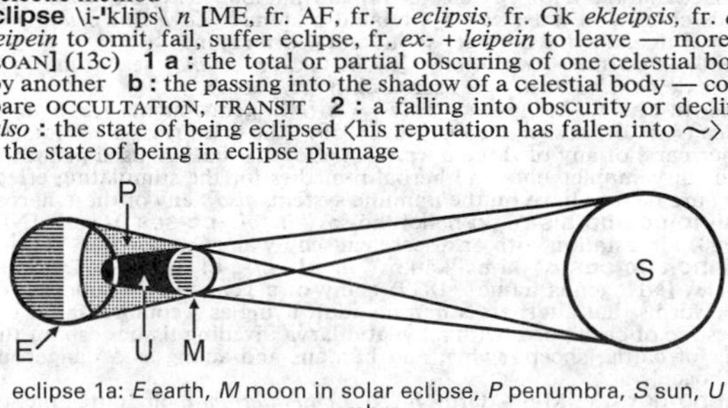

eclipse 1a: *E* earth, *M* moon in solar eclipse, *P* penumbra, *S* sun, *U* umbra

[2]**eclipse** *vt* **eclipsed; eclips·ing** (13c) **:** to cause an eclipse of: as **a :** OBSCURE, DARKEN **b :** to reduce in importance or repute **c :** SURPASS ⟨her score *eclipsed* the old record⟩

eclipse plumage *n* (1906) **:** comparatively dull plumage that is usu. of seasonal occurrence in birds exhibiting a distinct breeding plumage

[1]**eclip·tic** \i-ˈklip-tik\ *adj* [ME *ecliptik,* fr. LL *ecliptica linea,* lit., line of eclipses] (14c) **:** of or relating to the ecliptic or an eclipse

[2]**ecliptic** *n* (15c) **:** the great circle of the celestial sphere that is the apparent path of the sun among the stars or of the earth as seen from the sun **:** the plane of the earth's orbit extended to meet the celestial sphere

ec·logue \ˈek-ˌlȯg, -ˌläg\ *n* [ME *eclog,* fr. L *Eclogae,* title of Virgil's pastorals, lit., selections, pl. of *ecloga,* fr. Gk *eklogē,* fr. *eklegein* to select] (15c) **:** a poem in which shepherds converse

eclo·sion \i-ˈklō-zhən\ *n* [F *éclosion,* fr. *éclore* to hatch, fr. VL **exclaudere,* alter. of L *excludere* to hatch out, exclude] (ca. 1889) *of an insect* **:** the act of emerging from the pupal case or hatching from the egg

ECM *abbr* **1** electronic countermeasure **2** European Common Market

eco- *comb form* [LL *oeco-* household, fr. Gk *oik-, oiko-,* fr. *oikos* house — more at VICINITY] **1 :** habitat or environment ⟨*eco*species⟩ **2 :** ecological or environmental ⟨*eco*catastrophe⟩

eco·ca·tas·tro·phe \ˌē-(ˌ)kō-kə-ˈtas-trə-fē, ˌe-(ˌ)kō-\ *n* (1969) **:** a major destructive upset in the balance of nature esp. when caused by the action of humans

eco·cide \ˈē-kə-ˌsīd, ˈe-, -(ˌ)kō-\ *n* [*eco-* + *-cide*] (1969) **:** the destruction of large areas of the natural environment esp. as a result of deliberate human action — **eco·cid·al** \-ˈsī-d^{ə}l\ *adj*

eco–con·scious \ˈē-kō-ˌkän(t)-shəs, ˈe-\ *adj* (1988) **:** marked by or showing concern for the environment ⟨~ consumers⟩

eco·fem·i·nism \ˌē-kō-ˈfe-mə-ˌni-zəm, ˌe-kō-\ *n* (1980) **:** a movement or theory that applies feminist principles and ideas to ecological issues — **eco·fem·i·nist** \-nist\ *n or adj*

eco–friend·ly \ˌē-kō-ˈfren(d)-lē, ˌe-kō-\ *adj* (1989) **:** not environmentally harmful ⟨~ construction options⟩

ecol *abbr* ecological; ecology

E. coli \ˌē-ˈkō-ˌlī\ *n, pl* **E. coli** (1926) **:** an enterobacterium (*Escherichia coli*) that is used in public health as an indicator of fecal pollution (as of water or food) and in medicine and genetics as a research organism and that occurs in various strains that may live as harmless inhabitants of the human lower intestine or may produce a toxin causing intestinal illness

ecol·o·gy \i-ˈkä-lə-jē, e-\ *n, pl* **-gies** [G *Ökologie,* fr. *öko-* eco- + *-logie* -logy] (1873) **1 :** a branch of science concerned with the interrelationship of organisms and their environments **2 :** the totality or pattern of relations between organisms and their environment **3 :** HUMAN ECOLOGY **4 :** ENVIRONMENT, CLIMATE ⟨the moral ~⟩; *also* **:** an often delicate or intricate system or complex ⟨the ~ of language⟩ — **eco·log·i·cal** \ˌē-kə-ˈlä-ji-kəl, ˌe-kə-\ *also* **eco·log·ic** \-jik\ *adj* — **eco·log·i·cal·ly** \-ji-k(ə-)lē\ *adv* — **ecol·o·gist** \i-ˈkä-lə-jist, e-\ *n*

e–com·merce \ˈē-ˌkä-(ˌ)mərs\ *n, often attrib* (1993) **:** commerce conducted via the Internet

econ *abbr* economics; economist; economy

econo·box \i-ˈkä-nō-ˌbäks, ē-\ *n* [*econo*mical + [2]*box*] (1979) **:** a small economical car

econo·met·rics \i-ˌkä-nə-ˈme-triks, ē-ˌkä-\ *n pl but sing in constr* [blend of *economics* and *metric*] (1931) **:** the application of statistical methods to the study of economic data and problems — **econo·met·ric** \-trik\ *adj* — **econo·met·ri·cal·ly** \-tri-k(ə-)lē\ *adv* — **econo·me·tri·cian** \-mə-ˈtri-shən\ *n* — **econo·met·rist** \-ˈme-trist\ *n*

eco·nom·ic \ˌe-kə-ˈnä-mik, ˌē-kə-\ *adj* (1592) **1** *archaic* **:** of or relating to a household or its management **2 :** ECONOMICAL 2 **3 a :** of or relating to economics ⟨~ theories⟩ **b :** of, relating to, or based on the production, distribution, and consumption of goods and services ⟨~ growth⟩ **c :** of or relating to an economy ⟨a group of ~ advisers⟩ **4 :** having practical or industrial significance or uses **:** affecting material resources **5 :** PROFITABLE

eco·nom·i·cal \-ˈnä-mi-kəl\ *adj* (15c) **1** *archaic* **:** ECONOMIC 1 **2 :** marked by careful, efficient, and prudent use of resources **:** THRIFTY ⟨an ~ shopper⟩ **3 :** operating with little waste or at a saving ⟨an ~ car⟩ ***syn*** see SPARING

eco·nom·i·cal·ly \-ˈnä-mi-k(ə-)lē\ *adv* (1786) **:** in an economic or economical manner

economic rent *n* (1889) **:** the return for the use of a factor in excess of the minimum required to bring forth its service

eco·nom·ics \ˌe-kə-ˈnä-miks, ˌē-kə-\ *n pl but sing or pl in constr* (1792) **1 a :** a social science concerned chiefly with description and analysis of the production, distribution, and consumption of goods and services **b :** economic theory, principles, or practices ⟨sound ~⟩ **2 :** economic aspect or significance ⟨the ~ of building a new stadium⟩ **3 :** economic conditions ⟨current ~⟩

econ·o·mise *Brit var of* ECONOMIZE

econ·o·mist \i-ˈkä-nə-mist\ *n* (1586) **1** *archaic* **:** one who practices economy **2 :** a specialist in economics

econ·o·mize \-ˌmīz\ *vb* **-mized; -miz·ing** *vi* (1816) **:** to practice economy **:** be frugal ~ *vt* **:** to use frugally **:** SAVE — **econ·o·miz·er** *n*

[1]**econ·o·my** \i-ˈkä-nə-mē, ə-, ē-\ *n, pl* **-mies** [MF *yconomie,* fr. ML *oeconomia,* fr. Gk *oikonomia,* fr. *oikonomos* household manager, fr. *oikos* house + *nemein* to manage — more at VICINITY, NIMBLE] (15c) **1** *archaic* **:** the management of household or private affairs and esp. expenses **2 a :** thrifty and efficient use of material resources **:** frugality in expenditures; *also* **:** an instance or a means of economizing **:** SAVING **b :** efficient and concise use of nonmaterial resources (as effort, language, or motion) **3 a :** the arrangement or mode of operation of something **:** ORGANIZATION **b :** a system esp. of interaction and exchange ⟨an ~ of information⟩ **4 :** the structure or conditions of economic life in a country, area, or period; *also* **:** an economic system

[2]**economy** *adj* (ca. 1906) **:** designed to save money ⟨~ cars⟩

economy of scale (1944) **:** a reduction in the cost of producing something (as a car or a unit of electricity) brought about esp. by increased size of production facilities — usu. used in pl.

eco·phys·i·ol·o·gy \ˌē-kō-ˌfi-zē-ˈä-lə-jē, ˌe-kō-\ *n* (1962) **:** the science of the interrelationships between the physiology of organisms and their environment — **eco·phys·i·o·log·i·cal** \-zē-ə-ˈlä-ji-kəl\ *adj*

eco·sphere \ˈē-kō-ˌsfir, ˈe-kō-\ *n* (1953) **:** the parts of the universe habitable by living organisms; *esp* **:** BIOSPHERE 1

eco·sys·tem \-ˌsis-təm\ *n* (1935) **:** the complex of a community of organisms and its environment functioning as an ecological unit

eco·ter·ror·ism \ˌē-kō-ˈter-ər-i-zəm, ˌe-kō-\ *n* (1987) **1 :** sabotage intended to hinder activities that are considered damaging to the environment **2 :** political terrorism intended to damage an enemy's natural environment — **eco·ter·ror·ist** \-ər-ist\ *n or adj*

eco·tone \ˈē-kə-ˌtōn, ˈe-kə-\ *n* [*ec-* + Gk *tonos* tension — more at TONE] (1904) **:** a transition area between two adjacent ecological communities — **eco·ton·al** \-ˌtō-n^{ə}l\ *adj*

eco·tour·ism \ˌē-kō-ˈtu̇r-ˌi-zəm, ˌe-kō-\ *n* (1982) **:** the practice of touring natural habitats in a manner meant to minimize ecological impact — **eco·tour** \ˈē-kō-ˌtu̇r\ *n* — **eco·tour·ist** \ˌē-kō-ˈtu̇r-ist\ *n*

eco·tox·i·col·o·gy \-ˌtäk-si-ˈkä-lə-jē\ *n* (1977) **:** a scientific discipline combining the methods of ecology and toxicology in studying the effects of toxic substances and esp. pollutants on the environment — **eco·tox·i·co·log·i·cal** \-kə-ˈlä-ji-kəl\ *adj* — **eco·tox·i·col·o·gist** \-ˈkä-lə-jist\ *n*

eco·type \ˈē-kə-ˌtīp, ˈe-\ *n* (1922) **:** a population of a species that survives as a distinct group through environmental selection and isolation and that is comparable with a taxonomic subspecies — **eco·typ·ic** \ˌē-kə-ˈti-pik, ˌe-kə-\ *adj*

ecphrasis *var of* EKPHRASIS

ecru \ˈe-(ˌ)krü, ˈā-(ˌ)krü\ *n* [F *écru,* lit., unbleached, raw, fr. OF *escru,* fr. *es-* completely (fr. L *ex-*) + *cru* raw, fr. L *crudus* — more at RAW] (1836) **:** BEIGE 2 — **ecru** *adj*

ec·sta·sy \ˈek-stə-sē\ *n, pl* **-sies** [ME *extasie,* fr. MF, fr. LL *ecstasis,* fr. Gk *ekstasis,* fr. *existanai* to derange, fr. *ex-* out + *histanai* to cause to stand — more at EX-, STAND] (14c) **1 a :** a state of being beyond reason and self-control **b** *archaic* **:** SWOON **2 :** a state of overwhelming emotion; *esp* **:** rapturous delight **3 :** TRANCE; *esp* **:** a mystic or prophetic trance **4** *often cap* **:** a synthetic amphetamine analog $C_{11}H_{15}NO_2$ used illicitly for its mood-enhancing and hallucinogenic properties — called also *MDMA*

syn ECSTASY, RAPTURE, TRANSPORT mean intense exaltation of mind and feelings. ECSTASY and RAPTURE both suggest a state of trance or near immobility produced by an overpowering emotion. ECSTASY may apply to any strong emotion (as joy, fear, rage, adoration) ⟨religious *ecstasy*⟩. RAPTURE usu. implies intense bliss or beatitude ⟨in speechless *rapture*⟩. TRANSPORT applies to any powerful emotion that lifts one out of oneself and usu. provokes vehement expression or frenzied action ⟨in a *transport* of rage⟩.

[1]**ec·stat·ic** \ek-ˈsta-tik, ik-ˈsta-\ *adj* [ML *ecstaticus,* fr. Gk *ekstatikos,* fr. *existanai*] (1590) **:** of, relating to, or marked by ecstasy — **ec·stat·i·cal·ly** \-ˈsta-ti-k(ə-)lē\ *adv*

[2]**ecstatic** *n* (1659) **:** one that is subject to ecstasies

ECT *abbr* electroconvulsive therapy

ect- *or* **ecto-** *comb form* [NL, fr. Gk *ekto-,* fr. *ektos,* fr. *ex* out — more at EX-] **:** outside **:** external ⟨*ecto*derm⟩ — compare END-, EXO-

ec·to·derm \ˈek-tə-ˌdərm\ *n* [ISV] (1859) **1 :** the outer cellular membrane of a diploblastic animal (as a jellyfish) **2 a :** the outermost of the three primary germ layers of an embryo that is the source of various tissues and structures (as the epidermis, the nervous system, and the eyes and ears) **b :** a tissue (as neural tissue) derived from this germ layer — **ec·to·der·mal** \ˌek-tə-ˈdər-məl\ *adj*

ec·to·morph \ˈek-tə-ˌmȯrf\ *n* [*ecto*derm + *-morph*] (1940) **:** an ectomorphic individual

ec·to·mor·phic \ˌek-tə-ˈmȯr-fik\ *adj* [*ecto*derm + *-morphic;* fr. the predominance in such types of structures developed from the ectoderm] (1940) **1 :** of or relating to the component in W. H. Sheldon's classification of body types that measures the body's degree of slenderness, angularity, and fragility **2 :** characterized by a lean slender body build with slight muscular development

-ectomy *n comb form* [NL *-ectomia,* fr. Gk *ektemnein* to cut out, fr. *ec-, ex-* out + *temnein* to cut — more at TOME] **:** surgical removal ⟨gastr*ectomy*⟩

ec·to·par·a·site \ˌek-tō-ˈper-ə-ˌsīt, -ˈpa-rə-\ *n* [ISV] (1861) **:** a parasite that lives on the exterior of its host — **ec·to·par·a·sit·ic** \-ˌper-ə-ˈsi-tik, -pa-rə-\ *adj*

ec·top·ic \ek-ˈtä-pik\ *adj* [Gk *ektopos* out of place, fr. *ex-* out + *topos* place] (1873) **:** occurring in an abnormal position or in an unusual manner or form ⟨~ lesions⟩ — **ec·top·i·cal·ly** \-pi-k(ə-)lē\ *adv*

ectopic pregnancy *n* (1895) **:** development of a fertilized egg elsewhere than in the uterus (as in a fallopian tube or the peritoneal cavity)

ec·to·plasm \ˈek-tə-ˌpla-zəm\ *n* (1883) **1 :** the outer relatively rigid granule-free layer of the cytoplasm usu. held to be a gel reversibly convertible to a sol **2 :** a substance held to produce spirit materialization and telekinesis — **ec·to·plas·mic** \ˌek-tə-ˈplaz-mik\ *adj*

ec·to·therm \ˈek-tə-ˌthərm\ *n* (1940) **:** a cold-blooded animal **:** POIKILOTHERM — **ec·to·ther·mic** \ˌek-tə-ˈthər-mik\ *adj*

ec·to·tro·phic \ˌek-tə-ˈtrō-fik\ *adj* (ca. 1889) *of a mycorrhiza* **:** growing in a close web on the surface of the associated root — compare ENDOTROPHIC

[1]**ecu** \ˈā-ˌkyü, ā-ˈkᵫ\ *n, pl* **ecus** \-ˌkyüz, -ˈkᵫ\ [MF, lit., shield, fr. OF *escu,* fr. L *scutum;* from the device of a shield on the coin — more at ESQUIRE] (ca. 1593) **:** any of various old French units of value; *also* **:** a coin representing an ecu

[2]**ecu** \ˌē-(ˌ)sē-ˈyü\ *n, often cap E&C&U* [European Currency Unit (influenced by F *écu* ecu)] (1970) **:** a money of account based on the currency units of members of the European Union from 1979 up to the introduction of the euro in 1999

Ecua *abbr* Ecuador

ec·u·men·i·cal \ˌe-kyə-ˈme-ni-kəl, -kyü-\ *adj* [LL *oecumenicus,* fr. LGk *oikoumenikos,* fr. Gk *oikoumenē* the inhabited world, fr. fem. of *oikoumenos,* pres. pass. part. of *oikein* to inhabit, fr. *oikos* house — more at VICINITY] (ca. 1587) **1 :** worldwide or general in extent, influence, or application **2 a :** of, relating to, or representing the whole of a body of churches **b :** promoting or tending toward worldwide Christian unity or cooperation — **ec·u·men·i·cal·ly** \-k(ə-)lē\ *adv*

ec·u·men·i·cal·ism \-ˈme-ni-kə-ˌli-zəm\ *n* (1888) **:** ECUMENISM

ecumenical patriarch *n, often cap E&P* (1862) **:** the patriarch of Constantinople as the dignitary given first honor in the Eastern Orthodox Church

ec·u·men·i·cism \ˌe-kyə-ˈme-nə-ˌsi-zəm, -kyü-\ *n* (1961) **:** ECUMENISM — **ec·u·men·i·cist** \-sist\ *n*

ec·u·me·nic·i·ty \ˌe-kyə-mə-ˈni-sə-tē, -me-, -kyü-\ *n* (1840) **:** the quality or state of being drawn close to others through ecumenism

ec·u·men·ics \-ˈme-niks\ *n pl but sing in constr* (ca. 1945) **:** the study of the nature, mission, problems, and strategy of the Christian church from the perspective of its ecumenical character

ecu·me·nism \e-ˈkyü-mə-ˌni-zəm, i- *also* ˈe-kyə- *or* ˌe-kyə-ˈme-\ *n* (1948) **:** ecumenical principles and practices esp. as shown among religious groups (as Christian denominations) — **ecu·me·nist** \e-ˈkyü-mə-nist, i- *also* ˈe-kyə-mə-nist *or* ˌe-kyə-ˈme-nist\ *n*

ec·ze·ma \ig-ˈzē-mə, ˈeg-zə-mə, ˈek-sə-\ *n* [NL, fr. Gk *ekzema,* fr. *ekzein* to erupt, fr. *ex-* out + *zein* to boil — more at EX-, YEAST] (ca. 1753) **:** an inflammatory condition of the skin characterized by redness, itching, and oozing vesicular lesions which become scaly, crusted, or hardened — **ec·zem·a·tous** \ig-ˈze-mə-təs\ *adj*

[1]**ed** \ˈed\ *n* (1954) **:** EDUCATION ⟨driver's ~⟩ ⟨adult ~⟩

[2]**ed** *abbr* edited; edition; editor

ED *abbr* erectile dysfunction

[1]**-ed** \d *after a vowel or* b, g, j, l, m, n, ŋ, r, th, v, z, *or* zh; əd, id *after* d *or* t; t *after other sounds; exceptions are pronounced at their entries*\ *vb suffix or adj suffix* [ME, fr. OE *-ed, -od, -ad;* akin to OHG *-t,* pp. ending, L *-tus,* Gk *-tos,* suffix forming verbals] **1 —** used to form the past participle of regular weak verbs ⟨end*ed*⟩ ⟨fad*ed*⟩ ⟨tri*ed*⟩ ⟨patt*ed*⟩ **2 —** used to form adjectives of identical meaning from Latin-derived adjectives ending in *-ate* ⟨crenulat*ed*⟩ **3 a :** having **:** characterized by ⟨cultur*ed*⟩ ⟨two-legg*ed*⟩ **b :** having the characteristics of ⟨bigot*ed*⟩

[2]**-ed** *vb suffix* [ME *-ede, -de,* fr. OE *-de, -ede, -ode, -ade;* akin to OHG *-ta,* past ending (1st sing.) and prob. to OHG *-t,* pp. ending] — used to form the past tense of regular weak verbs ⟨judg*ed*⟩ ⟨deni*ed*⟩ ⟨dropp*ed*⟩

eda·cious \i-ˈdā-shəs\ *adj* [L *edac-, edax,* fr. *edere* to eat — more at EAT] (ca. 1798) **1** *archaic* **:** of or relating to eating **2 :** VORACIOUS — **edac·i·ty** \-ˈda-sə-tē\ *n*

Edam \ˈē-dəm, ˈē-ˌdam\ *n* [*Edam,* Netherlands] (1836) **:** a yellow pressed cheese of Dutch origin usu. made in flattened balls and often coated with red wax

ed·a·ma·me \ˌe-də-ˈmä-mā\ *n* [Jp, fr. *eda* branch + *mame* beans] (1951) **:** immature green soybeans usu. in the pod

edaph·ic \i-ˈda-fik\ *adj* [Gk *edaphos* bottom, ground] (ca. 1900) **1 :** of or relating to the soil **2 :** resulting from or influenced by the soil rather than the climate — compare CLIMATIC 2 — **edaph·i·cal·ly** \-ˈda-fi-k(ə-)lē\ *adv*

edaphic climax *n* (1926) **:** an ecological climax resulting from soil factors and commonly persisting through cycles of climatic and physiographic change — compare CLIMATIC CLIMAX

EDB *abbr* ethylene dibromide

EdD *abbr* doctor of education

EDD *abbr* English Dialect Dictionary

Ed·dic \ˈe-dik\ *adj* [ON *Edda,* a 13th cent. collection of mythological, heroic, and aphoristic poetry] (1868) **:** of, relating to, or resembling the Old Norse *Edda*

[1]**ed·dy** \ˈe-dē\ *n, pl* **eddies** [ME (Sc) *ydy,* prob. fr. ON *itha*] (15c) **1 a :** a current of water or air running contrary to the main current; *esp* **:** a circular current **:** WHIRLPOOL **b :** something moving similarly **2 :** a contrary or circular current (as of thought or policy)

[2]**eddy** *vb* **ed·died; ed·dy·ing** *vt* (1810) **:** to cause to move in an eddy ~ *vi* **:** to move in an eddy or in the manner of an eddy

eddy current *n* (1886) **:** an electric current induced by an alternating magnetic field

edel·weiss \ˈā-dᵊl-ˌvīs, -ˌwīs\ *n* [G, fr. *edel* noble + *weiss* white] (1862) **:** a small alpine perennial composite herb (*Leontopodium alpinum*) of central and southeast Europe that has a dense woolly white pubescence

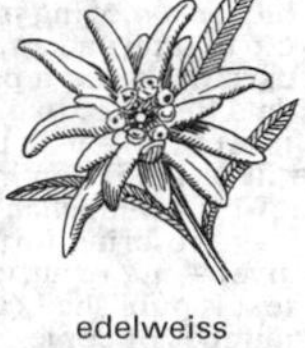

edelweiss

ede·ma \i-ˈdē-mə\ *n* [NL, fr. Gk *oidēma* swelling, fr. *oidein* to swell; akin to Arm *aytnu-* swell, OE *ātor* poison] (15c) **1 :** an abnormal infiltration and excess accumulation of serous fluid in connective tissue or in a serous cavity — called also *dropsy* **2 a :** watery swelling of plant organs or parts **b :** any of various plant diseases characterized by such swellings — **edem·a·tous** \-ˈde-mə-təs\ *adj*

Eden \ˈē-dᵊn\ *n* [LL, fr. Heb *ʽĒdhen*] (bef. 12c) **1 :** PARADISE 2 **2 :** the garden where according to the account in Genesis Adam and Eve first lived **3 :** a place of pristine or abundant natural beauty — **Eden·ic** \i-ˈde-nik, ē-\ *adj*

[1]**eden·tate** \(ˌ)ē-ˈden-ˌtāt\ *adj* [L *edentatus,* pp. of *edentare* to make toothless, fr. *e-* + *dent-, dens* tooth — more at TOOTH] (1828) **1 :** lacking teeth **2 :** being an edentate

[2]**edentate** *n* (1835) **:** any of an order (Edentata) of mammals having few or no teeth and including the sloths, armadillos, and New World anteaters and formerly also the pangolins and the aardvark

eden·tu·lous \(ˌ)ē-ˈden-chə-ləs\ *adj* [L *edentulus,* fr. *e-* + *dent-, dens*] (1782) **:** TOOTHLESS

Ed·gar \ˈed-gər\ *n* [*Edgar* Allan Poe, regarded as father of the detective story] (1947) **:** a statuette awarded annually by a professional organization for notable achievement in mystery-novel writing

[1]**edge** \ˈej\ *n* [ME *egge,* fr. OE *ecg;* akin to L *acer* sharp, Gk *akmē* point] (bef. 12c) **1 a :** the cutting side of a blade ⟨a razor's ~⟩ **b :** the sharpness of a blade ⟨a knife with no ~⟩ **c (1) :** FORCE, EFFECTIVENESS ⟨blunted the ~ of the legislation⟩ **(2) :** vigor or energy esp. of body ⟨maintains his hard ~⟩ **d (1) :** incisive or penetrating quality ⟨writing with a satirical ~⟩ **(2) :** a noticeably harsh or sharp quality ⟨her voice had an ~ to it⟩ **(3) :** a secondary but distinct quality ⟨rock music with a bluesy ~⟩ **e :** keenness or intensity of desire or enjoyment ⟨lost my competitive ~⟩ **2 a :** the line where an object or area begins or ends **:** BORDER ⟨on the ~ of a plain⟩ **b :** the narrow part adjacent to a border ⟨the ~ of the deck⟩ **c (1) :** a point near the beginning or the end; *esp* **:** BRINK, VERGE ⟨on the ~ of disaster⟩ **(2) :** the threshold of danger or ruin ⟨living on the ~⟩ **d :** a favorable margin **:** ADVANTAGE ⟨has an ~ on the competition⟩ **3 :** a line or line segment that is the intersection of two plane faces (as of a pyramid) or of two planes — **edge·less** *adj* — **on edge :** ANXIOUS, NERVOUS

[2]**edge** *vb* **edged; edg·ing** *vt* (14c) **1 a :** to give an edge to **b :** to be on an edge of ⟨trees *edging* the lake⟩ **2 :** to move or force gradually ⟨*edged* him off the road⟩ **3 :** to incline (a ski) sideways so that one edge cuts into the snow **4 :** to defeat by a small margin — often used with *out* ⟨*edged* out her opponent⟩ ~ *vi* **:** to advance by short moves

edge city *n* (1988) **:** a suburb that has developed its own political, economic, and commercial base independent of the central city

edged \ˈejd, ˈe-jid\ *adj* (bef. 12c) **1 :** having a specified kind of edge, boundary, or border or a specified number of edges ⟨rough-*edged*⟩ ⟨two-*edged*⟩ **2 :** SHARP, CUTTING ⟨an ~ knife⟩ ⟨an ~ remark⟩
edge effect *n* (1933) **:** the effect of an abrupt transition between two quite different adjoining ecological communities on the numbers and kinds of organisms in the marginal habitat
edge–grain \ˈej-ˌgrān\ *or* **edge–grained** \ˈej-ˌgrānd\ *adj* (1906) **:** QUARTERSAWN
edge in *vt* (1683) **:** to work in **:** INTERPOLATE ⟨*edged in* a few remarks⟩
edg·er \ˈe-jər\ *n* (1591) **:** one that edges; *esp* **:** a tool used to trim the edge of a lawn along a sidewalk or curb
edge tool *n* (14c) **:** a tool with a sharp cutting edge
edge·ways \ˈej-ˌwāz\ *adv* (1566) *chiefly Brit* **:** SIDEWAYS
edge·wise \-ˌwīz\ *adv* (1677) **1 :** SIDEWAYS **2 :** as if by an edge **:** BARELY — usu. used in the phrase *get a word in edgewise*
edg·ing *n* (1558) **:** something that forms an edge or border
edgy \ˈe-jē\ *adj* **edg·i·er; -est** (1775) **1 :** having an edge **:** SHARP **2 a :** being on edge **:** TENSE, IRRITABLE **b :** characterized by tension ⟨~ negotiations⟩ **3 :** having a bold, provocative, or unconventional quality ⟨an ~ film⟩ — **edg·i·ly** \ˈe-jə-lē\ *adv* — **edg·i·ness** \ˈe-jē-nəs\ *n*
edh *also* **eth** \ˈeth\ *n* [Icel *eth*] (1875) **:** the letter ð used in Old English to represent either of the fricatives \th\ or \th\ and in Icelandic and some phonetic alphabets to represent the fricative \th\
EDI *abbr* electronic data interchange
Edi·a·car·an \ˌē-dē-ˈa-k(ə-)rən, -ə-ˈka-rən\ *also* **Edi·a·cara** \-k(ə-)rə, -rə\ *adj* [*Ediacara* Hills, South Australia] (1966) **:** being or belonging to an assemblage of extinct multicellular marine organisms of the Late Precambrian era ⟨~ fauna⟩ — **Ediacaran** *n*
ed·i·ble \ˈe-də-bəl\ *adj* [LL *edibilis,* fr. L *edere* to eat — more at EAT] (1594) **:** fit to be eaten **:** EATABLE — **ed·i·bil·i·ty** \ˌe-də-ˈbi-lə-tē\ *n* — **edible** *n* — **ed·i·ble·ness** \ˈe-də-bəl-nəs\ *n*
edict \ˈē-ˌdikt\ *n* [ME, fr. L *edictum,* fr. neut. of *edictus,* pp. of *edicere* to decree, fr. *e-* + *dicere* to say — more at DICTION] (14c) **1 :** a proclamation having the force of law **2 :** ORDER, COMMAND ⟨we held firm to Grandmother's ~ —M. F. K. Fisher⟩ — **edic·tal** \i-ˈdik-tᵊl\ *adj*
ed·i·fi·ca·tion \ˌe-də-fə-ˈkā-shən\ *n* (14c) **:** an act or process of edifying
ed·i·fice \ˈe-də-fəs\ *n* [ME, fr. AF, fr. L *aedificium,* fr. *aedificare*] (14c) **1 :** BUILDING; *esp* **:** a large or massive structure **2 :** a large abstract structure ⟨holds together the social ~ —R. H. Tawney⟩
ed·i·fy \ˈe-də-ˌfī\ *vt* **-fied; -fy·ing** [ME, fr. AF *edifier,* fr. LL & L; LL *aedificare* to instruct or improve spiritually, fr. L, to erect a house, fr. *aedes* temple, house; akin to OE *ād* funeral pyre, L *aestas* summer] (14c) **1** *archaic* **a :** BUILD **b :** ESTABLISH **2 :** to instruct and improve esp. in moral and religious knowledge **:** UPLIFT; *also* **:** ENLIGHTEN, INFORM
[1]**ed·it** \ˈe-dət\ *vt* [back-formation fr. *editor*] (1791) **1 a :** to prepare (as literary material) for publication or public presentation **b :** to assemble (as a moving picture or tape recording) by cutting and rearranging **c :** to alter, adapt, or refine esp. to bring about conformity to a standard or to suit a particular purpose ⟨carefully ~*ed* the speech⟩ ⟨~ a data file⟩ **2 :** to direct the publication of ⟨~*s* the daily newspaper⟩ **3 :** DELETE — usu. used with *out* — **ed·it·able** \ˈe-də-tə-bəl\ *adj*
[2]**edit** *n* (1955) **:** an instance or result of editing
edi·tion \i-ˈdi-shən\ *n* [MF, fr. L *edition-, editio* publication, edition, fr. *edere* to bring forth, publish, fr. *e-* + *-dere* to put or *-dere* (fr. *dare* to give) — more at DO, DATE] (1555) **1 a :** the form or version in which a text is published ⟨a paperback ~⟩ ⟨the German ~⟩ **b (1) :** the whole number of copies published at one time **(2) :** a usu. special issue of a newspaper (as for a particular day or purpose) ⟨Sunday ~⟩ ⟨international ~⟩ **(3) :** one of the usu. several issues of a newspaper in a single day ⟨city ~⟩ ⟨late ~⟩ **2 a :** one of the forms in which something is presented ⟨this year's ~ of the annual charity ball⟩ **b :** the whole number of articles of one style put out at one time ⟨a limited ~ of collectors' pieces⟩ **3 :** COPY, VERSION
edi·tio prin·ceps \ā-ˌdi-tē-(ˌ)ō-ˈpriŋ-ˌkeps, i-ˌdi-shē-(ˌ)ō-ˈprin-ˌseps\ *n, pl* **edi·ti·o·nes prin·ci·pes** \ā-ˌdi-tē-ˈō-ˌnās-ˈpriŋ-kə-ˌpās, i-ˌdi-shē-ˈō-(ˌ)nēz-ˈprin(t)-sə-ˌpēz\ [NL, lit., first edition] (1802) **:** the first printed edition esp. of a work that circulated in manuscript before printing became common
ed·i·tor \ˈe-də-tər\ *n* (1649) **1 :** someone who edits esp. as an occupation **2 :** a device used in editing motion-picture film or magnetic tape **3 :** a computer program that permits the user to create or modify data (as text or graphics) esp. on a display screen — **ed·i·tor·ship** \-ˌship\ *n*
[1]**ed·i·to·ri·al** \ˌe-də-ˈtȯr-ē-əl\ *adj* (1744) **1 :** of or relating to an editor or editing ⟨an ~ office⟩ **2 :** being or resembling an editorial ⟨an ~ statement⟩ — **ed·i·to·ri·al·ly** \-ē-ə-lē\ *adv*
[2]**editorial** *n* (1830) **:** a newspaper or magazine article that gives the opinions of the editors or publishers; *also* **:** an expression of opinion that resembles such an article ⟨a television ~⟩
ed·i·to·ri·al·ist \-ē-ə-list\ *n* (1901) **:** a writer of editorials
ed·i·to·ri·al·ize \ˌe-də-ˈtȯr-ē-ə-ˌlīz\ *vi* **-ized; -iz·ing** (1856) **1 :** to express an opinion in the form of an editorial **2 :** to introduce opinion into the reporting of facts **3 :** to express an opinion (as on a controversial issue) — **ed·i·to·ri·al·i·za·tion** \-ˌtȯr-ē-ə-lə-ˈzā-shən\ *n* — **ed·i·to·ri·al·iz·er** *n*
editor in chief *n* (1873) **:** an editor who heads an editorial staff
ed·i·tress \ˈe-də-trəs\ *n* (1799) **:** a woman who is an editor
ed·i·trix \ˈe-də-ˌtriks\ *n, pl* **-trix·es** \-ˌtrik-səz\ *or* **-tri·ces** \ˌe-də-ˈtrī-(ˌ)sēz\ (1845) **:** EDITRESS
EdM *abbr* master of education
Edom·ite \ˈē-də-ˌmīt\ *n* [*Edom* (Esau), ancestor of the Edomites] (1534) **:** a member of a Semitic people living south of the Dead Sea in biblical times
EDP *abbr* electronic data processing
EdS *abbr* specialist in education
EDT *abbr* eastern daylight time
EDTA \ˌē-(ˌ)dē-(ˌ)tē-ˈā\ *n* [*e*thylene*d*iamine*t*etra*a*cetic acid] (1951) **:** a white crystalline acid $C_{10}H_{16}N_2O_8$ used esp. as a chelating agent, a preservative, and in medicine as an anticoagulant and in the treatment of lead poisoning
edu *abbr* educational institution — usu. preceded by a period; used in World Wide Web addresses
educ *abbr* education; educational
ed·u·ca·ble \ˈe-jə-kə-bəl\ *adj* (1845) **:** capable of being educated; *specif* **:** capable of some degree of learning — **ed·u·ca·bil·i·ty** \ˌe-jə-kə-ˈbi-lə-tē\ *n*
ed·u·cate \ˈe-jə-ˌkāt\ *vb* **-cat·ed; -cat·ing** [ME, to rear, fr. L *educatus,* pp. of *educare* to rear, educate, fr. *educere* to lead forth — more at EDUCE] *vt* (15c) **1 a :** to provide schooling for ⟨chose to ~ their children at home⟩ **b :** to train by formal instruction and supervised practice esp. in a skill, trade, or profession **2 a :** to develop mentally, morally, or aesthetically esp. by instruction **b :** to provide with information **:** INFORM ⟨*educating* themselves about changes in the industry⟩ **3 :** to persuade or condition to feel, believe, or act in a desired way ⟨~ the public to support our position⟩ ~ *vi* **:** to educate a person or thing
syn see TEACH
educated *adj* (1588) **1 :** having an education; *esp* **:** having an education beyond the average ⟨~ speakers⟩ **2 a :** giving evidence of training or practice **:** SKILLED ⟨~ hands⟩ **b :** befitting one that is educated ⟨~ taste⟩ **c :** based on some knowledge of fact ⟨an ~ guess⟩ — **ed·u·cat·ed·ness** *n*
ed·u·ca·tion \ˌe-jə-ˈkā-shən\ *n* (1531) **1 a :** the action or process of educating or of being educated; *also* **:** a stage of such a process **b :** the knowledge and development resulting from an educational process ⟨a person of little ~⟩ **2 :** the field of study that deals mainly with methods of teaching and learning in schools — **ed·u·ca·tion·al** \-shnəl, -shə-nᵊl\ *adj* — **ed·u·ca·tion·al·ly** \-ē\ *adv*
educational psychology *n* (1911) **:** psychology concerned with human maturation, school learning, teaching methods, guidance, and evaluation of aptitude and progress by standardized tests — **educational psychologist** *n*
educational television *n* (1951) **1 :** television that provides instruction esp. for students **2 :** public television
ed·u·ca·tion·ese \ˌe-jə-ˌkā-shə-ˈnēz, -ˈnēs\ *n* (1954) **:** the jargon used esp. by educational theorists
ed·u·ca·tion·ist \ˌe-jə-ˈkā-sh(ə-)nist\ *also* **ed·u·ca·tion·al·ist** \-shnə-list, -shə-nᵊl-ist\ *n* (1829) **1** *chiefly Brit* **:** a professional educator **2 :** an educational theorist
ed·u·ca·tive \ˈe-jə-ˌkā-tiv\ *adj* (1844) **1 :** tending to educate **:** INSTRUCTIVE ⟨an ~ experience⟩ **2 :** of or relating to education
ed·u·ca·tor \ˈe-jə-ˌkā-tər\ *n* (1673) **1 :** one skilled in teaching **:** TEACHER **2 a :** a student of the theory and practice of education **:** EDUCATIONIST 2 **b :** an administrator in education
educe \i-ˈdüs *also* -ˈdyüs\ *vt* **educed; educ·ing** [L *educere* to draw out, fr. *e-* + *ducere* to lead — more at TOW] (1603) **1 :** to bring out (as something latent) **2 :** DEDUCE — **educ·ible** \-ˈdü-sə-bəl *also* -ˈdyü-\ *adj* — **educ·tion** \-ˈdək-shən\ *n*
syn EDUCE, EVOKE, ELICIT, EXTRACT, EXTORT mean to draw out something hidden, latent, or reserved. EDUCE implies the bringing out of something potential or latent ⟨*educed* order out of chaos⟩. EVOKE implies a strong stimulus that arouses an emotion or an interest or recalls an image or memory ⟨a song that *evokes* warm memories⟩. ELICIT usu. implies some effort or skill in drawing forth a response ⟨careful questioning *elicited* the truth⟩. EXTRACT implies the use of force or pressure in obtaining answers or information ⟨*extracted* a confession from him⟩. EXTORT suggests a wringing or wresting from one who resists strongly ⟨*extorted* their cooperation by threatening to inform⟩.
educ·tor \i-ˈdək-tər\ *n* [LL, one that leads out, fr. L *educere*] (1796) **:** EJECTOR 2
ed·u·tain·ment \ˌe-jə-ˈtān-mənt, ˌe-dyü-\ *n* [*edu*cation + enter*tainment*] (1973) **:** entertainment (as by games, films, or shows) that is designed to be educational
Ed·war·di·an \e-ˈdwär-dē-ən, -ˈdwȯr-\ *adj* (1908) **:** of, relating to, or characteristic of Edward VII of England or his age; *esp, of clothing* **:** marked by the hourglass silhouette for women and long narrow fitted suits and high collars for men — **Edwardian** *n*
EE *abbr* electrical engineer
[1]**-ee** *n suffix* [ME *-e,* fr. AF *-é,* fr. *-é,* pp. ending, fr. L *-atus*] **1 :** recipient or beneficiary of (a specified action) ⟨appoint*ee*⟩ ⟨grant*ee*⟩ **2 :** person furnished with (a specified thing) ⟨patent*ee*⟩ **3 :** person that performs (a specified action) ⟨escap*ee*⟩
[2]**-ee** *n suffix* [prob. alter. of *-y*] **1 :** one associated with ⟨barg*ee*⟩ **2 :** a particular esp. small kind of ⟨boot*ee*⟩ **3 :** one resembling or suggestive of ⟨goat*ee*⟩
EEC *abbr* European Economic Community
EEG *abbr* electroencephalogram; electroencephalograph
eek \ˈēk\ *interj* (1951) — used to express surprise or dismay
eel \ˈēl\ *n* [ME *ele,* fr. OE *ǣl;* akin to OHG *āl* eel] (bef. 12c) **1 a :** any of numerous voracious elongate snakelike bony fishes (order Anguilliformes) that have a smooth slimy skin, lack pelvic fins, and have the median fins confluent around the tail — compare AMERICAN EEL **b :** any of numerous other elongate fishes (as of the order Synbranchiformes) **2 :** any of various nematodes (as the vinegar eel) — **eel·like** \ˈēl-ˌlīk\ *adj* — **eely** \ˈē-lē\ *adj*
eel·grass \ˈēl-ˌgras\ *n* (1790) **1 :** a submerged long-leaved monocotyledonous marine plant (*Zostera marina*) that is found esp. in coastal temperate waters and whose dried stems and leaves are used esp. as packing material in woven goods **2 :** TAPE GRASS
eel·pout \-ˌpau̇t\ *n* (bef. 12c) **1 :** any of various elongate tapered marine fishes (family Zoarcidae) usu. living on the bottom of cold seas **2 :** BURBOT
eel·worm \-ˌwərm\ *n* (1888) **:** a nematode worm; *esp* **:** any of various small free-living or plant-parasitic roundworms
-een *n suffix* [prob. fr. *ratteen*] **:** inferior fabric resembling (a specified fabric) **:** imitation ⟨velvet*een*⟩
e'en \ˈēn\ *adv* (ca. 1553) **:** EVEN
EENT *abbr* eye, ear, nose, and throat
EEO *abbr* equal employment opportunity
EEOC *abbr* Equal Employment Opportunity Commission
EEPROM *abbr* electronically erasable programmable read-only memory
-eer *n suffix* [MF *-ier,* fr. L *-arius* — more at -ARY] **:** one that is concerned with professionally, conducts, or produces ⟨auction*eer*⟩ ⟨pamphlet*eer*⟩ — often in words with derogatory meaning ⟨profit*eer*⟩
e'er \ˈer\ *adv* (13c) **:** EVER
ee·rie *also* **ee·ry** \ˈir-ē\ *adj* **ee·ri·er; -est** [ME (northern dial.) *eri*] (14c) **1** *chiefly Scot* **:** affected with fright **:** SCARED **2 :** so mysterious,

strange, or unexpected as to send a chill up the spine ⟨a coyote's ~ howl⟩ ⟨the similarities were ~⟩; *also* : seemingly not of earthly origin ⟨the flames cast an ~ glow⟩ *syn* see WEIRD — **ee·ri·ly** \ˈir-ə-lē\ *adv* — **ee·ri·ness** \ˈir-ē-nəs\ *n*

EEZ *abbr* exclusive economic zone

ef \ˈef\ *n* (bef. 12c) : the letter *f*

eff *abbr* efficiency

ef·face \i-ˈfās, e-\ *vt* **ef·faced; ef·fac·ing** [ME, fr. AF *esfacer, effacer,* fr. *e-* + *face* face] (15c) **1** : to eliminate or make indistinct by or as if by wearing away a surface ⟨coins with dates *effaced* by wear⟩; *also* : to cause to vanish ⟨daylight *effaced* the stars⟩ **2** : to make (oneself) modestly or shyly inconspicuous — **ef·face·able** \-ˈfā-sə-bəl\ *adj* — **ef·face·ment** \-ˈfās-mənt\ *n* — **ef·fac·er** *n*

[1]**ef·fect** \i-ˈfekt, e-, ē-, ə-\ *n* [ME, fr. AF & L; AF, fr. L *effectus,* fr. *efficere* to bring about, fr. *ex-* + *facere* to make, do — more at DO] (14c) **1 a** : PURPORT, INTENT **b** : basic meaning : ESSENCE **2** : something that inevitably follows an antecedent (as a cause or agent) **3** : an outward sign : APPEARANCE **4** : ACCOMPLISHMENT, FULFILLMENT **5** : power to bring about a result : INFLUENCE ⟨the content itself of television . . . is therefore less important than its ~ —*Current Biog.*⟩ **6** *pl* : movable property : GOODS ⟨personal ~*s*⟩ **7 a** : a distinctive impression ⟨the color gives the ~ of being warm⟩ **b** : the creation of a desired impression ⟨her tears were purely for ~⟩ **c (1)** : something designed to produce a distinctive or desired impression — usu. used in pl. **(2)** *pl* : SPECIAL EFFECTS **8** : the quality or state of being operative : OPERATION ⟨the law goes into ~ next week⟩ — **in effect** : in substance : VIRTUALLY ⟨the . . . committee agreed to what was *in effect* a reduction in the hourly wage —*Current Biog.*⟩ — **to the effect** : with the meaning ⟨issued a statement *to the effect* that he would resign⟩

[2]**effect** *vt* (1533) **1** : to cause to come into being **2 a** : to bring about often by surmounting obstacles : ACCOMPLISH ⟨~ a settlement of a dispute⟩ **b** : to put into operation ⟨the duty of the legislature to ~ the will of the citizens⟩ *syn* see PERFORM

usage *Effect* and *affect* are often confused because of their similar spelling and pronunciation. The verb [2]*affect* usu. has to do with pretense ⟨she *affected* a cheery disposition despite feeling down⟩. The more common [3]*affect* denotes having an effect or influence ⟨the weather *affected* everyone's mood⟩. The verb *effect* goes beyond mere influence; it refers to actual achievement of a final result ⟨the new administration hopes to *effect* a peace settlement⟩. The uncommon noun *affect,* which has a meaning relating to psychology, is also sometimes mistakenly used for the very common *effect.* In ordinary use, the noun you will want is *effect* ⟨waiting for the new law to take *effect*⟩ ⟨the weather had an *effect* on everyone's mood⟩.

[1]**ef·fec·tive** \i-ˈfek-tiv, e-, ē-, ə-\ *adj* (14c) **1 a** : producing a decided, decisive, or desired effect ⟨an ~ policy⟩ **b** : IMPRESSIVE, STRIKING ⟨a gold lamé fabric studded with ~ . . . precious stones —Stanley Marcus⟩ **2** : ready for service or action ⟨~ manpower⟩ **3** : ACTUAL ⟨the need to increase ~ demand for goods⟩ **4** : being in effect : OPERATIVE ⟨the tax becomes ~ next year⟩ **5** *of a rate of interest* : equal to the rate of simple interest that yields the same amount when the interest is paid once at the end of the interest period as a quoted rate of interest does when calculated at compound interest over the same period — compare NOMINAL 4 — **ef·fec·tive·ness** *n* — **ef·fec·tiv·i·ty** \ˌe-ˌfek-ˈti-və-tē, i-, ē-, ə-\ *n*

syn EFFECTIVE, EFFECTUAL, EFFICIENT, EFFICACIOUS mean producing or capable of producing a result. EFFECTIVE stresses the actual production of or the power to produce an effect ⟨an *effective* rebuttal⟩. EFFECTUAL suggests the accomplishment of a desired result esp. as viewed after the fact ⟨the measures to stop the pilfering proved *effectual*⟩. EFFICIENT suggests an acting or a potential for action or use in such a way as to avoid loss or waste of energy in effecting, producing, or functioning ⟨an *efficient* small car⟩. EFFICACIOUS suggests possession of a special quality or virtue that gives effective power ⟨a detergent that is *efficacious* in removing grease⟩.

[2]**effective** *n* (1722) : one that is effective; *esp* : a soldier equipped for duty

ef·fec·tive·ly \-lē\ *adv* (ca. 1536) **1** : in effect : VIRTUALLY ⟨by withholding further funds they ~ killed the project⟩ **2** : in an effective manner ⟨dealt with the problem ~⟩

ef·fec·tor \i-ˈfek-tər, -ˌtȯr\ *n* (1906) **1** : a bodily organ (as a gland or muscle) that becomes active in response to stimulation **2** : a molecule (as an inducer or a corepressor) that activates, controls, or inactivates a process or action (as protein synthesis)

ef·fec·tu·al \i-ˈfek-chə(-wə)l, -chü(-ə)l; -ˈfeksh-wəl\ *adj* (14c) : producing or able to produce a desired effect *syn* see EFFECTIVE — **ef·fec·tu·al·i·ty** \-ˌfek-chə-ˈwa-lə-tē, -chü-ˈa-\ *n* — **ef·fec·tu·al·ness** \-ˈfek-chə(-wə)l-nəs, -chü(-ə)l-; -ˈfeksh-wəl-\ *n*

ef·fec·tu·al·ly \i-ˈfek-chə(-wə)-lē, -chü(-ə)-; -ˈfek-shwə-\ *adv* (14c) **1** : in an effectual manner **2** : with great effect : COMPLETELY

ef·fec·tu·ate \i-ˈfek-chə-ˌwāt, -chü-ˌāt\ *vt* **-at·ed; -at·ing** (1580) : EFFECT 2 — **ef·fec·tu·a·tion** \-ˌfek-chə-ˈwā-shən, -chü-ˈā-\ *n*

ef·fem·i·na·cy \ə-ˈfe-mə-nə-sē\ *n* (1602) : the quality of being effeminate

[1]**ef·fem·i·nate** \-nət\ *adj* [ME, fr. L *effeminatus,* fr. pp. of *effeminare* to make effeminate, fr. *ex-* + *femina* woman — more at FEMININE] (15c) **1** : having feminine qualities untypical of a man : not manly in appearance or manner **2** : marked by an unbecoming delicacy or overrefinement ⟨~ art⟩ ⟨an ~ civilization⟩

[2]**effeminate** *n* (1597) : an effeminate person

ef·fen·di \e-ˈfen-dē, ə-\ *n* [Turk *efendi* master, fr. ModGk *aphentēs,* alter. of Gk *authentēs* — more at AUTHENTIC] (1614) : a man of property, authority, or education in an eastern Mediterranean country

ef·fer·ent \ˈe-fə-rənt, -ˌfer-, ˈē-\ *adj* [F *efférent,* fr. L *efferent-, efferens,* prp. of *efferre* to carry outward, fr. *ex-* + *ferre* to carry — more at BEAR] (1856) : conducting outward from a part or organ; *specif* : conveying nervous impulses to an effector ⟨~ neurons⟩ — compare AFFERENT — **efferent** *n* — **ef·fer·ent·ly** *adv*

ef·fer·vesce \ˌe-fər-ˈves\ *vi* **-vesced; -vesc·ing** [L *effervescere,* fr. *ex-* + *fervescere* to begin to boil, incho. of *fervēre* to boil — more at BREW] (1784) **1** : to bubble, hiss, and foam as gas escapes **2** : to show liveliness or exhilaration — **ef·fer·ves·cence** \-ˈve-sᵊn(t)s\ *n* — **ef·fer·ves·cent** \-sᵊnt\ *adj* — **ef·fer·ves·cent·ly** *adv*

ef·fete \e-ˈfēt, i-\ *adj* [L *effetus,* fr. *ex-* + *fetus* fruitful — more at FEMININE] (1660) **1** : no longer fertile **2 a** : having lost character, vitality, or strength ⟨the ~ monarchies . . . of feudal Europe —G. M. Trevelyan⟩ **b** : marked by weakness or decadence ⟨the ~ East⟩ **c** : soft or delicate from or as if from a pampered existence ⟨peddled . . . trendy tweeds to ~ Easterners —William Helmer⟩ ⟨~ tenderfeet⟩; *also* : characteristic of an effete person ⟨a wool scarf . . . a bit ~ on an outdoorsman —Nelson Bryant⟩ **3** : EFFEMINATE 1 ⟨a good-humored, ~ boy brought up by maiden aunts —Herman Wouk⟩ — **ef·fete·ly** *adv* — **ef·fete·ness** *n*

ef·fi·ca·cious \ˌe-fə-ˈkā-shəs\ *adj* [L *efficac-, efficax,* fr. *efficere*] (1528) : having the power to produce a desired effect ⟨an ~ remedy⟩ *syn* see EFFECTIVE — **ef·fi·ca·cious·ly** *adv* — **ef·fi·ca·cious·ness** *n*

ef·fi·cac·i·ty \ˌe-fə-ˈka-sə-tē\ *n* (15c) : EFFICACY

ef·fi·ca·cy \ˈe-fi-kə-sē\ *n, pl* **-cies** (13c) : the power to produce an effect

ef·fi·cien·cy \i-ˈfi-shən-sē\ *n, pl* **-cies** (1633) **1** : the quality or degree of being efficient **2 a** : efficient operation **b (1)** : effective operation as measured by a comparison of production with cost (as in energy, time, and money) **(2)** : the ratio of the useful energy delivered by a dynamic system to the energy supplied to it **3** : EFFICIENCY APARTMENT

efficiency apartment *n* (1930) : a small usu. furnished apartment with minimal kitchen and bath facilities

efficiency expert *n* (1913) : one who analyzes methods, procedures, and jobs in order to secure maximum efficiency — called also *efficiency engineer*

ef·fi·cient \i-ˈfi-shənt\ *adj* [ME, fr. MF or L; MF, fr. L *efficient-, efficiens,* fr. prp. of *efficere*] (14c) **1** : being or involving the immediate agent in producing an effect ⟨the ~ action of heat in changing water to steam⟩ **2** : productive of desired effects; *esp* : productive without waste ⟨an ~ worker⟩ *syn* see EFFECTIVE — **ef·fi·cient·ly** *adv*

ef·fi·gy \ˈe-fə-jē\ *n, pl* **-gies** [MF *effigie,* fr. L *effigies,* fr. *effingere* to form, fr. *ex-* + *fingere* to shape — more at DOUGH] (1539) : an image or representation esp. of a person; *esp* : a crude figure representing a hated person — **in effigy** : publicly in the form of an effigy ⟨the football coach was burned *in effigy*⟩

ef·flo·resce \ˌe-flə-ˈres\ *vi* **-resced; -resc·ing** [L *efflorescere,* fr. *ex-* + *florescere* to begin to blossom — more at FLORESCENCE] (1775) **1** : to burst forth : BLOOM **2 a** : to change to a powder from loss of water of crystallization **b** : to form or become covered with a powdery crust ⟨bricks may ~ owing to the deposition of soluble salts⟩

ef·flo·res·cence \-ˈre-sᵊn(t)s\ *n* (1626) **1 a** : the action or process of developing and unfolding as if coming into flower : BLOSSOMING ⟨periods of . . . intellectual and artistic ~ —Julian Huxley⟩ **b** : an instance of such development **c** : fullness of manifestation : CULMINATION **2** : the period or state of flowering **3** : the process or product of efflorescing chemically — **ef·flo·res·cent** \-sᵊnt\ *adj*

ef·flu·ence \ˈe-ˌflü-ən(t)s; e-ˈflü-, ə-ˈ\ *n* (1603) **1** : something that flows out **2** : an action or process of flowing out

[1]**ef·flu·ent** \-ənt\ *adj* [L *effluent-, effluens,* prp. of *effluere* to flow out, fr. *ex-* + *fluere* to flow — more at FLUID] (1726) : flowing out : EMANATING, OUTGOING ⟨an ~ river⟩

[2]**effluent** *n* (1859) : something that flows out: as **a** : an outflowing branch of a main stream or lake **b** : waste material (as smoke, liquid industrial refuse, or sewage) discharged into the environment esp. when serving as a pollutant

ef·flu·vi·um \e-ˈflü-vē-əm\ *also* **ef·flu·via** \-vē-ə\ *n, pl* **-via** *also* **-vi·ums** [L *effluvium* act of flowing out, fr. *effluere*] (1651) **1** : an invisible emanation; *esp* : an offensive exhalation or smell **2** : a by-product esp. in the form of waste

ef·flux \ˈe-ˌfləks\ *n* [ML *effluxus,* fr. *effluere*] (1647) **1** : something given off in or as if in a stream **2 a** : EFFLUENCE 2 **b** : a passing away : EXPIRATION — **ef·flux·ion** \e-ˈflək-shən\ *n*

ef·fort \ˈe-fərt, -ˌfȯrt\ *n* [MF, fr. OF *esforz, esfort,* fr. *esforcier* to force, fr. *ex-* + *forcier* to force] (15c) **1** : conscious exertion of power : hard work ⟨a job requiring time and ~⟩ **2** : a serious attempt : TRY ⟨making an ~ to reduce costs⟩ **3** : something produced by exertion or trying ⟨the novel was her most ambitious ~⟩ **4** : effective force as distinguished from the possible resistance called into action by such a force **5** : the total work done to achieve a particular end ⟨the war ~⟩

ef·fort·ful \-fərt-fəl\ *adj* (ca. 1895) : showing or requiring effort — **ef·fort·ful·ly** \-fə-lē\ *adv* — **ef·fort·ful·ness** \-fəl-nəs\ *n*

ef·fort·less \-fərt-ləs\ *adj* (1801) : showing or requiring little or no effort ⟨~ power⟩ *syn* see EASY — **ef·fort·less·ly** *adv* — **ef·fort·less·ness** *n*

ef·fron·tery \i-ˈfrən-tə-rē, e-\ *n, pl* **-ter·ies** [F *effronterie,* ultim. fr. ML *effront-, effrons* shameless, fr. L *ex-* + *front-, frons* forehead] (1697) : shameless boldness : INSOLENCE *syn* see TEMERITY

ef·ful·gence \i-ˈfu̇l-jən(t)s, e-, -ˈfəl-\ *n* [LL *effulgentia,* fr. L *effulgent-, effulgens,* prp. of *effulgēre* to shine forth, fr. *ex-* + *fulgēre* to shine — more at FULGENT] (1667) : radiant splendor : BRILLIANCE — **ef·ful·gent** \-jənt\ *adj*

[1]**ef·fuse** \i-ˈfyüz, e-\ *vb* **ef·fused; ef·fus·ing** [L *effusus,* pp. of *effundere,* fr. *ex-* + *fundere* to pour — more at FOUND] *vt* (1526) : to pour out (a liquid) ~ *vi* **1** : to flow out : EMANATE **2** : to make a great or excessive display of enthusiasm ⟨they *effused* about his accomplishments⟩

[2]**ef·fuse** \-ˈfyüs\ *adj* (ca. 1530) : DIFFUSE; *specif* : spread out flat without definite form ⟨~ lichens⟩

ef·fu·sion \i-ˈfyü-zhən, e-\ *n* (15c) **1** : an act of effusing **2** : unrestrained expression of words or feelings ⟨greeted her with great ~ —Olive H. Prouty⟩ **3 a (1)** : the escape of a fluid from anatomical vessels by rupture or exudation **(2)** : the flow of a gas through an aperture whose diameter is small as compared with the distance between the molecules of the gas **b** : the fluid that escapes

ef·fu·sive \i-ˈfyü-siv, e-, -ziv\ *adj* (1662) **1** : marked by the expression of great or excessive emotion or enthusiasm ⟨~ praise⟩ **2** *archaic*

\ə\ **abut** \ᵊ\ kitten, F table \ər\ **fur**ther \a\ **a**sh \ā\ **a**ce \ä\ m**o**p, m**a**r \au̇\ **ou**t \ch\ **ch**in \e\ b**e**t \ē\ **ea**sy \g\ **g**o \i\ h**i**t \ī\ **i**ce \j\ **j**ob \ŋ\ si**ng** \ō\ g**o** \ȯ\ l**aw** \ȯi\ b**oy** \th\ **th**in \t͟h\ **th**e \ü\ l**oo**t \u̇\ f**oo**t \y\ **y**et \zh\ vi**si**on, bei**ge** \k, ⁿ, œ,ue, ʸ\ *see* Guide to Pronunciation

: pouring freely **3 :** characterized or formed by a nonexplosive outpouring of lava ‹~ rocks› — **ef·fu·sive·ly** *adv* — **ef·fu·sive·ness** *n*

Ef·ik \ˈe-fik\ *n* (1849) **1 :** a member of a people of southeastern Nigeria **2 :** the language of the Efik people

eft \ˈeft\ *n* [ME *evete, ewte,* fr. OE *efete*] (bef. 12c) **:** NEWT; *esp* **:** the terrestrial phase of a predominantly aquatic newt

EFT *or* **EFTS** *abbr* electronic funds transfer (system)

eft·soons \eft-ˈsünz\ *adv* [ME *eftsones,* alter. of OE *eftsōna,* fr. OE *eft* after + *sōna* soon; akin to OE *æfter* after] (bef. 12c) *archaic* **:** soon after

e.g. *abbr* [L *exempli gratia*] for example

Eg *abbr* Egypt; Egyptian

egad \i-ˈgad\ *or* **egads** \-ˈgadz\ *interj* [prob. euphemism for *oh God*] (1673) — used as a mild oath

egal \ˈē-gəl\ *adj* [ME, fr. AF, fr. L *aequalis*] (14c) *obs* **:** EQUAL

egal·i·tar·i·an \i-ˌga-lə-ˈter-ē-ən\ *adj* [F *égalitaire,* fr. *égalité* equality, fr. L *aequalitat-, aequalitas,* fr. *aequalis* equal] (1885) **:** asserting, promoting, or marked by egalitarianism — **egalitarian** *n*

egal·i·tar·i·an·ism \-ē-ə-ˌni-zəm\ *n* (1905) **1 :** a belief in human equality esp. with respect to social, political, and economic affairs **2 :** a social philosophy advocating the removal of inequalities among people

éga·li·té \ā-gä-lē-tā\ *n* [F] (1794) **:** social or political equality

Ege·ria \i-ˈjir-ē-ə\ *n* [L, a nymph who advised the legendary Roman king Numa Pompilius] (1621) **:** a woman who is an adviser or a companion

eges·ta \i-ˈjes-tə\ *n pl* [NL, fr. L, neut. pl. of *egestus*] (1727) **:** egested material

eges·tion \i-ˈjes(h)-chən\ *n* [ME *egestioun,* fr. MF or L; MF *egestion,* fr. L *egestion-, egestio,* fr. *egerere* to carry outside, discharge, fr. *e-* + *gerere* to carry] (1547) **:** the act or process of discharging undigested or waste material from a cell or organism; *specif* **:** DEFECATION — **egest** \i-ˈjest\ *vt* — **eges·tive** \-ˈjes-tiv\ *adj*

EGF *abbr* epidermal growth factor

[1]**egg** \ˈeg, ˈāg\ *vt* [ME, fr. ON *eggja;* akin to OE *ecg* edge — more at EDGE] (13c) **:** to incite to action — usu. used with *on*

[2]**egg** *n, often attrib* [ME *egge,* fr. ON *egg;* akin to OE *ǣg* egg, L *ovum,* Gk *ōion*] (14c) **1 a :** the hard-shelled reproductive body produced by a bird and esp. by the common domestic chicken; *also* **:** its contents used as food **b :** an animal reproductive body consisting of an ovum together with its nutritive and protective envelopes and having the capacity to develop into a new individual capable of independent existence **c :** OVUM **2 :** something resembling an egg **3 :** PERSON, SORT ‹a good ~› — **egg·less** *adj* — **eggy** \ˈe-gē, ˈā-\ *adj* — **egg on one's face :** a state of embarrassment or humiliation

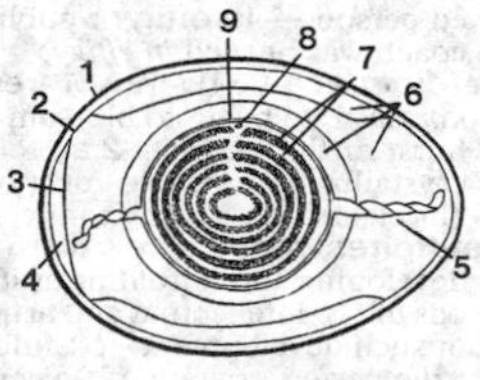

egg 1a: *1* shell, *2* outer shell membrane, *3* inner shell membrane, *4* air space, *5* chalaza, *6* albumen or white layers, *7* yolk layers, *8* blastodisc, *9* vitelline membrane

[3]**egg** *vt* (1833) **1 :** to cover with egg **2 :** to pelt with eggs

egg and dart *n* (ca. 1864) **:** a carved ornamental design in relief consisting of an egg-shaped figure alternating with a figure somewhat like an elongated javelin or arrowhead

egg·beat·er \ˈeg-ˌbē-tər, ˈāg-\ *n* (1828) **1 :** a hand-operated kitchen utensil used for beating, stirring, or whipping; *esp* **:** a rotary device for these purposes **2 :** HELICOPTER

egg case *n* (1847) **:** a protective case enclosing eggs **:** OOTHECA — called also *egg capsule*

egg cell *n* (1880) **:** OVUM

egg cream *n* (1906) **:** a sweetened drink made with milk or cream and other ingredients; *esp* **:** a drink consisting of milk, a flavoring syrup, and soda water

egg·cup \ˈeg-ˌkəp, ˈāg-\ *n* (1773) **:** a cup for holding an egg that is to be eaten from the shell

egg foo yong *or* **egg foo young** *or* **egg foo yung** \-ˈfü-ˈyəŋ\ *n* [Chin (Guangdong) *fùh yùhng* egg white, egg-coated ingredients, lit., a kind of hibiscus] (1917) **:** a fried egg patty containing vegetables (as bean sprouts) and sometimes meat

egg·head \-ˌhed\ *n, often attrib* (1952) **:** INTELLECTUAL, HIGHBROW

egg·head·ed \-ˈhe-dəd\ *adj* (1938) **:** having the characteristics of an egghead — **egg·head·ed·ness** *n*

egg·nog \-ˌnäg\ *n* (ca. 1775) **:** a drink consisting of eggs beaten with sugar, milk or cream, and often alcoholic liquor

egg·plant \-ˌplant\ *n* (1767) **1 a :** a widely cultivated perennial Asian herb (*Solanum melongena*) of the nightshade family yielding edible fruit **b :** the usu. smooth ovoid typically blackish-purple or white fruit of the eggplant **2 :** a dark grayish or blackish purple

egg roll *n* (1934) **:** a thin egg-dough casing filled with minced vegetables and often bits of meat (as shrimp or chicken) and usu. deep-fried

eggs Ben·e·dict \-ˈbe-nə-ˌdikt\ *n pl but sing or pl in constr* [prob. fr. the name *Benedict*] (1898) **:** poached eggs and broiled ham placed on toasted halves of English muffin and covered with hollandaise

[1]**egg·shell** \ˈeg-ˌshel, ˈāg-\ *n* (14c) **1 :** the hard exterior covering of an egg **2 :** something resembling an eggshell esp. in fragility

[2]**eggshell** *adj* (1835) **1 :** thin and fragile **2 :** slightly glossy **3 :** yellowish white

egg timer *n* (1884) **:** a small sandglass for timing the boiling of eggs

egg tooth *n* (1893) **:** a hard sharp prominence on the beak of an unhatched bird or the nose of an unhatched reptile that is used to break through the eggshell

egis *var of* AEGIS

eg·lan·tine \ˈe-glən-ˌtīn, -ˌtēn\ *n* [ME *eglentyn,* fr. AF *eglent,* fr. VL **aculentum,* fr. L *acus* needle; akin to L *acer* sharp — more at EDGE] (14c) **:** SWEETBRIAR

eglo·mi·se *also* **églo·mi·sé** \ˌā-glə-(ˌ)mē-ˈzā, ˌe-; ˈā-glə-(ˌ)mē-ˌ, ˈe-\ *adj* [F, pp. of *églomiser* to decorate a glass panel by painting on its back, fr. Jean-Baptiste *Glomy* †1786 Fr. decorator] (1877) **:** made of glass on the back of which is a painted picture that shows through

ego \ˈē-(ˌ)gō *also* ˈe-\ *n, pl* **egos** [NL, fr. L, I — more at I] (1789) **1 :** the self esp. as contrasted with another self or the world **2 a :** EGOTISM 2 **b :** SELF-ESTEEM 1 **3 :** the one of the three divisions of the psyche in psychoanalytic theory that serves as the organized conscious mediator between the person and reality esp. by functioning both in the perception of and adaptation to reality — compare ID, SUPEREGO — **ego·less** *adj*

ego·cen·tric \ˌē-gō-ˈsen-trik *also* ˌe-\ *adj* (1894) **1 :** concerned with the individual rather than society **2 :** taking the ego as the starting point in philosophy **3 a :** limited in outlook or concern to one's own activities or needs **b :** SELF-CENTERED, SELFISH — **egocentric** *n* — **ego·cen·tri·cal·ly** \-tri-k(ə-)lē\ *adv* — **ego·cen·tric·i·ty** \-ˌsen-ˈtri-sə-tē\ *n* — **ego·cen·trism** \-ˈsen-ˌtri-zəm\ *n*

ego ideal *n* (1922) **:** the standards, ideals, and ambitions that according to psychoanalytic theory are assimilated from the superego

ego·ism \ˈē-gə-ˌwi-zəm, -gō-ˌi- *also* ˈe-\ *n* (1800) **1 a :** a doctrine that individual self-interest is the actual motive of all conscious action **b :** a doctrine that individual self-interest is the valid end of all actions **2 :** excessive concern for oneself with or without exaggerated feelings of self-importance — compare EGOTISM 2

ego·ist \-gə-wist, -gō-ist\ *n* (1879) **1 :** a believer in egoism **2 :** an egocentric or egotistic person — **ego·is·tic** \ˌē-gə-ˈwis-tik, -gō-ˈis- *also* ˌe-\ *also* **ego·is·ti·cal** \-ti-kəl\ *adj* — **ego·is·ti·cal·ly** \-ti-k(ə-)lē\ *adv*

egoistic hedonism *n* (1874) **:** the ethical theory that achieving one's own happiness is the proper goal of all conduct

ego·ma·nia \ˌē-gō-ˈmā-nē-ə, -nyə\ *n* (1825) **:** the quality or state of being extremely egocentric — **ego·ma·ni·ac** \-nē-ˌak\ *n* — **ego·ma·ni·a·cal** \ˌmə ˈnī-ə-kəl\ *adj* — **ego·ma·ni·a·cal·ly** \-k(ə-)lē\ *adv*

ego·tism \ˈē-gə-ˌti-zəm *also* ˈe-\ *n* [L *ego* + E *-tism* (as in *idiotism*)] (1714) **1 a :** excessive use of the first person singular personal pronoun **b :** the practice of talking about oneself too much **2 :** an exaggerated sense of self-importance **:** CONCEIT — compare EGOISM 2 — **ego·tist** \-tist\ *n* — **ego·tis·tic** \ˌē-gə-ˈtis-tik *also* ˌe-\ *or* **ego·tis·ti·cal** \-ˈtis-ti-kəl\ *adj* — **ego·tis·ti·cal·ly** \-k(ə-)lē\ *adv*

ego trip *n* (1967) **:** an act or course of action that enhances and satisfies one's ego — **ego–trip** *vi* — **ego–trip·per** *n*

egre·gious \i-ˈgrē-jəs\ *adj* [L *egregius,* fr. *e-* + *greg-, grex* herd — more at GREGARIOUS] (ca. 1534) **1** *archaic* **:** DISTINGUISHED **2 :** CONSPICUOUS; *esp* **:** conspicuously bad **:** FLAGRANT ‹~ errors› — **egre·gious·ly** *adv* — **egre·gious·ness** *n*

[1]**egress** \ˈē-ˌgres\ *n* [L *egressus,* fr. *egredi* to go out, fr. *e-* + *gradi* to go — more at GRADE] (1538) **1 :** the action or right of going or coming out **2 :** a place or means of going out **:** EXIT

[2]**egress** \ē-ˈgres\ *vi* (1578) **:** to go or come out

egres·sion \ē-ˈgre-shən\ *n* (15c) **:** EGRESS, EMERGENCE

egret \ˈē-grət, -ˌgret *also* i-ˈgret, ˈeg-rət\ *n* [ME, fr. AF, fr. Old Occitan **aigreta,* of Gmc origin; akin to OHG *heigaro* heron] (14c) **:** any of various herons that bear long plumes during the breeding season

[1]**Egyp·tian** \i-ˈjip-shən\ *adj* (14c) **:** of, relating to, or characteristic of Egypt or the Egyptians

[2]**Egyptian** *n* (14c) **1 :** a native or inhabitant of Egypt **2 :** the Afro-Asiatic language of the ancient Egyptians from earliest times to about the third century A.D. **3** *often not cap* **:** a typeface having little contrast between thick and thin strokes and squared serifs

Egyptian alfalfa weevil *n* (1943) **:** an Old World weevil (*Hypera brunneipennis*) that is now a pest of alfalfa in western No. America

Egyptian clover *n* (ca. 1900) **:** BERSEEM

Egyptian cotton *n* (1877) **:** a fine long-staple often somewhat brownish cotton grown chiefly in Egypt

Egyp·tol·o·gy \ˌē-(ˌ)jip-ˈtä-lə-jē\ *n* (1841) **:** the study of Egyptian antiquities — **Egyp·to·log·i·cal** \-tə-ˈlä-jə-kəl\ *adj* — **Egyp·tol·o·gist** \-ˈtä-lə-jist\ *n*

eh \ˈā, ˈe, ˈa(i), *also with* h *preceding and/or with nasalization*\ *interj* [ME *ey*] (13c) — used to ask for confirmation or repetition or to express inquiry; used esp. in Canadian English in anticipation of the listener's or reader's agreement

EHF *abbr* extremely high frequency

ehr·lich·i·o·sis \er-ˌli-kē-ˈō-sis\ *n, pl* **-o·ses** \-ˌsēz\ [NL, fr. *Ehrlichia,* bacteria genus, fr. Paul *Ehrlich*] (1965) **:** infection with or disease caused by tick-borne bacteria (genus *Ehrlichia* of the family Anaplasmataceae)

EHV *abbr* extra high voltage

ei·cos·a·noid \ī-ˈkō-sə-ˌnȯid\ *n* [*eicosa-* containing 20 atoms (fr. Gk *eikosa-* twenty, fr. *eikosi*) + *-noic,* suffix used in names of fatty acids (fr. *-ane* + *-oic*) + [1]*-oid* — more at VIGESIMAL] (1980) **:** any of a class of compounds (as the prostaglandins) derived from polyunsaturated fatty acids (as arachidonic acid) and involved in cellular activity

ei·co·sa·pen·ta·e·no·ic acid \ˌī-kō-sə-ˌpen-tə-ē-ˈnō-ik-\ *n* [ISV *eicosa-* twenty (fr. Gk *eikosa-,* fr. *eikosi*) + *penta-* + *-ene* + *-oic* — more at VIGESIMAL] (1969) **:** an omega-3 fatty acid $C_{20}H_{30}O_2$ found esp. in fish oils

ei·der \ˈī-dər\ *n* [D, G, or Sw, fr. Icel *æthur,* fr. ON *æthr*] (1743) **1 :** any of several large northern sea ducks (genera *Somateria* and *Polysticta*) having fine soft down that is used by the female for lining the nest — called also *eider duck* **2 :** EIDERDOWN 1

ei·der·down \-ˌdau̇n\ *n* [prob. fr. G *Eiderdaune,* fr. Icel *æthardūnn,* fr. *æthur* + *dūnn* [1]down] (1774) **1 :** the down of the eider **2 :** a comforter filled with eiderdown **3 :** a soft lightweight clothing fabric knitted or woven and napped on one or both sides

ei·det·ic \ī-ˈde-tik\ *adj* [Gk *eidētikos* of a form, fr. *eidos* form — more at WISE] (ca. 1924) **:** marked by or involving extraordinarily accurate and vivid recall esp. of visual images ‹an ~ memory› — **ei·det·i·cal·ly** \-ti-k(ə-)lē\ *adv*

ei·do·lon \ī-ˈdō-lən\ *n, pl* **-lons** \-lənz\ *or* **-la** \-lə\ [Gk *eidōlon* — more at IDOL] (1828) **1 :** an unsubstantial image **:** PHANTOM **2 :** IDEAL

ei·gen·mode \ˈī-gən-ˌmōd\ *n* [*eigen-* (as in *eigenvector*) + [1]*mode*] (1972) **:** a normal mode of vibration of an oscillating system

ei·gen·val·ue \ˈī-gən-ˌval-(ˌ)yü\ *n* [part trans. of G *Eigenwert,* fr. *eigen* own, peculiar + *Wert* value] (1927) **:** a scalar associated with a given linear transformation of a vector space and having the property that there is some nonzero vector which when multiplied by the scalar is equal to the vector obtained by letting the transformation operate on the vector; *esp* **:** a root of the characteristic equation of a matrix

ei·gen·vec·tor \-ˌvek-tər\ *n* [ISV *eigen-* (fr. G *eigen*) + *vector*] (1941) **:** a nonzero vector that is mapped by a given linear transformation of a vector space onto a vector that is the product of a scalar multiplied by the original vector — called also *characteristic vector*

eight \ˈāt\ *n* [ME *eighte,* fr. *eighte,* adj., fr. OE *eahta;* akin to OHG *ahto* eight, L *octo,* Gk *oktō*] (bef. 12c) **1** — see NUMBER table **2 :** the eighth in a set or series ⟨the ~ of spades⟩ **3 :** something having eight units or members: as **a :** an 8-oared racing boat or its crew **b :** an 8-cylinder engine or automobile — **eight** *adj* — **eight** *pron, pl in constr*

eight ball *n* (1932) **1 :** a black pool ball numbered 8 **2 :** MISFIT — **behind the eight ball :** in a highly disadvantageous position

eigh·teen \(ˈ)ā(t)-ˈtēn\ *n* [ME *eightetene,* adj., fr. OE *eahtatīene,* fr. *eahta* + *-tīene;* akin to OE *tīen* ten] (bef. 12c) — see NUMBER table — **eighteen** *adj* — **eighteen** *pron, pl in constr* — **eigh·teenth** \-ˈtēn(t)th\ *adj or n*

18–wheel·er *or* **eigh·teen–wheel·er** \ˌā(t)-(ˌ)tēn-ˈwē-lər\ *n* (1934) **:** a trucking rig consisting of a tractor and a trailer and typically having eighteen wheels

eight·fold \ˈāt-ˌfōld, -ˈfōld\ *adj* (bef. 12c) **1 :** having eight units or members **2 :** being eight times as great or as many ⟨an ~ increase⟩ — **eight·fold** \-ˈfōld\ *adv*

eightfold way *n* (1961) **:** a unified theoretical scheme for classifying the relationship among strongly interacting elementary particles on the basis of isospin and hypercharge

eighth \ˈātth, ˈāth\ *n, pl* **eighths** \ˈāt(th)s, ˈāths\ (1557) **1** — see NUMBER table **2 :** OCTAVE — **eighth** *adj or adv*

eighth note *n* (ca. 1864) **:** a musical note with the time value of ⅛ of a whole note — see NOTE illustration

eighth rest *n* (ca. 1890) **:** a musical rest corresponding in time value to an eighth note

800 number \ˌāt-ˈhən-drəd-, -dərd-\ *n* (1971) **:** a toll-free telephone number for long-distance calls that is prefixed by the number 800

800–pound gorilla \ˈāt-ˈhən-drəd-ˈpau̇nd-, -dərd-\ *n* (1976) **:** one that is dominating or uncontrollable because of great size or power ⟨like it or not, the *800-pound gorilla* usually sets the standard —Daya Nadamuni⟩

eight·pen·ny nail \ˌāt-ˌpe-nē-\ *n* [fr. its original price per hundred] (15c) **:** a nail typically 2½ inches (6.35 centimeters) long

eighty \ˈā-tē\ *n, pl* **eight·ies** [ME *eighty,* adj., fr. OE *eahtatig,* short for *hundeahtatig,* n., group of eighty, fr. *hund-,* lit., hundred + *eahta* eight + *-tig* group of ten; akin to OE *tīen* ten] (bef. 12c) **1** — see NUMBER table **2** *pl* **:** the numbers 80 to 89; *specif* **:** the years 80 to 89 in a lifetime or century — **eight·i·eth** \ˈā-tē-əth\ *adj or n* — **eighty** *adj* — **eighty** *pron, pl in constr*

eighty–six *or* **86** \ˌā-tē-ˈsiks\ *vt* [prob. rhyming slang for [3]*nix*] (1959) *slang* **:** to refuse to serve (a customer); *also* **:** to get rid of **:** THROW OUT

ein·korn \ˈīn-ˌkȯrn\ *n* [G, fr. OHG, fr. *ein* one + *korn* grain — more at ONE, CORN] (ca. 1901) **:** an ancient wheat (*Triticum monococcum*) having one-grained spikelets and grown esp. formerly in poor soils in central and southern Europe and southwest Asia

ein·stei·ni·um \īn-ˈstī-nē-əm\ *n* [NL, fr. Albert *Einstein*] (1955) **:** a radioactive element produced artificially — see ELEMENT table

ei·re·nic *chiefly Brit var of* IRENIC

eis·ege·sis \ˌī-sə-ˈjē-səs, ˈī-sə-ˌ\ *n, pl* **-ege·ses** \-ˌsēz\ [Gk *eis* into (akin to Gk *en* in) + E *exegesis* — more at IN] (1892) **:** the interpretation of a text (as of the Bible) by reading into it one's own ideas — compare EXEGESIS

ei·stedd·fod \ī-ˈste<u>th</u>-ˌvȯd, ā-\ *n, pl* **-fods** \-ˌvȯdz\ *or* **-fod·au** \-ˌste<u>th</u>-ˈvȯ-ˌdī\ [W, lit., session, fr. *eistedd* to sit + *bod* being] (1822) **:** a usu. Welsh competitive festival of the arts esp. in poetry and singing — **ei·stedd·fod·ic** \ˌī-ˌste<u>th</u>-ˈvȯ-dik, ˌā-\ *adj*

eis·wein \ˈīs-ˌwīn, -ˌvīn\ *n, often cap* [G, fr. *Eis* ice + *Wein* wine] (1967) **:** a sweet German wine made from grapes that have frozen on the vine; *also* **:** a similar wine made elsewhere

[1]**ei·ther** \ˈē-<u>th</u>ər *also* ˈī-\ *adj* [ME, fr. OE *ǣghwæther* both, each, fr. *ā* always + *ge-,* collective prefix + *hwæther* which of two, whether — more at AYE, CO-] (bef. 12c) **1 :** being the one and the other of two **:** EACH ⟨flowers blooming on ~ side of the walk⟩ ⟨plays ~ instrument well⟩ **2 :** being the one or the other of two ⟨take ~ road⟩

[2]**either** *pron* (bef. 12c) **:** the one or the other ⟨take ~ of the two routes⟩

[3]**either** *conj* (bef. 12c) — used as a function word before two or more coordinate words, phrases, or clauses joined usu. by *or* to indicate that what immediately follows is the first of two or more alternatives ⟨can be used ~ as a guest room or as an office⟩

[4]**either** *adv* (15c) **1 :** LIKEWISE, MOREOVER — used for emphasis after a negative ⟨not smart or handsome ~⟩ **2 :** for that matter — used for emphasis after an alternative following a question or conditional clause esp. where negation is implied ⟨who answers for the Irish parliament? or army ~? —Robert Browning⟩

[1]**ei·ther–or** \ˌē-<u>th</u>ər-ˈȯr *also* ˌī-\ *n* (1922) **:** an unavoidable choice or exclusive division between only two alternatives

[2]**either–or** *adj* (1926) **:** of or marked by either-or **:** BLACK-AND-WHITE

[1]**ejac·u·late** \i-ˈja-kyə-ˌlāt\ *vb* **-lat·ed; -lat·ing** [L *ejaculatus,* pp. of *ejaculari* to throw out, fr. *e-* + *jaculari* to throw, fr. *jaculum* dart, fr. *jacere* to throw — more at JET] *vt* (1578) **1 :** to eject from a living body; *specif* **:** to eject (semen) in orgasm **2 :** to utter suddenly and vehemently ~ *vi* **:** to eject a fluid — **ejac·u·la·tor** \-ˌlā-tər\ *n*

[2]**ejac·u·late** \-lət\ *n* (1927) **:** the semen released by one ejaculation

ejac·u·la·tion \i-ˌja-kyə-ˈlā-shən\ *n* (1603) **1 :** an act of ejaculating; *specif* **:** a sudden discharging of a fluid from a duct **2 :** something ejaculated; *esp* **:** a short sudden emotional utterance

ejac·u·la·to·ry \i-ˈja-kyə-lə-ˌtȯr-ē\ *adj* (1644) **1 :** marked by or given to vocal ejaculation **2 :** casting or throwing out; *specif* **:** associated with or concerned in physiological ejaculation ⟨~ vessels⟩

ejaculatory duct *n* (1751) **:** a duct through which semen is ejaculated; *specif* **:** either of the paired ducts in the human male that are formed by the junction of the duct from the seminal vesicle with the vas deferens and that pass through the prostate to empty into the urethra

eject \i-ˈjekt\ *vt* [ME, fr. L *ejectus,* pp. of *eicere,* fr. *e-* + *jacere*] (15c) **1 a :** to throw out esp. by physical force, authority, or influence ⟨~*ed* the player from the game⟩ **b :** to evict from property **2 :** to throw out or off from within ⟨~*s* the empty cartridges⟩ — **eject·able** \-ˈjek-tə-bəl\ *adj* — **ejec·tion** \-ˈjek-shən\ *n* — **ejec·tive** \-ˈjek-tiv\ *adj*

syn EJECT, EXPEL, OUST, EVICT mean to drive or force out. EJECT carries an esp. strong implication of throwing or thrusting out from within as a physical action ⟨*ejected* an obnoxious patron from the bar⟩. EXPEL stresses a thrusting out or driving away esp. permanently which need not be physical ⟨a student *expelled* from college⟩. OUST implies removal or dispossession by power of the law or by force or compulsion ⟨police *ousted* the squatters⟩. EVICT chiefly applies to turning out of house and home ⟨*evicted* for nonpayment of rent⟩.

ejec·ta \i-ˈjek-tə\ *n pl but sing or pl in constr* [NL, fr. L, neut. pl. of *ejectus*] (1886) **:** material thrown out (as from a volcano)

ejection seat *n* (1945) **:** an emergency escape seat for propelling an occupant out and away from an airplane

eject·ment \i-ˈjek(t)-mənt\ *n* (1523) **1 :** the act or an instance of ejecting **:** DISPOSSESSION **2 :** an action for the recovery of possession of real property and damages and costs

ejec·tor \i-ˈjek-tər\ *n* (1640) **1 :** one that ejects; *esp* **:** a mechanism of a firearm that ejects an empty cartridge **2 :** a jet pump for withdrawing a gas, fluid, or powdery substance from a space

eka- *comb form* [ISV, fr. Skt *eka* one — more at ONE] **:** standing or assumed to stand next in order beyond (a specified element) in the same family of the periodic table — in names of chemical elements esp. when not yet discovered ⟨*eka*-lead is the hypothetical element 114⟩

[1]**eke** \ˈēk\ *adv* [ME, fr. OE *ēac;* akin to OHG *ouh* also, L *aut* or, Gk *au* again] (bef. 12c) *archaic* **:** ALSO

[2]**eke** *vt* **eked; ek·ing** [ME, fr. OE *īecan, ēcan;* akin to OHG *ouhhōn* to add, L *augēre* to increase, Gk *auxein*] (bef. 12c) **1** *archaic* **:** INCREASE, LENGTHEN **2 :** to get with great difficulty — usu. used with *out* ⟨~ out a living⟩

eke out *vt* (1596) **1 :** to make up for the deficiencies of **:** SUPPLEMENT ⟨*eked out* his income by getting a second job⟩ **2 :** to make (a supply) last by economy

EKG *abbr* [G *Elektrokardiogramm*] electrocardiogram; electrocardiograph

ekis·tics \i-ˈkis-tiks\ *n pl but sing in constr* [ModGk *oikistikē,* fr. fem. of *oikistikos* of settlement, fr. Gk, fr. *oikizein* to settle, colonize, fr. *oikos* house — more at VICINITY] (1958) **:** a science dealing with human settlements and drawing on the research and experience of professionals in various fields (as architecture, engineering, city planning, and sociology) — **ekis·tic** \-tik\ *adj*

ek·phra·sis *also* **ec·phra·sis** \ˈek-frə-səs\ *n, pl* **ek·phra·ses** *also* **ec·phra·ses** \-ˌsēz\ [Gk *ekphrasis,* lit., description, fr. *ekphrazein* to recount, describe, fr. *ex-* out + *phrazein* to point out, explain] (1715) **:** a literary description of or commentary on a visual work of art

[1]**el** \ˈel\ *n* (14c) **:** the letter *l*

[2]**el** *n, often cap* (ca. 1906) **:** an urban railway that operates chiefly on an elevated structure; *also* **:** a train belonging to such a railway

[3]**el** *abbr* elevation

[1]**elab·o·rate** \i-ˈla-b(ə-)rət\ *adj* [L *elaboratus,* fr. pp. of *elaborare* to work out, acquire by labor, fr. *e-* + *laborare* to work — more at LABORATORY] (1592) **1 :** planned or carried out with great care ⟨took ~ precautions⟩ **2 :** marked by complexity, fullness of detail, or ornateness ⟨~ prose⟩ — **elab·o·rate·ly** *adv* — **elab·o·rate·ness** *n*

[2]**elab·o·rate** \i-ˈla-bə-ˌrāt\ *vb* **-rat·ed; -rat·ing** *vt* (1611) **1 :** to produce by labor **2 :** to build up (as complex organic compounds) from simple ingredients **3 :** to work out in detail **:** DEVELOP ⟨~ a theory⟩ ~ *vi* **1 :** to become elaborate **2 :** to expand something in detail ⟨would you care to ~ on that statement⟩ — **elab·o·ra·tion** \-ˌla-bə-ˈrā-shən\ *n* — **elab·o·ra·tive** \-ˈla-bə-ˌrā-tiv\ *adj*

Elaine \i-ˈlān\ *n* (15c) **:** any of several women in Arthurian legend; *esp* **:** one who dies for unrequited love of Lancelot

Elam·ite \ˈē-lə-ˌmīt\ *n* (1874) **:** a language of unknown affinities used in Elam approximately from the 25th to the 4th centuries B.C.

élan \ā-ˈläⁿ\ *n* [F, fr. MF *eslan* rush, fr. *(s')eslancer* to rush, fr. *ex-* + *lancer* to hurl — more at LANCE] (1864) **:** vigorous spirit or enthusiasm

eland \ˈē-lənd, -ˌland\ *n, pl* **eland** *also* **elands** [Afrik, elk, fr. D, fr. obs. G *Elend,* prob. fr. obs. Lith *ellenis;* akin to OHG *elaho* elk — more at ELK] (1600) **:** either of two large African antelopes (*Taurotragus oryx* syn. *Tragelaphus oryx* and *Taurotragus derbianus* syn. *Tragelaphus derbianus*) bovine in form with short spirally twisted horns in both sexes

élan vi·tal \ā-läⁿ-vē-täl\ *n* [F] (1907) **:** the vital force or impulse of life; *esp* **:** a creative principle held by Bergson to be immanent in all organisms and responsible for evolution

el·a·pid \ˈe-lə-pəd\ *n* [NL *Elap-, Elaps,* genus of snakes, fr. MGk, a fish, alter. of Gk *elops*] (1885) **:** any of a family (Elapidae) of venomous snakes (as the cobras and coral snakes) with hollow fangs

[1]**elapse** \i-ˈlaps\ *vi* **elapsed; elaps·ing** [L *elapsus,* pp. of *elabi,* fr. *e-* + *labi* to slip — more at SLEEP] (1644) **:** PASS, GO BY ⟨four years *elapsed* before he returned⟩

[2]**elapse** *n* (ca. 1677) **:** PASSAGE ⟨returned after an ~ of 15 years⟩

elapsed time *n* (ca. 1909) **:** the actual time taken (as by a boat or automobile in traveling over a racecourse)

elas·mo·branch \i-ˈlaz-mə-ˌbraŋk\ *n, pl* **-branchs** [ultim. fr. Gk *elasmos* metal plate (fr. *elaunein*) + *branchia* gills] (1872) **:** any of a subclass (Elasmobranchii) of cartilaginous fishes that have five to seven lateral to ventral gill openings on each side and that comprise the sharks, rays, skates, and extinct related fishes — **elasmobranch** *adj*

elas·tase \i-ˈlas-ˌtās, -ˌtāz\ *n* [*elastin* + *-ase*] (1949) **:** an enzyme esp. of pancreatic juice that digests elastin

[1]**elas·tic** \i-ˈlas-tik\ *adj* [NL *elasticus,* fr. LGk *elastos* ductile, beaten, fr. Gk *elaunein* to drive, beat out; prob. akin to Gk *ēlythe* he went, OIr *luid*] (1674) **1 a** *of a solid* **:** capable of recovering size and shape after deformation **b :** relating to or being a collision between particles in which the total kinetic energy of the particles remains unchanged **2 :** capable of recovering quickly esp. from depression or disappointment ⟨my ~ spirits revived —Wilkie Collins⟩ **3 :** capable of being easily stretched or expanded and resuming former shape **:** FLEXIBLE ⟨an ~ bandage⟩ **4 a :** capable of ready change or easy expansion or contraction **:** not rigid or constricted ⟨an ~ concept⟩ **b :** receptive to new ideas **:** ADAPTABLE ⟨an ~ mind⟩ — **elas·ti·cal·ly** \-ti-k(ə-)lē\ *adv*

syn ELASTIC, RESILIENT, SPRINGY, FLEXIBLE, SUPPLE mean able to endure strain without being permanently injured. ELASTIC implies the property of resisting deformation by stretching ⟨an *elastic* waistband〉. RESILIENT implies the ability to recover shape quickly when the deforming force or pressure is removed 〈a *resilient* innersole〉. SPRINGY stresses both the ease with which something yields to pressure and the quickness of its return to original shape 〈the cake is done when the top is *springy*〉. FLEXIBLE applies to something which may or may not be resilient or elastic but which can be bent or folded without breaking 〈*flexible* plastic tubing〉. SUPPLE applies to something that can be readily bent, twisted, or folded without any sign of injury 〈*supple* leather〉.

[2]**elastic** *n* (1847) **1 a :** easily stretched rubber usu. prepared in cords, strings, or bands **b :** RUBBER BAND **2 a :** an elastic fabric usu. made of yarns containing rubber **b :** something made from this fabric

elastic fiber *n* (1849) **:** a thick very elastic smooth yellowish anastomosing fiber of connective tissue that contains elastin

elas·tic·i·ty \i-ˌlas-ˈti-sə-tē, ˌē-ˌlas-, -ˈtis-tē\ *n, pl* **-ties** (1664) **1 :** the quality or state of being elastic: as **a :** the capability of a strained body to recover its size and shape after deformation **:** SPRINGINESS **b :** RESILIENCE 2 **c :** the quality of being adaptable **2 :** the responsiveness of a dependent economic variable to changes in influencing factors 〈~ of demand〉 〈price ~〉

elas·ti·cized \i-ˈlas-tə-ˌsīzd\ *adj* (ca. 1909) **:** made with elastic thread or inserts 〈an ~ waistband〉

elastic limit *n* (1898) **:** the greatest stress that an elastic solid can sustain without undergoing permanent deformation

elastic modulus *n* (1904) **:** the ratio of the stress in a body to the corresponding strain

elastic scattering *n* (1933) **:** a scattering of particles as the result of an elastic collision

elas·tin \i-ˈlas-tən\ *n* [ISV, fr. NL *elasticus*] (1875) **:** a protein that is similar to collagen and is the chief constituent of elastic fibers

elas·to·mer \-tə-mər\ *n* [*elastic* + *-o-* + *-mer*] (ca. 1939) **:** any of various elastic substances resembling rubber 〈polyvinyl ~*s*〉 — **elas·to·mer·ic** \i-ˌlas-tə-ˈmer-ik\ *adj*

[1]**elate** \i-ˈlāt\ *vt* **elat·ed; elat·ing** [L *elatus* (pp. of *efferre* to carry out, elevate), fr. *e-* + *latus,* pp. of *ferre* to carry — more at TOLERATE, BEAR] (ca. 1619) **:** to fill with joy or pride

[2]**elate** *adj* (1647) **:** ELATED 〈I smiled to myself and felt ~ —Charlotte Brontë〉

elated *adj* (ca. 1619) **:** marked by high spirits **:** EXULTANT — **elat·ed·ly** *adv* — **elat·ed·ness** *n*

el·a·ter \ˈe-lə-tər\ *n* [NL, fr. Gk *elatēr* driver, fr. *elaunein* to drive] (1830) **:** a plant structure functioning in the dispersal of spores: as **a :** one of the elongated filaments among the spores in the capsule of a liverwort **b :** one of the filamentous appendages of the spores in the horsetails

ela·tion \i-ˈlā-shən\ *n* (14c) **1 :** the quality or state of being elated **2 :** pathological euphoria

E layer *n* (1933) **:** a layer of the ionosphere occurring about 65 miles (110 kilometers) above the earth's surface during daylight hours that is capable of reflecting shortwave frequencies

El·ba \ˈel-bə\ *n* [*Elba* (Mediterranean island), residence of Napoléon Bonaparte after his first abdication May 14, 1814 to Feb. 26, 1815] (1924) **:** a place or state of exile

[1]**el·bow** \ˈel-ˌbō\ *n* [ME *elbowe,* fr. OE *elboga,* fr. *el-* (akin to *eln* ell) + OE *boga* bow — more at ELL, BOW] (bef. 12c) **1 a :** the joint of the human arm **b :** a corresponding joint in the anterior limb of a lower vertebrate **2 :** something (as macaroni or an angular pipe fitting) resembling an elbow — **at one's elbow :** at one's side — **out at elbows** *or* **out at the elbows 1 :** shabbily dressed **2 :** short of funds

[2]**elbow** *vt* (1605) **1 a :** to push with the elbow **:** JOSTLE **b :** to shove aside by pushing with or as if with the elbow 〈people ~*ed* each other to get a better view〉 **2 :** to force (as one's way) by pushing with or as if with the elbow 〈~*ing* our way through the crowd〉 ~ *vi* **1 :** to advance by pushing with the elbow **2 :** to make an angle **:** TURN

elbow grease *n* (1672) **:** vigorously applied physical labor **:** hard work

el·bow room \ˈel-ˌbō-ˌrüm, -ˌru̇m\ *n* (ca. 1540) **1 a :** room for moving the elbows freely **b :** adequate space for work or operation 〈a lab with plenty of *elbow room*〉 **2 :** free scope 〈*elbow room* to try new ideas〉

el cheapo \(ˌ)el-ˈchē-(ˌ)pō, ˈel-\ *adj* [Sp *el* the + E *cheap* + Sp *-o* (masc. n. ending)] (1967) **:** CHEAP 3a, b

eld \ˈeld\ *n* [ME, fr. OE *ieldo;* akin to OE *eald* old — more at OLD] (bef. 12c) **1 :** old age **2** *archaic* **:** old times **:** ANTIQUITY

[1]**el·der** \ˈel-dər\ *n* [ME *eldre,* fr. OE *ellærn;* perh. akin to OE *alor* alder — more at ALDER] (bef. 12c) **:** ELDERBERRY 2

[2]**elder** *adj* [ME, fr. OE *ieldra,* compar. of *eald* old] (bef. 12c) **1 :** of earlier birth or greater age 〈his ~ brother〉 **2 :** of or relating to earlier times **:** FORMER **3** *archaic* **:** of or relating to a more advanced time of life **4 :** prior or superior in rank, office, or validity

[3]**elder** *n* (bef. 12c) **1 :** one living in an earlier period **2 a :** one who is older **:** SENIOR 〈a child trying to please her ~*s*〉 **b :** an aged person **3 :** one having authority by virtue of age and experience 〈the village ~*s*〉 **4 :** any of various officers of religious groups: as **a :** PRESBYTER 1 **b :** a permanent officer elected by a Presbyterian congregation and ordained to serve on the session and assist the pastor at communion **c :** MINISTER 2 **d :** a leader of the Shakers **e :** a Mormon ordained to the Melchizedek priesthood — **el·der·ship** \-ˌship\ *n*

el·der·ber·ry \ˈel-də(r)-ˌber-ē, -ˌbe-rē\ *n* (1589) **1 :** the edible black or red berrylike drupe of any of a genus (*Sambucus*) of shrubs or trees of the honeysuckle family bearing flat clusters of small white or pink flowers **2 :** a tree or shrub bearing elderberries

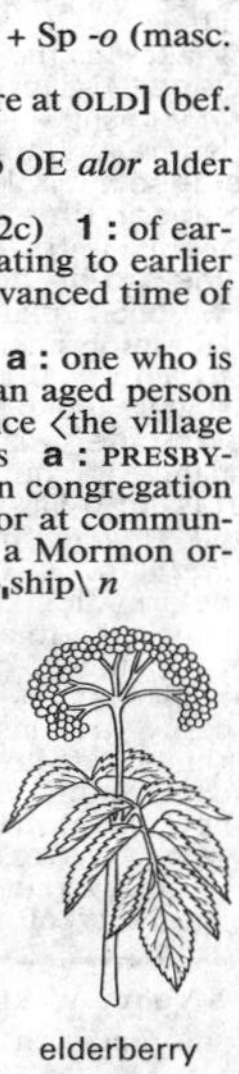
elderberry

[1]**el·der·ly** \ˈel-dər-lē\ *adj* (1611) **1 a :** rather old; *esp* **:** being past middle age **b :** OLD-FASHIONED **2 :** of, relating to, or characteristic of later life or elderly persons — **el·der·li·ness** *n*

[2]**elderly** *n, pl* **-ly** *or* **-lies** (1865) **:** an elderly person

elder statesman *n* (1904) **:** an eminent senior member of a group or organization; *esp* **:** a retired statesman who unofficially advises current leaders

el·dest \ˈel-dəst\ *adj* (bef. 12c) **:** of the greatest age or seniority **:** OLDEST 〈my ~ daughter〉

eldest hand *n* (ca. 1597) **:** the card player who first receives cards in the deal

El Do·ra·do \ˌel-də-ˈrä-(ˌ)dō, -ˈrā-\ *n* [Sp, lit., the gilded one] (1596) **1 :** a city or country of fabulous riches held by 16th century explorers to exist in So. America **2 :** a place of fabulous wealth or opportunity

el·dress \ˈel-drəs\ *n* (1640) **:** a woman who is an elder esp. of the Shakers

el·dritch \ˈel-drich\ *adj* [perh. fr. ME **elfriche* fairyland, fr. ME *elf* + *riche* kingdom, fr. OE *rīce* — more at RICH] (1508) **:** WEIRD, EERIE 〈whose voice had risen to a kind of ~ singsong —R. L. Stevenson〉

El·e·at·ic \ˌel-ē-ˈa-tik\ *adj* [L *Eleaticus,* fr. Gk *Eleatikos,* fr. *Elea* (Velia), ancient town in southern Italy] (1695) **:** of or relating to a school of Greek philosophers founded by Parmenides and developed by Zeno and marked by belief in the unity of being and the unreality of motion or change — **Eleatic** *n* — **El·e·at·i·cism** \-ˈa-tə-ˌsi-zəm\ *n*

elec *abbr* electric, electrical, electricity

ele·cam·pane \ˌe-li-ˌkam-ˈpān\ *n* [ME *elena campana,* fr. ML *enula campana,* lit., field elecampane, fr. *inula, enula* elecampane + *campana* of the field] (14c) **:** a large coarse Eurasian composite herb (*Inula helenium*) that has yellow ray flowers and is naturalized in the U.S.

[1]**elect** \i-ˈlekt\ *adj* [ME, fr. L *electus,* pp. of *eligere* to select, fr. *e-* + *legere* to choose — more at LEGEND] (15c) **1 :** carefully selected **:** CHOSEN **2 :** chosen for salvation through divine mercy **3 a :** chosen for office or position but not yet installed 〈the president-*elect*〉 **b :** chosen for marriage at some future time 〈the bride-*elect*〉

[2]**elect** *n, pl* **elect** (15c) **1 :** one chosen or set apart (as by divine favor) **2** *pl* **:** a select or exclusive group of people

[3]**elect** *vb* [ME, fr. L *electus*] *vt* (15c) **1 :** to select by vote for an office, position, or membership 〈~*ed* her class president〉 **2 :** to make a selection of 〈will ~ an academic program〉 **3 :** to choose (as a course of action) esp. by preference 〈might ~ to sell the business〉 ~ *vi* **:** to make a selection

elect·able \i-ˈlek-tə-bəl\ *adj* (1879) **:** capable of being elected (as to public office) — **elect·abil·i·ty** \-ˌlek-tə-ˈbi-lə-tē\ *n*

elec·tion \i-ˈlek-shən\ *n* (13c) **1 a :** an act or process of electing 〈the ~ of a new governor〉 **b :** the fact of being elected 〈her ~ to the Senate〉 **2 :** predestination to eternal life **3 :** the right, power, or privilege of making a choice

Election Day *n* (15c) **:** a day legally established for the election of public officials; *esp* **:** the first Tuesday after the first Monday in November in an even year designated for national elections in the U.S. and observed as a legal holiday in many states

elec·tion·eer \i-ˌlek-shə-ˈnir\ *vi* [*election* + *-eer* (as in *privateer,* v.)] (1760) **:** to take an active part in an election; *specif* **:** to work for the election of a candidate or party — **elec·tion·eer·er** *n*

[1]**elec·tive** \i-ˈlek-tiv\ *adj* (ca. 1531) **1 a :** chosen or filled by popular election 〈an ~ official〉 **b :** of or relating to election **c :** based on the right or principle of election 〈the presidency is an ~ office〉 **2 a :** permitting a choice **:** OPTIONAL 〈an ~ course in school〉 **b :** beneficial to the patient but not essential for survival 〈~ surgery〉 **3 a :** tending to operate on one substance rather than another 〈~ absorption〉 **b :** favorably inclined to one more than to another **:** SYMPATHETIC 〈an ~ affinity〉 — **elec·tive·ly** *adv* — **elec·tive·ness** *n*

[2]**elective** *n* (1850) **:** an elective course or subject

elec·tor \i-ˈlek-tər, -ˌtȯr\ *n* (15c) **1 :** one qualified to vote in an election **2 :** one entitled to participate in an election: as **a :** any of the German princes entitled to take part in choosing the Holy Roman Emperor **b :** a member of the electoral college in the U.S.

elec·tor·al \i-ˈlek-t(ə-)rəl, ˌē-lek-ˈtȯr-əl\ *adj* (1675) **1 :** of or relating to an elector 〈the ~ vote〉 **2 :** of or relating to election 〈an ~ system〉 — **elec·tor·al·ly** \-t(ə-)rə-lē, -ˈtȯr-ə-lē\ *adv*

electoral college *n* (1677) **:** a body of electors; *esp* **:** one that elects the president and vice president of the U.S.

elec·tor·ate \i-ˈlek-t(ə-)rət\ *n* (1620) **1 :** the territory, jurisdiction, or dignity of a German elector **2 :** a body of people entitled to vote

electr- *or* **electro-** *comb form* [NL *electricus*] **1 a :** electricity 〈*electrometer*〉 **b :** electric 〈*electrode*〉 **:** electric and 〈*electrochemical*〉 **:** electrically 〈*electropositive*〉 **2 :** electrolytic 〈*electroanalysis*〉 **3 :** electron 〈*electrophilic*〉

Elec·tra \i-ˈlek-trə\ *n* [L, fr. Gk *Ēlektra*] (1580) **:** a sister of Orestes who aids him in killing their mother Clytemnestra

Electra complex *n* (1913) **:** the Oedipus complex when it occurs in a female

elec·tress \i-ˈlek-trəs\ *n* (1618) **:** the wife or widow of a German elector

elec·tret \i-ˈlek-trət, -ˌtret\ *n* [*electricity* + *magnet*] (1885) **:** a dielectric body in which a permanent state of electric polarization has been set up

[1]**elec·tric** \i-ˈlek-trik, ē-\ *adj* [NL *electricus* produced from amber by friction, electric, fr. ML, of amber, fr. L *electrum* amber, electrum, fr. Gk *ēlektron;* akin to Gk *ēlektōr* beaming sun] (1675) **1** *or* **elec·tri·cal** \-tri-kəl\ **:** of, relating to, or operated by electricity 〈an ~ current〉 〈an ~ heater〉 **2 :** exciting as if by electric shock 〈an ~ performance〉 〈an ~ personality〉; *also* **:** charged with strong emotion 〈the room was ~ with tension〉 **3 a :** ELECTRONIC 3a **b :** amplifying sound by electronic means — used of a musical instrument 〈an ~ guitar〉 **4 :** very bright 〈~ blue〉 〈~ orange〉 — **elec·tri·cal·ly** \-tri-k(ə-)lē\ *adv*

[2]**electric** *n* (1646) **1** *archaic* **:** a nonconductor of electricity used to excite or accumulate electricity **2 :** something (as a light, automobile, or train) operated by electricity

electrical storm *n* (1934) **:** THUNDERSTORM — called also *electric storm*

electric chair *n* (1889) **1 :** a chair used in legal electrocution **2 :** the penalty of death by electrocution

electric eel *n* (1794) **:** a large eel-shaped fish (*Electrophorus electricus*) of the Orinoco and Amazon basins that is capable of giving a severe shock with its electric organs

electric eye *n* (1898) **:** PHOTOELECTRIC CELL

electric field *n* (ca. 1889) **:** a region associated with a distribution of electric charge or a varying magnetic field in which forces due to that charge or field act upon other electric charges

elec·tri·cian \i-ˌlek-ˈtri-shən, ē-ˌ\ *n* (1814) **:** one who installs, maintains, operates, or repairs electrical equipment

elec·tric·i·ty \i-ˌlek-ˈtri-sə-tē, ē-ˌ, -ˈtris-tē\ *n, pl* **-ties** (1646) **1 a :** a fundamental form of energy observable in positive and negative forms that occurs naturally (as in lightning) or is produced (as in a generator) and that is expressed in terms of the movement and interaction of electrons **b :** electric current or power **2 :** a science that deals with the phenom-

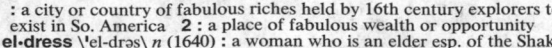

ena and laws of electricity **3 :** keen contagious excitement ⟨could feel the ~ in the room⟩

electric organ *n* (1773) **:** a specialized tract of tissue (as in the electric eel) in which electricity is generated

electric ray *n* (1774) **:** any of various round-bodied short-tailed rays (family Torpedinidae) of warm seas with a pair of electric organs

elec·tri·fi·ca·tion \i-ˌlek-trə-fə-ˈkā-shən, ē-ˌ\ *n* (1748) **1 :** an act or process of electrifying **2 :** the state of being electrified

elec·tri·fy \i-ˈlek-trə-ˌfī, ē-ˈ\ *vt* **-fied; -fy·ing** (1745) **1 a :** to charge with electricity **b** (1) **:** to equip for use of electric power (2) **:** to supply with electric power (3) **:** to amplify (music) electronically **2 :** to excite intensely or suddenly ⟨the news *electrified* the nation⟩

elec·tro·acous·tics \i-ˌlek-trō-ə-ˈküs-tiks\ *n pl but sing in constr* (1927) **:** a science that deals with the transformation of acoustic energy into electric energy or vice versa — **elec·tro·acous·tic** \-tik\ *adj*

elec·tro·anal·y·sis \-ə-ˈna-lə-səs\ *n* (1903) **:** chemical analysis by electrolytic methods — **elec·tro·an·a·lyt·i·cal** \-ˈlit-i-kəl\ *adj*

elec·tro·car·dio·gram \-ˈkär-dē-ə-ˌgram\ *n* (ca. 1904) **:** the tracing made by an electrocardiograph; *also* **:** the procedure for producing an electrocardiogram

elec·tro·car·dio·graph \-ˌgraf\ *n* (1913) **:** an instrument for recording the changes of electrical potential occurring during the heartbeat used esp. in diagnosing abnormalities of heart action — **elec·tro·car·dio·graph·ic** \-ˌkär-dē-ə-ˈgra-fik\ *adj* — **elec·tro·car·dio·graph·i·cal·ly** \-fi-k(ə-)lē\ *adv* — **elec·tro·car·di·og·ra·phy** \-dē-ˈä-grə-fē\ *n*

elec·tro·cau·tery \-ˈkȯ-tə-rē\ *n* (ca. 1884) **:** cauterization of tissue by means of an instrument heated by an electric current

elec·tro·chem·is·try \-ˈke-mə-strē\ *n* (1814) **:** a science that deals with the relation of electricity to chemical changes and with the interconversion of chemical and electrical energy — **elec·tro·chem·i·cal** \-ˈke-mi-kəl\ *adj* — **elec·tro·chem·i·cal·ly** \-k(ə-)lē\ *adv* — **elec·tro·chem·ist** \-ˈke-mist\ *n*

elec·tro·con·vul·sive \i-ˌlek-trō-kən-ˈvəl-siv\ *adj* (1947) **:** of, relating to, or involving convulsive response to electroshock ⟨~ shocks⟩

electroconvulsive therapy *n* (1948) **:** ELECTROSHOCK THERAPY

elec·tro·cor·ti·co·gram \i-ˌlek-trō-ˈkȯr-ti-kə-ˌgram\ *n* (1939) **:** an electroencephalogram made with the electrodes in direct contact with the brain

elec·tro·cute \i-ˈlek-trə-ˌkyüt\ *vt* **-cut·ed; -cut·ing** [*electr-* + *-cute* (as in *execute*)] (1889) **1 :** to execute (a criminal) by electricity **2 :** to kill by electric shock — **elec·tro·cu·tion** \-ˌlek-trə-ˈkyü-shən\ *n*

elec·trode \i-ˈlek-ˌtrōd\ *n* (1834) **1 :** a conductor used to establish electrical contact with a nonmetallic part of a circuit **2 :** an element in a semiconductor device (as a transistor) that emits or collects electrons or holes or controls their movements

[1]**elec·tro·de·pos·it** \i-ˌlek-trō-di-ˈpä-zət\ *n* (1864) **:** a deposit formed in or at an electrode by electrolysis

[2]**electrodeposit** *vt* (1882) **:** to deposit (as a metal or rubber) by electrolysis — **elec·tro·de·po·si·tion** \-ˌde-pə-ˈzi-shən, -ˌdē-pə-\ *n*

elec·tro·der·mal \i-ˌlek-trō-ˈdər-məl\ *adj* (1940) **:** of or relating to electrical activity in or electrical properties of the skin

elec·tro·des·ic·ca·tion \i-ˌlek-trō-ˌde-si-ˈkā-shən\ *n* (1919) **:** the drying up of tissue by a high-frequency electric current applied with a needle-shaped electrode — called also *fulguration*

elec·tro·di·al·y·sis \i-ˌlek-trō-dī-ˈa-lə-səs\ *n* (1921) **:** dialysis accelerated by an electromotive force applied to electrodes adjacent to the membranes — **elec·tro·di·a·lyt·ic** \-ˌdī-ə-ˈli-tik\ *adj*

elec·tro·dy·nam·ics \-dī-ˈna-miks\ *n pl but sing in constr* (1827) **:** a branch of physics that deals with the effects arising from the interactions of electric currents with magnets, with other currents, or with themselves — **elec·tro·dy·nam·ic** \-mik\ *adj*

elec·tro·en·ceph·a·lo·gram \-in-ˈse-f(ə-)lə-ˌgram\ *n* [ISV] (1934) **:** the tracing of brain waves made by an electroencephalograph

elec·tro·en·ceph·a·lo·graph \-ˌgraf\ *n* [ISV] (1936) **:** an apparatus for detecting and recording brain waves — **elec·tro·en·ceph·a·log·ra·pher** \-ˌse-fə-ˈlä-grə-fər\ *n* — **elec·tro·en·ceph·a·lo·graph·ic** \-ˌse-f(ə-)lə-ˈgra-fik\ *adj* — **elec·tro·en·ceph·a·lo·graph·i·cal·ly** \-fi-k(ə-)lē\ *adv* — **elec·tro·en·ceph·a·log·ra·phy** \-ˈlä-grə-fē\ *n*

elec·tro·fish·ing \i-ˈlek-trō-ˌfi-shiŋ\ *n* (1950) **:** fishing that employs a direct electric current to attract and usu. temporarily immobilize fish for easy capture

elec·tro·form \i-ˈlek-trə-ˌfȯrm\ *vt* (1931) **:** to form (shaped articles) by electrodeposition on a mold — **electroform** *n*

elec·tro·gen·ic \i-ˌlek-trə-ˈje-nik\ *adj* (ca. 1890) **:** of or relating to the production of electrical activity in living tissue ⟨an ~ pump⟩ — **elec·tro·gen·e·sis** \-ˈje-nə-sis\ *n*

elec·tro·gram \i-ˈlek-trə-ˌgram\ *n* (ca. 1935) **:** a tracing of the electrical potentials of a tissue (as the brain or heart) made by means of electrodes placed directly in the tissue instead of on the surface of the body

elec·tro·hy·drau·lic \i-ˌlek-trō-hī-ˈdrȯ-lik, -ˈdrä-\ *adj* (1922) **1 :** of or relating to a combination of electric and hydraulic mechanisms **2 :** involving or produced by the action of very brief but powerful pulse discharges of electricity under a liquid resulting in the generation of shock waves and highly reactive chemical species ⟨an ~ effect⟩

elec·tro·jet \i-ˈlek-trə-ˌjet\ *n* (1955) **:** a concentration of atmospheric electric current found in the regions of strong auroral displays and along the magnetic equator

elec·tro·ki·net·ic \i-ˌlek-trō-kə-ˈne-tik, -kī-\ *adj* (1873) **:** of or relating to the motion of particles or liquids that results from or produces a difference of electric potential

elec·tro·ki·net·ics \-tiks\ *n pl but sing in constr* (ca. 1925) **:** a branch of physics dealing with the motion of electric currents or charged particles

elec·tro·less \i-ˈlek-ˌtrō-ləs, -trə-\ *adj* (1947) **:** being or involving deposition of metal by chemical means instead of by electrodeposition

elec·trol·o·gist \i-ˌlek-ˈträ-lə-jist\ *n* [blend of *electrolysis* and *-logist* (fr. *-logy* + *-ist*)] (ca. 1902) **:** a person who removes hair by means of an electric current applied to the body with a needle-shaped electrode — **elec·trol·o·gy** \-lə-jē\ *n*

elec·tro·lu·mi·nes·cent \i-ˌlek-trō-ˌlü-mə-ˈne-sᵊnt\ *adj* (ca. 1909) **:** of or relating to luminescence resulting from a high-frequency discharge through a gas or from application of a current to a layer of phosphor — **elec·tro·lu·mi·nes·cence** \-sᵊn(t)s\ *n*

elec·trol·y·sis \i-ˌlek-ˈträ-lə-səs\ *n* (1834) **1 a :** the producing of chemical changes by passage of an electric current through an electrolyte **b :** subjection to this action **2 :** the destruction of hair roots by an electrologist using direct current

elec·tro·lyte \i-ˈlek-trə-ˌlīt\ *n* (1834) **1 :** a nonmetallic electric conductor in which current is carried by the movement of ions **2 a :** a substance that when dissolved in a suitable solvent or when fused becomes an ionic conductor **b :** any of the ions (as of sodium or calcium) that in biological fluid regulate or affect most metabolic processes (as the flow of nutrients into and waste products out of cells)

elec·tro·lyt·ic \i-ˌlek-trə-ˈli-tik\ *adj* (1842) **:** of or relating to electrolysis or an electrolyte ⟨an ~ cell⟩; *also* **:** produced by or used in electrolysis ⟨~ copper⟩ — **elec·tro·lyt·i·cal·ly** \-ti-k(ə-)lē\ *adv*

elec·tro·lyze \i-ˈlek-trə-ˌlīz\ *vt* **-lyzed; -lyz·ing** (1834) **:** to subject to electrolysis

elec·tro·mag·net \i-ˌlek-trō-ˈmag-nət\ *n* (1831) **:** a core of magnetic material (as iron) surrounded by a coil of wire through which an electric current is passed to magnetize the core

elec·tro·mag·net·ic \-mag-ˈne-tik\ *adj* (1821) **:** of, relating to, or produced by electromagnetism — **elec·tro·mag·net·i·cal·ly** \-ti-k(ə-)lē\ *adv*

electromagnetic pulse *n* (1963) **:** high-intensity electromagnetic radiation generated by a nuclear blast high above the earth's surface and held to disrupt electronic and electrical systems

electromagnetic radiation *n* (1902) **:** energy in the form of electromagnetic waves; *also* **:** a series of electromagnetic waves

electromagnetic spectrum *n* (ca. 1934) **:** the entire range of wavelengths or frequencies of electromagnetic radiation extending from gamma rays to the longest radio waves and including visible light

electromagnetic unit *n* (1855) **:** any of a system of electrical units based primarily on the magnetic properties of electrical currents

electromagnetic wave *n* (1906) **:** one of the waves that are propagated by simultaneous periodic variations of electric and magnetic field intensity and that include radio waves, infrared, visible light, ultraviolet, X-rays, and gamma rays

elec·tro·mag·ne·tism \i-ˌlek-trō-ˈmag-nə-ˌti-zəm\ *n* (1828) **1 :** magnetism developed by a current of electricity **2 a :** a fundamental physical force that is responsible for interactions between charged particles which occur because of their charge and for the emission and absorption of photons, that is about a hundredth the strength of the strong force, and that extends over infinite distances but is dominant over atomic and molecular distances — called also *electromagnetic force*; compare GRAVITY 3a(2), STRONG FORCE, WEAK FORCE **b :** a branch of physical science that deals with the physical relations between electricity and magnetism

elec·tro·me·chan·i·cal \-mə-ˈka-ni-kəl\ *adj* (1888) **:** of, relating to, or being a mechanical process or device actuated or controlled electrically; *esp* **:** being a transducer for converting electrical energy to mechanical energy — **elec·tro·me·chan·i·cal·ly** \-k(ə-)lē\ *adv*

elec·tro·met·al·lur·gy \-ˈme-tə-ˌlər-jē, *esp Brit* -mə-ˈta-lər-\ *n* (1840) **:** a branch of metallurgy that deals with the application of electric current either for electrolytic deposition or as a source of heat

elec·trom·e·ter \i-ˌlek-ˈträ-mə-tər\ *n* (1749) **:** any of various instruments for detecting or measuring potential differences or ionizing radiations by means of the forces of attraction or repulsion between charged bodies

elec·tro·mo·tive force \i-ˌlek-trō-ˌmō-tiv-, -trə-\ *n* (1827) **:** something that moves or tends to move electricity; *esp* **:** the apparent force that drives a current around an electrical circuit and that is equivalent to the potential difference between the terminals of the circuit

elec·tro·myo·gram \i-ˌlek-trō-ˈmī-ə-ˌgram\ *n* (1917) **:** a tracing made by an electromyograph

elec·tro·myo·graph \-ˌgraf\ *n* [*electr-* + *my-* + *-graph*] (1948) **:** an instrument that converts the electrical activity associated with functioning skeletal muscle into a visual record or into sound and is used to diagnose neuromuscular disorders and in biofeedback training — **elec·tro·myo·graph·ic** \-ˌmī-ə-ˈgra-fik\ *adj* — **elec·tro·myo·graph·i·cal·ly** \-fi-k(ə-)lē\ *adv* — **elec·tro·my·og·ra·phy** \-mī-ˈä-grə-fē\ *n*

elec·tron \i-ˈlek-ˌträn\ *n* [*electr-* + [2]*-on*] (1891) **:** an elementary particle consisting of a charge of negative electricity equal to about 1.602×10^{-19} coulomb and having a mass when at rest of about 9.109×10^{-31} kilogram or about $1/1836$ that of a proton

electron cloud *n* (1926) **:** the system of electrons surrounding the nucleus of an atom

elec·tro·neg·a·tive \i-ˌlek-trō-ˈne-gə-tiv\ *adj* (1813) **:** having a tendency to attract electrons — **elec·tro·neg·a·tiv·i·ty** \-ˌne-gə-ˈti-və-tē\ *n*

electron gas *n* (ca. 1929) **:** a population of free electrons in a vacuum or in a metallic conductor

electron gun *n* (1924) **:** an electron-emitting cathode and its surrounding assembly (as electromagnets in a cathode-ray tube) for directing, controlling, and focusing a beam of electrons

elec·tron·ic \i-ˌlek-ˈträ-nik\ *adj* (1902) **1 :** of or relating to electrons **2 a :** of, relating to, or utilizing devices constructed or working by the methods or principles of electronics ⟨~ fuel injection⟩ **b :** implemented on or by means of a computer **:** involving a computer ⟨~ banking⟩ **3 a :** generating musical tones by electronic means ⟨an ~ organ⟩ **b :** of, relating to, or being music that consists of sounds electronically generated or modified **4 :** of, relating to, or being a medium (as television) by which information is transmitted electronically ⟨~ journalism⟩ — **elec·tron·i·cal·ly** \-ni-k(ə-)lē\ *adv*

elec·tron·i·ca \i-ˌlek-ˈträ-ni-kə\ *n* [prob. fr. *New Electronica,* recording label of the Brit. firm Beechwood Music Ltd.] (1994) **:** dance music featuring extensive use of synthesizers, electronic percussion, and samples of recorded music or sound

electronic countermeasure *n* (1962) **:** the disruption of the operation of an enemy's equipment (as by jamming radio or radar signals)

electronic mail *n* (1975) **:** E-MAIL

electronic publishing *n* (1977) **:** publishing in which information is distributed by means of a computer network or is produced in a format for use with a computer

elec·tron·ics \i-ˌlek-ˈträ-niks\ *n pl* (1910) **1** *sing in constr* **:** a branch of physics that deals with the emission, behavior, and effects of electrons (as in electron tubes and transistors) and with electronic devices **2 :** electronic components, devices, or equipment

electron micrograph *n* (1934) **:** a micrograph made with an electron microscope — **electron micrography** \-mī-ˈkrä-grə-fē\ *n*

electron microscope *n* (1932) **:** an electron-optical instrument in which a beam of electrons is used to produce an enlarged image of a minute object — **electron microscopist** *n* — **electron microscopy** *n*

electron multiplier *n* (1936) **:** a device utilizing secondary emission of electrons for amplifying a current of electrons

electron optics *n pl but sing in constr* (1916) **:** a branch of physics in which the principles of optics are applied to beams of electrons — **elec·tron–op·ti·cal** \i-ˌlek-ˌträn-ˈäp-ti-kəl\ *adj*

electron probe *n* (1962) **:** a microprobe that uses an electron beam to induce X-ray emissions in a sample

electron transport *n* (1951) **:** the sequential transfer of electrons esp. by cytochromes in cellular respiration from an oxidizable substrate to molecular oxygen by a series of oxidation-reduction reactions

electron tube *n* (1922) **:** an electronic device in which conduction by electrons takes place through a vacuum or a gaseous medium within a sealed glass or metal container and which has various uses based on the controlled flow of electrons

electron volt *n* (1930) **:** a unit of energy equal to the energy gained by an electron in passing from a point of low potential to a point one volt higher in potential **:** 1.60×10^{-19} joule

elec·tro·oc·u·lo·gram \i-ˌlek-trō-ˈä-kyə-lə-ˌgram\ *n* [*electr-* + L *oculus* eye + E *-gram* — more at EYE] (1947) **:** a record of the difference in electrical charge between the front and back of the eye that is correlated with eyeball movement (as in REM sleep) and obtained by electrodes placed on the skin near the eye

elec·tro·oc·u·log·ra·phy \-ˌä-kyə-ˈlä-grə-fē\ *n, pl* **-phies** (1951) **:** the preparation and study of electrooculograms

elec·tro–op·ti·cal \i-ˌlek-trō-ˈäp-ti-kəl\ *or* **elec·tro–op·tic** \-ˈäp-tik\ *adj* (1879) **1 :** of or relating to electro-optics **2 a :** relating to or being a change in the refractive index of a material due to an electric field ⟨~ effect⟩ **b :** using or being a material that exhibits electro-optical properties ⟨an ~ crystal⟩ **3 :** relating to or being an electronic device for emitting, modulating, transmitting, or sensing light — **elec·tro–op·ti·cal·ly** \-k(ə-)lē\ *adv*

elec·tro–op·tics \-trō-ˈäp-tiks\ *n pl* (ca. 1889) **1** *sing in constr* **:** a branch of physics that deals with the effects of an electric field on light traversing it **2 :** electro-optical devices

elec·tro·os·mo·sis \i-ˌlek-trō-äz-ˈmō-səs, -äs-\ *n* (1906) **:** the movement of a liquid out of or through a porous material or a biological membrane under the influence of an electric field — **elec·tro·os·mot·ic** \-ˈmä-tik\ *adj*

elec·tro·phe·ro·gram \-trə-ˈfir-ə-ˌgram, -ˈfer-\ *n* [*electr-* + *phero-* (fr. Gk *pherein* to carry) + *-gram*] (1951) **:** ELECTROPHORETOGRAM

elec·tro·phile \i-ˈlek-trə-ˌfī(-ə)l\ *n* (1906) **:** an electrophilic substance (as an electron-accepting reagent)

elec·tro·phil·ic \i-ˌlek-trə-ˈfi-lik\ *adj* (1933) **1** *of an atom, ion, or molecule* **:** having an affinity for electrons **:** being an electron acceptor **2 :** involving an electrophilic species ⟨an ~ reaction⟩ — compare NUCLEOPHILIC — **elec·tro·phi·lic·i·ty** \-trō-fi-ˈli-sə-tē\ *n*

elec·tro·pho·re·sis \-trə-fə-ˈrē-səs\ *n* [NL] (1911) **:** the movement of suspended particles through a medium (as paper or gel) under the action of an electromotive force applied to electrodes in contact with the suspension — **elec·tro·pho·rese** \-ˈrēs, -ˈrēz\ *vt* — **elec·tro·pho·ret·ic** \-ˈre-tik\ *adj* — **elec·tro·pho·ret·i·cal·ly** \-ti-k(ə-)lē\ *adv*

elec·tro·pho·reto·gram \-ˈre-tə-ˌgram\ *n* [*electrophoretic* + *-o-* + *-gram*] (1954) **:** a record that consists of the separated components of a mixture (as of proteins) produced by electrophoresis in a supporting medium (as filter paper)

elec·troph·o·rus \i-ˌlek-ˈträ-fə-rəs\ *n, pl* **-ri** \-ˌrī, -ˌrē\ [NL, fr. *electr-* + *-phorus* -phore] (1778) **:** a device for producing electric charges consisting of a disk that is negatively electrified by friction and a metal plate that becomes charged by induction when placed on the disk

elec·tro·pho·tog·ra·phy \i-ˌlek-trō-fə-ˈtä-grə-fē\ *n* (1894) **:** photography in which images are produced by electrical means (as in xerography) — **elec·tro·pho·to·graph·ic** \-trə-ˌfō-tə-ˈgra-fik\ *adj*

elec·tro·phys·i·ol·o·gy \i-ˌlek-trō-ˌfi-zē-ˈä-lə-jē\ *n* (1838) **1 :** physiology that is concerned with the electrical aspects of physiological phenomena **2 :** electrical phenomena associated with a physiological process (as the function of a body or bodily part) ⟨~ of the eye⟩ — **elec·tro·phys·i·o·log·i·cal** \-zē-ə-ˈlä-ji-kəl\ *also* **elec·tro·phys·i·o·log·ic** \-jik\ *adj* — **elec·tro·phys·i·o·log·i·cal·ly** \-ji-k(ə-)lē\ *adv* — **elec·tro·phys·i·ol·o·gist** \-zē-ˈäl-ə-jist\ *n*

elec·tro·plate \i-ˈlek-trə-ˌplāt\ *vt* (1851) **:** to plate with an adherent continuous coating by electrodeposition

elec·tro·po·ra·tion \i-ˌlek-trə-pȯr-ˈā-shən\ *n* [*electr-* + ²*pore* + *-ation*] (1985) **:** the application of an electric current to a living surface (as the skin or a cell membrane) in order to open pores or channels through which something (as a drug or DNA) may pass

elec·tro·pos·i·tive \i-ˌlek-trō-ˈpä-zə-tiv, -ˈpäz-tiv\ *adj* (1813) **:** having a tendency to release electrons

elec·tro·re·cep·tor \-ri-ˈsep-tər\ *n* (1958) **:** a vertebrate organ found esp. in fish that contains sensory cells capable of detecting electric fields

elec·tro·ret·i·no·gram \-ˈre-tə-nə-ˌgram\ *n* (1936) **:** a graphic record of electrical activity of the retina used esp. in the diagnosis of retinal conditions

elec·tro·ret·i·no·graph \-ˌgraf\ *n* (1962) **:** an instrument for recording electrical activity in the retina — **elec·tro·ret·i·no·graph·ic** \-ˌre-tə-nə-ˈgra-fik\ *adj* — **elec·tro·ret·i·nog·ra·phy** \-tᵊn-ˈä-grə-fē\ *n*

elec·tro·scope \i-ˈlek-trə-ˌskōp\ *n* [prob. fr. F *électroscope*] (1810) **:** any of various instruments for detecting the presence of an electric charge on a body, for determining whether the charge is positive or negative, or for indicating and measuring intensity of radiation

elec·tro·shock \-trō-ˌshäk\ *n* (1941) **1 :** ³SHOCK 5 **2 :** ELECTROSHOCK THERAPY

electroshock therapy *n* (1942) **:** the treatment of mental disorder and esp. depression by the application of electric current to the head of a usu. anesthetized patient that induces unconsciousness and convulsive seizures in the brain — called also *electroconvulsive therapy*

elec·tro·stat·ic \i-ˌlek-trə-ˈsta-tik\ *adj* [ISV] (1856) **1 :** of or relating to static electricity or electrostatics **2 :** of or relating to painting with a spray that utilizes electrically charged particles to ensure complete coating — **elec·tro·stat·i·cal·ly** \-ˈsta-ti-k(ə-)lē\ *adv*

electrostatic generator *n* (ca. 1931) **:** VAN DE GRAAFF GENERATOR

electrostatic precipitator *n* (1949) **:** an electrostatic device in chimney flues that removes particles from escaping gases

elec·tro·stat·ics \i-ˌlek-trə-ˈsta-tiks\ *n pl but sing in constr* (1827) **:** physics that deals with phenomena due to attractions or repulsions of electric charges but not dependent upon their motion

elec·tro·sur·gery \i-ˌlek-trō-ˈsər-jə-rē\ *n* (ca. 1882) **:** surgery by means of diathermy — **elec·tro·sur·gi·cal** \-ˈsər-ji-kəl\ *adj*

elec·tro·ther·a·py \-ˈther-ə-pē\ *n* (1881) **:** the therapeutic use of electricity

elec·tro·ther·mal \-ˈthər-məl\ *adj* (1884) **:** relating to or combining electricity and heat; *specif* **:** relating to the generation of heat by electricity — **elec·tro·ther·mal·ly** \-mə-lē\ *adv*

elec·tro·ton·ic \i-ˌlek-trə-ˈtä-nik\ *adj* (1832) **1 :** of, induced by, relating to, or constituting electrotonus **2 :** of, relating to, or being the spread of electrical activity through living tissue or cells in the absence of repeated action potentials — **elec·tro·ton·i·cal·ly** \-ni-k(ə-)lē\ *adv*

elec·trot·o·nus \i-ˌlek-ˈträ-tə-nəs\ *n* [NL] (1878) **:** the altered sensitivity of a nerve when a constant current of electricity passes through any part of it

elec·tro·type \i-ˈlek-trə-ˌtīp\ *n* (1840) **1 :** a duplicate printing surface made by an electroplating process **2 :** a copy (as of a coin) made by an electroplating process — **electrotype** *vt* — **elec·tro·typ·er** \-ˌtī-pər\ *n*

elec·tro·weak \i-ˈlek-trō-ˌwēk\ *adj* (1978) **:** of, relating to, or being the unification of electromagnetism and the weak force

elec·tro·win·ning \i-ˈlek-trō-ˌwi-niŋ\ *n* (1924) **:** the recovery esp. of metals from solutions by electrolysis

elec·trum \i-ˈlek-trəm\ *n* [ME, fr. L — more at ELECTRIC] (14c) **:** a natural pale yellow alloy of gold and silver

elec·tu·ary \i-ˈlek-chə-ˌwer-ē, -chü-ˌer-\ *n, pl* **-ar·ies** [ME *electuarie*, fr. AF *eletuarie*, fr. LL *electuarium*, prob. fr. Gk *ekleikton*, fr. *ekleichein* to lick up, fr. *ex-* + *leichein* to lick — more at LICK] (14c) **:** CONFECTION 2b

el·e·doi·sin \ˌe-lə-ˈdȯi-sᵊn\ *n* [irreg. fr. NL *Eledone*, fr. Gk *eledōnē*, a kind of octopus] (1963) **:** a small protein $C_{54}H_{85}N_{13}O_{15}S$ from the salivary glands of several octopuses (genus *Eledone*) that is a powerful vasodilator and hypotensive agent

el·ee·mo·sy·nary \ˌe-li-ˈmä-sə-ˌner-ē, -ˈmō-; -ˈmä-zə-\ *adj* [ML *eleemosynarius*, fr. LL *eleemosyna* alms — more at ALMS] (ca. 1616) **:** of, relating to, or supported by charity

el·e·gance \ˈe-li-gən(t)s\ *n* (ca. 1510) **1 a :** refined grace or dignified propriety **:** URBANITY **b :** tasteful richness of design or ornamentation ⟨the sumptuous ~ of the furnishings⟩ **c :** dignified gracefulness or restrained beauty of style **:** POLISH ⟨the essay is marked by lucidity, wit, and ~⟩ **d :** scientific precision, neatness, and simplicity ⟨the ~ of a mathematical proof⟩ **2 :** something that is elegant

el·e·gan·cy \-gən(t)-sē\ *n, pl* **-cies** (15c) **:** ELEGANCE

el·e·gant \ˈe-li-gənt\ *adj* [MF or L; MF, fr. L *elegant-, elegans;* akin to L *eligere* to select — more at ELECT] (15c) **1 :** marked by elegance ⟨~ clothes⟩ ⟨an ~ solution⟩ **2 :** of a high grade or quality **:** SPLENDID ⟨~ gems priced at hundreds of thousands of dollars⟩ ***syn*** see CHOICE — **el·e·gant·ly** *adv*

ele·gi·ac \ˌe-lə-ˈjī-ək, -ˌak *also* i-ˈlē-jē-ˌak\ *also* **el·e·gi·a·cal** \ˌe-lə-ˈjī-ə-kəl\ *adj* [LL *elegiacus*, fr. Gk *elegeiakos*, fr. *elegeion*] (1542) **1 a :** of, relating to, or consisting of two dactylic hexameter lines the second of which lacks the arsis in the third and sixth feet **b (1) :** written in or consisting of elegiac couplets **(2) :** noted for having written poetry in such couplets **c :** of or relating to the period in Greece about the seventh century B.C. when poetry written in such couplets flourished **2 :** of, relating to, or comprising elegy or an elegy; *esp* **:** expressing sorrow often for something now past ⟨an ~ lament for departed youth⟩ — **elegiac** *n* — **el·e·gi·a·cal·ly** \ˌe-lə-ˈjī-ə-k(ə-)lē\ *adv*

ele·git \i-ˈlē-jət\ *n* [L, lit., he has chosen, fr. *eligere*] (1504) **:** a judicial writ of execution by which a defendant's goods and if necessary his or her lands are delivered for debt to the plaintiff until the debt is paid

el·e·gize \ˈe-lə-ˌjīz\ *vb* **-gized; -giz·ing** *vi* (1653) **:** to write an elegy ~ *vt* **:** to write an elegy on

el·e·gy \ˈe-lə-jē\ *n, pl* **-gies** [L *elegia* poem in elegiac couplets, fr. Gk *elegeia, elegeion*, fr. *elegos* song of mourning] (1501) **1 :** a poem in elegiac couplets **2 a :** a song or poem expressing sorrow or lamentation esp. for one who is dead **b :** something (as a speech) resembling such a song or poem **3 a :** a pensive or reflective poem that is usu. nostalgic or melancholy **b :** a short pensive musical composition

elem *abbr* elementary

el·e·ment \ˈe-lə-mənt\ *n* [ME, fr. AF & L; AF, fr. L *elementum*] (13c) **1 a :** any of the four substances air, water, fire, and earth formerly believed to compose the physical universe **b** *pl* **:** weather conditions; *esp* **:** violent or severe weather ⟨battling the ~*s*⟩ **c :** the state or sphere natural or suited to a person or thing ⟨at school she was in her ~⟩ **2 :** a constituent part: as **a** *pl* **:** the simplest principles of a subject of study **:** RUDIMENTS **b (1) :** a part of a geometric magnitude ⟨an infinitesimal ~ of volume⟩ **(2) :** a generator of a geometric figure; *also* **:** a line or line segment contained in the surface of a cone or cylinder **(3) :** a basic member of a mathematical or logical class or set **(4) :** one of the individual entries in a mathematical matrix or determinant **c :** a distinct group within a larger group or community ⟨the criminal ~ in the city⟩ **d (1) :** one of the necessary data or values on which calculations or conclusions are based **(2) :** one of the factors determining the outcome of a process **e :** any of the fundamental substances that consist of atoms of only one kind and that singly or in combination constitute all matter **f :** a distinct part of a composite device **g :** a subdivision of a military unit **3** *pl* **:** the bread and wine used in the Eucharist

syn ELEMENT, COMPONENT, CONSTITUENT, INGREDIENT mean one of the parts of a compound or complex whole. ELEMENT applies to any such part and often connotes irreducible simplicity ⟨the basic *elements* of geometry⟩. COMPONENT and CONSTITUENT may designate any of the substances (whether elements or compounds) or the qualities that enter into the makeup of a complex product; COMPONENT stresses its separate entity or distinguishable character ⟨the *components* of a stereo system⟩. CONSTITUENT stresses its essential and formative character ⟨the *constituents* of a chemical compound⟩. INGREDIENT applies to any of the substances which when combined form a particular mixture ⟨the *ingredients* of a cocktail⟩.

CHEMICAL ELEMENTS

ELEMENT	SYMBOL	ATOMIC NUMBER	ATOMIC WEIGHT[1]
actinium	Ac	89	(227)
aluminum	Al	13	26.98154
americium	Am	95	(243)
antimony	Sb	51	121.760
argon	Ar	18	39.948
arsenic	As	33	74.92160
astatine	At	85	(210)
barium	Ba	56	137.33
berkelium	Bk	97	(247)
beryllium	Be	4	9.012182
bismuth	Bi	83	208.98040
bohrium	Bh	107	(264)
boron	B	5	10.81
bromine	Br	35	79.904
cadmium	Cd	48	112.41
calcium	Ca	20	40.078
californium	Cf	98	(251)
carbon	C	6	12.011
cerium	Ce	58	140.116
cesium	Cs	55	132.90545
chlorine	Cl	17	35.453
chromium	Cr	24	51.996
cobalt	Co	27	58.93320
copernicium	Cn	112	(285)
copper	Cu	29	63.546
curium	Cm	96	(247)
darmstadtium	Ds	110	(269)
dubnium	Db	105	(262)
dysprosium	Dy	66	162.50
einsteinium	Es	99	(252)
erbium	Er	68	167.259
europium	Eu	63	151.964
fermium	Fm	100	(257)
fluorine	F	9	18.998403
francium	Fr	87	(223)
gadolinium	Gd	64	157.25
gallium	Ga	31	69.723
germanium	Ge	32	72.64
gold	Au	79	196.96657
hafnium	Hf	72	178.49
hassium	Hs	108	(277)
helium	He	2	4.002602
holmium	Ho	67	164.93032
hydrogen	H	1	1.0079
indium	In	49	114.818
iodine	I	53	126.90447
iridium	Ir	77	192.217
iron	Fe	26	55.845
krypton	Kr	36	83.80
lanthanum	La	57	138.90547
lawrencium	Lr	103	(262)
lead	Pb	82	207.2
lithium	Li	3	6.941
lutetium	Lu	71	174.967
magnesium	Mg	12	24.305
manganese	Mn	25	54.93805
meitnerium	Mt	109	(268)
mendelevium	Md	101	(258)
mercury	Hg	80	200.59
molybdenum	Mo	42	95.94
neodymium	Nd	60	144.242
neon	Ne	10	20.180
neptunium	Np	93	(237)
nickel	Ni	28	58.6934
niobium	Nb	41	92.90638
nitrogen	N	7	14.0067
nobelium	No	102	(259)
osmium	Os	76	190.23
oxygen	O	8	15.9994
palladium	Pd	46	106.42
phosphorus	P	15	30.973762
platinum	Pt	78	195.084
plutonium	Pu	94	(244)
polonium	Po	84	(209)
potassium	K	19	39.0983
praseodymium	Pr	59	140.90765
promethium	Pm	61	(145)
protactinium	Pa	91	(231)
radium	Ra	88	(226)
radon	Rn	86	(222)
rhenium	Re	75	186.207
rhodium	Rh	45	102.90550
roentgenium	Rg	111	(280)
rubidium	Rb	37	85.4678
ruthenium	Ru	44	101.07
rutherfordium	Rf	104	(261)
samarium	Sm	62	150.36
scandium	Sc	21	44.95591
seaborgium	Sg	106	(266)
selenium	Se	34	78.96
silicon	Si	14	28.0855
silver	Ag	47	107.8682
sodium	Na	11	22.989769
strontium	Sr	38	87.62
sulfur	S	16	32.07
tantalum	Ta	73	180.9479
technetium	Tc	43	(98)
tellurium	Te	52	127.60
terbium	Tb	65	158.92535
thallium	Tl	81	204.3833
thorium	Th	90	(232)
thulium	Tm	69	168.93421
tin	Sn	50	118.71
titanium	Ti	22	47.867
tungsten	W	74	183.84
uranium	U	92	(238)
vanadium	V	23	50.9415
xenon	Xe	54	131.29
ytterbium	Yb	70	173.04
yttrium	Y	39	88.90585
zinc	Zn	30	65.39
zirconium	Zr	40	91.224

[1]Weights are based on the naturally occurring isotope compositions and scaled to $^{12}C = 12$. For elements lacking stable isotopes, the mass number of the most stable nuclide is shown in parentheses.

el·e·men·tal \ˌe-lə-ˈmen-t²l\ *adj* (15c) **1 a** : of, relating to, or being an element; *specif* : existing as an uncombined chemical element **b** (1) : of, relating to, or being the basic or essential constituent of something : FUNDAMENTAL ⟨~ biological needs⟩ (2) : SIMPLE, UNCOMPLICATED ⟨~ food⟩ **c** : of, relating to, or dealing with the rudiments of something : ELEMENTARY ⟨taught ~ crafts to the children⟩ **d** : forming an integral part : INHERENT ⟨an ~ sense of rhythm⟩ **2** : of, relating to, or resembling a great force of nature ⟨the rains come with ~ violence⟩ ⟨~ passions⟩ — **elemental** *n* — **el·e·men·tal·ly** \-ˈt²l-ē\ *adv*
el·e·men·ta·ry \ˌe-lə-ˈmen-tə-rē, -ˈmen-trē\ *adj* (14c) **1 a** : of, relating to, or dealing with the simplest elements or principles of something **b** : of or relating to an elementary school **2** : ELEMENTAL 1a, b **3** : ELEMENTAL 2 — **el·e·men·ta·ri·ly** \ˌ-ˌmen-ˈter-ə-lē, -ˈmen-trə-lē\ *adv* — **el·e·men·ta·ri·ness** \-ˈmen-tə-rē-nəs, -ˈmen-trē-\ *n*
elementary particle *n* (1934) : any of the particles of which matter and energy are composed or which mediate the fundamental forces of nature; *esp* : one whose existence has not been attributed to the combination of other more fundamental entities
elementary school *n* (1818) : a school including usu. the first four to the first eight grades and often a kindergarten
el·e·mi \ˈe-lə-mē\ *n* [NL *elimi*, prob. fr. Ar *al lāmi* the elemi] (1543) : any of various fragrant oleoresins from tropical trees (family Burseraceae) used chiefly in varnishes, lacquers, and printing inks
elen·chus \i-ˈleŋ-kəs\ *n*, *pl* **-chi** \-ˌkī, -ˌ(ˌ)kē\ [L, fr. Gk *elenchos*] (1663) : REFUTATION; *esp* : one in syllogistic form
el·e·phant \ˈe-lə-fənt\ *n*, *pl* **elephants** *also* **elephant** *often attrib* [ME, fr. AF & L; AF *olifant, elefant*, fr. L *elephantus*, fr. Gk *elephant-, elephas*] (14c) **1** : any of a family (Elephantidae, the elephant family) of thickset usu. extremely large nearly hairless herbivorous mammals that have a snout elongated into a muscular trunk and two incisors in the upper jaw developed esp. in the male into large ivory tusks and that include two living forms and various extinct relatives: as **a** : a tall large-eared mammal (*Loxodonta africana*) of tropical Africa — called also *African elephant* **b** : a relatively small-eared mammal (*Elephas maximus*) of forests of southeastern Asia — called also *Asian elephant, Indian elephant* **2** : an animal or fossil related to the elephants **3** : one that is uncommonly large or hard to manage

elephant: *1* African, *2* Asian

elephant bird *n* (ca. 1889) : any of a group (genus *Aepyornis* or order Aepyornithiformes) of gigantic flightless ratite birds known only from remains found in Madagascar
elephant garlic *n* (ca. 1923) : an Old World herb (*Allium ampeloprasum*) of the lily family that is related to the leek and has a bulb that resembles that of garlic but is much larger; *also* : the mildly flavored bulb of the elephant garlic used esp. as a seasoning
elephant grass *n* (1832) **1** : an Old World cattail (*Typha elephantina*) used esp. in making baskets **2** : NAPIER GRASS

\ə\ **abut** \ᵊ\ **kitten, F table** \ər\ **further** \a\ **ash** \ā\ **ace** \ä\ **mop, mar**
\au̇\ **out** \ch\ **chin** \e\ **bet** \ē\ **easy** \g\ **go** \i\ **hit** \ī\ **ice** \j\ **job**
\ŋ\ **sing** \ō\ **go** \ȯ\ **law** \ȯi\ **boy** \th\ **thin** \t̠h\ **the** \ü\ **loot** \u̇\ **foot**
\y\ **yet** \zh\ **vision, beige** \k, ⁿ, œ, ᴜ, ᵊ\ *see* **Guide to Pronunciation**

el·e·phan·ti·a·sis \ˌe-lə-fən-ˈtī-ə-səs, -ˌfan-\ *n, pl* **-a·ses** \-ˌsēz\ [NL, fr. L, a kind of leprosy, fr. Gk, fr. *elephant-, elephas*] (1562) **1 :** enlargement and thickening of tissues; *specif* **:** the enormous enlargement of a limb or the scrotum caused by obstruction of lymphatics by filarial worms (esp. *Wuchereria bancrofti*) **2 :** an undesirable usu. enormous growth, enlargement, or overdevelopment ⟨~ of the imagination⟩

el·e·phan·tine \ˌe-lə-ˈfan-ˌtēn, -ˌtīn, ˈe-lə-fən-\ *adj* (1610) **1 a :** having enormous size or strength **:** MASSIVE **b :** CLUMSY, PONDEROUS ⟨~ verse⟩ **2 :** of or relating to an elephant

elephant in the room (1985) **:** an obvious major problem or issue that people avoid discussing or acknowledging

elephant seal *n* (1839) **:** either of two very large seals (genus *Mirounga* of the family Phocidae) characterized by a long inflatable proboscis: **a :** one (*M. angustirostris*) found in Pacific coastal waters from southeastern Alaska to Baja California **b :** one (*M. leonina*) found in coastal waters of subantarctic islands and Patagonia

elephant's ear *n* (1866) **:** any of several large-leaved plants of the arum family: as **a :** TARO **b :** any of a genus (*Alocasia*) of tropical Asian perennial herbs cultivated as ornamentals for their large heavily veined basal leaves

El·eu·sin·i·an \ˌel-yü-ˈsi-nē-ən\ *adj* (1591) **:** of or relating to ancient Eleusis or to the religious mysteries celebrated there in worship of Demeter and Persephone

elev *abbr* elevation

[1]**el·e·vate** \ˈe-lə-ˌvāt, -vət\ *adj* (14c) *archaic* **:** ELEVATED

[2]**el·e·vate** \-ˌvāt\ *vb* **-vat·ed; -vat·ing** [ME, fr. L *elevatus,* pp. of *elevare,* fr. *e-* + *levare* to raise — more at LEVER] *vt* (15c) **1 :** to lift up or make higher **:** RAISE ⟨~ a patient's leg⟩ ⟨exercises that ~ the heart rate⟩ **2 :** to raise in rank or status ⟨was *elevated* to chairman⟩ **3 :** to improve morally, intellectually, or culturally ⟨great books that both entertain and ~ their readers⟩ **4 :** to raise the spirits of **:** ELATE ~ *vi* **:** to become elevated **:** RISE ⟨his voice *elevated* to a shout⟩ ***syn*** see LIFT

[1]**el·e·vat·ed** \-ˌvā-təd\ *adj* (1553) **1 a :** raised esp. above the ground or other surface ⟨an ~ highway⟩ **b :** increased esp. abnormally (as in degree or amount) ⟨~ blood pressure⟩ **2 a :** being morally or intellectually on a high plane **:** REFINED ⟨~ conversation⟩ **b :** FORMAL, DIGNIFIED ⟨~ diction⟩ **3 :** exhilarated in mood or feeling

[2]**elevated** *n* (1881) **:** [2]EL

el·e·va·tion \ˌe-lə-ˈvā-shən\ *n* (14c) **1 :** the height to which something is elevated: as **a :** the angular distance of something (as a celestial object) above the horizon **b :** the degree to which a gun is aimed above the horizon **c :** the height above the level of the sea **:** ALTITUDE **2 :** a dancer's or an athlete's leap and seeming suspension in the air; *also* **:** the ability to achieve an elevation **3 :** an act or instance of elevating **4 :** something that is elevated: as **a :** an elevated place **b :** a swelling esp. on the skin **5 :** the quality or state of being elevated **6 :** a geometrical drawing that depicts one vertical plane of an object or structure ***syn*** see HEIGHT

el·e·va·tor \ˈe-lə-ˌvā-tər\ *n* (1646) **1 :** one that raises or lifts something up: as **a :** an endless belt or chain conveyor with cleats, scoops, or buckets for raising material **b :** a cage or platform and its hoisting machinery for conveying people or things to different levels **c :** GRAIN ELEVATOR **2 :** a movable airfoil usu. attached to the tailplane of an airplane for controlling pitch — see AIRPLANE illustration

elevator music *n* (1963) **:** instrumental arrangements of popular songs often piped in (as to an elevator or retail store)

elev·en \i-ˈle-vən\ *n* [ME *enleven,* fr. *enleven,* adj., fr. OE *endleofan,* fr. *end-* (alter. of *ān* one) + *-leofan;* akin to OE *lēon* to lend — more at ONE, LOAN] (bef. 12c) **1** — see NUMBER table **2 :** the 11th in a set or series **3 :** something having 11 units or members; *esp* **:** a football team — **eleven** *adj* — **eleven** *pron, pl in constr* — **elev·enth** \-vən(t)th\ *adj or n*

eleven–plus \i-ˌle-vən-ˈpləs\ *n* (1955) *Brit* **:** an examination taken by schoolchildren between the ages of 11 and 12 that determines the type of secondary education to which they are assigned

elev·ens·es \-vən-zəz\ *n pl but sometimes sing in constr* [double pl. of *eleven* (o'clock)] (ca. 1819) *Brit* **:** light refreshment (as a snack) taken in the middle of the morning

eleventh hour *n* (1821) **:** the latest possible time before it is too late ⟨still making changes at the *eleventh hour*⟩

el·e·von \ˈe-lə-ˌvän\ *n* [*elevator* + *aileron*] (1944) **:** an airplane control surface that combines the functions of elevator and aileron

elf \ˈelf\ *n, pl* **elves** \ˈelvz\ [ME, fr. OE *ælf;* akin to ON *alfr* elf & perh. to L *albus* white — more at ALB] (bef. 12c) **1 :** a small often mischievous fairy **2 :** a small lively creature; *also* **:** a usu. lively mischievous or malicious person — **elf·ish** \ˈel-fish\ *adj* — **elf·ish·ly** *adv*

ELF *abbr* extremely low frequency

elf·in \ˈel-fən\ *adj* [irreg. fr. *elf*] (1590) **1 a :** of, relating to, or produced by an elf **b :** resembling an elf esp. in its tiny size ⟨~ portions⟩ **2 :** having an otherworldly or magical quality or charm

elf·lock \ˈelf-ˌläk\ *n* (1592) **:** hair matted as if by elves — usu. used in pl.

elf owl *n* (1887) **:** a very small insectivorous owl (*Micrathene whitneyi*) of the southwestern U.S. and Mexico that roosts and nests in the cavities of trees and saguaro cacti

el·hi \(ˌ)el-ˈhī\ *adj* [*el*ementary (school) + *hi*gh (school)] (ca. 1948) **:** of, relating to, or designed for use in grades 1 to 12

Eli \ˈē-ˌlī\ *n* [Heb *ʿĒlī*] (14c) **:** a judge and priest of Israel who according to the account in I Samuel was entrusted with the care of the boy Samuel

Eli·as \i-ˈlī-əs\ *n* [LL, fr. Gk *Elias,* fr. Heb *Ēlīyāh*] (bef. 12c) **:** ELIJAH

elic·it \i-ˈli-sət\ *vt* [L *elicitus,* pp. of *elicere,* fr. *e-* + *lacere* to allure] (1605) **1 :** to draw forth or bring out (something latent or potential) ⟨hypnotism ~*ed* his hidden fears⟩ **2 :** to call forth or draw out (as information or a response) ⟨her remarks ~*ed* cheers⟩ ***syn*** see EDUCE — **elic·i·ta·tion** \i-ˌli-sə-ˈtā-shən, ˌē-\ *n* — **elic·i·tor** \i-ˈli-sə-tər\ *n*

elide \i-ˈlīd\ *vt* **elid·ed; elid·ing** [L *elidere* to strike out, fr. *e-* + *laedere* to injure by striking] (1796) **1 a :** to suppress or alter (as a vowel or syllable) by elision **b :** to strike out (as a written word) **2 a :** to leave out of consideration **:** OMIT **b :** CURTAIL, ABRIDGE

el·i·gi·ble \ˈe-lə-jə-bəl\ *adj* [ME, fr. LL *eligibilis,* fr. L *eligere* to choose — more at ELECT] (15c) **1 a :** qualified to participate or be chosen ⟨~ to retire⟩ **b :** permitted under football rules to catch a forward pass **2 :** worthy of being chosen ⟨an ~ young bachelor⟩ — **el·i·gi·bil·i·ty** \ˌe-lə-jə-ˈbi-lə-tē\ *n* — **eligible** *n* — **el·i·gi·bly** \ˈe-lə-jə-blē\ *adv*

Eli·jah \i-ˈlī-jə\ *n* [Heb *Ēlīyāh*] (1587) **:** a Hebrew prophet of the ninth century B.C. who according to the account in I Kings championed the worship of Jehovah as against Baal

elim·i·nate \i-ˈli-mə-ˌnāt\ *vb* **-nat·ed; -nat·ing** [L *eliminatus,* pp. of *eliminare,* fr. *e-* + *limin-, limen* threshold] *vt* (1568) **1 a :** to put an end to or get rid of **:** REMOVE ⟨~ errors⟩ **b :** to remove from consideration ⟨~ someone as a suspect⟩ **c :** to remove from further competition by defeating ⟨the team was *eliminated* in the first round of the playoffs⟩ **2 :** to expel (as waste) from the living body **3 :** to cause (as an unknown) to disappear by combining two or more mathematical equations ~ *vi* **:** to expel waste from the living body — **elim·i·na·tive** \-ˈli-mə-ˌnā-tiv\ *adj* — **elim·i·na·tor** \-ˌnā-tər\ *n*

elim·i·na·tion \i-ˌli-mə-ˈnā-shən\ *n, often attrib* (1627) **:** the act, process, or an instance of eliminating or discharging: as **a :** the act of discharging or excreting waste products from the body **b :** the removal from a molecule of the constituents of a simpler molecule ⟨ethylene is formed by the ~ of water from ethanol⟩ — compare ADDITION 4

ELISA \ē-ˈlī-sə, -zə\ *n* (1971) **:** ENZYME-LINKED IMMUNOSORBENT ASSAY

Eli·sha \i-ˈlī-shə\ *n* [Heb *Ēlīshāʿ*] (14c) **:** a Hebrew prophet and disciple and successor of Elijah

eli·sion \i-ˈli-zhən\ *n* [LL *elision-, elisio,* fr. L *elidere*] (1581) **1 a :** the use of a speech form that lacks a final or initial sound which a variant speech form has (as *'s* instead of *is* in *there's*) **b :** the omission of an unstressed vowel or syllable in a verse to achieve a uniform metrical pattern **2 :** the act or an instance of omitting something **:** OMISSION

elite \ā-ˈlēt, i-, ē-\ *n* [F *élite,* fr. OF *eslite,* fr. fem. of *eslit,* pp. of *eslire* to choose, fr. L *eligere*] (1823) **1 a** *sing or pl in constr* **:** the choice part **:** CREAM ⟨the ~ of the entertainment world⟩ **b** *sing or pl in constr* **:** the best of a class ⟨superachievers who dominate the computer ~ —Marilyn Chase⟩ **c** *sing or pl in constr* **:** the socially superior part of society ⟨how the French-speaking ~ . . . was changing —*Economist*⟩ **d :** a group of persons who by virtue of position or education exercise much power or influence ⟨members of the ruling ~⟩ **e :** a member of such an elite — usu. used in pl. ⟨the ~*s* . . . , pursuing their studies in Europe —Robert Wernick⟩ **2 :** a typewriter type providing 12 characters to the linear inch — **elite** *adj*

élite, élit·ism *chiefly Brit var of* ELITE, ELITISM

elit·ism \ā-ˈlē-ˌti-zəm, i-, ē-\ *n* (1947) **1 :** leadership or rule by an elite **2 :** the selectivity of the elite; *esp* **:** SNOBBERY **3 :** consciousness of being or belonging to an elite — **elit·ist** \-ˈlē-tist\ *n or adj*

elix·ir \i-ˈlik-sər\ *n* [ME, fr. ML, fr. Ar *al-iksīr* the elixir, fr. *al* the + *iksīr* elixir, prob. fr. Gk *xērion* desiccative powder, fr. *xēros* dry] (14c) **1 a (1) :** a substance held capable of changing base metals into gold **(2) :** a substance held capable of prolonging life indefinitely **b (1) :** CURE-ALL **(2) :** a medicinal concoction **2 :** a sweetened liquid usu. containing alcohol that is used in medication either for its medicinal ingredients or as a flavoring **3 :** the essential principle

Eliz·a·be·than \i-ˌli-zə-ˈbē-thən\ *adj* (1807) **:** of, relating to, or characteristic of Elizabeth I of England or her reign — **Elizabethan** *n*

elk \ˈelk\ *n, pl* **elks** [ME, prob. fr. OE *eolh;* akin to OHG *elaho* elk, Gk *elaphos* deer] (bef. 12c) **1** *pl usu* **elk a :** MOOSE 1 — used for one of the Old World **b :** a large gregarious deer (*Cervus elaphus*) of No. America, Europe, Asia, and northwestern Africa — called also *red deer, wapiti* **c :** any of various large Asian deer **2 :** soft tanned rugged leather **3** *cap* [Benevolent and Protective Order of *Elks*] **:** a member of a major benevolent and fraternal order

elk·horn coral \ˈelk-ˌhȯrn-\ *n* (1928) **:** a reef-building branching coral (*Acropora palmata*) of shallow waters of southern Florida and the West Indies

elk·hound \ˈelk-ˌhau̇nd, ˈel-ˌkau̇nd\ *n* (1889) **:** NORWEGIAN ELKHOUND

[1]**ell** \ˈel\ *n* [ME *eln,* fr. OE; akin to OHG *elina* ell, L *ulna* forearm, Gk *ōlenē* elbow, Skt *aratni*] (bef. 12c) **:** a former English unit of length (as for cloth) equal to 45 inches (about 1.14 meters); *also* **:** any of various units of length used similarly

[2]**ell** *n* [alter. of [1]*el*] (1773) **1 :** an extension at right angles to the length of a building **2 :** an elbow in a pipe or conduit

el·lag·ic acid \ə-ˈla-jik-, e-\ *n* [F *ellagique,* fr. *ellag,* anagram of *galle* gall] (1810) **:** a crystalline phenolic compound $C_{14}H_6O_8$ with two lactone groupings that is obtained esp. from oak galls and some tannins and is used medicinally as a hemostatic

el·lipse \i-ˈlips, e-\ *n* [Gk *elleipsis*] (ca. 1753) **1 a :** OVAL **b :** a closed plane curve generated by a point moving in such a way that the sums of its distances from two fixed points is a constant **:** a plane section of a right circular cone that is a closed curve **2 :** ELLIPSIS

el·lip·sis \i-ˈlip-səs, e-\ *n, pl* **el·lip·ses** \-ˌsēz\ [L, fr. Gk *elleipsis* ellipsis, ellipse, fr. *elleipein* to leave out, fall short, fr. *en* in + *leipein* to leave — more at IN, LOAN] (1540) **1 a :** the omission of one or more words that are obviously understood but that must be supplied to make a construction grammatically complete **b :** a sudden leap from one topic to another **2 :** marks or a mark (as . . .) indicating an omission (as of words) or a pause

el·lip·soid \i-ˈlip-ˌsȯid, e-\ *n* (1721) **:** a surface all plane sections of which are ellipses or circles — **el·lip·soi·dal** \i-ˌlip-ˈsȯi-dᵊl, (ˌ)e-\ *also* **ellipsoid** *adj*

el·lip·ti·cal \i-ˈlip-ti-kəl, e-\ *or* **el·lip·tic** \-tik\ *adj* [Gk *elleiptikos* defective, marked by ellipsis, fr. *elleipein*] (1656) **1 :** of, relating to, or shaped like an ellipse **2 a :** of, relating to, or marked by ellipsis or an ellipsis **b (1) :** of, relating to, or marked by extreme economy of speech or writing **(2) :** of or relating to deliberate obscurity (as of literary or conversational style) — **el·lip·ti·cal·ly** \-ti-k(ə-)lē\ *adv*

elliptical galaxy *n* (1948) **:** a galaxy that has a generally elliptical shape and that has no apparent internal structure or spiral arms — called also *elliptical*; compare SPIRAL GALAXY

elliptical trainer *n* (1997) **:** a stationary exercise device on which the user stands on two small rimmed platforms and moves them forward and back in an approximately elliptical path — called also *elliptical machine*

el·lip·tic·i·ty \i-ˌlip-ˈti-sə-tē, (ˌ)e-\ *n* (1753) **:** deviation of an ellipse or a spheroid from the form of a circle or a sphere

elm \ˈelm\ *n* [ME, fr. OE; akin to OHG *elme* elm, L *ulmus*] (bef. 12c) **1 :** any of a genus (*Ulmus* of the family Ulmaceae, the elm family) of usu. large deciduous north temperate-zone trees with alternate stipulate leaves and fruit that is a samara **2 :** the wood of an elm

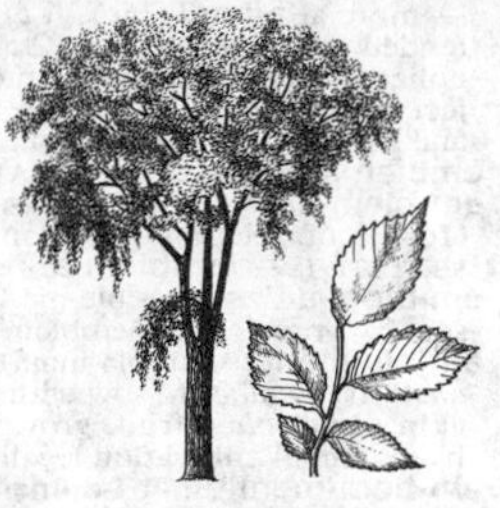

elm 1

elm bark beetle *n* (ca. 1909) **:** either of two beetles (family Scolytidae) that are vectors for the fungus causing Dutch elm disease: **a :** one (*Hylurgopinus rufipes*) native to eastern No. America **b :** one (*Scolytus multistriatus*) introduced from Europe into eastern No. America

elm leaf beetle *n* (1881) **:** a small yellow to greenish black-striped Old World chrysomelid beetle (*Pyrrhalta luteola*) that in the larval and adult stage is a leaf-eating pest of elms in eastern No. America

El Ni·ño \el-ˈnē-nyō\ *n, pl* **El Niños** [Sp, lit., the child (i.e., the Christ child); fr. the appearance of the flow at the Christmas season] (1896) **:** an irregularly recurring flow of unusually warm surface waters from the Pacific Ocean toward and along the western coast of South America that prevents upwelling of nutrient-rich cold deep water and that disrupts typical regional and global weather patterns — compare LA NIÑA

el·o·cu·tion \ˌe-lə-ˈkyü-shən\ *n* [ME *elocucioun,* fr. L *elocution-, elocutio,* fr. *eloqui*] (15c) **1 :** a style of speaking esp. in public **2 :** the art of effective public speaking — **el·o·cu·tion·ary** \-shə-ˌner-ē\ *adj* — **el·o·cu·tion·ist** \-sh(ə-)nist\ *n*

elo·dea \i-ˈlō-dē-ə\ *n* [NL, genus name, fr. Gk *helōdēs* marshy, fr. *helos* marsh; akin to Skt *saras* pond] (ca. 1868) **:** any of a small American genus (*Elodea*) of submerged aquatic monocotyledonous herbs

Elo·him \ˌe-lō-ˈhēm, e-ˈlō-ˌhim\ *n* [Heb *ĕlōhīm*] (1617) **:** GOD 1a — used esp. in the Hebrew Bible

eloign \i-ˈlȯin\ *vt* [ME *eloynen,* fr. AF *esloigner, eloigner,* fr. *es-* ex- (fr. L *ex-*) + *luin, loing* (adv.) far, fr. L *longe,* fr. *longus* long] (15c) **1** *archaic* **:** to take (oneself) far away **2** *archaic* **:** to remove to a distant or unknown place **:** CONCEAL

[1]**elon·gate** \i-ˈlȯŋ-ˌgāt, (ˌ)ē-, ˈē-ˌ\ *vb* **-gat·ed; -gat·ing** [LL *elongatus,* pp. of *elongare,* to withdraw, fr. L *e-* + *longus*] *vt* (1578) **:** to extend the length of ~ *vi* **:** to grow in length

[2]**elongate** *or* **elon·gat·ed** *adj* (1751) **1 :** stretched out **2 :** SLENDER

elon·ga·tion \(ˌ)ē-ˌlȯŋ-ˈgā-shən\ *n* (14c) **1 :** the angular distance of a celestial body from another around which it revolves or from a particular point in the sky **2 a :** the state of being elongated or lengthened; *also* **:** the process of elongating **b :** something that is elongated

elope \i-ˈlōp\ *vi* **eloped; elop·ing** [AF *aloper, esloper* to abduct, run away] (1628) **1 :** to slip away **:** ESCAPE ⟨might have mistaken him for . . . some scarecrow *eloped* from a cornfield —Washington Irving⟩ **2 a :** to run away from one's husband with a lover **b :** to run away secretly with the intention of getting married usu. without parental consent — **elope·ment** \-ˈlōp-mənt\ *n* — **elop·er** *n*

el·o·quence \ˈe-lə-kwən(t)s\ *n* (14c) **1 :** discourse marked by force and persuasiveness; *also* **:** the art or power of using such discourse **2 :** the quality of forceful or persuasive expressiveness

el·o·quent \-kwənt\ *adj* [ME, fr. AF, fr. L *eloquent-, eloquens,* fr. prp. of *eloqui* to speak out, fr. *e-* + *loqui* to speak] (14c) **1 :** marked by forceful and fluent expression ⟨an ~ preacher⟩ **2 :** vividly or movingly expressive or revealing ⟨an ~ monument⟩ — **el·o·quent·ly** *adv*

[1]**else** \ˈel(t)s\ *adv* [ME *elles,* fr. OE; akin to L *alius* other, *alter* other of two, Gk *allos* other] (bef. 12c) **1 a :** in a different manner or place or at a different time ⟨how ~ could he have acted⟩ ⟨here and nowhere ~⟩ **b :** in an additional manner or place or at an additional time ⟨where ~ is gold found⟩ **2 :** if not **:** OTHERWISE ⟨leave or ~ you'll be sorry⟩ — used absolutely to express a threat ⟨do what I tell you or ~⟩

[2]**else** *adj* (bef. 12c) **:** OTHER: **a :** being different in identity ⟨it must have been somebody ~⟩ **b :** being in addition ⟨what ~ did he say?⟩

else·where \-ˌ(h)wer\ *adv* [ME *elleswher,* fr. OE *elles hwǣr*] (bef. 12c) **:** in or to another place ⟨took my business ~⟩

el·u·ant *or* **el·u·ent** \ˈel-yə-wənt, -yü-ənt\ *n* [L *eluent-, eluens,* prp. of *eluere*] (1941) **:** a solvent used in eluting

el·u·ate \ˈel-yə-wət, -ˌwāt; -yü-ət, -ˌāt\ *n* [L *eluere* + E [1]*-ate*] (1932) **:** the washings obtained by eluting

elu·ci·date \i-ˈlü-sə-ˌdāt\ *vb* **-dat·ed; -dat·ing** [LL *elucidatus,* pp. of *elucidare,* fr. L *e-* + *lucidus* lucid] *vt* (ca. 1568) **:** to make lucid esp. by explanation or analysis ⟨~ a text⟩ ~ *vi* **:** to give a clarifying explanation ***syn*** see EXPLAIN — **elu·ci·da·tion** \-ˌlü-sə-ˈdā-shən\ *n* — **elu·ci·da·tive** \-ˈlü-sə-ˌdā-tiv\ *adj* — **elu·ci·da·tor** \-ˌdā-tər\ *n*

elude \ē-ˈlüd\ *vt* **elud·ed; elud·ing** [L *eludere,* fr. *e-* + *ludere* to play — more at LUDICROUS] (1667) **1 :** to avoid adroitly **:** EVADE ⟨the mice *eluded* the traps⟩ ⟨managed to ~ capture⟩ **2 :** to escape the perception, understanding, or grasp of ⟨subtletly simply ~*s* them⟩ ⟨victory continued to ~ us⟩ **3 :** DEFY 4 ⟨it ~*s* explanation⟩ ***syn*** see ESCAPE

Elul \e-ˈlül\ *n* [Heb *Ĕlūl*] (1535) **:** the 12th month of the civil year or the 6th month of the ecclesiastical year in the Jewish calendar — see MONTH table

elu·sion \ē-ˈlü-zhən\ *n* [ML *elusion-, elusio,* fr. LL, deception, fr. L *eludere*] (1617) **:** an act of eluding

elu·sive \ē-ˈlü-siv, -ˈlü-ziv\ *adj* (1719) **:** tending to elude: as **a :** tending to evade grasp or pursuit ⟨~ prey⟩ **b :** hard to comprehend or define **c :** hard to isolate or identify — **elu·sive·ly** *adv* — **elu·sive·ness** *n*

elute \ē-ˈlüt\ *vt* **elut·ed; elut·ing** [L *elutus,* pp. of *eluere* to wash out, fr. *e-* + *lavere* to wash — more at LYE] (1731) **:** EXTRACT; *specif* **:** to remove (adsorbed material) from an adsorbent by means of a solvent — **elu·tion** \-ˈlü-shən\ *n*

elu·tri·ate \ē-ˈlü-trē-ˌāt\ *vt* **-at·ed; -at·ing** [L *elutriatus,* pp. of *elutriare* to put in a vat, perh. fr. **elutrum* vat, fr. Gk *elytron* reservoir, lit., covering] (ca. 1727) **:** to purify, separate, or remove by washing — **elu·tri·a·tion** \ē-ˌlü-trē-ˈā-shən\ *n* — **elu·tri·a·tor** \ē-ˈlü-trē-ˌā-tər\ *n*

elu·vi·a·tion \(ˌ)ē-ˌlü-vē-ˈā-shən\ *n* [*eluvi*al of eluviation (fr. *e-* + *-luvial*—as in *alluvial*) + *-ation*] (1899) **:** the transportation of dissolved or suspended material within the soil by the movement of water when rainfall exceeds evaporation — **elu·vi·al** \ē-ˈlü-vē-əl\ *adj* — **elu·vi·at·ed** \-ˈlü-vē-ā-təd\ *adj*

el·ver \ˈel-vər\ *n* [alter. of *eelfare* migration of eels] (ca. 1640) **:** a young eel; *specif* **:** a small immature catadromous eel chiefly of fresh and brackish water

elves *pl of* ELF

el·vish \ˈel-vish\ *adj* (13c) **1 :** of or relating to elves **2 :** MISCHIEVOUS

ely·sian \i-ˈli-zhən\ *adj, often cap* (1579) **1 :** of or relating to Elysium **2 :** BLISSFUL, DELIGHTFUL ⟨~ peace⟩

elysian fields *n pl, often cap E* (1579) **:** ELYSIUM

Ely·si·um \i-ˈli-zhē-əm, -zē-\ *n, pl* **-si·ums** *or* **-sia** \-zhē-ə, -zē-\ [L, fr. Gk *Ēlysion*] (1567) **1 :** the abode of the blessed after death in classical mythology **2 :** PARADISE 2

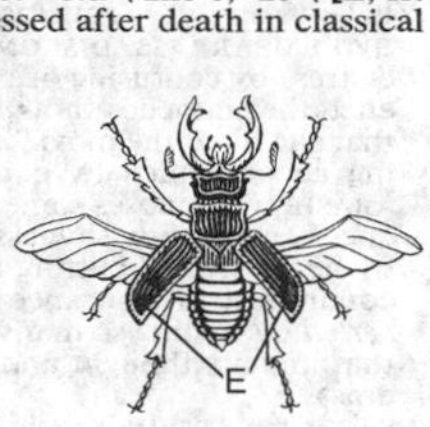

elytron *E*

el·y·tron \ˈe-lə-ˌträn\ *n, pl* **-tra** \-trə\ [NL, fr. Gk, sheath, wing cover, fr. *eilyein* to roll, wrap — more at VOLUBLE] (1774) **:** one of the anterior wings in beetles and some other insects that serve to protect the posterior pair of functional wings

em \ˈem\ *n* (13c) **1 :** the letter *m* **2 :** the width of a piece of type about as wide as it is tall used as a unit of measure of typeset matter

EM *abbr* **1** electromagnetic **2** electron microscope; electron microscopy **3** end matched **4** engineer of mines **5** enlisted man

em- — see EN-

'em \əm; *after* p,b,f, *or* v *often* ᵊm\ *pron* [ME *hem,* fr. OE *heom, him,* dat. pl. of *hē* he] (bef. 12c) **:** THEM

ema·ci·ate \i-ˈmā-shē-ˌāt\ *vb* **-at·ed; -at·ing** [L *emaciatus,* pp. of *emaciare,* fr. *e-* + *macies* leanness, fr. *macer* lean — more at MEAGER] *vi* (1646) **:** to waste away physically ~ *vt* **1 :** to cause to lose flesh so as to become very thin ⟨cattle *emaciated* by illness⟩ **2 :** to make feeble — **ema·ci·a·tion** \-ˌmā-s(h)ē-ˈā-shən\ *n*

e–mail \ˈē-ˌmāl\ *n* [electronic] (1982) **1 :** a means or system for transmitting messages electronically (as between computers on a network) ⟨communicating by ~⟩ **2 a :** messages sent and received electronically through an e-mail system ⟨receives a lot of ~⟩ **b :** an e-mail message ⟨sent him an ~⟩ — **e–mail** *vb* — **e–mail·er** \-ˌmā-lər\ *n*

emalangeni *pl of* LILANGENI

em·a·nate \ˈe-mə-ˌnāt\ *vb* **-nat·ed; -nat·ing** [L *emanatus,* pp. of *emanare,* fr. *e-* + *manare* to flow] *vi* (1756) **:** to come out from a source ⟨a sweet scent *emanating* from the blossoms⟩ ~ *vt* **:** EMIT ⟨she seems to ~ an air of serenity⟩ ***syn*** see SPRING

em·a·na·tion \ˌe-mə-ˈnā-shən\ *n* (1570) **1 a :** the action of emanating **b :** the origination of the world by a series of hierarchically descending radiations from the Godhead through intermediate stages to matter **2 a :** something that emanates or is produced by emanation **:** EFFLUENCE **b :** an isotope of radon produced by radioactive disintegration ⟨radium ~⟩ — **em·a·na·tive** \ˈe-mə-ˌnā-tiv\ *adj*

eman·ci·pate \i-ˈman(t)-sə-ˌpāt\ *vt* **-pat·ed; -pat·ing** [L *emancipatus,* pp. of *emancipare,* fr. *e-* + *mancipare* to transfer ownership of, fr. *mancip-, manceps* contractor, fr. *manus* hand + *capere* to take — more at MANUAL, HEAVE] (1613) **1 :** to free from restraint, control, or the power of another; *esp* **:** to free from bondage **2 :** to release from paternal care and responsibility and make sui juris **3 :** to free from any controlling influence (as traditional mores or beliefs) ***syn*** see FREE — **eman·ci·pa·tor** \-ˌpā-tər\ *n* — **eman·ci·pa·tory** \-pə-ˌtȯr-ē\ *adj*

eman·ci·pa·tion \i-ˌman(t)-sə-ˈpā-shən\ *n* (1631) **:** the act or process of emancipating — **eman·ci·pa·tion·ist** \-sh(ə-)nist\ *n*

emar·gin·ate \(ˌ)ē-ˈmär-jə-nət, -ˌnāt\ *adj* [L *emarginatus,* pp. of *emarginare* to deprive of a margin, fr. *e-* + *margin-, margo* margin] (1794) **:** having the margin notched — **emar·gi·na·tion** \(ˌ)ē-ˌmär-jə-ˈnā-shən\ *n*

emas·cu·late \i-ˈmas-kyə-ˌlāt\ *vt* **-lat·ed; -lat·ing** [L *emasculatus,* pp. of *emasculare,* fr. *e-* + *masculus* male — more at MALE] (1607) **1 :** to deprive of strength, vigor, or spirit **:** WEAKEN **2 :** to deprive of virility or procreative power **:** CASTRATE **3 :** to remove the androecium of (a flower) in the process of artificial cross-pollination ***syn*** see UNNERVE — **emas·cu·late** \-lət\ *adj* — **emas·cu·la·tion** \-ˌmas-kyə-ˈlā-shən\ *n* — **emas·cu·la·tor** \-ˈmas-kyə-ˌlā-tər\ *n*

em·balm \im-ˈbä(l)m, em-\ *vt* [ME *embaumen,* fr. AF *enbaumer, enbasmer,* fr. *en-* + *basme* balm — more at BALM] (14c) **1 :** to treat (a dead body) so as to protect from decay **2 :** to fill with sweet odors **:** PERFUME **3 :** to protect from decay or oblivion **:** PRESERVE ⟨~ a hero's memory⟩ **4 :** to fix in a static condition — **em·balm·er** *n* — **em·balm·ment** \-ˈbä(l)m-mənt, -ˈbäm-\ *n*

em·bank \im-ˈbaŋk\ *vt* (1576) **:** to enclose or confine by an embankment

em·bank·ment \-mənt\ *n* (1786) **1 :** a raised structure (as of earth or gravel) used esp. to hold back water or to carry a roadway **2 :** the action of embanking

em·bar·ca·de·ro \(ˌ)em-ˌbär-kə-ˈder-(ˌ)ō\ *n, pl* **-ros** [Sp, fr. *embarcado,* pp. of *embarcar* to embark, fr. *em-* (fr. L *in-*) + *barca* bark, fr. LL] (1846) *West* **:** a landing place esp. on an inland waterway

[1]**em·bar·go** \im-ˈbär-(ˌ)gō\ *n, pl* **-goes** [Sp, fr. *embargar* to bar, fr. VL **imbarricare,* fr. L *in-* + VL **barra* bar] (1593) **1 :** an order of a government prohibiting the departure of commercial ships from its ports **2 :** a legal prohibition on commerce ⟨a trade ~⟩ **3 :** STOPPAGE, IMPEDIMENT; *esp* **:** PROHIBITION ⟨I lay no ~ on anybody's words —Jane Austen⟩ **4 :** an order by a common carrier or public regulatory agency prohibiting or restricting freight transportation

[2]**embargo** *vt* **-goed; -go·ing** (1755) **:** to place an embargo on

em·bark \im-ˈbärk\ *vb* [MF *embarquer,* fr. Old Occitan *embarcar,* fr. *em-* (fr. L *in-*) + *barca* bark] *vi* (1533) **1 :** to go on board a vehicle for transportation ⟨the troops ~*ed* at noon⟩ **2 :** to make a start ⟨~*ed* on a new career⟩ ~ *vt* **1 :** to cause to go on board (as a boat or airplane) **2 :** to engage, enlist, or invest in an enterprise — **em·bar·ka·tion** \ˌem-ˌbär-ˈkā-shən, -bər-\ *n* — **em·bark·ment** \im-ˈbärk-mənt\ *n*

em·bar·rass \im-ˈber-əs, -ˈba-rəs\ *vb* [F *embarrasser,* fr. Sp *embarazar,* fr. Pg *embaraçar,* fr. *em-* (fr. L *in-*) + *baraça* noose] *vt* (1672) **1 a :** to place in doubt, perplexity, or difficulties **b :** to involve in financial difficulties **c :** to cause to experience a state of self-conscious distress ⟨bawdy stories *~ed* him⟩ **2 a :** to hamper the movement of **b :** HINDER, IMPEDE **3 :** to make intricate : COMPLICATE **4 :** to impair the activity of (a bodily function) or the function of (a bodily part) ⟨digestion *~ed* by overeating⟩ **~** *vi* **:** to become anxiously self-conscious ⟨he *~es* easily⟩ — **em·bar·rass·able** \-ə-sə-bəl\ *adj*

syn EMBARRASS, DISCOMFIT, ABASH, DISCONCERT, RATTLE mean to distress by confusing or confounding. EMBARRASS implies some influence that impedes thought, speech, or action ⟨*embarrassed* to admit that she liked the movie⟩. DISCOMFIT implies a hampering or frustrating accompanied by confusion ⟨hecklers *discomfited* the speaker⟩. ABASH presupposes some initial self-confidence that receives a sudden check, producing shyness, shame, or a feeling of inferiority ⟨*abashed* by her swift and cutting retort⟩. DISCONCERT implies an upsetting of equanimity or assurance producing uncertainty or hesitancy ⟨*disconcerted* by finding so many in attendance⟩. RATTLE implies an agitation that impairs thought and judgment ⟨*rattled* by all the television cameras⟩.

em·bar·rassed·ly \-əst-lē, -ə-səd-lē\ *adv* (1883) **:** with embarrassment

em·bar·rass·ing·ly \-ə-siŋ-lē\ *adv* (ca. 1864) **:** to an embarrassing degree : so as to cause embarrassment ⟨an **~** messy house⟩

em·bar·rass·ment \im-ˈber-ə-smənt, -ˈba-rəs-\ *n* (1729) **1 a :** something that embarrasses ⟨the scandal was a major **~**⟩ **b :** an excessive quantity from which to select — used esp. in the phrase *embarrassment of riches* **2 :** the state of being embarrassed: as **a :** confusion or disturbance of mind ⟨couldn't hide her **~**⟩ **b :** difficulty arising from the want of money to pay debts **c :** difficulty in functioning as a result of disease ⟨cardiac **~**⟩

em·bas·sage \ˈem-bə-sij\ *n* (1526) **1 :** the message or commission entrusted to an ambassador **2** *archaic* **:** EMBASSY

em·bas·sy \ˈem-bə-sē\ *n, pl* **-sies** [MF *ambassee,* ultim. of Gmc origin; akin to OHG *ambaht* service] (1534) **1 :** a body of diplomatic representatives; *specif* **:** one headed by an ambassador **2 a :** the function or position of an ambassador **b :** a mission abroad undertaken officially esp. by an ambassador **3 :** EMBASSAGE 1 **4 :** the official residence and offices of an ambassador

em·bat·tle \im-ˈba-tᵊl\ *vt* **em·bat·tled; em·bat·tling** \-ˈbat-liŋ, -tᵊl-iŋ\ [ME *embatailen,* fr. AF *embataillier,* fr. *en-* + *batailler* to battle] (14c) **1 :** to arrange in order of battle : prepare for battle **2 :** FORTIFY

embattled *adj* (15c) **1 a :** ready to fight : prepared to give battle ⟨here once the **~** farmers stood —R. W. Emerson⟩ **b :** engaged in battle, conflict, or controversy ⟨an **~** official accused of extortion⟩ **2 a :** being a site of battle, conflict, or controversy ⟨the **~** capital⟩ **b :** characterized by conflict or controversy ⟨an **~** presidency⟩

em·bat·tle·ment \-ˈba-tᵊl-mənt\ *n* (15c) **1 :** BATTLEMENT **2 :** the state of being embattled

em·bay \im-ˈbā\ *vt* (1582) **:** to trap or catch in or as if in a bay ⟨an *~ed* sailing ship⟩

em·bay·ment \-ˈbā-mənt\ *n* (1815) **1 :** formation of a bay **2 :** a bay or a conformation resembling a bay

Emb·den \ˈem-dən\ *n* [*Emden,* Germany] (1903) **:** any of a breed of large white domestic geese with an orange bill and deep orange shanks and toes

em·bed *also* **im·bed** \im-ˈbed\ *vb* **em·bed·ded** *also* **im·bed·ded; em·bed·ding** *also* **im·bed·ding** *vt* (ca. 1794) **1 a :** to enclose closely in or as if in a matrix ⟨fossils *embedded* in stone⟩ **b :** to make something an integral part of ⟨the prejudices *embedded* in our language⟩ **c :** to prepare (a microscopy specimen) for sectioning by infiltrating with and enclosing in a supporting substance **2 :** to surround closely ⟨a sweet pulp *~s* the plum seed⟩ **~** *vi* **:** to become embedded — **em·bed·ment** \-ˈbed-mənt\ *n*

em·bed·ded \im-ˈbe-dəd\ *adj* (1961) **:** occurring as a grammatical constituent (as a verb phrase or clause) within a like constituent — **em·bed·ding** \-diŋ\ *n*

em·bel·lish \im-ˈbe-lish\ *vt* [ME, fr. AF *embeliss-,* stem of *embelir,* fr. *en-* + *bel* beautiful — more at BEAUTY] (14c) **1 :** to make beautiful with ornamentation : DECORATE ⟨a book *~ed* with illustrations⟩ **2 :** to heighten the attractiveness of by adding decorative or fanciful details : ENHANCE ⟨*~ed* our account of the trip⟩ ***syn*** see ADORN — **em·bel·lish·er** *n*

em·bel·lish·ment \-lish-mənt\ *n* (1591) **1 :** the act or process of embellishing **2 :** something serving to embellish **3 :** ORNAMENT 5

em·ber \ˈem-bər\ *n* [ME *eymere,* fr. ON *eimyrja;* akin to OE *ǣmerge* ashes, L *urere* to burn] (14c) **1 :** a glowing fragment (as of coal) from a fire; *esp* **:** one smoldering in ashes **2** *pl* **:** the smoldering remains of a fire **3** *pl* **:** slowly dying or fading emotions, memories, ideas, or responses still capable of being revived ⟨the *~s* of his past⟩

ember day \ˈem-bər-\ *n* [ME, fr. OE *ymbrendæg,* fr. *ymbrene* circuit, anniversary + *dæg* day] (bef. 12c) **:** a Wednesday, Friday, or Saturday following the first Sunday in Lent, Whitsunday, September 14, or December 13 set apart for fasting and prayer in Western churches

em·bez·zle \im-ˈbe-zəl, em-\ *vt* **em·bez·zled; em·bez·zling** \-(ə-)liŋ\ [ME *embesilen,* fr. AF *embesiller* to make away with, fr. *en-* + *besiller* to steal, plunder] (15c) **:** to appropriate (as property entrusted to one's care) fraudulently to one's own use ⟨*embezzled* thousands of dollars⟩ — **em·bez·zle·ment** \-zəl-mənt\ *n* — **em·bez·zler** \-z(ə-)lər\ *n*

em·bit·ter \im-ˈbi-tər\ *vt* (15c) **1 :** to excite bitter feelings in ⟨*~ed* by divorce⟩ **2 :** to make bitter — **em·bit·ter·ment** \-mənt\ *n*

[1]**em·blaze** \im-ˈblāz\ *vt* **em·blazed; em·blaz·ing** (15c) **1 :** to illuminate esp. by a blaze **2 :** to set ablaze

[2]**emblaze** *vt* **em·blazed; em·blaz·ing** [*en-* + *blaze* to blazon] (1593) **1** *archaic* **:** EMBLAZON 1 **2 :** to adorn sumptuously ⟨with gems and golden luster rich *emblazed* —John Milton⟩

em·bla·zon \im-ˈblā-zᵊn\ *vt* **em·bla·zoned; em·bla·zon·ing** \-ˈblāz-niŋ, -ˈblā-zᵊn-iŋ\ (1589) **1 a :** to inscribe or adorn with or as if with heraldic bearings or devices **b :** to inscribe (as heraldic bearings) on a surface **2 :** CELEBRATE, EXTOL ⟨have his . . . deeds *~ed* by a poet —Thomas Nash⟩ — **em·bla·zon·er** \-ˈblāz-nər, -zᵊn-ər\ *n* — **em·bla·zon·ment** \-ˈblā-zᵊn-mənt\ *n*

em·bla·zon·ry \-zᵊn-rē\ *n* (1667) **1 :** emblazoned figures : brilliant decoration **2 :** the act or art of emblazoning

[1]**em·blem** \ˈem-bləm\ *n* [ME, fr. L *emblema* inlaid work, fr. Gk *emblēmat-, emblēma,* fr. *emballein* to insert, fr. *en-* + *ballein* to throw — more at DEVIL] (15c) **1 :** a picture with a motto or set of verses intended as a moral lesson **2 :** an object or the figure of an object symbolizing and suggesting another object or an idea **3 a :** a symbolic object used as a heraldic device **b :** a device, symbol, or figure adopted and used as an identifying mark

[2]**emblem** *vt* (1584) **:** EMBLEMATIZE

em·blem·at·ic \ˌem-blə-ˈma-tik\ *also* **em·blem·at·i·cal** \-ti-kəl\ *adj* (1645) **:** of, relating to, or constituting an emblem : SYMBOLIC, REPRESENTATIVE — **em·blem·at·i·cal·ly** \-ti-k(ə-)lē\ *adv*

em·blem·a·tize \em-ˈble-mə-ˌtīz\ *vt* **-tized; -tiz·ing** (1615) **:** to represent by or as if by an emblem : SYMBOLIZE

em·ble·ments \ˈem-blə-mən(t)s\ *n pl* [ME *emblayment,* fr. AF *emblaement,* fr. *emblaer* to sow with grain, fr. *en-* + *bleé* grain, of Gmc origin; akin to OE *blǣd* fruit, growth, leaf — more at BLADE] (15c) **:** crops from annual cultivation legally belonging to the tenant

em·bodi·ment \im-ˈbä-di-mənt\ *n* (1828) **1 :** one that embodies something ⟨the **~** of all our hopes⟩ **2 :** the act of embodying : the state of being embodied

em·body \im-ˈbä-dē\ *vt* **em·bod·ied; em·body·ing** (ca. 1548) **1 :** to give a body to (a spirit) : INCARNATE **2 a :** to deprive of spirituality **b :** to make concrete and perceptible **3 :** to cause to become a body or part of a body : INCORPORATE **4 :** to represent in human or animal form : PERSONIFY ⟨men who greatly *embodied* the idealism of American life —A. M. Schlesinger *b*1917⟩ — **em·bodi·er** *n*

em·bold·en \im-ˈbōl-dən\ *vt* (15c) **:** to instill with boldness or courage

em·bo·lec·to·my \ˌem-bə-ˈlek-tə-mē\ *n, pl* **-mies** (1923) **:** surgical removal of an embolus

em·bol·ic \em-ˈbä-lik, im-\ *adj* (1866) **:** of or relating to an embolus or embolism

em·bo·li·sa·tion *Brit var of* EMBOLIZATION

em·bo·lism \ˈem-bə-ˌli-zəm\ *n* [ME *embolisme,* fr. ML *embolismus,* fr. Gk *embol-* (fr. *emballein* to insert, intercalate) — more at EMBLEM] (14c) **1 :** the insertion of one or more days in a calendar : INTERCALATION **2 a :** the sudden obstruction of a blood vessel by an embolus **b :** EMBOLUS — **em·bo·lis·mic** \ˌem-bə-ˈliz-mik\ *adj*

em·bo·li·za·tion \ˌem-bə-lə-ˈzā-shən\ *n* (1942) **:** the process or state in which a blood vessel or organ is obstructed by the lodgment of a material mass (as an embolus)

em·bo·lus \ˈem-bə-ləs\ *n, pl* **-li** \-ˌlī\ [NL, fr. Gk *embolos* wedge-shaped object, stopper, fr. *emballein*] (1859) **:** an abnormal particle (as an air bubble) circulating in the blood — compare THROMBUS

em·bon·point \äⁿ-bōⁿ-ˈpwaⁿ\ *n* [F, fr. MF, fr. *en bon point* in good condition] (1670) **:** plumpness of person : STOUTNESS

em·bos·om \im-ˈbu̇-zəm *also* -ˈbü-\ *vt* (ca. 1590) **1** *archaic* **:** to take into or place in the bosom **2 :** to shelter closely : ENCLOSE ⟨his house *~ed* in the grove —Alexander Pope⟩

[1]**em·boss** \im-ˈbäs, -ˈbȯs\ *vt* [ME *embosen* to become exhausted from being hunted, ultim. fr. AF *bois* woods] (14c) *archaic* **:** to drive (as a hunted animal) to bay or to exhaustion

[2]**emboss** *vt* [ME *embosen,* fr. MF *embocer,* fr. *en-* + *boce* boss] (15c) **1 :** to raise the surface of into bosses; *esp* **:** to ornament with raised work **2 :** to raise in relief from a surface **3 :** ADORN, EMBELLISH — **em·boss·able** \-ˈbä-sə-bəl, -ˈbȯ-\ *adj* — **em·boss·er** \-sər\ *n* — **em·boss·ment** \-mənt\ *n*

em·bou·chure \ˈäm-bü-ˌshu̇r, ˌäm-bü-ˈ\ *n* [F, fr. (*s'*)*emboucher* to flow into, fr. *en-* + *bouche* mouth — more at DEBOUCH] (1760) **1 :** the position and use of the lips, tongue, and teeth in playing a wind instrument **2 :** the mouthpiece of a musical instrument

em·bour·geoise·ment \em-ˈbu̇rzh-ˌwäz-mənt, äm-; äⁿ-bu̇rzh-wäz-ˈmäⁿ\ *n* [F, fr. *embourgeoiser* to make bourgeois, fr. *em-* + *bourgeois*] (1937) **:** a shift to bourgeois values and practices

em·bowed \im-ˈbōd\ *adj* (15c) **:** bent like a bow : ARCHED

em·bow·el \im-ˈbau̇(-ə)l\ *vt* **-eled** *or* **-elled; -el·ing** *or* **-el·ling** (1521) **1 :** DISEMBOWEL **2** *obs* **:** ENCLOSE

em·bow·er \im-ˈbau̇(-ə)r\ *vt* (1580) **:** to shelter or enclose in or as if in a bower ⟨like a rose *~ed* in its own green leaves —P. B. Shelley⟩

[1]**em·brace** \im-ˈbrās\ *vb* **em·braced; em·brac·ing** [ME, fr. AF *embracer,* fr. *en-* + *brace* pair of arms — more at BRACE] *vt* (14c) **1 a :** to clasp in the arms : HUG **b :** CHERISH, LOVE **2 :** ENCIRCLE, ENCLOSE **3 a :** to take up esp. readily or gladly ⟨**~** a cause⟩ **b :** to avail oneself of : WELCOME ⟨*embraced* the opportunity to study further⟩ **4 a :** to take in or include as a part, item, or element of a more inclusive whole ⟨charity *~s* all acts that contribute to human welfare⟩ **b :** to be equal or equivalent to ⟨his assets *embraced* $10⟩ **~** *vi* **:** to participate in an embrace ***syn*** see ADOPT, INCLUDE — **embrace·able** \-ˈbrā-sə-bəl\ *adj* — **em·brace·ment** \-ˈbrās-mənt\ *n* — **em·brac·er** *n* — **em·brac·ing·ly** \-ˈbrā-siŋ-lē\ *adv*

[2]**embrace** *n* (1592) **1 :** a close encircling with the arms and pressure to the chest esp. as a sign of affection : HUG **2 :** GRIP, ENCIRCLEMENT ⟨in the **~** of terror⟩ **3 :** ACCEPTANCE ⟨her **~** of new ideas⟩

em·bra·ceor \im-ˈbrā-sər\ *n* [AF *embraseour,* fr. *embraser* to set on fire, fr. *en-* + *brase, brese* live coals, fr. OF *breze* — more at BRAISE] (15c) **:** one guilty of embracery

em·brac·ery \im-ˈbrā-sə-rē\ *n, pl* **-er·ies** [ME, fr. AF *embraceour*] (15c) **:** an attempt to influence a jury corruptly

em·brac·ive \-ˈbrā-siv\ *adj* (1855) **1 :** disposed to embrace **2 :** INCLUSIVE, COMPREHENSIVE

em·bran·gle \im-ˈbraŋ-gəl\ *vt* **-gled; -gling** \-g(ə-)liŋ\ [*en-* + *brangle* (squabble)] (1664) **:** EMBROIL — **em·bran·gle·ment** \-gəl-mənt\ *n*

em·bra·sure \im-ˈbrā-zhər\ *n* [F, fr. obs. *embraser* to widen an opening] (1702) **1 :** an opening with sides flaring outward in a wall or parapet of a fortification usu. for allowing the firing of cannon **2 :** a recess of a door or window

em·brit·tle \im-ˈbri-tᵊl\ *vb* **-brit·tled; -brit·tling** \-ˈbrit-liŋ, -tᵊl-iŋ\ *vt* (1902) **:** to make brittle **~** *vi* **:** to become brittle — **em·brit·tle·ment** \-ˈbri-tᵊl-mənt\ *n*

em·bro·ca·tion \ˌem-brə-ˈkā-shən\ *n* [ME *embrocacioun,* fr. MF *embrocacion,* fr. ML *embrocation-, embrocatio,* fr. LL *embrocare* to rub with lotion, fr. Gk *embroche* lotion, fr. *en-* + *brechein* to wet] (15c) **:** LINIMENT

em·broi·der \im-ˈbrȯi-dər\ *vb* **em·broi·dered; em·broi·der·ing** \-d(ə-)riŋ\ [alter. of ME *embroderen,* fr. AF *embrouder,* fr. *en-* + *brosder, brouder* to embroider, of Gmc origin; akin to OE *brord* point, *byrst* bristle] *vt* (14c) **1 a :** to ornament with needlework **b :** to form with

needlework **2 :** to elaborate on : EMBELLISH ⟨~ a story⟩ ~ *vi* **1 :** to make embroidery **2 :** to provide embellishments : ELABORATE — **em·broi·der·er** \-ˈbrȯi-dər-ər\ *n*
em·broi·dery \im-ˈbrȯi-d(ə-)rē\ *n, pl* **-der·ies** (14c) **1 a :** the art or process of forming decorative designs with hand or machine needlework **b :** a design or decoration formed by or as if by embroidery **c :** an object decorated with embroidery **2 :** elaboration by use of decorative and often fictitious detail **3 :** something pleasing or desirable but unimportant ⟨considered the humanities mere educational ~⟩
em·broil \im-ˈbrȯi(-ə)l\ *vt* [F *embrouiller,* fr. MF, fr. *en-* + *brouiller* to jumble, fr. OF *broilier,* fr. VL **brodiculare* — more at BROIL] (1603) **1 :** to throw into disorder or confusion **2 :** to involve in conflict or difficulties ⟨~*ed* in controversy⟩ — **em·broil·ment** \-mənt\ *n*
em·brown \im-ˈbrau̇n\ *vt* (1667) **1 :** DARKEN **2 :** to cause to turn brown
embrue *var of* IMBRUE
embry- *or* **embryo-** *comb form* [LL, fr. Gk, fr. *embryon*] : embryo ⟨*embryo*geny⟩
em·bryo \ˈem-brē-ˌō\ *n, pl* **em·bry·os** [ML *embryon-, embryo,* fr. Gk *embryon,* fr. *en-* + *bryein* to swell; akin to Gk *bryon* catkin] (1548) **1 a** *archaic* : a vertebrate at any stage of development prior to birth or hatching **b :** an animal in the early stages of growth and differentiation that are characterized by cleavage, the laying down of fundamental tissues, and the formation of primitive organs and organ systems; *esp* : the developing human individual from the time of implantation to the end of the eighth week after conception **2 :** the young sporophyte of a seed plant usu. comprising a rudimentary plant with plumule, radicle, and cotyledons **3 a :** something as yet undeveloped **b :** a beginning or undeveloped state of something ⟨productions seen in ~ during their out-of-town tryout period —Henry Hewes⟩
em·bryo·gen·e·sis \ˌem-brē-ō-ˈje-nə-səs\ *n* (1830) : the formation and development of the embryo — **em·bryo·ge·net·ic** \-jə-ˈne-tik\ *adj*
em·bry·og·e·ny \ˌem-brē-ˈä-jə-nē\ *n, pl* **-nies** (1835) : EMBRYOGENESIS — **em·bryo·gen·ic** \-brē-ō-ˈje-nik\ *adj*
em·bry·oid \ˈem-brē-ˌȯid\ *n* (ca. 1927) : a mass of plant or animal tissue that resembles an embryo — **embryoid** *adj*
em·bry·ol·o·gy \ˌem-brē-ˈä-lə-jē\ *n* [F *embryologie*] (ca. 1847) **1 :** a branch of biology dealing with embryos and their development **2 :** the features and phenomena exhibited in the formation and development of an embryo — **em·bry·o·log·i·cal** \-brē-ə-ˈlä-ji-kəl\ *adj* — **em·bry·o·log·i·cal·ly** \-ji-k(ə-)lē\ *adv* — **em·bry·ol·o·gist** \-brē-ˈä-lə-jist\ *n*
embryon- *or* **embryoni-** *comb form* [ML *embryon-, embryo*] : embryo ⟨*embryon*ic⟩
em·bry·o·nal \em-ˈbrī-ə-nᵊl\ *adj* (1652) : EMBRYONIC 1
em·bry·o·nat·ed \ˈem-brē-ə-ˌnā-təd\ *adj* (1687) : having an embryo
em·bry·on·ic \ˌem-brē-ˈä-nik\ *adj* (1740) **1 :** of or relating to an embryo **2 :** being in an early stage of development : INCIPIENT, RUDIMENTARY ⟨an ~ plan⟩ — **em·bry·on·i·cal·ly** \-ni-k(ə-)lē\ *adv*
embryonic disk *n* (ca. 1938) **1 a :** BLASTODISC **b :** BLASTODERM **2 :** the part of the inner cell mass of a blastocyst from which the embryo of a placental mammal develops — called also *embryonic shield*
embryonic membrane *n* (1947) : a structure (as the amnion) that derives from the fertilized ovum but does not form a part of the embryo
em·bryo·phyte \ˈem-brē-ə-ˌfīt\ *n* (ca. 1909) : any of a subkingdom (Embryophyta) of plants in which the embryo is retained within maternal tissue and which include the bryophytes and tracheophytes
embryo sac *n* (1844) : the female gametophyte of a seed plant consisting of a thin-walled sac within the nucellus that contains the egg nucleus and other nuclei which give rise to endosperm on fertilization
embryo transfer *n* (1966) : a procedure used esp. in animal breeding in which an embryo from a superovulated female is removed and reimplanted in the uterus of another female — called also *embryo transplant*
¹**em·cee** \ˌem-ˈsē\ *n* [*MC*] (1930) : MASTER OF CEREMONIES
²**emcee** *vb* **em·ceed; em·cee·ing** *vt* (1937) : to act as master of ceremonies of ⟨~ an awards dinner⟩ ~ *vi* : to act as master of ceremonies
-eme *n suffix* [F *-ème* (fr. *phonème* speech sound, phoneme)] : significantly distinctive unit of language structure ⟨tax*eme*⟩
emend \ē-ˈmend\ *vt* [ME, fr. L *emendare* — more at AMEND] (15c) : to correct usu. by textual alterations ⟨~*ed* the manuscript⟩ ***syn*** see CORRECT — **emend·able** \-ˈmen-də-bəl\ *adj* — **emend·er** *n*
emen·da·tion \ˌē-ˌmen-ˈdā-shən; ˌe-mən-, e-ˌmen-\ *n* (1536) **1 :** the act or practice of emending **2 :** an alteration designed to correct or improve
emer *abbr* emeritus
¹**em·er·ald** \ˈem-rəld, ˈe-mə-\ *n* [ME *emeralde,* fr. AF *esmeralde,* fr. VL **smaralda,* fr. L *smaragdus,* fr. Gk *smaragdos* — more at SMARAGD] (14c) **1 :** a rich green variety of beryl prized as a gemstone **2 :** any of various green gemstones (as synthetic corundum or demantoid)
²**emerald** *adj* (1508) : brightly or richly green
emerald ash borer *n* (2002) : a metallic-green Asian beetle (*Agrilus planipennis*) accidentally introduced into the U.S. and having a destructive larva that bores into the wood of ash trees
emerald cut *n* (1926) : a rectangular cut for a gem having a series of parallel facets on each side and at each corner
emerald green *n* (1646) **1 :** a clear bright green resembling that of the emerald **2 :** any of various strong greens
emerge \i-ˈmərj\ *vi* **emerged; emerg·ing** [L *emergere,* fr. *e-* + *mergere* to plunge — more at MERGE] (1563) **1 :** to become manifest : become known ⟨new problems *emerged*⟩ **2 :** to rise from or as if from an enveloping fluid : come out into view ⟨a diver *emerging* from the water⟩ **3 :** to rise from an obscure or inferior position or condition ⟨someone must ~ as a leader⟩ **4 :** to come into being through evolution
emer·gence \i-ˈmər-jən(t)s\ *n* (1704) **1 :** the act or an instance of emerging **2 :** any of various superficial outgrowths of plant tissue usu. formed from both epidermis and immediately underlying tissues **3 :** penetration of the soil surface by a newly germinated plant
emer·gen·cy \i-ˈmər-jənt-sē\ *n, pl* **-cies** *often attrib* (ca. 1631) **1 :** an unforeseen combination of circumstances or the resulting state that calls for immediate action **2 :** an urgent need for assistance or relief ⟨the mayor declared a state of ~ after the flood⟩ ***syn*** see JUNCTURE
emergency brake *n* (1900) : a brake (as on an automobile) that can be used for stopping in the event of failure of the main brakes and to keep the vehicle from rolling when parked
emergency medical technician *n* (1980) : EMT
emergency medicine *n* (1966) : a medical specialty concerned with the care and treatment of acutely ill or injured patients who need immediate medical attention
emergency room *n* (1964) : a hospital room or area staffed and equipped for the reception and treatment of persons requiring immediate medical care
¹**emer·gent** \i-ˈmər-jənt\ *adj* [ME, fr. L *emergent-, emergens,* prp. of *emergere*] (1593) **1 a :** arising unexpectedly **b :** calling for prompt action : URGENT ⟨~ danger⟩ **2 a :** rising out of or as if out of a fluid ⟨~ coastal islands⟩ **b :** rooted in shallow water and having most of its vegetative growth above water ⟨an ~ plant⟩ **3 :** arising as a natural or logical consequence **4 :** newly formed or prominent ⟨~ nations⟩
²**emergent** *n* (1620) **1 :** something emergent **2 a :** a tree that rises above the surrounding forest **b :** an emergent plant
emergent evolution *n* (1923) : evolution that according to some theories involves the appearance of new characters and qualities at complex levels of organization (as the cell or organism) which cannot be predicted solely from the study of less complex levels (as the atom or molecule) — compare CREATIVE EVOLUTION
emerging *adj* (1646) : EMERGENT 4 ⟨~ nations⟩ ⟨an ~ artist⟩
emer·i·ta \i-ˈmer-ə-tə\ *adj* [L, fem. of *emeritus*] (1842) : EMERITUS — used of a woman ⟨Professor *Emerita* Mary Smith⟩
¹**emer·i·tus** \i-ˈmer-ə-təs\ *n, pl* **-i·ti** \-ə-ˌtī, -ˌtē\ (1750) : one retired from professional life but permitted to retain as an honorary title the rank of the last office held
²**emeritus** *adj* [L, pp. of *emereri* to serve out one's term, fr. *e-* + *mereri, merēre* to earn, deserve, serve — more at MERIT] (1794) **1 :** holding after retirement an honorary title corresponding to that held last during active service **2 :** retired from an office or position ⟨professor ~⟩ — converted to *emeriti* after a plural ⟨professors *emeriti*⟩
emersed \(ˌ)ē-ˈmərst\ *adj* (1686) : standing out of or rising above a surface (as of a fluid) ⟨~ aquatic weeds⟩
emer·sion \(ˌ)ē-ˈmər-zhən, -shən\ *n* [L *emersus,* pp. of *emergere*] (1633) : an act of emerging : EMERGENCE
em·ery \ˈem-rē, ˈe-mə-\ *n, pl* **em·er·ies** *often attrib* [ME, fr. AF *esmeril,* fr. OIt *smiriglio,* fr. ML *smiriglum,* fr. Gk *smyrid-, smyris*] (15c) : a dark granular mineral that consists of corundum with iron oxide impurities (as magnetite) and is used as an abrasive; *also* : a hard abrasive powder
emery board *n* (1725) : a cardboard nail file covered with emery
eme·sis \ˈe-mə-səs, i-ˈmē-\ *n, pl* **eme·ses** \-ˌsēz\ [NL, fr. Gk, fr. *emein*] (ca. 1847) : an act or instance of vomiting
emet·ic \i-ˈme-tik\ *n* [L *emetica,* fr. Gk *emetikē,* fr. fem. of *emetikos* causing vomiting, fr. *emein* to vomit — more at VOMIT] (1657) : an agent that induces vomiting — **emetic** *adj*
em·e·tine \ˈe-mə-ˌtēn\ *n* (1819) : an emetic alkaloid $C_{29}H_{40}N_2O_4$ extracted from ipecac root and used esp. to treat amebiasis
émeute \ā-ˈmœt\ *n, pl* **émeutes** *same*\ [F, fr. OF *esmeute* act of starting, fr. fem. of *esmeut,* pp. of *esmovoir* to start — more at EMOTION] (1782) : UPRISING
emf *abbr* electromotive force
EMF *abbr* electromagnetic field
EMG *abbr* electromyogram; electromyograph; electromyography
-emia *n comb form* [NL *-emia, -aemia,* fr. Gk *-aimia,* fr. *haima* blood] **1 :** condition of having (such) blood ⟨leuk*emia*⟩ **2 :** condition of having (a specified thing) in the blood ⟨ur*emia*⟩
emic \ˈē-mik\ *adj* [phon*emic*] (1954) : of, relating to, or involving analysis of cultural phenomena from the perspective of one who participates in the culture being studied — compare ETIC
¹**em·i·grant** \ˈe-mi-grənt\ *n* (1735) **1 :** one who emigrates **2 :** a migrant plant or animal
²**emigrant** *adj* (1773) : departing or having departed from a country to settle elsewhere
em·i·grate \ˈe-mə-ˌgrāt\ *vi* **-grat·ed; -grat·ing** [L *emigratus,* pp. of *emigrare,* fr. *e-* + *migrare* to migrate] (1766) : to leave one's place of residence or country to live elsewhere ⟨*emigrated* from Canada to the United States⟩ — **em·i·gra·tion** \ˌe-mə-ˈgrā-shən\ *n*
émi·gré *also* **emi·gré** \ˈe-mi-ˌgrā, ˌe-mi-ˈ\ *n, often attrib* [F *émigré,* fr. pp. of *émigrer* to emigrate, fr. L *emigrare*] (1792) : EMIGRANT; *esp* : a person who emigrates for political reasons
em·i·nence \ˈe-mə-nən(t)s\ *n* (15c) **1 :** a position of prominence or superiority **2 :** one that is eminent, prominent, or lofty: as **a :** an anatomical protuberance (as on a bone) **b :** a person of high rank or attainments — often used as a title for a cardinal **c :** a natural elevation
émi·nence grise \ā-mē-näⁿs-ˈgrēz\ *n, pl* **éminences grises** *same*\ [F, lit., gray eminence, nickname of Père Joseph (François du Tremblay) †1638 Fr. monk and diplomat, confidant of Cardinal Richelieu who was known as *Éminence Rouge* red eminence; fr. the colors of their respective habits] (1925) **1 :** a confidential agent; *esp* : one exercising unsuspected or unofficial power **2 :** a respected authority; *specif* : ELDER STATESMAN ⟨the *éminence grise* of classical music⟩
em·i·nen·cy \ˈe-mə-nən(t)-sē\ *n, pl* **-cies** (1604) *archaic* : EMINENCE
em·i·nent \ˈe-mə-nənt\ *adj* [ME, fr. AF or L; AF, fr. L *eminent-, eminens,* prp. of *eminēre* to stand out, fr. *e-* + *-minēre;* akin to L *mont-, mons* mountain — more at MOUNT] (15c) **1 :** standing out so as to be readily perceived or noted : CONSPICUOUS **2 :** jutting out : PROJECTING **3 :** exhibiting eminence esp. in standing above others in some quality or position : PROMINENT ***syn*** see FAMOUS
eminent domain *n* (1783) : a right of a government to take private property for public use by virtue of the superior dominion of the sovereign power over all lands within its jurisdiction
em·i·nent·ly \-lē\ *adv* (1616) : to a high degree : VERY ⟨~ worthy⟩ ⟨an ~ sensible plan⟩
emir *or* **amir** *also* **ameer** \ə-ˈmir, ā-\ *n* [Ar *amīr* commander] (1595) : a ruler, chief, or commander in Islamic countries
emir·ate \ˈe-mə-rət, -ˌrāt\ *n* (1847) : the state or jurisdiction of an emir

em·is·sary \'e-mə-ˌser-ē, -ˌse-rē\ *n, pl* **-sar·ies** [L *emissarius,* fr. *emissus,* pp. of *emittere*] (1607) **1 :** one designated as the agent of another : REPRESENTATIVE **2 :** a secret agent

emis·sion \ē-'mi-shən\ *n* (1607) **1 a :** an act or instance of emitting : EMANATION **b** *archaic* : PUBLICATION **c :** a putting into circulation **2 a :** something sent forth by emitting: as (1) : electromagnetic radiation from an antenna or a celestial body (2) *usu pl* : substances discharged into the air (as by a smokestack or an automobile engine) **b** : EFFLUVIUM — **emis·sive** \-'mi-siv\ *adj*

emis·siv·i·ty \ˌe-mə-'si-və-tē, ˌē-ˌmi-'siv-\ *n, pl* **-ties** (1880) : the relative power of a surface to emit heat by radiation : the ratio of the radiant energy emitted by a surface to that emitted by a blackbody at the same temperature

emit \ē-'mit\ *vt* **emit·ted; emit·ting** [L *emittere* to send out, fr. *e-* + *mittere* to send] (1598) **1 a :** to throw or give off or out (as light or heat) **b :** to send out : EJECT **2 a :** to issue with authority; *esp* : to put (as money) into circulation **b** *obs* : PUBLISH **3 :** to give utterance or voice to ⟨*emitted* a groan⟩ — **emit·ter** *n*

emit·tance \ē-'mi-tᵊn(t)s\ *n* (1940) **1 :** the energy radiated by the surface of a body per second per unit area **2 :** EMISSIVITY

Emmanuel *var of* IMMANUEL

em·men·a·gogue \ə-'me-nə-ˌgäg, e-\ *n* [Gk *emmēna* menses (fr. neut. pl. of *emmēnos* monthly, fr. *en-* + *mēn* month) + E *-agogue* — more at MOON] (ca. 1732) : an agent that promotes the menstrual discharge

Em·men·ta·ler *or* **Em·men·tha·ler** \'e-mən-ˌtä-lər\ *or* **Em·men·tal** *or* **Em·men·thal** \-ˌtäl\ *n* [G, fr. *Emmental,* Switzerland] (1902) : SWISS CHEESE

em·mer \'e-mər\ *n* [G, fr. OHG *amari*] (ca. 1900) : an ancient tetraploid wheat (*Triticum dicoccum*) that has spikelets with two hard red kernels which remain in the glumes after threshing and that has been cultivated esp. in southwest Asia, northeast Africa, and Europe

em·met \'e-mət\ *n* [ME *emete,* fr. OE *æmette* ant — more at ANT] (bef. 12c) *chiefly dial* : ANT

Em·my \'e-mē\ *n, pl* **Emmys** [fr. alter. of *Immy,* nickname for *image orthicon* (a camera tube used in television)] (1949) : a statuette awarded annually by a professional organization for notable achievement in television

emo \'ē-(ˌ)mō\ *n* [short for *emotional*] (1993) : a style of rock music influenced by punk rock and featuring introspective and emotionally fraught lyrics

em·o·din \'e-mə-dən\ *n* [ISV *emodi-* (fr. NL *Rheum emodi,* species of rhubarb) + [1]*-in*] (1858) : an orange crystalline phenolic compound $C_{15}H_{10}O_5$ that is obtained from plants (as rhubarb and cascara buckthorn) and is used as a laxative

[1]**emol·lient** \i-'mäl-yənt\ *adj* [L *emollient-, emolliens,* prp. of *emollire* to soften, fr. *e-* + *mollis* soft — more at MOLLIFY] (1626) **1 :** making soft or supple; *also* : soothing esp. to the skin or mucous membrane ⟨an ~ hand lotion⟩ **2 :** making less intense or harsh : MOLLIFYING ⟨soothe us in our agonies with ~ words —H. L. Mencken⟩

[2]**emollient** *n* (1656) : something that softens or soothes

emol·u·ment \i-'mäl-yə-mənt\ *n* [ME, fr. L *emolumentum* advantage, fr. *emolere* to produce by grinding, fr. *e-* + *molere* to grind — more at MEAL] (15c) **1 :** the returns arising from office or employment usu. in the form of compensation or perquisites **2** *archaic* : ADVANTAGE

emote \i-'mōt\ *vi* **emot·ed; emot·ing** [back-formation fr. *emotion*] (1917) : to give expression to emotion esp. in acting — **emot·er** \-'mō-tər\ *n*

emo·ti·con \i-'mō-ti-ˌkän\ *n* [*emotion* + *icon*] (1987) : a group of keyboard characters (as :-)) that typically represents a facial expression or suggests an attitude or emotion and that is used esp. in computerized communications (as e-mail)

emo·tion \i-'mō-shən\ *n* [MF, fr. *emouvoir* to stir up, fr. OF *esmovoir,* fr. L *emovēre* to remove, displace, fr. *e-* + *movēre* to move] (1579) **1 a** *obs* : DISTURBANCE **b :** EXCITEMENT **2 a :** the affective aspect of consciousness : FEELING **b :** a state of feeling **c :** a conscious mental reaction (as anger or fear) subjectively experienced as strong feeling usu. directed toward a specific object and typically accompanied by physiological and behavioral changes in the body ***syn*** see FEELING

emo·tion·al \-shnəl, -shə-nᵊl\ *adj* (1834) **1 :** of or relating to emotion **2 :** dominated by or prone to emotion ⟨an ~ person⟩ **3 :** appealing to or arousing emotion **4 :** markedly aroused or agitated in feeling or sensibilities ⟨gets ~ at weddings⟩ — **emo·tion·al·i·ty** \-ˌmō-shə-'na-lə-tē\ *n* — **emo·tion·al·ly** \-'mō-shnə-lē, -shə-nᵊl-ē\ *adv*

emo·tion·al·ism \i-'mō-shnə-ˌli-zəm, -shə-nə-ˌliz-\ *n* (1865) **1 :** a tendency to regard things emotionally **2 :** undue indulgence in or display of emotion

emo·tion·al·ist \-shnə-list, -shə-nə-list\ *n* (1865) **1 :** one who bases a theory or policy on an emotional conviction **2 :** one prone to emotionalism — **emo·tion·al·is·tic** \-ˌmō-shnə-'lis-tik, -shə-nə-'lis-\ *adj*

emo·tion·al·ize \i-'mō-shnə-ˌlīz, -shə-nə-ˌlīz\ *vt* **-ized; -iz·ing** (1879) : to give an emotional quality to

emo·tion·less \i-'mō-shən-ləs\ *adj* (1843) : showing, having, or expressing no emotion ⟨an ~ stare⟩ — **emo·tion·less·ness** *n* — **emo·tion·less·ly** *adv*

emo·tive \i-'mō-tiv\ *adj* (1830) **1 :** of or relating to the emotions **2 :** appealing to or expressing emotion ⟨the ~ use of language⟩ — **emo·tive·ly** *adv* — **emo·tiv·i·ty** \i-ˌmō-'ti-və-tē, ˌē-ˌmō-\ *n*

emp *abbr* emperor; empress

EMP *abbr* electromagnetic pulse

em·pa·na·da \ˌem-pə-'nä-də\ *n* [AmerSp, fr. Sp, fem. of *empanado,* pp. of *empanar* to bread, fr. *em-* (fr. L *in-*) + *pan* bread, fr. L *panis* — more at FOOD] (1882) : a turnover with a sweet or savory filling

empanel *var of* IMPANEL

em·pa·thet·ic \ˌem-pə-'the-tik\ *adj* (1932) : involving, characterized by, or based on empathy — **em·pa·thet·i·cal·ly** \-ti-k(ə-)lē\ *adv*

em·path·ic \em-'pa-thik, im-\ *adj* (1909) : EMPATHETIC — **em·path·i·cal·ly** \-thi-k(ə-)lē\ *adv*

em·pa·thise *Brit var of* EMPATHIZE

em·pa·thize \'em-pə-ˌthīz\ *vi* **-thized; -thiz·ing** (ca. 1921) : to experience empathy ⟨*empathized* with his son's fears⟩ — **em·pa·thiz·er** \-ˌthī-zər\ *n*

em·pa·thy \'em-pə-thē\ *n* [Gk *empatheia,* lit., passion, fr. *empathēs* emotional, fr. *em-* + *pathos* feelings, emotion — more at PATHOS] (1850) **1 :** the imaginative projection of a subjective state into an object so that the object appears to be infused with it **2 :** the action of understanding, being aware of, being sensitive to, and vicariously experiencing the feelings, thoughts, and experience of another of either the past or present without having the feelings, thoughts, and experience fully communicated in an objectively explicit manner; *also* : the capacity for this

em·pen·nage \ˌäm-pə-'näzh, ˌem-\ *n* [F, feathers of an arrow, empennage, fr. *empenner* to feather an arrow, fr. *em-* [1]*en-* + *penne* feather, fr. MF — more at PEN] (1909) : the tail assembly of an airplane

em·per·or \'em-pər-ər, -prər\ *n* [ME, fr. AF *emperur,* fr. L *imperator,* lit., commander, fr. *imperare* to command, fr. *in-* + *parare* to prepare, order — more at PARE] (13c) : the sovereign or supreme male monarch of an empire — **em·per·or·ship** \-ˌship\ *n*

emperor penguin *n* (1885) : a penguin (*Aptenodytes forsteri*) that is the largest known and that is noted for the male's habit of incubating the egg between the feet and a fold of abdominal skin resembling a pouch — called also *emperor*

em·pery \'em-p(ə-)rē\ *n, pl* **em·per·ies** [ME *emperie,* fr. AF — more at EMPIRE] (1533) : wide dominion : EMPIRE

em·pha·sis \'em(p)-fə-səs\ *n, pl* **-pha·ses** \-ˌsēz\ [L, fr. Gk, exposition, emphasis, fr. *emphainein* to indicate, fr. *en-* + *phainein* to show — more at FANCY] (1573) **1 a :** force or intensity of expression that gives impressiveness or importance to something **b :** a particular prominence given in reading or speaking to one or more words or syllables **2 :** special consideration of or stress or insistence on something

em·pha·sise *Brit var of* EMPHASIZE

em·pha·size \'em(p)-fə-ˌsīz\ *vt* **-sized; -siz·ing** (ca. 1806) : to place emphasis on : STRESS ⟨*emphasized* the need for reform⟩

em·phat·ic \im-'fa-tik, em-\ *adj* [Gk *emphatikos,* fr. *emphainein*] (1635) **1 :** uttered with or marked by emphasis ⟨an ~ refusal⟩ **2 :** tending to express oneself in forceful speech or to take decisive action **3 :** attracting special attention **4 :** constituting or belonging to a set of tense forms in English consisting of the auxiliary *do* followed by an infinitive without *to* that are used to facilitate rhetorical inversion or to emphasize something — **em·phat·i·cal·ly** \-'fa-ti-k(ə-)lē\ *adv*

em·phy·se·ma \ˌem(p)-fə-'zē-mə, -'sē-\ *n* [NL, fr. Gk *emphysēma,* fr. *emphysan* to inflate, fr. *em-* [2]*en-* + *physan* to blow, fr. *physa* breath — more at PUSTULE] (1661) : a condition characterized by air-filled expansions of body tissues; *specif* : a condition of the lung marked by abnormal enlargement of the alveoli with loss of pulmonary elasticity that is characterized esp. by shortness of breath and may lead to impairment of heart action — **em·phy·se·ma·tous** \-'ze-mə-təs, -'se-, -'zē-, -'sē-\ *adj* — **em·phy·se·mic** \-'zē-mik, -'sē-\ *adj*

em·pire \'em-ˌpī(-ə)r\ *n* [ME, fr. AF *empire, empirie,* fr. L *imperium* absolute authority, empire, fr. *imperare* to command — more at EMPEROR] (14c) **1 a** (1) : a major political unit having a territory of great extent or a number of territories or peoples under a single sovereign authority *esp* : one having an emperor as chief of state (2) : the territory of such a political unit **b :** something resembling a political empire *esp* : an extensive territory or enterprise under single domination or control **2 :** imperial sovereignty, rule, or dominion **3** *cap* [*Empire* State, nickname for New York] : a juicy apple with dark red skin that is a cross between a McIntosh and a Red Delicious apple

Em·pire \'äm-ˌpir, 'em-ˌpī(-ə)r\ *adj* [F, fr. (*le premier*) *Empire* the first Empire of France] (1860) : of, relating to, or characteristic of a style (as of clothing or furniture) popular in early 19th century France

Em·pire Day \'em-ˌpī(-ə)r-\ *n* (1902) : COMMONWEALTH DAY — used before the official adoption of *Commonwealth Day* in 1958

em·pir·ic \im-'pir-ik, em-\ *n* [L *empiricus,* fr. Gk *empeirikos* doctor relying on experience alone, fr. *empeiria* experience, fr. *em-* [2]*en-* + *peiran* to attempt — more at FEAR] (1562) **1 :** CHARLATAN 2 **2 :** one who relies on practical experience

em·pir·i·cal \-i-kəl\ *also* **em·pir·ic** \-ik\ *adj* (1569) **1 :** originating in or based on observation or experience ⟨~ data⟩ **2 :** relying on experience or observation alone often without due regard for system and theory ⟨an ~ basis for the theory⟩ **3 :** capable of being verified or disproved by observation or experiment ⟨~ laws⟩ **4 :** of or relating to empiricism — **em·pir·i·cal·ly** \-i-k(ə-)lē\ *adv*

empirical formula *n* (1878) : a chemical formula showing the simplest ratio of elements in a compound rather than the total number of atoms in the molecule ⟨CH_2O is the *empirical formula* for glucose⟩

em·pir·i·cism \im-'pir-ə-ˌsi-zəm, em-\ *n* (1657) **1 a :** a former school of medical practice founded on experience without the aid of science or theory **b :** QUACKERY, CHARLATANRY **2 a :** the practice of relying on observation and experiment esp. in the natural sciences **b :** a tenet arrived at empirically **3 :** a theory that all knowledge originates in experience — **em·pir·i·cist** \-sist\ *n*

em·place \im-'plās\ *vt* [back-formation fr. *emplacement*] (1865) : to put into position ⟨missiles *emplaced* around the city⟩

em·place·ment \-'plā-smənt\ *n* [F, fr. MF *emplacer* to emplace, fr. *en-* + *place*] (1802) **1 :** the situation or location of something **2 :** a prepared position for weapons or military equipment ⟨radar ~*s*⟩ **3 :** a putting into position : PLACEMENT

emplane *var of* ENPLANE

[1]**em·ploy** \im-'plȯi, em-\ *vt* [ME *emploien,* fr. AF *empleier, emploier, emplier* to entangle, apply, make use of, fr. L *implicare* to enfold, involve, fr. *in-* + *plicare* to fold — more at PLY] (15c) **1 a :** to make use of (someone or something inactive) ⟨~ a pen for sketching⟩ **b :** to use (as time) advantageously ⟨a job that ~*ed* her skills⟩ **c** (1) : to use or engage the services of (2) : to provide with a job that pays wages or a salary **2 :** to devote to or direct toward a particular activity or person ⟨~*ed* all her energies to help the poor⟩ ***syn*** see USE — **em·ploy·er** *n*

[2]**em·ploy** \im-'plȯi, 'im-ˌ, 'em-ˌ\ *n* (1666) **1 a :** USE, PURPOSE **b :** OCCUPATION, JOB **2 :** the state of being employed ⟨in the city's ~⟩

[1]**em·ploy·able** \im-'plȯi-ə-bəl\ *adj* (1593) : capable of being employed — **em·ploy·abil·i·ty** \-ˌplȯi-ə-'bi-lə-tē\ *n*

[2]**employable** *n* (1934) : one who is employable

em·ploy·ee *also* **em·ploye** \im-ˌplȯ(i)-'ē, (ˌ)em-; im-'plȯ(i)-ˌē, em-\ *n* (1822) : one employed by another usu. for wages or salary and in a position below the executive level

em·ploy·ment \im-'plȯi-mənt\ *n* (15c) **1 :** USE, PURPOSE **2 a :** activity in which one engages or is employed ⟨seeking gainful ~⟩ **b :** an instance of such activity **3 :** the act of employing : the state of being employed ⟨~ of a pen in sketching⟩ ***syn*** see WORK

employment agency *n* (1888) : an agency whose business is to find jobs for people seeking them or to find people to fill jobs that are open

em·poi·son \im-ˈpȯi-zᵊn\ *vt* [ME *empoysonen,* fr. AF *empoisener,* fr. *en-* + *poison* poison] (14c) **1** *archaic* : POISON **2** : EMBITTER ⟨a look of ~*ed* acceptance —Saul Bellow⟩ — **em·poi·son·ment** \-mənt\ *n*

em·po·ri·um \im-ˈpȯr-ē-əm, em-\ *n, pl* **-ri·ums** *also* **-ria** \-ē-ə\ [L, fr. Gk *emporion,* fr. *emporos* traveler, trader, fr. *em-* [2]en- + *poros* passage, journey — more at FARE] (1586) **1 a** : a place of trade; *esp* : a commercial center **b** : a retail outlet ⟨a hardware ~⟩ ⟨a pizza ~⟩ **2** : a store carrying many different kinds of merchandise

em·pow·er \im-ˈpau̇(-ə)r\ *vt* (1648) **1** : to give official authority or legal power to ⟨~*ed* her attorney to act on her behalf⟩ **2** : ENABLE 1a **3** : to promote the self-actualization or influence of ⟨women's movement has been inspiring and ~*ing* women —Ron Hansen⟩ — **em·pow·er·ment** \-mənt\ *n*

em·press \ˈem-prəs\ *n* [ME *emperice,* fr. AF, fem. of *emperur* emperor] (12c) **1** : the wife or widow of an emperor **2** : a woman who is the sovereign or supreme monarch of an empire

em·presse·ment \ä^n-pres-ˈmä^n\ *n* [F, fr. (*s'*)*empresser* to hurry, fr. *en-* + *presser* to press] (1709) : demonstrative warmth or cordiality

em·prise \em-ˈprīz\ *n* [ME, undertaking, fr. AF, fr. *emprendre* to undertake, fr. VL **imprehendere,* fr. L *in-* + *prehendere* to seize — more at GET] (13c) : an adventurous, daring, or chivalric enterprise

[1]**emp·ty** \ˈem(p)-tē\ *adj* **emp·ti·er; -est** [ME, fr. OE *ǣmettig* unoccupied, fr. *ǣmetta* leisure, perh. fr. *ǣ-* without + *-metta* (prob. akin to *mōtan* to have to) — more at MUST] (bef. 12c) **1 a** : containing nothing ⟨~ shelves⟩ **b** : not occupied or inhabited ⟨an ~ building⟩ **c** : UNFREQUENTED **d** : not pregnant ⟨~ heifer⟩ **e** : NULL 4a ⟨the ~ set⟩ **2 a** : lacking reality, substance, meaning, or value : HOLLOW ⟨an ~ pleasure⟩ **b** : destitute of effect or force ⟨an ~ threat⟩ **c** : devoid of sense : FOOLISH **3** : HUNGRY **4 a** : IDLE ⟨~ hours⟩ **b** : having no purpose or result : USELESS **5** : marked by the absence of human life, activity, or comfort ⟨an ~ silence⟩ — **emp·ti·ly** \-tə-lē\ *adv* — **emp·ti·ness** \-tē-nəs\ *n*

syn EMPTY, VACANT, BLANK, VOID, VACUOUS mean lacking contents which could or should be present. EMPTY suggests a complete absence of contents ⟨an *empty* bucket⟩. VACANT suggests an absence of appropriate contents or occupants ⟨a *vacant* apartment⟩. BLANK stresses the absence of any significant, relieving, or intelligible features on a surface ⟨a *blank* wall⟩. VOID suggests absolute emptiness as far as the mind or senses can determine ⟨a statement *void* of meaning⟩. VACUOUS suggests the emptiness of a vacuum and esp. the lack of intelligence or significance ⟨a *vacuous* facial expression⟩. ***syn*** see in addition VAIN

[2]**empty** *vb* **emp·tied; emp·ty·ing** *vt* (1548) **1 a** : to make empty : remove the contents of ⟨~ a purse⟩ **b** : DEPRIVE, DIVEST ⟨a phrase *emptied* of all meaning⟩ **c** : to discharge (itself) of contents **d** : to fire (a repeating firearm) until empty **2** : to remove from what holds or encloses ~ *vi* **1** : to become empty ⟨the theater *emptied* quickly⟩ **2** : to discharge contents ⟨the river *empties* into the ocean⟩

[3]**empty** *n, pl* **emp·ties** (1865) : something (as a bottle or can) that is empty

empty calories *n pl* (1955) : calories from food that supplies energy but is not nutritionally balanced

emp·ty–hand·ed \ˌem(p)-tē-ˈhan-dəd\ *adj* (1589) **1** : having or bringing nothing **2** : having acquired or gained nothing ⟨came back ~⟩

emp·ty–head·ed \-ˈhe-dəd\ *adj* (1640) : VACUOUS 2

empty nest·er \-ˈnes-tər\ *n* (1962) : a parent whose children have grown and moved away from home

emp·ty–nest syndrome \ˌem(p)-tē-ˈnest-\ *n* (1972) : an emotional letdown often experienced by an empty nester

empty suit *n* (1950) : an ineffectual executive

em·pur·ple \im-ˈpər-pəl\ *vb* **em·pur·pled; em·pur·pling** \-ˈpər-p(ə-)liŋ\ *vt* (1590) : to tinge or color purple ~ *vi* : to become purple

em·py·ema \ˌem-ˌpī-ˈē-mə\ *n, pl* **-ema·ta** \-mə-tə\ *or* **-emas** [LL, fr. Gk *empyēma,* fr. *empyein* to suppurate, fr. *em-* [2]en- + *pyon* pus — more at FOUL] (ca. 1605) : the presence of pus in a bodily cavity — **em·py·emic** \-mik\ *adj*

em·py·re·al \ˌem-ˌpī-ˈrē-əl, -pə-; em-ˈpir-ē-əl, -ˈpī-rē-\ *adj* [LL *empyrius, empyreus,* fr. LGk *empyrios,* fr. Gk *em-* [2]en- + *pyr* fire] (15c) **1** : of or relating to the empyrean : CELESTIAL **2** : SUBLIME

[1]**em·py·re·an** \-ən\ *adj* (15c) : EMPYREAL

[2]**empyrean** *n* (ca. 1610) **1 a** : the highest heaven or heavenly sphere in ancient and medieval cosmology usu. consisting of fire or light **b** : the true and ultimate heavenly paradise **2** : FIRMAMENT, HEAVENS **3** : an ideal place or state

EMS *abbr* emergency medical service; emergency medical services

EMT \ˌē-(ˌ)em-ˈtē\ *n* [*e*mergency *m*edical *t*echnician] (1972) : a specially trained medical technician certified to provide basic emergency services (as cardiopulmonary resuscitation) before and during transportation to a hospital — compare PARAMEDIC 2

[1]**emu** \ˈē-(ˌ)myü, -mü\ *n* [modif. of Pg *ema* cassowary] (1656) : a swift-running Australian ratite bird (*Dromaius novae-hollandiae*) with undeveloped wings that is smaller than the ostrich

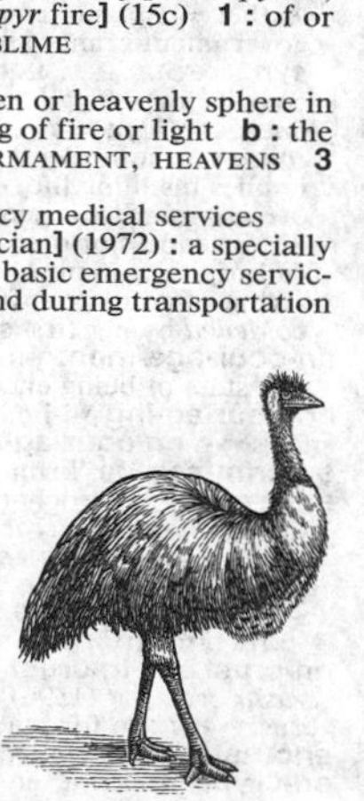

emu

[2]**emu** *abbr* electromagnetic unit

[1]**em·u·late** \ˈem-yə-ˌlāt, -yü-\ *vt* **-lat·ed; -lat·ing** [L *aemulatus,* pp. of *aemulari,* fr. *aemulus* rivaling] (1582) **1 a** : to strive to equal or excel **b** : IMITATE; *esp* : to imitate by means of an emulator **2** : to equal or approach equality with

[2]**em·u·late** \-lət\ *adj* (1602) *obs* : EMULOUS 1b ⟨pricked on by a most ~ pride —Shak.⟩

em·u·la·tion \ˌem-yə-ˈlā-shən, -yü-\ *n* (1542) **1** *obs* : ambitious or envious rivalry **2** : ambition or endeavor to equal or excel others (as in achievement) **3 a** : IMITATION **b** : the use of or technique of using an emulator — **em·u·la·tive** \ˈem-yə-ˌlā-tiv\ *adj* — **em·u·la·tive·ly** *adv*

em·u·la·tor \ˈem-yə-ˌlā-tər\ *n* (1589) **1** : one that emulates **2** : hardware or software that permits programs written for one computer to be run on another computer

em·u·lous \ˈem-yə-ləs\ *adj* (1535) **1 a** : inspired by or deriving from a desire to emulate **b** : ambitious or eager to emulate **2** *obs* : JEALOUS — **em·u·lous·ly** *adv* — **em·u·lous·ness** *n*

emul·si·fi·er \i-ˈməl-sə-ˌfī(-ə)r\ *n* (1888) : one that emulsifies; *esp* : a surface-active agent (as a soap) promoting the formation and stabilization of an emulsion

emul·si·fy \-ˌfī\ *vt* **-fied; -fy·ing** (1859) : to disperse (as an oil) in an emulsion; *also* : to convert (two or more immiscible liquids) into an emulsion — **emul·si·fi·able** \i-ˈməl-sə-ˌfī-ə-bəl\ *adj* — **emul·si·fi·ca·tion** \i-ˌməl-sə-fə-ˈkā-shən\ *n*

emul·sion \i-ˈməl-shən\ *n* [NL *emulsion-, emulsio,* fr. L *emulgēre* to milk out, fr. *e-* + *mulgēre* to milk; akin to OE *melcan* to milk, Gk *amelgein*] (1612) **1 a** : a system (as fat in milk) consisting of a liquid dispersed with or without an emulsifier in an immiscible liquid usu. in droplets of larger than colloidal size **b** : the state of such a system **2** : SUSPENSION 2b(3); *esp* : a suspension of a sensitive silver salt or a mixture of silver halides in a viscous medium (as a gelatin solution) forming a coating on photographic plates, film, or paper

en \ˈen\ *n* (1792) **1** : the width of a piece of type half the width of an em **2** : the letter *n*

[1]**en-** *also* **em-** \in *also* en; *sometimes only* in *is shown when* en *is infrequent*\ *prefix* [ME, fr. AF, fr. L *in-, im-,* fr. *in*] **1** : put into or onto ⟨*en*throne⟩ : cover with ⟨*en*shroud⟩ : go into or onto ⟨*en*plane⟩ — in verbs formed from nouns **2** : cause to be ⟨*en*slave⟩ — in verbs formed from adjectives or nouns **3** : provide with ⟨*em*power⟩ — in verbs formed from nouns **4** : so as to cover ⟨*en*wrap⟩ : thoroughly ⟨*en*tangle⟩ — in verbs formed from verbs; in all senses usu. *em-* before *b, m,* or *p*

[2]**en-** *also* **em-** *prefix* [ME, fr. L, fr. Gk, fr. *en* in — more at IN] : in : within ⟨*en*zootic⟩ — usu. *em-* before *b, m,* or *p* ⟨*em*pathy⟩

[1]**-en** *also* **-n** *adj suffix* [ME, fr. OE; akin to OHG *-īn* made of, L *-inus* of or belonging to, Gk *-inos* made of, of or belonging to] : made of : consisting of ⟨earth*en*⟩ ⟨leather*n*⟩

[2]**-en** *vb suffix* [ME *-nen,* fr. OE *-nian;* akin to OHG *-inōn* -en] **1 a** : cause to be ⟨sharp*en*⟩ **b** : cause to have ⟨length*en*⟩ **2 a** : come to be ⟨steep*en*⟩ **b** : come to have ⟨length*en*⟩

en·able \i-ˈnā-bəl\ *vt* **en·abled; en·abling** \-b(ə-)liŋ\ (15c) **1 a** : to provide with the means or opportunity ⟨training that ~*s* people to earn a living⟩ **b** : to make possible, practical, or easy ⟨a deal that would ~ passage of a new law⟩ **c** : to cause to operate ⟨software that ~*s* the keyboard⟩ **2** : to give legal power, capacity, or sanction to ⟨a law *enabling* admission of a state⟩

en·abler \i-ˈnā-blər, -bᵊl-ər\ *n* (1615) : one that enables another to achieve an end; *esp* : one who enables another to persist in self-destructive behavior (as substance abuse) by providing excuses or by making it possible to avoid the consequences of such behavior

en·act \i-ˈnakt\ *vt* (15c) **1** : to establish by legal and authoritative act; *specif* : to make (as a bill) into law **2** : ACT OUT ⟨~ a role⟩ — **en·actor** \-ˈnak-tər\ *n*

en·act·ment \-ˈnak(t)-mənt\ *n* (1792) **1** : the act of enacting : the state of being enacted **2** : something (as a law) that has been enacted

enal·a·pril \e-ˈna-lə-ˌpril\ *n* [perh. fr. ph*en*yl + *al*anyl + *-pril,* alter. of *proline*] (1982) : an antihypertensive drug $C_{20}H_{28}N_2O_5$ that is an ACE inhibitor administered orally in the form of its maleate

[1]**enam·el** \i-ˈna-məl\ *vt* **-eled** *or* **-elled; -el·ing** *or* **-el·ling** \-ˈnam-liŋ, -ˈna-mə-\ [ME, fr. AF *enameller,* fr. *en-* + *asmal, esmal* enamel, of Gmc origin; akin to OHG *smelzan* to melt — more at SMELT] (14c) **1** : to cover, inlay, or decorate with enamel **2** : to beautify with a colorful surface **3** : to form a glossy surface on (as paper, leather, or cloth) — **enam·el·er** *n* — **enam·el·ist** \-mə-list\ *n*

[2]**enamel** *n* (15c) **1** : a usu. opaque vitreous composition applied by fusion to the surface of metal, glass, or pottery **2** : a surface or outer covering that resembles enamel **3 a** : something that is enameled **b** : ENAMELWARE **4** : a cosmetic intended to give a smooth or glossy appearance **5** : a hard calcareous substance that forms a thin layer capping the teeth — see TOOTH illustration **6** : a paint that flows out to a smooth coat when applied and that dries with a glossy appearance

enam·el·ware \i-ˈna-məl-ˌwer\ *n* (1903) : metalware (as kitchen utensils) coated with enamel

en·amine \ˈe-nə-ˌmēn, ˈē-\ *n* [ISV *en-* (alter. of *-ene*) + *amine*] (1942) : an amine containing the double bond linkage C=C–N

en·am·or \i-ˈna-mər\ *vt* **-ored; -or·ing** \-mə-riŋ, -ˈnam-riŋ\ [ME *enamouren,* fr. AF *enamourer,* fr. *en-* + *amour* love — more at AMOUR] (14c) **1** : to inflame with love — usu. used in the passive with *of* **2** : to cause to feel a strong or excessive interest or fascination — usu. used in the passive with *of* or *with* ⟨baseball fans ~*ed* of statistics⟩

en·am·our *chiefly Brit var of* ENAMOR

en·an·tio·mer \i-ˈnan-tē-ə-mər\ *n* [Gk *enantios* + E *-mer*] (ca. 1929) : either of a pair of chemical compounds whose molecular structures have a nonsuperimposable mirror-image relationship to each other — compare DIASTEREOMER — **en·an·tio·mer·ic** \-ˌnan-tē-ə-ˈmer-ik\ *adj*

en·an·tio·morph \i-ˈnan-tē-ə-ˌmȯrf\ *n* [Gk *enantios* opposite (fr. *enanti* facing, fr. *en* in + *anti* against) + ISV *-morph* -morph] (1885) **1** : ENANTIOMER **2** : either of a pair of crystals (as of quartz) that are structural mirror images — **en·an·tio·mor·phic** \-ˌnan-tē-ə-ˈmȯr-fik\ *adj* — **en·an·tio·mor·phism** \-ˈmȯr-ˌfi-zəm\ *n* — **en·an·tio·mor·phous** \-ˈmȯr-fəs\ *adj*

ena·tion \i-ˈnā-shən\ *n* [L *enatus,* pp. of *enasci* to rise out of, fr. *e-* + *nasci* to be born — more at NATION] (ca. 1842) : an outgrowth from the surface of an organ ⟨a plant virus causing ~*s* on leaves⟩

en banc \ä^n-ˈbä^{n}k\ *adv or adj* [F, on the bench] (1863) : in full court : with full judiciary authority

en bloc \ä^n-ˈbläk\ *adv or adj* [F] (1861) : as a whole : in a mass

en bro·chette \ˌä^n-brō-ˈshet\ *adj* [F] (ca. 1909) *of food* : cooked or served on a skewer ⟨shrimp *en brochette*⟩

enc *or* **encl** *abbr* enclosure

en·cae·nia \en-ˈsē-nyə\ *n pl but sing or pl in constr, often cap* [NL, fr. L, dedication festival, fr. Gk *enkainia,* fr. *en* + *kainos* new — more at RECENT] (1691) **:** an annual university ceremony (as at Oxford) of commemoration with recital of poems and essays and conferring of degrees
en·cage \in-ˈkāj, en-\ *vt* (1592) **:** CAGE 1
en·camp \in-ˈkamp, en-\ *vi* (1563) **:** to set up or occupy a camp ~ *vt* **:** to place or establish in a camp
en·camp·ment \-mənt\ *n* (1598) **1 a :** the place where a group (as a body of troops) is encamped **b :** the individuals that make up an encampment **2 :** the act of encamping **:** the state of being encamped
en·cap·su·late \in-ˈkap-sə-ˌlāt, en-\ *vb* **-lat·ed; -lat·ing** *vt* (1872) **1 :** to enclose in or as if in a capsule ⟨a pilot *encapsulated* in the cockpit⟩ **2 :** EPITOMIZE, SUMMARIZE ⟨~ an era in an aphorism⟩ ~ *vi* **:** to become encapsulated — **en·cap·su·la·tion** \-ˌkap-sə-ˈlā-shən\ *n*
encapsulated *adj* (1894) **1 :** surrounded by a gelatinous or membranous envelope ⟨~ water bacteria⟩ **2 :** CONDENSED
en·cap·sule \in-ˈkap-səl, -(ˌ)sül, en-\ *vt* **-suled; -sul·ing** (1877) **:** ENCAPSULATE
en·case \in-ˈkās, en-\ *vt* (1633) **:** to enclose in or as if in a case
en·case·ment \in-ˈkā-smənt, en-\ *n* (1741) **:** the act or process of encasing **:** the state of being encased; *also* **:** CASE, COVERING
en·cash \in-ˈkash, en-\ *vt* (1861) *Brit* **:** CASH — **en·cash·able** \-ˈka-shə-bəl\ *adj, chiefly Brit* — **en·cash·ment** \-mənt\ *n, chiefly Brit*
en·caus·tic \in-ˈkȯ-stik\ *n* [*encaustic,* adj., fr. L *encausticus,* fr. Gk *enkaustikos,* fr. *enkaiein* to burn in, fr. *en-* + *kaiein* to burn] (1601) **:** a paint made from pigment mixed with melted beeswax and resin and after application fixed by heat; *also* **:** the method involving the use of encaustic or a work produced by this method — **encaustic** *adj*
-ence *n suffix* [ME, fr. AF, fr. L *-entia,* fr. *-ent-, -ens,* prp. ending + *-ia* ²-y] **1 :** action or process ⟨emergence⟩ **:** instance of an action or process ⟨reference⟩ **2 :** quality or state ⟨despondence⟩
[1]**en·ceinte** \äⁿ(n)-ˈsant\ *adj* [F, perh. fr. VL **incenta,* alter. of L *incient-, inciens* being with young, modif. of Gk *enkyos* pregnant, fr. *en-* + *kyein* to be pregnant — more at CYME] (1602) **:** PREGNANT 4
[2]**enceinte** *n* [F, fr. OF, enclosing wall, fr. *enceindre* to surround, fr. L *incingere,* fr. *in-* + *cingere* to gird — more at CINCTURE] (ca. 1708) **:** a line of fortification enclosing a castle or town; *also* **:** the area so enclosed
encephal- *or* **encephalo-** *comb form* [F *encéphal-,* fr. Gk *enkephal-,* fr. *enkephalos,* fr. *en-* + *kephalē* head — more at CEPHALIC] **:** brain ⟨*encephal*itis⟩ ⟨*encephalo*myocarditis⟩
en·ceph·a·li·tis \in-ˌse-fə-ˈlī-təs\ *n, pl* **-lit·i·des** \-ˈli-tə-ˌdēz\ (1843) **:** inflammation of the brain — **en·ceph·a·lit·ic** \-ˈli-tik\ *adj*
en·ceph·a·li·to·gen·ic \-ˌlī-tə-ˈje-nik\ *adj* (1923) **:** tending to cause encephalitis ⟨an ~ virus⟩ — **en·ceph·a·li·to·gen** \-ˈlī-tə-jən, -ˌjen\ *n*
en·ceph·a·lo·gram \in-ˈse-fə-lə-ˌgram\ *n* (1928) **:** an X-ray picture of the brain made by encephalography
en·ceph·a·lo·graph \-ˌgraf\ *n* (1928) **1 :** ENCEPHALOGRAM **2 :** ELECTROENCEPHALOGRAPH
en·ceph·a·log·ra·phy \in-ˌse-fə-ˈlä-grə-fē\ *n* (1922) **:** radiography of the brain after the cerebrospinal fluid has been replaced by a gas (as air)
en·ceph·a·lo·my·eli·tis \in-ˌse-fə-lō-ˌmī-ə-ˈlī-təs\ *n, pl* **-elit·i·des** \-ə-ˈli-tə-ˌdēz\ [NL] (1908) **:** concurrent inflammation of the brain and spinal cord; *specif* **:** EQUINE ENCEPHALITIS
en·ceph·a·lo·myo·car·di·tis \-ˌmī-ə-kär-ˈdī-təs\ *n* [NL] (1947) **:** an acute febrile disease esp. of swine and some nonhuman primates caused by a picornavirus (species *Encephalomyocarditis virus* of the genus *Cardiovirus*) and marked by degeneration and inflammation of skeletal and cardiac muscle and lesions of the central nervous system
en·ceph·a·lon \in-ˈse-fə-ˌlän, -lən\ *n, pl* **-la** \-lə\ [NL, fr. Gk *enkephalos*] (1741) **:** the vertebrate brain
en·ceph·a·lop·a·thy \in-ˌse-fə-ˈlä-pə-thē\ *n, pl* **-thies** (1866) **:** a disease of the brain; *esp* **:** one involving alterations of brain structure — **en·ceph·a·lo·path·ic** \-lə-ˈpa-thik\ *adj*
en·chain \in-ˈchān\ *vt* [ME *encheynen,* fr. AF *enchaener,* fr. *en-* + *chaene* chain] (14c) **:** to bind or hold with or as if with chains — **en·chain·ment** \-mənt\ *n*
en·chant \in-ˈchant, en-\ *vt* [ME, fr. AF *enchanter,* fr. L *incantare,* fr. *in-* + *cantare* to sing — more at CHANT] (14c) **1 :** to influence by or as if by charms and incantation **:** BEWITCH **2 :** to attract and move deeply **:** rouse to ecstatic admiration ⟨the scene *~ed* her to the point of tears —Elinor Wylie⟩ ***syn*** see ATTRACT
en·chant·er *n* (13c) **:** one that enchants; *esp* **:** SORCERER
en·chant·ing *adj* (1593) **:** CHARMING ⟨an ~ smile⟩ — **en·chant·ing·ly** *adv*
en·chant·ment \in-ˈchant-mənt, en-\ *n* (13c) **1 a :** the act or art of enchanting **b :** the quality or state of being enchanted **2 :** something that enchants ⟨the *~s* of sailing⟩
en·chant·ress \in-ˈchan-trəs, en-\ *n* (14c) **1 :** a woman who practices magic **:** SORCERESS **2 :** a fascinating or beautiful woman
en·chase \in-ˈchās\ *vt* [ME, to emboss, fr. AF *enchaser* to set (gems), fr. *en-* + *case, chase* case, box, shrine, fr. L *capsa* case — more at CASE] (15c) **1 :** ORNAMENT: as **a :** to cut or carve in relief **b :** INLAY **2 :** SET ⟨~ a gem⟩
en·chi·la·da \ˌen-chə-ˈlä-də\ *n* [AmerSp, fr. fem. of *enchilado,* pp. of *enchilar* to season with chili, fr. Sp *en-* ¹en- + *chile* chili] (1887) **1 :** a usu. corn tortilla rolled around a savory mixture, covered with chili sauce, and usu. baked **2 :** SCHMEAR, BALL OF WAX ⟨the whole ~⟩
en·chi·rid·i·on \ˌen-ˌkī-ˈri-dē-ən, -ˌki-\ *n, pl* **-rid·ia** \-dē-ə\ [LL, fr. Gk *encheiridion,* fr. *en* in + *cheir* hand — more at IN, CHIR-] (15c) **:** HANDBOOK, MANUAL
-enchyma *n comb form, pl* **-enchymata** *or* **-enchymas** [NL, fr. *parenchyma*] **:** cellular tissue ⟨coll*enchyma*⟩
en·ci·pher \in-ˈsī-fər, en-\ *vt* (1577) **:** to convert (a message) into cipher — **en·ci·pher·er** \-fər-ər\ *n* — **en·ci·pher·ment** \-fər-mənt\ *n*
en·cir·cle \in-ˈsər-kəl, en-\ *vt* [ME *enserclen*] (15c) **1 :** to form a circle around **:** SURROUND **2 :** to pass completely around — **en·cir·cle·ment** \-mənt\ *n*
en clair \äⁿ-ˈkler\ *adv or adj* [F, in clear] (ca. 1897) **:** in plain language ⟨a message sent *en clair*⟩
en·clasp \in-ˈklasp, en-\ *vt* (1584) **:** to seize and hold **:** EMBRACE
en·clave \ˈen-ˌklāv, ˈän-ˌklāv\ *n* [F, fr. MF, fr. *enclaver* to enclose, fr. VL **inclavare* to lock up, fr. L *in-* + *clavis* key — more at CLAVICLE] (1868) **:** a distinct territorial, cultural, or social unit enclosed within or as if within foreign territory ⟨ethnic *~s*⟩
en·clit·ic \en-ˈkli-tik\ *n* [LL *encliticus,* fr. Gk *enklitikos,* fr. *enklinesthai* to lean on, fr. *en-* + *klinein* to lean — more at LEAN] (ca. 1663) **:** a clitic that is associated with a preceding word — **enclitic** *adj*
en·close \in-ˈklōz, en-\ *also* **in·close** \in-\ *vt* [ME, prob. fr. *enclos* enclosed, fr. AF, pp. of *enclore* to enclose, fr. VL **inclaudere,* alter. of L *includere* — more at INCLUDE] (14c) **1 a** (1) **:** to close in **:** SURROUND ⟨~ a porch with glass⟩ (2) **:** to fence off (common land) for individual use **b :** to hold in **:** CONFINE **2 :** to include along with something else in a parcel or envelope ⟨a check is *enclosed* herewith⟩
en·clo·sure \in-ˈklō-zhər, en-\ *also* **in·clo·sure** \in-\ *n* (15c) **1 :** the act or action of enclosing **:** the quality or state of being enclosed **2 :** something that encloses **3 :** something enclosed ⟨a letter with two *~s*⟩
en·code \in-ˈkōd, en-\ *vt* (ca. 1919) **1 a :** to convert (as a body of information) from one system of communication into another; *esp* **:** to convert (a message) into code **b :** to convey symbolically ⟨the capacity of poetry to ~ ideology —J. D. Niles⟩ **2 :** to specify the genetic code for — **en·cod·er** *n*
en·co·mi·ast \en-ˈkō-mē-ˌast, -mē-əst\ *n* [Gk *enkōmiastēs,* fr. *enkōmiazein* to praise, fr. *enkōmion*] (1599) **:** one that praises **:** EULOGIST — **en·co·mi·as·tic** \-ˌkō-mē-ˈas-tik\ *adj*
en·co·mi·um \en-ˈkō-mē-əm\ *n, pl* **-mi·ums** *also* **-mia** \-mē-ə\ [L, fr. Gk *enkōmion,* fr. *en* in + *kōmos* revel, celebration] (1567) **:** glowing and warmly enthusiastic praise; *also* **:** an expression of this
syn ENCOMIUM, EULOGY, PANEGYRIC, TRIBUTE, CITATION mean a formal expression of praise. ENCOMIUM implies enthusiasm and warmth in praising a person or a thing ⟨received *encomiums* from literary critics⟩. EULOGY applies to a prepared speech or writing extolling the virtues and services of a person ⟨delivered the *eulogy* at the funeral service⟩. PANEGYRIC suggests an elaborate often poetic compliment ⟨her lyrical memoir was a *panegyric* to her mentor⟩. TRIBUTE implies deeply felt praise conveyed either through words or through a significant act ⟨the concert was a musical *tribute* to the early jazz masters⟩. CITATION applies to the formal praise of a person offered in a military dispatch or in awarding an honorary degree ⟨earned a *citation* for bravery⟩.
en·com·pass \in-ˈkəm-pəs, en- *also* -ˈkäm-\ *vt* [ME] (14c) **1 a :** to form a circle about **:** ENCLOSE **b** *obs* **:** to go completely around **2 a :** ENVELOP **b :** INCLUDE, COMPREHEND ⟨a plan that *~es* a number of aims⟩ **3 :** BRING ABOUT, ACCOMPLISH ⟨~ a task⟩ — **en·com·pass·ment** \-pə-smənt\ *n*
en·core \ˈän-ˌkȯr\ *n* [F, still, again] (1712) **1 :** a demand for repetition or reappearance made by an audience **2 a :** a reappearance or additional performance demanded by an audience **b :** a second achievement esp. that surpasses the first — **encore** *vb*
[1]**en·coun·ter** \in-ˈkau̇n-tər, en-\ *vb* **en·coun·tered; en·coun·ter·ing** \-ˈkau̇n-t(ə-)riŋ\ [ME *encountren,* fr. AF *encuntrer,* fr. ML *incontrare,* fr. LL *incontra* toward, fr. L *in-* + *contra* against — more at COUNTER] *vt* (14c) **1 a :** to meet as an adversary or enemy **b :** to engage in conflict with **2 :** to come upon face-to-face **3 :** to come upon or experience esp. unexpectedly ⟨~ difficulties⟩ ~ *vi* **:** to meet esp. by chance
[2]**encounter** *n* (14c) **1 :** a meeting between hostile factions or persons **:** a sudden often violent clash ⟨an ~ between the police and demonstrators⟩ **2 a :** a chance meeting ⟨an accidental ~⟩ **b :** a particular kind of meeting or experience with another person ⟨a romantic ~⟩ **3 :** a coming into the vicinity of a celestial body ⟨the Martian ~ of a spacecraft⟩
encounter group *n* (1967) **:** a usu. unstructured group that seeks to develop the capacity of the individual to express feelings and to form emotional ties by unrestrained confrontation of individuals
en·cour·age \in-ˈkər-ij, -ˈkə-rij, en-\ *vt* **-aged; -ag·ing** [ME *encoragen,* fr. AF *encorager,* fr. *en-* + *curage* courage] (15c) **1 a :** to inspire with courage, spirit, or hope **:** HEARTEN ⟨she was *encouraged* to continue by her early success⟩ **b :** to attempt to persuade **:** URGE ⟨they *encouraged* him to go back to school⟩ **2 :** to spur on **:** STIMULATE ⟨warm weather *~s* plant growth⟩ **3 :** to give help or patronage to **:** FOSTER ⟨government grants designed to ~ conservation⟩ — **en·cour·ag·er** *n*
syn ENCOURAGE, INSPIRIT, HEARTEN, EMBOLDEN mean to fill with courage or strength of purpose. ENCOURAGE suggests the raising of one's confidence esp. by an external agency ⟨the teacher's praise *encouraged* the students to greater efforts⟩. INSPIRIT, somewhat literary, implies instilling life, energy, courage, or vigor into something ⟨patriots *inspirited* the people to resist⟩. HEARTEN implies the lifting of dispiritedness or despondency by an infusion of fresh courage or zeal ⟨a hospital patient *heartened* by good news⟩. EMBOLDEN implies the giving of courage sufficient to overcome timidity or reluctance ⟨*emboldened* by her first success, she tried an even more difficult climb⟩.
en·cour·age·ment \-ij-mənt, -rij-\ *n* (1549) **1 :** the act of encouraging **:** the state of being encouraged **2 :** something that encourages
en·cour·ag·ing \-i-jiŋ, -ri-jiŋ\ *adj* (1593) **:** giving hope or promise ⟨~ news⟩ — **en·cour·ag·ing·ly** \-jiŋ-lē\ *adv*
en·crim·son \in-ˈkrim-zən\ *vt* (1597) **:** to make or dye crimson
en·croach \in-ˈkrōch, en-\ *vi* [ME *encrochen* to get, seize, fr. AF *encrocher,* fr. *en-* + *croc, croche* hook — more at CROCHET] (1528) **1 :** to enter by gradual steps or by stealth into the possessions or rights of another **2 :** to advance beyond the usual or proper limits ⟨the gradually *~ing* sea⟩ ***syn*** see TRESPASS — **en·croach·er** *n* — **en·croach·ment** \-ˈkrōch-mənt\ *n*
en·crust *also* **in·crust** \in-ˈkrəst, iŋ-\ *vb* [prob. fr. L *incrustare,* fr. *in-* + *crusta* crust] *vt* (1596) **:** to cover, line, or overlay with or as if with a crust ~ *vi* **:** to form a crust
encrustation *var of* INCRUSTATION
en·crypt \in-ˈkript, en-\ *vt* [*en-* + *crypt-* (as in *cryptogram*)] (1944) **1 :** ENCIPHER **2 :** ENCODE 1a — **en·cryp·tion** \-ˈkrip-shən\ *n*
en·cul·tur·a·tion \in-ˌkəl-chə-ˈrā-shən, (ˌ)en-\ *n* (1948) **:** the process by which an individual learns the traditional content of a culture and assimilates its practices and values — **en·cul·tur·ate** \-ˈkəl-chə-ˌrāt\ *vb*
en·cum·ber \in-ˈkəm-bər\ *vt* **-cum·bered; -cum·ber·ing** \-b(ə-)riŋ\ [ME *encombren,* fr. AF *encumbrer,* fr. *en-* + MF *combre* dam, weir] (14c) **1 :** WEIGH DOWN, BURDEN ⟨tourists *~ed* by heavy luggage⟩ **2**

: to impede or hamper the function or activity of : HINDER ⟨negotiations ~*ed* by a lack of trust⟩ **3 :** to burden with a legal claim (as a mortgage) ⟨~ an estate⟩

en·cum·brance \in-ˈkəm-brən(t)s\ *n* (1535) **1 :** something that encumbers : IMPEDIMENT, BURDEN **2 :** a claim (as a mortgage) against property

en·cum·branc·er \-brən(t)-sər\ *n* (1858) : one that holds an encumbrance

ency *or* **encyc** *abbr* encyclopedia

-ency *n suffix* [ME *-encie,* fr. L *-entia* — more at -ENCE] : quality or state ⟨despond*ency*⟩

¹en·cyc·li·cal \in-ˈsi-kli-kəl, en-\ *adj* [LL *encyclicus,* fr. Gk *enkyklios* circular, general, fr. *en* in + *kyklos* circle — more at IN, WHEEL] (1647) : addressed to all the individuals of a group : GENERAL

²encyclical *n* (1837) : an encyclical letter; *specif* : a papal letter to the bishops of the church as a whole or to those in one country

en·cy·clo·pae·dia, en·cy·clo·pae·dic *chiefly Brit var of* ENCYCLOPEDIA, ENCYCLOPEDIC

en·cy·clo·pe·dia \in-ˌsī-klə-ˈpē-dē-ə\ *n* [ML *encyclopaedia* course of general education, fr. Gk *enkyklios* + *paideia* education, child rearing, fr. *paid-, pais* child — more at FEW] (1644) : a work that contains information on all branches of knowledge or treats comprehensively a particular branch of knowledge usu. in articles arranged alphabetically often by subject

en·cy·clo·pe·dic \-ˈpē-dik\ *adj* (1824) : of, relating to, or suggestive of an encyclopedia or its methods of treating or covering a subject : COMPREHENSIVE ⟨an ~ mind⟩ ⟨an ~ collection of armor⟩ — **en·cy·clo·pe·di·cal·ly** \-di-k(ə-)lē\ *adv*

en·cy·clo·pe·dism \-ˈpē-ˌdi-zəm\ *n* (1833) : the quality or state of being encyclopedic

en·cy·clo·pe·dist \-ˈpē-dist\ *n* (1651) **1 :** one who compiles or writes for an encyclopedia **2** *often cap* : one of the writers of a French encyclopedia (1751–80) who were identified with the Enlightenment and advocated deism and scientific rationalism

en·cyst \in-ˈsist, en-\ *vt* (1720) : to enclose in a cyst ~ *vi* : to form or become enclosed in a cyst — **en·cyst·ment** \-ˈsis(t)-mənt\ *n*

¹end \ˈend\ *n* [ME *ende,* fr. OE; akin to OHG *enti* end, L *ante* before, Gk *anti* against] (bef. 12c) **1 a :** the part of an area that lies at the boundary **b (1) :** a point that marks the extent of something **(2) :** the point where something ceases to exist ⟨world without ~⟩ **c :** the extreme or last part lengthwise : TIP **d :** the terminal unit of something spatial that is marked off by units **e :** a player stationed at the extremity of a line (as in football) **2 a :** cessation of a course of action, pursuit, or activity **b :** DEATH, DESTRUCTION **c (1) :** the ultimate state **(2) :** RESULT, ISSUE **3 :** something incomplete, fragmentary, or undersized : REMNANT **4 a :** an outcome worked toward : PURPOSE ⟨the ~ of poetry is to be poetry —R. P. Warren⟩ **b :** the object by virtue of or for the sake of which an event takes place **5 a :** a share in an undertaking ⟨kept your ~ up⟩ **b :** a particular operation or aspect of an undertaking or organization ⟨the sales ~ of the business⟩ **6 :** something that is extreme : ULTIMATE — used with *the* **7 :** a period of action or turn in any of various sports events (as archery or lawn bowling) ***syn*** see INTENTION — **end·ed** \ˈen-dəd\ *adj* — **in the end :** AFTER ALL, ULTIMATELY ⟨will surely succeed *in the end*⟩ — **no end :** EXCEEDINGLY ⟨it pleases us *no end*⟩ — **on end :** without a stop or letup ⟨it rained for days *on end*⟩

²end *vt* (bef. 12c) **1 a :** to bring to an end **b :** DESTROY **2 :** to make up the end of ⟨a wedding scene ~*s* the film⟩ ~ *vi* **1 a :** to come to an end ⟨the meeting will ~ at noon⟩ **b :** to reach a specified ultimate rank, situation, or place — usu. used with *up* ⟨~*ed* up as a colonel⟩ **2 :** DIE ***syn*** see CLOSE

³end *adj* (13c) : FINAL, ULTIMATE ⟨~ results⟩ ⟨~ markets⟩

⁴end *vt* [prob. alter. of E dial. *in* to harvest] (1607) *dial Eng* : to put (grain or hay) into a barn or stack

end- *or* **endo-** *comb form* [F, fr. Gk, fr. *endon* within; akin to Gk *en* in, OL *indu,* Hitt *andan* within — more at IN] **1 :** within : inside ⟨*endo*skeleton⟩ — compare ECT-, EXO- **2 :** taking in ⟨*endo*thermic⟩

en·dam·age \in-ˈda-mij\ *vt* [ME] (14c) : to cause loss or damage to

en·dan·ger \in-ˈdān-jər, en-\ *vb* **-dan·gered; -dan·ger·ing** \-ˈdānj-riŋ, -ˈdān-jə-\ *vt* (1964) : to bring into danger or peril ⟨recklessly ~*ing* innocent lives⟩ ~ *vi* : to create a dangerous situation ⟨driving to ~⟩ — **en·dan·ger·ment** \-ˈdān-jər-mənt\ *n*

endangered *adj* (1964) : being or relating to an endangered species ⟨an ~ bird⟩ ⟨put on the ~ list⟩

endangered species *n* (1964) : a species threatened with extinction; *broadly* : anyone or anything whose continued existence is threatened

en·darch \ˈen-ˌdärk\ *adj* (1900) : formed or taking place from inner cells outward ⟨~ xylem⟩

end around *n* (1926) : a football play in which an offensive end comes behind the line of scrimmage to take a handoff and attempts to carry the ball around the opposite flank

end·ar·ter·ec·to·my \ˌen-ˌdär-tə-ˈrek-tə-mē\ *n, pl* **-mies** [NL *endarterium* intima of an artery (fr. *end-* + *arteria* artery) + E *-ectomy*] (1974) : surgical removal of the inner layer of an artery when thickened and atheromatous or occluded (as by intimal plaques)

end·brain \ˈen(d)-ˌbrān\ *n* (1927) : TELENCEPHALON

end brush *n* (ca. 1891) : END PLATE

end·cap \ˈend-ˌkap\ *n* (1983) : a display of products placed at the end of an aisle in a store

en·dear \in-ˈdir, en-\ *vt* (1580) **1** *obs* : to make higher in cost, value, or estimation **2 :** to cause to become beloved or admired ⟨her generosity has ~*ed* her to the public⟩ — **en·dear·ing·ly** \-iŋ-lē\ *adv*

en·dear·ment \in-ˈdir-mənt\ *n* (1610) **1 :** a word or an act (as a caress) expressing affection **2 :** the act or process of endearing

¹en·deav·or \in-ˈde-vər\ *vb* **en·deav·ored; en·deav·or·ing** \-v(ə-)riŋ\ [ME *endeveren* to exert oneself, fr. *en-* + *dever* duty — more at DEVOIR] *vt* (15c) **1** *archaic* : to strive to achieve or reach **2 :** to attempt (as the fulfillment of an obligation) by exertion of effort ⟨~*s* to finish the race⟩ ~ *vi* : to work with set purpose ***syn*** see ATTEMPT

²endeavor *n* (15c) **1 :** serious determined effort **2 :** activity directed toward a goal : ENTERPRISE ⟨fields of ~⟩

en·deav·our *chiefly Brit var of* ENDEAVOR

¹en·dem·ic \en-ˈde-mik, in-\ *adj* [F *endémique,* fr. *endémie* endemic disease, fr. Gk *endēmia* action of dwelling, fr. *endēmos* endemic, fr. *en* in + *dēmos* people, populace — more at DEMAGOGUE] (1759) **1 a :** belonging or native to a particular people or country **b :** characteristic of or prevalent in a particular field, area, or environment ⟨problems ~ to translation⟩ ⟨the self-indulgence ~ in the film industry⟩ **2 :** restricted or peculiar to a locality or region ⟨~ diseases⟩ ⟨an ~ species⟩ ***syn*** see NATIVE — **en·dem·i·cal·ly** \-ˈde-mi-k(ə-)lē\ *adv* — **en·de·mic·i·ty** \ˌen-ˌde-ˈmi-sə-tē, -də-ˈmi-\ *n* — **en·de·mism** \ˈen-də-ˌmi-zəm\ *n*

²endemic *n* (1926) : an endemic organism

end·er·gon·ic \ˌen-ˌdər-ˈgä-nik\ *adj* [*end-* + Gk *ergon* work — more at WORK] (1940) : ENDOTHERMIC 1 ⟨an ~ biochemical reaction⟩

end·ex·ine \(ˌ)en-ˈdek-ˌsēn, -ˌsīn\ *n* (1947) : an inner membranous layer of the exine

end·game \ˈen(d)-ˌgām\ *n* (1881) : the stage of a chess game after major reduction of forces; *also* : the final stage of some action or process

end·ing \ˈen-diŋ\ *n* (bef. 12c) : something that constitutes an end: as **a :** CONCLUSION ⟨a movie with a happy ~⟩ **b :** one or more letters or syllables added to a word base esp. in inflection

en·dive \ˈen-ˌdīv, ˌän-ˈdēv\ *n* [ME, fr. AF, fr. LL *endivia,* fr. LGk *entybion,* fr. L *intubus*] (14c) **1 :** an annual or biennial composite herb (*Cichorium endivia*) occurring in two forms: **a :** one having slightly bitter curly usu. dissected leaves used esp. in salads **b :** one having slightly bitter broad flat leaves used esp. cooked as a vegetable — called also *escarole* **2 :** BELGIAN ENDIVE

end·leaf \ˈend-ˌlēf\ *n* (1888) : ENDPAPER

end·less \ˈen(d)-ləs\ *adj* (bef. 12c) **1 :** being or seeming to be without end ⟨an ~ speech⟩ **2 :** extremely numerous ⟨all the multiplied, ~, nameless iniquities —Edmund Burke⟩ **3 :** joined at the ends ⟨an ~ chain⟩ — **end·less·ly** *adv* — **end·less·ness** *n*

end line *n* (1893) : a line marking an end or boundary esp. of a playing area: as **a :** a line at either end of a football field 10 yards beyond and parallel to the goal line **b :** a line at either end of a court (as in basketball or tennis) perpendicular to the sidelines

end·long \ˈend-ˌlȯŋ\ *adv* [ME *endelong,* alter. of *andlong,* fr. OE *andlang* along, fr. *andlang,* prep. — more at ALONG] (13c) *archaic* : LENGTHWISE

end man *n* (1865) : a man at each end of the line of performers in a minstrel show who engages in comic repartee with the interlocutor

end·most \ˈen(d)-ˌmōst\ *adj* (bef. 12c) : situated at the very end

end·note \ˈen(d)-ˌnōt\ *n* (1926) : a note placed at the end of the text

en·do·bi·ot·ic \ˌen-dō-ˌbī-ˈä-tik, -bē-\ *adj* [ISV] (ca. 1900) : dwelling within the cells or tissues of a host ⟨~ fungi⟩

en·do·car·di·al \ˌen-dō-ˈkär-dē-əl\ *adj* (ca. 1849) **1 :** situated within the heart **2 :** of or relating to the endocardium

en·do·car·di·tis \-ˌkär-ˈdī-təs\ *n* [NL] (ca. 1839) : inflammation of the lining of the heart and its valves

en·do·car·di·um \-ˈkär-dē-əm\ *n, pl* **-dia** \-dē-ə\ [NL] (ca. 1864) : a thin serous membrane lining the cavities of the heart

en·do·carp \ˈen-də-ˌkärp\ *n* [F *endocarpe*] (1830) : the inner layer of the pericarp of a fruit (as an apple or orange) when it consists of two or more layers of different texture or consistency

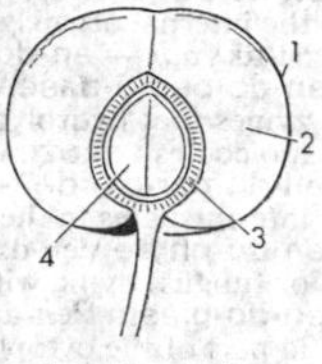

endocarp (cross section of a cherry): *1* exocarp, *2* mesocarp, *3* endocarp, *4* seed; *1, 2,* and *3* together form the pericarp

en·do·cast \ˈen-dō-ˌkast\ *n* (1949) : ENDOCRANIAL CAST

en·do·chon·dral \ˌen-də-ˈkän-drəl\ *adj* (1882) : relating to, formed by, or being ossification that takes place from centers arising in cartilage and involves deposition of lime salts in the cartilage matrix followed by secondary absorption and replacement by true bony tissue

en·do·cra·ni·al cast \ˌen-də-ˌkrā-nē-əl-\ *n* (1923) : a cast of the cranial cavity showing the approximate shape of the brain

¹en·do·crine \ˈen-də-krən, -ˌkrīn, -ˌkrēn\ *adj* [ISV *end-* + Gk *krinein* to separate — more at CERTAIN] (1914) **1 :** secreting internally; *specif* : producing secretions that are distributed in the body by way of the bloodstream ⟨hormones produced by the ~ system⟩ **2 :** of, relating to, affecting, or resembling an endocrine gland or secretion ⟨~ tumors⟩

²endocrine *n* (1922) **1 :** HORMONE 1 **2 :** ENDOCRINE GLAND

endocrine gland *n* (1914) : a gland (as the thyroid or the pituitary) that produces an endocrine secretion — called also *ductless gland*

en·do·cri·no·log·ic \ˌen-də-ˌkri-nə-ˈlä-jik, -ˌkrī-, -ˌkrē-\ *or* **en·do·cri·no·log·i·cal** \-ji-kəl\ *adj* (ca. 1934) : involving or relating to the endocrine glands or secretions or to endocrinology

en·do·cri·nol·o·gy \ˌen-də-kri-ˈnä-lə-jē, -ˌkrī-\ *n* [ISV] (ca. 1913) : a branch of medicine concerned with the structure, function, and disorders of the endocrine glands — **en·do·cri·nol·o·gist** \-jist\ *n*

en·do·cy·to·sis \-sī-ˈtō-səs\ *n* [NL, fr. *end-* + *-cytosis* (as in *phagocytosis*)] (1963) : incorporation of substances into a cell by phagocytosis or pinocytosis — **en·do·cy·tot·ic** \-ˈtä-tik\ *adj*

en·do·derm \ˈen-də-ˌdərm\ *n* [F *endoderme,* fr. *end-* + Gk *derma* skin — more at DERM-] (1861) : the innermost of the three primary germ layers of an embryo that is the source of the epithelium of the digestive tract and its derivatives and of the lower respiratory tract; *also* : a tissue derived from this layer — **en·do·der·mal** \ˌen-də-ˈdər-məl\ *adj*

en·do·der·mis \ˌen-də-ˈdər-məs\ *n* [NL] (1884) : the innermost tissue of the cortex in many roots and stems

end·odon·tics \-ˈdän-tiks\ *n pl but sing in constr* [*end-* + *odont-* + *-ics*] (1946) : a branch of dentistry concerned with diseases of the pulp — **end·odon·tic** \-ˈdän-tik\ *adj* — **end·odon·ti·cal·ly** \-ˈdän-ti-k(ə-)lē\ *adv* — **end·odon·tist** \-ˈdän-tist\ *n*

en·do·en·zyme \ˌen-dō-ˈen-ˌzīm\ *n* [ISV] (ca. 1909) : an enzyme that functions inside the cell

en·do·er·gic \ˌen-dō-ˈər-jik\ *adj* (1940) : absorbing energy : ENDOTHERMIC ⟨~ nuclear reactions⟩

\ə\ **abut** \ᵊ\ kitten, F table \ər\ **fur**ther \a\ **ash** \ā\ **ace** \ä\ mop, mar \au̇\ **out** \ch\ **ch**in \e\ **bet** \ē\ **easy** \g\ **go** \i\ **hit** \ī\ **ice** \j\ **job** \ŋ\ **sing** \ō\ **go** \ȯ\ **law** \ȯi\ **boy** \th\ **thin** \t͟h\ **the** \ü\ **loot** \u̇\ **foot** \y\ **yet** \zh\ vi**s**ion, beige \k̲, ⁿ, œ, ue, ʸ\ *see* Guide to Pronunciation

en·dog·a·my \en-ˈdä-gə-mē\ *n* (1865) **:** marriage within a specific group as required by custom or law — **en·dog·a·mous** \-məs\ *adj*
en·do·gen·ic \ˌen-də-ˈje-nik\ *adj* (ca. 1904) **1 :** of or relating to metamorphism taking place within a planet or moon **2 :** ENDOGENOUS
en·dog·e·nous \en-ˈdä-jə-nəs\ *adj* (1830) **1 :** growing or produced by growth from deep tissue ⟨~ plant roots⟩ **2 a :** caused by factors inside the organism or system ⟨suffered from ~ depression⟩ ⟨~ business cycles⟩ **b :** produced or synthesized within the organism or system ⟨an ~ hormone⟩ — **en·dog·e·nous·ly** *adv*
en·do·lith·ic \ˌen-də-ˈli-thik\ *adj* (1886) **:** living within or penetrating deeply into stony substances (as rocks or coral) ⟨~ lichens⟩
en·do·lymph \ˈen-də-ˌlim(p)f\ *n* [ISV] (ca. 1839) **:** the watery fluid in the membranous labyrinth of the ear — **en·do·lym·phat·ic** \ˌen-də-lim-ˈfa-tik\ *adj*
en·do·me·tri·osis \ˌen-dō-ˌmē-trē-ˈō-səs\ *n* [NL] (1925) **:** the presence and growth of functioning endometrial tissue in places other than the uterus that often results in severe pain and infertility
en·do·me·tri·tis \ˌen-dō-mə-ˈtrī-təs\ *n* [NL] (1872) **:** inflammation of the endometrium
en·do·me·tri·um \-ˈmē-trē-əm\ *n, pl* **-tria** \-trē-ə\ [NL, fr. *end-* + Gk *mētra* uterus, fr. *mētr-, mētēr* mother — more at MOTHER] (ca. 1882) **:** the mucous membrane lining the uterus — **en·do·me·tri·al** \-trē-əl\ *adj*
en·do·mi·to·sis \-mī-ˈtō-səs\ *n* [NL] (1942) **:** division of chromosomes not followed by nuclear division that results in an increased number of chromosomes in the cell — **en·do·mi·tot·ic** \-mī-ˈtä-tik\ *adj*
en·do·mix·is \-ˈmik-səs\ *n* [NL, fr. *end-* + Gk *mixis* act of mixing, fr. *mignynai* to mix — more at MIX] (1914) **:** a periodic nuclear reorganization in ciliated protozoans
en·do·morph \ˈen-də-ˌmȯrf\ *n* [*endo*derm + *-morph*] (1940) **:** an endomorphic individual
en·do·mor·phic \ˌen-də-ˈmȯr-fik\ *adj* [*endo*derm + *-morphic;* fr. the predominance in such types of structures developed from the endoderm] (1940) **1 :** of or relating to the component in W. H. Sheldon's classification of body types that measures the massiveness of the digestive viscera and the body's degree of roundedness and softness **2 :** having a heavy rounded body build often with a marked tendency to become fat — **en·do·mor·phy** \ˈen-də-ˌmȯr-fē\ *n*
en·do·mor·phism \ˌen-də-ˈmȯr-ˌfi-zəm\ *n* (1909) **:** a homomorphism that maps a mathematical set into itself — compare ISOMORPHISM
en·do·nu·cle·ase \ˌen-dō-ˈnü-klē-ˌās, -ˌāz, -ˈnyü-\ *n* (1962) **:** an enzyme that breaks down a nucleotide chain into two or more shorter chains by cleaving the internal covalent bonds linking nucleotides — compare EXONUCLEASE
en·do·nu·cleo·lyt·ic \-ˌnü-klē-ō-ˈli-tik, -ˌnyü-\ *adj* [*end-* + *nucleo-* + *-lytic*] (1967) **:** cleaving a nucleotide chain into two parts at an internal point ⟨~ nicks⟩
en·do·par·a·site \-ˈpa-rə-ˌsīt\ *n* [ISV] (ca. 1882) **:** a parasite that lives in the internal organs or tissues of its host — **en·do·par·a·sit·ic** \-ˌpa-rə-ˈsi-tik\ *adj* — **en·do·par·a·sit·ism** \-ˈpa-rə-ˌsī-ˌti-zəm, -sə-ˌti-\ *n*
en·do·pep·ti·dase \-ˈpep-tə-ˌdās, -ˌdāz\ *n* (1936) **:** any of a group of enzymes that hydrolyze peptide bonds within the long chains of protein molecules **:** PROTEASE — compare EXOPEPTIDASE
en·do·per·ox·ide \-pə-ˈräk-ˌsīd\ *n* (1962) **:** any of various biosynthetic intermediates in the formation of prostaglandins
en·do·phyte \ˈen-də-ˌfīt\ *n* [ISV] (1835) **:** an organism (as a bacterium or fungus) living within a plant — **en·do·phyt·ic** \ˌen-də-ˈfi-tik\ *adj*
en·do·plasm \ˈen-də-ˌpla-zəm\ *n* [ISV] (1882) **:** the inner relatively fluid part of the cytoplasm — **en·do·plas·mic** \ˌen-də-ˈplaz-mik\ *adj*
endoplasmic reticulum *n* (1947) **:** a system of interconnected vesicular and lamellar cytoplasmic membranes that functions esp. in the transport of materials within the cell and that is studded with ribosomes in some places — see CELL illustration
en·do·poly·ploidy \ˌen-dō-ˈpä-li-ˌplȯi-dē\ *n* (1945) **:** a polyploid state in which the chromosomes have divided repeatedly without subsequent division of the nucleus or cell — **en·do·poly·ploid** \-ˌplȯid\ *adj*
end organ *n* (1875) **:** a structure forming the end of a neural path and consisting of an effector or a receptor with its associated nerve terminations
en·dor·phin \en-ˈdȯr-fən\ *n* [ISV *endo*genous + *m*orphine] (1976) **:** any of a group of endogenous peptides (as enkephalin) found esp. in the brain that bind chiefly to opiate receptors and produce some pharmacological effects (as pain relief) like those of opiates; *specif* **:** BETA-ENDORPHIN
en·dorse \in-ˈdȯrs, en-\ *also* **in·dorse** \in-\ *vt* **-dorsed; -dors·ing** [alter. of obs. *endoss,* fr. ME *endosen,* fr. AF *endosser,* to put on, don, write on the back of, fr. *en-* + *dos* back, fr. L *dorsum*] (1581) **1 a :** to write on the back of; *esp* **:** to sign one's name as payee on the back of (a check) in order to obtain the cash or credit represented on the face **b :** to inscribe (one's signature) on a check, bill, or note **c :** to inscribe (as an official document) with a title or memorandum **d :** to make over to another (the value represented in a check, bill, or note) by inscribing one's name on the document **e :** to acknowledge receipt of (a sum specified) by one's signature on a document **2 a :** to approve openly ⟨~ an idea⟩; *esp* **:** to express support or approval of publicly and definitely ⟨~ a mayoral candidate⟩ **b :** to recommend (as a product or service) usu. for financial compensation ⟨shoes *endorsed* by a pro basketball player⟩ ***syn*** see APPROVE — **en·dors·able** \-ˈdȯr-sə-bəl\ *adj* — **en·dors·ee** \in-ˌdȯr-ˈsē, ˌen-\ *n* — **en·dors·er** \in-ˈdȯr-sər\ *n*
en·dorse·ment \in-ˈdȯr-smənt, en-\ *also* **in·dorse·ment** \in-\ *n* (1547) **1 :** the act or process of endorsing **2 a :** something that is written in the process of endorsing **b :** a provision added to an insurance contract altering its scope or application **3 :** SANCTION, APPROVAL ⟨went ahead without the ~ of his boss⟩ **4 :** money earned from a product recommendation ⟨made millions in salary and ~*s*⟩
en·do·scope \ˈen-də-ˌskōp\ *n* [ISV] (1861) **:** an illuminated usu. fiber-optic flexible or rigid tubular instrument for visualizing the interior of a hollow organ or part (as the bladder or esophagus) for diagnostic or therapeutic purposes that typically has one or more channels to enable passage of instruments (as forceps or scissors) — **en·dos·co·py** \en-ˈdäs-kə-pē\ *n*
en·do·scop·ic \ˌen-də-ˈskä-pik\ *adj* (1853) **:** of, relating to, or performed by means of an endoscope or endoscopy — **en·do·scop·i·cal·ly** \-pi-k(ə-)lē\ *adv*
en·do·skel·e·ton \ˌen-dō-ˈske-lə-tən\ *n* (ca. 1847) **:** an internal skeleton or supporting framework in an animal — **en·do·skel·e·tal** \-lə-tᵊl\ *adj*
en·do·some \ˈen-də-ˌsōm\ *n* (1887) **:** a vesicle formed by the invagination and pinching off of the cell membrane during endocytosis
en·do·sperm \ˈen-dō-ˌspərm\ *n* [F *endosperme,* fr. *end-* + Gk *sperma* seed — more at SPERM] (1819) **:** a nutritive tissue in seed plants formed within the embryo sac by division of the endosperm nucleus
endosperm nucleus *n* (ca. 1902) **:** the triploid nucleus formed in the embryo sac of a seed plant by fusion of a sperm nucleus with two polar nuclei or with a nucleus formed by the prior fusion of the polar nuclei
en·do·spore \ˈen-dō-ˌspȯr\ *n* [ISV] (1875) **:** an asexual spore developed within the cell esp. in bacteria
end·os·te·al \en-ˈdäs-tē-əl\ *adj* (ca. 1868) **1 :** of or relating to the endosteum **2 :** located within bone or cartilage — **end·os·te·al·ly** *adv*
end·os·te·um \en-ˈdäs-tē-əm\ *n, pl* **-tea** \-tē-ə\ [NL, fr. *end-* + Gk *osteon* bone — more at OSSEOUS] (ca. 1881) **:** the layer of vascular connective tissue lining the medullary cavities of bone
en·do·style \ˈen-dō-ˌstī(-ə)l\ *n* [ISV *end-* + Gk *stylos* pillar — more at STEER] (1854) **:** a pair of parallel longitudinal folds projecting into the pharyngeal cavity in lower chordates (as the tunicates) that secrete mucus for trapping food particles
en·do·sul·fan \ˌen-də-ˈsəl-fən, -ˌfan\ *n* [*endo-* + *sulf-* + ³*-an*] (1961) **:** a toxic crystalline chlorinated insecticide and acaricide $C_9H_6Cl_6O_3S$ used esp. on food crops
en·do·sym·bi·o·sis \ˌen-dō-ˌsim-bī-ˈō-səs, -bē-\ *n* (ca. 1940) **:** symbiosis in which a symbiont dwells within the body of its symbiotic partner — **en·do·sym·bi·ont** \-ˈsim-bī-ˌänt, -bē-\ *n* — **en·do·sym·bi·ot·ic** \-ˌsim-bī-ˈä-tik, -bē-\ *adj*
en·do·the·ci·um \ˌen-dō-ˈthē-sē-əm, -shē-\ *n, pl* **-cia** \-sē-ə, -shē-\ [NL] (1832) **:** the inner lining of a mature anther
en·do·the·li·o·ma \-ˌthē-lē-ˈō-mə\ *n, pl* **-mas** *or* **-ma·ta** \-mə-tə\ [NL] (1880) **:** a tumor developing from endothelial tissue
en·do·the·li·um \ˌen-də-ˈthē-lē-əm\ *n, pl* **-lia** \-lē-ə\ [NL, fr. *end-* + *-thelium* (as in *epithelium*)] (1872) **1 :** an epithelium of mesodermal origin composed of a single layer of thin flattened cells that lines internal body cavities and the lumens of vessels **2 :** the inner layer of the seed coat of some plants — **en·do·the·li·al** \-lē-əl\ *adj*
en·do·therm \ˈen-dō-ˌthərm\ *n* (1940) **:** a warm-blooded animal
en·do·ther·mic \ˌen-də-ˈthər-mik\ *adj* [ISV] (1884) **1 :** characterized by or formed with absorption of heat **2 :** WARM-BLOODED
en·do·ther·my \ˈen-də-ˌthər-mē\ *n* (1922) **:** physiological generation and regulation of body temperature by metabolic means **:** the property or state of being warm-blooded
en·do·tox·in \ˌen-dō-ˈtäk-sən\ *n* [ISV] (1904) **:** a toxic heat-stable lipopolysaccharide substance present in the outer membrane of gram-negative bacteria that is released from the cell upon lysis — **en·do·tox·ic** \-sik\ *adj*
en·do·tra·che·al \-ˈtrā-kē-əl\ *adj* (1910) **1 :** placed within the trachea ⟨an ~ tube⟩ **2 :** applied or effected through the trachea
en·do·tro·phic \ˌen-də-ˈtrō-fik\ *adj* (1899) *of a mycorrhiza* **:** penetrating into the associated root and ramifying between the cells — compare ECTOTROPHIC
en·dow \in-ˈdau̇, en-\ *vt* [ME, fr. AF *endower,* fr. *en-* + *dower, douer* to endow, fr. L *dotare,* fr. *dot-, dos* gift, dowry — more at DATE] (14c) **1 :** to furnish with an income; *esp* **:** to make a grant of money providing for the continuing support or maintenance of ⟨~ a hospital⟩ **2 :** to furnish with a dower **3 :** to provide with something freely or naturally ⟨~*ed* with a good sense of humor⟩
en·dow·ment \-mənt\ *n* (15c) **1 :** the act or process of endowing **2 :** something that is endowed; *specif* **:** the part of an institution's income derived from donations **3 :** natural capacity, power, or ability ⟨a person of great intellectual ~⟩
end·pa·per \ˈen(d)-ˌpā-pər\ *n* (1818) **:** a once-folded sheet of paper having one leaf pasted flat against the inside of the front or back cover of a book and the other pasted at the base to the first or last page
end plate *n* (1878) **:** a complex terminal treelike branching of the axon of a motor neuron that contacts with a muscle fiber
end point *n* (1899) **1 :** a point marking the completion of a process or stage of a process; *esp* **:** a point in a titration at which a definite effect (as a color change) is observed **2** *usu* **end·point :** either of two points or values that mark the ends of a line segment or interval; *also* **:** a point that marks the end of a ray
en·drin \ˈen-drən\ *n* [*end-* + diel*drin*] (1952) **:** a toxic chlorinated compound $C_{12}H_8Cl_6O$ that is a stereoisomer of dieldrin used esp. formerly as an insecticide
end run *n* (1902) **1 :** a football play in which the ballcarrier attempts to run wide around the end of the line; *specif* **:** SWEEP 3e **2 :** an evasive trick or maneuver ⟨made an *end run* around the regulations⟩
end–run *vt* (1952) **:** to avoid artfully ⟨*end-running* the law⟩
end–stage \ˈend-ˌstāj\ *adj* (1977) **:** being or occurring in the final stages of a terminal disease or condition ⟨~ renal disease⟩
end–stopped \ˈen(d)-ˌstäpt\ *adj* (1877) **:** marked by a logical or rhetorical pause at the end ⟨an ~ line of verse⟩ — compare RUN-ON
end table *n* (1851) **:** a small table usu. about the height of the arm of a chair that is used beside a larger piece of furniture (as a sofa)
end–time \ˈend-ˌtīm\ *n, often attrib* (1917) **:** the time of the prophesied end of the world **:** ARMAGEDDON
en·due \in-ˈdü, -ˈdyü, en-\ *or* **in·due** \in-\ *vt* **en·dued** *or* **in·dued; en·du·ing** *or* **in·du·ing** [ME, fr. AF *enduire* to introduce, imbue, fr. L *inducere* — more at INDUCE] (15c) **1 :** PROVIDE, ENDOW ⟨*endued* with the rights of a citizen⟩ **2 :** IMBUE, TRANSFUSE ⟨a mummy again *endued* with animation —Mary W. Shelley⟩ **3** [ME *induen;* influenced by L *induere* to put on] **:** PUT ON, DON
en·dur·able \in-ˈdu̇r-ə-bəl, -ˈdyu̇r-, en-\ *adj* (1796) **:** capable of being endured **:** BEARABLE — **en·dur·ably** \-blē\ *adv*
en·dur·ance \in-ˈdu̇r-ən(t)s, -ˈdyu̇r-, en-\ *n* (15c) **1 :** PERMANENCE, DURATION ⟨the ~ of the play's importance⟩ **2 :** the ability to withstand hardship or adversity; *esp* **:** the ability to sustain a prolonged stressful effort or activity ⟨a marathon runner's ~⟩ **3 :** the act or an instance of enduring or suffering ⟨~ of many hardships⟩

en·dure \in-ˈdu̇r, -ˈdyu̇r, en-\ *vb* **en·dured; en·dur·ing** [ME, fr. AF *endurer,* fr. VL **indurare,* fr. L, to harden, fr. *in-* + *durare* to harden, endure — more at DURING] *vt* (14c) **1 :** to undergo (as a hardship) esp. without giving in **:** SUFFER ⟨*endured* great pain⟩ **2 :** to regard with acceptance or tolerance ⟨could not ~ noisy children⟩ ~ *vi* **1 :** to continue in the same state **:** LAST ⟨the style *endured* for centuries⟩ **2 :** to remain firm under suffering or misfortune without yielding ⟨though it is difficult, we must ~⟩ ***syn*** see BEAR, CONTINUE

enduring *adj* (15c) **:** LASTING, DURABLE ⟨an ~ truth⟩ — **en·dur·ing·ly** *adv* — **en·dur·ing·ness** *n*

en·duro \in-ˈdu̇r-(ˌ)ō, -ˈdyu̇r-\ *n, pl* **en·dur·os** [*endur*ance + *-o* (It or Sp masc. n. ending)] (1935) **:** a long race (as for automobiles or motorcycles) stressing endurance rather than speed

end user *n* (ca. 1945) **:** the ultimate consumer of a finished product

end·ways \ˈend-ˌwāz\ *adv or adj* (ca. 1608) **1 :** in or toward the direction of the ends **:** LENGTHWISE ⟨~ pressure⟩ **2 :** with the end forward (as toward the observer) **3 :** on end **:** UPRIGHT ⟨boxes set ~⟩

end·wise \ˈend-ˌwīz\ *adv or adj* (1655) **:** ENDWAYS

En·dym·i·on \en-ˈdi-mē-ən\ *n* [L, fr. Gk *Endymiōn*] (1567) **:** a beautiful youth loved by Selene in Greek mythology

end zone *n* (ca. 1916) **:** the area at either end of a football field between the goal line and the end line

ENE *abbr* east-northeast

-ene *suffix* [ISV, fr. Gk *-ēnē,* fem. of *-ēnos,* adj. suffix] **:** unsaturated carbon compound ⟨benz*ene*⟩; *esp* **:** carbon compound with one double bond ⟨ethyl*ene*⟩

en·e·ma \ˈe-nə-mə\ *n, pl* **enemas** *also* **ene·ma·ta** \ˌe-nə-ˈmä-tə, ˈe-nə-mə-tə\ [LL, fr. Gk, fr. *enienai* to inject, fr. *en-* + *hienai* to send — more at JET] (15c) **1 :** the injection of liquid into the rectum and colon by way of the anus **2 :** material for injection as an enema

en·e·my \ˈe-nə-mē\ *n, pl* **-mies** [ME *enemi,* fr. AF, fr. L *inimicus,* fr. *in-* [1]in- + *amicus* friend — more at AMIABLE] (13c) **1 :** one that is antagonistic to another; *esp* **:** one seeking to injure, overthrow, or confound an opponent **2 :** something harmful or deadly ⟨alcohol was his greatest ~⟩ **3 a :** a military adversary **b :** a hostile unit or force

en·er·get·ic \ˌe-nər-ˈje-tik\ *adj* [Gk *energētikos,* fr. *energein* to be active, fr. *energos*] (1651) **1 :** operating with or marked by vigor or effect **2 :** marked by energy **:** STRENUOUS ⟨an ~ walk⟩ **3 :** of or relating to energy ***syn*** see VIGOROUS — **en·er·get·i·cal·ly** \-ti-k(ə-)lē\ *adv*

en·er·get·ics \-tiks\ *n pl but sing in constr* (1855) **1 :** a branch of mechanics that deals primarily with energy and its transformations **2 :** the total energy relations and transformations of a physical, chemical, or biological system ⟨the ~ of an ecological community⟩

en·er·gise *Brit var of* ENERGIZE

en·er·gize \ˈe-nər-ˌjīz\ *vb* **-gized; -giz·ing** *vt* (1750) **1 :** to make energetic, vigorous, or active ⟨*energized* by the coach's pep talk⟩ **2 :** to impart energy to ⟨sunlight ~*s* the chemical reactions⟩ **3 :** to apply voltage to ~ *vi* **:** to put forth energy **:** ACT — **en·er·gi·za·tion** \ˌe-nər-jī-ˈzā-shən\ *n* — **en·er·giz·er** *n*

en·er·gy \ˈe-nər-jē\ *n, pl* **-gies** [LL *energia,* fr. Gk *energeia* activity, fr. *energos* active, fr. *en* in + *ergon* work — more at WORK] (1599) **1 a :** dynamic quality ⟨narrative ~⟩ **b :** the capacity of acting or being active ⟨intellectual ~⟩ **c :** a usu. positive spiritual force ⟨the ~ flowing through all people⟩ **2 :** vigorous exertion of power **:** EFFORT ⟨investing time and ~⟩ **3 :** a fundamental entity of nature that is transferred between parts of a system in the production of physical change within the system and usu. regarded as the capacity for doing work **4 :** usable power (as heat or electricity); *also* **:** the resources for producing such power ***syn*** see POWER

energy drink *n* (1904) **:** a usu. carbonated beverage that typically contains caffeine and other ingredients (as taurine and ginseng) intended to increase the drinker's energy

energy level *n* (1910) **:** one of the stable states of constant energy that may be assumed by a physical system — used esp. of the quantum states of electrons in atoms and of nuclei; called also *energy state*

[1]ener·vate \i-ˈnər-vət\ *adj* (1603) **:** lacking physical, mental, or moral vigor **:** ENERVATED

[2]en·er·vate \ˈe-nər-ˌvāt\ *vt* **-vat·ed; -vat·ing** [L *enervatus,* pp. of *enervare,* fr. *e-* + *nervus* sinew — more at NERVE] (1605) **1 :** to reduce the mental or moral vigor of **2 :** to lessen the vitality or strength of ***syn*** see UNNERVE — **en·er·vat·ing·ly** \-ˌvā-tiŋ-lē\ *adv* — **en·er·va·tion** \ˌe-nər-ˈvā-shən\ *n*

en·fant ter·ri·ble \äⁿ-fäⁿ-te-ˈrēblᵊ\ *n, pl* **enfants terribles** *same*\ [F, lit., terrifying child] (1851) **1 a :** a child whose inopportune remarks cause embarrassment **b :** a person known for shocking remarks or outrageous behavior **2 :** a usu. young and successful person who is strikingly unorthodox, innovative, or avant-garde

en·fee·ble \in-ˈfē-bəl, en-\ *vt* **en·fee·bled; en·fee·bling** \-b(ə-)liŋ\ [ME *enfeblen,* fr. AF *enfebler, enfeblir,* fr. *en-* + *feble* feeble] (14c) **:** to make feeble **:** deprive of strength ***syn*** see WEAKEN — **en·fee·ble·ment** \-bəl-mənt\ *n*

en·feoff \in-ˈfef, -ˈfēf, en-\ *vt* [ME *enfeoffen,* fr. AF *enfeffer, enfeoffer,* fr. *en-* + *fé, fief* fief] (15c) **:** to invest with a fief or fee — **en·feoff·ment** \-mənt\ *n*

en·fet·ter \in-ˈfe-tər, en-\ *vt* (1599) **:** to bind in fetters **:** ENCHAIN

En·field rifle \ˈen-ˌfēld-\ *n* [*Enfield,* England] (1854) **:** a .30 caliber bolt-action repeating rifle used by U.S. and British troops in World War I

[1]en·fi·lade \ˈen-fə-ˌlād, -ˌläd\ *n* [F, fr. *enfiler* to thread, enfilade, fr. OF, to thread, fr. *en-* + *fil* thread — more at FILE] (ca. 1730) **1 :** an interconnected group of rooms arranged usu. in a row with each room opening into the next **2 :** gunfire directed from a flanking position along the length of an enemy battle line

[2]enfilade *vt* **-lad·ed; -lad·ing** (1706) **:** to rake or be in a position to rake with gunfire in a lengthwise direction

enflame *var of* INFLAME

en·fleu·rage \ˌäⁿ-ˌflər-ˈäzh\ *n* [F, fr. *enfleurer* to saturate with the perfume of flowers, fr. *en-* [1]en- + *fleur* flower, fr. OF *flor* — more at FLOWER] (1855) **:** a process of extracting perfumes by exposing absorbents to the exhalations of flowers

en·fold \in-ˈfōld, en-\ *vt* (1566) **1 a :** to cover with or as if with folds **:** ENVELOP **b :** to surround with a covering **:** CONTAIN **2 :** to clasp within the arms **:** EMBRACE

en·force \in-ˈfȯrs, en-\ *vt* [ME, fr. AF *enforcer,* fr. *en-* + *force* force] (14c) **1 :** to give force to **:** STRENGTHEN **2 :** to urge with energy ⟨~ arguments⟩ **3 :** CONSTRAIN, COMPEL ⟨~ obedience⟩ **4** *obs* **:** to effect or gain by force **5 :** to carry out effectively ⟨~ laws⟩ — **en·force·abil·i·ty** \-ˌfȯr-sə-ˈbi-lə-tē\ *n* — **en·force·able** \-ˈfȯr-sə-bəl\ *adj* — **en·force·ment** \-ˈfȯr-smənt\ *n*

en·forc·er \in-ˈfȯr-sər\ *n* (1580) **1 :** one that enforces **2 a :** a violent criminal employed by a crime syndicate; *esp* **:** HIT MAN 1 **b :** player (as in ice hockey) known for rough play and fighting

en·frame \in-ˈfrām\ *vt* (1615) **:** FRAME 6 — **en·frame·ment** \-ˈfrām-mənt\ *n*

en·fran·chise \in-ˈfran-ˌchīz, en-\ *vt* **-chised; -chis·ing** [ME, fr. AF *enfranchiss-,* stem of *enfranchir,* fr. *en-* + *franc* free — more at FRANK] (15c) **1 :** to set free (as from slavery) **2 :** to endow with a franchise: as **a :** to admit to the privileges of a citizen and esp. to the right of suffrage **b :** to admit (a municipality) to political privileges or rights — **en·fran·chise·ment** \-ˌchīz-mənt, -chəz-\ *n*

eng *abbr* **1** engine **2** engineer; engineering

en·gage \in-ˈgāj, en-\ *vb* **en·gaged; en·gag·ing** [ME, fr. AF *engager,* fr. *en-* + *gage* pledge, gage] *vt* (15c) **1 :** to offer (as one's word) as security for a debt or cause **2 a** *obs* **:** to entangle or entrap in or as if in a snare or bog **b :** to attract and hold by influence or power **c :** to interlock with **:** MESH; *also* **:** to cause (mechanical parts) to mesh ⟨~ the clutch⟩ **3 :** to bind (as oneself) to do something; *esp* **:** to bind by a pledge to marry **4 a :** to provide occupation for **:** INVOLVE ⟨~ him in a new project⟩ **b :** to arrange to obtain the use or services of **:** HIRE ⟨~ a lawyer⟩ **5 a :** to hold the attention of **:** ENGROSS ⟨her work ~*s* her completely⟩ **b :** to induce to participate ⟨*engaged* the shy boy in conversation⟩ **6 a :** to enter into contest or battle with ⟨~ the enemy⟩ **b :** to bring together or interlock (weapons) **7 :** to deal with esp. at length ~ *vi* **1 a :** to pledge oneself **:** PROMISE **b :** to make a guarantee ⟨he ~*s* for the honesty of his brother⟩ **2 a :** to begin and carry on an enterprise or activity — used with *in* ⟨*engaged* in trade for many years⟩ **b :** to do or take part in something — used with *in* ⟨~ in healthy activities⟩ ⟨~ in bad conduct⟩ **c :** to give attention to something **:** DEAL ⟨failing to ~ with the problem⟩ **3 :** to enter into conflict or battle **4 :** to come together and interlock ⟨the gears *engaged*⟩

en·ga·gé \ˌäⁿ-ˌgä-ˈzhā\ *adj* [F, pp. of *engager* to engage] (1946) **:** committed to or supportive of a cause

en·gaged \in-ˈgājd, en-\ *adj* (1629) **1 :** involved in activity **:** OCCUPIED, BUSY **2 :** pledged to be married **:** BETROTHED **3 :** greatly interested **:** COMMITTED **4 :** involved esp. in a hostile encounter **5 :** partly embedded in a wall ⟨an ~ column⟩ **6 :** being in gear **:** MESHED

en·gage·ment \in-ˈgāj-mənt, en-\ *n* (1601) **1 a :** an arrangement to meet or be present at a specified time and place ⟨a dinner ~⟩ **b :** a job or period of employment esp. as a performer **2 :** something that engages **:** PLEDGE **3 a :** the act of engaging **:** the state of being engaged **b :** emotional involvement or commitment ⟨seesaws between obsessive ~ and ambiguous detachment —Gary Taylor⟩ **c :** BETROTHAL **4 :** the state of being in gear **5 :** a hostile encounter between military forces

engaging *adj* (1673) **:** tending to draw favorable attention or interest **:** ATTRACTIVE ⟨an ~ smile⟩ — **en·gag·ing·ly** \-ˈgā-jiŋ-lē\ *adv*

En·gel·mann spruce \ˌeŋ-gəl-mən-\ *n* [George *Engelmann* †1884 Am. botanist] (1866) **:** a large spruce (*Picea engelmannii*) of the Rocky mountain region and British Columbia that yields a light-colored wood

en·gen·der \in-ˈjen-dər, en-\ *vb* **en·gen·dered; en·gen·der·ing** \-d(ə-)riŋ\ [ME *engendren,* fr. AF *engendrer,* fr. L *ingenerare,* fr. *in-* + *generare* to generate] *vt* (14c) **1 :** BEGET, PROCREATE **2 :** to cause to exist or to develop **:** PRODUCE ⟨policies that have ~*ed* controversy⟩ ~ *vi* **:** to assume form **:** ORIGINATE

en·gild \in-ˈgild, en-\ *vt* (15c) **:** to make bright with or as if with light

[1]en·gine \ˈen-jən\ *n* [ME *engin,* fr. AF, fr. L *ingenium* natural disposition, talent, fr. *in-* + *gignere* to beget — more at KIN] (13c) **1** *obs* **a :** INGENUITY **b :** evil contrivance **:** WILE **2 a :** something used to effect a purpose **:** AGENT, INSTRUMENT ⟨mournful and terrible ~ of horror and of crime —E. A. Poe⟩ **b :** something that produces a particular and usu. desirable result ⟨~*s* of economic growth⟩ **3 a :** a mechanical tool: as (1) **:** an instrument or machine of war (2) *obs* **:** a torture implement **b :** MACHINERY **c :** any of various mechanical appliances — often used in combination ⟨fire ~⟩ **4 :** a machine for converting any of various forms of energy into mechanical force and motion; *also* **:** a mechanism or object that serves as an energy source ⟨black holes may be the ~*s* for quasars⟩ **5 :** a railroad locomotive **6 :** computer software that performs a fundamental function esp. of a larger program — **en·gine·less** *adj*

[2]engine *vt* **en·gined; en·gin·ing** (1868) **:** to equip with engines

[1]en·gi·neer \ˌen-jə-ˈnir\ *n* [ME *engineour,* fr. AF, fr. *enginer* to devise, construct, fr. *engin*] (14c) **1 :** a member of a military group devoted to engineering work **2** *obs* **:** a crafty schemer **:** PLOTTER **3 a :** a designer or builder of engines **b :** a person who is trained in or follows as a profession a branch of engineering **c :** a person who carries through an enterprise by skillful or artful contrivance **4 :** a person who runs or supervises an engine or an apparatus

[2]engineer *vt* (1843) **1 :** to lay out, construct, or manage as an engineer ⟨~ a bridge⟩ **2 a :** to contrive or plan out usu. with more or less subtle skill and craft ⟨~ a business deal⟩ **b :** to guide the course of ⟨~ a rally⟩ **3 :** to modify or produce by genetic engineering ⟨corn ~*ed* to resist crop pests⟩ ***syn*** see GUIDE

en·gi·neer·ing \-ˈnir-iŋ\ *n* (1720) **1 :** the activities or function of an engineer **2 a :** the application of science and mathematics by which the properties of matter and the sources of energy in nature are made useful to people **b :** the design and manufacture of complex products ⟨software ~⟩ **3 :** calculated manipulation or direction (as of behavior) ⟨social ~⟩ — compare GENETIC ENGINEERING

en·gine·ry \ˈen-jən-rē\ *n* (1641) **:** instruments of war

en·gird \in-ˈgərd, en-\ *vt* (1566) *archaic* **:** GIRD, ENCOMPASS

en·gir·dle \in-ˈgər-dᵊl, en-\ *vt* (1596) **:** GIRDLE 1

\ə\ **abut** \ᵊ\ kitten, F table \ər\ **fur**ther \a\ **ash** \ā\ **ace** \ä\ **mop, mar** \au̇\ **out** \ch\ **ch**in \e\ **bet** \ē\ **easy** \g\ **go** \i\ **hit** \ī\ **ice** \j\ **job** \ŋ\ **sing** \ō\ **go** \ȯ\ **law** \ȯi\ **boy** \th\ **th**in \t͟h\ **the** \ü\ **loot** \u̇\ **foot** \y\ **y**et \zh\ **vision, beige** \k̟, ⁿ, œ, ue, ʸ\ *see* Guide to Pronunciation

[1]**En·glish** \ˈiŋ-glish, ˈiŋ-lish\ *adj* [ME, fr. OE *englisc,* fr. *Engle* (pl.) Angles] (bef. 12c) **:** of, relating to, or characteristic of England, the English people, or the English language — **En·glish·ness** *n*

[2]**English** *n* (bef. 12c) **1 a :** the language of the people of England and the U.S. and many areas now or formerly under British control **b :** a particular variety of English distinguished by peculiarities (as of pronunciation) **c :** English language, literature, or composition when a subject of study **2** *pl in constr* **:** the people of England **3 a :** an English translation **b :** idiomatic or intelligible English **4 :** spin around the vertical axis deliberately imparted to a ball that is driven or rolled — compare DRAW, FOLLOW, BODY ENGLISH

[3]**English** *vt* (14c) **1 :** to translate into English **2 :** to adopt into English **:** ANGLICIZE

English breakfast *n* (1807) **1 :** a substantial breakfast (as of eggs, ham or bacon, toast, and cereal) **2 :** CONGOU; *broadly* **:** any similar black tea

English cocker spaniel *n* (1948) **:** any of a breed of active friendly spaniels that have square muzzles, wide noses, and heads which are typically half muzzle and half skull with the forehead and skull arched and slightly flattened

English daisy *n* (1852) **:** DAISY 1a

English foxhound *n* (1845) **:** any of a breed of medium-sized foxhounds developed in England and characterized by a muscular body, bi- or tri-colored short coat, and lightly fringed tail

English holly *n* (1865) **:** a Eurasian holly (*Ilex aquifolium*) with glossy green leaves and persistent red berries that is widely planted in the U.S.

English horn *n* [trans. of It *corno inglese*] (1838) **:** a double-reed woodwind instrument resembling the oboe in design but having a longer tube and a range a fifth lower than that of the oboe

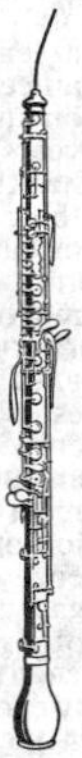
English horn

English ivy *n* (1624) **:** IVY 1

En·glish·man \ˈiŋ-glish-mən, ˈiŋ-lish-\ *n* (bef. 12c) **:** a native or inhabitant of England

English muffin *n* (1884) **:** bread dough rolled and cut into rounds, baked on a griddle, and split and toasted just before eating

English pea *n* (1634) *Southern* **:** PEA 1a, b

En·glish·ry \ˈiŋ-glish-rē, ˈiŋ-lish-\ *n* (1620) **:** the state, fact, or quality of being English **:** ENGLISHNESS

English saddle *n* (1739) **:** a saddle with long side bars, steel cantle and pommel, no horn, and a leather seat supported by webbing stretched between the saddlebow and cantle

English setter *n* (1845) **:** any of a breed of dogs often trained as bird dogs and characterized by a moderately long flat silky coat of white or white with color and by feathering on the tail and legs

English shepherd *n* (1950) **:** any of a breed of vigorous medium-sized working dogs with a long and glossy black coat usu. with tan to brown markings that was developed in England for herding sheep and cattle

English sonnet *n* (1890) **:** a sonnet consisting of three quatrains and a couplet with a rhyme scheme of *abab cdcd efef gg* — called also *Shakespearean sonnet*

English sparrow *n* (1876) **:** HOUSE SPARROW

English springer spaniel *n* (1929) **:** any of a breed of springer spaniels having a muscular build and a moderately long silky coat usu. of black-and-white or liver and white hair — called also *English springer*

English system *n* (1821) **:** the foot-pound-second system of units

English toy spaniel *n* (ca. 1934) **:** any of a breed of small blocky spaniels with well-rounded upper skull projecting forward toward the short turned-up nose

English walnut *n* (1760) **:** a Eurasian walnut (*Juglans regia*) with large edible nuts and hard richly figured wood; *also* **:** its nut or wood

En·glish·wom·an \ˈiŋ-glish-ˌwu̇-mən *also* ˈiŋ-lish-\ *n* (15c) **:** a woman of English birth, nationality, or origin

English yew *n* (1615) **:** YEW 1a(1)

en·gorge \in-ˈgȯrj, en-\ *vb* [MF *engorgier,* fr. OF, to devour, fr. *en-* + *gorge* throat — more at GORGE] *vt* (1515) **:** GORGE, GLUT; *esp* **:** to fill with blood to the point of congestion ~ *vi* **:** to suck blood to the limit of body capacity — **en·gorge·ment** \-mənt\ *n*

engr *abbr* **1** engineer **2** engraved; engraver; engraving

en·graft \in-ˈgraft, en-\ *vt* (1549) **1 :** to join or fasten as if by grafting **2 :** GRAFT 1 **3 :** GRAFT 3 ~ *vi* **1 :** to become grafted and begin functioning normally ⟨the transplanted bone marrow ~*ed* successfully⟩ — **en·graft·ment** \-ˈgraf(t)-mənt\ *n*

en·grailed \in-ˈgrāld, en-\ *adj* [ME *engreled,* fr. AF *engreslé,* lit., reduced, thinned, fr. *en-* + *gresle* slender, fr. L *gracilis*] (15c) **1 :** indented with small concave curves ⟨an ~ heraldic bordure⟩ **2 :** made of or bordered by a circle of raised dots ⟨an ~ coin⟩

engrain, engrained *var of* INGRAIN, INGRAINED

en·gram *also* **en·gramme** \ˈen-ˌgram\ *n* [ISV] (1908) **:** a hypothetical change in neural tissue postulated in order to account for persistence of memory

en·grave \in-ˈgrāv, en-\ *vt* **en·graved; en·grav·ing** [MF *engraver,* fr. *en-* + *graver* to grave, of Gmc origin; akin to OE *grafan* to grave] (1509) **1 a :** to impress deeply as if with a graver ⟨the incident was *engraved* in his memory⟩ **b :** to form by incision (as on wood or metal) **2 a :** to cut figures, letters, or designs on for printing; *also* **:** to print from an engraved plate ⟨an *engraved* invitation⟩ **b :** PHOTOENGRAVE — **en·grav·er** *n*

engraving *n* (1599) **1 :** the act or process of one that engraves **2 :** something that is engraved: as **a :** an engraved printing surface **b :** engraved work **3 :** an impression from an engraved printing surface

en·gross \in-ˈgrōs, en-\ *vt* [ME, fr. AF *engrosser* to put (a legal document) in final form, fr. ML *ingrossare,* fr. *in grossam* (put) into final form, lit., (written) in large (letter)] (15c) **1 a :** to copy or write in a large hand **b :** to prepare the usu. final handwritten or printed text of (an official document) **2** [ME, fr. AF *engrosser,* fr. *en gros* wholesale, in quantity] **a :** to purchase large quantities of (as for speculation) **b** *archaic* **:** AMASS, COLLECT **c :** to take or engage the whole attention of **:** occupy completely ⟨ideas that have ~*ed* the minds of scholars for generations⟩ — **en·gross·er** *n*

en·gross·ing \-ˈgrō-siŋ\ *adj* (1749) **:** taking up the attention completely **:** ABSORBING — **en·gross·ing·ly** \-siŋ-lē\ *adv*

en·gross·ment \in-ˈgrō-smənt, en-\ *n* (1526) **1 :** the act of engrossing **2 :** the state of being absorbed or occupied **:** PREOCCUPATION

en·gulf \in-ˈgəlf, en-\ *vt* (1555) **1 :** to flow over and enclose **:** OVERWHELM ⟨the mounting seas threatened to ~ the island⟩ **2 :** to take in (food) by or as if by flowing over and enclosing — **en·gulf·ment** \-mənt\ *n*

en·ha·lo \in-ˈhā-(ˌ)lō, en-\ *vt* (1842) **:** to surround with or as if with a halo ⟨a figure ~*ed* with misty light⟩

en·hance \in-ˈhan(t)s, en-\ *vt* **en·hanced; en·hanc·ing** [ME *enhauncen,* fr. AF *enhaucer, enhauncer,* fr. VL **inaltiare,* fr. L *in* + *altus* high — more at OLD] (13c) **1** *obs* **:** RAISE **2 :** HEIGHTEN, INCREASE; *esp* **:** to increase or improve in value, quality, desirability, or attractiveness ⟨*enhanced* the room with crown molding⟩ — **en·hance·ment** \-ˈhan(t)-smənt\ *n*

enhanced recovery *n* (1970) **:** the extraction of oil from a nearly exhausted well by methods more costly and complex than waterflooding alone

en·hanc·er \in-ˈhan(t)-sər, en-\ *n* (14c) **1 :** one that enhances **2 :** a nucleotide sequence that increases the rate of genetic transcription by preferentially increasing the activity of the nearest promoter on the same DNA molecule

en·har·mon·ic \ˌen-(ˌ)här-ˈmä-nik\ *adj* [F *enharmonique,* fr. MF, of a scale employing quarter tones, fr. Gk *enarmonios,* fr. *en* in + *harmonia* harmony, scale] (1794) **:** of, relating to, or being notes that are written differently (as A flat and G sharp) but sound the same in the tempered scale — **en·har·mon·i·cal·ly** \-ni-k(ə-)lē\ *adv*

enig·ma \i-ˈnig-mə, e-\ *n* [L *aenigma,* fr. Gk *ainigmat-, ainigma,* fr. *ainissesthai* to speak in riddles, fr. *ainos* fable] (1539) **1 :** an obscure speech or writing **2 :** something hard to understand or explain **3 :** an inscrutable or mysterious person ***syn*** see MYSTERY

enig·mat·ic \ˌe-(ˌ)nig-ˈma-tik *also* ˌē-(ˌ)nig-\ *also* **enig·mat·i·cal** \-ti-kəl\ *adj* (1609) **:** of, relating to, or resembling an enigma **:** MYSTERIOUS ***syn*** see OBSCURE — **enig·mat·i·cal·ly** \-ti-k(ə-)lē\ *adv*

en·isle \in-ˈī(-ə)l, en-\ *vt* (1612) **1 :** to place apart **:** ISOLATE **2 :** to make an island of

en·jamb·ment \in-ˈjam-mənt\ *also* **en·jambe·ment** *same or* ä^{n}-zhä^{n}b-ˈmä^{n}\ *n* [F *enjambement,* fr. MF, encroachment, fr. *enjamber* to straddle, encroach on, fr. *en-* + *jambe* leg — more at JAMB] (ca. 1839) **:** the running over of a sentence from one verse or couplet into another so that closely related words fall in different lines — compare RUN-ON

en·join \in-ˈjȯin, en-\ *vt* [ME, fr. AF *enjoindre,* fr. L *injungere,* fr. *in-* + *jungere* to join — more at YOKE] (13c) **1 :** to direct or impose by authoritative order or with urgent admonition ⟨~*ed* us to be careful⟩ **2 a :** FORBID, PROHIBIT ⟨was ~*ed* by conscience from telling a lie⟩ **b :** to prohibit by a judicial order **:** put an injunction on ⟨a book had been ~*ed* prior to publication —David Margolick⟩ ***syn*** see COMMAND

en·joy \in-ˈjȯi, en-\ *vb* [ME *enjoien,* fr. AF *enjoir, enjoier* to gladden, enjoy, fr. *en-* + *joie* joy] *vi* (15c) **:** to have a good time ~ *vt* **1 :** to have for one's use, benefit, or lot **:** EXPERIENCE ⟨~*ed* great success⟩ **2 :** to take pleasure or satisfaction in — **en·joy·able** \-ə-bəl\ *adj* — **en·joy·able·ness** *n* — **en·joy·ably** \-blē\ *adv* — **en·joy·er** *n* — **enjoy oneself :** to have a good time

en·joy·ment \in-ˈjȯi-mənt\ *n* (1553) **1 a :** the action or state of enjoying **b :** possession and use ⟨the ~ of civic rights⟩ **2 :** something that gives keen satisfaction ⟨the poorest life has its ~*s* and pleasures⟩

en·keph·a·lin \in-ˈke-fə-lən, -(ˌ)lin, en-\ *n* [*enkephal-* (alter. of *encephal-*) + *-in*] (1975) **:** either of two pentapeptides with opiate and analgesic activity that occur naturally esp. in the brain and have a marked affinity for opiate receptors — compare ENDORPHIN

en·kin·dle \in-ˈkin-d^{ə}l, en-\ *vt* (1542) **1 :** to set (as fuel) on fire **2 :** to make bright and glowing ~ *vi* **:** to take fire **:** FLAME

enl *abbr* **1** enlarged **2** enlisted

en·lace \in-ˈlās, en-\ *vt* [ME, fr. AF *enlacer* to ensnare, fr. *en-* + *lace* lace] (14c) **1 :** ENCIRCLE, ENFOLD **2 :** ENTWINE, INTERLACE

en·lace·ment \in-ˈlā-smənt, en-\ *n* (1830) **1 :** the process or result of interlacing **2 :** a pattern of interlacing elements

en·large \in-ˈlärj, en-\ *vb* **en·larged; en·larg·ing** [ME, fr. AF *enlarger, enlargir,* fr. *en-* + *large* broad, large] *vt* (14c) **1 :** to make larger **:** EXTEND ⟨*enlarged* the family fortune with new investments⟩ **2 :** to give greater scope to **:** EXPAND ⟨education may ~ one's view of the world⟩ **3 :** to set free (as a captive) ~ *vi* **1 :** to grow larger **2 :** to speak or write at length **:** ELABORATE ⟨let me ~ upon that point⟩ ***syn*** see INCREASE — **en·large·able** \-ˈlär-jə-bəl\ *adj* — **en·larg·er** *n*

en·large·ment \in-ˈlärj-mənt, en-\ *n* (1540) **1 :** an act or instance of enlarging **:** the state of being enlarged **2 :** a photographic print larger than the negative that is made by projecting the negative image through a lens onto a photographic printing surface

en·light·en \in-ˈlī-t^{ə}n, en-\ *vt* **en·light·ened; en·light·en·ing** \-ˈlīt-niŋ, -t^{ə}n-iŋ\ (1587) **1** *archaic* **:** ILLUMINATE **2 a :** to furnish knowledge to **:** INSTRUCT ⟨~*ed* us about the problem⟩ **b :** to give spiritual insight to

enlightened *adj* (1652) **1 :** freed from ignorance and misinformation ⟨an ~ people⟩ ⟨an ~ time⟩ **2 :** based on full comprehension of the problems involved ⟨issued an ~ ruling⟩

en·light·en·ment \in-ˈlī-t^{ə}n-mənt, en-\ *n* (1654) **1 :** the act or means of enlightening **:** the state of being enlightened **2** *cap* **:** a philosophic movement of the 18th century marked by a rejection of traditional social, religious, and political ideas and an emphasis on rationalism — used with *the* **3** *Buddhism* **:** a final blessed state marked by the absence of desire or suffering

en·list \in-ˈlist, en-\ *vt* (1599) **1 a :** to secure the support and aid of **:** employ in advancing an interest ⟨~ all the available resources⟩ ⟨~*ed* our help⟩ **b :** to win over **:** ATTRACT ⟨trying to ~ my sympathies⟩ **2 :** to engage (a person) for duty in the armed forces ~ *vi* **1 :** to enroll oneself in the armed forces ⟨will ~ for three years⟩ **2 :** to participate heartily (as in a cause, drive, or crusade) — **en·list·ee** \-ˌlis-ˈtē, -ˈlis-tē\ *n* — **en·list·ment** \-ˈlis(t)-mənt\ *n*

en·list·ed \-ˈlis-təd\ *adj* (1724) **:** of, relating to, or constituting the part of a military or naval force below commissioned or warrant officers

enlisted man *n* (1724) **:** a man or woman in the armed forces ranking below a commissioned or warrant officer; *specif* **:** one ranking below a noncommissioned officer or petty officer

en·liv·en \in-ˈlī-vən, en-\ *vt* (1604) **:** to give life, action, or spirit to **:** ANIMATE ⟨fresh flowers ~ the room⟩ ***syn*** see QUICKEN

en masse \ä^{n}(n)-ˈmas, -ˈmäs, en-\ *adv* [F] (1795) **:** in a body **:** as a whole ⟨moved the inmates *en masse* to the new prison⟩

en·mesh \in-ˈmesh, en-\ *also* **im·mesh** \i(m)-\ *vt* (1604) **:** to catch or entangle in or as if in meshes ⟨deeply ~*ed* in the plot⟩ — **en·mesh·ment** \-mənt\ *n*

en·mi·ty \ˈen-mə-tē\ *n, pl* **-ties** [ME *enmite,* fr. AF *enemité, enemisté,* fr. *enemi* enemy] (13c) **:** positive, active, and typically mutual hatred or ill will

syn ENMITY, HOSTILITY, ANTIPATHY, ANTAGONISM, ANIMOSITY, RANCOR, ANIMUS mean deep-seated dislike or ill will. ENMITY suggests positive hatred which may be open or concealed ⟨an unspoken *enmity*⟩. HOSTILITY suggests an enmity showing itself in attacks or aggression ⟨*hostility* between the two nations⟩. ANTIPATHY and ANTAGONISM imply a natural or logical basis for one's hatred or dislike, ANTIPATHY suggesting repugnance, a desire to avoid or reject, and ANTAGONISM suggesting a clash of temperaments leading readily to hostility ⟨a natural *antipathy* for self-seekers⟩ ⟨*antagonism* between the brothers⟩. ANIMOSITY suggests intense ill will and vindictiveness that threaten to kindle hostility ⟨*animosity* that led to revenge⟩. RANCOR is esp. applied to bitter brooding over a wrong ⟨*rancor* filled every line of his letters⟩. ANIMUS adds to animosity the implication of strong prejudice ⟨objections devoid of personal *animus*⟩.

en·ne·ad \ˈe-nē-ˌad\ *n* [Gk *ennead-, enneas,* fr. *ennea* nine — more at NINE] (1550) **:** a group of nine

en·no·ble \i-ˈnō-bəl, e-ˈnō-\ *vt* **en·no·bled; en·no·bling** \-b(ə-)liŋ\ [ME *ennobelen,* fr. MF *ennoblir,* fr. OF, fr. *en-* + *noble* noble] (15c) **1 :** to make noble **:** ELEVATE ⟨seemed *ennobled* by suffering⟩ **2 :** to raise to the rank of nobility — **en·no·ble·ment** \-bəl-mənt\ *n*

en·nui \ˌän-ˈwē\ *n* [F, fr. OF *enui* annoyance, fr. *enuier* to vex, fr. LL *inodiare* to make loathsome — more at ANNOY] (1732) **:** a feeling of weariness and dissatisfaction **:** BOREDOM

Enoch \ˈē-nək, -nik\ *n* [Gk *Enōch,* fr. Heb *Ḥănōkh*] (bef. 12c) **:** an Old Testament patriarch and father of Methuselah

eno·ki·da·ke \e-ˌnō-kē-ˈdä-kē\ *n* [Jp *enokitake,* fr. *enoki* Chinese hackberry (*Celtis sinensis*) + *take* mushroom] (ca. 1977) **:** ENOKI MUSHROOM

eno·ki mushroom \e-ˈnō-kē-\ *n* [Jp *enoki*] (1979) **:** a whitish cultivated agaric mushroom (*Flammulina velutipes* syn. *Collybia velutipes*) with a long thin stem and a small cap — called also *enoki*

enol \ˈē-ˌnȯl, -ˌnōl\ *n* [ISV *en-* (fr. *-ene*) + *-ol*] (1904) **:** an organic compound that contains a hydroxyl group bonded to a carbon atom having a double bond and that is usu. characterized by the grouping C=C(OH) — **eno·lic** \ē-ˈnō-lik, -ˈnä-lik\ *adj*

eno·lase \ˈē-nə-ˌlās, -ˌlāz\ *n* [ISV *enol* + *-ase*] (1937) **:** a crystalline enzyme that is found esp. in muscle and yeast and is important in the metabolism of carbohydrates

enol·o·gy *also* **oe·nol·o·gy** \ē-ˈnä-lə-jē\ *n* [Gk *oinos* wine + E *-logy* — more at WINE] (1814) **:** a science that deals with wine and wine making — **eno·log·i·cal** *also* **oe·no·log·i·cal** \ˌē-nə-ˈlä-ji-kəl\ *adj* — **enol·o·gist** *also* **oe·nol·o·gist** \ē-ˈnä-lə-jist\ *n*

enor·mi·ty \i-ˈnȯr-mə-tē\ *n, pl* **-ties** (15c) **1 :** an outrageous, improper, vicious, or immoral act ⟨the *enormities* of state power —Susan Sontag⟩ ⟨other *enormities* too juvenile to mention —Richard Freedman⟩ **2 :** the quality or state of being immoderate, monstrous, or outrageous; *esp* **:** great wickedness ⟨the ~ of the crimes committed during the Third Reich —G. A. Craig⟩ **3 :** the quality or state of being huge **:** IMMENSITY ⟨the inconceivable ~ of the universe⟩ **4 :** a quality of momentous importance or impact ⟨the ~ of the decision⟩

usage *Enormity,* some people insist, is improperly used to denote large size. They insist on *enormousness* for this meaning, and would limit *enormity* to the meaning "great wickedness." Those who urge such a limitation may not recognize the subtlety with which *enormity* is actually used. It regularly denotes a considerable departure from the expected or normal ⟨they awakened; they sat up; and then the *enormity* of their situation burst upon them. "How did the fire start?" —John Steinbeck⟩. When used to denote large size, either literal or figurative, it usu. suggests something so large as to seem overwhelming ⟨no intermediate zone of study. Either the *enormity* of the desert or the sight of a tiny flower —Paul Theroux⟩ ⟨the *enormity* of the task of teachers in slum schools —J. B. Conant⟩ and may even be used to suggest both great size and deviation from morality ⟨the *enormity* of existing stockpiles of atomic weapons —*New Republic*⟩. It can also emphasize the momentousness of what has happened ⟨the sombre *enormity* of the Russian Revolution —George Steiner⟩ or of its consequences ⟨perceived as no one in the family could the *enormity* of the misfortune —E. L. Doctorow⟩.

enor·mous \i-ˈnȯr-məs, ē-\ *adj* [L *enormis,* fr. *e, ex* out of + *norma* rule] (1531) **1 a** *archaic* **:** ABNORMAL, INORDINATE **b :** exceedingly wicked **:** SHOCKING ⟨an ~ sin⟩ **2 :** marked by extraordinarily great size, number, or degree; *esp* **:** exceeding usual bounds or accepted notions — **enor·mous·ly** *adv* — **enor·mous·ness** *n*

syn ENORMOUS, IMMENSE, HUGE, VAST, GIGANTIC, COLOSSAL, MAMMOTH mean exceedingly large. ENORMOUS and IMMENSE both suggest an exceeding of all ordinary bounds in size or amount or degree, but ENORMOUS often adds an implication of abnormality or monstrousness ⟨an *enormous* expense⟩ ⟨an *immense* shopping mall⟩. HUGE commonly suggests an immensity of bulk or amount ⟨incurred a *huge* debt⟩. VAST usu. suggests immensity of extent ⟨the *vast* Russian steppes⟩. GIGANTIC stresses the contrast with the size of others of the same kind ⟨a *gigantic* sports stadium⟩. COLOSSAL applies esp. to a human creation of stupendous or incredible dimensions ⟨a *colossal* statue of Lincoln⟩. MAMMOTH suggests both hugeness and ponderousness of bulk ⟨a *mammoth* boulder⟩.

eno·sis \i-ˈnō-səs\ *n* [ModGk *enōsis,* fr. Gk *henōsis* union, fr. *henoun* to unite, fr. *hen-, heis* one — more at SAME] (1928) **:** a movement to secure the political union of Greece and Cyprus

[1]**enough** \i-ˈnəf, ē-, ə-\ *adj* [ME *ynough,* fr. OE *genōg* (akin to OHG *ginuog* enough), fr. *ge-* (perfective prefix) + *-nōg;* akin to L *nancisci* to get, Gk *enenkein* to carry — more at CO-] (bef. 12c) **:** occurring in such quantity, quality, or scope as to fully meet demands, needs, or expectations ⟨~ food for everyone⟩ ***syn*** see SUFFICIENT

[2]**enough** *adv* (bef. 12c) **1 :** in or to a degree or quantity that satisfies or that is sufficient or necessary for satisfaction **:** SUFFICIENTLY **2 :** FULLY, QUITE ⟨he is qualified ~ for the position⟩ **3 :** in a tolerable degree ⟨she sang well ~⟩

[3]**enough** *pron* (bef. 12c) **:** a sufficient number, quantity, or amount ⟨~ were present to constitute a quorum⟩ ⟨had ~ of their foolishness⟩ — often used interjectionally

enounce \ē-ˈnau̇n(t)s\ *vt* **enounced; enounc·ing** [F *énoncer,* fr. L *enuntiare* to report — more at ENUNCIATE] (1788) **1 :** to set forth or state (as a proposition) **2 :** to pronounce distinctly **:** ARTICULATE

enow \i-ˈnau̇, i-ˈnō\ *adv or adj* [ME *inow,* fr. OE *genōg*] (bef. 12c) *archaic* **:** ENOUGH

en pas·sant \ˌä^{n}-ˌpä-ˈsä^{n}, -pə-\ *adv* [F] (1665) **1 :** in passing **2 —** used in chess of the capture of a pawn as it makes a first move of two squares by an enemy pawn that threatens the first of these squares

en·plane \in-ˈplān, en-\ *also* **em·plane** \im-, em-\ *vi* (1941) **:** to board an airplane

en prise \ä^{n}-ˈprēz\ *adj* [F, lit., engaged, within grasp] (1820) *of a chess piece* **:** exposed to capture

en·quire \in-ˈkwī(-ə)r\, **en·qui·ry** \ˈin-ˌkwī(-ə)r-ē, in-ˈ; ˈin-kwə-rē, ˈiŋ-\ *chiefly Brit var of* INQUIRE, INQUIRY

en·rage \in-ˈrāj, en-\ *vt* [MF *enrager* to become mad, fr. OF *enragier,* fr. *en-* + *rage* rage] (1575) **:** to fill with rage **:** ANGER

en·rapt \in-ˈrapt, en-\ *adj* (1606) **:** wholly absorbed with rapture

en·rap·ture \in-ˈrap-chər, en-\ *vt* **en·rap·tured; en·rap·tur·ing** \-ˈrap-chə-riŋ, -ˈrap-shriŋ\ (1740) **:** to fill with delight

en·reg·is·ter \in-ˈre-jə-stər, en-\ *vt* [MF *enregistrer,* fr. OF, fr. *en-* + *registre* register] (1523) **:** to put on record **:** REGISTER

en·rich \in-ˈrich, en-\ *vt* [ME, fr. AF *enrichir, enricher,* fr. *en-* + *riche* rich] (14c) **:** to make rich or richer esp. by the addition or increase of some desirable quality, attribute, or ingredient ⟨the experience will ~ your life⟩: as **a :** to add beauty to **:** ADORN **b :** to enhance the taste of ⟨butter will ~ the sauce⟩ **c :** to make (a soil) more fertile **d :** to improve the nutritive value of (a food) by adding nutrients (as vitamins or amino acids) and esp. by restoring part of the nutrients lost in processing ⟨~*ed* flour⟩ **e :** to process so as to add or increase the proportion of a desirable ingredient ⟨~*ed* uranium⟩ ⟨~*ed* natural gas⟩ — **en·rich·er** *n* — **en·rich·ment** \-ˈrich-mənt\ *n*

en·robe \in-ˈrōb, en-\ *vt* (1593) **1 :** to cover with or as if with a robe **2 :** COAT 2

en·roll *also* **en·rol** \in-ˈrōl, en-\ *vb* **en·rolled; en·roll·ing** [ME, fr. AF *enrouler,* fr. *en-* + *rolle* roll, register] *vt* (14c) **1 :** to insert, register, or enter in a list, catalog, or roll ⟨the school ~*s* about 800 pupils⟩ **2 :** to prepare a final perfect copy of (a bill passed by a legislature) in written or printed form **3 :** to roll or wrap up ~ *vi* **:** to enroll oneself or cause oneself to be enrolled ⟨we ~*ed* in the history course⟩ — **en·roll·ee** \-rō-ˈlē\ *n* — **en·roll·ment** *also* **en·rol·ment** \-ˈrōl-mənt\ *n*

en·root \in-ˈrüt, -ˈru̇t\ *vt* [ME] (15c) **:** ESTABLISH, IMPLANT

en route \ä^{n}(n)-ˈrüt, en-, in-, -ˈrau̇t\ *adv or adj* [F] (1779) **:** on or along the way ⟨he reads *en route*⟩ ⟨arrived early despite *en route* delays⟩

ENS *abbr* ensign

en·sam·ple \in-ˈsam-pəl\ *n* [ME, fr. AF *ensample, essample, example*] (13c) *archaic* **:** EXAMPLE, INSTANCE

en·san·guine \in-ˈsaŋ-gwən\ *vt* **-guined; -guin·ing** (1667) **1 :** to make bloody **2 :** CRIMSON

en·sconce \in-ˈskän(t)s\ *vt* **en·sconced; en·sconc·ing** [*en-* + [2]*sconce*] (1594) **1 :** SHELTER, CONCEAL ⟨*ensconced* themselves within the protection of three great elms —Mark Twain⟩ **2 :** ESTABLISH, SETTLE ⟨*ensconced* in a new job⟩

[1]**en·sem·ble** \än-ˈsäm-bəl, ä^{n}-\ *n* [F, fr. *ensemble* together, fr. OF, fr. L *insimul* at the same time, fr. *in-* + *simul* at the same time — more at SAME] (1750) **:** a group producing a single effect: as **a :** concerted music of two or more parts **b :** a complete costume of harmonizing or complementary clothing and accessories **c** (1) **:** the musicians engaged in the performance of a musical ensemble (2) **:** a group of supporting players, singers, or dancers; *esp* **:** CORPS DE BALLET

[2]**ensemble** *adj* (ca. 1911) **:** emphasizing the roles of all performers as a whole rather than a star performance ⟨~ acting⟩

en·serf \in-ˈsərf, en-\ *vt* (1882) **:** to make a serf of **:** deprive of liberty and personal rights — **en·serf·ment** \-mənt\ *n*

en·sheathe \in-ˈshēth, en-\ *vt* (1593) **:** to cover with or as if with a sheath

en·shrine \in-ˈshrīn, en-, *esp Southern* -ˈsrīn\ *vt* [ME] (14c) **1 :** to enclose in or as if in a shrine **2 :** to preserve or cherish as sacred — **enshrine·ment** \-mənt\ *n*

en·shri·nee \in-ˈshrī-nē, -ˌshrī-ˈnē, en-\ *n* (1968) **:** a person inducted into a Hall of Fame

en·shroud \in-ˈshrau̇d, en-, *esp Southern* -ˈsrau̇d\ *vt* (1583) **:** to cover or enclose with or as if with a shroud

en·si·form \ˈen(t)-sə-ˌfȯrm\ *adj* [F *ensiforme,* fr. L *ensis* sword + F *-forme* -form; akin to Skt *asi* sword] (1541) **:** having sharp edges and tapering to a slender point ⟨~ leaves⟩ — see LEAF illustration

en·sign \ˈen(t)-sən, *also* ˈen-ˌsīn *for 1, 2, & 3a*\ *n* [ME *ensigne,* sign, token, banner, fr. AF *enseigne,* fr. L *insignia* insignia, flags] (15c) **1 :** a flag that is flown (as by a ship) as the symbol of nationality and that may also be flown with a distinctive badge added to its design **2 a :** a badge of office, rank, or power **b :** EMBLEM, SIGN **3 a :** an infantry officer of what was formerly the lowest commissioned rank **b :** a commissioned officer in the navy or coast guard ranking above a chief warrant officer and below a lieutenant junior grade

en·si·lage \ˈen(t)-s(ə-)lij, *for 1 also* in-ˈsī-lij\ *n* [F, fr. *ensiler* to ensile, fr. *en-* + *silo* silo, fr. Sp] (1876) **1 :** the process of preserving fodder by ensiling **2 :** SILAGE

en·sile \en-ˈsī(-ə)l, in-\ *vt* **en·siled; en·sil·ing** (1883) **:** to prepare and store (fodder) so as to induce conversion to silage

\ə\ abut \ᵊ\ kitten, F table \ər\ further \a\ ash \ā\ ace \ä\ mop, mar
\au̇\ out \ch\ chin \e\ bet \ē\ easy \g\ go \i\ hit \ī\ ice \j\ job
\ŋ\ sing \ō\ go \ȯ\ law \ȯi\ boy \th\ thin \th\ the \ü\ loot \u̇\ foot
\y\ yet \zh\ vision, beige \k, n, œ, ue, y\ *see* Guide to Pronunciation

en·sky \in-ˈskī, en-\ *vt* (1603) : EXALT ⟨I hold you as a thing *enskied* and sainted —Shak.⟩
en·slave \in-ˈslāv, en-\ *vt* (1628) : to reduce to or as if to slavery : SUBJUGATE — **en·slave·ment** \-mənt\ *n* — **en·slav·er** *n*
en·snare \in-ˈsner, en-\ *vt* (1576) : to take in or as if in a snare ***syn*** see CATCH
en·snarl \in-ˈsnär(-ə)l, en-\ *vt* (15c) : to involve in a snarl
en·sor·cell *or* **en·sor·cel** \in-ˈsȯr-səl\ *vt* **-celled** *or* **-celed; -cell·ing** *or* **-cel·ing** [MF *ensorceler,* alter. of OF *ensorcerer,* fr. *en-* + *-sorcerer,* fr. *sorcier, sorcer* sorcerer — more at SORCERY] (ca. 1541) : BEWITCH, ENCHANT — **en·sor·cell·ment** \-mənt\ *n*
en·soul \in-ˈsōl, en-\ *vt* (1605) : to endow or imbue with a soul — **en·soul·ment** \-mənt\ *n*
en·sphere \in-ˈsfir, en-\ *vt* (1612) : to enclose in or as if in a sphere
en·sue \in-ˈsü, en-\ *vb* **en·sued; en·su·ing** [ME, fr. AF *ensivre* (3d sing. *ensiut*), fr. *en-* + *sivre* to follow — more at SUE] *vt* (14c) : to strive to attain : PURSUE ⟨I wander, seeking peace, and *ensuing* it —Rupert Brooke⟩ ~ *vi* : to take place afterward or as a result ***syn*** see FOLLOW
en suite \äⁿ-ˈswēt\ *adv or adj* [F] (1812) : so as to form a suite : CONNECTED ⟨bathroom *en suite*⟩; *also* : so as to make a matching set
en·sure \in-ˈshu̇r\ *vt* **en·sured; en·sur·ing** [ME, fr. AF *ensurer,* alter. of *assurer* — more at ASSURE] (1660) : to make sure, certain, or safe : GUARANTEE
syn ENSURE, INSURE, ASSURE, SECURE mean to make a thing or person sure. ENSURE, INSURE, and ASSURE are interchangeable in many contexts where they indicate the making certain or inevitable of an outcome, but ENSURE may imply a virtual guarantee ⟨the government has *ensured* the safety of the refugees⟩, while INSURE sometimes stresses the taking of necessary measures beforehand ⟨careful planning should *insure* the success of the party⟩, and ASSURE distinctively implies the removal of doubt and suspense from a person's mind ⟨I *assure* you that no harm will be done⟩. SECURE implies action taken to guard against attack or loss ⟨sent reinforcements to *secure* their position⟩.
en·swathe \in-ˈswäth, -ˈswȯth, -ˈswāth, en-\ *vt* (1597) : to enfold or enclose with or as if with a covering : SWATHE
ENT *abbr* ear, nose, and throat
ent- *or* **ento-** *comb form* [NL, fr. Gk *entos* within; akin to L *intus* within, Gk *en* in — more at IN] : inner : within ⟨*ento*derm⟩
en·tab·la·ture \in-ˈta-blə-ˌchu̇r, -chər, -ˌt(y)u̇r\ *n* [obs. F, modif. of It *intavolatura,* fr. *intavolare* to put on a board or table, fr. *in-* (fr. L) + *tavola* board, table, fr. L *tabula*] (1611) : a horizontal part in classical architecture that rests on the columns and consists of architrave, frieze, and cornice — see COLUMN illustration
[1]**en·tail** \in-ˈtāl, en-\ *vt* [ME *entailen, entaillen,* fr. ¹*en-* + *taile, taille* limitation — more at TAIL] (14c) **1 :** to restrict (property) by limiting the inheritance to the owner's lineal descendants or to a particular class thereof **2 a :** to confer, assign, or transmit as if by entail : FASTEN ⟨~*ed* on them indelible disgrace —Robert Browning⟩ **b :** to fix (a person) permanently in some condition or status ⟨~ him and his heirs unto the crown —Shak.⟩ **3 :** to impose, involve, or imply as a necessary accompaniment or result ⟨the project will ~ considerable expense⟩ — **en·tail·er** \-ˈtā-lər\ *n* — **en·tail·ment** \-ˈtāl-mənt\ *n*
[2]**en·tail** \ˈen-ˌtāl, in-ˈtāl\ *n* (14c) **1 a :** an entailing esp. of lands **b :** an entailed estate **2 :** something transmitted as if by entail
ent·amoe·ba \ˌen-tə-ˈmē-bə\ *n* [NL] (1914) : any of a genus (*Entamoeba*) of amoebas parasitic in vertebrates and including one (*E. histolytica*) that causes amebic dysentery in humans
en·tan·gle \in-ˈtaŋ-gəl, en-\ *vt* [ME, fr. AF *entangler* — more at TANGLE] (15c) **1 a :** to wrap or twist together : INTERWEAVE **b :** ENSNARE **2 a :** to involve in a perplexing or troublesome situation ⟨became *entangled* in a lawsuit⟩ **b :** to make complicated ⟨the story is *entangled* with legends⟩ — **en·tan·gler** \-g(ə-)lər\ *n*
en·tan·gle·ment \in-ˈtaŋ-gəl-mənt, en-\ *n* (1535) **1 a :** the action of entangling : the state of being entangled **b :** something that entangles, confuses, or ensnares ⟨a project delayed by legal ~*s*⟩ **2 :** the condition of being deeply involved ⟨their ~ in politics⟩
en·ta·sis \ˈen-tə-sis\ *n, pl* **-ta·ses** \-tə-ˌsēz\ [Gk, lit., distension, stretching, fr. *enteinen* to stretch tight, fr. *en-* ²en- + *teinein* to stretch — more at THIN] (1664) : a slight convexity esp. in the shaft of a column
en·tel·e·chy \en-ˈte-lə-kē, in-\ *n, pl* **-chies** [LL *entelechia,* fr. Gk *entelecheia,* fr. *entelēs* complete (fr. *en-* ²en- + *telos* end) + *echein* to have — more at TELOS, SCHEME] (1593) **1 :** the actualization of form-giving cause as contrasted with potential existence **2 :** a hypothetical agency not demonstrable by scientific methods that in some vitalist doctrines is considered an inherent regulating and directing force in the development and functioning of an organism
en·tente \än-ˈtänt\ *n* [F, fr. OF, intent, understanding — more at INTENT] (1854) **1 :** an international understanding providing for a common course of action **2** [F *entente cordiale*] **:** a coalition of parties to an entente
en·tente cor·diale \(ˌ)äⁿ-ˈtäⁿt-ˌkȯr-ˈdyäl\ *n* [F, lit., cordial understanding] (1844) **1 :** ENTENTE 1 **2 :** a friendly agreement or working relationship
en·ter \ˈen-tər\ *vb* **en·tered; en·ter·ing** \ˈen-t(ə-)riŋ\ [ME *entren,* fr. AF *entrer,* fr. L *intrare,* fr. *intra* within; akin to L *inter* between — more at INTER-] *vi* (13c) **1 :** to go or come in **2 :** to come or gain admission into a group : JOIN — often used with *into* **3 a :** to make a beginning ⟨~*ing* upon a career⟩ **b :** to begin to consider a subject — usu. used with *into* or *upon* **4 :** to go upon land for the purpose of taking possession **5 a :** to come onstage — usu. used in the subjunctive as a stage direction ⟨~ Hamlet reading⟩ **b :** to come into a preestablished situation or context like an actor coming onstage — usu. used in the subjunctive ⟨~ the new principal with her radical ideas⟩ **6 :** to play a part : be a factor ⟨other considerations ~ when money is involved⟩ ~ *vt* **1 :** to come or go into ⟨~ a room⟩ **2 :** INSCRIBE, REGISTER ⟨~ the names of qualified voters⟩ **3 :** to cause to be received or admitted ⟨~ a child at a school⟩ **4 :** to put in : INSERT ⟨~ the new data into the computer⟩ **5 a :** to make a beginning in ⟨~ politics⟩ **b :** to go into (a particular period of time) ⟨~ middle age⟩ **6 :** to become a member of or an active participant in ⟨~ the university⟩ ⟨~ a race⟩ **7 :** to make report of (a ship or its cargo) to customs authorities **8 :** to place in proper form before a court of law or upon record ⟨~ a writ⟩ **9 :** to go into or upon and take actual possession of (as land) **10 :** to put formally on record ⟨~*ing* a complaint⟩ — **en·ter·able** \ˈen-t(ə-)rə-bəl\ *adj* — **enter into 1 :** to make oneself a party to or in ⟨*enter into* an agreement⟩ **2 :** to form or be part of ⟨your prejudices shouldn't *enter into* it⟩ **3 :** to participate or share in ⟨*enter into* the spirit of the occasion⟩ — **enter the lists :** to engage in a fight or struggle
syn ENTER, PENETRATE, PIERCE, PROBE mean to make way into something. ENTER is the most general of these and may imply either going in or forcing a way in ⟨*entered* the city in triumph⟩. PENETRATE carries a strong implication of an impelling force or compelling power that achieves entrance ⟨the enemy *penetrated* the fortress⟩. PIERCE means an entering or cutting through with a sharp pointed instrument ⟨*pierced* the boil with a lancet⟩. PROBE implies penetration to investigate or explore something hidden from sight or knowledge ⟨*probed* the depths of the sea⟩.
enter- *or* **entero-** *comb form* [Gk, fr. *enteron* — more at INTER-] : intestine ⟨*enter*itis⟩
en·ter·al \ˈen-tə-rəl\ *adj* (1903) : ENTERIC — **en·ter·al·ly** \-rə-lē\ *adv*
en·ter·ic \en-ˈter-ik, in-\ *adj* (1833) **1 :** of, relating to, or affecting the intestines; *broadly* : ALIMENTARY **2 :** being or having a coating designed to pass through the stomach unaltered and disintegrate in the intestines ⟨~ aspirin⟩
enteric fever *n* (1862) : TYPHOID FEVER; *also* : PARATYPHOID
en·ter·i·tis \ˌen-tə-ˈrī-təs\ *n, pl* **en·ter·it·i·des** \-ˈri-tə-ˌdēz\ *also* **en·ter·i·tis·es** (1808) **1 :** inflammation of the intestines and esp. of the human ileum **2 :** a disease of domestic animals (as panleukopenia of cats) marked by enteritis and diarrhea
en·tero·bac·te·ri·um \ˌen-tə-rō-bak-ˈtir-ē-əm\ *n* [NL] (ca. 1951) : any of a family (Enterobacteriaceae) of gram-negative straight rod bacteria (as a salmonella, a shigella, or E. coli) that ferment glucose and include saprophytes as well as some serious plant and animal pathogens — **en·tero·bac·te·ri·al** \-ē-əl\ *adj*

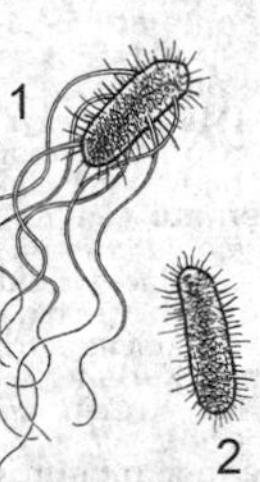

enterobacterium: *1* E. coli, *2* shigella

en·tero·bi·a·sis \-ˈbī-ə-səs\ *n, pl* **-a·ses** \-ˌsēz\ [NL, fr. *Enterobius,* genus name (fr. Gk *enter-* + *bios* mode of life) + *-iasis*] (ca. 1927) : infestation with or disease caused by pinworms (genus *Enterobius,* esp. *E. vermicularis*) that occurs esp. in children
en·tero·chro·maf·fin \-ˈkrō-mə-fən\ *adj* (ca. 1941) : of or relating to epithelial cells of the intestinal mucosa that stain esp. with chromium salts and usu. contain serotonin
en·tero·coc·cus \-ˈkä-kəs\ *n, pl* **-coc·ci** \-ˈkäk-ˌ(s)ī, -ˈkäk-(ˌ)(s)ē\ [NL, genus name] (1908) : any of a genus (*Enterococcus*) of gram-positive bacteria that resemble streptococci and were formerly classified with them; *esp* : a bacterium (*E. faecalis*) normally present in the intestine — **en·tero·coc·cal** \-ˈkä-kəl\ *adj*
en·tero·coele *or* **en·tero·coel** \ˈen-tə-rō-ˌsēl\ *n* (1877) : a coelom originating by outgrowth from the archenteron — **en·tero·coe·lous** \ˌen-tə-rō-ˈsē-ləs\ *adj* — **en·tero·coe·lic** \-lik\ *adj*
en·tero·co·li·tis \ˌen-tə-rō-kə-ˈlī-təs\ *n* [NL] (ca. 1857) : enteritis affecting both the large and small intestine
en·tero·gas·trone \-ˈgas-ˌtrōn\ *n* [*enter-* + *gastr-* + *-one* (as in *hormone*)] (ca. 1930) : a hormone that is produced by the duodenal mucosa and has an inhibitory action on gastric motility and secretion
en·tero·ki·nase \ˌen-tə-rō-ˈkī-ˌnās, -ˌnāz\ *n* [ISV] (ca. 1902) : an enzyme esp. of the duodenal mucosa that activates trypsinogen by converting it to trypsin
en·ter·on \ˈen-tə-ˌrän, -rən\ *n* [NL, fr. Gk, intestine — more at INTER-] (ca. 1842) : the alimentary canal or system — used esp. of the embryo
en·tero·patho·gen·ic \ˌen-tə-rō-ˌpa-thə-ˈje-nik\ *adj* (1961) : tending to produce disease in the intestinal tract ⟨~ bacteria⟩
en·ter·op·a·thy \ˌen-tə-ˈrä-pə-thē\ *n* (ca. 1889) : a disease of the intestinal tract
en·ter·os·to·my \ˌen-tə-ˈräs-tə-mē\ *n, pl* **-mies** [ISV] (1878) : a surgical formation of an opening into the intestine through the abdominal wall — **en·ter·os·to·mal** \-tə-məl\ *adj*
en·tero·toxi·gen·ic \ˌen-tə-rō-ˌtäk-sə-ˈjen-ik\ *adj* (1946) : producing enterotoxin ⟨~ strains of E. coli⟩
en·tero·tox·in \ˌen-tə-rō-ˈtäk-sən\ *n* (ca. 1928) : a toxin that is produced by microorganisms (as some staphylococci) and causes gastrointestinal symptoms (as in some forms of food poisoning or cholera)
en·tero·vi·rus \-ˈvī-rəs\ *n* [NL] (1957) : any of a genus (*Enterovirus*) of picornaviruses that occur esp. in the gastrointestinal tract but may infect other tissues (as nerve and muscle) and that include the poliovirus and several species with numerous serotypes named as Coxsackie viruses and echoviruses — **en·tero·vi·ral** \-rəl\ *adj*
en·ter·prise \ˈen-tə(r)-ˌprīz\ *n* [ME, fr. AF, fr. *entreprendre* to undertake, fr. *entre-* inter- + *prendre* to take — more at PRIZE] (15c) **1 :** a project or undertaking that is esp. difficult, complicated, or risky **2 :** readiness to engage in daring or difficult action : INITIATIVE ⟨showed great ~ in dealing with the crisis⟩ **3 a :** a unit of economic organization or activity; *esp* : a business organization **b :** a systematic purposeful activity ⟨agriculture is the main economic ~ among these people⟩
en·ter·pris·er \-ˌprī-zər\ *n* (1523) : ENTREPRENEUR
enterprise zone *n* (1978) : an economically depressed area in which business growth is encouraged by the government through tax relief and financial concessions
en·ter·pris·ing \-ˌprī-ziŋ\ *adj* (1611) : marked by an independent energetic spirit and by readiness to act ⟨an ~ young reporter⟩
en·ter·tain \ˌen-tər-ˈtān\ *vb* [ME *entertinen,* fr. MF *entretenir,* fr. *entre-* inter- + *tenir* to hold — more at TENABLE] *vt* (15c) **1 a** *archaic* : MAINTAIN **b** *obs* : RECEIVE **2 :** to show hospitality to ⟨~ guests⟩ **3 a :** to keep, hold, or maintain in the mind ⟨I ~ grave doubts about her sincerity⟩ **b :** to receive and take into consideration ⟨refused to ~ our plea⟩ **4 :** to provide entertainment for **5 :** to play against (an opposing team) on one's home field or court ~ *vi* : to provide entertainment esp. for guests ***syn*** see AMUSE — **en·ter·tain·er** *n*
en·ter·tain·ing \-ˈtā-niŋ\ *adj* (1676) : providing entertainment : DIVERTING ⟨an ~ book⟩ ⟨an ~ speaker⟩ — **en·ter·tain·ing·ly** \-ˈtā-niŋ-lē\ *adv*

en·ter·tain·ment \ˌen-tər-ˈtān-mənt\ *n* (15c) **1 :** the act of entertaining **2 a** *archaic* **:** MAINTENANCE, PROVISION **b** *obs* **:** EMPLOYMENT **3 a :** amusement or diversion provided esp. by performers ⟨hired a band to provide ~⟩ **b :** something diverting or engaging: as (1) **:** a public performance (2) **:** a usu. light comic or adventure novel

en·thal·py \ˈen-ˌthal-pē, en-ˈ\ *n* [*en-* + Gk *thalpein* to heat] (ca. 1924) **:** the sum of the internal energy of a body or system and the product of its volume multiplied by the pressure

en·thrall *or* **en·thral** \in-ˈthrȯl, en-\ *vt* **en·thralled; en·thrall·ing** [ME] (15c) **1 :** to hold in or reduce to slavery **2 :** to hold spellbound **:** CHARM — **en·thrall·ment** \-ˈthrȯl-mənt\ *n*

en·throne \in-ˈthrōn, en-\ *vt* (ca. 1593) **1 a :** to seat in a place associated with a position of authority or influence **b :** to seat ceremonially on a throne **2 :** to assign supreme virtue or value to **:** EXALT — **en·throne·ment** \-mənt\ *n*

en·thuse \in-ˈthüz, en-, *also* -ˈthyüz\ *vb* **en·thused; en·thus·ing** [back-formation fr. *enthusiasm*] *vt* (1827) **1 :** to make enthusiastic ⟨is *enthused* about the project⟩ **2 :** to express with enthusiasm ~ *vi* **:** to show enthusiasm ⟨a splendid performance, and I was *enthusing* over it —Julian Huxley⟩

usage *Enthuse* is apparently American in origin, although the earliest known example of its use occurs in a letter written in 1827 by a young Scotsman who spent about two years in the Pacific Northwest. It has been disapproved since about 1870. Current evidence shows it to be flourishing nonetheless on both sides of the Atlantic esp. in journalistic prose.

en·thu·si·asm \in-ˈthü-zē-ˌa-zəm, en-, *also* -ˈthyü-\ *n* [Gk *enthousiasmos,* fr. *enthousiazein* to be inspired, irreg. fr. *entheos* inspired, fr. *en-* + *theos* god] (1603) **1 a :** belief in special revelations of the Holy Spirit **b :** religious fanaticism **2 a :** strong excitement of feeling **:** ARDOR ⟨did her work with energy and ~⟩ **b :** something inspiring zeal or fervor ⟨his ~*s* include sailing and fishing⟩ ***syn*** see PASSION

en·thu·si·ast \-ˌast, -əst\ *n* (1570) **:** a person filled with enthusiasm: as **a :** one who is ardently attached to a cause, object, or pursuit ⟨a sports car ~⟩ **b :** one who tends to become ardently absorbed in an interest

en·thu·si·as·tic \in-ˌthü-zē-ˈas-tik, en-, *also* -ˌthyü-\ *adj* (1603) **:** filled with or marked by enthusiasm ⟨~ supporters⟩ ⟨an ~ recommendation⟩ — **en·thu·si·as·ti·cal·ly** \-ti-k(ə-)lē\ *adv*

en·thy·meme \ˈen(t)-thi-ˌmēm\ *n* [L *enthymema,* fr. Gk *enthymēma,* fr. *enthymeisthai* to keep in mind, fr. *en-* + *thymos* mind, soul] (1552) **:** a syllogism in which one of the premises is implicit

en·tice \in-ˈtīs, en-\ *vt* **en·ticed; en·tic·ing** [ME, fr. AF *enticer,* fr. VL **intitiare,* fr. L *in-* + *titio* firebrand] (14c) **:** to attract artfully or adroitly or by arousing hope or desire **:** TEMPT ***syn*** see LURE — **en·tice·ment** \-ˈtī-smənt\ *n* — **en·tic·ing·ly** \-ˈtī-siŋ-lē\ *adv*

[1]**en·tire** \in-ˈtī(-ə)r, ˈen-ˌ\ *adj* [ME *enter, entier, entire,* fr. AF *enter, entier,* fr. L *integer,* lit., untouched, fr. *in-* + *tangere* to touch — more at TANGENT] (14c) **1 :** having no element or part left out **:** WHOLE ⟨was alone the ~ day⟩ **2 :** complete in degree **:** TOTAL ⟨their ~ devotion to their family⟩ **3 a :** consisting of one piece **b :** HOMOGENEOUS, UNMIXED **c :** INTACT ⟨strove to keep the collection ~⟩ **4 :** not castrated **5 :** having the margin continuous or free from indentations ⟨an ~ leaf⟩ ***syn*** see WHOLE, PERFECT — **entire** *adv* — **en·tire·ness** *n*

[2]**entire** *n* (1597) **1** *archaic* **:** the whole **:** ENTIRETY **2 :** STALLION

en·tire·ly *adv* (14c) **1 :** to the full or entire extent **:** COMPLETELY ⟨I agree ~⟩ ⟨you are ~ welcome⟩ **2 :** to the exclusion of others **:** SOLELY ⟨~ by my own efforts⟩

en·tire·ty \in-ˈtī-rə-tē, -ˈtī(-ə)r-tē\ *n, pl* **-ties** (1548) **1 :** the state of being entire or complete **2 :** SUM TOTAL, WHOLE

en·ti·tle \in-ˈtī-t^{ə}l, en-\ *vt* **en·ti·tled; en·ti·tling** \-ˈtīt-liŋ, -^{ə}l-iŋ\ [ME, fr. AF *entitler,* fr. LL *intitulare,* fr. L *in-* + *titulus* title] (14c) **1 :** to give a title to **:** DESIGNATE **2 :** to furnish with proper grounds for seeking or claiming something ⟨this ticket ~*s* the bearer to free admission⟩

en·ti·tle·ment \-ˈtī-t^{ə}l-mənt\ *n* (1942) **1 a :** the state or condition of being entitled **:** RIGHT **b :** a right to benefits specified esp. by law or contract **2 :** a government program providing benefits to members of a specified group; *also* **:** funds supporting or distributed by such a program **3 :** belief that one is deserving of or entitled to certain privileges

en·ti·ty \ˈen-tə-tē, ˈe-nə-\ *n, pl* **-ties** [ML *entitas,* fr. L *ent-, ens* existing thing, fr. coined prp. of *esse* to be — more at IS] (1596) **1 a :** BEING, EXISTENCE; *esp* **:** independent, separate, or self-contained existence **b :** the existence of a thing as contrasted with its attributes **2 :** something that has separate and distinct existence and objective or conceptual reality **3 :** an organization (as a business or governmental unit) that has an identity separate from those of its members

ento- — see ENT-

en·to·derm \ˈen-tə-ˌdərm\ *n* (1879) **:** ENDODERM — **en·to·der·mal** \ˌen-tə-ˈdər-məl\ *adj*

en·toil \in-ˈtȯi(-ə)l\ *vt* (1581) **:** ENTRAP, ENMESH

entom- *or* **entomo-** *comb form* [F, fr. Gk *entomon*] **:** insect ⟨*entomo*phagous⟩

entom *or* **entomol** *abbr* entomological; entomology

en·tomb \in-ˈtüm, en-\ *vt* [ME *entoumben,* fr. MF *entomber,* fr. *en-* + *tombe* tomb] (1565) **1 :** to deposit in or as if in a tomb **:** BURY **2 :** to serve as a tomb for — **en·tomb·ment** \-ˈtüm-mənt\ *n*

en·to·mo·fau·na \ˌen-tə-mō-ˈfȯ-nə, -ˈfä-\ *n* [NL] (1951) **:** a fauna of insects **:** the insects of an environment or region

en·to·mol·o·gy \ˌen-tə-ˈmä-lə-jē\ *n* [F *entomologie,* fr. Gk *entomon* insect (fr. neut. of *entomos* cut up, fr. *en-* + *temnein* to cut) + F *-logie* -logy — more at TOME] (1766) **:** a branch of zoology that deals with insects — **en·to·mo·log·i·cal** \-mə-ˈlä-ji-kəl\ *adj* — **en·to·mo·log·i·cal·ly** \-k(ə-)lē\ *adv* — **en·to·mol·o·gist** \ˌen-tə-ˈmä-lə-jist\ *n*

en·to·moph·a·gous \ˌen-tə-ˈmä-fə-gəs\ *adj* (ca. 1847) **:** feeding on insects

en·to·moph·a·gy \-ˈmä-fə-jē\ *n* (1975) **:** the practice of eating insects

en·to·moph·i·lous \ˌen-tə-ˈmä-fə-ləs\ *adj* (1880) **:** normally pollinated by insects — compare ZOOPHILIC — **en·to·moph·i·ly** \-lē\ *n*

en·to·proct \ˈen-tə-ˌpräkt\ *n* [ultim. fr. *ent-* + Gk *prōktos* anus] (1940) **:** any of a phylum (Entoprocta) of chiefly marine animals that are very similar to bryozoans but lack a true coelom and have the anus located near the mouth inside a crown of tentacles

en·to·rhi·nal \ˌen-tə-ˈrī-n^{ə}l\ *adj* [*ent-* + *-rhinal;* fr. the rhinal sulcus, the furrow within which the entorhinal cortex is located] (1968) **:** of, relating to, or being the part of the cerebral cortex in the medial temporal lobe that serves as the main cortical input to the hippocampus

en·tou·rage \ˌän-tü-ˈräzh\ *n* [F, fr. MF, fr. *entourer* to surround, fr. *entour* around, fr. *en* in (fr. L *in*) + *tour* circuit — more at TURN] (ca. 1834) **1 :** one's attendants or associates **2 :** SURROUNDINGS

en·tr'acte \ˈä^{n}(n)-ˌtrakt, -ˌträkt, ä^{n}(n)-ˈ\ *n* [F, fr. *entre-* inter- + *acte* act] (ca. 1842) **1 :** a dance, piece of music, or interlude performed between two acts of a play **2 :** the interval between two acts of a play

en·trails \ˈen-ˌtrālz, -trəlz\ *n pl* [ME *entrailles,* fr. AF, fr. ML *intralia,* alter. of L *interanea,* pl. of *interaneum* intestine, fr. neut. of *interaneus* interior] (14c) **1 :** BOWELS, VISCERA; *broadly* **:** internal parts **2 :** the inner workings of something ⟨the ~ of the movie industry⟩

[1]**en·train** \in-ˈtrān\ *vt* [MF *entrainer,* fr. *en-* + *trainer* to draw, drag — more at TRAIN] (1568) **1 :** to draw along with or after oneself **2 :** to draw in and transport (as solid particles or gas) by the flow of a fluid **3 :** to incorporate (air bubbles) into concrete **4 :** to determine or modify the phase or period of ⟨circadian rhythms ~*ed* by a light cycle⟩ — **en·train·er** *n* — **en·train·ment** \-ˈtrān-mənt\ *n*

[2]**entrain** *vt* (1881) **:** to put aboard a train ~ *vi* **:** to go aboard a train

[1]**en·trance** \ˈen-trən(t)s\ *n* (15c) **1 :** power or permission to enter **:** ADMISSION **2 :** the act of entering **3 :** the means or place of entry **4 :** the point at which a voice or instrument part begins in ensemble music **5 :** the first appearance of an actor in a scene

[2]**en·trance** \in-ˈtran(t)s, en-\ *vt* **en·tranced; en·tranc·ing** (1541) **1 :** to put into a trance **2 :** to carry away with delight, wonder, or rapture ⟨we were *entranced* by the view⟩ — **en·trance·ment** \-ˈtran(t)-smənt\ *n*

en·trance·way \ˈen-trən(t)s-ˌwā\ *n* (1849) **:** ENTRYWAY

en·trant \ˈen-trənt\ *n* (1635) **:** one that enters; *esp* **:** one that enters a contest

en·trap \in-ˈtrap, en-\ *vt* [MF *entraper,* fr. *en-* + *trape* trap] (1534) **1 :** to catch in or as if in a trap **2 :** to lure into a compromising statement or act ***syn*** see CATCH

en·trap·ment \-mənt\ *n* (1597) **1 a :** the action or process of entrapping **b :** the condition of being entrapped **2 :** the action of luring an individual into committing a crime in order to prosecute the person for it

en·treat \in-ˈtrēt, en-\ *vb* [ME *entreten,* fr. AF *entreter,* fr. *en-* + *treter* to treat] *vi* (14c) **1** *obs* **a :** NEGOTIATE **b :** INTERCEDE **2 :** to make an earnest request **:** PLEAD ~ *vt* **1 :** to plead with esp. in order to persuade **:** ask urgently ⟨~*ed* his boss for another chance⟩ **2** *archaic* **:** to deal with **:** TREAT ***syn*** see BEG — **en·treat·ing·ly** \-trē-tiŋ-lē\ *adv* — **en·treat·ment** \-mənt\ *n*

en·treaty \-ˈtrē-tē\ *n, pl* **-treat·ies** (15c) **:** an act of entreating **:** PLEA

en·tre·chat \ˈä^{n}(n)-trə-ˌshä\ *n* [F, modif. of It *(capriola) intrecciata,* lit., intertwined caper] (1775) **:** a leap in which a ballet dancer repeatedly crosses the legs and sometimes beats them together

en·tre·côte *also* **en·tre·cote** \ˈä^{n}(n)-trə-ˌkōt\ *n* [F *entrecôte,* fr. *entre-* inter- + *côte* rib, fr. L *costa* — more at INTER-, COAST] (1841) **:** a steak cut from between the ribs

en·trée *or* **en·tree** \ˈän-ˌtrā *also* än-ˈ\ *n* [F *entrée,* fr. OF — more at ENTRY] (1725) **1 a :** the act or manner of entering **:** ENTRANCE **b :** freedom of entry or access **2 :** the main course of a meal in the U.S.

en·tre·mets *as sing* ˌä^{n}(n)-trə-ˈmā, *as pl* -ˈmā(z)\ *n pl but sing or pl in constr* [F, fr. OF *entremes,* fr. *entre* between + *mes* food, dish] (15c) **:** dishes served in addition to the main course of a meal; *esp* **:** DESSERT

en·trench \in-ˈtrench, en-\ *also* **in·trench** \in-\ *vt* (1548) **1 a :** to place within or surround with a trench esp. for defense **b :** to place (oneself) in a strong defensive position **c :** to establish solidly ⟨~*ed* themselves in the business⟩ **2 :** to cut into **:** FURROW; *specif* **:** to erode downward so as to form a trench ~ *vi* **1 :** to dig or occupy a trench for defensive purposes **2 :** to enter upon or take over something unfairly, improperly, or unlawfully **:** ENCROACH — used with *on* or *upon* — **en·trench·ment** \-mənt\ *n*

en·tre·pôt \ˈä^{n}(n)-trə-ˌpō\ *n* [F, fr. MF *entrepost,* fr. *entreposer* to put between, fr. *entre-* inter- + *poser* to pose, put] (1758) **:** an intermediary center of trade and transshipment

en·tre·pre·neur \ˌä^{n}n-trə-p(r)ə-ˈnər, -ˈn(y)u̇r\ *n* [F, fr. OF, fr. *entreprendre* to undertake — more at ENTERPRISE] (1852) **:** one who organizes, manages, and assumes the risks of a business or enterprise — **en·tre·pre·neur·ial** \-ˈn(y)u̇r-ē-əl, -ˈnər-\ *adj* — **en·tre·pre·neur·ial·ism** \-ē-ə-li-zəm\ *n* — **en·tre·pre·neur·ial·ly** \-ē-ə-lē\ *adv* — **en·tre·pre·neur·ship** \-ˈnər-ˌship, -ˈn(y)u̇r-\ *n*

en·tre·sol \ˈä^{n}(n)-trə-ˌsäl, -ˌsȯl\ *n* [F, fr. Sp *entresuelo,* fr. *entre* between + *suelo* ground, floor] (1711) **:** MEZZANINE

en·tro·pi·on \en-ˈtrō-pē-ˌän, -pē-ən\ *n* [NL, fr. *en-* [2]en- + *ectropion* turning out of the eyelid, fr. Gk *ektropion,* fr. *ektrepein* to turn out, fr. *ex-* out + *trepein* to turn] (ca. 1860) **:** the inversion or turning inward of the border of the eyelid against the eyeball

en·tro·py \ˈen-trə-pē\ *n, pl* **-pies** [ISV [2]*en-* + Gk *tropē* change, lit., turn, fr. *trepein* to turn] (1875) **1 :** a measure of the unavailable energy in a closed thermodynamic system that is also usu. considered to be a measure of the system's disorder, that is a property of the system's state, and that varies directly with any reversible change in heat in the system and inversely with the temperature of the system; *broadly* **:** the degree of disorder or uncertainty in a system **2 a :** the degradation of the matter and energy in the universe to an ultimate state of inert uniformity **b :** a process of degradation or running down or a trend to disorder **3 :** CHAOS, DISORGANIZATION, RANDOMNESS — **en·tro·pic** \en-ˈtrō-pik, -ˈträ-pik\ *adj* — **en·tro·pi·cal·ly** \-pi-k(ə-)lē\ *adv*

en·trust \in-ˈtrəst, en-\ *also* **in·trust** \in-\ *vt* (1593) **1 :** to confer a trust on; *esp* **:** to deliver something in trust to **2 :** to commit to another with confidence ***syn*** see COMMIT — **en·trust·ment** \-ˈtrəs(t)-mənt\ *n*

en·try \ˈen-trē\ *n, pl* **entries** [ME *entre,* fr. AF *entree,* fr. fem. of *entré,* pp. of *entrer* to enter] (13c) **1 :** the right or privilege of entering **:** ENTRÉE **2 :** the act of entering **:** ENTRANCE **3 :** a place of entrance: as **a :** VESTIBULE, PASSAGE **b :** DOOR, GATE **4 a :** the act of making or entering a record **b :** something entered: as (1) **:** a record or notation of an occurrence, transaction, or proceeding (2) **:** a descriptive record (as in a card catalog or an index) (3) **:** HEADWORD (4) **:** a headword with its definition or identification (5) **:** VOCABULARY ENTRY **5 :** a person, thing, or group entered into something (as a contest or market) ⟨the latest *entries* in the computer market⟩ ⟨judge the *entries* in the writing contest⟩

en·try–lev·el \ˈen-trē-ˌle-vəl\ *adj* (1970) **:** of or being at the lowest level of a hierarchy ⟨~ jobs⟩

en·try·way \-trē-ˌwā\ *n* (1746) **:** a passage for entrance

entry word *n* (ca. 1908) **:** HEADWORD

en·twine \in-ˈtwīn, en-\ *vt* (1590) **:** to twine together or around ~ *vi* **:** to become twisted or twined

en·twist \in-ˈtwist, en-\ *vt* (1590) **:** ENTWINE

enu·cle·ate \(ˌ)ē-ˈnü-klē-ˌāt, -ˈnyü-\ *vt* **-at·ed; -at·ing** [L *enucleatus,* pp. of *enucleare,* lit., to remove the kernel from, fr. *e-* + *nucleus* kernel — more at NUCLEUS] (1548) **1** *archaic* **:** EXPLAIN **2 :** to deprive of a nucleus **3 :** to remove without cutting into ⟨~ a tumor⟩ ⟨~ the eyeball⟩ — **enu·cle·ation** \(ˌ)ē-ˌn(y)ü-klē-ˈā-shən\ *n*

enu·mer·a·ble \i-ˈn(y)üm-rə-bəl, -ˈn(y)ü-mə-\ *adj* (ca. 1889) **:** COUNTABLE — **enu·mer·a·bil·i·ty** \-ˌn(y)üm-rə-ˈbi-lə-tē, -ˈn(y)ü-mə-\ *n*

enu·mer·ate \i-ˈn(y)ü-mə-ˌrāt\ *vt* **-at·ed; -at·ing** [L *enumeratus,* pp. of *enumerare,* fr. *e-* + *numerare* to count, fr. *numerus* number] (1616) **1 :** to ascertain the number of **:** COUNT **2 :** to specify one after another **:** LIST — **enu·mer·a·tion** \-ˌn(y)ü-mə-ˈrā-shən\ *n* — **enu·mer·a·tive** \-ˈn(y)ü-mə-ˌrā-tiv, -ˈn(y)üm-rə-, -ˈn(y)ü-mə-rə-\ *adj*

enu·mer·a·tor \-ˈn(y)ü-mə-ˌrā-tər\ *n* (1835) **:** one that enumerates; *esp* **:** a census taker

enun·ci·ate \ē-ˈnən(t)-sē-ˌāt\ *vb* **-at·ed; -at·ing** [L *enuntiatus,* pp. of *enuntiare* to report, declare, fr. *e-* + *nuntiare* to report — more at ANNOUNCE] *vt* (1623) **1 a :** to make a definite or systematic statement of **b :** ANNOUNCE, PROCLAIM ⟨*enunciated* the new policy⟩ **2 :** ARTICULATE, PRONOUNCE ⟨~ all the syllables⟩ ~ *vi* **:** to utter articulate sounds — **enun·cia·ble** \-ˈnən(t)-sē-ə-bəl, -ˈnən-ch(ē-)ə-\ *adj* — **enun·ci·a·tion** \-ˌnən(t)-sē-ˈā-shən\ *n* — **enun·ci·a·tor** \-ˈnən(t)-sē-ˌā-tər\ *n*

enure *var of* INURE

en·ure·sis \ˌen-yu̇-ˈrē-səs\ *n* [NL, fr. Gk *enourein* to urinate in, wet the bed, fr. *en-* + *ourein* to urinate — more at URINE] (ca. 1800) **:** the involuntary discharge of urine **:** incontinence of urine — **en·uret·ic** \-ˈre-tik\ *adj or n*

env *abbr* envelope

en·vel·op \in-ˈve-ləp, en-\ *vt* [ME *envolupen,* fr. AF *envoluper, envoleper,* fr. *en-* + *voluper* to wrap] (14c) **1 :** to enclose or enfold completely with or as if with a covering **2 :** to mount an attack on (an enemy's flank) — **en·vel·op·ment** \-mənt\ *n*

en·ve·lope \ˈen-və-ˌlōp, ˈän-\ *n* (ca. 1714) **1 :** a flat usu. paper container (as for a letter) **2 :** something that envelops **:** WRAPPER ⟨the ~ of air around the earth⟩ **3 a :** the outer covering of an aerostat **b :** the bag containing the gas in a balloon or airship **4 a :** a natural enclosing covering (as a membrane, shell, or integument) **b :** a lipoprotein unit membrane that forms the outer layer of some virions **5 a :** a curve tangent to each of a family of curves **b :** a surface tangent to each of a family of surfaces **6 :** a set of performance limits (as of an aircraft) that may not be safely exceeded; *also* **:** the set of operating parameters that exists within these limits **7 :** a conventionally accepted limit ⟨new computers that push the ~⟩

usage The \ˈen-\ and \ˈän-\ pronunciations are used with about equal frequency, and both are fully acceptable, though the \ˈän-\ version is sometimes decried as "pseudo-French." Actually \ˈän-\ is exactly what one would expect to hear when a French word like *entrepreneur* is becoming anglicized. *Envelope,* however, has been in English for nearly 300 years, plenty of time for it to become completely anglicized and for both of its pronunciations to win respectability.

en·ven·om \in-ˈve-nəm, en-\ *vt* [ME *envenimen,* fr. AF *envenimer,* fr. *en-* + *venim* venom] (13c) **1 :** to make poisonous **2 :** EMBITTER

en·ven·om·ation \in-ˌve-nə-ˈmā-shən, en-\ *n* (1923) **:** an act or instance of poisoning by venom (as of a snake or spider) — **en·ven·om·ate** \-ˈve-nə-ˌmāt\ *vt*

en·ven·om·i·za·tion \in-ˌve-nə-mə-ˈzā-shən, en-\ *n* (1960) **:** ENVENOMATION

en·vi·able \ˈen-vē-ə-bəl\ *adj* (1602) **:** highly desirable — **en·vi·able·ness** *n* — **en·vi·ably** \-blē\ *adv*

en·vi·er \ˈen-vē-ər\ *n* (15c) **:** one that envies

en·vi·ous \ˈen-vē-əs\ *adj* (13c) **1 :** feeling or showing envy ⟨~ of their neighbor's new car⟩ ⟨~ looks⟩ **2** *archaic* **a :** EMULOUS **b :** ENVIABLE — **en·vi·ous·ly** *adv* — **en·vi·ous·ness** *n*

en·vi·ro \in-ˈvī-rō\ *n, pl* **-ros** (1987) **:** ENVIRONMENTALIST

en·vi·ron \in-ˈvī-rən, -ˈvī(-ə)rn\ *vt* [ME *envirounen,* fr. AF *enviruner,* fr. *envirun* around, fr. *en* in (fr. L *in*) + *virun* circle, fr. *virer* to turn — more at VEER] (14c) **:** ENCIRCLE, SURROUND

en·vi·ron·ment \in-ˈvī-rə(n)-mənt, -ˈvī(-ə)r(n)-\ *n* (1827) **1 :** the circumstances, objects, or conditions by which one is surrounded **2 a :** the complex of physical, chemical, and biotic factors (as climate, soil, and living things) that act upon an organism or an ecological community and ultimately determine its form and survival **b :** the aggregate of social and cultural conditions that influence the life of an individual or community **3 :** the position or characteristic position of a linguistic element in a sequence **4 :** a computer interface from which various tasks can be performed ⟨a programming ~⟩ ***syn*** see BACKGROUND — **en·vi·ron·men·tal** \-ˌvī-rə(n)-ˈmen-tᵊl, -ˌvī(-ə)r(n)-\ *adj* — **en·vi·ron·men·tal·ly** \-tᵊl-ē\ *adv*

en·vi·ron·men·tal·ism \-ˌvī-rə(n)-ˈmen-tə-ˌli-zəm, -ˌvī(-ə)r(n)-\ *n* (ca. 1922) **1 :** a theory that views environment rather than heredity as the important factor in the development and esp. the cultural and intellectual development of an individual or group **2 :** advocacy of the preservation, restoration, or improvement of the natural environment; *esp* **:** the movement to control pollution

en·vi·ron·men·tal·ist \-tə-ləst\ *n* (1916) **1 :** an advocate of environmentalism **2 :** one concerned about environmental quality esp. of the human environment with respect to the control of pollution

en·vi·rons \in-ˈvī-rənz, -ˈvī(-ə)rnz\ *n pl* (1665) **1 :** the districts around a city **2 a :** environing things **:** SURROUNDINGS **b :** an adjoining region or space **:** VICINITY

en·vis·age \in-ˈvi-zij, en-\ *vt* **-aged; -ag·ing** [F *envisager,* fr. *en-* + *visage* face] (1660) **1 :** to view or regard in a certain way ⟨~*s* the slum as a hotbed of crime⟩ **2 :** to have a mental picture of esp. in advance of realization ⟨~*s* an entirely new system of education⟩ ***syn*** see THINK

en·vi·sion \in-ˈvi-zhən, en-\ *vt* (1855) **:** to picture to oneself ⟨~*s* a career dedicated to promoting peace⟩ ***syn*** see THINK

en·voi *or* **en·voy** \ˈen-ˌvȯi, ˈän-\ *n* [ME *envoye,* fr. MF *envoi,* lit., message, fr. OF *envei,* fr. *enveier* to send on one's way, fr. VL **inviare,* fr. L *in-* + *via* way — more at WAY] (14c) **:** the usu. explanatory or commendatory concluding remarks to a poem, essay, or book; *esp* **:** a short final stanza of a ballad serving as a summary or dedication

en·voy \ˈen-ˌvȯi, ˈän-\ *n* [F *envoyé,* fr. pp. of *envoyer* to send, fr. OF *enveier*] (1635) **1 a :** a minister plenipotentiary accredited to a foreign government who ranks between an ambassador and a minister resident — called also *envoy extraordinary* **b :** a person delegated to represent one government in its dealings with another **2 :** MESSENGER, REPRESENTATIVE

¹en·vy \ˈen-vē\ *n, pl* **envies** [ME *envie,* fr. AF, fr. L *invidia,* fr. *invidus* envious, fr. *invidēre* to look askance at, envy, fr. *in-* + *vidēre* to see — more at WIT] (13c) **1 :** painful or resentful awareness of an advantage enjoyed by another joined with a desire to possess the same advantage **2** *obs* **:** MALICE **3 :** an object of envious notice or feeling ⟨his new car made him the ~ of his friends⟩

²envy *vb* **en·vied; en·vy·ing** *vt* (14c) **1 :** to feel envy toward or on account of **2** *obs* **:** BEGRUDGE ~ *vi, obs* **:** to feel or show envy — **en·vy·ing·ly** \-vē-iŋ-lē\ *adv*

en·wheel \in-ˈhwēl, -ˈwēl, en-\ *vt* (1604) *obs* **:** ENCIRCLE

en·wind \in-ˈwīnd, en-\ *vt* **en·wound** \-ˈwau̇nd\; **en·wind·ing** (1631) **:** to wind in or about **:** ENFOLD

en·womb \in-ˈwüm, en-\ *vt* (1590) **:** to shut up as if in a womb

en·wrap \in-ˈrap, en-\ *vt* (14c) **1 :** to wrap in a covering **:** ENFOLD **2 a :** ENVELOP **b :** to preoccupy or absorb mentally **:** ENGROSS

en·wreathe \in-ˈrēth, en-\ *vt* (15c) **:** to encircle with or as if with a wreath **:** ENVELOP

en·zo·ot·ic \ˌen-zə-ˈwä-tik, -zō-ˈä-\ *adj* [*en-* + epizootic] (1882) *of animal diseases* **:** peculiar to or constantly present in a locality — **enzootic** *n*

en·zy·mat·ic \ˌen-zə-ˈma-tik\ *also* **en·zy·mic** \en-ˈzī-mik\ *adj* (1900) **:** of, relating to, or produced by an enzyme — **en·zy·mat·i·cal·ly** \ˌen-zə-ˈma-ti-k(ə-)lē\ *also* **en·zy·mi·cal·ly** \en-ˈzī-mi-k(ə-)lē\ *adv*

en·zyme \ˈen-ˌzīm\ *n* [G *Enzym,* fr. MGk *enzymos* leavened, fr. Gk *en-* + *zymē* leaven — more at JUICE] (1881) **:** any of numerous complex proteins that are produced by living cells and catalyze specific biochemical reactions at body temperatures

enzyme–linked immunosorbent assay *n* (1976) **:** an in vitro method for quantifying an antigen or antibody concentration in which the test material is immobilized on a surface and exposed either to a complex of an enzyme linked to an antibody specific for the antigen or an enzyme linked to an antigen specific for the antibody followed by reaction of the enzyme with a substrate to yield a colored product corresponding to the concentration of the test material — called also *ELISA*

en·zy·mol·o·gy \ˌen-ˌzī-ˈmä-lə-jē, -zə-\ *n* [ISV] (ca. 1900) **:** a branch of biochemistry that deals with the properties, activity, and significance of enzymes — **en·zy·mol·o·gist** \-jist\ *n*

EO *abbr* executive order

eo- *comb form* [Gk *ēō-* dawn, fr. *ēōs* — more at EAST] **:** earliest **:** oldest ⟨*eo*lithic⟩

Eo·cene \ˈē-ə-ˌsēn\ *adj* (1831) **:** of, relating to, or being an epoch of the Tertiary between the Paleocene and the Oligocene or the corresponding series of rocks — see GEOLOGIC TIME table — **Eocene** *n*

EOE *abbr* equal opportunity employer

eo·hip·pus \ˌē-ō-ˈhi-pəs\ *n* [NL, fr. *eo-* + Gk *hippos* horse — more at EQUINE] (ca. 1879) **:** any of a genus (*Hyracotherium* syn. *Eohippus*) of very small primitive horses from the Lower Eocene having 4-toed forefeet and 3-toed hind feet — called also *dawn horse*

eo·lian *also* **ae·o·lian** \ē-ˈō-lē-ən, -ˈōl-yən\ *adj* [L *Aeolus,* Aeolus] (1622) **:** borne, deposited, produced, or eroded by the wind

eo·lith \ˈē-ə-ˌlith\ *n* (1895) **:** a very crudely chipped flint

Eo·lith·ic \ˌē-ə-ˈli-thik\ *adj* (1890) **:** of or relating to the early period of the Stone Age marked by the use of eoliths

EOM *abbr* end of month

eon *var of* AEON

eo no·mi·ne \ˌē-ō-ˈnä-mə-nē\ [L] (1627) **:** by or under that name

Eos \ˈē-ˌäs\ *n* [Gk *Ēōs*] (1574) **:** the Greek goddess of dawn — compare AURORA

eo·sin \ˈē-ə-sən\ *also* **eo·sine** \-sən, -ˌsēn\ *n* [ISV, fr. Gk *ēōs* dawn] (1866) **1 :** a red fluorescent dye $C_{20}H_8Br_4O_5$ obtained by the action of bromine on fluorescein and used esp. in cosmetics and as a toner; *also* **:** its red to brown sodium or potassium salt used esp. as a biological stain for cytoplasmic structures **2 :** any of several dyes related to eosin

¹eo·sin·o·phil \ˌē-ə-ˈsi-nə-ˌfil\ *adj* (ca. 1882) **:** EOSINOPHILIC 1

²eosinophil *n* (ca. 1900) **:** a granulocyte readily stained by eosin that is present at sites of allergic reactions and parasitic infections

eo·sin·o·phil·ia \-ˌsi-nə-ˈfi-lē-ə\ *n* [NL] (1900) **:** abnormal increase in the number of eosinophils in the blood that is characteristic of allergic states and various parasitic infections

eo·sin·o·phil·ic \-ˌsi-nə-ˈfi-lik\ *adj* (ca. 1900) **1 :** staining readily with eosin **2 :** of, relating to, or characterized by eosinophilia

EP *abbr* **1** estimated position **2** European plan **3** extended play

EPA *abbr* **1** eicosapentaenoic acid **2** Environmental Protection Agency

epact \ˈē-ˌpakt, ˈe-\ *n* [MF *epacte,* fr. LL *epacta,* fr. Gk *epaktē,* fr. *epagein* to bring in, intercalate, fr. *epi-* + *agein* to drive — more at AGENT] (1588) **:** a period added to harmonize the lunar with the solar calendar

ep·ar·chy \ˈe-ˌpär-kē\ *n, pl* **-chies** [Gk *eparchia* province, fr. *eparchos* prefect, fr. *epi-* + *archos* ruler — more at ARCH-] (1796) **:** a diocese of an Eastern church

ep·au·let *also* **ep·au·lette** \ˌe-pə-ˈlet; ˈe-pə-ˌlet, -lət\ *n* [F *épaulette,* dim. of *épaule* shoulder, fr. OF *espalle,* fr. LL *spatula* shoulder blade, spoon, dim. of L *spatha* spoon, sword — more at SPADE] (1778) **:** something that ornaments or protects the shoulder: as **a :** an ornamental fringed shoulder pad formerly worn as part of a military uniform **b :** an ornamental strip or loop sewn across the shoulder of a dress or coat — **ep·au·let·ted** \ˌe-pə-ˈle-təd, ˈe-pə-ˌ\ *adj*

ep·a·zote \ˈe-pə-ˌzōt\ *n* [MexSp, fr. Nahuatl *epazōtl*] (1946) : WORMSEED b; *also* : the fresh or dried pungent-smelling leaves of wormseed used esp. in Mexican cooking

épée \ˈe-ˌpā, ā-ˈpā\ *n* [F, fr. OF *espee*, L *spatha*] (1889) **1** : a fencing or dueling sword having a bowl-shaped guard and a rigid blade of triangular section with no cutting edge that tapers to a sharp point blunted for fencing — compare [5]FOIL 1, SABER **2** : the art or sport of fencing with the épée

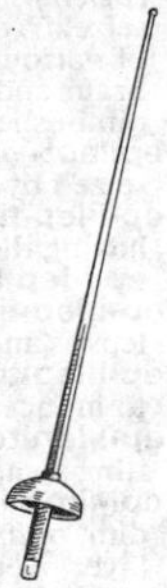

épée 1

épée·ist \-ist\ *n* (1910) : one who fences with an épée

ep·ei·rog·e·ny \ˌe-ˌpī-ˈrä-jə-nē\ *n, pl* **-nies** [Gk *ēpeiros* mainland, continent + E *-geny*] (1890) : the deformation of the earth's crust by which the broader features of relief are produced — **epei·ro·gen·ic** \i-ˌpī-rə-ˈje-nik\ *adj* — **epei·ro·gen·i·cal·ly** \-ni-k(ə-)lē\ *adv*

epen·the·sis \i-ˈpen(t)-thə-səs, e-\ *n, pl* **-the·ses** \-ˌsēz\ [LL, fr. Gk, fr. *epentithenai* to insert a letter, fr. *epi-* + *entithenai* to put in, fr. *en-* + *tithenai* to put — more at DO] (1543) : the insertion or development of a sound or letter in the body of a word (as \ə\ in \ˈa-thə-ˌlēt\ *athlete*) — **ep·en·thet·ic** \ˌe-pən-ˈthe-tik\ *adj*

epergne \i-ˈpərn, ā-\ *n* [prob. fr. F *épargne* saving] (1754) : an often ornate tiered centerpiece consisting typically of a frame of wrought metal (as silver or gold) bearing dishes, vases, or candle holders or a combination of these

ep·ex·e·ge·sis \ˌe-ˌpek-sə-ˈjē-səs\ *n, pl* **-ge·ses** \-ˌsēz\ [Gk *epexēgēsis*, fr. *epi-* + *exēgēsis* exegesis] (ca. 1577) : additional explanation or explanatory matter — **ep·ex·e·get·i·cal** \-ˈje-ti-kəl\ *or* **ep·ex·e·get·ic** \-ˈje-tik\ *adj* — **ep·ex·e·get·i·cal·ly** \-ˈje-ti-k(ə-)lē\ *adv*

Eph *or* **Ephes** *abbr* Ephesians

ephah \ˈē-fə, ˈe-fə\ *n* [ME *ephi*, fr. LL, fr. Heb *ēphāh*, fr. Egypt *ʾpt*] (1611) : an ancient Hebrew unit of dry measure equal to 1/10 homer or a little over a bushel

ephebe \ˈe-ˌfēb, i-ˈfēb\ *n* [L *ephebus*] (1880) : EPHEBUS; *also* : a young man : YOUTH

ephe·bic \i-ˈfē-bik\ *adj* (1865) : of, relating to, or characteristic of an ephebe or ephebus

ephe·bus \i-ˈfē-bəs, e-\ *n, pl* **-bi** \-ˌbī\ [L, fr. Gk *ephēbos*, fr. *epi-* + *hēbē* youth, puberty] (1627) : a youth of ancient Greece; *esp* : an Athenian 18 or 19 years old in training for full citizenship

ephe·dra \i-ˈfe-drə, ˈe-fə-drə\ *n* [NL, genus name, fr. L, equisetum, fr. Gk, fr. *ephedros* sitting upon, fr. *epi-* + *hedra* seat — more at SIT] (ca. 1889) **1** : any of a genus (*Ephedra* of the family Ephedraceae) of jointed nearly leafless shrubs of dry or desert regions with the leaves reduced to scales at the nodes **2** : an extract of ma huang containing ephedrine and related alkaloids and used as a dietary supplement

ephed·rine \i-ˈfe-drən, *Brit also* ˈe-fə-drən\ *n* [NL *Ephedra*] (1889) : a crystalline sympathomimetic alkaloid $C_{10}H_{15}NO$ extracted from Chinese ephedras or synthesized and usu. used in the form of a salt esp. as a bronchodilator and decongestant

ephem·era \i-ˈfe-mər-ə, -ˈfem-rə\ *n, pl* **ephemera** *also* **ephem·er·ae** \-mər-ē, -rē\ *or* **ephemeras** [NL, fr. Gk *ephēmera*, neut. pl. of *ephēmeros*] (1650) **1** : something of no lasting significance — usu. used in pl. **2** *ephemera pl* : paper items (as posters, broadsides, and tickets) that were orig. meant to be discarded after use but have since become collectibles

[1]**ephem·er·al** \i-ˈfem-rəl, -ˈfem-; -ˈfe-mə-, -ˈfē-\ *adj* [Gk *ephēmeros* lasting a day, daily, fr. *epi-* + *hēmera* day] (1576) **1** : lasting one day only ⟨an ~ fever⟩ **2** : lasting a very short time ⟨~ pleasures⟩ ***syn*** see TRANSIENT — **ephem·er·al·ly** \-rə-lē\ *adv*

[2]**ephemeral** *n* (1807) : something ephemeral; *specif* : a plant that grows, flowers, and dies in a few days

ephem·er·al·i·ty \i-ˌfe-mə-ˈra-lə-tē, -ˌfē-\ *n, pl* **-ties** (1822) **1** *pl* : ephemeral things **2** : the quality or state of being ephemeral

ephem·er·id \i-ˈfe-mə-rəd\ *n* [ultim. fr. Gk *ephēmeron*] (1872) : MAYFLY

ephem·er·is \-mə-rəs\ *n, pl* **eph·e·mer·i·des** \ˌe-fə-ˈmer-ə-ˌdēz\ [L, diary, ephemeris, fr. Gk *ephēmeris*, fr. *ephēmeros*] (1508) : a tabular statement of the assigned places of a celestial body for regular intervals

ephemeris time *n* (1950) : a uniform measure of time defined by the orbital motions of the planets

Ephe·sians \i-ˈfē-zhənz\ *n pl but sing in constr* [short for *Epistle to the Ephesians*] (1549) : a letter addressed to early Christians and included as a book in the New Testament — see BIBLE table

eph·od \ˈe-ˌfäd, ˈē-\ *n* [ME, fr. LL, fr. Heb *ēphōdh*] (14c) **1** : a linen apron worn in ancient Hebrew rites; *esp* : a vestment for the high priest **2** : an ancient Hebrew instrument of priestly divination

eph·or \ˈe-fər, -ˌfȯr\ *n* [L *ephorus*, fr. Gk *ephoros*, fr. *ephoran* to oversee, fr. *epi-* + *horan* to see — more at WARY] (1579) **1** : one of five ancient Spartan magistrates having power over the king **2** : a government official in modern Greece; *esp* : one who oversees public works — **eph·or·ate** \ˈe-fə-ˌrāt\ *n*

Ephra·im \ˈē-frē-əm\ *n* [Heb *Ephrayim*] (bef. 12c) : a son of Joseph and the traditional eponymous ancestor of one of the tribes of Israel

Ephra·im·ite \-frē-ə-ˌmīt\ *n* (1568) **1** : a member of the Hebrew tribe of Ephraim **2** : a native or inhabitant of the biblical northern kingdom of Israel

epi- *or* **ep-** *prefix* [L, fr. Gk, fr. *epi* on, at, besides, after; akin to OE *eofot* crime] **1** : upon ⟨*epi*phyte⟩ : besides ⟨*epi*phenomenon⟩ : attached to ⟨*epi*didymis⟩ : over ⟨*epi*center⟩ : outer ⟨*epi*blast⟩ : after ⟨*epi*genesis⟩ **2 a** : chemical entity related to (such) another ⟨*epi*mer⟩ **b** : chemical entity distinguished from (such) another by having a bridge connection ⟨*epi*chlorohydrin⟩

epi·blast \ˈe-pə-ˌblast\ *n* (1875) : the outer layer of the blastoderm : ECTODERM — **epi·blas·tic** \ˌe-pə-ˈblas-tik\ *adj*

epib·o·ly \i-ˈpi-bə-lē\ *n, pl* **-lies** [Gk *epibolē* addition, fr. *epiballein* to throw on, fr. *epi-* + *ballein* to throw — more at DEVIL] (1875) : the growing of one part about another; *esp* : such growth of the dorsal lip area during gastrulation — **ep·i·bol·ic** \ˌe-pə-ˈbä-lik\ *adj*

[1]**ep·ic** \ˈe-pik\ *adj* [L *epicus*, fr. Gk *epikos*, fr. *epos* word, speech, poem — more at VOICE] (1589) **1** : of, relating to, or having the characteristics of an epic ⟨an ~ poem⟩ **2 a** : extending beyond the usual or ordinary esp. in size or scope ⟨his genius was ~ —*Times Lit. Supp.*⟩ **b** : HEROIC — **ep·i·cal** \-pi-kəl\ *adj* — **ep·i·cal·ly** \-pi-k(ə-)lē\ *adv*

[2]**epic** *n* (1706) **1** : a long narrative poem in elevated style recounting the deeds of a legendary or historical hero ⟨the *Iliad* and the *Odyssey* are ~*s*⟩ **2** : a work of art (as a novel or drama) that resembles or suggests an epic **3** : a series of events or body of legend or tradition thought to form the proper subject of an epic ⟨the ~ of the winning of the West⟩

epi·ca·lyx \ˌe-pi-ˈkā-liks *also* -ˈka-liks\ *n* (1870) : an involucre resembling the calyx but consisting of a whorl of bracts that is exterior to the calyx or results from the union of the sepal appendages

epi·can·thic fold \ˌe-pə-ˈkan(t)-thik-\ *n* [NL *epicanthus* epicanthic fold, fr. *epi-* + *canthus* canthus] (1913) : a prolongation of a fold of the skin of the upper eyelid over the inner angle or both angles of the eye

epi·car·di·um \ˌe-pə-ˈkär-dē-əm\ *n, pl* **-dia** \-dē-ə\ [NL] (ca. 1865) : the inner layer of the pericardium that closely envelops the heart — **epi·car·di·al** \-dē-əl\ *adj*

epi·carp \ˈe-pi-ˌkärp\ *n* [F *épicarpe*, fr. *épi-* epi- + *-carpe* -carp] (1835) : EXOCARP

ep·i·cene \ˈe-pə-ˌsēn\ *adj* [ME, fr. L *epicoenus*, fr. Gk *epikoinos*, fr. *epi-* + *koinos* common — more at CO-] (15c) **1** *of a noun* : having but one form to indicate either sex **2 a** : having characteristics typical of the other sex : INTERSEXUAL **b** : EFFEMINATE **3** : lacking characteristics of either sex — **epicene** *n* — **ep·i·cen·ism** \-ˌsē-ˌni-zəm, ˌe-pə-ˈ\ *n*

epi·cen·ter \ˈe-pi-ˌsen-tər\ *n* [NL *epicentrum*, fr. *epi-* + L *centrum* center] (1887) **1** : the part of the earth's surface directly above the focus of an earthquake — compare HYPOCENTER 1 **2** : CENTER 2a, b, c ⟨the ~ of world finance⟩ — **epi·cen·tral** \ˌe-pi-ˈsen-trəl\ *adj*

epi·chlo·ro·hy·drin \ˌe-pi-ˌklȯr-ə-ˈhī-drən\ *n* (ca. 1891) : a volatile liquid toxic epoxide C_3H_5ClO having a chloroform odor and used esp. in making epoxy resins and rubbers

epi·con·ti·nen·tal \ˌe-pi-ˌkän-tə-ˈnen-tᵊl\ *adj* (1900) : lying upon a continent or a continental shelf ⟨~ seas⟩

epi·cot·yl \ˈe-pi-ˌkä-tᵊl\ *n* [*epi-* + *cotyle*don] (1880) : the portion of the axis of a plant embryo or seedling above the cotyledonary node

ep·i·crit·ic \ˌe-pə-ˈkri-tik\ *adj* [Gk *epikritikos* determinative, fr. *epikrinein* to decide, fr. *epi-* + *krinein* to judge — more at CERTAIN] (1905) : of, relating to, being, or mediating cutaneous sensory reception marked by accurate discrimination between small degrees of sensation

epic simile *n* (1931) : an extended simile that is used typically in epic poetry to intensify the heroic stature of the subject

ep·i·cure \ˈe-pi-ˌkyu̇r\ *n* [*Epicurus*] (1565) **1** *archaic* : one devoted to sensual pleasure : SYBARITE **2** : one with sensitive and discriminating tastes esp. in food or wine

syn EPICURE, GOURMET, GOURMAND, GASTRONOME mean one who takes pleasure in eating and drinking. EPICURE implies fastidiousness and voluptuousness of taste. GOURMET implies being a connoisseur in food and drink and the discriminating enjoyment of them. GOURMAND implies a hearty appetite for good food and drink, not without discernment, but with less than a gourmet's. GASTRONOME implies that one has studied extensively the history and rituals of haute cuisine.

ep·i·cu·re·an \ˌe-pi-kyu̇-ˈrē-ən, -ˈkyu̇r-ē-\ *adj* (1586) **1** *cap* : of or relating to Epicurus or Epicureanism **2** : of, relating to, or suited to an epicure

Epicurean *n* (14c) **1** : a follower of Epicurus **2** *often not cap* : EPICURE 2

ep·i·cu·re·an·ism \-ə-ˌni-zəm\ *n* (ca. 1751) **1** *cap* **a** : the philosophy of Epicurus who subscribed to a hedonistic ethics that considered an imperturbable emotional calm the highest good and whose followers held intellectual pleasures superior to transient sensualism **b** : a way of life in accord with Epicureanism **2** : EPICURISM

ep·i·cur·ism \ˈe-pi-ˌkyu̇r-ˌi-zəm, ˌe-pi-ˈ\ *n* (1586) : the practices or tastes of an epicure or an epicurean

epi·cu·ti·cle \ˌe-pi-ˈkyü-ti-kəl\ *n* (1929) : the outermost waxy layer of the arthropod exoskeleton — **epi·cu·tic·u·lar** \-kyü-ˈti-kyə-lər\ *adj*

epi·cy·cle \ˈe-pə-ˌsī-kəl\ *n* [ME *epicicle*, fr. LL *epicyclus*, fr. Gk *epikyklos*, fr. *epi-* + *kyklos* circle — more at WHEEL] (14c) **1** *in Ptolemaic astron* : a circle in which a planet moves and which has a center that is itself carried around at the same time on the circumference of a larger circle **2** : a process going on within a larger one — **epi·cy·clic** \ˌe-pə-ˈsī-klik, -ˈsi-klik\ *adj*

epicyclic train *n* (1869) : a train (as of gear wheels) designed to have one or more parts travel around the circumference of another fixed or revolving part

epi·cy·cloid \ˌe-pə-ˈsī-ˌklȯid\ *n* (ca. 1755) : a curve traced by a point on a circle that rolls on the outside of a fixed circle — **epi·cy·cloi·dal** \-sī-ˈklȯi-dᵊl\ *adj*

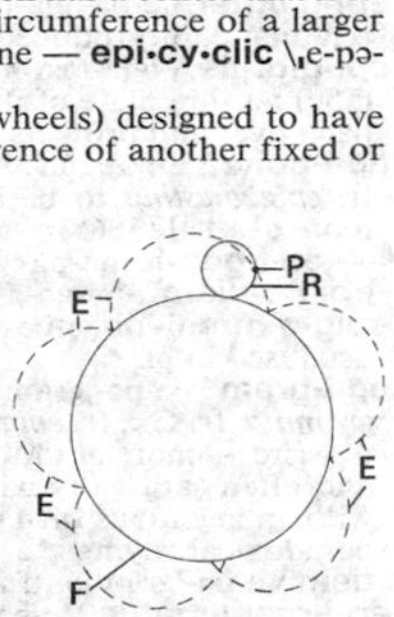

epicycloid *E*, traced by point *P*, on circle *R*, rolling on fixed circle *F*

[1]**ep·i·dem·ic** \ˌe-pə-ˈde-mik\ *adj* [F *épidémique*, fr. MF, fr. *epidemie*, n., epidemic, fr. LL *epidemia*, fr. Gk *epidēmia* visit, epidemic, fr. *epidēmos* visiting, epidemic, fr. *epi-* + *dēmos* people — more at DEMAGOGUE] (1603) **1** : affecting or tending to affect a disproportionately large number of individuals within a population, community, or region at the same time ⟨typhoid was ~⟩ **2 a** : excessively prevalent **b** : CONTAGIOUS 4 ⟨~ laughter⟩ **3** : of, relating to, or constituting an epidemic ⟨the practice had reached ~ proportions⟩ — **ep·i·dem·i·cal** \-ˈde-mi-kəl\ *adj* — **ep·i·dem·i·cal·ly** \-ˈde-mi-k(ə-)lē\ *adv* — **ep·i·de·mic·i·ty** \-də-ˈmi-sə-tē\ *n*

[2]**epidemic** *n* (1757) **1** : an outbreak of epidemic disease **2** : an outbreak or product of sudden rapid spread, growth, or development ⟨an ~ of bankruptcies⟩

ep·i·de·mi·ol·o·gy \ˌe-pə-ˌdē-mē-ˈä-lə-jē, -ˌde-mē-\ *n* [LL *epidemia* + ISV *-logy*] (ca. 1860) **1** : a branch of medical science that deals with the incidence, distribution, and control of disease in a population **2**

\ə\ **a**but \ᵊ\ kitten, F table \ər\ f**ur**ther \a\ **a**sh \ā\ **a**ce \ä\ m**o**p, m**ar** \au̇\ **ou**t \ch\ **ch**in \e\ b**e**t \ē\ **ea**sy \g\ **g**o \i\ h**i**t \ī\ **i**ce \j\ **j**ob \ŋ\ si**ng** \ō\ g**o** \ȯ\ l**aw** \ȯi\ b**oy** \th\ **th**in \t͟h\ **th**e \ü\ l**oo**t \u̇\ f**oo**t \y\ **y**et \zh\ vi**s**ion, beige \k, ⁿ, œ, ue, ʸ\ *see* Guide to Pronunciation

: the sum of the factors controlling the presence or absence of a disease or pathogen — **ep·i·de·mi·o·log·i·cal** \-ˌdē-mē-ə-ˈlä-ji-kəl, -ˌde-mē-\ *also* **ep·i·de·mi·o·log·ic** \-jik\ *adj* — **ep·i·de·mi·o·log·i·cal·ly** \-ji-k(ə-)lē\ *adv* — **ep·i·de·mi·ol·o·gist** \-ˌdē-mē-ˈä-lə-jist, -ˌde-mē-\ *n*

ep·i·den·drum \ˌe-pə-ˈden-drəm\ *n* [NL, fr. Gk *epi-* + *dendron* tree — more at DENDR-] (1791) : any of a large genus (*Epidendrum*) of chiefly epiphytic orchids found esp. in tropical America

epi·der·mal \ˌe-pə-ˈdər-məl\ *also* **epi·der·mic** \-mik\ *adj* (1816) : of, relating to, or arising from the epidermis

epidermal growth factor *n* (1966) : a polypeptide hormone that stimulates cell proliferation

epi·der·mis \ˌe-pə-ˈdər-məs\ *n* [LL, fr. Gk, fr. *epi-* + *derma* skin — more at DERM-] (1626) **1 a :** the outer epithelial layer of the external integument of the animal body that is derived from the embryonic epiblast; *specif* : the outer nonsensitive and nonvascular layer of the skin of a vertebrate that overlies the dermis **b :** any of various animal integuments **2 :** a thin surface layer of tissue in higher plants formed by growth of a primary meristem

epi·der·moid \-ˌmȯid\ *adj* (1836) : resembling epidermis or epidermal cells : made up of elements like those of epidermis ⟨an ~ cyst⟩

epi·dia·scope \ˌe-pə-ˈdī-ə-ˌskōp\ *n* [ISV] (1903) **1 :** a projector for images of both opaque objects and transparencies **2 :** EPISCOPE

ep·i·did·y·mis \ˌe-pə-ˈdi-də-məs\ *n, pl* **-mi·des** \-mə-ˌdēz\ [NL, fr. Gk, fr. *epi-* + *didymos* testicle, twin, fr. *dyo* two — more at TWO] (1610) : a system of ductules emerging posteriorly from the testis that holds sperm during maturation and that forms a tangled mass before uniting into a single coiled duct which is continuous with the vas deferens — **ep·i·did·y·mal** \-məl\ *adj*

epi·did·y·mi·tis \ˌe-pə-ˌdi-də-ˈmī-təs\ *n* [NL] (1852) : inflammation of the epididymis

ep·i·dote \ˈe-pə-ˌdōt\ *n* [F *épidote,* fr. Gk *epididonai* to give in addition, fr. *epi-* + *didonai* to give — more at DATE] (1808) : a yellowish-green mineral $Ca_2(Al,Fe)_3Si_3O_{12}OH$ usu. occurring in grains or columnar masses and sometimes used as a gemstone

[1]**epi·du·ral** \ˌe-pi-ˈd(y)u̇r-əl\ *adj* (1882) : situated upon or administered or placed outside the dura mater ⟨~ anesthesia⟩ ⟨an ~ abscess⟩

[2]**epidural** *n* (1970) : an injection of a local anesthetic into the space outside the dura mater of the spinal cord in the lower back region to produce loss of sensation esp. in the abdomen or pelvic region

epi·fau·na \-ˈfȯ-nə, -ˈfä-\ *n* [NL] (ca. 1914) : benthic fauna living on the substrate (as a hard sea floor) or on other organisms — compare INFAUNA — **epi·fau·nal** \-ˈfȯ-nᵊl, -ˈfä-\ *adj*

epi·gas·tric \ˌe-pi-ˈgas-trik\ *adj* (ca. 1678) **1 :** lying upon or over the stomach **2 a :** of, relating to, supplying, or draining the anterior walls of the abdomen **b :** of or relating to the abdominal region

epi·ge·al \ˌe-pi-ˈjē-əl\ *also* **epi·ge·an** \-ˈjē-ən\ *or* **epi·ge·ous** \-ˈjē-əs\ *or* **epi·ge·ic** \-ˈjē-ik\ *adj* [Gk *epigaios* upon the earth, fr. *epi-* + *gaia* earth] (1861) **1** *of a cotyledon* : forced above ground by elongation of the hypocotyl **2 :** marked by the production of epigeal cotyledons ⟨~ germination⟩ **3 :** living on or near the surface of the ground; *also* : relating to or being the environment near the surface of the ground

epi·gen·e·sis \ˌe-pə-ˈje-nə-səs\ *n* [NL] (1798) **1 :** development of a plant or animal from an egg or spore through a series of processes in which unorganized cell masses differentiate into organs and organ systems; *also* : the theory that plant and animal development proceeds in this way — compare PREFORMATION 2 **2 :** change in the mineral character of a rock owing to outside influences

epi·ge·net·ic \-jə-ˈne-tik\ *adj* (1883) **1 a :** of, relating to, or produced by the chain of developmental processes in epigenesis that lead from genotype to phenotype after the initial action of the genes **b :** relating to, being, or involving changes in gene function that do not involve changes in DNA sequence ⟨~ inheritance⟩ **2** *of a deposit or structure* : formed after the laying down of the enclosing rock — **epi·ge·net·i·cal·ly** \-ˈne-ti-k(ə-)lē\ *adv*

epi·ge·net·ics \ˌe-pə-jə-ˈne-tiks\ *n* (1942) : the study of heritable changes in gene function that do not involve changes in DNA sequence

epi·glot·tal \ˌe-pə-ˈglä-tᵊl\ *also* **epi·glot·tic** \-ˈglä-tik\ *adj* (1926) : of, relating to, or produced with the aid of the epiglottis

epi·glot·tis \-ˈglä-təs\ *n* [NL, fr. Gk *epiglōttis,* fr. *epi-* + *glōttis* glottis] (15c) : a thin plate of flexible cartilage in front of the glottis that folds back over and protects the glottis during swallowing

ep·i·gone \ˈe-pə-ˌgōn\ *n* [G, fr. L *epigonus* successor, fr. Gk *epigonos,* fr. *epigignesthai* to be born after, fr. *epi-* + *gignesthai* to be born — more at KIN] (1865) : FOLLOWER, DISCIPLE; *also* : an inferior imitator — **ep·i·gon·ic** \ˌe-pə-ˈgä-nik\ *or* **epig·o·nous** \i-ˈpi-gə-nəs, e-\ *adj* — **epig·o·nism** \-ˈpi-gə-ˌni-zəm\ *n*

epig·o·nus \i-ˈpi-gə-nəs, e-\ *n, pl* **-ni** \-ˌnī, -ˌnē\ [L] (1922) : EPIGONE — usu. used in pl.

ep·i·gram \ˈe-pə-ˌgram\ *n* [ME *epigrame,* fr. L *epigrammat-, epigramma,* fr. Gk, fr. *epigraphein* to write on, inscribe, fr. *epi-* + *graphein* to write — more at CARVE] (15c) **1 :** a concise poem dealing pointedly and often satirically with a single thought or event and often ending with an ingenious turn of thought **2 :** a terse, sage, or witty and often paradoxical saying **3 :** epigrammatic expression — **ep·i·gram·ma·tism** \ˌe-pə-ˈgra-mə-ˌti-zəm\ *n* — **ep·i·gram·ma·tist** \-ˈgra-mə-tist\ *n*

ep·i·gram·mat·ic \ˌe-pə-grə-ˈma-tik\ *adj* (1694) **1 :** of, relating to, or resembling an epigram **2 :** marked by or given to the use of epigrams — **ep·i·gram·mat·i·cal·ly** \-ˈma-ti-k(ə-)lē\ *adv*

ep·i·gram·ma·tize \-ˈgra-mə-ˌtīz\ *vb* **-tized; -tiz·ing** *vt* (1691) **1 :** to express in the form of an epigram **2 :** to make an epigram about ~ *vi* : to make an epigram — **ep·i·gram·ma·tiz·er** *n*

ep·i·graph \ˈe-pə-ˌgraf\ *n* [Gk *epigraphē,* fr. *epigraphein*] (1624) **1 :** an engraved inscription **2 :** a quotation set at the beginning of a literary work or one of its divisions to suggest its theme

epig·ra·pher \i-ˈpi-grə-fər, e-\ *n* (1887) : EPIGRAPHIST

ep·i·graph·ic \ˌe-pə-ˈgra-fik\ *also* **ep·i·graph·i·cal** \-fi-kəl\ *adj* (1858) : of or relating to epigraphs or epigraphy — **ep·i·graph·i·cal·ly** \-fi-k(ə-)lē\ *adv*

epig·ra·phist \i-ˈpi-grə-fist, e-\ *n* (ca. 1864) : a specialist in epigraphy

epig·ra·phy \-fē\ *n* (1851) **1 :** EPIGRAPHS, INSCRIPTIONS **2 :** the study of inscriptions; *esp* : the deciphering of ancient inscriptions

epig·y·nous \i-ˈpi-jə-nəs, e-\ *adj* (1830) **1** *of a floral organ* : adnate to the surface of the ovary and appearing to grow from the top of it **2 :** having epigynous floral organs — **epig·y·ny** \-nē\ *n*

ep·i·la·tion \ˌe-pə-ˈlā-shən\ *n* [F *épilation,* fr. *épiler* to remove hair, fr. *é-* e- + L *pilus* hair — more at PILE] (1878) : the loss or removal of hair

ep·i·lep·sy \ˈe-pə-ˌlep-sē\ *n, pl* **-sies** [ME *epilencie,* fr. AF & L; AF *epelempsie,* modif. of LL *epilepsia,* fr. Gk *epilēpsia,* fr. *epilambanein* to seize, fr. *epi-* + *lambanein* to take, seize — more at LATCH] (1543) : any of various disorders marked by abnormal electrical discharges in the brain and typically manifested by sudden brief episodes of altered or diminished consciousness, involuntary movements, or convulsions

epilept- *or* **epilepti-** *or* **epilepto-** *comb form* [Gk *epilēpt-,* fr. *epilēptos* seized by epilepsy, fr. *epilambanein*] : epilepsy ⟨*epilepto*id⟩

ep·i·lep·tic \ˌe-pə-ˈlep-tik\ *adj* (1605) : relating to, affected with, or having the characteristics of epilepsy ⟨an ~ seizure⟩ — **epileptic** *n* — **ep·i·lep·ti·cal·ly** \-ti-k(ə-)lē\ *adv*

ep·i·lep·ti·form \-ˈlep-tə-ˌfȯrm\ *adj* (ca. 1859) : resembling that of epilepsy ⟨an ~ convulsion⟩

ep·i·lep·to·gen·ic \-ˌlep-tə-ˈje-nik\ *adj* (ca. 1882) : inducing or tending to induce epilepsy ⟨an ~ drug⟩

ep·i·lep·toid \-ˈlep-ˌtȯid\ *adj* (ca. 1860) **1 :** EPILEPTIFORM **2 :** exhibiting symptoms resembling those of epilepsy ⟨the ~ person⟩

epi·lim·ni·on \ˌe-pə-ˈlim-nē-ˌän, -nē-ən\ *n* [NL, fr. *epi-* + Gk *limnion,* dim. of *limnē* marshy lake — more at LIMNETIC] (ca. 1910) : the water layer overlying the thermocline of a lake

ep·i·logue *also* **ep·i·log** \ˈe-pə-ˌlȯg, -ˌläg\ *n* [ME *epiloge,* fr. MF *epilogue,* fr. L *epilogus,* fr. Gk *epilogos,* fr. *epilegein* to say in addition, fr. *epi-* + *legein* to say — more at LEGEND] (15c) **1 :** a concluding section that rounds out the design of a literary work **2 a :** a speech often in verse addressed to the audience by an actor at the end of a play; *also* : the actor speaking such an epilogue **b :** the final scene of a play that comments on or summarizes the main action **3 :** the concluding section of a musical composition : CODA

epi·mer \ˈe-pi-mər\ *n* [*epi-* + *isomer*] (ca. 1911) : either of two stereoisomers that differ in the arrangement of groups on a single asymmetric carbon atom (as the first chiral center of a sugar's carbon chain) — **epi·mer·ic** \ˌe-pi-ˈmer-ik\ *adj*

epim·er·ase \i-ˈpi-mə-ˌrās, e-, -ˌrāz\ *n* (1960) : any of various isomerases that catalyze the inversion of asymmetric groups in a substrate with several centers of asymmetry

epi·my·si·um \ˌe-pə-ˈmi-zhē-əm, -zē-\ *n, pl* **-sia** \-zhē-ə, -zē-ə\ [NL, irreg. fr. *epi-* + Gk *mys* mouse, muscle — more at MOUSE] (1900) : the external connective-tissue sheath of a muscle

epi·nas·ty \ˈe-pə-ˌnas-tē\ *n* [ISV *epi-* + Gk *nastos* close-pressed (fr. *nassein* to press) + ISV [2]*-y*] (1880) : a nastic movement in which a plant part (as a flower petal) is bent outward and often downward

epi·neph·rine *also* **epi·neph·rin** \ˌe-pə-ˈne-frən\ *n* [ISV *epi-* + Gk *nephros* kidney — more at NEPHRITIS] (1899) : a colorless crystalline feebly basic sympathomimetic hormone $C_9H_{13}NO_3$ that is the principal blood-pressure raising hormone secreted by the adrenal medulla and is used medicinally esp. as a heart stimulant, a vasoconstrictor in controlling hemorrhages of the skin, and a muscle relaxant in bronchial asthma — called also *adrenaline*

epi·neu·ri·um \ˌe-pə-ˈn(y)u̇r-ē-əm\ *n* [NL] (ca. 1882) : the external connective-tissue sheath of a nerve trunk

epi·pe·lag·ic \ˌe-pi-pə-ˈla-jik\ *adj* (1940) : of, relating to, or constituting the part of the oceanic zone into which enough light penetrates for photosynthesis

ep·i·phan·ic \ˌe-pə-ˈfa-nik\ *adj* (1951) : of or having the character of an epiphany

epiph·a·nous \i-ˈpi-fə-nəs\ *adj* (1965) : EPIPHANIC

epiph·a·ny \i-ˈpi-fə-nē\ *n, pl* **-nies** [ME *epiphanie,* fr. AF, fr. LL *epiphania,* fr. LGk, pl., prob. alter. of Gk *epiphaneia* appearance, manifestation, fr. *epiphainein* to manifest, fr. *epi-* + *phainein* to show — more at FANCY] (14c) **1** *cap* : January 6 observed as a church festival in commemoration of the coming of the Magi as the first manifestation of Christ to the Gentiles or in the Eastern Church in commemoration of the baptism of Christ **2 :** an appearance or manifestation esp. of a divine being **3 a** (1) : a usu. sudden manifestation or perception of the essential nature or meaning of something (2) : an intuitive grasp of reality through something (as an event) usu. simple and striking (3) : an illuminating discovery, realization, or disclosure **b :** a revealing scene or moment

epi·phe·nom·e·nal \ˌe-pi-fi-ˈnä-mə-nᵊl\ *adj* (1899) : of or relating to an epiphenomenon : DERIVATIVE — **epi·phe·nom·e·nal·ly** \-nᵊl-ē\ *adv*

epi·phe·nom·e·nal·ism \-nə-ˌli-zəm\ *n* (1899) : a doctrine that mental processes are epiphenomena of brain processes

epi·phe·nom·e·non \-ˈnä-mə-ˌnän, -nən\ *n, pl* **-na** \-ˌnä, -nə\ (ca. 1706) : a secondary phenomenon accompanying another and caused by it; *specif* : a secondary mental phenomenon that is caused by and accompanies a physical phenomenon but has no causal influence itself

ep·i·phragm \ˈe-pə-ˌfram\ *n* [Gk *epiphragma* covering] (ca. 1854) : a closing membrane or septum (as of a snail shell or a moss capsule)

epiph·y·se·al \i-ˌpi-fə-ˈsē-əl\ *also* **ep·i·phys·i·al** \ˌe-pə-ˈfi-zē-əl\ *adj* (1842) : of or relating to an epiphysis

epiph·y·sis \i-ˈpi-fə-səs\ *n, pl* **-y·ses** \-ˌsēz\ [NL, fr. Gk, growth, fr. *epiphyesthai* to grow on, fr. *epi-* + *phyesthai* to grow, middle voice of *phyein* to bring forth — more at BE] (1634) **1 :** a part or process of a bone that ossifies separately and later becomes ankylosed to the main part of the bone; *esp* : an end of a long bone **2 :** PINEAL GLAND

epi·phyte \ˈe-pə-ˌfīt\ *n* (ca. 1847) : a plant that derives its moisture and nutrients from the air and rain and grows usu. on another plant

epi·phyt·ic \ˌe-pə-ˈfi-tik\ *adj* (1830) **1 :** of, relating to, or being an epiphyte **2 :** living on the surface of plants — **epi·phyt·i·cal·ly** \-ˈfi-ti-k(ə-)lē\ *adv* — **epi·phyt·ism** \ˈe-pə-ˌfī-ˌti-zəm\ *n*

ep·i·phy·tot·ic \-ˈtä-tik\ *adj* [*epi-* + *-phyte* + *-otic* (as in *epizootic*)] (ca. 1899) : of, relating to, or being a plant disease that tends to recur sporadically and to affect large numbers of susceptible plants — **epiphytotic** *n*

EPIRB *abbr* emergency position-indicating radio beacon

epi·scia \i-ˈpi-sh(ē-)ə\ *n* [NL, fr. Gk *episkios* shaded, fr. *epi-* + *skia* shadow — more at SHINE] (ca. 1868) : any of a genus (*Episcia*)

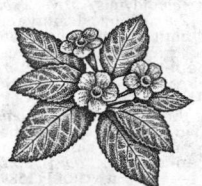

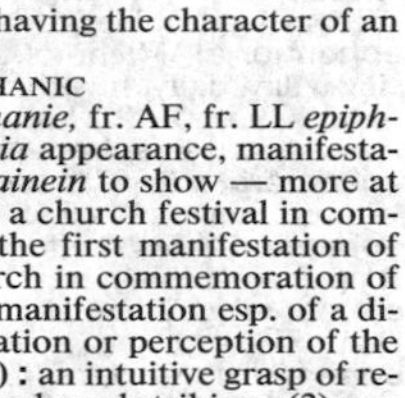
episcia

of tropical American herbs of the gesneriad family that have hairy foliage and are related to the African violet
epis·co·pa·cy \i-ˈpis-kə-pə-sē\ *n, pl* **-cies** (1641) **1 :** government of the church by bishops or by a hierarchy **2 :** EPISCOPATE
epis·co·pal \i-ˈpis-kə-pəl, -bəl\ *adj* [ME, fr. LL *episcopalis,* fr. *episcopus* bishop — more at BISHOP] (15c) **1 :** of or relating to a bishop **2 :** of, having, or constituting government by bishops **3** *cap* **:** of or relating to the Protestant Episcopal Church representing the Anglican communion in the U.S. — **epis·co·pal·ly** \-p(ə-)lē\ *adv*
Episcopal *n* (1752) **:** EPISCOPALIAN
Epis·co·pa·lian \i-ˌpis-kə-ˈpāl-yən\ *n* (1690) **1 :** an adherent of the episcopal form of church government **2 :** a member of an episcopal church (as the Protestant Episcopal Church) — **Episcopalian** *adj* — **Epis·co·pa·lian·ism** \-yə-ˌni-zəm\ *n*
epis·co·pate \i-ˈpis-kə-pət, -ˌpāt\ *n* (1641) **1 :** the rank or office of or term of as a bishop **2 :** DIOCESE **3 :** the body of bishops (as in a country)
epi·scope \ˈe-pə-ˌskōp\ *n* [ISV] (ca. 1909) **:** a projector for images of opaque objects (as photographs)
epi·si·ot·o·my \i-ˌpi-zē-ˈä-tə-mē, -ˌpē-\ *n* [ISV *episio-* vulva (fr. Gk *epision* pubic region) + *-tomy*] (1878) **:** surgical incision of the perineum to enlarge the vaginal opening for obstetrical purposes during the birth process
ep·i·sode \ˈe-pə-ˌsōd *also* -ˌzōd\ *n* [Gk *epeisodion,* fr. neut. of *epeisodios* coming in besides, fr. *epi-* + *eisodios* coming in, fr. *eis* into (akin to Gk *en* in) + *hodos* road, journey — more at IN] (1678) **1 :** a usu. brief unit of action in a dramatic or literary work: as **a :** the part of an ancient Greek tragedy between two choric songs **b :** a developed situation that is integral to but separable from a continuous narrative **:** INCIDENT **c :** one of a series of loosely connected stories or scenes **d :** the part of a serial presented at one performance **2 :** an event that is distinctive and separate although part of a larger series **3 :** a digressive subdivision in a musical composition ***syn*** see OCCURRENCE
ep·i·sod·ic \ˌe-pə-ˈsä-dik *also* -ˈzä-\ *also* **ep·i·sod·i·cal** \-di-kəl\ *adj* (1711) **1 :** made up of separate esp. loosely connected episodes **2 :** having the form of an episode **3 :** of or limited in duration or significance to a particular episode **:** TEMPORARY ⟨may be able to establish whether the sea-floor spreading is continuous or ~ —A. I. Hammond⟩ **4 :** occurring, appearing, or changing at usu. irregular intervals **:** OCCASIONAL ⟨an ~ illness⟩ — **ep·i·sod·i·cal·ly** \-di-k(ə-)lē\ *adv*
epi·some \ˈe-pə-ˌsōm, -ˌzōm\ *n* (ca. 1931) **:** a genetic determinant (as the DNA of some bacteriophages) that can replicate autonomously in bacterial cytoplasm or as an integral part of the chromosomes — **epi·som·al** \ˌe-pə-ˈsō-məl, -ˈzō-\ *adj* — **epi·som·al·ly** \-mə-lē\ *adv*
epis·ta·sis \i-ˈpis-tə-səs\ *n, pl* **-ta·ses** \-ˌsēz\ [NL, fr. Gk, act of stopping, fr. *ephistanai* to stop, fr. *epi-* + *histanai* to cause to stand — more at STAND] (ca. 1917) **:** suppression of the effect of a gene by a nonallelic gene — **ep·i·stat·ic** \ˌe-pə-ˈsta-tik\ *adj*
ep·i·stax·is \ˌe-pə-ˈstak-səs\ *n, pl* **-stax·es** \-ˌsēz\ [NL, fr. Gk, fr. *epistazein* to drip on, to bleed at the nose again, fr. *epi-* + *stazein* to drip] (1793) **:** NOSEBLEED
ep·i·ste·mic \ˌe-pə-ˈstē-mik, -ˈste-mik\ *adj* (1922) **:** of or relating to knowledge or knowing **:** COGNITIVE — **ep·i·ste·mi·cal·ly** \-mi-k(ə-)lē\ *adv*
epis·te·mol·o·gy \i-ˌpis-tə-ˈmä-lə-jē\ *n* [Gk *epistēmē* knowledge, fr. *epistanai* to understand, know, fr. *epi-* + *histanai* to cause to stand — more at STAND] (ca. 1856) **:** the study or a theory of the nature and grounds of knowledge esp. with reference to its limits and validity — **epis·te·mo·log·i·cal** \-mə-ˈlä-ji-kəl\ *adj* — **epis·te·mo·log·i·cal·ly** \-k(ə-)lē\ *adv* — **epis·te·mol·o·gist** \-ˈmä-lə-jist\ *n*
epis·tle \i-ˈpi-səl\ *n* [ME, letter, Epistle, fr. AF, fr. L *epistula, epistola* letter, fr. Gk *epistolē* message, letter, fr. *epistellein* to send to, fr. *epi-* + *stellein* to send] (13c) **1** *cap* **a :** one of the letters adopted as books of the New Testament **b :** a liturgical lection usu. from one of the New Testament Epistles **2 a :** LETTER; *esp* **:** a formal or elegant letter **b :** a composition in the form of a letter — **epis·tler** \-ˈpi-sə-lər\ *n*
¹**epis·to·lary** \i-ˈpis-tə-ˌler-ē, ˌe-pi-ˈstȯ-lə-rē\ *adj* (ca. 1656) **1 :** of, relating to, or suitable to a letter **2 :** contained in or carried on by letters ⟨an endless sequence of . . . ~ love affairs —*Times Lit. Supp.*⟩ **3 :** written in the form of a series of letters ⟨an ~ novel⟩
²**epistolary** *n, pl* **-lar·ies** (ca. 1900) **:** a lectionary containing a body of liturgical epistles
epis·to·ler \i-ˈpis-tə-lər\ *n* (1530) **:** the reader of the liturgical Epistle esp. in Anglican churches
ep·i·stome \ˈe-pə-ˌstōm\ *n* [NL *epistoma*] (1852) **:** any of several structures or regions situated above or covering the mouth of various invertebrates
epis·tro·phe \i-ˈpis-trə-(ˌ)fē\ *n* [Gk *epistrophē,* lit., turning about, fr. *epi-* + *strophē* turning — more at STROPHE] (ca. 1584) **:** repetition of a word or expression at the end of successive phrases, clauses, sentences, or verses esp. for rhetorical or poetic effect (as Lincoln's "of the people, by the people, for the people") — compare ANAPHORA
ep·i·taph \ˈe-pə-ˌtaf\ *n* [ME *epitaphe,* fr. AF & ML; AF, fr. ML *epitaphium,* fr. L, funeral oration, fr. Gk *epitaphion,* fr. *epi-* + *taphos* tomb, funeral] (14c) **1 :** an inscription on or at a tomb or a grave in memory of the one buried there **2 :** a brief statement commemorating or epitomizing a deceased person or something past — **ep·i·taph·ial** \ˌe-pə-ˈta-fē-əl\ *adj* — **ep·i·taph·ic** \-ˈta-fik\ *adj*
epit·a·sis \i-ˈpi-tə-səs\ *n, pl* **-a·ses** \-ˌsēz\ [Gk, increased intensity, fr. *epiteinein* to stretch tighter, fr. *epi-* + *teinein* to stretch — more at THIN] (1583) **:** the part of a play developing the main action and leading to the catastrophe
ep·i·taxy \ˈe-pə-ˌtak-sē\ *n* [ISV] (ca. 1931) **:** the growth on a crystalline substrate of a crystalline substance that mimics the orientation of the substrate — **ep·i·tax·i·al** \ˌe-pə-ˈtak-sē-əl\ *adj* — **ep·i·tax·i·al·ly** \-sē-ə-lē\ *adv*
ep·i·tha·la·mi·um \ˌe-pə-thə-ˈlā-mē-əm\ *or* **ep·i·tha·la·mi·on** \-mē-ən\ *n, pl* **-mi·ums** *or* **-mia** \-mē-ə\ [L & Gk; L *epithalamium,* fr. Gk *epithalamion,* fr. *epi-* + *thalamos* room, bridal chamber; perh. akin to Gk *tholos* rotunda] (1588) **:** a song or poem in honor of a bride and bridegroom — **ep·i·tha·lam·ic** \-ˈla-mik\ *adj*
ep·i·the·li·al \ˌe-pə-ˈthē-lē-əl\ *adj* (1845) **:** of or relating to epithelium
ep·i·the·li·al·i·za·tion \ˌe-pə-ˌthē-lē-ə-lə-ˈzā-shən\ *or* **ep·i·the·li·za·tion** \-ˌthē-lə-ˈzā-\ *n* (ca. 1934) **:** the process of becoming covered with or converted to epithelium — **ep·i·the·li·al·ize** \-ˈthē-lē-ə-ˌlīz\ *or* **ep·i·the·lize** \-ˈthē-ˌlīz\ *vt*
ep·i·the·li·oid \-lē-ˌȯid\ *adj* (1878) **:** resembling epithelium ⟨~ cells⟩
ep·i·the·li·o·ma \-ˌthē-lē-ˈō-mə\ *n, pl* **-mas** *also* **-ma·ta** \-mə-tə\ (1872) **:** a tumor derived from epithelial tissue — **ep·i·the·li·o·ma·tous** \-mə-təs\ *adj*
ep·i·the·li·um \ˌe-pə-ˈthē-lē-əm\ *n, pl* **-lia** \-lē-ə\ [NL, fr. *epi-* + Gk *thēlē* nipple — more at FEMININE] (1748) **1 :** a membranous cellular tissue that covers a free surface or lines a tube or cavity of an animal body and serves esp. to enclose and protect the other parts of the body, to produce secretions and excretions, and to function in assimilation **2 :** a usu. thin layer of parenchyma that lines a cavity or tube of a plant
ep·i·thet \ˈe-pə-ˌthet *also* -thət\ *n* [L *epitheton,* fr. Gk, fr. neut. of *epithetos* added, fr. *epitithenai* to put on, add, fr. *epi-* + *tithenai* to put — more at DO] (1579) **1 a :** a characterizing word or phrase accompanying or occurring in place of the name of a person or thing **b :** a disparaging or abusive word or phrase **c :** the part of a taxonomic name identifying a subordinate unit within a genus **2** *obs* **:** EXPRESSION — **ep·i·thet·ic** \ˌe-pə-ˈthe-tik\ *or* **ep·i·thet·i·cal** \-ti-kəl\ *adj*
epit·o·me \i-ˈpi-tə-mē\ *n* [L, fr. Gk *epitomē,* fr. *epitemnein* to cut short, fr. *epi-* + *temnein* to cut — more at TOME] (1520) **1 a :** a summary of a written work **b :** a brief presentation or statement of something **2 :** a typical or ideal example **:** EMBODIMENT ⟨the British monarchy itself is the ~ of tradition —Richard Joseph⟩ **3 :** brief or miniature form — usu. used with *in* — **ep·i·tom·ic** \ˌe-pə-ˈtä-mik\ *or* **ep·i·tom·i·cal** \-mi-kəl\ *adj*
epit·o·mise *Brit var of* EPITOMIZE
epit·o·mize \-ˌmīz\ *vt* **-mized; -miz·ing** (1594) **1 :** to make or give an epitome of **2 :** to serve as the typical or ideal example of
epi·tope \ˈe-pə-ˌtōp\ *n* [ISV, fr. *epi-* + Gk *topos* place] (1960) **:** a molecular region on the surface of an antigen capable of eliciting an immune response and of combining with the specific antibody produced by such a response — called also *determinant, antigenic determinant*
epi·zo·ic \ˌe-pə-ˈzō-ik\ *adj* (ca. 1857) **:** living upon the body of an animal ⟨an ~ plant⟩ — **epi·zo·ite** \-ˌīt\ *n*
epi·zo·ot·ic \ˌe-pə-zə-ˈwä-tik, -zō-ˈä-\ *n* [F *épizootique,* fr. *épizootie* such an outbreak, fr. *épi-* (as in *épidemie* epidemic) + Gk *zōiotēs* animal nature, fr. *zōē* life — more at QUICK] (1748) **:** an outbreak of disease affecting many animals of one kind at the same time; *also* **:** the disease itself — **epizootic** *adj*
epi·zo·ot·i·ol·o·gy \ˌe-pə-zə-ˌwä-tē-ˈä-lə-jē, -zō-ˌä-\ *n* (1910) **1 :** the sum of the factors controlling the occurrence of a disease or pathogen of animals **2 :** a science that deals with the character, ecology, and causes of outbreaks of animal diseases — **epi·zo·ot·i·o·log·i·cal** \-tē-ə-ˈlä-ji-kəl\ *also* **epi·zo·ot·i·o·log·ic** \-jik\ *adj*
EPO *abbr* erythropoietin
ep·och \ˈe-pək, ˈe-ˌpäk, *US also & Brit usu* ˈē-ˌpäk\ *n* [ML *epocha,* fr. Gk *epochē* cessation, fixed point, fr. *epechein* to pause, hold back, fr. *epi-* + *echein* to hold — more at SCHEME] (1614) **1 a :** an event or a time marked by an event that begins a new period or development **b :** a memorable event or date **2 a :** an extended period of time usu. characterized by a distinctive development or by a memorable series of events **b :** a division of geologic time less than a period and greater than an age **3 :** an instant of time or a date selected as a point of reference (as in astronomy) ***syn*** see PERIOD
ep·och·al \ˈe-pə-kəl, ˈe-ˌpä-kəl\ *adj* (1685) **1 :** of or relating to an epoch **2 :** uniquely or highly significant **:** MOMENTOUS ⟨during his three ~ years in the assembly —C. G. Bowers⟩; *also* **:** UNPARALLELED ⟨~ stupidity⟩ — **ep·och·al·ly** *adv*
ep·ode \ˈe-ˌpōd\ *n* [L *epodos,* fr. Gk *epōidos,* fr. *epōidos* sung or said after, fr. *epi-* + *aidein* to sing — more at ODE] (1598) **1 :** a lyric poem in which a long verse is followed by a shorter one **2 :** the third part of a triadic Greek ode following the strophe and the antistrophe
ep·onym \ˈe-pə-ˌnim\ *n* [Gk *epōnymos,* fr. *epōnymos* eponymous, fr. *epi-* + *onyma* name — more at NAME] (1846) **1 :** one for whom or which something is or is believed to be named **2 :** a name (as of a drug or a disease) based on or derived from an eponym — **ep·onym·ic** \ˌe-pə-ˈni-mik\ *adj*
epon·y·mous \i-ˈpä-nə-məs, e-\ *adj* (1846) **:** of, relating to, or being an eponym — **epon·y·mous·ly** *adv*
epon·y·my \-mē\ *n, pl* **-mies** (1865) **:** the explanation of a proper name (as of a town or tribe) by supposing a fictitious eponym
ep·o·pee \ˈe-pə-ˌpē\ *n* [F *épopée,* fr. Gk *epopoiia,* fr. *epos* + *poiein* to make — more at POET] (1697) **:** EPIC; *esp* **:** an epic poem
ep·os \ˈe-ˌpäs\ *n* [Gk, word, epic poem — more at VOICE] (ca. 1828) **1 :** EPIC 1 **2 :** a number of poems that treat an epic theme but are not formally united
ep·ox·i·da·tion \(ˌ)e-ˌpäk-sə-ˈdā-shən\ *n* (1944) **:** a conversion of a usu. unsaturated compound into an epoxide
ep·ox·ide \(ˌ)e-ˈpäk-ˌsīd\ *n* (1930) **:** an epoxy compound
ep·ox·i·dize \(ˌ)e-ˈpäk-sə-ˌdīz\ *vt* **-dized; -diz·ing** (1945) **:** to convert into an epoxide ⟨*epoxidized* esters⟩
¹**ep·oxy** \i-ˈpäk-sē\ *adj* [*epi-* + *oxy*] (1916) **1 :** containing oxygen attached to two different atoms already united in some other way; *specif* **:** containing a 3-membered ring consisting of one oxygen and two carbon atoms **2 :** of or relating to an epoxide
²**epoxy** *vt* **ep·ox·ied** *or* **ep·oxyed; ep·oxy·ing** (1966) **:** to glue, fill, or coat with epoxy resin
epoxy resin *n* (1950) **:** a flexible usu. thermosetting resin made by copolymerization of an epoxide with another compound having two hydroxyl groups and used chiefly in coatings and adhesives — called also *epoxy*
EPR *abbr* electron paramagnetic resonance
EPROM \ˈē-ˌpräm\ *n* [*e*rasable *p*rogrammable *r*ead-*o*nly *m*emory] (1977) **:** a read-only memory that can be erased (as by exposure to ultraviolet radiation) and usu. reprogrammed

\ə\ **abut** \ᵊ\ **kitten**, F table \ər\ **further** \a\ **ash** \ā\ **ace** \ä\ **mop, mar** \au̇\ **out** \ch\ **chin** \e\ **bet** \ē\ **easy** \g\ **go** \i\ **hit** \ī\ **ice** \j\ **job** \ŋ\ **sing** \ō\ **go** \ȯ\ **law** \ȯi\ **boy** \th\ **thin** \t͟h\ **the** \ü\ **loot** \u̇\ **foot** \y\ **yet** \zh\ **vision, beige** \k̲, ⁿ, œ, ue, ʸ\ *see* Guide to Pronunciation

ep·si·lon \'ep-sə-ˌlän, -lən\ *n* [Gk *e psilon,* lit., simple e] (15c) **1 :** the 5th letter of the Greek alphabet — see ALPHABET table **2 :** an arbitrarily small positive quantity in mathematical analysis — **ep·si·lon·ic** \ˌep-sə-'lä-nik\ *adj*
Ep·som salt \'ep-səm-\ *n* (1770) **:** EPSOM SALTS
Epsom salts *n pl but sing or pl in constr* [*Epsom,* England] (1828) **:** a bitter colorless or white crystalline salt $MgSO_4 \cdot 7H_2O$ that is a hydrated magnesium sulfate with cathartic properties
Ep·stein–Barr virus \ˌep-ˌstīn-'bär-\ *n* [Michael Anthony *Epstein* *b*1921 and Yvonne M. *Barr* *b*1932 Eng. pathologists] (1968) **:** a herpesvirus (species *Human herpesvirus 4* of the genus *Lymphocryptovirus*) that causes infectious mononucleosis and is associated with Burkitt's lymphoma and nasopharyngeal carcinoma — abbr. *EBV*
eq *abbr* **1** equal **2** equation
equa·ble \'e-kwə-bəl, 'ē-\ *adj* [L *aequabilis,* fr. *aequare* to make level or equal, fr. *aequus*] (1677) **1 :** marked by lack of variation or change **:** UNIFORM ⟨an ~ distance apart⟩ **2 :** marked by lack of noticeable, unpleasant, or extreme variation or inequality ⟨an ~ temperament⟩ ***syn*** see STEADY — **equa·bil·i·ty** \ˌe-kwə-'bi-lə-tē, ˌē-\ *n* — **equa·ble·ness** \'e-kwə-bəl-nəs, 'ē-\ *n* — **equa·bly** \-blē\ *adv*
[1]**equal** \'ē-kwəl\ *adj* [ME, fr. L *aequalis,* fr. *aequus* level, equal] (14c) **1 a (1) :** of the same measure, quantity, amount, or number as another **(2) :** identical in mathematical value or logical denotation **:** EQUIVALENT **b :** like in quality, nature, or status **c :** like for each member of a group, class, or society ⟨provide ~ employment opportunities⟩ **2 :** regarding or affecting all objects in the same way **:** IMPARTIAL **3 :** free from extremes: as **a :** tranquil in mind or mood **b :** not showing variation in appearance, structure, or proportion **4 a :** capable of meeting the requirements of a situation or a task **b :** SUITABLE ⟨bored with work not ~ to his abilities⟩ ***syn*** see SAME
[2]**equal** *n* (1573) **1 :** one that is equal ⟨insists that women can be absolute ~*s* with men —Anne Bernays⟩ **2 :** an equal quantity
[3]**equal** *vt* **equaled** *or* **equalled; equal·ing** *or* **equal·ling** (1590) **1 :** to be equal to; *esp* **:** to be identical in value to **2** *archaic* **:** EQUALIZE **3 :** to make or produce something equal to
equal–area *adj* (1901) *of a map projection* **:** maintaining constant ratio of size between quadrilaterals formed by the meridians and parallels and the quadrilaterals of the globe thereby preserving true areal extent of forms represented
equal·ise, equal·is·er *Brit var of* EQUALIZE, EQUALIZER
equal·i·tar·i·an \i-ˌkwä-lə-'ter-ē-ən\ *adj or n* (1799) **:** EGALITARIAN — **equal·i·tar·i·an·ism** \-ē-ə-ˌni-zəm\ *n*
equal·i·ty \i-'kwä-lə-tē\ *n, pl* **-ties** (15c) **1 :** the quality or state of being equal **2 :** EQUATION 2a
equal·ize \'ē-kwə-ˌlīz\ *vb* **-ized; -iz·ing** *vt* (1600) **1 :** to make equal **2 a :** to compensate for **b :** to make uniform; *esp* **:** to distribute evenly or uniformly ⟨~ the tax burden⟩ **c :** to adjust or correct the frequency characteristics of (an electronic signal) by restoring to their original level high frequencies that have been attenuated **~** *vi, chiefly Brit* **:** to tie the score — **equal·i·za·tion** \ˌē-kwə-lə-'zā-shən\ *n*
equal·iz·er \-ˌlī-zər\ *n* (1792) **:** one that equalizes: as **a :** a score that ties a game **b :** an electronic device (as in a sound-reproducing system) used to adjust response to different audio frequencies
equal·ly \'ē-kwə-lē\ *adv* (14c) **1 :** in an equal or uniform manner **:** EVENLY ⟨sharing the money ~⟩ **2 :** to an equal degree ⟨respected ~ by young and old⟩
equal opportunity employer *n* (1963) **:** an employer who agrees not to discriminate against any employee or job applicant because of race, color, religion, national origin, sex, physical or mental disability, or age
equal protection *n* (1953) **:** a guarantee under the 14th Amendment to the U.S. Constitution that a state must treat an individual or class of individuals the same as it treats other individuals or classes in like circumstances
equal sign *n* (ca. 1909) **:** a sign = indicating mathematical or logical equivalence — called also *equality sign, equals sign*
equa·nim·i·ty \ˌē-kwə-'ni-mə-tē, ˌe-kwə-\ *n, pl* **-ties** [L *aequanimitas,* fr. *aequo animo* with even mind] (ca. 1616) **1 :** evenness of mind esp. under stress ⟨nothing could disturb his ~⟩ **2 :** right disposition **:** BALANCE ⟨physical ~⟩
syn EQUANIMITY, COMPOSURE, SANGFROID mean evenness of mind under stress. EQUANIMITY suggests a habit of mind that is only rarely disturbed under great strain ⟨accepted her troubles with *equanimity*⟩. COMPOSURE implies the controlling of emotional or mental agitation by an effort of will or as a matter of habit ⟨maintaining his *composure* even under hostile questioning⟩. SANGFROID implies great coolness and steadiness under strain ⟨handled the situation with professional *sangfroid*⟩.
equate \i-'kwāt, 'ē-ˌ\ *vb* **equat·ed; equat·ing** [ME, fr. L *aequatus,* pp. of *aequare*] *vt* (15c) **1 a :** to make equal **:** EQUALIZE **b :** to make such an allowance or correction in as will reduce to a common standard or obtain a correct result **2 :** to treat, represent, or regard as equal, equivalent, or comparable ⟨~*s* disagreement with disloyalty⟩ **~** *vi* **:** to correspond as equal
equa·tion \i-'kwā-zhən *also* -shən\ *n* (14c) **1 a :** the act or process of equating **b (1) :** an element affecting a process **:** FACTOR **(2) :** a complex of variable factors **c :** a state of being equated; *specif* **:** a state of close association or identification ⟨bring governmental enterprises and payment for them into immediate ~ —R. G. Tugwell⟩ **2 a :** a usu. formal statement of the equality or equivalence of mathematical or logical expressions **b :** an expression representing a chemical reaction quantitatively by means of chemical symbols
equa·tion·al \i-'kwāzh-nəl, -'kwā-zhə-nᵊl *also* -'kwāsh-\ *adj* (1864) **1 :** of, using, or involving equation or equations **2 :** dividing into two equal parts — used esp. of the mitotic cell division usu. following reduction in meiosis — **equa·tion·al·ly** *adv*
equation of time (1667) **:** the difference between apparent time and mean time usu. expressed as a correction which is to be added to apparent time to give local mean time
equa·tor \i-'kwā-tər, 'ē-ˌ\ *n* [ME, fr. ML *aequator,* lit., equalizer, fr. L *aequare*] (14c) **1 :** the great circle of the celestial sphere whose plane is perpendicular to the axis of the earth **2 :** a great circle of the earth or a celestial body that is everywhere equally distant from the two poles and divides the surface into the northern and southern hemispheres **3 a :** a circle or circular band dividing the surface of a body into two usu. equal and symmetrical parts **b :** EQUATORIAL PLANE ⟨the ~ of a dividing cell⟩ **4 :** GREAT CIRCLE
equa·to·ri·al \ˌē-kwə-'tȯr-ē-əl, ˌe-kwə-\ *adj* (1664) **1 a :** of, relating to, or located at the equator or an equator; *also* **:** being in the plane of the equator ⟨a satellite in ~ orbit⟩ **b :** of, originating in, or suggesting the region around the geographic equator **2 a :** being or having a support that includes two axles at right angles to each other with one parallel to the earth's axis of rotation ⟨an ~ telescope mount⟩ **b :** extending in a direction essentially in the plane of a cyclic structure (as of cyclohexane) ⟨~ hydrogens⟩ — compare AXIAL
equatorial plane *n* (ca. 1892) **:** the plane perpendicular to the spindle of a dividing cell and midway between the poles
equatorial plate *n* (1882) **1 :** METAPHASE PLATE **2 :** EQUATORIAL PLANE
equa·tor·ward \i-'kwā-tər-wərd\ *adv or adj* (1875) **:** toward or near the equator ⟨currents flowing ~⟩ ⟨~ winds⟩
equer·ry \'e-kwə-rē, i-'kwer-ē\ *n, pl* **-ries** [modif. of MF *ecurie, escuyrie* squires (collectively), duties of a squire, care of horses, stable, fr. *escuier* squire — more at ESQUIRE] (1591) **1 :** an officer of a prince or noble charged with the care of horses **2 :** an officer of the British royal household in personal attendance upon the sovereign or a member of the royal family
[1]**eques·tri·an** \i-'kwes-trē-ən\ *adj* [L *equestr-, equester* of a horseman, fr. *eques* horseman, fr. *equus* horse — more at EQUINE] (ca. 1681) **1 a :** of, relating to, or featuring horseback riding ⟨~ Olympic events⟩ **b** *archaic* **:** riding on horseback **:** MOUNTED **c :** representing a person on horseback **2 :** of, relating to, or composed of knights
[2]**equestrian** *n* (1774) **:** one who rides on horseback
eques·tri·enne \i-ˌkwes-trē-'en\ *n* [[1]*equestrian* + *-enne* (as in *tragedienne*)] (1823) **:** a girl or woman who rides on horseback
equi- *comb form* [L *aequi-,* fr. *aequus* equal] **:** equal ⟨*equi*poise⟩ **:** equally ⟨*equi*probable⟩
equi·an·gu·lar \ˌē-kwi-'aŋ-gyə-lər, ˌe-kwi-\ *adj* (1660) **:** having all or corresponding angles equal ⟨mutually ~ parallelograms⟩
equi·ca·lor·ic \ˌē-kwə-kə-'lȯr-ik, ˌe-kwə-, -'lär-\ *adj* (1940) **:** capable of yielding equal amounts of energy in the body ⟨~ diets⟩
equid \'e-ˌkwid, 'ē-\ *n* [NL *Equidae,* family name, fr. *Equus,* genus name, fr. L, horse] (ca. 1889) **:** any of a family (Equidae) of perissodactyl mammals consisting of the horses, asses, zebras, and extinct related animals
equi·dis·tant \ˌē-kwə-'dis-tənt, ˌe-\ *adj* [MF or LL; MF, fr. LL *aequidistant-, aequidistans,* fr. L *aequi-* + *distant-, distans,* prp. of *distare* to stand apart — more at DISTANT] (1556) **1 :** equally distant ⟨a location ~ from two major cities⟩ **2 :** representing map distances true to scale in all directions — **equi·dis·tant·ly** *adv*
equi·lat·er·al \ˌē-kwə-'la-tə-rəl, ˌe-, -'la-trəl\ *adj* [LL *aequilateralis,* fr. L *aequi-* + *later-, latus* side — more at LATERAL] (1570) **1 :** having all sides equal ⟨an ~ triangle⟩ ⟨an ~ polygon⟩ — see TRIANGLE illustration **2 :** having all the faces equal ⟨an ~ polyhedron⟩
equilateral hyperbola *n* (1880) **:** a hyperbola with its asymptotes at right angles
equil·i·brant \i-'kwi-lə-brənt, ē-, *also* ˌē-kwə-'li-brənt\ *n* (1883) **:** a force that will balance one or more unbalanced forces
equil·i·brate \i-'kwi-lə-ˌbrāt\ *vb* **-brat·ed; -brat·ing** *vt* (1635) **:** to bring into or keep in equilibrium **:** BALANCE **~** *vi* **:** to bring about, come to, or be in equilibrium — **equil·i·bra·tion** \ˌē-ˌkwi-lə-'brā-shən\ *n* — **equil·i·bra·tor** \-'kwi-lə-ˌbrā-tər\ *n* — **equil·i·bra·to·ry** \-brə-ˌtōr-ē, -ˌtȯr-\ *adj*
equi·li·brist \ˌē-kwə-'li-brist, ˌe-; i-'kwi-lə-brist\ *n* (1760) **:** one (as a rope dancer) who performs difficult feats of balancing — **equil·i·bris·tic** \i-ˌkwi-lə-'bris-tik\ *adj*
equi·lib·ri·um \ˌē-kwə-'li-brē-əm, ˌe-\ *n, pl* **-ri·ums** *or* **-ria** \-brē-ə\ [L *aequilibrium,* fr. *aequilibris* being in equilibrium, fr. *aequi-* + *libra* weight, balance] (1608) **1 a :** a state of intellectual or emotional balance **:** POISE ⟨trying to recover his ~⟩ **b :** a state of adjustment between opposing or divergent influences or elements **2 :** a state of balance between opposing forces or actions that is either static (as in a body acted on by forces whose resultant is zero) or dynamic (as in a reversible chemical reaction when the rates of reaction in both directions are equal) **3 :** BALANCE 6a
equilibrium constant *n* (1929) **:** a number that expresses the relationship between the amounts of products and reactants present at equilibrium in a reversible chemical reaction at a given temperature
equi·mo·lar \-'mō-lər\ *adj* (1881) **1 :** of or relating to an equal number of moles ⟨an ~ mixture⟩ **2 :** having equal molar concentration
equine \'ē-ˌkwīn, 'e-\ *adj* [L *equinus,* fr. *equus* horse; akin to OE *eoh* horse, Gk *hippos,* Skt *aśva*] (1776) **:** of, relating to, or resembling a horse or the horse family — **equine** *n* — **equine·ly** *adv*
equine encephalitis *n* (1946) **:** any of three forms of encephalitis that attack chiefly equines and humans in various parts of No. and So. America and are caused by three togaviruses (species *Eastern equine encephalitis virus, Venezuelan equine encephalitis virus,* and *Western equine encephalitis virus* of the genus *Alphavirus*)
[1]**equi·noc·tial** \ˌē-kwə-'näk-shəl, ˌe-\ *adj* (1545) **1 :** relating to an equinox or to a state or the time of equal day and night **2 :** relating to the regions or climate on or near the equator **3 :** relating to the time when the sun passes an equinoctial point
[2]**equinoctial** *n* (1521) **1 :** EQUATOR 1 **2 :** an equinoctial storm
equi·nox \'ē-kwə-ˌnäks, 'e-\ *n* [ME, fr. AF or ML; AF *equinocce,* fr. ML *equinoxium,* alter. of L *aequinoctium,* fr. *aequi-* equi- + *noct-, nox* night — more at NIGHT] (14c) **1 :** either of the two points on the celestial sphere where the celestial equator intersects the ecliptic **2 :** either of the two times each year (as about March 21 and September 23) when the sun crosses the equator and day and night are everywhere on earth of approximately equal length
[1]**equip** \i-'kwip\ *vt* **equipped; equip·ping** [modif. of AF *eskiper, eschiper* to load on board a ship, embark, outfit, man, of Gmc origin; akin to OE *scipian* equip a ship, *scip* ship] (1523) **1 :** to furnish for service or action by appropriate provisioning ⟨~ an army⟩ **2 :** DRESS, ARRAY **3 :** to make ready **:** PREPARE ⟨wasn't *equipped* to handle the pressures of the job⟩ ***syn*** see FURNISH
[2]**equip** *abbr* equipment
eq·ui·page \'e-kwə-pij\ *n* (1573) **1 a :** material or articles used in equipment **:** OUTFIT **b** *archaic* **(1) :** a set of small articles (as for table

service) (2) : ETUI **c** : TRAPPINGS **2** *archaic* : RETINUE **3** : a horse-drawn carriage with its servants; *also* : such a carriage alone

equip·ment \i-ˈkwip-mənt\ *n* (1651) **1 a** : the set of articles or physical resources serving to equip a person or thing: as (1) : the implements used in an operation or activity : APPARATUS ⟨sports ~⟩ (2) : all the fixed assets other than land and buildings of a business enterprise (3) : the rolling stock of a railway **b** : a piece of such equipment **2 a** : the equipping of a person or thing **b** : the state of being equipped **3** : mental or emotional traits or resources : ENDOWMENT

[1]**equi·poise** \ˈe-kwə-ˌpȯiz, ˈē-\ *n* (1658) **1** : a state of equilibrium **2** : COUNTERBALANCE

[2]**equipoise** *vt* (1664) **1** : to serve as an equipoise to **2** : to put or hold in equipoise

equi·pol·lent \ˌē-kwə-ˈpä-lənt, ˌe-\ *adj* [ME, fr. AF, fr. L *aequipollent-, aequipollens,* fr. *aequi-* equi- + *pollent-, pollens,* prp. of *pollēre* to be able] (15c) **1** : equal in force, power, or validity **2** : the same in effect or signification — **equi·pol·lence** \-lən(t)s\ *n* — **equipollent** *n* — **equi·pol·lent·ly** *adv*

equi·pon·der·ant \-ˈpän-d(ə-)rənt\ *adj* [ML *aequiponderant-, aequiponderans,* prp. of *aequiponderare,* fr. L *aequi-* + *ponderare* to weigh — more at PONDER] (1630) : evenly balanced

equi·po·ten·tial \ˌē-kwə-pə-ˈten(t)-shəl, ˌe-\ *adj* (ca. 1865) : having the same potential : of uniform potential throughout ⟨~ points⟩

equi·prob·a·ble \-ˈprä-bə-bəl\ *adj* (1921) : having the same degree of logical or mathematical probability ⟨~ alternatives⟩

eq·ui·se·tum \ˌe-kwə-ˈsē-təm\ *n, pl* **-se·tums** *or* **-se·ta** \-ˈsē-tə\ [NL, fr. L *equisaetum* horsetail plant, fr. *equus* horse + *saeta* bristle] (1761) : HORSETAIL

eq·ui·ta·ble \ˈe-kwə-tə-bəl\ *adj* (1598) **1** : having or exhibiting equity : dealing fairly and equally with all concerned ⟨an ~ settlement of the dispute⟩ **2** : existing or valid in equity as distinguished from law ⟨an ~ defense⟩ ***syn*** see FAIR — **eq·ui·ta·bil·i·ty** \ˌe-kwə-tə-ˈbi-lə-tē\ *n* — **eq·ui·ta·ble·ness** \ˈe-kwə-tə-bəl-nəs\ *n* — **eq·ui·ta·bly** \-blē\ *adv*

eq·ui·ta·tion \ˌe-kwə-ˈtā-shən\ *n* [MF, fr. L *equitation-, equitatio,* fr. *equitare* to ride on horseback, fr. *equit-, eques* horseman, fr. *equus* horse] (1562) : the act or art of riding on horseback

eq·ui·ty \ˈe-kwə-tē\ *n, pl* **-ties** [ME *equite,* fr. AF *equité,* fr. L *aequitat-, aequitas,* fr. *aequus* equal, fair] (14c) **1 a** : justice according to natural law or right; *specif* : freedom from bias or favoritism **b** : something that is equitable **2 a** : a system of law originating in the English chancery and comprising a settled and formal body of legal and procedural rules and doctrines that supplement, aid, or override common and statute law and are designed to protect rights and enforce duties fixed by substantive law **b** : trial or remedial justice under or by the rules and doctrines of equity **c** : a body of legal doctrines and rules developed to enlarge, supplement, or override a narrow rigid system of law **3 a** : a right, claim, or interest existing or valid in equity **b** : the money value of a property or of an interest in a property in excess of claims or liens against it **c** : a risk interest or ownership right in property **d** : the common stock of a corporation

equity capital *n* (1942) : capital (as stock or surplus earnings) that is free of debt; *esp* : capital received for an interest in the ownership of a business

equiv *abbr* equivalency; equivalent

equiv·a·lence \i-ˈkwiv-lən(t)s, -ˈkwi-və-\ *n* (ca. 1541) **1 a** : the state or property of being equivalent **b** : the relation holding between two statements if they are either both true or both false so that to affirm one and to deny the other would result in a contradiction **2** : a presentation of terms as equivalent **3** : equality in metrical value of a regular foot and one in which there are substitutions

equivalence class *n* (1952) : a set for which an equivalence relation holds between every pair of elements

equivalence relation *n* (ca. 1949) : a relation (as equality) between elements of a set (as the real numbers) that is symmetric, reflexive, and transitive and for any two elements either holds or does not hold

equiv·a·len·cy \i-ˈkwiv-lən(t)-sē, -ˈkwi-və-\ *n, pl* **-cies** (1535) **1** : EQUIVALENCE **2** : a level of achievement equivalent to completion of an educational or training program ⟨a high school ~ certificate⟩

equiv·a·lent \-lənt\ *adj* [ME, fr. MF or LL; MF, fr. LL *aequivalent-, aequivalens,* prp. of *aequivalēre* to have equal power, fr. L *aequi-* + *valēre* to be strong — more at WIELD] (15c) **1** : equal in force, amount, or value; *also* : equal in area or volume but not superposable ⟨a square ~ to a triangle⟩ **2 a** : like in signification or import **b** : having logical equivalence ⟨~ statements⟩ **3** : corresponding or virtually identical esp. in effect or function **4** *obs* : equal in might or authority **5** : having the same chemical combining capacity ⟨~ quantities of two elements⟩ **6 a** : having the same solution set ⟨~ equations⟩ **b** : capable of being placed in one-to-one correspondence ⟨~ sets⟩ **c** : related by an equivalence relation ***syn*** see SAME — **equivalent** *n* — **equiv·a·lent·ly** *adv*

equivalent weight *n* (ca. 1855) : the mass of a substance esp. in grams that combines with or is chemically equivalent to eight grams of oxygen or one gram of hydrogen : the atomic or molecular weight divided by the valence

equiv·o·cal \i-ˈkwi-və-kəl\ *adj* [LL *aequivocus,* fr. *aequi-* equi- + *voc-, vox* voice — more at VOICE] (1599) **1 a** : subject to two or more interpretations and usu. used to mislead or confuse ⟨an ~ statement⟩ **b** : uncertain as an indication or sign ⟨~ evidence⟩ **2 a** : of uncertain nature or classification ⟨~ shapes⟩ **b** : of uncertain disposition toward a person or thing : UNDECIDED ⟨an ~ attitude⟩ **c** : of doubtful advantage, genuineness, or moral rectitude ⟨~ behavior⟩ ***syn*** see OBSCURE — **equiv·o·cal·i·ty** \-ˌkwi-və-ˈka-lə-tē\ *n* — **equiv·o·cal·ly** \-ˈkwi-və-k(ə-)lē\ *adv* — **equiv·o·cal·ness** \-kəl-nəs\ *n*

equiv·o·cate \i-ˈkwi-və-ˌkāt\ *vi* **-cat·ed; -cat·ing** (1590) **1** : to use equivocal language esp. with intent to deceive **2** : to avoid committing oneself in what one says ***syn*** see LIE — **equiv·o·ca·tion** \-ˌkwi-və-ˈkā-shən\ *n* — **equiv·o·ca·tor** \-ˈkwi-və-ˌkā-tər\ *n*

equi·voque *also* **equi·voke** \ˈe-kwə-ˌvōk, ˈē-\ *n* [F *équivoque,* fr. *équivoque* equivocal, fr. LL *aequivocus*] (1599) **1** : an equivocal word or phrase; *specif* : PUN **2 a** : double meaning **b** : WORDPLAY

er \ˈə, ˈä, *usu with prolonged vowel,* ÷ˈər\ *interj* (1862) — used to express hesitation

Er *symbol* erbium

ER *abbr* **1** earned run **2** emergency room

[1]**-er** *adj suffix or adv suffix* [ME *-er, -ere, -re,* fr. OE *-ra* (in adjectives), *-or* (in adverbs); akin to OHG *-iro,* adj. compar. suffix, L *-ior,* Gk *-iōn*] — used to form the comparative degree of adjectives and adverbs of one syllable ⟨hott*er*⟩ ⟨dri*er*⟩ and of some adjectives and adverbs of two or more syllables ⟨complet*er*⟩ ⟨beautifull*er*⟩

[2]**-er** *also* **-ier** *or* **-yer** *n suffix* [ME *-er, -ere, -ier, -iere;* partly fr. OE *-ere* (fr. L *-arius*); partly fr. OF *-ier, -iere,* fr. L *-arius, -aria, -arium* -ary; partly fr. AF *-ere,* fr. L *-ator* -or — more at -ARY, -OR] **1 a** : person occupationally connected with ⟨furri*er*⟩ ⟨law*yer*⟩ **b** : person or thing belonging to or associated with ⟨head*er*⟩ ⟨old-tim*er*⟩ **c** : native of : resident of ⟨cottag*er*⟩ ⟨New York*er*⟩ **d** : one that has ⟨three-deck*er*⟩ **e** : one that produces or yields ⟨pork*er*⟩ **2 a** : one that does or performs (a specified action) ⟨batt*er*⟩ — sometimes added to both elements of a compound ⟨build*er*-upp*er*⟩ **b** : one that is a suitable object of (a specified action) ⟨broil*er*⟩ **3** : one that is ⟨foreign*er*⟩ — in all senses *-yer* in a few words after *w, -ier* in a few other words, otherwise *-er*

era \ˈer-ə, ˈe-rə, ˈir-ə\ *n* [LL *aera,* fr. L, counters, pl. of *aer-, aes* copper, money — more at ORE] (1615) **1 a** : a fixed point in time from which a series of years is reckoned **b** : a memorable or important date or event; *esp* : one that begins a new period in the history of a person or thing **2** : a system of chronological notation computed from a given date as basis **3 a** : a period identified by some prominent figure or characteristic feature ⟨the ~ of the horse and buggy⟩ **b** : a stage in development (as of a person or thing) **c** : a large division of geologic time usu. shorter than an eon ⟨Paleozoic ~⟩ ***syn*** see PERIOD

ERA *abbr* **1** earned run average **2** Equal Rights Amendment

erad·i·cate \i-ˈra-də-ˌkāt\ *vt* **-cat·ed; -cat·ing** [L *eradicatus,* pp. of *eradicare,* fr. *e-* + *radic-, radix* root — more at ROOT] (1532) **1** : to pull up by the roots **2** : to do away with as completely as if by pulling up by the roots ⟨programs to ~ illiteracy⟩ ***syn*** see EXTERMINATE — **erad·i·ca·ble** \-ˈra-di-kə-bəl\ *adj* — **erad·i·ca·tion** \-ˌra-də-ˈkā-shən\ *n* — **erad·i·ca·tor** \-ˌkā-tər\ *n*

erase \i-ˈrās, *Brit* -ˈrāz\ *vb* **erased; eras·ing** [L *erasus,* pp. of *eradere,* fr. *e-* + *radere* to scratch, scrape — more at RODENT] *vt* (1605) **1 a** : to rub or scrape out (as written, painted, or engraved letters) ⟨~ an error⟩ **b** : to remove written or drawn marks from ⟨~ a blackboard⟩ **c** : to remove (recorded matter) from a magnetic medium; *also* : to remove recorded matter from ⟨~ a videotape⟩ **d** : to delete from a computer storage device ⟨~ a file⟩ **2 a** : to remove from existence or memory as if by erasing **b** : to nullify the effect or force of ~ *vi* : to yield to erasure — **eras·abil·i·ty** \-ˌrā-sə-ˈbi-lə-tē\ *n* — **eras·able** \-ˈrā-sə-bəl\ *adj*

eras·er \i-ˈrā-sər\ *n* (1790) : one that erases; *esp* : a device (as a piece of rubber or a felt pad) used to erase marks (as of ink or chalk)

Eras·tian \i-ˈras-tē-ən, -ˈras-chən\ *adj* [Thomas *Erastus* †1583 Swiss physician and Zwinglian theologian] (1773) : of, characterized by, or advocating the doctrine of state supremacy in ecclesiastical affairs — **Erastian** *n* — **Eras·tian·ism** \-ˌni-zəm\ *n*

era·sure \i-ˈrā-shər *also* -zhər\ *n* (1734) : an act or instance of erasing

Er·a·to \ˈer-ə-ˌtō\ *n* [Gk *Eratō*] (1557) : the Greek Muse of lyric and love poetry

er·bi·um \ˈər-bē-əm\ *n* [NL, fr. *Ytterby,* Sweden] (1843) : a metallic element of the rare-earth group — see ELEMENT table

[1]**ere** \ˈer\ *prep* [ME *er,* fr. OE *ǣr,* fr. *ǣr,* adv., early, soon; akin to OHG *ēr* earlier, Gk *ēri* early] (bef. 12c) : [2]BEFORE 2 ⟨~ nightfall⟩

[2]**ere** *conj* (bef. 12c) : [3]BEFORE

e–read·er \ˈē-ˌrē-dər\ *n* (1999) : a handheld electronic device designed to be used for reading e-books and similar material

Er·e·bus \ˈer-ə-bəs\ *n* [L, fr. Gk *Erebos*] (1578) **1** : a personification of darkness in Greek mythology **2** : a place of darkness in the underworld on the way to Hades

[1]**erect** \i-ˈrekt\ *adj* [ME, fr. L *erectus,* pp. of *erigere* to erect, fr. *e-* + *regere* to lead straight, guide — more at RIGHT] (14c) **1 a** : vertical in position; *also* : not spread out or decumbent ⟨an ~ plant stem⟩ ⟨columns still ~ in the ruins⟩ **b** : standing up or out from the body ⟨~ hairs⟩ **c** : characterized by firm or rigid straightness in bodily posture ⟨an ~ bearing⟩ **2** *archaic* : directed upward **3** *obs* : ALERT, WATCHFUL **4** : being in a state of physiological erection — **erect·ly** \-ˈrek-(t)lē\ *adv* — **erect·ness** \-ˈrek(t)-nəs\ *n*

[2]**erect** *vt* (15c) **1 a** (1) : to put up by the fitting together of materials or parts : BUILD (2) : to fix in an upright position (3) : to cause to stand up or stand out **b** *archaic* : to direct upward **c** : to change (an image) from an inverted to a normal position **2** : to elevate in status **3** : SET UP, ESTABLISH **4** *obs* : ENCOURAGE, EMBOLDEN **5** : to draw or construct (as a perpendicular or figure) upon a given base — **erect·able** \-ˈrek-tə-bəl\ *adj*

erec·tile \i-ˈrek-tᵊl, -ˌtī(-ə)l\ *adj* (1830) **1** : of, relating to, or capable of undergoing physiological erection ⟨~ tissue⟩ ⟨~ dysfunction⟩ **2** : capable of being raised to an upright position ⟨the ~ quills of a porcupine⟩ — **erec·til·i·ty** \-ˌrek-ˈti-lə-tē\ *n*

erec·tion \i-ˈrek-shən\ *n* (15c) **1 a** : the state marked by firm turgid form and erect position of a previously flaccid bodily part containing cavernous tissue when that tissue becomes dilated with blood **b** : an occurrence of such a state in the penis or clitoris **2** : the act or process of erecting something : CONSTRUCTION **3** : something erected

erec·tor \i-ˈrek-tər\ *n* (1538) : one that erects; *esp* : a muscle that raises or keeps a part erect

Erector *trademark* — used for a metal toy construction set

E region *n* (1930) : the part of the ionosphere occurring between about 55 and 80 miles (90 and 130 kilometers) above the surface of the earth and containing the daytime E layer and the sporadic E layer

ere·long \er-ˈlȯŋ\ *adv* (1553) *archaic* : BEFORE LONG, SOON

er·e·mite \ˈer-ə-ˌmīt\ *n* [ME — more at HERMIT] (13c) : HERMIT; *esp* : a religious recluse — **er·e·mit·ic** \ˌer-ə-ˈmi-tik\ *or* **er·e·mit·i·cal** \-ti-kəl\ *adj* — **er·e·mit·ism** \ˈer-ə-ˌmī-ˌti-zəm\ *n*

er·e·mu·rus \ˌer-ə-ˈmyu̇r-əs\ *n, pl* **-uri** \-ˈmyu̇r-ˌī\ [NL, fr. Gk *erēmos* solitary + *oura* tail — more at ASS] (1829) : any of a genus (*Eremurus*)

\ə\ **a**but \ᵊ\ kitten, F table \ər\ f**ur**ther \a\ **a**sh \ā\ **a**ce \ä\ m**o**p, m**a**r
\au̇\ **ou**t \ch\ **ch**in \e\ b**e**t \ē\ **ea**sy \g\ **g**o \i\ h**i**t \ī\ **i**ce \j\ **j**ob
\ŋ\ si**ng** \ō\ g**o** \ȯ\ l**aw** \ȯi\ b**oy** \th\ **th**in \th\ **th**e \ü\ l**oo**t \u̇\ f**oo**t
\y\ **y**et \zh\ vi**s**ion, beige \k, ⁿ, œ, ue, ʸ\ *see* Guide to Pronunciation

of perennial Asian herbs of the lily family that produce tall racemes of showy blooms — called also *foxtail lily*

ere·now \er-ˈnau̇\ *adv* (14c) *archaic* : HERETOFORE

erep·sin \i-ˈrep-sən\ *n* [ISV *er-* (prob. fr. L *eripere* to snatch away, fr. *e-* + *rapere* to seize) + *pepsin* — more at RAPID] (1902) : a mixture of exopeptidases obtained esp. from the intestinal juice

er·e·thism \ˈer-ə-ˌthi-zəm\ *n* [F *éréthisme,* fr. Gk *erethismos* irritation, fr. *erethizein* to irritate; akin to Gk *ornynai* to rouse — more at ORIENT] (1800) : abnormal irritability or responsiveness to stimulation

ere·while \er-ˈ(h)wī(-ə)l\ *also* **ere·whiles** \-ˈ(h)wī(-ə)lz\ *adv* (13c) *archaic* : a while before : FORMERLY

erg \ˈərg\ *n* [Gk *ergon* work — more at WORK] (1873) : a centimeter-gram-second unit of work equal to the work done by a force of one dyne acting through a distance of one centimeter and equivalent to 10^{-7} joule

erg- *or* **ergo-** *comb form* [Gk, fr. *ergon*] : work ⟨*ergo*meter⟩

er·gas·tic \(ˌ)ər-ˈgas-tik\ *adj* [Gk *ergastikos* able to work, fr. *ergazesthai* to work, fr. *ergon* work] (ca. 1896) : constituting the nonliving by-products of protoplasmic activity ⟨~ substances⟩

er·gas·to·plasm \-tə-ˌpla-zəm\ *n* [ISV] (1902) : ribosome-studded endoplasmic reticulum — **er·gas·to·plas·mic** \-ˌgas-tə-ˈplaz-mik\ *adj*

er·ga·tive \ˈər-gə-tiv\ *adj* [Gk *ergatēs* worker, fr. *ergon* work] (1939) : of, relating to, or being a language (as Inuit or Georgian) in which the objects of transitive verbs and subjects of intransitive verbs are typically marked by the same linguistic forms; *also* : being an inflectional morpheme that typically marks the subject of a transitive verb in an ergative language

-ergic *adj comb form* [*-ergy* work (fr. LL *-ergia,* fr. Gk, fr. *ergon* work) + *-ic* — more at WORK] : exhibiting or stimulating activity of ⟨dopamin*ergic*⟩

er·go \ˈer-(ˌ)gō, ˈər-\ *adv* [ME, fr. L, fr. OL, because of, fr. OL **e rogo* from the direction (of)] (14c) : THEREFORE, HENCE

ergo- *comb form* [F, fr. *ergot*] : ergot ⟨*ergo*sterol⟩

er·go·dic \(ˌ)ər-ˈgä-dik, -ˈgō-\ *adj* [ISV *erg-* + *-ode*] (1926) **1** : of or relating to a process in which every sequence or sizable sample is equally representative of the whole (as in regard to a statistical parameter) **2** : involving or relating to the probability that any state will recur; *esp* : having zero probability that any state will never recur — **er·go·dic·i·ty** \ˌər-gə-ˈdi-sə-tē\ *n*

er·go·gen·ic \ˌər-gə-ˈje-nik\ *adj* (1941) : enhancing physical performance ⟨athletic use of caffeine and other ~ aids⟩

er·go·graph \ˈər-gə-ˌgraf\ *n* [ISV] (1892) : an apparatus for measuring the work capacity of a muscle

er·gom·e·ter \(ˌ)ər-ˈgä-mə-tər\ *n* (ca. 1879) : an apparatus for measuring the work performed (as by a person exercising); *also* : an exercise machine equipped with an ergometer — **er·go·met·ric** \ˌər-gə-ˈme-trik\ *adj*

er·go·nom·ics \ˌər-gə-ˈnä-miks\ *n pl but sing or pl in constr* [*erg-* + *-nomics* (as in *economics*)] (1949) **1** : an applied science concerned with designing and arranging things people use so that the people and things interact most efficiently and safely — called also *biotechnology, human engineering, human factors* **2** : the design characteristics of an object resulting esp. from the application of the science of ergonomics — **er·go·nom·ic** \-mik\ *adj* — **er·go·nom·i·cal·ly** \-mi-k(ə-)lē\ *adv* — **er·gon·o·mist** \(ˌ)ər-ˈgä-nə-mist\ *n*

er·go·no·vine \ˌər-gə-ˈnō-ˌvēn\ *n* [*ergo-* + L *novus* new — more at NEW] (ca. 1936) : an alkaloid $C_{19}H_{23}N_3O_2$ derived from ergot and used esp. in the form of its maleate as an oxytocic

er·gos·ter·ol \(ˌ)ər-ˈgäs-tə-ˌrȯl, -ˌrōl\ *n* [ISV] (1906) : a crystalline steroid alcohol $C_{28}H_{44}O$ that occurs esp. in yeast, molds, and ergot and is converted by ultraviolet irradiation ultimately into vitamin D_2

er·got \ˈər-gət, -ˌgät\ *n* [F, lit., cock's spur] (1683) **1** : the black or dark purple sclerotium of fungi (genus *Claviceps*) that occurs as a club-shaped body replacing the seed of a grass (as rye); *also* : a fungus bearing ergots **2** : a disease of rye and other cereals caused by an ergot fungus **3 a** : the dried sclerotia of an ergot fungus grown on rye and containing several alkaloids (as ergonovine and ergotamine) **b** : any of such alkaloids used medicinally for their contractile effect on smooth muscle (as of the uterus and or blood vessels) — **er·got·ic** \(ˌ)ər-ˈgä-tik\ *adj*

er·got·a·mine \(ˌ)ər-ˈgä-tə-ˌmēn\ *n* [ISV] (1921) : an alkaloid $C_{33}H_{35}N_5O_5$ derived from ergot that is used chiefly in the form of its tartrate esp. in treating migraine

er·got·ism \ˈər-gə-ˌti-zəm\ *n* (ca. 1841) : a toxic condition produced by eating grain, grain products (as rye bread), or grasses infected with ergot fungus or by chronic excessive use of an ergot drug

er·got·ized \-ˌtīzd\ *adj* (1860) : infected with ergot ⟨~ grain⟩; *also* : poisoned by ergot ⟨~ cattle⟩

er·i·ca \ˈer-i-kə\ *n* [NL, fr. L *erice* heather, fr. Gk *ereikē* — more at BRIAR] (1826) : any of a large genus (*Erica*) of evergreen chiefly African plants of the heath family ranging from low shrubs to small trees

er·i·ca·ceous \ˌer-ə-ˈkā-shəs\ *adj* (ca. 1859) : of, relating to, or being a heath or the heath family

er·i·coid \ˈer-ə-ˌkȯid\ *adj* (1848) : resembling heath ⟨~ foliage⟩

Erie \ˈir-ē\ *n* [AmerF *Erie, Erié,* modif. of Huron *Eriehronon* the Erie people] (ca. 1909) **1** : a member of an American Indian people living south of Lake Erie in the 17th century **2** : the extinct and prob. Iroquoian language of the Erie people

erig·er·on \ə-ˈri-jə-ˌrän\ *n* [NL, fr. L, groundsel, fr. Gk *ērigerōn,* fr. *ēri* early + *gerōn* old man; fr. the hoary down of some species — more at ERE, GERONT-] (1601) : any of a widely distributed genus (*Erigeron*) of composite herbs with flower heads that resemble asters but have fewer and narrower involucral bracts

Eri·nys \i-ˈri-nəs, -ˈrī-\ *n, pl* **Eriny·es** \-ˈri-nē-ˌēz\ [Gk] (1567) : FURY 2a

er·i·o·phy·id \ˌer-ē-ˈä-fē-əd, -ē-ə-ˈfī-əd\ *n* [ultim. fr. Gk *erion* wool + *phyē* growth; akin to Gk *physis* growth — more at PHYSICS] (1942) : any of a large family (Eriophyidae) of minute plant-feeding wormlike mites that have two pairs of legs and include gall mites and rust mites — **eriophyid** *adj*

Eris \ˈer-is\ *n* [*Eris,* ancient Greek goddess of strife] (2006) : a dwarf planet with a mean distance from the sun of 67 astronomical units (6.2 billion miles) and a diameter of 1500 miles (2400 kilometers)

ERISA *abbr* Employee Retirement Income Security Act

1**eris·tic** \i-ˈris-tik, e-\ *also* **eris·ti·cal** \-ti-kəl\ *adj* [Gk *eristikos* fond of wrangling, fr. *erizein* to wrangle, fr. *eris* strife] (1637) : characterized by disputatious and often subtle and specious reasoning — **eris·ti·cal·ly** \-ti-k(ə-)lē\ *adv*

2**eristic** *n* (1659) **1** : a person devoted to logical disputation **2** : the art or practice of disputation and polemics

Er·len·mey·er flask \ˈər-lən-ˌmī(-ə)r-, ˈer-lən-\ *n* [Emil *Erlenmeyer*] (1886) : a flat-bottomed conical laboratory flask

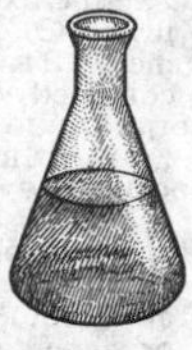

Erlenmeyer flask

er·mine \ˈər-mən\ *n, pl* **ermines** [ME, fr. AF *hermin,* of Gmc origin; akin to OHG *harmo* weasel] (12c) **1** *or pl* **ermine a** : any of several weasels whose coats become white in winter usu. with black on the tip of the tail; *esp* : a short-tailed weasel (*Mustela erminea*) of the forests and tundra of Eurasia and No. America **b** : the white fur of the ermine **2** : a rank or office whose ceremonial or official robe is ornamented with ermine

er·mined \-mənd\ *adj* (15c) : clothed or adorned with ermine

erne \ˈərn, ˈern\ *n* [ME, fr. OE *earn;* akin to OHG *arn* eagle, Gk *ornis* bird] (bef. 12c) : EAGLE; *esp* : a long-winged sea eagle (*Haliäetus albicilla*) with a short white wedge-shaped tail

erode \i-ˈrōd\ *vb* **erod·ed; erod·ing** [L *erodere* to eat away, fr. *e-* + *rodere* to gnaw — more at RODENT] *vt* (1612) **1** : to diminish or destroy by degrees: **a** : to eat into or away by slow destruction of substance (as by acid, infection, or cancer) **b** : to wear away by the action of water, wind, or glacial ice ⟨flooding *eroded* the hillside⟩ **c** : to cause to deteriorate or disappear as if by eating or wearing away ⟨inflation *eroding* buying power⟩ **2** : to produce or form by eroding ⟨glaciers ~ U-shaped valleys⟩ ~ *vi* : to undergo erosion ⟨where the land has *eroded* away⟩ — **erod·ibil·i·ty** \-ˌrō-də-ˈbi-lə-tē\ *n* — **erod·ible** *also* **erod·able** \-ˈrō-də-bəl\ *adj*

erog·e·nous \i-ˈrä-jə-nəs\ *adj* [Gk *erōs* + E *-genous, -genic*] (ca. 1889) **1** : producing sexual excitement or libidinal gratification when stimulated : sexually sensitive **2** : of, relating to, or arousing sexual feelings

Eros \ˈer-ˌäs, ˈir-\ *n* [Gk *Erōs,* fr. *erōs* sexual love; akin to Gk *erasthai* to love, desire] (14c) **1** : the Greek god of erotic love — compare CUPID **2** : the sum of life-preserving instincts that are manifested as impulses to gratify basic needs, as sublimated impulses, and as impulses to protect and preserve the body and mind — compare DEATH INSTINCT **3 a** : love conceived by Plato as a fundamental creative impulse having a sensual element **b** *often not cap* : erotic love or desire

erose \i-ˈrōs\ *adj* [L *erosus,* pp. of *erodere*] (1793) : IRREGULAR, UNEVEN; *specif* : having the margin irregularly notched ⟨an ~ leaf⟩

ero·sion \i-ˈrō-zhən\ *n* (1541) **1 a** : the action or process of eroding **b** : the state of being eroded **2** : an instance or product of erosion — **ero·sion·al** \-ˈrōzh-nəl, -ˈrō-zhə-nᵊl\ *adj* — **ero·sion·al·ly** \-ē\ *adv*

ero·sive \i-ˈrō-siv, -ziv\ *adj* (1830) : tending to erode or to induce or permit erosion; *also* : caused or marked by erosion ⟨~ arthritis⟩ — **ero·sive·ness** *n* — **ero·siv·i·ty** \i-ˌrō-ˈsi-və-tē\ *n*

erot·ic \i-ˈrä-tik\ *also* **erot·i·cal** \-ti-kəl\ *adj* [Gk *erōtikos,* fr. *erōt-, erōs*] (1651) **1** : of, devoted to, or tending to arouse sexual love or desire ⟨~ art⟩ **2** : strongly marked or affected by sexual desire — **erotic** *n* — **erot·i·cal·ly** \-ti-k(ə-)lē\ *adv*

erot·i·ca \i-ˈrä-ti-kə\ *n pl but sing or pl in constr* [NL, fr. Gk *erōtika,* neut. pl. of *erōtikos*] (1819) **1** : literary or artistic works having an erotic theme or quality **2** : depictions of things erotic

erot·i·cism \i-ˈrä-tə-ˌsi-zəm\ *n* (1881) **1** : an erotic theme or quality **2** : a state of sexual arousal **3** : insistent sexual impulse or desire — **erot·i·cist** \-sist\ *n*

erot·i·cize \-ˌsīz\ *vt* **-cized; -ciz·ing** (ca. 1914) : to make erotic ⟨~ the male image⟩ — **erot·i·ci·za·tion** \i-ˌrä-tə-sə-ˈzā-shən\ *n*

er·o·tism \ˈer-ə-ˌti-zəm\ *n* (1849) : EROTICISM

er·o·tize \ˈer-ə-ˌtīz\ *vt* **-tized; -tiz·ing** (1936) : to invest with erotic significance or sexual feeling — **er·o·ti·za·tion** \ˌer-ə-tə-ˈzā-shən\ *n*

eroto- *comb form* [NL, fr. Gk *erōto-,* fr. *erot-, eros*] : sexual desire ⟨*eroto*genic⟩

ero·to·gen·ic \i-ˌrō-tə-ˈje-nik, -ˌrä-\ *adj* (ca. 1909) : EROGENOUS

ero·to·ma·nia \i-ˌrō-tə-ˈmā-nē-ə, -ˌrä-\ *n* [NL] (1877) **1** : excessive sexual desire **2** : a psychological disorder marked by the delusional belief that one is the object of another person's love or sexual desire — **ero·to·ma·ni·ac** \-ˌak\ *n*

err \ˈer, ˈər\ *vi* [ME, fr. AF *errer,* fr. L *errare* to wander, err; akin to OE *ierre* wandering, perverse, Goth *airzeis* deceived] (14c) **1** *archaic* : STRAY **2 a** : to make a mistake ⟨~*ed* in his calculations⟩ ⟨~*ed* on the side of caution⟩ **b** : to violate an accepted standard of conduct

er·ran·cy \ˈer-ən(t)-sē, ˈe-rən(t)-\ *n, pl* **-cies** (1621) : the state or an instance of erring

er·rand \ˈer-ənd, ˈe-rənd\ *n* [ME *erend* message, business, fr. OE *ǣrend;* akin to OHG *ārunti* message] (bef. 12c) **1** *archaic* **a** : an oral message entrusted to a person **b** : EMBASSY, MISSION **2 a** : a short trip taken to attend to some business often for another ⟨was on an ~ for his mother⟩ **b** : the object or purpose of such a trip

er·rant \ˈer-ənt, ˈe-rənt\ *adj* [ME *erraunt,* fr. AF *errant,* prp. of *errer* to err & *errer* to travel, fr. LL *iterare,* fr. L *iter* road, journey — more at ITINERANT] (14c) **1** : traveling or given to traveling ⟨an ~ knight⟩ **2 a** : straying outside the proper path or bounds ⟨an ~ calf⟩ **b** : moving about aimlessly or irregularly ⟨an ~ breeze⟩ **c** : behaving wrongly ⟨an ~ child⟩ **d** : FALLIBLE — **errant** *n* — **er·rant·ly** *adv*

er·rant·ry \ˈer-ən-trē, ˈe-rən-\ *n, pl* **-ries** (1620) : the quality, condition, or fact of wandering; *esp* : a roving in search of chivalrous adventure

er·ra·ta \e-ˈrä-tə, -ˈrā-, -ˈra-\ *n* [L, pl. of *erratum*] (1573) : a list of corrigenda; *also* : a page bearing such a list

1**er·rat·ic** \i-ˈra-tik\ *adj* [ME, fr. L *erraticus,* fr. *erratus,* pp. of *errare*] (14c) **1 a** : having no fixed course : WANDERING ⟨an ~ comet⟩ **b** *archaic* : NOMADIC **2** : transported from an original resting place esp. by a glacier ⟨an ~ boulder⟩ **3 a** : characterized by lack of consistency, regularity, or uniformity ⟨~ dieting⟩ ⟨keeps ~ hours⟩ **b** : deviating from what is ordinary or standard : ECCENTRIC ⟨an ~ genius⟩ *syn* see STRANGE — **er·rat·i·cal** \-ti-kəl\ *adj* — **er·rat·i·cal·ly** \-ti-k(ə-)lē\ *adv* — **er·rat·i·cism** \-ˈa-tə-ˌsi-zəm\ *n*

2**erratic** *n* (ca. 1623) : one that is erratic; *esp* : an erratic boulder or block of rock

er·ra·tum \e-ˈrä-təm, -ˈrā-, -ˈra-\ *n, pl* **-ta** \-tə\ [L, fr. neut. of *erratus*] (1589) : ERROR; *esp* : CORRIGENDUM

er·ro·ne·ous \i-ˈrō-nē-əs, e-\ *adj* [ME, fr. L *erroneus,* fr. *erron-, erro* wanderer, fr. *errare*] (15c) **1 :** containing or characterized by error **:** MISTAKEN ⟨~ assumptions⟩ ⟨gave an ~ impression⟩ **2** *archaic* **:** WANDERING — **er·ro·ne·ous·ly** *adv* — **er·ro·ne·ous·ness** *n*

er·ror \ˈer-ər, ˈe-rər\ *n* [ME *errour,* fr. AF, fr. L *error,* fr. *errare*] (13c) **1 a :** an act or condition of ignorant or imprudent deviation from a code of behavior **b :** an act involving an unintentional deviation from truth or accuracy ⟨made an ~ in adding up the bill⟩ **c :** an act that through ignorance, deficiency, or accident departs from or fails to achieve what should be done ⟨an ~ in judgment⟩: as **(1) :** a defensive misplay other than a wild pitch or passed ball made by a baseball player when normal play would have resulted in an out or prevented an advance by a base runner **(2) :** the failure of a player (as in tennis) to make a successful return of a ball during play **d :** a mistake in the proceedings of a court of record in matters of law or of fact **2 a :** the quality or state of erring ⟨the map is in ~⟩ **b** *Christian Science* **:** illusion about the nature of reality that is the cause of human suffering **:** the contradiction of truth **c :** an instance of false belief **3 :** something produced by mistake ⟨a typographical ~⟩; *esp* **:** a postage stamp exhibiting a consistent flaw (as a wrong color) in its manufacture **4 a :** the difference between an observed or calculated value and a true value; *specif* **:** variation in measurements, calculations, or observations of a quantity due to mistakes or to uncontrollable factors **b :** the amount of deviation from a standard or specification **5 :** a deficiency or imperfection in structure or function ⟨an ~ of metabolism⟩ — **er·ror·less** \-ləs\ *adj*

syn ERROR, MISTAKE, BLUNDER, SLIP, LAPSE mean a departure from what is true, right, or proper. ERROR suggests the existence of a standard or guide and a straying from the right course through failure to make effective use of this ⟨procedural *errors*⟩. MISTAKE implies misconception or inadvertence and usu. expresses less criticism than *error* ⟨dialed the wrong number by *mistake*⟩. BLUNDER regularly imputes stupidity or ignorance as a cause and connotes some degree of blame ⟨diplomatic *blunders*⟩. SLIP stresses inadvertence or accident and applies esp. to trivial but embarrassing mistakes ⟨a *slip* of the tongue⟩. LAPSE stresses forgetfulness, weakness, or inattention as a cause ⟨a *lapse* in judgment⟩.

error bar *n* (1968) **:** the estimated uncertainty in experimental data

er·satz \ˈer-ˌsäts, -ˌzäts, er-ˈ; ˈər-ˌsats\ *adj* [G *ersatz-,* fr. *Ersatz,* n., substitute] (1875) **:** being a usu. artificial and inferior substitute or imitation ⟨~ turf⟩ ⟨~ intellectuals⟩ — **ersatz** *n*

Erse \ˈərs\ *n* [ME (Sc) *Erisch,* adj., Irish, alter. of *Irish*] (15c) **1 :** SCOTTISH GAELIC **2 :** IRISH GAELIC — **Erse** *adj*

erst \ˈərst\ *adv* [ME *erest* earliest, formerly, fr. OE *ǣrest,* superl. of *ǣr* early — more at ERE] (12c) *archaic* **:** ERSTWHILE

[1]**erst·while** \ˈərst-ˌ(h)wī(-ə)l\ *adv* (1569) **:** in the past **:** FORMERLY ⟨cultures, ~ unknown to each other —Robert Plank⟩

[2]**erstwhile** *adj* (1903) **:** FORMER, PREVIOUS ⟨~ enemies⟩

ERT *abbr* estrogen replacement therapy

eru·cic acid \i-ˈrü-sik-\ *n* [NL *Eruca,* genus of herbs, fr. L, colewort] (1869) **:** a crystalline fatty acid $C_{22}H_{42}O_2$ found in the form of glycerides esp. in rapeseed oil

eruct \i-ˈrəkt\ *vb* [L *eructare,* freq. of *erugere* to belch, disgorge; akin to OE *rocettan* to belch, Gk *ereugesthai*] (1596) **:** BELCH

eruc·ta·tion \i-ˌrək-ˈtā-shən, ˌē-\ *n* (15c) **:** an act or instance of belching

er·u·dite \ˈer-ə-ˌdīt, ˈer-yə-\ *adj* [ME *erudit,* fr. L *eruditus,* fr. pp. of *erudire* to instruct, fr. *e-* + *rudis* rude, ignorant] (15c) **:** possessing or displaying erudition **:** LEARNED ⟨an ~ scholar⟩ — **er·u·dite·ly** *adv*

er·u·di·tion \ˌer-ə-ˈdi-shən, ˌer-yə-\ *n* (15c) **:** extensive knowledge acquired chiefly from books **:** profound, recondite, or bookish learning ***syn*** see KNOWLEDGE

erupt \i-ˈrəpt\ *vb* [L *eruptus,* pp. of *erumpere* to burst forth, fr. *e-* + *rumpere* to break — more at REAVE] *vi* (1657) **1 a (1) :** to burst from limits or restraint **(2)** *of a tooth* **:** to emerge through the gum **b :** to force out or release suddenly and often violently something (as lava or steam) that is pent up **c :** to become active or violent esp. suddenly **:** break forth ⟨war could ~ at any moment⟩ ⟨the audience ~*ed* in applause⟩ **2 :** to break out with or as if with a skin eruption ~ *vt* **:** to force out or release usu. suddenly and violently ⟨a volcano ~*ing* lava and ash⟩ — **erupt·ible** \-ˈrəp-tə-bəl\ *adj* — **erup·tive** \-tiv\ *adj* — **erup·tive·ly** *adv*

erup·tion \i-ˈrəp-shən\ *n* (1555) **1 a :** an act, process, or instance of erupting **b :** the breaking out of a rash on the skin or mucous membrane **2 :** a product of erupting (as a skin rash)

-ery *n suffix, pl* **-eries** [ME *-erie,* fr. AF, fr. *-ier* -er + *-ie* -y] **1 :** qualities collectively **:** character **:** -NESS ⟨snobb*ery*⟩ **2 :** art **:** practice ⟨quack*ery*⟩ ⟨trick*ery*⟩ **3 :** place of doing, keeping, producing, or selling (the thing specified) ⟨fish*ery*⟩ ⟨bak*ery*⟩ ⟨eat*ery*⟩ **4 :** collection **:** aggregate ⟨fin*ery*⟩ ⟨green*ery*⟩ **5 :** state or condition ⟨slav*ery*⟩

eryn·go \i-ˈriŋ-(ˌ)gō\ *n, pl* **-goes** *or* **-gos** [modif. of L *eryngion* sea holly, fr. Gk *ēryngion*] (1543) **1 :** any of various plants (genus *Eryngium*) of the carrot family that have elongate spinulose-margined leaves and flowers in dense bracted heads **2 :** candied root of the sea holly formerly used as an aphrodisiac

ery·sip·e·las \ˌer-ə-ˈsi-p(ə-)ləs, ˌir-\ *n* [ME *erisipila,* fr. L *erysipelas,* fr. Gk, fr. *erysi-* (prob. akin to Gk *erythros* red) + *-pelas* (prob. akin to L *pellis* skin) — more at RED, FELL] (14c) **:** an acute febrile disease associated with intense edematous local inflammation of the skin and subcutaneous tissues caused by a hemolytic streptococcus

er·y·the·ma \ˌer-ə-ˈthē-mə\ *n* [NL, fr. Gk *erythēma,* fr. *erythainein* to redden, fr. *erythros*] (ca. 1783) **:** abnormal redness of the skin due to capillary congestion — **er·y·them·a·tous** \-ˈthe-mə-təs\ *adj*

erythema mi·grans \-ˈmī-grənz\ *or* **erythema chron·i·cum migrans** \-ˌkrä-nə-kəm-\ *n* [NL, lit., (chronic) migrating erythema] (1979) **:** a red spreading annular skin lesion that is an early symptom of Lyme disease and that develops at the site of the bite of a tick (as the deer tick) infected with the causative spirochete

er·y·thor·bate \ˌer-ə-ˈthȯr-ˌbāt\ *n* (1963) **:** a salt of erythorbic acid that is used in foods as an antioxidant

er·y·thor·bic acid \-ˌthȯr-bik-\ *n* [*erythr-* + *ascorbic acid*] (1963) **:** a diastereoisomer of ascorbic acid with optical activity

erythr- *or* **erythro-** *comb form* [Gk, fr. *erythros* — more at RED] **1 :** red ⟨*erythro*cyte⟩ **2 :** erythrocyte ⟨*erythr*oid⟩

er·y·thre·mia \ˌer-ə-ˈthrē-mē-ə\ *n* [NL] (1908) **:** POLYCYTHEMIA VERA

er·y·thrism \ˈer-ə-ˌthri-zəm\ *n* (1864) **:** a condition marked by exceptional prevalence of red pigmentation (as in hair or feathers) — **er·y·thris·tic** \ˌer-ə-ˈthris-tik\ *also* **er·y·thris·mal** \-ˈthriz-məl\ *adj*

er·y·thrite \ˈer-ə-ˌthrīt\ *n* (1844) **:** a usu. rose-colored mineral consisting of a hydrous cobalt arsenate occurring esp. in monoclinic crystals

eryth·ro·blast \i-ˈrith-rə-ˌblast\ *n* [ISV] (ca. 1890) **:** a polychromatic nucleated cell of red bone marrow that synthesizes hemoglobin and that is an intermediate in the initial stage of red blood cell formation; *broadly* **:** a cell ancestral to red blood cells — **eryth·ro·blas·tic** \-ˌrith-rə-ˈblas-tik\ *adj*

eryth·ro·blas·to·sis \i-ˌrith-rə-ˌblas-ˈtō-səs\ *n, pl* **-to·ses** \-ˌsēz\ [NL] (ca. 1923) **:** abnormal presence of erythroblasts in the circulating blood; *esp* **:** ERYTHROBLASTOSIS FETALIS

erythroblastosis fe·ta·lis \-fi-ˈta-ləs\ *n* [NL, fetal erythroblastosis] (ca. 1934) **:** a hemolytic disease of the fetus and newborn that occurs when the system of an Rh-negative mother produces antibodies to an antigen in the blood of an Rh-positive fetus which cross the placenta and destroy fetal erythrocytes and that is characterized by an increase in circulating erythroblasts and by jaundice

eryth·ro·cyte \i-ˈrith-rə-ˌsīt\ *n* [ISV] (ca. 1894) **:** RED BLOOD CELL — **eryth·ro·cyt·ic** \-ˌrith-rə-ˈsi-tik\ *adj*

ery·throid \i-ˈrith-ˌrȯid, ˈer-ə-ˌthrȯid\ *adj* (1927) **:** relating to erythrocytes or their precursors

eryth·ro·my·cin \i-ˌrith-rə-ˈmī-sᵊn\ *n* (1952) **:** a broad-spectrum antibiotic $C_{37}H_{67}NO_{13}$ produced by an actinomycete (*Streptomyces erythreus*) and administered orally or topically

eryth·ro·poi·e·sis \i-ˌrith-rō-pȯi-ˈē-səs\ *n* [NL] (1918) **:** the production of red blood cells (as from the bone marrow) — **eryth·ro·poi·et·ic** \-ˈe-tik\ *adj*

eryth·ro·poi·e·tin \-ˈpȯi-ə-tən\ *n* (1948) **:** a glycoprotein hormone formed esp. in the kidney and stimulating red blood cell formation

eryth·ro·sin \i-ˈrith-rə-sən\ *also* **eryth·ro·sine** \-sən, -ˌsēn\ *n* [ISV *erythr-* + *eosin*] (ca. 1882) **:** any of several dyes made from fluorescein that yield reddish shades

Es *symbol* einsteinium

[1]**-es** \əz, iz *after* s, z, sh, ch; z *after* v *or a vowel*\ *n pl suffix* [ME *-es, -s* — more at [1]-s] — used to form the plural of most nouns that end in *s* ⟨glass*es*⟩, *z* ⟨fuzz*es*⟩, *sh* ⟨bush*es*⟩, *ch* ⟨peach*es*⟩, or a final *y* that changes to *i* ⟨lad*ies*⟩ and of some nouns ending in *f* that changes to *v* ⟨loav*es*⟩; compare [1]-s

[2]**-es** *vb suffix* [ME — more at [3]-s] — used to form the third person singular present of most verbs that end in *s* ⟨bless*es*⟩, *z* ⟨fizz*es*⟩, *sh* ⟨hush*es*⟩, *ch* ⟨catch*es*⟩, or a final *y* that changes to *i* ⟨def*ies*⟩; compare [3]-s

Esau \ˈē-(ˌ)sȯ\ *n* [L, fr. Gk *Ēsau,* fr. Heb *ʿĒsāw*] (bef. 12c) **:** the elder son of Isaac and Rebekah who sold his birthright to his twin brother Jacob

ESB *abbr* electrical stimulation of the brain

es·ca·drille \ˈes-kə-ˌdril, -ˌdrē\ *n* [F, flotilla, escadrille, fr. Sp *escuadrilla,* dim. of *escuadra* squadron, squad — more at SQUAD] (1912) **:** a unit of a European air command containing usu. six airplanes

es·ca·lade \ˈes-kə-ˌlād, -ˌläd\ *n* [F, fr. It *scalata,* fr. *scalare* to scale, fr. *scala* ladder, fr. LL — more at SCALE] (1598) **:** an act of scaling esp. the walls of a fortification — **escalade** *vt* — **es·ca·lad·er** *n*

es·ca·late \ˈes-kə-ˌlāt, ÷-kyə-\ *vb* **-lat·ed; -lat·ing** [back-formation fr. *escalator*] *vi* (1944) **:** to increase in extent, volume, number, amount, intensity, or scope ⟨a little war threatens to ~ into a huge ugly one —Arnold Abrams⟩ ~ *vt* **:** EXPAND 2 — **es·ca·la·tion** \ˌes-kə-ˈlā-shən, ÷-kyə-\ *n* — **es·ca·la·to·ry** \ˈes-kə-lə-ˌtȯr-ē, ÷-kyə-\ *adj*

[1]**es·ca·la·tor** \ˈes-kə-ˌlā-tər, ÷-kyə-\ *n* [fr. *Escalator,* a trademark] (1900) **1 a :** a power-driven set of stairs arranged like an endless belt that ascend or descend continuously **b :** an upward course suggestive of an escalator ⟨a never-stopping ~ of economic progress —D. W. Brogan⟩ **2 :** an escalator clause or provision

[2]**escalator** *adj* (1930) **:** providing for a periodic proportional upward or downward adjustment (as of prices or wages) ⟨an ~ arrangement tying the base pay . . . to living costs —*N. Y. Times*⟩

es·ca·lope \ˈes-kə-ˌlōp\ *n* [F — more at SCALLOP] (1828) **:** SCALLOP 5

es·ca·pade \ˈes-kə-ˌpād\ *n* [F, action of escaping, fr. Sp. *escapada,* fr. *escapar* to escape, fr. VL **excappare*] (1667) **:** a usu. adventurous action that runs counter to approved or conventional conduct

[1]**es·cape** \is-ˈkāp, es-, *dial* iks-ˈkāp\ *vb* **es·caped; es·cap·ing** [ME, fr. AF *escaper, eschaper,* fr. VL **excappare,* fr. L *ex-* + LL *cappa* head covering, cloak] *vi* (13c) **1 a :** to get away (as by flight) ⟨*escaped* from prison⟩ **b :** to issue from confinement ⟨gas is *escaping*⟩ **c** *of a plant* **:** to run wild from cultivation **2 :** to avoid a threatening evil ⟨the boat sank but the crew *escaped*⟩ ~ *vt* **1 :** to get free of **:** break away from ⟨~ the jungle⟩ ⟨~ the solar system⟩ **2 :** to get or stay out of the way of **:** AVOID ⟨efforts to ~ poverty⟩ **3 :** to fail to be noticed or recallable by ⟨his name ~*s* me⟩ **4 a :** to issue from ⟨a smile *escaped* me⟩ **b :** to be uttered involuntarily by ⟨a sigh of relief *escaped* her⟩ — **es·cap·er** *n*

syn ESCAPE, AVOID, EVADE, ELUDE, SHUN, ESCHEW mean to get away or keep away from something. ESCAPE stresses the fact of getting away or being passed by not necessarily through effort or by conscious intent ⟨nothing *escapes* her sharp eyes⟩. AVOID stresses forethought and caution in keeping clear of danger or difficulty ⟨try to *avoid* past errors⟩. EVADE implies adroitness, ingenuity, or lack of scruple in escaping or avoiding ⟨*evaded* the question by changing the subject⟩. ELUDE implies a slippery or baffling quality in the person or thing that escapes ⟨what she sees in him *eludes* me⟩. SHUN often implies an avoiding as a matter of habitual practice or policy and may imply repugnance or abhorrence ⟨you have *shunned* your responsibilities⟩. ESCHEW implies an avoiding or abstaining from as unwise or distasteful ⟨a playwright who *eschews* melodrama⟩.

[2]**escape** *n* (14c) **1 :** an act or instance of escaping: as **a :** flight from confinement **b :** evasion of something undesirable **c :** leakage or outflow esp. of a fluid **d :** distraction or relief from routine or reality **2 :** a means of escape **3 :** a cultivated plant run wild

[3]**escape** *adj* (1817) **1 :** providing a means of escape ⟨~ literature⟩ **2 :** providing a means of evading a regulation, claim, or commitment ⟨an ~ clause in a contract⟩
escape artist *n* (1943) **:** one (as a performer or criminal) unusually adept at escaping from confinement
es·cap·ee \is-ˌkā-ˈpē, ˌes-(ˌ)kā-, ˌes-kə-\ *n* (ca. 1866) **:** one that has escaped; *esp* **:** an escaped prisoner
escape hatch *n* (1925) **1 :** a hatch providing an emergency exit from an enclosed space **2 :** a means of evading a difficulty, dilemma, or responsibility
escape mechanism *n* (1927) **:** a mode of behavior or thinking adopted to evade unpleasant facts or responsibilities
es·cape·ment \is-ˈkāp-mənt\ *n* (1779) **1 a :** a device in a timepiece which controls the motion of the train of wheelwork and through which the energy of the power source is delivered to the pendulum or balance by means of impulses that permit a tooth to escape from a pallet at regular intervals **b :** a ratchet device (as the spacing mechanism of a typewriter) that permits motion in one direction only in equal steps **2 a :** the act of escaping **b :** a way of escape **:** VENT
escape velocity *n* (1934) **:** the minimum velocity that a moving body (as a rocket) must have to escape from the gravitational field of a celestial body (as the earth) and move outward into space
es·cap·ism \is-ˈkā-ˌpi-zəm\ *n* (1933) **:** habitual diversion of the mind to purely imaginative activity or entertainment as an escape from reality or routine — **es·cap·ist** \-pist\ *adj or n*
es·cap·ol·o·gy \is-ˌkā-ˈpä-lə-jē, ˌes-(ˌ)\ *n* (1939) **:** the art or practice of escaping — **es·cap·ol·o·gist** \-jist\ *n*
es·car·got \ˌes-ˌkär-ˈgō\ *n, pl* **-gots** \-ˈgō(z)\ [F, snail, fr. MF, fr. Old Occitan *escaragol*] (ca. 1892) **:** a snail prepared for use as food
es·ca·role \ˈes-kə-ˌrōl\ *n* [F *escarole, scarole,* fr. OF *escariole,* fr. LL *escariola,* fr. L *escarius* of food, fr. *esca* food, fr. *edere* to eat — more at EAT] (1897) **:** ENDIVE 1b
es·carp·ment \i-ˈskärp-mənt\ *n* [F *escarpement,* fr. *escarper* to scarp, fr. MF, fr. *escarpe* scarp, fr. OIt *scarpa* — more at SCARP] (ca. 1802) **1 :** a steep slope in front of a fortification **2 :** a long cliff or steep slope separating two comparatively level or more gently sloping surfaces and resulting from erosion or faulting
-escence *n suffix* [MF, fr. L *-escentia,* fr. *-escent-, -escens* + *-ia* -y] **:** state or process of becoming ⟨obsol*escence*⟩
-escent *adj suffix* [MF, fr. L *-escent-, -escens,* prp. suffix of incho. verbs in *-escere*] **1 :** beginning **:** beginning to be **:** slightly ⟨frut*escent*⟩ **2 :** reflecting or emitting light (in a specified way) ⟨opal*escent*⟩
es·char \ˈes-ˌkär\ *n* [ME *escare* — more at SCAR] (1543) **:** a scab formed esp. after a burn
es·cha·rot·ic \ˌes-kə-ˈrä-tik\ *adj* [F or LL; F *escharotique,* fr. LL *escharoticus,* fr. Gk *escharōtikos,* fr. *escharoun* to form an eschar, fr. *eschara* eschar] (1612) **:** producing an eschar — **escharotic** *n*
es·cha·to·log·i·cal \(ˌ)es-ˌka-tə-ˈlä-ji-kəl, ˌes-kə-\ *adj* (1854) **1 :** of or relating to eschatology or an eschatology **2 :** of or relating to the end of the world or the events associated with it in eschatology — **es·cha·to·log·i·cal·ly** \-ji-k(ə-)lē\ *adv*
es·cha·tol·o·gy \ˌes-kə-ˈtä-lə-jē\ *n, pl* **-gies** [Gk *eschatos* last, farthest] (1844) **1 :** a branch of theology concerned with the final events in the history of the world or of humankind **2 :** a belief concerning death, the end of the world, or the ultimate destiny of humankind; *specif* **:** any of various Christian doctrines concerning the Second Coming, the resurrection of the dead, or the Last Judgment
[1]**es·cheat** \is-ˈchēt, ish-ˈchēt\ *n* [ME *eschete,* fr. AF, reversion of property, fr. *escheir* to fall, devolve, fr. VL **excadēre,* fr. L *ex-* + VL **cadēre* to fall, fr. L *cadere* — more at CHANCE] (14c) **1 :** escheated property **2 a :** the reversion of lands in English feudal law to the lord of the fee when there are no heirs capable of inheriting under the original grant **b :** the reversion of property to the crown in England or to the state in the U.S. when there are no legal heirs
[2]**escheat** *vt* (14c) **:** to cause to revert by escheat ~ *vi* **:** to revert by escheat — **es·cheat·able** \-ˈchē-tə-bəl\ *adj*
es·chew \e-ˈshü, i-; es-ˈchü, is-; *also* e-ˈskyü\ *vt* [ME, fr. AF *eschiver* (3d pres. *eschiu*) of Gmc origin; akin to OHG *sciuhen* to frighten off — more at SHY] (14c) **:** to avoid habitually esp. on moral or practical grounds **:** SHUN ***syn*** see ESCAPE — **es·chew·al** \-əl\ *n*
es·co·lar \ˌes-kə-ˈlär\ *n, pl* **escolar** *or* **escolars** [Sp, lit., scholar, fr. ML *scholaris* — more at SCHOLAR] (ca. 1890) **:** a large widely distributed rough-scaled scombroid fish (*Lepidocybium flavobrunneum*) that resembles a mackerel
[1]**es·cort** \ˈes-ˌkȯrt\ *n* [MF *escorte,* fr. It *scorta,* fr. *scorgere* to guide, fr. VL **excorrigere,* fr. L *ex-* + *corrigere* to make straight, correct — more at CORRECT] (1579) **1 a** (1) **:** a person or group of persons accompanying another to give protection or as a courtesy (2) **:** the man who goes on a date with a woman **b :** a protective screen of warships or fighter planes or a single ship or plane used to fend off enemy attack from one or more vulnerable craft **2 :** accompaniment by a person or an armed protector (as a ship)
[2]**es·cort** \is-ˈkȯrt, es-, ˈes-ˌ\ *vt* (1708) **:** to accompany as an escort
es·cot \is-ˈkät\ *vt* [AF *escoter,* fr. *escot* contribution, of Gmc origin; akin to ON *skot* contribution, shot — more at SHOT] (1602) *obs* **:** SUPPORT, MAINTAIN
es·cri·toire \ˈes-krə-ˌtwär\ *n* [obs. F, writing desk, scriptorium, fr. ML *scriptorium*] (1664) **:** a writing table or desk; *specif* **:** SECRETARY 4b
[1]**es·crow** \ˈes-ˌkrō, es-ˈ\ *n* [AF *escroue* scroll — more at SCROLL] (1594) **1 :** a deed, a bond, money, or a piece of property held in trust by a third party to be turned over to the grantee only upon fulfillment of a condition **2 :** a fund or deposit designed to serve as an escrow — **in escrow :** in trust as an escrow ⟨had $1000 *in escrow* to pay taxes⟩
[2]**es·crow** \es-ˈkrō, ˈes-ˌ\ *vt* (1946) **:** to place in escrow
es·cu·do \is-ˈkü-(ˌ)dō\ *n, pl* **-dos** [Sp & Pg, lit., shield, fr. L *scutum*] (ca. 1821) **1 :** any of various former gold or silver coins of Hispanic countries **2 a :** the basic monetary unit of Portugal from 1910 to 2001 **b** — see MONEY table **3 :** the basic monetary unit of Chile from 1960 to 1975
es·cu·lent \ˈes-kyə-lənt\ *adj* [L *esculentus,* fr. *esca* food, fr. *edere* to eat — more at EAT] (1626) **:** EDIBLE — **esculent** *n*
es·cutch·eon \is-ˈkə-chən\ *n* [ME *escochon,* fr. AF *escuchoun,* fr. VL **scution-, scutio,* fr. L *scutum* shield — more at ESQUIRE] (15c) **1 :** a defined area on which armorial bearings are displayed and which usu. consists of a shield **2 :** a protective or ornamental plate or flange (as around a keyhole) **3 :** the part of a ship's stern on which the name is displayed

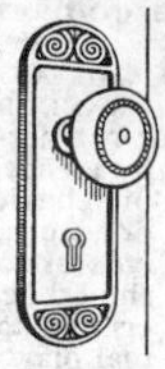

escutcheon 2

Esd *abbr* Esdras
Es·dras \ˈez-drəs\ *n* [LL, fr. Gk, fr. Heb *ʽEzrā*] (14c) **1 :** either of two books of the Roman Catholic canon of the Old Testament: **a :** EZRA 2 **b :** NEHEMIAH 2 **2 :** either of two uncanonical books of Scripture included in the Protestant Apocrypha — see BIBLE table
ESE *abbr* east-southeast
[1]**-ese** *adj suffix* [Pg *-ês* & It *-ese,* fr. L *-ensis*] **:** of, relating to, or originating in (a certain place or country) ⟨Japan*ese*⟩
[2]**-ese** *n suffix, pl* **-ese 1 :** native or resident of (a specified place or country) ⟨Chin*ese*⟩ **2 a :** language of (a particular place, country, or nationality) ⟨Canton*ese*⟩ **b :** speech, literary style, or diction peculiar to (a specified place, person, group, discipline, subject, or activity) — usu. in words applied in depreciation ⟨journal*ese*⟩ ⟨baseball*ese*⟩
es·em·plas·tic \ˌe-ˌsem-ˈplas-tik, -səm-\ *adj* [Gk *es hen* into one + E *plastic*] (1817) **:** shaping or having the power to shape disparate things into a unified whole ⟨the ~ power of the poetic imagination —W. H. Gardner⟩
es·er·ine \ˈe-sə-ˌrēn\ *n* [F *ésérine*] (1879) **:** PHYSOSTIGMINE
Esk *abbr* Eskimo
es·ker \ˈes-kər\ *n* [Ir *eiscir* ridge] (1848) **:** a long narrow ridge or mound of sand, gravel, and boulders deposited by a stream flowing on, within, or beneath a stagnant glacier
Es·ki·mo \ˈes-kə-ˌmō\ *n* [obs. *Esquimawe,* prob. fr. Sp *esquimao,* fr. Montagnais (Algonquian language of eastern Canada) *aiachkime8* Micmac, Eskimo; prob. akin to modern Montagnais *assime·w* she laces a snowshoe, Ojibwa *aškime·*] (1584) **1** *pl* **Eskimo** *or* **Eskimos :** a member of a group of peoples of northern Canada, Greenland, Alaska, and eastern Siberia **2 :** any of the languages of the Eskimo peoples — **Es·ki·mo·an** \ˌes-kə-ˈmō-ən\ *adj*
Es·ki·mo–Aleut \-ˈa-lē-ˌüt\ *n* (1921) **:** a language family including Eskimo and Aleut languages
Eskimo curlew *n* (1813) **:** an extremely rare New World curlew (*Numenius borealis*) that breeds in northern No. America and winters in So. America
Eskimo dog *n* (1774) **:** any of an American breed of spitz dogs with a thick white coat; *also* **:** any of a breed of Canadian sled dogs
ESL *abbr* English as a second language
ESOP \ˌē-ˌes-(ˌ)ō-ˈpē, ˈē-ˌsäp\ *n* [*e*mployee *s*tock *o*wnership *p*lan] (1975) **:** a program by which a corporation's employees acquire its stock
esoph·a·gi·tis \i-ˌsä-fə-ˈjī-təs, -ˈgī-\ *n, pl* **-git·i·des** \-ˈji-tə-ˌdēz, -ˈgi-\ [NL] (ca. 1900) **:** inflammation of the esophagus
esoph·a·gus \i-ˈsä-fə-gəs\ *n, pl* **-gi** \-ˌgī, -ˌjī\ [ME *ysophagus,* fr. ML *ysofagus,* fr. Gk *oisophagos,* fr. *oisein* to be going to carry + *phagein* to eat — more at BAKSHEESH] (14c) **:** a muscular tube that in humans is about nine inches (23 centimeters) long and passes from the pharynx down the neck between the trachea and the spinal column and behind the left bronchus where it pierces the diaphragm slightly to the left of the middle line and joins the cardiac end of the stomach — **esoph·a·ge·al** \i-ˌsä-fə-ˈjē-əl\ *adj*
es·o·ter·ic \ˌe-sə-ˈter-ik, -ˈte-rik\ *adj* [LL *esotericus,* fr. Gk *esōterikos,* fr. *esōterō,* compar. of *eisō, esō* within, fr. *eis* into; akin to Gk *en* in — more at IN] (ca. 1660) **1 a :** designed for or understood by the specially initiated alone ⟨a body of ~ legal doctrine —B. N. Cardozo⟩ **b :** requiring or exhibiting knowledge that is restricted to a small group ⟨~ terminology⟩; *broadly* **:** difficult to understand ⟨~ subjects⟩ **2 a :** limited to a small circle ⟨engaging in ~ pursuits⟩ **b :** PRIVATE, CONFIDENTIAL ⟨an ~ purpose⟩ **3 :** of special, rare, or unusual interest ⟨~ building materials⟩ — **es·o·ter·i·cal·ly** \-i-k(ə-)lē\ *adv*
es·o·ter·i·ca \-i-kə\ *n pl* [NL, fr. Gk *esōterika,* neut. pl. of *esōterikos*] (ca. 1929) **:** esoteric items
es·o·ter·i·cism \-ˈter-ə-ˌsi-zəm, -ˈte-rə-\ *n* (1846) **1 :** esoteric doctrines or practices **2 :** the quality or state of being esoteric
esp *abbr* especially
ESP \ˌē-ˌes-ˈpē\ *n* [*e*xtra*s*ensory *p*erception] (1934) **:** EXTRASENSORY PERCEPTION
es·pa·drille \ˈes-pə-ˌdril\ *n* [F, alter. of *espardille,* ultim. fr. L *spartum*] (1892) **:** a sandal usu. having a fabric upper and a flexible sole
[1]**es·pal·ier** \is-ˈpal-yər, -ˌyā\ *n* [F, ultim. fr. It *spalla* shoulder, fr. LL *spatula* shoulder blade — more at EPAULET] (1662) **1 :** a plant (as a fruit tree) trained to grow flat against a support (as a wall) **2 :** a railing or trellis on which fruit trees or shrubs are trained to grow flat
[2]**espalier** *vt* (1810) **1 :** to train as an espalier **2 :** to furnish with an espalier
es·par·to \is-ˈpär-(ˌ)tō\ *n, pl* **-tos** [Sp, fr. L *spartum,* fr. Gk *sparton* — more at SPIRE] (1845) **1 :** either of two Spanish and Algerian grasses (*Stipa tenacissima* and *Lygeum spartum*) used esp. to make cordage, shoes, and paper — called also *esparto grass* **2 :** the fiber of esparto
es·pe·cial \is-ˈpe-shəl\ *adj* [ME, fr. AF — more at SPECIAL] (14c) **:** being distinctive: as **a :** directed toward a particular individual, group, or end ⟨sent ~ greetings to his son⟩ ⟨took ~ care to speak clearly⟩ **b :** of special note or importance **:** unusually great or significant ⟨a decision of ~ relevance⟩ **c :** highly distinctive or personal **:** PECULIAR ⟨had an ~ dislike for music⟩ **d :** CLOSE, INTIMATE ⟨his ~ crony⟩ **e :** SPECIFIC, PARTICULAR ⟨had no ~ destination in mind⟩ ***syn*** see SPECIAL — **in especial :** in particular
es·pe·cial·ly \is-ˈpesh-lē, -ˈpe-shə-\ *adv* (15c) **1 :** SPECIALLY 1 **2 a :** in particular **:** PARTICULARLY ⟨food seems cheaper, ~ meats⟩ **b :** for a particular purpose ⟨built ~ for research⟩ **3 —** used as an intensive ⟨an ~ good essay⟩ ⟨nothing ~ radical in the remarks⟩
es·per·ance \ˈes-p(ə-)rən(t)s\ *n* [ME *esperaunce,* fr. MF *esperance*] (15c) *obs* **:** HOPE, EXPECTATION
Es·pe·ran·to \ˌes-pə-ˈrän-(ˌ)tō, -ˈran-(ˌ)tō\ *n* [Dr. *Esperanto,* pseudonym of L. L. Zamenhof †1917 Pol. oculist, its inventor] (1892) **:** an artificial international language based as far as possible on words common to the chief European languages — **Es·pe·ran·tist** \-ˈrän-tist, -ˈran-\ *n or adj*
es·pi·al \is-ˈpī(-ə)l\ *n* (14c) **1 :** OBSERVATION **2 :** an act of noticing **:** DISCOVERY

es·piè·gle \es-ˈpyegl°\ *adj* [F, after *Ulespiegle* (Till Eulenspiegel), peasant prankster] (1816) : FROLICSOME, ROGUISH
es·piè·gle·rie \es-pyeg-lə-ˈrē\ *n* [F, fr. *espiègle*] (1815) : the quality or state of being roguish or frolicsome
es·pi·o·nage \ˈes-pē-ə-ˌnäzh, -ˌnäj, -nij, *Canad also* -ˌnazh; ˌes-pē-ə-ˈnäzh; is-ˈpē-ə-nij\ *n* [F *espionnage,* fr. MF, fr. *espionner* to spy, fr. *espion* spy, fr. OIt *spione,* fr. *spia,* of Gmc origin; akin to OHG *spehōn* to spy — more at SPY] (1793) : the practice of spying or using spies to obtain information about the plans and activities esp. of a foreign government or a competing company ⟨industrial ~⟩
es·pla·nade \ˈes-plə-ˌnäd, ˌes-plə-ˈ *also* -ˈnād *or* -ˌnād\ *n* [MF, fr. It *spianata,* fr. *spianare* to level, fr. L *explanare* — more at EXPLAIN] (1591) : a level open stretch of paved or grassy ground; *esp* : one designed for walking or driving along a shore
ESPN *abbr* Entertainment and Sports Programming Network
es·pous·al \is-ˈpau̇-zəl *also* -səl\ *n* (14c) **1 a** : BETROTHAL **b** : WEDDING **c** : MARRIAGE **2** : a taking up or adopting of a cause or belief
es·pouse \is-ˈpau̇z *also* -ˈpau̇s\ *vt* **es·poused; es·pous·ing** [ME, fr. AF *espuser,* fr. LL *sponsare* to betroth, fr. L *sponsus* betrothed — more at SPOUSE] (15c) **1** : MARRY **2** : to take up and support as a cause : become attached to ***syn*** see ADOPT — **es·pous·er** *n*
espres·so \e-ˈspre-(ˌ)sō\ *also* **ex·pres·so** \ik-ˈspre-(ˌ)sō\ *n, pl* **-sos** [It (*caffè*) *espresso,* prob. lit., coffee made on the spot at the customer's request] (1945) **1** : coffee brewed by forcing steam or hot water through finely ground darkly roasted coffee beans **2** : a cup of espresso
es·prit \is-ˈprē\ *n* [F, fr. OF *espirit,* L *spiritus* spirit] (1573) **1** : vivacious cleverness or wit **2** : ESPRIT DE CORPS
es·prit de corps \is-ˌprē-də-ˈkȯr\ *n* [F] (1780) : the common spirit existing in the members of a group and inspiring enthusiasm, devotion, and strong regard for the honor of the group
es·py \is-ˈpī\ *vt* **es·pied; es·py·ing** [ME *espien,* fr. AF *espier* — more at SPY] (14c) : to catch sight of ⟨among the several horses . . . she *espied* the white mustang —Zane Grey⟩
Esq *also* **Esqr** *abbr* esquire
-esque *adj suffix* [F, fr. It *-esco,* of Gmc origin; akin to OHG *-isc* -ish — more at -ISH] : in the manner or style of : like ⟨statue*esque*⟩
Es·qui·mau \ˈes-kə-ˌmō\ *n, pl* **Esquimau** *or* **Es·qui·maux** \-ˌmō(z)\ [F, fr. Montagnais (Algonquian language)] (1744) : ESKIMO
es·quire \ˈes-ˌkwī(-ə)r, is-ˈ\ *n* [ME, fr. AF *esquier* squire, fr. LL *scutarius,* fr. L *scutum* shield; akin to OIr *sciath* shield] (15c) **1** : a member of the English gentry ranking below a knight **2** : a candidate for knighthood serving as shield bearer and attendant to a knight **3** — used as a title of courtesy usu. placed in its abbreviated form after the surname ⟨John R. Smith, *Esq.*⟩ **4** *archaic* : a landed proprietor
ess \ˈes\ *n* (1540) **1** : the letter *s* **2** : something resembling the letter *S* in shape; *esp* : an S-shaped curve in a road
-ess *n suffix* [ME *-esse,* fr. AF, fr. LL *-issa,* fr. Gk] : female ⟨giant*ess*⟩
[1]**es·say** \e-ˈsā, ə-ˈsā, ˈe-ˌsā\ *vt* (14c) **1** : to put to a test **2** : to make an often tentative or experimental effort to perform : TRY ***syn*** see ATTEMPT — **es·say·er** *n*
[2]**es·say** \ˈe-ˌsā; *senses 1, 2 & 4 also* e-ˈsā\ *n* [MF *essai,* ultim. fr. LL *exagium* act of weighing, fr. L *ex-* + *agere* to drive — more at AGENT] (14c) **1** : TRIAL, TEST **2 a** : EFFORT, ATTEMPT; *esp* : an initial tentative effort **b** : the result or product of an attempt **3 a** : an analytic or interpretative literary composition usu. dealing with its subject from a limited or personal point of view **b** : something resembling such a composition ⟨a photographic ~⟩ **4** : a proof of an unaccepted design for a stamp or piece of paper money
es·say·ist \ˈe-ˌsā-ist\ *n* (1601) : a writer of essays
es·say·is·tic \ˌe-(ˌ)sā-ˈis-tik\ *adj* (1862) **1** : of or relating to an essay or an essayist **2** : resembling an essay in quality or character
essay question *n* (1947) : an examination question that requires an answer in a sentence, paragraph, or short composition
es·sence \ˈe-s°n(t)s\ *n* [ME *essencia,* fr. L *essentia,* fr. *esse* to be — more at IS] (14c) **1 a** : the permanent as contrasted with the accidental element of being **b** : the individual, real, or ultimate nature of a thing esp. as opposed to its existence ⟨a painting that captures the ~ of the land⟩ **c** : the properties or attributes by means of which something can be placed in its proper class or identified as being what it is **2** : something that exists : ENTITY **3 a (1)** : a volatile substance or constituent (as of perfume) **(2)** : a constituent or derivative possessing the special qualities (as of a plant or drug) in concentrated form; *also* : a preparation of such an essence or a synthetic substitute **b** : ODOR, PERFUME **4** : one that possesses or exhibits a quality in abundance as if in concentrated form ⟨she was the ~ of punctuality⟩ **5** : the most significant element, quality, or aspect of a thing or person ⟨the ~ of the issue⟩ — **in essence** : in or by its very nature : ESSENTIALLY, BASICALLY ⟨was *in essence* an honest person⟩ — **of the essence** : of the utmost importance ⟨time is *of the essence*⟩
Es·sene \i-ˈsēn, ˈe-ˌsēn\ *n* [Gk *Essēnos*] (1553) : a member of a monastic brotherhood of Jews in Palestine from the second century B.C. to the second century A.D. — **Es·se·ni·an** \i-ˈsē-nē-ən, e-ˈse-\ *or* **Es·se·nic** \-ˈse-nik, -ˈsē-nik\ *adj* — **Es·se·nism** \-ˈsē-ˌni-zəm\ *n*
[1]**es·sen·tial** \i-ˈsen(t)-shəl\ *adj* (14c) **1** : of, relating to, or constituting essence : INHERENT **2 a** : of the utmost importance : BASIC, INDISPENSABLE, NECESSARY ⟨an ~ requirement for admission to college⟩ **b** : being a substance that is not synthesized by the body in a quantity sufficient for normal health and growth and that must be obtained from the diet ⟨dietary protein provides the body with ~ amino acids⟩ — compare NONESSENTIAL 2 **3** : IDIOPATHIC ⟨~ disease⟩ ⟨~ hypertension⟩ — **es·sen·tial·ly** \-ˈsench-lē, -ˈsen-chə-\ *adv* — **es·sen·tial·ness** \-ˈsen-chəl-nəs\ *n*

syn ESSENTIAL, FUNDAMENTAL, VITAL, CARDINAL mean so important as to be indispensable. ESSENTIAL implies belonging to the very nature of a thing and therefore being incapable of removal without destroying the thing itself or its character ⟨conflict is *essential* in drama⟩. FUNDAMENTAL applies to something that is a foundation without which an entire system or complex whole would collapse ⟨*fundamental* principles of algebra⟩. VITAL suggests something that is necessary to a thing's continued existence or operation ⟨cut off from *vital* supplies⟩. CARDINAL suggests something on which an outcome turns or depends ⟨a *cardinal* rule in buying a home⟩.

[2]**essential** *n* (15c) **1** : something basic ⟨the ~*s* of astronomy⟩ **2** : something necessary, indispensable, or unavoidable
es·sen·tial·ism \-ˌli-zəm\ *n* (1927) **1** : an educational theory that ideas and skills basic to a culture should be taught to all alike by time-tested methods — compare PROGRESSIVISM **2** : a philosophical theory ascribing ultimate reality to essence embodied in a thing perceptible to the senses — compare NOMINALISM **3** : the practice of regarding something (as a presumed human trait) as having innate existence or universal validity rather than as being a social, ideological, or intellectual construct — **es·sen·tial·ist** \-list\ *adj or n*
es·sen·ti·al·i·ty \i-ˌsen(t)-shē-ˈa-lə-tē\ *n, pl* **-ties** (1616) **1 a** : essential nature : ESSENCE **b** : an essential quality, property, or aspect **2** : the quality or state of being essential ⟨the ~ of freedom and justice —P. G. Hoffman⟩
es·sen·tial·ize \i-ˈsen(t)-shə-ˌlīz\ *vt* **-ized; -iz·ing** (1893) : to express or formulate in essential form : reduce to essentials
essential oil *n* (1674) : any of a class of volatile oils that give plants their characteristic odors and are used esp. in perfumes and flavorings, and for aromatherapy — compare FIXED OIL
es·soin \i-ˈsȯin\ *n* [ME *essoine,* fr. AF, fr. *essonier* to offer an essoin, fr. *es-* ex- + **soigne* legal excuse, of Gmc origin; akin to OS *sunnea* denial, OE *sōth* truth — more at SOOTH] (14c) **1** : an excuse for not appearing in an English law court at the appointed time **2** *obs* : EXCUSE, DELAY
essonite *var of* HESSONITE
est *abbr* **1** established **2** estimate; estimated
EST *abbr* eastern standard time
[1]**-est** *adj suffix or adv suffix* [ME, fr. OE *-st, -est, -ost;* akin to OHG *-isto* (adj. superl. suffix), Gk *-istos*] — used to form the superlative degree of adjectives and adverbs of one syllable ⟨fatt*est*⟩ ⟨lat*est*⟩, of some adjectives and adverbs of two syllables ⟨lucki*est*⟩ ⟨often*est*⟩, and less often of longer ones ⟨beggarli*est*⟩
[2]**-est** *or* **-st** *vb suffix* [ME, fr. OE *-est, -ast, -st;* akin to OHG *-ist, -ōst, -ēst,* 2d sing. ending] — used to form the archaic second person singular of English verbs (with *thou*) ⟨did*st*⟩ ⟨can*st*⟩
es·tab·lish \i-ˈsta-blish\ *vt* [ME *establissen,* fr. AF *establiss-,* stem of *establir,* fr. L *stabilire,* fr. *stabilis* stable] (14c) **1** : to institute (as a law) permanently by enactment or agreement **2** *obs* : SETTLE 7 **3 a** : to make firm or stable **b** : to introduce and cause to grow and multiply ⟨~ grass on pasturelands⟩ **4 a** : to bring into existence : FOUND ⟨~*ed* a republic⟩ **b** : BRING ABOUT, EFFECT ⟨~*ed* friendly relations⟩ **5 a** : to put on a firm basis : SET UP ⟨~ his son in business⟩ **b** : to put into a favorable position **c** : to gain full recognition or acceptance of ⟨the role ~*ed* her as a star⟩ **6** : to make (a church) a national or state institution **7** : to put beyond doubt : PROVE ⟨~*ed* my innocence⟩ — **es·tab·lish·able** \-shə-bəl\ *adj* — **es·tab·lish·er** \-shər\ *n*
established church *n* (ca. 1702) : a church recognized by law as the official church of a nation or state and supported by civil authority
establishing shot *n* (ca. 1948) : a usu. long shot in film or video used at the beginning of a sequence to establish an overview of the scene that follows
es·tab·lish·ment \i-ˈsta-blish-mənt\ *n* (15c) **1** : something established: as **a** : a settled arrangement; *esp* : a code of laws **b** : ESTABLISHED CHURCH **c** : a permanent civil or military organization **d** : a place of business or residence with its furnishings and staff **e** : a public or private institution **2** : an established order of society: as **a** *often cap* : a group of social, economic, and political leaders who form a ruling class (as of a nation) **b** *often cap* : a controlling group ⟨the literary ~⟩ **3 a** : the act of establishing **b** : the state of being established
es·tab·lish·men·tar·i·an \i-ˌsta-blish-mən-ˈter-ē-ən, -ˌmen-\ *adj* (1847) : of, relating to, or favoring the social or political establishment — **establishmentarian** *n* — **es·tab·lish·men·tar·i·an·ism** \-ē-ə-ˌni-zəm\ *n*
es·ta·mi·net \e-stä-mē-ˈnā\ *n, pl* **-nets** \-nā(z)\ [F] (1814) : a small café
es·tan·cia \e-ˈstän(t)-s(ˌ)yä\ *n* [AmerSp, fr. Sp, stay, room, fr. VL **stantia* — more at STANCE] (1704) : a So. American cattle ranch or stock farm
[1]**es·tate** \i-ˈstāt\ *n* [ME *estat,* fr. AF — more at STATE] (13c) **1** : STATE, CONDITION **2** : social standing or rank esp. of a high order **3** : a social or political class; *specif* : one of the great classes (as the nobility, the clergy, and the commons) formerly vested with distinct political powers **4 a** : the degree, quality, nature, and extent of one's interest in land or other property **b (1)** : POSSESSIONS, PROPERTY; *esp* : a person's property in land and tenements ⟨a man of small ~⟩ **(2)** : the assets and liabilities left by a person at death **c** : a landed property usu. with a large house on it **d** *Brit* : PROJECT 4 **5** *Brit* : STATION WAGON **6** : FARM, PLANTATION; *also* : VINEYARD
[2]**estate** *adj* (1978) : previously owned by another and usu. of high quality ⟨~ jewelry⟩
estate agent *n* (1856) *Brit* : a real estate broker or manager
estate–bottled *adj* (1940) *of a wine* : entirely produced and bottled by a single winery
estate car *n* (1948) *Brit* : STATION WAGON
estate tax *n* (1928) : a tax in the form of a percentage of the taxable estate that is imposed on a property owner's right to transfer the property to others after his or her death — compare INHERITANCE TAX 1
[1]**es·teem** \i-ˈstēm\ *n* (14c) **1** *archaic* : WORTH, VALUE **2** *archaic* : OPINION, JUDGMENT **3** : the regard in which one is held; *esp* : high regard ⟨the ~ we all feel for her⟩
[2]**esteem** *vt* [ME *estemen* to estimate, fr. AF *estimer,* fr. L *aestimare*] (15c) **1** *archaic* : APPRAISE **2 a** : to view as : CONSIDER ⟨~ it a privilege⟩ **b** : THINK, BELIEVE **3** : to set a high value on : regard highly and prize accordingly ⟨an ~*ed* guest⟩ ***syn*** see REGARD
es·ter \ˈes-tər\ *n* [G, fr. *Essigäther* ethyl acetate, fr. *Essig* vinegar + *Äther* ether] (ca. 1852) : any of a class of often fragrant organic compounds that can be represented by the formula RCOOR′ and that are usu. formed by the reaction between an acid and an alcohol with elimination of water

\ə\ **abut** \°\ kitten, F table \ər\ **further** \a\ **ash** \ā\ **ace** \ä\ **mop, mar**
\au̇\ **out** \ch\ **chin** \e\ **bet** \ē\ **easy** \g\ **go** \i\ **hit** \ī\ **ice** \j\ **job**
\ŋ\ **sing** \ō\ **go** \ȯ\ **law** \ȯi\ **boy** \th\ **thin** \th\ **the** \ü\ **loot** \u̇\ **foot**
\y\ **yet** \zh\ **vision, beige** \k, ⁿ, œ, ue, ʸ\ *see* Guide to Pronunciation

es·ter·ase \ˈes-tə-ˌrās, -ˌrāz\ *n* (1910) **:** an enzyme that accelerates the hydrolysis or synthesis of esters

es·ter·i·fy \e-ˈster-ə-ˌfī\ *vt* **-fied; -fy·ing** (1898) **:** to convert into an ester — **es·ter·i·fi·ca·tion** \-ˌster-ə-fə-ˈkā-shən\ *n*

Esth *abbr* Esther

Es·ther \ˈes-tər\ *n* [L, fr. Heb *Estēr*] (14c) **1 :** the Jewish heroine of the Old Testament book of Esther **2 :** a narrative book of canonical Jewish and Christian Scripture — see BIBLE table

esthete, esthetic, esthetical, esthetician, estheticism, estheticize *var of* AESTHETE, AESTHETIC, AESTHETICAL, AESTHETICIAN, AESTHETICISM, AESTHETICIZE

es·ti·ma·ble \ˈes-tə-mə-bəl\ *adj* (15c) **1 :** capable of being estimated ⟨an ~ amount⟩ **2** *archaic* **:** VALUABLE **3 :** worthy of esteem ⟨an ~ adversary⟩ — **es·ti·ma·ble·ness** *n* — **es·ti·ma·bly** \-blē\ *adv*

[1]**es·ti·mate** \ˈes-tə-ˌmāt\ *vt* **-mat·ed; -mat·ing** [L *aestimatus*, pp. of *aestimare* to value, estimate] (ca. 1532) **1** *archaic* **a :** ESTEEM **b :** APPRAISE **2 a :** to judge tentatively or approximately the value, worth, or significance of **b :** to determine roughly the size, extent, or nature of **c :** to produce a statement of the approximate cost of **3 :** JUDGE, CONCLUDE — **es·ti·ma·tive** \-ˌmā-tiv\ *adj*

syn ESTIMATE, APPRAISE, EVALUATE, VALUE, RATE, ASSESS mean to judge something with respect to its worth or significance. ESTIMATE implies a judgment, considered or casual, that precedes or takes the place of actual measuring or counting or testing out ⟨*estimated* the crowd at two hundred⟩. APPRAISE commonly implies the fixing by an expert of the monetary worth of a thing, but it may be used of any critical judgment ⟨having their house *appraised*⟩. EVALUATE suggests an attempt to determine relative or intrinsic worth in terms other than monetary ⟨*evaluate* a student's work⟩. VALUE equals APPRAISE but without implying expertness of judgment ⟨a watercolor *valued* by the donor at $500⟩. RATE adds to ESTIMATE the notion of placing a thing according to a scale of values ⟨a highly *rated* restaurant⟩. ASSESS implies a critical appraisal for the purpose of understanding or interpreting, or as a guide in taking action ⟨officials are trying to *assess* the damage⟩.

[2]**es·ti·mate** \ˈes-tə-mət\ *n* (1552) **1 :** the act of appraising or valuing **:** CALCULATION **2 :** an opinion or judgment of the nature, character, or quality of a person or thing ⟨had a high ~ of his abilities⟩ **3 a :** a rough or approximate calculation **b :** a numerical value obtained from a statistical sample and assigned to a population parameter **4 :** a statement of the cost of work to be done

es·ti·ma·tion \ˌes-tə-ˈmā-shən\ *n* (14c) **1 :** JUDGMENT, OPINION ⟨a poor choice in my ~⟩ **2 a :** the act of estimating something **b :** the value, amount, or size arrived at in an estimate **3 :** ESTEEM, HONOR

es·ti·ma·tor \ˈes-tə-ˌmā-tər\ *n* (1611) **1 :** one that estimates **2 :** ESTIMATE 3b; *also* **:** a statistical function whose value for a sample furnishes an estimate of a population parameter

es·ti·val *also* **aes·ti·val** \ˈes-tə-vəl\ *adj* [ME, fr. AF or L; AF, fr. L *aestivalis*, fr. *aestivus* of summer, fr. *aestas* summer — more at EDIFY] (14c) **:** of or relating to the summer

es·ti·vate *also* **aes·ti·vate** \-ˌvāt\ *vi* **-vat·ed; -vat·ing** (1626) **1 :** to spend the summer usu. at one place **2 :** to pass the summer in a state of torpor — compare HIBERNATE

es·ti·va·tion *also* **aes·ti·va·tion** \ˌes-tə-ˈvā-shən\ *n* (1625) **:** the state of one that estivates

Es·to·nian \e-ˈstō-nē-ən, -nyən\ *n* (1795) **1 :** a native or inhabitant of Estonia **2 :** the Finno-Ugric language of the Estonian people — **Estonian** *adj*

es·top \e-ˈstäp\ *vt* **es·topped; es·top·ping** [ME *estoppen*, fr. AF *estoper, estuper*, fr. VL **stuppare* to stop with a tow — more at STOP] (15c) **1** *archaic* **:** to stop up **2 :** BAR; *specif* **:** to impede by estoppel

es·top·pel \e-ˈstä-pəl\ *n* [prob. alter. of AF *estopere* stopping, fr. *estoper*] (1531) **:** a legal bar to alleging or denying a fact because of one's own previous actions or words to the contrary

estr- *or* **estro-** *comb form* **:** estrus ⟨*estrogen*⟩

es·tra·di·ol \ˌes-trə-ˈdī-ˌȯl, -ˌōl\ *n* [ISV *estra-* (fr. *estrane* parent compound of estradiol, fr. NL *estrus* + E *-ane*) + *di-* + [1]*-ol*] (1934) **:** a natural estrogenic hormone that is a phenolic alcohol $C_{18}H_{24}O_2$ secreted chiefly by the ovaries, that is the most potent of the naturally occurring estrogens, and that is administered in its natural or semisynthetic esterified form esp. to treat menopausal symptoms

es·tral cycle \ˈes-trəl-\ *n* (1941) **:** ESTROUS CYCLE

es·trange \i-ˈstrānj\ *vt* **es·tranged; es·trang·ing** [ME, fr. AF *estranger, estranger*, fr. ML *extraneare*, fr. L *extraneus* strange — more at STRANGE] (15c) **1 :** to remove from customary environment or associations **2 :** to arouse esp. mutual enmity or indifference in where there had formerly been love, affection, or friendliness **:** ALIENATE — **estrange·ment** \-mənt\ *n* — **es·trang·er** *n*

syn ESTRANGE, ALIENATE, DISAFFECT mean to cause one to break a bond of affection or loyalty. ESTRANGE implies the development of indifference or hostility with consequent separation or divorcement ⟨his *estranged* wife⟩. ALIENATE may or may not suggest separation but always implies loss of affection or interest ⟨managed to *alienate* all his coworkers⟩. DISAFFECT refers esp. to those from whom loyalty is expected and stresses the effects (as rebellion or discontent) of alienation without actual separation ⟨troops *disaffected* by hunger⟩.

[1]**es·tray** \i-ˈstrā\ *n* (ca. 1523) **:** STRAY 1

[2]**estray** *vi* [MF *estraier*] (1572) *archaic* **:** STRAY

es·tri·ol \ˈes-ˌtrī-ˌȯl, e-ˈstrī-, -ˌōl\ *n* [*estrane* + *tri-* + [1]*-ol*] (1933) **:** a relatively weak natural estrogenic hormone that is a glycol $C_{18}H_{24}O_3$ found in the body chiefly as a metabolite of estradiol, is the main estrogen secreted by the placenta during pregnancy, and is the estrogen typically found in the urine of pregnant women

es·tro·gen \ˈes-trə-jən\ *n* [NL *estrus* + ISV *-o-* + *-gen*] (1927) **:** any of various natural steroids (as estradiol) that are formed from androgen precursors, that are secreted chiefly by the ovaries, placenta, adipose tissue, and testes, and that stimulate the development of female secondary sex characteristics and promote the growth and maintenance of the female reproductive system; *also* **:** any of various synthetic or semisynthetic steroids (as ethinyl estradiol) that mimic the physiological effect of natural estrogens

es·tro·gen·ic \ˌes-trə-ˈje-nik\ *adj* (1930) **1 :** promoting estrus **2 :** of, relating to, caused by, or being an estrogen — **es·tro·gen·i·cal·ly** \-ni-k(ə-)lē\ *adv*

estrogen replacement therapy *n* (1967) **:** hormone replacement therapy involving the administration of estrogen without progestin

es·trone \ˈes-ˌtrōn\ *n* [*estrane*] (1933) **:** a natural estrogenic hormone that is a ketone $C_{18}H_{22}O_2$ found in the body chiefly as a metabolite of estradiol, that is also secreted esp. by the ovaries, and that is used to treat various conditions (as ovarian failure and menopausal symptoms) relating to estrogen deficiency

es·trous \ˈes-trəs\ *adj* (1900) **1 :** of, relating to, or characteristic of estrus **2 :** being in heat

estrous cycle *n* (1900) **:** the correlated phenomena of the endocrine and reproductive systems of a female mammal from the beginning of one period of estrus to the beginning of the next — called also *estral cycle, estrus cycle*

es·tru·al \ˈes-trə-wəl, -trü-əl\ *adj* (ca. 1857) **:** ESTROUS

es·trus \ˈes-trəs\ *n* [NL, fr. L *oestrus* gadfly, frenzy, fr. Gk *oistros* — more at IRE] (ca. 1890) **:** a regularly recurrent state of sexual excitability during which the female of most mammals will accept the male and is capable of conceiving **:** HEAT; *also* **:** a single occurrence of this state

es·tu·ar·i·al \ˌes-chə-ˈwer-ē-əl, ˌesh-\ *adj* (1883) **:** ESTUARINE

es·tu·a·rine \ˈes-chə-(wə-)ˌrīn, -ˌrēn, -ˌrin, ˈesh-\ *adj* (1846) **:** of, relating to, or formed in an estuary ⟨~ currents⟩ ⟨~ animals⟩

es·tu·ary \ˈes-chə-ˌwer-ē, ˈesh-\ *n, pl* **-ar·ies** [L *aestuarium*, fr. *aestus* boiling, tide; akin to L *aestas* summer — more at EDIFY] (1538) **:** a water passage where the tide meets a river current; *esp* **:** an arm of the sea at the lower end of a river

esu·ri·ence \i-ˈsu̇r-ē-ən(t)s, -ˈzu̇r-\ *n* (1825) **:** the quality or state of being esurient

esu·ri·ent \-ənt\ *adj* [L *esurient-, esuriens*, prp. of *esurire* to be hungry; akin to L *edere* to eat — more at EAT] (ca. 1672) **:** HUNGRY, GREEDY — **esu·ri·ent·ly** *adv*

et \ˈet\ *dial past and past part of* EAT

Et *abbr* ethyl

[1]**ET** \ˈē-ˈtē\ *n* (1981) **:** EXTRATERRESTRIAL

[2]**ET** *abbr* eastern time

[1]**-et** *n suffix* [ME, fr. AF *-et*, masc., & *-ete*, fem., fr. LL *-itus* & *-ita*] **:** small one ⟨*baronet*⟩ ⟨*cellaret*⟩

[2]**-et** *n suffix* [*duet*] **:** group ⟨*octet*⟩

eta \ˈā-tə, *chiefly Brit* ˈē-tə\ *n* [ME, fr. LL, fr. Gk *ēta*, of Sem origin; akin to Heb *ḥēth* heth] (15c) **:** the 7th letter of the Greek alphabet — see ALPHABET table

ETA *abbr* estimated time of arrival

éta·gère *or* **eta·gere** \ˌā-ˌtä-ˈzher, -tə-\ *n* [F, fr. MF *estagiere*, fr. *estage* floor of a building, station, fr. OF — more at STAGE] (1840) **:** a piece of furniture consisting of a set of open shelves for displaying small objects and sometimes having an enclosed cabinet as a base

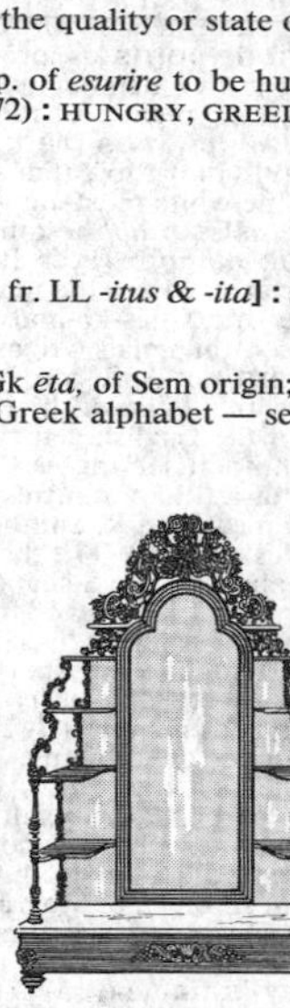

étagère

e–tail \ˈē-ˌtāl\ *n* [blend of *e-* and [2]*retail*] (1995) **:** retail business conducted online via the World Wide Web — **e–tail·er** *n* — **e–tail·ing** *n*

et al *abbr* [L *et alii* (masc.), *et aliae* (fem.), or *et alia* (neut.)] and others

et alia \(ˌ)et-ˈā-l(ē-)yə, -ˈā-, -ˈa-\ [L] (1953) **:** and others

eta·mine \ˈā-tə-ˌmēn\ *n* [F *étamine*] (1714) **:** a light cotton or worsted fabric with an open mesh

etat·ism \ā-ˈtä-ˌti-zəm\ *n* [F *étatisme*, fr. *état* state, fr. OF *estat* — more at STATE] (1923) **:** STATISM — **etat·ist** \-ˈtä-tist\ *adj*

etc *abbr* et cetera — usu. punctuated

et·cet·era \et-ˈse-tə-rə, -ˈse-trə *also* it-, ÷ek-, ÷ik-\ *n* (1597) **1 :** a number of unspecified additional persons or things **2** *pl* **:** unspecified additional items **:** ODDS AND ENDS

et cet·era \et-ˈse-tə-rə, -ˈse-trə *also* it-, ÷ek-, ÷ik-\ [L] (12c) **:** and others esp. of the same kind **:** and so forth

[1]**etch** \ˈech\ *vb* [D *etsen*, fr. G *ätzen* to etch, corrode, fr. OHG *azzen* to feed; akin to OHG *ezzan* to eat — more at EAT] *vt* (1634) **1 a :** to produce (as a pattern or design) on a hard material by eating into the material's surface (as by acid or laser beam) **b :** to subject to such etching **2 :** to delineate or impress clearly ⟨scenes ~*ed* in our minds⟩ ⟨pain was ~*ed* on his features⟩ ~ *vi* **:** to practice etching — **etch·er** *n*

[2]**etch** *n* (1896) **1 :** the action or effect of etching a surface **2 :** a chemical agent used in etching

etch·ant \ˈe-chənt\ *n* (1904) **:** ETCH 2

etch·ing \ˈe-chiŋ\ *n* (1634) **1 a :** the action or process of etching **b :** the art of producing pictures or designs by printing from an etched metal plate **2 a :** an etched design **b :** an impression from an etched plate

ETD *abbr* estimated time of departure

[1]**eter·nal** \i-ˈtər-nᵊl\ *adj* [ME, fr. MF, fr. LL *aeternalis*, fr. L *aeternus* eternal, fr. *aevum* age, eternity — more at AYE] (14c) **1 a :** having infinite duration **:** EVERLASTING ⟨~ damnation⟩ **b :** of or relating to eternity **c :** characterized by abiding fellowship with God ⟨good teacher, what must I do to inherit ~ life? —Mk 10:17(RSV)⟩ **2 a :** continued without intermission **:** PERPETUAL ⟨an ~ flame⟩ **b :** seemingly endless ⟨~ delays⟩ **3** *archaic* **:** INFERNAL ⟨some ~ villain . . . devised this slander —Shak.⟩ **4 :** valid or existing at all times **:** TIMELESS ⟨~ verities⟩ — **eter·nal·ize** \-nə-ˌlīz\ *vt* — **eter·nal·ly** \-nᵊl-ē\ *adv* — **eter·nal·ness** *n*

[2]**eternal** *n* (1573) **1** *cap* **:** GOD 1 — used with *the* **2 :** something eternal

eterne \i-ˈtərn\ *adj* [ME, fr. MF, fr. L *aeternus*] (14c) *archaic* **:** ETERNAL

eter·ni·ty \i-ˈtər-nə-tē\ *n, pl* **-ties** [ME *eternite*, fr. MF *eternité*, fr. L *aeternitat-, aeternitas*, fr. *aeternus*] (14c) **1 :** the quality or state of being eternal **2 :** infinite time ⟨lasting throughout ~⟩ **3** *pl* **:** AGE 3b **4 :** the state after death **:** IMMORTALITY **5 :** a seemingly endless or immeasurable time ⟨an ~ of delays⟩

eter·nize \i-ˈtər-ˌnīz\ *vt* **-nized; -niz·ing** (1566) **1 a :** to make eternal **b :** to prolong indefinitely **2 :** IMMORTALIZE — **eter·ni·za·tion** \-ˌtər-nə-ˈzā-shən\ *n*

Ete·sian \i-ˈtē-zhən\ *adj* [L *etesius,* fr. Gk *etēsios,* fr. *etos* year — more at WETHER] (1601) : recurring annually — used of summer winds that blow over the Mediterranean — **Etesian** *n*

eth \ˈet͟h\ *var of* EDH

eth- *comb form* [ISV] : ethyl ⟨*eth*ene⟩

[1]**-eth** *or* **-th** *vb suffix* [ME, fr. OE *-eth, -ath, -th;* akin to OHG *-it, -ōt, -ēt,* 3d sing. ending, L *-t, -it*] — used to form the archaic third person singular present of verbs ⟨do*th*⟩

[2]**-eth** — see [2]-TH

eth·a·cryn·ic acid \ˌe-thə-ˌkri-nik-\ *n* [prob. fr. *eth-* + *acryl*ic + phe*n-* + acet*ic* acid] (1963) : a potent synthetic diuretic $C_{13}H_{12}Cl_2O_4$ used esp. in the treatment of edema

eth·am·bu·tol \e-ˈtham-byu̇-ˌtȯl, -ˌtōl\ *n* [*eth*ylene + *am*ine + *but*anol] (1961) : a synthetic drug $C_{10}H_{24}N_2O_2$ used in the form of its hydrochloride esp. in the treatment of tuberculosis

eth·ane \ˈe-ˌthān, *Brit usu* ˈē-\ *n* [ISV, fr. *ethyl*] (1866) : a colorless odorless gaseous alkane C_2H_6 found in natural gas and used as a fuel

eth·a·nol \ˈe-thə-ˌnȯl, -ˌnōl, *Brit also* ˈē-\ *n* (1892) : a colorless volatile flammable liquid C_2H_5OH that is the intoxicating agent in liquors and is also used as a solvent and in fuel — called also *ethyl alcohol, grain alcohol*

eth·a·nol·amine \ˌe-thə-ˈnä-lə-ˌmēn, -ˈnō-, *Brit also* ˌē-\ *n* (1897) : a colorless liquid amino alcohol C_2H_7NO used esp. as a solvent in the synthesis of detergents and in gas purification

eth·ene \ˈe-ˌthēn\ *n* (1869) : ETHYLENE

eth·e·phon \ˈe-thə-ˌfän\ *n* [*eth*yl + phos*phon*ic acid (a dibasic organic acid)] (1971) : a synthetic plant growth regulator $C_2H_6ClO_3P$ that induces flowering and abscission by promoting the release of ethylene and has been used to cause early ripening (as of apples on the tree)

ether \ˈē-thər\ *n* [ME, fr. L *aether,* fr. Gk *aithēr,* fr. *aithein* to ignite, blaze; akin to OE *ād* pyre — more at EDIFY] (14c) **1 a :** the rarefied element formerly believed to fill the upper regions of space **b :** the upper regions of space : HEAVENS **2 a** *also* **ae·ther :** a medium that in the wave theory of light permeates all space and transmits transverse waves **b :** AIRWAVES **3 a :** a light volatile flammable liquid $C_4H_{10}O$ used chiefly as a solvent and esp. formerly as an anesthetic **b :** any of a class of organic compounds characterized by an oxygen atom attached to two carbon atoms — **ethe·ric** \i-ˈther-ik, -ˈthir-\ *adj*

ethe·re·al \i-ˈthir-ē-əl\ *adj* (1513) **1 a :** of or relating to the regions beyond the earth **b :** CELESTIAL, HEAVENLY **c :** UNWORLDLY, SPIRITUAL **2 a :** lacking material substance : IMMATERIAL, INTANGIBLE **b :** marked by unusual delicacy or refinement ⟨this smallest, most ~, and daintiest of birds —William Beebe⟩ **c :** suggesting the heavens or heaven **3 :** relating to, containing, or resembling a chemical ether — **ethe·re·al·i·ty** \-ˌthir-ē-ˈa-lə-tē\ *n* — **ethe·re·al·i·za·tion** \-ē-ə-lə-ˈzā-shən\ *n* — **ethe·re·al·ize** \-ˈthir-ē-ə-ˌlīz\ *vt* — **ethe·re·al·ly** \-ē-ə-lē\ *adv* — **ethe·re·al·ness** *n*

ether extract *n* (ca. 1900) : the part of a complex organic material that is soluble in ether and consists chiefly of fats and fatty acids

ether·ize \ˈē-thə-ˌrīz\ *vt* **-ized; -iz·ing** (1847) **1 :** to treat or anesthetize with ether **2 :** to make numb as if by anesthetizing — **ether·i·za·tion** \ˌē-thə-rə-ˈzā-shən\ *n* — **ether·iz·er** *n*

Ether·net \ˈē-thər-ˌnet\ *n* [fr. *Ethernet,* a trademark] 1976 : a computer network architecture consisting of various specified local-area network protocols, devices, and connection methods

eth·ic \ˈe-thik\ *n* [ME *ethik,* fr. MF *ethique,* fr. L *ethice,* fr. Gk *ēthikē,* fr. *ēthikos*] (14c) **1** *pl but sing or pl in constr* **:** the discipline dealing with what is good and bad and with moral duty and obligation **2 a :** a set of moral principles : a theory or system of moral values ⟨the present-day materialistic ~⟩ ⟨an old-fashioned work ~⟩ — often used in pl. but sing. or pl. in constr. ⟨an elaborate ~*s*⟩ ⟨Christian ~*s*⟩ **b** *pl but sing or pl in constr* **:** the principles of conduct governing an individual or a group ⟨professional ~*s*⟩ **c :** a guiding philosophy **d :** a consciousness of moral importance ⟨forge a conservation ~⟩ **3** *pl* **:** a set of moral issues or aspects (as rightness) ⟨debated the ~*s* of human cloning⟩

eth·i·cal \ˈe-thi-kəl\ *also* **eth·ic** \-thik\ *adj* [ME *etik,* fr. L *ethicus,* fr. Gk *ēthikos,* fr. *ēthos* character — more at SIB] (1588) **1 :** of or relating to ethics ⟨~ theories⟩ **2 :** involving or expressing moral approval or disapproval ⟨~ judgments⟩ **3 :** conforming to accepted standards of conduct ⟨~ behavior⟩ **4** *of a drug* **:** restricted to sale only on a doctor's prescription ***syn*** see MORAL — **eth·i·cal·i·ty** \ˌe-thə-ˈka-lə-tē\ *n* — **eth·i·cal·ly** \ˈe-thi-k(ə-)lē\ *adv* — **eth·i·cal·ness** \-kəl-nəs\ *n*

ethi·cian \e-ˈthi-shən\ *n* (1629) : ETHICIST

eth·i·cist \ˈe-thə-sist\ *n* (ca. 1890) : a specialist in ethics

ethid·ium bromide \e-ˈthi-dē-əm-\ *n* [*eth*yl + *-id* + *-ium*] (ca. 1959) : a fluorescent mutagenic biological dye $C_{21}H_{20}BrN_3$ that is used esp. to stain nucleic acids

ethi·nyl *also* **ethy·nyl** \e-ˈthī-nᵊl, ˈe-thə-ˌnil\ *n* [*ethine* ethyne + *-yl*] (1929) : a monovalent unsaturated radical HC≡C– derived from acetylene by removal of one hydrogen atom

ethinyl estradiol *n* (1939) : a very potent synthetic estrogen $C_{20}H_{24}O_2$ used esp. as an oral contraceptive

eth·i·on \ˈe-thē-ˌän\ *n* [blend of *eth-* and *thion-*] (ca. 1960) : a toxic organophosphate $C_9H_{22}O_4P_2S_4$ used as an insecticide and acaricide

eth·i·on·amide \ˌe-thē-ˈä-nə-ˌmīd\ *n* (1960) : a compound $C_8H_{10}N_2S$ used against mycobacteria (as in tuberculosis and leprosy)

ethi·o·nine \e-ˈthī-ə-ˌnēn\ *n* (1938) : an amino acid $C_6H_{13}NO_2S$ that is the ethyl homologue of methionine and is biologically antagonistic to methionine

Ethi·op \ˈē-thē-ˌäp\ *or* **Ethi·ope** \-ˌōp\ *n* [ME *Ethiope,* fr. AF, fr. L *Aethiops,* fr. Gk *Aithiops*] (13c) *archaic* **:** ETHIOPIAN

[1]**Ethi·o·pi·an** \ˌē-thē-ˈō-pē-ən\ *n* (13c) **1 :** a member of any of the mythical or actual peoples usu. described by the ancient Greeks as dark-skinned and living far to the south **2** *archaic* **:** a black person **3 :** a native or inhabitant of Ethiopia

[2]**Ethiopian** *adj* (1557) **1 :** of, relating to, or characteristic of the inhabitants or the country of Ethiopia **2 :** of, relating to, or being the biogeographic region that includes Africa south of the Sahara, southern Arabia, and sometimes Madagascar and the adjacent islands

[1]**Ethi·o·pic** \-ˈä-pik, -ˈō-pik\ *adj* (1631) **1 :** ETHIOPIAN **2 a :** of, relating to, or constituting Ethiopic **b :** of, relating to, or constituting a group of related Semitic languages spoken in Ethiopia

[2]**Ethiopic** *n* (1677) **1 :** a Semitic language formerly spoken in Ethiopia and still used as the liturgical language of the Christian church in Ethiopia **2 :** the Ethiopic group of Semitic languages

eth·moid \ˈeth-ˌmȯid\ *n* [F *ethmoïde,* fr. Gk *ēthmoeidēs,* lit., like a strainer, fr. *ēthmos* strainer] (1842) : a light spongy cubical bone forming much of the walls of the nasal cavity and part of those of the orbits — **ethmoid** *same*\ *or* **eth·moi·dal** \(ˌ)eth-ˈmȯi-dᵊl\ *adj*

[1]**eth·nic** \ˈeth-nik\ *adj* [ME, fr. LL *ethnicus,* fr. Gk *ethnikos* national, gentile, fr. *ethnos* nation, people; akin to Gk *ēthos* custom — more at SIB] (15c) **1 :** HEATHEN **2 a :** of or relating to large groups of people classed according to common racial, national, tribal, religious, linguistic, or cultural origin or background ⟨~ minorities⟩ ⟨~ enclaves⟩ **b :** being a member of a specified ethnic group ⟨an ~ German⟩ **c :** of, relating to, or characteristic of ethnics ⟨~ neighborhoods⟩ ⟨~ foods⟩

[2]**ethnic** *n* (1941) : a member of an ethnic group; *esp* : a member of a minority group who retains the customs, language, or social views of the group

eth·ni·cal \ˈeth-ni-kəl\ *adj* (15c) **1 :** ETHNIC **2 :** of or relating to ethnology : ETHNOLOGIC — **eth·ni·cal·ly** \-k(ə-)lē\ *adv*

ethnic cleansing *n* (1991) : the expulsion, imprisonment, or killing of an ethnic minority by a dominant majority in order to achieve ethnic homogeneity

eth·nic·i·ty \eth-ˈni-sə-tē\ *n, pl* **-ties** (1950) **1 :** ethnic quality or affiliation ⟨aspects of ~⟩ **2 :** a particular ethnic affiliation or group ⟨students of diverse *ethnicities*⟩

ethno- *comb form* [F, fr. Gk *ethno-, ethn-,* fr. *ethnos*] : race : people : cultural group ⟨*ethno*centric⟩

eth·no·bi·ol·o·gy \ˌeth-nō-bī-ˈä-lə-jē\ *n* (1940) : the interdisciplinary study of how human cultures interact with and use their native plants and animals — **eth·no·bi·o·log·i·cal** \-ˌbī-ə-ˈlä-ji-kəl\ *adj* — **eth·no·bi·ol·o·gist** \-bī-ˈä-lə-jist\ *n*

eth·no·bot·a·ny \ˌeth-nō-ˈbä-tə-nē, -ˈbät-nē\ *n* (1890) : the plant lore of indigenous cultures; *also* : the systematic study of such lore — **eth·no·bo·tan·i·cal** \-bə-ˈta-ni-kəl\ *adj* — **eth·no·bot·a·nist** \-ˈbä-tə-nist, -ˈbät-nist\ *n*

eth·no·cen·tric \ˌeth-nō-ˈsen-trik\ *adj* (1900) : characterized by or based on the attitude that one's own group is superior — **eth·no·cen·tric·i·ty** \-sen-ˈtri-sə-tē\ *n* — **eth·no·cen·trism** \-ˈsen-ˌtri-zəm\ *n*

eth·nog·ra·phy \eth-ˈnä-grə-fē\ *n* [F *ethnographie,* fr. *ethno-* + *-graphie* -graphy] (1834) : the study and systematic recording of human cultures; *also* : a descriptive work produced from such research — **eth·nog·ra·pher** \-fər\ *n* — **eth·no·graph·ic** \ˌeth-nə-ˈgra-fik\ *or* **eth·no·graph·i·cal** \-fi-kəl\ *adj* — **eth·no·graph·i·cal·ly** \-fi-k(ə-)lē\ *adv*

eth·no·his·to·ry \ˌeth-nō-ˈhis-t(ə-)rē\ *n* (1943) : a study of the development of cultures — **eth·no·his·to·ri·an** \-(h)is-ˈtȯr-ē-ən, -ˈtär-\ *n* — **eth·no·his·to·ric** \-(h)is-ˈtȯr-ik, -ˈtär-\ *or* **eth·no·his·to·ri·cal** \-i-kəl\ *adj*

eth·nol·o·gy \eth-ˈnä-lə-jē\ *n* (ca. 1828) **1 :** a science that deals with the division of human beings into races and their origin, distribution, relations, and characteristics **2 :** anthropology dealing chiefly with the comparative and analytical study of cultures : CULTURAL ANTHROPOLOGY — **eth·no·log·i·cal** \ˌeth-nə-ˈlä-ji-kəl\ *also* **eth·no·log·ic** \-jik\ *adj* — **eth·nol·o·gist** \eth-ˈnä-lə-jist\ *n*

eth·no·med·i·cine \ˌeth-nō-ˈme-də-sən, *Brit usu* -ˈmed-sən\ *n* (1971) : the comparative study of how different cultures view disease and how they treat or prevent it; *also* : the medical beliefs and practices of indigenous cultures — **eth·no·med·i·cal** \-ˈme-di-kəl\ *adj*

eth·no·meth·od·ol·o·gy \ˌeth-nō-ˌme-thə-ˈdä-lə-jē\ *n* (1967) : a branch of sociology dealing with nonspecialists' commonsense understanding of the structure and organization of society — **eth·no·meth·od·ol·o·gist** \-ˈdä-lə-jist\ *n*

eth·no·mu·si·col·o·gy \ˌeth-nō-ˌmyü-zi-ˈkä-lə-jē\ *n* (1950) **1 :** the study of music that is outside the European art tradition **2 :** the study of music in a sociocultural context — **eth·no·mu·si·co·log·i·cal** \-kə-ˈlä-ji-kəl\ *adj* — **eth·no·mu·si·col·o·gist** \-ˈkä-lə-jist\ *n*

eth·no·sci·ence \ˈeth-nō-ˌsī-ən(t)s\ *n* (1961) : the study of a culture's system of classifying knowledge (as its taxonomy of plants and animals); *also* : such a system in a particular culture

ethol·o·gy \ē-ˈthä-lə-jē\ *n* [Gk *ethos* + E *-logy*] (ca. 1843) **1 :** a branch of knowledge dealing with human character and with its formation and evolution **2 :** the scientific and objective study of animal behavior esp. under natural conditions — **etho·log·i·cal** \ˌē-thə-ˈlä-ji-kəl, ˌe-thə-\ *adj* — **ethol·o·gist** \ē-ˈthä-lə-jist\ *n*

ethos \ˈē-ˌthäs\ *n* [NL, fr. Gk *ēthos* custom, character — more at SIB] (1851) : the distinguishing character, sentiment, moral nature, or guiding beliefs of a person, group, or institution; *also* : ETHIC 2c

eth·oxy \e-ˈthäk-sē\ *adj* (ca. 1909) : relating to or containing the monovalent radical CH_3CH_2O– composed of ethyl united with oxygen

eth·yl \ˈe-thəl\ *n* [G *Ethyl* (now *Äthyl*), fr. *Äther* ether + *-yl*] (1838) : an alkyl radical CH_3CH_2– derived from ethane — **eth·yl·ic** \e-ˈthi-lik\ *adj*

ethyl acetate *n* (1874) : a colorless fragrant volatile flammable liquid ester $C_4H_8O_2$ used esp. as a solvent

ethyl alcohol *n* (1869) : ETHANOL

eth·yl·ben·zene \ˌe-thil-ˈben-ˌzēn\ *n* [ISV] (1871) : a liquid aromatic hydrocarbon C_8H_{10} used chiefly in the manufacture of styrene

ethyl cellulose *n* (1936) : any of various thermoplastic substances used esp. in plastics and lacquers

ethyl chloride *n* (1869) : a colorless pungent flammable gaseous or volatile liquid C_2H_5Cl used esp. as a topical anesthetic

eth·yl·ene \ˈe-thə-ˌlēn\ *n* (ca. 1852) **1 :** a colorless flammable gaseous unsaturated hydrocarbon C_2H_4 that is found in coal gas, can be produced by pyrolysis of petroleum hydrocarbons, and occurs in plants functioning esp. as a natural growth regulator that promotes the ripening of fruit **2 :** a divalent hydrocarbon group C_2H_4 derived from ethane — **eth·yl·enic** \ˌe-thə-ˈlē-nik, -ˈle-nik\ *adj*

eth·yl·ene·di·amine·tet·ra·ac·e·tate \ˌe-thə-ˌlēn-ˌdī-ə-ˌmēn-ˌte-trə-ˈa-sə-ˌtāt, -dī-ˌa-mən-\ *n* (1954) : a salt of EDTA

\ə\ abut \ᵊ\ kitten, F table \ər\ further \a\ ash \ā\ ace \ä\ mop, mar \au̇\ out \ch\ chin \e\ bet \ē\ easy \g\ go \i\ hit \ī\ ice \j\ job \ŋ\ sing \ō\ go \ȯ\ law \ȯi\ boy \th\ thin \t͟h\ the \ü\ loot \u̇\ foot \y\ yet \zh\ vision, beige \k̲, ⁿ, œ, ue, ʸ\ *see* Guide to Pronunciation

eth·yl·ene·di·amine·tet·ra·ace·tic acid \-(ə-)ˈsē-tik-\ *n* (1942) : EDTA
ethylene di·bro·mide \-(ˌ)dī-ˈbrō-ˌmīd\ *n* (1866) : a colorless toxic liquid compound $C_2H_4Br_2$ that is used chiefly as a fuel additive in leaded gasolines, that has been found to be strongly carcinogenic in laboratory animals, and that was used formerly in the U.S. as an agricultural pesticide — abbr. *EDB*
ethylene glycol *n* (ca. 1884) : a thick liquid diol $C_2H_6O_2$ used esp. as an antifreeze and in making polyester fibers
ethylene oxide *n* (ca. 1884) : a colorless flammable toxic compound C_2H_4O used esp. in synthesis (as of ethylene glycol) and in sterilization and fumigation
ethyl ether *n* (1878) : ETHER 3a
eth·yne \ˈe-ˌthīn, e-ˈ\ *n* [alter. of *ethine,* fr. *ethyl* + [2]*-ine*] (1877) : ACETYLENE
ethynyl *var of* ETHINYL
et·ic \ˈe-tik\ *adj* [phon*etic*] (1954) : of, relating to, or involving analysis of cultural phenomena from the perspective of one who does not participate in the culture being studied — compare EMIC
-etic *adj suffix* [L & Gk; L *-eticus,* fr. Gk *-etikos, -ētikos,* fr. *-etos, -ētos,* ending of certain verbals] : -IC ⟨limn*etic*⟩ — often in adjectives corresponding to nouns ending in *-esis* ⟨gen*etic*⟩
et·i·dro·nate \ˌē-tə-ˈdrō-ˌnāt, ˌe-\ *n* [etidronic acid (of which etidronate is a salt), perh. fr. *ethylid*ene (the radical CH_3CH) + hy*dr*- + phosph*onic acid* (an acid obtained from phosphine)] (1971) : a white sodium salt $C_2H_6Na_2O_7P_2$ that inhibits the formation, growth, and dissolution of hydroxyapatite crystals and is administered orally in the treatment of some bone diseases (as Paget's disease of bone) — called also *etidronate disodium*
eti·o·late \ˈē-tē-ə-ˌlāt\ *vt* **-lat·ed; -lat·ing** [F *étioler*] (1791) **1 :** to bleach and alter the natural development of (a green plant) by excluding sunlight **2 a :** to make pale **b :** to deprive of natural vigor : make feeble — **eti·o·la·tion** \ˌē-tē-ə-ˈlā-shən\ *n*
eti·o·log·ic \ˌē-tē-ə-ˈlä-jik\ *or* **eti·o·log·i·cal** \-ji-kəl\ *adj* (ca. 1753) **1 :** assigning or seeking to assign a cause **2 :** of or relating to etiology — **eti·o·log·i·cal·ly** \-ji-k(ə-)lē\ *adv*
eti·ol·o·gy \ˌē-tē-ˈä-lə-jē\ *n, pl* **-gies** [ML *aetiologia* statement of causes, fr. Gk *aitiologia,* fr. *aitia* cause] (ca. 1555) **1 :** CAUSE, ORIGIN; *specif* : the cause of a disease or abnormal condition **2 :** a branch of knowledge concerned with causes; *specif* : a branch of medical science concerned with the causes and origins of diseases
et·i·quette \ˈe-ti-kət, -ˌket\ *n* [F *étiquette,* lit., ticket — more at TICKET] (1750) : the conduct or procedure required by good breeding or prescribed by authority to be observed in social or official life
ETO *abbr* European theater of operations
Eton collar \ˌē-tᵊn-\ *n* [*Eton* College, English public school] (1887) : a large stiff turnover collar
Eto·ni·an \ē-ˈtō-nē-ən\ *n* (1658) : a student or former student of Eton College — **Etonian** *adj*
Eton jacket *n* (1881) : a short black jacket with long sleeves, wide lapels, and an open front
étouf·fée *also* **etouf·fee** \ˌā-tü-ˈfā\ *n* [LaF, fr. F *à l'étouffée* braised] (ca. 1933) : a Cajun stew of shellfish or chicken served over rice
Etru·ri·an \i-ˈtrůr-ē-ən\ *n* (1566) : ETRUSCAN — **Etrurian** *adj*
[1]**Etrus·can** \i-ˈtrəs-kən\ *adj* [L *etruscus;* akin to L *Etruria,* ancient country] (1584) : of, relating to, or characteristic of Etruria, the Etruscans, or the Etruscan language
[2]**Etruscan** *n* (1584) **1 :** the language of the Etruscans which is of uncertain affiliation **2 :** a native or inhabitant of ancient Etruria
et seq *abbr* [L *et sequens*] and the following one; [L *et sequentes* (masc. & fem. pl.) or *et sequentia* (neut. pl.)] and the following ones
-ette *n suffix* [F, fem. dim. suffix, fr. OF *-ete* — more at -ET] **1 :** little one ⟨kitchen*ette*⟩ **2 :** female ⟨farmer*ette*⟩
étude \ˈā-ˌtüd, -ˌtyüd\ *n* [F, lit., study, fr. MF *estude, estudie,* fr. OF — more at STUDY] (ca. 1837) **1 :** a piece of music for the practice of a point of technique **2 :** a composition built on a technical motive but played for its artistic value
etui \ā-ˈtwē, ˈā-ˌ\ *n, pl* **etuis** [F *étui*] (1611) : a small ornamental case
et ux *abbr* [L *et uxor*] and wife
ETV *abbr* educational television
et·y·mol·o·gise *Brit var of* ETYMOLOGIZE
et·y·mol·o·gist \ˌe-tə-ˈmä-lə-jist\ *n* (1635) : a specialist in etymology
et·y·mol·o·gize \-ˌjīz\ *vb* **-gized; -giz·ing** *vt* (ca. 1530) : to discover, formulate, or state an etymology for ~ *vi* : to study or formulate etymologies
et·y·mol·o·gy \-jē\ *n, pl* **-gies** [ME *ethimologie,* fr. AF, fr. L *etymologia,* fr. Gk, fr. *etymon* + *-logia* -logy] (14c) **1 :** the history of a linguistic form (as a word) shown by tracing its development since its earliest recorded occurrence in the language where it is found, by tracing its transmission from one language to another, by analyzing it into its component parts, by identifying its cognates in other languages, or by tracing it and its cognates to a common ancestral form in an ancestral language **2 :** a branch of linguistics concerned with etymologies — **et·y·mo·log·i·cal** \-mə-ˈlä-ji-kəl\ *adj* — **et·y·mo·log·i·cal·ly** \-k(ə-)lē\ *adv*
et·y·mon \ˈe-tə-ˌmän\ *n, pl* **-ma** \-mə\ *also* **-mons** [L, fr. Gk, literal meaning of a word according to its origin, fr. *etymos* true; akin to Gk *eteos* true — more at SOOTH] (ca. 1576) **1 a :** an earlier form of a word in the same language or an ancestral language **b :** a word in a foreign language that is the source of a particular loanword **2 :** a word or morpheme from which words are formed by composition or derivation
Eu *symbol* europium
EU *abbr* European Union
eu- *comb form* [L, fr. Gk, fr. *eu* well, fr. neut. of *eys* good; perh. akin to L *esse* to be] **1 a :** well : easily ⟨*eu*clase⟩ — compare DYS- **b :** good ⟨*eu*daemonism⟩ — compare DYS- **2 :** true ⟨*eu*chromatin⟩
eu·bac·te·ri·um \ˌyü-bak-ˈtir-ē-əm\ *n* [NL] (1913) : any of the bacteria excluding those included in the archaebacteria or the archaea — **eu·bac·te·ri·al** \-ē-əl\ *adj*
eu·ca·lypt \ˈyü-kə-ˌlipt\ *n* (1877) : EUCALYPTUS
eu·ca·lyp·tol *also* **eu·ca·lyp·tole** \ˌyü-kə-ˈlip-ˌtȯl, -ˌtōl\ *n* (1879) : a liquid $C_{10}H_{18}O$ with an odor of camphor that occurs in many essential oils (as of eucalyptus) and is used esp. as an expectorant and flavoring agent — called also *cineole*
eu·ca·lyp·tus \ˌyü-kə-ˈlip-təs\ *n, pl* **-ti** \-ˌtī, -ˌtē\ *or* **-tus·es** [NL, genus name, fr. *eu-* + Gk *kalyptos* covered, fr. *kalyptein* to conceal; fr. the conical covering of the buds — more at HELL] (1801) : any of a genus (*Eucalyptus*) of mostly Australian evergreen trees or rarely shrubs of the myrtle family that have rigid entire leaves and umbellate flowers and are widely cultivated for their gums, resins, oils, and woods
eucaryote *var of* EUKARYOTE
Eu·cha·rist \ˈyü-k(ə-)rəst\ *n* [ME *eukarist,* fr. AF *eukariste,* fr. LL *eucharistia,* fr. Gk, Eucharist, gratitude, fr. *eucharistos* grateful, fr. *eu-* + *charizesthai* to show favor, fr. *charis* favor, grace, gratitude; akin to Gk *chairein* to rejoice — more at YEARN] (14c) **1 :** COMMUNION 2a **2** *Christian Science* : spiritual communion with God — **eu·cha·ris·tic** \ˌyü-kə-ˈris-tik\ *adj, often cap*
[1]**eu·chre** \ˈyü-kər\ *n* [origin unknown] (1841) : a card game in which each player is dealt five cards and the player making trump must take three tricks to win a hand
[2]**euchre** *vt* **eu·chred; eu·chring** \-k(ə-)riŋ\ (1847) **1 :** to prevent from winning three tricks in euchre **2 :** CHEAT, TRICK ⟨*euchred* out of their life savings —Pete Martin⟩
eu·chro·ma·tin \(ˌ)yü-ˈkrō-mə-tən\ *n* [ISV] (1932) : the part of chromatin that is genetically active and is largely composed of genes — **eu·chro·mat·ic** \ˌyü-krō-ˈma-tik\ *adj*
eu·clase \ˈyü-ˌklās, -ˌklāz\ *n* [F, fr. *eu-* (fr. L) + Gk *klasis* breaking, fr. *klan* to break] (1804) : a mineral that consists of a brittle silicate of beryllium and aluminum in pale yellow, green, or blue prismatic crystals and is used esp. as a gemstone
eu·clid·e·an *also* **eu·clid·i·an** \yü-ˈkli-dē-ən\ *adj, often cap* (1660) : of, relating to, or based on the geometry of Euclid or a geometry with similar axioms
Euclidean algorithm *n* (ca. 1955) : a method of finding the greatest common divisor of two numbers by dividing the larger by the smaller, the smaller by the remainder, the first remainder by the second remainder, and so on until exact division is obtained whence the greatest common divisor is the exact divisor — called also *Euclid's algorithm*
euclidean geometry *n, often cap E* (ca. 1865) **1 :** geometry based on Euclid's axioms **2 :** the geometry of a euclidean space
euclidean space *n, often cap E* (1883) : a space in which Euclid's axioms and definitions (as of straight and parallel lines and angles of plane triangles) apply
eu·crite \ˈyü-ˌkrīt\ *n* [G *Eukrit,* fr. Gk *eukritos* easily discerned, fr. *eu-* + *kritos* separated, fr. *krinein* to separate — more at CERTAIN] (1881) **1 :** a stony meteorite composed essentially of plagioclase and pigeonite **2 :** a rock consisting of a very basic gabbro — **eu·crit·ic** \yü-ˈkri-tik\ *adj*
eu·dae·mo·nism \yü-ˈdē-mə-ˌni-zəm\ *or* **eu·dai·mo·nism** \-ˈdī-\ *n* [Gk *eudaimonia* happiness, fr. *eudaimōn* having a good attendant spirit, happy, fr. *eu-* + *daimōn* spirit — more at DEMON] (1827) : a theory that the highest ethical goal is happiness and personal well-being — **eu·dae·mo·nist** \-nist\ *n* — **eu·dae·mo·nis·tic** \-ˌdē-mə-ˈnis-tik\ *adj*
eu·di·om·e·ter \ˌyü-dē-ˈä-mə-tər\ *n* [modif. of It *eudiometro,* fr. Gk *eudia* fair weather (fr. *eu-* + *-dia* weather—akin to L *dies* day) + It *-metro* -meter, fr. Gk *metron* measure] (1777) : an instrument for the volumetric measurement and analysis of gases — **eu·dio·met·ric** \ˌyü-dē-ə-ˈme-trik\ *adj* — **eu·dio·met·ri·cal·ly** \-tri-k(ə-)lē\ *adv*
eu·gen·ic \yü-ˈje-nik\ *adj* [Gk *eugenēs* wellborn, fr. *eu-* + *-genēs* born — more at -GEN] (1883) **1 :** relating to or fitted for the production of good offspring **2 :** of or relating to eugenics — **eu·gen·i·cal·ly** \-ni-k(ə-)lē\ *adv*
eu·gen·i·cist \-ˈje-nə-sist\ *n* (ca. 1909) : a student or advocate of eugenics
eu·gen·ics \yü-ˈje-niks\ *n pl but sing in constr* (1883) : a science that deals with the improvement (as by control of human mating) of hereditary qualities of a race or breed
eu·gen·ist \yü-ˈje-nist\ *n* (1908) : EUGENICIST
eu·ge·nol \ˈyü-jə-ˌnȯl, -ˌnōl\ *n* [ISV *eugen-,* fr. NL *Eugenia,* genus of tropical trees] (1886) : a colorless aromatic liquid phenol $C_{10}H_{12}O_2$ found esp. in clove oil and used commercially in flavors and perfumes and in dentistry as an analgesic
eu·geo·syn·cline \(ˌ)yü-ˌjē-ō-ˈsin-ˌklīn\ *n* (1942) : a narrow rapidly subsiding geosyncline usu. with volcanic materials mingled with clastic sediments — **eu·geo·syn·cli·nal** \-(ˌ)sin-ˈklī-nᵊl\ *adj*
eu·gle·na \yü-ˈglē-nə\ *n* [NL, genus name, fr. *eu-* + Gk *glēnē* eyeball, socket of a joint] (ca. 1889) : any of a genus (*Euglena*) of green freshwater flagellates often classified as algae
eu·gle·noid \-ˌnȯid\ *n* (1885) : any of a taxon (Euglenoidina or Euglenophyta) of varied flagellates (as a euglena) that are typically green or colorless stigma-bearing solitary microorganisms with one or two flagella emerging from a well-defined gullet — **euglenoid** *adj*
euglenoid movement *n* (1940) : writhing usu. nonprogressive protoplasmic movement of plastic-bodied euglenoid flagellates
eu·glob·u·lin \yü-ˈglä-byə-lən\ *n* [ISV] (1904) : a simple protein that does not dissolve in pure water
eu·he·mer·ism \yü-ˈhē-mə-ˌri-zəm, -ˈhe-mə-\ *n* [*Euhemerus,* 4th cent. B.C. Greek mythographer] (1846) : interpretation of myths as traditional accounts of historical persons and events — **eu·he·mer·ist** \-rist\ *n* — **eu·he·mer·is·tic** \-ˌhē-mə-ˈris-tik, -ˌhe-mə-\ *adj*
eu·kary·ote *also* **eu·cary·ote** \(ˌ)yü-ˈker-ē-ˌōt, -ət, -ˈka-rē-\ *n* [NL *Eukaryotes,* proposed subdivision of protists, fr. *eu-* + *kary-* + *-otes,* pl. n. suffix, fr. Gk *-ōtos* — more at -OTIC] (1943) : any of a domain (Eukarya) or a higher taxonomic group (Eukaryota) above the kingdom that includes organisms composed of one or more cells containing visibly evident nuclei and organelles — compare ARCHAEA, BACTERIUM, PROKARYOTE — **eu·kary·ot·ic** \-ˌker-ē-ˈä-tik, -ˌka-rē-\ *adj*
eu·la·chon \ˈyü-lə-ˌkän, -li-kən\ *n, pl* **eulachon** *or* **eulachons** [Chinook Jargon *ulâkân,* prob. fr. Lower Chinook *u-ƛalχʷə̂n*] (1807) : CANDLEFISH
eu·lo·gise *Brit var of* EULOGIZE
eu·lo·gist \ˈyü-lə-jist\ *n* (1808) : one who eulogizes
eu·lo·gi·um \yü-ˈlō-jē-əm\ *n, pl* **-gia** \-jē-ə\ *or* **-gi·ums** [ML] (1621) : EULOGY
eu·lo·gize \ˈyü-lə-ˌjīz\ *vt* **-gized; -giz·ing** (1810) : to speak or write in high praise of : EXTOL — **eu·lo·giz·er** *n*
eu·lo·gy \ˈyü-lə-jē\ *n, pl* **-gies** [ME *euloge,* fr. ML *eulogium,* fr. Gk *eulogia* praise, fr. *eu-* + *-logia* -logy] (15c) **1 :** a commendatory oration

or writing esp. in honor of one deceased ⟨she delivered the ~ at his funeral⟩ **2 :** high praise ***syn*** see ENCOMIUM — **eu·lo·gis·tic** \ˌyü-lə-ˈjis-tik\ *adj* — **eu·lo·gis·ti·cal·ly** \-ti-k(ə-)lē\ *adv*

Eu·men·i·des \yü-ˈme-nə-ˌdēz\ *n pl* [L, fr. Gk, lit., the gracious ones] (1536) **:** the Furies in Greek mythology

eu·nuch \ˈyü-nək, -nik\ *n* [ME *eunuk,* fr. L *eunuchus,* fr. Gk *eunouchos,* fr. *eunē* bed + *echein* to have, have charge of — more at SCHEME] (15c) **1 :** a castrated man placed in charge of a harem or employed as a chamberlain in a palace **2 :** a man or boy deprived of the testes or external genitals **3 :** one that lacks virility or power ⟨political ~*s*⟩ — **eu·nuch·ism** \-nə-ˌki-zəm, -ni-\ *n*

eu·nuch·oid \-nə-ˌkȯid, -ni-\ *n* (1906) **:** a sexually deficient individual; *esp* **:** one lacking in sexual differentiation and tending toward the intersexual state — **eunuchoid** *adj*

eu·on·y·mus \yü-ˈä-nə-məs\ *n* [NL, genus name, fr. L *euonymos* spindle tree, fr. Gk *euōnymos,* fr. *euōnymos* having an auspicious name, fr. *eu-* + *onyma* name — more at NAME] (1736) **:** SPINDLE TREE

eu·pa·trid \yü-ˈpa-trəd, ˈyü-pə-\ *n, pl* **eu·pat·ri·dae** \yü-ˈpa-trə-ˌdē\ *often cap* [Gk *eupatridēs,* fr. *eu-* + *patr-, patēr* father — more at FATHER] (1836) **:** one of the hereditary aristocrats of ancient Athens

eu·pep·tic \yü-ˈpep-tik\ *adj* (1699) **1 :** of, relating to, or having good digestion **2 :** CHEERFUL, OPTIMISTIC

eu·phau·si·id \yü-ˈfȯ-zē-əd\ *n* [NL *Euphausia,* genus of crustaceans] (1885) **:** any of an order (Euphausiacea) of small usu. luminescent malacostracan crustaceans that resemble shrimps and in some areas form an important element in marine plankton — **euphausiid** *adj*

eu·phe·mise *Brit var of* EUPHEMIZE

eu·phe·mism \ˈyü-fə-ˌmi-zəm\ *n* [Gk *euphēmismos,* fr. *euphēmos* auspicious, sounding good, fr. *eu-* + *phēmē* speech, fr. *phanai* to speak — more at BAN] (ca. 1681) **:** the substitution of an agreeable or inoffensive expression for one that may offend or suggest something unpleasant; *also* **:** the expression so substituted — **eu·phe·mist** \-mist\ *n* — **eu·phe·mis·tic** \ˌyü-fə-ˈmis-tik\ *adj* — **eu·phe·mis·ti·cal·ly** \-ti-k(ə-)lē\ *adv*

eu·phe·mize \ˈyü-fə-ˌmīz\ *vt* **-mized; -miz·ing** (1857) **:** to express or describe euphemistically ⟨~ death⟩ — **eu·phe·miz·er** \-ˌmī-zər\ *n*

eu·phen·ics \yü-ˈfe-niks\ *n pl but sing in constr* [*eu-* + *phen-* (fr. *phenotype*) + *-ics;* after E *genotype : eugenics*] (1963) **:** the therapeutic techniques and procedures for amelioration of the deleterious phenotypic effects of a genetic defect esp. without altering the genetic makeup of the germplasm of the individual — **eu·phen·ic** \-nik\ *adj*

eu·pho·ni·ous \yü-ˈfō-nē-əs\ *adj* (1774) **:** pleasing to the ear — **eu·pho·ni·ous·ly** *adv* — **eu·pho·ni·ous·ness** *n*

eu·pho·ni·um \yü-ˈfō-nē-əm\ *n* [Gk *euphōnos* + E *-ium* (as in *harmonium*)] (1865) **:** a brass instrument smaller than but resembling a tuba and having a range from B flat below the bass staff upward for three octaves

eu·pho·ny \ˈyü-fə-nē\ *n, pl* **-nies** [F *euphonie,* fr. LL *euphonia,* fr. Gk *euphōnia,* fr. *euphōnos* sweet-voiced, musical, fr. *eu-* + *phōnē* voice — more at BAN] (1606) **1 :** pleasing or sweet sound; *esp* **:** the acoustic effect produced by words so formed or combined as to please the ear **2 :** a harmonious succession of words having a pleasing sound — **eu·phon·ic** \yu̇-ˈfä-nik\ *adj* — **eu·phon·i·cal·ly** \-ni-k(ə-)lē\ *adv*

eu·phor·bia \yü-ˈfȯr-bē-ə\ *n* [NL, alter. of L *euphorbea,* fr. *Euphorbus,* 1st cent. A.D. Greek physician] (14c) **:** any of a large genus (*Euphorbia*) of herbs, shrubs, and trees of the spurge family that have a milky juice and flowers lacking a calyx and included in an involucre which surrounds a group of several staminate flowers and a central pistillate flower with 3-lobed pistils; *broadly* **:** SPURGE

eu·pho·ria \yü-ˈfȯr-ē-ə\ *n* [NL, fr. Gk, fr. *euphoros* healthy, fr. *eu-* + *pherein* to bear — more at BEAR] (ca. 1751) **:** a feeling of well-being or elation — **eu·phor·ic** \-ˈfȯr-ik, -ˈfär-\ *adj* — **eu·phor·i·cal·ly** \-i-k(ə-)lē\ *adv*

eu·pho·ri·ant \yü-ˈfȯr-ē-ənt\ *n* (1947) **:** a drug that tends to induce euphoria — **euphoriant** *adj*

eu·pho·tic \yü-ˈfō-tik\ *adj* [ISV] (1909) **:** of, relating to, or constituting the upper layers of a body of water into which sufficient light penetrates to permit growth of green plants

Eu·phros·y·ne \yü-ˈfrä-sə-(ˌ)nē, -zə-\ *n* [L, fr. Gk *Euphrosynē*] (1579) **:** one of the three Graces

eu·phu·ism \ˈyü-fyə-ˌwi-zəm, -fyü-ˌi-\ *n* [*Euphues,* character in prose romances by John Lyly] (1592) **1 :** an elegant Elizabethan literary style marked by excessive use of balance, antithesis, and alliteration and by frequent use of similes drawn from mythology and nature **2 :** artificial elegance of language — **eu·phu·ist** \-wist, -ist\ *n* — **eu·phu·is·tic** \ˌyü-fyə-ˈwis-tik, -fyü-ˈis-\ *adj* — **eu·phu·is·ti·cal·ly** \-ti-k(ə-)lē\ *adv*

eu·ploid \ˈyü-ˌplȯid\ *adj* [ISV] (1926) **:** having a chromosome number that is an exact multiple of the monoploid number — compare ANEUPLOID — **euploid** *n* — **eu·ploi·dy** \-ˌplȯi-dē\ *n*

eup·nea *also* **eup·noea** \yüp-ˈnē-ə\ *n* [NL, fr. Gk *eupnoia,* fr. *eupnous* breathing freely, fr. *eu-* + *pnein* to breathe — more at SNEEZE] (ca. 1706) **:** normal respiration — **eup·ne·ic** \-ˈnē-ik\ *adj*

Eur *abbr* Europe; European

Eur- *or* **Euro-** *comb form* [*Europe*] **:** European and ⟨*Eur*american⟩ **:** European ⟨*Euro*centric⟩ **:** western European ⟨*Euro*communism⟩ **:** of the European Union ⟨*Euro*crat⟩

Eur·asian \yu̇r-ˈā-zhən, -shən, yər-\ *adj* (1844) **1 :** of a mixed European and Asian origin **2 :** of or relating to Europe and Asia — **Eurasian** *n*

[1]**eu·re·ka** \yu̇-ˈrē-kə\ *interj* [Gk *heurēka* I have found, fr. *heuriskein* to find; fr. the exclamation attributed to Archimedes on discovering a method for determining the purity of gold — more at HEURISTIC] (1603) — used to express triumph on a discovery

[2]**eureka** *adj* (1948) **:** marked by usu. sudden triumphant discovery ⟨a ~ moment⟩

[1]**eu·ro** \ˈyu̇r-(ˌ)ō\ *n, pl* **euros** [Adnyamathanha (Australian aboriginal language of South Australia) *yuru*] (1855) **:** WALLAROO

[2]**euro** *n, pl* **euros** *also* **euro** [short for the equivalent of *Europe* or *European* in the languages of the European Union] (1981) **:** the common basic monetary unit of most countries of the European Union — see MONEY table

Eu·ro \ˈyu̇r-(ˌ)ō\ *adj* (1963) **:** EUROPEAN — **Euro** *n*

[1]**Eu·ro–Amer·i·can** \ˌyu̇r-ō-ə-ˈmer-ə-kən\ *or* **Eur·amer·i·can** \ˌyu̇r-ə-ˈmer-ə-kən\ *adj* (1941) **1 :** WESTERN 2a, b **2 :** WESTERN 3

[2]**Euro–American** *n* (1949) **1 :** a person of both European and American ancestry **2 :** an American of European and esp. white European descent

Eu·ro·bond \ˈyu̇r-ō-ˌbänd\ *n* (1966) **:** a bond of a U.S. corporation that is sold outside the U.S. and that is denominated and paid for in dollars and yields interest in dollars

euro cent *n* (1995) **1 :** a monetary unit equal to 1/100 euro **2 :** a coin representing one euro cent

Eu·ro·cen·tric \ˌyu̇r-ə-ˈsen-trik\ *adj* (1963) **:** centered on Europe or the Europeans; *esp* **:** reflecting a tendency to interpret the world in terms of European or Anglo-American values and experiences — **Eu·ro·cen·trism** \-ˌtri-zəm\ *n* — **Eu·ro·cen·trist** \-ˈsen-trist\ *n*

Eu·ro·com·mu·nism \ˌyu̇r-ō-ˈkäm-yə-ˌni-zəm\ *n* (1976) **:** the communism esp. of western European Communist parties that was marked by a willingness to reach power through coalitions and by independence from Soviet leadership — **Eu·ro·com·mu·nist** *n or adj*

Eu·ro·crat \ˈyu̇r-ə-ˌkrat\ *n* (1961) **:** a staff member of the administrative commission of the European Union — **Eu·ro·cra·cy** \yu̇-ˈrä-krə-sē\ *n*

Eu·ro·cur·ren·cy \ˌyu̇r-ō-ˈkər-ən-sē, -ˈkə-rən-\ *n* (1963) **:** moneys (as of the U.S. and Japan) held outside their countries of origin and used in the money markets of Europe

Eu·ro·dol·lar \ˈyu̇r-ō-ˌdä-lər\ *n* (1960) **:** a U.S. dollar held as Eurocurrency

Eu·ro·pa \yu̇-ˈrō-pə\ *n* [L, fr. Gk *Eurōpē*] (14c) **:** a Phoenician princess carried off by Zeus in the form of a white bull and by him mother of Minos, Rhadamanthus, and Sarpedon

[1]**Eu·ro·pe·an** \ˌyu̇r-ə-ˈpē-ən, -ˈpēn\ *adj* (1603) **:** of, relating to, or characteristic of Europe or its people — **Eu·ro·pe·an·ness** *n*

[2]**European** *n* (1623) **1 :** a native or inhabitant of Europe **2 :** a person of European descent

European American *n* (1881) **:** EURO-AMERICAN

European bison *n* (1860) **:** WISENT

European chafer *n* (1947) **:** an Old World beetle (*Rhizotragus majalis* syn. *Amphimallon majalis*) established in parts of eastern No. America where its larva is a destructive pest on the roots of turf grasses

European corn borer *n* (1920) **:** an Old World moth (*Ostrinia nubilalis*) widespread in eastern and central No. America where its larva is a major pest in the stems, crowns, and fruits of crop plants and esp. corn

European flat *n* (1981) **:** a flat-shelled European oyster (*Ostrea edulis*)

Eu·ro·pe·an·ism \ˌyu̇r-ō-ˈpē-ə-ni-zəm\ *n* (1828) **1 :** attachment or allegiance to the traditions, interests, or ideals of Europeans **2 :** the ideal or advocacy of the political and economic integration of Europe

Eu·ro·pe·an·ist \ˌyu̇r-ō-ˈpē-ə-nist\ *n* (1948) **1 :** a specialist in European culture or history **2 :** an advocate for Europeanism

Eu·ro·pe·an·ize \yu̇r-ə-ˈpē-ə-ˌnīz\ *vt* **-ized; -iz·ing** (1844) **:** to cause to acquire or conform to European characteristics — **Eu·ro·pe·an·i·za·tion** \-ˌpē-ə-nə-ˈzā-shən\ *n*

European plan *n* (1834) **:** a hotel plan whereby the daily rates cover only the cost of the room — compare AMERICAN PLAN

European red mite *n* (1940) **:** a small bright red or brownish-red oval Old World mite (*Panonychus ulmi*) that is a destructive orchard pest

eu·ro·pi·um \yu̇-ˈrō-pē-əm\ *n* [NL, fr. *Europa* Europe] (1901) **:** a divalent and trivalent metallic element of the rare-earth group found esp. in monazite sand — see ELEMENT table

Eu·ro·po·cen·tric \yu̇-ˌrō-pə-ˈsen-trik\ *adj* (1926) **:** EUROCENTRIC — **Eu·ro·po·cen·trism** \-ˌtri-zəm\ *n*

eu·ro·zone \ˈyu̇r-ō-ˌzōn\ *n* (1995) **:** the geographical area comprising the countries that use the euro as the official currency

eury- *comb form* [NL, fr. Gk, fr. *eurys;* akin to Skt *uru* broad, wide] **:** broad **:** wide ⟨*eury*haline⟩

eu·ry·bath·ic \ˌyu̇r-i-ˈba-thik\ *adj* [*eury-* + Gk *bathos* depth] (1902) **:** capable of living on the bottom in both deep and shallow water

Eu·ryd·i·ce \yu̇-ˈri-də-(ˌ)sē\ *n* [L, fr. Gk *Eurydikē*] (15c) **:** the wife of Orpheus whom he attempts to bring back from Hades

eu·ry·ha·line \ˌyu̇r-i-ˈhā-ˌlīn, -ˈha-\ *adj* [ISV *eury-* + Gk *halinos* of salt, fr. *hals* salt — more at SALT] (1888) **:** able to live in waters of a wide range of salinity ⟨~ crabs⟩

eu·ryp·ter·id \yu̇-ˈrip-tə-rəd\ *n* [ultim. fr. Gk *eury-* + *pteron* wing — more at FEATHER] (1871) **:** any of an order (Eurypterida) of usu. large aquatic Paleozoic arthropods resembling scorpions and related to the horseshoe crabs — called also *sea scorpion* — **eurypterid** *adj*

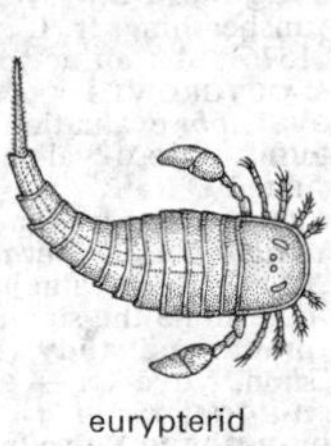
eurypterid

eu·ry·ther·mal \ˌyu̇r-i-ˈthər-məl\ *adj* [ISV] (1881) **:** tolerating a wide range of temperature ⟨~ animals⟩

eu·ry·ther·mic \-mik\ *adj* [ISV] (1903) **:** EURYTHERMAL

eu·ry·ther·mous \-məs\ *adj* [ISV] (1940) **:** EURYTHERMAL

eu·ryth·mic *or* **eu·rhyth·mic** \yu̇-ˈrith-mik\ *adj* (1855) **1 :** HARMONIOUS **2 :** of or relating to eurythmy or eurythmics

eu·ryth·mics *or* **eu·rhyth·mics** \-miks\ *n pl but sing or pl in constr* (1912) **:** the art of harmonious bodily movement esp. through expressive timed movements in response to improvised music

eu·ryth·my *or* **eu·rhyth·my** \-mē\ *n* [G *Eurhythmie,* fr. L *eurythmia* rhythmical movement, fr. Gk, fr. *eurythmos* rhythmical, fr. *eu-* + *rhythmos* rhythm] (1949) **:** a system of harmonious body movement to the rhythm of spoken words

eu·ry·top·ic \ˌyu̇r-i-ˈtä-pik\ *adj* [ISV *eury-* + Gk *topos* place] (1937) **:** tolerant of wide variation in one or more environmental factors

eu·so·cial \ˌyü-ˈsō-shəl\ *adj* (1966) **:** living in a cooperative group in which usu. one female and several males are reproductively active and the nonbreeding individuals care for the young or protect and provide for the group ⟨~ termites, ants, and naked mole rats⟩ — **eu·so·ci·al·i·ty** \-ˌsō-shē-ˈa-lə-tē\ *n*

eu·sta·chian tube \yü-ˈstā-sh(ē-)ən- *also* -ˈstā-kē-ən-\ *n, often cap E* [Bartolommeo *Eustachio*] (1741) : a bony and cartilaginous tube connecting the middle ear with the nasopharynx and equalizing air pressure on both sides of the tympanic membrane — called also *auditory tube;* see EAR illustration

eu·stat·ic \yü-ˈsta-tik\ *adj* [ISV] (1906) : relating to or characterized by worldwide change of sea level

eu·stele \ˈyü-ˌstēl, yü-ˈstē-lē\ *n* (1902) : a stele typical of dicotyledonous plants that consists of vascular bundles of xylem and phloem strands with parenchymal cells between the bundles

eu·tec·tic \yü-ˈtek-tik\ *adj* [Gk *eutēktos* easily melted, fr. *eu-* + *tēktos* melted, fr. *tēkein* to melt — more at THAW] (1884) **1** *of an alloy or solution* : having the lowest melting point possible **2** : of or relating to a eutectic alloy or solution or its melting or freezing point — **eutectic** *n* — **eu·tec·toid** \-ˌtȯid\ *adj or n*

Eu·ter·pe \yü-ˈtər-pē\ *n* [L, fr. Gk *Euterpē*] (15c) : the Greek Muse of music

eu·tha·na·sia \ˌyü-thə-ˈnā-zh(ē-)ə\ *n* [Gk, easy death, fr. *euthanatos,* fr. *eu-* + *thanatos* death — more at THANATOS] (1869) : the act or practice of killing or permitting the death of hopelessly sick or injured individuals (as persons or domestic animals) in a relatively painless way for reasons of mercy — **eu·tha·na·sic** \-zik, -sik\ *adj*

eu·tha·nize \ˈyü-thə-ˌnīz\ *also* **eu·than·a·tize** \yü-ˈtha-nə-ˌtīz\ *vt* **-nized** *also* **-tized; -niz·ing** *also* **-tiz·ing** [Gk *euthanatos*] (1873) : to subject to euthanasia

eu·then·ics \yü-ˈthe-niks\ *n pl but sing or pl in constr* [Gk *euthenein* to thrive] (1905) : a science that deals with development of human well-being by improvement of living conditions — **eu·the·nist** \yü-ˈthe-nist, ˈyü-thə-\ *n*

eu·the·ri·an \yü-ˈthir-ē-ən\ *adj* [ultim. fr. NL *eu-* + Gk *thērion* beast — more at TREACLE] (1880) : of or relating to a major division (Eutheria) of mammals comprising the placental mammals — **eutherian** *n*

eu·thy·roid \(ˌ)yü-ˈthī-ˌrȯid\ *adj* (1924) : characterized by normal thyroid function

eu·tro·phic \yü-ˈtrō-fik\ *adj* [prob. fr. G *Eutroph* eutrophic, fr. Gk *eutrophos* well-nourished, nourishing, fr. *eu-* + *trephein* to nourish] (1928) *of a body of water* : characterized by the state resulting from eutrophication — compare MESOTROPHIC, OLIGOTROPHIC — **eu·tro·phy** \ˈyü-trə-fē\ *n*

eu·tro·phi·ca·tion \yü-ˌtrō-fə-ˈkā-shən, ˌyü-trə-fə-\ *n* (1946) : the process by which a body of water becomes enriched in dissolved nutrients (as phosphates) that stimulate the growth of aquatic plant life usu. resulting in the depletion of dissolved oxygen

eV *abbr* electron volt

EV *abbr* electric vehicle

EVA *abbr* extravehicular activity

evac·u·ate \i-ˈva-kyə-ˌwāt, -kyü-ˌāt\ *vb* **-at·ed; -at·ing** [ME, to draw off morbid humors, fr. L *evacuatus,* pp. of *evacuare* to empty, fr. *e-* + *vacuus* empty] *vt* (15c) **1** : to remove the contents of : EMPTY **2** : to discharge from the body as waste : VOID **3** : to remove something (as gas or water) from esp. by pumping **4 a** : to remove esp. from a military zone or dangerous area **b** : to withdraw from military occupation of **c** : VACATE ⟨were ordered to ~ the building⟩ ~ *vi* **1** : to withdraw from a place in an organized way esp. for protection **2** : to pass urine or feces from the body — **evac·u·a·tive** \-ˌwā-tiv, -ˌā-\ *adj*

evac·u·a·tion \i-ˌva-kyə-ˈwā-shən, -kyü-ˈā-\ *n* (14c) **1** : the act or process of evacuating **2** : something evacuated or discharged

evac·u·ee \i-ˌva-kyə-ˈwē, -kyü-ˈē-\ *n* (1918) : an evacuated person

evade \i-ˈvād, ē-\ *vb* **evad·ed; evad·ing** [MF & L; MF *evader,* fr. L *evadere,* fr. *e-* + *vadere* to go, walk — more at WADE] *vi* (1513) **1** : to slip away **2** : to take refuge in escape or avoidance ~ *vt* **1** : to elude by dexterity or stratagem **2 a** : to avoid facing up to ⟨*evaded* the real issues⟩ **b** : to avoid the performance of : DODGE, CIRCUMVENT; *esp* : to fail to pay (taxes) **c** : to avoid answering directly : turn aside **3** : to be elusive to : BAFFLE ⟨the simple, personal meaning *evaded* them —C. D. Lewis⟩ ***syn*** see ESCAPE — **evad·able** \-ˈvā-də-bəl\ *adj* — **evad·er** *n*

evag·i·na·tion \i-ˌva-jə-ˈnā-shən\ *n* [LL *evagination-, evaginatio,* act of unsheathing, fr. L *evaginare* to unsheathe, fr. *e-* + *vagina* sheath] (ca. 1676) **1** : an act or instance of everting **2** : a product of eversion : OUTGROWTH

eval *abbr* evaluation

evalu·able \i-ˈval-yə-bəl, -yə-wə-bəl, -yü-ə-\ *adj* (1880) : able to be evaluated

eval·u·ate \i-ˈval-yə-ˌwāt, -yü-ˌāt\ *vt* **-at·ed; -at·ing** [back-formation fr. *evaluation,* fr. F *évaluation,* fr. MF *evaluacion,* fr. *esvaluer* to evaluate, fr. *e-* + *value* value] (1842) **1** : to determine or fix the value of **2** : to determine the significance, worth, or condition of usu. by careful appraisal and study ***syn*** see ESTIMATE — **eval·u·a·tion** \-ˌval-yə-ˈwā-shən, -yü-ˈā-\ *n* — **eval·u·a·tive** \-ˈval-yə-ˌwā-tiv, -yü-ˌā-\ *adj* — **eval·u·a·tor** \-tər\ *n*

ev·a·nesce \ˌe-və-ˈnes\ *vi* **-nesced; -nesc·ing** [L *evanescere* — more at VANISH] (1822) : to dissipate like vapor

ev·a·nes·cence \ˌe-və-ˈne-sᵊn(t)s\ *n* (1751) **1** : the process or fact of evanescing **2** : evanescent quality

ev·a·nes·cent \-sᵊnt\ *adj* [L *evanescent-, evanescens,* prp. of *evanescere*] (1717) : tending to vanish like vapor ***syn*** see TRANSIENT

[1]**evan·gel** \i-ˈvan-jəl\ *n* [ME *evangile,* fr. AF *evangile,* fr. LL *evangelium,* fr. Gk *euangelion* good news, gospel, fr. *euangelos* bringing good news, fr. *eu-* + *angelos* messenger] (14c) : GOSPEL

[2]**evangel** *n* (1614) : EVANGELIST

[1]**evan·gel·i·cal** \ˌē-ˌvan-ˈje-li-kəl, ˌe-vən-\ *also* **evan·gel·ic** \-ik\ *adj* (1531) **1** : of, relating to, or being in agreement with the Christian gospel esp. as it is presented in the four Gospels **2** : PROTESTANT **3** : emphasizing salvation by faith in the atoning death of Jesus Christ through personal conversion, the authority of Scripture, and the importance of preaching as contrasted with ritual **4 a** *cap* : of or relating to the Evangelical Church in Germany **b** *often cap* : of, adhering to, or marked by fundamentalism : FUNDAMENTALIST **c** *often cap* : LOW CHURCH **5** : marked by militant or crusading zeal : EVANGELISTIC ⟨the ~ ardor of the movement's leaders —Amos Vogel⟩ — **Evan·gel·i·cal·ism** \-li-kə-ˌli-zəm\ *n* — **evan·gel·i·cal·ly** \-li-k(ə-)lē\ *adv*

[2]**evangelical** *n, often cap* (1532) : one holding evangelical principles or belonging to an evangelical party or church

evan·ge·lism \i-ˈvan-jə-ˌli-zəm\ *n* (ca. 1626) **1** : the winning or revival of personal commitments to Christ **2** : militant or crusading zeal — **evan·ge·lis·tic** \-ˌvan-jə-ˈlis-tik\ *adj* — **evan·ge·lis·ti·cal·ly** \-ti-k(ə-)lē\ *adv*

evan·ge·list \i-ˈvan-jə-list\ *n* (13c) **1** *often cap* : a writer of any of the four Gospels **2** : a person who evangelizes; *specif* : a Protestant minister or layman who preaches at special services **3** : an enthusiastic advocate ⟨an ~ for physical fitness⟩

evan·ge·lize \i-ˈvan-jə-ˌlīz\ *vb* **-lized; -liz·ing** *vt* (14c) **1** : to preach the gospel to **2** : to convert to Christianity ~ *vi* : to preach the gospel — **evan·ge·li·za·tion** \-ˌvan-jə-lə-ˈzā-shən\ *n*

evap *abbr* evaporate

evap·o·rate \i-ˈva-p(ə-)ˌrāt\ *vb* **-rat·ed; -rat·ing** [ME, fr. L *evaporatus,* pp. of *evaporare,* fr. *e-* + *vapor* steam, vapor] *vt* (15c) **1 a** : to convert into vapor; *also* : to dissipate or draw off in vapor or fumes **b** : to deposit (as a metal) in the form of a film by sublimation **2 a** : to expel moisture from **b** : EXPEL ⟨~ electrons from a hot wire⟩ ~ *vi* **1 a** : to pass off in vapor or in minute particles **b** (1) : to pass off or away : DISAPPEAR ⟨her ardor *evaporated*⟩ (2) : to diminish quickly **2** : to give forth vapor — **evap·o·ra·tion** \-ˌva-pə-ˈrā-shən\ *n* — **evap·o·ra·tive** \-ˈva-pə-ˌrā-tiv\ *adj* — **evap·o·ra·tor** \-ˈva-pə-ˌrā-tər\ *n*

evaporated milk *n* (1870) : unsweetened milk concentrated by partial evaporation

evap·o·rite \i-ˈva-pə-ˌrīt\ *n* [*evaporation* + [1]*-ite*] (1924) : a sedimentary rock (as gypsum) that originates by evaporation of seawater in an enclosed basin — **evap·o·rit·ic** \-ˌva-pə-ˈri-tik\ *adj*

evapo·trans·pi·ra·tion \i-ˈva-pō-ˌtran(t)-spə-ˈrā-shən\ *n* [*evaporation* + *transpiration*] (1938) : loss of water from the soil both by evaporation and by transpiration from the plants growing thereon

eva·sion \i-ˈvā-zhən, ē-\ *n* [ME, fr. AF or LL; AF, fr. LL *evasion-, evasio,* fr. L *evadere* to evade] (15c) **1** : a means of evading : DODGE **2** : the act or an instance of evading : ESCAPE ⟨suspected of tax ~⟩

eva·sive \i-ˈvā-siv, -ziv, ē-\ *adj* (1637) : tending or intended to evade : EQUIVOCAL ⟨~ answers⟩ — **eva·sive·ly** *adv* — **eva·sive·ness** *n*

eve \ˈēv\ *n* [ME *eve, even*] (13c) **1** : EVENING **2** : the evening or the day before a special day **3** : the period immediately preceding

Eve \ˈēv\ *n* [OE *Ēfe,* fr. LL *Eva,* fr. Heb *Ḥawwāh*] (bef. 12c) : the first woman, the wife of Adam, and the mother of Cain and Abel

[1]**even** \ˈē-vən\ *n* [ME *even, eve,* fr. OE *ǣfen*] (bef. 12c) *archaic* : EVENING

[2]**even** *adj* [ME, fr. OE *efen;* akin to OHG *eban* even] (bef. 12c) **1 a** : having a horizontal surface : FLAT ⟨~ ground⟩ **b** : being without break, indentation, or irregularity : SMOOTH **c** : being in the same plane or line **2 a** : free from variation : UNIFORM ⟨his disposition was ~⟩ **b** : LEVEL 4 **3 a** : EQUAL, FAIR ⟨an ~ exchange⟩ **b** (1) : leaving nothing due on either side : SQUARE ⟨we will not be ~ until you repay my visit⟩ (2) : fully revenged **c** : being in equilibrium : BALANCED; *specif* : showing neither profit nor loss **d** *obs* : CANDID **4 a** : being any of the integers (as –2, 0, and +2) that are divisible by two without leaving a remainder **b** : marked by an even number **c** : being a mathematical function such that $f(x) = f(-x)$ where the value remains unchanged if the sign of the independent variable is reversed **5** : EXACT, PRECISE ⟨an ~ dollar⟩ **6** : as likely as not : FIFTY-FIFTY ⟨an ~ chance of winning⟩ ***syn*** see LEVEL, STEADY — **even·ly** *adv* — **even·ness** \-vən-nəs\ *n* — **on an even keel** *also* **on even keel** : in a sound or stable condition

[3]**even** *adv* [ME, fr. OE *efne,* fr. *efen,* adj.] (bef. 12c) **1 a** : EXACTLY, PRECISELY **b** : to a degree that extends : FULLY, QUITE ⟨faithful ~ unto death⟩ **c** : at the very time ⟨raining ~ as the sun came out⟩ **2 a** — used as an intensive to emphasize the identity or character of something ⟨forgot his car keys and ~ left the engine running⟩ **b** — used as an intensive to stress an extreme or highly unlikely condition or instance ⟨so simple ~ a child can do it⟩ **c** — used as an intensive to stress the comparative degree ⟨she did ~ better⟩ **d** — used as an intensive to indicate a small or minimum amount ⟨didn't ~ try⟩

[4]**even** *vb* **evened; even·ing** \ˈēv-niŋ, ˈē-və-\ *vt* (13c) : to make even ~ *vi* : to become even — **even·er** \-nər\ *n*

even·fall \ˈē-vən-ˌfȯl\ *n* (1814) : the beginning of evening : DUSK

even·hand·ed \ˌē-vən-ˈhan-dəd\ *adj* (1605) : FAIR, IMPARTIAL — **even·hand·ed·ly** *adv* — **even·hand·ed·ness** *n*

[1]**eve·ning** \ˈēv-niŋ\ *n, often attrib* [ME, fr. OE *ǣfnung,* fr. *ǣfnian* to grow toward evening, fr. *ǣfen* evening; akin to OHG *āband* evening and perh. to Gk *epi* on] (bef. 12c) **1 a** : the latter part and close of the day and early part of the night **b** *chiefly Southern & Midland* : AFTERNOON **c** : the period from sunset or the evening meal to bedtime **2** : the latter portion **3** : the period of an evening's entertainment

[2]**evening** *adj* (1797) : suitable for formal or semiformal evening social occasions ⟨~ dress⟩ ⟨~ clothes⟩

evening grosbeak *n* (1828) : a No. American grosbeak (*Coccothraustes vespertinus*) having conspicuous white wing patches with the male being chiefly yellowish with some black

evening prayer *n, often cap E&P* (1571) : the daily evening office of the Anglican liturgy

evening primrose *n* (1804) : any of several dicotyledonous plants of a family (Onagraceae, the evening-primrose family) and esp. of the type genus (*Oenothera*); *esp* : a coarse biennial herb (*O. biennis*) of No. America with yellow flowers that open in the evening

eve·nings \ˈēv-niŋz\ *adv* (1652) : in the evening repeatedly : on any evening ⟨goes bowling ~⟩

evening star *n* (1535) **1** : a bright planet (as Venus) seen esp. in the western sky at or after sunset **2** : a planet that rises before midnight

even–keeled \ˈē-vən-ˌkēld\ *adj* (1945) : characterized by stability or consistency

even money *n* (1880) : a situation in wagering in which the odds are even

even permutation *n* (ca. 1932) : a permutation that is produced by the successive application of an even number of interchanges of pairs of elements

even so *adv* (1930) : in spite of that : NEVERTHELESS

even·song \ˈē-vən-ˌsȯŋ\ *n, often cap* [ME, fr. OE *ǣfensang,* fr. *ǣfen* evening + *sang* song] (bef. 12c) **1** : VESPERS 1 **2** : EVENING PRAYER

event \i-ˈvent\ *n* [MF or L; MF, fr. L *eventus,* fr. *evenire* to happen, fr. *e-* + *venire* to come — more at COME] (1549) **1 a** *archaic* : OUTCOME **b** : the final outcome or determination of a legal action **c** : a postulated outcome, condition, or eventuality ⟨in the ~ that I am not there, call the house⟩ **2 a :** something that happens : OCCURRENCE **b :** a noteworthy happening **c :** a social occasion or activity **d :** an adverse or damaging medical occurrence ⟨a heart attack or other cardiac ~⟩ **3 :** any of the contests in a program of sports **4 :** the fundamental entity of observed physical reality represented by a point designated by three coordinates of place and one of time in the space-time continuum postulated by the theory of relativity **5 :** a subset of the possible outcomes of an experiment ***syn*** see OCCURRENCE — **event·less** \-ləs\ *adj* — **at all events :** in any case — **in any event :** in any case — **in the event** *chiefly Brit* : as it turns out

event·ful \i-ˈvent-fəl\ *adj* (1600) **1 :** full of or rich in events **2 :** MOMENTOUS — **event·ful·ly** \-fə-lē\ *adv* — **event·ful·ness** *n*

event horizon *n* (1969) : the surface of a black hole : the boundary of a black hole beyond which nothing can escape from within it

even·tide \ˈē-vən-ˌtīd\ *n* (bef. 12c) : the time of evening : EVENING

even·tu·al \i-ˈven(t)-sh(ə-)wəl, -ˈven-chəl, -chü-əl\ *adj* (1683) **1** *archaic* : CONTINGENT, CONDITIONAL **2 :** taking place at an unspecified later time : ultimately resulting ⟨they counted on our ~ success⟩

even·tu·al·i·ty \i-ˌven-chə-ˈwa-lə-tē\ *n, pl* **-ties** (1759) : a possible event or outcome : POSSIBILITY

even·tu·al·ly *adv* (ca. 1680) : at an unspecified later time : in the end

even·tu·ate \i-ˈven-chə-ˌwāt\ *vi* **-at·ed; -at·ing** (1789) : to come out finally : RESULT, COME ABOUT

ev·er \ˈe-vər\ *adv* [ME, fr. OE *ǣfre*] (bef. 12c) **1 :** ALWAYS ⟨~ striving to improve⟩ ⟨the *ever*-increasing population⟩ **2 a :** at any time ⟨more than ~ before⟩ **b :** in any way ⟨how can I ~ thank you⟩ **3 —** used as an intensive ⟨looks ~ so angry⟩ ⟨am I ~ happy to see you⟩ — **ever and anon :** from time to time : OCCASIONALLY

ev·er·bloom·ing \ˌe-vər-ˈblü-miŋ\ *adj* (1838) : blooming more or less continuously throughout the growing season

ev·er·dur·ing \ˌe-vər-ˈdu̇r-iŋ, -ˈdyu̇r-\ *adj* (15c) *archaic* : EVERLASTING

ev·er·glade \ˈe-vər-ˌglād\ *n* [the *Everglades,* Fla.] (1823) : a swampy grassland esp. in southern Florida usu. containing saw grass and at least seasonally covered by slowly moving water — usu. used in pl.

[1]**ev·er·green** \ˈe-vər-ˌgrēn\ *adj* (1574) **1 :** having foliage that remains green and functional through more than one growing season — compare DECIDUOUS 1 **2 :** retaining freshness or interest : PERENNIAL

[2]**evergreen** *n* (1644) **1 :** an evergreen plant; *also* : CONIFER **2** *pl* : twigs and branches of evergreen plants used for decoration **3 :** something that retains its freshness, interest, or popularity

evergreen oak *n* (1673) : any of various oaks (as a live oak, a holm oak, or a tan oak) with foliage that persists for two years so that the plant is more or less continuously green

[1]**ev·er·last·ing** \ˌe-vər-ˈlas-tiŋ\ *adj* (13c) **1 :** lasting or enduring through all time : ETERNAL **2 a (1) :** continuing for a long time or indefinitely **(2) :** having or being flowers or foliage that retain form or color for a long time when dried **b :** tediously persistent ⟨the ~ sympathy-seeker who demands attention —H. A. Overstreet⟩ **3 :** wearing indefinitely ⟨~ twill pants⟩ — **ev·er·last·ing·ly** \-tiŋ-lē\ *adv* — **ev·er·last·ing·ness** *n*

[2]**everlasting** *n* (14c) **1 :** ETERNITY ⟨from ~⟩ **2** *cap* : GOD 1 — used with *the* **3 a :** any of several chiefly composite plants (as cudweed) with flowers that can be dried without loss of form or color — compare PEARLY EVERLASTING **b :** the flower of an everlasting

ev·er·more \ˌe-vər-ˈmȯr\ *adv* (13c) **1 :** FOREVER, ALWAYS **2 :** in the future

ever·sion \i-ˈvər-zhən, -shən\ *n* (1751) **1 :** the act of turning inside out : the state of being turned inside out ⟨~ of the bladder⟩ **2 :** the condition (as of the foot) of being turned or rotated outward — **ever·si·ble** \-ˈvər-sə-bəl\ *adj*

evert \i-ˈvərt\ *vt* [L *evertere,* fr. *e-* + *vertere* to turn — more at WORTH] (1533) **1 :** OVERTHROW, UPSET **2 :** to subject to eversion

ev·ery \ˈev-rē\ *adj* [ME *everich, every,* fr. OE *ǣfre ǣlc,* fr. *ǣfre* ever + *ǣlc* each] (bef. 12c) **1 a :** being each individual or part of a group without exception **b :** being each in a series or succession ⟨~ few days⟩ ⟨~ once in a while⟩ **2** *obs* : being all taken severally **3 :** being each within a range of possibilities ⟨was given ~ chance⟩ **4 :** COMPLETE, ENTIRE ⟨we have ~ confidence in her⟩ — **every now and then** *or* **every now and again** *or* **every so often :** at intervals : OCCASIONALLY

ev·ery·body \ˈev-ri-ˌbə-dē, -ˌbä-\ *pron* (15c) : EVERYONE

ev·ery·day \ˈev-rē-ˌdā, ˌev-re-ˈ\ *adj* (ca. 1623) : encountered or used routinely or typically : ORDINARY ⟨~ clothes⟩ — **ev·ery·day·ness** \-ˈdā-nəs\ *n*

ev·ery·man \ˈev-rē-ˌman\ *n, often cap* [*Everyman,* allegorical character in *The Summoning of Everyman,* 15th cent. Eng. morality play] (1906) : the typical or ordinary person

ev·ery·one \-(ˌ)wən\ *pron* (13c) : every person : EVERYBODY

ev·ery·place \-ˌplās\ *adv* (ca. 1917) : EVERYWHERE

ev·ery·thing \ˈev-rē-ˌthiŋ\ *pron* (14c) **1 a :** all that exists **b :** all that relates to the subject **2 :** all that is important ⟨you mean ~ to me⟩ **3 :** all sorts of other things — used to indicate related but unspecified events, facts, or conditions ⟨all the pains and colds and ~ —E. B. White⟩

ev·ery·where \ˈev-rē-ˌ(h)wer\ *adv* (13c) : in every place or part

every which way *adv* [prob. by folk etymology fr. ME *everich way* every way] (1824) **1 :** in every direction **2 :** in a disorderly manner : IRREGULARLY ⟨toys scattered about *every which way*⟩

ev·ery·wom·an \ˈev-rē-ˌwu̇-mən\ *n, often cap* [after *everyman*] (1945) : the typical or ordinary woman

evg *abbr* evening

evict \i-ˈvikt\ *vt* [ME, fr. LL *evictus,* pp. of *evincere,* fr. L, to vanquish, win a point — more at EVINCE] (15c) **1 a :** to recover (property) from a person by legal process **b :** to put (a tenant) out by legal process **2 :** to force out : EXPEL ***syn*** see EJECT — **evic·tion** \-ˈvik-shən\ *n* — **evic·tor** \-ˈvik-tər\ *n*

evict·ee \i-ˌvik-ˈtē\ *n* (1879) : an evicted person

[1]**ev·i·dence** \ˈe-və-dən(t)s, -və-ˌden(t)s\ *n* (14c) **1 a :** an outward sign : INDICATION **b :** something that furnishes proof : TESTIMONY; *specif* : something legally submitted to a tribunal to ascertain the truth of a matter **2 :** one who bears witness; *esp* : one who voluntarily confesses a crime and testifies for the prosecution against his accomplices — **in evidence 1 :** to be seen : CONSPICUOUS ⟨trim lawns . . . are everywhere *in evidence —Amer. Guide Series: N.C.*⟩ **2 :** as evidence

[2]**evidence** *vt* **-denced; -denc·ing** (ca. 1610) : to offer evidence of : PROVE, EVINCE ***syn*** see SHOW

ev·i·dent \ˈe-və-dənt, -və-ˌdent\ *adj* [ME, fr. AF, fr. L *evident-, evidens,* fr. *e-* + *vident-, videns,* prp. of *vidēre* to see — more at WIT] (14c) : clear to the vision or understanding

syn EVIDENT, MANIFEST, PATENT, DISTINCT, OBVIOUS, APPARENT, PLAIN, CLEAR mean readily perceived or apprehended. EVIDENT implies presence of visible signs that lead one to a definite conclusion ⟨an *evident* fondness for sweets⟩. MANIFEST implies an external display so evident that little or no inference is required ⟨*manifest* hostility⟩. PATENT applies to a cause, effect, or significant feature that is clear and unmistakable once attention has been directed to it ⟨*patent* defects⟩. DISTINCT implies such sharpness of outline or definition that no unusual effort to see or hear or comprehend is required ⟨a *distinct* refusal⟩. OBVIOUS implies such ease in discovering that it often suggests conspicuousness or little need for perspicacity in the observer ⟨the *obvious* solution⟩. APPARENT is very close to EVIDENT except that it may imply more conscious exercise of inference ⟨for no *apparent* reason⟩. PLAIN suggests lack of intricacy, complexity, or elaboration ⟨her feelings about him are *plain*⟩. CLEAR implies an absence of anything that confuses the mind or obscures the pattern ⟨a *clear* explanation⟩.

ev·i·den·tial \ˌe-və-ˈden(t)-shəl\ *adj* (ca. 1641) : EVIDENTIARY 1 — **ev·i·den·tial·ly** *adv*

ev·i·den·tia·ry \ˌe-və-ˈden-chə-rē, -chē-ˌer-ē\ *adj* (1810) **1 :** being, relating to, or affording evidence ⟨photographs of ~ value⟩ **2 :** conducted so that evidence may be presented ⟨an ~ hearing⟩

ev·i·dent·ly \ˈe-və-dənt-lē, -ə-ˌdent-, *esp for 2 often* ˌev-ə-ˈdent-\ *adv* (1609) **1 :** in an evident manner : CLEARLY, OBVIOUSLY ⟨any style . . . so ~ bad or second-rate —T. S. Eliot⟩ **2 :** on the basis of available evidence ⟨he was born . . . ~ in Texas —Robert Coughlan⟩

[1]**evil** \ˈē-vəl, *Brit often & US also* ˈē-(ˌ)vil\ *adj* **evil·er** *or* **evil·ler; evil·est** *or* **evil·lest** [ME, fr. OE *yfel;* akin to OHG *ubil* evil] (bef. 12c) **1 a :** morally reprehensible : SINFUL, WICKED ⟨an ~ impulse⟩ **b :** arising from actual or imputed bad character or conduct ⟨a person of ~ reputation⟩ **2 a** *archaic* : INFERIOR **b :** causing discomfort or repulsion : OFFENSIVE ⟨an ~ odor⟩ **c :** DISAGREEABLE ⟨woke late and in an ~ temper⟩ **3 a :** causing harm : PERNICIOUS ⟨the ~ institution of slavery⟩ **b :** marked by misfortune : UNLUCKY — **evil** *adv, archaic* — **evil·ly** \-(l)ē\ *adv* — **evil·ness** \-nəs\ *n*

[2]**evil** *n* (bef. 12c) **1 a :** the fact of suffering, misfortune, and wrongdoing **b :** a cosmic evil force **2 :** something that brings sorrow, distress, or calamity

evil·do·er \ˌē-vəl-ˈdü-ər\ *n* (14c) : one who does evil

evil·do·ing \-ˈdü-iŋ\ *n* (14c) : the act or action of doing evil

evil eye *n* (bef. 12c) : an eye or glance held capable of inflicting harm; *also* : a person believed to have such an eye or glance

evil–mind·ed \ˌē-vəl-ˈmīn-dəd, -vil-\ *adj* (1531) : having an evil disposition or evil thoughts — **evil–mind·ed·ly** *adv* — **evil–mind·ed·ness** *n*

evince \i-ˈvin(t)s\ *vt* **evinced; evinc·ing** [L *evincere* to vanquish, win a point, fr. *e-* + *vincere* to conquer — more at VICTOR] (1604) **1 :** to constitute outward evidence of **2 :** to display clearly : REVEAL ***syn*** see SHOW — **evinc·ible** \-ˈvin(t)-sə-bəl\ *adj*

evis·cer·ate \i-ˈvi-sə-ˌrāt\ *vb* **-at·ed; -at·ing** [L *evisceratus,* pp. of *eviscerare,* fr. *e-* + *viscera* viscera] *vt* (1599) **1 a :** to take out the entrails of : DISEMBOWEL **b :** to deprive of vital content or force **2 :** to remove an organ from (a patient) or the contents of (an organ) ~ *vi* : to protrude through a surgical incision or suffer protrusion of a part through an incision — **evis·cer·a·tion** \-ˌvi-sə-ˈrā-shən\ *n*

ev·i·ta·ble \ˈe-və-tə-bəl\ *adj* [L *evitabilis,* fr. *evitare* to avoid, fr. *e-* + *vitare* to shun] (1502) : capable of being avoided

evo·ca·ble \ˈe-və-kə-bəl, i-ˈvō-kə-\ *adj* (1886) : capable of being evoked

evo·ca·tion \ˌē-vō-ˈkā-shən, ˌe-və-\ *n* [L *evocation-, evocatio,* fr. *evocare*] (1633) **1 :** the act or fact of evoking : SUMMONING: as **a :** the summoning of a spirit **b :** imaginative recreation ⟨an ~ of the past⟩ **2 :** INDUCTION 4e — **evo·ca·tor** \ˈē-vō-ˌkā-tər, ˈe-və-\ *n*

evoc·a·tive \i-ˈvä-kə-tiv\ *adj* (1657) : evoking or tending to evoke an esp. emotional response ⟨settings . . . so ~ that they bring tears to the eyes —Eric Malpass⟩ — **evoc·a·tive·ly** *adv* — **evoc·a·tive·ness** *n*

evoke \i-ˈvōk\ *vt* **evoked; evok·ing** [F *évoquer,* fr. L *evocare,* fr. *e-* + *vocare* to call — more at VOCATION] (ca. 1622) **1 :** to call forth or up: as **a :** CONJURE 2a ⟨~ evil spirits⟩ **b :** to cite esp. with approval or for support : INVOKE **c :** to bring to mind or recollection ⟨this place ~*s* memories⟩ **2 :** to re-create imaginatively ***syn*** see EDUCE

evo·lute \ˈe-və-ˌlüt *also* ˈē-və-\ *n* (ca. 1736) : the locus of the center of curvature or the envelope of the normals of a curve

evo·lu·tion \ˌe-və-ˈlü-shən, ˌē-və-\ *n* [L *evolution-, evolutio* unrolling, fr. *evolvere*] (1622) **1 :** one of a set of prescribed movements **2 a :** a process of change in a certain direction : UNFOLDING **b :** the action or an instance of forming and giving something off : EMISSION **c (1) :** a process of continuous change from a lower, simpler, or worse to a higher, more complex, or better state : GROWTH **(2) :** a process of gradual and relatively peaceful social, political, and economic advance **d :** something evolved **3 :** the process of working out or developing **4 a :** the historical development of a biological group (as a race or species) : PHYLOGENY **b :** a theory that the various types of animals and plants have their origin in other preexisting types and that the distinguishable differences are due to modifications in successive generations; *also* : the process described by this theory **5 :** the extraction of a mathematical root **6 :** a process in which the whole universe is a progression of interrelated phenomena — **evo·lu·tion·ari·ly** \-shə-ˌner-ə-lē\ *adv* — **evo·lu·tion·ary** \-shə-ˌner-ē\ *adj* — **evo·lu·tion·ism** \-shə-ˌni-zəm\ *n* — **evo·lu·tion·ist** \-sh(ə-)nist\ *n or adj*

evolutionary psychology *n* (1890) : the study of human cognition and behavior with respect to their evolutionary origins — **evolutionary psychologist** *n*

evolve \i-ˈvälv, -ˈvȯlv, ē- *also* -ˈväv *or* -ˈvȯv\ *vb* **evolved; evolv·ing** [L *evolvere* to unroll, fr. *e-* + *volvere* to roll — more at VOLUBLE] *vt* (1775) **1 :** EMIT **2 a :** DERIVE, EDUCE **b :** to produce by natural evolutionary processes **c :** DEVELOP, WORK OUT ⟨~ social, political, and literary philosophies —L. W. Doob⟩ ~ *vi* **:** to undergo evolutionary change — **evolv·able** \-ˈväl-və-bəl, -ˈvȯl- *also* -ˈvä-və- *or* -ˈvȯ-və-\ *adj* — **evolve·ment** \-ˈvälv-mənt, -ˈvȯlv- *also* -ˈväv- *or* -ˈvȯv-\ *n*

evul·sion \i-ˈvəl-shən\ *n* [L *evulsion-, evulsio,* fr. *evellere* to pluck out, fr. *e-* + *vellere* to pluck — more at VULNERABLE] (ca. 1611) **1 :** EXTRACTION **2 :** AVULSION

ev·zone \ˈev-ˌzōn\ *n* [ModGk *euzōnos,* fr. Gk, active, lit., well girt, fr. *eu-* + *zōnē* girdle — more at ZONE] (1897) **:** a member of a select Greek infantry unit often serving as a palace guard

EW *abbr* enlisted woman

e–waste \ˈē-ˌwāst\ *n* (2004) **:** waste consisting of discarded electronic products (as computers, televisions, and cell phones)

ewe \ˈyü, *in rural dials also* ˈyō\ *n* [ME, fr. OE *ēowu;* akin to OHG *ouwi* ewe, L *ovis* sheep, Gk *ois*] (bef. 12c) **:** the female of the sheep esp. when mature; *also* **:** the female of various related animals

Ewe \ˈā-ˌwā, ˈā-ˌvā\ *n, pl* **Ewe** *also* **Ewes** [Ewe *eβe, βe,* a self-designation] (1861) **:** a people of Ghana and Togo speaking a Kwa language; *also* **:** the language itself

ewe–neck \ˈyü-ˈnek\ *n* (1820) **:** a thin neck with a concave arch occurring as a defect in dogs and horses — **ewe–necked** \-ˈnekt\ *adj*

ew·er \ˈyü-ər, ˈyu̇-ər\ *n* [ME, fr. AF *ewer, ewier,* fr. L *aquarium* water source, neut. of *aquarius* of water, fr. *aqua* water — more at ISLAND] (14c) **:** a vase-shaped pitcher or jug

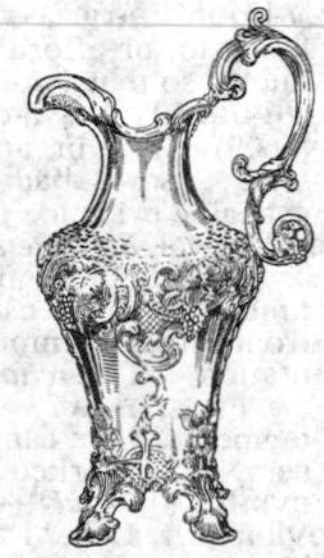
ewer

Ew·ing's sarcoma \ˈyü-iŋz-\ *n* [James *Ewing* †1943 Am. pathologist] (1927) **:** a malignant bone tumor esp. of a long bone or the pelvis

[1]**ex** \(ˈ)eks\ *prep* [L] (ca. 1755) **1 :** out of **:** FROM: as **a :** from a specified place or source **b :** from a specified dam ⟨a promising calf by Eric XVI ~ Heatherbell⟩ **2 :** free from **:** WITHOUT: as **a :** without an indicated value or right — used esp. of securities **b :** free of charges precedent to removal from the specified place with purchaser to provide means of subsequent transportation ⟨~ dock⟩

[2]**ex** *n* (1818) **:** the letter *x*

[3]**ex** *n* [ˈ*ex-*] (1827) **:** one that formerly held a specified position or place; *esp* **:** a former spouse

[4]**ex** *abbr* **1** example **2** exchange **3** executive **4** express **5** extra

Ex *abbr* Exodus

[1]**ex-** \e *also occurs in this prefix where only* i *is shown below (as in "express") and* ks *sometimes occurs where only* gz *is shown (as in "exact")*\ *prefix* [ME, fr. AF & L; AF, fr. L (also, prefix with perfective and causative value), fr. *ex* out of, from; akin to Gk *ex, ex-* out of, from OCS *iz*] **1 :** out of **:** outside ⟨*ex*clave⟩ **2 :** not ⟨*ex*stipulate⟩ **3** \(ˌ)eks, ˈeks\ [ME, fr. LL, fr. L] **:** former ⟨*ex*-president⟩

[2]**ex-** — see EXO-

exa- *comb form* [ISV, modif. of Gk *hexa-* hexa-] **:** quintillion (10^{18}) ⟨*exa*joule⟩

ex·ac·er·bate \ig-ˈza-sər-ˌbāt\ *vt* **-bat·ed; -bat·ing** [L *exacerbatus,* pp. of *exacerbare,* fr. *ex-* + *acerbus* harsh, bitter, fr. *acer* sharp — more at EDGE] (1660) **:** to make more violent, bitter, or severe ⟨the new law only ~*s* the problem⟩ — **ex·ac·er·ba·tion** \-ˌza-sər-ˈbā-shən\ *n*

[1]**ex·act** \ig-ˈzakt\ *vt* [ME, to require as payment, fr. L *exactus,* pp. of *exigere* to drive out, demand, measure, fr. *ex-* + *agere* to drive — more at AGENT] (1564) **1 :** to call for forcibly or urgently and obtain ⟨from them has been ~*ed* the ultimate sacrifice —D. D. Eisenhower⟩ **2 :** to call for as necessary or desirable ***syn*** see DEMAND — **ex·act·able** \-ˈzak-tə-bəl\ *adj* — **ex·ac·tor** *also* **ex·act·er** \-ˈzak-tər\ *n*

[2]**exact** *adj* [L *exactus*] (1533) **1 :** exhibiting or marked by strict, particular, and complete accordance with fact or a standard **2 :** marked by thorough consideration or minute measurement of small factual details ***syn*** see CORRECT — **ex·act·ness** \-ˈzak(t)-nəs\ *n*

ex·ac·ta \ig-ˈzak-tə\ *n* [AmerSp (*quiniela*) *exacta* exact quiniela] (1964) **:** PERFECTA

exact differential *n* (1825) **:** a differential expression of the form $X_1dx_1 + \ldots + X_ndx_n$ where the *X's* are the partial derivatives of a function $f(x_1, \ldots, x_n)$ with respect to $x_1, \ldots, x_n$ respectively

ex·act·ing \ig-ˈzak-tiŋ\ *adj* (1634) **1 :** tryingly or unremittingly severe in making demands **2 :** requiring careful attention and precision ***syn*** see ONEROUS — **ex·act·ing·ly** \-tiŋ-lē\ *adv* — **ex·act·ing·ness** *n*

ex·ac·tion \ig-ˈzak-shən\ *n* (15c) **1 a :** the act or process of exacting **b :** EXTORTION **2 :** something exacted; *esp* **:** a fee, reward, or contribution demanded or levied with severity or injustice

ex·ac·ti·tude \ig-ˈzak-tə-ˌtüd, -ˌtyüd\ *n* (1734) **:** the quality or an instance of being exact **:** EXACTNESS

ex·act·ly \ig-ˈzak-(t)lē\ *adv* (1612) **1 a :** in a manner or measure or to a degree or number that strictly conforms to a fact or condition ⟨it's ~ 3 o'clock⟩ ⟨these two pieces are ~ the same size⟩ **b :** in every respect **:** ALTOGETHER, ENTIRELY ⟨that was ~ the wrong thing to do⟩ ⟨not ~ what I had in mind⟩ **2 :** quite so — used to express agreement

exact science *n* (1843) **:** a science (as physics, chemistry, or astronomy) whose laws are capable of accurate quantitative expression

ex·ag·ger·ate \ig-ˈza-jə-ˌrāt\ *vb* **-at·ed; -at·ing** [L *exaggeratus,* pp. of *exaggerare,* lit., to heap up, fr. *ex-* + *agger* heap, fr. *aggerere* to carry toward, fr. *ad-* + *gerere* to carry] *vt* (1613) **1 :** to enlarge beyond bounds or the truth **:** OVERSTATE ⟨a friend ~*s* a man's virtues —Joseph Addison⟩ **2 :** to enlarge or increase esp. beyond the normal **:** OVEREMPHASIZE ~ *vi* **:** to make an overstatement — **ex·ag·ger·at·ed·ly** *adv* — **ex·ag·ger·at·ed·ness** *n* — **ex·ag·ger·a·tion** \-ˌza-jə-ˈrā-shən\ *n* — **ex·ag·ger·a·tive** \-ˈza-jə-ˌrā-tiv, -ˈzaj-rə-, -ˈza-jə-\ *adj* — **ex·ag·ger·a·tor** \-ˈza-jə-ˌrā-tər\ *n* — **ex·ag·ger·a·to·ry** \-ˈzaj-rə-ˌtȯr-ē, -ˈza-jə-\ *adj*

ex·alt \ig-ˈzȯlt\ *vb* [ME, fr. L *exaltare,* fr. *ex-* + *altus* high — more at OLD] *vt* (15c) **1 :** to raise in rank, power, or character **2 :** to elevate by praise or in estimation **:** GLORIFY **3** *obs* **:** ELATE **4 :** to raise high **:** ELEVATE **5 :** to enhance the activity of **:** INTENSIFY ⟨rousing and ~*ing* the imagination —George Eliot⟩ ~ *vi* **:** to induce exaltation — **ex·alt·ed·ly** *adv* — **ex·alt·er** *n*

ex·al·ta·tion \ˌeg-ˌzȯl-ˈtā-shən, ˌek-ˌsȯl-\ *n* (14c) **1 :** an act of exalting **:** the state of being exalted **2 :** an excessively intensified sense of well-being, power, or importance **3 :** an increase in degree or intensity ⟨~ of virulence of a virus⟩

ex·am \ig-ˈzam\ *n* (1872) **:** EXAMINATION

ex·a·men \ig-ˈzā-mən\ *n* [L, tongue of a balance, examination, fr. *exigere* — more at EXACT] (1606) **1 :** EXAMINATION **2 :** a critical study

ex·am·i·nant \-ˈza-mə-nənt\ *n* (1588) **1 :** EXAMINEE **2 :** one who examines **:** EXAMINER

ex·am·i·na·tion \ig-ˌza-mə-ˈnā-shən\ *n* (14c) **1 :** the act or process of examining **:** the state of being examined **2 :** an exercise designed to examine progress or test qualification or knowledge **3 :** a formal interrogation — **ex·am·i·na·tion·al** \-shnəl, -shə-nᵊl\ *adj*

ex·am·ine \ig-ˈza-mən\ *vb* **ex·am·ined; ex·am·in·ing** \-ˈzam-niŋ, -ˈza-mə-\ [ME, fr. AF *examiner,* fr. L *examinare,* fr. *examen*] *vt* (14c) **1 a :** to inspect closely **b :** to test the condition of **c :** to inquire into carefully **:** INVESTIGATE **2 a :** to interrogate closely ⟨~ a prisoner⟩ **b :** to test by questioning in order to determine progress, fitness, or knowledge ~ *vi* **:** to make or give an examination ***syn*** see SCRUTINIZE — **ex·am·in·able** \-ˈza-mə-nə-bəl\ *adj* — **ex·am·in·er** \-ˈzam-nər, -ˈza-mə-\ *n*

ex·am·in·ee \ig-ˌza-mə-ˈnē\ *n* (1788) **:** a person who is examined

[1]**ex·am·ple** \ig-ˈzam-pəl\ *n* [ME, fr. AF *essample, example,* fr. L *exemplum,* fr. *eximere* to take out, fr. *ex-* + *emere* to take — more at REDEEM] (14c) **1 :** one that serves as a pattern to be imitated or not to be imitated ⟨a good ~⟩ **2 :** a punishment inflicted on someone as a warning to others; *also* **:** an individual so punished **3 :** one that is representative of all of a group or type **4 :** a parallel or closely similar case esp. when serving as a precedent or model **5 :** an instance (as a problem to be solved) serving to illustrate a rule or precept or to act as an exercise in the application of a rule ***syn*** see INSTANCE, MODEL — **for example** \fər-ig-ˈzam-pəl, frig-\ **:** as an example ⟨there are many sources of air pollution; exhaust fumes, *for example*⟩

[2]**example** *vt* **ex·am·pled; ex·am·pling** \-p(ə-)liŋ\ (15c) **1 :** to serve as an example of **2** *archaic* **:** to be or set an example to

ex·an·i·mate \eg-ˈza-nə-mət\ *adj* [L *exanimatus,* pp. of *exanimare* to deprive of life or spirit, fr. *ex-* + *anima* breath, soul — more at ANIMATE] (ca. 1534) **1 :** lacking animation **:** SPIRITLESS **2 :** being or appearing lifeless

ex·an·them \eg-ˈzan(t)-thəm, ˈek-ˌsan-ˌthem\ *also* **ex·an·the·ma** \ˌeg-ˌzan-ˈthē-mə\ *n, pl* **-thems** *also* **-them·a·ta** \ˌeg-ˌzan-ˈthe-mə-tə\ *or* **-themas** [LL *exanthema,* fr. Gk *exanthēma,* fr. *exanthein* to bloom, break out, fr. *ex-* + *anthos* flower — more at ANTHOLOGY] (1656) **:** an eruptive disease (as measles) or its symptomatic eruption — **ex·an·them·a·tous** \ˌeg-ˌzan-ˈthe-mə-təs\ *or* **ex·an·the·mat·ic** \-ˌzan-thə-ˈma-tik\ *adj*

ex·ap·ta·tion \ˌeg-ˌzap-ˈtā-shən\ *n* [ˈ*ex-* + *adaptation*] (1981) **:** PREADAPTATION

[1]**ex·arch** \ˈek-ˌsärk\ *n* [LL *exarchus,* fr. LGk *exarchos,* fr. Gk, leader, fr. *exarchein* to begin, take the lead, fr. *ex-* + *archein* to rule, begin — more at ARCH-] (1588) **1 :** a Byzantine viceroy **2 :** an Eastern bishop ranking below a patriarch and above a metropolitan; *specif* **:** the head of an independent church — **ex·ar·chal** \ek-ˈsär-kəl\ *adj* — **ex·arch·ate** \ˈek-ˌsär-kət\ *n* — **ex·ar·chy** \ˈek-ˌsär-kē\ *n*

[2]**exarch** *adj* [*exo-* + *-arch*] (1891) **:** formed or taking place from the periphery toward the center ⟨~ xylem⟩

[1]**ex·as·per·ate** \ig-ˈzas-pə-ˌrāt\ *vt* **-at·ed; -at·ing** [L *exasperatus,* pp. of *exasperare,* fr. *ex-* + *asper* rough — more at ASPERITY] (1534) **1 a :** to excite the anger of **:** ENRAGE **b :** to cause irritation or annoyance to **2** *obs* **:** to make more grievous **:** AGGRAVATE ***syn*** see IRRITATE — **ex·as·per·at·ed·ly** *adv* — **ex·as·per·at·ing·ly** \-ˌrā-tiŋ-lē\ *adv*

[2]**ex·as·per·ate** \-p(ə-)rət\ *adj* (1541) **1 :** irritated or annoyed esp. to the point of injudicious action **:** EXASPERATED **2 :** roughened with irregular prickles or elevations ⟨~ seed coats⟩

ex·as·per·a·tion \ig-ˌzas-pə-ˈrā-shən\ *n* (1547) **1 :** the state of being exasperated **2 :** the act or an instance of exasperating

exc *abbr* **1** excellent **2** except

Ex·cal·i·bur \ek-ˈska-lə-bər\ *n* [ME *Excalaber,* fr. AF *Escalibor,* fr. ML *Caliburnus*] (15c) **:** the sword of King Arthur

ex ca·the·dra \ˌeks-kə-ˈthē-drə\ *adv or adj* [NL, lit., from the chair] (1693) **:** by virtue of or in the exercise of one's office or position ⟨*ex cathedra* pronouncements⟩

ex·ca·vate \ˈek-skə-ˌvāt\ *vb* **-vat·ed; -vat·ing** [L *excavatus,* pp. of *excavare,* fr. *ex-* + *cavare* to make hollow — more at CAVATINA] *vt* (1599) **1 :** to form a cavity or hole in **2 :** to form by hollowing out **3 :** to dig out and remove **4 :** to expose to view by or as if by digging away a covering ⟨~ the remains of a temple⟩ ~ *vi* **:** to make excavations

ex·ca·va·tion \ˌek-skə-ˈvā-shən\ *n* (ca. 1611) **1 :** the action or process of excavating **2 :** a cavity formed by cutting, digging, or scooping — **ex·ca·va·tion·al** \-shnəl, -shə-nᵊl\ *adj*

ex·ca·va·tor \ˈek-skə-ˌvā-tər\ *n* (ca. 1815) **:** one that excavates; *esp* **:** a power-operated shovel

ex·ceed \ik-ˈsēd\ *vb* [ME *exceden,* fr. MF *exceder,* fr. L *excedere,* fr. *ex-* + *cedere* to go] *vt* (14c) **1 :** to extend outside of ⟨the river will ~ its banks⟩ **2 :** to be greater than or superior to **3 :** to go beyond a limit set by ⟨~*ed* his authority⟩ ~ *vi* **1** *obs* **:** OVERDO **2 :** PREDOMINATE

syn EXCEED, SURPASS, TRANSCEND, EXCEL, OUTDO, OUTSTRIP mean to go or be beyond a stated or implied limit, measure, or degree. EXCEED implies going beyond a limit set by authority or established by custom or by prior achievement ⟨*exceed* the speed limit⟩. SURPASS suggests superiority in quality, merit, or skill ⟨the book *surpassed* our expectations⟩. TRANSCEND implies a rising or extending notably above or beyond ordinary limits ⟨*transcended* the values of their culture⟩. EXCEL implies preeminence in achievement or quality and may suggest superiority to all others ⟨*excels* in mathematics⟩. OUTDO applies to a bettering or exceeding what has been done before ⟨*outdid* herself this time⟩. OUTSTRIP suggests surpassing in a race or competition ⟨*outstripped* other firms in sales⟩.

ex·ceed·ance *also* **ex·ceed·ence** \ik-ˈsē-dᵊn(t)s\ *n* (ca. 1956) **:** an act or instance of exceeding esp. a limit or amount

ex·ceed·ing \-ˈsē-diŋ\ *adj* (15c) **:** exceptional in amount, quality, or degree

ex·ceed·ing·ly \-ˈsē-diŋ-lē\ *also* **ex·ceed·ing** *adv* (1535) **:** to an extreme degree **:** EXTREMELY

ex·cel \ik-ˈsel\ *vb* **ex·celled; ex·cel·ling** [ME *excellen,* fr. L *excellere,* fr. *ex-* + *-cellere* to rise, project; akin to L *collis* hill — more at HILL] *vt* (15c) **:** to be superior to **:** surpass in accomplishment or achievement ~ *vi* **:** to be distinguishable by superiority **:** surpass others ‹~ in sports› ‹*excelled* at lipreading› ***syn*** see EXCEED

ex·cel·lence \ˈek-s(ə-)lən(t)s\ *n* (14c) **1 :** the quality of being excellent **2 :** an excellent or valuable quality **:** VIRTUE **3 :** EXCELLENCY 2

ex·cel·len·cy \-s(ə-)lən(t)-sē\ *n, pl* **-cies** (15c) **1 :** EXCELLENCE; *esp* **:** outstanding or valuable quality — usu. used in pl. ‹so crammed, as he thinks, with *excellencies* —Shak.› **2 —** used as a title for high dignitaries of state (as a governor or an ambassador) or church (as a Roman Catholic archbishop or bishop)

ex·cel·lent \ˈek-s(ə-)lənt\ *adj* [ME, fr. AF, fr. L *excellent-, excellens,* fr. prp. of *excellere*] (14c) **1** *archaic* **:** SUPERIOR **2 :** very good of its kind **:** eminently good **:** FIRST-CLASS — **ex·cel·lent·ly** *adv*

ex·cel·si·or \ik-ˈsel-sē-ər, -ˌȯr\ *n* [trade name, fr. L, higher, compar. of *excelsus* high, fr. pp. of *excellere*] (1868) **:** fine curled wood shavings used esp. for packing fragile items

[1]**ex·cept** \ik-ˈsept\ *also* **ex·cept·ing** \-ˈsep-tiŋ\ *prep* (14c) **:** with the exclusion or exception of ‹daily ~ Sundays›

[2]**except** *vb* [ME, fr. AF *excepter,* fr. L *exceptare,* freq. of *excipere* to take out, except, fr. *ex-* + *capere* to take — more at HEAVE] *vt* (14c) **:** to take or leave out from a number or a whole **:** EXCLUDE ~ *vi* **:** to take exception **:** OBJECT — **ex·cep·tive** \-ˈsep-təv\ *adj*

[3]**except** *also* **excepting** *conj* (15c) **1 :** on any other condition than that **:** UNLESS ‹~ you repent› **2 :** with this exception, namely ‹was inaccessible ~ by boat› **3 :** ONLY — often followed by *that* ‹I would go ~ that it's too far›

except for *prep* (15c) **1 :** with the exception of ‹everyone was gone *except for* me› **2 :** were it not for ‹*except for* you I would be dead›

ex·cep·tion \ik-ˈsep-shən\ *n* (14c) **1 :** the act of excepting **:** EXCLUSION **2 :** one that is excepted; *esp* **:** a case to which a rule does not apply **3 :** QUESTION, OBJECTION ‹witnesses whose authority is beyond ~ —T. B. Macaulay› **4 :** an oral or written legal objection

ex·cep·tion·able \ik-ˈsep-sh(ə-)nə-bəl\ *adj* (1691) **:** being likely to cause objection **:** OBJECTIONABLE ‹visitors even drink the ~ beer —W. D. Howells› — **ex·cep·tion·abil·i·ty** \-ˌsep-sh(ə-)nə-ˈbi-lə-tē\ *n* — **ex·cep·tion·ably** \-ˈsep-sh(ə-)nə-blē\ *adv*

ex·cep·tion·al \ik-ˈsep-shnəl, -shə-nᵊl\ *adj* (1787) **1 :** forming an exception **:** RARE ‹an ~ number of rainy days› **2 :** better than average **:** SUPERIOR ‹~ skill› **3 :** deviating from the norm: as **a :** having above or below average intelligence **b :** physically disabled — **ex·cep·tion·al·i·ty** \-ˌsep-shə-ˈna-lə-tē\ *n* — **ex·cep·tion·al·ness** *n*

ex·cep·tion·al·ism \ik-ˈsep-shnə-ˌli-zəm, -shə-nə-\ *n* (1929) **:** the condition of being different from the norm; *also* **:** a theory expounding the exceptionalism esp. of a nation or region — **ex·cep·tion·al·ist** \-list\ *adj*

ex·cep·tion·al·ly \ik-ˈsep-shnə-lē, -shə-nᵊl-ē\ *adv* (1703) **:** in an exceptional manner **:** to an exceptional degree; *esp* **:** more than average or usual ‹an ~ difficult task›

[1]**ex·cerpt** \ek-ˈsərpt, eg-ˈzərpt, ˈek-ˌ, ˈeg-ˌ\ *vt* [L *excerptus,* pp. of *excerpere,* fr. *ex-* + *carpere* to gather, pluck — more at HARVEST] (15c) **1 :** to select (a passage) for quoting **:** EXTRACT **2 :** to take or publish extracts from (as a book) — **ex·cerp·tor** *or* **ex·cerpt·er** *n* — **ex·cerp·tion** \ek-ˈsərp-shən, eg-ˈzərp-\ *n*

[2]**ex·cerpt** \ˈek-ˌsərpt, ˈeg-ˌzərpt\ *n* (1627) **:** a passage (as from a book or musical composition) selected, performed, or copied **:** EXTRACT

[1]**ex·cess** \ik-ˈses, ˈek-ˌ\ *n* [ME, fr. AF or LL; AF *exces,* fr. LL *excessus,* fr. L, departure, projection, fr. *excedere* to exceed] (14c) **1 a :** the state or an instance of surpassing usual, proper, or specified limits **:** SUPERFLUITY **b :** the amount or degree by which one thing or quantity exceeds another ‹an ~ of 10 bushels› **2 :** undue or immoderate indulgence **:** INTEMPERANCE; *also* **:** an act or instance of intemperance ‹prevent *~es* and abuses by newly created local powers —Albert Shanker› — **in excess of :** to an amount or degree beyond **:** OVER

[2]**excess** *adj* (15c) **:** more than the usual, proper, or specified amount

[3]**excess** *vt* (1971) **:** to eliminate the position of ‹*~ed* several teachers because of budget cutbacks›

ex·ces·sive \ik-ˈse-siv\ *adj* (14c) **:** exceeding what is usual, proper, necessary, or normal — **ex·ces·sive·ly** *adv* — **ex·ces·sive·ness** *n*

syn EXCESSIVE, IMMODERATE, INORDINATE, EXTRAVAGANT, EXORBITANT, EXTREME mean going beyond a normal limit. EXCESSIVE implies an amount or degree too great to be reasonable or acceptable ‹*excessive* punishment›. IMMODERATE implies lack of desirable or necessary restraint ‹*immoderate* spending›. INORDINATE implies an exceeding of the limits dictated by reason or good judgment ‹*inordinate* pride›. EXTRAVAGANT implies an indifference to restraints imposed by truth, prudence, or good taste ‹*extravagant* claims for the product›. EXORBITANT implies a departure from accepted standards regarding amount or degree ‹*exorbitant* prices›. EXTREME may imply an approach to the farthest limit possible or conceivable but commonly means only to a notably high degree ‹*extreme* shyness›.

exch *abbr* exchange; exchanged

[1]**ex·change** \iks-ˈchānj, ˈeks-ˌ\ *n, often attrib* [ME *exchaunge,* fr. AF *eschange,* fr. *eschanger* to exchange, fr. VL **excambiare,* fr. L *ex-* + *cambiare* to exchange — more at CHANGE] (14c) **1 :** the act of giving or taking one thing in return for another **:** TRADE ‹an ~ of prisoners› **2 a :** the act or process of substituting one thing for another **b :** reciprocal giving and receiving **3 :** something offered, given, or received in an exchange **4 a :** funds payable currently at a distant point either in a foreign currency or in domestic currency **b (1) :** interchange or conversion of the money of two countries or of current and uncurrent money with allowance for difference in value **(2) :** EXCHANGE RATE **(3) :** the amount of the difference in value between two currencies or between values of a particular currency at two places **c :** instruments (as checks or bills of exchange) presented in a clearinghouse for settlement **5 :** a place where things or services are exchanged: as **a :** an organized market or center for trading in securities or commodities **b :** a store or shop specializing in merchandise usu. of a particular type **c :** a cooperative store or society **d :** a central office in which telephone lines are connected to permit communication — **in exchange :** as a substitute

[2]**exchange** *vb* **ex·changed; ex·chang·ing** *vt* (15c) **1 a :** to part with, give, or transfer in consideration of something received as an equivalent **b :** to have replaced by other merchandise ‹*exchanged* the shirt for one in a larger size› **2 :** to part with for a substitute ‹*exchanging* future security for immediate pleasure› **3 :** to give and receive reciprocally ‹~ gifts› ~ *vi* **1 :** to pass or become received in exchange **2 :** to engage in an exchange — **ex·change·abil·i·ty** \iks-ˌchān-jə-ˈbi-lə-tē\ *n* — **ex·change·able** \iks-ˈchān-jə-bəl\ *adj* — **ex·chang·er** \iks-ˈchān-jər, eks-ˌ\ *n*

exchange rate *n* (1855) **:** the ratio at which the principal unit of two currencies may be traded

exchange student *n* (ca. 1930) **:** a student from one country received into an institution in another country in exchange for one sent to an institution in the home country of the first

Ex·chang·ite \iks-ˈchān-ˌjīt\ *n* [*(National) Exchange (club)*] (ca. 1934) **:** a member of a major national service club

ex·che·quer \ˈeks-ˌche-kər, iks-ˈ\ *n* [ME *escheker,* fr. AF, chessboard, counting table, exchequer — more at CHECKER] (14c) **1** *cap* **:** a department or office of state in medieval England charged with the collection and management of the royal revenue and judicial determination of all revenue causes **2** *cap* **:** a former superior court having jurisdiction in England and Wales primarily over revenue matters and now merged with King's Bench **3** *often cap* **a :** the department or office of state in Great Britain and Northern Ireland charged with the receipt and care of the national revenue **b :** the national banking account of this realm **4 :** TREASURY; *esp* **:** a national or royal treasury **5 :** pecuniary resources **:** FUNDS

ex·ci·mer laser \ˈek-si-ˌmər-\ *n* [*excit*ed + *dimer*] (1973) **:** a laser that uses a noble-gas halide to generate radiation usu. in the ultraviolet region of the spectrum

ex·cip·i·ent \ik-ˈsi-pē-ənt\ *n* [L *excipient-, excipiens,* prp. of *excipere* to take out, take up — more at EXCEPT] (ca. 1753) **:** a usu. inert substance (as gum arabic or starch) that forms a vehicle (as for a drug)

ex·cis·able \ˈek-ˌsī-zə-bəl, -ˌsī-sə-, ek-ˈ\ *adj* (1689) **:** subject to excise

[1]**ex·cise** \ˈek-ˌsīz, -ˌsīs\ *n* [obs. D *excijs* (now *accijns*), fr. MD, prob. modif. of OF *assise* session, assessment — more at ASSIZE] (15c) **1 :** an internal tax levied on the manufacture, sale, or consumption of a commodity **2 :** any of various taxes on privileges often assessed in the form of a license or fee

[2]**ex·cise** \ˈek-ˌsīz, -ˌsīs, ik-ˈsīz\ *vt* **ex·cised; ex·cis·ing** (1652) **:** to impose an excise on

[3]**ex·cise** \ik-ˈsīz\ *vt* **ex·cised; ex·cis·ing** [L *excisus,* pp. of *excidere,* fr. *ex-* + *caedere* to cut] (1634) **:** to remove by or as if by excision

ex·cise·man \ˈek-ˌsīz-mən, -ˌsīs-, -ˌman, ek-ˈ\ *n* (1647) **:** an officer who inspects and rates articles liable to excise under British law

ex·ci·sion \ik-ˈsi-zhən\ *n* [MF, fr. L *excision-, excisio,* fr. *excidere*] (1541) **:** the act or procedure of removing by or as if by cutting out; *esp* **:** surgical removal or resection — **ex·ci·sion·al** \-ˈsizh-nəl, -zhə-nəl\ *adj*

ex·cit·able \ik-ˈsī-tə-bəl\ *adj* (1609) **1 :** capable of being readily roused into action or a state of excitement or irritability **2 :** capable of being activated by and reacting to stimuli ‹~ cells› — **ex·cit·abil·i·ty** \-ˌsī-tə-ˈbi-lə-tē\ *n* — **ex·cit·able·ness** \-ˈsī-tə-bəl-nəs\ *n*

ex·ci·tant \ik-ˈsī-tᵊnt, ˈek-sə-tənt\ *adj* (1607) **:** tending to excite or augment ‹~ drugs› — **excitant** *n*

ex·ci·ta·tion \ˌek-ˌsī-ˈtā-shən, ˌek-sə-\ *n* (14c) **:** EXCITEMENT; *esp* **:** the disturbed or altered condition resulting from stimulation of an individual, organ, tissue, or cell

ex·cit·ative \ik-ˈsī-tə-tiv\ *adj* (15c) **:** tending to induce excitation (as of a neuron) ‹~ substances›

ex·cit·ato·ry \ik-ˈsī-tə-ˌtȯr-ē\ *adj* (1803) **:** exhibiting, resulting from, related to, or producing excitement or excitation ‹~ nerve fibers›

ex·cite \ik-ˈsīt, ek-\ *vt* **ex·cit·ed; ex·cit·ing** [ME, fr. AF *exciter,* fr. L *excitare,* fr. *ex-* + *citare* to rouse — more at CITE] (14c) **1 a :** to call to activity **b :** to rouse to an emotional response ‹scenes to ~ the hardest man to pity› **c :** to arouse (as a strong emotional response) by appropriate stimuli ‹~ enthusiasm for the new regime —Arthur Knight› **2 a :** ENERGIZE ‹~ an electromagnet› **b :** to produce a magnetic field in ‹~ a dynamo› **3 :** to increase the activity of (as a living organism) **:** STIMULATE **4 :** to raise (as an atomic nucleus, an atom, or a molecule) to a higher energy level ***syn*** see PROVOKE — **ex·cit·ed·ly** \-ˈsī-təd-lē\ *adv*

excited state *n* (1927) **:** a state of a physical system (as an atomic nucleus, an atom, or a molecule) that is higher in energy than the ground state

ex·cite·ment \ik-ˈsīt-mənt\ *n* (1604) **1 :** something that excites or rouses **2 :** the action of exciting **:** the state of being excited

ex·cit·er \ik-ˈsī-tər\ *n* (14c) **1 :** one that excites **2 a :** a generator or battery that supplies the electric current used to produce the magnetic field in another generator or motor **b :** an electrical oscillator that generates the carrier frequency (as for a radio transmitter)

ex·cit·ing \ik-ˈsī-tiŋ\ *adj* (1647) **:** producing excitement — **ex·cit·ing·ly** \-iŋ-lē\ *adv*

ex·ci·ton \ˈek-sə-ˌtän, -ˌsī-\ *n* [ISV *excitation* + [2]*-on*] (1936) **:** a mobile combination of an electron and a hole in an excited crystal (as of a semiconductor) — **ex·ci·ton·ic** \ˌek-sə-ˈtä-nik, -ˌsī-\ *adj*

ex·ci·tor \ik-ˈsī-tər\ *n* (1816) **:** an afferent nerve arousing increased action of the part that it supplies

excl *abbr* exclude; excluded; excluding

ex·claim \iks-ˈklām\ *vb* [MF *exclamer,* fr. L *exclamare,* fr. *ex-* + *clamare* to cry out — more at CLAIM] *vi* (1566) **1 :** to cry out or speak in strong or sudden emotion ‹*~ed* in delight› **2 :** to speak loudly or vehemently ‹*~ed* against immorality› ~ *vt* **:** to utter sharply, passionately, or vehemently **:** PROCLAIM — **ex·claim·er** *n*

ex·cla·ma·tion \ˌeks-klə-ˈmā-shən\ *n* (14c) **1 :** a sharp or sudden utterance **2 :** vehement expression of protest or complaint

exclamation point *n* (1824) **1 :** a mark ! used esp. after an interjection or exclamation to indicate forceful utterance or strong feeling **2 :** a distinctive indication of major significance, interest, or contrast

\ə\ **a**but \ᵊ\ kitten, F table \ər\ **fur**ther \a\ **a**sh \ā\ **a**ce \ä\ m**o**p, m**a**r
\au̇\ **ou**t \ch\ **ch**in \e\ b**e**t \ē\ **ea**sy \g\ **g**o \i\ h**i**t \ī\ **i**ce \j\ **j**ob
\ŋ\ si**ng** \ō\ g**o** \ȯ\ l**aw** \ȯi\ b**oy** \th\ **th**in \t͟h\ **th**e \ü\ l**oo**t \u̇\ f**oo**t
\y\ **y**et \zh\ vi**s**ion, beige \k, ⁿ, œ, ue, ʸ\ *see* Guide to Pronunciation

⟨the game put an *exclamation point* on the season⟩ — called also *exclamation mark*
ex·clam·a·to·ry \iks-ˈkla-mə-ˌtȯr-ē\ *adj* (1593) **:** containing, expressing, using, or relating to exclamation ⟨an ~ phrase⟩
ex·clave \ˈeks-ˌklāv, -ˌkläv\ *n* [*ex-* + *-clave* (as in *enclave*)] (1888) **:** a portion of a country separated from the main part and constituting an enclave in respect to the surrounding territory
ex·clud·able *or* **ex·clud·ible** \iks-ˈklü-də-bəl\ *adj* (1916) **:** subject to exclusion ⟨~ income⟩ — **ex·clud·abil·i·ty** \-ˌklü-də-ˈbi-lə-tē\ *n*
ex·clude \iks-ˈklüd\ *vt* **ex·clud·ed; ex·clud·ing** [ME, fr. L *excludere,* fr. *ex-* + *claudere* to close — more at CLOSE] (14c) **1 a :** to prevent or restrict the entrance of **b :** to bar from participation, consideration, or inclusion **2 :** to expel or bar esp. from a place or position previously occupied — **ex·clud·er** *n*
ex·clu·sion \iks-ˈklü-zhən\ *n* [ME, fr. AF, fr. L *exclusion-, exclusio,* fr. *excludere*] (15c) **1 :** the act or an instance of excluding **2 :** the state of being excluded — **ex·clu·sion·ary** \-zhə-ˌner-ē\ *adj*
exclusionary rule *n* (1964) **:** a legal rule that bars unlawfully obtained evidence from being used in court proceedings
ex·clu·sion·ist \iks-ˈklüzh-nist, -ˈklü-zhə-\ *n* (1822) **:** one who would exclude another from some right or privilege — **exclusionist** *adj*
exclusion principle *n* (1926) **:** a principle in physics: no two particles (as electrons) in an atom or molecule can have the same set of quantum numbers — called also *Pauli exclusion principle*
1**ex·clu·sive** \iks-ˈklü-siv, -ziv\ *adj* (1515) **1 a :** excluding or having power to exclude **b :** limiting or limited to possession, control, or use by a single individual or group **2 a :** excluding others from participation **b :** snobbishly aloof **3 a :** accepting or soliciting only a socially restricted patronage (as of the upper class) **b :** STYLISH, FASHIONABLE **c :** restricted in distribution, use, or appeal because of expense **4 a :** SINGLE, SOLE ⟨~ jurisdiction⟩ **b :** WHOLE, UNDIVIDED ⟨his ~ attention⟩ — **ex·clu·sive·ly** *adv* — **ex·clu·sive·ness** *n*
2**exclusive** *n* (15c) **:** something exclusive: as **a :** a news story at first released to or reported by only one source **b :** an exclusive right (as to sell a particular product in a certain area)
exclusive disjunction *n* (1942) **:** a compound proposition in logic that is true when one and only one of its constituent statements is true — see TRUTH TABLE table
exclusive economic zone *n* (1975) **:** the area of sea and seabed extending from the shore of a country claiming exclusive rights to it
exclusive of *prep* (1722) **:** not taking into account ⟨there were four of us *exclusive of* the guide⟩
ex·clu·siv·ism \iks-ˈklü-sə-ˌvi-zəm, -ˈklü-zə-\ *n* (1834) **:** the practice of excluding or of being exclusive — **ex·clu·siv·ist** \-vist\ *n or adj*
ex·clu·siv·i·ty \ˌeks-ˌklü-ˈsi-və-tē, iks-, -ˈzi-\ *n, pl* **-ties** (1926) **1 :** the quality or state of being exclusive **2 :** exclusive rights or services
ex·cog·i·tate \ek-ˈskä-jə-ˌtāt\ *vt* [L *excogitatus,* pp. of *excogitare,* fr. *ex-* + *cogitare* to cogitate] (ca. 1530) **:** to think out **:** DEVISE — **ex·cog·i·ta·tion** \(ˌ)ek-ˌskä-jə-ˈtā-shən\ *n* — **ex·cog·i·ta·tive** \ek-ˈskä-jə-ˌtā-tiv\ *adj*
1**ex·com·mu·ni·cate** \ˌek-skə-ˈmyü-nə-ˌkāt\ *vt* [ME, fr. LL *excommunicatus,* pp. of *excommunicare,* fr. L *ex-* + LL *communicare* to communicate] (15c) **:** to subject to excommunication — **ex·com·mu·ni·ca·tor** \-ˌkā-tər\ *n*
2**ex·com·mu·ni·cate** \-ni-kət\ *adj* (1521) **:** excluded from the rights of church membership **:** EXCOMMUNICATED — **excommunicate** *n*
ex·com·mu·ni·ca·tion \-ˌmyü-nə-ˈkā-shən\ *n* (15c) **1 :** an ecclesiastical censure depriving a person of the rights of church membership **2 :** exclusion from fellowship in a group or community — **ex·com·mu·ni·ca·tive** \-ˈmyü-nə-ˌkā-tiv, -ni-kət-\ *adj*
ex·co·ri·ate \ek-ˈskȯr-ē-ˌāt\ *vt* **-at·ed; -at·ing** [ME, fr. LL *excoriatus,* pp. of *excoriare,* fr. L *ex-* + *corium* skin, hide — more at CUIRASS] (15c) **1 :** to wear off the skin of **:** ABRADE **2 :** to censure scathingly — **ex·co·ri·a·tion** \(ˌ)ek-ˌskȯr-ē-ˈā-shən\ *n*
ex·cre·ment \ˈek-skrə-mənt\ *n* [L *excrementum,* fr. *excernere*] (1533) **:** waste matter discharged from the body; *esp* **:** FECES — **ex·cre·men·tal** \ˌek-skrə-ˈmen-tᵊl\ *adj* — **ex·cre·men·ti·tious** \-ˌmen-ˈti-shəs, -mən-\ *adj*
ex·cres·cence \ik-ˈskre-sᵊn(t)s, ek-\ *n* (15c) **1 :** a projection or outgrowth esp. when abnormal ⟨warty ~*s* in the colon⟩ **2 :** a disfiguring, extraneous, or unwanted mark or part **:** BLOT **3 :** BY-PRODUCT 2
ex·cres·cen·cy \-sᵊn-sē\ *n, pl* **-cies** (1545) **:** EXCRESCENCE
ex·cres·cent \-sᵊnt\ *adj* [L *excrescent-, excrescens,* prp. of *excrescere* to grow out, fr. *ex-* + *crescere* to grow — more at CRESCENT] (1633) **1 :** forming an abnormal, excessive, or useless outgrowth **2 :** of, relating to, or constituting epenthesis — **ex·cres·cent·ly** *adv*
ex·cre·ta \ik-ˈskrē-tə\ *n pl* [NL, fr. L, neut. pl. of *excretus*] (1853) **:** waste matter (as feces) eliminated or separated from the body — **ex·cre·tal** \-ˈskrē-tᵊl\ *adj*
ex·crete \ik-ˈskrēt\ *vt* **ex·cret·ed; ex·cret·ing** [L *excretus,* pp. of *excernere* to sift out, discharge, fr. *ex-* + *cernere* to sift — more at CERTAIN] (1620) **:** to separate and eliminate or discharge (waste) from the blood, tissues, or organs or from the active protoplasm — **ex·cret·er** *n*
ex·cre·tion \ik-ˈskrē-shən\ *n* (1578) **1 :** the act or process of excreting **2 :** something excreted; *esp* **:** metabolic waste products (as urea and carbon dioxide) that are eliminated from the body
ex·cre·to·ry \ˈek-skrə-ˌtȯr-ē\ *adj* (ca. 1681) **:** of, relating to, or functioning in excretion ⟨~ ducts⟩
ex·cru·ci·ate \ik-ˈskrü-shē-ˌāt\ *vt* **-at·ed; -at·ing** [L *excruciatus,* pp. of *excruciare,* fr. *ex-* + *cruciare* to crucify, fr. *cruc-, crux* cross] (ca. 1570) **1 :** to inflict intense pain on **:** TORTURE **2 :** to subject to intense mental distress — **ex·cru·ci·a·tion** \-ˌskrü-shē-ˈā-shən, -sē-\ *n*
excruciating *adj* (1599) **1 :** causing great pain or anguish **:** AGONIZING ⟨the nation's most ~ dilemma —W. H. Ferry⟩ **2 :** very intense **:** EXTREME ⟨~ pain⟩ — **ex·cru·ci·at·ing·ly** \-ˌā-tiŋ-lē\ *adv*
ex·cul·pate \ˈek-(ˌ)skəl-ˌpāt, (ˌ)ek-ˈ\ *vt* **-pat·ed; -pat·ing** [ML *exculpatus,* pp. of *exculpare,* fr. L *ex-* + *culpa* blame] (ca. 1681) **:** to clear from alleged fault or guilt — **ex·cul·pa·tion** \ˌek-(ˌ)skəl-ˈpā-shən\ *n*
syn EXCULPATE, ABSOLVE, EXONERATE, ACQUIT, VINDICATE mean to free from a charge. EXCULPATE implies a clearing from blame or fault often in a matter of small importance ⟨*exculpating* himself from the charge of overenthusiasm⟩. ABSOLVE implies a release either from an obligation that binds the conscience or from the consequences of disobeying the law or committing a sin ⟨cannot be *absolved* of blame⟩. EXONERATE implies a complete clearance from an accusation or charge and from any attendant suspicion of blame or guilt ⟨*exonerated* by the investigation⟩. ACQUIT implies a formal decision in one's favor with respect to a definite charge ⟨voted to *acquit* the defendant⟩. VINDICATE may refer to things as well as persons that have been subjected to critical attack or imputation of guilt, weakness, or folly, and implies a clearing effected by proving the unfairness of such criticism or blame ⟨her judgment was *vindicated*⟩.
ex·cul·pa·to·ry \ek-ˈskəl-pə-ˌtȯr-ē\ *adj* (1781) **:** tending or serving to exculpate
ex·cur·rent \(ˌ)ek-ˈskər-ənt, -ˈskə-rənt\ *adj* [L *excurrent-, excurrens,* prp. of *excurrere* to run out, extend, fr. *ex-* + *currere* to run — more at CAR] (1826) **1 :** characterized by a current that flows outward ⟨the clam's ~ siphon⟩ **2 :** having the axis prolonged to form an undivided main stem or trunk (as in conifers) — compare DELIQUESCENT 2
ex·cur·sion \ik-ˈskər-zhən\ *n* [L *excursion-, excursio,* fr. *excurrere*] (ca. 1587) **1 a :** a going out or forth **:** EXPEDITION **b (1) :** a usu. brief pleasure trip **(2) :** a trip at special reduced rates **2 :** deviation from a direct, definite, or proper course; *esp* **:** DIGRESSION ⟨needless ~*s* into abstruse theory⟩ **3 :** a movement outward and back or from a mean position or axis; *also* **:** the distance traversed **:** AMPLITUDE ⟨the ~ of a piston⟩
ex·cur·sion·ist \-ˈskərzh-nist, -ˈskər-zhə-\ *n* (1830) **:** a person who goes on an excursion
ex·cur·sive \-ˈskər-siv\ *adj* (1659) **:** constituting a digression **:** characterized by digression — **ex·cur·sive·ly** *adv* — **ex·cur·sive·ness** *n*
ex·cur·sus \ik-ˈskər-səs\ *n, pl* **ex·cur·sus·es** *also* **ex·cur·sus** \-səs, -ˌsüs\ [L, digression, fr. *excurrere*] (1803) **:** an appendix or digression that contains further exposition of some point or topic
ex·cu·sa·to·ry \ik-ˈskyü-zə-ˌtȯr-ē\ *adj* (1535) **:** making or containing excuse
1**ex·cuse** \ik-ˈskyüz, *imperatively often* ˈskyüz\ *vt* **ex·cused; ex·cus·ing** [ME, fr. AF *escuser, excuser,* fr. L *excusare,* fr. *ex-* + *causa* cause, explanation] (13c) **1 a :** to make apology for **b :** to try to remove blame from **2 :** to forgive entirely or disregard as of trivial import **:** regard as excusable ⟨graciously *excused* his tardiness⟩ **3 a :** to grant exemption or release to ⟨was *excused* from jury duty⟩ **b :** to allow to leave ⟨*excused* the class⟩ **4 :** to serve as excuse for **:** JUSTIFY ⟨nothing can ~ such neglect⟩ — **ex·cus·able** \ik-ˈskyü-zə-bəl\ *adj* — **ex·cus·able·ness** *n* — **ex·cus·ably** \-blē\ *adv* — **ex·cus·er** *n*
syn EXCUSE, CONDONE, PARDON, FORGIVE mean to exact neither punishment nor redress. EXCUSE may refer to specific acts esp. in social or conventional situations or the person responsible for these ⟨*excuse* an interruption⟩ ⟨*excused* them for interrupting⟩. Often the term implies extenuating circumstances ⟨injustice *excuses* strong responses⟩. CONDONE implies that one overlooks without censure behavior (as dishonesty or violence) that involves a serious breach of a moral, ethical, or legal code, and the term may refer to the behavior or to the agent responsible for it ⟨a society that *condones* alcohol but not narcotics⟩. PARDON implies that one remits a penalty due for an admitted or established offense ⟨*pardon* a criminal⟩. FORGIVE implies that one gives up all claim to requital and to resentment or vengeful feelings ⟨could not *forgive* their rudeness⟩.
2**ex·cuse** \ik-ˈskyüs\ *n* (14c) **1 :** the act of excusing **2 a :** something offered as justification or as grounds for being excused **b** *pl* **:** an expression of regret for failure to do something **c :** a note of explanation of an absence **3 :** JUSTIFICATION, REASON ***syn*** see APOLOGY
ex–di·rec·to·ry \ˌeks-də-ˈrek-t(ə-)rē, -dī-\ *adj* [L *ex* out of — more at EX-] (1936) *Brit* **:** not listed in a telephone book **:** UNLISTED
ex·ec \ig-ˈzek\ *n* (1896) **1 :** EXECUTIVE OFFICER **2 :** EXECUTIVE
ex·e·cra·ble \ˈek-si-krə-bəl\ *adj* (14c) **1 :** deserving to be execrated **:** DETESTABLE ⟨~ crimes⟩ **2 :** very bad **:** WRETCHED ⟨~ hotel food⟩ — **ex·e·cra·ble·ness** *n* — **ex·e·cra·bly** \-blē\ *adv*
ex·e·crate \ˈek-sə-ˌkrāt\ *vt* **-crat·ed; -crat·ing** [L *exsecratus,* pp. of *exsecrari* to put under a curse, fr. *ex* + *sacr-, sacer* sacred] (1531) **1 :** to declare to be evil or detestable **:** DENOUNCE **2 :** to detest utterly — **ex·e·cra·tive** \-ˌkrā-tiv\ *adj* — **ex·e·cra·tor** \-ˌkrā-tər\ *n*
ex·e·cra·tion \ˌek-sə-ˈkrā-shən\ *n* (14c) **1 :** the act of cursing or denouncing; *also* **:** the curse so uttered **2 :** an object of curses **:** something detested
ex·ec·u·tant \ig-ˈze-k(y)ə-tənt\ *n* (1846) **:** one who executes or performs; *esp* **:** one skilled in the technique of an art **:** PERFORMER
ex·e·cute \ˈek-si-ˌkyüt\ *vb* **-cut·ed; -cut·ing** [ME, fr. AF *executer,* fr. *execucion* execution] *vt* (14c) **1 :** to carry out fully **:** put completely into effect ⟨~ a command⟩ **2 :** to do what is provided or required by ⟨~ a decree⟩ **3 :** to put to death esp. in compliance with a legal sentence **4 :** to make or produce (as a work of art) esp. by carrying out a design **5 :** to perform what is required to give validity to ⟨~ a deed⟩ **6 :** PLAY ⟨~ a piece of music⟩ ~ *vi* **1 :** to perform properly or skillfully the fundamentals of a sport or of a particular play ⟨never had a team ~ better —Bobby Knight⟩ **2 :** to perform indicated tasks according to encoded instructions — used of a computer program or routine ***syn*** see KILL, PERFORM — **ex·e·cut·able** \-ˌkyü-tə-bəl\ *adj*
ex·e·cu·tion \ˌek-si-ˈkyü-shən\ *n* [ME *execucion,* fr. AF, fr. L *exsecution-, exsecutio,* fr. *exsequi* to execute, fr. *ex-* + *sequi* to follow — more at SUE] (14c) **1 :** the act or process of executing **:** PERFORMANCE **2 :** a putting to death esp. as a legal penalty **3 :** the process of enforcing a legal judgment (as against a debtor); *also* **:** a judicial writ directing such enforcement **4 :** the act or mode or result of performance **5** *archaic* **:** effective or destructive action ⟨his brandished steel, which smoked with bloody ~ —Shak.⟩ — usu. used with *do* ⟨as soon as day came, we went out to see what ~ we had done —Daniel Defoe⟩
ex·e·cu·tion·er \-sh(ə-)nər\ *n* (1536) **:** one who executes; *esp* **:** one who puts to death
1**ex·ec·u·tive** \ig-ˈze-k(y)ə-tiv, -kyü-\ *adj* (1649) **1 a :** of or relating to the execution of the laws and the conduct of public and national affairs **b :** belonging to the branch of government that is charged with such powers as diplomatic representation, superintendence of the execution of the laws, and appointment of officials and that usu. has some power over legislation (as through veto) — compare JUDICIAL, LEGISLATIVE **2 a :** designed for or relating to execution or carrying into effect ⟨~ board⟩ **b :** having administrative or managerial responsibility ⟨~ director⟩ **3 :** of or relating to an executive ⟨the ~ offices⟩

[2]**executive** *n* (1774) **1 :** the executive branch of a government; *also* **:** the person or persons who constitute the executive magistracy of a state **2 :** a directing or controlling office of an organization **3 :** one that exercises administrative or managerial control
executive agreement *n* (1942) **:** an agreement between the U.S. and a foreign government made by the executive branch either alone or with Congressional approval and dealing usu. with routine matters
executive council *n* (1775) **1 :** a council constituted to advise or share in the functions of a political executive **2 :** a council that exercises supreme executive power
executive officer *n* (1776) **:** the officer second in command of a military or naval organization or vessel
executive order *n* (1862) **:** REGULATION 2b
executive privilege *n* (1909) **:** exemption from legally enforced disclosure of communications within the executive branch of government when such disclosure would adversely affect the functions and decision-making processes of the executive branch
executive secretary *n* (1915) **:** a secretary having administrative duties; *esp* **:** an official responsible for administering the activities and business affairs of an organization
executive session *n* (1840) **:** a usu. closed session (as of a legislative body) that functions as an executive council (as of the U.S. Senate when considering appointments or the ratification of treaties)
ex•ec•u•tor \ig-ˈze-k(y)ə-tər *or in sense 1* ˈek-sə-ˌkyü-\ *n* [ME, fr. AF, fr. L *exsecutor,* fr. *exsequi*] (13c) **1 a :** one who executes something **b** *obs* **:** EXECUTIONER **2 a :** the person appointed by a testator to execute a will **b :** LITERARY EXECUTOR — **ex•ec•u•to•ri•al** \ig-ˌze-k(y)ə-ˈtȯr-ē-əl\ *adj*
ex•ec•u•to•ry \ig-ˈze-k(y)ə-ˌtȯr-ē\ *adj* (1592) **1 :** designed or of such a nature as to be executed in time to come or to take effect on a future contingency **2 :** relating to administration
ex•ec•u•trix \ig-ˈze-k(y)ə-(ˌ)triks\ *n, pl* **ex•ec•u•tri•ces** \-ˌze-k(y)ə-ˈtrī-(ˌ)sēz\ *or* **ex•ec•u•trix•es** \-ˈze-k(y)ə-ˌtrik-səz\ (15c) **:** a woman who is an executor
ex•e•dra \ˈek-sə-drə\ *n, pl* **-drae** \-ˌdrē, -ˌdrī\ *or* **-dras** [L, fr. Gk, fr. *ex-* + *hedra* seat — more at SIT] (1659) **1 :** a room (as in a temple or house) in ancient Greece and Rome used for conversation and formed by an open or columned recess often semicircular in shape and furnished with seats **2 :** a large outdoor nearly semicircular seat with a solid back
ex•e•ge•sis \ˌek-sə-ˈjē-səs, ˈek-sə-ˌ\ *n, pl* **-ge•ses** \-ˈjē-(ˌ)sēz\ [NL, fr. Gk *exēgēsis,* fr. *exēgeisthai* to explain, interpret, fr. *ex-* + *hēgeisthai* to lead — more at SEEK] (1619) **:** EXPOSITION, EXPLANATION; *esp* **:** an explanation or critical interpretation of a text
ex•e•gete \ˈek-sə-ˌjēt\ *n* [Gk *exēgētēs,* fr. *exēgeisthai*] (ca. 1736) **:** one who practices exegesis
ex•e•get•i•cal \ˌek-sə-ˈje-ti-kəl\ *also* **ex•e•get•ic** \-tik\ *adj* [Gk *exēgētikos,* fr. *exēgeisthai*] (ca. 1623) **:** of or relating to exegesis **:** EXPLANATORY ⟨an ~ text⟩
ex•e•get•ist \-ˈjē-tist, -ˈje-\ *n* (1848) **:** EXEGETE
ex•em•plar \ig-ˈzem-ˌplär, -plər, eg-\ *n* [ME, fr. L, fr. *exemplum* example] (15c) **:** one that serves as a model or example: as **a :** an ideal model **b :** a typical or standard specimen ⟨an ~ of medieval architecture⟩ **c :** a copy of a book or writing **d :** IDEA 1a ***syn*** see MODEL
ex•em•pla•ry \ig-ˈzem-plə-rē\ *adj* (ca. 1507) **1 a :** serving as a pattern **b :** deserving imitation **:** COMMENDABLE ⟨his courage was ~⟩; *also* **:** deserving imitation because of excellence ⟨they serve ~ pastries —G. V. Higgins⟩ **2 :** serving as a warning **:** MONITORY ⟨given an ~ punishment⟩ **3 :** serving as an example, instance, or illustration — **ex•em•plar•i•ly** \ˌeg-ˌzem-ˈpler-ə-lē\ *adv* — **ex•em•pla•ri•ness** \ig-ˈzem-plə-rē-nəs\ *n* — **ex•em•plar•i•ty** \ˌeg-ˌzem-ˈpla-rə-tē\ *n*
ex•em•pli•fi•ca•tion \ig-ˌzem-plə-fə-ˈkā-shən\ *n* (1510) **1 a :** the act or process of exemplifying **b :** EXAMPLE, CASE IN POINT **2 :** an exemplified copy of a document
ex•em•pli•fy \ig-ˈzem-plə-ˌfī\ *vt* **-fied; -fy•ing** [ME *exemplifien,* fr. AF *exemplifier,* fr. ML *exemplificare,* fr. L *exemplum*] (15c) **1 :** to show or illustrate by example ⟨anecdotes ~*ing* those virtues⟩ **2 :** to make an attested copy or transcript of (a document) under seal **3 a :** to be an instance of or serve as an example of **:** EMBODY ⟨she *exemplifies* the qualities of a good leader⟩ **b :** to be typical of ⟨a dish that *exemplifies* French cuisine⟩
ex•em•pli gra•tia \ig-ˌzem-(ˌ)plē-ˈgrä-tē-ˌä, -ˈgrā-sh(ē-)ə\ *adv* [L] (1602) **:** for example
ex•em•plum \ig-ˈzem-pləm, eg-\ *n, pl* **-pla** \-plə\ [L] (1890) **1 :** EXAMPLE, MODEL ⟨an ~ of heroism⟩ **2 :** an anecdote or short narrative used to point a moral or sustain an argument
[1]**ex•empt** \ig-ˈzem(p)t\ *adj* [ME, fr. AF, fr. L *exemptus,* pp. of *eximere* to take out — more at EXAMPLE] (14c) **1** *obs* **:** set apart **2 :** free or released from some liability or requirement to which others are subject ⟨was ~ from jury duty⟩ ⟨the estate was ~ from taxes⟩
[2]**exempt** *vt* (15c) **:** to release or deliver from some liability or requirement to which others are subject ⟨~*ed* from military service⟩
[3]**exempt** *n* (1670) **:** one exempted or freed from duty
ex•emp•tion \ig-ˈzem(p)-shən\ *n* (14c) **1 :** the act of exempting or state of being exempt **:** IMMUNITY **2 :** one that exempts or is exempted; *esp* **:** a source or amount of income exempted from taxation
ex•en•ter•ate \ig-ˈzen-tə-ˌrāt\ *vt* **-at•ed; -at•ing** [L *exenteratus,* pp. of *exenterare* to disembowel, modif. of Gk *exenterizein,* fr. *ex-* + *enteron* intestine — more at INTER-] (1607) **:** to remove the contents of (as the orbit or pelvis) — **ex•en•ter•a•tion** \-ˌzen-tə-ˈrā-shən\ *n*
[1]**ex•er•cise** \ˈek-sər-ˌsīz\ *n* [ME, fr. AF *exercice,* fr. L *exercitium,* fr. *exercitare* to train, exercise, freq. of *exercēre* to train, occupy, fr. *ex-* + *arcēre* to enclose, hold off — more at ARK] (14c) **1 a :** the act of bringing into play or realizing in action **:** USE ⟨the ~ of self-control⟩ **b :** the discharge of an official function or professional occupation ⟨~ of his judicial duties⟩ **c :** the act or an instance of carrying out the terms of an agreement (as an option) — often used attributively ⟨an option's ~ price⟩ **2 a :** regular or repeated use of a faculty or bodily organ **b :** bodily exertion for the sake of developing and maintaining physical fitness ⟨trying to get more ~⟩ **3 :** something performed or practiced in order to develop, improve, or display a specific capability or skill ⟨arithmetic ~*s*⟩ ⟨vocal ~*s*⟩ **4 :** a performance or activity having a strongly marked secondary or ulterior aspect ⟨party politics has always been an ~ in compromise —H. S. Ashmore⟩ **5 a :** a maneuver, operation, or drill carried out for training and discipline ⟨naval ~*s*⟩ **b** *pl* **:** a program including speeches, announcements of awards and honors, and various traditional practices of secular or religious character ⟨commencement ~*s*⟩
[2]**exercise** *vb* **-cised; -cis•ing** *vt* (14c) **1 a :** to make effective in action **:** USE ⟨didn't ~ good judgment⟩ **b :** to bring to bear **:** EXERT ⟨~ influence⟩ **c :** to implement the terms of (as an option) **2 a :** to use repeatedly in order to strengthen or develop ⟨~ a muscle⟩ **b :** to train (as troops) by drills and maneuvers **c :** to put through exercises ⟨~ the horses⟩ **3 a :** to engage the attention and effort of **b :** to cause anxiety, alarm, or indignation in ⟨the issues *exercising* voters this year⟩ ~ *vi* **:** to take exercise — **ex•er•cis•able** \-ˌsī-zə-bəl\ *adj*
exercise bicycle *n* (1976) **:** STATIONARY BICYCLE
exercise bike *n* (1977) **:** STATIONARY BICYCLE
ex•er•cis•er \ˈek-sər-ˌsī-zər\ *n* (1552) **1 :** one that exercises **2 :** an apparatus for use in physical exercise
ex•er•ci•ta•tion \ig-ˌzər-sə-ˈtā-shən\ *n* [ME *exercitacioun,* fr. L *exercitation-, exercitatio,* fr. *exercitare*] (14c) **:** EXERCISE
Ex•er•cy•cle \ˈek-sər-ˌsī-kəl\ *trademark* — used for a stationary bicycle
ex•er•gon•ic \ˌek-(ˌ)sər-ˈgä-nik\ *adj* [*exo-* + Gk *ergon* work — more at WORK] (1940) **:** EXOTHERMIC ⟨an ~ biochemical reaction⟩
ex•ergue \ˈek-ˌsərg, ˈeg-ˌzərg\ *n* [F, fr. NL *exergum,* fr. Gk *ex* out of + *ergon* work] (1697) **:** a space on a coin, token, or medal usu. on the reverse below the central part of the design
ex•ert \ig-ˈzərt\ *vt* [L *exsertus,* pp. of *exserere* to thrust out, fr. *ex-* + *serere* to join — more at SERIES] (ca. 1630) **1 a :** to put forth (as strength) ⟨the force is ~*ed* sideways⟩ **b :** to put (oneself) into action or to tiring effort ⟨won't have to ~ himself moving the table⟩ **2 :** to bring to bear esp. with sustained effort or lasting effect ⟨~*ed* a bad influence on his students⟩ **3 :** EMPLOY, WIELD ⟨~*ed* her leadership abilities intelligently⟩
ex•er•tion \ig-ˈzər-shən\ *n* (1677) **:** the act or an instance of exerting; *esp* **:** a laborious or perceptible effort
ex•er•tion•al \ig-ˈzər-shnəl, -shə-nᵊl\ *adj* (1959) **:** precipitated by physical exertion ⟨~ chest pain⟩
ex•e•unt \ˈek-sē-(ˌ)ənt, -ˌu̇nt\ [L, they go out, fr. *exire* to go out — more at EXIT] (15c) — used as a stage direction to specify that all or certain named characters leave the stage
ex•fil•trate \eks-ˈfil-ˌtrāt, ˈeks-(ˌ)fil-\ *vb* **-trat•ed; -trat•ing** [ˈ*ex-* + in*filtrate*] *vt* (1947) **1 :** to remove (as soldiers) furtively from a hostile area **2 :** to steal (sensitive data) from a computer (as with a flash drive) ~ *vi* **:** to escape from a hostile area — **ex•fil•tra•tion** \ˌeks-(ˌ)fil-ˈtrā-shən\ *n*
ex•fo•liant \(ˌ)eks-ˈfō-lē-ənt, -ˈfōl-yənt\ *n* (1983) **:** a mechanical or chemical agent (as an abrasive skin wash or salicylic acid) that is applied to the skin to remove dead cells from the surface
ex•fo•li•ate \(ˌ)eks-ˈfō-lē-ˌāt\ *vb* **-at•ed; -at•ing** [LL *exfoliatus,* pp. of *exfoliare* to strip of leaves, fr. L *ex-* + *folium* leaf — more at BLADE] *vt* (1612) **1 :** to cast off in scales, laminae, or splinters **2 :** to remove the surface of in scales or laminae **3 :** to spread or extend by or as if by opening out leaves ~ *vi* **1 :** to split into or give off scales, laminae, or body cells **2 :** to come off in thin layers or scales **3 :** to grow by or as if by producing or unfolding leaves — **ex•fo•li•a•tion** \(ˌ)eks-ˌfō-lē-ˈā-shən\ *n* — **ex•fo•li•a•tive** \eks-ˈfō-lē-ˌā-tiv\ *adj*
ex•fo•li•a•tor \(ˌ)eks-ˈfō-lē-ˌā-tər\ *n* (1980) **:** EXFOLIANT
ex gra•tia \(ˌ)eks-ˈgrā-sh(ē-)ə\ *adj or adv* [NL] (1769) **:** as a favor **:** not compelled by legal right ⟨*ex gratia* pension payments⟩
ex•hal•ant *or* **ex•hal•ent** \eks-ˈhā-lənt, ek-ˈsā-\ *adj* (1771) **:** bearing out or outward **:** EMISSIVE ⟨an ~ siphon of a clam⟩
ex•ha•la•tion \ˌeks-hə-ˈlā-shən, ˌek-sə-\ *n* (14c) **1 :** something exhaled or given off **:** EMANATION **2 :** an act of exhaling
ex•hale \eks-ˈhāl, ek-ˈsāl\ *vb* **ex•haled; ex•hal•ing** [ME *exalen,* fr. L *exhalare,* fr. *ex-* + *halare* to breathe] *vi* (14c) **1 :** to rise or be given off as vapor **2 :** to emit breath or vapor ~ *vt* **1 a :** to breathe out ⟨she *exhaled* a sigh⟩ **b :** to give forth (gaseous matter) **:** EMIT **2** *archaic* **:** to cause to be emitted in vapor
[1]**ex•haust** \ig-ˈzȯst\ *vb* [L *exhaustus,* pp. of *exhaurire,* fr. *ex-* + *haurire* to draw; akin to MHG *œsen* to empty, Gk *auein* to take] *vt* (1531) **1 a :** to consume entirely **:** USE UP ⟨~*ed* our funds in a week⟩ **b :** to tire extremely or completely ⟨~*ed* by overwork⟩ **c :** to deprive of a valuable quality or constituent ⟨~ a soil of fertility⟩ **2 a :** to draw off or let out completely **b :** to empty by drawing off the contents; *specif* **:** to create a vacuum in **3 a :** to consider or discuss (a subject) thoroughly or completely **b :** to try out the whole number of ⟨~*ed* all the possibilities⟩ ~ *vi* **:** DISCHARGE, EMPTY ⟨the engine ~*s* through the muffler⟩ ***syn*** see DEPLETE, TIRE — **ex•haust•er** *n* — **ex•haust•ibil•i•ty** \-ˌzȯ-stə-ˈbi-lə-tē\ *n* — **ex•haust•ible** \-ˈzȯ-stə-bəl\ *adj*
[2]**exhaust** *n* (1848) **1 a :** the escape of used gas or vapor from an engine **b :** the gas or vapor thus escaping **2 a :** the conduit through which used gases escape **b :** an arrangement for removing fumes, dusts, or odors from an enclosure **3 :** EXHAUSTION
ex•haus•tion \ig-ˈzȯs-chən\ *n* (1615) **:** the act or process of exhausting **:** the state of being exhausted
ex•haus•tive \ig-ˈzȯ-stiv\ *adj* (ca. 1789) **:** including all possibilities **:** THOROUGH ⟨conducted an ~ search⟩ — **ex•haus•tive•ly** *adv* — **ex•haus•tive•ness** *n* — **ex•haus•tiv•i•ty** \-ˌzȯ-ˈsti-və-tē\ *n*
ex•haust•less \ig-ˈzȯst-ləs\ *adj* (1614) **:** not to be exhausted **:** INEXHAUSTIBLE — **ex•haust•less•ly** *adv* — **ex•haust•less•ness** *n*
exhbn *abbr* exhibition
[1]**ex•hib•it** \ig-ˈzi-bət\ *vb* [ME, fr. L *exhibitus,* pp. of *exhibēre,* fr. *ex-* + *habēre* to have, hold — more at GIVE] *vt* (15c) **1 :** to submit (as a document) to a court or officer in course of proceedings; *also* **:** to present or offer officially or in legal form **2 :** to present to view: as **a :** to show or display outwardly esp. by visible signs or actions ⟨~*ed* no fear⟩ **b :** to have as a readily discernible quality or feature ⟨in all cultures we know, men ~ an aesthetic sense —H. J. Muller⟩ **c :** to show publicly esp. for purposes of competition or demonstration ⟨~ a collection of artifacts⟩ ~ *vi* **:** to display something for public inspection

\ə\ **abut** \ᵊ\ **kitten, F table** \ər\ **further** \a\ **ash** \ā\ **ace** \ä\ **mop, mar**
\au̇\ **out** \ch\ **chin** \e\ **bet** \ē\ **easy** \g\ **go** \i\ **hit** \ī\ **ice** \j\ **job**
\ŋ\ **sing** \ō\ **go** \ȯ\ **law** \ȯi\ **boy** \th\ **thin** \t͟h\ **the** \ü\ **loot** \u̇\ **foot**
\y\ **yet** \zh\ **vision, beige** \k̲, ⁿ, œ, ue, ʸ\ *see* **Guide to Pronunciation**

syn see SHOW — **ex·hib·i·tive** \-bə-tiv\ *adj* — **ex·hib·i·tor** \-bə-tər\ *n* — **ex·hib·i·to·ry** \-bə-ˌtȯr-ē\ *adj*

[2]**exhibit** *n* (1626) **1 :** a document or material object produced and identified in court or before an examiner for use as evidence **2 :** something exhibited **3 :** an act or instance of exhibiting : EXHIBITION

ex·hi·bi·tion \ˌek-sə-ˈbi-shən\ *n* (14c) **1 :** an act or instance of exhibiting **2** *Brit* **:** a grant drawn from the funds of a school or university to help maintain a student **3 :** a public showing (as of works of art, objects of manufacture, or athletic skill) ⟨a one-man ~⟩ ⟨an ~ game⟩

ex·hi·bi·tion·er \-ˈbish-nər, -ˈbi-shə-\ *n* (1679) *Brit* **:** one who holds a grant from a school or university

ex·hi·bi·tion·ism \-ˈbi-shə-ˌni-zəm\ *n* (1893) **1 a :** a perversion in which sexual gratification is obtained from the indecent exposure of one's genitals (as to a stranger) **b :** an act of such exposure **2 :** the act or practice of behaving so as to attract attention to oneself — **ex·hi·bi·tion·ist** \-ˈbish-nist, -ˈbi-shə-\ *n or adj* — **ex·hi·bi·tion·is·tic** \-ˌbi-shə-ˈnis-tik\ *adj* — **ex·hi·bi·tion·is·ti·cal·ly** \-ti-k(ə-)lē\ *adv*

ex·hil·a·rate \ig-ˈzi-lə-ˌrāt\ *vt* **-rat·ed; -rat·ing** [L *exhilaratus,* pp. of *exhilarare,* fr. *ex-* + *hilarare* to gladden, fr. *hilarus* cheerful — more at HILARIOUS] (1540) **1 :** to make cheerful and excited : ENLIVEN, ELATE ⟨was *exhilarated* by her success⟩ **2 :** REFRESH, STIMULATE — **ex·hil·a·rat·ing·ly** \ig-ˈzi-lə-ˌrā-tiŋ-lē\ *adv* — **ex·hil·a·ra·tive** \-ˌrā-tiv\ *adj*

ex·hil·a·ra·tion \ig-ˌzi-lə-ˈrā-shən\ *n* (1622) **1 :** the action of exhilarating **2 :** the feeling or the state of being exhilarated

ex·hort \ig-ˈzȯrt\ *vb* [ME, fr. AF *exorter,* fr. L *exhortari,* fr. *ex-* + *hortari* to incite — more at YEARN] *vt* (15c) **:** to incite by argument or advice : urge strongly ⟨~*ing* voters to do the right thing⟩ ~ *vi* **:** to give warnings or advice : make urgent appeals — **ex·hort·er** *n*

ex·hor·ta·tion \ˌek-ˌsȯr-ˈtā-shən, -sər-; ˌeg-ˌzȯr-, -zər-\ *n* (14c) **1 :** an act or instance of exhorting **2 :** language intended to incite and encourage

ex·hor·ta·tive \ig-ˈzȯr-tə-tiv\ *adj* (15c) **:** serving to exhort

ex·hor·ta·to·ry \-tə-ˌtȯr-ē\ *adj* (15c) **:** using exhortation : EXHORTATIVE ⟨an ~ appeal⟩

ex·hume \ig-ˈzüm, igz-ˈyüm, iks-ˈ(h)yüm\ *vt* **ex·humed; ex·hum·ing** [ME, fr. ML *exhumare,* fr. L *ex* out of + *humus* earth — more at EX-, HUMBLE] (15c) **1 :** DISINTER ⟨~ a body⟩ **2 :** to bring back from neglect or obscurity ⟨*exhumed* a great deal of information from the archives⟩ — **ex·hu·ma·tion** \ˌeks-(h)yü-ˈmā-shən, ˌeg-zü-, ˌegz-yü-\ *n* — **ex·hum·er** \ig-ˈzü-mər, igz-ˈyü-, iks-ˈ(h)yü-\ *n*

ex hy·po·the·si \ˌeks-hī-ˈpä-thə-ˌsī\ *adv* [NL, from a hypothesis] (1603) **:** according to assumptions made : by hypothesis ⟨regard . . . all elites as *ex hypothesi* incompatible with democracy —P. G. J. Pulzer⟩

ex·i·gence \ˈek-sə-jən(t)s\ *n* (15c) **:** EXIGENCY

ex·i·gen·cy \ˈek-sə-jən(t)-sē, ig-ˈzi-jən(t)-\ *n, pl* **-cies** (1581) **1 :** that which is required in a particular situation — usu. used in pl. ⟨exceptionally quick in responding to the *exigencies* of modern warfare —D. B. Ottaway⟩ **2 a :** the quality or state of being exigent **b :** a state of affairs that makes urgent demands ⟨a leader must act in any sudden ~⟩ *syn* see JUNCTURE

ex·i·gent \ˈek-sə-jənt\ *adj* [L *exigent-, exigens,* prp. of *exigere* to demand — more at EXACT] (1629) **1 :** requiring immediate aid or action ⟨~ circumstances⟩ **2 :** requiring or calling for much : DEMANDING ⟨an ~ client⟩ — **ex·i·gent·ly** *adv*

ex·i·gu·ity \ˌek-zi-ˈgyü-ə-tē\ *n, pl* **-ities** (ca. 1626) **:** the quality or state of being exiguous : SCANTINESS

ex·ig·u·ous \ig-ˈzi-gyə-wəs\ *adj* [L *exiguus,* fr. *exigere*] (1651) **:** excessively scanty : INADEQUATE ⟨wrest an ~ existence from the land⟩ ⟨~ evidence⟩ — **ex·ig·u·ous·ly** *adv* — **ex·ig·u·ous·ness** *n*

[1]**ex·ile** \ˈeg-ˌzī(-ə)l, ˈek-ˌsī(-ə)l\ *n* [ME *exil,* fr. AF *essil, exil,* fr. L *exilium,* fr. *exul, exsul* an exile] (14c) **1 a :** the state or a period of forced absence from one's country or home **b :** the state or a period of voluntary absence from one's country or home **2 :** a person who is in exile — **ex·il·ic** \eg-ˈzi-lik\ *adj*

[2]**exile** *vt* **ex·iled; ex·il·ing** (14c) **:** to banish or expel from one's own country or home *syn* see BANISH

ex·im·i·ous \eg-ˈzi-mē-əs\ *adj* [L *eximius,* fr. *eximere* to take out — more at EXAMPLE] (1547) *archaic* **:** CHOICE, EXCELLENT

ex·ine \ˈek-ˌsēn, -ˌsīn\ *n* [ISV *ex-* + *in-* fibrous tissue, fr. Gk *in-, is* tendon] (ca. 1884) **:** the outer of the two major layers forming the walls of some spores and esp. pollen grains

ex·ist \ig-ˈzist\ *vi* [L *exsistere* to come into being, exist, fr. *ex-* + *sistere* to stand, stop; akin to L *stare* to stand — more at STAND] (ca. 1568) **1 a :** to have real being whether material or spiritual ⟨did unicorns ~⟩ ⟨the largest galaxy known to ~⟩ **b :** to have being in a specified place or with respect to understood limitations or conditions ⟨strange ideas ~*ed* in his mind⟩ **2 :** to continue to be ⟨racism still ~*s* in society⟩ **3 a :** to have life or the functions of vitality ⟨we cannot ~ without oxygen⟩ **b :** to live at an inferior level or under adverse circumstances ⟨the hungry ~*ing* from day to day⟩

ex·is·tence \ig-ˈzis-tən(t)s\ *n* (14c) **1 a** *obs* **:** reality as opposed to appearance **b :** reality as presented in experience **c (1) :** the totality of existent things **(2) :** a particular being ⟨all the fair ~*s* of heaven —John Keats⟩ **d :** sentient or living being : LIFE **2 a :** the state or fact of having being esp. independently of human consciousness and as contrasted with nonexistence ⟨the ~ of other worlds⟩ **b :** the manner of being that is common to every mode of being **c :** being with respect to a limiting condition or under a particular aspect **3 :** actual or present occurrence ⟨~ of a state of war⟩

ex·is·tent \-tənt\ *adj* [L *exsistent-, exsistens,* prp. of *exsistere*] (1561) **1 :** having being : EXISTING **2 :** existing now : PRESENT ⟨~ methods of flood control⟩ — **existent** *n*

ex·is·ten·tial \ˌeg-(ˌ)zis-ˈten(t)-shəl, ˌek-(ˌ)sis-\ *adj* (1693) **1 :** of, relating to, or affirming existence ⟨~ propositions⟩ **2 a :** grounded in existence or the experience of existence : EMPIRICAL **b :** having being in time and space **3** [trans. of Dan *eksistentiel* & G *existential*] **:** EXISTENTIALIST — **ex·is·ten·tial·ly** *adv*

ex·is·ten·tial·ism \-ˈten(t)-shə-ˌli-zəm\ *n* (1941) **:** a chiefly 20th century philosophical movement embracing diverse doctrines but centering on analysis of individual existence in an unfathomable universe and the plight of the individual who must assume ultimate responsibility for acts of free will without any certain knowledge of what is right or wrong or good or bad

[1]**ex·is·ten·tial·ist** \-list\ *n* (1942) **:** an adherent of existentialism

[2]**existentialist** *adj* (1946) **:** of or relating to existentialism or existentialists — **ex·is·ten·tial·is·tic** \-ˌten(t)-shə-ˈlis-tik\ *adj* — **ex·is·ten·tial·is·ti·cal·ly** \-ti-k(ə-)lē\ *adv*

existential quantifier *n* (1936) **:** a quantifier (as *for some* in "for some *x*, 2*x* + 5 = 8") that asserts that there exists at least one value of a variable — called also *existential operator*

[1]**ex·it** \ˈeg-zət, ˈek-sət\ [L, he goes out, fr. *exire* to go out, fr. *ex-* + *ire* to go — more at ISSUE] (1538) — used as a stage direction to specify who goes off stage

[2]**exit** *n* [L *exitus,* fr. *exire*] (1588) **1** [[1]*exit*] **:** a departure from a stage **2 a :** the act of going out or away ⟨made an early ~⟩ **b :** DEATH **3 :** a way out of an enclosed place or space **4 :** one of the designated points of departure from an expressway — **ex·it·less** *adj*

[3]**exit** *vi* (1607) **1 :** to go out or away : DEPART **2 :** DIE ~ *vt* **1 :** LEAVE 3a **2 :** to cause (a computer program or routine) to cease running

exit poll *n* (1980) **:** a poll taken (as by news media) of voters leaving the voting place that is usu. used for predicting the winners — **exit polling** *n*

ex li·bris \eks-ˈlē-brəs, -ˌbrēs\ *n, pl* **ex libris** [NL, from the books; used before the owner's name on bookplates] (1880) **:** BOOKPLATE

Ex·moor \ˈek-ˌsmu̇r, -ˌsmȯr\ *n* [*Exmoor,* England] (1808) **1 :** any of a breed of horned sheep of Devonshire in England valued esp. for mutton **2 :** any of a breed of hardy ponies native to the Exmoor district that have a brown, bay, or dun coat and a pale-colored muzzle

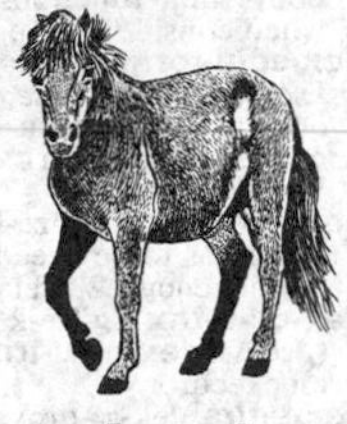
Exmoor 2

ex ni·hi·lo \(ˌ)eks-ˈnē-(h)ə-ˌlō, -ˈni-, -ˈnī-\ *adv or adj* [L] (1656) **:** from or out of nothing ⟨creation *ex nihilo*⟩

exo- *or* **ex-** *comb form* [Gk *exō* out, outside, fr. *ex* out of — more at EX-] **1 :** outside ⟨*exo*gamy⟩ : outer ⟨*exo*skeleton⟩ — compare ECT-, END- **2 :** turning out ⟨*exo*ergic⟩

exo·bi·ol·o·gy \ˌek-sō-bī-ˈä-lə-jē\ *n* (1960) **:** a branch of biology concerned with the search for life outside the earth and with the effects of extraterrestrial environments on living organisms — **exo·bi·o·log·i·cal** \-ˌbī-ə-ˈlä-ji-kəl\ *adj* — **exo·bi·ol·o·gist** \-bī-ˈä-lə-jist\ *n*

exo·carp \ˈek-sō-ˌkärp\ *n* [ISV] (ca. 1845) **:** the outermost layer of the pericarp of a fruit — see ENDOCARP illustration

exo·crine \ˈek-sə-krən, -ˌkrīn, -ˌkrēn\ *adj* [ISV *exo-* + Gk *krinein* to separate — more at CERTAIN] (ca. 1911) **:** producing, being, or relating to a secretion that is released outside its source ⟨~ pancreatic cells⟩

exocrine gland *n* (ca. 1927) **:** a gland (as a salivary gland or part of the pancreas) that releases a secretion external to or at the surface of an organ by means of a canal or duct

exo·cy·clic \ˌek-sō-ˈsī-klik, -ˈsi-\ *adj* (1913) **:** situated outside of a ring in a chemical structure

exo·cy·to·sis \ˌek-sō-sī-ˈtō-səs\ *n, pl* **-to·ses** \-ˌsēz\ [NL, fr. *exo-* + *cyt-* + *-osis*] (1963) **:** the release of cellular substances (as secretory products) contained in cell vesicles by fusion of the vesicular membrane with the plasma membrane and subsequent release of the contents to the exterior of the cell — **exo·cy·tot·ic** \-ˈtä-tik\ *adj*

Exod *abbr* Exodus

exo·der·mis \ˌek-sō-ˈdər-məs\ *n* [NL] (1889) **:** a layer of the outer living cortical cells of plants that takes over the functions of the epidermis in roots lacking secondary thickening

ex·odon·tia \ˌek-sə-ˈdän(t)-sh(ē-)ə\ *n* [NL, fr. [1]*ex-* + *-odontia*] (1913) **:** a branch of dentistry that deals with the extraction of teeth — **ex·odon·tist** \-ˈdän-tist\ *n*

ex·o·dus \ˈek-sə-dəs, ˈeg-zə-\ *n* [L, fr. Gk *Exodos,* lit., road out, fr. *ex-* + *hodos* road] (bef. 12c) **1** *cap* **:** the mainly narrative second book of canonical Jewish and Christian Scripture — see BIBLE table **2 :** a mass departure : EMIGRATION

exo·en·zyme \ˌek-sō-ˈen-ˌzīm\ *n* [ISV] (1908) **:** an extracellular enzyme

exo·er·gic \ˌek-sō-ˈər-jik\ *adj* (1942) **:** releasing energy : EXOTHERMIC

exo·eryth·ro·cyt·ic \ˌek-sō-i-ˌri-thrə-ˈsi-tik\ *adj* (1942) **:** occurring outside the red blood cells — used esp. of stages of malaria parasites

ex of·fi·cio \ˌek-sə-ˈfi-shē-ˌō, -sē-\ *adv or adj* [LL] (1533) **:** by virtue or because of an office ⟨the Vice President serves *ex officio* as president of the Senate⟩

ex·og·a·my \ek-ˈsä-gə-mē\ *n, pl* **-mies** (1865) **:** marriage outside of a specific group esp. as required by custom or law — **ex·og·a·mous** \ek-ˈsä-gə-məs\ *or* **exo·gam·ic** \ˌek-sə-ˈga-mik\ *adj*

ex·og·e·nous \ek-ˈsä-jə-nəs\ *adj* [F *exogène* exogenous, fr. *exo-* + *-gène* (fr. Gk *-genēs* born) — more at -GEN] (1830) **1 :** produced by growth from superficial tissue ⟨~ roots produced by leaves⟩ **2 a :** caused by factors (as food or a traumatic factor) or an agent (as a disease-producing organism) from outside the organism or system ⟨~ obesity⟩ ⟨~ psychic depression⟩ ⟨~ market fluctuations⟩ **b :** introduced from or produced outside the organism or system; *specif* **:** not synthesized within the organism or system — **ex·og·e·nous·ly** *adv*

ex·on \ˈek-ˌsän\ *n* [*e*xpressed sequence + [2]*-on*] (ca. 1978) **:** a polynucleotide sequence in a nucleic acid that codes information for protein synthesis and that is copied and spliced together with other such sequences to form messenger RNA — compare INTRON — **ex·on·ic** \ek-ˈsä-nik\ *adj*

ex·on·er·ate \ig-ˈzä-nə-ˌrāt, eg-\ *vt* **-at·ed; -at·ing** [ME, fr. L *exoneratus,* pp. of *exonerare* to unburden, fr. *ex-* + *oner-, onus* load] (1524) **1 :** to relieve of a responsibility, obligation, or hardship **2 :** to clear from accusation or blame *syn* see EXCULPATE — **ex·on·er·a·tion** \-ˌzä-nə-ˈrā-shən\ *n* — **ex·on·er·a·tive** \-ˈzä-nə-ˌrā-tiv\ *adj*

exo·nu·cle·ase \ˌek-sō-ˈnü-klē-ˌās, -ˈnyü-, -ˌāz\ *n* (1963) **:** an enzyme that breaks down a nucleic acid by removing nucleotides one by one from the end of a chain — compare ENDONUCLEASE

exo·nu·mia \ˌek-sə-ˈnü-mē-ə, -ˈnyü-\ *n pl* [NL, fr. *exo-* + E *numismatic* + NL *-ia*] (1962) **:** numismatic items (as tokens, medals, or scrip) other than coins and paper money

exo·pep·ti·dase \-ˈpep-tə-ˌdās, -ˌdāz\ *n* (1936) **:** any of a group of enzymes that hydrolyze peptide bonds formed by the terminal amino acids of peptide chains : PEPTIDASE — compare ENDOPEPTIDASE

ex·oph·thal·mos *also* **ex·oph·thal·mus** \ˌek-säf-ˈthal-məs, -səf-, -säp-\ *n* [NL, fr. Gk *exophthalmos* having prominent eyes, fr. *ex* out +

ophthalmos eye; akin to Gk *ōps* eye — more at EYE] (1872) : abnormal protrusion of the eyeball — **ex·oph·thal·mic** \-mik\ *adj*
exo·plan·et \ˈek-sō-ˌpla-nət, ˌek-sō-ˈpla-\ *n* (1996) : a planet orbiting a star that is not our sun
exor *abbr* executor
ex·or·bi·tance \ig-ˈzȯr-bə-tən(t)s\ *n* (1609) **1** : an exorbitant action or procedure; *esp* : excessive or gross deviation from rule, right, or propriety **2** : the tendency or disposition to be exorbitant
ex·or·bi·tant \-tənt\ *adj* [ME, fr. LL *exorbitant-, exorbitans,* prp. of *exorbitare* to deviate, fr. L *ex-* + *orbita* track of a wheel, rut, fr. *orbis* disk, hoop] (15c) **1** : not coming within the scope of the law **2** : exceeding the customary or appropriate limits in intensity, quality, amount, or size ***syn*** see EXCESSIVE — **ex·or·bi·tant·ly** *adv*
ex·or·cise *also* **ex·or·cize** \ˈek-ˌsȯr-ˌsīz, -sər-\ *vt* **-cised** *also* **-cized; -cis·ing** *also* **-ciz·ing** [ME, fr. AF *exorciser,* fr. LL *exorcizare,* fr. Gk *exorkizein,* fr. *ex-* + *horkizein* to bind by oath, adjure, fr. *horkos* oath] (1539) **1 a** : to expel (an evil spirit) by adjuration **b** : to get rid of (something troublesome, menacing, or oppressive) **2** : to free of an evil spirit — **ex·or·cis·er** *n*
ex·or·cism \-ˌsi-zəm\ *n* (14c) **1** : the act or practice of exorcising **2** : a spell or formula used in exorcising — **ex·or·cist** \-ˌsist, -səst\ *n* — **ex·or·cis·tic** \ˌek-ˌsȯr-ˈsis-tik, -sər-\ *or* **ex·or·cis·ti·cal** \-ti-kəl\ *adj*
ex·or·di·um \eg-ˈzȯr-dē-əm\ *n, pl* **-diums** *or* **-dia** \-dē-ə\ [L, fr. *exordiri* to begin, fr. *ex-* + *ordiri* to begin — more at ORDER] (1577) : a beginning or introduction esp. to a discourse or composition — **ex·or·di·al** \-dē-əl\ *adj*
exo·skel·e·ton \ˌek-sō-ˈske-lə-tən\ *n* (1847) **1** : an external supportive covering of an animal (as an arthropod) **2** : bony or horny parts of a vertebrate produced from epidermal tissues **3** : an artificial external supporting structure — **exo·skel·e·tal** \-lə-t^{ə}l\ *adj*
exo·sphere \ˈek-sō-ˌsfir\ *n* [ISV] (1949) : the outer fringe region of the atmosphere of the earth or a celestial body (as a planet) — **exo·spher·ic** \ˌek-sō-ˈsfir-ik, -ˈsfer-\ *adj*
exo·spore \ˈek-sə-ˌspȯr\ *n* [ISV] (1859) : an asexual spore cut off from a parent sporophore by the formation of septa
ex·os·to·sis \ˌek-(ˌ)säs-ˈtō-səs\ *n, pl* **-to·ses** \-ˌsēz\ [NL, fr. Gk *exostōsis,* fr. *ex* out of + *osteon* bone — more at EX-, OSSEOUS] (1736) : a spur or bony outgrowth from a bone or the root of a tooth
ex·o·ter·ic \ˌek-sə-ˈter-ik\ *adj* [L & Gk; L *exotericus,* fr. Gk *exōterikos,* lit., external, fr. *exōterō* more outside, compar. of *exō* outside — more at EXO-] (1660) **1 a** : suitable to be imparted to the public ⟨the ~ doctrine⟩ — compare ESOTERIC **b** : belonging to the outer or less initiate circle **2** : relating to the outside : EXTERNAL — **ex·o·ter·i·cal·ly** \-i-k(ə-)lē\ *adv*
exo·ther·mal \ˌek-sō-ˈthər-məl\ *adj* (1906) : EXOTHERMIC — **exo·ther·mal·ly** \-mə-lē\ *adv*
exo·ther·mic \-mik\ *adj* [ISV] (1884) : characterized by or formed with evolution of heat — **exo·ther·mi·cal·ly** \-mi-k(ə-)lē\ *adv* — **exo·ther·mi·ci·ty** \-ˌthər-ˈmis-ə-tē\ *n*
^{1}**ex·ot·ic** \ig-ˈzä-tik\ *adj* [L *exoticus,* fr. Gk *exōtikos,* fr. *exō*] (1599) **1** : introduced from another country : not native to the place where found ⟨~ plants⟩ **2** *archaic* : FOREIGN, ALIEN **3** : strikingly, excitingly, or mysteriously different or unusual ⟨~ flavors⟩ **4** : of or relating to striptease ⟨~ dancing⟩ — **ex·ot·i·cal·ly** \-ti-k(ə-)lē\ *adv* — **ex·ot·ic·ness** \-tik-nəs\ *n*
^{2}**exotic** *n* (1645) **1** : one (as a plant or animal) that is exotic **2** : STRIPTEASER **3** : EXOTIC SHORTHAIR
ex·ot·i·ca \ig-ˈzä-ti-kə\ *n pl* [NL, fr. L, neut. pl. of *exoticus*] (1828) : things excitingly different or unusual; *esp* : literary or artistic items having an exotic theme or nature
ex·ot·i·cism \ig-ˈzä-tə-ˌsi-zəm\ *also* **ex·o·tism** \ˈeg-zə-ˌti-zəm, ˈek-sə-\ *n* (1827) : the quality or state of being exotic
exotic shorthair *n* (1974) : any of a breed of stocky short-haired domestic cats developed in the U.S. by crossing American shorthairs and Persians
exo·tox·in \ˌek-sō-ˈtäk-sən\ *n* [ISV] (1920) : a soluble poisonous substance produced during growth of a microorganism and released into the surrounding medium
exp *abbr* **1** expense **2** experience **3** experiment; experimental **4** exponent **5** export **6** express
ex·pand \ik-ˈspand\ *vb* [ME *expaunden,* fr. L *expandere,* fr. *ex-* + *pandere* to spread — more at FATHOM] *vt* (15c) **1** : to open up : UNFOLD **2** : to increase the extent, number, volume, or scope of : ENLARGE **3 a** : to express at length or in greater detail **b** : to write out in full ⟨~ all abbreviations⟩ **c** : to subject to mathematical expansion ⟨~ a function in a power series⟩ ~ *vi* **1** : to open out : SPREAD **2** : to increase in extent, number, volume, or scope **3** : to speak or write fully or in detail ⟨~*ed* on the theme⟩ **4** : to feel generous or optimistic — **ex·pand·abil·i·ty** \-ˌspan-də-ˈbi-lə-tē\ *n* — **ex·pand·able** \-ˈspan-də-bəl\ *adj*
syn EXPAND, AMPLIFY, SWELL, DISTEND, INFLATE, DILATE mean to increase in size or volume. EXPAND may apply regardless of the manner of increase (as growth, unfolding, addition of parts) ⟨a business that *expands* every year⟩. AMPLIFY implies the extension or enlargement of something inadequate ⟨*amplify* the statement with details⟩. SWELL implies gradual expansion beyond a thing's original or normal limits ⟨the bureaucracy *swelled* to unmanageable proportions⟩. DISTEND implies outward extension caused by pressure from within ⟨a *distended* abdomen⟩. INFLATE implies expanding by introduction of air or something insubstantial and suggests a vulnerability to sudden collapse ⟨an *inflated* ego⟩. DILATE applies esp. to expansion of circumference ⟨*dilated* pupils⟩.
ex·pand·ed \-ˈspan-dəd\ *adj* (1875) *of a typeface* : EXTENDED
expanded metal *n* (1890) : sheet metal cut and expanded into a lattice and used esp. as lath
expanded plastic *n* (1945) : lightweight cellular plastic used esp. as insulation and protective packing material — called also *foamed plastic, plastic foam*
ex·pand·er \ik-ˈspan-dər\ *n* (1862) : one that expands; *specif* : any of several colloidal substances (as dextran) of high molecular weight used as a blood or plasma substitute for increasing the blood volume

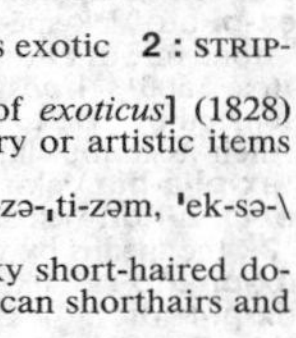

expanded metal

ex·panse \ik-ˈspan(t)s\ *n* [NL *expansum,* fr. L, neut. of *expansus,* pp. of *expandere*] (1637) **1** : FIRMAMENT **2** : great extent of something spread out ⟨an ~ of calm ocean⟩
ex·pan·si·ble \ik-ˈspan(t)-sə-bəl\ *adj* (ca. 1691) : capable of being expanded — **ex·pan·si·bil·i·ty** \-ˌspan(t)-sə-ˈbi-lə-tē\ *n*
ex·pan·sion \ik-ˈspan(t)-shən\ *n* (1611) **1** : EXPANSE **2** : the act or process of expanding ⟨territorial ~⟩ ⟨economic ~⟩ ⟨~ of the universe⟩ **3** : the quality or state of being expanded **4** : the increase in volume of working fluid (as steam) in an engine cylinder after cutoff or in an internal combustion engine after explosion **5 a** : an expanded part **b** : something that results from an act of expanding ⟨the book is an ~ of a lecture series⟩ **6** : the result of carrying out an indicated mathematical operation : the expression of a function in the form of a series — **ex·pan·sion·al** \-ˈpanch-nəl, -chə-n^{ə}l\ *adj*
ex·pan·sion·ary \ik-ˈspan(t)-shə-ˌner-ē\ *adj* (1936) : tending toward expansion ⟨an ~ economy⟩
expansion card *n* (1982) : a circuit board connecting to a motherboard which expands the capabilities of a computer
ex·pan·sion·ism \ik-ˈspan-(t)-shə-ˌni-zəm\ *n* (1899) : a policy or practice of expansion and esp. of territorial expansion by a nation — **ex·pan·sion·ist** \-ˈspan(t)-sh(ə-)nist\ *n* — **expansionist** *also* **ex·pan·sion·is·tic** \-ˌspan(t)-shə-ˈnis-tik\ *adj*
expansion slot *n* (1980) : a socket on the motherboard of a computer into which an expansion card may be inserted
ex·pan·sive \ik-ˈspan(t)-siv\ *adj* (1651) **1** : having a capacity or a tendency to expand **2** : causing or tending to cause expansion **3 a** : characterized by high spirits, generosity, or readiness to talk : OPEN ⟨grew ~ after dinner⟩ **b** : marked by or indicative of exaggerated euphoria and delusions of self-importance ⟨an ~ patient⟩ **4** : marked by expansion; *esp* : having a great expanse or extent : SIZABLE, EXTENSIVE ⟨an ~ interpretation of the law⟩ **5** : characterized by richness, abundance, or magnificence ⟨~ living⟩ ⟨~ taste⟩ — **ex·pan·sive·ly** *adv* — **ex·pan·sive·ness** *n*
ex·pan·siv·i·ty \ˌek-ˌspan-ˈsi-və-tē, ik-\ *n* (1837) : the quality or state of being expansive; *esp* : the capacity to expand
ex par·te \(ˌ)eks-ˈpär-tē\ *adv or adj* [ML] (1672) **1** : on or from one side or party only — used of legal proceedings **2** : from a one-sided or partisan point of view
ex·pat \ˈeks-ˌpat\ *n* (1962) *chiefly Brit* : an expatriate person : EXPATRIATE
ex·pa·ti·ate \ek-ˈspā-shē-ˌāt\ *vi* **-at·ed; -at·ing** [L *exspatiatus,* pp. of *exspatiari* to wander, digress, fr. *ex-* + *spatium* space, course] (1538) **1** : to move about freely or at will : WANDER **2** : to speak or write at length or in detail ⟨*expatiating* upon the value of the fabric —Thomas Hardy⟩ — **ex·pa·ti·a·tion** \(ˌ)ek-ˌspā-shē-ˈā-shən\ *n*
^{1}**ex·pa·tri·ate** \ek-ˈspā-trē-ˌāt\ *vb* **-at·ed; -at·ing** [ML *expatriatus,* pp. of *expatriare* to leave one's own country, fr. L *ex-* + *patria* native country, fr. fem. of *patrius* of a father, fr. *patr-, pater* father — more at FATHER] *vt* (1768) **1** : BANISH, EXILE **2** : to withdraw (oneself) from residence in or allegiance to one's native country ~ *vi* : to leave one's native country to live elsewhere; *also* : to renounce allegiance to one's native country — **ex·pa·tri·ate** \-ˌāt, -ət\ *n* — **ex·pa·tri·a·tion** \(ˌ)ek-ˌspā-trē-ˈā-shən\ *n*
^{2}**ex·pa·tri·ate** \ek-ˈspā-trē-ət, -trē-ˌāt\ *adj* (1812) : living in a foreign land
ex·pa·tri·a·tism \ek-ˈspā-trē-ə-ˌti-zəm\ *n* (1937) : the fact or state of being an expatriate
ex·pect \ik-ˈspekt\ *vb* [L *exspectare* to look forward to, fr. *ex-* + *spectare* to look at, freq. of *specere* to look — more at SPY] *vi* (1560) **1** *archaic* : WAIT, STAY **2** : to look forward **3** : to be pregnant : await the birth of one's child — used in progressive tenses ⟨she's ~*ing* next month⟩ ~ *vt* **1** *archaic* : AWAIT **2** : to anticipate or look forward to the coming or occurrence of ⟨we ~ them any minute now⟩ ⟨~*ed* a telephone call⟩ **3** : SUPPOSE, THINK **4 a** : to consider probable or certain ⟨~ to be forgiven⟩ ⟨~ that things will improve⟩ **b** : to consider reasonable, due, or necessary ⟨~*ed* hard work from the students⟩ **c** : to consider bound in duty or obligated ⟨they ~ you to pay your bills⟩ — **ex·pect·able** \-ˈspek-tə-bəl\ *adj* — **ex·pect·ably** \-blē\ *adv* — **ex·pect·ed·ly** *adv* — **ex·pect·ed·ness** *n*
syn EXPECT, HOPE, LOOK mean to await some occurrence or outcome. EXPECT implies a high degree of certainty and usu. involves the idea of preparing or envisioning ⟨*expects* to be finished by Tuesday⟩. HOPE implies little certainty but suggests confidence or assurance in the possibility that what one desires or longs for will happen ⟨*hopes* to find a job soon⟩. LOOK, with *to,* implies assurance that expectations will be fulfilled ⟨*looks* to a tidy profit from the sale⟩; with *for* it implies less assurance and suggests an attitude of expectancy and watchfulness ⟨*look* for rain when the wind shifts to the northeast⟩.
ex·pec·tance \ik-ˈspek-tən(t)s\ *n* (1603) : EXPECTANCY
ex·pec·tan·cy \-tən(t)-sē\ *n, pl* **-cies** (1600) **1 a** : the act, action, or state of expecting ⟨the strange ~ that getting on any train gives us —John Updike⟩ **b** : the state of being expected ⟨occurs with an ~ slightly greater than usual⟩ **2 a** : something expected ⟨their belief led to an ~⟩ **b** : the expected amount (as of the number of years of life) based on statistical probability ⟨life ~⟩
^{1}**ex·pec·tant** \-tənt\ *adj* (14c) **1** : characterized by expectation **2** : expecting the birth of a child ⟨~ mothers⟩ — **ex·pec·tant·ly** *adv*
^{2}**expectant** *n* (1609) : one who is looking forward to something
ex·pec·ta·tion \ˌek-ˌspek-ˈtā-shən, ik-\ *n* (1540) **1** : the act or state of expecting : ANTICIPATION ⟨in ~ of what would happen⟩ **2 a** : something expected ⟨not up to ~*s*⟩ ⟨~*s* for an economic recovery⟩ **b** : basis for expecting : ASSURANCE ⟨they have every ~ of success⟩ **c** : prospects of inheritance — usu. used in pl. **3** : the state of being expected **4 a** : EXPECTANCY 2b **b** : EXPECTED VALUE — **ex·pec·ta·tion·al** \-tā-shə-n^{ə}l, -shnəl\ *adj*
ex·pec·ta·tive \ik-ˈspek-tə-tiv\ *adj* (15c) : of, relating to, or constituting an object of expectation ⟨~ goals⟩

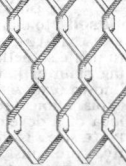

expected value *n* (1915) **1 :** the sum of the values of a random variable with each value multiplied by its probability of occurrence **2 :** the integral of the product of a probability density function of a continuous random variable and the random variable itself when taken over all possible values of the variable

ex·pec·to·rant \ik-ˈspek-t(ə-)rənt\ *n* (1782) **:** an agent that promotes the discharge or expulsion of mucus from the respiratory tract; *broadly* **:** an antitussive agent — **expectorant** *adj*

ex·pec·to·rate \-tə-ˌrāt\ *vb* **-rat·ed; -rat·ing** [L *expectoratus,* pp. of *expectorare* to banish from the mind (taken to mean lit. "to expel from the chest"), fr. *ex-* + *pector-, pectus* breast, soul — more at PECTORAL] *vt* (1601) **1 :** to eject from the throat or lungs by coughing or hawking and spitting **2 :** SPIT ∼ *vi* **1 :** to discharge matter from the throat or lungs by coughing or hawking and spitting **2 :** SPIT — **ex·pec·to·ra·tion** \-ˌspek-tə-ˈrā-shən\ *n*

ex·pe·di·ence \ik-ˈspē-dē-ən(t)s\ *n* (1548) **:** EXPEDIENCY

ex·pe·di·en·cy \-dē-ən(t)-sē\ *n, pl* **-cies** (1597) **1 :** the quality or state of being suited to the end in view **:** SUITABILITY, FITNESS **2** *obs* **a :** HASTE, DISPATCH **b :** an enterprise requiring haste or caution **3 :** adherence to expedient means and methods ⟨put more emphasis on ∼ than on principle —W. H. Jones⟩ **4 :** a means of achieving a particular end **:** EXPEDIENT — **ex·pe·di·en·tial** \-ˌspē-dē-ˈen-chəl\ *adj*

[1]**ex·pe·di·ent** \ik-ˈspē-dē-ənt\ *adj* [ME, fr. AF or L; AF, fr. L *expedient-, expendiens,* prp. of *expedire* to extricate, prepare, be useful, fr. *ex-* + *ped-, pes* foot — more at FOOT] (14c) **1 :** suitable for achieving a particular end in a given circumstance **2 :** characterized by concern with what is opportune; *esp* **:** governed by self-interest — **ex·pe·di·ent·ly** *adv*

syn EXPEDIENT, POLITIC, ADVISABLE mean dictated by practical or prudent motives. EXPEDIENT usu. implies what is immediately advantageous without regard for ethics or consistent principles ⟨a politically *expedient* decision⟩. POLITIC stresses judiciousness and tactical value but usu. implies some lack of candor or sincerity ⟨a *politic* show of interest⟩. ADVISABLE applies to what is practical, prudent, or advantageous but lacks the derogatory implication of EXPEDIENT and POLITIC ⟨sometimes it's *advisable* to say nothing⟩.

[2]**expedient** *n* (1630) **:** something expedient **:** a temporary means to an end ***syn*** see RESOURCE

ex·pe·dite \ˈek-spə-ˌdīt\ *vt* **-dit·ed; -dit·ing** [L *expeditus,* pp. of *expedire*] (15c) **1 :** to execute promptly **2 :** to accelerate the process or progress of **:** speed up **3 :** ISSUE, DISPATCH

ex·pe·dit·er *also* **ex·pe·di·tor** \-ˌdī-tər\ *n* (1891) **:** one that expedites; *specif* **:** one employed to ensure efficient movement of goods or supplies in a business

ex·pe·di·tion \ˌek-spə-ˈdi-shən\ *n* (15c) **1 a :** a journey or excursion undertaken for a specific purpose **b :** the group of persons making such a journey **2 :** efficient promptness **:** SPEED **3 :** a sending or setting forth ***syn*** see HASTE — **ex·pe·di·tion·er** \-sh(ə-)nər\ *n*

ex·pe·di·tion·ary \-ˈdi-shə-ˌner-ē\ *adj* (1817) **:** of, relating to, or being an expedition; *also* **:** sent on military service abroad ⟨an ∼ force⟩

ex·pe·di·tious \ˌek-spə-ˈdi-shəs\ *adj* (1599) **:** marked by or acting with prompt efficiency ***syn*** see FAST — **ex·pe·di·tious·ly** *adv* — **ex·pe·di·tious·ness** *n*

ex·pel \ik-ˈspel\ *vt* **ex·pelled; ex·pel·ling** [ME *expellen,* fr. L *expellere,* fr. *ex-* + *pellere* to drive — more at FELT] (14c) **1 :** to force out **:** EJECT ⟨*expelled* the smoke from her lungs⟩ **2 :** to force to leave (as a place or organization) by official action **:** take away rights or privileges of membership ⟨*expelled* from college⟩ ***syn*** see EJECT — **ex·pel·la·ble** \-ˈspe-lə-bəl\ *adj*

ex·pel·lee \ˌek-ˌspe-ˈlē, ik-\ *n* (1888) **:** a person who is expelled esp. from a native or adopted country

ex·pend \ik-ˈspend\ *vt* [ME, fr. L *expendere* to weigh out, expend, fr. *ex-* + *pendere* to weigh — more at SPIN] (15c) **1 :** to pay out **:** SPEND ⟨the social services upon which public revenue is ∼*ed* —J. A. Hobson⟩ **2 :** to make use of for a specific purpose **:** UTILIZE ⟨projects on which they ∼*ed* great energy⟩; *also* **:** USE UP — **ex·pend·er** *n*

[1]**ex·pend·able** \ik-ˈspen-də-bəl\ *adj* (1805) **:** that may be expended: as **a :** normally used up or consumed in service ⟨∼ supplies like pencils and paper⟩ **b :** more easily or economically replaced than rescued, salvaged, or protected — **ex·pend·abil·i·ty** \-ˌspen-də-ˈbi-lə-tē\ *n*

[2]**expendable** *n* (1942) **:** one that is expendable — usu. used in pl.

ex·pen·di·ture \ik-ˈspen-di-chər, -də-ˌchu̇r, -də-ˌt(y)u̇r\ *n* [irreg. fr. *expend*] (1769) **1 :** the act or process of expending ⟨an ∼ of energy⟩ **2 :** something expended **:** DISBURSEMENT, EXPENSE ⟨income should exceed ∼*s*⟩

[1]**ex·pense** \ik-ˈspen(t)s\ *n* [ME, fr. AF or LL; AF, fr. LL *expensa,* fr. L, fem. of *expensus,* pp. of *expendere*] (14c) **1** *archaic* **:** the act or an instance of expending **:** EXPENDITURE **2 a :** something expended to secure a benefit or bring about a result **b :** financial burden or outlay **:** COST ⟨built the monument at their own ∼⟩ **c :** an item of business outlay chargeable against revenue for a specific period **3 :** a cause or occasion of expenditure ⟨an estate is a great ∼⟩ **4 :** a loss, detriment, or embarrassment that results from some action or gain **:** SACRIFICE ⟨everyone had a good laugh at my ∼⟩ — usu. used in the phrase *at the expense of* ⟨develop a boy's physique at the ∼ of his intelligence —Bertrand Russell⟩

[2]**expense** *vt* **ex·pensed; ex·pens·ing** (ca. 1909) **1 :** to charge with expenses **2 a :** to charge to an expense account **b :** to write off as an expense

expense account *n* (1922) **:** an account of expenses reimbursable to an employee; *also* **:** the right of charging expenses to such an account

ex·pen·sive \ik-ˈspen(t)-siv\ *adj* (ca. 1610) **1 :** involving high cost or sacrifice ⟨an ∼ hobby⟩ **2 a :** commanding a high price and esp. one that is not based on intrinsic worth or is beyond a prospective buyer's means **b :** characterized by high prices ⟨∼ shops⟩ — **ex·pen·sive·ly** *adv* — **ex·pen·sive·ness** *n*

[1]**ex·pe·ri·ence** \ik-ˈspir-ē-ən(t)s\ *n* [ME, fr. AF, fr. L *experientia* act of trying, fr. *experient-, experiens,* prp. of *experiri* to try, fr. *ex-* + *-periri* (akin to *periculum* attempt) — more at FEAR] (14c) **1 a :** direct observation of or participation in events as a basis of knowledge **b :** the fact or state of having been affected by or gained knowledge through direct observation or participation **2 a :** practical knowledge, skill, or practice derived from direct observation of or participation in events or in a particular activity **b :** the length of such participation ⟨has 10 years' ∼ in the job⟩ **3 a :** the conscious events that make up an individual life **b :** the events that make up the conscious past of a community or nation or humankind generally **4 :** something personally encountered, undergone, or lived through **5 :** the act or process of directly perceiving events or reality

[2]**experience** *vt* **-enced; -enc·ing** (1580) **1 :** to learn by experience ⟨I have *experienced* that a landscape and the sky unfold the deepest beauty —Nathaniel Hawthorne⟩ **2 :** to have experience of **:** UNDERGO ⟨*experienced* severe hardships as a child⟩

ex·pe·ri·enced \-ən(t)st\ *adj* (1567) **:** made skillful or wise through experience **:** PRACTICED ⟨an ∼ driver⟩

ex·pe·ri·en·tial \ik-ˌspir-ē-ˈen(t)-shəl\ *adj* (1658) **:** relating to, derived from, or providing experience **:** EMPIRICAL ⟨∼ knowledge⟩ ⟨∼ lessons⟩ — **ex·pe·ri·en·tial·ly** \-ˈen(t)-sh(ə-)lē\ *adv*

[1]**ex·per·i·ment** \ik-ˈsper-ə-mənt *also* -ˈspir-\ *n* [ME, fr. AF *esperiment,* fr. L *experimentum,* fr. *experiri*] (14c) **1 a :** TEST, TRIAL ⟨make another ∼ of his suspicion —Shak.⟩ **b :** a tentative procedure or policy **c :** an operation or procedure carried out under controlled conditions in order to discover an unknown effect or law, to test or establish a hypothesis, or to illustrate a known law **2** *obs* **:** EXPERIENCE **3 :** the process of testing **:** EXPERIMENTATION

[2]**ex·per·i·ment** \-ˌment\ *vi* (1787) **:** to carry out experiments **:** try out a new procedure, idea, or activity — **ex·per·i·men·ta·tion** \ik-ˌsper-ə-mən-ˈtā-shən, -ˌmen- *also* -ˌspir-\ *n* — **ex·per·i·ment·er** \-ˈsper-ə-ˌmen-tər *also* -ˈspir-\ *n*

ex·per·i·men·tal \ik-ˌsper-ə-ˈmen-tᵊl *also* -ˌspir-\ *adj* (15c) **1 :** of, relating to, or based on experience or experiment **2 a :** serving the ends of or used as a means of experimentation ⟨an ∼ school⟩ **b :** relating to or having the characteristics of experiment **:** TENTATIVE ⟨still in the ∼ stage⟩ — **ex·per·i·men·tal·ly** \-tᵊl-ē\ *adv*

ex·per·i·men·tal·ism \-tə-ˌli-zəm\ *n* (ca. 1834) **:** reliance on or advocacy of experimental or empirical principles and procedures; *specif* **:** INSTRUMENTALISM

ex·per·i·men·tal·ist \-tə-ləst\ *n* (1762) **:** one who experiments; *specif* **:** a person conducting scientific experiments

experiment station *n* (1874) **:** an establishment for scientific research (as in agriculture) where experiments are carried out, studies of practical application are made, and information is disseminated

[1]**ex·pert** \ˈek-ˌspərt, ik-ˈ\ *adj* [ME, fr. AF & L; AF, fr. L *expertus,* fr. pp. of *experiri*] (14c) **1** *obs* **:** EXPERIENCED **2 :** having, involving, or displaying special skill or knowledge derived from training or experience ***syn*** see PROFICIENT — **ex·pert·ly** *adv* — **ex·pert·ness** *n*

[2]**ex·pert** \ˈek-ˌspərt\ *n* [MF, fr. *expert,* adj.] (1535) **:** one with the special skill or knowledge representing mastery of a particular subject

[3]**ex·pert** \ˈek-ˌspərt\ *vi* (ca. 1889) **:** to serve as an expert

ex·per·tise \ˌek-(ˌ)spər-ˈtēz, -ˈtēs\ *n* [F, fr. MF, expertness, fr. *expert*] (1868) **1 :** expert opinion or commentary **2 :** the skill of an expert

ex·pert·ism \ˈek-ˌspər-ˌti-zəm\ *n* (1886) **:** EXPERTISE 2

ex·pert·ize \ˈek-spər-ˌtīz\ *vb* **-ized; -iz·ing** *vi* (1889) **:** to give a professional opinion usu. after careful study ∼ *vt* **:** to examine and give expert judgment on

expert system *n* (1977) **:** computer software that attempts to mimic the reasoning of a human specialist

ex·pi·ate \ˈek-spē-ˌāt\ *vb* **-at·ed; -at·ing** [L *expiatus,* pp. of *expiare* to atone for, fr. *ex-* + *piare* to atone for, appease, fr. *pius* faithful, pious] *vt* (ca. 1500) **1** *obs* **:** to put an end to **2 a :** to extinguish the guilt incurred by **b :** to make amends for ⟨permission to ∼ their offences by their assiduous labours —Francis Bacon⟩ ∼ *vi* **:** to make expiation — **ex·pi·a·ble** \ˈek-spē-ə-bəl\ *adj* — **ex·pi·a·tor** \-spē-ˌā-tər\ *n*

ex·pi·a·tion \ˌek-spē-ˈā-shən\ *n* (15c) **1 :** the act of making atonement **2 :** the means by which atonement is made

ex·pi·a·to·ry \ˈek-spē-ə-ˌtȯr-ē\ *adj* (15c) **:** serving to expiate

ex·pi·ra·tion \ˌek-spə-ˈrā-shən\ *n* (1526) **1 a :** the last emission of breath **:** DEATH **b (1) :** the act or process of releasing air from the lungs through the nose or mouth **:** EXHALATION **(2) :** the escape of carbon dioxide from the body protoplasm (as through the blood and lungs or by diffusion) **2 :** the fact of coming to an end or the point at which something ends **:** TERMINATION

expiration date *n* (ca. 1946) **1 :** the date after which something (as a credit card) is no longer in effect **2 :** the date after which a product (as food or medicine) should not be sold because of an expected decline in quality or effectiveness

ex·pi·ra·to·ry \ik-ˈspī-rə-ˌtȯr-ē, ek-ˈ; ˈek-sp(ə-)rə-\ *adj* (ca. 1847) **:** of, relating to, or employed in the expiration of air from the lungs

ex·pire \ik-ˈspī(-ə)r, *oftenest for vi 3 and vt 2* ek-\ *vb* **ex·pired; ex·pir·ing** [ME, fr. MF or L; AF *espirer* to breathe out, fr. L *exspirare,* fr. *ex-* + *spirare* to breathe] *vi* (15c) **1 :** to breathe one's last breath **:** DIE **2 :** to come to an end **3 :** to emit the breath ∼ *vt* **1** *obs* **:** CONCLUDE **2 :** to breathe out from or as if from the lungs **3** *archaic* **:** EMIT

ex·pi·ry \ik-ˈspī(-ə)r-ē, ˈek-spə-rē\ *n, pl* **-ries** (1752) **:** EXPIRATION: as **a :** exhalation of breath **b :** DEATH **c :** TERMINATION; *esp* **:** the termination of a time or period fixed by law, contract, or agreement

ex·plain \ik-ˈsplān\ *vb* [ME *explanen,* fr. L *explanare,* lit., to make level, fr. *ex-* + *planus* level, flat — more at FLOOR] *vt* (15c) **1 a :** to make known ⟨∼ the secret of your success⟩ **b :** to make plain or understandable ⟨footnotes that ∼ the terms⟩ **2 :** to give the reason for or cause of ⟨unable to ∼ his strange conduct⟩ **3 :** to show the logical development or relationships of ⟨∼*ed* the new theory⟩ ∼ *vi* **:** to make something plain or understandable ⟨a report that suggests rather than ∼*s*⟩ — **ex·plain·able** \-ˈsplā-nə-bəl\ *adj* — **ex·plain·er** *n* — **explain oneself :** to clarify one's statements or the reasons for one's conduct

syn EXPLAIN, EXPOUND, EXPLICATE, ELUCIDATE, INTERPRET mean to make something clear or understandable. EXPLAIN implies a making plain or intelligible what is not immediately obvious or entirely known ⟨*explain* the rules⟩. EXPOUND implies a careful often elaborate explanation ⟨*expounding* a scientific theory⟩. EXPLICATE adds the idea of a developed or detailed analysis ⟨*explicate* a poem⟩. ELUCIDATE stresses the throwing of light upon as by offering details or motives previously unclear or only implicit ⟨*elucidate* an obscure passage⟩. INTERPRET adds to EXPLAIN the need for imagination or sympathy or special knowledge in dealing with something ⟨*interpreting* a work of art⟩.

explain away *vt* (1704) **1** : to get rid of by or as if by explanation **2** : to minimize the significance of by or as if by explanation ⟨explains his faults, but does not try to *explain* them *away* —M. K. Spears⟩
ex·pla·na·tion \ˌek-splə-ˈnā-shən\ *n* (14c) **1** : the act or process of explaining **2** : something that explains ⟨gave no ~⟩
ex·plan·a·tive \ik-ˈspla-nə-tiv\ *adj* (ca. 1616) : EXPLANATORY — **ex·plan·a·tive·ly** *adv*
ex·plan·a·to·ry \ik-ˈspla-nə-ˌtȯr-ē\ *adj* (1618) : serving to explain ⟨~ notes⟩ — **ex·plan·a·to·ri·ly** \-ˌspla-nə-ˈtȯr-ə-lē\ *adv*
[1]**ex·plant** \(ˌ)ek-ˈsplant\ *vt* [*ex-* + *-plant* (as in *implant*)] (1915) : to remove (living tissue) esp. to a medium for tissue culture — **ex·plan·ta·tion** \ˌek-ˌsplan-ˈtā-shən\ *n*
[2]**ex·plant** \ˈek-ˌsplant\ *n* (1917) : living tissue removed from an organism and placed in a medium for tissue culture
[1]**ex·ple·tive** \ˈek-splə-tiv\ *n* (1612) **1 a** : a syllable, word, or phrase inserted to fill a vacancy (as in a sentence or a metrical line) without adding to the sense; *esp* : a word (as *it* in "make it clear which you prefer") that occupies the position of the subject or object of a verb in normal English word order and anticipates a subsequent word or phrase that supplies the needed meaningful content **b** : an exclamatory word or phrase; *esp* : one that is obscene or profane **2** : one that serves to fill out or as a filling
[2]**expletive** *adj* [LL *expletivus,* fr. L *expletus,* pp. of *explēre* to fill out, fr. *ex-* + *plēre* to fill — more at FULL] (1666) **1** : serving to fill up ⟨~ phrases⟩ **2** : marked by the use of expletives
ex·ple·to·ry \ˈek-splə-ˌtȯr-ē\ *adj* (1672) : EXPLETIVE
ex·pli·ca·ble \ek-ˈspli-kə-bəl, ˈek-(ˌ)splik-\ *adj* (1556) : capable of being explained — **ex·pli·ca·bly** \-blē\ *adv*
ex·pli·cate \ˈek-splə-ˌkāt\ *vt* **-cat·ed; -cat·ing** [L *explicatus,* pp. of *explicare,* lit., to unfold, fr. *ex-* + *plicare* to fold — more at PLY] (1531) **1** : to give a detailed explanation of **2** : to develop the implications of : analyze logically ***syn*** see EXPLAIN — **ex·pli·ca·tion** \ˌek-splə-ˈkā-shən\ *n* — **ex·pli·ca·tor** \ˈek-splə-ˌkā-tər\ *n*
ex·pli·ca·tion de texte \ek-splē-kä-syōⁿ-də-ˈtekst\ *n, pl* **explications de texte** *same*\ [F, lit., explanation of text] (1935) : a method of literary criticism involving a detailed analysis of a work
ex·pli·ca·tive \ek-ˈspli-kə-tiv, ˈek-splə-ˌkāt-\ *adj* (1649) : serving to explicate; *specif* : serving to explain logically what is contained in the subject ⟨an ~ proposition⟩ — **ex·pli·ca·tive·ly** *adv*
ex·pli·ca·to·ry \ek-ˈspli-kə-ˌtȯr-ē, ˈek-(ˌ)spli-\ *adj* (1625) : EXPLICATIVE
ex·plic·it \ik-ˈspli-sət\ *adj* [F or ML; F *explicite,* fr. ML *explicitus,* fr. L, pp. of *explicare*] (1607) **1 a** : fully revealed or expressed without vagueness, implication, or ambiguity : leaving no question as to meaning or intent ⟨~ instructions⟩ **b** : open in the depiction of nudity or sexuality ⟨~ books and films⟩ **2** : fully developed or formulated ⟨an ~ plan⟩ ⟨an ~ notion of our objective⟩ **3** : unambiguous in expression ⟨was very ~ on how we are to behave⟩ **4** *of a mathematical function* : defined by an expression containing only independent variables — compare IMPLICIT 1c — **ex·plic·it·ly** *adv* — **ex·plic·it·ness** *n*
syn EXPLICIT, DEFINITE, EXPRESS, SPECIFIC mean perfectly clear in meaning. EXPLICIT implies such verbal plainness and distinctness that there is no need for inference and no room for difficulty in understanding ⟨*explicit* instructions⟩. DEFINITE stresses precise, clear statement or arrangement that leaves no doubt or indecision ⟨the law is *definite* in such cases⟩. EXPRESS implies both explicitness and direct and positive utterance ⟨her *express* wishes⟩. SPECIFIC applies to what is precisely and fully treated in detail or particular ⟨two *specific* criticisms⟩.
ex·plode \ik-ˈsplōd\ *vb* **ex·plod·ed; ex·plod·ing** [L *explodere* to drive off the stage by clapping, fr. *ex-* + *plaudere* to clap] *vt* (1605) **1** *archaic* : to drive from the stage by noisy disapproval **2** : to bring into disrepute or discredit ⟨~ a theory⟩ **3** : to cause to explode or burst noisily ⟨~ a bomb⟩ ~ *vi* **1** : to burst forth with sudden violence or noise from internal energy: as **a** : to undergo a rapid chemical or nuclear reaction with the production of noise, heat, and violent expansion of gases ⟨dynamite ~*s*⟩ **b** : to burst violently as a result of pressure from within **2 a** : to give forth a sudden strong and noisy outburst of emotion ⟨*exploded* in anger⟩ **b** : to move with sudden speed and force ⟨*exploded* from the starting gate⟩ **3** : to increase rapidly ⟨the population of the city *exploded*⟩ **4** : to suggest an explosion (as in appearance or effect) ⟨shrubs *exploded* with blossoms⟩ — **ex·plod·er** *n*
ex·plod·ed *adj* (1944) : showing the parts separated but in correct relationship to each other ⟨an ~ view of a carburetor⟩
[1]**ex·ploit** \ˈek-ˌsplȯit, ik-ˈ\ *n* [ME *espleit, expleit, exploit* furtherance, outcome, fr. AF, fr. L *explicitum,* neut. of *explicitus,* pp.] (ca. 1538) : DEED, ACT; *esp* : a notable or heroic act ***syn*** see FEAT
[2]**ex·ploit** \ik-ˈsplȯit, ˈek-ˌ\ *vt* (1838) **1** : to make productive use of : UTILIZE ⟨~*ing* your talents⟩ ⟨~ your opponent's weakness⟩ **2** : to make use of meanly or unfairly for one's own advantage ⟨~*ing* migrant farm workers⟩ — **ex·ploit·abil·i·ty** \ik-ˌsplȯi-tə-ˈbi-lə-tē\ *n* — **ex·ploit·able** \-ˈsplȯi-tə-bəl\ *adj* — **ex·ploit·er** *n*
ex·ploi·ta·tion \ˌek-ˌsplȯi-ˈtā-shən\ *n* (1803) : an act or instance of exploiting ⟨~ of natural resources⟩ ⟨~ of immigrant laborers⟩ ⟨clever ~ of the system⟩
ex·ploit·ative \ik-ˈsplȯi-tə-tiv, ek-ˌsplȯi-\ *adj* (1885) : exploiting or tending to exploit; *esp* : unfairly or cynically using another person or group for profit or advantage ⟨~ terms of employment⟩ ⟨an ~ film⟩ — **ex·ploit·ative·ly** *adv*
ex·ploit·ive \ik-ˈsplȯi-tiv\ *adj* (1921) : EXPLOITATIVE
ex·plo·ra·tion \ˌek-splə-ˈrā-shən, -ˌsplȯ-\ *n* (1537) : the act or an instance of exploring — **ex·plo·ra·tion·al** \-shnəl, -shə-nᵊl\ *adj*
ex·plor·ative \ik-ˈsplȯr-ə-tiv\ *adj* (1738) : EXPLORATORY — **ex·plor·ative·ly** *adv*
ex·plor·ato·ry \-ə-ˌtȯr-ē\ *adj* (1620) : of, relating to, or being exploration ⟨~ surgery⟩ ⟨~ drilling for oil⟩
ex·plore \ik-ˈsplȯr\ *vb* **ex·plored; ex·plor·ing** [L *explorare,* fr. *ex-* + *plorare* to cry out] *vt* (1585) **1 a** : to investigate, study, or analyze : look into ⟨~ the relationship between social class and learning ability⟩ — sometimes used with indirect questions ⟨to ~ where ethical issues arise —R. T. Blackburn⟩ **b** : to become familiar with by testing or experimenting ⟨~ new cuisines⟩ **2** : to travel over (new territory) for adventure or discovery **3** : to examine esp. for diagnostic purposes ⟨~ the wound⟩ ~ *vi* : to make or conduct a systematic search ⟨~ for oil⟩
ex·plor·er \ik-ˈsplȯr-ər\ *n* (1602) **1** : one that explores; *esp* : a person who travels in search of geographical or scientific information **2** *cap* : a member of a coed scouting program of the Boy Scouts of America for young people ages 14 to 20 focusing on career awareness
ex·plo·sion \ik-ˈsplō-zhən\ *n* [L *explosion-, explosio* act of driving off by clapping, fr. *explodere*] (1667) **1** : the act or an instance of exploding ⟨injured in a laboratory ~⟩ **2** : a large-scale, rapid, or spectacular expansion or bursting out or forth ⟨the ~ of suburbia⟩ ⟨an ~ of red hair⟩ **3** : the release of occluded breath that occurs in one kind of articulation of stop consonants
[1]**ex·plo·sive** \ik-ˈsplō-siv, -ziv\ *adj* (1667) **1 a** : relating to, characterized by, or operated by explosion ⟨an ~ hatch⟩ **b** : resulting from or as if from an explosion ⟨~ population growth⟩ **2 a** : tending to explode ⟨an ~ person⟩ **b** : likely to erupt in or produce hostile reaction or violence ⟨an ~ ghetto situation⟩ — **ex·plo·sive·ly** *adv* — **ex·plo·sive·ness** *n*
[2]**explosive** *n* (1849) **1** : an explosive substance **2** : a consonant characterized by explosion in its articulation when it occurs in certain environments : STOP
ex·po \ˈek-(ˌ)spō\ *n, pl* **expos** (1913) : EXPOSITION 3
ex·po·nent \ik-ˈspō-nənt, ˈek-ˌ\ *n* [L *exponent-, exponens,* prp. of *exponere* — more at EXPOSE] (1706) **1** : a symbol written above and to the right of a mathematical expression to indicate the operation of raising to a power **2 a** : one that expounds or interprets **b** : one that champions, practices, or exemplifies
ex·po·nen·tial \ˌek-spə-ˈnen-chəl\ *adj* (1704) **1** : of or relating to an exponent **2** : involving a variable in an exponent ⟨10^x is an ~ expression⟩ **3** : expressible or approximately expressible by an exponential function; *esp* : characterized by or being an extremely rapid increase (as in size or extent) ⟨an ~ growth rate⟩ — **ex·po·nen·tial·ly** \-ˈnench-(ə-)lē\ *adv*
exponential function *n* (1879) : a mathematical function in which an independent variable appears in one of the exponents — called also *exponential*
ex·po·nen·ti·a·tion \ˌek-spə-ˌnen(t)-shē-ˈā-shən\ *n* (1903) : the mathematical operation of raising a quantity to a power — called also *involution*
[1]**ex·port** \ek-ˈspȯrt, ˈek-ˌ\ *vb* [ME, fr. L *exportare,* fr. *ex-* + *portare* to carry — more at FARE] *vt* (15c) **1** : to carry away : REMOVE **2** : to carry or send (as a commodity) to some other place (as another country) ~ *vi* : to export something abroad — **ex·port·abil·i·ty** \(ˌ)ek-ˌspȯr-tə-ˈbi-lə-tē\ *n* — **ex·port·able** \ek-ˈspȯr-tə-bəl, ˈek-ˌ\ *adj*
[2]**ex·port** \ˈek-ˌspȯrt\ *n* (1671) **1** : something exported; *specif* : a commodity conveyed from one country or region to another for purposes of trade **2** : the act of exporting : EXPORTATION ⟨the ~ of wheat⟩
[3]**ex·port** \ˈek-ˌ\ *adj* (1795) : of or relating to exportation or exports ⟨~ duties⟩
ex·por·ta·tion \ˌek-ˌspȯr-ˈtā-shən, -spər-\ *n* (1601) : the act of exporting; *also* : a commodity exported
ex·port·er \ek-ˈspȯr-tər, ˈek-ˌ\ *n* (1623) : one that exports; *specif* : a wholesaler who sells to merchants or industrial consumers in foreign countries
ex·pose \ik-ˈspōz\ *vt* **ex·posed; ex·pos·ing** [ME, fr. AF *exposer,* fr. L *exponere* to set forth, explain (perf. indic. *exposui*), fr. *ex-* + *ponere* to put, place — more at POSITION] (15c) **1 a** : to deprive of shelter, protection, or care : subject to risk from a harmful action or condition ⟨~ troops needlessly⟩ ⟨has not yet been *exposed* to measles⟩ **b** : to submit or make accessible to a particular action or influence ⟨~ children to good books⟩; *esp* : to subject (a sensitive photographic film, plate, or paper) to radiant energy **c** : to abandon (an infant) esp. by leaving in the open **2 a** : to make known : bring to light (as something shameful) **b** : to disclose the faults or crimes of ⟨~ a murderer⟩ **3** : to cause to be visible or open to view : DISPLAY: as **a** : to offer publicly for sale **b** : to exhibit for public veneration **c** : to reveal the face of (a playing card) or the cards of (a player's hand) **d** : to engage in indecent exposure of (oneself) ***syn*** see SHOW — **ex·pos·er** *n*
ex·po·sé *also* **ex·po·se** \ˌek-spō-ˈzā, -spə-\ *n* [F *exposé,* fr. pp. of *exposer*] (1803) **1** : a formal statement of facts **2** : an exposure of something discreditable ⟨a newspaper ~ of government corruption⟩
ex·posed \ik-ˈspōzd\ *adj* (ca. 1623) **1** : open to view **2** : not shielded or protected; *also* : not insulated ⟨an ~ electric wire⟩ ***syn*** see LIABLE
ex·pos·it \ik-ˈspä-zət\ *vt* [L *expositus,* pp. of *exponere*] (1882) : EXPOUND
ex·po·si·tion \ˌek-spə-ˈzi-shən\ *n* (14c) **1** : a setting forth of the meaning or purpose (as of a writing) **2 a** : discourse or an example of it designed to convey information or explain what is difficult to understand **b** (1) : the first part of a musical composition in sonata form in which the thematic material of the movement is presented (2) : the opening section of a fugue **3** : a public exhibition or show — **ex·po·si·tion·al** \-ˈzish-nəl, -ˈzi-shə-nᵊl\ *adj*
ex·pos·i·tive \ik-ˈspä-zə-tiv\ *adj* (15c) : DESCRIPTIVE, EXPOSITORY
ex·pos·i·tor \-zə-tər\ *n* [ME *expositour,* fr. AF *expositur,* fr. LL *expositor,* fr. L *exponere*] (14c) : a person who explains : COMMENTATOR
ex·pos·i·to·ry \-zə-ˌtȯr-ē\ *adj* (1628) : of, relating to, or containing exposition ⟨~ writing⟩
[1]**ex post fac·to** \ˌeks-ˌpōs(t)-ˈfak-(ˌ)tō\ *adv* [LL, lit., from a thing done afterward] (1621) : after the fact : RETROACTIVELY
[2]**ex post facto** *adj* (1787) : done, made, or formulated after the fact : RETROACTIVE ⟨*ex post facto* approval⟩ ⟨*ex post facto* laws⟩
ex·pos·tu·late \ik-ˈspäs-chə-ˌlāt\ *vb* [L *expostulatus,* pp. of *expostulare* to demand, dispute, fr. *ex-* + *postulare* to ask for — more at POSTULATE] *vt* (1573) *obs* : DISCUSS, EXAMINE ~ *vi* : to reason earnestly with a person for purposes of dissuasion or remonstrance
ex·pos·tu·la·tion \ik-ˌspäs-chə-ˈlā-shən\ *n* (1540) : an act or instance of expostulating — **ex·pos·tu·la·to·ry** \-ˈspäs-chə-lə-ˌtȯr-ē\ *adj*
ex·po·sure \ik-ˈspō-zhər\ *n* (1605) **1** : the fact or condition of being exposed: as **a** : the condition of being presented to view or made

known ⟨a politician seeks a lot of ~⟩ **b :** the condition of being unprotected esp. from severe weather ⟨died of ~⟩ **c :** the condition of being subject to some effect or influence ⟨risk ~ to the flu⟩ **d :** the condition of being at risk of financial loss ⟨minimizes your ~ to market fluctuations⟩; *also* : an amount at risk **2 :** the act or an instance of exposing: as **a :** disclosure of something secret ⟨tried to prevent ~ of their past⟩ **b :** the treating of sensitized material (as film) to controlled amounts of radiant energy; *also* : the amount of such energy or length of such treatment ⟨a 3-second ~⟩ **3 a :** the manner of being exposed **b :** the position (as of a house) with respect to weather influences or compass points ⟨a room with a southern ~⟩ **4 :** a piece or section of sensitized material (as film) on which an exposure is or can be made ⟨36 ~*s* per roll⟩

exposure meter *n* (1891) : a device for indicating correct photographic exposure under varying conditions of illumination

ex·pound \ik-ˈspau̇nd\ *vb* [ME, fr. AF *espundre, expondre,* fr. L *exponere* to explain — more at EXPOSE] *vt* (14c) **1 a :** to set forth : STATE **b :** to defend with argument **2 :** to explain by setting forth in careful and often elaborate detail ⟨~ a law⟩ ~ *vi* : to make a statement : COMMENT ***syn*** see EXPLAIN — **ex·pound·er** *n*

[1]**ex·press** \ik-ˈspres\ *adj* [ME, fr. AF *expres,* fr. L *expressus,* pp. of *exprimere* to press out, express, fr. *ex-* + *premere* to press — more at PRESS] (14c) **1 a :** directly, firmly, and explicitly stated ⟨my ~ orders⟩ **b :** EXACT, PRECISE **2 a :** designed for or adapted to its purpose **b :** of a particular sort : SPECIFIC ⟨for that ~ purpose⟩ **3 a :** traveling at high speed; *specif* : traveling with few or no stops along the way ⟨~ train⟩ **b :** adapted or suitable for travel at high speed ⟨an ~ highway⟩ **c** *Brit* : designated to be delivered without delay by special messenger ***syn*** see EXPLICIT

[2]**express** *adv* (14c) **1** *obs* : EXPRESSLY **2 :** by express ⟨delivered ~⟩

[3]**express** *n* (1619) **1 a** *Brit* : a messenger sent on a special errand **b** *Brit* : a dispatch conveyed by a special messenger **c (1) :** a system for the prompt and safe transportation of parcels, money, or goods at rates higher than standard freight charges **(2) :** a company operating such a merchandise freight service **d** *Brit* : SPECIAL DELIVERY **2 :** an express vehicle

[4]**express** *vt* [ME, fr. AF & L; AF *espresser,* fr. *expres,* adj.] (14c) **1 a :** DELINEATE, DEPICT **b :** to represent in words : STATE **c :** to give or convey a true impression of : SHOW, REFLECT **d :** to make known the opinions or feelings of (oneself) **e :** to give expression to the artistic or creative impulses or abilities of (oneself) **f :** to represent by a sign or symbol : SYMBOLIZE **2 a :** to force out (as the juice of a fruit) by pressure **b :** to subject to pressure so as to extract something **3 :** to send by express **4 :** to cause (a gene) to manifest its effects in the phenotype; *also* : to manifest or produce (a character, molecule, or effect) by a genetic process — **ex·press·er** *n* — **ex·press·ible** \-ə-bəl\ *adj*

syn EXPRESS, VENT, UTTER, VOICE, BROACH, AIR mean to make known what one thinks or feels. EXPRESS suggests an impulse to reveal in words, gestures, actions, or what one creates or produces ⟨*expressed* her feelings in music⟩. VENT stresses a strong inner compulsion to express esp. in words ⟨a tirade *venting* his frustration⟩. UTTER implies the use of the voice not necessarily in articulate speech ⟨*utter* a groan⟩. VOICE does not necessarily imply vocal utterance but does imply expression or formulation in words ⟨an editorial *voicing* their concerns⟩. BROACH adds the implication of disclosing for the first time something long thought over or reserved for a suitable occasion ⟨*broached* the subject of a divorce⟩. AIR implies an exposing or parading of one's views often in order to gain relief or sympathy or attention ⟨publicly *airing* their differences⟩.

ex·press·age \ik-ˈspre-sij\ *n* (1857) : a carrying of parcels by express; *also* : a charge for such carrying

ex·pres·sion \ik-ˈspre-shən\ *n* (15c) **1 a :** an act, process, or instance of representing in a medium (as words) : UTTERANCE ⟨freedom of ~⟩ **b (1) :** something that manifests, embodies, or symbolizes something else ⟨this gift is an ~ of my admiration for you⟩ **(2) :** a significant word or phrase **(3) :** a mathematical or logical symbol or a meaningful combination of symbols **(4) :** the detectable effect of a gene; *also* : EXPRESSIVITY 1 **2 a :** a mode, means, or use of significant representation or symbolism; *esp* : felicitous or vivid indication or depiction of mood or sentiment ⟨read the poem with ~⟩ **b (1) :** the quality or fact of being expressive **(2) :** facial aspect or vocal intonation as indicative of feeling **3 :** an act or product of pressing out — **ex·pres·sion·al** \-ˈspresh-nəl, -ˈspre-shə-nᵊl\ *adj*

ex·pres·sion·ism \ik-ˈspre-shə-ˌni-zəm\ *n, often cap* (ca. 1901) : a theory or practice in art of seeking to depict the subjective emotions and responses that objects and events arouse in the artist — **ex·pres·sion·ist** \-ˈspre-shə-nist\ *n or adj, often cap* — **ex·pres·sion·is·tic** \-ˌspre-shə-ˈnis-tik\ *adj* — **ex·pres·sion·is·ti·cal·ly** \-ti-k(ə-)lē\ *adv*

ex·pres·sion·less \ik-ˈspre-shən-ləs\ *adj* (1831) : lacking expression ⟨an ~ face⟩ — **ex·pres·sion·less·ly** *adv* — **ex·pres·sion·less·ness** *n*

ex·pres·sive \ik-ˈspre-siv\ *adj* (15c) **1 :** of or relating to expression ⟨the ~ function of language⟩ **2 :** serving to express, utter, or represent ⟨foul and novel terms ~ of rage —H. G. Wells⟩ **3 :** effectively conveying meaning or feeling ⟨an ~ silence⟩ ⟨~ line drawings⟩ — **ex·pres·sive·ly** *adv* — **ex·pres·sive·ness** *n*

ex·pres·siv·i·ty \ˌek-ˌspre-ˈsi-və-tē\ *n, pl* **-ties** (1934) **1 :** the relative capacity of a gene to affect the phenotype of the organism of which it is a part **2 :** the quality of being expressive

ex·press·ly \ik-ˈspres-lē\ *adv* (14c) **1 :** in an express manner : EXPLICITLY ⟨~ rejected the proposal⟩ **2 :** for the express purpose : PARTICULARLY, SPECIFICALLY ⟨made ~ for me⟩

Express Mail *service mark* — used for overnight delivery of mail

ex·press·man \ik-ˈspres-ˌman, -mən\ *n* (1839) : a person employed in the express business

expresso *var of* ESPRESSO

ex·press·way \ik-ˈspres-ˌwā\ *n* (1944) : a high-speed divided highway for through traffic with access partially or fully controlled

ex·pro·pri·ate \ek-ˈsprō-prē-ˌāt\ *vt* **-at·ed; -at·ing** [ML *expropriatus,* pp. of *expropriare,* fr. L *ex-* + *proprius* own] (1611) **1 :** to deprive of possession or proprietary rights **2 :** to transfer (the property of another) to one's own possession — **ex·pro·pri·a·tor** \-ˌā-tər\ *n*

ex·pro·pri·a·tion \(ˌ)ek-ˌsprō-prē-ˈā-shən\ *n* (15c) : the act of expropriating or the state of being expropriated; *specif* : the action of the state in taking or modifying the property rights of an individual in the exercise of its sovereignty

expt *abbr* experiment

exptl *abbr* experimental

ex·pulse \ik-ˈspəls\ *vt* **ex·pulsed; ex·puls·ing** (15c) : EXPEL

ex·pul·sion \ik-ˈspəl-shən\ *n* [ME, fr. AF *expulsioun,* fr. L *expulsion-, expulsio,* fr. *expellere* to expel] (15c) : the act of expelling : the state of being expelled — **ex·pul·sive** \-ˈspəl-siv\ *adj*

ex·punc·tion \ik-ˈspəŋ(k)-shən\ *n* [L *expungere*] (1606) : the act of expunging : the state of being expunged : ERASURE

ex·punge \ik-ˈspənj\ *vt* **ex·punged; ex·pung·ing** [L *expungere* to mark for deletion by dots, fr. *ex-* + *pungere* to prick — more at PUNGENT] (1602) **1 :** to strike out, obliterate, or mark for deletion **2 :** to efface completely : DESTROY **3 :** to eliminate (as a memory) from one's consciousness — **ex·pung·er** *n*

ex·pur·gate \ˈek-spər-ˌgāt\ *vt* **-gat·ed; -gat·ing** [L *expurgatus,* pp. of *expurgare,* fr. *ex-* + *purgare* to purge] (1678) : to cleanse of something morally harmful, offensive, or erroneous; *esp* : to expunge objectionable parts from before publication or presentation ⟨an *expurgated* edition of the letters⟩ — **ex·pur·ga·tion** \ˌek-spər-ˈgā-shən\ *n* — **ex·pur·ga·tor** \ˈek-spər-ˌgā-tər\ *n*

ex·pur·ga·to·ri·al \(ˌ)ek-ˌspər-gə-ˈtȯr-ē-əl\ *adj* (1807) : relating to expurgation or an expurgator : EXPURGATORY

ex·pur·ga·to·ry \ek-ˈspər-gə-ˌtȯr-ē\ *adj* (1625) : serving to purify from something morally harmful, offensive, or erroneous

expwy *abbr* expressway

[1]**ex·qui·site** \ek-ˈskwi-zət, ˈek-(ˌ)\ *adj* [ME *exquisit,* fr. L *exquisitus,* pp. of *exquirere* to search out, fr. *ex-* + *quaerere* to seek] (15c) **1 :** carefully selected : CHOICE **2** *archaic* : ACCURATE **3 a :** marked by flawless craftsmanship or by beautiful, ingenious, delicate, or elaborate execution ⟨an ~ vase⟩ **b :** marked by nice discrimination, deep sensitivity, or subtle understanding ⟨~ taste⟩ **c :** ACCOMPLISHED, PERFECTED ⟨an ~ gentleman⟩ **4 a :** pleasing through beauty, fitness, or perfection ⟨an ~ white blossom⟩ **b :** ACUTE, INTENSE ⟨~ pain⟩ **c :** having uncommon or esoteric appeal ***syn*** see CHOICE — **ex·qui·site·ly** *adv* — **ex·qui·site·ness** *n*

[2]**exquisite** *n* (1819) : one who is overly fastidious in dress or ornament

exrx *abbr* executrix

ex·san·gui·na·tion \(ˌ)ek(s)-ˌsaŋ-gwə-ˈnā-shən\ *n* [L *exsanguinatus* drained of blood, fr. *ex-* + *sanguin-, sanguis* blood] (ca. 1909) : the action or process of draining or losing blood — **ex·san·gui·nate** \ek(s)-ˈsaŋ-gwə-ˌnāt\ *vt*

ex·scind \ek-ˈsind\ *vt* [L *exscindere,* fr. *ex-* + *scindere* to cut, tear — more at SHED] (1662) : to cut off or out : EXCISE

ex·sert \ek-ˈsərt\ *vt* [L *exsertus,* pp. of *exserere* — more at EXERT] (1816) : to thrust out — **ex·ser·tion** \-ˈsər-shən\ *n*

ex·sert·ed *adj* (1816) : projecting beyond an enclosing organ or part

ex·sic·cate \ˈek-si-ˌkāt\ *vt* **-cat·ed; -cat·ing** [ME, fr. L *exsiccatus,* pp. of *exsiccare,* fr. *ex-* + *siccare* to dry, fr. *siccus* dry — more at SACK] (15c) : to remove moisture from : DRY — **ex·sic·ca·tion** \ˌek-si-ˈkā-shən\ *n*

ex·so·lu·tion \ˌek-sə-ˈlü-shən\ *n* (1921) : the process of separating or precipitating from a solid crystalline phase

ext *abbr* **1** extension **2** exterior **3** external; externally **4** extra **5** extract

ex·tant \ˈek-stənt; ek-ˈstant, ˈek-ˌ\ *adj* [L *exstant-, exstans,* prp. of *exstare* to stand out, be in existence, fr. *ex-* + *stare* to stand — more at STAND] (1545) **1** *archaic* : standing out or above **2 a :** currently or actually existing ⟨the most charming writer ~ —G. W. Johnson⟩ **b :** still existing : not destroyed or lost ⟨~ manuscripts⟩

ex·tem·po·ral \ek-ˈstem-p(ə-)rəl\ *adj* [L *extemporalis,* fr. *ex tempore*] (1570) *archaic* : EXTEMPORANEOUS — **ex·tem·po·ral·ly** \-ē\ *adv*

ex·tem·po·ra·ne·ity \(ˌ)ek-ˌstem-pə-rə-ˈnē-ə-tē, -ˈnā-\ *n* (1937) : the quality or state of being extemporaneous

ex·tem·po·ra·ne·ous \(ˌ)ek-ˌstem-pə-ˈrā-nē-əs\ *adj* [LL *extemporaneus,* fr. L *ex tempore*] (1673) **1 a (1) :** composed, performed, or uttered on the spur of the moment : IMPROMPTU ⟨an ~ comment⟩ **(2) :** carefully prepared but delivered without notes or text **b :** skilled at or given to extemporaneous utterance **c :** happening suddenly and often unexpectedly and usu. without clearly known causes or relationships ⟨a great deal of criminal and delinquent behavior is . . . ~ —W. C. Reckless⟩ **2 :** provided, made, or put to use as an expedient : MAKESHIFT ⟨an ~ shelter⟩ — **ex·tem·po·ra·ne·ous·ly** *adv* — **ex·tem·po·ra·ne·ous·ness** *n*

ex·tem·po·rary \ik-ˈstem-pə-ˌrer-ē\ *adj* (1596) : EXTEMPORANEOUS — **ex·tem·po·rar·i·ly** \-ˌstem-pə-ˈrer-ə-lē\ *adv*

ex·tem·po·re \ik-ˈstem-pə-(ˌ)rē\ *adv or adj* [L *ex tempore,* fr. *ex* + *tempore,* abl. of *tempus* time] (ca. 1553) : in an extemporaneous manner ⟨speaking ~⟩

ex·tem·po·ri·sa·tion, ex·tem·po·rise *Brit var of* EXTEMPORIZATION, EXTEMPORIZE

ex·tem·po·ri·za·tion \ik-ˌstem-pə-rə-ˈzā-shən\ *n* (ca. 1860) **1 :** the act of extemporizing : IMPROVISATION **2 :** something extemporized

ex·tem·po·rize \ik-ˈstem-pə-ˌrīz\ *vb* **-rized; -riz·ing** *vi* (1592) **1 :** to do something extemporaneously : IMPROVISE; *esp* : to speak extemporaneously **2 :** to get along in a makeshift manner ~ *vt* : to compose, perform, or utter extemporaneously : IMPROVISE ⟨*extemporized* an after-dinner speech⟩ — **ex·tem·po·riz·er** *n*

ex·tend \ik-ˈstend\ *vb* [ME, fr. AF or L; AF *estendre,* fr. L *extendere,* fr. *ex-* + *tendere* to stretch — more at THIN] *vt* (14c) **1 :** to spread or stretch forth : UNBEND ⟨~*ed* both her arms⟩ **2 a :** to stretch out to fullest length **b :** to cause (as a horse) to move at full stride **c :** to exert (oneself) to full capacity ⟨could work long and hard without seeming to ~ himself⟩ **d (1) :** to increase the bulk of (as by adding a cheaper substance or a modifier) **(2) :** ADULTERATE **3** [ME, fr. ML *extendere* (fr. L) or AF *estendre,* fr. OF] **a** *Brit* : to take possession of (as lands) by a writ of extent **b** *obs* : to take by force **4 a :** to make the offer of : PROFFER ⟨~*ing* aid to the needy⟩ ⟨~*ing* their greetings⟩ **b :** to make available ⟨~*ing* credit to customers⟩ **5 a :** to cause to reach (as in distance or scope) ⟨national authority was ~*ed* over new territories⟩ **b :** to cause to be longer : PROLONG ⟨~ the side of a triangle⟩ ⟨~*ed* their visit another day⟩; *also* : to prolong the time of payment of **c :** ADVANCE, FURTHER ⟨~*ing* her potential through job training⟩ **6 a :** to cause to be of greater area or volume : ENLARGE

⟨~*ed* the patio to the back of the house⟩ **b :** to increase the scope, meaning, or application of **:** BROADEN ⟨beauty, I suppose, opens the heart, ~*s* the consciousness —Algernon Blackwood⟩ **c** *archaic* **:** EXAGGERATE ~ *vi* **1 :** to stretch out in distance, space, or time **:** REACH ⟨their jurisdiction ~*ed* over the whole area⟩ **2 :** to reach in scope or application ⟨his concern ~*s* beyond mere business to real service to his customers⟩ — **ex·tend·abil·i·ty** \-ˌsten-də-ˈbi-lə-tē\ *n* — **ex·tend·able** *also* **ex·tend·ible** \-ˈsten-də-bəl\ *adj*

syn EXTEND, LENGTHEN, PROLONG, PROTRACT mean to draw out or add to so as to increase in length. EXTEND and LENGTHEN imply a drawing out in space or time but EXTEND may also imply increase in width, scope, area, or range ⟨*extend* a vacation⟩ ⟨*extend* welfare services⟩ ⟨*lengthen* a skirt⟩ ⟨*lengthen* the workweek⟩. PROLONG suggests chiefly increase in duration esp. beyond usual limits ⟨*prolonged* illness⟩. PROTRACT adds to PROLONG implications of needlessness, vexation, or indefiniteness ⟨*protracted* litigation⟩.

ex·tend·ed \-ˈsten-dəd\ *adj* (15c) **1 :** drawn out in length esp. of time ⟨an ~ visit⟩ **2 a :** fully stretched out ⟨an ~ battle line⟩ **b** *of a horse's gait* **:** performed with a greatly lengthened stride but without a break — compare COLLECTED **c :** INTENSIVE ⟨~ efforts⟩ **3 :** having spatial magnitude **:** being larger than a point ⟨an ~ source of light⟩ **4 :** EXTENSIVE 1 ⟨made available ~ information —Ruth G. Strickland⟩ **5 :** DERIVATIVE 1, SECONDARY 2a ⟨an ~ sense of a word⟩ **6** *of a typeface* **:** having a wider face than that of a standard typeface — **ex·tend·ed·ly** *adv* — **ex·tend·ed·ness** *n*

extended family *n* (ca. 1935) **:** a family that includes in one household near relatives in addition to a nuclear family

ex·tend·er \ik-ˈsten-dər\ *n* (ca. 1529) **:** one that extends: as **a :** a substance added to a product esp. in the capacity of a diluent, adulterant, or modifier **b :** an added ingredient used to increase the bulk of a food (as soup or meat)

ex·ten·si·ble \ik-ˈsten(t)-sə-bəl\ *adj* (1603) **:** capable of being extended — **ex·ten·si·bil·i·ty** \-ˌsten(t)-sə-ˈbi-lə-tē\ *n*

ex·ten·sile \ik-ˈsten(t)-səl, -ˈsten-ˌsī(-ə)l\ *adj* (1744) **:** EXTENSIBLE

ex·ten·sion \ik-ˈsten(t)-shən\ *n* [ME, fr. LL *extension-, extensio,* fr. L *extendere*] (15c) **1 a :** the action of extending **:** state of being extended **b :** an enlargement in scope or operation ⟨tools are ~*s* of human hands⟩ **2 a :** the total range over which something extends **:** COMPASS **b :** DENOTATION 4 **3 a :** the stretching of a fractured or dislocated limb so as to restore it to its natural position **b :** an unbending movement around a joint in a limb (as the knee or elbow) that increases the angle between the bones of the limb at the joint — compare FLEXION 4a **4 :** a property whereby something occupies space **5 :** an increase in length of time; *specif* **:** an increase in time allowed under agreement or concession **6 :** a program that geographically extends the educational resources of an institution by special arrangements (as correspondence courses) to persons otherwise unable to take advantage of such resources **7 a :** a part constituting an addition **b :** a section or line segment forming an additional length **c :** an extra telephone connected to the principal line **d :** a length of natural or synthetic hair that is worn attached to one's natural hair **e :** a series of usu. three or four characters following a dot at the end of the name of a computer file that specifies the file's format or purpose **8 :** a mathematical set (as a field or group) that includes a given and similar set as a subset

extension agent *n* (1949) **:** COUNTY AGENT

ex·ten·sion·al \ik-ˈstench-nəl, -ˈsten(t)-shə-nᵊl\ *adj* (1647) **1 :** of, relating to, or marked by extension; *specif* **:** DENOTATIVE **2 :** concerned with objective reality — **ex·ten·sion·al·i·ty** \-ˌsten(t)-shə-ˈna-lə-tē\ *n* — **ex·ten·sion·al·ly** \-ˈstench-nə-lē, -ˈsten(t)-shə-nᵊl-ē\ *adv*

extension cord *n* (1944) **:** an electric cord fitted with a plug at one end and a receptacle at the other

ex·ten·si·ty \ik-ˈsten(t)-sə-tē\ *n, pl* **-ties** (ca. 1834) **1 a :** the quality of having extension **b :** degree of extension **:** RANGE **2 :** an attribute of sensation whereby space or size is perceived

ex·ten·sive \ik-ˈsten(t)-siv\ *adj* (1604) **1 :** having wide or considerable extent ⟨~ reading⟩ **2 :** EXTENSIONAL **3 :** of, relating to, or constituting farming in which large areas of land are utilized with minimum outlay and labor — **ex·ten·sive·ly** *adv* — **ex·ten·sive·ness** *n*

ex·ten·som·e·ter \ˌek-ˌsten-ˈsä-mə-tər\ *n* [*extens*ion + *-o-* + *-meter*] (1887) **:** an instrument for measuring minute deformations of test specimens caused by tension, compression, bending, or twisting

ex·ten·sor \ik-ˈsten(t)-sər\ *n* (1615) **:** a muscle serving to extend a bodily part (as a limb)

ex·tent \ik-ˈstent\ *n* [ME, fr. AF *estente, extente* land valuation, fr. *extendre, estendre* to survey, evaluate, lit., to extend] (14c) **1** *archaic* **:** valuation (as of land) in Great Britain esp. for taxation **2 a :** seizure (as of land) in execution of a writ of extent in Great Britain; *also* **:** the condition of being so seized **b :** a writ giving to a creditor temporary possession of his debtor's property **3 a :** the range over which something extends **:** SCOPE ⟨the ~ of her jurisdiction⟩ **b :** the point, degree, or limit to which something extends ⟨using talents to the greatest ~⟩ **c :** the amount of space or surface that something occupies or the distance over which it extends **:** MAGNITUDE ⟨the ~ of the forest⟩

ex·ten·u·ate \ik-ˈsten-yə-ˌwāt, -yü-ˌāt\ *vt* **-at·ed; -at·ing** [L *extenuatus,* pp. of *extenuare,* fr. *ex-* + *tenuis* thin — more at THIN] (1529) **1 a** *archaic* **:** to make light of **b :** to lessen or to try to lessen the seriousness or extent of by making partial excuses **:** MITIGATE ⟨*extenuating* circumstances⟩ **c** *obs* **:** DISPARAGE **2 a** *archaic* **:** to make thin or emaciated **b :** to lessen the strength or effect of — **ex·ten·u·a·tor** \-ˌ(w)ā-tər\ *n* — **ex·ten·u·a·to·ry** \-(w)ə-ˌtȯr-ē\ *adj*

ex·ten·u·a·tion \ik-ˌsten-yə-ˈwā-shən, -yü-ˈā-\ *n* (ca. 1543) **1 :** the act of extenuating or state of being extenuated; *esp* **:** partial justification **2 :** something extenuating; *esp* **:** a partial excuse

¹**ex·te·ri·or** \ek-ˈstir-ē-ər\ *adj* [L, compar. of *exter, exterus* being on the outside, foreign, fr. *ex*] (1528) **1 :** being on an outside surface **:** situated on the outside **2 :** observable by outward signs ⟨his ~ quietness is belied by an occasional nervous twitch —*Current Biog.*⟩ **3 :** suitable for use on outside surfaces — **ex·te·ri·or·ly** *adv*

²**exterior** *n* (1591) **1 a :** an exterior part or surface **:** OUTSIDE **b :** outward manner or appearance **2 :** a representation (as on stage or film) of an outdoor scene; *also* **:** a scene filmed outdoors

exterior angle *n* (1756) **1 :** the angle between a side of a polygon and an extended adjacent side **2 :** an angle formed by a transversal as it cuts one of two lines and situated on the outside of the line

ex·te·ri·or·ise *Brit var of* EXTERIORIZE

ex·te·ri·or·i·ty \(ˌ)ek-ˌstir-ē-ˈȯr-ə-tē, -ˈär-\ *n* (1611) **:** the quality or state of being exterior or exteriorized **:** EXTERNALITY

ex·te·ri·or·ize \ek-ˈstir-ē-ə-ˌrīz\ *vt* **-ized; -iz·ing** (1879) **1 :** EXTERNALIZE **2 :** to bring out of the body (as for surgery) — **ex·te·ri·or·iza·tion** \-ˌstir-ē-ə-rə-ˈzā-shən\ *n*

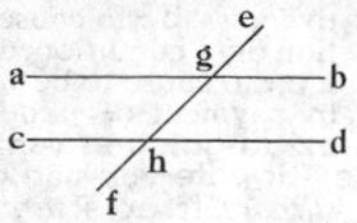

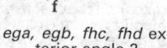

ega, egb, fhc, fhd exterior angle 2

ex·ter·mi·nate \ik-ˈstər-mə-ˌnāt\ *vt* **-nat·ed; -nat·ing** [L *exterminatus,* pp. of *exterminare,* fr. *ex-* + *terminus* boundary — more at TERM] (1591) **:** to get rid of completely usu. by killing off ⟨~ termites and cockroaches⟩ — **ex·ter·mi·na·tion** \-ˌstər-mə-ˈnā-shən\ *n* — **ex·ter·mi·na·tor** \-ˈstər-mə-ˌnā-tər\ *n*

syn EXTERMINATE, EXTIRPATE, ERADICATE, UPROOT mean to effect the destruction or abolition of something. EXTERMINATE implies complete and immediate extinction by killing off all individuals ⟨*exterminate* cockroaches⟩. EXTIRPATE implies extinction of a race, family, species, or sometimes an idea or doctrine by destruction or removal of its means of propagation ⟨many species have been *extirpated* from the area⟩. ERADICATE implies the driving out or elimination of something that has established itself ⟨a campaign to *eradicate* illiteracy⟩. UPROOT implies a forcible or violent removal and stresses displacement or dislodgment rather than immediate destruction ⟨the war *uprooted* thousands⟩.

ex·ter·mi·na·to·ry \ik-ˈstər-mə-nə-ˌtȯr-ē\ *adj* (1790) **:** of, relating to, or marked by extermination

ex·ter·mine \ik-ˈstər-mən\ *vt* **-mined; -min·ing** (1539) *obs* **:** EXTERMINATE

¹**ex·tern** \ek-ˈstərn, ˈek-ˌ\ *adj* [MF or L; MF *externe,* fr. L *externus*] (1530) *archaic* **:** EXTERNAL

²**ex·tern** *also* **ex·terne** \ˈek-ˌstərn\ *n* (1823) **:** a person connected with an institution but not living or boarding in it; *specif* **:** a nonresident doctor or medical student at a hospital

¹**ex·ter·nal** \ek-ˈstər-nᵊl\ *adj* [L *externus* external, fr. *exter* — more at EXTERIOR] (1542) **1 a :** capable of being perceived outwardly ⟨~ signs of a disease⟩ **b (1) :** having merely the outward appearance of something **:** SUPERFICIAL **(2) :** not intrinsic or essential ⟨~ circumstances⟩ **2 a :** of, relating to, or connected with the outside or an outer part ⟨the building's ~ features⟩ **b :** applied or applicable to the outside ⟨a lotion for ~ use⟩ **3 a (1) :** situated outside, apart, or beyond; *specif* **:** situated near or toward the surface of the body **(2) :** arising or acting from outside ⟨an ~ force⟩ **b :** of or relating to dealings or relationships with foreign countries **c :** having existence independent of the mind ⟨~ reality⟩ — **ex·ter·nal·ly** \-nᵊl-ē\ *adv*

²**external** *n* (ca. 1635) **:** something that is external: as **a :** an outer part **b :** an external feature or aspect — usu. used in pl.

external combustion engine *n* (1915) **:** a heat engine (as a steam engine) that derives its heat from fuel consumed outside the cylinder

external degree *n* (1928) **:** a degree conferred on a student who has not attended the university but has passed the qualifying examination

ex·ter·nal·i·sa·tion, ex·ter·nal·ise *Brit var of* EXTERNALIZATION, EXTERNALIZE

ex·ter·nal·ism \ek-ˈstər-nə-ˌli-zəm\ *n* (1856) **1 :** attention to externals; *esp* **:** excessive preoccupation with externals **2 :** EXTERNALITY 1

ex·ter·nal·i·ty \ˌek-ˌstər-ˈna-lə-tē\ *n, pl* **-ties** (1673) **1 :** the quality or state of being external or externalized **2 :** something that is external **3 :** a secondary or unintended consequence ⟨pollution and other *externalities* of manufacturing⟩

ex·ter·nal·i·za·tion \ek-ˌstər-nə-lə-ˈzā-shən\ *n* (1803) **1 a :** the action or process of externalizing **b :** the quality or state of being externalized **2 :** something externalized **:** EMBODIMENT

ex·ter·nal·ize \ek-ˈstər-nə-ˌlīz\ *vt* **-ized; -iz·ing** (1852) **1 :** to make external or externally manifest **2 :** to attribute to causes outside the self **:** RATIONALIZE ⟨*externalized* his lack of ability to succeed⟩

external respiration *n* (1940) **:** exchange of gases between the external environment and a distributing system of the animal body (as the lungs of higher vertebrates or the tracheal tubes of insects) or between the alveoli of the lungs and the blood — compare INTERNAL RESPIRATION

ex·tern·ship \ˈek-ˌstərn-ˌship\ *n* (1945) **:** a training program that is part of a course of study of an educational institution and is taken in private business

ex·tero·cep·tive \ˌek-stə-rō-ˈsep-tiv\ *adj* [*exter*ior + *-o-* + *-ceptive* (as in *receptive*)] (1906) **:** relating to, being, or activated by stimuli received by an organism from outside

ex·tero·cep·tor \-tər\ *n* (1906) **:** a sense organ excited by exteroceptive stimuli

ex·ter·ri·to·ri·al \ˌek-ˌster-ə-ˈtȯr-ē-əl\ *adj* (ca. 1880) **:** EXTRATERRITORIAL — **ex·ter·ri·to·ri·al·i·ty** \-ˌtȯr-ē-ˈa-lə-tē\ *n*

¹**ex·tinct** \ik-ˈstiŋ(k)t, ˈek-ˌ\ *adj* [ME, fr. L *exstinctus,* pp. of *exstinguere*] (15c) **1 a :** no longer burning **b :** no longer active ⟨an ~ volcano⟩ **2 :** no longer existing ⟨an ~ animal⟩ **3 a :** gone out of use **:** SUPERSEDED **b :** having no qualified claimant ⟨an ~ title⟩

²**extinct** *vt* (15c) *archaic* **:** EXTINGUISH

ex·tinc·tion \ik-ˈstiŋ(k)-shən\ *n* (15c) **1 :** the act of making extinct or causing to be extinguished **2 :** the condition or fact of being extinct or extinguished; *also* **:** the process of becoming extinct ⟨~ of a species⟩ **3 :** the process of eliminating or reducing a conditioned response by not reinforcing it

extinction coefficient *n* (1902) **:** a measure of the rate of diminution of transmitted light via scattering and absorption for a medium

ex·tinc·tive \ik-ˈstiŋ(k)-tiv\ *adj* (1600) **:** tending or serving to extinguish or make extinct

ex·tin·guish \ik-ˈstiŋ-(g)wish\ *vt* [L *exstinguere* (fr. *ex-* + *stinguere* to extinguish) + E *-ish* (as in *abolish*); akin to L *instigare* to incite — more at STICK] (ca. 1540) **1 a (1) :** to bring to an end **:** make an end of ⟨hope for their safety was slowly ~*ed*⟩ **(2) :** to reduce to silence or ineffectiveness **b** : to cause to cease burning : QUENCH **c** : to cause extinction of (a conditioned response) **d** : to dim the brightness of : ECLIPSE **2 a** : to cause to be void : NULLIFY ⟨~ a claim⟩ **b** : to get rid of usu. by payment ⟨~ a debt⟩ — **ex·tin·guish·able** \-(g)wi-shə-bəl\ *adj* — **ex·tin·guish·er** \-shər\ *n* — **ex·tin·guish·ment** \-mənt\ *n*

ex·tir·pate \'ek-stər-ˌpāt\ *vt* **-pat·ed; -pat·ing** [L *exstirpatus,* pp. of *exstirpare,* fr. *ex-* + *stirp-, stirps* trunk, root] (1535) **1 a** : to destroy completely : WIPE OUT **b** : to pull up by the root **2** : to cut out by surgery ***syn*** see EXTERMINATE — **ex·tir·pa·tion** \ˌek-stər-'pā-shən\ *n* — **ex·tir·pa·tor** \'ek-stər-ˌpā-tər\ *n*

ex·tol *also* **ex·toll** \ik-'stōl\ *vt* **ex·tolled; ex·tol·ling** [ME, fr. L *extollere,* fr. *ex-* + *tollere* to lift up — more at TOLERATE] (15c) : to praise highly : GLORIFY — **ex·tol·ler** *n* — **ex·tol·ment** \-'stōl-mənt\ *n*

ex·tort \ik-'stȯrt\ *vt* [L *extortus,* pp. of *extorquēre* to wrench out, extort, fr. *ex-* + *torquēre* to twist — more at TORTURE] (15c) : to obtain from a person by force, intimidation, or undue or illegal power : WRING; *also* : to gain esp. by ingenuity or compelling argument ***syn*** see EDUCE — **ex·tort·er** *n* — **ex·tor·tive** \-'stȯr-tiv\ *adj*

ex·tor·tion \ik-'stȯr-shən\ *n* (14c) **1** : the act or practice of extorting esp. money or other property; *esp* : the offense committed by an official engaging in such practice **2** : something extorted; *esp* : a gross overcharge — **ex·tor·tion·er** \-sh(ə-)nər\ *n* — **ex·tor·tion·ist** \-sh(ə-)nist\ *n*

ex·tor·tion·ary \-shə-ˌner-ē\ *adj* (1771) *archaic* : EXTORTIONATE 1

ex·tor·tion·ate \ik-'stȯr-sh(ə-)nət\ *adj* (1757) **1** : characterized by extortion **2** : EXCESSIVE, EXORBITANT ⟨~ prices⟩ — **ex·tor·tion·ate·ly** *adv*

[1]**ex·tra** \'ek-strə\ *adj* [prob. short for *extraordinary*] (1757) **1 a** : more than is due, usual, or necessary : ADDITIONAL ⟨~ work⟩ **b** : subject to an additional charge ⟨dessert is ~⟩ **2** : SUPERIOR ⟨~ quality⟩

[2]**extra** *n* (1793) **1** : one that is extra or additional: as **a** : a special edition of a newspaper **b** : an added charge **c** : an additional worker; *specif* : one hired to act in a group scene in a motion picture or stage production **d** : an attractive addition or accessory : FRILL ⟨cars loaded with ~*s*⟩ **2** : something of superior quality or grade

[3]**extra** *adv* (1807) : beyond the usual size, extent, or degree ⟨~ large⟩

extra- *prefix* [L, fr. *extra,* adv. & prep., outside, except, beyond, fr. *exter* being on the outside — more at EXTERIOR] : outside : beyond ⟨*extra*judicial⟩

extra–base hit *n* (ca. 1949) : a hit in baseball that lets the batter take more than one base

ex·tra·cel·lu·lar \ˌek-strə-'sel-yə-lər\ *adj* (1867) : situated or occurring outside a cell or the cells of the body ⟨~ digestion⟩ ⟨~ enzymes⟩ — **ex·tra·cel·lu·lar·ly** *adv*

ex·tra·chro·mo·som·al \-ˌkrō-mə-'sō-məl, -'zō-\ *adj* (1940) : situated or controlled by factors outside the chromosome ⟨~ inheritance⟩

ex·tra·cor·po·re·al \-kȯr-'pȯr-ē-əl\ *adj* (1865) : occurring or based outside the living body ⟨the heart-lung machine maintains ~ circulation during heart surgery⟩ — **ex·tra·cor·po·re·al·ly** \-ē-ə-lē\ *adv*

ex·tra·cra·ni·al \-'krā-nē-əl\ *adj* (ca. 1884) : situated or occurring outside the cranium

[1]**ex·tract** \ik-'strakt, *oftenest in sense* 5 'ek-ˌ\ *vt* [ME, fr. L *extractus,* pp. of *extrahere,* fr. *ex-* + *trahere* to draw] (15c) **1 a** : to draw forth (as by research) ⟨~ data⟩ **b** : to pull or take out forcibly ⟨~*ed* a wisdom tooth⟩ **c** : to obtain by much effort from someone unwilling ⟨~*ed* a confession⟩ **2 a** : to withdraw (as a juice or fraction) by physical or chemical process **b** : to treat with a solvent so as to remove a soluble substance **3** : to separate (a metal) from an ore **4** : to determine (a mathematical root) by calculation **5** : to select (excerpts) and copy out or cite ***syn*** see EDUCE — **ex·tract·abil·i·ty** \ik-ˌstrak-tə-'bi-lə-tē, (ˌ)ek-\ *n* — **ex·tract·able** \ik-'strak-tə-bəl, 'ek-ˌ\ *adj*

[2]**ex·tract** \'ek-ˌstrakt\ *n* (15c) **1** : a selection from a writing or discourse : EXCERPT **2** : a product (as an essence or concentrate) prepared by extracting; *esp* : a solution (as in alcohol) of essential constituents of a complex material (as meat or an aromatic plant)

ex·trac·tion \ik-'strak-shən\ *n* (15c) **1** : the act or process of extracting something **2** : ANCESTRY, ORIGIN ⟨a family of French ~⟩ **3** : something extracted

[1]**ex·trac·tive** \ik-'strak-tiv, 'ek-ˌ\ *adj* (1599) **1 a** : of, relating to, or involving extraction **b** : tending toward or resulting in withdrawal of natural resources by extraction with no provision for replenishment ⟨~ agriculture⟩ **2** : capable of being extracted — **ex·trac·tive·ly** *adv*

[2]**extractive** *n* (1810) : something extracted or extractable : EXTRACT

ex·trac·tor \ik-'strak-tər\ *n* (1597) : one that extracts; *esp* : the mechanism in a firearm that dislodges a spent cartridge from the chamber

ex·tra·cur·ric·u·lar \ˌek-strə-kə-'ri-kyə-lər\ *adj* (1925) **1** : not falling within the scope of a regular curriculum; *specif* : of or relating to officially or semiofficially approved and usu. organized student activities (as athletics) connected with school and usu. carrying no academic credit ⟨~ sports⟩ **2 a** : lying outside one's regular duties or routine **b** : EXTRAMARITAL — **extracurricular** *n*

ex·tra·dit·able \'ek-strə-ˌdī-tə-bəl\ *adj* (1881) **1** : subject or liable to extradition **2** : making one liable to extradition ⟨an ~ offense⟩

ex·tra·dite \'ek-strə-ˌdīt\ *vt* **-dit·ed; -dit·ing** [back-formation fr. *extradition*] (1864) **1** : to deliver up to extradition **2** : to obtain the extradition of

ex·tra·di·tion \ˌek-strə-'di-shən\ *n* [F, fr. *ex-* + L *tradition-, traditio* act of handing over — more at TREASON] (1839) : the surrender of an alleged criminal usu. under the provisions of a treaty or statute by one authority (as a state) to another having jurisdiction to try the charge

ex·tra·dos \'ek-strə-ˌdäs, -ˌdō; ek-'strā-ˌdäs\ *n, pl* **-dos·es** \-ˌdä-səz\ *or* **-dos** \-ˌdōz, -ˌdäs\ [F, fr. L *extra* + F *dos* back — more at DOSSIER] (1772) : the exterior curve of an arch — see ARCH illustration

ex·tra·em·bry·on·ic \ˌek-strə-ˌem-brē-'ä-nik\ *adj* (1901) : situated outside the embryo; *esp* : developed from the zygote but not part of the embryo ⟨~ membranes⟩

ex·tra·ga·lac·tic \ˌek-strə-gə-'lak-tik\ *adj* [ISV] (1851) : originating or existing outside the Milky Way galaxy; *also* : of or relating to extragalactic space ⟨~ astronomy⟩

ex·tra·he·pat·ic \-hi-'pa-tik\ *adj* (ca. 1923) : situated or originating outside the liver

ex·tra·ju·di·cial \-jü-'di-shəl\ *adj* (1630) **1 a** : not forming a valid part of regular legal proceedings ⟨an ~ investigation⟩ **b** : delivered without legal authority : PRIVATE 2a(2) ⟨the judge's ~ statements⟩ **2** : done in contravention of due process of law ⟨an ~ execution⟩ — **extra·ju·di·cial·ly** \-'dish-lē, -'di-shə-\ *adv*

ex·tra·le·gal \ˌek-strə-'lē-gəl\ *adj* (1644) : not regulated or sanctioned by law — **ex·tra·le·gal·ly** \-gə-lē\ *adv*

ex·tra·lim·it·al \-'li-mə-tᵊl\ *adj* (1874) : not present in a given area — used of kinds of organisms (as species)

ex·tra·lin·guis·tic \-liŋ-'gwis-tik\ *adj* (1927) : lying outside the province of linguistics — **ex·tra·lin·guis·ti·cal·ly** \-ti-kə-lē\ *adv*

ex·tra·lit·er·ary \-'li-tə-ˌrer-ē\ *adj* (1945) : lying outside the field of literature

ex·tral·i·ty \ek-'stra-lə-tē\ *n* [by contr.] (1925) : EXTRATERRITORIALITY

ex·tra·log·i·cal \ˌek-strə-'lä-ji-kəl\ *adj* (1833) : not guided or determined by considerations of logic

ex·tra·mar·i·tal \ˌek-strə-'ma-rə-tᵊl\ *adj* (1925) : of, relating to, or being sexual intercourse between a married person and someone other than his or her spouse : ADULTEROUS ⟨an ~ affair⟩

ex·tra·mun·dane \ˌek-strə-ˌmən-'dān, -'mən-ˌ\ *adj* [LL *extramundanus,* fr. L *extra* + *mundus* the world] (1665) : situated in or relating to a region beyond the material world

ex·tra·mu·ral \-'myu̇r-əl\ *adj* (1854) **1** : existing or functioning outside or beyond the walls, boundaries, or precincts of an organized unit (as a school or hospital) **2** *chiefly Brit* : of, relating to, or taking part in extension courses or facilities — **ex·tra·mu·ral·ly** \-ə-lē\ *adv*

ex·tra·mu·si·cal \-'myü-zi-kəl\ *adj* (1923) : lying outside the province of music

ex·tra·ne·ous \ek-'strā-nē-əs\ *adj* [L *extraneus* — more at STRANGE] (1638) **1** : existing on or coming from the outside ⟨~ light⟩ **2 a** : not forming an essential or vital part ⟨~ ornamentation⟩ **b** : having no relevance ⟨an ~ digression⟩ **3** : being a number obtained in solving an equation that is not a solution of the equation ⟨~ roots⟩ ***syn*** see EXTRINSIC — **ex·tra·ne·ous·ly** *adv* — **ex·tra·ne·ous·ness** *n*

ex·tra·net \'ek-strə-ˌnet\ *n* (1995) : a network (as of a company) similar to an intranet that also allows access by certain others (as customers or suppliers)

ex·tra·nu·cle·ar \ˌek-strə-'nü-klē-ər, -'nyü-, ÷-kyə-lər\ *adj* (1887) **1** : situated in or affecting the parts of a cell external to the nucleus : CYTOPLASMIC **2** : situated outside the nucleus of an atom

ex·tra·oc·u·lar muscle \ˌek-strə-'ä-kyə-lər-\ *n* (1939) : any of six small voluntary muscles that pass between the eyeball and the orbit and control the movement of the eyeball in relation to the orbit

ex·traor·di·naire \ik-ˌstrȯ(r)-də-'ner, ek-\ *adj* [F] (1940) : EXTRAORDINARY — used postpositively ⟨a chef ~⟩

ex·traor·di·nary \ik-'strȯr-də-ˌner-ē, ˌek-strə-'ȯr-\ *adj* [ME *extraordinarie,* fr. L *extraordinarius,* fr. *extra ordinem* out of course, fr. *extra* + *ordinem,* acc. of *ordin-, ordo* order] (15c) **1 a** : going beyond what is usual, regular, or customary ⟨~ powers⟩ **b** : exceptional to a very marked extent ⟨~ beauty⟩ **c** *of a financial transaction* : NONRECURRING **2** : employed for or sent on a special function or service ⟨an ambassador ~⟩ — **ex·traor·di·nari·ly** \ik-ˌstrȯr-də-'ner-ə-lē, ˌek-strə-ˌȯr-\ *adv* — **ex·traor·di·nari·ness** \ik-'strȯr-də-ˌner-ē-nəs, ˌek-strə-'ȯr-\ *n*

extra point *n* (ca. 1949) : a point gained on a conversion in football

ex·trap·o·late \ik-'stra-pə-ˌlāt\ *vb* **-lat·ed; -lat·ing** [L *extra* outside + E *-polate* (as in *interpolate*) — more at EXTRA-] *vt* (1874) **1** : to infer (values of a variable in an unobserved interval) from values within an already observed interval **2 a** : to project, extend, or expand (known data or experience) into an area not known or experienced so as to arrive at a usu. conjectural knowledge of the unknown area ⟨~*s* present trends to construct an image of the future⟩ **b** : to predict by projecting past experience or known data ⟨~ public sentiment on one issue from known public reaction on others⟩ ~ *vi* : to perform the act or process of extrapolating — **ex·trap·o·la·tion** \-ˌstra-pə-'lā-shən\ *n* — **ex·trap·o·la·tive** \-'stra-pə-ˌlā-tiv\ *adj* — **ex·trap·o·la·tor** \-ˌlā-tər\ *n*

ex·tra·py·ra·mi·dal \ˌek-strə-pə-'ra-mə-dᵊl, -ˌpir-ə-'mi-dᵊl\ *adj* (ca. 1902) : situated outside of the pyramidal tracts; *also* : involving descending nerve tracts other than the pyramidal tracts

ex·tra·sen·so·ry \ˌek-strə-'sen(t)s-rē, -'sen(t)-sə-\ *adj* (1934) : residing beyond or outside the ordinary senses

extrasensory perception *n* (1934) : perception (as in telepathy, clairvoyance, and precognition) that involves awareness of information about events external to the self not gained through the senses and not deducible from previous experience — called also *ESP*

ex·tra·so·lar \-'sō-lər, -ˌlär\ *adj* (1872) : originating or existing outside the solar system ⟨~ planets⟩

ex·tra·sys·to·le \-'sis-tə-(ˌ)lē\ *n* [NL] (ca. 1900) : a premature beat of one of the chambers of the heart that leads to momentary arrhythmia

[1]**ex·tra·ter·res·tri·al** \-tə-'res-trē-əl, -'res(h)-chəl\ *adj* (1848) : originating, existing, or occurring outside the earth or its atmosphere ⟨~ life⟩

[2]**extraterrestrial** *n* (1950) : an extraterrestrial being

ex·tra·ter·ri·to·ri·al \-ˌter-ə-'tȯr-ē-əl\ *adj* (1869) : existing or taking place outside the territorial limits of a jurisdiction

ex·tra·ter·ri·to·ri·al·i·ty \-ˌtȯr-ē-'a-lə-tē\ *n* (1836) : exemption from the application or jurisdiction of local law or tribunals

ex·tra·tex·tu·al \ˌek-strə-'teks-chə-wəl, -chəl\ *adj* (1961) : of, relating to, or being something outside a literary text

ex·tra·trop·i·cal cyclone \ˌek-strə-ˌträ-pi-kəl-\ *n* (1923) : a cyclone in the middle or high latitudes often containing a cold front that extends toward the equator for hundreds of miles

ex·tra·uter·ine \ˌek-strə-'yü-tə-rən, -ˌrīn\ *adj* (1709) : situated or occurring outside the uterus ⟨~ pregnancy⟩

ex·trav·a·gance \ik-'stra-vi-gən(t)s\ *n* (1640) **1 a** : an instance of excess or prodigality; *specif* : an excessive outlay of money **b** : something extravagant ⟨a new car is an ~ we can't afford⟩ **2** : the quality or fact of being extravagant ⟨the ~ of the decorations⟩

ex·trav·a·gan·cy \-gən(t)-sē\ *n, pl* **-cies** (1625) : EXTRAVAGANCE

ex·trav·a·gant \ik-'stra-vi-gənt\ *adj* [ME, fr. MF, fr. ML *extravagant-, extravagans,* fr. L *extra-* + *vagant-, vagans,* prp. of *vagari* to wander about, fr. *vagus* wandering] (15c) **1 a** *obs* : STRANGE, CURIOUS **b** *archaic* : WANDERING **2 a** : exceeding the limits of reason or necessity ⟨~ claims⟩ **b** : lacking in moderation, balance, and restraint ⟨~ praise⟩ **c** : extremely or excessively elaborate ⟨an ~ display⟩ **3 a** : spending much more than necessary ⟨has always been ~ with her money⟩ **b** : PROFUSE, LAVISH **4** : extremely or unreasonably high in price ⟨an ~ purchase⟩ ***syn*** see EXCESSIVE — **ex·trav·a·gant·ly** *adv*

ex·trav·a·gan·za \ik-ˌstra-və-ˈgan-zə\ *n* [It *estravaganza,* lit., extravagance, fr. *estravagante* extravagant, fr. ML *extravagant-, extravagans*] (1754) **1 :** a literary or musical work marked by extreme freedom of style and structure and usu. by elements of burlesque or parody **2 :** a lavish or spectacular show or event **3 :** something extravagant
ex·trav·a·gate \ik-ˈstra-və-ˌgāt\ *vi* **-gat·ed; -gat·ing** (ca. 1755) *archaic* **:** to go beyond proper limits
ex·trav·a·sate \ik-ˈstra-və-ˌsāt, -ˌzāt\ *vb* **-sat·ed; -sat·ing** [L *extra* + *vas* vessel] *vt* (1668) **:** to force out or cause to escape from a proper vessel or channel ~ *vi* **:** to pass by infiltration or effusion from a proper vessel or channel (as a blood vessel) into surrounding tissue — **ex·trav·a·sa·tion** \-ˌstra-və-ˈsā-shən, -ˈzā-\ *n*
ex·tra·vas·cu·lar \ˌek-strə-ˈvas-kyə-lər\ *adj* (1804) **:** not occurring or contained in body vessels ⟨~ tissue fluids⟩
ex·tra·ve·hic·u·lar \-vē-ˈhi-kyə-lər\ *adj* (1965) **:** taking place outside a vehicle (as a spacecraft) ⟨~ activity⟩
ex·tra–vir·gin \ˈek-strə-ˈvər-jən\ *adj* (1980) **:** being a virgin olive oil that is lowest in acidity and highest in quality
[1]**ex·treme** \ik-ˈstrēm\ *adj* [ME, fr. MF, fr. L *extremus,* superl. of *exter, exterus* being on the outside — more at EXTERIOR] (15c) **1 a :** existing in a very high degree ⟨~ poverty⟩ **b :** going to great or exaggerated lengths **:** RADICAL ⟨went on an ~ diet⟩ **c :** exceeding the ordinary, usual, or expected ⟨~ weather conditions⟩ **2** *archaic* **:** LAST **3 :** situated at the farthest possible point from a center ⟨the country's ~ north⟩ **4 a :** most advanced or thoroughgoing ⟨the ~ political left⟩ **b :** MAXIMUM **5 a :** of, relating to, or being an outdoor activity or a form of a sport (as skiing) that involves an unusually high degree of physical risk ⟨~ mountain biking down steep slopes⟩ **b :** involved in an extreme sport ⟨an ~ snowboarder⟩ ***syn*** see EXCESSIVE — **ex·treme·ness** *n*
[2]**extreme** *n* (1555) **1 a :** something situated at or marking one end or the other of a range ⟨~*s* of heat and cold⟩ **b :** the first term or the last term of a mathematical proportion **c :** the major term or minor term of a syllogism **2 a :** a very pronounced or excessive degree **b :** highest degree **:** MAXIMUM **3 :** an extreme measure or expedient ⟨going to ~*s*⟩ — **in the extreme :** to the greatest possible extent
ex·treme·ly *adv* (1509) **1 :** in an extreme manner **2 :** to an extreme extent
extremely high frequency *n* (1952) **:** a radio frequency in the highest range of the radio spectrum — see RADIO FREQUENCY table
extremely low frequency *n* (1966) **:** a radio frequency in the lowest range of the radio spectrum — see RADIO FREQUENCY table
extreme unction *n* (15c) **:** a sacrament in which a priest anoints and prays for the recovery and salvation of a critically ill or injured person
ex·trem·ism \ik-ˈstrē-ˌmi-zəm\ *n* (1865) **1 :** the quality or state of being extreme **2 :** advocacy of extreme measures or views **:** RADICALISM — **ex·trem·ist** \-mist\ *n or adj*
ex·trem·i·ty \ik-ˈstre-mə-tē\ *n, pl* **-ties** (14c) **1 a :** the farthest or most remote part, section, or point ⟨the island's westernmost ~⟩ **b :** a limb of the body; *esp* **:** a human hand or foot **2 a :** extreme danger or critical need **b :** a moment marked by imminent destruction or death **3 a :** an intense degree ⟨the ~ of his participation —*Saturday Rev.*⟩ **b :** the utmost degree (as of emotion or pain) **4 :** a drastic or desperate act or measure ⟨driven to *extremities*⟩
ex·trem·o·phile \ik-ˈstrē-mə-ˌfī(-ə)l\ *n* (1989) **:** an organism that lives under extreme environmental conditions (as in a hot spring or ice cap)
ex·tre·mum \ik-ˈstrē-məm\ *n, pl* **-ma** \-mə\ [NL, fr. L, neut. of *extremus*] (1904) **:** a maximum or a minimum of a mathematical function — called also *extreme value*
ex·tri·cate \ˈek-strə-ˌkāt\ *vt* **-cat·ed; -cat·ing** [L *extricatus,* pp. of *extricare,* fr. *ex-* + *tricae* trifles, perplexities] (1601) **1 a** *archaic* **:** UNRAVEL **b :** to distinguish from a related thing **2 :** to free or remove from an entanglement or difficulty — **ex·tri·ca·ble** \ik-ˈstri-kə-bəl, ek-ˈ, ˈek-(ˌ)\ *adj* — **ex·tri·ca·tion** \ˌek-strə-ˈkā-shən\ *n*

syn EXTRICATE, DISENTANGLE, UNTANGLE, DISENCUMBER, DISEMBARRASS mean to free from what binds or holds back. EXTRICATE implies the use of care or ingenuity in freeing from a difficult position or situation ⟨*extricated* himself from financial difficulties⟩. DISENTANGLE and UNTANGLE suggest painstaking separation of a thing from other things ⟨*disentangling* fact from fiction⟩ ⟨*untangle* a web of deceit⟩. DISENCUMBER implies a release from something that clogs or weighs down ⟨an article *disencumbered* of jargon⟩. DISEMBARRASS suggests a release from something that impedes or hinders ⟨*disembarrassed* herself of her advisers⟩.

ex·trin·sic \ek-ˈstrin-zik, -ˈstrin(t)-sik\ *adj* [F & LL; F *extrinsèque,* fr. LL *extrinsecus,* fr. L, adv., from without; akin to L *exter* outward and to L *sequi* to follow — more at EXTERIOR, SUE] (1613) **1 a :** not forming part of or belonging to a thing **:** EXTRANEOUS **b :** originating from or on the outside; *esp* **:** originating outside a part and acting upon the part as a whole ⟨~ muscles of the tongue⟩ **2 :** EXTERNAL — **ex·trin·si·cal·ly** \-zi-k(ə-)lē, -si-\ *adv*

syn EXTRINSIC, EXTRANEOUS, FOREIGN, ALIEN mean external to a thing, its essential nature, or its original character. EXTRINSIC applies to what is distinctly outside the thing in question or is not contained in or derived from its essential nature ⟨sentimental value that is *extrinsic* to the house's market value⟩. EXTRANEOUS applies to what is on or comes from the outside and may or may not be capable of becoming an essential part ⟨arguments *extraneous* to the issue⟩. FOREIGN applies to what is so different as to be rejected or repelled or to be incapable of becoming assimilated ⟨techniques *foreign* to French cuisine⟩. ALIEN is stronger than FOREIGN in suggesting opposition, repugnance, or irreconcilability ⟨a practice totally *alien* to her nature⟩.

extrinsic factor *n* (1938) **:** VITAMIN B_{12}
extro- *prefix* [alter. of L *extra-*] **:** outward ⟨*extro*vert⟩ — compare INTRO-
ex·trorse \ˈek-ˌstrȯrs\ *adj* [prob. fr. NL **extrorsus,* fr. LL, adv., outward, fr. L *extra-* + *-orsus* (as in *introrsus*) — more at INTRORSE] (1858) **:** facing outward ⟨an ~ anther⟩
ex·tro·ver·sion *or* **ex·tra·ver·sion** \ˌek-strə-ˈvər-zhən, -shən\ *n* [G *Extraversion,* fr. L *extra-* + *versus,* pp. of *vertere* to turn — more at WORTH] (1915) **:** the act, state, or habit of being predominantly concerned with and obtaining gratification from what is outside the self
ex·tro·vert *also* **ex·tra·vert** \ˈek-strə-ˌvərt\ *n* [modif. of G *extravertiert,* fr. L *extra-* + *vertere*] (1918) **:** one whose personality is characterized by extroversion; *broadly* **:** a gregarious and unreserved person — **extrovert** *also* **extravert** *adj* — **ex·tro·vert·ed** *also* **ex·tra·vert·ed** \-ˌvər-təd, ˌek-strə-ˈvər-\ *adj*
ex·trude \ik-ˈstrüd\ *vb* **ex·trud·ed; ex·trud·ing** [L *extrudere,* fr. *ex-* + *trudere* to thrust — more at THREAT] *vt* (1566) **1 :** to force, press, or push out **2 :** to shape (as metal or plastic) by forcing through a die ~ *vi* **:** to become extruded — **ex·trud·abil·i·ty** \-ˌstrü-də-ˈbi-lə-tē\ *n* — **ex·trud·able** \-ˈstrü-də-bəl\ *adj* — **ex·trud·er** \-ˈstrü-dər\ *n*
ex·tru·sion \ik-ˈstrü-zhən\ *n* [ML *extrusion-, extrusio,* fr. L *extrudere*] (1540) **:** the act or process of extruding; *also* **:** a form or product produced by this process
ex·tru·sive \ik-ˈstrü-siv, -ziv\ *adj* (1816) **:** relating to or formed by geological extrusion from the earth in a molten state or as volcanic ash
ex·u·ber·ance \ig-ˈzü-b(ə-)rən(t)s\ *n* (1631) **1 :** the quality or state of being exuberant ⟨youthful ~⟩ **2 :** an exuberant act or expression
ex·u·ber·ant \-b(ə-)rənt\ *adj* [ME, fr. MF, fr. L *exuberant-, exuberans,* prp. of *exuberare* to be abundant, fr. *ex-* + *uber* fruitful, fr. *uber* udder — more at UDDER] (15c) **1 :** extreme or excessive in degree, size, or extent ⟨~ prosperity⟩ **2 a :** joyously unrestrained and enthusiastic ⟨~ praise⟩ ⟨an ~ personality⟩ **b :** unrestrained or elaborate esp. in style **:** FLAMBOYANT ⟨~ architecture⟩ **3 :** produced in extreme abundance **:** PLENTIFUL ⟨~ foliage and vegetation⟩ ***syn*** see PROFUSE — **ex·u·ber·ant·ly** *adv*
ex·u·ber·ate \-bə-ˌrāt\ *vi* **-at·ed; -at·ing** (15c) **1** *archaic* **:** to have something in abundance **:** OVERFLOW **2 :** to become exuberant **:** show exuberance ⟨*exuberated* over his victory⟩
ex·u·date \ˈek-s(y)ü-ˌdāt, -shü-\ *n* (1876) **:** exuded matter
ex·u·da·tion \ˌek-s(y)ü-ˈdā-shən, -shü-\ *n* (1612) **1 :** the process of exuding **2 :** EXUDATE — **ex·u·da·tive** \ig-ˈzü-də-tiv; ˈek-s(y)ü-ˌdā-tiv, -shü-\ *adj*
ex·ude \ig-ˈzüd\ *vb* **ex·ud·ed; ex·ud·ing** [L *exsudare,* fr. *ex-* + *sudare* to sweat — more at SWEAT] *vi* (1574) **1 :** to ooze out **2 :** to undergo diffusion ~ *vt* **1 :** to cause to ooze or spread out in all directions **2 :** to display conspicuously or abundantly ⟨~*s* charm⟩
ex·ult \ig-ˈzəlt\ *vi* [MF *exulter,* fr. L *exsultare,* lit., to leap up, fr. *ex-* + *saltare* to leap — more at SALTATION] (1548) **1** *obs* **:** to leap for joy **2 :** to be extremely joyful **:** REJOICE ⟨the team ~*ed* in their victory⟩ — **ex·ult·ing·ly** \-ˈzəl-tiŋ-lē\ *adv*
ex·ul·tance \ig-ˈzəl-tᵊn(t)s\ *n* (1650) **:** EXULTATION
ex·ul·tan·cy \-ˈzəl-tᵊn(t)-sē\ *n* (1621) **:** EXULTATION
ex·ul·tant \ig-ˈzəl-tᵊnt\ *adj* (1653) **:** filled with or expressing great joy or triumph **:** JUBILANT ⟨an ~ cheer⟩ ⟨~ fans⟩ — **ex·ul·tant·ly** *adv*
ex·ul·ta·tion \ˌek-(ˌ)səl-ˈtā-shən, ˌeg-(ˌ)zəl-\ *n* (15c) **:** the act of exulting **:** the state of being exultant
ex·urb \ˈek-ˌsərb, ˈeg-ˌzərb\ *n* [*ex-* + sub*urb*] (1955) **:** a region or settlement that lies outside a city and usu. beyond its suburbs and that often is inhabited chiefly by well-to-do families — **ex·ur·ban** \ek-ˈsər-bən; eg-ˈzər-, ig-\ *adj*
ex·ur·ban·ite \ek-ˈsər-bə-ˌnīt; eg-ˈzər-, ig-\ *n* (1955) **:** one who lives in an exurb
ex·ur·bia \-bē-ə\ *n* (1955) **:** the generalized region of exurbs
ex·u·vi·ae \ig-ˈzü-vē-ˌē, -vē-ˌī\ *n pl* [L, fr. *exuere* to take off, fr. *ex-* + *-uere* to put on; akin to OCS *obuti* to put on (footwear)] (1653) **:** sloughed off natural animal coverings (as the skins of snakes) — **ex·u·vi·al** \-vē-əl\ *adj*
ex·u·vi·a·tion \-ˌzü-vē-ˈā-shən\ *n* (1839) **:** the process of molting
[1]**ex–vo·to** \(ˌ)eks-ˈvō-(ˌ)tō\ *n, pl* **ex–votos** [L *ex voto* according to a vow] (1787) **:** a votive offering
[2]**ex–voto** *adj* (1823) **:** VOTIVE
-ey — see -Y
ey·as \ˈī-əs\ *n* [ME, alter. (by incorrect division of *a neias*) of *neias,* fr. AF *niais* taken in the nest, fr. VL **nidax* nestling, fr. L *nidus* nest — more at NEST] (15c) **:** an unfledged bird; *specif* **:** a nestling hawk
[1]**eye** \ˈī\ *n* [ME, fr. OE *ēage;* akin to OHG *ouga* eye, L *oculus,* Gk *ōps* eye, face, Skt *akṣi* eye] (bef. 12c) **1 a :** a specialized light-sensitive sensory structure of animals that in nearly all vertebrates, most arthropods, and some mollusks is the image-forming organ of sight; *esp* **:** the nearly spherical usu. paired hollow organ of sight in vertebrates that is filled with a jellylike material, is lined with a photosensitive retina, and is lodged in a bony orbit in the skull **b :** all the visible structures within and surrounding the orbit and including eyelids, eyelashes, and eyebrows **c (1) :** the faculty of seeing with eyes **(2) :** the faculty of intellectual or aesthetic perception or appreciation ⟨an ~ for beauty⟩ **(3) :** skill or ability dependent upon eyesight ⟨a batter with a good ~⟩ **d :** LOOK, GLANCE ⟨cast an eager ~⟩ **e (1) :** an attentive look ⟨kept an ~ on his valuables⟩ **(2) :** ATTENTION, NOTICE ⟨caught his ~⟩ **(3) :** close observation **:** SCRUTINY ⟨works under the ~ of her boss⟩ ⟨in the public ~⟩ **f :** POINT OF VIEW, JUDGMENT ⟨beauty is in the ~ of the beholder⟩ — often used in pl. ⟨an offender in the ~*s* of the law⟩ **2 :** something having an appearance suggestive of an eye: as **a :** the hole through the head of a needle **b :** a usu. circular marking (as on a peacock's tail) **c :** LOOP; *esp* **:** a loop or catch to receive a hook **d :** an undeveloped bud (as on a potato) **e :** an area like a hole in the center of a tropical cyclone marked by only light winds or complete calm with no precipitation **f :** the center of a flower esp. when differently colored or marked; *specif* **:** the disk of a composite **g (1) :** a triangular piece of beef cut from between the top and bottom of a round **(2) :** the chief muscle of a

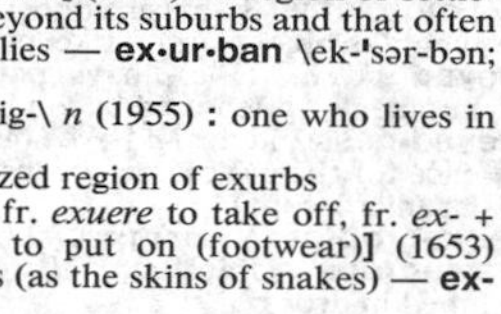

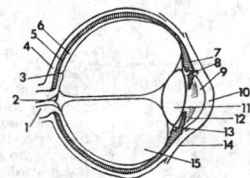

eye 1a: *1* optic nerve, *2* blind spot, *3* fovea, *4* sclera, *5* choroid, *6* retina, *7* ciliary body, *8* posterior chamber, *9* anterior chamber, *10* cornea, *11* lens, *12* iris, *13* suspensory ligament, *14* conjunctiva, *15* vitreous humor

chop (3) : a compact mass of muscular tissue usu. embedded in fat in a rib or loin cut of meat   **h** : a device (as a photoelectric cell) that functions in a manner analogous to human vision   **3** : something central : CENTER ⟨the ∼ of the problem —Norman Mailer⟩   **4** : the direction from which the wind is blowing — **eye·less** \ˈī-ləs\ adj — **eye·like** \-ˌlīk\ adj — **an eye for an eye** : retribution in kind — **my eye** — used to express mild disagreement or sometimes surprise ⟨a diamond, my eye! That's glass⟩ — **with an eye to** also **with an eye toward**   **1** : with awareness or contemplation of ⟨with an eye to the future⟩   **2** : with the object of ⟨built the house with an eye to adding on later⟩
²**eye** vb **eyed**; **eye·ing** or **ey·ing** vt (15c)   **1 a** (1) : to fix the eyes on : look at ⟨they eyed him suspiciously⟩   (2) : CONTEMPLATE, CONSIDER ⟨∼ing the choices⟩   **b** : to watch or study closely ⟨∼ing changes in the stock market⟩   **2** : to furnish with an eye ∼ vi, obs : SEEM, LOOK — **ey·er** \ˈī-(-ə)r\ n
¹**eye·ball** \ˈī-ˌbȯl\ n (1582)   **1** : the more or less globular capsule of the vertebrate eye formed by the sclera and cornea together with their contained structures   **2** pl : people who view something (as an advertisement) ⟨Web sites competing for ∼s⟩
²**eyeball** vt (1901) : to look at intently esp. in making an evaluation or choice ⟨diners ∼ing the menu⟩ ⟨∼ the competition⟩
³**eyeball** adj (1959) : based on observation ⟨∼ judgment⟩
eyeball–to–eyeball adv or adj (1962) : FACE-TO-FACE
eye bank n (1944) : a storage place for human corneas from the newly dead for transplant to the eyes of those blind from corneal defects
eye·bar \ˈī-ˌbär\ n (ca. 1889) : a metal bar having a closed loop at one or both ends
eye·blink \ˈī-ˌbliŋk\ n (1867)   **1** : a brief period of time : INSTANT   **2** : BLINK 3
eye·bolt \ˈī-ˌbōlt\ n (1769) : a bolt with a looped head
eye·bright \ˈī-ˌbrīt\ n (1533) : any of a genus (Euphrasia) of semiparasitic herbs of the snapdragon family with spikelike racemes
eye·brow \ˈī-ˌbrau̇\ n (15c) : the ridge over the eye or the hair growing on it
eyebrow pencil n (1881) : a cosmetic pencil for the eyebrows
eye candy n (1981) : something superficially attractive to look at
eye–catch·er \ˈī-ˌka-chər, -ˌke-\ n (1923) : something that arrests the eye — **eye–catch·ing** \-chiŋ\ adj — **eye–catch·ing·ly** \-chiŋ-lē\ adv
eye chart n (1943) : a chart read at a fixed distance for purposes of testing sight; esp : one with rows of letters or objects of decreasing size
eye contact n (1955) : visual contact with another person's eyes
eye·cup \ˈī-ˌkəp\ n (ca. 1874)   **1** : a small oval cup with a rim curved to fit the orbit of the eye used for applying liquid remedies to the eyes   **2** : OPTIC CUP   **3** : a usu. rubber cup at the eyepiece of an optical instrument (as binoculars) for keeping out extraneous light
eyed \ˈīd\ adj (14c) : having an eye or eyes esp. of a specified kind or number — often used in combination ⟨an almond-eyed girl⟩
eyed·ness \ˈīd-nəs\ n [-eyed (as in right-eyed, left-eyed)] (1924) : preference for the use of one eye instead of the other (as in using a monocular microscope)
eye·drop·per \ˈī-ˌdrä-pər\ n (1926) : DROPPER 2
eye·drops \-ˌdräps\ n pl (1926) : a medicated solution for the eyes applied in drops
eye·ful \ˈī-ˌfu̇l\ n (ca. 1864)   **1** : a full or completely satisfying view   **2** : one that is visually attractive; esp : a strikingly beautiful woman
eye·glass \ˈī-ˌglas\ n (1593)   **1 a** : EYEPIECE   **b** : a lens worn to aid vision; specif : MONOCLE   **c** pl : GLASSES, SPECTACLES   **2** : EYECUP 1
eye·hole \ˈī-ˌhōl\ n (1637)   **1** : ¹ORBIT   **2** : PEEPHOLE
eye·lash \ˈī-ˌlash\ n (1752)   **1** : the fringe of hair edging the eyelid — usu. used in pl.   **2** : a single hair of the eyelashes   **3** : HAIRBREADTH
eye lens n (1871) : the lens nearest the eye in an eyepiece
eye·let \ˈī-lət\ n [alter. of ME oilet, fr. AF oillet, dim. of oil eye, fr. L oculus] (14c)   **1 a** : a small hole designed to receive a cord or used for decoration (as in embroidery)   **b** : a small typically metal ring to reinforce an eyelet : GROMMET   **2** : PEEPHOLE, LOOPHOLE

eye·lid \ˈī-ˌlid\ n (13c) : either of the movable folds of skin and muscle that can be closed over the eyeball
eye lift n (1974) : BLEPHAROPLASTY
eye·lin·er \ˈī-ˌlī-nər\ n (1947) : makeup used to emphasize the contour of the eyes
ey·en \ˈī(-ə)n\ archaic pl of EYE
eye–open·er \ˈī-ˌōp-nər, -ˌō-pə-\ n (1817)   **1** : a drink intended to wake one up   **2** : something startling, surprising, or enlightening ⟨her biography is a real ∼⟩ — **eye–open·ing** \-niŋ\ adj
eye·piece \ˈī-ˌpēs\ n (1790) : the lens or combination of lenses at the eye end of an optical instrument
eye–pop·per \ˈī-ˌpä-pər\ n (1941) : something that excites, astonishes, or attracts the eye — **eye–pop·ping** \-ˌpä-piŋ\ adj
eye rhyme n (1871) : an imperfect rhyme that appears to have identical vowel sounds from similarity of spelling (as move and love)
eye·shade \ˈī-ˌshād\ n (1845) : a visor that shields the eyes from strong light and is fastened on with a headband
eye shadow n (1930) : a cosmetic cream or powder in one of various colors that is applied to the eyelids to accent the eyes
eye–shot \ˈī-ˌshät\ n (1599) : the range of the eye : VIEW
eye·sight \ˈī-ˌsīt\ n (13c)   **1** : SIGHT 4a   **2** archaic : OBSERVATION 1
eye socket n (ca. 1844) : ¹ORBIT
eyes only adj (1972) : to be read only by the person addressed
eye·sore \ˈī-ˌsȯr\ n (1530) : something offensive to view ⟨the old factory has become an ∼⟩
eye·spot \ˈī-ˌspät\ n (1862)   **1** : a spot of color   **2 a** : a simple visual organ of pigment or pigmented cells covering a sensory termination : OCELLUS   **b** : a small pigmented body of various unicellular algae   **3** : any of several fungal diseases of cultivated grasses (as corn, wheat, and sugarcane) characterized by yellowish oval lesions on the leaves and stem
eye·stalk \ˈī-ˌstȯk\ n (1854) : one of the movable peduncles bearing an eye at the tip in a decapod crustacean
eye·strain \ˈī-ˌstrān\ n (1874) : weariness or a strained state of the eye
eye·strings \ˈī-ˌstriŋz\ n pl (1590) obs : organic eye attachments formerly believed to break at death or blindness
eye·tooth \ˈī-ˈtüth\ n (ca. 1545) : a canine tooth of the upper jaw
eye view n (ca. 1771) : POINT OF VIEW ⟨an alien eye view⟩
eye·wash \ˈī-ˌwȯsh, -ˌwäsh\ n (ca. 1859)   **1** : an eye lotion   **2** : misleading or deceptive statements, actions, or procedures
eye·wear \ˈī-ˌwer\ n (1926) : corrective or protective devices (as glasses or contact lenses) for the eyes
eye·wink \ˈī-ˌwiŋk\ n (1598) : LOOK, GLANCE
eye·wit·ness \ˈī-ˈwit-nəs\ n (1539) : one who sees an occurrence or an object; esp : one who gives a report on what he or she has seen
eyre \ˈer\ n [ME eire, fr. AF, journey, eyre, fr. errer to travel — more at ERRANT] (14c) : a circuit traveled by an itinerant justice in medieval England or the court he presided over
ey·rie chiefly Brit var of AERIE
ey·rir \ˈā-ˌrir\ n, pl **au·rar** \ˈȯy-ˌrär\ [Icel, fr. ON, money (in pl.), prob. fr. L aureus a gold coin] (ca. 1927) — see krona at MONEY table
Ez or **Ezr** abbr Ezra
Ezech abbr Ezechiel
Eze·chiel \i-ˈzē-kyəl, -kē-əl\ n [LL] (bef. 12c) : EZEKIEL
Ezek abbr Ezekiel
Eze·kiel \i-ˈzē-kyəl, -kē-əl\ n [LL Ezechiel, fr. Heb Yĕḥezqēl] (1568)   **1** : a Hebrew priest and prophet of the sixth century B.C.   **2** : a prophetic book of canonical Jewish and Christian Scripture written by Ezekiel — see BIBLE table
e–zine \ˈē-ˌzēn\ n [²e- + -zine (as in fanzine)] (1992) : an electronic magazine (as on the World Wide Web)
Ez·ra \ˈez-rə\ n [LL, fr. Heb ʿEzrā] (1540)   **1** : a Hebrew priest, scribe, and reformer of Judaism of the fifth century B.C. in Babylon and Jerusalem   **2** : a narrative book of canonical Jewish and Christian Scripture — see BIBLE table

¹**f** \ˈef\ n, pl **f's** or **fs** \ˈefs\ often cap, often attrib (bef. 12c)   **1 a** : the 6th letter of the English alphabet   **b** : a graphic representation of this letter   **c** : a speech counterpart of orthographic f   **2** : the fourth tone of a C-major scale   **3** : a graphic device for reproducing the letter f   **4** : one designated f esp. as the sixth in order or class   **5 a** : a grade rating a student's work as failing   **b** : one graded or rated with an F   **6** : something shaped like the letter F
²**f** abbr   **1** failure   **2** false   **3** family   **4** faraday   **5** feast   **6** female   **7** feminine   **8** femto-   **9** fermi   **10** fine   **11** finish   **12** fluid; fluidness   **13** focal length   **14** folio   **15** [following] and the following one   **16** force   **17** forte   **18** fragile   **19** frequency   **20** from   **21** full
¹**F** abbr   **1** Fahrenheit   **2** farad   **3** French   **4** Friday
²**F** symbol fluorine
fa \ˈfä\ n [ME, fr. ML, fr. the syllable sung to this note in a medieval hymn to St. John the Baptist] (13c) : the fourth tone of the diatonic scale in solmization
FA abbr   **1** field artillery   **2** fielding average   **3** football association
FAA abbr   **1** Federal Aviation Administration   **2** free of all average

fab \ˈfab\ adj (1957) : FABULOUS
Fa·bi·an \ˈfā-bē-ən\ adj (1638)   **1 a** : of, relating to, or in the manner of the Roman general Quintus Fabius Maximus known for his defeat of Hannibal in the Second Punic War by the avoidance of decisive contests   **b** : CAUTIOUS, DILATORY   **2** [the Fabian Society; fr. the members' belief in slow rather than revolutionary change in government] : of, relating to, or being a society of socialists organized in England in 1884 to spread socialist principles gradually — **Fabian** n — **Fa·bi·an·ism** \-ə-ˌni-zəm\ n
¹**fa·ble** \ˈfā-bəl\ n [ME, fr. AF, fr. L fabula conversation, story, play, fr. fari to speak — more at BAN] (14c)   **1** : a fictitious narrative or statement: as   **a** : a legendary story of supernatural happenings   **b** : a narration intended to enforce a useful truth; esp : one in which animals speak and act like human beings   **c** : FALSEHOOD, LIE
²**fable** vb **fa·bled**; **fa·bling** \-b(ə-)liŋ\ vi (14c) archaic : to tell fables ∼ vt : to talk or write about as if true — **fa·bler** \-b(ə-)lər\ n
fabled adj (1602)   **1** : FICTITIOUS   **2** : told or celebrated in fables   **3** : RENOWNED, FAMOUS ⟨the team's ∼ coach⟩
fab·li·au \ˈfa-blē-ˌō\ n, pl **-aux** \-ˌō(z)\ [F, fr. OF, dim. of fable] (1804) : a short, usu. comic, frankly coarse, and often cynical tale in verse popular esp. in the 12th and 13th centuries
fab·ric \ˈfa-brik\ n [MF fabrique, fr. L fabrica workshop, structure]

(15c) **1 a :** STRUCTURE, BUILDING **b :** underlying structure : FRAMEWORK ⟨the ~ of society⟩ **2 :** an act of constructing : ERECTION; *specif* : the construction and maintenance of a church building **3 a :** structural plan or style of construction **b :** TEXTURE, QUALITY — used chiefly of textiles **c :** the arrangement of physical components (as of soil) in relation to each other **4 a :** CLOTH 1a **b :** a material that resembles cloth **5 :** the appearance or pattern produced by the shapes and arrangement of the crystal grains in a rock

fab·ri·cant \ˈfa-bri-kənt\ *n* (1757) : MANUFACTURER

fab·ri·cate \ˈfa-bri-ˌkāt\ *vt* **-cat·ed; -cat·ing** [ME, fr. L *fabricatus,* pp. of *fabricari,* fr. *fabrica*] (15c) **1 a :** INVENT, CREATE **b :** to make up for the purpose of deception ⟨accused of *fabricating* evidence⟩ **2 :** CONSTRUCT, MANUFACTURE; *specif* : to construct from diverse and usu. standardized parts — **fab·ri·ca·tor** \ˈfa-bri-ˌkā-tər\ *n*

fab·ri·ca·tion \ˌfa-bri-ˈkā-shən\ *n* (15c) **1 :** the act or process of fabricating **2 :** a product of fabrication; *esp* : LIE, FALSEHOOD

fabric softener *n* (1965) : a product used to make laundered fabrics softer and fluffier

fab·u·lar \ˈfa-byə-lər\ *adj* (1684) : of, relating to, or having the form of a fable

fab·u·list \ˈfa-byə-list\ *n* (1593) **1 :** a creator or writer of fables **2 :** LIAR — **fabulist** *or* **fab·u·lis·tic** \ˌfa-byə-ˈlis-tik\ *adj*

fab·u·lous \ˈfa-byə-ləs\ *adj* [ME, fr. L *fabulosus,* fr. *fabula*] (15c) **1 a :** resembling or suggesting a fable : of an incredible, astonishing, or exaggerated nature ⟨~ wealth⟩ **b :** WONDERFUL, MARVELOUS ⟨had a ~ time⟩ **2 :** told in or based on fable ***syn*** see FICTITIOUS — **fab·u·lous·ly** *adv* — **fab·u·lous·ness** *n*

fac *abbr* **1** facsimile **2** faculty

FAC *abbr* forward air controller

fa·cade *also* **fa·çade** \fə-ˈsäd\ *n* [F *façade,* fr. It *facciata,* fr. *faccia* face, fr. VL **facia*] (ca. 1681) **1 :** the front of a building; *also* : any face of a building given special architectural treatment ⟨a museum's east ~⟩ **2 :** a false, superficial, or artificial appearance or effect

facade 1

[1]face \ˈfās\ *n, often attrib* [ME, fr. AF, fr. VL **facia,* fr. L *facies* make, form, face, fr. *facere* to make, do — more at DO] (13c) **1 a :** the front part of the head that in humans extends from the forehead to the chin and includes the mouth, nose, cheeks, and eyes **b :** the face as a means of identification : COUNTENANCE ⟨would know that ~ anywhere⟩ **2** *archaic* : PRESENCE, SIGHT **3 a :** facial expression ⟨a friendly ~⟩ **b :** a facial expression of distaste or displeasure ⟨he made a ~ when he saw the test results⟩ **c :** MAKEUP 3a(1) **4 a (1) :** outward appearance ⟨put a good ~ on it⟩ **(2) :** the aspect of something that is perceptible or obvious upon superficial examination ⟨the theory is absurd on its ~ —Kim Neely⟩ **b :** DISGUISE, PRETENSE **c (1) :** ASSURANCE, CONFIDENCE ⟨maintaining a firm ~ in spite of adversity⟩ **(2) :** EFFRONTERY ⟨how anyone could have the ~ to ask that question⟩ **d :** DIGNITY, PRESTIGE ⟨afraid to lose ~⟩ **5 :** SURFACE: **a (1) :** a front, upper, or outer surface **(2) :** the front of something having two or four sides **(3) :** FACADE **(4) :** an exposed surface of rock **(5) :** any of the plane surfaces that bound a geometric solid **b :** a surface specially prepared: as **(1) :** the principal dressed surface (as of a disk) **(2) :** the right side (as of cloth or leather) **(3) :** an inscribed, printed, or marked side **c :** a striking surface (as of a tool) ⟨the ~ of the golf club⟩ ⟨the ~ of an anvil⟩ **d (1) :** the surface (as of type) that receives the ink and transfers it to the paper **(2) :** a style of type **6 :** the end or wall of a mine tunnel, drift, or excavation at which work is progressing **7 :** FACE VALUE **8 :** PERSON ⟨lots of new ~*s* around here⟩ — **in one's face :** directly and aggressively in one's presence ⟨dunked the ball *in his face*⟩ — often used with *get* to describe aggressively confrontational speech or behavior ⟨his boss got *in his face* about being late⟩ — **in the face of** *also* **in face of :** face-to-face with : DESPITE ⟨fearless *in the face of* danger⟩ — **to one's face :** in one's presence or so that one is fully aware of what is going on

[2]face *vb* **faced; fac·ing** *vt* (15c) **1 :** to confront impudently **2 a :** to line near the edge esp. with a different material **b :** to cover the front or surface of ⟨*faced* the building with marble⟩ **3 :** to meet face-to-face or in competition **4 a :** to stand or sit with the face toward **b :** to have the front oriented toward ⟨a house *facing* the park⟩ **5 a :** to recognize and deal with straightforwardly ⟨~ the facts⟩ **b :** to master by confronting with determination — used with *down* ⟨*faced* down his critics⟩ **6 a :** to have as a prospect : be confronted by ⟨~ a grim future⟩ **b :** to be a prospect or a source of concern for ⟨the problems that ~ us⟩ **c :** to bring face-to-face ⟨he was *faced* with ruin⟩ **7 :** to make the surface of (as a stone) flat or smooth **8 :** to cause (troops) to face in a particular direction on command ~ *vi* **1 :** to have the face or front turned in a specified direction **2 :** to turn the face in a specified direction — **face the music :** to meet an unpleasant situation, a danger, or the consequences of one's actions

face angle *n* (1913) : an angle formed by two edges of a polyhedral angle

face card *n* (1826) : a king, queen, or jack in a deck of cards

face–cen·tered \ˈfās-ˌsen-tərd\ *adj* (1913) : relating to or being a crystal space lattice in which each cubic unit cell has an atom at the center and at the corners of each face — compare BODY-CENTERED

face·cloth \ˈfās-ˌklȯth\ *n* (1602) : WASHCLOTH

face cord *n* (ca. 1926) : a unit of wood cut for fuel equal to a stack 4 × 8 feet with lengths of pieces from about 12 to 16 inches

-faced *adj comb form* : having (such) a face or (so many) faces ⟨rosy-*faced*⟩ ⟨two-*faced*⟩

face·down \ˌfās-ˈdau̇n\ *adv* (1830) : with the face down ⟨sliding ~⟩

face–first \ˌfās-ˈfərst\ *adv* (1880) : with the face foremost ⟨hit the wall ~⟩ — **face–first** *adj*

face fly *n* (1961) : a European dipteran fly (*Musca autumnalis*) that is similar to the housefly, is widely established in No. America, and causes distress to livestock by clustering about the face

face·less \ˈfās-ləs\ *adj* (1568) **1 a :** lacking character or individuality : NONDESCRIPT ⟨the ~ masses⟩ **b :** not identified : ANONYMOUS ⟨a ~ accuser⟩ **2 :** lacking a face — **face·less·ness** *n*

face–lift \ˈfās-ˌlift\ *n* (1934) **1 :** plastic surgery on the face and neck to remove defects and imperfections (as wrinkles or sagging skin) typical of aging **2 :** an alteration, restoration, or restyling (as of a building) intended esp. to modernize — **face–lift** *vt*

face mask *n* (1906) : a mask covering the face (as in football)

face–off \ˈfās-ˌȯf\ *n* (1896) **1 :** a method of beginning play (as in hockey or lacrosse) in which two opponents face each other and attempt to gain control of a puck or ball dropped or placed between them **2 :** CONFRONTATION

face off *vi* (1948) : to be in or come into opposition or competition ⟨politicians *facing off* against each other in a televised debate⟩

face–plant \ˈfās-ˌplant\ *n* (1982) : a sudden face-first fall

face·plate \ˈfās-ˌplāt\ *n* (1841) **1 :** a disk fixed with its face at right angles to the live spindle of a lathe for the attachment of the work **2 a :** a protective plate for a machine or device **b :** a protective cover for the human face (as of a diver) **3 :** the glass front of a cathode-ray tube on which the image is seen

fac·er \ˈfā-sər\ *n* (15c) **1 :** one that faces **2** *Brit* : a sudden often stunning check or obstacle

face–sav·er \ˈfā(s)-ˌsā-vər\ *n* (1923) : something (as a compromise) that saves face — **face–sav·ing** \-ˌsā-viŋ\ *adj or n*

fac·et \ˈfa-sət\ *n* [F *facette,* dim. of *face*] (1625) **1 :** a small plane surface (as on a cut gem) — see BRILLIANT illustration **2 :** any of the definable aspects that make up a subject (as of contemplation) or an object (as of consideration) **3 :** the external corneal surface of an ommatidium **4 :** a smooth flat circumscribed anatomical surface (as of a bone) — **fac·et·ed** *or* **fac·et·ted** \ˈfa-sə-təd\ *adj*

fa·cete \fə-ˈsēt\ *adj* [L *facetus*] (1603) *archaic* : FACETIOUS, WITTY

fa·ce·ti·ae \fə-ˈsē-shē-ˌē, -ˌī\ *n pl* [L, fr. pl. of *facetia* jest, fr. *facetus* elegant, witty] (1529) : witty or humorous writings or sayings

face time *n* (1978) **1 :** the amount of time one spends appearing on television **2 :** time spent in a face-to-face meeting with someone **3 :** time spent at one's place of employment esp. beyond normal work hours

fa·ce·tious \fə-ˈsē-shəs\ *adj* [MF *facetieux,* fr. *facetie* jest, fr. L *facetia*] (1599) **1 :** joking or jesting often inappropriately : WAGGISH ⟨just being ~⟩ **2 :** meant to be humorous or funny : not serious ⟨a ~ remark⟩ ***syn*** see WITTY — **fa·ce·tious·ly** *adv* — **fa·ce·tious·ness** *n*

face–to–face *adv or adj* (14c) **1 :** within each other's sight or presence ⟨met and talked ~⟩ ⟨a ~ consultation⟩ **2 :** in or into direct contact or confrontation ⟨came ~ with the problem⟩

face·up \ˈfās-ˈəp\ *adv* (1891) : with the face up

face up *vi* (1920) : to confront or deal directly with someone or something previously avoided — usu. used with *to* ⟨*faced up* to my fears⟩

face value *n* (1876) **1 :** the value indicated on the face (as of a postage stamp or a stock certificate) **2 :** the apparent value or significance ⟨if their remarks may be taken at *face value*⟩

facia *var of* FASCIA 3

[1]fa·cial \ˈfā-shəl\ *adj* (ca. 1818) **1 :** of or relating to the face ⟨~ expressions⟩ **2 :** concerned with or used in improving the appearance of the face — **fa·cial·ly** \-shə-lē\ *adv*

[2]facial *n* (1914) : a facial treatment

facial index *n* (ca. 1889) : the ratio of the breadth of the face to its length multiplied by 100

facial nerve *n* (ca. 1818) : either of the seventh pair of cranial nerves that supply motor fibers esp. to the muscles of the face and jaw and sensory and parasympathetic fibers to the tongue, palate, and fauces

-facient *adj comb form* [L *-facient-, -faciens* (as in *calefacient-, calefaciens* making warm, prp. of *calefacere* to warm)] : making : causing ⟨somni*facient*⟩

fa·cies \ˈfā-sh(ē-ˌ)ēz\ *n, pl* **facies** [NL, fr. L, face] (ca. 1736) **1 :** general appearance ⟨a plant species with a particularly distinct ~⟩ **2 :** an appearance and expression of the face characteristic of a particular condition esp. when abnormal ⟨adenoid ~⟩ **3 :** a part of a rock or group of rocks that differs from the whole formation (as in composition, age, or fossil content)

fac·ile \ˈfa-səl\ *adj* [MF, fr. L *facilis,* fr. *facere* to do — more at DO] (15c) **1 a (1) :** easily accomplished or attained ⟨a ~ victory⟩ **(2) :** SHALLOW, SIMPLISTIC ⟨I am not concerned . . . with offering any ~ solution for so complex a problem —T. S. Eliot⟩ **b :** used or comprehended with ease **c :** readily manifested and often lacking sincerity or depth ⟨~ tears⟩ **2** *archaic* : mild or pleasing in manner or disposition **3 a :** READY, FLUENT ⟨~ prose⟩ **b :** POISED, ASSURED ***syn*** see EASY — **fac·ile·ly** \-sə(l)-lē\ *adv* — **fac·ile·ness** \-səl-nəs\ *n*

fa·cil·i·tate \fə-ˈsi-lə-ˌtāt\ *vt* **-tat·ed; -tat·ing** (1611) : to make easier : help bring about ⟨~ growth⟩ — **fa·cil·i·ta·tive** \-ˌtā-tiv\ *adj*

fa·cil·i·ta·tion \fə-ˌsi-lə-ˈtā-shən\ *n* (1619) **1 :** the act of facilitating : the state of being facilitated **2 a :** the lowering of the threshold for reflex conduction along a particular neural pathway esp. from repeated use of that pathway **b :** the increasing of the ease or intensity of a response by repeated stimulation

fa·cil·i·ta·tor \fə-ˈsi-lə-ˌtā-tər\ *n* (1799) : one that facilitates; *esp* : one that helps to bring about an outcome (as learning, productivity, or communication) by providing indirect or unobtrusive assistance, guidance, or supervision ⟨the workshop's ~ kept discussion flowing smoothly⟩

fa·cil·i·ta·to·ry \fə-ˈsi-lə-tə-ˌtȯr-ē\ *adj* (1944) : inducing or involved in facilitation esp. of a reflex action

fa·cil·i·ty \fə-ˈsi-lə-tē\ *n, pl* **-ties** (1531) **1 :** the quality of being easily performed **2 :** ease in performance : APTITUDE **3 :** readiness of compliance **4 a (1) :** something that makes an action, operation, or course of conduct easier — usu. used in pl. ⟨*facilities* for study⟩ **(2) :** LAVATORY 2 — often used in pl. **b :** something (as a hospital) that is built, installed, or established to serve a particular purpose

\ə\ **abut** \ᵊ\ **kitten**, F **table** \ər\ **further** \a\ **ash** \ā\ **ace** \ä\ **mop, mar**
\au̇\ **out** \ch\ **chin** \e\ **bet** \ē\ **easy** \g\ **go** \i\ **hit** \ī\ **ice** \j\ **job**
\ŋ\ **sing** \ō\ **go** \ȯ\ **law** \ȯi\ **boy** \th\ **thin** \t͟h\ **the** \ü\ **loot** \u̇\ **foot**
\y\ **yet** \zh\ **vision, beige** \k̲, ⁿ, œ, ue, ʸ\ *see* Guide to Pronunciation

fac·ing \ˈfā-siŋ\ *n* (1566) **1 a :** a lining at the edge esp. of a garment **b** *pl* **:** the collar, cuffs, and trimmings of a uniform coat **2 :** an ornamental or protective layer **3 :** material for facing
fac·sim·i·le \fak-ˈsi-mə-lē\ *n* [L *fac simile* make similar] (1691) **1 :** an exact copy **2 :** a system of transmitting and reproducing graphic matter (as printing or still pictures) by means of signals sent over telephone lines ***syn*** see REPRODUCTION
fact \ˈfakt\ *n* [L *factum,* fr. neut. of *factus,* pp. of *facere*] (15c) **1 :** a thing done: as **a** *obs* **:** FEAT **b :** CRIME ⟨accessory after the ~⟩ **c** *archaic* **:** ACTION **2** *archaic* **:** PERFORMANCE, DOING **3 :** the quality of being actual **:** ACTUALITY ⟨a question of ~ hinges on evidence⟩ **4 a :** something that has actual existence ⟨space exploration is now a ~⟩ **b :** an actual occurrence ⟨prove the ~ of damage⟩ **5 :** a piece of information presented as having objective reality — **in fact :** in truth
fact–check \ˈfak(t)-ˌchek\ *vt* (1973) **:** to verify the factual accuracy of ⟨~ the article before publication⟩ — **fact–check·er** \-ˌche-kər\ *n*
fact finder *n* (1926) **:** one that tries to determine the realities of a case, situation, or relationship; *esp* **:** an impartial examiner designated by a government agency to appraise the facts underlying a particular matter (as a labor dispute) — **fact–find·ing** *n or adj*
fac·tic·i·ty \fak-ˈti-sə-tē\ *n* [F or G; F *facticité,* fr. G *Faktizität,* fr. *Factum* fact, fr. L *factum*] (1945) **:** the quality or state of being a fact
fac·tion \ˈfak-shən\ *n* [MF & L; MF, fr. L *faction-, factio* act of making, faction — more at FASHION] (1509) **1 :** a party or group (as within a government) that is often contentious or self-seeking **:** CLIQUE **2 :** party spirit esp. when marked by dissension — **fac·tion·al** \-shnəl, -shə-nᵊl\ *adj* — **fac·tion·al·ism** \-shnə-ˌli-zəm, -shə-nə-ˌliz-\ *n* — **fac·tion·al·ly** \-ē\ *adv*
-faction *n comb form* [L *-faction-, -factio* (as in *satisfaction-, satisfactio* satisfaction)] **:** making **:** -FICATION ⟨petri*faction*⟩
fac·tious \ˈfak-shəs\ *adj* [MF or L; MF *factieux,* fr. L *factiosus,* fr. *factio*] (1532) **:** of or relating to faction: as **a :** caused by faction ⟨~ disputes⟩ **b :** inclined to faction or the formation of factions **c :** SEDITIOUS — **fac·tious·ly** *adv* — **fac·tious·ness** *n*
fac·ti·tious \fak-ˈti-shəs\ *adj* [L *facticius,* fr. *factus,* pp. of *facere* to make, do — more at DO] (1646) **1 :** produced by humans rather than by natural forces **2 a :** formed by or adapted to an artificial or conventional standard **b :** produced by special effort **:** SHAM ⟨created a ~ demand by spreading rumors of shortage⟩ — **fac·ti·tious·ly** *adv* — **fac·ti·tious·ness** *n*
fac·ti·tive \ˈfak-tə-tiv\ *adj* [prob. fr. L *factitare* to do habitually, freq. of *facere*] (1846) **:** of, relating to, or being a transitive verb that in some constructions requires an objective complement as well as an object — **fac·ti·tive·ly** *adv*
-factive *adj comb form* [*-faction*] **:** making **:** causing ⟨putre*factive*⟩
fact of life (1849) **1 :** something that exists and must be taken into consideration **2** *pl* **:** the fundamental physiological processes and behavior involved in sex and reproduction
fac·toid \ˈfak-ˌtȯid\ *n* (1973) **1 :** an invented fact believed to be true because it appears in print **2 :** a briefly stated and usu. trivial fact
[1]**fac·tor** \ˈfak-tər\ *n* [ME, fr. MF *facteur,* fr. L *factor* doer, fr. *facere*] (15c) **1 :** one who acts or transacts business for another: as **a :** BROKER 1b **b :** one that lends money to producers and dealers (as on the security of accounts receivable) **2 a** (1) **:** one that actively contributes to the production of a result **:** INGREDIENT ⟨price wasn't a ~ in the decision⟩ (2) **:** a substance that functions in or promotes the function of a particular physiological process or bodily system **b :** a good or service used in the process of production **3 :** GENE **4 a :** any of the numbers or symbols in mathematics that when multiplied together form a product; *also* **:** a number or symbol that divides another number or symbol **b :** a quantity by which a given quantity is multiplied or divided in order to indicate a difference in measurement ⟨costs increased by a ~ of 10⟩ — **fac·tor·ship** \-ˌship\ *n*
[2]**factor** *vb* **fac·tored; fac·tor·ing** \-t(ə-)riŋ\ *vi* (1621) **:** to work as a factor ~ *vt* **1 :** to resolve into factors **2 a :** to include or admit as a factor — used with *in* or *into* ⟨~ inflation into our calculations⟩ **b :** to exclude as a factor — used with *out* — **fac·tor·able** \-t(ə-)rə-bəl\ *adj*
fac·tor·age \-t(ə-)rij\ *n* (1613) **1 :** the charges made by a factor for services **2 :** the business of a factor
factor analysis *n* (1931) **:** the analytical process of transforming statistical data (as measurements) into linear combinations of usu. independent variables — **factor analytic** *adj*
factor VIII \-ˈāt\ *n* (1954) **:** a glycoprotein clotting factor of blood plasma that is essential for blood clotting and is absent or inactive in hemophilia — called also *antihemophilic factor*
factor group *n* (1897) **:** QUOTIENT GROUP
[1]**fac·to·ri·al** \fak-ˈtȯr-ē-əl\ *adj* (1837) **:** of, relating to, or being a factor or a factorial
[2]**factorial** *n* (1869) **1 :** the product of all the positive integers from 1 to *n* — symbol *n!* **2 :** the quantity *0!* arbitrarily defined as equal to 1
fac·tor·i·za·tion \ˌfak-tə-rə-ˈzā-shən\ *n* (1886) **:** the operation of resolving a quantity into factors; *also* **:** a product obtained by factorization — **fac·tor·ize** \ˈfak-tə-ˌrīz\ *vt*
fac·to·ry \ˈfak-t(ə-)rē\ *n, pl* **-ries** (1582) **1 :** a station where factors reside and trade ⟨a colonial ~⟩ **2 a :** a building or set of buildings with facilities for manufacturing **b :** the seat of some kind of production ⟨the vice *factories* of the slums⟩ — **fac·to·ry·like** \-ˌlīk\ *adj*
factory farm *n* (1868) **:** a large industrialized farm; *esp* **:** a farm on which large numbers of livestock are raised indoors in conditions intended to maximize production at minimal cost — **factory farming** *n*
factory ship *n* (1851) **:** a ship equipped to process a whale or fish catch at sea
fac·to·tum \fak-ˈtō-təm\ *n* [NL, lit., do everything, fr. L *fac* (imper. of *facere* do) + *totum* everything] (1566) **1 :** a person having many diverse activities or responsibilities **2 :** a general servant
fac·tu·al \ˈfak-chə-wəl, -chəl, -chü-əl, ˈfaksh-wəl\ *adj* [*fact* + *-ual* (as in *actual*)] (ca. 1834) **1 :** of or relating to facts ⟨a ~ error⟩ **2 :** restricted to or based on fact ⟨a ~ statement⟩ — **fac·tu·al·i·ty** \ˌfak-chə-ˈwa-lə-tē\ *n* — **fac·tu·al·ly** \ˈfak-chə-wə-lē, -chə-lē, -chü(-ə)-lē, ˈfaksh-wə-\ *adv* — **fac·tu·al·ness** *n*
fac·tu·al·ism \ˈfak-chə-wə-ˌli-zəm, -chə-ˌli-, -chü-ə-ˌli-, ˈfaksh-wə-\ *n* (1936) **:** adherence or dedication to facts — **fac·tu·al·ist** \-list\ *n*
fac·ture \ˈfak-chər\ *n* [ME, fr. AF, fr. L *factura* action of making, fr. *factus*] (15c) **:** the manner in which something (as a painting) is made

fac·u·la \ˈfa-kyə-lə\ *n, pl* **-lae** \-ˌlē, -ˌlī\ [NL, fr. L, dim. of *fac-, fax* torch] (1706) **:** any of the bright regions of the sun's photosphere seen most easily near the sun's edge
fac·ul·ta·tive \ˈfa-kəl-ˌtā-tiv, *Brit* -tə-tiv\ *adj* (1820) **1 a :** of or relating to the grant of permission, authority, or privilege ⟨~ legislation⟩ **b :** OPTIONAL **2 :** of or relating to a mental faculty **3 a :** taking place under some conditions but not under others ⟨~ diapause⟩ **b :** exhibiting an indicated lifestyle under some environmental conditions but not under others ⟨~ anaerobes⟩ — **fac·ul·ta·tive·ly** *adv*
fac·ul·ty \ˈfa-kəl-tē\ *n, pl* **-ties** [ME *faculte,* fr. AF *faculté,* fr. ML & L; ML *facultat-, facultas* branch of learning or teaching, fr. L, ability, abundance, fr. *facilis* facile] (14c) **1 :** ABILITY, POWER: as **a :** innate or acquired ability to act or do **b :** an inherent capability, power, or function ⟨the ~ of hearing⟩ **c :** any of the powers of the mind formerly held by psychologists to form a basis for the explanation of all mental phenomena **d :** natural aptitude ⟨has a ~ for saying the right things⟩ **2 a :** a branch of teaching or learning in an educational institution **b** *archaic* **:** something in which one is trained or qualified **3 a :** the members of a profession **b :** the teaching and administrative staff and those members of the administration having academic rank in an educational institution **c faculty** *pl* **:** faculty members ⟨many ~ were present⟩ **4 :** power, authority, or prerogative given or conferred ***syn*** see GIFT
fad \ˈfad\ *n* [origin unknown] (1867) **:** a practice or interest followed for a time with exaggerated zeal **:** CRAZE ***syn*** see FASHION — **fad·dish** \ˈfa-dish\ *adj* — **fad·dish·ly** *adv* — **fad·dish·ness** *n* — **fad·dism** \ˈfa-ˌdi-zəm\ *n* — **fad·dist** \ˈfa-dist\ *n* — **fad·dy** \-dē\ *adj*
FAD \ˌef-ˌā-ˈdē\ *n* (1944) **:** FLAVIN ADENINE DINUCLEOTIDE
[1]**fade** \ˈfād\ *vb* **fad·ed; fad·ing** [ME, fr. AF **fader,* fr. *fade* feeble, insipid, fr. VL **fatidus,* alter. of L *fatuus* fatuous, insipid] *vi* (14c) **1 :** to lose freshness, strength, or vitality **:** WITHER ⟨*fading* flowers⟩ **2 :** to lose freshness or brilliance of color **3 :** to sink away **:** VANISH ⟨a *fading* memory⟩ **4 :** to change gradually in loudness, strength, or visibility — used of a motion-picture image or of an electronics signal and usu. with *in* or *out* **5** *of an automobile brake* **:** to lose braking power gradually **6 :** to move back from the line of scrimmage — used of a quarterback **7** *of a ball or shot* **:** to move in a slight to moderate slice ~ *vt* **:** to cause to fade — **fad·er** *n*
[2]**fade** *n* (1918) **1 a :** FADE-OUT **b :** a gradual changing of one picture to another in a motion-picture or television sequence **2 :** a fading of an automobile brake **3 :** a slight to moderate and usu. intentional slice in golf **4 :** a hairstyle similar to a crew cut in which the hair on top of the head stands high
[3]**fade** \ˈfäd\ *adj* [ME, fr. AF] (15c) **:** INSIPID, COMMONPLACE
fade·away \ˈfād-ə-ˌwā\ *n* (1909) **1 a :** SCREWBALL 1 **b :** a slide in which a base runner throws his or her body sideways to avoid the tag **2 :** an act or instance of fading away
fade–in \ˈfād-ˌin\ *n* (1917) **:** a gradual increase in a motion-picture or television image's visibility at the beginning of a sequence
fade·less \ˈfād-ləs\ *adj* (1652) **:** not susceptible to fading
fade–out \ˈfād-ˌau̇t\ *n* (1917) **:** an act or instance of fading out; *esp* **:** a gradual decrease in a motion-picture or television image's visibility at the end of a sequence
FADM *abbr* fleet admiral
fa·do \ˈfä-(ˌ)thü, ˈfa-\ *n, pl* **fados** [Pg, lit., fate, fr. L *fatum*] (1890) **:** a plaintive Portuguese folk song
fae·cal, fae·ces *chiefly Brit var of* FECAL, FECES
fa·e·na \fä-ˈā-(ˌ)nä\ *n* [Sp, lit., task, fr. obs. Catal, fr. L *facienda* things to be done, fr. *facere* to do — more at DO] (1927) **:** a series of final passes leading to the kill made by the matador in a bullfight
fa·er·ie *also* **fa·ery** \ˈfā-(ə-)rē, ˈfer-ē\ *n, pl* **fa·er·ies** [ME *fairie* — more at FAIRY] (1579) **1 :** FAIRYLAND **2 :** FAIRY 1 — **faery** *adj*
Faero·ese *or* **Faro·ese** \ˌfer-ə-ˈwēz, -ˈwēs\ *n, pl* **Faeroese** *or* **Faroese** (1854) **1 :** a member of the people inhabiting the Faeroes **2 :** the North Germanic language of the Faeroese people — **Faeroese** *adj*
Faf·nir \ˈfäv-nər, ˈfäf-, -ˌnir\ *n* [ON *Fāfnir*] (1850) **:** a dragon in Norse mythology that guards the Nibelungs' gold hoard until slain by Sigurd
[1]**fag** \ˈfag\ *vb* **fagged; fag·ging** [perh. fr. obs. *fag* to droop, fr. *fag* fag end] *vi* (1772) **:** to work hard **:** TOIL ~ *vt* **:** to tire by strenuous activity **:** EXHAUST ⟨*fagged* by the strenuous climb⟩ ***syn*** see TIRE
[2]**fag** *n* (1780) **1** *chiefly Brit* **:** TOIL, DRUDGERY **2 :** DRUDGE 1
[3]**fag** *n* [prob. short for *faggot*] (1785) **:** an English public-school boy who acts as servant to an older schoolmate
[4]**fag** *vi* (1806) **:** to serve as a fag esp. in an English public school ⟨*fagging* for older boys during his first year⟩
[5]**fag** *n* [*fag end*] (ca. 1888) **:** CIGARETTE
[6]**fag** *n* (1921) *usu disparaging* **:** FAGGOT — **fag·gy** \ˈfa-gē\ *adj, usu disparaging*
fag end *n* [earlier *fag,* fr. ME *fagge* flap] (1600) **1 a :** a poor or worn-out end **:** REMNANT **b :** the extreme end **2 a :** the last part or coarser end of a web of cloth **b :** the untwisted end of a rope
fag·got \ˈfa-gət\ *n* [earlier and dial., contemptuous word for a woman or child, prob. fr. [1]*fagot*] (1914) *usu disparaging* **:** a male homosexual — **fag·got·ry** \-gə-trē\ *n, usu disparaging* — **fag·goty** \-gə-tē\ *adj, usu disparaging*
fa·gin \ˈfā-gən\ *n, often cap* [*Fagin,* character in Charles Dickens' *Oliver Twist* (1839)] (1847) **:** an adult who instructs others (as children) in crime
[1]**fag·ot** *or* **fag·got** \ˈfa-gət\ *n* [ME *fagot,* fr. AF] (14c) **:** BUNDLE: as **a :** a bundle of sticks **b :** a bundle of pieces of wrought iron to be shaped by rolling or hammering at high temperature
[2]**fagot** *or* **faggot** *vt* (ca. 1598) **:** to make a fagot of **:** bind together into a bundle ⟨~*ed* sticks⟩
fag·ot·ing *or* **fag·got·ing** \ˈfa-gə-tiŋ\ *n* (1885) **1 :** an embroidery produced by pulling out horizontal threads from a fabric and tying the remaining cross threads into groups of an hourglass shape **2 :** an openwork stitch joining hemmed edges

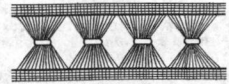

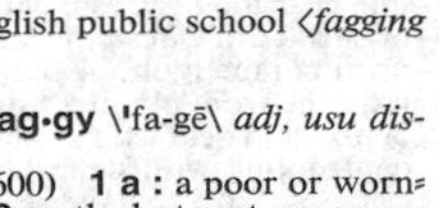
fagoting 1

Fah *or* **Fahr** *abbr* Fahrenheit
Fahr·en·heit \ˈfer-ən-ˌhīt\ *adj* [Daniel G. *Fahrenheit*] (1753) **:** relating or conforming to a thermometric scale on which under standard atmospheric pressure the boiling point of water

is at 212 degrees above the zero of the scale, the freezing point is at 32 degrees above zero, and the zero point approximates the temperature produced by mixing equal quantities by weight of snow and common salt — abbr. *F*

fa·ience *or* **fa·ïence** \fā-ˈän(t)s, fī-, -ˈä^{n}s\ *n* [F, fr. *Faenza,* Italy] (1714) **:** earthenware decorated with opaque colored glazes

[1]**fail** \ˈfāl\ *vb* [ME *failen,* fr. AF *faillir,* fr. VL **fallire,* alter. of L *fallere* to deceive, disappoint] *vi* (13c) **1 a :** to lose strength **:** WEAKEN ⟨her health was ~*ing*⟩ **b :** to fade or die away ⟨until our family line ~*s*⟩ **c :** to stop functioning normally ⟨the patient's heart ~*ed*⟩ **2 a :** to fall short ⟨~*ed* in his duty⟩ **b :** to be or become absent or inadequate ⟨the water supply ~*ed*⟩ **c :** to be unsuccessful ⟨the marriage ~*ed*⟩; *specif* **:** to be unsuccessful in achieving a passing grade ⟨took the exam and ~*ed*⟩ **d :** to become bankrupt or insolvent ~ *vt* **1 a :** to disappoint the expectations or trust of ⟨her friends ~*ed* her⟩ **b :** to miss performing an expected service or function for ⟨his wit ~*ed* him⟩ **2 :** to be deficient in **:** LACK ⟨never ~*ed* an invincible courage —Douglas MacArthur⟩ **3 :** to leave undone **:** NEGLECT ⟨~ to lock the door⟩ **4 a :** to be unsuccessful in passing ⟨~*ed* chemistry⟩ **b :** to grade (as a student) as not passing — **fail·ing·ly** \ˈfā-liŋ-lē\ *adv*

[2]**fail** *n* (13c) **1 :** FAILURE — usu. used in the phrase *without fail* **2 :** a failure (as by a security dealer) to deliver or receive securities within a prescribed period after purchase or sale

[1]**fail·ing** \ˈfā-liŋ\ *n* (1590) **:** a usu. slight or insignificant defect in character, conduct, or ability ***syn*** see FAULT

[2]**failing** *prep* (1810) **:** in absence or default of ⟨~ specific instructions, use your own judgment⟩

faille \ˈfī(-ə)l\ *n* [F, fr. OF] (1869) **:** a somewhat shiny closely woven silk, rayon, or cotton fabric characterized by slight ribs in the weft

[1]**fail–safe** \ˈfāl-ˌsāf\ *adj* (1946) **1 :** incorporating some feature for automatically counteracting the effect of an anticipated possible source of failure **2 :** being or relating to a safeguard that prevents continuing on a bombing mission according to a preconceived plan **3 :** having no chance of failure **:** infallibly problem-free ⟨the little black dress . . . has consistently been the ~ solution for night —*Vogue*⟩

[2]**fail–safe** *n* (1975) **:** a device or measure that makes something fail-safe

fail·ure \ˈfāl-yər\ *n* [alter. of earlier *failer,* fr. AF, fr. OF *faillir* to fail] (1643) **1 a :** omission of occurrence or performance; *specif* **:** a failing to perform a duty or expected action ⟨~ to pay the rent on time⟩ **b** (1) **:** a state of inability to perform a normal function ⟨kidney ~⟩ — compare HEART FAILURE (2) **:** an abrupt cessation of normal functioning ⟨a power ~⟩ **c :** a fracturing or giving way under stress ⟨structural ~⟩ **2 a :** lack of success **b :** a failing in business **:** BANKRUPTCY **3 a :** a falling short **:** DEFICIENCY ⟨a crop ~⟩ **b :** DETERIORATION, DECAY **4 :** one that has failed

[1]**fain** \ˈfān\ *adj* [ME *fagen, fayn,* fr. OE *fægen;* akin to OE *gefēon* to rejoice, OHG *gifehan,* ON *feginn* happy] (bef. 12c) **1** *archaic* **:** HAPPY, PLEASED **2** *archaic* **:** INCLINED, DESIROUS **3 a :** WILLING ⟨he was very ~, for the young widow was "altogether fair and lovely . . . " —Amy Kelly⟩ **b :** being obliged or constrained **:** COMPELLED ⟨Great Britain was ~ to devote its whole energy . . . to the business of slaying and being slain —G. M. Trevelyan⟩

[2]**fain** *adv* (12c) **1 :** with pleasure **:** GLADLY ⟨a speech of fire that ~ would blaze —Michael Billington⟩ **2 a :** by preference ⟨knew it, too, though he would ~ not admit it publicly —John Lukacs⟩ **b :** by desire ⟨I would ~ consult you —W. S. Gilbert⟩

[1]**fai·né·ant** \fā-nā-ˈä^n\ *n, pl* **fainéants** \-ˈä^n(z)\ [F, fr. MF *fait-nient,* lit., does nothing, by folk etymology fr. *faignant,* fr. prp. of *faindre, feindre* to feign] (1619) **:** an irresponsible idler

[2]**fai·né·ant** \fā-nā-ˈä^n\ *or* **fai·ne·ant** \ˈfā-nē-ənt\ *adj* (1854) **:** idle and ineffectual **:** INDOLENT

[1]**faint** \ˈfānt\ *adj* [ME *faint, feint,* fr. AF, fr. pp. of *feindre, faindre* to feign, lose heart — more at FEIGN] (14c) **1 :** lacking courage and spirit **:** COWARDLY ⟨~ of heart⟩ **2 :** weak, dizzy, and likely to faint **3 :** lacking strength or vigor **:** performed, offered, or accomplished weakly or languidly ⟨~ praise⟩ **4 :** producing a sensation of faintness **:** OPPRESSIVE ⟨the ~ atmosphere of a tropical port⟩ **5 a :** hardly perceptible **:** DIM ⟨~ handwriting⟩ **b :** VAGUE 2a ⟨haven't the *faintest* idea⟩ — **faint·ish** \ˈfān-tish\ *adj* — **faint·ish·ness** *n* — **faint·ly** *adv* — **faint·ness** *n*

[2]**faint** *vi* (14c) **1** *archaic* **:** to lose courage or spirit **2** *archaic* **:** to become weak **3 :** to lose consciousness because of a temporary decrease in the blood supply to the brain

[3]**faint** *n* (1792) **:** the physiological action of fainting; *also* **:** the resulting condition **:** SYNCOPE 1

faint·heart·ed \ˈfānt-ˈhär-təd\ *adj* (15c) **:** lacking courage or resolution **:** TIMID — **faint·heart·ed·ly** *adv* — **faint·heart·ed·ness** *n*

[1]**fair** \ˈfer\ *adj* [ME *fager, fair,* fr. OE *fæger;* akin to OHG *fagar* beautiful] (bef. 12c) **1 :** pleasing to the eye or mind esp. because of fresh, charming, or flawless quality **2 :** superficially pleasing **:** SPECIOUS ⟨she trusted his ~ promises⟩ **3 a :** CLEAN, PURE ⟨~ sparkling water⟩ **b :** CLEAR, LEGIBLE **4 :** not stormy or foul **:** FINE ⟨~ weather⟩ **5 :** AMPLE ⟨a ~ estate⟩ **6 a :** marked by impartiality and honesty **:** free from self-interest, prejudice, or favoritism ⟨a very ~ person to do business with⟩ **b** (1) **:** conforming with the established rules **:** ALLOWED (2) **:** consonant with merit or importance **:** DUE ⟨a ~ share⟩ **c :** open to legitimate pursuit, attack, or ridicule ⟨~ game⟩ **7 a :** PROMISING, LIKELY ⟨in a ~ way to win⟩ **b :** favorable to a ship's course ⟨a ~ wind⟩ **8** *archaic* **:** free of obstacles **9 :** not dark ⟨~ skin⟩ **10 a :** sufficient but not ample **:** ADEQUATE ⟨a ~ understanding of the work⟩ **b :** moderately numerous, large, or significant ⟨takes a ~ amount of time⟩ **11 :** being such to the utmost **:** UTTER ⟨a ~ treat to watch him —*New Republic*⟩ — **fair·ness** *n*

syn FAIR, JUST, EQUITABLE, IMPARTIAL, UNBIASED, DISPASSIONATE, OBJECTIVE mean free from favor toward either or any side. FAIR implies a proper balance of conflicting interests ⟨a *fair* decision⟩. JUST implies an exact following of a standard of what is right and proper ⟨a *just* settlement of territorial claims⟩. EQUITABLE implies a less rigorous standard than JUST and usu. suggests equal treatment of all concerned ⟨the *equitable* distribution of the property⟩. IMPARTIAL stresses an absence of favor or prejudice ⟨an *impartial* third party⟩. UNBIASED implies even more strongly an absence of all prejudice ⟨your *unbiased* opinion⟩. DISPASSIONATE suggests freedom from the influence of strong feeling and often implies cool or even cold judgment ⟨a *dispassionate* summation of the facts⟩. OBJECTIVE stresses a tendency to view events or persons as apart from oneself and one's own interest or feelings ⟨I can't be *objective* about my own child⟩. ***syn*** see in addition BEAUTIFUL

[2]**fair** *n* (bef. 12c) **1** *obs* **:** BEAUTY, FAIRNESS **2 :** something that is fair or fortunate **3** *archaic* **:** WOMAN; *esp* **:** SWEETHEART — **for fair :** to the greatest extent or degree **:** FULLY ⟨the rush is on *for fair*⟩ — **no fair :** something that is not according to the rules ⟨that's *no fair*⟩

[3]**fair** *adv* (bef. 12c) **1 :** in a fair manner ⟨play ~⟩ **2** *chiefly Brit* **:** FAIRLY 3 ⟨~ makes you want to cry⟩

[4]**fair** *vi* (1819) *of the weather* **:** CLEAR ~ *vt* **:** to join so that the external surfaces blend smoothly

[5]**fair** *n* [ME *feire,* fr. AF, fr. ML *feria* weekday, fair, fr. LL, festal day, fr. L *feriae* (pl.) holidays — more at FEAST] (13c) **1 :** a gathering of buyers and sellers at a particular place and time for trade **2 a :** a competitive exhibition usu. with accompanying entertainment and amusements ⟨an agricultural ~⟩ **b :** an exhibition designed to acquaint prospective buyers or the general public with a product ⟨a book ~⟩ **c :** an exposition that promotes the availability of services or opportunities ⟨health ~*s*⟩ ⟨job ~*s*⟩ **3 :** a sale of assorted articles usu. for a charitable purpose

fair ball *n* (1856) **:** a batted baseball that lands within the foul lines or that is within the foul lines when bounding to the outfield past first or third base or when going beyond the outfield for a home run

fair catch *n* (1867) **:** a catch of a kicked football by a player who gives a prescribed signal, may not advance the ball, and may not be tackled — **fair–catch** *vt*

fair copy *n* (ca. 1638) **:** a neat and exact copy esp. of a corrected draft

fair·go·er \ˈfer-ˌgō-ər\ *n* (1836) **:** one who attends a fair

fair·ground \ˈfer-ˌgrau̇nd\ *n* (1741) **:** an area where outdoor fairs, circuses, or exhibitions are held — often used in pl. with sing. constr. ⟨what a spot for a ~*s* —W. L. Gresham⟩

fair–haired \ˈfer-ˈherd\ *adj* (1909) **:** specially favored **:** WHITE-HEADED — used esp. in the phrase *fair-haired boy*

[1]**fair·ing** \ˈfer-iŋ\ *n* (1574) **1** *Brit* **a :** a present bought or given at a fair **b :** GIFT **2** *Brit* **:** [3]DESERT 2

[2]**fairing** *n* [[4]*fair*] (1914) **:** a member or structure whose primary function is to produce a smooth outline and to reduce drag (as on an airplane)

fair·ish \ˈfer-ish\ *adj* (ca. 1611) **:** fairly good — **fair·ish·ly** *adv*

Fair Isle *n* (1851) **:** a style of knitting originating in the Shetland Islands that is characterized by bands of multicolored geometric patterns; *also* **:** an article of clothing knitted in this style

fair·lead \ˈfer-ˌlēd\ *n* (ca. 1841) **1** *also* **fair·lead·er** \-ˌlē-dər\ **:** a block, ring, or strip of plank with holes that serves as a guide for the running rigging or any ship's rope and keeps it from chafing **2 :** a course of running ship's rope that avoids all chafing

fair·ly \ˈfer-lē\ *adv* (12c) **1 :** in a handsome manner ⟨a table ~ set⟩ **2** *obs* **a :** in a gentle manner **:** QUIETLY **b :** in a courteous manner **3 :** so to speak **:** NEARLY, PRACTICALLY ⟨~ bursting with pride⟩ **4 a :** in a proper or legal manner ⟨~ priced stocks⟩ **b :** without bias or distortion **:** IMPARTIALLY ⟨a story told ~ and objectively⟩ **5 :** to a full degree or extent **:** PLAINLY, DISTINCTLY ⟨had ~ caught sight of him⟩ **6 :** RATHER 5, MODERATELY ⟨a ~ easy job⟩

fair market value *n* (1901) **:** a price at which buyers and sellers with a reasonable knowledge of pertinent facts and not acting under any compulsion are willing to do business

fair–mind·ed \ˈfer-ˌmīn-dəd\ *adj* (1874) **:** marked by impartiality and honesty **:** JUST, UNPREJUDICED — **fair–mind·ed·ness** *n*

fairness doctrine *n* (1967) **:** a tenet of licensed broadcasting that ensures a reasonable opportunity for the airing of conflicting viewpoints on controversial issues

fair play *n* (1595) **:** equitable or impartial treatment **:** JUSTICE

fair shake *n* (1830) **:** a fair chance or fair treatment

fair–spo·ken \ˈfer-ˌspō-kən\ *adj* (15c) **:** pleasant and courteous in speech ⟨a ~ youth⟩

fair–trade \ˈfer-ˈtrād\ *vt* (1947) **:** to market (a commodity) in compliance with the provisions of a fair-trade agreement — **fair trader** *n*

fair trade *n* (1932) **1 :** trade in conformity with a fair-trade agreement **2 :** a movement whose goal is to help producers in developing countries to get a fair price for their products so as to reduce poverty, provide for the ethical treatment of workers and farmers, and promote environmentally sustainable practices

fair–trade agreement *n* (1937) **:** an agreement between a producer and a seller that commodities bearing a trademark, label, or brand name belonging to the producer be sold at or above a specified price

fair use *n* (1847) **:** a legal doctrine that portions of copyrighted materials may be used without permission of the copyright owner provided the use is fair and reasonable, does not substantially impair the value of the materials, and does not curtail the profits reasonably expected by the owner

fair·way \ˈfer-ˌwā\ *n* (1584) **1 a :** a navigable part of a river, bay, or harbor **b :** an open path or space **2 :** the closely mowed part of a golf course between a tee and a green

fair–weather *adj* (1736) **1 :** loyal only during a time of success ⟨a ~ friend⟩ **2 :** suitable for or done during fair weather ⟨a ~ sail⟩

fairy \ˈfer-ē\ *n, pl* **fair·ies** [ME *fairie* fairyland, enchantment, fr. AF *faerie,* fr. *fee* fairy, fr. L *Fata,* goddess of fate, fr. *fatum* fate] (14c) **1 :** a mythical being of folklore and romance usu. having diminutive human form and magic powers **2** *usu disparaging* **:** a male homosexual — **fairy** *adj* — **fairy·like** \-ˌlīk\ *adj*

fairy godmother *n* (1839) **:** a generous friend or benefactor

fairy·land \-ˌland\ *n* (1590) **1 :** the land of fairies **2 :** a place of delicate beauty or magical charm

fairy ring *n* [fr. the folk belief that such rings were dancing places of the fairies] (1599) **1 :** a ring of basidiomycetous mushrooms produced at the periphery of a body of mycelium which has grown outward from an initial growth point; *also* **:** a ring of luxuriant vegetation esp. when

\ə\ **abut** \ᵊ\ kitten, F table \ər\ **further** \a\ **ash** \ā\ **ace** \ä\ **mop, mar**
\au̇\ **out** \ch\ **chin** \e\ **bet** \ē\ **easy** \g\ **go** \i\ **hit** \ī\ **ice** \j\ **job**
\ŋ\ **sing** \ō\ **go** \ȯ\ **law** \ȯi\ **boy** \th\ **thin** \t͟h\ **the** \ü\ **loot** \u̇\ **foot**
\y\ **yet** \zh\ **vision, beige** \k̲, ^{n}, œ, ue, ^{y}\ *see* Guide to Pronunciation

associated with these mushrooms **2 :** a mushroom (esp. *Marasmius oreades*) that commonly grows in fairy rings
fairy shrimp *n* (1857) **:** any of several very small translucent freshwater branchiopod crustaceans (order Anostraca)
fairy–tale *adj* (1924) **:** characteristic of or suitable to a fairy tale; *esp* **:** marked by seemingly unreal beauty, perfection, luck, or happiness ⟨led a ~ life⟩ ⟨a store clerk's ~ romance⟩
fairy tale *n* (1749) **1 a :** a story (as for children) involving fantastic forces and beings (as fairies, wizards, and goblins) — called also *fairy story* **b :** a story in which improbable events lead to a happy ending **2 :** a made-up story usu. designed to mislead
fait ac·com·pli \ˌfā-tə-ˌkäm-ˈplē, ˈfe-, ˈfe-ˌta-, -ˌkō^{n}(m)-, *Brit usu* -ˈkäm-(ˌ)plē\ *n, pl* **faits accomplis** *same, or* -ˈplēz\ [F, accomplished fact] (1845) **:** a thing accomplished and presumably irreversible
[1]**faith** \ˈfāth\ *n, pl* **faiths** \ˈfāths, *sometimes* ˈfāthz\ [ME *feith,* fr. AF *feid, fei,* fr. L *fides;* akin to L *fidere* to trust — more at BIDE] (13c) **1 a :** allegiance to duty or a person **:** LOYALTY **b (1) :** fidelity to one's promises **(2) :** sincerity of intentions **2 a (1) :** belief and trust in and loyalty to God **(2) :** belief in the traditional doctrines of a religion **b (1) :** firm belief in something for which there is no proof **(2) :** complete trust **3 :** something that is believed esp. with strong conviction; *esp* **:** a system of religious beliefs ⟨the Protestant ~⟩ ***syn*** see BELIEF — **on faith :** without question ⟨took everything he said *on faith*⟩
[2]**faith** *vt* (15c) *archaic* **:** BELIEVE, TRUST
[1]**faith·ful** \ˈfāth-fəl\ *adj* (14c) **1** *obs* **:** full of faith **2 :** steadfast in affection or allegiance **:** LOYAL **3 :** firm in adherence to promises or in observance of duty **:** CONSCIENTIOUS **4 :** given with strong assurance **:** BINDING ⟨a ~ promise⟩ **5 :** true to the facts, to a standard, or to an original ⟨a ~ copy⟩ — **faith·ful·ly** \-fə-lē\ *adv* — **faith·ful·ness** *n*
syn FAITHFUL, LOYAL, CONSTANT, STAUNCH, STEADFAST, RESOLUTE mean firm in adherence to whatever one owes allegiance. FAITHFUL implies unswerving adherence to a person or thing or to the oath or promise by which a tie was contracted ⟨*faithful* to her promise⟩. LOYAL implies a firm resistance to any temptation to desert or betray ⟨remained *loyal* to the czar⟩. CONSTANT stresses continuing firmness of emotional attachment without necessarily implying strict obedience to promises or vows ⟨*constant* friends⟩. STAUNCH suggests fortitude and resolution in adherence and imperviousness to influences that would weaken it ⟨a *staunch* defender of free speech⟩. STEADFAST implies a steady and unwavering course in love, allegiance, or conviction ⟨*steadfast* in their support⟩. RESOLUTE implies firm determination to adhere to a cause or purpose ⟨a *resolute* ally⟩.
[2]**faithful** *n* (ca. 1533) **1** *pl in constr* **a :** church members in full communion and good standing — used with *the* **b :** the body of believers in Islam — used with *the* **2** *pl* **faithful** *or* **faithfuls :** one who is faithful; *esp* **:** a loyal follower, member, or fan ⟨party ~*s*⟩
faith healing *n* (1885) **:** a method of treating diseases by prayer and exercise of faith in God — **faith healer** *n*
faith·less \ˈfāth-ləs\ *adj* (14c) **1 :** not true to allegiance or duty **:** TREACHEROUS, DISLOYAL ⟨a ~ servant⟩ **2 :** not to be relied on **:** UNTRUSTWORTHY ⟨a ~ tool⟩ — **faith·less·ly** *adv* — **faith·less·ness** *n*
syn FAITHLESS, FALSE, DISLOYAL, TRAITOROUS, TREACHEROUS, PERFIDIOUS mean untrue to what should command one's fidelity or allegiance. FAITHLESS applies to any failure to keep a promise or pledge or any breach of allegiance or loyalty ⟨*faithless* allies⟩. FALSE stresses the fact of failing to be true in any manner ranging from fickleness to cold treachery ⟨betrayed by *false* friends⟩. DISLOYAL implies a lack of complete faithfulness to a friend, cause, leader, or country ⟨*disloyal* to their country⟩. TRAITOROUS implies either actual treason or a serious betrayal of trust ⟨*traitorous* acts punishable by death⟩. TREACHEROUS implies readiness to betray trust or confidence ⟨a *treacherous* adviser⟩. PERFIDIOUS adds to FAITHLESS the implication of an incapacity for fidelity or reliability ⟨a *perfidious* double-crosser⟩.
fai·tour \ˈfā-tər\ *n* [ME, fr. AF *faitour* maker, swindler, fr. L *factor* doer — more at FACTOR] (14c) *archaic* **:** CHEAT, IMPOSTER
fa·ji·ta \fə-ˈhē-tə, fä-\ *n* [AmerSp, dim. of Sp *faja* sash, belt, prob. fr. Catal *faixa,* fr. L *fascia* band — more at FASCIA] (1971) **:** a marinated strip usu. of beef or chicken grilled or broiled and served usu. with a flour tortilla and various savory fillings — usu. used in pl.
[1]**fake** \ˈfāk\ *vt* **faked; fak·ing** [ME] (15c) **:** to coil in fakes
[2]**fake** *n* (1627) **:** one loop of a coil (as of ship's rope or a fire hose) coiled free for running
[3]**fake** *adj* [origin unknown] (1775) **:** COUNTERFEIT, SHAM
[4]**fake** *n* (1827) **:** one that is not what it purports to be: as **a :** a worthless imitation passed off as genuine **b :** IMPOSTOR, CHARLATAN **c :** a simulated movement in a sports contest (as a pretended kick, pass, or jump or a quick movement in one direction before going in another) designed to deceive an opponent **d :** a device or apparatus used by a magician to achieve the illusion of magic in a trick ***syn*** see IMPOSTURE
[5]**fake** *vb* **faked; fak·ing** *vt* (1851) **1 :** to alter, manipulate, or treat so as to give a spuriously genuine appearance to **:** DOCTOR ⟨*faked* the lab results⟩ **2 :** COUNTERFEIT, SIMULATE, CONCOCT ⟨*faked* a heart attack⟩ **3 :** to deceive (an opponent) in a sports contest by means of a fake **4 :** IMPROVISE, AD-LIB ⟨whistle a few bars . . . and I'll ~ the rest —Robert Sylvester⟩ ~ *vi* **1 :** to engage in faking something **:** PRETEND — sometimes used with *it* ⟨if you don't have the answers, ~ it⟩ **2 :** to give a fake to an opponent — **fak·er** *n* — **fak·ery** \ˈfā-k(ə-)rē\ *n*
fake out *vt* (1949) **:** to deliberately mislead **:** FOOL, TRICK
fa·kir *n* [Ar *faqīr,* lit., poor man] (1609) **1** \fə-ˈkir, fä-, fa-; ˈfā-kər\ **a :** a Muslim mendicant **:** DERVISH **b :** an itinerant Hindu ascetic or wonder-worker **2** \ˈfā-kər\ **:** IMPOSTOR; *esp* **:** SWINDLER
fa la \fä-ˈlä\ *n* [*fa-la,* meaningless syllables often occurring in its refrain] (1597) **:** a 16th and 17th century part-song
fa·la·fel *also* **fe·la·fel** \fə-ˈlä-fəl\ *n, pl* **falafel** *also* **felafel** [Ar *falāfil*] (1949) **:** a spicy mixture of ground vegetables (as chick-peas or fava beans) formed into balls or patties and then fried
Fa·lan·gist \fə-ˈlan-jist, ˈfā-ˌ\ *n* [Sp *falangista,* fr. *Falange española* Spanish Phalanx, a fascist organization] (1936) **:** a member of the fascist political party governing Spain after the civil war of 1936–39
Fa·la·sha \fə-ˈlä-shə\ *n, pl* **-sha** *or* **-shas** [Amharic *fälaša*] (1710) **:** a member of a people of highland Ethiopia who practice a variety of Judaism
fal·cate \ˈfal-ˌkāt, ˈfȯl-\ *adj* [L *falcatus,* fr. *falc-, falx* sickle, scythe] (1826) **:** hooked or curved like a sickle
fal·chion \ˈfȯl-chən\ *n* [ME *fauchoun,* fr. AF *fauchun,* fr. *faucher* to mow, fr. VL **falcare,* fr. L *falc-, falx*] (14c) **1 :** a broad-bladed slightly curved sword of medieval times **2** *archaic* **:** SWORD

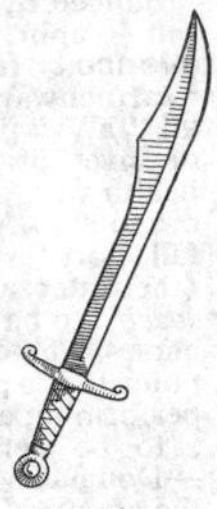
falchion 1

fal·ci·form \ˈfal-sə-ˌfȯrm, ˈfȯl-\ *adj* [L *falc-, falx* + E *-iform*] (1766) **:** having the shape of a scythe or sickle
fal·cip·a·rum malaria \fal-ˈsi-pə-rəm-\ *n* [NL, specific epithet, fr. L *falc-, falx* + *-parum,* neut. of *-parus* -parous] (1940) **:** extremely severe malaria caused by a sporozoan parasite (*Plasmodium falciparum*)
fal·con \ˈfal-kən, ˈfȯl- *also* ˈfō-kən\ *n* [ME *faucoun, falcon,* fr. AF *faucon,* fr. LL *falcon-, falco,* prob. fr. L *falc-, falx*] (13c) **1 :** any of various hawks trained for use in falconry; *esp* **:** PEREGRINE FALCON — used technically only of a female; compare TIERCEL **2 :** any of various hawks (family Falconidae) that have long pointed wings, a long tail, and a notched beak and that usu. inhabit open areas
fal·con·er \-kə-nər\ *n* (14c) **:** a person who breeds, trains, or hunts with hawks
fal·con·et \ˌfal-kə-ˈnet, ˌfȯl- *also* ˌfō-\ *n* (1559) **1 :** a very small cannon used in the 16th and 17th centuries **2 :** any of several very small falcons (genera *Microhierax, Polihierax,* and *Spiziapteryx*)
fal·con–gen·tle \-kən-ˈjen-t^{ə}l\ *n* [ME *faucon gentil* peregrine falcon, fr. AF, lit., noble falcon] (15c) **:** the female peregrine falcon
fal·con·ry \ˈfal-kən-rē, ˈfȯl- *also* ˈfō-kən-\ *n* (1575) **1 :** the art of training hawks to hunt in cooperation with a person **2 :** the sport of hunting with hawks
falderal *var of* FOLDEROL
fald·stool \ˈfȯl(d)-ˌstül\ *n* [ML *faldistolium,* of Gmc origin; akin to OHG *faltistuol* folding chair, fr. *falt* (akin to OHG *faldan* to fold) + *stuol* chair — more at FOLD, STOOL] (1603) **1 :** a folding stool or chair; *specif* **:** one used by a bishop **2 :** a folding stool or small desk at which one kneels during devotions; *esp* **:** one used by the sovereigns of England at their coronation **3 :** the desk from which the litany is read in Anglican churches
[1]**fall** \ˈfȯl\ *vb* **fell** \ˈfel\; **fall·en** \ˈfȯ-lən\; **fall·ing** [ME, fr. OE *feallan;* akin to OHG *fallan* to fall and perh. to Lith *pulti*] *vi* (bef. 12c) **1 a :** to descend freely by the force of gravity **b :** to hang freely ⟨her hair ~*s* over her shoulders⟩ **c :** to drop oneself to a lower position ⟨*fell* to his knees⟩ **d :** to come or go as if by falling ⟨darkness ~*s* early in the winter⟩ **2 :** to become born — usu. used of lambs **3 a :** to become lower in degree or level ⟨the temperature *fell* 10°⟩ **b :** to drop in pitch or volume ⟨their voices *fell* to a whisper⟩ **c :** ISSUE 1a, b ⟨wisdom that *fell* from his lips⟩ **d :** to become lowered ⟨her eyes *fell*⟩ **4 a :** to leave an erect position suddenly and involuntarily ⟨slipped and *fell* on the ice⟩ **b :** to enter as if unawares **:** STUMBLE, STRAY ⟨*fell* into error⟩ **c :** to drop down wounded or dead; *esp* **:** to die in battle **d :** to suffer military capture ⟨after a long siege the city *fell*⟩ **e :** to lose office ⟨the party *fell* from power⟩ **f :** to suffer ruin, defeat, or failure ⟨the deal *fell* through⟩ **5 :** to commit an immoral act; *esp* **:** to lose one's chastity **6 a :** to move or extend in a downward direction ⟨the land ~*s* away to the east⟩ **b :** SUBSIDE, ABATE ⟨the wind is ~*ing*⟩ **c :** to decline in quality, activity, or quantity ⟨production *fell* off⟩ **d :** to lose weight — used with *off* or *away* **e :** to assume a look of shame, disappointment, or dejection ⟨his face *fell*⟩ **f :** to decline in financial value or price ⟨stocks *fell* sharply⟩ **7 a :** to occur at a certain time ⟨her birthday ~*s* on a Monday this year⟩ **b :** to come by chance ⟨a job that *fell* into his hands⟩ **c :** to come or pass by lot, assignment, or inheritance **:** DEVOLVE ⟨it *fell* to him to break the news⟩ **d :** to have a certain or proper position, place, or station ⟨the accent ~*s* on the second syllable⟩ **8 :** to come within the limits, scope, or jurisdiction of something ⟨this word ~*s* into the class of verbs⟩ **9 :** to pass suddenly and passively into a state of body or mind or a new state or condition ⟨~ asleep⟩ ⟨~ in love⟩ **10 :** to set about heartily or actively ⟨*fell* to work⟩ **11 :** STRIKE, IMPINGE ⟨music ~*ing* on the ear⟩ ~ *vt* **:** FELL 1 — **fall all over oneself** *or* **fall over oneself** *or* **fall over backward :** to display great or excessive eagerness — **fall apart 1 :** DISINTEGRATE **2 :** to succumb to mental or emotional stress **:** BREAK DOWN — **fall behind 1 :** to lag behind **2 :** to be in arrears — **fall between two stools :** to fail because of inability to choose between or reconcile two alternative or conflicting courses of action — **fall flat :** to produce no response or result ⟨the joke *fell flat*⟩ — **fall for 1 :** to fall in love with **2 :** to become a victim of ⟨*fell for* the trick⟩ — **fall from grace :** BACKSLIDE 1 — **fall home :** to curve inward — used of the timbers or upper parts of a ship's side — **fall into line :** to comply with a certain course of action — **fall on** *or* **fall upon :** to meet with ⟨*fell on* hard times⟩ — **fall on one's face :** to fail utterly ⟨the movie *fell on its face* at the box office⟩ — **fall on one's sword :** to sacrifice one's pride or position — **fall short 1 :** to be deficient **2 :** to fail to attain something (as a goal or target)
[2]**fall** *n* (13c) **1 :** the act of falling by the force of gravity **2 a :** a falling out, off, or away **:** DROPPING ⟨the ~ of leaves⟩ ⟨a ~ of snow⟩ **b :** the season when leaves fall from trees **:** AUTUMN **c :** a thing or quantity that falls or has fallen ⟨a ~ of rock at the base of the cliff⟩; *esp* **:** one or more meteorites or their fragments that have fallen together **d (1) :** BIRTH **(2) :** the quantity born — usu. used of lambs **3 a :** a costume decoration of lace or thin fabric arranged to hang loosely and gracefully **b :** a very wide turned-down collar worn in the 17th century **c :** the part of a turnover collar from the crease to the outer edge **d :** a wide front flap on trousers (as those worn by sailors) **e :** the freely hanging lower edge of the skirt of a coat **f :** one of the three outer and often drooping segments of the flower of an iris **g :** long hair overhanging the face of dogs of some breeds **h :** a usu. long straight portion of hair that is attached to a person's own hair **4 :** a hoisting-tackle rope or chain; *esp* **:** the part of it to which the power is applied **5 a :** loss of greatness **:** COLLAPSE ⟨the ~ of the Roman Empire⟩ **b :** the surrender or capture of a besieged place ⟨the ~ of Troy⟩ **c :** lapse or departure from innocence or goodness **d :** loss of a woman's chastity **e :** the blame for a failure or misdeed ⟨took the ~ for the robbery⟩ **6 a :** the downward slope (as of a hill) **:** DECLIVITY **b :** a precipitous descent of water **:** WATERFALL — usu. used in pl. but sing.

or pl. in constr. **c** : a musical cadence **d** : a falling-pitch intonation in speech **7** : a decrease in size, quantity, degree, or value **8 a** : the distance which something falls **b** : INCLINATION, PITCH **9 a** : the act of felling something **b** : the quantity of trees cut down **c** (1) : an act of forcing a wrestler's shoulders to the mat for a specified time (as one second) (2) : a bout of wrestling **10** *Scot* : DESTINY, LOT

[3]**fall** *adj* (1677) : of, relating to, or suitable for autumn ⟨a new ~ coat⟩

fal·la·cious \fə-ˈlā-shəs\ *adj* (1509) **1** : embodying a fallacy ⟨a ~ conclusion⟩ **2** : tending to deceive or mislead : DELUSIVE — **fal·la·cious·ly** *adv* — **fal·la·cious·ness** *n*

fal·la·cy \ˈfa-lə-sē\ *n, pl* **-cies** [L *fallacia,* fr. *fallac-, fallax* deceitful, fr. *fallere* to deceive] (14c) **1 a** *obs* : GUILE, TRICKERY **b** : deceptive appearance : DECEPTION **2 a** : a false or mistaken idea ⟨popular *fallacies*⟩ **b** : erroneous character : ERRONEOUSNESS **3** : an often plausible argument using false or invalid inference

fal–lal \fa-ˈlal, ˈfa(l)-ˌlal\ *n* [perh. alter. of *falbala* furbelow, fr. F] (ca. 1706) : a fancy ornament esp. in dress — **fal·lal·ery** \fa-ˈla-lə-rē\ *n*

fall armyworm *n* (1881) : a migratory American noctuid moth (*Spodoptera frugiperda*) that is destructive to grains and grasses as a larva

fall·away \ˈfȯl-ə-ˌwā\ *adj* (1966) : made while moving away from the basket in basketball ⟨a ~ jump shot⟩ — **fallaway** *n*

fall away *vi* (1535) **1 a** : to withdraw friendship or support **b** : to renounce one's faith **2 a** : to diminish gradually in size **b** : to drift off a course

fall·back \ˈfȯl-ˌbak\ *n* (1851) **1** : something on which one can fall back : RESERVE — often used attributively ⟨a ~ career⟩ ⟨a ~ position⟩ **2** : a falling back : RETREAT **3** : something that falls back ⟨the ~ from an explosion⟩

fall back *vi* (1607) : RETREAT, RECEDE — **fall back on** *or* **fall back upon** : to have recourse to ⟨had to *fall back on* their reserves⟩

fall down *vi* (1873) : to fail to meet expectations or requirements ⟨*fell down* on the job⟩

fall·er \ˈfȯ-lər\ *n* (1677) **1** : a machine part that acts by falling **2** : a logger who fells trees

fall·fish \ˈfȯl-ˌfish\ *n* (ca. 1811) : a common silvery cyprinid fish (*Semotilus corporalis*) of the streams of northeastern No. America

fall guy *n* (1904) : SCAPEGOAT ⟨a *fall guy* for his boss's errors⟩

fal·li·bil·i·ty \ˌfa-lə-ˈbi-lə-tē\ *n* (1634) : liability to err

fal·li·ble \ˈfa-lə-bəl\ *adj* [ME, fr. ML *fallibilis,* fr. L *fallere*] (15c) **1** : liable to be erroneous ⟨a ~ generalization⟩ **2** : capable of making a mistake ⟨we're all ~⟩ — **fal·li·bly** \-blē\ *adv*

fall in *vi* (1719) **1** : to sink inward ⟨the roof *fell in*⟩ **2** : to take one's proper place in a military formation — **fall in with 1** : to concur with ⟨had to *fall in with* her wishes⟩ **2** : to harmonize with ⟨it *falls in* exactly *with* my views⟩ **3** : to begin associating with ⟨she *fell in with* a bad crowd⟩

falling diphthong *n* (1888) : a diphthong (as \ȯi\ in \ˈnȯiz\ *noise*) composed of a vowel followed by a less sonorous glide

fall·ing–out \ˌfȯ-liŋ-ˈau̇t\ *n, pl* **fallings–out** *or* **falling–outs** (1568) : an instance of falling out : QUARREL ⟨had a ~ with his parents⟩

falling rhythm *n* (1918) : rhythm with stress occurring regularly on the first syllable of each foot — compare RISING RHYTHM

falling star *n* (1563) : METEOR 2a

fall line *n* (1882) **1** : a line joining the waterfalls on numerous rivers that marks the point where each river descends from the upland to the lowland and the limit of the navigability of each river **2** : the natural downhill course (as for skiing) between two points on a slope

fall·off \ˈfȯl-ˌȯf\ *n* (1880) : a decline esp. in quantity or quality ⟨a ~ in exports⟩ ⟨a ~ of light intensity⟩

fall off *vi* (1613) **1** : TREND 1b **2** *of a ship* : to deviate to leeward of the point to which the bow was directed

fal·lo·pi·an tube \fə-ˈlō-pē-ən-\ *n, often cap F* [Gabriel *Fallopius* †1562 Ital. anatomist] (ca. 1696) : either of the pair of tubes that carry the egg from the ovary to the uterus

fall·out \ˈfȯl-ˌau̇t\ *n* (1949) **1 a** : the often radioactive particles stirred up by or resulting from a nuclear explosion and descending through the atmosphere; *also* : other polluting particles (as volcanic ash) descending likewise **b** : descent (as of fallout) through the atmosphere **2** : a secondary and often lingering effect, result, or set of consequences ⟨have to take a position and accept the political ~ —Andy Logan⟩

fall out *vi* (15c) **1** : QUARREL; *also* : to cut off relations over a quarrel ⟨former friends who have *fallen out*⟩ **2** : TURN OUT, HAPPEN ⟨expected to be in the States . . . , but things *fell out* otherwise —Mark Twain⟩ **3 a** : to leave one's place in the ranks **b** : to leave a building in order to take one's place in a military formation

[1]**fal·low** \ˈfa-(ˌ)lō\ *adj* [ME *falow,* fr. OE *fealu;* akin to OHG *falo* pale, fallow, L *pallēre* to be pale, Gk *polios* gray] (bef. 12c) : of a light yellowish-brown color

[2]**fallow** *n* [ME *falwe, falow,* fr. OE *fealg* — more at FELLY] (bef. 12c) **1** : usu. cultivated land that is allowed to lie idle during the growing season **2** *obs* : plowed land **3** : the state or period of being fallow **4** : the tilling of land without sowing it for a season

[3]**fallow** *vt* (15c) : to plow, harrow, and break up (land) without seeding to destroy weeds and conserve soil moisture

[4]**fallow** *adj* (15c) **1** : left untilled or unsown after plowing **2** : DORMANT, INACTIVE — used esp. in the phrase *to lie fallow* ⟨at this very moment there are probably important inventions lying ~ —*Harper's*⟩ — **fal·low·ness** *n*

fallow deer *n* [[1]*fallow*] (15c) : a deer (*Dama dama* syn. *Cervus dama*) of variable color with palmate antlers in the male and typically a yellow-brown coat spotted with white in the summer that was orig. of Mediterranean regions of Europe and Asia but has been introduced elsewhere

fall to *vi* (1575) : to begin doing something (as working or eating) esp. vigorously — often used in invitation or command

[1]**false** \ˈfȯls\ *adj* **fals·er; fals·est** [ME *fals, faus,* fr. AF & L; AF, fr. L *falsus,* fr. pp. of *fallere* to deceive] (12c) **1** : not genuine ⟨~ documents⟩ ⟨~ teeth⟩ **2 a** : intentionally untrue ⟨~ testimony⟩ **b** : adjusted or made so as to deceive ⟨~ scales⟩ ⟨a trunk with a ~ bottom⟩ **c** : intended or tending to mislead ⟨a ~ promise⟩ **3** : not true ⟨~ concepts⟩ **4 a** : not faithful or loyal : TREACHEROUS ⟨a ~ friend⟩ **b** : lacking naturalness or sincerity ⟨~ sympathy⟩ **5 a** : not essential or permanent — used of parts of a structure that are temporary or supplemental **b** : fitting over a main part to strengthen it, to protect it, or to disguise its appearance ⟨a ~ ceiling⟩ **6** : inaccurate in pitch ⟨a ~ note⟩ **7 a** : based on mistaken ideas ⟨~ pride⟩ **b** : inconsistent with the facts ⟨a ~ position⟩ ⟨a ~ sense of security⟩ **8** : threateningly sudden or deceptive ⟨don't make any ~ moves⟩ ***syn*** see FAITHLESS — **false·ly** *adv* — **false·ness** *n*

[2]**false** *adv* (13c) : in a false or faithless manner : TREACHEROUSLY ⟨his friends played him ~⟩

false alarm *n* (1578) **1** : an alarm (as a fire or burglar alarm) that is set off needlessly **2** : one causing alarm or excitement that proves to be unfounded

false arrest *n* (1715) : an arrest not justifiable under law

false color *n* (1968) : color in an image (as a photograph) of an object that does not actually appear in the object but is used to enhance, contrast, or distinguish details

false·hood \ˈfȯls-ˌhu̇d\ *n* (13c) **1** : an untrue statement : LIE **2** : absence of truth or accuracy **3** : the practice of lying : MENDACITY

false imprisonment *n* (14c) : imprisonment of a person contrary to law

false mi·ter·wort \-ˈmī-tər-ˌwərt, -ˌwȯrt\ *n* [*miterwort* fr. the resemblance of the plant's capsule to a bishop's miter] (1868) : FOAMFLOWER

false morel *n* (1942) : any of a genus (*Gyromitra*) of fungi that are often poisonous and have a cap with convolutions resembling a brain

false pregnancy *n* (ca. 1860) : PSEUDOCYESIS, PSEUDOPREGNANCY

false rib *n* (15c) : a rib whose cartilages unite indirectly or not at all with the sternum — compare FLOATING RIB

false Solomon's seal *n* (ca. 1856) : any of a genus (*Smilacina*) of herbs of the lily family that differ from Solomon's seal in having flowers in a terminal raceme or panicle — called also *false Solomonseal*

false start *n* (1815) **1** : a premature start (as of a race or football play) **2** : an unsuccessful attempt to begin something (as a career)

[1]**fal·set·to** \fȯl-ˈse-(ˌ)tō\ *n, pl* **-tos** [It, fr. dim. of *falso* false, fr. L *falsus*] (1721) **1** : an artificially high voice; *esp* : an artificially produced singing voice that overlaps and extends above the range of the full voice esp. of a tenor **2** : a singer who uses falsetto

[2]**falsetto** *adv* (1940) : in falsetto

false·work \ˈfȯls-ˌwərk\ *n* (ca. 1874) : temporary construction work on which a main work is wholly or partly built and supported until the main work is strong enough to support itself

fals·ie \ˈfȯl-sē\ *n* (ca. 1943) : an artificial addition to a bodily part worn to enhance appearance; *specif* : a breast-shaped usu. fabric or rubber cup used to pad a brassiere — usu. used in pl.

fal·si·fy \ˈfȯl-sə-ˌfī\ *vb* **-fied; -fy·ing** [ME *falsifien,* fr. MF *falsifier,* fr. ML *falsificare,* fr. L *falsus*] *vt* (15c) **1** : to prove or declare false : DISPROVE **2** : to make false: as **a** : to make false by mutilation or addition ⟨the accounts were *falsified* to conceal a theft⟩ **b** : to represent falsely : MISREPRESENT **3** : to prove unsound by experience ~ *vi* : to tell lies : LIE — **fal·si·fi·abil·i·ty** \ˌfȯl-sə-ˌfī-ə-ˈbi-lə-tē\ *n* — **fal·si·fi·able** \-ˈfī-ə-bəl\ *adj* — **fal·si·fi·ca·tion** \ˌfȯl-sə-fə-ˈkā-shən\ *n* — **fal·si·fi·er** \ˈfȯl-sə-ˌfī(-ə)r\ *n*

fal·si·ty \ˈfȯl-sə-tē\ *n, pl* **-ties** (13c) **1** : something false : LIE **2** : the quality or state of being false

Fal·staff \ˈfȯl-ˌstaf\ *n* (1596) : a fat, convivial, roguish character in Shakespeare's *Merry Wives of Windsor* and *Henry IV* — **Fal·staff·ian** \fȯl-ˈsta-fē-ən\ *adj*

[1]**fal·ter** \ˈfȯl-tər\ *vb* **fal·tered; fal·ter·ing** \-t(ə-)riŋ\ [ME] *vi* (14c) **1 a** : to walk unsteadily : STUMBLE **b** : to give way : TOTTER ⟨could feel my legs ~*ing*⟩ **c** : to move waveringly or hesitatingly **2** : to speak brokenly or weakly : STAMMER ⟨her voice ~*ed*⟩ **3 a** : to hesitate in purpose or action : WAVER ⟨he never ~*ed* in his determination⟩ **b** : to lose drive or effectiveness ⟨the business was ~*ing*⟩ ~ *vt* : to utter hesitatingly or brokenly ***syn*** see HESITATE — **fal·ter·er** \-tər-ər\ *n* — **fal·ter·ing·ly** \-t(ə-)riŋ-lē\ *adv*

[2]**falter** *n* (1834) : an act or instance of faltering

fam *abbr* **1** familiar **2** family

[1]**fame** \ˈfām\ *n* [ME, fr. AF, fr. L *fama* report, fame; akin to L *fari* to speak — more at BAN] (13c) **1 a** : public estimation : REPUTATION **b** : popular acclaim : RENOWN **2** *archaic* : RUMOR

[2]**fame** *vt* **famed; fam·ing** (14c) **1** *archaic* : REPORT, REPUTE **2** : to make famous

famed \ˈfāmd\ *adj* (ca. 1533) : known widely and well : FAMOUS

fa·mil·ial \fə-ˈmil-yəl, -ˈmi-lē-əl\ *adj* [F, fr. L *familia*] (ca. 1900) **1** : tending to occur in more members of a family than expected by chance alone ⟨a ~ disorder⟩ **2** : of, relating to, or suggestive of a family ⟨has ~ ties to the area⟩ ⟨a ~ atmosphere⟩

familial adenomatous pol·yp·o·sis \-ˌpä-li-ˈpō-səs\ *n* [*polyposis* presence of polyps, fr. NL, fr. *polypus* polyp + *-osis*] (1976) : an inherited disease of the large intestine marked by the formation esp. in the colon and rectum of numerous glandular polyps which typically become malignant if left untreated — called also *familial polyposis*

familial hypercholesterolemia *n* (1966) : an inherited metabolic disorder marked by excess accumulation of LDL cholesterol in the blood resulting esp. in atherosclerosis and irregular yellow skin lesions

[1]**fa·mil·iar** \fə-ˈmil-yər\ *n* (13c) **1** : a member of the household of a high official **2** : one that is familiar; *esp* : an intimate associate : COMPANION **3** : a spirit often embodied in an animal and held to attend and serve or guard a person **4 a** : one who is well acquainted with something **b** : one who frequents a place

[2]**familiar** *adj* [ME *familier,* fr. AF, fr. L *familiaris,* fr. *familia*] (14c) **1** : closely acquainted : INTIMATE ⟨a ~ family friend⟩ **2** *obs* : AFFABLE, SOCIABLE **3 a** : of or relating to a family ⟨remembering past ~ celebrations⟩ **b** : frequented by families ⟨a ~ resort⟩ **4 a** : being free and easy ⟨the ~ association of old friends⟩ **b** : marked by informality ⟨a ~ essay⟩ **c** : overly free and unrestrained : PRESUMPTUOUS ⟨grossly ~ behavior⟩ **d** : moderately tame ⟨~ animals⟩ **5 a** : frequently seen or experienced : easily recognized ⟨a ~ theme⟩ **b** : of everyday occurrence ⟨a ~ routine⟩ **c** : possibly known but imperfectly remembered ⟨her face looked ~⟩ **6** : having personal or inti-

mate knowledge — used with *with* ⟨~ with the facts of the case⟩ ***syn*** see COMMON — **fa·mil·iar·ly** *adv* — **fa·mil·iar·ness** *n*

fa·mil·iar·ise *Brit var of* FAMILIARIZE

fa·mil·iar·i·ty \fə-ˌmi-lē-ˈ(y)er-ə-tē, -ˈ(y)a-rə-; -ˌmil-ˈyer-, -ˌmil-ˈya-rə-\ *n, pl* **-ties** (13c) **1 a :** the quality or state of being familiar **b :** a state of close relationship : INTIMACY **2 a :** absence of ceremony : INFORMALITY **b :** an unduly informal act or expression : IMPROPRIETY **c :** a sexual liberty **3 :** close acquaintance with something

fa·mil·iar·ize \fə-ˈmil-yə-ˌrīz\ *vt* **-ized; -iz·ing** (1593) **1 :** to make known or familiar ⟨Shakespeare . . . ~*s* the wonderful —Samuel Johnson⟩ **2 :** to make well acquainted ⟨~ students with good literature⟩ — **fa·mil·iar·i·za·tion** \-ˌmil-yə-rə-ˈzā-shən\ *n*

familiar spirit *n* (1565) **1 :** a spirit or demon that serves or prompts an individual **2 :** the spirit of a dead person invoked by a medium to advise or prophesy

fam·i·lism \ˈfa-mə-ˌli-zəm\ *n* (1925) **:** a social pattern in which the family assumes a position of ascendance over individual interests — **fam·i·lis·tic** \ˌfa-mə-ˈlis-tik\ *adj*

fa·mille rose \fə-ˈmē-\ *n* [F, lit., rose family] (ca. 1898) **:** Chinese porcelain in the decoration of which a rose color predominates

fa·mille verte \fə-ˈmē-ˈvert\ *n* [F, lit., green family] (1872) **:** Chinese porcelain in the decoration of which green predominates

[1]**fam·i·ly** \ˈfam-lē, ˈfa-mə-\ *n, pl* **-lies** [ME *familie,* fr. L *familia* household (including servants as well as kin of the householder), fr. *famulus* servant] (15c) **1 :** a group of individuals living under one roof and usu. under one head : HOUSEHOLD **2 a :** a group of persons of common ancestry : CLAN **b :** a people or group of peoples regarded as deriving from a common stock : RACE **3 a :** a group of people united by certain convictions or a common affiliation : FELLOWSHIP **b :** the staff of a high official (as the President) **4 :** a group of things related by common characteristics: as **a :** a closely related series of elements or chemical compounds **b :** a group of soils with similar chemical and physical properties (as texture, pH, and mineral content) that comprise a category ranking above the series and below the subgroup in soil classification **c :** a group of related languages descended from a single ancestral language **5 a :** the basic unit in society traditionally consisting of two parents rearing their children; *also* **:** any of various social units differing from but regarded as equivalent to the traditional family ⟨a single-parent ~⟩ **b :** spouse and children ⟨want to spend more time with my ~⟩ **6 a :** a group of related plants or animals forming a category ranking above a genus and below an order and usu. comprising several to many genera **b** *in livestock breeding* **(1) :** the descendants or line of a particular individual esp. of some outstanding female **(2) :** an identifiable strain within a breed **7 :** a set of curves or surfaces whose equations differ only in parameters **8 :** a unit of a crime syndicate (as the Mafia) operating within a geographic area — **fam·i·ly·hood** \-ˌhu̇d\ *n*

[2]**family** *adj* (1602) **1 :** of or relating to a family **2 :** designed or suitable for both children and adults ⟨~ restaurants⟩ ⟨~ movies⟩

family Bible *n* (1740) **:** a large Bible usu. having special pages for recording births, marriages, and deaths

family court *n* (ca. 1931) **:** COURT OF DOMESTIC RELATIONS

family doctor *n* (1840) **1 :** a doctor regularly consulted by a family **2 :** a doctor specializing in family practice

family jewels *n pl* (ca. 1946) *slang* **:** a man's testicles

family leave *n* (1981) **:** a usu. unpaid leave of absence for an employee to attend to family concerns (as a serious illness or the care of an infant)

family man *n* (1856) **:** a man with a wife and children dependent on him; *esp* **:** a man devoted to his family

family name *n* (1699) **:** SURNAME 2

family physician *n* (1796) **:** FAMILY DOCTOR

family planning *n* (1939) **:** planning intended to determine the number and spacing of one's children through birth control

family practice *n* (1969) **:** a medical practice or specialty which provides continuing general medical care for the individual and family — called also *family medicine*

family practitioner *n* (1846) **:** FAMILY DOCTOR

family room *n* (1810) **:** a large room designed as a recreation center and informal gathering place for members of a family

family style *adv or adj* (1932) **:** with the food placed on the table in serving dishes from which those eating may help themselves

family tree *n* (ca. 1770) **1 :** GENEALOGY **2 :** a genealogical diagram

family values *n pl* (1916) **:** values esp. of a traditional or conservative kind which are held to promote the sound functioning of the family and to strengthen the fabric of society

family way *n* (1796) **:** condition of being pregnant — used with *in* and *the* or *a* ⟨she is in a *family way*⟩

fam·ine \ˈfa-mən\ *n* [ME, fr. AF, fr. *feim, faim* hunger, fr. L *fames*] (14c) **1 :** an extreme scarcity of food **2** *archaic* **:** STARVATION **3** *archaic* **:** a ravenous appetite **4 :** a great shortage

fam·ish \ˈfa-mish\ *vb* [ME, prob. alter. of *famen,* fr. AF *afamer,* fr. VL **affamare,* fr. L *ad-* + *fames*] *vt* (15c) **1 :** to cause to suffer severely from hunger **2** *archaic* **:** to cause to starve to death ~ *vi* **1** *archaic* **:** STARVE **2 :** to suffer for lack of something necessary ⟨a moment when French poetry in particular was ~*ing* for such invention —T. S. Eliot⟩ — **fam·ish·ment** \-mənt\ *n*

fam·ished \ˈfa-misht\ *adj* (15c) **:** intensely hungry; *also* **:** NEEDY 1

fa·mous \ˈfā-məs\ *adj* [ME, fr. AF, fr. L *famosus,* fr. *fama* fame] (14c) **1 a :** widely known **b :** honored for achievement **2 :** EXCELLENT, FIRST-RATE ⟨~ weather for a walk⟩ — **fa·mous·ness** *n*

syn FAMOUS, RENOWNED, CELEBRATED, NOTED, NOTORIOUS, DISTINGUISHED, EMINENT, ILLUSTRIOUS mean known far and wide. FAMOUS implies little more than the fact of being, sometimes briefly, widely and popularly known ⟨a *famous* actress⟩. RENOWNED implies more glory and acclamation ⟨one of the most *renowned* figures in sports history⟩. CELEBRATED implies notice and attention esp. in print ⟨the most *celebrated* beauty of her day⟩. NOTED suggests well-deserved public attention ⟨the *noted* mystery writer⟩. NOTORIOUS frequently adds to FAMOUS an implication of questionableness or evil ⟨a *notorious* gangster⟩. DISTINGUISHED implies acknowledged excellence or superiority ⟨a *distinguished* scientist who won the Nobel Prize⟩. EMINENT implies even greater prominence for outstanding quality or character ⟨the country's most *eminent* writers⟩. ILLUSTRIOUS stresses enduring honor and glory attached to a deed or person ⟨*illustrious* war heroes⟩.

fa·mous·ly *adv* (1546) **1 :** in a celebrated manner **2 :** in a superlative fashion **3 :** to an unusual degree : VERY

fam·u·lus \ˈfam-yə-ləs\ *n, pl* **-li** \-ˌlī, -ˌlē\ [G, assistant to a professor, fr. L, servant] (1825) **:** a private secretary or attendant

[1]**fan** \ˈfan\ *n* [ME, fr. OE *fann,* fr. L *vannus* — more at WINNOW] (bef. 12c) **1 :** any of various devices for winnowing grain **2 :** an instrument for producing a current of air: as **a :** a device that is held in the hand and moved back and forth to cool a person and that is usu. shaped like a segment of a circle and composed of material (as feathers or paper) mounted on thin rods or slats moving about a pivot so that the device may be closed compactly when not in use **b :** a device that consists of a series of vanes radiating from a hub rotated on its axle by a motor **c** *slang* **:** an airplane propeller **3 a :** something resembling an open fan **b :** a gently sloping fan-shaped body of detritus; *esp* **:** ALLUVIAL FAN — **fan·like** \-ˌlīk\ *adj*

[2]**fan** *vb* **fanned; fan·ning** *vt* (bef. 12c) **1 a :** to drive away the chaff of (grain) by means of a current of air **b :** to eliminate (as chaff) by winnowing **2 :** to move or impel (air) with a fan **3 :** to blow or breathe upon ⟨the breeze *fanning* her hair⟩ **4 a :** to direct a current of air upon with a fan **b :** to stir up to activity as if by fanning : STIMULATE ⟨*fanning* the fires of nationalism⟩ **5** *archaic* **:** WAVE **6** *slang* **:** SPANK **7 :** to spread like a fan ⟨the peacock *fanned* his tail⟩ **8 :** to strike (a batter) out in baseball **9 :** to fire a series of shots from (a single-action revolver) by holding the trigger back and successively striking the hammer to the rear with the free hand ~ *vi* **1 :** to move like a fan : FLUTTER **2 :** to spread like a fan — often used with *out* ⟨the searchers *fanned* out⟩ **3 :** STRIKE OUT 3 — **fan·ner** \ˈfa-nər\ *n*

[3]**fan** *n* [prob. short for *fanatic*] (1682) **1 :** an enthusiastic devotee (as of a sport or a performing art) usu. as a spectator **2 :** an ardent admirer or enthusiast (as of a celebrity or a pursuit) ⟨science-fiction ~*s*⟩

fa·nat·ic \fə-ˈna-tik\ *or* **fa·nat·i·cal** \-ti-kəl\ *adj* [L *fanaticus* inspired by a deity, frenzied, fr. *fanum* temple — more at FEAST] (1550) **:** marked by excessive enthusiasm and often intense uncritical devotion ⟨they're ~ about politics⟩ — **fanatic** *n* — **fa·nat·i·cal·ly** \fə-ˈna-ti-k(ə-)lē\ *adv* — **fa·nat·i·cal·ness** \-kəl-nəs\ *n*

fa·nat·i·cism \fə-ˈna-tə-ˌsi-zəm\ *n* (1652) **:** fanatic outlook or behavior

fa·nat·i·cize \-ˌsīz\ *vt* **-cized; -ciz·ing** (1812) **:** to cause to become fanatic

fan·boy \ˈfan-ˌbȯi\ *n* (1919) **:** a boy or man who is an extremely or overly enthusiastic fan of someone or something

fan·ci·er \ˈfan(t)-sē-ər\ *n* (1751) **1 :** one that has a special liking or interest **2 :** a person who breeds or grows a particular animal or plant for points of excellence ⟨a pigeon ~⟩

fan·ci·ful \ˈfan(t)-si-fəl\ *adj* (ca. 1627) **1 :** marked by fancy or unrestrained imagination rather than by reason and experience ⟨a ~ person⟩ **2 :** existing in fancy only ⟨a ~ notion⟩ **3 :** marked by or as if by fancy or whim ⟨gave their children ~ names⟩ ***syn*** see IMAGINARY — **fan·ci·ful·ly** \-f(ə-)lē\ *adv* — **fan·ci·ful·ness** \-fəl-nəs\ *n*

fan·ci·fy \ˈfan(t)-sə-ˌfī\ *vt* **-fied; -fy·ing** (1823) **:** to make ornate, elaborate, or fancy ⟨a *fancified* hamburger⟩

[1]**fan·cy** \ˈfan(t)-sē\ *vt* **fan·cied; fan·cy·ing** (14c) **1 :** to have a fancy for : LIKE **2 :** to form a conception of : IMAGINE ⟨~ our embarrassment⟩ **3 a :** to believe mistakenly or without evidence **b :** to believe without being certain ⟨she *fancied* she had met him before⟩ **4 :** to visualize or interpret as ⟨*fancied* myself a child again⟩ ***syn*** see THINK

[2]**fancy** *n, pl* **fancies** [ME *fantasie, fantsy* imagination, image, illusion, preference, fr. AF *fantasie* illusion, fr. L *phantasia,* fr. Gk, appearance, imagination, fr. *phantazein* to present to the mind (middle voice, to imagine), fr. *phainein* to show; akin to OE *gebōned* polished, Gk *phōs* light] (15c) **1 a :** a liking formed by caprice rather than reason : INCLINATION ⟨took a ~ to the mutt⟩ **b :** amorous fondness : LOVE **2 a :** NOTION, WHIM **b :** an image or representation of something formed in the mind **3** *archaic* **:** fantastic quality or state **4 a :** imagination esp. of a capricious or delusive sort **b :** the power of conception and representation used in artistic expression (as by a poet) **5 :** TASTE, JUDGMENT **6 a :** devotees of some particular art, practice, or amusement **b :** the object of interest of such a fancy; *esp* **:** [1]BOXING

[3]**fancy** *adj* **fan·ci·er; -est** (1646) **1 :** dependent or based on fancy : WHIMSICAL **2 a (1) :** not plain : ORNAMENTAL ⟨a ~ hairdo⟩ **(2) :** SWANKY 2, POSH ⟨a ~ restaurant⟩ **b (1) :** of particular excellence or highest grade ⟨~ tuna⟩ **(2) :** IMPRESSIVE ⟨posted some ~ numbers⟩ **c** *of an animal or plant* **:** bred esp. for bizarre or ornamental qualities that lack practical utility **3 :** based on conceptions of the fancy ⟨~ sketches⟩ **4 a :** dealing in fancy goods **b :** EXTRAVAGANT ⟨paying ~ prices⟩ **5 :** executed with technical skill and style ⟨~ footwork⟩ ⟨~ diving⟩ **6 :** PARTI-COLOR ⟨~ carnations⟩ — **fan·ci·ly** \ˈfan(t)-sə-lē\ *adv* — **fan·ci·ness** \-sē-nəs\ *n*

fancy–dan \ˈfan(t)-sē-ˈdan, -ˌdan\ *adj, often cap D* (1938) **:** SHOWY 2, FANCY ⟨~ basketball players hotdogging on the court⟩

fancy Dan *n, often cap F* (ca. 1943) **:** one given to flamboyant display esp. of technique or dress

fancy dress *n* (1770) **:** a costume (as for a masquerade) chosen to suit the wearer's fancy

fan·cy–free \ˌfan(t)-sē-ˈfrē\ *adj* (1590) **1 :** free from amorous attachment or engagement ⟨footloose and ~⟩ **2 :** free to imagine or fancy

fancy man *n* (ca. 1811) **:** a woman's paramour; *also* **:** PIMP

fancy–pants *adj* (1945) **:** overly elegant or refined : LA-DI-DA

fancy up *vt* (1934) **:** to add superficial adornment to

fancy woman *n* (1812) **:** a woman of questionable morals; *specif* **:** PROSTITUTE

fan·cy·work \ˈfan(t)-sē-ˌwərk\ *n* (1791) **:** decorative needlework

F and A *abbr* fore and aft

fan·dan·go \fan-ˈdaŋ-(ˌ)gō\ *n, pl* **-gos** [Sp] (1770) **1 :** a lively Spanish or Spanish-American dance in triple time that is usu. performed by a man and a woman to the accompaniment of guitar and castanets; *also* **:** music for this dance **2 :** TOMFOOLERY

fan·dom \ˈfan-dəm\ *n* (1903) **1 :** all the fans (as of a sport) **2 :** the state or attitude of being a fan

fane \ˈfān\ *n* [ME, fr. L *fanum* — more at FEAST] (15c) **1 :** TEMPLE **2 :** CHURCH

fan·fare \ˈfan-ˌfer\ *n* [F] (1605) **1 :** a short and lively sounding of trumpets **2 :** a showy outward display

fan·far·o·nade \ˌfan-ˌfa-rə-ˈnād, -ˈnäd\ *n* [F *fanfaronnade,* fr. Sp *fanfarronada,* fr. *fanfarrón* braggart] (1652) **:** empty boasting **:** BLUSTER
fan fiction *n* (1944) **:** stories involving popular fictional characters that are written by fans and often posted on the Internet — called also *fanfic* \-ˈfik\
fan·fold \ˈfan-ˌfōld\ *n* (1925) **:** paper (as business forms or tape) made from a web and folded like a fan lengthwise and sometimes crosswise — **fanfold** *vt*
fang \ˈfaŋ\ *n* [ME, that which is taken, fr. OE; akin to OHG *fang* seizure, OE *fōn* to seize — more at PACT] (1555) **1 a :** a long sharp tooth: as **(1) :** one by which an animal's prey is seized and held or torn **(2) :** one of the long hollow or grooved and often erectile teeth of a venomous snake **b :** one of the chelicerae of a spider at the tip of which a poison gland opens **2 :** the root of a tooth or one of the processes or prongs into which a root divides **3 :** a projecting tooth or prong — **fanged** \ˈfaŋd\ *adj*
Fang \ˈfaŋ, ˈfäŋ\ *also* **Fan** \ˈfan, ˈfän\ *n, pl* **Fang** *or* **Fangs** *also* **Fan** *or* **Fans** (1861) **1 :** a member of a Bantu-speaking people of northern Gabon, mainland Equatorial Guinea, and southern Cameroon **2 :** the language of the Fang people
fan·girl \ˈfan-ˌgər(-ə)l\ *n* (1934) **:** a girl or woman who is an extremely or overly enthusiastic fan of someone or something
fan–jet \ˈfan-ˌjet\ *n* (1962) **:** a jet engine having a fan that operates in a duct and draws in extra air whose compression and expulsion provide extra thrust; *also* **:** an airplane powered by a fan-jet engine
fan letter *n* (1932) **:** a letter sent to a public figure by an admirer
fan·light \ˈfan-ˌlīt\ *n* (1819) **:** a semicircular window with radiating bars like the ribs of a fan that is placed over a door or window

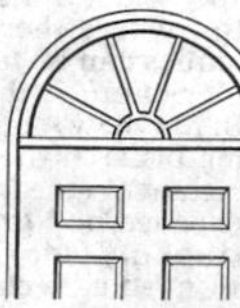
fanlight

fan mail *n* (1924) **:** FAN LETTERS
fan·ny \ˈfa-nē\ *n, pl* **fannies** [perh. fr. *Fanny,* nickname of *Frances*] (ca. 1840) **1** *slang Brit* **:** VULVA **2 :** BUTTOCKS
fanny pack *n* (1967) **:** a pack that straps to the waist and is used for carrying personal articles
fan·tab·u·lous \fan-ˈta-byə-ləs\ *adj* [blend of *fantastic* and *fabulous*] (1957) *slang* **:** marvelously good
fan·tail \ˈfan-ˌtāl\ *n* (1728) **1 :** a fan-shaped tail or end **2 :** a domestic pigeon having a broad rounded tail often with 30 or 40 feathers **3 :** an architectural part resembling a fan **4 :** a counter or after overhang of a ship shaped like a duck's bill
fan–tan \ˈfan-ˌtan\ *n* [Chin (Guangdong) *fāantāan*] (1878) **1 :** a Chinese gambling game in which the banker divides a pile of objects (as beans) into fours and players bet on what number will be left at the end of the count **2 :** a card game in which players must build in sequence upon sevens and attempt to be the first one out of cards
fan·ta·sia \fan-ˈtā-zhə, -z(h)ē-ə; ˌfan-tə-ˈzē-ə\ *n* [It, lit., fancy, fr. L *phantasia* — more at FANCY] (1724) **1 :** a free usu. instrumental composition not in strict form **2 a :** a work (as a poem or play) in which the author's fancy roves unrestricted **b :** something possessing grotesque, bizarre, or unreal qualities
fan·ta·sied \ˈfan-tə-sēd, -zēd\ *adj* (1561) **1 :** existing only in the imagination **:** FANCIED **2** *obs* **:** full of fancies or strange whims
fan·ta·sise *Brit var of* FANTASIZE
fan·ta·sist \-sist, -zist\ *n* (1896) **:** one who creates fantasias or fantasies
fan·ta·size \-ˌsīz\ *vb* **-sized; -siz·ing** *vi* (1926) **:** to indulge in reverie **:** create or develop imaginative and often fantastic views or ideas ⟨doing things I'd *fantasized* about in my sheltered childhood —Diane Arbus⟩ ~ *vt* **:** to portray in the mind **:** FANCY ⟨likes to ~ herself as very wealthy⟩ — **fan·ta·siz·er** \-ˌsī-zər\ *n*
fantasm *var of* PHANTASM
fan·tast \ˈfan-ˌtast\ *n* [G, fr. ML *fantasta,* prob. back-formation fr. LL *phantasticus*] (1588) **1 :** VISIONARY **2 :** a fantastic or eccentric person **3 :** FANTASIST
[1]**fan·tas·tic** \fan-ˈtas-tik, fən-\ *also* **fan·tas·ti·cal** \-ti-kəl\ *adj* [ME *fantastic, fantastical,* fr. MF & LL; MF *fantastique,* fr. LL *phantasticus,* fr. Gk *phantastikos* producing mental images, fr. *phantazein* to present to the mind — more at FANCY] (14c) **1 a :** based on fantasy **:** not real **b :** conceived or seemingly conceived by unrestrained fancy **c :** so extreme as to challenge belief **:** UNBELIEVABLE; *broadly* **:** exceedingly large or great **2 :** marked by extravagant fantasy or extreme individuality **:** ECCENTRIC **3** *fantastic* **:** EXCELLENT, SUPERLATIVE ⟨a ~ meal⟩ — **fan·tas·ti·cal·i·ty** \(ˌ)fan-ˌtas-tə-ˈka-lə-tē, fən-\ *n* — **fan·tas·ti·cal·ness** \-ˈtas-tə-kəl-nəs\ *n*
syn FANTASTIC, BIZARRE, GROTESQUE mean conceived, made, or carried out without adherence to truth or reality. FANTASTIC may connote extravagance in conception or ingenuity of decorative invention ⟨dreamed up *fantastic* rumors⟩. BIZARRE applies to the sensationally strange and implies violence of contrast or incongruity of combination ⟨a *bizarre* medieval castle in the heart of a modern city⟩. GROTESQUE may apply to what is conventionally ugly but artistically effective or it may connote ludicrous awkwardness or incongruity often with sinister or tragic overtones ⟨*grotesque* statues on the cathedral⟩ ⟨though grieving, she made a *grotesque* attempt at a smile⟩. ***syn*** see in addition IMAGINARY
[2]**fantastic** *n* (1598) **:** ECCENTRIC 2
fan·tas·ti·cal·ly \fan-ˈtas-ti-k(ə-)lē, fən-\ *adv* (1543) **1 :** in a fantastic manner **2 :** to a fantastic degree **:** EXTREMELY ⟨~ expensive clothes⟩
fan·tas·ti·co \fan-ˈtas-ti-ˌkō, fən-\ *n, pl* **-coes** [It, fantastic (adj.), fr. LL *phantasticus*] (1596) **:** a ridiculously fantastic individual
[1]**fan·ta·sy** *also* **phan·ta·sy** \ˈfan-tə-sē, -zē\ *n, pl* **-sies** [ME *fantasie* — more at FANCY] (14c) **1** *obs* **:** HALLUCINATION **2 :** FANCY; *esp* **:** the free play of creative imagination **3 :** a creation of the imaginative faculty whether expressed or merely conceived: as **a :** a fanciful design or invention **b :** a chimerical or fantastic notion **c :** FANTASIA 1 **d :** imaginative fiction featuring esp. strange settings and grotesque characters — called also *fantasy fiction* **4 :** CAPRICE **5 :** the power or process of creating esp. unrealistic or improbable mental images in response to psychological need ⟨an object of ~⟩; *also* **:** a mental image or a series of mental images (as a daydream) so created ⟨sexual *fantasies*⟩ **6** *often attrib* **:** a coin usu. not intended for circulation as currency and often issued by a dubious authority (as a government-in-exile)
[2]**fantasy** *vb* **-sied; -sy·ing** (15c) **:** FANTASIZE
[3]**fantasy** *adj* (1984) **:** of, relating to, or being a game in which participants create and manage imaginary teams consisting of players from a particular sport and scoring is based on the statistical performances of the actual players ⟨~ football⟩
fan·ta·sy·land \-ˌland\ *n* (1967) **:** an imaginary or ideal place or situation
fan·toc·ci·ni \ˌfän-tə-ˈchē-nē, ˌfan-\ *n pl* [It, pl. of *fantoccino,* dim. of *fantoccio* doll, aug. of *fante* child, fr. L *infant-, infans* infant] (1771) **:** a puppet show using puppets operated by strings or mechanical devices; *also* **:** such puppets
fan·tod \ˈfan-ˌtäd\ *n* [perh. alter. of E dial. *fantique, fanteeg,* perh. blend of *fantastic* and *fatigue*] (1839) **1** *pl* **a :** a state of irritability and tension **b :** FIDGETS **2 :** an emotional outburst **:** FIT
fan vault *n* (ca. 1901) **:** a Gothic vault in which the ribs from each springer spread out like the vanes of a fan — **fan vaulting** *n*
fan·wise \ˈfan-ˌwīz\ *adv or adj* (1882) **:** in the manner or position of the slats of an open fan ⟨boats anchored ~ at the pier⟩
fan·zine \ˈfan-ˌzēn\ *n* [[3]*fan* + maga*zine*] (1942) **:** a magazine written by and for fans ⟨a sci-fi ~⟩ ⟨a punk rocker with her own ~⟩
FAO *abbr* Food and Agriculture Organization of the United Nations
[1]**FAQ** \ˈfak, ˌef-ˌā-ˈkyü\ *n* [*f*requently *a*sked *q*uestions] (1991) **:** a document (as on a Web site) that provides answers to a list of typical questions that users might ask regarding a particular subject ⟨check the ~⟩; *also* **:** a question included in such a document ⟨a list of ~*s*⟩
[2]**FAQ** *abbr* fair average quality
[1]**far** \ˈfär\ *adv* **far·ther** \-t͟hər\ *or* **fur·ther** \ˈfər-\; **far·thest** *or* **fur·thest** \-t͟həst\ [ME *fer,* fr. OE *feorr;* akin to OHG *ferro* far, OE *faran* to go — more at FARE] (bef. 12c) **1 :** at or to a considerable distance in space ⟨wandered ~ from home⟩ **2 a :** to a great extent **:** MUCH ⟨~ better methods⟩ **b :** by a broad interval **:** WIDELY ⟨the ~ distant future⟩ **3 :** to or at a definite distance, point, or degree ⟨as ~ as I know⟩ **4 :** to an advanced point or extent ⟨a bright student will go ~⟩ ⟨worked ~ into the night⟩ **5 :** at a considerable distance in time ⟨not ~ from the year 1870⟩ — **by far :** far and away ⟨is *by far* the best runner⟩ — **far be it from :** it would be inappropriate or impossible for ⟨*far be it from* me to complain⟩ — **far from :** of a distinctly different and esp. opposite quality than ⟨the trip was *far from* a failure⟩ — **how far :** to what extent, degree, or distance ⟨didn't know *how far* to trust them⟩ — **so far 1 :** to a certain extent, degree, or distance ⟨when the water rose *so far,* we fled⟩ **2 :** up to the present ⟨has written one novel *so far*⟩ — **thus far :** so far ⟨*thus far* the results are negative⟩
[2]**far** *adj* **farther** *or* **further; farthest** *or* **furthest** (bef. 12c) **1 a :** remote in space **b :** distinctly different in quality or relationship **c :** remote in time **2 a :** LONG ⟨a ~ journey⟩ **b :** of notable extent **:** COMPREHENSIVE ⟨a man of ~ vision⟩ **3 :** the more distant of two ⟨the ~ end⟩ **4 :** EXTREME ⟨the ~ left⟩ ⟨a ~ right political organization⟩
FAR *abbr* federal air regulation
far·ad \ˈfer-ˌad, -əd; ˈfa-ˌrad, -ˌrəd\ *n* [Michael *Faraday*] (1873) **:** the unit of capacitance equal to the capacitance of a capacitor between whose plates there appears a potential of one volt when it is charged by one coulomb of electricity
far·a·day \ˈfer-ə-ˌdā, -dē; ˈfa-rə-\ *n* [Michael *Faraday*] (1904) **:** the quantity of electricity transferred in electrolysis per equivalent weight of an element or ion equal to about 96,500 coulombs
fa·rad·ic \fə-ˈra-dik, fa-ˈra-\ *also* **far·a·da·ic** \ˌfer-ə-ˈdā-ik, ˌfa-rə-\ *adj* (1875) **:** of or relating to an asymmetric alternating current of electricity produced by an induction coil ⟨~ stimulation of the muscles⟩
far and away *adv* (1852) **:** by a considerable margin ⟨was *far and away* the better team⟩
far·an·dole \ˈfer-ən-ˌdōl, ˈfa-rən-\ *n* [F *farandole,* fr. Occitan *farandoulo*] (1863) **1 :** a lively Provençal dance in which men and women hold hands, form a chain, and follow a leader through a serpentine course **2 :** music in sextuple time for a farandole
far and wide *adv* (bef. 12c) **:** in every direction **:** EVERYWHERE ⟨searched *far and wide*⟩
far·away \ˈfär-ə-ˌwā\ *adj* (1735) **1 :** lying at a great distance **:** REMOTE ⟨~ lands⟩ **2 :** DREAMY, ABSTRACTED ⟨a ~ look in her eyes⟩
[1]**farce** \ˈfärs\ *vt* **farced; farc·ing** [ME *farsen,* fr. AF *farsir,* fr. L *farcire*] (14c) **1 :** STUFF **2 :** to improve as if by stuffing
[2]**farce** *n* [ME *farse,* fr. MF *farce,* fr. VL **farsa,* fr. L, fem. of *farsus,* pp. of *farcire*] (14c) **1 :** a savory stuffing **:** FORCEMEAT **2 :** a light dramatic composition marked by broadly satirical comedy and improbable plot **3 :** the broad humor characteristic of farce **4 :** an empty or patently ridiculous act, proceeding, or situation ⟨the trial became a ~⟩
far·ceur \fär-ˈsər\ *n* [F, fr. MF, fr. *farcer* to joke, fr. OF, fr. *farce*] (1781) **1 :** JOKER, WAG **2 :** a writer or actor of farce
far·ci *or* **far·cie** \fär-ˈsē\ *adj* [F, fr. pp. of *farcir*] (1903) **:** stuffed esp. with forcemeat ⟨oysters ~⟩
far·ci·cal \ˈfär-si-kəl\ *adj* (1710) **1 :** of, relating to, or resembling farce **:** LUDICROUS **2 :** laughably inept **:** ABSURD — **far·ci·cal·i·ty** \ˌfär-sə-ˈka-lə-tē\ *n* — **far·ci·cal·ly** \ˈfär-si-k(ə-)lē\ *adv*
far cry *n* (1817) **1 :** a long distance **2 :** something notably different ⟨the effects of the new law were a *far cry* from what was intended⟩
far·cy \ˈfär-sē\ *n* [ME *farsin, farsi,* fr. AF *farcin,* fr. LL *farcimen,* fr. L, sausage, fr. *farcire*] (15c) **:** GLANDERS; *esp* **:** cutaneous glanders
fard \ˈfärd\ *vt* [ME, fr. AF *farder,* of Gmc origin; akin to OHG *faro* colored — more at PERCH] (15c) **1 :** to paint (the face) with cosmetics **2** *archaic* **:** to gloss over — **fard** *n, archaic*
far·del \ˈfär-dᵊl\ *n* [ME, fr. AF, ultim. fr. Ar *farda* part, bundle] (14c) **1 :** BUNDLE **2 :** BURDEN
[1]**fare** \ˈfer\ *vi* **fared; far·ing** [ME *faren,* fr. OE *faran;* akin to OHG *faran* to go, L *portare* to carry, Gk *peran* to pass through, *poros* passage, journey] (bef. 12c) **1 :** GO, TRAVEL **2 :** GET ALONG, SUCCEED ⟨how did you ~ on your exam?⟩ **3 :** EAT, DINE
[2]**fare** *n* [ME, journey, passage, supply of food, fr. OE *faru, fær;* akin to OE *faran* to go] (15c) **1 a :** range of food **:** DIET **b :** material provided for use, consumption, or enjoyment **2 a :** the price charged to transport a person **b :** a paying passenger on a public conveyance

\ə\ **abut** \ᵊ\ **kitten,** F **table** \ər\ **further** \a\ **ash** \ā\ **ace** \ä\ **mop, mar** \au̇\ **out** \ch\ **chin** \e\ **bet** \ē\ **easy** \g\ **go** \i\ **hit** \ī\ **ice** \j\ **job** \ŋ\ **sing** \ō\ **go** \ȯ\ **law** \ȯi\ **boy** \th\ **thin** \t͟h\ **the** \ü\ **loot** \u̇\ **foot** \y\ **yet** \zh\ **vision, beige** \k̲, ⁿ, œ, ue, ʸ\ *see* Guide to Pronunciation

fare–thee–well \ˈfer-(ˌ)t͟hē-ˌwel\ *also* **fare–you–well** \-yə-, -yü-, -yē-\ *n* (1884) **1 :** the utmost degree ⟨researched the story to a ~⟩ **2 :** a state of perfection ⟨imitated the speaker's pompous manner to a ~⟩
[1]**fare·well** \fer-ˈwel\ *vb imper* (14c) **:** get along well — used interjectionally to or by one departing
[2]**farewell** *n* (14c) **1 :** a wish of well-being at parting **:** GOOD-BYE **2 a :** an act of departure **:** LEAVE-TAKING **b :** a formal occasion honoring a person about to leave or retire
[3]**fare·well** *vt* (1580) *chiefly Austral & NewZeal* **:** to bid farewell to
[4]**fare·well** \ˈfer-ˌwel\ *adj* (1669) **:** of or relating to leave-taking **:** FINAL ⟨a ~ performance⟩
far·fal·le \fär-ˈfä-(ˌ)lā, -lē\ *n* [It, pl. of *farfalla,* lit., butterfly] (1941) **:** butterfly-shaped pasta
far·fel *or* **far·fal** \ˈfär-fəl\ *n* [Yiddish *farfl* (pl.), fr. MHG *varveln* noodles, noodle soup] (1892) **:** noodles in the form of pellets or granules
far–fetched \ˈfär-ˈfecht\ *adj* (1548) **1 :** brought from a remote time or place **2 :** not easily or naturally deduced or introduced **:** IMPROBABLE ⟨a ~ story⟩ — **far·fetched·ness** \-ˈfech(t)-nəs, -ˈfe-chəd-nəs\ *n*
far–flung \-ˈfləŋ\ *adj* (1849) **1 :** widely spread or distributed ⟨a ~ empire⟩ **2 :** REMOTE ⟨a ~ correspondent⟩
fa·ri·na \fə-ˈrē-nə\ *n* [L, meal, flour, fr. *far* spelt — more at BARLEY] (14c) **1 :** a fine meal of vegetable matter (as cereal grains) used chiefly for puddings or as a breakfast cereal **2 :** any of various powdery or mealy substances
far·i·na·ceous \ˌfer-ə-ˈnā-shəs, ˌfa-rə-\ *adj* (1646) **1 :** having a mealy texture or surface **2 :** containing or rich in starch
far–in·fra·red \ˈfär-ˌin-frə-ˈred\ *adj* (1923) **:** of or relating to the longer wavelengths of radiation in the infrared spectrum and esp. to those between 10 and 1000 micrometers
fa·ri·nha \fə-ˈrēn-yə\ *n* [Pg, flour, cassava meal, fr. L *farina*] (1726) **:** cassava meal
far·kle·ber·ry \ˈfär-kəl-ˌber-ē\ *n* [origin unknown] (1765) **:** a shrub or small tree (*Vaccinium arboreum*) of the heath family of the southeastern U.S. having a small hard black berry with stony seeds
farl \ˈfär(-ə)l\ *n* [contr. of Sc *fardel,* lit., fourth part, fr. ME (Sc), fr. *ferde del,* fr. *ferde* fourth + *del* part] (1686) *Scot* **:** a small thin triangular cake or biscuit made esp. with oatmeal or wheat flour
[1]**farm** \ˈfärm\ *n, often attrib* [ME *ferme,* fr. AF, fr. *fermer* to fix, rent, fr. L *firmare* to make firm, fr. *firmus* firm] (14c) **1** *obs* **:** a sum or due fixed in amount and payable at fixed intervals **2 :** a letting out of revenues or taxes for a fixed sum to one authorized to collect and retain them **3 :** a district or division of a country leased out for the collection of government revenues **4 :** a tract of land devoted to agricultural purposes **5 a :** a plot of land devoted to the raising of animals and esp. domestic livestock **b :** a tract of water reserved for the artificial cultivation of some aquatic life form ⟨a fish ~⟩ **6 :** a minor-league team (as in baseball) associated with a major-league team as a subsidiary **7 :** an area containing a number of similar structures or objects (as radio antennas or storage tanks)
[2]**farm** *vt* (15c) **1** *obs* **:** RENT **2 :** to collect and take the fees or profits of (an occupation or business) on payment of a fixed sum **3 :** to give up (as an estate or a business) to another on condition of receiving in return a fixed sum **4 a :** to devote to agriculture **b :** to manage and cultivate as a farm **c :** to grow or cultivate in quantity ⟨~ trees for fuel⟩ ⟨~ salmon⟩ ~ *vi* **:** to engage in raising crops or animals
farm·er \ˈfär-mər\ *n* (14c) **1 :** a person who pays a fixed sum for some privilege or source of income **2 :** a person who cultivates land or crops or raises animals (as livestock or fish) **3 :** YOKEL, BUMPKIN
farmer cheese *n* (1949) **:** a pressed unripened cheese similar to but drier and firmer than cottage cheese
farm·er·ette \ˌfär-mə-ˈret\ *n* (1902) **:** a woman who is a farmer or farmhand
farmer's lung *n* (1945) **:** an acute pulmonary disorder characterized by sudden onset, fever, cough, expectoration, and breathlessness that results from the inhalation of spores in dust from moldy hay or straw
farm·hand \ˈfärm-ˌhand\ *n* (1843) **1 :** a farm laborer; *esp* **:** a hired laborer on a farm **2 :** a player on a farm team
farm·house \-ˌhau̇s\ *n* (1598) **:** a dwelling on a farm
farm·ing *n* (1659) **:** the practice of agriculture or aquaculture
farm·land \ˈfärm-ˌland\ *n* (1638) **:** land used or suitable for farming
farm out *vt* (ca. 1600) **1 :** to turn over (as a job) for performance by another usu. under contract **2 a :** to put (as children) into the hands of another for care **b :** to send (as a baseball player) to a farm team **3 :** to exhaust (land) by farming esp. by continuously raising one crop
farm·stead \ˈfärm-ˌsted\ *n* (1807) **:** the buildings and adjacent service areas of a farm; *broadly* **:** a farm with its buildings
farm·wife \ˈfärm-ˌwīf\ *n* (1874) **:** a farmer's wife
farm·work·er \ˈfärm-ˌwər-kər\ *n* (1941) **:** FARMHAND 1 — **farm·work** \-ˌwərk\ *n*
farm·yard \-ˌyärd\ *n* (1723) **:** land around or enclosed by farm buildings; *esp* **:** BARNYARD
faro \ˈfer-(ˌ)ō\ *n, pl* **far·os** [prob. alter. of earlier *pharaoh,* trans. of F *pharaon*] (1731) **:** a gambling game in which players bet on cards drawn from a dealing box
Faroese *var of* FAEROESE
far–off \ˈfär-ˌȯf\ *adj* (15c) **:** remote in time or space
fa·rouche \fə-ˈrüsh\ *adj* [F, wild, shy, fr. OF, alter. of *forasche,* fr. LL *forasticus* living outside, fr. L *foras* outdoors; akin to L *fores* door — more at DOOR] (1765) **1 :** WILD **2 :** marked by shyness and lack of social graces
far–out \ˈfär-ˌau̇t\ *adj* (1954) **:** marked by a considerable departure from the conventional or traditional ⟨~ clothes⟩ — **far–out·ness** *n*
far·rag·i·nous \fə-ˈra-jə-nəs\ *adj* (1615) **:** consisting of a farrago
far·ra·go \fə-ˈrä-(ˌ)gō, -ˈrā-\ *n, pl* **-goes** [L *farragin-, farrago* mixed fodder, mixture, fr. *far* spelt — more at BARLEY] (1632) **:** a confused mixture **:** HODGEPODGE
far–reach·ing \ˈfär-ˈrē-chiŋ\ *adj* (ca. 1590) **:** having a wide range or effect
far–red \-ˈred\ *adj* (1951) **:** NEAR-INFRARED
far·ri·er \ˈfer-ē-ər, ˈfa-rē-\ *n* [alter. of ME *ferrour,* fr. AF *ferrour* blacksmith, fr. *ferrer* to shoe (horses), fr. VL **ferrare,* fr. L *ferrum* iron] (15c) **:** a person who shoes horses
[1]**far·row** \ˈfer-(ˌ)ō, ˈfa-(ˌ)rō\ *vb* [ME *farwen,* fr. OE **feargian,* fr. OE *fearh* young pig; akin to OHG *farah* young pig, L *porcus* pig] *vt* (13c) **:** to give birth to (a farrow) ~ *vi, of swine* **:** to bring forth young — often used with *down*
[2]**farrow** *n* (1577) **1 :** a litter of pigs **2 :** an act of farrowing
[3]**farrow** *adj* [ME (Sc) *ferow*] (15c) *of a cow* **:** not pregnant
far·see·ing \ˈfär-ˌsē-iŋ\ *adj* (1598) **:** FARSIGHTED 1
Far·si \ˈfär-sē\ *n* [Pers *fārsī,* fr. *Fārs* Persia] (1878) **:** PERSIAN 2b
far·side *n* (15c) **:** the farther side; *esp* **:** the side of the moon away from the earth — **on the far side of :** BEYOND ⟨just *on the far side of* 40⟩
far·sight·ed \ˈfär-ˌsī-təd\ *adj* (1609) **1 a :** seeing or able to see to a great distance **b :** having or showing foresight or good judgment **:** SAGACIOUS **2 :** affected with hyperopia — **far·sight·ed·ly** *adv*
far·sight·ed·ness *n* (ca. 1829) **1 :** the quality or state of being farsighted **2 :** HYPEROPIA
[1]**fart** \ˈfärt\ *vi* [ME *ferten, farten;* akin to OHG *ferzan* to break wind, ON *freta,* Gk *perdesthai,* Skt *pardate* he breaks wind] (13c) *often vulgar* **:** to expel intestinal gas from the anus
[2]**fart** *n* (14c) **1** *often vulgar* **:** an expulsion of intestinal gas **2** *often vulgar* **:** a foolish or contemptible person ⟨couldn't stand the old ~⟩
[1]**far·ther** \ˈfär-t͟hər\ *adv* [ME *ferther,* alter. of *further*] (14c) **1 :** at or to a greater distance or more advanced point ⟨got no ~ than the first page⟩ ⟨nothing could be ~ from the truth⟩ **2 :** to a greater degree or extent ⟨see to it that I do not have to act any ~ in the matter —Bernard DeVoto⟩

usage *Farther* and *further* have been used more or less interchangeably throughout most of their history, but currently they are showing signs of diverging. As adverbs they continue to be used interchangeably whenever spatial, temporal, or metaphorical distance is involved. But where there is no notion of distance, *further* is used ⟨our techniques can be *further* refined⟩. *Further* is also used as a sentence modifier ⟨*further,* the workshop participants were scarcely optimistic —L. B. Mayhew⟩, but *farther* is not. A polarizing process appears to be taking place in their adjective use. *Farther* is taking over the meaning of distance ⟨the *farther* shore⟩ and *further* the meaning of addition ⟨needed no *further* invitation⟩.

[2]**farther** *adj* (14c) **1 :** more distant **:** REMOTER ⟨the ~ side of town⟩ **2 :** FURTHER 2 ⟨clearing his throat preparatory to ~ revelations —Edith Wharton⟩
far·ther·most \-ˌmōst\ *adj* (15c) **:** most distant **:** FARTHEST
[1]**far·thest** \ˈfär-t͟həst\ *adj* (14c) **:** most distant esp. in space or time ⟨the ~ frontier⟩ ⟨the seat ~ from the door⟩
[2]**farthest** *adv* (15c) **1 :** to or at the greatest distance in space or time ⟨who can jump the ~⟩ **2 :** to the most advanced point ⟨goes ~ toward answering the question⟩ **3 :** by the greatest degree or extent **:** MOST ⟨the painting ~ removed from reality⟩
far·thing \ˈfär-t͟hiŋ\ *n* [ME *ferthing,* fr. OE *fēorthung* (akin to MHG *vierdunc* fourth part), fr. OE *fēortha* fourth] (bef. 12c) **1 a :** a former British monetary unit equal to ¼ of a penny **b :** a coin representing this unit **2 :** something of small value **:** MITE
far·thin·gale \ˈfär-t͟hən-ˌgāl, -t͟hiŋ-\ *n* [modif. of MF *verdugale,* fr. OSp *verdugado,* fr. *verdugo* young shoot of a tree, fr. *verde* green, fr. L *viridis* — more at VERDANT] (1552) **:** a support (as of hoops) worn esp. in the 16th century beneath a skirt to expand it at the hipline
far–ultraviolet *adj* (1947) **:** of, relating to, or being the shortest wavelengths of radiation in the ultraviolet spectrum and esp. those between 100 and 300 nanometers
FAS *abbr* **1** fetal alcohol syndrome **2** firsts and seconds **3** free alongside ship
fasc *abbr* fascicle
fas·ces \ˈfas-ˌēz\ *n pl but sing or pl in constr* [L, fr. pl. of *fascis* bundle; akin to L *fascia*] (1598) **:** a bundle of rods and among them an ax with projecting blade borne before ancient Roman magistrates as a badge of authority

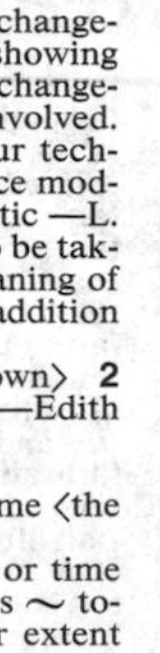
fasces

fas·cia *1 & 3 are usu* ˈfā-sh(ē-)ə, *2 is usu* ˈfa-\ *n, pl* **-ci·ae** \-shē-ˌē\ *or* **-cias** [It, fr. L, band, bandage; akin to MIr *basc* necklace] (1563) **1 :** a flat usu. horizontal member of a building having the form of a flat band or broad fillet: as **a :** a flat piece used as a molding **b :** a horizontal piece (as a board) covering the joint between the top of a wall and the projecting eaves — called also *fascia board* **c :** a nameplate over the front of a shop **2 :** a sheet of connective tissue covering or binding together body structures (as muscles); *also* **:** tissue of this character **3** *or* **fa·cia** \ˈfā-sh(ē-)ə\ *Brit* **:** the dashboard of an automobile — **fas·cial** \ˈfa-sh(ē-)əl\ *adj*
fas·ci·at·ed \ˈfa-shē-ˌā-təd\ *adj* (ca. 1835) **1 :** exhibiting fasciation **2 :** arranged in fascicles
fas·ci·a·tion \ˌfa-s(h)ē-ˈā-shən\ *n* (1677) **:** a malformation of plant stems commonly manifested as enlargement and flattening as if several stems were fused
fas·ci·cle \ˈfa-si-kəl\ *n* [L *fasciculus,* dim. of *fascis*] (15c) **1 :** a small or slender bundle (as of pine needles or nerve fibers) **2 :** one of the divisions of a book published in parts — **fas·ci·cled** \-kəld\ *adj*
fas·cic·u·lar \fə-ˈsi-kyə-lər, fa-\ *adj* (1816) **:** of, relating to, or consisting of fascicles or fasciculi — **fas·cic·u·lar·ly** *adv*
fas·cic·u·late \-lət\ *also* **fas·cic·u·lat·ed** \-ˌlā-təd\ *adj* (1794) **:** FASCICULAR
fas·cic·u·la·tion \fə-ˌsi-kyə-ˈlā-shən, fa-\ *n* (1938) **:** muscular twitching involving the simultaneous contraction of contiguous groups of muscle fibers
fas·ci·cule \ˈfa-si-ˌkyül\ *n* [F, fr. L *fasciculus*] (1880) **:** FASCICLE 2
fas·cic·u·lus \fə-ˈsi-kyə-ləs, fa-\ *n, pl* **-li** \-ˌlī\ [NL, fr. L] (1713) **1 :** a slender bundle of anatomical fibers (as nerve fibers) **2 :** FASCICLE 2
fas·ci·i·tis \ˌfa-shē-ˈī-təs, -sē-\ *also* **fas·ci·tis** \fa-ˈshī-təs, -ˈsī-\ *n* [NL] (1893) **:** inflammation of a fascia (as from infection or injury) — compare NECROTIZING FASCIITIS
fas·ci·nate \ˈfa-sə-ˌnāt\ *vb* **fas·ci·nat·ed; fas·ci·nat·ing** \ˈfas-ˌnā-tiŋ, ˈfa-sə-ˌnā-\ [L *fascinatus,* pp. of *fascinare,* fr. *fascinum* evil spell] *vt* (1598) **1** *obs* **:** BEWITCH **2 a :** to transfix and hold spellbound by an irresistible power ⟨believed that the serpent could ~ its prey⟩ **b :** to command the interest of **:** ALLURE ⟨was *fascinated* by carnivals⟩ ~ *vi* **:** to be irresistibly attractive ⟨the novel's flamboyant cover ~*s*⟩ ***syn*** see ATTRACT
fascinating *adj* (1638) **:** extremely interesting or charming **:** CAPTIVATING — **fas·ci·nat·ing·ly** \-ˌā-tiŋ-lē\ *adv*

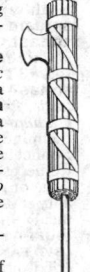

fas·ci·na·tion \ˌfa-sə-ˈnā-shən\ *n* (1605) **1 a :** the quality or power of fascinating **b :** something fascinating **2 :** the state of being fascinated : the state of feeling an intense interest in something

fas·ci·na·tor \ˈfa-sə-ˌnā-tər\ *n* (1750) **1 :** one that fascinates **2 :** a woman's lightweight head scarf usu. of crochet or lace

fas·cine \fa-ˈsēn, fə-\ *n* [F, fr. L *fascina,* fr. *fascis*] (ca. 1688) **:** a long bundle of sticks of wood bound together and used for such purposes as filling ditches and making revetments for riverbanks

fa·sci·o·li·a·sis \fə-ˌsē-ə-ˈlī-ə-səs, -ˌsī-\ *n, pl* **-a·ses** \-ˌsēz\ [NL, fr. *Fasciola,* genus of flukes + *-iasis*] (1890) **:** infestation with or disease caused by liver flukes (*Fasciola hepatica* or *F. gigantica*)

fas·cism \ˈfa-ˌshi-zəm *also* ˈfa-ˌsi-\ *n* [It *fascismo,* fr. *fascio* bundle, fasces, group, fr. L *fascis* bundle & *fasces* fasces] (1921) **1** *often cap* **:** a political philosophy, movement, or regime (as that of the Fascisti) that exalts nation and often race above the individual and that stands for a centralized autocratic government headed by a dictatorial leader, severe economic and social regimentation, and forcible suppression of opposition **2 :** a tendency toward or actual exercise of strong autocratic or dictatorial control ⟨early instances of army ~ and brutality —J. W. Aldridge⟩ — **fas·cist** \-shist *also* -sist\ *n or adj, often cap* — **fas·cis·tic** \fa-ˈshis-tik *also* -ˈsis-\ *adj, often cap* — **fas·cis·ti·cal·ly** \-ti-k(ə-)lē\ *adv, often cap*

Fa·sci·sta \fä-ˈshē-(ˌ)stä\ *n, pl* **-sti** \-(ˌ)stē\ [It, fr. *fascio*] (1921) **:** a member of an Italian political organization under Mussolini governing Italy 1922–1943 according to the principles of fascism

fash \ˈfash\ *vb* [MF *fascher,* fr. VL **fastidiare* to disgust, fr. L *fastidium* disgust — more at FASTIDIOUS] (1533) *chiefly Scot* **:** VEX — **fash** *n, chiefly Scot*

[1]**fash·ion** \ˈfa-shᵊn\ *n* [ME *facioun, fasoun* shape, manner, fr. AF *façun, fauschoun,* fr. L *faction-, factio* act of making, faction, fr. *facere* to make — more at DO] (14c) **1 a :** the make or form of something **b** *archaic* **:** KIND, SORT **2 a :** a distinctive or peculiar and often habitual manner or way ⟨he will, after his sour ~, tell you —Shak.⟩ **b :** mode of action or operation ⟨assembled in an orderly ~⟩ **3 a :** a prevailing custom, usage, or style **b (1) :** the prevailing style (as in dress) during a particular time **(2) :** a garment in such a style ⟨always wears the latest ~*s*⟩ **c :** social standing or prominence esp. as signalized by dress or conduct ⟨men and women of ~⟩ — **after a fashion :** in an approximate or rough way ⟨became an artist *after a fashion*⟩

syn FASHION, STYLE, MODE, VOGUE, FAD, RAGE, CRAZE mean the usage accepted by those who want to be up-to-date. FASHION is the most general term and applies to any way of dressing, behaving, writing, or performing that is favored at any one time or place ⟨the current *fashion*⟩. STYLE often implies a distinctive fashion adopted by people of taste ⟨a media baron used to traveling in *style*⟩. MODE suggests the fashion of the moment among those anxious to appear elegant and sophisticated ⟨slim bodies are the *mode* at this resort⟩. VOGUE stresses the wide acceptance of a fashion ⟨short skirts are back in *vogue*⟩. FAD suggests caprice in taking up or in dropping a fashion ⟨last year's *fad* is over⟩. RAGE and CRAZE stress intense enthusiasm in adopting a fad ⟨Cajun food was the *rage* nearly everywhere for a time⟩ ⟨crossword puzzles once seemed just a passing *craze* but have lasted⟩. ***syn*** see in addition METHOD

[2]**fashion** *vt* **fash·ioned; fash·ion·ing** \ˈfash-niŋ, ˈfa-shᵊn-iŋ\ (15c) **1 a :** to give shape or form to **:** MOLD **b :** ALTER, TRANSFORM **c :** to mold into a particular character by influencing or training **d :** to make or construct usu. with the use of imagination and ingenuity ⟨~ a lamp from an old churn⟩ **2 :** FIT, ADAPT **3** *obs* **:** CONTRIVE — **fash·ion·er** \ˈfash-nər, ˈfa-shə-nər\ *n*

[1]**fash·ion·able** \ˈfash-nə-bəl, ˈfa-shə-nə-\ *adj* (ca. 1580) **1 :** conforming to the custom, fashion, or established mode **2 :** of or relating to the world of fashion — **fash·ion·abil·i·ty** \ˌfash-nə-ˈbi-lə-tē, ˌfa-shə-nə-\ *n* — **fash·ion·able·ness** \ˈfash-nə-bəl-nəs, ˈfa-shə-\ *n* — **fash·ion·ably** \-blē\ *adv*

[2]**fashionable** *n* (ca. 1800) **:** a fashionable person

fash·ion·is·ta \ˌfa-shə-ˈnēs-tə\ *n* [[1]*fashion* + *-ista* (as in *Sandinista*)] (1993) **:** a designer, promoter, or follower of the latest fashions

fash·ion·mon·ger \ˈfa-shᵊn-ˌmäŋ-gər, -ˌməŋ-\ *n* (1599) **:** one that studies, imitates, or sets the fashion

fashion plate *n* (1851) **1 :** an illustration of a clothing style **2 :** a person who dresses in the latest fashions

[1]**fast** \ˈfast\ *adj* [ME, fr. OE *fæst;* akin to OHG *festi* firm, ON *fastr,* Arm *hast*] (bef. 12c) **1 a :** firmly fixed ⟨roots ~ in the ground⟩ **b :** tightly shut ⟨the drawers were ~⟩ **c :** adhering firmly **d :** not easily freed **:** STUCK ⟨a ball ~ in the mouth of the cannon⟩ **e :** STABLE ⟨movable items were made ~ to the deck⟩ **2 :** firmly loyal ⟨became ~ friends⟩ **3 a :** characterized by quick motion, operation, or effect: **(1) :** moving or able to move rapidly **:** SWIFT **(2) :** taking a comparatively short time **(3) :** imparting quickness of motion ⟨a ~ bowler⟩ **(4) :** accomplished quickly **(5) :** agile of mind; *esp* **:** quick to learn ⟨a class for ~ students⟩ **b :** conducive to rapidity of play or action **c (1)** *of a timepiece or weighing device* **:** indicating in advance of what is correct **(2) :** according to or being daylight saving time **d :** contributing to a shortening of exposure time ⟨~ film⟩ **e :** acquired with unusually little effort and often by shady or dishonest methods ⟨had a keen eye for a ~ buck —R. A. Keith⟩ **4 a :** securely attached ⟨a rope ~ to the wharf⟩ **b :** TENACIOUS ⟨a ~ hold on her purse⟩ **5 a** *archaic* **:** sound asleep **b** *of sleep* **:** not easily disturbed **6 :** not fading or changing color readily **7 a :** WILD ⟨a pretty ~ crowd⟩ **b :** sexually promiscuous **8 :** resistant to change (as from destructive action or fading) ⟨~ dyes⟩ — often used in combination ⟨sun*fast*⟩ ⟨acid-*fast* bacteria⟩

syn FAST, RAPID, SWIFT, FLEET, QUICK, SPEEDY, HASTY, EXPEDITIOUS mean moving, proceeding, or acting with celerity. FAST and RAPID are very close in meaning, but FAST applies particularly to the thing that moves ⟨*fast* horses⟩ and RAPID to the movement itself ⟨*rapid* current⟩. SWIFT suggests great rapidity coupled with ease of movement ⟨returned the ball with one *swift* stroke⟩. FLEET adds the implication of lightness and nimbleness ⟨*fleet* runners⟩. QUICK suggests promptness and the taking of little time ⟨a *quick* wit⟩. SPEEDY implies quickness of successful accomplishment ⟨*speedy* delivery of mail⟩ and may also suggest unusual velocity. HASTY suggests hurry and precipitousness and often connotes carelessness ⟨a *hasty* inspection⟩. EXPEDITIOUS suggests efficiency together with rapidity of accomplishment ⟨the *expeditious* handling of an order⟩.

[2]**fast** *adv* (bef. 12c) **1 :** in a firm or fixed manner ⟨stuck ~⟩ **2 :** in a sound manner **:** DEEPLY ⟨~ asleep⟩ **3 a :** in a rapid manner **:** QUICKLY **b :** in quick succession **4 :** in a reckless or dissipated manner **5 :** ahead of a correct time or schedule **6** *archaic* **:** CLOSE, NEAR

[3]**fast** *vi* [ME, fr. OE *fæstan*] (bef. 12c) **1 :** to abstain from food **2 :** to eat sparingly or abstain from some foods

[4]**fast** *n* (bef. 12c) **1 :** the practice of fasting **2 :** a time of fasting

[5]**fast** *n* [alter. of ME *fest,* fr. ON *festr* rope, mooring cable, fr. *fastr* firm] (15c) **:** something that fastens (as a mooring line) or holds a fastening

fast and loose *adv* (1580) **1 :** in a reckless or irresponsible manner ⟨played *fast and loose* with the public purse strings —Paul Stuewe⟩ **2 :** in a craftily deceitful way ⟨manipulated evidence . . . and played *fast and loose* with the truth —C. V. Woodward⟩

fast·back \ˈfas(t)-ˌbak\ *n* (1954) **:** an automobile with a roof having a long curving downward slope to the rear; *also* **:** the back of such an automobile

fast·ball \ˈfas(t)-ˌbȯl\ *n* (1899) **:** a baseball pitch thrown at full speed and often rising slightly as it nears the plate — **fast·ball·er** \-ˌbȯ-lər\ *n*

fast break *n* (1938) **:** a quick offensive drive toward a goal (as in basketball) in an attempt to score before the opponent's defense is set up — **fast–break** *vi*

fas·ten \ˈfa-sᵊn\ *vb* **fas·tened; fas·ten·ing** \ˈfas-niŋ, ˈfa-sᵊn-iŋ\ [ME *fastnen,* fr. OE *fæstnian* to make fast; akin to OHG *festinōn* to make fast, OE *fæst* fast] *vt* (bef. 12c) **1 a :** to attach esp. by pinning, tying, or nailing **b :** to make fast and secure **c :** to fix firmly or securely **d :** to secure against opening **2 :** to fix or set steadily ⟨~*ed* her attention on the main problem⟩ **3 :** to take a firm grip with ⟨the dog ~*ed* its teeth in the shoe⟩ **4 a :** to attach (oneself) persistently and usu. objectionably **b :** to place forcefully **:** IMPOSE ⟨~*ed* the blame on the wrong person⟩ ~ *vi* **1 :** to become fast or fixed **2 a :** to take a firm grip or hold **b :** to focus attention — **fas·ten·er** \ˈfas-nər, ˈfa-sᵊn-ər\ *n*

syn FASTEN, FIX, ATTACH, AFFIX mean to make something stay firmly in place. FASTEN implies an action such as tying, buttoning, nailing, locking, or otherwise securing ⟨*fasten* the reins to a post⟩. FIX usu. implies a driving in, implanting, or embedding ⟨*fixed* the stake in the ground⟩. ATTACH suggests a connecting or uniting by a bond, link, or tie in order to keep things together ⟨*attach* the W-2 form here⟩. AFFIX implies an imposing of one thing on another by gluing, impressing, or nailing ⟨*affix* your address label here⟩.

fastening *n* (12c) **:** something that fastens **:** FASTENER

fast–food \ˈfas(t)-ˌfüd\ *adj* (1951) **1 :** of, relating to, or specializing in food that can be prepared and served quickly ⟨a ~ restaurant⟩ **2 :** designed for ready availability, use, or consumption and with little consideration given to quality or significance ⟨~ TV programming⟩ — **fast food** *n*

[1]**fast–for·ward** \ˌfas(t)-ˈfȯr-wərd\ *n, often attrib* (1948) **1 :** a function of an electronic device that advances a recording at a higher than normal speed **2 :** a state or an instance of rapid advancement ⟨put her career in *fast-forward*⟩

[2]**fast–forward** *vt* (1974) **1 :** to advance (a magnetic tape) using the fast-forward of a tape player **2 :** to bypass (as a commercial) by fast-forwarding ~ *vi* **1 :** to advance a magnetic tape using the fast-forward **2 :** to proceed rapidly forward esp. in time ⟨~ to the future⟩

fas·tid·i·ous \fa-ˈsti-dē-əs, fə-\ *adj* [ME, fr. L *fastidiosus,* fr. *fastidium* disgust, prob. fr. *fastus* arrogance (prob. akin to L *fastigium* top) + *taedium* irksomeness — more at TEDIUM] (15c) **1** *archaic* **:** SCORNFUL **2 a :** having high and often capricious standards **:** difficult to please ⟨critics . . . so ~ that they can talk only to a small circle of initiates —Granville Hicks⟩ **b :** showing or demanding excessive delicacy or care **c :** reflecting a meticulous, sensitive, or demanding attitude ⟨~ workmanship⟩ **3 :** having complex nutritional requirements ⟨~ microorganisms⟩ — **fas·tid·i·ous·ly** *adv* — **fas·tid·i·ous·ness** *n*

fas·ti·gi·ate \fa-ˈsti-jē-ət\ *adj* [prob. fr. NL **fastigiatus,* fr. L *fastigium* — more at BRISTLE] (1662) **:** narrowing toward the top; *esp* **:** having upright usu. clustered branches ⟨~ trees⟩

fast lane *n* (1933) **1 :** a traffic lane intended for vehicles traveling at higher speeds **2 :** a way of life marked by a fast pace and usu. the pursuit of immediate gratification **3 :** FAST TRACK — **fast–lane** *adj*

fast·ness \ˈfas(t)-nəs\ *n* (bef. 12c) **1 :** the quality or state of being fast: as **a :** the quality or state of being fixed **b :** the quality or state of being swift **c :** colorfast quality **d :** resistance (as of an organism) to the action of a usu. toxic substance **2 a :** a fortified or secure place **b :** a remote and secluded place ⟨vacationed in their mountain ~⟩

Fast of Esther (1887) **:** a Jewish fast day observed the day before Purim in commemoration of a fast proclaimed by Queen Esther

fast–pitch \ˈfas(t)-ˌpich\ *n* (1967) **:** softball which is played with 9 or 10 players on each side and in which pitches are thrown with speed and base stealing is allowed — compare SLOW-PITCH

fast–talk \ˈfas(t)-ˌtȯk\ *vt* (1946) **:** to influence or persuade by fluent, facile, and usu. deceptive or tricky talk ⟨~*ed* him into buying a lemon⟩ — **fast–talk·er** *n*

[1]**fast–track** \ˈfas(t)-ˌtrak\ *adj* (1967) **1 :** of, relating to, or moving along a fast track ⟨~ executives⟩ **2 :** of, relating to, or being a construction procedure in which work on a building begins before designs are completed **3 :** of or relating to authority granted to the President of the U.S. by Congress that allows the President to negotiate trade agreements which Congress must confirm or reject in their entirety

[2]**fast–track** *vt* (1971) **:** to speed up the processing, production, or construction of in order to meet a goal — **fast–track·er** *n*

fast track *n* (1975) **1 :** a course leading to rapid advancement or success **2 :** a course of expedited consideration or approval

fast–twitch \ˈfas(t)-ˌtwich\ *adj* (1970) **:** of, relating to, or being muscle fiber that contracts quickly esp. during brief high-intensity physical activity requiring strength — compare SLOW-TWITCH

fas·tu·ous \ˈfas-chə-wəs\ *adj* [L *fastuosus,* fr. *fastus* arrogance] (1638) **1 :** HAUGHTY, ARROGANT ⟨a ~ air of finality —Carl Van Vechten⟩ **2 :** OSTENTATIOUS, SHOWY ⟨disdained ~ ceremonies⟩

\ə\ **a**but \ᵊ\ kitt**e**n, F ta**b**le \ər\ f**ur**th**er** \a\ **a**sh \ā\ **a**ce \ä\ m**o**p, m**a**r \au̇\ **ou**t \ch\ **ch**in \e\ b**e**t \ē\ **ea**sy \g\ **g**o \i\ h**i**t \ī\ **i**ce \j\ **j**ob \ŋ\ si**ng** \ō\ g**o** \ȯ\ l**aw** \ȯi\ b**oy** \th\ **th**in \th\ **th**e \ü\ l**oo**t \u̇\ f**oo**t \y\ **y**et \zh\ vi**si**on, bei**ge** \k, ⁿ, œ, ue, ʸ\ *see* Guide to Pronunciation

[1]fat \ˈfat\ *adj* **fat·ter; fat·test** [ME, fr. OE *fǣtt,* pp. of *fǣtan* to cram; akin to OHG *feizit* fat] (bef. 12c) **1 :** notable for having an unusual amount of fat: **a :** PLUMP **b :** OBESE **c** *of a meat animal* **:** fattened for market **d** *of food* **:** OILY, GREASY **2 a :** well filled out **:** THICK, BIG ⟨a ~ book⟩ **b :** full in tone and quality **:** RICH ⟨a gorgeous ~ bass voice —*Irish Digest*⟩ **c :** well stocked ⟨a ~ larder⟩ **d :** PROSPEROUS, WEALTHY ⟨grew ~ on the war —*Time*⟩ **e :** being substantial and impressive ⟨a ~ bank account⟩ **3 a :** richly rewarding or profitable ⟨a ~ part in a movie⟩ ⟨a ~ contract⟩ **b :** practically nonexistent ⟨a ~ chance⟩ **4 :** PRODUCTIVE, FERTILE ⟨a ~ year for crops⟩ **5 :** STUPID, FOOLISH **6 :** being swollen ⟨got a ~ lip from the fight⟩ **7** *of a baseball pitch* **:** easy to hit — **fat·ness** *n*

[2]fat *vt* **fat·ted; fat·ting** (bef. 12c) **:** to make fat **:** FATTEN

[3]fat *n* (14c) **1 :** animal tissue consisting chiefly of cells distended with greasy or oily matter **2 a :** oily or greasy matter making up the bulk of adipose tissue and often abundant in seeds **b :** any of various compounds of carbon, hydrogen, and oxygen that are glycerides of fatty acids, are the chief constituents of plant and animal fat, are a major class of energy-rich food, and are soluble in organic solvents but not in water **c :** a solid or semisolid fat as distinguished from an oil **3 :** the best or richest part **4 :** OBESITY **5 :** something in excess **:** SUPERFLUITY ⟨trim the ~ from the news operation —Ray Olson⟩ — **fat·less** \-ləs\ *adj*

fa·tal \ˈfā-tᵊl\ *adj* [ME, fr. L *fatalis,* fr. *fatum* fate] (14c) **1** *obs* **:** FATED **2 :** FATEFUL ⟨a ~ hour⟩ **3 a :** of or relating to fate **b :** resembling fate in proceeding according to a fixed sequence **c :** determining one's fate **4 a :** causing death **b :** bringing ruin ⟨a ~ attraction to gambling⟩ **c :** causing failure ⟨a ~ design flaw⟩ ***syn*** see DEADLY

fa·tal·ism \-tə-ˌli-zəm\ *n* (1678) **:** a doctrine that events are fixed in advance so that human beings are powerless to change them; *also* **:** a belief in or attitude determined by this doctrine — **fa·tal·ist** \-list\ *n* — **fa·tal·is·tic** \ˌfā-tə-ˈlis-tik\ *adj* — **fa·tal·is·ti·cal·ly** \-ti-k(ə-)lē\ *adv*

fa·tal·i·ty \fā-ˈta-lə-tē, fə-\ *n, pl* **-ties** [MF *fatalité,* fr. LL *fatalitat-, fatalitas,* fr. L *fatalis*] (15c) **1 a :** the quality or state of causing death or destruction **b :** the quality or condition of being destined for disaster **2 :** something established by fate **3 a :** FATE 1 **b :** FATALISM **4 :** the agent or agency of fate **5 a :** death resulting from a disaster **b :** one that experiences a fatal outcome

fa·tal·ly *adv* (15c) **1 :** in a way determined by fate **2 :** in a manner suggesting fate or an act of fate: as **a :** in a manner resulting in death **:** MORTALLY ⟨~ wounded⟩ **b :** beyond repair **:** IRREVOCABLY **c :** in a manner resulting in ruin or evil ⟨it is ~ easy to pass off our prejudices as our opinions —W. F. Hambly⟩ **d :** in a manner that cannot be easily resisted ⟨thinks she is ~ attractive —J. W. Krutch⟩

fa·ta mor·ga·na \ˌfä-tə-mȯr-ˈgä-nə, -ˈga-\ *n* [It, lit., Morgan le Fay (sorceress of Arthurian legend)] (1801) **:** MIRAGE

fat·back \ˈfat-ˌbak\ *n* (1903) **:** the strip of fat from the back of a hog carcass usu. cured by drying and salting

fat body *n* (1869) **:** a fatty tissue esp. of nearly mature insect larvae that serves as a food reserve

fat cat *n* (1928) **1 a :** a wealthy contributor to a political campaign fund **b :** a wealthy and privileged person **c :** BIG SHOT **2 :** a lethargic complacent person — **fat–cat** \ˈfat-ˌkat\ *adj*

fat cell *n* (1845) **:** one of the fat-laden cells making up adipose tissue

fat depot *n* (1946) **:** ADIPOSE TISSUE

[1]fate \ˈfāt\ *n* [ME, fr. MF or L; MF, fr. L *fatum,* lit., what has been spoken, fr. neut. of *fatus,* pp. of *fari* to speak — more at BAN] (14c) **1 :** the will or principle or determining cause by which things in general are believed to come to be as they are or events to happen as they do **:** DESTINY **2 a :** an inevitable and often adverse outcome, condition, or end **b :** DISASTER; *esp* **:** DEATH **3 a :** final outcome **b :** the expected result of normal development ⟨prospective ~ of embryonic cells⟩ **c :** the circumstances that befall someone or something ⟨did not know the ~ of her former classmates⟩ **4** *pl, cap* **:** the three goddesses who determine the course of human life in classical mythology

syn FATE, DESTINY, LOT, PORTION, DOOM mean a predetermined state or end. FATE implies an inevitable and usu. an adverse outcome ⟨the *fate* of the submarine is unknown⟩. DESTINY implies something foreordained and often suggests a great or noble course or end ⟨the country's *destiny* to be a model of liberty to the world⟩. LOT and PORTION imply a distribution by fate or destiny, LOT suggesting blind chance ⟨it was her *lot* to die childless⟩, PORTION implying the apportioning of good and evil ⟨remorse was his daily *portion*⟩. DOOM distinctly implies a grim or calamitous fate ⟨if the rebellion fails, his *doom* is certain⟩.

[2]fate *vt* **fat·ed; fat·ing** (1601) **:** DESTINE; *also* **:** DOOM

fated *adj* (1542) **:** decreed, controlled, or marked by fate

fate·ful \ˈfāt-fəl\ *adj* (ca. 1720) **1 :** having a quality of ominous prophecy ⟨a ~ remark⟩ **2 a :** involving momentous consequences **:** DECISIVE ⟨made his ~ decision to declare war —W. L. Shirer⟩ **b :** DEADLY, CATASTROPHIC **3 :** controlled by fate **:** FOREORDAINED ***syn*** see OMINOUS — **fate·ful·ly** \-fə-lē\ *adv* — **fate·ful·ness** *n*

fat farm *n* (1969) **:** a health spa that specializes in weight reduction

fath *abbr* fathom

fat·head \ˈfat-ˌhed\ *n* (1842) **:** a stupid person — **fat·head·ed** \-ˈhe-dəd\ *adj* — **fat·head·ed·ly** *adv* — **fat·head·ed·ness** *n*

[1]fa·ther \ˈfä-thər\ *n* [ME *fader,* fr. OE *fæder;* akin to OHG *fater* father, L *pater,* Gk *patēr*] (bef. 12c) **1 a :** a man who has begotten a child; *also* **:** SIRE 3 **b** *cap* (1) **:** GOD 1 (2) **:** the first person of the Trinity **2 :** FOREFATHER **3 a :** one related to another in a way suggesting that of father to child **b :** an old man — used as a respectful form of address **4** *often cap* **:** a pre-Scholastic Christian writer accepted by the church as an authoritative witness to its teaching and practice — called also *church father* **5 a :** one that originates or institutes ⟨the ~ of modern science⟩ **b :** SOURCE ⟨the sun, the ~ of warmth and light —Lena M. Whitney⟩ **c :** PROTOTYPE **6 :** a priest of the regular clergy; *broadly* **:** PRIEST — used esp. as a title **7 :** one of the leading men (as of a city) — usu. used in pl. — **fa·ther·hood** \-ˌhu̇d\ *n* — **fa·ther·less** \-ləs\ *adj* — **fa·ther·like** \-ˌlīk\ *adj or adv*

[2]father *vb* **fa·thered; fa·ther·ing** \ˈfäth-riŋ, ˈfä-thə-\ *vt* (15c) **1 a :** BEGET **b :** to be the founder, producer, or author of ⟨~*ed* the improvement plan⟩ **c :** to accept responsibility for **2 a :** to fix the paternity or origin of **b :** to place responsibility for the origin or cause of ⟨collected gossip and ~*ed* it on responsible men —J. A. Williamson⟩ **3 :** FOIST, IMPOSE ~ *vi* **:** to care for or look after someone as a father might

Father Christmas *n* (1658) *Brit* **:** SANTA CLAUS

father figure *n* (1934) **:** a person often of particular power or influence who serves as an emotional substitute for a father

father image *n* (1937) **:** an idealization of one's father often projected onto someone to whom one looks for guidance and protection

father–in–law \ˈfä-thə-rən-ˌlȯ, -thərn-ˌlȯ\ *n, pl* **fa·thers–in–law** \-thər-zən-\ (14c) **1 :** the father of one's spouse **2** *archaic* **:** STEPFATHER

fa·ther·land \ˈfä-thər-ˌland\ *n* (12c) **1 :** the native land or country of one's father or ancestors **2 :** one's native land or country

fa·ther·ly \ˈfä-thər-lē\ *adj* (15c) **1 :** of, relating to, or befitting a father ⟨~ responsibilities⟩ **2 :** resembling a father (as in affection or care) ⟨a ~ old man⟩ — **fa·ther·li·ness** \-lē-nəs\ *n* — **fatherly** *adv*

Father's Day *n* (1927) **:** the third Sunday in June appointed for the honoring of fathers

Father Time *n* (1590) **:** time personified esp. as a bearded old man holding a scythe and an hourglass

[1]fath·om \ˈfa-thəm\ *n* [ME *fadme,* fr. OE *fæthm* outstretched arms, length of the outstretched arms; akin to ON *fathmr* fathom, L *patēre* to be open, *pandere* to spread out, Gk *petannynai*] (bef. 12c) **1 :** a unit of length equal to six feet (1.83 meters) used esp. for measuring the depth of water — sometimes used in the singular when qualified by a number ⟨five ~ deep⟩ **2 :** COMPREHENSION

[2]fathom *vi* (1607) **1 :** PROBE **2 :** to take soundings ~ *vt* **1 :** to measure by a sounding line **2 :** to penetrate and come to understand ⟨couldn't ~ the problem⟩ — **fath·om·able** \ˈfa-thə-mə-bəl\ *adj*

Fa·thom·e·ter \fa-ˈthä-mə-tər, ˈfa-thə-ˌmē-\ *trademark* — used for a sonic depth finder

fath·om·less \ˈfa-thəm-ləs\ *adj* (1638) **:** incapable of being fathomed **:** IMMEASURABLE ⟨~ powers of gravity and chemistry —R. W. Emerson⟩ — **fath·om·less·ly** *adv* — **fath·om·less·ness** *n*

fa·tid·ic \fā-ˈti-dik, fə-\ *or* **fa·tid·i·cal** \-di-kəl\ *adj* [L *fatidicus,* fr. *fatum* fate + *dicere* to say — more at DICTION] (1607) **:** of or relating to prophecy

fa·ti·ga·ble \fə-ˈtē-gə-bəl, ˈfa-ti-gə-\ *adj* (1556) **:** susceptible to fatigue — **fa·ti·ga·bil·i·ty** \fə-ˌtē-gə-ˈbi-lə-tē, ˌfa-ti-gə-\ *n*

[1]fa·tigue \fə-ˈtēg\ *n* [F, fr. MF, fr. *fatiguer* to fatigue, fr. L *fatigare;* akin to L *affatim* sufficiently] (1669) **1 a :** LABOR **b :** manual or menial work performed by military personnel **c** *pl* **:** the uniform or work clothing worn on fatigue and in the field **2 a :** weariness or exhaustion from labor, exertion, or stress **b :** the temporary loss of power to respond that is induced in a sensory receptor or motor end organ by continued stimulation **3 :** the tendency of a material to break under repeated stress ⟨metal ~⟩

[2]fatigue *vb* **fa·tigued; fa·tigu·ing** *vt* (1693) **1 :** to weary with labor or exertion **2 :** to induce a condition of fatigue in ~ *vi* **:** to suffer fatigue ***syn*** see TIRE — **fa·tigu·ing·ly** \-ˈtē-giŋ-lē\ *adv*

[3]fatigue *adj* (1774) **1 :** consisting of, done, or used in fatigue ⟨~ detail⟩ **2 :** belonging to fatigues ⟨a ~ cap⟩

fat·ling \ˈfat-liŋ\ *n* (ca. 1534) **:** a young animal fattened for slaughter

fat·ly *adv* (15c) **1 :** RICHLY **2 :** in the manner of one that is fat ⟨waddled ~⟩ **3 :** in a smug manner **:** COMPLACENTLY ⟨snickered ~⟩

fats·hed·era \fats-ˈhe-d(ə-)rə, ˈfat-ˈse-\ *n* [NL *Fatsia,* genus of shrubs + *Hedera,* genus of vines (fr. L, ivy)] (1948) **:** an ornamental foliage plant (× *Fatshedera lizei*) with lobed glossy palmate leaves that is a hybrid between plants of two different genera of the ginseng family

fat·so \ˈfat-(ˌ)sō\ *n, pl* **fat·soes** [prob. fr. *Fats,* nickname for a fat person + *-o*] (1944) *often disparaging* **:** a fat person

fat·stock \-ˌstäk\ *n* (1812) *chiefly Brit* **:** livestock that is fat and ready for market

fat–tailed sheep \ˈfat-ˌtāld-\ *n* (1842) **:** a coarse-wooled mutton sheep that has great quantities of fat on each side of the tail bones

fat·ten \ˈfa-tᵊn\ *vb* **fat·tened; fat·ten·ing** \ˈfat-niŋ, ˈfa-tə-niŋ\ *vt* (ca. 1552) **1 :** to make fat, fleshy, or plump; *esp* **:** to feed (as a stock animal) for slaughter **b :** to make more substantial **2 :** to make fertile ~ *vi* **:** to become fat — **fat·ten·er** \ˈfat-nər, ˈfa-tə-nər\ *n*

fat·tish \ˈfa-tish\ *adj* (14c) **:** somewhat fat

Fat Tuesday *n* (1866) **:** MARDI GRAS 1a

[1]fat·ty \ˈfa-tē\ *adj* **fat·ti·er; -est** (14c) **1 :** containing fat esp. in unusual amounts ⟨~ foods⟩; *also* **:** unduly stout **:** CORPULENT **2 :** GREASY **3 :** derived from or chemically related to fat — **fat·ti·ness** *n*

[2]fatty *n, pl* **fat·ties** (1797) **:** one that is fat; *esp* **:** an overweight person

fatty acid *n* (1838) **1 :** any of numerous saturated aliphatic monocarboxylic acids $C_nH_{2n+1}COOH$ (as acetic acid) including many that occur naturally usu. in the form of esters in fats, waxes, and essential oils **2 :** any of the saturated or unsaturated monocarboxylic acids (as palmitic acid) usu. with an even number of carbon atoms that occur naturally in the form of glycerides in fats and fatty oils

fatty liver *n* (ca. 1839) **:** an abnormal condition of the liver marked by excess lipid accumulation in the hepatocytes and caused by injury, malnutrition, or toxins; *also* **:** a liver affected with fatty liver

fa·tu·i·ty \fə-ˈtü-ət-ē, fa-, -ˈchü-, -ˈtyü-\ *n, pl* **-ities** [MF *fatuité* foolishness, fr. L *fatuitat-, fatuitas,* fr. *fatuus*] (1538) **1 a :** something foolish or stupid **b :** STUPIDITY, FOOLISHNESS **2** *archaic* **:** IMBECILITY, DEMENTIA

fat·u·ous \ˈfa-chü-əs, -tyü-\ *adj* [L *fatuus* foolish] (1633) **:** complacently or inanely foolish **:** SILLY ⟨a ~ remark⟩ ***syn*** see SIMPLE — **fat·u·ous·ly** *adv* — **fat·u·ous·ness** *n*

fat·wa \ˈfət-wə, ˈfät-wä\ *n* [Ar *fatwā*] (ca. 1889) **:** a legal opinion or decree handed down by an Islamic religious leader

fat–wit·ted \ˈfat-ˌwi-təd\ *adj* (1596) **:** STUPID, IDIOTIC

fat·wood \ˈfat-ˌwu̇d\ *n* (1904) *chiefly Southern* **:** LIGHTWOOD

fau·bourg \fō-ˈbu̇r\ *n* [ME *fabour,* fr. MF *fauxbourg,* alter. of *forsbourg,* fr. OF *forsborc,* fr. *fors* outside + *borc* town — more at BOURG] (15c) **1 :** SUBURB; *esp* **:** a suburb of a French city **2 :** a city quarter

fau·ces \ˈfȯ-ˌsēz\ *n pl but sing or pl in constr* [L, pl., throat, fauces] (15c) **:** the narrow passage from the mouth to the pharynx between the soft palate and the base of the tongue — **fau·cial** \ˈfȯ-shəl\ *adj*

fau·cet \ˈfȯ-sət, ˈfä-\ *n* [ME, bung, faucet, fr. MF *fausset* bung, perh. fr. *fausser* to damage, fr. LL *falsare* to falsify, fr. L *falsus* false] (15c) **:** a fixture for drawing or regulating the flow of liquid esp. from a pipe

faugh *a strong* p-*sound or lip trill; often read as* ˈfȯ(k)\ *interj* (1542) — used to express contempt, disgust, or abhorrence

[1]**fault** \ˈfȯlt, *in poetry also* ˈfȯt\ *n* [ME *faute, falte,* fr. AF, fr. VL **fallita,* fr. fem. of *fallitus,* pp. of L *fallere* to deceive, disappoint] (13c) **1** *obs* **:** LACK **2 a :** WEAKNESS, FAILING; *esp* **:** a moral weakness less serious than a vice **b :** a physical or intellectual imperfection or impairment **:** DEFECT **c :** an error esp. in service in a net or racket game **3 a :** MISDEMEANOR **b :** MISTAKE **4 :** responsibility for wrongdoing or failure ⟨the accident was the driver's ~⟩ **5 :** a fracture in the crust of a planet (as the earth) or moon accompanied by a displacement of one side of the fracture with respect to the other usu. in a direction parallel to the fracture — **at fault 1 :** unable to find the scent and continue chase **2 :** open to blame **:** RESPONSIBLE ⟨you were really *at fault*⟩ — **to a fault :** to an excessive degree ⟨precise *to a fault*⟩

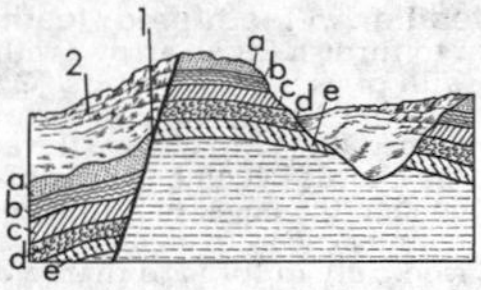

fault 5: *1* fault with displaced strata *a, b, c, d, e;* *2* scarp

syn FAULT, FAILING, FRAILTY, FOIBLE, VICE mean an imperfection or weakness of character. FAULT implies a failure, not necessarily culpable, to reach some standard of perfection in disposition, action, or habit ⟨a writer of many virtues and few *faults*⟩. FAILING suggests a minor shortcoming in character ⟨being late is a *failing* of mine⟩. FRAILTY implies a general or chronic proneness to yield to temptation ⟨human *frailties*⟩. FOIBLE applies to a harmless or endearing weakness or idiosyncrasy ⟨an eccentric's charming *foibles*⟩. VICE can be a general term for any imperfection or weakness, but it often suggests violation of a moral code or the giving of offense to the moral sensibilities of others ⟨compulsive gambling was his *vice*⟩.

[2]**fault** *vi* (15c) **1 :** to commit a fault **:** ERR **2 :** to fracture so as to produce a geologic fault ~ *vt* **1 :** to find a fault in ⟨easy to praise this book and to ~ it —H. G. Roepke⟩ **2 :** to produce a geologic fault in **3 :** BLAME, CENSURE ⟨can't ~ them for not coming⟩

fault·find·er \ˈfȯlt-ˌfīn-dər\ *n* (1558) **:** one given to faultfinding

[1]**fault·find·ing** \-diŋ\ *adj* (1622) **:** disposed to find fault **:** captiously critical ***syn*** see CRITICAL

[2]**faultfinding** *n* (ca. 1611) **:** petty, nagging, or unreasonable criticism

fault·less \ˈfȯlt-ləs\ *adj* (14c) **:** having no fault **:** IRREPROACHABLE ⟨~ workmanship⟩ — **fault·less·ly** *adv* — **fault·less·ness** *n*

fault line *n* (1869) **:** something resembling a fault **:** SPLIT, RIFT ⟨a major conceptual *fault line* in foreign policy —Morton Kondracke⟩

fault–tol·er·ant \ˈfȯlt-ˌtä-lə-rənt\ *adj* (1975) **:** relating to or being a computer or program with a self-contained backup system that allows continued operation when major components fail — **fault tolerance** *n*

faulty \ˈfȯl-tē\ *adj* **fault·i·er; -est** (14c) **:** marked by fault or defect **:** IMPERFECT — **fault·i·ly** \-tə-lē\ *adv* — **fault·i·ness** \-tē-nəs\ *n*

faun \ˈfȯn, ˈfän\ *n* [ME, fr. L *faunus,* fr. *Faunus*] (14c) **:** a figure in Roman mythology similar to but gentler than the satyr

fau·na \ˈfȯ-nə, ˈfä-\ *n, pl* **faunas** *also* **fau·nae** \-ˌnē, -ˌnī\ [NL, fr. L *Fauna,* sister of Faunus] (1771) **:** animal life; *esp* **:** the animals characteristic of a region, period, or special environment — compare FLORA — **fau·nal** \-nᵊl\ *adj* — **fau·nal·ly** *adv*

fau·nis·tic \fȯ-ˈnis-tik, fä-\ *adj* (1881) **:** of or relating to zoogeography **:** FAUNAL — **fau·nis·ti·cal·ly** \-ti-k(ə-)lē\ *adv*

Fau·nus \ˈfȯ-nəs, ˈfä-\ *n* [L] (1581) **:** the Roman god of animals

Faust \ˈfau̇st\ *or* **Fau·stus** \ˈfau̇-stəs, ˈfȯ-\ *n* [G] (1589) **:** a magician of German legend who enters into a compact with the devil

Faust·ian \ˈfau̇-stē-ən, ˈfȯ-\ *adj* (1876) **:** of, relating to, resembling, or suggesting Faust; *esp* **:** made or done for present gain without regard for future cost or consequences ⟨a ~ bargain⟩

faute de mieux \ˌfōt-də-ˈmyə(r), -ˈmyœ\ *adv* [F] (1766) **:** for lack of something better or more desirable ⟨sherry made him dopey but he drank it *faute de mieux* —F. T. Marsh⟩

fau·teuil \fō-ˈtœy; ˈfō-ˌtil\ *n, pl* **fau·teuils** \fō-ˈtœy; -ˌtilz\ [F, fr. OF *faudestuel,* of Gmc origin; akin to OHG *faltistuol* folding chair — more at FALDSTOOL] (1744) **:** ARMCHAIR; *esp* **:** an upholstered chair with open arms

[1]**fauve** \ˈfōv\ *n, often cap* [F, lit., wild animal, fr. *fauve* tawny, wild, fr. OF *falve* tawny, of Gmc origin; akin to OHG *falo* fallow — more at FALLOW] (1931) **:** a painter practicing fauvism **:** FAUVIST

[2]**fauve** *adj* (1945) **1** *often cap* **:** of or relating to the fauves **2 :** vivid in color

fau·vism \ˈfō-ˌvi-zəm\ *n, often cap* (1922) **:** a movement in painting typified by the work of Matisse and characterized by vivid colors, free treatment of form, and a resulting vibrant and decorative effect — **fau·vist** \-vist\ *n or adj, often cap*

faux \ˈfō\ *adj* [F, false] (1975) **:** IMITATION, ERSATZ ⟨~ marble⟩

faux–na·ïf *or* **faux–na·if** \ˌfō-nä-ˈēf\ *adj* [F, lit., falsely naive] (1948) **:** spuriously or affectedly childlike **:** artfully simple ⟨~ prose⟩

faux pas \ˈfō-ˌpä, fō-ˈ\ *n, pl* **faux pas** \-ˌpä(z), -ˈpä(z)\ [F, lit., false step] (1676) **:** BLUNDER; *esp* **:** a social blunder

fa·va bean \ˈfä-və-\ *n* [It, fr. L *faba* bean] (1928) **:** BROAD BEAN

fave \ˈfāv\ *n* (1938) **:** FAVORITE — **fave** *adj*

fa·ve·la *also* **fa·vel·la** \fə-ˈve-lə\ *n* [Brazilian Pg *favela,* perh. fr. *Favela,* hill outside Rio de Janeiro] (1946) **:** a settlement of jerry-built shacks lying on the outskirts of a Brazilian city

fav·ism \ˈfä-ˌvi-zəm\ *n* (ca. 1927) **:** a condition esp. of males of Mediterranean descent that is marked by the development of hemolytic anemia upon consumption of broad beans or inhalation of broad bean pollen and is caused by a usu. inherited deficiency of glucose-6-phosphate

fa·vo·ni·an \fə-ˈvō-nē-ən\ *adj* [L *favonianus,* fr. *Favonius,* the west wind] (ca. 1681) **:** of or relating to the west wind **:** MILD

[1]**fa·vor** \ˈfā-vər\ *n* [ME, fr. AF, fr. L, fr. *favēre* to be favorable; perh. akin to OHG *gouma* attention, OCS *gověti* to revere] (14c) **1 a** (1) **:** friendly regard shown toward another esp. by a superior (2) **:** approving consideration or attention **:** APPROBATION **b :** PARTIALITY **c** *archaic* **:** LENIENCY **d** *archaic* **:** PERMISSION **e :** POPULARITY **2** *archaic* **a :** APPEARANCE **b** (1) **:** FACE (2) **:** a facial feature **3 a :** gracious kindness; *also* **:** an act of such kindness ⟨did you a ~⟩ **b** *archaic* **:** AID, ASSISTANCE **c** *pl* **:** effort in one's behalf or interest **:** ATTENTION **4 a :** a token of love (as a ribbon) usu. worn conspicuously **b :** a small gift or decorative item given out at a party **c :** BADGE **5 a :** a special privilege or right granted or conceded **b :** sexual privileges — usu. used in pl. **6** *archaic* **:** LETTER **7 :** BEHALF, INTEREST — **in favor of 1 a :** in accord or sympathy with **b :** to the benefit of **:** in support of ⟨a verdict *in favor of* the accused⟩ **2 :** to the order of **3 :** in order to choose **:** out of preference for ⟨turned down the scholarship *in favor of* a pro career⟩ — **in one's favor 1 :** in one's good graces **2 :** to one's advantage — **out of favor :** UNPOPULAR, DISLIKED

[2]**favor** *vt* **fa·vored; fa·vor·ing** \ˈfā-v(ə-)riŋ\ (14c) **1 a :** to regard or treat with favor **b** (1) **:** to do a kindness for **:** OBLIGE (2) **:** ENDOW **c :** to treat gently or carefully ⟨~*ed* her injured leg⟩ **2 :** to show partiality toward **:** PREFER **3 a :** to give support or confirmation to **:** SUSTAIN **b :** to afford advantages for success to **:** FACILITATE ⟨good weather ~*ed* the outing⟩ **4 :** to bear a resemblance to ⟨he ~*s* his father⟩ — **fa·vor·er** \ˈfā-vər-ər\ *n*

fa·vor·able \ˈfā-v(ə-)rə-bəl, ˈfā-vər-bəl\ *adj* (14c) **1 a :** disposed to favor **:** PARTIAL **b :** expressing approval **:** COMMENDATORY **c :** giving a result that is in one's favor ⟨a ~ comparison⟩ **d :** AFFIRMATIVE ⟨a ~ reply⟩ **2 :** winning approval **:** PLEASING ⟨a ~ impression⟩ **3 a :** tending to promote or facilitate **:** ADVANTAGEOUS ⟨a ~ wind⟩ **b :** marked by success — **fa·vor·abil·i·ty** \ˌfā-v(ə-)rə-ˈbi-lə-tē, ˌfā-vər-\ *n* — **fa·vor·able·ness** *n* — **fa·vor·ably** \ˈfā-v(ə-)rə-blē, ˈfā-vər-blē\ *adv*

syn FAVORABLE, AUSPICIOUS, PROPITIOUS mean pointing toward a happy outcome. FAVORABLE implies that the persons involved are approving or helpful or that the circumstances are advantageous ⟨*favorable* weather conditions⟩. AUSPICIOUS applies to something taken as a sign or omen promising success before or at the start of an event ⟨an *auspicious* beginning⟩. PROPITIOUS may also apply to beginnings but often implies a continuing favorable condition ⟨a *propitious* time for starting a business⟩.

fa·vored \ˈfā-vərd\ *adj* (15c) **1 :** having an appearance or features of a particular kind ⟨hard-*favored*⟩ **2 :** endowed with special advantages or gifts **3 :** providing preferential treatment ⟨~ rates of credit⟩

[1]**fa·vor·ite** \ˈfā-v(ə-)rət, ˈfā-vərt, *chiefly dial* ˈfā-və-ˌrīt\ *n* [It *favorito,* pp. of *favorire* to favor, fr. *favore* favor, fr. L *favor*] (1583) **1 :** one that is treated or regarded with special favor or liking; *esp* **:** a person who is specially loved, trusted, or provided with favors by someone of high rank or authority **2 :** a competitor judged most likely to win

[2]**favorite** *adj* (1692) **:** constituting a favorite; *esp* **:** markedly popular

favorite son *n* (1788) **1 :** one favored by the delegates of his state as presidential candidate at a national political convention **2 :** a famous person who is popular with hometown people

fa·vor·it·ism \ˈfā-v(ə-)rə-ˌti-zəm, ˈfā-vər-\ *n* (1763) **1 :** the showing of special favor **:** PARTIALITY **2 :** the state or fact of being a favorite

fa·vour *chiefly Brit var of* FAVOR

fa·vus \ˈfā-vəs\ *n* [NL, fr. L, honeycomb] (ca. 1543) **:** any of several contagious skin diseases caused by ascomycetous fungi (as *Trichophyton schoenleinii*) and occurring in humans and many domestic animals

[1]**fawn** \ˈfȯn, ˈfän\ *vi* [ME *faunen,* fr. OE *fagnian* to rejoice, fr. *fægen, fagan* glad — more at FAIN] (13c) **1 :** to show affection — used esp. of a dog **2 :** to court favor by a cringing or flattering manner — **fawn·er** *n* — **fawn·ing·ly** \ˈfȯ-niŋ-lē, ˈfä-\ *adv*

syn FAWN, TOADY, TRUCKLE, CRINGE, COWER mean to behave abjectly before a superior. FAWN implies seeking favor by servile flattery or exaggerated attention ⟨waiters *fawning* over a celebrity⟩. TOADY suggests the attempt to ingratiate oneself by an abjectly menial or subservient attitude ⟨*toadying* to his boss⟩. TRUCKLE implies the subordination of oneself and one's desires or judgment to those of a superior ⟨*truckling* to a powerful lobbyist⟩. CRINGE suggests a bowing or shrinking in fear or servility ⟨a *cringing* sycophant⟩. COWER suggests a display of abject fear in the company of threatening or domineering people ⟨*cowering* before a bully⟩.

[2]**fawn** *n* [ME *foun,* fr. AF *feun, foon* young of an animal, fr. VL **feton-, feto,* fr. L *fetus* offspring — more at FETUS] (14c) **1 :** a young deer; *esp* **:** one still unweaned or retaining a distinctive baby coat **2 :** KID 1 **3 :** a light grayish brown — **fawny** \ˈfȯ-nē, ˈfä-\ *adj*

fawn lily *n* (ca. 1894) **:** DOGTOOTH VIOLET

fax \ˈfaks\ *n* [by shortening & alter.] (1948) **1 :** FACSIMILE 2 **2 :** a device used to send or receive facsimile communications **3 :** a facsimile communication — **fax** *vb*

fax modem *n* (1986) **:** a computer peripheral capable of sending data to or receiving data from a fax machine or another computer esp. over phone lines

[1]**fay** \ˈfā\ *vb* [ME *feien,* fr. OE *fēgan;* akin to OHG *fuogen* to fit, L *pangere* to fasten — more at PACT] (bef. 12c) **:** to fit or join closely or tightly

[2]**fay** *n* [ME *fai, fei,* fr. AF *feid, fei* — more at FAITH] (13c) *obs* **:** FAITH

[3]**fay** *n* [ME *faie,* fr. AF *fee* — more at FAIRY] (14c) **:** FAIRY, ELF

[4]**fay** *adj* (14c) **:** resembling an elf

[5]**fay** *n* (1927) **:** OFAY

faze \ˈfāz\ *vt* **fazed; faz·ing** [alter. of *feeze* to drive away, frighten, fr. ME *fesen,* fr. OE *fēsian* to drive away] (1830) **:** to disturb the composure of **:** DISCONCERT, DAUNT ⟨nothing *fazed* her⟩

FB *abbr* **1** foreign body **2** freight bill

FBI *abbr* Federal Bureau of Investigation

f–bomb \ˈef-ˌbäm\ *n* (1988) **:** the word *fuck* — used metaphorically as a euphemism ⟨accidentally dropped an ~ on television —Tim Kurkjian⟩

FC *abbr* **1** fire control **2** follow copy **3** *often not cap* foot-candle

FCA *abbr* Farm Credit Administration

FCC *abbr* Federal Communications Commission

F clef *n* (1596) **:** BASS CLEF

FD *abbr* fire department

FDA *abbr* Food and Drug Administration

FDIC *abbr* Federal Deposit Insurance Corporation

F distribution *n* [Sir Ronald Fisher †1962 Eng. geneticist and statistician] (1947) **:** a probability density function that is used esp. in analysis of variance and is a function of the ratio of two independent random variables each of which has a chi-square distribution and is divided by its number of degrees of freedom

\ə\ **abut** \ᵊ\ **kitten, F table** \ər\ **further** \a\ **ash** \ā\ **ace** \ä\ **mop, mar**
\au̇\ **out** \ch\ **chin** \e\ **bet** \ē\ **easy** \g\ **go** \i\ **hit** \ī\ **ice** \j\ **job**
\ŋ\ **sing** \ō\ **go** \ȯ\ **law** \ȯi\ **boy** \th\ **thin** \t͟h\ **the** \ü\ **loot** \u̇\ **foot**
\y\ **yet** \zh\ **vision, beige** \ḵ, ⁿ, œ, ue, ʸ\ *see* Guide to Pronunciation

Fe *symbol* [L *ferrum*] iron

fe·al·ty \ˈfē(-ə)l-tē\ *n, pl* **-ties** [ME *feute, fealtye,* fr. AF *feelté, fealté,* fr. L *fidelitat-, fidelitas* — more at FIDELITY] (14c) **1 a :** the fidelity of a vassal or feudal tenant to his lord **b :** the obligation of such fidelity **2 :** intense fidelity ***syn*** see FIDELITY

[1]**fear** \ˈfir\ *vt* [ME *feren,* fr. OE *fǣran,* fr. *fǣr*] (bef. 12c) **1** *archaic* **:** FRIGHTEN **2** *archaic* **:** to feel fear in (oneself) **3 :** to have a reverential awe of ⟨~ God⟩ **4 :** to be afraid of **:** expect with alarm ⟨~ the worst⟩ ~ *vi* **:** to be afraid or apprehensive ⟨~*ed* for their lives⟩ — **fear·er** *n*

[2]**fear** *n* [ME *fer,* fr. OE *fǣr* sudden danger; akin to OHG *fāra* ambush and perh. to L *periculum* attempt, peril, Gk *peiran* to attempt] (12c) **1 a :** an unpleasant often strong emotion caused by anticipation or awareness of danger **b (1) :** an instance of this emotion **(2) :** a state marked by this emotion **2 :** anxious concern **:** SOLICITUDE **3 :** profound reverence and awe esp. toward God **4 :** reason for alarm **:** DANGER

syn FEAR, DREAD, FRIGHT, ALARM, PANIC, TERROR, TREPIDATION mean painful agitation in the presence or anticipation of danger. FEAR is the most general term and implies anxiety and usu. loss of courage ⟨*fear* of the unknown⟩. DREAD usu. adds the idea of intense reluctance to face or meet a person or situation and suggests aversion as well as anxiety ⟨faced the meeting with *dread*⟩. FRIGHT implies the shock of sudden, startling fear ⟨*fright* at being awakened suddenly⟩. ALARM suggests a sudden and intense awareness of immediate danger ⟨view the situation with *alarm*⟩. PANIC implies unreasoning and overmastering fear causing hysterical activity ⟨the news caused widespread *panic*⟩. TERROR implies the most extreme degree of fear ⟨immobilized with *terror*⟩. TREPIDATION adds to DREAD the implications of timidity, trembling, and hesitation ⟨raised the subject with *trepidation*⟩.

fear·ful \ˈfir-fəl\ *adj* (14c) **1 :** causing or likely to cause fear, fright, or alarm esp. because of dangerous quality ⟨a ~ storm⟩ **2 a :** full of fear ⟨~ for his safety⟩ **b :** indicating or arising from fear ⟨a ~ glance⟩ **c :** inclined to fear **:** TIMOROUS **3 :** very great or bad — used as an intensive ⟨a ~ waste⟩ ⟨~ slum conditions⟩ — **fear·ful·ly** \-f(ə-)lē\ *adv* — **fear·ful·ness** \-fəl-nəs\ *n*

syn FEARFUL, APPREHENSIVE, AFRAID mean disturbed by fear. FEARFUL implies often a timorous or worrying temperament ⟨the child is *fearful* of loud noises⟩. APPREHENSIVE suggests a state of mind and implies a premonition of evil or danger ⟨*apprehensive* of being found out⟩. AFRAID often suggests weakness or cowardice and regularly implies inhibition of action or utterance ⟨*afraid* to speak the truth⟩.

fear·less \ˈfir-ləs\ *adj* (1540) **:** free from fear **:** BRAVE — **fear·less·ly** *adv* — **fear·less·ness** *n*

fear·mon·ger \ˈfir-ˌməŋ-gər, -ˌmäŋ-\ *n* (1939) **:** SCAREMONGER — **fear·mon·ger·ing** \-g(ə-)riŋ\ *n*

fear·some \ˈfir-səm\ *adj* (1768) **1 a :** causing fear ⟨a ~ monster⟩ **b :** INTENSE, EXTREME ⟨~ determination⟩ **2 :** TIMID, TIMOROUS — **fear·some·ly** *adv* — **fear·some·ness** *n*

fea·si·ble \ˈfē-zə-bəl\ *adj* [ME *faisible,* fr. AF *faisable,* fr. *fais-,* stem of *faire* to make, do, fr. L *facere* — more at DO] (15c) **1 :** capable of being done or carried out ⟨a ~ plan⟩ **2 :** capable of being used or dealt with successfully **:** SUITABLE **3 :** REASONABLE, LIKELY ***syn*** see POSSIBLE — **fea·si·bil·i·ty** \ˌfē-zə-ˈbi-lə-tē\ *n* — **fea·si·bly** \ˈfē-zə-blē\ *adv*

[1]**feast** \ˈfēst\ *n* [ME *feste,* fr. AF, fr. L *festa,* pl. of *festum* festival, fr. neut. of *festus* solemn, festal; akin to L *feriae* holidays, *fanum* temple] (13c) **1 a :** an elaborate and usu. abundant meal often accompanied by a ceremony or entertainment **:** BANQUET **b (1) :** something that gives unusual or abundant enjoyment ⟨a visual ~⟩ **(2) :** ABUNDANCE, PROFUSION ⟨an unprecedented ~ of corruption, gargantuan in scale —Neil Sheehan⟩ **2 :** a periodic religious observance commemorating an event or honoring a deity, person, or thing

[2]**feast** *vi* (14c) **1 :** to take part in a feast **2 :** to enjoy some unusual pleasure or delight ~ *vt* **1 :** to give a feast for **2 :** DELIGHT, GRATIFY ⟨~*ing* our eyes on the scenery⟩ — **feast·er** *n*

Feast of Tabernacles (14c) **:** SUKKOTH

[1]**feat** \ˈfēt\ *n* [ME *fait, fet,* fr. AF, fr. L *factum,* fr. neut. of *factus,* pp. of *facere* to make, do — more at DO] (14c) **1 :** ACT, DEED **2 a :** a deed notable esp. for courage **b :** an act or product of skill, endurance, or ingenuity

syn FEAT, EXPLOIT, ACHIEVEMENT mean a remarkable deed. FEAT implies strength or dexterity or daring ⟨an acrobatic *feat*⟩. EXPLOIT suggests an adventurous or heroic act ⟨his *exploits* as a spy⟩. ACHIEVEMENT implies hard-won success in the face of difficulty or opposition ⟨her *achievements* as a chemist⟩.

[2]**feat** *adj* [ME *fete, fayt,* fr. AF *fait,* pp. of *faire*] (15c) **1** *archaic* **:** BECOMING, NEAT **2** *archaic* **:** SMART, DEXTEROUS

[1]**feath·er** \ˈfe-t͟hər\ *n* [ME *fether,* fr. OE; akin to OHG *federa* wing, L *petere* to go to, seek, Gk *petesthai* to fly, *piptein* to fall, *pteron* wing] (bef. 12c) **1 a :** any of the light horny epidermal outgrowths that form the external covering of the body of birds and that consist of a shaft bearing on each side a series of barbs which bear barbules which in turn bear barbicels commonly ending in hooked hamuli and interlocking with the barbules of an adjacent barb to link the barbs into a continuous vane **b** *archaic* **:** PLUME 2a **c :** the vane of an arrow **2 a :** PLUMAGE **b :** KIND, NATURE ⟨birds of a ~ flock together⟩ **c :** ATTIRE, DRESS **d :** CONDITION, MOOD ⟨woke up in fine ~⟩ **e** *pl* **:** COMPOSURE ⟨some ~*s* had been ruffled —D. J. Blum⟩ **3 :** FEATHERING 2 **4 :** a projecting strip, rib, fin, or flange **5 :** a feathery flaw in the eye or in a precious stone **6 :** the act of feathering an oar — **feath·ered** \-t͟hərd\ *adj* — **feath·er·less** *adj* — **a feather in one's cap :** a mark of distinction **:** HONOR

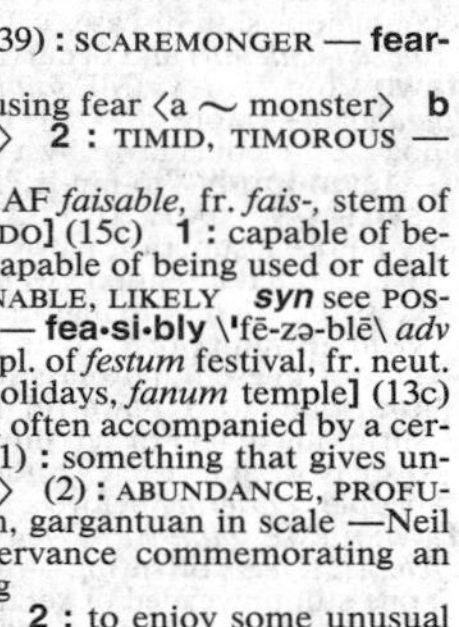

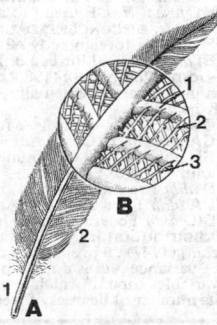

feather 1a: *A: 1* quill, *2* vane; *B: 1* barb, *2* barbule, *3* barbicel with hamulus

[2]**feather** *vb* **feath·ered; feath·er·ing** \ˈfet͟h-riŋ, ˈfe-t͟hə-\ *vt* (13c) **1 a :** to furnish (as an arrow) with a feather **b :** to cover, clothe, or adorn with or as if with feathers **2 a :** to turn (an oar blade) almost horizontal when lifting from the water at the end of a stroke to reduce air resistance **b (1) :** to change the angle of (airplane propeller blades) so that the chords become approximately parallel to the line of flight; *also* **:** to change the angle of airplane propeller blades of (an engine) in such a manner **(2) :** to change the angle of (a rotor blade of a rotorcraft) periodically in forward flight **3 :** to reduce the edge of to a featheredge **4 :** to cut (as air) with or as if with a wing **5 :** to join by a tongue and groove **6 :** to hit, throw, pass, or shoot softly and usu. with precision ⟨~*ed* a perfect lob over the net⟩ ~ *vi* **1 :** to grow or form feathers **2 :** to have or take on the appearance of a feather or something feathered **3 :** to soak in and spread **:** BLUR — used of ink or a printed impression **4 :** to feather an oar or an airplane propeller blade — **feather one's nest :** to provide for oneself esp. financially by unethically exploiting a position of trust

[1]**feath·er·bed** \ˈfe-t͟hər-ˌbed\ *adj* (1938) **:** calling for, sanctioning, or resulting from featherbedding ⟨a ~ rule⟩ ⟨a ~ job⟩

[2]**featherbed** *vi* (1949) **1 a :** to require that more workers be hired than are needed **b :** to limit production under a featherbed rule **2 :** to do featherbed work or put in time under a featherbed rule ~ *vt* **1 :** to bring under a featherbed rule **2 :** to assist (as an industry) by government aid

feather bed *n* (bef. 12c) **1 :** a feather mattress **2 :** a bed having a feather mattress

feath·er·bed·ding \-ˌbe-diŋ\ *n* (1921) **:** the requiring of an employer usu. under a union rule or safety statute to hire more employees than are needed or to limit production

feath·er·brain \-ˌbrān\ *n* (1668) **:** a foolish scatterbrained person — **feath·er·brained** \-ˌbrānd\ *adj*

feath·er·edge \ˈfe-t͟hər-ˌej, ˌfe-t͟hər-ˈ\ *n* (1616) **:** a very thin sharp edge; *esp* **:** one that is easily broken or bent over — **featheredge** *vt*

feath·er·head \ˈfe-t͟hər-ˌhed\ *n* (1788) **:** a foolish person **:** FEATHERBRAIN — **feath·er·head·ed** \ˌfe-t͟hər-ˈhe-dəd\ *adj*

feath·er·ing \ˈfet͟h-riŋ, ˈfe-t͟hər-iŋ\ *n* (1721) **1 :** a covering of feathers **:** PLUMAGE **2 :** a fringe of hair (as on the legs of a dog) — see DOG illustration

feath·er·light \ˈfe-t͟hər-ˈlīt\ *adj* (ca. 1837) **:** extremely light

feather star *n* (1862) **:** any of an order (Comatulida) of free-swimming stalkless crinoids

feath·er·stitch \ˈfe-t͟hər-ˌstich\ *n* (1835) **:** an embroidery stitch consisting of a line of diagonal blanket stitches worked alternately to the left and right — **featherstitch** *vb*

feath·er·weight \-ˌwāt\ *n* (1812) **1 :** one that is very light in weight; *esp* **:** a boxer in a weight division having a maximum limit of 126 pounds for professionals and 125 pounds for amateurs — compare BANTAMWEIGHT, LIGHTWEIGHT **2 :** LIGHTWEIGHT 2 — **featherweight** *adj*

feath·ery \ˈfet͟h-rē, ˈfe-t͟hər-ē\ *adj* (1580) **:** resembling, suggesting, or covered with feathers; *esp* **:** extremely light

[1]**feat·ly** \ˈfēt-lē\ *adv* [ME *fetly,* fr. *fete* feat (adj.)] (14c) **1 :** in a graceful manner **:** NIMBLY **2 :** in a suitable manner **:** PROPERLY **3 :** with skill and ingenuity

[2]**featly** *adj* (1801) **:** GRACEFUL, NEAT

[1]**fea·ture** \ˈfē-chər\ *n* [ME *feture,* fr. AF, fr. L *factura* act of making, fr. *factus,* pp. of *facere* to make — more at DO] (14c) **1 a :** the structure, form, or appearance esp. of a person **b** *obs* **:** physical beauty **2 a :** the makeup or appearance of the face or its parts **b :** a part of the face **:** LINEAMENT **3 a :** a prominent part or characteristic **b :** any of the properties (as voice or gender) that are characteristic of a grammatical element (as a phoneme or morpheme); *esp* **:** one that is distinctive **4 :** a special attraction: as **a :** a featured motion picture **b :** a featured article, story, or department in a newspaper or magazine **c :** something offered to the public or advertised as particularly attractive ⟨one of the car's most popular ~*s*⟩ — **fea·ture·less** \-ləs\ *adj*

[2]**feature** *vb* **fea·tured; fea·tur·ing** \ˈfēch-riŋ, ˈfē-chər-iŋ\ *vt* (ca. 1755) **1** *chiefly dial* **:** to resemble in features **2 :** to picture or portray in the mind **:** IMAGINE **3 a :** to give special prominence to ⟨the exhibit ~*s* local artists⟩ **b :** to have as a characteristic or feature ⟨a menu *featuring* many options⟩ ~ *vi* **:** to play an important part

fea·tured \ˈfē-chərd\ *adj* (15c) **1 :** having facial features of a particular kind — used in combination ⟨a heavy-*featured* lout⟩ **2 :** displayed, advertised, or presented as a special attraction

fea·tur·ette \ˈfē-chər-ˌet, ˌfē-chər-ˈ\ *n* (1940) **:** a short film; *esp* **:** a short documentary film about the making of a full-length movie

Feb *abbr* February

febri- *comb form* [LL, fr. L *febris*] **:** fever ⟨*febrific*⟩

fe·brif·ic \fi-ˈbrif-ik\ *adj* (1710) *archaic* **:** FEVERISH

feb·ri·fuge \ˈfe-brə-ˌfyüj\ *n* [F *fébrifuge,* prob. fr. NL **febrifuga,* fr. LL *febrifuga, febrifugia* centaury, fr. *febri-* + LL *-fuga* -fuge] (1686) **:** ANTIPYRETIC — **febrifuge** *adj*

fe·brile \ˈfe-ˌbrī(-ə)l *also* ˈfē-\ *adj* [ML *febrilis,* fr. L *febris* fever] (1651) **:** marked or caused by fever **:** FEVERISH

Feb·ru·ary \ˈfe-b(y)ə-ˌwer-ē, ˈfe-brə-\ *n, pl* **-ar·ies** *or* **-ar·ys** [ME *Februarie,* fr. OE *Februarius,* fr. L, fr. *Februa,* pl., feast of purification] (bef. 12c) **:** the second month of the Gregorian calendar

usage Dissimilation may occur when a word contains two identical or closely related sounds, resulting in the change or loss of one of them. This happens regularly in *February,* which is more often pronounced \ˈfe-b(y)ə-ˌwer-ē\ than \ˈfe-brə-ˌwer-ē\, though all of these variants are in frequent use and widely accepted. The \y\ heard from many speakers is not an intrusion but rather a common pronunciation of the vowel *u* after a consonant, as in *January* and *annual.*

fec *abbr* [L *fecit*] he made it

fe·cal \ˈfē-kəl\ *adj* (1541) **:** of, relating to, or constituting feces

fe·ces \ˈfē-(ˌ)sēz\ *n pl* [ME, fr. L *faec-, faex* (sing.) dregs] (14c) **:** bodily waste discharged through the anus **:** EXCREMENT

feck·less \ˈfek-ləs\ *adj* [Sc, fr. *feck* effect, majority, fr. ME (Sc) *fek,* alter. of ME *effect*] (ca. 1585) **1 :** WEAK, INEFFECTIVE **2 :** WORTHLESS, IRRESPONSIBLE — **feck·less·ly** *adv* — **feck·less·ness** *n*

feck·ly \ˈfek-lē\ *adv* [*feck* + *-ly*] (1768) *chiefly Scot* **:** ALMOST, NEARLY

fec·u·lent \ˈfe-kyə-lənt\ *adj* [ME, fr. L *faeculentus,* fr. *faec-, faex*] (15c) **:** foul with impurities **:** FECAL — **fe·cu·lence** \-lən(t)s\ *n*

fe·cund \ˈfe-kənd, ˈfē-\ *adj* [ME, fr. AF, fr. L *fecundus* — more at FEMININE] (15c) **1** : fruitful in offspring or vegetation : PROLIFIC **2** : intellectually productive or inventive to a marked degree ⟨a ~ imagination⟩ ***syn*** see FERTILE — **fe·cun·di·ty** \fi-ˈkən-də-tē, fe-\ *n*

fe·cun·date \ˈfe-kən-ˌdāt, ˈfē-\ *vt* **-dat·ed; -dat·ing** [L *fecundatus,* pp. of *fecundare,* fr. *fecundus*] (ca. 1631) **1** : to make fecund **2** : IMPREGNATE — **fe·cun·da·tion** \ˌfe-kən-ˈdā-shən, ˌfē-\ *n*

fed *abbr* federal; federation

Fed \ˈfed\ *n* [short for *federal*] (1916) **1** *often not cap* : a federal agent, officer, or official — usu. used in pl. **2 a** : FEDERAL RESERVE BOARD **b** : FEDERAL RESERVE SYSTEM

fe·da·yee \fi-ˌda-ˈ(y)ē, -ˌdä-\ *n, pl* **fe·da·yeen** \-ˈ(y)ēn\ [Ar *fidāʾī,* lit., one who sacrifices himself] (1955) : a member of an Arab commando group operating esp. against Israel — usu. used in pl.

fed·er·al \ˈfe-d(ə-)rəl\ *adj* [L *foeder-, foedus* compact, league; akin to L *fidere* to trust — more at BIDE] (1660) **1** *archaic* : of or relating to a compact or treaty **2 a** : formed by a compact between political units that surrender their individual sovereignty to a central authority but retain limited residuary powers of government **b** : of or constituting a form of government in which power is distributed between a central authority and a number of constituent territorial units **c** : of or relating to the central government of a federation as distinguished from the governments of the constituent units **3** *cap* : advocating or friendly to the principle of a federal government with strong centralized powers; *esp* : of or relating to the American Federalists **4** *often cap* : of, relating to, or loyal to the federal government or the Union armies of the U.S. in the American Civil War **5** *cap* : being or belonging to a style of architecture and decoration current in the U.S. following the American Revolution — **fed·er·al·ly** \-d(ə-)rə-lē\ *adv*

Federal *n* (1861) **1** : a supporter of the U.S. government in the Civil War; *esp* : a soldier in the federal armies **2** : FED 1 — usu. used in pl.

federal case *n* (1955) : BIG DEAL ⟨don't make a *federal case* out of it⟩

federal court *n* (1789) : a court established by a federal government; *esp* : one established under the constitution and laws of the U.S.

federal district *n* (ca. 1934) : a district set apart as the seat of the central government of a federation

federal district court *n* (1948) : a district trial court of law and equity that hears cases under federal jurisdiction

fed·er·al·ese \ˌfe-d(ə-)rə-ˈlēz, -ˈlēs; ˈfe-d(ə-)rə-ˌ\ *n* (1944) : BUREAUCRATESE

federal funds *n pl* (1950) : reserve funds lent overnight by one Federal Reserve bank to another

fed·er·al·ism \ˈfe-d(ə-)rə-ˌli-zəm\ *n* (1787) **1 a** *often cap* : the distribution of power in an organization (as a government) between a central authority and the constituent units — compare CENTRALISM **b** : support or advocacy of this principle **2** *cap* : Federalist principles

fed·er·al·ist \-list\ *n* (1774) **1** : an advocate of federalism: as **a** *often cap* : an advocate of a federal union between the American colonies after the Revolution and of the adoption of the U.S. Constitution **b** *often cap* : WORLD FEDERALIST **2** *cap* : a member of a major political party in the early years of the U.S. favoring a strong centralized national government — **federalist** *adj, often cap*

fed·er·al·i·za·tion \ˌfe-d(ə-)rə-lə-ˈzā-shən\ *n* (ca. 1860) **1** : the act of federalizing **2** : the state of being federalized

fed·er·al·ize \ˈfe-d(ə-)rə-ˌlīz\ *vt* **-ized; -iz·ing** (1801) **1** : to unite in or under a federal system **2** : to bring under the jurisdiction of a federal government

Federal Reserve bank *n* (1914) : one of 12 reserve banks set up under the Federal Reserve Act to hold reserves and discount commercial paper for affiliated banks in their respective districts

Federal Reserve Board *n* (1920) : a 7-member board of governors overseeing the Federal Reserve System

Federal Reserve System *n* (1919) : the central banking system of the U.S. consisting of 12 districts with a Federal Reserve bank in the principal commercial city of each district

[1]**fed·er·ate** \ˈfe-d(ə-)rət\ *adj* [L *foederatus,* fr. *foeder-, foedus*] (1710) : united in an alliance or federation : FEDERATED

[2]**fed·er·ate** \ˈfe-də-ˌrāt\ *vt* **-at·ed; -at·ing** (1580) : to join in a federation

federated church *n* (1898) : a local church uniting two or more congregations that maintain different denominational ties — compare UNION CHURCH

fed·er·a·tion \ˌfe-də-ˈrā-shən\ *n* (1787) **1** : an encompassing political or societal entity formed by uniting smaller or more localized entities: as **a** : a federal government **b** : a union of organizations **2** : the act of creating or becoming a federation; *esp* : the forming of a federal union

fed·er·a·tive \ˈfe-də-ˌrā-tiv, ˈfe-d(ə-)rə-\ *adj* (1690) : of, relating to, or formed by federation ⟨a ~ republic⟩ — **fed·er·a·tive·ly** *adv*

fedn *abbr* federation

fe·do·ra \fi-ˈdȯr-ə\ *n* [*Fédora* (1882), drama by V. Sardou] (1891) : a low soft felt hat with the crown creased lengthwise

fed up *adj* (1900) : tired, sated, or disgusted beyond endurance

[1]**fee** \ˈfē\ *n* [ME, fr. AF *fé, fief,* of Gmc origin; akin to OE *feoh* cattle, property, OHG *fihu* cattle; akin to L *pecus* cattle, *pecunia* money] (14c) **1 a (1)** : an estate in land held in feudal law from a lord on condition of homage and service **(2)** : a piece of land so held **b** : an inherited or heritable estate in land **2 a** : a fixed charge **b** : a sum paid or charged for a service — **in fee** : in absolute and legal possession

[2]**fee** *vt* **feed; fee·ing** (15c) **1** *chiefly Scot* : HIRE **2** : [9]TIP 2

fee·ble \ˈfē-bəl\ *adj* **fee·bler** \-b(ə-)lər\; **fee·blest** \-b(ə-)ləst\ [ME *feble,* fr. AF, fr. L *flebilis* lamentable, wretched, fr. *flēre* to weep — more at BLEAT] (12c) **1 a** : markedly lacking in strength **b** : indicating weakness **2 a** : deficient in qualities or resources that indicate vigor, authority, force, or efficiency **b** : INADEQUATE, INFERIOR ***syn*** see WEAK — **fee·ble·ness** \-bəl-nəs\ *n* — **fee·bly** \-blē\ *adv*

fee·ble·mind·ed \ˌfē-bəl-ˈmīn-dəd\ *adj* (1534) **1** *obs* : IRRESOLUTE, VACILLATING **2** : mentally deficient **3** : FOOLISH, STUPID — **fee·ble·mind·ed·ly** *adv* — **fee·ble·mind·ed·ness** *n*

fee·blish \ˈfē-b(ə-)lish\ *adj* (1674) : somewhat feeble

[1]**feed** \ˈfēd\ *vb* **fed** \ˈfed\; **feed·ing** [ME *feden,* fr. OE *fēdan;* akin to OE *fōda* food — more at FOOD] *vt* (bef. 12c) **1 a** : to give food to **b** : to give as food **2 a** : to furnish something essential to the development, sustenance, maintenance, or operation of ⟨reading ~*s* the mind⟩ **b** : to supply (material to be operated on) to a machine **3** : to produce or provide food for **4 a** : SATISFY, GRATIFY **b** : SUPPORT, ENCOURAGE **5 a (1)** : to supply for use or consumption **(2)** : CHANNEL, ROUTE **b (1)** : to supply (a signal) to an electronic circuit **(2)** : to send (as by wire or satellite) to a transmitting station for broadcast **6** : to supply (a fellow actor) with cues and situations that make a role more effective **7** : to pass a ball or puck to (a teammate) esp. for a shot at the goal ~ *vi* **1 a** : to consume food : EAT **b** : PREY — used with *on, upon,* or *off* **2** : to become nourished or satisfied or sustained as if by food **3 a** : to become channeled or directed **b** : to move into a machine or opening in order to be used or processed

[2]**feed** *n* (1576) **1 a** : an act of eating **b** : MEAL; *esp* : a large meal **2 a** : food for livestock; *specif* : a mixture or preparation for feeding livestock **b** : the amount given at each feeding **3 a** : material supplied (as to a furnace or machine) **b** : a mechanism by which the action of feeding is effected **c** : the motion or process of carrying forward the material to be operated upon (as in a machine) **d** : the act or process of feeding a signal (as an audio or video transmission); *also* : the signal being fed **4** : the action of passing a ball or puck to a team member who is in position to score

feed·back \ˈfēd-ˌbak\ *n* (1919) **1** : the return to the input of a part of the output of a machine, system, or process (as for producing changes in an electronic circuit that improve performance or in an automatic control device that provide self-corrective action) **2 a** : the partial reversion of the effects of a process to its source or to a preceding stage **b** : the transmission of evaluative or corrective information about an action, event, or process to the original or controlling source; *also* : the information so transmitted **3** : a rumbling, whining, or whistling sound resulting from an amplified or broadcast signal (as music or speech) that has been returned as input and retransmitted

feedback inhibition *n* (1960) : inhibition of an enzyme controlling an early stage of a series of biochemical reactions by the end product when it reaches a critical concentration

feed dog *n* (1858) : a notched piece of metal on a sewing machine that feeds material into position under the needle

feed·er \ˈfē-dər\ *n, often attrib* (14c) **1** : one that feeds: as **a** : one that fattens livestock for slaughter **b** : a device or apparatus for supplying food **2** : one that eats or takes nourishment; *esp* : an animal being fattened or one suitable for fattening **3 a** : one that supplies, replenishes, or connects **b** : TRIBUTARY 2 **c** : a heavy wire conductor supplying electricity at some point of an electric distribution system (as from a substation) **d** : BRANCH; *esp* : a branch transportation line **e** : a road that provides access to a major artery

feeding frenzy *n* (1973) : a frenzy of eating; *also* : the excited pursuit of something by a group

feeding tube *n* (1882) : a flexible tube passed into the stomach for introducing fluids and liquid food into the stomach

feed·lot \ˈfēd-ˌlät\ *n* (1889) : a plot of land on which livestock are fattened for market

feed·stock \-ˌstäk\ *n* (1932) : raw material supplied to a machine or processing plant

feed·stuff \-ˌstəf\ *n* (1856) : FEED 2a; *also* : any of the constituent nutrients of an animal ration

fee–for–service *n, often attrib* (1945) : separate payment to a health-care provider for each medical service rendered to a patient

[1]**feel** \ˈfēl\ *vb* **felt** \ˈfelt\; **feel·ing** [ME *felen,* fr. OE *fēlan;* akin to OHG *fuolen* to feel, L *palpare* to caress] *vt* (bef. 12c) **1 a** : to handle or touch in order to examine, test, or explore some quality **b** : to perceive by a physical sensation coming from discrete end organs (as of the skin or muscles) **2 a** : to undergo passive experience of **b** : to have one's sensibilities markedly affected by **3** : to ascertain by cautious trial — usu. used with *out* **4 a** : to be aware of by instinct or inference **b** : BELIEVE, THINK ⟨say what you really ~⟩ ~ *vi* **1 a** : to receive or be able to receive a tactile sensation **b** : to search for something by using the sense of touch **2 a** : to be conscious of an inward impression, state of mind, or physical condition **b** : to have a marked sentiment or opinion ⟨~*s* strongly about it⟩ **3** : SEEM ⟨it ~*s* like spring today⟩ **4** : to have sympathy or pity ⟨I ~ for you⟩ — **feel like** : to have an inclination for ⟨*feel like* a walk?⟩

[2]**feel** *n* (13c) **1** : SENSATION, FEELING **2** : the sense of touch **3 a** : the quality of a thing as imparted through or as if through touch **b** : typical or peculiar quality or atmosphere; *also* : an awareness of such a quality or atmosphere **4** : intuitive knowledge or ability

feel·er \ˈfē-lər\ *n* (1526) : one that feels: as **a** : a tactile process (as a tentacle) of an animal **b** : something (as a proposal) ventured to ascertain the views of others

feeler gauge *n* (1925) : a thin metal strip or wire of known thickness used as a gauge

feel–good \ˈfēl-ˌgu̇d\ *adj* (1977) **1** : relating to or promoting an often specious sense of satisfaction or well-being ⟨a ~ reform program that makes no changes⟩ **2** : cheerfully sentimental ⟨a ~ movie⟩

[1]**feel·ing** \ˈfē-liŋ\ *n* (12c) **1 a (1)** : the one of the basic physical senses of which the skin contains the chief end organs and of which the sensations of touch and temperature are characteristic : TOUCH **(2)** : a sensation experienced through this sense **b** : generalized bodily consciousness or sensation **c** : appreciative or responsive awareness or recognition **2 a** : an emotional state or reaction ⟨a kindly ~ toward the boy⟩ **b** *pl* : susceptibility to impression : SENSITIVITY ⟨the remark hurt her ~*s*⟩ **3 a** : the undifferentiated background of one's awareness considered apart from any identifiable sensation, perception, or thought **b** : the overall quality of one's awareness **c** : conscious recognition : SENSE **4 a** : often unreasoned opinion or belief : SENTIMENT **b** : PRESENTIMENT **5** : capacity to respond emotionally esp. with the higher emotions **6** : the character ascribed to something : ATMOSPHERE **7 a** : the quality of a work of art that conveys the emotion of the artist **b** : sympathetic aesthetic response **8** : FEEL 4

syn FEELING, EMOTION, AFFECTION, SENTIMENT, PASSION mean a subjective response to a person, thing, or situation. FEELING denotes

\ə\ **a**but \ᵊ\ kitten, F table \ər\ **fur**ther \a\ **a**sh \ā\ **a**ce \ä\ m**o**p, m**ar**
\au̇\ **ou**t \ch\ **ch**in \e\ b**e**t \ē\ **ea**sy \g\ **g**o \i\ h**i**t \ī\ **i**ce \j\ **j**ob
\ŋ\ si**ng** \ō\ g**o** \ȯ\ l**aw** \ȯi\ b**oy** \th\ **th**in \t͟h\ **th**e \ü\ l**oo**t \u̇\ f**oo**t
\y\ **y**et \zh\ vi**si**on, bei**ge** \k̲, ⁿ, œ, ue, ʸ\ *see* Guide to Pronunciation

any partly mental, partly physical response marked by pleasure, pain, attraction, or repulsion; it may suggest the mere existence of a response but imply nothing about the nature or intensity of it ⟨the *feelings* that once moved me are gone⟩. EMOTION carries a strong implication of excitement or agitation but, like FEELING, encompasses both positive and negative responses ⟨the drama portrays the *emotions* of adolescence⟩. AFFECTION applies to feelings that are also inclinations or likings ⟨a memoir of childhood filled with *affection* for her family⟩. SENTIMENT often implies an emotion inspired by an idea ⟨her feminist *sentiments* are well known⟩. PASSION suggests a very powerful or controlling emotion ⟨revenge became his ruling *passion*⟩.

²**feeling** *adj* (14c) **1 a :** SENTIENT, SENSITIVE **b :** easily moved emotionally **2** *obs* **:** deeply felt **3 :** expressing emotion or sensitivity — **feel·ing·ly** \-liŋ-lē\ *adv* — **feel·ing·ness** *n*

feel up *vt* (1930) **:** to touch or fondle (someone) for sexual pleasure

fee simple *n, pl* **fees simple** (14c) **:** a fee without limitation to any class of heirs or restrictions on transfer of ownership

fee splitting *n* (1943) **:** payment by a specialist (as a doctor or a lawyer) of a part of his or her fee to the person who made the referral

feet *pl of* FOOT

fee tail *n, pl* **fees tail** [ME *fee taille,* fr. AF *fé taillé* entailed fee] (15c) **:** a fee limited to a particular class of heirs

feet–first \ˌfēt-ˈfərst\ *adv* (ca. 1833) **:** with the feet foremost

feet of clay [fr. the feet of the idol in Dan 2:33] (1814) **:** a character flaw that is usu. not readily apparent

feeze \ˈfēz, ˈfāz\ *n* [ME *veze,* fr. *fesen, vesen* to drive away — more at FAZE] (14c) **1** *chiefly dial* **:** RUSH **2** *dial* **:** a state of alarm or excitement

Feh·ling's solution \ˈfā-liŋ(z)-\ *n* [Hermann *Fehling* †1885 Ger. chemist] (1873) **:** a blue solution of Rochelle salt and copper sulfate used as an oxidizing agent in a test for sugars and aldehydes

feign \ˈfān\ *vb* [ME, fr. AF *feign-,* stem of *feindre,* fr. L *fingere* to shape, feign — more at DOUGH] *vi* (13c) **:** PRETEND, DISSEMBLE ~ *vt* **1 a :** to give a false appearance of **:** induce as a false impression ⟨~ death⟩ **b :** to assert as if true **:** PRETEND **2** *archaic* **a :** INVENT, IMAGINE **b :** to give fictional representation to **3** *obs* **:** DISGUISE, CONCEAL ***syn*** see ASSUME — **feign·er** *n*

feigned *adj* (14c) **1 :** FICTITIOUS **2 :** not genuine or real

fei·joa \fā-ˈyō-ə, -ˈhō-ə\ *n* [NL, genus name, fr. João da Silva *Feijó* †1824 Brazilian naturalist] (1898) **:** the green round or oval juicy fruit of a shrub or small tree (*Feijoa sellowiana*) of the myrtle family that is native to So. America and is grown commercially esp. in New Zealand; *also* **:** the tree or shrub

¹**feint** \ˈfānt\ *n* [F *feinte,* fr. OF, fr. *feint,* pp. of *feindre*] (1644) **:** something feigned; *specif* **:** a mock blow or attack on or toward one part in order to distract attention from the point one really intends to attack ***syn*** see TRICK

²**feint** *vi* (1741) **:** to make a feint ~ *vt* **1 :** to lure or deceive with a feint **2 :** to make a pretense of

fei·rie \ˈfē-rē\ *adj* [ME (Sc) *fery,* fr. OE *fēre* able to go; akin to OE *faran* to travel, fare] (bef. 12c) *Scot* **:** NIMBLE, STRONG

feist \ˈfīst\ *also* **fice** *or* **fyce** \ˈfīs\ *n* [obs. *fisting hound,* fr. obs. *fist* to break wind] (1770) *chiefly dial* **:** a small dog

feisty \ˈfī-stē\ *adj* **feist·i·er; -est** (1896) **1** *chiefly Southern & Midland* **a :** full of nervous energy **:** FIDGETY **b :** TOUCHY, QUARRELSOME **c :** exuberantly frisky **2 :** having or showing a lively aggressiveness **:** SPUNKY ⟨the movie's ~ heroine⟩ — **feist·i·ness** *n*

felafel *var of* FALAFEL

feld·sher \ˈfel(d)-shər\ *n* [Russ *fel'dsher,* fr. G *Feldscher, Feldscherer* field surgeon, fr. *Feld* field + *Scherer* barber, surgeon] (1877) **:** a medical or surgical practitioner without full professional qualifications or status in some east European countries and esp. Russia

feld·spar \ˈfel(d)-ˌspär\ *n* [modif. of obs. G *Feldspath* (now *Feldspat*), fr. G *Feld* field + obs. G *Spath* (now *Spat*) spar] (1772) **:** any of a group of crystalline minerals that consist of aluminum silicates with either potassium, sodium, calcium, or barium and that are an essential constituent of nearly all crystalline rocks

feld·spath·ic \fel(d)-ˈspa-thik\ *adj* [*feldspath* (var. of *feldspar*), fr. obs. G] (ca. 1828) **:** relating to or containing feldspar

fe·li·cif·ic \ˌfē-lə-ˈsi-fik\ *adj* [L *felic-, felix*] (1865) **:** causing or intended to cause happiness

felicific calculus *n* (1945) **:** a method of determining the rightness of an action by balancing the probable pleasures and pains that it would produce

¹**fe·lic·i·tate** \fi-ˈli-sə-ˌtāt\ *adj* [LL *felicitatus,* pp. of *felicitare* to make happy, fr. L *felicitas*] (1605) *obs* **:** made happy

²**felicitate** *vt* **-tat·ed; -tat·ing** (1628) **1** *archaic* **:** to make happy **2 a :** to consider happy or fortunate **b :** to offer congratulations to — **fe·lic·i·ta·tion** \-ˌli-sə-ˈtā-shən\ *n* — **fe·lic·i·ta·tor** \-ˈli-sə-ˌtā-tər\ *n*

fe·lic·i·tous \fi-ˈli-sə-təs\ *adj* (1789) **1 :** very well suited or expressed **:** APT ⟨a ~ remark⟩ **2 :** PLEASANT, DELIGHTFUL ⟨~ weather⟩ ***syn*** see FIT — **fe·lic·i·tous·ly** *adv* — **fe·lic·i·tous·ness** *n*

fe·lic·i·ty \fi-ˈli-sə-tē\ *n, pl* **-ties** [ME *felicite,* fr. AF *felicité,* fr. L *felicitat-, felicitas,* fr. *felic-, felix* fruitful, happy — more at FEMININE] (14c) **1 a :** the quality or state of being happy; *esp* **:** great happiness ⟨marital ~⟩ **b :** an instance of happiness **2 :** something that causes happiness **3 :** a pleasing manner or quality esp. in art or language ⟨a ~ with words⟩ **4 :** an apt expression

fe·lid \ˈfē-ləd\ *n* [NL *Felidae,* family name, fr. *Felis,* genus of cats, fr. L, cat] (ca. 1889) **:** CAT 1b — **felid** *adj*

fe·line \ˈfē-ˌlīn\ *adj* [L *felinus,* fr. *felis*] (1681) **1 :** of, relating to, or affecting cats or the cat family **2 :** resembling a cat: as **a :** sleekly graceful **b :** SLY, TREACHEROUS **c :** STEALTHY — **feline** *n* — **fe·line·ly** *adv* — **fe·lin·i·ty** \fē-ˈli-nə-tē\ *n*

feline distemper *n* (1942) **:** PANLEUKOPENIA

feline panleukopenia *n* (ca. 1943) **:** PANLEUKOPENIA

¹**fell** \ˈfel\ *n* [ME, fr. OE; akin to OHG *fel* skin, L *pellis*] (bef. 12c) **1 :** SKIN, HIDE, PELT **2 :** a thin tough membrane covering a carcass directly under the hide

²**fell** *vt* [ME, fr. OE *fellan;* akin to OE *feallan* to fall — more at FALL] (bef. 12c) **1 a :** to cut, knock, or bring down ⟨~ a tree⟩ **b :** KILL **2 :** to sew (a seam) by folding one raw edge under the other and sewing flat on the wrong side — **fell·able** \ˈfe-lə-bəl\ *adj* — **fell·er** *n*

³**fell** *past of* FALL

⁴**fell** *adj* [ME *fel,* fr. AF — more at FELON] (14c) **1 a :** FIERCE, CRUEL, TERRIBLE **b :** SINISTER, MALEVOLENT ⟨a ~ purpose⟩ **c :** very destructive **:** DEADLY ⟨a ~ disease⟩ **2** *Scot* **:** SHARP, PUNGENT — **fell·ness** *n* — **fel·ly** \ˈfel-lē\ *adv*

⁵**fell** *n* [ME, fr. ON *fell, fjall* mountain; akin to OHG *felis* rock] (14c) *dial Brit* **:** a high barren field or moor

fel·la \ˈfe-lə\ *n* [alter. of *fellow*] (1816) **:** FELLOW, MAN

fel·lah \ˈfe-lə, fə-ˈlä\ *n, pl* **fel·la·hin** *also* **fel·la·heen** \ˌfel-ə-ˈhēn, fə-ˌlä-ˈhēn\ [Ar *fallāḥ*] (1743) **:** a peasant or agricultural laborer in an Arab country (as Egypt)

fel·late \ˈfe-ˌlāt, fə-ˈlāt\ *vb* **fel·lat·ed; fel·lat·ing** [back-formation fr. *fellatio*] *vt* (1941) **:** to perform fellatio on ~ *vi* **:** to fellate someone — **fel·la·tor** \-ˌlā-tər, -ˈlā-tər\ *n*

fel·la·tio \fə-ˈlā-shē-ˌō, fe-\ *also* **fel·la·tion** \-ˈlā-shən\ *n* [NL *fellation-, fellatio,* fr. L *felare, fellare,* lit., to suck — more at FEMININE] (ca. 1893) **:** oral stimulation of the penis

fell·mon·ger \ˈfel-ˌməŋ-gər, -ˌmäŋ-\ *n* [¹*fell*] (1530) *Brit* **:** one who removes hair or wool from hides in preparation for leather making — **fell·mon·gered** \-gərd\ *adj, Brit* — **fell·mon·ger·ing** \-g(ə-)riŋ\ *n, Brit* — **fell·mon·gery** \-g(ə-)rē\ *n, Brit*

fel·low \ˈfe-(ˌ)lō\ *n, often attrib* [ME *felawe,* fr. OE *fēolaga,* fr. ON *fēlagi,* fr. *fēlag* partnership, fr. *fē* cattle, money + *lag* act of laying] (bef. 12c) **1 :** COMRADE, ASSOCIATE **2 a :** an equal in rank, power, or character **:** PEER **b :** one of a pair **:** MATE **3 :** a member of a group having common characteristics; *specif* **:** a member of an incorporated literary or scientific society **4 a** *obs* **:** a person of one of the lower social classes **b** *archaic* **:** a worthless man or boy **c :** MAN, BOY **d :** BOYFRIEND, BEAU **5 :** an incorporated member of a college or collegiate foundation esp. in a British university **6 :** a person appointed to a position granting a stipend and allowing for advanced study or research

fellow feeling *n* (1686) **:** a feeling of community of interest or of mutual understanding

fel·low·ly \-lō-lē, -lə-lē\ *adj* (13c) **:** SOCIABLE — **fellowly** *adv*

fellow man *n* (1667) **:** a kindred human being

fellow servant *n* (1900) **:** an employee working with another employee under such circumstances that each one if negligent may expose the other to harm which the employer cannot reasonably be expected to guard against or be held legally liable for

¹**fel·low·ship** \ˈfe-lə-ˌship, -lō-\ *n* (bef. 12c) **1 :** COMPANIONSHIP, COMPANY **2 a :** community of interest, activity, feeling, or experience **b :** the state of being a fellow or associate **3 :** a company of equals or friends **:** ASSOCIATION **4 :** the quality or state of being comradely **5** *obs* **:** MEMBERSHIP, PARTNERSHIP **6 a :** the position of a fellow (as of a university) **b :** the stipend of a fellow **c :** a foundation for the providing of such a stipend

²**fellowship** *vb* **-shipped** *also* **-shiped** \-ˌshipt\; **-ship·ping** *also* **-ship·ing** \-ˌshi-piŋ\ *vi* (14c) **:** to join in fellowship esp. with a church member ~ *vt* **:** to admit to fellowship (as in a church)

fellow traveler *n* [trans. of Russ *poputchik*] (1925) **:** a person who sympathizes with and often furthers the ideals and program of an organized group (as the Communist party) without membership in the group or regular participation in its activities; *broadly* **:** a sympathetic supporter of another's cause — **fel·low–trav·el·ing** *adj*

fel·ly \ˈfe-lē\ *or* **fel·loe** \-(ˌ)lō\ *n, pl* **fellies** *or* **felloes** [ME *fely, felive,* fr. OE *felg;* akin to OHG *felga* felly, OE *fealg* piece of plowed land] (bef. 12c) **:** the exterior rim or a segment of the rim of a wheel supported by the spokes

fe·lo–de–se \ˌfe-lō-də-ˈsā, -ˈsē\ *n, pl* **fe·lo·nes–de–se** \fə-ˌlō-(ˌ)nēz-də-\ *or* **fe·los–de–se** \ˌfe-lōz-də-\ [ML *felo de se, fello de se,* lit., evildoer in respect to oneself] (1607) **1 :** a person who commits suicide or who dies from the effects of having committed an unlawful malicious act **2 :** an act of deliberate self-destruction **:** SUICIDE

¹**fel·on** \ˈfe-lən\ *n* [ME, fr. AF *felun, fel* evildoer, prob. of Gmc origin; akin to OHG *fillen* to beat, whip, *fel* skin — more at FELL] (13c) **1 :** one who has committed a felony **2** *archaic* **:** VILLAIN **3 :** WHITLOW

²**felon** *adj* (13c) **1** *archaic* **a :** CRUEL **b :** EVIL **2** *archaic* **:** WILD

fe·lo·ni·ous \fə-ˈlō-nē-əs\ *adj* (1567) **1** *archaic* **:** very evil **:** VILLAINOUS **2 :** of, relating to, or having the nature of a felony ⟨~ assault⟩ — **fe·lo·ni·ous·ly** *adv* — **fe·lo·ni·ous·ness** *n*

fel·on·ry \ˈfe-lən-rē\ *n* (1837) **:** FELONS; *esp* **:** the convict population of a penal colony

fel·o·ny \ˈfe-lə-nē\ *n, pl* **-nies** (14c) **1 :** an act on the part of a feudal vassal involving the forfeiture of his fee **2 a :** a grave crime formerly differing from a misdemeanor under English common law by involving forfeiture in addition to any other punishment **b :** a grave crime declared to be a felony by the common law or by statute regardless of the punishment actually imposed **c :** a crime declared a felony by statute because of the punishment imposed **d :** a crime for which the punishment in federal law may be death or imprisonment for more than one year

fel·site \ˈfel-ˌsīt\ *n* [*felspar* + *-ite*] (1794) **:** a dense igneous rock consisting almost entirely of feldspar and quartz — **fel·sit·ic** \fel-ˈsi-tik\ *adj*

fel·spar \ˈfel-ˌspär\ *chiefly Brit var of* FELDSPAR

¹**felt** \ˈfelt\ *n* [ME, fr. OE; akin to OHG *filz* felt, L *pellere* to drive, beat] (bef. 12c) **1 a :** a cloth made of wool and fur often mixed with natural or synthetic fibers through the action of heat, moisture, chemicals, and pressure **b :** a firm woven cloth of wool or cotton heavily napped and shrunk **2 :** an article made of felt **3 :** a material resembling felt: as **a :** a heavy paper of organic or asbestos fibers impregnated with asphalt and used in building construction **b :** semirigid pressed fiber insulation used in building — **felt·like** *adj*

²**felt** *vt* (14c) **1 :** to make out of or cover with felt **2 :** to cause to adhere and mat together **3 :** to make into felt or a similar substance

³**felt** *past and past part of* FEEL

felt·ing \ˈfel-tiŋ\ *n* (1686) **1 :** the process of making felt **2 :** FELT

felt–tip \ˈfel(t)-ˌtip\ *n* (1956) **:** a pen having a writing point made of felt — **felt–tip** *also* **felt–tipped** \-ˌtipt\ *adj*

fe·luc·ca \fə-ˈlü-kə, -ˈlə-kə\ *n* [It *feluca*] (1615) **:** a narrow fast lateen-rigged sailing vessel chiefly of the Mediterranean area

fem *abbr* female; feminine

FEMA *abbr* Federal Emergency Management Agency

¹**fe·male** \ˈfē-ˌmāl\ *adj* (14c) **1 a (1) :** of, relating to, or being the sex that bears young or produces eggs **(2) :** PISTILLATE **b (1) :** composed of members of the female sex ⟨the ~ population⟩ **(2) :** characteristic

of girls or women ⟨composed for ~ voices⟩ ⟨a ~ name⟩ **2** : having some quality (as gentleness) associated with the female sex **3** : designed with a hollow or groove into which a corresponding male part fits ⟨the ~ coupling of a hose⟩ — **fe·male·ness** *n*

[2]**female** *n* [ME, alter. of *femel, femelle,* fr. AF & ML; AF *femele,* fr. ML *femella,* fr. L, girl, dim. of *femina*] (14c) **1 a** : a female person : a woman or a girl **b** : an individual that bears young or produces large usu. immobile gametes (as eggs) that are fertilized by small usu. motile gametes of a male **2** : a pistillate plant

female genital mutilation *n* (1979) : a procedure performed esp. as a cultural rite that typically includes the total or partial excision of the female external genitalia and esp. the clitoris and labia minora and that is now outlawed in many nations including the U.S. — abbr. *FGM*; called also *female circumcision*; compare INFIBULATION

fem·i·na·zi \ˈfe-mə-ˌnät-sē\ *n* [blend of *feminist* and *Nazi*] (1989) *usu disparaging* : an extreme or militant feminist

[1]**fem·i·nine** \ˈfe-mə-nən\ *adj* [ME, fr. AF *feminin,* fr. L *femininus,* fr. *femina* woman; akin to OE *delu* nipple, L *filius* son, *felix, fetus, & fecundus* fruitful, *felare* to suck, Gk *thēlē* nipple] (14c) **1** : FEMALE 1a(1) **2** : characteristic of or appropriate or unique to women ⟨~ beauty⟩ ⟨a ~ perspective⟩ **3** : of, relating to, or constituting the gender that ordinarily includes most words or grammatical forms referring to females ⟨a ~ noun⟩ **4 a** : being an unstressed and usu. hypermetric final syllable ⟨a ~ ending⟩ **b** *of rhyme* : having an unstressed final syllable **c** : having the final chord occurring on a weak beat ⟨music in ~ cadences⟩ — **fem·i·nine·ly** *adv* — **fem·i·nine·ness** \-nə(n)-nəs\ *n*

[2]**feminine** *n* (15c) **1 a** : a noun, pronoun, adjective, or inflectional form or class of the feminine gender **b** : the feminine gender **2** : the embodiment or conception of a timeless or idealized feminine nature

fem·i·nin·i·ty \ˌfe-mə-ˈni-nə-tē\ *n* (14c) **1** : the quality or nature of the female sex **2** : EFFEMINACY **3** : WOMEN, WOMANKIND

fem·i·nise *Brit var of* FEMINIZE

fem·i·nism \ˈfe-mə-ˌni-zəm\ *n* (1895) **1** : the theory of the political, economic, and social equality of the sexes **2** : organized activity on behalf of women's rights and interests — **fem·i·nist** \-nist\ *n or adj* — **fem·i·nis·tic** \ˌfe-mə-ˈnis-tik\ *adj*

fe·min·i·ty \fe-ˈmi-nə-tē, fə-\ *n* (14c) : FEMININITY

fem·i·nize \ˈfe-mə-ˌnīz\ *vt* **-nized; -niz·ing** (1652) **1** : to give a feminine quality to **2** : to cause (a male or castrate) to take on feminine characters (as by implantation of ovaries or administration of estrogens) — **fem·i·ni·za·tion** \ˌfe-mə-nə-ˈzā-shən\ *n*

femme *also* **fem** \ˈfem\ *n* [prob. fr. F *femme* woman, fr. OF *feme,* fr. L *femina*] (1957) **1** : WOMAN 1a **2** : a lesbian who is notably or stereotypically feminine in appearance and manner

femme fa·tale \ˌfem-fə-ˈtal, ˌfam-, -ˈtäl\ *n, pl* **femmes fa·tales** \-ˈtal(z), -ˈtäl(z)\ [F, lit., disastrous woman] (1912) **1** : a seductive woman who lures men into dangerous or compromising situations **2** : a woman who attracts men by an aura of charm and mystery

fem·o·ral \ˈfe-mə-rəl, ˈfem-rəl\ *adj* (ca. 1771) : of or relating to the femur or thigh

femoral artery *n* (ca. 1771) : the chief artery of the thigh lying in its anterior inner part

femto- *comb form* [ISV, fr. Dan or Norw *femten* fifteen, fr. ON *fimmtān;* akin to OE *fīftēne* fifteen] : one quadrillionth (10^{-15}) part of ⟨*femto*second⟩

fem·to·sec·ond \ˈfem(p)-tə-ˌse-kənd, -kənt, -tō-\ *n* (1976) : one quadrillionth of a second

fe·mur \ˈfē-mər\ *n, pl* **fe·murs** *or* **fem·o·ra** \ˈfe-mə-rə, ˈfem-rə\ [NL *femor-, femur,* fr. L, thigh] (ca. 1726) **1** : the proximal bone of the hind or lower limb that extends from the hip to the knee — called also *thighbone* **2** : the segment of an insect's leg that is third from the body

[1]**fen** \ˈfen\ *n* [ME, fr. OE *fenn;* akin to OHG *fenna* fen, Skt *paṅka* mud] (bef. 12c) : low land that is covered wholly or partly with water unless artificially drained and that usu. has peaty alkaline soil and characteristic flora (as of sedges and reeds)

[2]**fen** \ˈfən\ *n, pl* **fen** [Chin (Beijing) *fēn*] (1916) — see *yuan* at MONEY table

[1]**fence** \ˈfen(t)s\ *n, often attrib* [ME *fens,* short for *defens* defense] (14c) **1** *archaic* : a means of protection : DEFENSE **2 a** : a barrier intended to prevent escape or intrusion or to mark a boundary; *esp* : such a barrier made of posts and wire or boards **b** : an immaterial barrier or boundary line ⟨on the other side of the ~ in the argument⟩ **3** : FENCING 1 **4 a** : a receiver of stolen goods **b** : a place where stolen goods are bought — **fence·less** \-ləs\ *adj* — **fence·less·ness** *n* — **on the fence** : in a position of neutrality or indecision

[2]**fence** *vb* **fenced; fenc·ing** *vt* (15c) **1 a** : to enclose with a fence **b** (1) : to keep in or out with a fence (2) : to ward off **2** : to provide a defense for **3** : to sell (stolen property) to a fence ~ *vi* **1 a** : to practice fencing **b** (1) : to use tactics of attack and defense resembling those of fencing (2) : to parry arguments by shifting ground **2** *archaic* : to provide protection — **fenc·er** *n*

fence–mend·ing \ˈfen(t)s-ˌmen-diŋ\ *n* (1947) : the rehabilitating of a deteriorated political relationship

fence·row \ˈfen(t)s-ˌrō\ *n* (1842) : the land occupied by a fence including the uncultivated area on each side

fence–sit·ting \ˈfen(t)s-ˌsi-tiŋ\ *n* (1904) : a state of indecision or neutrality with respect to conflicting positions — **fence–sit·ter** *n*

fencing *n* (1578) **1** : the art or practice of attack and defense with the foil, épée, or saber **2 a** (1) : FENCE 2a (2) : the fences of a property or region **b** : material used for building fences

[1]**fend** \ˈfend\ *vb* [ME *fenden,* short for *defenden*] *vt* (14c) **1** : DEFEND **2** : to keep or ward off : REPEL — often used with *off* ⟨~ off an invader⟩ **3** *dial Brit* : to provide for : SUPPORT ~ *vi* **1** *dial Brit* : to make an effort : STRUGGLE **2 a** : to try to get along without help : SHIFT ⟨had to ~ for themselves⟩ **b** : to provide a livelihood

[2]**fend** *n* (1721) *chiefly Scot* : an effort or attempt esp. for oneself

fend·er \ˈfen-dər\ *n* (13c) : a device that protects: as **a** (1) : a cushion (as foam rubber or a wood float) between a boat and a dock or between two boats that lessens shock and prevents chafing (2) : a pile or a row or cluster of piles placed to protect a dock or bridge pier from damage by ships or floating objects **b** : RAILING **c** : a device in front of locomotives and streetcars to lessen injury to animals or pedestrians in case of collision **d** : a guard over the wheel of a motor vehicle **e** : a low metal frame or a screen before an open fireplace **f** : an oblong or triangular shield of leather attached to the stirrup leather of a saddle to protect a rider's legs — **fend·ered** \-dərd\ *adj* — **fend·er·less** *adj*

fender bender *n* (ca. 1962) : a minor automobile accident

fe·nes·tra \fə-ˈnes-trə\ *n, pl* **-trae** \-ˌtrē, -ˌtrī\ [NL, fr. L, window] (ca. 1737) **1** : a small anatomical opening (as in a bone): as **a** : OVAL WINDOW — called also *fenestra ova·lis* \-ō-ˈvā-ləs\, *fenestra ves·tib·u·li* \-ves-ˈti-byə-(ˌ)lē\ **b** : ROUND WINDOW — called also *fenestra cochleae, fenestra ro·tun·da* \-rō-ˈtən-də\ **2** : an opening cut in bone — **fe·nes·tral** \-trəl\ *adj*

fe·nes·trate \fə-ˈnes-ˌtrāt, ˈfe-nə-ˌstrāt\ *adj* [L *fenestratus,* fr. *fenestra*] (1835) : FENESTRATED

fen·es·trat·ed \ˈfe-nə-ˌstrā-təd\ *adj* (ca. 1852) : having one or more openings or pores ⟨~ blood capillaries⟩

fen·es·tra·tion \ˌfe-nə-ˈstrā-shən\ *n* (1846) **1** : the arrangement, proportioning, and design of windows and doors in a building **2** : an opening in a surface (as a wall or membrane) **3** : the operation of cutting an opening in the bony labyrinth between the inner ear and tympanum to replace natural fenestrae that are not functional

fen·flur·amine \ˌfen-ˈflu̇r-ə-ˌmēn\ *n* [*fen-* (alter. of *phen-*) + *-flur-* (alter. of *fluor-*) + *amine*] (1965) : an anorectic amphetamine derivative $C_{12}H_{16}F_3N$ with little stimulant effect on the central nervous system formerly used in the form of its hydrochloride to treat obesity but no longer used due to its association with heart valve disease — see FEN=PHEN

feng shui \ˈfəŋ-ˈshwē, -ˈshwā\ *n* [Chin (Beijing) *fēngshuǐ* geomantic omen, lit., wind-water] (1797) : a Chinese geomantic practice in which a structure or site is chosen or configured so as to harmonize with the spiritual forces that inhabit it; *also* : orientation, placement, or arrangement according to the precepts of feng shui

Fe·ni·an \ˈfē-nē-ən\ *n* [*Fen-* (prob. in part fr. MIr *Féni* freeholders, legendary settlers of Ireland, in part fr. Ir *fiann,* gen. sing. *féinne* band of warriors) + *-ian*] (1816) **1** : a member of a legendary band of warriors defending Ireland in the second and third centuries A.D. **2** : a member of a secret 19th century Irish and Irish-American organization dedicated to the overthrow of British rule in Ireland — **Fenian** *adj* — **Fe·ni·an·ism** \-ə-ˌni-zəm\ *n*

fen·ing \ˈfe-niŋ\ *n, pl* **fen·inga** \-niŋ-ə\ *also* **fening** *or* **fen·ings** [Bosnian, Croatian & Serbian (gen. pl. *feninga*), fr. G *Pfennig* pfennig] (1998) — see *mark* at MONEY table

fen·land \ˈfen-ˌland\ *n* (bef. 12c) : an area of low often marshy ground

fen·nec \ˈfe-nik\ *n* [Ar *fanak*] (1790) : a small pale-fawn fox (*Vulpes zerda* syn. *Fennecus zerda*) with large ears that inhabits the deserts of northern Africa and Arabia

fen·nel \ˈfe-nᵊl\ *n* [ME *fenel,* fr. OE *finugl,* fr. VL **fenuculum,* fr. L *feniculum* fennel, irreg. dim. of *fenum* hay] (bef. 12c) : a perennial European herb (*Foeniculum vulgare*) of the carrot family having two cultivated forms: **a** : the commonly cultivated form (*F. vulgare dulce*) having aromatic leaves and seeds **b** : FLORENCE FENNEL

fen·ny \ˈfe-nē\ *adj* (bef. 12c) **1** : having the characteristics of a fen : BOGGY **2** *archaic* : peculiar to or found in a fen

fen–phen \ˈfen-ˌfen\ *n* [*fen*fluramine + *phen*termine] (1994) : a former diet drug combination of phentermine with either fenfluramine or dexfenfluramine — called also *phen-fen*

fen·ta·nyl \ˈfen-tə-ˌnil\ *n* [prob. alter. of *phenethyl,* a monovalent radical derived from ethylbenzine, fr. *phen-* + *ethyl*] (1964) : a synthetic opioid narcotic analgesic $C_{22}H_{28}N_2O$ with pharmacological action similar to morphine that is administered esp. in the form of its citrate

fenu·greek \ˈfen-yə-ˌgrēk\ *n* [ME *fenugrek,* fr. AF *fenugrec,* fr. L *fenum Graecum,* lit., Greek hay] (14c) : a leguminous annual Eurasian herb (*Trigonella foenum-graecum*) with aromatic seeds; *also* : its seeds

feoff·ee \fe-ˈfē, fē-ˈfē\ *n* (15c) : one to whom a feoffment is made

feoff·ment \ˈfef-mənt, ˈfēf-\ *n* [ME *feffement,* fr. AF, fr. *feffer, feoffer* to invest with a fee, fr. *fieu, fé* fee] (14c) : the granting of a fee

feof·for \ˈfe-fər, ˈfē-; fe-ˈfȯr, fē-\ *or* **feoff·er** \ˈfe-fər, ˈfē-\ *n* (15c) : one who makes a feoffment

FEPA *abbr* Fair Employment Practices Act

FEPC *abbr* Fair Employment Practices Commission

-fer *n comb form* [F & L; F *-fère,* fr. L *-fer* bearing, one that bears, fr. *ferre* to carry — more at BEAR] : one that bears ⟨aqui*fer*⟩

fe·rae na·tu·rae \ˈfer-ˌī-nə-ˈtu̇r-ˌī\ *adj* [L, of a wild nature] (ca. 1661) : wild by nature and not usu. tamed

fe·ral \ˈfir-əl, ˈfer-; ˈfe-rəl\ *adj* [ML *feralis,* fr. L *fera* wild animal, fr. fem. of *ferus* wild — more at FIERCE] (1604) **1** : of, relating to, or suggestive of a wild beast ⟨~ teeth⟩ ⟨~ instincts⟩ **2 a** : not domesticated or cultivated : WILD **b** : having escaped from domestication and become wild ⟨~ cats⟩ ***syn*** see BRUTAL — **feral** *n*

fer–de–lance \ˈfer-də-ˈlan(t)s, -ˈlän(t)s\ *n, pl* **fer–de–lance** [F, lit., lance iron, spearhead] (1880) : a large extremely venomous pit viper (*Bothrops atrox*) of Central and So. America

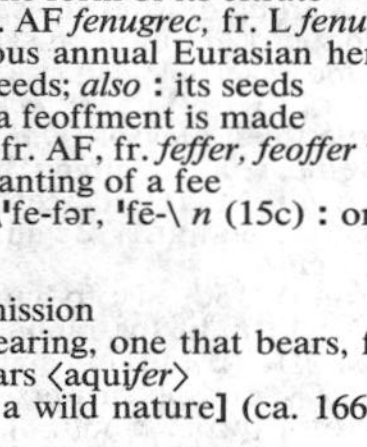

fer-de-lance

fere \ˈfir\ *n* [ME, fr. OE *gefēra;* akin to OE *faran* to go, travel — more at FARE] (bef. 12c) **1** *archaic* : COMPANION 1 **2** *archaic* : SPOUSE

[1]**fe·ria** \ˈfir-ē-ə, ˈfer-\ *n* [ML — more at FAIR] (15c) : a weekday of a church calendar on which no feast falls — **fe·ri·al** \-ē-əl\ *adj*

[2]**fe·ria** \ˈfer-ē-ə, -ē-ˌä\ *n* [Sp, fair, market, fr. ML — more at FAIR] (1844) : a Hispanic market festival often in observance of a religious holiday

fe·rine \ˈfir-ˌīn\ *adj* [L *ferinus,* fr. *fera*] (1640) : FERAL

fer·lie *also* **fer·ly** \ˈfer-lē\ *n, pl* **fer·lies** [ME, fr. *ferly* strange, fr. OE *fǣrlīc* unexpected, fr. *fǣr* sudden danger — more at FEAR] (13c) *Scot* : WONDER

fer·ma·ta \fer-ˈmä-tə\ *n* [It, lit., stop, fr. *fermare* to stop, fr. L *firmare* to make firm] (ca. 1859) : a prolongation at the discretion of the performer of a musical note, chord, or rest beyond its given time value; *also* : the sign 𝄐 denoting such a prolongation — called also *hold*

Fer·mat's last theorem \fer-ˈmäz-\ *n* [Pierre de *Fermat*] (1847) : a theorem in number theory: the equation $x^n + y^n = z^n$ has no solutions when *x, y, z,* and *n* are all positive integers and *n* is greater than 2

[1]**fer·ment** \(ˌ)fər-ˈment\ *vi* (14c) **1** : to undergo fermentation **2** : to be in a state of agitation or intense activity ~ *vt* **1** : to cause to undergo fermentation **2** : to work up (as into a state of agitation) : FOMENT — **fer·ment·able** \-ˈmen-tə-bəl\ *adj*

[2]**fer·ment** \ˈfər-ˌment *also* (ˌ)fər-ˈ\ *n* [ME, fr. L *fermentum* yeast — more at BARM] (15c) **1 a** : a living organism (as a yeast) that causes fermentation by virtue of its enzymes **b** : ENZYME **2 a** : a state of unrest : AGITATION **b** : a process of active often disorderly development ⟨the great period of creative ~ in literature —William Barrett⟩

fer·men·ta·tion \ˌfər-mən-ˈtā-shən, -ˌmen-\ *n* (1601) **1 a** : a chemical change with effervescence **b** : an enzymatically controlled anaerobic breakdown of an energy-rich compound (as a carbohydrate to carbon dioxide and alcohol or to an organic acid); *broadly* : an enzymatically controlled transformation of an organic compound **2** : FERMENT 2

fer·men·ta·tive \(ˌ)fər-ˈmen-tə-tiv\ *adj* (1661) **1** : causing or producing a substance that causes fermentation ⟨~ organisms⟩ **2** : of, relating to, or produced by fermentation

fer·men·ter \(ˌ)fər-ˈmen-tər\ *n* (1918) **1** : an organism that causes fermentation **2** *or* **fer·men·tor** : an apparatus for carrying out fermentation

fer·mi \ˈfer-(ˌ)mē, ˈfər-\ *n* [Enrico *Fermi*] (1955) : a unit of length equal to 10^{-13} centimeter

fer·mi·on \ˈfer-mē-ˌän, ˈfər-\ *n* [Enrico *Fermi* + E [2]*-on*] (1947) : a particle (as an electron, proton, or neutron) whose spin quantum number is an odd multiple of ½ — compare BOSON — **fer·mi·on·ic** \ˌfer-mē-ˈä-nik, ˌfər-\ *adj*

fer·mi·um \ˈfer-mē-əm, ˈfər-\ *n* [Enrico *Fermi*] (1955) : a radioactive metallic element produced artificially (as by bombardment of plutonium with neutrons) — see ELEMENT table

fern \ˈfərn\ *n* [ME, fr. OE *fearn;* akin to OHG *farn* fern, Skt *parṇa* wing, leaf] (bef. 12c) : any of a division (Filicophyta) or class (Filicopsida) of flowerless spore-producing vascular plants having alternating sporophyte and gametophyte generations; *esp* : any of an order (Filicales) of homosporous plants possessing roots, stems, and leaflike fronds — compare SEED FERN — **fern·like** \-ˌlīk\ *adj* — **ferny** \ˈfər-nē\ *adj*

fern bar *n* (1976) : a bar or restaurant fashionably decorated with green plants and esp. ferns

fern·ery \ˈfər-nə-rē\ *n, pl* **-er·ies** (1840) **1** : a place or stand where ferns grow **2** : a collection of growing ferns

fern seed *n* (1596) : the dustlike asexual spores of ferns formerly thought to be seeds and believed to make the possessor invisible

fe·ro·cious \fə-ˈrō-shəs\ *adj* [L *feroc-, ferox,* lit., fierce looking, fr. *ferus* + *-oc-, -ox* (akin to Gk *ōps* eye) — more at EYE] (1646) **1** : exhibiting or given to extreme fierceness and unrestrained violence and brutality ⟨a ~ predator⟩ **2** : extremely intense ⟨~ heat⟩ ***syn*** see FIERCE — **fe·ro·cious·ly** *adv* — **fe·ro·cious·ness** *n*

fe·roc·i·ty \fə-ˈrä-sə-tē\ *n* (1606) : the quality or state of being ferocious

-ferous *adj comb form* [ME, fr. AF & L; AF *-fere* -fer, fr. L *-fer*] : bearing : producing ⟨carboni*ferous*⟩

fer·re·dox·in \ˌfer-ə-ˈdäk-sən\ *n* [L *fer*rum + E *redox* + *-in*] (1962) : any of a group of iron- and sulfur-containing proteins that function as electron carriers in photosynthetic and nitrogen-fixing organisms and in some anaerobic bacteria

[1]**fer·ret** \ˈfer-ət\ *n* [ME *furet, ferret,* fr. AF *firet, furet,* fr. VL **furittus,* lit., little thief, dim. of L *fur* thief — more at FURTIVE] (14c) **1 a** : a domesticated usu. albino, brownish, or silver-gray animal (*Mustela putorius furo*) that is descended from the European polecat **b** : BLACK-FOOTED FERRET **2** : an active and persistent searcher — **fer·rety** \-ə-tē\ *adj*

[2]**ferret** *vi* (15c) **1** : to hunt with ferrets **2** : to search about ~ *vt* **1 a** (1) : to hunt (as rabbits) with ferrets (2) : to force out of hiding : FLUSH **b** : to find and bring to light by searching — usu. used with *out* ⟨~ out the answers⟩ **2** : HARRY, WORRY — **fer·ret·er** *n*

[3]**ferret** *n* [prob. modif. of It *fioretti* floss silk, fr. pl. of *fioretto,* dim. of *fiore* flower, fr. L *flor-, flos* — more at BLOW] (1649) : a narrow cotton, silk, or wool tape — called also *ferreting*

ferri- *comb form* [L, fr. *ferrum*] **1** : iron ⟨*ferri*ferous⟩ **2** : ferric iron ⟨*ferri*cyanide⟩

fer·ri·age \ˈfer-ē-ij\ *n* [ME] (14c) **1** : the fare paid for a ferry passage **2** : the act or business of transporting by ferry

fer·ric \ˈfer-ik, ˈfe-rik\ *adj* (1799) **1** : of, relating to, or containing iron **2** : being or containing iron usu. with a valence of three

ferric ammonium citrate *n* (ca. 1924) : a complex salt containing varying amounts of iron and used esp. for making blueprints

ferric chloride *n* (1869) : a deliquescent dark salt $FeCl_3$ that readily hydrates to the yellow-orange form and that is used esp. for etching, in sewage treatment, and as an astringent

ferric oxide *n* (1851) : the red or black oxide of iron Fe_2O_3 found in nature as hematite and as rust and also obtained synthetically and used esp. in magnetic materials, as a pigment, and for polishing

fer·ri·cy·a·nide \ˌfer-ˌī-ˈsī-ə-ˌnīd, ˌfer-i-\ *n* [ISV] (1845) **1** : the trivalent anion $Fe(CN)_6{}^{3-}$ **2** : a compound containing the ferricyanide anion; *esp* : the red salt $K_3Fe(CN)_6$ used in making blue pigments

fer·rif·er·ous \fə-ˈri-f(ə-)rəs, fe-\ *adj* (1811) : containing or yielding iron

fer·ri·mag·net·ic \ˈfer-ˌī-mag-ˈne-tik, ˌfer-i-\ *adj* (1951) : of or relating to a substance (as ferrite) characterized by magnetization in which two types of ions of unequal magnetic moment are polarized in opposite directions — **fer·ri·mag·net** \ˈfer-ˌī-ˌmag-nət, ˈfer-i-\ *n* — **fer·ri·mag·net·i·cal·ly** \ˈfer-ˌī-mag-ˈne-ti-k(ə-)lē, ˌfer-i-\ *adv* — **fer·ri·mag·ne·tism** \-ˈmag-nə-ˌti-zəm\ *n*

Fer·ris wheel \ˈfer-əs-, ˈfe-rəs-\ *n* [G. W. G. *Ferris* †1896 Am. engineer] (1893) : an amusement device consisting of a large upright power-driven wheel carrying seats that remain horizontal around its rim

fer·rite \ˈfer-ˌīt\ *n* (1851) **1** : any of several magnetic substances that consist essentially of ferric oxide combined with the oxides of one or more other metals (as manganese, nickel, or zinc), have high magnetic permeability and high electrical resistivity, and are used esp. in electronic devices **2** : a solid solution in which alpha iron is the solvent — **fer·rit·ic** \fə-ˈri-tik, fe-\ *adj*

fer·ri·tin \ˈfer-ə-tən\ *n* [ISV, alter. of *ferratin,* iron-containing protein, fr. L *ferrat*us bound with iron (fr. *ferrum*) + ISV *-in*] (1937) : a crystalline iron-containing protein that functions in the storage of iron and is found esp. in the liver and spleen

ferro- *comb form* [ML, fr. L *ferrum*] **1** : iron ⟨*ferro*concrete⟩ **2** : ferrous iron ⟨*ferro*cyanide⟩

fer·ro–ce·ment \ˌfer-ō-si-ˈment\ *n* (1956) : a building material made of thin cement slabs reinforced with steel mesh

fer·ro·cene \ˈfer-ō-ˌsēn\ *n* [*ferro-* + cycl- + *-ene*] (1952) : a crystalline stable organometallic coordination compound $(C_5H_5)_2Fe$; *also* : an analogous compound with a heavy metal (as chromium)

fer·ro·con·crete \ˌfer-ō-ˈkän-ˌkrēt, -kän-ˈ\ *n* (1900) : REINFORCED CONCRETE

fer·ro·cy·a·nide \-ˈsī-ə-ˌnīd\ *n* (ca. 1826) **1** : the tetravalent anion $Fe(CN)_6{}^{4-}$ **2** : a compound containing the ferrocyanide anion; *esp* : the salt $K_4Fe(CN)_6$ used in making blue pigments (as Prussian blue)

fer·ro·elec·tric \ˌfer-ō-i-ˈlek-trik\ *adj* (1935) : of or relating to crystalline substances having spontaneous electric polarization reversible by an electric field — **ferroelectric** *n* — **fer·ro·elec·tric·i·ty** \-ˌlek-ˈtri-sə-tē, -ˈtris-tē\ *n*

fer·ro·mag·ne·sian \-mag-ˈnē-zhən, -shən\ *adj* (1852) : containing iron and magnesium ⟨~ minerals⟩

fer·ro·mag·net·ic \-ˈne-tik\ *adj* (1896) : of or relating to substances with an abnormally high magnetic permeability, a definite saturation point, and appreciable residual magnetism and hysteresis — **fer·ro·mag·net** \ˈfer-ə-ˌmag-nət\ *n* — **fer·ro·mag·ne·tism** \ˌfer-ō-ˈmag-nə-ˌti-zəm\ *n*

fer·ro·man·ga·nese \-ˈmaŋ-gə-ˌnēz, -ˌnēs\ *n* (1864) : an alloy of iron and manganese containing usu. about 80 percent manganese and used in the manufacture of steel

fer·ro·sil·i·con \-ˈsi-li-kən, -lə-ˌkän\ *n* (1882) : an alloy of iron and silicon containing 15 to 95 percent silicon and used for deoxidizing molten steel and making silicon steel and high-silicon cast iron

fer·ro·type \ˈfer-ə-ˌtīp\ *n* (1844) **1** : a positive photograph made by a collodion process on a thin iron plate having a darkened surface — called also *tintype* **2** : the process by which a ferrotype is made

fer·rous \ˈfer-əs, ˈfe-rəs\ *adj* [NL *ferrosus,* fr. L *ferrum*] (1851) **1** : of, relating to, or containing iron **2** : being or containing divalent iron

ferrous sulfate *n* (1865) : a salt obtained usu. in its bluish-green hydrated form $FeSO_4{\cdot}7H_2O$ that is used esp. in making inks, pigments, and other iron salts and in medicine for treating anemia caused by iron deficiency

fer·ru·gi·nous \fə-ˈrü-jə-nəs, fe-\ *adj* [L *ferrugineus, ferruginus,* fr. *ferrugin-, ferrugo* iron rust, fr. *ferrum*] (ca. 1661) **1** : of, relating to, or containing iron ⟨a ~ soil⟩ **2** : resembling iron rust in color

ferruginous hawk *n* : a large hawk (*Buteo regalis*) of western No. America that is typically rust-colored above and white below with long tapered wings

fer·rule \ˈfer-əl, ˈfe-rəl\ *n* [alter. of ME *virole,* fr. AF, fr. L *viriola,* dim. of *viria* bracelet, of Celtic origin; akin to OIr *fiar* oblique] (1611) **1** : a ring or cap usu. of metal put around a slender shaft (as a cane or a tool handle) to strengthen it or prevent splitting **2** : a usu. metal sleeve used esp. for joining or binding one part to another (as pipe sections or the bristles and handle of a brush) — **fer·ruled** *adj*

[1]**fer·ry** \ˈfer-ē, ˈfe-rē\ *vb* **fer·ried; fer·ry·ing** [ME *ferien,* fr. OE *ferian* to carry, convey; akin to OE *faran* to go — more at FARE] *vt* (bef. 12c) **1 a** : to carry by boat over a body of water **b** : to cross by a ferry **2 a** : to convey (as by aircraft or motor vehicle) from one place to another : TRANSPORT **b** : to fly (an airplane) from the factory or other shipping point to a designated delivery point or from one base to another ~ *vi* : to cross water in a boat

[2]**ferry** *n, pl* **fer·ries** (15c) **1** : a place where persons or things are carried across a body of water (as a river) in a boat **2** : FERRYBOAT **3** : a franchise or right to operate a ferry service across a body of water **4** : an organized service and route for flying airplanes esp. across a sea or continent for delivery to the user

fer·ry·boat \-ˌbōt\ *n* (15c) : a boat used to ferry passengers, vehicles, or goods

fer·ry·man \-mən\ *n* (15c) : a person who operates a ferry

fer·tile \ˈfər-tᵊl\ *adj* [ME, fr. MF & L; MF, fr. L *fertilis,* fr. *ferre* to carry, bear — more at BEAR] (15c) **1 a** : producing or bearing fruit in great quantities : PRODUCTIVE **b** : characterized by great resourcefulness of thought or imagination : INVENTIVE ⟨a ~ mind⟩ **c** *obs* : PLENTIFUL **2 a** (1) : capable of sustaining abundant plant growth ⟨~ soil⟩ (2) : affording abundant possibilities for growth or development ⟨damp bathrooms are ~ ground for fungi —*Consumer Reports*⟩ ⟨a ~ area for research⟩ **b** : capable of growing or developing ⟨a ~ egg⟩ **c** (1) : capable of producing fruit (2) *of an anther* : containing pollen (3) : developing spores or spore-bearing organs **d** : capable of breeding or reproducing **3** : capable of being converted into fissionable material ⟨~ uranium 238⟩ — **fer·tile·ly** \-tᵊl-(l)ē\ *adv* — **fer·tile·ness** \-tᵊl-nəs\ *n*

syn FERTILE, FECUND, FRUITFUL, PROLIFIC mean producing or capable of producing offspring or fruit. FERTILE implies the power to reproduce in kind or to assist in reproduction and growth ⟨*fertile* soil⟩; applied figuratively, it suggests readiness of invention and development ⟨a *fertile* imagination⟩. FECUND emphasizes abundance or rapidity in bearing fruit or offspring ⟨a *fecund* herd⟩. FRUITFUL adds to FERTILE and FECUND the implication of desirable or useful results ⟨*fruitful* research⟩. PROLIFIC stresses rapidity of spreading or multiplying by or as if by natural reproduction ⟨a *prolific* writer⟩.

fer·til·i·ty \(ˌ)fər-ˈti-lə-tē\ *n* (15c) **1** : the quality or state of being fertile **2** : the birthrate of a population

fer·til·i·za·tion \ˌfər-tə-lə-ˈzā-shən\ *n* (ca. 1787) : an act or process of making fertile: as **a** : the application of fertilizer **b** (1) : an act or process of fecundation, insemination, or pollination — not used technically (2) : the process of union of two gametes whereby the somatic chromosome number is restored and the development of a new individual is initiated

fertilization membrane *n* (1931) : a resistant membranous layer in eggs of many animals that forms following fertilization by the thickening and separation of the vitelline membrane from the cell surface and that prevents multiple fertilization

fer·til·ize \ˈfər-tə-ˌlīz\ *vt* **-ized; -iz·ing** (1621) **:** to make fertile: as **a :** to apply a fertilizer to ⟨~ land⟩ **b :** to cause the fertilization of — **fer·til·iz·able** \-ˌlī-zə-bəl\ *adj*

fer·til·iz·er \-ˌlī-zər\ *n* (ca. 1661) **:** one that fertilizes; *specif* **:** a substance (as manure or a chemical mixture) used to make soil more fertile

fer·ule \ˈfer-əl, ˈfe-rəl\ *also* **fer·u·la** \ˈfer-(y)ə-lə\ *n* [L *ferula* giant fennel, ferule] (1566) **1 :** an instrument (as a flat piece of wood like a ruler) used to punish children **2 :** school discipline

fe·ru·lic acid \fə-ˈrü-lik-\ *n* [*ferula*] (1879) **:** a white crystalline acid that is structurally related to vanillin and is obtained esp. from plant sources (as aspen bark)

fer·ven·cy \ˈfər-vən(t)-sē\ *n, pl* **-cies** (15c) **:** FERVOR

fer·vent \ˈfər-vənt\ *adj* [ME, fr. AF & L; AF, fr. L *fervent-, fervens,* prp. of *fervēre* to boil, froth — more at BARM] (14c) **1 :** very hot **:** GLOWING **2 :** exhibiting or marked by great intensity of feeling **:** ZEALOUS ⟨~ prayers⟩ ***syn*** see IMPASSIONED — **fer·vent·ly** *adv*

fer·vid \ˈfər-vəd\ *adj* [L *fervidus,* fr. *fervēre*] (1599) **1 :** very hot **:** BURNING **2 :** marked by often extreme fervor ⟨a ~ crusader⟩ ***syn*** see IMPASSIONED — **fer·vid·ly** *adv* — **fer·vid·ness** *n*

fer·vor \ˈfər-vər\ *n* [ME *fervour,* fr. AF & L; AF *fervur,* fr. L *fervor,* fr. *fervēre*] (14c) **1 :** intensity of feeling or expression ⟨booing and cheering with almost equal ~ —Alan Rich⟩ **2 :** intense heat ***syn*** see PASSION

fer·vour *chiefly Brit var of* FERVOR

fes·cen·nine \ˈfe-sə-ˌnīn, -ˌnēn\ *adj* [L *fescennini* (*versus*), ribald songs sung at rustic weddings, prob. fr. *Fescinninus* of Fescennium, fr. *Fescennium,* town in Etruria] (1601) **:** SCURRILOUS, OBSCENE

fes·cue \ˈfes-(ˌ)kyü\ *n* [ME *festu* stalk, straw, fr. AF, fr. LL *festucum,* fr. L *festuca*] (1589) **1 :** a small pointer (as a stick) used to point out letters to children learning to read **2 :** any of a genus (*Festuca*) of tufted perennial grasses with panicled spikelets

fescue foot *n* (1949) **:** a disease of the feet of cattle resembling ergotism that is associated with feeding on fescue grass and esp. tall fescue

[1]**fess** *also* **fesse** \ˈfes\ *n* [ME *fesse,* fr. AF *faisse* band, fr. L *fascia* — more at FASCIA] (15c) **1 :** a broad horizontal bar across the middle of a heraldic field **2 :** the center point of an armorial escutcheon

[2]**fess** \ˈfes\ *vi* [short for *confess*] (1840) **:** to own up **:** CONFESS — usu. used with *up*

fest \ˌfest\ *n* [G, fr. *Fest* celebration, fr. L *festum* — more at FEAST] (1889) **:** a gathering, event, or show having a specified focus ⟨a music ~⟩ — often used in combination ⟨a gab*fest*⟩

fes·tal \ˈfes-tᵊl\ *adj* [L *festum*] (15c) **:** of or relating to a feast or festival **:** FESTIVE — **fes·tal·ly** \-tᵊl-ē\ *adv*

[1]**fes·ter** \ˈfes-tər\ *n* [ME, fr. AF *festre,* fr. L *fistula* pipe, fistulous ulcer] (14c) **:** a suppurating sore **:** PUSTULE

[2]**fester** *vb* **fes·tered; fes·ter·ing** \-t(ə-)riŋ\ *vi* (14c) **1 :** to generate pus **2 :** PUTREFY, ROT **3 a :** to cause increasing poisoning, irritation, or bitterness **:** RANKLE ⟨dissent ~*ed* unchecked⟩ **b :** to undergo or exist in a state of progressive deterioration ⟨allowed slums to ~⟩ ~ *vt* **:** to make inflamed or corrupt

[1]**fes·ti·nate** \ˈfes-tə-ˌnāt\ *vb* **-nat·ed; -nat·ing** (1596) **:** HASTEN

[2]**fes·ti·nate** \-nət, -ˌnāt\ *adj* [L *festinatus,* pp. of *festinare* to hasten; perh. akin to MIr *bras* forceful, W *brys* haste] (1605) **:** HASTY ⟨a most ~ preparation —Shak.⟩ — **fes·ti·nate·ly** *adv*

[1]**fes·ti·val** \ˈfes-tə-vəl\ *adj* [ME, fr. AF, fr. L *festivus* festive] (14c) **:** of, relating to, appropriate to, or set apart as a festival

[2]**festival** *n* (1528) **1 a :** a time of celebration marked by special observances **b :** FEAST 2 **2 :** an often periodic celebration or program of events or entertainment having a specified focus ⟨a daffodil ~⟩ ⟨a Greek ~⟩ **3 :** GAIETY, CONVIVIALITY

fes·ti·val·go·er \-ˌgō-ər\ *n* (1959) **:** one who attends a festival

fes·tive \ˈfes-tiv\ *adj* [L *festivus,* fr. *festum*] (1613) **1 :** of, relating to, or suitable for a feast or festival ⟨a ~ occasion⟩ **2 :** JOYFUL, GAY ⟨a ~ mood⟩ — **fes·tive·ly** *adv* — **fes·tive·ness** *n*

fes·tiv·i·ty \fes-ˈti-və-tē, fəs-\ *n, pl* **-ties** (14c) **1 :** FESTIVAL 1 **2 :** the quality or state of being festive **:** GAIETY **3 :** festive activity

[1]**fes·toon** \fes-ˈtün\ *n* [F *feston,* fr. It *festone,* fr. *festa* festival, fr. L — more at FEAST] (1630) **1 :** a decorative chain or strip hanging between two points **2 :** a carved, molded, or painted ornament representing a decorative chain

[2]**festoon** *vt* (1765) **1 :** to hang or form festoons on **2 :** to shape into festoons **3 :** DECORATE, ADORN; *also* **:** COVER 4b

fes·toon·ery \fes-ˈtü-nə-rē\ *n* (1836) **:** an arrangement of festoons

Fest·schrift \ˈfes(t)-ˌshrift\ *n, pl* **Fest·schrif·ten** \-ˌshrif-tən\ *or* **Festschrifts** [G, fr. *Fest* celebration + *Schrift* writing] (1898) **:** a volume of writings by different authors presented as a tribute or memorial esp. to a scholar

FET *abbr* **1** Federal excise tax **2** field-effect transistor

fe·ta \ˈfe-tə, ˈfe-ˌtä\ *n, often cap* [ModGk (*tyri*) *pheta,* fr. *tyri* cheese + *pheta* slice, fr. It *fetta* — more at FETTUCCINE] (1915) **:** a white moderately hard and crumbly Greek cheese made from sheep's or goat's milk and cured in brine

fe·tal \ˈfē-tᵊl\ *adj* (1811) **:** of, relating to, or being a fetus

fetal alcohol syndrome *n* (1974) **:** a highly variable group of birth defects including mental retardation, deficient growth, and malformations of the skull and face that tend to occur in the offspring of women who consume large amounts of alcohol during pregnancy

fetal hemoglobin *n* (1950) **:** a hemoglobin variant that predominates in the blood of a newborn and persists in increased proportions in some forms of anemia (as thalassemia)

fetal position *n* (1963) **:** a position (as of a sleeping person) in which the body lies curled up on one side with the arms and legs drawn up and the head bowed forward and which is assumed in some forms of psychic regression

[1]**fetch** \ˈfech\ *vb* [ME *fecchen,* fr. OE *fetian, feccan;* perh. akin to OE *fōt* foot — more at FOOT] *vt* (bef. 12c) **1 a :** to go or come after and bring or take back ⟨~ a doctor⟩ **b :** DERIVE, DEDUCE **2 a :** to cause to come **b :** to bring in (as a price) **:** REALIZE **c :** INTEREST, ATTRACT **3 a :** to give (a blow) by striking **:** DEAL **b** *chiefly dial* **:** BRING ABOUT, ACCOMPLISH **c** (1) **:** to take in (as a breath) **:** DRAW (2) **:** to bring forth (as a sound) **:** HEAVE ⟨~ a sigh⟩ **4 a :** to reach by sailing esp. against the wind or tide **b :** to arrive at **:** REACH ~ *vi* **1 :** to get and bring something; *specif* **:** to retrieve killed game **2 :** to take a roundabout way **:** CIRCLE **3 a :** to hold a course on a body of water **b :** VEER — **fetch·er** *n*

[2]**fetch** *n* (ca. 1530) **1 :** TRICK, STRATAGEM **2 :** an act or instance of fetching **3 a :** the distance along open water or land over which the wind blows **b :** the distance traversed by waves without obstruction

[3]**fetch** *n* [origin unknown] (ca. 1787) **:** DOPPELGÄNGER 1

fetch·ing \ˈfe-chiŋ\ *adj* (1880) **:** ATTRACTIVE, PLEASING ⟨a ~ smile⟩ — **fetch·ing·ly** \-chiŋ-lē\ *adv*

fetch up *vt* (1599) **1 :** to bring up or out **:** PRODUCE **2 :** to make up (as lost time) **3 :** to bring to a stop ~ *vi* **:** to reach a standstill, stopping place, or goal **:** end up ⟨may have *fetched up* running a village store —Geoffrey Household⟩

[1]**fete** *or* **fête** \ˈfāt, ˈfet\ *n* [ME *fete,* fr. MF, fr. OF *feste* — more at FEAST] (15c) **1 :** FESTIVAL **2 a :** a lavish often outdoor entertainment **b :** a large elaborate party

[2]**fete** *or* **fête** *vt* **fet·ed** *or* **fêt·ed; fet·ing** *or* **fêt·ing** (1814) **1 :** to honor or commemorate with a fete **2 :** to pay high honor to

fête cham·pê·tre \ˌfāt-ˌshäⁿ(m)-ˈpetrᵊ, ˌfet-\ *n, pl* **fêtes champêtres** *same*\ [F, lit., rural festival] (1774) **:** an outdoor entertainment

fe·ti·cide \ˈfē-tə-ˌsīd\ *n* (1842) **:** the act of causing the death of a fetus

fet·id \ˈfe-təd, *esp Brit* ˈfē-tid\ *adj* [ME, fr. L *foetidus,* fr. *foetēre* to stink] (15c) **:** having a heavy offensive smell ⟨a ~ swamp⟩ ***syn*** see MALODOROUS — **fet·id·ly** *adv* — **fet·id·ness** *n*

fe·tish *also* **fe·tich** \ˈfe-tish *also* ˈfē-\ *n* [F & Pg; F *fétiche,* fr. Pg *feitiço,* fr. *feitiço* artificial, false, fr. L *facticius* factitious] (1613) **1 a :** an object (as a small stone carving of an animal) believed to have magical power to protect or aid its owner; *broadly* **:** a material object regarded with superstitious or extravagant trust or reverence **b :** an object of irrational reverence or obsessive devotion **:** PREPOSSESSION **c :** an object or bodily part whose real or fantasied presence is psychologically necessary for sexual gratification and that is an object of fixation to the extent that it may interfere with complete sexual expression **2 :** a rite or cult of fetish worshipers **3 :** FIXATION

fe·tish·ism *also* **fe·tich·ism** \-tish-ˌi-zəm\ *n* (1801) **1 :** belief in magical fetishes **2 :** extravagant irrational devotion **3 :** the pathological displacement of erotic interest and satisfaction to a fetish — **fe·tish·ist** \-tish-ist\ *n* — **fe·tish·is·tic** \ˌfe-ti-ˈshis-tik *also* ˌfē-\ *adj* — **fe·tish·is·ti·cal·ly** \-ti-k(ə-)lē\ *adv*

fe·tish·ize \-ti-ˌshīz\ *vt* **-ized; -iz·ing** (1920) **:** to make a fetish of **:** treat or regard with fetishism

fet·lock \ˈfet-ˌläk\ *n* [ME *fitlok, fetlak;* akin to OE *fōt* foot] (14c) **1 a :** a projection bearing a tuft of hair on the back of the leg above the hoof of a horse or similar animal — see HORSE illustration **b :** the tuft of hair itself **2 :** the joint of the limb at the fetlock

feto- *or* **feti-** *comb form* [NL *fetus*] **:** fetus ⟨*feticide*⟩

fe·tol·o·gy \fē-ˈtä-lə-jē\ *n* (1965) **:** a branch of medical science concerned with the study and treatment of the fetus in the uterus — **fe·tol·o·gist** \-jist\ *n*

fe·to·pro·tein \ˌfē-tō-ˈprō-ˌtēn, -ˈprō-tē-ən\ *n* (1965) **:** any of several fetal antigens present in the adult in some abnormal conditions

fe·tor \ˈfē-tər, ˈfē-ˌtȯr\ *n* [ME *fetoure,* fr. L *foetor,* fr. *foetēre*] (15c) **:** a strong offensive smell **:** STENCH

fe·to·scope \ˈfē-tə-ˌskōp\ *n* (1972) **1 :** an endoscope for visual examination of the pregnant uterus **2 :** a stethoscope for listening to the fetal heartbeat — **fe·tos·co·py** \fē-ˈtäs-kə-pē\ *n*

[1]**fet·ter** \ˈfe-tər\ *n* [ME *feter,* fr. OE; akin to OE *fōt* foot] (bef. 12c) **1 :** a chain or shackle for the feet **2 :** something that confines **:** RESTRAINT

[2]**fetter** *vt* (bef. 12c) **1 :** to put fetters on **:** SHACKLE **2 :** to restrain from motion, action, or progress ***syn*** see HAMPER

[1]**fet·tle** \ˈfe-tᵊl\ *n* [[2]*fettle*] (1740) **:** state or condition of health, fitness, wholeness, spirit, or form — often used in the phrase *in fine fettle*

[2]**fettle** *vt* **fet·tled; fet·tling** \ˈfet-liŋ, ˈfe-tᵊl-iŋ\ [Brit. dial., to set in order, get ready, fr. ME *fetlen* to shape, prepare; perh. akin to OE *fetian* to fetch — more at FETCH] (1881) **:** to cover or line the hearth of (as a reverberatory furnace) with loose material (as sand or gravel)

fet·tuc·ci·ne *or* **fet·tuc·ci·ni** *or* **fet·tu·ci·ne** *or* **fet·tu·ci·ni** \ˌfe-tə-ˈchē-nē\ *n pl but sing or pl in constr* [It, pl. of *fettuccina,* dim. of *fettuccia* small slice, ribbon, dim. of *fetta* slice, prob. alter. of **offetta,* fr. *offa* flour cake, fr. L] (1912) **:** pasta in the form of narrow ribbons; *also* **:** a dish of which fettuccine forms the base

fettuccine Al·fre·do \-(ˌ)al-ˈfrā-(ˌ)dō, -(ˌ)äl-\ *n* [fr. *Alfredo all'Augusteo,* restaurant in Rome where it originated] (1961) **:** a dish consisting of fettuccine with butter, Parmesan cheese, cream, and seasonings — called also *fettuccine all'Alfredo* \-ˌal-(ˌ)al-, -ˌäl-(ˌ)äl-\

fe·tus \ˈfē-təs\ *n* [ME, fr. L, act of bearing young, offspring; akin to L *fetus* newly delivered, fruitful — more at FEMININE] (14c) **:** an unborn or unhatched vertebrate esp. after attaining the basic structural plan of its kind; *specif* **:** a developing human from usu. two months after conception to birth — compare EMBRYO 1b

[1]**feud** \ˈfyüd\ *n* [alter. of ME *feide,* fr. AF **faide,* of Gmc origin; akin to OHG *fēhida* hostility, feud, OE *fāh* hostile — more at FOE] (15c) **:** a mutual enmity or quarrel that is often prolonged or inveterate; *esp* **:** BLOOD FEUD — **feud** *vi*

[2]**feud** *n* [ML *feodum, feudum,* alter. (prob. influenced by ML *alodum, allodium* land not subject to rent or service) of *feo, feus,* of Gmc origin; akin to OHG *fihu* cattle — more at FEE] (1614) **:** FEE 1a

feu·dal \ˈfyü-dᵊl\ *adj* (1602) **1 :** of, relating to, or having the characteristics of a medieval fee **2 :** of, relating to, or suggestive of feudalism ⟨~ law⟩ — **feu·dal·ly** \-dᵊl-ē\ *adv*

feu·dal·ism \ˈfyü-də-ˌli-zəm\ *n* (ca. 1818) **1 :** the system of political organization prevailing in Europe from the 9th to about the 15th centuries having as its basis the relation of lord to vassal with all land held in fee and as chief characteristics homage, the service of tenants under arms and in court, wardship, and forfeiture **2 :** any of various political or social systems similar to medieval feudalism — **feu·dal·ist** \-də-list\ *n* — **feu·dal·is·tic** \ˌfyü-dᵊl-ˈis-tik\ *adj*

---

feu·dal·i·ty \fyü-ˈda-lə-tē\ *n, pl* **-ties** (1790) **1 :** the quality or state of being feudal **2 :** a feudal holding, domain, or concentration of power

feu·dal·ize \ˈfyü-də-ˌlīz\ *vt* **-ized; -iz·ing** (1828) **:** to make feudal — **feu·dal·i·za·tion** \ˌfyü-dᵊl-ə-ˈzā-shən\ *n*

[1]**feu·da·to·ry** \ˈfyü-də-ˌtȯr-ē\ *adj* [ML *feudatorius,* fr. *feudare* to enfeoff, fr. *feudum*] (1592) **1 :** owing feudal allegiance **2 :** being under the overlordship of a foreign state

[2]**feudatory** *n, pl* **-ries** (1644) **1 :** a dependent lordship **:** FEE **2 :** one holding lands by feudal tenure

[1]**feud·ist** \ˈfyü-dist\ *n* (1607) **:** a specialist in feudal law

[2]**feudist** *n* (1901) **:** one who feuds

feuil·le·ton \ˌfə-yə-ˈtōⁿ, ˌfər-, ˌfœ-\ *n* [F, fr. *feuillet* sheet of paper, fr. OF *foillet,* dim. of *foille* leaf — more at FOIL] (1845) **1 :** a part of a European newspaper or magazine devoted to material designed to entertain the general reader **2 :** something (as an installment of a novel) printed in a feuilleton **3 a :** a novel printed in installments **b :** a work of fiction catering to popular taste **4 :** a short literary composition often having a familiar tone and reminiscent content — **feuil·le·ton·ism** \-ˈtō(ⁿ)-ˌni-zəm\ *n* — **feuil·le·ton·ist** \-nist\ *n*

Feul·gen \ˈfȯil-gən\ *adj* (1928) **:** of, relating to, utilizing, or staining by the Feulgen reaction ⟨positive ~ mitochondria⟩

Feulgen reaction *n* [Robert *Feulgen* †1955 Ger. physiologist] (1928) **:** the development of a brilliant purple color by DNA in a microscopic preparation stained with a modified Schiff's reagent

[1]**fe·ver** \ˈfē-vər\ *n* [ME, fr. OE *fēfer,* fr. L *febris*] (bef. 12c) **1 a :** a rise of body temperature above the normal **b :** any of various diseases of which fever is a prominent symptom **2 a :** a state of heightened or intense emotion or activity **b :** a contagious usu. transient enthusiasm **:** CRAZE

[2]**fever** *vb* **fe·vered; fe·ver·ing** \ˈfē-vriŋ, ˈfe-vər-iŋ\ *vt* (1606) **:** to throw into a fever **:** AGITATE ~ *vi* **:** to contract or be in a fever **:** become feverish

fever blister *n* (1845) **:** COLD SORE

fe·ver·few \ˈfē-vər-ˌfyü\ *n* [ME, fr. OE *feferfuge,* fr. LL *febrifugia* centaury — more at FEBRIFUGE] (15c) **:** a perennial European composite herb (*Chrysanthemum parthenium*) widely cultivated as an ornamental

fe·ver·ish \ˈfē-vrish, ˈfe-vər-ish\ *adj* (14c) **1 a :** tending to cause fever **b :** having the symptoms of a fever **c :** indicating or relating to fever **2 :** marked by intense emotion, activity, or instability ⟨~ excitement⟩ — **fe·ver·ish·ly** *adv* — **fe·ver·ish·ness** *n*

fe·ver·ous \ˈfē-vrəs, ˈfe-vər-əs\ *adj* (14c) **:** FEVERISH

fever pitch *n* (1846) **:** a state of intense excitement and agitation

fever tree *n* (1868) **:** any of several shrubs or trees that are thought to indicate regions free from fever or that yield remedies for fever; *esp* **:** an African acacia (*Acacia xanthlophloea*)

fe·ver·wort \ˈfē-vər-ˌwərt, -ˌwȯrt\ *n* (ca. 1814) **:** a coarse American herb (*Triosteum perfoliatum*) of the honeysuckle family — called also *horse gentian*

[1]**few** \ˈfyü\ *pron, pl in constr* [ME *fewe,* pron. & adj., fr. OE *fēawa;* akin to OHG *fō* little, L *paucus* little, *pauper* poor, Gk *paid-, pais* child, Skt *putra* son] (bef. 12c) **:** not many persons or things ⟨~ were present⟩ ⟨~ of his stories are true⟩

[2]**few** *adj* (bef. 12c) **1 :** consisting of or amounting to only a small number ⟨one of our ~ pleasures⟩ **2 :** at least some but indeterminately small in number — used with *a* ⟨caught a ~ fish⟩ — **few·ness** *n* — **few and far between :** few in number and infrequently met **:** RARE

[3]**few** *n, pl in constr* (bef. 12c) **1 :** a small number of units or individuals ⟨a ~ of them⟩ **2 :** a special limited number ⟨the discriminating ~⟩

[1]**few·er** \ˈfyü-ər, ˈfyu̇r\ *pron, pl in constr* (bef. 12c) **:** a smaller number of persons or things

[2]**fewer** *adj, comparative of* FEW ***usage*** see LESS

few·trils \ˈfyü-trəlz\ *n pl* [origin unknown] (ca. 1750) *dial Eng* **:** things of little value **:** TRIFLES

fey \ˈfā\ *adj* [ME *feye,* fr. OE *fǣge;* akin to OHG *feigi* doomed and perh. to OE *fāh* hostile, outlawed — more at FOE] (bef. 12c) **1 a** *chiefly Scot* **:** fated to die **:** DOOMED **b :** marked by a foreboding of death or calamity **2 a :** able to see into the future **:** VISIONARY **b :** marked by an otherworldly air or attitude **c :** CRAZY, TOUCHED **3 a :** excessively refined **:** PRECIOUS **b :** quaintly unconventional **:** CAMPY — **fey·ly** *adv* — **fey·ness** *n*

fez \ˈfez\ *n, pl* **fez·zes** *also* **fez·es** [F, fr. *Fez,* Morocco] (ca. 1803) **:** a brimless cone-shaped flat-crowned hat that usu. has a tassel, is usu. made of red felt, and is worn esp. by men in eastern Mediterranean countries — **fezzed** \ˈfezd\ *adj*

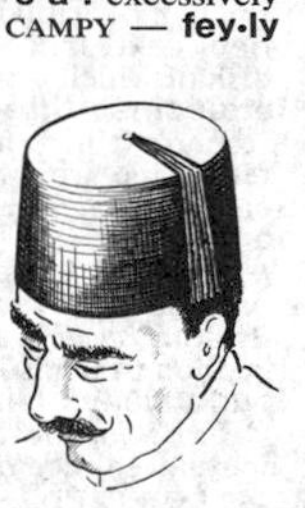

fez

ff *abbr* **1** folios **2** [*f*ollowing] and the following ones **3** fortissimo

FGM *abbr* female genital mutilation

FHA *abbr* Federal Housing Administration

fi·acre \fē-ˈäkrᵊ\ *n, pl* **fi·acres** *same, or* -ˈäk-rəz\ [F, fr. the Hotel St. *Fiacre,* Paris] (1698) **:** a small hackney coach

fi·an·cé \ˌfē-ˌän-ˈsā, fē-ˈän-ˌ\ *n* [F, fr. MF, fr. pp. of *fiancer* to promise, betroth, fr. OF *fiancier,* fr. *fiance* promise, trust, fr. *fier* to trust, fr. VL **fidare,* alter. of L *fidere* — more at BIDE] (1838) **:** a man engaged to be married

fi·an·cée \ˌfē-ˌän-ˈsā, fē-ˈän-ˌ\ *n* [F, fem. of *fiancé*] (1835) **:** a woman engaged to be married

fi·an·chet·to \ˌfē-ən-ˈke-(ˌ)tō, -ˈche-\ *vb* [*fianchetto* an opening in chess, fr. It, dim. of *fianco* side, flank, fr. OF *flanc* — more at FLANK] *vt* (1927) **:** to develop (a bishop) in a chess game to the second square on the adjacent knight's file ~ *vi* **:** to fianchetto a bishop

[1]**fi·as·co** \fē-ˈas-(ˌ)kō *also* -ˈäs-\ *n, pl* **-coes** [F, fr. It, fr. *fare fiasco,* lit., to make a bottle] (ca. 1854) **:** a complete failure

[2]**fi·as·co** \fē-ˈäs-(ˌ)kō, -ˈas-\ *n, pl* **-coes** *also* **fi·as·chi** \-(ˌ)kē\ [It, fr. LL *flasco* bottle — more at FLASK] (1887) **:** BOTTLE, FLASK; *esp* **:** a bulbous long-necked straw-covered bottle for wine

fi·at \ˈfē-ət, -ˌat, -ˌät; ˈfī-ət, -ˌat\ *n* [L, let it be done, 3d sing. pres. subj. of *fieri* to become, be done — more at BE] (ca. 1631) **1 :** a command or act of will that creates something without or as if without further effort **2 :** an authoritative determination **:** DICTATE ⟨a ~ of conscience⟩ **3 :** an authoritative or arbitrary order **:** DECREE ⟨government by ~⟩

fiat money *n* (1876) **:** money (as paper currency) not convertible into coin or specie of equivalent value

[1]**fib** \ˈfib\ *n* [perh. by shortening & alter. fr. *fable*] (1611) **:** a trivial or childish lie

[2]**fib** *vi* **fibbed; fib·bing** (1675) **:** to tell a fib ***syn*** see LIE — **fib·ber** *n*

[3]**fib** *vb* **fibbed; fib·bing** [origin unknown] (ca. 1665) *Brit* **:** PUMMEL, BEAT

fi·ber \ˈfī-bər\ *n* [MF *fibre,* fr. L *fibra*] (1540) **1 :** a thread or a structure or object resembling a thread: as **a** (1) **:** a slender root (as of a grass) (2) **:** an elongated tapering thick-walled plant cell void at maturity that imparts elasticity, flexibility, and tensile strength **b** (1) **:** a strand of nerve tissue **:** AXON, DENDRITE (2) **:** one of the filaments composing most of the intercellular matrix of connective tissue (3) **:** one of the elongated contractile cells of muscle tissue **c :** a slender and greatly elongated natural or synthetic filament (as of wool, cotton, asbestos, gold, glass, or rayon) typically capable of being spun into yarn **d :** mostly indigestible material in food that stimulates the intestine to peristalsis — called also *bulk, roughage* **2 :** material made of fibers; *esp* **:** VULCANIZED FIBER **3 a :** an element that gives texture or substance **b :** basic toughness **:** STRENGTH, FORTITUDE **c :** essential structure or character ⟨the very ~ of a person's being⟩ — **fi·bered** \-bərd\ *adj*

fi·ber·board \-ˌbȯrd\ *n* (1897) **:** a material made by compressing fibers (as of wood) into stiff sheets; *also* **:** CARDBOARD

fi·ber·fill \-ˌfil\ *n* (1962) **:** synthetic fibers used as a filling material (as for cushions)

[1]**fi·ber·glass** \-ˌglas\ *n* (1937) **1 :** glass in fibrous form used in making various products (as glass wool for insulation) **2 :** a composite structural material of plastic and fiberglass

[2]**fiberglass** *vt* (1967) **:** to protect or repair by applying fiberglass

fi·ber·ize \ˈfī-bə-ˌrīz\ *vt* **-ized; -iz·ing** (1925) **:** to make or break down into fibers — **fi·ber·i·za·tion** \ˌfī-b(ə-)rə-ˈzā-shən\ *n*

fi·ber–op·tic \ˈfī-bər-ˌäp-tik\ *adj* (1961) **:** of, relating to, or using fiber optics

fiber optics *n pl* (1956) **1 :** thin transparent fibers of glass or plastic that are enclosed by material of a lower refractive index and that transmit light throughout their length by internal reflections; *also* **:** a bundle of such fibers used in an instrument (as for viewing body cavities) **2** *sing in constr* **:** the technique of the use of fiber optics

fi·ber·scope \ˈfī-bər-ˌskōp\ *n* (1954) **:** a flexible instrument utilizing fiber optics and used for examination of inaccessible areas

Fi·bo·nac·ci number \ˌfē-bə-ˈnä-chē-, ˌfi-bə-\ *n* [Leonardo *Fibonacci* †*ab*1250 Ital. mathematician] (1914) **:** an integer in the infinite sequence 1, 1, 2, 3, 5, 8, 13, . . . of which the first two terms are 1 and 1 and each succeeding term is the sum of the two immediately preceding

fibr- *or* **fibro-** *comb form* [L *fibra*] **:** fiber **:** fibrous tissue ⟨*fibr*oid⟩ **:** fibrous and ⟨*fibro*vascular⟩

fi·branne \ˈfī-ˌbran, fī-ˈ\ *n* [F, viscose rayon, fr. *fibre*] (1941) **:** a fabric made of spun-rayon yarn

fi·bre *chiefly Brit var of* FIBER

fi·bril \ˈfi-brəl, ˈfī-\ *n* [NL *fibrilla,* dim. of L *fibra*] (1664) **:** a small filament or fiber: as **a :** ROOT HAIR **b** (1) **:** one of the fine threads into which a striated muscle fiber can be longitudinally split (2) **:** NEUROFIBRIL — **fi·bril·lar** \ˈfi-brə-lər, ˈfī-\ *adj*

fi·bril·late \ˈfi-brə-ˌlāt, ˈfī-\ *vb* **-lat·ed; -lat·ing** *vi* (ca. 1847) **:** to undergo or exhibit fibrillation ~ *vt* **:** to cause to undergo fibrillation

fi·bril·la·tion \ˌfi-brə-ˈlā-shən, ˌfī-\ *n* (1845) **1 :** an act or process of forming fibers or fibrils **2 a :** a muscular twitching involving individual muscle fibers acting without coordination **b :** very rapid irregular contractions of the muscle fibers of the heart resulting in a lack of synchronism between heartbeat and pulse

fi·brin \ˈfī-brən\ *n* (1800) **:** a white insoluble fibrous protein formed from fibrinogen by the action of thrombin esp. in the clotting of blood — **fi·bri·nous** \-brə-nəs\ *adj*

fi·brin·o·gen \fī-ˈbri-nə-jən\ *n* [ISV] (1872) **:** a plasma protein that is produced in the liver and is converted into fibrin during blood clot formation

fi·bri·noid \ˈfi-brə-ˌnȯid, ˈfī-\ *n, often attrib* (1910) **:** a homogeneous acidophilic refractile material that somewhat resembles fibrin and is formed in the walls of blood vessels and in connective tissue in some pathological conditions and normally in the placenta

fi·bri·no·ly·sin \ˌfī-brə-nə-ˈlī-sᵊn\ *n* [ISV] (1915) **:** any of several proteolytic enzymes that promote the dissolution of blood clots; *esp* **:** PLASMIN

fi·bri·no·ly·sis \-ˈī-səs, -brə-ˈnä-lə-səs\ *n* [NL] (1907) **:** the usu. enzymatic breakdown of fibrin — **fi·bri·no·lyt·ic** \-brə-nə-ˈli-tik\ *adj*

fi·bri·no·pep·tide \ˌfī-brə-nō-ˈpep-ˌtīd\ *n* (1960) **:** any of the vertebrate polypeptides that are cleaved from fibrinogen by thrombin during clot formation

fi·bro·blast \ˈfī-brə-ˌblast, ˈfi-\ *n* [ISV] (1876) **:** a connective-tissue cell of mesenchymal origin that secretes proteins and esp. molecular collagen from which the extracellular fibrillar matrix of connective tissue forms — **fi·bro·blas·tic** \ˌfī-brə-ˈblas-tik, ˌfi-\ *adj*

fibroblast growth factor *n* (1974) **:** any of several protein growth factors that stimulate the proliferation esp. of endothelial cells and that promote angiogenesis

fi·bro·cys·tic \ˌfī-brə-ˈsis-tik, ˌfi-\ *adj* (1854) **:** characterized by the presence or development of fibrous tissue and cysts

[1]**fi·broid** \ˈfī-brȯid, ˈfi-\ *adj* (1852) **:** resembling, forming, or consisting of fibrous tissue ⟨a ~ tumor⟩

[2]**fibroid** *n* (ca. 1860) **:** a benign tumor that consists of fibrous and muscular tissue and occurs esp. in the uterine wall

fi·bro·in \ˈfī-brə-wən, ˈfi-, -brō-ən\ *n* [F *fibroïne,* fr. *fibr-* + *-ine* -in] (1878) **:** an insoluble protein comprising the filaments of the raw silk fiber

fi·bro·ma \fī-ˈbrō-mə\ *n, pl* **-mas** *also* **-ma·ta** \-mə-tə\ (ca. 1849) **:** a benign tumor consisting mainly of fibrous tissue — **fi·bro·ma·tous** \-mə-təs\ *adj*

fi·bro·my·al·gia \ˌfī-brō-ˌmī-ˈal-j(ē)ə\ *n* [NL] (1983) **:** a chronic disorder characterized by widespread pain, tenderness, and stiffness of muscles and associated connective tissue structures that is typically accompanied by fatigue, headache, and sleep disturbances

fi·bro·nec·tin \ˌfī-brə-ˈnek-tən\ *n* [*fibr-* + L *nectere* to tie, bind + E *-in*] (1976) **:** any of a group of glycoproteins of cell surfaces, blood plasma, and connective tissue that promote cellular adhesion and migration
fi·bro·sar·co·ma \ˌfī-brə-sär-ˈkō-mə, ˌfi-\ *n* (1878) **:** a sarcoma of relatively low malignancy consisting chiefly of spindle-shaped cells that tend to form collagenous fibrils
fi·bro·sis \fī-ˈbrō-səs\ *n* [NL] (1873) **:** a condition marked by increase of interstitial fibrous tissue — **fi·brot·ic** \-ˈbrä-tik\ *adj*
fi·bro·si·tis \ˌfī-brə-ˈsī-təs, ˌfi-\ *n* [NL, fr. *fibrosus* fibrous, fr. ISV *fibrous*] (1904) **:** a rheumatic disorder of fibrous tissue; *esp* **:** FIBROMYALGIA
fi·brous \ˈfī-brəs\ *adj* [modif. of MF *fibreux,* fr. *fibre* fiber] (1597) **1 a :** containing, consisting of, or resembling fibers **b :** characterized by fibrosis **c :** capable of being separated into fibers ⟨a ~ mineral⟩ **2 :** TOUGH, SINEWY ⟨~ texture⟩
fibrous root *n* (1626) **:** a root (as in most grasses) that has no prominent central axis and that branches in all directions
fi·bro·vas·cu·lar \ˌfī-brō-ˈvas-kyə-lər, ˌfi-\ *adj* (1845) **:** having or consisting of fibers and conducting cells
fibrovascular bundle *n* (1875) **:** VASCULAR BUNDLE
fib·u·la \ˈfi-byə-lə\ *n, pl* **-lae** \-lē, -lī\ *or* **-las** [L, pin, clasp; akin to L *figere* to fasten] (1578) **1 :** the outer and usu. smaller of the two bones between the knee and ankle in the hind or lower limbs of vertebrates **2 :** a clasp resembling a safety pin used esp. by the ancient Greeks and Romans — **fib·u·lar** \-lər\ *adj*

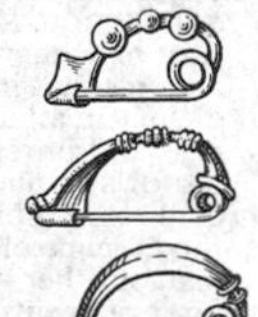
fibula 2

-fic *adj suffix* [L *-ficus,* fr. *facere* to make — more at DO] **:** making **:** causing ⟨felici*fic*⟩
FICA *abbr* Federal Insurance Contributions Act
-fication *n comb form* [L *-fication-, -ficatio,* fr. *-ficare* to make, fr. *-ficus*] **:** making **:** production ⟨rei*fication*⟩
fice *var of* FEIST
fiche \ˈfēsh *also* ˈfish\ *n, pl* **fiche** *also* **fiches** (1951) **:** MICROFICHE
fi·chu \ˈfi-(ˌ)shü, ˈfē-\ *n* [F, fr. pp. of *ficher* to stick in, throw on, fr. VL **figicare,* fr. L *figere* to fasten, pierce] (1803) **:** a woman's light triangular scarf that is draped over the shoulders and fastened in front or worn to fill in a low neckline
fi·cin \ˈfī-sᵊn\ *n* [L *ficus* fig] (1930) **:** a protease obtained from the latex of fig trees and used as an anthelmintic and protein digestive
fick·le \ˈfi-kəl\ *adj* [ME *fikel* deceitful, inconstant, fr. OE *ficol* deceitful; akin to OE *befician* to deceive, and prob. to OE *fāh* hostile — more at FOE] (13c) **:** marked by lack of steadfastness, constancy, or stability **:** given to erratic changeableness ***syn*** see INCONSTANT — **fick·le·ness** *n* — **fick·ly** \ˈfi-k(ə-)lē\ *adv*
fi·co \ˈfē-(ˌ)kō\ *n, pl* **ficoes** [obs. *fico,* obscene gesture of contempt, modif. of It *fica* fig, vulva, gesture of contempt, fr. VL **fica* fig — more at FIG] (1585) *archaic* **:** FIG 2
fict *abbr* fiction; fictitious
fic·tile \ˈfik-tᵊl, -ˌtī(-ə)l\ *adj* [L *fictilis* molded of clay, fr. *fingere*] (1626) **1** *archaic* **:** PLASTIC 2a **2 :** of or relating to pottery **3 :** MALLEABLE 2a
fic·tion \ˈfik-shən\ *n* [ME *ficcioun,* fr. MF *fiction,* fr. L *fiction-, fictio* act of fashioning, fiction, fr. *fingere* to shape, fashion, feign — more at DOUGH] (14c) **1 a :** something invented by the imagination or feigned; *specif* **:** an invented story **b :** fictitious literature (as novels or short stories) **c :** a work of fiction; *esp* **:** NOVEL **2 a :** an assumption of a possibility as a fact irrespective of the question of its truth ⟨a legal ~⟩ **b :** a useful illusion or pretense **3 :** the action of feigning or of creating with the imagination — **fic·tion·al** \-shnəl, -shə-nᵊl\ *adj* — **fic·tion·al·i·ty** \ˌfik-shə-ˈna-lə-tē\ *n* — **fic·tion·al·ly** \ˈfik-shnə-lē, -shə-nᵊl-ē\ *adv*
fic·tion·al·ise *Brit var of* FICTIONALIZE
fic·tion·al·ize \ˈfik-shnə-ˌlīz, -shə-nə-ˌlīz\ *vt* **-ized; -iz·ing** (1918) **:** to make into or treat in the manner of fiction ⟨~ a biography⟩ — **fic·tion·al·i·za·tion** \ˌfik-shnə-lə-ˈzā-shən, -shə-nə-lə-\ *n*
fic·tion·eer \ˌfik-shə-ˈnir\ *n* (1923) **:** one who writes fiction esp. in quantity and without high standards — **fic·tion·eer·ing** *n*
fic·tion·ist \ˈfik-sh(ə-)nist\ *n* (1829) **:** a writer of fiction; *esp* **:** NOVELIST
fic·tion·ize \ˈfik-shə-ˌnīz\ *vt* **-ized; -iz·ing** (1831) **:** FICTIONALIZE — **fic·tion·i·za·tion** \ˌfik-shə-nə-ˈzā-shən\ *n*
fic·ti·tious \fik-ˈti-shəs\ *adj* [L *ficticius* artificial, feigned, fr. *fictus*] (ca. 1633) **1 :** of, relating to, or characteristic of fiction **:** IMAGINARY **2 a :** conventionally or hypothetically assumed or accepted ⟨a ~ concept⟩ **b** *of a name* **:** FALSE, ASSUMED **3 :** not genuinely felt — **fic·ti·tious·ly** *adv* — **fic·ti·tious·ness** *n*
syn FICTITIOUS, FABULOUS, LEGENDARY, MYTHICAL, APOCRYPHAL mean having the nature of something imagined or invented. FICTITIOUS implies fabrication and suggests artificiality or contrivance more than deliberate falsification or deception ⟨*fictitious* characters⟩. FABULOUS stresses the marvelous or incredible character of something without necessarily implying impossibility or actual nonexistence ⟨a land of *fabulous* riches⟩. LEGENDARY suggests the elaboration of invented details and distortion of historical facts produced by popular tradition ⟨the *legendary* exploits of Davy Crockett⟩. MYTHICAL implies a purely fanciful explanation of facts or the creation of beings and events out of the imagination ⟨*mythical* creatures⟩. APOCRYPHAL implies an unknown or dubious source or origin or may imply that the thing itself is dubious or inaccurate ⟨a book that repeats many *apocryphal* stories⟩.
fic·tive \ˈfik-tiv\ *adj* (1612) **1 :** not genuine **:** FEIGNED **2 :** of, relating to, or capable of imaginative creation **3 :** of, relating to, or having the characteristics of fiction **:** FICTIONAL — **fic·tive·ly** *adv* — **fic·tive·ness** *n*
fi·cus \ˈfī-kəs\ *n, pl* **ficus** *or* **fi·cus·es** [NL, fr. L, fig] (1693) **:** FIG 1b
fid \ˈfid\ *n* [origin unknown] (1615) **:** a tapered usu. wooden pin used in opening the strands of a rope
-fid *adj comb form* [L *-fidus,* fr. *findere* to split — more at BITE] **:** divided into (so many) parts or (such) parts ⟨pinnati*fid*⟩
[1]**fid·dle** \ˈfi-dᵊl\ *n* [ME *fidel,* fr. OE **fithele,* prob. fr. ML *vitula*] (13c) **1 :** VIOLIN **2 :** a device (as a slat, rack, or light railing) to keep objects from sliding off a table aboard ship **3 :** FIDDLESTICKS — used as an interjection **4** [[2]*fiddle*] *chiefly Brit* **:** SWINDLE
[2]**fiddle** *vb* **fid·dled; fid·dling** \ˈfid-liŋ, ˈfi-dᵊl-iŋ\ *vi* (14c) **1 :** to play on a fiddle **2 a :** to move the hands or fingers restlessly **b :** to spend time in aimless or fruitless activity **:** PUTTER, TINKER ⟨*fiddled* around with the engine for hours⟩ **c :** MEDDLE, TAMPER **d :** to make minor manual movements esp. to adjust something ⟨*fiddled* with the radio knobs⟩ ~ *vt* **1 :** to play (as a tune) on a fiddle **2 :** CHEAT, SWINDLE **3 :** to alter or manipulate deceptively for fraudulent gain ⟨accountants *fiddling* the books —Stanley Cohen⟩ — **fid·dler** \ˈfid-lər, ˈfi-dᵊl-ər\ *n*
fiddle away *vt* (1667) **:** to fritter away ⟨*fiddling away* the time⟩
fid·dle·back \ˈfi-dᵊl-ˌbak\ *n* (1890) **:** something resembling a fiddle
fid·dle–fad·dle \ˈfi-dᵊl-ˌfa-dᵊl\ *n* [redupl. of *fiddle* (fiddlesticks)] (1577) **:** NONSENSE — often used as an interjection
fid·dle–foot·ed \ˌfi-dᵊl-ˈfu̇-təd\ *adj* (1941) **1 :** SKITTISH, JUMPY ⟨a ~ horse⟩ **2 :** prone to wander ⟨the nameless ~ drifters, the shifty riders who traveled the back trails —Luke Short⟩
fid·dle·head \ˈfi-dᵊl-ˌhed\ *n* (1882) **:** one of the young unfurling fronds of some ferns that are often eaten as greens — called also *fiddlehead fern*
fiddler crab *n* (1843) **:** any of a genus (*Uca*) of burrowing crabs in which the male has one claw that is greatly enlarged
fid·dle·stick \ˈfi-dᵊl-ˌstik\ *n* (15c) **1 :** a violin bow **2 a :** something of little value **:** TRIFLE ⟨didn't care a ~ for that⟩ **b** *pl* **:** NONSENSE — used as an interjection
fiddling *adj* (1652) **:** TRIFLING, PETTY ⟨a ~ excuse⟩
fid·dly \ˈfi-dᵊl-ē\ *adj* (1926) *chiefly Brit* **:** requiring close attention to detail **:** FUSSY; *esp* **:** requiring an annoying amount of close attention ⟨the tiny control buttons on the back are ~ —M. J. McNamara⟩
fi·de·ism \ˈfē-(ˌ)dā-ˌi-zəm\ *n* [prob. fr. F *fidéisme,* fr. L *fides*] (1885) **:** reliance on faith rather than reason in pursuit of religious truth — **fi·de·ist** \-ˌdā-ist\ *n* — **fi·de·is·tic** \ˌfē-(ˌ)dā-ˈis-tik\ *adj*
Fi·del·is·ta \ˌfē-də-ˈlē-stə\ *n* [AmerSp, fr. *Fidel* Castro + *-ista* -ist] (1960) **:** an adherent of Castroism
fi·del·i·ty \fə-ˈde-lə-tē, fī-\ *n, pl* **-ties** [ME *fidelite,* fr. MF & L; MF *fidelité,* fr. L *fidelitat-, fidelitas,* fr. *fidelis* faithful, fr. *fides* faith, fr. *fidere* to trust — more at BIDE] (15c) **1 a :** the quality or state of being faithful **b :** accuracy in details **:** EXACTNESS **2 :** the degree to which an electronic device (as a record player, radio, or television) accurately reproduces its effect (as sound or picture)
syn FIDELITY, ALLEGIANCE, FEALTY, LOYALTY, DEVOTION, PIETY mean faithfulness to something to which one is bound by pledge or duty. FIDELITY implies strict and continuing faithfulness to an obligation, trust, or duty ⟨marital *fidelity*⟩. ALLEGIANCE suggests an adherence like that of citizens to their country ⟨pledging *allegiance*⟩. FEALTY implies a fidelity acknowledged by the individual and as compelling as a sworn vow ⟨*fealty* to the truth⟩. LOYALTY implies a faithfulness that is steadfast in the face of any temptation to renounce, desert, or betray ⟨valued the *loyalty* of his friends⟩. DEVOTION stresses zeal and service amounting to self-dedication ⟨a painter's *devotion* to her art⟩. PIETY stresses fidelity to obligations regarded as natural and fundamental ⟨filial *piety*⟩.
fidge \ˈfij\ *vi* **fidged; fidg·ing** [prob. alter. of E dial. *fitch,* fr. ME *fichen*] (1575) *chiefly Scot* **:** FIDGET
[1]**fidg·et** \ˈfi-jət\ *n* [irreg. fr. *fidge*] (1674) **1 :** uneasiness or restlessness as shown by nervous movements — usu. used in pl. **2** [[2]*fidget*] **:** one that fidgets
[2]**fidget** *vi* (1754) **:** to move or act restlessly or nervously ~ *vt* **:** to cause to move or act nervously
fidg·ety \ˈfi-jə-tē\ *adj* (ca. 1736) **1 :** inclined to fidget **2 :** making unnecessary fuss **:** FUSSY — **fidg·et·i·ness** *n*
fi·do \ˈfī-(ˌ)dō\ *n, pl* **fidos** [*f*reaks + *i*rregulars + *d*efects + *o*ddities] (1967) **:** a coin having a minting error
fi·du·cial \fə-ˈdü-shəl, -ˈdyü-, fī-\ *adj* (1571) **1 :** taken as standard of reference ⟨a ~ mark⟩ **2 :** founded on faith or trust **3 :** having the nature of a trust **:** FIDUCIARY — **fi·du·cial·ly** \-shə-lē\ *adv*
[1]**fi·du·cia·ry** \-ˈdü-shē-ˌer-ē, -shə-rē, -ˈdyü-\ *n, pl* **-ries** (1631) **:** one that holds a fiduciary relation or acts in a fiduciary capacity
[2]**fiduciary** *adj* [L *fiduciarius,* fr. *fiducia* confidence, trust, fr. *fidere*] (ca. 1641) **:** of, relating to, or involving a confidence or trust: as **a :** held or founded in trust or confidence **b :** holding in trust **c :** depending on public confidence for value or currency ⟨~ fiat money⟩
fie \ˈfī\ *interj* [ME *fi,* fr. AF] (14c) — used to express disgust or disapproval
fief \ˈfēf\ *n* [F, fr. OF — more at FEE] (ca. 1611) **1 :** a feudal estate **:** FEE **2 :** something over which one has rights or exercises control ⟨a politician's ~⟩ — **fief·dom** \-dəm\ *n*
[1]**field** \ˈfēld\ *n* [ME, fr. OE *feld;* akin to OHG *feld* field, OE *flōr* floor — more at FLOOR] (bef. 12c) **1 a** (1) **:** an open land area free of woods and buildings (2) **:** an area of land marked by the presence of particular objects or features ⟨dune ~*s*⟩ **b** (1) **:** an area of cleared enclosed land used for cultivation or pasture ⟨a ~ of wheat⟩ (2) **:** land containing a natural resource (3) **:** AIRFIELD **c :** the place where a battle is fought; *also* **:** BATTLE **d :** a large unbroken expanse (as of ice) **2 a :** an area or division of an activity, subject, or profession **b :** the sphere of practical operation outside a base (as a laboratory, office, or factory) ⟨geologists working in the ~⟩ **c :** an area for military exercises or maneuvers **d** (1) **:** an area constructed, equipped, or marked for sports (2) **:** the portion of an indoor or outdoor sports area enclosed by the running track and on which field events are conducted (3) **:** any of the three sections of a baseball outfield ⟨hits to all ~*s*⟩ **3 :** a space on which something is drawn or projected: as **a :** the space on the surface of a coin, medal, or seal that does not contain the design **b :** the ground of each division in a flag **c :** the whole surface of an escutcheon **4 :** the individuals that make up all or part of the participants in a contest; *esp* **:** all participants with the exception of the favorite or the winner in a contest where more than two are entered **5 :** the area visible through the lens of an optical instrument **6 a :** a region or space in which a given effect (as magnetism) exists **b :** a region of em-

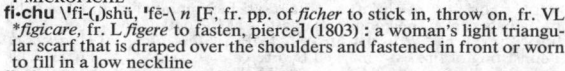

bryonic tissue capable of a particular type of differentiation ⟨a morphogenetic ~⟩ **7** : a set of mathematical elements that is subject to two binary operations the second of which is distributive relative to the first and that constitutes a commutative group under the first operation and also under the second if the zero or unit element under the first is omitted **8** : a complex of forces that serve as causative agents in human behavior **9** : a series of drain tiles and an absorption area for septic-tank outflow **10** : a particular area (as of a record in a database) in which the same type of information is regularly recorded — **from the field** : in field goals as opposed to free throws ⟨made 40 percent of his shots *from the field*⟩

[2]**field** *adj* (12c) : of or relating to a field: as **a** : growing in or inhabiting the fields or open country **b** : made, conducted, or used in the field **c** : operating or active in the field

[3]**field** *vt* (1823) **1 a** : to catch or pick up (as a batted ball) and usu. throw to a teammate **b** : to take care of or respond to (as a telephone call or a request) **c** : to give an impromptu answer or solution to ⟨the senator ~*ed* the reporters' questions⟩ **2** : to put into the field ⟨~ an army⟩ ⟨~ a team⟩; *also* : to enter in competition ~ *vi* : to play as a fielder

field artillery *n* (1644) : artillery other than antiaircraft artillery used with armies in the field

field bed *n* (1590) : a four-poster with a canopy arched at the center

field corn *n* (1856) : an Indian corn (as dent corn or flint corn) with starchy kernels grown for feeding livestock or for market grain

field crop *n* (1860) : an agricultural crop (as hay, grain, or cotton) grown on large areas

field day *n* (1747) **1 a** : a day for military exercises or maneuvers **b** : an outdoor meeting or social gathering **c** : a day of sports and athletic competition **2** : a time of extraordinary pleasure or opportunity ⟨the newspaper had a *field day* with the scandal⟩

field–ef·fect transistor \ˈfēld-ə-ˌfekt-\ *n* (1953) : a transistor in which the output current is controlled by a variable electric field

field·er \ˈfēl-dər\ *n* (1832) : one that fields; *esp* : a defensive player stationed in the field (as in baseball)

fielder's choice *n* (1902) : a situation in baseball in which a batter reaches base safely because the fielder attempts to put out another base runner on the play

field event *n* (1899) : an event (as weight-throwing or jumping) in a track-and-field meet other than a race

field·fare \ˈfēl(d)-ˌfer\ *n* [ME *feldefare,* fr. OE, fr. *feld* + *-fare;* prob. akin to OE *fara* companion; akin to OE *faran* to go — more at FARE] (bef. 12c) : a medium-sized Eurasian thrush (*Turdus pilaris*) with an ash-colored head and chestnut wings and back

field glass *n* (1836) : a binocular without prisms esp. for use outdoors — usu. used in pl.

field goal *n* (1902) **1** : a score of three points in football made by drop-kicking or place-kicking the ball over the crossbar from ordinary play **2** : a goal in basketball made while the ball is in play

field grade *n* (1944) : the rank of a field officer

field guide *n* (1934) : an illustrated manual for identifying natural objects, flora, or fauna found in nature

field hand *n* (1826) : an outdoor farm laborer

field hockey *n* (1903) : a game played on a turfed field between two teams of 11 players each whose object is to direct a ball into the opponent's goal with a hockey stick

field house *n* (1895) **1** : a building at an athletic field for housing equipment or providing dressing facilities **2** : a building enclosing a large area suitable for various forms of athletics and usu. providing seats for spectators

fielding percentage *n* (1972) : the average (as of a baseball fielder) determined by dividing the number of putouts and assists by the number of chances — called also *fielding average*; compare BATTING AVERAGE

field judge *n* (ca. 1929) : a football official whose duties include covering action on kicks and forward passes and timing intermission periods and time-outs

field lens *n* (1837) : the lens in a compound eyepiece that is nearer the objective

field magnet *n* (1883) : a magnet for producing and maintaining a magnetic field esp. in a generator or electric motor

field marshal *n* (1614) : the highest ranking military officer (as in the British army)

field mouse *n* (15c) : any of various mice and voles that inhabit fields

field mushroom *n* (1832) : MEADOW MUSHROOM

field officer *n* (1656) : a commissioned officer in the army, air force, or marine corps of the rank of colonel, lieutenant colonel, or major — compare COMPANY OFFICER, GENERAL OFFICER

field of force (1850) : FIELD 6a

field of honor (1824) **1** : BATTLEFIELD **2** : a place where a duel is fought

field of view (ca. 1816) : FIELD 5

field of vision (1862) : VISUAL FIELD

field pea *n* (1709) **1** : a small-seeded pea (*Pisum sativum* var. *arvense*) widely grown for forage, food, and green manure; *also* : its usu. dried green or yellow seed — compare SPLIT PEA **2** : COW PEA

field·piece \ˈfēl(d)-ˌpēs\ *n* (1590) : a gun or howitzer for use in the field

field spaniel *n* (1867) : any of a breed of medium-sized hunting and retrieving spaniels developed in England that have a flat dense usu. black, liver, red, or roan coat

field·stone \ˈfēl(d)-ˌstōn\ *n* (1799) : stone (as in building) in usu. unaltered form as taken from the field

field·strip \-ˌstrip\ *vt* (1947) : to take apart (a weapon) to the extent authorized for routine cleaning, lubrication, and minor repairs

field–test \-ˌtest\ *vt* (1948) : to test (as a procedure or product) in actual situations reflecting intended use — **field test** *n*

field theory *n* (1901) : any theory in physics consisting of a detailed mathematical description of the assumed physical properties of a region under some influence (as gravitation)

field trial *n* (1849) **1** : a trial of sporting dogs in actual performance **2** : a trial of a new product in actual situations for which it is intended

field trip *n* (1926) : a visit (as to a factory, farm, or museum) made (as by students and a teacher) for purposes of firsthand observation

field winding *n* (1893) : the winding of a field magnet

field·work \ˈfēld-ˌwərk\ *n* (1819) **1** : a temporary fortification thrown up by an army in the field **2** : work done in the field (as by students) to gain practical experience and knowledge through firsthand observation **3** : the gathering of anthropological or sociological data through the interviewing and observation of subjects in the field — **field–work·er** *n*

fiend \ˈfēnd\ *n* [ME, fr. OE *fēond;* akin to OHG *fīant* enemy, Skt *pīyati* he reviles, blames] (bef. 12c) **1 a** : DEVIL 1 **b** : DEMON **c** : a person of great wickedness or maliciousness **2** : a person extremely devoted to a pursuit or study : FANATIC ⟨a golf ~⟩ **3** : ADDICT 1 ⟨a dope ~⟩ **4** : WIZARD 3 ⟨a ~ at mathematics⟩

fiend·ish \ˈfēn-dish\ *adj* (1529) **1** : perversely diabolical ⟨took a ~ pleasure in hurting people⟩ **2** : extremely cruel or wicked **3** : excessively bad, unpleasant, or difficult ⟨~ weather⟩ — **fiend·ish·ly** *adv* — **fiend·ish·ness** *n*

fierce \ˈfirs\ *adj* **fierc·er; fierc·est** [ME *fiers,* fr. AF *fer, fers, fiers,* fr. L *ferus* wild, savage; akin to Gk *thēr* wild animal] (14c) **1 a** : violently hostile or aggressive in temperament **b** : given to fighting or killing : PUGNACIOUS **2 a** : marked by unrestrained zeal or vehemence ⟨a ~ argument⟩ **b** : extremely vexatious, disappointing, or intense ⟨~ pain⟩ **3** : furiously active or determined ⟨make a ~ effort⟩ **4** : wild or menacing in appearance — **fierce·ness** *n*

syn FIERCE, FEROCIOUS, BARBAROUS, SAVAGE, CRUEL mean showing fury or malignity in looks or actions. FIERCE applies to humans and animals that inspire terror because of their wild and menacing aspect or fury in attack ⟨*fierce* warriors⟩. FEROCIOUS implies extreme fierceness and unrestrained violence and brutality ⟨a *ferocious* dog⟩. BARBAROUS implies a ferocity or mercilessness regarded as unworthy of civilized people ⟨*barbarous* treatment of prisoners⟩. SAVAGE implies the absence of inhibitions restraining civilized people filled with rage, lust, or other violent passion ⟨a *savage* criminal⟩. CRUEL implies indifference to suffering and even positive pleasure in inflicting it ⟨the *cruel* jokes of schoolboys⟩.

fierce·ly *adv* (14c) **1** : in a fierce or vehement manner ⟨~ competitive⟩ **2** : to a high degree : VERY ⟨~ expensive⟩

fi·eri fa·cias \ˌfī-(ə-)rē-ˈfā-sh(ē-)əs\ *n* [L, cause (it) to be done] (15c) : a writ authorizing the sheriff to obtain satisfaction of a judgment in debt or damages from the goods and chattels of the defendant

fi·ery \ˈfī(-ə)-rē\ *adj* **fi·er·i·er; -est** [ME, fr. *fire, fier* fire] (13c) **1 a** : consisting of fire **b** : marked by fire ⟨a ~ crash⟩ **c** : using or carried out with fire **d** : liable to catch fire or explode : FLAMMABLE ⟨a ~ vapor⟩ **2 a** : hot like a fire **b** (1) : being in an inflamed state or condition ⟨a ~ boil⟩ (2) : feverish and flushed ⟨a ~ forehead⟩ **3** : of the color of fire : RED ⟨a ~ sunset⟩ **4 a** : full of or exuding emotion or spirit ⟨a ~ sermon⟩ **b** : easily provoked : IRRITABLE ⟨a ~ temper⟩ — **fi·eri·ly** \ˈfī-rə-lē\ *adv* — **fi·eri·ness** \ˈfī-rē-nəs\ *n* — **fiery** *adv*

fi·es·ta \fē-ˈes-tə\ *n* [Sp, fr. L *festa* — more at FEAST] (1844) : FESTIVAL; *specif* : a saint's day celebrated in Spain and Latin America with processions and dances

fi fa *abbr* fieri facias

fife \ˈfīf\ *n* [G *Pfeife* pipe, fife, fr. OHG *pfīfa,* fr. VL **pipa* pipe — more at PIPE] (1539) : a small transverse flute with six to eight finger holes and usu. no keys

fife rail *n* (ca. 1800) : a rail about the mast near the deck to which rigging is belayed

FIFO *abbr* first in, first out

fif·teen \ˌfif-ˈtēn, ˈfif-ˌ\ *n* [ME *fiftene,* adj., fr. OE *fīftēne,* fr. *fīf* five + *-tīene* (akin to OE *tīen* ten) — more at FIVE, TEN] (bef. 12c) **1** — see NUMBER table **2** : the first point scored by a side in a game of tennis — called also *five* — **fifteen** *adj* — **fifteen** *pron, pl in constr* — **fif·teenth** \-ˈtēn(t)th, -ˌtēn(t)th\ *adj or n*

fifth \ˈfith, ˈfif(t)th, ˈfift\ *n, pl* **fifths** \ˈfiths, ˈfif(t)ths, ˈfif(t)s\ [ME *fifte, fifthe,* fr. OE *fīfta,* fr. *fīf* five] (bef. 12c) **1** — see NUMBER table **2 a** : the musical interval embracing five diatonic degrees **b** : a tone at this interval; *specif* : DOMINANT 1 **c** : the harmonic combination of two tones at this interval **3** : a unit of measure for liquor equal to one fifth of a U.S. gallon (0.757 liter) **4** *cap* : the Fifth Amendment of the U.S. Constitution; *also* : the right accorded by the Fifth Amendment to refuse to testify against oneself — usu. used in the phrase *take the Fifth* — **fifth** *adj or adv* — **fifth·ly** *adv*

fifth column *n* [name applied to rebel sympathizers in Madrid in 1936 when four rebel columns were advancing on the city] (1936) : a group of secret sympathizers or supporters of an enemy that engage in espionage or sabotage within defense lines or national borders — **fifth col·um·nism** \-ˈkä-ləm-ˌ(n)i-zəm\ *n* — **fifth col·um·nist** \-(n)ist\ *n*

fifth disease *n* [fr. its enumeration as the fifth of five exanthematous childhood diseases known at the time of its description] (ca. 1941) : an acute virus disease esp. of children caused by a parvovirus (species *Human parvovirus B19* of the genus *Erythrovirus*) and manifested by a blotchy red rash on the cheeks which spreads to the extremities and is usu. accompanied by fever and malaise

fifth wheel *n* (ca. 1874) **1 a** : a horizontal wheel or segment of a wheel that consists of two parts rotating on each other above the fore axle of a carriage and that forms support to prevent tipping **b** : a similar coupling between tractor and trailer of a semitrailer **2** : one that is superfluous, unnecessary, or burdensome

fif·ty \ˈfif-tē\ *n, pl* **fifties** [ME, fr. *fifty,* adj., fr. OE *fīftig,* fr. *fīftig,* n., group of 50, fr. *fīf* five + *-tig* group of ten; akin to *tīen* ten] (bef. 12c) **1** — see NUMBER table **2** *pl* : the numbers 50 to 59; *specif* : the years 50 to 59 in a lifetime or century **3** : a 50-dollar bill — **fif·ti·eth** \-tē-əth\ *adj or n* — **fifty** *adj* — **fifty** *pron, pl in constr* — **fif·ty·ish** \-tē-ish\ *adj*

fif·ty–fif·ty \ˌfif-tē-ˈfif-tē\ *adj* (1913) **1** : shared, assumed, or borne equally ⟨a ~ proposition⟩ **2** : half favorable and half unfavorable ⟨a ~ chance⟩ — **fifty–fifty** *adv*

[1]**fig** \ˈfig\ *n* [ME *fige,* fr. AF, fr. Old Occitan *figa,* fr. VL **fica,* fr. L *ficus* fig tree, fig] (13c) **1 a** : an oblong or pear-shaped syconium fruit of a tree (genus *Ficus*) of the mulberry family **b** : a tree bearing figs; *esp* : a widely

fig 1

cultivated tree (*F. carica*) that produces edible figs **2 :** a worthless trifle : the least bit ⟨doesn't care a ~⟩

²fig *n* [*fig,* vb., to adorn] (1835) : DRESS, ARRAY ⟨a young woman in dazzling royal full ~ —Mollie Panter-Downes⟩

³fig *abbr* figurative; figuratively; figure

¹fight \ˈfīt\ *vb* **fought** \ˈfȯt\; **fight·ing** [ME, fr. OE *feohtan;* akin to OHG *fehtan* to fight and perh. to L *pectere* to comb — more at PECTINATE] *vi* (bef. 12c) **1 a :** to contend in battle or physical combat; *esp* **:** to strive to overcome a person by blows or weapons **b :** to engage in boxing **2 :** to put forth a determined effort ~ *vt* **1 a** (1) **:** to contend against in or as if in battle or physical combat (2) **:** to box against in the ring **b** (1) **:** to attempt to prevent the success or effectiveness of ⟨the company *fought* the takeover attempt⟩ (2) **:** to oppose the passage or development of ⟨~ a bill in Congress⟩ **2 a :** WAGE, CARRY ON ⟨~ a battle⟩ **b :** to take part in (as a boxing match) **3 :** to struggle to endure or surmount ⟨~ a cold⟩ **4 a :** to gain by struggle ⟨~*s* his way through⟩ **b :** to resolve by struggle ⟨*fought* out their differences in court⟩ **5 a :** to manage (a ship) in a battle or storm **b :** to cause to struggle or contend **c :** to manage in an unnecessarily rough or awkward manner — **fight shy of :** to avoid facing or meeting

²fight *n* (bef. 12c) **1 a :** a hostile encounter : BATTLE, COMBAT **b :** a boxing match **c :** a verbal disagreement : ARGUMENT **2 :** a struggle for a goal or an objective ⟨a ~ for justice⟩ **3 :** strength or disposition for fighting : PUGNACITY ⟨still full of ~⟩

fight·er \ˈfī-tər\ *n* (13c) **:** one that fights: as **a** (1) **:** WARRIOR, SOLDIER (2) **:** a pugnacious or game individual (3) **:** ¹BOXER 1 **b :** an airplane of high speed and maneuverability with armament designed to destroy enemy aircraft

fight·er–bomb·er \-ˈbä-mər\ *n* (1936) **:** a fighter aircraft fitted to carry bombs and rockets in addition to its normal armament

fighting chair *n* (1950) **:** a chair from which a salt-water angler plays a hooked fish

fighting chance *n* (1889) **:** a chance that may be realized by a struggle ⟨the patient had a *fighting chance* to live⟩

fighting word *n* (1917) **:** a word likely to provoke a fight

fight–or–flight *adj* (1973) **:** relating to, being, or causing physiological changes in the body (as an increase in heart rate or dilation of bronchi) in response to stress ⟨epinephrine is a ~ hormone⟩ ⟨a ~ reaction⟩

fight song *n* (1954) **:** a song used to inspire enthusiasm usu. during an athletic competition

fig leaf *n* (14c) **1 :** the leaf of a fig tree **2** [fr. the use by Adam and Eve of fig leaves to cover their nakedness after eating the forbidden fruit (Gen. 3:7)] **:** something that conceals or camouflages usu. inadequately or dishonestly

fig·ment \ˈfig-mənt\ *n* [ME, fr. L *figmentum,* fr. *fingere* to shape — more at DOUGH] (15c) **:** something made up or contrived

fig·ur·al \ˈfi-g(y)ə-rəl\ *adj* (15c) **1 :** FIGURATIVE 2a **2 :** of, relating to, or consisting of human or animal figures ⟨a ~ composition⟩

fig·u·ra·tion \ˌfi-g(y)ə-ˈrā-shən\ *n* (14c) **1 :** FORM, OUTLINE **2 :** the act or process of creating or providing a figure **3 :** an act or instance of representation in figures and shapes ⟨cubism was explained as a synthesis of colored ~*s* of objects —Janet Flanner⟩ **4 :** ornamentation of a musical passage by using decorative and usu. repetitive figures

fig·u·ra·tive \ˈfi-g(y)ə-rə-tiv\ *adj* (14c) **1 a :** representing by a figure or resemblance : EMBLEMATIC **b :** of or relating to representation of form or figure in art ⟨~ sculpture⟩ **2 a :** expressing one thing in terms normally denoting another with which it may be regarded as analogous : METAPHORICAL ⟨~ language⟩ **b :** characterized by figures of speech ⟨a ~ description⟩ — **fig·u·ra·tive·ly** *adv* — **fig·u·ra·tive·ness** *n*

¹fig·ure \ˈfi-gyər, *Brit & often US* ˈfi-gər\ *n* [ME, fr. AF, fr. L *figura,* fr. *fingere*] (13c) **1 a :** a number symbol : NUMERAL, DIGIT **b** *pl* **:** arithmetical calculations ⟨good at ~*s*⟩ **c :** a written or printed character **d :** value esp. as expressed in numbers : SUM, PRICE ⟨sold at a low ~⟩ **e** *pl* **:** digits representing an amount (as of money earned or points scored) ⟨made six ~*s* last year⟩ ⟨a score in double ~*s*⟩ **2 a :** a geometric form (as a line, triangle, or sphere) esp. when considered as a set of geometric elements (as points) in space of a given number of dimensions ⟨a square is a plane ~⟩ **b :** bodily shape or form esp. of a person ⟨a slender ~⟩ **c :** an object noticeable only as a shape or form ⟨~*s* moving in the dusk⟩ **3 a :** the graphic representation of a form esp. of a person or geometric entity **b :** a diagram or pictorial illustration of textual matter **4 :** a person, thing, or action representative of another **5 a :** FIGURE OF SPEECH **b :** an intentional deviation from the ordinary form or syntactical relation of words **6 :** the form of a syllogism with respect to the relative position of the middle term **7 :** an often repetitive pattern or design in a manufactured article (as cloth) or natural product (as wood) ⟨a polka-dot ~⟩ **8 :** appearance made : impression produced ⟨the couple cut quite a ~⟩ **9 a :** a series of movements in a dance **b :** an outline representation of a form traced by a series of evolutions (as with skates on an ice surface or by an airplane in the air) **10 :** a prominent personality : PERSONAGE ⟨great ~*s* of history⟩ **11 :** a short coherent group of notes or chords that may constitute part of a phrase, theme, or composition

²figure *vb* **fig·ured; fig·ur·ing** \ˈfi-gyə-riŋ, ˈfi-g(ə-)riŋ\ *vt* (14c) **1 :** to represent by or as if by a figure or outline **2 :** to decorate with a pattern; *also* **:** to write figures over or under (the bass) in order to indicate the accompanying chords **3 :** to indicate or represent by numerals **4 a :** CALCULATE **b :** CONCLUDE, DECIDE ⟨*figured* there was no use in further effort⟩; *also* **:** ASSUME ⟨~ it will rain⟩ **c :** REGARD, CONSIDER **d :** to appear likely ⟨~*s* to win⟩ ~ *vi* **1 a :** to be or appear important or conspicuous **b :** to be involved or implicated ⟨*figured* in a robbery⟩ **2 :** to perform a figure in dancing **3 :** COMPUTE, CALCULATE **4 :** to seem rational, normal, or expected ⟨that ~*s*⟩ **5 :** to make sense of something — used interjectionally in the phrase *go figure* to suggest that something is surprising or perplexing ⟨why do they think women will buy this lie? Go ~ —Ellen Bravo⟩ — **fig·ur·er** \-g(y)ər-ər\ *n* — **figure on 1 :** to take into consideration ⟨*figuring on* the extra income⟩ **2 :** to rely on **3 :** PLAN ⟨I *figure on* going into town⟩

figured *adj* (15c) **1 :** adorned with, formed into, or marked with a figure ⟨~ muslin⟩ ⟨~ wood⟩ **2 :** being represented : PORTRAYED **3 :** indicated by figures

figured bass *n* (1801) **:** CONTINUO

figure eight *n* (1748) **:** something resembling the Arabic numeral eight in form or shape: as **a :** a small knot — see KNOT illustration **b :** an embroidery stitch **c :** a dance pattern **d :** a skater's figure — called also *figure-of-eight*

fig·ure·head \ˈfi-g(y)ər-ˌhed\ *n* (1765) **1 :** the figure on a ship's bow **2 :** a head or chief in name only

figure in *vt* (ca. 1934) **:** to include esp. in a reckoning

figure of merit (ca. 1865) **:** a numerical quantity based on one or more characteristics of a system or device that represents a measure of efficiency or effectiveness

figure of speech (1751) **:** a form of expression (as a simile or metaphor) used to convey meaning or heighten effect often by comparing or identifying one thing with another that has a meaning or connotation familiar to the reader or listener

figure out *vt* (1600) **1 :** DISCOVER, DETERMINE ⟨try to *figure out* a way to do it⟩ **2 :** SOLVE, FATHOM ⟨*figure out* a problem⟩

figure skating *n* (1852) **:** skating characterized by the performance of various jumps, spins, and dance movements and formerly by the tracing of prescribed figures — **figure skater** *n*

fig·u·rine \ˌfi-g(y)ə-ˈrēn\ *n* [F, fr. It *figurina,* dim. of *figura* figure, fr. L — more at FIGURE] (1854) **:** a small carved or molded figure : STATUETTE

fig wasp *n* (1883) **:** a minute wasp (*Blastophaga psenes* of the family Agaontidae) that breeds in the caprifig and is the agent of caprification; *broadly* **:** any wasp of the same family

fig·wort \ˈfig-ˌwərt, -ˌwȯrt\ *n* (1548) **:** any of a genus (*Scrophularia*) of chiefly herbaceous often fetid plants of the snapdragon family with terminal cymes of small purple, yellow, or greenish flowers

Fi·ji·an \ˈfē-(ˌ)jē-ən, fi-ˈ\ *n* (1809) **1 :** a member of a Melanesian people of Fiji **2 :** the Austronesian language of the Fijians — **Fijian** *adj*

fil·a·ment \ˈfi-lə-mənt\ *n* [MF, fr. ML *filamentum,* fr. LL *filare* to spin — more at FILE] (1594) **:** a single thread or a thin flexible threadlike object, process, or appendage: as **a :** a tenuous conductor (as of carbon or metal) made incandescent by the passage of an electric current; *specif* **:** a cathode in the form of a metal wire in an electron tube **b** (1) **:** a thin and fine elongated constituent part of a gill (2) **:** an elongated thin series of cells attached one to another or a very long thin cylindrical single cell (as of some algae, fungi, or bacteria) **c :** the anther-bearing stalk of a stamen — see FLOWER illustration — **fil·a·men·ta·ry** \ˌfil-ə-ˈmen-t(ə-)rē\ *adj* — **fil·a·men·tous** \-ˈmen-təs\ *adj*

fi·lar \ˈfī-lər\ *adj* [L *filum* thread] (ca. 1859) **:** of or relating to a thread or line; *esp* **:** having threads across the field of view ⟨a ~ eyepiece⟩

fi·lar·ia \fə-ˈler-ē-ə\ *n, pl* **-i·ae** \-ē-ˌē, -ē-ˌī\ [NL, genus name, fr. L *filum*] (1833) **:** any of numerous slender filamentous nematodes (*Filaria* and related genera) that as adults are parasites in the blood or tissues of mammals and as larvae usu. develop in biting insects — **fi·lar·i·al** \-ē-əl\ *adj* — **fi·lar·i·id** \-ē-əd\ *adj or n*

fil·a·ri·a·sis \ˌfi-lə-ˈrī-ə-səs\ *n, pl* **-a·ses** \-ˌsēz\ [NL] (1879) **:** infestation with or disease caused by filariae

fil·a·ture \ˈfil-ə-ˌchu̇r, -chər, -ˌt(y)u̇r\ *n* [F, fr. LL *filatus,* pp. of *filare*] (1759) **:** a factory where silk is reeled

fil·bert \ˈfil-bərt\ *n* [ME, fr. AF *philber,* fr. St. *Philibert* †684 Frankish abbot whose feast day falls in the nutting season] (14c) **1 :** either of two Eurasian hazels (*Corylus avellana* and *C. maxima*) **2 :** the sweet thick-shelled nut of the filbert; *broadly* **:** HAZELNUT

filch \ˈfilch\ *vt* [ME] (1561) **:** to appropriate furtively or casually ⟨~ a cookie⟩ ***syn*** see STEAL

¹file \ˈfī(-ə)l\ *n* [ME, fr. OE *fēol;* akin to OHG *fīla* file] (bef. 12c) **1 :** a tool usu. of hardened steel with cutting ridges for forming or smoothing surfaces esp. of metal **2 :** a shrewd or crafty person

²file *vt* **filed; fil·ing** (13c) **:** to rub, smooth, or cut away with or as if with a file

³file *vt* **filed; fil·ing** [ME, fr. OE *fȳlan,* fr. *fūl* foul] (bef. 12c) *chiefly dial* **:** DEFILE, CORRUPT

⁴file *vb* **filed; fil·ing** [ME, fr. ML *filare* to string documents on a string or wire, fr. *filum* file of documents, lit., thread, fr. L; akin to Arm *ǰil* sinew] *vt* (15c) **1 :** to arrange in order for preservation and reference ⟨~ letters⟩ **2 a :** to place among official records as prescribed by law ⟨~ a mortgage⟩ **b :** to send (copy) to a newspaper ⟨*filed* a story⟩ **c :** to return to the office of the clerk of a court without action on the merits **3 :** to initiate (as a legal action) through proper formal procedure ⟨threatened to ~ charges⟩ ~ *vi* **1 :** to register as a candidate esp. in a primary election **2 :** to place items in a file **3 :** to submit documents necessary to initiate a legal proceeding ⟨~ for bankruptcy⟩ — **fil·er** \ˈfī-lər\ *n*

⁵file *n* (1525) **1 :** a device (as a folder, case, or cabinet) by means of which papers are kept in order **2 a** *archaic* **:** ROLL, LIST **b :** a collection of papers or publications usu. arranged or classified **c** (1) **:** a collection of related data records (as for a computer) (2) **:** a complete collection of data (as text or a program) treated by a computer as a unit esp. for purposes of input and output — **on file :** in or as if in a file for ready reference

⁶file *n* [MF, fr. *filer* to spin, draw out, fr. LL *filare,* fr. L *filum*] (1598) **1 :** SINGLE FILE **2 :** any of the rows of squares that extend across a chessboard from one player's side to the other player's side

⁷file *vi* **filed; filing** (1614) **:** to march or proceed in single file

fi·lé *also* **fi·le** \fə-ˈlā, (ˌ)fē-ˈlā, ˈfē-(ˌ)lā\ *n* [LaF, fr. F, pp. of *filer* to twist, spin] (1806) **:** powdered young leaves of sassafras used to thicken soups or stews

file clerk *n* (1919) **:** a clerk who works on files

file·fish \ˈfī(-ə)l-ˌfish\ *n* (1681) **:** any of various small-mouthed bony fishes (family Monacantidae, esp. genera *Aluterus, Cantherhines,* and *Monacanthus*) with rough granular leathery skin

fi·let \fi-ˈlā\ *n* [F, lit., net] (1838) **:** a lace with a square mesh and geometric designs

\ə\ **abut** \ᵊ\ **kitten,** F **table** \ər\ **further** \a\ **ash** \ā\ **ace** \ä\ **mop, mar**
\au̇\ **out** \ch\ **chin** \e\ **bet** \ē\ **easy** \g\ **go** \i\ **hit** \ī\ **ice** \j\ **job**
\ŋ\ **sing** \ō\ **go** \ȯ\ **law** \ȯi\ **boy** \th\ **thin** \t͟h\ **the** \ü\ **loot** \u̇\ **foot**
\y\ **yet** \zh\ **vision, beige** \k̲, ⁿ, œ, ue, ʸ\ *see* Guide to Pronunciation

fi·let mi·gnon \ˌfi-(ˌ)lā-mēn-ˈyō^n, fi-ˌlā-\ *n, pl* **filets mignons** \ˌfi-(ˌ)lā-mēn-ˈyō^{n}z, fi-ˌlā-\ [F, lit., dainty fillet] (1835) : a thick slice of beef cut from the narrow end of a beef tenderloin

fili- *or* **filo-** *comb form* [L *filum*] : thread ⟨*fili*form⟩

fil·ial \ˈfi-lē-əl, ˈfil-yəl\ *adj* [ME, fr. LL *filialis,* fr. L *filius* son — more at FEMININE] (14c) **1** : of, relating to, or befitting a son or daughter ⟨~ obedience⟩ **2** : having or assuming the relation of a child or offspring — **fil·ial·ly** \-lē-ə-lē, -yə-lē\ *adv*

filial generation *n* (1902) : a generation in a breeding experiment that is successive to a mating between parents of two distinctively different but usu. relatively pure genotypes

fil·i·a·tion \ˌfi-lē-ˈā-shən\ *n* (15c) **1 a** : filial relationship esp. of a son to his father **b** : the adjudication of paternity **2 a** : descent or derivation esp. from a culture or language **b** : the act or process of determining such relationship

[1]fil·i·bus·ter \ˈfi-lə-ˌbəs-tər\ *n* [Sp *filibustero,* lit., freebooter] (1851) **1** : an irregular military adventurer; *specif* : an American engaged in fomenting insurrections in Latin America in the mid-19th century **2** [[2]*filibuster*] **a** : the use of extreme dilatory tactics in an attempt to delay or prevent action esp. in a legislative assembly **b** : an instance of this practice

[2]filibuster *vb* **-tered; -ter·ing** \-t(ə-)riŋ\ *vi* (1851) **1** : to carry out insurrectionist activities in a foreign country **2** : to engage in a filibuster ~ *vt* : to subject to a filibuster — **fil·i·bus·ter·er** \-tər-ər\ *n*

fil·i·cide \ˈfi-lə-ˌsīd\ *n* [L *filius* son & *filia* daughter + E *-cide*] (1665) : the murder of one's own daughter or son

fi·li·form \ˈfi-lə-ˌfȯrm, ˈfī-\ *adj* (1757) : shaped like a filament

[1]fil·i·gree \ˈfi-lə-ˌgrē\ *n* [modif. of F *filigrane,* fr. It *filigrana,* fr. L *filum* + *granum* grain — more at CORN] (1693) **1** : ornamental work esp. of fine wire of gold, silver, or copper applied chiefly to gold and silver surfaces **2 a** : ornamental openwork of delicate or intricate design **b** : a pattern or design resembling such openwork ⟨a ~ of frost⟩ **c** : ORNAMENTATION, EMBELLISHMENT ⟨writings . . . heavy with late Victorian ~ —Jack Beatty⟩

filigree 2a

[2]filigree *vt* **fil·i·greed; fil·i·gree·ing** (1831) : to adorn with or as if with filigree

[1]fil·ing \ˈfī-liŋ\ *n* (14c) **1** : an act or instance of using a file **2** : a fragment rubbed off in filing ⟨iron ~*s*⟩

[2]filing *n* (1712) **1** : an act or instance of filing something **2** : a document filed

fil·io·pi·etis·tic \ˈfi-lē-ō-ˌpī-ə-ˈtis-tik\ *adj* [*fil*ial + *-o-* + *pietistic*] (1893) : of or relating to an often excessive veneration of ancestors or tradition — **fil·io·pi·e·tism** \ˌfi-lē-ō-ˈpī-ə-ˌti-zəm\ *n*

Fil·i·pi·na \ˌfi-lə-ˈpē-nə\ *n* [Sp] (1899) : a Filipino girl or woman

Fil·i·pi·no \-ˈpē-(ˌ)nō\ *n, pl* **Filipinos** [Sp] (ca. 1889) **1** : a native of the Philippine Islands **2** : a citizen of the Republic of the Philippines **3** : the Tagalog-based official language of the Republic of the Philippines — **Filipino** *adj*

[1]fill \ˈfil\ *vb* [ME, fr. OE *fyllan;* akin to OE *full* full] *vt* (bef. 12c) **1 a** : to put into as much as can be held or conveniently contained ⟨~ a cup with water⟩ **b** : to supply with a full complement ⟨the class is ~*ed*⟩ **c (1)** : to cause to swell or billow ⟨wind ~*ed* the sails⟩ **(2)** : to trim (a sail) to catch the wind **d** : to raise the level of with fill ⟨~*ed* land⟩ **e** : to repair the cavities of (teeth) **f** : to stop up : OBSTRUCT ⟨wreckage ~*ed* the channel⟩ **g** : to stop up the interstices, crevices, or pores of (as cloth, wood, or leather) with a foreign substance **2 a** : FEED, SATIATE **b** : SATISFY, FULFILL ⟨~*s* all requirements⟩ **c** : MAKE OUT, COMPLETE — used with *out* or *in* ⟨~ out a form⟩ ⟨~ in the blanks⟩ **d** : to draw the playing cards necessary to complete (as a straight or flush in poker) **3 a** : to occupy the whole of ⟨smoke ~*ed* the room⟩ **b** : to spread through ⟨music ~*ed* the air⟩ **c** : to make full ⟨a mind ~*ed* with fantasies⟩ **4 a** : to possess and perform the duties of : HOLD ⟨~ an office⟩ **b** : to place a person in ⟨~ a vacancy⟩ **5** : to supply as directed ⟨~ a prescription⟩ **6** : to cover the surface of with a layer of precious metal ~ *vi* : to become full — **fill one's shoes** : to take over one's job, position, or responsibilities

[2]fill *n* (bef. 12c) **1** : a full supply; *esp* : a quantity that satisfies or satiates ⟨eat your ~⟩ **2** : something that fills: as **a** : material used to fill a receptacle, cavity, passage, or low place **b** : a bit of instrumental music that fills the pauses between phrases (as of a vocalist or soloist) **c** : artificial light used in photography to reduce or eliminate shadows — often used attributively ⟨~ flash⟩

fill away *vi* (1645) **1** : to trim a sail to catch the wind **2** : to proceed on the course esp. after being brought up in the wind

[1]fill·er \ˈfi-lər\ *n* (15c) : one that fills: as **a** : a substance added to a product (as to increase bulk, weight, viscosity, opacity, or strength) **b** : a composition used to fill the pores and grain esp. of a wood surface before painting or varnishing **c** : a piece used to cover or fill in a space between two parts of a structure **d** : tobacco used to form the core of a cigar **e** : material used to fill extra space in a column or page of a newspaper or magazine or to increase the size of a work (as a book) **f** : a pack of paper for a loose-leaf notebook **g** : a sound, word, or phrase (as "you know?") used to fill pauses in speaking

[2]fil·ler \ˈfi-ˌler\ *n, pl* **filler** *also* **fillers** [Hung *fillér*] (1904) — see *forint* at MONEY table

[1]fil·let \ˈfi-lət, *in sense 2b also* fi-ˈlā, ˈfi-(ˌ)lā\ *also* **fi·let** \fi-ˈlā, ˈfi-(ˌ)lā\ *n* [ME *filet,* fr. AF, dim. of *fil* thread, fr. L *filum* — more at FILE] (14c) **1** : a ribbon or narrow strip of material used esp. as a headband **2 a** : a thin narrow strip of material **b** : a piece or slice of boneless meat or fish; *esp* : the tenderloin of beef **3 a** : a concave junction formed where two surfaces meet (as at an angle) **b** : a strip that gives a rounded appearance to such a junction; *also* : a strip to reinforce the corner where two surfaces meet **4** : a narrow flat architectural member: **a** : a flat molding separating others **b** : the space between two flutings in a shaft

[2]fil·let \ˈfi-lət, *in sense 2 also* fi-ˈlā, ˈfi-(ˌ)lā\ *vt* (1604) **1** : to bind, furnish, or adorn with or as if with a fillet **2** : to cut into fillets

fillet weld *n* (1926) : a weld of approximately triangular cross section used to join two pieces esp. perpendicularly

fill–in \ˈfil-ˌin\ *n* (1917) : someone or something that fills in

fill in *vt* (1840) **1** : to enrich (as a design) with detail **2** : to give necessary or recently acquired information to ⟨I'll *fill* you *in*⟩ ~ *vi* : to fill a vacancy usu. temporarily ⟨interns *filled in* for regular staffers⟩

fill·ing \ˈfi-liŋ\ *n* (14c) **1** : an act or instance of filling **2** : something used to fill a cavity, container, or depression **3** : something that completes: as **a** : the yarn interlacing the warp in a fabric; *also* : yarn for the shuttle **b** : a food mixture used to fill pastry or sandwiches

filling station *n* (1921) : GAS STATION

[1]fil·lip \ˈfi-ləp\ *vt* [prob. of imit. origin] (15c) **1 a** : to make a filliping motion with **b** : to strike or tap with a fillip ⟨~*ed* him on the nose⟩ **2** : to project quickly by or as if by a fillip ⟨~ crumbs off the table⟩ **3** : STIMULATE ⟨with this to ~ his spirits —Robert Westerby⟩

[2]fillip *n* (1519) **1 a** : a blow or gesture made by the sudden forcible straightening of a finger curled up against the thumb **b** : a short sharp blow : BUFFET **2** : something tending to arouse or excite: as **a** : STIMULUS ⟨just the ~ my confidence needed⟩ ⟨lent a ~ of danger to the sport⟩ **b** : a trivial addition : EMBELLISHMENT ⟨showy ~*s* of language⟩ **c** : a significant and often unexpected development : WRINKLE ⟨plot twists and ~*s*⟩

fill out *vi* (1856) : to put on flesh

fill–up \ˈfil-ˌəp\ *n* (1853) : an action or instance of filling up something (as a gas tank)

fil·ly \ˈfi-lē\ *n, pl* **fillies** [ME *fyly,* fr. ON *fylja;* akin to OE *fola* foal] (15c) **1** : a young female horse usu. of less than four years **2** : a young woman : GIRL

[1]film \ˈfilm, *Southern also* ˈfi(ə)m\ *n, often attrib* [ME *filme,* fr. OE *filmen;* akin to Gk *pelma* sole of the foot, OE *fell* skin — more at FELL] (bef. 12c) **1 a** : a thin skin or membranous covering : PELLICLE **b** : an abnormal growth on or in the eye **2** : a thin covering or coating ⟨a ~ of ice⟩ **3 a** : an exceedingly thin layer : LAMINA **b (1)** : a thin flexible transparent sheet (as of plastic) used esp. as a wrapping **(2)** : a thin sheet of cellulose acetate or nitrocellulose coated with a radiation-sensitive emulsion for taking photographs **4** : MOTION PICTURE — **film·less** \-ləs\ *adj*

[2]film *vt* (1602) **1** : to cover with or as if with a film **2** : to make a motion picture of or from ⟨~ a scene⟩ ~ *vi* **1** : to become covered or obscured with or as if with a film **2** : to make a motion picture — **film·able** \ˈfil-mə-bəl\ *adj*

film badge *n* (1945) : a small pack of sensitive photographic film worn as a badge for indicating exposure to radiation

film·dom \ˈfilm-dəm\ *n* (1914) : the motion-picture industry

film·go·er \-ˌgō-ər\ *n* (1919) : one who frequently attends films

film·ic \ˈfil-mik\ *adj* (ca. 1930) : of, relating to, or resembling motion pictures — **film·i·cal·ly** \-mi-k(ə-)lē\ *adv*

film·land \ˈfilm-ˌland\ *n* (1913) : FILMDOM

film·mak·er \ˈfilm-ˌmā-kər\ *n* (1908) : one who makes motion pictures

film·mak·ing \-ˌmā-kiŋ\ *n* (1913) : the making of motion pictures

film noir \-ˈnwär\ *n, pl* **film noirs** \-ˈnwär(z)\ *or* **films noir** *or* **films noirs** \-ˈnwär\ [F, lit., black film] (1958) : a type of crime film featuring cynical malevolent characters in a sleazy setting and an ominous atmosphere that is conveyed by shadowy photography and foreboding background music; *also* : a film of this type

film·og·ra·phy \fil-ˈmä-grə-fē\ *n, pl* **-phies** [*film* + *-ography* (as in *bibliography*)] (1957) : a list of motion pictures featuring the work of a prominent film figure or relating to a particular topic

film·set·ting \ˈfilm-ˌse-tiŋ\ *n* (1954) : PHOTOCOMPOSITION — **film·set·ter** *n*

film·strip \ˈfilm-ˌstrip\ *n* (1930) : a strip of film bearing a sequence of images for projection as still pictures

filmy \ˈfil-mē\ *adj* **film·i·er; -est** (1584) **1** : of, resembling, or composed of film : GAUZY ⟨~ draperies⟩ **2** : covered with a haze or film — **film·i·ly** \-mə-lē\ *adv* — **film·i·ness** \-mē-nəs\ *n*

filo *also* **fillo** *var of* PHYLLO

filo- — see FILI-

fi·lo·vi·rus \ˈfī-lō-ˌvī-rəs\ *n* [NL, fr. L *filum* thread + NL *-o-* + *virus*] (1989) : any of a family (*Filoviridae*) of single-stranded chiefly filamentous RNA viruses that infect vertebrates and include the Marburg virus and the Ebola viruses

[1]fils \ˈfēs\ *n* [F, fr. OF *fils, fiz, fil,* fr. L *filius* — more at FEMININE] (1786) : SON — used after a family name to distinguish a son from his father

[2]fils \ˈfils\ *n, pl* **fils** [Ar] (1931) — see *dinar, dirham, rial* at MONEY table

[1]fil·ter \ˈfil-tər\ *n* [ME *filtre,* fr. ML *filtrum* piece of felt used as a filter, of Gmc origin; akin to OHG *filz* felt — more at FELT] (1563) **1 a** : a porous article or mass (as of paper or sand) through which a gas or liquid is passed to separate out matter in suspension **b** : an apparatus containing a filter medium **2 a** : a device or material for suppressing or minimizing waves or oscillations of certain frequencies (as of electricity, light, or sound) **b** : a transparent material (as colored glass) that absorbs light of certain wavelengths or colors selectively and is used for modifying light that reaches a sensitized photographic material — called also *color filter* **3** : something that has the effect of a filter (as by holding back elements or modifying the appearance of something) ⟨his work is too often viewed through the ~ of race —Brent Staples⟩ **4** : software for sorting or blocking access to certain online material

[2]filter *vb* **fil·tered; fil·ter·ing** \-t(ə-)riŋ\ *vt* (1576) **1** : to subject to the action of a filter **2** : to remove by means of a filter ~ *vi* **1** : to pass or move through or as if through a filter **2** : to come or go in small units over a period of time ⟨people began ~*ing* in⟩

fil·ter·able *also* **fil·tra·ble** \ˈfil-t(ə-)rə-bəl\ *adj* (1908) : capable of being filtered or of passing through a filter — **fil·ter·abil·i·ty** \ˌfil-t(ə-)rə-ˈbi-lə-tē\ *n*

filterable virus *n* (1911) : any of the infectious agents that pass through a filter of diatomite or unglazed porcelain with the filtrate and remain virulent and that include the viruses as presently understood and various other groups (as the mycoplasmas and rickettsias) which were orig. considered viruses before their cellular nature was established

filter bed *n* (ca. 1874) : a sand or gravel bed for filtering water or sewage

filter feeder *n* (1928) : an animal (as a clam or baleen whale) that obtains its food by filtering organic matter or minute organisms from a current of water that passes through some part of its system

filter paper *n* (ca. 1846) : porous unsized paper used esp. for filtering

filter tip *n* (1932) **:** a cigar or cigarette tip designed to filter the smoke before it enters the smoker's mouth; *also* **:** a cigar or cigarette provided with such a tip — **fil·ter–tipped** \ˌfil-tər-ˈtipt\ *adj*

filth \ˈfilth\ *n* [ME, fr. OE *fȳlth,* fr. *fūl* foul] (bef. 12c) **1 :** foul or putrid matter; *esp* **:** loathsome dirt or refuse **2 a :** moral corruption or defilement **b :** something that tends to corrupt or defile

[1]filthy \ˈfil-thē\ *adj* **filth·i·er; -est** (14c) **1 :** covered with, containing, or characterized by filth **2 a :** UNDERHAND, VILE **b :** OBSCENE ⟨~ language⟩ ***syn*** see DIRTY — **filth·i·ly** \-thə-lē\ *adv* — **filth·i·ness** \-thē-nəs\ *n*

[2]filthy *adv* (1940) **:** in a filthy manner ⟨~ dirty⟩ ⟨~ rich⟩

fil·trate \ˈfil-ˌtrāt\ *n* (ca. 1846) **:** fluid that has passed through a filter

fil·tra·tion \fil-ˈtrā-shən\ *n* (1605) **1 :** the process of filtering **2 :** the process of passing through or as if through a filter; *also* **:** DIFFUSION

fim·bria \ˈfim-brē-ə\ *n, pl* **-bri·ae** \-brē-ˌē, -ˌī\ [NL, fr. L, fringe] (1752) **1 :** a bordering fringe esp. at the entrance of the fallopian tubes **2 :** a pilus of a bacterium — **fim·bri·al** \-brē-əl\ *adj*

fim·bri·at·ed \ˈfim-brē-ˌā-təd\ *also* **fim·bri·ate** \-ˌāt\ *adj* (15c) **:** having the edge or extremity bordered by slender processes **:** FRINGED — **fim·bri·a·tion** \ˌfim-brē-ˈā-shən\ *n*

[1]fin \ˈfin\ *n* [ME *finn,* fr. OE] (bef. 12c) **1 :** an external membranous process of an aquatic animal (as a fish) used in propelling or guiding the body — see FISH illustration **2 :** something resembling a fin: as **a :** HAND, ARM **b (1) :** an appendage of a boat (as a submarine) **(2) :** an airfoil attached to an airplane for directional stability **c :** FLIPPER 1b **d :** any of the projecting ribs on a radiator or an engine cylinder — **fin·like** \-ˌlīk\ *adj* — **finned** \ˈfind\ *adj*

[2]fin *vb* **finned; fin·ning** *vt* (1933) **:** to equip with fins ~ *vi* **1 :** to show the fins above the water **2 :** to move through water propelled by fins

[3]fin *n* [Yiddish *finf* five, fr. MHG, fr. OHG — more at FIVE] (1916) *slang* **:** a 5-dollar bill

[4]fin *abbr* **1** finance; financial **2** finish

fi·na·gle \fə-ˈnā-gəl\ *vb* **fi·na·gled; fi·na·gling** \-g(ə-)liŋ\ [perh. alter. of *fainaigue* to renege] *vt* (ca. 1924) **1 :** to obtain by indirect or involved means ⟨~ a ride home⟩ **2 :** to obtain by trickery ⟨*finagled* his way into the concert⟩ ~ *vi* **:** to use devious or dishonest methods to achieve one's ends — **fi·na·gler** \-g(ə-)lər\ *n*

[1]fi·nal \ˈfī-nᵊl\ *adj* [ME, fr. AF, fr. L *finalis,* fr. *finis* boundary, end] (14c) **1 a :** not to be altered or undone ⟨all sales are ~⟩ **b :** of or relating to a concluding court action or proceeding ⟨~ decree⟩ **2 :** coming at the end **:** being the last in a series, process, or progress ⟨the ~ chapter⟩ **3 :** of or relating to the ultimate purpose or result of a process ⟨our ~ goal⟩ ***syn*** see LAST — **fi·nal·ly** \ˈfī-nᵊl-ē, ˈfīn-lē\ *adv*

[2]final *n* (1609) **:** something that is final: as **a :** a deciding match, game, heat, or trial — usu. used in pl. **b :** the last examination in a course — often used in pl.

fi·na·le \fə-ˈna-lē, fi-ˈnä-\ *n* [It, fr. *finale,* adj., final, fr. L *finalis*] (1774) **:** the close or termination of something: as **a :** the last section of an instrumental musical composition **b :** the closing part, scene, or number in a public performance **c :** the last and often climactic event or item in a sequence

fi·nal·ise *Brit var of* FINALIZE

fi·nal·ist \ˈfī-nə-list\ *n* (1898) **:** a contestant in a competition finals

fi·nal·i·ty \fī-ˈna-lə-tē, fə-\ *n, pl* **-ties** (1833) **1 a :** the character or condition of being final, settled, irrevocable, or complete **b :** the condition of being at an ultimate point esp. of development or authority **2 :** something final; *esp* **:** a fundamental fact, action, or belief

fi·nal·ize \ˈfī-nə-ˌlīz\ *vt* **-ized; -iz·ing** (1901) **1 :** to put in final or finished form ⟨soon my conclusion will be *finalized* —D. D. Eisenhower⟩ **2 :** to give final approval to ⟨*finalizing* the papers prepared . . . by his staff —*Newsweek*⟩ — **fi·nal·i·za·tion** \ˌfī-nə-lə-ˈzā-shən\ *n*

usage *Finalize* has been frequently castigated as an unnecessary neologism or as U.S. government gobbledygook. It appears to have first gained currency in Australia (where it has been acceptable all along) in the early 1920s. The U.S. Navy picked it up in the late 20s, and from there it came into widespread use. It is a standard formation (see -IZE). Currently, it is most frequently used in government and business dealings; it usu. is not found in belles-lettres.

final solution *n, often cap F&S* (1947) **:** the Nazi program for extermination of all Jews in Europe

[1]fi·nance \fə-ˈnan(t)s, ˈfī-ˌ, fī-ˈ\ *n* [ME, ending, payment, fr. AF, fr. *finer* to end, pay, fr. *fin* end — more at FINE] (1739) **1** *pl* **:** money or other liquid resources of a government, business, group, or individual **2 :** the system that includes the circulation of money, the granting of credit, the making of investments, and the provision of banking facilities **3 :** the science or study of the management of funds **4 :** the obtaining of funds or capital **:** FINANCING

[2]finance *vt* **fi·nanced; fi·nanc·ing** (1866) **1 a :** to raise or provide funds or capital for ⟨~ a new house⟩ **b :** to furnish with necessary funds ⟨~ a son through college⟩ **2 :** to sell something to on credit

finance company *n* (ca. 1924) **:** a company that makes usu. small short-term loans usu. to individuals

fi·nan·cial \fə-ˈnan(t)-shəl, fī-\ *adj* (1769) **:** relating to finance or financiers ⟨~ aid⟩ ⟨the ~ district⟩ — **fi·nan·cial·ly** \-ˈnan(t)-sh(ə-)lē\ *adv*

fi·nan·cials \-shəlz\ *n pl* (1972) **:** financial statistics ⟨reviewed the company's ~⟩

fi·nan·cier \ˌfi-nən-ˈsir; fə-ˌnan-, ˌfī-\ *n* (1618) **1 :** one who specializes in raising and expending public moneys **2 :** one who deals with finance and investment on a large scale

financing *n* (1827) **:** the act or process or an instance of raising or providing funds; *also* **:** the funds thus raised or provided

fi·nas·te·ride \fə-ˈnas-tə-ˌrīd\ *n* [*fina-* (of unknown origin) + testo*sterone* + am*ide*] (1989) **:** a nitrogenous steroid derivative $C_{23}H_{36}N_2O_2$ that is used esp. to treat symptoms of benign prostatic hyperplasia and to increase hair growth in male-pattern baldness

fin·back \ˈfin-ˌbak\ *n* (1725) **:** FIN WHALE

fin·ca \ˈfiŋ-kə\ *n* [Sp] (1878) **:** a rural property, ranch, or farm in Spain or Spanish America

finch \ˈfinch\ *n* [ME, fr. OE *finc;* akin to OHG *fincho* finch and perh. to Gk *spiza* chaffinch] (bef. 12c) **:** any of numerous passerine songbirds (families Fringillidae, Estrildidae, Emberizidae, and Cardinalidae) having a short stout usu. conical bill adapted for crushing seeds

[1]find \ˈfīnd\ *vb* **found** \ˈfau̇nd\; **find·ing** [ME, fr. OE *findan;* akin to OHG *findan* to find, L *pont-, pons* bridge, Gk *pontos* sea, Skt *patha* way, course] *vt* (bef. 12c) **1 a :** to come upon often accidentally **:** ENCOUNTER **b :** to meet with (a particular reception) ⟨hoped to ~ favor⟩ **2 a :** to come upon by searching or effort ⟨must ~ a suitable person for the job⟩ **b :** to discover by study or experiment ⟨~ an answer⟩ **c :** to obtain by effort or management ⟨~ the time to study⟩ **d :** ATTAIN, REACH ⟨the bullet *found* its mark⟩ **3 a :** to discover by the intellect or the feelings **:** EXPERIENCE ⟨~ much pleasure in your company⟩ **b :** to perceive (oneself) to be in a certain place or condition **c :** to gain or regain the use or power of ⟨trying to ~ his tongue⟩ **d :** to bring (oneself) to a realization of one's powers or of one's proper sphere of activity ⟨must help the student to ~ himself as an individual —N. M. Pusey⟩ **4 a :** PROVIDE, SUPPLY **b :** to furnish (room and board) esp. as a condition of employment **5 :** to determine and make a statement about ⟨~ a verdict⟩ ⟨*found* her guilty⟩ ~ *vi* **:** to determine a case judicially by a verdict ⟨~ for the defendant⟩ — **find·able** \ˈfīn-də-bəl\ *adj* — **find fault :** to criticize unfavorably

[2]find *n* (1825) **1 :** an act or instance of finding **2 :** something found: as **a :** a valuable discovery ⟨an archaeological ~⟩ **b :** a person whose ability proves to be unexpectedly good

find·er \ˈfīn-dər\ *n* (14c) **1 :** one that finds **2 :** a small astronomical telescope of low power and wide field attached to a larger telescope for finding an object **3 :** VIEWFINDER

fin de siè·cle \ˌfan-də-sē-ˈe-kᵊl; faⁿ-də-ˈsyeklᵊ\ *adj* [F, end of the century] (1890) **1 :** of, relating to, or characteristic of the close of the 19th century and esp. its literary and artistic climate of sophistication, world-weariness, and fashionable despair **2 :** of or relating to the end of a century — **fin de siècle** *n*

finding *n* (14c) **1 a :** the act of one that finds **b :** FIND 2 **2** *pl* **:** small tools and supplies used by an artisan (as a dressmaker, jeweler, or shoemaker) **3 a :** the result of a judicial examination or inquiry **b :** the results of an investigation — usu. used in pl.

find out *vt* (13c) **1 :** to learn by study, observation, or search **:** DISCOVER **2 a :** to catch in an offense (as a crime) ⟨the culprits were soon *found out*⟩ **b :** to ascertain the true character or identity of ⟨the informer was *found out*⟩ ~ *vi* **:** to discover, learn, or verify something ⟨I don't know, but I'll *find out* for you⟩

[1]fine \ˈfīn\ *n* [ME, fr. AF *fin, fine,* fr. L *finis* boundary, end] (13c) **1** *obs* **:** END, CONCLUSION **2 :** a compromise of a fictitious suit used as a form of conveyance of lands **3 a :** a sum imposed as punishment for an offense **b :** a forfeiture or penalty paid to an injured party in a civil action — **in fine :** in short

[2]fine *vt* **fined; fin·ing** (1559) **:** to impose a fine on **:** punish by a fine

[3]fine *adj* **fin·er; fin·est** [ME *fin,* fr. AF, fr. L *finis,* n., end, limit] (13c) **1 a :** free from impurity **b** *of a metal* **:** having a stated proportion of pure metal in the composition expressed in parts per thousand ⟨a gold coin .9166 ~⟩ **2 a (1) :** very thin in gauge or texture ⟨~ thread⟩ **(2) :** not coarse ⟨~ sand⟩ **(3) :** very small ⟨~ print⟩ **(4) :** KEEN ⟨a knife with a ~ edge⟩ **(5) :** very precise or accurate ⟨a ~ adjustment⟩ ⟨trying to be too ~ with his pitches⟩ **b :** physically trained or hardened close to the limit of efficiency — used of an athlete or animal **3 :** delicate, subtle, or sensitive in quality, perception, or discrimination ⟨a ~ distinction⟩ **4 :** superior in kind, quality, or appearance **:** EXCELLENT ⟨a ~ job⟩ ⟨a ~ day⟩ ⟨~ wines⟩ **5 a :** ORNATE 1 ⟨~ writing⟩ **b :** marked by or affecting elegance or refinement ⟨~ manners⟩ **6 a :** very well ⟨feel ~⟩ **b :** ALL RIGHT ⟨that's ~ with me⟩ **7** — used as an intensive ⟨the leader, in a ~ frenzy, beheaded one of his wives —Brian Crozier⟩ — **fine·ness** \ˈfīn-nəs\ *n*

[4]fine *adv* (14c) **1 :** FINELY: as **a :** very well **b :** ALL RIGHT **2 :** with a very narrow margin of time or space ⟨she had not intended to cut her escape so ~ —Melinda Beck *et al.*⟩

[5]fine *vb* **fined; fin·ing** *vt* (14c) **1 :** PURIFY, CLARIFY ⟨~ and filter wine⟩ **2 :** to make finer in quality or size ~ *vi* **1 :** to become pure or clear ⟨the ale will ~⟩ **2 :** to become smaller in lines or proportions

[6]fi·ne \ˈfē-(ˌ)nā\ *n* [It, fr. L *finis* end] (ca. 1798) **:** END — used as a direction in music to mark the closing point after a repeat

fine art *n* (1739) **1 a :** art (as painting, sculpture, or music) concerned primarily with the creation of beautiful objects — usu. used in pl. **b :** objects of fine art **2 :** an activity requiring a fine skill

fine·ly \ˈfīn-lē\ *adv* (14c) **:** in a fine manner: as **a :** extremely well **:** EXCELLENTLY ⟨plays the hero very ~ —*New Yorker*⟩ **b :** with close discrimination **:** PRECISELY **c :** with delicacy or subtlety **:** SENSITIVELY ⟨a leader ~ attuned to the needs of the people⟩ **d :** MINUTELY ⟨~ ground meal⟩

fine print *n* (1951) **:** something thoroughly and often deliberately obscure; *esp* **:** a part of an agreement or document spelling out restrictions and limitations often in small type or obscure language

fin·ery \ˈfīn-rē, ˈfī-nə-\ *n, pl* **-er·ies** (1680) **:** ORNAMENT, DECORATION; *esp* **:** dressy or showy clothing and jewels

fines \ˈfīnz\ *n pl* [[3]*fine*] (1880) **:** finely crushed or powdered material (as ore); *also* **:** very small particles in a mixture of various sizes

fines herbes \fēn-ˈzerb, fē-ˈnerb\ *n pl* [F, lit., fine herbs] (1845) **:** a mixture of herbs used as a seasoning or garnish

fine·spun \ˈfīn-ˈspən\ *adj* (1642) **:** developed with extreme care or delicacy; *also* **:** developed in excessively fine or subtle detail

[1]fi·nesse \fə-ˈnes\ *n* [ME, fr. MF, fr. *fin*] (1528) **1 :** refinement or delicacy of workmanship, structure, or texture **2 :** skillful handling of a situation **:** adroit maneuvering **3 :** the withholding of one's highest card or trump in the hope that a lower card will take the trick because the only opposing higher card is in the hand of an opponent who has already played

[2]finesse *vb* **fi·nessed; fi·ness·ing** *vi* (1746) **:** to make a finesse in playing cards ~ *vt* **1 :** to play (a card) in a finesse **2 a :** to bring about, direct, or manage by adroit maneuvering ⟨~ his way through tight places —Marquis James⟩ **b :** EVADE, SKIRT ⟨~ the hard issues⟩

finest *n, pl in constr* [superl. of [3]*fine*] (1951) **:** POLICE OFFICERS — usu. used with the possessive form of a city or area ⟨the city's ~⟩

\ə\ **abut** \ᵊ\ **kitten,** F **table** \ər\ **further** \a\ **ash** \ā\ **ace** \ä\ **mop, mar**
\au̇\ **out** \ch\ **chin** \e\ **bet** \ē\ **easy** \g\ **go** \i\ **hit** \ī\ **ice** \j\ **job**
\ŋ\ **sing** \ō\ **go** \ȯ\ **law** \ȯi\ **boy** \th\ **thin** \t͟h\ **the** \ü\ **loot** \u̇\ **foot**
\y\ **yet** \zh\ **vision, beige** \k͟, ⁿ, œ, ue, ʸ\ *see* Guide to Pronunciation

fine structure *n* (1935) : microscopic structure of a biological entity or one of its parts esp. as studied in preparations for the electron microscope — **fine structural** *adj*
fine–tooth comb \ˈfīn-ˌtüth-\ *n* (1836) **1** : a comb with close-set teeth used esp. for clearing parasites or foreign matter from the hair **2** : an attitude or system of thorough searching or scrutinizing ⟨went over the report with a *fine-tooth comb*⟩
fine–tune \ˈfīn-ˈtün\ *vt* (1967) **1 a** : to adjust precisely so as to bring to the highest level of performance or effectiveness ⟨~ a TV set⟩ ⟨~ the format⟩ **b** : to improve through minor alteration or revision ⟨~ the temperature of the room⟩ **2** : to stabilize (an economy) by small-scale fiscal and monetary manipulations
fin·fish \ˈfin-ˌfish\ *n* (ca. 1890) : FISH 1b — compare SHELLFISH
[1]fin·ger \ˈfiŋ-gər\ *n* [ME, fr. OE; akin to OHG *fingar* finger] (bef. 12c) **1** : any of the five terminating members of the hand : a digit of the forelimb; *esp* : one other than the thumb **2 a** : something that resembles a finger ⟨a narrow ~ of land⟩ **b** : a part of a glove into which a finger is inserted **c** : a projecting piece (as a pawl for a ratchet) brought into contact with an object to affect its motion **3** : the breadth of a finger **4** : INTEREST, SHARE — often used in the phrase *have a finger in the pie* **5** : BIRD 10 — usu. used with *the* — **fin·ger·like** \-ˌlīk\ *adj*
[2]finger *vb* **fin·gered; fin·ger·ing** \-g(ə-)riŋ\ *vt* (15c) **1** : to touch or feel with the fingers **2 a** : to play (a musical instrument) with the fingers **b** : to play (as notes or chords) with a specific fingering **c** : to mark the notes of (a music score) as a guide in playing **3** : to point out : IDENTIFY **4** : to extend into or penetrate in the shape of a finger ~ *vi* **1** : to touch or handle something **2 a** : to use the fingers in playing a musical instrument **b** : to have a certain fingering — used of a musical instrument **3** : to extend in the shape or manner of a finger
fin·ger·board \ˈfiŋ-gər-ˌbȯrd\ *n* (ca. 1672) : the part of a stringed instrument against which the fingers press the strings to vary the pitch — see VIOLIN illustration
finger bowl *n* (1838) : a small water bowl for rinsing the fingers at the table
fingered *adj* (ca. 1529) **1** : having fingers esp. of a specified kind or number — used in combination ⟨stubby-*fingered*⟩ ⟨five-*fingered*⟩ **2** : having projections or processes like fingers ⟨the ~ roots of giant trees⟩
finger food *n* (1928) : a food that is to be held with the fingers for eating
fin·ger·hold \ˈfiŋ-gər-ˌhōld\ *n* (1909) **1** : a hold or place of support for the fingers **2** : a tenuous hold or support
finger hole *n* (1815) **1** : any of several holes in the side of a wind instrument (as a recorder) which may be covered or left open by the fingers to change the pitch of the tone **2** : a hole (as in a telephone dial or a bowling ball) into which the finger is placed to provide a grip
fingering *n* (14c) **1 a** : the act or method of using the fingers in playing an instrument **b** : the marking (as by figures on a musical score) of the method of fingering **2** : the act or process of handling or touching with the fingers
fin·ger·ling \ˈfiŋ-gər-liŋ\ *n* (1834) : a small fish esp. up to one year of age
fin·ger·nail \ˈfiŋ-gər-ˌnāl, ˌfiŋ-gər-ˈnāl\ *n* (13c) : the nail of a finger
finger painting *n* (1937) : a technique of spreading pigment on paper chiefly with the fingers; *also* : a picture so produced
fin·ger·pick·ing \ˈfiŋ-gər-ˌpi-kiŋ\ *n* (1956) : a method of playing a stringed instrument (as a guitar) with the thumb and tips of the fingers rather than with a pick — **fin·ger·pick** *vb*
fin·ger–point·ing \-ˌpȯin-tiŋ\ *n* (1949) : the act of making explicit and often unfair accusations of blame
fin·ger·post \ˈfiŋ-gər-ˌpōst\ *n* (1785) **1** : a post bearing one or more signs often terminating in a pointing finger **2** : something serving as a guide to understanding or knowledge
fin·ger·print \-ˌprint\ *n* (1859) **1** : the impression of a fingertip on any surface; *also* : an ink impression of the lines upon the fingertip taken for the purpose of identification **2** : something that identifies: as **a** : a trait, trace, or characteristic revealing origin or responsibility **b** : analytical evidence (as a spectrogram) that characterizes an object or substance; *esp* : the chromatogram or electrophoretogram obtained by cleaving a protein by enzymatic action and subjecting the resulting collection of peptides to two-dimensional chromatography or electrophoresis **c** : the base-pair pattern in an individual's DNA obtained by DNA fingerprinting — **fingerprint** *vt* — **fin·ger·print·ing** *n*
finger spelling *n* (1918) : communication by signs made with the fingers — called also *dactylology*
[1]fin·ger·tip \-ˌtip\ *n* (1826) **1** : the tip of a finger **2** : a protective covering for the end of a finger — **at one's fingertips** : instantly or readily available
[2]fingertip *adj* (1926) **1** : readily accessible : being within easy reach ⟨~ information⟩ ⟨~ controls⟩ **2** : extending from head or shoulders to mid-thigh — used of clothing
finger wave *n* (ca. 1934) : a method of setting hair by dampening with water or wave solution and forming waves or curls with the fingers and a comb
fin·i·al \ˈfi-nē-əl\ *n* [ME, fr. *final, finial* final] (15c) **1** : a usu. foliated ornament forming an upper extremity esp. in Gothic architecture **2** : a crowning ornament or detail (as a decorative knob)
fin·i·cal \ˈfi-ni-kəl\ *adj* [prob. fr. [3]*fine*] (1592) : FINICKY — **fin·i·cal·ly** \-k(ə-)lē\ *adv* — **fin·i·cal·ness** \-kəl-nəs\ *n*
fin·ick·ing \-kiŋ, -kən\ *adj* [alter. of *finical*] (1661) : FINICKY
fin·icky \ˈfi-ni-kē\ *adj* [alter. of *finicking*] (ca. 1825) **1** : extremely or excessively particular, exacting, or meticulous in taste or standards ⟨a ~ eater⟩ **2** : requiring much care, precision, or attentive effort ⟨a ~ recipe⟩ — **fin·ick·i·ness** *n*
fi·nis \ˈfi-nəs, ˈfī-nəs; fə-ˈnē\ *n* [ME, fr. L] (15c) : END, CONCLUSION
[1]fin·ish \ˈfi-nish\ *vb* [ME *finisshen,* fr. AF *finiss-,* stem of *finir,* fr. L *finire,* fr. *finis*] *vi* (14c) **1 a** : to come to an end : TERMINATE **b** : END 1b **2 a** : to come to the end of a course, task, or undertaking **b** : to end relations — used with *with* ⟨decided to ~ with him for good⟩ **3** : to end a competition in a specified manner or position ⟨~*ed* third in the race⟩ ~ *vt* **1 a** : to bring to an end : TERMINATE ⟨~*ed* the speech and sat down⟩ **b** : to use or dispose of entirely ⟨her sandwich ~*ed* the loaf⟩ **2 a** : to bring to completion or issue ⟨hope to ~ their new home before winter⟩ **b** : to provide with a finish; *esp* : to put a final coat or surface on ⟨~ a table with varnish⟩ **3 a** : to defeat or ruin utterly and finally ⟨the scandal ~*ed* his career⟩ **b** : to bring about the death of *syn* see CLOSE — **fin·ish·er** *n*
[2]finish *n* (1779) **1** : something that completes or perfects: as **a** : the fine or decorative work required for a building or one of its parts **b** : a finishing material used in painting **c** : the final treatment or coating of a surface **d** : the taste in the mouth after swallowing a beverage (as wine) **2 a** : final stage : END **b** : the cause of one's ruin **3** : the result or product of a finishing process ⟨a glossy ~⟩ **4** : the quality or state of being perfected
fin·ished \-nisht\ *adj* (1693) : marked by the highest quality : CONSUMMATE ⟨~ workmanship⟩
finishing school *n* (1832) : a private school for girls that emphasizes cultural studies and prepares students esp. for social activities
finish line *n* (1899) : a line marking the end of a racecourse
fi·nite \ˈfī-ˌnīt\ *adj* [ME *finit,* fr. L *finitus,* pp. of *finire*] (15c) **1 a** : having definite or definable limits ⟨a ~ number of possibilities⟩ **b** : having a limited nature or existence ⟨~ beings⟩ **2** : completely determinable in theory or in fact by counting, measurement, or thought ⟨the ~ velocity of light⟩ **3 a** : less than an arbitrary positive integer and greater than the negative of that integer **b** : having a finite number of elements ⟨a ~ set⟩ **4** : of, relating to, or being a verb or verb form that can function as a predicate or as the initial element of one and that is limited (as in tense, person, and number) — **finite** *n* — **fi·nite·ly** *adv* — **fi·nite·ness** *n*
finite difference *n* (1807) : any of a sequence of differences obtained by incrementing successively the dependent variable of a function by a fixed amount; *esp* : any of such differences obtained from a polynomial function using successive integral values of its dependent variable
fi·ni·tude \ˈfī-nə-ˌtüd, -ˌtyüd, ˈfin-ə-\ *n* (1644) : finite quality or state
[1]fink \ˈfiŋk\ *n* [origin unknown] (1894) **1** : one who is disapproved of or is held in contempt **2** : STRIKEBREAKER **3** : INFORMER 2
[2]fink *vi* (ca. 1925) : to turn informer : SQUEAL
fink out *vi* (1956) : BACK OUT, COP OUT
Fin·land·isa·tion *Brit var of* FINLANDIZATION
Fin·land·i·za·tion \ˌfin-lən-də-ˈzā-shən, (ˌ)fin-ˌlan-\ *n* [*Finland*] (1969) : a foreign policy of neutrality under the influence of the Soviet Union; *also* : the conversion to such a policy — **Fin·land·ize** \ˈfin-lən-ˌdīz, (ˌ)fin-ˈlan-\ *vt*
Finn \ˈfin\ *n* [Sw *Finne,* fr. OSw; akin to ON *Finnar* Finns, OE *Finnas*] (bef. 12c) **1** : a member of a people speaking Finnish or a Finnic language **2 a** : a native or inhabitant of Finland **b** : one who is of Finnish descent
fin·nan had·die \ˌfi-nən-ˈha-dē\ *n* [alter. of *findon haddock,* fr. *Findon,* village in Scotland] (1848) : smoked haddock — called also *finnan haddock*
Finn·ic \ˈfi-nik\ *adj* (1668) **1** : of or relating to the Finns **2** : of, relating to, or constituting the branch of the Finno-Ugric subfamily that includes Finnish, Estonian, and Sami
[1]Finn·ish \ˈfi-nish\ *adj* (1699) : of, relating to, or characteristic of Finland, the Finns, or Finnish
[2]Finnish *n* (ca. 1845) : the Finno-Ugric language of the Finns
Fin·no–Ugri·an \ˌfi-(ˌ)nō-ˈ(y)ü-grē-ən\ *adj* (1880) : FINNO-UGRIC — **Finno–Ugrian** *n*
Fin·no–Ugric \ˌfi-nō-ˈ(y)ü-grik\ *adj* (1879) **1** : of, relating to, or constituting a subfamily of the Uralic family of languages comprising various languages spoken in Hungary, Lapland, Finland, Estonia, and parts of western Russia **2** : of or relating to any of the peoples speaking Finno-Ugric languages — **Finno–Ugric** *n*
fin·ny \ˈfi-nē\ *adj* (1590) **1** : provided with or characterized by fins **2** : relating to or being fish
fino \ˈfē-(ˌ)nō\ *n, pl* **finos** [Sp, fr. *fino* fine, fr. *fin* end, fr. L *finis*] (1846) : a very dry Spanish sherry
fi·noc·chio \fi-ˈnō-kē-ˌō\ *n* [It, fr. VL **fenuculum* — more at FENNEL] (1941) : FLORENCE FENNEL
fin whale *n* (1885) : a baleen whale (*Balaenoptera physalus*) that may attain a length of over 70 feet (21 meters) and is found chiefly in subtropical to arctic and antarctic waters worldwide — called also *finback*
FIO *abbr* free in and out
fiord *var of* FJORD
fio·ri·tu·ra \fē-ˌȯr-ə-ˈtu̇r-ə\ *n, pl* **-tu·re** \-ˈtu̇r-ē\ [It, lit., flowering, fr. *fiorito,* pp. of *fiorire* to flower, fr. VL **florire* — more at FLOURISH] (1836) : ORNAMENT 5
fip·ple flute \ˈfi-pəl-\ *n* [origin unknown] (1911) : any of a group of wind instruments (as a flageolet or recorder) having a straight tubular shape, a whistle mouthpiece, and finger holes
fir \ˈfər\ *n* [ME, fr. OE *fyrh;* akin to OHG *forha* fir, L *quercus* oak] (bef. 12c) **1** : any of a genus (*Abies*) of north temperate evergreen trees of the pine family that have flattish leaves, circular leaf scars, and erect female cones and are valued for their wood; *also* : any of various conifers (as the Douglas fir) of other genera **2** : the wood of a fir
[1]fire \ˈfī(-ə)r\ *n, often attrib* [ME, fr. OE *fȳr;* akin to OHG *fiur* fire, Gk *pyr*] (bef. 12c) **1 a (1)** : the phenomenon of combustion manifested in light, flame, and heat **(2)** : one of the four elements of the alchemists **b (1)** : burning passion : ARDOR **(2)** : liveliness of imagination : INSPIRATION **2 a** : fuel in a state of combustion (as on a hearth) **b** *Brit* : a small gas or electric space heater **3 a** : a destructive burning (as of a building) **b (1)** : death or torture by fire **(2)** : severe trial or ordeal **4** : BRILLIANCY, LUMINOSITY ⟨the ~ of a gem⟩ **5 a** : the firing of weapons (as firearms, artillery, or missiles) **b** : intense verbal attack or criticism **c** : a rapidly delivered series (as of remarks) — **fire·less** \-ləs\ *adj* — **on fire 1** : being consumed by fire : AFLAME **2** : EAGER, BURNING — **under fire 1** : exposed to fire from an enemy's weapons **2** : under attack
[2]fire *vb* **fired; fir·ing** *vt* (13c) **1 a** : to set on fire : KINDLE; *also* : IGNITE ⟨~ a rocket engine⟩ **b (1)** : to give life or spirit to : INSPIRE ⟨the description *fired* his imagination⟩ **(2)** : to fill with passion or enthusiasm — often used with *up* **c** : to light up as if by fire **d** : to cause to start operating — usu. used with *up* ⟨*fired* up the engine⟩ **2 a** : to drive out or away by or as if by fire **b** : to dismiss from a position **3 a (1)** : to cause to explode : DETONATE **(2)** : to propel from or as if from a gun : DISCHARGE, LAUNCH ⟨~ a rocket⟩ **(3)** : SHOOT 1b ⟨~ a gun⟩ **(4)** : to score (a number) in a game or contest **b** : to throw with speed or force ⟨*fired* the ball to first base⟩ ⟨~ a left jab⟩ **c** : to utter with force

and rapidity 4 : to apply fire or fuel to: as **a** : to process by applying heat ⟨~ pottery⟩ **b** : to feed or serve the fire of ⟨~ a boiler⟩ ~ *vi* **1 a** : to take fire : KINDLE, IGNITE **b** : to begin operation : START ⟨the engine *fired*⟩ **c** : to operate esp. as the result of the application of an electrical impulse ⟨the spark plug ~*s*⟩ **2 a** : to become irritated or angry — often used with *up* **b** : to become filled with excitement or enthusiasm **3 a** : to discharge a firearm ⟨~ at close range⟩ **b** : to emit or let fly an object **4** : to tend a fire **5** : to transmit a nerve impulse ⟨the rate at which a neuron ~*s*⟩ — **fire·able** \ˈfī(-ə)r-ə-bəl, ˈfī-rə-\ *adj* — **fir·er** *n*

FIRE *abbr* finance, insurance, and real estate

fire and brimstone *n* (13c) : the torments suffered by sinners in hell — **fire–and–brimstone** *adj*

fire ant *n* (1796) : any of a genus (*Solenopsis*) of fiercely stinging omnivorous ants; *esp* : IMPORTED FIRE ANT

fire·arm \ˈfī(-ə)r-ˌärm\ *n* (1646) : a weapon from which a shot is discharged by gunpowder — usu. used of small arms

fire away *vi* (1756) : to speak without hesitation — usu. used as an imperative

fire·back \-ˌbak\ *n* (1847) : an often decorated cast-iron plate lining the back wall of a fireplace

fire·ball \ˈfī(-ə)r-ˌbȯl\ *n* (1555) **1** : a ball of fire; *also* : something resembling such a ball ⟨the primordial ~ associated with the beginning of the universe —*Scientific American*⟩ **2** : a brilliant meteor that may trail bright sparks **3** : the highly luminous cloud of vapor and dust created by a nuclear explosion **4** : a highly energetic person

fire·ball·er \-ˌbȯ-lər\ *n* (1946) : a baseball pitcher known for throwing fastballs — **fire·ball·ing** \-liŋ\ *adj*

fire·base \-ˌbās\ *n* (1968) : a secured site from which field artillery can lay down interdicting fire

fire blight *n* (1750) : a destructive infectious disease esp. of apples, pears, and related fruits caused by a bacterium (*Erwinia amylovora*)

fire·boat \ˈfī(-ə)r-ˌbōt\ *n* (1849) : a ship equipped with firefighting apparatus

fire·bomb \-ˌbäm\ *n* (1895) : an incendiary bomb — **firebomb** *vt*

fire·box \-ˌbäks\ *n* (1791) **1** : a chamber (as of a furnace or steam boiler) that contains a fire **2** : a box containing an apparatus for transmitting an alarm to a fire station

fire·brand \-ˌbrand\ *n* (13c) **1** : a piece of burning wood **2** : one that creates unrest or strife (as in aggressively promoting a cause) : AGITATOR

fire·brat \-ˌbrat\ *n* (1895) : a wingless insect (*Thermobia domestica*) related to the silverfish and found in warm moist places

fire·break \-ˌbrāk\ *n* (1841) : a barrier of cleared or plowed land intended to check a forest or grass fire

fire–breath·ing \-ˌbrē-t͟hiŋ\ *adj* (1933) : intimidatingly or violently aggressive in speech and manner ⟨a ~ orator⟩ — **fire–breath·er** \-t͟hər\ *n*

fire·brick \-ˌbrik\ *n* (1793) : a refractory brick capable of sustaining high temperatures that is used esp. for lining furnaces or fireplaces

fire brigade *n* (1838) : a body of firefighters: as **a** : a usu. private or temporary firefighting organization **b** *Brit* : FIRE DEPARTMENT

fire·bug \-ˌbəg\ *n* (1872) : INCENDIARY, PYROMANIAC

fire chief *n* (1889) : the head of a fire department

fire·clay \-ˌklā\ *n* (1800) : clay capable of withstanding high temperatures that is used esp. for firebrick and crucibles

fire control *n* (ca. 1864) : the planning, preparation, and delivery of fire on targets

fire coral *n* (1953) : a colonial coralline hydrozoan (genus *Millepora*) having nematocysts that inflict a painful and burning sting

fire·crack·er \-ˌkra-kər\ *n* (1829) : a usu. paper cylinder containing an explosive and a fuse and set off to make a noise

fired *adj* (1889) : using a specified fuel — usu. used in combination ⟨oil-*fired* power plant⟩

fire·damp \ˈfī(-ə)r-ˌdamp\ *n* (1677) : a combustible mine gas that consists chiefly of methane; *also* : the explosive mixture of this gas with air

fire department *n* (1825) **1** : an organization for preventing or extinguishing fires; *esp* : a government division (as in a municipality) having these duties **2** : the members of a fire department

fire·dog \-ˌdȯg\ *n* (1763) *chiefly Southern & Midland* : ANDIRON

fire·drake \-ˌdrāk\ *n* [ME *firdrake,* fr. OE *fȳrdraca,* fr. *fȳr* + *draca* dragon, fr. L *draco* — more at DRAGON] (bef. 12c) : a fire-breathing dragon esp. in Germanic mythology

fire drill *n* (ca. 1890) : a practice drill in extinguishing fires or in the conduct and manner of exit in case of fire

fire–eat·er \-ˌē-tər\ *n* (1672) **1** : a performer who pretends to eat fire **2 a** : a violent or pugnacious person **b** : a person who displays very militant or aggressive partisanship

fire–eat·ing \-ˌē-tiŋ\ *adj* (1819) : violent or highly militant in disposition, bearing, or policy ⟨a ~ radical⟩

fire engine *n* (ca. 1680) : a usu. mobile apparatus for directing an extinguishing agent upon fires; *esp* : FIRE TRUCK

fire–en·gine red \-ˌen-jən-\ *n* (1954) : a bright red

fire escape *n* (1788) : a device for escape from a burning building; *esp* : a metal stairway attached to the outside of a building

fire extinguisher *n* (1849) : a portable or wheeled apparatus for putting out small fires by ejecting extinguishing chemicals

fire·fight \ˈfī(-ə)r-ˌfīt\ *n* (1899) **1 a** : a usu. brief intense exchange of fire between opposing military units **b** : a hostile confrontation that involves gunfire **2** : SKIRMISH 2b

fire·fight·er \-ˌfī-tər\ *n* (1903) : a person who fights fires : FIREMAN 2 — **firefighting** *n*

fire·fly \-ˌflī\ *n* (1658) : any of various winged nocturnal beetles (esp. family Lampyridae) that produce a bright soft intermittent light by oxidation of luciferin esp. for courtship purposes

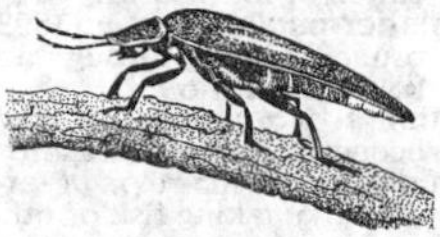

firefly

fire·guard \-ˌgärd\ *n* (1833) **1** : a person who watches for the outbreak of fire; *also* : a person whose duty is to extinguish fires **2** : FIRE SCREEN **3** : FIREBREAK

fire hall *n* (1881) *chiefly Canad* : FIRE STATION

fire·house \-ˌhau̇s\ *n* (1901) : FIRE STATION

fire irons *n pl* (1646) : utensils (as tongs) for tending a fire esp. in a fireplace

fire·light \-ˌlīt\ *n* (bef. 12c) : the light of a fire (as in a fireplace) — **fire·lit** \-ˌlit\ *adj*

fire line *n* (1901) : FIREBREAK

fire·lock \-ˌläk\ *n* (1547) **1** : a gun's lock employing a slow match to ignite the powder charge; *also* : a gun having such a lock **2 a** : FLINTLOCK **b** : WHEEL LOCK

fire·man \-mən\ *n* (14c) **1** : a person who tends or feeds fires : STOKER **2** : a member of a fire department : FIREFIGHTER **3** : an enlisted man in the navy who works with engineering machinery **4** : a relief pitcher in baseball

fire off *vt* (1888) : to write and send usu. in haste or anger ⟨*fired off* a memo⟩

fire opal *n* (1816) : GIRASOLE 2

fire·place \-ˌplās\ *n* (1669) **1** : a framed opening made in a chimney to hold an open fire : HEARTH; *also* : a metal container with a smoke pipe used for the same purpose **2** : an outdoor structure of brick, stone, or metal for an open fire — **fire·placed** \-ˌplāst\ *adj*

fire·plug \-ˌpləg\ *n* (1713) : HYDRANT

fire·pot \-ˌpät\ *n* (ca. 1625) **1** : a clay pot filled with combustibles formerly used as a missile in war **2** : a vessel used in eastern Asian cuisine for cooking foods in broth at the table; *also* : the food cooked in it

fire·pow·er \-ˌpau̇(-ə)r\ *n* (1913) **1 a** : the capacity (as of a military unit) to deliver effective fire on a target **b** : effective fire **2 a** : effective power or force ⟨intellectual ~⟩ **b** : the scoring ability of a team or player

1**fire·proof** \-ˌprüf\ *adj* (1610) : proof against or resistant to fire

2**fireproof** *vt* (1867) : to make fireproof

fire–sale *adj* (1953) : heavily discounted ⟨~ prices⟩

fire sale *n* (1891) : a sale of merchandise damaged in a fire; *also* : a sale at very low prices

fire screen *n* (15c) : a protective screen before a fireplace

fire·ship \ˈfī(-ə)r-ˌship\ *n* (1588) : a ship carrying combustibles or explosives sent burning among the enemy's ships or works to set them on fire

1**fire·side** \-ˌsīd\ *n* (1563) **1** : a place near the fire or hearth **2** : HOME

2**fireside** *adj* (1740) : having an informal or intimate quality ⟨a ~ chat⟩

fire station *n* (1877) : a building housing fire apparatus and usu. firefighters

fire·stone \ˈfī(-ə)r-ˌstōn\ *n* (bef. 12c) **1** : pyrite formerly used for striking fire; *also* : FLINT **2** : a stone that will endure high heat

fire–stop \-ˌstäp\ *n* (1897) : material used to close open parts esp. of a building for preventing the spread of fire — **fire–stop** *vt*

fire·storm \-ˌstȯrm\ *n* (1945) **1** : a large usu. stationary fire characterized by very high temperatures in which the central column of rising heated air induces strong inward winds which supply oxygen to the fire **2 a** : a sudden or violent outburst ⟨a ~ of public protest⟩ **b** : a raging controversy ⟨a political ~⟩

fire·thorn \-ˌthȯrn\ *n* (ca. 1900) : PYRACANTHA; *esp* : a European semievergreen shrub (*P. coccinea*) with orange-red berries

fire tower *n* (1827) : a tower (as in a forest) from which a watch for fires is maintained

fire·trap \-ˌtrap\ *n* (1881) : a place (as a building) apt to catch on fire or difficult to escape from in case of fire

fire truck *n* (1935) : an automotive vehicle equipped with firefighting apparatus

fire wall *n* (1759) **1** : a wall constructed to prevent the spread of fire **2** *usu* **fire·wall** \ˈfī(-ə)r-ˌwȯl\ : computer hardware or software that prevents unauthorized access to private data (as on a company's local area network or intranet) by outside computer users (as of the Internet)

fire·wa·ter \ˈfī(-ə)r-ˌwȯ-tər, -ˌwä-\ *n* (1817) : strong alcoholic liquor

fire·weed \-ˌwēd\ *n* (1784) : any of several plants that grow esp. in clearings or burned districts: as **a** : a weedy annual composite (*Erechtites hieracifolia*) of eastern No. America having flower heads of whitish tubular disk flowers enveloped by green bracts **b** : a tall perennial (*Epilobium angustifolium*) of the evening-primrose family that has long spikes of pinkish-purple flowers and is an important honey plant in some areas — called also *willow herb*

fire·wood \-ˌwu̇d\ *n* (14c) : wood used for fuel

fire·work \-ˌwərk\ *n* (1575) **1** : a device for producing a striking display by the combustion of explosive or flammable compositions **2** *pl* : a display of fireworks **3** *pl* **a** : a display of temper or intense conflict **b** : a spectacular display ⟨the ~*s* of autumn leaves⟩

fir·ing \ˈfī(-ə)r-iŋ\ *n* (14c) **1** : the act or process of one that fires **2** : the process of maturing ceramic products by the application of heat

firing line *n* (1881) **1** : a line from which fire is delivered against a target **2** : the forefront of an activity — used esp. in the phrase *on the firing line*

firing pin *n* (1874) : the pin that strikes the cartridge primer in the breech mechanism of a firearm

firing squad *n* (1864) **1** : a detachment detailed to fire volleys over the grave of one buried with military honors **2** : a detachment detailed to carry out a sentence of death by shooting

fir·kin \ˈfər-kən\ *n* [ME, ultim. fr. MD *veerdel* fourth, fr. *veer* four; akin to OE *fēower* — more at FOUR] (14c) **1** : a small wooden vessel or cask **2** : any of various British units of capacity usu. equal to ¼ barrel

1**firm** \ˈfərm\ *adj* [ME *ferm,* fr. AF, fr. L *firmus;* akin to Gk *thronos* chair, throne] (14c) **1 a** : securely or solidly fixed in place **b** : not weak or uncertain : VIGOROUS **c** : having a solid or compact structure that resists stress or pressure **2 a** (1) : not subject to change or revision (2) : not subject to price weakness : STEADY **b** : not easily moved or disturbed : STEADFAST **c** : WELL-FOUNDED **3** : indicating firmness or resolution ⟨a ~ mouth⟩ — **firm·ly** *adv* — **firm·ness** *n*

2**firm** *adv* (14c) : in a firm manner : STEADFASTLY, FIXEDLY

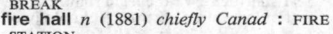

[3]**firm** *vt* (14c) **1 a :** to make secure or fast : TIGHTEN ⟨~*ing* her grip on the racquet⟩ — often used with *up* **b :** to make solid or compact ⟨~ the soil⟩ **2 :** to put into final form : SETTLE ⟨~ a contract⟩ ⟨~ up plans⟩ **3 :** to give additional support to : STRENGTHEN — usu. used with *up* ~ *vi* **1 :** to become firm : HARDEN — often used with *up* **2 :** to recover from a decline : IMPROVE ⟨the market is ~*ing*⟩

[4]**firm** *n* [G *Firma,* fr. It, signature, ultim. fr. L *firmare* to make firm, confirm, fr. *firmus*] (1744) **1 :** the name or title under which a company transacts business **2 :** a partnership of two or more persons that is not recognized as a legal person distinct from the members composing it **3 :** a business unit or enterprise

fir·ma·ment \ˈfər-mə-mənt\ *n* [ME, fr. LL & L; LL *firmamentum,* fr. L, support, fr. *firmare*] (13c) **1 :** the vault or arch of the sky : HEAVENS **2** *obs* : BASIS **3 :** the field or sphere of an interest or activity ⟨the international fashion ~⟩ — **fir·ma·men·tal** \ˌfər-mə-ˈmen-tᵊl\ *adj*

fir·mer chisel \ˈfər-mər-\ *n* [F *fermoir* chisel, alter. of MF *formoir,* fr. *former* to form, fr. OF *forme* form] (1823) **:** a woodworking chisel with a thin flat blade

firm·ware \ˈfərm-ˌwer\ *n* (1967) **:** computer programs contained permanently in a hardware device (as a read-only memory)

firn \ˈfirn\ *n* [G, fr. OHG *firni* old; akin to OE *faran*] (1853) **:** NÉVÉ

[1]**first** \ˈfərst\ *adj* [ME, fr. OE *fyrst;* akin to OHG *furist* first, OE *faran* to go — more at FARE] (bef. 12c) **:** preceding all others in time, order, or importance: as **a :** EARLIEST **b :** being the lowest forward gear or speed of a motor vehicle **c :** having the highest or most prominent part among a group of similar voices or instruments ⟨~ violins⟩

[2]**first** *adv* (bef. 12c) **1 a :** before another in time, space, or importance **b :** in the first place — often used with *of all* **c :** for the first time **2 :** in preference to something else : SOONER

[3]**first** *n* (13c) **1** — see NUMBER table **2 :** something that is first: as **a :** the first occurrence or item of a kind **b :** the first forward gear or speed of a motor vehicle **c :** the highest or chief voice or instrument of a group **d :** an article of commerce of the finest grade **e :** the winning or highest place in a competition, examination, or contest **3 :** FIRST BASE — **at first :** at the beginning : INITIALLY

first aid *n* (1882) **:** emergency care or treatment given to an ill or injured person before regular medical aid can be obtained

first base *n* (1845) **1 :** the base that must be touched first by a base runner in baseball **2 :** the player position for defending the area around first base **3 :** the first step or stage in a course of action ⟨plans never got to *first base*⟩ — **first base·man** \-ˈbā-smən\ *n*

first·born \ˈfərs(t)-ˈbȯrn\ *adj* (14c) **:** first brought forth : ELDEST — **firstborn** *n*

first cause *n* (14c) **:** the self-created ultimate source of all being

first–class \ˈfərs(t)-ˈklas\ *adj* (ca. 1838) **1 :** of or relating to first class **2 :** of the highest quality ⟨a ~ meal⟩ — **first–class** *adv*

first class *n* (1750) **:** the first or highest group in a classification: as **a :** the highest of usu. three classes of travel accommodations **b :** a class of mail that comprises letters, postcards, or matter sealed against inspection

first cousin *n* (1649) **:** COUSIN 1a

first day cover *n* (1932) **:** a philatelic cover franked with a newly issued postage stamp and bearing the postmark of the first day of issue and an officially chosen place of issue

first–degree burn *n* (ca. 1929) **:** a mild burn characterized by heat, pain, and reddening of the burned surface but not exhibiting blistering or charring of tissues

first down *n* (ca. 1897) **1 :** the first of a series of usu. four downs in which a football team must net a 10-yard gain to retain possession of the ball **2 :** a gain of a total of 10 or more yards within usu. four downs giving the team the right to start a new series of downs

first edition *n* (1568) **:** the copies of a literary work first printed from the same type and issued at the same time; *also* **:** a single copy from a first edition

first estate *n, often cap F&E* (1935) **:** the first of the traditional political estates; *specif* **:** CLERGY

first floor *n* (15c) **1 :** GROUND FLOOR 1 **2** *chiefly Brit* **:** the floor next above the ground floor

first·fruits \ˈfərs(t)-ˈfrüts\ *n pl* (14c) **1 :** the earliest gathered fruits offered to the Deity in acknowledgment of the gift of fruitfulness **2 :** the earliest products or results of an endeavor

first·hand \ˈfərst-ˈhand\ *adj* (1748) **:** obtained by, coming from, or being direct personal observation or experience ⟨a ~ account of the war⟩ — **firsthand** *adv*

first lady *n, often cap F&L* (1834) **1 :** the wife or hostess of the chief executive of a country or jurisdiction **2 :** the leading woman of an art or profession

first lieutenant *n* (1706) **1 :** a commissioned officer in the army, air force, or marine corps ranking above a second lieutenant and below a captain **2 :** a naval officer responsible for a ship's upkeep

first–line \ˈfərst-ˈlīn\ *adj* (1925) **:** being the preferred, standard, or first choice ⟨~ treatment of tuberculosis⟩ — compare SECOND-LINE

first·ling \ˈfərst-liŋ\ *n* (1535) **1 :** the first of a class or kind **2 :** the first offspring or result of something

first·ly \-lē\ *adv* (ca. 1532) **:** in the first place : FIRST

first mortgage *n* (1728) **:** a mortgage that has priority as a lien over all mortgages and liens except those imposed by law

first name *n* (13c) **:** the name that stands first in one's full name

first night *n* (1698) **:** the night on which a theatrical production is first performed at a given place; *also* **:** the performance itself

first–night·er \ˈfərs(t)-ˈnī-tər\ *n* (1882) **:** a spectator at a first-night performance

first off *adv* (1880) **:** in the first place : before anything else

first offender *n* (1849) **:** one convicted of an offense for the first time

first papers *n pl* (1912) **:** papers declaring intention filed by an applicant for citizenship as the first step in the naturalization process

first person *n* (1520) **1 a :** a set of linguistic forms (as verb forms, pronouns, and inflectional affixes) referring to the speaker or writer of the utterance in which they occur **b :** a linguistic form belonging to such a set **c :** reference of a linguistic form to the speaker or writer of the utterance in which it occurs **2 :** a style of discourse marked by general use of verbs and pronouns of the first person

[1]**first–rate** \ˈfərs(t)-ˈrāt\ *adj* (1671) **:** of the first order of size, importance, or quality — **first–rate·ness** *n* — **first–rat·er** \-ˈrā-tər\ *n*

[2]**first–rate** *adv* (1844) **:** very well ⟨is getting along ~ —Mark Twain⟩

First Reader *n* (1895) **:** a Christian Scientist chosen to conduct meetings for a specified time and specif. to read aloud from the writings of Mary Baker Eddy

first reading *n* (1660) **:** the first submitting of a bill before a quorum of a legislative assembly usu. by title or number only

first responder *n* (1970) **:** a person (as a police officer or an EMT) who is among those responsible for going immediately to the scene of an accident or emergency to provide assistance

first–run \ˈfərs(t)-ˈrən\ *adj* (1912) **:** available for public viewing for the first time ⟨~ movies⟩; *also* **:** exhibiting first-run movies ⟨~ theaters⟩

first sergeant *n* (ca. 1860) **1 :** a noncommissioned officer serving as the chief assistant to the commander of a military unit (as a company or squadron) **2 :** the rank of a first sergeant; *specif* **:** a rank in the army above a sergeant first class and below a sergeant major and in the marine corps above a gunnery sergeant and below a master gunnery sergeant

first strike *n* (1960) **:** a preemptive nuclear attack — **first–strike** *adj*

first–string \ˈfərs(t)-ˈstriŋ\ *adj* (1917) **1 :** being a regular as distinguished from a substitute (as on a team) **2 :** FIRST-RATE — **first–string·er** \-ˈstriŋ-ər\ *n*

first water *n* (1753) **1 :** the purest luster — used of gems **2 :** the highest grade, degree, or quality

first world *n, often cap F&W* [after *third world*] (1967) **:** the highly developed industrialized nations often considered the westernized countries of the world

firth \ˈfərth\ *n* [ME, fr. ON *fjǫrthr* — more at FORD] (14c) **:** ESTUARY

fisc \ˈfisk\ *n* [L *fiscus*] (1598) **:** a state or royal treasury

[1]**fis·cal** \ˈfis-kəl\ *adj* [L *fiscalis,* fr. *fiscus* basket, treasury] (1563) **1 :** of or relating to taxation, public revenues, or public debt ⟨~ policy⟩ **2 :** of or relating to financial matters — **fis·cal·ly** \-kə-lē\ *adv*

[2]**fiscal** *n* (1869) **1 :** REVENUE STAMP **2 :** FISCAL YEAR

fiscal year *n* (1843) **:** an accounting period of 12 months

[1]**fish** \ˈfish\ *n, pl* **fish** *or* **fish·es** *often attrib* [ME, fr. OE *fisc;* akin to OHG *fisc* fish, L *piscis*] (bef. 12c) **1 a :** an aquatic animal — usu. used in combination ⟨star*fish*⟩ ⟨cuttle*fish*⟩ **b :** any of numerous cold-blooded strictly aquatic craniate vertebrates that include the bony fishes and usu. the cartilaginous and jawless fishes and that have typically an elongated somewhat spindle-shaped body terminating in a broad caudal fin, limbs in the form of fins when present at all, and a 2-chambered heart by which blood is sent through thoracic gills to be oxygenated **2 :** the flesh of fish used as food **3 a :** a person who is caught or is wanted (as in a criminal investigation) **b :** FELLOW, PERSON ⟨an odd ~⟩ **c :** SUCKER 5a **4 :** something that resembles a fish: as **a** *pl, cap* **:** PISCES 1; *also* **:** PISCES 2a **b :** TORPEDO 2b — **fish·less** \ˈfish-ləs\ *adj* — **fish·like** \-ˌlīk\ *adj* — **fish out of water :** a person who is in an unnatural or uncomfortable sphere or situation — **fish to fry :** concerns or interests to pursue — usu. used with *other* — **neither fish nor fowl :** one that does not belong to a particular class or category

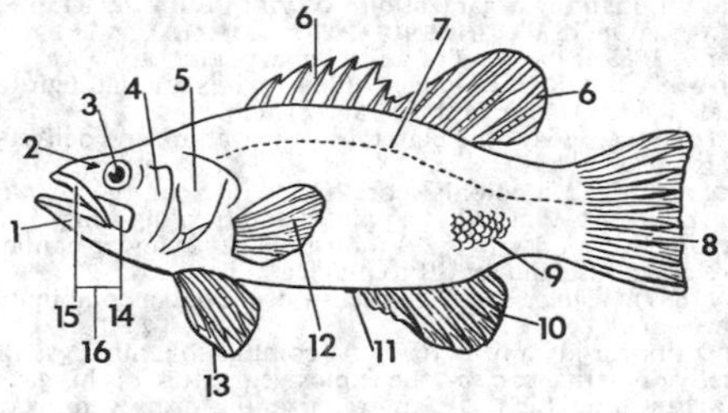

fish 1b: *1* mandible, *2* nasal opening, *3* eye, *4* cheek, *5* operculum, *6* dorsal fins, *7* lateral line, *8* caudal fin, *9* scales, *10* anal fin, *11* anus, *12* pectoral fin, *13* pelvic fin, *14* maxilla, *15* premaxilla, *16* upper jaw

[2]**fish** *vi* (bef. 12c) **1 :** to attempt to catch fish **2 :** to seek something by roundabout means ⟨~*ing* for a compliment⟩ **3 a :** to search for something underwater ⟨~ for pearls⟩ **b :** to engage in a search by groping or feeling ⟨~*ing* around in her purse for her keys⟩ ~ *vt* **1 a :** to try to catch fish in **b :** to fish with : use (as a boat, net, or bait) in fishing **2 a :** to go fishing for ⟨~ salmon⟩ **b :** to pull or draw as if fishing ⟨~*ed* the ball from under the car⟩ ⟨~ wires through a conduit⟩ — **fish·abil·i·ty** \ˌfi-shə-ˈbi-lə-tē\ *n* — **fish·able** \ˈfi-shə-bəl\ *adj* — **fish or cut bait :** to make a choice between alternatives

fish–and–chips \ˌfi-shᵊn-ˈchips\ *n pl* (1876) **:** fried fish and french fried potatoes

fish·bowl \ˈfish-ˌbōl\ *n* (1906) **1 :** a bowl for the keeping of live fish **2 :** a place or condition that affords no privacy

fish cake *n* (1854) **:** a round fried cake made of shredded fish and mashed potato

fish duck *n* (1858) **:** MERGANSER

fish·er \ˈfi-shər\ *n* (bef. 12c) **1 :** one that fishes **2 a :** a dark brown No. American carnivorous mammal (*Martes pennanti*) of the weasel family **b :** the fur or pelt of this animal

fish·er·folk \ˈfi-shər-ˌfōk\ *n pl* (1822) **:** people who fish esp. for a living

fish·er·man \-mən\ *n* (15c) **1 :** one who engages in fishing as an occupation or for pleasure **2 :** a ship used in commercial fishing

fisherman's bend *n* (1823) **:** a knot made by passing the end twice round a spar or through a ring and then back under both turns — see KNOT illustration

fish·er·wo·man \ˈfi-shər-ˌwu̇-mən\ *n* (1816) **:** a woman who fishes as an occupation or for pleasure

fish·ery \ˈfi-shə-rē\ *n, pl* **-er·ies** (1528) **1 :** the occupation, industry, or season of taking fish or other sea animals (as sponges, shrimp, or seals) **:** FISHING **2 :** a place for catching fish or taking other sea animals **3 :** a fishing establishment; *also* **:** its fishermen **4 :** the legal right to take fish at a particular place or in particular waters **5 :** the technology of fishery — usu. used in pl.

fish–eye \ˈfish-ˌī\ *adj* (1943) : being, having, or produced by a wide-angle photographic lens that has a highly curved protruding front, that covers an angle of about 180 degrees, and that gives a circular image
fish farm *n* (1865) : a commercial facility for raising aquatic animals for human food — **fish–farm** \ˈfish-ˌfärm\ *vt*
fish finger *n* (1962) *Brit* : FISH STICK
fish fry *n* (1824) **1** : a picnic or supper featuring fried fish **2** : fried fish
fish hawk *n* (1709) : OSPREY 1
fish•hook \ˈfish-ˌhu̇k\ *n* (14c) : a usu. barbed hook for catching fish
fish•ing \ˈfi-shiŋ\ *n* (13c) **1** : the sport or business of catching fish **2** : a place for catching fish
fishing expedition *n* (1874) **1** : a legal interrogation or examination to discover information for a later proceeding **2** : an investigation that does not stick to a stated objective but hopes to uncover incriminating or newsworthy evidence
fish ladder *n* (1864) : a series of pools arranged like steps by which fish can pass over a dam in going upstream
fish meal *n* (1854) : ground dried fish and fish waste used as fertilizer and animal food
fish•mong•er \ˈfish-ˌmäŋ-gər, -ˌməŋ-\ *n* (15c) *chiefly Brit* : a fish dealer
fish•net \-ˌnet\ *n* (bef. 12c) **1** : netting fitted with floats and weights or a supporting frame for catching fish **2** : a coarse open-mesh fabric
fish oil *n* (1785) : a fatty oil from the bodies of various fishes (as menhaden or sardines) that contains large amounts of unsaturated fatty acids and is used in making various products (as cosmetics and paints)
fish out *vt* (1892) : to exhaust the supply of fish in by fishing
fish•plate \-ˌplāt\ *n* (1855) : a steel plate used to lap a butt joint
fish•pond \-ˌpänd\ *n* (14c) : a pond stocked with fish
fish protein concentrate *n* (1961) : a protein-rich food additive made from ground whole fish
fish stick *n* (1953) : a small elongated breaded fillet of fish
fish story *n* [fr. the traditional exaggeration by fishermen of the size of fish almost caught] (1819) : an extravagant or incredible story
fish•tail \ˈfish-ˌtāl\ *vi* (1927) **1** : to swing the tail of an airplane from side to side to reduce speed esp. when landing **2** : to have the rear end slide from side to side out of control while moving forward ⟨the car ~*ed* on the icy curve⟩
fish•way \-ˌwā\ *n* (1845) : a contrivance for enabling fish to pass around a fall or dam in a stream; *specif* : FISH LADDER
fish•wife \-ˌwīf\ *n* [ME] (15c) **1** : a woman who sells fish **2** : a vulgar abusive woman
fishy \ˈfi-shē\ *adj* **fish•i•er; -est** (15c) **1** : of or resembling fish esp. in taste or odor **2** : creating doubt or suspicion : QUESTIONABLE
fis•sile \ˈfi-səl, ˈfi-ˌsī(-ə)l\ *adj* [L *fissilis,* fr. *findere*] (1661) **1** : capable of or prone to being split or divided in the direction of the grain or along natural planes of cleavage ⟨~ wood⟩ ⟨~ crystals⟩ **2** : capable of undergoing fission — **fis•sil•i•ty** \fi-ˈsi-lə-tē\ *n*
[1]**fis•sion** \ˈfi-shən, -zhən\ *n* [L *fission-, fissio,* fr. *findere* to split — more at BITE] (ca. 1617) **1** : a splitting or breaking up into parts **2** : reproduction by spontaneous division of the body into two or more parts each of which grows into a complete organism **3** : the splitting of an atomic nucleus resulting in the release of large amounts of energy — **fis•sion•al** \-shə-nəl, -zhə-\ *adj*
[2]**fission** *vi* (1929) : to undergo fission ~ *vt* : to cause to undergo fission
fis•sion•able \ˈfi-shə-nə-bəl, -zhə-; ˈfish-nə-, ˈfizh-\ *adj* (1945) : FISSILE 2 — **fis•sion•abil•i•ty** \ˌfi-shə-nə-ˈbi-lə-tē, -zhə-; ˌfish-nə-, ˌfizh-\ *n*
fis•sip•a•rous \fi-ˈsi-p(ə-)rəs\ *adj* [L *fissus,* pp. of *findere* + E *-parous*] (1874) : tending to break up into parts : DIVISIVE ⟨~ tendencies within a political party⟩ — **fis•sip•a•rous•ness** *n*
[1]**fis•sure** \ˈfi-shər\ *n* [ME, fr. MF, fr. L *fissura,* fr. *fissus*] (14c) **1** : a narrow opening or crack of considerable length and depth usu. occurring from some breaking or parting **2 a** : a natural cleft between body parts or in the substance of an organ **b** : a break or slit in tissue usu. at the junction of skin and mucous membrane **3** : a separation or disagreement in thought or viewpoint : SCHISM ⟨~*s* in a political party⟩
[2]**fissure** *vb* **fis•sured; fis•sur•ing** *vt* (1656) : to break into fissures : CLEAVE ~ *vi* : CRACK, DIVIDE
[1]**fist** \ˈfist\ *n* [ME, fr. OE *fȳst;* akin to OHG *fūst* fist, Pol *pięść,* and prob. to OE *fīf* five] (bef. 12c) **1** : the hand clenched with the fingers doubled into the palm and the thumb doubled inward across the fingers **2** : the hand closed as in grasping : CLUTCH **3** : INDEX 5
[2]**fist** *vt* (1607) **1** : to grip with the fist : HANDLE **2** : to clench into a fist
fist bump *n* (1996) : a gesture in which two people bump their fists together (as in greeting or celebration) — **fist–bump** *vb*
-fisted *comb form* : having (such or so many) fists ⟨tight*fisted*⟩
fist•fight \ˈfist-ˌfīt\ *n* (1603) : a usu. spontaneous fight with bare fists
fist•ful \-ˌfu̇l\ *n* (1611) **1** : HANDFUL ⟨a ~ of coins⟩ **2** : a considerable number or amount ⟨a whole ~ of musicians —Thomas Lask⟩
fist•ic \ˈfis-tik\ *adj* (1806) : of or relating to boxing or to fighting with the fists ⟨~ prowess⟩
fist•i•cuffs \ˈfis-ti-ˌkəfs\ *n pl* [alter. of *fisty cuff,* fr. *fisty* fistic + *cuff*] (1605) : a fight with the fists
fist•note \ˈfis(t)-ˌnōt\ *n* (ca. 1934) : matter in a text to which attention is directed by means of an index mark
fist pump *n* (1981) : a celebratory gesture (as by a sports player) in which the fist is raised in front of the body and then quickly and vigorously drawn back
fis•tu•la \ˈfis(h)-chə-lə\ *n, pl* **-las** *or* **-lae** \-ˌlē, -ˌlī\ [ME, fr. L, pipe, fistula] (14c) : an abnormal passage that leads from an abscess or hollow organ or part to the body surface or from one hollow organ or part to another and that may be surgically created to permit passage of fluids or secretions
fis•tu•lous \-ləs\ *adj* (15c) **1** : of, relating to, or having the form or nature of a fistula **2** : hollow like a pipe or reed
[1]**fit** \ˈfit\ *n* [ME, fr. OE *fitt;* akin to OS *fittea* division of a poem, OHG *fizza* skein] (bef. 12c) *archaic* : a division of a poem or song
[2]**fit** *adj* **fit•ter; fit•test** [ME; akin to ME *fitten*] (14c) **1 a** (1) : adapted to an end or design : suitable by nature or by art (2) : adapted to the environment so as to be capable of surviving **b** : acceptable from a particular viewpoint (as of competence or morality) : PROPER ⟨a movie ~ for the whole family⟩ **2 a** : put into a suitable state : made ready ⟨get the house ~ for company⟩ **b** : being in such a state as to be or seem ready to do or suffer something ⟨fair ~ to cry I was —Bryan MacMahon⟩ ⟨laughing ~ to burst⟩ **3** : sound physically and mentally : HEALTHY — **fit•ly** *adv* — **fit to be tied** : extremely angry or irritated — **fit to kill** : in a striking manner ⟨dressed *fit to kill*⟩
syn FIT, SUITABLE, MEET, PROPER, APPROPRIATE, FITTING, APT, HAPPY, FELICITOUS mean right with respect to some end, need, use, or circumstance. FIT stresses adaptability and sometimes special readiness for use or action ⟨*fit* for battle⟩. SUITABLE implies an answering to requirements or demands ⟨clothes *suitable* for camping⟩. MEET suggests a just proportioning ⟨*meet* payment⟩. PROPER suggests a suitability through essential nature or accordance with custom ⟨*proper* acknowledgement⟩. APPROPRIATE implies eminent or distinctive fitness ⟨an *appropriate* gift⟩. FITTING implies harmony of mood or tone ⟨a *fitting* end⟩. APT connotes a fitness marked by nicety and discrimination ⟨*apt* quotations⟩. HAPPY suggests what is effectively or successfully appropriate ⟨a *happy* choice of words⟩. FELICITOUS suggests an aptness that is opportune, telling, or graceful ⟨a *felicitous* phrase⟩.
[3]**fit** *n* [ME, fr. OE *fitt* strife] (ca. 1541) **1 a** : a sudden violent attack of a disease (as epilepsy) esp. when marked by convulsions or unconsciousness : PAROXYSM **b** : a sudden but transient attack of a physical disturbance **2** : a sudden burst or flurry (as of activity) ⟨cleaned the whole house in a ~ of efficiency⟩ **3** : an emotional reaction (as in anger or frustration) ⟨has a ~ when I show up late⟩ — **by fits** *or* **by fits and starts** *or* **in fits and starts** : in an impulsive and irregular manner ⟨construction proceeded *by fits and starts*⟩
[4]**fit** *vb* **fit•ted** *or* **fit; fit•ting** [ME *fitten* to marshal troops, fr. or akin to MD *vitten* to be suitable] *vt* (15c) **1 a** : to be suitable for or to : harmonize with **b** *archaic* : to be seemly or proper for ⟨it ~*s* us then to be as provident as fear may teach us —Shak.⟩ **2 a** : to conform correctly to the shape or size of ⟨it doesn't ~ me anymore⟩ **b** (1) : to insert or adjust until correctly in place ⟨~ the mechanism into the box⟩ (2) : to make or adjust to the right shape and size ⟨*fitting* the jacket to the customer⟩ (3) : to measure for determining the specifications of something to be worn by ⟨*fitted* him for a new suit⟩ **c** : to make a place or room for : ACCOMMODATE **3** : to be in agreement or accord with ⟨the theory ~*s* all the facts⟩ **4 a** : to put into a condition of readiness **b** : to cause to conform to or suit something **5** : SUPPLY, EQUIP ⟨*fitted* the ship with new engines⟩ — often used with *out* **6** : to adjust (a smooth curve of a specified type) to a given set of points ~ *vi* **1** *archaic* : to be seemly, proper, or suitable **2** : to conform to a particular shape or size; *also* : to be accommodated ⟨will we all ~ into the car?⟩ **3** : to be in harmony or accord : BELONG — often used with *in* — **fit•ter** *n*
[5]**fit** *n* (1823) : the fact, condition, or manner of fitting or being fitted: as **a** : the way clothing fits the wearer **b** : the degree of closeness between surfaces in an assembly of parts **c** : GOODNESS OF FIT
[6]**fit** *dial past and past part of* FIGHT
fitch \ˈfich\ *or* **fitch•ew** \ˈfi-(ˌ)chü\ *n* [ME *fiche, ficheux,* fr. MF or MD; MF *fichau,* fr. MD *vitsau*] (15c) **1** : POLECAT 1 **2** : the fur or pelt of the polecat
fitch•et \ˈfi-chət\ *n* (1535) : POLECAT 1
fit•ful \ˈfit-fəl\ *adj* (1592) **1** *obs* : characterized by fits or paroxysms **2** : having an erratic or intermittent character : IRREGULAR — **fit•ful•ly** \-fə-lē\ *adv* — **fit•ful•ness** *n*
syn FITFUL, SPASMODIC, CONVULSIVE mean lacking steadiness or regularity in movement. FITFUL implies intermittence, a succession of starts and stops or risings and fallings ⟨*fitful* sleep⟩. SPASMODIC adds to FITFUL the implication of rapid or violent activity alternating with inactivity ⟨*spasmodic* growth⟩. CONVULSIVE suggests the breaking of regularity or quiet by uncontrolled movement ⟨*convulsive* shocks⟩.
fit•ment \ˈfit-mənt\ *n* [⁴*fit*] (1851) *chiefly Brit* : FURNISHING 2, FIXTURE, CABINETRY — usu. used in pl.
fit•ness \ˈfit-nəs\ *n* (1580) **1** : the quality or state of being fit **2** : the capacity of an organism to survive and transmit its genotype to reproductive offspring as compared to competing organisms; *also* : the contribution of an allele or genotype to the gene pool of subsequent generations as compared to that of other alleles or genotypes
fitted *adj* (1652) **1** : FIT, SUITABLE **2** : shaped for a precise fit ⟨a ~ sheet⟩; *esp* : shaped to conform to the lines of the body ⟨a ~ shirt⟩
[1]**fitting** *adj* (15c) : of a kind appropriate to the situation : SUITABLE *syn* see FIT — **fit•ting•ly** \-tiŋ-lē\ *adv* — **fit•ting•ness** *n*
[2]**fitting** *n* (1607) **1** : an action or act of one that fits; *specif* : a trying on of clothes which are in the process of being made or altered **2** : something used in fitting up : ACCESSORY **3** : a small often standardized part ⟨an electrical ~⟩
five \ˈfīv\ *n* [ME, fr. *five,* adj., fr. OE *fīf;* akin to OHG *finf* five, L *quinque,* Gk *pente*] (bef. 12c) **1** — see NUMBER table **2** *pl* : a British handball game **3** : the fifth in a set or series ⟨the ~ of clubs⟩ **4** : something having five units or members; *esp* : a basketball team **5** : a 5-dollar bill **6** : FIFTEEN 2 **7** : a gesture in which two people slap each other's extended hands (as in greeting or celebration) — usu. used in phrases with *give* or *slap* ⟨so I slapped him ~ and hugged him —J. R. Burke⟩ — **five** *adj* — **five** *pron, pl in constr*
five–and–ten \ˌfīv-ən-ˈten\ *n* [fr. the fact that all articles in such stores were formerly priced at either 5 or 10 cents] (1880) : a retail store that carries chiefly inexpensive merchandise (as notions and household goods) — called also *five-and-dime*
five–fin•ger \ˈfīv-ˌfiŋ-gər\ *n* (bef. 12c) : CINQUEFOIL 1
five•fold \ˈfīv-ˌfōld, -ˈfōld\ *adj* (bef. 12c) **1** : having five units or members **2** : being five times as great or as many — **five•fold** \-ˈfōld\ *adv*
5–HT \ˈfīv-(ˌ)āch-ˈtē\ *n* [*5-h*ydroxy*t*ryptamine] (1958) : SEROTONIN
five of a kind (1897) : four cards of the same rank plus a wild card in one hand — see POKER illustration
fiv•er \ˈfī-vər\ *n* (1843) **1** *slang* : a 5-dollar bill **2** *Brit* : a 5-pound note
five–spice powder \ˈfīv-ˈspīs-\ *n* (1970) : a blend of spices typically including anise, pepper, fennel, cloves, and cinnamon that is used in Chinese cooking
five–star \ˈfīv-ˈstär\ *adj* (1913) : of first class or quality ⟨a ~ hotel⟩

\ə\ **abut** \ᵊ\ kitten, F table \ər\ **fur**ther \a\ **ash** \ā\ **ace** \ä\ **mop, mar**
\au̇\ **out** \ch\ **chin** \e\ **bet** \ē\ **easy** \g\ **go** \i\ **hit** \ī\ **ice** \j\ **job**
\ŋ\ **sing** \ō\ **go** \ȯ\ **law** \ȯi\ **boy** \th\ **thin** \th\ **the** \ü\ **loot** \u̇\ **foot**
\y\ yet \zh\ **vi**sion, beige \k, ⁿ, œ, ue, ʸ\ *see* Guide to Pronunciation

[1]**fix** \ˈfiks\ *vb* [ME, fr. L *fixus,* pp. of *figere* to fasten; akin to Lith *dygti* to sprout, break through] *vt* (14c) **1 a :** to make firm, stable, or stationary **b :** to give a permanent or final form to: as (1) **:** to change into a stable compound or available form ⟨bacteria that ~ nitrogen⟩ (2) **:** to kill, harden, and preserve for microscopic study (3) **:** to make the image of (a photographic film) permanent by removing unused salts **c :** AFFIX, ATTACH **2 a :** to hold or direct steadily ⟨~*es* his eyes on the horizon⟩ **b :** to capture the attention of ⟨~*ed* her with a stare⟩ **3 a :** to set or place definitely **:** ESTABLISH **b :** to make an accurate determination of **:** DISCOVER ⟨~*ing* our location on the chart⟩ **c :** ASSIGN ⟨~ the blame⟩ **4 :** to set in order **:** ADJUST **5 :** to get ready **:** PREPARE ⟨~ lunch⟩ **6 a :** REPAIR, MEND ⟨~ the clock⟩ **b :** RESTORE, CURE ⟨the doctor ~*ed* him up⟩ **c :** SPAY, CASTRATE **7 a :** to get even with **b :** to influence the actions, outcome, or effect of by improper or illegal methods ⟨the race had been ~*ed*⟩ ~ *vi* **1 :** to become firm, stable, or fixed **2 :** to get set **:** be on the verge ⟨we're ~*ing* to leave soon⟩ **3 :** to direct one's attention or efforts **:** FOCUS; *also* **:** DECIDE, SETTLE — usu. used with *on* ⟨had ~*ed* on the first Saturday in June⟩ ***syn*** see FASTEN — **fix•able** \ˈfik-sə-bəl\ *adj*

[2]**fix** *n* (1809) **1 :** a position of difficulty or embarrassment **:** PREDICAMENT **2 a :** the position (as of a ship) determined by bearings, observations, or radio; *also* **:** a determination of one's position **b :** an accurate determination or understanding esp. by observation or analysis **3 :** an act or instance of improper or illegal fixing ⟨the ~ was in⟩ **4 :** a supply or dose of something strongly desired or craved ⟨a coffee ~⟩; *esp* **:** a shot of a narcotic **5 :** FIXATION **6 :** something that fixes or restores **:** SOLUTION ⟨an easy ~⟩

fix•ate \ˈfik-ˌsāt\ *vb* **fix•at•ed; fix•at•ing** *vt* (1885) **1 :** to make fixed, stationary, or unchanging **2 :** to focus one's gaze on **3 :** to direct (the libido) toward an infantile form of gratification ~ *vi* **1 :** to focus or concentrate one's gaze or attention intently or obsessively **2 :** to undergo arrestment at a stage of development

fixated *adj* (1926) **:** arrested in development or adjustment; *esp* **:** arrested at a pregenital level of psychosexual development

fix•a•tion \fik-ˈsā-shən\ *n* (14c) **:** the act, process, or result of fixing, fixating, or becoming fixated: as **a :** a persistent concentration of libidinal energies upon objects characteristic of psychosexual stages of development preceding the genital stage **b :** stereotyped behavior (as in response to frustration) **c :** an obsessive or unhealthy preoccupation or attachment

fix•a•tive \ˈfik-sə-tiv\ *n* (ca. 1859) **:** something that fixes or sets: as **a :** a substance added to a perfume esp. to prevent too rapid evaporation **b :** a substance used to fix living tissue **c :** a varnish used esp. for the protection of drawings (as in pastel or charcoal) — **fixative** *adj*

fixed \ˈfikst\ *adj* (14c) **1 a :** securely placed or fastened **:** STATIONARY **b** (1) **:** NONVOLATILE (2) **:** formed into a chemical compound **c** (1) **:** not subject to change or fluctuation ⟨a ~ income⟩ (2) **:** firmly set in the mind ⟨a ~ idea⟩ (3) **:** having a final or crystallized form or character (4) **:** recurring on the same date from year to year ⟨~ holidays⟩ **d :** IMMOBILE, CONCENTRATED ⟨a ~ stare⟩ **2 :** supplied with something (as money) needed ⟨comfortably ~⟩ — **fixed•ly** \ˈfik-səd-lē, ˈfikst-lē\ *adv* — **fixed•ness** \ˈfik-səd-nəs, ˈfiks(t)-nəs\ *n*

fixed charge *n* (ca. 1901) **:** a regularly recurring expense (as rent, taxes, or interest) that must be met when due

fixed oil *n* (ca. 1791) **:** a nonvolatile oil; *esp* **:** a fatty oil — compare ESSENTIAL OIL

fixed–point *adj* (1948) **:** involving or being a mathematical notation (as in a decimal system) in which the point separating whole numbers and fractions is fixed — compare FLOATING-POINT

fixed star *n* (1551) **:** a star so distant that its motion can be measured only by very precise observations over long periods

fix•er \ˈfik-sər\ *n* (1601) **:** one that fixes: as **a :** a person who intervenes to enable someone to circumvent the law or obtain a political favor **b :** a person who adjusts matters or disputes by negotiation **c :** SODIUM THIOSULFATE; *also* **:** a solution of sodium thiosulfate

fix•er–up•per \ˈfik-sər-ˌə-pər\ *n* (ca. 1977) **:** something (as a house or car) that needs fixing up

fix•ing \-siŋ\ *n* (1605) **1 :** the act or process of one that fixes **2** *pl* *often* -sənz\ **:** customary accompaniments **:** TRIMMINGS ⟨a turkey dinner with all the ~*s*⟩

fix•i•ty \ˈfik-sə-tē\ *n, pl* **-ties** (1666) **1 :** the quality or state of being fixed or stable **2 :** something that is fixed

fix•ture \ˈfiks-chər\ *n* [modif. of LL *fixura,* fr. L *fixus*] (1598) **1 :** the act or process of fixing **:** the state of being fixed **2 a :** something that is fixed or attached (as to a building) as a permanent appendage or as a structural part ⟨a plumbing ~⟩ **b :** a device for supporting work during machining **c :** an item of movable property so incorporated into real property that it may be regarded as legally a part of it **3 :** a familiar or invariably present element or feature in some particular setting; *esp* **:** a person long associated with a place or activity **4 :** a settled date or time esp. for a sporting or festive event; *also* **:** such an event esp. as a regularly scheduled affair

fix up *vt* (1764) **1 :** REFURBISH ⟨*fix up* the attic⟩ **2 :** to set right **:** SETTLE ⟨*fixed up* their dispute⟩ **3 :** to provide with something needed or wanted; *esp* **:** to arrange a date for

[1]**fizz** \ˈfiz\ *vi* [prob. of imit. origin] (1685) **1 :** to make a hissing or sputtering sound **:** EFFERVESCE **2 :** to show excitement or exhilaration

[2]**fizz** *n* (1842) **1 a :** a hissing sound **b :** SPIRIT, LIVELINESS **2 :** an effervescent beverage — **fizzy** \ˈfi-zē\ *adj*

[1]**fiz•zle** \ˈfi-zəl\ *vi* **fiz•zled; fiz•zling** \-z(ə-)liŋ\ [perh. alter. of *fist* to break wind] (1840) **1 :** FIZZ **2 :** to fail or end feebly esp. after a promising start — often used with *out*

[2]**fizzle** *n* (1846) **:** an abortive effort **:** FAILURE

fjord *also* **fiord** \fē-ˈȯrd, ˈfē-ˌ; ˈfyȯrd\ *n* [Norw *fjord,* fr. ON *fjǫrthr* — more at FORD] (1674) **:** a narrow inlet of the sea between cliffs or steep slopes

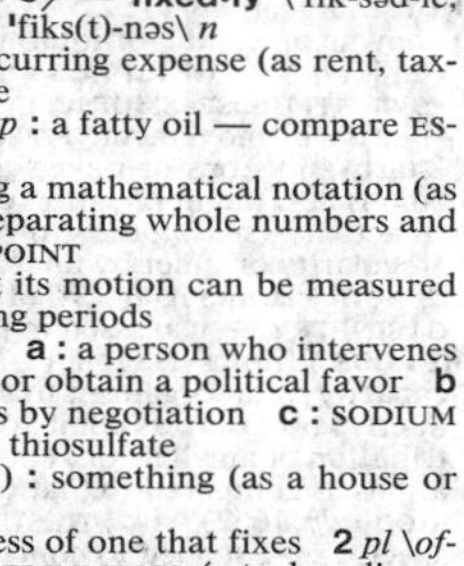

fjord

fl *abbr* **1** flanker **2** floor **3** florin **4** [L *floruit*] flourished **5** fluid

FL *abbr* **1** Florida **2** focal length **3** foreign language

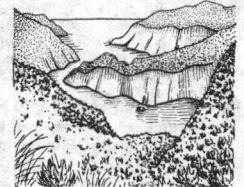

Fla *abbr* Florida

flab \ˈflab\ *n* [back-formation fr. *flabby*] (1951) **:** soft flabby body tissue

flab•ber•gast \ˈfla-bər-ˌgast\ *vt* [origin unknown] (1772) **:** to overwhelm with shock, surprise, or wonder **:** DUMBFOUND ***syn*** see SURPRISE — **flab•ber•gast•ing•ly** \-ˌgas-tiŋ-lē\ *adv*

flab•by \ˈfla-bē\ *adj* **flab•bi•er; -est** [alter. of *flappy*] (1694) **1 :** lacking resilience or firmness **:** FLACCID **2 :** weak and ineffective **:** FEEBLE — **flab•bi•ly** \ˈfla-bə-lē\ *adv* — **flab•bi•ness** \ˈfla-bē-nəs\ *n*

flac•cid \ˈfla-səd *also* ˈflak-səd\ *adj* [L *flaccidus,* fr. *flaccus* flabby] (1620) **1 a :** not firm or stiff; *also* **:** lacking normal or youthful firmness ⟨~ muscles⟩ **b** *of a plant part* **:** deficient in turgor **2 :** lacking vigor or force ⟨~ leadership⟩ — **flac•cid•i•ty** \fla(k)-ˈsi-də-tē\ *n* — **flac•cid•ly** \ˈfla(k)-səd-lē\ *adv*

[1]**flack** \ˈflak\ *n* [origin unknown] (1939) **:** one who provides publicity; *esp* **:** PRESS AGENT — **flack•ery** \ˈfla-k(ə-)rē\ *n*

[2]**flack** *var of* FLAK

[3]**flack** *vi* (1965) **:** to provide publicity **:** engage in press-agentry

fla•con \ˈfla-kən, -ˌkän; fla-ˈkōⁿ\ *n* [F, fr. MF, bottle — more at FLAGON] (1824) **:** a small usu. ornamental bottle with a tight cap

[1]**flag** \ˈflag *also* ˈflāg\ *n* [ME *flagge* reed, rush] (14c) **:** any of various monocotyledonous plants with long ensiform leaves: as **a :** IRIS; *esp* **:** a wild iris **b :** SWEET FLAG

[2]**flag** *n, often attrib* [prob. akin to *fag* end of cloth — more at FAG END] (1530) **1 :** a usu. rectangular piece of fabric of distinctive design that is used as a symbol (as of a nation), as a signaling device, or as a decoration **2 a :** the tail of some dogs (as a setter or hound); *also* **:** the long hair fringing a dog's tail **b :** the tail of a deer **3 a :** something used like a flag to signal or attract attention **b :** one of the cross strokes of a musical note less than a quarter note in value **4 :** something represented by a flag: as **a :** FLAGSHIP **b :** an admiral functioning in his office of command **c :** NATIONALITY; *esp* **:** the nationality of registration of a ship or aircraft

[3]**flag** *vt* **flagged; flag•ging** (1856) **1 :** to signal with or as if with a flag; *esp* **:** to signal to stop ⟨*flagged* the train⟩ — often used with *down* **2 :** to mark or identify with or as if with a flag ⟨*flagged* potential problems in the proposal⟩ **3 :** to call a penalty on **:** PENALIZE ⟨a lineman *flagged* for being offside⟩

[4]**flag** *vi* **flagged; flag•ging** [prob. fr. [2]*flag*] (1545) **1 :** to hang loose without stiffness **2 a :** to become unsteady, feeble, or spiritless **b :** to decline in interest, attraction, or value ⟨*flagging* stock prices⟩

[5]**flag** *n* [ME *flagge* turf, perh. fr. ON *flaga* slab; akin to OE *flōh* chip] (1604) **:** a hard evenly stratified stone that splits into flat pieces suitable for paving; *also* **:** a piece of such stone

[6]**flag** *vt* **flagged; flag•ging** (1615) **:** to lay (as a pavement) with flags

flag day *n* (1894) **1** *cap F&D* **:** June 14 observed in various states in commemoration of the adoption in 1777 of the official U.S. flag **2** *Brit* **:** a day on which charitable contributions are solicited in exchange for small flags

fla•gel•lant \ˈfla-jə-lənt, flə-ˈje-lənt\ *n* (ca. 1587) **1 :** a person who scourges himself or herself as a public penance **2 :** a person who responds sexually to being beaten by or to beating another person — **flagellant** *adj* — **fla•gel•lant•ism** \-lən-ˌti-zəm\ *n*

fla•gel•lar \flə-ˈje-lər, ˈfla-jə-lər\ *adj* (ca. 1889) **:** of or relating to a flagellum

[1]**flag•el•late** \ˈfla-jə-ˌlāt\ *vt* **-lat•ed; -lat•ing** [L *flagellatus,* pp. of *flagellare,* fr. *flagellum,* dim. of *flagrum* whip; perh. akin to ON *blaka* to wave] (ca. 1623) **1 :** WHIP, SCOURGE **2 :** to drive or punish as if by whipping

[2]**fla•gel•late** \ˈfla-jə-lət, -ˌlāt; flə-ˈje-lət\ *adj* [NL *flagellatus,* fr. *flagellum*] (ca. 1859) **1 a** *or* **flag•el•lat•ed** \ˈfla-jə-ˌlā-təd\ **:** having flagella **b :** shaped like a flagellum **2** [[3]*flagellate*] **:** of, relating to, or caused by flagellates ⟨~ diarrhea⟩

[3]**flagellate** *same as* [2]\ *n* [NL *Flagellata,* class of unicellular organisms, fr. neut. pl. of *flagellatus*] (1879) **:** a flagellate protozoan or alga

flag•el•la•tion \ˌfla-jə-ˈlā-shən\ *n* (15c) **:** the act or practice of flagellating; *esp* **:** the practice of a flagellant

fla•gel•lin \flə-ˈje-lən\ *n* [*flagell*um + [1]-*in*] (1955) **:** a polymeric protein that is the chief constituent of bacterial flagella and that determines the specificity of the flagellum in eliciting an immune response

fla•gel•lum \flə-ˈje-ləm\ *n, pl* **-la** \-lə\ *also* **-lums** [NL, fr. L, whip, shoot of a plant] (1852) **:** any of various elongated filiform appendages of plants or animals: as **a :** the slender distal part of an antenna **b :** a long tapering process that projects singly or in groups from a cell and is the primary organ of motion of many microorganisms

[1]**fla•geo•let** \ˌfla-jə-ˈlet, -ˈlā\ *n* [F, fr. OF *flajolet,* fr. *flajol* flute, fr. VL **flabeolum,* fr. L *flare* to blow — more at BLOW] (1659) **:** a small fipple flute resembling the treble recorder

[2]**flageolet** *n* [F, dim. of *flageolle* kidney bean, modif. of It *fagiolo,* fr. L *phaseolus* — more at FRIJOLE] (1877) **:** a green kidney bean used in French cuisine

flag football *n* (1954) **:** a variation of football in which a player must remove a flag attached to the ballcarrier's clothing to stop the play

flagging *adj* (1545) **1 :** LANGUID, WEAK **2 :** becoming progressively less **:** DWINDLING — **flag•ging•ly** *adv*

fla•gi•tious \flə-ˈji-shəs\ *adj* [ME *flagicious,* fr. L *flagitiosus,* fr. *flagitium* shameful thing] (14c) **:** marked by scandalous crime or vice **:** VILLAINOUS — **fla•gi•tious•ly** *adv* — **fla•gi•tious•ness** *n*

flag•man \ˈflag-mən\ *n* (1832) **:** a person who signals with a flag

flag of convenience (1956) **:** registry of a merchant ship under a foreign flag in order to profit from less restrictive regulations

flag officer *n* [fr. such officers being entitled to display a flag with one or more stars indicating rank] (1665) **:** any of the officers in the navy or coast guard above captain — compare GENERAL OFFICER

flag of truce (1582) **:** a white flag carried or displayed to an enemy as an invitation to conference or parley

flag•on \ˈfla-gən\ *n* [ME, fr. MF *flascon, flacon* bottle, fr. LL *flascon-, flasco* — more at FLASK] (15c) **1 a :** a large usu. metal or pottery vessel (as for wine) with handle and spout and often a lid **b :** a large bulging short-necked bottle **2 :** the contents of a flagon

flag•pole \ˈflag-ˌpōl\ *n* (1854) **:** a pole on which to raise a flag

fla•grance \ˈflā-grən(t)s *also* ˈfla-\ *n* (ca. 1615) **:** FLAGRANCY

fla•gran•cy \ˈflā-grən(t)-sē *also* ˈfla-\ *n* (1599) **:** the quality or state of being flagrant

flag rank *n* (1894) **:** the rank of a flag officer

fla·grant \ˈflā-grənt *also* ˈfla-\ *adj* [L *flagrant-, flagrans,* prp. of *flagrare* to burn — more at BLACK] (1513) **1** *archaic* : fiery hot : BURNING **2** : conspicuously offensive ⟨~ errors⟩; *esp* : so obviously inconsistent with what is right or proper as to appear to be a flouting of law or morality ⟨~ violations of human rights⟩ — **fla·grant·ly** *adv*

syn FLAGRANT, GLARING, GROSS, RANK mean conspicuously bad or objectionable. FLAGRANT applies usu. to offenses or errors so bad that they can neither escape notice nor be condoned ⟨*flagrant* abuse of the office of president⟩. GLARING implies painful or damaging obtrusiveness of something that is conspicuously wrong, faulty, or improper ⟨*glaring* errors⟩. GROSS implies the exceeding of reasonable or excusable limits ⟨*gross* carelessness⟩. RANK applies to what is openly and extremely objectionable and utterly condemned ⟨*rank* heresy⟩.

flagrante delicto *adv* (1826) : IN FLAGRANTE DELICTO

flag·ship \ˈflag-ˌship\ *n* (1672) **1** : the ship that carries the commander of a fleet or subdivision of a fleet and flies the commander's flag **2** : the finest, largest, or most important one of a series, network, or chain ⟨the company's ~ store⟩

flag·staff \-ˌstaf\ *n* (ca. 1613) : a staff on which a flag is hoisted

flag·stick \-ˌstik\ *n* (1926) : a staff for a flag marking the location of the cup on a golf putting green

flag·stone \-ˌstōn\ *n* (1730) : [5]FLAG

flag stop *n* (1941) : a point at which a vehicle in public transportation stops only on prearrangement or signal

flag–wav·er \ˈflag-ˌwā-vər\ *n* (1894) **1** : one who is intensely and conspicuously patriotic **2** : one who waves a flag in signaling **3** : a song intended to rouse patriotic sentiment

flag–wav·ing \-viŋ\ *n* (1892) : passionate appeal to patriotic or partisan sentiment : CHAUVINISM

[1]**flail** \ˈflāl\ *n* [ME *fleil, flail,* partly fr. OE **flegel* (whence OE *fligel*), fr. LL *flagellum* flail, fr. L, whip & partly fr. AF *flael,* fr. LL *flagellum* — more at FLAGELLATE] (bef. 12c) : a hand threshing implement consisting of a wooden handle at the end of which a stouter and shorter stick is so hung as to swing freely

[2]**flail** *vt* (15c) **1 a** : to strike with or as if with a flail ⟨arms ~*ing* the water⟩ **b** : to move, swing, or beat as if wielding a flail ⟨~*ing* a club to drive away the insects⟩ **2** : to thresh (grain) with a flail ~ *vi* : to move, swing, or beat like a flail

flair \ˈfler\ *n* [F, lit., sense of smell, fr. OF, odor, fr. *flairier* to give off an odor, fr. LL *flagrare,* alter. of L *fragrare*] (1881) **1** : a skill or instinctive ability to appreciate or make good use of something : TALENT ⟨a ~ for color⟩; *also* : INCLINATION, TENDENCY ⟨a ~ for the dramatic⟩ **2** : a uniquely attractive quality : STYLE ⟨fashionable dresses with a ~ all their own⟩

flak *also* **flack** \ˈflak\ *n, pl* **flak** *also* **flack** [G, fr. *Fliegerabwehrkanonen,* fr. *Flieger* flyer + *Abwehr* defense + *Kanonen* cannons] (1938) **1** : antiaircraft guns **2** : the bursting shells fired from flak **3** *also* **flack** : CRITICISM, OPPOSITION

[1]**flake** \ˈflāk\ *n* [ME; akin to OE *flacor* flying (of arrows), ON *flakna* to flake off, split] (14c) **1** : a small loose mass or bit ⟨~*s* of snow⟩ **2** : a thin flattened piece or layer : CHIP **3** *slang* : COCAINE **4** : FLAKE TOOL

[2]**flake** *vb* **flaked; flak·ing** *vt* (1602) **1** : to cover with or as if with flakes **2** : to form or break into flakes : CHIP ~ *vi* : to separate into flakes; *also* : to peel in flakes

[3]**flake** *n* [ME *flake, fleke* hurdle; akin to MD *vlāke, vlaec* hurdle, ON *flaki*] (1623) : a stage, platform, or tray for drying fish or produce

[4]**flake** *n* [perh. fr. *flake out*] (1964) : a person who is flaky : ODDBALL

flake out *vi* [prob. fr. dial. *flake* to lie, bask] (1939) **1** *slang* : to fall asleep **2** *slang* : to be overcome esp. by exhaustion

flake tool *n* (ca. 1947) : a Stone-Age tool that is a flake of stone struck off from a larger piece — called also *flake*

flak jacket *n* (1950) : a jacket containing metal plates for protection against flak; *broadly* : a bulletproof vest — called also *flak vest*

[1]**flaky** *also* **flak·ey** \ˈflā-kē\ *adj* **flak·i·er; -est** (1580) **1** : consisting of flakes ⟨~ snow⟩ **2** : tending to flake ⟨a ~ crust⟩ — **flak·i·ness** *n*

[2]**flaky** *adj* **flak·i·er; -est** [[4]*flake*] (ca. 1963) : markedly odd or unconventional : OFFBEAT, WACKY — **flak·i·ness** *n*

flam \ˈflam\ *n* [prob. imit.] (1744) : a drumbeat of two strokes of which the first is a very quick grace note

[1]**flam·bé** \fläm-ˈbā, flä^{n}-\ *adj* [F *flambé,* fr. pp. of *flamber* to flame, singe, fr. OF, fr. *flambe* flame] (1914) : dressed or served covered with flaming liquor — usu. used postpositively ⟨crepes suzette ~⟩

[2]**flambé** *vt* **flam·béed; flam·bé·ing** (ca. 1946) : to douse with a liquor (as brandy, rum, or cognac) and ignite

flam·beau \ˈflam-ˌbō\ *n, pl* **flam·beaux** \-ˌbōz\ *or* **flambeaus** [F, fr. MF, fr. *flambe* flame] (1632) : a flaming torch; *broadly* : TORCH

flam·boy·ance \flam-ˈbȯi-ən(t)s\ *n* (1891) : the quality or state of being flamboyant

flam·boy·an·cy \-ən(t)-sē\ *n* (ca. 1889) : FLAMBOYANCE

[1]**flam·boy·ant** \-ənt\ *adj* [F, fr. prp. of *flamboyer* to flame, fr. OF, fr. *flambe*] (1832) **1** *often cap* : characterized by waving curves suggesting flames ⟨~ tracery⟩ ⟨~ architecture⟩ **2** : marked by or given to strikingly elaborate or colorful display or behavior ⟨a ~ performer⟩ — **flam·boy·ant·ly** *adv*

[2]**flamboyant** *n* (1879) : ROYAL POINCIANA

[1]**flame** \ˈflām\ *n* [ME *flaume, flaumbe,* fr. AF *flame* (fr. L *flamma*) & *flambe, flamble,* fr. L *flammula,* dim. of *flamma* flame; akin to L *flagrare* to burn — more at BLACK] (14c) **1** : the glowing gaseous part of a fire **2 a** : a state of blazing combustion ⟨the car burst into ~⟩ **b** : a condition or appearance suggesting a flame or burning: as (1) : burning zeal or passion (2) : a strong reddish-orange color **3** : BRILLIANCE, BRIGHTNESS **4** : SWEETHEART **5** : the memory, reputation, or beliefs of a deceased person; *broadly* : MEMORY ⟨keeper of the ~⟩ **6** : an angry, hostile, or abusive electronic message

[2]**flame** *vb* **flamed; flam·ing** *vi* (14c) **1** : to burn with a flame : BLAZE **2 a** : to burst or break out violently or passionately ⟨*flaming* with indignation⟩ **b** : to send an angry, hostile, or abusive electronic message **3** : to shine brightly : GLOW ⟨color *flaming* up in her cheeks⟩ ~ *vt* **1** : to send or convey by means of flame ⟨~ a message by signal fires⟩ **2** : to treat or affect with flame: as **a** : to sear, sterilize, or destroy by fire **b** : FLAMBÉ **3** : to send an angry, hostile, or abusive electronic message to or about — **flam·er** *n*

flame cell *n* (1888) : a hollow cell that has a tuft of vibratile cilia and is part of some lower invertebrate excretory systems (as of a platyhelminthic worm)

fla·men \ˈflā-mən\ *n, pl* **flamens** *or* **flam·i·nes** \ˈfla-mə-ˌnēz\ [ME *flamin,* fr. L *flamin-, flamen*] (14c) : a priest esp. in ancient Rome

fla·men·co \flə-ˈmeŋ-(ˌ)kō\ *n, pl* **-cos** [Sp, fr. *flamenco* of the Gypsies, lit., Flemish, fr. MD *Vlaminc* Fleming] (1896) **1** : a vigorous rhythmic dance style of the Andalusian Gypsies; *also* : a dance in flamenco style **2** : music or song suitable to accompany a flamenco dance

flame·out \ˈflām-ˌau̇t\ *n* (1950) **1** : the unintentional cessation of operation of a jet airplane engine **2** : a sudden downfall, failure, or cessation **3** : a person whose successful career ends abruptly

flame out *vi* (1951) : to fail spectacularly and esp. prematurely

flame photometer *n* (1945) : a spectrophotometer in which a spray of metallic salts in solution is vaporized in a very hot flame and subjected to quantitative analysis by measuring the intensities of the spectral lines of the metals present — **flame photometric** *adj* — **flame photometry** *n*

flame·proof \ˈflām-ˌprüf\ *adj* (1886) : resistant to damage or burning on contact with flame — **flameproof** *vt* — **flame·proof·er** *n*

flame–retardant *adj* (1947) : made or treated so as to resist burning

flame stitch *n* (1936) : a needlepoint stitch that produces a pattern resembling flames

flame·throw·er \-ˌthrō-ər\ *n* (1917) **1** : a device that expels from a nozzle a burning stream of liquid or semiliquid fuel under pressure **2** : a pitcher who throws hard : a fastball pitcher

flame tree *n* (1860) : any of several trees or shrubs with showy scarlet or yellow flowers: as **a** : a tree (*Brachychiton acerifolium* of the family Sterculiaceae) of southern Australia with panicles of brilliant scarlet flowers **b** : ROYAL POINCIANA

flaming *adj* (14c) **1** : resembling or suggesting a flame in color, brilliance, or wavy outline ⟨the ~ sunset sky⟩ ⟨~ red hair⟩ **2** : being on fire : BLAZING ⟨a ~ torch⟩ **3** : INTENSE, PASSIONATE ⟨~ youth⟩ **4** — used as an intensive ⟨you ~ idiot⟩ — **flam·ing·ly** *adv*

fla·min·go \flə-ˈmiŋ-(ˌ)gō\ *n, pl* **-gos** *also* **-goes** [obs. Sp *flamengo* (now *flamenco*), lit., Fleming, German (conventionally thought of as ruddy-complexioned)] (1565) : any of several large aquatic birds (family Phoenicopteridae) with long legs and neck, webbed feet, a broad lamellate bill resembling that of a duck but abruptly bent downward, and usu. rosy-white plumage with scarlet wing coverts and black wing quills

flam·ma·bil·i·ty \ˌfla-mə-ˈbi-lə-tē\ *n* (1646) : ability to support combustion; *esp* : a high capacity for combustion

flam·ma·ble \ˈfla-mə-bəl\ *adj* [L *flammare* to flame, set on fire, fr. *flamma*] (1813) : capable of being easily ignited and of burning quickly — **flammable** *n*

flan \ˈflan, ˈflän\ *n* [F, fr. OF *flaon,* fr. LL *fladon-, flado* flat cake, of Gmc origin; akin to OHG *flado* flat cake] (1846) **1 a** : an open pie containing any of various sweet or savory fillings **b** : custard baked with a caramel glaze **2** : the metal disk of a coin, token, or medal as distinguished from the design and lettering stamped on it

fla·neur *also* **flâ·neur** \flä-ˈnər\ *n* [F *flâneur*] (1854) : an idle man-about-town

[1]**flange** \ˈflanj\ *n* [perh. alter. of *flanch* a curving charge on a heraldic shield] (ca. 1735) **1** : a rib or rim for strength, for guiding, or for attachment to another object ⟨a ~ on a pipe⟩ ⟨a ~ on a wheel⟩ **2** : a projecting edge of cloth used for decoration on clothing ⟨a jacket with ~ shoulders⟩

[2]**flange** *vt* **flanged; flang·ing** (ca. 1859) : to furnish with a flange

[1]**flank** \ˈflaŋk\ *n* [ME, fr. OF *flanc,* of Gmc origin; akin to OHG *hlanca* loin, flank — more at LANK] (bef. 12c) **1 a** : the fleshy part of the side between the ribs and the hip; *broadly* : the side of a quadruped **b** : a cut of meat from this part of an animal — see BEEF illustration **2 a** : SIDE **b** : the right or left of a formation **3** : the area along either side of a heraldic shield

[2]**flank** *vt* (1594) **1 a** : to be situated at the side of; *esp* : to be situated on both sides of ⟨a road ~*ed* with linden trees⟩ **b** : to place something on each side of **2** : to protect a flank of **3** : to attack or threaten the flank of (as a body of troops)

flan·ken \ˈfläŋ-kən\ *n* [Yiddish, pl. of *flank,* lit., flank, ultim. fr. OF *flanc*] (1950) : beef flank cooked esp. by boiling

flank·er \ˈflaŋ-kər\ *n* (1940) : a football player stationed wide of the formation slightly behind the line of scrimmage as a pass receiver — called also *flanker back*

flank steak *n* (1902) : a pear-shaped muscle of the beef flank; *also* : a steak cut from this muscle — see BEEF illustration

flan·nel \ˈfla-nᵊl\ *n* [ME *flaunneol* woolen cloth or garment] (1503) **1 a** : a soft twilled wool or worsted fabric with a loose texture and a slightly napped surface **b** : a napped cotton fabric of soft yarns simulating the texture of wool flannel **c** : a stout cotton fabric usu. napped on one side **2** *pl* **a** : flannel underwear **b** : outer garments of flannel; *esp* : men's trousers **3** *Brit* : WASHCLOTH **4** *Brit* : flattering or evasive talk; *also* : NONSENSE, RUBBISH — **flannel** *adj* — **flan·nel·ly** \-nᵊl-ē\ *adj*

flan·nel·ette \ˌfla-nə-ˈlet\ *n* (ca. 1882) : a lightweight cotton flannel

flan·nel·mouthed \ˈfla-nᵊl-ˌmau̇tht, -ˌmau̇t͟hd\ *adj* (1853) **1** : speaking in a tricky or ingratiating way **2** : speaking indistinctly

[1]**flap** \ˈflap\ *n* [ME *flappe*] (14c) **1** : a stroke with something broad : SLAP **2** *obs* : something broad and flat used for striking **3** : something that is broad, limber, or flat and usu. thin and that hangs loose or projects freely: as **a** : a piece on a garment that hangs free **b** : a part of a book jacket that folds under the book's cover **c** : a piece of tissue partly severed from its place of origin for use in surgical grafting **d** : an extended part forming the closure (as of an envelope or carton) **4** : the motion of something broad and limber (as a sail or wing) **5** : a movable auxiliary airfoil usu. attached to an airplane wing's trailing edge to increase lift or drag — see AIRPLANE illustration **6 a** : a state

\ə\ **abut** \ᵊ\ **kitten**, F table \ər\ **further** \a\ **ash** \ā\ **ace** \ä\ **mop**, **mar**
\au̇\ **out** \ch\ **chin** \e\ **bet** \ē\ **easy** \g\ **go** \i\ **hit** \ī\ **ice** \j\ **job**
\ŋ\ **sing** \ō\ **go** \ȯ\ **law** \ȯi\ **boy** \th\ **thin** \t͟h\ **the** \ü\ **loot** \u̇\ **foot**
\y\ **yet** \zh\ **vision, beige** \k̲, ⁿ, œ, ue, ʸ\ *see* Guide to Pronunciation

of excitement or agitation : TIZZY, UPROAR **b** : something that generates an uproar **7** : a consonant (as the sound \d\ in *ladder* and \t\ in *latter*) characterized by a single rapid contact of the tongue or lower lip against another point in the mouth — called also *tap*

[2]**flap** *vb* **flapped; flap·ping** *vt* (14c) **1** : to beat with or as if with a flap **2** : to toss sharply : FLING **3** : to move or cause to move in flaps ~ *vi* **1** : to sway loosely usu. with a noise of striking and esp. when moved by wind **2 a** : to beat or pulsate wings or something suggesting wings **b** : to progress by flapping **c** : to flutter ineffectively **3** : to talk foolishly and persistently

flap·doo·dle \ˈflap-ˌdü-dᵊl\ *n* [origin unknown] (1878) : NONSENSE

flap·jack \-ˌjak\ *n* (ca. 1600) : PANCAKE

flap·pa·ble \ˈfla-pə-bəl\ *adj* (1968) : easily upset

flap·per \ˈfla-pər\ *n* (ca. 1570) **1 a** : something used in flapping or striking **b** : one that flaps **c** : FLIPPER 1 **2** : a young woman; *specif* : a young woman of the period of World War I and the following decade who showed freedom from conventions (as in conduct)

flap·py \ˈfla-pē\ *adj* (1858) : flapping or tending to flap

[1]**flare** \ˈfler\ *n* [origin unknown] (1580) **1 a** : a fire or blaze of light used esp. to signal, illuminate, or attract attention; *also* : a device or composition used to produce such a flare **2** : an unsteady glaring light **b** : SOLAR FLARE; *also* : a sudden increase and decrease in the brightness of a star often amounting to a difference of several magnitudes **3 a** : a sudden outburst (as of excitement or anger) **b** : FLARE-UP 3 **4 a** : a spreading outward; *also* : a place or part that spreads **b** : an area of skin flush **5** : light resulting from reflection (as between lens surfaces) or an effect of this light (as a fogged or dense area in a photographic negative) **6 a** : a short pass in football thrown to a back who is running toward the sideline **b** : a weakly hit fly ball in baseball ⟨a ~ into short right field⟩ **7** *pl* : pants that flare toward the bottom

[2]**flare** *vb* **flared; flar·ing** *vi* (1616) **1 a** : to burn with an unsteady flame **b** : to stream in the wind **2 a** : to shine with a sudden light ⟨a match ~*s* in the darkness⟩ **b** (1) : to become suddenly excited or angry — usu. used with *up* (2) : to break out or intensify usu. suddenly or violently — often used with *up* **c** : to express strong emotion (as anger) **3** : to open or spread outward ⟨the pants ~ at the bottom⟩ ~ *vt* **1** : to display conspicuously ⟨*flaring* her scarf to attract attention⟩ **2** : to cause to flare ⟨the breeze ~*s* the candle⟩ **3** : to signal with a flare or by flaring **4** : to burn (a jet of waste gas) in the open air

flare–up \-ˌəp\ *n* (1839) **1** : a sudden outburst or intensification **2** : a sudden bursting (as of a smoldering fire) into flame or light **3** : a sudden outburst of or increase in the symptoms of a disease or condition

flar·ing \ˈfler-iŋ\ *adj* (1566) **1 a** : flaming or as if flaming brightly or unsteadily **b** : GAUDY ⟨a ~ resort hotel⟩ **2** : opening or spreading outward ⟨~ nostrils⟩ — **flar·ing·ly** \-iŋ-lē\ *adv*

[1]**flash** \ˈflash\ *vb* [ME *flaschen,* of imit. origin] *vi* (13c) **1** : RUSH, DASH — used of flowing water **2** : to break forth in or like a sudden flame or flare **3 a** : to appear suddenly ⟨an idea ~*es* into her mind⟩ **b** : to move with great speed ⟨the days ~ by⟩ **4 a** : to break forth or out so as to make a sudden display **b** : to act or speak vehemently and suddenly esp. in anger **5 a** : to give off light suddenly or in transient bursts **b** : to glow or gleam esp. with animation or passion ⟨her eyes ~*ed* with anger⟩ **6** : to change suddenly or violently into vapor **7** : to expose one's breasts or genitals usu. suddenly and briefly in public **8** : to have sudden insight — often used with *on* ~ *vt* **1 a** *archaic* : SPLASH **b** : to fill by a sudden inflow of water **2 a** : to cause the sudden appearance of (light) **b** : to cause to burst violently into flame **c** (1) : to cause (light) to reflect (2) : to cause (as a mirror) to reflect light (3) : to cause (a lamp) to flash **d** : to convey by means of flashes of light **3 a** : to make known or cause to appear with great speed ⟨~ a message on the screen⟩ **b** : to display obtrusively and ostentatiously ⟨always ~*ing* a roll of bills⟩ **c** : to expose to view usu. suddenly and briefly ⟨~*ed* a badge⟩ **4** : to cover with or form into a thin layer: as **a** : to protect against rain by covering with sheet metal or a substitute **b** : to coat (as glass) with a thin layer (as of metal or a differently colored glass) **5** : to subject (an exposed photographic negative or positive) to a supplementary uniform exposure to light before development in order to modify detail or tone **6** : to expose one's breasts or genitals usu. suddenly and briefly to ⟨~*ed* the audience⟩

syn FLASH, GLEAM, GLINT, SPARKLE, GLITTER, GLISTEN, GLIMMER, SHIMMER mean to send forth light. FLASH implies a sudden outburst of bright light ⟨lightning *flashed*⟩. GLEAM suggests a steady light seen through an obscuring medium or against a dark background ⟨lights *gleamed* in the valley⟩. GLINT implies a cold glancing light ⟨*glinting* steel⟩. SPARKLE suggests innumerable moving points of bright light ⟨the *sparkling* waters⟩. GLITTER connotes a brilliant sparkling or gleaming ⟨*glittering* diamonds⟩. GLISTEN applies to the soft sparkle from a wet or oily surface ⟨*glistening* wet sidewalk⟩. GLIMMER suggests a faint or wavering gleam ⟨a distant *glimmering* light⟩. SHIMMER means shining with a wavering light ⟨a *shimmering* satin dress⟩.

[2]**flash** *n* (1549) **1 a** : a sudden burst of light **b** : a movement of a flag in signaling **2** : a sudden and often brilliant burst ⟨a ~ of wit⟩ **3** : a brief time **4 a** : SHOW, DISPLAY; *esp* : a vulgar ostentatious display **b** *archaic* : a showy ostentatious person **c** : one that attracts notice; *esp* : an outstanding athlete **d** : PIZZAZZ **5** *obs* : thieves' slang **6** : something flashed: as **a** : GLIMPSE, LOOK **b** : SMILE **c** : a first brief news report **d** : FLASHLIGHT 2 **e** : a quick-spreading flame or momentary intense outburst of radiant heat **f** (1) : FLASHLIGHT 1 (2) : a device for producing a flashlight for taking photographs **7** : RUSH 7a **8** : the rapid conversion of a liquid into vapor

[3]**flash** *adj* (ca. 1700) **1 a** : FLASHY, SHOWY **b** : of, relating to, or characteristic of flashy people or things ⟨~ behavior⟩ **c** : of, relating to, or characteristic of persons considered social outcasts ⟨~ language⟩ **2** : of sudden origin and short duration ⟨a ~ fire⟩ **3** : having or using a solid-state data storage technology that retains data even without a connection to a power source ⟨~ memory⟩

[4]**flash** *adv* (1970) : by very brief exposure to an intense altering agent (as heat or cold) ⟨~ fry⟩ ⟨~ freeze⟩

flash·back \ˈflash-ˌbak\ *n* (1903) **1** : a recession of flame to an unwanted position (as into a blowpipe) **2 a** : interruption of chronological sequence (as in a film or literary work) by interjection of events of earlier occurrence; *also* : an instance of flashback **b** : a past incident recurring vividly in the mind

flash back *vi* (1944) **1** : to focus one's mind on or vividly remember a past time or incident — usu. used with *to* ⟨*flashed back* to my childhood⟩ **2** : to employ a flashback (as in a film) — usu. used with *to*

flash·board \-ˌbȯrd\ *n* (ca. 1774) : one or more boards projecting above the top of a dam to increase the depth of the water

flash·bulb \-ˌbəlb\ *n* (1935) : an electric bulb that can be used only once to produce a brief and very bright flash for taking photographs

flash card *n* (1923) : a card bearing words, numbers, or pictures that is briefly displayed (as by a teacher to a class) usu. as a learning aid

flash drive *n* (1992) : a data storage device that uses flash memory; *specif* : a small rectangular device that is designed to be plugged directly into a USB port on a computer and is often used for transferring files from one computer to another — called also *jump drive, thumb drive*

flash·er \ˈfla-shər\ *n* (1686) : one that flashes: as **a** : a light (as a traffic signal or automobile light) that flashes to catch attention **b** : a device for automatically flashing a light **c** : an exhibitionist who flashes

flash flood *n* (1940) : a local flood of short duration generally resulting from heavy rainfall in the immediate vicinity — **flash flood** *vb*

flash–for·ward \ˈflash-ˈfȯr-wərd\ *n* (1949) : interruption of chronological sequence (as in a film or novel) by interjection of events of future occurrence; *also* : an instance of flash-forward — **flash forward** *vi*

flash·gun \-ˌgən\ *n* (1925) : a device for producing a bright flash of light for photography

flash·ing \ˈfla-shiŋ\ *n* (1782) : sheet metal used in waterproofing (as at roof valleys or hips or the angle between a chimney and a roof)

flash in the pan [fr. the firing of the priming in the pan of a flintlock musket without discharging the piece] (1706) **1** : a sudden spasmodic effort that accomplishes nothing **2** : one that appears promising but turns out to be disappointing or worthless

flash·lamp \ˈflash-ˌlamp\ *n* (1890) : a lamp for producing a brief but intense flash of light (as for taking photographs)

flash·light \ˈflash-ˌlīt\ *n* (1886) **1 a** : a sudden bright artificial light used in taking photographic pictures **b** : a photograph taken by such a light **2** : a small battery-operated portable electric light

flash mob *n* (2003) : a group of people summoned (as by e-mail or text message) to a designated location at a specified time to perform an indicated action before dispersing

flash·over \-ˌō-vər\ *n* (1892) **1** : an abnormal electrical discharge (as through the air to the ground from a high potential source or between two conducting portions of a structure) **2** : the sudden spread of flame over an area when it becomes heated to the flash point

flash point *n* (1878) **1** : the lowest temperature at which vapors above a volatile combustible substance ignite in air when exposed to flame **2** : a point at which someone or something bursts suddenly into action or being **3** : TINDERBOX 2

flash·tube \ˈflash-ˌt(y)üb\ *n* (1945) : a gas discharge tube that produces very brief intense flashes of light and is used esp. in photography

flashy \ˈfla-shē\ *adj* **flash·i·er; -est** (1593) **1** *chiefly dial* : lacking in substance or flavor : INSIPID **2** : momentarily dazzling **3 a** : superficially attractive or impressive **b** : ostentatious or showy often beyond the bounds of good taste; *esp* : marked by gaudy brightness ***syn*** see GAUDY — **flash·i·ly** \ˈfla-shə-lē\ *adv* — **flash·i·ness** \ˈfla-shē-nəs\ *n*

flask \ˈflask, ˈfläsk\ *n* [MF *flasque* powder flask, ultim. fr. LL *flascon-, flasco* bottle, prob. of Gmc origin; akin to OHG *flaska* bottle] (1549) : a container often somewhat narrowed toward the outlet and often fitted with a closure: as **a** : a broad flattened necked vessel used esp. to carry alcoholic beverages on the person **b** *Brit* : THERMOS

[1]**flat** \ˈflat\ *adj* **flat·ter; flat·test** [ME, fr. ON *flatr;* akin to OHG *flaz* flat, and prob. to Gk *platys* broad — more at PLACE] (14c) **1 a** : lying at full length or spread out upon the ground : PROSTRATE **b** : utterly ruined or destroyed **c** : resting with a surface against something **2 a** : having a continuous horizontal surface **b** : being or characterized by a horizontal line or tracing without peaks or depressions ⟨a ~ EEG⟩ **3** : having a relatively smooth or even surface **4** : arranged or laid out so as to be level or even **5 a** : having the major surfaces essentially parallel and distinctly greater than the minor surfaces ⟨a ~ piece of wood⟩ **b** *of a shoe heel* : very low and broad **6 a** : clearly unmistakable ⟨a ~ denial⟩ **b** (1) : not varying : FIXED ⟨a ~ rate⟩ (2) : having no fraction either lacking or in excess : EXACT ⟨in a ~ 10 seconds⟩ (3) *of a frequency response* : not varying significantly throughout its range **7 a** : lacking in animation, zest, or vigor : DULL **b** : lacking flavor : TASTELESS **c** : lacking effervescence or sparkle ⟨~ ginger ale⟩ **d** : commercially inactive; *also* : characterized by no significant rise or decline from one period to another ⟨sales were ~⟩ **e** *of a tire* : lacking air : DEFLATED **f** *chiefly Brit, of a battery* : DEAD 3c, DISCHARGED **8 a** (1) *of a tone* : lowered a half step in pitch (2) : lower than the proper pitch **b** *of the vowel a* : pronounced as in *bad* or *bat* **9 a** : having a low trajectory **b** *of a tennis stroke* : made so as to give little or no spin to the ball **10** : not having an inflectional ending ⟨~ adverbs⟩ **11** *of a sail* : TAUT **12 a** : uniform in hue or shade **b** : having little or no illusion of depth **c** *of a photograph or negative* : lacking contrast **d** *of lighting conditions* : lacking shadows or contours **e** : free from gloss ⟨a ~ paint⟩ **f** : TWO-DIMENSIONAL 3 ⟨~ characters⟩ **13** : of, relating to, or used in competition on the flat ⟨a ~ horse⟩ **14** *of a universe* : having a mass such that expansion halts only after infinite time and collapse never occurs ***syn*** see LEVEL, INSIPID — **flat·ly** *adv* — **flat·ness** *n* — **flat·tish** \ˈfla-tish\ *adj*

[2]**flat** *n* (14c) **1 a** : a level surface of land — usu. used in pl. ⟨sagebrush ~*s*⟩ ⟨tidal ~*s*⟩ **b** : a stretch of land without obstacles; *esp* : a track or course for a flat race — usu. used with *the* ⟨has won twice on the ~⟩ **2** : a flat part or surface ⟨the ~ of one's hand⟩ **3 a** : a musical note or tone one half step lower than a specified note or tone **b** : a character ♭ on a line or space of the musical staff indicating a half step drop in pitch **4** : something flat: as **a** : a shallow container for shipping produce **b** : a shallow box in which seedlings are started **c** : a flat piece of theatrical scenery **d** : a shoe or slipper having a flat heel or no heel **5** *chiefly Brit* : an apartment on one floor **6** : a deflated tire **7** : the area to either side of an offensive football formation

[3]**flat** *adv* (1531) **1** : in a flat manner : DIRECTLY, POSITIVELY **2** : in a complete manner : ABSOLUTELY ⟨~ broke⟩ **3** : below the proper musical pitch **4** : without interest charge; *esp* : without allowance or charge for accrued interest ⟨bonds sold ~⟩

[4]**flat** *vb* **flat·ted; flat·ting** *vt* (ca. 1604) **1** : FLATTEN **2** : to lower in pitch esp. by a half step ~ *vi* : to sing or play below the true pitch

1**flat·bed** \ˈflat-ˌbed\ *adj* (1892) **:** having a horizontal bed on which the work rests ⟨a ~ printing press⟩ ⟨a ~ scanner⟩

2**flatbed** *n* (1944) **:** a motortruck or trailer with a body in the form of a platform or shallow box

flat·boat \-ˌbōt\ *n* (1653) **:** a boat with a flat bottom and square ends used for transportation of bulky freight esp. in shallow waters

flat·car \-ˌkär\ *n* (1861) **:** a railroad freight car without permanent raised sides, ends, or covering

flat–coated retriever \ˈflat-ˌkō-təd-\ *n* (1929) **:** any of an English breed of medium-sized sporting dogs that have a dense smooth black or liver-colored coat

flat–earth·er \ˌflat-ˈər-thər\ *also* **flat–earth·ist** \-thist\ *n* (1926) **:** a person who believes that the planet Earth is flat

flat·fish \ˈflat-ˌfish\ *n* (1710) **:** any of an order (Heterosomata) of marine typically bottom-dwelling bony fishes (as the halibuts, flounders, turbots, and soles) that as adults swim on one side of the laterally compressed body and have both eyes on the upper side

flat·foot \-ˌfu̇t (*always so in sense 3*), ˌflat-ˈ\ *n, pl* **flat·feet** \-ˌfēt, -ˈfēt\ (1860) **1 :** a condition in which the arch of the instep is flattened so that the entire sole rests upon the ground **2 :** a foot affected with flatfoot **3 a** *or pl* **flatfoots** *slang* **:** POLICE OFFICER; *esp* **:** a patrolman walking a regular beat **b** *slang* **:** SAILOR

1**flat–foot·ed** \ˈflat-ˌfu̇-təd, ˌflat-ˈ\ *adj* (1601) **1 :** affected with flatfoot; *broadly* **:** walking with a dragging or shambling gait **2 a :** firm and well balanced on the feet **b :** free from reservation **:** FORTHRIGHT ⟨had an honest ~ way of saying a thing⟩ **3 :** not ready **:** UNPREPARED — used chiefly in the phrase *catch one flat-footed* **4 :** proceeding in a plodding or unimaginative way **:** PEDESTRIAN ⟨~ prose⟩ — **flat–foot·ed·ly** *adv* — **flat–foot·ed·ness** *n*

2**flat–footed** *adv* (1828) **1 :** in an open and determined manner **:** FLATLY **2 :** with the feet flat on a surface (as the ground)

flat–hat \ˈflat-ˌhat\ *vi* [fr. an alleged incident in which a pedestrian's hat was crushed by a low-flying plane] (1940) **:** to fly low in an airplane in a reckless manner **:** HEDGEHOP — **flat–hat·ter** *n*

Flat·head \-ˌhed\ *n, pl* **Flatheads** *or* **Flathead** (1709) **1 :** a member of any of several No. American Indian peoples that practiced head-flattening **2 :** an American Indian people of Montana **3** *not cap* **:** any of a family (Platycephalidae) of mostly Australian and East Indian marine food fishes that resemble sculpins

flat·head catfish \ˈflat-ˌhed-\ *n* (1945) **:** a large yellowish catfish (*Pylodictis olivaris*) of the central and Gulf states of the U.S. with the sides and back heavily mottled with brown or black

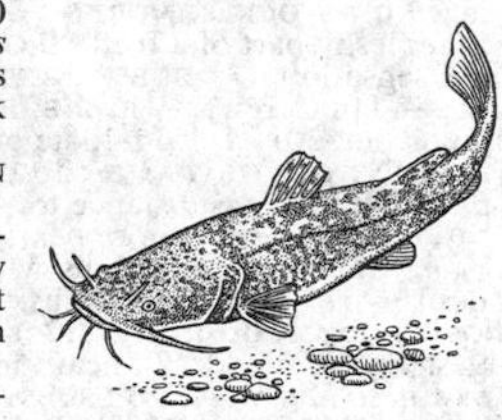
flathead catfish

flat·iron \ˈflat-ˌī(-ə)rn\ *n* (1743) **:** IRON 2c

flat·land \ˈflat-ˌland\ *n* (1735) **1 :** a region in which the land is predominantly flat — usu. used in pl. **2 :** land that lacks significant variation in elevation — **flat·land·er** \-ˌlan-dər\ *n*

flat·let \ˈflat-lət\ *n* (1925) *Brit* **:** EFFICIENCY APARTMENT

flat·line \ˈflat-ˌlīn\ *vi* (1980) **1 a :** to register on an electronic monitor as having no brain waves or heartbeat **b :** DIE **2 a :** to be in a state of no progress or advancement **b :** to come to an end — **flat·lin·er** *n*

flat·ling \ˈflat-liŋ\ *or* **flat·lings** \-liŋz\ *adv* (15c) *dial Brit* **:** with a flat side or edge

flat·mate \ˈflat-ˌmāt\ *n* (1955) *chiefly Brit* **:** one of two or more persons sharing the same flat

flat–out \ˈflat-ˌau̇t\ *adj* (1906) **1 :** being or going at maximum effort or speed **2 :** OUT-AND-OUT, DOWNRIGHT ⟨it was a ~ lie⟩

flat out *adv* (1932) **1 :** in a blunt and direct manner **:** OPENLY ⟨called *flat out* for revolution —*Nat'l Review*⟩ **2 :** at top speed or peak performance ⟨the car does 180 m.p.h. *flat out*⟩ **3** *usu* **flat–out :** ABSOLUTELY, DOWNRIGHT — usu. used as an intensive ⟨is just *flat-out* confusing⟩

flat–pan·el \ˈflat-ˈpa-nᵊl\ *adj* (1977) **:** relating to or being a thin flat video display (as for a portable computer)

flat–picking \ˈflat-ˌpi-kiŋ\ *n* (1970) **:** a method of playing a stringed instrument (as a guitar) with a plectrum held between the thumb and index finger

flat race *n* (1848) **:** a race (as for horses) on a level course without obstacles (as hurdles) — compare STEEPLECHASE — **flat racing** *n*

flat tax *n* (1952) **:** PROPORTIONAL TAX

flat·ten \ˈfla-tᵊn\ *vb* **flat·tened; flat·ten·ing** \ˈflat-niŋ, ˈfla-tə-\ *vt* (1630) **:** to make flat: as **a :** to make level or smooth **b :** to knock down; *also* **:** to defeat decisively **c :** to make dull or uninspired — often used with *out* **d :** to make (as paint) lusterless **e :** to stabilize esp. at a lower level ~ *vi* **:** to become flat or flatter: as **a :** to become dull or spiritless **b :** to extend in or into a flat position or form **c :** to become uniform or stabilized often at a new lower level — usu. used with *out* — **flat·ten·er** \-nər\ *n*

1**flat·ter** \ˈfla-tər\ *vb* [ME *flateren,* fr. AF *flater* to lap, flatter, of Gmc origin; akin to OHG *flaz* flat] *vt* (13c) **1 :** to praise excessively esp. from motives of self-interest **2 a** *archaic* **:** BEGUILE 4 **b :** to encourage or gratify esp. with the assurance that something is right ⟨I ~ myself that my interpretation is correct⟩ **3 a :** to portray too favorably ⟨the portrait ~*s* him⟩ **b :** to display to advantage ⟨candlelight often ~*s* the face⟩ ~ *vi* **:** to use flattery — **flat·ter·er** \-tər-ər\ *n* — **flat·ter·ing·ly** \-tər-iŋ-lē\ *adv*

2**flatter** *n* (1714) **:** one that flattens; *esp* **:** a flat-faced swage used in smithing

flat·tery \ˈfla-tə-rē\ *n, pl* **-ter·ies** (14c) **1 a :** the act or practice of flattering **b** (1) **:** something that flatters (2) **:** insincere or excessive praise **2** *obs* **:** a pleasing self-deception

flat·top \ˈflat-ˌtäp\ *n* (1940) **:** something with a flat or flattened upper surface: as **a :** AIRCRAFT CARRIER **b :** a modified crew cut

flat·u·lence \ˈfla-chə-lən(t)s\ *n* (1711) **1 :** the quality or state of being flatulent **2 :** flatus expelled through the anus

flat·u·len·cy \-lən(t)-sē\ *n* (1660) **:** FLATULENCE 1

flat·u·lent \-lənt\ *adj* [MF, fr. L *flatus* act of blowing, wind, fr. *flare* to blow — more at BLOW] (1599) **1 a :** likely to cause gas **b :** marked by or affected with gas generated in the intestine or stomach **2 :** pompously or portentously overblown — **flat·u·lent·ly** *adv*

fla·tus \ˈflā-təs\ *n* [L, act of blowing, act of breaking wind] (1651) **:** gas generated in the stomach or bowels

flat·ware \ˈflat-ˌwer\ *n* (1746) **:** relatively flat tableware; *esp* **:** eating and serving utensils (as knives, forks, and spoons) — compare HOLLOWWARE

flat·ways \-ˌwāz\ *adv* (1692) **:** FLATWISE

flat·wise \-ˌwīz\ *adv* (1601) **:** with the flat surface presented in some expressed or implied position

flat·work \-ˌwərk\ *n* (1925) **:** laundry that can be finished mechanically and does not require hand ironing

flat·worm \-ˌwərm\ *n* (1874) **:** any of a phylum (Platyhelminthes) of soft-bodied usu. much flattened acoelomate worms (as the planarians, flukes, and tapeworms) — called also *platyhelminth*

flaunt \ˈflȯnt, ˈflänt\ *vb* [perh. of Scand origin; akin to ON *flana* to rush around] *vi* (1566) **1 :** to display or obtrude oneself to public notice ⟨a great ~*ing* crowd —Charles Dickens⟩ **2 :** to wave or flutter showily ⟨the flag ~*s* in the breeze⟩ ~ *vt* **1 :** to display ostentatiously or impudently **:** PARADE ⟨~*ing* his superiority⟩ **2 :** to treat contemptuously ⟨~*ed* the rules —Louis Untermeyer⟩ ***syn*** see SHOW — **flaunt** *n* — **flaunt·ing·ly** \ˈflȯn-tiŋ-lē, ˈflän-\ *adv* — **flaunty** \-tē\ *adj*

usage Although transitive sense 2 of *flaunt* undoubtedly arose from confusion with *flout,* the contexts in which it appears cannot be called substandard ⟨meting out punishment to the occasional mavericks who operate rigged games, tolerate rowdyism, or otherwise *flaunt* the law —Oscar Lewis⟩ ⟨observed with horror the *flaunting* of their authority in the suburbs, where men . . . put up buildings that had no place at all in a Christian commonwealth —Marchette Chute⟩ ⟨in our profession . . . very rarely do we publicly chastise a colleague who has *flaunted* our most basic principles —R. T. Blackburn, *AAUP Bull.*⟩. If you use it, however, you should be aware that many people will consider it a mistake. Use of *flout* in the sense of *flaunt* 1 is found occasionally ⟨"The proper pronunciation," the blonde said, *flouting* her refined upbringing, "is pree feeks" —Mike Royko⟩.

flau·ta \ˈflau̇-tə\ *n* [Amer Sp, lit., flute] (1976) **:** a usu. corn tortilla rolled tightly around a filling (as of meat) and deep-fried

flau·tist \ˈflȯ-tist, ˈflau̇-\ *n* [It *flautista,* fr. *flauto* flute, fr. Old Occitan *flaut*] (1860) **:** FLUTIST

fla·va·none \ˈflā-və-ˌnōn\ *n* [L *flavus* + ISV *-ane* + *-one*] (1949) **:** any of various aromatic ketones that often occur in plants as glycosides and that constitute a subset of the flavonoids

fla·vin \ˈflā-vən\ *n* [ISV, fr. L *flavus* yellow — more at BLUE] (1933) **:** any of a class of yellow water-soluble nitrogenous pigments derived from isoalloxazine and occurring in the form of nucleotides as coenzymes of flavoproteins; *esp* **:** RIBOFLAVIN

flavin adenine dinucleotide *n* (1954) **:** a coenzyme $C_{27}H_{33}N_9O_{15}P_2$ of some flavoproteins

fla·vine \ˈflā-ˌvēn\ *n* [ISV, fr. L *flavus*] (ca. 1853) **:** any of a series of yellow acridine dyes (as acriflavine) having antiseptic properties

flavin mononucleotide *n* (ca. 1953) **:** FMN

fla·vi·vi·rus \ˈflā-vi-ˌvī-rəs\ *n* [NL, fr. L *flavus* yellow + NL -i- + *virus* — more at VIRUS] (1974) **:** any of a family (*Flaviviridae* and esp. genus *Flavivirus*) of single-stranded RNA viruses transmitted esp. by ticks and mosquitoes and including the causative agents of dengue, hepatitis C, hog cholera, Saint Louis encephalitis, West Nile fever, and yellow fever

fla·vone \ˈflā-ˌvōn\ *n* [ISV, fr. L *flavus*] (1897) **:** a colorless crystalline aromatic ketone $C_{15}H_{10}O_2$ found in the leaves, stems, and seed capsules of many primroses; *also* **:** any of the derivatives of this ketone many of which occur as yellow plant pigments in the form of glycosides and are used as dyestuffs

fla·vo·noid \ˈflā-və-ˌnȯid\ *n* [*flavone* + *-oid*] (1947) **:** any of a group of oxygen-containing aromatic antioxidant compounds that includes many common pigments (as the anthocyanins and flavones)

fla·vo·nol \ˈflā-və-ˌnȯl, -ˌnōl\ *n* (1898) **:** any of various hydroxy derivatives of flavone

fla·vo·pro·tein \ˌflā-vō-ˈprō-ˌtēn, -ˈprō-tē-ən\ *n* [ISV *flavin* + *-o-* + *protein*] (1934) **:** a dehydrogenase that contains a flavin and often a metal and plays a major role in biological oxidations

1**fla·vor** \ˈflā-vər\ *n* [ME *flavour,* modif. of AF *flaur, flour,* fr. VL **flator,* alter. of L *flatus* breath, act of blowing — more at FLATULENT] (14c) **1 a** *archaic* **:** ODOR, FRAGRANCE **b :** the quality of something that affects the sense of taste **c :** the blend of taste and smell sensations evoked by a substance in the mouth ⟨the ~ of apples⟩ **2 :** a substance that flavors ⟨artificial ~*s*⟩ **3 a :** characteristic or predominant quality ⟨the ethnic ~ of a neighborhood⟩ **b :** a distinctive appealing or enlivening quality ⟨her performance adds ~ to the show⟩ **4 a :** VARIETY 3a **b :** a property that distinguishes different types of elementary particles (as quarks or neutrinos); *also* **:** any of the different types of particles that are distinguished by flavor **5 :** VERSION 3 ⟨~*s* of software⟩ **6 :** one that is in the center of public attention for a limited time — usu. used in phrases like *flavor of the month* — **fla·vored** \-vərd\ *adj* — **fla·vor·ful** \-vər-fəl\ *adj* — **fla·vor·ful·ly** \-fə-lē\ *adv* — **fla·vor·less** \-vər-ləs\ *adj* — **fla·vor·some** \-səm\ *adj*

2**flavor** *vt* **fla·vored; fla·vor·ing** \ˈflā-v(ə-)riŋ\ (1542) **:** to give or add flavor to

flavoring *n* (1845) **:** FLAVOR 2

fla·vor·ist \ˈflā-vər-ist\ *n* (1964) **:** a specialist in the creation of artificial flavors

fla·vour *chiefly Brit var of* FLAVOR

1**flaw** \ˈflȯ\ *n* [of Scand origin; akin to Norw *flaga* gust, squall] (1513) **1 :** a sudden brief burst of wind; *also* **:** a spell of stormy weather **2** *obs* **:** an outburst esp. of passion

2**flaw** *n* [ME, flake, fr. ON *flaga* stone slab, moldar*flaga* thin layer of turf; akin to OE *flōh* flat stone] (1586) **1 a :** a defect in physical structure or form ⟨a diamond with a ~⟩ **b :** an imperfection or weakness and esp. one that detracts from the whole or hinders effectiveness ⟨vanity was the ~ in his character⟩ ⟨a ~ in the book's plot⟩ **2** *obs* **:** FRAG-

MENT — **flawed** \'flȯd\ *adj* — **flaw·less** \-ləs\ *adj* — **flaw·less·ly** *adv* — **flaw·less·ness** *n*

[3]**flaw** *vt* (1610) : to make flaws in : MAR ~ *vi* : to become defective

flax \'flaks\ *n, often attrib* [ME, fr. OE *fleax;* akin to OHG *flahs* flax, L *plectere* to braid — more at PLY] (bef. 12c) **1 :** any of a genus (*Linum* of the family Linaceae, the flax family) of herbs; *esp* **:** a slender erect annual (*L. usitatissimum*) with blue flowers commonly cultivated for its bast fiber and seed **2 :** the fiber of the flax plant esp. when prepared for spinning **3 :** any of several plants resembling flax — **flaxy** \'flak-sē\ *adj*

flax·en \'flak-sən\ *adj* (15c) **1 :** made of flax **2 :** resembling flax esp. in pale soft strawy color ⟨~ hair⟩

flax·seed \'flak(s)-ˌsēd\ *n* (1562) **:** the small seed of flax (esp. *Linum usitatissimum*) used esp. as a source of oil, as a demulcent and emollient, and as a dietary supplement — called also *linseed*

flay \'flā\ *vt* [ME *flen,* fr. OE *flēan;* akin to ON *flā* to flay, Lith *plėšti* to tear] (bef. 12c) **1 :** to strip off the skin or surface of : SKIN **2 :** to criticize harshly : EXCORIATE **3 :** LASH 1b ⟨the wind whipped up to gale fury, *~ing* his face —Richard Kent⟩

F layer *n* (1928) : the highest and most densely ionized regular layer of the ionosphere occurring at night within the F region

fl dr *abbr* fluid dram

flea \'flē\ *n* [ME *fle,* fr. OE *flēa;* akin to OHG *flōh* flea] (bef. 12c) **:** any of an order (Siphonaptera) of small wingless bloodsucking insects that have a hard laterally compressed body and legs adapted to leaping and that feed on warm-blooded animals — **flea in one's ear :** REBUKE ⟨sent him away with a *flea in his ear*⟩

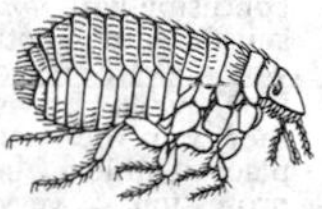
flea

flea·bag \'flē-ˌbag\ *n* (1839) : an inferior hotel or rooming house

flea·bane \-ˌbān\ *n* (1548) : any of various composite plants (esp. of the genus *Erigeron*) that were once believed to drive away fleas

flea beetle *n* (1842) : any of a subfamily (Alticinae, esp. genera *Alticia* and *Epitrix*) of small chrysomelid beetles with legs adapted for leaping that feed on foliage and include some that are agricultural pests

flea·bite \'flē-ˌbīt\ *n* (1570) **1 :** the bite of a flea; *also* **:** the red spot caused by such a bite **2 :** a trifling pain or annoyance

flea–bit·ten \-ˌbi-tᵊn\ *adj* (1570) **1** *of a horse* **:** having a white or gray coat flecked with a darker color **2 :** bitten by or infested with fleas

flea collar *n* (1953) : a collar for animals (as dogs and cats) that contains insecticide for killing fleas

flea–flick·er \-ˌfli-kər\ *n* (1927) : any of various offensive plays in football involving a combination of handoffs and forward or lateral passes

flea·hop·per \-ˌhä-pər\ *n* (1902) : any of several small jumping bugs that feed on cultivated plants

flea market *n* [trans. of F *Marché aux puces,* a market in Paris] (1922) : a usu. open-air market for secondhand articles and antiques

flea·pit \-ˌpit\ *n* (1937) *Brit* : a dilapidated building usu. housing a movie theater

flea·wort \'flē-ˌwərt, -ˌwȯrt\ *n* (bef. 12c) : any of three Old World plantains (esp. *Plantago psyllium*) whose seeds are sometimes used as a mild laxative — compare PSYLLIUM

flèche \'flāsh, 'flesh\ *n* [F, lit., arrow, fr. OF *fleche,* of Gmc origin; akin to MD *vlieke* arrow, OE *flēogan* to fly] (1848) : SPIRE; *esp* : a slender spire above the intersection of the nave and transepts of a church

flé·chette \flā-'shet, fle-\ *n* [F, fr. dim. of *flèche* arrow] (1915) : a small dart-shaped projectile that is clustered in an explosive warhead, dropped as a missile from an airplane, or fired from a handheld gun

[1]**fleck** \'flek\ *vt* [back-formation fr. *flecked* spotted, fr. ME; akin to OHG *flec* spot, ON *flekkr*] (14c) **1 :** STREAK, SPOT ⟨whitecaps *~ed* the blue sea⟩ **2 :** to color as if by sprinkling with flecks ⟨his wit is *~ed* with sarcasm —James Atlas⟩

[2]**fleck** *n* (1598) **1 :** SPOT, MARK ⟨a brown tweed with *~s* of yellow⟩ **2 :** FLAKE, PARTICLE ⟨*~s* of snow drifted down⟩

fledge \'flej\ *vb* **fledged; fledg·ing** [*fledge* capable of flying, fr. ME *flegge,* fr. OE *-flycge;* akin to OHG *flucki* capable of flying, OE *flēogan* to fly — more at FLY] *vi* (1566) *of a young bird* **:** to acquire the feathers necessary for flight or independent activity; *also* **:** to leave the nest after acquiring such feathers ~ *vt* **1 :** to rear until ready for flight or independent activity **2 :** to cover with or as if with feathers or down **3 :** to furnish (as an arrow) with feathers

fledg·ling \'flej-liŋ\ *n, often attrib* (1830) **1 :** a young bird just fledged **2 :** an immature or inexperienced person **3 :** one that is new ⟨a ~ company⟩

flee \'flē\ *vb* **fled** \'fled\; **flee·ing** [ME *flen,* fr. OE *flēon;* akin to OHG *fliohan* to flee] *vi* (bef. 12c) **1 a :** to run away often from danger or evil : FLY **b :** to hurry toward a place of security **2 :** to pass away swiftly : VANISH ~ *vt* **:** to run away from : SHUN

[1]**fleece** \'flēs\ *n* [ME *flees,* fr. OE *flēos;* akin to MHG *vlius* fleece and perh. to L *pluma* feather, down] (bef. 12c) **1 a :** the coat of wool covering a wool-bearing animal (as a sheep) **b :** the wool obtained from a sheep at one shearing **2 a :** any of various soft or woolly coverings **b :** a soft bulky deep-piled knitted or woven fabric used chiefly for clothing

[2]**fleece** *vt* **fleeced; fleec·ing** (1537) **1 a :** to strip of money or property by fraud or extortion **b :** to charge excessively for goods or services **2 :** to remove the fleece from : SHEAR **3 :** to dot or cover with fleecy masses

fleeced \'flēst\ *adj* (1580) **1 :** covered with or as if with a fleece **2** *of a textile* **:** having a soft nap

fleecy \'flē-sē\ *adj* **fleec·i·er; -est** (1590) : covered with, made of, or resembling fleece ⟨a ~ winter coat⟩

[1]**fleer** \'flir\ *vi* [ME *fleryen,* of Scand origin; akin to Norw *flire* to giggle] (15c) : to laugh or grimace in a coarse derisive manner : SNEER ***syn*** see SCOFF — **fleer·ing·ly** \-iŋ-lē\ *adv*

[2]**fleer** *n* (1604) : a word or look of derision or mockery

[1]**fleet** \'flēt\ *vb* [ME *fleten,* fr. OE *flēotan;* akin to OHG *fliozzan* to float, OE *flōwan* to flow] *vi* (bef. 12c) **1** *obs* **:** DRIFT **2 a** *archaic* **:** FLOW **b :** to fade away : VANISH **3** [[3]*fleet*] **:** to fly swiftly ~ *vt* **:** to cause (time) to pass usu. quickly or imperceptibly

[2]**fleet** *n* [ME *flete,* fr. OE *flēot* ship, fr. *flēotan*] (13c) **1 :** a number of warships under a single command; *specif* **:** an organization of ships and aircraft under the command of a flag officer **2 :** GROUP 2a, b; *esp* **:** a group (as of ships, planes, or trucks) operated under unified control

[3]**fleet** *adj* [prob. fr. [1]*fleet*] (ca. 1529) **1 :** swift in motion : NIMBLE **2 :** FLEETING ***syn*** see FAST — **fleet·ly** *adv* — **fleet·ness** *n*

fleet admiral *n* (1942) : an admiral of the highest rank in the navy whose insignia is five stars

fleet–foot·ed \-ˌfu̇-təd\ *adj* (ca. 1743) : able to run fast

fleet·ing \'flē-tiŋ\ *adj* (1563) : passing swiftly : TRANSITORY ***syn*** see TRANSIENT — **fleet·ing·ly** \'flē-tiŋ-lē\ *adv* — **fleet·ing·ness** *n*

Fleet Street \'flēt-\ *n* [*Fleet Street,* London, England, center of the London newspaper district] (1882) : the London press — **Fleet Street·er** *n*

fleh·men \'flā-mən\ *n* [G, fr. *flehmen* (of animals) to curl the upper lip] (1976) : a mammalian behavior (as of horses or cats) in which the animal inhales with the mouth open and upper lip curled to facilitate exposure of the vomeronasal organ to a scent or pheromone — **flehmen** *vi*

flei·shig \'flā-shik\ *adj* [Yiddish *fleyshik,* fr. MHG *vleischic* meaty, fr. *vleisch* flesh, meat, fr. OHG *fleisk*] (1943) : made of, prepared with, or used for meat or meat products — compare MILCHIG, PAREVE

Flem·ing \'fle-miŋ\ *n* [ME, fr. MD *Vlaminc* (akin to MD *Vlander* Flanders)] (12c) : a member of the Germanic people inhabiting northern Belgium and a small section of northern France

[1]**Flem·ish** \'fle-mish\ *adj* (14c) : of, relating to, or characteristic of Flanders or the Flemings or their language

[2]**Flemish** *n* (ca. 1741) **1 :** the Germanic language of the Flemings that is made up of dialects of Dutch **2** *pl in constr* **:** FLEMINGS

Flemish giant *n* (1898) : any of a breed of very large solid-colored rabbits prob. of Belgian origin

flense \'flen(t)s\ *vt* **flensed; flens·ing** [D *flensen* or Dan & Norw *flense*] (1820) : to strip (as a whale) of blubber or skin

[1]**flesh** \'flesh\ *n* [ME, fr. OE *flǣsc;* akin to OHG *fleisk* flesh and perh. to OE *flēan* to flay — more at FLAY] (bef. 12c) **1 a :** the soft parts of the body of an animal and esp. of a vertebrate; *esp* **:** the parts composed chiefly of skeletal muscle as distinguished from internal organs, bone, and integument **b :** the condition of having ample fat on the body ⟨cattle in good ~⟩ **c :** SKIN **2 a :** edible parts of an animal **b :** flesh of a mammal or fowl eaten as food **3 a :** the physical nature of human beings ⟨the spirit indeed is willing, but the ~ is weak —Mt 26:41(AV)⟩ **b :** HUMAN NATURE **4 a :** human beings : HUMANKIND **b :** living beings **c :** STOCK, KINDRED **5 :** a fleshy plant part used as food; *also* **:** the fleshy part of a fruit **6** *Christian Science* **:** an illusion that matter has sensation **7 :** SUBSTANCE ⟨insights buried in the ~ of the narrative —Jan Carew⟩ — **in the flesh :** in person and alive

[2]**flesh** *vt* (1530) **1 :** to initiate or habituate esp. by giving a foretaste **2** *archaic* **:** GRATIFY **3 a :** to clothe or cover with or as if with flesh; *broadly* **:** to give substance to — usu. used with *out* ⟨~ out a plan⟩ **b :** to make fuller or more nearly complete — used with *out* ⟨museums *~ing* out their collections with borrowed works⟩ **4 :** to free from flesh ~ *vi* **:** to become fleshy — often used with *up* or *out*

flesh and blood *n* (bef. 12c) **1 :** corporeal nature as composed of flesh and of blood **2 :** near kindred — used chiefly in the phrase *one's own flesh and blood* **3 :** SUBSTANCE, REALITY

fleshed \'flesht\ *adj* (15c) : having flesh esp. of a specified kind — often used in combination ⟨pink-*fleshed*⟩ ⟨thick-*fleshed*⟩

flesh fly *n* (14c) : a dipteran fly whose maggots feed on flesh; *esp* : any of a family (Sarcophagidae) of flies some of which cause myiasis

flesh·ly \'flesh-lē\ *adj* (bef. 12c) **1 a :** CORPOREAL, BODILY **b :** of, relating to, or characterized by indulgence of bodily appetites; *esp* **:** LASCIVIOUS ⟨~ desires⟩ **c :** not spiritual : WORLDLY **2 :** FLESHY 1a **3 :** having a sensuous quality ⟨~ art⟩ ***syn*** see CARNAL

flesh·ment \'flesh-mənt\ *n* [[2]*flesh*] (1605) *obs* : excitement associated with a successful beginning

flesh·pot \'flesh-ˌpät\ *n* (1592) **1** *pl* **:** bodily comfort : LUXURY **2 :** a place of lascivious entertainment — usu. used in pl.

flesh–press·ing \'flesh-ˌpre-siŋ\ *n* (1969) : the act of greeting and shaking hands with people esp. while campaigning for political office

flesh wound *n* (1655) : an injury involving penetration of the body musculature without damage to bones or internal organs

fleshy \'fle-shē\ *adj* **flesh·i·er; -est** (14c) **1 a :** marked by, consisting of, or resembling flesh **b :** marked by abundant flesh; *esp* **:** CORPULENT **2 a :** SUCCULENT, PULPY ⟨the ~ texture of a melon⟩ **b :** not thin, dry, or membranous ⟨~ fungi⟩ — **flesh·i·ness** *n*

fleshy fruit *n* (1829) : a fruit (as a berry, drupe, or pome) consisting largely of soft succulent tissue

fletch \'flech\ *vt* [back-formation fr. *fletcher*] (ca. 1656) : FEATHER 1a

fletch·er \'fle-chər\ *n* [ME *flecchere,* fr. AF *flecher,* fr. *fleche* arrow — more at FLÈCHE] (14c) : a maker of arrows

fletch·ing \-chiŋ\ *n* (ca. 1930) : the feathers on an arrow; *also* : the arrangement of such feathers

fleur de coin \ˌflər-də-'kwaⁿ\ *adj* [F *à fleur de coin,* lit., with the bloom of the die] (ca. 1889) : being in the preserved mint condition

fleur–de–lis *also* **fleur–de–lys** \ˌflər-də-'lē, ˌflu̇r-\ *n, pl* **fleurs–de–lis** *or* **fleur–de–lis** *also* **fleurs–de–lys** *or* **fleur–de–lys** \ˌflər-də-'lē(z), ˌflu̇r-\ [ME *flourdelis,* fr. AF *flur de lis,* lit., lily flower] (14c) **1 :** IRIS **3 2 :** a conventionalized iris in artistic design and heraldry

fleu·ry \'flu̇r-ē\ *adj* [alter. of ME *flory,* fr. AF *floré,* flowered fr. *flur, flor* flower — more at FLOWER] (15c) *of a heraldic cross* **:** having the ends of the arms broadening out into the heads of fleurs-de-lis — see CROSS illustration

flew *past of* FLY

flews \'flüz\ *n pl* [origin unknown] (1575) : the pendulous lateral parts of a dog's upper lip — see DOG illustration

[1]**flex** \'fleks\ *vb* [L *flexus,* pp. of *flectere* to bend] *vt* (ca. 1521) **1 :** to bend esp. repeatedly **2 a :** to move muscles so as to cause flexion of (a joint) **b :** to move or tense (a muscle) by contraction **3 :** USE, DEMONSTRATE ⟨*~ing* her skills as a singer⟩ ~ *vi* **:** BEND — **flex one's muscles :** to demonstrate one's strength ⟨an exaggerated need to *flex his* political *muscles* —J. P. Lash⟩

[2]**flex** *n* [short for *flexible cord*] (1905) *chiefly Brit* : an electric cord

[3]**flex** *n* (ca. 1934) : an act or instance of flexing

flex–cuff \'fleks-ˌkəf\ *n* (1981) : a plastic strip that can be fastened as a restraint around a person's wrists or ankles — **flex–cuff** *vt*

flex·i·ble \'flek-sə-bəl\ *adj* (15c) **1 :** capable of being flexed : PLIANT **2 :** yielding to influence : TRACTABLE **3 :** characterized by a ready capability to adapt to new, different, or changing requirements ⟨a ~ foreign policy⟩ ⟨a ~ schedule⟩ ***syn*** see ELASTIC — **flex·i·bil·i·ty** \ˌflek-sə-ˈbi-lə-tē\ *n* — **flex·i·bly** \ˈflek-sə-blē\ *adv*

flex·ile \ˈflek-səl, -ˌsī(-ə)l\ *adj* (1613) : FLEXIBLE

flex·ion \ˈflek-shən\ *n* [L *flexion-, flexio,* fr. *flectere*] (1615) **1 :** the act of flexing or bending **2 :** a part bent : BEND **3 :** INFLECTION 3 **4 a :** a bending movement around a joint in a limb (as the knee or elbow) that decreases the angle between the bones of the limb at the joint — compare EXTENSION 3b **b :** a forward raising of the arm or leg by a movement at the shoulder or hip joint

flex·i·tar·i·an \ˌflek-sə-ˈter-ē-ən\ *n* [*flex*ible + vege*tarian*] (1998) : one whose normally meatless diet occasionally includes meat or fish — **flexitarian** *adj*

flex·og·ra·phy \flek-ˈsä-grə-fē\ *n* [*flex*ible + *-o-* + *-graphy*] (1954) : a process of rotary letterpress printing using flexible plates and fast-drying inks — **flexo·graph·ic** \ˌflek-sə-ˈgra-fik\ *adj* — **flexo·graph·i·cal·ly** \-fi-k(ə-)lē\ *adv*

flex·or \ˈflek-sər, -ˌsȯr\ *n* (1615) : a muscle serving to bend a body part (as a limb)

flex·time \ˈfleks-ˌtīm\ *also* **flexi·time** \ˈflek-si-ˌtīm\ *n* (1972) : a system that allows employees to choose their own times for starting and finishing work within a broad range of available hours

flex·u·ous \ˈflek-sh(ə-)wəs\ *adj* [L *flexuosus,* fr. *flexus* bend, fr. *flectere*] (1605) **1 :** having curves, turns, or windings **2 :** lithe or fluid in action or movement

flex·ur·al \ˈflek-sh(ə-)rəl\ *adj* (1877) **1 :** of, relating to, or resulting from flexure **2 :** characterized by flexure

flex·ure \ˈflek-shər\ *n* (1592) **1 :** the quality or state of being flexed : FLEXION **2 :** TURN, BEND, FOLD

fley \ˈflā\ *vt* [ME *flayen,* fr. OE *āflēgan,* fr. *ā-,* perfective prefix + *-flēgan* to put to flight] (13c) *Scot* : FRIGHTEN

flib·ber·ti·gib·bet \ˌfli-bər-tē-ˈji-bət\ *n* [ME *flepergebet*] (15c) : a silly flighty person — **flib·ber·ti·gib·bety** \-bə-tē\ *adj*

flic \ˈflēk\ *n* [F] (1899) : a French police officer

[1]**flick** \ˈflik\ *n* [imit.] (15c) **1 :** a light sharp jerky stroke or movement ⟨a ~ of the wrist⟩ **2 :** a sound produced by a flick **3 :** [2]FLICKER 1

[2]**flick** *vt* (1629) **1 a :** to move or propel with or as if with a flick ⟨~*ed* her hair back over her shoulder⟩ **b :** to activate, deactivate, or change by or as if by flicking a switch ⟨~ off the radio⟩ **2 a :** to strike lightly with a quick sharp motion **b :** to remove with light blows ⟨~*ed* an ash off her sleeve⟩ ~ *vi* **1 :** to go or pass quickly or abruptly ⟨~*ing* through some papers⟩ **2 :** to direct flicks at something

[3]**flick** *n* [short for [2]*flicker*] (1926) : MOVIE

[1]**flick·er** \ˈfli-kər\ *vb* **flick·ered; flick·er·ing** \-k(ə-)riŋ\ [ME *flikeren,* fr. OE *flicorian*] *vi* (bef. 12c) **1 :** to move irregularly or unsteadily : FLUTTER **2 :** to burn or shine fitfully or with a fluctuating light ⟨a candle ~*ing* in the window⟩ **3 :** to appear briefly ~ *vt* **1 :** to cause to flicker **2 :** to produce by flickering — **flick·er·ing·ly** \-k(ə-)riŋ-lē\ *adv*

[2]**flicker** *n* (1822) **1 a :** an act of flickering **b :** a sudden brief movement **c :** a momentary quickening ⟨a ~ of anger⟩ **d :** a slight indication : HINT **2 a :** a wavering light **b :** a repeated momentary defect in a cathode-ray tube image caused esp. by slow scanning of the screen **3 :** MOVIE — often used in pl. — **flick·ery** \ˈfli-k(ə-)rē\ *adj*

[3]**flicker** *n* [prob. imit. of its call] (1809) : a large barred and spotted No. American woodpecker (*Colaptes auratus*) with a brown back that commonly forages on the ground for ants — compare RED-SHAFTED FLICKER, YELLOW-SHAFTED FLICKER

flick–knife \ˈflik-ˌnīf\ *n* (1957) *Brit* : SWITCHBLADE

flied *past and past part of* [3]FLY

fli·er *also* **fly·er** \ˈflī(-ə)r\ *n* (15c) **1 :** one that flies; *specif* : AIRMAN **2 :** a reckless or speculative venture — usu. used in the phrase *take a flier* **3** *usu flyer* : an advertising circular

[1]**flight** \ˈflīt\ *n, often attrib* [ME, fr. OE *flyht;* akin to MD *vlucht* flight, OE *flēogan* to fly] (bef. 12c) **1 a :** an act or instance of passing through the air by the use of wings ⟨the ~ of a bee⟩ **b :** the ability to fly ⟨~ is natural to birds⟩ **2 a :** a passing through the air or through space outside the earth's atmosphere **b :** the distance covered in such a flight **c :** swift movement **3 a :** a trip made by or in an airplane or spacecraft **b :** a scheduled airplane trip **4 :** a group of similar beings or objects flying through the air together **5 :** a brilliant, imaginative, or unrestrained exercise or display ⟨a ~ of fancy⟩ **6 a :** a continuous series of stairs from one landing or floor to another **b :** a series (as of terraces or conveyors) resembling a flight of stairs **7 :** a unit of the U.S. Air Force below a squadron — **flight·less** \-ləs\ *adj*

[2]**flight** *vt* (1571) : FLUSH ~ *vi* : to rise, settle, or fly in a flock ⟨geese ~*ing* on the marsh⟩

[3]**flight** *n* [ME *fluht, fliht;* akin to OHG *fluht* flight, OE *flēon* to flee] (13c) : an act or instance of running away

flight attendant *n* (1947) : a person who attends passengers on an airplane

flight bag *n* [[1]*flight*] (1943) **1 :** a lightweight traveling bag with zippered outside pockets **2 :** a small canvas satchel

flight deck *n* (1924) **1 :** the uppermost complete deck of an aircraft carrier **2 :** the forward compartment in some airplanes

flight engineer *n* (1938) : a flight crewman responsible for mechanical operation

flight feather *n* (1735) : one of the quills of a bird's wing or tail that support it in flight — compare CONTOUR FEATHER

flight lieutenant *n* (1914) : a commissioned officer in the British air force who ranks with a captain in the army

flight line *n* (1943) : a parking and servicing area for airplanes

flight path *n* (1908) : the path in the air or space made or followed by something (as a particle, an airplane, or a spacecraft) in flight

flight pay *n* (1928) : an additional allowance paid to military personnel who take part in regular authorized aircraft flights

flight plan *n* (ca. 1936) : a usu. written statement (as by a pilot) of the details of an intended flight (as of an airplane or spacecraft) usu. filed with an authority

flight recorder *n* (1939) : a crashworthy instrument for recording flight data (as airspeed and altitude)

flight suit *n* (1944) : a usu. one-piece garment esp. of fire-resistant fabric worn esp. by a member of a military aircrew

flight surgeon *n* (1925) : a military medical officer specializing in aerospace medicine

flight–test \ˈflīt-ˌtest\ *vt* (1930) : to test (as an airplane or spacecraft) in flight

flighty \ˈflī-tē\ *adj* **flight·i·er; -est** (1552) **1 :** SWIFT **2 :** lacking stability or steadiness: **a :** easily upset : VOLATILE ⟨a ~ temper⟩ **b :** easily excited : SKITTISH ⟨a ~ horse⟩ **c :** CAPRICIOUS, SILLY — **flight·i·ly** \ˈflī-tə-lē\ *adv* — **flight·i·ness** \ˈflī-tē-nəs\ *n*

[1]**flim·flam** \ˈflim-ˌflam\ *n* [perh. of Scand origin; akin to ON *flim* mockery] (ca. 1570) **1 :** deceptive nonsense **2 :** DECEPTION, FRAUD

[2]**flimflam** *vt* **flim·flammed; flim·flam·ming** (1660) : to subject to a flimflam — **flim·flam·mer** *n* — **flim·flam·mery** \-ˌfla-mə-rē\ *n*

[1]**flim·sy** \ˈflim-zē\ *adj* **flim·si·er; -est** [perh. alter. of [1]*film* + *-sy* (as in *tricksy*)] (ca. 1702) **1 a :** lacking in physical strength or substance ⟨~ silks⟩ **b :** of inferior materials and workmanship **2 :** having little worth or plausibility ⟨a ~ excuse⟩ — **flim·si·ly** \-zə-lē\ *adv* — **flim·si·ness** \-zē-nəs\ *n*

[2]**flimsy** *n, pl* **flim·sies** (1814) *chiefly Brit* : a lightweight paper used esp. for multiple copies; *also* : a document printed on flimsy

flinch \ˈflinch\ *vi* [MF *flenchir* to bend, of Gmc origin; akin to MHG *lenken* to bend, OHG *hlanca* flank — more at LANK] (1578) : to withdraw or shrink from or as if from pain : WINCE; *also* : to tense the muscles involuntarily in anticipation of discomfort ***syn*** see RECOIL — **flinch** *n* — **flinch·er** *n*

flin·ders \ˈflin-dərz\ *n pl* [ME *flendris*] (15c) : SPLINTERS, FRAGMENTS

[1]**fling** \ˈfliŋ\ *vb* **flung** \ˈfləŋ\; **fling·ing** \ˈfliŋ-iŋ\ [ME, perh. of Scand origin; akin to ON *flengja* to whip] *vi* (14c) **1 :** to move in a brusque or headlong manner ⟨*flung* out of the room in a rage⟩ **2** *of an animal* : to kick or plunge vigorously **3** *Scot* : CAPER ~ *vt* **1 a :** to throw forcefully, impetuously, or casually ⟨*flung* herself down on the sofa⟩ ⟨clothes were *flung* on the floor⟩ **b :** to cast as if by throwing ⟨*flung* off all restraint⟩ **2 :** to place or send suddenly and unceremoniously ⟨was arrested and *flung* into prison⟩ **3 :** to give unrestrainedly ⟨*flung* himself into music⟩ ***syn*** see THROW — **fling·er** \ˈfliŋ-ər\ *n*

[2]**fling** *n* (1556) **1 :** an act or instance of flinging **2 a :** a casual try or involvement **b :** a casual or brief love affair **3 :** a period devoted to self-indulgence

flint \ˈflint\ *n* [ME, fr. OE; akin to OHG *flins* pebble, hard stone] (bef. 12c) **1 :** a massive hard dark quartz that produces a spark when struck by steel **2 :** an implement of flint used in prehistoric cultures **3 a :** a piece of flint **b :** a material used for producing a spark; *esp* : an alloy (as of iron and cerium) used in lighters **4 :** something resembling flint in hardness — **flint·like** \-ˌlīk\ *adj*

flint corn *n* (1705) : corn of a variety (*Zea mays indurata*) having kernels with a very hard smooth seed coat enclosing a small amount of soft endosperm

flint glass *n* (1683) : heavy brilliant glass that contains lead oxide, has a relatively high refractive index, and is used in lenses and prisms

flint·lock \ˈflint-ˌläk\ *n* (1683) **1 :** a lock for a gun or pistol having a flint in the hammer for striking a spark to ignite the charge **2 :** a firearm fitted with a flintlock

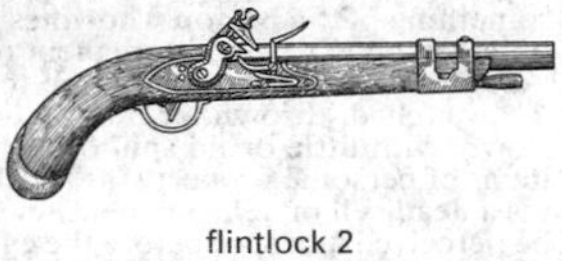

flintlock 2

flinty \ˈflin-tē\ *adj* **flint·i·er; -est** (1536) **1 :** resembling flint; *esp* : STERN, UNYIELDING ⟨~ determination⟩ **2 :** composed of or covered with flint — **flint·i·ly** \ˈflin-tə-lē\ *adv* — **flint·i·ness** \ˈflin-tē-nəs\ *n*

[1]**flip** \ˈflip\ *vb* **flipped; flip·ping** [prob. imit.] *vt* (ca. 1567) **1 :** to toss so as to cause to turn over in the air ⟨~ a coin⟩; *also* : TOSS ⟨~ me the ball⟩ ⟨~ one end of the scarf over your shoulder⟩ **2 a :** to cause to turn and esp. to turn over ⟨*flipped* the car⟩ ⟨*flipping* the pages of a book⟩ **b :** to move with a small quick motion ⟨~ a switch⟩ **3 :** to buy and usu. renovate (real estate) so as to quickly resell at a higher price ~ *vi* **1 :** to make a twitching or flicking movement ⟨the fish *flipped* and flopped on the deck⟩; *also* : to change from one position to another and esp. turn over ⟨the car *flipped*⟩ **2 :** LEAF 2 ⟨*flipped* through the pages⟩ **3** *slang* **a :** to lose one's mind or composure — often used with *out* **b :** to become very enthusiastic

[2]**flip** *n* (1695) **1 :** a mixed drink usu. consisting of a sweetened spiced liquor with beaten eggs **2 :** an act or instance of flipping **3 :** the motion used in flipping **4 :** a somersault esp. in the air

[3]**flip** *adj* (1823) : FLIPPANT, IMPERTINENT

flip–flop \ˈflip-ˌfläp\ *n* (1600) **1 :** the sound or motion of something flapping loosely **2 a :** a backward handspring **b :** a sudden reversal (as of policy or strategy) **3 :** a usu. electronic device or a circuit (as in a computer) capable of assuming either of two stable states **4 :** a rubber sandal loosely fastened to the foot by a thong — **flip–flop** *vi*

flip off *vt* (1982) : to hold up the middle finger as an obscene gesture of contempt to ⟨*flipped off* the other driver⟩

flip·pan·cy \ˈfli-pən(t)-sē\ *n, pl* **-cies** (1746) : unbecoming levity or pertness esp. in respect to grave or sacred matters

flip·pant \ˈfli-pənt\ *adj* [prob. fr. [1]*flip*] (1599) **1** *archaic* : GLIB, TALKATIVE **2 :** lacking proper respect or seriousness — **flip·pant·ly** *adv*

flip·per \ˈfli-pər\ *n* (1822) **1 a :** a broad flat limb (as of a seal or cetacean) adapted for swimming **b :** a flat rubber shoe with the front expanded into a paddle used in skin diving **2 :** one that flips

flip·py \ˈfli-pē\ *adj* (1967) : loose and flaring at the bottom ⟨a ~ skirt⟩

flip side *n* (1949) **1 :** the reverse and usu. less popular side of a phonograph record **2 :** a reverse or opposite side, aspect, or result ⟨the *flip side* of deficient saving . . . is overconsumption —R. S. Gay⟩

[1]**flirt** \ˈflərt\ *vi* [origin unknown] (1580) **1 :** to move erratically : FLIT **2 a :** to behave amorously without serious intent **b :** to show superficial or casual interest or liking ⟨~*ed* with the idea⟩; *also* : EXPERIMENT ⟨a novelist ~*ing* with poetry⟩ **3 :** to come close to reaching or experiencing something — used with *with* ⟨~*ing* with disaster⟩ ~ *vt* **1 :** FLICK **2 :** to move in a jerky manner ***syn*** see TRIFLE — **flir·ta·tion** \ˌflər-ˈtā-shən\ *n* — **flirt·er** *n* — **flirty** \ˈflər-tē\ *adj*

[2]flirt *n* (ca. 1590) **1 :** an act or instance of flirting **2 :** a person who flirts

flir·ta·tious \ˌflər-ˈtā-shəs\ *adj* (1834) **:** inclined to flirt **:** COQUETTISH — **flir·ta·tious·ly** *adv* — **flir·ta·tious·ness** *n*

flit \ˈflit\ *vi* **flit·ted; flit·ting** [ME *flitten,* of Scand origin; akin to ON *flytjask* to move, OE *flēotan* to float] (13c) **1 :** to pass quickly or abruptly from one place or condition to another **2** *archaic* **:** ALTER, SHIFT **3 :** to move in an erratic fluttering manner — **flit** *n*

flitch \ˈflich\ *n* [ME *flicche,* fr. OE *flicce;* akin to OHG *fleisk* flesh — more at FLESH] (bef. 12c) **1 :** a side of cured meat; *esp* **:** a side of bacon **2 :** a longitudinal section of a log

[1]flit·ter \ˈfli-tər\ *vi* [freq. of *flit*] (15c) **:** FLUTTER, FLICKER

[2]flitter *n* (1554) **:** one that flits

fliv·ver \ˈfli-vər\ *n* [origin unknown] (1910) **:** a small cheap usu. old automobile

[1]float \ˈflōt\ *n* [ME *flote* boat, float, fr. OE *flota* ship; akin to OHG *flōz* raft, stream, OE *flēotan* to float — more at FLEET] (bef. 12c) **1 :** an act or instance of floating **2 :** something that floats in or on the surface of a fluid: as **a :** a device (as a cork) buoying up the baited end of a fishing line **b :** a floating platform anchored near a shoreline for use by swimmers or boats **c :** a hollow ball that floats at the end of a lever in a cistern, tank, or boiler and regulates the liquid level **d :** a sac containing air or gas and buoying up the body of a plant or animal **e :** a watertight structure giving an airplane buoyancy on water **3 :** a tool or apparatus for smoothing a surface (as of wet concrete) **4 :** a government grant of a fixed amount of land not yet located by survey out of a larger specific tract **5 :** a vehicle with a platform used to carry an exhibit in a parade; *also* **:** the vehicle and exhibit together **6 a :** an amount of money represented by checks outstanding and in process of collection **b :** the time between a transaction (as the writing of a check or a purchase on credit) and the actual withdrawal of funds to cover it **c :** the volume of a company's shares available for active trading in the auction market **7 :** a soft drink with ice cream floating in it

[2]float *vi* (bef. 12c) **1 :** to rest on the surface of or be suspended in a fluid **2 a :** to drift on or through or as if on or through a fluid ⟨yellow leaves ~*ed* down⟩ **b :** WANDER **3** *of a currency* **:** to find a level in the international exchange market in response to the law of supply and demand and without any restrictive effect of artificial support or control ~ *vt* **1 a :** to cause to float in or on the surface of a fluid **b :** to cause to float as if in a fluid **2 :** FLOOD ⟨~ a cranberry bog⟩ **3 :** to smooth (as plaster or cement) with a float **4 a :** to put forth (as a proposal) for acceptance **b :** to place (an issue of securities) on the market **c :** to obtain money for the establishment or development of (an enterprise) by issuing and selling securities **d :** NEGOTIATE ⟨~ a loan⟩

floatation *var of* FLOTATION

float·er \ˈflō-tər\ *n* (1717) **1 a :** one that floats **b :** a person who floats something **2 :** a person who votes illegally in various polling places **3 a :** a person without a permanent residence or regular employment **b :** a worker who moves from job to job; *esp* **:** one without fixed duties **4 :** a pitched, thrown, or hit ball that moves through the air relatively slowly with little or no spin or rotation **5 :** a policy insuring specific items of personal property (as jewelry or art) **6 :** a bit of optical debris (as a dead cell or cell fragment) in the vitreous humor or lens that may be perceived as a spot before the eye; *also* **:** a spot in the visual field due to such debris — usu. used in pl.

float glass *n* (1959) **:** flat glass produced by solidifying molten glass on the surface of a bath of molten tin

float·ing \ˈflō-tiŋ\ *adj* (1600) **1 :** buoyed on or in a fluid **2 :** located out of the normal position ⟨a ~ kidney⟩ **3 a :** continually drifting or changing position ⟨the ~ population⟩ **b :** not presently committed or invested ⟨~ capital⟩ **c :** short-term and usu. not funded ⟨~ debt⟩ **d :** having no fixed value or rate ⟨~ currencies⟩ ⟨~ interest rates⟩ **4 :** connected or constructed so as to operate and adjust smoothly ⟨a ~ axle⟩

floating dock *n* (1866) **:** a dock that floats on the water and can be partly submerged to permit entry of a ship and raised to keep the ship high and dry — called also *floating drydock*

floating island *n* (1771) **:** a dessert consisting of custard with floating masses of beaten egg whites

floating–point *adj* (1948) **:** expressed in, using, or being a mathematical notation in which a number is represented (as in a computer display) by an integer or a decimal fraction multiplied by a power of the number base indicated by an exponent (as in 4.52E2 for 452) — compare FIXED-POINT

floating rib *n* (1831) **:** a rib (as one of either of the last two pairs in humans) that has no attachment to the sternum — compare FALSE RIB

float·plane \ˈflōt-ˌplān\ *n* (1922) **:** a seaplane supported on the water by one or more floats

floaty \ˈflō-tē\ *adj* **float·i·er; -est** (ca. 1608) **1 :** tending to float **:** BUOYANT **2 :** light and billowy ⟨a ~ gown⟩

floc \ˈfläk\ *n* [short for *floccule*] (1921) **:** a flocculent mass

floc·cu·late \ˈflä-kyə-ˌlāt\ *vb* **-lat·ed; -lat·ing** *vt* (1877) **:** to cause to aggregate into a flocculent mass ⟨~ clay particles⟩ ~ *vi* **:** to become flocculent — **floc·cu·lant** \-lənt\ *n* — **floc·cu·la·tion** \ˌflä-kyə-ˈlā-shən\ *n* — **floc·cu·la·tor** \ˈflä-kyə-ˌlā-tər\ *n*

floc·cule \ˈflä-(ˌ)kyül\ *n* [LL *flocculus*] (ca. 1846) **:** FLOC

floc·cu·lent \ˈflä-kyə-lənt\ *adj* [L *flocc*us + E *-ulent*] (1800) **1 :** resembling wool esp. in loose fluffy organization **2 :** containing, consisting of, or occurring in the form of loosely aggregated particles or soft flakes ⟨a ~ precipitate⟩

floc·cu·lus \-ləs\ *n, pl* **-li** \-ˌlī, -ˌlē\ [LL, dim. of L *floccus* tuft of wool] (1799) **1 :** a small loosely aggregated mass **2 :** a bright or dark patch on the sun

[1]flock \ˈfläk\ *n* [ME, fr. OE *flocc* crowd, band; akin to ON *flokkr* crowd, band] (13c) **1 :** a group of animals (as birds or sheep) assembled or herded together **2 :** a group under the guidance of a leader; *esp* **:** a church congregation **3 :** a large number ⟨a ~ of tourists⟩

[2]flock *vi* (14c) **:** to gather or move in a flock ⟨they ~*ed* to the beach⟩

[3]flock *n* [ME *flok,* fr. AF, fr. L *floccus*] (13c) **1 :** a tuft of wool or cotton fiber **2 :** woolen or cotton refuse used for stuffing furniture and mattresses **3 :** very short or pulverized fiber used esp. to form a velvety pattern on cloth or paper or a protective covering on metal **4 :** FLOC

[4]flock *vt* (1530) **1 :** to fill with flock **2 :** to decorate with flock

flock·ing \ˈflä-kiŋ\ *n* (ca. 1874) **:** a design in flock

floe \ˈflō\ *n* [prob. fr. Norw *flo* flat layer] (1817) **1 :** floating ice formed in a large sheet on the surface of a body of water **2 :** ICE FLOE

flog \ˈfläg\ *vb* **flogged; flog·ging** [perh. modif. of L *flagellare* to whip — more at FLAGELLATE] *vt* (ca. 1676) **1 a :** to beat with or as if with a rod or whip **b :** to criticize harshly **2 :** to force or urge into action **:** DRIVE **3 a** *chiefly Brit* **:** to sell (as stolen goods) illegally ⟨*flogged* their employers' petrol to ordinary motorists —*Economist*⟩ **b :** SELL 7 ⟨traveled by horse, *flogging* encyclopedias —Robert Darnton⟩ **c :** to promote aggressively **:** PLUG ⟨flying around the world *flogging* your movies —Peter Bogdanovich⟩ **4** *Brit* **:** STEAL 1 ~ *vi* **1 :** FLAP, FLUTTER ⟨sails *flogging*⟩ **2** *Brit* **:** to move along with difficulty **:** SLOG — **flog·ger** *n*

flo·ka·ti rug \flō-ˈkä-tē-\ *n* [ModGk *phlokatē*] (1967) **:** a hand-woven Greek woolen rug with a thick shaggy pile — called also *flokati*

[1]flood \ˈfləd\ *n* [ME, fr. OE *flōd;* akin to OHG *fluot* flood, OE *flōwan* to flow] (bef. 12c) **1 a :** a rising and overflowing of a body of water esp. onto normally dry land; *also* **:** a condition of overflowing ⟨rivers in ~⟩ **b** *cap* **:** a flood described in the Bible as covering the earth in the time of Noah **2 :** the flowing in of the tide **3 :** an overwhelming quantity or volume; *also* **:** a state of abundant flow or volume — often used in the phrase *in full flood* ⟨a debate in full ~⟩ **4 :** FLOODLIGHT

[2]flood *vt* (1663) **1 :** to cover with a flood **:** INUNDATE **2 a :** to fill abundantly or excessively ⟨~ the market⟩ **b :** to supply an excess of fuel to (as an engine or its carburetor) so that engine operation is hampered ~ *vi* **1 :** to pour forth, go, or come in a flood **2 :** to become filled with a flood — **flood·er** *n*

flood·gate \ˈfləd-ˌgāt\ *n* [ME *flodgate*] (13c) **1 :** a gate for shutting out, admitting, or releasing a body of water **:** SLUICE **2 :** something serving to restrain an outburst ⟨opened the ~*s* of criticism⟩

[1]flood·light \-ˌlīt\ *n* (1922) **1 a :** artificial illumination in a broad beam **b :** a source of such illumination **2 :** a lighting unit for projecting a broad beam of light

[2]floodlight *vt* **-lit** \-ˌlit\ *also* **-light·ed; -light·ing** (1923) **:** to illuminate by means of one or more floodlights

flood·plain \ˈfləd-ˌplān\ *n* (1873) **1 :** level land that may be submerged by floodwaters **2 :** a plain built up by stream deposition

flood tide *n* (1719) **1 :** a rising tide **2 a :** an overwhelming quantity **b :** a high point **:** PEAK

flood·wa·ter \-ˌwȯ-tər, -ˌwä-\ *n* (1791) **:** the water of a flood

flood·way \-ˌwā\ *n* (1928) **:** a channel for diverting floodwaters

floo·ey \ˈflü-ē\ *adj* [origin unknown] (1905) **:** AWRY, ASKEW ⟨go ~⟩

[1]floor \ˈflȯr\ *n, often attrib* [ME *flor,* fr. OE *flōr;* akin to OHG *fluor* meadow, L *planus* level, and perh. to Gk *planasthai* to wander] (bef. 12c) **1 :** the level base of a room **2 a :** the lower inside surface of a hollow structure (as a cave or bodily part) **b :** a ground surface ⟨the ocean ~⟩ **3 a :** a structure dividing a building into stories; *also* **:** STORY **b :** the occupants of such a floor **4 :** the surface of a structure on which one travels ⟨the ~ of a bridge⟩ **5 a :** a main level space (as in a stock exchange or legislative chamber) distinguished from a platform or gallery **b :** the specially prepared or marked area on which indoor sports events take place **c :** the members of an assembly ⟨took questions from the ~⟩ **d :** the right to address an assembly ⟨the senator from Utah has the ~⟩ **6 :** a lower limit **:** BASE — **floored** *adj* — **from the floor :** in field goals as opposed to free throws ⟨made 16 of 18 shots *from the floor*⟩

[2]floor *vt* (15c) **1 :** to cover with a floor or flooring **2 a :** to knock or bring down **b :** FLABBERGAST, DUMBFOUND **3 :** to press (the accelerator of a vehicle) to the floorboard; *also* **:** to accelerate rapidly ⟨~*ed* the van⟩ — **floor·er** *n*

floor·board \ˈflȯr-ˌbȯrd\ *n* (1881) **1 :** a board in a floor **2 :** the floor of an automobile

floor·cloth \-ˌklȯth\ *n, pl* **-cloths** \-ˌklȯt͟hz, -ˌklȯths\ (1746) **:** a usu. decorated heavy cloth (as of canvas) used for a floor covering

floor exercise *n* (1957) **:** an event in gymnastics competition consisting of various ballet and tumbling movements (as jumps, somersaults, and handstands) performed without apparatus

floor·ing \ˈflȯr-iŋ\ *n* (1624) **1 :** FLOOR, BASE **2 :** material for floors

floor lamp *n* (1892) **:** a tall lamp that stands on the floor

floor leader *n* (1899) **:** a member of a legislative body chosen by a party to have charge of its organization and strategy on the floor

floor–length *adj* (1939) **:** reaching to the floor ⟨a ~ gown⟩

floor manager *n* (1887) **:** a person who directs something from the floor (as of a nominating convention)

floor show *n* (1927) **:** a series of acts presented in a nightclub

floor–through \ˈflȯr-ˌthrü\ *n* (1967) **:** an apartment that occupies an entire floor of a building

floor·walk·er \ˈflȯr-ˌwȯ-kər\ *n* (1876) **:** a person employed in a retail store to oversee the salespeople and aid customers

floo·zy *or* **floo·zie** \ˈflü-zē\ *n, pl* **floozies** [origin unknown] (1911) **:** a usu. young woman of loose morals

[1]flop \ˈfläp\ *vb* **flopped; flop·ping** [alter. of [2]*flap*] *vi* (1602) **1 :** to swing or move loosely **:** FLAP **2 :** to throw or move oneself in a heavy, clumsy, or relaxed manner ⟨*flopped* into the chair⟩ **3 :** to change or turn suddenly **4 :** to go to bed ⟨a place to ~ at night⟩ **5 :** to fail completely ⟨the play *flopped*⟩ ~ *vt* **:** to move or drop heavily or noisily **:** cause to flop ⟨*flopped* the bundles down⟩ — **flop·per** *n*

[2]flop *adv* (1728) **:** RIGHT, SQUARELY ⟨fell ~ on my face⟩

[3]flop *n* (1823) **1 :** an act or sound of flopping **2 :** a complete failure ⟨the movie was a ~⟩ **3** *slang* **:** a place to sleep; *esp* **:** FLOPHOUSE **4 :** DUNG ⟨cow ~⟩; *also* **:** a piece of dung

flop·house \ˈfläp-ˌhau̇s\ *n* (1916) **:** a cheap rooming house or hotel

[1]flop·py \ˈflä-pē\ *adj* **flop·pi·er; -est** (1858) **:** tending to flop; *esp* **:** being both soft and flexible — **flop·pi·ly** \ˈflä-pə-lē\ *adv* — **flop·pi·ness** \ˈflä-pē-nəs\ *n*

[2]floppy *n, pl* **floppies** (1974) **:** FLOPPY DISK

floppy disk *n* (1972) **:** a thin plastic disk coated with magnetic material on which data for a computer can be stored

flop sweat *n* (1953) **:** nervous sweat (as of a performer) caused esp. by the fear of failing

flo·ra \ˈflȯr-ə\ *n, pl* **floras** *also* **flo·rae** \ˈflȯr-ˌē, -ˌī\ [NL, fr. L *Flora,* Roman goddess of flowers, fr. L *flor-, flos*] (1777) **1 :** a treatise on or list of the plants of an area or period **2 :** plant or bacterial life; *esp* **:** such life characteristic of a region, period, or special environment ⟨fossil ~⟩ ⟨intestinal ~⟩ — compare FAUNA

1**flo·ral** \ˈflȯr-əl\ *adj* [L *flor-, flos* flower — more at BLOW] (1753) **1 :** of, relating to, or depicting flowers ⟨a ~ display⟩ ⟨a ~ design⟩ **2 :** of or relating to a flora ⟨~ diversity⟩

2**floral** *n* (1897) **:** a design or picture in which flowers predominate

floral envelope *n* (ca. 1829) **:** PERIANTH

Flor·ence fennel \ˈflȯr-ən(t)s-, ˈflär-\ *n* [*Florence,* Italy] (1942) **:** a fennel (*Foeniculum vulgare azoricum*) cultivated for its edible bulbous stem base — called also *finocchio*

Flor·ence flask \ˈflȯr-ən(t)s-, ˈflär-\ *n* [*Florence,* Italy; fr. the use of flasks of this shape for certain Italian wines] (1744) **:** a round usu. flat-bottomed laboratory vessel with a long neck

Flor·en·tine \ˈflȯr-ən-ˌtēn, ˈflär-, -ˌtīn\ *adj* [ML *Florentinus*] (1568) **1 a :** of or relating to Florence, Italy **b :** MACHIAVELLIAN ⟨~ politics⟩ **2 :** served or dressed with spinach ⟨poached eggs ~⟩ **3 :** having a matte brushed finish ⟨~ gold⟩

flo·res·cence \flȯ-ˈre-sᵊn(t)s, flə-\ *n* [NL *florescentia,* fr. L *florescent-, florescens,* prp. of *florescere,* incho. of *florēre* to blossom, flourish — more at FLOURISH] (1793) **:** a state or period of flourishing — **flo·res·cent** \-sᵊnt\ *adj*

flo·ret \ˈflȯr-ət\ *n* [ME *flourette,* fr. AF **floret,* dim. of *flur* flower] (1671) **1 :** a small flower; *esp* **:** one of the small flowers forming the head of a composite plant **2 :** a cluster of flower buds separated from a head esp. when used as food ⟨broccoli ~*s*⟩

flori- *comb form* [L, fr. *flor-, flos*] **:** flower or flowers ⟨*flori*culture⟩

flo·ri·at·ed \ˈflȯr-ē-ˌā-təd\ *adj* (1845) **:** having floral ornaments or a floral form — **flo·ri·a·tion** \ˌflȯr-ē-ˈā-shən\ *n*

flo·ri·bun·da \ˌflȯr-ə-ˈbən-də\ *n* [NL, fem. of *floribundus* flowering freely] (1898) **:** any of various bush roses with large flowers in open clusters that derive from crosses of polyantha and tea roses

flo·ri·cul·ture \ˈflȯr-ə-ˌkəl-chər\ *n* (1822) **:** the cultivation and management of ornamental and esp. flowering plants — **flo·ri·cul·tur·al** \ˌflȯr-ə-ˈkəlch-rəl, -ˈkəl-chə-\ *adj* — **flo·ri·cul·tur·ist** \-rist\ *n*

flor·id \ˈflȯr-əd, ˈflär-\ *adj* [L *floridus* blooming, flowery, fr. *florēre*] (1651) **1 a** *obs* **:** covered with flowers **b :** very flowery in style **:** ORNATE ⟨~ prose⟩ ⟨~ declamations⟩; *also* **:** having a florid style ⟨a ~ writer⟩ **c :** elaborately decorated ⟨a ~ interior⟩ **2 a :** tinged with red **:** RUDDY ⟨a ~ complexion⟩ **b :** marked by emotional or sexual fervor ⟨a ~ secret life⟩ ⟨a ~ sensibility⟩ **3** *archaic* **:** HEALTHY **4 :** fully developed **:** manifesting a complete and typical clinical syndrome ⟨the ~ stage of a disease⟩ — **flo·rid·i·ty** \flə-ˈri-də-tē, flȯ-\ *n* — **flor·id·ly** \ˈflȯr-əd-lē, ˈflär-\ *adv* — **flor·id·ness** \-nəs\ *n*

Flor·i·da panther \ˈflȯr-ə-də-, ˈflär-\ *n* (1948) **:** a highly endangered cougar (*Felis concolor coryi*) whose range is now limited to southern Florida

flo·rif·er·ous \flȯ-ˈri-f(ə-)rəs\ *adj* [L *florifer,* fr. *flori-* + *-fer* fer] (1678) **:** bearing flowers; *esp* **:** blooming freely — **flo·rif·er·ous·ness** *n*

flo·ri·gen \ˈflȯr-ə-jən\ *n* [ISV] (1936) **:** a hormone or hormonal agent that promotes flowering — **flo·ri·gen·ic** \ˌflȯr-ə-ˈje-nik\ *adj*

flo·ri·le·gium \ˌflȯr-ə-ˈlē-j(ē-)əm\ *n, pl* **-gia** \-j(ē-)ə\ [NL, fr. L *florilegus* culling flowers, fr. *flori-* + *legere* to gather — more at LEGEND] (1647) **:** a volume of writings **:** ANTHOLOGY

flo·rin \ˈflȯr-ən, ˈflär-\ *n* [ME, fr. AF, fr. OIt *fiorino,* fr. *fiore* flower, fr. L *flor-, flos;* fr. the lily on the coins] (14c) **1 a :** an old gold coin first struck at Florence in 1252 **b :** any of various European gold coins patterned after the Florentine florin **2 a :** a British silver coin worth two shillings **b :** any of several similar coins issued in parts of the Commonwealth of Nations **3 :** GULDEN

flo·rist \ˈflȯr-ist, ˈflär-\ *n* (1623) **:** a person who sells or grows for sale flowers and ornamental plants — **flo·rist·ry** \-ə-strē\ *n*

flo·ris·tic \flȯ-ˈris-tik\ *adj* (1898) **:** of or relating to flowers, a flora, or the phytogeographical study of plants and plant groups — **flo·ris·ti·cal·ly** \-ti-k(ə-)lē\ *adv*

flo·ru·it \ˈflȯr-(y)ə-wət, ˈflär-\ *n* [L, he flourished, fr. *florēre* to flourish] (1843) **:** a period of flourishing (as of a person or movement)

1**floss** \ˈfläs, ˈflȯs\ *n* [prob. modif. of F *floche* soft, weak (of silk fiber), fr. Gascon, fr. L *fluxus,* lit., loose, flowing, pp. of *fluere* to flow — more at FLUID] (1759) **1 a :** soft thread of silk or mercerized cotton for embroidery **b :** DENTAL FLOSS **2 :** fluffy fibrous material

2**floss** *vt* (1974) **:** to use dental floss on ~ *vi* **:** to use dental floss

flossy \ˈflä-sē, ˈflȯ-\ *adj* **floss·i·er; -est** (1839) **1 :** of, relating to, or having the characteristics of floss **2 :** stylish or glamorous esp. at first impression ⟨~ new hotels⟩ — **floss·i·ly** \ˈflä-sə-lē\ *adv*

flo·ta \ˈflō-tə\ *n* [Sp] (1527) **:** a fleet of Spanish ships

flo·ta·tion *also* **float·a·tion** \flō-ˈtā-shən\ *n* [2*float*] (1806) **1 :** the act, process, or state of floating **2 :** an act or instance of financing (as an issue of stock) **3 :** the separation of the particles of a mass of pulverized ore according to their relative capacity for floating on a given liquid; *also* **:** any of various similar processes involving the relative capacity of materials for floating **4 :** the ability (as of a tire or snowshoes) to stay on the surface of soft ground or snow

flo·til·la \flō-ˈti-lə\ *n* [Sp, dim. of *flota* fleet, fr. OF *flote,* fr. ON *floti;* akin to OE *flota* ship, fleet — more at FLOAT] (1711) **1 :** a fleet of ships or boats; *esp* **:** a navy organizational unit consisting of two or more squadrons of small warships **2 :** an indefinite large number ⟨a ~ of changes⟩

flot·sam \ˈflät-səm\ *n* [AF *floteson,* fr. *floter* to float, of Gmc origin; akin to OE *flotian* to float, *flota* ship] (ca. 1607) **1 :** floating wreckage of a ship or its cargo; *broadly* **:** floating debris **2 a :** a floating population (as of emigrants or castaways) ⟨human ~⟩ **b :** miscellaneous or unimportant material ⟨a notebook filled with ~ and jetsam⟩ **c :** DEBRIS, REMAINS ⟨the village . . . built on the ~ of war —Stan Sesser⟩

1**flounce** \ˈflau̇n(t)s\ *vi* **flounced; flounc·ing** [perh. of Scand origin; akin to Norw *flunsa* to hurry] (1542) **1 a :** to move with exaggerated jerky or bouncy motions ⟨*flounced* about the room, jerking her shoulders, gesticulating —Agatha Christie⟩; *also* **:** to move so as to draw attention to oneself ⟨*flounced* into the lobby⟩ **b :** to go with sudden determination ⟨*flounced* out in a huff⟩ **2 :** FLOUNDER, STRUGGLE

2**flounce** *n* (1583) **:** an act or instance of flouncing — **flouncy** \ˈflau̇n(t)-sē\ *adj*

3**flounce** *vt* **flounced; flounc·ing** [alter. of earlier *frounce,* fr. ME *frouncen* to curl] (1711) **:** to trim with flounces

4**flounce** *n* (1713) **:** a strip of fabric attached by one edge; *also* **:** a wide ruffle — **flouncy** \ˈflau̇n(t)-sē\ *adj*

flouncing *n* (1862) **:** material used for flounces

1**floun·der** \ˈflau̇n-dər\ *n, pl* **flounder** *or* **flounders** [ME, of Scand origin; akin to Norw *flundra* flounder] (15c) **:** FLATFISH; *esp* **:** a marine fish of either of two families (Pleuronectidae and Bothidae) that include important food fishes

2**flounder** *vi* **floun·dered; floun·der·ing** \-d(ə-)riŋ\ [prob. alter. of *founder*] (1592) **1 :** to struggle to move or obtain footing **:** thrash about wildly **2 :** to proceed or act clumsily or ineffectually

1**flour** \ˈflau̇(-ə)r\ *n* [ME — more at FLOWER] (13c) **1 :** a product consisting of finely milled wheat; *also* **:** a similar product made from another grain or food product (as dried potatoes or fish) **2 :** a fine soft powder — **flour·less** *adj* — **floury** \-ē\ *adj*

2**flour** *vt* (ca. 1657) **:** to coat with or as if with flour ~ *vi* **:** to break up into particles

flour beetle *n* (1888) **:** any of various small darkling beetles (esp. *Tribolium confusum* and *T. castaneum*) that typically feed on and lay eggs in stored grain and grain products

1**flour·ish** \ˈflər-ish, ˈflə-rish\ *vb* [ME *florisshen,* fr. AF *fluriss-,* stem of *flurir, florir,* fr. VL **florire,* alter. of L *florēre,* fr. *flor-, flos* flower] *vi* (14c) **1 :** to grow luxuriantly **:** THRIVE **2 a :** to achieve success **:** PROSPER ⟨a ~*ing* business⟩ **b :** to be in a state of activity or production ⟨~*ed* around 1850⟩ **c :** to reach a height of development or influence **3 :** to make bold and sweeping gestures ~ *vt* **:** to wield with dramatic gestures **:** BRANDISH ***syn*** see SWING — **flour·ish·er** *n* — **flour·ish·ing·ly** \-i-shiŋ-lē\ *adv*

2**flourish** *n* (ca. 1552) **1 :** an act or instance of brandishing or waving **2 a :** a florid bit of speech or writing ⟨rhetorical ~*es*⟩ **b :** an ornamental stroke in writing or printing **c :** a decorative or finishing detail ⟨a house with clever little ~*es*⟩ **3 :** FANFARE **4 a :** a period of thriving **b :** a luxuriant growth or profusion ⟨a ~ of white hair⟩ ⟨a springtime ~ of color⟩ **5 :** showiness in the doing of something ⟨opened the door with a ~⟩ **6 :** a sudden burst ⟨a ~ of activity⟩

1**flout** \ˈflau̇t\ *vb* [prob. fr. ME *flouten* to play the flute, fr. *floute* flute] *vt* (1551) **:** to treat with contemptuous disregard **:** SCORN ⟨~*ing* the rules⟩ ~ *vi* **:** to indulge in scornful behavior ***syn*** see SCOFF ***usage*** see FLAUNT — **flout·er** *n*

2**flout** *n* (1566) **:** JEER

1**flow** \ˈflō\ *vb* [ME, fr. OE *flōwan;* akin to OHG *flouwen* to rinse, wash, L *pluere* to rain, Gk *plein* to sail, float] *vi* (bef. 12c) **1 a** (1) **:** to issue or move in a stream (2) **:** CIRCULATE **b :** to move with a continual change of place among the constituent particles ⟨molasses ~*s* slowly⟩ **2 :** RISE ⟨the tide ebbs and ~*s*⟩ **3 :** ABOUND ⟨a land ~*ing* with natural resources⟩ **4 a :** to proceed smoothly and readily ⟨conversation ~*ed* easily⟩ **b :** to have a smooth continuity **5 :** to hang loose and billowing ⟨her gown ~*ed* around her⟩ **6 :** to derive from a source **:** COME ⟨the wealth that ~*s* from trade⟩ **7 :** to deform under stress without cracking or rupturing — used esp. of minerals and rocks **8 :** MENSTRUATE ~ *vt* **1 :** to cause to flow **2 :** to discharge in a flow ***syn*** see SPRING — **flow·ing·ly** \-iŋ-lē\ *adv*

2**flow** *n* (15c) **1 :** an act of flowing **2 a :** FLOOD 1a **b :** FLOOD 2 ⟨the tide's ebb and ~⟩ **3 a :** a smooth uninterrupted movement or progress ⟨a ~ of information⟩ **b :** STREAM; *also* **:** a mass of material which has flowed when molten ⟨an old lava ~⟩ **c :** the direction of movement or development ⟨go with the ~⟩ **4 :** the quantity that flows in a certain time ⟨a gauge that measures fuel ~⟩ **5 :** MENSTRUATION **6 a :** the motion characteristic of fluids **b :** a continuous transfer of energy

flow·age \ˈflō-ij\ *n* (1830) **1 a :** an overflowing onto adjacent land **b :** a body of water formed by overflowing or damming **c :** floodwater esp. of a stream **2 :** gradual deformation of a body of plastic solid (as rock) by intermolecular shear

flow·chart \-ˌchärt\ *n* (1920) **:** a diagram that shows step-by-step progression through a procedure or system esp. using connecting lines and a set of conventional symbols — **flow·chart·ing** \-ˌchär-tiŋ\ *n*

flow cy·tom·e·try \-sī-ˈtä-mə-trē\ *n* (1978) **:** a technique for identifying and sorting cells and their components (as DNA) by staining with a fluorescent dye and detecting the fluorescence usu. by laser beam illumination — **flow cy·tom·e·ter** \-sī-ˈtä-mə-tər\ *n*

flow diagram *n* (1943) **:** FLOWCHART

1**flow·er** \ˈflau̇(-ə)r\ *n* [ME *flour* flower, best of anything, flour, fr. AF *flur, flour, flaur,* fr. L *flor-, flos* — more at BLOW] (13c) **1 a :** the part of a seed plant that normally bears reproductive organs **:** BLOSSOM, INFLORESCENCE **b :** a shoot of the sporophyte of a higher plant that is modified for reproduction and consists of a shortened axis bearing modified leaves; *esp* **:** one of a seed plant differentiated into a calyx, corolla, stamens, and carpels **c :** a plant cultivated for its blossoms **2 a :** the best part or example ⟨the ~ of our youth⟩ **b :** the finest most vigorous period **c :** a state of blooming or flourishing ⟨in full ~⟩ **3** *pl* **:** a finely divided powder produced esp. by condensation or sublimation ⟨~*s* of sulfur⟩ — **flow·ered** \ˈflau̇(-ə)rd\ *adj* — **flow·er·ful** \ˈflau̇(-ə)r-fəl\ *adj* — **flow·er·less** \-ləs\ *adj* — **flow·er·like** \-ˌlīk\ *adj*

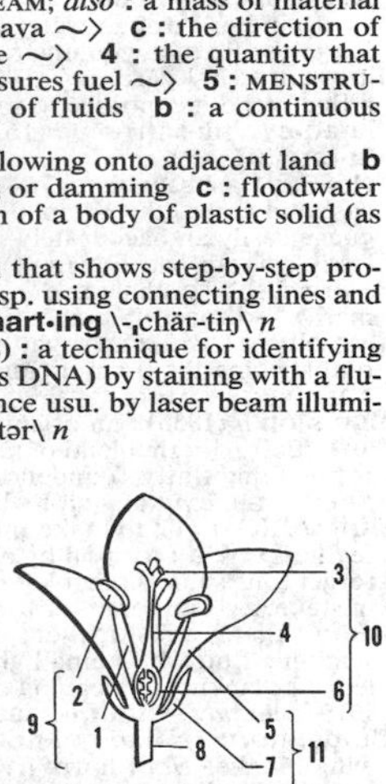

cross section of flower 1b: *1* filament, *2* anther, *3* stigma, *4* style, *5* petal, *6* ovary, *7* sepal, *8* pedicel, *9* stamen, *10* pistil, *11* perianth

2**flower** *vi* (13c) **1 a :** DEVELOP ⟨~*ed* into young womanhood⟩ **b :** FLOURISH 2 **2 :** to produce flowers **:** BLOSSOM ~ *vt* **1 :** to cause to bear flowers **2 :** to decorate with flowers or floral designs — **flow·er·er** \ˈflau̇(-ə)r-ər\ *n*

\ə\ **abut** \ᵊ\ **kitten,** F **table** \ər\ **further** \a\ **ash** \ā\ **ace** \ä\ **mop, mar** \au̇\ **out** \ch\ **chin** \e\ **bet** \ē\ **easy** \g\ **go** \i\ **hit** \ī\ **ice** \j\ **job** \ŋ\ **sing** \ō\ **go** \ȯ\ **law** \ȯi\ **boy** \th\ **thin** \t͟h\ **the** \ü\ **loot** \u̇\ **foot** \y\ **yet** \zh\ **vision, beige** \ḵ, ⁿ, œ, ue, ʸ\ *see* Guide to Pronunciation

flow·er·age \ˈflau̇(-ə)r-ij\ *n* (1840) **:** a flowering process, state, or condition
flower bud *n* (1703) **:** a plant bud that produces only a flower
flower bug *n* (ca. 1889) **:** any of various small mostly black-and-white predaceous bugs (family Anthocoridae) that frequent flowers and feed on pest insects (as aphids and thrips)
flower child *n* (1967) **:** a hippie who advocates love, beauty, and peace
flow·er·et *also* **flow·er·ette** \ˈflau̇(-ə)r-ət\ *n* (15c) **:** FLORET
flower girl *n* (1902) **:** a little girl who carries flowers at a wedding
flower head *n* (1842) **:** a capitulum (as of a composite) having sessile flowers so arranged that the whole inflorescence looks like a single flower
flowering dogwood *n* (1843) **:** a common spring-flowering usu. white-bracted dogwood (*Cornus florida*)
flowering plant *n* (1745) **:** ANGIOSPERM
flower people *n pl* (1967) **:** FLOWER CHILDREN
flow·er·pot \ˈflau̇(-ə)r-ˌpät\ *n* (1583) **:** a pot in which to grow plants
flower power *n* (1967) **:** a nonviolent ethic as advocated by hippies
flow·ery \ˈflau̇(-ə)r-ē\ *adj* (14c) **1 :** of, relating to, or resembling flowers **2 :** marked by or given to rhetorical elegance ⟨~ speeches⟩ — **flow·er·i·ly** \ˈflau̇(-ə)r-ə-lē\ *adv* — **flow·er·i·ness** *n*
flow·me·ter \ˈflō-ˌmē-tər\ *n* (1915) **:** an instrument for measuring one or more properties (as velocity or pressure) of a flow (as of a liquid in a pipe)
¹**flown** \ˈflōn\ *past part of* FLY
²**flown** *adj* [archaic pp. of ¹*flow*] (1626) **:** filled to excess
flow sheet *n* (1912) **:** FLOWCHART
flow·stone \ˈflō-ˌstōn\ *n* (1925) **:** calcite deposited by a thin sheet of flowing water usu. along the walls or floor of a cave
fl oz *abbr* fluid ounce
FLSA *abbr* Fair Labor Standards Act
flu \ˈflü\ *n* [by shortening] (1839) **1 :** INFLUENZA **2 :** any of several virus diseases marked esp. by respiratory or intestinal symptoms — **flu-like** \ˈflü-ˌlīk\ *adj*
¹**flub** \ˈfləb\ *vb* **flubbed; flub·bing** [origin unknown] *vt* (1904) **:** to make a mess of **:** BOTCH ⟨*flubbed* my lines⟩ ~ *vi* **:** BLUNDER
²**flub** *n* (1900) **:** an act or instance of flubbing **:** BLUNDER
flub·dub \ˈfləb-ˌdəb\ *n* [origin unknown] (1888) **:** BUNKUM, BALDERDASH
flu·con·a·zole \flü-ˈkä-nə-ˌzōl\ *n* [*fluor-* + *-conazole* (as in *miconazole*)] (1985) **:** an antifungal agent $C_{13}H_{12}F_2N_6O$ used orally to treat cryptococcal meningitis and systemic candida infections
fluc·tu·ant \ˈflək-chə-wənt, -chü-ənt\ *adj* (1560) **1 :** moving in waves **2 :** VARIABLE, UNSTABLE **3 :** being movable and compressible ⟨a ~ abscess⟩
fluc·tu·ate \ˈflək-chə-ˌwāt, -chü-ˌāt\ *vb* **-at·ed; -at·ing** [L *fluctuatus*, pp. of *fluctuare*, fr. *fluctus* flow, wave, fr. *fluere* — more at FLUID] *vi* (1634) **1 :** to shift back and forth uncertainly **2 :** to ebb and flow in waves ~ *vt* **:** to cause to fluctuate *syn* see SWING — **fluc·tu·a·tion** \ˌflək-chə-ˈwā-shən, -chü-ˈā-\ *n* — **fluc·tu·a·tion·al** \-shnəl, -shə-nᵊl\ *adj*
flue \ˈflü\ *n* [origin unknown] (1582) **:** an enclosed passageway for directing a current: as **a :** a channel in a chimney for conveying flame and smoke to the outer air **b :** a pipe for conveying flame and hot gases around or through water in a steam boiler **c :** an air channel leading to the lip of a wind instrument **d :** FLUE PIPE
flue–cured \-ˌkyu̇rd\ *adj* (1905) **:** cured with heat transmitted through a flue without exposure to smoke or fumes ⟨~ tobacco⟩
flu·en·cy \ˈflü-ən(t)-sē\ *n* (1636) **:** the quality or state of being fluent
flu·ent \ˈflü-ənt\ *adj* [L *fluent-, fluens*, prp. of *fluere* — more at FLUID] (1585) **1 a :** capable of flowing **:** FLUID **b :** capable of moving with ease and grace ⟨the ~ body of a dancer⟩ **2 a :** capable of using a language easily and accurately ⟨~ in Spanish⟩ ⟨a ~ writer⟩ **b :** effortlessly smooth and flowing **:** POLISHED ⟨a ~ performance⟩ ⟨spoke in ~ English⟩ **c :** having or showing mastery of a subject or skill ⟨~ in math⟩ — **flu·ent·ly** *adv*
flue pipe *n* (1852) **:** an organ pipe whose tone is produced by an air current striking the lip and causing the air within to vibrate — compare REED PIPE
flue stop *n* (1855) **:** an organ stop made up of flue pipes
¹**fluff** \ˈfləf\ *n* [perh. blend of *flue* (fluff) and *puff*] (1790) **1 :** ⁷DOWN 1 **2 :** something fluffy ⟨dandelion ~⟩ **3 :** something inconsequential **4 :** BLUNDER; *esp* **:** an actor's lapse of memory
²**fluff** *vt* (1835) **1 :** to make fluffy ⟨~ the pillows⟩ ⟨birds ~*ing* up their feathers⟩ **2 a :** to spoil by a mistake **:** BOTCH **b :** to deliver badly or forget (one's lines) in a play ~ *vi* **1 :** to become fluffy **2 :** to make a mistake; *esp* **:** to forget or bungle one's lines in a play
fluffy \ˈflə-fē\ *adj* **fluff·i·er; -est** (ca. 1825) **1 a :** covered with or resembling fluff **b :** being light and soft or airy **:** puffed up ⟨a ~ omelet⟩ **2 :** lacking in meaning or substance **:** SUPERFICIAL 2c — **fluff·i·ly** \ˈflə-fə-lē\ *adv* — **fluff·i·ness** \ˈflə-fē-nəs\ *n*
flü·gel·horn *or* **flue·gel·horn** \ˈflü-gəl-ˌhȯrn, ˈflœ-\ *n* [G, fr. *Flügel* wing, flank + *Horn* horn; fr. its use to signal the flanking drivers in a battue] (1854) **:** a valved brass instrument resembling a cornet but having a larger bore — **flü·gel·horn·ist** \-ˌhȯr-nist\ *n*
¹**flu·id** \ˈflü-əd\ *adj* [F or L; F *fluide*, fr. L *fluidus*, fr. *fluere* to flow; akin to Gk *phlyzein* to boil over] (1603) **1 a :** having particles that easily move and change their relative position without a separation of the mass and that easily yield to pressure **:** capable of flowing **b :** subject to change or movement ⟨boundaries became ~⟩ **2 :** characterized by or employing a smooth easy style ⟨the ballerina's ~ movements⟩ ⟨~ recitation of his lines⟩ **3 a :** available for various uses ⟨a ~ computer program⟩ **b :** LIQUID 4 ⟨~ assets⟩ — **flu·id·ly** *adv* — **flu·id·ness** *n*
²**fluid** *n* (1661) **:** a substance (as a liquid or gas) tending to flow or conform to the outline of its container — **flu·id·al** \ˈflü-ə-dᵊl\ *adj* — **flu·id·al·ly** \-dᵊl-ē\ *adv* — **flu·id·like** \-ˌlīk\ *adj*
fluid dram *or* **flu·i·dram** \ˌflü-ə(d)-ˈdram\ *n* (ca. 1860) **:** a unit of liquid capacity equal to ⅛ fluid ounce — see WEIGHT table
flu·id·ex·tract \ˌflü-əd-ˈek-ˌstrakt\ *n* (1851) **:** an alcohol preparation of a plant-derived drug containing the active constituents of one gram of the dry drug in each milliliter
flu·id·ic \flü-ˈi-dik\ *adj* (1960) **:** of, relating to, or being a device (as an amplifier or control) that depends for operation on the pressures and flows of a fluid in precisely shaped channels — **fluidic** *n* — **flu·id·ics** \-diks\ *n pl but sing in constr*
flu·id·i·ty \flü-ˈi-də-tē\ *n* (1603) **1 :** the quality or state of being fluid **2 :** the physical property of a substance that enables it to flow
flu·id·ize \ˈflü-ə-ˌdīz\ *vt* **-ized; -iz·ing** (ca. 1855) **1 :** to cause to flow like a fluid **2 :** to suspend (as solid particles) in a rapidly moving stream of gas or vapor to induce flowing motion of the whole — **flu·id·i·za·tion** \ˌflü-ə-də-ˈzā-shən\ *n* — **flu·id·iz·er** \ˈflü-ə-ˌdī-zər\ *n*
fluidized bed *n* (1949) **:** a bed of small solid particles (as in a coal burning furnace) suspended and kept in motion by an upward flow of a fluid (as a gas) — called also *fluid bed*
fluid mechanics *n pl but sing or pl in constr* (1937) **:** a branch of mechanics dealing with the properties of liquids and gases
fluid ounce *n* (1811) **1 :** a U.S. unit of liquid capacity equal to ¹⁄₁₆ pint — see WEIGHT table **2 :** a British unit of liquid capacity equal to ¹⁄₂₀ pint — see WEIGHT table
¹**fluke** \ˈflük\ *n* [ME *floke, fluke*, fr. OE *flōc;* akin to OE *flōh* chip, OHG *flah* smooth, Gk *plax* flat surface, and prob. to OE *flōr* floor — more at FLOOR] (bef. 12c) **1 :** FLATFISH **2 :** a flattened digenetic trematode worm; *broadly* **:** TREMATODE — compare LIVER FLUKE
²**fluke** *n* [perh. fr. ¹*fluke*] (1561) **1 :** the part of an anchor that fastens in the ground — see ANCHOR illustration **2 :** one of the lobes of a whale's tail
³**fluke** *n* [origin unknown] (1857) **1 :** an accidentally successful stroke at billiards or pool **2 :** a stroke of luck ⟨the discovery was a ~⟩
fluky *also* **fluk·ey** \ˈflü-kē\ *adj* **fluk·i·er; -est** (1867) **1 :** happening by or depending on chance **2 :** being unsteady or uncertain — used esp. of wind
flume \ˈflüm\ *n* [prob. fr. ME *flum* river, fr. AF, fr. L *flumen*, fr. *fluere* — more at FLUID] (1748) **1 :** an inclined channel for conveying water (as for power) **2 :** a ravine or gorge with a stream running through it
flum·mery \ˈfləm-rē, ˈflə-mə-\ *n, pl* **-mer·ies** [W *llymru*] (1623) **1 a :** a soft jelly or porridge made with flour or meal **b :** any of several sweet desserts **2 :** MUMMERY, MUMBO JUMBO
flum·mox \ˈflə-məks, -miks\ *vt* [origin unknown] (1837) **:** CONFUSE
¹**flump** \ˈfləmp\ [imit.] *vi* (1729) **:** to move or fall suddenly and heavily ⟨~*ed* down into the chair⟩ ~ *vt* **:** to place or drop with a flump
²**flump** *n* (1767) **:** a dull heavy sound (as of a fall)
flung *past and past part of* FLING
¹**flunk** \ˈfləŋk\ *vb* [perh. blend of *flinch* and *funk*] *vi* (1823) **:** to fail esp. in an examination or course ~ *vt* **1 :** to give a failing grade to **2 :** to get a failing grade or result in — **flunk·er** *n*
²**flunk** *n* (1846) **:** an act or instance of flunking
flunk out *vi* (1920) **:** to be dismissed from a school or college for failure ~ *vt* **:** to dismiss from a school or college for failure
flun·ky *or* **flun·key** *or* **flun·kie** \ˈfləŋ-kē\ *n, pl* **flunkies** *also* **flunkeys** [Sc, of unknown origin] (ca. 1782) **1 a :** a liveried servant **b :** one performing menial or miscellaneous duties **2 :** YES-MAN
flu·o·cin·o·lone ac·e·to·nide \ˌflü-ə-ˈsi-nə-ˌlōn-ˌa-sə-ˈtō-ˌnīd\ *n* [*fluor-* + *-cinolone* (as in *triamcinolone*)] (1963) **:** a glucocorticoid steroid $C_{24}H_{30}F_2O_6$ used esp. as an anti-inflammatory agent in the treatment of skin diseases
flu·or \ˈflü-ˌȯr, ˈflü-ər\ *n* [NL, mineral belonging to a group used as fluxes and including fluorite, fr. L, flow, fr. *fluere* — more at FLUID] (1661) **:** FLUORITE
fluor- *or* **fluoro-** *comb form* [F] **1 :** fluorine ⟨*fluor*ide⟩ **2** *also* **fluori-** **:** fluorescence ⟨*fluoro*scope⟩ ⟨*fluori*meter⟩
fluo·resce \flu̇-ˈres, flȯ-\ *vi* **-resced; -resc·ing** [back-formation fr. *fluorescence*] (1874) **:** to produce, undergo, or exhibit fluorescence — **fluo·resc·er** *n*
fluo·res·ce·in \-ˈre-sē-ən\ *n* (1871) **:** a yellow or red crystalline dye $C_{20}H_{12}O_5$ with a bright yellow-green fluorescence in alkaline solution
fluo·res·cence \-ˈre-sᵊn(t)s\ *n* [*fluor*spar + opal*escence*] (1852) **:** luminescence that is caused by the absorption of radiation at one wavelength followed by nearly immediate reradiation usu. at a different wavelength and that ceases almost at once when the incident radiation stops; *also* **:** the radiation emitted — compare PHOSPHORESCENCE
fluo·res·cent \-sᵊnt\ *adj* (1853) **1 :** having or relating to fluorescence **2 :** bright and glowing as a result of fluorescence ⟨~ inks⟩; *broadly* **:** very bright in color — **fluorescent** *n* — **fluo·res·cent·ly** *adv*
fluorescent lamp *n* (1896) **:** a usu. tubular electric lamp having a coating of fluorescent material on its inner surface and containing mercury vapor whose bombardment by electrons from the cathode provides ultraviolet light which causes the material to emit visible light
fluo·ri·date \ˈflu̇r-ə-ˌdāt, ˈflȯr-\ *vt* **-dat·ed; -dat·ing** (1949) **:** to add a fluoride to (as drinking water) to reduce tooth decay — **fluo·ri·da·tion** \ˌflu̇r-ə-ˈdā-shən, ˌflȯr-\ *n*
fluo·ride \ˈflȯr-ˌīd, ˈflu̇r-\ *n, often attrib* (1826) **1 :** a compound of fluorine **2 :** the monovalent anion of fluorine
fluo·ri·nate \ˈflȯr-ə-ˌnāt, ˈflu̇r-\ *vt* **-nat·ed; -nat·ing** (ca. 1929) **:** to treat or cause to combine with fluorine or a compound of fluorine — **fluo·ri·na·tion** \ˌflȯr-ə-ˈnā-shən, ˌflu̇r-\ *n*
fluo·rine \ˈflu̇r-ˌēn, ˈflȯr-\ *n* [F, fr. NL *fluor*] (1813) **:** a nonmetallic halogen element that is isolated as a pale yellowish flammable irritating toxic diatomic gas — see ELEMENT table
fluo·rite \ˈflu̇r-ˌīt, ˈflȯr-\ *n* [It, fr. NL *fluor*] (1868) **:** a transparent or translucent mineral of different colors that consists of the fluoride of calcium and is used esp. as a steelmaking flux and in the making of opalescent and opaque glasses
fluo·ro·car·bon \ˌflu̇r-ō-ˈkär-bən, ˌflȯr-\ *n* (1937) **:** any of various chemically inert compounds containing carbon and fluorine used chiefly as lubricants, refrigerants, nonstick coatings, and formerly aerosol propellants and in making resins and plastics; *also* **:** CHLOROFLUOROCARBON
fluo·ro·chrome \ˈflu̇r-ə-ˌkrōm, ˌflȯr-\ *n* (1943) **:** any of various fluorescent substances used in biological staining to produce fluorescence in a specimen
fluo·rog·ra·phy \flu̇-ˈrä-grə-fē, flȯ-\ *n* (1941) **:** the photography of the image produced on a fluorescent screen by X rays — **fluo·ro·graph·ic** \ˌflu̇r-ə-ˈgra-fik, ˌflȯr-\ *adj*
fluo·rom·e·ter \flu̇-ˈrä-mə-tər, flȯ-\ *or* **fluo·rim·e·ter** \-ˈri-\ *n* (1897) **:** an instrument for measuring fluorescence and related phenomena (as intensity of radiation) — **fluo·ro·met·ric** *or* **fluo·ri·met·ric** \ˌflu̇r-ə-

ˈme-trik, ˌflȯr-\ *adj* — **fluo·rom·e·try** \flu̇-ˈrä-mə-trē, flȯ-\ *or* **fluo·rim·e·try** \-ˈri-mə-trē\ *n*

flu·o·ro·quin·o·lone \ˌflu̇r-ō-ˈkwi-nə-ˌlōn\ *n* (1984) : any of a group of fluorinated derivatives of quinolone that are used as antibacterial drugs

[1]**fluo·ro·scope** \ˈflu̇r-ə-ˌskōp, ˈflȯr-\ *n* [ISV] (1896) : an instrument used for observing the internal structure of an opaque object (as the living body) by means of X-rays — **fluo·ro·scop·ic** \ˌflu̇r-ə-ˈskä-pik, ˌflȯr-\ *adj* — **fluo·ro·scop·i·cal·ly** \-pi-k(ə-)lē\ *adv* — **fluo·ros·co·pist** \flu̇-ˈräs-kə-pist, flȯ-\ *n* — **fluo·ros·co·py** \-pē\ *n*

[2]**fluoroscope** *vt* **-scoped; -scop·ing** (1898) : to examine by fluoroscopy

fluo·ro·sis \flu̇-ˈrō-səs, flȯ-\ *n* [NL] (1927) : an abnormal condition (as mottling of the teeth) caused by fluorine or its compounds — **fluo·rot·ic** \-ˈrä-tik\ *adj*

fluo·ro·ura·cil \ˌflu̇r-ō-ˈyu̇r-ə-ˌsil, -ˌsəl, ˌflȯr-\ *n* [*fluor-* + *uracil*] (ca. 1958) : a fluorine-containing pyrimidine base $C_4H_3FN_2O_2$ used as a neoplastic agent to treat some kinds of cancer

fluor·spar \ˈflu̇r-ˌspär, ˈflȯr-\ *n* (1794) : FLUORITE

flu·ox·e·tine \flü-ˈäk-sə-ˌtēn\ *n* [ISV, prob. fr. *fluor-* + *oxy* + *m*ethyl + *amine*] (1975) : an antidepressant drug $C_{17}H_{18}F_3NO$ that is administered in the form of its hydrochloride and enhances serotonin activity

flu·phen·azine \flü-ˈfe-nə-ˌzēn\ *n* [*fluor-* + *phenazine*] (1959) : a tranquilizer $C_{22}H_{26}F_3N_3OS$ used esp. in the form of its hydrochloride

[1]**flur·ry** \ˈflər-ē, ˈflə-rē\ *n, pl* **flurries** [prob. fr. *flurr* to throw scatteringly] (1686) **1 a :** a gust of wind **b :** a brief light snowfall **2 a :** a brief period of commotion or excitement **b :** a sudden occurrence of many things at once : BARRAGE 2 ⟨a ~ of insults⟩ **3 :** a brief advance or decline in prices : a short-lived outburst of trading activity

[2]**flurry** *vb* **flur·ried; flur·ry·ing** *vt* (1749) : to cause to become agitated and confused ~ *vi* : to move in an agitated or confused manner

[1]**flush** \ˈfləsh\ *vb* [ME *flusshen*] *vi* (13c) : to fly away suddenly ~ *vt* **1** : to cause (as a bird) to flush **2 :** to expose or chase from a place of concealment ⟨~*ed* the boys from their hiding place⟩

[2]**flush** *n* [MF *flus, fluz,* fr. L *fluxus* flow, flux] (ca. 1529) **1 :** a hand of playing cards all of the same suit; *specif* : a poker hand containing five cards of the same suit but not in sequence — see POKER illustration **2** : a series of three or more slalom gates set vertically on a slope

[3]**flush** *n* [perh. modif. of L *fluxus*] (1529) **1 :** a sudden flow (as of water); *also* : a rinsing or cleansing with or as if with a flush of water **2 a** : a sudden increase or expansion; *esp* : sudden and usu. abundant new plant growth ⟨the spring ~ of grass⟩ **b :** a surge of emotion ⟨felt a ~ of anger at the insult⟩ **3 a :** a tinge of red : BLUSH **b :** a fresh and vigorous state ⟨in the first ~ of womanhood⟩ **4 :** a transitory sensation of extreme heat — compare HOT FLASH

[4]**flush** *vi* (1548) **1 :** to flow and spread suddenly and freely **2 a :** to glow brightly **b :** BLUSH **3 :** to produce new growth ⟨the plants ~ twice during the year⟩ ~ *vt* **1 a :** to cause to flow **b :** to pour liquid over or through; *esp* : to cleanse or wash out with or as if with a rush of liquid ⟨~ the toilet⟩ ⟨~ the lungs with air⟩ **2 :** INFLAME, EXCITE — usu. used passively ⟨~*ed* with pride⟩ **3 :** to cause to blush

[5]**flush** *adj* (ca. 1568) **1 a :** of a ruddy healthy color **b :** full of life and vigor : LUSTY **2 a :** filled to overflowing **b :** AFFLUENT **3 :** readily available : ABUNDANT **4 a :** having or forming a continuous plane or unbroken surface ⟨~ paneling⟩ **b :** directly abutting or immediately adjacent: as **(1)** : set even with an edge of a type page or column : having no indention **(2)** : arranged edge to edge so as to fit snugly — **flush·ness** *n*

[6]**flush** *adv* (1700) **1 :** in a flush manner **2 :** SQUARELY ⟨hit him ~ on the chin⟩

[7]**flush** *vt* (ca. 1842) : to make flush ⟨~ the headings on a page⟩

flush·able \ˈflə-shə-bəl\ *adj* (1973) : suitable for disposal by flushing down a toilet

[1]**flus·ter** \ˈfləs-tər\ *vb* **flus·tered; flus·ter·ing** \-t(ə-)riŋ\ [prob. of Scand origin; akin to Icel *flaustur* hurry] *vt* (1604) **1 :** to make tipsy **2 :** to put into a state of agitated confusion : UPSET ~ *vi* : to move or behave in an agitated or confused manner ***syn*** see DISCOMPOSE — **flus·tered·ly** *adv*

[2]**fluster** *n* (1712) : a state of agitated confusion

[1]**flute** \ˈflüt\ *n* [ME *floute,* fr. AF *floute, fleute,* fr. OF *flaüte,* prob. of imit. origin] (14c) **1 a :** RECORDER 3 **b :** a keyed woodwind instrument consisting of a cylindrical tube which is stopped at one end and which has a side hole over which air is blown to produce the tone and having a range from middle C upward for three octaves **2 :** something long and slender: as **a :** a tall slender wineglass **b :** a grooved pleat (as on a hat brim) **3** : a rounded groove; *specif* : one of the vertical parallel grooves on a classical architectural column — **flute·like** \-ˌlīk\ *adj* — **fluty** *or* **flut·ey** \ˈflü-tē\ *adj*

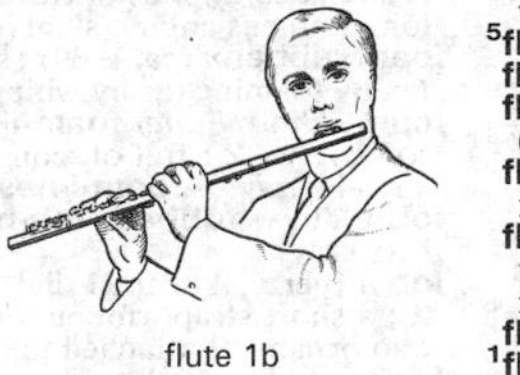

flute 1b

[2]**flute** *vb* **flut·ed; flut·ing** *vi* (14c) **1 :** to play a flute **2 :** to produce a flutelike sound ~ *vt* **1 :** to utter with a flutelike sound **2 :** to form flutes in — **flut·er** *n*

flut·ed *adj* (1611) : having or marked by grooves

fluting *n* (1611) **1 :** a series of flutes ⟨the ~ of a column⟩ **2 :** fluted material

flut·ist \ˈflü-tist\ *n* (1603) : one who plays a flute

[1]**flut·ter** \ˈflə-tər\ *vb* [ME *floteren* to float, flutter, fr. OE *floterian,* freq. of *flotian* to float; akin to OE *flēotan* to float — more at FLEET] *vi* (bef. 12c) **1 :** to flap the wings rapidly **2 a :** to move with quick wavering or flapping motions **b :** to vibrate in irregular spasms **3 :** to move about or behave in an agitated aimless manner ~ *vt* : to cause to flutter — **flut·ter·er** \-tər-ər\ *n* — **flut·tery** \-tə-rē\ *adj*

[2]**flutter** *n* (1641) **1 :** an act of fluttering **2 a :** a state of nervous confusion or excitement **b :** FLURRY, COMMOTION **c :** abnormal spasmodic fluttering of a body part ⟨treatment of atrial ~⟩ **3 a :** a distortion in reproduced sound similar to but of a higher pitch than wow **b** : fluctuation in the brightness of a television image **4 :** an unwanted oscillation (as of an aileron or a bridge) set up by natural forces **5** *chiefly Brit* : a small speculative venture or gamble

flutter kick *n* (ca. 1934) : an alternating whipping motion of the legs used in various swimming styles (as the crawl)

flutter sleeve *n* (1973) : a loose-fitting tapered sleeve falling in folds over the upper arm

flu·vi·al \ˈflü-vē-əl\ *adj* [ME, fr. L *fluvialis,* fr. *fluvius* river, fr. *fluere*] (14c) **1 :** of, relating to, or living in a stream or river **2 :** produced by the action of a stream ⟨a ~ plain⟩

flu·vi·a·tile \ˈflü-vē-ə-ˌtī(-ə)l\ *adj* [MF, fr. L *fluviatilis,* fr. *fluvius*] (1599) : FLUVIAL

[1]**flux** \ˈfləks\ *n* [ME, fr. AF & ML; AF, fr. ML *fluxus,* fr. L, flow, fr. *fluere* to flow — more at FLUID] (14c) **1 :** a flowing of fluid from the body: as **a :** DIARRHEA **b :** DYSENTERY **2 :** a continuous moving on or passing by (as of a stream) **3 :** a continued flow : FLOOD **4 a :** INFLUX **b :** CHANGE, FLUCTUATION ⟨in a state of ~⟩ **5 :** a substance used to promote fusion (as of metals or minerals); *esp* : one (as rosin) applied to surfaces to be joined by soldering, brazing, or welding to clean and free them from oxide and promote their union **6 :** the rate of transfer of fluid, particles, or energy across a given surface

[2]**flux** *vt* (15c) **1 :** to cause to become fluid **2 :** to treat with a flux ~ *vi* : to become fluid : FUSE

flux·gate \ˈfləks-ˌgāt\ *n* (1944) : a device used to indicate the direction and intensity of the magnetic field (as on a planet)

flux·ion \ˈflək-shən\ *n* (1599) **1 :** the action of flowing or changing; *also* : something subjected to such action **2 :** DERIVATIVE 3 — compare METHOD OF FLUXIONS — **flux·ion·al** \-shnəl, -shə-nᵊl\ *adj*

[1]**fly** \ˈflī\ *vb* **flew** \ˈflü\; **flown** \ˈflōn\; **fly·ing** [ME *flien,* fr. OE *flēogan;* akin to OHG *fliogan* to fly and prob. to OE *flōwan* to flow] *vi* (bef. 12c) **1 a :** to move in or pass through the air with wings **b :** to move through the air or before the wind or through outer space **c :** to float, wave, or soar in the air ⟨flags ~*ing* at half-mast⟩ **2 a :** to take flight : FLEE **b :** to fade and disappear : VANISH **3 a :** to move, pass, or spread quickly ⟨rumors were ~*ing*⟩ **b :** to be moved with sudden extreme emotion ⟨*flew* into a rage⟩ **c :** to seem to pass quickly ⟨the time simply *flew*⟩ **4 :** to become expended or dissipated rapidly **5 :** to operate or travel in an airplane or spacecraft **6 :** to work successfully : win popular acceptance ⟨knew . . . a pure human-rights approach would not ~ —Charles Brydon⟩ ~ *vt* **1 a :** to cause to fly, float, or hang in the air ⟨~*ing* a kite⟩ **b :** to operate (as a balloon, aircraft, rocket, or spacecraft) in flight **c :** to journey over or through by flying **2 a :** to flee or escape from **b :** AVOID, SHUN **3 :** to transport by aircraft or spacecraft — **fly at :** to assail suddenly and violently — **fly blind :** to fly an airplane solely by instruments — **fly high :** to be elated — **fly in the face of** *or* **fly in the teeth of :** to stand or act forthrightly or brazenly in defiance or contradiction of

[2]**fly** *n, pl* **flies** (bef. 12c) **1 :** the action or process of flying : FLIGHT **2 a :** a device consisting of two or more radial vanes capable of rotating on a spindle to act as a fan or to govern the speed of clockwork or very light machinery **b :** FLYWHEEL **3** *pl* : the space over a theater stage where scenery and equipment can be hung **4 :** something attached by one edge: as **a :** a garment closing concealed by a fold of cloth extending over the fastener **b (1)** : the length of an extended flag from its staff or support **(2)** : the outer or loose end of a flag **5 :** a baseball hit high into the air **6 :** FLYLEAF **7 :** a sheet of material (as canvas) that is attachable to a tent for use as a double top or as a rooflike extension **8 :** a football pass pattern in which the receiver runs straight downfield — **on the fly 1 :** in motion : BUSY **2 :** while still in the air : without the ball bouncing ⟨the home run carried 450 feet *on the fly*⟩ **3 :** in a hurry and often without preparation : HASTILY, SPONTANEOUSLY ⟨making decisions *on the fly*⟩ **4 :** simultaneously with another task ⟨software that handles formatting *on the fly*⟩

[3]**fly** *vi* **flied; fly·ing** (1893) : to hit a fly in baseball

[4]**fly** *n, pl* **flies** [ME *flie,* fr. OE *flēoge;* akin to OHG *flioga* fly, OE *flēogan* to fly] (bef. 12c) **1 :** a winged insect — usu. used in combination ⟨may*flies*⟩ ⟨butter*fly*⟩ **2 a :** any of a large order (Diptera) of winged or rarely wingless insects (as the housefly, mosquito, or gnat) that have the anterior wings functional, the posterior wings reduced to halteres, and segmented often headless, eyeless, and legless larvae — compare MAGGOT **b :** a large stout-bodied fly **3 :** a fishhook dressed (as with feathers or tinsel) to suggest an insect — **fly in the ointment :** a detracting factor or element

[5]**fly** *adj* [prob. fr. [1]*fly*] (1811) *chiefly Brit* : KEEN, ARTFUL

fly·able \ˈflī-ə-bəl\ *adj* (ca. 1909) : suitable for flying or for being flown

fly agaric *n* (1788) : a medium to large poisonous amanita mushroom (*Amanita muscaria*) with a usu. bright red cap

fly ash *n* (1931) : fine solid particles of ashes, dust, and soot carried out from burning fuel (as coal or oil) by the draft

fly·away \ˈflī-ə-ˌwā\ *adj* (1844) **1 :** loose and flowing esp. because of unconfined fullness at the back ⟨a ~ jacket⟩ **2 :** of, relating to, or being an aircraft that is ready to fly ⟨the plane's ~ price⟩

fly ball *n* (1865) : [2]FLY 5

[1]**fly·blow** \-ˌblō\ *n* (1556) : FLY-STRIKE

[2]**flyblow** *vt* **-blew; -blown** (1603) **1 :** TAINT, CONTAMINATE **2 :** to deposit eggs or young larvae of a flesh fly or blowfly in

fly·blown \ˈflī-ˌblōn\ *adj* (ca. 1529) **1 a :** not pure : TAINTED ⟨a world ~ with the vices of irresponsible power —V. L. Parrington⟩ **b :** not bright and new : SEEDY, MOTH-EATEN **c :** TRITE, HACKNEYED ⟨a long list of ~ metaphors —*Horizon*⟩ **2 a :** infested with eggs or young larvae of a flesh fly or blowfly **b :** covered with flyspecks

fly·boy \ˈflī-ˌbȯi\ *n* (1937) : a member of the air force; *esp* : an aircraft pilot

fly·bridge \ˈflī-ˌbrij\ *n* (1962) : an open deck on a cabin cruiser located above the bridge on the cabin roof and usu. having a duplicate set of navigating equipment

fly·by \ˈflī-ˌbī\ *n, pl* **flybys** (1953) **1 :** a prearranged usu. low-altitude flight by one or more airplanes over a public gathering (as an air show) **2 a :** a flight of a spacecraft past a celestial body (as Mars) close enough to obtain scientific data **b :** a spacecraft that makes a flyby

\ə\ **a**but \ᵊ\ kitten, F table \ər\ **f**ur**ther** \a\ **a**sh \ā\ **a**ce \ä\ m**o**p, m**a**r
\au̇\ **ou**t \ch\ **ch**in \e\ b**e**t \ē\ **ea**sy \g\ **g**o \i\ h**i**t \ī\ **i**ce \j\ **j**ob
\ŋ\ si**ng** \ō\ g**o** \ȯ\ l**aw** \ȯi\ b**oy** \th\ **th**in \t͟h\ **th**e \ü\ l**oo**t \u̇\ f**oo**t
\y\ **y**et \zh\ vi**si**on, bei**ge** \ḵ, ⁿ, œ, ue, ʸ\ *see* Guide to Pronunciation

[1]**fly–by–night** \ˈflī-bī-ˌnīt\ *n* (1822) **1 :** one that seeks to evade responsibilities and esp. creditors by flight **2 :** one without established reputation or standing; *esp* **:** a shaky business enterprise
[2]**fly–by–night** *adj* (1914) **1 :** given to making a quick profit usu. by shady or irresponsible acts **2 :** TRANSITORY, PASSING ⟨~ fashions⟩
fly–by–night·er \ˌflī-bī-ˈnī-tər\ *n* (1946) **:** FLY-BY-NIGHT
fly–by–wire \ˈflī-bī-ˌwī(-ə)r\ *adj* (1968) **:** of, relating to, being, or utilizing a flight-control system in which controls are operated electrically rather than mechanically
fly casting *n* (ca. 1889) **:** the casting of artificial flies in fly-fishing or as a competitive sport
fly·catch·er \ˈflī-ˌka-chər, -ˌke-\ *n* (1678) **:** any of various passerine birds (families Muscicapidae and Tyrannidae) that feed on insects taken on the wing
fly dope *n* (1897) **:** an insect repellent
flyer *var of* FLIER
fly fisherman *n* (1886) **:** an angler who uses the technique of fly-fishing
fly–fish·ing \ˈflī-ˌfi-shiŋ\ *n* (1653) **:** a method of fishing in which an artificial fly is cast by use of a fly rod, a reel, and a relatively heavy oiled or treated line — **fly–fish** \ˈflī-ˌfish\ *vi*
fly front *n* (1843) **:** a concealed closing on the front of a coat, skirt, shirt, dress, or pants — **fly–front** \ˈflī-ˌfrənt\ *adj*
fly gallery *n* (1888) **:** a narrow raised platform at the side of a theater stage from which flying scenery lines are operated
[1]**flying** *adj* (bef. 12c) **1 a :** moving or capable of moving in the air **b :** moving or made by moving rapidly ⟨~ feet⟩ ⟨a ~ leap⟩ **c :** very brief **2 :** intended for ready movement or action ⟨a ~ squad car⟩ **3 :** having stylized wings — used esp. of livestock brand marks **4 :** of or relating to the operation of aircraft ⟨a ~ club⟩ **5 :** traversed or to be traversed (as in speed-record trials) after a running start ⟨a ~ kilometer⟩ — **with flying colors :** with complete or eminent success
[2]**flying** *n* (1548) **1 :** travel by air **2 :** the operation of an aircraft or spacecraft
flying boat *n* (1913) **:** a seaplane with a hull designed for floating
flying bomb *n* (1944) *chiefly Brit* **:** BUZZ BOMB
flying bridge *n* (ca. 1909) **1 :** the highest navigational bridge on a ship **2 :** FLYBRIDGE
flying buttress *n* (1669) **:** a masonry structure that typically consists of a straight inclined bar carried on an arch and a solid pier or buttress against which it abuts and that receives the thrust of a roof or vault

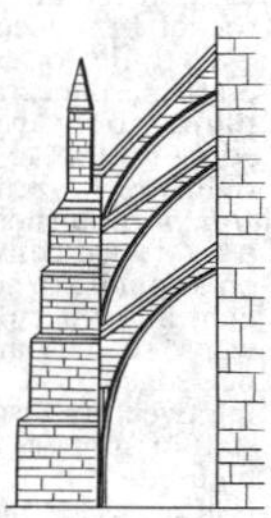
flying buttress

Flying Dutchman *n* (1813) **1 :** a legendary Dutch mariner condemned to sail the seas until Judgment Day **2 :** a spectral ship that according to legend haunts the seas near the Cape of Good Hope
flying fish *n* (ca. 1511) **:** any of numerous bony fishes (family Exocoetidae) chiefly of tropical and warm seas that are capable of long gliding flights out of water by spreading their large pectoral fins like wings
flying fox *n* (1759) **:** FRUIT BAT
flying gurnard *n* (1792) **:** any of several marine fishes (family Dactylopteridae) that resemble gurnards and have large pectoral fins allowing them to glide above the water for short distances
flying jib *n* (1711) **:** a sail outside the jib on an extension of the jibboom — see SAIL illustration
flying lemur *n* (1883) **:** either of two East Indian or Philippine arboreal nocturnal mammals (*Cynocephalus volans* and *C. variegatus*) that are about the size of a cat, that make long gliding leaps using a broad fold of skin on each side attached to and extending between the limbs, and that are placed in a separate order (Dermoptera)
flying machine *n* (1736) **:** an apparatus for navigating the air
flying mare *n* (1754) **:** a wrestling maneuver in which an opponent is seized by the wrist and thrown to the ground by being pulled over the back of the aggressor
flying officer *n* (1913) **:** a commissioned officer in the British air force who ranks with a first lieutenant in the army
flying saucer *n* (1947) **:** any of various unidentified flying objects usu. described as being saucer-shaped or disk-shaped
flying spot *n* (1933) **:** a spot of light moved over a surface (as one bearing printing or an image) so that light reflected from or transmitted by different parts of the surface is translated into electrical signals for transmission (as in television or computers)
flying squad *n* (1925) **:** a usu. small standby group of people ready to move or act swiftly; *esp* **:** a police unit formed to respond quickly in an emergency
flying squirrel *n* (1591) **:** either of two small nocturnal No. American squirrels (*Glaucomys volans* and *G. sabrinus*) with folds of skin connecting the forelegs and hind legs that enable it to make long gliding leaps; *also* **:** any of various squirrels that possess a patagium
flying start *n* (1851) **1 :** a start in racing in which the participants are already moving when they cross the starting line or receive the starting signal **2 :** a favorable start of something
flying wedge *n* (1909) **:** a moving formation (as of guards or police) resembling a wedge
fly·leaf \ˈflī-ˌlēf\ *n, pl* **fly·leaves** \-ˌlēvz\ (1832) **:** one of the free endpapers of a book
fly·man \-mən, -ˌman\ *n* (1881) **:** a worker in the flies of a theater who manipulates curtains and scenery
fly net *n* (bef. 12c) **:** a net to exclude or keep off insects (as from a harness horse)
fly–on–the–wall *adj* (1974) **:** having or involving an inconspicuous but effective point of observation ⟨~ observations of aspects of daily life —Will Manley⟩
fly·over \ˈflī-ˌō-vər\ *n* (1901) **1** *Brit* **:** OVERPASS **2 :** FLYBY 1
fly·pa·per \-ˌpā-pər\ *n* (1846) **:** paper coated with a sticky often poisonous substance for killing flies
fly·past \-ˌpast\ *n* (1914) *chiefly Brit* **:** FLYBY 1
fly rod *n* (1684) **:** a light springy fishing rod used in fly casting — **fly-rod·der** \ˈflī-ˌrä-dər\ *n*
flysch \ˈflish\ *n* [G, fr. G dial.] (1853) **:** a thick and extensive deposit largely of sandstone that is formed in a geosyncline adjacent to a rising mountain belt and is esp. common in the Alpine region of Europe
fly sheet *n* (1825) **1 :** a small loose advertising sheet **:** HANDBILL **2 :** a sheet of a folder, booklet, or catalog giving directions for the use of or information about the material that follows
fly·speck \ˈflī-ˌspek\ *n* (1723) **1 :** a speck made by fly excrement **2 :** something small and insignificant — **flyspeck** *vt*
fly–strike \-ˌstrīk\ *n* (1940) *Brit* **:** infestation with fly maggots — **fly-struck** \-ˌstrək\ *adj, Brit*
fly·swat·ter \-ˌswä-tər\ *n* (1917) **:** a device for killing insects that consists of a flat piece of perforated rubber or plastic or fine-mesh wire netting attached to a handle
fly·ti·er \ˈflī-ˌtī(-ə)r\ *n* [*fly* + *tier* (one that ties)] (1881) **:** a person who makes flies for fishing
flyt·ing \ˈflī-tiŋ\ *n* [Sc, lit., contention, gerund of *flyte* to contend, argue, fr. ME *fliten,* fr. OE *flītan;* akin to OHG *flīzan* to argue] (1508) **:** a dispute or exchange of personal abuse in verse form
fly·way \ˈflī-ˌwā\ *n* (1891) **:** an established air route of migratory birds
fly·weight \-ˌwāt\ *n* (1911) **:** a boxer in a weight division having a maximum limit of 112 pounds — compare BANTAMWEIGHT
fly·wheel \-ˌhwēl, -ˌwēl\ *n* (1784) **:** a heavy wheel for opposing and moderating by its inertia any fluctuation of speed in the machinery with which it revolves; *also* **:** a similar wheel used for storing kinetic energy (as for motive power)
fly whisk *n* (1841) **:** a whisk for brushing away flies
fm *abbr* fathom
Fm *symbol* fermium
[1]**FM** \ˈef-ˌem\ *n, often attrib* [*f*requency *m*odulation] (1940) **:** a broadcasting system using frequency modulation; *also* **:** a radio receiver of such a system
[2]**FM** *abbr* field manual
FMN \ˌef-ˌem-ˈen\ *n* [*f*lavin *mon*o*n*ucleotide] (ca. 1953) **:** a yellow crystalline phosphoric ester $C_{17}H_{21}N_4O_9P$ of riboflavin that is a coenzyme of several flavoprotein enzymes
fMRI *abbr* functional magnetic resonance imaging
fn *abbr* footnote
f–num·ber \ˈef-ˌnəm-bər\ *n* [*f*ocal length] (ca. 1903) **1 :** the ratio of the focal length to the aperture in an optical system **2 :** a number following the symbol f/ that expresses the effectiveness of the aperture of a camera lens in relation to brightness of image so that the smaller the number the brighter the image and therefore the shorter the exposure required
fo *or* **fol** *abbr* folio
FO *abbr* **1** field officer **2** field order **3** finance officer **4** flight officer **5** foreign office **6** forward observer
[1]**foal** \ˈfōl\ *n* [ME *fole,* fr. OE *fola;* akin to L *pullus* young of an animal, Gk *pais* child — more at FEW] (bef. 12c) **:** a young animal of the horse family; *esp* **:** one under one year — **in foal :** PREGNANT 4
[2]**foal** *vi* (14c) **:** to give birth to a foal ~ *vt* **:** to give birth to (a foal)
[1]**foam** \ˈfōm\ *n* [ME *fome,* fr. OE *fām;* akin to OHG *feim* foam, L *spuma* foam, *pumex* pumice] (bef. 12c) **1 :** a light frothy mass of fine bubbles formed in or on the surface of a liquid or from a liquid: as **a :** a frothy mass formed in salivating or sweating **b :** a stabilized froth produced chemically or mechanically and used esp. in fighting oil fires **c :** a material in a lightweight cellular form resulting from introduction of gas bubbles during manufacture **2 :** SEA **3 :** something resembling foam — **foam·less** \-ləs\ *adj*
[2]**foam** *vi* (bef. 12c) **1 a :** to produce or form foam **b :** to froth at the mouth esp. in anger; *broadly* **:** to be angry **2 :** to gush out in foam **3 :** to become covered with or as if with foam ⟨streets . . . ~*ing* with life —Thomas Wolfe⟩ ~ *vt* **1 :** to cause to foam; *specif* **:** to cause air bubbles to form in **2 :** to convert (as a plastic) into a foam — **foam·able** \ˈfō-mə-bəl\ *adj* — **foam·er** \ˈfō-mər\ *n*
foam cell *n* (1926) **:** a swollen vacuolated phagocytic cell filled with lipid inclusions that often accummulates along arterial walls and is characteristic of some conditions of disturbed lipid metabolism
foamed plastic *n* (1945) **:** EXPANDED PLASTIC
foam·flow·er \ˈfōm-ˌflau̇(-ə)r\ *n* (1895) **:** a spring-flowering herb (*Tiarella cordifolia*) of eastern No. America that has white flowers with long stamens and no stem leaves — called also *false miterwort*
foam rubber *n* (ca. 1939) **:** spongy rubber of fine texture made from latex by foaming (as by whipping) before vulcanization
foamy \ˈfō-mē\ *adj* **foam·i·er; -est** (bef. 12c) **1 :** covered with foam **:** FROTHY **2 :** full of, consisting of, or resembling foam — **foam·i·ly** \-mə-lē\ *adv* — **foam·i·ness** \-mē-nəs\ *n*
[1]**fob** \ˈfäb\ *vt* **fobbed; fob·bing** [ME *fobben*] (14c) *archaic* **:** DECEIVE, CHEAT
[2]**fob** *n* [perh. akin to G dial. *Fuppe* pocket] (1630) **1 :** WATCH POCKET **2 :** a short strap, ribbon, or chain attached esp. to a pocket watch **3 :** an ornament attached to a fob chain
FOB *abbr* free on board
fob off *vt* (1597) **1 :** to put off with a trick, excuse, or inferior substitute **2 :** to pass or offer (something spurious) as genuine **3 :** to put aside ⟨now *fob off* what once they would have welcomed eagerly —Walter Lippmann⟩
FOC *abbr* free of charge
fo·cac·cia \fō-ˈkä-ch(ē-)ə\ *n* [It, fr. LL *focacia* (neut. pl.), fr. L *focus* hearth] (1881) **:** a flat Italian bread typically seasoned with herbs and olive oil
fo·cal \ˈfō-kəl\ *adj* (1693) **:** of, relating to, being, or having a focus — **fo·cal·ly** \-kə-lē\ *adv*
focal infection *n* (ca. 1923) **:** a persistent bacterial infection of some organ or region; *esp* **:** one causing symptoms elsewhere in the body
fo·cal·ize \ˈfō-kə-ˌlīz\ *vb* **-ized; -iz·ing** *vt* (1845) **1 :** to bring to a focus **2 :** LOCALIZE ~ *vi* **1 :** to come to a focus **:** CONCENTRATE **2 :** LOCALIZE — **fo·cal·i·za·tion** \ˌfō-kə-lə-ˈzā-shən\ *n*
focal length *n* (1693) **:** the distance of a focus from the surface of a lens or curved mirror
focal plane *n* (1889) **:** a plane that is perpendicular to the axis of a lens or mirror and passes through the focus
focal point *n* (1713) **1 :** FOCUS 1a **2 :** FOCUS 5a
focal ratio *n* (1926) **:** F-NUMBER
fo'c'sle *var of* FORECASTLE

¹fo·cus \'fō-kəs\ *n, pl* **fo·ci** \'fō-ˌsī *also* -ˌkī\ *also* **fo·cus·es** [NL, fr. L, hearth] (1644) **1 a :** a point at which rays (as of light, heat, or sound) converge or from which they diverge or appear to diverge; *specif* : the point where the geometrical lines or their prolongations conforming to the rays diverging from or converging toward another point intersect and give rise to an image after reflection by a mirror or refraction by a lens or optical system **b :** a point of convergence of a beam of particles (as electrons) **2 a :** FOCAL LENGTH **b :** adjustment for distinct vision; *also* : the area that may be seen distinctly or resolved into a clear image **c :** a state or condition permitting clear perception or understanding ⟨tried to bring the issues into ∼⟩ **3 :** DIRECTION 6c ⟨the team lost ∼⟩ **3 :** one of the fixed points that with the corresponding directrix defines a conic section **4 :** a localized area of disease or the chief site of a generalized disease or infection **5 a :** a center of activity, attraction, or attention ⟨the ∼ of the meeting was drug abuse⟩ **b :** a point of concentration **6 :** the place of origin of an earthquake or moonquake **7 :** directed attention : EMPHASIS — **fo·cus·less** \-ləs\ *adj* — **in focus :** having or giving the proper sharpness of outline due to good focusing — **out of focus :** not in focus

²focus *vb* **fo·cused** *also* **fo·cussed; fo·cus·ing** *also* **fo·cus·sing** (1775) **1 a :** to bring into focus **b :** to adjust the focus of (as the eye or a lens) **2 :** to cause to be concentrated ⟨∼ed their attention on the most urgent problems⟩ **3 :** to bring (as light rays) to a focus : CONCENTRATE ∼ *vi* **1 :** to come to a focus : CONVERGE **2 :** to adjust one's eye or a camera to a particular range **3 :** to concentrate attention or effort — **fo·cus·able** \-kə-sə-bəl\ *adj* — **fo·cus·er** *n*

focus group *n* (1985) : a small group of people whose response to something (as a new product or a politician's image) is studied to determine the response that can be expected from a larger population

fod·der \'fä-dər\ *n* [ME, fr. OE *fōdor;* akin to OHG *fuotar* food — more at FOOD] (bef. 12c) **1 :** something fed to domestic animals; *esp* : coarse food for cattle, horses, or sheep **2 :** inferior or readily available material used to supply a heavy demand ⟨∼ for tabloids⟩ — **fod·der** *vt*

fod·gel \'fä-jəl\ *adj* [origin unknown] (1724) *Scot* : BUXOM

foe \'fō\ *n* [ME *fo,* fr. OE *fāh,* fr. *fāh,* adj., hostile; akin to OHG *gifēh* hostile] (bef. 12c) **1 :** one who has personal enmity for another **2 a :** an enemy in war **b :** ADVERSARY, OPPONENT **3 :** one who opposes on principle ⟨a ∼ of needless expenditures⟩ **4 :** something prejudicial or injurious

FOE *abbr* Fraternal Order of Eagles

foehn *or* **föhn** \'fā(r)n, 'fœn, 'fān\ *n* [G *Föhn*] (1861) : a warm dry wind blowing down the side of a mountain

foe·man \'fō-mən\ *n* (bef. 12c) : FOE 2

foe·tal, foe·tus *chiefly Brit var of* FETAL, FETUS

foe·tid *chiefly Brit var of* FETID

foeto- *or* **foeti-** *chiefly Brit var of* FETO-

¹fog \'fòg, fäg\ *n* [prob. back-formation fr. *foggy*] (1544) **1 a :** vapor condensed to fine particles of water suspended in the lower atmosphere that differs from cloud only in being near the ground **b :** a fine spray or a foam for firefighting **2 :** a murky condition of the atmosphere or a substance causing it **3 a :** a state of confusion or bewilderment ⟨spent the morning in a ∼⟩ **b :** something that confuses or obscures ⟨hid behind a ∼ of rhetoric⟩ **4 :** cloudiness or partial opacity in a developed photographic image caused by chemical action or stray radiation — **fog·less** \-ləs\ *adj*

²fog *vb* **fogged; fog·ging** *vt* (1599) **1 :** to cover, envelop, or suffuse with or as if with fog ⟨the barns with pesticide⟩ **2 :** to make obscure or confusing ⟨accusations which *fogged* the real issues⟩ **3 :** to make confused **4 :** to produce fog on (as a photographic film) during development ∼ *vi* **1 :** to become covered or thick with fog **2 a :** to become blurred by a covering of fog or mist **b :** to become indistinct through exposure to light or radiation

fog·bound \'fòg-ˌbaùnd, 'fäg-\ *adj* (1814) **1 :** unable to move because of fog ⟨a ∼ ship⟩ **2 :** covered by fog ⟨a ∼ coast⟩

fog·bow \-ˌbō\ *n* (1831) : a nebulous arc or circle of white or yellowish light sometimes seen in fog

fog·gage \'fò-gij, 'fä-\ *n* [Sc, fr. ME (Sc) *fogage,* fr. ML *fogagium,* fr. ME *fogge* second growth of grass (prob. of Scand origin; akin to Norw *fogg* long grass on damp ground) + ML *-agium* -age] (1775) *Scot* : a second growth of grass

fog·ger \'fò-gər, 'fä-\ *n* (1953) : an apparatus for spreading a fog of pesticide

fog·gy \'fò-gē, 'fä-\ *adj* **fog·gi·er; -est** [earlier, marshy, thick, prob. fr. *fog* second growth of grass, fr. ME *fogge*] (15c) **1 a :** filled or abounding with fog **b :** covered or made opaque by moisture or grime **2 :** blurred or obscured as if by fog ⟨hadn't the *foggiest* notion⟩ — **fog·gi·ly** \'fò-gə-lē, 'fä-\ *adv* — **fog·gi·ness** \'fò-gē-nəs, 'fä-\ *n*

Foggy Bottom *n* [*Foggy Bottom,* district in Washington, D.C.] (1951) : the U.S. Department of State

fog·horn \'fòg-ˌhòrn, 'fäg-\ *n* (1848) **1 :** a horn (as on a ship) sounded in a fog to give warning **2 :** a loud hoarse voice

fo·gy *also* **fo·gey** \'fō-gē\ *n, pl* **fogies** *also* **fogeys** [origin unknown] (1780) : a person with old-fashioned ideas — usu. used with *old* — **fo·gy·ish** *or* **fo·gey·ish** \-gē-ish\ *adj* — **fo·gy·ism** *or* **fo·gey·ism** \-gē-ˌi-zəm\ *n*

FOIA *abbr* Freedom of Information Act

foi·ble \'fòi-bəl\ *n* [obs. F (now *faible*), fr. obs. *foible* weak, fr. OF *feble* feeble] (ca. 1648) **1 :** the part of a sword or foil blade between the middle and point **2 :** a minor flaw or shortcoming in character or behavior : WEAKNESS ⟨admired their teacher despite his ∼s⟩ *syn* see FAULT

foie gras \fwä-'grä\ *n* [F, lit., fat liver] (1818) : the fatted liver of an animal and esp. of a goose usu. served as a pâté

¹foil \'fòi(-ə)l\ *vt* [ME, alter. of *fullen* to full cloth, fr. AF *foller* — more at FULL] (14c) **1** *obs* : TRAMPLE **2 a :** to prevent from attaining an end : DEFEAT ⟨always able to ∼ her enemies⟩ **b :** to bring to naught : THWART ⟨∼ed the plot⟩ *syn* see FRUSTRATE

²foil *n* (15c) **1** *archaic* : DEFEAT **2** *archaic* : the track or trail of an animal

³foil *n* [ME, leaf, fr. AF *fuille, foille* (fr. L *folia,* pl. of *folium*) & *fuil,* fr. L *folium* — more at BLADE] (14c) **1 :** very thin sheet metal ⟨aluminum ∼⟩ **2 :** a thin piece of material (as metal) put under an inferior or paste stone to add color or brilliance **3 :** someone or something that serves as a contrast to another ⟨acted as a ∼ for a comedian⟩ **4 a :** an indentation between cusps in Gothic tracery **b :** one of several arcs that enclose a complex figure **5 :** HYDROFOIL 1

⁴foil *vt* (1611) **1 :** to back or cover with foil **2 :** to enhance by contrast

⁵foil *n* [origin unknown] (1594) **1 :** a light fencing sword having a usu. circular guard and a flexible blade of rectangular section tapering to a blunted point — compare ÉPÉE, SABER **2 :** the art or sport of fencing with the foil — often used in pl.

foiled \'fòi(-ə)ld\ *adj* (1835) : ornamented with foils ⟨a ∼ arch⟩

foils·man \'fòi(-ə)lz-mən\ *n* (1927) : a person who fences with a foil

¹foin \'fòin\ *n* [ME, fr. *foin* fork for spearing fish, fr. AF *fuin*] (14c) *archaic* : to thrust with a pointed weapon : LUNGE

²foin *n* (15c) *archaic* : a pass in fencing : LUNGE

foi·son \'fòi-zᵊn\ *n* [ME *foisoun,* fr. AF *fuisun, foison,* fr. L *fusion-, fusio* outpouring — more at FUSION] (14c) **1** *archaic* : rich harvest **2** *chiefly Scot* : physical energy or strength **3** *pl, obs* : RESOURCES

foist \'fòist\ *vt* [prob. fr. obs. D *vuisten* to take into one's hand, fr. MD *vuysten,* fr. *vuyst* fist; akin to OE *fȳst* fist] (ca. 1587) **1 a :** to introduce or insert surreptitiously or without warrant **b :** to force another to accept esp. by stealth or deceit **2 :** to pass off as genuine or worthy ⟨∼ costly and valueless products on the public —Jonathan Spivak⟩

fo·la·cin \'fō-lə-sən\ *n* [*folic acid* + *-in*] (1949) : FOLIC ACID

fo·late \'fō-ˌlāt\ *n* (1951) : FOLIC ACID

¹fold \'fōld\ *n* [ME, fr. OE *falod;* akin to OS *faled* enclosure] (bef. 12c) **1 :** an enclosure for sheep **2 a :** a flock of sheep **b :** a group of people or institutions that share a common faith, belief, activity, or enthusiasm

²fold *vt* (bef. 12c) : to pen up or confine (as sheep) in a fold

³fold *vb* [ME, fr. OE *fealdan;* akin to OHG *faldan* to fold, Gk *diplasios* twofold] *vt* (bef. 12c) **1 :** to lay one part over another part of ⟨∼ a letter⟩ **2 :** to reduce the length or bulk of by doubling over ⟨∼ a tent⟩ **3 :** to clasp together : ENTWINE ⟨∼ the hands⟩ **4 :** to clasp or enwrap closely : EMBRACE **5 :** to bend (as a layer of rock) into folds **6 a :** to incorporate (a food ingredient) into a mixture by repeated gentle overturnings without stirring or beating **b :** to incorporate closely ∼ *vi* **1 :** to concede defeat by withdrawing (one's cards) from play (as in poker) **2 :** to bring to an end ∼ *vi* **1 :** to become doubled or pleated **2 :** to fail completely : COLLAPSE; *esp* : to go out of business **3 :** to fold one's cards (as in poker) — **fold·able** \'fōl-də-bəl\ *adj*

⁴fold *n* (13c) **1 :** a part doubled or laid over another part : PLEAT **2 :** something that is folded together or that enfolds **3 a :** a bend or flexure produced in rock by forces operative after the depositing or consolidation of the rock **b** *chiefly Brit* : an undulation in the landscape **4 :** a margin apparently formed by the doubling upon itself of a flat anatomical structure (as a membrane) **5 :** a crease made by folding something (as a newspaper)

fold 3a

-fold *suffix* [ME, fr. OE *-feald;* akin to OHG *-falt* -fold, L *-plex, -plus,* OE *fealdan*] **1 :** multiplied by (a specified number) : times — in adjectives ⟨a six*fold* increase⟩ and adverbs ⟨repay you ten*fold*⟩ **2 :** having (so many) parts ⟨three*fold* aspect of the problem⟩

fold·away \'fōld-ə-ˌwā\ *adj* (1948) : designed to be folded for storage or portability ⟨∼ doors⟩ ⟨a ∼ bed⟩ ⟨a ∼ table⟩

fold·boat \'fōld(-d)-ˌbōt\ *n* [trans. of G *Faltboot*] (1938) : a small collapsible canoe made of rubberized sailcloth stretched over a framework

fold·er \'fōl-dər\ *n* (1552) **1 :** one that folds **2 :** a folded printed circular **3 a :** a folded cover or large envelope for holding or filing loose papers **b :** an organizational element of a computer operating system used to group files or other folders together

fol·de·rol \'fäl-də-ˌräl\ *also* **fal·de·ral** \'fal-də-ˌral\ *n* [*fol-de-rol,* a nonsense refrain in songs] (ca. 1820) **1 :** a useless ornament or accessory : TRIFLE **2 :** NONSENSE

fold·ing \'fōl-diŋ\ *adj* (15c) : capable of being folded into a more compact shape ⟨∼ chairs⟩ ⟨a ∼ door⟩

folding money *n* (ca. 1930) : PAPER MONEY

fold·out \'fōld-ˌaùt\ *n, often attrib* (1950) : a folded leaf in a publication (as a book) that is larger in some dimension than the page ⟨a ∼ map⟩

Fo·ley \'fō-lē\ *n, often attrib* [Jack D. Foley †1967 Am. sound technician] (1984) : sound effects created for a film ⟨a ∼ artist⟩

fo·li·a·ceous \ˌfō-lē-'ā-shəs\ *adj* [L *foliaceus,* fr. *folium* leaf + *-aceus* -aceous] (1658) : of, relating to, or resembling an ordinary green leaf as distinguished from a modified leaf (as a petal, bract, or scale)

fo·liage \'fō-lē-ij *also* -lyij; ÷'fō-lij, ÷'fō-lij\ *n* [MF *fuellage,* fr. *foille* leaf — more at FOIL] (1598) **1 :** a representation of leaves, flowers, and branches for architectural ornamentation **2 :** the aggregate of leaves of one or more plants **3 :** a cluster of leaves, flowers, and branches — **fo·liaged** \-lē-ijd *also* -lyijd; ÷'fō-lijd, ÷'fō-lijd\ *adj*

usage The disyllabic pronunciation \'fō-lij\ is very common. Some commentators insist that *foliage* requires a trisyllabic pronunciation because of its spelling, but words of a similar pattern such as *carriage* and *marriage* do not fall under their prescription. The pronunciation \'fō-lij\ is disapproved because it suggests the transposition of the *l* and *i* in the spelling. It is not as common as \'fō-lij\ and may be associated with the nonstandard spelling *foilage.*

foliage plant *n* (1862) : a plant grown primarily for its decorative foliage

fo·li·ar \'fō-lē-ər\ *adj* [F *foliaire,* fr. L *foliaire,* fr. L *folium* leaf + F *-aire* -ar] (ca. 1859) : of, relating to, or applied to leaves ⟨∼ sprays⟩ ⟨∼ diseases⟩

fo·li·ate \'fō-lē-ət, -ˌāt\ *adj* [L *foliatus* leafy, fr. *folium* leaf — more at BLADE] (ca. 1658) **1 :** shaped like a leaf ⟨a ∼ sponge⟩ **2 :** FOLIATED

fo·li·at·ed \-ˌā-təd\ *adj* (1650) **1 :** composed of or separable into layers ⟨a ∼ rock⟩ **2 :** ornamented with foils or a leaf design

fo·li·a·tion \ˌfō-lē-'ā-shən\ *n* (ca. 1623) **1 a :** the process of forming into a leaf **b :** the state of being in leaf : VERNATION **2 :** the numbering of the leaves of a manuscript or early printed book **3 a :** orna-

\ə\ abut \ᵊ\ kitten, F table \ər\ further \a\ ash \ā\ ace \ä\ mop, mar \aù\ out \ch\ chin \e\ bet \ē\ easy \g\ go \i\ hit \ī\ ice \j\ job \ŋ\ sing \ō\ go \ò\ law \òi\ boy \th\ thin \th\ the \ü\ loot \ù\ foot \y\ yet \zh\ vision, beige \k, ⁿ, œ, ᵫ, �\ *see* Guide to Pronunciation

mentation with foliage **b :** a decoration resembling a leaf **4 :** the enrichment of an opening by foils **5 :** foliated texture

fo·lic acid \ˌfō-lik-\ *n* [L *folium*] (1941) **:** a crystalline vitamin $C_{19}H_{19}N_7O_6$ of the B complex that is used esp. in the treatment of nutritional anemias — called also *pteroylglutamic acid*

fo·lie à deux \fȯ-lē-ä-ˈdœ, ˌfä-lē-ˌä-ˈdə(r)\ *n* [F, lit., double madness] (ca. 1892) **:** the presence of the same or similar delusional ideas in two persons closely associated with one another

[1]**fo·lio** \ˈfō-lē-ˌō\ *n, pl* **fo·li·os** [ME, fr. L, abl. of *folium*] (15c) **1 a :** a leaf esp. of a manuscript or book **b :** a leaf number **c :** a page number **d :** an identifying reference in accounting used in posting **2 a :** a sheet of paper folded once **b :** a case or folder for loose papers **3 a :** the size of a piece of paper cut two from a sheet; *also* **:** paper or a page of this size **b :** a book printed on folio pages **c :** a book of the largest size **4 :** a certain number of words taken as a unit or division in a document for purposes of measurement or reference

[2]**folio** *vt* (1858) **:** to put a serial number on each leaf or page of

fo·li·ose \ˈfō-lē-ˌōs\ *adj* [L *foliosus* leafy] (1758) **:** having a flat, thin, and usu. lobed thallus attached to the substratum ⟨∼ lichens⟩ — compare CRUSTOSE, FRUTICOSE

[1]**folk** \ˈfōk\ *n, pl* **folk** *or* **folks** [ME, fr. OE *folc;* akin to OHG *folc* people] (bef. 12c) **1** *archaic* **:** a group of kindred tribes forming a nation **:** PEOPLE **2 :** the great proportion of the members of a people that determines the group character and that tends to preserve its characteristic form of civilization and its customs, arts and crafts, legends, traditions, and superstitions from generation to generation **3** *pl* **:** a certain kind, class, or group of people ⟨old ∼*s*⟩ ⟨just plain ∼⟩ ⟨country ∼⟩ ⟨media ∼⟩ **4** *pl* **:** people generally **5** *folks pl* **:** the persons of one's own family; *esp* **:** PARENTS **6 :** folk music

[2]**folk** *adj* (bef. 12c) **1 :** originating or traditional with the common people of a country or region and typically reflecting their lifestyle ⟨∼ hero⟩ ⟨∼ music⟩ **2 :** of or relating to the common people or to the study of the common people ⟨∼ sociology⟩

folk art *n* (1911) **:** the traditional typically anonymous art of usu. untrained people

folk etymology *n* (1882) **:** the transformation of words so as to give them an apparent relationship to other better-known or better-understood words (as in the change of Spanish *cucaracha* to English *cockroach*)

[1]**folk·ie** *also* **folky** \ˈfō-kē\ *n, pl* **folkies** (1965) **:** a folk singer or instrumentalist

[2]**folkie** *or* **folky** *adj* (1965) **:** of or relating to folk music

folk·ish \ˈfō-kish\ *adj* (1938) **:** FOLKLIKE — **folk·ish·ness** *n*

folk·life \ˈfōk-ˌlīf\ *n* (1864) **:** the traditions, activities, skills, and products (as handicrafts) of a particular people or group

folk·like \ˈfōk-ˌlīk\ *adj* (1939) **:** having a folk character

folk·lore \ˈfōk-ˌlȯr\ *n* (1846) **1 :** traditional customs, tales, sayings, dances, or art forms preserved among a people **2 :** a branch of knowledge that deals with folklore **3 :** an often unsupported notion, story, or saying that is widely circulated — **folk·lor·ic** \-ˌlȯr-ik\ *adj* — **folk·lor·ish** \-ish\ *adj* — **folk·lor·ist** \-ist\ *n* — **folk·lor·is·tic** \ˌfōk-ˌlȯr-ˈis-tik\ *adj*

folk mass *n* (1966) **:** a mass in which traditional liturgical music is replaced by folk music

folk medicine *n* (1878) **:** traditional medicine as practiced nonprofessionally esp. by people isolated from modern medical services and usu. involving the use of plant-derived remedies on an empirical basis

folk·moot \ˈfōk-ˌmüt\ *or* **folk·mote** \-ˌmōt\ *n* [alter. of OE *folcmōt, folcgemōt,* fr. *folc* people + *mōt, gemōt* meeting — more at MOOT] (bef. 12c) **:** a general assembly of the people (as of a shire) in early England

folk·sing·er \-ˌsiŋ-ər\ *n* (1884) **:** one who sings folk songs or sings in a style associated with folk songs — **folk·sing·ing** \-ˌsiŋ-iŋ\ *n*

folk song *n* (1847) **:** a traditional or composed song typically characterized by stanzaic form, refrain, and simplicity of melody

folksy \ˈfōk-sē\ *adj* **folks·i·er; -est** (1852) **1 :** SOCIABLE, FRIENDLY **2 :** informal, casual, or familiar in manner or style ⟨∼ humor⟩ — **folks·i·ly** \-sə-lē\ *adv* — **folks·i·ness** \-sē-nəs\ *n*

folk·tale \ˈfōk-ˌtāl\ *n* (1852) **:** a characteristically anonymous, timeless, and placeless tale circulated orally among a people

folk·way \ˈfōk-ˌwā\ *n* (ca. 1906) **:** a mode of thinking, feeling, or acting common to a given group of people; *esp* **:** a traditional social custom

fol·li·cle \ˈfä-li-kəl\ *n* [NL *folliculus,* fr. L, dim. of *follis* bag — more at FOOL] (1646) **1 a :** a small anatomical cavity or deep narrow-mouthed depression **b :** a small lymph node **c :** a vesicle in the mammalian ovary that contains a developing egg surrounded by a covering of cells; *esp* **:** GRAAFIAN FOLLICLE **2 :** a dry dehiscent one-celled many-seeded fruit (as of the milkweed) that has a single carpel and opens along one suture — **fol·lic·u·lar** \fə-ˈli-kyə-lər, fä-\ *adj*

follicle mite *n* (1925) **:** any of several minute mites (genus *Demodex*) parasitic in hair follicles

follicle–stimulating hormone *n* (ca. 1943) **:** a hormone produced by the anterior lobe of the pituitary gland that stimulates the growth of the ovum-containing follicles in the ovary and activates sperm-forming cells — abbr. *FSH*

fol·lic·u·li·tis \fə-ˌli-kyə-ˈlī-təs\ *n* [NL, fr. *folliculus* + *-itis*] (ca. 1860) **:** inflammation of one or more follicles esp. of the hair

[1]**fol·low** \ˈfä-(ˌ)lō\ *vb* [ME *folwen,* fr. OE *folgian;* akin to OHG *folgēn* to follow] *vt* (bef. 12c) **1 :** to go, proceed, or come after ⟨∼*ed* the guide⟩ **2 a :** to engage in as a calling or way of life **:** PURSUE ⟨wheat-growing is generally ∼*ed* here⟩ **b :** to walk or proceed along ⟨∼ a path⟩ **3 a :** to be or act in accordance with ⟨∼ directions⟩ **b :** to accept as authority **:** OBEY ⟨∼*ed* his conscience⟩ **4 a :** to pursue in an effort to overtake **b :** to seek to attain ⟨∼ knowledge⟩ **5 :** to come into existence or take place as a result or consequence of ⟨disaster ∼*ed* the blunder⟩ **6 a :** to come or take place after in time, sequence, or order **b :** to cause to be followed ⟨∼*ed* dinner with a liqueur⟩ **7 :** to copy after **:** IMITATE **8 a :** to watch steadily ⟨∼*ed* the flight of the ball⟩ **b :** to keep the mind on ⟨∼ a speech⟩ **c :** to attend closely to **:** keep abreast of ⟨∼*ed* his career with interest⟩ **d :** to understand the sense or logic of (as a line of thought) ∼ *vi* **1 :** to go or come after a person or thing in place, time, or sequence **2 :** to result or occur as a consequence, effect, or inference — **as follows :** as comes next — used impersonally — **follow one's nose 1 :** to go in a straight or obvious course **2 :** to proceed without plan or reflection **:** obey one's instincts — **follow suit 1 :** to play a card of the same suit as the card led **2 :** to follow an example set

syn FOLLOW, SUCCEED, ENSUE, SUPERVENE mean to come after something or someone. FOLLOW may apply to a coming after in time, position, or logical sequence ⟨speeches *followed* the dinner⟩. SUCCEED implies a coming after immediately in a sequence determined by natural order, inheritance, election, or laws of rank ⟨she *succeeded* her father as head of the business⟩. ENSUE commonly suggests a logical consequence or naturally expected development ⟨after the talk a general discussion *ensued*⟩. SUPERVENE suggests the following or beginning of something unforeseen or unpredictable ⟨unable to continue because of *supervening* circumstances⟩. ***syn*** see in addition CHASE

[2]**follow** *n* (1661) **1 :** the act or process of following **2 :** forward spin given to a ball by striking it above center — compare DRAW, ENGLISH

fol·low·er \ˈfä-lə-wər\ *n* (bef. 12c) **1 a :** one in the service of another **:** RETAINER **b :** one that follows the opinions or teachings of another **c :** one that imitates another **2** *archaic* **:** one that chases **3 :** a sheet added to the first sheet of an indenture or other deed **4 :** a machine part that receives motion from another part **5 :** a spring-loaded plate at the bottom of a firearm's magazine that angles cartridges for proper insertion into the chamber **6 :** FAN, DEVOTEE

syn FOLLOWER, ADHERENT, DISCIPLE, PARTISAN mean one who gives full loyalty and support to another. FOLLOWER may apply to people who attach themselves either to the person or beliefs of another ⟨an evangelist and his *followers*⟩. ADHERENT suggests a close and persistent attachment ⟨*adherents* to Marxism⟩. DISCIPLE implies a devoted allegiance to the teachings of one chosen as a master ⟨*disciples* of Gandhi⟩. PARTISAN suggests a zealous often prejudiced attachment ⟨*partisans* of the President⟩.

fol·low·er·ship \-ˌship\ *n* (ca. 1928) **1 :** FOLLOWING **2 :** the capacity or willingness to follow a leader

[1]**fol·low·ing** \ˈfä-lə-wiŋ\ *adj* (15c) **1 :** being next in order or time ⟨the ∼ day⟩ **2 :** listed or shown next ⟨trains will leave at the ∼ times⟩

[2]**following** *n* (15c) **:** a group of followers, adherents, or partisans

[3]**following** *prep* (ca. 1926) **:** SUBSEQUENT TO ⟨∼ the lecture tea was served⟩

fol·low–on \ˈfä-lō-ˌȯn, -ˌän\ *adj* (1960) **:** being or relating to something that follows as a natural or logical consequence, development, or progression — **follow–on** *n*

follow out *vt* (1658) **1 :** to follow to the end or to a conclusion **2 :** CARRY OUT, EXECUTE ⟨*followed out* their orders⟩

follow shot *n* (ca. 1909) **1 :** a shot in billiards or pool made by striking the cue ball above its center to cause it to continue forward after striking the object ball **2 :** a camera shot in which the camera follows the movement of the subject

fol·low–through \ˈfä-lō-ˌthrü, ˌfä-lō-ˈ, -lə-\ *n* (1897) **1 :** the part of the stroke following the striking of a ball **2 :** the act or an instance of following through

follow through *vi* (1895) **1 :** to continue a stroke or motion to the end of its arc **2 :** to press on in an activity or process esp. to a conclusion

[1]**fol·low–up** \ˈfä-lō-ˌəp\ *n* (1916) **1 a :** the act or an instance of following up **b :** something that follows up **2 :** maintenance of contact with or reexamination of a person (as a patient) esp. following treatment **3 :** a news story presenting new information on a story published earlier

[2]**follow–up** *adj* (1912) **1 :** of, relating to, or being something that follows up ⟨∼ action by the police —Frank Faulkner⟩ **2 :** done, conducted, or administered in the course of following up persons ⟨∼ care for discharged hospital patients⟩

follow up *vt* (1767) **1 :** to follow with something similar, related, or supplementary ⟨*following up* his convictions with action —G. P. Merrill⟩ **2 :** to maintain contact with (a person) so as to monitor the effects of earlier activities or treatments **3 :** to pursue in an effort to take further action ⟨the police are *following up* leads⟩ ∼ *vi* **:** to take appropriate action ⟨*follow up* on complaints⟩

fol·ly \ˈfä-lē\ *n, pl* **follies** [ME *folie,* fr. AF, fr. *fol* fool] (13c) **1 :** lack of good sense or normal prudence and foresight **2 a :** criminally or tragically foolish actions or conduct **b** *obs* **:** EVIL, WICKEDNESS; *esp* **:** lewd behavior **3 :** a foolish act or idea **4 :** an excessively costly or unprofitable undertaking **5 :** an often extravagant picturesque building erected to suit a fanciful taste

Fol·som \ˈfōl-səm\ *adj* [*Folsom,* town in New Mexico] (1928) **:** of, relating to, or characteristic of a prehistoric culture of No. America on the east side of the Rocky Mountains that is characterized by flint projectile points having a concave base with side projections and a longitudinal groove on each face

fo·ment \ˈfō-ˌment, fō-ˈ\ *vt* [ME, to apply a warm substance to, fr. LL *fomentare,* fr. L *fomentum* compress, fr. *fovēre* to heat, soothe; akin to Lith *degti* to burn, Skt *dahati* it burns] (ca. 1613) **:** to promote the growth or development of **:** ROUSE, INCITE ⟨∼ a rebellion⟩ ***syn*** see INCITE — **fo·ment·er** *n*

fo·men·ta·tion \ˌfō-mən-ˈtā-shən, -ˌmen-\ *n* (14c) **1 a :** the application of hot moist substances to the body to ease pain **b :** the material so applied **2 :** the act of fomenting **:** INSTIGATION

fo·mite \ˈfō-ˌmīt\ *n, pl* **fo·mites** \ˈfō-ˌmīts; ˈfä-mə-ˌtēz, ˈfō-\ [back-formation fr. *fomites,* fr. NL, pl. of *fomit-, fomes,* fr. L, kindling wood; akin to L *fovēre* to heat — more at FOMENT] (1803) **:** an object (as a dish or an article of clothing) that may be contaminated with infectious organisms and serve in their transmission

[1]**fond** \ˈfänd\ *adj* [ME *fonned, fond,* fr. *fonne* fool] (14c) **1 :** FOOLISH, SILLY ⟨∼ pride⟩ **2 a :** prizing highly **:** DESIROUS — used with *of* ⟨∼ of praise⟩ **b :** having an affection or liking — used with *of* ⟨∼ of music⟩ **3 a :** foolishly tender **:** INDULGENT ⟨a ∼ mother⟩ **b :** AFFECTIONATE, LOVING ⟨absence makes the heart grow ∼*er*⟩ **4 :** cherished with great affection **:** doted on ⟨our ∼*est* hopes⟩

[2]**fond** *vi* (1530) *obs* **:** to lavish affection **:** DOTE

[3]**fond** \ˈfōⁿ\ *n, pl* **fonds** \ˈfōⁿ(z)\ [F, fr. OF *fons, font,* fr. L *fundus* bottom, piece of property — more at BOTTOM] (1664) **1 :** BACKGROUND, BASIS **2** *obs* **:** FUND

fon·dant \ˈfän-dənt\ *n* [F, fr. prp. of *fondre* to melt — more at FOUND] (1877) **1 :** a soft creamy preparation of sugar, water, and flavorings that is used as a basis for candies or icings **2 :** a candy consisting chiefly of fondant

fon·dle \ˈfän-dᵊl\ *vb* **fon·dled; fon·dling** \-(d)liŋ, -dᵊl-iŋ\ [freq. of obs. *fond* to fondle] *vt* (1694) **1** *obs* : PAMPER **2** : to handle tenderly, lovingly, or lingeringly : CARESS ~ *vi* : to show affection or desire by caressing — **fon·dler** \-(d)lər, -dᵊl-ər\ *n*

fond·ly \ˈfän-(d)lē\ *adv* (14c) **1** *archaic* : in a foolish manner : FOOLISHLY **2** : in a fond manner : AFFECTIONATELY ⟨spoke of her ~⟩ **3** : in a willingly credulous manner ⟨it would stun, I ~ hoped, the reader —Annie Dillard⟩

fond·ness \ˈfän(d)-nəs\ *n* (14c) **1** *obs* : FOOLISHNESS, FOLLY **2** : tender affection **3** : APPETITE, RELISH ⟨had a ~ for argument⟩

fon·due *also* **fon·du** \fän-ˈdü, -ˈdyü, ˈfän-ˌ\ *n* [F *fondue,* fr. fem. of *fondu,* pp. of *fondre* to melt, fr. OF — more at FOUND] (1829) **1** : a dish similar to a soufflé usu. made with cheese and bread crumbs **2 a** (1) : a preparation of melted cheese (as Swiss cheese and Gruyère) usu. flavored with white wine and kirsch (2) : a dish that consists of small pieces of food (as meat or fruit) cooked in or dipped into a hot liquid ⟨beef ~⟩ ⟨chocolate ~⟩ **b** : a chafing dish in which fondue is made

F_1 layer \ˈef-ˈwən-\ *n* (1933) : the lower of the two layers into which the F region of the ionosphere splits in the daytime that occurs at varying heights from about 80 to 120 miles (130 to 200 kilometers) above the earth's surface

[1]**font** \ˈfänt\ *n* [ME, fr. OE, fr. LL *font-, fons,* fr. L, fountain] (bef. 12c) **1 a** : a receptacle for baptismal water **b** : a receptacle for holy water **c** : a receptacle for various liquids **2** : SOURCE, FOUNTAIN ⟨a ~ of information⟩ — **font·al** \ˈfän-tᵊl\ *adj*

[2]**font** *n* [F *fonte,* fr. MF, act of founding, fr. VL **fundita,* fem. of *funditus,* pp. of L *fundere* to found, pour — more at FOUND] (ca. 1688) : an assortment or set of type or characters all of one style and sometimes one size

fon·ta·nel *or* **fon·ta·nelle** \ˌfän-tə-ˈnel, ˈfän-tə-ˌ\ *n* [ME *fontinelle* a bodily hollow or pit, fr. AF *funtainele,* dim. of *funtaine* fountain] (1741) : a membrane-covered opening in bone or between bones; *specif* : any of the spaces closed by membranous structures between the uncompleted angles of the parietal bones and the neighboring bones of a fetal or young skull

fon·ti·na \fän-ˈtē-nə\ *n, often cap* [It] (1938) : a cheese that is semisoft to hard in texture and mild to medium sharp in flavor

food \ˈfüd\ *n, often attrib* [ME *fode,* fr. OE *fōda;* akin to OHG *fuotar* food, fodder, L *panis* bread, *pascere* to feed] (bef. 12c) **1 a** : material consisting essentially of protein, carbohydrate, and fat used in the body of an organism to sustain growth, repair, and vital processes and to furnish energy; *also* : such food together with supplementary substances (as minerals, vitamins, and condiments) **b** : inorganic substances absorbed by plants in gaseous form or in water solution **2** : nutriment in solid form **3** : something that nourishes, sustains, or supplies ⟨~ for thought⟩ — **food·less** \-ləs\ *adj* — **food·less·ness** *n*

food chain *n* (1920) **1** : an arrangement of the organisms of an ecological community according to the order of predation in which each uses the next usu. lower member as a food source **2** : a hierarchy based on power or importance ⟨at the top of the corporate *food chain*⟩

food court *n* (1982) : an area within a building (as a shopping mall) set apart for food concessions

food·ie \ˈfü-dē\ *n* (1982) : a person having an avid interest in the latest food fads

foo dog *or* **fu dog** \ˈfü-\ *n, often cap F* [Chin (Beijing) *fó* Buddha; fr. the use of such figures in ceramic or stone as guardians of Buddhist temples] (1953) : a mythical lion-dog used as a decorative motif in Far Eastern art

food poisoning *n* (1886) : an acute gastrointestinal disorder caused by bacteria or their toxic products or by chemical residues in food

food processor *n* (1974) : an electric kitchen appliance with a set of interchangeable blades revolving inside a container

food pyramid *n* (1949) : an ecological hierarchy of food relationships in which a chief predator is at the top, each level preys on the next lower level, and usu. green plants are at the bottom

food stamp *n* (1939) : a government-issued coupon that is sold or given to low-income persons and is redeemable for food

food·stuff \ˈfüd-ˌstəf\ *n* (1872) : a substance with food value; *specif* : the raw material of food before or after processing

food vacuole *n* (ca. 1889) : a membrane-bound vacuole (as in an amoeba) in which ingested food is digested — see AMOEBA illustration

food·ways \ˈfüd-ˌwāz\ *n pl* (1946) : the eating habits and culinary practices of a people, region, or historical period

food web *n* (1949) : the totality of interacting food chains in an ecological community

foo·fa·raw \ˈfü-fə-ˌrȯ\ *n* [origin unknown] (1934) **1** : frills and flashy finery **2** : a disturbance or to-do over a trifle : FUSS

[1]**fool** \ˈfül\ *n* [ME, fr. AF *fol,* fr. LL *follis,* fr. L, bellows, bag; akin to OHG *bolla* blister, *balg* bag — more at BELLY] (13c) **1** : a person lacking in judgment or prudence **2 a** : a retainer formerly kept in great households to provide casual entertainment and commonly dressed in motley with cap, bells, and bauble **b** : one who is victimized or made to appear foolish : DUPE **3 a** : a harmlessly deranged person or one lacking in common powers of understanding **b** : one with a marked propensity or fondness for something ⟨a dancing ~⟩ ⟨a ~ for candy⟩ **4** : a cold dessert of pureed fruit mixed with whipped cream or custard

[2]**fool** *adj* (13c) : FOOLISH, SILLY ⟨barking its ~ head off⟩

[3]**fool** *vi* (1593) **1 a** : to behave foolishly ⟨told the children to stop their ~*ing*⟩ — often used with *around* **b** : to meddle, tamper, or experiment esp. thoughtlessly or ignorantly ⟨don't ~ with that gun⟩ — often used with *around* **2 a** : to play or improvise a comic role **b** : to speak in jest : JOKE ⟨I was only ~*ing*⟩ **3** : to contend or fight without serious intent or with less than full strength : TOY ⟨a dangerous man to ~ with⟩ ~ *vt* **1** : to make a fool of : DECEIVE **2** *obs* : INFATUATE **3** : to spend on trifles or without advantage : FRITTER — used with *away*

fool around *vi* (1837) **1** : to spend time idly, aimlessly, or frivolously **2** : to engage in casual sexual activity

fool·ery \ˈfül-rē, ˈfü-lə-\ *n, pl* **-er·ies** (1552) **1** : a foolish act, utterance, or belief **2** : foolish behavior

fool·har·dy \ˈfül-ˌhär-dē\ *adj* (13c) : foolishly adventurous and bold : RASH ***syn*** see ADVENTUROUS — **fool·har·di·ly** \-ˌhär-dᵊl-ē\ *adv* — **fool·har·di·ness** \-ˌhär-dē-nəs\ *n*

fool·ish \ˈfü-lish\ *adj* (13c) **1** : lacking in sense, judgment, or discretion **2 a** : ABSURD, RIDICULOUS **b** : marked by a loss of composure : NONPLUSSED **3** : INSIGNIFICANT, TRIFLING ***syn*** see SIMPLE — **fool·ish·ly** *adv*

fool·ish·ness *n* (15c) **1** : foolish behavior **2** : a foolish act or idea

fool·proof \ˈfül-ˌprüf\ *adj* (1902) : so simple, plain, or reliable as to leave no opportunity for error, misuse, or failure ⟨a ~ plan⟩

fools·cap *also* **fool's cap** \ˈfülz-ˌkap\ *n* (1602) **1** : a cap or hood usu. with bells worn by jesters **2** : a conical cap for slow or lazy students **3** *usu foolscap* [fr. the watermark of a foolscap formerly applied to such paper] : a size of paper formerly standard in Great Britain; *broadly* : a piece of writing paper

fool's gold *n* (1872) : PYRITE; *broadly* : any of various pyritic minerals resembling gold

fool's paradise *n* (15c) : a state of delusory happiness

fool's parsley *n* (1755) : a poisonous European weed (*Aethusa cynapium*) of the carrot family that resembles parsley and is naturalized in the northern U.S. and southern Canada

foos·ball \ˈfüz-ˌbȯl\ *n, often cap* [prob. modif. of G *Tischfussball,* fr. *Tisch* table + *Fussball* soccer, fr. *Fuss* foot + *Ball* ball] (1977) : a table game resembling soccer in which the ball is moved by manipulating rods to which small figures of players are attached — called also *table soccer*

[1]**foot** \ˈfu̇t\ *n, pl* **feet** \ˈfēt\ *also* **foot** [ME *fot,* fr. OE *fōt;* akin to OHG *fuot* foot, L *ped-, pes,* Gk *pod-, pous*] (bef. 12c) **1** : the terminal part of the vertebrate leg upon which an individual stands **2** : an invertebrate organ of locomotion or attachment; *esp* : a ventral muscular surface or process of a mollusk **3** : any of various units of length based on the length of the human foot; *esp* : a unit equal to ⅓ yard and comprising 12 inches — pl. *foot* used between a number and a noun ⟨a 10-*foot* pole⟩; pl. *feet* or *foot* used between a number and an adjective ⟨6 *feet* tall⟩; see WEIGHT table **4** : the basic unit of verse meter consisting of any of various fixed combinations or groups of stressed and unstressed or long and short syllables **5 a** : motion or power of walking or running : STEP ⟨fleet of ~⟩ **b** : SPEED, SWIFTNESS ⟨showed early ~⟩ **6** : something resembling a foot in position or use: as **a** : the lower end of the leg of a chair or table **b** (1) : the basal portion of the sporophyte in mosses (2) : a specialized outgrowth by which the embryonic sporophyte esp. of many bryophytes absorbs nourishment from the gametophyte **c** : a piece on a sewing machine that presses the cloth against the feed **7** *foot pl, chiefly Brit* : INFANTRY **8** : the lower edge (as of a sail) **9** : the lowest part : BOTTOM ⟨the ~ of the hill⟩ **10 a** : the end that is lower or opposite the head ⟨the ~ of the bed⟩ **b** : the part (as of a stocking) that covers the foot **11 foots** *pl but sing or pl in constr* : material deposited esp. in aging or refining : DREGS **12 foots** *pl* : FOOTLIGHTS — **at one's feet** : under one's spell or influence — **foot in the door** : the initial step toward a goal — **off one's feet** : in a sitting or lying position — **on foot** : by walking or running ⟨tour the campus *on foot*⟩ — **on one's feet** **1** : in a standing position **2** : in an established position or state **3** : in a recovered condition (as from illness) ⟨back *on my feet*⟩ **4** : in an extemporaneous manner : while in action ⟨good debaters can think *on their feet*⟩ — **to one's feet** : to a standing position ⟨brought the crowd *to its feet*⟩

[2]**foot** *vi* (15c) **1** : DANCE **2** : to go on foot **3** *of a sailboat* : to make speed : MOVE ~ *vt* **1 a** : to perform the movements of (a dance) **b** : to walk, run, or dance on, over, or through **2** *archaic* **a** : KICK **b** : REJECT **3** *archaic* : ESTABLISH **4 a** : to add up **b** : to pay or stand credit for ⟨~ the bill⟩ **5** : to make or renew the foot of (as a stocking)

foot·age \ˈfu̇-tij\ *n* (1892) : length or quantity expressed in feet: as **a** : BOARD FEET **b** : the total number of running feet of motion-picture film used (as for a scene or subject); *also* : the material contained on such footage

foot–and–mouth disease *n* (1862) : an acute contagious febrile disease esp. of cloven-footed animals that is caused by serotypes of a picornavirus (species *Foot-and-mouth disease virus* of the genus *Aphthovirus*) and is marked by ulcerating vesicles in the mouth, about the hooves, and on the udder and teats — called also *foot-and-mouth, hoof-and-mouth disease*; compare HAND, FOOT AND MOUTH DISEASE

foot·ball \ˈfu̇t-ˌbȯl\ *n* (15c) **1** : any of several games played between two teams on a usu. rectangular field having goalposts or goals at each end and whose object is to get the ball over a goal line, into a goal, or between goalposts by running, passing, or kicking: as **a** *Brit* : SOCCER **b** *Brit* : RUGBY **c** : an American game played between two teams of 11 players each in which the ball is in possession of one side at a time and is advanced by running or passing **d** *Austral* : AUSTRALIAN RULES FOOTBALL **e** *Canad* : CANADIAN FOOTBALL **2 a** : an inflated oval ball used in the game of football **b** *Brit* : a soccer ball **3** : something treated roughly esp. as the subject of a prolonged dispute ⟨the issue became a political ~ in Congress⟩ — **foot·ball·er** \-ˌbȯ-lər\ *n*

foot·bath \ˈfu̇t-ˌbath, -ˌbäth\ *n* (1599) : a bath for cleansing, warming, soothing, or disinfecting the feet

foot·board \ˈfu̇t-ˌbȯrd\ *n* (1751) **1** : a narrow platform on which to stand or brace the feet **2** : a board forming the foot of a bed

foot·boy \-ˌbȯi\ *n* (1585) : a serving boy : PAGE, ATTENDANT

foot·bridge \ˈfu̇t-ˌbrij\ *n* (14c) : a bridge for pedestrians

foot–can·dle \-ˈkan-dᵊl\ *n* (1906) : a unit of illuminance on a surface that is everywhere one foot from a uniform point source of light of one candle and equal to one lumen per square foot

foot·cloth \-ˌklȯth\ *n* (14c) **1** *archaic* : an ornamental cloth draped over the back of a horse to reach the ground on each side **2** *archaic* : CARPET

foot·drag·ger \-ˌdra-gər\ *n* (1957) : one who engages in foot-dragging

foot–drag·ging \-ˌdra-giŋ\ *n* (1952) : failure to act with the necessary promptness or vigor

foot·ed \ˈfu̇-təd\ *adj* (14c) : having a foot or feet esp. of a specified kind or number — often used in combination ⟨a four-*footed* animal⟩

foot·er \ˈfu̇-tər\ *n* (1608) **1** *archaic* : PEDESTRIAN **2** : information (as a page number) printed at the bottom of each page of a document

---

-footer *n comb form* : one that is a specified number of feet in height, length, or breadth ⟨a six-*footer*⟩
foot·fall \ˈfu̇t-ˌfȯl\ *n* (1610) : the sound of a footstep
foot fault *n* (1886) : an infraction of the service rules (as in tennis, racquetball, or volleyball) that results from illegal placement of the server's feet — **foot-fault** \ˈfu̇t-ˌfȯlt\ *vi*
foot·gear \ˈfu̇t-ˌgir\ *n* (1837) : FOOTWEAR
foot·hill \-ˌhil\ *n* (1850) **1** : a hill at the foot of higher hills **2** *pl* : a hilly region at the base of a mountain range
foot·hold \-ˌhōld\ *n* (ca. 1609) **1** : a hold for the feet : FOOTING **2** : a position usable as a base for further advance
foot·ing \ˈfu̇-tiŋ\ *n* (14c) **1** : a stable position or placing of the feet **2** : a surface or its condition with respect to one walking or running on it; *esp* : the condition of a racetrack **3** : the act of moving on foot : STEP, TREAD **4 a** : a place or position providing a base of operations : FOOTHOLD **b** : established position : STATUS; *esp* : position or rank in relation to others ⟨they all started off on an equal ~⟩ **5** : BASIS **6** : terms of social intercourse **7** : an enlargement at the lower end of a foundation wall, pier, or column to distribute the load **8** : the sum of a column of figures
foot·lam·bert \ˈfu̇t-ˌlam-bərt\ *n* (1925) : a unit of luminance equal to the luminance of a perfectly diffusing surface that emits or reflects one lumen per square foot
foo·tle \ˈfü-tᵊl\ *vi* **foo·tled; foo·tling** \-tᵊl-iŋ, ˈfüt-liŋ\ [prob. alter. of *footer* to waste time] (1892) **1** : to talk or act foolishly **2** : to waste time : TRIFLE, FOOL — **footle** *n* — **foo·tler** \-tᵊl-ər, ˈfüt-lər\ *n*
foot·less \ˈfu̇t-ləs\ *adj* (14c) **1 a** : having no feet **b** : lacking foundation : UNSUBSTANTIAL **2** : STUPID, INEPT — **foot·less·ly** *adv* — **foot·less·ness** *n*
foot·lights \-ˌlīts\ *n pl* (ca. 1839) **1** : a row of lights set across the front of a stage floor **2** : the stage as a profession ⟨the lure of the ~⟩
foo·tling \ˈfü-tᵊl-iŋ, ˈfüt-liŋ\ *adj* [*footle*] (ca. 1897) **1** : lacking judgment or ability : INEPT ⟨~ amateurs who understand nothing —E. R. Bentley⟩ **2** : lacking use or value : TRIVIAL ⟨~ matters⟩
foot·lock·er \ˈfu̇t-ˌlä-kər\ *n* (1942) : a small trunk designed to be placed at the foot of a bed (as in a barracks)
foot·loose \-ˌlüs\ *adj* (1873) : having no ties : free to move about
foot·man \-mən\ *n* (14c) **1 a** *archaic* : a traveler on foot : PEDESTRIAN **b** : INFANTRYMAN **2 a** : a servant in livery formerly attending a rider or required to run in front of his master's carriage **b** : a servant who serves at table, tends the door, and runs errands
foot·mark \-ˌmärk\ *n* (1799) : FOOTPRINT
1**foot·note** \-ˌnōt\ *n* (1607) **1** : a note of reference, explanation, or comment usu. placed below the text on a printed page **2 a** : one that is a relatively subordinate or minor part (as of an event, work, or field) ⟨a movement now regarded as a ~ to architectural history⟩ **b** : COMMENTARY 3a
2**footnote** *vt* (1864) : to furnish with a footnote : ANNOTATE
foot·pace \ˈfu̇t-ˌpās\ *n* (1538) **1** : a walking pace **2** : PLATFORM, DAIS
1**foot·pad** \-ˌpad\ *n* [*foot* + *pad* highwayman, prob. fr. 3*pad*] (1678) : a criminal who robs pedestrians
2**footpad** *n* [*foot* + 1*pad*] (1966) : a flattish foot on the leg of a spacecraft for distributing weight to minimize sinking into a surface
foot·path \ˈfu̇t-ˌpath, -ˌpäth\ *n* (1526) : a narrow path for pedestrians
foot–pound \-ˈpau̇nd\ *n, pl* **foot–pounds** (1850) : a unit of work equal to the work done by a force of one pound acting through a distance of one foot in the direction of the force
foot–pound–second *adj* (1892) : being or relating to a system of units based upon the foot as the unit of length, the pound as the unit of weight, and the second as the unit of time — abbr. *fps*
foot·print \ˈfu̇t-ˌprint\ *n* (1552) **1** : an impression of the foot on a surface **2 a** : the area on a surface covered by something ⟨a tire with a wide ~⟩ ⟨the ~ of a laser beam⟩ **b** : range of operation (as of a service) ⟨a global ~⟩ **3** : a marked effect, impression, or impact ⟨left a ~ in the field of research⟩ **4** : something that identifies ⟨a genetic ~⟩
foot·race \-ˌrās\ *n* (1616) : a race run by humans on foot
foot·rest \-ˌrest\ *n* (1861) : a support for the feet
foot·rope \-ˌrōp\ *n* (1769) **1** : the part of a boltrope sewed to the lower edge of a sail **2** : a rope rigged below a yard for crew members to stand on
foot rot *n* (1708) **1** : a progressive inflammation of the feet of sheep, goats, or cattle that is associated with bacterial infection **2** : a plant disease marked by rot of the stem near the ground
foot·sie *or* **foot·sy** \ˈfu̇t-sē\ *n* [dim. of 1*foot*] (1944) **1** : a furtive flirtatious caressing with the feet (as under a table) **2** : a usu. surreptitious cooperation or negotiation with someone supposed hostile to one's own interests — usu. used with *play*
foot·slog \ˈfu̇t-ˌsläg\ *vi* (1899) : to march or tramp through mud — **foot·slog·ger** *n*
foot soldier *n* (1622) **1** : INFANTRYMAN **2** : a person likened to an infantryman esp. in doing active and usu. unglamorous work in support of an organization or movement ⟨*foot soldiers* in the war against drugs⟩
foot·sore \ˈfu̇t-ˌsȯr\ *adj* (1719) : having sore or tender feet (as from much walking) — **foot·sore·ness** *n*
foot·step \-ˌstep\ *n* (13c) **1** : the mark of the foot : TRACK **2 a** : TREAD **b** : distance covered by a step : PACE **3** : a step on which to ascend or descend **4** : a way of life, conduct, or action ⟨followed in his father's ~*s*⟩
foot·stone \-ˌstōn\ *n* (1724) : a stone placed at the foot of a grave
foot·stool \-ˌstül\ *n* (1530) : a low stool used to support the feet
foot·wall \-ˌwȯl\ *n* (1860) **1** : the lower underlying wall of a vein, ore deposit, or coal seam in a mine **2** : the lower wall of an inclined fault
foot·way \-ˌwā\ *n* (15c) : a narrow way or path for pedestrians
foot·wear \-ˌwer\ *n* (1881) : wearing apparel (as shoes or boots) for the feet
foot·work \-ˌwərk\ *n* (1859) **1** : the activity of moving from place to place ⟨the investigation entailed a lot of ~⟩ **2** : the management of the feet (as in boxing); *also* : the work done with them **3** : active and adroit maneuvering to achieve an end ⟨fancy political ~⟩
1**foo·zle** \ˈfü-zəl\ *n* (1890) : an act of foozling; *esp* : a bungling golf stroke
2**foozle** *vt* **foo·zled; foo·zling** \ˈfüz-liŋ, ˈfü-zə-\ [perh. fr. G dial. *fuseln* to work carelessly] (1888) : to manage or play awkwardly : BUNGLE
1**fop** \ˈfäp\ *n* [ME; akin to ME *fobben* to deceive, MHG *voppen*] (15c) **1** *obs* : a foolish or silly person **2** : a man who is devoted to or vain about his appearance or dress : COXCOMB, DANDY
2**fop** *vt* **fopped; fop·ping** (ca. 1590) *obs* : FOOL, DUPE
fop·pery \ˈfä-p(ə-)rē\ *n, pl* **-per·ies** (1546) **1** : foolish character or action : FOLLY **2** : the behavior or dress of a fop
fop·pish \ˈfä-pish\ *adj* (1599) **1** *obs* : FOOLISH, SILLY **2 a** : characteristic of a fop ⟨a ~ dressing gown⟩ **b** : behaving or dressing in the manner of a fop — **fop·pish·ly** *adv* — **fop·pish·ness** *n*
1**for** \fər, (ˈ)fȯr, *Southern also* (ˈ)fär\ *prep* [ME, fr. OE; akin to L *per* through, *prae* before, *pro* before, for, ahead, Gk *pro*, OE *faran* to go — more at FARE] (bef. 12c) **1 a** — used as a function word to indicate purpose ⟨a grant ~ studying medicine⟩ **b** — used as a function word to indicate an intended goal ⟨left ~ home⟩ ⟨acted ~ the best⟩ **c** — used as a function word to indicate the object or recipient of a perception, desire, or activity ⟨now ~ a good rest⟩ ⟨run ~ your life⟩ ⟨an eye ~ a bargain⟩ **2 a** : as being or constituting ⟨taken ~ a fool⟩ ⟨eggs ~ breakfast⟩ **b** — used as a function word to indicate an actual or implied enumeration or selection ⟨~ one thing, the price is too high⟩ **3** : because of ⟨can't sleep ~ the heat⟩ **4** — used as a function word to indicate suitability or fitness ⟨it is not ~ you to choose⟩ ⟨ready ~ action⟩ **5 a** : in place of ⟨go to the store ~ me⟩ **b** (1) : on behalf of : REPRESENTING ⟨speaks ~ the court⟩ (2) : in favor of ⟨all ~ the plan⟩ **6** : in spite of — usu. used with *all* ⟨~ all his large size, he moves gracefully⟩ **7** : with respect to : CONCERNING ⟨a stickler ~ detail⟩ ⟨heavy ~ its size⟩ **8 a** — used as a function word to indicate equivalence in exchange ⟨$10 ~ a hat⟩, equality in number or quantity ⟨point ~ point⟩, or correspondence or correlation ⟨~ every one that works, you'll find five that don't⟩ **b** — used as a function word to indicate number of attempts ⟨0 ~ 4⟩ **9** — used as a function word to indicate duration of time or extent of space ⟨gone ~ two days⟩ **10** : in honor of : AFTER ⟨named ~ her grandmother⟩
2**for** *conj* (12c) : for the reason that : on this ground : BECAUSE
3**for** *abbr* **1** foreign **2** forestry
FOR *abbr* free on rail
for- *prefix* [ME, fr. OE; akin to OHG *far-* for-, OE *for*] **1** : so as to involve prohibition, exclusion, omission, failure, neglect, or refusal ⟨*forbid*⟩ **2** : destructively or detrimentally ⟨*fordo*⟩ **3** : completely : excessively : to exhaustion : to pieces ⟨*forspent*⟩
fora *pl of* FORUM
1**for·age** \ˈfȯr-ij, ˈfär-\ *n* [ME, fr. AF, fr. *fuerre, foer* fodder, straw, of Gmc origin; akin to OHG *fuotar* food, fodder — more at FOOD] (14c) **1** : food for animals esp. when taken by browsing or grazing **2** [2*forage*] : the act of foraging : search for provisions
2**forage** *vb* **for·aged; for·ag·ing** *vt* (15c) **1** : to strip of provisions : collect forage from **2** : to secure by foraging ⟨*foraged* a chicken for the feast⟩ ~ *vi* **1** : to wander in search of forage or food **2** : to secure forage (as for horses) by stripping the country **3** : RAVAGE, RAID **4** : to make a search : RUMMAGE — **for·ag·er** *n*
fo·ram \ˈfȯr-əm\ *n* (1927) : FORAMINIFER
fo·ra·men \fə-ˈrā-mən\ *n, pl* **fo·ram·i·na** \-ˈra-mə-nə\ *or* **fo·ra·mens** \-ˈrā-mənz\ [L *foramin-, foramen*, fr. *forare* to bore — more at BORE] (1671) : a small opening, perforation, or orifice : FENESTRA — **fo·ram·i·nal** \fə-ˈra-mə-nᵊl\ *or* **fo·ram·i·nous** \-mə-nəs\ *adj*
fo·ra·men mag·num \fə-ˌrā-mən-ˈmag-nəm\ *n* [NL, lit., large opening] (1857) : the opening in the skull through which the spinal cord passes to become the medulla oblongata
foramen ova·le \-ō-ˈva-lē, -ˈvä-, -ˈvā-\ *n* [NL, lit., oval opening] (ca. 1860) : an opening in the septum between the two atria of the heart that is normally present only in the fetus
for·a·min·i·fer \ˌfȯr-ə-ˈmi-nə-fər, ˌfär-\ *n* (ca. 1842) : any of an order (Foraminifera) of large chiefly marine rhizopod protozoans usu. having calcareous shells that often are perforated with minute holes for protrusion of slender pseudopodia and form the bulk of chalk and nummulitic limestone — **fo·ra·mi·nif·er·al** \fə-ˌra-mə-ˈni-f(ə-)rəl; ˌfȯr-ə-mə-ˈni-, ˌfär-\ *adj*

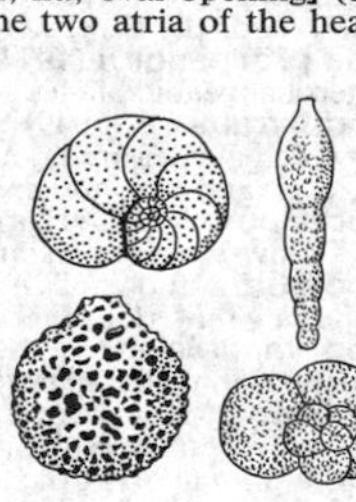
foraminifer shells

fo·ra·mi·nif·era \fə-ˌra-mə-ˈni-f(ə-)rə; ˌfȯr-ə-mə-ˈni-, ˌfär-\ *n pl* [NL, fr. L *foramin-, foramen* + *-fera*, neut. pl. of *-fer* -fer] (ca. 1836) : organisms that are foraminifers
fo·ra·mi·nif·er·an \-f(ə-)rən\ *n* (1920) : FORAMINIFER
for and *conj* (ca. 1529) *obs* : and also
for·as·much as \ˈfȯr-əz-ˌmə-chəz\ *conj* (13c) : in view of the fact that
1**for·ay** \ˈfȯr-ˌā, ˈfär- *also* fȯ-ˈrā *or* fə-ˈ\ *vb* [ME *forrayen*, fr. AF *forreyer, foreer*, prob. back-formation fr. **forrier*, **forreour* forager, raider, fr. *fuerre, foer* provender — more at FORAGE] *vt* (14c) *archaic* : to ravage in search of spoils : PILLAGE ~ *vi* : to make a raid or brief invasion ⟨~*ed* into enemy territory⟩ — **for·ay·er** *n*
2**foray** *n* (14c) **1** : a sudden or irregular invasion or attack for war or spoils : RAID **2** : a brief excursion or attempt esp. outside one's accustomed sphere ⟨the novelist's ~ into nonfiction⟩
forb \ˈfȯrb\ *n* [Gk *phorbē* fodder, food, fr. *pherbein* to graze] (1924) : an herb other than grass
1**for·bear** \fȯr-ˈber, fər-\ *vb* **-bore** \-ˈbȯr\; **-borne** \-ˈbȯrn\; **-bear·ing** [ME *forberen*, fr. OE *forberan* to endure, do without, fr. *for-* + *beran* to bear] *vt* (bef. 12c) **1** *obs* : to do without **2** : to hold oneself back from esp. with an effort ⟨*forbore* mentioning the incident⟩ **3** *obs* : to leave alone : SHUN ⟨~ his presence —Shak.⟩ ~ *vi* **1** : HOLD BACK, ABSTAIN ⟨have *forborne* from taking part in any controversy —Abraham Lincoln⟩ **2** : to control oneself when provoked : be patient — **for·bear·er** *n*
2**forbear** *var of* FOREBEAR
for·bear·ance \fȯr-ˈber-ən(t)s, fər-\ *n* (1576) **1** : a refraining from the enforcement of something (as a debt, right, or obligation) that is due **2** : the act of forbearing : PATIENCE **3** : the quality of being forbearing : LENIENCY
1**for·bid** \fər-ˈbid, fȯr-\ *vt* **-bade** \-ˈbad, -ˈbād\ *also* **-bad** \-ˈbad\; **-bid·den** \-ˈbi-dᵊn\; **-bid·ding** [ME *forbidden*, fr. OE *forbēodan*, fr. *for-* +

bēodan to bid — more at BID] (bef. 12c) **1 :** to proscribe from or as if from the position of one in authority : command against ⟨the law ~*s* stores to sell liquor to minors⟩ ⟨her mother ~*s* her to go⟩ **2 :** to hinder or prevent as if by an effectual command ⟨space ~*s* further treatment here⟩ — **for·bid·der** *n*

syn FORBID, PROHIBIT, INTERDICT, INHIBIT mean to debar one from doing something or to order that something not be done. FORBID implies that the order is from one in authority and that obedience is expected ⟨smoking is *forbidden* in the building⟩. PROHIBIT suggests the issuing of laws, statutes, or regulations ⟨*prohibited* the sale of liquor⟩. INTERDICT implies prohibition by civil or ecclesiastical authority usu. for a given time or a declared purpose ⟨practices *interdicted* by the church⟩. INHIBIT implies restraints or restrictions that amount to prohibitions, not only by authority but also by the exigencies of the time or situation ⟨conditions *inhibiting* the growth of free trade⟩.

[2]**forbid** *adj* (1606) *archaic* : ACCURSED ⟨he shall live a man ~ —Shak.⟩

for·bid·dance \fər-ˈbi-dᵊn(t)s, fȯr-\ *n* (ca. 1611) : the act of forbidding

for·bid·den \-ˈbi-dᵊn\ *adj* (13c) **1 :** not permitted or allowed **2 :** not conforming to the usual selection principles — used of quantum phenomena ⟨~ transition⟩ ⟨~ radiation⟩ ⟨~ spectral line⟩

forbidden fruit *n* [fr. the forbidden fruit of the Garden of Eden in Gen 3:2–19] (1605) : an immoral or illegal pleasure

forbidding *adj* (1599) **1 :** such as to make approach or passage difficult or impossible ⟨~ walls⟩ **2 :** DISAGREEABLE, REPELLENT ⟨a ~ task⟩ **3 :** GRIM, MENACING ⟨a dark ~ sky⟩ — **for·bid·ding·ly** \-ˈbi-diŋ-lē\ *adv*

forbode *var of* FOREBODE

[1]**for·by** *or* **for·bye** \fȯr-ˈbī\ *prep* [ME *forby,* prep. & adv., fr. *fore-* + *by*] (14c) **1** *archaic* **a :** PAST **b :** NEAR **2** *chiefly Scot* : BESIDES

[2]**forby** *or* **forbye** *adv* (1590) *chiefly Scot* : BESIDES : in addition

[1]**force** \ˈfȯrs\ *n* [ME, fr. AF, fr. VL **fortia,* fr. L *fortis* strong] (14c) **1 a** (1) **:** strength or energy exerted or brought to bear : cause of motion or change : active power ⟨the ~*s* of nature⟩ ⟨the motivating ~ in her life⟩ (2) *cap* — used with a number to indicate the strength of the wind according to the Beaufort scale ⟨a *Force* 10 hurricane⟩ **b :** moral or mental strength **c :** capacity to persuade or convince ⟨the ~ of the argument⟩ **2 a :** military strength **b** (1) **:** a body (as of troops or ships) assigned to a military purpose (2) *pl* **:** the whole military strength (as of a nation) **c :** a body of persons or things available for a particular end ⟨a labor ~⟩ ⟨the missile ~⟩ **d :** an individual or group having the power of effective action ⟨join ~*s* to prevent violence⟩ ⟨a ~ in politics⟩ **e** *often cap* : POLICE FORCE — usu. used with *the* **3 :** violence, compulsion, or constraint exerted upon or against a person or thing **4 a :** an agency or influence that if applied to a free body results chiefly in an acceleration of the body and sometimes in elastic deformation and other effects **b :** any of the natural influences (as electromagnetism, gravity, the strong force, and the weak force) that exist esp. between particles and determine the structure of the universe **5 :** the quality of conveying impressions intensely in writing or speech ⟨stated the objectives with ~⟩ ***syn*** see POWER — **force·less** \-ləs\ *adj* — **in force 1 :** in great numbers ⟨picnickers were out *in force*⟩ **2 :** VALID, OPERATIVE ⟨the ban remains *in force*⟩

[2]**force** *vt* **forced; forc·ing** (14c) **1 :** to do violence to; *esp* : RAPE **2 :** to compel by physical, moral, or intellectual means **3 :** to make or cause esp. through natural or logical necessity ⟨*forced* to admit my error⟩ ⟨the last minute goal *forced* overtime⟩ **4 a :** to press, drive, pass, or effect against resistance or inertia ⟨~ your way through⟩ **b :** to impose or thrust urgently, importunately, or inexorably ⟨~ unwanted attentions on a coworker⟩ **5 :** to achieve or win by strength in struggle or violence: as **a :** to win one's way into ⟨~ a castle⟩ ⟨*forced* the mountain passes⟩ **b :** to break open or through ⟨~ a lock⟩ **6 a :** to raise or accelerate to the utmost ⟨*forcing* the pace⟩ **b :** to produce only with unnatural or unwilling effort ⟨*forced* a smile⟩ **c :** to wrench, strain, or use (language) with marked unnaturalness and lack of ease **7 a :** to hasten the rate of progress or growth of **b :** to bring (as plants) to maturity out of the normal season ⟨*forcing* lilies for Easter⟩ **8 :** to induce (as a particular bid or play by another player) in a card game by some conventional act, play, bid, or response **9 a :** to cause (a runner in baseball) to be put out on a force-out **b :** to cause (a run) to be scored in baseball by giving a base on balls when the bases are full — **forc·er** *n* — **force one's hand :** to cause one to act precipitously : force one to reveal one's purpose or intention

syn FORCE, COMPEL, COERCE, CONSTRAIN, OBLIGE mean to make someone or something yield. FORCE is the general term and implies the overcoming of resistance by the exertion of strength, power, or duress ⟨*forced* to flee for their lives⟩. COMPEL typically suggests overcoming of resistance or unwillingness by an irresistible force ⟨*compelled* to admit my mistake⟩. COERCE suggests overcoming resistance or unwillingness by actual or threatened violence or pressure ⟨*coerced* into signing over the rights⟩. CONSTRAIN suggests the effect of a force or circumstance that limits freedom of action or choice ⟨*constrained* by conscience⟩. OBLIGE implies the constraint of necessity, law, or duty ⟨felt *obliged* to go⟩.

forced *adj* (ca. 1537) **1 :** compelled by force or necessity : INVOLUNTARY ⟨a ~ landing⟩ **2 :** done or produced with effort, exertion, or pressure ⟨a ~ laugh⟩ — **forc·ed·ly** \ˈfȯr-səd-lē\ *adv*

force–feed *vt* **-fed; -feed·ing** (1901) **1 :** to feed (as an animal) by forcible administration of food **2 :** to force to take in ⟨~ students the classics⟩ — also used with a single object ⟨~ the classics to students⟩ ⟨~ students with the classics⟩

force field *n* (1920) **1 :** FIELD 6a **2 :** a special charm, aura, or spirit that can influence anyone in its presence **3 :** something resembling a force field esp. in intensity that restricts or impedes movement toward an area or object

force·ful \ˈfȯrs-fəl\ *adj* (1571) : possessing or filled with force : EFFECTIVE ⟨a ~ argument⟩ — **force·ful·ly** \-fə-lē\ *adv* — **force·ful·ness** *n*

force ma·jeure \ˌfȯrs-mä-ˈzhər, -mə-\ *n* [F, superior force] (1883) **1 :** superior or irresistible force **2 :** an event or effect that cannot be reasonably anticipated or controlled — compare ACT OF GOD

force·meat \ˈfȯrs-ˌmēt\ *n* [*force* (alter. of [2]*farce*) + *meat*] (ca. 1688) **:** finely chopped and highly seasoned meat or fish that is either served alone or used as a stuffing — called also *farce*

force of habit (1796) : behavior made involuntary or automatic by repeated practice

force of nature (1975) : FORCE 4b

force–out \ˈfȯrs-ˌau̇t\ *n* (1896) : a play in baseball in which a runner is put out by being forced to advance to the next base but failing to do so safely

force play *n* (1912) : FORCE-OUT

for·ceps \ˈfȯr-səps, -ˌseps\ *n, pl* **forceps** [L, tongs, perh. fr. *formus* warm + *capere* to take — more at THERM, HEAVE] (1634) : an instrument for grasping, holding firmly, or exerting traction upon objects esp. for delicate operations (as by jewelers or surgeons) — **for·ceps·like** \-ˌlīk\ *adj*

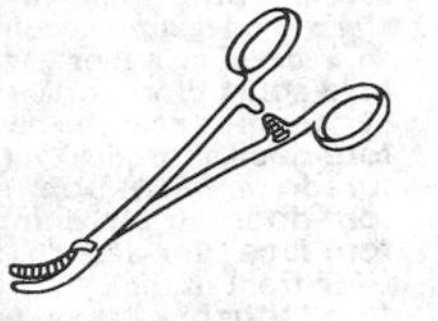

forceps

force pump *n* (1659) : a pump with a solid piston for drawing and forcing through valves a liquid (as water) to a considerable height above the pump or under a considerable pressure

forc·ible \ˈfȯr-sə-bəl\ *adj* (15c) **1 :** effected by force used against opposition or resistance **2 :** characterized by force, efficiency, or energy : POWERFUL — **forc·ible·ness** *n* — **forc·ibly** \-blē\ *adv*

[1]**ford** \ˈfȯrd\ *n* [ME, fr. OE; akin to ON *fjǫrthr* fjord, L *portus* port, OE *faran* to go — more at FARE] (bef. 12c) : a shallow part of a body of water that may be crossed by wading

[2]**ford** *vt* (1614) : to cross (a body of water) by wading — **ford·able** \ˈfȯr-də-bəl\ *adj*

for·do *also* **fore·do** \fȯr-ˈdü\ *vt* **-did** \-ˈdid\; **-done** \-ˈdən\; **-do·ing** \-ˈdü-iŋ\ [ME *fordon,* fr. OE *fordōn,* fr. *for-* + *dōn* to do] (bef. 12c) **1** *archaic* : to do away with : DESTROY **2 :** to overcome with fatigue — used only as past participle ⟨quite *fordone* with the heat⟩

[1]**fore** \ˈfȯr\ *adv* [ME, fr. OE; akin to OE *for*] (bef. 12c) **1** *obs* : at an earlier time or period **2 :** in, toward, or near the front : FORWARD

[2]**fore** *also* **'fore** *prep* (bef. 12c) **1** *chiefly dial* : BEFORE **2 :** in the presence of

[3]**fore** *adj* [*fore-*] (15c) **1 :** situated in front of something else : FORWARD **2 :** prior in order of occurrence : FORMER

[4]**fore** *n* (1637) : something that occupies a front position — **to the fore :** in or into a position of prominence : FORWARD

[5]**fore** *interj* [prob. short for *before*] (ca. 1878) — used by a golfer to warn anyone within range of the probable line of flight of the ball

fore- *comb form* [ME *for-, fore-,* fr. OE *fore-,* fr. *fore,* adv.] **1 a :** earlier : beforehand ⟨*fore*see⟩ **b :** occurring earlier : occurring beforehand ⟨*fore*shock⟩ **2 a :** situated at the front : in front ⟨*fore*leg⟩ **b :** front part of (something specified) ⟨*fore*arm⟩ **c :** foremast ⟨*fore*top⟩

fore–and–aft \ˌfȯr-ə-ˈnaft\ *adj* (1820) **1 :** lying, running, or acting in the general line of the length of a construction (as a ship or a house) : LONGITUDINAL **2 :** having no square sails

fore and aft *adv* (ca. 1618) **1 :** lengthwise of a ship : from stem to stern **2 :** in, at, or toward both the bow and stern **3 :** in or at the front and back or the beginning and end

fore–and–aft·er \-ˈnaf-tər\ *n* (1823) : a ship with a fore-and-aft rig; *esp* : SCHOONER

fore–and–aft rig *n* (1879) : a sailing-ship rig in which most or all of the sails are not attached to yards but are bent to gaffs or set on the masts or on stays in a fore-and-aft line

[1]**fore·arm** \(ˌ)fȯr-ˈärm\ *vt* (1584) : to arm in advance : PREPARE

[2]**fore·arm** \ˈfȯr-ˌärm\ *n* (1741) : the part of the human arm between the elbow and the wrist; *also* : the corresponding part in other vertebrates

fore·bay \ˈfȯr-ˌbā\ *n* (1770) : a reservoir or canal from which water is taken to run equipment (as a waterwheel or turbine)

fore·bear *also* **for·bear** \-ˌber\ *n* [ME (Sc), fr. *fore-* + *-bear* (fr. *been* to be)] (15c) : ANCESTOR, FOREFATHER; *also* : PRECURSOR — usu. used in pl.

fore·bear·er \ˈfȯr-ˌber-ər\ *n* (1852) : ANCESTOR, FOREFATHER

fore·bode *also* **for·bode** \(ˌ)fȯr-ˈbōd\ *vt* (1603) **1 :** to have an inward conviction of (as coming ill or misfortune) **2 :** FORETELL, PORTEND ~ *vi* : AUGUR, PREDICT — **fore·bod·er** *n*

[1]**fore·bod·ing** \-ˈbō-diŋ\ *n* (14c) : the act of one who forebodes; *also* : an omen, prediction, or presentiment esp. of coming evil : PORTENT

[2]**foreboding** *adj* (1630) : indicative of or marked by foreboding — **fore·bod·ing·ly** \-diŋ-lē\ *adv* — **fore·bod·ing·ness** *n*

fore·brain \ˈfȯr-ˌbrān\ *n* (1879) : the anterior of the three primary divisions of the developing vertebrate brain or the corresponding part of the adult brain that includes esp. the cerebral hemispheres, the thalamus, and the hypothalamus and that esp. in higher vertebrates is the main control center for sensory and associative information processing, visceral functions, and voluntary motor functions — called also *prosencephalon*; compare DIENCEPHALON, TELENCEPHALON

fore·cad·die \-ˌka-dē\ *n* (1792) : a golf caddie who is stationed in the fairway and who indicates the position of balls on the course

[1]**fore·cast** \-ˌkast; fȯr-ˈkast\ *vb* **forecast** *also* **fore·cast·ed; fore·cast·ing** *vt* (15c) **1 a :** to calculate or predict (some future event or condition) usu. as a result of study and analysis of available pertinent data; *esp* : to predict (weather conditions) on the basis of correlated meteorological observations **b :** to indicate as likely to occur **2 :** to serve as a forecast of : PRESAGE ⟨such events may ~ peace⟩ ~ *vi* : to calculate the future ***syn*** see FORETELL — **fore·cast·able** \-ˌkas-tə-bəl\ *adj* — **fore·cast·er** *n*

[2]**fore·cast** \ˈfȯr-ˌkast\ *n* (1527) **1** *archaic* : foresight of consequences and provision against them : FORETHOUGHT **2 :** a prophecy, estimate, or prediction of a future happening or condition

fore·cas·tle \ˈfōk-səl; ˈfȯr-ˌka-səl\ *or* **fo'·c'sle** \ˈfōk-səl\ *n* (15c) **1 :** the forward part of the upper deck of a ship **2 :** the crew's quarters usu. in a ship's bow

fore·check \ˈfȯr-ˌchek\ *vi* (1951) : to check an opponent in ice hockey in the opponent's defensive zone — **fore·check·er** \-ˌche-kər\ *n*

fore·close \(ˌ)fȯr-ˈklōz\ *vb* [ME, fr. AF *forclos,* pp. of *forclore, forsclore,* fr. *fors* outside (fr. L *foris*) + *clore* to close — more at FORUM] *vt* (15c) **1** : to shut out : PRECLUDE **2** : to hold exclusively **3** : to deal with or close in advance **4** : to subject to foreclosure proceedings ~ *vi* : to foreclose a mortgage

fore·clo·sure \-ˈklō-zhər\ *n* (1713) : an act or instance of foreclosing; *specif* : a legal proceeding that bars or extinguishes a mortgagor's right of redeeming a mortgaged estate

fore·court \ˈfȯr-ˌkȯrt\ *n* (1535) **1** : an open court in front of a building **2** : the area near the net in a court game

fore·deck \ˈfȯr-ˌdek\ *n* (1565) : the forepart of a ship's main deck

foredo *var of* FORDO

fore·doom \(ˌ)fȯr-ˈdüm\ *vt* (1559) : DOOM 2

fore·face \ˈfȯr-ˌfās\ *n* (1545) : the part of the head of a quadruped that is in front of the eyes

fore·fa·ther \-ˌfä-t͟hər\ *n* (14c) **1** : ANCESTOR 1a **2** : a person of an earlier period and common heritage

fore·feel \(ˌ)fȯr-ˈfēl\ *vt* **-felt** \-ˈfelt\; **-feel·ing** (1580) : to have a presentiment of

forefend *var of* FORFEND

fore·fin·ger \ˈfȯr-ˌfiŋ-gər\ *n* (15c) : INDEX FINGER

fore·foot \-ˌfu̇t\ *n* (14c) **1 a** : one of the anterior feet esp. of a quadruped **b** : the front part of the human foot; *also* : the front part of a shoe **2** : the forward part of a ship where the stem and keel meet

fore·front \-ˌfrənt\ *n* (15c) : the foremost part or place

foregather *var of* FORGATHER

[1]fore·go \fȯr-ˈgō\ *vt* **-went** \-ˈwent\; **-gone** \-ˈgȯn *also* -ˈgän\; **-go·ing** \-ˈgō-iŋ, -ˈgȯ(-)iŋ\ (bef. 12c) : to go before : PRECEDE — **fore·go·er** \-ˈgō-ər\ *n*

[2]forego *var of* FORGO

fore·go·ing \-ˈgō-iŋ, -ˈgȯ(-)iŋ\ *adj* (15c) : listed, mentioned, or occurring before ⟨the ~ statement can be proven⟩ ***syn*** see PRECEDING

fore·gone \ˈfȯr-ˌgȯn *also* -ˌgän\ *adj* (1575) : PREVIOUS, PAST

foregone conclusion *n* (1604) **1** : a conclusion that has preceded argument or examination **2** : an inevitable result : CERTAINTY ⟨the victory was a *foregone conclusion*⟩

[1]fore·ground \ˈfȯr-ˌgrau̇nd\ *n* (1695) **1** : the part of a scene or representation that is nearest to and in front of the spectator **2** : a position of prominence : FOREFRONT **3** : a level of computer processing at which the processor responds immediately to input to a designated high-priority task — compare BACKGROUND

[2]foreground *vt* (1892) : to bring to the foreground; *esp* : to give prominence or emphasis to

fore·gut \ˈfȯr-ˌgət\ *n* (ca. 1889) : the anterior part of the alimentary canal of a vertebrate embryo that develops into the pharynx, esophagus, stomach, and extreme anterior part of the intestine

[1]fore·hand \-ˌhand\ *n* (1557) **1** *archaic* : superior position : ADVANTAGE **2** : the part of a horse that is before the rider **3** : a forehand stroke (as in tennis or racquets); *also* : the side on which such strokes are made

[2]forehand *adj* (1599) **1** *obs* : done or given in advance : PRIOR **2** : made with the palm of the hand turned in the direction in which the hand is moving ⟨a ~ tennis stroke⟩

[3]forehand *adv* (1925) : with a forehand stroke

fore·hand·ed \(ˌ)fȯr-ˈhan-dəd\ *adj* (1650) **1 a** : mindful of the future : PRUDENT **b** : WELL-TO-DO **2** : FOREHAND 2 — **fore·hand·ed·ly** *adv* — **fore·hand·ed·ness** *n*

fore·head \ˈfär-əd, ˈfȯr-; ˈfȯr-ˌhed *also* -ˌed\ *n* (bef. 12c) **1** : the part of the face above the eyes **2** : the front or forepart of something ⟨flames in the ~ of the morning sky —John Milton⟩

fore·hoof \ˈfȯr-ˌhu̇f, -ˌhüf\ *n* (1726) : the hoof of a forefoot

for·eign \ˈfȯr-ən, ˈfär-\ *adj* [ME *forein,* fr. AF, fr. LL *foranus* on the outside, fr. L *foris* outside — more at FORUM] (13c) **1** : situated outside a place or country; *esp* : situated outside one's own country **2** : born in, belonging to, or characteristic of some place or country other than the one under consideration **3** : of, relating to, or proceeding from some other person or material thing than the one under consideration **4** : alien in character : not connected or pertinent **5** : related to or dealing with other nations **6 a** : occurring in an abnormal situation in the living body and often introduced from outside ⟨a ~ body lodged in the esophagus⟩ **b** : not recognized by the immune system as part of the self ⟨~ proteins⟩ **7** : not being within the jurisdiction of a political unit (as a state) ***syn*** see EXTRINSIC — **for·eign·ness** \-ən-nəs\ *n*

foreign affairs *n pl* (1611) : matters having to do with international relations and with the interests of the home country in foreign countries

foreign aid *n* (1947) : assistance (as economic aid) provided by one nation to another

foreign bill *n* (1682) : a bill of exchange that is drawn in one jurisdiction (as a country or state) and payable within another

for·eign–born \ˌfȯr-ən-ˈbȯrn, ˌfär-\ *adj* (1692) : foreign by birth

foreign correspondent *n* (1801) : a correspondent employed to send news or comment from a foreign country

for·eign·er \ˈfȯr-ə-nər, ˈfär-\ *n* (15c) **1** : a person belonging to or owing allegiance to a foreign country **2** *chiefly dial* : one not native to a place or community : STRANGER 1c

foreign exchange *n* (1691) **1** : a process of settling accounts or debts between persons residing in different countries **2** : foreign currency or current short-term credit instruments payable in such currency

for·eign·ism \ˈfȯr-ə-ˌni-zəm, ˈfär-\ *n* (1855) : something peculiar to a foreign language or people; *specif* : a foreign idiom or custom

foreign minister *n* (1678) : a governmental minister for foreign affairs

foreign office *n* (1820) : a government office (as a ministry) that deals with foreign affairs

foreign policy *n* (1804) : the policy of a sovereign state in its interaction with other sovereign states

foreign service *n* (1870) : the field force of a foreign office comprising diplomatic and consular personnel

[1]fore·judge \fər-ˈjəj, fȯr-\ *vt* [ME *forjuggen,* fr. AF *forjuger, forsjugger,* fr. *fors* outside (fr. L *foris*) + *juger* to judge] (15c) : to expel, oust, or put out by judgment of a court

[2]fore·judge \(ˌ)fȯr-ˈjəj\ *vt* (1561) : PREJUDGE

fore·know \(ˌ)fȯr-ˈnō\ *vt* **-knew** \-ˈnü, -ˈnyü\; **-known** \-ˈnōn\; **-know·ing** (14c) : to have previous knowledge of : know beforehand esp. by paranormal means or by revelation ***syn*** see FORESEE — **fore·knowl·edge** \ˈfȯr-ˌnä-lij, (ˌ)fȯr-ˈnä-\ *n*

fore·la·dy \ˈfȯr-ˌlā-dē\ *n* (ca. 1889) : FOREWOMAN

fore·land \ˈfȯr-lənd\ *n* (14c) : PROMONTORY, HEADLAND

fore·leg \ˈfȯr-ˌleg, -ˌlāg\ *n* (15c) : a front leg

fore·limb \-ˌlim\ *n* (ca. 1796) : a limb (as an arm, wing, fin, or leg) that is situated anteriorly ⟨the ~ of a bat⟩

fore·lock \-ˌläk\ *n* (1589) : a lock of hair growing from the front of the head

fore·man \ˈfȯr-mən\ *n* (15c) : a first or chief person: as **a** : a member of a jury who acts as chairman and spokesman **b (1)** : a chief and often specially trained worker who works with and usu. leads a gang or crew **(2)** : a person in charge of a group of workers, a particular operation, or a section of a plant — **fore·man·ship** \-ˌship\ *n*

fore·mast \ˈfȯr-ˌmast, -məst\ *n* (1582) : the mast nearest the bow of a ship

[1]fore·most \-ˌmōst\ *adj* [ME *formest,* fr. OE, superl. of *forma* first; akin to OHG *fruma* advantage, OE *fore* fore] (bef. 12c) **1** : first in a series or progression **2** : of first rank or position : PREEMINENT

[2]foremost *adv* (bef. 12c) **1** : in the first place **2** : most importantly ⟨first and ~⟩

fore·moth·er \ˈfȯr-ˌmə-t͟hər\ *n* (1582) : a female ancestor

fore·name \-ˌnām\ *n* (1533) : a name that precedes one's surname

fore·named \-ˌnāmd\ *adj* (13c) : named previously : AFORESAID

fore·noon \ˈfȯr-ˌnün, fȯr-ˈ\ *n* (15c) : the early part of the day ending with noon : MORNING

[1]fo·ren·sic \fə-ˈren(t)-sik, -ˈren-zik\ *adj* [L *forensis* public, forensic, fr. *forum* forum] (1659) **1** : belonging to, used in, or suitable to courts of judicature or to public discussion and debate **2** : ARGUMENTATIVE, RHETORICAL **3** : relating to or dealing with the application of scientific knowledge to legal problems ⟨~ medicine⟩ ⟨~ science⟩ ⟨~ pathologist⟩ ⟨~ experts⟩ — **fo·ren·si·cal·ly** \-si-k(ə-)lē, -zi-\ *adv*

[2]forensic *n* (1814) **1** : an argumentative exercise **2** *pl but sing or pl in constr* : the art or study of argumentative discourse **3** *pl but sing or pl in constr* : the application of scientific knowledge to legal problems; *esp* : scientific analysis of physical evidence (as from a crime scene)

fore·or·dain \ˌfȯr-ȯr-ˈdān\ *vt* (15c) : to dispose or appoint in advance : PREDESTINE — **fore·or·di·na·tion** \-ˌȯr-də-ˈnā-shən\ *n*

fore·part \ˈfȯr-ˌpärt\ *n* (14c) **1** : the anterior part of something **2** : the earlier part of a period of time

fore·passed *or* **fore·past** \-ˌpast\ *adj* (1557) : BYGONE

fore·paw \-ˌpȯ\ *n* (1782) : the paw of a foreleg

fore·peak \-ˌpēk\ *n* (1693) : the extreme forward lower compartment or tank usu. used for trimming or storage in a ship

fore·play \-ˌplā\ *n* (1929) **1** : erotic stimulation preceding sexual intercourse **2** : action or behavior that precedes an event

fore·quar·ter \-ˌkwȯ(r)-tər, -ˌkȯr-\ *n* (15c) : the front half of a lateral half of the body or carcass of a quadruped ⟨a ~ of beef⟩

fore·reach \fȯr-ˈrēch\ *vi* (1644) *of a ship* : to gain ground in tacking ~ *vt* : to gain on or go ahead of (a ship) when close-hauled

fore·run \-ˈrən\ *vt* **-ran** \-ˈran\; **-run; -run·ning** (bef. 12c) **1** : to run before **2** : to come before as a token of something to follow **3** : FORESTALL, ANTICIPATE

fore·run·ner \ˈfȯr-ˌrə-nər\ *n* (13c) **1** : one that precedes and indicates the approach of another: as **a** : a premonitory sign or symptom **b** : a skier who runs the course before the start of a race **2** : PREDECESSOR, ANCESTOR

syn FORERUNNER, PRECURSOR, HARBINGER, HERALD mean one that goes before or announces the coming of another. FORERUNNER is applicable to anything that serves as a sign or presage ⟨the blockade was the *forerunner* of war⟩. PRECURSOR applies to a person or thing paving the way for the success or accomplishment of another ⟨18th century poets like Burns were *precursors* of the Romantics⟩. HARBINGER and HERALD both apply, chiefly figuratively, to one that proclaims or announces the coming or arrival of a notable event ⟨their early victory was the *harbinger* of a winning season⟩ ⟨the *herald* of a new age in medicine⟩.

fore·said \-ˌsed\ *adj* (bef. 12c) *archaic* : AFORESAID

fore·sail \ˈfȯr-ˌsāl, -səl\ *n* (15c) **1** : the lowest sail set on the foremast of a square-rigged ship or schooner — see SAIL illustration **2** : the sole or principal headsail (as of a sloop, cutter, or schooner)

fore·see \fȯr-ˈsē\ *vt* **-saw** \-ˈsȯ\; **-seen** \-ˈsēn\; **-see·ing** (bef. 12c) : to see (as a development) beforehand — **fore·seer** \fȯr-ˈsē-ər, -ˈsir\ *n*

syn FORESEE, FOREKNOW, DIVINE, ANTICIPATE mean to know beforehand. FORESEE implies nothing about how the knowledge is derived and may apply to ordinary reasoning and experience ⟨economists should have *foreseen* the recession⟩. FOREKNOW usu. implies supernatural assistance, as through revelation ⟨if only we could *foreknow* our own destinies⟩. DIVINE adds to FORESEE the suggestion of exceptional wisdom or discernment ⟨was able to *divine* Europe's rapid recovery from the war⟩. ANTICIPATE implies taking action about or responding emotionally to something before it happens ⟨the waiter *anticipated* our every need⟩.

fore·see·able \-ˈsē-ə-bəl\ *adj* (1804) **1** : being such as may be reasonably anticipated ⟨~ problems⟩ **2** : lying within the range for which forecasts are possible ⟨in the ~ future⟩ — **fore·see·abil·i·ty** \-ˌsē-ə-ˈbi-lə-tē\ *n*

fore·shad·ow \-ˈsha-(ˌ)dō\ *vt* (1577) : to represent, indicate, or typify beforehand : PREFIGURE — **fore·shad·ow·er** \-də-wər\ *n*

fore·shank \ˈfȯr-ˌshaŋk\ *n* (1924) : the upper part of the foreleg of cattle; *also* : meat cut from this part

fore·sheet \-ˌshēt\ *n* (1667) **1** : one of the sheets of a foresail **2** *pl* : the forward part of an open boat

fore·shock \-ˌshäk\ *n* (1902) : any of the usu. minor tremors commonly preceding the principal shock of an earthquake

fore·shore \-ˌshȯr\ *n* (1764) **1** : a strip of land margining a body of water **2** : the part of a seashore between high-water and low-water marks

fore·short·en \fȯr-ˈshȯr-tᵊn\ *vt* (1606) **1** : to shorten by proportionately contracting in the direction of depth so that an illusion of projection or extension in space is obtained **2** : to make more compact : ABRIDGE, SHORTEN

fore·side \ˈfȯr-ˌsīd\ *n* (14c) : the front side or part : FRONT

fore·sight \ˈfȯr-ˌsīt\ *n* (14c) **1** : an act or the power of foreseeing : PRESCIENCE **2** : provident care : PRUDENCE ⟨had the ~ to invest his money wisely⟩ **3** : an act of looking forward; *also* : a view forward — **fore·sight·ed** \-ˌsī-təd\ *adj* — **fore·sight·ed·ly** *adv* — **fore·sight·ed·ness** *n* — **fore·sight·ful** \-ˌsīt-fəl\ *adj*

fore·skin \-ˌskin\ *n* (1530) : a fold of skin that covers the glans of the penis — called also *prepuce*

fore·speak \fȯr-ˈspēk\ *vt* **-spoke** \-ˈspōk\; **-spo·ken** \-ˈspō-kən\; **-speak·ing** (14c) **1** *archaic* : FORETELL, PREDICT **2** *archaic* : to arrange for in advance

[1]**for·est** \ˈfȯr-əst, ˈfär-\ *n, often attrib* [ME, fr. AF, fr. LL *forestis (silva)* unenclosed (woodland), fr. L *foris* outside — more at FORUM] (13c) **1** : a dense growth of trees and underbrush covering a large tract **2** : a tract of wooded land in England formerly owned by the sovereign and used for game **3** : something resembling a forest esp. in profusion or lushness ⟨a ~ of microphones⟩ ⟨a kelp ~⟩ — **for·est·al** \-əs-tᵊl\ *or* **fo·res·tial** \fə-ˈres-tē-əl, fō-, -ˈres(h)-chəl\ *adj* — **for·est·ed** \ˈfȯr-ə-stəd, ˈfär-\ *adj*

[2]**forest** *vt* (ca. 1828) : to cover with trees or forest ⟨land densely ~*ed* with firs⟩ — **for·es·ta·tion** \ˌfȯr-ə-ˈstā-shən, ˌfär-\ *n*

fore·stage \ˈfȯr-ˌstāj\ *n* (1923) : APRON 2e

fore·stall \fȯr-ˈstȯl\ *vt* [ME, fr. *forstall* act of waylaying, fr. OE *foresteall,* fr. *fore-* + *steall* position, stall] (bef. 12c) **1** : to prevent the normal trading in by buying or diverting goods or by persuading persons to raise prices **2** *archaic* : INTERCEPT **3** *obs* : OBSTRUCT, BESET **4** : to exclude, hinder, or prevent by prior occupation or measures **5** : to get ahead of : ANTICIPATE ***syn*** see PREVENT — **fore·stall·er** *n* — **fore·stall·ment** \-ˈstȯl-mənt\ *n*

fore·stay \ˈfȯr-ˌstā\ *n* (13c) : a stay from the foremast to the foredeck or bow of a ship

fore·stay·sail \-ˌsāl, -səl\ *n* (1742) : the triangular aftermost headsail of a schooner, ketch, or yawl set on the forestay — see SAIL illustration

for·est·er \ˈfȯr-ə-stər, ˈfär-\ *n* [ME *forster, forester,* fr. AF *forester,* fr. *forest*] (14c) **1** : a person trained in forestry **2** : an inhabitant of a forest **3** : any of various noctuid woodland moths (subfamily Agaristinae) **4** *cap* : a member of a major benevolent and fraternal order

forest floor *n* (1849) : the richly organic layer of soil and debris characteristic of forested land

forest green *n* (1810) : a dark yellowish or moderate olive green

for·est·land \ˈfȯr-əst-ˌland, ˈfär-\ *n* (1649) : land covered with forest or reserved for the growth of forests

forest ranger *n* (1830) : an officer charged with the patrolling and guarding of a forest; *esp* : one in charge of the management and protection of a portion of a public forest

for·est·ry \ˈfȯr-ə-strē, ˈfär-\ *n* (1823) **1** : FORESTLAND **2 a** : the science of developing, caring for, or cultivating forests **b** : the management of growing timber

forest tent caterpillar *n* (1854) : a moth (*Malacosoma disstria* of the family Lasiocampidae) whose orange-marked larva is a tent caterpillar and a serious defoliator of deciduous trees

foreswear, foresworn *var of* FORSWEAR, FORSWORN

[1]**fore·taste** \ˈfȯr-ˌtāst\ *n* (15c) **1** : a small anticipatory sample **2** : an advance indication or warning ***syn*** see PROSPECT

[2]**fore·taste** \fȯr-ˈtāst, ˈfȯr-ˌ\ *vt* (15c) : to taste beforehand : ANTICIPATE

fore·tell \fȯr-ˈtel\ *vt* **-told** \-ˈtōld\; **-tell·ing** (14c) : to tell beforehand : PREDICT — **fore·tell·er** *n*

syn FORETELL, PREDICT, FORECAST, PROPHESY, PROGNOSTICATE mean to tell beforehand. FORETELL applies to the telling of the coming of a future event by any procedure or any source of information ⟨seers *foretold* the calamity⟩. PREDICT commonly implies inference from facts or accepted laws of nature ⟨astronomers *predicted* an eclipse⟩. FORECAST adds the implication of anticipating eventualities and differs from PREDICT in being usually concerned with probabilities rather than certainties ⟨*forecast* snow⟩. PROPHESY connotes inspired or mystic knowledge of the future esp. as the fulfilling of divine threats or promises ⟨*prophesying* a new messiah⟩. PROGNOSTICATE is used less often than the other words; it may suggest learned or skilled interpretation, but more often it is simply a colorful substitute for PREDICT OR PROPHESY ⟨*prognosticating* the future⟩.

[1]**fore·thought** \ˈfȯr-ˌthȯt\ *n* (14c) **1** : a thinking or planning out in advance : PREMEDITATION **2** : consideration for the future

[2]**forethought** *adj* (15c) *archaic* : AFORETHOUGHT

fore·thought·ful \-fəl\ *adj* (ca. 1810) : full of or having forethought — **fore·thought·ful·ly** \-fə-lē\ *adv* — **fore·thought·ful·ness** *n*

fore·time \ˈfȯr-ˌtīm\ *n* (ca. 1540) : former or past time : the time before the present

[1]**fore·to·ken** \ˈfȯr-ˌtō-kən\ *n* (bef. 12c) : a premonitory sign

[2]**fore·to·ken** \fȯr-ˈtō-kən\ *vt* **fore·to·kened; fore·to·ken·ing** \-ˈtōk-niŋ, -ˈtō-kə-\ (15c) : to indicate or warn of in advance

fore·top \ˈfȯr-ˌtäp, -təp\ *n* (1509) : the platform at the head of a ship's foremast

fore·top·man \ˈfȯr-ˌtäp-mən, -təp-\ *n* (1816) : a sailor on duty on the foremast and above

fore–top·mast \ˈfȯr-ˌtäp-məst, -təp-ˌmast\ *n* (1626) : a mast next above the foremast

[1]**for·ev·er** \fə-ˈrev-ər, fō-; *Southern often* fə-ˈe-və\ *adv* (ca. 1500) **1** : for a limitless time ⟨wants to live ~⟩ **2** : at all times : CONTINUALLY ⟨is ~ making bad puns⟩

[2]**forever** *n* (1858) : a seemingly interminable time : excessively long ⟨it took her ~ to find the answer⟩

for·ev·er·more \-ˌre-və(r)-ˈmȯr\ *adv* (1641) : FOREVER 1

for·ev·er·ness \-ˈre-vər-nəs\ *n* (1945) : ETERNITY

fore·warn \fȯr-ˈwȯrn\ *vt* (14c) : to warn in advance

fore·warn·ing \fȯr-ˈwȯr-niŋ\ *n* (1548) **1** : a warning given in advance **2** : the state of being warned in advance

fore·wing \ˈfȯr-ˌwiŋ\ *n* (ca. 1889) : either of the anterior wings of a 4-winged insect

fore·wom·an \ˈfȯr-ˌwu̇-mən\ *n* (1620) : a woman who is a foreman

fore·word \ˈfȯr-(ˌ)wərd\ *n* (1842) : prefatory comments (as for a book) esp. when written by someone other than the author

fore·worn *archaic var of* FORWORN

[1]**for·feit** \ˈfȯr-fət\ *n* [ME *forfait,* fr. AF, fr. pp. of *forfaire, forsfaire* to commit a crime, forfeit, fr. *fors* outside (fr. L *foris*) + *faire* to do, fr. L *facere* — more at FORUM, DO] (14c) **1** : something forfeited or subject to being forfeited (as for a crime, offense, or neglect of duty) : PENALTY **2** : forfeiture esp. of civil rights **3 a** : something deposited (as for making a mistake in a game) and then redeemed on payment of a fine **b** *pl* : a game in which forfeits are exacted

[2]**forfeit** *vt* (14c) **1** : to lose or lose the right to esp. by some error, offense, or crime **2** : to subject to confiscation as a forfeit; *also* : ABANDON, GIVE UP — **for·feit·able** \-fə-tə-bəl\ *adj* — **for·feit·er** *n*

[3]**forfeit** *adj* (14c) : forfeited or subject to forfeiture

for·fei·ture \ˈfȯr-fə-ˌchu̇r, -chər, -ˌt(y)u̇r\ *n* (14c) **1** : the act of forfeiting : the loss of property or money because of a breach of a legal obligation **2** : something (as money or property) that is forfeited : PENALTY

for·fend \fȯr-ˈfend\ *vt* (14c) **1 a** *archaic* : FORBID **b** : to ward off : PREVENT **2** : PROTECT, PRESERVE

for·gath·er *or* **fore·gath·er** \fȯr-ˈga-t͟hər\ *vi* (1513) **1** : to come together : ASSEMBLE **2** : to meet someone usu. by chance

[1]**forge** \ˈfȯrj\ *n* [ME, fr. AF, fr. L *fabrica,* fr. *fabr-, faber* smith] (13c) **1** : a furnace or a shop with its furnace where metal is heated and wrought : SMITHY **2** : a workshop where wrought iron is produced or where iron is made malleable

[2]**forge** *vb* **forged; forg·ing** *vt* (14c) **1 a** : to form (as metal) by heating and hammering **b** : to form (metal) by a mechanical or hydraulic press with or without heat **2** : to make or imitate falsely esp. with intent to defraud : COUNTERFEIT ⟨~ a document⟩ ⟨~ a signature⟩ **3** : to form or bring into being esp. by an expenditure of effort ⟨working to ~ party unity⟩ ~ *vi* **1** : to work at a forge **2** : to commit forgery — **forge·abil·i·ty** \ˌfȯr-jə-ˈbi-lə-tē\ *n* — **forge·able** \ˈfȯr-jə-bəl\ *adj*

[3]**forge** *vi* **forged; forg·ing** [origin unknown] (1611) **1** : to move forward slowly and steadily ⟨the ship *forged* ahead through heavy seas⟩ **2** : to move with a sudden increase of speed and power ⟨*forged* into the lead⟩ ⟨*forged* ahead in marketing the product⟩

forg·er \ˈfȯr-jər\ *n* ([2]*forge*) (14c) **1** : one that forges metals **2 a** : a person who falsifies; *esp* : a creator of false tales **b** : a person guilty of forgery

forg·ery \ˈfȯrj-rē, ˈfȯr-jə-\ *n, pl* **-er·ies** (1583) **1** *archaic* : INVENTION **2** : something forged **3** : an act of forging; *esp* : the crime of falsely and fraudulently making or altering a document (as a check)

for·get \fər-ˈget, fȯr-\ *vb* **-got** \-ˈgät\; **-got·ten** \-ˈgä-tᵊn\ *or* **-got; -get·ting** [ME, fr. OE *forgietan,* fr. *for-* + *-gietan* (akin to ON *geta* to get)] *vt* (bef. 12c) **1 a** : to lose the remembrance of : be unable to think of or recall ⟨I ~ his name⟩ **b** *obs* : to cease from doing **2** : to treat with inattention or disregard ⟨*forgot* their old friends⟩ **3 a** : to disregard intentionally : OVERLOOK — usu. used in the imperative ⟨I shouldn't have said that, so just ~ it⟩ **b** : to give up hope for or expectation of — usu. used in the imperative ⟨as for prompt service, ~ it⟩ ~ *vi* **1** : to cease remembering or noticing ⟨forgive and ~⟩ **2** : to fail to become mindful at the proper time ⟨*forgot* about paying the bill⟩ ***syn*** see NEGLECT — **for·get·ter** *n* — **forget oneself** : to lose one's dignity, temper, or self-control

for·get·ful \-ˈget-fəl\ *adj* (14c) **1** : likely to forget **2** : characterized by negligent failure to remember : NEGLECTFUL **3** : inducing oblivion ⟨~ sleep⟩ — **for·get·ful·ly** \-fə-lē\ *adv* — **for·get·ful·ness** *n*

for·ge·tive \ˈfȯr-jə-tiv\ *adj* [prob. fr. [2]*forge* + *-tive* (as in *inventive*)] (1597) *archaic* : INVENTIVE, IMAGINATIVE

for·get–me–not \fər-ˈget-mē-ˌnät, fȯr-\ *n* (1532) : any of a genus (*Myosotis*) of small herbs of the borage family having usu. bright blue or white flowers usu. arranged in a curving spike

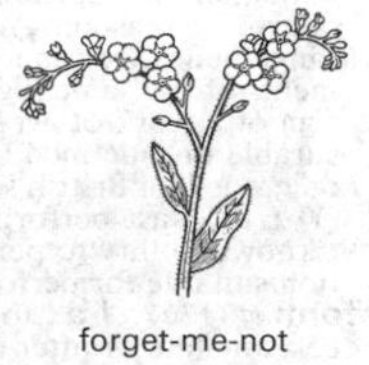
forget-me-not

for·get·ta·ble \fər-ˈge-tə-bəl, fȯr-\ *adj* (1845) : fit or likely to be forgotten ⟨a ~ movie⟩

forging *n* (14c) **1** : the art or process of forging **2** : a piece of forged work **3** : FORGERY 3

for·give \fər-ˈgiv, fȯr-\ *vb* **-gave** \-ˈgāv\; **-giv·en** \-ˈgi-vən\; **-giv·ing** [ME, fr. OE *forgifan,* fr. *for-* + *gifan* to give] *vt* (bef. 12c) **1 a** : to give up resentment of or claim to requital for ⟨~ an insult⟩ **b** : to grant relief from payment of ⟨~ a debt⟩ **2** : to cease to feel resentment against (an offender) : PARDON ⟨~ one's enemies⟩ ~ *vi* : to grant forgiveness ***syn*** see EXCUSE — **for·giv·able** \-ˈgi-və-bəl\ *adj* — **for·giv·ably** \-blē\ *adv* — **for·giv·er** *n*

for·give·ness \-ˈgiv-nəs\ *n* (bef. 12c) : the act of forgiving

forgiving *adj* (1623) **1** : willing or able to forgive **2** : allowing room for error or weakness ⟨designed to be a ~ tennis racquet⟩ — **for·giv·ing·ly** \-ˈgi-viŋ-lē\ *adv* — **for·giv·ing·ness** *n*

for·go *also* **fore·go** \fȯr-ˈgō\ *vt* **-went** \-ˈwent\; **-gone** \-ˈgȯn *also* -ˈgän\; **-go·ing** \-ˈgō-iŋ, -ˈgȯ(-)iŋ\ [ME, fr. OE *forgān* to pass by, forgo, fr. *for-* + *gān* to go] (bef. 12c) **1** : to give up the enjoyment or advantage of : do without **2** *archaic* : FORSAKE — **for·go·er** \-ˈgō-ər\ *n*

forgotten man *n* (1925) : a person or category of persons that receives less attention than is merited

for instance \fə-ˈrin(t)-stənts, ˈfrin(t)-\ *n* (1959) : EXAMPLE ⟨I'll give you a *for instance*⟩

fo·rint \ˈfȯr-ˌint\ *n, pl* **forints** *also* **forint** [Hung] (1946) — see MONEY table

[1]**fork** \ˈfȯrk\ *n* [ME *forke,* fr. OE & AF; OE *forca* & AF *furke,* fr. L *furca*] (bef. 12c) **1** : an implement with two or more prongs used esp. for taking up (as in eating), pitching, or digging **2** : a forked part, tool, or piece of equipment **3 a** : a division into branches or the place where something divides into branches **b** : CONFLUENCE **4** : one of the branches into which something forks **5** : an attack by one chess piece (as a knight) on two pieces simultaneously — **fork·ful** \-ˌfu̇l\ *n*

[2]**fork** *vi* (15c) **1** : to divide into two or more branches ⟨where the road ~*s*⟩ **2 a** : to use or work with a fork **b** : to turn into a fork ~ *vt* **1** : to give the form of a fork to ⟨~*ing* her fingers⟩ **2** : to attack (two chessmen) simultaneously **3** : to raise, pitch, dig, or work with a fork

⟨~ hay⟩ **4 :** PAY, CONTRIBUTE — used with *over, out,* or *up* ⟨had to ~ over $5000⟩ — **fork·er** *n*

fork·ball \ˈfȯrk-ˌbȯl\ *n* (1936) **:** a baseball pitch in which the ball is gripped between the forked index and middle fingers

forked \ˈfȯrkt, ˈfȯr-kəd\ *adj* (13c) **1 :** resembling a fork esp. in having one end divided into two or more branches or points ⟨~ lightning⟩ **2 :** shaped like a fork or having a forked part ⟨a ~ road⟩

forked tongue *n* (1833) **:** intent to mislead or deceive — usu. used in the phrase *to speak with forked tongue*

fork·lift \ˈfȯrk-ˌlift\ *n* (1944) **:** a self-propelled machine for hoisting and transporting heavy objects by means of steel fingers inserted under the load

fork–ten·der \ˈfȯrk-ˈten-dər\ *adj* (1973) **:** tender enough to be easily pierced or cut with a fork ⟨~ filet mignon⟩

forky \ˈfȯr-kē\ *adj* **fork·i·er; -est** (1695) **:** FORKED ⟨a ~ beard⟩

for·lorn \fər-ˈlȯrn, fȯr-\ *adj* [ME *forloren,* fr. OE, pp. of *forlēosan* to lose, fr. *for-* + *lēosan* to lose — more at LOSE] (bef. 12c) **1 a :** BEREFT, FORSAKEN ⟨left quite ~ of hope⟩ **b :** sad and lonely because of isolation or desertion **:** DESOLATE ⟨a ~ landscape⟩ **2 :** being in poor condition **:** MISERABLE, WRETCHED ⟨~ tumbledown buildings⟩ **3 :** nearly hopeless ⟨a ~ attempt⟩ ***syn*** see ALONE — **for·lorn·ly** *adv* — **for·lorn·ness** \-ˈlȯrn-nəs\ *n*

forlorn hope *n* [by folk etymology fr. D *verloren hoop,* lit., lost band] (1579) **1 :** a body of men selected to perform a perilous service **2 :** a desperate or extremely difficult enterprise

[1]**form** \ˈfȯrm\ *n* [ME *forme,* fr. AF *furme, forme,* fr. L *forma* form, beauty] (13c) **1 a :** the shape and structure of something as distinguished from its material **b :** a body (as of a person) esp. in its external appearance or as distinguished from the face **:** FIGURE **c** *archaic* **:** BEAUTY **2 :** the essential nature of a thing as distinguished from its matter: as **a :** IDEA 1a **b :** the component of a thing that determines its kind **3 a :** established method of expression or proceeding **:** procedure according to rule or rote; *also* **:** a standard or expectation based on past experience **:** PRECEDENT ⟨true to ~, the champions won again⟩ **b :** a prescribed and set order of words **:** FORMULA ⟨the ~ of the marriage service⟩ **4 :** a printed or typed document with blank spaces for insertion of required or requested information ⟨tax ~*s*⟩ **5 a (1) :** conduct regulated by extraneous controls (as of custom or etiquette) **:** CEREMONY **(2) :** show without substance **b :** manner or conduct as tested by a prescribed or accepted standard ⟨rudeness is simply bad ~⟩ **c :** manner or style of performing or accomplishing according to recognized standards of technique ⟨a strong swimmer but weak on ~⟩ **6 a :** the resting place or nest of a hare **b :** a long seat **:** BENCH **7 a :** a supporting frame model of the human figure or part (as the torso) of the human figure usu. used for displaying apparel **b :** a proportioned and often adjustable model for fitting clothes **c :** a mold in which concrete is placed to set **8 :** the printing type or other matter arranged and secured in a chase ready for printing **9 a :** one of the different modes of existence, action, or manifestation of a particular thing or substance **:** KIND ⟨one ~ of respiratory disorder⟩ ⟨a ~ of art⟩ **b :** a distinguishable group of organisms **c :** LINGUISTIC FORM **d :** one of the different aspects a word may take as a result of inflection or change of spelling or pronunciation ⟨verbal ~*s*⟩ **e :** a mathematical expression of a particular type ⟨a bilinear ~⟩ ⟨a polynomial ~⟩ **10 a (1) :** orderly method of arrangement (as in the presentation of ideas) **:** manner of coordinating elements (as of an artistic production or course of reasoning) **(2) :** a particular kind or instance of such arrangement ⟨the sonnet is a poetical ~⟩ **b :** PATTERN, SCHEMA ⟨arguments of the same logical ~⟩ **c :** the structural element, plan, or design of a work of art — compare CONTENT 2c **d :** a visible and measurable unit defined by a contour **:** a bounded surface or volume **11 :** a grade in a British school or in some American private schools **12 a (1) :** the past performance of a race horse **(2) :** RACING FORM **b :** known ability to perform ⟨a singer at the top of her ~⟩ **c :** condition suitable for performing (as in athletic competition) ⟨back on ~⟩

[2]**form** *vt* (13c) **1 a :** to give a particular shape to **:** shape or mold into a certain state or after a particular model ⟨~ the dough into a ball⟩ ⟨a state ~*ed* along republican lines⟩ **b :** to arrange themselves in ⟨the dancers ~*ed* a line⟩ **c :** to model by instruction and discipline ⟨a mind ~*ed* by classical education⟩ **2 :** to give form or shape to **:** FASHION, CONSTRUCT **3 :** to serve to make up or constitute **:** be an essential or basic element of **4 :** DEVELOP, ACQUIRE ⟨~ a habit⟩ **5 :** to arrange in order **:** DRAW UP **6 a :** to assume an inflection so as to produce (as a tense) ⟨~*s* the past in *-ed*⟩ **b :** to combine to make (a compound word) ~ *vi* **1 :** to become formed or shaped **2 :** to take form **:** come into existence **:** ARISE **3 :** to take on a definite form, shape, or arrangement — **form·abil·i·ty** \ˌfȯr-mə-ˈbi-lə-tē\ *n* — **form·able** \ˈfȯr-mə-bəl\ *adj* — **form on :** to take up a formation next to

form- *or* **formo-** *comb form* [*formic*] **:** formic acid ⟨*formate*⟩

-form *adj comb form* [F & L; F *-forme,* fr. L *-formis,* fr. *forma*] **:** in the form or shape of **:** resembling ⟨fili*form*⟩

[1]**for·mal** \ˈfȯr-məl\ *adj* [ME, fr. L *formalis,* fr. *forma*] (14c) **1 a :** belonging to or constituting the form or essence of a thing ⟨~ cause⟩ **b :** relating to or involving the outward form, structure, relationships, or arrangement of elements rather than content ⟨~ logic⟩ ⟨a ~ style of painting⟩ ⟨a ~ approach to comparative linguistics⟩ **2 a :** following or according with established form, custom, or rule ⟨lacked ~ schooling⟩ ⟨a ~ dinner party⟩ ⟨~ attire⟩ **b :** done in due or lawful form ⟨a ~ contract⟩ ⟨received ~ recognition⟩ **3 a :** characterized by punctilious respect for form **:** METHODICAL ⟨very ~ in all his dealings⟩ **b :** rigidly ceremonious **:** PRIM **4 :** having the appearance without the substance ⟨~ Christians who go to church only at Easter⟩ ***syn*** see CEREMONIAL — **for·mal·ly** \-mə-lē\ *adv* — **for·mal·ness** *n*

[2]**formal** *n* (1605) **:** something (as a dance or a dress) formal in character

[3]**formal** *adj* [*form*ula + [1]*-al*] (ca. 1934) **:** [3]MOLAR

form·al·de·hyde \fȯr-ˈmal-də-ˌhīd, fər-\ *n* [ISV *form-* + *aldehyde*] (1872) **:** a colorless pungent irritating gas CH_2O used chiefly in aqueous solution as a disinfectant and preservative and in chemical synthesis

for·ma·lin \ˈfȯr-mə-lən, -ˌlēn\ *n* [*Formalin,* a trademark] (1893) **:** a clear aqueous solution of formaldehyde containing a small amount of methanol used esp. as a preservative

for·mal·ise *Brit var of* FORMALIZE

for·mal·ism \ˈfȯr-mə-ˌli-zəm\ *n* (1839) **1 :** the practice or the doctrine of strict adherence to prescribed or external forms (as in religion or art); *also* **:** an instance of this **2 :** marked attention to arrangement, style, or artistic means (as in art or literature) usu. with corresponding de-emphasis of content — **for·mal·ist** \-list\ *n or adj* — **for·mal·is·tic** \ˌfȯr-mə-ˈlis-tik\ *adj*

for·mal·i·ty \fȯr-ˈma-lə-tē\ *n, pl* **-ties** (1597) **1 :** compliance with formal or conventional rules **:** CEREMONY **2 :** the quality or state of being formal **3 :** an established form or procedure that is required or conventional ⟨the interview was just a ~⟩

for·mal·ize \ˈfȯr-mə-ˌlīz\ *vt* **-ized; -iz·ing** (1646) **1 :** to give a certain or definite form to **:** SHAPE **2 a :** to make formal **b :** to give formal status or approval to — **for·mal·iz·able** \-ˌlī-zə-bəl\ *adj* — **for·mal·i·za·tion** \ˌfȯr-mə-lə-ˈzā-shən\ *n* — **for·mal·iz·er** \ˈfȯr-mə-ˌlī-zər\ *n*

form·am·ide \fȯr-ˈma-ˌmīd; ˈfȯr-mə-ˌmīd, -məd\ *n* [ISV *form-* + *amide*] (1852) **:** a colorless hygroscopic liquid $CHONH_2$ used chiefly as a solvent

for·mant \ˈfȯr-mənt, -ˌmant\ *n* (1901) **:** a characteristic component of the quality of a speech sound; *specif* **:** any of several resonance bands held to determine the phonetic quality of a vowel

[1]**for·mat** \ˈfȯr-ˌmat\ *n* [F or G; F, fr. G, fr. L *formatus,* pp. of *formare* to form, fr. *forma*] (1840) **1 :** the shape, size, and general makeup (as of something printed) **2 :** general plan of organization, arrangement, or choice of material (as for a television show) **3 :** a method of organizing data (as for storage) ⟨various file ~*s*⟩

[2]**format** *vt* **for·mat·ted; for·mat·ting** (1964) **1 :** to arrange (as material to be printed or stored data) in a particular format **2 :** to prepare (as a computer disk) for storing data in a particular format — **for·mat·ter** *n*

for·mate \ˈfȯr-ˌmāt\ *n* (1807) **:** a salt or ester of formic acid

for·ma·tion \fȯr-ˈmā-shən\ *n* (15c) **1 :** an act of giving form or shape to something or of taking form **:** DEVELOPMENT **2 :** something that is formed ⟨new word ~*s*⟩ **3 :** the manner in which a thing is formed **:** STRUCTURE ⟨the peculiar ~ of the heart⟩ **4 :** a major kind of plant growth (as forest, grassland, or tundra) characteristic of a broad ecological region **5 a :** any igneous, sedimentary, or metamorphic rock represented as a unit **b :** any sedimentary bed or consecutive series of beds sufficiently homogeneous or distinctive to be a unit **6 :** an arrangement of a body or group of persons or things in some prescribed manner or for a particular purpose ⟨flying in ~⟩

[1]**for·ma·tive** \ˈfȯr-mə-tiv\ *adj* (15c) **1 a :** giving or capable of giving form **:** CONSTRUCTIVE ⟨a ~ influence⟩ **b :** used in word formation or inflection **2 :** capable of alteration by growth and development; *also* **:** producing new cells and tissues **3 :** of, relating to, or characterized by formative effects or formation ⟨~ years⟩ — **for·ma·tive·ly** *adv*

[2]**formative** *n* (1816) **:** the element (as a suffix) in a word that serves to give the word appropriate form and is not part of the base

form class *n* (1921) **:** a class of linguistic forms that can be used in the same position in a construction and that have one or more morphological or syntactical features in common

form–critical *adj* (1933) **:** based on or applying form criticism

form criticism *n* (1928) **:** a method of criticism for determining the sources and historicity of biblical writings through analysis of the writings in terms of ancient literary forms and oral traditions (as love poems, parables, and proverbs) — **form critic** *n*

forme \ˈfȯm, ˈfȯrm\ *n* (15c) *Brit* **:** FORM 8

formed \ˈfȯrmd\ *adj* (1565) **:** organized in a way characteristic of living matter ⟨mitochondria are ~ bodies of the cell⟩

for·mée \ˈfȯr-ˌmā, fȯr-ˈ\ *adj* [F, fem. pp. of *former* to form, fr. OF, fr. L *formare*] (15c) *of a heraldic cross* **:** having the arms narrow at the center and expanding toward the ends — see CROSS illustration

[1]**for·mer** \ˈfȯr-mər\ *adj* [ME, fr. *forme* first, fr. OE *forma* — more at FOREMOST] (12c) **1 a :** coming before in time **b :** of, relating to, or occurring in the past ⟨~ correspondence⟩ **2 :** preceding in place or arrangement **:** FOREGOING ⟨the ~ part of the chapter⟩ **3 :** first in order of two or more things cited or understood ⟨of the two given, the ~ spelling is more common⟩ ⟨of the two spellings, the ~ is more common⟩ **4 :** having been previously **:** ONETIME ⟨a ~ athlete⟩ ***syn*** see PRECEDING

[2]**form·er** \ˈfȯr-mər\ *n* (14c) **1 :** one that forms **2** *chiefly Brit* **:** a member of a school form — usu. used in combination ⟨sixth ~⟩

for·mer·ly \ˈfȯr-mə(r)-lē\ *adv* (1534) **1 :** at an earlier time **:** PREVIOUSLY **2** *obs* **:** just before

form·fit·ting \ˈfȯrm-ˌfi-tiŋ\ *adj* (1897) **:** conforming to the outline of the body **:** fitting snugly ⟨a ~ sweater⟩

form·ful \ˈfȯrm-fəl\ *adj* (1753) **:** exhibiting or notable for form

form genus *n* (1873) **:** an artificial taxonomic category established for organisms (as imperfect fungi) of obscure true relationships

For·mi·ca \fȯr-ˈmī-kə, fər-\ *trademark* — used for any of various laminated plastic products used esp. for surface finish

for·mic acid \ˈfȯr-mik-\ *n* [irreg. fr. L *formica* ant — more at PISMIRE] (1790) **:** a colorless pungent fuming vesicant liquid acid CH_2O_2 found esp. in ants and in many plants and used chiefly in dyeing and finishing textiles

for·mi·cary \ˈfȯr-mə-ˌker-ē\ *n, pl* **-car·ies** [ML *formicarium,* fr. L *formica*] (1816) **:** an ant nest

for·mi·da·ble \ˈfȯr-mə-də-bəl; fȯr-ˈmi-, fər-ˈmi-\ *adj* [ME, fr. L *formidabilis,* fr. *formidare* to fear, fr. *formido* terror, bogey; akin to Gk *mormō* bogey] (15c) **1 :** causing fear, dread, or apprehension ⟨a ~ prospect⟩ **2 :** having qualities that discourage approach or attack **3 :** tending to inspire awe or wonder **:** IMPRESSIVE — **for·mi·da·bil·i·ty** \ˌfȯr-mə-də-ˈbi-lə-tē; fȯr-ˌmi-, fər-ˌ\ *n* — **for·mi·da·ble·ness** \ˈfȯr-mə-də-bəl-nəs; fȯr-ˈmi-, fər-ˈ\ *n* — **for·mi·da·bly** \-blē\ *adv*

form·less \ˈfȯrm-ləs\ *adj* (1591) **1 :** having no regular form or shape **2 :** lacking order or arrangement **3 :** having no physical existence — **form·less·ly** *adv* — **form·less·ness** *n*

form letter *n* (1909) **1 :** a letter on a subject of frequent recurrence that can be sent to different people without essential change except in the address **2 :** a letter for mass circulation that is printed in many copies and has a very general salutation (as *Dear Friend*)

formo- — see FORM-

For·mo·san termite \fȯr-ˈmō-sᵊn-, fər-, -zᵊn-\ *n* [*Formosa* (Taiwan)] (1968) **:** a large termite (*Coptotermes formosanus* of the family Rhinotermitidae) native to Taiwan and nearby areas and introduced into Hawaii, California, and some southern U.S. states where it is a destructive pest of wooden structures — called also *Formosan subterranean termite*

¹for·mu·la \ˈfȯr-myə-lə\ *n, pl* **-las** *or* **-lae** \-ˌlē, -ˌlī\ [L, dim. of *forma* form] (1618) **1 a :** a set form of words for use in a ceremony or ritual **b :** a conventionalized statement intended to express some fundamental truth or principle esp. as a basis for negotiation or action **2 a** (1) **:** RECIPE (2) **:** PRESCRIPTION **b :** a milk mixture or substitute for feeding an infant **3 a :** a general fact, rule, or principle expressed in usu. mathematical symbols **b :** a symbolic expression of the chemical composition or constitution of a substance **c :** a group of symbols (as letters and numbers) associated to express facts or data (as the number and kinds of teeth in the jaw) concisely **d :** a combination of signs in a logical calculus **4 :** a customary or set form or method allowing little room for originality — **for·mu·la·ic** \ˌfȯr-myə-ˈlā-ik\ *adj* — **for·mu·la·ical·ly** \-ˈlā-ə-k(ə-)lē\ *adv*

²formula *adj* (1951) **:** of, relating to, or being an open-wheel open-cockpit rear-engine racing car conforming to prescribed specifications as to size, weight, and engine displacement

for·mu·la·rize \ˈfȯr-myə-lə-ˌrīz\ *vt* **-rized; -riz·ing** (1852) **:** to state in or reduce to a formula **:** FORMULATE — **for·mu·la·ri·za·tion** \ˌfȯr-myə-lə-rə-ˈzā-shən\ *n* — **for·mu·la·riz·er** \ˈfȯr-myə-lə-ˌrī-zər\ *n*

for·mu·lary \ˈfȯr-myə-ˌler-ē\ *n, pl* **-lar·ies** (1541) **1 :** a collection of prescribed forms (as oaths or prayers) **2 :** FORMULA 1 **3 :** a book listing medicinal substances and formulas — **formulary** *adj*

for·mu·late \ˈfȯr-myə-ˌlāt\ *vt* **-lat·ed; -lat·ing** (1855) **1 a :** to reduce to or express in a formula **b :** to put into a systematized statement or expression **c :** DEVISE ⟨~ a policy⟩ **2 a :** to develop a formula for the preparation of (as a soap or plastic) **b :** to prepare according to a formula — **for·mu·la·tor** \-ˌlā-tər\ *n*

for·mu·la·tion \ˌfȯr-myə-ˈlā-shən\ *n* (ca. 1873) **:** an act or the product of formulating

formula weight *n* (ca. 1920) **:** MOLECULAR WEIGHT — used esp. of ionic compounds

for·mu·lize \ˈfȯr-myə-ˌlīz\ *vt* **-lized; -liz·ing** (1842) **:** FORMULATE 1

form word *n* (1875) **:** FUNCTION WORD

form·work \ˈfȯrm-ˌwərk\ *n* (1918) **:** a set of forms in place to hold wet concrete until it sets

for·myl \ˈfȯr-ˌmil\ *n* [ISV] (ca. 1859) **:** the radical HCO– of formic acid that is also characteristic of aldehydes

for·ni·cate \ˈfȯr-nə-ˌkāt\ *vb* **-cat·ed; -cat·ing** [LL *fornicatus*, pp. of *fornicare* to have intercourse with prostitutes, fr. L *fornic-, fornix* arch, vault, brothel] *vi* (1552) **:** to commit fornication ~ *vt* **:** to commit fornication with — **for·ni·ca·tor** \-ˌkā-tər\ *n*

for·ni·ca·tion \ˌfȯr-nə-ˈkā-shən\ *n* (14c) **:** consensual sexual intercourse between two persons not married to each other — compare ADULTERY

for·nix \ˈfȯr-niks\ *n, pl* **for·ni·ces** \-nə-ˌsēz\ [NL, fr. L] (1681) **:** an anatomical arch or fold

for–prof·it \ˈfȯr-ˈprä-fət\ *adj* (1972) **:** established, maintained, or conducted for the purpose of making a profit ⟨~ businesses⟩

for·rad·er *also* **for·rard·er** \ˈfär-ə-dər\ *adv* [E dial., compar. of E *forward*] (1888) *chiefly Brit* **:** further ahead

for·sake \fər-ˈsāk, fȯr-\ *vt* **for·sook** \-ˈsu̇k\; **for·sak·en** \-ˈsā-kən\; **for·sak·ing** [ME, fr. OE *forsacan*, fr. *for-* + *sacan* to dispute; akin to OE *sacu* action at law — more at SAKE] (bef. 12c) **:** to renounce or turn away from entirely ⟨friends have *forsaken* her⟩ ⟨*forsook* the theater for politics⟩ ***syn*** see ABANDON

for·sooth \fər-ˈsüth\ *adv* [ME *for soth*, fr. OE *forsōth*, fr. *for* + *sōth* sooth] (bef. 12c) **:** in truth **:** INDEED — often used to imply contempt or doubt

for·spent \fər-ˈspent, fȯr-\ *adj* (1563) *archaic* **:** WORN-OUT, EXHAUSTED

for·swear *also* **fore·swear** \fȯr-ˈswer\ *vb* **-swore** \-ˈswȯr\; **-sworn** \-ˈswȯrn\; **-swear·ing** [ME *forsweren*, fr. OE *forswerian*, fr. *for-* + *swerian* to swear] *vt* (bef. 12c) **1 :** to make a liar of (oneself) under or as if under oath **2 a :** to reject or renounce under oath **b :** to renounce earnestly **3 :** to deny under oath ~ *vi* **:** to swear falsely ***syn*** see ABJURE

for·sworn *also* **fore·sworn** \-ˈswȯrn\ *adj* (bef. 12c) **1 :** guilty of perjury **2 :** marked by perjury

for·syth·ia \fər-ˈsi-thē-ə, *chiefly Brit* -ˈsī-\ *n, pl* **-ias** *also* **-ia** [NL, fr. William *Forsyth* †1804 Brit. botanist] (ca. 1814) **:** any of a genus (*Forsythia*) of ornamental shrubs of the olive family with opposite leaves and yellow bell-shaped flowers appearing before the leaves in early spring

fort \ˈfȯrt\ *n* [ME *forte*, fr. AF *fort*, fr. *fort*, adj., strong, fr. L *fortis*] (15c) **1 :** a strong or fortified place; *esp* **:** a fortified place occupied only by troops and surrounded with such works as a ditch, rampart, and parapet **:** FORTIFICATION **2 :** a permanent army post — often used in place names

for·ta·lice \ˈfȯr-tə-ləs\ *n* [ME, fr. ML *fortalitia* — more at FORTRESS] (15c) **1** *archaic* **:** FORTRESS **2** *archaic* **:** a small fort

¹forte \ˈfȯrt; *2 is often* ˈfȯr-ˌtā *or* fȯr-ˈtā *or* ˈfȯr-tē\ *n* [F *fort*, fr. *fort*, adj., strong] (ca. 1648) **1 :** the part of a sword or foil blade that is between the middle and the hilt and that is the strongest part of the blade **2 :** one's strong point

usage In *forte* we have a word derived from French that in its "strong point" sense has no entirely satisfactory pronunciation. Usage writers have denigrated \ˈfȯr-ˌtā\ and \ˈfȯr-tē\ because they reflect the influence of the Italian-derived ²*forte*. Their recommended pronunciation \ˈfȯrt\, however, does not exactly reflect French either: the French would write the word *le fort* and would rhyme it with English *for*. So you can take your choice, knowing that someone somewhere will dislike whichever variant you choose. All are standard, however. In British English \ˈfȯ-ˌtā\ and \ˈfȯt\ predominate; \ˈfȯr-ˌtā\ and \fȯr-ˈtā\ are prob. the most frequent pronunciations in American English.

²for·te \ˈfȯr-ˌtā, ˈfȯr-tē\ *adv or adj* [It, fr. *forte* strong, fr. L *fortis*] (ca. 1724) **:** LOUD — used as a direction in music

³for·te \ˈfȯr-ˌtā, ˈfȯr-tē\ *n* (1759) **:** a tone or passage played forte

for·te·pia·no \ˌfȯr-ˌtā-pē-ˈa-(ˌ)nō *also* -ˈä-(ˌ)nō\ *n* [F or It; F, fr. It, fr. *forte* loud + *piano* soft] (1771) **:** an early form of the piano originating in the 18th and early 19th centuries and having a smaller range and softer timbre than a modern piano

for·te–pi·a·no \ˌfȯr-ˌtā-pē-ˈä-(ˌ)nō, ˌfȯr-tē-\ *adv or adj* (1823) **:** loud then immediately soft — used as a direction in music

¹forth \ˈfȯrth\ *adv* [ME, fr. OE; akin to OE *for*] (bef. 12c) **1 :** onward in time, place, or order **:** FORWARD ⟨from that day ~⟩ **2 :** out into notice or view ⟨put ~ leaves⟩ **3** *obs* **:** AWAY, ABROAD

²forth *prep* (ca. 1575) *archaic* **:** forth from **:** OUT OF

forth·com·ing \fȯrth-ˈkə-miŋ, ˈfȯrth-\ *adj* [obs. *forthcome* to come forth] (ca. 1532) **1 :** being about to appear or to be produced or made available ⟨the ~ holidays⟩ ⟨your ~ novel⟩ ⟨funds are ~⟩ **2 a :** RESPONSIVE, OUTGOING ⟨a ~ and courteous man⟩ **b :** characterized by openness, candidness, and forthrightness ⟨not ~ about his memories of medical school —Mark Kramer⟩

forth of *prep* (13c) *archaic* **:** out from **:** OUT OF

¹forth·right \ˈfȯrth-ˌrīt\ *adv* [ME, fr. OE *forthriht*, fr. *forth* + *riht* right] (bef. 12c) **1** *archaic* **a :** directly forward **b :** without hesitation **:** FRANKLY **2** *archaic* **:** at once

²forthright *adj* (bef. 12c) **1** *archaic* **:** proceeding straight on **2 :** free from ambiguity or evasiveness **:** going straight to the point ⟨a ~ critic⟩ ⟨was ~ in appraising the problem⟩ **3 :** notably simple in style or quality ⟨~ furniture⟩ — **forth·right·ly** *adv* — **forth·right·ness** *n*

³forthright *n* (1606) *archaic* **:** a straight path

forth·with \(ˌ)fȯrth-ˈwith *also* -ˈwith\ *adv* (14c) **:** IMMEDIATELY

for·ti·fi·ca·tion \ˌfȯr-tə-fə-ˈkā-shən\ *n* (15c) **1 :** an act or process of fortifying **2 :** something that fortifies, defends, or strengthens; *esp* **:** works erected to defend a place or position

fortified wine *n* (1874) **:** a wine (as sherry) to which alcohol usu. in the form of grape brandy has been added during or after fermentation

for·ti·fy \ˈfȯr-tə-ˌfī\ *vb* **-fied; -fy·ing** [ME *fortifien*, fr. AF *fortifier*, fr. LL *fortificare*, fr. L *fortis* strong] *vt* (15c) **:** to make strong: as **a :** to strengthen and secure (as a town) by forts or batteries **b :** to give physical strength, courage, or endurance to ⟨*fortified* by a hearty meal⟩ **c :** to add mental or moral strength to **:** ENCOURAGE ⟨*fortified* by prayer⟩ **d :** to add material to for strengthening or enriching ⟨*fortified* milk⟩ ~ *vi* **:** to erect fortifications — **for·ti·fi·er** \-ˌfī(-ə)r\ *n*

for·tis \ˈfȯr-təs\ *adj* [NL, fr. L, strong] (1897) **:** produced with relatively great articulatory tenseness and strong expiration ⟨\t\ in *toe* is ~, \d\ in *doe* is lenis⟩

¹for·tis·si·mo \fȯr-ˈti-sə-ˌmō\ *adv or adj* [It, superl. of *forte*] (1724) **:** very loud — used esp. as a direction in music

²fortissimo *n, pl* **-mos** *or* **-mi** \-ˌmē\ (1856) **:** a very loud passage, sound, or tone

for·ti·tude \ˈfȯr-tə-ˌtüd, -ˌtyüd\ *n* [ME, fr. L *fortitudin-, fortitudo*, fr. *fortis*] (12c) **1 :** strength of mind that enables a person to encounter danger or bear pain or adversity with courage **2** *obs* **:** STRENGTH

fort·night \ˈfȯrt-ˌnīt\ *n* [ME *fourtenight*, alter. of *fourtene night*, fr. OE *fēowertȳne niht* fourteen nights] (bef. 12c) **:** a period of 14 days **:** two weeks

¹fort·night·ly \-lē\ *adj* (1800) **:** occurring or appearing once in a fortnight

²fortnightly *adv* (1820) **:** once in a fortnight **:** every fortnight

³fortnightly *n, pl* **-lies** (1940) **:** a publication issued fortnightly

FOR·TRAN *or* **For·tran** \ˈfȯr-ˌtran\ *n* [*for*mula *tran*slation] (1956) **:** a computer programming language that resembles algebra in its notation and is widely used for scientific applications

for·tress \ˈfȯr-trəs\ *n* [ME *forteresse*, fr. AF *fortelesce, forteresse*, fr. ML *fortalitia*, fr. L *fortis* strong] (14c) **:** a fortified place **:** STRONGHOLD; *esp* **:** a large and permanent fortification sometimes including a town — **for·tress·like** \-ˌlīk\ *adj*

for·tu·itous \fȯr-ˈtü-ə-təs, -ˈtyü-, fər-\ *adj* [L *fortuitus*; akin to L *fort-, fors* chance — more at FORTUNE] (1653) **1 :** occurring by chance **2 a :** FORTUNATE, LUCKY ⟨from a cost standpoint, the company's timing is ~ —*Business Week*⟩ **b :** coming or happening by a lucky chance ⟨belted down the stairs, and there was a ~ train —Doris Lessing⟩ ***syn*** see ACCIDENTAL — **for·tu·itous·ly** *adv* — **for·tu·itous·ness** *n*

usage Sense 2a has been influenced in meaning by *fortunate*. It has been in standard if not elevated use for some 70 years, but is still disdained by some critics. Sense 2b, a blend of 1 and 2a, is virtually unnoticed by the critics. Sense 1 is the only sense commonly used in negative constructions.

for·tu·ity \-ə-tē\ *n, pl* **-ities** (ca. 1747) **1 :** the quality or state of being fortuitous **2 :** a chance event or occurrence

for·tu·nate \ˈfȯrch-nət, ˈfȯr-chə-\ *adj* (14c) **1 :** bringing some good thing not foreseen as certain **:** AUSPICIOUS **2 :** receiving some unexpected good ***syn*** see LUCKY — **for·tu·nate·ness** *n*

for·tu·nate·ly \-lē\ *adv* (1548) **1 :** in a fortunate manner **2 :** it is fortunate that ⟨~, no one was hurt⟩

¹for·tune \ˈfȯr-chən\ *n* [ME, fr. AF, fr. L *fortuna*; akin to L *fort-, fors* chance, luck, and perh. to *ferre* to carry — more at BEAR] (14c) **1** *often cap* **:** a hypothetical force or personified power that unpredictably determines events and issues favorably or unfavorably **2** *obs* **:** ACCIDENT, INCIDENT **3 a :** prosperity attained partly through luck **:** SUCCESS **b :** LUCK 1 **c** *pl* **:** the turns and courses of luck accompanying one's progress (as through life) ⟨her ~*s* varied but she never gave up⟩ **4 :** DESTINY, FATE ⟨can tell your ~⟩; *also* **:** a prediction of fortune **5 a :** RICHES, WEALTH ⟨a man of ~⟩ **b :** a store of material possessions ⟨the family ~⟩ **c :** a very large sum of money ⟨spent a ~ redecorating⟩

²fortune *vb* **for·tuned; for·tun·ing** *vt* (14c) **1** *obs* **:** to give good or bad fortune to **2** *archaic* **:** to endow with a fortune ~ *vi, archaic* **:** HAPPEN, CHANCE

fortune cookie *n* (1940) **:** a thin cookie folded to contain a slip of paper on which is printed a fortune, proverb, or humorous statement

fortune hunter *n* (1689) **:** a person who seeks wealth esp. by marriage

for·tune–tell·er \-ˌte-lər\ *n* (1590) **:** one that professes to foretell future events — **for·tune–tell·ing** \-liŋ\ *n or adj*

for·ty \ˈfȯr-tē\ *n, pl* **forties** [ME *fourty*, adj., fr. OE *fēowertig*, fr. *fēowertig* group of 40, fr. *fēower* four + *-tig* group of 10; akin to OE *tien* ten] (bef. 12c) **1 —** see NUMBER table **2** *pl* **:** the numbers 40 to 49; *specif* **:** the years 40 to 49 in a lifetime or century **3 :** the third point scored by a side in a game of tennis — **for·ti·eth** \ˈfȯr-tē-əth\ *adj or n* — **forty** *adj* — **forty** *pron, pl in constr* — **for·ty·ish** \-tē-ish\ *adj*

for·ty–five \ˌfȯr-tē-ˈfīv\ *n* (ca. 1623) **1** — see NUMBER table **2 :** a .45 caliber handgun — usu. written .45 **3 :** a phonograph record designed to be played at 45 revolutions per minute — usu. written 45 — **forty–five** *adj* — **forty–five** *pron, pl in constr*
Forty Hours *n pl but sing or pl in constr* (1759) **:** a Roman Catholic devotion in which the churches of a diocese in 2-day turns have the Blessed Sacrament exposed on the altar for continuous daytime veneration
for·ty–nin·er \ˌfȯr-tē-ˈnī-nər\ *n* (1853) **:** one taking part in the rush to California for gold in 1849
forty winks *n pl but sing or pl in constr* (1828) **:** a short sleep **:** NAP
fo·rum \ˈfȯr-əm\ *n, pl* **forums** *also* **fo·ra** \-ə\ [L; akin to L *foris* outside, *fores* door — more at DOOR] (15c) **1 a :** the marketplace or public place of an ancient Roman city forming the center of judicial and public business **b :** a public meeting place for open discussion **c :** a medium (as a newspaper or online service) of open discussion or expression of ideas **2 :** a judicial body or assembly **:** COURT **3 a :** a public meeting or lecture involving audience discussion **b :** a program (as on radio or television) involving discussion of a problem usu. by several authorities
1**for·ward** \ˈfȯr-wərd, *also* ˈfō- *or* ˈfȯ-, *Southern also* ˈfär-\ *adj* [ME, fr. OE *foreweard,* fr. *fore-* + *-weard* -ward] (bef. 12c) **1 a :** near, being at, or belonging to the forepart **b :** situated in advance **2 a :** strongly inclined **:** READY **b :** lacking modesty or reserve **:** BRASH **3 :** notably advanced or developed **:** PRECOCIOUS **4 :** moving, tending, or leading toward a position in front; *also* **:** moving toward an opponent's goal **5 a :** advocating an advanced policy in the direction of what is considered progress **b :** EXTREME, RADICAL **6 :** of, relating to, or getting ready for the future ⟨~ buying of produce⟩ — **for·ward·ly** *adv* — **for·ward·ness** *n*
2**forward** *adv* (bef. 12c) **:** to or toward what is ahead or in front ⟨from that time ~⟩ ⟨moved slowly ~⟩
3**forward** *vt* (1596) **1 :** to help onward **:** PROMOTE ⟨~*ed* his friend's career⟩ **2 a :** to send forward **:** TRANSMIT ⟨will ~ the goods on receipt of your check⟩ **b :** to send or ship onward from an intermediate post or station in transit ⟨~ mail⟩ ***syn*** see ADVANCE
4**forward** *n* (1879) **:** a player who plays at the front of his team's formation near the goal at which his team is attempting to score
forward air controller *n* (1952) **:** a military officer who directs from a forward position on the ground or in the air the action of combat aircraft engaged in close air support of land forces
for·ward·er \-wər-dər\ *n* (1549) **:** one that forwards; *esp* **:** an agent who performs services (as receiving, transshipping, or delivering) designed to move goods to their destination
for·ward–look·ing \ˈfȯr-wərd-ˌlu̇-kiŋ\ *adj* (1800) **:** concerned with or planning for the future
forward pass *n* (1890) **:** a pass (as in football) made in the direction of the opponents' goal
for·wards \ˈfȯr-wərdz\ *adv* (15c) **:** FORWARD
forwent *past of* FORGO
for·worn \fər-ˈwȯrn\ *adj* (1508) *archaic* **:** WORN-OUT
forz *abbr* forzando
for·zan·do \fȯrt-ˈsän-(ˌ)dō\ *adj or adv* [It] (1801) **:** SFORZANDO
fos·car·net \fäs-ˈkär-nət\ *n* [prob. fr. ISV *fos-* (alter. of *phosph-*) + *carb-* + *-net* (of unknown origin)] (1981) **:** a hydrated sodium salt $Na_3CO_5 \cdot 6H_2O$ that is administered intravenously to individuals infected with HIV to treat retinitis caused by a cytomegalovirus
1**fos·sa** \ˈfä-sə\ *n, pl* **fos·sae** \-ˌsē, -ˌsī\ [NL, fr. L, ditch] (1733) **:** an anatomical pit, groove, or depression
2**fossa** *n* [Malagasy] (1838) **:** a slender long-tailed carnivorous mammal (*Cryptoprocta ferox*) of Madagascar that has retractile claws and is often grouped with the mongooses or placed in a related family (Eupleridae)

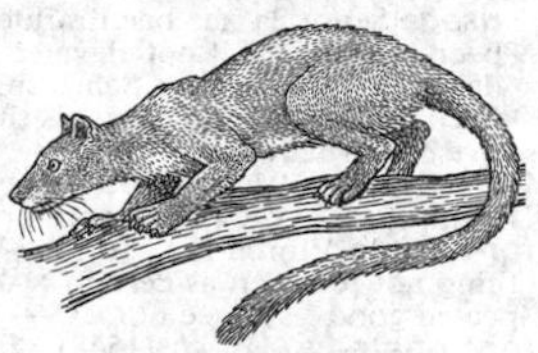
2fossa

fosse *or* **foss** \ˈfäs\ *n* [ME *fosse,* fr. AF, fr. L *fossa,* fr. fem. of *fossus*] (15c) **:** DITCH, MOAT
fos·sick \ˈfä-sik\ *vb* [E dial. *fossick* to ferret out] *vi* (1852) **1** *Austral & NewZeal* **:** to search for gold or gemstones typically by picking over abandoned workings **2** *chiefly Austral & NewZeal* **:** to search about **:** RUMMAGE ~ *vt, chiefly Austral & NewZeal* **:** to search for by or as if by rummaging **:** ferret out — **fos·sick·er** *n, chiefly Austral & NewZeal*
1**fos·sil** \ˈfä-səl\ *adj* [L *fossilis* obtained by digging, fr. *fodere* to dig — more at BED] (1604) **1 :** preserved from a past geologic age ⟨~ plants⟩ ⟨~ water in an underground reservoir⟩ **2 :** being or resembling a fossil **3 :** of or relating to fossil fuel
2**fossil** *n* (1736) **1 :** a remnant, impression, or trace of an organism of past geologic ages that has been preserved in the earth's crust — compare LIVING FOSSIL **2 a :** a person whose views are outmoded **:** FOGY **b :** something (as a theory) that has become rigidly fixed **3 :** an old word or word element preserved only by idiom (as *fro* in *to and fro*)
fossil fuel *n* (1835) **:** a fuel (as coal, oil, or natural gas) formed in the earth from plant or animal remains — **fos·sil–fueled** \-ˌfyü(-ə)ld\ *adj*
fos·sil·if·er·ous \ˌfä-sə-ˈli-f(ə-)rəs\ *adj* (1830) **:** containing fossils
fos·sil·ise *chiefly Brit var of* FOSSILIZE
fos·sil·ize \ˈfä-sə-ˌlīz\ *vb* **-ized; -iz·ing** *vt* (1794) **1 :** to convert into a fossil **2 :** to make outmoded, rigid, or fixed ~ *vi* **:** to become changed into a fossil — **fos·sil·i·za·tion** \ˌfä-sə-lə-ˈzā-shən\ *n*
fos·so·ri·al \fä-ˈsȯr-ē-əl\ *adj* [ML *fossorius* used for digging, fr. L *fossor* digger, fr. *fodere*] (1837) **:** adapted to digging ⟨a ~ foot⟩
1**fos·ter** \ˈfȯs-tər, ˈfäs-\ *adj* [ME, fr. OE *fōstor-,* fr. *fōstor* food, feeding; akin to OE *fōda* food] (bef. 12c) **:** affording, receiving, or sharing nurture or parental care though not related by blood or legal ties
2**foster** *vt* **fos·tered; fos·ter·ing** \-t(ə-)riŋ\ (12c) **1 :** to give parental care to **:** NURTURE **2 :** to promote the growth or development of **:** ENCOURAGE ⟨~*ed* the college in its early years⟩ — **fos·ter·er** \-tər-ər\ *n*
fos·ter·age \-tə-rij\ *n* (1614) **1 :** the act of fostering **2 :** a custom once prevalent in Ireland, Wales, and Scotland of entrusting one's child to foster parents to be brought up
foster home *n* (1886) **:** a household in which an orphaned, neglected, or delinquent child is placed for care
fos·ter·ling \-tər-liŋ\ *n* (bef. 12c) **:** a foster child
fou \ˈfü\ *adj* [ME (Sc) *fow* full, fr. ME *full*] (1535) *Scot* **:** DRUNK 1a
Fou·caul·di·an \fü-ˈkō-dē-ən\ *also* **Fou·cault·ian** \-ˈkō-ē-ən\ *adj* (1981) **:** of, relating to, or characteristic of the philosophy of Michel Foucault
Fou·cault pendulum \ˌfü-ˈkō-\ *n* [J. B. L. *Foucault*] (1931) **:** a freely swinging pendulum that consists of a heavy weight hung by a long wire and that swings in a constant direction which appears to change showing that the earth rotates
fouet·té \(ˌ)fwe-ˈtā\ *n* [F, fr. pp. of *fouetter* to whip, fr. MF, fr. *fouet* whip, fr. OF, fr. *fou* beech, fr. L *fagus* — more at BEECH] (1830) **:** a quick whipping movement of the raised leg in ballet usu. accompanying a pirouette
fought *past and past part of* FIGHT
1**foul** \ˈfau̇(-ə)l\ *adj* [ME, fr. OE *fūl;* akin to OHG *fūl* rotten, L *pus* pus, *putēre* to stink, Gk *pyon* pus] (bef. 12c) **1 a :** offensive to the senses **:** LOATHSOME **b :** filled or covered with offensive matter **2 :** full of dirt or mud **3 a :** morally or spiritually odious **:** DETESTABLE ⟨a ~ crime⟩ **b :** notably unpleasant or distressing **:** WRETCHED, HORRID ⟨in a ~ mood⟩ **4 :** OBSCENE, ABUSIVE ⟨~ language⟩ **5 a :** being wet and stormy **b :** obstructive to navigation ⟨a ~ tide⟩ **6** *dial Brit* **:** HOMELY, UGLY **7 a :** TREACHEROUS, DISHONORABLE ⟨fair means or ~⟩ **b :** constituting an infringement of rules in a game or sport ⟨a ~ blow in boxing⟩ **8 :** containing marked-up corrections ⟨a ~ manuscript⟩ ⟨~ proofs⟩ **9 :** encrusted, clogged, or choked with a foreign substance ⟨the chimney was ~ and smoked badly⟩ **10 :** being odorous and impure **:** POLLUTED ⟨~ air⟩ **11 :** placed in a situation that impedes physical movement **:** ENTANGLED **12 :** being outside the foul lines in baseball ***syn*** see DIRTY — **foul·ly** \ˈfau̇(l)-lē\ *adv* — **foul·ness** *n*
2**foul** *n* (bef. 12c) **1** *archaic* **:** something foul **2 :** an entanglement or collision esp. in angling or sailing **3 a :** an infringement of the rules in a game or sport **b :** FREE THROW **4 :** FOUL BALL
3**foul** *vi* (bef. 12c) **1 :** to become or be foul: as **a :** DECOMPOSE, ROT **b :** to become encrusted, clogged, or choked with a foreign substance **c :** to become entangled or come into collision **2 :** to commit a violation of the rules in a sport or game **3 :** to hit a foul ball ~ *vt* **1 :** to make foul: as **a :** to make dirty **:** POLLUTE **b :** to tangle or come into collision with **c :** to encrust with a foreign substance ⟨a ship's bottom ~*ed* with barnacles⟩ **d :** OBSTRUCT, BLOCK **2 :** DISHONOR, DISCREDIT **3 :** to commit a foul against **4 :** to hit (a baseball) foul
4**foul** *adv* (13c) **:** in a foul manner **:** so as to be foul
fou·lard \fu̇-ˈlärd\ *n* [F] (1830) **1 a :** a lightweight plain-woven or twilled silk usu. decorated with a printed pattern **b :** an imitation of this fabric **2 :** an article of clothing made of foulard
foul ball *n* (1860) **:** a baseball batted into foul territory
foul·brood \ˈfau̇(-ə)l-ˌbrüd\ *n* (1863) **:** a destructive disease of honeybee larvae caused by bacteria (as *Bacillus larvae*)
foul·ing *n* (14c) **:** DEPOSIT, INCRUSTATION ⟨~ on a ship's bottom⟩
foul line *n* (1870) **1 :** either of two straight lines extending from the rear corner of home plate through the outer corners of first and third base respectively and prolonged to the boundary of a baseball field **2 :** a line across a bowling alley that a player must not step over when delivering the ball **3 :** either of two lines on a basketball court parallel to and 15 feet from the backboards behind which a player must stand while shooting a free throw
foul·mouthed \ˈfau̇(-ə)l-ˌmau̇t͟hd, -ˌmau̇tht\ *adj* (1593) **:** given to the use of obscene, profane, or abusive language
foul of *prep* (1627) **:** AFOUL OF ⟨he fell *foul of* the law⟩ ⟨ran *foul of* a hidden reef⟩
foul out *vi* (1948) **:** to be put out of a basketball game for exceeding the number of fouls permitted
foul play *n* (15c) **:** VIOLENCE; *esp* **:** MURDER
foul shot *n* (1905) **:** FREE THROW
foul tip *n* [1*foul* + *tip* (tap)] (1870) **:** a pitched ball in baseball that is slightly deflected by the bat; *specif* **:** a tipped pitch legally caught by the catcher and counting as a full strike with the ball remaining in play
foul–up \ˈfau̇(-ə)l-ˌəp\ *n* (1950) **1 :** a state of confusion or an error caused by ineptitude, carelessness, or mismanagement ⟨~*s* in transportation⟩ **2 :** a mechanical difficulty
foul up *vt* (1947) **1 :** to make dirty **:** CONTAMINATE **2 :** to spoil by making mistakes or using poor judgment **:** CONFUSE **3 :** ENTANGLE, BLOCK ⟨*fouled up* communications⟩ ~ *vi* **:** to cause a foul-up **:** BUNGLE ⟨it was his fault. He had *fouled up* —Pat Frank⟩
1**found** \ˈfau̇nd\ *past and past part of* FIND
2**found** *adj* (1793) **1 :** having all usual, standard, or reasonably expected equipment ⟨the boat comes fully ~, ready to go —*Holiday*⟩ **2 :** presented as or incorporated into an artistic work essentially as found ⟨sculpture of fabric, wood, and other ~ materials —Hilton Kramer⟩
3**found** *n* (1830) **:** free food and lodging in addition to wages ⟨they're paid $175 a month and ~ —*New Yorker*⟩
4**found** *vt* [ME, fr. AF *funder, fonder,* fr. L *fundare,* fr. *fundus* bottom — more at BOTTOM] (13c) **1 :** to take the first steps in building **2 :** to set or ground on something solid **:** BASE **3 :** to establish (as an institution) often with provision for future maintenance
5**found** *vt* [MF *fondre* to pour, melt, fr. L *fundere;* akin to OE *gēotan* to pour, Gk *chein*] (1562) **:** to melt (as metal) and pour into a mold
foun·da·tion \fau̇n-ˈdā-shən\ *n* (14c) **1 :** the act of founding **2 :** a basis (as a tenet, principle, or axiom) upon which something stands or is supported ⟨the ~*s* of geometry⟩ ⟨the rumor is without ~ in fact⟩ **3 a :** funds given for the permanent support of an institution **:** ENDOWMENT **b :** an organization or institution established by endowment with provision for future maintenance **4 :** an underlying base or support; *esp* **:** the whole masonry substructure of a building **5 a :** a body or ground upon which something is built up or overlaid **b :** a woman's supporting undergarment **:** CORSET **c :** a cosmetic usu. used as a base for makeup — **foun·da·tion·al** \-shnəl, -shə-nᵊl\ *adj* — **foun·da·tion·al·ly** *adv* — **foun·da·tion·less** \-shən-ləs\ *adj*
foundation stone *n* (1628) **1 :** a stone in the foundation of a building; *esp* **:** such a stone laid with public ceremony — compare CORNERSTONE **2 :** BASIS, GROUNDWORK
1**found·er** \ˈfau̇n-dər\ *n* [4*found*] (14c) **:** one that founds or establishes

[2]**foun·der** \ˈfau̇n-dər\ *vb* **foun·dered; foun·der·ing** \-d(ə-)riŋ\ [ME *foundren* to fall to the ground, sink, fr. AF *fondrer,* alter. of *fondre,* fr. L *fundere* to pour, cast, disperse, lay low, slay — more at FOUND] *vi* (14c) **1** : to become disabled; *esp* : to go lame **2** : to give way : COLLAPSE **3** : to become submerged : SINK **4** : to come to grief : FAIL ~ *vt* : to disable (an animal) esp. by excessive feeding

[3]**foun·der** *n* (ca. 1547) : LAMINITIS

[4]**found·er** *n* [[5]*found*] (15c) : one that founds metal; *esp* : TYPEFOUNDER

founder effect *n* (1970) : the effect on the resulting gene pool that occurs when a new isolated population is founded by a small number of individuals possessing limited genetic variation relative to the larger population from which they have migrated

founding father *n* (1914) **1** : an originator of an institution or movement : FOUNDER **2** *often cap both Fs* : a leading figure in the founding of the U.S.; *specif* : a member of the American Constitutional Convention of 1787

found·ling \ˈfau̇n(d)-liŋ\ *n* (14c) : an infant found after its unknown parents have abandoned it

found object *n* (1950) : OBJET TROUVÉ

found poem *n* (1966) : a poem consisting of words found in a nonpoetic context (as a product label) and usu. broken into lines that convey a verse rhythm

found·ry \ˈfau̇n-drē\ *n, pl* **foundries** (1536) **1** : an establishment where founding is carried on **2** : the act, process, or art of casting metals

[1]**fount** \ˈfau̇nt\ *n* [ME, fr. AF *funte, founte,* fr. L *font-, fons*] (15c) : FOUNTAIN, SOURCE

[2]**fount** \ˈfänt, ˈfau̇nt\ *n* [F *fonte,* fr. MF — more at FONT] (ca. 1683) *Brit* : a type font

[1]**foun·tain** \ˈfau̇n-tᵊn\ *n* [ME, fr. AF *funtaine, fontaine,* fr. LL *fontana,* fr. L, fem. of *fontanus* of a spring, fr. *font-, fons*] (14c) **1** : the source from which something proceeds or is supplied **2** : a spring of water issuing from the earth **3** : an artificially produced jet of water; *also* : the structure from which it rises **4** : a reservoir containing a liquid that can be drawn off as needed **5** : SODA FOUNTAIN 2

[2]**fountain** *vi* (1903) : to flow or spout like a fountain ~ *vt* : to cause to flow like a fountain

fountain grass *n* (1905) : any of several ornamental grasses (genus *Pennisetum*) having tufted stems and spikes of feathery flower clusters

foun·tain·head \-ˌhed\ *n* (1585) **1** : a spring that is the source of a stream **2** : principal source : ORIGIN

fountain pen *n* (1710) : a pen containing a reservoir that automatically feeds the writing point with ink

four \ˈfȯr\ *n* [ME, fr. *four* adj., fr. OE *fēower;* akin to OHG *fior* four, L *quattuor,* Gk *tessares, tettares*] (bef. 12c) **1** — see NUMBER table **2** : the fourth in a set or series ⟨the ~ of hearts⟩ **3** : something having four units or members: as **a** : a 4-oared racing shell or its crew **b** : a 4-cylinder engine or automobile — **four** *adj* — **four** *pron, pl in constr*

four–bag·ger \-ˈba-gər\ *n* (1926) : HOME RUN 1

four–ball \-ˌbȯl\ *n* (1904) : a golf match in which the best individual score of one partnership is matched against the best individual score of another partnership for each hole

4x4 *also* **four–by–four** \ˈfȯr-bī-ˌfȯr\ *n* (1942) : a four-wheel automotive vehicle (as a pickup) equipped with four-wheel drive

four·chée \fu̇r-ˈshā\ *adj* [F (fem.), lit., forked] (1706) *of a heraldic cross* : having the end of each arm forked — see CROSS illustration

four–dimensional *adj* (1880) : relating to or having four dimensions ⟨~ space-time continuum⟩; *esp* : consisting of or relating to elements requiring four coordinates to determine them

four·dri·nier \ˌfȯr-drə-ˈnir; fu̇r-ˈdri-nē-ər, fȯr-\ *n, often cap* [Henry & Sealy *Fourdrinier*] (1839) : a machine for making paper in an endless web

four–eyed \ˈfȯr-ˌīd\ *adj* (1926) : wearing glasses

4–F \ˈfȯr-ˈef\ *n* (1942) : classification as unfit for military service; *also* : a person having this classification

four–flush *vi* (1896) : to bluff in poker holding a four flush; *broadly* : to make a false claim : BLUFF — **four–flush·er** \-ˈflə-shər\ *n*

four flush *n* (1887) : four cards of the same suit in a 5-card poker hand

four·fold \ˈfȯr-ˌfōld, -ˈfōld\ *adj* [ME, fr. OE *fēowerfeald,* fr. *fēower* + *-feald* -fold] (bef. 12c) **1** : being four times as great or as many **2** : having four units or members — **four·fold** \-ˈfōld\ *adv*

four–foot·ed \-ˈfu̇-təd\ *adj* (14c) : having four feet : QUADRUPED

4–H \ˈfȯr-ˈāch\ *adj* [fr. the fourfold aim of improving the head, heart, hands, and health] (1926) : of or relating to a program set up by the U.S. Department of Agriculture orig. in rural areas to help young people become productive citizens by instructing them in useful skills (as in agriculture, animal husbandry, and carpentry), community service, and personal development — **4–H'·er** *also* **4–H·er** \-ˈā-chər\ *n*

four–hand \ˈfȯr-ˌhand\ *adj* (ca. 1909) : FOUR-HANDED

four–hand·ed \-ˈhan-dəd\ *adj* (ca. 1770) **1** : engaged in by four persons ⟨a ~ card game⟩ **2** : designed for four hands ⟨a ~ piano piece⟩

Four Horsemen *n pl* [fr. the apocalyptic vision in Rev 6:2–8] (1918) : war, famine, pestilence, and death personified as the four major plagues of humankind

Four Hundred *or* **400** *n* (1888) : the exclusive social set of a community — used with *the*

Fou·ri·er analysis \ˈfu̇r-ē-ˌā-\ *n* [Baron J.B.J. *Fourier* †1830 Fr. geometrician & physicist] (ca. 1928) : the process of using the terms of a Fourier series to find a function that approximates periodic data

Fou·ri·er·ism \ˈfu̇r-ē-ə-ˌri-zəm, -ē-ˌā-ˌi-\ *n* [F *fouriérisme,* fr. F.M.C. *Fourier*] (1843) : a system for reorganizing society into cooperative communities of small self-sustaining groups — **Fou·ri·er·ist** \-ē-ə-rist, -ē-ˌā-ist\ *n*

Fourier series *n* [Baron J.B.J. *Fourier*] (1877) : an infinite series in which the terms are constants multiplied by sine or cosine functions of integer multiples of the variable and which is used in the analysis of periodic functions

Fourier's theorem *n* (1834) : a theorem in mathematics: under suitable conditions any periodic function can be represented by a Fourier series

Fourier transform *n* (1923) : any of various functions (as $F(u)$) that under suitable conditions can be obtained from given functions (as $f(x)$) by multiplying by e^{iux} and integrating over all values of x and that in scientific instrumentation describe the dependence of the average of a series of measurements (as of a spectrum) on a quantity of interest (as brightness) esp. of a very small magnitude — called also *Fourier transformation*

four–in–hand \ˈfȯr-ən-ˌhand\ *n* (1793) **1 a** : a vehicle drawn by a team of four horses driven by one person **b** : such a team of four horses **2** : a necktie tied in a slipknot with long ends overlapping vertically in front

four–letter *adj* (1897) : of, relating to, or being four-letter words

four–letter word *n* (1897) : any of a group of vulgar or obscene words typically made up of four letters; *broadly* : a taboo word or topic ⟨tax is a *four-letter word* to him⟩

four–o'clock \ˈfȯr-ə-ˌkläk\ *n* (1756) : any of a genus (*Mirabilis*) of chiefly American annual or perennial herbs (family Nyctaginaceae, the four-o'clock family) having apetalous flowers with a showy involucre simulating a calyx; *esp* : a garden plant (*M. jalapa*) with fragrant yellow, red, or white flowers opening late in the afternoon

four of a kind (ca. 1934) : four cards of the same rank in one hand — see POKER illustration

411 \ˈfȯr-ˈwən-ˈwən\ *n* [fr. the telephone number *411* used to reach directory assistance] (1985) *slang* : relevant information : SKINNY ⟨fiber-optic ~ fed 24/7 in satellite real time —Jeff MacGregor⟩

401(k) \ˌfȯr-(ˌ)ō-(ˌ)wən-ˈkā\ *n* [fr. the section of the Internal Revenue Code that established it] (1989) : a retirement account to which employee and employer contribute, on which taxes are deferred until withdrawal, and for which the employee usu. selects the types of investments

four–peat \ˈfȯr-ˌpēt\ *n* [*four* + three-*peat*] (1989) : a fourth consecutive championship — **four–peat** *vi*

four·plex \ˈfȯr-ˌpleks\ *n* (1952) : a building that contains four separate apartments

four–post·er \ˌfȯr-ˈpō-stər\ *n* (1837) : a bed with tall often carved corner posts orig. designed to support curtains or a canopy

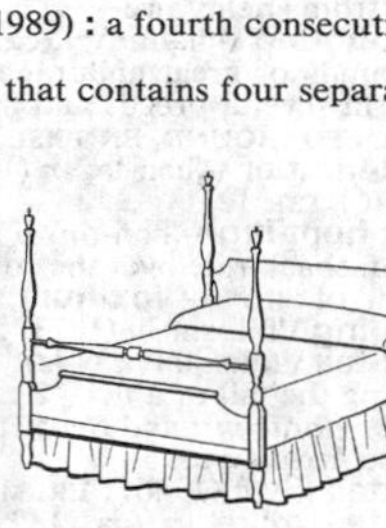
four-poster

four·ra·gère \ˌfu̇r-ə-ˈzher\ *n* [F, fr. fem. of *fourrager* of forage, fr. *fourrage* forage] (1919) : a braided cord worn usu. around the left shoulder; *esp* : such a cord awarded as a decoration to a military unit

four·score \ˈfȯr-ˈskȯr\ *adj* (13c) : being four times twenty : EIGHTY

four·some \ˈfȯr-səm\ *n* (14c) **1 a** : a group of four persons or things : QUARTET **b** : two couples **2** : a golf match in which two players compete against two others with players on each side taking turns playing one ball; *broadly* : any golf match involving four players

four·square \-ˈskwer\ *adj* (14c) **1** : SQUARE **2** : marked by boldness and conviction : FORTHRIGHT ⟨a ~ hero⟩ — **foursquare** *adv*

four–star \-ˈstär\ *adj* [fr. the number of asterisks used to denote relative excellence in guidebooks] (1921) : of a superior degree of excellence ⟨a ~ French restaurant⟩

four·teen \fȯr-ˈtēn, ˈfȯr(t)-\ *n* [ME *fourtene,* fr. OE *fēowertīene,* fr. *fēowertīene,* adj., fr. *fēower* + *-tīene;* akin to OE *tīen* ten] (bef. 12c) — see NUMBER table — **fourteen** *adj* — **fourteen** *pron, pl in constr* — **four·teenth** \-ˈtēn(t)th; -ˌtēn(t)th\ *adj or n*

four·teen·er \-ˈtē-nər\ *n* (1884) **1** : a verse consisting of 14 syllables or esp. of 7 iambic feet **2** : a mountain that is at least 14,000 feet high

fourth \ˈfȯrth\ *n, pl* **fourths** \ˈfȯr(th)s\ (bef. 12c) **1** — see NUMBER table **2 a** : a musical interval embracing four tones of the diatonic scale **b** : a tone at this interval; *specif* : SUBDOMINANT 1 **c** : the harmonic combination of two tones a fourth apart **3** : the fourth forward gear or speed of a motor vehicle **4** *cap* : INDEPENDENCE DAY — used with *the* — **fourth** *adj or adv* — **fourth·ly** *adv*

fourth dimension *n* (1875) **1** : a dimension in addition to length, breadth, and depth; *specif* : a coordinate in addition to three rectangular coordinates esp. when interpreted as the time coordinate in a space-time continuum **2** : something outside the range of ordinary experience — **fourth–dimensional** *adj*

fourth estate *n, often cap F&E* (1837) : the public press

Fourth of July (1779) : INDEPENDENCE DAY

fourth wall *n* (1807) : an imaginary wall (as at the opening of a modern stage proscenium) that keeps performers from recognizing or directly addressing their audience

fourth world *n, often cap F&W* (1974) : a group of nations esp. in Africa and Asia characterized by extremely low per capita income and an absence of valuable natural resources

four–way \ˈfȯr-ˈwā\ *adj* (1824) **1 a** : allowing or affecting passage in any of four directions **b** : applicable to traffic from each of four directions ⟨a ~ stop⟩ **2** : including four participants

4WD *abbr* four-wheel drive

four–wheel \ˈfȯr-ˌhwēl, -ˌwēl\ *or* **four–wheeled** \-ˌhwēld, -ˌwēld\ *adj* (1740) **1** : having four wheels **2** : acting on or by means of four wheels of an automotive vehicle ⟨~ disc brakes⟩

four–wheel drive *n* (1926) : an automotive drive mechanism that acts on all four wheels of the vehicle; *also* : a vehicle equipped with such a drive

four–wheel·er \-ˌhwē-lər, -ˌwē-\ *n* (1846) : a vehicle with four wheels

fo·vea \ˈfō-vē-ə\ *n, pl* **fo·ve·ae** \-vē-ˌē, -vē-ˌī\ [NL, fr. L, pit] (1849) **1** : a small fossa **2** : a small rodless area of the retina that affords acute vision — see EYE illustration — **fo·ve·al** \-vē-əl\ *adj* — **fo·ve·ate** \-vē-ˌāt, -ət\ *adj*

fovea cen·tra·lis \-sen-ˈtra-ləs, -ˈträ-, -ˈtrā-\ *n* [NL, central fovea] (1858) : FOVEA 2

[1]**fowl** \ˈfau̇(-ə)l\ *n, pl* **fowl** *or* **fowls** [ME *foul,* fr. OE *fugel;* akin to OHG *fogal* bird, and prob. to OE *flēogan* to fly — more at FLY] (bef. 12c) **1** : a bird of any kind — compare WATERFOWL, WILDFOWL **2 a** : a cock

\ə\ **abut** \ᵊ\ kitten, F table \ər\ **further** \a\ **ash** \ā\ **ace** \ä\ **mop, mar** \au̇\ **out** \ch\ **chin** \e\ **bet** \ē\ **easy** \g\ **go** \i\ **hit** \ī\ **ice** \j\ **job** \ŋ\ **sing** \ō\ **go** \ȯ\ **law** \ȯi\ **boy** \th\ **thin** \t͟h\ **the** \ü\ **loot** \u̇\ **foot** \y\ **yet** \zh\ **vision, beige** \k̲, ⁿ, œ, ue, ʸ\ *see* Guide to Pronunciation

or hen of the domestic chicken (*Gallus gallus*); *esp* : an adult hen **b** : any of several domesticated or wild gallinaceous birds — compare GUINEA FOWL, JUNGLE FOWL **3** : the meat of fowls used as food

²fowl *vi* (bef. 12c) : to seek, catch, or kill wildfowl — **fowl·er** *n*

fowling piece *n* (1596) : a shotgun for shooting birds or small animals

¹fox \ˈfäks\ *n, pl* **fox·es** *also* **fox** *often attrib* [ME, fr. OE; akin to OHG *fuhs* fox and perh. to Skt *puccha* tail] (bef. 12c) **1 a** : any of various carnivorous mammals (esp. genus *Vulpes*) of the dog family related to but smaller than wolves with shorter legs, more pointed muzzle, large erect ears, and long bushy tail **b** : the fur of a fox **2** : a clever crafty person **3** *archaic* : SWORD **4** *cap* : a member of an American Indian people formerly living in what is now Wisconsin **5** : a good-looking young woman or man

²fox *vt* (1611) **1** *obs* : INTOXICATE **2 a** : to trick by ingenuity or cunning : OUTWIT **b** : BAFFLE ⟨~*ed* by his behavior⟩

foxed \ˈfäkst\ *adj* (1847) : discolored with foxing ⟨~ pages⟩

fox fire *n* (15c) : an eerie phosphorescent light (as of decaying wood); *also* : a luminous fungus (as *Armillaria mellea*) that causes decaying wood to glow

fox·glove \ˈfäks-ˌgləv\ *n* (bef. 12c) : any of a genus (*Digitalis*) of erect herbs of the snapdragon family; *esp* : a common European biennial or perennial (*D. purpurea*) cultivated for its showy racemes of dotted white or purple tubular flowers and as a source of digitalis

fox grape *n* (1657) : any of several native grapes (esp. *Vitis labrusca*) of eastern No. America with sour or musky fruit

fox·hole \ˈfäks-ˌhōl\ *n* (1919) : a pit dug usu. hastily for individual cover from enemy fire

fox·hound \-ˌhau̇nd\ *n* (ca. 1763) : any of various large swift powerful hounds of great endurance used in hunting foxes and developed to form several breeds and many distinctive strains — compare AMERICAN FOXHOUND, ENGLISH FOXHOUND

fox·hunt·er \-ˌhən-tər\ *n* (1692) **1** : one who engages in foxhunting **2** : HUNTER 1c

fox·hunt·ing \-ˌhən-tiŋ\ *n* (1674) : a pastime in which participants on horseback ride over the countryside following a pack of hounds on the trail of a fox — **fox·hunt** \-ˌhənt\ *vi*

fox·ing \ˈfäk-siŋ\ *n* (1873) : brownish spots on old paper

fox·tail \ˈfäks-ˌtāl\ *n* (14c) **1 a** : the tail of a fox **b** : something resembling the tail of a fox **2** : any of several grasses (esp. genera *Alopecurus, Hordeum,* and *Setaria*) with spikes resembling brushes — called also *foxtail grass*

foxtail lily *n* (1946) : EREMURUS

foxtail millet *n* (ca. 1899) : a coarse drought-resistant but frost-sensitive annual grass (*Setaria italica*) grown for grain, hay, and forage

fox terrier *n* (1823) : a small lively terrier of either of two breeds formerly used to dig out foxes: **a** : SMOOTH FOX TERRIER **b** : WIRE FOX TERRIER

Fox·trot \ˈfäks-ˌträt\ (1952) — a communications code word for the letter *f*

¹fox–trot \ˈfäks-ˌträt\ *n* (1872) **1** : a short broken slow trotting gait in which the hind foot of the horse hits the ground a trifle before the diagonally opposite forefoot **2** : a ballroom dance in duple time with slow walking steps, quick running steps, and the step of the two-step

²fox–trot *vi* (1916) : to dance the fox-trot

foxy \ˈfäk-sē\ *adj* **fox·i·er; -est** (1528) **1** : resembling or suggestive of a fox ⟨a narrow ~ face⟩: as **a** : cunningly shrewd **b** : of a warm reddish-brown color ⟨~ eyebrows⟩ **2** : having a sharp brisk flavor ⟨~ grapes⟩ **3** : physically attractive ⟨a ~ lady⟩ ***syn*** see SLY — **fox·i·ly** \ˈfäk-sə-lē\ *adv* — **fox·i·ness** \-sē-nəs\ *n*

foy \ˈfȯi\ *n* [D dial. *fooi* feast at end of the harvest] (ca. 1645) *chiefly Scot* : a farewell feast or gift

foy·er \ˈfȯi(-ə)r, ˈfȯi-ˌ(y)ā *also* ˈfwä-ˌyā\ *n* [F, lit., fireplace, fr. VL **focarium,* fr. L *focus* hearth] (1833) : an anteroom or lobby esp. of a theater; *also* : an entrance hallway : VESTIBULE

fp *abbr* freezing point

FP *abbr* fielding percentage

FPC *abbr* fish protein concentrate

fpm *abbr* feet per minute

FPO *abbr* fleet post office

fps *abbr* **1** feet per second **2** foot-pound-second **3** frames per second

fr *abbr* **1** father **2** franc **3** friar **4** from

¹Fr *abbr* **1** France; French **2** Friday

²Fr *symbol* francium

Fra \ˈfrä\ *n* [It, short for *frate,* fr. L *frater* — more at BROTHER] (1722) — used as a title equivalent to *brother* preceding the name of an Italian monk or friar

fra·cas \ˈfrā-kəs, ˈfra-, *Brit* ˈfra-ˌkä\ *n, pl* **fra·cas·es** \-kə-səz\ *or Brit* **frac·as** \-ˌkäz\ [F, din, row, fr. It *fracasso,* fr. *fracassare* to shatter] (1716) : a noisy quarrel : BRAWL

frack·ing \ˈfra-kiŋ\ *n* [by shortening & alter. fr. (*hydraulic*) *fracturing*] (1953) : the injection of fluid into shale beds at high pressure in order to free up petroleum resources (such as oil or natural gas) — **frack** \ˈfrak\ *vb*

frac·tal \ˈfrak-tᵊl\ *n* [F *fractale,* fr. L *fractus* broken, uneven (pp. of *frangere* to break) + F *-ale* -al (n. suffix)] (1975) : any of various extremely irregular curves or shapes for which any suitably chosen part is similar in shape to a given larger or smaller part when magnified or reduced to the same size — **fractal** *adj*

fract·ed \ˈfrak-təd\ *adj* [L *fractus*] (1547) *obs* : BROKEN

frac·tion \ˈfrak-shən\ *n* [ME *fraccioun,* fr. LL *fraction-, fractio* act of breaking, fr. L *frangere* to break — more at BREAK] (14c) **1 a** : a numerical representation (as ¾, ⅝, or 3.234) indicating the quotient of two numbers **b** (1) : a piece broken off : FRAGMENT (2) : a discrete unit : PORTION **2** : one of several portions (as of a distillate) separable by fractionation **3** : BIT, LITTLE ⟨a ~ closer⟩

frac·tion·al \-shnəl, -shə-nᵊl\ *adj* (1650) **1** : of, relating to, or being a fraction **2** : of, relating to, or being fractional currency **3** : relatively small : INCONSIDERABLE **4** : of, relating to, or involving a process for separating components of a mixture through differences in physical or chemical properties ⟨~ distillation⟩ — **frac·tion·al·ly** *adv*

fractional currency *n* (1862) **1** : paper money in denominations of less than one dollar issued by the U.S. 1863–76 **2** : currency in denominations less than the basic monetary unit

frac·tion·al·ize \ˈfrak-shnə-ˌlīz, -shə-nə-ˌlīz\ *vt* **-ized; -iz·ing** (1924) : to break up into parts or sections — **frac·tion·al·i·za·tion** \ˌfrak-shnə-lə-ˈzā-shən, -shə-nə-lə-ˈzā-\ *n*

frac·tion·ate \ˈfrak-shə-ˌnāt\ *vt* **-at·ed; -at·ing** (1867) **1** : to separate (as a mixture) into different portions esp. by a fractional process **2** : to divide or break up — **frac·tion·ation** \ˌfrak-shə-ˈnā-shən\ *n* — **frac·tion·ator** \ˈfrak-shə-ˌnā-tər\ *n*

frac·tious \ˈfrak-shəs\ *adj* [*fraction* (discord) + *-ous*] (1714) **1** : tending to be troublesome : UNRULY ⟨a ~ crowd⟩ **2** : QUARRELSOME, IRRITABLE — **frac·tious·ly** *adv* — **frac·tious·ness** *n*

¹frac·ture \ˈfrak-chər, -shər\ *n* [ME, fr. L *fractura,* fr. *fractus*] (15c) **1** : the result of fracturing : BREAK **2 a** : the act or process of breaking or the state of being broken; *esp* : the breaking of hard tissue (as bone) **b** : the rupture (as by tearing) of soft tissue ⟨kidney ~⟩ **3** : the general appearance of a freshly broken surface of a mineral

²fracture *vb* **frac·tured; frac·tur·ing** \-chə-riŋ, -shriŋ\ *vt* (1612) **1 a** : to cause a fracture in : BREAK ⟨~ a rib⟩ **b** : RUPTURE, TEAR **2 a** : to damage or destroy as if by rupturing **b** : to cause great disorder in **c** : to break up : FRACTIONATE **d** : to go beyond the limits of (as rules) : VIOLATE ⟨*fractured* the English language with malaprops —Goodman Ace⟩ ~ *vi* : to undergo fracture

fracture zone *n* (1946) : an area of suboceanic crust characterized by fractures

frae \ˈfrā\ *prep* [ME (northern) *fra, frae,* fr. ON *frā;* akin to OE *fram* from] (ca. 1585) *Scot* : FROM

frag·ile \ˈfra-jəl, -ˌjī(-ə)l\ *adj* [MF, fr. L *fragilis* — more at FRAIL] (1521) **1 a** : easily broken or destroyed ⟨a ~ vase⟩ **b** : constitutionally delicate : lacking in vigor ⟨a ~ child⟩ **2** : TENUOUS, SLIGHT ⟨~ hope⟩ — **fra·gil·i·ty** \frə-ˈji-lə-tē\ *n*

syn FRAGILE, FRANGIBLE, BRITTLE, CRISP, FRIABLE mean breaking easily. FRAGILE implies extreme delicacy of material or construction and need for careful handling ⟨a *fragile* antique chair⟩. FRANGIBLE implies susceptibility to being broken without implying weakness or delicacy ⟨*frangible* stone used for paving⟩. BRITTLE implies hardness together with lack of elasticity or flexibility or toughness ⟨*brittle* bones⟩. CRISP implies a firmness and brittleness desirable esp. in some foods ⟨*crisp* lettuce⟩. FRIABLE applies to substances that are easily crumbled or pulverized ⟨*friable* soil⟩. ***syn*** see in addition WEAK

fragile X syndrome *n* (1979) : an X-linked inherited disorder that is characterized esp. by moderate to severe mental retardation, by a long face and large ears, and by large testes in males and that often has limited or no effect in heterozygous females — called also *fragile X*

¹frag·ment \ˈfrag-mənt\ *n* [ME, fr. L *fragmentum,* fr. *frangere* to break — more at BREAK] (15c) : a part broken off, detached, or incomplete ***syn*** see PART

²frag·ment \-ˌment\ *vi* (1818) : to fall to pieces ~ *vt* : to break up or apart into fragments

frag·men·tal \frag-ˈmen-tᵊl\ *adj* (1798) : FRAGMENTARY — **frag·men·tal·ly** \-tᵊl-ē\ *adv*

frag·men·tary \ˈfrag-mən-ˌter-ē\ *adj* (1611) : consisting of fragments : INCOMPLETE ⟨~ evidence⟩ ⟨a ~ account⟩ — **frag·men·tari·ly** \ˌfrag-mən-ˈter-ə-lē\ *adv* — **frag·men·tari·ness** \-ˌter-ē-nəs\ *n*

frag·men·ta·tion \ˌfrag-mən-ˈtā-shən, -ˌmen-\ *n* (1881) **1** : the act or process of fragmenting or making fragmentary **2** : the state of being fragmented or fragmentary — **frag·men·tate** \ˈfrag-mən-ˌtāt\ *vb*

fragmentation bomb *n* (1918) : a bomb or shell whose casing is splintered upon explosion and thrown in fragments in all directions

frag·men·tize \ˈfrag-mən-ˌtīz\ *vt* **-tized; -tiz·ing** (1815) : FRAGMENT

fra·grance \ˈfrā-grən(t)s\ *n* (1667) **1 a** : a sweet or delicate odor (as of fresh flowers, pine trees, or perfume) **b** : something (as a perfume) compounded to give off a sweet or pleasant odor **2** : the quality or state of having a sweet odor

syn FRAGRANCE, PERFUME, SCENT, REDOLENCE mean a sweet or pleasant odor. FRAGRANCE suggests the odors of flowers or other growing things ⟨the *fragrance* of pine⟩. PERFUME may suggest a stronger or heavier odor ⟨the *perfume* of lilacs⟩. SCENT is very close to PERFUME but of wider application because more neutral in connotation ⟨*scent*-free soaps⟩. REDOLENCE implies a mixture of fragrant or pungent odors ⟨the *redolence* of a forest after a rain⟩.

fra·gran·cy \-grən(t)-sē\ *n* (1578) : FRAGRANCE

fra·grant \ˈfrā-grənt\ *adj* [ME, fr. L *fragrant-, fragrans,* fr. prp. of *fragrare* to be fragrant] (15c) : having a sweet or pleasant smell ***syn*** see ODOROUS — **fra·grant·ly** *adv*

frail \ˈfrāl\ *adj* [ME, fr. AF *fraile,* fr. L *fragilis* fragile, fr. *frangere*] (14c) **1** : easily led into evil ⟨~ humanity⟩ **2** : easily broken or destroyed : FRAGILE **3 a** : physically weak **b** : SLIGHT, UNSUBSTANTIAL ***syn*** see WEAK — **frail·ly** \ˈfrā(l)-lē\ *adv* — **frail·ness** *n*

frail·ty \ˈfrāl-tē\ *n, pl* **frailties** (14c) **1** : the quality or state of being frail **2** : a fault due to weakness esp. of moral character ***syn*** see FAULT

fraise \ˈfrāz\ *n* [F] (1775) : an obstacle of pointed stakes driven into the ramparts of a fortification in a horizontal or inclined position

Frak·tur *also* **Frac·tur** \fräk-ˈtu̇r\ *n* [G, fr. L *fractura* fracture] (1904) **1** : a German style of black letter **2** *often not cap* : a Pennsylvania German document (as a birth or wedding certificate) that is written in calligraphy and illuminated with decorative motifs (as tulips, birds, and scrolls)

fram·be·sia \fram-ˈbē-zh(ē-)ə\ *n* [NL, fr. F *framboise* raspberry; fr. the appearance of the lesions] (1803) : YAWS

fram·boise \fräⁿ-ˈbwäz\ *n* [F, lit., raspberry, fr. OF, of Gmc origin; akin to D *braambes* blackberry, lit., bramble berry, OHG *brāmberi* — more at BROOM, BERRY] (ca. 1945) : a brandy or liqueur made from raspberries

¹frame \ˈfrām\ *vb* **framed; fram·ing** [ME, to benefit, construct, fr. OE *framian* to benefit, make progress; akin to ON *fram* forward, OE *fram* from] *vt* (14c) **1** : to construct by fitting and uniting the parts of the skeleton of (a structure) **2 a** : PLAN, CONTRIVE ⟨*framed* a new method of achieving their purpose⟩ **b** : SHAPE, CONSTRUCT **c** : to give expression to : FORMULATE **d** : to draw up (as a document) **3 a** : to devise falsely (as a criminal charge) **b** : to contrive the evidence against (an innocent person) so that a verdict of guilty is assured **c** : FIX 7b **4** : to fit or adjust esp. to something or for an end : ARRANGE **5** *obs* : PRODUCE **6** : to enclose in a frame; *also* : to enclose as if in a frame

~ *vi* **1** *archaic* : PROCEED, GO **2** *obs* : MANAGE — **fram·able** *or* **frame·able** \ˈfrā-mə-bəl\ *adj* — **fram·er** *n*

[2]**frame** *n* (14c) **1 a :** something composed of parts fitted together and united **b :** the physical makeup of an animal and esp. a human body : PHYSIQUE, FIGURE **2 a :** the underlying constructional system or structure that gives shape or strength (as to a building) **b :** a frame dwelling **3** *obs* **:** the act or manner of framing **4 a :** a machine built upon or within a framework ⟨a spinning ~⟩ **b :** an open case or structure made for admitting, enclosing, or supporting something ⟨a window ~⟩ **c (1) :** a part of a pair of glasses that holds one of the lenses **(2)** *pl* **:** that part of a pair of glasses other than the lenses **d :** a structural unit in an automobile chassis supported on the axles and supporting the rest of the chassis and the body **5 a :** an enclosing border **b :** the matter or area enclosed in such a border: as **(1) :** one of the squares in which scores for each round are recorded (as in bowling); *also* **:** a round in bowling **(2) :** an individual drawing in a comic strip usu. enclosed by a bordering line **(3) :** one picture of the series on a length of film **(4) :** a complete image for display (as on a television set) **c :** an inning in baseball **d (1) :** FRAMEWORK 1a **(2) :** CONTEXT, FRAME OF REFERENCE **e :** an event that forms the background for the action of a novel or play **6 :** FRAME-UP

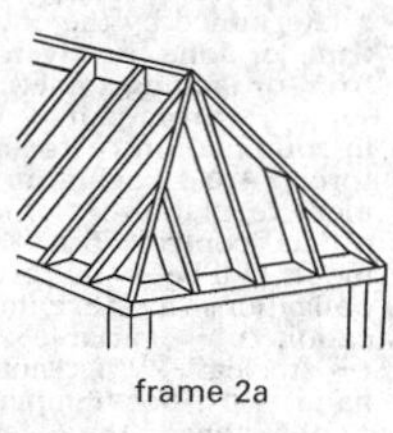
frame 2a

[3]**frame** *adj* (1753) **:** having a wood frame ⟨~ houses⟩

frame of mind (1665) **:** mental attitude or outlook **:** MOOD

frame of reference (1897) **1 :** an arbitrary set of axes with reference to which the position or motion of something is described or physical laws are formulated **2 :** a set of ideas, conditions, or assumptions that determine how something will be approached, perceived, or understood ⟨a Marxian *frame of reference*⟩

frame·shift \ˈfrām-ˌshift\ *adj* (1967) **:** relating to, being, or causing a mutation in which a number of nucleotides not divisible by three is inserted or deleted so as to change the reading frame of some triplet codons during genetic translation — **frameshift** *n*

frame–up \ˈfrām-ˌəp\ *n* (1889) **1 :** an act or series of actions in which someone is framed **2 :** an action that is framed

frame·work \ˈfrām-ˌwərk\ *n* (1578) **1 a :** a basic conceptional structure (as of ideas) ⟨the ~ of the U.S. Constitution⟩ **b :** a skeletal, openwork, or structural frame **2 :** FRAME OF REFERENCE **3 :** the larger branches of a tree that determine its shape

fram·ing \ˈfrā-miŋ\ *n* (1703) **:** FRAME, FRAMEWORK

franc \ˈfraŋk\ *n* [F] (14c) **1 :** any of various former basic monetary units (as in Belgium, France, and Luxembourg) **2 —** see MONEY table

[1]**fran·chise** \ˈfran-ˌchīz\ *n* [ME, fr. AF, fr. *franchir* to free, fr. *franc* free — more at FRANK] (14c) **1 :** freedom or immunity from some burden or restriction vested in a person or group **2 a :** a special privilege granted to an individual or group; *esp* **:** the right to be and exercise the powers of a corporation **b :** a constitutional or statutory right or privilege; *esp* **:** the right to vote **c (1) :** the right or license granted to an individual or group to market a company's goods or services in a particular territory; *also* **:** a business granted such a right or license **(2) :** the territory involved in such a right **3 a :** the right of membership in a professional sports league **b :** a team and its operating organization having such membership

[2]**franchise** *vt* **fran·chised; fran·chis·ing** (14c) **1** *archaic* **:** FREE **2 :** to grant a franchise to

fran·chi·see \ˌfran-ˌchī-ˈzē, -chə-\ *n* (1954) **:** one granted a franchise

fran·chis·er \ˈfran-ˌchī-zər\ *n* [in sense 1, fr. [1]*franchise;* in sense 2, fr. [2]*franchise*] (1843) **1 :** FRANCHISEE **2 :** FRANCHISOR

fran·chi·sor \ˌfran-ˌchī-ˈzȯr, -chə-\ *n* [[2]*franchise* + [1]*-or*] (1967) **:** one that grants a franchise

Fran·cis·can \fran-ˈsis-kən\ *n* [ML *Franciscus* Francis] (1536) **:** a member of the Order of Friars Minor founded by St. Francis of Assisi in 1209 and dedicated esp. to preaching, missions, and charities — **Franciscan** *adj*

fran·ci·um \ˈfran(t)-sē-əm\ *n* [NL, fr. *France*] (1946) **:** a short-lived radioactive element of the alkali-metal group occurring naturally as a disintegration product of actinium and also produced artificially — see ELEMENT table

fran·co \ˈfräŋ-(ˌ)kō, ˈfraŋ-\ *n* [Sp, fr. F *franc*] (1989) **:** the frank of Equatorial Guinea — see MONEY table

Franco- *comb form* [ML, fr. *Francus* Frenchman, fr. LL, Frank] **1 :** French and ⟨*Franco*-American⟩ **2 :** French ⟨*Franco*phile⟩

Fran·co–Amer·i·can \ˌfraŋ-kō-ə-ˈmer-ə-kən\ *n* (1859) **:** an American of French or esp. French-Canadian descent — **Franco–American** *adj*

fran·co·lin \ˈfraŋ-k(ə-)lən\ *n* [F, fr. It *francolino*] (1653) **:** any of a genus (*Francolinus*) of partridges of chiefly southern Asia and Africa

Fran·co·phile \ˈfraŋ-kə-ˌfī(-ə)l, -kō-\ *or* **Fran·co·phil** \-ˌfil\ *adj* (1887) **:** markedly friendly to France or French culture — **Francophile** *n* — **Fran·co·phil·ia** \ˌfraŋ-kə-ˈfi-lē-ə, -lyə, -kō-\ *n*

Fran·co·phobe \-ˌfōb\ *adj* (1855) **:** marked by a fear or strong dislike of France or French culture or customs — **Francophobe** *n* — **Franco·pho·bia** \ˌfraŋ-kə-ˈfō-bē-ə, -kō-\ *n*

fran·co·phone \-ˌfōn\ *adj, often cap* (1962) **:** of, having, or belonging to a population using French as its first or sometimes second language — **Francophone** *n*

franc–ti·reur \ˌfräⁿ-(ˌ)tē-ˈrər\ *n* [F, fr. *franc* free + *tireur* shooter] (1808) **:** a civilian and esp. a guerrilla fighter or sniper

fran·gi·ble \ˈfran-jə-bəl\ *adj* [ME, fr. MF & ML; MF, fr. ML *frangibilis,* fr. L *frangere* to break — more at BREAK] (15c) **:** readily or easily broken *syn* see FRAGILE — **fran·gi·bil·i·ty** \ˌfran-jə-ˈbi-lə-tē\ *n*

fran·gi·pane \ˈfran-jə-ˌpān, fräⁿ-zhē-ˈpän\ *n* [F, frangipani (perfume), fragipane, fr. It] (1858) **:** a custard usu. flavored with almonds

fran·gi·pa·ni *also* **fran·gi·pan·ni** \ˌfran-jə-ˈpa-nē, -ˈpä-\ *n, pl* **-pani** *also* **-panni** [modif. of It *frangipane,* fr. Muzio *Frangipane,* 16th cent. Ital. nobleman] (1675) **1 :** a perfume derived from or imitating the odor of the flower of a frangipani (*Plumeria rubra*) **2 :** any of a genus (*Plumeria*) of shrubs or small trees of the dogbane family that are native to the American tropics and widely cultivated as ornamentals

fran·glais \fräⁿ-ˈglā\ *n, often cap* [F, blend of *français* French and *anglais* English] (1952) **:** French marked by a considerable number of borrowings from English ⟨banning ~ from French broadcasts⟩

[1]**frank** \ˈfraŋk\ *adj* [ME, free, fr. AF *franc,* fr. ML *francus,* fr. LL *Francus* Frank] (1535) **1 :** marked by free, forthright, and sincere expression ⟨a ~ reply⟩ **2 a :** unmistakably evident ⟨~ materialism⟩ **b :** clinically evident and unmistakable ⟨~ pus⟩ — **frank·ness** *n*

syn FRANK, CANDID, OPEN, PLAIN mean showing willingness to tell what one feels or thinks. FRANK stresses lack of shyness or secretiveness or of evasiveness from considerations of tact or expedience ⟨*frank* discussions⟩. CANDID suggests expression marked by sincerity and honesty esp. in offering unwelcome criticism or opinion ⟨a *candid* appraisal⟩. OPEN implies frankness but suggests more indiscretion than FRANK and less earnestness than CANDID ⟨*open* in saying what they think⟩. PLAIN suggests outspokenness and freedom from affectation or subtlety in expression ⟨*plain* talk⟩.

[2]**frank** *vt* (1701) **1 a :** to mark (a piece of mail) with an official signature or sign indicating the right of the sender to free mailing **b :** to mail free **c :** to affix to (mail) a stamp or a marking indicating the payment of postage **2 :** to enable to pass or go freely or easily — **frank·able** \ˈfraŋ-kə-bəl\ *adj* — **frank·er** *n*

[3]**frank** *n* (1713) **1 a :** the signature of the sender on a piece of franked mail serving in place of a postage stamp **b :** a mark or stamp on a piece of mail indicating postage paid **c :** a franked envelope **2 :** the privilege of sending mail free of charge

[4]**frank** *n* (1904) **:** FRANKFURTER

Frank \ˈfraŋk\ *n* [ME, partly fr. OE *Franca;* partly fr. AF *Franc,* fr. LL *Francus,* of Gmc origin; akin to OHG *Franko* Frank, OE *Franca*] (bef. 12c) **:** a member of a West Germanic tribal confederacy that entered the Roman provinces in A.D. 253, occupied the Netherlands and most of Gaul, and established themselves along the Rhine

Fran·ken·food \ˈfraŋ-kən-ˌfüd\ *n* [*Franken-* (as in *Frankenstein*) + *food*] (1992) **:** genetically engineered food

Fran·ken·stein \ˈfraŋ-kən-ˌstīn *also* -ˌstēn\ *n* (1818) **1 a :** the title character in Mary W. Shelley's novel *Frankenstein* who creates a monster that ruins his life **b :** a monster in the shape of a man esp. in popularized versions of the Frankenstein story **2 :** a monstrous creation; *esp* **:** a work or agency that ruins its originator — **Fran·ken·stein·ian** \ˌfraŋ-kən-ˈstī-nē-ən, -ˈsti-\ *adj*

frank·furt·er \ˈfraŋk-fə(r)t-ər, -ˌfərt-\ *or* **frank·furt** \-fərt\ *n* [G *Frankfurter* of Frankfurt, fr. *Frankfurt am Main,* Germany] (1887) **:** a cured cooked sausage (as of beef or beef and pork) that may be skinless or stuffed in a casing

frank·in·cense \ˈfraŋ-kən-ˌsen(t)s\ *n* [ME *fraunk encense,* fr. AF *franc encens,* fr. *franc* (perh. in sense "of high quality") + *encens* incense] (14c) **:** a fragrant gum resin from trees of a genus (*Boswellia* of the family Burseraceae) of Somalia and southern coastal Arabia that is an important incense resin and has been used in religious rites, perfumery, and embalming

[1]**Frank·ish** \ˈfraŋ-kish\ *adj* (14c) **:** of or relating to the Franks

[2]**Frankish** *n* (14c) **:** the Germanic language of the Franks

frank·lin \ˈfraŋ-klən\ *n* [ME *frankeleyn,* fr. AF *franclein,* fr. *franc*] (14c) **:** a medieval English landowner of free but not noble birth

Franklin stove *n* [Benjamin *Franklin,* its inventor] (1776) **:** a metal heating stove resembling an open fireplace but designed to be set out in a room

frank·ly \ˈfraŋ-klē\ *adv* (1537) **1 :** in a frank manner ⟨spoke ~⟩ **2 :** in truth **:** INDEED ⟨~, I don't know⟩ ***usage*** see HOPEFULLY

frank·pledge \ˈfraŋk-ˌplej\ *n* [ME *frankeplegge,* fr. AF *francplege* (prob. trans. of ME *friborg* peace pledge), fr. *franc* free + *plege* pledge] (15c) **:** an Anglo-Saxon system under which each adult male member of a tithing was responsible for the good conduct of the others; *also* **:** the member himself or the tithing

fran·tic \ˈfran-tik\ *adj* [ME *frenetik, frantik* — more at FRENETIC] (14c) **1 a** *archaic* **:** mentally deranged **b :** emotionally out of control **2 :** marked by fast and nervous, disordered, or anxiety-driven activity — **fran·ti·cal·ly** \-ti-k(ə-)lē\ *adv* — **fran·tic·ness** \-tik-nəs\ *n*

frap \ˈfrap\ *vt* **frapped; frap·ping** [ME, to strike, beat, fr. AF *fraper*] (1548) **:** to draw tight (as with ropes or cables) ⟨~ a sail⟩

[1]**frap·pé** \fra-ˈpā\ *adj* [F, fr. pp. of *frapper* to strike, chill, fr. OF *fraper* to strike] (1848) **:** chilled or partly frozen

[2]**frap·pé** \fra-ˈpā\ *or* **frappe** \ˈfrap, fra-ˈpā\ *n* (1903) **1 a :** a partly frozen drink (as of fruit juice) **b :** a liqueur served over shaved ice **2 :** a thick milk shake

Fra·ser fir \ˈfrā-zər-\ *n* [John *Fraser* †1811 Brit. botanist] (1897) **:** a southern Appalachian fir (*Abies fraseri*) that resembles the balsam fir

frass \ˈfras\ *n* [G, insect damage, lit., eating away, fr. OHG *vrāz* food, fr. *frezzan* to devour — more at FRET] (1854) **:** debris or excrement produced by insects

frat \ˈfrat\ *n* (ca. 1895) **:** FRATERNITY 1c

fra·ter·nal \frə-ˈtər-nᵊl\ *adj* [ME, fr. ML *fraternalis,* fr. L *fraternus,* fr. *frater* brother — more at BROTHER] (15c) **1 a :** of, relating to, or involving brothers **b :** of, relating to, or being a fraternity or society ⟨a ~ order⟩ **2 :** derived from two ova **:** DIZYGOTIC ⟨~ twins⟩ **3 :** FRIENDLY, BROTHERLY — **fra·ter·nal·ism** \-nə-ˌliz-əm\ *n* — **fra·ter·nal·ly** \-nᵊl-ē\ *adv*

fra·ter·ni·ty \frə-ˈtər-nə-tē\ *n, pl* **-ties** (14c) **1 :** a group of people associated or formally organized for a common purpose, interest, or pleasure: as **a :** a fraternal order **b :** GUILD 1 **c :** a men's student organization formed chiefly for social purposes having secret rites and a name consisting of Greek letters **d :** a student organization for scholastic, professional, or extracurricular activities ⟨a debating ~⟩ **2 :** the quality or state of being brothers **:** BROTHERLINESS **3 :** persons of the same class, profession, character, or tastes ⟨the racetrack ~⟩

frat·er·nize \ˈfra-tər-ˌnīz\ *vi* **-nized; -niz·ing** (1611) **1 :** to associate or mingle as brothers or on fraternal terms **2 a :** to associate on close terms with members of a hostile group esp. when contrary to military orders **b :** to be friendly or amiable — **frat·er·ni·za·tion** \ˌfra-tər-nə-ˈzā-shən\ *n* — **frat·er·niz·er** \ˈfra-tər-ˌnī-zər\ *n*

frat·ri·cide \ˈfra-trə-ˌsīd\ *n* [in sense 1, fr. ME, fr. MF or L; MF, fr. L *fratricida,* fr. *fratr-, frater* brother + *-cida* -cide; in sense 2, fr. MF or L; MF, fr. L *fratricidium,* fr. *fratr-, frater* + *-cidium* -cide] (15c) **1 :** one that murders or kills his or her own brother or sister or an individual (as a countryman) having a relationship like that of a brother or sister **2 :** the act of a fratricide — **frat·ri·cid·al** \ˌfra-trə-ˈsī-dᵊl\ *adj*

Frau \ˈfrau̇\ *n, pl* **Frau·en** \ˈfrau̇(-ə)n\ [G, woman, wife, fr. OHG *frouwa* mistress, lady; akin to OE *frēa* lord, OHG *fruma* advantage — more at FOREMOST] (ca. 1813) **:** a German married woman **:** WIFE — used as a title equivalent to *Mrs.*

fraud \ˈfrȯd\ *n* [ME *fraude,* fr. AF, fr. L *fraud-, fraus*] (14c) **1 a :** DECEIT, TRICKERY; *specif* **:** intentional perversion of truth in order to induce another to part with something of value or to surrender a legal right **b :** an act of deceiving or misrepresenting **:** TRICK **2 a :** a person who is not what he or she pretends to be **:** IMPOSTOR; *also* **:** one who defrauds **:** CHEAT **b :** one that is not what it seems or is represented to be ***syn*** see DECEPTION, IMPOSTURE

fraud·ster \ˈfrȯd-stər\ *n* (1960) *chiefly Brit* **:** a person who engages in fraud **:** CHEAT

fraud·u·lence \ˈfrȯ-jə-lən(t)s\ *n* (1601) **:** the quality or state of being fraudulent

fraud·u·lent \-lənt\ *adj* (15c) **:** characterized by, based on, or done by fraud **:** DECEITFUL — **fraud·u·lent·ly** *adv* — **fraud·u·lent·ness** *n*

1**fraught** \ˈfrȯkt\ *n* [ME, freight, load, fr. MD or MLG *vracht, vrecht*] (14c) *chiefly Scot* **:** LOAD, CARGO

2**fraught** *vt* **fraught·ed** *or* **fraught; fraught·ing** [ME *fraughten,* fr. *1fraught*] (14c) *chiefly Scot* **:** LOAD, FREIGHT

3**fraught** \ˈfrȯt\ *adj* [ME, fr. pp. of *fraughten*] (14c) **1** *archaic* **a :** LADEN **b :** well supplied or provided **2 :** full of or accompanied by something specified — used with *with* ⟨a situation ~ with danger⟩ **3 :** causing or characterized by emotional distress or tension **:** UNEASY ⟨a ~ relationship⟩

fräu·lein \ˈfrȯi-ˌlīn\ *n* [G, dim. of *Frau*] (ca. 1689) **1** *cap* **:** an unmarried German woman — used as a title equivalent to *Miss* **2 :** a German governess

frax·i·nel·la \ˌfrak-sə-ˈne-lə\ *n* [NL, dim. of L *fraxinus* ash tree — more at BIRCH] (1611) **:** a Eurasian perennial herb (*Dictamnus albus*) of the rue family with flowers that emit an aromatic flammable vapor in hot weather — called also *gas plant*

1**fray** \ˈfrā\ *vt* [ME *fraien,* short for *affraien* to affray] (14c) *archaic* **:** SCARE; *also* **:** to frighten away

2**fray** *n* (14c) **:** a usu. disorderly or protracted fight, struggle, or dispute

3**fray** *vb* [ME *fraien,* fr. AF *freier, froier* to rub, fr. L *fricare* — more at FRICTION] *vt* (15c) **1 a :** to wear (as an edge of cloth) by or as if by rubbing **:** FRET **b :** to separate the threads at the edge of **2 :** STRAIN, IRRITATE ⟨tempers became a bit *~ed*⟩ ~ *vi* **1 :** to wear out or into shreds **2 :** to show signs of strain ⟨*~ing* nerves⟩

4**fray** *n* (1630) **:** a raveled place or worn spot (as on fabric)

fray·ing *n* (1637) **:** something rubbed or worn off by fraying

1**fraz·zle** \ˈfra-zəl\ *vb* **fraz·zled; fraz·zling** \ˈfraz-liŋ, ˈfra-zə-\ [alter. of E dial. *fazle* to tangle, fray] *vt* (ca. 1825) **1 :** 3FRAY **2 a :** to put in a state of extreme physical or nervous fatigue **b :** UPSET ~ *vi* **:** to become frazzled

2**frazzle** *n* (1865) **1 :** the state of being frazzled **2 :** a condition of fatigue or nervous exhaustion ⟨worn to a ~⟩

FRB *abbr* Federal Reserve Board

1**freak** \ˈfrēk\ *n* [origin unknown] (1563) **1 a :** a sudden and odd or seemingly pointless idea or turn of the mind **b :** a seemingly capricious action or event **2** *archaic* **:** a whimsical quality or disposition **3 :** one that is markedly unusual or abnormal: as **a :** a person or animal having a physical oddity and appearing in a circus sideshow **b** *slang* (1) **:** a sexual deviate (2) **:** a person who uses an illicit drug **c :** HIPPIE **d :** an atypical postage stamp usu. caused by a unique defect in paper (as a crease) or a unique event in the manufacturing process (as a speck of dirt on the plate) that does not produce a constant or systematic effect **4 a :** an ardent enthusiast ⟨film *~s*⟩ **b :** a person who is obsessed with something ⟨a control ~⟩

2**freak** *adj* (ca. 1887) **:** having the character of a freak ⟨a ~ accident⟩

3**freak** *vt* (1964) **1 :** to make greatly distressed, astonished, or discomposed — often used with *out* ⟨the news *~ed* them out⟩ **2 :** to put under the influence of a psychedelic drug — often used with *out* ~ *vi* **1 :** to withdraw from reality esp. by taking drugs — often used with *out* **2 :** to experience nightmarish hallucinations as a result of taking drugs — often used with *out* **3 a :** to behave irrationally or unconventionally under the influence of drugs — often used with *out* **b :** to react with extreme or irrational distress or discomposure — often used with *out* — **freaked** *adj* — **freaked–out** *adj*

4**freak** *vt* [perh. fr. or akin to *1freckle*] (1637) **:** to streak esp. with color ⟨silver and mother-of-pearl *~ing* the intense azure —Robert Bridges †1930⟩

freak·ing \ˈfrē-kᵊn, -kiŋ\ *adj or adv* [euphemism for *frigging* or *fucking*] (1928) **:** DAMNED — used as an intensive

freak·ish \ˈfrē-kish\ *adj* (1653) **1 :** WHIMSICAL, CAPRICIOUS **2 :** markedly strange or abnormal ⟨~ appearance⟩ — **freak·ish·ly** *adv* — **freak·ish·ness** *n*

freak of nature (1879) **:** FREAK 3a

freak–out \ˈfrēk-ˌau̇t\ *n* (1966) **1 :** an act or instance of freaking out **2 :** a gathering of hippies

freak show *n* (1887) **:** an exhibition (as a sideshow) featuring freaks of nature

freaky \ˈfrē-kē\ *adj* **freak·i·er; -est** (1824) **:** FREAKISH — **freak·i·ness** *n*

1**freck·le** \ˈfre-kəl\ *n* [ME *freken, frekel,* of Scand origin; akin to ON *freknōttr* freckled] (14c) **:** any of the small brownish spots in the skin due to augmented melanin production that increase in number and intensity on exposure to sunlight — **freck·ly** \ˈfre-k(ə-)lē\ *adj*

2**freckle** *vb* **freck·led; freck·ling** \ˈfre-k(ə-)liŋ\ *vt* (1613) **:** to sprinkle or mark with freckles or small spots ~ *vi* **:** to become marked with freckles

1**free** \ˈfrē\ *adj* **fre·er; fre·est** [ME, fr. OE *frēo;* akin to OHG *frī* free, W *rhydd,* Skt *priya* own, dear] (bef. 12c) **1 a :** having the legal and political rights of a citizen **b :** enjoying civil and political liberty ⟨~ citizens⟩ **c :** enjoying political independence or freedom from outside domination **d :** enjoying personal freedom **:** not subject to the control or domination of another **2 a :** not determined by anything beyond its own nature or being **:** choosing or capable of choosing for itself **b :** determined by the choice of the actor or performer ⟨~ actions⟩ **c :** made, done, or given voluntarily or spontaneously **3 a :** relieved from or lacking something and esp. something unpleasant or burdensome ⟨~ from pain⟩ ⟨a speech ~ of political rhetoric⟩ — often used in combination ⟨error-*free*⟩ **b :** not bound, confined, or detained by force **4 a :** having no trade restrictions **b :** not subject to government regulation **c** *of foreign exchange* **:** not subject to restriction or official control **5 a :** having no obligations (as to work) or commitments ⟨I'll be ~ this evening⟩ **b :** not taken up with commitments or obligations ⟨a ~ evening⟩ **6 :** having a scope not restricted by qualification ⟨a ~ variable⟩ **7 a :** not obstructed, restricted, or impeded ⟨~ to leave⟩ **b :** not being used or occupied ⟨waved with his ~ hand⟩ **c :** not hampered or restricted in its normal operation **8 a :** not fastened ⟨the ~ end of the rope⟩ **b :** not confined to a particular position or place ⟨in twelve-tone music, no note is wholly ~ for it must hold its place in the series —J. L. Stewart⟩ **c :** capable of moving or turning in any direction ⟨a ~ particle⟩ **d :** performed without apparatus ⟨~ tumbling⟩ **e :** done with artificial aids (as pitons) used only for protection against falling and not for support ⟨a ~ climb⟩ **9 a :** not parsimonious ⟨~ spending⟩ **b :** OUTSPOKEN **c :** availing oneself of something without stint **d :** FRANK, OPEN **e :** overly familiar or forward in action or attitude **f :** LICENTIOUS **10 :** not costing or charging anything **11 a** (1) **:** not united with, attached to, combined with, or mixed with something else **:** SEPARATE ⟨~ ores⟩ ⟨a ~ surface of a bodily part⟩ (2) **:** FREESTANDING ⟨a ~ column⟩ **b :** chemically uncombined ⟨~ oxygen⟩ ⟨~ acids⟩ **c :** not permanently attached but able to move about ⟨a ~ electron in a metal⟩ **d :** capable of being used alone as a meaningful linguistic form ⟨the word *hats* is a ~ form⟩ — compare 5BOUND 7 **12 a :** not literal or exact ⟨~ translation⟩ **b :** not restricted by or conforming to conventional forms ⟨~ skating⟩ **13 :** FAVORABLE — used of a wind blowing from a direction more than six points from dead ahead **14 :** not allowing slavery **15 :** open to all comers — **free·ness** \-nəs\ *n* — **for free :** without charge

syn FREE, INDEPENDENT, SOVEREIGN, AUTONOMOUS mean not subject to the rule or control of another. FREE stresses the complete absence of external rule and the full right to make all of one's own decisions ⟨you're *free* to do as you like⟩. INDEPENDENT implies a standing alone; applied to a state it implies lack of connection with any other having power to interfere with its citizens, laws, or policies ⟨the colony's struggle to become *independent*⟩. SOVEREIGN stresses the absence of a superior power and implies supremacy within a thing's own domain or sphere ⟨separate and *sovereign* armed services⟩. AUTONOMOUS stresses independence in matters pertaining to self-government ⟨in this denomination each congregation is regarded as *autonomous*⟩.

2**free** *vt* **freed; free·ing** (bef. 12c) **1 a :** to cause to be free **b :** to relieve or rid of what restrains, confines, restricts, or embarrasses ⟨~ a person from debt⟩ — often used with *up* ⟨~ up space on the hard drive⟩ **c :** DISENTANGLE, CLEAR **2** *obs* **:** BANISH — **fre·er** *n*

syn FREE, RELEASE, LIBERATE, EMANCIPATE, MANUMIT mean to set loose from restraint or constraint. FREE implies a usu. permanent removal from whatever binds, confines, entangles, or oppresses ⟨*freed* the animals from their cages⟩. RELEASE suggests a setting loose from confinement, restraint, or a state of pressure or tension, often without implication of permanent liberation ⟨*released* his anger on a punching bag⟩. LIBERATE stresses particularly the resulting state of liberty ⟨*liberated* their country from the tyrant⟩. EMANCIPATE implies the liberation of a person from subjection or domination ⟨labor-saving devices *emancipated* us from household drudgery⟩. MANUMIT implies emancipation from slavery ⟨the document *manumitted* the slaves⟩.

3**free** *adv* (1559) **1 :** in a free manner **2 :** without charge **3 :** with the wind more than six points from dead ahead ⟨sailing ~⟩

free agent *n* (1955) **:** a professional athlete (as a baseball player) who is free to negotiate a contract with any team — **free agency** *n*

free alongside ship *adv or adj* (1888) **:** with delivery at the side of the ship free of charges and the buyer's liability then beginning

free and easy *adj* (1699) **1 :** marked by informality and lack of constraint ⟨the *free and easy,* open-air life of the plains —Allan Murray⟩ **2 :** not observant of strict demands ⟨too *free and easy* in accepting political contributions⟩ — **free–and–eas·i·ness** \ˌfrē-ən(d)-ˈē-zē-nəs\ *n* — **free and easy** *adv*

free association *n* (1899) **1 a :** the expression (as by speaking or writing) of the content of consciousness without censorship as an aid in gaining access to unconscious processes esp. in psychoanalysis **b :** the reporting of the first thought that comes to mind in response to a given stimulus (as a word) **2 :** an idea or image elicited by free association **3 :** a method using free association — **free–as·so·ci·ate** \ˌfrē-ə-ˈsō-s(h)ē-ˌāt\ *vi* — **free–as·so·ci·at·ive** \-s(h)ē-ˌā-tiv, -shə-tiv\ *adj*

1**free·base** \ˈfrē-ˌbās\ *vi* (1980) **:** to prepare or use freebase cocaine ~ *vt* **:** to prepare or use (cocaine) as freebase — **free·bas·er** *n*

2**freebase** *n* (1980) **:** a purified solid form of cocaine (as crack) that is obtained by treating the powdered hydrochloride of cocaine with an alkaloid base (as sodium bicarbonate) and that can be smoked or heated to produce vapors for inhalation; *specif* **:** a form derived from treatment of the hydrochloride of cocaine with ammonia or similar alkaloid solution followed by extraction with a solvent (as ether)

free beach *n* (1975) **:** a beach at which nudity is permitted

free·bie *or* **free·bee** \ˈfrē-bē\ *n* [by alter. fr. obs. *freeby* gratis, irreg. fr. *free*] (1928) **:** something (as a theater ticket) given without charge

free·board \ˈfrē-ˌbȯrd\ *n* (1726) **1 :** the distance between the waterline and the main deck or weather deck of a ship or between the level of the water and the upper edge of the side of a small boat **2 :** the height above the recorded high-water mark of a structure (as a dam) associated with the water

free·boo·ter \ˈfrē-ˌbü-tər\ *n* [by folk etymology fr. D *vrijbuiter,* fr. *vrijbuit* plunder, fr. *vrij* free + *buit* booty] (1570) **:** PIRATE, PLUNDERER — **free·boot** \-ˌbüt\ *vi*

free·born \ˈfrē-ˈbȯrn\ *adj* (13c) **1 :** not born in vassalage or slavery **2 :** of, relating to, or befitting one that is freeborn

free–climb \ˈfrē-ˌklīm\ *vt* (1969) **:** to climb (as a rock face) without using aids for support ~ *vi* **:** to free-climb something — **free climber** *n*

free diver *n* (1953) **:** one who engages in skin diving — **free diving** *n*

freed•man \ˈfrēd-mən, -ˌman\ *n* (1591) **:** a person freed from slavery
free•dom \ˈfrē-dəm\ *n* (bef. 12c) **1 :** the quality or state of being free: as **a :** the absence of necessity, coercion, or constraint in choice or action **b :** liberation from slavery or restraint or from the power of another **:** INDEPENDENCE **c :** the quality or state of being exempt or released usu. from something onerous ⟨∼ from care⟩ **d :** EASE, FACILITY ⟨spoke the language with ∼⟩ **e :** the quality of being frank, open, or outspoken ⟨answered with ∼⟩ **f :** improper familiarity **g :** boldness of conception or execution **h :** unrestricted use ⟨gave him the ∼ of their home⟩ **2 a :** a political right **b :** FRANCHISE, PRIVILEGE
syn FREEDOM, LIBERTY, LICENSE mean the power or condition of acting without compulsion. FREEDOM has a broad range of application from total absence of restraint to merely a sense of not being unduly hampered or frustrated ⟨*freedom* of the press⟩. LIBERTY suggests release from former restraint or compulsion ⟨the released prisoner had difficulty adjusting to his new *liberty*⟩. LICENSE implies freedom specially granted or conceded and may connote an abuse of freedom ⟨freedom without responsibility may degenerate into *license*⟩.
freedom fighter *n* (1942) **:** a person who takes part in a resistance movement against an oppressive political or social establishment
freedom of the seas (1917) **:** the right of a merchant ship to travel any waters except territorial waters either in peace or war
freedom ride *n, often cap F&R* (1961) **:** a ride made by civil rights workers through states of the southern U.S. to ascertain whether public facilities (as bus terminals) are desegregated — **freedom rider** *n*
freed•wom•an \ˈfrēd-ˌwu̇-mən\ *n* (1862) **:** a woman freed from slavery
free–elec•tron laser \ˈfrē-i-ˈlek-ˌträn-\ *n* (1978) **:** a laser that can be tuned over a wide range of frequencies and that produces electromagnetic radiation by the motion of electrons moving at relativistic velocities in a magnetic field
free enterprise *n* (1890) **:** freedom of private business to organize and operate for profit in a competitive system without interference by government beyond regulation necessary to protect public interest and keep the national economy in balance
free enterpriser *n* (1943) **:** a supporter or advocate of free enterprise
free fall *n* (1919) **1 :** the condition of unrestrained motion in a gravitational field; *also* **:** such motion **2 a :** the part of a parachute jump before the parachute opens **b :** a rapid and continuing drop or decline ⟨a *free fall* in stock prices⟩ — **free–fall** *vi*
free–fire zone \ˈfrē-ˌfī-(ə)-r-\ *n* (1967) **:** a combat area in which any moving thing is a legitimate target
free–float•ing \-ˈflō-tiŋ\ *adj* (1921) **1 a :** floating freely ⟨∼ vegetation⟩ **b :** lacking specific attachment, direction, or purpose ⟨∼ ideas⟩ **2 :** felt as an emotion without apparent cause ⟨∼ anxiety⟩
free–flow•ing \-ˌflō-iŋ\ *adj* (1875) **:** characterized by easy freedom in movement, progression, or style ⟨a ∼ essay⟩
free–for–all \ˈfrē-fə-ˌrȯl\ *n* (1881) **:** a competition, dispute, or fight open to all comers and usu. with no rules **:** BRAWL; *also* **:** a chaotic situation resembling a free-for-all esp. in lacking rules or structure ⟨the press conference deteriorated into a ∼⟩ — **free–for–all** *adj*
free–form \ˈfrē-ˈfȯrm\ *adj* (1950) **1 :** having or being an irregular or asymmetrical shape or design ⟨∼ furniture⟩ **2 :** FREE 12b ⟨∼ dancing⟩
free•gan \ˈfrē-gən\ *n* (2006) **:** an activist who scavenges for free food (as in waste receptacles at stores and restaurants) as a means of reducing consumption of resources — **free•gan•ism** \ˈfrē-gə-ˌni-zəm\ *n*
free•hand \ˈfrē-ˌhand\ *adj* (ca. 1862) **:** done without mechanical aids or devices ⟨∼ drawing⟩ — **freehand** *adv*
free hand \-ˈhand\ *n* (1890) **:** freedom of action or decision
free•hand•ed \ˈfrē-ˈhan-dəd\ *adj* (1592) **:** GENEROUS, OPENHANDED — **free•hand•ed•ly** *adv* — **free•hand•ed•ness** *n*
free•heart•ed \-ˈhär-təd\ *adj* (14c) **1 :** FRANK, UNRESERVED **2 :** GENEROUS — **free•heart•ed•ly** *adv*
free•hold \ˈfrē-ˌhōld\ *n* (15c) **1 :** a tenure of real property by which an estate in fee simple or fee tail or an estate for life is held; *also* **:** an estate held by such tenure — compare FEE 1 **2** *Brit* **:** an estate held in fee simple — **freehold** *adj or adv* — **free•hold•er** \-ˌhōl-dər\ *n*
free jazz *n* (1972) **:** free-form jazz marked esp. by an abandonment of preset chord progression and a lack of melodic pattern
free kick *n* (1882) **:** a kick (as in football, soccer, or rugby) with which an opponent may not interfere; *esp* **:** such a kick in any direction awarded because of an infraction of the rules by an opponent
¹free•lance \ˈfrē-ˌlan(t)s\ *n* (1820) **1 a** *usu* **free lance :** a mercenary soldier esp. of the Middle Ages **:** CONDOTTIERE **b :** a person who acts independently without being affiliated with or authorized by an organization **2 :** a person who pursues a profession without a long-term commitment to any one employer
²freelance *adj* (1901) **1 a :** of, relating to, or being a freelance **:** INDEPENDENT ⟨a ∼ writer⟩ **b :** done by a freelance ⟨∼ reviewing⟩ **2 :** not sponsored by an organization ⟨∼ terrorists⟩ — **freelance** *adv*
³freelance *vi* (1902) **:** to act or work as a freelance ∼ *vt* **:** to produce as a freelance ⟨*freelancing* magazine articles⟩
free•lanc•er \ˈfrē-ˌlan(t)-sər\ *n* (1937) **1 :** FREELANCE 1b **2 :** FREELANCE 2
free–liv•ing \ˈfrē-ˈli-viŋ\ *adj* (1818) **1 :** marked by more than usual freedom in the gratification of appetites **2 a :** not fixed to the substrate but capable of motility ⟨a ∼ protozoan⟩ **b :** being metabolically independent **:** neither parasitic nor symbiotic ⟨a ∼ adult hairworm⟩
free•load \-ˌlōd\ *vi* (ca. 1934) **:** to impose upon another's generosity or hospitality without sharing in the cost or responsibility involved **:** SPONGE — **free•load•er** *n*
free love *n* (1822) **1 :** living openly with a sexual partner without marriage **2 :** sexual relations with no commitments by either partner
free lunch *n* (1949) **:** something one does not have to pay for; *also* **:** FREE RIDE
free•ly \ˈfrē-lē\ *adv* (bef. 12c) **:** in a free manner: as **a :** of one's own accord ⟨left home ∼⟩ **b :** with freedom from external control ⟨a ∼ elected government⟩ **c :** without restraint or reservation ⟨spent ∼ on clothes⟩ **d :** without hindrance ⟨a gate swinging ∼⟩ **e :** not strictly following a model, convention, or rule ⟨∼ translated⟩
free•man \ˈfrē-mən, -ˌman\ *n* (bef. 12c) **1 :** one enjoying civil or political liberty **2 :** one having the full rights of a citizen
free market *n* (1897) **:** an economy operating by free competition
free marketeer *also* **free marketer** *n* (1954) **:** a proponent of a free-market economy
free•mar•tin \ˈfrē-ˌmär-tᵊn\ *n* [origin unknown] (1681) **:** a sexually imperfect usu. sterile female calf twinborn with a male
Free•ma•son \-ˈmā-sᵊn\ *n* (1646) **:** a member of a major fraternal organization called Free and Accepted Masons or Ancient Free and Accepted Masons that has certain secret rituals
free•ma•son•ry \-rē\ *n* (1730) **1** *cap* **:** the principles, institutions, or practices of Freemasons — called also *Masonry* **2 :** natural fellowship based on some common experience
free on board *adv or adj* (1668) **:** without charge for delivery to and placing on board a carrier at a specified point
free port *n* (1711) **:** an enclosed port or section of a port where goods are received and shipped free of customs duty
freer *comparative of* FREE
free radical *n* (1900) **:** an esp. reactive atom or group of atoms that has one or more unpaired electrons; *esp* **:** one that is produced in the body by natural biological processes or introduced from an outside source (as tobacco smoke, toxins, or pollutants) and that can damage cells, proteins, and DNA by altering their chemical structure
free–range \ˈfrē-ˌrānj\ *adj* (1960) **:** allowed to range and forage with relative freedom ⟨∼ chickens⟩; *also* **:** of, relating to, or produced by free-range animals ⟨∼ eggs⟩
free reed *n* (1855) **:** a reed in a musical instrument (as a harmonica) that vibrates in an air opening just large enough to allow the reed to move freely — compare BEATING REED
free rein *n* (1952) **:** unrestricted liberty of action or decision
free ride *n* (1882) **:** a benefit obtained at another's expense or without the usual cost or effort; *also* **:** soft or easy treatment — **free ride** *vi* — **free rider** *n*
free safety *n* (1971) **:** a safety in football who has no particular receiver to cover in a man-to-man defense
free•sia \ˈfrē-zh(ē-)ə, -zē-ə\ *n* [NL, fr. F. H. T. *Freese* †1876 Ger. physician] (ca. 1882) **:** any of a genus (*Freesia*) of sweet-scented African herbs of the iris family with usu. red, pink, white, or yellow flowers
free–soil *adj* (1846) **1 :** characterized by free soil ⟨∼ states⟩ **2** *cap F&S* **:** opposing the extension of slavery into U.S. territories and the admission of slave states into the Union prior to the Civil War; *specif* **:** of, relating to, or being a minor U.S. political party with these aims — **Free–Soil•er** \-ˈsȯi-lər\ *n* — **Free–Soil•ism** \-ˈsȯi(-ə)-ˌli-zəm\ *n*
free soil *n* (1827) **:** U.S. territory where prior to the Civil War slavery was prohibited
free speech *n* (1781) **:** speech that is protected by the First Amendment to the U.S. Constitution; *also* **:** the right to such speech ⟨an unconstitutional restraint on *free speech* —*Nat'l Law Jour.*⟩
free spirit *n* (1970) **:** NONCONFORMIST 2 — **free–spir•it•ed** \ˈfrē-ˈspir-ə-təd\ *adj*
free–spo•ken \ˈfrē-ˈspō-kən\ *adj* (1625) **:** speaking freely **:** OUTSPOKEN
freest *superlative of* FREE
free•stand•ing \ˈfrē-ˈstan-diŋ\ *adj* (1876) **1 :** standing alone or on its own foundation free of support or attachment ⟨a ∼ wall⟩ **2 :** INDEPENDENT 1; *esp* **:** not being part of or affiliated with another organization ⟨a ∼ clinic⟩ ⟨a ∼ city⟩ ⟨a ∼ computer store⟩
Free State *n* (1819) **:** a state of the U.S. in which slavery was prohibited before the Civil War
free•stone \ˈfrē-ˌstōn\ *n* (13c) **1 :** a stone that may be cut freely without splitting **2 a :** a fruit stone to which the flesh does not cling **b :** a fruit having such a stone
free•style \ˈfrē-ˌstī(-ə)l\ *n, often attrib* (ca. 1934) **1 :** a competition in which the contestant is given more latitude than in related events; *esp* **:** swimming competition in which the swimmer may use any stroke **2 :** CRAWL 2 — **free•styl•er** *n*
free–swim•ming \-ˈswi-miŋ\ *adj* (1869) **:** able to swim about **:** not attached ⟨the ∼ larva of the barnacle⟩
free–swing•ing \-ˈswiŋ-iŋ\ *adj* (1949) **:** bold, forthright, and heedless of personal consequences ⟨a ∼ soldier of fortune —Will Herberg⟩
free–tailed bat \ˈfrē-ˌtāld-\ *n* (1895) **:** any of a family (Molossidae) of bats characterized by a tail that projects beyond the posterior part of the flight membrane and found in warm regions of the world
free•think•er \-ˈthiŋ-kər\ *n* (1692) **:** one who forms opinions on the basis of reason independently of authority; *esp* **:** one who doubts or denies religious dogma — **free•think•ing** \-kiŋ\ *n or adj*
free thought *n* (1711) **:** unorthodox attitudes or beliefs; *specif* **:** 18th century deism
free throw *n* (1891) **:** an unhindered shot in basketball made from behind a set line and awarded because of a foul by an opponent
free throw lane *n* (ca. 1929) **:** a 12 or 16 foot wide lane on a basketball court that extends from underneath the goal to a line 15 feet in front of the backboard and that players may not enter during a free throw
free trade *n* (1655) **:** trade based on the unrestricted international exchange of goods with tariffs used only as a source of revenue
free trader *n* (1832) **:** one that practices or advocates free trade
free verse *n* (1908) **:** verse whose meter is irregular in some respect or whose rhythm is not metrical
free•ware \ˈfrē-ˌwer\ *n* (1983) **:** software that is available for use at no cost or for a nominal usu. voluntary fee
free•way \ˈfrē-ˌwā\ *n* (ca. 1930) **1 :** an expressway with fully controlled access **2 :** a highway without toll fees
¹free•wheel \-ˈ(h)wēl\ *n* (1930) **:** a clutch fitted in the rear hub of a bicycle that permits the rear wheel to run on free from the rear sprocket when the pedals are stopped
²freewheel *vi* (1903) **1 :** to roll along freely independent of a gear **2 :** to move, live, or play freely or irresponsibly — **free•wheel•er** *n*
free•wheel•ing \ˌfrē-ˈhwē-liŋ, -ˈwē-\ *adj* (1931) **:** free and loose in form or manner: as **a :** heedless of social norms or niceties ⟨the raider style of his ∼ father —Garry Wills⟩ **b :** not repressed or restrained ⟨∼ promiscuity⟩ ⟨a ∼ competitive spirit⟩ **c :** not bound by formal rules,

procedures, or guidelines ⟨a ~ investigation⟩ **d :** loose and undisciplined : not defensive ⟨a ~ style of hockey⟩ — **free·wheel·ing·ly** *adv*
free·will \ˈfrē-ˌwil\ *adj* (1535) : VOLUNTARY, SPONTANEOUS
free will *n* (13c) **1 :** voluntary choice or decision ⟨I do this of my own *free will*⟩ **2 :** freedom of humans to make choices that are not determined by prior causes or by divine intervention
Freewill Baptist *n* (1732) : a member of a Baptist group holding to Arminian doctrine and practicing open communion
free world *n, often cap F&W* (1949) : the part of the world where democracy and capitalism or moderate socialism rather than totalitarian or Communist political and economic systems prevail
free·writ·ing \ˈfrē-ˈrī-tiŋ\ *n* (1980) : automatic writing done esp. as a classroom exercise — **free·write** \ˈfrē-ˌrīt\ *vi*
1**freeze** \ˈfrēz\ *vb* **froze** \ˈfrōz\; **fro·zen** \ˈfrō-zᵊn\; **freez·ing** [ME *fresen,* fr. OE *frēosan;* akin to OHG *friosan* to freeze, L *pruina* hoarfrost, OE *frost* frost] *vi* (bef. 12c) **1 a :** to become congealed into ice by cold **b :** to solidify as a result of abstraction of heat **c :** to withstand freezing ⟨the bread ~*s* well⟩ **2 :** to become chilled with cold ⟨almost *froze* to death⟩ **3 :** to adhere solidly by or as if by freezing ⟨pressure caused the metals to ~⟩ **4 :** to become fixed or motionless; *esp* : to become incapable of acting or speaking **5 :** to become clogged with ice ⟨the water pipes *froze*⟩ ~ *vt* **1 a :** to harden into ice **b :** to convert from a liquid to a solid by cold **2 :** to make extremely cold : CHILL **3 a :** to act on usu. destructively by frost **b :** to anesthetize by cold **4 :** to cause to grip tightly or remain in immovable contact **5 a :** to cause to become fixed, immovable, unavailable, or unalterable ⟨~ interest rates⟩ **b :** to immobilize by governmental regulation the expenditure, withdrawal, or exchange of ⟨~ foreign assets⟩ **c :** to render motionless ⟨a fake *froze* the defender⟩ **6 :** to attempt to retain continuous possession of (a ball or puck) without an attempt to score usu. in order to protect a small lead — **freez·ing·ly** *adv*
2**freeze** *n* (15c) **1 a :** an act or instance of freezing **b :** the state of being frozen **2 :** a state of weather marked by low temperature esp. when below the freezing point **3 :** a halt in the production, testing, and deployment of military weapons ⟨a nuclear ~⟩
freeze–dried \-ˈdrīd\ *adj* (1946) : being in a state produced by or as if by freeze-drying
freeze–dry \-ˈdrī\ *vt* (1949) : to dry (as food) in a frozen state under high vacuum esp. for preservation
freeze–etch·ing \ˈfrēz-ˌe-chiŋ\ *n* (1968) : FREEZE FRACTURE
freeze fracture *n* (1973) : preparation of a specimen (as of tissue) for examination by an electron microscope after freezing, fracturing along natural structural lines, and preparing a replica (as by simultaneous vapor deposition of carbon and platinum) — **freeze–frac·ture** *adj*
freeze–frame \ˈfrēz-ˈfrām\ *n* (1948) **1 a :** a frame of a motion-picture film that is repeated so as to give the illusion of a static picture **b :** a static picture produced esp. from a videodisc or videotape recording **2 :** something resembling a freeze-frame esp. in unchanging quality — **freeze–frame** *vt*
freeze out *vt* (1861) : EXCLUDE — **freeze–out** \ˈfrēz-ˌau̇t\ *n*
freez·er \ˈfrē-zər\ *n* (1843) : one that freezes or keeps cool; *esp* : a compartment, room, or device for freezing food or keeping it frozen
freezer burn *n* (1926) : light-colored spots developed in frozen foods as a result of surface evaporation and drying when inadequately wrapped or packaged
freezing point *n* (1747) : the temperature at which a liquid solidifies
free zone *n* (1900) : an area within which goods may be received and stored without payment of duty
F region *n* (1923) : the highest region of the ionosphere occurring from 80 miles (130 kilometers) to more than 300 miles (500 kilometers)
1**freight** \ˈfrāt\ *n, often attrib* [ME, fr. MD or MLG *vracht, vrecht*] (15c) **1 a :** the compensation paid for the transportation of goods **b :** COST ⟨help pay the ~⟩ **2 a :** goods to be shipped : CARGO **b :** LOAD, BURDEN **c :** MEANING 3, SIGNIFICANCE **3 a :** the ordinary transportation of goods by a common carrier and distinguished from express **b :** a train designed or used for such transportation
2**freight** *vt* (15c) **1 a :** to load with goods for transportation **b :** BURDEN, CHARGE ⟨~*ed* with memories⟩ **2 :** to transport or ship by freight
freight·age \ˈfrā-tij\ *n* (1694) : FREIGHT
freight·er \-tər\ *n* (1622) **1 :** one that loads or charters and loads a ship **2 :** SHIPPER **3 :** a ship or airplane used chiefly to carry freight
frem·i·tus \ˈfre-mə-təs\ *n* [NL, fr. L, murmur, fr. *fremere* to murmur; akin to OE *bremman* to roar] (1862) : a sensation felt by a hand placed on a part of the body (as the chest) that vibrates during speech
french \ˈfrench\ *vt, often cap* (ca. 1895) **1 :** to trim the meat from the end of the bone of (as a chop) **2 :** to cut (green beans) in thin lengthwise strips before cooking
1**French** \ˈfrench\ *adj* [ME, fr. OE *frencisc,* fr. *Franca* Frank] (bef. 12c) **1 :** of, relating to, or characteristic of France, its people, or their language **2 :** of or relating to the overseas descendants of the French people — **French·ness** *n*
2**French** *n* (12c) **1 :** a Romance language that developed out of the Vulgar Latin spoken in northern and central Transalpine Gaul and that became the literary and official language of France **2** *pl in constr* : the French people **3 :** strong language ⟨pardon my ~⟩
French bean *n* (1552) **1** *chiefly Brit* : a bean (as a green bean) of which the whole young pod is eaten **2** *chiefly Brit* : KIDNEY BEAN 2
French bread *n* (15c) : a crusty white bread baked usu. in long thin loaves
French bulldog *n* (1875) : any of a breed of small compact heavy-boned dogs developed in France and having erect ears
French Canadian *n* (1758) : one of the descendants of French settlers in Lower Canada — **French–Canadian** *adj*
French chalk *n* (ca. 1728) : a soft white granular variety of steatite used esp. for drawing lines on cloth and for removing grease in dry cleaning
French cuff *n* (1916) : a soft double cuff that is made by turning back half of a wide cuff band and fastening with cuff links
french curve *n, often cap F* (1885) : a curved piece of flat often plastic material used as a guide in drawing curves
French door *n* (1917) : a door with rectangular glass panes extending the full length; *also* : FRENCH WINDOW
French dressing *n* (1876) **1 :** a salad dressing made with oil and vinegar or lemon juice, and spices **2 :** a commercial salad dressing that is tomato-flavored and of creamy consistency
1**french fry** *n, often cap 1st F* (1918) : a strip of potato fried in deep fat — usu. used in pl.
2**french fry** *vt, often cap 1st F* (ca. 1930) : to fry (as strips of potato) in deep fat until brown
French horn *n* (1682) : a circular valved brass instrument having a conical bore, a funnel-shaped mouthpiece, and a usual range from B below the bass staff upward for more than three octaves

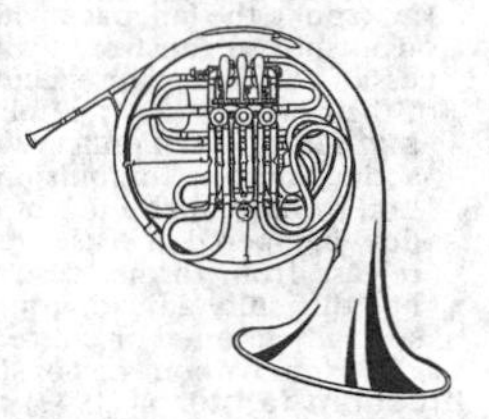
French horn

french·ify \ˈfren-chə-ˌfī\ *vt* **-ified; -ify·ing** *often cap* (1592) : to make French in qualities, traits, or typical practices — **french·i·fi·ca·tion** \ˌfren-chə-fi-ˈkā-shən\ *n, often cap*
French kiss *n* (ca. 1923) : an open-mouth kiss usu. involving tongue-to-tongue contact — **French–kiss** *vb*
French leave *n* [fr. an 18th cent. French custom of leaving a reception without taking leave of the host or hostess] (1771) : an informal, hasty, or secret departure
French letter *n* (ca. 1856) *chiefly Brit* : CONDOM 1
French·man \ˈfrench-mən\ *n* (bef. 12c) **1 :** a native or inhabitant of France **2 :** a person who is of French descent
French pastry *n* (1847) : a rich pastry filled esp. with custard or fruit
French press *n* (1986) : a coffeepot in which ground beans are infused and then pressed to the bottom by means of a plunger
French provincial *n, often cap P* (1945) : a style of furniture, architecture, or fabric originating in or characteristic of the 17th and 18th century French provinces
French seam *n* (ca. 1890) : a strong seam stitched on both sides of the fabric to enclose all raw edges
French telephone *n* (1932) : HANDSET
French toast *n* (1871) : bread dipped in a mixture of egg and milk and sautéed
French twist *n* (1855) : a woman's hairstyle in which the hair is coiled at the rear and secured in place
French window *n* (1801) : a pair of casement windows that reaches to the floor, opens in the middle, and is placed in an exterior wall
French·wom·an \ˈfrench-ˌwu̇-mən\ *n* (1592) **1 :** a woman who is a native or inhabitant of France **2 :** a woman of French descent
fren·e·my \ˈfre-nə-mē\ *n, pl* **-mies** [blend of *friend* and *enemy*] (1977) : one who pretends to be a friend but is actually an enemy
fre·net·ic \fri-ˈne-tik\ *adj* [ME *frenetik* insane, fr. AF, fr. L *phreneticus,* modif. of Gk *phrenitikos,* fr. *phrenitis* inflammation of the brain, fr. *phren-, phrēn* diaphragm, mind] (14c) : FRENZIED, FRANTIC — **fre·net·i·cal·ly** \-ti-k(ə-)lē\ *adv* — **fre·net·i·cism** \-ˈne-tə-ˌsi-zəm\ *n*
fren·u·lum \ˈfren-yə-ləm\ *n, pl* **-la** \-lə\ [NL, dim. of L *frenum*] (ca. 1706) **1 :** a connecting fold of membrane serving to support or restrain a part (as the tongue) **2 :** a bristle or group of bristles on the front edge of the posterior wings of some lepidoptera that unites the wings by interlocking with a catch on the posterior part of the forewings
fre·num \ˈfrē-nəm\ *n, pl* **frenums** *or* **fre·na** \-nə\ [NL, fr. L, bridle, reins, and bit; prob. akin to L *frendere* to grind — more at GRIND] (1741) : FRENULUM 1
frenzied *adj* (1651) : feeling or showing great or abnormal excitement or emotional disturbance ⟨~ dancing⟩ — **fren·zied·ly** *adv*
1**fren·zy** \ˈfren-zē\ *n, pl* **frenzies** [ME *frenesie,* fr. MF, fr. ML *phrenesia,* alter. of L *phrenesis,* fr. *phreneticus*] (14c) **1 a :** a temporary madness **b :** a violent mental or emotional agitation **2 :** intense usu. wild and often disorderly compulsive or agitated activity ⟨a shopping ~⟩
2**frenzy** *vt* **fren·zied; fren·zy·ing** (1791) : to affect with frenzy
Fre·on \ˈfrē-ˌän\ *trademark* — used for any of various fluorocarbons
freq *abbr* **1** frequency **2** frequent; frequently **3** frequentative
fre·quence \ˈfrē-kwən(t)s\ *n* (1603) : FREQUENCY
fre·quen·cy \ˈfrē-kwən(t)-sē\ *n, pl* **-cies** (1600) **1 :** the fact or condition of occurring frequently **2 a :** the number of times that a periodic function repeats the same sequence of values during a unit variation of the independent variable **b :** the number, proportion, or percentage of items in a particular category in a set of data **3 :** the number of repetitions of a periodic process in a unit of time: as **a :** the number of complete alternations per second of an alternating current **b :** the number of complete oscillations per second of energy (as sound or electromagnetic radiation) in the form of waves
frequency distribution *n* (1895) : an arrangement of statistical data that exhibits the frequency of the occurrence of the values of a variable
frequency modulation *n* (1922) : modulation of the frequency of the carrier wave in accordance with speech or a signal; *also* : FM
frequency response *n* (1926) : the ability of a device (as an audio amplifier) to handle the frequencies applied to it; *also* : a graph representing this ability
1**fre·quent** \frē-ˈkwent, ˈfrē-kwənt\ *vt* (15c) **1 :** to associate with, be in, or resort to often or habitually ⟨a bar ~*ed* by sports fans⟩ **2** *archaic* : to read systematically or habitually — **fre·quen·ta·tion** \ˌfrē-ˌkwen-ˈtā-shən, -kwən-\ *n* — **fre·quent·er** *n*
2**fre·quent** \ˈfrē-kwənt\ *adj* [ME, ample, fr. MF or L; MF, crowded, fr. L *frequent-, frequens*] (1531) **1 a :** COMMON, USUAL **b :** happening at short intervals : often repeated or occurring ⟨a bus making ~ stops⟩ **2** *obs* : FULL, THRONGED **3 :** acting or returning regularly or often ⟨a ~ visitor⟩ **4** *archaic* : INTIMATE, FAMILIAR — **fre·quent·ness** *n*
fre·quen·ta·tive \frē-ˈkwen-tə-tiv\ *adj* (1533) : denoting repeated or recurrent action or state — used of a verb aspect, verb form, or meaning — **frequentative** *n*
fre·quent–fli·er *also* **fre·quent–fly·er** \ˈfrē-kwənt-ˈflī-ər\ *adj* : of, relating to, or being an airline program that offers awards for specified numbers of air miles traveled
fre·quent·ly \ˈfrē-kwənt-lē\ *adv* (1531) : at frequent or short intervals
fres·co \ˈfres-(ˌ)kō\ *n, pl* **frescoes** [It, fr. *fresco* fresh, of Gmc origin; akin to OHG *frisc* fresh] (1598) **1 :** the art of painting on freshly spread moist lime plaster with water-based pigments **2 :** a painting executed in fresco — **fresco** *vt*

[1]**fresh** \ˈfresh\ *adj* [ME, fr. AF *fresch, freis,* of Gmc origin; akin to OHG *frisc* fresh; akin to OE *fersc* fresh] (13c) **1 a :** having its original qualities unimpaired: as **(1) :** full of or renewed in vigor **:** REFRESHED ⟨rose ~ from a good night's sleep⟩ **(2) :** not stale, sour, or decayed ⟨~ bread⟩ **(3) :** not faded ⟨lessons ~ in her memory⟩ **(4) :** not worn or rumpled ⟨a ~ white shirt⟩ **b :** not altered by processing ⟨~ vegetables⟩ **2 a :** not salt **b (1) :** free from taint **:** PURE ⟨~ air⟩ **(2)** *of wind* **:** moderately strong **3 a (1) :** experienced, made, or received newly or anew **(2) :** ADDITIONAL, ANOTHER ⟨a ~ start⟩ **b :** ORIGINAL, VIVID ⟨a ~ portrayal⟩ **c :** lacking experience **:** RAW **d :** just come or arrived ⟨~ from school⟩ **e :** having the milk flow recently established ⟨a ~ cow⟩ **4** [prob. by folk etymology fr. G *frech*] **:** disposed to take liberties **:** IMPUDENT ⟨don't get ~ with me⟩ **5** *slang* **:** FASHIONABLE, COOL ***syn*** see NEW — **fresh·ly** *adv* — **fresh·ness** *n*

[2]**fresh** *adv* (14c) **:** just recently **:** NEWLY ⟨we're ~ out of eggs⟩

[3]**fresh** *n* (1538) **1 :** an increased flow or rush (as of water) **:** FRESHET **2** *archaic* **:** a stream, spring, or pool of freshwater

fresh breeze *n* (1846) **:** wind having a speed of 19 to 24 miles per hour (30 to 39 kilometers per hour) — see BEAUFORT SCALE table

fresh·en \ˈfre-shən\ *vb* **fresh·ened; fresh·en·ing** \-sh(ə-)niŋ\ *vi* (1697) **1 :** to grow or become fresh: as **a** *of wind* **:** to increase in strength **b :** to become fresh in appearance or vitality — usu. used with *up* ⟨~ up with a shower⟩ **2** *of a milk animal* **:** to begin lactating ~ *vt* **:** to make fresh; *also* **:** REFRESH, REVIVE — **fresh·en·er** \-sh(ə-)nər\ *n*

fresh·et \ˈfre-shət\ *n* (1596) **1** *archaic* **:** STREAM 1 **2 a :** a great rise or overflowing of a stream caused by heavy rains or melted snow **b :** a swelling quantity **:** INFLUX ⟨summer brings a ~ of tourists⟩

fresh gale *n* (1582) **:** wind having a speed of 39 to 46 miles per hour (62 to 74 kilometers per hour) — see BEAUFORT SCALE table

fresh·man \ˈfresh-mən\ *n, often attrib* (1552) **1 :** a first-year student **2 :** BEGINNER, NEWCOMER

[1]**fresh·wa·ter** \ˈfresh-ˈwȯ-tər, -ˈwä-\ *n* (14c) **:** water that is not salty esp. when considered as a natural resource

[2]**freshwater** *adj* (1528) **1 :** of, relating to, being, or living in freshwater **2 :** accustomed to navigating only in inland waters ⟨a ~ sailor⟩; *also* **:** UNSKILLED **3 :** inland and usu. provincial ⟨a ~ college⟩

freshwater drum *n* (1879) **:** a croaker (*Aplodinotus grunniens*) of the Great Lakes and Mississippi River valley that may attain a weight of 50 pounds (23 kilograms) or more — called also *sheepshead, white perch*

freshwater pearl *n* (1918) **:** a usu. very small pearl produced by a freshwater mollusk

Fres·nel lens \ˈfrez-nəl-, frā-ˈnel-\ *n* [Augustin J. *Fresnel*] (1865) **:** a lens that has a surface consisting of a concentric series of simple lens sections so that a thin lens with a short focal length and large diameter is possible and that is used esp. for spotlights

[1]**fret** \ˈfret\ *vb* **fret·ted; fret·ting** [ME, to devour, fret, fr. OE *fretan* to devour; akin to OHG *frezzan* to devour, *ezzan* to eat — more at EAT] *vt* (12c) **1 a :** to eat or gnaw into **:** CORRODE; *also* **:** FRAY **b :** RUB, CHAFE **c :** to make by wearing away a substance ⟨the stream *fretted* a channel⟩ **2 :** to cause to suffer emotional strain **:** VEX **3 :** to pass (as time) in fretting **4 :** AGITATE, RIPPLE ~ *vi* **1 a :** to eat into something **b :** to affect something as if by gnawing or biting **:** GRATE **2 a :** WEAR, CORRODE **b :** CHAFE **c :** FRAY 1 **3 a :** to become vexed or worried **b** *of running water* **:** to become agitated

[2]**fret** *n* (15c) **1 a :** the action of wearing away **:** EROSION **b :** a worn or eroded spot **2 :** an agitation of mind **:** IRRITATION

[3]**fret** *vt* **fret·ted; fret·ting** [ME, back-formation fr. *fret, fretted* adorned, interwoven, fr. AF *fretté,* pp. of *fretter* to tie, prob. fr. VL **firmitare,* fr. L *firmus* firm] (14c) **1 a :** to decorate with interlaced designs **b :** to form a pattern upon **2 :** to enrich with embossed or carved patterns

[4]**fret** *n* (14c) **1 :** an ornamental network; *esp* **:** a medieval metallic or jeweled net for a woman's headdress **2 :** an ornament or ornamental work often in relief consisting of small straight bars intersecting one another in right or oblique angles

[5]**fret** *n* [perh. fr. MF *frete* ferrule, fr. *freter*] (ca. 1500) **:** one of a series of ridges fixed across the fingerboard of a stringed musical instrument (as a guitar) — **fret·less** *adj* — **fret·ted** *adj*

[6]**fret** *vt* **fret·ted; fret·ting** (1602) **:** to press (the strings of a stringed instrument) against the frets

fret·ful \ˈfret-fəl\ *adj* (1594) **:** disposed to fret **:** IRRITABLE, RESTLESS — **fret·ful·ly** \-fə-lē\ *adv* — **fret·ful·ness** *n*

fret·saw \ˈfret-ˌsȯ\ *n* (1865) **:** a saw that resembles a coping saw but usu. has a deeper frame and is used for cutting curved outlines

fret·work \-ˌwərk\ *n* (1601) **1 :** decoration consisting of work adorned with frets **2 :** ornamental openwork or work in relief

Freud·ian \ˈfrȯi-dē-ən\ *adj* (1910) **:** of, relating to, or according with the psychoanalytic theories or practices of Sigmund Freud — **Freudian** *n* — **Freud·ian·ism** \-ə-ˌni-zəm\ *n*

Freudian slip *n* (1941) **:** a slip of the tongue that is motivated by and reveals some unconscious aspect of the mind

Frey \ˈfrā\ *n* [ON *Freyr*] (1851) **:** the Norse god of fertility, crops, peace, and prosperity

Freya \ˈfrā-ə\ *n* [ON *Freyja*] (1691) **:** the Norse goddess of love and beauty

FRG *abbr* Federal Republic of Germany

Fri *abbr* Friday

fri·a·ble \ˈfrī-ə-bəl\ *adj* [MF or L; MF, fr. L *friabilis,* fr. *friare* to crumble — more at FRICTION] (1563) **:** easily crumbled or pulverized ⟨~ soil⟩ ***syn*** see FRAGILE — **fri·a·bil·i·ty** \ˌfrī-ə-ˈbi-lə-tē\ *n*

fri·ar \ˈfrī(-ə)r\ *n* [ME *frere, fryer,* fr. AF *frere, friere, fraire* lit., brother, fr. L *fratr-, frater* — more at BROTHER] (13c) **:** a member of a mendicant order

fri·ar·ly \-lē\ *adj* (1549) **:** resembling a friar **:** relating to friars

friar's lantern *n* (1632) *obs* **:** IGNIS FATUUS

fri·ary \ˈfrī(-ə)r-ē\ *n, pl* **-ar·ies** (1538) **:** a monastery of friars

[1]**frib·ble** \ˈfri-bəl\ *vb* **frib·bled; frib·bling** \-b(ə-)liŋ\ [origin unknown] *vt* (1633) **:** to trifle or fool away ~ *vi* **1 :** TRIFLE **2** *obs* **:** DODDER

[2]**fribble** *n* (1664) **:** a frivolous person, thing, or idea — **frib·ble** *adj*

fric·an·deau \ˈfri-kən-ˌdō\ *n* [F, fr. MF, prob. fr. *fricasser* + *-ande* (as in *viande* meat) + *-eau,* n. suffix] (1706) **:** larded veal roasted and glazed

[1]**fric·as·see** *also* **fric·as·sée** \ˈfri-kə-ˌsē, ˌfri-kə-ˈ\ *n* [MF, fr. fem. of *fricassé,* pp. of *fricasser* to fricassee] (1568) **:** a dish of pieces of meat (as chicken) or vegetables stewed in stock and served in a white sauce

[2]**fricassee** *vt* **-seed; -see·ing** (1657) **:** to cook as a fricassee

fric·a·tive \ˈfri-kə-tiv\ *n* [L *fricatus,* pp. of *fricare*] (1863) **:** a consonant characterized by frictional passage of the expired breath through a narrowing at some point in the vocal tract — **fricative** *adj*

frick·ing \ˈfri-kiŋ, -kən\ *adj or adv* [alter. of *frigging,* pres. part. of *frig*] (ca. 1936) *often vulgar* **:** DAMNED — used as an intensive

fric·tion \ˈfrik-shən\ *n* [earlier, therapeutic rubbing of the limbs, fr. MF, fr. L *friction-, frictio,* fr. *fricare* to rub; akin to L *friare* to crumble, and perh. to Skt *bhriṇanti* they injure] (1704) **1 a :** the rubbing of one body against another **b :** the force that resists relative motion between two bodies in contact **2 :** the clashing between two persons or parties of opposed views **:** DISAGREEMENT **3 :** sound produced by the movement of air through a narrow constriction in the mouth or glottis — **fric·tion·less** \-ləs\ *adj* — **fric·tion·less·ly** *adv*

fric·tion·al \ˈfrik-shnəl, -shə-nᵊl\ *adj* (1850) **1 :** of or relating to friction **2 :** moved or produced by friction — **fric·tion·al·ly** *adv*

friction clutch *n* (ca. 1842) **:** a clutch in which connection is made through sliding friction

friction drive *n* (1907) **:** a power-transmission system that transmits motion by surface friction instead of teeth

friction tape *n* (1920) **:** a usu. cloth tape impregnated with water-resistant insulating material and an adhesive and used esp. to protect, insulate, and support electrical conductors

Fri·day \ˈfrī-(ˌ)dā, -dē\ *n* [ME, fr. OE *frīgedæg* (akin to OHG *frīatag* Friday), fr. **Frīg* Frigga + *dæg* day, prehistoric trans. of L *dies Veneris* Venus' day] (bef. 12c) **:** the sixth day of the week — **Fri·days** \-(ˌ)dāz, -dēz\ *adv*

fridge *also* **frig** \ˈfrij\ *n* [by shortening & alter.] (1926) **:** REFRIGERATOR

fried *adj* (1926) **:** INTOXICATED, HIGH

fried·cake \ˈfrīd-ˌkāk\ *n* (1836) **:** DOUGHNUT, CRULLER

fried rice *n* (1958) **:** a dish of boiled or steamed rice that is stir-fried typically with soy sauce, beaten egg, chopped meat, and vegetables

[1]**friend** \ˈfrend\ *n* [ME *frend,* fr. OE *frēond;* akin to OHG *friunt* friend, OE *frēon* to love, *frēo* free] (bef. 12c) **1 a :** one attached to another by affection or esteem **b :** ACQUAINTANCE **2 a :** one that is not hostile **b :** one that is of the same nation, party, or group **3 :** one that favors or promotes something (as a charity) **4 :** a favored companion **5** *cap* **:** a member of a Christian sect that stresses Inner Light, rejects sacraments and an ordained ministry, and opposes war — called also *Quaker* — **friend·less** \ˈfren(d)-ləs\ *adj* — **friend·less·ness** *n* — **be friends with :** to have a friendship or friendly relationship with

[2]**friend** *vt* (13c) **1 :** to act as the friend of **:** BEFRIEND **2 :** to include (someone) in a list of designated friends on a person's social networking site

[1]**friend·ly** \ˈfren(d)-lē\ *adj* **friend·li·er; -est** (bef. 12c) **1 :** of, relating to, or befitting a friend: as **a :** showing kindly interest and goodwill **b :** not hostile ⟨a ~ merger offer⟩; *also* **:** involving or coming from actions of one's own forces ⟨~ fire⟩ **c :** CHEERFUL, COMFORTING ⟨the ~ glow of the fire⟩ **2 :** serving a beneficial or helpful purpose **3 :** easy to use or understand ⟨~ computer software⟩ — often used in combination ⟨a reader-*friendly* layout⟩ **4 :** COMPATIBLE, ACCOMMODATING ⟨environmentally ~ packaging⟩ — often used in combination ⟨a kid-*friendly* restaurant⟩ ***syn*** see AMICABLE — **friend·li·ly** \ˈfren(d)-lə-lē\ *adv* — **friend·li·ness** *n*

[2]**friendly** *adv* (bef. 12c) **:** in a friendly manner **:** AMICABLY

[3]**friendly** *n, pl* **friendlies** (1861) **1 :** one that is friendly; *esp* **:** a native who is friendly to settlers or invaders **2** *chiefly Brit* **:** a match between sports teams and esp. international teams that has no connection with league or championship play

friendly society *n* (1703) *Brit* **:** a mutual association for providing life and health insurance and old-age pension benefits to members

friend of the court (1776) **:** AMICUS CURIAE

friend·ship \ˈfren(d)-ˌship\ *n* (bef. 12c) **1 :** the state of being friends **2 :** the quality or state of being friendly **:** FRIENDLINESS **3** *obs* **:** AID

friend with benefits (1997) **:** a friend with whom one has casual sexual relations without commitments

frier *var of* FRYER

Frie·sian \ˈfrē-zhən\ *n* [var. of *Frisian*] (1923) *chiefly Brit* **:** HOLSTEIN

[1]**frieze** \ˈfrēz *or* frē-ˈzā\ *n* [ME *frise,* fr. AF, fr. MD *vriese*] (15c) **1 :** a heavy durable coarse wool and shoddy fabric with a rough surface **2 :** a pile surface of uncut loops or of patterned cut and uncut loops

[2]**frieze** \ˈfrēz\ *n* [MF *frise,* perh. fr. ML *phrygium, frisium* embroidered cloth, fr. L *phrygium,* fr. neut. of *Phrygius* Phrygian, fr. *Phrygia*] (1563) **1 :** the part of an entablature between the architrave and the cornice **2 :** a sculptured or richly ornamented band (as on a building or piece of furniture) **3 :** a band, line, or series suggesting a frieze ⟨a constant ~ of visitors wound its way around the . . . ruins —Mollie Panter-Downes⟩ — **frieze·like** *adj*

frig \ˈfrig\ *vi* **frigged; frig·ging** [ME *fryggen* to wriggle] (ca. 1610) *often vulgar* **:** COPULATE — often used in the present participle as a meaningless intensive

frig·ate \ˈfri-gət\ *n* [MF, fr. OIt *fregata*] (1583) **1 :** a light boat propelled orig. by oars but later by sails **2 :** a square-rigged war vessel intermediate between a corvette and a ship of the line **3 :** a modern warship that is smaller than a destroyer

frigate bird *n* (1738) **:** any of a family (Fregatidae, containing a single genus *Fregata*) of tropical seabirds having a forked tail and large wingspans that are noted for aggressively taking food from other birds

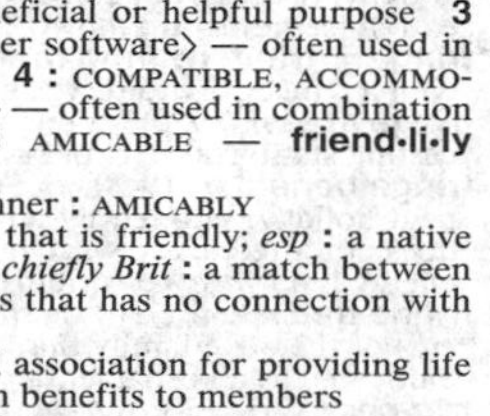

frigate bird

Frig·ga \ˈfri-gə\ *n* [ON *Frigg*] (1597) **:** the wife of Odin and Norse goddess of married love and of the hearth

[1]**fright** \ˈfrīt\ *n* [ME, fr. OE *fyrhto, fryhto;* akin to OHG *forhta* fear] (bef. 12c) **1 :** fear excited by sudden danger **2 :** ALARM ⟨gave me quite a ~⟩

\ə\ **abut** \ᵊ\ **kitten,** F **table** \ər\ **further** \a\ **ash** \ā\ **ace** \ä\ **mop, mar** \au̇\ **out** \ch\ **chin** \e\ **bet** \ē\ **easy** \g\ **go** \i\ **hit** \ī\ **ice** \j\ **job** \ŋ\ **sing** \ō\ **go** \ȯ\ **law** \ȯi\ **boy** \th\ **thin** \t͟h\ **the** \ü\ **loot** \u̇\ **foot** \y\ **yet** \zh\ **vision, beige** \k̲, ⁿ, œ, ue, ʸ\ *see* Guide to Pronunciation

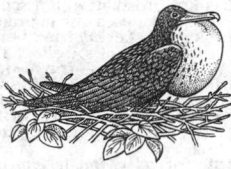

: something strange, ugly, or shocking **syn** see FEAR
[2]**fright** *vt* (bef. 12c) : to alarm suddenly : FRIGHTEN
fright·en \ˈfrī-tᵊn\ *vb* **fright·ened; fright·en·ing** \ˈfrī-tᵊn-iŋ, ˈfrīt-niŋ\ *vt* (1630) **1** : to make afraid : TERRIFY **2** : to drive or force by frightening ⟨~*ed* the boy into confessing⟩ ~ *vi* : to become frightened — **fright·en·ing·ly** \-tᵊn-iŋ-lē, -niŋ-lē\ *adv*
fright·ful \ˈfrīt-fəl\ *adj* (1607) **1** : causing intense fear or alarm : TERRIFYING **2** : startling esp. in being bad or objectionable ⟨a ~ novel⟩ **3** : EXTREME ⟨~ thirst⟩ — **fright·ful·ly** \-fə-lē\ *adv* — **fright·ful·ness** *n*
fright wig *n* (1886) : a wig with hair that stands out from the head
frig·id \ˈfri-jəd\ *adj* [L *frigidus,* fr. *frigēre* to be cold; akin to L *frigus* frost, cold, Gk *rhigos*] (1619) **1 a** : intensely cold **b** : lacking warmth or ardor : INDIFFERENT **2** : lacking imaginative qualities : INSIPID **3 a** : abnormally averse to sexual intercourse — used esp. of women **b** *of a female* : unable to achieve orgasm during sexual intercourse — **frig·id·ly** *adv* — **frig·id·ness** *n*
Frig·i·daire \ˌfri-jə-ˈder\ *trademark* — used for an electric refrigerator
fri·gid·i·ty \fri-ˈji-də-tē\ *n* (15c) : the quality or state of being frigid; *specif* : marked or abnormal sexual indifference esp. in a woman
frigid zone *n* (1620) : the area or region between the arctic circle and the north pole or between the antarctic circle and the south pole
frig·o·rif·ic \ˌfri-gə-ˈri-fik\ *adj* [L *frigorificus,* fr. *frigor-, frigus* frost] (1667) : causing cold : CHILLING
fri·jo·le \frē-ˈhō-lē\ *also* **fri·jol** \frē-ˈhōl, ˈfrē-ˌ\ *n, pl* **fri·jo·les** \frē-ˈhō-lēz, ˈfrē-ˌ\ [AmerSp *frijol,* fr. Sp, kidney bean, fr. earlier *fesol, fresol,* prob. modif. of Galician *feijoo,* fr. L *phaseolus,* dim. of *phaselus* cowpea, fr. Gk *phasēlos*] (1577) : any of various beans used in Mexican style cooking — usu. used in pl.
[1]**frill** \ˈfril\ *vt* (1574) : to provide or decorate with a frill
[2]**frill** *n* [perh. fr. D dial. (Brabant) *frul* ribbon bow, trifle] (1591) **1 a** : a gathered, pleated, or bias-cut fabric edging used on clothing **b** : a strip of paper curled at one end and rolled to be slipped over the bone end (as of a chop) in serving **2** : a ruff of hair or feathers or a wing or cartilaginous projection about the neck of an animal **3 a** : AFFECTATION, AIR — usu. used in pl. ⟨intellectual ~*s* and fustian —Joseph Epstein⟩ **b** : something decorative or useful and desirable but not essential : LUXURY — **frilly** \ˈfri-lē\ *adj*
[1]**fringe** \ˈfrinj\ *n, often attrib* [ME *frenge,* fr. AF, fr. VL **frimbia,* fr. L *fimbriae* (pl.)] (14c) **1** : an ornamental border consisting of short straight or twisted threads or strips hanging from cut or raveled edges or from a separate band **2 a** : something resembling a fringe : EDGE, PERIPHERY — often used in pl. ⟨operated on the ~*s* of the law⟩ **b** *chiefly Brit* : [4]BANG **c** : one of various light or dark bands produced by the interference or diffraction of light **d** : an area bordering a putting green on a golf course with grass trimmed longer than on the green itself **3 a** : something that is marginal, additional, or secondary to some activity, process, or subject ⟨a ~ sport⟩ **b** : a group with marginal or extremist views **c** : FRINGE BENEFIT — **fringy** \ˈfrin-jē\ *adj*
[2]**fringe** *vt* **fringed; fring·ing** \ˈfrin-jiŋ\ (15c) **1** : to furnish or adorn with a fringe **2** : to serve as a fringe for : BORDER
fringe area *n* (1950) : a region in which reception from a given broadcasting station is weak or subject to serious distortion
fringe benefit *n* (1948) **1** : an employment benefit (as a pension or a paid holiday) granted by an employer that has a monetary value but does not affect basic wage rates **2** : any additional benefit ⟨increased energy is a *fringe benefit* of regular exercise⟩
fringe tree *n* (ca. 1730) : a small eastern U.S. tree (*Chionanthus virginicus*) of the olive family that has clusters of white flowers and is widely cultivated as an ornamental
frip·pery \ˈfri-p(ə-)rē\ *n, pl* **-per·ies** [MF *friperie,* alter. of OF *freperie,* fr. *frepe* old garment] (1568) **1** *obs* **a** : cast-off clothes **b** *archaic* : a place where old clothes are sold **2 a** : FINERY; *also* : an elegant or showy garment **b** : something showy, frivolous, or nonessential **c** : OSTENTATION; *esp* : something foolish or affectedly elegant
Fris·bee \ˈfriz-bē\ *trademark* — used for a plastic disk for tossing between players
Frise aileron \ˈfrēz-\ *n* [Leslie George *Frise b*1897 Eng. engineer] (ca. 1934) : an aileron having a nose portion projecting ahead of the hinge axis and a lower surface in line with the lower surface of the wing
fri·sée *also* **fri·sé** \frē-ˈzā\ *n* [F, short for *chicorée frisée* curly chicory] (1982) : curly leaves of endive (sense 1) that have finely dissected edges and are used in salads — called also *curly endive, frisée lettuce*
[1]**Fri·sian** \ˈfri-zhən, ˈfrē-\ *adj* [L *Frisius* Frisian; akin to OE *Frīsa, Frēsa* a Frisian] (1598) : of, relating to, or characteristic of Friesland, the Frisians, or Frisian
[2]**Frisian** *n* (1601) **1** : a member of a people that inhabit principally the Netherlands province of Friesland and the Frisian islands in the North Sea **2** : the Germanic language of the Frisian people
[1]**frisk** \ˈfrisk\ *vb* [obs. *frisk* lively] *vi* (1519) : to leap, skip, or dance in a lively or playful way : GAMBOL ~ *vt* : to search (a person) for something (as a concealed weapon) by running the hand rapidly over the clothing and through the pockets — **frisk·er** *n*
[2]**frisk** *n* (1525) **1 a** *archaic* : CAPER **b** : GAMBOL, ROMP **c** : DIVERSION **2** : an act of frisking
fris·ket \ˈfris-kət\ *n* [F *frisquette,* fr. MF] (ca. 1898) : a masking device or material used esp. in printing or graphic arts
frisky \ˈfris-kē\ *adj* **frisk·i·er; -est** (ca. 1500) : inclined to frisk : PLAYFUL ⟨~ puppies⟩; *also* : LIVELY ⟨a ~ performance⟩ — **frisk·i·ly** \ˈfris-kə-lē\ *adv* — **frisk·i·ness** \-kē-nəs\ *n*
fris·son \frē-ˈsōⁿ\ *n, pl* **frissons** \-ˈsōⁿ(z)\ [F, shiver, fr. OF *friçon,* fr. LL *friction-, frictio,* fr. L, lit., friction (taken in LL as derivative of *frigēre* to be cold)] (1777) : a brief moment of emotional excitement : SHUDDER, THRILL ⟨produce a genuine ~ of disquiet —Patricia Craig⟩
[1]**frit** \ˈfrit\ *n* [It *fritta,* fr. fem. of *fritto,* pp. of *friggere* to fry, fr. L *frigere* to roast — more at FRY] (1662) **1** : the calcined or partly fused materials of which glass is made **2** : any of various chemically complex glasses used ground esp. to introduce soluble or unstable ingredients into glazes or enamels
[2]**frit** *vt* **frit·ted; frit·ting** (1832) **1** : to prepare (materials for glass) by heat : FUSE **2** : to convert into a frit
frith \ˈfrith\ *n* (14c) *archaic* : ESTUARY
frit·il·lar·ia \ˌfri-tə-ˈler-ē-ə, -ˈar-\ *n* [NL, fr. L *fritillus* dice cup; fr. the markings of the petals] (1664) : any of a widespread genus (*Fritillaria*) of bulbous herbs of the lily family with variably colored and often mottled or checkered flowers
frit·il·lary \ˈfri-tə-ˌler-ē\ *n, pl* **-lar·ies** [NL *fritillaria*] (1633) **1** : FRITILLARIA **2** : any of numerous nymphalid butterflies (*Argynnis, Speyeria,* and related genera) that usu. are orange with black spots on the upper side of both wings and silver spotted on the underside of the hind wing
frit·ta·ta \frē-ˈtä-tə\ *n* [It, fr. *fritto* fried — more at FRIT] (1877) : an unfolded omelet often containing chopped vegetables or meats
fritted *adj* [[2]*frit*] (1879) : being porous glass made of sintered powdered glass or fiberglass
[1]**frit·ter** \ˈfri-tər\ *n* [ME *fritour,* fr. AF *friture,* fr. VL **frictura,* fr. L *frictus,* pp. of *frigere* to roast] (14c) : a small mass of fried or sautéed batter often containing fruit or meat
[2]**fritter** *vb* [*fritter,* n. (fragment, shred)] *vt* (1728) **1** : to spend or waste bit by bit, on trifles, or without commensurate return — usu. used with *away* **2** : to break into small fragments ~ *vi* : DISSIPATE, DWINDLE — **frit·ter·er** \-tər-ər\ *n*
frit·to mi·sto \ˈfrē-(ˌ)tō-ˈmē-(ˌ)stō\ *n* [It, lit., mixed fried (food)] (1903) : small morsels of meat, seafood, or vegetables coated with batter and deep fried
fritz \ˈfrits\ *n* [origin unknown] (1902) : a state of disorder or disrepair — used in the phrase *on the fritz*
friv·ol \ˈfri-vəl\ *vi* **-oled** *or* **-olled; -ol·ing** *or* **-ol·ling** \-vᵊl-iŋ, -və-liŋ\ [back-formation fr. *frivolous*] (1866) : to act frivolously : TRIFLE — **friv·ol·er** *or* **friv·ol·ler** \-və-lər\ *n*
fri·vol·i·ty \fri-ˈvä-lə-tē\ *n, pl* **-ties** (1764) **1** : the quality or state of being frivolous **2** : a frivolous act or thing
friv·o·lous \ˈfri-və-ləs\ *adj* [ME, fr. L *frivolus*] (15c) **1 a** : of little weight or importance **b** : having no sound basis (as in fact or law) ⟨a ~ lawsuit⟩ **2 a** : lacking in seriousness **b** : marked by unbecoming levity — **friv·o·lous·ly** *adv* — **friv·o·lous·ness** *n*
[1]**frizz** \ˈfriz\ *vb* [F *friser*] *vt* (1660) : to form into small tight curls ~ *vi, of hair* : to form a mass of tight curls
[2]**frizz** *n* (1668) **1** : a tight curl **2** : hair that is tightly curled
[3]**frizz** *vb* [alter. of [1]*fry*] *vt* (1835) : to fry or sear with a sizzling noise ~ *vi* : SIZZLE
friz·zies \ˈfri-zēz\ *n pl* (1979) : frizzy hair — often used with *the* ⟨a bad case of the ~⟩
[1]**friz·zle** \ˈfri-zᵊl\ *vb* **friz·zled; friz·zling** \-zᵊl-iŋ, -zə-liŋ\ [prob. akin to OFris *frīsle* curl] (1573) : FRIZZ, CURL
[2]**frizzle** *n* (1613) : a crisp curl
[3]**frizzle** *vb* **friz·zled; friz·zling** [[1]*fry* + *sizzle*] *vt* (1813) **1** : to fry until crisp and curled **2** : BURN, SCORCH ~ *vi* : to cook with a sizzling noise
frizzy \ˈfri-zē\ *adj* **frizz·i·er; -est** (ca. 1864) *of hair* : not smooth and neat because individual shafts are variably wavy and do not align together — **frizz·i·ness** *n*
FRM *abbr* fixed rate mortgage
[1]**fro** \frə, ˈfrō\ *prep* [ME, fr. ON *frā;* akin to OE *fram* from] (13c) *dial Brit* : FROM
[2]**fro** \ˈfrō\ *adv* (14c) : BACK, AWAY — used in the phrase *to and fro*
[1]**frock** \ˈfräk\ *n* [ME *frok,* fr. AF *froc,* of Gmc origin; akin to OHG *hroch* mantle, coat] (14c) **1** : an outer garment worn by monks and friars : HABIT **2** : an outer garment worn chiefly by men: **a** : a long loose mantle **b** : a workman's outer shirt; *esp* : SMOCK FROCK **c** : a woolen jersey worn esp. by sailors **3** : a woman's dress
[2]**frock** *vt* (1828) **1** : to clothe in a frock **2** : to make a cleric of
frock coat *n* (1823) : a man's knee-length usu. double-breasted coat
froe *also* **frow** \ˈfrō\ *n* [perh. alter. of obs. *froward* turned away, fr. ME; fr. the position of the handle] (1574) : a cleaving tool for splitting cask staves and shingles from the block
frog \ˈfrȯg, ˈfräg\ *n* [ME *frogge,* fr. OE *frogga;* akin to OHG *frosk* frog; senses 2, 3, 5, 7, 8 unclearly derived & perh. of distinct origin] (bef. 12c) **1** : any of various largely aquatic leaping anuran amphibians (as ranids) that have slender bodies with smooth moist skin and strong long hind legs with webbed feet — compare TOAD **2** : the triangular elastic horny pad in the middle of the sole of the foot of a horse — see HOOF illustration **3 a** : a loop attached to a belt to hold a weapon or tool **b** : an ornamental braiding for fastening the front of a garment that consists of a button and a loop through which it passes **4** *often cap, usu offensive* : FRENCHMAN **5** : a device permitting the wheels on one rail of a track to cross an intersecting rail **6** : a condition in the throat that produces hoarseness ⟨had a ~ in his throat⟩ **7** : the nut of a violin bow **8** : a small holder (as of metal, glass, or plastic) with perforations or spikes for holding flowers in place in a bowl or vase
frog·eye \-ˌī\ *n* (ca. 1909) : any of various fungal leaf diseases characterized by concentric rings about the diseased spots
frog·hop·per \-ˌhä-pər\ *n* (1711) : SPITTLEBUG
frog kick *n* (1940) : a breaststroke kick executed with the knees primarily turned outward and the legs alternately separated and closed
frog·let \ˈfrȯg-lət, ˈfräg-\ *n* (1874) : a young frog; *specif* : one that has recently metamorphosed from a tadpole
frog·man \ˈfrȯg-ˌman, ˈfräg-, -mən\ *n* (1945) : a person equipped (as with face mask, flippers, and air supply) for extended periods of underwater swimming; *esp* : a person so equipped for military reconnaissance and demolition
frog–march \-ˌmärch\ *vt* (1923) : to seize from behind roughly and forcefully propel forward ⟨~*ed* him out the door⟩
frog spit *n* (ca. 1825) : CUCKOO SPIT 1
[1]**frol·ic** \ˈfrä-lik\ *adj* [D *vroolijk,* fr. MD *vrolijc,* fr. *vro* happy; akin to OHG *frō* happy] (1538) : full of fun : MERRY
[2]**frolic** *vi* **frol·icked; frol·ick·ing** (1593) **1** : to amuse oneself : make merry **2** : to play and run about happily : ROMP — **frol·ick·er** *n*
[3]**frolic** *n* (1616) **1** : a playful or mischievous action **2 a** : an occasion or scene of fun : PARTY **b** : FUN, MERRIMENT
frol·ic·some \ˈfrä-lik-səm\ *adj* (1699) : full of gaiety : PLAYFUL, SPORTIVE
from \ˈfrəm, ˈfräm *also* fəm\ *prep* [ME, fr. OE *from, fram;* akin to OHG *fram,* adv., forth, away, OE *faran* to go — more at FARE] (bef. 12c) **1 a** — used as a function word to indicate a starting point of a physical movement or a starting point in measuring or reckoning or in a statement of limits ⟨came here ~ the city⟩ ⟨a week ~ today⟩ ⟨cost ~ $5 to $10⟩ **b** — used as a function word to indicate the starting or focal

point of an activity ⟨called me ~ a pay phone⟩ ⟨ran a business ~ her home⟩ **2** — used as a function word to indicate physical separation or an act or condition of removal, abstention, exclusion, release, subtraction, or differentiation ⟨protection ~ the sun⟩ ⟨relief ~ anxiety⟩ **3** — used as a function word to indicate the source, cause, agent, or basis ⟨we conclude ~ this⟩ ⟨a call ~ my lawyer⟩ ⟨inherited a love of music ~ his father⟩ ⟨worked hard ~ necessity⟩

frond \ˈfränd\ *n* [L *frond-, frons* foliage] (1785) **1 :** a large leaf (esp. of a palm or fern) usu. with many divisions **2 :** a thallus or thalloid shoot (as of a lichen or seaweed) resembling a leaf — **frond•ed** \ˈfrän-dəd\ *adj*

fron•deur \frō^{n}-ˈdər\ *n* [F, lit., slinger, participant in a 17th cent. revolt in which the rebels were compared to schoolboys using slings only when the teacher was not looking] (1798) **:** REBEL, MALCONTENT

[1]**front** \ˈfrənt\ *n* [ME, fr. AF *frunt, front,* fr. L *front-, frons*] (13c) **1 a :** FOREHEAD; *also* **:** the whole face **b :** external and often feigned appearance esp. in the face of danger or adversity **2 a** (1) **:** VANGUARD (2) **:** a line of battle (3) **:** a zone of conflict between armies **b** (1) **:** a stand on an issue **:** POLICY (2) **:** an area of activity or interest ⟨progress on the educational ~⟩ (3) **:** a movement linking divergent elements to achieve common objectives; *esp* **:** a political coalition **3 :** a side of a building; *esp* **:** the side that contains the principal entrance **4 a :** the forward part or surface **b** (1) **:** FRONTAGE (2) **:** a beach promenade at a seaside resort **c :** DICKEY 1a **d :** the boundary between two dissimilar air masses **5** *archaic* **:** BEGINNING **6 a** (1) **:** a position ahead of a person or of the foremost part of a thing (2) — used as a call by a hotel desk clerk in summoning a bellhop **b :** a position of leadership or superiority **7 a :** a person, group, or thing used to mask the identity or true character or activity of the actual controlling agent **b :** a person who serves as the nominal head or spokesman of an enterprise or group to lend it prestige — **in front of :** directly before or ahead of — **out front :** in the audience

[2]**front** *vi* (1523) **1 :** to have the front or principal side adjacent to something; *also* **:** to have frontage on something ⟨a ten-acre plot *~ing* on a lake —*Current Biog.*⟩ **2 :** to serve as a front ⟨*~ing* for special interests⟩ ~ *vt* **1 a :** CONFRONT ⟨went to the woods because I wished . . . to ~ only the essential facts of life —H. D. Thoreau⟩ **b :** to appear before ⟨daily *~ed* him in some fresh splendor —Alfred Tennyson⟩ **2 a :** to be in front of ⟨a lawn *~ing* the house⟩ **b :** to be the leader of (a musical group) ⟨appeared as a soloist and *~ed* bands⟩ **3 :** to face toward or have frontage on ⟨the house *~s* the street⟩ **4 :** to supply a front to ⟨*~ed* the building with bricks⟩ **5 a :** to articulate (a sound) with the tongue farther forward **b :** to move (a word or phrase) to the beginning of a sentence **6** *basketball* **:** to play in front of (an opposing player) rather than between the player and the basket **7 :** ADVANCE 7 ⟨*~ed* him the cash⟩

[3]**front** *adj* (1600) **1 a :** of, relating to, or situated at the front **b :** acting as a front ⟨~ company⟩ **2 :** articulated at or toward the front of the oral passage ⟨~ vowels⟩ **3 :** constituting the first nine holes of an 18-hole golf course — **front** *adv*

[4]**front** *abbr* frontispiece

front•age \ˈfrən-tij\ *n* (1622) **1 a :** a piece of land that lies adjacent (as to a street or the ocean) **b :** the land between the front of a building and the street **c :** the length of a frontage **2 :** the act or fact of facing a given way **3 :** the front side of a building

frontage road *n* (1949) **:** a local street that parallels an expressway or through street and that provides access to property near the expressway — called also *service road*

[1]**fron•tal** \ˈfrən-t^{ə}l\ *n* (14c) **1** [ME *frontel,* fr. ML *frontellum,* dim. of L *front-, frons*] **:** a cloth hanging over the front of an altar **2 :** FACADE 1

[2]**frontal** *adj* [NL *frontalis,* fr. L *front-, frons*] (1656) **1 :** of, relating to, or adjacent to the forehead or the frontal bone **2 a :** of, relating to, or situated at the front **b :** directed against the front or at the main point or issue **:** DIRECT ⟨~ assault⟩ **3 :** parallel to the main axis of the body and at right angles to the sagittal plane **4 :** of or relating to a meteorological front — **fron•tal•ly** \-t^{ə}l-ē\ *adv*

frontal bone *n* (1741) **:** a bone that forms the forehead and roofs over most of the orbits and nasal cavity and that at birth consists of two halves separated by a suture

fron•tal•i•ty \ˌfrən-ˈta-lə-tē\ *n* (1905) **1** *sculpture* **:** a schematic composition of the front view that is complete without lateral movement **2** *painting* **:** the depiction of an object, figure, or scene in a plane parallel to the plane of the picture surface

frontal lobe *n* (1879) **:** the anterior division of each cerebral hemisphere

front and center *adv* (1951) **:** in or to the forefront of activity or consideration

front bench *n* (ca. 1889) **:** either of the two benches nearest the chair in a British legislature (as the House of Commons) occupied by government and opposition leaders; *also* **:** the leaders themselves — compare BACKBENCH — **front–bench•er** \-ˈben-chər\ *n*

front burner *n* (1973) **:** the condition of being in active consideration or development **:** a position of priority — usu. used in the phrase *on the front burner*; compare BACK BURNER — **front–burner** *adj*

front•court \ˈfrənt-ˈkȯrt\ *n* (ca. 1949) **1 :** a basketball team's offensive half of the court **2 :** the positions of the forwards and center on a basketball team; *also* **:** the forwards and center themselves

front dive *n* (ca. 1934) **:** a dive from a position facing the water

front–end *adj* (1962) **:** relating to or required at the beginning of an undertaking ⟨no ~ charge at the time of investment⟩

front end *n* (1973) **1 :** a unit in a computer system devoted to controlling the data communications link between terminals and the main computer and often to the preliminary processing of data **2 :** a software interface (as a graphical user interface) designed to enable user-friendly interaction with a computer

front–end load *n* (1962) **:** the part of the total commission and expenses taken out of early payments under a contract plan for the periodic purchase of investment-company shares

front–end loader *n* (1954) **:** a usu. wheeled vehicle with a hydraulically operated scoop in front for excavating and loading loose material — called also *front loader*

fron•tier \ˌfrən-ˈtir, ˈfrən-ˌ, frän-ˈ, ˈfrän-ˌ\ *n* [ME *fronter,* fr. AF *fraunture, fronter,* fr. *front*] (15c) **1 a :** a border between two countries **b** *obs* **:** a stronghold on a frontier **2 a :** a region that forms the margin of settled or developed territory **b :** the farthermost limits of knowledge or achievement in a particular subject **c :** a line of division between different or opposed things ⟨the *~s* separating science and the humanities —R. W. Clark⟩ **d :** a new field for exploitative or developmental activity — **frontier** *adj*

fron•tiers•man \ˌfrən-ˈtirz-mən, frän-\ *n* (1814) **:** a person who lives or works on a frontier

fron•tis•piece \ˈfrən-tə-ˌspēs\ *n* [MF *frontispice,* fr. LL *frontispicium* facade, fr. L *front-, frons* + *-i-* + *specere* to look at — more at SPY] (ca. 1598) **1 a :** the principal front of a building **b :** a decorated pediment over a portico or window **2 :** an illustration preceding and usu. facing the title page of a book or magazine

front•less \ˈfrənt-ləs\ *adj* (1605) *archaic* **:** SHAMELESS

front•let \-lət\ *n* [ME *frontlette,* fr. MF *frontelet,* dim. of *frontel,* fr. L *frontale,* fr. *front-, frons*] (15c) **1 :** a band or phylactery worn on the forehead **2 :** the forehead esp. of an animal

front•line \ˈfrənt-ˌlīn\ *adj* (1915) **1 :** relating to, being, or involved in a front line ⟨~ ambulances⟩ **2 :** FIRST-RATE ⟨~ teachers⟩; *also* **:** FIRST-STRING ⟨a ~ goalie⟩

front line *n* (ca. 1797) **1 a :** a military line formed by the most advanced tactical combat units; *also* **:** FRONT 2a(2) **b :** an area of potential or actual conflict or struggle **2 :** the most advanced, responsible, or visible position in a field or activity

front–load *vt* (1976) **:** to assign costs or benefits to the early stages of (as a contract, project, or time period)

front man *n* (1932) **1 :** a person serving as a front or figurehead **2 :** the lead performer in a musical group

front matter *n* (ca. 1909) **:** matter preceding the main text of a book

front money *n* (ca. 1928) **:** money that is paid in advance for a promised service or product

fronto- *comb form* [[1]*front*] **:** boundary of an air mass ⟨*fronto*genesis⟩

front office *n* (1900) **:** the policy-making officials of an organization — usu. hyphenated when used attributively ⟨the *front-office* staff⟩

front•o•gen•e•sis \ˌfrən-tō-ˈje-nə-səs\ *n* [NL] (1931) **:** the coming together into a distinct front of two dissimilar air masses that commonly react upon each other to induce cloud and precipitation

front•ol•y•sis \ˌfrən-ˈtä-lə-səs\ *n* [NL] (1934) **:** a process tending to destroy a meteorological front

fron•ton \ˈfrän-ˌtän\ *n* [Sp *frontón* gable, wall of a pelota court, fronton, fr. aug. of *frente* forehead, fr. L *front-, frons*] (1896) **:** a jai alai arena

[1]**front–page** \ˈfrənt-ˈpāj\ *adj* (1917) **:** printed on the front page of a newspaper; *also* **:** very newsworthy

[2]**front–page** *vt* (1929) **:** to print or report on the front page

front room *n* (1781) **:** LIVING ROOM, PARLOR

front–run•ner \ˈfrənt-ˌrə-nər\ *n* (1914) **1 :** a contestant who runs best when in the lead **2 :** a leading contestant in or as if in a rivalry or competition ⟨a political ~⟩

front•ward \ˈfrənt-wərd\ *or* **front•wards** \-wərdz\ *adv or adj* (1865) **:** toward the front

frore \ˈfrȯr\ *adj* [ME *froren,* fr. OE, pp. of *frēosan* to freeze] (13c) **:** FROSTY, FROZEN

frosh \ˈfräsh\ *n, pl* **frosh** [by shortening & alter.] (ca. 1915) **:** FRESHMAN

[1]**frost** \ˈfrȯst\ *n* [ME, fr. OE; akin to OHG *frost* — more at FREEZE] (bef. 12c) **1 a :** the process of freezing **b :** a covering of minute ice crystals on a cold surface; *also* **:** ice particles formed from a gas **c :** the temperature that causes freezing **2 a :** coldness of deportment or temperament **:** an indifferent, reserved, or unfriendly manner **b :** FAILURE ⟨the play was . . . a most dreadful ~ —Arnold Bennett⟩

[2]**frost** *vt* (1635) **1 a :** to cover with or as if with frost; *esp* **:** to put icing on (cake) **b :** to produce a fine-grained slightly roughened surface on (as metal or glass) **2 :** to injure or kill (as plants) by frost **3 :** to make angry or irritated ⟨that really *~s* me⟩ ~ *vi* **:** to become frosted

[1]**frost•bite** \ˈfrȯs(t)-ˌbīt\ *vt* **-bit** \-ˌbit\; **-bit•ten** \-ˌbi-t^{ə}n\; **-bit•ing** \-ˌbī-tiŋ\ (1593) **:** to affect or injure by frost or frostbite

[2]**frostbite** *n* (1813) **:** the superficial or deep freezing of the tissues of some part of the body (as the feet or hands); *also* **:** the damage to tissues caused by freezing — compare FROSTNIP

[3]**frostbite** *adj* (1941) **:** done in cold weather ⟨~ sailing⟩; *also* **:** of or relating to cold-weather sailing ⟨~ sailors⟩

frost•bit•ing \-ˌbī-tiŋ\ *n* (1965) **:** the sport of sailing in cold weather

frost•ed \ˈfrȯ-stəd\ *adj* (1947) **:** having undergone frosting ⟨~ hair⟩

frost heave *n* (1941) **:** an upthrust of ground or pavement caused by freezing of moist soil — called also *frost heaving*

frost•ing \ˈfrȯs-tiŋ\ *n* (1858) **1 a :** ICING **b :** TRIMMING, ORNAMENTATION **2 :** lusterless finish of metal or glass **:** MAT; *also* **:** a white finish produced on glass (as by etching) **3 :** the lightening (as by chemicals) of small strands of hair throughout the entire head to produce a two-tone effect — compare STREAKING

frost•nip \ˈfrȯs(t)-ˌnip\ *n* (1967) **:** the reversible freezing of superficial skin layers that is usu. marked by numbness and whiteness of the skin

frost•work \ˈfrȯs(t)-ˌwərk\ *n* (1729) **:** the figures that moisture sometimes forms in freezing (as on a windowpane)

frosty \ˈfrȯ-stē\ *adj* **frost•i•er; -est** (bef. 12c) **1 a :** attended with or producing frost **:** FREEZING **b :** briskly cold **:** CHILLY **2 :** covered or appearing as if covered with frost **:** HOARY ⟨a man of 65, with ~ eyebrows and hair —Nan Robertson⟩ **3 :** marked by coolness or extreme reserve in manner ⟨his smile was distinctly ~ —Erle Stanley Gardner⟩ — **frost•i•ly** \-stə-lē\ *adv* — **frost•i•ness** \-stē-nəs\ *n*

[1]**froth** \ˈfrȯth\ *n, pl* **froths** \ˈfrȯths, ˈfrȯt͟hz\ [ME, fr. ON *frotha;* akin to OE *āfrēothan* to froth] (14c) **1 a :** bubbles formed in or on a liquid **:** FOAM **b :** a foamy slaver sometimes accompanying disease or exhaustion **2 :** something resembling froth (as in being unsubstantial, worthless, or light and airy)

[2]**froth** \ˈfrȯth, ˈfrȯt͟h\ *vi* (14c) **1 :** to foam at the mouth **2 :** to throw froth out or up **3 :** to become covered with or as if with froth ⟨whole

groves ~ with nodding blossoms —Amy Lovejoy〉 ~ *vt* **1 :** to cause to foam **2 :** to cover with froth **3 :** VENT, VOICE
frothy \ˈfrȯ-thē, -t͟hē\ *adj* **froth·i·er; -est** (15c) **1 :** full of or consisting of froth **2 a :** gaily frivolous or light in content or treatment : INSUBSTANTIAL 〈a ~ comedy〉 **b :** made of light thin material — **froth·i·ly** \-thə-lē, -t͟hə-\ *adv* — **froth·i·ness** \-thē-nəs, -t͟hē-\ *n*
frot·tage \frȯ-ˈtäzh\ *n* [F, fr. *frotter* to rub] (1935) **1 :** the technique of creating a design by rubbing (as with a pencil) over an object placed underneath the paper; *also* **:** a composition so made **2 :** the act of obtaining sexual stimulation by rubbing against a person or object
frou·frou \ˈfrü-(ˌ)frü\ *n* [F, of imit. origin] (1870) **1 :** a rustling esp. of a woman's skirts **2 :** showy or frilly ornamentation
frow *var of* FROE
fro·ward \ˈfrō-(w)ərd\ *adj* [ME, turned away, froward, fr. *fro* from + *-ward* -ward] (13c) **1 :** habitually disposed to disobedience and opposition **2** *archaic* **:** ADVERSE — **fro·ward·ly** *adv* — **fro·ward·ness** *n*
[1]frown \ˈfrau̇n\ *vb* [ME *frounen,* fr. MF *frogner* to snort, frown, of Celt origin; akin to W *ffroen* nostril, OIr *srón* nose] *vi* (14c) **1 :** to contract the brow in displeasure or concentration **2 :** to give evidence of displeasure or disapproval by or as if by facial expression 〈critics ~ on the idea〉 ~ *vt* **:** to show displeasure with or disapproval of esp. by facial expression — **frown·er** *n* — **frown·ing·ly** \ˈfrau̇-niŋ-lē\ *adv*
[2]frown *n* (1581) **1 :** an expression of displeasure **2 :** a wrinkling of the brow in displeasure or concentration
frows·ty \ˈfrau̇-stē\ *adj* **frowst·i·er; -est** [alter. of *frowsy*] (1865) **1** *chiefly Brit* **:** MUSTY **2** *chiefly Brit* **:** FROWSY 2
frow·sy *or* **frow·zy** \ˈfrau̇-zē\ *adj* **frow·si·er** *or* **frow·zi·er; -est** [origin unknown] (1681) **1 :** MUSTY, STALE 〈a ~ smell of stale beer and stale smoke —W. S. Maugham〉 **2 :** having a slovenly or uncared-for appearance 〈a couple of ~ stuffed chairs —R. M. Williams〉
froze *past of* FREEZE
fro·zen \ˈfrō-zᵊn\ *adj* (14c) **1 a :** treated, affected, or crusted over by freezing **b :** subject to long and severe cold 〈the ~ north〉 **2 a :** incapable of being changed, moved, or undone : FIXED; *specif* **:** debarred by official action from movement or from change in status 〈~ wages〉 **b :** not available for present use 〈~ capital〉 **c (1) :** drained or incapable of emotion **(2) :** expressing or characterized by cold unfriendliness — **fro·zen·ly** *adv* — **fro·zen·ness** \-zᵊn-(n)əs\ *n*
FRS *abbr* Federal Reserve System
frt *abbr* freight
fruc·ti·fi·ca·tion \ˌfrək-tə-fə-ˈkā-shən, ˌfru̇k-\ *n* (1753) **:** the reproductive organs or fruit of a plant; *esp* **:** SPOROPHORE
fruc·ti·fy \ˈfrək-tə-ˌfī, ˈfru̇k-\ *vb* **-fied; -fy·ing** [ME *fructifien,* fr. AF *fructefier,* fr. L *fructificare,* fr. *fructus* fruit] *vi* (14c) **:** to bear fruit 〈its seeds shall ~ —Amy Lowell〉 〈no partnership can ~ without candor on both sides —D. M. Ogilvy〉 ~ *vt* **:** to make fruitful or productive
fruc·tose \ˈfrək-ˌtōs, ˈfru̇k-, ˈfru̇k-, -ˌtōz\ *n* [ISV *fruct-* (fr. L *fructus* fruit) + [2]*-ose*] (ca. 1864) **1 :** a crystalline sugar $C_6H_{12}O_6$ sweeter and more soluble than glucose **2 :** the very sweet levorotatory D-form of fructose that occurs esp. in fruit juices and honey — called also *fruit sugar, levulose*
fruc·tu·ous \ˈfrək-chə-wəs, ˈfru̇k, -chü-əs\ *adj* (14c) **:** FRUITFUL 〈a ~ land〉
fru·gal \ˈfrü-gəl\ *adj* [MF or L; MF, fr. L *frugalis* virtuous, frugal, fr. *frug-, frux* fruit, value; akin to L *frui* to enjoy] (1590) **:** characterized by or reflecting economy in the use of resources ***syn*** see SPARING — **fru·gal·i·ty** \frü-ˈga-lə-tē\ *n* — **fru·gal·ly** \ˈfrü-gə-lē\ *adv*
fru·giv·o·rous \frü-ˈji-və-rəs\ *adj* [L *frug-, frux* + E *-vorous*] (1713) **:** feeding on fruit — **fru·gi·vore** \ˈfrü-ji-ˌvȯr\ *n*
[1]fruit \ˈfrüt\ *n, often attrib* [ME, fr. AF *frut, fruit,* fr. L *fructus* fruit, use, fr. *frui* to enjoy, have the use of — more at BROOK] (12c) **1 a :** a product of plant growth (as grain, vegetables, or cotton) 〈the ~*s* of the field〉 **b (1) :** the usu. edible reproductive body of a seed plant; *esp* **:** one having a sweet pulp associated with the seed 〈the ~ of the tree〉 **(2) :** a succulent plant part (as the petioles of a rhubarb plant) used chiefly in a dessert or sweet course **c :** a dish, quantity, or diet of fruits 〈live on ~〉 **d :** a product of fertilization in a plant with its modified envelopes or appendages; *specif* **:** the ripened ovary of a seed plant and its contents **e :** the flavor or aroma of fresh fruit in mature wine **2 :** OFFSPRING, PROGENY **3 a :** the state of bearing fruit 〈a tree in ~〉 **b :** the effect or consequence of an action or operation : PRODUCT, RESULT 〈the ~*s* of our labor〉 **4** *usu disparaging* **:** a male homosexual — **fruit·ed** \ˈfrü-təd\ *adj*
[2]fruit *vi* (14c) **:** to bear fruit ~ *vt* **:** to cause to bear fruit
fruit·age \ˈfrü-tij\ *n* (15c) **1 a :** FRUIT **b :** the condition or process of bearing fruit **2 :** the product or result of an action
frui·tar·i·an \(ˌ)frü(t)-ˈter-ē-ən\ *n* (1893) **:** a person who lives on fruit
fruit bat *n* (1877) **:** any of a family (Pteropodidae of the suborder Megachiroptera) of often large tropical and subtropical Old World bats that feed on ripe fruit, pollen, and nectar and that usu. use visual navigation rather than echolocation — called also *flying fox*

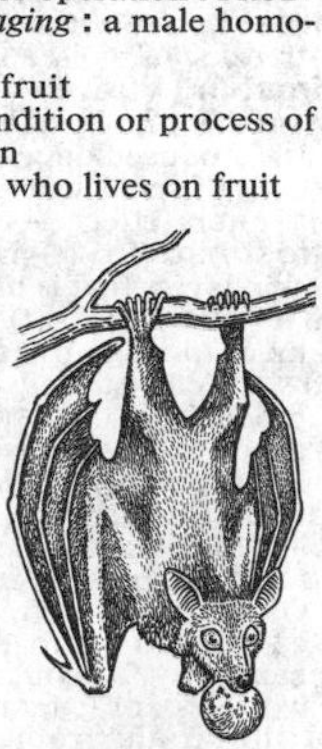

fruit bat with fruit

fruit·cake \ˈfrüt-ˌkāk\ *n* (1848) **1 :** a rich cake containing nuts, dried or candied fruits, and spices **2 :** NUT 6a
fruit·er·er \ˈfrü-tər-ər\ *n* [ME, modif. of AF *fruiter,* fr. *fruit*] (15c) *chiefly Brit* **:** a person who deals in fruit
fruit fly *n* (ca. 1753) **:** any of various small dipteran flies (as a drosophila) whose larvae feed on fruit or decaying vegetable matter
fruit·ful \ˈfrüt-fəl\ *adj* (14c) **1 a :** yielding or producing fruit **b :** conducive to an abundant yield **2 :** abundantly productive 〈a ~ discussion〉 ***syn*** see FERTILE — **fruit·ful·ly** \-fə-lē\ *adv* — **fruit·ful·ness** *n*
fruiting body *n* (1918) **:** a plant organ specialized for producing spores; *esp* **:** SPOROPHORE
fru·ition \frü-ˈi-shən\ *n* [ME *fruicioun,* fr. AF or LL; AF *fruicion,* fr. LL *fruition-, fruitio,* fr. L *frui*] (15c) **1 :** pleasurable use or possession : ENJOYMENT **2 a :** the state of bearing fruit **b :** REALIZATION
fruit·less \ˈfrüt-ləs\ *adj* (14c) **1 :** UNSUCCESSFUL 〈a ~ attempt〉 **2 :** lacking or not bearing fruit ***syn*** see FUTILE — **fruit·less·ly** *adv* — **fruit·less·ness** *n*
fruit·let \-lət\ *n* (1881) **1 :** a small fruit **2 :** a unit of a collective fruit
fruit machine *n* (1933) *Brit* **:** SLOT MACHINE 2
fruit sugar *n* (ca. 1872) **:** FRUCTOSE 2
fruit·wood \ˈfrüt-ˌwu̇d\ *n, often attrib* (1927) **:** the wood of a fruit tree (as the apple, cherry, or pear) 〈~ furniture〉
fruity \ˈfrü-tē\ *adj* **fruit·i·er; -est** (1657) **1 a :** relating to, made with, or resembling fruit **b :** having the flavor or aroma of ripe fruit **2 a :** extremely effective, interesting, or enjoyable **b :** sweet or sentimental esp. to excess **c** *of a voice* **:** rich and deep **3** *slang* **:** CRAZY, SILLY — **fruit·i·ly** *adv* — **fruit·i·ness** *n*
fru·men·ty \ˈfrü-mən-tē\ *also* **fur·mi·ty** \ˈfər-mə-tē\ *n, pl* **-ties** [ME *frumente, furmente,* fr. AF *furmenté,* fr. *furment, frument* grain, fr. L *frumentum,* fr. *frui* to enjoy — more at BROOK] (14c) **:** a dish of wheat boiled in milk and usu. sweetened and spiced
frump \ˈfrəmp\ *n* [prob. fr. *frumple* to wrinkle] (1817) **1 :** a dowdy unattractive girl or woman **2 :** a staid, drab, old-fashioned person
frump·ish \ˈfrəm-pish\ *adj* (ca. 1847) **:** DOWDY, DRAB
frumpy \ˈfrəm-pē\ *adj* **frump·i·er; -est** (ca. 1840) **:** DOWDY, DRAB
[1]frus·trate \ˈfrəs-ˌtrāt\ *vt* **frus·trat·ed; frus·trat·ing** [ME, fr. L *frustratus,* pp. of *frustrare* to deceive, frustrate, fr. *frustra* in error, in vain] (15c) **1 a :** to balk or defeat in an endeavor **b :** to induce feelings of discouragement in **2 a (1) :** to make ineffectual : bring to nothing **(2) :** IMPEDE, OBSTRUCT **b :** to make invalid or of no effect
syn FRUSTRATE, THWART, FOIL, BAFFLE, BALK mean to check or defeat another's plan or block achievement of a goal. FRUSTRATE implies making vain or ineffectual all efforts however vigorous or persistent 〈*frustrated* attempts at government reform〉. THWART suggests frustration or checking by crossing or opposing 〈the army *thwarted* his attempt at a coup〉. FOIL implies checking or defeating so as to discourage further effort 〈*foiled* by her parents, he stopped trying to see her〉. BAFFLE implies frustration by confusing or puzzling 〈*baffled* by the maze of rules and regulations〉. BALK suggests the interposing of obstacles or hindrances 〈officials felt that legal restrictions had *balked* their efforts to control crime〉.
[2]frustrate *adj* (15c) **:** characterized by frustration
frustrating *adj* (1871) **:** tending to produce or characterized by frustration 〈a ~ delay〉 — **frus·trat·ing·ly** \-tiŋ-lē\ *adv*
frus·tra·tion \(ˌ)frəs-ˈtrā-shən\ *n* (ca. 1555) **1 :** the act of frustrating **2 a :** the state or an instance of being frustrated **b :** a deep chronic sense or state of insecurity and dissatisfaction arising from unresolved problems or unfulfilled needs **3 :** something that frustrates
frus·tule \ˈfrəs-(ˌ)chül, -(ˌ)t(y)ül\ *n* [F, fr. L *frustulum,* dim. of *frustum*] (1848) **:** the 2-valved siliceous shell of a diatom
frus·tum \ˈfrəs-təm\ *n, pl* **frustums** *or* **frus·ta** \-tə\ [NL, fr. L, piece, bit — more at BRUISE] (1658) **:** the basal part of a solid cone or pyramid formed by cutting off the top by a plane parallel to the base; *also* **:** the part of a solid intersected between two usu. parallel planes
fru·ti·cose \ˈfrü-ti-ˌkōs\ *adj* [L *fruticosus,* fr. *frutic-, frutex* shrub] (1882) **:** having a shrubby often branched thallus that grows perpendicular to the substrate 〈~ lichens〉 — compare CRUSTOSE, FOLIOSE
frwy *abbr* freeway
[1]fry \ˈfrī\ *vb* **fried; fry·ing** [ME *frien,* fr. AF *frire,* fr. L *frigere* to roast; akin to Gk *phrygein* to roast, fry, Skt *bhṛjjati* he roasts] *vt* (13c) **1 :** to cook in a pan or on a griddle over heat esp. with the use of fat **2** *slang* **:** ELECTROCUTE 1 **3 :** to damage or destroy (an electrical device or its circuitry) by overheating esp. as a result of unusually high voltage ~ *vi* **1 :** to undergo frying **2 :** to get very hot or burn as if being fried 〈bodies ~*ing* on the beach〉
[2]fry *n, pl* **fries** (1833) **1 :** a social gathering or picnic where food is fried and eaten 〈a fish ~〉 **2 a :** a dish of something fried **b :** FRENCH FRY — usu. used in pl. 〈a burger and *fries*〉
[3]fry *n, pl* **fry** [ME, AF *frie,* fr. *freier, frier* to rub, spawn — more at FRAY] (14c) **1 a :** recently hatched or juvenile fishes **b :** the young of other animals **2 :** very small adult fishes **3 :** members of a group or class : INDIVIDUALS 〈small ~〉
fry bread *n* (1950) **:** quick bread cooked (as by American Indians) by deep-frying
fry·er *also* **fri·er** \ˈfrī(-ə)r\ *n* (1851) **:** something intended for or used in frying: as **a :** a young chicken **b :** a deep utensil for frying foods
frying pan *n* (14c) **:** a metal pan with a handle that is used for frying foods — called also *fry pan* — **out of the frying pan into the fire :** clear of one difficulty only to fall into a greater one
fry–up \ˈfrī-ˌəp\ *n* (1967) *Brit* **:** a dish or meal of fried food
fs *abbr* femtosecond
FS *abbr* **1** filmstrip **2** Foreign Service
FSH *abbr* follicle-stimulating hormone
FSLIC *abbr* Federal Savings and Loan Insurance Corporation
FSO *abbr* Foreign Service Officer
f–stop \ˈef-ˌstäp\ *n* (1946) **:** a camera lens aperture setting indicated by an f-number
ft *abbr* **1** feet; foot **2** fort
FT *abbr* **1** Fourier transform **2** free throw **3** full time
FTC *abbr* Federal Trade Commission
FTE *abbr* full-time equivalent
fth *abbr* fathom
ft lb *abbr* foot-pound
F2F *abbr* face-to-face
FTP \ˌef-(ˌ)tē-ˈpē\ *n* [*f*ile *t*ransfer *p*rotocol] (1986) **:** a system for transferring computer files esp. via the Internet — **FTP** *vt*
F_2 layer \ˈef-ˈtü-\ *n* (1933) **:** the upper of the two layers into which the F region of the ionosphere splits in the daytime at varying heights from about 120 miles (200 kilometers) to more than 300 miles (500 kilometers) above the earth
fubsy \ˈfəb-zē\ *adj* [obs. E *fubs* chubby person] (1780) **:** chubby and somewhat squat
fuch·sia \ˈfyü-shə\ *n* [NL, fr. Leonhard *Fuchs* †1566 Ger. botanist] (1789) **1 :** any of a genus (*Fuchsia*) of ornamental shrubs of the evening-primrose family having showy nodding flowers usu. in deep pinks, reds, and purples **2 :** a vivid reddish purple

fuch·sin *or* **fuch·sine** \ˈfyük-sən, -ˌsēn\ *n* [F *fuchsine,* prob. fr. NL *Fuchsia;* fr. its color] (1865) **:** a dye that is produced by oxidation of a mixture of aniline and toluidines and yields a brilliant bluish red

[1]**fuck** \ˈfək\ *vb* [akin to D *fokken* to breed (cattle), Sw dial. *fokka* to copulate] *vi* (ca. 1503) **1** *usu obscene* **:** COPULATE **2** *usu vulgar* **:** MESS 3 — used with *with* ~ *vt* **1** *usu obscene* **:** to engage in coitus with — sometimes used interjectionally with an object (as a personal or reflexive pronoun) to express anger, contempt, or disgust **2** *usu vulgar* **:** to deal with unfairly or harshly **:** CHEAT, SCREW

[2]**fuck** *n* (1680) **1** *usu obscene* **:** an act of copulation **2** *usu obscene* **:** a sexual partner **3 a** *usu vulgar* **:** DAMN 2 **b** *usu vulgar* — used esp. with *the* as a meaningless intensive ⟨what the ~ do they want from me⟩ **4** *usu vulgar* **:** FUCKER

fucked–up \ˈfəkt-ˈəp\ *adj* (1939) *usu vulgar* **:** thoroughly confused, disordered, or damaged

fuck·er \ˈfə-kər\ *n* (1598) *usu vulgar* **:** one that fucks — often used as a generalized term of abuse

fuck·ing \ˈfə-kiŋ, -kin\ *adj or adv* (1893) *usu vulgar* **:** DAMNED — used as an intensive

fuck off *vi* (1929) *usu vulgar* **:** SCRAM — usu. used as a command

fuck up *vi* (1942) *usu vulgar* **:** to act foolishly or stupidly **:** BLUNDER ~ *vt, usu vulgar* **:** to ruin or spoil esp. through stupidity or carelessness **:** BUNGLE — **fuck–up** \ˈfək-ˌəp\ *n, usu vulgar*

[1]**fu·coid** \ˈfyü-ˌkȯid\ *adj* [NL *Fucus,* fr. L] (1839) **:** relating to or resembling the rockweeds

[2]**fucoid** *n* (ca. 1841) **:** a fucoid seaweed or fossil

fu·cose \ˈfyü-ˌkōs, -ˌkōz\ *n* [ISV *fuc-* (fr. L *fucus*) + *-ose*] (ca. 1909) **:** an aldose sugar that occurs in bound form in the dextrorotatory form in various glycosides and in the levorotatory form in some brown algae and in mammalian polysaccharides typical of some blood groups

fu·co·xan·thin \ˌfyü-kō-ˈzan-thən\ *n* (1873) **:** a brown carotenoid pigment $C_{40}H_{60}O_6$ occurring esp. in the chloroplasts of brown algae

fu·cus \ˈfyü-kəs\ *n* [L, seaweed, archil, dye obtained from archil, fr. Gk *phykos*] (1591) **1** *obs* **:** a face paint **2** [NL, genus name, fr. L] **:** any of a genus (*Fucus*) of leathery marine brown algae of rocky intertidal zones that are a source of algin and have been used as fertilizer; *broadly* **:** any of various brown algae — compare ROCKWEED

fud \ˈfəd\ *n* (1913) **:** FUDDY-DUDDY

FUD *abbr* fear, uncertainty, doubt

fud·dle \ˈfə-dᵊl\ *vb* **fud·dled; fud·dling** \ˈfəd-liŋ, ˈfə-dᵊl-iŋ\ [origin unknown] *vi* (1588) **:** BOOZE, TIPPLE ~ *vt* **1 :** to make drunk **:** INTOXICATE **2 :** to make confused **:** MUDDLE ⟨corridors, archways, recesses . . . combined to ~ any sense of direction —Elizabeth Bowen⟩

fud·dy–dud·dy \ˈfə-dē-ˌdə-dē\ *n, pl* **-dies** [origin unknown] (ca. 1904) **:** one that is old-fashioned, unimaginative, or conservative — **fuddy–duddy** *adj*

[1]**fudge** \ˈfəj\ *vb* **fudged; fudg·ing** [origin unknown] *vt* (1674) **1 a :** to devise as a substitute **:** FAKE **b :** FALSIFY ⟨*fudged* the figures⟩ **2 :** to fail to come to grips with **:** DODGE ⟨*fudged* the issue⟩ ~ *vi* **1 :** to exceed the proper bounds or limits of something ⟨feel that the author has *fudged* a little on the . . . rules for crime fiction —*Newsweek*⟩; *also* **:** CHEAT ⟨*fudging* on an exam⟩ **2 :** to fail to perform as expected **3 :** to avoid commitment **:** HEDGE ⟨the government's tendency to ~ on delicate matters of policy —Claire Sterling⟩

[2]**fudge** *n* (1766) **1 :** foolish nonsense — often used interjectionally to express annoyance, disappointment, or disbelief **2 :** a soft creamy candy made typically of sugar, milk, butter, and flavoring **3 :** something that is fudged; *esp* **:** a bending of rules or a compromise

fudge factor *n* (1962) **:** an arbitrary mathematical term inserted into a calculation in order to arrive at an expected solution or to allow for errors esp. of underestimation; *broadly* **:** any arbitrary unspecified factor

fu dog *often cap F, var of* FOO DOG

[1]**fu·el** \ˈfyü(-ə)l\ *n, often attrib* [ME *fewel,* fr. AF *fuail, feuaile,* fr. VL **focalia,* fr. L *focus* hearth] (13c) **1 a :** a material used to produce heat or power by burning **b :** nutritive material **c :** a material from which atomic energy can be liberated esp. in a reactor **2 :** a source of sustenance or incentive **:** REINFORCEMENT

[2]**fuel** *vb* **-eled** *or* **-elled; -el·ing** *or* **-el·ling** *vt* (1592) **1 :** to provide with fuel **2 :** SUPPORT, STIMULATE ⟨movement is ~*ed* by massive grants-in-aid —Allen Schick⟩ ~ *vi* **:** to take in fuel — often used with *up*

fuel cell *n* (1922) **:** a device that continuously changes the chemical energy of a fuel (as hydrogen) and an oxidant directly into electrical energy

fuel injection *n* (1900) **:** a usu. electronically-controlled system for injecting a precise amount of atomized fuel into the cylinders or the intake airstream of an internal combustion engine — **fuel–in·ject·ed** \ˈfyül-in-ˈjek-təd\ *adj*

fuel oil *n* (1893) **:** an oil that is used for fuel and that usu. has a higher flash point than kerosene

fuel·wood \ˈfyü(-ə)l-ˌwu̇d\ *n* (14c) **:** wood grown or used for fuel

[1]**fug** \ˈfəg\ *n* [perh. alter. of [1]*fog*] (1888) **:** the stuffy atmosphere of a poorly ventilated space; *also* **:** a stuffy or malodorous emanation — **fug·gy** \ˈfə-gē\ *adj*

[2]**fug** *vb* **fugged; fug·ging** *vi* (ca. 1889) **:** to loll indoors in a stuffy atmosphere ~ *vt* **:** to make stuffy and odorous

fu·ga·cious \fyü-ˈgā-shəs\ *adj* [L *fugac-, fugax,* fr. *fugere*] (1634) **:** lasting a short time **:** EVANESCENT

fu·gac·i·ty \fyü-ˈga-sə-tē\ *n* [*fugacious*] (1902) **:** the vapor pressure of a vapor assumed to be an ideal gas obtained by correcting the determined vapor pressure and useful as a measure of the escaping tendency of a substance from a heterogeneous system

fu·gal \ˈfyü-gəl\ *adj* (1854) **:** of, relating to, or being in the style of a musical fugue — **fu·gal·ly** \-gə-lē\ *adv*

-fuge *n comb form* [F, fr. LL *-fuga,* fr. L *fugare* to put to flight, fr. *fuga*] **:** one that drives away ⟨febri*fuge*⟩

[1]**fu·gi·tive** \ˈfyü-jə-tiv\ *adj* [ME, fr. MF & L; MF *fugitif,* fr. L *fugitivus,* fr. *fugitus,* pp. of *fugere* to flee; akin to Gk *pheugein* to flee] (14c) **1 :** running away or intending flight ⟨a ~ slave⟩ ⟨a ~ debtor⟩ **2 :** moving from place to place **:** WANDERING **3 a :** being of short duration **b :** difficult to grasp or retain **:** ELUSIVE **c :** likely to evaporate, deteriorate, change, fade, or disappear ⟨dyed with ~ colors⟩ **4 :** being of transient interest ⟨~ essays⟩ ***syn*** see TRANSIENT — **fu·gi·tive·ly** *adv* — **fu·gi·tive·ness** *n*

[2]**fugitive** *n* (14c) **1 :** a person who flees or tries to escape; *esp* **:** REFUGEE **2 :** something elusive or hard to find

fu·gle·man \ˈfyü-gəl-mən\ *n* [modif. of G *Flügelmann,* fr. *Flügel* wing + *Mann* man] (1804) **1 :** a trained soldier formerly posted in front of a line of soldiers at drill to serve as a model in their exercises **2 :** one at the head or forefront of a group or movement

fu·gu \ˈf(y)ü-(ˌ)gü\ *n* [Jp] (1909) **:** any of various very poisonous puffer fishes (family Tetraodontidae) that contain tetrodotoxin and that are used as food in Japan after the toxin-containing parts are removed

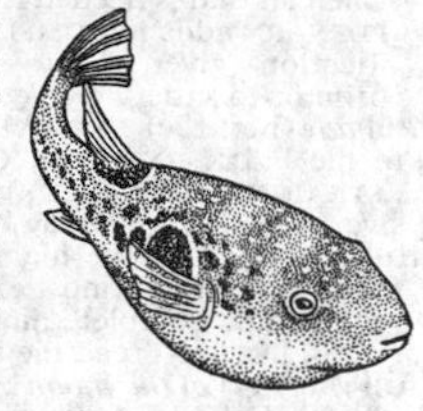

fugu

fugue \ˈfyüg\ *n* [prob. fr. It *fuga* flight, fugue, fr. L, flight, fr. *fugere*] (1597) **1 a :** a musical composition in which one or two themes are repeated or imitated by successively entering voices and contrapuntally developed in a continuous interweaving of the voice parts **b :** something that resembles a fugue esp. in interweaving repetitive elements **2 :** a disturbed state of consciousness in which the one affected seems to perform acts in full awareness but upon recovery cannot recollect the acts performed — **fugue** *vb* — **fugu·ist** \ˈfyü-gist\ *n*

füh·rer *or* **fueh·rer** \ˈfyu̇r-ər, ˈfir-\ *n* [G (*der*) *Führer,* lit., the leader (title assumed by Adolf Hitler), fr. MHG *vüerer,* fr. *vüeren* to lead, bear, fr. OHG *fuoren* to lead; akin to OE *faran* to go — more at FARE] (1934) **:** LEADER 2; *esp* **:** TYRANT

fu·ji \ˈfü-(ˌ)jē\ *n* [*Fuji,* mountain in Japan] (1925) **:** a spun silk clothing fabric in plain weave orig. made in Japan

[1]**-ful** *adj suffix, sometimes* **-ful·ler** *sometimes* **-ful·lest** [ME, fr. OE, fr. *full,* adj] **1 :** full of ⟨pride*ful*⟩ **2 :** characterized by ⟨peace*ful*⟩ **3 :** having the qualities of ⟨master*ful*⟩ **4 :** tending, given, or liable to ⟨help*ful*⟩

[2]**-ful** *n suffix* **:** number or quantity that fills or would fill ⟨room*ful*⟩

Fu·la *or* **Fu·lah** \ˈfü-lə\ *n, pl* **Fula** *or* **Fulas** *or* **Fulah** *or* **Fulahs** (1799) **1 :** a member of a mainly pastoral African people dispersed over savanna and desert from Senegal to eastern Sudan **2 :** the language of the Fula people

Fu·la·ni \ˈfü-ˌlä-nē, fü-ˈ\ *n, pl* **-ni** *or* **-nis** (1855) **1 :** FULA 1; *esp* **:** the Fula of northern Nigeria and adjacent areas **2 :** FULA 2

ful·crum \ˈfu̇l-krəm, ˈfəl-\ *n, pl* **fulcrums** *or* **ful·cra** \-krə\ [LL, fr. L, bedpost, fr. *fulcire* to prop — more at BALK] (1668) **1 a :** PROP; *specif* **:** the support about which a lever turns **b :** one that supplies capability for action **2 :** a part of an animal that serves as a hinge or support

ful·fill *or* **ful·fil** \fu̇(l)-ˈfil *also* fə(l)-\ *vt* **ful·filled; ful·fill·ing** [ME *fulfillen,* fr. OE *fullfyllan,* fr. *full* + *fyllan* to fill] (bef. 12c) **1** *archaic* **:** to make full **:** FILL ⟨her subtle, warm, and golden breath . . . ~*s* him with beatitude —Alfred Tennyson⟩ **2 a :** to put into effect **:** EXECUTE **b :** to meet the requirements of (a business order) **c :** to bring to an end **d :** to measure up to **:** SATISFY **3 a :** to convert into reality **b :** to develop the full potentialities of ***syn*** see PERFORM — **ful·fill·er** *n*

ful·fill·ment *or* **ful·fil·ment** \fu̇(l)-ˈfil-mənt *also* fə(l)-\ *n* (ca. 1775) **1 :** the act or process of fulfilling **2 :** the act or process of delivering a product (as a publication) to a customer

ful·gent \ˈfu̇l-jənt, ˈfəl-\ *adj* [ME, fr. L *fulgent-, fulgens,* prp. of *fulgēre* to shine; akin to L *flagrare* to burn — more at BLACK] (15c) **:** dazzlingly bright **:** RADIANT — **ful·gent·ly** *adv*

ful·gu·rant \ˈfu̇l-g(y)ə-rənt, ˈfu̇l-jə-, ˈfəl-\ *adj* (1647) **:** flashing like lightning; *also* **:** BRILLIANT

ful·gu·ra·tion \ˌfu̇l-g(y)ə-ˈrā-shən, ˌfu̇l-jə-, fəl-\ *n* [L *fulguration-, fulguratio* sheet lightning, fr. *fulgurare* to flash with lightning, fr. *fulgur* lightning, fr. *fulgēre*] (1633) **1 :** the act or process of flashing like lightning **2 :** ELECTRODESICCATION — **ful·gu·rate** \ˈfu̇l-g(y)ə-ˌrāt, ˈfu̇l-jə-, ˈfəl-\ *vt*

ful·gu·rite \ˈfu̇l-g(y)ə-ˌrīt, ˈfu̇l-jə-, ˈfəl-\ *n* [ISV, fr. L *fulgur*] (1834) **:** an often tubular vitrified crust produced by the fusion of sand or rock by lightning

ful·gu·rous \-rəs\ *adj* [L *fulgur*] (1865) **:** flashing with lightning

ful·ham \ˈfu̇-ləm\ *n* [alter. of earlier *fullan,* perh. fr. [1]*full* + [3]*one*] (ca. 1592) *archaic* **:** a loaded die

fu·lig·i·nous \fyu̇-ˈli-jə-nəs\ *adj* [LL *fuliginosus,* fr. L *fuligin-, fuligo* soot; akin to Lith *dūlis* cloud, vapor, and prob. to L *fumus* smoke — more at FUME] (1621) **1 a :** SOOTY **b :** OBSCURE, MURKY **2 :** having a dark or dusky color — **fu·lig·i·nous·ly** *adv*

[1]**full** \ˈfu̇l *also* ˈfəl\ *adj* [ME, fr. OE; akin to OHG *fol* full, L *plenus* full, *plēre* to fill, Gk *plērēs* full, *plēthein* to be full] (bef. 12c) **1 :** containing as much or as many as is possible or normal ⟨a bin ~ of corn⟩ **2 a :** complete esp. in detail, number, or duration ⟨a ~ report⟩ ⟨gone a ~ hour⟩ ⟨my ~ share⟩ **b :** lacking restraint, check, or qualification ⟨~ retreat⟩ ⟨~ support⟩ **c :** having all distinguishing characteristics **:** enjoying all authorized rights and privileges ⟨~ member⟩ ⟨~ professor⟩ **d :** not lacking in any essential **:** PERFECT ⟨in ~ control of your senses⟩ **e (1) :** completely occupied by runners ⟨came to bat with the bases ~⟩ **(2) :** having three balls and two strikes ⟨a ~ count⟩ **3 a :** being at the highest or greatest degree **:** MAXIMUM ⟨~ speed⟩ ⟨~ strength⟩ **b :** being at the height of development ⟨~ bloom⟩ **c :** being a full moon **:** completely illuminated ⟨the moon is ~ tonight⟩ **4 :** rounded in outline ⟨a ~ figure⟩ **5 a :** possessing or containing a great number or amount — used with *of* ⟨a room ~ of pictures⟩ ⟨~ of hope⟩ **b :** having an abundance of material esp. in the form of gathered, pleated, or flared parts ⟨a ~ skirt⟩ **c :** rich in experience ⟨a ~ life⟩ **6 a :** satisfied esp. with food or drink **b :** large enough to satisfy ⟨a ~ meal⟩ **7** *archaic* **:** completely weary **8 :** having both parents in common ⟨~ sisters⟩ **9 :** having volume or depth of sound ⟨~ tones⟩ **10 :** completely occupied esp. with a thought or plan ⟨~ of

his own concerns⟩ **11 :** possessing a rich or pronounced quality ⟨a food of ~ flavor⟩ — **full of it :** not to be believed

syn FULL, COMPLETE, PLENARY, REPLETE mean containing all that is wanted or needed or possible. FULL implies the presence or inclusion of everything that is wanted or required by something or that can be held, contained, or attained by it ⟨a *full* schedule⟩. COMPLETE applies when all that is needed is present ⟨a *complete* picture of the situation⟩. PLENARY adds to COMPLETE the implication of fullness without qualification ⟨given *plenary* power⟩. REPLETE implies being filled to the brim or to satiety ⟨*replete* with delightful details⟩.

[2]**full** *adv* (bef. 12c) **1 a :** VERY, EXTREMELY ⟨knew ~ well they had lied to me⟩ **b :** ENTIRELY ⟨swung ~ around —Morley Callaghan⟩ **2 :** STRAIGHT, SQUARELY ⟨got hit ~ in the face⟩ **3** — used as an intensive ⟨wound up winning by a ~ four strokes —William Johnson⟩

[3]**full** *n* (14c) **1 :** the highest or fullest state or degree ⟨the ~ of the moon⟩ **2 :** the utmost extent ⟨enjoy to the ~⟩ — **in full 1 :** to the requisite or complete amount ⟨paid *in full*⟩ **2 :** to the fullest extent **:** COMPLETELY ⟨read the book *in full*⟩

[4]**full** *vi* (1794) *of the moon* **:** to become full ~ *vt* **:** to make full in sewing

[5]**full** *vt* [ME, fr. AF *fuller, fouler* to full, trample underfoot, fr. ML *fullare,* fr. L *fullo* fuller] (14c) **:** to shrink and thicken (woolen cloth) by moistening, heating, and pressing

full•back \ˈfu̇l-ˌbak\ *n* (1887) **1 :** an offensive football back used primarily for line plunges and blocking **2 :** a primarily defensive player usu. stationed nearest the defended goal (as in soccer or field hockey)

full blast *adv* (1909) **:** at full capacity **:** with great intensity

[1]**full–blood** \ˈfu̇l-ˌbləd\ *adj* (1812) **:** FULL-BLOODED 1

[2]**full–blood** *n* (1846) **:** a full-blooded individual

full–blood•ed \ˈfu̇l-ˌblə-dəd\ *adj* (1774) **1 :** of unmixed ancestry **:** PUREBRED **2 :** FLORID, RUDDY ⟨of ~ face⟩ **3 :** FORCEFUL ⟨~ prose style⟩ **4 a :** lacking no particulars **:** GENUINE **b :** containing fullness of substance **:** RICH — **full–blood•ed•ness** *n*

full–blown \-ˈblōn\ *adj* (1601) **1 a :** fully mature **b :** being at the height of bloom **c :** FULL-FLEDGED **2 :** possessing or exhibiting all the usual or necessary features or symptoms ⟨a general philosophy, if not a ~ ideology, is emerging —W. H. Jones⟩ ⟨developed ~ AIDS⟩

full–bod•ied \-ˌbä-dēd\ *adj* (1686) **1 :** having a large body **2** *of a beverage* **:** imparting to the palate the general impression of substantial weight and rich texture **3 :** having importance, significance, or meaningfulness ⟨~ study of literature⟩

full–bore \ˈfu̇l-ˈbȯr\ *adj* (1974) **1 :** FULL-BLOWN 2 ⟨a ~ crisis⟩ **2 :** made with maximum effort ⟨a ~ attempt to succeed⟩

full bore *adv* (1927) **:** with maximum effort or speed ⟨runners sprinting *full bore*⟩

full circle *adv* (1878) **:** through a series of developments that lead back to the original source, position, or situation or to a complete reversal of the original position — usu. used in the phrase *come full circle*

full–court press *n* (1952) **1 :** a press employed in basketball on both halves of the court **2 :** an all-out effort or offensive

full–dress *adj* (1761) **:** involving attention to every detail in preparation or execution ⟨a ~ rehearsal⟩ ⟨a ~ investigation⟩

full dress *n* (1748) **:** the style of dress prescribed for ceremonial or formal social occasions

[1]**full•er** \ˈfu̇-lər\ *n* [ME, fr. OE *fullere,* fr. L *fullo*] (bef. 12c) **:** one that fulls cloth

[2]**ful•ler** \ˈfu̇-lər\ *n* [*fuller* to form a groove in] (ca. 1864) **:** a blacksmithing hammer for grooving and spreading iron

ful•ler•ene \ˌfu̇-lə-ˈrēn\ *n* [R. Buckminster *Fuller;* fr. the resemblance of the molecules to the geodesic domes designed by Fuller] (1987) **:** any of a class of closed hollow aromatic carbon compounds whose structures are made up of twelve pentagonal and differing numbers of hexagonal faces; *esp* **:** one having a roughly spherical shape

fuller's earth *n* [[1]*fuller;* fr. its earlier use as fulling agent] (15c) **:** an earthy substance that consists chiefly of clay mineral but lacks plasticity and that is used as an adsorbent, a filter medium, and a carrier for catalysts

ful•ler's teasel *n* (15c) **:** TEASEL 1a

full–fash•ioned \ˈfu̇l-ˈfa-shənd\ *adj* (1883) **:** employing or produced by a knitting process for shaping to conform to body lines ⟨~ hosiery⟩

full–fledged \-ˈflejd\ *adj* (1833) **1 :** fully developed **:** TOTAL, COMPLETE ⟨a ~ biography⟩ **2 :** having attained complete status ⟨~ lawyer⟩ **3 :** FULL-BLOWN 2 ⟨a ~ reunion⟩

full house *n* (1887) **:** a poker hand containing three of a kind and a pair — see POKER illustration

full–length \ˈfu̇l-ˌleŋ(k)th\ *adj* (1760) **1 :** showing or adapted to the entire length esp. of the human figure ⟨a ~ mirror⟩ ⟨a ~ dress⟩ **2 :** having a length as great as that which is normal or standard for one of its kind ⟨a ~ play⟩

full marks *n pl* (1916) *chiefly Brit* **:** due credit or commendation

full moon *n* (bef. 12c) **:** the moon with its whole apparent disk illuminated

full•mouthed \ˈfu̇l-ˈmau̇t͟hd, -ˈmau̇tht\ *adj* (1577) **1 :** having a full complement of teeth ⟨~ ewes⟩ **2 :** uttered loudly

full nelson *n* (1900) **:** a wrestling hold gained from behind an opponent by thrusting the arms under the opponent's arms and clasping the hands behind the opponent's head — compare HALF NELSON

full•ness *also* **ful•ness** \ˈfu̇l-nəs\ *n* (14c) **:** the quality or state of being full — **in the fullness of time :** at some point **:** EVENTUALLY

full–on \ˈfu̇l-ˌȯn-, -ˌän\ *adj* (1970) **:** COMPLETE, FULL-FLEDGED

full–out \-ˌau̇t\ *adj* (14c) **:** COMPLETE, TOTAL ⟨a ~ effort⟩

full–scale \-ˌskāl\ *adj* (1933) **1 :** identical to an original in proportion and size ⟨~ drawing⟩ **2 a :** involving full use of available resources ⟨a ~ biography⟩ ⟨~ war⟩ **b :** TOTAL, COMPLETE ⟨a ~ musical renaissance —*Current Biog.*⟩

full–ser•vice \-ˈsər-vəs\ *adj* (1934) **:** providing comprehensive service of a particular kind ⟨a ~ bank⟩

full–size \-ˌsīz\ *adj* (1832) **1 :** having the usual or normal size of its kind **2 :** having the dimensions 54 by 75 inches (about 1.4 by 1.9 meters) — used of a bed; compare KING-SIZE, QUEEN-SIZE, TWIN-SIZE

full stop *n* (1596) *chiefly Brit* **:** PERIOD 5a

full–term \ˈfu̇l-ˌtərm\ *adj* (1907) **:** retained in the uterus for the normal period of gestation before birth ⟨a ~ newborn⟩

full tilt *adv* [[2]*tilt*] (1679) **:** at high speed ⟨running *full tilt*⟩

full–time *adj* (1898) **1 :** employed for or involving full time ⟨~ employees⟩ ⟨~ work⟩ **2 :** devoting one's full attention and energies to something ⟨a ~ gambler⟩ — **full–time** *adv*

full time *n* (1898) **:** the amount of time considered the normal or standard amount for working during a given period

full–tim•er \ˈfu̇l-ˈtī-mər\ *n* (1868) **:** a person who works full-time

ful•ly \ˈfu̇(l)-lē\ *adv* (bef. 12c) **1 :** in a full manner or degree **:** COMPLETELY **2 :** at least ⟨~ nine tenths of us⟩ ***usage*** see PLENTY

ful•mar \ˈfu̇l-mər, -ˌmär\ *n* [of Scand origin; akin to ON *fūlmār* fulmar, fr. *fūll* foul + *mār* gull — more at MEW] (1698) **:** a seabird (*Fulmarus glacialis*) of colder northern seas closely related to the petrels; *also* **:** a related bird (*F. glacialoides*) of circumpolar distribution in colder southern seas

ful•mi•nant \ˈfu̇l-mə-nənt, ˈfəl-\ *adj* (1602) **:** coming on suddenly and with great severity ⟨~ disease⟩

[1]**ful•mi•nate** \-ˌnāt\ *vb* **-nat•ed; -nat•ing** [ME, fr. ML *fulminatus,* pp. of *fulminare,* fr. L, to strike (of lightning), fr. *fulmin-, fulmen* lightning; akin to L *flagrare* to burn — more at BLACK] *vt* (15c) **:** to utter or send out with denunciation ⟨~ a decree⟩ ~ *vi* **:** to send forth censures or invectives — **ful•mi•na•tion** \ˌfu̇l-mə-ˈnā-shən, ˌfəl-\ *n*

[2]**fulminate** *n* [*fulminic acid,* fr. L *fulmin-, fulmen*] (1826) **:** an often explosive salt (as mercury fulminate) containing the group –CNO

fulminating *adj* (1626) **1 :** hurling denunciations or menaces **2 :** EXPLOSIVE **3 :** FULMINANT

ful•mine \ˈfu̇l-mən, ˈfəl-\ *vb* (1623) *archaic* **:** FULMINATE

ful•some \ˈfu̇l-səm\ *adj* [ME *fulsom* copious, cloying, fr. *full* + *-som* -some] (13c) **1 a :** characterized by abundance **:** COPIOUS ⟨describes in ~ detail —G. N. Shuster⟩ ⟨~ bird life. The feeder overcrowded —Maxine Kumin⟩ **b :** generous in amount, extent, or spirit ⟨the passengers were ~ in praise of the plane's crew —Don Oliver⟩ ⟨a ~ victory for the far left —Bruce Rothwell⟩ ⟨the greetings have been ~, the farewells tender —Simon Gray⟩ **c :** being full and well developed ⟨she was in generally ~, limpid voice —Thor Eckert, Jr.⟩ **2 :** aesthetically, morally, or generally offensive ⟨~ lies and nauseous flattery —William Congreve⟩ ⟨the devil take thee for a . . . ~ rogue —George Villiers⟩ **3 :** exceeding the bounds of good taste **:** OVERDONE ⟨the ~ chromium glitter of the escalators dominating the central hall —Lewis Mumford⟩ **4 :** excessively complimentary or flattering **:** EFFUSIVE ⟨an admiration whose extent I did not express, lest I be thought ~ —A. J. Liebling⟩ — **ful•some•ly** *adv* — **ful•some•ness** *n*

usage The senses shown above are the chief living senses of *fulsome.* Sense 2, which was a generalized term of disparagement in the late 17th century, is the least common of these. *Fulsome* became a point of dispute when sense 1, thought to be obsolete in the 19th century, began to be revived in the 20th. The dispute was exacerbated by the fact that the large dictionaries of the first half of the century missed the beginnings of the revival. Sense 1 has not only been revived but has spread in its application and continues to do so. The chief danger for the user of *fulsome* is ambiguity. Unless the context is made very clear, the reader or hearer cannot be sure whether such an expression as "fulsome praise" is meant in sense 1b or in sense 4.

ful•vous \ˈfu̇l-vəs, ˈfəl-\ *adj* [L *fulvus;* perh. akin to L *flavus* yellow — more at BLUE] (1664) **:** of a dull brownish yellow **:** TAWNY

Fu Man•chu mustache \ˌfü-(ˌ)man-ˈchü-\ *n* [*Fu Manchu,* Chinese villain in stories by "Sax Rohmer" (A. S. Ward †1955)] (1968) **:** a long mustache with ends that turn down to the chin

fu•ma•rase \ˈfyü-mə-ˌrās, -ˌrāz\ *n* (1936) **:** an enzyme that catalyzes the interconversion (as in the Krebs cycle) of fumaric acid and malic acid or their salts

fu•ma•rate \-ˌrāt\ *n* (1864) **:** a salt or ester of fumaric acid

fu•mar•ic acid \fyu̇-ˈmer-ik-, -ˈma-rik-\ *n* [ISV, fr. NL *Fumaria,* genus of herbs, fr. LL, fumitory, fr. L *fumus*] (ca. 1864) **:** a crystalline acid $C_4H_4O_4$ found in various plants or made synthetically

fu•ma•role \ˈfyü-mə-ˌrōl\ *n* [It *fumarola,* fr. It dial. (Neapolitan), fr. LL *fumariolum* vent, fr. L *fumarium* smoke chamber for aging wine, fr. *fumus*] (1811) **:** a hole in a volcanic region from which hot gases and vapors issue — **fu•ma•rol•ic** \ˌfyü-mə-ˈrō-lik\ *adj*

[1]**fum•ble** \ˈfəm-bəl\ *vb* **fum•bled; fum•bling** \-b(ə-)liŋ\ [prob. of Scand origin; akin to Sw *fumla* to fumble] *vi* (1534) **1 a :** to grope for or handle something clumsily or aimlessly **b :** to make awkward attempts to do or find something ⟨*fumbled* in his pocket for a coin⟩ **c :** to search by trial and error **d :** BLUNDER **2 :** to feel one's way or move awkwardly **3 a :** to drop or juggle or fail to play cleanly a grounder **b :** to lose hold of a football while handling or running with it ~ *vt* **1 :** to bring about by clumsy manipulation **2 a :** to feel or handle clumsily **b :** to deal with in a blundering way **:** BUNGLE **3 :** to make (one's way) in a clumsy manner **4 a :** MISPLAY ⟨~ a grounder⟩ **b :** to lose hold of (a football) while handling or running — **fum•bler** \-b(ə-)lər\ *n* — **fum•bling•ly** \-b(ə-)liŋ-lē\ *adv*

[2]**fumble** *n* (1634) **1 :** an act or instance of fumbling **2 :** a fumbled ball

[1]**fume** \ˈfyüm\ *n* [ME, fr. AF *fum,* fr. L *fumus;* akin to OHG *toumen* to be fragrant, Skt *dhūma* smoke, OCS *dymŭ*] (14c) **1 a :** a smoke, vapor, or gas esp. when irritating or offensive ⟨engine exhaust ~*s*⟩ **b :** an often noxious suspension of particles in a gas (as air) **2 :** something (as an emotion) that impairs one's reasoning ⟨sometimes his head gets a little hot with the ~*s* of patriotism —Matthew Arnold⟩ **3 :** a state of excited irritation or anger — usu. used in the phrase *in a fume* — **fumy** \ˈfyü-mē\ *adj* — **on fumes :** with little of the original strength or energy remaining ⟨tired ballplayers running *on fumes*⟩

[2]**fume** *vb* **fumed; fum•ing** *vt* (14c) **1 :** to expose to or treat with fumes **2 :** to give off in fumes ⟨*fuming* thick black smoke⟩ **3 :** to utter while in a state of excited irritation or anger ~ *vi* **1 a :** to emit fumes **b :** to be in a state of excited irritation or anger ⟨fretted and *fumed* over the delay⟩ **2 :** to rise in or as if in fumes

fu•met \fyü-ˈmā, ˈfyü-mət\ *n* [F, lit., pleasant aroma (of meat cooking), fr. MF, fr. *fumer* to give off smoke or steam, fr. L *fumare,* fr. *fumus*] (1906) **:** a reduced and seasoned fish, meat, or vegetable stock

fu•mi•gant \ˈfyü-mi-gənt\ *n* (1940) **:** a substance used in fumigating

fu•mi•gate \ˈfyü-mə-ˌgāt\ *vt* **-gat•ed; -gat•ing** [L *fumigatus,* pp. of *fumigare,* fr. *fumus* + *-igare* (akin to L *agere* to drive) — more at AGENT] (1781) **:** to apply smoke, vapor, or gas to esp. for the purpose of disinfecting or of destroying pests — **fu•mi•ga•tion** \ˌfyü-mə-ˈgā-shən\ *n* — **fu•mi•ga•tor** \ˈfyü-mə-ˌgā-tər\ *n*

fu·mi·to·ry \ˈfyü-mə-ˌtȯr-ē\ *n* [ME *fumeterre,* fr. AF, fr. ML *fumus terrae,* lit., smoke of the earth, fr. L *fumus* + *terrae,* gen. of *terra* earth — more at TERRACE] (14c) : any of a genus (*Fumaria* of the family Fumariaceae, the fumitory family) of erect or climbing herbs; *esp* : a common European herb (*F. officinalis*)

¹**fun** \ˈfən\ *n* [E dial. *fun* to hoax, perh. alter. of ME *fonnen,* fr. *fonne* dupe] (1727) **1** : what provides amusement or enjoyment; *specif* : playful often boisterous action or speech ⟨full of ∼⟩ **2** : a mood for finding or making amusement ⟨all in ∼⟩ **3 a** : AMUSEMENT, ENJOYMENT ⟨sickness takes all the ∼ out of life⟩ **b** : derisive jest : SPORT, RIDICULE ⟨a figure of ∼⟩ **4** : violent or excited activity or argument
syn FUN, JEST, SPORT, GAME, PLAY mean action or speech that provides amusement or arouses laughter. FUN usu. implies laughter or gaiety but may imply merely a lack of serious or ulterior purpose ⟨played cards just for *fun*⟩. JEST implies lack of earnestness and may suggest a hoaxing or teasing ⟨hurt by remarks said only in *jest*⟩. SPORT applies esp. to the arousing of laughter against someone ⟨teasing begun in *sport* led to anger⟩. GAME is close to SPORT, and often stresses mischievous or malicious fun ⟨made *game* of their poor relations⟩. PLAY stresses the opposition to *earnest* without implying any malice or mischief ⟨pretended to strangle his brother in *play*⟩.

²**fun** *vi* **funned; fun·ning** (1833) : to indulge in banter or play : JOKE

³**fun** *adj, sometimes* **fun·ner**; *sometimes* **fun·nest** (ca. 1846) **1** : providing entertainment, amusement, or enjoyment ⟨a ∼ party⟩ ⟨a ∼ person to be with⟩ **2** : full of fun : PLEASANT ⟨have a ∼ time⟩

fu·nam·bu·lism \fyu̇-ˈnam-byə-ˌli-zəm\ *n* [L *funambulus* ropewalker, fr. *funis* rope + *ambulare* to walk] (1824) **1** : tightrope walking **2** : a show esp. of mental agility — **fu·nam·bu·list** \-list\ *n*

fun and games *n pl but sing or pl in constr* (1920) : light amusement

¹**func·tion** \ˈfəŋ(k)-shən\ *n* [L *function-, functio* performance, fr. *fungi* to perform; prob. akin to Skt *bhuṅkte* he enjoys] (1533) **1** : professional or official position : OCCUPATION **2** : the action for which a person or thing is specially fitted or used or for which a thing exists : PURPOSE **3** : any of a group of related actions contributing to a larger action; *esp* : the normal and specific contribution of a bodily part to the economy of a living organism **4** : an official or formal ceremony or social gathering **5 a** : a mathematical correspondence that assigns exactly one element of one set to each element of the same or another set **b** : a variable (as a quality, trait, or measurement) that depends on and varies with another ⟨height is a ∼ of age⟩; *also* : RESULT ⟨illnesses that are a ∼ of stress⟩ **6** : characteristic behavior of a chemical compound due to a particular reactive unit; *also* : FUNCTIONAL GROUP **7** : a computer subroutine; *specif* : one that performs a calculation with variables provided by a program and supplies the program with a single result — **func·tion·less** \-ləs\ *adj*
syn FUNCTION, OFFICE, DUTY, PROVINCE mean the acts or operations expected of a person or thing. FUNCTION implies a definite end or purpose or a particular kind of work ⟨the *function* of language is two-fold: to communicate emotion and to give information —Aldous Huxley⟩. OFFICE is typically applied to the function or service associated with a trade or profession or a special relationship to others ⟨they exercise the *offices* of the judge, the priest, the counsellor —W. E. Gladstone⟩. DUTY applies to a task or responsibility imposed by one's occupation, rank, status, or calling ⟨it is the judicial *duty* of the court, to examine the whole case —R. B. Taney⟩. PROVINCE applies to a function, office, or duty that naturally or logically falls to one ⟨I felt it was not my *province* to inquire —Anne Brontë⟩.

²**function** *vi* **func·tioned; func·tion·ing** \-sh(ə-)niŋ\ (1856) **1** : to have a function : SERVE ⟨an attributive noun ∼*s* as an adjective⟩ **2** : to carry on a function or be in action : OPERATE

func·tion·al \ˈfəŋ(k)-shnəl, -shə-nᵊl\ *adj* (1631) **1 a** : of, connected with, or being a function **b** : affecting physiological or psychological functions but not organic structure ⟨∼ heart disease⟩ **2** : used to contribute to the development or maintenance of a larger whole ⟨∼ and practical school courses⟩; *also* : designed or developed chiefly from the point of view of use **3** : performing or able to perform a regular function — **func·tion·al·ly** \ˈfəŋ(k)-shnə-lē, -shə-nᵊl-ē\ *adv*

functional calculus *n* (1933) : PREDICATE CALCULUS

functional food *n* (1988) : NUTRACEUTICAL

functional genomics *n* (1995) : a branch of genomics that uses various techniques (as RNA interference and mass spectrometry) to analyze the function of genes and the proteins they produce

functional group *n* (1906) : a characteristic reactive unit of a chemical compound esp. in organic chemistry

functional illiterate *n* (1946) : a person who has had some schooling but does not meet a minimum standard of literacy — **functional illiteracy** *n* — **functionally illiterate** *adj*

func·tion·al·ism \ˈfəŋ(k)-shnə-ˌli-zəm, -shə-nə-ˌli-\ *n* (1914) **1** : a late 19th century to early 20th century American school of psychology concerned esp. with how the mind functions to adapt the individual to the environment — compare STRUCTURALISM 1 **2** : a philosophy of design (as in architecture) holding that form should be adapted to use, material, and structure **3** : a theory that stresses the interdependence of the patterns and institutions of a society and their interaction in maintaining cultural and social unity **4** : a doctrine or practice that emphasizes practical utility or functional relations — **func·tion·al·ist** \-shnə-list, -shə-nə-list\ *n* — **functionalist** *or* **func·tion·al·is·tic** \ˌfəŋ(k)-shnə-ˈlis-tik, -shə-nə-ˈlis-\ *adj*

func·tion·al·i·ty \ˌfəŋ(k)-shə-ˈna-lə-tē\ *n, pl* **-ties** (1871) : the quality or state of being functional; *esp* : the set of functions or capabilities associated with computer software or hardware or an electronic device

functional magnetic resonance imaging *n* (1989) : magnetic resonance imaging used to detect physical changes (as of blood flow) in the brain resulting from increased neuronal activity — called also *functional MRI*

functional shift *n* (1942) : the process by which a word or form comes to be used in another grammatical function

func·tion·ary \ˈfəŋ(k)-shə-ˌner-ē\ *n, pl* **-ar·ies** (1791) **1** : one who serves in a certain function **2** : one holding office in a government or political party

function key *n* (ca. 1964) : any of a set of keys on a computer keyboard that have or can be programmed to have special functions

function word *n* (1940) : a word (as a preposition, auxiliary verb, or conjunction) that expresses primarily a grammatical relationship

func·tor \ˈfəŋ(k)-tər\ *n* (1935) : something that performs a function or an operation

¹**fund** \ˈfənd\ *n* [L *fundus* bottom, country estate — more at BOTTOM] (1694) **1 a** : a sum of money or other resources whose principal or interest is set apart for a specific objective **b** : money on deposit on which checks or drafts can be drawn — usu. used in pl. **c** : CAPITAL **d** *pl* : the stock of the British national debt — usu. used with *the* **2** : an available quantity of material or intangible resources : SUPPLY **3** *pl* : available pecuniary resources **4** : an organization administering a special fund

²**fund** *vt* (1789) **1 a** : to make provision of resources for discharging the interest or principal of **b** : to provide funds for ⟨a federally ∼*ed* program⟩ **2** : to place in a fund : ACCUMULATE **3** : to convert into a debt that is payable either at a distant date or at no definite date and that bears a fixed interest ⟨∼ a floating debt⟩ — **fund·er** \ˈfən-dər\ *n*

³**fund** *abbr* fundamental

fun·da·ment \ˈfən-də-mənt\ *n* [ME *foundement,* fr. AF, fr. L *fundamentum,* fr. *fundare* to found, fr. *fundus*] (13c) **1** : an underlying ground, theory, or principle **2 a** : BUTTOCKS **b** : ANUS **3** : the part of a land surface that has not been altered by human activities

¹**fun·da·men·tal** \ˌfən-də-ˈmen-tᵊl\ *adj* (15c) **1 a** : serving as an original or generating source : PRIMARY ⟨a discovery ∼ to modern computers⟩ **b** : serving as a basis supporting existence or determining essential structure or function : BASIC **2 a** : of or relating to essential structure, function, or facts : RADICAL ⟨∼ change⟩; *also* : of or dealing with general principles rather than practical application ⟨∼ science⟩ **b** : adhering to fundamentalism **3** : of, relating to, or produced by the lowest component of a complex vibration **4** : of central importance : PRINCIPAL ⟨∼ purpose⟩ **5** : belonging to one's innate or ingrained characteristics : DEEP-ROOTED ⟨her ∼ good humor⟩ ***syn*** see ESSENTIAL — **fun·da·men·tal·ly** \-tᵊl-ē\ *adv*

²**fundamental** *n* (1637) **1** : something fundamental; *esp* : one of the minimum constituents without which a thing or a system would not be what it is **2 a** : the principal musical tone produced by vibration (as of a string or column of air) on which a series of higher harmonics is based **b** : the root of a chord **3** : the harmonic component of a complex wave that has the lowest frequency and commonly the greatest amplitude

fundamental group *n* (1957) : a set that is a subset of all paths defined on a set of points each pair of which is joined by a path and that is the quotient group of the group of all paths beginning and ending in a given point

fun·da·men·tal·ism \-tə-ˌli-zəm\ *n* (1922) **1 a** *often cap* : a movement in 20th century Protestantism emphasizing the literally interpreted Bible as fundamental to Christian life and teaching **b** : the beliefs of this movement **c** : adherence to such beliefs **2** : a movement or attitude stressing strict and literal adherence to a set of basic principles ⟨Islamic ∼⟩ ⟨political ∼⟩ — **fun·da·men·tal·ist** \-tə-list\ *n* — **fundamentalist** *or* **fun·da·men·tal·is·tic** \-ˌmen-tə-ˈlis-tik\ *adj*

fundamental law *n* (1622) : the organic or basic law of a political unit as distinguished from legislative acts; *specif* : CONSTITUTION

fundamental particle *n* (1947) : ELEMENTARY PARTICLE

fun·dic \ˈfən-dik\ *adj* (ca. 1927) : of or relating to a fundus

fund–rais·er \ˈfənd-ˌrā-zər\ *n* (1957) **1** : a person employed to raise funds **2** : a social event (as a cocktail party) held for the purpose of raising funds

fund–rais·ing \-ziŋ\ *n, often attrib* (1940) : the organized activity of raising funds (as for an institution or political cause)

fun·dus \ˈfən-dəs\ *n, pl* **fun·di** \-ˌdī, -ˌdē\ [NL, fr. L, bottom] (1764) : the bottom of or part opposite the aperture of the internal surface of a hollow organ: as **a** : the greater curvature of the stomach **b** : the lower back part of the bladder **c** : the large upper end of the uterus **d** : the part of the eye opposite the pupil

¹**fu·ner·al** \ˈfyün-rəl, ˈfyü-nə-\ *adj* [ME, fr. LL *funeralis,* fr. L *funer-, funus* funeral (n.)] (14c) **1** : of, relating to, or constituting a funeral **2** : FUNEREAL 2

²**funeral** *n* [ME *funerelles* (pl.), fr. MF *funerailles* (pl.), fr. ML *funeralia* (pl.), fr. LL, neut. pl. of *funeralis,* adj.] (ca. 1512) **1** : the observances held for a dead person usu. before burial or cremation **2** *chiefly dial* : a funeral sermon **3** : a funeral procession **4** : an end of something's existence **5** : a matter of concern to one : WORRY ⟨if you flunk, it's your ∼⟩

funeral director *n* (1886) : one whose profession is the management of funerals and who is usu. an embalmer

funeral home *n* (1926) : an establishment with facilities for the preparation of the dead for burial or cremation, for the viewing of the body, and for funerals — called also *funeral parlor*

fu·ner·ary \ˈfyü-nə-ˌrer-ē\ *adj* (ca. 1693) : of, used for, or associated with burial ⟨a pharaoh's ∼ chamber⟩

fu·ne·re·al \fyu̇-ˈnir-ē-əl\ *adj* [L *funereus,* fr. *funer-, funus*] (1725) **1** : of or relating to a funeral **2** : befitting or suggesting a funeral (as in solemnity) — **fu·ne·re·al·ly** \-ə-lē\ *adv*

fun·fair \ˈfən-ˌfer\ *n* (1925) *chiefly Brit* : AMUSEMENT PARK

fun·gal \ˈfəŋ-gəl\ *adj* (1835) **1** : of, relating to, or having the characteristics of fungi **2** : caused by a fungus ⟨a ∼ skin disease⟩

fungi- *comb form* [L *fungus*] : fungus ⟨*fungi*form⟩

¹**fun·gi·ble** \ˈfən-jə-bəl\ *n* (ca. 1765) : something that is fungible — usu. used in pl.

²**fungible** *adj* [NL *fungibilis,* fr. L *fungi* to perform — more at FUNCTION] (1818) **1** : being of such a nature that one part or quantity may be replaced by another equal part or quantity in the satisfaction of an obligation ⟨oil, wheat, and lumber are ∼ commodities⟩ **2** : INTERCHANGEABLE **3** : FLEXIBLE 3 — **fun·gi·bil·i·ty** \ˌfən-jə-ˈbi-lə-tē\ *n*

fun·gi·cid·al \ˌfən-jə-ˈsī-dᵊl, ˌfəŋ-gə-\ *adj* (1905) : ANTIFUNGAL — **fun·gi·cid·al·ly** \-dᵊl-ē\ *adv*

fun·gi·cide \ˈfən-jə-ˌsīd, ˈfəŋ-gə-\ *n* [ISV] (1889) : an agent that destroys fungi or inhibits their growth

\ə\ **abut** \ᵊ\ **kitten, F table** \ər\ **further** \a\ **ash** \ā\ **ace** \ä\ **mop, mar**
\au̇\ **out** \ch\ **chin** \e\ **bet** \ē\ **easy** \g\ **go** \i\ **hit** \ī\ **ice** \j\ **job**
\ŋ\ **sing** \ō\ **go** \ȯ\ **law** \ȯi\ **boy** \th\ **thin** \t͟h\ **the** \ü\ **loot** \u̇\ **foot**
\y\ **yet** \zh\ **vision, beige** \k, ⁿ, œ, ue, ʸ\ *see* **Guide to Pronunciation**

fun·gi·form \ˈfən-jə-ˌfȯrm, ˈfəŋ-gə-\ *adj* (1823) **:** shaped like a mushroom

fun·gi·stat·ic \ˌfən-jə-ˈsta-tik\ *adj* (1922) **:** inhibiting the growth of fungi without destroying them

fun·go \ˈfəŋ-(ˌ)gō\ *n, pl* **fungoes** [origin unknown] (ca. 1867) **1 :** a fly ball hit esp. for practice fielding by a player who tosses a ball in the air and hits it as it comes down **2 :** FUNGO BAT

fungo bat *n* (1926) **:** a long thin bat used for hitting fungoes

fun·goid \ˈfəŋ-ˌgȯid\ *adj* (ca. 1836) **:** resembling, characteristic of, caused by, or being a fungus ⟨a ~ growth⟩ — **fungoid** *n*

fun·gous \ˈfəŋ-gəs\ *adj* (15c) **:** FUNGAL

fun·gus \ˈfəŋ-gəs\ *n, pl* **fun·gi** \ˈfən-ˌjī, ˈfəŋ-ˌgī\ *also* **fun·gus·es** \ˈfəŋ-gə-səz\ *often attrib* [L] (1527) **:** any of a kingdom (Fungi) of saprophytic and parasitic spore-producing eukaryotic typically filamentous organisms formerly classified as plants that lack chlorophyll and include molds, rusts, mildews, smuts, mushrooms, and yeasts

fungus gnat *n* (1884) **:** any of various small dipteran flies (families Mycetophilidae and Sciaridae) resembling mosquitoes and having larvae that feed on fungi and decaying organic matter

fun house *n* (1936) **:** a building in an amusement park that contains various devices designed to startle or amuse

[1]**fu·nic·u·lar** \fyu̇-ˈni-kyə-lər, fə-\ *adj* [L *funiculus*] (1664) **1 :** having the form of or associated with a cord usu. under tension **2** [NL *funiculus*] **:** of, relating to, or being a funiculus **3 :** of, relating to, or being a funicular ⟨a ~ system⟩

[2]**funicular** *n* (1911) **:** a cable railway ascending a mountain; *esp* **:** one in which an ascending car counterbalances a descending car

fu·nic·u·lus \-ləs\ *n, pl* **-li** \-ˌlī, -ˌlē\ [NL, fr. L, dim. of *funis* rope] (1826) **1 :** a bodily structure suggesting a cord; *esp* **:** a bundle of nerve fibers **2 :** the stalk of a plant ovule

[1]**funk** \ˈfəŋk\ *n* [prob. ultim. fr. F dial. (Picard) *funquer* to give off smoke] (1623) **:** a strong offensive smell

[2]**funk** *vi* (ca. 1739) **:** to become frightened and shrink back ~ *vt* **1 :** to be afraid of **:** DREAD **2 :** to shrink from undertaking or facing

[3]**funk** *n* [perh. fr. obs. D dial. (Flanders) *fonck*] (1743) **1 a :** a state of paralyzing fear **b :** a depressed state of mind **2 :** one that funks **:** COWARD **3 :** SLUMP 1 ⟨an economic ~⟩ ⟨the team went into a ~⟩

[4]**funk** *n* [back-formation fr. [2]*funky*] (1959) **1 :** music that combines elements of rhythm and blues and soul music and that is characterized by a percussive vocal style, static harmonies, and a strong bass line with heavy downbeats **2 :** the quality or state of being funky ⟨jeans . . . have lost much of their ~ —Tom Wolfe⟩

funk hole *n* (1900) **1 :** DUGOUT 2 **2 :** a place of safe retreat

fun·kia \ˈfəŋ-kē-ə, ˈfu̇ŋ-\ *n* [NL, genus name, fr. C. H. *Funck* †1839 Ger. botanist] (1839) **:** HOSTA

[1]**funky** \ˈfəŋ-kē\ *adj* (1845) **:** being in a funk **:** PANICKY

[2]**funky** *adj* **funk·i·er; -est** [*funk* offensive odor] (1784) **1 :** having an offensive odor **:** FOUL **2 :** having an earthy unsophisticated style and feeling; *esp* **:** having the style and feeling of older black American music (as blues or gospel) or of funk ⟨a ~ beat⟩ **3 a :** odd or quaint in appearance or feeling **b :** lacking style or taste **c :** unconventionally stylish **:** HIP — **funk·i·ly** *adv* — **funk·i·ness** *n*

[1]**fun·nel** \ˈfə-nᵊl\ *n* [ME *fonel,* fr. AF *fonyle,* fr. Old Occitan *fonilh,* fr. ML *fundibulum,* short for L *infundibulum,* fr. *infundere* to pour in, fr. *in-* + *fundere* to pour — more at FOUND] (15c) **1 a :** a utensil that is usu. a hollow cone with a tube extending from the smaller end and that is designed to catch and direct a downward flow **b :** something shaped like a funnel **2 :** a stack or flue for the escape of smoke or for ventilation (as on a ship)

[2]**funnel** *vb* **-neled** *also* **-nelled; -nel·ing** *also* **-nel·ling** *vi* (1594) **1 :** to have or take the shape of a funnel **2 :** to pass through or as if through a funnel or conduit ⟨the crowd ~*s* through the doors⟩ ~ *vt* **1 :** to form in the shape of a funnel ⟨~*ed* his hands and shouted through them⟩ **2 :** to move to a focal point or into a conduit or central channel ⟨contributions were ~*ed* into one account⟩

funnel cloud *n* (ca. 1909) **:** a funnel-shaped cloud that projects from the base of a thundercloud and that often precedes the formation of a tornado; *also* **:** TORNADO 2b

fun·nel·form \ˈfə-nᵊl-ˌfȯrm\ *adj* (ca. 1828) **:** having the form of a funnel or cone ⟨~ flowers⟩

[1]**fun·ny** \ˈfə-nē\ *adj* **fun·ni·er; -est** (1756) **1 a :** affording light mirth and laughter **:** AMUSING **b :** seeking or intended to amuse **:** FACETIOUS **2 :** differing from the ordinary in a suspicious, perplexing, quaint, or eccentric way **:** PECULIAR — often used as a sentence modifier ⟨~, things didn't turn out the way we planned⟩ **3 :** involving trickery or deception ⟨told his prisoner not to try anything ~⟩ — **fun·ni·ly** \ˈfə-nə-lē\ *adv* — **fun·ni·ness** \ˈfə-nē-nəs\ *n* — **funny** *adv*

[2]**funny** *n, pl* **fun·nies** (1852) **1 :** one that is funny; *esp* **:** JOKE **2** *pl* **:** comic strips or the comic section of a periodical — usu. used with *the*

funny bone *n* [fr. the tingling felt when it is struck] (1840) **1 :** the place at the back of the elbow where the ulnar nerve rests against a prominence of the humerus **2 :** a sense of humor

funny book *n* (1947) **:** COMIC BOOK

funny car *n* (1969) **:** a specialized dragster that has a one-piece molded body resembling the body of a mass-produced car

funny farm *n* (1963) *slang* **:** a psychiatric hospital

fun·ny·man \ˈfə-nē-ˌman\ *n* (1852) **:** COMEDIAN 2, HUMORIST

funny money *n* (1938) **1 :** artificially inflated currency **2 :** counterfeit money

funny paper *n* (1918) **:** a comic section of a newspaper

Fun·plex \ˈfən-ˌpleks\ *service mark* — used for an entertainment complex with facilities for sports and games and often restaurants

FUO *abbr* fever of undetermined origin; fever of unknown origin

[1]**fur** \ˈfər\ *vb* **furred; fur·ring** [ME *furren,* fr. AF *furrer* to stuff, fill, line, fr. *fuerre* sheath, of Gmc origin; akin to OHG *fuotar* sheath; akin to Gk *pōma* lid, cover, Skt *pāti* he protects] *vt* (14c) **1 :** to cover, line, trim, or clothe with fur **2 :** to coat or clog as if with fur **3 :** to apply furring to ~ *vi* **:** to become coated or clogged as if with fur

[2]**fur** *n, often attrib* (14c) **1 :** a piece of the dressed pelt of an animal used to make, trim, or line wearing apparel **2 :** an article of clothing made of or with fur **3 :** the hairy coat of a mammal esp. when fine, soft, and thick; *also* **:** such a coat with the skin **4 :** a coating resembling fur: as **a :** a coat of epithelial debris on the tongue **b :** the thick pile of a fabric (as chenille) — **fur·less** \ˈfər-ləs\ *adj*

[3]**fur** *abbr* furlong

fu·ran \ˈfyu̇r-ˌan, fyu̇-ˈran\ *also* **fu·rane** \ˈfyu̇r-ˌān, fyu̇-ˈrān\ *n* [ISV, fr. *furfural*] (1894) **:** a cyclic flammable liquid compound C_4H_4O that is obtained from wood oils of pines or made synthetically and is used esp. in organic synthesis; *also* **:** any of various derivatives of furan

fu·ra·nose \ˈfyu̇r-ə-ˌnōs, -ˌnōz\ *n* (1927) **:** a sugar having an oxygen-containing ring of five atoms

fu·ran·o·side \fyu̇-ˈra-nə-ˌsīd\ *n* (1932) **:** a glycoside containing the ring characteristic of furanose

fu·ra·zol·i·done \ˌfyu̇r-ə-ˈzä-lə-ˌdōn\ *n* [*fur*fural + *azole* + *-ide* + *-one*] (1955) **:** an antimicrobial drug $C_8H_7N_3O_5$ used against bacteria and some protozoa esp. in infections of the gastrointestinal tract

fur·bear·er \ˈfər-ˌber-ər\ *n* (1875) **:** an animal that bears fur esp. of a commercially desired quality

fur·be·low \ˈfər-bə-ˌlō\ *n* [by folk etymology fr. F dial. *farbella*] (1702) **1 :** a pleated or gathered piece of material; *esp* **:** a flounce on women's clothing **2 :** something that suggests a furbelow esp. in being showy or superfluous — **furbelow** *vt*

fur·bish \ˈfər-bish\ *vt* [ME *furbisshen,* fr. AF *furbiss-,* stem of *furbir,* of Gmc origin; akin to OHG *furben* to polish] (14c) **1 :** to make lustrous **:** POLISH **2 :** to give a new look to **:** RENOVATE — often used with *up* — **fur·bish·er** *n*

fur·ca·tion \ˌfər-ˈkā-shən\ *n* [ML *furcation-, furcatio,* fr. *furcare* to branch, fr. L *furca* fork] (1646) **1 :** something that is branched **:** FORK **2 :** the act or process of branching

fur·cu·la \ˈfər-kyə-lə\ *n, pl* **-lae** \-ˌlē, -ˌlī\ [NL, fr. L, forked prop, dim. of *furca*] (1859) **:** a forked process or part: as **a :** WISHBONE **b :** the forked leaping appendage arising from the fourth abdominal segment of a springtail

fur·fu·ral \ˈfər-f(y)ə-ˌral\ *n* [L *furfur* bran + ISV [3]*-al*] (1879) **:** a liquid aldehyde $C_5H_4O_2$ of penetrating odor that is usu. made from plant materials and used esp. in making furan or phenolic resins and as a solvent

fu·ri·o·so \ˌfyu̇r-ē-ˈō-(ˌ)sō, -(ˌ)zō\ *adv or adj* [It, lit., furious] (ca. 1823) **:** with great force or vigor — used as a direction in music

fu·ri·ous \ˈfyu̇r-ē-əs\ *adj* [ME, fr. MF & L; MF *furieus,* fr. L *furiosus,* fr. *furia* madness, fury] (14c) **1 a** (1) **:** exhibiting or goaded by anger (2) **:** indicative of or proceeding from anger **b :** giving a stormy or turbulent appearance ⟨~ bursts of flame⟩ **c :** marked by noise, excitement, activity, or rapidity **2 :** INTENSE 1a ⟨the ~ growth of tropical vegetation⟩ — **fu·ri·ous·ly** *adv*

[1]**furl** \ˈfər(-ə)l\ *vb* [AF *ferlier* to fasten, fr. *fer, ferm* tight (fr. L *firmus* firm) + *lier* to tie, fr. L *ligare* — more at LIGATURE] *vt* (1556) **:** to wrap or roll (as a sail or a flag) close to or around something ~ *vi* **:** to curl or fold as in being furled

[2]**furl** *n* (1643) **1 :** a furled coil **2 :** the act of furling

fur·long \ˈfər-ˌlȯŋ\ *n* [ME, fr. OE *furlang,* fr. *furh* furrow + *lang* long] (14c) **:** a unit of distance equal to 220 yards (about 201 meters)

[1]**fur·lough** \ˈfər-(ˌ)lō\ *n* [D *verlof,* lit., permission, fr. MD, fr. *ver-* for- + *lof* permission; akin to MHG *loube* permission — more at FOR-, LEAVE] (1625) **:** a leave of absence from duty granted esp. to a soldier; *also* **:** a document authorizing such a leave of absence

[2]**furlough** *vt* (1781) **1 :** to grant a furlough to **2 :** to lay off from work

furmity *var of* FRUMENTY

fur·nace \ˈfər-nəs\ *n* [ME *furnas,* fr. AF *forneise,* fr. L *fornac-, fornax;* akin to L *formus* warm — more at THERM] (13c) **:** an enclosed structure in which heat is produced (as for heating a house or for reducing ore)

fur·nish \ˈfər-nish\ *vt* [ME *furnisshen,* fr. AF *furniss-,* stem of *furnir, fournir* to complete, equip, of Gmc origin; akin to OHG *frummen* to further, *fruma* advantage — more at FOREMOST] (15c) **1 :** to provide with what is needed; *esp* **:** to equip with furniture **2 :** SUPPLY, GIVE ⟨~*ed* food and shelter for the refugees⟩ — **fur·nish·er** *n*

syn FURNISH, EQUIP, OUTFIT, APPOINT, ACCOUTRE mean to supply one with what is needed. FURNISH implies the provision of any or all essentials for performing a function ⟨a sparsely *furnished* apartment⟩. EQUIP suggests the provision of something making for efficiency in action or use ⟨a fully *equipped* kitchen⟩. OUTFIT implies provision of a complete list or set of articles as for a journey, an expedition, or a special occupation ⟨*outfitted* the family for a ski trip⟩. APPOINT implies provision of complete and usu. elegant or elaborate equipment or furnishings ⟨a lavishly *appointed* apartment⟩. ACCOUTRE suggests the supplying of personal dress or equipment for a special activity ⟨fully *accoutred* members of a polar expedition⟩.

fur·nish·ing \ˈfər-ni-shiŋ\ *n* (1594) **1 :** an article or accessory of dress — usu. used in pl. **2 :** an object that tends to increase comfort or utility; *esp* **:** an article of furniture for the interior of a building — usu. used in pl.

fur·ni·ture \ˈfər-ni-chər\ *n* [MF *fourniture,* fr. *fournir*] (1542) **:** equipment that is necessary, useful, or desirable: as **a** *archaic* **:** the trappings of a horse **b :** movable articles used in readying an area (as a room or patio) for occupancy or use

furniture beetle *n* (1915) **:** a widespread beetle (*Anobium punctatum* of the family Anobiidae) that bores in and damages furniture and seasoned wood

fu·ror \ˈfyu̇r-ˌȯr, -ər\ *n* [MF & L; MF, fr. L, fr. *furere* to rage] (15c) **1 :** an angry or maniacal fit **:** RAGE **2 :** FURY 4 **3 :** a fashionable craze **:** VOGUE **4 a :** furious or hectic activity **b :** an outburst of public excitement or indignation **:** UPROAR

fu·rore \ˈfyu̇r-ˌȯr, -ər, *esp Brit* fyu̇-ˈrȯ-ri\ *n* [It, fr. L *furor*] (1790) **1 :** FUROR 3 **2 :** FUROR 4b

fu·ro·se·mide \fyu̇-ˈrō-sə-ˌmīd\ *n* [*fur*fural + *-o-* + *sulf-* + *-emide,* prob. alter. of *amide*] (1965) **:** a powerful diuretic $C_{12}H_{11}ClN_2O_5S$ used esp. to treat edema and hypertension

furred \ˈfərd\ *adj* [ME] (14c) **1 :** lined, trimmed, or faced with fur **2 :** coated as if with fur; *specif* **:** having a coating consisting chiefly of mucus and dead epithelial cells ⟨a ~ tongue⟩ **3 :** bearing or wearing fur **4 :** provided with furring ⟨~ wall⟩

fur·ri·er \ˈfər-ē-ər, ˈfə-rē-\ *n* [alter. of ME *furrer,* fr. AF *furrere,* fr. *furrer* to fur — more at FUR] (14c) **1 :** a fur dealer **2 a :** one that dresses furs **b :** one that makes, repairs, alters, or cleans fur garments

fur·ri·ery \-ə-rē\ *n* (ca. 1864) **1 :** the fur business **2 :** fur craftsmanship

fur·rin·er \ˈfər-ə-nər\ *n* [by alter.] (1838) **:** FOREIGNER 2 — used to represent a dial. pronunc.

fur·ring \ˈfər-iŋ\ *n* (14c) **1** : a fur trimming or lining **2 a** : the application of thin wood, brick, or metal to joists, studs, or walls to form a level surface (as for attaching wallboard) or an air space **b** : the material used in this process

1fur·row \ˈfər-(ˌ)ō, ˈfə-(ˌ)rō\ *n* [ME *furgh, forow,* fr. OE *furh;* akin to OHG *furuh* furrow, L *porca*] (bef. 12c) **1 a** : a trench in the earth made by a plow **b** : plowed land : FIELD **2** : something that resembles the track of a plow: as **a** : a marked narrow depression : GROOVE **b** : a deep wrinkle ⟨~*s* in his brow⟩

2furrow *vt* (15c) : to make furrows, grooves, wrinkles, or lines in ~ *vi* : to make or form furrows, grooves, wrinkles, or lines

fur·ry \ˈfər-ē\ *adj* **fur·ri·er; -est** (ca. 1674) **1** : consisting of or resembling fur ⟨animals with ~ coats⟩ **2** : covered with fur **3** : thick in quality ⟨spoke with a ~ voice⟩

fur seal *n* (1775) : any of two genera (*Callorhinus* and *Arctocephalus*) of eared seals that have a double coat with a dense soft underfur

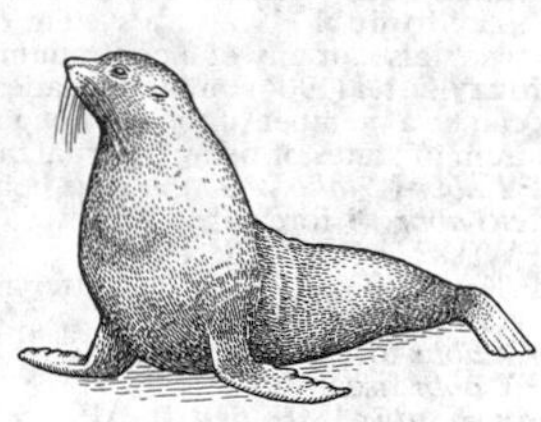
fur seal

1fur·ther \ˈfər-t͟hər\ *adv* [ME, fr. OE *furthor* (akin to OHG *furthar* further), compar., fr. the base of OE *forth* forth] (bef. 12c) **1** : FARTHER 1 ⟨my ponies are tired, and I have ~ to go —Thomas Hardy⟩ **2** : in addition : MOREOVER **3** : to a greater degree or extent ⟨~ annoyed by a second intrusion⟩ ***usage*** see FARTHER

2further *vt* **fur·thered; fur·ther·ing** \ˈfərt͟h-riŋ, ˈfər-t͟hə-\ (bef. 12c) : to help forward : PROMOTE ***syn*** see ADVANCE — **fur·ther·er** \ˈfər-t͟hər-ər\ *n*

3further *adj* (13c) **1** : FARTHER 1 ⟨rode . . . across the valley and up the ~ slopes —T. E. Lawrence⟩ **2** : going or extending beyond : ADDITIONAL ⟨~ volumes⟩ ⟨~ education⟩ ***usage*** see FARTHER

fur·ther·ance \ˈfərt͟h-rən(t)s, ˈfər-t͟hə-\ *n* (15c) : the act of furthering : ADVANCEMENT

further education *n* (1937) *Brit* : ADULT EDUCATION

fur·ther·more \ˈfər-t͟hə(r)-ˌmōr\ *adv* (13c) : in addition to what precedes : BESIDES

fur·ther·most \-t͟hər-ˌmōst\ *adj* (15c) : most distant : FARTHEST

fur·thest \ˈfər-t͟həst\ *adv or adj* (14c) : FARTHEST

fur·tive \ˈfər-tiv\ *adj* [F or L; F *furtif,* fr. L *furtivus,* fr. *furtum* theft, fr. *fur* thief, fr. or akin to Gk *phōr* thief; akin to Gk *pherein* to carry — more at BEAR] (1612) **1 a** : done by stealth : SURREPTITIOUS **b** : expressive of stealth : SLY ⟨had a ~ look about him⟩ **2** : obtained underhandedly : STOLEN ***syn*** see SECRET — **fur·tive·ly** *adv* — **fur·tive·ness** *n*

fu·run·cle \ˈfyu̇r-ˌəŋ-kəl\ *n* [L *furunculus* petty thief, boil, dim. of *furon-, furo* ferret, thief, fr. *fur*] (1676) : 2BOIL

fu·run·cu·lo·sis \fyu̇-ˌrəŋ-kyə-ˈlō-səs\ *n, pl* **-lo·ses** \-ˌsēz\ [NL] (1886) **1** : the condition of having or tending to develop multiple furuncles **2** : a highly infectious disease of various salmonoid fishes (as trout) that is caused by a bacterium (*Aeromonas salmonicida*) and is esp. virulent in dense fish populations (as in hatcheries)

fu·ry \ˈfyu̇r-ē\ *n, pl* **furies** [ME *furie,* fr. L *furia,* fr. *furere* to rage] (14c) **1** : intense, disordered, and often destructive rage **2 a** *cap* : any of the avenging deities in Greek mythology who torment criminals and inflict plagues **b** : an avenging spirit **c** : one who resembles an avenging spirit; *esp* : a spiteful woman **3** : extreme fierceness or violence **4** : a state of inspired exaltation : FRENZY ***syn*** see ANGER

furze \ˈfərz\ *n* [ME *firse,* fr. OE *fyrs;* akin to Russ *pyreĭ* quack grass, Gk *pyros* wheat] (bef. 12c) : GORSE — **furzy** \ˈfər-zē\ *adj*

fu·sar·i·um \fyü-ˈzer-ē-əm\ *n* [NL, fr. L *fusus* spindle] (1907) : any of a genus (*Fusarium*) of ascomycetous fungi having curved septate conidia which includes forms that are important agents of plant disease and others that produce mycotoxins implicated in human and animal disease; *also* : a plant disease (as wilt or dry rot) caused by a fusarium

fus·cous \ˈfəs-kəs\ *adj* [L *fuscus* — more at DUSK] (1662) : of any of several colors averaging a brownish gray

1fuse \ˈfyüz\ *vb* **fused; fus·ing** [L *fusus,* pp. of *fundere* to pour, melt — more at FOUND] *vt* (1592) **1** : to reduce to a liquid or plastic state by heat **2** : to blend thoroughly by or as if by melting together : COMBINE **3** : to stitch by applying heat and pressure with or without the use of an adhesive ~ *vi* **1 a** : to become fluid with heat **b** *Brit* : to fail because of the blowing of a fuse **2** : to become blended or joined by or as if by melting together ***syn*** see MIX

2fuse *n* (1868) : an electrical safety device consisting of or including a wire or strip of fusible metal that melts and interrupts the circuit when the current exceeds a particular amperage

3fuse *n* [It *fuso* spindle, fr. L *fusus,* of unknown origin] (1644) **1** : a continuous train of a combustible substance enclosed in a cord or cable for setting off an explosive charge by transmitting fire to it **2** *also* **fuze** : a mechanical or electrical detonating device for setting off the bursting charge of a projectile, bomb, or torpedo

4fuse *also* **fuze** \ˈfyüz\ *vt* **fused** *also* **fuzed; fus·ing** *also* **fuz·ing** (1802) : to equip with a fuse

fused quartz *n* (1925) : QUARTZ GLASS — called also *fused silica*

fu·see \fyü-ˈzē\ *n* [F *fusée,* lit., spindleful of yarn, fr. OF, fr. *fus* spindle, fr. L *fusus*] (1622) **1** : a conical spirally grooved pulley in a timepiece from which a cord or chain unwinds onto a cylinder containing the mainspring and which by its increasing diameter compensates for the lessening power of the spring **2** : a red signal flare used esp. for protecting stalled trains and trucks

fu·se·lage \ˈfyü-sə-ˌläzh, -zə-\ *n* [F, fr. *fuselé* spindle-shaped, fr. MF, fr. *fusel,* dim. of *fus*] (1909) : the central body portion of an aircraft designed to accommodate the crew and the passengers or cargo — see AIRPLANE illustration

fu·sel oil \ˈfyü-zəl-\ *n* [G *Fusel* bad liquor] (1850) : an acrid oily liquid occurring in insufficiently distilled alcoholic liquors, consisting chiefly of amyl alcohol, and used esp. as a source of alcohols and as a solvent

fus·ible \ˈfyü-zə-bəl\ *adj* (14c) : capable of being fused and esp. liquefied by heat ⟨~ alloy⟩ — **fus·ibil·i·ty** \ˌfyü-zə-ˈbi-lə-tē\ *n*

fu·si·form \ˈfyü-zə-ˌfȯrm\ *adj* [L *fusus* spindle] (1746) : tapering toward each end ⟨~ bacteria⟩

1fu·sil \ˈfyü-zəl\ *or* **fu·sile** \ˈfyü-zəl, -ˌzī(-ə)l\ *adj* [ME, fr. L *fusilis,* fr. *fundere*] (14c) **1** *archaic* **a** : made by melting and pouring into forms : CAST **b** : liquefied by heat **2** *archaic* : FUSIBLE

2fusil *n* [F, lit., steel for striking fire, fr. OF *foisil,* fr. VL **focilis,* fr. LL *focus* fire — more at FUEL] (1680) : a light flintlock musket

fu·sil·ier *or* **fu·sil·eer** \ˌfyü-zə-ˈlir\ *n* [F *fusilier,* fr. *fusil*] (1680) **1** : a soldier armed with a fusil **2** : a member of a British regiment formerly armed with fusils

fu·sil·lade \ˈfyü-sə-ˌläd, -ˌlād, ˌfyü-sə-ˈ, -zə-\ *n* [F, fr. *fusiller* to shoot, fr. *fusil*] (1801) **1 a** : a number of shots fired simultaneously or in rapid succession **b** : something that gives the effect of a fusillade ⟨a ~ of rocks and bottles⟩ **2** : a spirited outburst esp. of criticism

fu·sil·li \fyü-ˈsi-lē, -ˈsē-\ *n* [It, pl. of *fusillo,* fr. It dial. (southern Italy), dim. of *fuso* spindle, fr. L *fusus*] (1948) : spiral-shaped pasta

fu·sion \ˈfyü-zhən\ *n, often attrib* [L *fusion-, fusio,* fr. *fundere*] (14c) **1** : the act or process of liquefying or rendering plastic by heat **2** : a union by or as if by melting: as **a** : a merging of diverse, distinct, or separate elements into a unified whole **b** : a political partnership : COALITION **c** : popular music combining different styles (as jazz and rock) **d** : food prepared using techniques and ingredients of two or more ethnic or regional cuisines — called also *fusion cuisine* **3** : the union of atomic nuclei to form heavier nuclei resulting in the release of enormous quantities of energy when certain light elements unite

fu·sion·ist \ˈfyü-zhə-nist\ *n* (1851) : a person involved in a political fusion or in musical fusion

1fuss \ˈfəs\ *n* [origin unknown] (1701) **1 a** : needless bustle or excitement **b** : a show of flattering attention ⟨made a big ~ over his favorite niece⟩ **2 a** : a state of agitation esp. over a trivial matter **b** : OBJECTION, PROTEST **c** : an often petty controversy or quarrel

2fuss *vi* (1792) **1 a** : to create or be in a state of restless activity; *esp* : to shower flattering attentions ⟨~*ing* over the grandchildren⟩ **b** : to pay close or undue attention to small details ⟨~*ed* with her hair⟩ **2 a** : to become upset : WORRY **b** : to express annoyance or pique : COMPLAIN ~ *vt* : AGITATE, UPSET — **fuss·er** *n*

fuss·bud·get \ˈfəs-ˌbə-jət\ *n* (ca. 1904) : one who fusses or is fussy esp. about trifles — **fuss·bud·gety** \-jə-tē\ *adj*

fuss·pot \ˈfəs-ˌpät\ *n* (1921) : FUSSBUDGET

fussy \ˈfə-sē\ *adj* **fuss·i·er; -est** (1831) **1** : easily upset : IRRITABLE **2** : overly decorative ⟨a ~ wallpaper pattern⟩ **3 a** : requiring or giving close attention to details ⟨~ bookkeeping procedures⟩ **b** : revealing a sometimes extreme concern for niceties : FASTIDIOUS, PICKY — **fuss·i·ly** \ˈfə-sə-lē\ *adv* — **fuss·i·ness** \ˈfə-sē-nəs\ *n*

fus·tian \ˈfəs-chən\ *n* [ME, fr. AF *fustian, fustayn,* fr. ML *fustaneum,* prob. fr. *fustis* tree trunk, fr. L, stick, cudgel] (13c) **1 a** : a strong cotton and linen fabric **b** : a class of cotton fabrics usu. having a pile face and twill weave **2** : high-flown or affected writing or speech; *broadly* : anything high-flown or affected in style — **fustian** *adj*

fus·tic \ˈfəs-tik\ *n* [ME *fustyk* smoke tree, fr. MF *fustoc,* fr. Ar *fustuq,* fr. Gk *pistakē* pistachio tree — more at PISTACHIO] (15c) : the wood of a tropical American tree (*Chlorophora tinctoria*) of the mulberry family that yields a yellow dye; *also* : any of several similar dyewoods

fus·ti·gate \ˈfəs-tə-ˌgāt\ *vt* **-gat·ed; -gat·ing** [LL *fustigatus,* pp. of *fustigare,* fr. L *fustis* + *-igare* (as in *fumigare* to fumigate)] (ca. 1661) **1** : CUDGEL **2** : to criticize severely — **fus·ti·ga·tion** \ˌfəs-tə-ˈgā-shən\ *n*

fus·ty \ˈfəs-tē\ *adj* **fus·ti·er; -est** [prob. alter. of ME *foisted, foist* musty, fr. *foist* wine cask, fr. AF *fust, fuist* wood, tree trunk, cask, fr. ML *fustis*] (14c) **1** *Brit* : impaired by age or dampness : MOLDY **2** : saturated with dust and stale odors : MUSTY **3** : rigidly old-fashioned or reactionary ***syn*** see MALODOROUS — **fus·ti·ly** \-tə-lē\ *adv* — **fus·ti·ness** \-tē-nəs\ *n*

fu·su·li·nid \ˌfyü-zə-ˈlī-nid, -ˈlē-, -ˈli-\ *n* [NL *Fusulinidae,* fr. *Fusulina,* a genus, fr. L *fusus* spindle + *-ulus* -ule + NL *-ina,* dim. suffix] (1941) : any of a family (Fusulinidae) of extinct marine foraminifers

fut *abbr* future

fu·thark \ˈfü-ˌthärk\ *also* **fu·thorc** *or* **fu·thork** \-ˌthȯrk\ *n* [fr. the first six letters, *f, u, þ (th), o* (or *a*), *r, c* (=k)] (1851) : the runic alphabet — see RUNE illustration

fu·tile \ˈfyü-tᵊl, ˈfyü-ˌtī(-ə)l\ *adj* [MF or L; MF, fr. L *futilis* brittle, pointless, prob. fr. *fu-* (akin to *fundere* to pour) — more at FOUND] (ca. 1555) **1** : serving no useful purpose : completely ineffective ⟨efforts to convince him were ~⟩ **2** : occupied with trifles : FRIVOLOUS — **fu·tile·ly** \-tᵊl-(l)ē, -ˌtī(-ə)l-lē\ *adv* — **fu·tile·ness** \-tᵊl-nəs, -ˌtī(-ə)l-nəs\ *n*

syn FUTILE, VAIN, FRUITLESS mean producing no result. FUTILE may connote completeness of failure or unwisdom of undertaking ⟨resistance had proved so *futile* that surrender was the only choice left⟩. VAIN usu. implies simple failure to achieve a desired result ⟨a *vain* attempt to get the car started⟩. FRUITLESS comes close to VAIN but often suggests long and arduous effort or severe disappointment ⟨*fruitless* efforts to obtain a lasting peace⟩.

fu·til·i·tar·i·an \fyü-ˌti-lə-ˈter-ē-ən\ *n* [blend of *futile* and *utilitarian*] (1827) : one who believes that human striving is futile — **futilitarian** *adj* — **fu·til·i·tar·i·an·ism** \-ē-ə-ˌni-zəm\ *n*

fu·til·i·ty \fyü-ˈti-lə-tē\ *n, pl* **-ties** (ca. 1623) **1** : the quality or state of being futile : USELESSNESS **2** : a useless act or gesture ⟨the *futilities* of debate for its own sake —W. A. White⟩

fu·ton \ˈfü-ˌtän\ *n, pl* **futons** *also* **futon** [Jp] (1876) : a usu. cotton-filled mattress used on the floor or in a frame as a bed, couch, or chair

fut·tock \ˈfə-tək\ *n* [ME *votek, futtek,* perh. modif. of MD *voetkijn,* dim. of *voet* foot] (13c) : one of the curved timbers scarfed together to form the lower part of the compound rib of a ship

futtock shroud *n* (1817) : a short iron rod connecting the topmast rigging with the lower mast

1fu·ture \ˈfyü-chər\ *adj* [ME, fr. AF & L; AF, fr. L *futurus* about to be — more at BE] (14c) **1** : that is to be; *specif* : existing after death **2** : of,

\ə\ **abut** \ᵊ\ **kitten**, F **table** \ər\ **further** \a\ **ash** \ā\ **ace** \ä\ **mop, mar**
\au̇\ **out** \ch\ **chin** \e\ **bet** \ē\ **easy** \g\ **go** \i\ **hit** \ī\ **ice** \j\ **job**
\ŋ\ **sing** \ō\ **go** \ȯ\ **law** \ȯi\ **boy** \th\ **thin** \t͟h\ **the** \ü\ **loot** \u̇\ **foot**
\y\ **yet** \zh\ **vision, beige** \k̲, ⁿ, œ, ue, ʸ\ *see* Guide to Pronunciation

relating to, or constituting a verb tense expressive of time yet to come **3** : existing or occurring at a later time ⟨met his ∼ wife⟩

²**future** n (15c) **1 a** : time that is to come **b** : what is going to happen **2** : an expectation of advancement or progressive development **3** : something (as a bulk commodity) bought for future acceptance or sold for future delivery — usu. used in pl. ⟨grain ∼s⟩ **4 a** : the future tense of a language **b** : a verb form in the future tense

fu·ture·less \'fyü-chǝr-lǝs\ adj (1863) : having no future — **fu·ture·ness** n

future perfect adj (ca. 1898) : of, relating to, or constituting a verb tense that is traditionally formed in English with will have and shall have and that expresses completion of an action by a specified time that is yet to come — **future perfect** n

future shock n (1965) : the physical and psychological distress suffered by one who is unable to cope with the rapidity of social and technological changes

fu·tur·ism \'fyü-chǝ-,ri-zǝm\ n (1909) **1** : a movement in art, music, and literature begun in Italy about 1909 and marked esp. by an effort to give formal expression to the dynamic energy and movement of mechanical processes **2** : a point of view that finds meaning or fulfillment in the future rather than in the past or present

fu·tur·ist \'fyü-chǝ-rist\ n (ca. 1846) **1** : one who studies and predicts the future esp. on the basis of current trends **2** : one who advocates or practices futurism — **futurist** adj

fu·tur·is·tic \,fyü-chǝ-'ris-tik\ adj (1915) : of, relating to, or characteristic of the future, futurism, or futurology; also : very modern — **fu·tur·is·ti·cal·ly** \-ti-k(ǝ-)lē\ adv

fu·tur·is·tics \-tiks\ n pl but sing in constr (1969) : FUTUROLOGY

fu·tu·ri·ty \fyü-'tùr-ǝ-tē, -'tyùr-, -'chùr-\ n, pl **-ties** (1604) **1** : time to come : FUTURE **2** : the quality or state of being future **3** pl : future events or prospects **4 a** : a horse race usu. for two-year-olds in which the competitors are nominated at birth or before **b** : a race or competition for which entries are made well in advance of the event

fu·tur·ol·o·gy \,fyü-chǝ-'rä-lǝ-jē\ n (1946) : a study that deals with future possibilities based on current trends — **fu·tur·olog·i·cal** \-rǝ-'läji-kǝl\ adj — **fu·tur·ol·o·gist** \-'rä-lǝ-jist\ n

futz \'fǝts\ vi [perh. part modif., part trans. of Yiddish arumfartsn zikh, lit., to fart around] (ca. 1930) slang : FOOL AROUND 1 — often used with around ⟨∼ around without producing any worthwhile music —John Koegel⟩

fuze var of FUSE

¹**fuzz** \'fǝz\ n [prob. back-formation fr. fuzzy] (1674) **1** : fine light particles or fibers (as of down or fluff) **2** : a blurred effect

²**fuzz** vi (ca. 1702) **1** : to fly off in or become covered with fluffy particles **2** : to become blurred ⟨her frame of reference ∼ing at the edges —Jane O'Reilly⟩ ∼ vt **1** : to make fuzzy **2** : to envelop in a haze

³**fuzz** n [origin unknown] (1927) : POLICE; also : a police officer

fuzzy \'fǝ-zē\ adj **fuzz·i·er; -est** [perh. fr. LG fussig loose, spongy] (1713) **1** : marked by or giving a suggestion of fuzz ⟨a ∼ covering of felt⟩ **2** : lacking in clarity or definition ⟨moving the camera causes ∼ photos⟩ **3** : being, relating to, or invoking pleasant and usu. sentimental emotions ⟨warm and ∼ feelings⟩ — **fuzz·i·ly** \'fǝ-zǝ-lē\ adv — **fuzz·i·ness** \'fǝ-zē-nǝs\ n

fuzzy logic n (1969) : a system of logic in which a statement can be true, false, or any of a continuum of values in between

fuzzy set n (1964) : a mathematical set with the property that an object can be a member of the set, not a member of the set, or any of a continuum of states of being a partial member of the set

FV abbr [L folio verso the page being turned] on the back of the page

fwd abbr **1** foreword **2** forward

FWD abbr front-wheel drive

F/X or FX \,ef-'eks\ n pl [letter names ef and ex representing effects] (1985) : SPECIAL EFFECTS

FX abbr foreign exchange

FY abbr fiscal year

-fy vb suffix [ME -fien, fr. AF -fier, fr. L -ficare, fr. -ficus -fic] **1** : make : form into ⟨dandify⟩ **2** : invest with the attributes of : make similar to ⟨citify⟩

fyce var of FEIST

FYI abbr for your information

fyke \'fīk\ n [D fuik] (1832) : a long bag net kept open by hoops

fyl·fot \'fil-,fät\ n [ME, device used to fill the lower part of a painted glass window (fr. a conjectural MS reading)] (1842) : SWASTIKA

fyn·bos \'fän-,bòs\ n [Afrik, fr. fyn fine, delicate + bos bush] (1936) : a biome of southern coastal South Africa characterized by a diverse richness of endemic plant species (as of the heath, protea, composite, iris, and lily families), by soil that is acidic and nutrient-poor, and by a climate marked by cold wet winters and hot dry summers; also : the type of vegetation characteristic of this biome

---

¹**g** \'jē\ n, pl **g's or gs** \'jēz\ often cap, often attrib (bef. 12c) **1 a** : the 7th letter of the English alphabet **b** : a graphic representation of this letter **c** : a speech counterpart of orthographic g **2** : the fifth tone of a C-major scale **3** : a graphic device for reproducing the letter g **4** : one designated g esp. as the seventh in order or class **5** [gravity] : ACCELERATION OF GRAVITY; also : a unit of force that is equal to the force exerted by gravity on a body at rest and is used to indicate the force to which a body is subjected when undergoing acceleration **6** [grand] slang : a sum of $1000 **7** : something shaped like the letter G

²**g** abbr **1** acceleration of gravity; gravity **2** game **3** gauge **4** gelding **5** gender **6** good **7** gram

¹**G** abbr **1** German **2** giga- **3** guanine **4** Gulf

²**G** certification mark — used to certify that a motion picture is of such a nature that persons of all ages may be allowed admission; compare NC-17, PG, PG-13, R

ga abbr gauge

¹**Ga** abbr Georgia

²**Ga** symbol gallium

GA abbr **1** Gamblers Anonymous **2** general agent **3** general assembly **4** general average **5** general of the army **6** Georgia

GAAP abbr generally accepted accounting principles

¹**gab** \'gab\ vi **gabbed; gab·bing** [prob. short for gabble] (1786) : to talk in a rapid or thoughtless manner : CHATTER — **gab·ber** n

²**gab** n (1790) : TALK; esp : idle talk

³**gab** n (1939) : GABARDINE 2

GABA abbr gamma-aminobutyric acid

gab·ar·dine \'ga-bǝr-,dēn\ n [MF gaverdine] (1520) **1** : GABERDINE 1 **2 a** : a firm hard-finish durable fabric (as of wool or rayon) twilled with diagonal ribs on the right side **b** : a garment of gabardine

gab·ble \'ga-bǝl\ vb **gab·bled; gab·bling** \-b(ǝ-)liŋ\ [prob. of imit. origin] vi (1577) **1** : to talk fast or foolishly : JABBER **2** : to utter inarticulate or animal sounds ∼ vt : to say with incoherent rapidity : BABBLE — **gabble** n — **gab·bler** \-b(ǝ-)lǝr\ n

gab·bro \'ga-(,)brō\ n, pl **gabbros** [It, prob. modif. of L glaber smooth — more at GLAD] (ca. 1828) : a granular igneous rock composed essentially of calcic plagioclase, a ferromagnesian mineral, and accessory minerals — **gab·bro·ic** \ga-'brō-ik\ adj

gab·by \'ga-bē\ adj **gab·bi·er; -est** (1719) : TALKATIVE, GARRULOUS

ga·belle \gǝ-'bel\ n [ME gabell, fr. gabelle, fr. OIt gabella tax, fr. Ar qabāla] (15c) : a tax on salt levied in France prior to 1790

gab·er·dine \'ga-bǝr-,dēn\ n [MF gaverdine] (1520) **1** : a long loose outer garment worn in medieval times and associated esp. with Jews since the 16th century **2** : GABARDINE 2

gab·fest \'gab-,fest\ n (1897) **1** : an informal gathering for general talk ⟨political ∼s⟩ **2** : an extended conversation

ga·bi·on \'gā-bē-ǝn, 'ga-\ n [MF, fr. OIt gabbione, lit., large cage, aug. of gabbia cage, fr. L cavea — more at CAGE] (1573) : a basket or cage filled with earth or rocks and used esp. in building a support or abutment

ga·ble \'gā-bǝl\ n [ME, fr. AF, prob. fr. ML gabulum gibbet, of Celt origin; akin to OIr gabul forked stick] (14c) **1 a** : the vertical triangular end of a building from cornice or eaves to ridge **b** : the similar end of a gambrel roof **c** : the end wall of a building **2** : a triangular part or structure — **ga·bled** \-bǝld\ adj

1 gable 1a

gable roof n (1850) : a double-sloping roof that forms a gable at each end

gab·oon \gä-'bün, gǝ-\ n [alter. of ¹gob + -oon (as in spittoon)] (1929) dial : SPITTOON

Ga·bri·el \'gā-brē-ǝl\ n [Heb Gabhrī'ēl] (bef. 12c) : one of the four archangels named in Hebrew tradition

ga·by \'gā-bē\ n, pl **gabies** [origin unknown] (ca. 1796) dial chiefly Eng : SIMPLETON

¹**gad** \'gad\ n [ME, spike, fr. ON gaddr; akin to OE geard rod — more at YARD] (1671) **1** : a chisel or pointed iron or steel bar for loosening ore or rock **2** chiefly dial : a long stick

²**gad** vi **gad·ded; gad·ding** [ME gadden] (15c) : to be on the go without a specific aim or purpose — usu. used with about

³**gad** interj [euphemism for God] (1608) — used as a mild oath

Gad \'gad\ n [Heb Gādh] (bef. 12c) : a son of Jacob and the traditional eponymous ancestor of one of the tribes of Israel — **Gad·ite** \'ga-,dīt\ n

gad·about \'ga-dǝ-,baùt\ n (1837) : a person who flits about in social activity — **gadabout** adj

gad·a·rene \'ga-dǝ-,rēn\ adj, often cap [fr. the demon-possessed Gadarene swine in Mt 8:28 that rushed into the sea] (1922) : HEADLONG, PRECIPITATE ⟨a ∼ rush to the cities⟩

gad·fly \'gad-,flī\ n [¹gad] (1593) **1** : any of various flies (as a horsefly, botfly, or warble fly) that bite or annoy livestock **2** : a person who stimulates or annoys esp. by persistent criticism

gad·get \'ga-jǝt\ n [origin unknown] (1886) : an often small mechanical or electronic device with a practical use but often thought of as a novelty — **gad·ge·teer** \,ga-jǝ-'tir\ n — **gad·get·ry** \'ga-jǝ-trē\ n — **gad·gety** \-jǝ-tē\ adj

ga·doid \'gā-,dòid, 'ga-\ adj [NL Gadus, genus of fishes, fr. Gk gados, a fish] (ca. 1842) : resembling or related to the cods — **gadoid** n

gad·o·lin·ite \'ga-dǝ-lǝ-,nīt\ n [G Gadolinit, fr. Johann Gadolin †1852 Finn. chemist] (1802) : a black or brown mineral that is a source of rare earths and consists of a silicate esp. of iron, beryllium, yttrium, cerium, and erbium

gad·o·lin·i·um \ˌga-də-ˈli-nē-əm\ *n* [NL, fr. J. *Gadolin*] (1886) : a magnetic metallic element of the rare-earth group occurring in combination in gadolinite and several other minerals — see ELEMENT table

ga·droon \gə-ˈdrün\ *n* [F *godron* round plait, gadroon] (ca. 1724) **1** : the ornamental notching or carving of a rounded molding **2** : a short often oval fluting or reeding used in decoration — **gadroon** *vt* — **ga·droon·ing** *n*

gad·wall \ˈgad-ˌwȯl\ *n, pl* **gadwalls** *or* **gadwall** [origin unknown] (1666) : a grayish-brown medium-sized dabbling duck (*Anas strepera*)

gad·zook·ery \gad-ˈzü-kə-rē, -ˈzu̇-\ *n* (1955) *Brit* : the use of archaisms (as in a historical novel)

gad·zooks \gad-ˈzüks, -ˈzu̇ks\ *interj, often cap* [perh. fr. *God's hooks,* the nails of the Crucifixion] (1694) *archaic* — used as a mild oath

Gaea \ˈjē-ə\ *n* [Gk *Gaia*] (1833) : the Greek earth goddess and mother of the Titans

Gael \ˈgāl\ *n* [ScGael *Gàidheal* & Ir *Gaedheal*] (1753) **1** : a Scottish Highlander **2** : a Celtic esp. Gaelic-speaking inhabitant of Ireland, Scotland, or the Isle of Man — **Gael·dom** \-dəm\ *n*

Gael·ic \ˈgā-lik, ˈga-, ˈgä-\ *adj* [ScGael *Gàidhlig* the Scottish Gaelic language, fr. *Gàidheal* Gael] (1741) **1** : of or relating to the Gaels and esp. the Celtic Highlanders of Scotland **2** : of, relating to, or constituting the Goidelic speech of the Celts in Ireland, the Isle of Man, and the Scottish Highlands — **Gaelic** *n*

Gael·tacht \ˈgāl-təkt\ *n* [Ir, fr. *Gael,* spelling var. of *Gaedheal* Irishman, Gael] (1929) : any of the Irish-speaking regions remaining in Ireland

[1]**gaff** \ˈgaf\ *n* [F *gaffe,* fr. Occitan *gaf*] (ca. 1656) **1 a** : a spear or spearhead for taking fish or turtles **b** : a handled hook for holding or lifting heavy fish **c** : a metal spur for a gamecock **d** : a butcher's hook **e** : a climbing iron or its steel point used by a telephone lineman **2** : the spar on which the head of a fore-and-aft sail is extended **3** : GAFFE

[2]**gaff** *vt* (1844) **1** : to strike or secure with a gaff **2** : to fit (a gamecock) with a gaff

[3]**gaff** *n* [origin unknown] (1812) *Brit* : a cheap theater or music hall

[4]**gaff** *n* [origin unknown] (1896) **1 a** : something painful or difficult to bear : ORDEAL — usu. used in the phrase *stand the gaff*; *esp* : persistent raillery or criticism **b** : rough treatment : ABUSE **2 a** : HOAX, FRAUD **b** : GIMMICK, TRICK

[5]**gaff** *vt* (1933) **1** : DECEIVE, TRICK; *also* : FLEECE **2** : to fix for the purpose of cheating ⟨~ the dice⟩

gaffe \ˈgaf\ *n* [F, gaff, gaffe] (1909) **1** : a social or diplomatic blunder **2** : a noticeable mistake

gaf·fer \ˈga-fər\ *n* [alter. of *godfather*] (1589) **1** : an old man — compare GAMMER **2** *Brit* **a** : FOREMAN, OVERSEER **b** : EMPLOYER **3** : a head glassblower **4** : a lighting electrician on a motion-picture or television set

gaff–top·sail \ˈgaf-ˈtäp-ˌsāl, -səl\ *n* (1794) : a usu. triangular topsail with its foot extended upon the gaff — see SAIL illustration

[1]**gag** \ˈgag\ *vb* **gagged; gag·ging** [ME *gaggen* to strangle, of imit. origin] *vt* (1509) **1 a** : to restrict use of the mouth of by inserting a gag **b** : to prevent from exercising freedom of speech or expression **c** : to pry or hold open with a gag **2** : to provide or write quips or pranks for ⟨~ a show⟩ **3** : to choke or cause to retch ~ *vi* **1 a** : CHOKE; *also* : to suffer a throat spasm that makes swallowing or breathing difficult **b** : RETCH **2** : to be unable to endure something : BALK **3** : to make quips — **gag·ger** *n*

[2]**gag** *n* (1530) **1** : something thrust into the mouth to keep it open or to prevent speech or outcry **2** : an official check or restraint on debate or free speech ⟨a ~ rule⟩ **3** : a laugh-provoking remark or act **4** : PRANK, TRICK

ga·ga \ˈgä-(ˌ)gä\ *adj* [F, fr. *gaga* fool, of imit. origin] (1917) **1** : CRAZY, FOOLISH **2** : marked by wild enthusiasm : INFATUATED, DOTING

ga·ga·ku \gä-ˈgä-(ˌ)kü\ *n* [Jp, fr. *ga* elegance + *gaku* music] (1929) : the ancient court music of Japan

[1]**gage** \ˈgāj\ *n* [ME, pledge, reward, fr. AF — more at WAGE] (14c) **1** : a token of defiance; *specif* : a glove or cap cast on the ground to be taken up by an opponent as a pledge of combat **2** : something deposited as a pledge of performance

[2]**gage** *vt* (15c) **1** *archaic* : PLEDGE **2** *archaic* : STAKE, RISK

[3]**gage** *var of* GAUGE

[4]**gage** *n* (1847) : GREENGAGE

gag·gle \ˈga-gəl\ *n* [ME *gagyll,* fr. *gagelen* to cackle] (15c) **1** : FLOCK; *esp* : a flock of geese when not in flight — compare SKEIN **2** : a group, aggregation, or cluster lacking organization ⟨a ~ of reporters and photographers⟩ **3** : an indefinite number ⟨participated in a ~ of petty crimes⟩

gag·man \ˈgag-ˌman\ *n* (1928) **1** : a gag writer **2** : COMEDIAN 2

gag order *n* (1952) : a judicial ruling barring public disclosure or discussion (as by the press) of information related to a case; *broadly* : a similar nonjudicial prohibition against the release of confidential information or against public discussion of a sensitive matter

gag·ster \ˈgag-stər\ *n* (1935) : GAGMAN; *also* : one who plays practical jokes

gahn·ite \ˈgä-ˌnīt\ *n* [G *Gahnit,* fr. J. G. *Gahn* †1818 Swed. chemist] (ca. 1808) : a usu. dark green mineral consisting of an oxide of zinc and aluminum

Gaia \ˈgī-ə\ *n* [Gk, Gaea] (1975) : the hypothesis that the living and nonliving components of earth function as a single system in such a way that the living component regulates and maintains conditions (as the temperature of the ocean or composition of the atmosphere) so as to be suitable for life; *also* : this system regarded as a single organism

gai·ety *also* **gay·ety** \ˈgā-ə-tē\ *n, pl* **-eties** [F *gaieté*] (1634) **1** : MERRYMAKING; *also* : festive activity — often used in pl. **2** : high spirits : MERRIMENT **3** : ELEGANCE, FINERY

gai·jin \ˈgī-(ˌ)jēn, -(ˌ)jin\ *n, pl* **gaijin** [Jp, fr. *gai-* outer, foreign + *-jin* person] (1964) : a foreigner in Japan

gail·lar·dia \gə-ˈlär-d(ē-)ə\ *n* [NL, fr. *Gaillard* de Marentonneau, 18th cent. Fr. botanist] (1879) : any of a genus (*Gaillardia*) of American composite herbs with showy flower heads — called also *blanketflower*

gai·ly *also* **gay·ly** \ˈgā-lē\ *adv* (14c) : in a gay manner : marked by gaiety

[1]**gain** \ˈgān\ *n* [ME *gayne,* fr. AF *gaigne, gain,* fr. *gaaigner* to till, earn, gain, of Gmc origin; akin to OHG *weidanōn* to hunt for food, OE *wāth* pursuit, hunt] (14c) **1** : resources or advantage acquired or increased : PROFIT ⟨made substantial ~*s* last year⟩ **2** : the act or process of gaining **3 a** : an increase in amount, magnitude, or degree ⟨a ~ in efficiency⟩ **b** : the increase (as of voltage or signal intensity) caused by an amplifier; *esp* : the ratio of output over input **c** : the signal-gathering ability of an antenna

[2]**gain** *vt* (14c) **1 a** : to acquire or get possession of usu. by industry, merit, or craft ⟨~ an advantage⟩ ⟨he stood to ~ a fortune⟩ **b** : to win in competition or conflict ⟨the troops ~*ed* enemy territory⟩ **c** (1) : to arrive at : REACH, ATTAIN ⟨~*ed* the river that night⟩ (2) : TRAVERSE, COVER ⟨~*ed* 10 yards on the play⟩ **d** : to get by a natural development or process ⟨~ strength⟩ **e** : to establish a specific relationship with ⟨~ a friend⟩ **2 a** : to make an increase of (a specified amount) ⟨~*ed* three percent in the past month⟩ **b** : to increase in (a particular quality) ⟨~ momentum⟩ **3** : to win to one's side : PERSUADE ⟨~ adherents to a cause⟩ **4** : to cause to be obtained or given : ATTRACT ⟨~ attention⟩ **5** *of a timepiece* : to run fast by the amount of ⟨the clock ~*s* a minute a day⟩ ~ *vi* **1** : to get advantage : PROFIT ⟨hoped to ~ by the deal⟩ **2 a** : INCREASE ⟨the day was ~*ing* in warmth⟩ **b** : to increase in weight **c** : to improve in health or ability **3** *of a timepiece* : to run fast **4** : to get closer to something pursued — usu. used with *on* or *upon* — **gain·er** *n* — **gain ground** : to make progress

gain·ful \ˈgān-fəl\ *adj* (1553) : productive of gain : PROFITABLE ⟨~ employment⟩ — **gain·ful·ly** \-fə-lē\ *adv* — **gain·ful·ness** *n*

gain·giv·ing \ˈgān-ˌgi-viŋ, ˌgān-ˈ\ *n* [*gain-* (against) + *giving*] (1602) *archaic* : MISGIVING

gain·say \ˌgān-ˈsā\ *vt* **-said** \-ˈsād, -ˈsed\; **-say·ing** \-ˈsā-iŋ\; **-says** \-ˈsāz, -ˈsez\ [ME *gainsayen,* fr. *gain-* against (fr. OE *gēan-*) + *sayen* to say — more at AGAIN] (14c) **1** : to declare to be untrue or invalid **2** : CONTRADICT, OPPOSE ***syn*** see DENY — **gain·say·er** *n*

[1]**gait** \ˈgāt\ *n* [ME *gait, gate* gate, way] (1509) **1** : a manner of walking or moving on foot **2** : a sequence of foot movements (as a walk, trot, pace, or canter) by which a horse or a dog moves forward **3** : a manner or rate of movement or progress ⟨the leisurely ~ of summer⟩

[2]**gait** *vt* (ca. 1900) **1** : to train (a horse or a dog) to use a particular gait or set of gaits **2** : to lead (a show dog) before a judge to display carriage and movement ~ *vi* : to walk with a particular gait

gait·ed \ˈgā-təd\ *adj* (1588) : having a particular gait or so many gaits ⟨slow-*gaited*⟩ ⟨a 3-*gaited* horse⟩

gai·ter \ˈgā-tər\ *n* [F *guêtre*] (1775) **1** : a cloth or leather leg covering reaching from the instep to above the ankle or to mid-calf or knee **2 a** : an overshoe with fabric upper **b** : an ankle-high shoe with elastic gores in the sides

[1]**gal** \ˈgal\ *n* [by alter.] (1795) : GIRL, WOMAN

[2]**gal** *n* [*Galileo* Galilei] (1914) : a unit of acceleration equivalent to one centimeter per second per second — used esp. for values of gravity

[3]**gal** *abbr* **1** gallery **2** gallon

Gal *abbr* Galatians

ga·la \ˈgā-lə, ˈga-, ˈgä-\ *n* [It, fr. MF *gale* festivity, pleasure — more at GALLANT] (1777) **1** : a festive celebration; *esp* : a public entertainment marking a special occasion **2** *cap* : a medium-sized apple with crisp yellowish-white sweet flesh and a red skin or a golden skin with red striping — **gala** *adj*

ga·la·bia *or* **ga·la·bi·eh** *or* **ga·la·bi·ya** \gə-ˈlä-b(ē-)ə\ *n* [Ar dial. (Egypt) *gallābīya*] (1725) : DJELLABA

galact- *or* **galacto-** *comb form* [L *galact-,* fr. Gk *galakt-, galakto-,* fr. *galakt-, gala* — more at GALAXY] **1** : milk ⟨*galacto*rrhea⟩ **2** : related to galactose ⟨*galacto*semia⟩

ga·lac·tic \gə-ˈlak-tik\ *adj* (1839) **1** : of or relating to a galaxy and esp. the Milky Way galaxy **2** : HUGE ⟨a ~ sum of money⟩

ga·lac·tor·rhea \gə-ˌlak-tə-ˈrē-ə\ *n* (ca. 1860) : a spontaneous flow of milk from the nipple

ga·lac·tos·amine \gə-ˌlak-ˈtō-sə-ˌmēn, -zə-\ *n* (1900) : an amino derivative $C_6H_{13}O_5N$ of galactose that occurs in cartilage

ga·lac·tose \gə-ˈlak-ˌtōs, -ˌtōz\ *n* [F, fr. *galact-*] (1866) : a sugar $C_6H_{12}O_6$ less soluble and less sweet than glucose

ga·lac·to·semia \gə-ˌlak-tə-ˈsē-mē-ə\ *n* (1934) : a metabolic disorder that is inherited as an autosomal recessive trait and in which galactose accumulates in the blood due to deficiency of an enzyme catalyzing its conversion to glucose — **ga·lac·to·semic** \-mik\ *adj*

ga·lac·to·si·dase \gə-ˌlak-ˈtō-sə-ˌdās, -zə-ˌdāz\ *n* (1917) : an enzyme (as lactase) that hydrolyzes a galactoside

ga·lac·to·side \gə-ˈlak-tə-ˌsīd\ *n* (1862) : a glycoside that yields galactose on hydrolysis

ga·lac·to·syl \gə-ˈlak-tə-ˌsil\ *n* (1950) : a glycosyl radical $C_6H_{11}O_5$– that is derived from galactose

ga·lact·uron·ic acid \gə-ˌlak-tu̇-ˈrä-nik-, -tyu̇-\ *n* [ISV] (1917) : a crystalline aldehyde-acid $C_6H_{10}O_7$ that occurs esp. in polymerized form in pectin

ga·la·go \gə-ˈlā-(ˌ)gō, -ˈlä-\ *n, pl* **-gos** [NL, perh. fr. Wolof *golo* monkey] (1840) : BUSH BABY

ga·lah \gə-ˈlä\ *n* [Yuwaalaraay (Australian aboriginal language of northern New South Wales) *gilaa*] (1862) : a pink-breasted Australian cockatoo (*Eolophus roseicapillus* syn. *Cacatua roseicapilla*) that is sometimes a pest in wheat-growing areas and is often kept as a cage bird

Gal·a·had \ˈga-lə-ˌhad\ *n* (14c) **1** : the knight of the Round Table who successfully seeks the Holy Grail **2** : one who is pure, noble, and unselfish

ga·lan·ga \gə-ˈlaŋ-gə\ *n* [ME, fr. OE & ML; ME, fr. OE *gallengar,* fr. ML *galanga, gallingar*] (bef. 12c) : GALANGAL

gal·an·gal \ˈga-lən-ˌgal, -liŋ-\ *n* [ME *galingale,* fr. AF, fr. ML *galingala, galanga,* fr. Ar *khalanjān, khulūnjān*] (13c) **1** : either of two eastern Asian perennial herbs (*Alpinia galanga* and *A. officinarum*) of the ginger family with dark green sword-shaped leaves and pungent aromatic rhizomes **2 :** the fresh, dried, or ground rhizome of a galangal used in cookery as a spice and in medicine

gal·an·tine \ˈga-lən-ˌtēn\ *n* [F, fr. OF *galentine, galatine* fish sauce, fr. ML *galatina,* prob. fr. L *gelatus,* pp. of *gelare* to congeal, freeze — more at COLD] (1725) **:** a cold dish consisting of boned meat or fish that has been stuffed, poached, and covered with aspic

Gal·a·tea \ˌga-lə-ˈtē-ə\ *n* [L, fr. Gk *Galateia*] (14c) **:** a female figure sculpted by Pygmalion and given life by Aphrodite in fulfillment of his prayer

Ga·la·tians \gə-ˈlā-shənz\ *n pl but sing in constr* (1587) **:** an argumentative letter of St. Paul written to the Christians of Galatia and included as a book in the New Testament — see BIBLE table

galavant *var of* GALLIVANT

ga·lax \ˈgā-ˌlaks\ *n* [NL] (ca. 1753) **:** an evergreen herb (*Galax urceolata* syn. *G. aphylla* of the order Diapensiales) of the southeastern U.S. that has glossy leaves and is related to the heaths (order Ericales)

gal·axy \ˈga-lək-sē\ *n, pl* **-ax·ies** [ME *galaxie, galaxias,* fr. LL *galaxias,* fr. Gk, fr. *galakt-, gala* milk; akin to L *lac* milk] (14c) **1 a** *often cap* **:** MILKY WAY GALAXY — used with *the* **b :** any of the very large groups of stars and associated matter that are found throughout the universe **2 a :** an assemblage of brilliant or notable persons or things ⟨a ~ of artists⟩ **b :** WORLD 11 ⟨remained *galaxies* apart on the issue —*Newsweek*⟩

gal·ba·num \ˈgal-bə-nəm, ˈgȯl-\ *n* [ME, fr. L, fr. Gk *chalbanē,* of Sem origin; akin to Heb *ḥelbĕnāh* galbanum] (14c) **:** a yellowish to green or brown aromatic bitter gum resin derived from several Asian plants (as *Ferula galbaniflua*) and used in incense

gale \ˈgāl\ *n* [origin unknown] (ca. 1547) **1 a :** a strong current of air: (1) **:** a wind from 32 to 63 miles per hour (about 51 to 102 kilometers per hour) (2) **:** FRESH GALE — see BEAUFORT SCALE table **b** *archaic* **:** BREEZE **2 :** an emotional outburst ⟨~*s* of laughter⟩

ga·lea \ˈgā-lē-ə\ *n* [NL, fr. L, helmet] (1823) **:** an anatomical part suggesting a helmet

ga·le·na \gə-ˈlē-nə\ *n* [L, lead ore] (1671) **:** a bluish-gray cubic mineral with metallic luster consisting of lead sulfide and constituting the principal ore of lead

ga·len·i·cal \gə-ˈle-ni-kəl, gā-\ *n* [*Galen* + [1]*-ic* + [1]*-al*] (1768) **:** a medicine prepared by extracting one or more active constituents of a plant

ga·lère \ga-ˈler\ *n* [F, galley, fr. MF, fr. Catal *galera,* fr. MGk *galea*] (1756) **:** a group of people having an attribute in common

ga·lette \gə-ˈlet\ *n* [F, fr. OF, fr. *galet* rounded pebble, fr. OF dial. (Picard), dim. of *gal* pebble] (1775) **1 :** a flat round cake of pastry often topped with fruit **2 :** a food prepared and served in the shape of a flat round cake ⟨a ~ of potatoes⟩

gal Friday *n* (1958) **:** GIRL FRIDAY

Gal·i·le·an \ˌga-lə-ˈlē-ən, -ˈlā-\ *adj* (ca. 1751) **:** of, relating to, or discovered by Galileo Galilei ⟨~ satellites⟩

gal·i·lee \ˈga-lə-ˌlē\ *n* [AF, fr. ML *galilaea,* prob. fr. L *Galilaea* Galilee, fr. L] (15c) **:** a chapel or porch at the entrance of an English church

gal·in·gale \ˈga-lən-ˌgāl, -liŋ-\ *n* [ME, fr. AF, galangal] (1578) **1 :** an Old World sedge (*Cyperus longus*); *broadly* **:** any of various other sedges of the same genus **2 :** GALANGAL

galiot *var of* GALLIOT

[1]**gall** \ˈgȯl\ *n* [ME, fr. OE *gealla;* akin to Gk *cholē, cholos* gall, wrath, OE *geolu* yellow — more at YELLOW] (bef. 12c) **1 a :** BILE; *esp* **:** bile obtained from an animal and used in the arts or medicine **b :** something bitter to endure **c :** bitterness of spirit **:** RANCOR **2 :** brazen boldness coupled with impudent assurance and insolence ***syn*** see TEMERITY

[2]**gall** *n* [ME *galle,* fr. OE *gealla,* fr. L *galla* gallnut] (bef. 12c) **1 a :** a skin sore caused by chronic irritation **b :** a cause or state of exasperation **2** *archaic* **:** FLAW

[3]**gall** *vt* (14c) **1 :** to fret and wear away by friction **:** CHAFE ⟨the loose saddle ~*ed* the horse's back⟩ ⟨the ~*ing* of a metal bearing⟩ **2 :** IRRITATE, VEX ⟨sarcasm ~*s* her⟩ ~ *vi* **1 :** to become sore or worn by rubbing **2 :** SEIZE 2

[4]**gall** *n* [ME *galle,* fr. AF, fr. L *galla*] (14c) **:** an abnormal outgrowth of plant tissue usu. due to insect or mite parasites or fungi and sometimes forming an important source of tannin — see GALL WASP illustration

Gal·la \ˈga-lə\ *n, pl* **Galla** *or* **Gallas** [Geez & Amharic] (1875) **:** OROMO

gal·la·mine tri·eth·io·dide \ˈga-lə-ˌmēn-ˌtrī-ˌe-ˈthī-ə-ˌdīd\ *n* [*pyrogallol* + *amine* + *tri-* + *eth-* + *iodide*] (1951) **:** a substituted ammonium salt $C_{30}H_{60}I_3N_3O_3$ that is used to produce muscle relaxation esp. during anesthesia — called also *gallamine*

[1]**gal·lant** \gə-ˈlant, gə-ˈlänt, ˈga-lənt\ *n* (14c) **1 :** a young man of fashion **2 a :** LADIES' MAN **b :** SUITOR **c :** PARAMOUR

[2]**gal·lant** \ˈga-lənt *(usu in sense 2);* gə-ˈlant, gə-ˈlänt *(usu in sense 3)*\ *adj* [ME *galaunt,* fr. MF *galant,* fr. prp. of *galer* to have a good time, fr. OF, fr. *gale* pleasure, of Gmc origin; akin to OE *wela* weal — more at WEAL] (15c) **1 :** showy in dress or bearing **:** SMART **2 a :** SPLENDID, STATELY ⟨a ~ ship⟩ **b :** SPIRITED, BRAVE ⟨~ efforts against the enemy⟩ **c :** nobly chivalrous and often self-sacrificing **3 :** courteously and elaborately attentive esp. to ladies ***syn*** see CIVIL — **gal·lant·ly** *adv*

[3]**gal·lant** \gə-ˈlant, -ˈlänt\ *vt* (1672) **1 :** to pay court to (a lady) **:** ATTEND ⟨used to ~ her in his youth —Washington Irving⟩ **2** *obs* **:** to manipulate (a fan) in a modish manner ~ *vi* **:** to pay court to ladies

gal·lant·ry \ˈga-lən-trē\ *n, pl* **-ries** (1613) **1** *archaic* **:** gallant appearance **2 a :** an act of marked courtesy **b :** courteous attention to a lady **c :** amorous attention or pursuit **3 :** spirited and conspicuous bravery

gal·late \ˈga-ˌlāt, ˈgȯ-\ *n* (1788) **:** a salt or ester of gallic acid

gall·blad·der \ˈgȯl-ˌbla-dər\ *n* (1676) **:** a membranous muscular sac in which bile from the liver is stored

gal·le·ass \ˈga-lē-əs\ *n* [MF *galeasse,* fr. OF *galie* galley] (1544) **:** a large fast galley used esp. as a warship by Mediterranean countries in the 16th and 17th centuries and having both sails and oars but usu. propelled chiefly by rowing

gal·le·on \ˈga-lē-ən\ *n* [OSp *galeón,* fr. MF *galion,* fr. OF *galie*] (1529) **:** a heavy square-rigged sailing ship of the 15th to early 18th centuries used for war or commerce esp. by the Spanish

gal·le·ria \ˌga-lə-ˈrē-ə\ *n* [It, gallery, fr. ML *galeria*] (ca. 1901) **:** a roofed and usu. glass-enclosed promenade or court (as at a mall)

gal·lery \ˈga-lə-rē, ˈgal-rē\ *n, pl* **-ler·ies** [ME *galerie,* fr. ML *galeria,* prob. alter. of *galilaea* galilee] (15c) **1 a :** a roofed promenade **:** COLONNADE **b :** CORRIDOR 1 **2 a :** an outdoor balcony **b** *Southern & Midland* **:** PORCH, VERANDA **c :** a platform at the quarters or stern of a ship **3 a :** a long and narrow passage, apartment, or corridor **b :** a subterranean passageway in a cave or military mining system; *also* **:** a working drift or level in mining **c :** an underground passage made by a mole or ant or a passage made in wood by an insect (as a beetle) **4 a :** a room or building devoted to the exhibition of works of art **b :** an institution or business exhibiting or dealing in works of art **c :** COLLECTION, AGGREGATION ⟨the rich ~ of characters in this novel —H. S. Canby⟩ **5 a :** a structure projecting from one or more interior walls (as of an auditorium or church) to accommodate additional people; *esp* **:** the highest balcony in a theater commonly having the cheapest seats **b :** the part of a theater audience seated in the top gallery **c :** the undiscriminating general public **d :** the spectators at a sporting event (as a tennis or golf match) **6 :** a small ornamental barrier or railing (as along the edge of a table or shelf) **7 :** a photographer's studio — **gal·ler·ied** \-rēd\ *adj* — **gal·lery·ite** \-rē-ˌīt\ *n*

gallery forest *n* (1920) **:** a forest growing along a watercourse in a region otherwise devoid of trees

gal·lery·go·er \ˈga-lə-rē-ˌgō(-ə)r, ˈgal-rē-\ *n* (1888) **:** one who frequently goes to art galleries

ga·lle·ta \gə-ˈye-tə, gī-ˈe-tə\ *n* [Sp, hardtack] (1872) **:** either of two perennial grasses (*Hilaria rigida* and *H. jamesii* syn. *Pleuraphis rigida* and *P. jamesii*) chiefly of the southwestern U.S. and Mexico used for forage

gal·ley \ˈga-lē\ *n, pl* **galleys** [ME *galeie,* fr. AF *galie, galee,* ultim. fr. MGk *galea*] (13c) **1 :** a ship or boat propelled solely or chiefly by oars: as **a :** a long low ship used for war and trading esp. in the Mediterranean Sea from the Middle Ages to the 19th century; *also* **:** GALLEASS **b :** a warship of classical antiquity — compare BIREME, TRIREME **c :** a large open boat (as a gig) formerly used in England **2 :** the kitchen and cooking apparatus esp. of a ship or airplane **3 a :** an oblong tray to hold esp. a single column of set type **b :** a proof of typeset matter esp. in a single column before being made into pages

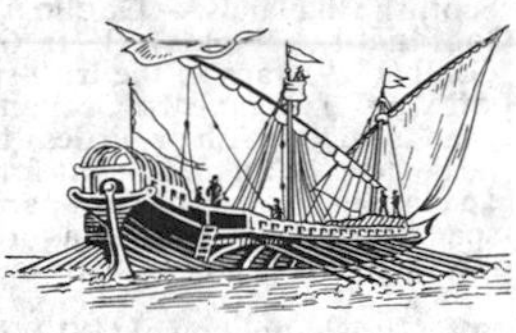

galley 1a

gal·ley–west \ˌga-lē-ˈwest\ *adv* [prob. alter. of E dial. *collywest* badly askew] (1875) **:** into destruction or confusion ⟨was knocked ~⟩

gall·fly \ˈgȯl-ˌflī\ *n* (ca. 1834) **:** an insect (as a gall wasp) that deposits its eggs in plants causing the formation of galls in which the larvae feed

[1]**gal·liard** \ˈgal-yərd\ *adj* [ME *gaillard* strong, lively, fr. AF, bold, stalwart] (14c) *archaic* **:** GAY, LIVELY

[2]**galliard** *n* (1533) **:** a sprightly dance with five steps to a phrase popular in the 16th and 17th centuries

Gal·lic \ˈga-lik\ *adj* [L *Gallicus,* fr. *Gallia* Gaul] (1635) **:** of or relating to Gaul or France

gal·li·ca \ˈga-li-kə\ *n, often cap* [NL, fem. of *Gallicus* Gallic, French, fr. L] (1848) **:** a compact fragrant European rose (*Rosa gallica*) having usu. pink, red, or crimson flowers that yield an oil used esp. in perfumery

gal·lic acid \ˈga-lik-, ˈgȯ-lik-\ *n* [F *gallique,* fr. *galle* gall] (1788) **:** a white crystalline acid $C_7H_6O_5$ found widely in plants or combined in tannins and used esp. in dyes and as a photographic developer

Gal·li·can \ˈga-li-kən\ *adj* (14c) **1 :** GALLIC **2** *often not cap* **:** of or relating to Gallicanism — **Gallican** *n*

Gal·li·can·ism \-kə-ˌni-zəm\ *n* (1805) **:** a movement originating in France and advocating administrative independence from papal control for the Roman Catholic Church in each nation

gal·li·cism \ˈga-lə-ˌsi-zəm\ *n, often cap* (ca. 1656) **1 :** a characteristic French idiom or expression appearing in another language **2 :** a French trait

gal·li·cize \-ˌsīz\ *vt* **-cized; -ciz·ing** *often cap* (1773) **:** to cause to conform to a French mode or idiom — **gal·li·ci·za·tion** \ˌga-lə-sə-ˈzā-shən\ *n, often cap*

gal·li·gas·kins \ˌga-li-ˈgas-kənz\ *n pl* [prob. modif. of MF *garguesques,* fr. OSp *gregüescos,* fr. *griego* Greek, fr. L *Graecus*] (1577) **1 a :** loose wide hose or breeches worn in the 16th and 17th centuries **b :** very loose trousers **2** *dial chiefly Brit* **:** LEGGINGS

gal·li·mau·fry \ˌga-lə-ˈmȯ-frē\ *n, pl* **-fries** [MF *galimafree* stew] (ca. 1556) **:** HODGEPODGE ⟨a ~ of opinions⟩

gal·li·na·ceous \ˌga-lə-ˈnā-shəs\ *adj* [L *gallinaceus* of domestic fowl, fr. *gallina* hen, fr. *gallus* cock] (1693) **:** of or relating to an order (Galliformes) of heavy-bodied largely terrestrial birds including the pheasants, turkeys, grouse, and the common domestic chicken

gall·ing \ˈgȯ-liŋ\ *adj* [[3]*gall*] (1583) **:** markedly irritating **:** VEXING ⟨a most ~ defeat⟩ — **gall·ing·ly** \-liŋ-lē\ *adv*

gal·li·nip·per \ˈga-lə-ˌni-pər\ *n* [origin unknown] (1709) *chiefly Southern & Midland* **:** any of various insects (as a large mosquito or crane fly)

gal·li·nule \ˈga-lə-ˌnül, -ˌnyül\ *n* [NL *Gallinula,* genus of birds, fr. L, pullet, dim. of *gallina*] (1776) **:** any of several aquatic birds of the rail family with long thin feet and a platelike frontal area on the head: as **a :** MOORHEN **b :** one (*Porphyrula martinica*) found from the southern U.S. to Argentina that is purplish blue with olive-green upperparts, a red and yellow bill, and a light blue frontal area

gal·li·ot *or* **gal·i·ot** \ˈga-lē-ət\ *n* [ME *galiot,* fr. AF, fr. ML *galeota,* dim. of *galea* galley, fr. MGk] (14c) **1 :** a small swift galley formerly used in the Mediterranean **2** [D *galjoot,* fr. MF *galiot*] **:** a long narrow shallow-draft Dutch merchant sailing ship

gal·li·pot \ˈga-li-ˌpät\ *n* [ME *galy pott*] (15c) **1 :** a small usu. ceramic vessel **2** *archaic* **:** DRUGGIST

gal·li·um \ˈga-lē-əm\ *n* [NL, fr. L *gallus* cock (intended as trans. of surname of Paul *Lecoq* de Boisbaudran †1912 Fr. chemist)] (1875) **:** a bluish-white metallic element obtained esp. as a by-product in refining various ores and used esp. in semiconductors and optoelectronic devices — see ELEMENT table

gallium arsenide *n* (ca. 1961) **:** a synthetic compound GaAs used esp. as a semiconducting material

gal·li·vant *also* **gal·a·vant** \ˈga-lə-ˌvant\ *vi* [perh. alter. of [3]*gallant*] (1823) **1 :** to go about usu. ostentatiously or indiscreetly with members of the opposite sex **2 :** to travel, roam, or move about for pleasure

gall midge *n* (ca. 1889) **:** any of numerous minute dipteran flies (family Cecidomyiidae) most of which cause gall formation in plants

gall mite *n* (1881) **:** any of various minute 4-legged mites (family Eriophyidae) that form galls on plants

gall·nut \ˈgȯl-ˌnət\ *n* [[4]*gall*] (1572) **:** a gall resembling a nut

gal·lon \ˈga-lən\ *n* [ME *galon,* a liquid measure, fr. AF *galun, jalun,* ultim. fr. ML *galeta* pail, a liquid measure] (13c) **:** a unit of liquid capacity equal to 231 cubic inches or four quarts — see WEIGHT table

gal·lon·age \ˈga-lə-nij\ *n* (ca. 1909) **:** amount in gallons

gal·loon \gə-ˈlün\ *n* [F *galon*] (1604) **:** a narrow trimming (as of lace or braid with metallic threads) having both edges scalloped

[1]**gal·lop** \ˈga-ləp\ *vi* (15c) **1 :** to progress or ride at a gallop **2 :** to run fast ~ *vt* **1 :** to cause to gallop **2 :** to transport at a gallop — **gal·lop·er** *n*

[2]**gallop** *n* [MF *galop*] (1523) **1 :** a bounding gait of a quadruped; *specif* **:** a fast natural usu. 4-beat gait of the horse — compare [3]CANTER, RUN **2 :** a ride or run at a gallop **3 :** a stretch of land suitable for galloping horses **4 :** a rapid or hasty progression or pace

gal·lo·pade \ˌga-lə-ˈpād, -ˈpäd\ *n* (1828) **:** GALOP

Gal·lo·phile \ˈga-lə-ˌfī(-ə)l\ *adj* [L *Gallus* Gaul + E *-phile*] (1880) **:** FRANCOPHILE — **Gallophile** *n*

gal·lop·ing \ˈga-lə-piŋ\ *adj* (1567) **:** progressing, developing, or increasing rapidly ⟨~ inflation⟩ ⟨a ~ farce⟩ ⟨~ alcoholism⟩

Gal·lo–Ro·mance \ˌga-lō-rō-ˈman(t)s, -rə-; -ˈrō-ˌman(t)s\ *n* [L *Gallus* inhabitant of Gaul] (1946) **:** the Romance speech that developed out of the spoken Latin of Transalpine Gaul

Gal·lo·way \ˈga-lə-ˌwā\ *n* [*Galloway,* Scotland] (1805) **:** any of a breed of hardy medium-sized hornless chiefly black beef cattle native to southwestern Scotland

gal·low·glass \ˈga-lō-ˌglas\ *n* [modif. of Ir *gallóglach,* fr. *gall* foreigner + *óglach* young man, warrior] (ca. 1515) **1 :** a mercenary or retainer of an Irish chief **2 :** an armed Irish foot soldier

[1]**gal·lows** \ˈga-(ˌ)lōz, -ləz, *in sense 3 also* -ləs\ *n, pl* **gallows** *or* **gal·lows·es** [ME *galwes,* pl. of *galwe,* fr. OE *galga, gealga;* akin to ON *gelgja* pole, stake, Arm *jałk* twig] (bef. 12c) **1 a :** a frame usu. of two upright posts and a transverse beam from which criminals are hanged — called also *gallows tree* **b :** the punishment of hanging **2 :** a structure consisting of an upright frame with a crosspiece **3 :** SUSPENDER 2a

[2]**gallows** *adj* (15c) **:** deserving the gallows

gallows bird *n* (ca. 1785) **:** a person who deserves hanging

gallows humor *n* (1901) **:** humor that makes fun of a life-threatening, disastrous, or terrifying situation

gall·stone \ˈgȯl-ˌstōn\ *n* (1758) **:** a calculus (as of cholesterol) formed in the gallbladder or biliary passages

gal·lus \ˈga-ləs\ *n* [alter. of [1]*gallows*] (1836) **:** SUSPENDER 2a — usu. used in pl.

gal·lused \ˈga-ləst\ *adj* (1927) **:** wearing galluses

gall wasp *n* (1879) **:** any of a family (Cynipidae) of hymenopterous gallflies

gal·ly \ˈga-lē\ *vt* **gal·lied; gal·ly·ing** [origin unknown] (1605) *chiefly dial* **:** FRIGHTEN, TERRIFY

Ga·lois theory \(ˌ)gal-ˈwä-, ˈgal-ˌwä-\ *n* [Évariste *Galois*] (1893) **:** a part of the theory of mathematical groups concerned esp. with the conditions under which a solution to a polynomial equation with coefficients in a given mathematical field can be obtained in the field by the repetition of operations and the extraction of nth roots

ga·loot \gə-ˈlüt\ *n* [origin unknown] (ca. 1818) *slang* **:** FELLOW; *esp* **:** one who is strange or foolish

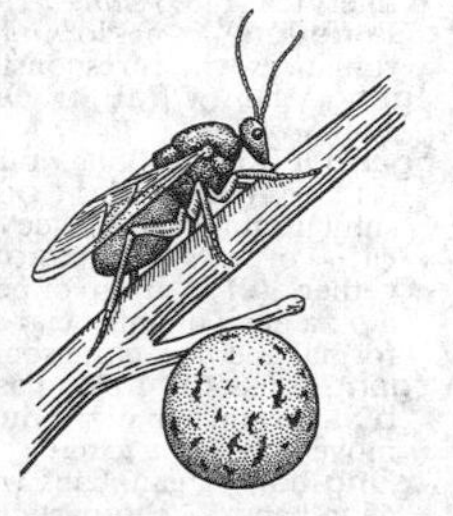

gall wasp and gall

ga·lop \ˈga-ləp, ga-ˈlō\ *n* [F] (1830) **:** a lively dance in duple measure; *also* **:** the music of a galop

ga·lore \gə-ˈlȯr\ *adj* [Ir *go leor* enough] (1628) **:** ABUNDANT, PLENTIFUL — used postpositively ⟨bargains ~⟩

ga·losh \gə-ˈläsh\ *n* [ME *galoche,* fr. MF] (14c) **1** *obs* **:** a shoe with a heavy sole **2 :** a high overshoe worn esp. in snow and slush — **ga·loshed** \-ˈläsht\ *adj*

ga·lumph \gə-ˈləm(p)f\ *vi* [prob. alter. of [1]*gallop*] (1872) **:** to move with a clumsy heavy tread

gal·van·ic \gal-ˈva-nik\ *adj* (1797) **1 :** of, relating to, or producing a direct current of electricity ⟨a ~ cell⟩ **2 a :** having an electric effect **:** intensely exciting ⟨a ~ performance⟩ **b :** produced as if by an electric shock ⟨had a ~ effect on the audience⟩ — **gal·van·i·cal·ly** \-ni-k(ə-)lē\ *adv*

galvanic skin response *n* (1942) **:** a change in the electrical resistance of the skin that is a physiochemical response to emotional arousal which increases sympathetic nervous system activity

gal·va·nise *Brit var of* GALVANIZE

gal·va·nism \ˈgal-və-ˌni-zəm\ *n* [F or It; F *galvanisme,* fr. It *galvanismo,* fr. Luigi *Galvani*] (1797) **1 :** a direct current of electricity esp. when produced by chemical action **2 :** the therapeutic use of direct electric current (as for pain relief) **3 :** vital or forceful activity

gal·va·nize \ˈgal-və-ˌnīz\ *vb* **-nized; -niz·ing** *vt* (1802) **1 a :** to subject to the action of an electric current esp. for the purpose of stimulating physiologically ⟨~ a muscle⟩ **b :** to stimulate or excite as if by an electric shock ⟨an issue that would ~ public opinion⟩ **2 :** to coat (iron or steel) with zinc; *esp* **:** to immerse in molten zinc to produce a coating of zinc-iron alloy ~ *vi* **:** to react as if stimulated by an electric shock ⟨they *galvanized* into action⟩ — **gal·va·ni·za·tion** \ˌgal-və-nə-ˈzā-shən\ *n* — **gal·va·niz·er** \ˈgal-və-ˌnī-zər\ *n*

galvano- *comb form* [*galvanic*] **:** galvanic current ⟨*galvano*meter⟩

gal·va·nom·e·ter \ˌgal-və-ˈnä-mə-tər\ *n* (1802) **:** an instrument for detecting or measuring a small electric current by movements of a magnetic needle or of a coil in a magnetic field — **gal·va·no·met·ric** \-nō-ˈme-trik\ *adj*

gal·va·no·scope \gal-ˈva-nə-ˌskōp, ˈgal-və-nə-\ *n* (1832) **:** an instrument for detecting the presence and direction of an electric current by the deflection of a magnetic needle

[1]**gam** \ˈgam\ *n* [prob. ultim. fr. Lingua Franca *gamba* leg, fr. It, fr. LL] (ca. 1785) *slang* **:** LEG

[2]**gam** *n* [perh. short for obs. *gammon* talk] (1846) **1 :** a visit or friendly conversation at sea or ashore esp. between whalers **2 :** a school of whales

[3]**gam** *vb* **gammed; gam·ming** *vi* (1849) **:** to engage in a gam ~ *vt* **1 :** to have a gam with **2 :** to spend or pass (as time) talking

gama grass \ˈga-mə-\ *n* [prob. alter. of *grama*] (1833) **:** a tall coarse American grass (*Tripsacum dactyloides*) valuable for forage

ga·may \ga-ˈmā, ˈga-ˌmā\ *n, often cap* [F, fr. *Gamay,* village in Burgundy] (ca. 1941) **:** a light dry red table wine made from the same grape used for French Beaujolais ⟨~ rosé⟩; *also* **:** the grape

gam·ba \ˈgäm-bə, ˈgam-\ *n* (1598) **:** VIOLA DA GAMBA

[1]**gam·ba·do** \gam-ˈbā-(ˌ)dō\ *n, pl* **-does** *also* **-dos** [perh. modif. of It *gambale,* fr. *gamba* leg] (ca. 1656) **:** a horseman's legging

[2]**gambado** *n, pl* **-does** *also* **-dos** [modif. of F *gambade* — more at GAMBOL] (1820) **1 :** a spring of a horse **2 :** CAPER, GAMBOL

gam·bier *also* **gam·bir** \ˈgam-ˌbir\ *n* [Malay *gambir*] (1830) **:** a yellowish catechu that is obtained from a tropical southeast Asian woody vine (*Uncaria gambir*) of the madder family and is used for chewing with the betel nut and for tanning and dyeing

gam·bit \ˈgam-bət\ *n* [It *gambetto,* lit., act of tripping someone, fr. *gamba* leg, fr. LL *gamba, camba,* fr. Gk *kampē* bend; prob. akin to Goth *hamfs* maimed, Lith *kampas* corner] (1656) **1 :** a chess opening in which a player risks one or more pawns or a minor piece to gain an advantage in position **2 a** (1) **:** a remark intended to start a conversation or make a telling point (2) **:** TOPIC **b :** a calculated move **:** STRATAGEM

[1]**gam·ble** \ˈgam-bəl\ *vb* **gam·bled; gam·bling** \-b(ə-)liŋ\ [prob. back-formation fr. *gambler,* prob. alter. of obs. *gamner,* fr. obs. *gamen* to play] *vi* (1772) **1 a :** to play a game for money or property **b :** to bet on an uncertain outcome **2 :** to stake something on a contingency **:** take a chance ~ *vt* **1 :** to risk by gambling **:** WAGER **2 :** VENTURE, HAZARD — **gam·bler** \-blər\ *n*

[2]**gamble** *n* (1823) **1 a :** an act having an element of risk **b :** something chancy **2 :** the playing of a game of chance for stakes

gam·boge \gam-ˈbōj, -ˈbüzh\ *n* [NL *gambogium,* alter. of *cambugium,* fr. or akin to Pg *Camboja* Cambodia] (1712) **1 :** an orange to brown gum resin from southeast Asian trees (genus *Garcinia*) of the Saint-John's-wort family that is used as a yellow pigment and cathartic **2 :** a strong yellow

[1]**gam·bol** \ˈgam-bəl\ *vi* **-boled** *or* **-bolled; -bol·ing** *or* **-bol·ling** \-bə-liŋ *also* -bliŋ\ (1508) **:** to skip about in play **:** FRISK, FROLIC

[2]**gambol** *n* [modif. of MF *gambade* spring of a horse, gambol, prob. fr. Old Occitan *camba* leg, fr. LL] (ca. 1510) **:** a skipping or leaping about in play

gam·brel \ˈgam-brəl\ *n* [perh. fr. MF dial. (Norman) *gamberel,* fr. *gambe* leg, fr. LL *gamba*] (1547) **:** a stick or iron for suspending slaughtered animals

gambrel roof *n* (1765) **:** a roof with a lower steeper slope and an upper less steep one on each of its two sides — see ROOF illustration

gam·bu·sia \gam-ˈbü-zh(ē-)ə, -ˈbyü-\ *n* [NL, modif. of AmerSp *gambusino* gambusia] (ca. 1889) **:** any of a genus (*Gambusia*) of live-bearers (family Poeciliidae) including some introduced as exterminators of mosquito larvae in warm freshwaters — compare MOSQUITO FISH

[1]**game** \ˈgām\ *n* [ME, fr. OE *gamen;* akin to OHG *gaman* amusement] (bef. 12c) **1 a** (1) **:** activity engaged in for diversion or amusement **:** PLAY (2) **:** the equipment for a game **b :** often derisive or mocking jesting **:** FUN, SPORT ⟨make ~ of a nervous player⟩ **2 a :** a procedure or strategy for gaining an end **:** TACTIC **b :** an illegal or shady scheme or maneuver **:** RACKET **3 a** (1) **:** a physical or mental competition conducted according to rules with the participants in direct opposition to each other (2) **:** a division of a larger contest (3) **:** the number of points necessary to win (4) **:** points scored in certain card games (as in all fours) by a player whose cards count up the highest (5) **:** the manner of playing in a contest (6) **:** the set of rules governing a game (7) **:** a particular aspect or phase of play in a game or sport ⟨a football team's kicking ~⟩ **b** *pl* **:** organized athletics **c** (1) **:** a field of gainful activity **:** LINE ⟨the newspaper ~⟩ (2) **:** any activity undertaken or regarded as a contest involving rivalry, strategy, or struggle ⟨the dating ~⟩ ⟨the ~ of politics⟩; *also* **:** the course or period of such an activity ⟨got into aviation early in the ~⟩ (3) **:** area of expertise **:** SPECIALTY 3 ⟨comedy is not my ~⟩ **4 a** (1) **:** animals under pursuit or taken in hunting; *esp* **:** wild animals hunted for sport or food (2) **:** the flesh of game animals **b** *archaic* **:** PLUCK **c :** a target or object esp. of ridicule or attack — often used in the phrase *fair game* ***syn*** see FUN — **game·like** \-ˌlīk\ *adj*

[2]**game** *vb* **gamed; gam·ing** *vi* (1512) **:** to play for a stake ~ *vt* **1** *archaic* **:** to lose or squander by gambling **2 :** to take dishonest advantage of **:** CHEAT ⟨~ the tax system⟩

[3]**game** *adj* (1610) **1 a :** having or showing a resolute unyielding spirit **b :** willing or ready to proceed ⟨were ~ for anything⟩ **2 :** of or relating to game ⟨~ laws⟩ — **game·ly** *adv* — **game·ness** *n*

[4]**game** *adj* [origin unknown] (ca. 1787) **:** LAME ⟨a ~ leg⟩

game ball *n* (1966) **:** a ball (as a football) presented to a player or coach in recognition of an outstanding contribution to a team victory

game bird *n* (1840) **:** a bird that may be legally hunted according to the laws esp. of a state of the U.S.

game changer *n* (1993) **:** a newly introduced element or factor that changes an existing situation or activity in a significant way

game·cock \ˈgām-ˌkäk\ *n* (1646) **:** a rooster of the domestic chicken trained for fighting

game face *n* (1965) **:** a look of intense determination on the face of a game player

game fish *n* (1862) **1 :** a fish of a family (Salmonidae) including salmons, trouts, chars, and whitefishes **2 :** SPORT FISH; *esp* **:** a fish made a legal catch by law

game hen *n* (1975) : an immature domestic hen weighing usu. less than two pounds and used esp. for roasting ⟨a Cornish *game hen*⟩

game·keep·er \ˈgām-ˌkē-pər\ *n* (1659) : a person in charge of the breeding and protection of game animals or birds on a private preserve

gam·elan \ˈga-mə-ˌlan, -ˌlän\ *n* [Jav] (1817) : an Indonesian orchestra made up esp. of percussion instruments (as gongs, xylophones, and drums)

game of chance (1790) : a game (as a dice game) in which chance rather than skill determines the outcome

game pad *n* (1991) : a device having buttons and a joystick that is used for controlling images in video games — called also *joypad*

game plan *n* (1941) : a strategy for achieving an objective — **game–plan** *vi*

game point *n* (1903) : a situation (as in tennis) in which one player will win the game by winning the next point; *also* : the point itself

gam·er \ˈgā-mər\ *n* (ca. 1630) **1** : a player who is game; *esp* : an athlete who relishes competition **2** : a person who plays games; *esp* : a person who regularly plays computer or video games

game show *n* (1958) : a television program on which contestants compete for prizes in a game (as a quiz)

games·man \ˈgāmz-mən, -ˌman\ *n* (1947) : one who practices gamesmanship; *also* : one who plays games

games·man·ship \ˈgāmz-mən-ˌship\ *n* (1947) **1** : the art or practice of winning games by questionable expedients without actually violating the rules **2** : the use of ethically dubious methods to gain an objective

game·some \ˈgām-səm\ *adj* [ME] (14c) : MERRY, FROLICSOME

game·ster \ˈgām-stər\ *n* (1553) : one who plays games; *esp* : GAMBLER

gamet- *or* **gameto-** *comb form* [NL, fr. *gameta*] : gamete ⟨*gameto*phore⟩

gam·etan·gi·um \ˌga-mə-ˈtan-jē-əm\ *n, pl* **-gia** \-jē-ə\ [NL, fr. *gamet-* + Gk *angeion* vessel — more at ANGI-] (1886) : a cell or organ (as of an alga, fern, or fungus) in which gametes are developed

gam·ete \ˈga-ˌmēt *also* gə-ˈmēt\ *n* [NL *gameta*, fr. Gk *gametēs* husband, fr. *gamein* to marry] (1886) : a mature male or female germ cell usu. possessing a haploid chromosome set and capable of initiating formation of a new diploid individual by fusion with a gamete of the opposite sex — **ga·met·ic** \gə-ˈme-tik, -ˈmē-\ *adj* — **ga·met·i·cal·ly** \-ti-k(ə-)lē\ *adv*

gamete in·tra·fal·lo·pi·an transfer \-ˌin-trə-fə-ˈlō-pē-ən-\ *n* (1984) : a method of assisting reproduction in cases of infertility that involves obtaining eggs from an ovary, mixing them with sperm, and inserting them into a fallopian tube by a laparoscope — abbr. *GIFT*; called also *gamete intrafallopian tube transfer*

game theory *n* (ca. 1947) : the analysis of a situation involving conflicting interests (as in business or military strategy) in terms of gains and losses among opposing players — **game theorist** *n*

ga·me·to·cyte \gə-ˈmē-tə-ˌsīt\ *n* [ISV] (1899) : a cell (as of a protozoan causing malaria) that divides to produce gametes

ga·me·to·gen·e·sis \gə-ˌmē-tə-ˈje-nə-səs, ˌga-mə-tə-\ *n* [NL] (ca. 1900) : the production of gametes — **ga·me·to·gen·ic** \-ˈje-nik\ *or* **gam·etog·e·nous** \ˌga-mə-ˈtä-jə-nəs\ *adj*

ga·me·to·phore \gə-ˈmē-tə-ˌfȯr\ *n* (1895) : a modified branch (as of a moss) bearing gametangia

ga·me·to·phyte \gə-ˈmē-tə-ˌfīt\ *n* [ISV] (ca. 1889) : the haploid multicellular individual or generation of a plant or alga with alternation of generations that begins with a haploid spore, produces gametes by mitotic division, and ends with fertilization producing a diploid zygote and that constitutes the visibly dominant form in mosses and algae, exists as an independent plant body in ferns and their relatives, and is reduced to a microscopic or rudimentary state in seed plants — compare SPOROPHYTE — **ga·me·to·phyt·ic** \-ˌmē-tə-ˈfi-tik\ *adj*

-gamic *adj comb form* [ISV, fr. Gk *-gamos* -gamous] : having (such) reproductive organs ⟨cleisto*gamic*⟩

gam·i·fi·ca·tion \ˌgā-mə-fə-ˈkā-shən\ *n* [1*game* + *-ification*] (2010) : the process of adding games or gamelike elements to something (as a task) so as to encourage participation

gam·in \ˈga-mən\ *n* [F] (1840) **1** : a boy who hangs around on the streets : URCHIN **2** : GAMINE 2

1**ga·mine** \ga-ˈmēn, ˈga-ˌmēn\ *n* [F, fem. of *gamin*] (1889) **1** : a girl who hangs around on the streets **2** : a small playfully mischievous girl

2**gamine** *adj* (1925) : of, relating to, or suggesting a gamine

gaming *n* (1501) **1** : the practice of gambling **2 a** : the playing of games that simulate actual conditions (as of business or war) esp. for training or testing purposes **b** : the playing of video games

1**gam·ma** \ˈga-mə\ *n* [ME, fr. LL, fr. Gk, of Sem origin; akin to Heb *gīmel* gimel] (15c) **1** : the 3d letter of the Greek alphabet — see ALPHABET table **2** : the degree of contrast of a developed photographic image or of a video image **3** : a unit of magnetic flux density equal to one nanotesla **4** : GAMMA RAY ⟨~ counter⟩ **5** : MICROGRAM

2**gamma** *adj* (1896) **1** : of, relating to, or being one of three or more closely related chemical substances **2** : third in position in the structure of an organic molecule from a particular group or atom — symbol γ

gam·ma–ami·no·bu·tyr·ic acid \ˌga-mə-ə-ˌmē-(ˌ)nō-byü-ˈtir-ik-, ˌga-mə-ˌa-mə-(ˌ)nō-\ *n* (1957) : an amino acid $C_4H_9NO_2$ that is a neurotransmitter which induces inhibition of postsynaptic neurons

gamma camera *n* (1953) : a camera that detects the radiation from a radioactive tracer injected into the body and is used esp. in medical diagnostic scanning

gamma globulin *n* (1937) **1** : a protein fraction of blood rich in antibodies **2** : a sterile solution of gamma globulin from pooled human blood administered esp. for passive immunity against measles, German measles, infectious hepatitis, or poliomyelitis

gamma hy·droxy·bu·ty·rate \-hī-ˌdräk-sē-ˈbyü-tə-ˌrāt\ *n* (1964) : GHB

gamma interferon *n* (1980) : an interferon that is produced by T cells, regulates the immune response, and in a form produced by recombinant DNA technology is used esp. to control infections due to inability of white blood cells to destroy certain bacteria and fungi — compare ALPHA INTERFERON, BETA INTERFERON

Gamma Knife *trademark* — used for a medical device that emits a highly focused beam of gamma radiation

gamma radiation *n* (1904) : radiation composed of gamma rays

gamma ray *n* (1903) : a photon emitted spontaneously by a radioactive substance; *also* : a photon of higher energy than that of an X-ray

gam·mer \ˈga-mər\ *n* [alter. of *godmother*] (1575) *archaic* : an old woman — compare GAFFER

1**gam·mon** \ˈga-mən\ *n* [AF *gambon* ham, fr. *gambe, jambe* leg, fr. LL *gamba* — more at GAMBIT] (15c) **1** *chiefly Brit* : HAM 2 **2** *chiefly Brit* **a** : a side of bacon **b** : the lower end of a side of bacon

2**gammon** *n* [perh. alter. of ME *gamen* game] (ca. 1734) **1** *archaic* : BACKGAMMON **2** : the winning of a backgammon game before the loser removes any men from the board

3**gammon** *vt* (1735) : to beat by scoring a gammon

4**gammon** *vi* (1789) **1** : to talk gammon **2** : PRETEND, FEIGN ~ *vt* : DECEIVE, FOOL

5**gammon** *n* [perh. fr. argot *to give (someone) gammon* to distract a victim during a robbery] (1805) : talk intended to deceive

gam·my \ˈga-mē\ *adj* [perh. fr. 4*game*] (1870) *Brit* : LAME, GAME

-gamous *adj comb form* [Gk *-gamos*, fr. *gamos* marriage, fr. *gamein* to marry] **1** : characterized by having or practicing (such) a marriage or (so many) marriages ⟨exo*gamous*⟩ **2** : -GAMIC ⟨hetero*gamous*⟩

gam·ut \ˈga-mət\ *n* [ML *gamma*, lowest note of a medieval scale (fr. LL, 3d letter of the Greek alphabet) + *ut* ut] (15c) **1** : the whole series of recognized musical notes **2** : an entire range or series ⟨ran the ~ from praise to contempt⟩ ***syn*** see RANGE

gamy *or* **gam·ey** \ˈgā-mē\ *adj* **gam·i·er; -est** (1844) **1** : BRAVE, PLUCKY — used esp. of animals **2 a** : having the flavor of game; *esp* : having the flavor of game near tainting **b** : SMELLY **3 a** : SORDID, SCANDALOUS ⟨gave us all the ~ details⟩ **b** : CORRUPT, DISREPUTABLE ⟨a ~ character⟩ **c** : sexually suggestive : RACY ⟨~ witticisms⟩ — **gam·i·ly** \-mə-lē\ *adv* — **gam·i·ness** \-mē-nəs\ *n*

-gamy *n comb form* [ME *-gamie*, fr. LL *-gamia*, fr. Gk, fr. *gamein* to marry] **1** : marriage ⟨exo*gamy*⟩ **2** : union for propagation or reproduction ⟨allo*gamy*⟩ **3** : possession of (such) reproductive organs or (such) a mode of fertilization ⟨cleisto*gamy*⟩

gan *past of* GIN

ga·nache \(ˌ)gä-ˈnäsh, gə-\ *n* [F, lit., jowl, fr. It *ganascia*, modif. of Gk *gnathos* jaw — more at -GNATHOUS] (1977) : a sweet creamy chocolate mixture used esp. as a filling or frosting

gan·ci·clo·vir \gan-ˈsī-klə-(ˌ)vir\ *n* [perh. fr. *guanosine* + *-ciclovir*, alter. of *-cyclovir* (as in *acyclovir*)] (1986) : an antiviral drug $C_9H_{13}N_5O_4$ related to acyclovir and used esp. to treat cytomegalovirus retinitis in immunocompromised individuals

Gan·da \ˈgan-də, ˈgän-\ *n, pl* **Ganda** *or* **Gandas** (1934) **1** : a member of a Bantu-speaking people of Uganda **2** : LUGANDA

1**gan·der** \ˈgan-dər\ *n* [ME, fr. OE *gandra*; akin to OE *gōs* goose] (bef. 12c) **1** : an adult male goose **2** : SIMPLETON

2**gander** *n* [prob. fr. 1*gander*; fr. the outstretched neck of a person craning to look at something] (ca. 1914) : LOOK, GLANCE ⟨take a ~⟩

gan·dy dancer \ˈgan-dē-\ *n* [origin unknown] (1915) **1** : a laborer in a railroad section gang **2** : an itinerant or seasonal laborer

ga·nef *or* **gon·if** *also* **gon·iff** \ˈgä-nəf\ *n* [Yiddish, fr. Heb *gannābh* thief] (ca. 1839) *slang* : THIEF, RASCAL

Ga·ne·lon \ˌga-nə-ˈlōⁿ\ *n* [F] (ca. 1533) : the traitor in the Charlemagne romances who is responsible for the death of Roland

1**gang** \ˈgaŋ\ *vi* [ME, fr. OE *gangan*; akin to Lith *žengti* to stride] (bef. 12c) *Scot* : GO

2**gang** *n* [ME, walking, journey, fr. OE; akin to OE *gangan*] (15c) **1 a** (1) : a set of articles : OUTFIT ⟨a ~ of oars⟩ (2) : a combination of similar implements or devices arranged for convenience to act together ⟨a ~ of saws⟩ **b** : GROUP: as (1) : a group of persons working together (2) : a group of persons working to unlawful or antisocial ends; *esp* : a band of antisocial adolescents **2** : a group of persons having informal and usu. close social relations ⟨watching TV with the ~⟩

3**gang** *vt* (1856) **1 a** : to assemble or operate simultaneously as a group **b** : to arrange in or produce as a gang **2** : to attack in a gang ~ *vi* : to move or act as a gang

gang·bang \ˈgaŋ-ˌbaŋ\ *vi* (1949) **1** *often vulgar* : to participate in a gang bang **2** : to participate in esp. violent gang activity ~ *vt, often vulgar* : to subject to a gang bang

gang bang *n* (1945) **1** *often vulgar* : copulation by several persons in succession with the same passive partner **2** *often vulgar* : GANG RAPE

gang·bang·er \ˈgaŋ-ˌbaŋ-ər\ *n* (1969) : a member of a street gang

gang·bust·er \ˈgaŋ-ˌbəs-tər\ *n* (1940) : one engaged in the aggressive breakup of organized criminal gangs — **like gangbusters** : with great or excessive force or aggressiveness ⟨came on *like gangbusters*⟩; *also* : with great speed or success ⟨was selling *like gangbusters*⟩

gangbusters *also* **gangbuster** *adj* (1971) : outstandingly excellent or successful ⟨a ~ ballplayer⟩ — **gangbusters** *adv*

gang·er \ˈgaŋ-ər\ *n* (1849) *Brit* : the foreman of a gang of workers

gang hook *n* (1877) : two or three fishhooks with their shanks joined together

gang·land \ˈgaŋ-ˌland, -lənd\ *n, often attrib* (1912) : the world of organized crime ⟨a ~ killing⟩

gan·gling \ˈgaŋ-gliŋ, -glən\ *adj* [perh. alter. of Sc *gangrel* vagrant, lanky person] (1764) : loosely and awkwardly built : LANKY

gan·gli·on \ˈgaŋ-glē-ən\ *n, pl* **-glia** \-glē-ə\ *also* **-gli·ons** [LL, fr. Gk] (ca. 1681) **1** : a small cystic tumor connected either with a joint membrane or tendon sheath **2 a** : a mass of nerve tissue containing cell bodies of neurons external to the brain or spinal cord; *also* : NUCLEUS 2b **b** : something likened to a nerve ganglion ⟨a ~ of cables and wires⟩ — **gan·gli·on·at·ed** \ˈgaŋ-glē-ə-ˌnā-təd\ *adj* — **gan·gli·on·ic** \ˌgaŋ-glē-ˈä-nik\ *adj*

gan·gli·o·side \ˈgaŋ-glē-ə-ˌsīd\ *n* [ISV *ganglion* + 2*-ose* + *-ide*] (1943) : any of a group of glycolipids that yield a hexose sugar on hydrolysis and are found esp. in the plasma membrane of cells of the gray matter

gang·ly \ˈgaŋ-glē\ *adj* **gan·gli·er; -est** (1872) : GANGLING

gang·plank \ˈgaŋ-ˌplaŋk\ *n* (1846) : a movable bridge used in boarding or leaving a ship at a pier

gang rape *n* (1900) : rape of one person by several attackers in succession — **gang–rape** *vt*

gang·rel \ˈgaŋ-(ə-)rəl\ *n* [ME, fr. *gangen* to go, fr. OE *gangan*] (14c) *Scot* : VAGRANT

1**gan·grene** \ˈgaŋ-ˌgrēn, gaŋ-ˈ, ˈgan-ˌ, gan-ˈ\ *n* [L *gangraena*, fr. Gk *gangraina*; akin to Gk *gran* to gnaw] (1543) **1** : local death of soft tissues due to loss of blood supply **2** : pervasive decay or corruption : ROT ⟨moral ~⟩ — **gan·gre·nous** \ˈgaŋ-grə-nəs\ *adj*

[2]**gan·grene** *vb* **gan·grened; gan·gren·ing** *vt* (1607) : to make gangrenous ~ *vi* : to become gangrenous

gang·sta \ˈgaŋ(k)-stə\ *n, often attrib* [alter. of *gangster*] (1988) **1** : a member of an urban street gang **2** : a performer of gangsta rap

gangsta rap *n* (1990) : rap music with lyrics explicitly portraying the violence and drug use of urban gang life and typically expressing hostility toward whites, women, and civil authority — **gangsta rapper** *n*

gang·ster \ˈgaŋ-stər\ *n* (1886) : a member of a gang of criminals : RACKETEER — **gang·ster·dom** \-dəm\ *n* — **gang·ster·ish** \-stə-rish\ *adj* — **gang·ster·ism** \-stə-ˌri-zəm\ *n*

gang–tackle \ˈgaŋ-ˌta-kəl\ *vt* (1951) : to bring down (a ballcarrier in football) with several tacklers

gangue \ˈgaŋ\ *n* [F, fr. G *Gang* vein of metal, fr. OHG, act of going] (1809) : the worthless rock or vein matter in which valuable metals or minerals occur

gang up *vi* (1925) **1** : to make a joint assault ⟨*ganged up* on him and beat him up⟩ **2** : to combine for a specific purpose ⟨*ganged up* to raise prices⟩ **3** : to exert group pressure ⟨*ganged up* against the boss⟩

gang·way \ˈgaŋ-ˌwā\ *n* (bef. 12c) **1** : PASSAGEWAY; *esp* : a temporary way of planks **2 a** : either of the sides of the upper deck of a ship **b** : the opening by which a ship is boarded **c** : GANGPLANK **3** *Brit* : AISLE **4 a** : a cross aisle dividing the front benches from the backbenches in the British House of Commons **b** : an aisle in the British House of Commons that separates government and opposition benches **5** : a clear passage through a crowd — often used as an interjection

gan·is·ter *also* **gan·nis·ter** \ˈga-nə-stər\ *n* [origin unknown] (1811) : a fine-grained quartzite used in the manufacture of refractory brick

gan·ja \ˈgän-jə, ˈgan-\ *n* [Hindi *gā̃jā* & Urdu *gānjā*, fr. Skt *gañjā* hemp] (1689) : a potent and selected preparation of marijuana used esp. for smoking; *broadly* : MARIJUANA

gan·net \ˈga-nət\ *n, pl* **gannets** *also* **gannet** [ME *ganet*, fr. OE *ganot;* akin to OE *gōs* goose] (bef. 12c) : any of a genus (*Morus* of the family Sulidae, the gannet family) of large fish-eating seabirds that breed in colonies chiefly on offshore islands

[1]**gan·oid** \ˈga-ˌnȯid\ *adj* [ultim. fr. Gk *ganos* brightness; akin to Gk *gēthein* to rejoice — more at JOY] (ca. 1847) : of, having, or being fish scales consisting of bone and an outer shiny layer resembling enamel; *also* : relating to or being fish with ganoid scales

[2]**ganoid** *n* (ca. 1839) : a fish (as a sturgeon or gar) with ganoid scales

gante·lope *or* **gant·lope** \ˈgant-ˌlōp\ *n* [modif. of Sw *gatlopp*, fr. OSw *gatulop*, fr. *gata* road + *lop* course] (1646) *archaic* : [2]GAUNTLET

gantlet *var of* GAUNTLET

gan·try \ˈgan-trē\ *n, pl* **gantries** [ME *ganter, gauntree*, fr. AF *ganter, fr. OF dial. (Artois) *gantier*, fr. L *cantherius* horse of poor quality, rafter, trellis] (15c) **1** : a frame for supporting barrels **2** : a frame structure raised on side supports so as to span over or around something: as **a** : a platform made to carry a traveling crane and supported by towers or side frames running on parallel tracks; *also* : a movable structure with platforms at different levels used for erecting and servicing rockets before launching **b** : a structure spanning several railroad tracks and displaying signals for each

Gan·y·mede \ˈga-ni-ˌmēd\ *n* [L *Ganymedes*, fr. Gk *Ganymēdēs*] (1565) : a beautiful youth in classical mythology carried off to Olympus to be the cupbearer of the gods

GAO *abbr* General Accounting Office; Government Accountability Office

gaol \ˈjāl\, **gaol·er** \ˈjā-lər\ *chiefly Brit var of* JAIL, JAILER

[1]**gap** \ˈgap\ *n* [ME, fr. ON, chasm, hole; akin to ON *gapa* to gape] (14c) **1 a** : a break in a barrier (as a wall, hedge, or line of military defense) **b** : an assailable position **2 a** : a mountain pass **b** : RAVINE **3** : SPARK GAP **4 a** : a separation in space **b** : an incomplete or deficient area ⟨a ~ in her knowledge⟩ **5** : a break in continuity : HIATUS **6** : a break in the vascular cylinder of a plant where a vascular trace departs from the central cylinder **7** : lack of balance : DISPARITY ⟨the ~ between imports and exports⟩ **8** : a wide difference in character or attitude ⟨the generation ~⟩ **9** : a problem caused by some disparity ⟨a communication ~⟩ ⟨credibility ~⟩ — **gap·py** \ˈga-pē\ *adj*

[2]**gap** *vb* **gapped; gap·ping** *vt* (1879) **1** : to make an opening in **2** : to adjust the space between the electrodes of (a spark plug) ~ *vi* : to fall or stand open

[1]**gape** \ˈgāp *sometimes* ˈgap\ *vi* **gaped; gap·ing** [ME, fr. ON *gapa;* perh. akin to L *hiare* to gape, yawn — more at YAWN] (13c) **1 a** : to open the mouth wide **b** : to open or part widely ⟨holes *gaped* in the pavement⟩ **2** : to gaze stupidly or in openmouthed surprise or wonder **3** : YAWN — **gap·ing·ly** \ˈgā-piŋ-lē, ˈga-piŋ-\ *adv*

[2]**gape** *n* (1535) **1** : an act of gaping: **a** : YAWN **b** : an openmouthed stare **2** : an unfilled space or extent **3 a** : the median margin-to-margin length of the open mouth **b** : the line along which the mandibles of a bird close **c** : the width of an opening **4** *pl but sing in constr* **a** : a disease of birds and esp. young birds in which gapeworms invade and irritate the trachea **b** : a fit of yawning

gap·er \ˈgā-pər *sometimes* ˈga-pər\ *n* (ca. 1637) **1** : one that gapes **2** : any of several large sluggish burrowing clams (families Myacidae and Mactridae) including several used for food

gape·worm \ˈgāp-ˌwərm *sometimes* ˈgap-\ *n* (1873) : a nematode worm (*Syngamus trachea*) that causes gapes in birds

gaping *adj* (1588) : wide open ⟨a ~ hole⟩

gap junction *n* (1967) : an area of contact between adjacent cells characterized by modification of the plasma membranes for intercellular communication or transfer of low molecular-weight substances

gapped scale *n* (1910) : a musical scale derived from a larger system of tones by omitting certain tones

gap–toothed \ˈgap-ˌtütht\ *adj* (1567) : having gaps between the teeth

gap year *n* (1985) : a one-year hiatus from academic studies to allow for nonacademic activities

[1]**gar** \ˈgär\ *interj* [euphemism for *God*] (1598) — used as a mild oath in the phrase *by gar*

[2]**gar** *n* [short for *garfish*] (1765) : any of various fishes that have an elongate body resembling that of a pike and long narrow jaws: as **a** : NEEDLEFISH 1 **b** : any of several predaceous No. American freshwater bony fishes (family Lepisosteidae) with heavy ganoid scales

[3]**gar** *abbr* garage

GAR *abbr* Grand Army of the Republic

[1]**ga·rage** \gə-ˈräzh, -ˈräj; *Canad also* -ˈrazh, -ˈraj; *Brit usu* ˈga-(ˌ)räzh, -(ˌ)räj, -rij\ *n* [F, act of docking, garage, fr. *garer* to dock, fr. MF *garrer*, prob. ultim. fr. ON *vara* to beware, take care; akin to OHG *biwarōn* to protect — more at WARE] (1902) **1** : a shelter or repair shop for automotive vehicles **2** : a cabinet with a vertical rolling door that is used for storing a small kitchen appliance

[2]**garage** *vt* **ga·raged; ga·rag·ing** (1905) : to keep or put in a garage

garage band *n* (1972) : an amateur rock band typically holding its rehearsals in a garage and usu. having only a local audience

ga·rage·man \-ˌman\ *n* (1919) : a person who works in a garage

garage sale *n* (1964) : a sale of used household or personal articles (as furniture, tools, or clothing) held on the seller's own premises

ga·ram ma·sa·la \gä-ˈräm-mə-ˈsä-lə\ *n* [Hindi & Urdu *garam masālā*, lit., hot spices] (1954) : a pungent and aromatic mixture of ground spices used in Indian cooking

Ga·rand rifle \gə-ˈrand-, ˈga-rənd-\ *n* [John C. *Garand*] (1931) : M1 RIFLE

[1]**garb** \ˈgärb\ *n* [MF or OIt; MF *garbe* graceful contour, grace, fr. OIt *garbo* grace] (1599) **1** *obs* : FASHION, MANNER **2 a** : a style of apparel **b** : outward form : APPEARANCE

[2]**garb** *vt* (1846) : to cover with or as if with clothing

gar·bage \ˈgär-bij\ *n* [ME, offal] (15c) **1 a** : food waste **b** : discarded or useless material **2 a** : TRASH 1b **b** : inaccurate or useless data

gar·bage·man \-ˌman\ *n* (1888) : one who collects and hauls away garbage

gar·ban·zo \gär-ˈbän-(ˌ)zō, *also* -ˈban-\ *n, pl* **-zos** [Sp] (1759) : CHICKPEA

garbanzo bean *n* (1944) : CHICKPEA

[1]**gar·ble** \ˈgär-bəl\ *vt* **gar·bled; gar·bling** \-b(ə-)liŋ\ [ME *garbelen*, fr. OIt *garbellare* to sift, fr. Ar *gharbala*, fr. LL *cribellare*, fr. *cribellum* sieve; akin to L *cernere* to sift — more at CERTAIN] (15c) **1** *archaic* : CULL 1 **2** : to sift impurities from **3 a** : to so alter or distort as to create a wrong impression or change the meaning ⟨~ a story⟩ **b** : to introduce textual error into (a message) by inaccurate encipherment, transmission, or decipherment — **gar·bler** \-b(ə-)lər\ *n*

[2]**garble** *n* (1502) **1** : the impurities removed from spices in sifting **2** : an act or an instance of garbling

gar·board \ˈgär-ˌbȯrd\ *n* [obs. D *gaarboord*] (1627) : the strake next to a ship's keel

gar·boil \-ˌbȯi(-ə)l\ *n* [MF *garbouil*, fr. OIt *garbuglio*] (1548) *archaic* : a confused disordered state : TURMOIL

gar·bol·o·gy \gär-ˈbä-lə-jē\ *n* [*garbage* + *-ology* (as in *geology*)] (1975) : the study of modern culture through the analysis of what is thrown away as garbage — **gar·bol·o·gist** \-jist\ *n*

gar·çon \gär-ˈsō^{n}\ *n, pl* **garçons** \-ˈsō^{n}(z)\ [F, boy, servant, fr. OF, of Gmc origin; akin to OHG *hrechjo* fugitive — more at WRETCH] (1788) : WAITER

gar·da \ˈgär-də\ *n, pl* **gar·dai** \ˌgär-ˈdē\ *often cap* [Ir *garda* (pl. *gardaí*), short for *garda síochána*, lit., guardian of the peace] (1934) : a police officer in the Republic of Ireland

garde–man·ger \ˌgärd-ˌmä^{n}-ˈzhā\ *n, pl* **garde–mangers** \-ˈzhā(z)\ [F, lit., one who keeps food] (1928) : a cook who specializes in the preparation of cold foods (as meats, fish, and salads)

[1]**gar·den** \ˈgär-dᵊn\ *n* [ME *gardin*, fr. AF *gardin, jardin*, of Gmc origin; akin to OHG *gart* enclosure — more at YARD] (13c) **1 a** : a plot of ground where herbs, fruits, flowers, or vegetables are cultivated **b** : a rich well-cultivated region **c** : a container (as a window box) planted with usu. a variety of small plants **2 a** : a public recreation area or park usu. ornamented with plants and trees ⟨a botanical ~⟩ **b** : an open-air eating or drinking place **c** : a large hall for public entertainment — **gar·den·ful** \-ˌfu̇l\ *n*

[2]**garden** *vb* **gar·dened; gar·den·ing** \ˈgär-də-niŋ, ˈgärd-niŋ\ *vi* (1577) : to lay out or work in a garden ~ *vt* **1** : to make into a garden **2** : to ornament with gardens — **gar·den·er** \ˈgär-də-nər, ˈgärd-nər\ *n*

[3]**garden** *adj* (15c) **1** : of, relating to, used in, or frequenting a garden **2 a** : of a kind grown in the open as distinguished from one more delicate ⟨~ plant⟩ **b** : commonly found : GARDEN-VARIETY

garden apartment *n* (1946) : a multiple-unit low-rise dwelling having considerable lawn or garden space

garden city *n* (1898) : a planned residential community with park and planted areas

garden cress *n* (1577) : an annual herb (*Lepidium sativum*) of the mustard family sometimes cultivated for its pungent basal leaves

garden heliotrope *n* (ca. 1902) : a tall rhizomatous Old World valerian (*Valeriana officinalis*) widely cultivated for its fragrant tiny flowers and for its roots which yield the drug valerian

gar·de·nia \gär-ˈdē-nyə\ *n* [NL, fr. Alexander *Garden* †1791 Scot. naturalist] (1760) : any of a large genus (*Gardenia*) of Old World tropical trees and shrubs of the madder family with showy fragrant white or yellow flowers

Garden of Eden (1535) : EDEN

garden rocket *n* (1597) : ARUGULA

garden–variety *adj* (1928) : ORDINARY, COMMONPLACE

garde·robe \ˈgär-ˌdrōb\ *n* [ME, fr. OF, from *garder* to watch, guard + *robe* clothing] (15c) **1** : a wardrobe or its contents **2** : a private room : BEDROOM **3** : PRIVY 1

gar·dy·loo \ˌgär-dē-ˈlü\ *interj* [perh. fr. F *garde à l'eau!* look out for the water!] (1622) — used in Edinburgh as a warning cry when it was customary to throw slops from the windows into the streets

Gar·eth \ˈga-rəth\ *n* (15c) : a knight of the Round Table and nephew of King Arthur

gar·fish \ˈgär-ˌfish\ *n* [ME *garfysshe*] (15c) : GAR

Gar·gan·tua \gär-ˈgan(t)-sh(ə-)wə\ *n* [F] (1571) : a gigantic king in Rabelais's *Gargantua* having a great capacity for food and drink

gar·gan·tuan \-wən\ *adj, often cap* [*Gargantua*] (1596) : tremendous in size, volume, or degree : GIGANTIC, COLOSSAL ⟨~ waterfalls⟩

[1]**gar·gle** \ˈgär-gəl\ *vb* **gar·gled; gar·gling** \-g(ə-)liŋ\ [MF *gargouiller*, of imit. origin] *vt* (1527) **1 a** : to hold (a liquid) in the mouth or throat

and agitate with air from the lungs **b :** to cleanse or disinfect (the oral cavity) in this manner **2 :** to utter with a gargling sound ∼ *vi* **1 :** to use a gargle **2 :** to speak or sing as if gargling

[2]**gargle** *n* (1629) **1 :** a liquid used in gargling **2 :** a sound of or like that of gargling

gar·goyle \ˈgär-ˌgȯi(-ə)l\ *n* [ME *gargule, gargoyl,* fr. OF *gargoule*] (13c) **1 a :** a spout in the form of a grotesque human or animal figure projecting from a roof gutter to throw rainwater clear of a building **b :** a grotesquely carved figure **2 :** a person with an ugly face — **gar·goyled** \-ˌgȯi(-ə)ld\ *adj*

gar·i·bal·di \ˌgar-ə-ˈbȯl-dē\ *n* (1862) **:** a woman's blouse copied from the red shirt worn by the Italian patriot Garibaldi

Ga·ri·fu·na \ˌgä-rē-ˈfü-nə\ *n, pl* **Garifuna** *or* **Ga·ri·fu·nas** [Garifuna *garífuna,* a self-designation; akin to Taino *caribe, caribi* Carib, Island Carib (Arawakan language of the Lesser Antilles) *Callípona,* a self-designation, Guianan Carib *kariʔna* Carib, person] (1977) **:** a member of a people of African and American Indian descent that live mainly along the Caribbean coast of northern Central America — called also *Black Carib; also* **:** the Arawakan language containing many Cariban elements spoken by the Garifunas

ga·rigue \gə-ˈrēg\ *n* [F] (1896) **:** a low open scrubland with many evergreen shrubs, low trees, aromatic herbs, and bunchgrasses found in poor or dry soil in the Mediterranean region

gar·ish \ˈger-ish\ *adj* [origin unknown] (1545) **1 :** clothed in vivid colors **2 a :** excessively or disturbingly vivid ⟨∼ colors⟩ ⟨∼ imagery⟩ **b :** offensively or distressingly bright **:** GLARING **3 :** tastelessly showy **:** FLASHY ***syn*** see GAUDY — **gar·ish·ly** *adv* — **gar·ish·ness** *n*

[1]**gar·land** \ˈgär-lənd\ *n* [ME, fr. AF *garlande*] (14c) **1 :** a circular or spiral arrangement of intertwined material (as flowers or leaves) **2 :** ANTHOLOGY, COLLECTION

[2]**garland** *vt* (15c) **1 :** to form into a garland **2 :** to adorn with or as if with a garland

gar·lic \ˈgär-lik\ *n* [ME *garlek,* fr. OE *gārlēac,* fr. *gār* spear + *lēac* leek — more at GORE] (bef. 12c) **1 :** a European allium (*Allium sativum*) widely cultivated for its pungent compound bulbs much used in cookery; *broadly* **:** ALLIUM **2 :** a bulb of garlic — **gar·licky** \-li-kē\ *adj*

garlic chive *n* (1969) **:** a perennial allium (*Allium tuberosum*) native to southeastern Asia but widely cultivated for its garlic-flavored stems, leaves, buds, and flower heads — usu. used in pl.; called also *Chinese chive*

gar·licked \ˈgär-likt\ *adj* (1950) **:** containing or prepared with garlic

garlic salt *n* (1927) **:** a seasoning of ground dried garlic and salt

[1]**gar·ment** \ˈgär-mənt\ *n* [ME, fr. AF *garnement,* fr. *garnir* to equip — more at GARNISH] (14c) **:** an article of clothing

[2]**garment** *vt* (ca. 1547) **:** to clothe with or as if with a garment

garment bag *n* (1927) **:** a bag used by travelers that folds in half and has a center handle for easy carrying

gar·ner \ˈgär-nər\ *vt* **gar·nered; gar·ner·ing** \ˈgärn-riŋ, ˈgär-nə-\ [ME (Sc), fr. ME *gerner, garner* granary, fr. AF *gerner, grenier,* fr. L *granarium,* fr. *granum* grain — more at CORN] (14c) **1 a :** to gather into storage **b :** to deposit as if in a granary ⟨volumes in which he has ∼*ed* the fruits of his lifetime labors —Reinhold Niebuhr⟩ **2 a :** to acquire by effort **:** EARN **b :** ACCUMULATE, COLLECT

gar·net \ˈgär-nət\ *n* [ME *gernet,* fr. AF *gernete,* fr. *gernet* dark red, fr. *pume gernete* pomegranate] (14c) **1 :** a brittle and more or less transparent usu. red silicate mineral that has a vitreous luster, occurs mainly in crystals but also in massive form and in grains, is found commonly in gneiss and mica schist, and is used as a semiprecious stone and as an abrasive **2 :** a variable color averaging a dark red — **gar·net·if·er·ous** \ˌgär-nə-ˈti-f(ə-)rəs\ *adj*

garnet paper *n* (ca. 1902) **:** an abrasive paper with crushed garnet as the abrasive

gar·ni·er·ite \ˈgär-nē-ə-ˌrīt\ *n* [Jules *Garnier* †1904 Fr. geologist] (1875) **:** a soft mineral consisting of hydrous nickel magnesium silicate and constituting an important ore of nickel

[1]**gar·nish** \ˈgär-nish\ *vt* [ME, fr. AF *garniss-,* stem of *garnir* to warn, equip, garnish, of Gmc origin; akin to OHG *warnōn* to take heed — more at WARN] (14c) **1 a :** DECORATE, EMBELLISH **b :** to add decorative or savory touches to (food or drink) **2 :** to equip with accessories **:** FURNISH **3 :** GARNISHEE ***syn*** see ADORN

[2]**garnish** *n* (1596) **1 :** EMBELLISHMENT, ORNAMENT **2 :** something (as lemon wedges or parsley) used to garnish food or drink **3 a :** an unauthorized fee formerly extorted from a new inmate of an English jail **b :** a similar payment required of a new worker

[1]**gar·nish·ee** \ˌgär-nə-ˈshē\ *n* (1627) **:** a person who is served with a legal process of garnishment

[2]**garnishee** *vt* **-eed; -ee·ing** (1846) **1 :** to serve with a garnishment **2 :** to take (as a debtor's wages) by legal authority

gar·nish·ment \ˈgär-nish-mənt\ *n* (1550) **1 :** ORNAMENT, GARNISH **2 :** a legal summons or warning concerning the attachment of property to satisfy a debt **3 :** a stoppage of a specified sum from wages to satisfy a creditor or a legal obligation (as child support)

gar·ni·ture \ˈgär-ni-chər, -nə-ˌchu̇r\ *n* [MF, equipment, alter. of OF *garnesture,* fr. *garnir*] (1558) **1 :** EMBELLISHMENT, TRIMMING **2 :** a set of decorative objects (as vases, urns, or clocks)

gar·pike \ˈgär-ˌpīk\ *n* (1776) **:** GAR b

gar·ret \ˈger-ət, ˈga-rət\ *n* [ME *garite* watchtower, turret, fr. AF, fr. *garir*] (14c) **:** a room or unfinished part of a house just under the roof

[1]**gar·ri·son** \ˈger-ə-sən, ˈga-rə-\ *n* [ME *garisoun* protection, fr. AF *garisun* healing, protection, fr. *garir* to heal, protect, of Gmc origin; akin to OHG *werien* to defend — more at WEIR] (15c) **1 :** a military post; *esp* **:** a permanent military installation **2 :** the troops stationed at a garrison

[2]**garrison** *vt* **gar·ri·soned; gar·ri·son·ing** \-s(ə-)niŋ\ (1569) **1 :** to station troops in **2 a :** to assign as a garrison **b :** to occupy with troops

garrison cap *n* (1944) **:** a visorless folding cap worn as part of a military uniform — compare SERVICE CAP

Gar·ri·son finish \ˈga-rə-sən-\ *n* [Edward H. "Snapper" *Garrison,* †1930 Am. jockey] (1890) **:** a finish in which the winner comes from behind at the end

garrison house *n* (1676) **1 :** a house fortified against attack **2 :** BLOCKHOUSE **3 :** a house having the second story overhanging the first in the front

garrison state *n* (1937) **:** a state organized to serve primarily its own need for military security; *also* **:** a state maintained by military power

gar·ron \ˈga-rən, gə-ˈrȯn\ *n* [Ir *gearrán* & ScGael *gearran,* gelding] (1540) *Scot & Irish* **:** a small sturdy workhorse

[1]**gar·rote** *or* **ga·rotte** \gə-ˈrät, -ˈrōt; ˈger-ət, ˈga-rət\ *n* [Sp *garrote*] (1622) **1 a :** a method of execution by strangulation **b :** the apparatus used **2 :** an implement (as a wire with a handle at each end) for strangulation

[2]**garrote** *or* **garotte** *vt* **gar·rot·ed** *or* **ga·rott·ed; gar·rot·ing** *or* **ga·rott·ing** (1851) **:** to strangle with or as if with a garrote — **gar·rot·er** *n*

gar·ru·li·ty \gə-ˈrü-lə-tē, ga-\ *n* (1581) **:** the quality or state of being garrulous

gar·ru·lous \ˈger-ə-ləs, ˈga-rə- *also* ˈger-yə-\ *adj* [L *garrulus,* fr. *garrire* to chatter — more at CARE] (ca. 1611) **1 :** given to prosy, rambling, or tedious loquacity **:** pointlessly or annoyingly talkative **2 :** WORDY 1 ⟨∼ speeches⟩ ***syn*** see TALKATIVE — **gar·ru·lous·ly** *adv* — **gar·ru·lous·ness** *n*

[1]**gar·ter** \ˈgär-tər\ *n* [ME, fr. AF *gareter,* fr. *garet* thigh, shank, of Celt origin; akin to W *gar* shank] (14c) **1 a :** a band worn to hold up a stocking or sock **b :** a band worn to hold up a shirt sleeve **c :** a strap hanging from a girdle or corset to support a stocking **2** *cap* **a :** the British Order of the Garter; *also* **:** the blue velvet garter that is its badge **b :** membership in the order

[2]**garter** *vt* (15c) **:** to support with or as if with a garter

garter snake *n* (1743) **:** any of a genus (*Thamnophis*) of harmless viviparous American snakes with longitudinal stripes on the back

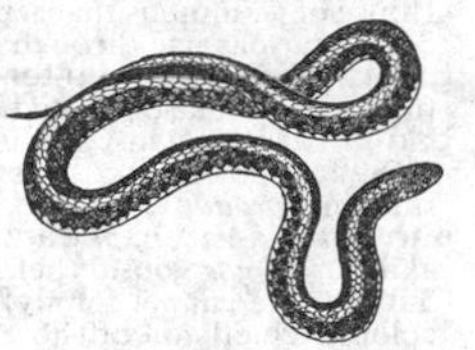

garter snake

garth \ˈgärth\ *n* [ME, fr. ON *garthr* yard; akin to OHG *gart* enclosure — more at YARD] (14c) **:** a small yard or enclosure **:** CLOSE

gar·vey \ˈgär-vē\ *n, pl* **garveys** [prob. fr. the name *Garvey*] (ca. 1896) **:** a small scow esp. of the New Jersey coast

[1]**gas** \ˈgas\ *n, pl* **gas·es** *also* **gas·ses** [NL, alter. of L *chaos* space, chaos] (1779) **1 :** a fluid (as air) that has neither independent shape nor volume but tends to expand indefinitely **2 a :** a combustible gas or gaseous mixture for fuel or lighting; *esp* **:** NATURAL GAS **b :** a gaseous product of digestion; *also* **:** discomfort from this **c :** a gas or gaseous mixture used to produce anesthesia **d :** a substance that can be used to produce a poisonous, asphyxiating, or irritant atmosphere **3 :** empty talk **:** BOMBAST **4 :** GASOLINE; *also* **:** the accelerator pedal of an automotive vehicle **5 :** driving force **:** ENERGY ⟨I was young, and full of ∼ —H. L. Mencken⟩ ⟨ran out of ∼ in the seventh inning⟩ **6** *slang* **:** something that gives pleasure **:** DELIGHT ⟨the party was a ∼⟩

[2]**gas** *vb* **gassed; gas·sing** *vi* (1852) **1 :** to talk idly or garrulously **2 :** to give off gas **3 :** to fill the tank (as of an automobile) with gasoline — usu. used with *up* ∼ *vt* **1 :** to supply with gas or esp. gasoline ⟨∼ up the car⟩ **2 a :** to treat chemically with gas **b :** to poison or otherwise affect adversely with gas **3** *slang* **:** to please greatly

gas·bag \ˈgas-ˌbag\ *n* (1827) **1 :** a bag for holding gas **2 :** an idle or garrulous talker

gas chamber *n* (1933) **:** a chamber in which prisoners are executed by poison gas

gas chromatograph *n* (1958) **:** an instrument used to separate a sample into components in gas chromatography

gas chromatography *n* (1952) **:** chromatography in which the sample mixture is vaporized and injected into a stream of carrier gas (as nitrogen or helium) moving through a column containing a stationary phase composed of a liquid or particulate solid and is separated into its component compounds according to their affinity for the stationary phase — **gas chromatographic** *adj*

gas·con \ˈgas-kən\ *n* (14c) **1** *cap* **a :** a native of Gascony **b :** the Romance speech of Gascony **2 :** a boastful swaggering person — **Gascon** *adj*

gas·co·nade \ˌgas-kə-ˈnād\ *n* [F *gasconnade,* fr. *gasconner* to boast, fr. *gascon* Gascon, boaster] (1709) **:** BRAVADO, BOASTING — **gasconade** *vi* — **gas·con·ad·er** *n*

gas·eous \ˈga-sē-əs, ˈga-shəs\ *adj* (1799) **1 :** having the form of or being gas; *also* **:** of or relating to gases **2 a :** lacking substance or solidity **b :** GASSY 3 ⟨trick phrases and ∼ circumlocutions —Edwin Newman⟩ — **gas·eous·ness** *n*

gas fitter *n* (1849) **:** a worker who installs or repairs gas pipes and appliances

gas gangrene *n* (1914) **:** progressive gangrene marked by impregnation of the dead and dying tissue with gas and caused by one or more toxin-producing clostridia

gas–guz·zler \ˈgas-ˈgəz-lər, -ˈgə-zə-\ *n* (1973) **:** a usu. large automobile that gets relatively poor mileage — **gas–guz·zling** \-liŋ\ *adj*

[1]**gash** \ˈgash\ *n* (1548) **1 :** a deep long cut in flesh **2 :** a deep narrow depression or cut ⟨cut a ∼ through the forest⟩ ⟨a ∼ in the hull⟩

[2]**gash** *vb* [alter. of ME *garsen,* fr. AF *garser* to nip, scratch, fr. VL **charissare,* fr. Gk *charassein* to scratch, engrave] *vt* (1566) **:** to make a gash in ∼ *vi* **:** to make a gash **:** CUT

[3]**gash** *adj* [origin unknown] (1706) **1** *chiefly Scot* **:** KNOWING, WITTY **2** *chiefly Scot* **:** well-dressed **:** TRIM

gas·hold·er \ˈgas-ˌhōl-dər\ *n* (1802) **:** a container for gas; *esp* **:** a huge cylindrical tank for storing fuel gas under pressure

gas·house \-ˌhau̇s\ *n* (1840) **:** GASWORKS

gas·i·fi·ca·tion \ˌga-sə-fə-ˈkā-shən\ *n* (1812) **:** conversion into gas; *esp* **:** conversion of coal into natural gas

gas·i·fy \ˈga-sə-ˌfī\ *vb* **-i·fied; -i·fy·ing** *vt* (ca. 1828) **:** to convert into gas ⟨∼ coal⟩ ∼ *vi* **:** to become gaseous — **gas·ifi·er** \ˈga-sə-ˌfī(-ə)r\ *n*

gas·ket \ˈgas-kət\ *n* [perh. modif. of F *garcette*] (ca. 1889) **:** a material (as rubber) or a part (as an O-ring) used to make a joint fluid-tight

gas·kin \ˈgas-kən\ *n* [prob. short for *galligaskins*] (1573) **1** *pl, obs* **:** HOSE, BREECHES **2 :** a part of the hind leg of a quadruped between the stifle and the hock — see HORSE illustration

gas·light \ˈgas-ˌlīt, -ˈlīt\ *n* (1808) **1 :** light made by burning illuminating gas **2 a :** a gas flame **b :** a gas lighting fixture

gas–liquid chromatography *n* (1952) **:** gas chromatography in which the stationary phase is a liquid — **gas–liquid chromatographic** *adj*

gas·lit \-ˌlit, -ˈlit\ *adj* (1837) **:** illuminated by gaslight
gas log *n* (1871) **:** a hollow perforated imitation log used as a gas burner in a fireplace
gas mask *n* (1915) **:** a mask connected to a chemical air filter and used to protect the face and lungs from toxic gases; *broadly* **:** RESPIRATOR 1
gas·o·gene \ˈga-sə-ˌjēn\ *or* **gaz·o·gene** \ˈga-zə-\ *n* [F *gazogène,* fr. *gaz* gas (fr. NL *gas*) + *-o-* + *-gène* -gen] (ca. 1853) **1 :** a portable apparatus for carbonating liquids **2 :** an apparatus carried by a vehicle to produce gas for fuel by partial burning of charcoal or wood
gas·o·hol \ˈga-sə-ˌhȯl\ *n* [blend of *gasoline* and *alcohol*] (1975) **:** a fuel consisting of a blend usu. of 10 percent ethanol and 90 percent gasoline
gas oil *n* (1901) **:** a hydrocarbon oil used as a fuel oil; *esp* **:** a petroleum distillate intermediate in boiling range and viscosity between kerosene and lubricating oil
gas·olier \ˌga-sə-ˈlir\ *n* [alter. of *gaselier,* fr. *gas* + *-elier* (as in *chandelier*)] (1849) **:** a gaslight chandelier
gas·o·line *also* **gas·o·lene** \ˈga-sə-ˌlēn, ˌga-sə-ˈ *also* -zə-\ *n* [[1]*gas* + [2]*-ol* + [2]*-ine* or *-ene*] (1865) **:** a volatile flammable liquid hydrocarbon mixture used as a fuel esp. for internal combustion engines and usu. blended from several products of natural gas and petroleum — **gas·o·lin·ic** \ˌga-sə-ˈlē-nik, -ˈli-\ *adj*
gas·om·e·ter \ga-ˈsä-mə-tər\ *n* [F *gazomètre,* fr. *gaz* + *-o-* + *-mètre* -meter] (1808) **1 :** GASHOLDER **2 :** a laboratory apparatus for holding and measuring gases
gas–operated *adj* (1944) *of a firearm* **:** using part of the force of expanding propellant gases to operate the action
gasp \ˈgasp\ *vb* [ME; akin to ON *geispa* to yawn] *vi* (14c) **1 :** to catch the breath convulsively and audibly (as with shock) **2 :** to breathe laboriously ~ *vt* **:** to utter in a gasping manner — **gasp** *n*
gasp·er \ˈgäs-pə(r)\ *n* (1914) *slang Brit* **:** CIGARETTE
gas plant *n* (ca. 1909) **:** FRAXINELLA
gas ring *n* (1878) **:** a ring-shaped portable gas burner for cooking
gassed \ˈgast\ *adj* (1919) **1** *slang* **:** DRUNK 1a **2** *slang* **:** drained of energy **:** SPENT, EXHAUSTED
gas·ser \ˈga-sər\ *n* (ca. 1944) *slang* **:** something outstanding
gas station *n* (1925) **:** a retail station for servicing motor vehicles esp. with gasoline and oil — called also *service station*
gas·sy \ˈga-sē\ *adj* **gas·si·er; -est** (1757) **1 :** full of or containing gas **2 :** having the characteristics of gas **3 :** characterized by many words but little content **:** emptily verbose — **gas·si·ly** \ˈga-sə-lē\ *adv* — **gas·si·ness** *n*
gast \ˈgast\ *vt* [ME, fr. *gast, gost* ghost — more at GHOST] (14c) *obs* **:** SCARE ⟨~*ed* by the noise I made, full suddenly he fled —Shak.⟩
gas·ter \ˈgas-tər\ *n* [Gk *gastēr*] (ca. 1909) **:** the enlarged part of the abdomen behind the pedicel in hymenopterous insects (as ants)
gas·tight \ˈgas-ˈtīt\ *adj* (1831) **:** impervious to gas — **gas·tight·ness** *n*
gast·ness \ˈgas(t)-nəs\ *n* (14c) *obs* **:** FRIGHT, TERROR
gastr- *or* **gastro-** *also* **gastri-** *comb form* [Gk, fr. *gastr-, gastēr*] **1 :** stomach ⟨*gastr*ectomy⟩ **2 :** gastric and ⟨*gastro*intestinal⟩
gas·trec·to·my \ga-ˈstrek-tə-mē\ *n, pl* **-mies** [ISV] (1886) **:** surgical removal of all or part of the stomach
gas·tric \ˈgas-trik\ *adj* [Gk *gastr-, gastēr,* alter. of **grastēr,* fr. *gran* to gnaw, eat] (1656) **:** of or relating to the stomach
gastric bypass *n* (1972) **:** a surgical bypass operation that involves reducing the size of the stomach and reconnecting the smaller stomach to bypass the first portion of the small intestine so as to restrict food intake and reduce caloric absorption in cases of severe obesity
gastric gland *n* (1836) **:** any of various glands in the walls of the stomach that secrete gastric juice
gastric juice *n* (ca. 1736) **:** a thin watery acid digestive fluid secreted by glands in the mucous membrane of the stomach
gastric ulcer *n* (1877) **:** a peptic ulcer situated in the stomach
gas·trin \ˈgas-trən\ *n* (1905) **:** any of various polypeptide hormones that are secreted by the gastric mucosa and induce secretion of gastric juice
gas·tri·tis \ga-ˈstrī-təs\ *n* (1806) **:** inflammation esp. of the mucous membrane of the stomach
gas·troc·ne·mi·us \ˌgas-(ˌ)träk-ˈnē-mē-əs, -trək-\ *n, pl* **-mii** \-mē-ˌī\ [NL, fr. Gk *gastroknēmē* calf of the leg, fr. *gastr-* + *knēmē* shank — more at HAM] (1676) **:** the largest and most superficial muscle of the calf of the leg arising by two heads from the condyles of the femur and attaching to a tendon that becomes part of the Achilles tendon
gas·tro·du·o·de·nal \ˌgas-trō-ˌd(y)ü-ə-ˈdē-nᵊl, -d(y)u̇-ˈä-də-nəl\ *adj* (1854) **:** of, relating to, or involving the stomach and the duodenum
gas·tro·en·ter·i·tis \ˌgas-trō-ˌen-tə-ˈrī-təs\ *n* (ca. 1829) **:** inflammation of the lining membrane of the stomach and the intestines characterized esp. by nausea, vomiting, diarrhea, and cramps
gas·tro·en·ter·ol·o·gy \-ˌen-tə-ˈrä-lə-jē\ *n* [ISV] (ca. 1904) **:** a branch of medicine concerned with the structure, functions, diseases, and pathology of the stomach and intestines — **gas·tro·en·ter·o·log·i·cal** \-rə-ˈlä-ji-kəl\ *adj* — **gas·tro·en·ter·ol·o·gist** \-ˌen-tə-ˈrä-lə-jist\ *n*
gas·tro·esoph·a·ge·al \ˈgas-trō-i-ˌsä-fə-ˈjē-əl\ *adj* (ca. 1889) **:** of, relating to, or involving the stomach and esophagus
gastroesophageal reflux *n* (1966) **:** backward flow of the contents of the stomach into the esophagus due to malfunctioning of a sphincter at the lower end of the esophagus and resulting esp. in heartburn
gas·tro·in·tes·ti·nal \ˌgas-trō-in-ˈtes-tə-nᵊl, -ˈtes(t)-nəl\ *adj* (1831) **:** of, relating to, affecting, or including both stomach and intestine
gas·tro·lith \ˈgas-trə-ˌlith\ *n* (1854) **:** a stone or pebble ingested by an animal and functioning to grind food in gastric digestion
gas·tro·nome \ˈgas-trə-ˌnōm\ *n* [F, back-formation fr. *gastronomie*] (1823) **:** a lover of good food; *esp* **:** one with a serious interest in gastronomy ***syn*** see EPICURE
gas·tron·o·mist \ga-ˈsträ-nə-mist\ *n* (1825) **:** GASTRONOME
gas·tron·o·my \-mē\ *n* [F *gastronomie,* fr. Gk *Gastronomia,* title of a 4th cent. B.C. poem, fr. *gastro-* gastr- + *-nomia* -nomy] (1814) **1 :** the art or science of good eating **2 :** culinary customs or style — **gas·tro·nom·ic** \ˌgas-trə-ˈnä-mik\ *also* **gas·tro·nom·i·cal** \-mi-kəl\ *adj* — **gas·tro·nom·i·cal·ly** \ˌgas-trə-ˈnä-mi-k(ə-)lē\ *adv*
gas·tro·pod \ˈgas-trə-ˌpäd\ *n* [NL *Gastropoda,* class name] (1826) **:** any of a large class (Gastropoda) of mollusks (as snails and slugs) usu. with a univalve shell or none and a distinct head bearing sensory organs — **gastropod** *adj*
gas·tro·pub \ˈga-strō-ˌpəb\ *n* (1996) **:** a pub, bar, or tavern that offers meals of high quality
gas·tro·scope \ˈgas-trə-ˌskōp\ *n* [ISV] (1888) **:** an endoscope for viewing the interior of the stomach — **gas·tro·scop·ic** \ˌgas-trə-ˈskä-pik\ *adj* — **gas·tros·co·pist** \ga-ˈsträs-kə-pist\ *n* — **gas·tros·co·py** \-pē\ *n*
gas·tro·trich \ˈgas-trə-ˌtrik\ *n* [ultim. fr. Gk *gastr-* + *trich-, thrix* hair — more at TRICH-] (1940) **:** any of a phylum (Gastrotricha) of minute aquatic pseudocoelomate animals that usu. have a spiny or scaly cuticle and cilia on the ventral surface
gas·tro·vas·cu·lar \ˌgas-trō-ˈvas-kyə-lər\ *adj* [ISV] (1876) **:** functioning in both digestion and circulation ⟨the ~ cavity of a coelenterate⟩
gas·tru·la \ˈgas-trə-lə\ *n, pl* **-las** *or* **-lae** \-ˌlē, -ˌlī\ [NL, fr. *gastr-*] (1876) **:** an early metazoan embryo in which the ectoderm, mesoderm, and endoderm are established either by invagination of the blastula (as in fish and amphibians) to form a multilayered cellular cup with a blastopore opening into the archenteron or by differentiation of the blastodisc (as in reptiles, birds, and mammals) and inward cellular migration — compare BLASTULA, MORULA — **gas·tru·lar** \-lər\ *adj*
gas·tru·la·tion \ˌgas-trə-ˈlā-shən\ *n* (1879) **:** the process of becoming or of forming a gastrula — **gas·tru·late** \ˈgas-trə-ˌlāt\ *vi*
gas turbine *n* (1904) **:** an internal combustion engine in which expanding gases from the combustion chamber drive the blades of a turbine
gas·works \ˈgas-ˌwərks\ *n pl but sing or pl in constr* (1819) **:** a plant for manufacturing gas and esp. illuminating gas
[1]**gat** \ˈgat\ *archaic past of* GET
[2]**gat** *n* [prob. fr. D, lit., hole; akin to OE *geat* gate] (1723) **:** a natural or artificial channel or passage
[3]**gat** *n* [short for *Gatling gun*] (1897) *slang* **:** HANDGUN
[1]**gate** \ˈgāt\ *n* [ME, fr. OE *geat;* akin to ON *gat* opening] (bef. 12c) **1 :** an opening in a wall or fence **2 :** a city or castle entrance often with defensive structures (as towers) **3 a :** the frame or door that closes a gate **b :** a movable barrier (as at a grade crossing) **4 a :** a means of entrance or exit **b :** STARTING GATE **c :** an area (as at a railroad station or an airport) for departure or arrival **d :** a space between two markers through which a competitor must pass in the course of a slalom race **5 a :** a door, valve, or other device for controlling the passage esp. of a fluid **b (1) :** an electronic switch that allows or prevents the flow of current in a circuit **(2) :** an electrode in a field-effect transistor that modulates the current flowing through the transistor according to the voltage applied to the electrode — compare DRAIN, SOURCE **c :** a device (as in a computer) that outputs a signal when specified input conditions are met ⟨logic ~⟩ **d :** a molecule or part of a molecule that acts (as by a change in conformation) in response to a stimulus to permit or block passage (as of ions) through a cell membrane **6** *slang* **:** DISMISSAL ⟨gave him the ~⟩ **7 :** the total admission receipts or the number of spectators (as at a sports event)
[2]**gate** *vt* **gat·ed; gat·ing** (1835) **1** *Brit* **:** to confine to a campus or dormitory **2 :** to supply with a gate **3 :** to control with a gate
[3]**gate** *n* [ME, fr. ON *gata* road; akin to OHG *gazza* road] (13c) **1** *archaic* **:** WAY, PATH **2** *dial* **:** METHOD, STYLE
-gate \ˌgāt\ *n comb form* [Water*gate*] **:** usu. political scandal often involving the concealment of wrongdoing ⟨Iran*gate*⟩
gâ·teau *or* **ga·teau** \(ˌ)gä-ˈtō\ *n, pl* **gâ·teaux** *or* **ga·teaux** \-ˈtō(z)\ *also* **gateaus** [F, fr. OF *gastel,* prob. of Gmc origin; akin to OE *wist* sustenance, food] (1764) **1 :** food baked or served in the form of a cake ⟨eggplant ~⟩ **2 :** a rich or fancy cake
gate–crash·er \ˈgāt-ˌkra-shər\ *n* (1921) **:** a person who enters, attends, or participates without ticket or invitation — **gate–crash** *vb*
gated *adj* (1581) **1 :** having or controlled by a gate ⟨a ~ entrance⟩ **2 :** designed to restrict entrance usu. by means of physical barriers, a private security force, and a controlled gate ⟨~ communities⟩
gate·fold \-ˌfōld\ *n* (1946) **:** FOLDOUT; *esp* **:** one with a single fold that opens out like a gate
gate·house \-ˌhau̇s\ *n* (14c) **:** a building or house connected or associated with a gate
gate·keep·er \-ˌkē-pər\ *n* (1572) **1 :** one that tends or guards a gate **2 :** a person who controls access — **gate·keep·ing** \-piŋ\ *n*
gate·leg table \ˈgāt-ˌleg-, -ˌlāg-\ *n* (1926) **:** a table with drop leaves supported by movable paired legs

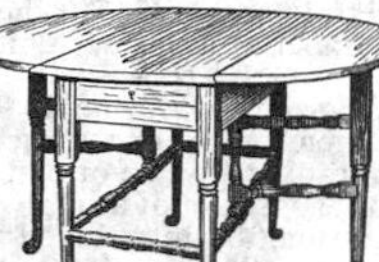
gateleg table

gate·post \ˈgāt-ˌpōst\ *n* (1522) **:** the post to which a gate is hung or the one against which it closes
gate·way \-ˌwā\ *n* (1707) **1 :** an opening for a gate **2 :** GATE 4a
gateway drug *n* (1982) **:** a drug (as alcohol or marijuana) whose use is thought to lead to the use of and dependence on a harder drug (as cocaine or heroin)
[1]**gath·er** \ˈga-t͟hər *also* ˈge-\ *vb* **gath·ered; gath·er·ing** \ˈgat͟h-riŋ, ˈga-t͟hə-\ [ME *gaderen,* fr. OE *gaderian;* akin to MHG *gadern* to unite — more at GOOD] *vt* (bef. 12c) **1 :** to bring together **:** COLLECT ⟨tried to ~ a crowd⟩ ⟨~*ed* firewood⟩ **2 a :** PICK, HARVEST ⟨~ flowers⟩ **b :** to pick up or amass as if by harvesting ⟨~*ing* ideas for the project⟩ **c :** to scoop up or take up from a resting place ⟨~*ed* the child up in his arms⟩ **3 :** to serve as an attraction for **:** ACCUMULATE ⟨books ~*ing* dust⟩ **4 :** to effect the collection of ⟨~ contributions⟩ **5 a :** to summon up ⟨~*ed* his courage⟩ **b :** to gain by gradual increase ⟨~ speed⟩ **c :** to prepare (as oneself) by mustering strength **d :** to gain or regain control of ⟨~*ed* his wits⟩ **6 :** to reach a conclusion often intuitively from hints or through inferences ⟨I ~ that you want to leave⟩ **7 a :** to pull (fabric) along a line of stitching so as to draw into puckers **b :** to draw about or close to something ⟨~*ing* her cloak about her⟩ **c :** to bring together the parts of ⟨~*ed* her hair into a ponytail⟩ **d :** to assemble (the signatures of a book) in proper sequence for binding **e :** to haul in ⟨the sailors ~*ed* the sails⟩ ~ *vi* **1 a :** to come together in a body **b :** to cluster around a focus of attraction **2 a :** to

swell and fill with pus **b :** GROW, INCREASE ⟨the ~*ing* crisis⟩ — **gath·er·er** \-thər-ər\ *n*

syn GATHER, COLLECT, ASSEMBLE, CONGREGATE mean to come or bring together into a group, mass, or unit. GATHER is the most general term for bringing or coming together from a spread-out or scattered state ⟨a crowd quickly *gathered*⟩. COLLECT often implies careful selection or orderly arrangement ⟨*collected* books on gardening⟩. ASSEMBLE implies an ordered union or organization of persons or things often for a definite purpose ⟨experts *assembled* for a conference⟩. CONGREGATE implies a spontaneous flocking together into a crowd or huddle ⟨*congregating* under a shelter⟩. *syn* see in addition INFER

[2]**gather** *n* (1555) **1 :** something gathered: as **a :** a puckering in cloth made by gathering **b :** a mass of molten glass collected for use in glassblowing **2 :** an act or instance of gathering

gathering *n* (bef. 12c) **1 :** ASSEMBLY, MEETING **2 :** a suppurating swelling **:** ABSCESS **3 :** the collecting of food or raw materials from the wild **4 :** COLLECTION, COMPILATION **5 :** a gather in cloth

Gat·ling gun \ˈgat-liŋ-\ *n* [Richard J. *Gatling* †1903 Am. inventor] (1867) **:** a machine gun with a revolving cluster of barrels fired once each per revolution

ga·tor \ˈgā-tər\ *n* (1844) **:** ALLIGATOR

Gats·by·esque \ˌgats-bē-ˈesk\ *adj* (1977) **:** resembling or characteristic of the title character or the world of the novel *The Great Gatsby* by F. Scott Fitzgerald

GATT *abbr* General Agreement on Tariffs and Trade

gauche \ˈgōsh\ *adj, sometimes* **gauch·er;** *sometimes* **gauch·est** [F, lit., left] (1751) **1 a :** lacking social experience or grace; *also* **:** not tactful **:** CRUDE ⟨it would be ~ to mention the subject⟩ **b :** crudely made or done ⟨a ~ turn of phrase⟩ **2 :** not planar ⟨~ conformation of molecules⟩ *syn* see AWKWARD — **gauche·ly** *adv* — **gauche·ness** *n*

gau·che·rie \ˌgō-sh(ə-)ˈrē\ *n* [F] (1810) **:** a tactless or awkward act

Gau·cher's disease \(ˌ)gō-ˈshāz-\ *n* [Philippe C. E. *Gaucher* †1918 Fr. physician] (1902) **:** a rare hereditary disorder of lipid metabolism caused by an enzyme deficiency and characterized by enlargement of the spleen and liver, bone lesions, and neurological impairment

gau·cho \ˈgau̇-(ˌ)chō\ *n, pl* **gauchos** [AmerSp] (1824) **:** a cowboy of the So. American pampas

gaud \ˈgȯd, ˈgäd\ *n* [ME *gaude*] (15c) **:** ORNAMENT, TRINKET

gaud·ery \ˈgȯ-də-rē, ˈgä-\ *n* (ca. 1598) **:** showy ornamentation; *esp* **:** personal finery

[1]**gau·dy** \ˈgȯ-dē, ˈgä-\ *adj* **gaud·i·er; -est** (1582) **1 :** ostentatiously or tastelessly ornamented **2 :** marked by extravagance or sometimes tasteless showiness **:** OUTLANDISH ⟨~ lies⟩ ⟨~ claims⟩; *also* **:** EXCEPTIONAL ⟨a ~ batting average⟩ — **gaud·i·ly** \ˈgȯ-də-lē, ˈgä-\ *adv* — **gaud·i·ness** \ˈgȯ-dē-nəs, ˈgä-\ *n*

syn GAUDY, TAWDRY, GARISH, FLASHY, MERETRICIOUS mean vulgarly or cheaply showy. GAUDY implies a tasteless use of overly bright, often clashing colors or excessive ornamentation ⟨circus performers in *gaudy* costumes⟩. TAWDRY applies to what is at once gaudy and cheap and sleazy ⟨*tawdry* saloons⟩. GARISH describes what is distressingly or offensively bright ⟨*garish* neon signs⟩. FLASHY implies an effect of brilliance quickly and easily seen to be shallow or vulgar ⟨a *flashy* nightclub act⟩. MERETRICIOUS stresses falsity and may describe a tawdry show that beckons with a false allure or promise ⟨a *meretricious* wasteland of casinos and bars⟩.

[2]**gaudy** *n, pl* **gaudies** [prob. fr. L *gaudium* joy — more at JOY] (1651) **:** a feast or entertainment esp. in the form of an annual college dinner at a British university

gauffer *var of* GOFFER

[1]**gauge** *also* **gage** \ˈgāj\ *n* [ME *gauge,* fr. AF] (15c) **1 a :** a measurement (as of linear dimension) according to some standard or system: as (1) **:** the distance between the rails of a railroad (2) **:** the size of a shotgun barrel's inner diameter nominally expressed as the number of lead balls each just fitting that diameter required to make a pound ⟨a 12-*gauge* shotgun⟩ (3) **:** the thickness of a thin material (as sheet metal or plastic film) (4) **:** the diameter of a slender object (as wire or a hypodermic needle) (5) **:** the fineness of a knitted fabric expressed by the number of loops per unit width **b :** DIMENSIONS, SIZE **c :** MEASURE 1 ⟨surveys are a ~ of public sentiment⟩ **2 :** an instrument for or a means of measuring or testing: as **a :** an instrument for measuring a dimension or for testing mechanical accuracy **b :** an instrument with a graduated scale or dial for measuring or indicating quantity **3 :** relative position of a ship with reference to another ship and the wind **4 :** a function introduced into a field equation to produce a convenient form of the equation but having no observable physical consequences *syn* see STANDARD

[2]**gauge** *also* **gage** *vt* **gauged** *also* **gaged; gaug·ing** *also* **gag·ing** (15c) **1 a :** to measure precisely the size, dimensions, or other measurable quantity of **b :** to determine the capacity or contents of **c :** ESTIMATE, JUDGE ⟨hard to ~ his moods⟩ **2 a :** to check for conformity to specifications or limits **b :** to measure off or set out

gauged \ˈgājd\ *adj* (1823) *of masonry* **:** dressed to size

gaug·er \ˈgā-jər\ *n* (15c) **1 :** one that gauges **2** *chiefly Brit* **:** an exciseman who inspects dutiable bulk goods

gauge theory *n* (1973) **:** any of several theories in physics that explain the transmission of a fundamental force between two interacting particles by the exchange of an elementary particle

Gaul \ˈgȯl\ *n* (1625) **1 :** a Celt of ancient Gaul **2 :** FRENCHMAN

gau·lei·ter \ˈgau̇-ˌlī-tər\ *n* [G, fr. *Gau* party district in Nazi Germany + *Leiter* leader] (1936) **1 a :** a district leader in Nazi Germany who served as a provincial governor **b :** a subordinate political official resembling a Nazi gauleiter in function or in autocratic manner **2 :** a person with an arrogant overbearing outlook or manner

[1]**Gaul·ish** \ˈgȯ-lish\ *adj* (1659) **:** of or relating to the Gauls or their language or land

[2]**Gaulish** *n* (1668) **:** the Celtic language of the ancient Gauls — see INDO-EUROPEAN LANGUAGES table

Gaull·ism \ˈgō-ˌli-zəm, ˈgȯ-\ *n* [Charles de *Gaulle*] (1943) **1 :** a French political movement during World War II led by Charles de Gaulle in opposition to the Vichy regime **2 :** a postwar French political movement led by Charles de Gaulle — **Gaull·ist** \-list\ *adj or n*

gault \ˈgȯlt\ *n* [perh. of Scand origin; akin to ON *gald* hard-packed snow] (1575) *chiefly Brit* **:** a heavy thick clay soil

gaum \ˈgȯm, ˈgäm\ *vt* [origin unknown] (1656) *dial* **:** SMUDGE, SMEAR

gaunt \ˈgȯnt, ˈgänt\ *adj* [ME] (15c) **1 :** excessively thin and angular ⟨a long ~ face⟩ **2 :** BARREN, DESOLATE *syn* see LEAN — **gaunt·ly** *adv* — **gaunt·ness** *n*

[1]**gaunt·let** *also* **gant·let** \ˈgȯnt-lət, ˈgänt-\ *n* [ME, fr. MF *gantelet,* dim. of *gant* glove, fr. OF, of Gmc origin; akin to MD *want* glove, ON *vǫttr*] (15c) **1 :** a glove worn with medieval armor to protect the hand **2 :** any of various protective gloves used esp. in industry **3 :** an open challenge (as to combat) — used in phrases like *throw down the gauntlet* **4 :** a dress glove extending above the wrist — **gaunt·let·ed** \-lə-təd\ *adj*

[2]**gauntlet** *also* **gantlet** *n* [by folk etymology fr. *gantelope*] (1645) **1 a :** a double file of men facing each other and armed with clubs or other weapons with which to strike at an individual who is made to run between them — used with *run* **b :** a line, series, or assemblage; *esp* **:** one that poses some sort of ordeal ⟨a ~ of autograph-seekers⟩ **2 :** a severe trial **:** ORDEAL ⟨ran the ~ of criticism and censure⟩

gaur \ˈgau̇(-ə)r\ *n* [Hindi, fr. Skt *gaura;* akin to Skt *go* bull, cow — more at COW] (1806) **:** a large wild ox (*Bos gaurus*) of India and southeast Asia with a broad forehead and short thick curved horns

gauss \ˈgau̇s\ *n, pl* **gauss** *also* **gauss·es** [Karl F. *Gauss*] (1882) **:** the centimeter-gram-second unit of magnetic flux density that is equal to 1×10^{-4} tesla

Gauss·ian \ˈgau̇-sē-ən\ *adj* [Karl F. *Gauss*] (1905) **:** being or having the shape of a normal curve or a normal distribution

Gaussian curve *n* (1905) **:** NORMAL CURVE

Gaussian distribution *n* (1905) **:** NORMAL DISTRIBUTION

gauze \ˈgȯz\ *n* [MF *gaze*] (1561) **1 a :** a thin often transparent fabric used chiefly for clothing or draperies **b :** a loosely woven cotton surgical dressing **c :** a firm woven fabric of metal or plastic filaments **2 :** HAZE — **gauze·like** \-ˌlīk\ *adj* — **gauz·i·ly** \ˈgȯ-zə-lē\ *adv*

gauzy \ˈgȯ-zē\ *adj* **gauz·i·er; -est** (1760) **1 :** made of or resembling gauze ⟨~ wings⟩ **2 :** marked by vagueness, elusiveness, or fuzziness ⟨his ~ memory of the events⟩ ⟨a ~ melody⟩ **3 :** tending to be or make romantic ⟨~ optimism⟩

ga·vage \gə-ˈväzh, gä-\ *n* [F, fr. *gaver* to stuff, force-feed, fr. MF dial. (Picardy) *gave* gullet, crop] (1889) **:** introduction of material into the stomach by a tube

gave *past of* GIVE

[1]**gav·el** \ˈga-vəl\ *n* [ME, fr. OE *gafol;* akin to OE *giefan* to give] (bef. 12c) **:** rent or tribute in medieval England

[2]**gavel** *n* [origin unknown] (1835) **:** a mallet used (as by a presiding officer or auctioneer) for commanding attention or confirming an action (as a vote or sale)

[3]**gavel** *vt* **-eled** *or* **-elled; -el·ing** *or* **-el·ling** \ˈgav-liŋ, ˈga-və-\ (1925) **:** to bring or force by use of a gavel ⟨~*ed* the audience to silence⟩

gav·el·kind \ˈga-vəl-ˌkīnd\ *n* [ME *gavelkynde,* fr. [1]*gavel* + *kinde* kind] (14c) **:** a tenure of land existing chiefly in Kent from Anglo-Saxon times until 1925 and providing for division of an intestate's estate equally among the sons or other heirs

gavel–to–gavel *adj* (1968) **:** extending from the beginning to the end of a meeting or session ⟨~ television coverage⟩

ga·vi·al \ˈgā-vē-əl\ *n* [F, modif. of Bengali *ghāṛiyal* or Hindi *ghaṛyal* — more at GHARIAL] (ca. 1825) **:** GHARIAL

ga·votte \gə-ˈvät\ *n* [F, fr. MF, fr. Old Occitan *gavato,* fr. *gavot* Alpine dweller] (1696) **1 :** a dance of French peasant origin marked by the raising rather than sliding of the feet **2 :** a tune for the gavotte in moderately quick 4/4 time — **gavotte** *vi*

Ga·wain \gə-ˈwān, ˈgä-ˌwān, ˈgau̇-ən\ *n* (14c) **:** a knight of the Round Table and nephew of King Arthur

[1]**gawk** \ˈgȯk\ *n* [prob. fr. E dial. *gawk* left-handed] (1757) **:** a clumsy stupid person **:** LOUT

[2]**gawk** *vi* [perh. alter. of obs. *gaw* to stare] (1785) **:** to gape or stare stupidly — **gawk·er** *n*

gawk·ish \ˈgȯ-kish\ *adj* (1840) **:** GAWKY — **gawk·ish·ly** *adv* — **gawk·ish·ness** *n*

gawky \ˈgȯ-kē\ *adj* **gawk·i·er; -est** (1759) **:** AWKWARD, CLUMSY ⟨a ~ adolescent⟩ — **gawk·i·ly** \-kə-lē\ *adv* — **gawk·i·ness** *n* — **gawky** *n*

gawp \ˈgȯp, ˈgäp\ *vi* [E dial. *gawp* to yawn, gape, fr. obs. *galp,* fr. ME] (1855) *chiefly Brit* **:** GAWK — **gawp·er** \ˈgȯ-pər, ˈgä-\ *n*

[1]**gay** \ˈgā\ *adj* [ME, fr. AF *gai,* of Gmc origin; akin to OHG *gāhi* quick, sudden] (14c) **1 a :** happily excited **:** MERRY ⟨in a ~ mood⟩ **b :** keenly alive and exuberant **:** having or inducing high spirits ⟨a bird's ~ spring song⟩ **2 a :** BRIGHT, LIVELY ⟨~ sunny meadows⟩ **b :** brilliant in color **3 :** given to social pleasures; *also* **:** LICENTIOUS **4 a :** HOMOSEXUAL ⟨~ men⟩ **b :** of, relating to, or used by homosexuals ⟨the ~ rights movement⟩ ⟨a ~ bar⟩ *syn* see LIVELY — **gay** *adv* — **gay·ness** *n*

[2]**gay** *n* (1953) **:** HOMOSEXUAL; *esp* **:** a homosexual male

gay·dar \ˈgā-ˌdär\ *n* [blend of *gay* and *radar*] (1982) *slang* **:** the ability to recognize homosexuals through observation or intuition

gayety, gayly *var of* GAIETY, GAILY

gaz *abbr* gazette

ga·za·nia \gə-ˈzā-nē-ə, -nyə\ *n* [NL, fr. Theodorus *Gaza* †1478 Greek scholar] (1813) **:** any of a genus (*Gazania*) of So. African composite herbs often cultivated for their brightly colored flowers

ga·zar \gə-ˈzär\ *n* [origin unknown] (1967) **:** a silk organza

[1]**gaze** \ˈgāz\ *vi* **gazed; gaz·ing** [ME] (14c) **:** to fix the eyes in a steady intent look often with eagerness or studious attention — **gaz·er** *n*

[2]**gaze** *n* (1566) **:** a fixed intent look

ga·ze·bo \gə-ˈzē-(ˌ)bō *also* -ˈzā-\ *n, pl* **-bos** [perh. fr. [1]*gaze* + L *-ebo* (as in *videbo* I shall see)] (1752) **1 :** BELVEDERE **2 :** a freestanding roofed structure usu. open on the sides

gaze·hound \ˈgāz-ˌhau̇nd\ *n* (1610) **:** SIGHTHOUND

ga·zelle \gə-ˈzel\ *n, pl* **gazelles** *also* **gazelle** [F, fr. MF, fr. Ar *ghazāl*] (1600) **:** any of numerous small to medium graceful and swift African and Asian antelopes (*Gazella* and related genera)

[1]**ga·zette** \gə-ˈzet\ *n* [F, fr. It *gazetta*] (ca. 1598) **1 :** NEWSPAPER **2 :** an official journal **3** *Brit* **:** an announcement in an official gazette

[2]**gazette** *vt* **ga·zett·ed; ga·zett·ing** (1678) **1** *chiefly Brit* **:** to announce or publish in a gazette **2** *Brit* **:** to announce the appointment or status of in an official gazette

gaz·et·teer \ˌga-zə-ˈtir\ *n* (1611) **1** *archaic* **:** JOURNALIST, PUBLICIST **2** [*The Gazetteer's: or, Newsman's Interpreter,* a geographical index edited by Laurence Echard] : a geographical dictionary; *also* : a book in which a subject is treated esp. in regard to geographic distribution and regional specialization

ga·zil·lion \gə-ˈzil-yən\ *n* [alter. of *zillion*] (1977) : ZILLION — **gazil·lion** *adj* — **ga·zil·lionth** \-yən(t)th\ *adj*

ga·zil·lion·aire \gə-ˌzil-yə-ˈner, -ˈzil-yə-ˌ\ *n* (1980) : ZILLIONAIRE

gazogene *var of* GASOGENE

ga·zoo \gə-ˈzü\ *n, pl* **gazoos** [origin unknown] (1965) *slang* : WAZOO

gaz·pa·cho \gəz-ˈpä-(ˌ)chō, gə-ˈspä-\ *n, pl* **-chos** [Sp] (1775) : a spicy soup that is usu. made from chopped raw vegetables (as tomato, onion, pepper, and cucumber) and that is served cold

[1]**GB** \ˌjē-ˈbē\ *n* [code name] (1961) : SARIN

[2]**GB** *abbr* **1** gigabyte **2** Great Britain

GC *abbr* gas chromatograph; gas chromatography

GCA *abbr* ground-controlled approach

GCB *abbr* Knight Grand Cross of the Bath

GCD *abbr* greatest common divisor

GCF *abbr* greatest common factor

G clef *n* (1596) : TREBLE CLEF

gd *abbr* good

Gd *symbol* gadolinium

GDP *abbr* gross domestic product

GDR *abbr* German Democratic Republic

ge *abbr* gilt edges

Ge *symbol* germanium

[1]**gear** \ˈgir\ *n* [ME *gere,* fr. ON *gervi, gǫrvi;* akin to OE *gearwe* equipment, clothing, *gearu* ready — more at YARE] (14c) **1 a** : CLOTHING, GARMENTS **b** : movable property : GOODS **2** : EQUIPMENT, PARAPHERNALIA ⟨fishing ~⟩ **3 a** : the rigging of a ship or boat **b** : the harness esp. of horses **4** *dial chiefly Brit* : absurd talk : NONSENSE **5** *dial chiefly Brit* : DOINGS **6 a** (1) : a mechanism that performs a specific function in a complete machine ⟨steering ~⟩ (2) : a toothed wheel (3) : working relation, position, order, or adjustment ⟨got her career in ~⟩ (4) : a level or pace of functioning ⟨kicked their performance into high ~⟩ **b** : one of two or more adjustments of a transmission (as of a bicycle or motor vehicle) that determine mechanical advantage, relative speed, and direction of travel — **gear·less** \-ləs\ *adj*

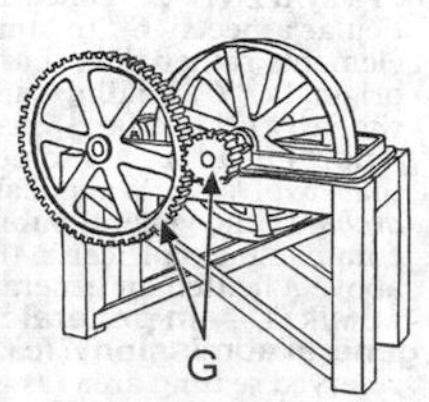

G gear 6a(2)

[2]**gear** *vt* (1851) **1 a** : to provide (as machinery) with gearing **b** : to connect by gearing **2 a** : to make ready for effective operation **b** : to adjust so as to match, blend with, or satisfy something ⟨~*ing* wages to productivity⟩ ~ *vi* **1 a** *Brit, of machinery* : to be in gear : MESH **b** : SHIFT 1c ⟨~ down⟩ **2** : to become adjusted so as to match, blend, or harmonize

gear·box \ˈgir-ˌbäks\ *n* (1887) **1** : GEARING 2 **2** : TRANSMISSION 3

gear·change \-ˌchānj\ *n* (1927) *Brit* : GEARSHIFT

gear·head \ˈgir-ˌhed\ *n* (1974) : a person who pursues mechanical or technological interests (as in automobiles or computers)

gear·ing \ˈgir-iŋ\ *n* (1833) **1** : the act or process of providing or fitting with gears **2** : the parts by which motion is transmitted from one portion of machinery to another; *esp* : a train of gears

gear·shift \ˈgir-ˌshift\ *n* (ca. 1924) : a mechanism by which the transmission gears in a power-transmission system are engaged and disengaged; *also* : a lever for controlling such a mechanism

gear up *vi* (1943) : to get ready ⟨are *gearing up* for the big game⟩

gear·wheel \ˈgir-ˌhwēl, -ˌwēl\ *n* (ca. 1874) : GEAR 6a(2)

Geat \ˈgēt, ˈgā-ət, *OE* ˈyaət\ *n* [OE *Gēat*] (bef. 12c) : a member of a Scandinavian people of southern Sweden to which the legendary hero Beowulf belonged — **Geat·ish** \ˈgē-tish, ˈgā-, *OE* ˈyaə-\ *adj*

gecko \ˈge-(ˌ)kō\ *n, pl* **geck·os** *also* **geck·oes** [perh. fr. Malay dial. *geʔkok*] (1774) : any of numerous small chiefly tropical and nocturnal insectivorous lizards (family Gekkonidae)

[1]**GED** \ˌjē-ˌē-ˈdē\ *service mark* — used for educational testing services designed to provide a high school equivalency credential

[2]**GED** *abbr* general equivalency diploma

ge·dank·en·ex·per·i·ment \gə-ˈdäŋ-kən-ik-ˌsper-ə-mənt *also* -ˌspir-\ *n* [G, fr. *Gedanke* thought + *Experiment* experiment] (1941) : an experiment carried out in thought only

[1]**gee** \ˈjē\ *vb* [origin unknown] *vb imper* (1628) — used as a direction to turn to the right or move ahead; compare [5]HAW ~ *vi* **geed; gee·ing** : to turn to the right side

[2]**gee** *n* (1818) **1** : the letter *g* **2** [grand] *slang* : a thousand dollars

[3]**gee** *interj* [euphemism for *Jesus*] (1884) — used as an introductory expletive or to express surprise or enthusiasm

geegaw *var of* GEWGAW

geek \ˈgēk\ *n* [prob. fr. E dial. *geek, geck* fool, fr. LG *geck,* fr. MLG] (1914) **1** : a carnival performer often billed as a wild man whose act usu. includes biting the head off a live chicken or snake **2** : a person often of an intellectual bent who is disliked **3** : an enthusiast or expert esp. in a technological field or activity ⟨computer ~⟩ — **geek·dom** \ˈgēk-dəm\ *n* — **geek·i·ness** *n* — **geeky** \ˈgē-kē\ *adj*

geeked \ˈgēkt\ *adj* (1984) *slang* : filled with excitement or enthusiasm

geese *pl of* GOOSE

gee–whiz \ˈjē-ˌhwiz, -ˌwiz\ *adj* (1934) **1** : designed to arouse wonder or excitement or to amplify the merits or significance of something esp. by the use of clever or sensational language ⟨play-by-play specialists who wallow in ~ banality —Jack Gould⟩ **2** : marked by spectacular or astonishing qualities or achievement ⟨~ technology⟩ **3** : characterized by wide-eyed enthusiasm, excitement, and wonder

gee whiz \(ˌ)jē-ˈ\ *interj* (1876) : [3]GEE

geez *var of* JEEZ

Ge·ez \gē-ˈez; ˈgē-(ˌ)ez, ˈgā-\ *n* [Geez *gəʿəz*] (1790) : a Semitic language formerly spoken in northern highland Ethiopia and still used as the liturgical language of the Christian church in Ethiopia

gee·zer \ˈgē-zər\ *n* [prob. alter. of Sc *guiser* one in disguise] (1884) : a queer, odd, or eccentric person — used esp. of elderly men — **gee·zer·hood** \-ˌhu̇d\ *n*

ge·fil·te fish \gə-ˈfil-tə-\ *n* [Yiddish, lit., stuffed fish] (1892) : balls or cakes of seasoned minced fish usu. simmered in a fish stock or baked in a tomato sauce

ge·gen·schein \ˈgā-gən-ˌshīn\ *n, often cap* [G, fr. *gegen* against, counter- + *Schein* shine] (1877) : a faint light about 20° across on the celestial sphere opposite the sun probably caused by backscatter of sunlight by solar-system dust

Ge·hen·na \gi-ˈhe-nə\ *n* [LL, fr. Gk *Geenna,* fr. Heb *Gē' Hinnōm,* lit., valley of Hinnom] (ca. 1534) **1** : a place or state of misery **2** : HELL 1a(2)

Gei·ger counter \ˈgī-gər-\ *n* [Hans *Geiger* †1945 Ger. physicist] (1924) : an instrument for detecting the presence and intensity of radiations (as cosmic rays or particles from a radioactive substance) by means of their ionizing effect on an enclosed gas which results in a pulse that is amplified and fed to a device giving a visible or audible indication

Gei·ger–Mül·ler counter \-ˈmyü-lər, -ˈmi-, -ˈmə-\ *n* [W. *Müller,* 20th cent. Ger. physicist] (1932) : GEIGER COUNTER

gei·sha \ˈgā-shə, *also* ˈgē-\ *n, pl* **geisha** *or* **geishas** [Jp, fr. *gei* art + *-sha* person] (1881) : a Japanese girl or woman who is trained to provide entertaining and lighthearted company esp. for a man or a group of men

[1]**gel** \ˈjel\ *n* [*gelatin*] (1899) **1** : a colloid in a more solid form than a sol; *broadly* : JELLY 2 **2** : a thin colored transparent sheet used over a stage light to color it **3** : a gelatinous preparation used in styling hair

[2]**gel** *vi* **gelled; gel·ling** (1917) **1** : to change into or take on the form of a gel : SET **2** : JELL 2 — **gel·able** \ˈje-lə-bəl\ *adj*

gel·a·da baboon \ˈje-lə-də-, ˈge-; jə-ˈlä-də-\ *n* [Amharic *č̣ällada*] (1871) : a large long-haired chiefly herbivorous monkey (*Theropithecus gelada*) of Ethiopia that feeds esp. on grasses and resembles the related baboon — called also *gelada*

ge·län·de·sprung \gə-ˈlen-də-ˌshpru̇ŋ, -ˌspru̇ŋ\ *n* [G, fr. *Gelände* open fields + *Sprung* jump] (1931) : a jump usu. over an obstacle in skiing that is made from a low crouch with the aid of both ski poles

gel·ate \ˈje-ˌlāt\ *vi* **gel·at·ed; gel·at·ing** (1915) : GEL

gel·a·tin *also* **gel·a·tine** \ˈje-lə-tən\ *n* [F *gélatine* edible jelly, gelatin, fr. It *gelatina,* fr. *gelato,* pp. of *gelare* to freeze, fr. L — more at COLD] (1800) **1** : glutinous material obtained from animal tissues by boiling; *esp* : a colloidal protein used as a food, in photography, and in medicine **2 a** : any of various substances (as agar) resembling gelatin **b** : an edible jelly made with gelatin **3** : GEL 2

ge·la·ti·ni·za·tion \jə-ˌla-tə-nə-ˈzā-shən, ˌje-lə-tə-\ *n* (1843) : the process of converting into a gelatinous form or into a jelly — **ge·la·ti·nize** \jə-ˈla-tə-ˌnīz, ˈje-lə-tə-\ *vb*

ge·lat·i·nous \jə-ˈlat-nəs, -ˈla-tə-nəs\ *adj* (1712) **1** : resembling gelatin or jelly : VISCOUS ⟨a ~ precipitate⟩ **2** : of, relating to, or containing gelatin — **ge·lat·i·nous·ly** *adv* — **ge·lat·i·nous·ness** *n*

[1]**ge·la·tion** \ji-ˈlā-shən\ *n* [L *gelation-, gelatio,* fr. *gelare*] (1854) : the action or process of freezing

[2]**gel·ation** \je-ˈlā-shən\ *n* [[1]*gel* + *-ation*] (1915) : the formation of a gel from a sol

ge·la·to \je-ˈlä-(ˌ)tō\ *n, pl* **-ti** \-tē\ *also* **-tos** [It, lit., frozen] (1929) : a soft rich ice cream containing little or no air

gel·cap \ˈjel-ˌkap\ *n* (1986) : a capsule-shaped tablet coated with gelatin for easy swallowing

[1]**geld** \ˈgeld\ *vt* [ME, fr. ON *gelda;* akin to OE *gelde* sterile] (14c) **1** : CASTRATE **2** : to deprive of a natural or essential part ⟨the legislation was pretty much ~*ed* by the time it was passed⟩

[2]**geld** *n* [OE *gield, geld* service, tribute; akin to OE *gieldan* to pay, yield — more at YIELD] (1610) : the crown tax paid under Anglo-Saxon and Norman kings

geld·ing \ˈgel-diŋ\ *n* [ME, fr. ON *geldingr,* fr. *gelda*] (14c) **1** : a castrated animal; *specif* : a castrated male horse **2** *archaic* : EUNUCH

ge·lée \zhə-ˈlā\ *n* [F, jelly, fr. MF — more at JELLY] (1966) : a cosmetic gel

gel electrophoresis *n* (1955) : electrophoresis in which molecules (as proteins and nucleic acids) migrate through a gel and esp. a polyacrylamide gel and separate into bands according to size

gel ice *n* (1983) : a gel matrix in a solution that is frozen in a pack esp. for use in preserving perishable products

gel·id \ˈje-ləd\ *adj* [L *gelidus,* fr. *gelu* frost, cold — more at COLD] (1599) : extremely cold : ICY ⟨~ water⟩ ⟨a man of ~ reserve —*New Yorker*⟩ — **ge·lid·i·ty** \jə-ˈli-də-tē, je-\ *n* — **gel·id·ly** \ˈje-ləd-lē\ *adv*

gel·ig·nite \ˈje-lig-ˌnīt\ *n* [*gel*atin + L *ign*is fire + E *-ite* — more at IGNEOUS] (1889) : a dynamite in which the adsorbent base is largely potassium nitrate or a similar nitrate usu. with some wood pulp

gel·lant \ˈje-lənt\ *n* (1956) : a substance used to produce gelling

gel permeation chromatography *n* (1966) : chromatography in which macromolecules (as polymers) in a solution are separated by size on a column packed with a gel (as of polystyrene)

gelt \ˈgelt\ *n* [D & G *geld* & Yiddish *gelt;* all akin to OE *geld* [2]geld] (ca. 1529) : MONEY

[1]**gem** \ˈjem\ *n* [ME *gemme,* fr. AF, fr. L *gemma* bud, gem] (14c) **1 a** : JEWEL **b** : a precious or sometimes semiprecious stone cut and polished for ornament **2 a** : something prized esp. for great beauty or perfection **b** : a highly prized or well-beloved person **3** : MUFFIN

[2]**gem** *vt* **gemmed; gem·ming** (1610) : to adorn with or as if with gems

GEM *abbr* ground-effect machine

Ge·ma·ra \gə-ˈmär-ə, -ˈmȯr-\ *n* [Aram *gĕmārā* completion] (1613) : a commentary on the Mishnah forming the second part of the Talmud — **Ge·ma·ric** \-ik\ *adj* — **Ge·ma·rist** \-ist\ *n*

ge·mein·schaft \gə-ˈmīn-ˌshäft\ *n* [G, community, fr. *gemein* common, general (fr. OHG *gimeini*) + *-schaft* -ship — more at MEAN] (1937) : a spontaneously arising organic social relationship characterized by strong reciprocal bonds of sentiment and kinship within a common tradition; *also* : a community or society characterized by this relationship — compare GESELLSCHAFT

gem·fi·bro·zil \jem-ˈfi-brə-(ˌ)zil, -ˈfi-\ *n* [origin unknown] (1976) : a drug $C_{15}H_{22}O_3$ that regulates blood serum lipids and is used esp. to lower the levels of triglycerides and increase the levels of HDLs

\ə\ abut \ᵊ\ kitten, F table \ər\ further \a\ ash \ā\ ace \ä\ mop, mar
\au̇\ out \ch\ chin \e\ bet \ē\ easy \g\ go \i\ hit \ī\ ice \j\ job
\ŋ\ sing \ō\ go \ȯ\ law \ȯi\ boy \th\ thin \t͟h\ the \ü\ loot \u̇\ foot
\y\ yet \zh\ vision, beige \k̲, ⁿ, œ, ue, ʸ\ see Guide to Pronunciation

gem·i·nal \ˈje-mə-nᵊl\ *adj* [L *geminus* twin] (1967) : relating to or characterized by two usu. similar substituents on the same atom — **gem·i·nal·ly** \-nᵊl-ē\ *adv*

[1]**gem·i·nate** \ˈje-mə-nət, -ˌnāt\ *adj* [L *geminatus,* pp. of *geminare* to double, fr. *geminus* twin] (15c) **1 :** arranged in pairs : DUPLICATE **2 :** being a sequence of identical speech sounds (as in *meanness* or Italian *notte* \ˈnȯt-te\ "night")

[2]**gem·i·nate** \-ˌnāt\ *vb* **-nat·ed; -nat·ing** *vt* (ca. 1637) : to make geminate ~ *vi* : to be or become geminate — **gem·i·na·tion** \ˌje-mə-ˈnā-shən\ *n*

Gem·i·ni \ˈje-mə-(ˌ)nē, -ˌnī; ˈge-mə-ˌnē\ *n pl but sing in constr* [L (gen. *Geminorum*), lit., the twins (Castor and Pollux)] (14c) **1 :** the third zodiacal constellation pictorially represented as the twins Castor and Pollux sitting together and located on the opposite side of the Milky Way from Taurus and Orion **2 a :** the third sign of the zodiac in astrology — see ZODIAC table **b :** one born under the sign of Gemini

gem·ma \ˈje-mə\ *n, pl* **gem·mae** \-ˌmē\ [L] (ca. 1741) : BUD; *broadly* : an asexual reproductive body that becomes detached from a parent plant

gem·ma·tion \je-ˈmā-shən\ *n* (ca. 1839) : reproduction by gemmae

gem·mule \ˈjem-(ˌ)yül\ *n* [F, fr. L *gemmula,* dim. of *gemma*] (ca. 1828) : a small bud: **a :** a theoretical particle proposed in the theory of pangenesis that is shed by a somatic cell and contains all the information necessary to reproduce that cell type (as in an offspring) **b :** a reproductive bud produced by freshwater and some marine sponges that consists of a usu. hardened aggregate of cells

gem·my \ˈje-mē\ *adj* (15c) **1 :** having the characteristics desired in a gemstone **2 :** BRIGHT, GLITTERING

gem·ol·o·gist *also* **gem·mol·o·gist** \je-ˈmä-lə-jist, jə-\ *n* (1931) : a specialist in gems; *specif* : one who appraises gems

gem·ol·o·gy *or* **gem·mol·o·gy** \-jē\ *n* [L *gemma* gem] (1811) : the science of gems — **gem·olog·i·cal** \ˌje-mə-ˈlä-ji-kəl\ *adj*

ge·mot *or* **ge·mote** \gə-ˈmōt, yə-\ *n* [OE *gemōt,* fr. *ge-,* perfective prefix + *mōt* assembly — more at CO-, MOOT] (bef. 12c) : a judicial or legislative assembly in Anglo-Saxon England

gems·bok \ˈgemz-ˌbäk\ *n* [Afrik, fr. G *Gemsbock* male chamois, fr. *Gems* chamois + *Bock* male goat] (1777) : a large and strikingly marked oryx (*Oryx gazella*) formerly abundant in southern Africa

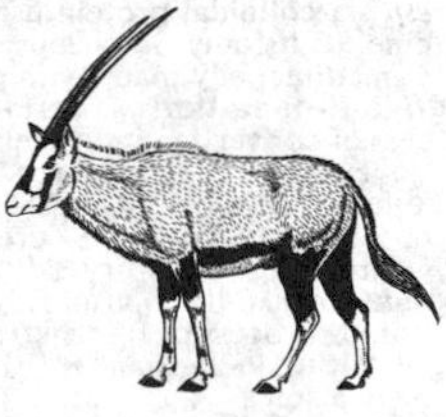

gemsbok

gem·stone \ˈjem-ˌstōn\ *n* (bef. 12c) : a mineral or petrified material that when cut and polished can be used in jewelry

ge·müt·lich \gə-ˈmu̇et-lik, -ˈmüt-lik\ *adj* [G, fr. MHG *gemüetlich* pleasant, fr. *gemüete* mentality, mind] (1852) : agreeably pleasant : COMFORTABLE

ge·müt·lich·keit \gə-ˈmu̇et-lik-ˌkīt, -ˈmüt-lik-\ *n* [G, fr. *gemütlich* + *-keit,* alter. of *-heit* -hood] (1892) : CORDIALITY, FRIENDLINESS

[1]**gen** \ˈjen\ *n* [perh. fr. *general* information] (1940) *chiefly Brit* : INFORMATION 2a

[2]**gen** *abbr* **1** general **2** genitive **3** genus

Gen *abbr* Genesis

gen- *or* **geno-** *comb form* [Gk *genos* birth, race, kind — more at KIN] **1 :** offspring : race ⟨*gen*ocide⟩ **2 :** genus : kind ⟨*geno*type⟩

-gen *also* **-gene** *n comb form* [F *-gène,* fr. Gk *-genēs* born; akin to Gk *genos* birth] **1 :** producer ⟨andro*gen*⟩ **2 :** one that is (so) produced ⟨culti*gen*⟩

Gen AF *abbr* general of the air force

gen·darme \ˈzhän-ˌdärm *also* ˈjän-\ *n* [F, fr. MF, back-formation fr. *gensdarmes,* pl. of *gent d'armes,* lit., armed people] (1793) **1 :** a member of a body of soldiers esp. in France serving as an armed police force for the maintenance of public order **2 :** POLICE OFFICER

gen·dar·mer·ie *or* **gen·dar·mery** \zhän-ˈdär-mə-rē, jän-\ *n, pl* **-mer·ies** [F *gendarmerie,* fr. *gendarme*] (1795) : a body of gendarmes

[1]**gen·der** \ˈjen-dər\ *n* [ME *gendre,* fr. AF *genre, gendre,* fr. L *gener-, genus* birth, race, kind, gender — more at KIN] (14c) **1 a :** a subclass within a grammatical class (as noun, pronoun, adjective, or verb) of a language that is partly arbitrary but also partly based on distinguishable characteristics (as shape, social rank, manner of existence, or sex) and that determines agreement with and selection of other words or grammatical forms **b :** membership of a word or a grammatical form in such a subclass **c :** an inflectional form showing membership in such a subclass **2 a :** SEX ⟨the feminine ~⟩ **b :** the behavioral, cultural, or psychological traits typically associated with one sex

[2]**gender** *vb* **gen·dered; gen·der·ing** \-d(ə-)riŋ\ [ME *gendren,* fr. AF *gendrer,* fr. L *generare* — more at GENERATE] (14c) : ENGENDER

gender bender *n* (1980) : a person who dresses and behaves like a member of the opposite sex — **gender–bending** *adj or n*

gendered *adj* (1972) : reflecting the experience, prejudices, or orientations of one sex more than the other ⟨~ language⟩; *also* : reflecting or involving gender differences or stereotypical gender roles

gen·der·less \ˈjen-dər-ləs\ *adj* (ca. 1879) **1 :** lacking qualities typically associated with either sex **2 :** suitable to or for either sex; *also* : not reflective of the experiences, prejudices, or orientations of one sex more than the other ⟨~ language⟩ — **gen·der·less·ness** *n*

gene \ˈjēn\ *n* [G *Gen,* short for *Pangen,* fr. *pan-* + *-gen*] (1911) : a specific sequence of nucleotides in DNA or RNA that is located usu. on a chromosome and that is the functional unit of inheritance controlling the transmission and expression of one or more traits by specifying the structure of a particular polypeptide and esp. a protein or controlling the function of other genetic material

ge·ne·al·o·gist \ˌjē-nē-ˈä-lə-jist *also* -ˈa-lə- *also* ˌje-nē-\ *n* (1605) : a person who traces or studies the descent of persons or families

ge·ne·al·o·gy \-jē\ *n, pl* **-gies** [ME *genealogie,* fr. AF, fr. LL *genealogia,* fr. Gk, fr. *genea* race, family + *-logia* -logy; akin to Gk *genos* race] (14c) **1 :** an account of the descent of a person, family, or group from an ancestor or from older forms **2 :** regular descent of a person, family, or group of organisms from a progenitor or older form : PEDIGREE **3 :** the study of family pedigrees **4 :** an account of the origin and historical development of something — **ge·ne·a·log·i·cal** \ˌjē-nē-ə-ˈlä-ji-kəl, ˌje-nē-\ *adj* — **ge·ne·a·log·i·cal·ly** \-k(ə-)lē\ *adv*

gene conversion *n* (1955) : a genetic process that involves nonreciprocal meiotic recombination in heterozygotes in which a mismatched DNA sequence from one heteroduplex DNA strand is replaced with a sequence complementary to the other strand resulting in aberrant gametic ratios (as 3:1) and that is observed esp. in ascomycetous fungi

gene flow *n* (1947) : the passage and establishment of genes typical of one breeding population into the gene pool of another

gene frequency *n* (1930) : the ratio of the number of a specified allele in a population to the total of all alleles at its genetic locus

gene mutation *n* (1925) : mutation due to fundamental intramolecular reorganization of a gene — compare POINT MUTATION

gene pool *n* (1946) : the collection of genes in an interbreeding population that includes each gene at a certain frequency in relation to its alleles : the genetic information of a population of interbreeding organisms ⟨the human *gene pool*⟩

genera *pl of* GENUS

gen·er·a·ble \ˈjen-rə-bəl, ˈje-nə-\ *adj* (15c) : capable of being generated

[1]**gen·er·al** \ˈjen-rəl, ˈje-nə-\ *adj* [ME, fr. AF, fr. L *generalis,* fr. *gener-, genus* kind, class — more at KIN] (14c) **1 :** involving, applicable to, or affecting the whole **2 :** involving, relating to, or applicable to every member of a class, kind, or group ⟨the ~ equation of a straight line⟩ **3 :** not confined by specialization or careful limitation **4 :** belonging to the common nature of a group of like individuals : GENERIC **5 a :** applicable to or characteristic of the majority of individuals involved : PREVALENT **b :** concerned or dealing with universal rather than particular aspects **6 :** relating to, determined by, or concerned with main elements rather than limited details ⟨bearing a ~ resemblance to the original⟩ **7 :** holding superior rank or taking precedence over others similarly titled ⟨the ~ manager⟩

[2]**general** *n* (14c) **1 :** something (as a concept, principle, or statement) that involves or is applicable to the whole **2 :** SUPERIOR GENERAL **3** *archaic* : the general public : PEOPLE **4 a :** GENERAL OFFICER **b :** a commissioned officer in the army, air force, or marine corps who ranks above a lieutenant general and whose insignia is four stars — compare ADMIRAL — **in general :** for the most part : GENERALLY

general admission *n* (ca. 1949) : a fee paid for admission to a usu. unreserved seating area (as in an auditorium or stadium)

general agent *n* (1812) **1 :** one employed to transact generally all legal business entrusted by a principal **2 :** an insurance company agent working within a specified area

general anesthesia *n* (1881) : anesthesia affecting the entire body and accompanied by loss of consciousness — **general anesthetic** *n*

general assembly *n* (ca. 1572) **1 :** the highest governing body in a religious denomination (as the United Presbyterian Church) **2 :** a legislative assembly; *esp* : a U.S. state legislature **3** *cap G&A* : the supreme deliberative body of the United Nations

general aviation *n* (1966) : the operation of civilian aircraft not under the control of a common carrier; *also* : such aircraft collectively

General Court *n* (1628) : a legislative assembly; *specif* : the state legislature in Massachusetts and New Hampshire

general delivery *n* (1846) : a department of a post office that handles the delivery of mail at a post office window to persons who call for it

general election *n* (ca. 1687) : an election usu. held at regular intervals in which candidates are elected in all or most constituencies of a nation or state

gen·er·al·i·sa·tion, gen·er·al·ise, gen·er·al·ised *Brit var of* GENERALIZATION, GENERALIZE, GENERALIZED

gen·er·a·lis·si·mo \ˌjen-rə-ˈli-sə-ˌmō, ˌje-nə-\ *n, pl* **-mos** [It, fr. *generale* general] (1621) : the chief commander of an army

gen·er·al·ist \ˈjen-rə-list, ˈje-nə-\ *n* (1611) : one whose skills, interests, or habits are varied or unspecialized

gen·er·al·i·ty \ˌje-nə-ˈra-lə-tē\ *n, pl* **-ties** (15c) **1 :** the quality or state of being general **2 a :** GENERALIZATION 2 **b :** a vague or inadequate statement **3 :** the greatest part : BULK ⟨the ~ of the population⟩

gen·er·al·i·za·tion \ˌjen-rə-lə-ˈzā-shən, ˌje-nə-\ *n* (1761) **1 :** the act or process of generalizing **2 :** a general statement, law, principle, or proposition **3 :** the act or process whereby a learned response is made to a stimulus similar to but not identical with the conditioned stimulus

gen·er·al·ize \ˈjen-rə-ˌlīz, ˈje-nə-\ *vb* **-ized; -iz·ing** *vt* (ca. 1751) **1 :** to give a general form to **2 a :** to derive or induce (a general conception or principle) from particulars **b :** to draw a general conclusion from **3 :** to give general applicability to ⟨~ a law⟩; *also* : to make indefinite ~ *vi* **1 :** to form generalizations; *also* : to make vague or indefinite statements **2 :** to spread or extend throughout the body — **gen·er·al·iz·abil·i·ty** \ˌjen-rə-ˌlī-zə-ˈbi-lə-tē, ˌje-nə-\ *n* — **gen·er·al·iz·able** \-ˌlī-zə-bəl\ *adj* — **gen·er·al·iz·er** *n*

generalized *adj* (1813) : made general; *esp* : not highly differentiated biologically nor strictly adapted to a particular environment

gen·er·al·ly \ˈjen-rə-lē, ˈje-nə-, ˈje-nər-lē\ *adv* (14c) : in a general manner: as **a :** in disregard of specific instances and with regard to an overall picture ⟨~ speaking⟩ **b :** as a rule : USUALLY

general officer *n* (1681) : any of the officers in the army, air force, or marine corps above colonel — compare COMPANY OFFICER, FIELD OFFICER, FLAG OFFICER

general of the air force (1949) : a general of the highest rank in the air force whose insignia is five stars

general of the army (1945) : a general of the highest rank in the army whose insignia is five stars

general paresis *n* (1874) : insanity caused by syphilitic alteration of the brain that leads to dementia and paralysis — called also *general paralysis of the insane*

general partner *n* (1822) : a partner whose liability for partnership debts and obligations is unlimited

general practitioner *n* (1810) : a physician or veterinarian whose practice is not limited to a specialty; *broadly* : GENERALIST

general–purpose *adj* (1894) : suitable to be used for two or more basic purposes

general quarters *n pl* (1850) : a condition of maximum readiness of a warship for action

general relativity *n* (1916) : RELATIVITY 3b

general semantics *n pl but sing or pl in constr* (1933) : a doctrine and educational discipline intended to improve habits of response of human beings to their environment and one another esp. by training in the more critical use of words and other symbols

gen•er•al•ship \ˈjen-rəl-ˌship, ˈje-nə-\ *n* (1610) **1 :** office or tenure of office of a general **2 :** LEADERSHIP **3 :** military skill in a high commander

general store *n* (1835) **:** a retail store located usu. in a small or rural community that carries a wide variety of goods including groceries but is not divided into departments

general theory of relativity (1921) **:** RELATIVITY 3b

general will *n* (1792) **:** the collective will of a community that is the embodiment or expression of its common interest

gen•er•ate \ˈje-nə-ˌrāt\ *vt* **-at•ed; -at•ing** [L *generatus,* pp. of *generare,* fr. *gener-, genus* descent, birth — more at KIN] (1509) **1 :** to bring into existence: as **a :** PROCREATE, BEGET **b :** to originate by a vital, chemical, or physical process **:** PRODUCE ⟨~ electricity⟩ **2 :** to be the cause of (a situation, action, or state of mind) ⟨these stories . . . ~ a good deal of psychological suspense —*Atlantic*⟩ **3 :** to define or originate (as a mathematical or linguistic set or structure) by the application of one or more rules or operations; *esp* **:** to trace out (as a curve) by a moving point or trace out (as a surface) by a moving curve

gen•er•a•tion \ˌje-nə-ˈrā-shən\ *n* (14c) **1 a :** a body of living beings constituting a single step in the line of descent from an ancestor **b :** a group of individuals born and living contemporaneously **c :** a group of individuals having contemporaneously a status (as that of students in a school) which each one holds only for a limited period **d :** a type or class of objects usu. developed from an earlier type ⟨first of the . . . new ~ of powerful supersonic fighters —Kenneth Koyen⟩ **2 a :** the action or process of producing offspring **:** PROCREATION **b :** the process of coming or bringing into being ⟨~ of income⟩ **c :** origination by a generating process **:** PRODUCTION; *esp* **:** formation of a geometric figure by motion of another **3 :** the average span of time between the birth of parents and that of their offspring — **gen•er•a•tion•al** \-shnəl, -shə-nᵊl\ *adj* — **gen•er•a•tion•al•ly** \-shnə-lē, shə-nᵊl-ē\ *adv*

Generation X *n* (1989) **:** the generation of Americans born in the 1960s and 1970s — **Generation Xer** \-ˈek-sər\ *n*

Generation Y *n* (1992) **:** the generation of Americans born in the 1980s and 1990s **:** the millennials

gen•er•a•tive \ˈjen-rə-tiv, ˈje-nə-, -ˌrā-tiv\ *adj* (14c) **:** having the power or function of generating, originating, producing, or reproducing

generative cell *n* (1868) **:** a sexual reproductive cell **:** GAMETE

generative grammar *usu* ˈje-nə-rə-tiv-\ *n* (1959) **1 :** a description in the form of a set of rules for producing the grammatical sentences of a language **2 :** TRANSFORMATIONAL GRAMMAR

generative nucleus *n* (ca. 1892) **:** the one of the two nuclei resulting from the first division in the pollen grain of a seed plant that gives rise to sperm nuclei — compare TUBE NUCLEUS

generative semantics *usu* ˈje-nə-rə-tiv-\ *n pl but usu sing in constr* (1970) **:** a description of a language emphasizing a semantic deep structure that is logical in form, that provides syntactic structure, and that is related to surface structure by transformations

gen•er•a•tor \ˈje-nə-ˌrā-tər\ *n* (1646) **1 :** one that generates: as **a :** an apparatus in which vapor or gas is formed **b :** a machine by which mechanical energy is changed into electrical energy **2 :** a mathematical entity that when subjected to one or more operations yields another mathematical entity or its elements; *specif* **:** GENERATRIX

gen•er•a•trix \ˌje-nə-ˈrā-triks\ *n, pl* **-er•a•tri•ces** \-trə-ˌsēz, -ə-rə-ˈtrī-(ˌ)sēz\ (1840) **:** a point, line, or surface whose motion generates a line, surface, or solid

[1]**ge•ner•ic** \jə-ˈner-ik, -ˈne-rik\ *adj* [F *générique,* fr. L *gener-, genus* birth, kind, class] (1676) **1 a :** relating to or characteristic of a whole group or class **:** GENERAL **b :** being or having a nonproprietary name ⟨~ drugs⟩ **c :** having no particularly distinctive quality or application ⟨~ restaurants⟩ **2 :** relating to or having the rank of a biological genus — **ge•ner•i•cal•ly** \-i-k(ə-)lē\ *adv* — **ge•ner•ic•ness** *n*

[2]**generic** *n* (1967) **:** a generic product (as a drug)

gen•er•os•i•ty \ˌje-nə-ˈrä-sə-tē, -ˈräs-tē\ *n, pl* **-ties** (1566) **1 a :** the quality or fact of being generous **b :** a generous act **2 :** ABUNDANCE ⟨great ~ of spirit⟩

gen•er•ous \ˈjen-rəs, ˈje-nə-\ *adj* [MF or L; MF *genereus,* fr. L *generosus,* fr. *gener-, genus*] (1583) **1** *archaic* **:** HIGHBORN **2 a :** characterized by a noble or kindly spirit **:** MAGNANIMOUS **b :** liberal in giving ⟨a ~ benefactor⟩ **c :** marked by abundance or ample proportions ⟨wide overhangs and ~ verandas —Lewis Mumford⟩ ***syn*** see LIBERAL — **gen•er•ous•ly** *adv* — **gen•er•ous•ness** *n*

gen•e•sis \ˈje-nə-səs\ *n, pl* **-e•ses** \-ˌsēz\ [L, fr. Gk, fr. *gignesthai* to be born — more at KIN] (ca. 1604) **:** the origin or coming into being of something ⟨the ~ of a new political movement⟩

Genesis *n* [Gk] (bef. 12c) **:** the mainly narrative first book of canonical Jewish and Christian Scriptures — see BIBLE table

gene–splic•ing \ˈjēn-ˌsplī-siŋ\ *n* (ca. 1978) **:** the process of preparing recombinant DNA

gen•et \ˈje-nət\ *n* [ME *genete,* fr. AF, ultim. fr. Ar *jarnayṭ*] (15c) **:** any of a genus (*Genetta*) of small Old World usu. carnivorous viverrid mammals related to the civets and having retractile claws, spotted or striped fur, and a ringed tail

gene therapy *n* (1971) **:** the insertion of usu. genetically altered genes into cells esp. to replace defective genes in the treatment of genetic disorders or to provide a specialized disease-fighting function — **gene therapist** *n*

ge•net•ic \jə-ˈne-tik\ *also* **ge•net•i•cal** \-ti-kəl\ *adj* [*genesis*] (1831) **1 :** relating to or determined by the origin, development, or causal antecedents of something **2 a :** of, relating to, or involving genetics **b :** of, relating to, caused by, or controlled by genes ⟨a ~ disease⟩ ⟨~ variation⟩ — **ge•net•i•cal•ly** \-ti-k(ə-)lē\ *adv*

-genetic *adj comb form* **1 :** -GENIC 1 ⟨organo*genetic*⟩ **2 :** -GENIC 2 ⟨psycho*genetic*⟩

genetic code *n* (1961) **:** the biochemical basis of heredity consisting of codons in DNA and RNA that determine the specific amino acid sequence in proteins and appear to be uniform for nearly all known forms of life

genetic counseling *n* (1955) **:** guidance relating to genetic disorders that is provided by a medical professional typically to individuals with an increased risk of having a child with such a disorder

genetic drift *n* (1945) **:** random changes in gene frequency esp. in small populations when leading to preservation or extinction of particular genes

genetic engineering *n* (1951) **:** the group of applied techniques of genetics and biotechnology used to cut up and join together genetic material and esp. DNA from one or more species of organism and to introduce the result into an organism in order to change one or more of its characteristics — **genetically engineered** *adj* — **genetic engineer** *n*

genetic fingerprinting *n* (1984) **:** DNA FINGERPRINTING — **genetic fingerprint** *n*

genetic load *n* (1965) **:** the decrease in fitness of the average individual in a population relative to the fittest genotype due to the presence of deleterious genes in the gene pool

genetic map *n* (1957) **:** MAP 3

genetic marker *n* (1950) **:** a readily recognizable genetic trait, gene, DNA segment, or gene product used for identification esp. when closely linked to a trait or genetic material that is difficult to identify

ge•net•ics \jə-ˈne-tiks\ *n pl but sing in constr* (1905) **1 :** a branch of biology that deals with the heredity and variation of organisms **2 :** the genetic makeup and phenomena of an organism, type, group, or condition — **ge•net•i•cist** \-ˈne-tə-sist\ *n*

ge•ne•va \jə-ˈnē-və\ *n* [modif. of obs. D *genever* (now *jenever*), lit., juniper, fr. MD, fr. OF *geneivre,* ultim. fr. L *juniperus*] (1705) **:** a highly aromatic bitter gin orig. made in the Netherlands

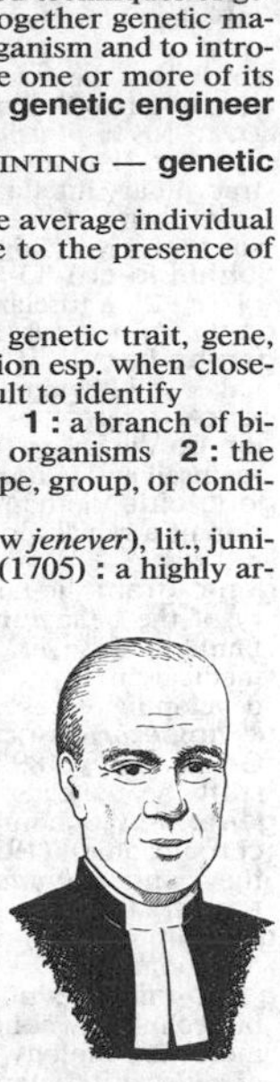
Geneva bands

Ge•ne•va bands \jə-ˈnē-və-\ *n pl* [*Geneva,* Switzerland; fr. their use by the Calvinist clergy of Geneva] (1636) **:** two strips of white cloth suspended from the front of a clerical collar and sometimes worn by Protestant clergymen — called also *Geneva tabs*

Geneva convention *n* (1880) **:** one of a series of agreements concerning the treatment of prisoners of war and of the sick, wounded, and dead in battle first made at Geneva, Switzerland in 1864 and subsequently accepted in later revisions by most nations

Geneva cross *n* [fr. its adoption by the Geneva convention] (ca. 1889) **:** RED CROSS

Geneva gown *n* [fr. its use by the Calvinist clergy of Geneva] (1820) **:** a loose large-sleeved black academic gown widely used as a vestment by members of the Protestant clergy

Ge•ne•van \jə-ˈnē-vən\ *adj* (1573) **1 :** of or relating to Geneva, Switzerland **2 :** of or relating to Calvinism — **Genevan** *n*

[1]**ge•nial** \ˈjēn-yəl, ˈjē-nē-əl\ *adj* [L *genialis,* fr. *genius*] (1566) **1** *obs* **:** of or relating to marriage or generation ⟨the ~ bed —John Milton⟩ **2** *obs* **:** INBORN, NATIVE **3 a :** favorable to growth or comfort **:** MILD ⟨~ sunshine⟩ **b :** marked by or diffusing sympathy or friendliness ⟨your ~ host⟩ **4 :** displaying or marked by genius ***syn*** see GRACIOUS — **ge•nial•i•ty** \ˌjē-nē-ˈa-lə-tē, jēn-ˈyal-\ *n* — **ge•nial•ly** \ˈjēn-yə-lē\ *adv*

[2]**ge•ni•al** \ji-ˈnī(-ə)l\ *adj* [Gk *geneion* chin, fr. *genys* jaw — more at CHIN] (1831) **:** of or relating to the chin

gen•ic \ˈjē-nik, ˈje-\ *adj* [*gene* + [1]*-ic*] (1918) **:** GENETIC 2b — **gen•i•cal•ly** \-ni-k(ə-)lē\ *adv*

-genic *adj comb form* [ISV *-gen & -geny* + [1]*-ic*] **1 :** producing **:** forming ⟨carcino*genic*⟩ **2 :** produced by **:** formed from ⟨bio*genic*⟩ **3** [*photogenic*] **:** suitable for production or reproduction by (such) a medium ⟨tele*genic*⟩

ge•nic•u•late \jə-ˈni-kyə-lət\ *or* **ge•nic•u•lat•ed** \-ˌlā-təd\ *adj* [L *geniculatus,* fr. *geniculum,* dim. of *genu* knee — more at KNEE] (1657) **:** bent abruptly at an angle like a bent knee

ge•nie \ˈjē-nē\ *n, pl* **ge•nies** *also* **ge•nii** \ˈjē-nē(-ˌī)\ [F *génie,* fr. Ar *jinnī*] (1748) **1 :** JINNI 1 **2 :** a magic spirit believed to take human form and serve the person who calls it

ge•nis•tein \jə-ˈnis-tē-ən, -ˈnis-ˌtēn\ *n* [*genist-* (fr. NL *Genista tinctoria,* a species of broom) + *-ein,* alter. of [1]*-in*] (1900) **:** an isoflavone $C_{15}H_{10}O_5$ found esp. in soybeans and shown in laboratory experiments to have antitumor activity

gen•i•tal \ˈje-nə-tᵊl\ *adj* [ME, fr. L *genitalis,* fr. *genitus,* pp. of *gignere* to beget — more at KIN] (14c) **1 :** GENERATIVE **2 :** of, relating to, or being a sexual organ **3 :** of, relating to, or characterized by the stage of psychosexual development in psychoanalytic theory during which oral and anal impulses are subordinated to adaptive interpersonal mechanisms — **gen•i•tal•ly** \-tə-lē\ *adv*

genital herpes *n* (1968) **:** herpes simplex of the type typically affecting the genitalia

gen•i•ta•lia \ˌje-nə-ˈtāl-yə\ *n pl* [L, fr. neut. pl. of *genitalis*] (1876) **:** the organs of the reproductive system; *esp* **:** the external genital organs — **gen•i•ta•lic** \-ˈta-lik, -ˈtā-\ *adj*

gen•i•tals \ˈje-nə-tᵊlz\ *n pl* (14c) **:** GENITALIA

genital wart *n* (1954) **:** a wart on the skin or adjoining mucous membrane on or near the genital organs or the anus and caused by any of several human papillomaviruses

gen•i•ti•val \ˌje-nə-ˈtī-vəl\ *adj* (1818) **:** of, relating to, or formed with or from the genitive case — **gen•i•ti•val•ly** \-və-lē\ *adv*

gen•i•tive \ˈje-nə-tiv\ *adj* [ME, fr. L *genetivus, genitivus,* lit., of generation (erroneous translation of Gk *genikos* genitive), fr. *genitus*] (14c) **1 :** of, relating to, or constituting a grammatical case marking typically a relationship of possessor or source — compare POSSESSIVE **2 :** expressing a relationship that in some inflected languages is often marked by a genitive case — used esp. of English prepositional phrases introduced by *of* — **genitive** *n*

genito- *comb form* [*genital*] **:** genital and ⟨*genito*urinary⟩

gen•i•to•uri•nary \ˌje-nə-tō-ˈyůr-ə-ˌner-ē\ *adj* (ca. 1836) **:** of or relating to the genital and urinary organs or functions ⟨~ disorders⟩

gen•i•ture \ˈje-nə-ˌchůr, -chər, -ˌt(y)ůr\ *n* (15c) **:** NATIVITY, BIRTH

ge•nius \ˈjēn-yəs, ˈjē-nē-əs\ *n, pl* **ge•nius•es** *or* **ge•nii** \-nē-ˌī\ [L, tutelary spirit, natural inclinations, fr. *gignere* to beget] (1513) **1 a** *pl genii*

: an attendant spirit of a person or place **b** *pl usu* **genii** : a person who influences another for good or bad **2** : a strong leaning or inclination : PENCHANT **3 a** : a peculiar, distinctive, or identifying character or spirit **b** : the associations and traditions of a place **c** : a personification or embodiment esp. of a quality or condition **4** *pl usu* **genii** : SPIRIT, JINNI **5** *pl usu* **geniuses** **a** : a single strongly marked capacity or aptitude ⟨had a ∼ for getting along with boys —Mary Ross⟩ **b** : extraordinary intellectual power esp. as manifested in creative activity **c** : a person endowed with transcendent mental superiority; *esp* : a person with a very high IQ *syn* see GIFT

genius lo·ci \-ˈlō-ˌsī, -ˌkē\ *n* [L] (1605) **1** : the pervading spirit of a place **2** : a tutelary deity of a place

genl *abbr* general

gen·na·ker \ˈje-ni-kər\ *n* [blend of *genoa* and *spinnaker*] (1983) : a spinnaker sail having an asymmetrical shape

geno- — see GEN-

gen·oa \ˈje-nə-wə\ *n* [*Genoa*, Italy] (1932) : a large jib that overlaps the mainsail and is used esp. in racing

geno·cide \ˈje-nə-ˌsīd\ *n* (1944) : the deliberate and systematic destruction of a racial, political, or cultural group — **geno·cid·al** \ˌje-nə-ˈsī-dᵊl\ *adj*

gen·o·gram \ˈje-nə-ˌgram, ˈjē-\ *n* (1978) : a diagram outlining the history of the behavior patterns (as of divorce, abortion, or suicide) of a family over several generations; *also* : a similar diagram detailing the medical history of a family in order to assess a family member's risk of developing disease

ge·noise *or* **gé·noise** \zhā-ˈnwäz\ *n* [F *génoise*, fr. fem. of *génois* of Genoa, Italy] (1892) : a sponge cake containing butter and leavened by stiffly beaten eggs

ge·nome \ˈjē-ˌnōm\ *n* [G *Genom*, fr. *Gen* gene + *-om* (as in *Chromosom* chromosome)] (1930) : one haploid set of chromosomes with the genes they contain; *broadly* : the genetic material of an organism — compare PROTEOME

ge·no·mic \ji-ˈnō-mik, -ˈnä-\ *adj* (1934) : of or relating to a genome or to genomics

ge·no·mics \jē-ˈnō-miks, jə-\ *n pl but sing in constr* (1987) : a branch of biotechnology concerned with applying the techniques of genetics and molecular biology to the genetic mapping and DNA sequencing of sets of genes or the complete genomes of selected organisms, with organizing the results in databases, and with applications of the data (as in medicine or biology) — compare PROTEOMICS

ge·no·type \ˈjē-nə-ˌtīp, ˈje-\ *n* (1897) **1** [ISV *gen-*] : TYPE SPECIES **2** [ISV *gene*] : all or part of the genetic constitution of an individual or group — compare PHENOTYPE — **ge·no·typ·ic** \ˌjē-nə-ˈti-pik, ˌje-\ *also* **ge·no·typ·i·cal** \-pi-kəl\ *adj* — **ge·no·typ·i·cal·ly** \-pi-k(ə-)lē\ *adv*

-genous *adj comb form* [*-gen* + *-ous*] **1** : producing : yielding ⟨*erogenous*⟩ **2** : having (such) an origin ⟨*terrigenous*⟩

genre \ˈzhän-rə, ˈzhäⁿ-; ˈzhäⁿr; ˈjän-rə\ *n* [F, fr. MF, kind, gender — more at GENDER] (1770) **1** : a category of artistic, musical, or literary composition characterized by a particular style, form, or content **2** : KIND, SORT **3** : painting that depicts scenes or events from everyday life usu. realistically

gen·ro \ˈgen-ˈrō\ *n pl, often cap* [Jp *genrō*] (1876) : the elder statesmen of Japan who formerly advised the emperor

gens \ˈjenz, ˈgen(t)s\ *n, pl* **gen·tes** \ˈjen-ˌtēz, ˈgen-ˌtās\ [L *gent-*, *gens* — more at GENTLE] (1846) **1** : a Roman clan embracing the families of the same stock in the male line with the members having a common name and worshipping a common ancestor **2** : CLAN; *esp* : a patrilineal clan **3** : a distinguishable group of related organisms

¹**gent** \ˈjent\ *adj* [ME, noble, graceful, fr. AF, fr. L *genitus*, pp. of *gignere* to beget — more at KIN] (13c) *archaic* : PRETTY, GRACEFUL

²**gent** *n* (1564) : GENTLEMAN

gen·ta·mi·cin \ˌjen-tə-ˈmī-sᵊn\ *n* [alter. of earlier *gentamycin*, fr. *gentian* violet + kan*amycin*; fr. the color of the actinomycete] (1963) : a broad-spectrum antibiotic mixture derived from an actinomycete (*Micromonospora purpurea* or *M. echinospora*) and extensively used as the sulfate in treating infections (as of the urinary tract)

gen·teel \jen-ˈtēl\ *adj* [MF *gentil* gentle] (1599) **1 a** : having an aristocratic quality or flavor : STYLISH **b** : of or relating to the gentry or upper class **c** : elegant or graceful in manner, appearance, or shape **d** : free from vulgarity or rudeness : POLITE **2 a** : maintaining or striving to maintain the appearance of superior or middle-class social status or respectability **b** (1) : marked by false delicacy, prudery, or affectation (2) : conventionally or insipidly pretty ⟨timid and ∼ artistic style⟩ — **gen·teel·ly** \-ˈtē(l)-lē\ *adv* — **gen·teel·ness** *n*

gen·teel·ism \-ˈtē(l)-ˌli-zəm\ *n* (1926) : a word believed by its user to be more polite or less vulgar than a common synonym; *also* : the use of genteelisms

gen·tian \ˈjen(t)-shən\ *n* [ME *gencian*, fr. AF *genciane*, fr. L *gentiana*] (14c) **1** : any of numerous herbs (family Gentianaceae, the gentian family, and esp. genus *Gentiana*) with opposite smooth leaves and showy usu. blue flowers **2** : the rhizome and roots of a yellow=flowered gentian (*Gentiana lutea*) of southern Europe that is used as a tonic, stomachic, and flavoring in vermouth

gentian violet *n, often cap G&V* (1897) : any of several dyes or dye mixtures consisting of one or more methyl derivatives of pararosaniline; *esp* : a dark green or greenish mixture used esp. as a bactericide, fungicide, and anthelmintic

¹**gen·tile** \ˈjen-ˌtī(-ə)l\ *n* [ME, fr. LL *gentilis*, fr. L *gent-*, *gens* nation] (14c) **1** *often cap* : a person of a non-Jewish nation or of non-Jewish faith; *esp* : a Christian as distinguished from a Jew **2** : HEATHEN, PAGAN **3** *often cap* : a non-Mormon

²**gentile** *adj* (15c) **1** *often cap* **a** : of or relating to the nations at large as distinguished from the Jews; *also* : of or relating to Christians as distinguished from the Jews **b** : of or relating to non-Mormons **2** : HEATHEN, PAGAN **3** [L *gentilis*] : relating to a tribe or clan

gen·ti·lesse \ˌjen-tə-ˈles\ *n* [ME, fr. AF, fr. *gentil*] (14c) : decorum of conduct befitting a member of the gentry

gen·til·i·ty \jen-ˈti-lə-tē\ *n, pl* **-ties** (14c) **1 a** : the condition of belonging to the gentry **b** : GENTLEFOLK, GENTRY **2 a** (1) : decorum of conduct : COURTESY (2) : attitudes or activity marked by false delicacy, prudery, or affectation **b** : superior social status or prestige evidenced by manners, possessions, or mode of life

¹**gen·tle** \ˈjen-tᵊl\ *adj* **gen·tler** \ˈjent-lər, -tᵊl-ər\; **gen·tlest** \ˈjent-ləst, -tᵊl-əst\ [ME *gentil*, fr. AF, fr. L *gentilis* of a gens, of one's family, fr. *gent-*, *gens* gens, nation; akin to L *gignere* to beget — more at KIN] (13c) **1 a** : belonging to a family of high social station **b** *archaic* : CHIVALROUS **c** : HONORABLE, DISTINGUISHED; *specif* : of or relating to a gentleman **d** : KIND, AMIABLE — used esp. in address as a complimentary epithet ⟨∼ reader⟩ **e** : suited to a person of high social station **2 a** : TRACTABLE, DOCILE **b** : free from harshness, sternness, or violence **3** : SOFT, DELICATE **4** : MODERATE — **gent·ly** \ˈjent-lē\ *adv*

²**gentle** *n* (14c) : a person of gentle birth or status

³**gentle** *vb* **gen·tled; gen·tling** \ˈjent-liŋ, ˈjen-tᵊl-iŋ\ *vt* (14c) **1** : to raise from the commonalty : ENNOBLE **2 a** : to make gentler **b** : to make (an animal) tame and docile **c** : MOLLIFY, PLACATE **d** : to stroke soothingly : PET ∼ *vi* : to become gentle ⟨the wind *gentled*⟩

gentle breeze *n* (ca. 1881) : wind having a speed of 8 to 12 miles per hour (about 12 to 19 kilometers per hour) — see BEAUFORT SCALE table

gen·tle·folk \ˈjen-tᵊl-ˌfōk\ *also* **gen·tle·folks** \-ˌfōks\ *n pl* (1594) : persons of gentle or good family and breeding

gen·tle·man \ˈjen-tᵊl-mən, ˈje-nᵊl-, *in rapid speech also* ˈjen-tə-mən, ˈje-nə-\ *n, often attrib* [ME *gentilman*] (12c) **1 a** : a man of noble or gentle birth **b** : a man belonging to the landed gentry **c** (1) : a man who combines gentle birth or rank with chivalrous qualities (2) : a man whose conduct conforms to a high standard of propriety or correct behavior **d** (1) : a man of independent means who does not engage in any occupation or profession for gain (2) : a man who does not engage in a menial occupation or in manual labor for gain **2** : VALET — often used in the phrase *gentleman's gentleman* **3** : a man of any social class or condition — often used in a courteous reference ⟨show this ∼ to a seat⟩ or usu. in the pl. in address ⟨ladies and *gentlemen*⟩ — **gen·tle·man·like** \-mən-ˌlīk\ *adj* — **gen·tle·man·like·ness** *n*

gentleman–at–arms *n, pl* **gentlemen–at–arms** (1859) : one of a military corps of 40 gentlemen who attend the British sovereign on state occasions

gentleman–commoner *n, pl* **gentlemen–commoners** (1687) : any of a privileged class of commoners formerly required to pay higher fees than ordinary commoners at the universities of Oxford and Cambridge

gentleman farmer *n, pl* **gentlemen farmers** (1749) : a man who farms mainly for pleasure rather than for profit

gen·tle·man·ly \-lē\ *adj* (15c) : characteristic of or having the character of a gentleman — **gen·tle·man·li·ness** *n*

gentleman of fortune (1743) : ADVENTURER

gentleman's agreement *or* **gentlemen's agreement** *n* (1886) : an agreement secured only by the honor of the participants

gentleman's club *n* (1990) : a nightclub for men that features scantily clad women dancers or stripteasers

gen·tle·ness \ˈjen-tᵊl-nəs\ *n* (14c) : the quality or state of being gentle; *esp* : mildness of manners or disposition

gen·tle·per·son \ˈjen-tᵊl-ˌpər-sᵊn\ *n* (1943) : a gentleman or lady

gentle sex *n* (1583) : the female sex : women in general

gen·tle·wom·an \ˈjen-tᵊl-ˌwu̇-mən\ *n* (13c) **1 a** : a woman of noble or gentle birth **b** : a woman who is an attendant upon a lady of rank **2** : a woman of refined manners or good breeding : LADY

Gen·too \ˈjen-(ˌ)tü\ *n, pl* **Gentoos** [Pg *gentio*, lit., gentile, fr. LL *gentilis*] (1638) *archaic* : HINDU

gentoo penguin \ˈjen-(ˌ)tü-\ *n* [perh. fr. *Gentoo*] (1860) : a penguin (*Pygoscelis papua*) of Antarctica and nearby islands with a gray back and throat, white underparts, and white spots above the eyes — called also *gentoo*

gen·trice \ˈjen-trəs\ *n* [ME *gentrise*, fr. AF *genterise*, alter. of *gentelise*, fr. *gentil* gentle] (14c) *archaic* : gentility of birth : RANK

gen·tri·fi·ca·tion \ˌjen-trə-fə-ˈkā-shən\ *n* (1964) : the process of renewal and rebuilding accompanying the influx of middle-class or affluent people into deteriorating areas that often displaces poorer residents

gen·tri·fy \ˈjen-trə-ˌfī\ *vb* **-fied; -fy·ing** *vt* (1972) : to attempt or accomplish the gentrification of ∼ *vi* : to become gentrified — **gen·tri·fi·er** \-ˌfī(-ə)r\ *n*

gen·try \ˈjen-trē\ *n, pl* **gentries** [ME *gentrie*, alter. of *gentrise*] (14c) **1 a** *obs* : the qualities appropriate to a person of gentle birth; *esp* : COURTESY **b** : the condition or rank of a gentleman **2 a** : upper or ruling class : ARISTOCRACY **b** : a class whose members are entitled to bear a coat of arms though not of noble rank; *esp* : the landed proprietors having such status **3** : people of a specified class or kind : FOLKS ⟨no real heroes or heroines among the academic ∼ —R. G. Hanvey⟩

gents \ˈjen(t)s\ *n, often cap* (1938) *chiefly Brit* : MEN'S ROOM

gen·u·flect \ˈjen-yə-ˌflekt\ *vi* [LL *genuflectere*, fr. L *genu* knee + *flectere* to bend — more at KNEE] (1630) **1 a** : to bend the knee **b** : to touch the knee to the floor or ground esp. in worship **2** : to be servilely obedient or respectful — **gen·u·flec·tion** \ˌjen-yə-ˈflek-shən\ *n*

gen·u·ine \ˈjen-yə-wən, -(ˌ)win, ÷-ˌwīn\ *adj* [L *genuinus* innate, genuine; akin to L *gignere* to beget — more at KIN] (ca. 1639) **1 a** : actually having the reputed or apparent qualities or character ⟨∼ vintage wines⟩ **b** : actually produced by or proceeding from the alleged source or author ⟨the signature is ∼⟩ **c** : sincerely and honestly felt or experienced ⟨a deep and ∼ love⟩ **d** : ACTUAL, TRUE ⟨a ∼ improvement⟩ **2** : free from hypocrisy or pretense : SINCERE *syn* see AUTHENTIC — **gen·u·ine·ly** *adv* — **gen·u·ine·ness** \-wə(n)-nəs\ *n* *usage* The objection which some commentators make to the pronunciation \ˈjen-yə-ˌwīn\ is perhaps occasioned by the fact that it is more frequent among those with less schooling. However, this variant is heard in the speech of cultured or highly educated speakers sufficiently frequently for it to be recognized as a widespread pronunciation at all social levels. This variant was recorded as early as 1890 and appears to be simply a long-standing spelling pronunciation.

ge·nus \ˈjē-nəs, ˈje-\ *n, pl* **gen·era** \ˈje-nə-rə\ *also* **ge·nus·es** [L *gener-*, *genus* birth, race, kind — more at KIN] (1551) **1** : a class, kind, or group marked by common characteristics or by one common characteristic; *specif* : a category of biological classification ranking between the family and the species, comprising structurally or phylogenetically related species or an isolated species exhibiting unusual differentiation, and being designated by a Latin or latinized capitalized singular noun **2** : a class of objects divided into several subordinate species

Gen X \ˈjen-ˈeks\ *n* (1992) : GENERATION X — often hyphenated in attributive use ⟨a *Gen-X* celebrity⟩ — **Gen Xer** \-ˈek-sər\ *n*

-geny *n comb form* [Gk *-geneia* act of being born, fr. *-genēs* born — more at -GEN] : generation : production ⟨phylo*geny*⟩

geo- *comb form* [L, fr. Gk *geō-*, fr. *gē*] **1** : earth : ground : soil ⟨*geo*phyte⟩ **2** : geographic : geography and ⟨*geo*politics⟩

geo·bot·a·ny \ˌjē-ō-ˈbä-tə-nē, -ˈbät-nē\ *n* (1904) : PHYTOGEOGRAPHY — **geo·bot·an·i·cal** \-bə-ˈta-ni-kəl\ *also* **geo·bo·tan·ic** \-nik\ *adj* — **geo·bot·a·nist** \-ˈbät-ə-nist, -ˈbät-nist\ *n*

geo·cach·ing \ˈjē-ō-ˌka-shiŋ\ *n* (2000) : a game in which players are given the geographical coordinates of a cache of items which they search for with a GPS device — **geo·cach·er** \-shər\ *n*

geo·cen·tric \ˌjē-ō-ˈsen-trik\ *adj* (1686) **1 a** : relating to, measured from, or as if observed from the earth's center — compare TOPOCENTRIC **b** : having or relating to the earth as center — compare HELIOCENTRIC **2** : taking or based on the earth as the center of perspective and valuation — **geo·cen·tri·cal·ly** \-tri-k(ə-)lē\ *adv*

geo·chem·is·try \ˌjē-ō-ˈke-mə-strē\ *n* (1902) **1** : a science that deals with the chemical composition of and chemical changes in the solid matter of the earth or a celestial body (as the moon) **2** : the related chemical and geological properties of a substance — **geo·chem·i·cal** \-ˈke-mi-kəl\ *adj* — **geo·chem·i·cal·ly** \-k(ə-)lē\ *adv* — **geo·chem·ist** \-ˈke-mist\ *n*

geo·chro·nol·o·gy \-krə-ˈnä-lə-jē\ *n* (1893) **1** : the chronology of the past as indicated by geologic data **2** : the study of geochronology — **geo·chro·no·log·i·cal** \-ˌkrä-nə-ˈlä-ji-kəl, -ˌkrō-\ *also* **geo·chro·no·log·ic** \-ˈä-jik\ *adj* — **geo·chro·no·log·i·cal·ly** \-ji-k(ə-)lē\ *adv* — **geo·chro·nol·o·gist** \-krə-ˈnä-lə-jist\ *n*

ge·ode \ˈjē-ˌōd\ *n* [L *geodes*, a gem, fr. Gk *geōdēs* earthlike, fr. *gē* earth] (ca. 1732) **1** : a nodule of stone having a cavity lined with crystals or mineral matter **2** : the cavity in a geode

¹**geo·de·sic** \ˌjē-ə-ˈde-sik, -ˈdē-, -zik\ *adj* (1821) **1** : GEODETIC **2** : made of light straight structural elements mostly in tension ⟨a ~ dome⟩

²**geodesic** *n* (1883) : the shortest line between two points that lies in a given surface

ge·od·e·sy \jē-ˈä-də-sē\ *n* [Gk *geōdaisia*, fr. *geō-* ge- + *daiesthai* to divide — more at TIDE] (1853) : a branch of applied mathematics concerned with the determination of the size and shape of the earth and the exact positions of points on its surface and with the description of variations of its gravity field — **ge·od·e·sist** \-də-sist\ *n*

geo·det·ic \ˌjē-ə-ˈde-tik\ *also* **geo·det·i·cal** \-ti-kəl\ *adj* [*geodesy*; after

such pairs as *heresy* : *heretic*] (ca. 1828) : of, relating to, or determined by geodesy

geodetic survey *n* (1880) : a survey of a large land area in which corrections are made for the curvature of the earth's surface

geo·duck \ˈgü-ē-ˌdək\ *n* [Lushootseed (Salishan language of the Puget Sound region) *gʷídəq*] (1881) : a large edible burrowing clam (*Panopea generosa* syn. *P. abrupta*) of the Pacific coast of No. America that usu. weighs two to three pounds (about one kilogram)

geo·eco·nom·ics \ˌjē-ō-ˌe-kə-ˈnä-miks, -ˌē-kə-\ *n* (1981) **1** : the combination of economic and geographic factors relating to international trade **2** : a governmental policy guided by geoeconomics — **geo·eco·nom·ic** \-mik\ *adj*

geog *abbr* geographic; geographical; geography

ge·og·ra·pher \jē-ˈä-grə-fər\ *n* (1542) : a specialist in geography

geo·graph·ic \ˌjē-ə-ˈgra-fik\ *or* **geo·graph·i·cal** \-fi-kəl\ *adj* (1559) **1** : of or relating to geography **2** : belonging to or characteristic of a particular region — **geo·graph·i·cal·ly** \-fi-k(ə-)lē\ *adv*

ge·og·ra·phy \jē-ˈä-grə-fē\ *n, pl* **-phies** [L *geographia*, fr. Gk *geōgraphia*, fr. *geōgraphein* to describe the earth's surface, fr. *geō-* + *graphein* to write — more at CARVE] (15c) **1** : a science that deals with the description, distribution, and interaction of the diverse physical, biological, and cultural features of the earth's surface **2** : the geographic features of an area **3** : a treatise on geography **4 a** : a delineation or systematic arrangement of constituent elements : CONFIGURATION **b** : MAKEUP 1 ⟨her emotional ~⟩

geo·hy·drol·o·gy \ˌjē-ō-hī-ˈdrä-lə-jē\ *n* (ca. 1909) : a science that deals with the character, source, and mode of occurrence of underground water — **geo·hy·dro·log·ic** \-ˌhī-drə-ˈlä-jik\ *adj* — **geo·hy·drol·o·gist** \-hī-ˈdrä-lə-jist\ *n*

ge·oid \ˈjē-ˌóid\ *n* [G, fr. Gk *geoeidēs* earthlike, fr. *gē*] (1881) : the surface within or around the earth that is everywhere normal to the direction of gravity and coincides with mean sea level in the oceans — **ge·oi·dal** \jē-ˈói-d°l\ *adj*

geol *abbr* geologic; geological; geology

geo·log·ic \ˌjē-ə-ˈlä-jik\ *or* **geo·log·i·cal** \-ji-kəl\ *adj* (1791) : of, relating to, or based on geology — **geo·log·i·cal·ly** \-ji-k(ə-)lē\ *adv*

geologic time *n* (1861) : the long period of time occupied by the earth's geologic history

ge·ol·o·gize \jē-ˈä-lə-ˌjīz\ *vi* **-gized; -giz·ing** (1826) : to study geology or make geologic investigations

GEOLOGIC TIME

EONS	ERAS	PERIODS AND SYSTEMS	EPOCHS AND SERIES	BEGINNING OF INTERVAL*	BIOLOGICAL FORMS
Phanerozoic	Cenozoic	Quaternary	Holocene	0.01	
			Pleistocene	1.8	Earliest humans
		Tertiary	Pliocene	5	
			Miocene	24	Earliest hominids
			Oligocene	34	
			Eocene	55	Earliest grasses
			Paleocene	65	Earliest large mammals
Cretaceous-Tertiary boundary (65 million years ago): extinction of dinosaurs					
	Mesozoic	Cretaceous	Upper	98	
			Lower	144	Earliest flowering plants; dinosaurs in ascendancy
		Jurassic		208	Earliest birds
		Triassic		248	Earliest dinosaurs & mammals
	Paleozoic	Permian		286	
		Carboniferous			
		Pennsylvanian		320	Earliest reptiles
		Mississippian		360	Earliest winged insects
		Devonian		410	Earliest amphibians & bony fish
		Silurian		438	Earliest land plants & insects
		Ordovician		505	Earliest corals
		Cambrian		544	Earliest fish
Proterozoic	Precambrian			2500	Earliest colonial algae & soft-bodied invertebrates
Archean				3800	Earliest surviving microfossils of primitive single-celled organisms
Hadean				4600	No surviving fossils

*Approximate, in millions of years before the present

ge·ol·o·gy \jē-ˈä-lə-jē\ *n, pl* **-gies** [NL *geologia,* fr. *ge-* + *-logia* -logy] (1735) **1 a :** a science that deals with the history of the earth and its life esp. as recorded in rocks **b :** a study of the solid matter of a celestial body (as the moon) **2 :** geologic features **3 :** a treatise on geology — **ge·ol·o·gist** \-jist\ *n*

geom *abbr* geometric; geometrical; geometry

geo·mag·net·ic \ˌjē-ō-mag-ˈne-tik\ *adj* (1904) **:** of or relating to terrestrial magnetism — **geo·mag·net·i·cal·ly** \-ti-k(ə-)lē\ *adv* — **geo·mag·ne·tism** \-ˈmag-nə-ˌti-zəm\ *n*

geomagnetic storm *n* (1941) **:** MAGNETIC STORM

geo·man·cy \ˈjē-ə-ˌman(t)-sē\ *n* [ME *geomancie,* fr. AF, fr. ML *geomantia,* fr. LGk *geōmanteia,* fr. Gk *geō-* + *-manteia* -mancy] (14c) **:** divination by means of figures or lines or geographic features — **geo·man·cer** \-sər\ *n* — **geo·man·tic** \ˌjē-ə-ˈman-tik\ *adj*

ge·om·e·ter \jē-ˈä-mə-tər\ *n* (15c) **1 :** a specialist in geometry **2 :** GEOMETRID

geo·met·ric \ˌjē-ə-ˈme-trik\ *or* **geo·met·ri·cal** \-ˈme-tri-kəl\ *adj* (14c) **1 a :** of, relating to, or according to the methods or principles of geometry **b :** increasing in a geometric progression ⟨~ population growth⟩ **2** *cap* **:** of or relating to a style of ancient Greek pottery characterized by geometric decorative motifs **3 a :** utilizing rectilinear or simple curvilinear motifs or outlines in design **b :** of or relating to art based on simple geometric shapes (as straight lines, circles, or squares) ⟨~ abstractions⟩ — **geo·met·ri·cal·ly** \-tri-k(ə-)lē\ *adv*

geo·me·tri·cian \(ˌ)jē-ˌä-mə-ˈtri-shən, ˌjē-ə-mə-\ *n* (15c) **:** GEOMETER 1

geometric mean *n* (1879) **:** the nth root of the product of *n* numbers; *specif* **:** a number that is the second term of three consecutive terms of a geometric progression ⟨the *geometric mean* of 9 and 4 is 6⟩

geometric progression *n* (ca. 1856) **:** a sequence (as 1, ½, ¼) in which the ratio of a term to its predecessor is always the same — called also *geometrical progression, geometric sequence*

geo·met·rics \ˌjē-ə-ˈme-triks\ *n pl* (1977) **:** decorative patterns or designs based on geometric shapes

geometric series *n* (ca. 1909) **:** a series (as $1 + x + x^2 + x^3 + \ldots$) whose terms form a geometric progression

ge·om·e·trid \jē-ˈä-mə-trəd, ˌjē-ə-ˈme-trəd\ *n* [ultim. fr. Gk *geōmetrēs* geometer, fr. *geōmetrein*] (1876) **:** any of a family (Geometridae) of usu. medium-sized moths with large wings and larvae that are loopers — **geometrid** *adj*

ge·om·e·trise *Brit var of* GEOMETRIZE

ge·om·e·trize \jē-ˈä-mə-ˌtrīz\ *vb* **-trized; -triz·ing** *vi* (1603) **:** to work by or as if by geometric methods or laws ~ *vt* **1 :** to represent geometrically **2 :** to make conform to geometric principles and laws — **ge·om·e·tri·za·tion** \-ˌä-mə-trə-ˈzā-shən\ *n*

ge·om·e·try \jē-ˈä-mə-trē\ *n, pl* **-tries** [ME *geometrie,* fr. AF, fr. L *geometria,* fr. Gk *geōmetria,* fr. *geōmetrein* to measure the earth, fr. *geō-* ge- + *metron* measure — more at MEASURE] (14c) **1 a :** a branch of mathematics that deals with the measurement, properties, and relationships of points, lines, angles, surfaces, and solids; *broadly* **:** the study of properties of given elements that remain invariant under specified transformations **b :** a particular type or system of geometry **2 a :** CONFIGURATION **b :** surface shape **3 :** an arrangement of objects or parts that suggests geometric figures

geo·mor·phic \ˌjē-ə-ˈmȯr-fik\ *adj* (1893) **:** GEOMORPHOLOGICAL

geo·mor·pho·log·i·cal \-ˌmȯr-fə-ˈlä-ji-kəl\ *adj* (1896) **:** of or relating to the form or surface features of the earth or another celestial body

geo·mor·phol·o·gy \-mȯr-ˈfä-lə-jē\ *n, pl* **-gies** [ISV] (1893) **1 :** a science that deals with the relief features of the earth or of another celestial body (as the moon) and seeks a genetic interpretation of them **2 :** the features dealt with in geomorphology — **geo·mor·phol·o·gist** \-mȯr-ˈfä-lə-jist\ *n*

ge·oph·a·gy \jē-ˈä-fə-jē\ *n* [ISV] (1850) **:** the practice of eating earthy substances (as clay) that in humans is performed esp. to augment a scanty or mineral-deficient diet or as part of a cultural tradition — compare ¹PICA

geo·phone \ˈjē-ə-ˌfōn\ *n* (1919) **:** an instrument for detecting vibrations passing through rocks, soil, or ice

geo·phys·ics \ˌjē-ə-ˈfi-ziks\ *n pl but sing or pl in constr* [ISV] (ca. 1889) **:** a branch of earth science dealing with the physical processes and phenomena occurring esp. in the earth and in its vicinity — **geo·phys·i·cal** \-zi-kəl\ *adj* — **geo·phys·i·cal·ly** \-zi-k(ə-)lē\ *adv* — **geo·phys·i·cist** \-ˈfi-zə-sist\ *n*

geo·phyte \ˈjē-ə-ˌfīt\ *n* (ca. 1900) **:** a perennial plant that bears its perennating buds below the surface of the soil

geo·pol·i·ti·cian \ˌjē-ō-ˌpä-lə-ˈti-shən\ *n* (1941) **:** a specialist in geopolitics

geo·pol·i·tics \-ˈpä-lə-ˌtiks\ *n pl but sing in constr* (1904) **1 :** a study of the influence of such factors as geography, economics, and demography on the politics and esp. the foreign policy of a state **2 :** a governmental policy guided by geopolitics **3 :** a combination of political and geographic factors relating to something (as a state or particular resources) — **geo·po·lit·i·cal** \-pə-ˈli-ti-kəl\ *adj* — **geo·po·lit·i·cal·ly** \-ti-k(ə-)lē\ *adv*

geo·pres·sured \ˌjē-ō-ˈpre-shərd\ *adj* (1968) **:** subjected to great pressure from geologic forces ⟨~ methane⟩

Geor·die \ˈjȯr-dē\ *n* [fr. *Geordie,* dim. of the name *George*] (1866) *chiefly Brit* **:** an inhabitant of Newcastle upon Tyne or its environs; *also* **:** the dialect of English spoken by Geordies

George \ˈjȯrj\ *n* [St. *George*] (1506) **1 :** either of two of the insignia of the British Order of the Garter **2 :** a British coin bearing the image of St. George

geor·gette \jȯr-ˈjet\ *n* [fr. *Georgette,* a trademark] (1915) **:** a sheer crepe woven from hard-twisted yarns to produce a dull pebbly surface

¹**Geor·gian** \ˈjȯr-jən\ *n* (15c) **1 :** a native or inhabitant of Georgia in the Caucasus **2 :** the language of the Georgian people

²**Georgian** *adj* (1607) **:** of, relating to, or constituting Georgia in the Caucasus, the Georgians, or Georgian

³**Georgian** *n* (1741) **:** a native or resident of the state of Georgia

⁴**Georgian** *adj* (1762) **:** of, relating to, or characteristic of the state of Georgia or its people

⁵**Georgian** *adj* (ca. 1855) **1 :** of, relating to, or characteristic of the reigns of the first four Georges of Great Britain **2 :** of, relating to, or characteristic of the reign of George V of Great Britain

⁶**Georgian** *n* (1901) **1 :** one belonging to either of the Georgian periods; *esp* **:** a poet of the second decade of the 20th century **2 :** Georgian taste or style esp. in architecture

¹**geor·gic** \ˈjȯr-jik\ *n* [the *Georgics,* poem by Virgil, fr. L *georgicus*] (1513) **:** a poem dealing with agriculture

²**georgic** *adj* [L *georgicus,* fr. Gk *geōrgikos,* fr. *geōrgos* farmer, fr. *geō-* ge- + *ergon* work — more at WORK] (ca. 1720) **:** AGRICULTURAL

geo·sci·ence \ˌjē-ō-ˈsī-ən(t)s\ *n* (1942) **1 :** the sciences (as geology, geophysics, and geochemistry) dealing with the earth **2 :** any of the geosciences — compare EARTH SCIENCE — **geo·sci·en·tist** \-ən-tist\ *n*

geo·sta·tion·ary \-ˈstā-shə-ˌner-ē\ *adj* (1961) **:** being or having an equatorial orbit at an altitude of about 22,300 miles (35,900 kilometers) requiring an angular velocity the same as that of the earth so that the position of a satellite in such an orbit is fixed with respect to the earth

geo·strat·e·gy \-ˈstra-tə-jē\ *n* (1942) **1 :** a branch of geopolitics that deals with strategy **2 :** the combination of geopolitical and strategic factors characterizing a particular geographic region **3 :** the use by a government of strategy based on geopolitics — **geo·stra·te·gic** \-strə-ˈtē-jik\ *adj* — **geo·strat·e·gist** \-ˈstra-tə-jist\ *n*

geo·stroph·ic \ˌjē-ə-ˈsträ-fik\ *adj* [*ge-* + Gk *strophikos* turned, fr. *strophē* turning — more at STROPHE] (1916) **:** of, relating to, or arising from the Coriolis force — **geo·stroph·i·cal·ly** \-fi-k(ə-)lē\ *adv*

geo·syn·chro·nous \ˌjē-ō-ˈsiŋ-krə-nəs, -ˈsin-\ *adj* (1968) **:** being or having an orbit around the earth with a period equal to one sidereal day; *specif* **:** GEOSTATIONARY

geo·syn·cline \-ˈsin-ˌklīn\ *n* (1895) **:** a great downward flexure of the earth's crust — **geo·syn·cli·nal** \-ˌsin-ˈklī-nəl\ *adj*

geo·tac·tic \ˌjē-ō-ˈtak-tik\ *adj* (1899) **:** of or relating to geotaxis

geo·tax·is \-ˈtak-səs\ *n* [NL] (1899) **:** a taxis in which the force of gravity is the directive factor

geo·tech·ni·cal \-ˈtek-ni-kəl\ *adj* (1947) **:** of or relating to geotechnical engineering

geotechnical engineering *n* (1974) **:** a science that deals with the application of geology to engineering

geo·tec·ton·ic \-tek-ˈtä-nik\ *adj* (1882) **:** of or relating to the form, arrangement, and structure of rock masses of the earth's crust resulting from folding or faulting — **geo·tec·ton·i·cal·ly** \-ni-k(ə-)lē\ *adv*

geo·ther·mal \-ˈthər-məl\ *adj* [ISV] (1875) **:** of, relating to, or utilizing the heat of the earth's interior; *also* **:** produced or permeated by such heat ⟨~ steam⟩ ⟨~ regions⟩ — **geo·ther·mal·ly** \-mə-lē\ *adv*

geo·tro·pic \ˌjē-ə-ˈtrō-pik, -ˈträ-\ *adj* (1875) **:** of or relating to geotropism — **geo·tro·pi·cal·ly** \-ˈtrō-pi-k(ə-)lē, -ˈträ-\ *adv*

ge·ot·ro·pism \jē-ˈä-trə-ˌpi-zəm\ *n* [ISV] (1875) **:** a tropism (as of plant roots) in which gravity is the orienting factor

ger *abbr* gerund

Ger *abbr* German; Germany

ge·rah \ˈgir-ə\ *n* [Heb *gērāh*] (1530) **:** an ancient Hebrew unit of weight equal to ¹⁄₂₀ shekel

ge·ra·ni·ol \jə-ˈrā-nē-ˌȯl, -ˌōl\ *n* [ISV, fr. NL *Geranium*] (1871) **:** a fragrant liquid unsaturated alcohol $C_{10}H_{18}O$ used chiefly in perfumes and soap

ge·ra·ni·um \jə-ˈrā-nē-əm, -nyəm\ *n* [NL, fr. L, geranium, fr. Gk *geranion,* fr. dim. of *geranos* crane — more at CRANE] (1548) **1 :** any of a widely distributed genus (*Geranium* of the family Geraniaceae, the geranium family) of plants having regular usu. white, pink, or purple flowers with elongated styles and glands that alternate with the petals — called also *cranesbill* **2 :** PELARGONIUM **3 :** a vivid or strong red

ge·rar·dia \jə-ˈrär-dē-ə\ *n* [NL, fr. John *Gerard* †1612 Eng. botanist] (1851) **:** any of a genus (*Agalinis* syn. *Gerardia*) of often root-parasitic herbs of the snapdragon family having pink, purple, or white flowers

ger·bera \ˈgər-bə-rə, ˈjər-\ *n* [NL, fr. Traugott *Gerber* †1743 Ger. naturalist] (1889) **:** any of a genus (*Gerbera*) of Asian and African composite herbs that have basal tufted leaves and are often cultivated for their showy heads of yellow, pink, or orange flowers with prominent rays

ger·bil *also* **ger·bille** \ˈjər-bəl\ *n* [F *gerbille,* fr. NL *Gerbillus,* dim. of *gerboa, jerboa* jerboa] (1849) **:** any of numerous Old World burrowing desert rodents (*Gerbillus* and related genera) with long hind legs adapted for leaping

GERD *abbr* gastroesophageal reflux disease

ge·rent \ˈjir-ənt\ *n* [L *gerent-, gerens,* prp. of *gerere* to bear, carry on] (1576) **:** one that rules or manages

ge·re·nuk \ˈger-ə-ˌnu̇k, gə-ˈre-nək\ *n, pl* **gerenuk** *or* **gerenuks** [Somali *gáránúug*] (1895) **:** a large-eyed antelope (*Litocranius walleri*) of eastern Africa with a long neck and limbs

¹**ger·i·at·ric** \ˌjer-ē-ˈa-trik, ˌjir-\ *n* (1909) **1** *pl but sing in constr* **:** a branch of medicine that deals with the problems and diseases of old age and aging people — compare GERONTOLOGY **2 :** an aged person

²**geriatric** *adj* [Gk *gēras* old age + E *-iatric*] (1926) **1 a :** of or relating to geriatrics or the process of aging **b :** of, relating to, or appropriate for elderly people ⟨the ~ set⟩ **2 a :** OLD, ELDERLY ⟨a ~ dachshund⟩ **b :** being old and outmoded ⟨~ airplanes⟩

ger·i·a·tri·cian \ˌjer-ē-ə-ˈtri-shən, ˌjir-\ *n* (1926) **:** a specialist in geriatrics

germ \ˈjərm\ *n* [F *germe,* fr. L *germin-, germen,* fr. *gignere* to beget — more at KIN] (1644) **1 a :** a small mass of living substance capable of developing into an organism or one of its parts **b :** the embryo with the scutellum of a cereal grain that is usu. separated from the starchy endosperm during milling **2 :** something that initiates development or serves as an origin **:** RUDIMENTS, BEGINNING **3 :** MICROORGANISM; *esp* **:** a microorganism causing disease

¹**ger·man** \ˈjər-mən\ *adj* [ME *germain,* fr. AF, fr. L *germanus* having the same parents, fr. *germen*] (14c) **:** having the same parents or the same grandparents on either the maternal or paternal side — usu. used after the noun which it modifies and joined to it by a hyphen ⟨brother-german⟩ ⟨cousin-german⟩

²**german** *n* (15c) *obs* **:** a near relative

¹**Ger·man** \ˈjər-mən\ *n* [ME, fr. ML *Germanus,* fr. L] (14c) **1 :** a member of any of the Germanic peoples inhabiting western Europe in Roman times **2 a :** a native or inhabitant of Germany **b :** a person of German descent **c :** one whose native language is German and who is a native of a country other than Germany **3 a :** the Germanic language spoken mainly in Germany, Austria, and parts of Switzerland **b :** the literary and official language of Germany **4** *often not cap* **a :** a dance consisting of intricate figures that are improvised and intermin-

gled with waltzes **b** *chiefly Midland* : a dancing party; *specif* : one at which the german is danced

[2]**German** *adj* (15c) : of, relating to, or characteristic of Germany, the Germans, or German

German cockroach *n* (1896) : a small active winged cockroach (*Blattella germanica*) prob. of African origin that is a common household pest in the U.S. — called also *Croton bug*

ger·man·der \(ˌ)jər-ˈman-dər\ *n* [ME, ultim. fr. Gk *chamaidrys,* fr. *chamai* on the ground + *drys* tree — more at HUMBLE, TREE] (15c) : any of a genus (*Teucrium*) of plants of the mint family with flowers having four projecting stamens, a short corolla tube, and a prominent lower lip

ger·mane \(ˌ)jər-ˈmān\ *adj* [ME *germain,* lit., having the same parents, fr. AF] (14c) **1** *obs* : closely akin **2 :** being at once relevant and appropriate : FITTING ⟨omit details that are not ~ to the discussion⟩ ***syn*** see RELEVANT — **ger·mane·ly** *adv*

[1]**Ger·man·ic** \(ˌ)jər-ˈma-nik\ *adj* (1633) **1 :** GERMAN **2 :** of, relating to, or characteristic of the Germanic-speaking peoples **3 :** of, relating to, or constituting Germanic

[2]**Germanic** *n* (1892) : a branch of the Indo-European language family containing English, German, Dutch, Afrikaans, Frisian, the Scandinavian languages, and Gothic — see INDO-EUROPEAN LANGUAGES table

Ger·man·ism \ˈjər-mə-ˌni-zəm\ *n* (1611) **1 :** a characteristic feature of German occurring in another language **2 :** partiality for Germany or German customs **3 :** the practices or objectives characteristic of the Germans

Ger·man·ist \-nist\ *n* (1831) : a specialist in German or Germanic language, literature, or culture

ger·ma·ni·um \(ˌ)jər-ˈmā-nē-əm\ *n* [NL, fr. ML *Germania* Germany] (1886) : a grayish-white hard brittle metalloid element that resembles silicon and is used esp. in optical and semiconductor materials and as a catalyst — see ELEMENT table

ger·man·ize \ˈjər-mə-ˌnīz\ *vb* **-ized; -iz·ing** *often cap, vt* (1598) **1** *archaic* : to translate into German **2 :** to cause to acquire German characteristics ~ *vi* : to have or acquire German customs or leanings — **ger·man·i·za·tion** \ˌjər-mə-nə-ˈzā-shən\ *n, often cap*

German measles *n pl but sing or pl in constr* (ca. 1875) : an acute contagious virus disease that is caused by a togavirus (species *Rubella virus* of the genus *Rubivirus*) and is milder than typical measles but is damaging to the fetus when occurring early in pregnancy — called also *rubella*

Germano- *comb form* : German ⟨*Germano*phile⟩

[1]**Ger·mano·phile** \(ˌ)jər-ˈma-nə-ˌfī(-ə)l\ *adj* (1898) : approving or favoring the German people and their institutions and customs

[2]**Germanophile** *n* (1911) : one that is Germanophile

German shepherd *n* (1926) : any of a breed of working dogs of German origin that are intelligent and responsive and are often used in police work and as guide dogs for the blind — called also *Alsatian*

German shorthaired pointer *n* (1931) : any of a breed of gundogs of German origin that have a liver or liver and white short coat

German silver *n* (1830) : a silver-white alloy of copper, zinc, and nickel

German wirehaired pointer *n* (ca. 1964) : any of a breed of gundogs of German origin that have a liver or liver and white flat-lying wiry coat

germ cell *n* (1851) : a gamete (as an egg or sperm cell) or one of its antecedent cells

ger·men \ˈjər-mən\ *n* [L] (1605) *archaic* : GERM 1a, 2

germ·free \ˈjərm-ˌfrē\ *adj* (1904) : free of microorganisms : AXENIC

ger·mi·cid·al \ˌjər-mə-ˈsī-dᵊl\ *adj* (1885) : of or relating to a germicide; *also* : destroying germs

ger·mi·cide \ˈjər-mə-ˌsīd\ *n* (1877) : an agent that destroys germs

ger·mi·na·bil·i·ty \ˌjər-mə-nə-ˈbi-lə-tē\ *n* (1896) : the capacity to germinate

ger·mi·nal \ˈjərm-nəl, ˈjer-mə-nᵊl\ *adj* [F, fr. L *germin-, germen* — more at GERM] (1808) **1 a :** being in the earliest stage of development **b :** CREATIVE, PRODUCTIVE **2 :** of, relating to, or having the characteristics of a germ cell or early embryo — **ger·mi·nal·ly** *adv*

germinal vesicle *n* (ca. 1839) : the enlarged nucleus of the egg before completion of meiosis

ger·mi·nate \ˈjər-mə-ˌnāt\ *vb* **-nat·ed; -nat·ing** [L *germinatus,* pp. of *germinare* to sprout, fr. *germin-, germen* bud, germ] *vt* (1610) : to cause to sprout or develop ~ *vi* **1 :** to come into being : EVOLVE ⟨before Western civilization began to ~ —A. L. Kroeber⟩ **2 :** to begin to grow : SPROUT — **ger·mi·na·tion** \ˌjər-mə-ˈnā-shən\ *n* — **ger·mi·na·tive** \ˈjər-mə-ˌnā-tiv, -mə-nə-\ *adj*

germ layer *n* (1877) : any of the three primary layers of cells differentiated in most embryos during and immediately following gastrulation

germ line *n* (1925) : the cellular lineage of a sexually reproducing organism from which eggs and sperm are derived; *also* : the genetic material contained in this cellular lineage which can be passed to the next generation

germ·o·phobe \ˈjər-mə-ˌfōb\ *n* (1922) : a person who has an abnormal fear of germs — **germ·o·pho·bic** \ˌjər-mə-ˈfō-bik\ *adj*

germ·plasm \ˈjərm-ˌpla-zəm\ *n* (1889) **1 :** germ cells and their precursors serving as the bearers of heredity and being fundamentally independent of other cells **2 :** the hereditary material of the germ cells : GENES

germ·proof \ˈjərm-ˌprüf\ *adj* (1879) : impervious to the penetration or action of germs

germ theory *n* (1870) : a theory in medicine: infections, contagious diseases, and various other conditions result from the action of microorganisms

germ warfare *n* (1938) : the use of harmful microorganisms (as bacteria) as weapons in war

germy \ˈjər-mē\ *adj* **germ·i·er; -est** (1912) : full of germs

geront- *or* **geronto-** *comb form* [F *géront-, géronto-,* fr. Gk *geront-, geronto-,* fr. *geront-, gerōn* old man; akin to Gk *gēras* old age, Skt *jarati* he grows old] : aged one : old age ⟨*geronto*logy⟩

ge·ron·tic \jə-ˈrän-tik\ *adj* (1885) : of or relating to decadence or old age

ger·on·toc·ra·cy \ˌjer-ən-ˈtä-krə-sē\ *n, pl* **-cies** [F *gérontocratie,* fr. *géronto-* geront- + *-cratie* -cracy] (1830) : rule by elders; *specif* : a form of social organization in which a group of old men or a council of elders dominates or exercises control — **ge·ron·to·crat** \jə-ˈrän-tə-ˌkrat\ *n* — **ge·ron·to·crat·ic** \-ˌrän-tə-ˈkra-tik\ *adj*

ger·on·tol·o·gy \ˌjer-ən-ˈtä-lə-jē\ *n* [ISV] (1903) : the comprehensive study of aging and the problems of the aged — compare GERIATRIC 1 — **ge·ron·to·log·i·cal** \jə-ˌrän-tə-ˈlä-ji-kəl\ *also* **ge·ron·to·log·ic** \-jik\ *adj* — **ger·on·tol·o·gist** \ˌjer-ən-ˈtä-lə-jist\ *n*

[1]**ger·ry·man·der** \ˈjer-ē-ˌman-dər, *also* ˈger-; *orig* ˈger-\ *n* [Elbridge *Gerry* + sala*mander;* fr. the shape of an election district formed during Gerry's governorship of Mass.] (1812) **1 :** the act or method of gerrymandering **2 :** a district or pattern of districts varying greatly in size or population as a result of gerrymandering

[2]**gerrymander** *vt* **-dered; -der·ing** \-d(ə-)riŋ\ (1812) **1 :** to divide (a territorial unit) into election districts to give one political party an electoral majority in a large number of districts while concentrating the voting strength of the opposition in as few districts as possible **2 :** to divide (an area) into political units to give special advantages to one group ⟨~ a school district⟩

ger·und \ˈjer-ənd, ˈje-rənd\ *n* [LL *gerundium,* fr. L **gerundus,** gerundive of *gerere* to bear, carry on] (1513) **1 :** a verbal noun in Latin that expresses generalized or uncompleted action **2 :** any of several linguistic forms analogous to the Latin gerund in languages other than Latin; *esp* : the English verbal noun ending in *-ing* that has the function of a substantive and at the same time shows the verbal features of tense, voice, and capacity to take adverbial qualifiers and to govern objects

ge·run·dive \jə-ˈrən-div\ *n* (15c) **1 :** the Latin future passive participle that functions as the verbal adjective, that expresses the fitness or necessity of the action to be performed, and that has the same suffix as the gerund **2 :** a verbal adjective in a language other than Latin analogous to the gerundive

ge·sell·schaft \gə-ˈzel-ˌshäft\ *n* [G, companionship, society] (1928) : a rationally developed mechanistic type of social relationship characterized by impersonally contracted associations between persons; *also* : a community or society characterized by this relationship — compare GEMEINSCHAFT

ges·ne·ri·ad \ges-ˈnir-ē-ˌad\ *n* [NL *Gesneria,* genus name, fr. Konrad *Gesner* †1565 Swiss naturalist] (1882) : any of a family (Gesneriaceae) of tropical or subtropical herbs (as an African violet or gloxinia) with chiefly opposite leaves and highly zygomorphic flowers

ges·so \ˈje-(ˌ)sō\ *n, pl* **gessoes** [It, lit., gypsum, fr. L *gypsum*] (1596) **1 :** plaster of paris or gypsum prepared with glue for use in painting or making bas-reliefs **2 :** a paste prepared by mixing whiting with size or glue and spread upon a surface to fit it for painting or gilding — **gessoed** \-(ˌ)sōd\ *adj*

gest *or* **geste** \ˈjest\ *n* [ME *geste* — more at JEST] (13c) **1 :** a tale of adventures; *esp* : a romance in verse **2 :** ADVENTURE, EXPLOIT

ge·stalt \gə-ˈstält, -ˈshtält, -ˈstȯlt, -ˈshtȯlt\ *n, pl* **ge·stalts** *also* **ge·stalten** \-ˈstäl-tᵊn, -ˈshtäl-, -ˈstȯl-, -ˈshtȯl-\ [G, lit., shape, form] (1922) : a structure, configuration, or pattern of physical, biological, or psychological phenomena so integrated as to constitute a functional unit with properties not derivable by summation of its parts

ge·stalt·ist \-ˈstäl-tist, -ˈshtäl-, -ˈstȯl-, -ˈshtȯl-\ *n, often cap* (1931) : a specialist in Gestalt psychology

Gestalt psychology *n* (1924) : the study of perception and behavior from the standpoint of an individual's response to configurational wholes with stress on the uniformity of psychological and physiological events and rejection of analysis into discrete events of stimulus, percept, and response

ge·sta·po \gə-ˈstä-(ˌ)pō\ *n, pl* **-pos** [G, fr. *Ge*heime *Sta*ats*po*lizei, lit., secret state police] (1934) : a secret-police organization employing underhanded and terrorist methods against persons suspected of disloyalty

ges·tate \ˈjes-ˌtāt\ *vb* **ges·tat·ed; ges·tat·ing** [back-formation fr. *gestation*] *vt* (1858) **1 :** to carry in the uterus during pregnancy **2 :** to conceive and gradually develop in the mind ~ *vi* : to be in the process of gestation

ges·ta·tion \je-ˈstā-shən\ *n* [L *gestation-, gestatio,* fr. *gestare* to bear, freq. of *gerere* to bear] (1615) **1 :** the carrying of young in the uterus : PREGNANCY **2 :** conception and development esp. in the mind — **ges·ta·tion·al** \-shnəl, -shə-nᵊl\ *adj*

geste *also* **gest** \ˈjest\ *n* [ME *geste,* fr. AF, fr. L *gestus,* fr. *gerere*] (14c) **1** *archaic* : DEPORTMENT **2** *archaic* : GESTURE

ges·tic \ˈjes-tik\ *adj* (1764) : relating to or consisting of bodily movements or gestures

ges·tic·u·lant \je-ˈsti-kyə-lənt\ *adj* (1877) : making gesticulations ⟨the little wiry man ~ and wild —William Faulkner⟩

ges·tic·u·late \je-ˈsti-kyə-ˌlāt\ *vi* **-lat·ed; -lat·ing** [L *gesticulatus,* pp. of *gesticulari,* fr. *gesticulus, dim. of gestus] (ca. 1609) : to make gestures esp. when speaking — **ges·ti·cu·la·tive** \je-ˈsti-kyə-ˌlā-tiv\ *adj* — **ges·tic·u·la·tor** \-ˌlā-tər\ *n* — **ges·tic·u·la·to·ry** \-lə-ˌtȯr-ē\ *adj*

ges·tic·u·la·tion \je-ˌsti-kyə-ˈlā-shən\ *n* (15c) **1 :** the act of making gestures **2 :** GESTURE; *esp* : an expressive gesture made in showing strong feeling or in enforcing an argument

ges·tur·al \ˈjes-chə-rəl, ˈjesh-\ *adj* (1613) **1 :** of, relating to, or consisting of gestures **2 :** of, relating to, or characterized by vigorous application of paint and expressive brushwork ⟨~ expressionism⟩ — **ges·tur·al·ly** \-chə-rə-lē\ *adv*

[1]**ges·ture** \ˈjes-chər, ˈjesh-\ *n* [ME, fr. AF, fr. ML *gestura* mode of action, fr. L *gestus,* pp. of *gerere*] (15c) **1** *archaic* : CARRIAGE, BEARING **2 :** a movement usu. of the body or limbs that expresses or emphasizes an idea, sentiment, or attitude **3 :** the use of motions of the limbs or body as a means of expression **4 :** something said or done by way of formality or courtesy, as a symbol or token, or for its effect on the attitudes of others ⟨a political ~ to draw popular support —V. L. Parrington⟩

[2]**gesture** *vb* **ges·tured; ges·tur·ing** *vi* (1542) : to make a gesture ~ *vt* : to express or direct by a gesture

gesture language *n* (1855) : communication by gestures; *esp* : SIGN LANGUAGE — called also *gestural language*

\ə\ **abut** \ᵊ\ **kitten**, F table \ər\ **further** \a\ **ash** \ā\ **ace** \ä\ **mop**, **mar** \au̇\ **out** \ch\ **chin** \e\ **bet** \ē\ **easy** \g\ **go** \i\ **hit** \ī\ **ice** \j\ **job** \ŋ\ **sing** \ō\ **go** \ȯ\ **law** \ȯi\ **boy** \th\ **thin** \th\ **the** \ü\ **loot** \u̇\ **foot** \y\ **yet** \zh\ **vision, beige** \k, ⁿ, œ, ue, ʸ\ *see* Guide to Pronunciation

ge·sund·heit \gə-ˈzu̇nt-ˌhīt\ *interj* [G, lit., health, fr. *gesund* healthy (fr. OHG *gisunt*) + *-heit* -hood — more at SOUND] (1914) — used to wish good health esp. to one who has just sneezed

[1]**get** \ˈget, ÷ˈgit\ *vb* **got** \ˈgät\; **got** *or* **got·ten** \ˈgä-tᵊn\; **get·ting** [ME, fr. ON *geta* to get, beget; akin to OE *bigietan* to beget, L *prehendere* to seize, grasp, Gk *chandanein* to hold, contain] *vt* (13c) **1 a :** to gain possession of **b :** to receive as a return : EARN ⟨he *got* a bad reputation for carelessness⟩ **2 a :** to obtain by concession or entreaty ⟨~ your mother's permission to go⟩ **b :** to become affected by (a disease or bodily condition) : CATCH ⟨*got* measles from his sister⟩ **3 a :** to seek out and obtain ⟨hoped to ~ dinner at the inn⟩ **b :** to obtain and bring where wanted or needed ⟨~ a pencil from the desk⟩ **4 :** BEGET **5 a :** to cause to come or go ⟨quickly *got* his luggage through customs⟩ **b :** to cause to move ⟨~ it out of the house⟩ **c :** to cause to be in a certain position or condition ⟨*got* his feet wet⟩ **d :** to make ready : PREPARE ⟨~ breakfast⟩ **6 a :** to be subjected to ⟨*got* a bad fall⟩ **b :** to receive by way of punishment **c :** to suffer a specified injury to ⟨*got* my nose broken⟩ **7 a :** to achieve as a result of military activity **b :** to obtain or receive by way of benefit or advantage ⟨he *got* little for his trouble⟩ ⟨~ the better of an enemy⟩ **8 a :** SEIZE **b :** OVERCOME **c :** to have an emotional effect on ⟨the final scene always ~*s* me⟩ **d :** IRRITATE ⟨the delays were starting to ~ her⟩ **e :** PUZZLE **f :** to take vengeance on; *specif* : KILL **g :** HIT **9 :** to prevail on : CAUSE ⟨finally *got* them to tidy up their room⟩ **10 a :** HAVE — used in the present perfect tense form with present meaning ⟨I've *got* no money⟩ **b :** to have as an obligation or necessity — used in the present perfect tense form with present meaning ⟨you have *got* to come⟩ **11 a :** to find out by calculation ⟨~ the answer to a problem⟩ **b :** MEMORIZE ⟨*got* the verse by heart⟩ **c :** HEAR **d :** UNDERSTAND ⟨he *got* the joke⟩ **12 :** to establish communication with **13 :** to put out in baseball **14 :** DELIVER 6b ⟨the car ~*s* 20 miles to the gallon⟩ ~ *vi* **1 a :** to succeed in coming or going : to bring or move oneself ⟨~ away to the country⟩ ⟨*got* into the car⟩ **b :** to reach or enter into a certain condition ⟨*got* to sleep after midnight⟩ **c :** to make progress ⟨hasn't *gotten* far with the essay⟩ **2 :** to acquire wealth **3 a :** to be able ⟨never *got* to go to college⟩ **b :** to come to be — often used with following present participle ⟨*got* talking about old times⟩ **4 a :** to succeed in becoming : BECOME ⟨how to ~ clear of all the debts I owe —Shak.⟩ **b :** to become involved ⟨people who ~ into trouble with the law⟩ **5 :** to leave immediately ⟨told them to ~⟩ ~ *verbal auxiliary* — used with the past participle of transitive verbs as a passive voice auxiliary ⟨they *got* caught in the act⟩ — **get after :** to pursue with exhortation, reprimand, or attack — **get ahead :** to achieve success ⟨determined to *get ahead* in life⟩ — **get a life :** to stop wasting time on trivial or hopeless matters — **get a move on :** HURRY — **get at 1 :** to reach effectively **2 :** to influence corruptly : BRIBE **3 :** to turn one's attention to **4 :** to try to prove or make clear ⟨what is he *getting at*⟩ — **get away with :** to avoid criticism or punishment for or the consequences of (as a reprehensible act) — **get cracking :** to make a start : get going ⟨ought to *get cracking* on that assignment⟩ — **get even :** to get revenge — **get even with :** to repay in kind — **get going :** to make a start — **get into :** to become strongly involved with or deeply interested in — **get it :** to receive a scolding or punishment — **get it on 1 :** to become enthusiastic, energetic, or excited **2 :** to engage in sexual intercourse — **get on 1 :** to produce an unfortunate effect on : UPSET ⟨the noise *got on* my nerves⟩ **2 :** to criticize insistently ⟨the fans *got on* him for losing the game⟩ — **get one's act together 1 :** to put one's life, thoughts, or emotions in order : cease to be confused or misdirected **2 :** to begin to function in a skillful or efficient manner ⟨the company finally *got its act together*⟩ — **get one's goat :** to make one angry or annoyed — **get over 1 a :** OVERCOME, SURMOUNT **b :** to recover from **c :** to reconcile oneself to : become accustomed to **2 :** to move or travel across — **get real :** to stop deceiving oneself or fooling around : face reality — **get religion 1 :** to undergo religious conversion **2 :** to turn to or adopt an enlightened course of action or point of view — **get somewhere :** to be successful — **get there :** to be successful — **get through :** to reach the end of : COMPLETE — **get to 1 a :** BEGIN ⟨*gets to* worrying over nothing at all⟩ **b :** to be ready to begin or deal with ⟨I'll *get to* the accounts as soon as I can⟩ **2 :** to have an effect on: as **a :** INFLUENCE **b :** BOTHER — **get together 1 :** to bring together : ACCUMULATE **2 :** to come together : ASSEMBLE, MEET **3 :** to reach agreement — **get wind of :** to become aware of — **get with it :** to become alert or aware : show sophisticated consciousness

usage The pronunciation \ˈgit\ has been noted as a feature of some British and American dialects since the 16th century. In the phonetic spelling of his own speech Benjamin Franklin records *git.* However, since at least 1687 some grammarians and teachers have disapproved this pronunciation. It nonetheless remains in widespread and unpredictable use in many dialects, often, but not exclusively, when *get* is a passive auxiliary (as in *get married*) or an imperative (as in *get up!*).

[2]**get** \ˈget\ *n* (14c) **1 a :** something begotten: (1) : OFFSPRING (2) : the entire progeny of a male animal **b :** LINEAGE **2 :** a return of a difficult shot in a game (as tennis)

[3]**get** \ˈget\ *n, pl* **git·tin** \gē-ˈtēn, ˈgi-tin\ [LHeb *gēṭ*] (1892) **1 :** a document of release from obligation in Jewish law; *specif* : a bill of divorce **2 :** a religious divorce by Jewish law

ge·ta \ˈge-(ˌ)tä, -tə\ *n, pl* **geta** *or* **getas** [Jp] (1884) : a Japanese wooden clog for outdoor wear

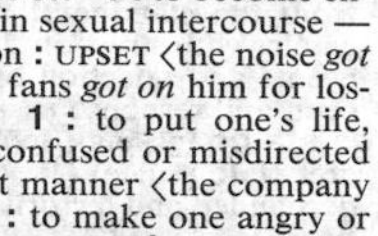
geta

get about *vi* (1793) **1 :** to become current : CIRCULATE **2 :** to be up and about : begin to walk ⟨able to *get about* again⟩

get across *vi* (1913) : to become clear or convincing ~ *vt* : to make clear or convincing ⟨we couldn't *get* our point *across*⟩

get along *vi* (1705) **1 a :** to proceed toward a destination : PROGRESS **b :** to approach an advanced stage; *esp* : to approach old age **2 :** to meet one's needs : MANAGE ⟨we *got along* on a minimum of clothing⟩ **3 :** to be or remain on congenial terms

get around *vt* (1835) **1 :** CIRCUMVENT, EVADE **2 :** to get the better of ~ *vi* **1 a :** to find or take the necessary time or effort — used with *to* **b :** to give attention or consideration — used with *to* **2 :** to go from place to place **3 :** to become known or current ⟨word *got around* that he was resigning⟩

get·at·able \get-ˈa-tə-bəl\ *adj* (1799) : ACCESSIBLE, APPROACHABLE

get·away \ˈge-tə-ˌwā\ *n* (1890) **1 :** an act or instance of getting away: as **a :** ESCAPE **b :** START **2 :** a place suitable for a vacation **3 :** a vacation esp. of brief duration

get back *vi* (1605) **1 :** to come or go again to a person, place, or condition : RETURN, REVERT ⟨*getting back* to the main topic of the lecture⟩ **2 :** to gain revenge : RETALIATE — usu. used with *at* ~ *vt* : to regain possession of : RECOVER

get by *vi* (1841) **1 :** to succeed with the least possible effort or accomplishment **2 :** to make ends meet : SURVIVE **3 :** to proceed without being discovered, criticized, or punished

get down *vt* (1647) **1 :** to manage to swallow **2 :** to cause to be physically, mentally, or emotionally exhausted : DEPRESS ⟨the weather was *getting* her *down*⟩ **3 :** to commit to writing : DESCRIBE ~ *vi* **1 :** to alight esp. from a vehicle : DESCEND **2 :** to give one's attention or consideration — used with *to* ⟨*get down* to business⟩ **3 a :** to perform music or dance effectively and infectiously **b :** to have a good time partying

get–go \ˈgit-ˌgō, ˈget-\ *also* **git–go** \ˈgit-\ *n* (1966) : the very beginning — used in the phrase *from the get-go* ⟨didn't like me from the ~⟩

Geth·sem·a·ne \geth-ˈse-mə-nē\ *n* [Gk *Gethsēmanē*] (ca. 1534) **1 :** the garden outside Jerusalem mentioned in Mk 14 as the scene of the agony and arrest of Jesus **2 :** a place or occasion of great mental or spiritual suffering

get in *vi* (ca. 1533) **1 a :** ENTER **b :** ARRIVE **2 a :** to become friendly **b :** to become involved **3 :** to become accepted for membership or chosen for office ~ *vt* **1 :** to succeed in doing, making, or delivering **2 :** to include in one's schedule **3 :** INVOLVE 2a, b

get off *vi* (1606) **1 :** to avoid the most serious consequences of a dangerous situation or punishment ⟨*got off* with a light sentence⟩ **2 :** START, LEAVE ⟨*got off* on the trip early⟩ **3 :** to leave work with permission or as scheduled **4 :** to get high on a drug **5 :** to experience orgasm **6 :** to experience great pleasure — often used with *on* ~ *vt* **1 :** to secure the release of or procure a modified penalty for ⟨his lawyers *got* him *off*⟩ **2 a :** UTTER ⟨*get off* a joke⟩ **b :** to write and send **3 :** to succeed in doing, making, or delivering **4 :** to cause to get off

get on *vi* (1816) **1 :** GET ALONG ⟨was *getting on* in years⟩ ⟨*got on* well with the boss⟩ ⟨*get on* with the game⟩ **2 :** to gain knowledge or understanding ⟨*got on* to the racket⟩

get out *vi* (14c) **1 :** LEAVE, ESCAPE ⟨doubted that he would *get out* alive⟩ **2 :** to become known : leak out ⟨their secret *got out*⟩ ~ *vt* **1 :** to cause to leave or escape **2 :** to bring before the public; *esp* : PUBLISH

get round *vi* (1748) : GET AROUND

get·ter \ˈge-tər\ *n* (15c) **1 :** one that gets **2 :** a substance introduced into a vacuum tube or electric lamp to remove traces of gas

get through *vi* (1619) **1 :** to reach a destination **2 :** to gain approval or a desired outcome **3 a :** to become clear or understood ⟨our warnings finally *got through* to him⟩ **b :** to complete a communications connection

get–to·geth·er \ˈget-tə-ˌge-t͟hər\ *n* (1911) : MEETING; *esp* : an informal social gathering

get·up \ˈget-ˌəp\ *n* (1847) **1 :** OUTFIT, COSTUME **2 :** general composition or structure

get up *vi* (14c) **1 a :** to arise from bed **b :** to rise to one's feet **c :** CLIMB, ASCEND **2 :** to go ahead or faster — used in the imperative as a command esp. to driven animals ~ *vt* **1 :** to make preparations for : ORGANIZE ⟨*got up* a party for the newcomers⟩ **2 :** to arrange as to external appearance : DRESS **3 :** to acquire a knowledge of **4 :** to create in oneself ⟨cannot *get up* the courage to tell them⟩

get–up–and–go \ˌget-ˌəp-ᵊn-ˈgō, ˌgit-, -ᵊm-, -ᵊŋ-\ *n* (1906) : ENERGY, DRIVE

ge·um \ˈjē-əm\ *n* [L] (ca. 1548) : AVENS

GeV *abbr* giga-electron-volt

gew·gaw \ˈg(y)ü-(ˌ)gȯ\ *also* **gee·gaw** \ˈjē-, ˈgē-\ *n* [origin unknown] (ca. 1529) : a showy trifle : BAUBLE, TRINKET

ge·würz·tra·mi·ner \gə-ˈvu̇rt-ˌstra-mə-nər, -ˈvərt-, -ˌsträ; -strə-ˈmē-nər\ *n, often cap* [G, variety of grape, fr. *Gewürz* spice + *Traminer,* variety of grape, fr. *Tramin* (Termeno, Italy)] (ca. 1950) : a light dry Alsatian white wine with a spicy bouquet; *also* : a similar wine made elsewhere

gey \ˈgā\ *adv* [alter. of *gay,* adv.] (1796) *chiefly Scot* : VERY, QUITE

gey·ser \ˈgī-zər, *Brit sometimes* ˈgā- *or* ˈgē- *for 1 & usu* ˈgē- *for 2*\ *n* [Icel *Geysir,* hot spring in Iceland, fr. *geysa* to rush forth, fr. ON; akin to OE *gēotan* to pour — more at FOUND] (1780) **1 :** a spring that throws forth intermittent jets of heated water and steam **2** *Brit* : an apparatus for heating water rapidly with a gas flame (as for a bath)

gey·ser·ite \-zə-ˌrīt\ *n* [F *geysérite,* fr. *geyser,* fr. Icel *Geysir*] (ca. 1814) : a variety of opal that is deposited around some hot springs and geysers in white or grayish concretions

g–fac·tor \ˈjē-ˌfak-tər\ *n* (1942) : GYROMAGNETIC RATIO

g–force \ˈjē-ˌfȯrs\ *n* (1903) : the force of gravity or acceleration on a body ⟨pilots experiencing strong ~*s* during takeoff⟩

GH *abbr* growth hormone

gha·ri·al \ˈger-ē-əl\ *n* [Hindi & Urdu *ghaṛyāl, ghaṛiyāl,* ultim. fr. Skt *ghaṇṭika* crocodilian] (ca. 1809) : a large long-snouted crocodilian (*Gavialis gangeticus* of the family Gavialidae) of India

ghar·ry \ˈga-rē, ˈgär-ē\ *n, pl* **gharries** [Hindi & Urdu *gāṛī*] (1810) : a horse-drawn cab used esp. in India and Egypt

ghast \ˈgast\ *adj* (1622) *archaic* : GHASTLY

ghast·ful \-fəl\ *adj* (14c) *archaic* : FRIGHTFUL — **ghast·ful·ly** *adv, archaic*

ghast·ly \ˈgast-lē\ *adj* **ghast·li·er; -est** [ME *gastly,* fr. *gasten* to terrify — more at GAST] (14c) **1 a :** terrifyingly horrible to the senses : FRIGHTENING ⟨a ~ crime⟩ **b :** intensely unpleasant, disagreeable, or objectionable ⟨such a life seems ~ in its emptiness and sterility —Aldous Huxley⟩ **2 :** resembling a ghost **3** *obs* : filled with fear **4 :** very great ⟨a ~ mistake⟩ — **ghast·li·ness** *n* — **ghastly** *adv*

syn GHASTLY, GRISLY, GRUESOME, MACABRE, LURID mean horrifying and repellent in appearance or aspect. GHASTLY suggests the terrifying aspects of corpses and ghosts ⟨a *ghastly* accident⟩. GRISLY and GRUESOME suggest additionally the results of extreme violence or cruelty ⟨an unusually *grisly* murder⟩ ⟨suffered a *gruesome* death⟩. MACABRE implies a morbid preoccupation with the physical aspects of death ⟨a *macabre* tale of premature burial⟩. LURID adds to GRUESOME the suggestion of shuddering fascination with violent death and esp. with murder ⟨the *lurid* details of a crime⟩.

ghat \ˈgȯt, ˈgät\ *n* [Hindi & Urdu *ghāṭ*, fr. Skt *ghaṭṭa*] (1783) : a broad flight of steps that is situated on an Indian riverbank and that provides access to the water esp. for bathing

GHB \ˌjē-(ˌ)āch-ˈbē\ *n* (1964) : a metabolite $C_4H_8O_3$ of gamma-aminobutyric acid that is a depressant of the central nervous system and is used illicitly in the form of its synthetic sodium salt to produce sedative and euphoric effects or to stimulate release of growth hormone to increase muscle mass — called also *gamma hydroxybutyrate*

ghee *or* **ghi** \ˈgē\ *n* [Hindi & Urdu *ghī*, fr. Skt *ghṛta*] (1665) : a semifluid clarified butter made esp. in India

gher·kin \ˈgər-kən\ *n* [D *gurken*, pl. of *gurk* cucumber, ultim. fr. MGk *agouros*] (1661) **1 a :** a small prickly fruit used for pickling; *also* : a pickle made from this fruit **b :** the slender annual vine (*Cucumis anguria*) of the gourd family that bears gherkins **2 :** the immature fruit of the cucumber esp. when used for pickling

¹ghet·to \ˈge-(ˌ)tō\ *n, pl* **ghettos** *also* **ghettoes** [It, fr. Venetian dial. *ghèto* island where Jews were forced to live, lit., foundry (located on the island), fr. *ghetàr* to cast, fr. L *jactare* to throw — more at JET] (1611) **1 :** a quarter of a city in which Jews were formerly required to live **2 :** a quarter of a city in which members of a minority group live esp. because of social, legal, or economic pressure **3 a :** an isolated group ⟨a geriatric ~⟩ **b :** a situation that resembles a ghetto esp. in conferring inferior status or limiting opportunity ⟨the pink-collar ~⟩

²ghetto *vt* (1936) : GHETTOIZE

ghetto blaster *n* (1981) : BOOM BOX

ghet·to·ize \ˈge-tō-ˌīz\ *vt* **-ized; -iz·ing** (1939) : to isolate in or as if in a ghetto — **ghet·to·i·za·tion** \ˌge-tō-ə-ˈzā-shən\ *n*

Ghib·el·line \ˈgi-bə-ˌlēn, -ˌlīn, -lən\ *n* [It *Ghibellino*] (1573) : a member of an aristocratic political party in medieval Italy supporting the authority of the German emperors — compare GUELF

ghillie *var of* GILLIE

¹ghost \ˈgōst\ *n* [ME *gost, gast*, fr. OE *gāst*; akin to OHG *geist* spirit, Skt *heḍa* anger] (bef. 12c) **1 :** the seat of life or intelligence : SOUL ⟨give up the ~⟩ **2 :** a disembodied soul; *esp* : the soul of a dead person believed to be an inhabitant of the unseen world or to appear to the living in bodily likeness **3 :** SPIRIT, DEMON **4 a :** a faint shadowy trace ⟨a ~ of a smile⟩ **b :** the least bit ⟨not a ~ of a chance⟩ **5 :** a false image in a photographic negative or on a television screen caused esp. by reflection **6 :** one who ghostwrites **7 :** a red blood cell that has lost its hemoglobin — **ghost·like** \-ˌlīk\ *adj* — **ghosty** \ˈgō-stē\ *adj*

²ghost *vt* (1606) **1 :** to haunt like a ghost **2 :** GHOSTWRITE ~ *vi* **1 a :** to move silently like a ghost **b :** to sail quietly in light winds **2 :** GHOSTWRITE

Ghost Dance *n* (1890) : a group dance of a late 19th century American Indian messianic cult believed to promote the return of the dead and the restoration of traditional ways of life

ghost·ing \ˈgōs-tiŋ\ *n* (ca. 1957) : a faint double image on a television screen; *also* : the formation of such images

ghost·ly \ˈgōst-lē\ *adj* **ghost·li·er; -est** (bef. 12c) **1 :** of or relating to the soul : SPIRITUAL **2 :** of, relating to, or having the characteristics of a ghost : SPECTRAL — **ghost·li·ness** *n* — **ghostly** *adv*

ghost story *n* (1819) **1 :** a story about ghosts **2 :** a tale based on imagination rather than fact

ghost town *n* (1931) : a once-flourishing town wholly or nearly deserted usu. as a result of the exhaustion of some natural resource

ghost word *n* (1886) : a word form never in established usage

ghost·write \ˈgōs(t)-ˌrīt\ *vb* **-wrote** \-ˌrōt\; **-writ·ten** \-ˌri-tᵊn\ [back-formation fr. *ghostwriter*] *vi* (1927) : to write for and in the name of another ~ *vt* : to write (as a speech) for another who is the presumed author — **ghost·writ·er** *n*

ghoul \ˈgül\ *n* [Ar *ghūl*] (1786) **1 :** a legendary evil being that robs graves and feeds on corpses **2 :** one suggestive of a ghoul; *esp* : one who shows morbid interest in things considered shocking or repulsive — **ghoul·ish** \ˈgü-lish\ *adj* — **ghoul·ish·ly** *adv* — **ghoul·ish·ness** *n*

ghou·lie \ˈgü-lē\ *n* (1928) : GHOUL 1

GHQ *abbr* general headquarters

GHz *abbr* gigahertz

gi *abbr* gill

¹GI \ˌjē-ˈī\ *adj* [galvanized *iron*; fr. abbr. used in listing such articles as garbage cans, but taken as abbr. for *government issue*] (ca. 1935) **1 :** provided by an official U.S. military supply department ⟨~ shoes⟩ **2 :** of, relating to, or characteristic of U.S. military personnel **3 :** conforming to military regulations or customs ⟨a ~ haircut⟩

²GI *n, pl* **GIs** *or* **GI's** \-ˈīz\ (1943) : a member or former member of the U.S. armed forces; *esp* : a man enlisted in the army

³GI *adv* (1949) : in a strictly regulation manner

⁴GI *vt* **GI'd** \-ˈīd\; **GI'·ing** \-ˈī-iŋ\ (1951) : to clean thoroughly (as floors) in preparation for or as if for a military inspection

⁵GI *abbr* **1** galvanized iron **2** gastrointestinal **3** general issue; government issue

¹gi·ant \ˈjī-ənt\ *n* [ME *giaunt*, fr. AF *geant*, fr. L *gigant-, gigas*, fr. Gk] (14c) **1 :** a legendary humanlike being of great stature and strength **2 a :** a living being of great size **b :** a person of extraordinary powers **3 :** something unusually large or powerful — **gi·ant·like** \-ˌlīk\ *adj*

²giant *adj* (15c) : having extremely large size, proportion, or power

giant anteater *n* (1940) : a large bushy-tailed anteater (*Myrmecophaga tridactyla*) of Central and So. America

giant cactus *n* (ca. 1884) : SAGUARO

giant clam *n* (ca. 1889) : a very large clam (*Tridacna gigas*) found on the coral reefs of the Indian and Pacific oceans that sometimes weighs more than 500 pounds (227 kilograms)

gi·ant·ess \ˈjī-ən-təs\ *n* (14c) : a female giant

gi·ant·ism \ˈjī-ən-ˌti-zəm\ *n* (1639) **1 :** the quality or state of being a giant ⟨~ in industry⟩ **2 :** GIGANTISM 2

giant panda *n* (1920) : PANDA 2

giant reed *n* (1851) : a tall perennial grass (*Arundo donax*) native to Mediterranean regions that has woody stems used esp. in making baskets, shelters, and reeds for woodwind instruments

giant schnauzer *n* (ca. 1934) : any of a breed of powerful heavyset schnauzers that attain a height of 23½ to 27½ inches (60 to 70 centimeters)

giant sequoia *n* (ca. 1931) : an evergreen tree (*Sequoiadendron giganteum*) of the bald cypress family that grows on the western slopes of the Sierra Nevada mountain range and sometimes exceeds 270 feet (about 82 meters) in height — called also *big tree, sequoia*

giant slalom *n* (1952) : a slalom race for skiers on a longer and steeper course than that used for the regular slalom

giant squid *n* (ca. 1890) : any of a genus (*Architeuthis*) of extremely large squids that may attain a length of 60 feet (18 meters) and include the largest mollusks known

giant star *n* (1912) : a star of great luminosity and of large mass

giant tortoise *n* (ca. 1909) : any of various large long-lived herbivorous land tortoises (genus *Geochelone*) formerly common on the islands of the western Indian Ocean and on the Galápagos Islands

giant water bug *n* (1901) : any of a family (Belostomatidae and esp. genus *Lethocerus*) of very large predatory aquatic bugs capable of inflicting a painful bite

giaour \ˈjau̇(-ə)r\ *n* [F, fr. It dial. (Venetian) *giaur*, fr. Turk *gâvur*, fr. Pers *gawr, gabr*] (1564) : one outside the Islamic faith : INFIDEL 2a

giar·dia \jē-ˈär-dē-ə, ˈjär-\ *n* [NL, fr. Alfred M. *Giard* †1908 Fr. biologist] (1918) : any of a genus (*Giardia*) of flagellate protozoans inhabiting the intestines of various mammals and including one (*G. lamblia* syn. *G. intestinalis*) that is associated with diarrhea in humans

giar·di·a·sis \(ˌ)jē-ˌär-ˈdī-ə-səs, jē-ər-, jär-\ *n, pl* **-a·ses** \-ˌsēz\ [NL] (1919) : infestation with or disease caused by a giardia

¹gib \ˈgib\ *n* [ME, fr. *Gib*, nickname for *Gilbert*] (1561) : a male cat; *specif* : a castrated male cat

²gib *n* [origin unknown] (1795) : a plate of metal or other material machined to hold other parts in place, to afford a bearing surface, or to provide means for overcoming looseness

Gib *or* **Gibr** *abbr* Gibraltar

gib·ber \ˈji-bər\ *vi* **gib·bered; gib·ber·ing** \-b(ə-)riŋ\ [imit.] (1604) : to speak rapidly, inarticulately, and often foolishly — **gibber** *n*

gib·ber·el·lic acid \ˌji-bə-ˈre-lik-\ *n* (1954) : a crystalline acid $C_{19}H_{22}O_6$ that is a gibberellin used esp. in the malting of barley

gib·ber·el·lin \-ˈre-lən\ *n* [NL *Gibberella fujikoroi*, fungus from which it was first isolated] (1939) : any of several growth-regulating plant hormones that promote cell elongation and activity of the cambium, induce parthenocarpy, and stimulate synthesis of nucleic acids and proteins

gib·ber·ish \ˈji-b(ə-)rish, ˈgi-\ *n* [prob. fr. *gibber*] (ca. 1554) : unintelligible or meaningless language: **a :** a technical or esoteric language **b :** pretentious or needlessly obscure language

¹gib·bet \ˈji-bət\ *n* [ME *gibet*, fr. AF] (13c) **1 :** GALLOWS 1a **2 :** an upright post with a projecting arm for hanging the bodies of executed criminals as a warning

²gibbet *vt* (1646) **1 a :** to expose to infamy or public scorn **b :** to hang on a gibbet **2 :** to execute by hanging on a gibbet

gib·bon \ˈgi-bən\ *n* [F] (1774) : any of a genus (*Hylobates* of the family Hylobatidae) of agile brachiating tailless apes of southeastern Asia that are the smallest and most arboreal anthropoid apes

gib·bos·i·ty \ji-ˈbä-sə-tē, gi-\ *n, pl* **-ties** (14c) : PROTUBERANCE, SWELLING

gib·bous \ˈji-bəs, ˈgi-\ *adj* [ME, fr. LL *gibbosus* humpbacked, fr. L *gibbus* hump] (14c) **1 a :** marked by convexity or swelling **b** *of the moon or a planet* : seen with more than half but not all of the apparent disk illuminated **2 :** having a hump : HUMPBACKED

gibe *or* **jibe** \ˈjīb\ *vb* **gibed** *or* **jibed; gib·ing** *or* **jib·ing** [perh. fr. MF *giber* to shake, handle roughly] *vi* (1567) : to utter taunting words ~ *vt* : to deride or tease with taunting words ***syn*** see SCOFF — **gibe** *or* **jibe** *n* — **gib·er** *or* **jib·er** *n*

gib·lets \ˈjib-ləts *also* ˈgib-\ *n pl* [ME *gibelet* giblets piece, nonessential bit, fr. AF *gibelot*, fr. OF (Picard) *giblé* stew of wildfowl] (15c) : the edible viscera of a fowl

Gi·bral·tar \jə-ˈbrȯl-tər\ *n* [*Gibraltar*, fortress in the Brit. colony of Gibraltar] (1776) : an impregnable stronghold

Gib·son \ˈgib-sən\ *n* [fr. the name *Gibson*] (1948) : a martini garnished with a cocktail onion

Gibson girl *adj* [Charles D. *Gibson*] (1936) : of or relating to a style esp. in women's clothing characterized by high necks, full sleeves, and wasp waists

gid \ˈgid\ *n* [back-formation fr. *giddy*] (1601) : a disease esp. of sheep caused by the larva of a tapeworm (*Multiceps multiceps*) in the brain

¹gid·dy \ˈgi-dē\ *adj* **gid·di·er; -est** [ME *gidy* mad, foolish, fr. OE *gydig* possessed, mad; akin to OE *god* god] (14c) **1 a :** DIZZY ⟨~ from the unaccustomed exercise⟩ **b :** causing dizziness ⟨a ~ height⟩ **c :** whirling rapidly **2 a :** lightheartedly silly : FRIVOLOUS **b :** joyfully elated : EUPHORIC — **gid·di·ly** \ˈgi-də-lē\ *adv* — **gid·di·ness** \ˈgi-dē-nəs\ *n*

²giddy *vb* **gid·died; gid·dy·ing** *vt* (1602) : to make giddy ~ *vi* : to become giddy

gid·dy·ap \ˌgi-dē-ˈap, -ˈəp\ *or* **gid·dy·up** \-ˈəp\ *also* **gid·dap** \gi-ˈdap, -ˈdep\ *vb imper* [alter. of *get up*] (ca. 1897) — a command (as to a horse) to go ahead or go faster

Gid·e·on \ˈgi-dē-ən\ *n* [Heb *Gidhʿōn*] (1535) **1 :** an early Hebrew hero noted for his defeat of the Midianites **2 :** a member of an interdenominational organization whose activities include the placing of Bibles in hotel rooms

gie \ˈgē\ *chiefly Scot var of* GIVE

Gi·em·sa stain \gē-ˈem-zə-\ *n* [Gustav *Giemsa* †1948 Ger. chemotherapist] (ca. 1909) : a stain consisting of eosin and a blue dye and used chiefly in the differential staining of blood films — called also *Giemsa, Giemsa's stain* — **Gi·em·sa–stained** \-ˌstānd\ *adj*

\ə\ **abut** \ᵊ\ **kitten**, F **table** \ər\ **further** \a\ **ash** \ā\ **ace** \ä\ **mop, mar**
\au̇\ **out** \ch\ **chin** \e\ **bet** \ē\ **easy** \g\ **go** \i\ **hit** \ī\ **ice** \j\ **job**
\ŋ\ **sing** \ō\ **go** \ȯ\ **law** \ȯi\ **boy** \th\ **thin** \t͟h\ **the** \ü\ **loot** \u̇\ **foot**
\y\ **yet** \zh\ **vision, beige** \k̲, ⁿ, œ, ue, ʸ\ *see* Guide to Pronunciation

GIF \ˈgif, ˈjif\ *n* [graphic *i*nterchange *f*ormat] (1987) **:** a computer file format for the compression and storage of digital video images; *also* **:** such an image itself

[1]**gift** \ˈgift\ *n* [ME, fr. ON, something given, talent; akin to OE *giefan* to give] (12c) **1 :** a notable capacity, talent, or endowment **2 :** something voluntarily transferred by one person to another without compensation **3 :** the act, right, or power of giving

syn GIFT, FACULTY, APTITUDE, BENT, TALENT, GENIUS, KNACK mean a special ability for doing something. GIFT often implies special favor by God or nature ⟨the *gift* of singing beautifully⟩. FACULTY applies to an innate or less often acquired ability for a particular accomplishment or function ⟨a *faculty* for remembering names⟩. APTITUDE implies a natural liking for some activity and the likelihood of success in it ⟨a mechanical *aptitude*⟩. BENT is nearly equal to APTITUDE but it stresses inclination perhaps more than specific ability ⟨a family with an artistic *bent*⟩. TALENT suggests a marked natural ability that needs to be developed ⟨has enough *talent* to succeed⟩. GENIUS suggests impressive inborn creative ability ⟨has no great *genius* for poetry⟩. KNACK implies a comparatively minor but special ability making for ease and dexterity in performance ⟨the *knack* of getting along⟩.

[2]**gift** *vt* (ca. 1550) **1 :** to endow with some power, quality, or attribute **2 :** PRESENT ⟨~*ed* her with flowers⟩ — **gift·ee** \ˌgif-ˈtē\ *n*

GIFT *abbr* gamete intrafallopian transfer; gamete intrafallopian tube transfer

gift card *n* (1991) **:** a card entitling the recipient to receive goods or services of a specified value from the issuer

gift certificate *n* (1942) **:** a certificate entitling the recipient to receive goods or services of a specified value from the issuer

gift·ed \ˈgif-təd\ *adj* (1644) **1 :** having great natural ability **:** TALENTED ⟨~ children⟩ **2 :** revealing a special gift ⟨~ voices⟩ — **gift·ed·ly** *adv* — **gift·ed·ness** *n*

gift of gab (1839) **:** the ability to talk glibly and persuasively

gift of tongues [fr. the gifts of the Spirit in 1 Cor 12:1–13] (1560) **:** a charisma identified by ecstatic usu. unintelligible speech

gift·ware \ˈgift-ˌwer\ *n* (1904) **:** wares or goods suitable for gifts

gift wrap *vt* (1936) **:** to wrap (merchandise intended as a gift) decoratively

[1]**gig** \ˈgig\ *n* [ME *-gyge* (in *whyrlegyge* whirligig), of unknown origin] (1570) **1 :** something that whirls or is whirled: as **a** *obs* **:** TOP, WHIRLIGIG **b :** a 3-digit selection in a numbers game **2 :** a person of odd or grotesque appearance **3 a :** a long light ship's boat **b :** a rowboat designed for speed rather than for work **4 :** a light 2-wheeled one-horse carriage

[2]**gig** *vi* **gigged; gig·ging** (1807) **:** to travel in a gig

[3]**gig** *n* [short for earlier *fizgig, fishgig,* of unknown origin] (1722) **1 :** a pronged spear for catching fish **2 :** an arrangement of hooks to be drawn through a school of fish in order to hook their bodies

[4]**gig** *vb* **gigged; gig·ging** *vt* (1803) **1 :** to spear with a gig **2 a** *chiefly West* **:** SPUR, JAB **b :** GOAD, PROVOKE ~ *vi* **:** to fish with a gig

[5]**gig** *n* [origin unknown] (1926) **:** a job usu. for a specified time; *esp* **:** an entertainer's engagement

[6]**gig** *vi* **gigged; gig·ging** (1939) **:** to work as a musician ⟨*gigged* with various bands —*Downbeat*⟩

[7]**gig** *n* [origin unknown] (ca. 1941) **:** a military demerit

[8]**gig** *vt* **gigged; gig·ging** (ca. 1941) **:** to give a military gig to

[9]**gig** *n* (1987) **:** GIGABYTE

giga- \ˈji-gə, ˈgi-\ *comb form* [ISV, fr. Gk *gigas* giant] **:** billion (10^9) ⟨*giga*hertz⟩ ⟨*giga*watt⟩

giga·bit \-ˌbit\ *n* (1970) **:** one billion bits

giga·byte \-ˌbīt\ *n* (1975) **:** 1024 megabytes or 1,073,741,824 bytes; *also* **:** one billion bytes

giga·flop \-ˌfläp\ *n* [*fl*oating-point *op*eration] (1976) **:** a unit of measure for the calculating speed of a computer equal to one billion floating-point operations per second

giga·hertz \-ˌhərts, -ˌherts\ *n* (1964) **:** a unit of frequency equal to one billion hertz

gi·gan·tesque \ˌjī-ˌgan-ˈtesk, -gən-\ *adj* (1821) **:** of enormous or grotesquely large proportions

gi·gan·tic \jī-ˈgan-tik, jə-\ *adj* [Gk *gigantikos,* fr. *gigant-, gigas* giant] (1630) **:** exceeding the usual or expected (as in size, force, or prominence) *syn* see ENORMOUS — **gi·gan·ti·cal·ly** \-ti-k(ə-)lē\ *adv*

gi·gan·tism \jī-ˈgan-ˌti-zəm, jə-; ˈjī-gən-\ *n* (ca. 1885) **1 :** GIANTISM 1 **2 :** development to abnormally large size **3 :** excessive vegetative growth often accompanied by the inhibiting of reproduction

giga·watt \ˈji-gə-ˌwät, ˈgi-\ *n* (ca. 1962) **:** a unit of power equal to one billion watts

[1]**gig·gle** \ˈgi-gəl\ *vb* **gig·gled; gig·gling** \-g(ə-)liŋ\ [imit.] *vi* (1509) **:** to laugh with repeated short catches of the breath ~ *vt* **:** to utter with a giggle — **gig·gler** \-g(ə-)lər\ *n* — **gig·gling·ly** \-g(ə-)liŋ-lē\ *adv* — **gig·gly** \-g(ə-)lē\ *adj*

[2]**giggle** *n* (ca. 1677) **1 :** the act of giggling **2** *chiefly Brit* **:** a source of amusement

GIGO *abbr* garbage in, garbage out

gig·o·lo \ˈji-gə-ˌlō, ˈzhi-\ *n, pl* **-los** [F] (1922) **1 :** a man supported by a woman usu. in return for his attentions **2 :** a professional dancing partner or male escort

gi·got \ˈji-gət, zhē-ˈgō\ *n, pl* **gi·gots** \-gəts, -ˈgō(z)\ [MF, dim. of *gigue* fiddle; fr. its shape — more at JIG] (1526) **1 :** a leg of meat (as lamb) esp. when cooked **2 :** a leg-of-mutton sleeve

gigue \ˈzhēg\ *n* [F, fr. E *jig*] (1685) **:** a lively dance movement (as of a suite) having compound triple rhythm and composed in fugal style

Gi·la monster \ˈhē-lə-\ *n* [*Gila* River, Ariz.] (1877) **:** a large orange and black venomous lizard (*Heloderma suspectum*) of the southwestern U.S.; *also* **:** a related lizard (*H. horridum*) of Mexico

gil·bert \ˈgil-bərt\ *n* [William *Gilbert*] (1893) **:** the centimeter-gram-second unit of magnetomotive force equivalent to $10 \div 4\pi$ ampere-turn

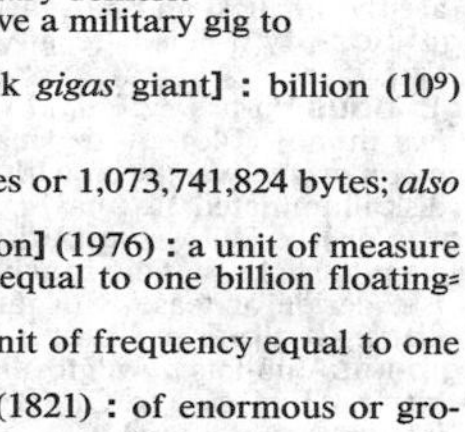

Gila monster

[1]**gild** \ˈgild\ *vt* **gild·ed** \ˈgil-dəd\ *or* **gilt** \ˈgilt\; **gild·ing** [ME, fr. OE *gyldan;* akin to OE *gold* gold] (14c) **1 :** to overlay with or as if with a thin covering of gold **2 a :** to give money to **b :** to give an attractive but often deceptive appearance to **c** *archaic* **:** to make bloody — **gild·er** *n* — **gild the lily :** to add unnecessary ornamentation to something beautiful in its own right

[2]**gild** *var of* GUILD

Gil·ga·mesh \ˈgil-gə-ˌmesh, gil-ˈgä-\ *n* (1894) **:** a legendary Sumerian king and hero of the *Gilgamesh Epic*

[1]**gill** \ˈjil\ *n* [ME *gille,* fr. ML *gillus,* fr. LL *gillo, gello* water pot] (14c) — see WEIGHT table

[2]**gill** \ˈgil\ *n* [ME *gile,* of Scand origin; akin to Sw *gäl* gill, ON *gjǫlnar* lips; akin to Gk *chelynē* lip, jawbone] (14c) **1 :** an organ (as of a fish) for obtaining oxygen from water **2 a :** [3]WATTLE **b :** the flesh under or about the chin or jaws — usu. used in pl. **c :** one of the radiating plates forming the undersurface of the cap of a mushroom fungus — **gilled** \ˈgild\ *adj* — **to the gills :** as full or as much as possible ⟨a suitcase packed *to the gills*⟩

[3]**gill** \ˈgil\ *vt* (1884) **:** GILLNET ~ *vi, of fish* **:** to become entangled in a gill net — **gill·er** *n*

[4]**gill** \ˈgil\ *n* [ME *gille,* fr. ON *gil;* akin to OHG *gil* hernia] (14c) **1** *Brit* **:** RAVINE **2** *Brit* **:** a narrow stream or rivulet

[5]**gill** \ˈjil\ *n, often cap* [ME, fr. *Gill,* nickname for *Gillian*] (15c) **:** GIRL, SWEETHEART

gill arch *n* (1879) **1 :** any of the bony or cartilaginous arches or curved bars extending dorsoventrally and placed one behind the other on each side of the pharynx and supporting the gills of fishes and amphibians **2 :** any of the rudimentary ridges in the embryos of all higher vertebrates that correspond to the gill arches

gill cleft *n* (ca. 1889) **1 :** GILL SLIT 1 **2 :** GILL SLIT 2

gill cover *n* (1776) **:** OPERCULUM 1b

gil·lie *or* **ghil·lie** \ˈgi-lē\ *n* [ScGael *gille* & Ir *giolla* youth, gillie] (1705) **1 :** a male attendant on a Scottish Highland chief; *broadly* **:** ATTENDANT **2** *chiefly Scot & Irish* **:** a fishing and hunting guide **3 :** a shoe with a low top and decorative lacing

gill·net \ˈgil-ˌnet\ *vt* (1949) **:** to catch (fish) with a gill net

gill net *n* (1796) **:** a flat net suspended vertically in the water with meshes that allow the head of a fish to pass but entangle the gills upon withdrawal

gill·net·ter \-ˌne-tər\ *n* (ca. 1889) **:** a boat equipped for or engaged in fishing with gill nets; *also* **:** a person who fishes with a gill net

gill raker *n* (1880) **:** any of the bony processes on a gill arch that divert solid substances away from the gills

gill slit *n* (1854) **1 :** any of the openings or clefts between the gill arches in vertebrates that breathe by gills through which water taken in at the mouth passes to the exterior and so bathes the gills **2 :** any of the rudimentary grooves in the neck region of the embryos of air-breathing vertebrates that correspond to the gill slits **3 :** the external opening to the cavity containing the gills when a protective covering of the gills is present

gil·ly·flow·er \ˈji-lē-ˌflau̇(-ə)r\ *n* [by folk etymology fr. ME *gilofre* clove, fr. AF, alter. of OF *girofle,* fr. L *caryophyllum,* fr. Gk *karyophyllon,* fr. *karyon* nut + *phyllon* leaf — more at CAREEN, BLADE] (1551) **:** CARNATION 2

Gil·son·ite \ˈgil-sə-ˌnīt\ *trademark* — used for asphalt

[1]**gilt** \ˈgilt\ *adj* [ME, fr. pp. of *gilden* to gild] (14c) **:** covered with gold or gilt **:** of the color of gold

[2]**gilt** *n* (15c) **1 :** gold or something that resembles gold laid on a surface **2** *slang* **:** MONEY **3 :** superficial brilliance **4 :** a bond issued by the government of the United Kingdom

[3]**gilt** *n* [ME *gylte,* fr. ON *gyltr;* akin to OE *gelde* sterile — more at GELD] (14c) **:** a young female swine

gilt–edged \ˈgilt-ˌejd\ *or* **gilt–edge** \-ˈej\ *adj* (1818) **1 :** having a gilt edge **2 :** of the best quality or rating ⟨~ securities⟩

[1]**gim·bal** \ˈgim-bəl, ˈjim-\ *n* [alter. of obs. *gemel* double ring, fr. ME, fr. AF *gemel, jomel,* fr. L *gemellus,* dim. of *geminus*] (ca. 1780) **:** a device that permits a body to incline freely in any direction or suspends it so that it will remain level when its support is tipped — usu. used in pl.; called also *gimbal ring*

[2]**gimbal** *vt* **-balled** *or* **-baled; -bal·ling** *or* **-bal·ing** (1875) **:** to provide with or support on gimbals

[1]**gim·crack** \ˈjim-ˌkrak\ *n* [origin unknown] (1676) **:** a showy object of little use or value **:** GEWGAW — **gim·crack·ery** \-ˌkra-k(ə-)rē\ *n*

[2]**gimcrack** *adj* (1715) **:** CHEAP, SHODDY

gim·el \ˈgi-məl\ *n* [Heb *gīmel*] (ca. 1567) **:** the 3d letter of the Hebrew alphabet — see ALPHABET table

[1]**gim·let** \ˈgim-lət\ *n* [ME, fr. AF *guimbelet,* fr. MF (Picard), modif. of MD *wimmelkijn,* fr. *wimmel* wimble] (14c) **:** a small tool with a screw point, grooved shank, and cross handle for boring holes

[2]**gimlet** *adj* (1752) **:** having a piercing or penetrating quality

[3]**gimlet** *vt* (1840) **:** to pierce as if with a gimlet

[4]**gimlet** *n* [prob. fr. [1]*gimlet*] (1928) **:** a drink consisting of sweetened lime juice and gin or vodka and sometimes carbonated or plain water

gim·let–eyed \-ˈīd\ *adj* (1752) **:** SHARP-SIGHTED

gim·mal \ˈgi-məl, ˈji-\ *n* [alter. of obs. *gemel* double ring — more at GIMBAL] (1598) **1** *pl* **:** joined work (as in a clock) whose parts move within each other **2 :** a finger ring consisting of a pair or series of interlocked rings

gim·me \ˈgi-mē\ *n, pl* **gimmes** [fr. *gimme,* contr. of *give me*] (1929) **1 :** a short putt in golf conceded to an opponent in casual or match play **2 :** something easily achieved or won esp. in a contest

gimme cap *n* (1978) **:** an adjustable visored cap that often features a corporate logo or slogan

[1]**gim·mick** \ˈgi-mik\ *n* [origin unknown] (1922) **1 a :** a mechanical device for secretly and dishonestly controlling gambling apparatus **b :** an ingenious or novel mechanical device **:** GADGET **2 a :** an important feature that is not immediately apparent **:** CATCH **b :** an ingenious and usu. new scheme or angle **c :** a trick or device used to attract business or attention ⟨a marketing ~⟩ — **gim·micky** \-mi-kē\ *adj*

[2]**gimmick** *vt* (1922) **1 :** to alter or influence by means of a gimmick **2 :** to provide with a gimmick — often used with *up*

gim·mick·ry \ˈgi-mi-krē\ *n, pl* **-ries** (1948) **:** an array or profusion of gimmicks; *also* **:** use of gimmicks

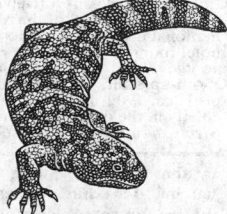

gimp • give 529

[1]**gimp** \ˈgimp\ *n* [perh. fr. D] (1664) **:** an ornamental flat braid or round cord used as a trimming
[2]**gimp** *n* [perh. fr. *gimp* fish line strengthened with wire] (1893) **:** SPIRIT, VIM
[3]**gimp** *n* [origin unknown] (1925) **1 :** CRIPPLE 1a **2 :** LIMP ‹walks with a ~ —Damon Runyon› — **gimpy** \ˈgim-pē\ *adj*
[4]**gimp** *vi* (ca. 1931) **:** LIMP, HOBBLE ‹~*ing* up the stairs›
[1]**gin** \ˈgin\ *vb* **gan** \ˈgan\; **gin·ning** [ME *ginnen,* short for *beginnen*] (13c) *archaic* **:** BEGIN
[2]**gin** \ˈjin\ *n* [ME *gin,* fr. AF, short for *engin* — more at ENGINE] (13c) **:** any of various tools or mechanical devices: as **a :** a snare or trap for game **b :** COTTON GIN
[3]**gin** \ˈjin\ *vt* **ginned; gin·ning** (1606) **1 :** SNARE **2 :** to separate (cotton fiber) from seeds and waste material **3 :** to come up with **:** GENERATE — usu. used with *up* ‹~ up enthusiasm› — **gin·ner** *n*
[4]**gin** \ˈgin\ *conj* [perh. by contr. fr. dial. *gif* if + *an* if] (1580) *dial* **:** IF
[5]**gin** \ˈjin\ *n* [by shortening & alter. fr. *geneva*] (1713) **1 :** a colorless alcoholic beverage made from distilled or redistilled neutral grain spirits flavored with juniper berries and aromatics (as anise and caraway seeds) **2 a :** GIN RUMMY **b :** the act of laying down a full hand of matched cards in gin rummy — **gin·ny** \ˈjin-ē\ *adj*
[1]**gin·ger** \ˈjin-jər\ *n* [ME, alter. of OE *gingifer,* fr. ML *gingiber,* alter. of L *zingiber,* fr. Gk *zingiberi,* of Indo-Aryan origin; akin to Pali *siṅgivēra* ginger] (bef. 12c) **1 a** (1) **:** a thickened pungent aromatic rhizome that is used as a spice and sometimes medicinally (2) **:** the spice usu. prepared by drying and grinding ginger **b :** any of a genus (*Zingiber* of the family Zingiberaceae, the ginger family) of herbs with pungent aromatic rhizomes; *esp* **:** a widely cultivated tropical herb (*Z. officinale*) that supplies most commercial ginger — compare WILD GINGER **2 :** PEP ‹the ~ to . . . work hard —Willa Cather› **3 :** a light reddish or reddish-brown color ‹~ hair› — **gin·gery** \ˈjinj-rē, ˈjin-jə-\ *adj*
[2]**ginger** *vt* **gin·gered; gin·ger·ing** \ˈjinj-riŋ, ˈjin-jə-\ (1849) **:** to make lively **:** pep up ‹~ up the tourist trade —*N.Y. Times*›
ginger ale *n* (ca. 1864) **:** a sweetened carbonated nonalcoholic beverage flavored mainly with ginger extract
ginger beer *n* (1809) **:** a sweetened carbonated nonalcoholic beverage heavily flavored with ginger or capsicum or both
gin·ger·bread \ˈjin-jər-ˌbred\ *n* (15c) **1 :** a cake whose ingredients include molasses and ginger **2** [fr. the fancy shapes and gilding formerly often applied to gingerbread] **:** lavish or superfluous ornament esp. in architecture — **gingerbread** *adj* — **gin·ger·bread·ed** \-ˌbre-dəd\ *adj* — **gin·ger·bready** \-dē\ *adj*
ginger group *n* (1925) *chiefly Brit* **:** a group that serves as an energizing force within a larger body (as a political party)
gin·ger·ly \ˈjin-jər-lē\ *adj* [perh. fr. [1]*ginger*] (1604) **:** very cautious or careful — **gin·ger·li·ness** *n* — **gingerly** *adv*
ginger nut *n* (1842) *Brit* **:** GINGERSNAP
gin·ger·root \ˈjin-jər-ˌ(r)üt, -ˌ(r)u̇t\ *n* (1831) **:** GINGER 1a(1)
gin·ger·snap \-ˌsnap\ *n* (1805) **:** a thin brittle cookie sweetened with molasses and flavored with ginger
ging·ham \ˈgiŋ-əm\ *n* [modif. of Malay *genggang* striped cloth] (1615) **:** a clothing fabric usu. of yarn-dyed cotton in plain weave
gin·gi·va \ˈjin-jə-və, jin-ˈjī-\ *n, pl* **-vae** \-ˌvē\ [L] (ca. 1889) **:** [1]GUM — **gin·gi·val** \ˈjin-jə-vəl\ *adj*
gin·gi·vec·to·my \ˌjin-jə-ˈvek-tə-mē\ *n, pl* **-mies** (ca. 1927) **:** surgical removal of a portion of the gingiva
gin·gi·vi·tis \ˌjin-jə-ˈvī-təs\ *n* (1874) **:** inflammation of the gums
gink \ˈgiŋk\ *n* [origin unknown] (1906) *slang* **:** PERSON, GUY
gink·go *also* **ging·ko** \ˈgiŋ-(ˌ)kō *also* ˈgiŋk-(ˌ)gō\ *n, pl* **ginkgoes** *or* **ginkgos** *also* **gingkos** *or* **gingkoes** [NL *Ginkgo,* fr. Jp *ginkyō*] (1773) **1 :** a gymnospermous dioecious tree (*Ginkgo biloba*) of eastern China that is widely grown as an ornamental or shade tree and has fan-shaped leaves and foul-smelling yellowish fleshy seed coats — called also *maidenhair tree* **2 :** GINKGO BILOBA
ginkgo bi·lo·ba \-ˌbī-ˈlō-bə\ *n* [NL, lit., bilobed ginkgo] (1980) **:** an extract of the leaves of ginkgo that is held to enhance mental functioning by increasing blood circulation to the brain
gin mill *n* (1865) **:** BAR, SALOON
gi·nor·mous \jī-ˈnȯr-məs\ *adj* [*gi*gantic + e*normous*] (ca. 1948) **:** extremely large **:** HUMONGOUS
gin rummy *n* [[5]*gin*] (1940) **:** a rummy game for two players in which each player is dealt 10 cards and in which a player may win a hand by matching all the cards in it or may end play when the unmatched cards count up to 10 points or less
gin·seng \ˈjin-ˌseŋ, -ˌsiŋ\ *n* [Chin (Beijing) *rénshēn*] (1654) **1 a :** a Chinese perennial herb (*Panax ginseng* syn. *P. schinseng* of the family Araliaceae, the ginseng family) having five leaflets on each leaf, scarlet berries, and an aromatic root valued esp. locally as a medicine **b :** any of several plants related to ginseng; *esp* **:** a No. American herb (*P. quinquefolius*) **2 :** the root of a ginseng

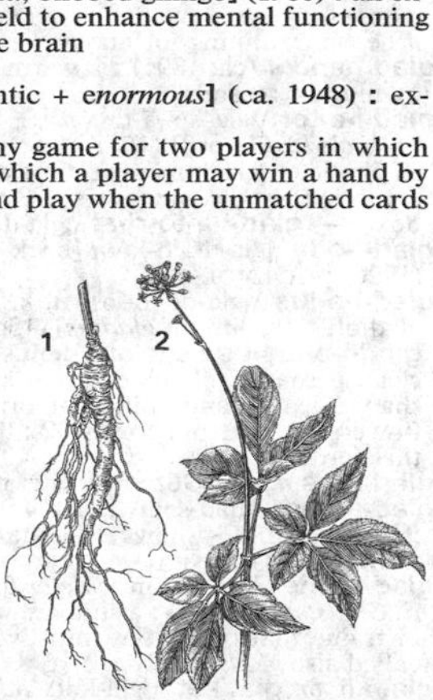

ginseng: *1* root, *2* leaves and flowers

Gip·sy *chiefly Brit var of* GYPSY
gi·raffe \jə-ˈraf\ *n, pl* **giraffes** [It *giraffa,* fr. Ar *zirāfa*] (ca. 1600) **1** *or pl* **giraffe :** a large fleet African ruminant mammal (*Giraffa camelopardalis*) that is the tallest of living quadrupeds and has a very long neck and a short coat with dark blotches separated by pale lines **2** *cap* **:** CAMELOPARDALIS — **gi·raff·ish** \-ˈra-fish\ *adj*
gir·an·dole \ˈjir-ən-ˌdōl\ *n* [F & It; F, fr. It *girandola,* fr. *girare* to turn, fr. LL *gyrare,* fr. L *gyrus* gyre] (1749) **1 :** a radiating and showy composition (as a cluster of skyrockets fired together) **2 :** an ornamental branched candlestick **3 :** a pendant earring usu. with three ornaments hanging from a central piece
gir·a·sole *also* **gir·a·sol** \ˈjir-ə-ˌsȯl, -ˌsōl, -ˌsäl\ *n* [It *girasole* sunflower, fr. *girare* + *sole* sun, fr. L *sol* — more at SOLAR] (ca. 1586) **1 :** JERUSALEM ARTICHOKE **2** *usu girasol* **:** an opal of varying color that gives out fiery reflections in bright light
[1]**gird** \ˈgərd\ *vb* **gird·ed** \ˈgər-dəd\ *or* **girt** \ˈgərt\; **gird·ing** [ME, fr. OE *gyrdan;* akin to OE *geard* yard — more at YARD] *vt* (bef. 12c) **1 a :** to encircle or bind with a flexible band (as a belt) **b :** to make fast (as a sword by a belt or clothing with a cord) **c :** SURROUND **2 :** PROVIDE, EQUIP; *esp* **:** to invest with the sword of knighthood **3 :** to prepare (oneself) for action ~ *vi* **:** to prepare for action — **gird one's loins :** to prepare for action **:** muster up one's resources
[2]**gird** *vb* [ME, to strike, thrust] *vt* (1546) **:** to sneer at **:** MOCK ~ *vi* **:** GIBE, RAIL
[3]**gird** *n* (1566) **:** a sarcastic remark
gird·er \ˈgər-dər\ *n* [[1]*gird*] (1611) **:** a horizontal main structural member (as in a building or bridge) that supports vertical loads and that consists of a single piece or of more than one piece bound together
[1]**gir·dle** \ˈgər-dᵊl\ *n* [ME *girdel,* fr. OE *gyrdel;* akin to OHG *gurtil* girdle, OE *gyrdan* to gird] (bef. 12c) **1 :** something that encircles or confines: as **a :** an article of dress encircling the body usu. at the waist **b :** a woman's close-fitting undergarment often boned and usu. elasticized that extends from the waist to below the hips **c** (1) **:** SHOULDER GIRDLE (2) **:** PELVIC GIRDLE **2 :** the edge of a brilliant that is grasped by the setting — see BRILLIANT illustration
[2]**girdle** *vt* **gir·dled; gir·dling** \ˈgər-dᵊl-iŋ\ (1582) **1 :** to encircle with or as if with a girdle **2 :** to cut away the bark and cambium in a ring around (a plant) usu. to kill by interrupting the circulation of water and nutrients **3 :** to move around **:** CIRCLE ‹*girdled* the world›
girl \ˈgər(-ə)l\ *n* [ME *gurle, girle* young person of either sex] (14c) **1 a :** a female child from birth to adulthood **b :** DAUGHTER **c :** a young unmarried woman **d** *sometimes offensive* **:** a single or married woman of any age **2 a :** SWEETHEART **b** *sometimes offensive* **:** a female servant or employee — **girl·hood** \-ˌhu̇d\ *n*
girl Friday *n* [*girl* + *Friday* (as in *man Friday*)] (1940) **:** a female assistant (as in an office) entrusted with a wide variety of tasks
girl·friend \ˈgər(-ə)l-ˌfrend\ *n* (1859) **1 :** a female friend **2 :** a frequent or regular female companion in a romantic or sexual relationship
Girl Guide *n* (1909) **:** a member of a worldwide scouting movement for girls 7 to 18 years of age that is equivalent to the Girl Scouts in the U.S.
girl·ie *or* **girly** \ˈgər-lē\ *adj* (1886) **1 :** GIRLISH **2** *usu girlie* **:** featuring scantily clothed women ‹~ magazines› ‹~ show›
girl·ish \ˈgər-lish\ *adj* (1565) **:** of, relating to, or having the characteristics of a girl or girlhood — **girl·ish·ly** *adv* — **girl·ish·ness** *n*
Girl Scout *n* (1919) **:** a member of any of the scouting programs of the Girl Scouts of the United States of America for girls ages 5 through 17
girn \ˈgirn\ *vi* [ME, alter. of *grinnen* to grin, snarl] (12c) *chiefly Scot* **:** SNARL — **girn** *n, chiefly Scot*
gi·ro \ˈjir-(ˌ)ō, ˈzhir-; ˈjē-(ˌ)rō, ˈzhē-, *esp Brit* ˈjī-\ *n* [G, circulation (of currency), fr. It, fr. L *gyrus* gyre] (1890) **:** a service of many European banks that permits authorized direct transfer of funds among account holders as well as conventional transfers by check
gi·rolle \zhē-ˈrōl, -ˈrȯl\ *n* [F] (1949) **:** CHANTERELLE
Gi·ron·din \jə-ˈrän-din, zhə-\ *n* [F, fr. *girondin* of Gironde] (1837) **:** GIRONDIST
Gi·rond·ist \-dist\ *n* [F *girondiste,* fr. *Gironde,* a political party, fr. *Gironde,* department of France represented by its leaders] (1795) **:** a member of the moderate republican party in the French legislative assembly in 1791
girt \ˈgərt\ *vb* [ME *girten,* alter. of *girden*] *vt* (15c) **1 :** GIRD **2 :** to fasten by means of a girth ~ *vi* **:** to measure in girth
[1]**girth** \ˈgərth\ *n* [ME, fr. ON *gjǫrth;* akin to OE *gyrdan* to gird] (13c) **1 :** a band or strap that encircles the body of an animal to fasten something (as a saddle) on its back **2 a :** a measure around a body ‹a man of more than average ~› ‹the ~ of a tree› **b :** SIZE, DIMENSIONS
[2]**girth** *vt* (15c) **1 :** ENCIRCLE **2 :** to bind or fasten with a girth **3 :** to measure the girth of
gi·sarme \gi-ˈzärm\ *n* [ME, fr. AF] (13c) **:** a medieval weapon consisting of a blade mounted on a long staff and carried by foot soldiers
gist \ˈjist\ *n* [AF, it lies, fr. *gisir* to lie, ultim. fr. L *jacēre* — more at ADJACENT] (ca. 1711) **1 :** the ground of a legal action **2 :** the main point or part **:** ESSENCE ‹the ~ of an argument›
[1]**git** \ˈgit\ *n* [var. of *get,* term of abuse, fr. [2]*get*] (1929) *Brit* **:** a foolish or worthless person
[2]**git** *dial var of* GET
git–go *var of* GET-GO
git·tern \ˈgi-tərn\ *n* [ME *giterne,* fr. MF *guiterne,* modif. of OSp *guitarra* guitar] (14c) **:** a medieval guitar
[1]**give** \ˈgiv\ *vb* **gave** \ˈgāv\; **giv·en** \ˈgi-vən\; **giv·ing** [ME, of Scand origin; akin to OSw *giva* to give; akin to OE *giefan, gifan* to give, and perh. to L *habēre* to have, hold] *vt* (13c) **1 :** to make a present of ‹~ a doll to a child› **2 a :** to grant or bestow by formal action ‹the law ~*s* citizens the right to vote› **b :** to accord or yield to another ‹*gave* him her confidence› **3 a :** to put into the possession of another for his or her use ‹*gave* me his phone number› **b** (1) **:** to administer as a sacrament (2) **:** to administer as a medicine **c :** to commit to another as a trust or responsibility and usu. for an expressed reason **d :** to transfer from one's authority or custody ‹the sheriff *gave* the prisoner to the warden› **e :** to execute and deliver ‹all employees must ~ bond› **f :** to convey to another ‹~ them my regards› **4 a :** to offer to the action of another **:** PROFFER ‹*gave* her his hand› **b :** to yield (oneself) to a man in sexual intercourse **5 a :** to present in public performance ‹~ a concert› **b :** to present to view or observation ‹*gave* the signal to start› **6 :** to provide by way of entertainment ‹~ a party› **7 :** to propose as a toast **8 a :** to designate as a share or portion **:** ALLOT ‹all the earth to thee and to thy race I ~ —John Milton› **b :** to make assignment of (a name) **c :** to set forth as an actual or hypothetical datum ‹~ the dimensions of the room› **d :** to attribute in thought or utterance **:** ASCRIBE ‹*gave* the credit to you› **9 a :** to yield as a product, conse-

\ə\ **abut** \ᵊ\ kitten, F table \ər\ **fur**ther \a\ **ash** \ā\ **ace** \ä\ **mop, mar**
\au̇\ **out** \ch\ **chin** \e\ **bet** \ē\ **easy** \g\ **go** \i\ **hit** \ī\ **ice** \j\ **job**
\ŋ\ **sing** \ō\ **go** \ȯ\ **law** \ȯi\ **boy** \th\ **thin** \t͟h\ **the** \ü\ **loot** \u̇\ **foot**
\y\ **yet** \zh\ **vision, beige** \k̲, ⁿ, œ, ue, ʸ\ *see* Guide to Pronunciation

quence, or effect : PRODUCE ⟨cows ~ milk⟩ ⟨84 divided by 12 ~*s* 7⟩ **b** : to bring forth : BEAR **10 a** : to yield possession of by way of exchange : PAY **b** : to dispose of for a price : SELL **11 a** : to deliver by some bodily action ⟨*gave* him a push⟩ **b** : to carry out (as a bodily movement) ⟨*gave* a cynical smile⟩ **c** : to inflict as punishment **d** : to award by formal verdict ⟨judgment was *given* against the plaintiff⟩ **12** : to offer for consideration, acceptance, or use ⟨~*s* no reason for his absence⟩ **13 a** : to suffer the loss of : SACRIFICE **b** : to offer as appropriate or due esp. to something higher or more worthy ⟨*gave* his spirit to God⟩ **c** : to apply freely or fully : DEVOTE ⟨*gave* themselves to their work⟩ **d** : to offer as a pledge ⟨I ~ you my word⟩ **14 a** : to cause one to have or receive ⟨mountains always *gave* him pleasure⟩ **b** : to cause a person to catch by contagion, infection, or exposure **15 a** : to allow one to have or take ⟨~ me time⟩ **b** : to lead or attempt to lead — used with an infinitive ⟨you *gave* me to understand you'd be late⟩ **16** : to care to the extent of ⟨didn't ~ a hoot⟩ ~ *vi* **1** : to make gifts or presents **2 a** : to yield to physical force or strain **b** : to collapse from the application of force or pressure **c** : to undergo or submit to change ⟨for the strike to be settled, something has to ~⟩ **3** : to afford a view or passage : OPEN ⟨the window ~*s* onto the terrace⟩ **4** : to enter wholeheartedly into an activity **5** *slang* : to be happening ⟨wants to know what ~*s*⟩ — **give a good account of** : to acquit (oneself) well — **give birth** : to have a baby ⟨*gave birth* last Thursday⟩ — **give birth to 1** : to produce as offspring ⟨*gave birth to* a son⟩ **2** : to be the source of — **give chase** : to set off in pursuit — **give ground** : to withdraw before superior force : RETREAT — **give of** : to make available : provide generously ⟨freely *gave of* their time⟩ — **give or take** : as an estimate accurate within (an amount to be added or subtracted) — **give place to** : to be replaced or succeeded by ⟨optimism *gave place to* worry⟩ — **give rise to** : to be the cause or source of : PRODUCE — **give the gun** : to open the throttle of : speed up — **give the lie to 1** : to accuse of falsehood **2** : to show to be false, inaccurate, or invalid — **give tongue** *of hounds* : to begin barking on the scent — **give way 1 a** : RETREAT **b** : to yield the right of way **2** : to yield oneself without restraint or control **3 a** : to yield to or as if to physical stress **b** : to yield to entreaty or insistence **4** : to yield place **5** : to begin to row

syn GIVE, PRESENT, DONATE, BESTOW, CONFER, AFFORD mean to convey to another as a possession. GIVE, the general term, is applicable to any passing over of anything by any means ⟨*give* alms⟩ ⟨*gave* her a ride on a pony⟩ ⟨*give* my love to your mother⟩. PRESENT carries a note of formality and ceremony ⟨*present* an award⟩. DONATE is likely to imply a publicized giving (as to charity) ⟨*donate* a piano to the orphanage⟩. BESTOW implies the conveying of something as a gift and may suggest condescension on the part of the giver ⟨*bestow* unwanted advice⟩. CONFER implies a gracious giving (as of a favor or honor) ⟨*confer* an honorary degree⟩. AFFORD implies a giving or bestowing usu. as a natural or legitimate consequence of the character of the giver ⟨the trees *afford* shade⟩ ⟨a development that *affords* us some hope⟩.

[2]**give** *n* (1868) **1** : capacity or tendency to yield to force or strain : FLEXIBILITY **2** : the quality or state of being springy

give–and–go \ˌgiv-ən-ˈgō\ *n* (1965) : a play (as in basketball or hockey) in which a player passes to a teammate and immediately cuts toward the net or goal to receive a return pass

give–and–take \ˌgiv-ən-ˈtāk\ *n* (1679) **1** : the practice of making mutual concessions : COMPROMISE **2** : a usu. good-natured exchange (as of ideas or comments)

give•away \ˈgiv-ə-ˌwā\ *n* (1882) **1** : an unintentional revelation or betrayal **2 a** : something given away free; *specif* : PREMIUM 1d **b** : the act of giving something away free ⟨staging a promotional ~⟩ **3** : a radio or television program on which prizes are given away

give away *vt* (14c) **1** : to make a present of **2** : to deliver (a bride) ceremonially to the bridegroom at a wedding **3 a** : BETRAY **b** : DISCLOSE, REVEAL **4** : to give (as weight) by way of a handicap

give•back \ˈgiv-ˌbak\ *n* (1978) : a previous gain (as an increase in wages or benefits) given back to management by workers (as in a labor contract)

give back *vi* (1548) : RETIRE, RETREAT ~ *vt* : to send in return or reply : RESTORE, RETURN

give in *vt* (1602) : DELIVER, SUBMIT ⟨*gave in* his resignation⟩ ~ *vi* : to yield under insistence or entreaty : SURRENDER

[1]**giv•en** \ˈgi-vən\ *adj* (14c) **1** : PRONE, DISPOSED ⟨~ to swearing⟩ **2** : presented as a gift : bestowed without compensation **3 a** : PARTICULAR, SPECIFIED ⟨at a ~ time⟩ **b** : assumed as actual or hypothetical : GRANTED ⟨~ that all are equal before the law⟩ **4** *of an official document* : having been executed : DATED **5** : immediately present in experience

[2]**given** *n* (1879) : something given; *esp* : something taken for granted : a basic condition or assumption

[3]**given** *prep* (1904) : in view of : CONSIDERING ⟨~ what she knew about others' lives, how could she complain about her own? —Marilyn French⟩

given name *n* (1717) : a name that precedes one's surname; *esp* : FIRST NAME

give off *vt* (1831) **1** : to send out as a branch **2** : EMIT ⟨*gave off* an unpleasant smell⟩ ~ *vi* : to branch off

give out *vt* (14c) **1 a** : DECLARE, PUBLISH ⟨*giving out* that the doctor . . . required a few days of complete rest —Charles Dickens⟩ **b** : to read aloud the words of (a hymn or psalm) for congregational singing **2** : EMIT ⟨*gave out* a constant hum⟩ **3** : ISSUE ⟨*gave out* new uniforms⟩ ~ *vi* **1** : BREAK DOWN, FAIL **2** : to become exhausted : COLLAPSE

give over *vt* (14c) **1** : CEASE **2** : ENTRUST **3 a** : to yield without restraint or control : ABANDON ⟨*gave* themselves *over* to laughter⟩ **b** : to set apart for a particular purpose or use **4** *archaic* : to pronounce incurable ~ *vi, Brit* : to cease an activity : STOP ⟨told him to *give over* and let me alone —Brendan Behan⟩

giv•er \ˈgi-vər\ *n* (14c) : one that gives : DONOR

give up *vt* (13c) **1** : to yield control or possession of : SURRENDER ⟨forced to *give up* his job⟩ **2** : to desist from : ABANDON ⟨refused to *give up* her efforts⟩ **3** : to declare incurable or insoluble **4 a** : to abandon (oneself) to a particular feeling, influence, or activity ⟨*gave* himself *up* to despair⟩ **b** : to devote to a particular purpose or use **5** : to despair of seeing ⟨we'd *given* you *up*⟩ **6** : to allow (a hit or run in baseball) while pitching ~ *vi* : to cease doing or attempting something esp. as an admission of defeat : QUIT — often used with *on* ⟨don't *give up* on the project⟩ — **give up the ghost** : to cease to live or function : DIE

giz•mo *also* **gis•mo** \ˈgiz-(ˌ)mō\ *n, pl* **gizmos** *also* **gismos** [origin unknown] (1943) : GADGET

giz•zard \ˈgi-zərd\ *n* [alter. of ME *giser* gizzard, liver, fr. AF *gesir, giser,* fr. L *gigeria* (pl.) giblets] (1565) **1 a** : the muscular enlargement of the alimentary canal of birds that has usu. thick muscular walls and a tough horny lining for grinding the food and when the crop is present follows it and the proventriculus **b** : a thickened part of the alimentary canal in some animals (as an insect or an earthworm) that is similar in function to the crop of a bird **2** : INNARDS

gla•bel•la \glə-ˈbe-lə\ *n, pl* **-bel•lae** \-ˈbe-(ˌ)lē, -ˌlī\ [NL, fr. L, fem. of *glabellus* hairless, dim. of *glaber*] (ca. 1823) : the smooth prominence between the eyebrows — **gla•bel•lar** \-ˈbe-lər\ *adj*

gla•brous \ˈglā-brəs\ *adj* [L *glabr-, glaber* smooth, bald — more at GLAD] (1640) : SMOOTH; *esp* : having a surface without hairs or projections ⟨~ skin⟩ ⟨~ leaves⟩

gla•cé \gla-ˈsā\ *adj* [F, fr. pp. of *glacer* to freeze, ice, glaze, fr. L *glaciare,* fr. *glacies*] (1845) **1** : made or finished so as to have a smooth glossy surface ⟨~ silk⟩ **2** *also* **gla•céed** \-ˈsād\ : coated with a glaze : CANDIED ⟨~ cherries⟩

gla•cial \ˈglā-shəl\ *adj* [L *glacialis,* fr. *glacies*] (1656) **1** : suggestive of ice: as **a** : extremely cold : FRIGID ⟨a ~ wind⟩ **b** : devoid of warmth and cordiality ⟨a ~ handshake⟩ **c** : coldly imperturbable ⟨maintained a ~ calm⟩ **2** : of a purity marked by the tendency to readily solidify in the form of ice-like crystals ⟨~ acetic acid⟩ **3 a (1)** : of, relating to, or being any of those parts of geologic time from Precambrian onward when a much larger portion of the earth was covered by glaciers than at present **(2)** *cap* : PLEISTOCENE **b** : of, relating to, or produced by glaciers **c** : suggestive of the very slow movement of glaciers ⟨progress on the bill has been ~⟩ — **gla•cial•ly** \-shə-lē\ *adv*

gla•ci•ate \ˈglā-shē-ˌāt, -sē-\ *vt* **-at•ed; -at•ing** (ca. 1623) **1** : FREEZE **2 a** : to subject to glacial action; *also* : to produce glacial effects in or on **b** : to cover with a glacier — **gla•ci•a•tion** \ˌglā-shē-ˈā-shən, -sē-\ *n*

gla•cier \ˈglā-shər *also* -zhər, *esp Brit* ˈgla-sē-ər *or* ˈglā-sē-\ *n* [F, fr. MF dial. (Franco-Provençal), fr. *glace* ice, fr. L *glacies;* akin to L *gelu* frost — more at COLD] (1744) : a large body of ice moving slowly down a slope or valley or spreading outward on a land surface

gla•ci•ol•o•gy \ˌglā-shē-ˈä-lə-jē, -sē-\ *n* [L *glacies* + ISV *-logy*] (1889) : any of the branches of science dealing with snow or ice accumulation, glaciation, or glacial epochs — **gla•ci•o•log•i•cal** \-ə-ˈlä-ji-kəl\ *adj* — **gla•ci•ol•o•gist** \-ˈä-lə-jist\ *n*

gla•cis \gla-ˈsē, ˈgla-sē\ *n, pl* **glacis** \-ˈsēz, -sēz\ [F, fr. *glacer* to freeze, slide] (1672) **1 a** : a gentle slope : INCLINE **b** : a slope that runs downward from a fortification **2** : BUFFER STATE; *also* : BUFFER ZONE

[1]**glad** \ˈglad\ *adj* **glad•der; glad•dest** [ME, shining, glad, fr. OE *glæd;* akin to OHG *glat* shining, smooth, L *glaber* smooth, bald] (bef. 12c) **1** *archaic* : having a cheerful or happy disposition by nature **2 a** : experiencing pleasure, joy, or delight : made happy **b** : made pleased, satisfied, or grateful — often used with *of* ⟨was ~ of their help⟩ **c** : very willing ⟨~ to do it⟩ **3 a** : marked by, expressive of, or caused by happiness and joy ⟨a ~ shout⟩ **b** : causing happiness and joy : PLEASANT ⟨~ tidings⟩ **4** : full of brightness and cheerfulness ⟨a ~ spring morning⟩ — **glad•ly** *adv* — **glad•ness** *n*

[2]**glad** *vb* **glad•ded; glad•ding** (bef. 12c) *archaic* : GLADDEN

[3]**glad** *n* (1923) : GLADIOLUS 1

glad•den \ˈgla-dᵊn\ *vb* **glad•dened; glad•den•ing** \ˈgla-dᵊn-iŋ\ *vi* (13c) *archaic* : to be glad ~ *vt* : to make glad

glade \ˈglād\ *n* [perh. fr. [1]*glad*] (1529) : an open space surrounded by woods — **glady** \ˈglā-dē\ *adj*

glad–hand \ˈglad-ˌhand\ *vt* (1903) : to extend a glad hand to ⟨candidates ~*ing* everyone they meet⟩ ~ *vi* : to extend a glad hand ⟨~*ing* as if he were running for mayor⟩ — **glad–hand•er** \ˈglad-ˌhan-dər\ *n*

glad hand *n* (ca. 1895) : a warm welcome or greeting often prompted by ulterior reasons

glad•i•a•tor \ˈgla-dē-ˌā-tər\ *n* [L, fr. *gladius* sword, of Celt origin; akin to W *cleddyf* sword] (15c) **1** : a person engaged in a fight to the death as public entertainment for ancient Romans **2** : a person engaging in a public fight or controversy **3** : a trained fighter; *esp* : a professional boxer — **glad•i•a•to•ri•al** \ˌgla-dē-ə-ˈtōr-ē-əl\ *adj*

glad•i•o•la \ˌgla-dē-ˈō-lə\ *n* [back-formation fr. *gladiolus,* taken as a pl.] (1926) : GLADIOLUS 1

glad•i•o•lus \ˌgla-dē-ˈō-ləs\ *n, pl* **-li** \-(ˌ)lē, -ˌlī\ [NL, fr. L, gladiolus, fr. dim. of *gladius*] (15c) **1** *or pl* **gladiolus** *also* **glad•i•o•lus•es** : any of a genus (*Gladiolus*) of chiefly African perennial plants of the iris family with erect sword-shaped leaves and spikes of brilliantly colored irregular flowers arising from corms **2** : the large middle portion of the sternum

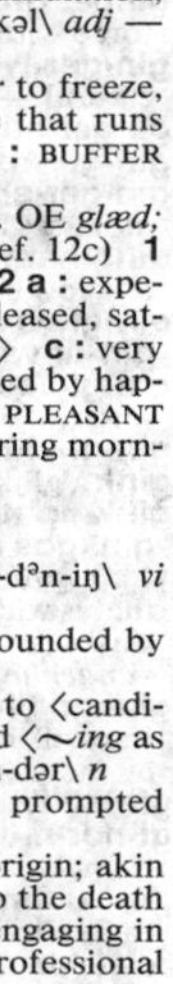

gladiolus 1

glad rags *n pl* (1896) : dressy clothes

glad•some \ˈglad-səm\ *adj* (14c) : giving or showing joy : CHEERFUL ⟨~ news⟩ — **glad•some•ly** *adv* — **glad•some•ness** *n*

glad•stone \ˈglad-ˌstōn, *chiefly Brit* -stən\ *n, often cap* [W. E. *Gladstone*] (1887) : a suitcase with flexible sides on a rigid frame that opens flat into two equal compartments — called also *gladstone bag*

glai•kit *or* **glai•ket** \ˈglā-kət\ *adj* [ME (Sc) *glaikit*] (15c) *chiefly Scot* : FOOLISH, GIDDY

glair *or* **glaire** \ˈgler\ *n* [ME *gleyre* egg white, fr. AF *gleire,* fr. VL **claria,* fr. L *clarus* clear — more at CLEAR] (13c) **1** : a sizing liquid made from egg white **2** : a viscid substance suggestive of an egg white

glairy \-ē\ *adj* **glair•i•er; -est** (1662) : having the characteristics of or overlaid with glair

glaive \ˈglāv\ *n* [ME, fr. AF, sword, lance, fr. L *gladius* sword] (15c) *archaic* : SWORD; *esp* : BROADSWORD

glam \ˈglam\ *n* (1963) **1** : extravagantly showy glamour **2** : GLITTER ROCK — **glam** *adj*

glam•or•ise *Brit var of* GLAMORIZE

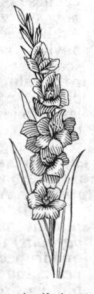

glam·or·ize *also* **glam·our·ize** \ˈgla-mə-ˌrīz\ *vt* **-ized; -iz·ing** (1936) **1 :** to look upon or depict as glamorous : ROMANTICIZE ⟨the novel ~*s* war⟩ **2 :** to make glamorous ⟨~ the living room⟩ — **glam·or·i·za·tion** \ˌgla-mə-rə-ˈzā-shən\ *n* — **glam·or·iz·er** \ˈgla-mə-ˌrī-zər\ *n*

glam·or·ous *also* **glam·our·ous** \ˈglam-rəs, ˈgla-mə-\ *adj* (1861) **:** full of glamour : excitingly attractive ⟨a ~ actress⟩ ⟨a ~ life⟩ — **glam·or·ous·ly** *adv* — **glam·or·ous·ness** *n*

glam·our *also* **glam·or** \ˈgla-mər\ *n* [Sc *glamour,* alter. of E *grammar;* fr. the popular association of erudition with occult practices] (1715) **1 :** a magic spell ⟨the girls appeared to be under a ~ —Llewelyn Powys⟩ **2 :** an exciting and often illusory and romantic attractiveness ⟨the ~ of Hollywood⟩; *esp* **:** alluring or fascinating attraction — often used attributively ⟨~ stock⟩ ⟨~ girls⟩ ⟨whooping cranes and . . . other ~ birds —R. T. Peterson⟩ — **glamour** *vt* — **glam·our·less** \-ləs\ *adj*

glam·our–puss \-ˌpu̇s\ *n* (1941) **:** a glamorously attractive person

[1]**glance** \ˈglan(t)s\ *vb* **glanced; glanc·ing** [ME *glencen, glenchen*] *vi* (15c) **1 :** to strike a surface obliquely so as to go off at an angle ⟨the bullet *glanced* off the wall⟩ **2 a :** to make sudden quick movements ⟨dragonflies *glancing* over the pond⟩ **b :** to flash or gleam with quick intermittent rays of light ⟨brooks *glancing* in the sun⟩ **3 :** to touch on a subject or refer to it briefly or indirectly ⟨the work ~*s* at the customs of ancient cultures⟩ **4 a** *of the eyes* **:** to move swiftly from one thing to another **b :** to take a quick look at something ⟨*glanced* at his watch⟩ ~ *vt* **1** *archaic* **a :** to take a quick look at **b :** to catch a glimpse of **2 :** to give an oblique path of direction to: **a :** to throw or shoot so that the object glances from a surface **b** *archaic* **:** to aim (as an innuendo) indirectly : INSINUATE — **glanc·er** *n*

[2]**glance** *n* (1503) **1 a :** a quick intermittent flash or gleam **b** *archaic* **:** a sudden quick movement **2 a** *archaic* **:** a rapid oblique movement **b :** a deflected impact or blow **3 a :** a swift movement of the eyes **b :** a quick or cursory look **4** *archaic* **a :** a brief satirical reference to something : GIBE **b :** ALLUSION — **at first glance :** on first consideration ⟨*at first glance* the subject seems harmless enough⟩

glanc·ing \ˈglan(t)-siŋ\ *adj* (ca. 1541) **1 :** hitting so as to glance off ⟨a ~ blow⟩ **2 :** INCIDENTAL, INDIRECT ⟨made ~ allusions to her past⟩ — **glanc·ing·ly** \-siŋ-lē\ *adv*

[1]**gland** \ˈgland\ *n* [F *glande,* fr. OF, glandular swelling on the neck, gland, ultim. fr. L *gland-, glans* acorn; akin to Gk *balanos* acorn] (1692) **1 a :** a specialized cell, group of cells, or organ of endothelial origin that selectively removes materials from the blood, concentrates or alters them, and secretes them for further use in the body or for elimination from the body — compare ENDOCRINE GLAND, EXOCRINE GLAND **b :** any of various animal structures suggestive of glands though not secretory in function **2 :** any of various secreting organs (as a nectary) of plants — **gland·less** \ˈgland-ləs\ *adj*

[2]**gland** *n* [origin unknown] (1839) **1 :** a device for preventing leakage of fluid past a joint in machinery **2 :** the movable part of a stuffing box by which the packing is compressed

glan·dered \ˈglan-dərd\ *adj* (1667) **:** affected with glanders

glan·ders \-dərz\ *n pl but sing or pl in constr* [MF *glandre* glandular swelling on the neck, fr. L *glandulae,* fr. pl. of *glandula,* dim. of *gland-, glans*] (1523) **:** a contagious and destructive disease esp. of horses caused by a bacterium (*Burkholderia mallei* syn. *Pseudomonas mallei*) and characterized by caseating nodular lesions esp. on the respiratory mucosae and lungs that tend to break down and form ulcers

glan·du·lar \ˈglan-jə-lər\ *adj* (ca. 1740) **1 a :** of, relating to, or involving glands, gland cells, or their products **b :** having the characteristics or function of a gland **2 a :** INNATE, INHERENT ⟨the almost ~ . . . instinct for adventure and romance —*Newsweek*⟩ **b :** PHYSICAL, SEXUAL — **glan·du·lar·ly** *adv*

glandular fever *n* (1902) **:** INFECTIOUS MONONUCLEOSIS

glans \ˈglanz\ *n, pl* **glan·des** \ˈglan-ˌdēz\ [L *gland-, glans,* lit., acorn] (1650) **1 :** a conical vascular body forming the extremity of the penis — called also *glans penis* **2 :** a structure of the clitoris similar to the glans penis — called also *glans cli·to·ri·dis* \-klə-ˈtȯr-ə-dəs\

[1]**glare** \ˈgler\ *vb* **glared; glar·ing** [ME *glaren;* akin to OE *glæs* glass] *vi* (13c) **1 a :** to shine with a harsh uncomfortably brilliant light **b :** STAND OUT, OBTRUDE **2 :** to stare angrily or fiercely ~ *vt* **1 :** to express (as hostility) by staring angrily **2** *archaic* **:** to cause to be sharply reflected

[2]**glare** *n* (15c) **1 a :** a harsh uncomfortably bright light ⟨the ~ of a neon sign⟩ ⟨the ~ of publicity⟩; *esp* **:** painfully bright sunlight **b :** cheap showy brilliance : GARISHNESS **2 :** an angry or fierce stare **3 :** a surface or sheet of smooth and slippery ice

glaring *adj* (14c) **1 :** having a fixed look of hostility, fierceness, or anger **2 a :** shining with or reflecting an uncomfortably bright light **b** (1) **:** GARISH (2) **:** vulgarly ostentatious **3 :** obtrusively and often painfully obvious ⟨a ~ error⟩ ***syn*** see FLAGRANT — **glar·ing·ly** \-iŋ-lē\ *adv* — **glar·ing·ness** *n*

glary \ˈgler-ē\ *adj* **glar·i·er; -est** (1578) **:** having a dazzling brightness

glas·nost \ˈglaz-(ˌ)nōst, ˈglas-, ˈgläz-, ˈgläs-\ *n* [Russ *glasnost',* lit., publicity, fr. *glasnyĭ* public, fr. *glas* voice, fr. OCS *glasŭ* — more at CALL] (1986) **:** a Soviet policy permitting open discussion of political and social issues and freer dissemination of news and information

[1]**glass** \ˈglas, ˈgläs\ *n, often attrib* [ME *glas,* fr. OE *glæs;* akin to OE *geolu* yellow — more at YELLOW] (bef. 12c) **1 :** any of various amorphous materials formed from a melt by cooling to rigidity without crystallization: as **a :** a usu. transparent or translucent material consisting typically of a mixture of silicates **b :** a material (as obsidian) produced by fast cooling of magma **2 a :** something made of glass: as (1) **:** TUMBLER; *also* **:** GLASSWARE (2) **:** MIRROR (3) **:** BAROMETER (4) **:** HOURGLASS (5) **:** BACKBOARD 1 **b** (1) **:** an optical instrument or device that has one or more lenses and is designed to aid in the viewing of objects not readily seen (2) **:** FIELD GLASSES, BINOCULARS — usu. used in pl. **c** *pl* **:** a device used to correct defects of vision or to protect the eyes that consists typically of a pair of glass or plastic lenses and the frame by which they are held in place — called also *eyeglasses, spectacles* **3 :** the quantity held by a glass container **4 :** FIBERGLASS — **glass·ful** \ˈglas-ˌfu̇l\ *n* — **glass·less** \-ləs\ *adj*

[2]**glass** *vt* (14c) **1 a :** to provide with glass : GLAZE 1 **b :** to enclose, case, or wall with glass ⟨the sunroom was ~*ed* in⟩ **2 :** to make glassy **3 a :** REFLECT **b :** to see mirrored **4 :** to look at through an optical instrument (as binoculars) ~ *vi* **:** [1]GLAZE 1

glass·blow·ing \-ˌblō-iŋ\ *n* (ca. 1829) **:** the art of shaping a mass of glass that has been softened by heat by blowing air into it through a tube — **glass·blow·er** \-ˌblō(-ə)r\ *n*

glass ceiling *n* (1984) **:** an intangible barrier within a hierarchy that prevents women or minorities from obtaining upper-level positions

glass closet *n* (1991) **:** the state in which the sexual orientation of a homosexual person is known to many but not publicly acknowledged

glass eye *n* (1651) **1 :** an artificial eye made of glass **2 :** an eye having a pale, whitish, or colorless iris — **glass–eyed** \-ˌīd\ *adj*

glass fiber *n* (1882) **:** FIBERGLASS

glass harmonica *n* (ca. 1909) **:** a musical instrument consisting of a series of rotating glass bowls of differing sizes played by touching the dampened edges with a finger

glass·house \ˈglas-ˌhau̇s\ *n* (14c) **1 :** a place where glass is made **2** *chiefly Brit* **:** GREENHOUSE **3** *Brit* **:** a military prison

glass·ie \ˈgla-sē\ *or* **glassy** *n, pl* **glass·ies** (1887) **:** a playing marble made of glass

glass·ine \gla-ˈsēn\ *n* (1916) **:** a thin dense transparent or semitransparent paper highly resistant to the passage of air and grease

glass jaw *n* (1940) **:** vulnerability (as of a boxer) to knockout punches

glass·mak·er \ˈglas-ˌmā-kər\ *n* (1576) **:** one that makes glass — **glass·mak·ing** \-kiŋ\ *n*

glass snake *n* (1709) **:** any of a genus (*Ophisaurus*) of limbless snakelike lizards of the southern U.S., Eurasia, and Africa with a fragile tail that readily breaks off from the body often in pieces

glass sponge *n* (1875) **:** any of a class (Hexactinellida syn. Hyalospongiae) of chiefly deep-water siliceous marine sponges with 6-rayed spicules and a skeleton often resembling glass when dried

glass·ware \ˈglas-ˌwer\ *n* (1722) **:** articles made of glass

glass wool *n* (1879) **:** glass fibers in a mass resembling wool and being used esp. for thermal insulation and air filters

glass·work \ˈglas-ˌwərk\ *n* (1611) **1 a :** the manufacture of glass or glassware; *also* **:** glaziers' work **b** *pl* **:** GLASSHOUSE 1 **2 :** GLASSWARE — **glass·work·er** \-ˌwər-kər\ *n*

glass·wort \-ˌwərt, -ˌwȯrt\ *n* [fr. its former use in the manufacture of glass] (1597) **:** any of a genus (*Salicornia*) of woody jointed succulent herbs of the goosefoot family with leaves reduced to fleshy sheaths — called also *pickleweed*

glassy \ˈgla-sē\ *adj* **glass·i·er; -est** (14c) **1 :** resembling or made of glass **2 :** having little animation : DULL, LIFELESS ⟨~ eyes⟩ — **glass·i·ly** \ˈgla-sə-lē\ *adv* — **glass·i·ness** \ˈgla-sē-nəs\ *n*

glassy–eyed \-ˌīd\ *adj* (1847) **:** marked by or having glassy eyes

Glau·ber's salt \ˈglau̇-bər(z)-\ *n* [Johann R. *Glauber* †1668 Ger. chemist] (1736) **:** a colorless crystalline sulfate of sodium $Na_2SO_4 \cdot 10H_2O$ used esp. in dyeing, as a cathartic, and in solar energy systems — sometimes used in pl.; called also *Glauber salt*

glau·co·ma \glau̇-ˈkō-mə, glȯ-\ *n* [L, cataract, fr. Gk *glaukōma,* fr. *glaukoun* to have a cataract, fr. *glaukos*] (1885) **:** a disease of the eye marked by increased pressure within the eyeball that can result in damage to the optic disk and gradual loss of vision

glau·co·nite \ˈglȯ-kə-ˌnīt\ *n* [G *Glaukonit,* irreg. fr. Gk *glaukos*] (1836) **:** a mineral consisting of a dull green earthy iron potassium silicate occurring in greensand — **glau·co·nit·ic** \ˌglȯ-kə-ˈni-tik\ *adj*

glau·cous \ˈglȯ-kəs\ *adj* [L *glaucus,* fr. Gk *glaukos* gleaming, gray] (1671) **1 a :** of a pale yellow-green color **b :** of a light bluish-gray or bluish-white color **2 :** having a powdery or waxy coating that gives a frosted appearance and tends to rub off — **glau·cous·ness** *n*

[1]**glaze** \ˈglāz\ *vb* **glazed; glaz·ing** [ME *glasen,* fr. *glas* glass] *vt* (14c) **1 :** to furnish or fit with glass **2 a :** to coat with or as if with a glaze ⟨the storm *glazed* trees with ice⟩ **b :** to apply a glaze to ⟨~ doughnuts⟩ **3 :** to give a smooth glossy surface to ~ *vi* **1 :** to become glazed or glassy ⟨my eyes *glazed* over⟩ **2 :** to form a glaze — **glaz·er** *n*

[2]**glaze** *n* (1752) **1 :** a smooth slippery coating of thin ice **2 a** (1) **:** a liquid preparation applied to food on which it forms a firm glossy coating (2) **:** a mixture mostly of oxides (as silica and alumina) applied to the surface of ceramic wares to form a moisture-impervious and often lustrous or ornamental coating **b :** a transparent or translucent color applied to modify the effect of a painted surface **c :** a smooth glossy or lustrous surface or finish **3 :** a glassy film

[3]**glaze** *vi* **glazed; glaz·ing** [prob. blend of *glare* and *gaze*] (1601) *archaic* **:** STARE

glazed \ˈglāzd\ *adj* (15c) **1 :** covered with or as if with a glassy film ⟨~ eyes⟩ **2 :** marked by lack of expression

gla·zier \ˈglā-zhər, -zē-ər\ *n* (14c) **:** one who sets glass — **gla·ziery** \ˈglā-zh(ə-)rē, ˈglā-zē-ə-rē\ *n*

glaz·ing \ˈglā-ziŋ\ *n* (15c) **1 :** the action, process, or trade of fitting windows with glass **2 a :** GLASSWORK **b :** GLAZE **3 :** transparent material (as glass) used for windows

GLBT *abbr* gay, lesbian, bisexual, and transgender

[1]**gleam** \ˈglēm\ *n* [ME *gleem,* fr. OE *glǣm;* akin to OE *geolu* yellow — more at YELLOW] (15c) **1 a :** a transient appearance of subdued or partly obscured light ⟨the ~ of dawn in the east⟩ **b** (1) **:** a small bright light ⟨the ~ of a match⟩ (2) **:** GLINT ⟨a ~ in his eyes⟩ **2 :** a brief or faint appearance ⟨a ~ of hope⟩ — **gleamy** \ˈglē-mē\ *adj*

[2]**gleam** *vi* (1508) **1 :** to shine with or as if with subdued steady light or moderate brightness **2 :** to appear briefly or faintly ⟨a light ~*ed* in the distance⟩ ~ *vt* **:** to cause to gleam ***syn*** see FLASH

glean \ˈglēn\ *vb* [ME *glenen,* fr. AF *glener,* fr. LL *glennare,* of Celtic origin; akin to OIr *doglenn* he selects] *vi* (14c) **1 :** to gather grain or other produce left by reapers **2 :** to gather information or material bit by bit ~ *vt* **1 a :** to pick up after a reaper **b :** to strip (as a field) of the leavings of reapers **2 a :** to gather (as information) bit by bit **b :** to pick over in search of relevant material ⟨~*ing* old files for information⟩ **3 :** FIND OUT — **glean·able** \ˈglē-nə-bəl\ *adj* — **glean·er** *n*

glean·ings \ˈglē-niŋz\ *n pl* (15c) **:** things acquired by gleaning

glebe \ˈglēb\ *n* [L *gleba* clod, land] (14c) **1** *archaic* **:** LAND; *specif* **:** a plot of cultivated land **2 :** land belonging or yielding revenue to a parish church or ecclesiastical benefice

glee \ˈglē\ *n* [ME, fr. OE *glēo* entertainment, music; akin to ON *glȳ* joy, and perh. to Gk *chleuē* joke] (bef. 12c) **1** : exultant high-spirited joy : MERRIMENT **2** : a part-song for usu. male voices
glee club *n* (1814) : a chorus organized for singing usu. short pieces
gleed \ˈglēd\ *n* [ME, fr. OE *glēd;* akin to OE *glōwan* to glow] (bef. 12c) *archaic* : a glowing coal
glee·ful \ˈglē-fəl\ *adj* (1586) : full of glee : MERRY ⟨~ laughter⟩ — **glee·ful·ly** \-fə-lē\ *adv* — **glee·ful·ness** *n*
gleek \ˈglēk\ *vi* [origin unknown] (1590) *archaic* : GIBE, JOKE
glee·man \ˈglē-mən\ *n* [ME *gleman,* fr. OE *glēoman,* fr. *glēo* + *man* man] (bef. 12c) : JONGLEUR
glee·some \ˈglē-səm\ *adj* (1590) *archaic* : GLEEFUL
gleet \ˈglēt\ *n* [ME *glet* slimy or mucous matter, fr. AF *glette,* fr. L *glittus* viscous; akin to L *gluten* glue — more at CLAY] (14c) : a chronic inflammation (as gonorrhea) of a bodily orifice usu. accompanied by an abnormal discharge; *also* : the discharge itself
gleg \ˈgleg\ *adj* [ME, fr. ON *gløggr* clear-sighted] (14c) *Scot* : marked by quickness of perception or movement
glei·za·tion \glā-ˈzā-shən\ *n* (1938) : development of or conversion into gley
glen \ˈglen\ *n* [ME (Sc), valley, fr. ScGael & Ir *gleann,* fr. OIr *glenn*] (15c) : a secluded narrow valley
glen·gar·ry \glen-ˈga-rē\ *n, pl* **-ries** *often cap* [*Glengarry,* valley in Scotland] (1841) : a woolen cap of Scottish origin — called also *glengarry bonnet*
glen plaid \ˈglen-\ *n* [short for *glenurquhart plaid,* fr. *Glen Urquhart,* valley in Inverness-shire, Scotland] (1926) : a twill pattern of broken checks; *also* : a fabric woven in this pattern — called also *glen check*
gley \ˈglā\ *n, often attrib* [Ukrainian *gleĭ* clayey earth; akin to OE *clǣg* clay — more at CLAY] (1927) : a sticky clay soil or soil layer formed under the surface of some waterlogged soils — **gleyed** *adj*
gley·ing \ˈglā-iŋ\ *n* (1949) : GLEIZATION
glia \ˈglē-ə, ˈglī-ə\ *n, pl* **glia** [NL, fr. MGk, glue — more at CLAY] (1891) : supporting tissue intermingled with the essential elements of nervous tissue esp. in the brain, spinal cord, and ganglia
gli·a·din \ˈglī-ə-dən\ *n* [It *gliadina,* fr. MGk *glia*] (ca. 1828) : PROLAMIN; *esp* : one obtained by alcoholic extraction of gluten from wheat and rye
gli·al \ˈglē-əl, ˈglī-\ *adj* (1888) : of, relating to, or constituting glia ⟨~ cells⟩
glib \ˈglib\ *adj* **glib·ber; glib·best** [prob. modif. of LG *glibberig* slippery] (1584) **1 a** : marked by ease and informality : NONCHALANT **b** : showing little forethought or preparation : OFFHAND ⟨~ answers⟩ **c** : lacking depth and substance : SUPERFICIAL ⟨~ solutions to knotty problems⟩ **2** *archaic* : SMOOTH, SLIPPERY **3** : marked by ease and fluency in speaking or writing often to the point of being insincere or deceitful ⟨a ~ politician⟩ — **glib·ly** *adv* — **glib·ness** *n*
[1]**glide** \ˈglīd\ *vb* **glid·ed; glid·ing** [ME, fr. OE *glīdan;* akin to OHG *glītan* to glide] *vi* (bef. 12c) **1** : to move smoothly, continuously, and effortlessly ⟨swans *gliding* over the lake⟩ **2** : to go or pass imperceptibly ⟨hours *glided* by⟩ **3 a** *of an airplane* : to descend gradually in controlled flight **b** : to fly in a glider **4** : to produce a glide (as in music or speech) ~ *vt* : to cause to glide
[2]**glide** *n* (1584) **1** : a calm stretch of shallow water flowing smoothly **2** : the act or action of gliding **3** : PORTAMENTO **4 a** : a less prominent vowel sound produced by the passing of the vocal organs to or from the articulatory position of a speech sound — compare DIPHTHONG **b** : SEMIVOWEL **5** : a device for facilitating movement of something; *esp* : a circular usu. metal button attached to the bottom of furniture legs to provide a smooth surface
glide path *n* (1936) : GLIDE SLOPE
glid·er \ˈglī-dər\ *n* (15c) **1** : one that glides: as **a** : an aircraft similar to an airplane but without an engine **b** : a porch seat suspended from an upright framework **2** : something that aids gliding
glide slope *n* (ca. 1949) **1** : the proper path of descent for an aircraft preparing to land; *esp* : such a path indicated by a radio beam **2** : the radio beam that marks a glide slope
glim \ˈglim\ *n* [perh. short for [2]*glimmer*] (ca. 1700) : something that furnishes light (as a lantern or candle); *also* : illumination given off by such a source
[1]**glim·mer** \ˈgli-mər\ *vi* **glim·mered; glim·mer·ing** \ˈglim-riŋ, ˈgli-mə-\ [ME *glimeren;* akin to OE *glǣm* gleam] (15c) **1 a** : to shine faintly or unsteadily **b** : to give off a subdued unsteady reflection **2** : to appear indistinctly with a faintly luminous quality ***syn*** see FLASH
[2]**glimmer** *n* (1590) **1 a** : a feeble or intermittent light **b** : a subdued unsteady shining or sparkle **2 a** : a dim perception or faint idea : INKLING **b** : HINT, SPARK ⟨a ~ of intelligence⟩
glimmering *n* (15c) : GLIMMER
[1]**glimpse** \ˈglim(p)s\ *vb* **glimpsed; glimps·ing** [ME *glimsen;* akin to MHG *glimsen* to glimmer, OE *glǣm* gleam] *vi* (14c) **1** *archaic* : GLIMMER **2** : to look briefly ~ *vt* : to get a brief look at — **glimps·er** *n*
[2]**glimpse** *n* (ca. 1540) **1** *archaic* : GLIMMER **2** : a fleeting view or look
[1]**glint** \ˈglint\ *vb* [ME, to dart obliquely, glint, alter. of *glenten,* of Scand origin; akin to Sw dial. *glänta* to clear up; akin to OHG *glanz* bright, OE *geolu* yellow — more at YELLOW] *vi* (14c) **1 a** *archaic* : to glance off an object **b** *of rays of light* : to be reflected at an angle from a surface **2** : to give off reflection in brilliant flashes; *also* : GLEAM **3** : to look quickly or briefly : GLANCE **4** : to appear briefly or faintly ~ *vt* : to cause to glint ***syn*** see FLASH
[2]**glint** *n* (14c) **1** : a tiny bright flash of light **2** : a brief or faint manifestation : GLIMMER ⟨a ~ of recognition⟩; *also* : a trace of emotion expressed through the eyes ⟨a steely ~ in his eye⟩
glio·blas·to·ma \ˌglī-ō-ˌbla-ˈstō-mə\ *n, pl* **-mas** *also* **-ma·ta** \-mə-tə\ [NL, fr. *glia* glia + *blast-* + *-oma*] (ca. 1923) : a malignant rapidly growing astrocytoma of the central nervous system and usu. of a cerebral hemisphere — called also *glioblastoma mul·ti·for·me* \-ˌməlt-ə-ˈfȯrm-ē\
gli·o·ma \glē-ˈō-mə, glī-\ *n, pl* **-mas** *also* **-ma·ta** \-mə-tə\ [NL, fr. *glia*] (1870) : a tumor arising from glial cells
[1]**glis·sade** \gli-ˈsäd, -ˈsād\ *vi* **glis·sad·ed; glis·sad·ing** [F, n., slide, glissade, fr. *glisser* to slide, fr. OF *glicier,* alter. of *glier,* of Gmc origin; akin to OHG *glītan* to glide] (1837) **1** : to perform a ballet glissade **2** : to slide in a standing or squatting position down a snow-covered slope without the aid of skis — **glis·sad·er** *n*
[2]**glissade** *n* (1843) **1** : a gliding step in ballet **2** : the action of glissading
glis·san·do \gli-ˈsän-(ˌ)dō\ *n, pl* **-di** \-(ˌ)dē\ *or* **-dos** [prob. modif. of F *glissade*] (ca. 1854) : a rapid sliding up or down the musical scale
[1]**glis·ten** \ˈgli-sᵊn\ *vi* **glis·tened; glis·ten·ing** \ˈgli-sᵊn-iŋ\ [ME *glistnen,* fr. OE *glisnian;* akin to OE *glisian* to glitter, *geolu* yellow — more at YELLOW] (bef. 12c) : to give off a sparkling or lustrous reflection of or as if of a moist or polished surface ***syn*** see FLASH
[2]**glisten** *n* (1840) : GLITTER, SPARKLE
glis·ter \ˈglis-tər\ *vi* **glis·tered; glis·ter·ing** \-t(ə-)riŋ\ [ME *glistren;* akin to OE *glisian*] (14c) : GLITTER — **glister** *n*
glitch \ˈglich\ *n* [perh. fr. Yiddish *glitsh* slippery place, fr. *glitshn* (*zikh*) to slide, glide; akin to OHG *glītan* to glide — more at GLIDE] (1962) **1 a** : a usu. minor malfunction ⟨a ~ in a spacecraft's fuel cell⟩; *also* : [2]BUG 2 **b** : a minor problem that causes a temporary setback : SNAG **2** : a false or spurious electronic signal — **glitchy** \ˈgli-chē\ *adj*
[1]**glit·ter** \ˈgli-tər\ *vi* [ME *gliteren,* perh. fr. ON *glitra;* akin to OE *geolu* yellow] (14c) **1 a** : to shine by reflection with many small flashes of brilliant light : SPARKLE ⟨sequins ~*ed* in the spotlight⟩ **b** : to shine with strong emotion : FLASH ⟨eyes ~*ing* in anger⟩ **2** : to be brilliantly attractive, lavish, or spectacular; *also* : to be superficially attractive or exciting ***syn*** see FLASH — **glit·ter·ing·ly** \-tə-riŋ-lē\ *adv*
[2]**glitter** *n* (1593) **1 a** : sparkling brilliance of something that glitters **b** : a bright usu. superficial attractiveness **c** : the quality of being spectacular **2** : small glittering objects used for ornamentation — **glittery** \ˈgli-tə-rē\ *adj*
glit·te·ra·ti \ˌgli-tə-ˈrä-tē\ *n pl* [blend of [2]*glitter* and *literati*] (1940) : CELEBRITIES, BEAUTIFUL PEOPLE
glitter rock *n* (1972) : rock music characterized by performers wearing glittering costumes and bizarre often grotesque makeup
[1]**glitz** \ˈglits\ *n* [perh. modif. of G *glitzern* to glitter, fr. MHG *glitzen;* akin to ON *glitra* to glitter] (1971) : extravagant showiness : GLITTER, OSTENTATION — **glitz·i·ness** \ˈglit-sē-nəs\ *n* — **glitzy** \ˈglit-sē\ *adj*
[2]**glitz** *vt* (1956) : to make flashy or extravagant in appearance — often used with *up* ⟨she got ~*ed* up for the party⟩
gloam \ˈglōm\ *n* [Sc *gloam* to become twilight, back-formation fr. *gloaming*] (ca. 1821) *archaic* : TWILIGHT
gloam·ing \ˈglō-miŋ\ *n* [ME (Sc) *gloming,* fr. OE *glōming,* fr. *glōm* twilight; akin to OE *glōwan* to glow] (bef. 12c) : TWILIGHT, DUSK
[1]**gloat** \ˈglōt\ *vi* [akin to ME *glouten* to scowl and perh. to ON *glotta* to grin scornfully] (1605) **1** *obs* : to look or glance admiringly or amorously **2** : to observe or think about something with triumphant and often malicious satisfaction, gratification, or delight ⟨~ over an enemy's misfortune⟩ — **gloat·er** *n* — **gloat·ing·ly** *adv*
[2]**gloat** *n* (1899) : the act or feeling of one who gloats
glob \ˈgläb\ *n* [perh. blend of *globe* and *blob*] (1900) **1** : a small drop : BLOB **2** : a usu. large and rounded mass — **glob·by** \ˈglä-bē\ *adj*
glob·al \ˈglō-bəl\ *adj* (1640) **1** : SPHERICAL **2** : of, relating to, or involving the entire world : WORLDWIDE ⟨a ~ system of communication⟩; *also* : of or relating to a celestial body (as the moon) **3** : of, relating to, or applying to a whole (as a mathematical function or a computer program) : UNIVERSAL ⟨a ~ search of a file⟩ — **glob·al·ly** \ˈglō-bə-lē\ *adv*
glob·al·i·sa·tion, glob·al·ise *Brit var of* GLOBALIZATION, GLOBALIZE
glob·al·ism \ˈglō-bə-ˌli-zəm\ *n* (1943) : a national policy of treating the whole world as a proper sphere for political influence — compare IMPERIALISM, INTERNATIONALISM — **glob·al·ist** \-list\ *n*
glob·al·i·za·tion \ˌglō-bə-lə-ˈzā-shən\ *n* (1951) : the act or process of globalizing : the state of being globalized; *esp* : the development of an increasingly integrated global economy marked esp. by free trade, free flow of capital, and the tapping of cheaper foreign labor markets
glob·al·ize \ˈglō-bə-ˌlīz\ *vt* **-ized; -iz·ing** (1944) : to make global; *esp* : to make worldwide in scope or application
Global Positioning System *n* (1974) : GPS
global village *n* (1960) : the world viewed as a community in which distance and isolation have been dramatically reduced by electronic media (as television and the Internet)
global warm·ing \-ˈwȯr-miŋ\ *n* (1969) : an increase in the earth's atmospheric and oceanic temperatures widely predicted to occur due to an increase in the greenhouse effect resulting esp. from pollution
[1]**globe** \ˈglōb\ *n* [MF, fr. L *globus*] (15c) : something spherical or rounded: as **a** : a spherical representation of the earth, a celestial body, or the heavens **b** : EARTH 4 **c** : ORB 5
[2]**globe** *vt* **globed; glob·ing** (1641) *archaic* : to form into a globe
globe amaranth *n* (1733) : an annual herb (*Gomphrena globosa*) of the amaranth family often cultivated as an ornamental for its dense globe-shaped flower heads which can be dried with nearly full retention of their color
globe artichoke *n* (1846) : ARTICHOKE 1
globe·fish \ˈglōb-ˌfish\ *n* (1668) : PUFFER FISH 1
globe·flow·er \-ˌflau̇(-ə)r\ *n* (1597) : any of a genus (*Trollius*) of plants of the buttercup family usu. with globose yellow or orange flowers
globe mallow *n* (1900) : any of a genus (*Sphaeralcea*) of coarse herbs of the mallow family found in arid regions of No. and So. America and often having clusters of cup-shaped pink or scarlet flowers
globe thistle *n* (1597) : any of a genus (*Echinops*) of widely cultivated Asian and Mediterranean composite herbs with spiky globose blue or white flowers
globe–trot·ter \-ˌträ-tər\ *n* (1875) : a person who travels widely — **globe–trot·ting** \-ˌträ-tiŋ\ *n or adj*
glo·bin \ˈglō-bən\ *n* [ISV, fr. *hemoglobin*] (1877) : a colorless protein obtained by removal of heme from a conjugated protein and esp. hemoglobin
glo·boid \ˈglō-ˌbȯid\ *adj* (1887) : shaped like a sphere
glo·bose \ˈglō-ˌbōs\ *adj* (15c) : GLOBULAR 1a(1) ⟨~ pollen⟩
glob·u·lar \ˈglä-byə-lər, *1b is also* ˈglō-\ *adj* [partly fr. L *globus* + E *-ular;* partly fr. L *globulus* + E *-ar*] (1654) **1 a** (1) : having the shape of a globe or globule (2) : composed of compactly folded polypeptide chains arranged in a spherical form ⟨~ proteins⟩ **b** : GLOBAL **2** : having or consisting of globules
globular cluster *n* (1859) : any of various approximately spherical clusters of gravitationally associated stars that typically populate galactic halos — called also *globular*

glob·ule \ˈglä-(ˌ)byül\ *n* [F, fr. L *globulus,* dim. of *globus*] (1661) **:** a tiny globe or ball esp. of a liquid ⟨~*s* of mercury⟩

glob·u·lin \ˈglä-byə-lən\ *n* (1845) **:** any of a class of simple proteins (as myosin) that are insoluble in pure water but are soluble in dilute salt solutions and that occur widely in plant and animal tissues — compare ALPHA GLOBULIN, BETA GLOBULIN, GAMMA GLOBULIN

glo·chid·i·um \glō-ˈki-dē-əm\ *n, pl* **-ia** \-dē-ə\ [NL, fr. Gk *glōchis* projecting point + NL *-idium*] (1875) **:** the larva of a freshwater mussel (family Unionidae) that develops as an external parasite on fish

glock·en·spiel \ˈglä-kən-ˌspēl, -ˌshpēl\ *n* [G, fr. *Glocke* bell + *Spiel* play] (ca. 1834) **:** a percussion instrument consisting of a series of graduated metal bars tuned to the chromatic scale and played with two hammers

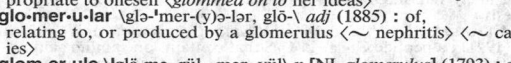

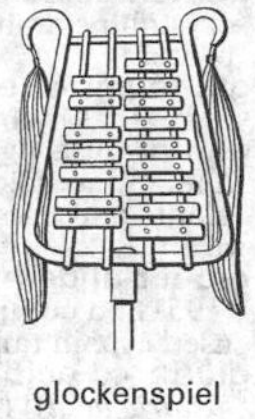
glockenspiel

glogg *or* **glögg** \ˈgləg, ˈglœg, ˈglu̇g\ *n* [Sw *glögg,* fr. *glödga* to burn, mull, fr. *glöd* glowing coal, fr. ON *glōth;* akin to OE *glēd* glowing coal — more at GLEED] (1927) **:** a hot spiced wine and liquor punch served in Scandinavian countries as a Christmas drink

glom \ˈgläm\ *vt* **glommed; glom·ming** [alter. of E dial. *glaum* to grab] (1907) **1 :** TAKE, STEAL **2 :** SEIZE, CATCH — **glom on to :** to grab hold of **:** appropriate to oneself ⟨*glommed on to* her ideas⟩

glo·mer·u·lar \glə-ˈmer-(y)ə-lər, glō-\ *adj* (1885) **:** of, relating to, or produced by a glomerulus ⟨~ nephritis⟩ ⟨~ capillaries⟩

glom·er·ule \ˈglä-mə-ˌrül, -mər-ˌyül\ *n* [NL *glomerulus*] (1793) **:** a compacted cyme of almost sessile and usu. small flowers

glo·mer·u·lo·ne·phri·tis \glə-ˌmer-(y)ə-lō-ni-ˈfrī-təs\ *n, pl* **-phrit·i·des** \-ˈfri-tə-ˌdēz\ (ca. 1886) **:** nephritis marked by inflammation of the capillaries of the renal glomeruli

glo·mer·u·lus \glə-ˈmer-(y)ə-ləs, glō-\ *n, pl* **-li** \-ˌlī, -ˌlē\ [NL, glomerulus, glomerule, dim. of L *glomer-, glomus* ball; akin to L *globus* globe] (1856) **:** a small convoluted or intertwined mass; *esp* **:** a tuft of capillaries at the point of origin of each vertebrate nephron that passes a protein-free filtrate to the surrounding Bowman's capsule

glo·mus \ˈglō-məs\ *n, pl* **glo·mera** \ˈglä-mə-rə, ˈglō-\ [NL, fr. L *glomer-, glomus*] (ca. 1847) **:** a small arteriovenous anastomosis together with its supporting structures

[1]**gloom** \ˈglüm\ *vb* [ME *gloumen*] *vi* (14c) **1 :** to look, feel, or act sullen or despondent **2 :** to be or become overcast **3 :** to loom up dimly ~ *vt* **:** to make dark, murky, or somber **:** make gloomy

[2]**gloom** *n* (1629) **1 a :** partial or total darkness **b :** a dark or shadowy place **2 a :** lowness of spirits **:** DEJECTION **b :** an atmosphere of despondency ⟨a ~ fell over the household⟩

gloomy \ˈglü-mē\ *adj* **gloom·i·er; -est** (1588) **1 a :** partially or totally dark; *esp* **:** dismally and depressingly dark ⟨~ weather⟩ **b :** having a frowning or scowling appearance **:** FORBIDDING ⟨a ~ countenance⟩ **c :** low in spirits **:** MELANCHOLY **2 a :** causing gloom **:** DEPRESSING ⟨a ~ story⟩ ⟨a ~ landscape⟩ **b :** lacking in promise or hopefulness **:** PESSIMISTIC ⟨~ prophecies⟩ ⟨a ~ future⟩ ***syn*** see DISMAL, SULLEN — **gloom·i·ly** \-mə-lē\ *adv* — **gloom·i·ness** \-mē-nəs\ *n*

Gloomy Gus \-ˈgəs\ *n, pl* **Gloomy Gus·es** *also* **Gloomy Gus·ses** *often not cap 1st G* [fr. a comic-strip character created by Frederick Burr Opper †1937 Am. cartoonist] (1904) **:** a person who is habitually gloomy

glop \ˈgläp\ *n* [origin unknown] (ca. 1944) **1 :** a thick semiliquid substance (as food) that is usu. unattractive in appearance **2 :** tasteless or worthless material — **glop·py** \ˈglä-pē\ *adj*

Glo·ria \ˈglȯr-ē-ə\ *n* [L, glory] (13c) **1 :** GLORIA IN EXCELSIS **2 :** GLORIA PATRI

Gloria in Ex·cel·sis \-ˌin-eks-ˈchel-səs, -ek-ˈshel-\ [LL, glory (be to God) on high] (14c) **:** a Christian liturgical hymn having the verse form of the Psalms

Gloria Pa·tri \-ˈpä-(ˌ)trē\ *n* [LL, glory (be) to the Father] (13c) **:** a 2-verse doxology to the Trinity

glo·ri·fy \ˈglȯr-ə-ˌfī\ *vt* **-fied; -fy·ing** [ME *glorifien,* fr. AF *glorifier,* fr. LL *glorificare,* fr. *gloria*] (14c) **1 a :** to make glorious by bestowing honor, praise, or admiration **b :** to elevate to celestial glory **2 :** to light up brilliantly **3 a :** to represent as glorious **:** EXTOL ⟨a song ~*ing* romantic love⟩ **b :** to cause to be or seem to be better than the actual condition ⟨the new position is just a *glorified* version of the old stockroom job⟩ **4 :** to give glory to (as in worship) — **glo·ri·fi·ca·tion** \ˌglȯr-ə-fə-ˈkā-shən\ *n* — **glo·ri·fi·er** \ˈglȯr-ə-ˌfī(-ə)r\ *n*

glo·ri·o·sa daisy \ˌglȯr-ē-ˈō-sə-, -zə-\ *n* [*gloriosa* fr. NL, lit., glorious] (1962) **:** a black-eyed Susan (*Rudbeckia hirta*) of either of two tetraploid cultivars with large single or double yellow, orange, maroon, or bicolored flowers

glo·ri·ous \ˈglȯr-ē-əs\ *adj* [ME, fr. AF & L; AF *glorios,* fr. L *gloriosus* glorious, vainglorious, fr. *gloria*] (13c) **1 a :** possessing or deserving glory **:** ILLUSTRIOUS **b :** entitling one to glory ⟨a ~ victory⟩ **2 :** marked by great beauty or splendor **:** MAGNIFICENT ⟨a ~ sunset⟩ **3 :** DELIGHTFUL, WONDERFUL ⟨had a ~ weekend⟩ ***syn*** see SPLENDID — **glo·ri·ous·ly** *adv* — **glo·ri·ous·ness** *n*

[1]**glo·ry** \ˈglȯr-ē\ *n, pl* **glories** [ME *glorie,* fr. AF & L; AF, fr. L *gloria*] (14c) **1 a :** praise, honor, or distinction extended by common consent **:** RENOWN **b :** worshipful praise, honor, and thanksgiving ⟨giving ~ to God⟩ **2 a :** something that secures praise or renown ⟨the ~ of a brilliant career⟩ **b :** a distinguished quality or asset **3 a (1) :** great beauty and splendor **:** MAGNIFICENCE ⟨the ~ that was Greece and the grandeur that was Rome —E. A. Poe⟩ **(2) :** something marked by beauty or resplendence ⟨a perfect ~ of a day⟩ **b :** the splendor and beatific happiness of heaven; *broadly* **:** ETERNITY **4 a :** a state of great gratification or exaltation ⟨when she's acting she's in her ~⟩ **b :** a height of prosperity or achievement **5 :** a ring or spot of light: as **a :** AUREOLE **b :** a halo appearing around the shadow of an object

[2]**glory** *vi* **glo·ried; glo·ry·ing** (14c) **:** to rejoice proudly — used with *in*

[3]**glory** *or* **glory be** *interj* (1816) — used to express surprise or delight

glory–of–the–snow *n* (ca. 1890) **:** any of a genus (*Chionodoxa*) of hardy spring-flowering chiefly Mediterranean bulbous herbs of the lily family with basal leaves and racemes of blue, white, or pink flowers

[1]**gloss** \ˈgläs, ˈglȯs\ *n* [akin to MHG *glosen* to glow, shine; akin to OE *geolu* yellow] (1538) **1 :** a surface luster or brightness **:** SHINE **2 a :** a deceptively attractive appearance ⟨selfishness that had a ~ of humanitarianism about it⟩ **b :** bright often superficial attractiveness ⟨show-biz ~⟩ **3 :** a transparent cosmetic preparation for adding shine and usu. color to the lips

[2]**gloss** *vt* (1656) **1 a :** to mask the true nature of **:** give a deceptively attractive appearance to — used with *over* ⟨the misery was general, where not ~*ed* over by liberal application of alcohol —Marston Bates⟩ **b :** to deal with (a subject or problem) too lightly or not at all — used with *over* ⟨~*es* over scholarly controversies rather than confronting them head-on —John Israel⟩ **2 :** to give a gloss to

[3]**gloss** *n* [alter. of *gloze,* fr. ME *glose,* fr. AF, fr. ML *glosa, glossa,* fr. Gk *glōssa, glōtta* tongue, language, obscure word; akin to Gk *glōchis* projecting point] (1548) **1 a :** a brief explanation (as in the margin or between the lines of a text) of a difficult or obscure word or expression **b :** a false and often willfully misleading interpretation (as of a text) **2 a :** GLOSSARY **b :** an interlinear translation **c :** a continuous commentary accompanying a text **3 :** COMMENTARY, INTERPRETATION

[4]**gloss** *vt* (1603) **1 a :** to provide a gloss for **:** EXPLAIN, DEFINE **b :** INTERPRET **2 :** to dispose of by false or perverse interpretation ⟨trying to ~ away the irrationalities of the universe —Irwin Edman⟩

gloss- *or* **glosso-** *comb form* [L, fr. Gk *glōss-, glōsso-,* fr. *glōssa*] **1 :** tongue ⟨*gloss*itis⟩ **2 :** language ⟨*glosso*lalia⟩

glos·sa \ˈglä-sə, ˈglȯ-\ *n, pl* **glos·sae** \-ˌsē, -ˌsī\ *also* **glossas** [NL, fr. Gk *glōssa*] (ca. 1852) **:** a tongue or lingual structure esp. in an insect; *esp* **:** the median distal lobe of the labium of an insect

glos·sa·rist \ˈglä-sə-rist, ˈglȯ-\ *n* (1774) **:** GLOSSATOR

glos·sa·ry \-sə-rē\ *n, pl* **-ries** (14c) **:** a collection of textual glosses or of specialized terms with their meanings — **glos·sar·i·al** \glä-ˈser-ē-əl, glȯ-\ *adj*

glos·sa·tor \ˈglä-ˌsā-tər, ˈglȯ-\ *n* (14c) **1 :** one that makes textual glosses **2 :** a compiler of a glossary

glos·si·tis \glä-ˈsī-təs, ˈglȯ-\ *n* (ca. 1834) **:** inflammation of the tongue

glos·sog·ra·pher \glä-ˈsä-grə-fər, glȯ-\ *n* [Gk *glōssographos,* fr. *glōssa* + *graphein* to write — more at CARVE] (1607) **:** GLOSSATOR

glos·so·la·lia \ˌglä-sə-ˈlā-lē-ə, ˌglȯ-\ *n* [NL] (1879) **:** TONGUE 4c — **glos·so·la·list** \-ˈlā-list\ *n*

glos·so·pha·ryn·geal nerve \ˌglä-sō-ˌfer-ən-ˈjē-əl-, ˌglȯ-, -fə-ˈrin-j(ē-)əl-\ *n* (ca. 1823) **:** either of the ninth pair of cranial nerves that are mixed nerves and supply chiefly the pharynx, posterior tongue, and parotid gland — called also *glossopharyngeal*

[1]**glossy** \ˈglä-sē, ˈglȯ-\ *adj* **gloss·i·er; -est** (1556) **1 :** having a surface luster or brightness ⟨rich ~ leather⟩ ⟨~ paper⟩ **2 :** attractive in an artificially opulent, sophisticated, or smoothly captivating manner **:** SLICK ⟨lots of ~ and phony chatter⟩ ***syn*** see SLEEK — **gloss·i·ly** \-sə-lē\ *adv* — **gloss·i·ness** \-sē-nəs\ *n*

[2]**glossy** *n, pl* **gloss·ies** (1928) **1 :** a photograph printed on smooth shiny paper **2** *chiefly Brit* **:** SLICK 4

glott- *or* **glotto-** *comb form* [Gk *glōtt-, glōtto-* tongue, fr. *glōssa, glōtta*] **:** language ⟨*glotto*chronology⟩

glot·tal \ˈglä-tᵊl\ *adj* (ca. 1846) **:** of, relating to, or produced in or by the glottis ⟨~ constriction⟩

glottal stop *n* (1888) **:** the interruption of the breath stream during speech by closure of the glottis

glot·tis \ˈglä-təs\ *n, pl* **glot·tis·es** *or* **glot·ti·des** \-tə-ˌdēz\ [Gk *glōttid-, glōttis,* fr. *glōtta* tongue — more at GLOSS] (1578) **:** the elongated space between the vocal cords; *also* **:** the structures that surround this space — compare EPIGLOTTIS

glot·to·chro·nol·o·gy \ˌglä-tō-krə-ˈnä-lə-jē\ *n* (1953) **:** a linguistic method that uses the rate of vocabulary replacement to estimate the date of divergence for distinct but genetically related languages — **glot·to·chro·no·log·i·cal** \-ˌkrä-nə-ˈlä-ji-kəl, -ˌkrō-\ *adj*

Gloucs *abbr* Gloucestershire

glout \ˈglüt, ˈglau̇t\ *vi* [ME — more at GLOAT] (14c) *archaic* **:** FROWN, SCOWL

[1]**glove** \ˈgləv\ *n* [ME, fr. OE *glōf;* akin to ON *glōfi* glove] (bef. 12c) **1 a :** a covering for the hand having separate sections for each of the fingers and the thumb and often extending part way up the arm **b :** [1]GAUNTLET 1 **2 a (1) :** a padded leather covering for the hand used in baseball to catch a thrown or batted ball; *specif* **:** one having individual thumb and finger sections usu. connected with a lacing or webbing — compare MITT **(2) :** fielding ability ⟨he's got a good ~ at three positions and can pinch-hit —Casey Stengel⟩ **b :** BOXING GLOVE **3 a :** [1]GAUNTLET 3 **b** *pl* **:** the restraints of civility ⟨the ~*s* came off for the interview⟩

[2]**glove** *vt* **gloved; glov·ing** (15c) **1 a :** to cover with or as if with a glove **b :** to furnish with gloves **2 :** to catch (as a baseball) in one's gloved hand

glove box *n* (1946) **1 :** GLOVE COMPARTMENT **2 :** a sealed protectively lined compartment having holes to which are attached gloves for use in handling esp. dangerous materials inside the compartment

glove compartment *n* (1939) **:** a small storage cabinet in the dashboard of an automobile

glove leather *n* (1721) **:** a soft lightweight leather

glov·er \ˈglə-vər\ *n* (14c) **:** one that makes or sells gloves

[1]**glow** \ˈglō\ *vi* [ME, fr. OE *glōwan;* akin to OE *geolu* yellow — more at YELLOW] (bef. 12c) **1 a :** to shine with or as if with an intense heat ⟨embers ~*ing* in the darkness⟩ **b (1) :** to have a rich warm typically ruddy color ⟨cheeks ~*ing* with health⟩ **(2) :** FLUSH, BLUSH ⟨the children ~*ed* with excitement⟩ **2 a :** to experience a sensation of or as if of heat ⟨~*ing* with rage⟩ **b :** to show exuberance or elation ⟨~ with pride⟩ — **glow·ing·ly** \-iŋ-lē\ *adv*

[2]**glow** *n* (1600) **1 :** brightness or warmth of color; *esp* **:** REDNESS **2 a :** warmth of feeling or emotion **b :** a sensation of warmth ⟨the drug produces a sustained ~⟩ **3 a :** the state of glowing with heat and light **b :** light such as is emitted by a solid body heated to luminosity **:** INCANDESCENCE

glow discharge *n* (1844) **:** a luminous electrical discharge without sparks through a gas

[1]glow·er \'glau̇(-ə)r, ÷'glō(-ə)r\ *vi* [ME (Sc) *glowren;* akin to MLG *glūren* to be overcast, MD *gloeren* to leer] (15c) **:** to look or stare with sullen annoyance or anger

[2]glower *n* (1715) **:** a sullen brooding look of annoyance or anger

glow lamp *n* (1884) **:** a gas-discharge electric lamp in which most of the light proceeds from the glow of the gas near the cathode

glow plug *n* (ca. 1941) **:** a heating element in a diesel-engine cylinder to preheat the air and facilitate starting; *also* **:** a similar element for ignition in other internal combustion engines

glow·worm \'glō-ˌwərm\ *n* [ME] (14c) **:** any of various luminous insect larvae or adults with wings rudimentary or lacking; *esp* **:** a larva or wingless female of a firefly (family Lampyridae) that emits light from the abdomen

glox·in·ia \gläk-'si-nē-ə\ *n* [NL, fr. B. P. *Gloxin* 18th cent. Ger. botanist] (ca. 1820) **:** any of a genus (*Sinningia*) of tuberous herbaceous gesneriads found from Mexico to Argentina; *esp* **:** a Brazilian plant (*S. speciosa*) widely cultivated for its bell-shaped or slipper-shaped flowers

[1]gloze \'glōz\ *vt* **glozed; gloz·ing** [ME *glosen* to gloss, flatter, fr. *glose* gloss] (14c) *archaic* **:** [4]GLOSS 1

[2]gloze *vt* **glozed; gloz·ing** (14c) **:** [2]GLOSS 1 — often used with *over*

gluc- *or* **gluco-** *comb form* [ISV] **:** glucose ⟨*gluco*kinase⟩

glu·ca·gon \'glü-kə-ˌgän\ *n* [*gluc-* + *-agon* (perh. fr. Gk *agōn,* prp. of *agein* to lead, drive) — more at AGENT] (1923) **:** a protein hormone that is produced esp. by the islets of Langerhans and that promotes an increase in the sugar content of the blood by increasing the rate of glycogen breakdown in the liver

glu·can \'glü-ˌkan, -kən\ *n* (1941) **:** a polysaccharide (as glycogen or cellulose) that is a polymer of glucose

glu·co·cor·ti·coid \ˌglü-kō-'kȯr-ti-ˌkȯid\ *n* (1950) **:** any of a group of corticosteroids (as cortisol) that are involved esp. in carbohydrate, protein, and fat metabolism, that are anti-inflammatory and immunosuppressive, and that are used widely in medicine (as to alleviate the symptoms of rheumatoid arthritis) — compare MINERALOCORTICOID

glu·co·ki·nase \-'kī-ˌnās, -ˌnāz\ *n* (1950) **:** a hexokinase found esp. in the liver that catalyzes the phosphorylation of glucose

glu·co·nate \'glü-kə-ˌnāt\ *n* (1884) **:** a salt or ester of gluconic acid

glu·co·neo·gen·e·sis \ˌglü-kə-ˌnē-ə-'je-nə-səs\ *n* [NL] (1912) **:** formation of glucose within the animal body esp. by the liver from substances (as fats and proteins) other than carbohydrates

glu·con·ic acid \(ˌ)glü-'kä-nik-\ *n* [ISV, irreg. fr. *glucose* + *-ic*] (1871) **:** a crystalline acid $C_6H_{12}O_7$ obtained by oxidation of glucose

glu·cos·amine \glü-'kō-sə-ˌmēn, -zə-\ *n* (1884) **:** an amino derivative $C_6H_{13}NO_5$ of glucose that occurs esp. as a constituent of various polysaccharides that are components of structural substances (as chitin and cartilage)

glu·cose \'glü-ˌkōs, -ˌkōz\ *n* [F, modif. of Gk *gleukos* must, sweet wine; akin to Gk *glykys* sweet — more at DULCET] (1840) **1 :** a crystalline sugar $C_6H_{12}O_6$; *specif* **:** the sweet colorless soluble dextrorotatory form that occurs widely in nature and is the usual form in which carbohydrate is assimilated by animals **2 :** a light-colored syrup made from cornstarch

glucose–1–phosphate *n* [fr. the position at which the phosphate group is attached] (1938) **:** an ester $C_6H_{13}O_9P$ that reacts in the presence of a phosphorylase with aldoses and ketoses to yield disaccharides or with itself in liver and muscle to yield glycogen and phosphoric acid

glucose phosphate *n* (1912) **:** a phosphate ester of glucose: as **a :** GLUCOSE-1-PHOSPHATE **b :** GLUCOSE-6-PHOSPHATE

glucose–6–phosphate *n* [fr. the position at which the phosphate group is attached] (1953) **:** an ester $C_6H_{13}O_9P$ that is formed from glucose and ATP in the presence of a glucokinase and that is an essential early stage in glucose metabolism

glucose–6–phosphate dehydrogenase *n* (1954) **:** an enzyme found esp. in red blood cells that dehydrogenates glucose-6-phosphate in a glucose degradation pathway alternative to the Krebs cycle

glu·co·si·dase \glü-'kō-sə-ˌdās, -zə-ˌdāz\ *n* (1909) **:** an enzyme (as maltase) that hydrolyzes a glucoside

glu·co·side \'glü-kə-ˌsīd\ *n* (1855) **:** GLYCOSIDE; *esp* **:** a glycoside that yields glucose on hydrolysis — **glu·co·sid·ic** \ˌglü-kə-'si-dik\ *adj*

glu·cu·ron·ic acid \ˌglü-kyə-'rä-nik-\ *n* [*gluc-* + *-uronic*] (1911) **:** a compound $C_6H_{10}O_7$ that occurs esp. as a constituent of mucopolysaccharides (as hyaluronic acid) and combined as a glucuronide

glu·cu·ron·i·dase \-'rä-nə-ˌdās, -ˌdāz\ *n* (1945) **:** an enzyme that hydrolyzes a glucuronide; *esp* **:** one that occurs widely (as in liver and spleen) and hydrolyzes the beta form of a glucuronide

glu·cu·ro·nide \glü-'kyu̇r-ə-ˌnīd\ *n* (1934) **:** any of various derivatives of glucuronic acid that are formed esp. as combinations with often toxic aromatic hydroxyl compounds and are excreted in the urine

[1]glue \'glü\ *n* [ME *glu,* fr. AF, fr. LL *glut-, glus;* akin to L *gluten* glue — more at CLAY] (14c) **1 a :** any of various strong adhesive substances; *esp* **:** a hard protein chiefly gelatinous substance that absorbs water to form a viscous solution with strong adhesive properties and that is obtained by cooking down collagenous materials (as hides or bones) **b :** a solution of glue used for sticking things together **2 :** something that binds together ⟨enough social ~ . . . to satisfy the human desire for community —E. D. Hirsch, Jr.⟩ — **glu·ey** \'glü-ē\ *adj* — **glu·i·ly** \'glü-ə-lē\ *adv*

[2]glue *vt* **glued; glu·ing** *also* **glue·ing** (14c) **1 :** to cause to stick tightly with or as if with glue ⟨*gluing* the parts together⟩ ⟨used that war to ~ together a frail story —Gloria Emerson⟩ **2 :** to cause to remain continuously or to be fixed steadily — usu. used with *to* ⟨the spectators were *glued* to their seats⟩ ⟨all eyes *glued* to the TV screen⟩

glüh·wein *also* **gluh·wein** \'glue-ˌvīn\ *n* [G *Glühwein,* fr. *glühen* to mull, glow + *Wein* wine] (1898) **:** mulled wine

glum \'gləm\ *adj* **glum·mer; glum·mest** [akin to ME *gloumen* to gloom] (1547) **1 :** broodingly morose ⟨became ~ when they heard the news⟩ **2 :** DREARY, GLOOMY ⟨a ~ countenance⟩ ***syn*** see SULLEN — **glum·ly** *adv* — **glum·ness** *n*

glume \'glüm\ *n* [NL *gluma,* fr. L, hull, husk; akin to L *glubere* to peel — more at CLEAVE] (1789) **:** a chaffy bract; *specif* **:** either of two empty bracts at the base of the spikelet in grasses

glu·on \'glü-ˌän\ *n* ['*glue* + [2]*-on*] (1971) **:** a hypothetical neutral massless particle held to bind together quarks to form hadrons

[1]glut \'glət\ *vb* **glut·ted; glut·ting** [ME *glouten,* prob. fr. AF *glutir* to swallow, fr. L *gluttire* — more at GLUTTON] *vt* (14c) **1 :** to fill esp. with food to satiety **2 :** to flood (the market) with goods so that supply exceeds demand ~ *vi* **:** to eat gluttonously ***syn*** see SATIATE

[2]glut *n* (ca. 1546) **1 :** an excessive quantity **:** OVERSUPPLY **2** *archaic* **:** the act or process of glutting

[3]glut *vt* **glut·ted; glut·ting** [prob. fr. obs. *glut,* n., swallow] (1600) *archaic* **:** to swallow greedily

glu·ta·mate \'glü-tə-ˌmāt\ *n* (1876) **:** a salt or ester of glutamic acid; *specif* **:** a salt or ester of levorotatory glutamic acid that functions as an excitatory neurotransmitter — compare MONOSODIUM GLUTAMATE

glu·tam·ic acid \(ˌ)glü-'ta-mik-\ *n* [ISV *glut*en + *am*ino + *-ic*] (1871) **:** a crystalline amino acid $C_5H_9NO_4$ widely distributed in plant and animal proteins

glu·ta·min·ase \'glü-tə-mə-ˌnās, glü-'ta-mə-, -ˌnāz\ *n* (1938) **:** an enzyme that hydrolyzes glutamine to glutamic acid and ammonia

glu·ta·mine \'glü-tə-ˌmēn\ *n* [ISV *glut*en + *amine*] (ca. 1885) **:** a crystalline amino acid $C_5H_{10}N_2O_3$ that is found both free and in proteins in plants and animals and that yields glutamic acid and ammonia on hydrolysis

glu·tar·al·de·hyde \ˌglü-tə-'ral-də-ˌhīd\ *n* [*glutar*ic acid + *aldehyde*] (1951) **:** a compound $C_5H_8O_2$ that contains two aldehyde groups and is used esp. in tanning leather and in the fixation of biological tissues

glu·tar·ic acid \glü-'ter-ik-, -'ta-rik-\ *n* [prob. fr. *glut*en + *-aric* (as in *tartaric acid*)] (ca. 1885) **:** a crystalline acid $C_5H_8O_4$ used esp. in organic synthesis

glu·ta·thi·one \ˌglü-tə-'thī-ˌōn\ *n* [ISV *gluta-* (fr. *glutamic acid*) + *thi-* + *-one*] (1921) **:** a peptide $C_{10}H_{17}N_3O_6S$ that contains one amino acid residue each of glutamic acid, cysteine, and glycine, that occurs widely in plant and animal tissues, and that plays an important role in biological oxidation-reduction processes and as a coenzyme

glute \'glüt\ *n* (1984) **:** GLUTEUS — usu. used in pl.

glu·te·al \'glü-tē-əl, glü-'tē-\ *adj* (1804) **:** of or relating to the gluteus muscles

glu·ten \'glü-tᵊn\ *n* [L *glutin-, gluten* glue — more at CLAY] (1803) **:** a tenacious elastic protein substance esp. of wheat flour that gives cohesiveness to dough — **glu·ten·ous** \'glüt-nəs, 'glü-tᵊn-əs\ *adj*

glu·teth·i·mide \glü-'te-thə-ˌmīd, -məd\ *n* [*gluten* + *eth-* + *imide*] (1955) **:** a sedative-hypnotic drug $C_{13}H_{15}NO_2$ that is a derivative of piperidine and has pharmacological properties similar to those of barbiturates

glu·te·us \'glü-tē-əs, glü-'tē-\ *n, pl* **glu·tei** \'glü-tē-ˌī, -tē-ˌē; glü-'tē-ˌī\ [NL *glutaeus, gluteus,* fr. Gk *gloutos* buttock — more at CLOUD] (ca. 1681) **:** any of the large muscles of the buttocks; *esp* **:** GLUTEUS MAXIMUS

gluteus max·i·mus \-'mak-sə-məs\ *n, pl* **glutei max·i·mi** \-'mak-sə-ˌmī\ [NL, lit., largest gluteus] (1831) **:** the outermost muscle of the three glutei found in each of the human buttocks

glu·ti·nous \'glüt-nəs, 'glü-tə-nəs\ *adj* [ME, fr. L *glutinosus,* fr. *glutin-, gluten*] (15c) **:** having the quality of glue **:** GUMMY — **glu·ti·nous·ly** *adv*

glutinous rice *n* (1900) **:** the seeds of a short-grained cultivated rice (*Oryza sativa glutinosa*) that are plump and sticky when cooked

glut·ton \'glə-tᵊn\ *n* [ME *glotoun,* fr. AF *glutun, glotun,* fr. L *glutton-, glutto;* akin to L *gluttire* to swallow, *gula* throat, OE *ceole*] (13c) **1 a :** one given habitually to greedy and voracious eating and drinking **b :** one that has a great capacity for accepting or enduring something ⟨a ~ for punishment⟩ **2 :** WOLVERINE 1a

glut·ton·ous \'glət-nəs, 'glə-tə-nəs\ *adj* (14c) **:** marked by or given to gluttony ⟨a ~ appetite⟩ ***syn*** see VORACIOUS — **glut·ton·ous·ly** *adv* — **glut·ton·ous·ness** *n*

glut·tony \'glət-nē, 'glə-tə-nē\ *n, pl* **-ton·ies** (13c) **1 :** excess in eating or drinking **2 :** greedy or excessive indulgence

glyc- *or* **glyco-** *comb form* [ISV, fr. Gk *glyk-* sweet, fr. *glykys*] **1 :** carbohydrate and esp. sugar ⟨*glyco*protein⟩ **2 :** glycine ⟨*glyc*yl⟩

gly·can \'glī-ˌkan\ *n* (1950) **:** POLYSACCHARIDE

gly·ce·mia \glī-'sē-mē-ə\ *n* [NL] (1901) **:** the presence of glucose in the blood — **gly·ce·mic** \-'sē-mik\ *adj*

glycemic index *n* (1981) **:** a measure of the rate at which ingested food causes the level of glucose in the blood to rise; *also* **:** a ranking of foods according to the glycemic index

glyc·er·al·de·hyde \ˌgli-sə-'ral-də-ˌhīd\ *n* [*glycer*ic acid + *aldehyde*] (1882) **:** a sweet crystalline compound $C_3H_6O_3$ that is formed as an intermediate in carbohydrate metabolism by the breakdown of sugars and that yields glycerol on reduction

gly·cer·ic acid \gli-'ser-ik-\ *n* [ISV, fr. *glycerin*] (1838) **:** a syrupy acid $C_3H_6O_4$ obtainable by oxidation of glycerol or glyceraldehyde

glyc·er·ide \'gli-sə-ˌrīd\ *n* (ca. 1864) **:** an ester of glycerol esp. with fatty acids — **glyc·er·id·ic** \ˌgli-sə-'ri-dik\ *adj*

glyc·er·in *or* **glyc·er·ine** \'glis-rən, 'gli-sə-\ *n* [F *glycérine,* fr. Gk *glykeros* sweet; akin to Gk *glykys*] (1830) **:** GLYCEROL

glyc·er·in·ate \'glis-rə-ˌnāt, 'gli-sə-\ *vt* **-at·ed; -at·ing** (1897) **:** to treat with or preserve in glycerin

glyc·er·ol \'gli-sə-ˌrȯl, -ˌrōl\ *n* [*glycer*in + *-ol*] (1880) **:** a sweet syrupy hygroscopic trihydroxy alcohol $C_3H_8O_3$ usu. obtained by the saponification of fats

glyc·er·yl \'glis-rəl, 'gli-sə-\ *n* (1845) **:** a radical derived from glycerol by removal of hydroxide; *esp* **:** a trivalent radical CH_2CHCH_2

gly·cine \'glī-ˌsēn, 'glī-sᵊn\ *n* (1851) **:** a sweet crystalline amino acid $C_2H_5NO_2$ obtained esp. by hydrolysis of proteins

gly·co·al·ka·loid \ˌglī-kō-'al-kə-ˌlȯid\ *n* (1949) **:** a bitter compound (as solanine) occurring in various plants and consisting of a glycoside of an alkaloid

gly·co·gen \'glī-kə-jən\ *n* (ca. 1864) **:** a white amorphous tasteless polysaccharide $(C_6H_{10}O_5)_x$ that is the principal form in which glucose is stored in animal tissues and esp. muscle and liver tissue

gly·co·gen·e·sis \ˌglī-kə-'je-nə-səs\ *n* [NL] (ca. 1886) **:** the formation and storage of glycogen

gly·co·gen·ol·y·sis \ˌglī-kə-jə-'nä-lə-səs\ *n, pl* **-y·ses** \-ˌsēz\ [NL] (1909) **:** the breakdown of glycogen esp. to glucose in the animal body — **gly·co·gen·o·lyt·ic** \-jə-nə-'li-tik, -ˌje-\ *adj*

gly·col \'glī-ˌkȯl, -ˌkōl\ *n* [ISV *glyc-* + *-ol*] (1857) **:** DIOL; *esp* **:** ETHYLENE GLYCOL

gly·col·ic acid *or* **gly·col·lic acid** \(ˌ)glī-'kä-lik-\ *n* [ISV *glycol* + [1]*-ic*] (1852) **:** an alpha hydroxy acid $C_2H_4O_3$ found esp. in unripe grapes and sugar beets and used esp. in textile and leather processing and in skin-care treatments esp. as an exfoliant

gly·co·lip·id \ˌglī-kō-ˈli-pəd\ *n* (1936) **:** a lipid (as a ganglioside or a cerebroside) that contains a carbohydrate radical

gly·col·y·sis \glī-ˈkä-lə-səs\ *n* [NL] (1892) **:** the enzymatic breakdown of a carbohydrate (as glucose) by way of phosphate derivatives with the production of pyruvic or lactic acid and energy stored in high-energy phosphate bonds of ATP — **gly·co·lyt·ic** \ˌglī-kə-ˈli-tik\ *adj*

gly·co·pep·tide \ˌglī-kō-ˈpep-ˌtīd\ *n* (1959) **:** GLYCOPROTEIN

gly·co·pro·tein \-ˈprō-ˌtēn, -ˈprō-tē-ən\ *n* (ca. 1908) **:** a conjugated protein in which the nonprotein group is a carbohydrate

gly·cos·ami·no·gly·can \ˌglī-kō-sə-ˌmē-nō-ˈglī-ˌkan, -kō-ˌsa-mə-nō-\ *n* [*glyc-* + hex*osamine* (amine derived from a hexose) + *-o-* + *glycan*] (1962) **:** any of various polysaccharides derived from an amino hexose that are constituents of mucoproteins, glycoproteins, and blood-group substances — called also *mucopolysaccharide*

gly·co·si·dase \glī-ˈkō-sə-ˌdās, -zə-ˌdāz\ *n* (1941) **:** an enzyme that catalyzes the hydrolysis of a bond joining a sugar of a glycoside to an alcohol or another sugar unit

gly·co·side \ˈglī-kə-ˌsīd\ *n* [alter. of *glucoside*] (1855) **:** any of numerous sugar derivatives that contain a nonsugar group bonded to an oxygen or nitrogen atom and that on hydrolysis yield a sugar (as glucose) — **gly·co·sid·ic** \ˌglī-kə-ˈsi-dik\ *adj* — **gly·co·sid·i·cal·ly** \-di-k(ə-)lē\ *adv*

gly·cos·uria \ˌglī-kō-ˈshu̇r-ē-ə, ˌglī-kəs-ˈyu̇r-\ *n* [NL, fr. ISV *glycose* glucose + NL *-uria*] (1860) **:** the presence in the urine of abnormal amounts of sugar

gly·co·syl \ˈglī-kə-ˌsil\ *n* [ISV *glycose* glucose] (1945) **:** a monovalent radical derived from a cyclic form of glucose by removal of the hemiacetal hydroxyl group

gly·co·syl·a·tion \ˌglī-kō-sə-ˈlā-shən\ *n* (1945) **:** the process of adding glycosyl radicals to a protein to form a glycoprotein — **gly·co·sy·late** \ˌglī-kō-ˈsī-ˌlāt\ *vt*

gly·cyl \ˈglī-səl\ *n* (1901) **:** the monovalent acyl radical NH_2CH_2CO– of glycine

glyph \ˈglif\ *n* [Gk *glyphē* carved work, fr. *glyphein* to carve — more at CLEAVE] (1775) **1 :** an ornamental vertical groove esp. in a Doric frieze **2 :** a symbolic figure or a character (as in the Mayan system of writing) usu. incised or carved in relief **3 :** a symbol (as a curved arrow on a road sign) that conveys information nonverbally — **glyph·ic** \ˈgli-fik\ *adj*

glyph·o·sate \ˈgli-fə-ˌsāt, ˈglī-\ *n* [perh. fr. ISV *gly*cine + *phos*ph- + [1]*-ate*] (1972) **:** a systemic organophosphate herbicide $C_3H_8NO_5P$ used to control herbaceous and woody weeds esp. on croplands

Glyp·tal \ˈglip-tᵊl\ *trademark* — used for an alkyd

glyp·tic \ˈglip-tik\ *n* [prob. fr. F *glyptique*, fr. Gk *glyptikē*, fr. *glyphein*] (ca. 1818) **:** the art or process of carving or engraving esp. on gems

gm *abbr* gram

GM *abbr* **1** general manager **2** genetically modified **3** grand master **4** guided missile

G–man \ˈjē-ˌman\ *n* [prob. fr. *g*overnment *man*] (1928) **:** a special agent of the Federal Bureau of Investigation

GMO *abbr* genetically modified organism

GMT *abbr* Greenwich mean time

GMW *abbr* gram molecular weight

gn *abbr* guinea

gnar *or* **gnarr** \ˈnär\ *vi* **gnarred; gnar·ring** [imit.] (15c) **:** SNARL, GROWL

[1]**gnarl** \ˈnär(-ə)l\ *vi* [prob. freq. of *gnar*] (1593) **:** SNARL, GROWL

[2]**gnarl** *vt* [back-formation fr. *gnarled*] (1814) **:** to twist into a state of deformity

[3]**gnarl** *n* (1805) **:** a hard protuberance with twisted grain on a tree

gnarled \ˈnär(-ə)ld\ *adj* [prob. alter. of *knurled*] (1603) **1 :** full of knots or gnarls **:** KNOTTY ⟨~ hands⟩ **2 :** crabbed in disposition, aspect, or character

gnarly \ˈnär-lē\ *adj* **gnarl·i·er; gnarl·i·est** (1773) **1 :** GNARLED **2** *slang* **a :** DIFFICULT, HAIRY ⟨skidded around ~ hairpin turns —Austin Murphy⟩ **b :** BAD, NASTY ⟨has some pretty ~ karma coming —Drew Barrymore⟩ **c :** COOL, GOOD

gnash \ˈnash\ *vt* [alter. of ME *gnasten*] (15c) **:** to strike or grind (as the teeth) together — **gnash** *n*

gnat \ˈnat\ *n* [ME, fr. OE *gnætt;* akin to OE *gnagan* to gnaw] (bef. 12c) **:** any of various small usu. biting dipteran flies — **gnat·ty** \-ē\ *adj*

gnat·catch·er \ˈnat-ˌka-chər, -ˌke-\ *n* (1839) **:** any of a genus (*Polioptila*) of several small No. and So. American insectivorous oscine birds

gnath·ic \ˈna-thik\ *also* **gna·thal** \ˈnā-thəl, ˈna-\ *adj* [Gk *gnathos* jaw] (1882) **:** of or relating to the jaw

-gnathous *adj comb form* [NL *-gnathus,* fr. Gk *gnathos;* akin to Gk *genys* jaw — more at CHIN] **:** having (such) a jaw ⟨pro*gnathous*⟩

gnaw \ˈnȯ\ *vb* [ME *gnawen,* fr. OE *gnagan;* akin to OHG *gnagan* to gnaw] *vt* (bef. 12c) **1 a :** to bite or chew on with the teeth; *esp* **:** to wear away by persistent biting or nibbling ⟨a dog ~*ing* a bone⟩ **b :** to make by gnawing ⟨rats ~*ed* a hole⟩ **2 a :** to be a source of vexation to **:** PLAGUE ⟨anxiety always ~*ing* him⟩ **b :** to affect like gnawing ⟨hunger ~*ing* her vitals⟩ **3 :** ERODE, CORRODE ~ *vi* **1 :** to bite or nibble persistently ⟨~*ing* at his underlip⟩ **2 :** to produce an effect of or as if of gnawing ⟨waves ~*ing* away at the cliffs⟩ — **gnaw·er** \ˈnȯ(-ə)r\ *n*

gneiss \ˈnīs\ *n* [G *Gneis,* alter. of MHG *gneiste* spark, fr. OHG *gneisto;* akin to OE *fȳrgnāst* spark] (1757) **:** a foliated metamorphic rock corresponding in composition to a feldspathic plutonic rock (as granite) — **gneiss·ic** \ˈnī-sik\ *adj* — **gneiss·oid** \-ˌsȯid\ *adj* — **gneiss·ose** \-ˌsōs\ *adj*

GNMA *abbr* Government National Mortgage Association

gnoc·chi \ˈnō-kē, ˈnyō-, ˈnä-\ *n pl* [It, pl. of *gnocco,* fr. It dial. (Veneto), prob. of Gmc origin; akin to MHG *knöchel* knuckle, *knoche* bone — more at KNUCKLE] (1891) **:** dumplings usu. made with potato or semolina and served with sauce

[1]**gnome** \ˈnōm\ *n* [Gk *gnōmē,* fr. *gignōskein* to know — more at KNOW] (1577) **:** MAXIM, APHORISM

[2]**gnome** *n* [F, fr. NL *gnomus*] (1661) **1 :** an ageless and often deformed dwarf of folklore who lives in the earth and usu. guards treasure **2 :** an elemental being in the theory of Paracelsus that inhabits earth — **gnome·like** \-ˌlīk\ *adj* — **gnom·ish** \ˈnō-mish\ *adj*

gno·mic \ˈnō-mik\ *adj* (1815) **1 :** characterized by aphorism ⟨~ utterances⟩ **2 :** given to the composition of gnomic writing ⟨a ~ poet⟩

gno·mon \ˈnō-mən, -ˌmän\ *n* [L, fr. Gk *gnōmōn* interpreter, pointer on a sundial, fr. *gignōskein*] (1546) **1 :** an object that by the position or length of its shadow serves as an indicator esp. of the hour of the day: as **a :** the pin of a sundial **b :** a column or shaft erected perpendicular to the horizon **2 :** the remainder of a parallelogram after the removal of a similar parallelogram containing one of its corners

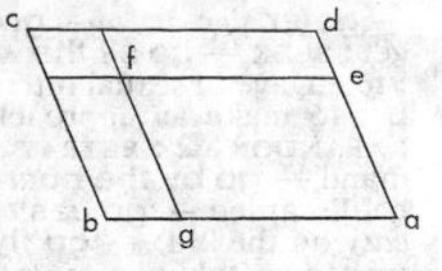

bcdefg gnomon 2

gno·sis \ˈnō-səs\ *n* [Gk *gnōsis,* lit., knowledge, fr. *gignōskein*] (1703) **:** esoteric knowledge of spiritual truth held by the ancient Gnostics to be essential to salvation

gnos·tic \ˈnäs-tik\ *n, often cap* [LL *gnosticus,* fr. Gk *gnōstikos* of knowledge, fr. *gignōskein*] (ca. 1587) **:** an adherent of gnosticism — **gnostic** *adj, often cap*

gnos·ti·cism \ˈnäs-tə-ˌsi-zəm\ *n, often cap* (1664) **:** the thought and practice esp. of various cults of late pre-Christian and early Christian centuries distinguished by the conviction that matter is evil and that emancipation comes through gnosis

gno·to·bi·ot·ic \ˌnō-tō-bī-ˈä-tik, -bē-\ *adj* [Gk *gnōtos* known (fr. *gignōskein* to know) + *biotē* life, way of life — more at KNOW, BIOTA] (1949) **:** of, relating to, living in, or being a controlled environment containing one or a few kinds of organisms; *also* **:** AXENIC — **gno·to·bi·ot·i·cal·ly** \-ti-k(ə-)lē\ *adv*

GNP *abbr* gross national product

GnRH *abbr* gonadotropin-releasing hormone

gnu \ˈnü *also* ˈnyü\ *n, pl* **gnu** *or* **gnus** [Khoikhoi *t'gnu*] (1777) **:** WILDEBEEST

[1]**go** \ˈgō\ *vb* **went** \ˈwent\; **gone** \ˈgȯn *also* ˈgän\; **go·ing** \ˈgō-iŋ, ˈgȯ(-)iŋ; *"going to" in sense 13 is often* ˈgō-nə *or* ˈgȯ-nə\; **goes** \ˈgōz\ [ME *gon,* fr. OE *gān;* akin to OHG *gān* to go, Gk *kichanein* to reach, attain] *vi* (bef. 12c) **1 :** to move on a course **:** PROCEED ⟨~ slow⟩ ⟨*went* by train⟩ — compare STOP **2 :** to move out of or away from a place expressed or implied **:** LEAVE, DEPART ⟨*went* from school to the party⟩ ⟨~*ing* away for vacation⟩ **3 a :** to take a certain course or follow a certain procedure ⟨reports ~ through channels to the president⟩ **b :** to pass by means of a process like journeying ⟨the message *went* by wire⟩ **c :** to proceed without delay and often in a thoughtless or reckless manner — used esp. to intensify a complementary verb ⟨why did you ~ and spoil it⟩ ⟨~ jump in a lake⟩ **d** (1) **:** to extend from point to point or in a certain direction ⟨the road ~*es* to the lake⟩ (2) **:** to give access **:** LEAD ⟨that door ~*es* to the cellar⟩ **4** *obs* **:** WALK **5 :** to be habitually in a certain state or condition ⟨~ bareheaded⟩ **6 a :** to become lost, consumed, or spent ⟨our time has *gone*⟩ **b :** DIE **c :** to slip away **:** ELAPSE ⟨the evening *went* quickly⟩ **d :** to come to be given up or discarded ⟨these slums have to ~⟩ **e :** to pass by sale ⟨*went* for a good price⟩ **f :** to become impaired or weakened ⟨his hearing started to ~⟩ **g :** to give way esp. under great force or pressure **:** BREAK ⟨the roof *went*⟩ **7 a :** to move along in a specified manner **:** FARE ⟨everything was ~*ing* well⟩ **b :** to be in general or on an average ⟨cheap, as yachts ~⟩ **c :** to be or become esp. as the result of a contest ⟨the election *went* in her favor⟩ **d :** to turn out well **:** SUCCEED ⟨worked hard to make the party ~⟩ **8 a :** to apply oneself ⟨*went* to work on the problem⟩ **b :** to put or subject oneself ⟨*went* to unnecessary expense⟩ **c** *chiefly Southern & Midland* **:** INTEND ⟨I didn't ~ to do it⟩ **9 :** to have recourse to another for corroboration, vindication, or decision **:** RESORT ⟨~ to court to recover damages⟩ **10 a :** to begin an action or motion ⟨here ~*es*⟩ **b :** to maintain or perform a certain action or motion ⟨still ~*ing* strong⟩ **c :** to function in the proper or expected manner **:** RUN ⟨the motor won't ~⟩ **11 :** to be known ⟨~*es* by an alias⟩ **12 a :** to act in accordance or harmony ⟨a good rule to ~ by⟩ **b :** to come to be determined ⟨dreams ~ by contraries⟩ **c :** to come to be applied or appropriated ⟨all proceeds ~ to charity⟩ **d :** to pass by award, assignment, or lot ⟨the prize *went* to a sophomore⟩ **e** (1) **:** to contribute to an end or result ⟨qualities that ~ to make a hero⟩ (2) **:** to be of advantage ⟨has a lot ~*ing* for her⟩ **13 :** to be about, intending, or expecting something — used in a progressive tense before an infinitive ⟨is ~*ing* to leave town⟩ **14 a :** EXTEND ⟨his knowledge fails to ~ very deep⟩ **b :** to come or arrive at a certain state or condition ⟨~ to sleep⟩ **c :** to come to be **:** BECOME ⟨the tire *went* flat⟩ — often used to express conversion to specified values or a specified state ⟨*gone* Hollywood⟩ ⟨~ condo⟩ **d :** to undergo a change ⟨leaves ~ from green to red⟩ **15 a :** to be in phrasing or expression **:** READ ⟨as the story ~*es*⟩ **b :** to be capable of being sung or played ⟨the tune ~*es* like this⟩ **16 :** to be compatible, suitable, or becoming **:** HARMONIZE ⟨the tie ~*es* with his suit⟩ **17 a :** to be capable of passing, extending, or being contained or inserted ⟨will these clothes ~ in your suitcase⟩ **b :** to have a usual or proper place or position **:** BELONG ⟨these books ~ on the top shelf⟩ **18 :** to have a tendency **:** CONDUCE ⟨it ~*es* to show⟩ **19 a** (1) **:** to carry authority ⟨what she said *went*⟩ (2) **:** to be acceptable, satisfactory, or adequate ⟨anything ~*es* here⟩ **b :** to hold true **:** be valid ⟨the rule ~*es* for you, too⟩ **20 :** to empty the bladder or bowels ~ *vt* **1 :** to proceed along or according to **:** FOLLOW ⟨if I were ~*ing* his way⟩ ⟨*went* the conventional route⟩ **2 :** to travel through or along **:** TRAVERSE ⟨*went* the length of the street⟩ **3 a :** to make a wager of **:** BET ⟨~ a dollar on the outcome⟩ **b :** to make an offer of **:** BID ⟨willing to ~ $50 for the clock⟩ **4 a :** to assume the function or obligation of ⟨promised to ~ bail for his friend⟩ **b :** to participate to the extent of ⟨decided to ~ halves on the winnings⟩ **5 :** YIELD, WEIGH ⟨this fish ~*es* ten pounds⟩ **6 a :** to put up with **:** TOLERATE ⟨couldn't ~ the noise⟩ **b :** AFFORD ⟨can't ~ the price⟩ **c :** ENJOY ⟨I could ~ a soda⟩ **7 a :** to cause (a characteristic sound) to occur ⟨the gun *went* bang⟩ **b :** SAY — used chiefly in oral narration of speech **8 :** to engage in ⟨don't ~ telling everyone⟩ **9** *of a sports team or player* **:** to have a record of ⟨*went* 11-0 last season⟩

— **go·er** \ˈgō-ər\ *n* — **go about** : to set about — **go after** : to try to get : SEEK — **go all the way** 1 : to enter into complete agreement 2 : to engage in sexual intercourse — **go at** 1 a : to make an attack on b : to make an approach to 2 : UNDERTAKE — **go back on** 1 : ABANDON 2 : BETRAY 3 : FAIL — **go begging** : to be in little demand — **go by the board** 1 : to be carried over a ship's side 2 : to be discarded — **go easy** : to be sparing ⟨*go easy* with the sugar⟩ ⟨*go easy* on the kid⟩ — **go fly a kite** : to stop being an annoyance or disturbance ⟨told him to *go fly a kite*⟩ — **go for** 1 : to pass for or serve as 2 : to try to secure or attain (as a goal) ⟨*go for* the prize⟩ 3 a : FAVOR, ACCEPT ⟨cannot *go for* your idea⟩ b : to have an interest in or liking for ⟨she *went for* him in a big way —Chandler Brossard⟩ 4 : ATTACK, ASSAIL ⟨my dog *went for* the intruder⟩ — **go for broke** : to put forth all one's strength or resources — **go great guns** : to achieve great success — **go hang** : to cease to be of interest or concern — **go into** : to be contained in ⟨5 *goes into* 60 12 times⟩ — **go it** 1 : to behave in a reckless, excited, or impromptu manner 2 : to proceed in a rapid or furious manner 3 : to conduct one's affairs : ACT ⟨insists on *going it* alone⟩ — **go missing** *chiefly Brit* : to become lost : DISAPPEAR — **go one better** : OUTDO, SURPASS — **go over** 1 : EXAMINE 2 a : REPEAT b : STUDY, REVIEW — **go places** : to be on the way to success — **go public** : to make a public disclosure — **go steady** : to date one person exclusively and frequently — **go through** 1 : to subject to thorough examination, consideration, or study 2 : EXPERIENCE, UNDERGO ⟨had to *go through* quite an ordeal⟩ 3 : CARRY OUT, PERFORM ⟨*went through* his work in a daze⟩ — **go to bat for** : to give active support or assistance to : DEFEND, CHAMPION — **go to bed with** : to have sexual intercourse with — **go to one's head** 1 : to cause one to become confused, excited, or dizzy 2 : to cause one to become conceited or overconfident — **go to pieces** : to become shattered (as in nerves or health) — **go to the mat** : to make an all-out combative effort (as in support of a position) — **go to town** 1 : to work or act rapidly or efficiently 2 : to be markedly successful 3 : to indulge oneself excessively — **go with** 1 : DATE 2 : CHOOSE 2 ⟨*went with* an iron off the tee⟩ — **go without saying** : to be self-evident — **go with the flow** : CONFORM 2b — **to go** 1 : still remaining ⟨ten minutes *to go*⟩ 2 *of prepared food* : sold for consumption off the premises

2**go** \ˈgō\ *n, pl* **goes** (1727) 1 : the act or manner of going 2 : the height of fashion : RAGE ⟨elegant shawls labeled . . . "quite the ~" —R. S. Surtees⟩ 3 : an often unexpected turn of affairs : OCCURRENCE 4 : the quantity used or furnished at one time ⟨you can obtain a ~ of brandy for sixpence —C. B. Fairbanks⟩ 5 : ENERGY, VIGOR 6 a : a turn in an activity (as a game) ⟨it's your ~⟩ b : ATTEMPT, TRY ⟨have a ~ at painting⟩ 7 : a spell of activity ⟨finished the job at one ~⟩ 8 : SUCCESS ⟨made a ~ of the business⟩ 9 : permission to proceed : GO-AHEAD ⟨gave the astronauts a ~ for another orbit⟩ — **no go** : to no avail : USELESS — **on the go** : constantly or restlessly active

3**go** *adj* (1961) : functioning properly : being in good and ready condition ⟨declared all systems ~⟩

4**go** *n, often cap* [Jp] (1890) : a game played between two players who alternately place black and white stones on a board checkered by 19 vertical lines and 19 horizontal lines in an attempt to enclose the larger area on the board

1**goad** \ˈgōd\ *n* [ME *gode,* fr. OE *gād* spear, goad; akin to Langobardic *gaida* spear, and perh. to Skt *hinoti* he urges on] (bef. 12c) 1 a : something that pains as if by pricking : THORN b : something that urges or stimulates into action : SPUR 2 : a pointed rod used to urge on an animal ***syn*** see MOTIVE

2**goad** *vt* (1579) 1 : to incite or rouse as if with a goad 2 : to drive (as cattle) with a goad

1**go–ahead** \ˈgō-ə-ˌhed\ *adj* (1834) 1 : marked by energy and enterprise : PROGRESSIVE ⟨a vigorous ~ company⟩ 2 : indicating that one may proceed ⟨~ signal⟩ 3 : being a score that gives a team the lead in a game ⟨drove in the ~ run⟩

2**go–ahead** *n* (1840) 1 a : ENERGY, SPIRIT b : one possessing go-ahead 2 : a sign, signal, or authority to proceed : GREEN LIGHT

goal \ˈgōl, *chiefly Northern esp in 1b & 3a also* ˈgül\ *n* [ME *gol* boundary, limit] (1531) 1 a : the terminal point of a race b : an area to be reached safely in children's games 2 : the end toward which effort is directed : AIM 3 a : an area or object toward which players in various games attempt to advance a ball or puck and usu. through or into which it must go to score points b : the act or action of causing a ball or puck to go through or into such a goal c : the score resulting from such an act ***syn*** see INTENTION — **goal** *vi* — **goal·less** \ˈgō(l)-ləs\ *adj*

goal·ie \ˈgō-lē\ *n* (1921) : GOALKEEPER

goal·keep·er \ˈgōl-ˌkē-pər\ *n* (1658) : a player who defends the goal in any of various games (as hockey, lacrosse, or soccer)

goal kick *n* (1891) : a free kick in soccer awarded to a defensive player when the ball is driven out of bounds over the end line by an opposing player

goal line *n* (1864) : a line at either end and usu. running the width of a playing area on which a goal or goalpost is situated

goal·mouth \ˈgōl-ˌmau̇th\ *n* (1882) : the area directly in front of the goal (as in soccer or hockey)

go along *vi* (1535) 1 : to move along : PROCEED 2 : to go or travel as a companion 3 : to act in cooperation or express agreement ⟨*go along* with the crowd⟩

goal·post \ˈgōl-ˌpōst\ *n* (1857) : one of usu. two vertical posts that with or without a crossbar constitute the goal in various games

goal·tend·er \ˈgōl-ˌten-dər\ *n* (ca. 1909) : GOALKEEPER

goal·tend·ing \-diŋ\ *n* (1968) 1 : the act of guarding a goal (as in hockey) 2 : a violation in basketball that involves touching or deflecting a ball that is on its downward path toward the basket or on or within the rim of the basket

goal·ward \ˈgōl-wərd\ *adv or adj* (1949) : toward a goal

go·an·na \gō-ˈa-nə\ *n* [alter. of *iguana*] (1831) : any of several large Australian monitor lizards (genus *Varanus* of the family Varanidae)

go–around \ˈgō-ə-ˌrau̇nd\ *n* (ca. 1929) 1 : RUNAROUND ⟨gave me the ~⟩ 2 a : ROUND ⟨reached an agreement during the first ~⟩ b : a heated argument or struggle ⟨had a real ~ with her about it⟩ 3 : an act or instance of going around (as in an air traffic pattern)

go around *vi* (ca. 1520) 1 a : to pass from place to place : go here and there b : to have currency : CIRCULATE ⟨an amusing story is *going around*⟩ 2 : to satisfy demand : fill the need ⟨not enough jobs to *go around*⟩

goat \ˈgōt\ *n, pl* **goats** [ME *gote,* fr. OE *gāt;* akin to OHG *geiz* goat, ON *geit,* L *haedus* kid] (bef. 12c) 1 a *or pl* **goat** : any of various hollow-horned ruminant mammals (esp. of the genus *Capra*) related to the sheep but of lighter build and with backwardly arching horns, a short tail, and usu. straight hair; *esp* : one (*Capra hircus*) long domesticated for its milk, wool, and flesh b *cap* : CAPRICORN 2 : a licentious man : LECHER 3 : SCAPEGOAT 2 — **goat·ish** \ˈgō-tish\ *adj* — **goat·like** \-ˌlīk\ *adj*

goat cheese *n* (1893) : any of various cheeses made from goat's milk

goa·tee \gō-ˈtē\ *n* [fr. its resemblance to the beard of a he-goat] (1844) : a small pointed or tufted beard on a man's chin — **goa·teed** \-ˈtēd\ *adj*

goat·fish \ˈgōt-ˌfish\ *n* (ca. 1639) : any of a family (Mullidae) of medium-sized often brightly colored bony fishes having two long barbels under the chin, and elongate body, and two widely separated dorsal fins — compare RED MULLET

goat·herd \-ˌhərd\ *n* [ME *goteherd,* fr. OE *gāthyrd*] (bef. 12c) : a person who tends goats

goat·skin \-ˌskin\ *n* (14c) 1 : the skin of a goat 2 : leather made from goatskin

goat·suck·er \-ˌsə-kər\ *n* (1611) : NIGHTJAR

1**gob** \ˈgäb\ *n* [ME *gobbe,* prob. back-formation fr. *gobet*] (14c) 1 : LUMP 2 : a large amount — usu. used in pl. ⟨~*s* of money⟩

2**gob** \ˈgȯb, ˈgäb\ *n* [prob. fr. ScGael, mouth & Ir, beak, pursed mouth] (ca. 1550) *chiefly Brit* : MOUTH

3**gob** \ˈgäb, ˈgȯb\ *n* [origin unknown] (1915) : SAILOR

gob·bet \ˈgä-bət\ *n* [ME *gobet,* fr. AF] (14c) 1 : a piece or portion (as of meat) 2 : LUMP, MASS 3 : a small fragment or extract ⟨a ~ of information⟩ 4 : a small quantity of liquid : DROP

1**gob·ble** \ˈgä-bəl\ *vt* **gob·bled; gob·bling** \-b(ə-)liŋ\ [prob. irreg. fr. 1*gob*] (1601) 1 : to swallow or eat greedily 2 : to take eagerly : GRAB — usu. used with *up* 3 : to read rapidly or greedily — usu. used with *up*

2**gobble** *vi* **gob·bled; gob·bling** \-b(ə-)liŋ\ [imit.] (1680) 1 : to make the natural guttural noise of a male turkey 2 : to make a sound resembling the gobble of a turkey — **gobble** *n*

gob·ble·dy·gook *also* **gob·ble·de·gook** \ˈgä-bəl-dē-ˌgu̇k, -ˌgük\ *n* [irreg. fr. *gobble,* n.] (1944) : wordy and generally unintelligible jargon

1**gob·bler** \ˈgä-blər\ *n* (ca. 1737) : a male turkey

2**gobbler** *n* (ca. 1755) : one that gobbles

Go·be·lin \ˈgō-bə-lən, ˌgō-bə-ˈlaⁿ\ *adj* [*Gobelin* dye and tapestry works, Paris, France] (1788) : of, relating to, or characteristic of tapestry produced at the Gobelin works in Paris — **Gobelin** *n*

go–be·tween \ˈgō-bə-ˌtwēn\ *n* (1598) : an intermediate agent : BROKER

gob·let \ˈgäb-lət\ *n* [ME *gobelet,* fr. AF *goblet*] (14c) 1 *archaic* : a bowl-shaped drinking vessel without handles 2 : a drinking vessel (as of glass) with a foot and stem — compare TUMBLER

goblet cell *n* [fr. its shape] (1878) : a mucus-secreting epithelial cell (as of intestinal columnar epithelium) that is distended at the free end

gob·lin \ˈgäb-lən\ *n* [ME *gobelin,* fr. AF, fr. ML *gobelinus,* ultim. fr. Gk *kobalos* rogue] (14c) : an ugly or grotesque sprite that is usu. mischievous and sometimes evil and malicious

go·bo \ˈgō-(ˌ)bō\ *n, pl* **gobos** *also* **goboes** [origin unknown] (ca. 1930) 1 : a dark strip (as of wallboard) to shield a motion-picture or television camera from light 2 : a device to shield a microphone from sound

go·by \ˈgō-bē\ *n, pl* **gobies** *also* **goby** [L *gobius* gudgeon, fr. Gk *kōbios*] (1769) : any of numerous spiny-finned fishes (family Gobiidae) that usu. have the pelvic fins united to form a ventral sucking disk

go by *vi* (1508) : PASS 3b ⟨as time *goes by*⟩

go–cart \ˈgō-ˌkärt\ *n* (1689) 1 a : WALKER b : STROLLER 2 : HANDCART 3 : a light open carriage

1**god** \ˈgäd *also* ˈgȯd\ *n* [ME, fr. OE; akin to OHG *got* god] (bef. 12c) 1 *cap* : the supreme or ultimate reality: as a : the Being perfect in power, wisdom, and goodness who is worshipped as creator and ruler of the universe b *Christian Science* : the incorporeal divine Principle ruling over all as eternal Spirit : infinite Mind 2 : a being or object believed to have more than natural attributes and powers and to require human worship; *specif* : one controlling a particular aspect or part of reality 3 : a person or thing of supreme value 4 : a powerful ruler

2**god** *vt* **god·ded; god·ding** (1595) : to treat as a god : IDOLIZE, DEIFY

god–aw·ful \gäd-ˈȯ-fəl\ *adj* [*god*damned + *awful*] (1878) : extremely unpleasant or disagreeable : ABOMINABLE ⟨~ weather⟩

god·child \ˈgäd-ˌchīld *also* ˈgȯd-\ *n* (13c) : a person for whom another person becomes sponsor at baptism

1**god·damn** *or* **god·dam** \ˈgä(d)-ˈdam\ *n, often cap* (1640) : DAMN ⟨they were in no mood to give a good ~ about anything —Robert Lowry⟩

2**goddamn** *or* **goddam** *vb, often cap* (1928) : DAMN

god·damned \ˌgä(d)-ˌdamd\ *or* **god·damn** *or* **god·dam** \-ˌdam\ *adj or adv* (1918) : DAMNED

god·daugh·ter \ˈgäd-ˌdȯ-tər *also* ˈgȯd-\ *n* (bef. 12c) : a female godchild

god·dess \ˈgä-dəs *also* ˈgȯ-\ *n* (14c) 1 : a female god 2 : a woman whose great charm or beauty arouses adoration

Go·del's theorem \ˈgō-dəlz-, ˈgər-, ˈgœ-\ *n* [Kurt *Gödel* †1978 Am. mathematician] (1933) : a theorem in advanced logic: in any logical system as complex as or more complex than the arithmetic of the integers there can always be found either a statement which can be shown to be both true and false or a statement whose truth or falsity cannot be deduced from other statements in the system — called also *Godel's incompleteness theorem*

go·det \gō-ˈdet, ˈgō-ˌdā\ *n, often attrib* [F, fr. *goder* to form creases, prob. fr. *god-* (as in *godron* rounded pleat on a ruffle, gadroon)] (1872) : an inset of cloth placed in a seam to give fullness (as at the bottom of a skirt)

go·de·tia \gō-ˈdē-sh(ē-)ə\ *n* [NL, fr. C.H. *Godet* †1879 Swiss botanist] (ca. 1840) : CLARKIA

go–dev·il \ˈgō-ˌde-vəl\ *n* (1852) : any of various devices: as a : a cultivator with wooden runners b : a weight formerly dropped in a bored hole (as of an oil well) to set off an explosive c : a cleaning scraper propelled through a pipeline **d** : a handcar or small gasoline car used on a railroad **e** : a child's sled

1**god·fa·ther** \ˈgäd-ˌfä-t͟hər *also* ˈgȯd-\ *n* (bef. 12c) **1** : a man who sponsors a person at baptism **2** : one having a relation to someone or something analogous to that of a male sponsor to his godchild: as **a** : one that founds, supports, or inspires ⟨made him the ~ of a whole generation of rebels —*Times Lit. Supp.*⟩ **b** : the leader of an organized crime syndicate

2**godfather** *vt* (1780) : to act as godfather to

God–fear·ing \-ˌfir-iŋ\ *adj* (1835) : having a reverent feeling toward God : DEVOUT

god·for·sak·en \-fər-ˌsā-kən\ *adj* (1860) **1** : REMOTE, DESOLATE **2** : neglected and miserable in appearance or circumstances

god·head \-ˌhed\ *n* [ME *godhed,* fr. *god* + *-hed* -hood; akin to ME *-hod* -hood] (13c) **1** : divine nature or essence **2** *cap* **a** : GOD 1 **b** : the nature of God esp. as existing in three persons — used with *the*

god·hood \-ˌhu̇d\ *n* (1563) : DIVINITY

Go·di·va \gə-ˈdī-və\ *n* (1785) : an English earl's wife who in legend rode naked through Coventry to save its citizens from a tax

god·less \ˈgäd-ləs *also* ˈgȯd-\ *adj* (1528) : not acknowledging a deity or divine law — **god·less·ness** *n*

god·like \-ˌlīk\ *adj* (bef. 12c) : resembling or having the qualities of God or a god : DIVINE — **god·like·ness** *n*

god·ling \-liŋ\ *n* (ca. 1500) : an inferior or local god

god·ly \-lē\ *adj* **god·li·er; -est** (14c) **1** : DIVINE **2** : PIOUS, DEVOUT — **god·li·ness** *n* — **godly** *adv, archaic*

god·moth·er \-ˌmə-t͟hər\ *n* (bef. 12c) : a woman who sponsors a person at baptism

go·down \ˈgō-ˌdau̇n\ *n* [by folk etymology fr. Malay *gudang*] (1552) : a warehouse in a country of southern or eastern Asia

go down *vi* (14c) **1 a** : to go below the horizon : SET ⟨the sun *went down*⟩ **b** : to fall to or as if to the ground ⟨the plane *went down* in flames⟩ **c** : to become submerged : SINK ⟨the ship *went down* with all hands⟩ **2** : to admit of being swallowed ⟨the medicine *went down* easily⟩ **3 a** : to find acceptance ⟨will the plan *go down* with the farmers⟩ **b** : to come to be remembered esp. in posterity ⟨will he *go down* in history as a great president⟩ **4** *Brit* : to leave a university **5 a** : to undergo defeat or failure **b** *chiefly Brit* : to become incapacitated ⟨*went down* with . . . acute tonsillitis —Helen Cathcart⟩ **6** *slang* : to take place : HAPPEN — **go down on** : to perform fellatio or cunnilingus on

god·par·ent \ˈgäd-ˌper-ənt *also* ˈgȯd-\ *n* (1865) : a sponsor at baptism

God's acre *n* (1617) : CHURCHYARD

god·send \ˈgäd-ˌsend *also* ˈgȯd-\ *n* [back-formation fr. *god-sent*] (1820) : a desirable or needed thing or event that comes unexpectedly

god·son \-ˌsən\ *n* (bef. 12c) : a male godchild

God·speed \-ˈspēd\ *n* [ME *god speid,* fr. the phrase *God spede you* God prosper you] (15c) : a prosperous journey : SUCCESS ⟨bade him ~⟩

god·wit \ˈgäd-ˌwit\ *n* [origin unknown] (1552) : any of a genus (*Limosa*) of shorebirds that are related to the curlews and sandpipers and have a long slender slightly upturned or straight bill

goes *pres 3d sing of* GO *pl of* GO

goe·thite \ˈgə(r)-ˌtīt\ *n* [G *Göthit,* fr. J. W. von *Goethe*] (ca. 1823) : a common brown mineral that consists of an iron hydrogen oxide and is the commonest constituent of many forms of natural rust

go·fer *or* **go·pher** \ˈgō-fər\ *n* [alter. of *go for*] (1967) : an employee whose duties include running errands : LACKEY

gof·fer *or* **gauf·fer** *also* ˈgō-\ *vt* [F *gaufrer,* fr. *gaufre* honeycomb, waffle, fr. OF, of Gmc origin; akin to MD *wafel* waffle] (1706) : to crimp, plait, or flute (as linen or lace) esp. with a heated iron — **goffer** *n*

go–get·ter \ˈgō-ˈge-tər, -ˌge-\ *n* (1919) : an aggressively enterprising person — **go–get·ting** \-ˌge-tiŋ\ *adj or n*

1**gog·gle** \ˈgä-gəl\ *vi* **gog·gled; gog·gling** [ME *gogelen* to squint] (1742) : to stare with wide or protuberant eyes — **gog·gler** \ˈgä-gə-lər\ *n*

2**goggle** *adj* (1540) : PROTUBERANT, STARING ⟨~ eyes⟩ — **gog·gly** \ˈgä-gə-lē\ *adj*

gog·gle–eye \ˈgä-gəl-ˌī\ *n* (1840) **1** : ROCK BASS **2** : WARMOUTH

gog·gle–eyed \-ˌīd\ *adj* (1711) : having bulging or rolling eyes

gog·gles \ˈgä-gəlz\ *n pl* (1715) **1** : protective glasses set in a flexible frame (as of rubber or plastic) that fits snugly against the face **2** : an electronic apparatus that covers the eyes and is used to enhance vision (as at night) or to produce images (as of a virtual reality) — **gog·gled** \-gəld\ *adj*

go–go \ˈgō-(ˌ)gō\ *adj* [partly fr. *a-go-go,* partly fr. redupl. of 1*go*] (1965) **1 a** : employed to entertain in a disco ⟨~ dancers⟩ **b** : of, relating to, or being a disco or the music or dances performed there **2** : marked by spirited or aggressive action ⟨~ baseball⟩ **3 a** : relating to or dealing in popular often speculative investment expected to yield high returns ⟨~ mutual funds⟩ **b** : relating to, involved in, or marked by business growth and prosperity and aggressive efforts to turn a quick profit ⟨~ bankers and entrepreneurs . . . who put together the megabuck deals —Ken Auletta⟩

1**Goi·del·ic** \gȯi-ˈde-lik\ *adj* [MIr *Goídel* Gael, Irishman] (1896) **1** : of, relating to, or characteristic of the Gaels **2** : of, relating to, or constituting Goidelic

2**Goidelic** *n* (1882) : the branch of the Celtic languages that includes Irish, Scottish Gaelic, and Manx — see INDO-EUROPEAN LANGUAGES table

go in *vi* (1812) **1** : to make an approach (as in attacking) **2 a** : to take part in a game or contest **b** : to call the opening bet in poker : STAY **3** *of a celestial body* : to become obscured by a cloud **4** : to form a union or alliance : JOIN — often used with *with* ⟨asked us to *go in* with them⟩ — **go in for 1** : to give support to : ADVOCATE **2** : to have or show an interest in or a liking for **3** : to engage in : take part in

1**go·ing** \ˈgō-iŋ, ˈgȯ(-)iŋ\ *n* (14c) **1** : an act or instance of going **2** *pl* : BEHAVIOR, ACTIONS ⟨for his eyes are upon the ways of man, and he seeth all his ~*s* —Job 34:21 (AV)⟩ **3** : the condition of the ground (as for walking) **4** : advance toward an objective ⟨when the ~ gets tough⟩

2**going** *adj* (14c) **1 a** : that goes — often used in combination ⟨easy*going*⟩ ⟨out*going*⟩ **b** : WORKING, MOVING ⟨everything was in ~ order⟩ **2** : LIVING, EXISTING ⟨the best novelist ~⟩ **3** : CURRENT, PREVAILING ⟨~ price⟩ **4** : conducting business with the expectation of indefinite continuance ⟨a ~ concern⟩ — **going on** : drawing near to : APPROACHING ⟨is six years old *going on* seven⟩

go·ing–over \ˌgō-iŋ-ˈō-vər, ˌgȯ(-)iŋ-\ *n, pl* **go·ings–over** (1872) **1 a** : a severe scolding **b** : BEATING **2** : a thorough examination

go·ings–on \ˌgō-iŋ-ˈzȯn, ˌgȯ(-)iŋ-, -ˈzän\ *n pl* (1775) **1** : ACTIONS, EVENTS **2** : irregular or reprehensible happenings or conduct

goi·ter \ˈgȯi-tər\ *n* [F *goitre,* fr. MF, back-formation fr. *goitron* throat, fr. VL **guttrion-, guttrio,* fr. L *guttur*] (1625) : an enlargement of the thyroid gland visible as a swelling of the front of the neck — compare HYPERTHYROIDISM, HYPOTHYROIDISM — **goi·trous** \ˈgȯi-trəs, ˈgȯi-tə-rəs\ *adj*

goi·tre *chiefly Brit var of* GOITER

goi·tro·gen \ˈgȯi-trə-jən\ *n* [*goiter* + *-o-* + *-gen*] (1946) : a substance (as thiourea or thiouracil) that induces goiter formation

goi·tro·gen·ic \ˌgȯi-trə-ˈje-nik\ *adj* (1929) : producing or tending to produce goiter — **goi·tro·ge·nic·i·ty** \ˌgȯi-trə-jə-ˈni-sə-tē\ *n*

go·ji \ˈgō-ˈjē\ *n* [modif. of Chin (Beijing) *gǒuqǐ* the shrub *Lycium chinense*] (2003) : the dark red mildly tart berry of a thorny chiefly Asian shrub (*Lycium barbarum*) that is typically dried and used in beverages

go–kart \ˈgō-ˌkärt\ *n* [alter. of *go-cart*] (1959) : a small motorized vehicle used esp. for racing

Gol·con·da \gäl-ˈkän-də\ *n* [*Golconda,* India, famous for its diamonds] (1884) : a rich mine; *broadly* : a source of great wealth

1**gold** \ˈgōld\ *n, often attrib* [ME, fr. OE; akin to OHG *gold* gold, OE *geolu* yellow — more at YELLOW] (bef. 12c) **1** : a yellow malleable ductile metallic element that occurs chiefly free or in a few minerals and is used esp. in coins, jewelry, and dentures — see ELEMENT table **2 a** (1) : gold coins (2) : a gold piece **b** : MONEY **c** : GOLD STANDARD 1 **3** : a variable color averaging deep yellow **4** : something resembling gold; *esp* : something valued as the finest of its kind ⟨a heart of ~⟩ **5** : a medal awarded as the first prize in a competition : a gold medal

2**gold** *adj* (1969) : qualifying for a gold record — **go gold** : to have enough sales to qualify for a gold record ⟨the album *went gold*⟩

1**gold·brick** \ˈgōl(d)-ˌbrik\ *n* (1881) **1 a** : a worthless brick that appears to be of gold **b** : something that appears to be valuable but is actually worthless **2** : a person who shirks assigned work

2**goldbrick** *vt* (1902) : SWINDLE ~ *vi* : to shirk duty or responsibility

gold·bug \-ˌbəg\ *n* (1878) **1** : a supporter of the gold standard **2** : a person who invests in or hoards gold

gold coast *n, often cap G&C* (1877) : an exclusive residential district

gold digger *n* (1830) **1** : one who digs for gold **2** : a person who uses charm to extract money or gifts from others

gold·en \ˈgōl-dən\ *adj* [ME] (13c) **1** : consisting of, relating to, or containing gold **2 a** : being or having the color gold or the color of gold **b** : BLOND 1 **3** : LUSTROUS, SHINING **4** : of a high degree of excellence : SUPERB **5** : PROSPEROUS, FLOURISHING ⟨~ days⟩ **6 a** : radiantly youthful and vigorous **b** : having talents that promise great success — often used with *boy* **c** : highly favored : POPULAR **7** : FAVORABLE, ADVANTAGEOUS ⟨a ~ opportunity⟩ **8** : of, relating to, or being a 50th anniversary or its celebration **9** : MELLOW, RESONANT ⟨a smooth ~ tenor⟩ — **gold·en·ly** *adv* — **gold·en·ness** \-də(n)-nəs\ *n*

golden age *n* (1555) : a period of great happiness, prosperity, and achievement

gold·en–ag·er \ˈgōl-dən-ˈā-jər\ *n* (1961) : an elderly and often retired person usu. engaging in club activities

golden al·ex·an·ders \-ˌa-lig-ˈzan-dərz, -ˌe-lig-\ *n pl but sing or pl in constr, often cap A* [*alexander* any of various herbs of the carrot family, ultim. fr. ML *alexandrum*] (ca. 1923) : a No. American yellow-flowered perennial herb (*Zizia aurea*) of the carrot family occurring in moist woods and meadows; *also* : any of several related herbs

golden–brown alga *n* (ca. 1957) : any of a division (Chrysophyta) of marine and freshwater algae (as diatoms) containing yellowish-green to golden-brown pigments that obscure the chlorophyll — called also *chrysophyte, golden alga*

golden club *n* (1837) : a No. American aquatic plant (*Orontium aquaticum*) of the arum family with a spadix of tiny yellow flowers

golden eagle *n* (1809) : a dark brown eagle (*Aquila chrysaetos*) of the northern hemisphere with gold-colored feathers on the back of the head and neck, a gray beak, and yellow legs and feet

gold·en·eye \ˈgōl-dən-ˌī\ *n* (ca. 1678) **1** : either of two diving ducks (genus *Bucephala*) with small yellow eyes; *esp* : a large-headed swift-flying Holarctic diving duck (*B. clangula*) with the male having a green head and striking black-and-white markings **2** : a lacewing (family Chrysopidae) with yellow eyes

Golden Fleece *n* (14c) : a fleece of gold placed by the king of Colchis in a dragon-guarded grove and recovered by the Argonauts

golden glow *n* (1902) : a tall branching composite herb (*Rudbeckia laciniata hortensia*) with showy yellow flower heads

golden hamster *n* (1939) : a small tawny hamster (*Mesocricetus auratus*) native chiefly to Syria and often kept as a pet or used as a laboratory animal — called also *Syrian hamster*

golden handcuffs *n pl* (1976) : special benefits offered to an employee as an inducement to continue service

golden handshake *n* (1960) : a generous severance agreement given esp. as an inducement to early retirement

Golden Horde *n* (1863) : a body of Mongols that overran eastern Europe in the 13th century and dominated Russia until 1486

golden lion tamarin *n* (1975) : a tamarin (*Leontopithecus rosalia*) with a reddish-gold coat and mane that occurs in remnants of tropical forest in southeastern Brazil

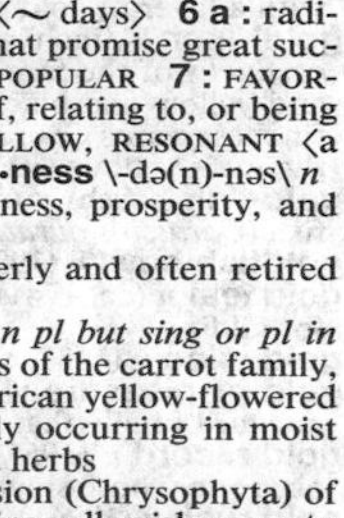
golden lion tamarin

golden mean *n* (1587) : the medium between extremes : MODERATION

golden nematode *n* (1946) : a small yellowish nematode worm (*Globodera rostochiensis* syn.

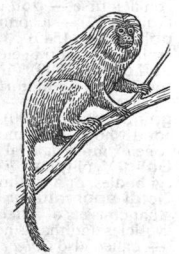

Heterodera rostochiensis) prob. of So. American origin that is a pest of solanaceous crops and esp. potatoes

golden oldie *n* (1970) **:** one that was a hit or favorite in the past

golden parachute *n* (1981) **:** a generous severance agreement for a corporate executive in the event of a sudden dismissal (as because of a merger)

golden plover *n* (1785) **:** any of three plovers (genus *Pluvialis*) having dark upperparts spotted with gold; *esp* **:** one (*P. dominica*) that breeds chiefly in arctic America and winters in So. America

golden rain tree *n* (1923) **:** an Asian tree (*Koelreuteria paniculata* of the family Sapindaceae) that has a rounded crown with very long showy clusters of yellow flowers

golden retriever *n* (1919) **:** any of a breed of medium-sized retrievers having a flat moderately long golden coat

gold·en·rod \ˈgōl-dən-ˌräd\ *n* (1568) **:** any of numerous chiefly No. American composite perennial herbs (genus *Solidago*) with small heads of usu. yellow late-blooming flowers often clustered in panicles — compare *rayless goldenrod*

golden rule *n* (1753) **1** *cap G&R* **:** a rule of ethical conduct referring to Mt 7:12 and Lk 6:31: do to others as you would have them do to you **2 :** a guiding principle

gold·en·seal \ˈgōl-dən-ˌsēl\ *n* (1839) **:** a perennial No. American herb (*Hydrastis canadensis*) of the buttercup family with large leaves and a thick knotted yellow rhizome sometimes used medicinally

golden section *n* (1875) **:** a proportion (as one involving a line divided into two segments or the length and width of a rectangle and their sum) in which the ratio of the whole to the larger part is the same as the ratio of the larger part to the smaller

golden shiner *n* (ca. 1889) **:** a small common cyprinid fish (*Notemigonus crysoleucas*) of eastern No. America having silvery sides with bright golden reflections and often used as bait

golden shower *n* (1968) **:** the act of urinating on another person usu. as part of a sex act

golden syrup *n* (1860) *chiefly Brit* **:** TREACLE 2b

golden trout *n* (1945) **:** a brightly colored golden-yellow trout (*Oncorhynchus aguabonita* syn. *Salmo aguabonita*) with red markings on the sides and belly that is native to waters of the southern Sierra Nevada but has been introduced in other upland waters of western No. America

golden years *n pl* (1964) **:** the advanced years in a lifetime ⟨active well into their *golden years*⟩

gold·field \ˈgōl(d)-ˌfēld\ *n* (1851) **:** a gold-mining district

gold–filled \-ˈfild\ *adj* (ca. 1903) **:** consisting of a base metal covered with a layer of gold ⟨a ~ bracelet⟩

gold·finch \-ˌfinch\ *n* (bef. 12c) **1 :** a small Palearctic finch (*Carduelis carduelis* of the family Fringillidae) with a red, white, and black head and yellow and black wings **2 :** any of three small related American finches (genus *Carduelis*, esp. *C. tristis*) having the breeding plumage of the male yellow with black markings on the wings, tail, and crown

gold·fish \-ˌfish\ *n* (1791) **:** a small usu. golden-orange Asian cyprinid fish (*Carassius auratus*) often kept as an aquarium and pond fish

goldfish bowl *n* (1935) **:** a place or situation offering no privacy

gold leaf *n* (ca. 1741) **:** an extremely thin sheet of gold that is used esp. for gilding

gold mine *n* (1637) **:** a rich source of something desired

gold of pleasure (1597) **:** a European herb (*Camelina sativa*) of the mustard family that is cultivated for its oil-rich seeds

gold record *n* (1957) **:** a gold phonograph record awarded to a singer or group whose single record or album has sold at least 500,000 copies

gold rush *n* (1876) **1 :** a rush to newly discovered goldfields in pursuit of riches **2 :** the headlong pursuit of sudden wealth in a new or lucrative field — **gold rush·er** \-ˈrə-shər\ *n*

gold·smith \ˈgōl(d)-ˌsmith\ *n* (bef. 12c) **:** one who makes or deals in articles of gold

gold standard *n* (1831) **1 :** a monetary standard under which the basic unit of currency is defined by a stated quantity of gold and which is usu. characterized by the coinage and circulation of gold, unrestricted convertibility of other money into gold, and the free export and import of gold for settling of international obligations **2 :** BENCHMARK 2b

gold·stone \ˈgōl(d)-ˌstōn\ *n* (ca. 1889) **:** aventurine glass spangled close and fine with particles of gold-colored material

go·lem \ˈgō-ləm, ˈgȯi-, ˈgā-\ *n* [Yiddish *goylem*, fr. Heb *gōlem* shapeless mass] (1897) **1 :** an artificial human being in Hebrew folklore endowed with life **2 :** something or someone resembling a golem: as **a :** AUTOMATON **b :** BLOCKHEAD

golf \ˈgälf, ˈgȯlf, ˈgäf, ˈgȯf *sometimes* ˈgəlf\ *n, often attrib* [ME (Sc)] (15c) **:** a game in which a player using special clubs attempts to sink a ball with as few strokes as possible into each of the 9 or 18 successive holes on a course — **golf** *vi* — **golf·er** *n*

Golf (1952) — a communications code word for the letter *g*

golf ball *n* (1545) **1 :** a small hard dimpled ball used in golf **2 :** the spherical printing element of an electric typewriter or printer

golf cart *n* (1899) **1 :** a small cart for wheeling a golf bag around a golf course **2 :** a motorized cart for carrying golfers and their equipment over a golf course — called also *golf car*

golf course *n* (1890) **:** an area of land laid out for golf with a series of 9 or 18 holes each including tee, fairway, and putting green and often one or more natural or artificial hazards — called also *golf links*

Gol·gi \ˈgȯl-(ˌ)jē\ *adj* (1891) **:** of or relating to the Golgi apparatus, Golgi bodies, or a method of staining nerve tissue ⟨~ vesicles⟩

Golgi apparatus *n* [Camillo *Golgi*] (1916) **:** a cytoplasmic organelle that consists of a stack of smooth membranous saccules and associated vesicles and that is active in the modification and transport of proteins — called also *Golgi complex*; see CELL illustration

Golgi body *n* (1925) **:** GOLGI APPARATUS; *also* **:** DICTYOSOME

go·liard \ˈgōl-yərd, -ˌyärd\ *n* [MF] (15c) **:** a wandering student of the 12th or 13th century given to the writing of satiric Latin verse and to convivial living and minstrelsy — **go·liar·dic** \gōl-ˈyär-dik\ *adj*

Go·li·ath \gə-ˈlī-əth\ *n* [Heb *Golyath*] (14c) **1 :** a Philistine champion who in I Samuel 17 is killed by David **2 :** GIANT

gol·li·wog *also* **gol·ly·wog** *or* **gol·li·wogg** \ˈgä-lē-ˌwäg\ *n* [*Golliwogg*, an animated doll in children's fiction by Bertha Upton †1912 Am. writer] (1895) **1 :** a grotesque black doll **2 :** a person resembling a golliwog

gol·ly \ˈgä-lē\ *interj* [euphemism for *God*] (1775) — used as a mild oath or to express surprise; usu. used in the phrase *by golly*

Go·mor·rah \gə-ˈmȯr-ə\ *n* [fr. *Gomorrah*, ancient city destroyed by God for its wickedness in Gen 19] (1850) **:** a place notorious for vice and corruption

gon- *or* **gono-** *comb form* [Gk, fr. *gonos* procreation, seed, fr. *gignesthai* to be born — more at KIN] **:** sexual **:** generative **:** semen **:** seed ⟨*gono*cyte⟩

-gon *n comb form* [NL *-gonum*, fr. Gk *-gōnon*, fr. *gōnia* angle; akin to Gk *gony* knee — more at KNEE] **:** figure having (so many) angles ⟨deca*gon*⟩

go·nad \ˈgō-ˌnad\ *n* [NL *gonad-*, *gonas*, fr. Gk *gonos*] (1880) **:** a reproductive gland (as an ovary or testis) that produces gametes — **go·nad·al** \gō-ˈna-dᵊl\ *adj*

go·nad·ec·to·my \ˌgō-nə-ˈdek-tə-mē\ *n, pl* **-mies** (1915) **:** surgical removal of an ovary or testis — **go·nad·ec·to·mized** \-ˌmīzd\ *adj*

go·nad·o·trop·ic \gō-ˌna-də-ˈträ-pik\ *also* **go·nad·o·tro·phic** \-ˈtrō-fik, -ˈträ-\ *adj* (ca. 1923) **:** acting on or stimulating the gonads

go·nad·o·tro·pin \-ˈtrō-pən\ *also* **go·nad·o·tro·phin** \-fən\ *n* (1931) **:** a gonadotropic hormone (as follicle-stimulating hormone)

gonadotropin–releasing hormone *n* (1974) **:** a hormone secreted by the hypothalamus that stimulates the anterior lobe of the pituitary gland to release gonadotropins (as luteinizing hormone and follicle-stimulating hormone) — abbr. *GnRH*; called also *luteinizing hormone-releasing hormone*

Gond \ˈgänd\ *n* (1801) **:** a member of a Dravidian or pre-Dravidian people of central India

Gondi \ˈgän-dē\ *n* (1848) **:** the Dravidian language of the Gonds

gon·do·la \ˈgän-də-lə (*usual for sense 1*), gän-ˈdō-\ *n* [It dial. (Venetian), prob. fr. MGk *kontoura* small vessel] (1549) **1 :** a long narrow flat-bottomed boat with a high prow and stern used on the canals of Venice **2 :** a heavy flat-bottomed boat used on New England rivers and on the Ohio and Mississippi rivers **3 :** a railroad car with no top, a flat bottom, and fixed sides that is used chiefly for hauling heavy bulk commodities **4 a :** an elongated car attached to the underside of an airship **b :** an often spherical airtight enclosure suspended from a balloon for carrying passengers or instruments **c :** an enclosed car suspended from a cable and used for transporting passengers; *esp* **:** one used as a ski lift

gon·do·lier \ˌgän-də-ˈlir\ *n* (1603) **:** one who propels a Venetian gondola

gone \ˈgȯn *also* ˈgän\ *adj* [fr. pp. of *go*] (1598) **1 a :** LOST, RUINED ⟨lost looks and ~ faculties —Penelope Gilliatt⟩ **b :** DEAD **c :** characterized by sinking or dropping ⟨the empty or ~ feeling in the abdomen so common in elevators —H. G. Armstrong⟩ **2 a :** INVOLVED, ABSORBED ⟨far ~ in hysteria⟩ **b :** possessed with a strong attachment or a foolish or unreasoning love or desire **:** INFATUATED — often used with *on* ⟨was real ~ on that man —Pete Martin⟩ **c :** PREGNANT ⟨she's six months ~⟩ **3 :** PAST ⟨memories of ~ summers —John Cheever⟩ **4** *slang* **:** GREAT ⟨a real ~ fashion reporter —Inez Robb⟩

G_1 phase \ˌjē-ˈwən-\ *n* [growth] (1966) **:** the period in the cell cycle from the end of cell division to the beginning of DNA replication — compare G_2 PHASE, M PHASE, S PHASE

gon·er \ˈgȯ-nər *also* ˈgä-nər\ *n* (1850) **:** one whose case is hopeless

gon·fa·lon \ˈgän-fə-ˌlän, -lən\ *n* [It *gonfalone*] (1595) **1 :** the ensign of certain princes or states (as the medieval republics of Italy) **2 :** a flag that hangs from a crosspiece or frame

gong \ˈgäŋ, ˈgȯŋ\ *n* [Malay & Jav, of imit. origin] (ca. 1590) **1 :** a disk-shaped percussion instrument that produces a resounding tone when struck with a usu. padded hammer **2 a :** a saucer-shaped bell (as in a fire alarm) that is struck by a mechanical hammer **b :** a wire rod wound in a flat spiral for sounding the time or chime or alarm (as in a clock) **3** *Brit* **:** MEDAL — **gong** *vi*

Gon·go·rism \ˈgäŋ-gə-ˌri-zəm\ *n* [Sp *gongorismo*, fr. Luis de *Góngora* y Argote †1627 Span. poet] (1813) **:** a literary style characterized by studied obscurity and by the use of various ornate devices — **gon·go·ris·tic** \ˌgäŋ-gə-ˈris-tik\ *adj*

go·nid·i·um \gō-ˈni-dē-əm\ *n, pl* **-ia** \-dē-ə\ [NL, fr. *gon-* + *-idium*] (1882) **:** an asexual reproductive cell or group of cells esp. in algae (as volvox)

gonif, goniff *var of* GANEF

go·ni·om·e·ter \ˌgō-nē-ˈä-mə-tər\ *n* [Gk *gōnia* angle] (1766) **1 :** an instrument for measuring angles **2 :** DIRECTION FINDER — **go·nio·met·ric** \-nē-ə-ˈme-trik\ *adj* — **go·ni·om·e·try** \-nē-ˈä-mə-trē\ *n*

-gonium *n comb form* [NL, fr. Gk *gonos*] **1 :** germ cell ⟨spermato*gonium*⟩ **2 :** reproductive structure of a plant or fungus ⟨oo*gonium*⟩

gon·o·coc·cus \ˌgä-nə-ˈkä-kəs\ *n, pl* **-coc·ci** \-ˈkäk-ˌsī, -(ˌ)sē; -ˈkä-ˌkī, -(ˌ)kē\ [NL] (1889) **:** a pus-producing bacterium (*Neisseria gonorrhoeae*) that causes gonorrhea — **gon·o·coc·cal** \-ˈkä-kəl\ *adj*

go–no–go \ˈgō-ˈnō-ˌgō\ *adj* (ca. 1945) **1 :** being or relating to a required decision to continue or stop a course of action **2 :** being or relating to a point at which a go-no-go decision must be made

gon·o·phore \ˈgä-nə-ˌfȯr\ *n* [ISV] (1859) **:** an attached reproductive zooid of a hydroid colony

gon·o·pore \ˈgä-nə-ˌpȯr\ *n* (1897) **:** a genital pore in some invertebrates and esp. some insects

gon·or·rhea \ˌgä-nə-ˈrē-ə\ *n* [NL, fr. LL, morbid loss of semen, fr. Gk *gonorrhoia*, fr. *gon-* + *-rrhoia* -rrhea] (ca. 1526) **:** a contagious inflammation of the genital mucous membrane caused by the gonococcus — called also *clap* — **gon·or·rhe·al** \-ˈrē-əl\ *adj*

-gony *n comb form* [L *-gonia*, fr. Gk, fr. *gonos*] **:** generation **:** reproduction **:** manner of coming into being ⟨iso*gony*⟩

gon·zo \ˈgän-(ˌ)zō\ *adj* [origin unknown] (1971) **1 :** idiosyncratically subjective but engagé ⟨~ journalism⟩ **2 :** BIZARRE **3 :** freewheeling or unconventional esp. to the point of outrageousness ⟨a ~ comedian⟩

goo \ˈgü\ *n* [perh. short for *burgoo*] (1900) **1 :** a viscid or sticky substance **2 :** sentimental tripe — **goo·ey** \-ē\ *adj* — **goo·ey·ness** \-nəs\ *n*

[1]**goo·ber** \ˈgü-bər, ˈgu̇-\ *n* [of Bantu origin; akin to Kimbundu *ŋguba* peanut] (1834) *Southern & Midland* **:** PEANUT

[2]**goober** *n* [earlier slang *goob*, *goober* kiss, pimple, penis, prob. of imit. origin] (1980) *slang* **:** a naive, ignorant, or foolish person

[1]**good** \ˈgu̇d\ *adj* **bet·ter** \ˈbe-tər\; **best** \ˈbest\ [ME, fr. OE *gōd;* akin to OHG *guot* good, MHG *gatern* to unite, Skt *gadhya* what one clings to]

(bef. 12c) **1 a** (1) : of a favorable character or tendency ⟨~ news⟩ (2) : BOUNTIFUL, FERTILE ⟨~ land⟩ (3) : HANDSOME, ATTRACTIVE ⟨~ looks⟩ **b** (1) : SUITABLE, FIT ⟨~ to eat⟩ (2) : free from injury or disease ⟨one ~ arm⟩ (3) : not depreciated ⟨bad money drives out ~⟩ (4) : commercially sound ⟨a ~ risk⟩ (5) : that can be relied on ⟨~ for another year⟩ ⟨~ for a hundred dollars⟩ ⟨always ~ for a laugh⟩ (6) : PROFITABLE, ADVANTAGEOUS ⟨made a very ~ deal⟩ **c** (1) : AGREEABLE, PLEASANT ⟨had a ~ time⟩ (2) : SALUTARY, WHOLESOME ⟨~ for a cold⟩ (3) : AMUSING, CLEVER ⟨a ~ joke⟩ **d** (1) : of a noticeably large size or quantity : CONSIDERABLE ⟨won by a ~ margin⟩ ⟨a ~ bit of the time⟩ (2) : FULL ⟨waited a ~ hour⟩ (3) — used as an intensive ⟨a ~ many of us⟩ **e** (1) : WELL-FOUNDED, COGENT ⟨~ reasons⟩ (2) : TRUE ⟨holds ~ for society at large⟩ (3) : deserving of respect : HONORABLE ⟨in ~ standing⟩ (4) : legally valid or effectual ⟨~ title⟩ **f** (1) : ADEQUATE, SATISFACTORY ⟨~ care⟩ — often used in faint praise ⟨his serve is only ~ —Frank Deford⟩ (2) : conforming to a standard ⟨~ English⟩ (3) : CHOICE, DISCRIMINATING ⟨~ taste⟩ (4) : containing less fat and being less tender than higher grades — used of meat and esp. of beef **2 a** (1) : VIRTUOUS, RIGHT, COMMENDABLE ⟨a ~ person⟩ ⟨~ conduct⟩ (2) : KIND, BENEVOLENT ⟨~ intentions⟩ **b** : UPPER-CLASS ⟨a ~ family⟩ **c** : COMPETENT, SKILLFUL ⟨a ~ doctor⟩ **d** (1) : LOYAL ⟨a ~ party man⟩ ⟨a ~ Catholic⟩ (2) : CLOSE ⟨a ~ friend⟩ **e** : free from infirmity or sorrow ⟨I feel ~⟩ — **good•ish** \ˈgu̇-dish\ *adj* — **as good as** : in effect : VIRTUALLY ⟨*as good as* dead⟩ — **as good as gold** **1** : of the highest worth or reliability ⟨his promise is *as good as gold*⟩ **2** : well-behaved ⟨the child was *as good as gold*⟩ — **good and** \ˌgu̇-dᵊn\ : VERY, ENTIRELY ⟨was *good and* mad⟩

usage An old notion that it is wrong to say "I feel good" in reference to health still occas. appears in print. The origins of this notion are obscure, but they seem to combine someone's idea that *good* should be reserved to describe virtue and uncertainty about whether an adverb or an adjective should follow *feel.* Today nearly everyone agrees that both *good* and *well* can be predicate adjectives after *feel.* Both are used to express good health, but *good* may connote good spirits in addition to good health.

[2]**good** *n* (bef. 12c) **1 a** : something that is good **b** (1) : something conforming to the moral order of the universe (2) : praiseworthy character : GOODNESS **c** : a good element or portion **2 a** : advancement of prosperity or well-being ⟨the ~ of the community⟩ ⟨it's for your own ~⟩ **b** : something useful or beneficial ⟨it's no ~ trying⟩ **3 a** : something that has economic utility or satisfies an economic want **b** *pl* : personal property having intrinsic value but usu. excluding money, securities, and negotiable instruments **c** *pl* : CLOTH **d** *pl* : something manufactured or produced for sale : WARES, MERCHANDISE ⟨canned ~*s*⟩ **e** *pl, Brit* : FREIGHT **4** : good persons — used with *the* **5** *pl* **a** : the qualities required to achieve an end **b** : proof of wrongdoing ⟨didn't have the ~*s* on him —T. G. Cooke⟩ — **for good** *also* **for good and all** : FOREVER, PERMANENTLY — **in good with** : in a favored position with — **to the good** **1** : for the best : BENEFICIAL ⟨efforts to restrict credit were all *to the good* —*Time*⟩ **2** : in a position of net gain or profit ⟨wound up $10 *to the good*⟩

[3]**good** *adv* (13c) **1** : WELL ⟨he showed me how ~ I was doing —Herbert Gold⟩ **2** — used as an intensive ⟨a ~ long time⟩

usage Adverbial *good* has been under attack from the schoolroom since the 19th century. Insistence on *well* rather than *good* has resulted in a split in connotation: *well* is standard, neutral, and colorless, while *good* is emotionally charged and emphatic. This makes *good* the adverb of choice in sports ⟨"I'm seeing the ball real *good*" is what you hear —Roger Angell⟩. In such contexts as ⟨listen up. And listen *good* —Alex Karras⟩ ⟨lets fly with his tomatoes before they can flee. He gets Clarence *good* —Charles Dickinson⟩ *good* cannot be adequately replaced by *well.* Adverbial *good* is primarily a spoken form; in writing it occurs in reported and fictional speech and in generally familiar or informal contexts.

good book *n, often cap G&B* (1651) : BIBLE

good–bye *or* **good–by** \gu̇d-ˈbī, gə(d)-\ *n* [alter. of *God be with you*] (ca. 1580) **1** : a concluding remark or gesture at parting — often used interjectionally **2** : a taking of leave ⟨a tearful ~⟩

good cholesterol *n* (1980) : HDL

good deal *n* (bef. 12c) : a considerable quantity or extent : LOT ⟨knows a *good deal* about disease⟩ ⟨a *good deal* faster⟩

good faith *n* (1755) : honesty or lawfulness of purpose

good fellow *n* (13c) : an affable companionable person — **good–fel•low•ship** \ˌgu̇d-ˈfe-lō-ˌship, -ˈfe-lə-\ *n*

good–for–noth•ing \ˈgu̇d-fər-ˌnə-thiŋ\ *adj* (1533) : of no use or value — **good–for–nothing** *n*

Good Friday *n* [fr. its special sanctity] (13c) : the Friday before Easter observed in churches as the anniversary of the crucifixion of Christ and in some states of the U.S. as a legal holiday

good–heart•ed \ˈgu̇d-ˈhär-təd\ *adj* (1552) : having a kindly generous disposition — **good–heart•ed•ly** *adv* — **good–heart•ed•ness** *n*

good–hu•mored \-ˈ(h)yü-mərd\ *adj* (1662) : GOOD-NATURED, CHEERFUL — **good–hu•mored•ly** *adv* — **good–hu•mored•ness** *n*

good life *n* (1942) : a life marked by a high standard of living

good–look•ing \ˈgu̇d-ˈlu̇-kiŋ\ *adj* (1762) : having a pleasing or attractive appearance — **good–look•er** \-ˈlu̇-kər\ *n*

good•ly \ˈgu̇d-lē\ *adj* **good•li•er; -est** (bef. 12c) **1** : pleasantly attractive **2** : significantly large : CONSIDERABLE ⟨a ~ number⟩

good•man \ˈgu̇d-mən\ *n* (13c) **1** *archaic* : the master of a household **2** *archaic* : MR.

good–na•tured \-ˈnā-chərd\ *adj* (1577) : of a pleasant and cooperative disposition ***syn*** see AMIABLE — **good–na•tured•ly** *adv* — **good–na•tured•ness** *n*

good–neighbor *adj* (1936) : marked by principles of friendship, cooperation, and noninterference in the internal affairs of another country ⟨a ~ policy⟩

good•ness \ˈgu̇d-nəs\ *n* (bef. 12c) **1** : the quality or state of being good **2** — used interjectionally or in phrases esp. to express mild surprise or shock ⟨oh, my ~!⟩ ⟨~ knows⟩ **3** : the nutritious, flavorful, or beneficial part of something

goodness of fit (1895) : the conformity between an experimental result and theoretical expectation or between data and an approximating curve

good offices *n pl* (1681) : services as a mediator

good old boy *or* **good ol' boy** *or* **good ole boy** \ˈgu̇d-ōl(d)-ˌbȯi\ *n* (ca. 1967) : a usu. white Southerner who conforms to the values, culture, or behavior of his peers

Good Samaritan *n* (1679) : SAMARITAN 2

good–tem•pered \ˈgu̇d-ˈtem-pərd\ *adj* (1768) : not easily angered or upset — **good–tem•pered•ly** *adv* — **good–tem•pered•ness** *n*

good•wife \ˈgu̇d-ˌwīf\ *n* (13c) **1** *archaic* : the mistress of a household **2** *archaic* : MRS.

good•will \ˌgu̇d-ˈwil\ *n* (bef. 12c) **1 a** : a kindly feeling of approval and support : benevolent interest or concern **b** (1) : the favor or advantage that a business has acquired esp. through its brands and its good reputation (2) : the value of projected earnings increases of a business esp. as part of its purchase price (3) : the excess of the purchase price of a company over its book value which represents the value of goodwill as an intangible asset for accounting purposes **2 a** : cheerful consent **b** : willing effort — **good•willed** \-ˈwild\ *adj*

[1]**goody** \ˈgu̇-dē\ *n* [alter. of *goodwife*] (1559) *archaic* : a usu. married woman of lowly station — used as a title preceding a surname

[2]**goody** *or* **good•ie** *n, pl* **good•ies** (1756) **1** : something that is particularly attractive, pleasurable, good, or desirable **2** *chiefly Brit* : one that is good; *esp* : an opponent of the villain (as in a motion picture)

goody–goody \ˌgu̇-dē-ˈgu̇-dē\ *adj* (1871) : affectedly or ingratiatingly good or proper — **goody–goody** *n*

Goody Two–shoes \ˈgu̇-dē-ˈtü-ˌshüz\ *n, often cap S* [fr. *Goody Two-Shoes,* heroine of a children's story perh. by Oliver Goldsmith] (1934) : a person who is goody-goody; *also* : a person who is uncommonly good — **goody–two–shoes** *adj*

[1]**goof** \ˈgüf\ *n* [prob. alter. of E dial. *goff* simpleton] (1915) **1** : a silly or stupid person **2** : BLUNDER

[2]**goof** *vi* (1932) **1 a** : to spend time idly or foolishly — usu. used with *off* ⟨~*ing* off instead of working⟩ **b** : to engage in playful activity — usu. used with *around* ⟨~*ing* around after school⟩ **2** : to make a usu. foolish or careless mistake : BLUNDER — often used with *up* ~ *vt* : to make a mess of : BUNGLE — usu. used with *up* ⟨~*ed* up the assignment⟩ — **goof on** *slang* : to make fun of : KID, PUT ON ⟨you're *goofing on* me, right?⟩

goof•ball \ˈgüf-ˌbȯl\ *n* (1950) **1** *slang* : a barbiturate sleeping pill **2** : a goofy person

go off *vi* (1579) **1** : EXPLODE **2** : to burst forth or break out suddenly or noisily **3** : to go forth, out, or away : LEAVE **4** : to undergo decline or deterioration **5** : to follow the expected or desired course : PROCEED ⟨the party *went off* well⟩ **6** : to make a characteristic noise : SOUND ⟨could hear the alarm *going off*⟩ — **go off the deep end** **1** : to enter recklessly on a course **2** : to become very much excited

goof–off \ˈgüf-ˌȯf\ *n* (1953) : one who evades work or responsibility

goofy \ˈgü-fē\ *adj* **goof•i•er; -est** (1921) : being crazy, ridiculous, or mildly ludicrous : SILLY ⟨a ~ sense of humor⟩ ⟨that hat looks ~⟩ — **goof•i•ly** \-fə-lē\ *adv* — **goof•i•ness** \-fē-nəs\ *n*

goo•gle \ˈgü-gəl\ *vt* **goo•gled; goo•gling** \-g(ə-)liŋ\ *often cap* [*Google,* trademark for a search engine] (2001) : to use the Google search engine to obtain information about (as a person) on the World Wide Web

goo•gly–eyed \ˈgü-glē-ˌīd\ *adj* [by alter.] (1926) : GOGGLE-EYED

goo•gol \ˈgü-ˌgȯl\ *n* [coined by Milton Sirotta *b ab* 1929 nephew of Edward Kasner †1955 Am. mathematician] (1938) : the figure 1 followed by 100 zeros equal to 10^{100}

goo•gol•plex \-ˌpleks\ *n* (1938) : the figure 1 followed by a googol of zeros equal to

$$10^{googol} \text{ or } 10^{10^{100}}$$

[1]**goo–goo** \ˈgü-(ˌ)gü\ *adj* [perh. alter. of [2]*goggle*] (1900) : LOVING, ENTICING — used chiefly in the phrase *goo-goo eyes*

[2]**goo–goo** *n, pl* **goo–goos** [fr. *good* government] (1912) : a member or advocate of a political reform movement

[1]**gook** \ˈgük\ *n* [origin unknown] (1920) *usu offensive* : a nonwhite or non-American person; *specif* : ASIAN

[2]**gook** *var of* GUCK

goom•bah \ˈgüm-ˌbä\ *n* [It dial. (Campania) *cumbà,* voc. form of *cumbare* respected older man, lit., godfather, fr. ML *compater* — more at COMPEER] (1968) **1** : a close friend or associate — used esp. among Italian-American men **2** : a member of a secret chiefly Italian-American crime organization : MAFIOSO; *broadly* : GANGSTER **3** : a macho Italian-American man

goon \ˈgün\ *n* [prob. short for E dial. *gooney* simpleton] (1921) **1** : a stupid person **2 a** : a man hired to terrorize or eliminate opponents **b** : ENFORCER 2b

go on *vi* (15c) **1 a** : to continue on or as if on a journey ⟨life *goes on*⟩ ⟨*went on* to greater things⟩ **b** : to keep on : CONTINUE ⟨*went on* smoking⟩ **c** : PROCEED ⟨*went on* to win the election⟩ **2** : to take place : HAPPEN ⟨what's *going on*⟩ **3** : to talk esp. in an effusive manner ⟨the way people *go on* about their ancestors —Hamilton Basso⟩

goo•ney *or* **goo•ny** \ˈgü-nē\ *n, pl* **gooneys** *or* **goonies** [prob. fr. E dial. *gooney* simpleton] (1895) : BLACK-FOOTED ALBATROSS; *broadly* : ALBATROSS

goop \ˈgüp\ *n* [prob. alter. of *goo*] (ca. 1918) : GOO, GUNK — **goopy** \ˈgü-pē\ *adj*

goo•san•der \gü-ˈsan-dər\ *n* [origin unknown] (1766) : the common merganser (*Mergus merganser*) of the northern hemisphere

[1]**goose** \ˈgüs\ *n, pl* **geese** \ˈgēs\ [ME *gos,* fr. OE *gōs;* akin to OHG *gans* goose, L *anser,* Gk *chēn*] (bef. 12c) **1 a** : any of numerous large waterfowl (family Anatidae) that are intermediate between the swans and ducks and have long necks, feathered lores, and reticulate tarsi **b** : a female goose as distinguished from a gander **2** : SIMPLETON, DOLT **3** *pl* **goos•es** : a tailor's smoothing iron with a gooseneck handle **4** *pl* **goos•es** : a poke between the buttocks

[2]**goose** *vt* **goosed; goos·ing** (ca. 1880) **1 :** to poke between the buttocks with an upward thrust **2 :** to increase the activity, speed, power, intensity, or amount of : SPUR ⟨an effort to ~ newsstand sales⟩

goose·ber·ry \'güs-ˌber-ē, 'güz-, -b(ə-)rē, *chiefly Brit* 'güz-\ *n* (1573) **1 a :** the acid usu. prickly fruit of any of several shrubs (genus *Ribes,* esp. *R. hirtellum* of the U.S. and *R. uva-crispa* of Europe) grouped esp. formerly in the saxifrage family but now often placed in a separate family (Grossulariaceae, the gooseberry family) **b :** a shrub bearing gooseberries **2 :** CURRANT 2

goose bumps *n pl* (1933) **:** a roughness of the skin produced by erection of its papillae esp. from cold, fear, or a sudden feeling of excitement

goose egg *n* (1866) **:** ZERO, NOTHING; *esp* **:** a score of zero in a game or contest

goose·fish \'güs-ˌfish\ *n* (1807) **:** any of a family (Lophiidae) of pediculate fishes with a large flattened head, a fringe of flaps along each side of the lower jaw, head, and body, and a long stalk on the head with a flap of flesh at the tip for attracting prey; *esp* **:** MONKFISH

goose·flesh \'güs-ˌflesh\ *n* (ca. 1810) **:** GOOSE BUMPS

goose·foot \-ˌfu̇t\ *n, pl* **goose·foots** (1548) **:** any of a genus (*Chenopodium*) or family (Chenopodiaceae, the goosefoot family) of glabrous herbs with fruit that is a utricle

goose·grass \-ˌgras\ *n* (1530) **1 :** CLEAVERS **2 :** YARD GRASS

goose·neck \'güs-ˌnek\ *n, often attrib* (1688) **1 :** something (as a flexible jointed metal pipe) curved like the neck of a goose or U-shaped **2 :** a truck trailer (as for transporting livestock) with a projecting front end designed to attach to the bed of a pickup truck — **goose·necked** \-ˌnekt\ *adj*

goose pimples *n pl* (ca. 1889) **:** GOOSE BUMPS

goose–step \'güs-ˌstep\ *vi* (1879) **1 :** to march in a goose step **2 :** to practice an unthinking conformity

goose step *n* (1806) **:** a straight-legged stiff-kneed step used by troops of some armies when passing in review

goos·ey \'gü-sē\ *adj* **goos·i·er; -est** (1811) **1 :** resembling a goose **2 a :** affected with goose bumps **:** SCARED **b :** very nervous **c :** reacting strongly when goosed or startled

go out *vi* (bef. 12c) **1 a :** to go forth, abroad, or outdoors; *specif* **:** to leave one's house **b** (1) **:** to take the field as a soldier (2) **:** to participate as a principal in a duel **c :** to travel as or as if a colonist or immigrant **d :** to work away from home **2 a :** to come to an end **b :** to give up office **:** RESIGN **c :** to become obsolete or unfashionable **d** (1) **:** to play the last card of one's hand (2) **:** to reach or exceed the total number of points required for game in cards **3 :** to take part in social activities **4 :** to go on strike **5 :** BREAK, COLLAPSE **6 :** to become a candidate ⟨*went out* for the football team⟩

go over *vi* (1645) **1 :** to make one's way ⟨*going over* to the store for supplies⟩ **2 :** to become converted **3 a :** to win approval **:** SUCCEED ⟨glad it *went over*⟩ **b :** to be received ⟨the film *went over* well⟩

GOP *abbr* Grand Old Party (Republican)

GOPer \ˌjē-(ˌ)ō-'pē-ər\ *n* (1951) **:** a member of the GOP

[1]**go·pher** \'gō-fər\ *n* [origin unknown] (1791) **1 :** a burrowing land tortoise (*Gopherus polyphemus*) of the southern U.S.; *broadly* **:** any of several related land tortoises — called also *gopher tortoise* **2 a :** any of a family (Geomyidae) of burrowing rodents of western No. America, Central America, and the southern U.S. that are the size of a large rat and have large cheek pouches opening beside the mouth — called also *pocket gopher* **b :** any of several small ground squirrels (genus *Spermophilus*) of the prairie region of No. America **3 :** GOPHER BALL

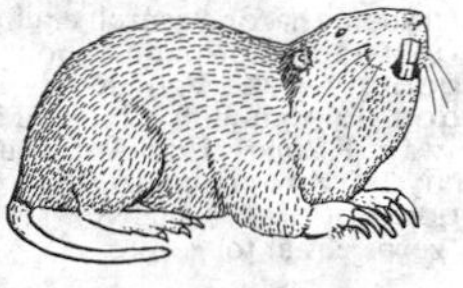

gopher 2a

[2]**gopher** *var of* GOFER

gopher ball *n* (ca. 1949) **:** a pitched baseball hit for a home run

gopher snake *n* (1837) **1 :** INDIGO SNAKE **2 :** BULL SNAKE

go·pik \gō-'pēk, -'pik\ *n, pl* **gopik** [Azerbaijani *gəpik* kopeck, fr. Russ *kopeĭka*] (1992) — see *manat* at MONEY table

Gor·di·an knot \'gȯr-dē-ən-\ *n* (1579) **1 :** an intricate problem; *esp* **:** a problem insoluble in its own terms — often used in the phrase *cut the Gordian knot* **2 :** a knot tied by Gordius, king of Phrygia, held to be capable of being untied only by the future ruler of Asia, and cut by Alexander the Great with his sword

gor·di·ta \gȯr-'dē-tə\ *n* [MexSp, dim. of *gorda* thick tortilla, fr. Sp, fem. of *gordo* fat, thick, fr. LL *gurdus* dull, blunt] (1945) **:** a deep-fried pocket of cornmeal dough filled with a savory mixture

Gor·don setter \'gȯr-dᵊn-\ *n* [Alexander, 4th Duke of *Gordon* †1827 Scot. sportsman] (1865) **:** any of a breed of large bird dogs of Scottish origin that have a long flat black-and-tan coat

[1]**gore** \'gȯr\ *n* [ME, fr. OE *gāra;* akin to OE *gār* spear, and perh. to Gk *chaion* shepherd's staff] (bef. 12c) **1 :** a small usu. triangular piece of land **2 a :** a tapering or triangular piece (as of cloth in a skirt) **b :** an elastic gusset for providing a snug fit in a shoe

[2]**gore** *vt* **gored; gor·ing** (1548) **1 :** to cut into a tapering triangular form **2 :** to provide with a gore

[3]**gore** *vt* **gored; gor·ing** [ME, prob. fr. *gore* spear, sword, fr. OE *gār* spear] (15c) **:** to pierce or wound with something pointed (as a horn or knife) ⟨*gored* by a bull⟩

[4]**gore** *n* [ME, filth, fr. OE *gor*] (1563) **1 :** BLOOD; *esp* **:** clotted blood **2 :** gruesomeness depicted in vivid detail

[1]**gorge** \'gȯrj\ *n* [ME, fr. AF, fr. LL *gurga,* alter. of *gurges,* fr. L, whirlpool — more at VORACIOUS] (14c) **1 :** THROAT — often used with *rise* to indicate revulsion accompanied by a sensation of constriction ⟨my ~ rises at the sight of blood⟩ **2 a :** a hawk's crop **b :** STOMACH, BELLY **3 :** the entrance into an outwork (as a bastion) of a fort **4 :** a narrow passage through land; *esp* **:** a narrow steep-walled canyon or part of a canyon **5 :** a primitive device used instead of a fishhook that consists of an object (as a piece of bone attached in the middle of a line) easy to swallow but difficult to eject **6 :** a mass choking a passage ⟨a river dammed by an ice ~⟩ **7 :** the line on the front of a coat or jacket formed by the crease of the lapel and collar

[2]**gorge** *vb* **gorged; gorg·ing** *vi* (14c) **:** to eat greedily or to repletion; *also* **:** to partake of something in large amounts ⟨*gorging* on books⟩ ~ *vi* **1 a :** to stuff to capacity **:** GLUT **b :** to fill completely or to the point of distension ⟨veins *gorged* with blood⟩ **2 :** to consume greedily ***syn*** see SATIATE — **gorg·er** *n*

[3]**gorge** *n* (1854) **:** the act or an instance of gorging

gor·geous \'gȯr-jəs\ *adj* [ME *gorgeouse,* fr. MF *gorgias* elegant, perh. fr. *gorgias* wimple, fr. *gorge* throat] (15c) **:** splendidly or showily brilliant or magnificent ***syn*** see SPLENDID — **gor·geous·ly** *adv* — **gor·geous·ness** *n*

gor·get \'gȯr-jət\ *n* [ME, fr. MF, fr. *gorge*] (15c) **1 :** a piece of armor protecting the throat — see ARMOR illustration **2 a :** an ornamental collar **b :** a part of a wimple covering the throat and shoulders **c :** a specially colored patch on the throat

gor·gon \'gȯr-gən\ *n* [L *Gorgon-, Gorgo,* fr. Gk *Gorgōn*] (14c) **1** *cap* **:** any of three snake-haired sisters in Greek mythology whose appearance turns the beholder to stone **2 :** an ugly or repulsive woman — **Gor·go·ni·an** \gȯr-'gō-nē-ən\ *adj*

gor·go·ni·an \gȯr-'gō-nē-ən\ *n* [NL *Gorgonia,* a coral genus, fr. L, coral, fr. *Gorgon-, Gorgo*] (1835) **:** any of an order (Gorgonacea) of colonial anthozoans with a usu. horny and branching axial skeleton — **gorgonian** *adj*

gor·gon·ize \'gȯr-gə-ˌnīz\ *vt* **-ized; -iz·ing** (1609) **:** to have a paralyzing or mesmerizing effect on **:** STUPEFY, PETRIFY

Gor·gon·zo·la \ˌgȯr-gən-'zō-lə\ *n* [It, fr. *Gorgonzola,* Italy] (1878) **:** a pungent blue cheese of Italian origin

go·ril·la \gə-'ri-lə\ *n* [NL, fr. Gk *Gorillai,* pl., a tribe of hairy women mentioned in an account of a voyage around Africa] (1847) **1 :** a very large typically black-colored anthropoid ape (*Gorilla gorilla*) of equatorial Africa that has a stocky body with broad shoulders and long arms and is less erect and has smaller ears than the chimpanzee **2 a :** an ugly or brutal man **b :** THUG, GOON

gor·man·dise *chiefly Brit var of* GORMANDIZE

gor·man·dize \'gȯr-mən-ˌdīz\ *vb* **-dized; -diz·ing** [*gormand,* alter. of *gourmand*] *vi* (1548) **:** to eat gluttonously or ravenously ~ *vt* **:** to eat greedily **:** DEVOUR — **gor·man·diz·er** *n*

gorm·less \'gȯrm-ləs\ *adj* [alter. of E dial. *gaumless,* fr. *gaum* attention, understanding (fr. ME *gome,* fr. ON *gaum, gaumr*) + *-less*] (1883) *chiefly Brit* **:** lacking intelligence **:** STUPID — **gorm·less·ness** *n, chiefly Brit*

go–round \'gō-ˌrau̇nd\ *n* (1891) **:** one of a series of recurring actions or events **:** ROUND

gorp \'gȯrp\ *n* [origin unknown] (1968) **:** a snack consisting of high-energy food (as raisins and nuts)

gorse \'gȯrs\ *n* [ME *gorst,* fr. OE; akin to OHG *gersta* barley, L *hordeum*] (bef. 12c) **:** a spiny yellow-flowered European shrub (*Ulex europaeus*) of the legume family; *broadly* **:** any of several related plants (genera *Ulex* and *Genista*) — **gorsy** \'gȯr-sē\ *adj*

gory \'gȯr-ē\ *adj* **gor·i·er; -est** (15c) **1 :** covered with gore **:** BLOODSTAINED **2 :** BLOODCURDLING, SENSATIONAL ⟨wanted to hear the ~ details⟩ ***syn*** see BLOODY

gosh \'gäsh, 'gȯsh\ *interj* [euphemism for *God*] (1757) — used as a mild oath or to express surprise

gos·hawk \'gäs-ˌhȯk\ *n* [ME *goshawke,* fr. OE *gōshafoc,* fr. *gōs* goose + *hafoc* hawk] (bef. 12c) **:** any of several long-tailed hawks with short rounded wings; *esp* **:** a large accipiter (*Accipiter gentilis*) of the northern hemisphere that is grayish-blue above with a barred white-and-gray underside and has a white stripe above and behind the eye

gos·ling \'gäz-liŋ, 'gȯz-, -lən\ *n* [ME, fr. *gos* goose] (14c) **1 :** a young goose **2 :** a foolish or callow person

go–slow \ˌgō-'slō\ *n* (1926) *Brit* **:** SLOWDOWN

[1]**gos·pel** \'gäs-pəl\ *n* [ME, fr. OE *gōdspel* (trans. of LL *evangelium*), fr. *gōd* good + *spell* tale — more at SPELL] (bef. 12c) **1 a** *often cap* **:** the message concerning Christ, the kingdom of God, and salvation **b** *cap* **:** one of the first four New Testament books telling of the life, death, and resurrection of Jesus Christ; *also* **:** a similar apocryphal book **c :** an interpretation of the Christian message ⟨the social ~⟩ **2** *cap* **:** a lection from one of the New Testament Gospels **3 :** the message or teachings of a religious teacher **4 :** something accepted or promoted as infallible truth or as a guiding principle or doctrine ⟨took her words as ~⟩ ⟨spreading the ~ of conservation —R. M. Hodesh⟩ **5 :** gospel music — **gos·pel·ly** \'gäs-pə-lē\ *adj*

[2]**gospel** *adj* (bef. 12c) **1 a :** having a basis in or being in accordance with the gospel **:** EVANGELICAL ⟨ordained to the ~ ministry —*Christian Century*⟩ **b :** marked by special or fervid emphasis on the gospel ⟨a ~ meeting⟩ **2 :** of, relating to, or being religious songs of American origin associated with evangelism and popular devotion and marked by simple melody and harmony and elements of folk songs and blues

gos·pel·er *or* **gos·pel·ler** \'gäs-p(ə-)lər\ *n* (1506) **1 :** a person who reads or sings the liturgical Gospel **2 :** a person who preaches or propounds a gospel

gospel side *n, often cap G* [fr. the custom of reading the Gospel from this side] (1891) **:** the left side of an altar or chancel as one faces it

[1]**gos·sa·mer** \'gä-sə-mər *also* 'gäz-mər, 'gä-zə-\ *n* [ME *gossomer,* fr. *gos* goose + *somer* summer] (14c) **1 :** a film of cobwebs floating in air in calm clear weather **2 :** something light, delicate, or insubstantial ⟨the ~ of youth's dreams —Andrea Parke⟩ — **gos·sa·mery** \-mə-rē\ *adj*

[2]**gossamer** *adj* (ca. 1807) **:** extremely light, delicate, or tenuous

gos·san \'gä-sᵊn\ *n* [Corn *gossen,* fr. *gōs* blood] (1776) **:** decomposed rock or vein material of reddish or rusty color that results from oxidized pyrites

[1]**gos·sip** \'gä-səp\ *n* [ME *gossib,* fr. OE *godsibb,* fr. *god* god + *sibb* kinsman, fr. *sibb* related — more at SIB] (bef. 12c) **1 a** *dial Brit* **:** GODPARENT **b :** COMPANION, CRONY **c :** a person who habitually reveals personal or sensational facts about others **2 a :** rumor or report of an intimate nature **b :** a chatty talk **c :** the subject matter of gossip — **gos·sip·ry** \-sə-prē\ *n*

[2]**gossip** *vi* (1627) **:** to relate gossip — **gos·sip·er** *n*

gos·sip·mon·ger \'gä-səp-ˌməŋ-gər, -ˌmäŋ-\ *n* (1836) **:** a person who starts or spreads gossip

gos·sipy \'gä-sə-pē\ *adj* (1818) **:** characterized by, full of, or given to gossip ⟨a ~ letter⟩ ⟨~ neighbors⟩

gos·sy·pol \'gä-sə-ˌpȯl, -ˌpōl\ *n* [ISV, ultim. fr. L *gossypion* cotton] (1899) **:** a toxic phenolic pigment $C_{30}H_{30}O_8$ in cottonseed

got *past and past part of* GET

got·cha \ˈgä-chə\ *n* [alter. of *got you*] (1974) **:** an unexpected usu. disconcerting challenge, revelation, or catch; *also* **:** an attempt to embarrass, expose, or disgrace someone (as a politician) with a gotcha

1Goth \ˈgäth\ *n* [ME *Gothes, Gotes* (pl.), partly fr. OE *Gotan* (pl.); partly fr. LL *Gothi* (pl.)] (14c) **1 :** a member of a Germanic people that overran the Roman Empire in the early centuries of the Christian era **2** *often not cap* **a :** rock music marked by dark and morbid lyrics **b :** a fan or performer of goth **3 :** a person who wears mostly black clothing, uses dark dramatic makeup, and often has dyed black hair

2Goth *abbr* Gothic

1Goth·ic \ˈgä-thik\ *adj* (1591) **1 a :** of, relating to, or resembling the Goths, their civilization, or their language **b :** TEUTONIC, GERMANIC **c :** MEDIEVAL 1 **d :** UNCOUTH, BARBAROUS **2 a :** of, relating to, or having the characteristics of a style of architecture developed in northern France and spreading through western Europe from the middle of the 12th century to the early 16th century that is characterized by the converging of weights and strains at isolated points upon slender vertical piers and counterbalancing buttresses and by pointed arches and vaulting **b :** of or relating to an architectural style reflecting the influence of the medieval Gothic **3** *often not cap* **:** of or relating to a style of fiction characterized by the use of desolate or remote settings and macabre, mysterious, or violent incidents — **goth·i·cal·ly** \-thi-k(ə-)lē\ *adv* — **Goth·ic·ness** \-thik-nəs\ *n*

2Gothic *n* (1691) **1 a :** BLACK LETTER **b :** SANS SERIF **2 :** Gothic art style or decoration; *specif* **:** the Gothic architectural style **3 :** the East Germanic language of the Goths — see INDO-EUROPEAN LANGUAGES table **4** *often not cap* **:** a novel, film, or play in the gothic style

Gothic arch *n* (1739) **:** a pointed arch; *esp* **:** one with a joint instead of a keystone at its apex

Goth·i·cism \ˈgä-thə-ˌsi-zəm\ *n* (1710) **1 :** barbarous lack of taste or elegance **2 :** conformity to or practice of Gothic style — **Goth·i·cist** \-sist\ *n*

goth·i·cize \-ˌsīz\ *vt* **-cized; -ciz·ing** *often cap* (1712) **:** to make Gothic

Goth·ick *chiefly Brit var of* GOTHIC

Gothic Revival *n* (1869) **:** an artistic style or movement of the 18th and 19th centuries inspired by and imitative of the Gothic style esp. in architecture

go through *vi* (1513) **1 :** to continue firmly or obstinately to the end ⟨I was *going through* with it if it killed me —A. W. Long⟩ **2 a :** to receive approval or sanction **:** PASS **b :** to come to a desired or satisfactory conclusion

go–to \ˈgō-ˌtü\ *adj* (1985) **:** relied on for expert knowledge or skill ⟨the company's ~ guy⟩

go to *vi* (15c) **1** *archaic* — used interjectionally as an exhortation ⟨and they said one to another, *go to,* let us make brick —Gen 11:3(AV)⟩ **2** *archaic* — used interjectionally to express disapproval or disbelief ⟨*go to, go to;* you have known what you should not —Shak.⟩

gotten *past part of* GET

Göt·ter·däm·mer·ung \ˌgə(r)-tər-ˈde-mə-ˌrüŋ, -ˈda-\ *n* [G, lit., twilight of the gods, fr. *Götter* (pl. of *Gott* god) + *Dämmerung* twilight] (1909) **:** a collapse (as of a society or regime) marked by catastrophic violence and disorder; *broadly* **:** DOWNFALL ⟨the ~ of Communism⟩

gouache \ˈgwäsh\ *n* [F, fr. It *guazzo,* lit., puddle, prob. fr. L *aquatio* watering place, fr. *aquari* to fetch water, fr. *aqua* water — more at ISLAND] (1882) **1 :** a method of painting with opaque watercolors **2 a :** a picture painted by gouache **b :** the pigment used in gouache

Gou·da \ˈgü-də\ *n* [*Gouda,* Netherlands] (1885) **:** a mild cheese of Dutch origin that is similar to Edam but contains more fat

1gouge \ˈgau̇j\ *n* [ME *gowge,* fr. MF *gouge,* fr. LL *gulbia*] (14c) **1 :** a chisel with a concavo-convex cross section **2 a :** the act of gouging **b :** a groove or cavity scooped out **3 :** an excessive or improper exaction **:** EXTORTION

2gouge *vt* **gouged; goug·ing** (1570) **1 :** to scoop out with or as if with a gouge **2 a :** to force out (an eye) with the thumb **b :** to thrust the thumb into the eye of **3 :** to subject to extortion or undue exaction **:** OVERCHARGE — **goug·er** *n*

gou·lash \ˈgü-ˌläsh, -ˌlash\ *n* [Hung *gulyás,* short for *gulyáshús,* lit., herdsman's meat] (1866) **1 :** a stew made with meat (as beef), assorted vegetables, and paprika **2 :** a round in bridge played with hands produced by a redistribution of previously dealt cards **3 :** a mixture of heterogeneous elements **:** JUMBLE

go under *vi* (1848) **:** to be overwhelmed, destroyed, or defeated **:** FAIL

go up *vi* (15c) **1** *chiefly Brit* **:** to attend a university **2** *of an actor* **:** to become confused **3 :** to be built or erected ⟨a new sign *went up*⟩ — **go up in flames :** BURN — **go up in smoke :** to be destroyed by or as if by burning

gou·ra·mi \gü-ˈrä-mē\ *n, pl* **-mi** *or* **-mis** *also* **-mies** [Malay dial. (Java), fr. Jav *graméh*] (1878) **:** any of numerous African and Asian tropical freshwater bony fishes (order Perciformes): as **a :** a large Asian food fish (*Osphronemus goramy* of the family Osphronemidae) **b :** any of various small fishes (families Belontiidae and Helostomatidae) often kept in aquariums

gourd \ˈgōrd, ˈgu̇rd\ *n* [ME *gourde,* fr. AF *gurde, gourde,* fr. L *cucurbita*] (14c) **1 :** any of a family (Cucurbitaceae, the gourd family) of chiefly herbaceous tendril-bearing vines including the cucumber, melon, squash, and pumpkin **2 :** the fruit of a gourd **:** PEPO; *esp* **:** any of various hard-rinded inedible fruits of plants of two genera (*Lagenaria* and *Cucurbita*) often used for ornament or for vessels and utensils — **out of one's gourd** *also* **off one's gourd :** CRAZY

gourde \ˈgu̇rd\ *n* [AmerF] (ca. 1858) — see MONEY table

gour·mand \ˈgu̇r-ˌmänd, -mənd\ *n* [ME *gourmaunt,* fr. MF *gourmant*] (15c) **1 :** one who is excessively fond of eating and drinking **2 :** one who is heartily interested in good food and drink ***syn*** see EPICURE — **gour·mand·ism** \ˈgu̇r-ˌmän-ˌdi-zəm, -mən-\ *n* — **gour·man·dize** \-ˌdīz\ *vi*

gour·man·dise \ˌgu̇r-män-ˈdēz\ *n* [F, fr. MF, fr. *gourmant*] (15c) **:** appreciation of or interest in good food and drink **:** GOURMANDISM

gour·met \ˈgu̇r-ˌmā, gu̇r-ˈ\ *n* [F, fr. MF, alter. of *gromet* boy servant, vintner's assistant, prob. ultim. fr. ME *grom* groom] (1820) **:** a connoisseur of food and drink; *broadly* **:** CONNOISSEUR 2 ⟨a film ~⟩ ***syn*** see EPICURE — **gourmet** *adj*

gout \ˈgau̇t\ *n* [ME *goute,* fr. AF *gute* drop, gout, fr. L *gutta* drop] (13c) **1 :** a metabolic disease marked by a painful inflammation of the joints, deposits of urates in and around the joints, and usu. an excessive amount of uric acid in the blood **2 :** a mass or aggregate esp. of something fluid often gushing or bursting forth — **gouty** \-ē\ *adj*

gov *abbr* **1** government; governor **2** governmental institution — usu. preceded by a period; used in World Wide Web addresses

gov·ern \ˈgə-vərn\ *vb* [ME, fr. AF *governer,* fr. L *gubernare* to steer, govern, fr. Gk *kybernan*] *vt* (14c) **1 a :** to exercise continuous sovereign authority over; *esp* **:** to control and direct the making and administration of policy in **b :** to rule without sovereign power and usu. without having the authority to determine basic policy **2 a** *archaic* **:** MANIPULATE **b :** to control the speed of (as a machine) esp. by automatic means **3 a :** to control, direct, or strongly influence the actions and conduct of **b :** to exert a determining or guiding influence in or over ⟨income must ~ expenditure⟩ **c :** to hold in check **:** RESTRAIN **4 :** to require (a word) to be in a certain case **5 :** to serve as a precedent or deciding principle for ⟨customs that ~ human decisions⟩ ~ *vi* **1 :** to prevail or have decisive influence **:** CONTROL **2 :** to exercise authority — **gov·ern·able** \-vər-nə-bəl\ *adj*

gov·er·nance \ˈgə-vər-nən(t)s\ *n* (14c) **:** GOVERNMENT

gov·ern·ess \ˈgə-vər-nəs\ *n* (15c) **1 :** a woman who governs **2 :** a woman who cares for and supervises a child esp. in a private household

gov·ern·essy \ˈgə-vər-ni-sē\ *adj* (1872) **:** characteristic of or resembling a governess (as in primness)

gov·ern·ment \ˈgə-vər(n)-mənt, -və-mənt; ˈgə-bᵊm-ənt, -vᵊm-\ *n, often attrib* (14c) **1 :** the act or process of governing; *specif* **:** authoritative direction or control **2** *obs* **:** moral conduct or behavior **:** DISCRETION **3 a :** the office, authority, or function of governing **b** *obs* **:** the term during which a governing official holds office **4 :** the continuous exercise of authority over and the performance of functions for a political unit **:** RULE **5 a :** the organization, machinery, or agency through which a political unit exercises authority and performs functions and which is usu. classified according to the distribution of power within it **b :** the complex of political institutions, laws, and customs through which the function of governing is carried out **6 :** the body of persons that constitutes the governing authority of a political unit or organization: as **a :** the officials comprising the governing body of a political unit and constituting the organization as an active agency **b** *cap* **:** the executive branch of the U.S. federal government **c** *cap* **:** a small group of persons holding simultaneously the principal political executive offices of a nation or other political unit and being responsible for the direction and supervision of public affairs: (1) **:** such a group in a parliamentary system constituted by the cabinet or by the ministry (2) **:** ADMINISTRATION 4b **7 :** POLITICAL SCIENCE — **gov·ern·men·tal** \ˌgə-vər(n)-ˈmen-tᵊl\ *adj* — **gov·ern·men·tal·ize** \-tə-ˌlīz\ *vt* — **gov·ern·men·tal·ly** \-tᵊl-ē\ *adv*

gov·ern·men·tal·ism \ˌgə-vər(n)-ˈmen-tə-ˌli-zəm\ *n* (1848) **1 :** a theory advocating extension of the sphere and degree of government activity **2 :** the tendency toward extension of the role of government — **gov·ern·men·tal·ist** \-tə-list\ *n*

gov·ern·men·tese \ˌgə-vər-mən-ˈtēz\ *n* (1944) **:** jargon held to be characteristic of government officials

gov·er·nor \ˈgə-vᵊn-ər *also* ˈgə-vər-nər\ *n* (14c) **1 :** one that governs: as **a :** one that exercises authority esp. over an area or group **b :** an official elected or appointed to act as ruler, chief executive, or nominal head of a political unit **c :** COMMANDING OFFICER **d :** the managing director and usu. the principal officer of an institution or organization **e :** a member of a group that directs or controls an institution or society **2 :** TUTOR **3 a** *slang* **:** one looked upon as governing **b :** MISTER, SIR — usu. used as a term of address **4 a :** an attachment to a machine (as a gasoline engine) for automatic control or limitation of speed **b :** a device giving automatic control (as of pressure or temperature) — **gov·er·nor·ate** \-ət, -ˌāt\ *n*

governor–general *n, pl* **governors–general** *or* **governor–generals** (1586) **:** a governor of high rank; *esp* **:** one who governs a large territory or has deputy governors under him

gov·er·nor·ship \ˈgə-vᵊn-ər-ˌship *also* ˈgə-vər-nər-\ *n* (1658) **1 :** the office of governor **2 :** the period of incumbency of a governor

govt *abbr* government

gow·an \ˈgau̇-ən\ *n* [prob. alter. of ME *gollan*] (1570) *chiefly Scot* **:** DAISY 1; *broadly* **:** a white or yellow field flower — **gow·any** \-ə-nē\ *adj, chiefly Scot*

gown \ˈgau̇n\ *n* [ME, fr. AF *gune, goune,* fr. LL *gunna,* a fur or leather garment] (14c) **1 a :** a loose flowing outer garment formerly worn by men **b :** a distinctive robe worn by a professional or academic person **c :** a woman's dress **d** (1) **:** DRESSING GOWN (2) **:** NIGHTGOWN **e :** a coverall worn in an operating room **2 :** the body of students and faculty of a college or university ⟨rivalry between town and ~⟩ — **gown** *vt*

gowns·man \ˈgau̇nz-mən\ *n* (1627) **:** a professional or academic person

goy \ˈgȯi\ *n, pl* **goy·im** \ˈgȯi-əm\ *also* **goys** [Yiddish, fr. Heb *gōy* people, nation] (1841) *sometimes disparaging* **:** GENTILE 1 — **goy·ish** \ˈgȯi-ish\ *adj, sometimes disparaging*

gp *abbr* group

GP *abbr* **1** general practice; general practitioner **2** geometric progression

GPA *abbr* grade point average

GPD *abbr* gallons per day

GPH *abbr* gallons per hour

GPM *abbr* gallons per minute

GPO *abbr* **1** general post office **2** Government Printing Office

gp120 \ˌjē-(ˌ)pē-ˌwən-ˈtwen-tē\ *n* [*glycoprotein*] (1985) **:** a glycoprotein protruding from the outer surface of the HIV virion that has a molecular weight of 120 and must bind to a CD4 receptor on a T cell bearing such receptors before infection of the cell can occur

G protein *n* [*guanosine triphosphate-binding protein*] (1967) **:** any of a class of cell membrane proteins that are coupled to cell surface receptors and upon stimulation of the receptor by an extracellular signaling molecule (as a hormone or neurotransmitter) bind to GTP to form an

\ə\ **abut** \ᵊ\ **kitten,** F **table** \ər\ **further** \a\ **ash** \ā\ **ace** \ä\ **mop, mar**
\au̇\ **out** \ch\ **chin** \e\ **bet** \ē\ **easy** \g\ **go** \i\ **hit** \ī\ **ice** \j\ **job**
\ŋ\ **sing** \ō\ **go** \ȯ\ **law** \ȯi\ **boy** \th\ **thin** \t͟h\ **the** \ü\ **loot** \u̇\ **foot**
\y\ **yet** \zh\ **vision, beige** \k̲, ⁿ, œ, ue, ʸ\ *see* Guide to Pronunciation

active complex which mediates an intracellular event (as activation of adenylate cyclase)

[1]**GPS** \ˌjē-(ˌ)pē-ˈes\ *n* [*G*lobal *P*ositioning *S*ystem] (1975) : a navigational system using satellite signals to fix the location of a radio receiver on or above the earth's surface; *also* : the radio receiver so used

[2]**GPS** *abbr* gallons per second

GQ *abbr* general quarters

gr *abbr* **1** grade **2** grain **3** gram **4** gravity **5** gross

Gr *abbr* Greece; Greek

graaf·ian follicle \ˌgrä-fē-ən-, ˌgra-\ *n, often cap G* [Regnier de *Graaf* †1673 Du. anatomist] (1883) : a mature liquid-filled cavity in a mammalian ovary that ruptures during ovulation to release an egg

[1]**grab** \ˈgrab\ *vb* **grabbed; grab·bing** [obs. D or LG *grabben*] *vt* (ca. 1581) **1** : to take or seize by or as if by a sudden motion or grasp ⟨~ up an ax⟩ ⟨*grabbed* the opportunity⟩ ⟨~ attention⟩ **2** : to obtain unscrupulously ⟨~ public lands⟩ **3** : to take hastily ⟨~ a bite to eat⟩ ⟨~ a cab⟩ **4 a** : to seize the attention of ⟨the technique of *grabbing* an audience —Pauline Kael⟩ **b** : to impress favorably and deeply ~ *vi* : to make a grab ***syn*** see TAKE — **grab·ber** *n*

[2]**grab** *adj* (1608) **1** : intended to be grabbed ⟨a ~ rail⟩ **2** : taken at random ⟨~ samples of rocks⟩

[3]**grab** *n* (1777) **1 a** : something grabbed **b** : a sudden snatch **c** : an unlawful or unscrupulous seizure **2** *chiefly Brit* **a** : a device for clutching an object **b** : CLAMSHELL 2a — **up for grabs** : available for anyone to take, win, or settle

grab bag *n* (1855) **1** : a receptacle (as a bag) containing small articles which are to be drawn (as at a party or fair) without being seen **2** : a miscellaneous collection : POTPOURRI

grab·ble \ˈgra-bəl\ *vi* **grab·bled; grab·bling** \-b(ə-)liŋ\ [D *grabbelen,* fr. MD, freq. of *grabben*] (ca. 1580) **1** : to search with the hand : GROPE **2** : to lie or fall prone : SPRAWL — **grab·bler** \-b(ə-)lər\ *n*

grab·by \ˈgra-bē\ *adj* **grab·bi·er; -est** (1910) **1** : tending to grab : GRASPING, GREEDY ⟨~ hands⟩ ⟨taught the children not to be ~⟩ **2** : having the power to grab the attention ⟨~ ads⟩

gra·ben \ˈgrä-bən\ *n* [G, ditch, fr. OHG *grabo,* fr. *graban* to dig — more at GRAVE] (1896) : a depressed segment of the crust of the earth or a celestial body (as the moon) bounded on at least two sides by faults

[1]**grace** \ˈgrās\ *n* [ME, fr. AF, fr. L *gratia* favor, charm, thanks, fr. *gratus* pleasing, grateful; akin to Skt *gṛṇāti* he praises] (12c) **1 a** : unmerited divine assistance given humans for their regeneration or sanctification **b** : a virtue coming from God **c** : a state of sanctification enjoyed through divine grace **2 a** : APPROVAL, FAVOR ⟨stayed in his good ~*s*⟩ **b** *archaic* : MERCY, PARDON **c** : a special favor : PRIVILEGE ⟨each in his place, by right, not ~, shall rule his heritage —Rudyard Kipling⟩ **d** : disposition to or an act or instance of kindness, courtesy, or clemency **e** : a temporary exemption : REPRIEVE **3 a** : a charming or attractive trait or characteristic **b** : a pleasing appearance or effect : CHARM ⟨all the ~ of youth —John Buchan⟩ **c** : ease and suppleness of movement or bearing **4** — used as a title of address or reference for a duke, a duchess, or an archbishop **5** : a short prayer at a meal asking a blessing or giving thanks **6** *pl, cap* : three sister goddesses in Greek mythology who are the givers of charm and beauty **7** : a musical trill, turn, or appoggiatura **8 a** : sense of propriety or right ⟨had the ~ not to run for elective office —Calvin Trillin⟩ **b** : the quality or state of being considerate or thoughtful ***syn*** see MERCY

[2]**grace** *vt* **graced; grac·ing** (1585) **1** : to confer dignity or honor on **2** : ADORN, EMBELLISH ⟨graveled walks *graced* with statues —J. A. Michener⟩

grace·ful \ˈgrās-fəl\ *adj* (1557) : displaying grace in form or action : pleasing or attractive in line, proportion, or movement — **grace·ful·ly** \-fə-lē\ *adv* — **grace·ful·ness** *n*

grace·less \ˈgrās-ləs\ *adj* (14c) **1** : lacking in divine grace : IMMORAL, UNREGENERATE **2 a** : lacking a sense of propriety ⟨a ~ accusation⟩ **b** : devoid of attractive qualities **3** : artistically inept or unbeautiful ⟨~ dancing⟩ — **grace·less·ly** *adv* — **grace·less·ness** *n*

grace note *n* (ca. 1823) **1** : a musical note added as an ornament; *esp* : APPOGGIATURA **2** : a small addition or embellishment

grace period *n* (1945) : a period of time beyond a due date during which a financial obligation may be met without penalty or cancellation

grac·ile \ˈgra-səl, -ˌsī(-ə)l\ *adj* [L *gracilis*] (1623) **1** : SLENDER, SLIGHT **2** : GRACEFUL **3** : of, relating to, resembling, or being a relatively small slender australopithecine (genus *Australopithecus*) characterized esp. by molars and incisors of similar size that are adapted to a diet including both plant matter and animal flesh — compare ROBUST 5 — **grac·ile·ness** *n* — **gra·cil·i·ty** \gra-ˈsi-lə-tē\ *n*

gra·ci·o·so \ˌgrä-sē-ˈō-(ˌ)sō, -(ˌ)zō\ *n, pl* **-sos** [Sp, fr. *gracioso,* adj., agreeable, amusing, fr. L *gratiosus*] (1749) : a buffoon in Spanish comedy

gra·cious \ˈgrā-shəs\ *adj* [ME, fr. AF *gracieus,* fr. L *gratiosus* enjoying favor, agreeable, fr. *gratia*] (14c) **1 a** *obs* : GODLY **b** *archaic* : PLEASING, ACCEPTABLE **2 a** : marked by kindness and courtesy ⟨a ~ host⟩ **b** : GRACEFUL **c** : marked by tact and delicacy : URBANE **d** : characterized by charm, good taste, generosity of spirit, and the tasteful leisure of wealth and good breeding ⟨~ living⟩ **3** : MERCIFUL, COMPASSIONATE — used conventionally of royalty and high nobility — **gra·cious·ly** *adv* — **gra·cious·ness** *n*

syn GRACIOUS, CORDIAL, AFFABLE, GENIAL, SOCIABLE mean markedly pleasant and easy in social intercourse. GRACIOUS implies courtesy and kindly consideration ⟨the *gracious* award winner thanked her colleagues⟩. CORDIAL stresses warmth and heartiness ⟨our host was *cordial* as he greeted us⟩. AFFABLE implies easy approachability and readiness to respond pleasantly to conversation or requests or proposals ⟨though wealthy, she was *affable* to all⟩. GENIAL stresses cheerfulness and even joviality ⟨a *genial* companion with a ready quip⟩. SOCIABLE suggests a genuine liking for the companionship of others ⟨*sociable* people who enjoy entertaining⟩.

grack·le \ˈgra-kəl\ *n* [NL *Gracula,* genus name, alter. of L *graculus* jackdaw] (1772) **1** : any of a genus (*Quiscalus* of the family Icteridae) of large American blackbirds having iridescent black plumage **2** : any of various Asian starlings (as the hill mynahs)

[1]**grad** \ˈgrad\ *n or adj* [by shortening] (ca. 1871) : GRADUATE

[2]**grad** *n* [F *grade* degree, fr. L *gradus*] (1898) : one hundredth of a right angle

[3]**grad** *abbr* graduated

gra·da·tion \grā-ˈdā-shən, grə-\ *n* (1549) **1 a** : a series forming successive stages **b** : a step or place in an ordered scale **2** : an advance by regular degrees **3** : a gradual passing from one tint or shade to another **4** : the act or process of grading **5** : ABLAUT — **gra·da·tion·al** \-shnəl, -shə-nᵊl\ *adj* — **gra·da·tion·al·ly** *adv*

[1]**grade** \ˈgrād\ *n* [L *gradus* step, degree, fr. L *gradi* to step, go; akin to Lith *gridyti* to go, wander] (1526) **1 a** (1) : a position in a scale of ranks or qualities (2) : a stage in a process **b** : a degree of severity in illness ⟨~ III carcinoma⟩ **c** : a class organized for the work of a particular year of a school course **d** : a military or naval rank **2 a** : a class of things of the same stage or degree **b** : a mark indicating a degree of accomplishment in school **c** : a standard of food quality **3 a** : the degree of inclination of a road or slope; *also* : a sloping road **b** : a datum or reference level; *esp* : ground level **4** : a domestic animal with one parent purebred and the other of inferior breeding **5** *pl* : the elementary school system — **grade·less** \-ləs\ *adj*

[2]**grade** *vb* **grad·ed; grad·ing** *vt* (1659) **1 a** : to arrange in grades : SORT **b** : to arrange in a scale or series **c** : to assign to a grade or assign a grade to **2** : to level off to a smooth horizontal or sloping surface ~ *vi* **1 a** : to form a series **b** : BLEND **2** : to be of a particular grade — **grad·able** \ˈgrā-də-bəl\ *adj*

[3]**grade** *adj* (1852) : being, involving, or yielding domestic animals of improved but not pure stock ⟨~ ewes⟩ ⟨~ breeding⟩

-grade *adj comb form* [F, fr. L *-gradus,* fr. *gradi*] : walking ⟨planti*grade*⟩

grade crossing *n* (ca. 1890) : a crossing of highways, railroad tracks, or pedestrian walks or combinations of these on the same level

grade inflation *n* (1975) : a rise in the average grade assigned to students; *esp* : the assigning of grades higher than previously assigned for given levels of achievement

grade point *n* (1951) : one of the points assigned to each course credit (as in a college) in accordance with the letter grade earned in the course — called also *quality point*

grade point average *n* (1966) : the average obtained by dividing the total number of grade points earned by the total number of credits attempted — called also *quality point average*

grad·er \ˈgrā-dər\ *n* (1832) **1** : one that grades **2** : a machine for leveling earth **3** : a pupil in a school grade ⟨a fifth ~⟩

grade school *n* (1869) : ELEMENTARY SCHOOL — **grade–school·er** \ˈgrād-ˌskü-lər\ *n*

grade separation *n* (1935) : a highway or railroad crossing using an underpass or overpass

grade up *vt* (1903) : to improve by breeding females to purebred males

gra·di·ent \ˈgrā-dē-ənt\ *n* [L *gradient-, gradiens,* prp. of *gradi*] (1835) **1 a** : the rate of regular or graded ascent or descent : INCLINATION **b** : a part sloping upward or downward **2** : change in the value of a quantity (as temperature, pressure, or concentration) with change in a given variable and esp. per unit distance in a specified direction **3** : the vector sum of the partial derivatives with respect to the three coordinate variables *x, y,* and *z* of a scalar quantity whose value varies from point to point **4** : a graded difference in physiological activity along an axis (as of the body or an embryonic field) **5** : change in response with distance from the stimulus

gra·di·om·e·ter \ˌgrā-dē-ˈä-mə-tər\ *n* [*gradient* + *-o-* + *-meter*] (1899) : an instrument for measuring the gradient of a physical quantity (as the earth's magnetic field)

[1]**grad·u·al** \ˈgra-jə-wəl, -jəl, ˈgraj-wəl\ *n, often cap* [ME, fr. ML *graduale,* fr. L *gradus* step; fr. its being sung on the steps of the altar] (15c) **1** : a book containing the choral parts of the Mass **2** : a pair of verses (as from the Psalms) proper after the Epistle in the Mass

[2]**gradual** *adj* [ML *gradualis,* fr. L *gradus*] (1658) **1** : proceeding by steps or degrees **2** : moving, changing, or developing by fine or often imperceptible degrees — **grad·u·al·ly** *adv* — **grad·u·al·ness** *n*

grad·u·al·ism \-jə-wə-ˌli-zəm, -jə-ˌli-\ *n* (1835) **1** : the policy of approaching a desired end by gradual stages **2** : the evolution of new species by gradual accumulation of small genetic changes over long periods of time; *also* : a theory or model of evolution emphasizing this — compare PUNCTUATED EQUILIBRIUM — **grad·u·al·ist** \-list\ *n or adj* — **grad·u·al·is·tic** \ˌgra-jə(-wə)-ˈlis-tik\ *adj*

grad·u·and \ˌgra-jə-ˈwand\ *n* [ML *graduandus,* gerundive of *graduare*] (1882) *Brit* : one about to graduate : a candidate for a degree

[1]**grad·u·ate** \ˈgra-jə-wət, -ˌwāt, ˈgraj-wət\ *n* (15c) **1** : a holder of an academic degree or diploma **2** : a graduated cup, cylinder, or flask

[2]**graduate** *adj* (15c) **1** : holding an academic degree or diploma **2** : of, relating to, or engaged in studies beyond the first or bachelor's degree ⟨~ school⟩ ⟨a ~ student⟩

[3]**grad·u·ate** \ˈgra-jə-ˌwāt\ *vb* **-at·ed; -at·ing** [ME, fr. ML *graduatus,* pp. of *graduare,* fr. L *gradus* step, degree] *vt* (15c) **1 a** : to grant an academic degree or diploma to **b** : to be graduated from **2 a** : to mark with degrees of measurement **b** : to divide into grades or intervals **3** : to admit to a particular standing or grade ~ *vi* **1** : to receive an academic degree or diploma **2** : to pass from one stage of experience, proficiency, or prestige to a usu. higher one **3** : to change gradually — **grad·u·a·tor** \-ˌwā-tər\ *n*

usage In the 19th century the transitive sense (1a) was prescribed; the intransitive ⟨I *graduated* from college⟩ was condemned. The intransitive prevailed nonetheless, and today it is the sense likely to be prescribed and the newer transitive sense (1b) ⟨she *graduated* high school⟩ the one condemned. All three are standard. The intransitive is currently the most common, the new transitive the least common.

graduated *adj* (1861) *of a tax* : increasing in rate with increase in taxable base : PROGRESSIVE ⟨a ~ income tax⟩

graduated cylinder *n* (1948) : a tall narrow container with a volume scale used esp. for measuring liquids

grad·u·a·tion \ˌgra-jə-ˈwā-shən\ *n* (1594) **1** : a mark on an instrument or vessel indicating degrees or quantity; *also* : these marks **2 a** : the award or acceptance of an academic degree or diploma **b** : COMMENCEMENT **3** : arrangement in degrees or ranks

Graeco- — see GRECO-

[1]**graf·fi·ti** \grə-ˈfē-(ˌ)tē, gra-, grä-\ *vt* **-tied; -ti·ing** \-(ˌ)tē-iŋ\ *also* **-ting** \-ˈfē-tiŋ\ (1964) : to draw graffiti on : to deface with graffiti ⟨~*ed* walls⟩

[2]**graffiti** *n* [It, pl. of *graffito*] (1945) : usu. unauthorized writing or drawing on a public surface
usage *Graffiti*, which also serves as the plural of *graffito*, is commonly used as a singular mass noun ⟨*graffiti* . . . was depressing people who rode the subways —*New Yorker*⟩ ⟨*graffiti* comes in various styles —S. K. Oberbeck⟩. This use is well established although not yet as well established as the mass-noun use of *data*. Use of *graffiti* as a singular count noun is still quite rare and is not standard.

graf•fi•to \grə-ˈfē-(ˌ)tō, gra-, grä-\ *n, pl* **-ti** [It, incised inscription, fr. *graffiare* to scratch, prob. fr. *grafio* stylus, fr. L *graphium*] (1851) : an inscription or drawing made on some public surface (as a rock or wall); *also* : a message or slogan written as or as if as a graffito — **graf•fi•tist** \-ˈfē-tist\ *n*

[1]**graft** \ˈgraft\ *n* [ME *graffe, grafte*, fr. AF *greffe, graife* stylus, graph, fr. ML *graphium*, fr. L, stylus, fr. Gk *grapheion*, fr. *graphein* to write — more at CARVE] (14c) **1 a** : a grafted plant **b** : SCION 1 **c** : the point of insertion of a scion upon a stock **2 a** : the act of grafting **b** : something grafted; *specif* : living tissue used in grafting

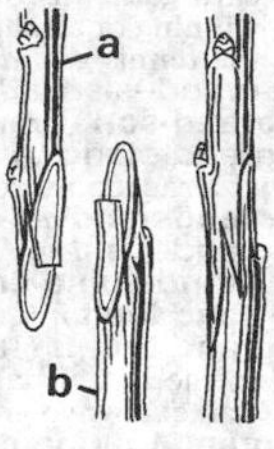

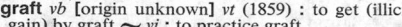

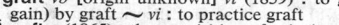

graft 1c: *a* scion, *b* stock

[2]**graft** *vt* (14c) **1 a** : to cause (a scion) to unite with a stock; *also* : to unite (plants or scion and stock) to form a graft **b** : to propagate (a plant) by grafting **2 a** : to join or unite as if by grafting **b** : to attach (a chemical unit) to a main molecular chain **3** : to implant (living tissue) surgically ~ *vi* **1** : to become grafted **2** : to perform grafting — **graft•er** *n*

[3]**graft** *n* [E dial. *graft*, vb., to work] (1853) *chiefly Brit* : WORK, LABOR

[4]**graft** *vb* [origin unknown] *vt* (1859) : to get (illicit gain) by graft ~ *vi* : to practice graft

[5]**graft** *n* (1865) : the acquisition of gain (as money) in dishonest or questionable ways; *also* : illegal or unfair gain

graft•age \ˈgraf-tij\ *n* (ca. 1895) : the principles and practice of grafting

graft–versus–host disease *n* (1965) : a potentially fatal bodily condition that results when T cells from a tissue or organ transplant and esp. a bone marrow transplant react immunologically against the recipient's antigens attacking cells and tissues

gra•ham cracker \ˈgram-, ˈgrā-əm-\ *n* [*graham flour*] (1837) : a slightly sweet cracker made of whole wheat flour

graham flour *n* [Sylvester *Graham* †1851 Am. dietary reformer] (1834) : whole wheat flour

grail \ˈgrāl\ *n* [ME *greal, graal*, fr. MF, bowl, grail, fr. ML *gradalis*] **1** *cap* : the cup or platter used according to medieval legend by Christ at the Last Supper and thereafter the object of knightly quests **2** : the object of an extended or difficult quest

[1]**grain** \ˈgrān\ *n* [ME, partly fr. AF *grain* cereal grain, fr. L *granum*; partly fr. AF *graine* seed, kermes, fr. L *grana*, pl. of *granum* — more at CORN] (14c) **1 a** (1) *obs* : a single small hard seed (2) : a seed or fruit of a cereal grass : CARYOPSIS **b** : the seeds or fruits of various food plants including the cereal grasses and in commercial and statutory usage other plants (as the soybean) **c** : plants producing grain **2 a** (1) : a small hard particle or crystal (2) : any of the particles produced in a photographic material by its development; *also* : the size of such grains in the aggregate (3) : an individual crystal in a metal **b** : a minute portion or particle **c** : the least amount possible ⟨a ~ of truth⟩ **3 a** : kermes or a scarlet dye made from it **b** : cochineal or a brilliant scarlet dye made from it **c** : a fast dye **d** *archaic* : COLOR, TINT **4 a** : a granulated surface or appearance **b** : the outer or hair side of a skin or hide **5** : a unit of weight based on the weight of a grain of wheat taken as an average of the weight of grains from the middle of the ear — see WEIGHT table **6 a** : the stratification of the wood fibers in a piece of wood **b** : a texture due to constituent particles or fibers ⟨the ~ of a rock⟩ **c** : the direction of threads in cloth **7** : tactile quality **8 a** : natural disposition : TEMPER ⟨lying goes against my ~⟩ **b** : a basic or characteristic quality **c** : a prevalent ideology or convention ⟨teaching against the ~⟩ — **grained** \ˈgrānd\ *adj* — **grain•less** *adj*

[2]**grain** *vt* (1530) **1** : INGRAIN **2** : to form into grains : GRANULATE **3** : to paint in imitation of the grain of wood or stone **4** : to feed with grain ~ *vi* : to become granular : GRANULATE — **grain•er** *n*

grain alcohol *n* (1883) : ETHANOL

grain elevator *n* (1852) : a building for elevating, storing, discharging, and sometimes processing grain

grain of salt (1647) : a skeptical attitude

grains of paradise (15c) : the pungent seeds of a West African plant (*Aframomum melegueta*) of the ginger family that are used as a spice

grain sorghum *n* (1920) : any of several sorghums cultivated primarily for grain — compare SORGO

grainy \ˈgrā-nē\ *adj* **grain•i•er; -est** (15c) **1** : resembling or having some characteristic of grain : not smooth or fine **2** *of a photograph* : appearing to be composed of grain-like particles — **grain•i•ness** *n*

[1]**gram** \ˈgram\ *n* [obs. Pg (now spelled *grão*), grain, fr. L *granum*] (1702) : any of several leguminous plants (as a chickpea) grown esp. for their seed; *also* : their seeds

[2]**gram** \ˈgram\ *n* [F *gramme*, fr. LL *gramma*, a small weight, fr. Gk *grammat-, gramma* letter, writing, a small weight, fr. *graphein* to write — more at CARVE] (1810) **1** : a metric unit of mass equal to 1/1000 kilogram and nearly equal to the mass of one cubic centimeter of water at its maximum density — see METRIC SYSTEM table **2** : the weight of a gram under the acceleration of gravity

[3]**gram** *n* [by shortening & alter.] (ca. 1934) : GRANDMOTHER

[4]**gram** *abbr* grammar; grammatical

-gram *n comb form* [L *-gramma*, fr. Gk, fr. *gramma*] : drawing : writing : record ⟨chrono*gram*⟩ ⟨tele*gram*⟩

grama \ˈgra-mə\ *n* [Sp, fr. L *gramina*, pl. of *gramen* grass] (1828) : any of several pasture grasses (genus *Bouteloua*) of the western U.S.

gram–atomic weight *n* (1927) : the mass of one mole of an element equal in grams to the atomic weight — called also *gram-atom*

gram calorie *n* (1902) : CALORIE 1a

gram equivalent *n* (ca. 1897) : the quantity of an element, group, or compound that has a mass in grams equal to the equivalent weight

gra•mer•cy \grə-ˈmər-sē\ *interj* [ME *grand mercy*, fr. AF *grand merci* great thanks] (14c) *archaic* — used to express gratitude or surprise

gram•i•ci•din \ˌgra-mə-ˈsī-dᵊn\ *n* [*gram*-positive + *-i-* + *-cide* + [1]*-in*] (1940) : any of several toxic crystalline polypeptide antibiotics produced by a soil bacterium (*Bacillus brevis*) and used against gram-positive bacteria in local infections

gra•min•e•ous \grə-ˈmi-nē-əs\ *adj* [L *gramineus*, fr. *gramin-, gramen* grass] (ca. 1658) : of or relating to a grass

gram•i•niv•o•rous \ˌgra-mə-ˈni-v(ə-)rəs\ *adj* [L *gramin-, gramen*] (1739) : feeding on grass or the seeds of grass ⟨~ locusts⟩ ⟨~ birds⟩

gram•mar \ˈgra-mər\ *n* [ME *gramere*, fr. AF *gramaire*, modif. of L *grammatica*, fr. Gk *grammatikē*, fr. fem. of *grammatikos* of letters, fr. *grammat-, gramma* — more at GRAM] (14c) **1 a** : the study of the classes of words, their inflections, and their functions and relations in the sentence **b** : a study of what is to be preferred and what avoided in inflection and syntax **2 a** : the characteristic system of inflections and syntax of a language **b** : a system of rules that defines the grammatical structure of a language **3 a** : a grammar textbook **b** : speech or writing evaluated according to its conformity to grammatical rules **4** : the principles or rules of an art, science, or technique ⟨a ~ of the theater⟩; *also* : a set of such principles or rules — **gram•mar•i•an** \grə-ˈmer-ē-ən\ *n*

grammar school *n* (14c) **1 a** : a secondary school emphasizing Latin and Greek in preparation for college **b** : a British college preparatory school **2** : a school intermediate between primary school and high school **3** : ELEMENTARY SCHOOL

gram•mat•i•cal \grə-ˈma-ti-kəl\ *adj* (1530) **1** : of or relating to grammar **2** : conforming to the rules of grammar ⟨a ~ sentence⟩ — **gram•mat•i•cal•i•ty** \-ˌma-tə-ˈka-lə-tē\ *n* — **gram•mat•i•cal•ly** \-ˈma-ti-k(ə-)lē\ *adv* — **gram•mat•i•cal•ness** \-kəl-nəs\ *n*

grammatical meaning *n* (1769) : the part of meaning that varies from one inflectional form to another (as from *plays* to *played* to *playing*) — compare LEXICAL MEANING

gramme *chiefly Brit var of* [2]GRAM

gram molecular weight *n* (ca. 1902) : the mass of one mole of a compound equal in grams to the molecular weight — called also *gram-molecule*

Gram•my \ˈgra-mē\ *service mark* — used for the annual presentation of a statuette for notable achievement in the recording industry

gram–neg•a•tive \ˈgram-ˈne-gə-tiv\ *adj* (1907) : not holding the purple dye when stained by Gram's stain — used chiefly of bacteria

gram•o•phone \ˈgra-mə-ˌfōn\ *n* [fr. *Gramophone*, a trademark] (1887) : PHONOGRAPH

gram–pos•i•tive \ˈgram-ˈpä-zə-tiv, -ˈpäz-tiv\ *adj* (1907) : holding the purple dye when stained by Gram's stain — used chiefly of bacteria

gramps \ˈgram(p)s\ *or* **gramp** \ˈgramp\ *n, pl* **gramps** [by shortening & alter.] (ca. 1900) : GRANDFATHER 1a

gram•pus \ˈgram-pəs\ *n* [alter. of ME *graspey, grapay*, fr. AF *graspeis*, fr. *gras* fat (fr. L *crassus*) + *peis* fish, fr. L *piscis* — more at CRASS, FISH] (ca. 1529) **1** : a dolphin (*Grampus griseus*) of temperate and tropical seas; *also* : any of various small cetaceans **2** : the giant whip scorpion (*Mastigoproctus giganteus*) of the southern U.S.

Gram's stain \ˈgramz-\ *or* **Gram stain** \ˈgram-\ *n* [Hans C. J. *Gram* †1938 Dan. physician] (1903) **1** : a method for the differential staining of bacteria by treatment with a watery solution of iodine and the iodide of potassium after staining with a triphenylmethane dye (as crystal violet) — called also *Gram's method* **2** : the chemicals used in Gram's stain

gram–vari•able \ˈgram-ˈver-ē-ə-bəl\ *adj* (1956) : staining irregularly or inconsistently by Gram's stain

gran \ˈgran\ *n* (1863) : GRANDMOTHER 1

grana *pl of* GRANUM

gran•a•dil•la \ˌgra-nə-ˈdi-lə, -ˈdē-(y)ə\ *n* [Sp, dim. of *granada* pomegranate, fr. LL *granata* — more at GRENADE] (1613) **1** : any of various usu. egg-shaped to football-shaped passion fruits (esp. of *Passiflora quadrangularis* and *P. edulis*) that have juicy aromatic pulp : a passionflower that produces granadillas

gra•na•ry \ˈgrā-nə-rē, ˈgra-\ *n, pl* **-ries** [L *granarium*, fr. *granum* grain] (1570) **1 a** : a storehouse for threshed grain **b** : a region producing grain in abundance **2** : a chief source or storehouse

[1]**grand** \ˈgrand\ *adj* [AF *grant, grand*, large, great, grand, fr. L *grandis*] (1548) **1 a** : having more importance than others : FOREMOST **b** : having higher rank than others bearing the same general designation ⟨the ~ champion⟩ **2 a** : INCLUSIVE, COMPREHENSIVE ⟨the ~ total of all money paid out⟩ **b** : DEFINITIVE, INCONTROVERTIBLE ⟨~ example⟩ **3** : CHIEF, PRINCIPAL **4** : large and striking in size, scope, extent, or conception ⟨~ design⟩ **5 a** : LAVISH, SUMPTUOUS ⟨a ~ celebration⟩ **b** : marked by a regal form and dignity **c** : fine or imposing in appearance or impression **d** : LOFTY, SUBLIME ⟨writing in the ~ style⟩ **6 a** : pretending to social superiority : SUPERCILIOUS **b** : intended to impress ⟨a person of ~ gestures⟩ **7** : very good : WONDERFUL ⟨a ~ time⟩ — **grand•ly** \ˈgran-(d)lē\ *adv* — **grand•ness** \ˈgran(d)-nəs\ *n*
syn GRAND, MAGNIFICENT, IMPOSING, STATELY, MAJESTIC, GRANDIOSE mean large and impressive. GRAND adds to greatness of size the implications of handsomeness and dignity ⟨a *grand* staircase⟩. MAGNIFICENT implies an impressive largeness proportionate to scale without sacrifice of dignity or good taste ⟨*magnificent* paintings⟩. IMPOSING implies great size and dignity but esp. stresses impressiveness ⟨an *imposing* edifice⟩. STATELY may suggest poised dignity, erectness of bearing, handsomeness of proportions, ceremonious deliberation of movement ⟨the *stately* procession⟩. MAJESTIC combines the implications of IMPOSING and STATELY and usu. adds a suggestion of solemn grandeur ⟨a *majestic* waterfall⟩. GRANDIOSE implies a size or scope exceeding ordinary experience ⟨*grandiose* hydroelectric projects⟩ but is most commonly applied derogatorily to inflated pretension or absurd exaggeration ⟨*grandiose* schemes⟩.

[2]**grand** *n* (1840) **1** : GRAND PIANO **2** *pl* **grand** *slang* : a thousand dollars

gran·dam \'gran-ˌdam, -dəm\ *n* [ME *graundam,* fr. AF *graund dame,* lit., great lady] (13c) **1** *or* **gran·dame** \-ˌdām\ **a** : GRANDMOTHER **b** : an old woman **2** *or* **grand·dam** \-ˌdam, -dəm\ : a dam's or sire's dam — used of an animal

grand·aunt \'grand-'ant, -'änt\ *n* (1826) : the aunt of one's father or mother — called also *great-aunt*

grand·ba·by \'gran(d)-ˌbā-bē\ *n* (1916) : an infant grandchild

grand·child \-ˌchī(-ə)ld\ *n* (1587) : the child of one's son or daughter

grand·dad *or* **gran·dad** \'gran-ˌdad\ *n* (1782) : GRANDFATHER 1a

grand·dad·dy \-ˌda-dē\ *also* **gran·dad·dy** *n* (1769) **1** : GRANDFATHER 1a **2** : one that is the first, earliest, or most venerable of its kind

grand·daugh·ter \-ˌdȯ-tər\ *n* (1611) : the daughter of one's son or daughter

grand duchess *n* (ca. 1757) **1** : a woman who rules a grand duchy in her own right **2** : the wife or widow of a grand duke

grand duchy *n* (1826) : the territory or dominion of a grand duke or grand duchess

grand duke *n* (1609) **1** : the sovereign duke of any of various European states **2** : a male descendant of a Russian czar in the male line

grande dame \'grän-'däm\ *n, pl* **grandes dames** \-'däm(z)\ *also* **grande dames** *same*\ [F, lit., great lady] (1775) **1** : a usu. elderly woman of great prestige or ability **2** : GRANDDADDY 2

gran·dee \gran-'dē\ *n* [Sp *grande,* fr. *grande,* adj., large, great, fr. L *grandis*] (1598) : a man of elevated rank or station; *esp* : a Spanish or Portuguese nobleman of the first rank

gran·deur \'gran-jər, -ˌju̇r, -ˌd(y)u̇r, -d(y)ər\ *n* [F, fr. OF, fr. *grand*] (1600) **1** : the quality or state of being grand : MAGNIFICENCE ⟨the glory that was Greece and the ~ that was Rome —E. A. Poe⟩ **2** : an instance or example of grandeur

[1]**grand·fa·ther** \'gran(d)-ˌfä-t͟hər\ *n* (15c) **1 a** : the father of one's father or mother **b** : ANCESTOR 1a **2** : GRANDDADDY 2 — **grand·fa·ther·ly** \-lē\ *adj*

[2]**grandfather** *vt* (1953) : to permit to continue under a grandfather clause

grandfather clause *n* (1900) : a clause creating an exemption based on circumstances previously existing; *esp* : a provision in several southern state constitutions designed to enfranchise poor whites and disenfranchise blacks by waiving high voting requirements for descendants of men voting before 1867

grandfather clock *n* [fr. the song *My Grandfather's Clock* (1876) by Henry C. Work †1884 Am. songwriter] (1909) : a tall pendulum clock that stands on the floor — called also *grandfather, grandfather's clock*

grand finale *n* (1800) : a climactic finale (as of an opera)

grand fir *n* (1897) : a lofty fir tree (*Abies grandis*) of the northwestern chiefly Pacific coastal region of No. America with cylindrical greenish cones and soft wood

Grand Gui·gnol \ˌgrä^{n}-gēn-'yȯl, -'yōl\ *n* [*Le Grand Guignol,* small theater in Montmartre, Paris, that specialized in such performances] (1908) : dramatic entertainment featuring the gruesome or horrible — **Grand Guignol** *adj*

gran·di·flo·ra \ˌgran-də-'flȯr-ə\ *n* [NL, fr. L *grandis* great + *flor-, flos* flower — more at BLOW] (1944) : a bush rose derived from crosses of floribunda and hybrid tea roses and characterized by production of blooms both singly and in clusters on the same plant

gran·dil·o·quence \gran-'di-lə-kwən(t)s\ *n* [prob. fr. MF, fr. L *grandiloquus* using lofty language, fr. *grandis* + *loqui* to speak] (1589) : a lofty, extravagantly colorful, pompous, or bombastic style, manner, or quality esp. in language — **gran·dil·o·quent** \-kwənt\ *adj* — **gran·dil·o·quent·ly** *adv*

gran·di·ose \'gran-dē-ˌōs, ˌgran-dē-'\ *adj* [F, fr. It *grandioso,* fr. *grande* great, fr. L *grandis*] (1838) **1** : characterized by affectation of grandeur or splendor or by absurd exaggeration **2** : impressive because of uncommon largeness, scope, effect, or grandeur ***syn*** see GRAND — **gran·di·ose·ly** *adv* — **gran·di·ose·ness** *n* — **gran·di·os·i·ty** \ˌgran-dē-'ä-sə-tē\ *n*

gran·di·o·so \ˌgrän-dē-'ō-(ˌ)sō, ˌgran-, -(ˌ)zō\ *adv or adj* [It] (1832) : in a broad and noble style — used as a direction in music

grand jury *n* (15c) : a jury that examines accusations against persons charged with crime and if the evidence warrants makes formal charges on which the accused persons are later tried — **grand juror** *n*

grand·kid \'gran(d)-ˌkid\ *n* (1927) : GRANDCHILD

Grand Lama *n* (1807) : DALAI LAMA

grand larceny *n* (1828) : larceny of property of a value greater than that fixed as constituting petit larceny

grand·ma \'gran(d)-ˌmä, -ˌmȯ; 'gra-ˌmä, -ˌmȯ\ *n* (1867) : GRANDMOTHER 1

grand mal \'grän(d)-ˌmäl, 'grä^{n}-ˌmäl, -ˌmal; 'gran(d)-ˌmal\ *n* [F, lit., great illness] (1897) : severe epilepsy characterized by seizures which are initially tonic and then become clonic and by loss of consciousness; *also* : a seizure characteristic of grand mal

grand manner *n* (1775) : an elevated or grand style (as in music or literature)

grand march *n* (1872) : an opening ceremony at a ball that consists of a march participated in by all the guests

grand marshal *n* (1951) : a person honored as the ceremonial marshal of a parade

grand master *n* (1724) **1** : the chief officer of a principal lodge in various fraternal orders (as Freemasonry) **2** : an expert player (as of chess) who has consistently scored high in international competition

grand·moth·er \'gran(d)-ˌmə-t͟hər\ *n* (15c) **1** : the mother of one's father or mother **2** : a female ancestor — **grand·moth·er·ly** \-lē\ *adj*

grand·neph·ew \'gran(d)-'nef-(ˌ)yü, *chiefly Brit* -'nev-\ *n* (ca. 1639) : a grandson of one's brother or sister

grand·niece \-'nēs\ *n* (1804) : a granddaughter of one's brother or sister

grand old man *n* (1887) : a venerated practitioner or former practitioner of an art, profession, or sport ⟨the *grand old man* of jazz⟩

grand opera *n* (1803) : opera in which the plot is serious or tragic and the entire text is set to music

grand·pa \'gran(d)-ˌpä, -ˌpȯ; 'gram-ˌpä, -ˌpȯ\ *n* (1883) : GRANDFATHER 1a

grand·par·ent \'gran(d)-ˌper-ənt\ *n* (1632) : a parent of one's father or mother — **grand·pa·ren·tal** \ˌgran(d)-pə-'ren-tᵊl\ *adj* — **grand·par·ent·hood** \'gran(d)-'per-ent-ˌhu̇d\ *n*

grand piano *n* (1803) : a piano with horizontal frame and strings — compare UPRIGHT PIANO

grand prix \'grä^{n}-'prē\ *n, pl* **grand prix** *also* **grands prix** \-'prē(z)\ *often cap G&P, often attrib* [F *Grand Prix de Paris,* an international horse race established 1863, lit., grand prize of Paris] (1863) **1** : the highest level of international equestrian competition; *also* : a contest at this level **2** : one of a series of international formula car races; *also* : a high-level competition in another sport (as sailing) that is often part of a series

grand·sire \'gran(d)-ˌsī(-ə)r\ *n* [ME] (14c) **1** *or* **grand·sir** \'gran(t)-sər\ *dial* : GRANDFATHER 1a **2** *archaic* : FOREFATHER **3** *archaic* : an aged man **4** : a dam's or sire's sire — used of an animal

grand slam *n* (1814) **1** : the winning of all the tricks in one hand of a card game (as bridge) **2** : a clean sweep or total success; *specif* : the winning of all the major or specified tournaments on a tour ⟨twice won the tennis *grand slam*⟩ **3** : a home run hit with the bases loaded — **grand–slam** *adj*

grand·son \'gran(d)-ˌsən\ *n* (1586) : the son of one's son or daughter

[1]**grand·stand** \-ˌstand\ *n* (1831) **1** : a usu. roofed stand for spectators at a racecourse or stadium **2** : AUDIENCE

[2]**grandstand** *adj* (1888) : done for show or to impress onlookers

[3]**grandstand** *vi* (1900) : to play or act so as to impress onlookers — **grand·stand·er** *n*

grand theft *n* (ca. 1930) : GRAND LARCENY

grand tour *n* (1670) **1** : an extended tour of the Continent that was formerly a usual part of the education of young British gentlemen **2** : an extensive and usu. educational tour

grand touring car *n* (1970) : a usu. 2-passenger coupe

grand·un·cle \'grand-'əŋ-kəl\ *n* (15c) : an uncle of one's father or mother

grand unified theory *n* (1978) : any of several theories that seek to unite in a single mathematical framework the electromagnetic and weak forces with the strong force or with the strong force and gravity — called also *grand unification theory*

grange \'grānj\ *n* [ME, fr. AF, fr. ML *granica,* fr. L *granum* grain] (14c) **1** *archaic* : GRANARY, BARN **2** : FARM; *esp* : a farmhouse with outbuildings **3** *cap* : one of the lodges of a national fraternal association orig. made up of farmers; *also* : the association itself

grang·er \'grān-jər\ *n* (1873) **1** *cap* : a member of a Grange **2** *chiefly West* : FARMER, HOMESTEADER

grang·er·ism \'grān-jə-ˌri-zəm\ *n* (1875) : the policy or methods of the grangers

gra·ni·ta \grə-'nē-tə\ *n* [It, fr. fem. of *granito,* pp. of *granire*] (1869) : a coarse-textured ice confection typically made from fruit

gran·ite \'gra-nət\ *n* [It *granito,* fr. pp. of *granire* to granulate, fr. *grano* grain, fr. L *granum*] (1646) **1** : a very hard natural igneous rock formation of visibly crystalline texture formed essentially of quartz and orthoclase or microcline and used esp. for building and for monuments **2** : unyielding firmness or endurance ⟨the cold ~ of Puritan formalism —V. L. Parrington⟩ — **gran·ite·like** \-ˌlīk\ *adj* — **gra·nit·ic** \gra-'ni-tik\ *adj* — **gran·it·oid** \'gra-nə-ˌtȯid\ *adj*

gran·ite·ware \'gra-nət-ˌwer\ *n* (1878) : ironware with grayish or bluish mottled enamel

gra·niv·o·rous \grə-'niv-rəs, grā-, -'ni-və-\ *adj* [L *granum* grain] (1646) : feeding on seeds or grain ⟨~ rodents⟩

gran·ny *or* **gran·nie** \'gra-nē\ *n, pl* **grannies** [by shortening & alter.] (1663) **1 a** : GRANDMOTHER 1 **b** : a fussy person **2** *chiefly Southern & south Midland* : MIDWIFE

granny dress *n* (1909) : a long loose-fitting dress usu. with high neck and long sleeves

granny flat *n* [fr. its use by parents of the family living in the house] (1965) *chiefly Brit* : an apartment that is adjacent to the main living quarters of a house

granny glasses *n pl* (1966) : spectacles with usu. small oval, round, or square lenses and metal frames

granny knot *n* (1853) : an insecure knot often made instead of a square knot — see KNOT illustration

Granny Smith \-'smith\ *n* [Maria Ann *Smith* †1870 who cultivated it near Sydney, Australia] (1895) : a tart green apple of Australian origin

grano- *comb form* [G, fr. *granit,* fr. It *granito*] : granite : granitic ⟨*granodiorite*⟩

grano·di·o·rite \ˌgra-nō-'dī-ə-ˌrīt\ *n* (1893) : a granular intrusive quartzose igneous rock intermediate between granite and quartz-containing diorite with plagioclase predominant over orthoclase — **grano·di·o·rit·ic** \-ˌdī-ə-'ri-tik\ *adj*

gra·no·la \grə-'nō-lə\ *n* [fr. *Granola,* a trademark] (1970) : a mixture typically of rolled oats and various added ingredients (as brown sugar, raisins, coconut, and nuts) that is eaten esp. for breakfast or as a snack

grano·lith·ic \ˌgra-nə-'li-thik\ *adj* (1881) : relating to or composed of a mixture of crushed granite and cement

grano·phyre \'gra-nə-ˌfī(-ə)r\ *n* [ISV, fr. *grano-* + F *-phyre* (as in *porphyre* porphyry)] (1882) : a porphyritic igneous rock chiefly of feldspar and quartz with granular groundmass — **grano·phyr·ic** \ˌgran-ə-'fir-ik\ *adj*

[1]**grant** \'grant\ *vt* [ME, fr. AF *granter, graanter,* fr. VL **credentare,* fr. L *credent-, credens,* prp. of *credere* to believe — more at CREED] (13c) **1 a** : to consent to carry out for a person : allow fulfillment of ⟨~ a request⟩ **b** : to permit as a right, privilege, or favor ⟨luggage allowances ~*ed* to passengers⟩ **2** : to bestow or transfer formally ⟨~ a scholarship to a student⟩; *specif* : to give the possession or title of by a deed **3 a** : to be willing to concede **b** : to assume to be true ⟨~*ing* that you are correct⟩ — **grant·able** \'gran-tə-bəl\ *adj* — **grant·er** \-tər\ *n* — **grant·or** \'gran-tər, -ˌtȯr; gran-'tȯr\ *n*

syn GRANT, CONCEDE, VOUCHSAFE, ACCORD, AWARD mean to give as a favor or a right. GRANT implies giving to a claimant or petitioner something that could be withheld ⟨*granted* them a new hearing⟩. CONCEDE implies yielding something reluctantly in response to a rightful or compelling claim ⟨even her critics *concede* she can be charming⟩. VOUCHSAFE implies granting something as a courtesy or an act of gracious condescension ⟨*vouchsafed* the secret to only a few chosen disciples⟩. ACCORD implies giving to another what is due or proper ⟨*accorded* all the honors befitting a head of state⟩. AWARD implies giving what is deserved or merited usu. after a careful weighing of pertinent factors ⟨*awarded* the company a huge defense contract⟩.

[2]**grant** *n* (13c) **1 :** the act of granting **2 :** something granted; *esp* **:** a gift (as of land or money) for a particular purpose **3 a :** a transfer of property by deed or writing **b :** the instrument by which such a transfer is made; *also* **:** the property so transferred **4 :** a minor territorial division of Maine, New Hampshire, or Vermont orig. granted by the state to an individual or institution

grant•ee \gran-ˈtē\ *n* (15c) **:** one to whom a grant is made

grant–in–aid \ˌgrant-ᵊn-ˈād\ *n, pl* **grants–in–aid** \ˌgran(t)s-ᵊn-ˈād\ (1851) **1 :** a grant or subsidy for public funds paid by a central to a local government in aid of a public undertaking **2 :** a grant or subsidy to a school or individual for an educational or artistic project

Grant's gazelle \ˈgran(t)s-\ *n* [James A. *Grant* †1892 Brit. explorer] (1912) **:** a large tan gazelle (*Gazella granti*) of eastern Africa from the Sudan and Ethiopia to Kenya and Uganda with long graceful horns and a white rump bordered with black

grants•man \ˈgran(t)-smən\ *n* (1966) **:** a specialist in grantsmanship

grants•man•ship \-ˌship\ *n* (1961) **:** the art of obtaining grants

granul- *or* **granuli-** *or* **granulo-** *comb form* [LL *granulum*] **:** granule ⟨*granulo*cyte⟩

gran•u•lar \ˈgran-yə-lər\ *adj* (1762) **1 :** consisting of or appearing to consist of granules **:** GRAINY **2 :** finely detailed ⟨~ reports⟩ — **gran•u•lar•i•ty** \ˌgran-yə-ˈler-ə-tē\ *n*

gran•u•late \ˈgran-yə-ˌlāt\ *vb* **-lat•ed; -lat•ing** *vt* (1666) **:** to form or crystallize into grains or granules ~ *vi* **:** to form granulations ⟨an open *granulating* wound⟩ — **gran•u•la•tor** \-ˌlā-tər\ *n*

gran•u•la•tion \ˌgran-yə-ˈlā-shən\ *n* (1612) **1 :** the act or process of granulating **:** the condition of being granulated **2 :** one of the minute red granules of new capillaries formed on the surface of a wound in healing **3 :** GRANULE 2

granulation tissue *n* (1873) **:** tissue made up of granulations that temporarily replaces lost tissue in a wound

gran•ule \ˈgran-(ˌ)yül\ *n* [LL *granulum,* dim. of L *granum* grain] (1652) **1 :** a small particle; *esp* **:** one of numerous particles forming a larger unit **2 :** any of the small short-lived brilliant spots on the sun's photosphere

gran•u•lite \ˈgran-yə-ˌlīt\ *n* (1849) **:** a granular metamorphic rock consisting mainly of feldspar and quartz — **gran•u•lit•ic** \ˌgran-yə-ˈli-tik\ *adj*

gran•u•lo•cyte \ˈgran-yə-lō-ˌsīt\ *n* [ISV] (1906) **:** a polymorphonuclear white blood cell with granule-containing cytoplasm — **gran•u•lo•cyt•ic** \ˌgran-yə-lō-ˈsi-tik\ *adj*

gran•u•lo•cy•to•poi•e•sis \ˈgran-yə-lō-ˌsī-tə-pȯi-ˈē-səs\ *n* [NL] (1944) **:** the formation of blood granulocytes typically in the bone marrow

gran•u•lo•ma \ˌgran-yə-ˈlō-mə\ *n, pl* **-mas** *also* **-ma•ta** \-mə-tə\ (1861) **:** a mass or nodule of chronically inflamed tissue with granulations that is usu. associated with an infective process — **gran•u•lo•ma•tous** \-mə-təs\ *adj*

granuloma in•gui•na•le \-ˌiŋ-gwə-ˈna-lē, -ˈnä-, -ˈnā-\ *n* [NL, lit., inguinal granuloma] (1918) **:** a sexually transmitted disease characterized by ulceration and formation of granulations on the genitalia and in the groin area and caused by a bacterium (*Calymmatobacterium granulomatis* syn. *Donovania granulomatis*)

gran•u•lo•sa cell \ˌgran-yə-ˈlō-sə-\ *n* [NL *granulosa,* fr. fem. of *granulosus* granulose] (1936) **:** one of the estrogen-secreting cells of the epithelial lining of a graafian follicle or its follicular precursor

gran•u•lose \ˈgran-yə-ˌlōs\ *adj* (1852) **:** GRANULAR; *esp* **:** having the surface roughened with granules

gran•u•lo•sis \ˌgran-yə-ˈlō-səs\ *n, pl* **-lo•ses** \-ˌsēz\ [NL] (1949) **:** any of several diseases of lepidopteran larvae marked by minute granular inclusions in infected cells and caused by viruses (genus *Granulovirus* of the family *Baculoviridae*)

gra•num \ˈgrā-nəm\ *n, pl* **gra•na** \-nə\ [NL, fr. L, grain — more at CORN] (1894) **:** one of the lamellar stacks of chlorophyll-containing thylakoids found in plant chloroplasts

grape \ˈgrāp\ *n, often attrib* [ME, fr. AF *grape* grape stalk, bunch of grapes, grape, of Gmc origin; akin to OHG *krāpfo* hook] (14c) **1 :** a smooth-skinned juicy greenish-white to deep red or purple berry eaten dried or fresh as a fruit or fermented to produce wine **2 :** any of numerous woody vines (genus *Vitis* of the family Vitaceae, the grape family) that usu. climb by tendrils, produce grapes, and are nearly cosmopolitan in cultivation **3 :** GRAPESHOT — **grape•like** \-ˌlīk\ *adj*

grape•fruit \ˈgrāp-ˌfrüt\ *n* (1814) **1** *pl* **grapefruit** *or* **grapefruits :** a large citrus fruit with a bitter yellow rind and inner skin and a highly flavored somewhat acid juicy pulp **2 :** a small roundheaded tree (*Citrus paradisi*) of the rue family that produces grapefruit

grape hyacinth *n* (1673) **:** any of several small bulbous spring-flowering herbs (genus *Muscari*) of the lily family with racemes of usu. blue flowers

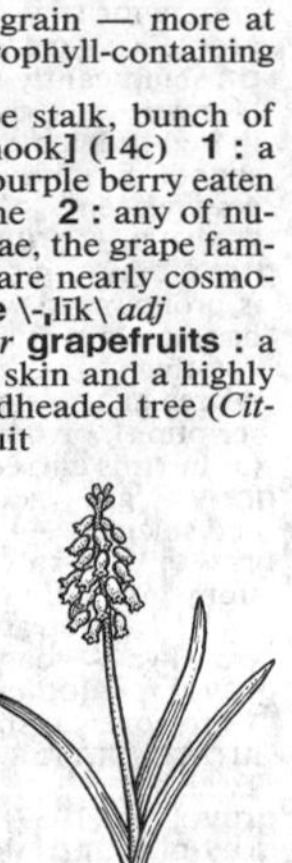

grape hyacinth

grape•shot \ˈgrāp-ˌshät\ *n* (1745) **:** an antipersonnel weapon consisting of a cluster of small iron balls shot from a cannon

grape sugar *n* (1831) **:** DEXTROSE

grape•vine \ˈgrāp-ˌvīn\ *n* (ca. 1736) **1 :** GRAPE 2 **2 a :** an informal person-to-person means of circulating information or gossip ⟨heard it through the ~⟩ **b :** a secret source of information

grapey *var of* GRAPY

[1]**graph** \ˈgraf\ *n* [short for *graphic formula*] (1886) **1 :** the collection of all points whose coordinates satisfy a given relation (as a function) **2 :** a diagram (as a series of one or more points, lines, line segments, curves, or areas) that represents the variation of a variable in comparison with that of one or more other variables **3 :** a collection of vertices and edges that join pairs of vertices

[2]**graph** *vt* (1898) **1 :** to represent by a graph **2 :** to plot on a graph

[3]**graph** *n* [prob. fr. *-graph*] (1933) **1 :** a written or printed representation of a basic unit of speech (as a phoneme or syllable); *esp* **:** GRAPHEME 1 **2 :** a single occurrence of a letter of an alphabet in any of its various shapes

-graph *n comb form* [L *-graphum,* fr. Gk *-graphon,* fr. neut. of *-graphos* written, fr. *graphein* to write — more at CARVE] **1 :** something written or drawn ⟨mono*graph*⟩ **2** [F *-graphe,* fr. LL *-graphus*] **:** instrument for making or transmitting records or images ⟨chrono*graph*⟩

graph•eme \ˈgra-ˌfēm\ *n* [*-graph* + *-eme*] (1932) **1 :** a unit (as a letter or digraph) of a writing system **2 :** the set of units of a writing system (as letters and letter combinations) that represent a phoneme — **gra•phe•mic** \gra-ˈfē-mik\ *adj* — **gra•phe•mi•cal•ly** \-mi-k(ə-)lē\ *adv*

gra•phe•mics \gra-ˈfē-miks\ *n pl but sing or pl in constr* (1951) **:** the study and analysis of a writing system in terms of graphemes

[1]**graph•ic** \ˈgra-fik\ *also* **graph•i•cal** \-fi-kəl\ *adj* [L *graphicus,* fr. Gk *graphikos,* fr. *graphein*] (1637) **1 a :** of or relating to the pictorial arts; *also* **:** PICTORIAL **b :** of, relating to, or involving such reproductive methods as those of engraving, etching, lithography, photography, serigraphy, and woodcut **c :** of or relating to the art of printing **d :** relating or according to graphics **2 :** formed by writing, drawing, or engraving **3** *usu graphic* **a :** marked by clear lifelike or vividly realistic description **b :** vividly or plainly shown or described ⟨a ~ sex scene⟩ **4** *usu graphical* **:** of, relating to, or represented by a graph **5 :** of or relating to the written or printed word or the symbols or devices used in writing or printing to represent sound or convey meaning — **graph•i•cal•ly** \-fi-k(ə-)lē\ *adv* — **graph•ic•ness** \-fik-nəs\ *n*

syn GRAPHIC, VIVID, PICTURESQUE mean giving a clear visual impression in words. GRAPHIC stresses the evoking of a clear lifelike picture ⟨a *graphic* account of combat⟩. VIVID suggests an impressing on the mind of the vigorous aliveness of something ⟨a *vivid* re-creation of an exciting event⟩. PICTURESQUE suggests the presentation of a striking or effective picture composed of features notable for their distinctness and charm ⟨a *picturesque* account of his travels⟩.

[2]**graphic** *n* (1944) **1 a :** a product of graphic art **b** *pl* **:** the graphic media **2 a :** a graphic representation (as a picture, map, or graph) used esp. for illustration **b :** a pictorial image displayed on a computer screen ⟨the program's ~*s* are impressive⟩ **c** *pl but sing or pl in constr* **:** the art or science of drawing a representation of an object on a two-dimensional surface according to mathematical rules of projection **3** *pl but sing or pl in constr* **:** the process whereby a computer displays graphics **4 :** a printed message superimposed on a television picture

-graphic *or* **-graphical** *adj comb form* [LL *-graphicus,* fr. Gk *-graphikos,* fr. *graphikos*] **:** written or transmitted in a (specified) way ⟨stylo*graphic*⟩ ⟨tele*graphic*⟩

graph•i•ca•cy \ˈgra-fə-kə-sē\ *n* [*graphic* + *-acy* (as in *literacy*)] (1965) **:** the ability to understand, use, or generate graphic images (as maps and diagrams)

graphical user interface *n* (1981) **:** a computer program designed to allow a computer user to interact easily with the computer typically by making choices from menus or groups of icons

graphic arts *n pl* (1858) **:** the fine and applied arts of representation, decoration, and writing or printing on flat surfaces together with the techniques and crafts associated with them

graphic design *n* (1935) **:** the art or profession of using design elements (as typography and images) to convey information or create an effect; *also* **:** a product of this art — **graphic designer** *n*

graphic equalizer *n* (1969) **:** an electronic device for adjusting the frequency response of an audio system by means of a number of controls each of which adjusts the response for a band centered on a particular frequency

graphic novel *n* (1978) **:** a fictional story that is presented in comic-strip format and published as a book

graphics tablet *n* (1980) **:** a device by which pictorial information is entered into a computer in a manner similar to drawing

graph•ite \ˈgra-ˌfīt\ *n* [G *Graphit,* fr. Gk *graphein* to write] (1796) **1 :** a soft black lustrous form of carbon that conducts electricity and is used in lead pencils and electrolytic anodes, as a lubricant, and as a moderator in nuclear reactors **2 :** a composite material in which carbon fibers are the reinforcing material — **gra•phit•ic** \gra-ˈfi-tik\ *adj*

graph•i•tize \ˈgra-fə-ˌtīz, -ˌfīt-ˌīz\ *vt* **-tized; -tiz•ing** (1899) **:** to convert into graphite — **graph•i•tiz•able** \-ˌtī-zə-bəl, -ˌfīt-ˌī-\ *adj* — **graph•i•ti•za•tion** \ˌgra-fə-tə-ˈzā-shən, -ˌfī-\ *n*

grapho- *comb form* [F, fr. MF, fr. Gk, fr. *graphē,* fr. *graphein* to write] **:** writing ⟨*grapho*lect⟩

graph•o•lect \ˈgra-fə-ˌlekt\ *n* [*grapho-* + *-lect* (as in *dialect*)] (1977) **:** a standard written language

gra•phol•o•gist \gra-ˈfä-lə-jist\ *n* (1885) **:** a specialist in graphology

gra•phol•o•gy \-jē\ *n* [F *graphologie,* fr. *grapho-* + *-logie* -logy] (1882) **:** the study of handwriting esp. for the purpose of character analysis — **graph•o•log•i•cal** \ˌgra-fə-ˈlä-ji-kəl\ *adj*

graph paper *n* (1927) **:** paper ruled for drawing graphs

graph theory *n* (1947) **:** a branch of mathematics concerned with the study of graphs

-graphy *n comb form* [L *-graphia,* fr. Gk, fr. *graphein*] **1 :** writing or representation in a (specified) manner or by a (specified) means or of a (specified) object ⟨steno*graphy*⟩ ⟨photo*graphy*⟩ **2 :** writing on a (specified) subject or in a (specified) field ⟨hagio*graphy*⟩

grap•nel \ˈgrap-nᵊl\ *n* [ME *grapenel,* fr. AF *grapinel,* dim. of MF *grapin,* dim. of OF *grape* hook, grape stalk, bunch of grapes — more at GRAPE] (14c) **:** a small anchor with usu. four or five flukes used esp. to recover a sunken object or to anchor a small boat — see ANCHOR illustration

grap•pa \ˈgrä-pə\ *n* [It, fr. It dial., grape stalk, of Gmc origin; akin to OHG *krāpfo* hook] (ca. 1893) **:** a dry colorless brandy distilled from fermented grape pomace

[1]**grap•ple** \ˈgra-pəl\ *n* [ME *grappel* grappling hook, fr. OF **grappelle,* dim. of *grape* hook — more at GRAPE] (1601) **1 a :** the act or an instance of grappling **b :** a hand-to-hand struggle **c :** a contest for superiority or mastery **2 :** a bucket similar to a clamshell but usu. having more jaws

[2]**grapple** *vb* **grap•pled; grap•pling** \ˈgra-p(ə-)liŋ\ *vt* (1530) **1 :** to seize with or as if with a grapple **2 :** to come to grips with **:** WRESTLE **3 :** to bind closely ~ *vi* **1 :** to make a ship fast with a grappling hook **2 :** to come to grips **3 :** to use a grapple — **grap•pler** \-p(ə-)lər\ *n*

grappling *n* (1582) **1 :** GRAPNEL **2 :** GRAPPLING HOOK

grappling hook *n* (1581) **:** a hook usu. with multiple prongs that is typically attached to a rope and is used for grabbing, grappling, or gripping — called also *grappling iron*

grap·to·lite \ˈgrap-tə-ˌlīt\ *n* [Gk *graptos* painted (fr. *graphein* to write, paint) + E *-lite* — more at CARVE] (1841) **:** any of an extinct class (Graptolithina) of hemichordate colonial marine animals of the Paleozoic era with zooids contained in conical cups along a chitinous support

grapy *or* **grap·ey** \ˈgrā-pē\ *adj* **grap·i·er; -est** (1594) **:** of or relating to grapes; *esp, of wine* **:** having the taste or aroma of fresh grapes — **grap·i·ness** \-nəs\ *n*

GRAS *abbr* generally recognized as safe; generally regarded as safe

1**grasp** \ˈgrasp\ *vb* [ME *graspen*] *vi* (14c) **:** to make the motion of seizing **:** CLUTCH ~ *vt* **1 :** to take or seize eagerly **2 :** to clasp or embrace esp. with the fingers or arms **3 :** to lay hold of with the mind **:** COMPREHEND ***syn*** see TAKE — **grasp·able** \ˈgras-pə-bəl\ *adj* — **grasp·er** *n* — **grasp at straws :** to reach for or try anything in desperation — **grasp the nettle :** to act boldly

2**grasp** *n* (1561) **1 a :** HANDLE **b :** EMBRACE **2 :** HOLD, CONTROL **3 a :** the reach of the arms **b :** the power of seizing and holding or attaining ⟨success lay within their ~⟩ **4 :** mental hold or comprehension esp. when broad ⟨a remarkable ~ of the subject⟩

grasp·ing \ˈgras-piŋ\ *adj* (1710) **:** desiring material possessions urgently and excessively and often to the point of ruthlessness ***syn*** see COVETOUS — **grasp·ing·ly** \ˈgras-piŋ-lē\ *adv* — **grasp·ing·ness** *n*

1**grass** \ˈgras\ *n, often attrib* [ME *gras,* fr. OE *græs;* akin to OHG *gras* grass, OE *grōwan* to grow] (bef. 12c) **1 :** herbage suitable or used for grazing animals **2 :** any of a large family (Gramineae syn. Poaceae) of monocotyledonous mostly herbaceous plants with jointed stems, slender sheathing leaves, and flowers borne in spikelets of bracts **3 :** land (as a lawn or a turf racetrack) covered with growing grass ⟨keep off the ~⟩ ⟨the horse had never won on ~⟩ **4** *pl* **:** leaves or plants of grass **5 :** a state or place of retirement ⟨put out to ~⟩ **6** [short for *grasshopper,* rhyming slang for *copper*] *slang Brit* **:** a police informer **7 :** electronic noise on a radarscope that takes the form of vertical lines resembling lawn grass **8 :** MARIJUANA — **grass·less** \-ləs\ *adj* — **grass·like** \-ˌlīk\ *adj*

2**grass** *vt* (ca. 1500) **1 :** to feed (livestock) on grass sometimes without grain or other concentrates **2 :** to cover with grass; *esp* **:** to seed to grass ~ *vi* **1 :** to produce grass **2** *slang Brit* **:** INFORM 2 — often used with *on*

grass carp *n* (1885) **:** an herbivorous cyprinid fish (*Ctenopharyngodon idella*) of eastern Asia that has been introduced elsewhere to control aquatic weeds — called also *white amur*

grass cloth *n* (1857) **:** a lustrous plain textile of usu. loosely woven fibers

grass court *n* (1883) **:** a tennis court with a grass surface

grass·hop·per \ˈgras-ˌhä-pər\ *n* (14c) **1 :** any of numerous plant-eating orthopterous insects (Acrididae, Tettigoniidae, and some related families) having the hind legs adapted for leaping and sometimes engaging in migratory flights in which whole regions may be stripped of vegetation **2 :** a cocktail made with crème de menthe, crème de cacao, and light cream

grasshopper sparrow *n* (1898) **:** a small American sparrow (*Ammodramus savannarum*) that is grayish brown above with a pale belly and has a high-pitched buzzing song that resembles the stridulation of grasshoppers

grass·land \-ˌland\ *n* (1682) **1 :** farmland occupied chiefly by forage plants and esp. grasses **2 a :** land on which the natural dominant plant forms are grasses and forbs **b :** an ecological community in which the characteristic plants are grasses

grass·roots \ˈgras-ˌrüts, -ˌru̇ts\ *also* **grass·root** \-ˌrüt, -ˌru̇t\ *adj* (1907) **1 :** BASIC, FUNDAMENTAL ⟨the ~ factor in deciding to buy a house⟩ **2 :** being, originating, or operating in or at the grass roots ⟨a ~ organization⟩ ⟨~ political support⟩ **3 :** not adapted from or added to an existing facility or operation **:** totally new ⟨a ~ refinery⟩

grass roots *n pl but sing or pl in constr* (1901) **1 :** the very foundation or source **2 :** the basic level of society or of an organization esp. as viewed in relation to higher or more centralized positions of power

grass tree *n* (1802) **:** any of a genus (*Xanthorrhoea*) of Australian plants of the lily family with a thick woody trunk bearing a cluster of stiff linear leaves and a terminal spike of small flowers

grass widow *n* (1528) **1** *chiefly dial* **a :** a discarded mistress **b :** a woman who has had an illegitimate child **2 a :** a woman whose husband is temporarily away from her **b :** a woman divorced or separated from her husband

grass widower *n* (1862) **1 :** a man divorced or separated from his wife **2 :** a man whose wife is temporarily away from him

grassy \ˈgra-sē\ *adj* **grass·i·er; -est** (15c) **1 a :** covered or abounding with grass ⟨~ lawns⟩ **b :** having a flavor or odor of grass ⟨~ tea⟩ ⟨wine with a ~ bouquet⟩ **2 :** resembling grass esp. in color

grat *past of* GREET

1**grate** \ˈgrāt\ *vb* **grat·ed; grat·ing** [ME, fr. AF *grater* to scratch, of Gmc origin; akin to OHG *krazzōn* to scratch] *vt* (14c) **1** *archaic* **:** ABRADE **2 :** to reduce to small particles by rubbing on something rough ⟨~ cheese⟩ **3 :** FRET, IRRITATE **4 a :** to gnash or grind noisily **b :** to cause to make a rasping sound **c :** to utter in a harsh voice ~ *vi* **1 :** to rub or rasp noisily **2 :** to cause irritation **:** JAR ⟨a voice that ~*s* on the nerves⟩ — **grat·er** *n* — **grat·ing·ly** \ˈgrā-tiŋ-lē\ *adv*

2**grate** *n* [ME, fr. ML *crata, grata* hurdle, alter. of L *cratis* — more at HURDLE] (14c) **1 a :** a barred frame for cooking over a fire **b :** a frame or bed of iron bars to hold a stove or furnace fire **c :** FIREPLACE **2 :** GRATING 2 **3** *obs* **:** CAGE, PRISON

3**grate** *vt* **grat·ed; grat·ing** (1547) **:** to furnish with a grate

G-rat·ed \ˈjē-ˈrā-təd\ *adj* (1975) **1 :** having a rating of G; *broadly* **:** relating to or characterized by a lack of violence, obscenity, or sexual explicitness ⟨a ~ novel⟩ **2 :** INNOCENT, CLEAN ⟨~ fun⟩

grate·ful \ˈgrāt-fəl\ *adj* [obs. *grate* pleasing, thankful, fr. L *gratus* — more at GRACE] (1552) **1 a :** appreciative of benefits received **b :** expressing gratitude ⟨~ thanks⟩ **2 a :** affording pleasure or contentment **:** PLEASING **b :** pleasing by reason of comfort supplied or discomfort alleviated — **grate·ful·ly** \-fə-lē\ *adv* — **grate·ful·ness** *n*

grat·i·cule \ˈgra-tə-ˌkyül\ *n* [F, fr. L *craticula* fine latticework, dim. of *cratis* wickerwork, hurdle] (1914) **1 :** RETICLE **2 :** the network of lines of latitude and longitude upon which a map is drawn

grat·i·fi·ca·tion \ˌgra-tə-fə-ˈkā-shən\ *n* (1576) **1 :** REWARD, RECOMPENSE; *esp* **:** GRATUITY **2 :** the act of gratifying **:** the state of being gratified **3 :** a source of satisfaction or pleasure

grat·i·fy \ˈgra-tə-ˌfī\ *vt* **-fied; -fy·ing** [MF *gratifier,* fr. L *gratificari* to show kindness to, fr. *gratus* + *-ificari,* pass. of *-ificare* -ify] (1539) **1** *archaic* **:** REMUNERATE, REWARD **2 :** to be a source of or give pleasure or satisfaction to ⟨it *gratified* him to have his wife wear jewels —Willa Cather⟩ **3 :** to give in to **:** INDULGE, SATISFY ⟨~ a whim⟩

grat·i·fy·ing *adj* (ca. 1611) **:** giving pleasure or satisfaction **:** PLEASING ⟨a ~ result⟩ — **grat·i·fy·ing·ly** \-iŋ-lē\ *adv*

gra·tin \ˈgra-tᵊn, ˈgrä-\ *n* [F, fr. MF, fr. *grater* to scratch] (1806) **1 :** a brown crust formed on food that has been cooked au gratin; *also* **:** a dish so cooked **2 :** UPPER CRUST ⟨the ~ of London society⟩

gra·ti·né *or* **gra·ti·née** \ˌgra-tə-ˈnā, ˌgrä-\ *adj* [F, fr. pp. of *gratiner* to cook au gratin, fr. *gratin*] (1931) **:** AU GRATIN

gra·ti·née *or* **gra·ti·nee** \ˌgra-tə-ˈnā, ˌgrä-\ *vt, past & past part* **gra·ti·néed** *or* **gra·ti·need** (1974) **:** to cook au gratin

grating *n* (1622) **1 :** a wooden or metal lattice used to close or floor an opening **2 :** a partition, covering, or frame of parallel bars or crossbars **3 :** a system of close equidistant and parallel lines or bars ruled on a polished surface to produce spectra by diffraction

gra·tis \ˈgra-təs, ˈgrā-\ *adv or adj* [ME, fr. L *gratiis, gratis,* fr. abl. pl. of *gratia* favor — more at GRACE] (15c) **:** without charge or recompense **:** FREE ⟨the food was supplied ~⟩

grat·i·tude \ˈgra-tə-ˌtüd, -ˌtyüd\ *n* [ME, fr. AF or ML; AF, fr. ML *gratitudo,* fr. L *gratus* grateful] (1523) **:** the state of being grateful **:** THANKFULNESS

gra·tu·itous \grə-ˈtü-ə-təs, -ˈtyü-\ *adj* [L *gratuitus,* fr. *gratus*] (1656) **1 a :** given unearned or without recompense **b :** not involving a return benefit, compensation, or consideration **c :** costing nothing **:** FREE **2 :** not called for by the circumstances **:** UNWARRANTED ⟨~ insolence⟩ ⟨a ~ assumption⟩ — **gra·tu·itous·ly** *adv* — **gra·tu·itous·ness** *n*

gra·tu·ity \grə-ˈtü-ə-tē, -ˈtyü-\ *n, pl* **-ities** (1540) **:** something given voluntarily or beyond obligation usu. for some service; *esp* **:** TIP

grat·u·late \ˈgra-chə-ˌlāt\ *vt* [L *gratulatus,* pp. of *gratulari* — more at CONGRATULATE] (1566) *archaic* **:** CONGRATULATE — **grat·u·la·tion** \ˌgra-chə-ˈlā-shən\ *n* — **grat·u·la·to·ry** \ˈgra-chə-lə-ˌtȯr-ē\ *adj*

grau·pel \ˈgrau̇-pəl\ *n* [G] (1889) **:** granular snow pellets — called also *soft hail*

Grau·stark \ˈgrau̇-ˌstärk, ˈgrȯ-\ *n* [*Graustark,* imaginary country in the novel *Graustark* (1901) by George B. McCutcheon †1928 Am. novelist] (1941) **:** an imaginary land of high romance; *also* **:** a highly romantic piece of writing — **Grau·stark·ian** \grau̇-ˈstär-kē-ən, grȯ-\ *adj*

gra·va·men \grə-ˈvā-mən\ *n, pl* **-va·mens** *or* **-vam·i·na** \-ˈva-mə-nə\ [LL, burden, fr. L *gravare* to burden, fr. *gravis*] (1602) **:** the material or significant part of a grievance or complaint

1**grave** \ˈgrāv\ *vt* **graved; grav·en** \ˈgrā-vən\ *or* **graved; grav·ing** [ME, fr. OE *grafan;* akin to OHG *graban* to dig, OCS *pogreti* to bury] (bef. 12c) **1** *archaic* **:** DIG, EXCAVATE **2 a :** to carve or shape with a chisel **:** SCULPTURE **b :** to carve or cut (as letters or figures) into a hard surface **:** ENGRAVE **3 :** to impress or fix (as a thought) deeply

2**grave** *n* [ME, fr. OE *græf;* akin to OHG *grab* grave, OE *grafan* to dig] (bef. 12c) **1 :** an excavation for burial of a body; *broadly* **:** a burial place **2 a :** DEATH 1a **b :** DEATH 4

3**grave** *vt* **graved; grav·ing** [ME *graven*] (15c) **:** to clean and pay with pitch ⟨~ a ship's bottom⟩

4**grave** \ˈgrāv, *in sense 5 often* ˈgräv\ *adj* **grav·er; grav·est** [MF, fr. L *gravis* heavy, grave — more at GRIEVE] (1539) **1 a** *obs* **:** AUTHORITATIVE, WEIGHTY **b :** meriting serious consideration **:** IMPORTANT ⟨~ problems⟩ **c :** likely to produce great harm or danger ⟨a ~ mistake⟩ **d :** significantly serious **:** CONSIDERABLE, GREAT ⟨~ importance⟩ **2 :** having a serious and dignified quality or demeanor ⟨a ~ and thoughtful look⟩ **3 :** drab in color **:** SOMBER **4 :** low-pitched in sound **5 a** *of an accent mark* **:** having the form ` **b :** marked with a grave accent **c :** of the variety indicated by a grave accent ***syn*** see SERIOUS — **grave·ly** *adv* — **grave·ness** *n*

5**grave** \ˈgrāv, ˈgräv\ *n* (1609) **:** a grave accent ` used to show that a vowel is pronounced with a fall of pitch (as in ancient Greek), that a vowel has a certain quality (as *è* in French), that a final *e* is stressed and close and that a final *o* is stressed and low (as in Italian), that a syllable has a degree of stress between maximum and minimum (as in phonetic transcription), or that the *e* of the English ending *-ed* is to be pronounced (as in "this cursèd day")

6**gra·ve** \ˈgrä-(ˌ)vā\ *adv or adj* [It, lit., grave, fr. L *gravis*] (1683) **:** slowly and solemnly — used as a direction in music

1**grav·el** \ˈgra-vəl\ *n* [ME, fr. AF *gravele,* dim. of *grave, greve* river bank, stony ground] (13c) **1** *obs* **:** SAND **2 a :** loose rounded fragments of rock **b :** a stratum or deposit of gravel; *also* **:** a surface covered with gravel ⟨a ~ road⟩ **3 :** small calculi in the kidneys and urinary bladder

2**gravel** *vt* **-eled** *or* **-elled; -el·ing** *or* **-el·ling** \ˈgrav-liŋ, ˈgra-və-\ (1543) **1 :** to cover or spread with gravel **2 a :** PERPLEX, CONFOUND **b :** IRRITATE, NETTLE ⟨disappointed . . . and ~*ed* him a good deal —Mark Twain⟩

3**gravel** *adj* (1939) **:** GRAVELLY 2 — used of the human voice

grav·el–blind \ˈgra-vəl-ˌblīnd\ *adj* [suggested by *sand-blind*] (1596) **:** having very weak vision

grave·less \ˈgrāv-ləs\ *adj* (1606) **1 :** not buried ⟨these ~ bones⟩ **2 :** not requiring graves **:** DEATHLESS ⟨the ~ home of the blessed⟩

grav·el·ly \ˈgrav-lē, ˈgra-və-\ *adj* (14c) **1 :** of, containing, or covered with gravel **2 :** having a rough or grating sound ⟨a ~ voice⟩

graven image *n* [*graven,* pp. of 1*grave*] (14c) **:** an object of worship carved usu. from wood or stone **:** IDOL

grav·er \ˈgrā-vər\ *n* [ME] (13c) **1 :** SCULPTOR, ENGRAVER **2 :** any of various cutting or shaving tools used in graving or in hand metal-turning

Graves' disease \ˈgrāvz-\ *n* [Robert J. *Graves* †1853 Irish physician] (1868) **:** a common form of hyperthyroidism characterized by goiter and often a slight protrusion of the eyeballs

grave·side \ˈgrāv-ˌsīd\ *n* (1838) **:** the area beside a grave ⟨at ~⟩

grave·stone \ˈgrāv-ˌstōn\ *n* (14c) **:** a burial monument

grave·yard \-ˌyärd\ *n* (1761) **1 :** CEMETERY **2 :** something resembling a graveyard ⟨an automobile ~⟩
graveyard shift *n* (1908) **:** a work shift beginning late at night (as 11 o'clock); *also* **:** the workers on such a shift
gravi- *comb form* [L, fr. *gravis*] **:** weight ⟨*gravi*metric⟩
grav·id \ˈgra-vəd\ *adj* [L *gravidus,* fr. *gravis* heavy] (1597) **1 :** PREGNANT **2 :** distended with or full of eggs ⟨a ~ fish⟩ — **gra·vid·i·ty** \gra-ˈvi-də-tē\ *n*
grav·i·da \ˈgra-və-də\ *n, pl* **-i·das** *or* **-i·dae** \-və-ˌdē\ [L, fr. fem. of *gravidus*] (1926) **:** a pregnant woman — often used with a number to indicate the number of pregnancies a woman has had ⟨a ~ 4⟩
gra·vi·me·ter \gra-ˈvi-mə-tər, ˈgra-və-ˌmē-\ *n* [F *gravimètre,* fr. *gravi-* + *-mètre* -meter] (1932) **:** a sensitive weighing instrument for measuring variations in a gravitational field (as of a planet)
gravi·met·ric \ˌgra-və-ˈme-trik\ *adj* (1850) **1 :** of or relating to measurement by weight **2 :** of or relating to variations in the gravitational field determined by means of a gravimeter — **gravi·met·ri·cal·ly** \-tri-k(ə-)lē\ *adv*
gra·vim·e·try \gra-ˈvi-mə-trē\ *n* (1858) **:** the measurement of weight, a gravitational field, or density
graving dock *n* (1840) **:** DRY DOCK
grav·i·tas \ˈgra-və-ˌtäs, -ˌtas\ *n* [L] (1869) **:** high seriousness (as in a person's bearing or in the treatment of a subject)
grav·i·tate \ˈgra-və-ˌtāt\ *vi* **-tat·ed; -tat·ing** (1692) **1 :** to move under the influence of gravitation **2 a :** to move toward something **b :** to be drawn or attracted esp. by natural inclination ⟨youngsters . . . ~ toward a strong leader —Rose Friedman⟩
grav·i·ta·tion \ˌgra-və-ˈtā-shən\ *n* (ca. 1645) **1 :** a force manifested by acceleration toward each other of two free material particles or bodies or of radiant-energy quanta **:** GRAVITY 3a(2) **2 :** the action or process of gravitating — **grav·i·ta·tion·al** \-shnəl, -shə-nᵊl\ *adj* — **grav·i·ta·tion·al·ly** *adv* — **grav·i·ta·tive** \ˈgra-və-ˌtā-tiv\ *adj*
gravitational lens *n* (1937) **:** a massive celestial object (as a galaxy) that bends and focuses the light of another more distant object (as a quasar) by gravity and that is usu. detected by the multiple images it forms of the second object
gravitational radiation *n* (1938) **:** a series of gravitational waves; *also* **:** the generation of such waves (as by a celestial object)
gravitational wave *n* (1906) **:** a hypothetical wave held to travel at the speed of light and to propagate the gravitational field
grav·i·ti·no \ˌgra-və-ˈtē-nō\ *n* [*graviton* + *-ino* (as in *neutrino*)] (1977) **:** a hypothetical fermion that is associated with the graviton in theories of supergravity
grav·i·ton \ˈgra-və-ˌtän\ *n* [ISV *gravity* + [2]*-on*] (1942) **:** a hypothetical particle with zero charge and rest mass that is held to be the quantum of the gravitational field
grav·i·ty \ˈgra-və-tē\ *n, pl* **-ties** *often attrib* [MF or L; MF *gravité,* fr. L *gravitat-, gravitas,* fr. *gravis*] (1505) **1 a :** dignity or sobriety of bearing **b :** IMPORTANCE, SIGNIFICANCE; *esp* **:** SERIOUSNESS **c :** a serious situation or problem **2 :** WEIGHT **3 a (1) :** the gravitational attraction of the mass of the earth, the moon, or a planet for bodies at or near its surface **(2) :** a fundamental physical force that is responsible for interactions which occur because of mass between particles, between aggregations of matter (as stars and planets), and between particles (as photons) and aggregations of matter, that is 10^{-39} times the strength of the strong force, and that extends over infinite distances but is dominant over macroscopic distances esp. between aggregations of matter — called also *gravitation, gravitational force;* compare ELECTROMAGNETISM 2a, STRONG FORCE, WEAK FORCE **b :** ACCELERATION OF GRAVITY **c :** SPECIFIC GRAVITY
gravity wave *n* (1877) **1 :** a wave in a fluid (as the ocean or the atmosphere) which is propagated because of the tendency of gravity to maintain a uniform level or in which gravity is the restoring force **2 :** GRAVITATIONAL WAVE
grav·lax *or* **grav·laks** \ˈgräv-ˌläks\ *n* [Sw *gravlax* or Norw *gravlaks,* fr. *grav* pit, hole, grave + Sw *lax,* Norw *laks* salmon] (1848) **:** salmon usu. cured with salt, pepper, dill, and aquavit
gra·vure \grə-ˈvyu̇r, grā-\ *n* [F, fr. *graver* to cut, engrave, fr. OF, to make a line, of Gmc origin; akin to OHG *graban* to dig, engrave — more at GRAVE] (1893) **:** PHOTOGRAVURE
gra·vy \ˈgrā-vē\ *n, pl* **gravies** [ME *gravey,* fr. AF *gravé* broth, stew] (14c) **1 :** a sauce made from the thickened and seasoned juices of cooked meat **2 a :** something additional or unexpected that is pleasing or valuable ⟨with expenses now paid, future money is pure ~ —K. Crossen⟩ **b :** unearned or illicit gain **:** [5]GRAFT
gravy train *n* (1914) **:** a much exploited source of easy money; *also* **:** GRAVY 2a
[1]**gray** *also* **grey** \ˈgrā\ *adj* [ME, fr. OE *grǣg;* akin to OHG *gris, grāo* gray] (bef. 12c) **1 a :** of the color gray **b :** tending toward gray ⟨blue-*gray* eyes⟩ **c :** dull in color **2 :** having the hair gray **:** HOARY **3 :** clothed in gray **4 a :** lacking cheer or brightness in mood, outlook, style, or flavor; *also* **:** DISMAL, GLOOMY ⟨a ~ day⟩ **b :** prosaically ordinary **:** DULL, UNINTERESTING **5 :** having an intermediate and often vaguely defined position, condition, or character ⟨an ethically ~ area⟩ — **gray·ly** *adv* — **gray·ness** *n*
[2]**gray** *also* **grey** *n* (13c) **1 :** something (as an animal, garment, cloth, or spot) of a gray color **2 :** any of a series of neutral colors ranging between black and white **3 a :** a soldier in the Confederate army during the American Civil War **b** *often cap* **:** the Confederate army
[3]**gray** *also* **grey** *vt* (14c) **:** to make gray ~ *vi* **1 :** to become gray **2 :** AGE; *also* **:** to contain an increasing percentage of older people
[4]**gray** *n* [Louis H. *Gray* †1965 Brit. radiobiologist] (1975) **:** the mks unit of absorbed dose of ionizing radiation equal to an energy of one joule per kilogram of irradiated material — abbr. *Gy*
gray·beard \ˈgrā-ˌbird\ *n* (1565) **:** an old man
gray birch *n* (1840) **1 :** a small birch (*Betula populifolia*) of northeastern No. America that has many lateral branches, grayish-white bark, triangular leaves, and soft weak wood and that occurs esp. in old fields reverting to woodland **2 :** YELLOW BIRCH
gray eminence *n* [trans. of F *Éminence grise,* nickname of Père Joseph (François Joseph du Tremblay) †1638 Fr. monk and diplomat who was confidant of Cardinal Richelieu, styled *Éminence rouge* (red eminence); fr. the colors of their respective habits] (1941) **:** a person who exercises power behind the scenes
gray·fish \ˈgrā-ˌfish\ *n* (1917) **:** DOGFISH
gray fox *n* (ca. 1679) **:** a fox (*Urocyon cinereoargenteus*) with coarse gray hair and white underparts that occurs from southern Canada to northern So. America
gray·ish \ˈgrā-ish\ *adj* (1562) **1 :** somewhat gray **2** *of a color* **:** low in saturation
gray·ling \ˈgrā-liŋ\ *n, pl* **grayling** *also* **graylings** (15c) **:** any of several freshwater salmonoid fishes (genus *Thymallus*) valued as food and sport fishes
gray literature *n* (1975) **:** written material (as a report) that is not published commercially or is not generally accessible
gray market *n* (1946) **:** a market employing irregular but not illegal methods; *esp* **:** a market that legally circumvents authorized channels of distribution to sell goods at prices lower than those intended by the manufacturer
gray matter *n* (1840) **1 :** neural tissue esp. of the brain and spinal cord that contains nerve-cell bodies as well as nerve fibers and has a brownish-gray color **2 :** BRAINS, INTELLECT
gray scale *n* (ca. 1939) **:** a series of regularly spaced tones ranging from black to white through intermediate shades of gray; *also* **:** an image composed solely of gray scale tones — **gray·scale** \ˈgrā-ˌskāl\ *adj*
gray squirrel *n* (1674) **:** a common light gray to black squirrel (*Sciurus carolinensis*) that is native to eastern No. America and has been introduced into Great Britain and So. Africa
gray·wacke \ˈgrā-ˌwak, -ˌwa-kə\ *n* [partial trans. of G *Grauwacke*] (1811) **:** a coarse usu. dark gray sandstone or fine-grained conglomerate composed of firmly cemented fragments (as of quartz or feldspar)
gray water *n* (1977) **:** household wastewater (as from a sink or bath) that does not contain serious contaminants (as from toilets or diapers)
gray whale *n* (1860) **:** a large baleen whale (*Eschrichtius robustus*) of the northern Pacific having short jaws and no dorsal fin
gray wolf *n* (1814) **:** a large usu. gray Holarctic wolf (*Canis lupus*) now rare in the more southern parts of its range — called also *timber wolf*

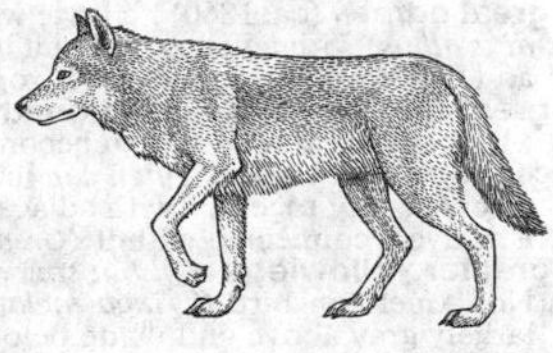
gray wolf

[1]**graze** \ˈgrāz\ *vb* **grazed; graz·ing** [ME *grasen,* fr. OE *grasian,* fr. *græs* grass] *vi* (bef. 12c) **1 :** to feed on growing herbage, attached algae, or phytoplankton **2 :** to eat small portions of food throughout the day ~ *vt* **1 a :** to crop and eat in the field **b :** to feed on the herbage of **2 a :** to put to graze **b :** to put cattle to graze on **3 :** to supply herbage for the grazing of — **graze·able** *or* **graz·able** \ˈgrā-zə-bəl\ *adj* — **graz·er** *n*
[2]**graze** *n* (1857) **1 :** an act of grazing **2 :** herbage for grazing
[3]**graze** *vb* **grazed; graz·ing** [perh. fr. [1]*graze*] *vt* (1604) **1 :** to touch lightly in passing **2 :** ABRADE, SCRATCH ⟨*grazed* her knee when she fell⟩ ~ *vi* **:** to touch or rub against something in passing
[4]**graze** *n* (1847) **:** a scraping along a surface or an abrasion made by it; *esp* **:** a superficial abrasion of the skin
gra·zier \ˈgrā-zhər\ *n* (15c) **1 :** a person who grazes cattle; *broadly* **:** RANCHER **2** *Austral* **:** a sheep raiser
grazing *n* (1517) **:** herbage or land for grazing
GRE \ˌjē-ˌär-ˈē\ *trademark* — used for a series of standardized tests for evaluating qualification for admission to graduate education programs
[1]**grease** \ˈgrēs\ *n* [ME *grese,* fr. AF *gresse, greisse, creisse,* fr. VL **crassia,* fr. L *crassus* fat] (13c) **1 a :** rendered animal fat **b :** oily matter **c :** a thick lubricant **2 :** wool as it comes from the sheep retaining the natural oils or fats — **grease·less** \ˈgrēs-ləs\ *adj* — **grease·proof** \ˈgrēs-ˈprüf\ *adj* — **in the grease** *of wool or fur* **:** in the natural uncleaned condition
[2]**grease** \ˈgrēs, ˈgrēz\ *vt* **greased; greas·ing** (14c) **1 :** to smear or daub with grease **2 :** to lubricate with grease **3 :** to soil with grease **4 :** to hasten the process or progress of; *also* **:** FACILITATE — **grease the hand of** *or* **grease the palm of :** BRIBE
grease·ball \ˈgrēs-ˌbȯl\ *n* (ca. 1922) *usu offensive* **:** a person of Hispanic or Mediterranean descent
grease monkey *n* (1928) **:** MECHANIC
grease·paint \ˈgrēs-ˌpānt\ *n* (1886) **1 :** a melted tallow or grease used in theater makeup **2 :** theater makeup
grease pencil *n* (1944) **:** a pencil in which the marking substance is pigment and grease
greaseproof paper *n* (1900) *Brit* **:** a heavy stiff waxed paper — called also *greaseproof*
greas·er \ˈgrē-zər, -sər\ *n* (1641) **1 :** one that greases **2** *usu offensive* **:** a native or inhabitant of Latin America or a Mediterranean land; *esp* **:** MEXICAN **3 :** an aggressive swaggering young white male usu. of working-class background
grease·wood \ˈgrēs-ˌwu̇d\ *n* (1838) **:** a low stiff shrub (*Sarcobatus vermiculatus*) of the goosefoot family common in alkaline soils in the western U.S.; *also* **:** any of various related or similar shrubs
greasy \ˈgrē-sē, -zē\ *adj* **greas·i·er; -est** (1514) **1 a :** smeared or soiled with grease ⟨~ clothes⟩ **b :** oily in appearance, texture, or manner ⟨his ~ smile —Jack London⟩ **c :** SLIPPERY **2 :** containing an unusual amount of grease ⟨~ food⟩ — **greas·i·ly** \-sə-lē, -zə-\ *adv* — **greas·i·ness** \-sē-nəs, -zē-\ *n*
greasy spoon *n* (1902) **:** a dingy small cheap restaurant
[1]**great** \ˈgrāt, *Southern also* ˈgre(ə)t\ *adj* [ME *grete,* fr. OE *grēat;* akin to OHG *grōz* large] (bef. 12c) **1 a :** notably large in size **:** HUGE **b :** of a kind characterized by relative largeness — used in plant and animal names **c :** ELABORATE, AMPLE ⟨~ detail⟩ **2 a :** large in number or measure **:** NUMEROUS ⟨~ multitudes⟩ **b :** PREDOMINANT ⟨the ~ majority⟩ **3 :** remarkable in magnitude, degree, or effectiveness ⟨~ bloodshed⟩ **4 :** full of emotion ⟨~ with anger⟩ **5 a :** EMINENT, DIS-

TINGUISHED ⟨a ~ poet⟩ **b** : chief or preeminent over others — often used in titles ⟨Lord *Great* Chamberlain⟩ **c** : ARISTOCRATIC, GRAND ⟨~ ladies⟩ **6** : long continued ⟨a ~ while⟩ **7** : PRINCIPAL, MAIN ⟨a reception in the ~ hall⟩ **8** : more remote in a family relationship by a single generation than a specified relative ⟨*great*-grandfather⟩ **9** : markedly superior in character or quality; *esp* : NOBLE ⟨~ of soul⟩ **10 a** : remarkably skilled ⟨~ at tennis⟩ **b** : marked by enthusiasm : KEEN ⟨~ on science fiction⟩ **11** — used as a generalized term of approval ⟨had a ~ time⟩ ⟨it was just ~⟩ — **great·ness** *n*

[2]**great** *adv* (13c) : in a great manner : SUCCESSFULLY, WELL ⟨things are going ~⟩

[3]**great** *n, pl* **great** *or* **greats** (13c) : an outstandingly superior or skillful person ⟨a tribute to the ~*s* of baseball⟩

great ape *n* (1913) : any of several large primates (as the orangutan, gorilla, or chimpanzee) that are either placed in the same family (Hominidae) as humans or are grouped in a separate family (Pongidae)

great auk *n* (ca. 1828) : an extinct large flightless auk (*Pinguinus impennis*) formerly abundant along No. Atlantic coasts

great–aunt *n* (1637) : GRANDAUNT

Great Bear *n* (1639) : URSA MAJOR

great blue heron *n* (1835) : a large slaty-blue American heron (*Ardea herodias*) with a crested head

great circle *n* (1594) : a circle formed on the surface of a sphere by the intersection of a plane that passes through the center of the sphere; *specif* : such a circle on the surface of the earth an arc of which connecting two terrestrial points constitutes the shortest distance on the earth's surface between them

great·coat \ˈgrāt-ˌkōt\ *n* (ca. 1685) : a heavy overcoat

Great Dane *n* (1774) : any of a breed of tall massive powerful smooth-coated dogs

great divide *n* [the *Great Divide,* No. Am. watershed] (1868) : a significant point of division; *esp* : DEATH

great egret *n* (ca. 1860) : a large white heron (*Ardea alba* syn. *Casmerodius albus*) with a yellow bill and black legs and feet that occurs in New and Old World temperate and tropical regions

great·en \ˈgrā-tᵊn\ *vb* **great·ened; great·en·ing** \ˈgrā-tᵊn-iŋ\ *vt* (1614) : to make greater ~ *vi* : to become greater

great·er \ˈgrā-tər\ *adj, often cap* [compar. of *great*] (1882) : consisting of a central city together with adjacent areas that are naturally or administratively connected with it ⟨*Greater* London⟩

greater yellowlegs *n pl but sing or pl in constr* (ca. 1909) : a common No. American bird (*Tringa melanoleuca*) of marsh and shore that is largely gray above and white below with black or dark gray flecks and yellow legs — compare LESSER YELLOWLEGS

greatest common divisor *n* (1851) : the largest integer or the polynomial of highest degree that is an exact divisor of each of two or more integers or polynomials — called also *greatest common factor*

great group *n* (1960) : a category below the suborder and above the subgroup in the hierarchy of soil classification comprising one or more subgroups based on similarities in horizons or characteristics of moisture or temperature — called also *great soil group*

great·heart·ed \ˈgrāt-ˌhär-təd\ *adj* (14c) **1** : characterized by bravery : COURAGEOUS **2** : GENEROUS, MAGNANIMOUS — **great·heart·ed·ly** *adv* — **great·heart·ed·ness** *n*

great horned owl *n* (1812) : a large American owl (*Bubo virginianus*) with conspicuous ear tufts

great house *n* (1633) : the main house of an estate or plantation

great laurel *n* (ca. 1736) : a large-leaved evergreen rhododendron (*Rhododendron maximum*) of eastern No. America with rosy bell-shaped flowers more or less speckled with green — called also *rosebay rhododendron*

great·ly \ˈgrāt-lē\ *adv* (13c) **1** : to a great extent or degree : very much ⟨contributed ~ to improved relations⟩ ⟨not ~ bothered⟩ **2** : in a great manner : NOBLY, MAGNANIMOUSLY ⟨a man may live ~ in the law —O. W. Holmes †1935⟩

Great Mogul *n* (1588) : the sovereign of the empire founded in India by the Moguls in the 16th century

great–nephew *n* (1581) : GRANDNEPHEW

great–niece *n* (1884) : GRANDNIECE

great northern bean *n* (1969) : a large white kidney bean

great power *n, often cap G&P* (1887) : one of the nations that figure most decisively in international affairs : SUPERPOWER

Great Pyr·e·nees \-ˈpir-ə-ˌnēz\ *n, pl* **Great Pyrenees** (1938) : any of a breed of large heavy-coated white dogs often used to guard livestock

great room *n* (1639) : a large room in a residence usu. serving several functions (as of a dining room, living room, and family room)

Great Russian *n* (1854) : RUSSIAN 1b — **Great Russian** *adj*

great seal *n* (15c) : a large seal that constitutes an emblem of sovereignty and is used esp. for the authentication of important documents

great skua *n* (ca. 1954) : a large seabird (*Stercorarius skua* syn. *Catharacta skua*) that is related to the jaegers, has dusky plumage and broad rounded wings, breeds chiefly along arctic and antarctic shores, and forages over most cold and temperate seas

great–uncle *n* (ca. 1547) : GRANDUNCLE

great vowel shift *n, often cap G&V&S* (1909) : a change in pronunciation of the long vowels of Middle English that began in the 15th century and continued into the 16th century in which the high vowels were diphthongized and the other vowels were raised

great white shark *n* (1833) : a large mackerel shark (*Carcharodon carcharias*) of warm seas that is bluish when young but becomes whitish with age and has been known to attack humans — called also *white shark*; see SHARK illustration

great year *n* (ca. 1741) : the period of about 25,800 years required for one complete cycle of the equinoxes around the ecliptic

greave \ˈgrēv\ *n* [ME *greve,* fr. AF] (14c) : armor for the shin

grebe \ˈgrēb\ *n* [F *grèbe*] (1766) : any of a family (Podicipedidae) of swimming and diving birds closely related to the loons but having lobed toes — compare DABCHICK

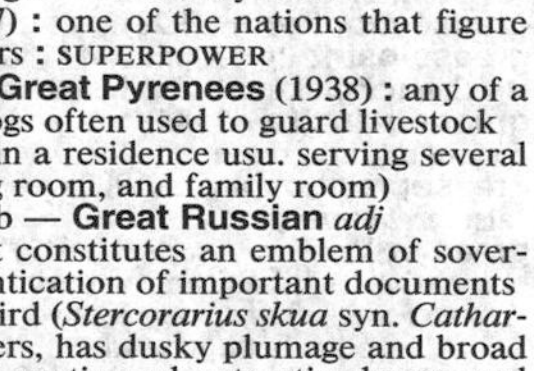

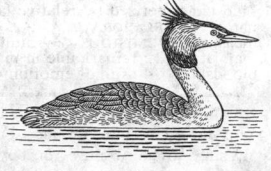

grebe

Gre·cian \ˈgrē-shən\ *adj* [ME *greciane,* ultim. fr. L *Graecia* Greece] (15c) : GREEK 1 — **Grecian** *n* — **gre·cian·ize** \-shə-ˌnīz\ *vt, often cap*

Gre·cism \ˈgrē-ˌsi-zəm\ *n* (1570) **1** : a Greek idiom **2** : a quality or style imitative of Greek art or culture

gre·cize \-ˌsīz\ *vt* **gre·cized; gre·ciz·ing** *often cap* (1692) : to make Greek or Hellenistic in character

Gre·co- \ˈgre-kō, ˈgrē-\ *or* **Grae·co-** \ˈgre-kō\ *comb form* [L *Graeco-,* fr. *Graecus*] **1** : Greece : Greeks ⟨*Grecophile*⟩ **2** : Greek and ⟨*Graeco*-Roman⟩

[1]**gree** \ˈgrē\ *n* [ME, fr. AF *gree, gré* step, degree, fr. L *gradus* — more at GRADE] (14c) *Scot* : MASTERY, SUPERIORITY

[2]**gree** *vb* **greed; gree·ing** [ME *green,* short for *agreen*] (14c) *dial* : AGREE

greed \ˈgrēd\ *n* [back-formation fr. *greedy*] (1609) : a selfish and excessive desire for more of something (as money) than is needed

greedy \ˈgrē-dē\ *adj* **greed·i·er; -est** [ME *gredy,* fr. OE *grǣdig;* akin to OHG *grātac* greedy] (bef. 12c) **1** : having a strong desire for food or drink **2** : marked by greed : having or showing a selfish desire for wealth and possessions **3** : EAGER, KEEN ⟨~ for fame⟩ ***syn*** see COVETOUS — **greed·i·ly** \ˈgrē-də-lē\ *adv* — **greed·i·ness** \ˈgrē-dē-nəs\ *n*

[1]**Greek** \ˈgrēk\ *n* [ME *Greke,* fr. OE *Grēca,* fr. L *Graecus,* fr. Gk *Graikos*] (bef. 12c) **1 a** : a native or inhabitant of ancient or modern Greece **b** : a person of Greek descent **2 a** : the language used by the Greeks from prehistoric times to the present constituting a branch of Indo-European — see INDO-EUROPEAN LANGUAGES table **b** : ancient Greek as used from the time of the earliest records to the end of the second century A.D. — see INDO-EUROPEAN LANGUAGES table **c** *often not cap* [trans. of L *Graecum* (in the medieval phrase *Graecum est; non potest legi* It is Greek; it cannot be read)] : something unintelligible ⟨it's ~ to me⟩ **3** : a member of a Greek-letter fraternity or sorority

[2]**Greek** *adj* (14c) **1** : of, relating to, or characteristic of Greece, the Greeks, or Greek ⟨~ architecture⟩ **2 a** : EASTERN ORTHODOX **b** : of or relating to an Eastern church using the Byzantine rite in Greek **c** : of or relating to the established Orthodox church of Greece **3** : of or relating to fraternities or sororities ⟨the ~ system⟩

Greek Catholic *n* (1837) **1** : a member of an Eastern rite of the Roman Catholic Church **2** : a member of an Eastern church

Greek cross *n* (1725) : a cross having an upright and a transverse shaft equal in length and intersecting at their middles — see CROSS illustration

Greek fire *n* (1788) : an incendiary composition used in warfare by the Byzantine Greeks that is said to have burst into flame on wetting

Greek·less \ˈgrēk-ləs\ *adj* (1891) : not proficient in Greek

Greek Orthodox *adj* (ca. 1900) : EASTERN ORTHODOX; *specif* : GREEK 2c

Greek Revival *n* (1918) **1** : a style of architecture in the first half of the 19th century marked by the use or imitation of Greek orders **2** : a style of decoration (as of furniture) using or imitating the decorative motifs of ancient Greece

[1]**green** \ˈgrēn\ *adj* [ME *grene,* fr. OE *grēne;* akin to OE *grōwan* to grow] (bef. 12c) **1** : of the color green **2 a** : covered by green growth or foliage ⟨~ fields⟩ **b** *of winter* : MILD, CLEMENT **c** : consisting of green plants and usu. edible herbage ⟨a ~ salad⟩ **3** : pleasantly alluring **4** : YOUTHFUL, VIGOROUS **5** : not ripened or matured ⟨~ apples⟩ **6** : FRESH, NEW **7 a** : marked by a pale, sickly, or nauseated appearance **b** : ENVIOUS 1 — used esp. in the phrase *green with envy* **8 a** : not fully processed or treated: as (1) : not aged ⟨~ liquor⟩ (2) : not dressed or tanned ⟨~ hides⟩ (3) : freshly sawed **b** : not in condition for a particular use **9 a** : deficient in training, knowledge, or experience ⟨~ recruits⟩ **b** : deficient in sophistication and savoir faire : NAIVE **c** : not fully qualified for or experienced in a particular function **10 a** *often cap* : relating to or being an environmentalist political movement **b** : concerned with or supporting environmentalism **c** : tending to preserve environmental quality (as by being recyclable, biodegradable, or nonpolluting) — **green·ish** \ˈgrē-nish\ *adj* — **green·ish·ness** *n* — **green·ly** *adv* — **green·ness** \ˈgrē(n)-nəs\ *n* — **green around the gills** : pale or sickly in appearance

[2]**green** *vi* (bef. 12c) : to become green ~ *vt* **1** : to make green **2** : REJUVENATE, REVITALIZE

[3]**green** *n* (13c) **1** : a color whose hue is somewhat less yellow than that of growing fresh grass or of the emerald or is that of the part of the spectrum lying between blue and yellow **2** : something of a green color **3** : green vegetation: as **a** *pl* : leafy parts of plants for use as decoration **b** *pl* (1) : leafy herbs (as spinach, dandelions, or Swiss chard) that are cooked as a vegetable (2) : GREEN VEGETABLES **4** : a grassy plain or plot: as **a** : a common or park in the center of a town or village **b** : PUTTING GREEN **5** : MONEY; *esp* : GREENBACKS **6** *often cap* : ENVIRONMENTALIST; *esp* : a member of an activist political party focusing on environmental and social issues — **greeny** \ˈgrē-nē\ *adj*

green alga *n* (1849) : any of a division (Chlorophyta) of green-colored algae that have chloroplasts and occur esp. in freshwater

green·back \ˈgrēn-ˌbak\ *n* (1862) : a legal-tender note issued by the U.S. government

green·back·er \-ˌba-kər\ *n* (1876) **1** *cap* : a member of a post-Civil War American political party opposing reduction in the amount of paper money in circulation **2** : one who advocates a paper currency backed only by the U.S. government — **green·back·ism** \-ˌki-zəm\ *n*

green bean *n* (1842) : a kidney bean that is used as a snap bean when the pods are colored green

green·belt \ˈgrēn-ˌbelt\ *n* (1932) : a belt of parkways, parks, or farmlands that encircles a community

Green Beret *n* [fr. the beret worn by Special Forces soldiers] (1955) : a member of the U.S. Army Special Forces

green·bri·er \-ˌbrī(-ə)r\ *n* (ca. 1785) : any of a genus (*Smilax*) of woody or herbaceous vines of the lily family; *esp* : a prickly vine (*S. rotundifolia*) of the eastern U.S. with umbels of small greenish flowers

green·bug \-ˌbəg\ *n* (1712) : a green aphid (*Schizaphis graminum*) that is a pest esp. of cereal and forage grasses

green card *n* [fr. the fact that it was formerly colored green] (1969) : an identity card attesting the permanent resident status of an alien in the U.S. — **green–carder** *n*

green–collar \ˈgrēn-ˈkä-lər\ *adj* (1990) : of, relating to, or involving actions for protecting the natural environment ⟨~ jobs⟩

green corn *n* (1645) : the young tender ears of corn

green dragon *n* (ca. 1818) : a No. American herb (*Arisaema dracontium*) of the arum family with digitate leaves, slender green spathe, and elongated spadix

greener pastures *n pl* (1970) : a better or more promising situation

green·ery \'grēn-rē, 'grē-nə-rē\ *n, pl* **-er·ies** (1797) **1** : green foliage or plants **2** : GREEN 3a

green–eyed \'grēn-ˌīd\ *adj* (1596) : JEALOUS

green–eyed monster *n* (1604) : JEALOUSY

green–field \'grēn-ˌfēld\ *n, often attrib* (1962) : land (as a potential industrial site) not previously developed or polluted

green·finch \-ˌfinch\ *n* (15c) : a very common European finch (*Carduelis chloris*) having olive-green and yellow plumage

green fingers *n pl* (1934) : GREEN THUMB

green flash *n* (1912) : a momentary green appearance of the uppermost part of the sun's disk at sunrise or sunset that results from atmospheric refraction

green–fly \'grēn-ˌflī\ *n* (ca. 1750) *Brit* : APHID; *esp* : GREEN PEACH APHID

green·gage \-ˌgāj\ *n* [*green* + Sir William *Gage* †1820 Eng. botanist] (1724) : any of several rather small rounded greenish or greenish-yellow cultivated plums

green gland *n* (ca. 1890) : one of a pair of large green glands in some crustaceans (as crayfishes) that have an excretory function and open at the bases of the larger antennae

green·gro·cer \'grēn-ˌgrō-sər, -shər\ *n* (1723) *chiefly Brit* : a retailer of fresh vegetables and fruit — **green·gro·cery** \-ˌgrō-sə-rē, -ˌgrōsh-rē\ *n*

green·head \'grēn-ˌhed\ *n* (1837) : any of several green-eyed horseflies (as *Tabanus nigrovittatus*)

green·heart \-ˌhärt\ *n* (1756) : a tropical So. American evergreen tree (*Ocotea rodiaei* syn. *Nectandra rodiaei*) of the laurel family with a hard greenish wood; *also* : its wood

green heron *n* (1785) : a small yellow-legged American heron (*Butorides virescens* syn. *B. striatus*) with a greenish back and chestnut neck and chest — called also *green-backed heron*

green·horn \-ˌhȯrn\ *n* [obs. *greenhorn* animal with green or young horns] (1682) **1** : an inexperienced or naive person **2** : a newcomer (as to a country) unacquainted with local manners and customs

¹green·house \-ˌhau̇s\ *n* (1664) **1** : a structure enclosed (as by glass) and used for the cultivation or protection of tender plants **2** : a clear plastic shell (as a canopy) covering a section of an airplane; *also* : a compartment (as for a bombardier) enclosed by such a shell

²greenhouse *adj* (1937) : of, relating to, contributing to, or caused by the greenhouse effect ⟨~ warming⟩ ⟨~ gases⟩

greenhouse effect *n* (1937) : warming of the surface and lower atmosphere of a planet (as Earth or Venus) that is caused by conversion of solar radiation into heat in a process involving selective transmission of short wave solar radiation by the atmosphere, its absorption by the planet's surface, and reradiation as infrared which is absorbed and partly reradiated back to the surface by atmospheric gases

green·ing \'grē-niŋ\ *n* (1664) : any of several green-skinned apples

green·keep·er \'grēn-ˌkē-pər\ *or* **greens·keep·er** \'grēnz-\ *n* (ca. 1730) : a person responsible for the care and upkeep of a golf course

green·let \'grēn-lət\ *n* (1831) : VIREO

green light *n* [fr. the green traffic light which signals permission to proceed] (1937) : authority or permission to proceed — **green–light** \'grēn-ˌlīt\ *vt*

green·ling \'grēn-liŋ\ *n* (ca. 1898) : any of several bony fishes (family Hexagrammidae) of the rocky coasts of the northern Pacific; *esp* : a common food and sport fish (*Hexagrammos decagrammus*)

green·mail \'grēn-ˌmāl\ *n* (1983) : the practice of buying enough of a company's stock to threaten a hostile takeover and reselling it to the company at a price above market value; *also* : the money paid for such stock — **greenmail** *vt* — **green·mail·er** \-ˌmā-lər\ *n*

green manure *n* (1842) : an herbaceous crop (as clover) plowed under while green to enrich the soil — **green–manure** *vt*

green mold *n* (1857) : a green or green-spored mold (as of the genera *Penicillium* or *Aspergillus*)

green monkey *n* (1840) : a long-tailed monkey of any of several African subspecies of a guenon (*Cercopithecus aethiops* syn. *Chloroebus aethiops*) having greenish-appearing hair and often used in medical research — called also *vervet*

green·nock·ite \'grēn-ə-ˌkīt\ *n* [Charles M. Cathcart, Lord *Greenock* †1859 Eng. soldier] (1844) : a mineral consisting of native cadmium sulfide occurring esp. in yellow translucent hexagonal crystals

green onion *n* (ca. 1740) : a young onion pulled before the bulb has enlarged and used esp. in salads

green paper *n, often cap G&P* (1967) *Brit* : a government document that proposes and invites discussion on approaches to a problem

green peach aphid *n* (1922) : a nearly cosmopolitan yellowish-green aphid (*Myzus persicae*) that is frequently a vector of plant virus diseases

green pepper *n* (1700) : a sweet pepper before it turns red at maturity

green revolution *n* (1969) : the great increase in production of food grains (as rice and wheat) due to the introduction of high-yielding varieties, to the use of pesticides, and to better management techniques

green·room \'grēn-ˌrüm, -ˌru̇m\ *n* (1701) : a room (as in a theater or studio) where performers can relax before or after appearances

green·sand \-ˌsand\ *n* (1699) : a sedimentary deposit that consists largely of dark greenish grains of glauconite often mingled with clay or sand

greens fee \'grēnz-\ *n* (1909) : a fee paid for the privilege of playing on a golf course — called also *green fee*

green·shank \'grēn-ˌshaŋk\ *n* (1766) : an Old World sandpiper (*Tringa nebularia*) with greenish legs and a slightly upturned bill

green·sick·ness \-ˌsik-nəs\ *n* (1583) : CHLOROSIS — **green·sick** *adj*

green snake *n* (1709) : either of two bright green harmless largely insectivorous No. American colubrid snakes (*Opheodrys vernalis* and *O. aestivus*)

green soap *n* (ca. 1840) : a soft soap made from vegetable oils and used esp. in the treatment of skin diseases

green·stick fracture \'grēn-ˌstik-\ *n* (ca. 1885) : a bone fracture in a young individual in which the bone is partly broken and partly bent

green·stone \-ˌstōn\ *n* (ca. 1784) **1** : NEPHRITE **2** : any of numerous usu. altered dark green compact rocks (as diorite)

green·stuff \-ˌstəf\ *n* (1851) : green vegetation used as foodstuff

green sunfish *n* (ca. 1896) : a sunfish (*Lepomis cyanellus*) of the Great Lakes region and southwestward to the Rio Grande that is largely greenish above with a blue spot on many of the scales

green·sward \-ˌswȯrd\ *n* (1600) : turf that is green with growing grass

green tea *n* (1704) : tea that is light in color and made from leaves that have not been oxidized before drying

green thumb *n* (1943) : an unusual ability to make plants grow — **green–thumbed** \'grēn-ˈthəmd\ *adj*

green turtle *n* (1657) : a large usu. herbivorous sea turtle (*Chelonia mydas*) of warm waters with a smooth greenish or olive-colored shell

green vegetable *n* (1826) : a vegetable whose foliage or foliage-bearing stalks are the chief edible part

green·wash·ing \'grēn-ˌwȯ-shiŋ, -ˌwä-\ *n* [*green* (environmentalist) + brain*washing*] (1989) : expressions of environmentalist concerns esp. as a cover for products, policies, or activities

green·way \-ˌwā\ *n* (1966) : a corridor of undeveloped land preserved for recreational use or environmental protection

Green·wich mean time \'gri-nij-, 'gre-, -nich-\ *n, often cap M&T* [*Greenwich*, England] (1863) : the mean solar time of the meridian of Greenwich used historically as the prime basis of standard time throughout the world — called also *Greenwich time*; compare COORDINATED UNIVERSAL TIME

green·wing \'grēn-ˌwiŋ\ *n* (ca. 1889) : GREEN-WINGED TEAL

green–winged teal \'grēn-ˌwiŋ(d)-\ *n* (1792) : a small Holarctic dabbling duck (*Anas crecca*) the male of which has a chestnut head with a green eye patch and a metallic green area on the wing speculum

green·wood \'grēn-ˌwu̇d\ *n* (14c) : a forest that is green with foliage

¹greet \'grēt\ *vt* [ME *greten*, fr. OE *grētan*; akin to OE *grǣtan* to weep] (bef. 12c) **1** : to address with expression of kind wishes upon meeting or arrival ⟨~*ed* guests at the door⟩ **2 a** : to meet or react to in a specified manner ⟨~*ed* him with boos⟩ **b** : to occur as a response to ⟨apathy ~*ed* the plan⟩ **3** : to appear to the perception of ⟨a surprising sight ~*ed* her eyes⟩ — **greet·er** *n*

²greet *vi* **grat** \'grat\; **gru*t*·ten** \'grə-tᵊn\ [ME *greten*, fr. OE *grētan*; akin to ON *grāta* to weep] (bef. 12c) *Scot* : WEEP, LAMENT

greet·ing *n* (bef. 12c) **1** : a salutation at meeting **2** : an expression of good wishes : REGARDS — usu. used in plural ⟨holiday ~*s*⟩

greeting card *n* (1898) : a piece of paper or thin cardboard having of a variety of shapes and formats and bearing a greeting or message of sentiment

greg·a·rine \'gre-gə-ˌrīn\ *n* [ultim. fr. L *gregarius*] (1867) : any of a subclass (Gregarinia) of parasitic vermiform sporozoan protozoans that occur esp. in insects and other invertebrates — **gregarine** *adj*

gre·gar·i·ous \gri-'ger-ē-əs\ *adj* [L *gregarius* of a flock or herd, fr. *greg-, grex* flock, herd] (1668) **1 a** : tending to associate with others of one's kind : SOCIAL **b** : marked by or indicating a liking for companionship : SOCIABLE **c** : of or relating to a social group **2 a** *of a plant* : growing in a cluster or a colony **b** : living in contiguous nests but not forming a true colony — used esp. of wasps and bees — **gre·gar·i·ous·ly** *adv* — **gre·gar·i·ous·ness** *n*

¹Gre·go·ri·an \gri-'gȯr-ē-ən\ *adj* (1592) : of or relating to Pope Gregory XIII or the Gregorian calendar

²Gregorian *adj* (1653) **1** : of or relating to Pope Gregory I **2** : of, relating to, or having the characteristics of Gregorian chant

³Gregorian *adj* [St. *Gregory* the Illuminator †332, apostle of Armenia] (1902) : of or relating to the Armenian national church

Gregorian calendar *n* (ca. 1771) : a calendar in general use introduced in 1582 by Pope Gregory XIII as a revision of the Julian calendar, adopted in Great Britain and the American colonies in 1752, marked by the suppression of 10 days or after 1700 11 days, and having leap years in every year divisible by four with the restriction that centesimal years are leap years only when divisible by 400 — see MONTH table

Gregorian chant *n* (1727) : a monodic and rhythmically free liturgical chant of the Roman Catholic Church

greige \'grā(zh)\ *adj* [F *grège* raw (of silk), fr. It *greggio*] (1926) : being in an unbleached undyed state as taken from a loom — used of textiles

grei·sen \'grī-zᵊn\ *n* [G] (1878) : a crystalline rock consisting of quartz and mica that is common in Cornwall and Saxony

grem·lin \'grem-lən\ *n* [origin unknown] (1941) : a cause of error or equipment malfunction (as in aircraft) conceived of as a small mischievous gnome

gre·nade \grə-'nād\ *n* [MF, lit., pomegranate, fr. LL *granata*, fr. L, fem. of *granatus* seedy, fr. *granum* grain — more at CORN] (1591) : a small missile that contains an explosive or a chemical agent (as tear gas, a flame producer, or a smoke producer) and that is thrown by hand or projected (as by a rifle or special launcher)

gren·a·dier \gre-nə-'dir\ *n* [F, fr. *grenade* grenade] (1676) **1 a** : a soldier who carries and throws grenades **b** : a member of a special regiment or corps formerly armed with grenades **2** : any of various deep-sea fishes (family Macrouridae) that are related to the cods and have an elongate tapering body and compressed pointed tail

gren·a·dine \ˌgre-nə-'dēn, 'gre-nə-ˌ\ *n* [F, fr. *grenade* coarse silk fabric, pomegranate] (1852) **1** : an open-weave fabric of various fibers **2** : a moderate reddish orange **3** : a syrup flavored with pomegranates and used in mixed drinks

Gren·del \'gren-dᵊl\ *n* [OE] (bef. 12c) : a monstrous man-eating descendant of Cain slain by Beowulf in the Old English poem *Beowulf*

Gresh·am's law \'gre-shəmz-\ *n* [Sir Thomas *Gresham*] (1858) : an observation in economics: when two coins are equal in debt-paying value but unequal in intrinsic value, the one having the lesser intrinsic value tends to remain in circulation and the other to be hoarded or exported as bullion; *broadly* : any process by which inferior products or practices drive out superior ones

Gret·na Green \ˌgret-nə-'grēn\ *n* [*Gretna Green*, village in Scotland] (1813) : a place where many eloping couples are married

Gre·vy's zebra \(ˌ)grā-'vēz-\ *n* [Jules *Grévy*] (1891) : a zebra (*Equus grevyi*) of eastern Africa with narrow stripes and a white belly

---

\ə\ abut \ᵊ\ kitten, F table \ər\ further \a\ ash \ā\ ace \ä\ mop, mar
\au̇\ out \ch\ chin \e\ bet \ē\ easy \g\ go \i\ hit \ī\ ice \j\ job
\ŋ\ sing \ō\ go \ȯ\ law \ȯi\ boy \th\ thin \t͟h\ the \ü\ loot \u̇\ foot
\y\ yet \zh\ vision, beige \k, ⁿ, œ, ɶ, �2 see Guide to Pronunciation

grew *past of* GROW
grewsome *var of* GRUESOME
grey *var of* GRAY
grey friar *n, often cap G&F* (14c) **:** a Franciscan friar
grey•hound \ˈgrā-ˌhau̇nd\ *n* [ME *grehound,* fr. OE *grīghund,* fr. *grīg-* (akin to ON *grey* bitch) + *hund* hound] (bef. 12c) **:** any of a breed of tall slender graceful smooth-coated dogs characterized by swiftness and keen sight and used for coursing game and racing; *also* **:** any of several related dogs — compare ITALIAN GREYHOUND
grey•lag \-ˌlag\ *n* [perh. fr. *gray* + [1]*lag*] (ca. 1713) **:** the common gray wild goose (*Anser anser*) of Europe from which most domestic breeds of geese are descended
grib•ble \ˈgri-bəl\ *n* [perh. alter. of [2]*grub*] (1838) **:** either of two small wood-boring marine isopods (*Limnoria lignorum* and *L. tripunctata*)
grid \ˈgrid\ *n* [back-formation fr. *gridiron*] (1839) **1 :** GRATING **2 a** (1) **:** a perforated or ridged metal plate used as a conductor in a storage battery (2) **:** an electrode consisting of a mesh or a spiral of fine wire in an electron tube (3) **:** a network of conductors for distribution of electric power; *also* **:** a network of radio or television stations **b :** a network of uniformly spaced horizontal and perpendicular lines (as for locating points on a map); *also* **:** something resembling such a network ⟨a road ~⟩ **c :** GRIDIRON 3; *broadly* **:** FOOTBALL **3 :** the starting positions of cars on a racecourse **4 :** a device in a photocomposer on which are located the characters to be exposed as the text is composed
grid•der \ˈgri-dər\ *n* (1928) **:** a football player
grid•dle \ˈgri-dᵊl\ *n* [ME *gredil* gridiron, fr. AF *greil, gredile,* fr. L *craticulum,* dim. of *cratis* wickerwork — more at HURDLE] (14c) **:** a flat stone or metal surface on which food is baked or fried
griddle cake *n* (1783) **:** PANCAKE
grid•iron \ˈgrid-ˌī(-ə)rn\ *n* [ME *gredire,* alter. of *gridel, gredil* griddle] (14c) **1 :** a grate for broiling food **2 :** something consisting of or covered with a network **3 :** a football field
grid•lock \-ˌläk\ *n* (1980) **1 :** a traffic jam in which a grid of intersecting streets is so completely congested that no vehicular movement is possible **2 :** a situation resembling gridlock (as in congestion or lack of movement) ⟨political ~⟩ — **gridlock** *vt*
grief \ˈgrēf\ *n* [ME *gref,* fr. AF *gref, grief* injustice, calamity, fr. *gref,* adj. heavy, grievous, fr. VL **grevis,* alter. of L *gravis*] (15c) **1** *obs* **:** GRIEVANCE 3 **2 a :** deep and poignant distress caused by or as if by bereavement **b :** a cause of such suffering **3 a :** an unfortunate outcome **:** DISASTER — used chiefly in the phrase *come to grief* **b :** MISHAP, MISADVENTURE **c :** TROUBLE, ANNOYANCE ⟨enough ~ for one day⟩ **d :** annoying or playful criticism ⟨getting ~ from his friends⟩ ***syn*** see SORROW
griev•ance \ˈgrē-vən(t)s\ *n* (14c) **1** *obs* **:** SUFFERING, DISTRESS **2 :** a cause of distress (as an unsatisfactory working condition) felt to afford reason for complaint or resistance **3 :** the formal expression of a grievance **:** COMPLAINT ***syn*** see INJUSTICE
griev•ant \-vənt\ *n* (1958) **:** one who submits a grievance for arbitration
grieve \ˈgrēv\ *vb* **grieved; griev•ing** [ME *greven,* fr. AF *grever,* fr. L *gravare* to burden, fr. *gravis* heavy, grave; akin to Gk *barys* heavy, Skt *guru*] *vt* (13c) **1 :** to cause to suffer **:** DISTRESS ⟨it ~*s* me to see him this way⟩ **2 :** to feel or show grief over ⟨*grieving* the death of her son⟩ **3 :** to submit a formal grievance concerning ⟨~ a dismissal⟩ ~ *vi* **:** to feel grief **:** SORROW — **griev•er** *n*
griev•ous \ˈgrē-vəs\ *adj* (13c) **1 :** causing or characterized by severe pain, suffering, or sorrow ⟨a ~ wound⟩ ⟨a ~ loss⟩ **2 :** OPPRESSIVE, ONEROUS ⟨~ costs of war⟩ **3 :** SERIOUS, GRAVE ⟨~ fault⟩ — **griev•ous•ly** *adv* — **griev•ous•ness** *n*
grif•fin *or* **grif•fon** *also* **gryph•on** \ˈgri-fən\ *n* [ME *griffon,* fr. AF *grif, griffun,* fr. L *gryphus,* fr. Gk *gryp-, gryps*] (14c) **:** a mythical animal typically having the head, forepart, and wings of an eagle and the body, hind legs, and tail of a lion
grif•fon \ˈgri-fən\ *n* [F, lit., griffin] (1882) **1 :** BRUSSELS GRIFFON **2 :** WIREHAIRED POINTING GRIFFON
grift \ˈgrift\ *vb* [*grift,* n., perh. alter. of *graft*] *vt* (1915) **:** to obtain (money) illicitly (as in a confidence game) ~ *vi* **:** to acquire money or property illicitly — **grift** *n* — **grift•er** *n*
grig \ˈgrig\ *n* [ME *grege*] (1566) **:** a lively lighthearted usu. small or young person
grigri *var of* GRIS-GRIS
[1]**grill** \ˈgril\ *vt* (1668) **1 :** to broil on a grill; *also* **:** to fry or toast on a griddle **2 a :** to torment as if by broiling **b :** to question intensely ⟨the police ~*ed* the suspect⟩ — **grill•er** *n*
[2]**grill** *n* [F *gril,* fr. OF *greil,* fr. L *craticulum* — more at GRIDDLE] (1685) **1 :** a cooking utensil of parallel bars on which food is exposed to heat (as from charcoal or electricity) **2 :** food that is broiled usu. on a grill — compare MIXED GRILL **3 :** a usu. informal restaurant or dining room
gril•lage \ˈgril-lij\ *n* [F, fr. *griller* to supply with grillwork, fr. *gril*] (1776) **1 :** a framework of timber or steel for support in marshy or treacherous soil **2 :** a framework for supporting a load (as a column)
grille *or* **grill** \ˈgril\ *n* [F *grille,* fr. OF *graille,* fr. L *craticula,* dim. of *cratis* wickerwork — more at HURDLE] (1686) **1 :** a grating forming a barrier or screen; *esp* **:** an ornamental one at the front end of an automobile **2 :** an opening covered with a grille **3** *usu grill* **:** a set of metallic covers for the teeth
grill•room \ˈgril-ˌrüm, -ˌru̇m\ *n* (1883) **:** GRILL 3
grill•work \ˈgril-ˌwərk\ *n* (1896) **:** work constituting or resembling a grille
grilse \ˈgrils\ *n, pl* **grilse** [ME *grills*] (15c) **:** a young Atlantic salmon returning to its native river to spawn for the first time after one winter at sea; *broadly* **:** any of various salmon at such a stage of development
grim \ˈgrim\ *adj* **grim•mer; grim•mest** [ME, fr. OE *grimm;* akin to OHG *grimm* fierce, Gk *chremetizein* to neigh] (bef. 12c) **1 :** fierce in disposition or action **:** SAVAGE **2 a :** stern or forbidding in action or appearance ⟨a ~ taskmaster⟩ **b :** SOMBER, GLOOMY **3 :** ghastly, repellent, or sinister in character ⟨a ~ tale⟩ **4 :** UNFLINCHING, UNYIELDING ⟨~ determination⟩ — **grim•ly** *adv* — **grim•ness** *n*
gri•mace \ˈgri-məs, gri-ˈmās\ *n* [F, fr. MF, alter. of *grimache,* of Gmc origin; akin to OE *grīma* mask] (1651) **:** a facial expression usu. of disgust, disapproval, or pain — **grimace** *vi* — **gri•mac•er** *n*
gri•mal•kin \gri-ˈmȯ(l)-kən, -ˈmal-\ *n* [*gray* + *malkin*] (1630) **:** a domestic cat; *esp* **:** an old female cat
grime \ˈgrīm\ *n* [MD *grime* soot, mask; akin to OE *grīma* mask] (14c) **:** soot, smut, or dirt adhering to or embedded in a surface; *broadly* **:** accumulated dirtiness and disorder — **grime** *vt*
Grimm's law \ˈgrimz-\ *n* [Jacob *Grimm*] (1838) **:** a statement in historical linguistics: Proto-Indo-European voiceless stops became Proto-Germanic voiceless fricatives (as in Greek *pyr, treis, kardia* compared with English *fire, three, heart*), Proto-Indo-European voiced stops became Proto-Germanic voiceless stops (as in Latin *duo, genus* compared with English *two, kin*), and Proto-Indo-European voiced aspirated stops became Proto-Germanic voiced fricatives (as in Sanskrit *nābhi, madhya* "mid" compared with English *navel,* Old Norse *mithr* "mid")
grim reaper *n, often cap G&R* (ca. 1927) **:** death esp. when personified as a man or skeleton with a scythe
grimy \ˈgrī-mē\ *adj* **grim•i•er; -est** (1612) **:** full of or covered with grime **:** DIRTY — **grim•i•ness** *n*
grin \ˈgrin\ *vi* **grinned; grin•ning** [ME *grennen,* fr. OE *grennian;* akin to OHG *grennen* to snarl] (bef. 12c) **:** to draw back the lips so as to show the teeth esp. in amusement or laughter; *broadly* **:** SMILE — **grin** *n* — **grin•ner** *n* — **grin•ning•ly** \ˈgri-niŋ-lē\ *adv*
grinch \ˈgrinch\ *n* [fr. the *Grinch,* character in the children's story *How the Grinch Stole Christmas* (1957) by Dr. Seuss (Theodor Geisel)] (1966) **:** KILLJOY, SPOILSPORT
[1]**grind** \ˈgrīnd\ *vb* **ground** \ˈgrau̇nd\; **grind•ing** [ME, fr. OE *grindan;* akin to L *frendere* to crush, grind] *vt* (bef. 12c) **1 :** to reduce to powder or small fragments by friction (as in a mill or with the teeth) **2 :** to wear down, polish, or sharpen by friction ⟨~ an ax⟩ **3 a :** OPPRESS, HARASS **b :** to weaken or destroy gradually — usu. used with *down* ⟨poverty *ground* her spirit down⟩ **4 a :** to press together with a rotating motion ⟨~ the teeth⟩ **b :** to rub or press harshly ⟨*ground* the cigarette out⟩ **5 :** to operate or produce by turning a crank ⟨~ a hand organ⟩ ~ *vi* **1 :** to perform the operation of grinding **2 :** to become pulverized, polished, or sharpened by friction **3 :** to move with difficulty or friction esp. so as to make a grating noise ⟨gears ~*ing*⟩ **4 :** DRUDGE; *esp* **:** to study hard ⟨~ for an exam⟩ **5 :** to rotate the hips in an erotic manner — **grind•ing•ly** \ˈgrīn-diŋ-lē\ *adv*
[2]**grind** *n* (13c) **1 a :** an act of grinding **b :** the sound of grinding **2 a :** dreary, monotonous, or difficult labor, study, or routine **b :** one who works or studies excessively **3 :** the result of grinding; *also* **:** material ground to a particular degree of fineness ⟨a drip ~ of coffee⟩ **4 :** the act of rotating the hips in an erotic manner ***syn*** see WORK
grind•er \ˈgrīn-dər\ *n* (14c) **1 a :** MOLAR **b** *pl* **:** TEETH **2 :** one that grinds **3 :** a machine or device for grinding **4 :** SUBMARINE 2 **5 :** an athlete who succeeds through hard work and determination rather than exceptional skill
grind house *n* (1927) **:** an often shabby movie theater having continuous showings esp. of pornographic or violent films
grind out *vt* (1868) **:** to produce in a mechanical way
grind•stone \ˈgrīn-ˌstōn\ *n* (13c) **1 :** MILLSTONE 1 **2 :** a flat circular stone of natural sandstone that revolves on an axle and is used for grinding, shaping, or smoothing

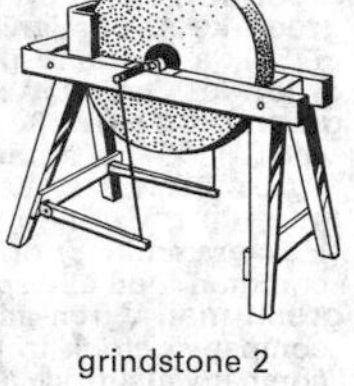
grindstone 2

grin•go \ˈgriŋ-(ˌ)gō\ *n, pl* **gringos** [Sp, alter. of *griego* Greek, stranger, fr. L *Graecus* Greek] (1849) *often disparaging* **:** a foreigner in Spain or Latin America esp. when of English or American origin; *broadly* **:** a non-Hispanic person
gri•ot \ˈgrē-ˌō\ *n* [F] (1820) **:** any of a class of musician-entertainers of western Africa whose performances include tribal histories and genealogies; *broadly* **:** STORYTELLER
[1]**grip** \ˈgrip\ *vt* **gripped; grip•ping** [ME *grippen,* fr. OE *grippan;* akin to OE *grīpan*] (bef. 12c) **1 :** to seize or hold firmly **2 :** to hold the interest of strongly ⟨a story that ~*s* the reader⟩ — **grip•per** *n* — **grip•ping•ly** \ˈgri-piŋ-lē\ *adv*
[2]**grip** *n* (bef. 12c) **1 a :** a strong or tenacious grasp **b :** strength in gripping **c :** manner or style of gripping **2 a :** a firm tenacious hold typically giving control, mastery, or understanding **b :** mental grasp **3 :** a part or device for gripping **4 :** a part by which something is grasped; *esp* **:** HANDLE **5 :** SUITCASE **6 :** STAGEHAND
[1]**gripe** \ˈgrīp\ *vb* **griped; grip•ing** [ME, fr. OE *grīpan;* akin to OHG *grīfan* to grasp, Lith *griebti*] *vt* (bef. 12c) **1** *archaic* **:** SEIZE, GRASP **2 a :** AFFLICT, DISTRESS **b :** IRRITATE, VEX **3 :** to cause pinching and spasmodic pain in the bowels of ~ *vi* **1 :** to experience gripes **2 :** to complain with grumbling — **grip•er** *n*
[2]**gripe** *n* (13c) **1** *archaic* **:** CLUTCH, GRASP; *broadly* **:** CONTROL, MASTERY **2 :** a pinching spasmodic intestinal pain — usu. used in pl. **3 :** GRIEVANCE, COMPLAINT
grip•man \ˈgrip-mən, -ˌman\ *n* (1886) **:** a cable car operator
grippe \ˈgrip\ *n* [F, lit., seizure] (1776) **:** an acute febrile contagious virus disease; *esp* **:** INFLUENZA 1
grip•sack \ˈgrip-ˌsak\ *n* (1877) **:** SUITCASE
gri•saille \gri-ˈzī, -ˈzāl\ *n* [F, fr. *gris* gray, fr. MF — more at GRIZZLE] (1848) **:** decoration in tones of a single color and esp. gray designed to produce a three-dimensional effect
Gri•sel•da \gri-ˈzel-də\ *n* [ME, fr. It] (14c) **:** a woman of humble origins in medieval legend who endures tests of wifely patience laid on her by her wellborn husband
gris•eo•ful•vin \ˌgri-zē-ō-ˈfu̇l-vən, ˌgri-sē-, -ˈfəl-\ *n* [NL *griseofulvum,* specific epithet of *Penicillium griseofulvum,* mold from which it is obtained] (1939) **:** an antibiotic $C_{17}H_{17}ClO_6$ used systematically in treating superficial fungal infections
gri•sette \gri-ˈzet\ *n* [F, grisette, cheap unbleached cloth, fr. *gris*] (1723) **1 :** a young French working-class woman **2 :** a young woman combining part-time prostitution with some other occupation
gris–gris *also* **gri•gri** \ˈgrē-(ˌ)grē\ *n, pl* **gris–gris** \-(ˌ)grēz\ *also* **grigri** [F] (1698) **:** an amulet or incantation used chiefly by people of black African ancestry
gris•ly \ˈgriz-lē\ *adj* **gris•li•er; -est** [ME, fr. OE *grislic,* fr. *gris-* (akin to OE *āgrīsan* to fear); akin to OHG *grisenlīh* terrible] (12c) **1 :** inspiring horror or intense fear ⟨houses that were dark and ~ under the blank, cold sky —D. H. Lawrence⟩ **2 :** inspiring disgust or distaste ⟨a ~ account of the fire⟩ ***syn*** see GHASTLY — **gris•li•ness** *n*

grist \ˈgrist\ *n* [ME, fr. OE *grīst;* akin to OE *grindan* to grind] (bef. 12c) **1 a :** grain or a batch of grain for grinding **b :** the product obtained from a grist of grain including the flour or meal and the grain offals **2 :** a required or usual amount **3 :** matter of interest or value forming the basis of a story or analysis **4 :** something turned to advantage or use — used esp. in the phrase *grist for one's mill*
gris•tle \ˈgri-səl, -zəl\ *n* [ME *gristil,* fr. OE *gristle;* akin to MLG *gristel* gristle] (bef. 12c) **:** CARTILAGE; *broadly* **:** tough cartilaginous, tendinous, or fibrous matter esp. in table meats
gris•tly \ˈgri-sə-lē, ˈgris-lē, ˈgriz-\ *adj* **gris•tli•er; -est** (14c) **:** consisting of or containing gristle ⟨~ steak⟩ — **gris•tli•ness** *n*
grist•mill \ˈgrist-ˌmil\ *n* (1602) **:** a mill for grinding grain
[1]**grit** \ˈgrit\ *n* [ME *grete,* fr. OE *grēot;* akin to OHG *grioz* sand] (bef. 12c) **1 a :** SAND, GRAVEL **b :** a hard sharp granule (as of sand); *also* **:** material (as many abrasives) composed of such granules **2 :** any of several sandstones **3 a :** the structure of a stone that adapts it to grinding **b :** the size of abrasive particles usu. expressed as their mesh **4 :** firmness of mind or spirit **:** unyielding courage in the face of hardship or danger **5** *cap* **:** a Liberal in Canadian politics
[2]**grit** *vb* **grit•ted; grit•ting** *vi* (1762) **:** to give forth a grating sound ~ *vt* **1 :** to cause (as one's teeth) to grind or grate **2 :** to cover or spread with grit; *esp* **:** to smooth (as marble) with a coarse abrasive
grith \ˈgrith\ *n* [ME, fr. OE, fr. ON, security] (bef. 12c) **:** peace, security, or sanctuary imposed or guaranteed in early medieval England under various special conditions
grits \ˈgrits\ *n pl but sing or pl in constr* [perh. partly fr. [1]*grit,* partly fr. dial. *grit* coarse meal, fr. OE *grytt;* akin to OE *grēot*] (1579) **:** coarsely ground hulled grain; *esp* **:** ground hominy with the germ removed
grit•ty \ˈgri-tē\ *adj* **grit•ti•er; -est** (1598) **1 :** containing or resembling grit **2 :** courageously persistent **:** PLUCKY ⟨a ~ heroine⟩ **3 :** having strong qualities of tough uncompromising realism ⟨a ~ novel⟩ — **grit•ti•ly** \ˈgri-tə-lē\ *adv* — **grit•ti•ness** \ˈgri-tē-nəs\ *n*
[1]**griz•zle** \ˈgri-zəl\ *n* [ME *grisel,* adj., gray, fr. AF, fr. *gris,* of Gmc origin; akin to OHG *grīs* gray] (1601) **1** *archaic* **:** gray hair **2 a :** a roan coat pattern or color **b :** a gray or roan animal
[2]**grizzle** *vb* **griz•zled; griz•zling** \ˈgriz-liŋ, ˈgri-zə-\ *vt* (1740) **:** to make grayish ~ *vi* **1 :** GRIPE, GRUMBLE **2 :** to become grayish
griz•zled \ˈgri-zəld\ *adj* (15c) **:** sprinkled or streaked with gray **:** GRAYING ⟨a ~ beard⟩; *also* **:** having gray hair ⟨a ~ veteran⟩
griz•zly \ˈgriz-lē\ *adj* **griz•zli•er; -est** (1594) **:** GRIZZLED
grizzly bear *n* (1791) **:** a very large brown bear (*Ursus arctos*) found from the northwestern U.S. to Alaska — called also *grizzly*
gro *abbr* gross
groan \ˈgrōn\ *vb* [ME *gronen,* fr. OE *grānian;* akin to OHG *grīnan* to growl] *vi* (bef. 12c) **1 :** to utter a deep moan indicative of pain, grief, or annoyance **2 :** to make a harsh sound (as of creaking) under sudden or prolonged strain ~ *vt* **:** to utter or express with groaning — **groan** *n*
groan•er \ˈgrō-nər\ *n* (1795) **1 :** one that groans **2 :** a stale or corny joke, observation, or story
[1]**groat** \ˈgrōt\ *n* [ME *grotes,* pl., fr. OE *grotan,* pl. of *grot;* akin to OE *grēot* grit] (12c) **1** *usu pl but sing or pl in constr* **:** hulled grain broken into fragments larger than grits **2 :** a grain (as of oats) exclusive of the hull
[2]**groat** *n* [ME *groot,* fr. MD] (14c) **:** an old British coin worth four pennies
gro•cer \ˈgrō-sər, -shər\ *n* [ME, fr. AF *groser* wholesaler, fr. *gros* coarse, wholesale — more at GROSS] (15c) **:** a dealer in staple foodstuffs, meats, produce, and dairy products and usu. household supplies
gro•cery \ˈgrōs-rē, ˈgrō-sə-; ˈgrōsh-rē\ *n, pl* **-cer•ies** (15c) **1** *pl* **:** commodities sold by a grocer — usu. sing. in Brit. usage **2 :** a grocer's store
grog \ˈgräg\ *n* [*Old Grog,* nickname of Edward Vernon †1757 Eng. admiral responsible for diluting the sailors' rum] (1756) **1 :** alcoholic liquor; *esp* **:** liquor (as rum) cut with water and now often served hot with lemon juice and sugar sometimes added **2 :** refractory materials (as crushed pottery and firebricks) used in the manufacture of refractory products (as crucibles) to reduce shrinkage in drying and firing
grog•gy \ˈgrä-gē\ *adj* **grog•gi•er; -est** [*grog*] (1832) **:** weak and unsteady on the feet or in action — **grog•gi•ly** \ˈgrä-gə-lē\ *adv* — **grog•gi•ness** \ˈgrä-gē-nəs\ *n*
gro•gram \ˈgrä-grəm, ˈgrō-\ *n* [MF *gros grain* coarse texture] (1562) **:** a coarse loosely woven fabric of silk, silk and mohair, or silk and wool — compare GROSGRAIN
grog•shop \ˈgräg-ˌshäp\ *n* (1790) *chiefly Brit* **:** a usu. low-class barroom
[1]**groin** \ˈgrȯin\ *n* [alter. of ME *grynde,* fr. OE, abyss; akin to OE *grund* ground] (ca. 1532) **1 :** the fold or depression marking the juncture of the lower abdomen and the inner part of the thigh; *also* **:** the region of this line **2 a :** the projecting curved line along which two intersecting vaults meet **b :** a rib that covers this edge **3 :** a rigid structure built out from a shore to protect the shore from erosion, to trap sand, or to direct a current for scouring a channel

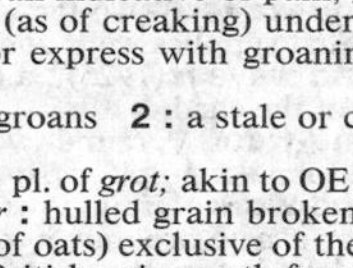
groin 2a

[2]**groin** *vt* (ca. 1816) **:** to build or equip with groins
grok \ˈgräk\ *vt* **grokked; grok•king** [coined by Robert A. Heinlein †1988 Am. author] (1961) **:** to understand profoundly and intuitively
grom•met \ˈgrä-mət, ˈgrə-\ *n* [obs. F *gormette* curb of a bridle] (1626) **1 :** a flexible loop that serves as a fastening, support, or reinforcement **2 :** an eyelet of firm material to strengthen or protect an opening or to insulate or protect something passed through it
grom•well \ˈgräm-ˌwel, -wəl\ *n* [ME *gromil,* fr. AF *grumel, gromel*] (14c) **:** any of a genus (*Lithospermum*) of plants of the borage family having smooth glossy hard white nutlets
[1]**groom** \ˈgrüm, ˈgru̇m\ *n* [ME *grom*] (14c) **1** *archaic* **:** MAN, FELLOW **2 a** (1) *archaic* **:** MANSERVANT (2) **:** one of several officers of the English royal household **b :** a person responsible for the feeding, exercising, and stabling of horses **3 :** BRIDEGROOM
[2]**groom** *vt* (1809) **1 :** to clean and maintain the appearance of (as the coat of a horse or dog) **2 :** to make neat or attractive ⟨an impeccably ~*ed* woman⟩ **3 :** to get into readiness for a specific objective **:** PREPARE ⟨was being ~*ed* as a presidential candidate⟩ ~ *vi* **:** to groom oneself
groom•er \ˈgrü-mər\ *n* (ca. 1890) **:** one who grooms (as dogs)
grooms•man \ˈgrümz-mən, ˈgru̇mz-\ *n* (1698) **:** a male friend who attends a bridegroom at his wedding
[1]**groove** \ˈgrüv\ *n* [ME *grove* pit, cave, fr. MD *groeve;* akin to OHG *gruoba* pit, cave, OE *grafan* to dig — more at GRAVE] (1659) **1 :** a long narrow channel or depression **2 a :** a fixed routine **:** RUT **b :** a situation suited to one's abilities or interests **:** NICHE **3 :** top form ⟨a great talker when he is in the ~⟩ **4 :** the middle of the strike zone in baseball where a pitch is most easily hit ⟨a fastball right in the ~⟩ **5 :** an enjoyable or exciting experience **6 :** a pronounced enjoyable rhythm
[2]**groove** *vb* **grooved; groov•ing** *vt* (1686) **1 a :** to make a groove in **b :** to join by a groove **2 :** to perfect by repeated practice ⟨*grooved* her golf swing⟩ **3 :** to throw (a pitch) in the groove ~ *vi* **1 :** to become joined or fitted by a groove **2 :** to form a groove **3 :** to enjoy oneself intensely **4 :** to interact harmoniously ⟨contemporary minds and rock ~ together —Benjamin DeMott⟩ — **groov•er** *n*
groovy \ˈgrü-vē\ *adj* **groov•i•er; -est** (ca. 1937) **1 :** MARVELOUS, WONDERFUL, EXCELLENT ⟨felt that this poetry was . . . enjoyable, not to mention ~ —R. M. Muccigrosso⟩ **2 :** HIP, TRENDY ⟨a younger and *groovier* audience —Robert MacKenzie⟩
grope \ˈgrōp\ *vb* **groped; grop•ing** [ME, fr. OE *grāpian;* akin to OE *grīpan* to seize] *vi* (bef. 12c) **1 :** to feel about blindly or uncertainly in search ⟨~ for the light switch⟩ **2 :** to look for something blindly or uncertainly ⟨~ for the right words⟩ **3 :** to feel one's way ~ *vt* **1 :** FEEL UP **2 :** to find (as one's way) by groping — **grope** *n* — **grop•er** *n*
gros•beak \ˈgrōs-ˌbēk\ *n* [part trans. of F *grosbec,* fr. *gros* thick + *bec* beak] (ca. 1678) **:** any of several finches (esp. families Cardinalidae and Fringillidae) of Europe and America having large stout conical bills
gro•schen \ˈgrō-shən, ˈgrȯ-\ *n, pl* **groschen** [G] (1925) **:** a former Austrian monetary unit equal to 1/100 schilling
gros•grain \ˈgrō-ˌgrān\ *n* [F *gros grain* coarse texture] (1868) **:** a strong close-woven corded fabric usu. of silk or rayon and often with cotton filler — compare GROGRAM
[1]**gross** \ˈgrōs\ *adj* [ME *grosse,* fr. AF & LL; AF *gros* large, thick, whole, fr. LL *grossus* coarse] (14c) **1 a** *archaic* **:** immediately obvious **b** (1) **:** glaringly noticeable usu. because of inexcusable badness or objectionableness ⟨a ~ error⟩ (2) **:** OUT-AND-OUT, UTTER ⟨a ~ injustice⟩ **c :** visible without the aid of a microscope **2 a :** BIG, BULKY; *esp* **:** excessively fat **b :** growing or spreading with excessive luxuriance **3 a :** of, relating to, or dealing with general aspects or broad distinctions **b :** consisting of an overall total exclusive of deductions ⟨~ income⟩ — compare NET **4 :** made up of material or perceptible elements **5** *archaic* **:** not fastidious in taste **:** UNDISCRIMINATING **6 a :** coarse in nature or behavior **:** UNREFINED **b :** gravely deficient in civility or decency **:** crudely vulgar ⟨merely ~, a scatological rather than a pornographic impropriety —Aldous Huxley⟩ **c :** inspiring disgust or distaste ⟨that sandwich looks ~⟩ **7 :** deficient in knowledge **:** IGNORANT, UNTUTORED ***syn*** see COARSE, FLAGRANT — **gross•ly** *adv* — **gross•ness** *n*
[2]**gross** *n* (1579) **1** *obs* **:** AMOUNT, SUM **2 :** overall total exclusive of deductions
[3]**gross** *vt* (1884) **:** to earn or bring in (an overall total) exclusive of deductions (as for taxes or expenses) — **gross•er** *n*
[4]**gross** *n, pl* **gross** [ME *gros,* prob. fr. AF *grosse* sum, whole, fr. fem. of *gros*] (14c) **:** an aggregate of 12 dozen things ⟨a ~ of pencils⟩
gross anatomy *n* (1888) **:** a branch of anatomy that deals with the macroscopic structure of tissues and organs
gross domestic product *n* (1970) **:** the gross national product excluding the value of net income earned abroad
gross national product *n* (1923) **:** the total value of the goods and services produced by the residents of a nation during a specified period (as a year)
gross–out \ˈgrōs-ˌau̇t\ *n, often attrib* (ca. 1968) **:** something inspiring disgust or distaste
gross out *vt* (1965) **:** to offend, insult, or disgust by something gross
gross ton *n* (ca. 1923) **:** LONG TON
gros•su•lar \ˈgräs-yə-lər\ *n* [NL *Grossularia,* genus name of the gooseberry] (1819) **:** a variety of garnet that is most commonly green and consists of calcium aluminum silicate
gros•su•la•rite \-lə-ˌrīt\ *n* [G *Grossularit,* fr. NL *Grossularia*] (ca. 1847) **:** GROSSULAR
grosz \ˈgrȯsh\ *n, pl* **gro•szy** \ˈgrȯ-shē\ [Pol] (1916) — see *zloty* at MONEY table
grot \ˈgrät\ *n* [MF *grotte,* fr. It *grotta*] (1506) **:** GROTTO
[1]**gro•tesque** \grō-ˈtesk\ *n* [MF & OIt; MF, fr. OIt (*pittura*) *grottesca,* lit., cave painting, fem. of *grottesco* of a cave, fr. *grotta*] (1561) **1 a :** a style of decorative art characterized by fanciful or fantastic human and animal forms often interwoven with foliage or similar figures that may distort the natural into absurdity, ugliness, or caricature **b :** a piece of work in this style **2 :** one that is grotesque **3 :** SANS SERIF
[2]**grotesque** *adj* (1603) **:** of, relating to, or having the characteristics of the grotesque: as **a :** FANCIFUL, BIZARRE **b :** absurdly incongruous **c :** departing markedly from the natural, the expected, or the typical ***syn*** see FANTASTIC — **gro•tesque•ly** *adv* — **gro•tesque•ness** *n*
gro•tes•que•rie *also* **gro•tes•que•ry** \grō-ˈtes-kə-rē\ *n, pl* **-ries** [*grotesque* + F *-erie* -ery] (ca. 1666) **1 :** something that is grotesque **2 :** the quality or state of being grotesque **:** GROTESQUENESS
grot•to \ˈgrä-(ˌ)tō\ *n, pl* **grottoes** *also* **grottos** [It *grotta, grotto,* fr. L *crypta* cavern, crypt] (1617) **1 :** CAVE **2 :** an artificial recess or structure made to resemble a natural cave
grot•ty \ˈgrä-tē\ *adj* **grot•ti•er; -est** [origin unknown] (1964) *chiefly Brit* **:** wretchedly shabby **:** of poor quality; *also* **:** FILTHY, GROSS

\ə\ **abut** \ᵊ\ kitten, F table \ər\ **fur**ther \a\ **ash** \ā\ **ace** \ä\ mop, mar \au̇\ **out** \ch\ **chin** \e\ bet \ē\ **easy** \g\ **go** \i\ **hit** \ī\ **ice** \j\ **job** \ŋ\ **sing** \ō\ **go** \ȯ\ **law** \ȯi\ **boy** \th\ **thin** \t͟h\ **the** \ü\ **loot** \u̇\ **foot** \y\ yet \zh\ vision, beige \k, ⁿ, œ, ue, ʸ\ *see* Guide to Pronunciation

grouch \ˈgrau̇ch\ *n* [prob. alter. of *grutch* grudge; fr. ME *grucche, grugge,* fr. *grucchen* — more at GRUDGE] (ca. 1895) **1 a :** a fit of bad temper **b :** GRUDGE, COMPLAINT **2 :** a habitually irritable or complaining person **:** GRUMBLER — **grouch** *vi*

grouchy \ˈgrau̇-chē\ *adj* **grouch·i·er; -est** (ca. 1895) **:** given to grumbling **:** PEEVISH — **grouch·i·ly** \-chə-lē\ *adv* — **grouch·i·ness** \-chē-nəs\ *n*

[1]**ground** \ˈgrau̇nd\ *n, often attrib* [ME, fr. OE *grund;* akin to OHG *grunt* ground] (bef. 12c) **1 a :** the bottom of a body of water **b** *pl* **(1) :** SEDIMENT 1 **(2) :** ground coffee beans after brewing **2 a :** a basis for belief, action, or argument ⟨~ for complaint⟩ — often used in pl. ⟨sufficient ~*s* for divorce⟩ **b (1) :** a fundamental logical condition **(2) :** a basic metaphysical cause **3 a :** a surrounding area **:** BACKGROUND **b :** material that serves as a substratum **4 a :** the surface of the earth **b :** an area used for a particular purpose ⟨the parade ~⟩ ⟨fishing ~*s*⟩ **c** *pl* **:** the area around and belonging to a house or other building **d :** an area to be won or defended in or as if in battle **e :** an area of knowledge or special interest ⟨covered a lot of ~ in his lecture⟩ **5 a :** SOIL, EARTH **b :** a special soil **6 a :** an object that makes an electrical connection with the earth **b :** a large conducting body (as the earth) used as a common return for an electric circuit and as an arbitrary zero of potential **c :** electric connection with a ground **7 :** a football offense utilizing primarily running plays — **from the ground up 1 :** entirely new or afresh **2 :** from top to bottom **:** THOROUGHLY — **into the ground :** beyond what is necessary or tolerable **:** to exhaustion ⟨labored an issue *into the ground* —*Newsweek*⟩ — **off the ground :** in or as if in flight **:** off to a good start ⟨the program never got *off the ground*⟩ — **on the ground :** at the scene of action — **to ground 1 :** into a burrow ⟨the fox went *to ground*⟩ **2 :** into hiding ⟨might need to make a run for it and go *to ground* someplace —Edward Hoagland⟩

[2]**ground** *vt* (13c) **1 a :** to bring to or place on the ground **b :** to cause to run aground **2 a :** to provide a reason or justification for ⟨our fears about technological change may be well ~*ed* —L. K. Williams⟩ **b :** to furnish with a foundation of knowledge **:** BASE ⟨an understanding . . . that is ~*ed* in fact —Michael Kimmelman⟩ **3 :** to connect electrically with a ground **4 a :** to restrict to the ground ⟨~ a pilot⟩ **b :** to prohibit from taking part in some usual activities ⟨~*ed* her for a week⟩ **5 :** to throw (a football) intentionally to the ground to avoid being tackled for a loss ~ *vi* **1 :** to have a ground or basis **:** RELY **2 :** to run aground **3 :** to hit a grounder ⟨~*ed* back to the pitcher⟩

[3]**ground** *past and past part of* GRIND

ground ball *n* (1857) **:** a batted baseball that bounds or rolls along the ground

ground bass *n* (1696) **:** a short bass passage continually repeated below constantly changing melody and harmony

ground beetle *n* (1848) **:** any of a large cosmopolitan family (Carabidae) of soil-inhabiting usu. carnivorous often shiny black or metallic beetles commonly having fused elytra

ground·break·er \ˈgrau̇n(d)-ˌbrā-kər\ *n* (1940) **:** one that innovates **:** PIONEER

ground·break·ing \-ˌbrā-kiŋ\ *adj* (1907) **:** markedly innovative ⟨has written a ~ work⟩

ground·burst \-ˌbərst\ *n* (ca. 1951) **:** the detonation of a nuclear warhead at ground level

ground–cher·ry \ˈgrau̇n(d)-ˈcher-ē\ *n* (1807) **:** any of various chiefly New World herbs (genus *Physalis*) of the nightshade family with pulpy fruits in papery husks; *also* **:** the fruit of the ground-cherry

ground cloth *n* (1931) **:** a waterproof sheet placed on the ground for protection (as of a sleeping bag) against soil moisture

ground cover *n* (1900) **1 :** the small plants on a forest floor except young trees **2 a :** a planting of low plants (as ivy) that covers the ground in place of turf **b :** a plant adapted for use as ground cover

ground crew *n* (1934) **:** the mechanics and technicians who maintain and service an airplane

ground·ed \ˈgrau̇n-dəd\ *adj* (1958) **:** mentally and emotionally stable **:** admirably sensible, realistic, and unpretentious ⟨remains ~ despite all the praise and attention⟩

ground–effect machine *n* [fr. the lift provided by compression of air between the vehicle and the ground] (1962) **:** HOVERCRAFT

ground·er \ˈgrau̇n-dər\ *n* (1867) **:** GROUND BALL

ground·fish \ˈgrau̇n(d)-ˌfish\ *n* (1795) **:** a bottom fish; *esp* **:** a marine fish (as a cod, haddock, pollack, or flounder) of commercial importance

ground floor *n* (1601) **1 :** the floor of a building most nearly on a level with the ground — compare FIRST FLOOR **2 :** a favorable position or privileged opportunity usu. obtained by early participants — used esp. in the phrase *in on the ground floor*

ground glass *n* (1848) **:** glass with a light-diffusing surface produced by etching or abrading

ground·hog \ˈgrau̇n(d)-ˌhȯg, -ˌhäg\ *n* (1742) **:** WOODCHUCK

Groundhog Day *n* [fr. the legend that a groundhog emerging from its burrow returns to hibernate if it sees its shadow on this day] (1871) **:** February 2 observed traditionally as a day that indicates six more weeks of winter if sunny or an early spring if cloudy

ground·ing \ˈgrau̇n-diŋ\ *n* (1644) **:** training or instruction in the fundamentals of a field of knowledge

ground ivy *n* (14c) **:** a trailing European mint (*Glechoma hederacea*) naturalized in No. America with rounded leaves and purplish flowers

ground·less \ˈgrau̇n(d)-ləs\ *adj* (1602) **:** having no ground or foundation ⟨~ fears⟩ — **ground·less·ly** *adv* — **ground·less·ness** *n*

ground·ling \ˈgrau̇n(d)-liŋ\ *n* (1602) **1 a :** a spectator who stood in the pit of an Elizabethan theater **b :** a person of unsophisticated taste **2 :** one that lives or works on or near the ground

ground loop *n* (1928) **:** a sharp uncontrollable turn made by an aircraft on the ground and usu. caused by an unbalanced drag (as from a wingtip touching the ground)

ground·mass \ˈgrau̇n(d)-ˌmas\ *n* (1879) **:** the fine-grained or glassy base of a porphyry in which the larger distinct crystals are embedded

ground meristem *n* (1938) **:** the part of a primary apical meristem remaining after differentiation of protoderm and procambium

ground·nut \ˈgrau̇n(d)-ˌnət\ *n* (1602) **1 a :** any of several plants having edible tuberous roots; *esp* **:** a No. American leguminous vine (*Apios americana*) with pinnate leaves and clusters of brownish-purple fragrant flowers **b :** the root of a groundnut **2** *chiefly Brit* **:** PEANUT

ground·out \ˈgrau̇nd-ˌau̇t\ *n* (1965) **:** a play in baseball in which a batter is put out after hitting a grounder to an infielder

ground pine *n* (1551) **1 :** a yellow-flowered European bugle (*Ajuga chamaepitys*) with a resinous odor **2 :** any of several club mosses (esp. *Lycopodium clavatum* and *L. complanatum*) with long creeping stems and erect branches

ground plan *n* (1731) **1 :** a plan of a floor of a building as distinguished from an elevation **2 :** a first or basic plan

ground rent *n* (1667) **:** the rent paid by a lessee for the use of land esp. for building

ground rule *n* (1890) **1 :** a sports rule adopted to modify play on a particular field, court, or course **2 :** a rule of procedure ⟨*ground rules* for selecting a superintendent —*Amer. School Board Jour.*⟩

ground·sel \ˈgrau̇n(d)-səl\ *n* [ME *groundeswele,* fr. OE *grundeswelge,* fr. *grund* ground + *swelgan* to swallow — more at SWALLOW] (bef. 12c) **:** any of various senecios (as the nearly cosmopolitan European weed *Senecio vulgaris*)

ground·sheet \ˈgrau̇n(d)-ˌshēt\ *n* (1907) **:** GROUND CLOTH

grounds·keep·er \ˈgrau̇n(d)z-ˌkē-pər\ *n* (1903) **:** a person who cares for the grounds of a usu. large property (as a sports field)

ground sloth *n* (1860) **:** any of various often huge extinct American edentates related to the recent sloths

grounds·man \ˈgrau̇n(d)z-mən\ *n* (1886) *chiefly Brit* **:** GROUNDSKEEPER

ground speed *n* (1917) **:** the speed (as of an airplane) with relation to the ground — compare AIRSPEED

ground squirrel *n* (1688) **:** any of various burrowing No. American and Eurasian rodents (esp. genus *Spermophilus*) of the squirrel family that often live in colonies esp. in open areas (as grasslands) — called also *spermophile*

ground state *n* (1926) **:** the state of a physical system (as of an atomic nucleus or an atom) having the least energy of all the possible states — called also *ground level*

ground stroke *n* (1895) **:** a stroke made (as in tennis) by hitting a ball that has rebounded from the ground — compare VOLLEY

ground substance *n* (1882) **:** a more or less homogeneous matrix in which the specific differentiated elements of a system are suspended: **a :** the intercellular substance of tissues **b :** CYTOSOL

ground·swell \ˈgrau̇nd-ˌswel\ *n* (1786) **1** *usu* **ground swell :** a broad deep undulation of the ocean caused by an often distant gale or seismic disturbance **2 :** a rapid spontaneous growth (as of political opinion) ⟨a ~ of support⟩

ground·wa·ter \-ˌwȯ-tər, -ˌwä-\ *n* (ca. 1889) **:** water within the earth esp. that supplies wells and springs

ground wave *n* (1925) **:** a radio wave that is propagated along the surface of the earth

ground·wood \ˈgrau̇nd-ˌwu̇d\ *n* [[3]*ground*] (1885) **:** wood ground up and used to make pulp for paper

ground·work \ˈgrau̇nd-ˌwərk\ *n* (15c) **:** FOUNDATION, BASIS ⟨laid the ~ for a new program⟩; *also* **:** preparation made beforehand ⟨the ~ was done before the winter tour —Susan Reiter⟩

ground zero *n* (1946) **1 :** the point directly above, below, or at which a nuclear explosion occurs **2 :** the center or origin of rapid, intense, or violent activity or change; *broadly* **:** CENTER 2a ⟨the party town that served as *ground zero* for those corporate . . . bashes —Rich Eisen⟩ **3 :** the very beginning **:** SQUARE ONE

[1]**group** \ˈgrüp\ *n, often attrib* [F *groupe,* fr. It *gruppo,* by-form of *groppo* knot, tangle, of Gmc origin; akin to OHG *kropf* craw — more at CROP] (1686) **1 :** two or more figures forming a complete unit in a composition **2 a :** a number of individuals assembled together or having some unifying relationship **b :** an assemblage of objects regarded as a unit **c (1) :** a military unit consisting of a headquarters and attached battalions **(2) :** a unit of the U.S. Air Force higher than a squadron and lower than a wing **3 a :** an assemblage of related organisms — often used to avoid taxonomic connotations when the kind or degree of relationship is not clearly defined **b (1) :** two or more atoms joined together or sometimes a single atom forming part of a molecule; *esp* **:** FUNCTIONAL GROUP ⟨a methyl ~⟩ **(2) :** an assemblage of elements forming one of the vertical columns of the periodic table **c :** a stratigraphic division comprising rocks deposited during an era **4 :** a mathematical set that is closed under a binary associative operation, contains an identity element, and has an inverse for every element

[2]**group** *vt* (1718) **1 :** to combine in a group **2 :** to assign to a group **:** CLASSIFY ~ *vi* **1 :** to form a group **2 :** to belong to a group **3 :** to make groups of closely spaced hits on a target ⟨the gun ~*ed* beautifully —R. C. Ruark⟩ — **group·able** \ˈgrü-pə-bəl\ *adj*

Group A *n* (1945) **:** any of various strains of a streptococcus (*Streptococcus pyogenes*) that include the causative agents of pharyngitis, scarlet fever, septicemia, some skin infections, rheumatic fever, and glomerulonephritis ⟨*Group A* strep throat⟩

Group B *n* (1965) **:** any of various strains of a streptococcus (*Streptococcus agalactiae*) that include the causative agents of certain infections (as pneumonia and meningitis) esp. of newborn infants ⟨*Group B* streptococcal infections⟩

group captain *n* (1919) **:** a commissioned officer in the British air force who ranks with a colonel in the army

group dynamics *n pl but sing or pl in constr* (1939) **:** the interacting forces within a small human group; *also* **:** the sociological study of these forces

grou·per \ˈgrü-pər\ *n, pl* **groupers** *also* **grouper** [Pg *garoupa*] (1671) **:** any of numerous fishes (family Serranidae and esp. genera *Epinephelus* and *Mycteroperca*) that are typically large solitary bottom-dwelling fishes of warm seas and include important food fishes

group home *n* (1967) **:** a residence for persons requiring care or supervision

group·ie \ˈgrü-pē\ *n* (1966) **1 :** a fan of a rock group who usu. follows the group around on concert tours **2 :** an admirer of a celebrity who attends as many of his or her public appearances as possible **3 :** ENTHUSIAST, AFICIONADO ⟨a political ~⟩ ⟨golf ~*s*⟩

group·ing \ˈgrü-piŋ\ *n* (1748) **1 :** the act or process of combining in groups **2 :** a set of objects combined in a group ⟨a furniture ~⟩

group practice *n* (1942) : medicine practiced by a group of associated physicians or dentists (as specialists in different fields) working as partners or as partners and employees
group theory *n* (1898) : a branch of mathematics concerned with finding all mathematical groups and determining their properties
group therapy *n* (1943) : therapy in the presence of a therapist in which several patients discuss and share their personal problems — called also *group psychotherapy* — **group therapist** *n*
group·think \'grüp-ˌthiŋk\ *n* ['*group* + *-think* (as in *doublethink*)] (1952) : a pattern of thought characterized by self-deception, forced manufacture of consent, and conformity to group values and ethics
grou·pus·cule \grü-'pəs-ˌkyül\ *n* [F, fr. *groupe* group + *-uscule* (as in *corpuscule* corpuscle)] (1969) : a small group of political activists
group·ware \'grüp-ˌwer\ *n* (1980) : software that enables users to work collaboratively on projects or files via a network
1grouse \'grau̇s\ *n, pl* **grouse** *or* **grouses** [origin unknown] (1531) : any of various chiefly ground-dwelling birds (family Tetraonidae) that are usu. of reddish-brown or other protective color and have feathered legs and that include many important game birds
2grouse *vi* **groused; grous·ing** [origin unknown] (1887) : COMPLAIN, GRUMBLE — **grous·er** *n*
3grouse *n* (1918) : COMPLAINT
1grout \'grau̇t\ *n* [ME, coarse meal, fr. OE *grūt;* akin to OE *grēot* grit] (1638) **1 a** : thin mortar used for filling spaces (as the joints in masonry); *also* : any of various other materials (as a mixture of cement and water or chemicals that solidify) used for a similar purpose **b** : PLASTER **2** : LEES
2grout *vt* (1838) **1** : to fill up or finish with grout **2** : to fix in place by means of grout ⟨~ a bolt into a wall⟩ — **grout·er** *n*
grove \'grōv\ *n* [ME, fr. OE *grāf*] (bef. 12c) **1** : a small wood without underbrush ⟨a picnic ~⟩ **2** : a planting of fruit or nut trees
grov·el \'grä-vəl, 'grə-\ *vi* **-eled** *or* **-elled; -el·ing** *or* **-el·ling** [back-formation fr. *groveling* prone, fr. *groveling,* adv., fr. ME, fr. *gruf,* adv., on the face (fr. ON *á grūfu*) + *-ling*] (1552) **1** : to creep with the face to the ground : CRAWL **2 a** : to lie or creep with the body prostrate in token of subservience or abasement **b** : to abase oneself **3** : to give oneself over to what is base or unworthy : WALLOW ⟨~*ing* in self-pity⟩ — **grov·el·er** \-vəl-ər\ *n* — **grov·el·ing·ly** \-vəl-iŋ-lē\ *adv*
groves of academe *often cap A* (1768) : the academic world
grow \'grō\ *vb* **grew** \'grü\; **grown** \'grōn\; **grow·ing** [ME, fr. OE *grōwan;* akin to OHG *gruowan* to grow] *vi* (bef. 12c) **1 a** : to spring up and develop to maturity **b** : to be able to grow in some place or situation ⟨trees that ~ in the tropics⟩ **c** : to assume some relation through or as if through a process of natural growth ⟨ferns ~*ing* from the rocks⟩ **2 a** : to increase in size by assimilation of material into the living organism or by accretion of material in a nonbiological process (as crystallization) **b** : INCREASE, EXPAND ⟨~*s* in wisdom⟩ **3** : to develop from a parent source ⟨the book *grew* out of a series of lectures⟩ **4 a** : to pass into a condition : BECOME ⟨*grew* pale⟩ **b** : to have an increasing influence ⟨habit ~*s* on a person⟩ **c** : to become increasingly acceptable or attractive ⟨didn't like it at first, but it *grew* on him⟩ ~ *vt* **1 a** : to cause to grow ⟨~ wheat⟩ **b** : to let grow on the body ⟨*grew* a beard⟩ **2** : to promote the development of ⟨start a business and ~ it successfully —J. L. Deckter⟩ — **grow·er** \'grō(-ə)r\ *n* — **grow·ing·ly** \'grō-iŋ-lē\ *adv*
growing pains *n pl* (1810) **1** : pains in the legs of growing children having no demonstrable relation to growth **2** : the stresses and strains attending a new project or development
growing point *n* (1835) : the undifferentiated end of a plant shoot from which additional shoot tissues differentiate
1growl \'grau̇(-ə)l\ *vb* [ME *groulen, grollen*] *vi* (14c) **1 a** : RUMBLE ⟨his stomach ~*ed*⟩ **b** : to utter a growl ⟨the dog ~*ed* at the stranger⟩ **2** : to complain angrily ~ *vt* : to utter with a growl : utter angrily
2growl *n* (1715) : a deep guttural inarticulate sound
growl·er \'grau̇-lər\ *n* (1753) **1** : one that growls **2** : a container (as a can or pitcher) for beer bought by the measure **3** : a small iceberg
growl·ing \'grau̇-liŋ\ *adj* (1752) : marked by a growl ⟨a low ~ voice⟩ ⟨listened to the ~ thunder⟩ — **growl·ing·ly** \-liŋ-lē\ *adv*
growly \'grau̇-lē\ *adj* **growl·i·er; -est** (1843) : resembling a growl ⟨a ~ voice⟩ — **growl·i·ness** *n*
grown \'grōn\ *adj* (1645) **1** : fully grown : MATURE ⟨~ men and women⟩ **2** : covered or surrounded with vegetation ⟨land well ~ with trees⟩ **3 a** : cultivated or produced in a specified way or locality — used in combination ⟨shade-*grown* tobacco⟩ **b** : overgrown with — used in combination ⟨a weed-*grown* patio⟩
1grown–up \'grōn-ˌəp\ *adj* (1633) **1** : not childish or immature : ADULT **2** : of, for, or characteristic of adults ⟨insisted on wearing ~ clothes⟩
2grown–up *n* (1813) : ADULT
growth \'grōth\ *n* (1557) **1 a (1)** : a stage in the process of growing : SIZE **(2)** : full growth **b** : the process of growing **c** : progressive development : EVOLUTION **d** : INCREASE, EXPANSION ⟨the ~ of the oil industry⟩ **2 a** : something that grows or has grown **b** : an abnormal proliferation of tissue (as a tumor) **c** : OUTGROWTH **d** : the result of growth : PRODUCT **3** : a producing esp. by growing ⟨fruits of his own ~⟩ **4** : anticipated progressive growth esp. in capital value and income ⟨some investors prefer ~ to immediate income⟩
growth company *n* (1959) : a company that grows at a greater rate than the economy as a whole and that usu. directs a relatively high proportion of income back into the business
growth cone *n* (1970) : the specialized motile tip of an axon of a growing or regenerating neuron
growth factor *n* (1926) : a substance (as a vitamin B_{12} or an interleukin) that promotes growth and esp. cellular growth
growth hormone *n* (1924) **1** : a vertebrate polypeptide hormone that is secreted by the anterior lobe of the pituitary gland and regulates growth; *also* : a recombinant version of this hormone — called also *somatotropin* **2** : GROWTH REGULATOR
growth industry *n* (1954) : a business that has become increasingly popular or profitable; *also* : an interest or activity that is increasingly popular or trendy
growth regulator *n* (1936) : any of various synthetic or naturally occurring plant substances (as an auxin or gibberellin) that regulate growth
growth ring *n* (1907) : a layer of wood (as an annual ring) produced during a single period of growth
growthy \'grō-thē\ *adj* **growth·i·er; -est** (1884) *of livestock* : exceptionally fast in growing and gaining weight — **growth·i·ness** \-nəs\ *n*
grow up *vi* (1535) : to grow toward or arrive at full stature or physical or mental maturity ⟨*growing up* intellectually, socially, and physically⟩
groyne \'grȯin\ *n* [by alter.] (1582) : GROIN 3
GRP *abbr* glass-reinforced plastic
GRU *abbr* [Russ *Glavnoe razvedyvatel'-noe upravlenie*] Chief Intelligence Directorate
1grub \'grəb\ *vb* **grubbed; grub·bing** [ME *grubben;* akin to OE *grafan* to dig — more at GRAVE] *vt* (14c) **1** : to clear by digging up roots and stumps **2** : to dig up by or as if by the roots ~ *vi* **1 a** : to dig in the ground esp. for something that is difficult to find or extract **b** : to search about ⟨*grubbed* in the countryside for food —*Lamp*⟩ **2** : TOIL, DRUDGE ⟨*grubbing* along at newspaper jobs —Walter Kirn⟩ — **grub·ber** *n*
2grub *n* [ME *grubbe,* fr. *grubben*] (15c) **1** : a soft thick wormlike larva of an insect (as a beetle) **2 a** : one who does menial work : DRUDGE **b** : a slovenly person **3** : FOOD
grub·by \'grə-bē\ *adj* **grub·bi·er; -est** (1725) **1** : infested with fly maggots **2 a** : DIRTY, GRIMY ⟨~ hands⟩ **b** : SLOVENLY, SLOPPY **3** : worthy of contempt : BASE ⟨~ political motives⟩ — **grub·bi·ly** \'grə-bə-lē\ *adv* — **grub·bi·ness** \'grə-bē-nəs\ *n*
1grub·stake \'grəb-ˌstāk\ *n* (1863) **1** : supplies or funds furnished a mining prospector on promise of a share in his discoveries **2** : material assistance (as a loan) provided for launching an enterprise or for a person in difficult circumstances
2grubstake *vt* (1879) : to provide with a grubstake — **grub·stak·er** *n*
Grub Street \'grəb-\ *n* [*Grub Street,* London, formerly inhabited by literary hacks] (1630) : the world or category of needy literary hacks
1grudge \'grəj\ *vt* **grudged; grudg·ing** [ME *grucchen, grudgen* to grumble, complain, fr. AF *grucer, grucher,* of Gmc origin; akin to MHG *grogezen* to howl] (14c) : to be unwilling to give or admit : give or allow reluctantly or resentfully ⟨didn't ~ the time⟩ — **grudg·er** *n*
2grudge *n* (15c) : a feeling of deep-seated resentment or ill will *syn* see MALICE
grudging *adj* (ca. 1533) **1** : UNWILLING, RELUCTANT **2** : done, given, or allowed unwillingly, reluctantly, or sparingly ⟨~ compliance⟩ — **grudg·ing·ly** *adv*
gru·el \'grü-əl\ *n* [ME *grewel,* fr. AF *gruel,* of Gmc origin; akin to OE *grūt* grout] (14c) **1** : a thin porridge **2** [fr. *to get one's gruel* to accept punishment] *chiefly Brit* : PUNISHMENT **3** : something that lacks substance or significance ⟨the argument was thin ~⟩
gru·el·ing *or* **gru·el·ling** \'grü-ə-liŋ\ *adj* [fr. prp. of obs. *gruel* to exhaust, punish, fr. *gruel,* n.] (1852) : trying or taxing to the point of exhaustion : PUNISHING ⟨a ~ race⟩ — **gru·el·ing·ly** \-liŋ-lē\ *adv*
grue·some *also* **grew·some** \'grü-səm\ *adj* [alter. of earlier *growsome,* fr. E dial. *grow, grue* to shiver, fr. ME *gruen,* prob. fr. MD *grūwen;* akin to OHG in*grūēn* to shiver] (ca. 1700) : inspiring horror or repulsion : GRISLY *syn* see GHASTLY — **grue·some·ly** *adv* — **grue·some·ness** *n*
1gruff \'grəf\ *adj* [D *grof;* akin to OHG *grob* coarse, *hruf* scurf — more at DANDRUFF] (1691) **1** : rough, brusque, or stern in manner, speech, or aspect ⟨a ~ reply⟩ **2** : being deep and harsh : HOARSE ⟨a ~ voice⟩ *syn* see BLUFF — **gruff·ly** *adv* — **gruff·ness** *n*
2gruff *vt* (1706) : to utter in a gruff voice or manner
grum·ble \'grəm-bəl\ *vb* **grum·bled; grum·bling** \-b(ə-)liŋ\ [prob. fr. MF *grommeler,* ultim. fr. MD *grommen;* akin to OHG *grimm* grim] *vi* (1580) **1** : to mutter in discontent **2** : GROWL, RUMBLE ~ *vt* : to express with grumbling — **grumble** *n* — **grum·bler** \-b(ə-)lər\ *n* — **grum·bling·ly** \-b(ə-)liŋ-lē\ *adv* — **grum·bly** \-b(ə-)lē\ *adj*
grummet *var of* GROMMET
1grump \'grəmp\ *n* [obs. E *grumps* snubs, slights] (1844) **1** : a fit of ill humor or sulkiness — usu. used in pl. **2** : a person given to complaining
2grump *vi* (1875) **1** : SULK **2** : GRUMBLE, COMPLAIN ~ *vt* : to utter in a grumpy manner
grumpy \'grəm-pē\ *adj* **grump·i·er; -est** (1778) : moodily cross : SURLY — **grump·i·ly** \-pə-lē\ *adv* — **grump·i·ness** \-pē-nəs\ *n*
grunge \'grənj\ *n* [back-formation fr. *grungy*] (1965) **1** : one that is grungy **2** : rock music incorporating elements of punk rock and heavy metal; *also* : the untidy fashions typical of fans of grunge — **grung·er** \'grən-jər\ *n*
grun·gy \'grən-jē\ *adj* **grun·gi·er; -est** [origin unknown] (1965) **1** : shabby or dirty in character or condition **2** : characteristic of grunge music or fashion
grun·ion \'grən-yən\ *n* [prob. fr. Sp *gruñón* grunter] (1917) : a silverside (*Leuresthes tenuis*) of the California coast notable for the regularity with which it comes inshore to spawn at nearly full moon
1grunt \'grənt\ *vb* [ME, fr. OE *grunnettan,* freq. of *grunian,* of imit. origin] *vi* (bef. 12c) : to utter a grunt ~ *vt* : to utter with a grunt — **grunt·er** *n*
2grunt *n* (1553) **1 a** : the deep short sound characteristic of a hog **b** : a similar sound **2** [fr. the noise it makes when taken from the water] : any of a family (Haemulidae syn. Pomadasyidae) of chiefly tropical marine bony fishes **3** : a dessert made by dropping biscuit dough on top of boiling berries and steaming ⟨blueberry ~⟩ **4 a** : a U.S. army or marine foot soldier esp. in the Vietnam War **b** : one who does routine unglamorous work — often used attributively ⟨~ work⟩
grun·tle \'grən-tᵊl\ *vt* **grun·tled; grun·tling** \'grənt-liŋ, 'grən-tᵊl-iŋ\ [back-formation fr. *disgruntle*] (1926) : to put in a good humor ⟨were *gruntled* with a good meal and good conversation —W. P. Webb⟩
grutch \'grəch\ *vt* [ME *grucchen*] (14c) *obs* : BEGRUDGE
grutten *past part of* GREET

\ə\ **abut** \ᵊ\ kitten, F table \ər\ **further** \a\ **ash** \ā\ **ace** \ä\ **mop, mar** \au̇\ **out** \ch\ **chin** \e\ **bet** \ē\ **easy** \g\ **go** \i\ **hit** \ī\ **ice** \j\ **job** \ŋ\ **sing** \ō\ **go** \ȯ\ **law** \ȯi\ **boy** \th\ **thin** \t͟h\ **the** \ü\ **loot** \u̇\ **foot** \y\ **yet** \zh\ **vision, beige** \k̲, ⁿ, œ, ue, ʸ\ *see* Guide to Pronunciation

Gru·yère \grü-'yer, grē-\ *n* [*Gruyère,* district in Switzerland] (1802) **1** : a firm cheese with small holes and a nutty flavor that is of Swiss origin **2** : a process cheese made from natural Gruyère
gr wt *abbr* gross weight
gryphon *var of* GRIFFIN
GS *abbr* **1** general staff **2** giant slalom **3** government service **4** ground speed
GSA *abbr* **1** General Services Administration **2** Girl Scouts of America
GSC *abbr* general staff corps
GSL *abbr* Guaranteed Student Loan
GSM *abbr* [F *Groupe spéciale mobile,* team appointed by European telecommunications administrations in 1982 to develop standards for wireless networks] global system for mobile communications
GSO *abbr* general staff officer
G–spot \'jē-ˌspät\ *n* [Grafenberg *spot,* fr. Ernst *Grafenberg* †1957 Am. (Ger.-born) gynecologist] (1982) : a mass of tissue that is held to exist on the anterior vaginal wall and to be highly erogenous
GSR *abbr* galvanic skin response
G–string \'jē-ˌstriŋ\ *n* [origin unknown] (1878) : a strip of cloth passed between the legs and supported by a waist cord that is worn esp. by striptease dancers
G suit *n* [gravity *suit*] (1944) : a suit designed to counteract the physiological effects of acceleration on an aviator or astronaut
GSUSA *abbr* Girl Scouts of the United States of America
gt *abbr* **1** great **2** [L *gutta*] drop
1**GT** \ˌjē-'tē\ *n* [It Gran Turismo] (1963) : GRAND TOURING CAR
2**GT** *abbr* gross ton
Gt Brit *abbr* Great Britain
gtd *abbr* guaranteed
GTP \ˌjē-(ˌ)tē-'pē\ *n* [guanosine *tri*phosphate] (1961) : an energy-rich nucleotide analogous to ATP that is composed of guanine, ribose, and three phosphate groups and is necessary for peptide-bond formation during protein synthesis — called also *guanosine triphosphate*
Gtr Man *abbr* Greater Manchester
gtt *abbr* [L *gutta,* pl. *guttae*] drops
G_2 phase \ˌjē-'tü-\ *n* [growth] (1968) : the period in the cell cycle from the completion of DNA replication to the beginning of cell division — compare G_1 PHASE, M PHASE, S PHASE
GU *abbr* **1** genitourinary **2** Guam
gua·ca·mo·le \ˌgwä-kə-'mō-lē\ *n* [MexSp, fr. Nahuatl *āhuacamōlli,* fr. *āhuacatl* avocado + *mōlli* sauce] (1920) : pureed or mashed avocado seasoned with condiments
gua·cha·ro \'gwä-chə-ˌrō\ *n, pl* **-ros** *or* **-roes** [AmerSp *guácharo*] (1818) : OILBIRD
guai·ac \'gwī-ˌak, 'gī-\ *n* [NL *Guaiacum*] (1750) : GUAIACUM 2
guai·a·cum \'gwī-ə-kəm, 'gī-\ *n* [NL, fr. Sp *guayaco,* fr. Taino *guayacan*] (1553) **1** : any of a genus (*Guaiacum*) of the caltrop family of tropical American evergreen trees and shrubs having pinnate leaves, usu. blue flowers, and capsular fruit **2 a** : the hard greenish-brown wood of a guaiacum (esp. *Guaiacum officinale*) **b** : a resin with a faint balsamic odor that is obtained from the trunk of two guaiacums (*G. officinale* and *G. sanctum*) and often used as a clinical reagent
guan \'gwän\ *n* [alter. of earlier *quam,* prob. fr. Kuna (Chibchan language of Panama) *kwama*] (1743) : any of various large gregarious neotropical birds (family Cracidae) that are chiefly arboreal forest-dwellers and that somewhat resemble turkeys
gua·na·co \gwə-'nä-(ˌ)kō\ *n, pl* **-cos** *also* **-co** [Sp, fr. Quechua *wanaku*] (1604) : a So. American mammal (*Lama guanicoe*) of dry open country that has a soft thick fawn-colored coat and is related to the camel but lacks a dorsal hump — compare ALPACA, LLAMA

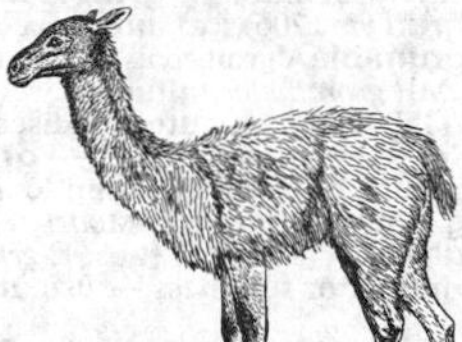
guanaco

gua·neth·i·dine \gwä-'ne-thə-ˌdēn\ *n* [*guanidine* + *eth-*] (1959) : a drug $C_{10}H_{22}N_4$ used esp. in the form of its sulfate to treat hypertension
gua·ni·dine \'gwä-nə-ˌdēn\ *n* [ISV, fr. *guanine*] (ca. 1864) : a base CH_5N_3 derived from guanine that in the form of its hydrochloride acts as a parasympathetic stimulant and is used esp. to denature proteins
gua·nine \'gwä-ˌnēn\ *n* [*guano* + *-ine;* fr. its being found esp. in guano] (1850) : a purine base $C_5H_5N_5O$ that codes genetic information in the polynucleotide chain of DNA or RNA — compare ADENINE, CYTOSINE, THYMINE, URACIL
gua·no \'gwä-(ˌ)nō\ *n* [Sp, fr. Quechua *wanu* fertilizer, dung] (1604) : a fertilizer containing the accumulated excrement of seabirds or bats; *broadly* : excrement esp. of seabirds or bats
gua·no·sine \'gwä-nə-ˌsēn\ *n* [*guan-* (as in *guanine*) + *ribose* + *-ine*] (1909) : a nucleoside $C_{10}H_{13}N_5O_5$ composed of guanine and ribose
guanosine triphosphate *n* (ca. 1962) : GTP
guar \'gwär\ *n* [Hindi *gvār* & Urdu *guār*] (1882) : a drought-tolerant legume (*Cyamopsis tetragonoloba*) cultivated in warm regions as a vegetable, for forage, and for its seeds which produce guar gum
gua·ra·na \ˌgwä-rə-'nä\ *n* [Pg *guaraná,* fr. Nhengatu (Tupi-based lingua franca of Amazonia), fr. Sateré-Mawé (Tupian language of the middle Amazon River basin) *warana*] (1838) : a dried paste that is made from the seeds of a So. American climbing shrub (*Paullinia cupana*) of the soapberry family, that contains caffeine and tannin, and that is used as a stimulant; *also* : this plant
gua·ra·ni \ˌgwär-ə-'nē\ *n* [Sp *guaraní*] (1797) **1** *cap* **a** *pl* **guarani** *or* **guaranis** : a member of a Tupi-Guaranian people of Bolivia, Paraguay, and southern Brazil **b** : the language of the Guarani **2** *pl* **guaranies** *also* **guaranis** — see MONEY table
1**guar·an·tee** \ˌger-ən-'tē, ˌgär-, ˌga-rən- *also* 'ger-ən-ˌ *or* 'gär-ən-ˌ, 'ga-rən-ˌ\ *n* [prob. alter. of 1*guaranty*] (1680) **1** : GUARANTOR **2** : GUARANTY 1 **3** : an assurance for the fulfillment of a condition: as **a** : an agreement by which one person undertakes to secure another in the possession or enjoyment of something **b** : an assurance of the quality of or of the length of use to be expected from a product offered for sale often with a promise of reimbursement **4** : GUARANTY 4
2**guarantee** *vt* **-teed; -tee·ing** (1731) **1** : to undertake to answer for the debt, default, or miscarriage of ⟨~ a loan⟩ **2** : to engage for the existence, permanence, or nature of : undertake to do or secure ⟨~ the winning of three tricks⟩ **3** : to give security to ⟨*guaranteed* her against loss⟩ **4** : to assert confidently ⟨I ~ you'll like it⟩
guar·an·tor \ˌger-ən-'tȯr, ˌgär-, ˌga-rən-; 'ger-ən-tər, 'gär-, 'ga-rən-\ *n* (ca. 1828) **1** : one that gives a guaranty **2** : one that guarantees
1**guar·an·ty** \'ger-ən-tē, 'gär-, 'ga-rən-\ *n, pl* **-ties** [AF *garantie,* fr. *garantir, warentir* to protect, warrant, guarantee — more at WARRANT] (1592) **1** : an undertaking to answer for the payment of a debt or the performance of a duty of another in case of the other's default or miscarriage **2** : GUARANTEE 3 **3** : GUARANTOR **4** : something given as security : PLEDGE **5** : the protection of a right afforded by legal provision (as in a constitution)
2**guaranty** *vt* **-tied; -ty·ing** (1737) : GUARANTEE
1**guard** \'gärd\ *n* [ME *garde,* fr. AF *garde, guarde, warde,* fr. *garder, guarder, warder,* to guard, defend, of Gmc origin; akin to OHG *wartēn* to watch, take care — more at WARD] (15c) **1** : one assigned to protect or oversee another: as **a** : a person or a body of persons on sentinel duty **b** *pl* : troops attached to the person of the sovereign **c** *Brit* : CONDUCTOR b **2 a** : a defensive state or attitude ⟨asked him out when his ~ was down⟩ **b** : a defensive position (as in boxing) **3 a** : the act or duty of protecting or defending **b** : the state of being protected : PROTECTION **4** : a protective or safety device; *specif* : a device for protecting a machine part or the operator of a machine **5** *archaic* : PRECAUTION **6 a** : a position or player next to the center in a football line **b** : a player stationed in the backcourt in basketball — **off guard** : in an unprepared or unsuspecting state — **on guard** : defensively watchful : ALERT
2**guard** *vt* (1500) **1** : to protect an edge of with an ornamental border **2 a** : to protect from danger esp. by watchful attention : make secure ⟨police ~*ing* our cities⟩ **b** : to stand at the entrance of as if on guard or as a barrier **c** : to tend to carefully : PRESERVE, PROTECT ⟨~*ed* their privacy⟩ **3** *archaic* : ESCORT **4 a** : to watch over so as to prevent escape, disclosure, or indiscretion **b** : to attempt to prevent (an opponent) from playing effectively or scoring ~ *vi* : to watch by way of caution or defense : stand guard ***syn*** see DEFEND — **guard·er** *n*
1**guar·dant** \'gär-d^{ə}nt\ *adj* [MF *gardant,* prp. of *garder* to guard, look at] (1572) : having the head turned toward the spectator — used of a heraldic animal whose body is seen from the side ⟨a lion passant ~⟩
2**guardant** *n* (1591) *obs* : GUARDIAN
guard cell *n* (1875) : one of the two crescent-shaped epidermal cells that border and open and close a plant stoma
guard·ed \'gär-dəd\ *adj* (1709) **1** : CAUTIOUS, CIRCUMSPECT **2** : being an extremely serious condition with uncertain outcome ⟨was in ~ condition after the crash⟩ — **guard·ed·ly** *adv* — **guard·ed·ness** *n*
guard hair *n* (1913) : one of the usu. long coarse hairs forming a protective coating over the undercoat of a mammal
guard·house \'gärd-ˌhau̇s\ *n* (1592) **1** : a building occupied by a guard or used as a headquarters by soldiers on guard duty **2** : a military jail
guard·ian \'gär-dē-ən\ *n* [ME *gardein, wardein* — more at WARDEN] (15c) **1** : one that guards : CUSTODIAN **2** : a superior of a Franciscan monastery **3** : one who has the care of the person or property of another — **guard·ian·ship** \-ˌship\ *n*
guardian angel *n* (ca. 1631) : an angel believed to have special care of a particular individual; *broadly* : SAVIOR 1, PROTECTOR
guard of honor (1816) : HONOR GUARD
guard·rail \'gärd-ˌrāl\ *n* (1860) : a railing guarding usu. against danger; *esp* : a barrier placed along the edge of a highway at dangerous points
guard·room \'gärd-ˌrüm, -ˌru̇m\ *n* (1671) **1** : a room occupied by a military guard during its term of duty **2** : a room where military prisoners are confined
guards·man \'gärdz-mən\ *n* (1648) : a member of a military body called *guard* or *guards*
guar gum *n* (1950) : a gum obtained from the endosperm of guar seeds and used esp. as a thickening agent and as a sizing material for paper and textiles
Guar·ne·ri·us \gwär-'nir-ē-əs, -'ner-\ *n* [NL, fr. It *Guarneri*] (1866) : a violin made by one of the Italian Guarneri family in the 17th and 18th centuries
gua·va \'gwä-və\ *n* [Sp *guaba, guayaba,* perh. fr. Taino] (1604) **1** : any of several tropical American shrubs or small trees (genus *Psidium*) of the myrtle family; *esp* : a shrubby tree (*P. guajava*) widely cultivated for its sweet acid yellow or pink fruit **2** : the roundish to pear-shaped fruit of a guava
gua·ya·bera \ˌgwī-ə-'ber-ə\ *n* [AmerSp] (1947) : a usu. short-sleeved lightweight sport shirt designed to be worn untucked
gua·yu·le \gwī-'ü-lē, wī-\ *n* [AmerSp, fr. Nahuatl *cuauholli* or *huauholli*] (1906) : a much-branched composite shrub (*Parthenium argentatum*) of Mexico and the southwestern U.S. that has been cultivated as a source of rubber
gu·ber·na·to·ri·al \ˌgü-bə(r)-nə-'tȯr-ē-əl, ˌgyü-, ˌgu̇-\ *adj* [L *gubernator* governor, steersman, fr. *gubernare* to govern — more at GOVERN] (1734) : of or relating to a governor
guck \'gək\ *or* **gook** \'gu̇k, 'gük\ *n* [perh. alter. of *goo*] (1949) : oozy sloppy dirt or debris; *broadly* : GOO, GUNK
1**gud·geon** \'gə-jən\ *n* [ME *gojoun,* fr. MF *goujon*] (15c) **1** : PIVOT 1, JOURNAL **2** : a socket for a rudder pintle
2**gudgeon** *n* [ME *gojune,* fr. AF *gojoun,* fr. L *gobion-, gobio,* alter. of *gobius* — more at GOBY] (15c) : a small European freshwater fish (*Gobio gobio*) related to the carps and often used for food or bait
gudgeon pin *n* (1891) : WRIST PIN
Gud·run \'gu̇d-ˌrün\ *n* [ON *Guthrūn*] (1842) : the wife of Sigurd and later of Atli in Norse mythology
guel·der rose \'gel-də(r)-\ *n* [*Guelderland, Gelderland,* Netherlands] (1597) : HIGHBUSH CRANBERRY; *esp* : a cultivated form of the cranberry bush with large roundish heads of sterile flowers
Guelf *or* **Guelph** \'gwelf\ *n* [It *Guelfo*] (1566) : a member of a papal and popular political party in medieval Italy that opposed the authority of the German emperors in Italy — compare GHIBELLINE
gue·non \'gwe-nən, gə-'nō^{n}\ *n* [F] (1838) : any of various long-tailed chiefly arboreal African monkeys (esp. genera *Cercopithecus* and *Erythrocebus*)

guer·don \ˈgər-d^{ə}n\ *n* [ME, fr. AF *guerdun,* of Gmc origin; akin to OHG *widarlōn* reward] (14c) : REWARD, RECOMPENSE — **guerdon** *vt*

gue·ri·don \gā-rē-ˈdō^{n}\ *n* [F *guéridon,* fr. *Gueridon,* character in 17th cent. farces and popular songs] (1853) : a small usu. ornately carved and embellished stand or table

Guern·sey \ˈgərn-zē\ *n, pl* **Guernseys** [*Guernsey,* Channel Islands] (1834) : any of a breed of usu. reddish-brown and white dairy cattle that are larger than the Jersey and produce rich yellowish milk

[1]**guer·ril·la** *or* **gue·ril·la** \gə-ˈri-lə, ge-, g(y)i-\ *n* [Sp *guerrilla,* fr. dim. of *guerra* war, of Gmc origin; akin to OHG *werra* strife — more at WAR] (1809) : a person who engages in irregular warfare esp. as a member of an independent unit carrying out harassment and sabotage

[2]**guerrilla** *adj* (1811) : of, relating to, or suggestive of guerrillas esp. in being aggressive, radical, or unconventional

guerrilla theater *n* (1968) : STREET THEATER

[1]**guess** \ˈges\ *vb* [ME *gessen,* perh. of Scand origin; akin to Norw & Sw *gissa* to guess, MD *gissen, gessen,* ON *geta* to get, guess — more at GET] *vt* (14c) **1** : to form an opinion of from little or no evidence **2** : BELIEVE, SUPPOSE ⟨I ~ you're right⟩ **3** : to arrive at a correct conclusion about by conjecture, chance, or intuition ⟨~ the answer⟩ ~ *vi* : to make a guess — **guess·able** \ˈge-sə-bəl\ *adj* — **guess·er** *n*

[2]**guess** *n* (14c) : CONJECTURE, SURMISE

guess·ti·mate \ˈges-tə-mət\ *n* [blend of *guess* and *estimate*] (1923) : an estimate usu. made without adequate information — **guess·ti·mate** \-ˌmāt\ *vt*

guess·work \ˈges-ˌwərk\ *n* (1725) : work performed or results obtained by guess : CONJECTURE

[1]**guest** \ˈgest\ *n* [ME *gest,* fr. ON *gestr;* akin to OE *giest* guest, stranger, L *hostis* stranger, enemy] (13c) **1 a** : a person entertained in one's house **b** : a person to whom hospitality is extended **c** : a person who pays for the services of an establishment (as a hotel or restaurant) **2** : an organism (as an insect) sharing the dwelling of another; *esp* : INQUILINE **3** : a substance that is incorporated in a host substance **4** : a usu. prominent person not a regular member of a cast or organization who appears in a program or performance

[2]**guest** *vt* (14c) : to receive as a guest ~ *vi* : to appear as a guest

guest·house \ˈgest-ˌhau̇s\ *n* (15c) : a building used for guests (as on an estate); *esp* : a house run as a boardinghouse or bed-and-breakfast

guest worker *n* (1960) : a foreign laborer working temporarily in an industrialized usu. European country

guff \ˈgəf\ *n* [prob. imit.] (1880) **1** : NONSENSE, HUMBUG **2** : verbal abuse ⟨doesn't take any ~⟩

guf·faw \(ˌ)gə-ˈfȯ, ˈgə-ˌfȯ\ *n* [imit.] (1720) : a loud or boisterous burst of laughter — **guf·faw** \(ˌ)gə-ˈfȯ\ *vi*

gug·gle \ˈgə-gəl\ *vi* **gug·gled; gug·gling** \-g(ə-)liŋ\ [imit.] (1611) : GURGLE — **guggle** *n*

GUI *abbr* graphical user interface

guid·able \ˈgī-də-bəl\ *adj* (1676) : capable of being guided

guid·ance \ˈgī-d^{ə}n(t)s\ *n* (1590) **1** : the act or process of guiding **2 a** : the direction provided by a guide **b** : advice on vocational or educational problems given to students **3** : the process of controlling the course of a projectile by a built-in mechanism

[1]**guide** \ˈgīd\ *n* [ME *gide, guide,* fr. AF, fr. Old Occitan *guida,* of Gmc origin; akin to OE *wītan* to look after, *witan* to know — more at WIT] (14c) **1 a** : one that leads or directs another's way **b** : a person who exhibits and explains points of interest **c** : something that provides a person with guiding information **d** : SIGNPOST 1 **e** : a person who directs another's conduct or course of life **2 a** : a device for steadying or directing the motion of something **b** : a ring or loop for holding the line of a fishing rod in position **c** : a sheet or a card with projecting tab for labeling inserted in a card index to facilitate reference **3** : a member of a unit on whom the movements or alignments of a military command are regulated — used esp. in commands ⟨~ right⟩

[2]**guide** *vb* **guid·ed; guid·ing** *vt* (14c) **1** : to act as a guide to : direct in a way or course **2 a** : to direct, supervise, or influence usu. to a particular end **b** : to superintend the training or instruction of ~ *vi* : to act or work as a guide — **guid·er** *n*

syn GUIDE, LEAD, STEER, PILOT, ENGINEER mean to direct in a course or show the way to be followed. GUIDE implies intimate knowledge of the way and of all its difficulties and dangers ⟨*guided* the scouts through the cave⟩. LEAD implies showing the way and often keeping those that follow under control and in order ⟨*led* his team to victory⟩. STEER implies an ability to keep to a course and stresses the capacity of maneuvering correctly ⟨*steered* the ship through a narrow channel⟩. PILOT suggests guidance over a dangerous or complicated course ⟨*piloted* the bill through the Senate⟩. ENGINEER implies finding ways to avoid or overcome difficulties in achieving an end or carrying out a plan ⟨*engineered* his son's election to the governorship⟩.

guide·book \ˈgīd-ˌbu̇k\ *n* (1814) : HANDBOOK 1; *esp* : a book of information for travelers

guided missile *n* (1945) : a missile whose course may be altered during flight (as by a target-seeking radar device)

guide dog *n* (1932) : a dog trained to lead the blind

guide·line \ˈgīd-ˌlīn\ *n* (1785) : a line by which one is guided: as **a** : a cord or rope to aid a passer over a difficult point or to permit retracing a course **b** : an indication or outline of policy or conduct

guide·post \-ˌpōst\ *n* (1738) **1** : INDICATION, SIGN **2** : GUIDELINE b

guide·way \-ˌwā\ *n* (1876) : a channel or track for controlling the line of motion of something

guide word *n* (ca. 1928) : either of the terms at the head of a page of an alphabetical reference work (as a dictionary) indicating the alphabetically first and last words on the page

gui·don \ˈgī-ˌdän, -d^{ə}n\ *n* [MF, fr. *guide*] (1530) **1** : a small flag; *esp* : one borne by a military unit as a unit marker **2** : one who carries a guidon

guid·will·ie \gœd-ˈwi-lē, gid-\ *adj* [Sc *guidwill* goodwill] (1788) *Scot* : CORDIAL, CHEERING

guild *also* **gild** \ˈgild\ *n* [ME *gilde,* fr. ON *gildi* payment, guild; akin to OE *gield* tribute, guild — more at GELD] (14c) **1** : an association of people with similar interests or pursuits; *esp* : a medieval association of merchants or craftsmen **2** : a group of organisms that use the same ecological resource in a similar way ⟨a feeding ~⟩ — **guild·ship** \ˈgil(d)-ˌship\ *n*

guil·der \ˈgil-dər\ *n* [ME *gylder, gyldren,* modif. of MD *gulden*] (15c) : GULDEN

guild·hall \ˈgild-ˌhȯl\ *n* (14c) : a hall where a guild or corporation usu. assembles

guilds·man \ˈgil(d)z-mən\ *n* (1873) **1** : a guild member **2** : an advocate of guild socialism

guild socialism *n* (1912) : an early 20th century English socialistic theory advocating state ownership of industry with control and management by guilds of workers

guile \ˈgī(-ə)l\ *n* [ME *gile,* fr. AF, prob. of Gmc origin; akin to OE *wigle* divination — more at WITCH] (13c) **1** : deceitful cunning : DUPLICITY **2** *obs* : STRATAGEM, TRICK — **guile·ful** \-fəl\ *adj* — **guile·ful·ly** \-fə-lē\ *adv* — **guile·ful·ness** *n*

guile·less \ˈgī(-ə)l-ləs\ *adj* (ca. 1616) : INNOCENT, NAIVE — **guile·less·ly** *adv* — **guile·less·ness** *n*

Guil·lain–Bar·ré syndrome \ˌgē-ˌlan-ˌbä-ˈrā-, ˌgē-ya^{n}-\ *n* [Georges *Guillain* †1961 Fr. physician and Jean A. *Barré* †1967 Fr. neurologist] (1939) : a polyneuritis of unknown cause characterized esp. by muscle weakness and paralysis

guil·le·met \ˌgē-(y)ə-ˈmā, ˌgi-lə-ˈmet\ *n* [F, fr. dim. of *Guillaume* William (perh. a printer's name)] (ca. 1905) : either of the marks « or » used as quotation marks in French writing

guil·le·mot \ˈgi-lə-ˌmät\ *n* [F, fr. MF, dim. of *Guillaume* William] (ca. 1672) **1** *Brit* : a common murre (*Uria aalge*) **2** : any of a genus (*Cepphus*) of narrow-billed auks of northern seas

guil·loche \gi-ˈlōsh, gē-ˈ(y)ōsh\ *n* [F *guillochis*] (ca. 1842) **1** : an architectural ornament formed of two or more interlaced bands with openings containing round devices **2** : a pattern (as on metalwork) made by interlacing curved lines

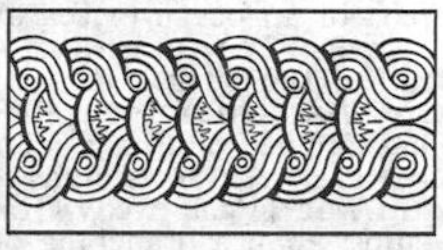

guilloche 2

guil·lo·tine \ˈgi-lə-ˌtēn; ˌgē-(y)ə-ˈ, ˈgē-(y)ə-ˌ\ *n* [F, fr. Joseph *Guillotin* †1814 Fr. physician] (1790) **1** : a machine for beheading by means of a heavy blade that slides down in vertical guides **2** : a shearing machine or instrument (as a paper cutter) that in action resembles a guillotine **3** *chiefly Brit* : closure by the imposition of a predetermined time limit on the consideration of specific sections of a bill or portions of other legislative business — **guillotine** *vt*

guilt \ˈgilt\ *n* [ME, delinquency, guilt, fr. OE *gylt* delinquency] (bef. 12c) **1** : the fact of having committed a breach of conduct esp. violating law and involving a penalty; *broadly* : guilty conduct **2 a** : the state of one who has committed an offense esp. consciously **b** : feelings of culpability esp. for imagined offenses or from a sense of inadequacy : SELF-REPROACH **3** : a feeling of culpability for offenses

guilt·less \ˈgilt-ləs\ *adj* (13c) : INNOCENT — **guilt·less·ly** *adv* — **guilt·less·ness** *n*

guilt–trip \ˈgil(t)-ˌtrip\ *vt* (1977) : to cause feelings of guilt in ⟨*guilt-tripped* them into helping⟩

guilty \ˈgil-tē\ *adj* **guilt·i·er; -est** (bef. 12c) **1** : justly chargeable with or responsible for a usu. grave breach of conduct or a crime **2** *obs* : justly liable to or deserving of a penalty **3 a** : suggesting or involving guilt **b** : aware of or suffering from guilt ⟨~ consciences⟩ ***syn*** see BLAMEWORTHY — **guilt·i·ly** \-tə-lē\ *adv* — **guilt·i·ness** \-tē-nəs\ *n*

guilty pleasure *n* (1907) : something pleasurable that induces a usu. minor feeling of guilt

guimpe \ˈgamp, ˈgimp\ *n* [F, fr. OF *guimple,* of Gmc origin; akin to OE *wimpel* wimple] (1831) **1** : a blouse worn under a jumper or pinafore **2** : a wide cloth used by some nuns to cover the neck and shoulders **3** [by alter.] : [1]GIMP

guin·ea \ˈgi-nē\ *n* [*Guinea,* Africa, supposed source of the gold from which it was made] (1664) **1** : an English gold coin issued from 1663 to 1813 and fixed in 1717 at 21 shillings **2** : a unit of value equal to one pound and one shilling

guinea fowl *n* (1749) : an African bird (*Numida meleagris*) related to the pheasants, raised for food in many parts of the world, and marked by a bare neck and head and slaty plumage speckled with white; *broadly* : any of several related birds

guinea grass *n* (1756) : a tall African forage grass (*Panicum maximum*) introduced into tropical America and the southern U.S.

guinea hen *n* (1599) : a female guinea fowl; *broadly* : GUINEA FOWL

guinea pepper *n* (1839) : GRAINS OF PARADISE

guinea pig *n* (1664) **1** : a small stout-bodied short-eared tailless domesticated rodent (*Cavia porcellus*) of So. American origin often kept as a pet and widely used in biological research — called also *cavy* **2** : a subject of research, experimentation, or testing

guinea worm *n* (1699) : a slender nematode worm (*Dracunculus medinensis*) of tropical regions that is parasitic in humans, has no known animal reservoir, and has an adult female that infests subcutaneous tissues and may attain a length of several feet

guinea worm disease *n* (1980) : DRACUNCULIASIS

Guin·e·vere \ˈgwi-nə-ˌvir, *Brit also* ˈgi-\ *n* (15c) : the wife of King Arthur and mistress of Lancelot

gui·pure \gi-ˈpyu̇r, -ˈpu̇r\ *n* [F] (1843) : a heavy large-patterned decorative lace

gui·ro \ˈwē-(ˌ)rō, ˈgwir-(ˌ)ō\ *n* [AmerSp *güiro,* lit., calabash] (1898) : a percussion instrument of Latin-American origin made of a serrated gourd and played by scraping a stick along its surface

gui·sard \ˈgī-zərd\ *n* [obs. Sc *gyze* to disguise, fr. ME *gyzen* to dress, fr. *guise, gyze* guise] (1626) *chiefly Scot* : MASKER, MUMMER

guise \ˈgīz\ *n* [ME *gise, guise,* fr. AF, of Gmc origin; akin to OHG *wīsa* manner — more at WISE] (13c) **1** : a form or style of dress : COSTUME **2 a** *obs* : MANNER, FASHION **b** *archaic* : a customary way of speaking or behaving **3 a** : external appearance : SEMBLANCE **b** : PRETEXT

gui·tar \gə-ˈtär, gi-, *esp Southern & Midland also* ˈgi-ˌtär\ *n* [F *guitare,* fr. Sp *guitarra,* fr. Ar *qītār,* fr. Gk *kithara* cithara] (1668) : a flat-bodied stringed instrument with a long fretted neck and usu. six strings played with a pick or with the fingers — **gui·tar·ist** \-ist\ *n*

gui·tar·fish \-ˌfish\ *n* (ca. 1900) **:** any of several viviparous rays (family Rhinobatidae) somewhat like a guitar in shape viewed from above

Gu·ja·ra·ti \ˌgü-jə-ˈrä-tē, ˌgu̇-\ *n* [Hindi *gujarātī*, fr. *Gujarāt* Gujarat] (1808) **1** *or* **Gu·je·ra·ti** *same*\ **:** the Indo-Aryan language of Gujarat and neighboring regions in northwestern India **2** *or* **Guj·ra·ti** \güj-ˈrä-, gu̇j-ˈrä-\ **:** a member of a people chiefly of Gujarat speaking the Gujarati language

gul \ˈgül\ *n* [Pers] (1813) *archaic* **:** ROSE 1

gu·lag \ˈgü-ˌläg\ *n, often cap* [Russ, fr. *G*lavnoe *u*pravlenie ispravitel'notrudovykh *lag*ereĭ chief administration of corrective labor camps] (1974) **:** the penal system of the U.S.S.R. consisting of a network of labor camps; *also* **:** LABOR CAMP 1

gu·lar \ˈg(y)ü-lər\ *adj* [L *gula* throat — more at GLUTTON] (1828) **:** of, relating to, or situated on the throat

gulch \ˈgəlch\ *n* [perh. fr. E dial. *gulch* to gulp, fr. ME *gulchen*] (1832) **:** a deep or precipitous cleft **:** RAVINE; *esp* **:** one occupied by a torrent

gul·den \ˈgül-dən, ˈgu̇l-\ *n, pl* **guldens** *or* **gulden** [ME (Sc), fr. MD *gulden florijn* golden florin] (15c) **1 :** the basic monetary unit of the Netherlands until 2002 **2 :** the basic monetary unit of Suriname until 2004

gules \ˈgyülz\ *n, pl* **gules** [ME *goules*, fr. AF] (14c) **:** the heraldic color red

[1]**gulf** \ˈgəlf\ *n* [ME *goulf*, fr. MF *golfe*, fr. It *golfo*, fr. LL *colpus*, fr. Gk *kolpos* bosom, gulf; akin to OE *hwealf* vault, OHG *walbo*] (15c) **1 :** a part of an ocean or sea extending into the land **2 :** a deep chasm **:** ABYSS **3 :** WHIRLPOOL **4 :** a wide gap ⟨the ~ between generations⟩

[2]**gulf** *vt* (1807) **:** ENGULF

Gulf War syndrome *n* (1992) **:** a syndrome of uncertain cause including fatigue, joint pain, memory loss, skin rash, and headache that has been reported in veterans of the war fought in the Persian Gulf in 1991

gulf·weed \ˈgəlf-ˌwēd\ *n* [*Gulf* of Mexico] (1674) **:** any of several sargassums; *esp* **:** a branching olive-brown seaweed (*Sargassum natans*) of tropical American seas with numerous berrylike air vesicles

[1]**gull** \ˈgəl\ *n* [ME, of Celt origin; akin to W *gwylan* gull] (15c) **:** any of numerous long-winged web-footed aquatic birds (subfamily Larinae of the family Laridae); *esp* **:** a usu. gray and white bird (esp. of the genus *Larus*) differing from a tern in usu. larger size, stouter build, thicker somewhat hooked bill, less pointed wings, and short unforked tail

[2]**gull** *vt* [obs. *gull* gullet, fr. ME *golle*, fr. AF *gule, gole*] (ca. 1550) **:** to take advantage of (one who is foolish or unwary) **:** DECEIVE

[3]**gull** *n* (1594) **:** a person who is easily deceived or cheated **:** DUPE

Gul·lah \ˈgə-lə\ *n* (1822) **1 :** a member of a group of blacks inhabiting the sea islands and coastal districts of So. Carolina, Georgia, and northeastern Florida **2 :** an English-based creole spoken by the Gullahs that is marked by vocabulary and grammatical elements from various African languages

gul·let \ˈgə-lət\ *n* [ME *golet*, fr. AF, dim. of *gule* throat, fr. L *gula* — more at GLUTTON] (14c) **1 :** ESOPHAGUS; *broadly* **:** THROAT **2 :** an invagination of the protoplasm in various protozoans (as a paramecium) that sometimes functions in the intake of food **3 :** the space between the tips of adjacent saw teeth

gull·ible *also* **gull·able** \ˈgə-lə-bəl\ *adj* (1818) **:** easily duped or cheated — **gull·ibil·i·ty** \ˌgə-lə-ˈbi-lə-tē\ *n* — **gull·ibly** \ˈgə-lə-blē\ *adv*

Gul·li·ver \ˈgə-lə-vər\ *n* (1726) **:** an Englishman in Jonathan Swift's satire *Gulliver's Travels* who makes voyages to the imaginary lands of the Lilliputians, Brobdingnagians, Laputans, and Houyhnhnms

[1]**gul·ly** \ˈgu̇-lē, ˈgə-\ *n, pl* **gullies** [short for E dial. *gully knife*] (1582) *dial Brit* **:** a large knife

[2]**gul·ly** *also* **gul·ley** \ˈgə-lē\ *n, pl* **gullies** [obs. E *gully* gullet, prob. alter. of ME *golet* ravine, throat] (1637) **1 :** a trench which was orig. worn in the earth by running water and through which water often runs after rains **2 :** a small valley or gulch

[3]**gul·ly** \ˈgə-lē\ *vb* **gul·lied; gul·ly·ing** *vt* (1754) **:** to make gullies in ~ *vi* **:** to undergo erosion **:** form gullies

gully erosion *n* (1928) **:** soil erosion produced by running water

gu·los·i·ty \g(y)ü-ˈlä-sə-tē\ *n* [ME *gulosite*, fr. AF, fr. LL *gulositas*, fr. L *gulosus* gluttonous, fr. *gula* gullet] (15c) **:** excessive appetite **:** GREEDINESS

gulp \ˈgəlp\ *vb* [ME, fr. a MD or MLG word akin to D & Fris *gulpen* to bubble forth, drink deep; akin to OE *gielpan* to boast — more at YELP] *vt* (14c) **1 :** to swallow hurriedly or greedily or in one swallow **2 :** to keep back as if by swallowing ⟨~ down a sob⟩ **3 :** to take in readily as if by swallowing ⟨~ down knowledge⟩ ~ *vi* **:** to catch the breath as if in taking a long drink — **gulp** *n* — **gulp·er** *n*

[1]**gum** \ˈgəm\ *n* [ME *gome*, fr. OE *gōma* palate; akin to OHG *guomo* palate, and perh. to Gk *chaos* abyss] (bef. 12c) **:** the tissue that surrounds the necks of teeth and covers the alveolar parts of the jaws; *broadly* **:** the alveolar portion of a jaw with its enveloping soft tissues

[2]**gum** *vt* **gummed; gum·ming** (1777) **1 :** to enlarge gullets of (a saw) **2 :** to chew with the gums

[3]**gum** *n* [ME *gomme*, fr. MF, fr. L *cummi, gummi*, fr. Gk *kommi*, fr. Egypt *qmyt*] (14c) **1 a :** any of numerous colloidal polysaccharide substances of plant origin that are gelatinous when moist but harden on drying and are salts of complex organic acids — compare MUCILAGE 1 **b :** any of various plant exudates (as an oleoresin or gum resin) **2 :** a substance or deposit resembling a plant gum (as in sticky or adhesive quality) **3 a :** a tree (as a black gum) that yields gum **b** *Austral* **:** EUCALYPTUS **4 :** the wood or lumber of a gum; *esp* **:** that of the sweet gum **5 :** CHEWING GUM

[4]**gum** *vb* **gummed; gum·ming** *vt* (1597) **:** to clog, impede, or damage with or as if with gum ⟨~ up the works⟩ ~ *vi* **1 :** to exude or form gum **2 :** to become gummy — **gum·mer** *n*

gum arabic *n* (14c) **:** a water-soluble gum obtained from several acacias (esp. *Acacia senegal*) and used esp. in the manufacture of inks, adhesives, pharmaceuticals, and confections

[1]**gum·bo** \ˈgəm-(ˌ)bō\ *n, pl* **gumbos** [AmerF *gombo*, of Bantu origin; akin to Umbundu *ochinggômbo* okra] (1805) **1 :** a soup thickened with okra pods or filé and containing meat or seafoods and usu. vegetables **2 :** OKRA 1 **3 a :** any of various fine-grained silty soils esp. of the central U.S. that when wet become impervious and soapy or waxy and very sticky **b :** a heavy sticky mud **4 :** MIXTURE, MÉLANGE — **gumbo** *adj*

[2]**gumbo** *n, often cap* [AmerF *gombo*, perh. fr. Kongo *nkômbô* runaway slave] (1838) **:** CREOLE 4a

gum·boil \ˈgəm-ˌbȯi(-ə)l\ *n* (1753) **:** an abscess in the gum

gum·bo–lim·bo \ˌgəm-bō-ˈlim-(ˌ)bō\ *n* [origin unknown] (1837) **:** a tree (*Bursera simaruba* of the family Burseraceae) of southern Florida and the American tropics that has a smooth coppery bark and supplies a reddish resin used locally in cements and varnishes

gum boot *n* (1850) **:** a rubber boot

gum·drop \ˈgəm-ˌdräp\ *n* (1860) **:** a sugar-coated candy made usu. from corn syrup with gelatin or gum arabic

gum·ma \ˈgə-mə\ *n, pl* **gummas** *also* **gum·ma·ta** \ˈgə-mə-tə\ [NL *gummat-, gumma*, fr. LL, gum, alter. of L *gummi* gum] (ca. 1722) **:** a tumor of gummy or rubbery consistency that is characteristic of the tertiary stage of syphilis — **gum·ma·tous** \-mə-təs\ *adj*

gum·mite \ˈgə-ˌmīt\ *n* (1868) **:** a yellow to reddish-brown mixture of hydrous oxides of uranium, thorium, and lead

gum·mo·sis \ˌgə-ˈmō-səs\ *n* [NL] (1882) **:** a pathological production of gummy exudate in a plant; *also* **:** a plant disease marked by gummosis

gum·mous \ˈgə-məs\ *adj* (1669) **:** resembling or composed of gum

gum·my \ˈgə-mē\ *adj* **gum·mi·er; -est** (14c) **1 :** VISCOUS, STICKY **2 a :** consisting of or containing gum **b :** covered with gum — **gum·mi·ness** *n*

gump·tion \ˈgəm(p)-shən\ *n* [origin unknown] (1719) **1** *chiefly dial* **:** COMMON SENSE, HORSE SENSE **2 :** ENTERPRISE, INITIATIVE ⟨lacked the ~ to try⟩

gum resin *n* (1712) **:** a product consisting essentially of a mixture of gum and resin usu. obtained by making an incision in a plant and allowing the juice which exudes to solidify

[1]**gum·shoe** \ˈgəm-ˌshü\ *n* (1913) **:** DETECTIVE

[2]**gumshoe** *vi* **gum·shoed; gum·shoe·ing** (1930) **:** to engage in detective work

gum tragacanth *n* (1573) **:** TRAGACANTH

gum tree *n* (1676) **:** [3]GUM 3

gum turpentine *n* (1884) **:** TURPENTINE 2a

gum·wood \ˈgəm-ˌwu̇d\ *n* (1709) **:** [3]GUM 4

[1]**gun** \ˈgən\ *n* [ME *gonne, gunne*] (14c) **1 a :** a piece of ordnance usu. with high muzzle velocity and comparatively flat trajectory **b :** a portable firearm (as a rifle or handgun) **c :** a device that throws a projectile **2 a :** a discharge of a gun esp. as a salute or signal **b :** a signal marking a beginning or ending **3 a :** HUNTER **b :** GUNMAN **4 :** something suggesting a gun in shape or function **5 :** THROTTLE — **gunned** \ˈgənd\ *adj* — **under the gun :** under pressure or attack

[2]**gun** *vb* **gunned; gun·ning** *vt* (1622) **1 a :** to fire on **b :** SHOOT ⟨*gunned* down by a hit man⟩ **2 a :** to open up the throttle of so as to increase speed ⟨~ the engine⟩ **b :** FIRE 3b ⟨*gunned* the ball to first base⟩ ~ *vi* **:** to hunt with a gun — **gun for :** to aim at or go after with determination or effort

gun·boat \ˈgən-ˌbōt\ *n* (1777) **:** an armed ship of shallow draft

gunboat diplomacy *n* (1927) **:** diplomacy backed by the use or threat of military force

gun control *n* (1964) **:** regulation of the selling, owning, and use of guns

gun·cot·ton \-ˌkä-tᵊn\ *n* (1846) **:** NITROCELLULOSE; *esp* **:** an explosive highly nitrated product used chiefly in smokeless powder

gun·dog \-ˌdȯg\ *n* (1744) **:** a dog trained to work with hunters by locating and retrieving game

gun·fight \-ˌfīt\ *n* (1659) **:** a hostile encounter in which antagonists with guns shoot at each other — **gun·fight·er** \-ˌfī-tər\ *n*

gun·fire \-ˌfī(-ə)r\ *n* (1801) **:** the firing of guns

gun·flint \-ˌflint\ *n* (1731) **:** a small sharp flint fashioned to ignite the priming in a flintlock

gung ho \ˈgəŋ-ˈhō\ *adj* [*Gung ho!*, motto (interpreted as meaning "work together") adopted by certain U.S. marines, fr. Chin (Beijing) *gōnghé*, short for *Zhōngguó Gōngyè Hézuò Shè* Chinese Industrial Cooperative Society] (1941) **:** extremely or overly zealous or enthusiastic

gun·ite \ˈgə-ˌnīt\ *n* [fr. *Gunite*, a trademark] (1914) **:** a building material consisting of a mixture of cement, sand, and water that is sprayed onto a mold

gunk \ˈgəŋk\ *n* [fr. *Gunk*, trademark for a cleaning solvent] (1943) **:** filthy, sticky, or greasy matter — **gunky** \ˈgəŋ-kē\ *adj*

gun lap *n* (ca. 1949) **:** the final lap of a race in track signaled by the firing of a gun as the leader begins the lap

gun·man \-mən\ *n* (1624) **1 :** a man armed with a gun; *esp* **:** a professional killer **2 :** a man noted for speed or skill in handling a gun

gun·met·al \ˈgən-ˌme-tᵊl\ *n* (1541) **1 :** a metal used for guns; *specif* **:** a bronze formerly much used as a material for cannon **2 :** an alloy or metal treated to imitate nearly black tarnished copper-alloy gunmetal **3 :** a bluish-gray color

gun moll \-ˌmäl, -ˌmȯl\ *n* [argot *gun* thief, rascal, by shortening & alter. fr. *gonoph, ganef* thief — more at GANEF] (ca. 1908) *slang* **:** MOLL 2b

Gun·nar \ˈgu̇-ˌnär, ˈgü-, -nər\ *n* [ON *Gunnarr*] (1842) **:** the king of the Nibelungs and husband of Brynhild in Norse mythology

[1]**gunnel** *var of* GUNWALE

[2]**gunnel** *n* [origin unknown] (1740) **:** a small slimy eellike bony fish (*Pholis gunnellus*) of the No. Atlantic; *broadly* **:** any fish of the family (Pholidae) to which the gunnel belongs

gun·ner \ˈgə-nər\ *n* (14c) **1 :** a soldier or airman who operates or aims a gun **2 :** one who hunts with a gun **3 :** a warrant officer who supervises ordnance and ordnance stores

gun·nery \ˈgən-rē, ˈgə-nə-\ *n* (1605) **:** the use of guns; *esp* **:** the science of the flight of projectiles and of the effective use of guns

gunnery sergeant *n* (ca. 1961) **:** a noncommissioned officer in the marine corps ranking above a staff sergeant and below a master sergeant or first sergeant

gun·ny·sack \ˈgə-nē-ˌsak\ *n* [*gunny* coarse fabric, of Indo-Aryan origin; akin to Hindi *gon* sack, Punjabi *gūṇī*] (1799) **:** a sack made of a coarse heavy fabric (as burlap)

gun·play \ˈgən-ˌplā\ *n* (1881) **:** the shooting of small arms with intent to scare or kill

gun·point \-ˌpȯint\ *n* (1951) **:** the muzzle of a gun — **at gunpoint :** under a threat of death by being shot

gun·pow·der \-ˌpau̇-dər\ *n* (15c) **:** an explosive mixture of potassium nitrate, charcoal, and sulfur used in gunnery and blasting; *broadly* **:** any of various powders used in guns as propelling charges

gun room *n* (1626) : quarters on a British warship orig. used by the gunner and his mates but now by midshipmen and junior officers
gun·run·ner \ˈgən-ˌrə-nər\ *n* (1899) : one that traffics in contraband arms and ammunition — **gun·run·ning** \-ˌrə-niŋ\ *n*
gun·sel \ˈgən(t)-səl\ *n* [argot *gunsel* catamite, perh. modif. of Yiddish *gendzl* gosling] (1943) *slang* : GUNMAN
gun·ship \ˈgən-ˌship\ *n* (1966) : a helicopter or cargo aircraft armed with rockets and machine guns
gun·shot \ˈgən-ˌshät\ *n* (15c) **1** : shot or a projectile fired from a gun **2** : the range of a gun **3** : the firing of a gun
gun–shy \-ˌshī\ *adj* (1884) **1** : afraid of loud noise (as that of a gun) **2** : markedly distrustful, afraid, or cautious
gun·sling·er \-ˌsliŋ-ər\ *n* (1927) : a person noted for speed and skill in handling and shooting a gun esp. in the American West
gun·sling·ing \-ˌsliŋ-iŋ\ *n* (ca. 1944) : the shooting of a gun esp. in a gunfight
gun·smith \-ˌsmith\ *n* (1588) : one who designs, makes, or repairs small firearms — **gun·smith·ing** \-ˌsmi-thiŋ\ *n*
Gun·ter's chain \ˈgən-tərz-\ *n* [Edmund *Gunter*] (ca. 1679) : a chain 66 feet (20.1 meters) long that is the unit of length for surveys of U.S. public lands
Gun·ther \ˈgu̇n-tər\ *n* [G] (1907) : a Burgundian king and husband of Brunhild in Germanic legend
gun·wale *also* **gun·nel** \ˈgə-nᵊl\ *n* [ME *gonne-wale,* fr. *gonne* gun + [1]*wale;* fr. its former use as a support for guns] (15c) : the upper edge of a ship's or boat's side — **to the gunwales** : as full as possible
gup·py \ˈgə-pē\ *n, pl* **guppies** [R.J.L. *Guppy* †1916 Trinidadian naturalist] (1925) : a small bony fish (*Poecilia reticulata* of the family Poeciliidae) esp. of Barbados, Trinidad, and Venezuela that is a live-bearer and is often kept as an aquarium fish
gur·gle \ˈgər-gəl\ *vi* **gur·gled; gur·gling** \-g(ə-)liŋ\ [prob. imit.] (1596) **1** : to flow in a broken irregular current ⟨the brook *gurgling* over the rocks⟩ **2** : to make a sound like that of a gurgling liquid ⟨the baby *gurgling* in his crib⟩ — **gurgle** *n*
Gur·kha \ˈgu̇r-kə, ˈgər-\ *n* [*Ghurka,* member of a Rajput clan who dominated Nepal in the 18th cent.] (1811) : a soldier from Nepal in the British or Indian army
gur·nard \ˈgər-nərd\ *n, pl* **gurnard** *or* **gurnards** [ME, fr. AF *gurenard,* irreg. fr. OF *grognier* to grunt, fr. L *grunnire,* of imit. origin] (14c) : SEA ROBIN — compare FLYING GURNARD
gur·ney \ˈgər-nē\ *n, pl* **gurneys** [prob. ultim. fr. *Gurney cab* type of horse-drawn cab with a rear entrance, fr. J. Theodore *Gurney,* who patented such a cab in Boston in 1883] (1939) : a wheeled cot or stretcher
gur·ry \ˈgər-ē, ˈgə-rē\ *n* [origin unknown] (1850) : fishing offal
gu·ru \ˈgu̇r-(ˌ)ü, ˈgü-(ˌ)rü\ *also* gə-ˈrü\ *n, pl* **gurus** [ultim. fr. Skt *guru,* fr. *guru,* adj., heavy, venerable — more at GRIEVE] (1613) **1** : a personal religious teacher and spiritual guide in Hinduism **2 a** : a teacher and esp. intellectual guide in matters of fundamental concern **b** : one who is an acknowledged leader or chief proponent **c** : a person with knowledge or expertise : EXPERT
[1]**gush** \ˈgəsh\ *vb* [ME *guschen*] *vi* (15c) **1** : to issue copiously or violently **2** : to emit a sudden copious flow **3** : to make an effusive display of affection or enthusiasm ⟨an aunt ~*ing* over the baby⟩ ~ *vt* **1** : to emit in a copious free flow **2** : to say or write effusively — **gush·ing·ly** \ˈgə-shiŋ-lē\ *adv*
[2]**gush** *n* (ca. 1682) **1 a** : a sudden outpouring **b** : something emitted in a gushing forth **2** : an effusive display or outpouring
gush·er \ˈgə-shər\ *n* (1864) : one that gushes; *specif* : an oil well with a copious natural flow
gushy \ˈgə-shē\ *adj* **gush·i·er; -est** (1845) : marked by effusive sentimentality — **gush·i·ly** \ˈgə-shə-lē\ *adv* — **gush·i·ness** \ˈgə-shē-nəs\ *n*
gus·set \ˈgə-sət\ *n* [ME, piece of armor covering the joints in a suit of armor, fr. AF *goussete*] (ca. 1570) **1** : a usu. diamond-shaped or triangular insert in a seam (as of a sleeve, pocketbook, or shoe upper) to provide expansion or reinforcement **2** : a plate or bracket for strengthening an angle in framework (as in a building or bridge) — **gusset** *vt*
gus·sy up \ˈgə-sē-ˈəp\ *vt* **gus·sied up; gus·sy·ing up** [origin unknown] (1952) : DRESS UP, EMBELLISH
[1]**gust** \ˈgəst\ *n* [ME *guste,* fr. L *gustus;* akin to L *gustare* to taste — more at CHOOSE] (15c) **1** *obs* **a** : the sensation of taste **b** : INCLINATION, LIKING **2** : keen delight

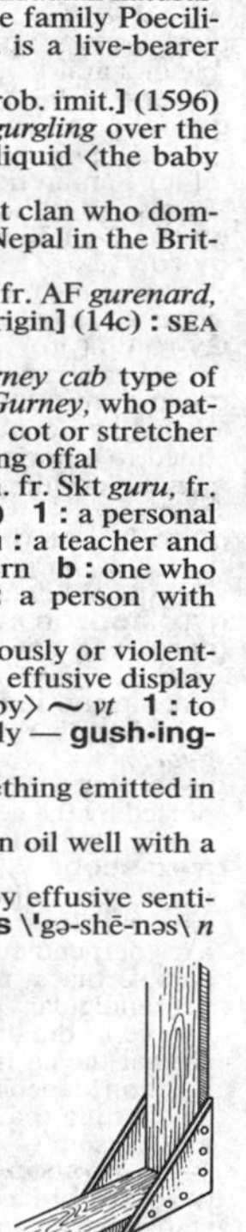

gusset 2

[2]**gust** *n* [prob. fr. ON *gustr;* akin to OHG *gussa* flood, and perh. to OE *gēotan* to pour — more at FOUND] (1588) **1** : a sudden brief rush of wind **2** : a sudden outburst : SURGE ⟨a ~ of emotion⟩ — **gust·i·ly** \ˈgəs-tə-lē\ *adv* — **gust·i·ness** \-tē-nəs\ *n* — **gusty** \-tē\ *adj*
[3]**gust** *vi* (1813) : to blow in gusts ⟨winds ~*ing* up to 40 mph⟩
gus·ta·tion \ˌgəs-ˈtā-shən\ *n* [L *gustation-, gustatio,* fr. *gustare*] (1599) : the act or sensation of tasting
gus·ta·to·ry \ˈgəs-tə-ˌtȯr-ē\ *adj* (1684) : relating to or associated with eating or the sense of taste — **gus·ta·to·ri·ly** \ˌgəs-tə-ˈtȯr-ə-lē\ *adv*
gus·to \ˈgəs-(ˌ)tō\ *n, pl* **gustoes** [It, fr. L *gustus,* pp.] (1620) **1 a** : an individual or special taste ⟨different ~*es*⟩ **b** : enthusiastic and vigorous enjoyment or appreciation **c** : vitality marked by an abundance of vigor and enthusiasm **2** *archaic* : artistic style
[1]**gut** \ˈgət\ *n* [ME, fr. OE *guttas,* pl.; prob. akin to OE *gēotan* to pour] (bef. 12c) **1 a (1)** : BOWELS, ENTRAILS — usu. used in pl. **(2)** : the basic visceral or emotional part of a person **b** : ALIMENTARY CANAL; *also* : part of the alimentary canal and esp. the intestine or stomach **c** : BELLY, ABDOMEN **d** : CATGUT **2** *pl* : the inner essential parts ⟨the ~*s* of a car⟩ **3** : a narrow passage; *also* : a narrow waterway or small creek **4** : the sac of silk taken from a silkworm ready to spin its cocoon and drawn out into a thread for use as a snell **5** *pl* : fortitude and stamina in coping with what alarms, repels, or discourages : COURAGE, PLUCK **6** : GUT COURSE
[2]**gut** *vt* **gut·ted; gut·ting** (14c) **1 a** : EVISCERATE **b** : to extract all the essential passages or portions from **2 a** : to destroy the inside of ⟨fire *gutted* the building⟩ **b** : to destroy the essential power or effectiveness of ⟨inflation *gutting* the economy⟩ — **gut it out** : PERSEVERE
[3]**gut** *adj* (1964) **1** : arising from one's inmost self : VISCERAL ⟨a ~ reaction⟩ **2** : having strong impact or immediate relevance ⟨~ issues⟩
GUT *abbr* grand unified theory; grand unification theory
gut·buck·et \ˈgət-ˌbə-kət\ *n* (1929) **1** : BARRELHOUSE 2 **2** : a homemade bass fiddle consisting of a stick attached to an inverted washtub and having a single string
gut check *n* (1972) : a test or assessment of courage, character, or determination
gut course *n* (1948) : a course (as in college) that is easily passed
gut·less \ˈgət-ləs\ *adj* (1900) **1** : lacking courage : COWARDLY **2** : lacking significance or vitality — **gut·less·ness** *n*
gutsy \ˈgət-sē\ *adj* **guts·i·er; -est** (ca. 1893) **1** : marked by courage, pluck, or determination ⟨a ~ little fighter⟩ ⟨a ~ decision⟩ **2 a** : expressing or characterized by basic physical senses or passions ⟨~ macho talk⟩ ⟨~ country blues⟩ **b** : rough or plain in style : not bland or sophisticated ⟨a ~ soup⟩ — **gut·si·ly** \-sə-lē\ *adv* — **guts·i·ness** *n*
gut·ta \ˈgə-tə, ˈgu̇-tə\ *n, pl* **gut·tae** \ˈgə-ˌtē, ˈgu̇-, -ˌtī\ [L, lit., drop] (1563) : one of a series of ornaments in the Doric entablature that is usu. in the form of a frustum of a cone
gut·ta–per·cha \ˌgə-tə-ˈpər-chə\ *n* [Malay *gĕtah-pĕrcha,* fr. *gĕtah* sap, latex + *pĕrcha* scrap, rag] (1845) : a tough plastic substance from the latex of several Malaysian trees (genera *Payena* and *Palaquium*) of the sapodilla family that resembles rubber but contains more resin and is used esp. as insulation and in dentistry in temporary fillings
gut·ta·tion \ˌgə-ˈtā-shən\ *n* [L *gutta* drop] (ca. 1889) : the exudation of liquid water from the uninjured surface of a plant leaf
[1]**gut·ter** \ˈgə-tər\ *n* [ME *goter,* fr. AF *gutere, goter,* fr. *gute* drop, fr. L *gutta*] (14c) **1 a** : a trough along the eaves to catch and carry off rainwater **b** : a low area (as at the edge of a street) to carry off surface water (as to a sewer) **c** : a trough or groove to catch and direct something ⟨the ~*s* of a bowling alley⟩ **2** : a white space formed by the adjoining inside margins of two facing pages (as of a book) **3** : the lowest or most vulgar level or condition of human life
[2]**gutter** *vt* (14c) **1** : to cut or wear gutters in **2** : to provide with a gutter ~ *vi* **1 a** : to flow in rivulets **b** *of a candle* : to melt away through a channel out of the side of the cup hollowed out by the burning wick **2** : to incline downward in a draft ⟨the candle flame ~*ing*⟩
[3]**gutter** *adj* (15c) : of, relating to, or characteristic of the gutter; *esp* : marked by extreme vulgarity, cheapness, or indecency ⟨~ politics⟩
gut·ter·ing \-iŋ\ *n* (1703) **1** : material for gutters **2** : GUTTER 1a
gutter out *vi* (1875) **1** : to become gradually weaker and then go out ⟨the candle *guttered out*⟩ **2** : to end feebly or undramatically ⟨his screen career had slowly *guttered out*⟩
gut·ter·snipe \ˈgə-tər-ˌsnīp\ *n* (ca. 1869) **1** : a homeless vagabond and esp. an outcast boy or girl in the streets of a city **2** : a person of the lowest moral or economic station — **gut·ter·snip·ish** \-ˌsnī-pish\ *adj*
gut·tur·al \ˈgə-tə-rəl, ˈgə-trəl\ *adj* [MF, prob. fr. ML *gutturalis,* fr. L *guttur* throat] (1594) **1** : articulated in the throat ⟨~ sounds⟩ **2** : VELAR **3** : being or marked by utterance that is strange, unpleasant, or disagreeable — **guttural** *n* — **gut·tur·al·ism** \ˈgə-tə-rə-ˌli-zəm, ˈgə-trə-\ *n*
gut·ty \ˈgə-tē\ *adj* **gut·ti·er; -est** (1942) **1** : GUTSY 1 ⟨a ~ quarterback⟩ **2** : having a vigorous challenging quality ⟨~ realism⟩
gut–wrench·ing \ˈgət-ˌren-chiŋ\ *adj* (1974) : causing mental or emotional anguish
[1]**guy** \ˈgī\ *n* [prob. fr. D *gei* brail] (1623) : a rope, chain, rod, or wire attached to something as a brace or guide — called also *guyline*
[2]**guy** *vt* (1712) : to steady or reinforce with a guy
[3]**guy** *n* [*Guy* Fawkes] (1806) **1** *often cap* : a grotesque effigy of Guy Fawkes traditionally displayed and burned in England on Guy Fawkes Day **2** *chiefly Brit* : a person of grotesque appearance **3 a** : MAN, FELLOW **b** : PERSON — used in pl. to refer to the members of a group regardless of sex ⟨saw her and the rest of the ~*s*⟩ **4** : INDIVIDUAL, CREATURE ⟨the other dogs pale in companion to this little ~⟩
[4]**guy** *vt* (1854) : to make fun of : RIDICULE
Guy Fawkes Day \ˈgī-ˈfȯks-\ *n* (1825) : November 5 observed in England in commemoration of the seizure of Guy Fawkes in 1605 for an attempt to blow up the houses of parliament
guy·ot \ˈgē-(ˌ)ō\ *n* [Arnold H. *Guyot* †1884 Am. geographer & geologist] (1946) : a flat-topped seamount
guz·zle \ˈgə-zəl\ *vb* **guz·zled; guz·zling** \ˈgəz-liŋ, ˈgə-zə-\ [origin unknown] *vi* (1567) : to drink esp. liquor greedily, continually, or habitually ~ *vt* **1** : to drink greedily or habitually ⟨~ beer⟩ **2** : CONSUME, USE UP ⟨devices that ~ electricity⟩ — **guz·zler** \ˈgəz-lər, ˈgə-zə-\ *n*
GVHD *abbr* graft-versus-host disease
GW *abbr* gross weight
Gy *abbr* gray
gybe *var of* JIBE
gym \ˈjim\ *n* (ca. 1871) **1** : GYMNASIUM **2** : PHYSICAL EDUCATION **3** : a usu. metal frame supporting an assortment of outdoor play equipment (as a swing, seesaw, and rings)
gym·kha·na \jim-ˈkä-nə, -ˈka-\ *n* [prob. modif. of Hindi *gẽdkhānā* & Urdu *gendkhāna,* lit., ball court] (1877) : a meet featuring sports contests or athletic skills: as **a** : competitive games on horseback **b** : a timed contest for automobiles featuring a series of events designed to test driving skill
gym·na·si·um *sense 1* jim-ˈnā-zē-əm, -zhəm; *sense 2 usu* gim-ˈnä-zē-əm\ *n, pl* **-na·si·ums** *or* **-na·sia** \-ˈnā-zē-ə, -ˈnā-zhə; -ˈnä-zē-ə\ [L, exercise ground, school, fr. Gk *gymnasion,* fr. *gymnazein* to exercise naked, fr. *gymnos* naked — more at NAKED] (1598) **1 a** : a large room used for various indoor sports (as basketball or boxing) and usu. equipped with gymnastic apparatus **b** : a building (as on a college campus) containing space and equipment for various indoor sports activities and usu. including spectator accommodations, locker and shower rooms, offices, classrooms, and a swimming pool **2** [G, fr. L, school] : a European secondary school that prepares students for the university
gym·nast \ˈjim-ˌnast, -nəst\ *n* [MF *gymnaste,* fr. Gk *gymnastēs* trainer, fr. *gymnazein*] (1594) : a person trained in gymnastics
[1]**gym·nas·tic** \jim-ˈnas-tik\ *adj* (1574) : of or relating to gymnastics : ATHLETIC — **gym·nas·ti·cal·ly** \-ti-k(ə-)lē\ *adv*

²**gymnastic** *n* (1652)   **1** *pl but sing in constr*   **a** : physical exercises designed to develop strength and coordination   **b** : a competitive sport in which individuals perform optional and prescribed acrobatic feats mostly on special apparatus in order to demonstrate strength, balance, and body control   **2** : an exercise in intellectual or artistic dexterity ⟨my earlier philosophic study had been an intellectual ∼ —John Dewey⟩ ⟨mental ∼*s*⟩   **3** : a physical feat or contortion ⟨the ∼*s* necessary for the killer to have swung from the fire escape —E. D. Radin⟩

gym·nos·o·phist \jim-'nä-sə-fist\ *n* [L *gymnosophista,* fr. Gk *gymnosophistēs,* fr. *gymnos* + *sophistēs* wise man, sophist] (15c) : any of a sect of ascetics in ancient India who went naked and practiced meditation

gym·no·sperm \'jim-nə-₁spərm\ *n* [ultim. fr. Gk *gymnos* + *sperma* seed — more at SPERM] (ca. 1838) : any of a group of vascular plants that produce naked seeds not enclosed in an ovary, that were formerly considered a class (Gymnospermae) of seed plants, but that are now considered polyphyletic in origin and divided into several extinct divisions and four divisions with surviving members typified by the cycadophytes, conifers, ginkgo, and ephedras — compare ANGIOSPERM — **gym·no·sper·mous** \₁jim-nə-'spər-məs\ *adj* — **gym·no·sper·my** \'jim-nə-₁spər-mē\ *n*

gyn *or* **gynecol** *abbr* gynecology

gyn- *or* **gyno-** *comb form* [Gk *gyn-,* fr. *gynē* woman — more at QUEEN] : female reproductive organ : ovary ⟨*gynophore*⟩

gy·nae·col·o·gy *chiefly Brit var of* GYNECOLOGY

gyn·an·dro·morph \₁gīn-'an-drə-₁mörf, ₁jin-\ *n* [ISV, fr. Gk *gynandros* + *-morph*] (ca. 1890) : an abnormal individual exhibiting characters of both sexes in various parts of the body : a sexual mosaic — **gyn·an·dro·mor·phic** \(₁)gīn-₁an-drə-'mór-fik, (₁)jin-\ *adj* — **gyn·an·dro·mor·phism** \-₁fi-zəm\ *n* — **gyn·an·dro·mor·phy** \₁gīn-'an-drə-₁mòr-fē, ₁jin-\ *n*

gyn·an·drous \₁gīn-'an-drəs, ₁jin-\ *adj* [Gk *gynandros* of doubtful sex, fr. *gynē* woman + *andr-, anēr* man — more at ANDR-] (1807) : having the androecium and gynoecium united in a column

-gyne *n comb form* [Gk *gynē*] : female reproductive organ ⟨*trichogyne*⟩

gynec- *or* **gyneco-** *also* **gynaec-** *or* **gynaeco-** *comb form* [Gk *gynaik-, gynaiko-,* fr. *gynaik-, gynē* woman — more at QUEEN] : woman ⟨*gynecology*⟩

gy·ne·coc·ra·cy \₁gī-ni-'kä-krə-sē, ₁ji-\ *n, pl* **-cies** [Gk *gynaikokratia,* fr. *gynaik-* + *-kratia* -cracy] (1612) : political supremacy of women — **gy·ne·co·crat·ic** \₁gī-ni-kō-'kra-tik, ₁ji-\ *adj*

gy·ne·coid \'gī-ni-₁kóid, 'ji-\ *adj* (1907) : typical or characteristic of the human female ⟨∼ pelvis⟩

gy·ne·col·o·gy \₁gī-nə-'kä-lə-jē, ₁ji-\ *n* [ISV] (ca. 1847) : a branch of medicine that deals with the diseases and routine physical care of the reproductive system of women — **gy·ne·co·log·ic** \₁gī-ni-kə-'lä-jik, ₁ji-\ *or* **gy·ne·co·log·i·cal** \-ji-kəl\ *adj* — **gy·ne·col·o·gist** \₁gī-nə-'kä-lə-jist, ₁ji-\ *n*

gy·ne·co·mas·tia \₁gī-nə-kō-'mas-tē-ə\ *n* [NL, fr. *gynec-* + Gk *mastos* breast + NL *-ia*] (1881) : excessive development of the breast in the male

gy·no·cen·tric \₁gī-nə-'sen-trik\ *adj* (1976) : dominated by or emphasizing feminine interests or a feminine point of view

gy·noe·ci·um \jī-'nē-shē-əm, gī-, -sē-\ *n, pl* **-cia** \-shē-ə, -sē-\ [NL, alter. of L *gynaeceum* women's apartments, fr. Gk *gynaikeion,* fr. *gynaik-, gynē*] (1832) : the aggregate of carpels or pistils in a flower

gy·no·gen·e·sis \₁gī-nə-'je-nə-səs\ *n* [NL] (1925) : development in which the embryo contains only maternal chromosomes due to activation of an egg by a sperm that degenerates without fusing with the egg nucleus — **gy·no·ge·net·ic** \-jə-'ne-tik\ *adj*

gy·no·phore \'gī-nə-₁fór, 'ji-\ *n* (1821) : a prolongation of the receptacle (as in a caper flower) with the gynoecium at its apex

-gynous *adj comb form* [NL *-gynus,* fr. Gk *-gynos,* fr. *gynē* woman — more at QUEEN]   **1** : of, relating to, or having (such or so many) wives ⟨*monogynous*⟩   **2** : situated (in a specified place) in relation to a female organ of a plant ⟨*hypogynous*⟩

-gyny *n comb form*   **1** : existence of or condition of having (such or so many) wives ⟨*polygyny*⟩   **2** : condition of being situated (in a specified place) in relation to a female organ of a plant ⟨*epigyny*⟩

¹**gyp** \'jip\ *n* [prob. short for *gypsy*] (1750)   **1** *Brit* : a college servant   **2**   **a** : CHEAT, SWINDLER   **b** : FRAUD, SWINDLE

²**gyp** *vb* **gypped; gyp·ping** (1880) : CHEAT

gyp·se·ous \'jip-sē-əs\ *adj* (1661) : resembling, containing, or consisting of gypsum ⟨∼ clay loam⟩

gyp·soph·i·la \jip-'sä-fə-lə\ *n* [NL, fr. L *gypsum* + NL *-phila* -phil] (1771) : any of a large genus (*Gypsophila*) of Old World herbs of the pink family having small delicate usu. paniculate flowers

gyp·sum \'jip-səm\ *n* [L, fr. Gk *gypsos*] (14c)   **1** : a widely distributed mineral consisting of hydrous calcium sulfate that is used esp. as a soil amendment and in making plaster of paris   **2** : DRYWALL

gyp·sy \'jip-sē\ *vi* **gyp·sied; gyp·sy·ing** (ca. 1627) : to live or roam like a Gypsy

Gyp·sy \'jip-sē\ *n, pl* **Gypsies** [by shortening & alter. fr. *Egyptian*] (1537)   **1** : a member of a traditionally itinerant people who originated in northern India and now live chiefly in south and southwest Asia, Europe, and No. America   **2** : ROMANY 2   **3** *not cap* : one that resembles a Gypsy; *esp* : WANDERER

gypsy cab *n* (1964) : a taxicab licensed only to answer calls; *esp* : such a cab that cruises in search of passengers illegally

gypsy moth *n* (1819) : an Old World tussock moth (*Lymantria dispar*) that was introduced about 1869 into the U.S. and has a grayish-brown mottled hairy caterpillar which is a destructive defoliator of many trees

gyr- *or* **gyro-** *comb form* [Gk *gyros* rounded]   **1** : ring : circle : spiral ⟨*gyromagnetic*⟩   **2** : gyroscope ⟨*gyrocompass*⟩

gyr·ase \'jī-₁rās\ *n* [*gyr-* + *-ase*] (1976) : a bacterial enzyme that catalyzes the breaking and rejoining of bonds linking adjacent nucleotides in circular DNA to generate supercoiled DNA helices

¹**gy·rate** \'jī-₁rāt\ *adj* (1830) : winding or coiled around : CONVOLUTED ⟨∼ branches of a tree⟩

²**gyrate** *vi* **gy·rat·ed; gy·rat·ing** (1830)   **1** : to revolve around a point or axis   **2** : to oscillate with or as if with a circular or spiral motion — **gy·ra·tor** \-₁rā-tər\ *n* — **gy·ra·to·ry** \'jī-rə-₁tór-ē\ *adj*

gy·ra·tion \jī-'rā-shən\ *n* (1615)   **1** : an act or instance of gyrating   **2** : something (as a coil of a shell) that is gyrate — **gy·ra·tion·al** \-shnəl, -shə-nᵉl\ *adj*

¹**gyre** \'jī(-ə)r\ *n* [L *gyrus,* fr. Gk *gyros*] (1566) : a circular or spiral motion or form; *esp* : a giant circular oceanic surface current — **gy·ral** \'jī-rəl\ *adj*

²**gyre** *vi* **gyred; gyr·ing** [LL *gyrare,* fr. L *gyrus*] (1593) : to move in a circle or spiral

gy·rene \jī-'rēn\ *n* [origin unknown] (ca. 1894) *slang* : a U.S. marine

gyr·fal·con \'jər-₁fal-kən, -₁fól- *also* -₁fó-kən\ *n* [ME *gerfaucun,* fr. AF *girfauc, girfaucon,* prob. fr. *gir* vulture (fr. OHG *gīr*) + *faucon* falcon] (14c) : an arctic falcon (*Falco rusticolus*) that occurs in several color forms and is the largest of all falcons

¹**gy·ro** \'jī-(₁)rō\ *n, pl* **gyros** (1910)   **1** : GYROCOMPASS   **2** : GYROSCOPE

²**gy·ro** \'yē-₁rō, 'zhir-ō\ *n, pl* **gyros** [ModGk *gyros* turn, fr. Gk; fr. the rotation of the meat on a spit] (1971) : a sandwich esp. of lamb and beef, tomato, onion, and yogurt sauce on pita bread

Gy·ro \'jī-(₁)rō\ *n, pl* **Gyros** [*Gyro* International (association)] (1971) : a member of a major international service club

gy·ro·com·pass \'jī-rō-₁kəm-pəs *also* -₁käm-\ *n* (1910) : a compass consisting of a continuously driven gyroscope whose spinning axis is confined to a horizontal plane so that the earth's rotation causes it to assume a position parallel to the earth's axis and thus point to the true north

gy·ro·fre·quen·cy \-₁frē-kwən(t)-sē\ *n* (1938) : the frequency with which a charged particle (as an electron) executes spiral gyrations in moving obliquely across a magnetic field

gyro horizon *n* (1938) : ARTIFICIAL HORIZON

gy·ro·mag·net·ic \₁jī-rō-mag-'ne-tik\ *adj* (1922) : of or relating to the magnetic properties of a rotating electrical particle

gyromagnetic ratio *n* (1922) : the ratio of the magnetic moment of a spinning charged particle to its angular momentum — called also *g-factor*

gy·ro·plane \'jī-rə-₁plān\ *n* [ISV] (1907) : an airplane balanced and supported by the aerodynamic forces acting on rapidly rotating horizontal or slightly inclined airfoils

gy·ro·scope \'jī-rə-₁skōp, *Brit also* 'gī-\ *n* [F] (1856) : a wheel or disk mounted to spin rapidly about an axis and also free to rotate about one or both of two axes perpendicular to each other and to the axis of spin so that a rotation of one of the two mutually perpendicular axes results from application of torque to the other when the wheel is spinning and so that the entire apparatus offers considerable opposition depending on the angular momentum to any torque that would change the direction of the axis of spin — **gy·ro·scop·ic** \₁jī-rə-'skä-pik\ *adj* — **gy·ro·scop·i·cal·ly** \-pi-k(ə-)lē\ *adv*

gyroscope

gy·ro·sta·bi·liz·er \₁jī-rō-'stā-bə-₁lī-zər\ *n* (1921) : a stabilizing device (as for a ship or airplane) that consists of a continuously driven gyro spinning about a vertical axis and pivoted so that its axis of spin may be tipped fore-and-aft in the vertical plane and that serves to oppose sideways motion — called also *gy·ro·stat* \'jī-rə-₁stat\

gy·rus \'jī-rəs\ *n, pl* **gy·ri** \'jī-₁rī\ [NL, fr. L, circle — more at GYRE] (ca. 1842) : a convoluted ridge between anatomical grooves; *esp* : CONVOLUTION 2

Gy Sgt *abbr* gunnery sergeant

gyve \'jīv, 'gīv\ *n* [ME] (13c) : FETTER, SHACKLE — **gyve** *vt*

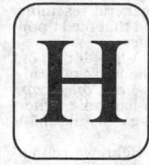

H

[1]**h** \ˈāch\ *n, pl* **h's** *or* **hs** \ˈā-chəz\ *often cap, often attrib* (bef. 12c) **1 a** : the 8th letter of the English alphabet **b** : a graphic representation of this letter **c** : a speech counterpart of orthographic *h* **2** : a graphic device for reproducing the letter *h* **3** : one designated *h* esp. as the eighth in order or class **4** : something shaped like the letter H

[2]**h** *abbr* **1** half **2** harbor **3** hard; hardness **4** hect-; hecto- **5** height **6** high **7** hit **8** horse **9** hour **10** humidity **11** hundred **12** husband

[1]**H** *abbr* **1** Hamiltonian **2** henry **3** heroin

[2]**H** *symbol* hydrogen

[1]**ha** *or* **hah** \ˈhä\ *interj* [ME, fr. OE] (bef. 12c) — used esp. to express surprise, joy, or triumph

[2]**ha** *abbr* hectare

HA *abbr* hour angle

Hab *abbr* Habacuc; Habakkuk

Ha·ba·cuc \ˈha-bə-ˌkək, hə-ˈba-kək\ *n* [LL, fr. Heb *Ḥăbhaqqūq*] (ca. 1600) : HABAKKUK

Ha·bak·kuk \ˈha-bə-ˌkək, hə-ˈba-kək\ *n* [Heb *Ḥăbhaqqūq*] (1621) **1** : a Hebrew prophet of seventh century B.C. Judah who prophesied an imminent Chaldean invasion **2** : a prophetic book of canonical Jewish and Christian Scripture — see BIBLE table

ha·ba·ne·ra \ˌ(h)ä-bə-ˈner-ə\ *n* [Sp (*danza*) *habanera,* lit., Havanan dance] (1878) **1** : a Cuban dance in slow duple time **2** : the music for the habanera

ha·ba·ne·ro *also* **ha·ba·ñe·ro** \ˌ(h)ä-bə-ˈn(y)er-ō\ *n* [AmerSp (*chile*) *habanero,* lit., Havanan chili] (1987) : a very hot roundish chili pepper (*Capsicum chinense*) that is usu. orange when mature

hab corp *abbr* habeas corpus

habdalah *var of* HAVDALAH

ha·be·as cor·pus \ˈhā-bē-əs-ˈkȯr-pəs\ *n* [ME, fr. ML, lit., you should have the body (the opening words of the writ)] (15c) **1** : any of several common-law writs issued to bring a party before a court or judge; *esp* : HABEAS CORPUS AD SUBJICIENDUM **2** : the right of a citizen to obtain a writ of habeas corpus as a protection against illegal imprisonment

habeas corpus ad sub·ji·ci·en·dum \-ˌad-səb-ˌji-sē-ˈen-dəm, -ˌji-shē-; -ˌäd-sùb-ˌyi-kē-ˈen-dùm\ *n* [NL, lit., you should have the body for submitting] (1768) : a writ for inquiring into the lawfulness of the restraint of a person who is imprisoned or detained in another's custody

hab·er·dash·er \ˈha-bə(r)-ˌda-shər\ *n* [ME *haberdassher,* fr. modif. of AF *hapertas* kind of cloth] (14c) **1** *Brit* : a dealer in notions **2** : a dealer in men's clothing and accessories

hab·er·dash·ery \-ˌda-sh(ə-)rē\ *n, pl* **-er·ies** (1547) **1** : goods sold by a haberdasher **2** : a haberdasher's shop

hab·er·geon \ˈha-bər-jən; hə-ˈbər-jē-ən, -jən\ *n* [ME *haubergeoun,* fr. AF *haubergeon,* dim. of *hauberc* hauberk] (14c) **1** : a medieval jacket of mail shorter than a hauberk **2** : HAUBERK

Ha·ber process \ˈhä-bər-\ *n* [Fritz *Haber* †1934 Ger. chemist] (1916) : a catalytic process for synthesizing ammonia from nitrogen and hydrogen

hab·ile \ˈha-bəl, -ˌbī(-ə)l\ *adj* [ME (Sc) *habyll,* fr. MF *habile,* fr. L *habilis* — more at ABLE] (15c) : having general skill : ABLE, SKILLFUL

ha·bil·i·ment \hə-ˈbi-lə-mənt\ *n* [ME *abiliments, habilementes,* fr. MF *abillement, habillemens,* fr. OF *abiller* to prepare, equip, fr. *bille* trimmed wood, log — more at BILLET] (15c) **1** *pl* : characteristic apparatus : TRAPPINGS ⟨the ∼*s* of civilization —W. P. Webb⟩ **2 a** : the dress characteristic of an occupation or occasion — usu. used in pl. **b** : CLOTHES — usu. used in pl.

ha·bil·i·tate \hə-ˈbi-lə-ˌtāt\ *vb* **-tat·ed; -tat·ing** [LL *habilitatus,* pp. of *habilitare,* fr. L *habilitas* ability — more at ABILITY] *vt* (1604) **1** : to make fit or capable (as for functioning in society) **2** : CLOTHE, DRESS ∼ *vi* : to qualify oneself — **ha·bil·i·ta·tion** \-ˌbi-lə-ˈtā-shən\ *n*

[1]**hab·it** \ˈha-bət\ *n* [ME, fr. AF, fr. L *habitus* condition, character, fr. *habēre* to have, hold — more at GIVE] (13c) **1** *archaic* : CLOTHING **2 a** : a costume characteristic of a calling, rank, or function ⟨a nun's ∼⟩ **b** : a costume worn for horseback riding **3** : manner of conducting oneself : BEARING **4** : bodily appearance or makeup ⟨a man of fleshy ∼⟩ **5** : the prevailing disposition or character of a person's thoughts and feelings : mental makeup **6** : a settled tendency or usual manner of behavior ⟨her ∼ of taking a morning walk⟩ **7 a** : a behavior pattern acquired by frequent repetition or physiologic exposure that shows itself in regularity or increased facility of performance **b** : an acquired mode of behavior that has become nearly or completely involuntary ⟨got up early from force of ∼⟩ **c** : ADDICTION ⟨a drug ∼⟩ **8** : characteristic mode of growth or occurrence ⟨a grass similar to Indian corn in ∼⟩ **9** *of a crystal* : characteristic assemblage of forms at crystallization leading to a usual appearance : SHAPE

syn HABIT, PRACTICE, USAGE, CUSTOM, WONT mean a way of acting fixed through repetition. HABIT implies a doing unconsciously and often compulsively ⟨had a *habit* of tapping his fingers⟩. PRACTICE suggests an act or method followed with regularity and usu. through choice ⟨our *practice* is to honor all major credit cards⟩. USAGE suggests a customary action so generally followed that it has become a social norm ⟨western-style dress is now common *usage* in international business⟩. CUSTOM applies to a practice or usage so steadily associated with an individual or group as to have almost the force of unwritten law ⟨the *custom* of wearing black at funerals⟩. WONT usu. applies to an habitual manner, method, or practice of an individual or group ⟨as was her *wont,* she slept until noon⟩.

[2]**habit** *vt* (1594) : CLOTHE, DRESS

hab·it·able \ˈha-bə-tə-bəl *also* hə-ˈbi-tə-\ *adj* (14c) : capable of being lived in : suitable for habitation — **hab·it·abil·i·ty** \ˌha-bə-tə-ˈbi-lə-tē\ *n* — **hab·it·able·ness** \ˈha-bə-tə-bəl-nes\ *n* — **hab·it·ably** \-blē\ *adv*

ha·bi·tant *n* (15c) **1** \ˈha-bə-tənt\ : INHABITANT, RESIDENT **2** \ˌ(h)a-bi-ˈtäⁿ\ *also* **ha·bi·tan** \-ˈtäⁿ\ : a settler or descendant of a settler of French origin working as a farmer in Canada

hab·i·tat \ˈha-bə-ˌtat\ *n* [L, it inhabits, fr. *habitare*] (1796) **1 a** : the place or environment where a plant or animal naturally or normally lives and grows **b** : the typical place of residence of a person or a group **c** : a housing for a controlled physical environment in which people can live under surrounding inhospitable conditions (as under the sea) **2** : the place where something is commonly found

hab·i·ta·tion \ˌha-bə-ˈtā-shən\ *n* [ME *habitacioun,* fr. AF *habitaciun,* fr. L *habitation-, habitatio,* fr. *habitare* to inhabit, freq. of *habēre*] (14c) **1** : the act of inhabiting : OCCUPANCY ⟨not fit for human ∼⟩ **2** : a dwelling place **3** : SETTLEMENT, COLONY

hab·it–form·ing \ˈha-bət-ˌfȯr-miŋ\ *adj* (1913) : inducing the formation of an addiction ⟨a ∼ drug⟩

ha·bit·u·al \hə-ˈbi-ch(ə-)wəl, ha-, -ˈbi-chəl\ *adj* (1603) **1** : having the nature of a habit : CUSTOMARY ⟨∼ candor⟩ ⟨∼ behavior⟩ **2** : doing, practicing, or acting in some manner by force of habit ⟨∼ drunkards⟩ **3** : resorted to on a regular basis ⟨our ∼ diet⟩ **4** : inherent in an individual ⟨∼ grace⟩ ***syn*** see USUAL — **ha·bit·u·al·ly** *adv* — **ha·bit·u·al·ness** *n*

ha·bit·u·ate \hə-ˈbi-chə-ˌwāt, ha-, -chü-ˌāt\ *vb* **-at·ed; -at·ing** *vt* (15c) **1** : to make used to something : ACCUSTOM **2** : FREQUENT 1 ∼ *vi* **1** : to cause habituation **2** : to undergo habituation ⟨∼ to a stimulus⟩

ha·bit·u·a·tion \-ˌbi-chə-ˈwā-shən, -chü-ˈā-\ *n* (15c) **1** : the process of habituating : the state of being habituated **2 a** : tolerance to the effects of a drug acquired through continued use **b** : psychological dependence on a drug after a period of use — compare ADDICTION **3** : decrease in responsiveness upon repeated exposure to a stimulus

hab·i·tude \ˈha-bə-ˌtüd, -ˌtyüd\ *n* (14c) **1** *archaic* : native or essential character **2** *obs* : habitual association **3 a** : habitual disposition or mode of behavior or procedure **b** : CUSTOM

ha·bi·tué *also* **ha·bi·tue** \hə-ˈbi-chə-ˌwā, ha-, -ˌbi-chə-ˈ\ *n* [F, fr. pp. of *habituer* to frequent, fr. LL *habituare* to habituate, fr. L *habitus*] (1818) **1** : a person who may be regularly found in or at a particular place or kind of place ⟨café ∼*s*⟩ **2** : DEVOTEE ⟨an Internet ∼⟩

hab·i·tus \ˈha-bə-təs\ *n, pl* **habitus** \-təs, -ˌtüs\ [NL, fr. L] (1886) : HABIT; *specif* : body build and constitution esp. as related to predisposition to disease

ha·boob \hə-ˈbüb\ *n* [Ar *habūb* violent storm] (1897) : a violent dust storm or sandstorm esp. of Sudan

Habsburg *var of* HAPSBURG

ha·ček \ˈhä-ˌchek\ *n* [Czech *háček,* lit., little hook] (1953) : a diacritic ˇ placed over a letter (as in *č*) to modify it : an inverted circumflex

ha·cen·da·do \ˌ(h)ä-sᵊn-ˈdä-(ˌ)dō\ *also* **ha·ci·en·da·do** \ˌhä-sē-en-\ *n, pl* **-dos** [Sp, fr. *hacienda*] (1840) : the owner or proprietor of a hacienda

[1]**ha·chure** \ha-ˈshu̇r\ *n* [F, fr. *hacher* to chop up, hash] (1858) : a short line used for shading and denoting surfaces in relief (as in map drawing) and drawn in the direction of slope

[2]**hachure** *vt* **ha·chured; ha·chur·ing** (ca. 1859) : to shade with or show by hachures

ha·ci·en·da \ˌ(h)ä-sē-ˈen-də\ *n* [Sp, fr. OSp *facienda,* fr. L, lit., things to be done, neut. pl. of *faciendus,* gerundive of *facere* to do — more at DO] (ca. 1772) **1** : a large estate esp. in a Spanish-speaking country : PLANTATION **2** : the main dwelling of a hacienda

[1]**hack** \ˈhak\ *vb* [ME *hakken,* fr. OE *-haccian;* akin to OHG *hacchōn* to hack, OE *hōc* hook] *vt* (13c) **1 a** : to cut or sever with repeated irregular or unskillful blows **b** : to cut or shape by or as if by crude or ruthless strokes ⟨∼*ing* out new election districts⟩ **c** : ANNOY, VEX — often used with *off* **2** : to clear or make by or as if by cutting away vegetation ⟨∼*ed* his way through the brush⟩ **3 a** : to manage successfully ⟨just couldn't ∼ the new job⟩ **b** : TOLERATE ⟨I can't ∼ all this noise⟩ ∼ *vi* **1 a** : to make chopping strokes or blows ⟨∼*ed* at the weeds⟩; *also* : to make cuts as if by chopping ⟨∼*ing* away at the work force⟩ *b* : to play inexpert golf **2** : to cough in a short dry manner **3** : LOAF — usu. used with *around* **4 a** : to write computer programs for enjoyment **b** : to gain access to a computer illegally — **hack it 1** : COPE 2b ⟨I can't *hack it* any longer⟩ **2** : to be successful ⟨couldn't *hack it* in the world of professional sports⟩

[2]**hack** *n* (14c) **1** : an implement for hacking **2** : NICK, NOTCH **3** : a short dry cough **4** : a hacking stroke or blow **5** : restriction to quarters as punishment for naval officers — usu. used in the phrase *under hack* **6** : a usu. creative solution to a computer hardware or programming problem or limitation

[3]**hack** *n* [short for *hackney*] (1672) **1 a** : HACKNEY **b (1)** : TAXICAB **(2)** : CABDRIVER **2 a (1)** : a horse let out for common hire **(2)** : a horse used in all kinds of work **b** : a horse worn out in service : JADE **c** : a light easy saddle horse; *esp* : a three-gaited saddle horse **d** : a ride on a horse **3 a** : a person who works solely for mercenary reasons : HIRELING ⟨party ∼*s*⟩ **b** : a writer who works on order; *also* : a writer who aims solely for commercial success **c** : HACKER 2

[4]**hack** *adj* (ca. 1734) **1** : working for hire esp. with mediocre professional standards ⟨a ∼ journalist⟩ **2** : performed by, suited to, or characteristic of a hack ⟨∼ writing⟩ **3** : HACKNEYED, TRITE

[5]**hack** *vi* (1857) **1** : to ride or drive at an ordinary pace or over the roads esp. as distinguished from racing or hunting **2** : to operate a taxicab ∼ *vt* : to ride (a horse) at an ordinary pace

[6]**hack** *vt* [*hack, n.,* board on which a hawk is fed, state of partial liberty, prob. alter. of ME *hache, heche, heck* lower door, hatch] (1883) : to rear (a young hawk) in a state of partial liberty esp. prior to the acquisition of flight and hunting capabilities

[7]**hack** *n* [origin unknown] (ca. 1914) *slang* : a guard esp. at a prison

hack·a·more \ˈha-kə-ˌmȯr\ *n* [by folk etymology fr. Sp *jáquima* bridle] (1850) : a bridle with a loop capable of being tightened about the nose in place of a bit or with a slip noose passed over the lower jaw

hack·ber·ry \ˈhak-ˌber-ē\ *n* [alter. of *hagberry* a cherry resembling the chokecherry] (1779) : any of a genus (*Celtis*) of trees and shrubs of the elm family with small often edible berries; *also* : its wood

hack·er \ˈha-kər\ *n* (14c) **1** : one that hacks **2** : a person who is inexperienced or unskilled at a particular activity ⟨a tennis ∼⟩ **3** : an expert at programming and solving problems with a computer **4** : a person who illegally gains access to and sometimes tampers with information in a computer system

hack·ie \ˈha-kē\ *n* (ca. 1926) : CABDRIVER

\ə\ **abut** \ᵊ\ kitten, F table \ər\ **further** \a\ ash \ā\ ace \ä\ mop, mar \au̇\ **out** \ch\ **chin** \e\ bet \ē\ **easy** \g\ **go** \i\ **hit** \ī\ **ice** \j\ **job** \ŋ\ **sing** \ō\ **go** \ȯ\ **law** \ȯi\ **boy** \th\ **thin** \t͟h\ **the** \ü\ **loot** \u̇\ **foot** \y\ yet \zh\ vision, beige \k͟, ⁿ, œ, ue, ʸ\ *see* Guide to Pronunciation

[1]**hack·le** \ˈha-kəl\ *n* [ME *hakell;* akin to OHG *hāko* hook — more at HOOK] (15c) **1 a :** one of the long narrow feathers on the neck or saddle of a bird **b :** the neck plumage of the domestic fowl **2 :** a comb or board with long metal teeth for dressing flax, hemp, or jute **3** *pl* **a :** erectile hairs along the neck and back esp. of a dog **b :** TEMPER, DANDER ⟨the issue raised some ∼*s*⟩ **4 a :** an artificial fishing fly made chiefly of the filaments of a cock's neck feathers **b :** filaments of cock feather projecting from the head of an artificial fly

[2]**hackle** *vt* **hack·led; hack·ling** \ˈha-k(ə-)liŋ\ (1616) **:** to comb out with a hackle — **hack·ler** \-k(ə-)lər\ *n*

hack·ly \ˈha-k(ə-)lē\ *adj* (1796) **:** having the appearance of something hacked **:** JAGGED

hack·man \ˈhak-mən\ *n* (1796) **:** CABDRIVER

hack·ma·tack \ˈhak-mə-ˌtak\ *n* [earlier *hakmantak,* prob. fr. Western Abenaki (Algonquian language of New Hampshire and Vermont)] (1792) **:** TAMARACK

[1]**hack·ney** \ˈhak-nē\ *n, pl* **hack·neys** [ME *hakeney*] (14c) **1 a :** a horse suitable for ordinary riding or driving **b :** a trotting horse used chiefly for driving **c** *often cap* **:** any of an English breed of rather compact usu. chestnut, bay, or brown high-stepping horses **2** *obs* **:** one that works for hire **3 :** a carriage or automobile kept for hire

[2]**hackney** *adj* (1589) **1 :** kept for public hire **2 :** HACKNEYED **3** *archaic* **:** done or suitable for doing by a drudge

[3]**hackney** *vt* **hack·neyed; hack·ney·ing** (1596) **1 a :** to make common or frequent use of **b :** to make trite, vulgar, or commonplace **2** *archaic* **:** to make sophisticated or jaded

hackney coach *n* (1619) **:** a coach kept for hire; *esp* **:** a four-wheeled carriage drawn by two horses and having seats for six persons

hack·neyed \ˈhak-nēd\ *adj* (1735) **:** lacking in freshness or originality ⟨∼ slogans⟩ ***syn*** see TRITE

hack·saw \ˈhak-ˌsȯ\ *n* (1654) **:** a fine-tooth saw with a blade under tension in a frame that is used for cutting hard materials (as metal) — **hacksaw** *vb*

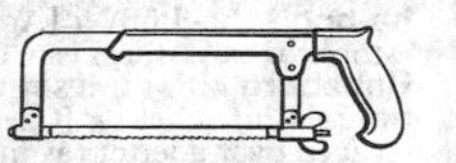
hacksaw

hack·work \-ˌwərk\ *n* (1851) **:** literary, artistic, or professional work done on order usu. according to formula and in conformity with commercial standards

had *past and past part of* HAVE

ha·dal \ˈhā-dᵊl\ *adj* [F, fr. *Hadès* Hades] (1959) **:** of, relating to, or being the parts of the ocean below 6000 meters (about 20,000 feet)

had·dock \ˈha-dək\ *n, pl* **haddock** *also* **haddocks** [ME *haddok*] (14c) **:** an important food fish (*Melanogrammus aeglefinus* syn. *Gadus aeglefinus*) of the cod family occurring on both sides of the No. Atlantic that has a black lateral line and dark patch above the pectoral fin

Ha·de·an \ˈhā-ˌdē-ən, hā-ˈdē-ən\ *adj* [*Hades*] (1984) **:** of, relating to, or being the aeon of history between the formation of the solar system and the formation of the first rocks on the earth — see GEOLOGIC TIME table — **Hadean** *n*

Ha·des \ˈhā-(ˌ)dēz\ *n* [Gk *Aidēs, Āidēs, Haidēs*] (1597) **1 :** PLUTO **2 :** the underground abode of the dead in Greek mythology **3 :** SHEOL **4** *often not cap* **:** HELL 1a

ha·dith \hə-ˈdēth\ *n, pl* **hadith** *or* **hadiths** *often cap* [Ar *ḥadīth,* lit., speech, report] (ca. 1817) **1 :** a narrative record of the sayings or customs of Muhammad and his companions **2 :** the collective body of traditions relating to Muhammad and his companions

hadj, hadji *var of* HAJJ, HAJJI

Had·ley cell \ˈhad-lē-\ *n* [George *Hadley* †1768 Eng. scientific writer] (1955) **:** a pattern of atmospheric circulation in which warm air rises near the equator, cools as it travels poleward at high altitude, sinks as cold air, and warms as it travels equatorward; *also* **:** a similar atmospheric circulation pattern on another planet (as Mars)

hadn't \ˈha-dᵊnt, -dᵊn, *dial also* ˈha-tᵊn(t) *or* ˈhant\ (1675) **:** had not

had·ron \ˈha-ˌdrän\ *n* [ISV *hadr-* thick, heavy (fr. Gk. *hadros* thick) + [2]*-on*] (1962) **:** any of the subatomic particles (as protons and neutrons) that are made up of quarks and are subject to the strong force — **ha·dron·ic** \ha-ˈdrä-nik\ *adj*

had·ro·saur \ˈha-drə-ˌsȯr\ *n* [NL *Hadrosaurus,* genus name, fr. Gk *hadros* thick, bulky + *sauros* lizard] (1877) **:** any of a family (Hadrosauridae) of medium-sized bipedal herbivorous dinosaurs of the Upper Cretaceous with long flat snouts and an often crested skull

hadst \ˈhadst, hədst, *or* t *for* d\ *archaic past 2d sing of* HAVE

hae \ˈhā\ *chiefly Scot var of* HAVE

haem *chiefly Brit var of* HEME

haem- *or* **haemo-** *chiefly Brit var of* HEM-

haema- *chiefly Brit var of* HEMA-

haemat- *or* **haemato-** *chiefly Brit var of* HEMAT-

hae·ma·tite *Brit var of* HEMATITE

-haemia *chiefly Brit var of* -EMIA

haet \ˈhāt\ *n* [contr. of Sc *hae it* (as in *Deil hae it!* Devil take it!)] (1603) *chiefly Scot* **:** a small quantity **:** WHIT, BIT

haf·fet \ˈha-fət\ *n* [ME (Sc) *halfheid,* fr. ME *half* half + *hed* head] (1513) *Scot* **:** CHEEK, TEMPLE

haf·ni·um \ˈhaf-nē-əm\ *n* [NL, fr. *Hafnia* (Copenhagen), Denmark] (1923) **:** a metallic element that resembles zirconium in its chemical properties, occurs esp. in zirconium minerals, and readily absorbs neutrons — see ELEMENT table

[1]**haft** \ˈhaft\ *n* [ME, fr. OE *hæft;* akin to OE *hebban* to lift — more at HEAVE] (bef. 12c) **:** the handle of a weapon or tool

[2]**haft** *vt* (15c) **:** to set in or furnish with a haft

haf·ta·rah *or* **haf·to·rah** \häf-ˈtȯr-ə, ˌhäf-tə-ˈrä\ *n* [Heb *haphṭārāh* conclusion] (1723) **:** one of the biblical selections from the Books of the Prophets read after the parashah in the Jewish synagogue service

[1]**hag** \ˈhag\ *n* [ME *hagge* demon, old woman] (14c) **1 :** an ugly, slatternly, or evil-looking old woman **2** *archaic* **a :** a female demon **b :** an evil or frightening spirit **:** HOBGOBLIN **3 :** WITCH — **hag·gish** \ˈha-gish\ *adj*

[2]**hag** *n* [Sc, break in a moor, fr. ON *hǫgg* cut, cleft; akin to OE *hēawan* to hew] (1662) **1** *Brit* **:** QUAGMIRE, BOG **2** *Brit* **:** a firm spot in a bog

Hag *abbr* Haggai

Ha·gar \ˈhā-ˌgär, -gər\ *n* [Heb *Hāghār*] (bef. 12c) **:** a concubine of Abraham driven into the desert with her son Ishmael because of Sarah's jealousy according to the account in Genesis

hag·fish \ˈhag-ˌfish\ *n* (1611) **:** any of a family (Myxinidae) of marine cyclostomes that are related to the lampreys and in general resemble eels but have a round mouth surrounded by barbels and that feed upon other fishes and invertebrates by boring into their bodies

Hag·ga·dah \hə-ˈgä-də, hä-, -ˈgȯ-\ *n, pl* **Hag·ga·doth** \-ˈgä-ˌdōt, -ˈgȯ-, -ˌdōth\ [Heb *haggādhāh*] (1856) **1 :** AGGADAH **2 :** the book of readings for the seder service — **hag·ga·dic** \-ˈgä-dik, -ˈgȯ-\ *adj, often cap*

hag·ga·dist \-ˈgä-dist, -ˈgȯ-\ *n, often cap* (1882) **1 :** a haggadic writer **2 :** a student of the Haggadah — **hag·ga·dis·tic** \ˌha-gə-ˈdis-tik, ˌhä-\ *adj, often cap*

Hag·gai \ˈha-gē-ˌī, ˈha-ˌgī\ *n* [Heb *Ḥaggai*] (14c) **1 :** a Hebrew prophet who flourished about 500 B.C. and who advocated that the Temple in Jerusalem be rebuilt **2 :** a prophetic book of canonical Jewish and Christian Scriptures — see BIBLE table

[1]**hag·gard** \ˈha-gərd\ *adj* [MF *hagard*] (1567) **1** *of a hawk* **:** not tamed **2 a :** wild in appearance **b :** having a worn or emaciated appearance **:** GAUNT ⟨∼ faces looked up sadly from out of the straw —W. M. Thackeray⟩ — **hag·gard·ly** *adv* — **hag·gard·ness** *n*

[2]**haggard** *n* (1567) **1 :** an adult hawk caught wild **2** *obs* **:** an intractable person

hag·gis \ˈha-gəs\ *n* [ME *hagese*] (15c) **:** a traditionally Scottish dish that consists of the heart, liver, and lungs of a sheep or a calf minced with suet, onions, oatmeal, and seasonings and boiled in the stomach of the animal

[1]**hag·gle** \ˈha-gəl\ *vb* **hag·gled; hag·gling** \-g(ə-)liŋ\ [freq. of *hag* to hew] *vt* (1599) **1 :** to cut roughly or clumsily **:** HACK **2** *archaic* **:** to annoy or exhaust with wrangling ∼ *vi* **:** BARGAIN, WRANGLE ⟨*haggling* over the price⟩ — **hag·gler** \-g(ə-)lər\ *n*

[2]**haggle** *n* (1858) **:** an act or instance of haggling

hagi- *or* **hagio-** *comb form* [LL, fr. Gk, fr. *hagios*] **1 :** holy ⟨*hagioscope*⟩ **2 :** saints ⟨*hagiography*⟩

Ha·gi·og·ra·pha \ˌha-gē-ˈä-grə-fə, ˌhā-, -jē-\ *n pl but sing or pl in constr* [LL, fr. LGk, fr. *hagio-* + *graphein* to write — more at CARVE] (1583) **:** WRITINGS

ha·gi·og·ra·pher \-fər\ *n* (1849) **:** a writer of hagiography

ha·gio·graph·ic \ˌha-gē-ə-ˈgra-fik, ˌhā-, -jē-\ *also* **ha·gio·graph·i·cal** \-fi-kəl\ *adj* (1819) **1 :** of, relating to, or being hagiography; *esp* **:** excessively flattering ⟨a ∼ biography⟩ **2 :** of or relating to the Hagiographa

ha·gi·og·ra·phy \-gē-ˈä-grə-fē, -jē-\ *n* (1821) **1 :** biography of saints or venerated persons **2 :** idealizing or idolizing biography

ha·gi·ol·o·gy \-gē-ˈä-lə-jē, -jē-\ *n* (1807) **1 :** literature dealing with venerated persons or writings **2 :** a list of venerated figures — **ha·gi·o·log·ic** \-gē-ə-ˈlä-jik, -jē-\ *or* **ha·gi·o·log·i·cal** \-ji-kəl\ *adj*

ha·gio·scope \ˈha-gē-ə-ˌskōp, ˈhā-jē-\ *n* (ca. 1840) **:** an opening in the interior walls of a cruciform church so placed as to afford a view of the altar to those in the transept — **ha·gio·scop·ic** \ˌha-gē-ə-ˈskä-pik, ˌhā-, -jē-\ *adj*

hag·ride \ˈhag-ˌrīd\ *vt* **-rode** \-ˌrōd\; **-rid·den** \-ˌri-dᵊn\ (1680) **:** HARASS, TORMENT

hah *var of* HA

[1]**ha–ha** \(ˈ)hä-ˈhä\ *interj* [ME, fr. OE *ha ha*] (bef. 12c) — used to express amusement or derision

[2]**ha–ha** \ˈhä-ˌhä\ *n* [F *haha*] (1749) **:** SUNK FENCE

hahn·ium \ˈhä-nē-əm\ *n* [NL, fr. Otto *Hahn*] (1970) **:** DUBNIUM

Hai·da \ˈhī-də\ *n, pl* **Haida** *or* **Haidas** [Haida (northern dial.) *ẖàˑt'eˑ, ẖàˑdeˑ,* a self-designation] (1841) **1 :** a member of an American Indian people of the Queen Charlotte Islands, British Columbia, and Prince of Wales Island, Alaska **2 :** the language of the Haida people

haik \ˈhīk\ *n* [Ar *ḥā'ik*] (1713) **:** a voluminous piece of usu. white cloth worn as an outer garment in northern Africa

hai·ku \ˈhī-(ˌ)kü\ *n, pl* **haiku** [Jp] (1902) **:** an unrhymed verse form of Japanese origin having three lines containing usu. five, seven, and five syllables respectively; *also* **:** a poem in this form usu. having a seasonal reference — compare TANKA

[1]**hail** \ˈhāl\ *n* [ME, fr. OE *hægl;* akin to OHG *hagal* hail] (bef. 12c) **1 :** precipitation in the form of small balls or lumps usu. consisting of concentric layers of clear ice and compact snow **2 :** something that gives the effect of a shower of hail ⟨a ∼ of rifle fire⟩

[2]**hail** *vi* (bef. 12c) **1 :** to precipitate hail ⟨it was ∼*ing* hard⟩ **2 :** to pour down or strike like hail

[3]**hail** *interj* [ME, fr. ON *heill,* fr. *heill* healthy — more at WHOLE] (13c) **1** *archaic* — used as a salutation **2** — used to express acclamation ⟨∼ to the chief —Sir Walter Scott⟩

[4]**hail** *vt* (13c) **1 a :** SALUTE, GREET **b :** to greet with enthusiastic approval **:** ACCLAIM **2 :** to greet or summon by calling ⟨∼ a taxi⟩ ∼ *vi* **:** to call out; *esp* **:** to call a greeting to a passing ship — **hail·er** \ˈhā-lər\ *n* — **hail from :** to be or have been native to or a resident of

[5]**hail** *n* (1500) **1 :** an exclamation of greeting or acclamation **2 :** a calling to attract attention **3 :** hearing distance ⟨stayed within ∼⟩

hail–fel·low \ˈhāl-ˌfe-(ˌ)lō\ *adj* (1580) **:** HAIL-FELLOW-WELL-MET — **hail–fellow** *n*

hail–fel·low–well–met \-lō-ˌwel-ˈmet, -lə-ˌwel-\ *adj* [fr. the archaic salutation "Hail, fellow! Well met!"] (1581) **:** heartily friendly and informal **:** COMRADELY — **hail–fellow–well–met** *n*

Hail Mary *n* [trans. of ML *Ave, Maria,* fr. the opening words] (15c) **1 :** a Roman Catholic prayer to the Virgin Mary that consists of salutations and a plea for her intercession **2 :** a long forward pass in football thrown into or near the end zone in a last-ditch attempt to score as time runs out

hail·stone \ˈhāl-ˌstōn\ *n* (bef. 12c) **:** a pellet of hail

hail·storm \-ˌstȯrm\ *n* (15c) **:** a storm accompanied by hail

hair \ˈher\ *n, often attrib* [ME, fr. OE *hǣr;* akin to OHG *hār* hair] (bef. 12c) **1 a :** a slender threadlike outgrowth of the epidermis of an animal; *esp* **:** one of the usu. pigmented filaments that form the characteristic coat of a mammal **b :** the

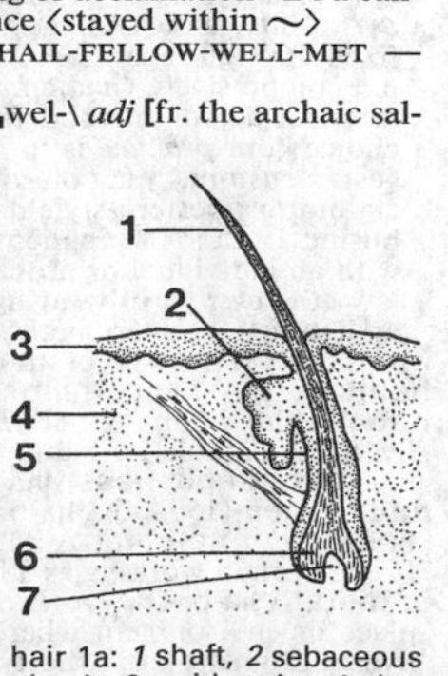

hair 1a: *1* shaft, *2* sebaceous gland, *3* epidermis, *4* dermis, *5* hair follicle, *6* bulb, *7* papilla

hairy covering of an animal or a body part; *esp* : the coating of hairs on a human head **2** : HAIRCLOTH **3 a** : a minute distance or amount ⟨won by a ~⟩ **b** : a precise degree ⟨aligned to a ~⟩ **4** *obs* : NATURE, CHARACTER **5** : a filamentous structure that resembles hair ⟨leaf ~⟩ — **hair·less** *adj* — **hair·less·ness** *n* — **hair·like** \-ˌlīk\ *adj* — **in one's hair** : persistently and annoyingly in one's presence ⟨can't work with you *in my hair* all day⟩ — **out of one's hair** : out of one's way : not in one's hair ⟨keep the children *out of his hair* for a while⟩

hair ball *n* (1712) : a compact mass of hair formed in the stomach esp. of a shedding animal (as a cat) that cleanses its coat by licking

[1]**hair·breadth** \ˈher-ˌbretth, -ˌbreth, -ˌbredth\ *or* **hairs·breadth** \ˈherz-\ *n* (1561) : a very small distance or margin

[2]**hairbreadth** *adj* (1604) : very narrow : CLOSE ⟨a ~ escape⟩

hair·brush \ˈher-ˌbrəsh\ *n* (1599) : a brush for the hair

hair cell *n* (ca. 1890) : a cell with hairlike processes; *esp* : one of the sensory cells in the auditory epithelium of the organ of Corti

hair·cloth \ˈher-ˌklȯth\ *n* (1500) : any of various stiff wiry fabrics esp. of horsehair or camel hair used for upholstery or for stiffening in garments

hair·cut \-ˌkət\ *n* (1899) **1** : the act or process of cutting and shaping the hair **2** : HAIRDO — **hair·cut·ter** \-ˌkə-tər\ *n* — **hair·cut·ting** \-ˌkə-tiŋ\ *n*

hair·do \-ˌdü\ *n, pl* **hairdos** (1932) : a way of wearing the hair : COIFFURE

hair·dress·er \-ˌdre-sər\ *n* (1764) **1** : a person whose occupation is the dressing or cutting of hair **2** *Brit* : BARBER

hair·dress·ing \-ˌdre-siŋ\ *n* (1771) **1 a** : the action or process of washing, cutting, curling, or arranging the hair **b** : the occupation of a hairdresser **2** : a preparation for grooming and styling the hair

haired \ˈherd\ *adj* (14c) : having hair esp. of a specified kind — usu. used in combination ⟨dark-*haired*⟩

hair follicle *n* (1838) : the tubular epithelial sheath that surrounds the lower part of the hair shaft and encloses at the bottom a vascular papilla supplying the growing basal part of the hair with nourishment — see HAIR illustration

hair·line \-ˈlīn\ *n* (1846) **1** : a very slender line: as **a** : a tiny line or crack on a surface ⟨a ~ bone fracture⟩ **b** : a fine line connecting thicker strokes in a printed letter **2** : HAIRBREADTH **3 a** : a textile design consisting of lengthwise or crosswise lines usu. one thread wide **b** : a fabric with such a design **4 a** : the outline of scalp hair esp. on the forehead **b** : the way the hair frames the face — **hairline** *adj*

hair·net \-ˌnet\ *n* (1852) : a net worn over the hair to keep it in place

hair·piece \-ˌpēs\ *n* (1926) **1** : supplementary hair (as a switch) used in some feminine coiffures **2** : TOUPEE 2

[1]**hair·pin** \-ˌpin\ *n* (1771) **1** : a pin to hold the hair in place; *specif* : a long U-shaped pin **2** : something shaped like a hairpin; *specif* : a sharp U-shaped turn in a road

[2]**hairpin** *adj* (1887) : having the shape of a hairpin ⟨a ~ turn⟩; *also* : having hairpin turns ⟨a steep ~ road⟩

hair–rais·er \ˈher-ˌrā-zər\ *n* (1897) : THRILLER

hair–rais·ing \-ˌrā-ziŋ\ *adj* (1900) : causing terror, excitement, or astonishment ⟨~ stories⟩ — **hair–rais·ing·ly** \-ziŋ-lē\ *adv*

hair seal *n* (1824) : any of a family (Phocidae) of seals having a coarse hairy coat, the hind limbs reduced to swimming flippers, and no external ears — called also *true seal*; compare EARED SEAL

hair shirt *n* (14c) **1** : a shirt made of rough animal hair worn next to the skin as a penance **2** : one that irritates like a hair shirt

hair·split·ter \ˈher-ˌspli-tər\ *n* (1849) : one that makes excessively fine distinctions in reasoning — **hair·split·ting** \-ˌspli-tiŋ\ *adj or n*

hair spray \-ˌsprā\ *n* (1958) : a liquid sprayed on the hair to keep it in place after styling

hair·spring \-ˌspriŋ\ *n* (1830) : a slender spiraled recoil spring that regulates the motion of the balance wheel of a timepiece

hair·streak \-ˌstrēk\ *n* (1815) : any of a subfamily (Theclinae of the family Lycaenidae) of small butterflies usu. having striped markings on the underside of the wings and thin filamentous projections from the hind wings

hair·style \ˈher-ˌstī(-ə)l\ *n* (1913) : HAIRDO

hair·styl·ing \-ˌstī-liŋ\ *n* (1936) : the work of a hairstylist

hair·styl·ist \-ˌstī-list\ *n* (1935) : HAIRDRESSER; *esp* : a person who does creative styling of coiffures

hair–trigger *adj* (1834) **1** : immediately responsive to the slightest stimulus ⟨a ~ temper⟩ **2** : delicately adjusted or easily disrupted

hair trigger *n* (1802) : a gun trigger so adjusted as to permit the firearm to be fired by a very slight pressure

hair·worm \ˈher-ˌwərm\ *n* (1658) **1** : any of a phylum (Nematomorpha) of elongated worms that have separate sexes, are parasitic in arthropods as larvae, and are free-living in water as adults — called also *horsehair worm* **2** : any of a genus (*Capillaria*) of nematode worms that include serious parasites of the alimentary tract of fowls and tissue and organ parasites of mammals

hairy \ˈher-ē\ *adj* **hair·i·er; -est** (14c) **1 a** : covered with hair or hairlike material **b** : having a downy fuzz on the stems and leaves **2** : made of or resembling hair **3 a** : tending to cause nervous tension (as from danger) ⟨a ~ adventure⟩ **b** : difficult to deal with or comprehend ⟨a ~ math problem⟩ — **hair·i·ness** \ˈher-ē-nəs\ *n*

hairy cell leukemia *n* (1970) : a chronic leukemia that is usu. of B cell origin and is characterized by malignant cells with a ciliated appearance

hairy–chest·ed \-ˌches-təd\ *adj* (ca. 1937) : characterized by esp. exaggerated or stereotypical manliness

hairy vetch *n* (1901) : a Eurasian vetch (*Vicia villosa*) extensively cultivated as a cover and early forage crop

hairy woodpecker *n* (ca. 1728) : a common No. American woodpecker (*Picoides villosus*) closely resembling the downy woodpecker but larger with a longer bill

Hai·tian \ˈhā-shən *also* ˈhā-tē-ən\ *n* (1805) **1** : a native or inhabitant of Haiti **2** : HAITIAN CREOLE — **Haitian** *adj*

Haitian Creole *n* (ca. 1938) : a French-based creole spoken by Haitians

hajj *also* **hadj** \ˈhaj\ *n* [Ar *ḥajj*] (1673) : the pilgrimage to Mecca prescribed as a religious duty for Muslims

hajji *also* **hadji** \ˈha-jē\ *n* [Ar *ḥajjī*, fr. *ḥajj*] (1609) : one who has made a pilgrimage to Mecca — often used as a title

hake \ˈhāk\ *n* [ME] (14c) : any of several marine food fishes (as of the genera *Merluccius* and *Urophycis*) related to the Atlantic cod

[1]**ha·kim** \ˈhä-kəm\ *n* [Ar *ḥākim*] (1611) : an administrator in a Muslim country

[2]**ha·kim** \hə-ˈkēm\ *n* [Ar *ḥakīm*, lit., wise one] (1638) : a physician in a Muslim country

hal- *or* **halo-** *comb form* [F, fr. Gk, fr. *hals* — more at SALT] **1** : salt ⟨*halo*phyte⟩ **2** [ISV, fr. *halogen*] : halogen ⟨*hal*ide⟩

ha·la·cha *also* **ha·la·kha** \hä-ˈlä-k̲ə, ˌhä-lə-ˈk̲ä\ *n, often cap* [Heb *hălākhāh*, lit., way] (1856) : the body of Jewish law supplementing the scriptural law and forming esp. the legal part of the Talmud — **ha·lach·ic** *also* **ha·lakh·ic** \hə-ˈla-kik, hä-ˈlä-\ *adj, often cap*

ha·lal \hə-ˈläl\ *adj* [Ar *ḥalāl* permissible] (1858) **1** : sanctioned by Islamic law; *esp* : ritually fit for use ⟨~ foods⟩ **2** : selling or serving food ritually fit according to Islamic law ⟨a ~ restaurant⟩

ha·la·la *or* **ha·la·lah** \hə-ˈlä-lə\ *n, pl* **halala** *or* **halalas** *or* **halalah** *or* **ha·la·lahs** [Ar] (1961) — see *riyal* at MONEY table

ha·la·tion \hā-ˈlā-shən\ *n* [*halo* + *-ation*] (1859) **1** : the spreading of light beyond its proper boundaries in a developed photographic image **2** : a bright ring that sometimes surrounds a bright object on a television screen

hal·berd \ˈhal-bərd, ˈhȯl-\ *also* **hal·bert** \-bərt\ *n* [ME, fr. MF *hallebarde*, fr. MHG *helmbarte*, fr. *helm* handle + *barte* ax] (15c) : a weapon esp. of the 15th and 16th centuries consisting typically of a battle-ax and pike mounted on a handle about six feet long

[1]**hal·cy·on** \ˈhal-sē-ən\ *n* [ME *alceon*, fr. L *halcyon*, fr. Gk *alkyōn*, *halkyōn*] (14c) **1** : a bird identified with the kingfisher and held in ancient legend to nest at sea about the time of the winter solstice and to calm the waves during incubation **2** : KINGFISHER

[2]**halcyon** *adj* (1601) **1** : of or relating to the halcyon or its nesting period **2 a** : CALM, PEACEFUL **b** : HAPPY, GOLDEN **c** : PROSPEROUS, AFFLUENT

[1]**hale** \ˈhāl\ *adj* [partly fr. ME (northern) *hale*, fr. OE *hāl*; partly fr. ME *hail*, fr. ON *heill* — more at WHOLE] (bef. 12c) : free from defect, disease, or infirmity : SOUND; *also* : retaining exceptional health and vigor ⟨a ~ and hearty old man⟩ ***syn*** see HEALTHY

[2]**hale** *vt* **haled; hal·ing** [ME *halen*, fr. AF *haler*, *aler* — more at HAUL] (13c) **1** : HAUL, PULL **2** : to compel to go

ha·ler \ˈhä-lər, -ˌler\ *n, pl* **ha·le·ru** \ˈhä-lə-ˌrü\ [Czech *haléř*, gen. pl. *haléřů*] (1930) — see *koruna* at MONEY table

[1]**half** \ˈhaf, ˈhäf\ *n, pl* **halves** \ˈhavz, ˈhävz\ [ME, fr. OE *healf*; akin to OHG *halb* half] (bef. 12c) **1 a** : either of two equal parts that compose something; *also* : a part approximately equal to one of these ⟨~ the distance⟩ ⟨the larger ~ of the fortune⟩ **b** : half an hour — used in designation of time **2** : one of a pair: as **a** : PARTNER **b** : SEMESTER, TERM **c** : either of the two equal periods that together make up the playing time of some games (as football); *also* : the midpoint in playing time ⟨the score was tied at the ~⟩ **3** : HALF-DOLLAR **4** : HALFBACK — **by half** : by a great deal — **by halves** : in part : HALFHEARTEDLY — **half again as** : one-and-a-half times as ⟨*half again as* many⟩ — **in half** : into two equal or nearly equal parts

[2]**half** *adj* (bef. 12c) **1 a** : being one of two equal parts ⟨a ~ share⟩ ⟨a ~ sheet of paper⟩ **b** (1) : amounting to approximately half ⟨a ~ mile⟩ ⟨a ~ million⟩ (2) : falling short of the full or complete thing : PARTIAL ⟨~ measures⟩ ⟨a ~ smile⟩ **2** : extending over or covering only half ⟨a ~ window⟩ ⟨a ~ mask⟩ — **half·ness** *n*

[3]**half** *adv* (12c) **1 a** : in an equal part or degree ⟨the crowd was ~ jeering, ~ respectful⟩ **b** : not completely : PARTIALLY ⟨~ persuaded⟩ **2** : by any means : AT ALL ⟨her singing isn't ~ bad⟩

half–and–half \ˌhaf-ᵊn-ˈhaf, ˌhäf-ᵊn-ˈhäf\ *n* (1756) : something that is approximately half one thing and half another: as **a** : a mixture of two malt beverages (as dark and light beer) **b** : a mixture of cream and whole milk — **half–and–half** *adj or adv*

half–assed \ˈhaf-ˈast, ˈhäf-ˈäst\ *adj* (ca. 1932) **1** *often vulgar* : lacking significance, adequacy, or completeness **2** *often vulgar* : lacking intelligence, character, or effectiveness — **half–assed** *adv, often vulgar*

half·back \ˈhaf-ˌbak, ˈhäf-\ *n* (1882) **1** : one of the backs stationed near either flank in football **2** : a player stationed immediately behind the forward line (as in field hockey, soccer, or rugby)

half–baked \-ˈbākt\ *adj* (1621) **1 a** : poorly developed or carried out ⟨a ~ idea⟩ ⟨~ research⟩ **b** : lacking adequate planning or forethought ⟨a ~ scheme for getting rich⟩ **c** : lacking in judgment, intelligence, or common sense **2** : imperfectly baked : UNDERDONE

half bath *n* (1951) : a bathroom containing a sink and toilet but no bathtub or shower

half·beak \-ˌbēk\ *n* (1880) : any of various narrow-bodied fishes of warm waters that have an elongated lower jaw and are grouped with the flying fishes (family Exocoetidae) or placed in their own family (Hemiramphidae)

half–blood \-ˈbləd\ *or* **half–blood·ed** \-ˈblə-dəd\ *adj* (1605) : having half blood or being a half blood

half blood *n* (1553) **1 a** : the relation between persons having only one parent in common **b** : a person so related to another **2** : HALF-BREED **3** : GRADE 4

half boot *n* (1771) : a boot with a top reaching above the ankle and ending below the knee

half–bound \ˈhaf-ˌbau̇nd, ˈhäf-\ *adj* (1768) *of a book* : bound in material of two qualities with the material of better quality on the spine and corners — **half binding** *n*

half–bred \-ˌbred\ *adj* (1701) : having one purebred parent — **half–bred** *n*

half–breed \-ˌbrēd\ *n* (1760) *often offensive* : the offspring of parents of different races; *esp* : the offspring of an American Indian and a white person — **half–breed** *adj, often offensive*

half brother *n* (14c) : a brother related through one parent only

half–caste \ˈhaf-ˌkast, ˈhäf-\ *n* (1789) *often offensive* : one of mixed racial descent : HALF-BREED — **half–caste** *adj, often offensive*

\ə\ **a**but \ᵊ\ kitt**e**n, F ta**b**l**e** \ər\ f**ur**ther \a\ **a**sh \ā\ **a**ce \ä\ m**o**p, m**a**r
\au̇\ **ou**t \ch\ **ch**in \e\ b**e**t \ē\ **ea**sy \g\ **g**o \i\ h**i**t \ī\ **i**ce \j\ **j**ob
\ŋ\ si**ng** \ō\ g**o** \ȯ\ l**aw** \ȯi\ b**oy** \th\ **th**in \t̲h̲\ **th**e \ü\ l**oo**t \u̇\ f**oo**t
\y\ **y**et \zh\ vi**s**ion, beige \k̲, ⁿ, œ, ue, ʸ\ *see* Guide to Pronunciation

half cock *n* (1745) **1 :** the position of the hammer of a firearm when about half retracted and held by the sear so that it cannot be operated by a pull on the trigger **2** *chiefly Brit* **:** a state of inadequate preparation or mental confusion ⟨go off at *half cock*⟩
half–cocked \ˈhaf-ˈkäkt, ˈhäf-\ *adj* (1809) **1 :** being at half cock **2 :** lacking adequate preparation or forethought ⟨go off ~⟩
half–court \ˈhaf-ˈkȯrt, ˈhäf-\ *n* (1888) **:** a dividing line that separates a playing court into equal halves (as in basketball); *also* **:** the area comprising each half
half crown *n* (1542) **:** a British coin worth two shillings and sixpence used as legal tender until 1970
half dime *n* (1792) **:** a silver 5-cent coin struck by the U.S. mint in 1792 and from 1794 to 1873
half disme *n* (1792) **:** a half dime struck in 1792
half–dol·lar \ˈhaf-ˈdä-lər, ˈhäf-\ *n* (1786) **1 :** a coin representing one half of a dollar **2 :** the sum of 50 cents
half duplex *n* (1950) **:** a mode of communication esp. with a computer via telephone line in which information can be sent in only one direction at a time — compare DUPLEX
half eagle *n* (1786) **:** a 5-dollar gold piece issued by the U.S. from 1795 to 1916 and in 1929
half–glass·es \ˈhaf-ˈgla-səz\ *n pl* (1971) **:** eyeglasses for reading that have about half the vertical dimension of typical eyeglasses
half–hardy *adj* (1824) *of a plant* **:** able to withstand a moderately low temperature but injured by severe freezing and surviving the winter in cold climates only if carefully protected
half·heart·ed \ˈhaf-ˈhär-təd, ˈhäf-\ *adj* (15c) **:** lacking heart, spirit, or interest — **half·heart·ed·ly** *adv* — **half·heart·ed·ness** *n*
half hitch *n* (1769) **:** a simple knot tied by passing the end of a line around an object, across the main part of the line, and then through the resulting loop — see KNOT illustration
half hour *n* (15c) **1 :** thirty minutes **2 :** the middle point of an hour — **half–hour·ly** \ˈhaf-ˈau̇(-ə)r-lē, ˈhäf-\ *adv or adj*
half–knot \ˈhaf-ˌnät, ˈhäf-\ *n* (1913) **:** a knot intertwining the ends of two cords and used in tying other knots
half–length \ˈhaf-ˈleŋ(k)th, ˈhäf-\ *n* (1699) **:** something (as a portrait) that is or represents only half the complete length
half–life \-ˌlīf\ *n* (1907) **1 :** the time required for half of something to undergo a process: as **a :** the time required for half of the atoms of a radioactive substance to become disintegrated **b :** the time required for half the amount of a substance (as a drug, radioactive tracer, or pesticide) in or introduced into a living system or ecosystem to be eliminated or disintegrated by natural processes **2 :** a period of usefulness or popularity preceding decline or obsolescence ⟨slang usually has a short ~⟩
half–light \-ˌlīt\ *n* (1577) **:** dim grayish light
half line *n* (ca. 1914) **:** a straight line extending from a point indefinitely in one direction only
[1]**half–mast** \-ˈmast\ *n* (1588) **:** a point some distance but not necessarily halfway down below the top of a mast or staff or the peak of a gaff
[2]**half–mast** *vt* (1891) **:** to cause to hang at half-mast ⟨~ a flag⟩
half–moon \ˈhaf-ˌmün, ˈhäf-\ *n* (15c) **1 :** the moon when half its disk appears illuminated **2 :** something shaped like a crescent **3 :** the lunule of a fingernail — **half–moon** *adj*
half nelson *n* (1889) **:** a wrestling hold in which one arm is thrust under the corresponding arm of an opponent and the hand placed on the back of the opponent's neck — compare FULL NELSON
half note *n* (1576) **:** a musical note with the time value of ½ of a whole note — see NOTE illustration
half·pen·ny \ˈhāp-nē, ˈhā-pə-, *US also* ˈhaf-ˌpe-nē, ˈhäf-\ *n* (13c) **1** *pl* **halfpence** \ˈhā-pən(t)s, *US also* ˈhaf-ˌpen(t)s, ˈhäf-\ *or* **halfpennies :** a formerly used British coin representing one half of a penny **2 :** the sum of half a penny **3 :** a small amount — **halfpenny** *adj*
[1]**half–pint** \ˈhaf-ˌpīnt, ˈhäf-\ *n* (15c) **1 :** half a pint **2 :** a short, small, or inconsequential person
[2]**half–pint** *adj* (1931) **:** of less than average size **:** DIMINUTIVE
half–pipe \ˈhaf-ˌpīp, ˈhäf-\ *n* (1978) **:** a U-shaped high-sided ramp or runway used esp. in snowboarding, skateboarding, or in-line skating
half plane *n* (1891) **:** the part of a plane on one side of an indefinitely extended straight line drawn in the plane
half rest *n* (ca. 1899) **:** a musical rest corresponding in time value to a half note
half shell *n* (1860) **:** either of the valves of a bivalve — **on the half shell :** served in a half shell ⟨oysters *on the half shell*⟩
half sister *n* (13c) **:** a sister related through one parent only
half–slip \ˈhaf-ˌslip, ˈhäf-\ *n* (ca. 1948) **:** a topless slip with an elasticized waistband
half–sole *vt* (1795) **:** to put half soles on
half sole *n* (1865) **:** a shoe sole extending from the shank forward
half sovereign *n* (ca. 1504) **:** a British gold coin worth 10 shillings
half–space \ˈhaf-ˌspās, ˈhäf-\ *n* (1962) **:** the part of three-dimensional euclidean space lying on one side of a plane
half–staff \-ˈstaf\ *n* (1708) **:** HALF-MAST
half step *n* (1904) **1 :** a walking step of 15 inches or in double time of 18 inches **2 :** a musical interval (as E-F or B-C) equivalent to ¹⁄₁₂ of an octave — called also *semitone*
half–timber *or* **half–tim·bered** \ˈhaf-ˈtim-bərd, ˈhäf-\ *adj* (1788) *of a building* **:** constructed of wood framing with spaces filled with masonry — **half–tim·ber·ing** \-b(ə-)riŋ\ *n*
half·time \-ˌtīm\ *n* (1871) **:** an intermission between halves of a game or contest (as in football or basketball)
half–time *adj* (1861) **:** involving or working half the standard hours — **half–time** *adv*
half title *n* (1879) **:** the title of a book appearing alone on a right-hand page immediately preceding the title page; *also* **:** the page itself
half·tone \ˈhaf-ˌtōn, ˈhäf-\ *n* (1651) **1 :** HALF STEP 2 **2 a :** any of the shades of gray between the darkest and the lightest parts of a photographic image **b (1) :** a photoengraving made from an image photographed through a screen and then etched so that the details of the image are reproduced in dots **(2) :** an image (as one printed on an offset press or laser printer) that renders smooth variations of color in an original by means of dots assigned to areas of the image electronically — **halftone** *adj*
half–track \-ˌtrak\ *n* (1935) **1 :** an endless chain-track drive system that propels a vehicle supported in front by a pair of wheels **2 :** a motor vehicle propelled by half-tracks; *specif* **:** one lightly armored for military use — **half–track** *or* **half–tracked** \-ˌtrakt\ *adj*
half–truth \-ˌtrüth\ *n* (1658) **1 :** a statement that is only partially true **2 :** a statement that mingles truth and falsehood with deliberate intent to deceive
half volley *n* (1843) **:** a stroke of a ball (as in tennis) at the instant it rebounds from the ground — **half–volley** *vb*
half·way \ˈhaf-ˈwā, ˈhäf-\ *adj* (1694) **1 :** midway between two points **2 :** PARTIAL — **halfway** *adv*
halfway house *n* (1694) **1 a :** a place to stop midway on a journey **b :** a halfway place in a progression **2 :** a residence for individuals after release from institutionalization (as for mental disorder, drug addiction, or criminal activity) that is designed to facilitate their readjustment to private life
half–wit \ˈhaf-ˌwit, ˈhäf-\ *n* (1640) **:** a foolish or imbecilic person — **half–wit·ted** \-ˈwi-təd\ *adj* — **half–wit·ted·ness** *n*
half–world \-ˌwərld\ *n* (1870) **:** DEMIMONDE
hal·i·but \ˈha-lə-bət *also* ˈhä-\ *n, pl* **halibut** *also* **halibuts** [ME *halybutte*, fr. *haly, holy* holy + *butte* flatfish, fr. MD or MLG *but;* fr. its being eaten on holy days] (14c) **:** any of several marine flatfishes (esp. *Hippoglossus hippoglossus* of the Atlantic and *H. stenolepis* of the Pacific) that are widely used for food and include some of the largest bony fishes
ha·lide \ˈha-ˌlīd, ˈhā-\ *n* (1855) **:** a binary compound of a halogen with a more electropositive element or radical
hal·i·dom \ˈha-lə-dəm\ *or* **hal·i·dome** \-lə-ˌdōm\ *n* [ME, fr. OE *hāligdōm*, fr. *hālig* holy + *-dōm* -dom] (bef. 12c) *archaic* **:** something held sacred
ha·lier \ˈhäl-ˌyer\ *n, pl* **ha·lier·ov** \ˈhäl-ˌyer-ō\ [Slovak, gen. pl. *halierov*] (1993) **:** a former monetary unit equal to ¹⁄₁₀₀ Slovakian koruna
ha·lite \ˈha-ˌlīt, ˈhā-\ *n* (1868) **:** ROCK SALT
hal·i·to·sis \ˌha-lə-ˈtō-səs\ *n* [NL, fr. L *halitus* breath, fr. *halare* to breathe — more at EXHALE] (1874) **:** a condition of having fetid breath
hall \ˈhȯl\ *n* [ME *halle*, fr. OE *heall;* akin to OHG *halla* hall, L *cella* small room, *celare* to conceal — more at HELL] (bef. 12c) **1 a :** the castle or house of a medieval king or noble **b :** the chief living room in such a structure **2 :** the manor house of a landed proprietor **3 :** a large usu. imposing building for public or semipublic purposes **4 a (1) :** a building used by a college or university for some special purpose **(2) :** DORMITORY **b :** a college or a division of a college at some universities **c (1) :** the common dining room of an English college **(2) :** a meal served there **5 a :** the entrance room of a building **:** LOBBY **b :** a corridor or passage in a building **6 :** a large room for assembly **:** AUDITORIUM **7 :** a place used for public entertainment
hallah *var of* CHALLAH
Hall effect \ˈhȯl-\ *n* [Edwin H. *Hall* †1938 Am. physicist] (ca. 1889) **:** a potential difference observed between the edges of a conducting strip carrying a longitudinal current when placed in a magnetic field perpendicular to the plane of the strip
Hal·lel \hä-ˈlāl\ *n* [Heb *hallēl* praise] (1702) **:** a selection comprising Psalms 113–118 chanted during Jewish feasts (as the Passover)
[1]**hal·le·lu·jah** \ˌha-lə-ˈlü-yə\ *interj* [Heb *hallĕlūyāh* praise (ye) the Lord] (14c) — used to express praise, joy, or thanks
[2]**hallelujah** *n* (13c) **:** a shout or song of praise or thanksgiving
[1]**hall·mark** \ˈhȯl-ˌmärk\ *n* [Goldsmiths' *Hall*, London, England, where gold and silver articles were assayed and stamped] (1721) **1 a :** an official mark stamped on gold and silver articles in England to attest their purity **b :** a mark or device placed or stamped on an article of trade to indicate origin, purity, or genuineness **2 :** a distinguishing characteristic, trait, or feature ⟨the dramatic flourishes which are the ~ of the trial lawyer —Marion K. Sanders⟩
[2]**hallmark** *vt* (1773) **:** to stamp with a hallmark
hallo *or* **halloo** *var of* HOLLO
Hall of Fame (ca. 1853) **1 :** a structure housing memorials to famous or illustrious individuals usu. chosen by a group of electors **2 :** a group of individuals in a particular category (as a sport) who have been selected as particularly illustrious — **Hall of Fam·er** \-ˈfā-mər\
hal·low \ˈha-(ˌ)lō\ *vt* [ME *halowen*, fr. OE *hālgian*, fr. *hālig* holy — more at HOLY] (bef. 12c) **1 :** to make holy or set apart for holy use **2 :** to respect greatly **:** VENERATE ***syn*** see DEVOTE
hal·lowed \ˈha-(ˌ)lōd, ˈha-ləd, *in the Lord's Prayer often* ˈha-lə-wəd\ *adj* (bef. 12c) **1 :** HOLY, CONSECRATED ⟨the church stands on ~ ground⟩ **2 :** SACRED, REVERED ⟨the university's ~ halls⟩ ⟨~ customs⟩
Hal·low·een *also* **Hal·low·e'en** \ˌha-lə-ˈwēn, ˌhä-\ *n* [short for *All Hallow Even* (All Saints' Eve)] (ca. 1700) **:** October 31 observed esp. with dressing up in disguise, trick-or-treating, and displaying jack-o'-lanterns during the evening
Hal·low·mas \ˈha-lō-ˌmas, ˈha-lə-, -məs\ *n* [short for ME *Alholowmesse*, fr. OE *ealra halgena mæsse*, lit., all saints' mass] (14c) **:** ALL SAINTS' DAY
halls of ivy [fr. the traditional training of ivy on the walls of older college buildings] (1965) **:** UNIVERSITY, COLLEGE
Hall·statt *also* **Hall·stadt** \ˈhȯl-ˌstat; ˈhäl-ˌshtät, -ˌstät\ *adj* [*Hallstatt*, Austria] (1899) **:** of or relating to the earlier period of the Iron Age in Europe
hal·lu·ci·nate \hə-ˈlü-sə-ˌnāt\ *vb* **-nat·ed; -nat·ing** [L *hallucinatus*, pp. of *hallucinari, allucinari* to prate, dream, modif. of Gk *alyein* to be distressed, to wander] *vt* (ca. 1834) **1 :** to affect with visions or imaginary perceptions **2 :** to perceive or experience as a hallucination ~ *vi* **:** to have hallucinations — **hal·lu·ci·na·tor** \-ˌnā-tər\ *n*
hal·lu·ci·na·tion \hə-ˌlü-sə-ˈnā-shən\ *n* (1629) **1 a :** perception of objects with no reality usu. arising from disorder of the nervous system or in response to drugs (as LSD) **b :** the object so perceived **2 :** an unfounded or mistaken impression or notion **:** DELUSION ***syn*** see DELUSION
hal·lu·ci·na·to·ry \hə-ˈlü-sə-nə-ˌtȯr-ē, -ˈlüs-nə-\ *adj* (1830) **1 :** tending to produce hallucination ⟨~ drugs⟩ **2 :** resembling, involving, or being a hallucination ⟨~ dreams⟩ ⟨a ~ figure⟩
hal·lu·ci·no·gen \hə-ˈlü-sə-nə-jən\ *n* [*hallucination* + *-o-* + *-gen*] (1954) **:** a substance that induces hallucinations — **hal·lu·ci·no·gen·ic** \-ˌlü-sə-nə-ˈje-nik\ *adj or n*
hal·lu·ci·no·sis \hə-ˌlü-sə-ˈnō-səs\ *n* [NL] (1905) **:** a pathological mental state characterized by hallucinations

hal·lux \ˈha-ləks\ *n, pl* **hal·lu·ces** \ˈha-lə-ˌsēz, ˈhal-yə-\ [NL, fr. L *hallus, hallux*] (1831) : the innermost digit (as the big toe) of a hind or lower limb

hall·way \ˈhȯl-ˌwā\ *n* (1876) **1** : an entrance hall **2** : CORRIDOR 1

hal·ma \ˈhal-mə\ *n* [Gk, leap, fr. *hallesthai* to leap — more at SALLY] (1889) : a game played on a square board and having rules similar to those of Chinese checkers

[1]**ha·lo** \ˈhā-(ˌ)lō\ *n, pl* **halos** *or* **haloes** [L *halos,* fr. Gk *halōs* threshing floor, disk, halo] (1603) **1** : a circle of light appearing to surround the sun or moon and resulting from refraction or reflection of light by ice particles in the atmosphere **2** : something resembling a halo: as **a** : NIMBUS **b** : a region of space surrounding a galaxy that is sparsely populated with luminous objects (as globular clusters) but is believed to contain a great deal of dark matter **c** : a differentiated zone surrounding a central zone or object **d** : an orthopedic device used to immobilize the head and neck (as to treat fracture of neck vertebrae) that consists of a metal band placed around the head and fastened to the skull usu. with metal pins and that is attached by extensions to an inflexible vest — called also *halo brace* **3** : the aura of glory, veneration, or sentiment surrounding an idealized person or thing

[2]**halo** *vt* (1801) : to form into or surround with a halo ⟨rainbows ~*ed* the waterfalls —Michael Crawford⟩

halo- — see HAL-

hal·o·car·bon \ˈha-lə-ˌkär-bən\ *n* (1950) : any of various compounds of carbon and one or more halogens

hal·o·cline \ˈha-lə-ˌklīn\ *n* (1960) : a usu. vertical gradient in salinity (as of the ocean)

halo effect *n* (ca. 1928) : generalization from the perception of one outstanding personality trait to an overly favorable evaluation of the whole personality

[1]**hal·o·gen** \ˈha-lə-jən\ *n* [Sw, fr. *hal-* + *-gen*] (1842) : any of the five elements fluorine, chlorine, bromine, iodine, and astatine that form part of group VIIA of the periodic table and exist in the free state normally as diatomic molecules — **ha·log·e·nous** \ha-ˈlä-jə-nəs\ *adj*

[2]**halogen** *adj* (1880) : containing, using, or being a halogen ⟨a ~ lamp⟩

ha·lo·ge·nate \ˈha-lə-jə-ˌnāt, ha-ˈlä-jə-\ *vt* **-nat·ed; -nat·ing** (1882) : to treat or cause to combine with a halogen — **ha·lo·ge·na·tion** \ˌha-lə-jə-ˈnā-shən, ha-ˌlä-jə-\ *n*

hal·o·ge·ton \ˌha-lə-ˈjē-ˌtän\ *n* [NL, fr. *hal-* + Gk *geitōn* neighbor] (1943) : a coarse annual Asian herb (*Halogeton glomeratus*) of the goosefoot family that is a noxious weed in western U.S. ranges

hal·o·mor·phic \ˌha-lə-ˈmȯr-fik\ *adj* (ca. 1938) *of a soil* : developed in the presence of neutral or alkali salts or both

ha·lon \ˈhā-ˌlän\ *n* [ISV *hal-* + [3]*-on*] (ca. 1951) : a halocarbon that contains esp. bromine

hal·o·per·i·dol \ˌha-lō-ˈper-ə-ˌdȯl, -ˌdōl\ *n* [*hal-* + pi*perid*ine + [1]*-ol*] (1960) : a depressant $C_{21}H_{23}ClFNO_2$ of the central nervous system used esp. as an antipsychotic drug

hal·o·phile \ˈha-lə-ˌfī(-ə)l\ *n* [ISV] (1923) : an organism that flourishes in a salty environment — **hal·o·phil·ic** \ˌha-lə-ˈfi-lik\ *adj*

hal·o·phyte \ˈha-lə-ˌfīt\ *n* [ISV] (ca. 1886) : a plant (as saltbush or sea lavender) that grows in salty soil and usu. has a physiological resemblance to a true xerophyte — **hal·o·phyt·ic** \ˌha-lə-ˈfi-tik\ *adj*

hal·o·thane \ˈha-lə-ˌthān\ *n* [*halo-* + *ethane*] (1957) : a potent inhalational anesthetic $C_2HBrClF_3$ that is nonexplosive and nonflammable

[1]**halt** \ˈhȯlt\ *adj* [ME, fr. OE *healt;* akin to OHG *halz* lame] (bef. 12c) : LAME

[2]**halt** *vi* (bef. 12c) **1** : to walk or proceed lamely : LIMP **2** : to stand in perplexity or doubt between alternate courses : WAVER **3** : to display weakness or imperfection : FALTER

[3]**halt** *n* [G, fr. MHG, fr. *halt,* imper. of *halten* to hold, fr. OHG *haltan* — more at HOLD] (ca. 1598) : STOP

[4]**halt** *vi* (1656) **1** : to cease marching or journeying **2** : DISCONTINUE, TERMINATE ⟨the project ~*ed* for lack of funds⟩ ~ *vt* **1** : to bring to a stop ⟨the strike ~*ed* subways and buses⟩ **2** : to cause the discontinuance of : END ⟨~ hostilities⟩

[1]**hal·ter** \ˈhȯl-tər\ *n* [ME, fr. OE *hælftre;* akin to OHG *halftra* halter, OE *hielfe* helve] (bef. 12c) **1 a** : a rope or strap for leading or tying an animal **b** : a headstall usu. with noseband and throatlatch to which a lead may be attached **2** : a rope for hanging criminals : NOOSE; *also* : death by hanging **3** : a woman's blouse or top that leaves the back, arms, and midriff bare and that is typically held in place by straps around the neck and across the back

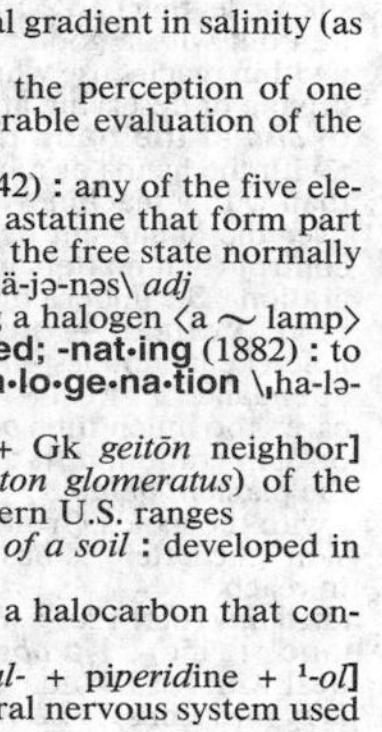
halter 1b

[2]**halter** *vt* **hal·tered; hal·ter·ing** \-t(ə-)riŋ\ (14c) **1 a** : to catch with or as if with a halter; *also* : to put a halter on **b** : HANG **2** : to put restraint upon : HAMPER

hal·ter·break \ˈhȯl-tər-ˌbrāk\ *vt* **-broke** \-ˌbrōk\; **-bro·ken** \-ˌbrō-kən\; **-break·ing** (1837) : to break (as a colt) to a halter

hal·tere \ˈhȯl-ˌtir, ˈhal-\ *n, pl* **hal·teres** \ˈhȯl-ˌtirz, ˈhal-; hȯl-ˈtir-ēz, hal-\ [NL *halter,* fr. L, jumping weight, fr. Gk *haltēr,* fr. *hallesthai* to leap — more at SALLY] (ca. 1823) : one of a pair of club-shaped organs in a dipteran fly that are the modified second pair of wings and function as sensory flight stabilizers

halt·ing \ˈhȯl-tiŋ\ *adj* (1585) : marked by a lack of sureness or effectiveness ⟨spoke in a ~ manner⟩ — **halt·ing·ly** \-tiŋ-lē\ *adv*

hal·vah *or* **hal·va** \häl-ˈvä; ˈhäl-(ˌ)vä, -və\ *n* [Yiddish *halva,* fr. Rom, fr. Turk *helva,* fr. Ar *ḥalwā* sweetmeat] (1846) : a flaky confection of crushed sesame seeds in a base of syrup (as of honey)

halve \ˈhav, ˈhäv\ *vt* **halved; halv·ing** [ME, fr. *half* half] (13c) **1 a** : to divide into two equal parts **b** : to reduce to one half ⟨*halving* the present cost⟩ **c** : to share equally **2** : to play (as a hole in golf) in the same number of strokes as one's opponent

halv·ers \ˈha-vərz, ˈhä-\ *n pl* (1517) : half shares : HALVES

halves *pl of* HALF

hal·yard \ˈhal-yərd\ *n* [ME *halier,* prob. fr. AF **halier,* fr. *haler* to haul — more at HALE] (14c) : a rope or tackle for hoisting and lowering something (as sails)

[1]**ham** \ˈham\ *n* [ME *hamme,* fr. OE *hamm;* akin to OHG *hamma* ham, Gk *knēmē* shinbone, OIr *cnáim* bone] (bef. 12c) **1 a** : the hollow of the knee **b** : a buttock with its associated thigh — usu. used in pl. **2** : a cut of meat consisting of a thigh; *esp* : one from a hog **3** [short for *hamfatter,* fr. "The *Ham-fat* Man," minstrel song] **a** : a showy performer; *esp* : an actor performing in an exaggerated theatrical style **b** : a licensed operator of an amateur radio station **4** : a cushion used esp. by tailors for pressing curved areas of garments — **ham** *adj*

[2]**ham** *vb* **hammed; ham·ming** *vt* (1933) : to execute with exaggerated speech or gestures : OVERACT ⟨~ it up for the camera⟩ ~ *vi* : to overplay a part

Ham \ˈham\ *n* [Heb] (bef. 12c) : a son of Noah held to be the progenitor of the Egyptians, Nubians, and Canaanites

hama·dry·ad \ˌha-mə-ˈdrī-əd, -ˌad\ *n* [L *hamadryad-, hamadryas,* fr. Gk, fr. *hama* together with + *dryad-, dryas* dryad — more at SAME] (14c) **1** : WOOD NYMPH **2** : KING COBRA

hama·dry·as baboon \ˌha-mə-ˈdrī-əs-\ *n* [NL *hamadryas,* fr. L] (ca. 1890) : a baboon (*Papio hamadryas*) that has a reddish-pink muzzle and a large bare patch of pink skin on each buttock and that was venerated by the ancient Egyptians — called also *sacred baboon*

ha·mal *also* **ham·mal** \hə-ˈmäl\ *n* [Ar *ḥammāl* porter] (ca. 1760) : a porter in countries of southwest Asia (as Turkey)

Ha·man \ˈhā-mən\ *n* [Heb *Hāmān*] (14c) : a Persian minister in the book of Esther who is hanged after plotting a foiled massacre of the Jews

ha·man·tasch \ˈhä-mən-ˌtäsh, ˈhȯ-, -ˌtȯsh\ *n, pl* **-tasch·en** \-ˌtä-shən, -ˌtȯ-\ [Yiddish *homentash,* fr. *Homen* Haman + *tash* pocket, bag] (1927) : a 3-cornered pastry with a filling (as of poppy seeds or prunes) traditionally eaten during the Jewish holiday Purim

ha·mar·tia \ˌhä-ˌmär-ˈtē-ə\ *n* [Gk, fr. *hamartanein* to miss the mark, err] (1913) : TRAGIC FLAW

ha·mate \ˈhā-ˌmāt\ *n* [L *hamatus* hooked, fr. *hamus* hook] (1924) : a bone on the inner side of the second row of the carpus in mammals

ham·burg·er \ˈham-ˌbər-gər\ *or* **ham·burg** \-ˌbərg\ *n* [G *Hamburger* of Hamburg, Germany] (1884) **1 a** : ground beef **b** : a patty of ground beef **2** : a sandwich consisting of a patty of hamburger in a split typically round bun

[1]**hame** \ˈhām\ *n* [ME] (14c) : one of two curved supports attached to the collar of a draft horse to which the traces are fastened

[2]**hame** *Scot var of* HOME

ham–fist·ed \ˈham-ˌfis-təd\ *adj* (1928) : HAM-HANDED

ham–hand·ed \-ˌhan-dəd\ *adj* (1918) : lacking dexterity or grace : HEAVY-HANDED — **ham–hand·ed·ly** \-lē\ *adv* — **ham–hand·ed·ness** \-dəd-nəs\ *n*

Ham·il·to·ni·an \ˌha-məl-ˈtō-nē-ən\ *n* [Sir William *Hamilton* †1865 Irish mathematician] (1926) : a function that is used to describe a dynamic system (as the motion of a particle) in terms of components of momentum and coordinates of space and time and that is equal to the total energy of the system when time is not explicitly part of the function — compare LAGRANGIAN

Ham·il·to·ni·an·ism \-nē-ə-ˌni-zəm\ *n* (1901) : the political principles and ideas held by or associated with Alexander Hamilton that center around a belief in a strong central government, broad interpretation of the federal constitution, encouragement of an industrial and commercial economy, and a general distrust of the political capacity or wisdom of the common man — **Hamiltonian** \-ˈtō-nē-ən\ *adj or n*

Ham·ite \ˈha-ˌmīt\ *n* [*Ham*] (1854) : a member of a Hamitic-speaking people

[1]**Ham·it·ic** \ha-ˈmi-tik, hə-\ *adj* (1844) : of, relating to, or characteristic of the Hamites or one of the Hamitic languages

[2]**Hamitic** *n* (1886) : HAMITIC LANGUAGES

Hamitic languages *n pl* (ca. 1890) : any of various groupings of non-Semitic Afro-Asiatic languages (as Berber, Egyptian, and Cushitic) that were formerly thought to make up a single branch of the Afro-Asiatic family

Ham·i·to–Se·mit·ic \ˌha-mə-(ˌ)tō-sə-ˈmi-tik, hə-ˈmi-tō-\ *adj* (1879) : of, relating to, or constituting the Afro-Asiatic languages — **Hamito–Semitic** *n*

ham·let \ˈham-lət\ *n* [ME, fr. AF *hamelet,* dim. of *ham* village, of Gmc origin; akin to OE *hām* village, home] (bef. 12c) : a small village

Ham·let \ˈham-lət\ *n* : a legendary Danish prince and hero of Shakespeare's play *Hamlet*

ham·mam \hə-ˈmäm\ *n* [Turk, Pers & Ar; Turk *hamam* bath, fr. Pers *hammām,* fr. Ar *ḥammām*] (1625) : TURKISH BATH

[1]**ham·mer** \ˈha-mər\ *n* [ME *hamer,* fr. OE *hamor;* akin to OHG *hamar* hammer, and perh. to OCS *kamen-, kamy* stone, Gk *akmē* point, edge — more at EDGE] (bef. 12c) **1 a** : a hand tool consisting of a solid head set crosswise on a handle and used for pounding **b** : a power tool that often substitutes a metal block or a drill for the hammerhead **2** : something that resembles a hammer in form or action: as **a** : a lever with a striking head for ringing a bell or striking a gong **b** (1) : an arm that strikes the cap in a percussion lock to ignite the propelling charge (2) : a part of the action of a modern gun that strikes the primer of the cartridge in firing or that strikes the firing pin to ignite the cartridge **c** : MALLEUS **d** : GAVEL **e** (1) : a padded mallet in a piano action for striking a string (2) : a hand mallet for playing on various percussion instruments (as a xylophone) **3** : a metal sphere thrown for distance in the hammer throw **4** : ACCELERATOR b — **under the hammer** : for sale at auction

[2]**hammer** *vb* **ham·mered; ham·mer·ing** \ˈha-mər-iŋ, ˈham-riŋ\ *vi* (14c) **1** : to strike blows esp. repeatedly with or as if with a hammer : POUND **2** : to make repeated efforts; *esp* : to reiterate an opinion or attitude ⟨the lectures all ~*ed* away at the same points⟩ ~ *vt* **1 a** : to beat, drive, or shape with repeated blows of a hammer **b** : to fasten or build with a hammer **2** : to strike or drive with a force suggesting a hammer blow or repeated blows ⟨~*ed* the ball over the fence⟩ ⟨tried to ~ me

\ə\ **abut** \ᵊ\ **kitten,** F **table** \ər\ **further** \a\ **ash** \ā\ **ace** \ä\ **mop, mar** \au̇\ **out** \ch\ **chin** \e\ **bet** \ē\ **easy** \g\ **go** \i\ **hit** \ī\ **ice** \j\ **job** \ŋ\ **sing** \ō\ **go** \ȯ\ **law** \ȯi\ **boy** \th\ **thin** \t͟h\ **the** \ü\ **loot** \u̇\ **foot** \y\ **yet** \zh\ **vision, beige** \k̲, ⁿ, œ, ue, ʸ\ *see* Guide to Pronunciation

into submission⟩ **3 :** to criticize severely — **ham·mer·er** \ˈha-mər-ər\ *n*

hammer and sickle *n* (1921) **:** an emblem consisting of a crossed hammer and sickle used esp. as a symbol of Soviet Communism

hammer and tongs *adv* (ca. 1780) **:** with great force, vigor, or violence ⟨went at it *hammer and tongs*⟩ — **hammer–and–tongs** *adj*

hammer dulcimer *n* (1953) **:** DULCIMER 1 — called also *hammered dulcimer*

hammered *adj* (1522) **1 :** having surface indentations produced or appearing to have been produced by hammering ⟨~ copper⟩ **2** *slang* **:** DRUNK 1a

ham·mer·head \ˈha-mər-ˌhed\ *n* (1562) **1 :** the striking part of a hammer **2 :** BLOCKHEAD **3 :** any of a family (Sphyrnidae) of active voracious medium-sized sharks that have the eyes at the ends of lateral extensions of the flattened head — see SHARK illustration

ham·mer·less \-ləs\ *adj* (1875) **:** having the hammer concealed ⟨a ~ revolver⟩

ham·mer·lock \-ˌläk\ *n* (1897) **:** a wrestling hold in which an opponent's arm is held bent behind the back; *broadly* **:** a strong hold

hammer mill *n* (1610) **:** a grinder or crusher in which materials are broken up by hammers

hammer out *vt* (ca. 1632) **:** to produce or bring about as if by repeated blows ⟨*hammered out* an agreement⟩

hammer price *n* [fr. the hammer used by the auctioneer to signal the auction's end] (1900) **:** the price at which an item is sold at auction

ham·mer·stone \ˈha-mər-ˌstōn\ *n* (1872) **:** a prehistoric hammering implement consisting of a rounded stone

hammer throw *n* (1898) **:** a field event in which a usu. 16-pound metal sphere attached to a flexible handle is thrown for distance

ham·mer·toe \ˈha-mər-ˌtō\ *n* (ca. 1885) **:** a deformed claw-shaped toe and esp. the second that results from permanent angular flexion between one or both phalangeal joints

[1]**ham·mock** \ˈha-mək\ *n* [Sp *hamaca,* fr. Taino] (1626) **:** a swinging couch or bed usu. made of netting or canvas and slung by cords from supports at each end

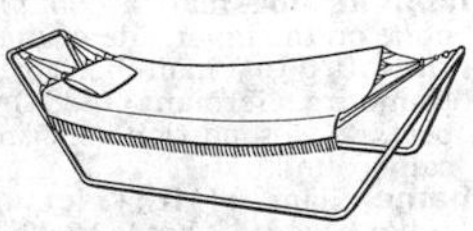
[1]hammock

[2]**hammock** *n* [earlier *hammok, hommoke, humock;* akin to MLG *hummel* small height, *hump* bump — more at HUMP] (1556) **1 :** HUMMOCK **2 :** a fertile area in the southern U.S. and esp. Florida that is usu. higher than its surroundings and that is characterized by hardwood vegetation and deep humus-rich soil

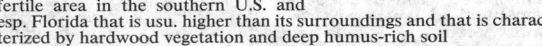

ham·my \ˈha-mē\ *adj* **ham·mi·er; -est** (1929) **:** marked by exaggerated and usu. self-conscious theatricality — **ham·mi·ly** \ˈha-mə-lē\ *adv* — **ham·mi·ness** \ˈha-mē-nəs\ *n*

[1]**ham·per** \ˈham-pər\ *vt* **ham·pered; ham·per·ing** \-p(ə-)riŋ\ [ME] (14c) **1 a :** to restrict the movement of by bonds or obstacles **:** IMPEDE **b :** to interfere with the operation of **:** DISRUPT **2 a :** CURB, RESTRAIN **b :** to interfere with **:** ENCUMBER

syn HAMPER, TRAMMEL, CLOG, FETTER, SHACKLE, MANACLE mean to hinder or impede in moving, progressing, or acting. HAMPER may imply the effect of any impeding or restraining influence ⟨*hampered* the investigation by refusing to cooperate⟩. TRAMMEL suggests entangling by or confining within a net ⟨rules that *trammel* the artist's creativity⟩. CLOG usu. implies a slowing by something extraneous or encumbering ⟨a court system *clogged* by frivolous suits⟩. FETTER suggests a restraining so severe that freedom to move or progress is almost lost ⟨a nation *fettered* by an antiquated class system⟩. SHACKLE and MANACLE are stronger than FETTER and suggest total loss of freedom ⟨a mind *shackled* by stubborn prejudice⟩ ⟨a people *manacled* by tyranny⟩.

[2]**hamper** *n* [ME *hamper, hanaper,* lit., case to hold goblets, fr. AF *hanaper,* fr. *hanap* goblet, of Gmc origin; akin to OE *hnæpp* bowl] (14c) **:** a large basket usu. with a cover for packing, storing, or transporting articles (as food or laundry)

Hamp·shire \ˈham(p)-ˌshir, -shər\ *n* [*Hampshire,* England] (1918) **1 :** any of a British breed of large hornless black-faced mutton-producing sheep — called also *Hampshire Down* **2 :** any of an American breed of black white-belted swine

ham·ster \ˈham(p)-stər\ *n* [G, fr. OHG *hamustro,* of Slavic origin; akin to ORuss *chomĕstorŭ* hamster, of Iranian origin; akin to Av *hamaēstar-* oppressor] (1607) **:** any of a subfamily (Cricetinae) of small Old World rodents having very large cheek pouches

[1]**ham·string** \ˈham-ˌstriŋ\ *n* (1565) **1 a :** either of two groups of tendons at the back of the human knee **b :** any of three muscles at the back of the thigh that function to flex and rotate the leg and extend the thigh **2 :** a large tendon above and behind the hock of a quadruped

[2]**hamstring** *vt* **-strung** \-ˌstrəŋ\; **-string·ing** \-ˌstriŋ-iŋ\ (1641) **1 :** to make ineffective or powerless **:** CRIPPLE ⟨*hamstrung* by guilt⟩ **2 :** to cripple by cutting the leg tendons

ham·u·lus \ˈham-yə-ləs\ *n, pl* **-u·li** \-ˌlī, -ˌlē\ [NL, fr. L, dim. of *hamus* hook] (ca. 1751) **:** a hook or hooked process (as of a bone)

ham·za *or* **ham·zah** \ˈham-zə, ˈhäm-\ *n* [Ar *hamza,* lit., compression] (1813) **:** the sign for a glottal stop in Arabic orthography usu. represented in English by an apostrophe

Han \ˈhän\ *n* [Chin (Beijing) *Hàn*] (1736) **1 :** a Chinese dynasty dated 206B.C.–A.D.220 and marked by centralized control through an appointive bureaucracy, a revival of learning, and the penetration of Buddhism **2 :** the Chinese peoples esp. as distinguished from non-Chinese (as Mongolian) elements in the population

Han·a·fi \ˈha-nə-(ˌ)fē\ *adj* [Ar *ḥanafī,* fr. Abū *Ḥanīfa* †767 Muslim jurist] (1913) **:** of or relating to an orthodox school of Sunni Muslim jurisprudence followed esp. in southern and central Asia

[1]**hand** \ˈhand\ *n, often attrib* [ME, fr. OE; akin to OHG *hant* hand] (bef. 12c) **1 a (1) :** the terminal part of the vertebrate forelimb when modified (as in humans) as a grasping organ **(2) :** the forelimb segment (as the terminal section of a bird's wing) of a vertebrate higher than the fishes that corresponds to the hand irrespective of its form or functional specialization **b :** a part serving the function of or resembling a hand: as **(1) :** the hind foot of an ape **(2) :** the chela of a crustacean **c :** something resembling a hand: as **(1) :** an indicator or pointer on a dial ⟨the ~s of a clock⟩ **(2) :** INDEX 5 **(3) :** a cluster of bananas developed from a single flower group **(4) :** a branched rootstock of ginger **(5) :** a bunch of large leaves (as of tobacco) tied together usu. with another leaf **2 a :** personal possession — usu. used in pl. ⟨the documents fell into the ~s of the enemy⟩ **b :** CONTROL, SUPERVISION — usu. used in pl. ⟨left the matter in her ~s⟩ **3 a :** SIDE, DIRECTION ⟨men fighting on either ~⟩ **b :** one of two sides or aspects of an issue or argument ⟨on the one ~ we can appeal for peace, and on the other, declare war⟩ **4 :** a pledge esp. of betrothal or bestowal in marriage **5 a :** style of penmanship **:** HANDWRITING ⟨wrote in a fancy ~⟩ **b :** SIGNATURE **6 a :** SKILL, ABILITY ⟨tried her ~ at sailing⟩ **b :** an instrumental part ⟨had a ~ in the victory⟩ **7 :** a unit of measure equal to 4 inches (10.2 centimeters) used esp. for the height of horses **8 a :** assistance or aid esp. involving physical effort ⟨lend a ~⟩ **b :** PARTICIPATION, INTEREST ⟨had no ~ in the decision⟩ **c :** a round of applause **9 a (1) :** a player in a card game or board game **(2) :** the cards or pieces held by a player **b :** a single round in a game **c :** the force or solidity of one's position (as in negotiations) ⟨trying to strengthen their ~⟩ **10 a :** a person who performs or executes a particular work ⟨two portraits by the same ~⟩ **b (1) :** a person employed at manual labor or general tasks ⟨a ranch ~⟩ **(2) :** WORKER, EMPLOYEE ⟨employed over a hundred ~s⟩ **c :** a member of a ship's crew ⟨all ~s on deck⟩ **d :** a person skilled in a particular action or pursuit **e :** a specialist or veteran in a usu. designated activity or region ⟨a China ~⟩ **11 a :** HANDIWORK, DOINGS **b :** style of execution **:** WORKMANSHIP ⟨the ~ of a master⟩ **c :** the feel of or tactile reaction to something (as silk or leather) **12 :** a punch made with a specified hand ⟨knocked him out with a good right ~⟩ — **at hand 1 :** near in time or place **:** within reach ⟨use whatever ingredients are *at hand*⟩ **2 :** currently receiving or deserving attention ⟨the business *at hand*⟩ — **at the hands of** *also* **at the hand of :** by or through the action of — **by hand 1 :** with the hands or a hand-worked implement (as a tool or pen) rather than with a machine **2 :** from one individual directly to another ⟨deliver the document *by hand*⟩ — **in hand 1 :** in one's possession or control ⟨had matters well *in hand*⟩ ⟨with money *in hand*⟩ **2 :** in preparation **3 :** under consideration — **on all hands** *or* **on every hand :** EVERYWHERE — **on hand 1 :** in present possession or readily available ⟨kept supplies *on hand*⟩ **2 :** about to appear **:** PENDING **3 :** in attendance **:** PRESENT — **on one's hands :** in one's possession or care ⟨too much time *on my hands*⟩ — **out of hand 1 :** without delay or deliberation; *also* **:** in a summary or peremptory manner ⟨rejected the plan *out of hand*⟩ **2 :** done with **:** FINISHED **3 :** out of control **4 :** with the hands ⟨fruit eaten *out of hand*⟩ — **to hand 1 :** into possession ⟨the letter . . . has come *to hand* —George Washington⟩ **2 :** within reach

[2]**hand** *adv* (bef. 12c) **:** with the hands rather than by machine

[3]**hand** *vt* (15c) **1 a** *obs* **:** to touch or manage with the hands; *also* **:** to deal with **b :** FURL **2 :** to lead, guide, or assist with the hand ⟨~ a lady into a bus⟩ **3 a :** to give, pass, or transmit with the hand ⟨~ a letter to her⟩ **b :** to present or provide with ⟨~*ed* him a surprise⟩ — **hand it to :** to give credit to **:** concede the excellence of

hand and foot *adv* (bef. 12c) **:** TOTALLY, ASSIDUOUSLY

hand ax *n* (13c) **1 :** a short-handled ax intended for use with one hand **2 :** a prehistoric stone tool having one end pointed for cutting and the other end rounded for holding in the hand

hand·bag \ˈhan(d)-ˌbag\ *n* (1862) **1 :** SUITCASE **2 :** a bag held in the hand or hung from a shoulder strap and used for carrying small personal articles and money

hand·ball \-ˌbȯl\ *n* (1873) **1 :** a game played in a walled court or against a single wall or board by two or four players who use their hands to strike the ball **2 :** a small rubber ball used in handball

hand·bar·row \-ˌba-(ˌ)rō\ *n* (15c) **:** a flat rectangular frame with handles at both ends that is carried by two persons

hand·bas·ket \-ˌbas-kət\ *n* (15c) **:** a small portable basket — usu. used in the phrase *to hell in a handbasket* denoting rapid and utter ruination

hand·bell \-ˌbel\ *n* (bef. 12c) **:** a small bell with a handle; *esp* **:** one of a set tuned in a scale for musical performance

hand·bill \-ˌbil\ *n* (1753) **:** a small printed sheet to be distributed (as for advertising) by hand

hand blender *n* (1975) **:** IMMERSION BLENDER

hand·blown \-ˈblōn\ *adj* (1925) **:** made by glassblowing and molded by hand

hand·book \-ˌbu̇k\ *n* (bef. 12c) **1 a :** a book capable of being conveniently carried as a ready reference **:** MANUAL **b :** a concise reference book covering a particular subject **2 a :** a bookmaker's book of bets **b :** a place where bookmaking is carried on

hand brake *n* (1854) **:** an emergency brake operated by a hand lever

hand·breadth \-ˌbretth, -ˌbreth, -ˌbredth\ *or* **hands·breadth** \ˈhan(d)z-\ *n* (bef. 12c) **:** any of various units of length varying from about 2½ to 4 inches based on the breadth of a hand

hand·car \ˈhan(d)-ˌkär\ *n* (1850) **:** a small four-wheeled railroad car propelled by a hand-operated mechanism or by a small motor

hand·cart \-ˌkärt\ *n* (1640) **:** a cart drawn or pushed by hand

hand·clasp \ˈhan(d)-ˌklasp\ *n* (1582) **:** HANDSHAKE

[1]**hand·craft** \-ˌkraft\ *n* (bef. 12c) **:** HANDICRAFT

[2]**handcraft** *vt* (1947) **:** to fashion by handicraft

hand·crafts·man \-ˌkraf(t)-smən\ *n* (15c) **:** a person who is skilled in handicraft — **hand·crafts·man·ship** \-ˌship\ *n*

[1]**hand·cuff** \-ˌkəf\ *n* (1695) **:** a metal fastening that can be locked around a wrist and is usu. connected by a chain or bar with another such fastening — usu. used in pl.

[2]**handcuff** *vt* (1691) **1 :** to apply handcuffs to **:** MANACLE **2 :** to hold in check **:** make ineffective or powerless ⟨~*ed* by strict regulations⟩

hand down *vt* (1685) **1 :** to transmit in succession (as from father to son) **2 :** to make official formulation of and express (the opinion of a court)

hand·ed \ˈhan-dəd\ *adj* (15c) **1 :** having a hand or hands esp. of a specified kind or number — usu. used in combination ⟨a large-*handed* man⟩ **2 :** using a specified hand or number of hands — used in combination ⟨right-*handed*⟩ ⟨a one-*handed* catch⟩

hand·ed·ness \-nəs\ *n* (1915) **1 :** a tendency to use one hand rather than the other **2 a :** the property of an object (as a molecule) of not being identical with its mirror image **:** CHIRALITY **b :** either of the two configurations of an object that may exist in forms which are nonidentical mirror images

hand·fast \ˈhan(d)-ˌfast\ *n* [ME, fr. OE *handfæst*] (1611) *archaic* **:** a contract or covenant esp. of betrothal or marriage

hand–feed \ˈhan(d)-ˈfēd\ *vt* **-fed** \-ˈfed\; **-feed·ing** (1805) **:** to feed (as animals) by hand

hand, foot and mouth disease *n* (1966) **:** a usu. mild contagious disease esp. of young children that is caused by an enterovirus (species *Human enterovirus A,* esp. serotype Human coxsackievirus A16) and is characterized by vesicular lesions chiefly in the mouth and on the hands and feet — compare FOOT-AND-MOUTH DISEASE

hand·ful \ˈhan(d)-ˌfu̇l\ *n, pl* **handfuls** \-ˌfu̇lz\ *also* **hands·ful** \ˈhan(d)z-ˌfu̇l\ (bef. 12c) **1 :** as much or as many as the hand will grasp **2 :** a small quantity or number ⟨a ~ of people⟩ **3 :** as much as one can manage ⟨the kids are quite a ~⟩

hand glass *n* (1875) **:** a small mirror with a handle

hand·grip \ˈhan(d)-ˌgrip\ *n* (bef. 12c) **1 :** a grasping with the hand **2 :** HANDLE **3** *pl* **:** hand-to-hand combat

hand·gun \-ˌgən\ *n* (15c) **:** a firearm (as a revolver or pistol) designed to be held and fired with one hand

hand·held \-ˌheld, -ˈheld\ *adj* (1923) **:** held in the hand; *esp* **:** designed to be operated while being held in the hand ⟨~ computers⟩ — **handheld** \-ˌheld\ *n*

hand·hold \ˈhand-ˌhōld\ *n* (1643) **1 :** HOLD, GRIP **2 :** something to hold on to (as in mountain climbing)

hand–hold·ing \-ˌhōl-diŋ\ *n* (1967) **:** solicitous attention, support, or instruction (as in servicing clients) — **hand–hold·er** \-ˌhōl-dər\ *n*

1**hand·i·cap** \ˈhan-di-ˌkap, -dē-\ *n* [obs. E *handicap,* a game in which forfeit money was held in a cap, fr. *hand in cap*] (1754) **1 a :** a race or contest in which an artificial advantage is given or disadvantage imposed on a contestant to equalize chances of winning **b :** an advantage given or disadvantage imposed usu. in the form of points, strokes, weight to be carried, or distance from the target or goal **2 a :** a disadvantage that makes achievement unusually difficult **b** *sometimes offensive* **:** a physical disability

2**handicap** *vt* **-capped; -cap·ping** (1852) **1 a :** to give a handicap to **b :** to assess the relative winning chances of (contestants) or the likely winner of (a contest) **2 :** to put at a disadvantage

handicapped *adj* (1891) *sometimes offensive* **:** having a physical or mental disability; *also* **:** of or reserved for handicapped persons ⟨~ parking spaces⟩

hand·i·cap·per \-ˌka-pər\ *n* (1754) **1 :** a person who assigns handicaps **2 :** a person who predicts the winners in a contest (as a horse race) **3 :** a person who competes with a (specified) handicap (as in golf) — usu. used in combination ⟨a 5-*handicapper*⟩

hand·i·craft \ˈhan-di-ˌkraft, -dē-\ *n* [ME *handi-crafte,* alter. of *handcraft*] (13c) **1 a :** manual skill **b :** an occupation requiring skill with the hands **2 :** the articles fashioned by those engaged in handicraft — **hand·i·craft·er** \-ˌkraf-tər\ *n*

hand·i·crafts·man \-ˌkraf(t)-smən\ *n* (1551) **:** a person who engages in a handicraft **:** ARTISAN

hand·i·ly \ˈhan-də-lē\ *adv* (1665) **1 :** in a dexterous manner **2 :** EASILY ⟨defeated the other candidate ~⟩ **3 :** conveniently nearby

hand in *vt* (1837) **:** SUBMIT 2 ⟨*hand in* your homework⟩

hand in glove *or* **hand and glove** *adv* (1664) **:** in extremely close relationship or agreement ⟨working *hand in glove* with the police⟩

hand in hand *adv* (15c) **1 :** with hands clasped (as in intimacy or affection) **2 :** in close association **:** TOGETHER

hand·i·work \ˈhan-di-ˌwərk, -dē-\ *n* [ME *handiwerk,* fr. OE *handgeweorc,* fr. *hand* + *geweorc,* fr. *ge-* (collective prefix) + *weorc* work — more at CO-] (bef. 12c) **1 a :** work done by the hands **b :** work done personally ⟨recognized her ~⟩ **2 :** the product of handiwork

hand·ker·chief \ˈhaŋ-kər-chəf, -(ˌ)chif, -ˌchēf\ *n, pl* **-chiefs** *also* **-chieves** \-chəfs, -(ˌ)chifs, -ˌchēvz, -ˌchēfs, -chəvz, -(ˌ)chivz\ (1530) **1 :** a small usu. square piece of cloth used for usu. personal purposes (as blowing the nose) or as a clothing accessory **2 :** KERCHIEF 1

1**han·dle** \ˈhan-dᵊl\ *n* [ME *handel,* fr. OE *handle;* akin to OE *hand*] (bef. 12c) **1 :** a part that is designed esp. to be grasped by the hand **2 :** something that resembles a handle **3 a :** TITLE 8 **b :** NAME; *also* **:** NICKNAME **4 :** HAND 11c **5 :** the total amount of money bet on a race, game, or event **6 :** a means of understanding or controlling ⟨can't quite get a ~ on things⟩ — **han·dled** \-dᵊld\ *adj* — **han·dle·less** \-dᵊl-(l)əs\ *adj* — **off the handle :** into a state of sudden and violent anger — usu. used with *fly*

2**handle** *vb* **han·dled; han·dling** \ˈhan(d)-liŋ, ˈhan-dᵊl-iŋ\ *vt* (bef. 12c) **1 a :** to try or examine (as by touching, feeling, or moving) with the hand ⟨~ silk to judge its weight⟩ **b :** to manage with the hands ⟨~ a horse⟩ **2 a :** to deal with in writing or speaking or in the plastic arts **b :** to have overall responsibility for supervising or directing **:** MANAGE ⟨a lawyer ~*s* all my affairs⟩ **c :** to train and act as second for (a boxer) **d :** to put up with **:** STAND ⟨can't ~ the heat⟩ **3 :** to act on or perform a required function with regard to ⟨~ the day's mail⟩ **4 :** to engage in the buying, selling, or distributing of (a commodity) ~ *vi* **:** to act, behave, or respond in a certain way when handled or directed ⟨a car that ~*s* well⟩ — **han·dle·able** \-dᵊl-ə-bəl\ *adj*

han·dle·bar \ˈhan-dᵊl-ˌbär\ *n* (1886) **:** a straight or bent bar with a handle at each end; *specif* **:** one used to steer a bicycle or similar vehicle — usu. used in pl.

handlebar mustache *n* (1896) **:** a heavy mustache with long sections that curve upward at each end

hand lens *n* (1930) **:** a magnifying glass to be held in the hand

han·dler \ˈhan(d)-lər, ˈhan-dᵊl-ər\ *n* (14c) **1 :** one that handles something **2 a :** a person in immediate physical charge of an animal; *esp* **:** a person who exhibits dogs at shows or field trials **b :** a person who trains or acts as second for a boxer **c :** a manager of a political or public figure or campaign

hand·less \ˈhan(d)-ləs\ *adj* (15c) **1 :** having no hands **2 :** inefficient in manual tasks **:** CLUMSY

handling *n* (bef. 12c) **1 a :** the action of one that handles something **b :** a process by which something is handled in a commercial transaction; *esp* **:** the packaging and shipping of an object or material (as to a consumer) **2 :** the manner in which something is treated (as in a musical, literary, or art work)

hand·list \ˈhan(d)-ˌlist\ *n* (1859) **:** a list (as of books) for purposes of reference or checking

hand·made \ˈhan(d)-ˈmād\ *adj* (1603) **:** made by hand or by a hand process

hand·maid·en \-ˌmā-dᵊn\ *also* **hand·maid** \-ˌmād\ *n* (13c) **1 :** a personal maid or female servant **2 :** something whose essential function is to serve or assist ⟨criticism is not the enemy of art but rather its ~ —Gary Michael⟩

hand–me–down \ˈhan(d)-mē-ˌdau̇n\ *adj* (1827) **1 :** put in use by one person or group after being used, discarded, or handed down by another ⟨~ clothes⟩ ⟨~ anecdotes⟩ **2 :** ready-made and usu. cheap and shoddy — **hand–me–down** *n*

hand off *vt* (1949) **:** to hand (a football) to a nearby teammate on a play ~ *vi* **:** to hand off a football — **hand·off** \ˈhand-ˌȯf\ *n*

hand on *vt* (1865) **:** HAND DOWN

hand organ *n* (1770) **:** a barrel organ operated by a hand crank

hand·out \ˈhand-ˌau̇t\ *n* (1882) **1 :** a portion of food, clothing, or money given to or as if to a beggar **2 :** a folder or circular of information for free distribution **3 :** a prepared statement released to the news media

hand out *vt* (ca. 1860) **1 a :** to give without charge **b :** to give freely **2 :** ADMINISTER ⟨*handed out* a severe punishment⟩

hand over *vt* (1864) **:** to yield control of — **hand·over** \ˈhan-ˌdō-vər\ *n*

hand over fist *adv* (1825) **:** quickly and in large amounts ⟨making money *hand over fist*⟩

hand·pick \ˈhan(d)-ˈpik\ *vt* (1831) **1 :** to pick by hand as opposed to a machine process **2 :** to select personally or for personal ends

hand·press \-ˌpres\ *n* (1679) **:** a hand-operated press

hand·print \-ˌprint\ *n* (1886) **:** an impression of a hand on a surface

hand puppet *n* (1937) **:** PUPPET 1a

hand·rail \ˈhan(d)-ˌrāl\ *n* (1725) **:** a narrow rail for grasping with the hand as a support

hand running *adv* (1828) *dial* **:** in unbroken succession

hand·saw \ˈhan(d)-ˌsȯ\ *n* (14c) **:** a saw designed to be used with one hand

handsbreadth *var of* HANDBREADTH

hands down \ˈhan(d)z-ˈdau̇n\ *adv* (1867) **1 :** without much effort **:** EASILY **2 :** without question — **hands–down** \ˈhan(d)z-ˌdau̇n\ *adj*

1**hand·sel** \ˈhan(t)-səl\ *n* [ME *hansell*] (14c) **1 :** a gift made as a token of good wishes or luck esp. at the beginning of a new year **2 :** something received first (as in a day of trading) and taken to be a token of good luck **3 a :** a first installment **:** earnest money **b :** EARNEST, FORETASTE

2**handsel** *vt* **-seled** *or* **-selled; -sel·ing** *or* **-sel·ling** \-s(ə-)liŋ\ (15c) **1 :** to give a handsel to **2 :** to inaugurate with a token or gesture of luck or pleasure **3 :** to use or do for the first time

hand·set \ˈhan(d)-ˌset\ *n* (ca. 1919) **:** a combined telephone transmitter and receiver mounted on a handheld device

hand·shake \-ˌshāk\ *n* (1871) **:** a clasping usu. of right hands by two people (as in greeting or farewell)

hands–off \ˈhan(d)z-ˈȯf\ *adj* (1902) **:** characterized by noninterference ⟨a ~ policy toward the internal affairs of other nations⟩

hand·some \ˈhan(t)-səm\ *adj* **hand·som·er; -est** [ME *handsom* easy to manipulate] (1530) **1** *chiefly dial* **:** APPROPRIATE, SUITABLE **2 :** moderately large **:** SIZABLE ⟨a painting that commanded a ~ price⟩ **3 :** marked by skill or cleverness **:** ADROIT **4 :** marked by graciousness or generosity **:** LIBERAL ⟨~ contributions to charity⟩ **5 :** having a pleasing and usu. impressive or dignified appearance ***syn*** see BEAUTIFUL — **hand·some·ly** *adv* — **hand·some·ness** *n*

hands–on \ˈhan(d)z-ˈȯn, -ˈän\ *adj* (1969) **1 :** relating to, being, or providing direct practical experience in the operation or functioning of something ⟨~ training⟩; *also* **:** involving or allowing use of or touching with the hands ⟨a ~ museum display⟩ **2 :** characterized by active personal involvement ⟨a ~ manager⟩

hand·spike \ˈhan(d)-ˌspīk\ *n* [by folk etymology fr. D *handspaak,* fr. *hand* hand + *spaak* pole; akin to OE *spāca* spoke] (1615) **:** a bar used as a lever

hand·spring \-ˌspriŋ\ *n* (1875) **:** an acrobatic feat in which the body turns forward or backward in a full circle from a standing position and lands first on the hands and then on the feet

hand·stand \-ˌstand\ *n* (1899) **:** an act of supporting the body on the hands with the trunk and legs balanced in the air

hand–to–hand \ˈhan-tə-ˈhand, -də-\ *adj* (1836) **:** involving physical contact or close enough range for physical contact ⟨~ fighting⟩

hand to hand *adv* (ca. 1533) **:** at very close range

hand–to–mouth \-ˈmau̇th\ *adj* (1748) **:** having or providing nothing to spare beyond basic necessities ⟨a ~ existence⟩ — **hand to mouth** *adv*

hand truck *n* (1920) **:** a small hand-propelled truck; *esp* **:** TRUCK 3b

hand up *vt* (1970) *of a jury* **:** to deliver (an indictment) to a judge or higher judicial authority

hand·wheel \ˈhan(d)-ˌ(h)wēl\ *n* (ca. 1889) **:** a wheel worked by hand

hand·work \ˈhand-ˌwərk\ *n* (bef. 12c) **:** work done with the hands and not by machines **:** HANDIWORK — **hand·work·er** \-ˌwər-kər\ *n*

hand·wo·ven \-ˈwō-vən\ *adj* (1880) **1 :** produced on a hand-operated loom **2 :** woven by hand ⟨~ baskets⟩

hand–wring·ing \-ˌriŋ-iŋ\ *n* (1922) **:** an overwrought expression of concern or guilt — **hand·wring·er** *n*

hand·write \-ˌrīt\ *vt* **-wrote** \-ˌrōt\; **-writ·ten** \-ˌri-tᵊn\; **-writ·ing** \-ˌrī-tiŋ\ [back-formation fr. *handwriting*] (ca. 1853) **:** to write by hand

hand·writ·ing \ˈhand-ˌrī-tiŋ\ *n* (15c) **1 :** writing done by hand; *esp* **:** the form of writing peculiar to a particular person **2 :** something written by hand — **handwriting on the wall :** an omen of one's unpleasant fate

hand·wrought \ˈhand-ˈrȯt\ *adj* (1876) **:** fashioned by hand or chiefly by hand processes ⟨~ silver⟩

handy \ˈhan-dē\ *adj* **hand·i·er; -est** (1650) **1 a :** conveniently near **b :** convenient for use **c** *of a ship* **:** easily handled **2 :** clever in using the hands esp. in a variety of useful ways ⟨~ with a hammer as well as with a paintbrush⟩ — **hand·i·ness** *n*

handy·man \-dē-ˌman\ *n* (1872) **1 :** a person who does odd jobs **2 :** one competent in a variety of small skills or inventive or ingenious in repair or maintenance work — called also *handyperson*

[1]**hang** \ˈhaŋ\ *vb* **hung** \ˈhəŋ\ *also* **hanged** \ˈhaŋd\; **hang·ing** \ˈhaŋ-iŋ\ [partly fr. ME *hon,* fr. OE *hōn,* v.t.; partly fr. ME *hangen,* fr. OE *hangian,* v.i. & v.t.; both akin to OHG *hāhan,* v.t., to hang, *hangēn,* v.i. — more at CUNCTATION] *vt* (bef. 12c) **1 a :** to fasten to some elevated point without support from below : SUSPEND **b :** to suspend by the neck until dead — often *hanged* in the past; often used as a mild oath ⟨I'll be ~*ed*⟩ **c :** to fasten so as to allow free motion within given limits upon a point of suspension ⟨~ a door⟩ **d :** to adjust the hem of (a skirt) so as to hang evenly and at a proper height **2 :** to furnish with hanging decorations (as flags or bunting) **3 :** to hold or bear in a suspended or inclined manner ⟨*hung* his head in shame⟩ **4 :** to apply to a wall ⟨~ wallpaper⟩ **5 :** to display (pictures) in a gallery **6 :** to throw (as a curveball) so that it fails to break properly **7 :** to make (a turn) esp. while driving ⟨~ a right⟩ ⟨*hung* a quick U-turn —Tom Clancy⟩ **8 :** BASE, FOUND ⟨something to ~ our hopes on⟩ ~ *vi* **1 a :** to remain suspended or fastened to some point above without support from below : DANGLE **b :** to die by hanging — often *hanged* in the past ⟨he ~*ed* for his crimes⟩ **c :** to be connected as something relevant or related ⟨thereby ~*s* a tale —Shak.⟩ **2 :** to remain poised or stationary in the air ⟨clouds ~*ing* low overhead⟩ **3 :** LINGER, PERSIST **4 :** to be imminent : IMPEND ⟨doom *hung* over the nation⟩ **5 :** to fall or droop from a usu. tense or taut position **6 :** DEPEND ⟨election ~*s* on one vote⟩ **7 a** (1) **:** to take hold for support : CLING ⟨she *hung* on his arm⟩ (2) **:** to keep persistent contact ⟨dogs *hung* to the trail⟩ (3) **:** to maintain or continue holding a position ⟨~ behind⟩ (4) **:** to stay even : KEEP UP — usu. used with *with* ⟨trying to ~ with the leader⟩ **b :** to be burdensome or oppressive ⟨time ~*s* on his hands⟩ **8 :** to be uncertain or in suspense ⟨the decision is still ~*ing*⟩ **9 :** to lean, incline, or jut over or downward **10 :** to be in a state of rapt attention ⟨*hung* on her every word⟩ **11 :** to fit or fall from the figure in easy lines ⟨the coat ~*s* loosely⟩ **12 :** to pass time idly or in relaxing or socializing ⟨~*ing* at the beach⟩ — often used with *around* or *out* ⟨*hung* out with friends⟩ **13** *of a thrown ball* **:** to fail to break or drop as intended — **hang·able** \ˈhaŋ-ə-bəl\ *adj* — **hang fire 1 :** to be slow in the explosion of a charge after its primer has been discharged **2 :** DELAY, HESITATE **3 :** to remain unsettled or unresolved — **hang it up :** to cease an activity or effort — **hang loose :** to remain calm or relaxed — **hang one on 1 :** to inflict a blow on **2** *slang* **:** to get very drunk — **hang out to dry :** to subject to ruin by abandonment — **hang one's hat 1 :** to situate oneself in (as a residence or place of employment) **2 :** to have or use as a source of support ⟨need a career to *hang my hat* on⟩ — **hang ten :** to ride a surfboard with the toes of both feet turned over the front edge — **hang tough :** to remain resolute in the face of adversity : HANG IN

usage For both transitive and intransitive senses 1b the past and past participle *hung,* as well as *hanged,* is standard. *Hanged* is most appropriate for official executions ⟨he was to be *hanged,* cut down whilst still alive . . . and his bowels torn out —Louis Allen⟩ but *hung* is also used ⟨gave orders that she should be *hung* —Peter Quennell⟩. *Hung* is more appropriate for less formal hangings ⟨by morning I'll be *hung* in effigy —Ronald Reagan⟩.

[2]**hang** *n* (ca. 1797) **1 :** the manner in which a thing hangs **2 :** DECLIVITY, SLOPE; *also* **:** DROOP **3 :** facility with or an understanding of something ⟨can't get the ~ of this⟩ **4 :** a hesitation or slackening in motion or in a course — **give a hang** *or* **care a hang :** to be the least bit concerned or worried

hang about *vi* (1781) *Brit* **:** HANG 12

[1]**han·gar** \ˈhaŋ-ər, ˈhaŋ-gər\ *n* [F] (1852) **:** SHELTER, SHED; *esp* **:** a covered and usu. enclosed area for housing and repairing aircraft

[2]**hangar** *vt* (1943) **:** to place or store in a hangar

hang around *vt* (1847) **:** to pass time or stay aimlessly in or at ⟨*hung around* the house all day⟩

hang back *vi* (1581) **1 :** to drag behind others **2 :** to be reluctant

[1]**hang·dog** \ˈhaŋ-ˌdȯg\ *adj* (1677) **1 :** SAD, DEJECTED **2 :** SHEEPISH

[2]**hangdog** *n* (1687) **:** a despicable or miserable person

hang·er \ˈhaŋ-ər\ *n* (15c) **1 :** one that hangs or causes to be hung or hanged **2 :** something that hangs, overhangs, or is suspended: as **a :** a decorative strip of cloth **b :** a small sword formerly used by seamen **c** *chiefly Brit* **:** a small wood on steeply sloping land **3 :** a device by which or to which something is hung or hangs: as **a :** a strap on a sword belt by which a sword or dagger can be suspended **b :** a loop by which a garment is hung up **c :** a device that fits inside or around a garment for hanging from a hook or rod

hang·er–on \-ˌȯn, -ˌän\ *n, pl* **hangers–on** (1542) **:** one that hangs around a person, place, or institution esp. for personal gain

hanger steak *n* (1977) **:** a steak cut from the beef diaphragm

hang glider *n* (1930) **:** a kitelike glider from which a harnessed rider hangs while gliding down from a cliff or hill — **hang glide** *vi* — **hang glid·ing** *n*

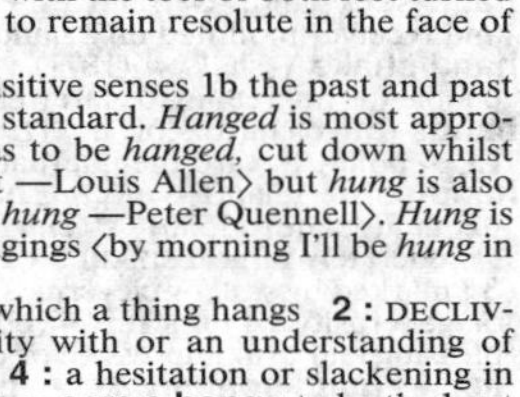

hang glider

hang in *vi* (1966) **:** to refuse to be discouraged or intimidated : show pluck ⟨*hang in* there⟩

[1]**hanging** *adj* (12c) **1 :** situated or lying on steeply sloping ground **2 a :** jutting out : OVERHANGING ⟨a ~ rock⟩ **b :** supported only by the wall on one side ⟨a ~ staircase⟩ **3** *archaic* **:** downcast in appearance **4 :** adapted for sustaining a hanging object **5 :** deserving, likely to cause, or prone to inflict death by hanging

[2]**hanging** *n* (14c) **1 :** an execution by strangling or breaking the neck by a suspended noose **2 :** something hung: as **a :** CURTAIN **b :** a covering (as a tapestry) for a wall **3 :** a downward slope : DECLIVITY

hanging indention *n* (1904) **:** indention of all the lines of a paragraph except the first

hang·man \ˈhaŋ-mən\ *n* (14c) **1 :** one who hangs a condemned person; *also* **:** a public executioner **2 :** a game in which the object is for one player to guess the letters of an unknown word before the player who knows the word creates a stick figure of a hanged man by drawing one line for each incorrect guess

hang·nail \-ˌnāl\ *n* [by folk etymology fr. *agnail* inflammation about the nail, fr. ME, corn on the foot or toe, fr. OE *angnægl,* fr. *ang-* (akin to *enge* tight, painful) + *nægl* nail — more at ANGER] (1678) **:** a bit of skin hanging loose at the side or root of a fingernail

hang off *vi* (1641) **:** HANG BACK

hang on *vi* (ca. 1719) **1 :** to keep hold : hold onto something **2 :** to persist tenaciously ⟨a cold that *hung on* all spring⟩ **3 :** HOLD ON 2 — **hang on to :** to hold, grip, or keep tenaciously

hang·out \ˈhaŋ-ˌau̇t\ *n* (ca. 1893) **:** a favorite place for spending time; *also* **:** a place frequented for entertainment or for socializing

hang out *vi* (14c) **1 :** to protrude and droop **2** *slang* **:** LIVE, RESIDE ~ *vt* **:** to display outside as an announcement to the public — used chiefly in the phrase *hang out one's shingle*

hang·over \ˈhaŋ-ˌō-vər\ *n* (1894) **1 :** something (as a surviving custom) that remains from what is past **2 a :** disagreeable physical effects following heavy consumption of alcohol or the use of drugs **b :** a letdown following great excitement or excess

hang·tag \ˈhaŋ-ˌtag\ *n* (1952) **:** a tag attached to an article of merchandise giving information about its material and proper care

hang time *n* (1971) **:** the amount of time a kicked football remains in the air; *also* **:** the length of time a leaping athlete is in the air

hang together *vi* (1551) **1 :** to remain united : stand by one another **2 :** to have unity : form a consistent or coherent whole

Hang·town fry \ˈhaŋ-ˌtau̇n-\ *n, often cap F* [*Hangtown,* nickname for Placerville, Calif.] (1949) **:** an omelet or scrambled eggs containing oysters

han·gul \ˈhän-ˌgül\ *n, often cap* [Korean *hangŭl*] (1946) **:** the alphabetic script in which Korean is written

hang–up \ˈhaŋ-ˌəp\ *n* (1952) **:** a source of mental or emotional difficulty; *broadly* **:** PROBLEM

hang up *vt* (12c) **1 a :** to place on a hook or hanger designed for the purpose ⟨*hang up* your coat⟩ **b :** to replace (a telephone receiver) on the cradle so that the connection is broken **2 :** to keep delayed, suspended, or held up **3 :** to cause to stick or snag immovably ⟨the ship was *hung up* on a sandbar⟩ ~ *vi* **1 :** to break a telephone connection **2 :** to become stuck or snagged so as to be immovable

ha·ni·wa \ˈhä-nə-ˌwä\ *n pl, often cap* [Jp] (1931) **:** large hollow baked clay sculptures placed on ancient Japanese burial mounds

hank \ˈhaŋk\ *n* [ME, of Scand origin; akin to ON *hǫnk* hank; akin to OE *hangian* to hang] (14c) **1 :** COIL, LOOP; *specif* **:** a coiled or looped bundle (as of yarn) usu. containing a definite yardage **2 :** any of a series of rings or clips by which a jib or staysail is attached to a stay

han·ker \ˈhaŋ-kər\ *vi* **han·kered; han·ker·ing** \-k(ə-)riŋ\ [prob. fr. D dial. *hankeren*] (1627) **:** to have a strong or persistent desire : YEARN — often used with *for* or *after* ***syn*** see LONG — **han·ker·er** \-kər-ər\ *n*

han·kie *or* **han·ky** \ˈhaŋ-kē\ *n, pl* **hankies** [*hand*kerchief + *-ie*] (1878) **:** HANDKERCHIEF

han·ky–pan·ky \ˌhaŋ-kē-ˈpaŋ-kē\ *n* [origin unknown] (1841) **1 :** questionable or underhanded activity **2 :** sexual dalliance

[1]**Han·o·ve·ri·an** \ˌha-nə-ˈvir-ē-ən, -ˈver-\ *adj* [*Hanover,* Germany] (1753) **1 :** of, relating to, or supporting the German ducal house of Hanover **2 :** of or relating to the British royal house that ruled from 1714 to 1901

[2]**Hanoverian** *n* (1730) **1 :** a member or supporter of the ducal or of the British royal Hanoverian house **2 :** any of a breed of horses of German origin bred to excel in equestrian competition (as dressage and jumping)

Han·sa \ˈhan(t)-sə, ˈhän-(ˌ)zä\ *or* **Hanse** \ˈhan(t)s, ˈhän-zə\ *n* [*Hansa* fr. ML, fr. MLG *hanse; Hanse* fr. ME *Hanze,* fr. AF *hanse,* fr. MLG] (15c) **1 :** a league orig. constituted of merchants of various free German cities dealing abroad in the medieval period and later of the cities themselves and organized to secure greater safety and privileges in trading **2 :** a medieval merchant guild or trading association — **Han·se·at·ic** \ˌhan(t)-sē-ˈa-tik\ *n or adj*

Han·sard \ˈhan(t)-sərd, ˈhan-ˌsärd\ *n* [Luke *Hansard*] (ca. 1859) **:** the official published report of debates in the parliament of a member of the Commonwealth of Nations

hansel *var of* HANDSEL

Han·sen's disease \ˈhan(t)-sənz-\ *n* [Armauer *Hansen* †1912 Norw. physician] (1938) **:** LEPROSY

han·som \ˈhan(t)-səm\ *n* [Joseph A. *Hansom* †1882 Eng. architect] (1847) **:** a light 2-wheeled covered carriage with the driver's seat elevated behind — called also *hansom cab*

hant \ˈhant\ *dial var of* HAUNT

han·ta·vi·rus \ˈhän-tə-ˌvī-rəs, ˈhən-, ˈhan-\ *n* [NL, fr. *hanta-* (fr. *Hantaan,* river in South Korea near where rodents carrying the virus were collected 1974–78) + *virus*] (1984) **:** any of a genus (*Hantavirus*) of bunyaviruses transmitted esp. by rodent feces and urine and including viruses causing serious pulmonary disease or hemorrhagic fevers marked by renal necrosis

Hants *abbr* Hampshire

Ha·nuk·kah *also* **Cha·nu·kah** *or* **Ha·nu·kah** \ˈhä-nə-kə, ˈkä-\ *n* [Heb *ḥănukkāh* dedication] (1843) **:** an 8-day Jewish holiday beginning on the 25th of Kislev and commemorating the rededication of the Temple of Jerusalem after its defilement by Antiochus of Syria

hao \ˈhau̇\ *n, pl* **hao** [Vietnamese *hào*] (1948) **:** a monetary unit of Vietnam equal to ¹⁄₁₀ dong

hao·le \ˈhau̇-lē, -(ˌ)lā\ *n* [Hawaiian] (1834) *sometimes disparaging* **:** one who is not descended from the aboriginal Polynesian inhabitants of Hawaii; *esp* **:** WHITE

[1]**hap** \ˈhap\ *n* [ME, fr. ON *happ* good luck; akin to OE *gehæp* suitable, OCS *kobĭ* lot, fate] (13c) **1 :** HAPPENING 1 **2 :** CHANCE, FORTUNE

[2]**hap** *vi* **happed; hap·ping** (14c) **:** HAPPEN

[3]**hap** *vt* **happed; hap·ping** [ME *happen*] (14c) *dial* **:** CLOTHE, COVER

[4]**hap** *n* (1724) *dial* **:** something (as a bed quilt or cloak) that serves as a covering or wrap

ha·pa hao·le \ˌhä-pə-ˈhau̇-lē, -(ˌ)lā\ *adj* [Hawaiian, fr. *hapa* half (fr. E *half*) + *haole*] (1919) **:** of part-white ancestry or origin; *esp* **:** of white and Hawaiian ancestry

ha·pax le·go·me·non \ˌha-ˌpaks-li-ˈgä-mə-ˌnän, ˌhä-ˌpäks-, -nən\ *n, pl* **hapax le·go·me·na** \-nə\ [Gk, something said only once] (1882) **:** a word or form occurring only once in a document or corpus

ha'·pen·ny \ˈhāp-nē, ˈhā-pə-\ *n* [by contr.] (13c) **:** HALFPENNY

[1]**hap·haz·ard** \(ˌ)hap-ˈha-zərd\ *n* [[1]*hap* + *hazard*] (1575) : CHANCE 1
[2]**haphazard** *adj* (1671) : marked by lack of plan, order, or direction ***syn*** see RANDOM — **haphazard** *adv* — **hap·haz·ard·ly** *adv* — **hap·haz·ard·ness** *n* — **hap·haz·ard·ry** \-zər-drē\ *n*
hap·ki·do \ˌhäp-ˈkē-dō\ *n* [Korean, fr. *hap-* together, joined + *ki* breath, energy + *to* way, art] (1973) : a Korean martial art based on kicking motions and incorporating elements of aikido
hapl- *or* **haplo-** *comb form* [NL, fr. Gk, fr. *haploos,* fr. *ha-* one (akin to *homos* same) + *-ploos* multiplied by; akin to L *-plex* -fold — more at SAME, -FOLD] **1 :** single ⟨*haplo*logy⟩ **2 :** haploid ⟨*hapl*ont⟩
hap·less \ˈha-pləs\ *adj* (14c) : having no luck : UNFORTUNATE — **hap·less·ly** *adv* — **hap·less·ness** *n*
hap·loid \ˈha-ˌplȯid\ *adj* [ISV, fr. Gk *haploeidēs* single, fr. *haploos*] (1908) : having the gametic number of chromosomes typically including one of each pair of homologous chromosomes — compare DIPLOID — **haploid** *n* — **hap·loi·dy** \-ˌplȯi-dē\ *n*
hap·lol·o·gy \ha-ˈplä-lə-jē\ *n* (1895) : contraction of a word by omission of one or more similar sounds or syllables (as in *mineralogy* for hypothetical *mineralology* or \ˈprä-blē\ for *probably*)
hap·lont \ˈha-ˌplänt\ *n* [ISV] (1920) : an organism (as some primitive algae) having a diploid zygote that undergoes meiosis to produce haploid cells — **hap·lon·tic** \ha-ˈplän-tik\ *adj*
hap·lo·type \ˈha-plō-ˌtīp\ *n* (1969) : a group of alleles of different genes (as of the major histocompatibility complex) on a single chromosome that are closely enough linked to be inherited usu. as a unit
hap·ly \ˈha-plē\ *adv* (14c) : by chance, luck, or accident
hap·pen \ˈha-pən, -pᵊm\ *vi* **hap·pened; hap·pen·ing** \ˈhap-niŋ, ˈha-pə-\ [ME, fr. *hap*] (14c) **1 :** to occur by chance — often used with *it* ⟨*it* so ∼*s* I'm going your way⟩ **2 :** to come into being or occur as an event, process, or result ⟨mistakes will ∼⟩ **3 :** to do, encounter, or attain something by or as if by chance ⟨I ∼ to know the answer⟩ **4 a :** to meet or discover something by chance ⟨∼*ed* upon a system that worked —Richard Corbin⟩ **b :** to come or go casually : make a chance appearance ⟨he might ∼ by at any time⟩ **5 :** to come esp. by way of injury or harm ⟨I promise nothing will ∼ to you⟩
hap·pen·chance \ˈha-pən-ˌchan(t)s, ˈha-pᵊm-\ *n* (1876) : HAPPENSTANCE
[1]**happening** *n* (1551) **1 :** something that happens : OCCURRENCE **2 :** an event or series of events designed to evoke a spontaneous reaction to sensory, emotional, or spiritual stimuli **3 :** something (as an event) that is particularly interesting, entertaining, or important
[2]**happening** *adj* (1977) **1 :** very fashionable : IN ⟨a ∼ hairstyle⟩ **2 :** offering much stimulating activity ⟨a ∼ dance club⟩
hap·pen·stance \ˈha-pən-ˌstan(t)s, ˈha-pᵊm-\ *n* [*happen* + *circumstance*] (1897) : a circumstance esp. that is due to chance — **hap·pen·stance** *adj*
hap·pi·ly \ˈha-pə-lē\ *adv* (14c) **1 a :** in a fortunate manner **b :** as it fortunately happens ⟨∼, some boyhood pleasures don't change —P. A. Witteman⟩ **2** *archaic* **:** by chance **3 :** in a happy manner or state **4 :** in an adequate or fitting manner : SUCCESSFULLY
hap·pi·ness \ˈha-pē-nəs\ *n* (15c) **1** *obs* **:** good fortune : PROSPERITY **2 a :** a state of well-being and contentment : JOY **b :** a pleasurable or satisfying experience **3 :** FELICITY, APTNESS
hap·py \ˈha-pē\ *adj* **hap·pi·er; -est** [ME, fr. *hap*] (14c) **1 :** favored by luck or fortune : FORTUNATE ⟨a ∼ coincidence⟩ **2 :** notably fitting, effective, or well adapted : FELICITOUS ⟨a ∼ choice⟩ **3 a :** enjoying or characterized by well-being and contentment ⟨is the *happiest* person I know⟩ ⟨a ∼ childhood⟩ **b :** expressing, reflecting, or suggestive of happiness ⟨a ∼ ending⟩ **c :** GLAD, PLEASED ⟨I'm ∼ to meet you⟩ **d :** having or marked by an atmosphere of good fellowship : FRIENDLY ⟨a ∼ office⟩ **4 a :** characterized by a dazed irresponsible state ⟨a punch-*happy* boxer⟩ **b :** impulsively or obsessively quick to use or do something ⟨trigger-*happy*⟩ **c :** enthusiastic about something to the point of obsession : OBSESSED ⟨education-conscious and statistic-*happy* —Helen Rowen⟩ ***syn*** see LUCKY, FIT
happy camper *n* (1984) : one who is content
hap·py–go–lucky \ˌha-pē-gō-ˈlə-kē\ *adj* (1856) : blithely unconcerned : CAREFREE
happy hour *n* (1959) : a period of time during which the price of drinks (as at a bar) is reduced or hors d'oeuvres are served free
happy hunting ground *n* (1837) **1 :** the paradise of some American Indian tribes to which the souls of warriors and hunters pass after death to spend a happy hereafter in hunting and feasting **2 :** a choice or profitable area of activity or exploitation
happy talk *n* (1973) **1 :** informal talk among the participants in a television news broadcast; *also* **:** a broadcast format featuring such talk **2 :** optimistic talk
Haps·burg *or* **Habs·burg** \ˈhaps-ˌbərg, ˈhäps-ˌbu̇rg\ *adj* [*Habsburg,* Aargau, Switzerland] (ca. 1861) : of or relating to the German royal house to which belong the rulers of Austria from 1278 to 1918, the rulers of Spain from 1516 to 1700, and many of the Holy Roman emperors — **Hapsburg** *n*
hap·ten \ˈhap-ˌten\ *n* [G, fr. Gk *haptein* to fasten] (1921) : a small separable part of an antigen that reacts specif. with an antibody but is incapable of stimulating antibody production except in combination with a carrier protein molecule — **hap·ten·ic** \hap-ˈte-nik\ *adj*
hap·tic \ˈhap-tik\ *adj* [ISV, fr. Gk *haptesthai* to touch] (ca. 1890) **1 :** relating to or based on the sense of touch **2 :** characterized by a predilection for the sense of touch ⟨a ∼ person⟩
hap·to·glo·bin \ˈhap-tə-ˌglō-bən\ *n* [ISV, fr. Gk *haptein* + ISV hemo*globin*] (1941) : any of several forms of an alpha globulin found in blood serum that can combine with free hemoglobin in the plasma and thereby prevent the loss of iron into the urine
hara–kiri *also* **hari–kari** \ˌha-ri-ˈkir-ē, -ˈka-rē\ *n* [Jp *harakiri,* fr. *hara* belly + *kiri* cutting] (1840) **1 :** ritual suicide by disembowelment practiced by the Japanese samurai or formerly decreed by a court in lieu of the death penalty **2 :** SUICIDE 1b
ha·ram \hä-ˈräm\ *adj* [Ar *ḥarām*] (1979) : forbidden by Islamic law ⟨∼ foods⟩
[1]**ha·rangue** \hə-ˈraŋ\ *n* [MF *arenge,* fr. OIt *aringa,* fr. *aringare* to speak in public, fr. *aringo* public assembly, of Gmc origin; akin to OHG *hring* ring] (ca. 1533) **1 :** a speech addressed to a public assembly **2 :** a ranting speech or writing **3 :** LECTURE
[2]**harangue** *vb* **ha·rangued; ha·rangu·ing** *vi* (1640) : to make a harangue : DECLAIM ∼ *vt* : to address in a harangue ⟨*haranguing* me . . . on the folly of my ways —Jay Jacobs⟩ — **ha·rangu·er** *n*
ha·rass \hə-ˈras; ˈher-əs, ˈha-rəs\ *vt* [F *harasser,* fr. MF, fr. *harer* to set a dog on, fr. OF *hare,* interj. used to incite dogs, of Gmc origin; akin to OHG *hier* here — more at HERE] (1617) **1 a :** EXHAUST, FATIGUE **b** (1) **:** to annoy persistently (2) **:** to create an unpleasant or hostile situation for esp. by uninvited and unwelcome verbal or physical conduct **2 :** to worry and impede by repeated raids ⟨∼*ed* the enemy⟩ ***syn*** see WORRY — **ha·rass·er** *n* — **ha·rass·ment** \-mənt\ *n*
[1]**har·bin·ger** \ˈhär-bən-jər\ *n* [ME *herbergere,* fr. AF, host, fr. *herberge* camp, lodgings, of Gmc origin; akin to OHG *heriberga*] (14c) **1** *archaic* **:** a person sent ahead to provide lodgings **2 a :** one that pioneers in or initiates a major change : PRECURSOR **b :** one that presages or foreshadows what is to come ***syn*** see FORERUNNER
[2]**harbinger** *vt* (1646) : to be a harbinger of : PRESAGE
[1]**har·bor** \ˈhär-bər\ *n* [ME *herberge, herberwe,* fr. OE *herebeorg* military quarters, fr. *here* army (akin to OHG *heri*) + *beorg* refuge; akin to OE *burg* fortified town — more at HARRY, BOROUGH] (12c) **1 :** a place of security and comfort : REFUGE **2 :** a part of a body of water protected and deep enough to furnish anchorage; *esp* **:** one with port facilities — **har·bor·ful** \-ˌfu̇l\ *n* — **har·bor·less** \-ləs\ *adj*
[2]**harbor** *vb* **har·bored; har·bor·ing** \-b(ə-)riŋ\ *vt* (12c) **1 a :** to give shelter or refuge to **b :** to be the home or habitat of ⟨the ledges still ∼ rattlesnakes⟩; *broadly* **:** CONTAIN 2 **2 :** to hold esp. persistently in the mind : CHERISH ⟨∼*ed* a grudge⟩ ∼ *vi* **1 :** to take shelter in or as if in a harbor **2 :** LIVE — **har·bor·er** \-bər-ər\ *n*
har·bor·age \-bə-rij\ *n* (15c) : SHELTER, HARBOR
har·bor·mas·ter \ˈhär-bər-ˌmas-tər\ *n* (1769) : an officer who executes the regulations respecting the use of a harbor
harbor seal *n* (1766) : a small hair seal (*Phoca vitulina*) of oceanic coasts in the northern hemisphere that often ascends rivers
har·bor·side \ˈhär-bər-ˌsīd\ *adj* (1924) : located next to a harbor
har·bour *chiefly Brit var of* HARBOR
[1]**hard** \ˈhärd\ *adj* [ME, fr. OE *heard;* akin to OHG *hart* hard, Gk *kratos* strength] (bef. 12c) **1 a :** not easily penetrated : not easily yielding to pressure **b** *of cheese* **:** not capable of being spread : very firm **2 a** *of liquor* (1) **:** having a harsh or acid taste (2) **:** strongly alcoholic **b :** characterized by the presence of salts (as of calcium or magnesium) that prevent lathering with soap ⟨∼ water⟩ **3 a :** of or relating to radiation of relatively high penetrating power : having high energy ⟨∼ X rays⟩ **b :** having or producing relatively great photographic contrast ⟨a ∼ negative⟩ **4 a :** metallic as distinct from paper ⟨∼ money⟩ **b** *of currency* **:** convertible into gold : stable in value **c :** usable as currency ⟨paid in ∼ cash⟩ **d** *of currency* **:** readily acceptable in international trade **e :** being high and firm ⟨∼ prices⟩ **5 a :** firmly and closely twisted ⟨∼ yarns⟩ **b :** having a smooth close napless finish ⟨a ∼ worsted⟩ **6 a :** physically fit ⟨in good ∼ condition⟩ **b :** resistant to stress or disease **c :** free of weakness or defects **7 a** (1) **:** FIRM, DEFINITE ⟨reached a ∼ agreement⟩ (2) **:** not speculative or conjectural : FACTUAL ⟨∼ evidence⟩ (3) **:** important or informative rather than sensational or entertaining ⟨∼ news⟩ **b :** CLOSE, SEARCHING ⟨gave a ∼ look⟩ **c :** free from sentimentality or illusion : REALISTIC ⟨good ∼ sense⟩ **d :** lacking in responsiveness : OBDURATE, UNFEELING ⟨a ∼ heart⟩ **8 a** (1) **:** difficult to bear or endure ⟨∼ luck⟩ ⟨∼ times⟩ (2) **:** OPPRESSIVE, INEQUITABLE ⟨sales taxes are ∼ on the poor⟩ ⟨a ∼ restriction⟩ **b** (1) **:** lacking consideration, compassion, or gentleness : CALLOUS ⟨a ∼ greedy landlord⟩ (2) **:** INCORRIGIBLE, TOUGH ⟨a ∼ gang⟩ **c** (1) **:** harsh, severe, or offensive in tendency or effect ⟨said some ∼ things⟩ (2) **:** RESENTFUL ⟨∼ feelings⟩ (3) **:** STRICT, UNRELENTING ⟨drives a ∼ bargain⟩ **d :** INCLEMENT ⟨∼ winter⟩ **e** (1) **:** intense in force, manner, or degree ⟨∼ blows⟩ (2) **:** demanding the exertion of energy : calling for stamina and endurance ⟨∼ work⟩ (3) **:** performing or carrying on with great energy, intensity, or persistence ⟨a ∼ worker⟩ **f :** most unyielding or thoroughgoing ⟨the ∼ political right⟩ **9 a :** characterized by sharp or harsh outline, rigid execution, and stiff drawing **b :** sharply defined : STARK ⟨∼ shadows⟩ **c :** lacking in shading, delicacy, or resonance ⟨∼ singing tones⟩ **d :** sounding as in *arcing* and *geese* respectively — used of *c* and *g* **e :** suggestive of toughness or insensitivity ⟨∼ eyes⟩ **10 a** (1) **:** difficult to accomplish or resolve : TROUBLESOME ⟨∼ problems⟩ ⟨the true story was ∼ to come by⟩ (2) **:** difficult to comprehend or explain ⟨a ∼ concept⟩ **b :** having difficulty in doing something ⟨∼ of hearing⟩ **c :** difficult to magnetize or demagnetize **11 :** being at once addictive and gravely detrimental to health ⟨such ∼ drugs as heroin⟩ **12 :** resistant to biodegradation ⟨∼ detergents⟩ ⟨∼ pesticides such as DDT⟩ **13 :** being, schooled in, or using the methods of the natural sciences and esp. of the physical sciences ⟨a ∼ scientist⟩ **14** *of money* **:** contributed (as by individuals or political action committees) directly to a particular candidate or campaign
syn HARD, DIFFICULT, ARDUOUS mean demanding great exertion or effort. HARD implies the opposite of all that is easy ⟨farming is *hard* work⟩. DIFFICULT implies the presence of obstacles to be surmounted or puzzles to be resolved and suggests the need of skill or courage ⟨the *difficult* ascent of the mountain⟩. ARDUOUS stresses the need of laborious and persevering exertion ⟨the *arduous* task of rebuilding⟩.
[2]**hard** *adv* (bef. 12c) **1 a :** with great or utmost effort or energy : STRENUOUSLY ⟨were ∼ at work⟩ **b :** in a violent manner : FIERCELY **c :** to the full extent — usu. used in nautical directions ⟨steer ∼ aport⟩ **d :** to an immoderate degree **e :** in a searching, close, or concentrated manner ⟨stared ∼ at me⟩ **2 a :** in such a manner as to cause hardship, difficulty, or pain **b :** with rancor, bitterness, or grief ⟨took the defeat ∼⟩ **3 :** in a firm manner : TIGHTLY **4 :** to the point of hardness ⟨frozen ∼⟩ **5 :** close in time or space ⟨stands ∼ by the river⟩
hard–and–fast \ˌhärd-ᵊn-ˈfast\ *adj* (1867) : not to be modified or evaded : STRICT ⟨a ∼ rule⟩
hard–ass \ˈhärd-ˌas\ *n* (1961) *often vulgar* **:** a tough, demanding, or uncompromising person — **hard–assed** \-ˌast\ *adj, often vulgar*

\ə\ **abut** \ᵊ\ **kitten,** F table \ər\ **further** \a\ **ash** \ā\ **ace** \ä\ **mop, mar**
\au̇\ **out** \ch\ **chin** \e\ **bet** \ē\ **easy** \g\ **go** \i\ **hit** \ī\ **ice** \j\ **job**
\ŋ\ **sing** \ō\ **go** \ȯ\ **law** \ȯi\ **boy** \th\ **thin** \th\ **the** \ü\ **loot** \u̇\ **foot**
\y\ **yet** \zh\ **vision, beige** \k, ⁿ, œ, ue, ʸ\ *see* Guide to Pronunciation

hard·back \ˈhärd-ˌbak\ *n* (1952) **:** a book bound in hard covers

hard·ball \-ˌbȯl\ *n* (ca. 1883) **1 :** BASEBALL **2 :** forceful uncompromising methods employed to gain an end ⟨played political ~⟩

hard–bit·ten \-ˈbi-tᵊn\ *adj* (1784) **1 :** inclined to bite hard **2 :** seasoned or steeled by difficult experience **:** TOUGH

hard·board \ˈhärd-ˌbȯrd\ *n* (1925) **:** a very dense fiberboard usu. having one smooth face

hard–boil \-ˈbȯi(-ə)l\ *vt* [back-formation fr. *hard-boiled*] (1895) **:** to cook (an egg) in the shell until both white and yolk have solidified

hard–boiled \-ˈbȯi(-ə)ld\ *adj* (1886) **1 a :** devoid of sentimentality **:** TOUGH ⟨a ~ drill sergeant⟩ **b :** of, relating to, or being a detective story featuring a tough unsentimental protagonist and a matter-of-fact attitude towards violence **2 :** HARDHEADED, PRACTICAL ⟨~ business decisions⟩

hard·boot \-ˌbüt\ *n* (1922) **:** an esp. small-time horseman

hard·bound \-ˌbau̇nd\ *adj* (1926) **:** HARDCOVER

hard candy *n* (1878) **:** a candy made of sugar and corn syrup boiled without crystallizing

hard·case \ˈhärd-ˈkās\ *adj* (1896) **:** HARD-BITTEN, TOUGH

hard case \-ˌkās\ *n* (1836) **:** a tough or hardened person

hard cheese *n* (1861) *chiefly Brit* **:** tough luck — often used interjectionally

hard cider *n* (1789) **:** fermented apple juice

hard clam *n* (1846) **:** a clam with a thick hard shell; *specif* **:** QUAHOG

hard coal *n* (1721) **:** ANTHRACITE

hard–coat·ed \ˈhärd-ˈkō-təd\ *adj* (ca. 1898) *of a dog* **:** having a harsh-textured coat ⟨~ terriers⟩

hard copy *n* (1954) **:** a copy of textual or graphic information (as from microfilm or computer storage) produced on paper in normal size

hard–core \-ˈkȯr\ *adj* (1940) **1 a :** of, relating to, or being part of a hard core ⟨~ poverty⟩ ⟨the ~ unemployed⟩ **b :** CONFIRMED, DIEHARD ⟨~ rock fans⟩ ⟨a ~ liberal⟩ **2** *of pornography* **:** containing explicit descriptions of sex acts or scenes of actual sex acts — compare SOFT-CORE **3 :** characterized by or being the purest or most basic form of something **:** FUNDAMENTAL ⟨a room gussied up in ~ French provincial style —John Canaday⟩

hard core *n* (1936) **1 :** a central or fundamental and usu. enduring group or part: as **a :** a relatively small enduring core of society marked by apparent resistance to change or inability to escape a persistent wretched condition (as poverty or chronic unemployment) **b :** a militant or fiercely loyal faction **2** *usu* **hard·core** \-ˌkōr, -ˌkȯr\ *chiefly Brit* **:** hard material in pieces (as broken bricks or stone) used as a bottom (as in making roads and in foundations)

hard·cov·er \ˈhärd-ˈkə-vər\ *adj* (1949) **1 :** having rigid boards on the sides covered in cloth or paper ⟨~ books⟩ **2 :** of or relating to hardcover books ⟨~ sales⟩ — **hardcover** *n*

hard disk *n* (1978) **:** a rigid metal disk coated with a magnetic material on which data for a computer can be stored; *also* **:** HARD DRIVE

hard drive *n* (1983) **:** a data-storage device consisting of a drive and one or more hard disks

hard–driv·ing \ˈhär(d)-ˈdrī-viŋ\ *adj* (1936) **:** intensely ambitious, energetic, or hardworking

hard–edge \ˈhärd-ˈej\ *adj* (1961) **:** of or relating to abstract painting characterized by geometric forms with clearly defined boundaries

hard–edged \-ˈejd\ *adj* (1954) **:** having a tough, driving, or sharp quality ⟨~ stories about life in the city⟩

hard·en \ˈhär-dᵊn\ *vb* **hard·ened; hard·en·ing** \ˈhärd-niŋ, ˈhär-dᵊn-iŋ\ *vt* (13c) **1 :** to make hard or harder **2 :** to confirm in disposition, feelings, or action; *esp* **:** to make callous ⟨~*ed* his heart⟩ **3 a :** INURE, TOUGHEN ⟨~ troops⟩ **b :** to inure to unfavorable environmental conditions (as cold) — often used with *off* ⟨~ off seedlings before transplanting⟩ **4 :** to protect from blast, heat, or radiation (as by a thick barrier or placement underground) ~ *vi* **1 :** to become hard or harder **2 a :** to become firm, stable, or settled **b :** to assume an appearance of harshness or severity ⟨her face ~*ed* at the thought⟩ **3 :** to become gradually acclimatized to unfavorable conditions — often used with *off* ⟨plants ~*ed* off before the first frost⟩

hard·en·er \ˈhärd-nər, ˈhär-dᵊn-ər\ *n* (1611) **:** one that hardens; *esp* **:** a substance added (as to a paint or varnish) to harden the film

hard·en·ing *n* (1953) **:** SCLEROSIS 1 ⟨~ of the arteries⟩

hard–eyed \ˈhärd-ˌīd\ *adj* (ca. 1844) **:** hard or cold in manner or approach **:** DISPASSIONATE ⟨a ~ view of the candidates⟩

hard·fist·ed \ˈhärd-ˈfis-təd\ *adj* (ca. 1656) **1 :** STINGY, CLOSEFISTED **2 :** HARDHANDED 2

hard goods *n pl* (1934) **:** DURABLES

hard·hack \ˈhärd-ˌhak\ *n* (1814) **:** a No. American spirea (*Spiraea tomentosa*) with dense terminal panicles of pink or occas. white flowers and leaves having a hairy and yellow to rust-colored underside

hard·hand·ed \-ˈhan-dəd\ *adj* (1590) **1 :** having hands made hard by labor **2 :** STRICT, OPPRESSIVE — **hard·hand·ed·ness** *n*

hard hat *usu* -ˈhat *for 1 and* -ˌhat *for 1b & 2*\ *n* (1926) **1 a :** a protective hat made of rigid material (as metal or fiberglass) and worn esp. by construction workers **b :** a construction worker **2 :** a conservative who is intolerant of opposing views

hard·head \ˈhärd-ˌhed\ *n* (15c) **1 a :** a hardheaded person **b :** BLOCKHEAD **2** *pl* **hardheads** *also* **hardhead :** any of several fishes esp. with a spiny or bony head; *esp* **:** ATLANTIC CROAKER

hard·head·ed \-ˈhe-dəd\ *adj* (1583) **1 :** STUBBORN, WILLFUL **2 :** concerned with or involving practical considerations **:** SOBER, REALISTIC ⟨some ~ advice⟩ ⟨a ~ observer of winds and tides⟩ — **hard·head·ed·ly** *adv* — **hard·head·ed·ness** *n*

hard–heart·ed \-ˈhär-təd\ *adj* (13c) **:** lacking in sympathetic understanding **:** UNFEELING, PITILESS — **hard–heart·ed·ly** *adv* — **hard–heart·ed·ness** *n*

hard–hit \ˈhärd-ˌhit\ *adj* (1826) **:** profoundly stricken **:** affected in an esp. negative way ⟨one of the industries particularly ~ during the downturn⟩

hard–hit·ting \-ˈhi-tiŋ\ *adj* (1926) **:** strikingly effective in force or result ⟨a ~ exposé⟩ ⟨plain ~ English⟩

har·di·hood \ˈhär-dē-ˌhu̇d\ *n* (1570) **1 a :** resolute courage and fortitude **b :** resolute and self-assured audacity often carried to the point of impudent insolence **2 :** VIGOR, ROBUSTNESS ***syn*** see TEMERITY

har·di·ment \-mənt\ *n* [ME, fr. AF *hardiement,* fr. *hardi* bold, hardy] (14c) **1** *archaic* **:** HARDIHOOD **2** *obs* **:** a bold deed

har·ding grass \ˈhär-diŋ-\ *n, often cap* [R. R. *Harding fl ab* 1900 Australian botanist] (1917) **:** a perennial Mediterranean grass (*Phalaris aquatica* syn. *P. tuberosa*) widely used as a forage grass

hard knocks *n pl* (1849) **:** rough unsparing treatment (as in use or in life) — often used in the phrase *school of hard knocks*

hard labor *n* (1682) **:** compulsory labor of imprisoned criminals as a part of the prison discipline

hard–line \ˈhärd-ˈlīn\ *adj* (1962) **:** advocating or involving a rigidly uncompromising course of action — **hard–lin·er** \-ˈlī-nər\ *n*

hard lines *n pl* (1824) *chiefly Brit* **:** hard luck — often used interjectionally

hard–luck \ˈhärd-ˌlək\ *adj* (1899) **:** marked by, relating to, or experiencing bad luck or difficulty ⟨another loss for the team's ~ pitcher⟩ ⟨~ stories⟩

hard·ly \ˈhärd-lē\ *adv* (bef. 12c) **1 :** with force **:** VIGOROUSLY **2 :** in a severe manner **:** HARSHLY **3 :** with difficulty **:** PAINFULLY **4 a —** used to emphasize a minimal amount ⟨I ~ knew her⟩ ⟨almost new — ~ a scratch on it⟩ **b —** used to soften a negative ⟨you can't ~ tell who anyone is —G. B. Shaw⟩ **5 :** certainly not ⟨that news is ~ surprising⟩

usage *Hardly* in sense 5 is used sometimes with *not* for emphasis ⟨just another day at the office? Not *hardly*⟩. In sense 4b with a negative verb (as *can't, wouldn't, didn't*) it does not make a double negative but softens the negative. In "you can't hardly find a red one," the sense is that you can find a red one, but only with difficulty; in "you can't find a red one," the sense is that red ones are simply not available. Use of *hardly* with a negative verb is a speech form; it is most commonly heard in Southern and Midland speech areas. In other speech areas and in all discursive prose, *hardly* is normally used with a positive ⟨you can *hardly* find a red one⟩.

hard maple *n* (1790) **:** SUGAR MAPLE

hard·mouthed \ˈhärd-ˈmau̇t͟hd, -ˈmau̇tht\ *adj* (1617) **1** *of a horse* **:** not sensitive to the bit **2 :** OBSTINATE, STUBBORN

hard·ness \-nəs\ *n* (bef. 12c) **1 :** the quality or state of being hard **2 a :** the cohesion of the particles on the surface of a mineral as determined by its capacity to scratch another or be itself scratched — compare MOHS' SCALE **b :** resistance of metal to indentation under a static load or to scratching

hard·nose \ˈhärd-ˌnōz\ *n* (ca. 1960) **:** a hard-nosed person

hard–nosed \ˈhärd-ˈnōzd\ *adj* (ca. 1927) **1 :** being tough, stubborn, or uncompromising **2 :** HARDHEADED 2, TOUGH-MINDED

hard of hearing *adj* (1564) **:** relating to or having a defective but functional sense of hearing

hard–on \ˈhärd-ˌȯn, -ˌän\ *n, pl* **hard–ons** (1888) *sometimes vulgar* **:** an erection of the penis

hard·pack \ˈhärd-ˌpak\ *n* (1967) **:** compacted snow

hard palate *n* (ca. 1847) **:** the bony anterior part of the palate forming the roof of the mouth

hard·pan \ˈhärd-ˌpan\ *n* (1817) **1 :** a cemented or compacted and often clayey layer in soil that is impenetrable by roots **2 :** a fundamental part **:** BEDROCK

hard–paste porcelain \ˈhärd-ˌpāst-\ *n* (ca. 1931) **:** PORCELAIN 1

hard pine *n* (1865) **:** a pine (as longleaf pine or pitch pine) that has hard wood and leaves usu. in groups of two or three; *also* **:** the wood of a hard pine

hard–pressed \ˈhärd-ˈprest\ *adj* (1825) **:** HARD PUT; *also* **:** being under financial strain

hard put *adj* (1893) **:** barely able **:** faced with difficulty or perplexity ⟨was *hard put* to find an explanation⟩

hard rock *n* (1967) **:** rock music marked by a heavy regular beat, high amplification, and usu. frenzied performances

hard rubber *n* (1860) **:** a firm rubber or rubber product; *esp* **:** a normally black horny substance made by vulcanizing natural rubber with high percentages of sulfur

hard sauce *n* (1872) **:** a creamed mixture of butter and powdered sugar often with added cream and flavoring (as vanilla or rum)

hard·scape \ˈhärd-ˌskāp\ *n* (1984) **:** structures (as fountains, benches, or gazebos) that are incorporated into a landscape

hard·scrab·ble \ˈhärd-ˌskra-bəl\ *adj* (1804) **1 a :** being or relating to a place of barren or barely arable soil ⟨a ~ farm⟩ ⟨~ prairies⟩ **b :** getting a meager living from poor soil ⟨a ~ farmer⟩ **2 :** marked by poverty ⟨a ~ cotton town⟩ ⟨a ~ childhood⟩

hard sell *n* (1952) **:** aggressive high-pressure salesmanship — compare SOFT SELL

hard–set \ˈhärd-ˈset\ *adj* (1813) **:** RIGID, FIXED

hard–shell \-ˌshel\ *or* **hard–shelled** \-ˌsheld\ *adj* (1838) **:** FUNDAMENTAL 2b, FUNDAMENTALIST ⟨a ~ preacher⟩ ⟨~ Baptists⟩; *also* **:** UNCOMPROMISING, HIDEBOUND ⟨a ~ conservative⟩

hard–shell clam *n* (1799) **:** QUAHOG — called also *hard-shelled clam*

hard–shell crab *n* (1902) **:** a crab that has not recently shed its shell — called also *hard-shelled crab*

hard·ship \ˈhärd-ˌship\ *n* (13c) **1 :** PRIVATION, SUFFERING **2 :** something that causes or entails suffering or privation

hard·stand \-ˌstand\ *n* (1944) **:** a paved area for parking an airplane

hard·stand·ing \-ˌstan-diŋ\ *n* (1944) *chiefly Brit* **:** HARDSTAND; *also* **:** PARKING LOT

hard stone *n* (1931) **:** an opaque usu. semiprecious stone that can be shaped or carved (as for jewelery or mosaics)

hard·tack \-ˌtak\ *n, pl* **hardtack** *or* **hardtacks** (1836) **1 :** a saltless hard biscuit, bread, or cracker **2 :** any of several mountain mahoganies (esp. *Cercocarpus betuloides*)

hard–times token *n* (1922) **:** any of the tokens issued during the controversy between the Jackson administration and the bank of the U.S.

hard·top \ˈhärd-ˌtäp\ *n* (1950) **:** an automobile or a motorboat having a permanent rigid top; *also* **:** such an automobile styled to resemble a convertible

hard up *adj* (1821) **1 :** short of money **2 :** poorly provided ⟨*hard up* for friends⟩

hard·ware \ˈhärd-ˌwer\ *n* (ca. 1515) **1 :** ware (as fittings, cutlery, tools, utensils, or parts of machines) made of metal **2 :** major items of equipment or their components used for a particular purpose ⟨educational ~⟩: as **a :** military equipment **b :** the physical components (as electronic and electrical devices) of a vehicle (as a spacecraft) or an

apparatus (as a computer) **3 :** an award (as a trophy, medal, or cup) given in a sports competition
hardware cloth *n* (ca. 1914) **:** rugged galvanized screening
hard wheat *n* (1787) **:** a wheat with hard kernels that are high in gluten and that yield a flour esp. suitable for bread and macaroni
hard·wired \ˈhärd-ˌwī(-ə)rd\ *adj* (1968) **1 :** implemented in the form of permanent electronic circuits; *also* **:** connected or incorporated by or as if by permanent electrical connections ⟨a ~ phone⟩ ⟨concepts of attractiveness may be universal and ~ into the human brain —Jane E. Brody⟩ **2 :** genetically or innately determined **:** INBORN ⟨creature whose every action is a reflexive, ~ response —Natalie Angier⟩; *also* **:** genetically or innately predisposed ⟨a human being who is ~ to be sociable —*Forbes*⟩
hard–won \-ˈwən\ *adj* (1818) **:** gained by great effort
[1]**hard·wood** \ˈhärd-ˌwu̇d\ *n* (1568) **1 :** the wood of an angiospermous tree as distinguished from that of a coniferous tree **2 :** a tree that yields hardwood **3 :** a basketball court
[2]**hardwood** *adj* (ca. 1817) **1 :** having or made of hardwood ⟨~ floors⟩ **2 :** consisting of mature woody tissue ⟨~ cuttings⟩
hard·work·ing \ˈhärd-ˈwər-kiŋ\ *adj* (1772) **:** INDUSTRIOUS, DILIGENT
har·dy \ˈhär-dē\ *adj* **har·di·er; -est** [ME *hardi,* fr. AF, fr. OF **hardir* to make hard, of Gmc origin; akin to OE *heard* hard] (13c) **1 :** BOLD, BRAVE **2 :** AUDACIOUS, BRAZEN **3 a :** inured to fatigue or hardships **:** ROBUST **b :** capable of withstanding adverse conditions ⟨~ outdoor furniture⟩ ⟨~ plants⟩ ⟨~ cattle⟩ — **har·di·ly** \ˈhär-dᵊl-ē\ *adv* — **har·di·ness** \ˈhär-dē-nəs\ *n*
Har·dy–Wein·berg law \ˌhär-dē-ˈwīn-ˌbərg-\ *n* [G. H. *Hardy* †1947 Eng. mathematician and W. *Weinberg* †1937 Ger. physician] (1950) **:** a fundamental principle of population genetics: population gene frequencies and genotype frequencies remain constant from generation to generation if mating is random and if mutation, selection, immigration, and emigration do not occur — called also *Hardy-Weinberg principle*
[1]**hare** \ˈher\ *n, pl* **hare** *or* **hares** [ME, fr. OE *hara;* akin to OHG *haso* hare, Skt *śaśa,* OE *hasu* gray] (bef. 12c) **:** any of various swift long-eared lagomorph mammals (family Leporidae and esp. genus *Lepus*) that are usu. solitary or sometimes live in pairs and have the young open-eyed and furred at birth — compare RABBIT 1a
[2]**hare** *vi* **hared; har·ing** (1719) **:** to go swiftly **:** [3]TEAR
hare and hounds *n* (1840) **:** a game in which some of the players leave a trail and others try to follow the trail to find and catch them
hare·bell \ˈher-ˌbel\ *n* (1636) **:** a slender blue-flowered herb (*Campanula rotundifolia*) with linear leaves on the stem

harebell

hare·brained \-ˈbrānd\ *adj* (1534) **1 :** FOOLISH 1 **2 :** ABSURD, RIDICULOUS
Ha·re Krish·na \ˈhär-ē-ˈkrish-nə, ˈher-, ˈha-rē-\ *n, pl* **Hare Krishna** *or* **Hare Krishnas** [fr. *Hare Krishna,* phrase in a chant, fr. Hindi *hare Kṛṣṇa* O Krishna!] (1969) **:** a member of a religious group dedicated to the worship of the Hindu god Krishna
hare·lip \ˈher-ˈlip\ *n* (1567) *sometimes offensive* **:** CLEFT LIP
har·em \ˈher-əm\ *n* [ultim. fr. Ar *ḥarīm,* lit., something forbidden & *ḥaram,* lit., sanctuary] (1623) **1 a :** a usu. secluded house or part of a house allotted to women in a Muslim household **b :** the wives, concubines, female relatives, and servants occupying a harem **2 :** a group of women associated with one man **3 :** a group of females associated with one male — used of polygamous animals
harem pants *n* [fr. their resemblance to traditional women's attire in some Muslim countries] (1952) **:** women's loose trousers that fit closely at the ankle
har·i·cot \ˈ(h)er-i-ˌkō, ˈ(h)a-ri-\ *n* [F] (1653) **:** the ripe seed or the unripe pod of any of several beans (genus *Phaseolus*) and esp. the kidney bean (*P. vulgaris*)
har·i·cot vert \ˌär-ē-kō-ˈver\ *n, pl* **har·i·cots verts** *same*\ *also* **haricot verts** \-ˈver(z)\ [F, green haricot] (1873) **:** a thin green bean
ha·ri·jan \ˌhär-i-ˈjän\ *n, often cap* [Skt *harijana* one belonging to the god Vishnu, fr. *Hari* Vishnu + *jana* person] (1932) **:** a member of the outcaste group in India **:** UNTOUCHABLE
hari–kari *var of* HARA-KIRI
hark \ˈhärk\ *vi* [ME *herkien;* akin to OHG *hōrechen* to listen, OE *hīeran* to hear] (14c) **:** to pay close attention **:** LISTEN
hark back *vi* (1824) **1 :** to turn back to an earlier topic or circumstance **2 :** to go back to something as an origin or source
hark·en *vi* (bef. 12c) **1 :** HEARKEN **2 :** HARK BACK — usu. used with *back*
har·le·quin \ˈhär-li-k(w)ən\ *n* [ultim. fr. It *arlecchino,* fr. MF *Helquin,* a demon] (1590) **1 a** *cap* **:** a character in comedy and pantomime with a shaved head, masked face, variegated tights, and wooden sword **b :** BUFFOON **2 a :** a variegated pattern (as of a textile) **b :** a combination of patches on a solid ground of contrasting color (as in the coats of some dogs)
har·le·quin·ade \ˌhär-li-k(w)ə-ˈnād\ *n* (1781) **:** a play or pantomime in which Harlequin has a leading role
har·lot \ˈhär-lət\ *n* [ME, rogue, buffoon, female prostitute, fr. AF *herlot* beggar, vagabond] (15c) **:** PROSTITUTE
har·lot·ry \-lə-trē\ *n, pl* **-ries** (14c) **1 :** sexual profligacy **:** PROSTITUTION **2 :** an unprincipled or immoral woman ⟨he sups tonight with a ~ —Shak.⟩
[1]**harm** \ˈhärm\ *n* [ME, fr. OE *hearm;* akin to OHG *harm* injury, OCS *sramŭ* shame] (bef. 12c) **1 :** physical or mental damage **:** INJURY **2 :** MISCHIEF, HURT
[2]**harm** *vt* (bef. 12c) **:** to cause harm to ***syn*** see INJURE — **harm·er** *n*
har·mat·tan \ˌhär-mə-ˈtan, här-ˈma-tᵊn\ *n, often cap* [fr. or akin to Twi *haramata*] (1671) **:** a dust-laden wind on the Atlantic coast of Africa in some seasons
harm·ful \ˈhärm-fəl\ *adj* (14c) **:** of a kind likely to be damaging **:** INJURIOUS — **harm·ful·ly** \-fə-lē\ *adv* — **harm·ful·ness** *n*
harm·less \ˈhärm-ləs\ *adj* (14c) **1 :** free from harm, liability, or loss **2 :** lacking capacity or intent to injure **:** INNOCUOUS ⟨a ~ joke⟩ — **harm·less·ly** *adv* — **harm·less·ness** *n*
[1]**har·mon·ic** \här-ˈmä-nik\ *adj* (1570) **1 :** MUSICAL **2 :** of or relating to musical harmony or a harmonic **3 :** pleasing to the ear **:** HARMONIOUS **4 :** of an integrated nature **:** CONGRUOUS — **har·mon·i·cal·ly** \-ni-k(ə-)lē\ *adv*
[2]**harmonic** *n* (1777) **1 a :** OVERTONE; *esp* **:** one whose vibration frequency is an integral multiple of that of the fundamental **b :** a flutelike tone produced on a stringed instrument by touching a vibrating string at a nodal point **2 :** a component frequency of a complex wave (as of electromagnetic energy) that is an integral multiple of the fundamental frequency
har·mon·i·ca \här-ˈmä-ni-kə\ *n* [It *armonica,* fem. of *armonico* harmonious] (1762) **1 :** GLASS HARMONICA **2 :** a small rectangular wind instrument with free reeds recessed in air slots from which tones are sounded by exhaling and inhaling — **har·mon·i·cist** \-nə-sist\ *n*
harmonic analysis *n* (1867) **:** the expression of a periodic function as a sum of sines and cosines and specif. by a Fourier series
harmonic mean *n* (1856) **:** the reciprocal of the arithmetic mean of the reciprocals of a finite set of numbers
harmonic motion *n* (1867) **:** a periodic motion (as of a sounding violin string or swinging pendulum) that has a single frequency or amplitude or is composed of two or more such simple periodic motions
harmonic progression *n* (1671) **:** a sequence of numbers whose reciprocals form an arithmetic progression
harmonic series *n* (1866) **:** a series of the form

$$1 + \frac{1}{2^\alpha} + \frac{1}{3^\alpha} + \frac{1}{4^\alpha} \cdots$$

which diverges for $0 \leq \alpha \leq 1$ and converges for $\alpha > 1$
har·mo·ni·ous \här-ˈmō-nē-əs\ *adj* (1530) **1 :** musically concordant **2 :** having the parts agreeably related **:** CONGRUOUS ⟨blended into a ~ whole⟩ **3 :** marked by accord in sentiment or action — **har·mo·ni·ous·ly** *adv* — **har·mo·ni·ous·ness** *n*
har·mo·nise *Brit var of* HARMONIZE
har·mo·ni·um \här-ˈmō-nē-əm\ *n* [F, fr. MF *harmonie, armonie*] (1847) **:** REED ORGAN
har·mo·nize \ˈhär-mə-ˌnīz\ *vb* **-nized; -niz·ing** *vi* (15c) **1 :** to play or sing in harmony **2 :** to be in harmony ~ *vt* **1 :** to bring into consonance or accord **2 :** to provide or accompany with harmony — **har·mo·ni·za·tion** \ˌhär-mə-nə-ˈzā-shən\ *n* — **har·mo·niz·er** \ˈhär-mə-ˌnī-zər\ *n*
har·mo·ny \ˈhär-mə-nē\ *n, pl* **-nies** [ME *armony,* fr. AF *armonie,* fr. L *harmonia,* fr. Gk, joint, harmony, fr. *harmos* joint — more at ARM] (14c) **1** *archaic* **:** tuneful sound **:** MELODY **2 a :** the combination of simultaneous musical notes in a chord **b :** the structure of music with respect to the composition and progression of chords **c :** the science of the structure, relation, and progression of chords **3 a :** pleasing or congruent arrangement of parts ⟨a painting exhibiting ~ of color and line⟩ **b :** CORRESPONDENCE, ACCORD ⟨lives in ~ with her neighbors⟩ **c :** internal calm **:** TRANQUILLITY **4 a :** an interweaving of different accounts into a single narrative **b :** a systematic arrangement of parallel literary passages (as of the Gospels) for the purpose of showing agreement or harmony
harm's way *n* (1631) **:** a dangerous place or situation ⟨was placed in *harm's way*⟩ ⟨got them out of *harm's way*⟩
[1]**har·ness** \ˈhär-nəs\ *n* [ME *herneis* baggage, gear, fr. AF *harneis, herneis,* prob. fr. ON **hernest,* fr. *herr* army + *nest* provisions] (14c) **1 a :** the gear other than a yoke of a draft animal **b :** GEAR, EQUIPMENT; *esp* **:** military equipment for a horse or man **2 a :** occupational surroundings or routine ⟨get back into ~ after a vacation⟩ **b :** close association ⟨ability to work in ~ with others —R. P. Brooks⟩ **3 a :** something that resembles a harness (as in holding or fastening something) ⟨a parachute ~⟩ **b :** prefabricated wiring with insulation and terminals ready to be attached **4 :** a part of a loom which holds and controls the heddles
[2]**harness** *vt* (14c) **1 a :** to put a harness on **b :** to attach by means of a harness **2 :** to tie together **:** YOKE **3 :** UTILIZE ⟨~ the computer's potential⟩
harness horse *n* (1861) **:** a horse for racing or working in harness
harness racing *n* (1901) **:** the sport of racing standardbred horses harnessed to 2-wheeled sulkies
[1]**harp** \ˈhärp\ *n* [ME, fr. OE *hearpe;* akin to OHG *harpha* harp] (bef. 12c) **1 :** a plucked stringed instrument consisting of a resonator, an arched or angled neck that may be supported by a post, and strings of graded length that are perpendicular to the soundboard **2 :** something resembling a harp **3 :** HARMONICA 2 — **harp·ist** \ˈhär-pist\ *n*

harp 1

[2]**harp** *vi* (bef. 12c) **1 :** to play on a harp **2 :** to dwell on or recur to a subject tiresomely or monotonously — usu. used with *on*
harp·er \ˈhär-pər\ *n* (bef. 12c) **1 :** a harp player **2 :** one that harps
har·poon \här-ˈpün\ *n* [prob. fr. D *harpoen,* fr. MD, fr. OF *harpon* brooch, fr. *harper* to grapple] (1625) **:** a barbed spear or javelin used esp. in hunting large fish or whales — **harpoon** *vt* — **har·poon·er** *n*
harp seal *n* [fr. the shape of its markings] (1766) **:** a dark-faced seal (*Phoca groenlandicus*) of the No. Atlantic that is a variable light gray with the male usu. having a dark crescent on its back and sides
harp·si·chord \ˈhärp-si-ˌkȯrd\ *n* [modif. of It *arpicordo,* fr. *arpa* harp + *corda* string] (1611) **:** a stringed instrument resembling a grand piano but usu. having two keyboards and two or more strings for each note and producing tones by the plucking of strings with plectra — **harp·si·chord·ist** \-ˌkȯr-dist\ *n*

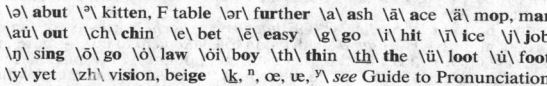

har·py \ˈhär-pē\ *n, pl* **harpies** [L *Harpyia,* fr. Gk] (1513) **1** *cap* **:** a foul malign creature in Greek mythology that is part woman and part bird **2 a :** a predatory person **:** LEECH **b :** a shrewish woman

harpy eagle *n* (1830) **:** a large powerful crested eagle (*Harpia harpyja*) of Central and So. America that is black above and chiefly white below

har·que·bus \ˈhär-kwi-(ˌ)bəs, -kə-bəs\ *or* **ar·que·bus** \ˈär-\ *n* [MF *harquebuse, arquebuse,* modif. of MD *hakebusse,* fr. *hake* hook + *busse* tube, box, gun, fr. LL *buxis* box] (1532) **:** a matchlock gun invented in the 15th century which was portable but heavy and was usu. fired from a support — **har·que·bus·ier** \ˌhär-kwi-(ˌ)bə-ˈsir, -kə-bə-\ *n*

har·ri·dan \ˈher-ə-dən, ˈha-rə-\ *n* [perh. modif. of F *haridelle* old horse, gaunt woman] (1678) **:** SHREW 2

harried *adj* (1609) **:** beset by problems **:** HARASSED

[1]**har·ri·er** \ˈher-ē-ər, ˈha-rē-\ *n* [irreg. fr. [1]*hare*] (1542) **1 :** any of a breed of hunting dogs resembling a small English foxhound and orig. bred for hunting rabbits **2 :** a runner on a cross-country team

[2]**harrier** *n* [alter. of *harrower,* fr. [1]*harrow*] (1556) **:** any of a genus (*Circus*) of slender hawks having long angled wings and long legs and feeding chiefly on small mammals, reptiles, and insects

[3]**harrier** *n* (1596) **:** one that harries

Har·ris's hawk \ˈha-rə-səz-\ *n* [Edward *Harris* †1863 Am. naturalist] (1909) **:** a black hawk (*Parabuteo unicinctus*) found from the southwestern U.S. to So. America that has brown shoulders and conspicuous white markings on the rump and tail — called also *Harris hawk*

[1]**har·row** \ˈher-(ˌ)ō, ˈha-(ˌ)rō\ *vt* [ME *harwen,* fr. OE *hergian*] (bef. 12c) *archaic* **:** PILLAGE, PLUNDER

[2]**harrow** *n* [ME *harwe;* akin to ON *hervi* harrow, MD *harke* rake] (14c) **:** a cultivating implement set with spikes, spring teeth, or disks and used primarily for pulverizing and smoothing the soil

[3]**harrow** *vt* (14c) **1 :** to cultivate with a harrow **2 :** TORMENT, VEX — **har·row·er** \ˈher-ə-wər, ˈha-rə-\ *n*

har·rumph \hə-ˈrəm(p)f\ *vb* [imit.] *vi* (1942) **1 :** to clear the throat in a pompous way **2 :** to comment disapprovingly ~ *vt* **:** to utter (a comment) disapprovingly — **harrumph** *n*

har·ry \ˈher-ē, ˈha-rē\ *vt* **har·ried; har·ry·ing** [ME *harien,* fr. OE *hergian;* akin to OHG *heriōn* to lay waste, *heri* army, Gk *koiranos* ruler] (bef. 12c) **1 :** to make a pillaging or destructive raid on **:** ASSAULT **2 :** to force to move along by harassing ⟨~*ing* the terrified horses down out of the mountains —R. A. Sokolov⟩ **3 :** to torment by or as if by constant attack ***syn*** see WORRY

harsh \ˈhärsh\ *adj* [ME *harsk,* of Scand origin; akin to Norw *harsk* harsh] (14c) **1 :** having a coarse uneven surface that is rough or unpleasant to the touch **2 a :** causing a disagreeable or painful sensory reaction **:** IRRITATING **b :** physically discomforting **:** PAINFUL **3 :** unduly exacting **:** SEVERE **4 :** lacking in aesthetic appeal or refinement **:** CRUDE ***syn*** see ROUGH — **harsh·ly** *adv* — **harsh·ness** *n*

harsh·en \ˈhär-shən\ *vb* **harsh·ened; harsh·en·ing** \-sh(ə-)niŋ\ *vt* (1824) **:** to make (as a voice) harsh ~ *vi* **:** to become harsh ⟨saw the grain of his skin ~*ing* over face bones —Elizabeth Bowen⟩

hart \ˈhärt\ *n* [ME *hert,* fr. OE *heort;* akin to L *cervus* hart, Gk *keras* horn — more at HORN] (bef. 12c) *chiefly Brit* **:** the male of the red deer esp. when over five years old **:** STAG — compare HIND

harte·beest \ˈhär-tə-ˌbēst\ *n* [obs. Afrik (now *hartbees*), fr. D, fr. *hart* deer + *beest* beast] (1786) **:** either of two large African antelopes (*Alcelaphus buselaphus* and *Sigmoceros lichtensteinii*) with long faces and short annulate divergent horns; *also* **:** a smaller antelope (*Damaliscus hunteri*) of eastern Africa having a horizontal white line between the eyes

harts·horn \ˈhärts-ˌhȯrn\ *n* [fr. the earlier use of hart's horns as the chief source of ammonia] (1685) **:** a preparation of ammonia used as smelling salts

har·um–scar·um \ˌher-əm-ˈsker-əm\ *adj* [perh. fr. archaic *hare* to harass + *scare*] (1751) **:** RECKLESS, IRRESPONSIBLE — **harum–scarum** *adv*

ha·rus·pex \hə-ˈrəs-ˌpeks, ˈha-rəs-\ *n, pl* **ha·rus·pi·ces** \hə-ˈrəs-pə-ˌsēz\ [L, fr. *haru-* (akin to *chordē* gut, cord) + *-spex,* fr. *specere* to look — more at YARN, SPY] (1584) **:** a diviner in ancient Rome basing his predictions on inspection of the entrails of sacrificial animals

ha·rus·pi·ca·tion \hə-ˌrəs-pə-ˈkā-shən\ *n* (1871) *chiefly Brit* **:** an act or instance of foretelling something

[1]**har·vest** \ˈhär-vəst\ *n, often attrib* [ME *hervest,* fr. OE *hærfest;* akin to L *carpere* to pluck, gather, Gk *karpos* fruit] (bef. 12c) **1 :** the season for gathering in agricultural crops **2 :** the act or process of gathering in a crop **3 a :** a mature crop (as of grain or fruit) **:** YIELD **b :** the quantity of a natural product gathered in a single season ⟨deer ~⟩ ⟨ice ~⟩ **4 :** an accumulated store or productive result ⟨a ~ of revenue⟩

[2]**harvest** *vt* (15c) **1 a :** to gather in (a crop) **:** REAP **b :** to gather, catch, hunt, or kill (as salmon, oysters, or deer) for human use, sport, or population control **c :** to remove or extract (as living cells, tissues, or organs) from culture or from a living or recently deceased body esp. for transplanting **2 a :** to accumulate a store of ⟨has now ~*ed* this new generation's scholarly labors —M. J. Wiener⟩ **b :** to win by achievement ⟨the team ~*ed* several awards⟩ ~ *vi* **:** to gather in a crop esp. for food — **har·vest·able** \-və-stə-bəl\ *adj* — **har·vest·er** *n*

harvest fly *n* (ca. 1753) **:** CICADA

harvest home *n* (1573) **1 :** a feast at the close of the harvest **2 :** the gathering or the time of the harvest **3 :** a song sung by the reapers at the close of the harvest

har·vest·man \ˈhär-vəs(t)-mən\ *n* (1847) **:** DADDY LONGLEGS 2

harvest mite *n* (1873) **:** CHIGGER 2

harvest moon *n* (1706) **:** the full moon nearest the time of the September equinox

har·vest·time \ˈhär-vəs(t)-ˌtīm\ *n* (14c) **:** the time during which an annual crop (as wheat) is harvested

has *pres 3d sing of* HAVE

has–been \ˈhaz-ˌbin, -ˌben, *chiefly Brit* -ˌbēn\ *n* (1606) **:** one that has passed the peak of effectiveness or popularity

ha·sen·pfef·fer \ˈhä-zᵊn-ˌ(p)fe-fər, ˈhä-sᵊn-\ *n* [G, fr. *Hase* hare + *Pfeffer* pepper] (1892) **:** a highly seasoned stew made of marinated rabbit meat

[1]**hash** \ˈhash\ *vt* [F *hacher,* fr. OF *hachier,* fr. *hache* battle-ax, of Gmc origin; akin to OHG *hāppa* sickle; akin to Gk *koptein* to cut — more at CAPON] (1590) **1 a :** to chop (as meat and potatoes) into small pieces **b :** CONFUSE, MUDDLE **2 :** to talk about **:** REVIEW — often used with *over* or *out* ⟨~ over a problem⟩ ⟨~*ing* out their differences⟩

[2]**hash** *n* (ca. 1663) **1 :** chopped food; *specif* **:** chopped meat mixed with potatoes and browned **2 :** a restatement of something that is already known ⟨the same old ~⟩ **3 a :** HODGEPODGE, JUMBLE **b :** a confused muddle ⟨made a ~ of the whole project⟩ **4 :** POUND SIGN 2

[3]**hash** *n* (1955) **:** HASHISH

hash browns *n pl* (1951) **:** boiled potatoes that have been diced, mixed with chopped onions and shortening, and fried usu. until they form a browned cake — called also *hash brown potatoes, hashed brown potatoes, hashed browns*

Hash·em·ite *or* **Hash·im·ite** \ˈha-shə-ˌmīt\ *n* [*Hashim,* great-grandfather of Muhammad] (1697) **:** a member of an Arab family having common ancestry with Muhammad and founding dynasties in countries of the eastern Mediterranean

hash house *n* (1869) **:** an inexpensive eating place

hash·ish \ˈha-ˌshēsh, ha-ˈshēsh\ *n* [Ar *ḥashīsh*] (1598) **:** the concentrated resin from the flowering tops of female hemp plants (*Cannabis sativa* or *C. indica*) that is smoked, chewed, or drunk for its intoxicating effect — called also *charas;* compare BHANG, MARIJUANA

hash mark *n* (1907) **1 :** SERVICE STRIPE **2 :** INBOUNDS LINE **3 :** POUND SIGN 2

hash·tag \ˈhash-ˌtag\ *n* (2008) **:** a word or phrase preceded by the symbol # that classifies or categorizes the accompanying text (such as a tweet)

Ha·sid *also* **Cha·sid** *or* **Chas·sid** \ˈha-səd, ˈkä-\ *n, pl* **Ha·si·dim** *also* **Cha·si·dim** *or* **Chas·si·dim** \ˈha-sə-dəm, kä-ˈsē-\ [Heb *ḥasīdh* pious] (1812) **1 :** a member of a Jewish sect of the second century B.C. opposed to Hellenism and devoted to the strict observance of the ritual law **2** *also* **Has·sid :** a member of a Jewish mystical sect founded in Poland about 1750 in opposition to rationalism and ritual laxity — **Ha·sid·ic** *also* **Has·sid·ic** *or* **Cha·sid·ic** *or* **Chas·sid·ic** \ha-ˈsi-dik, hä-, kä-\ *adj*

Ha·si·dism \ˈha-sə-ˌdi-zəm, ˈhä-, ˈkä-\ *n* (1893) **1 :** the practices and beliefs of the Hasidim **2 :** the Hasidic movement

Has·mo·nae·an *or* **Has·mo·ne·an** \ˌhaz-mə-ˈnē-ən\ *n* [LL *Asmonaeus* Hasmon, ancestor of the Maccabees, fr. Gk *Asamōnaios*] (1620) **:** a member of the Maccabees — **Hasmonaean** *or* **Hasmonean** *adj*

hasn't \ˈha-zᵊnt, -zᵊn\ (1746) **:** has not

hasp \ˈhasp\ *n* [ME, alter. fr. OE *hæpse;* akin to MHG *haspe* hasp] (bef. 12c) **:** any of several devices for fastening; *esp* **:** a fastener esp. for a door or lid consisting of a hinged metal strap that fits over a staple and is secured by a pin or padlock — **hasp** *vt*

has·si·um \ˈha-sē-əm\ *n* [NL, fr. *Hassia* Hesse (German state), location of the laboratory that first produced the element] (1992) **:** a short-lived radioactive metallic element produced artificially — see ELEMENT table

[1]**has·sle** \ˈha-səl\ *n* (1945) **1 :** a heated often protracted argument **:** WRANGLE **2 :** a violent skirmish **:** FIGHT **3 a :** a state of confusion **:** TURMOIL **b :** an annoying or troublesome concern

[2]**hassle** *vb* **has·sled; has·sling** \-s(ə-)liŋ\ [perh. blend of *harass* and *hustle*] *vi* (1951) **:** ARGUE, FIGHT ⟨*hassled* with the umpire⟩ ~ *vt* **:** to annoy persistently or acutely **:** HARASS ⟨gets *hassled* by the cops⟩

has·sock \ˈha-sək\ *n* [ME, sedge, fr. OE *hassuc*] (bef. 12c) **1 :** TUSSOCK **2 a :** a cushion for kneeling ⟨a church ~⟩ **b :** a padded cushion or low stool that serves as a seat or leg rest

hast \ˈhast, (h)əst\ *archaic pres 2d sing of* HAVE

HAST *abbr* Hawaii-Aleutian standard time

has·tate \ˈhas-ˌtāt\ *adj* [NL *hastatus,* fr. L *hasta* spear — more at YARD] (1788) **1 :** triangular with sharp basal lobes spreading away from the base of the petiole ⟨~ leaves⟩ — see LEAF illustration **2 :** shaped like a spear or the head of a spear ⟨a ~ spot of a bird⟩

[1]**haste** \ˈhāst\ *n* [ME, fr. AF, of Gmc origin; akin to OE *hǣst* violence] (14c) **1 :** rapidity of motion **:** SWIFTNESS **2 :** rash or headlong action **:** PRECIPITATENESS ⟨the beauty of speed uncontaminated by ~ —*Harper's*⟩ **3 :** undue eagerness to act

syn HASTE, HURRY, SPEED, EXPEDITION, DISPATCH mean quickness in movement or action. HASTE applies to personal action and implies urgency and precipitancy and often rashness ⟨marry in *haste*⟩. HURRY often has a strong suggestion of agitated bustle or confusion ⟨in the *hurry* of departure she forgot her toothbrush⟩. SPEED suggests swift efficiency in movement or action ⟨exercises to increase your reading *speed*⟩. EXPEDITION and DISPATCH both imply speed and efficiency in handling affairs but EXPEDITION stresses ease or efficiency of performance and DISPATCH stresses promptness in concluding matters ⟨the case came to trial with *expedition*⟩ ⟨paid bills with *dispatch*⟩.

[2]**haste** *vb* **hast·ed; hast·ing** *vt* (14c) *archaic* **:** to urge on **:** HASTEN ~ *vi* **:** to move or act swiftly

has·ten \ˈhā-sᵊn\ *vb* **has·tened; has·ten·ing** \ˈhās-niŋ, ˈhā-sᵊn-iŋ\ *vi* (1568) **:** to move or act quickly ~ *vt* **1 :** to urge on ⟨~*ed* her to the door —A. J. Cronin⟩ **2 :** ACCELERATE ⟨~ the coming of a new order —D. W. Brogan⟩ — **has·ten·er** \ˈhās-nər, ˈhā-sᵊn-ər\ *n*

hast·i·ly \ˈhā-stə-lē\ *adv* (14c) **:** in haste **:** HURRIEDLY

hasty \ˈhā-stē\ *adj* **hast·i·er; -est** (14c) **1 a** *archaic* **:** rapid in action or movement **:** SPEEDY **b :** done or made in a hurry **c :** fast and typically superficial ⟨made a ~ examination of the wound⟩ **2 :** EAGER, IMPATIENT **3 :** PRECIPITATE, RASH **4 :** prone to anger **:** IRRITABLE ***syn*** see FAST — **hast·i·ness** *n*

hasty pudding *n* (1599) **1** *Brit* **:** a porridge of oatmeal or flour boiled in water **2** *NewEng* **a :** cornmeal mush **b :** INDIAN PUDDING

[1]**hat** \ˈhat\ *n* [ME, fr. OE *hæt;* akin to OHG *huot* head covering — more at HOOD] (bef. 12c) **1 :** a covering for the head usu. having a shaped crown and brim **2 a :** a distinctive head covering worn as a symbol of office **b :** an office, position, or role assumed by or as if by the wearing of a special hat ⟨wore many ~*s* in her career⟩ — **hat·less** \-ləs\ *adj* — **under one's hat :** not disclosed ⟨kept the news *under his hat*⟩

[2]**hat** *vb* **hat·ted; hat·ting** *vt* (15c) **:** to furnish or provide with a hat ~ *vi* **:** to make or supply hats

hat·band \ˈhat-ˌband\ *n* (15c) **:** a band (as of fabric, leather, or cord) around the crown of a hat just above the brim

hat·box \-ˌbäks\ *n* (1794) **1 :** a box for holding or storing a hat **2 :** a usu. round piece of luggage designed esp. for carrying hats

[1]**hatch** \ˈhach\ *n* [ME *hache,* fr. OE *hæc;* akin to MD *hecke* trapdoor] (bef. 12c) **1 :** a small door or opening (as in an airplane or spaceship) ⟨an escape ~⟩ **2 a :** an opening in the deck of a ship or in the floor or

roof of a building **b :** the covering for such an opening **c :** HATCHWAY **d :** COMPARTMENT **3 :** FLOODGATE

[2]**hatch** *vb* [ME *hacchen;* akin to MHG *hecken* to mate] *vi* (13c) **1 :** to produce young by incubation **2 a :** to emerge from an egg, chrysalis, or pupa **b :** to give forth young or imagoes **3 :** to incubate eggs **:** BROOD ~ *vt* **1 a :** to produce (young) from an egg by applying natural or artificial heat **b :** INCUBATE 1a **2 :** to bring into being **:** ORIGINATE; *esp* **:** to concoct in secret ⟨~ a plot⟩ — **hatch·abil·i·ty** \ˌha-chə-ˈbi-lə-tē\ *n* — **hatch·able** \ˈha-chə-bəl\ *adj* — **hatch·er** *n*

[3]**hatch** *n* (1601) **1 :** an act or instance of hatching **2 :** a brood of hatched young

[4]**hatch** *vt* [MF *hacher* to chop, slice up, incise with fine lines, fr. OF *hachier* — more at HASH] (15c) **1 :** to inlay with narrow bands of distinguishable material ⟨a silver handle ~*ed* with gold⟩ **2 :** to mark (as a drawing or engraving) with fine closely spaced lines

[5]**hatch** *n* (1658) **:** LINE; *esp* **:** one used to give the effect of shading

hatch·back \ˈhach-ˌbak\ *n* (1970) **:** an automobile the back of which consists of a hatch that opens upward; *also* **:** the back itself

hat·check \ˈhat-ˌchek\ *adj* (1917) **:** employed in checking hats and articles of outdoor clothing ⟨a ~ girl⟩

hatch·ery \ˈha-chə-rē\ *n, pl* **-er·ies** (1880) **:** a place for hatching eggs (as of poultry or fish)

hatch·et \ˈha-chət\ *n* [ME *hachet,* fr. AF *hachette,* dim. of *hache* battle-ax — more at HASH] (14c) **1 :** a short-handled ax often with a hammerhead to be used with one hand **2 :** TOMAHAWK

hatchet face *n* (ca. 1666) **:** a thin sharp face — **hatch·et–faced** \ˈha-chət-ˌfāst\ *adj*

hatchet job *n* (1944) **:** a forceful or malicious verbal attack

hatchet man *n* (1880) **1 :** one hired for murder, coercion, or attack **2 a :** a writer specializing in invective **b :** a person hired to perform underhanded or unscrupulous tasks (as ruin reputations)

hatchet work *n* (1944) **:** the work of a hatchet man

hatch·ing \ˈha-chiŋ\ *n* (1662) **:** the engraving or drawing of fine lines in close proximity esp. to give an effect of shading; *also* **:** the pattern so made

hatch·ling \ˈhach-liŋ\ *n* (1899) **:** a recently hatched animal

hatch·ment \ˈhach-mənt\ *n* [perh. alter. of *achievement*] (1548) **:** a panel on which a coat of arms of a deceased person is temporarily displayed

hatch·way \ˈhach-ˌwā\ *n* (1626) **:** a passage giving access usu. by a ladder or stairs to an enclosed space (as a cellar); *also* **:** HATCH 2a

[1]**hate** \ˈhāt\ *n, often attrib* [ME, fr. OE *hete;* akin to OHG *haz* hate, Gk *kēdos* care] (bef. 12c) **1 a :** intense hostility and aversion usu. deriving from fear, anger, or sense of injury **b :** extreme dislike or antipathy **:** LOATHING ⟨had a great ~ of hard work⟩ **2 :** an object of hatred ⟨a generation whose finest ~ had been big business —F. L. Paxson⟩

[2]**hate** *vb* **hat·ed; hat·ing** *vt* (bef. 12c) **1 :** to feel extreme enmity toward ⟨~*s* his country's enemies⟩ **2 :** to have a strong aversion to **:** find very distasteful ⟨*hated* to have to meet strangers⟩ ⟨~ hypocrisy⟩ ~ *vi* **:** to express or feel extreme enmity or active hostility — **hat·er** *n* — **hate one's guts :** to hate someone with great intensity

syn HATE, DETEST, ABHOR, ABOMINATE, LOATHE mean to feel strong aversion or intense dislike for. HATE implies an emotional aversion often coupled with enmity or malice ⟨*hated* the enemy with a passion⟩. DETEST suggests violent antipathy ⟨*detests* cowards⟩. ABHOR implies a deep often shuddering repugnance ⟨a crime *abhorred* by all⟩. ABOMINATE suggests strong detestation and often moral condemnation ⟨*abominates* all forms of violence⟩. LOATHE implies utter disgust and intolerance ⟨*loathed* the mere sight of them⟩.

hate crime *n* (1984) **:** any of various crimes (as assault or defacement of property) when motivated by hostility to the victim as a member of a group (as one based on color, creed, gender, or sexual orientation)

hate·ful \ˈhāt-fəl\ *adj* (14c) **1 :** full of hate **:** MALICIOUS **2 :** deserving of or arousing hate — **hate·ful·ly** \-fə-lē\ *adv* — **hate·ful·ness** *n*

hath \ˈhath, (h)əth\ *archaic pres 3d sing of* HAVE

hatha yo·ga \ˈha-tə-ˈyō-gə, ˈhä-\ *n* [Skt *haṭha* force + *yoga* yoga] (1890) **:** a system of physical exercises for the control and perfection of the body that constitutes one of the four chief Hindu disciplines

hat in hand *adv* (1851) **:** in an attitude of respectful humility ⟨have to go *hat in hand* to apologize⟩

hat·mak·er \ˈhat-ˌmā-kər\ *n* (15c) **:** one who makes hats

ha·tred \ˈhā-trəd\ *n* [ME, fr. *hate* + OE *rǣden* condition — more at KINDRED] (12c) **1 :** HATE **2 :** prejudiced hostility or animosity ⟨old racial prejudices and national ~*s* —Peter Thomson⟩

hat·ter \ˈha-tər\ *n* (14c) **:** one that makes, sells, or cleans and repairs hats

hat trick *n* [prob. fr. the former practice of rewarding the feat with the gift of a hat] (1877) **1 :** the retiring of three batsmen with three consecutive balls by a bowler in cricket **2 :** the scoring of three goals in one game (as of hockey or soccer) by a single player **3 :** a series of three victories, successes, or related accomplishments ⟨scored a *hat trick* when her three best steers corralled top honors —*People*⟩

hau·berk \ˈhȯ-(ˌ)bərk\ *n* [ME, fr. AF *hauberc,* of Gmc origin; akin to OE *healsbeorg* neck armor] (14c) **:** a tunic of chain mail worn as defensive armor from the 12th to the 14th century

1 hauberk

haugh \ˈhȯ(k)\ *n* [ME (Sc) *halch,* fr. OE *healh* corner of land; akin to OE *holh* hole] (bef. 12c) *Scot* **:** a low-lying meadow by the side of a river

haugh·ty \ˈhȯ-tē, ˈhä-\ *adj* **haugh·ti·er; -est** [obs. *haught,* fr. ME *haute,* fr. AF *halt, haut,* lit., high, fr. L *altus* — more at OLD] (15c) **:** blatantly and disdainfully proud *syn* see PROUD — **haugh·ti·ly** \ˈhȯ-tə-lē, ˈhä-\ *adv* — **haugh·ti·ness** \ˈhȯ-tē-nəs, ˈhä-\ *n*

[1]**haul** \ˈhȯl\ *vb* [ME *halen* to pull, fr. AF *haler,* of Gmc origin; akin to MD *halen* to pull; akin to OE *geholian* to obtain] *vt* (13c) **1 a :** to exert traction on **:** DRAW ⟨~ a wagon⟩ **b :** to obtain or move by or as if by hauling ⟨was ~*ed* to parties night after night by his wife⟩ **c :** to transport in a vehicle **:** CART **2 :** to change the course of (a ship) esp. so as to sail closer to the wind **3 :** to bring before an authority for interrogation or judgment **:** HALE ⟨~ traffic violators into court⟩ ~ *vi* **1 :** to exert traction **:** PULL **2 :** to move along **:** PROCEED **3 :** to furnish transportation **4** *of the wind* **:** SHIFT — **haul ass** *often vulgar* **:** to move quickly

[2]**haul** *n* (1670) **1 a :** the act or process of hauling **:** PULL **b :** a device for hauling **2 a :** the result of an effort to obtain, collect, or win ⟨the burglar's ~⟩ **b :** the quantity of fish taken in a single draft of a net **3 a :** transportation by hauling **b :** the length or course of a transportation route ⟨a long ~⟩ **c :** a quantity transported **:** LOAD

haul·age \ˈhȯ-lij\ *n* (1826) **1 :** the act or process of hauling **2 :** a charge made for hauling

haul·er \ˈhȯ-lər\ *n* (1674) **:** one that hauls: as **a :** a commercial establishment or worker whose business is hauling **b :** an automotive vehicle for hauling goods or material

haul·ier \ˈhȯl-yər\ *Brit var of* HAULER

haulm \ˈhȯm\ *n* [ME *halm,* fr. OE *healm;* akin to OHG *halm* stem, L *culmus* stalk, Gk *kalamos* reed] (bef. 12c) **:** the stems or tops of crop plants (as peas or potatoes) esp. after the crop has been gathered

haul off *vi* (1843) **:** to get ready — used with *and* and a following verb describing a usu. sudden and violent act ⟨I *hauled off* and hit him⟩

haunch \ˈhȯnch, ˈhänch\ *n* [ME *haunche,* fr. AF *hanche, haunche,* of Gmc origin; akin to MD *hanke* haunch] (13c) **1 a :** HIP 1a **b :** HINDQUARTER 2 — usu. used in pl. **2 :** HINDQUARTER 1 **3 :** either side of an arch between the springing and the crown — **on one's haunches :** in a squatting position

[1]**haunt** \ˈhȯnt, ˈhänt\ *vb* [ME, fr. AF *hanter,* prob. fr. ON *heimta* to lead home, pull, claim, fr. *heimr* home] *vt* (14c) **1 a :** to visit often **:** FREQUENT **b :** to continually seek the company of **2 a :** to have a disquieting or harmful effect on **:** TROUBLE ⟨problems we ignore now will come back to ~ us⟩ **b :** to recur constantly and spontaneously to ⟨the tune ~*ed* her⟩ **c :** to reappear continually in ⟨a sense of tension that ~*s* his writing⟩ **3 :** to visit or inhabit as a ghost ~ *vi* **1 :** to stay around or persist **:** LINGER **2 :** to appear habitually as a ghost — **haunt·er** *n* — **haunt·ing·ly** \ˈhȯn-tiŋ-lē, ˈhän-\ *adv*

[2]**haunt** \ˈhȯnt, ˈhänt, *2 is usu* ˈhant\ *n* (14c) **1 :** a place habitually frequented **2** *chiefly dial* **:** GHOST

Hau·sa \ˈhau̇-sə, -zə\ *n, pl* **Hausa** *or* **Hausas** [Hausa *Hausā*] (1853) **1 :** the Chadic language of the Hausa people widely used in western Africa as a trade language **2 :** a member of a black people of northern Nigeria and southern Niger

haus·frau \ˈhau̇s-ˌfrau̇\ *n* [G, fr. *Haus* house + *Frau* woman, wife] (1798) **:** HOUSEWIFE

haus·tel·lum \hȯ-ˈste-ləm\ *n, pl* **-la** \-lə\ [NL, dim. of L *haustrum* scoop on a waterwheel, fr. *haurire* to drink, draw — more at EXHAUST] (1816) **:** a proboscis (as of an insect) adapted to suck blood or juices of plants

haus·to·ri·al \hȯ-ˈstȯr-ē-əl\ *adj* (1894) **:** of, relating to, or having a haustorium

haus·to·ri·um \-ē-əm\ *n, pl* **-ria** \-ē-ə\ [NL, fr. L *haurire*] (1875) **:** a food-absorbing outgrowth of a plant organ (as a hypha or stem)

haut·bois *or* **haut·boy** \ˈ(h)ō-ˌbȯi\ *n, pl* **hautbois** \-ˌbȯiz\ *or* **hautboys** [MF *hautbois,* fr. *haut* high + *bois* wood] (1575) **:** OBOE

haute \ˈōt\ *also* **haut** \ˈōt, ˈō\ *adj* [F] (1787) **:** FASHIONABLE, HIGH-CLASS ⟨~ interior decorators⟩ ⟨a store filled with ~ kitsch⟩

haute cou·ture \ˌōt-kü-ˈtür\ *n* [F, lit., high sewing] (1908) **:** the houses or designers that create exclusive and often trend-setting fashions for women; *also* **:** the fashions created

haute cui·sine \-kwi-ˈzēn\ *n* [F, lit., high cooking] (1928) **:** artful or elaborate cuisine; *esp* **:** traditionally elaborate French cuisine

haute école \-ā-ˈkȯl, -ˈkəl\ *n* [F, lit., high school] (1858) **:** a highly stylized form of classical riding **:** advanced dressage

hau·teur \hȯ-ˈtər, (h)ō-\ *n* [F, fr. *haut* high — more at HAUGHTY] (ca. 1628) **:** ARROGANCE, HAUGHTINESS

haut monde \ō-ˈmänd, ō-ˈmōⁿd\ *also* **haute monde** \ōt-\ *n* [F, lit., high world] (1864) **:** high society

Ha·vana \hə-ˈva-nə\ *n* [prob. fr. Sp *habano,* fr. *habano* of Havana, fr. La *Habana* (Havana), Cuba] (1826) **1 :** a cigar made from Cuban tobacco **2 :** a tobacco orig. grown in Cuba

Ha·var·ti \hə-ˈvär-tē\ *n* [Dan, fr. *Havarthi*gård, farm of Hanne Nielsen †1903 Dan. cheese maker] (1957) **:** a semisoft Danish cheese having a porous texture and usu. a mild flavor

hav·da·lah *also* **hab·da·lah** \ˌhäv-də-ˈlä, häv-ˈdȯ-lə\ *n, often cap* [Heb *habhdālāh* separation] (1733) **:** a Jewish ceremony marking the close of a Sabbath or holy day

[1]**have** \ˈhav, (h)əv, v; *in "have to" meaning "must" usu* ˈhaf\ *vb* **had** \ˈhad, (h)əd, d\; **hav·ing** \ˈha-viŋ\; **has** \ˈhaz, (h)əz, z, s; *in "has to" meaning "must" usu* ˈhas\ [ME, fr. OE *habban;* akin to OHG *habēn* to have, and perh. to *hevan* to lift — more at HEAVE] *vt* (bef. 12c) **1 a :** to hold or maintain as a possession, privilege, or entitlement ⟨they ~ a new car⟩ ⟨I ~ my rights⟩ **b :** to hold in one's use, service, regard, or at one's disposal ⟨the group will ~ enough tickets for everyone⟩ ⟨we don't ~ time to stay⟩ **c :** to hold, include, or contain as a part or whole ⟨the car *has* power brakes⟩ ⟨April *has* 30 days⟩ **2 :** to feel obligation in regard to — usu. used with an infinitive with *to* ⟨we ~ things to do⟩ ⟨~ a deadline to meet⟩ **3 :** to stand in a certain relationship to ⟨*has* three fine children⟩ ⟨we will ~ the wind at our backs⟩ **4 a :** to acquire or get possession of **:** OBTAIN ⟨these shoes are the best to be *had*⟩ **b :** RECEIVE ⟨*had* news⟩ **c :** ACCEPT; *specif* **:** to accept in marriage **d :** to copulate with **5 a :** to be marked or characterized by (a quality, attribute, or faculty) ⟨both ~ red hair⟩ ⟨*has* a way with words⟩ **b :** EXHIBIT, SHOW ⟨*had* the gall to refuse⟩ **c :** USE, EXERCISE ⟨~ mercy on us⟩ **6 a :** to experience esp. by submitting to, undergoing, or suffering ⟨I ~ a cold⟩ **b :** to make the effort to perform (an action) or engage in (an activity) ⟨~ a look at that cut⟩ **c :** to entertain in the mind ⟨~ an opinion⟩ **7 a :** to cause or command to do something — used with the infinitive without *to* ⟨~ the children stay⟩ **b :** to cause to be in a certain place or state ⟨*has* people around at all times⟩ **8 :** ALLOW ⟨we'll ~ no more of that⟩ **9 :** to be competent in ⟨*has* only a little French⟩ **10 a :** to hold in a position of disadvantage or certain defeat ⟨we ~ him now⟩ **b :** to take advantage of **:** TRICK, FOOL ⟨been *had*

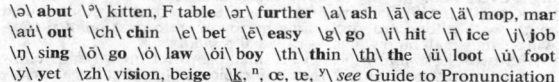

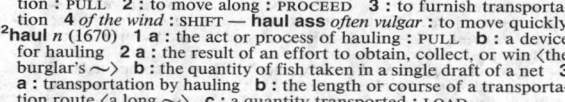

by a partner⟩ **11 :** BEAR 2a ⟨~ a baby⟩ **12 :** to partake of ⟨~ dinner⟩ ⟨~ a piece⟩ **13 :** BRIBE, SUBORN ⟨can be *had* for a price⟩ ~ *verbal auxiliary* **1** — used with the past participle to form the present perfect, past perfect, or future perfect ⟨*has* gone home⟩ ⟨*had* already eaten⟩ ⟨will ~ finished dinner by then⟩ **2 :** to be compelled, obliged, or required — used with an infinitive with *to* or *to* alone ⟨we *had* to go⟩ ⟨do what you *have* to⟩ ⟨it *has* to be said⟩ — **had better** *or* **had best :** would be wise to — **have at :** to go at or deal with : ATTACK — **have coming :** to deserve or merit what one gets, benefits by, or suffers ⟨he *had* that *coming*⟩ — **have done :** FINISH, STOP — **have done with :** to bring to an end : have no further concern with ⟨let us *have done with* name-calling⟩ — **have had it 1 :** to have had or have done all one is going to be allowed to **2 :** to have experienced, endured, or suffered all one can — **have it :** ASSERT, CLAIM ⟨rumor *has it* that he was drunk⟩ — **have it in for :** to intend to do harm to — **have it out :** to settle a matter of contention by discussion or a fight — **have none of :** to refuse to have anything to do with — **have one's eye on 1 a :** to look at **b :** to watch constantly and attentively **2 :** to have as an objective — **have to do with 1 :** to deal with ⟨the story *has to do with* real people —Alice M. Jordan⟩ **2 :** to have a specified relationship with or effect on ⟨the size of the brain *has* nothing *to do with* intelligence —Ruth Benedict⟩

[2]**have** \ˈhav\ *n* (1836) **:** one that is well-endowed esp. in material wealth

have·lock \ˈhav-ˌläk, -lək\ *n* [Sir Henry *Havelock*] (1861) **:** a covering attached to a cap to protect the neck from the sun or bad weather

ha·ven \ˈhā-vən\ *n* [ME, fr. OE *hæfen;* akin to MHG *habene* harbor] (bef. 12c) **1 :** HARBOR, PORT **2 :** a place of safety : REFUGE **3 :** a place offering favorable opportunities or conditions ⟨a ~ for artists⟩ — **haven** *vt*

have–not \ˈhav-ˌnät, -ˈnät\ *n* (1836) **:** one that is poor esp. in material wealth

haven't \ˈha-vənt, ˈha-bᵊm(t)\ (1777) **:** have not

have on *vt* (bef. 12c) **1 :** WEAR ⟨*has on* a new suit⟩ **2** *chiefly Brit* **:** to trick or deceive intentionally : PUT ON 5 **3 :** to have plans for ⟨what do you *have on* for tomorrow⟩

ha·ver \ˈhā-vər\ *vi* [origin unknown] (1866) *chiefly Brit* **:** to hem and haw

hav·er·sack \ˈha-vər-ˌsak\ *n* [F *havresac,* fr. G *Habersack* bag for oats, fr. *Haber* oats + *Sack* bag] (1749) **:** a bag similar to a knapsack but worn over one shoulder

ha·ver·sian canal \hə-ˈvər-zhən-\ *n, often cap H* [Clopton *Havers* †1702 Eng. physician & anatomist] (1842) **:** any of the small canals through which the blood vessels ramify in bone

haversian system *n, often cap H* (ca. 1846) **:** a haversian canal with the concentrically arranged laminae of bone that surround it

[1]**hav·oc** \ˈha-vək, -vik\ *n* [ME *havok,* fr. AF, modif. of OF *havot* plunder] (15c) **1 :** wide and general destruction : DEVASTATION **2 :** great confusion and disorder ⟨the blackout caused ~ in the city⟩

[2]**havoc** *vt* **hav·ocked; hav·ock·ing** (1577) **:** to lay waste : DESTROY

[1]**haw** \ˈhȯ\ *n* [ME *hawe,* fr. OE *haga* — more at HEDGE] (bef. 12c) **1 :** a hawthorn berry **2 :** HAWTHORN

[2]**haw** *n* [origin unknown] (15c) **:** NICTITATING MEMBRANE; *esp* **:** an inflamed nictitating membrane of a domesticated mammal

[3]**haw** *interj* (1600) — often used to indicate a vocalized pause in speaking

[4]**haw** *vi* [imit.] (1632) **1 :** to utter the sound represented by *haw* ⟨hemmed and ~*ed* before answering⟩ **2 :** EQUIVOCATE ⟨the administration hemmed and ~*ed* over the students' demands⟩

[5]**haw** *vb* [origin unknown] *vb imper* (1777) — used as a direction to turn to the left; compare GEE ~ *vi* **:** to turn to the near or left side

Hawaii–Aleutian time *n* (1983) **:** the time of the 10th time zone west of Greenwich that includes the Hawaiian Islands and the Aleutians west of the Fox group

Ha·wai·ian \hə-ˈwä-yən, -ˈwī-(y)ən, -ˈwȯ-yən\ *n* (1840) **1 :** a native or resident of Hawaii; *esp* **:** one of Polynesian ancestry **2 :** the Polynesian language of the Hawaiians — **Hawaiian** *adj*

Hawaiian goose *n* (ca. 1909) **:** NENE

Hawaiian guitar *n* (1928) **:** a usu. electric stringed instrument having a long fretted neck and six to eight steel strings that are plucked while being pressed with a movable steel bar for a glissando effect

Hawaiian shirt *n* (1952) **:** a usu. short-sleeved sport shirt with a colorful pattern

haw·finch \ˈhȯ-ˌfinch\ *n* [[1]*haw*] (ca. 1674) **:** an Old World finch (*Coccothraustes coccothraustes* of the family Fringillidae) with a large heavy bill and short thick neck and the male marked with black, white, and brown

[1]**hawk** \ˈhȯk\ *n* [ME *hauk,* fr. OE *hafoc;* akin to OHG *habuh* hawk, Russ *kobets* a falcon] (bef. 12c) **1 :** any of numerous diurnal birds of prey belonging to a suborder (Falcones of the order Falconiformes) and including all the smaller members of this group; *esp* **:** ACCIPITER **2 :** a small board or metal sheet with a handle on the underside used to hold mortar **3 :** one who takes a militant attitude and advocates immediate vigorous action; *esp* **:** a supporter of a war or warlike policy — compare DOVE — **hawk·ish** \ˈhȯ-kish\ *adj* — **hawk·ish·ly** *adv* — **hawk·ish·ness** *n*

[2]**hawk** *vi* (14c) **1 :** to hunt birds by means of a trained hawk **2 :** to soar and strike like a hawk ~ *vt* **:** to hunt on the wing like a hawk

[3]**hawk** *vb* [imit.] *vt* (1581) **:** to raise by trying to clear the throat ⟨~ up phlegm⟩ ~ *vi* **:** to utter a harsh guttural sound in or as if in hawking

[4]**hawk** *n* (1604) **:** an audible effort to force up phlegm from the throat

[5]**hawk** *vt* [back-formation fr. [2]*hawker*] (1713) **:** to offer for sale by calling out in the street ⟨~*ing* newspapers⟩; *broadly* **:** SELL

[1]**hawk·er** \ˈhȯ-kər\ *n* [ME, fr. OE *hafocere,* fr. *hafoc*] (bef. 12c) **:** FALCONER

[2]**hawker** *n* [by folk etymology fr. LG *höker,* fr. MLG *hōker,* fr. *hōken* to squat, peddle — more at HUNKER] (1512) **:** one who hawks wares

Hawk·eye \ˈhȯk-ˌī\ *n* (1823) **:** a native or resident of Iowa — used as a nickname

hawk–eyed \ˈhȯk-ˌīd\ *adj* (1795) **:** having keen sight

hawk moth *n* (1785) **:** any of a family (Sphingidae) of stout-bodied moths with a long proboscis, long narrow more or less pointed forewings, and small hind wings — called also *sphinx*

hawks·bill \ˈhȯks-ˌbil\ *n* (1712) **:** a small brown or brown and yellow sea turtle (*Eretmochelys imbricata*) of tropical waters that has a narrow pointed beak and a carapace of overlapping plates — compare TORTOISESHELL 1

hawk·shaw \ˈhȯk-ˌshȯ\ *n* [fr. *Hawkshaw,* detective in the play *The Ticket of Leave Man* (1863) by Tom Taylor] (1888) **:** DETECTIVE

hawk·weed \ˈhȯk-ˌwēd\ *n* (1562) **:** any of a genus (*Hieracium*) of perennial often apomictic composite herbs having usu. yellow flowers — compare ORANGE HAWKWEED

hawse \ˈhȯz\ *n* [alter. of ME *halse,* fr. ON *hals* neck, hawse; akin to OE *heals,* neck — more at COLLAR] (14c) **1 a :** the part of a ship's bow that contains the hawseholes **b :** HAWSEHOLE **2 :** the distance between a ship's bow and her anchor

hawse·hole \-ˌhōl\ *n* (1664) **:** a hole in the bow of a ship through which a cable passes

haw·ser \ˈhȯ-zər\ *n* [ME, fr. AF *haucer,* fr. AF *halcer, haucer* to raise, hoist, fr. VL **altiare,* fr. L *altus* high — more at OLD] (13c) **:** a large rope for towing, mooring, or securing a ship

haw·ser–laid \ˈhȯ-zər-ˌlād\ *adj* (1769) **:** composed of three ropes laid together right-handed with each containing three strands twisted together

haw·thorn \ˈhȯ-ˌthȯrn\ *n* [ME *hawethorn,* fr. OE *hagathorn,* fr. *haga* hawthorn + *thorn* — more at HEDGE] (bef. 12c) **:** any of a genus (*Crataegus*) of spring-flowering spiny shrubs or small trees of the rose family with glossy and often lobed leaves, white or pink fragrant flowers, and small red fruits

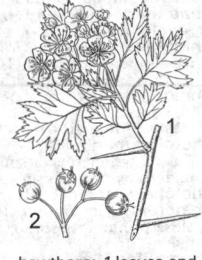

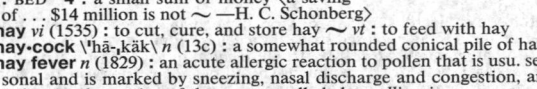

hawthorn: *1* leaves and flowers, *2* fruits

Haw·thorne effect \ˈhȯ-ˌthȯrn-\ *n* [fr. the *Hawthorne* Works of the Western Electric Co., Cicero, Ill., where its existence was established by experiment] (1962) **:** the stimulation to output or accomplishment that results from the mere fact of being under observation; *also* **:** such an increase in output or accomplishment

[1]**hay** \ˈhā\ *n* [ME *hey,* fr. OE *hīeg;* akin to OHG *hewi* hay, OE *hēawan* to hew] (bef. 12c) **1 :** herbage and esp. grass mowed and cured for fodder **2 :** REWARD **3** *slang* **:** BED **4 :** a small sum of money ⟨a saving of . . . $14 million is not ~ —H. C. Schonberg⟩

[2]**hay** *vi* (1535) **:** to cut, cure, and store hay ~ *vt* **:** to feed with hay

hay·cock \ˈhā-ˌkäk\ *n* (13c) **:** a somewhat rounded conical pile of hay

hay fever *n* (1829) **:** an acute allergic reaction to pollen that is usu. seasonal and is marked by sneezing, nasal discharge and congestion, and itching and watering of the eyes — called also *pollinosis*

hay·lage \ˈhā-lij\ *n* [*hay* + *silage*] (ca. 1958) **:** a stored forage that is essentially a grass silage wilted to 35 to 50 percent moisture

hay·loft \ˈhā-ˌlȯft\ *n* (1530) **:** a loft esp. for storing hay

hay·mak·er \-ˌmā-kər\ *n* (1902) **:** a powerful blow

hay·mow \-ˌmau̇\ *n* (15c) **:** a mow esp. of or for hay

hay·rack \-ˌrak\ *n* (1753) **1 :** a feeding rack that holds hay for livestock **2 :** a frame mounted on the running gear of a wagon and used esp. in hauling hay or straw; *also* **:** a wagon equipped with a hayrack

hay·rick \-ˌrik\ *n* (15c) **:** a relatively large sometimes thatched outdoor pile of hay : HAYSTACK

hay·ride \-ˌrīd\ *n* (1896) **:** a pleasure ride usu. at night by a group in a wagon, sleigh, or open truck partly filled with straw or hay

hay–scent·ed fern \ˈhā-ˌsen-təd-\ *n* (1915) **:** a common fern (*Dennstaedtia punctilobula*) of eastern No. America with fragrant finely divided pale green fronds

hay·seed \ˈhā-ˌsēd\ *n, pl* **hayseed** *or* **hayseeds** (1577) **1 a :** seed shattered from hay **b :** clinging bits of straw or chaff from hay **2** *pl* *hayseeds* **:** BUMPKIN, YOKEL

hay·stack \-ˌstak\ *n* (15c) **1 :** a stack of hay **2 :** a vertical standing wave in turbulent river waters

hay·wire \-ˌwī(-ə)r\ *adv or adj* [fr. the use of baling wire for makeshift repairs] (1929) **1 :** being out of order or having gone wrong ⟨the radio went ~⟩ **2 :** emotionally or mentally upset or out of control : CRAZY ⟨is going ~ with grief⟩

ha·zan \kə-ˈzän, ˈkä-zᵊn\ *n, pl* **ha·za·nim** \kə-ˈzä-nəm\ [LHeb *ḥazzān*] (1650) **1 :** an official of a Jewish synagogue or community of the period when the Talmud was compiled **2 :** CANTOR 2

[1]**haz·ard** \ˈha-zərd\ *n* [ME, fr. AF *hasard,* fr. OSp *azar,* fr. Ar *al-zahr* the die] (14c) **1 :** a game of chance like craps played with two dice **2 :** a source of danger **3 a :** CHANCE, RISK **b :** a chance event : ACCIDENT **4** *obs* **:** STAKE 3a **5 :** a golf-course obstacle — **at hazard :** at stake

[2]**hazard** *vt* (1530) **:** VENTURE, RISK ⟨~ a guess as to the outcome⟩

haz·ard·ous \ˈha-zər-dəs\ *adj* (1585) **1 :** depending on hazard or chance **2 :** involving or exposing one to risk (as of loss or harm) ⟨a ~ occupation⟩ ⟨disposing of ~ waste⟩ *syn* see DANGEROUS — **haz·ard·ous·ly** *adv* — **haz·ard·ous·ness** *n*

[1]**haze** \ˈhāz\ *n* [prob. back-formation fr. *hazy*] (1706) **1 a :** fine dust, smoke, or light vapor causing lack of transparency of the air **b :** a cloudy appearance in a transparent liquid or solid; *also* **:** a dullness of finish (as on furniture) **2 :** something suggesting atmospheric haze; *esp* **:** vagueness of mind or mental perception

[2]**haze** *vb* **hazed; haz·ing** *vt* (1801) **:** to make hazy, dull, or cloudy ~ *vi* **:** to become hazy or cloudy

[3]**haze** *vt* **hazed; haz·ing** [origin unknown] (1840) **1 a :** to harass by exacting unnecessary or disagreeable work **b :** to harass by banter, ridicule, or criticism **2 :** to haze by way of initiation ⟨~ the fraternity pledges⟩ **3** *West* **:** to drive (as cattle or horses) from horseback — **haz·er** *n*

[1]**ha·zel** \ˈhā-zəl\ *n* [ME *hasel,* fr. OE *hæsel;* akin to OHG *hasal* hazel, L *corulus*] (bef. 12c) **1 :** any of a genus (*Corylus* and esp. the American *C. americana* and the European *C. avellana*) of shrubs or small trees of the birch family bearing nuts enclosed in a leafy involucre **2 :** a light brown to strong yellowish brown

[2]**hazel** *adj* (14c) **1 :** consisting of hazels or of the wood of the hazel **2 a :** of the color hazel **b** *of eyes* **:** of a variable color averaging light greenish-grayish brown

hazel hen *n* (1661) **:** a European woodland grouse (*Bonasa bonasia*) related to the ruffed grouse — called also *hazel grouse*

ha·zel·nut \ˈhā-zəl-ˌnət\ *n* (bef. 12c) **:** the brown nut of a hazel

hazing *n* (ca. 1855) **:** the action of hazing; *esp* **:** an initiation process involving harassment

haz·mat \ˈhaz-ˌmat\ *n, often attrib* [*haz*ardous *mat*erial] (1980) **:** a material (as flammable or poisonous material) that would be a danger to life or to the environment if released without precautions

hazy \ˈhā-zē\ *adj* **haz·i·er; -est** [origin unknown] (1582) **1 :** obscured or made dim or cloudy by or as if by haze **2 :** VAGUE, INDEFINITE ⟨has only a ~ recollection⟩; *also* **:** UNCERTAIN ⟨I'm ~ on that point⟩ — **haz·i·ly** \-zə-lē\ *adv* — **haz·i·ness** \-zē-nəs\ *n*

Hb *abbr* hemoglobin

HBM *abbr* Her Britannic Majesty; His Britannic Majesty

H–bomb \ˈāch-ˌbäm\ *n* (1950) **:** HYDROGEN BOMB

HC *abbr* **1** Holy Communion **2** House of Commons **3** hydrocarbon

HCA *abbr* heterocyclic amine

HCF *abbr* highest common factor

HCFC *abbr* hydrochlorofluorocarbon

HCG *abbr* human chorionic gonadotropin

HCL *abbr* high cost of living

hd *abbr* head

HD *abbr* **1** heavy-duty **2** high definition

HDL \ˌāch-(ˌ)dē-ˈel\ *n* [*h*igh-*d*ensity *l*ipoprotein] (ca. 1965) **:** a lipoprotein of blood plasma that is composed of a high proportion of protein with little triglyceride and cholesterol and that is correlated with reduced risk of atherosclerosis — called also *good cholesterol*; compare LDL

HDMI \ˌāch-ˌdē-ˌem-ˈī\ *trademark* — used for a digital video interface capable of transmitting information in high definition

HDPE *abbr* high-density polyethylene

HDTV *abbr* high-definition television

hdwd *abbr* hardwood

1**he** \ˈhē, ē\ *pron* [ME, fr. OE *hē*; akin to OE *hēo* she, *hit* it, OHG *hē* he, L *cis, citra* on this side, Gk *ekeinos* that person] (bef. 12c) **1 :** that male one who is neither speaker nor hearer ⟨~ is my father⟩ — compare HIM, HIS, IT, SHE, THEY **2 —** used in a generic sense or when the sex of the person is unspecified ⟨~ that hath ears to hear, let him hear —Mt 11:15(AV)⟩ ⟨one should do the best ~ can⟩

2**he** \ˈhē\ *n* (bef. 12c) **1 :** a male person or animal **2 :** one that is strongly masculine or has strong masculine appeal — usu. used in combination ⟨that's what I call *he*-literature —Sinclair Lewis⟩

3**he** \ˈhā\ *n* [Heb *hēʾ*] (ca. 1567) **:** the 5th letter of the Hebrew alphabet — see ALPHABET table

He *symbol* helium

HE *abbr* **1** Her Excellency; His Excellency **2** high explosive **3** His Eminence

1**head** \ˈhed\ *n* [ME *hed,* fr. OE *hēafod;* akin to OHG *houbit* head, L *caput*] (bef. 12c) **1 :** the upper or anterior division of the animal body that contains the brain, the chief sense organs, and the mouth **2 a :** the seat of the intellect **:** MIND ⟨two ~*s* are better than one⟩ **b :** a person with respect to mental qualities ⟨let wiser ~*s* prevail⟩ **c :** natural aptitude or talent ⟨a good ~ for figures⟩ **d :** mental or emotional control **:** POISE ⟨a level ~⟩ **e :** HEADACHE **3 :** the obverse of a coin — usu. used in pl. **4 a :** PERSON, INDIVIDUAL ⟨count ~*s*⟩ **b** *pl* **head :** one of a number (as of domestic animals) **5 a :** the end that is upper or higher or opposite the foot ⟨the ~ of the table⟩ ⟨~ of a sail⟩ **b :** the source of a stream **c :** either end of something (as a drum) whose two ends need not be distinguished **6 :** DIRECTOR, LEADER: as **a :** HEADMASTER **b :** one in charge of a division or department in an office or institution **7 a :** CAPITULUM 2 **b :** the foliaged part of a plant esp. when consisting of a compact mass of leaves or close fructification ⟨a ~ of lettuce⟩ **8 a :** the leading element of a military column or a procession **b :** HEADWAY **9 a :** the uppermost extremity or projecting part of an object **:** TOP **b :** the striking part of a weapon, tool, or implement **c :** the rounded proximal end of a long bone (as the humerus) **d :** the end of a muscle nearest the origin **e :** the oval part of a printed musical note **10 a :** a body of water kept in reserve at a height; *also* **:** the containing bank, dam, or wall **b :** a mass of water in motion **11 a :** the difference in elevation between two points in a body of fluid **b :** the resulting pressure of the fluid at the lower point expressible as this height; *broadly* **:** pressure of a fluid **12 a :** the bow and adjacent parts of a ship **b :** a ship's toilet; *broadly* **:** TOILET 3 **13 :** the approximate length of the head of a horse ⟨won by a ~⟩ **14 :** the place of leadership, honor, or command ⟨at the ~ of her class⟩ **15 a** (1) **:** a word or series of words often in larger letters placed at the beginning of a passage or at the top of a page in order to introduce or categorize (2) **:** a separate part or topic **b :** a portion of a page or sheet that is above the first line of printing **16 :** the foam or scum that rises on a fermenting or effervescing liquid (as beer) **17 a :** the part of a boil, pimple, or abscess at which it is likely to break **b :** culminating point of action **:** CRISIS ⟨events came to a ~⟩ **18 a :** a part or attachment of a machine or machine tool containing a device (as a cutter or drill); *also* **:** the part of an apparatus that performs the chief function or a particular function **b :** an electromagnet used as a transducer in magnetic recording for recording on, reading, or erasing a magnetic medium (as tape or a disk) **19 :** an immediate constituent of a construction that can have the same grammatical function as the whole (as *man* in "an old man", "a very old man", or "the man in the street") **20 a :** one who uses a drug — often used in combination ⟨pot*head*⟩ **b :** a devoted enthusiast **:** AFICIONADO — often used in combination ⟨computer*head*⟩ **21** *often vulgar* **:** FELLATIO, CUNNILINGUS — usu. used with *give* — **by the head :** drawing the greater depth of water forward — **off one's head :** CRAZY, DISTRACTED — **out of one's head :** DELIRIOUS — **over one's head 1 :** beyond one's comprehension or competence ⟨the most awful intellectual detail, all of it *over my head* —E. B. White⟩ **2 :** so as to pass over one's superior standing or authority ⟨went *over my head* to complain⟩

2**head** *adj* (bef. 12c) **1 :** of, relating to, or intended for the head **2 :** PRINCIPAL, CHIEF ⟨~ cook⟩ **3 :** situated at the head **4 :** coming from in front ⟨~ sea⟩

3**head** *vt* (14c) **1 :** BEHEAD **2 a :** to put a head on **:** fit a head to ⟨~ an arrow⟩ **b :** to form the head or top of ⟨tower ~*ed* by a spire⟩ **3 :** to act as leader or head to ⟨~ a revolt⟩ **4 a :** to get in front of so as to hinder, stop, or turn back **b :** to take a lead over (as a racehorse) **:** SURPASS **c :** to pass (a stream) by going round above the source **5 a :** to put something at the head of (as a list) **b :** to stand as the first or leading member of ⟨~*s* the list of heroes⟩ **6 :** to set the course of ⟨~ a ship northward⟩ **7 :** to drive (as a soccer ball) with the head ~ *vi* **1 :** to form a head ⟨this cabbage ~*s* early⟩ **2 :** to point or proceed in a certain direction ⟨~*ed* south⟩ **3 :** to have a source **:** ORIGINATE

head·ache \ˈhed-ˌāk\ *n* (bef. 12c) **1 :** pain in the head **2 :** a vexatious or baffling situation or problem ⟨meetings had become a giant ~ —Franklin Foer⟩ — **head·achy** *also* **head·achey** \-ˌā-kē\ *adj*

head and shoulders *adv* (ca. 1864) **:** beyond comparison **:** by far ⟨*head and shoulders* above the competition⟩

head·band \ˈhed-ˌband\ *n* (1535) **1 :** a band worn on or around the head **2 :** a narrow strip of cloth sewn or glued by hand to a book at the extreme ends of the spine

head·bang·er \ˈhed-ˌbaŋ-ər\ *n* (1979) **:** a musician who performs hard rock; *also* **:** a fan of hard rock

head·board \-ˌbȯrd\ *n* (1730) **:** a board forming the head (as of a bed)

head case *n* (1966) **:** NUT 6a

head·cheese \-ˌchēz\ *n* (1831) **:** a jellied loaf or sausage made from edible parts of the head, feet, and sometimes the tongue and heart esp. of a pig

head cold *n* (1936) **:** a common cold centered in the nasal passages and adjacent mucous tissues

head·dress \ˈhed-ˌdres\ *n* (1702) **:** an often elaborate covering for the head

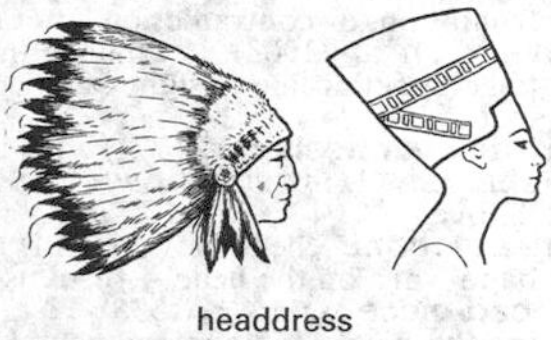
headdress

head·ed \ˈhe-dəd\ *adj* (13c) **1 :** having a head or a heading **2 :** having a head or heads of a specified kind or number — used in combination ⟨became light-*headed* from the fever⟩ ⟨a round-*headed* screw⟩

head·end \ˈhed-ˌend\ *n* (1971) **:** equipment or a facility which receives communications signals (as cable television broadcasts) for distribution to a local region

head·er \ˈhe-dər\ *n* (15c) **1 :** one that removes heads; *esp* **:** a grain-harvesting machine that cuts off the grain heads and elevates them to a wagon **2 a :** a brick or stone laid in a wall with its end toward the face of the wall **b :** a beam fitted at one side of an opening to support free ends of floor joists, studs, or rafters **c :** a horizontal structural or finish piece over an opening **:** LINTEL **d :** a conduit (as an exhaust pipe for a many-cylindered engine) into which a number of smaller conduits open **e :** a mounting plate through which electrical terminals pass from a sealed device (as a transistor) **3 :** a fall or dive headfirst **4 :** a shot or pass in soccer made by heading the ball **5 :** HEAD 15a(1)

head·first \ˈhed-ˈfərst\ *adv* (ca. 1828) **1 :** with the head foremost ⟨dove ~ into the waves⟩ **2 :** HEADLONG 2 — **headfirst** *adj*

head·fore·most \-ˈfōr-ˌmōst, -ˈfȯr-\ *adv* (1697) **:** HEADFIRST

head game *n* (1977) **:** MIND GAME

head·gate \ˈhed-ˌgāt\ *n* (1832) **:** a gate for controlling the water flowing into a channel (as an irrigation ditch)

head·gear \-ˌgir\ *n* (15c) **1 :** a covering or protective device for the head **2 :** a harness for a horse's head

head·hunt \ˈhed-ˌhənt\ *vt* (1969) **:** to recruit (personnel and esp. executives) for top-level jobs ~ *vi* **:** to recruit personnel for top-level jobs

head·hunt·er \-ˌhən-tər\ *n* (1853) **1 :** one that engages in head-hunting **2 :** a recruiter of personnel esp. at the executive level **3 :** an athlete who intentionally seeks to harm an opponent

head–hunt·ing \-ˌhən-tiŋ\ *n* (1853) **1 :** the act or custom of seeking out, decapitating, and preserving the heads of enemies as trophies **2 :** a seeking to deprive usu. political enemies of position or influence

head·ing \ˈhe-diŋ\ *n* (1676) **1 a :** something that forms or serves as a head; *esp* **:** an inscription, headline, or title standing at the top or beginning (as of a letter or chapter) **b :** the address and date at the beginning of a letter showing its place and time of origin **2 :** the compass direction in which the longitudinal axis of a ship or aircraft points; *broadly* **:** DIRECTION **3 :** DRIFT 6

head–in–the–sand *adj* (1970) **:** unwilling to recognize or acknowledge a problem or situation ⟨the government's usual ~ response⟩

head·lamp \-ˌlamp\ *n* (1885) **:** HEADLIGHT

head·land \ˈhed-lənd, -ˌland\ *n* (bef. 12c) **1 :** unplowed land at the ends of furrows or near a fence **2 :** a point of usu. high land jutting out into a body of water **:** PROMONTORY

head·less \-ləs\ *adj* (bef. 12c) **1 a :** having no head **b :** having the head cut off **:** BEHEADED **2 :** having no chief **3 :** lacking good sense or prudence **:** FOOLISH — **head·less·ness** *n*

head·light \-ˌlīt\ *n* (1861) **1 :** a light with a reflector and special lens mounted on the front of a vehicle to illuminate the road ahead; *also* **:** the beam cast by a headlight **2 :** a light worn on the forehead (as of a miner or physician)

1**head·line** \-ˌlīn\ *n* (1824) **1 :** words set at the head of a passage or page to introduce or categorize **2 a :** a head of a newspaper story or article usu. printed in large type and giving the gist of the story or article that follows **b** *pl* **:** front-page news ⟨the scandal made ~*s*⟩

2**headline** *vt* (1891) **1 :** to provide with a headline **2 :** to publicize highly **3 :** to be engaged as a leading performer in (a show)

3**headline** *adj* (1939) **:** deserving mention in a headline **:** very noteworthy ⟨the ~ abduction of a diplomat⟩

head·lin·er \ˈhed-ˌlī-nər\ *n* (1896) **1 :** the principal performer in a show **:** STAR; *broadly* **:** PERSONALITY 4b **2 :** fabric covering the inside of the roof of an automobile

head linesman *n* (ca. 1949) **:** a football linesman

head·lock \ˈhed-ˌläk\ *n* (1905) **:** a hold in which a wrestler encircles an opponent's head with one arm

1**head·long** \-ˈlȯŋ\ *adv* [ME *hedlong,* alter. of *hedling,* fr. *hed* head] (14c) **1 :** HEADFIRST 1 **2 :** without deliberation **:** RECKLESSLY ⟨rushes ~ into danger⟩ **3 :** without pause or delay

[2]**head·long** \-ˌlȯŋ\ *adj* (ca. 1550) **1** *archaic* **:** STEEP, PRECIPITOUS **2 :** lacking in calmness or restraint **:** PRECIPITATE ⟨a ~ torrent of emotion⟩ **3 :** plunging headfirst ***syn*** see PRECIPITATE

head louse *n* (1547) **:** a sucking louse (*Pediculus humanus capitis*) that lives on the human scalp

head·man *n* (bef. 12c) **1 a** \ˈhed-ˈman\ **:** FOREMAN, OVERSEER **b** \-ˈman, -ˌman\ **:** a lesser chief of a primitive community **2** \-mən\ **:** HEADSMAN

head·mas·ter \ˈhed-ˌmas-tər, -ˈmas-\ *n* (1576) **:** a man heading the staff of a private school **:** PRINCIPAL — **head·mas·ter·ly** \-lē\ *adj* — **head·mas·ter·ship** \-ˌship\ *n*

head·mis·tress \-ˌmis-trəs, -ˈmis-\ *n* (1872) **:** a woman heading the staff of a private school

head·most \ˈhed-ˌmōst\ *adj* (1628) **:** most advanced **:** LEADING

head·note \-ˌnōt\ *n* (1855) **1 :** a prefixed note of comment or explanation **2 :** a note prefixed to the report of a decided legal case

head off *vt* (1841) **:** to turn back or turn aside **:** BLOCK, PREVENT ⟨*head* them *off* at the pass⟩ ⟨attempts to *head off* the imminent crisis⟩

head of steam (1972) **:** strong driving force **:** MOMENTUM ⟨frequent rallies helped the movement develop a *head of steam*⟩

[1]**head–on** \ˈhed-ˈȯn, -ˈän\ *adv* (1840) **1 :** with the head or front making the initial contact ⟨the cars collided ~⟩ **2 :** in direct opposition, confrontation, or contradiction ⟨met the problem ~⟩

[2]**head–on** *adj* (1903) **1 :** having the front facing in the direction of initial contact or line of sight ⟨a ~ collision⟩ **2 :** FRONTAL 2b ⟨a ~ confrontation⟩

head over heels *adv* (1771) **1 a :** in or as if in a somersault **:** HELTER-SKELTER **b :** UPSIDE DOWN **2 :** very much **:** DEEPLY ⟨*head over heels* in love⟩

head·phone \ˈhed-ˌfōn\ *n* (1914) **:** an earphone held over the ear by a band worn on the head — usu. used in pl.

head·piece \-ˌpēs\ *n* (1535) **1 a :** a protective or defensive covering for the head **b :** an ornamental, ceremonial, or traditional covering for the head **2 :** BRAINS, INTELLIGENCE **3 :** an ornament esp. at the beginning of a chapter

head·pin \-ˌpin\ *n* (1927) **:** a bowling pin that stands foremost in the arrangement of pins

head·quar·ter \ˈhed-ˌkwȯ(r)-tər, -ˌkȯr-, (ˈ)hed-ˈ\ *vt* (1903) **:** to place in headquarters ~ *vi* **:** to make one's headquarters

head·quar·ters \-tərz\ *n pl but sing or pl in constr* (1647) **1 :** a place from which a commander performs the functions of command **2 :** the administrative center of an enterprise

head·rest \-ˌrest\ *n* (1853) **1 :** a support for the head **2 :** HEAD RESTRAINT

head restraint *n* (1967) **:** a resilient pad at the top of the back of an automobile seat esp. for preventing whiplash

head rhyme *n* (ca. 1943) **:** ALLITERATION

head·room \ˈhed-ˌrüm, -ˌru̇m\ *n* (1841) **:** vertical space in which to stand, sit, or move

head·sail \-ˌsāl, -səl\ *n* (1627) **:** a sail set forward of the foremast

head–scratch·er \ˈhed-ˌskra-chər\ *n* (1971) **:** PUZZLE, MYSTERY

head–scratch·ing \ˈhed-ˌskra-chiŋ\ *n* (1926) **:** puzzled contemplation ⟨a lot of ~ going on⟩; *also* **:** CONFUSION

head·set \-ˌset\ *n* (1921) **1 :** an attachment for holding an earphone and transmitter at one's head **2 :** a pair of headphones

head·ship \-ˌship\ *n* (1582) **:** the position, office, or dignity of a head

head shop *n* (1968) **:** a shop specializing in articles (as hashish pipes and roach clips) of interest to drug users

head·shrink·er \-ˌshriŋ-kər, *esp Southern* -ˌsriŋ-\ *n* (1950) **:** SHRINK 3

heads·man \ˈhedz-mən\ *n* (1600) **:** one that beheads **:** EXECUTIONER

head·space \ˈhed-ˌspās\ *n* (1936) **:** the volume above a liquid or solid in a closed container

head·spring \ˈhed-ˌspriŋ\ *n* (14c) **:** FOUNTAINHEAD, SOURCE

head·stall \-ˌstȯl\ *n* (14c) **:** a part of a bridle or halter that encircles the head

head·stand \-ˌstand\ *n* (ca. 1934) **:** the gymnastic feat of standing on one's head usu. with support from the hands

head start *n* (1886) **1 :** an advantage granted or achieved at the beginning of a race, a chase, or a competition ⟨a 10-minute *head start*⟩ **2 :** a favorable or promising beginning

head·stock \ˈhed-ˌstäk\ *n* (1688) **:** a bearing or pedestal for a revolving or moving part; *specif* **:** a part of a lathe that holds the revolving spindle and its attachments

head·stone \-ˌstōn\ *n* (1775) **:** a memorial stone at the head of a grave

head·stream \-ˌstrēm\ *n* (14c) **:** a stream that is the source of a river

head·strong \-ˌstrȯŋ\ *adj* (14c) **1 :** not easily restrained **:** impatient of control, advice, or suggestions ⟨a ~ businessman⟩ **2 :** directed by ungovernable will ⟨violent ~ actions⟩ ***syn*** see UNRULY

[1]**heads–up** \ˈhedz-ˈəp\ *adj* (1947) **:** ALERT, RESOURCEFUL ⟨~ football⟩

[2]**heads–up** *n* (1987) **:** a message that alerts or prepares **:** WARNING ⟨gave him a ~ that an investigation was pending⟩

heads up *interj* (ca. 1941) — used as a warning to look out for danger esp. overhead or to clear a passageway

head–to–head *adv or adj* (ca. 1728) **:** in a direct confrontation or encounter usu. between individuals

head·wait·er \ˈhed-ˈwā-tər\ *n* (1786) **:** the head of the dining-room staff of a restaurant or hotel

head·wa·ter \-ˌwȯ-tər, -ˌwä-\ *n* (1787) **:** the source of a stream — usu. used in pl.

head·way \-ˌwā\ *n* (1748) **1 a :** motion or rate of motion in a forward direction **b :** ADVANCE, PROGRESS **2 :** headroom (as under an arch) sufficient to allow passage **3 :** the time interval between two vehicles traveling in the same direction on the same route

head·wind \ˈhed-ˌwind\ *n* (1926) **:** a wind having the opposite general direction to a course of movement (as of an aircraft)

head·word \ˈhed-ˌwərd\ *n* (ca. 1823) **1 :** a word or term placed at the beginning (as of a chapter or an entry in an encyclopedia) **2 :** HEAD 19

head·work \-ˌwərk\ *n* (1837) **:** mental labor; *esp* **:** clever thinking

heady \ˈhe-dē\ *adj* **head·i·er; -est** (14c) **1 a :** WILLFUL, RASH ⟨~ opinions⟩ **b :** VIOLENT, IMPETUOUS **2 a :** tending to intoxicate or make giddy or elated ⟨~ wine⟩ ⟨being in such distinguished company was a ~ experience⟩ **b :** GIDDY, EXHILARATED ⟨~ with his success⟩ **c :** RICH ⟨a ~ sauce⟩ ⟨a ~ variety⟩ **d :** IMPRESSIVE ⟨a man of ~ accomplishments⟩ **3 a :** marked by or showing good judgment **:** SHREWD, INTELLIGENT **b :** intellectually stimulating or demanding — **head·i·ly** \ˈhe-də-lē\ *adv* — **head·i·ness** \ˈhe-dē-nəs\ *n*

heal \ˈhēl\ *vb* [ME *helen,* fr. OE *hǣlan;* akin to OHG *heilen* to heal, OE *hāl* whole — more at WHOLE] *vt* (bef. 12c) **1 a :** to make sound or whole ⟨~ a wound⟩ **b :** to restore to health **2 a :** to cause (an undesirable condition) to be overcome **:** MEND ⟨the troubles . . . had not been forgotten, but they had been ~*ed* —William Power⟩ **b :** to patch up (a breach or division) ⟨~ a breach between friends⟩ **3 :** to restore to original purity or integrity ⟨~*ed* of sin⟩ ~ *vi* **:** to return to a sound state

heal·er \ˈhē-lər\ *n* (12c) **1 :** one that heals **2 :** a Christian Science practitioner

health \ˈhelth *also* ˈheltth\ *n, often attrib* [ME *helthe,* fr. OE *hǣlth,* fr. *hāl*] (bef. 12c) **1 a :** the condition of being sound in body, mind, or spirit; *esp* **:** freedom from physical disease or pain **b :** the general condition of the body ⟨in poor ~⟩ ⟨enjoys good ~⟩ **2 a :** flourishing condition **:** WELL-BEING ⟨defending the ~ of the beloved oceans —Peter Wilkinson⟩ **b :** general condition or state ⟨poor economic ~⟩ **3 :** a toast to someone's health or prosperity

health care *n* (1940) **:** efforts made to maintain or restore health esp. by trained and licensed professionals — usu. hyphenated when used attributively

health club *n* (1961) **:** a usu. commercial establishment having members who pay a fee to use its health and fitness facilities and equipment

health food *n* (1882) **:** a food promoted as highly conducive to health

health·ful \ˈhelth-fəl *also* ˈheltth-\ *adj* (14c) **1 :** beneficial to health of body or mind **2 :** HEALTHY ⟨he felt incapable of looking into the girl's pretty, ~ face —Saul Bellow⟩ — **health·ful·ly** *adv* — **health·ful·ness** *n*

syn HEALTHFUL, WHOLESOME, SALUBRIOUS, SALUTARY mean favorable to the health of mind or body. HEALTHFUL implies a positive contribution to a healthy condition ⟨a *healthful* diet⟩. WHOLESOME applies to what benefits, builds up, or sustains physically, mentally, or spiritually ⟨*wholesome* foods⟩ ⟨the movie is *wholesome* family entertainment⟩. SALUBRIOUS applies chiefly to the helpful effects of climate or air ⟨cool and *salubrious* weather⟩. SALUTARY describes something corrective or beneficially effective, even though it may in itself be unpleasant ⟨a *salutary* warning that resulted in increased production⟩.

health insurance *n* (1901) **:** insurance against loss through illness of the insured; *esp* **:** insurance providing compensation for medical expenses

health maintenance organization *n* (1973) **:** HMO

health spa *n* (1960) **1 :** SPA 4; *esp* **:** one emphasizing health and fitness **2 :** HEALTH CLUB

healthy \ˈhel-thē *also* ˈhelt-\ *adj* **health·i·er; -est** (1552) **1 :** enjoying health and vigor of body, mind, or spirit **:** WELL **2 :** evincing health ⟨a ~ complexion⟩ **3 :** conducive to health ⟨walk three miles every day . . . a beastly bore, but ~ —G. S. Patton⟩ **4 a :** PROSPEROUS, FLOURISHING **b :** not small or feeble **:** CONSIDERABLE — **health·i·ly** \-thə-lē\ *adv* — **health·i·ness** \-thē-nəs\ *n*

syn HEALTHY, SOUND, WHOLESOME, ROBUST, HALE, WELL mean enjoying or indicative of good health. HEALTHY implies full strength and vigor as well as freedom from signs of disease ⟨a *healthy* family⟩. SOUND emphasizes the absence of disease, weakness, or malfunction ⟨a *sound* heart⟩. WHOLESOME implies appearance and behavior indicating soundness and balance ⟨a face with a *wholesome* glow⟩. ROBUST implies the opposite of all that is delicate or sickly ⟨a lively, *robust* little boy⟩. HALE applies particularly to robustness in old age ⟨still *hale* at the age of eighty⟩. WELL implies merely freedom from disease or illness ⟨she has never been a *well* person⟩.

[1]**heap** \ˈhēp\ *n* [ME *heep,* fr. OE *hēap;* akin to OHG *houf* heap] (bef. 12c) **1 :** a collection of things thrown one on another **:** PILE **2 :** a great number or large quantity **:** LOT

[2]**heap** *vt* (bef. 12c) **1 a :** to throw or lay in a heap **:** pile or collect in great quantity ⟨his sole object was to ~ up riches⟩ **b :** to form or round into a heap ⟨~*ed* the dirt into a mound⟩ **c :** to form a heap on **:** load heavily ⟨~ the plates with food⟩ **2 :** to accord or bestow lavishly or in large quantities ⟨~*ed* honors upon them⟩

hear \ˈhir\ *vb* **heard** \ˈhərd\; **hear·ing** \ˈhir-iŋ\ [ME *heren,* fr. OE *hīeran;* akin to OHG *hōren* to hear, and prob. to L *cavēre* to be on guard, Gk *akouein* to hear] *vt* (bef. 12c) **1 :** to perceive or apprehend by the ear **2 :** to gain knowledge of by hearing **3 a :** to listen to with attention **:** HEED **b :** ATTEND ⟨~ mass⟩ **4 a :** to give a legal hearing to **b :** to take testimony from ⟨~ witnesses⟩ ~ *vi* **1 :** to have the capacity of apprehending sound **2 a :** to gain information **:** LEARN **b :** to receive communication ⟨haven't *heard* from her lately⟩ **3 :** to entertain the idea — used in the negative ⟨wouldn't ~ of it⟩ **4** — often used in the expression *Hear! Hear!* to express approval (as during a speech) — **hear·er** \ˈhir-ər\ *n*

hearing *n* (13c) **1 a :** the process, function, or power of perceiving sound; *specif* **:** the special sense by which noises and tones are received as stimuli **b :** EARSHOT **2 a :** opportunity to be heard, to present one's side of a case, or to be generally known or appreciated **b** (1) **:** a listening to arguments (2) **:** a preliminary examination in criminal procedure **c :** a session (as of a legislative committee) in which testimony is taken from witnesses **3** *chiefly dial* **:** a piece of news

hearing aid *n* (1922) **:** an electronic device usu. worn in or behind the ear of a hearing-impaired person for amplifying sound

hearing dog *n* (1952) **:** a dog trained to alert its deaf or hearing-impaired owner to sounds (as of a doorbell, alarm, or telephone) — called also *hearing ear dog*

heark·en \ˈhär-kən\ *vb* **heark·ened; heark·en·ing** \ˈhärk-niŋ, ˈhär-kə-\ [ME *herknen,* fr. OE *heorcnian;* akin to OHG *hōrechen* to listen, OE *hīeran* to hear] *vi* (bef. 12c) **1 :** LISTEN **2 :** to give respectful attention ~ *vt, archaic* **:** to give heed to **:** HEAR

hearken back *vi* (1900) **:** HARK BACK

hear·say \ˈhir-ˌsā\ *n* (ca. 1532) **1 :** RUMOR **2 :** HEARSAY EVIDENCE

hearsay evidence *n* (1753) **:** evidence based not on a witness's personal knowledge but on another's statement not made under oath

[1]**hearse** \ˈhərs\ *n* [ME *herse,* fr. AF *herce* harrow, frame for holding candles, fr. L *hirpic-, hirpex* harrow] (14c) **1 a :** an elaborate framework erected over a coffin or tomb to which memorial verses or epitaphs are

attached **b** : a triangular candelabra for 15 candles used esp. at Tenebrae **2 a** *archaic* : COFFIN **b** *obs* : BIER 2 **3** : a vehicle for conveying the dead to the grave

[2]**hearse** *vt* **hearsed; hears·ing** (1592) **1 a** *archaic* : to place on or in a hearse **b** : to convey in a hearse **2** : BURY

[1]**heart** \ˈhärt\ *n* [ME *hert,* fr. OE *heorte;* akin to OHG *herza* heart, L *cord-, cor,* Gk *kardia*] (bef. 12c) **1 a** : a hollow muscular organ of vertebrate animals that by its rhythmic contraction acts as a force pump maintaining the circulation of the blood **b** : a structure in an invertebrate animal functionally analogous to the vertebrate heart **c** : BREAST, BOSOM **d** : something resembling a heart in shape; *specif* : a stylized representation of a heart **2 a** : a playing card marked with a stylized figure of a red heart **b** *pl* : the suit comprising cards marked with hearts **c** *pl but sing or pl in constr* : a game in which the object is to avoid taking tricks containing hearts **3 a** : PERSONALITY, DISPOSITION ⟨a cold ~⟩ **b** *obs* : INTELLECT **4** : the emotional or moral as distinguished from the intellectual nature: as **a** : generous disposition : COMPASSION ⟨a leader with ~⟩ **b** : LOVE, AFFECTION ⟨won her ~⟩ **c** : COURAGE, ARDOR ⟨never lost ~⟩ **5** : one's innermost character, feelings, or inclinations ⟨knew it in his ~⟩ ⟨a man after my own ~⟩ **6 a** : the central or innermost part : CENTER **b** : the essential or most vital part of something **c** : the younger central compact part of a leafy rosette (as a head of lettuce) — **at heart** : in essence : BASICALLY, ESSENTIALLY — **by heart** : by rote or from memory — **to heart** : with deep concern

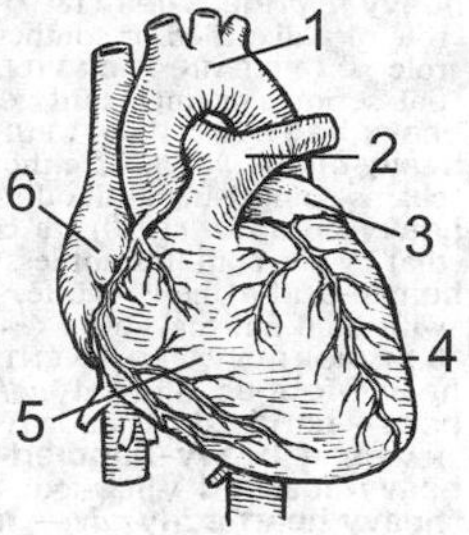

heart 1a: *1* aorta, *2* pulmonary artery, *3* left atrium, *4* left ventricle, *5* right ventricle, *6* right atrium

[2]**heart** *vt* (bef. 12c) **1** *archaic* : HEARTEN **2** *archaic* : to fix in the heart

heart·ache \ˈhärt-ˌāk\ *n* (1602) : anguish of mind : SORROW

heart attack *n* (1928) : an acute episode of heart disease marked by the death or damage of heart muscle due to insufficient blood supply to the heart usu. as a result of a coronary thrombosis or a coronary occlusion and that is characterized esp. by chest pain — called also *myocardial infarction*

heart·beat \ˈhärt-ˌbēt\ *n* (1850) **1** : one complete pulsation of the heart **2** : the vital center or driving impulse **3** : a brief space of time : FLASH — used chiefly in the phrase *in a heartbeat*

heart block *n* (1903) : incoordination of the heartbeat in which the atria and ventricles beat independently and which is marked by decreased cardiac output

heart·break \ˈhärt-ˌbrāk\ *n* (14c) : crushing grief, anguish, or distress

heart·break·er \-ˌbrā-kər\ *n* (1863) : one that causes heartbreak

heart·break·ing \-ˌbrā-kiŋ\ *adj* (1586) **1 a** : causing intense sorrow or distress **b** : extremely trying or difficult **2** : producing an intense emotional reaction or response ⟨~ beauty⟩ — **heart·break·ing·ly** \-kiŋ-lē\ *adv*

heart·bro·ken \-ˌbrō-kən\ *adj* (ca. 1586) : overcome by sorrow

heart·burn \-ˌbərn\ *n* (1597) : a burning discomfort behind the lower part of the sternum due esp. to spasmodic reflux of acid from the stomach into the esophagus

heart·burn·ing \-ˌbər-niŋ\ *n* (1513) : intense or rancorous jealousy or resentment

heart disease *n* (1850) : an abnormal organic condition of the heart or of the heart and circulation

heart·ed \ˈhär-təd\ *adj* (13c) **1** : having a heart esp. of a specified kind — usu. used in combination ⟨a faint*hearted* leader⟩ ⟨a light*hearted* wanderer⟩ **2** : seated in the heart

heart·en \ˈhär-tᵊn\ *vt* **heart·ened; heart·en·ing** \ˈhärt-niŋ, ˈhär-tᵊn-iŋ\ (1526) : to give heart to : CHEER ***syn*** see ENCOURAGE — **heart·en·ing·ly** \-niŋ-lē, -tᵊn-iŋ-\ *adv*

heart failure *n* (1894) **1** : a condition in which the heart is unable to pump blood at an adequate rate or in adequate volume **2** : cessation of heartbeat : DEATH

heart·felt \ˈhärt-ˌfelt\ *adj* (1722) : deeply felt : EARNEST ***syn*** see SINCERE

heart–free \ˈhärt-ˌfrē\ *adj* (1726) : not in love

hearth \ˈhärth\ *n* [ME *herth,* fr. OE *heorth;* akin to OHG *herd* hearth, and prob. to Skt *kūḍayāti* he scorches] (bef. 12c) **1 a** : a brick, stone, or concrete area in front of a fireplace **b** : the floor of a fireplace; *also* : FIREPLACE **c** : the lowest section of a furnace; *esp* : the section of a furnace on which the ore or metal is exposed to the flame or heat **2** : HOME **3** : a vital or creative center ⟨the central ~ of occidental civilization —A. L. Kroeber⟩

heart–healthy \ˈhärt-ˌhel-thē\ *adj* (1980) : conducive to a healthy heart and circulatory system ⟨~ exercise⟩ ⟨a ~ diet⟩

hearth·stone \-ˌstōn\ *n* (14c) **1** : stone forming a hearth **2** : HOME

heart·i·ly \ˈhär-tə-lē\ *adv* (14c) **1** : in a hearty manner **2 a** : with all sincerity : WHOLEHEARTEDLY **b** : with zest or gusto **3** : WHOLLY, THOROUGHLY ⟨~ sick of all this talk⟩

heart·land \ˈhärt-ˌland\ *n* (1904) : a central area: as **a** : a central land area (as northern Eurasia) having strategic advantages **b** : the central geographical region of the U.S. in which mainstream or traditional values predominate **c** : a region where something (as an industry or activity) most strongly thrives ⟨the ~ of high technology⟩

heart·less \-ləs\ *adj* (14c) **1** *archaic* : SPIRITLESS **2** : lacking feeling : CRUEL — **heart·less·ly** *adv* — **heart·less·ness** *n*

heart–lung machine *n* (1953) : a mechanical pump that maintains circulation during heart surgery by shunting blood away from the heart, oxygenating it, and returning it to the body

heart pine *n* (1838) : LONGLEAF PINE

heart·rend·ing \ˈhärt-ˌren-diŋ\ *adj* (1594) : HEARTBREAKING 1a — **heart·rend·ing·ly** \-diŋ-lē\ *adv*

hearts·ease \ˈhärts-ˌēz\ *n* (15c) **1** : peace of mind : TRANQUILLITY **2** : any of various violas; *esp* : JOHNNY-JUMP-UP

heart·sick \ˈhärt-ˌsik\ *adj* (1526) : very despondent : DEPRESSED — **heart·sick·ness** *n*

heart·some \ˈhert-səm, ˈhärt-\ *adj* (1596) *chiefly Scot* : giving spirit or vigor : ANIMATING, ENLIVENING — **heart·some·ly** *adv, chiefly Scot*

heart·sore \ˈhärt-ˌsȯr\ *adj* (1591) : HEARTSICK

heart–stop·ping \ˈhärt-ˌstä-piŋ\ *adj* (1943) : extremely shocking or exciting ⟨a ~ adventure⟩ ⟨~ views⟩ — **heart–stop·per** \-pər\ *n*

heart·string \-ˌstriŋ\ *n* (15c) **1** *obs* : a nerve once believed to sustain the heart **2** : the deepest emotions or affections ⟨pulled at his ~*s*⟩

heart·throb \-ˌthräb\ *n* (1839) **1** : the throb of a heart **2 a** : sentimental emotion : PASSION **b** : SWEETHEART; *also* : a usu. renowned man (as an entertainer) noted for his sex appeal ⟨teen ~*s*⟩

[1]**heart–to–heart** \ˈhärt-tə-ˈhärt\ *adj* (1867) : SINCERE, FRANK ⟨a ~ talk⟩

[2]**heart–to–heart** *n* (1910) : a heart-to-heart conversation

heart·warm·ing \ˈhärt-ˌwȯr-miŋ\ *adj* (1743) : inspiring sympathetic feeling : CHEERING — **heart–warm·er** *n*

heart–whole \-ˌhōl\ *adj* (1600) **1** : HEART-FREE **2** : SINCERE, GENUINE

heart·wood \-ˌwu̇d\ *n* (1810) : the older harder nonliving central wood of trees that is usu. darker, denser, less permeable, and more durable than the surrounding sapwood

heart·worm \-ˌwərm\ *n* (1888) : a filarial worm (*Dirofilaria immitis*) that is a parasite esp. in the right heart of dogs and is transmitted by mosquitoes; *also* : infestation or disease caused by the heartworm

[1]**hearty** \ˈhär-tē\ *adj* **heart·i·er; -est** (14c) **1 a** : giving unqualified support ⟨a ~ endorsement⟩ **b** : enthusiastically or exuberantly cordial : JOVIAL **c** : expressed unrestrainedly **2 a** : exhibiting vigorous good health **b** (1) : having a good appetite (2) : abundant, rich, or flavorful enough to satisfy the appetite **3** : VIGOROUS, VEHEMENT ⟨a ~ pull⟩ ***syn*** see SINCERE — **heart·i·ness** *n*

[2]**hearty** *n, pl* **heart·ies** (1803) : a hearty fellow; *also* : SAILOR

[1]**heat** \ˈhēt\ *vb* [ME *heten,* fr. OE *hǣtan;* akin to OE *hāt* hot] *vi* (bef. 12c) **1** : to become warm or hot **2** : to start to spoil from heat ~ *vt* **1** : to make warm or hot **2** : EXCITE — **heat·able** \ˈhē-tə-bəl\ *adj*

[2]**heat** *n* [ME *hete,* fr. OE *hǣte, hǣtu;* akin to OE *hāt* hot] (bef. 12c) **1 a** (1) : a condition of being hot : WARMTH (2) : a marked or notable degree of hotness **b** : pathological excessive bodily temperature **c** : a hot place or situation **d** (1) : a period of heat (2) : a single complete operation of heating; *also* : the quantity of material so heated **e** (1) : added energy that causes substances to rise in temperature, fuse, evaporate, expand, or undergo any of various other related changes, that flows to a body by contact with or radiation from bodies at higher temperatures, and that can be produced in a body (as by compression) (2) : the energy associated with the random motions of the molecules, atoms, or smaller structural units of which matter is composed **f** : appearance, condition, or color of a body as indicating its temperature **2 a** : intensity of feeling or reaction : PASSION **b** : the height or stress of an action or condition ⟨in the ~ of battle⟩ **c** : sexual excitement esp. in a female mammal; *specif* : ESTRUS **3** : a single continuous effort: as **a** : a single round of a contest (as a race) having two or more rounds for each contestant **b** : one of several preliminary contests held to eliminate less competent contenders **4** : pungency of flavor **5 a** *slang* (1) : the intensification of law-enforcement activity or investigation (2) : POLICE **b** : PRESSURE, COERCION **c** : ABUSE, CRITICISM ⟨took ~ for her mistakes⟩ **6** : SMOKE 8 **7** *slang* : GUN 1b — **heat·less** \ˈhēt-ləs\ *adj* — **heat·proof** \-ˌprüf\ *adj*

heat cramps *n pl* (1938) : a condition that is marked by sudden development of cramps in skeletal muscles and that results from prolonged work or exercise in high temperatures accompanied by profuse perspiration with loss of sodium chloride from the body

heat·ed \ˈhē-təd\ *adj* (1886) : marked by anger or passion ⟨a ~ argument⟩ — **heat·ed·ly** *adv*

heat engine *n* (ca. 1895) : a mechanism (as an internal combustion engine) for converting heat energy into mechanical or electrical energy

heat·er \ˈhē-tər\ *n* (15c) **1** : one that heats; *esp* : a device that imparts heat or holds something to be heated **2** : FASTBALL

heat exchanger *n* (1902) : a device (as an automobile radiator) for transferring heat from one fluid to another without allowing them to mix

heat exhaustion *n* (1939) : a condition marked by weakness, nausea, dizziness, and profuse sweating that results from physical exertion in a hot environment — called also *heat prostration*; compare HEATSTROKE

heath \ˈhēth\ *n* [ME *heth,* fr. OE *hǣth;* akin to OHG *heida* heather, OW *coit* forest] (bef. 12c) **1 a** : a tract of wasteland **b** : an extensive area of rather level open uncultivated land usu. with poor coarse soil, inferior drainage, and a surface rich in peat or peaty humus **2 a** : any of a family (Ericaceae, the heath family) of shrubby dicotyledonous and often evergreen plants that thrive on open barren usu. acid and ill-drained soil; *esp* : an evergreen subshrub of either of two genera (*Erica* and *Calluna*) with whorls of needlelike leaves and clusters of small flowers **b** : any of various plants that resemble true heaths — **heath·less** \-ləs\ *adj* — **heath·like** \-ˌlīk\ *adj* — **heathy** \ˈhē-thē\ *adj*

[1]**hea·then** \ˈhē-t͟hən\ *adj* [ME *hethen,* fr. OE *hǣthen;* akin to OHG *heidan* heathen, and prob. to OE *hǣth* heath] (bef. 12c) **1** : of or relating to heathens, their religions, or their customs **2** : STRANGE, UNCIVILIZED

[2]**heathen** *n, pl* **heathens** *or* **heathen** (bef. 12c) **1** : an unconverted member of a people or nation that does not acknowledge the God of the Bible **2** : an uncivilized or irreligious person — **hea·then·dom** \-dəm\ *n* — **hea·then·ism** \-t͟hə-ˌni-zəm\ *n* — **hea·then·ize** \-t͟hə-ˌnīz\ *vt*

hea·then·ish \ˈhē-t͟hə-nish\ *adj* (1567) : resembling or characteristic of heathens : BARBAROUS — **hea·then·ish·ly** *adv*

[1]**heath·er** \ˈhe-t͟hər\ *n* [ME (northern) *hather*] (14c) : HEATH 2a; *esp* : a common Eurasian heath (*Calluna vulgaris*) of northern and alpine regions that has small crowded sessile leaves and racemes of tiny usu. purplish-pink flowers and is naturalized in the northeastern U.S.

[2]**heather** *adj* (1615) : HEATHERY

heath·ery \ˈheth-rē, ˈhe-thə-\ *adj* (1535) **1 :** of, relating to, or resembling heather **2 :** having flecks of various colors ⟨a soft ~ tweed⟩

heath hen *n* (1644) **:** a now extinct grouse (*Tympanuchus cupido cupido*) of the northeastern U.S. — compare PRAIRIE CHICKEN

heath·land \ˈhēth-ˌland\ *n* (1819) **:** HEATH 1

heat lightning *n* (1810) **:** vivid and extensive flashes of electric light without thunder seen near the horizon esp. at the close of a hot day and ascribed to far-off lightning reflected by high clouds

heat pump *n* (1894) **:** an apparatus for heating or cooling (as a building) by transferring heat by mechanical means from or to an external reservoir (as the ground, water, or outside air)

heat rash *n* (1887) **:** PRICKLY HEAT

heat shield *n* (1962) **:** a barrier of ablative material to protect a space capsule from heat on its entry into an atmosphere

heat–shock protein *n* (1978) **:** any of a group of proteins that are produced esp. in cells subjected to stressful conditions (as high temperature), that serve to ensure proper protein folding, and that are held to comprise a class of molecular chaperones

heat sink *n* (1936) **:** a substance or device that absorbs or dissipates esp. unwanted heat (as from a process or an electronic device)

heat·stroke \ˈhēt-ˌstrōk\ *n* (1874) **:** a condition marked esp. by cessation of sweating, extremely high body temperature, and collapse that results from prolonged exposure to high temperature — compare HEAT EXHAUSTION

heat–treat \ˈhēt-ˌtrēt\ *vt* (1907) **:** to subject to heat; *esp* **:** to treat (as metals) by heating and cooling in a way that will produce desired properties — **heat treater** *n* — **heat treatment** *n*

heat wave *n* (1893) **:** a period of unusually hot weather

[1]**heave** \ˈhēv\ *vb* **heaved** *or* **hove** \ˈhōv\; **heav·ing** [ME *heven,* fr. OE *hebban;* akin to OHG *hevan* to lift, L *capere* to take] *vt* (bef. 12c) **1** *obs* **:** ELEVATE **2 :** LIFT, RAISE ⟨*heaved* the trunk onto the table⟩ **3 :** THROW, CAST ⟨*heaving* rocks⟩ **4 a :** to cause to swell or rise **b :** to displace (as a rock stratum) esp. by a fault **5 :** to utter with obvious effort or with a deep breath ⟨~ a sigh of relief⟩ **6 :** HAUL, DRAW ~ *vi* **1 :** LABOR, STRUGGLE **2 :** RETCH **3 a :** to rise and fall rhythmically **b :** PANT **4 a :** PULL, PUSH ⟨*heaving* on a rope⟩ **b :** to move a ship in a specified direction or manner **c** *past usu hove* **:** to move in an indicated way ⟨the ship *hove* into view⟩ **5 :** to rise or become thrown or raised up ***syn*** see LIFT — **heav·er** *n* — **heave to :** to halt the headway of a ship (as by positioning a sailboat with the jib aback and the rudder turned sharply to windward)

[2]**heave** *n* (ca. 1571) **1 a :** an effort to heave or raise **b :** HURL, CAST **2 :** an upward motion **:** RISING; *esp* **:** a rhythmical rising **3 :** horizontal displacement esp. by the faulting of a rock **4** *pl but sing or pl in constr* **:** chronic pulmonary emphysema of the horse resulting in difficult expiration, heaving of the flanks, and a persistent cough

heave–ho \ˈhēv-ˈhō\ *n* [fr. *heave ho!,* interjection used when heaving on a rope] (1947) **:** DISMISSAL ⟨gave him the old ~⟩

heav·en \ˈhe-vən\ *n* [ME *heven,* fr. OE *heofon;* akin to OHG *himil* heaven] (bef. 12c) **1 :** the expanse of space that seems to be over the earth like a dome **:** FIRMAMENT — usu. used in pl. **2 a** *often cap* **:** the dwelling place of the Deity and the blessed dead **b :** a spiritual state of everlasting communion with God **3** *cap* **:** GOD 1 **4 :** a place or condition of utmost happiness **5** *Christian Science* **:** a state of thought in which sin is absent and the harmony of divine Mind is manifest

heav·en·ly \-lē\ *adj* (bef. 12c) **1 :** of or relating to heaven or the heavens **:** CELESTIAL ⟨the ~ choirs⟩ ⟨use a telescope to study the ~ bodies⟩ **2 a :** suggesting the blessed state of heaven **:** BEATIFIC ⟨~ peace⟩ **b :** DELIGHTFUL — **heav·en·li·ness** *n*

heav·en–sent \-ˌsent\ *adj* (1612) **:** PROVIDENTIAL

heav·en·ward \-wərd\ *adv or adj* (13c) **:** toward heaven

heav·en·wards \-wərdz\ *adv* (1650) **:** HEAVENWARD

heavier–than–air *adj* (1903) **:** of greater weight than the air displaced

heavi·ly \ˈhe-və-lē\ *adv* (bef. 12c) **1 :** to a great degree **:** SEVERELY **2 :** slowly and laboriously **:** DULLY **3** *archaic* **:** with sorrow **:** GRIEVOUSLY **4 :** in a heavy manner

Heav·i·side layer \ˈhe-vē-ˌsīd-\ *n* [Oliver *Heaviside*] (1912) **:** IONOSPHERE

[1]**heavy** \ˈhe-vē\ *adj* **heavi·er; -est** [ME *hevy,* fr. OE *hefig;* akin to OHG *hebīc* heavy, OE *hebban* to lift — more at HEAVE] (bef. 12c) **1 a :** having great weight; *also* **:** characterized by mass or weight ⟨how ~ is it?⟩ **b :** having a high specific gravity **:** having great weight in proportion to bulk **c** (1) *of an isotope* **:** having or being atoms of greater than normal mass for that element (2) *of a compound* **:** containing heavy isotopes **2 :** hard to bear; *specif* **:** GRIEVOUS, AFFLICTIVE ⟨a ~ sorrow⟩ **3 :** of weighty import **:** SERIOUS ⟨~ consequences⟩ **4 :** DEEP, PROFOUND ⟨a ~ silence⟩ **5 a :** borne down by something oppressive **:** BURDENED **b :** PREGNANT; *esp* **:** approaching parturition **6 a :** slow or dull from loss of vitality or resiliency **:** SLUGGISH ⟨a tired ~ step⟩ **b :** lacking sparkle or vivacity **:** DRAB **c :** lacking mirth or gaiety **:** DOLEFUL **d :** characterized by declining prices **7 :** dulled with weariness **:** DROWSY **8 :** greater in quantity or quality than the average of its kind or class: as **a :** of unusually large size or amount ⟨a ~ turnout⟩ ⟨~ traffic⟩ **b :** of great force ⟨~ seas⟩ **c :** threatening to rain or snow **d** (1) **:** impeding motion (2) **:** full of clay and inclined to hold water **e :** coming as if from a depth **:** LOUD ⟨~ breathing⟩ **f :** THICK, COARSE ⟨~ syrup⟩ **g :** OPPRESSIVE ⟨a ~ odor⟩ ⟨~ weather⟩ ⟨rule with a ~ hand⟩ **h :** STEEP, ACUTE **i :** LABORIOUS, DIFFICULT ⟨~ going⟩ **j :** IMMODERATE ⟨a ~ smoker⟩ **k :** more powerful than usual for its kind ⟨a ~ cavalry⟩ ⟨a ~ cruiser⟩ **l :** of large capacity or output **9 a :** very rich and hard to digest ⟨~ desserts⟩ **b :** not properly raised or leavened ⟨~ bread⟩ **10 :** producing goods (as coal, steel, or chemicals) used in the production of other goods ⟨~ industry⟩ **11 a :** having stress ⟨a ~ rhythm⟩ — used esp. of syllables in accentual verse **b :** being the strongest degree of stress in speech **12 :** relating to theatrical parts of a grave or somber nature **13 :** LONG 9 ⟨~ on ideas⟩ **14 :** IMPORTANT, PROMINENT ⟨a ~ politician⟩ — **heavi·ness** *n*

syn HEAVY, WEIGHTY, PONDEROUS, CUMBROUS, CUMBERSOME mean having great weight. HEAVY implies that something has greater density or thickness than the average of its kind or class ⟨a *heavy* child for his age⟩. WEIGHTY suggests having actual and not just relative weight ⟨a load of *weighty* boxes⟩. PONDEROUS implies having great weight because of size and massiveness with resulting great inertia ⟨*ponderous* elephants in a circus parade⟩. CUMBROUS and CUMBERSOME imply heaviness and bulkiness that make for difficulty in grasping, moving, carrying, or manipulating ⟨wrestled with the *cumbrous* furniture⟩ ⟨early cameras were *cumbersome* and inconvenient⟩.

[2]**heavy** *adv* (bef. 12c) **:** in a heavy manner **:** HEAVILY

[3]**heavy** *n, pl* **heav·ies** (1897) **1 :** HEAVYWEIGHT 2 **2 a :** a theatrical role of a dignified or somber character; *also* **:** an actor playing such a role **b :** VILLAIN 4 **c :** VILLAIN 5 **d :** someone or something influential, serious, or important **e :** ELITE 1b

heavy bag *n* (ca. 1949) **:** PUNCHING BAG 1

heavy chain *n* (1964) **:** either of the two larger of the four polypeptide chains comprising antibodies — compare LIGHT CHAIN

heavy cream *n* (1930) **:** a cream that is markedly thick; *esp* **:** cream that by law contains not less than 36 percent butterfat

heavy–du·ty \ˌhe-vē-ˈdü-tē, -ˈdyü-\ *adj* (1914) **1 :** able or designed to withstand unusual strain ⟨~ trucks⟩ **2 :** INTENSIVE ⟨~ bargaining⟩ **3 :** IMPORTANT, PROMINENT ⟨~ lawyers⟩

heavy–foot·ed \-ˈfu̇-təd\ *adj* (1625) **:** heavy and slow in movement

heavy–hand·ed \-ˈhan-dəd\ *adj* (1647) **1 :** CLUMSY **2 :** OPPRESSIVE, HARSH — **heavy–hand·ed·ly** *adv* — **heavy–hand·ed·ness** *n*

heavy·heart·ed \-ˈhär-təd\ *adj* (14c) **:** DESPONDENT, SADDENED — **heavy·heart·ed·ly** *adv* — **heavy·heart·ed·ness** *n*

heavy hitter *n* (1976) **:** BIG SHOT, HEAVY

heavy hydrogen *n* (1933) **:** DEUTERIUM

heavy lifting *n* (1980) **:** a burdensome or laborious duty

heavy metal *n* (1973) **:** energetic and highly amplified electronic rock music having a hard beat

heavy·set \ˌhe-vē-ˈset\ *adj* (1922) **:** stocky and compact and sometimes tending to stoutness in build

heavy water *n* (1933) **1 :** the compound D_2O composed of deuterium and oxygen — called also *deuterium oxide* **2 :** water enriched in deuterium

heavy·weight \ˈhe-vē-ˌwāt\ *n, often attrib* (1857) **1 :** one that is above average in weight **2 :** one in the usu. heaviest class of contestants: as **a :** a boxer in an unlimited weight division — compare LIGHT HEAVYWEIGHT **b :** a weight lifter weighing more than 198 pounds **3 :** one that possesses great power, prominence, or stature

Heb *abbr* Hebrew; Hebrews

heb·do·mad \ˈheb-də-ˌmad\ *n* [L *hebdomad-, hebdomas,* fr. Gk, fr. *hebdomos* seventh, fr. *hepta* seven — more at SEVEN] (1545) **1 :** a group of seven **2 :** a period of seven days **:** WEEK

heb·dom·a·dal \heb-ˈdä-mə-dᵊl\ *adj* (1711) **:** WEEKLY — **heb·dom·a·dal·ly** \-dᵊl-ē\ *adv*

hebe \ˈhēb\ *n, often cap* [short for *Hebrew*] (1926) *usu offensive* **:** JEW

He·be \ˈhē-bē\ *n* [L, fr. Gk *Hēbē*] (1561) **:** the Greek goddess of youth and a cupbearer to the gods

he·be·phre·nia \ˌhē-bə-ˈfrē-nē-ə, -ˈfre-nē-\ *n* [NL, irreg. fr. Gk *hēbētēs* young adult (fr. *hēbē* youth) + E *-phrenia;* fr. the childish behavior which is often found with it] (1883) **:** a form of schizophrenia characterized esp. by incoherence, delusions lacking an underlying theme, and affect that is usu. flat, inappropriate, or silly — **he·be·phre·nic** \-ˈfre-nik, -ˈfrē-nik\ *adj or n*

heb·e·tate \ˈhe-bə-ˌtāt\ *vt* **-tat·ed; -tat·ing** [L *hebetatus,* pp. of *hebetare,* fr. *hebet-, hebes* dull] (1574) **:** to make dull or obtuse — **heb·e·ta·tion** \ˌhe-bə-ˈtā-shən\ *n*

heb·e·tude \ˈhe-bə-ˌtüd, -ˌtyüd\ *n* [LL *hebetudo,* fr. L *hebēre* to be dull; akin to L *hebes* dull] (ca. 1621) **:** LETHARGY, DULLNESS — **heb·e·tu·di·nous** \ˌhe-bə-ˈtü-dᵊn-əs, -ˈtyü-\ *adj*

He·bra·ic \hi-ˈbrā-ik\ *adj* [ME *Ebrayke,* fr. LL *Hebraicus,* fr. Gk *Hebraikos,* fr. *Hebraios*] (14c) **:** of, relating to, or characteristic of the Hebrews or their language or culture — **He·bra·i·cal·ly** \-ˈbrā-ə-k(ə-)lē\ *adv*

He·bra·ism \ˈhē-(ˌ)brā-ˌi-zəm\ *n* (1570) **1 :** a characteristic feature of Hebrew occurring in another language **2 :** the thought, spirit, or practice characteristic of the Hebrews **3 :** a moral theory or emphasis attributed to the Hebrews

He·bra·ist \-ˌbrā-ist\ *n* (1751) **:** a specialist in Hebrew and Hebraic studies

He·bra·is·tic \ˌhē-brā-ˈis-tik\ *adj* (1690) **1 :** marked by Hebraisms **2 :** HEBRAIC

he·bra·ize \ˈhē-brā-ˌīz\ *vb* **-ized; -iz·ing** *often cap, vi* (1645) **:** to use Hebraisms ~ *vt* **:** to make Hebraic in character or form — **he·bra·i·za·tion** \ˌhē-ˌbrā-ə-ˈzā-shən\ *n, often cap*

He·brew \ˈhē-(ˌ)brü\ *n* [ME *Ebreu,* fr. AF, fr. LL *Hebraeus,* fr. L, adj., fr. Gk *Hebraios,* fr. Aram *ʽEbrai*] (13c) **1 a :** the Semitic language of the ancient Hebrews **b :** any of various later forms of this language **2 :** a member of or descendant from one of a group of northern Semitic peoples including the Israelites; *esp* **:** ISRAELITE — **Hebrew** *adj*

He·brews \ˈhē-(ˌ)brüz\ *n pl but sing in constr* (14c) **:** a theological treatise addressed to early Christians and included as a book in the New Testament — see BIBLE table

Hec·ate \ˈhe-kə-tē, ˈhe-kət\ *n* [L, fr. Gk *Hekatē*] (1567) **:** a Greek goddess associated esp. with the underworld, night, and witchcraft

hec·a·tomb \ˈhe-kə-ˌtōm\ *n* [L *hecatombe,* fr. Gk *hekatombē,* fr. *hekaton* hundred + *-bē;* akin to Gk *bous* cow — more at HUNDRED, COW] (ca. 1592) **1 :** an ancient Greek and Roman sacrifice of 100 oxen or cattle **2 :** the sacrifice or slaughter of many victims

heck \ˈhek\ *n* [euphemism] (1887) **1 :** HELL 2 ⟨all ~ breaks loose⟩ **2 :** HELL 4 ⟨a ~ of a lot of money⟩

heck·le \ˈhe-kəl\ *vt* **heck·led; heck·ling** \-k(ə-)liŋ\ [ME *hekelen* to dress flax, scratch, fr. *heckele* hackle; akin to OHG *hāko* hook — more at HOOK] (ca. 1825) **:** to harass and try to disconcert with questions, challenges, or gibes **:** BADGER ***syn*** see BAIT — **heck·ler** \-k(ə-)lər\ *n*

hect- *or* **hecto-** *comb form* [F, irreg. fr. Gk *hekaton*] **:** hundred ⟨*hect*are⟩

hect·are \ˈhek-ˌter, -ˌtär\ *n* [F, fr. *hect-* + *are* [2]are] (1810) — see METRIC SYSTEM table

hec·tic \ˈhek-tik\ *adj* [ME *etyk,* fr. AF *etique,* fr. LL *hecticus,* fr. Gk *hektikos* habitual, consumptive, fr. *echein* to have — more at SCHEME] (14c) **1 :** of, relating to, or being a fluctuating but persistent fever (as in tuberculosis) **2 :** having a hectic fever **3 :** RED, FLUSHED **4 :** characterized by activity, excitement, or confusion ⟨the ~ days before the holidays⟩ — **hec·ti·cal·ly** \-ti-k(ə-)lē\ *adv*

hec·to·gram \ˈhek-tə-ˌgram\ *n* [F *hectogramme,* fr. *hect-* + *gramme* gram] (1810) — see METRIC SYSTEM table

hec·to·graph \-ˌgraf\ *n* [G *Hektograph,* fr. *hekto-* hect- + *-graph* -graph] (1880) : a machine for making copies of a writing or drawing produced on a gelatin surface — **hectograph** *vt*

hec·to·li·ter \ˈhek-tə-ˌlē-tər\ *n* [F *hectolitre,* fr. *hect-* + *litre* liter] (1810) — see METRIC SYSTEM table

hec·to·me·ter \ˈhek-tə-ˌmē-tər, hek-ˈtä-mə-tər\ *n* [F *hectomètre,* fr. *hect-* + *mètre* meter] (1810) — see METRIC SYSTEM table

[1]**hec·tor** \ˈhek-tər\ *n* [L, fr. Gk *Hektōr*] (14c) **1** *cap* : a son of Priam, husband of Andromache, and Trojan champion slain by Achilles **2** : BULLY, BRAGGART

[2]**hector** *vb* **hec·tored; hec·tor·ing** \-t(ə-)riŋ\ *vi* (1660) : to play the bully : SWAGGER ~ *vt* : to intimidate or harass by bluster or personal pressure ***syn*** see BAIT — **hec·tor·ing·ly** \-t(ə-)riŋ-lē\ *adv*

Hec·u·ba \ˈhe-kyə-bə\ *n* [L, fr. Gk *Hekabē*] : the wife of Priam in Homer's *Iliad*

he'd \ˈhēd, ēd\ (1599) : he had : he would

hed·dle \ˈhe-dᵊl\ *n* [prob. alter. of ME *helde,* fr. OE *hefeld;* akin to ON *hafald* heddle, OE *hebban* to lift — more at HEAVE] (1513) : one of the sets of parallel cords or wires that with their mounting compose the harness used to guide warp threads in a loom

he·der *also* **che·der** \ˈkā-dər, ˈke-\ *n* [Yiddish *kheyder,* fr. Heb *ḥedher* room] (1882) : an elementary Jewish school in which children are taught to read the Torah and other books in Hebrew

[1]**hedge** \ˈhej\ *n* [ME *hegge,* fr. OE *hecg;* akin to OE *haga* hedge, hawthorn] (bef. 12c) **1 a** : a fence or boundary formed by a dense row of shrubs or low trees **b** : BARRIER, LIMIT **2** : a means of protection or defense (as against financial loss) **3** : a calculatedly noncommittal or evasive statement

[2]**hedge** *vb* **hedged; hedg·ing** *vt* (14c) **1** : to enclose or protect with or as if with a hedge : ENCIRCLE **2** : to hem in or obstruct with or as if with a barrier : HINDER ‹*hedged* about by special regulations and statutes —Sandi Rosenbloom› **3** : to protect oneself from losing or failing by a counterbalancing action ‹~ a bet› ~ *vi* **1** : to plant, form, or trim a hedge **2** : to evade the risk of commitment esp. by leaving open a way of retreat : TRIM **3** : to protect oneself financially: as **a** : to buy or sell commodity futures as a protection against loss due to price fluctuation **b** : to minimize the risk of a bet — **hedg·er** *n* — **hedg·ing·ly** \ˈhe-jiŋ-lē\ *adv*

[3]**hedge** *adj* (14c) **1** : of, relating to, or designed for a hedge **2** : born, living, or made near or as if near hedges : ROADSIDE **3** : INFERIOR 3

hedge fund *n* (1966) : an investing group usu. in the form of a limited partnership that employs speculative techniques in the hope of obtaining large capital gains

hedge·hog \ˈhej-ˌhȯg, -ˌhäg\ *n* (15c) **1 a** : any of a subfamily (Erinaceinae) of Eurasian and African nocturnal insectivores that have both hair and spines which they present outwardly by rolling themselves up when threatened **b** : any of several spiny mammals (as a porcupine) **2 a** : a military defensive obstacle (as of barbed wire) **b** : a well-fortified military stronghold

hedge·hop \-ˌhäp\ *vi* [back-formation fr. *hedgehopper*] (1926) : to fly an airplane close to the ground and rise over obstacles as they appear — **hedge·hop·per** *n*

hedge·pig \-ˌpig\ *n* (1605) : HEDGEHOG

hedge·row \-ˌrō\ *n* (bef. 12c) : a row of shrubs or trees enclosing or separating fields

he·don·ic \hi-ˈdä-nik\ *adj* (1656) **1** : of, relating to, or characterized by pleasure **2** : of, relating to, or characterized by hedonism — **he·don·i·cal·ly** \-ni-k(ə-)lē\ *adv*

he·do·nism \ˈhē-də-ˌni-zəm\ *n* [Gk *hēdonē* pleasure; akin to Gk *hēdys* sweet — more at SWEET] (1856) **1** : the doctrine that pleasure or happiness is the sole or chief good in life **2** : a way of life based on or suggesting the principles of hedonism — **he·do·nist** \-nist\ *n* — **he·do·nis·tic** \ˌhē-də-ˈnis-tik\ *adj* — **he·do·nis·ti·cal·ly** \-ti-k(ə-)lē\ *adv*

-hedral *adj comb form* [NL *-hedron*] : having (such) a surface or (such or so many) surfaces ‹di*hedral*›

-hedron *n comb form, pl* **-hedrons** *or* **-hedra** [NL, fr. Gk *-edron,* fr. *hedra* seat — more at SIT] : crystal or geometrical figure having a (specified) form or number of surfaces ‹penta*hedron*› ‹trapezo*hedron*›

hee·bie–jee·bies \ˌhē-bē-ˈjē-bēz\ *n pl* [coined by Billy DeBeck †1942 Am. cartoonist] (1923) : JITTERS, CREEPS

[1]**heed** \ˈhēd\ *vb* [ME, fr. OE *hēdan;* akin to OHG *huota* guard, OE *hōd* hood] *vi* (bef. 12c) : to pay attention ~ *vt* : to give consideration or attention to : MIND ‹~ what he says› ‹~ the call›

[2]**heed** *n* (14c) : ATTENTION, NOTICE

heed·ful \ˈhēd-fəl\ *adj* (1540) : taking heed : ATTENTIVE ‹~ of what they were doing› — **heed·ful·ly** \-fə-lē\ *adv* — **heed·ful·ness** *n*

heed·less \-ləs\ *adj* (1565) : not taking heed : INCONSIDERATE, THOUGHTLESS ‹~ follies of unbridled youth —John DeBruyn› — **heed·less·ly** *adv* — **heed·less·ness** *n*

hee–haw \ˈhē-ˌhȯ, -ˈhȯ\ *n* [imit.] (1815) **1** : the bray of a donkey **2** : a loud rude laugh : GUFFAW — **hee–haw** *vi*

[1]**heel** \ˈhēl\ *n* [ME, fr. OE *hēla;* akin to ON *hæll* heel, OE *hōh* — more at HOCK] (bef. 12c) **1 a** : the back of the human foot below the ankle and behind the arch **b** : the part of the hind limb of other vertebrates that is homologous with the human heel **2** : an anatomical structure suggestive of the human heel; *esp* : the part of the palm of the hand nearest the wrist **3** : one of the crusty ends of a loaf of bread **4 a** : the part (as of a shoe) that covers the human heel **b** : a solid attachment of a shoe or boot forming the back of the sole under the heel of the foot **5** : a rear, low, or bottom part: as **a** : the after end of a ship's keel or the lower end of a mast **b** : the base of a tuber or cutting of a plant used for propagation **c** : the base of a ladder **6** : a contemptible person — **heel·less** \ˈhēl-ləs\ *adj* — **by the heels** : in a tight grip — **down at heel** *or* **down at the heel** : in or into a run-down or shabby condition — **on the heels of** : immediately following — **to heel 1** : close behind **2** : into agreement or line — **under heel** : under control or subjection

[2]**heel** *vt* (1605) **1 a** : to furnish with a heel **b** : to supply esp. with money **2 a** : to exert pressure on, propel, or strike with the heel ‹~*ed* her horse› **b** : to urge (as a lagging animal) by following closely or by nipping at the heels ‹dogs ~*ing* cattle› ~ *vi* : to move along at someone's heels

[3]**heel** *vb* [alter. of ME *heelden,* fr. OE *hieldan;* akin to OHG *hald* inclined, Lith *šalis* side, region] *vi* (1575) : to lean to one side : TIP; *esp, of a boat or ship* : to lean temporarily (as from the action of wind or waves) — compare LIST ~ *vt* : to cause (a boat) to heel

[4]**heel** *n* (1760) : a tilt (as of a boat) to one side; *also* : the extent of such a tilt

heel–and–toe \ˌhēl-ən-ˈtō\ *adj* (1827) : marked by a stride in which the heel of one foot touches the ground before the toe of the other foot leaves it ‹~ walking›

heel·ball \ˈhēl-ˌbȯl\ *n* (1822) : a composition of wax and lampblack used by shoemakers for polishing and by antiquarians for making rubbings of inscriptions

heel·er \ˈhē-lər\ *n* (1647) **1 a** : one that heels **b** : AUSTRALIAN CATTLE DOG **2 a** : a henchman of a local political boss **b** : a worker for a local party organization; *esp* : WARD HEELER

heel fly *n* (1878) : CATTLE GRUB

heel·piece \ˈhēl-ˌpēs\ *n* (1705) : a piece designed for or forming the heel (as of a shoe)

heel·tap \-ˌtap\ *n* (1780) : a small quantity of alcoholic beverage remaining (as in a glass after drinking)

[1]**heft** \ˈheft\ *n* [fr. *heave,* after such pairs as *weave : weft*] (15c) **1 a** : WEIGHT, HEAVINESS **b** : IMPORTANCE, INFLUENCE **2** *archaic* : the greater part of something : BULK

[2]**heft** *vt* (ca. 1661) **1** : to heave up : HOIST **2** : to test the weight of by lifting ‹~*ing* the rod . . . to get the feel of it —*Consumer Reports*›

hefty \ˈhef-tē\ *adj* **heft·i·er; -est** (1863) **1** : quite heavy **2 a** : marked by bigness, bulk, and usu. strength ‹a ~ football player› **b** : POWERFUL, MIGHTY **c** : impressively large : SUBSTANTIAL ‹~ portions› — **heft·i·ly** \-tə-lē\ *adv* — **heft·i·ness** \-tē-nəs\ *n*

he·gari \hi-ˈga-rē, -ˈga-rə; ˈhī-ˌgir\ *n* [Ar dial. (Sudan) *ḥijērī,* perh. alter. of Ar *ḥijārī* stony] (1919) : any of several Sudanese grain sorghums having chalky white seeds including one grown in the southwestern U.S.

[1]**He·ge·li·an** \hā-ˈgā-lē-ən, hi-\ *adj* (1838) : of, relating to, or characteristic of Hegel, his philosophy, or his dialectic method

[2]**Hegelian** *n* (1843) : a follower of Hegel : an adherent of Hegelianism

He·ge·li·an·ism \-lē-ə-ˌni-zəm\ *n* (1846) : the philosophy of Hegel that places ultimate reality in ideas rather than in things and that uses dialectic to comprehend an absolute idea behind phenomena

heg·e·mon \ˈhe-jə-ˌmän, ˈhē-\ *n* [Gk *hēgemōn*] (1904) : one (as a political state) possessing hegemony

he·gem·o·ny \hi-ˈje-mə-nē, -ˈge-; ˈhe-jə-ˌmō-nē\ *n* [Gk *hēgemonia,* fr. *hēgemōn* leader, fr. *hēgeisthai* to lead — more at SEEK] (1567) **1** : preponderant influence or authority over others : DOMINATION ‹battled for ~ in Asia› **2** : the social, cultural, ideological, or economic influence exerted by a dominant group — **heg·e·mon·ic** \ˌhe-jə-ˈmä-nik, ˌhe-gə-\ *adj*

he·gi·ra *also* **he·ji·ra** \hi-ˈjī-rə, ˈhe-jə-rə\ *n* [the *Hegira,* flight of Muhammad from Mecca in A.D. 622, fr. ML, fr. Ar *hijra,* lit., departure] (1753) : a journey esp. when undertaken to escape from a dangerous or undesirable situation : EXODUS

Hei·del·berg man \ˌhī-dᵊl-ˌbərg-, -ˌberg-\ *n* [*Heidelberg,* Germany] (1920) : an early Pleistocene hominid known from a massive fossilized jaw with distinctly human dentition and classified with the direct ancestor (*Homo erectus*) of modern humans

heif·er \ˈhe-fər\ *n* [ME *hayfare,* fr. OE *hēahfore*] (bef. 12c) : a young cow; *esp* : one that has not had a calf

heigh–ho \ˈhī-ˈhō, ˈhā-\ *interj* (ca. 1520) — used typically to express boredom, weariness, or sadness or sometimes as a cry of encouragement

height \ˈhīt, ÷ˈhītth\ *n* [ME *heighthe,* fr. OE *hīehthu;* akin to OHG *hōhida* height, OE *hēah* high] (bef. 12c) **1 a** : the highest part : SUMMIT **b** : highest or most advanced point : ZENITH ‹at the ~ of his powers› **2 a** : the distance from the bottom to the top of something standing upright **b** : the extent of elevation above a level **3** : the condition of being tall or high **4 a** : an extent of land rising to a considerable degree above the surrounding country **b** : a high point or position **5** *obs* : an advanced social rank

syn HEIGHT, ALTITUDE, ELEVATION mean vertical distance either between the top and bottom of something or between a base and something above it. HEIGHT refers to something measured vertically whether high or low ‹a wall two meters in *height*›. ALTITUDE and ELEVATION apply to height as measured by angular measurement or atmospheric pressure; ALTITUDE is preferable when referring to vertical distance above the surface of the earth or above sea level; ELEVATION is used esp. in reference to vertical height on land ‹fly at an *altitude* of 10,000 meters› ‹Denver is a city with a high *elevation*›.

height·en \ˈhī-tᵊn\ *vb* **height·ened; height·en·ing** \ˈhīt-niŋ, ˈhī-tᵊn-iŋ\ *vt* (1523) **1 a** : to increase the amount or degree of : AUGMENT **b** : to make brighter or more intense : DEEPEN **c** : to bring out more strongly : point up **d** : to make more acute : SHARPEN **2 a** : to raise high or higher : ELEVATE **b** : to raise above the ordinary or trite **3** *obs* : ELATE ~ *vi* **1** *archaic* : GROW, RISE **2 a** : to become great or greater in amount, degree, or extent **b** : to become brighter or more intense

height to paper (1771) : the height of printing type standardized at 0.9186 inch (2.333 centimeters) in English-speaking countries

Heim·lich maneuver \ˈhīm-lik-\ *n* [Henry J. *Heimlich b*1920 Am. surgeon] (1974) : the manual application of sudden upward pressure on the upper abdomen of a choking victim to force a foreign object from the trachea

hei·nie \ˈhī-nē\ *n* [alter. of [2]*hinder*] (1921) *slang* : BUTTOCKS

hei·nous \ˈhā-nəs\ *adj* [ME, fr. AF *hainus, heinous,* fr. *haine* hate, fr. *hair* to hate, of Gmc origin; akin to OHG *haz* hate — more at HATE] (14c) : hatefully or shockingly evil : ABOMINABLE — **hei·nous·ly** *adv* — **hei·nous·ness** *n*

[1]**heir** \ˈer\ *n* [ME, fr. AF *eir, heir,* fr. L *hered-, heres;* akin to Gk *chēros*

\ə\ **abut** \ᵊ\ kitten, F table \ər\ **further** \a\ **ash** \ā\ **ace** \ä\ **mop, mar**
\au̇\ **out** \ch\ **chin** \e\ **bet** \ē\ **easy** \g\ **go** \i\ **hit** \ī\ **ice** \j\ **job**
\ŋ\ **sing** \ō\ **go** \ȯ\ **law** \ȯi\ **boy** \th\ **thin** \th\ **the** \ü\ **loot** \u̇\ **foot**
\y\ **yet** \zh\ **vision, beige** \k, ⁿ, œ, ue, ʸ\ *see* Guide to Pronunciation

bereaved] (13c) **1 :** one who inherits or is entitled to inherit property **2 :** one who inherits or is entitled to succeed to a hereditary rank, title, or office ⟨~ to the throne⟩ **3 :** one who receives or is entitled to receive some endowment or quality from a parent or predecessor — **heir·less** \ˈer-ləs\ *adj* — **heir·ship** \-ˌship\ *n*

[2]**heir** *vt* (14c) *chiefly dial* **:** INHERIT

heir apparent *n, pl* **heirs apparent** (14c) **1 :** an heir whose right to an inheritance is indefeasible except by exclusion under a valid will if he or she survives the ancestor **2 :** HEIR PRESUMPTIVE **3 :** one whose succession esp. to a position or role appears certain under existing circumstances

heir at law (1684) **:** HEIR 1

heir·ess \ˈer-əs\ *n* (1607) **:** a woman who is an heir esp. to great wealth

heir·loom \ˈer-ˌlüm\ *n* [ME *heirlome,* fr. *heir* + *lome* implement — more at LOOM] (15c) **1 :** a piece of property that descends to the heir as an inseparable part of an inheritance of real property **2 :** something of special value handed on from one generation to another **3 :** a horticultural variety that has survived for several generations usu. due to the efforts of private individuals

heir presumptive *n, pl* **heirs presumptive** (ca. 1737) **:** an heir whose legal right to an inheritance may be defeated (as by the birth of a nearer relative)

Hei·sen·berg uncertainty principle \ˈhī-zᵊn-ˌbərg-, -ˌbərk-\ *n* [Werner *Heisenberg*] (1939) **:** UNCERTAINTY PRINCIPLE — called also *Heisenberg's uncertainty principle*

[1]**heist** \ˈhīst\ *vt* [var. of [1]*hoist*] (1865) **1** *chiefly dial* **:** HOIST **2 a :** to commit armed robbery on **b :** STEAL 1a

[2]**heist** *n* (1930) **:** armed robbery **:** HOLDUP; *also* **:** THEFT

Hel \ˈhel\ *n* [ON] (1844) **:** the Norse goddess of the dead and queen of the underworld

hela cell \ˈhe-lə-\ *n, often cap H & 1st L* [*H*enrietta *La*cks †1951 patient from whom the cells were taken] (1953) **:** a cell of a continuously cultured strain isolated from a human uterine cervical carcinoma in 1951 and used in biomedical research esp. to culture viruses

held *past and past part of* HOLD

hel·den·te·nor \ˈhel-dən-ˌtā-ˌnȯr, -ˌte-nər\ *n, often cap* [G, fr. *Held* hero + *Tenor* tenor] (ca. 1903) **:** a tenor with a powerful dramatic voice well suited to heroic (as Wagnerian) roles

Helen of Troy \ˌhe-lən-əv-ˈtrȯi\ (1510) **:** the wife of Menelaus whose abduction by Paris brings about the Trojan War

[1]**heli-** *or* **helio-** *comb form* [L, fr. Gk *hēli-, hēlio-,* fr. *hēlios* — more at SOLAR] **:** sun ⟨*helio*centric⟩

[2]**heli-** *comb form* [by shortening] **:** helicopter ⟨*heli*port⟩

he·li·a·cal \hi-ˈlī-ə-kəl\ *adj* [LL *heliacus,* fr. Gk *hēliakos,* fr. *hēlios*] (1545) **:** relating to or near the sun — used esp. of the last setting of a star before and its first rising after invisibility due to conjunction with the sun — **he·li·a·cal·ly** \-k(ə-)lē\ *adv*

helic- *or* **helico-** *comb form* [Gk *helik-, heliko-,* fr. *helik-, helix* spiral — more at HELIX] **:** helix **:** spiral ⟨*helic*al⟩

he·li·cal \ˈhe-li-kəl, ˈhē-\ *adj* (1591) **:** of, relating to, or having the form of a helix; *broadly* **:** SPIRAL 1a — **he·li·cal·ly** \-k(ə-)lē\ *adv*

he·li·coid \ˈhe-lə-ˌkȯid, ˈhē-\ *or* **he·li·coi·dal** \ˌhe-lə-ˈkȯi-dᵊl, ˌhē-\ *adj* (ca. 1704) **1 :** forming or arranged in a spiral **2 :** having the form of a flat coil or flattened spiral ⟨~ snail shell⟩

hel·i·con \ˈhe-lə-ˌkän, -i-kən\ *n* [prob. fr. Gk *helik-, helix* + E *-on* (as in *bombardon*); fr. its tube's forming a spiral encircling the player's body] (ca. 1875) **:** a large circular tuba similar to a sousaphone but lacking an adjustable bell

hel·i·co·nia \ˌhe-lə-ˈkō-nē-ə, -nyə\ *n* [NL, ultim. fr. Gk *Helikōnios,* fr. *Helikōn* Helicon, mountain in Greece] (1838) **:** any of a genus (*Heliconia* of the family Heliconiaceae) of perennial herbs of tropical America and islands of the western Pacific having showy brightly colored bracts and large leaves

[1]**he·li·cop·ter** \ˈhe-lə-ˌkäp-tər, ˈhē-\ *n* [F *hélicoptère,* fr. Gk *heliko-* + *pteron* wing — more at FEATHER] (1887) **:** an aircraft whose lift is derived from the aerodynamic forces acting on one or more powered rotors turning about substantially vertical axes

[2]**helicopter** *vi* (1952) **:** to travel by helicopter ~ *vt* **:** to transport by helicopter

helicopter parent *n* (1989) **:** a parent who is overly involved in the life of his or her child

he·lio·cen·tric \ˌhē-lē-ō-ˈsen-trik\ *adj* (1685) **1 :** referred to or measured from the sun's center or appearing as if seen from it **2 :** having or relating to the sun as center — compare GEOCENTRIC

he·lio·graph \-ˌgraf\ *n* [ISV] (1877) **:** an apparatus for telegraphing by means of the sun's rays flashed from a mirror — **heliograph** *vt*

he·lio·graph·ic \ˌhē-lē-ə-ˈgra-fik\ *adj* (1706) **:** measured on the sun's disk ⟨~ latitude⟩

he·li·ol·a·try \ˌhē-lē-ˈä-lə-trē\ *n* (ca. 1828) **:** sun worship — **he·li·ol·a·trous** \-trəs\ *adj*

he·li·om·e·ter \ˌhē-lē-ˈä-mə-tər\ *n* [F *héliomètre,* fr. *hélio-* [1]heli- + *-mètre* -meter] (1753) **:** a visual telescope that has a divided objective designed for measuring the apparent diameter of the sun but also used for measuring angles between celestial bodies or between points on the moon — **he·lio·met·ric** \ˌhē-lē-ō-ˈme-trik\ *adj* — **he·lio·met·ri·cal·ly** \-tri-k(ə-)lē\ *adv*

He·li·os \ˈhē-lē-əs, -(ˌ)ōs\ *n* [Gk *Hēlios*] (1829) **:** the god of the sun in Greek mythology — compare SOL

he·li·o·sphere \ˈhē-lē-ə-ˌsfir, -ō-\ *n* [ISV] (1976) **:** the region in space influenced by the sun or solar wind — **he·li·o·spher·ic** \ˌhē-lē-ə-ˈsfir-ik, -ˈsfer-, -lē-ō-\ *adj*

he·lio·stat \ˈhē-lē-ə-ˌstat\ *n* [NL *heliostata,* fr. [1]*heli-* + Gk *-statēs* -stat] (1747) **:** an instrument consisting of a mirror mounted on an axis moved by clockwork by which a sunbeam is steadily reflected in one direction

he·lio·trope \ˈhē-lē-ə-ˌtrōp, ˈhēl-yə-, *Brit also* ˈhel-yə-\ *n* [L *heliotropium,* fr. Gk *hēliotropion,* fr. *hēlio-* [1]heli- + *tropos* turn; fr. its flowers' turning toward the sun — more at TROPE] (1605) **1 :** any of a genus (*Heliotropium*) of herbs or shrubs of the borage family — compare GARDEN HELIOTROPE **2 :** BLOODSTONE **3 :** a variable color averaging a moderate to reddish purple

he·li·ot·ro·pism \ˌhē-lē-ˈä-trə-ˌpi-zəm\ *n* (ca. 1854) **:** phototropism in which sunlight is the orienting stimulus — **he·lio·tro·pic** \-lē-ə-ˈtrō-pik, -ˈträ-\ *adj*

he·lio·zo·an \ˌhē-lē-ə-ˈzō-ən\ *n* [NL *Heliozoa,* fr. [1]*heli-* + *-zoa*] (ca. 1889) **:** any of a class (Heliozoa) of free-living spherical usu. freshwater protozoans that reproduce by binary fission or budding

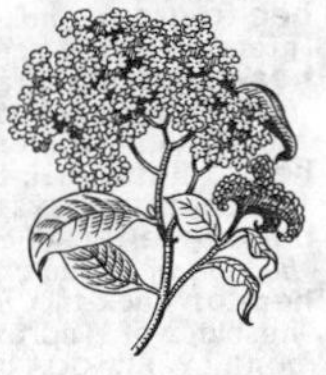

heliotrope 1

he·li·pad \ˈhe-lə-ˌpad, ˈhē-\ *n* (1960) **:** HELIPORT

he·li·port \-ˌpȯrt\ *n* (1948) **:** a landing and takeoff place for a helicopter

he·li–ski·ing \-ˌskē-iŋ\ *n* (1976) **:** downhill skiing on remote mountains reached by helicopter

he·li·um \ˈhē-lē-əm, ˈhēl-yəm\ *n* [NL, fr. Gk *hēlios*] (1872) **:** a light colorless inert gaseous element found esp. in natural gases and used chiefly for inflating airships and balloons, in lamps, in cryogenic research, and as a component of inert atmospheres (as in welding) — see ELEMENT table

he·lix \ˈhē-liks\ *n, pl* **he·li·ces** \ˈhe-lə-ˌsēz, ˈhē-\ *also* **he·lix·es** \ˈhē-lik-səz\ [L, fr. Gk; akin to Gk *eilyein* to roll, wrap — more at VOLUBLE] (1563) **1 :** something spiral in form: as **a :** an ornamental volute **b :** a coil formed by winding wire around a uniform tube **2 :** the incurved rim of the external ear **3 :** a curve traced on a cylinder or cone by the rotation of a point crossing its right sections at a constant oblique angle; *broadly* **:** SPIRAL 1b

hell \ˈhel\ *n* [ME, fr. OE; akin to OE *helan* to conceal, OHG *helan,* L *celare,* Gk *kalyptein*] (bef. 12c) **1 a** (1) **:** a nether world in which the dead continue to exist **:** HADES (2) **:** the nether realm of the devil and the demons in which the damned suffer everlasting punishment — often used in curses ⟨go to ~⟩ or as a generalized term of abuse ⟨the ~ with it⟩ **b** *Christian Science* **:** ERROR 2b, SIN **2 a :** a place or state of misery, torment, or wickedness ⟨war is ~ —W. T. Sherman⟩ **b :** a place or state of turmoil or destruction ⟨all ~ broke loose⟩ **c :** a severe scolding; *also* **:** FLAK, GRIEF ⟨gave me ~ for coming in late⟩ **d :** unrestrained fun or sportiveness ⟨the kids were full of ~⟩ — often used in the phrase *for the hell of it* esp. to suggest action on impulse or without a serious motive ⟨decided to go for the ~ of it⟩ **e :** an extremely unpleasant and often inescapable situation ⟨rush-hour ~⟩ **3** *archaic* **:** a tailor's receptacle **4** — used as an interjection ⟨~, I don't know!⟩ or as an intensive ⟨hurts like ~⟩ ⟨funny as ~⟩; often used in the phrase *hell of a* ⟨it was one ~ of a good fight⟩ or *hell out of* ⟨scared the ~ out of him⟩ or with *the* or *in* ⟨moved way the ~ up north⟩ ⟨what in ~ is wrong, now?⟩ — **from hell :** being the worst or most dreadful of its kind — **hell on :** very hard on or destructive to ⟨the constant traveling is *hell on* your digestive system⟩ — **hell or high water :** difficulties of whatever kind or size ⟨will stand by her convictions come *hell or high water*⟩ — **hell to pay :** dire consequences ⟨if he's late there'll be *hell to pay*⟩ — **what the hell** — used interjectionally to express a lack of concern about consequences or risks ⟨it might cost him half his estate . . . but *what the hell* —N. W. Aldrich *b*1935⟩

he'll \ˈhēl, ˈhil, ēl, il\ (1579) **:** he will **:** he shall

hel·la·cious \ˌhe-ˈlā-shəs\ *adj* [*hell* + *-acious* (as in *audacious*)] (1929) **1 :** exceptionally powerful or violent **2 :** remarkably good **3 :** extremely difficult **4 :** extraordinarily large — **hel·la·cious·ly** *adv*

hell·ben·der \ˈhel-ˌben-dər\ *n* (1812) **:** a large aquatic usu. brownish-gray salamander (*Cryptobranchus alleganiensis*) of streams of the eastern and central U.S.

hell–bent \-ˌbent\ *adj* (1835) **:** stubbornly and often recklessly determined or intent ⟨~ on winning⟩ — **hell–bent** *adv*

hell·broth \-ˌbrȯth\ *n* (1605) **:** a brew for working black magic

hell·cat \-ˌkat\ *n* (ca. 1605) **1 :** WITCH 2 **2 :** a violently temperamental person; *esp* **:** an ill-tempered woman

hel·le·bore \ˈhe-lə-ˌbȯr\ *n* [ME *elebre,* fr. AF, fr. L *elleborus, helleborus,* fr. Gk *helleboros*] (15c) **1 :** any of a genus (*Helleborus*) of poisonous Eurasian herbs of the buttercup family having showy flowers with petaloid sepals; *also* **:** the dried rhizome of a hellebore (as *H. niger*) formerly used in medicine **2 :** a poisonous herb (genus *Veratrum*) of the lily family; *also* **:** the dried rhizome of a hellebore (*V. album* or *V. viride*) that is used as an insecticide and contains toxic alkaloids that are cardiac and respiratory depressants

Hel·lene \ˈhe-ˌlēn\ *n* [Gk *Hellēn*] (1662) **:** GREEK 1a

[1]**Hel·len·ic** \he-ˈle-nik, hə-\ *adj* (1644) **:** of or relating to Greece, its people, or its language; *specif* **:** of or relating to ancient Greek history, culture, or art before the Hellenistic period

[2]**Hellenic** *n* (1847) **:** GREEK 2a

Hel·le·nism \ˈhe-lə-ˌni-zəm\ *n* (1609) **1 :** GRECISM 1 **2 :** devotion to or imitation of ancient Greek thought, customs, or styles **3 :** Greek civilization esp. as modified in the Hellenistic period by influences from southwestern Asia **4 :** a body of humanistic and classical ideals associated with ancient Greece and including reason, the pursuit of knowledge and the arts, moderation, civic responsibility, and bodily development

Hel·le·nist \-nist\ *n* (1613) **1 :** a person living in Hellenistic times who was Greek in language, outlook, and way of life but was not Greek in ancestry; *esp* **:** a hellenized Jew **2 :** a specialist in the language or culture of ancient Greece

Hel·le·nis·tic \ˌhe-lə-ˈnis-tik\ *adj* (ca. 1706) **1 :** of or relating to Greek history, culture, or art after Alexander the Great **2 :** of or relating to the Hellenists — **Hel·le·nis·ti·cal·ly** \-ti-k(ə-)lē\ *adv*

hel·le·nize \ˈhe-lə-ˌnīz\ *vb* **-nized; -niz·ing** *often cap, vi* (1613) **:** to become Greek or Hellenistic ~ *vt* **:** to make Greek or Hellenistic in form or culture — **hel·le·ni·za·tion** \ˌhe-lə-nə-ˈzā-shən\ *n, often cap*

hell·er \ˈhe-lər\ *n* (ca. 1895) **:** HELLION

hell·fire \ˈhel-ˌfī(-ə)r\ *n* (bef. 12c) **:** the eternal fire of hell that tortures sinners — **hellfire** *adj*

[1]**hell–for–leather** *adv* (1889) **:** in a hell-for-leather manner **:** at full speed ⟨rode ~ down the trail⟩

[2]**hell–for–leather** *adj* (1920) **:** marked by determined recklessness, great speed, or lack of restraint ⟨a cocky, ~ fighting man —H. H. Martin⟩

hell·gram·mite \ˈhel-grə-ˌmīt\ *n* [origin unknown] (1866) **:** a carnivorous aquatic No. American insect larva that is the young form of a dobsonfly (esp. *Corydalis cornutus*) and is used for fish bait

hell·hole \ˈhel-ˌhōl\ *n* (1866) **:** a place of extreme misery or squalor

hell·hound \-ˌhau̇nd\ *n* (bef. 12c) **1 :** a dog represented in mythology as a guardian of the underworld **2 :** a fiendish person

hel·lion \ˈhel-yən\ *n* [prob. alter. (influenced by *hell*) of *hallion* scamp] (1787) **:** a troublesome or mischievous person

hell·ish \ˈhe-lish\ *adj* (ca. 1530) : of, resembling, or befitting hell; *broadly* : TERRIBLE — **hell·ish·ly** *adv* — **hell·ish·ness** *n*

hel·lo \hə-ˈlō, he-\ *n, pl* **hellos** [alter. of *hollo*] (1877) : an expression or gesture of greeting — used interjectionally in greeting, in answering the telephone, or to express surprise

hell–rais·er \ˈhel-ˌrā-zər\ *n* (1914) : one given to wild, boisterous, or intemperate behavior — **hell–rais·ing** \-ˌrā-ziŋ\ *n or adj*

[1]**helm** \ˈhelm\ *n* [ME, fr. OE] (bef. 12c) : HELMET 1

[2]**helm** *vt* (bef. 12c) : to cover or furnish with a helmet

[3]**helm** *n* [ME *helme,* fr. OE *helma;* akin to OHG *helmo* tiller] (bef. 12c) **1 a** : a lever or wheel controlling the rudder of a ship for steering; *broadly* : the entire apparatus for steering a ship **b** : position of the helm with respect to the amidships position ⟨turn the ~ hard alee⟩ **2** : a position of control : HEAD ⟨a new dean is at the ~ of the medical school⟩

[4]**helm** *vt* (1603) **1** : to direct with or as if with a helm : STEER **2** : DIRECT, CONTROL ⟨the director has ~*ed* many action movies⟩

hel·met \ˈhel-mət\ *n* [ME, fr. MF, dim. of *helme* helmet, of Gmc origin; akin to OE *helm* helmet, OHG *helan* to conceal — more at HELL] (15c) **1** : a covering or enclosing headpiece of ancient or medieval armor — see ARMOR illustration **2** : any of various protective head coverings usu. made of a hard material to resist impact **3** : something resembling a helmet — **hel·met·ed** \-mə-təd\ *adj* — **hel·met·like** \-mət-ˌlīk\ *adj*

hel·minth \ˈhel-ˌmin(t)th\ *n* [Gk *helminth-, helmis*] (1852) : a parasitic worm (as a tapeworm, liver fluke, ascarid, or leech); *esp* : an intestinal worm — **hel·min·thic** \hel-ˈmin(t)-thik\ *adj*

hel·min·thi·a·sis \ˌhel-mən-ˈthī-ə-səs\ *n, pl* **-a·ses** \-ə-ˌsēz\ [NL] (ca. 1811) : infestation with or disease caused by parasitic worms

hel·min·thol·o·gy \-ˈthä-lə-jē\ *n* (1819) : a branch of zoology concerned with helminths; *esp* : the study of parasitic worms

helms·man \ˈhelmz-mən\ *n* (1590) : the person at the helm : STEERSMAN — **helms·man·ship** \-ˌship\ *n*

helms·per·son \ˈhelmz-ˌpər-sᵊn\ *n* (1981) : HELMSMAN

he·lo \ˈhē-(ˌ)lō\ *n, pl* **helos** [by shortening & alter.] (1968) : HELICOPTER

hel·ot \ˈhe-lət\ *n* [L *Helotes,* pl., fr. Gk *Heilōtes*] (1579) **1** *cap* : a member of a class of serfs in ancient Sparta **2** : SERF, SLAVE — **hel·ot·ry** \ˈhe-lə-trē\ *n*

[1]**help** \ˈhelp; *Southern often* ˈhep *also* ˈheəp\ *vb* [ME, fr. OE *helpan;* akin to OHG *helfan* to help, and perh. to Lith *šelpti*] *vt* (bef. 12c) **1** : to give assistance or support to ⟨~ a child with homework⟩ **2 a** : to make more pleasant or bearable : IMPROVE, RELIEVE ⟨bright curtains will ~ the room⟩ ⟨took an aspirin to ~ her headache⟩ **b** *archaic* : RESCUE, SAVE **3 a** : to be of use to : BENEFIT **b** : to further the advancement of : PROMOTE **4 a** : to change for the better **b** : to refrain from : AVOID ⟨we couldn't ~ laughing⟩ **c** : to keep from occurring : PREVENT ⟨they couldn't ~ the accident⟩ **d** : to restrain (oneself) from doing something ⟨knew they shouldn't go but couldn't ~ themselves⟩ **5** : to serve with food or drink esp. at a meal ⟨told the guests to ~ themselves⟩ **6** : to appropriate something for (oneself) ⟨~*ed* himself to the car keys⟩ ~ *vi* **1** : give assistance or support — often used with *out* ⟨~*s* out with the housework⟩ **2** : to be of use or benefit ***syn*** see IMPROVE — **so help me** : upon my word : believe it or not

[2]**help** *n* (bef. 12c) **1** : AID, ASSISTANCE **2** : a source of aid ⟨printed ~*s* to the memory —C. S. Braden⟩ **3** : REMEDY, RELIEF ⟨there was no ~ for it⟩ **4 a** : one who serves or assists another (as in housework) : HELPER **b** : EMPLOYEE ⟨~ wanted⟩ — often used collectively ⟨the hired ~⟩

help·er \ˈhel-pər\ *n* (13c) : one that helps; *esp* : a relatively unskilled worker who assists a skilled worker usu. by manual labor

helper T cell *n* (1974) : a T cell that participates in an immune response by recognizing a foreign antigen and secreting lymphokines to activate T cell and B cell proliferation and that usu. carries CD4 molecular markers on its cell surface — called also *helper cell, T-helper cell*

help·ful \ˈhelp-fəl; *Southern often* ˈhep- *also* ˈheəp-\ *adj* (14c) : of service or assistance : USEFUL ⟨~ advice⟩ — **help·ful·ly** \-fə-lē\ *adv* — **help·ful·ness** *n*

help·ing \ˈhel-piŋ\ *n* (1883) **1** : a portion of food : SERVING **2** : DOSE 3 ⟨large ~*s* of reportage and interviews —Stefan Kanfer⟩

helping hand *n* (15c) : HAND 8a

helping verb *n* (1711) : an auxiliary verb

help·less \ˈhel-pləs; *Southern often* ˈhep-ləs *also* ˈheəp-\ *adj* (bef. 12c) **1** : lacking protection or support : DEFENSELESS **2 a** : marked by an inability to act or react ⟨the crowd looked on in ~ horror —*Current Biog.*⟩ **b** : not able to be controlled or restrained ⟨~ laughter⟩ — **help·less·ly** *adv* — **help·less·ness** *n*

help·mate \ˈhelp-ˌmāt; *Southern often* ˈhep- *also* ˈheəp-\ *n* [by folk etymology fr. *helpmeet*] (1696) : one who is a companion and helper; *esp* : WIFE

help·meet \-ˌmēt\ *n* [[2]*help* + *meet,* adj.] (1673) : HELPMATE

[1]**hel·ter–skel·ter** \ˌhel-tər-ˈskel-tər\ *adv* [perh. fr. ME *skelten* to come, go] (1593) **1** : in undue haste, confusion, or disorder ⟨ran ~, getting in each other's way —F. V. W. Mason⟩ **2** : in a haphazard manner

[2]**helter–skelter** *n* (1713) **1** : a disorderly confusion : TURMOIL **2** *Brit* : a spiral slide around a tower at an amusement park

[3]**helter–skelter** *adj* (1708) **1** : confusedly hurried : PRECIPITATE **2** : marked by a lack of order or plan : HAPHAZARD ⟨the ~ arrangement of the papers, all mussed and frayed —Jean Stafford⟩

helve \ˈhelv\ *n* [ME, fr. OE *hielfe;* prob. akin to OE *helma* helm] (bef. 12c) : a handle of a tool or weapon : HAFT

Hel·ve·tii \hel-ˈvē-shē-ˌī\ *n pl* [L] (1781) : an early Celtic people in the area of western Switzerland at the time of Julius Caesar

[1]**hem** \ˈhem\ *n* [ME, fr. OE; akin to MHG *hemmen* to hem in, Arm *kamel* to press] (bef. 12c) **1** : a border of a cloth article doubled back and stitched down **2** : RIM, MARGIN ⟨bright green ~ of reeds about the ponds —R. M. Lockley⟩

[2]**hem** *vb* **hemmed; hem·ming** *vt* (14c) **1 a** : to finish with a hem **b** : BORDER, EDGE **2** : to surround in a restrictive manner : CONFINE — usu. used with *in* ⟨*hemmed* in by enemy troops⟩ ~ *vi* : to make a hem in sewing — **hem·mer** *n*

[3]**hem** \ˈhem\ *vi* **hemmed; hem·ming** (15c) **1** : to utter the sound represented by *hem* ⟨*hemmed* and hawed before answering⟩ **2** : EQUIVOCATE ⟨the administration *hemmed* and hawed over the students' demands⟩

[4]**hem** *usu read as* ˈhem\ *interj* [imit.] — often used to indicate a vocalized pause in speaking

hem- *or* **hemo-** *comb form* [L *haem-, haemo-,* fr. Gk *haim-, haimo-,* fr. *haima*] : blood ⟨*hem*agglutination⟩ ⟨*hemo*flagellate⟩

hema- *comb form* [NL, fr. Gk *haima*] : HEM- ⟨*hema*cytometer⟩

he·ma·cy·tom·e·ter \ˌhē-mə-sī-ˈtä-mə-tər\ *n* (1877) : an instrument for counting blood cells

hem·ag·glu·ti·na·tion \ˌhē-mə-ˌglü-tə-ˈnā-shən\ *n* (1907) : agglutination of red blood cells — **hem·ag·glu·ti·nate** \-ˈglü-tᵊn-ˌāt\ *vt*

hem·ag·glu·ti·nin \-ˈglü-tə-nən\ *n* [ISV] (ca. 1903) : an agglutinin (as an antibody or viral capsid protein) that causes hemagglutination

he–man \ˈhē-ˌman\ *n* (1758) : a strong virile man

hem·an·gi·o·ma \ˌhē-ˌman-jē-ˈō-mə\ *n* [NL, fr. *hem-* + *angioma*] (ca. 1890) : a usu. benign tumor made up of blood vessels that typically occurs as a purplish or reddish slightly elevated area of skin

hemat- *or* **hemato-** *comb form* [L *haemat-, haemato-,* fr. Gk *haimat-, haimato-,* fr. *haimat-, haima*] : HEM- ⟨*hemato*genous⟩

he·ma·tin \ˈhē-mə-tən\ *n* (1845) : a brownish-black or bluish-black derivative $C_{34}H_{33}N_4O_5Fe$ of oxidized heme; *also* : any of several similar compounds

he·ma·tin·ic \ˌhē-mə-ˈti-nik\ *n* (1855) : an agent that tends to stimulate blood cell formation or to increase the hemoglobin in the blood — **hematinic** *adj*

he·ma·tite \ˈhē-mə-ˌtīt\ *n* (1540) : a reddish-brown to black mineral consisting of ferric oxide, constituting an important iron ore, and occurring in crystals or as earthy red ocher — **he·ma·ti·tic** \ˌhē-mə-ˈti-tik\ *adj*

he·mat·o·crit \hi-ˈma-tə-krət, -ˌkrit\ *n* [ISV *hemat-* + Gk *kritēs* judge, fr. *krinein* to judge — more at CERTAIN] (ca. 1903) : the ratio of the volume of red blood cells to the total volume of blood as determined by separation of red blood cells from the plasma usu. by centrifugation

he·ma·tog·e·nous \ˌhē-mə-ˈtä-jə-nəs\ *adj* (1886) **1** : producing blood **2** : involving, spread by, or arising in the blood ⟨~ spread of infection⟩

he·ma·to·log·ic \ˌhē-mə-tə-ˈlä-jik\ *also* **he·ma·to·log·i·cal** \-ji-kəl\ *adj* (1854) : of or relating to blood or to hematology

he·ma·tol·o·gy \ˌhē-mə-ˈtä-lə-jē\ *n* (ca. 1811) : a medical science that deals with the blood and blood-forming organs — **he·ma·tol·o·gist** \-jist\ *n*

he·ma·to·ma \-ˈtō-mə\ *n, pl* **-mas** *also* **-ma·ta** \-mə-tə\ [NL] (ca. 1849) : a mass of usu. clotted blood that forms in a tissue, organ, or body space as a result of a broken blood vessel

he·ma·toph·a·gous \-ˈtä-fə-gəs\ *adj* [ISV] (ca. 1854) : feeding on blood ⟨~ mosquitoes⟩

he·ma·to·poi·e·sis \hi-ˌma-tə-pȯi-ˈē-səs, ˌhē-mə-tō-\ *n* [NL] (ca. 1854) : the formation of blood or of blood cells in the living body — **he·ma·to·poi·et·ic** \-ˈe-tik\ *adj*

he·ma·to·por·phy·rin \-ˈpȯr-fə-rən\ *n* [ISV] (1885) : any of several isomeric porphyrins $C_{34}H_{38}O_6N_4$ that are hydrated derivatives of protoporphyrins; *esp* : the deep red crystalline pigment obtained by treating hematin or heme with acid

he·ma·tox·y·lin \ˌhē-mə-ˈtäk-sə-lən\ *n* [ISV, fr. NL *Haematoxylon,* plant genus] (ca. 1847) : a crystalline phenolic compound $C_{16}H_{14}O_6$ found in logwood and used chiefly in biological staining

he·ma·tu·ria \-ˈtu̇r-ē-ə, -ˈtyu̇r-\ *n* [NL] (ca. 1811) : the presence of blood or blood cells in the urine

heme \ˈhēm\ *n* [ISV, fr. *hematin*] (1925) : the deep red iron-containing prosthetic group $C_{34}H_{32}N_4O_4Fe$ of hemoglobin and myoglobin

hem·el·y·tron \he-ˈme-lə-ˌträn\ *n, pl* **-tra** \-trə\ [NL, fr. *hemi-* + *elytron*] (ca. 1889) : one of the basally thickened anterior wings of various insects (as true bugs)

hem·ero·cal·lis \ˌhe-mə-rō-ˈka-ləs\ *n* [NL, fr. Gk *hēmerokalles,* fr. *hēmera* day + *kallos* beauty] (1625) : DAYLILY

hem·er·y·thrin \hē-ˈmer-ə-thrən\ *n* [*hem-* + *erythr-* + [1]*-in*] (1903) : an iron-containing respiratory pigment in the blood of various chiefly marine invertebrates (as some brachiopods)

hemi- *prefix* [ME, fr. L, fr. Gk *hēmi-* — more at SEMI-] : half ⟨*hemi*hedral⟩

-hemia — see -EMIA

hemi·ac·e·tal \ˌhe-mē-ˈa-sə-ˌtal\ *n* (1893) : any of a class of compounds characterized by the grouping C(OH)(OR) where R is an alkyl group and usu. formed as intermediates in the preparation of acetals from aldehydes or ketones

he·mic \ˈhē-mik\ *adj* (1857) : of, relating to, or produced by the blood or the circulation of blood ⟨a ~ murmur⟩

hemi·cel·lu·lose \ˌhe-mi-ˈsel-yə-ˌlōs, -ˌlōz\ *n* [ISV] (1891) : any of various plant polysaccharides less complex than cellulose and easily hydrolyzable to monosaccharides and other products

hemi·chor·date \-ˈkȯr-dət, -ˈkȯr-ˌdāt\ *n* [NL *Hemichordata,* fr. *hemi-* + *Chordata* chordates] (1885) : any of a phylum (Hemichordata) of wormlike marine animals (as an acorn worm) that have in the proboscis an outgrowth of the pharyngeal wall which superficially resembles the notochord of chordates

hemi·cy·cle \ˈhe-mi-ˌsī-kəl\ *n* [L *hemicyclium,* fr. Gk *hēmikyklion,* fr. *hēmi-* + *kyklos* circle — more at CYCLE] (15c) : a curved or semicircular structure or arrangement

hemi·demi·semi·qua·ver \ˌhe-mi-ˌde-mi-ˈse-mi-ˌkwā-vər\ *n* (1853) : SIXTY-FOURTH NOTE

hemi·he·dral \ˌhe-mi-ˈhē-drəl\ *adj* [*hemi-* + *-hedron*] (1837) *of a crystal* : having half the faces required by complete symmetry — compare HOLOHEDRAL, TETARTOHEDRAL

hemi·hy·drate \-ˈhī-ˌdrāt\ *n* (ca. 1901) : a hydrate (as plaster of paris) containing half a mole of water to one mole of the compound forming the hydrate — **hemi·hy·drat·ed** \-ˌdrā-təd\ *adj*

hemi·me·tab·o·lous \ˌhe-mi-mə-ˈta-bə-ləs\ *adj* [ultim. fr. Gk *hemi-* + *metabolos* changeable, fr. *metabolē* change — more at METABOLISM]

\ə\ **abut** \ᵊ\ **kitten,** F **table** \ər\ **further** \a\ **ash** \ā\ **ace** \ä\ **mop, mar**
\au̇\ **out** \ch\ **chin** \e\ **bet** \ē\ **easy** \g\ **go** \i\ **hit** \ī\ **ice** \j\ **job**
\ŋ\ **sing** \ō\ **go** \ȯ\ **law** \ȯi\ **boy** \th\ **thin** \t͟h\ **the** \ü\ **loot** \u̇\ **foot**
\y\ **yet** \zh\ **vision, beige** \ḵ, ⁿ, œ, ue, ʸ\ *see* Guide to Pronunciation

(1870) : characterized by incomplete metamorphosis ⟨∼ insects⟩ — compare HOLOMETABOLOUS

hemi·mor·phic \ˌhe-mi-ˈmȯr-fik\ *adj* [ISV] (ca. 1859) *of a crystal* : having different crystalline forms at each end of a crystallographic axis — **hemi·mor·phism** \-ˌfi-zəm\ *n*

he·min \ˈhē-mən\ *n* [ISV] (ca. 1857) : a red-brown to blue-black crystalline salt $C_{34}H_{32}N_4O_4FeCl$ derived from oxidized heme but usu. obtained in a characteristic crystalline form from hemoglobin

hemi·o·la \ˌhe-mē-ˈō-lə\ *n* [LL *hemiolia*, fr. Gk *hēmiolia* ratio of one and a half to one, fr. *hēmi-* + *holos* whole — more at SAFE] (ca. 1934) : a musical rhythmic alteration in which six equal notes may be heard as two groups of three or three groups of two

hemi·ple·gia \ˌhe-mi-ˈplē-j(ē-)ə\ *n* [NL, fr. MGk *hēmiplēgia* paralysis, fr. Gk *hēmi-* + *-plēgia* -plegia] (1600) : total or partial paralysis of one side of the body that results from disease of or injury to the motor centers of the brain — **hemi·ple·gic** \-jik\ *adj or n*

he·mip·ter·an \hi-ˈmip-tə-rən\ *n* [ultim. fr. Gk *hēmi-* + *pteron* wing — more at FEATHER] (ca. 1864) : any of a large order (Hemiptera) of hemimetabolous insects (as the true bugs) that have hemelytra and mouthparts adapted to piercing and sucking — **he·mip·ter·ous** \-rəs\ *adj*

hemi·sphere \ˈhe-mə-ˌsfir\ *n* [ME *hemispere*, fr. L *hemisphaerium*, fr. Gk *hēmisphairion*, fr. *hēmi-* + *sphairion*, dim. of *sphaira* sphere] (14c) **1 a** : a half of the celestial sphere as divided into two halves by the horizon, the celestial equator, or the ecliptic **b** : half of a spherical or roughly spherical body (as a planet); *specif* : the northern or southern half of the earth as divided by the equator or the eastern or western half as divided by a meridian **c** : the inhabitants of a terrestrial hemisphere **2** : REALM, PROVINCE **3** : one of two half spheres formed by a plane through the sphere's center **4** : a map or projection of a celestial or terrestrial hemisphere **5** : CEREBRAL HEMISPHERE — **hemi·spher·ic** \ˌhe-mə-ˈsfir-ik, -ˈsfer-\ *or* **hemi·spher·i·cal** \-ˈsfir-i-kəl, -ˈsfer-\ *adj*

hemi·spher·ec·to·my \ˌhe-mi-sfi-ˈrek-tə-mē\ *n, pl* **-mies** (ca. 1941) : surgical removal of a cerebral hemisphere

hemi·stich \ˈhe-mi-ˌstik\ *n* [L *hemistichium*, fr. Gk *hēmistichion*, fr. *hēmi-* + *stichos* line, verse; akin to Gk *steichein* to go — more at STAIR] (1575) : half a poetic line of verse usu. divided by a caesura

hemi·zy·gous \ˌhe-mi-ˈzī-gəs\ *adj* (ca. 1921) : having or characterized by one or more genes (as in a genetic deficiency or in an X chromosome paired with a Y chromosome) that have no allelic counterparts

hem·line \ˈhem-ˌlīn\ *n* (1923) : the line formed by the lower edge of a dress, skirt, or coat

hem·lock \ˈhem-ˌläk\ *n* [ME *hemlok*, fr. OE *hemlic*] (bef. 12c) **1 a** : any of several poisonous herbs (as a poison hemlock or a water hemlock) of the carrot family having finely cut leaves and small white flowers **b** : a drug or lethal drink prepared from the poison hemlock **2** : any of a genus (*Tsuga*) of evergreen coniferous trees of the pine family; *also* : the soft light splintery wood of a hemlock

hemo- — see HEM-

he·mo·chro·ma·to·sis \ˌhē-mə-ˌkrō-mə-ˈtō-səs\ *n* [NL, fr. *hem-* + *chromat-* + *-osis*] (1899) : a hereditary disorder of metabolism involving the deposition of iron-containing pigments in the tissues that is characterized esp. by joint or abdominal pain, weakness, and fatigue and that may lead to bronzing of the skin, arthritis, diabetes, cirrhosis, or heart disease if untreated

he·mo·coel \ˈhē-mə-ˌsēl\ *n* (1839) : a body cavity (as in arthropods or some mollusks) that contains blood or hemolymph and functions as part of the circulatory system

he·mo·cy·a·nin \ˌhē-mō-ˈsī-ə-nən\ *n* [ISV *hem-* + *cyan-* + ¹*-in*] (1885) : a copper-containing respiratory pigment in the circulatory fluid of various arthropods and mollusks

he·mo·cyte \ˈhē-mə-ˌsīt\ *n* [ISV] (ca. 1903) : a blood cell esp. of an invertebrate animal

he·mo·cy·tom·e·ter \ˌhē-mə-sī-ˈtä-mə-tər\ *n* [ISV] (1877) : HEMACYTOMETER

he·mo·di·al·y·sis \ˌhē-mō-dī-ˈa-lə-səs\ *n* (1947) : DIALYSIS 2

he·mo·di·lu·tion \-dī-ˈlü-shən, -də-\ *n* (1939) : decreased concentration of cells and solids in the blood resulting from gain of fluid

he·mo·dy·nam·ic \-dī-ˈna-mik, -də-\ *adj* (1907) **1** : of, relating to, or involving hemodynamics **2** : relating to or functioning in the mechanics of blood circulation — **he·mo·dy·nam·i·cal·ly** \-mi-k(ə-)lē\ *adv*

he·mo·dy·nam·ics \-miks\ *n pl but sing or pl in constr* (ca. 1857) **1** : a branch of physiology that deals with the circulation of the blood **2** : the forces or mechanisms involved in circulation

he·mo·fla·gel·late \ˌhē-mə-ˈfla-jə-lət, -ˌlāt; -ˌflə-ˈje-lət\ *n* (1909) : a flagellate (as a trypanosome) that is a blood parasite

he·mo·glo·bin \ˈhē-mə-ˌglō-bən\ *n* [ISV, short for earlier *hematoglobulin*] (1869) **1** : an iron-containing respiratory pigment of vertebrate red blood cells that consists of a globin composed of four subunits each of which is linked to a heme molecule, that functions in oxygen transport to the tissues after conversion to oxygenated form in the gills or lungs, and that assists in carbon dioxide transport back to the gills or lungs after surrender of its oxygen **2** : any of numerous iron-containing respiratory pigments of various organisms (as invertebrates and yeasts)

he·mo·glo·bin·op·a·thy \ˌhē-mə-ˌglō-bə-ˈnä-pə-thē\ *n, pl* **-thies** (1957) : a blood disorder (as sickle-cell anemia) caused by a genetically determined change in the molecular structure of hemoglobin

hemoglobin S *n* (1954) : an abnormal hemoglobin that occurs in the red blood cells in sickle-cell anemia and sickle-cell trait

he·mo·glo·bin·uria \ˌhē-mə-ˌglō-bə-ˈnu̇r-ē-ə, -ˈnyu̇r-\ *n* [NL] (1866) : the presence of free hemoglobin in the urine — **he·mo·glo·bin·uric** \-ˈnu̇r-ik, -ˈnyu̇r-\ *adj*

he·mo·lymph \ˈhē-mə-ˌlim(p)f\ *n* (1885) : the circulatory fluid of various invertebrate animals that is functionally comparable to the blood and lymph of vertebrates

he·mo·ly·sin \ˌhē-mə-ˈlī-sᵊn\ *n* [ISV] (1900) : a substance that causes the dissolution of red blood cells

he·mo·ly·sis \hi-ˈmä-lə-səs, ˌhē-mə-ˈlī-səs\ *n* [NL] (1890) : lysis of red blood cells with liberation of hemoglobin — **he·mo·lyt·ic** \ˌhē-mə-ˈli-tik\ *adj*

hemolytic anemia *n* (1938) : anemia caused by excessive destruction (as in infection or sickle-cell anemia) of red blood cells

hemolytic disease of the newborn (1948) : ERYTHROBLASTOSIS FETALIS

hemolytic uremic syndrome *n* (1965) : any of a group of rare disorders occurring esp. in young children that are characterized by hemolytic anemia, thrombocytopenia, and varying degrees of kidney failure and that are precipitated by various factors (as infection with E. coli)

he·mo·lyze \ˈhē-mə-ˌlīz\ *vb* **-lyzed; -lyz·ing** [irreg. fr. *hemolysis*] *vt* (1902) : to cause hemolysis of ∼ *vi* : to undergo hemolysis

he·mo·phil·ia \ˌhē-mə-ˈfi-lē-ə\ *n* [NL] (1872) : a sex-linked hereditary blood defect that occurs almost exclusively in males and is characterized by delayed clotting of the blood and consequent difficulty in controlling hemorrhage even after minor injuries

¹**he·mo·phil·i·ac** \-ˈfi-lē-ˌak\ *adj* (1896) : of, resembling, or affected with hemophilia

²**hemophiliac** *n* (1897) : one affected with hemophilia — called also *bleeder*

he·mo·phil·ic \-ˈfi-lik\ *n or adj* (1864) : HEMOPHILIAC

he·mo·poi·e·sis \ˌhē-mə-pȯi-ˈē-səs\ *n* [NL] (ca. 1900) : HEMATOPOIESIS — **he·mo·poi·et·ic** \-ˈe-tik\ *adj*

he·mo·pro·tein \-ˈprō-ˌtēn, -ˌprō-tē-ən\ *n* (1948) : a conjugated protein (as hemoglobin or cytochrome) whose prosthetic group is a porphyrin combined with iron

he·mop·ty·sis \hi-ˈmäp-tə-səs\ *n* [NL, fr. *hem-* + Gk *ptysis* act of spitting, fr. *ptyein* to spit — more at SPEW] (1646) : expectoration of blood from some part of the respiratory tract

¹**hem·or·rhage** \ˈhem-rij, ˈhe-mə-\ *n* [L *haemorrhagia*, fr. Gk *haimorrhagia*, fr. *haimo-* hem- + *-rrhagia*] (1671) **1** : a copious discharge of blood from the blood vessels **2** : a rapid and uncontrollable loss or outflow ⟨a financial ∼⟩ — **hem·or·rhag·ic** \ˌhe-mə-ˈra-jik\ *adj*

²**hemorrhage** *vb* **-rhaged; -rhag·ing** *vi* (1928) : to undergo heavy or uncontrollable bleeding ∼ *vt* : to lose rapidly and uncontrollably ⟨∼ money⟩

hemorrhagic fever *n* (1948) : any of a diverse group of virus diseases (as Lassa fever and Ebola) that are usu. transmitted by arthropods or rodents and are characterized by a sudden onset, fever, aching, bleeding in the internal organs, petechiae, and shock

hem·or·rhoid \ˈhem-ˌrȯid, ˈhe-mə-\ *n* [ME *emeroides*, pl., fr. AF *emorroides*, fr. L *haemorrhoidae*, fr. Gk *haimorrhoides*, fr. *haimorrhoos* flowing with blood, fr. *haimo-* hem- + *rhein* to flow — more at STREAM] (14c) : a mass of dilated veins in swollen tissue at the margin of the anus or nearby within the rectum — usu. used in pl.; called also *piles*

¹**hem·or·rhoid·al** \ˌhem-ˈrȯi-dᵊl, ˌhe-mə-\ *n* (15c) : a hemorrhoidal part (as an artery or vein)

²**hemorrhoidal** *adj* (1651) **1** : of, relating to, or involving hemorrhoids **2** : RECTAL

he·mo·sid·er·in \ˌhē-mō-ˈsi-də-rən\ *n* [ISV *hem-* + *sider-* + ¹*-in*] (ca. 1885) : a yellowish-brown granular intracellular pigment that is formed in some phagocytic cells (as macrophages) by the breakdown of hemoglobin and is prob. essentially a denatured form of ferritin

he·mo·sta·sis \ˌhē-mə-ˈstā-səs\ *n* [NL, fr. Gk *haimostasis* styptic, fr. *haimo-* hem- + *-stasis*] (1843) : arrest of bleeding

he·mo·stat \ˈhē-mə-ˌstat\ *n* (ca. 1900) : HEMOSTATIC; *esp* : an instrument for compressing a bleeding vessel

¹**he·mo·stat·ic** \ˌhē-mə-ˈsta-tik\ *n* (ca. 1706) : a hemostatic agent

²**hemostatic** *adj* (1834) **1** : of or caused by hemostasis **2** : serving to check bleeding

hemp \ˈhemp\ *n* [ME, fr. OE *hænep;* akin to OHG *hanaf* hemp, Gk *kannabis*] (bef. 12c) **1 a** : a tall widely cultivated Asian herb (*Cannabis sativa* of the family Cannabaceae, the hemp family) that has a tough bast fiber used esp. for cordage and that is often separated into a tall loosely branched species (*C. sativa*) and a low-growing densely branched species (*C. indica*) **b** : the fiber of hemp **c** : a psychoactive drug (as marijuana or hashish) from hemp **2** : a fiber (as jute) from a plant other than the true hemp; *also* : a plant yielding such fiber

hemp·en \ˈhem-pən\ *adj* (14c) : composed of hemp

hemp nettle *n* (1801) : any of a genus (*Galeopsis*) of coarse Old World herbs of the mint family; *esp* : a bristly Eurasian herb (*G. tetrahit*) naturalized in No. America as a weed

¹**hem·stitch** \ˈhem-ˌstich\ *vt* (1839) : to decorate (as a border) with hemstitch — **hem·stitch·er** *n*

²**hemstitch** *n* (1853) **1** : decorative needlework similar to drawnwork that is used esp. on or next to the stitching line of hems **2** : a stitch used in hemstitching

hen \ˈhen\ *n* [ME, fr. OE *henn;* akin to OE *hana* rooster — more at CHANT] (bef. 12c) **1 a** : a female chicken esp. over a year old; *broadly* : a female bird **b** : the female of various mostly aquatic animals (as lobsters or fish) **2** : WOMAN; *esp* : a fussy middle-aged woman

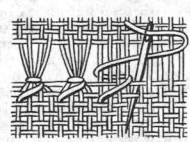

hemstitch

hen and chickens *n* (1884) : any of several plants having offsets, runners, or flowers that send out shoots; *esp* : HOUSELEEK

hen·bane \ˈhen-ˌbān\ *n* (14c) : a poisonous fetid Eurasian herb (*Hyoscyamus niger*) of the nightshade family with yellowish-brown flowers and sticky hairy leaves that yield hyoscyamine and scopolamine

hen·bit \ˈhen-ˌbit\ *n* (1597) : a Eurasian herb (*Lamium amplexicaule*) of the mint family that has small scalloped leaves and purplish flowers and is naturalized in No. America

hence \ˈhen(t)s\ *adv* [ME *hennes*, *henne*, fr. OE *heonan;* akin to OHG *hinnan* away, OE *hēr* here] (13c) **1** : from this place : AWAY **2 a** *archaic* : HENCEFORTH **b** : from this time ⟨four years ∼⟩ **3** : because of a preceding fact or premise : THEREFORE **4** : from this source or origin — **from hence** *archaic* : from this place : from this time

hence·forth \ˈhen(t)s-ˌfȯrth, hen(t)s-ˈ\ *adv* (14c) : from this point on

hence·for·ward \ˈhen(t)s-ˈfȯr-wərd\ *adv* (14c) : HENCEFORTH

hench·man \ˈhench-mən\ *n* [ME *henshman*, *hengestman* groom, fr. *hengest* stallion (fr. OE) + *man;* akin to OHG *hengist* gelding] (15c) **1** *obs* : a squire or page to a person of high rank **2 a** : a trusted follower : a right-hand man **b** : a political follower whose support is chiefly for personal advantage **c** : a member of a gang

hen·deca·syl·lab·ic \(ˌ)hen-ˌde-kə-sə-ˈla-bik\ *adj* [L *hendecasyllabus,* fr. Gk *hendeka* eleven (fr. *hen-, heis* one + *deka* ten) + *syllabē* syllable — more at SAME, TEN] (ca. 1751) **:** consisting of 11 syllables or composed of verses of 11 syllables — **hendecasyllabic** *n* — **hen·deca·syl·la·ble** \hen-ˈde-kə-ˌsi-lə-bəl, (ˌ)hen-ˌde-kə-ˈ\ *n*

hen·di·a·dys \hen-ˈdī-ə-dəs\ *n* [LL *hendiadys, hendiadyoin,* modif. of Gk *hen dia dyoin,* lit., one through two] (ca. 1577) **:** the expression of an idea by the use of usu. two independent words connected by *and* (as *nice and warm*) instead of the usual combination of independent word and its modifier (as *nicely warm*)

hen·e·quen \ˈhe-ni-kən, ˌhe-ni-ˈken\ *n* [Sp *henequén*] (1880) **:** a strong yellowish or reddish hard fiber obtained from the leaves of a tropical American agave (*Agave fourcroydes*) found chiefly in Yucatán and used esp. in making twine and rope; *also* **:** a plant that yields henequen

hen·house \ˈhen-ˌhau̇s\ *n* (1509) **:** a house or shelter for fowl

Hen·le's loop \ˈhen-lēz-\ *n* (ca. 1890) **:** LOOP OF HENLE

[1]**hen·na** \ˈhe-nə\ *n* [Ar *ḥinnāʾ*] (1600) **1 :** a reddish-brown dye obtained from leaves of the henna plant and used esp. on hair **2 :** an Old World tropical shrub or small tree (*Lawsonia inermis*) of the loosestrife family with small opposite leaves and panicles of fragrant usu. white flowers

[2]**henna** *vt* (1919) **:** to dye (as hair) with henna

hen·nery \ˈhe-nə-rē\ *n, pl* **-ner·ies** (1850) **:** a poultry farm; *also* **:** an enclosure for poultry

heno·the·ism \ˈhe-nə-(ˌ)thē-ˌi-zəm\ *n* [G *Henotheismus,* fr. Gk *hen-, heis* one + *theos* god — more at SAME] (1860) **:** the worship of one god without denying the existence of other gods — **heno·the·ist** \-ˌthē-ist\ *n* — **heno·the·is·tic** \ˌhe-nə-thē-ˈis-tik\ *adj*

hen party *n* (ca. 1885) **:** a party for women only

hen·peck \ˈhen-ˌpek\ *vt* (1671) **:** to subject (one's husband) to persistent nagging and domination

hen·ry \ˈhen-rē\ *n, pl* **henrys** *or* **henries** [Joseph *Henry*] (ca. 1890) **:** the practical meter-kilogram-second unit of inductance equal to the self-inductance of a circuit or the mutual inductance of two circuits in which the variation of one ampere per second results in an induced electromotive force of one volt

hent \ˈhent\ *vt* [ME, fr. OE *hentan*] (bef. 12c) *archaic* **:** SEIZE

hen track *n* (1878) **:** an illegible or scarcely legible mark intended as handwriting — called also *hen scratch*

[1]**hep** \ˈhep, ˈhəp, ˈhət\ *interj* [origin unknown] (1862) — used to mark a marching cadence

[2]**hep** \ˈhep\ *adj* [origin unknown] (1903) **:** [4]HIP

HEPA \ˈhe-pə\ *adj* [*h*igh-*e*fficiency *p*articulate *a*ir (filter)] (1983) **:** being, using, or containing a filter usu. designed to remove 99.97% of airborne particles measuring 0.3 micrometers or greater in diameter passing through it

hep·a·rin \ˈhe-pə-rən\ *n* [ISV, fr. Gk *hēpar* liver] (1918) **:** a mucopolysaccharide sulfuric acid ester that is found esp. in the liver and lungs, that prolongs the clotting time of blood, and that is used medically in the form of its sodium salt — **hep·a·rin·ized** \-rə-ˌnīzd\ *adj*

hepat- *or* **hepato-** *comb form* [L, fr. Gk *hēpat-, hēpato-,* fr. *hēpat-, hēpar;* akin to L *jecur* liver] **1 :** liver ⟨*hepat*ectomy⟩ ⟨*hepato*toxic⟩ **2 :** hepatic and ⟨*hepato*cellular⟩

hep·a·tec·to·my \ˌhe-pə-ˈtek-tə-mē\ *n, pl* **-mies** (ca. 1890) **:** excision of the liver or of part of the liver — **hep·a·tec·to·mized** \-ˌmīzd\ *adj*

[1]**he·pat·ic** \hi-ˈpa-tik\ *adj* [L *hepaticus,* fr. Gk *hēpatikos,* fr. *hēpat-, hēpar*] (1599) **:** of, relating to, affecting, associated with, supplying, or draining the liver ⟨a ~ complaint⟩ ⟨~ arteries⟩

[2]**hepatic** *n* (1900) **:** LIVERWORT

he·pat·i·ca \hi-ˈpa-ti-kə\ *n* [NL, fr. ML, liverwort, fr. L, fem. of *hepaticus*] (1578) **:** any of a genus (*Hepatica*) of herbs of the buttercup family with lobed leaves and delicate flowers

hep·a·ti·tis \ˌhe-pə-ˈtī-təs\ *n, pl* **-tit·i·des** \-ˈti-tə-ˌdēz\ *also* **-ti·tis·es** \-ˈtī-tə-səz\ [NL] (ca. 1751) **1 :** inflammation of the liver **2 :** a disease or condition (as hepatitis A or hepatitis B) marked by inflammation of the liver

hepatitis A *n* (1972) **:** an acute usu. benign hepatitis caused by a picornavirus (species *Hepatitis A virus* of the genus *Hepatovirus*) that does not persist in the blood serum and is transmitted esp. in food and water contaminated with infected fecal matter — called also *infectious hepatitis*

hepatitis B *n* (1971) **:** a sometimes fatal hepatitis caused by a double-stranded DNA virus (species *Hepatitis B virus* of the genus *Orthohepadnavirus,* family *Hepadnaviridae*) that tends to persist in the blood serum and is transmitted esp. by contact with infected blood or other bodily fluids (as semen) — called also *serum hepatitis*

hepatitis C *n* (1978) **:** a hepatitis caused by a flavivirus (species *Hepatitis C virus* of the genus *Hepacivirus*) that tends to persist in the blood serum and is usu. transmitted by contact with infected blood (as by transfusion or by illicit intravenous drug use)

he·pa·to·cel·lu·lar \ˌhe-pə-tō-ˈsel-yə-lər, hi-ˌpa-tə-ˈsel-\ *adj* (1940) **:** of or involving hepatocytes ⟨~ carcinoma⟩

he·pa·to·cyte \hi-ˈpa-tə-ˌsīt, ˈhe-pə-tə-\ *n* (1965) **:** an epithelial parenchymatous cell of the liver

hep·a·to·ma \ˌhe-pə-ˈtō-mə\ *n, pl* **-mas** *also* **-ma·ta** \-mə-tə\ [NL] (1905) **:** a usu. malignant tumor of the liver

he·pa·to·meg·a·ly \ˌhe-pə-tō-ˈme-gə-lē, hi-ˌpa-tə-ˈme-\ *n, pl* **-lies** (ca. 1901) **:** enlargement of the liver

he·pa·to·pan·cre·as \-ˈpaŋ-krē-əs, -ˈpan-\ *n* (1884) **:** a glandular structure (as of a crustacean) that combines the digestive functions of the vertebrate liver and pancreas

hep·a·to·tox·ic \-ˈtäk-sik\ *adj* (1926) **:** relating to or causing injury to the liver ⟨~ drugs⟩

hep·a·to·tox·ic·i·ty \-täk-ˈsi-sə-tē\ *n* (1952) **1 :** a state of toxic damage to the liver **2 :** a tendency or capacity to cause hepatotoxicity

hep·cat \ˈhep-ˌkat\ *n* (1937) **:** HIPSTER

He·phaes·tus \hi-ˈfes-təs, -ˈfēs-\ *n* [L, fr. Gk *Hēphaistos*] (1658) **:** the Greek god of fire and metalworking — compare VULCAN

hepped up *adj* [alter. of [3]*hipped*] (1939) **:** ENTHUSIASTIC

Hep·ple·white \ˈhe-pəl-ˌhwīt, -ˌwīt\ *adj* [George *Hepplewhite*] (1897) **:** of, relating to, or imitating a style of furniture originating in late 18th century England

hepta- *or* **hept-** *comb form* [Gk, fr. *hepta* — more at SEVEN] **1 :** seven ⟨*hepta*meter⟩ **2 :** containing seven atoms, groups, or equivalents ⟨*hept*ane⟩

hep·ta·chlor \ˈhep-t-əˌklȯr\ *n* [*hepta-* + *chlor*ine] (1949) **:** a cyclodiene chlorinated hydrocarbon pesticide $C_{10}H_5Cl_7$ that causes liver disease in animals and is a suspected human carcinogen

hep·tad \ˈhep-ˌtad\ *n* [Gk *heptad-, heptas,* fr. *hepta*] (1660) **:** a group of seven

hep·ta·gon \ˈhep-tə-ˌgän\ *n* [Gk *heptagōnos* heptagonal, fr. *hepta* + *gōnia* angle — more at -GON] (1570) **:** a polygon of seven angles and seven sides — **hep·tag·o·nal** \hep-ˈta-gə-nᵊl\ *adj*

hep·tam·e·ter \hep-ˈta-mə-tər\ *n* (ca. 1849) **:** a line of verse consisting of seven metrical feet

hep·tane \ˈhep-ˌtān\ *n* (1877) **:** any of several isomeric alkanes C_7H_{16}; *esp* **:** the liquid normal isomer occurring in petroleum and used esp. as a solvent and in determining octane numbers

hep·tar·chy \ˈhep-ˌtär-kē\ *n* (1576) **:** a hypothetical confederacy of seven Anglo-Saxon kingdoms of the seventh and eighth centuries

Hep·ta·teuch \ˈhep-tə-ˌtük, -ˌtyük\ *n* [LL *heptateuchos,* fr. Gk, fr. *hepta* + *teuchos* book — more at PENTATEUCH] (1678) **:** the first seven books of the canonical Jewish and Christian Scriptures

hep·tath·lete \hep-ˈtath-ˌlēt\ *n* [blend of *heptathlon* and *athlete*] (1981) **:** an athlete who competes in a heptathlon

hep·tath·lon \hep-ˈtath-lən, -ˌlän, ÷-ˈta-thə-\ *n* [*hept-* + *-athlon* (as in *decathlon*)] (1977) **:** a 7-event athletic contest; *specif* **:** a composite contest for female athletes that consists of the 100-meter hurdles, the high jump, the shot put, the 200-meter dash, the long jump, the javelin throw, and the 800-meter run

hep·tose \ˈhep-ˌtōs, -ˌtōz\ *n* (1890) **:** any of various monosaccharides $C_7H_{14}O_7$ containing seven carbon atoms in a molecule

[1]**her** \(h)ər, ˈhər\ *adj* [ME *hire,* fr. OE *hiere,* gen. of *hēo* she — more at HE] (bef. 12c) **:** of or relating to her or herself esp. as possessor, agent, or object of an action ⟨~ house⟩ ⟨~ research⟩ — compare [1]SHE

[2]**her** *pron, objective case of* SHE

[3]**her** *abbr* heraldry

He·ra \ˈhir-ə, ˈhe-rə, ˈher-ə\ *n* [Gk *Hēra, Hērē*] (1584) **:** the sister and consort of Zeus — compare JUNO

Her·a·cles \ˈher-ə-ˌklēz-, ˈhe-rə-\ *n* [Gk *Hēraklēs*] (1846) **:** HERCULES

[1]**her·ald** \ˈher-əld, ˈhe-rəld\ *n* [ME, fr. AF *heraud, herald,* fr. Frankish **heriwald-,* lit., leader of an armed force, fr. **heri-* army + **wald-* rule; akin to OHG *heri-* army, *waltan* to rule — more at HARRY, WIELD] **1 a :** an official at a tournament of arms with duties including the making of announcements and the marshaling of combatants **b :** an officer with the status of ambassador acting as official messenger between leaders esp. in war **c (1) :** OFFICER OF ARMS **(2) :** an officer of arms ranking above a pursuivant and below a king of arms **2 :** an official crier or messenger **3 a :** one that precedes or foreshadows **b :** one that conveys news or proclaims **:** ANNOUNCER **c :** one who actively promotes or advocates **:** EXPONENT ***syn*** see FORERUNNER

[2]**herald** *vt* (14c) **1 :** to give notice of **:** ANNOUNCE **2 a :** to greet esp. with enthusiasm **:** HAIL ⟨doctors are ~*ing* a new drug⟩ **b :** PUBLICIZE **3 :** to signal the approach of **:** FORESHADOW

he·ral·dic \he-ˈral-dik, hə-\ *adj* (1772) **:** of or relating to heralds or heraldry — **he·ral·di·cal·ly** \-di-k(ə-)lē\ *adv*

her·ald·ry \ˈher-əl-drē, ˈhe-rəl-\ *n, pl* **-ries** (1572) **1 :** the practice of devising, blazoning, and granting armorial insignia and of tracing and recording genealogies **2 :** an armorial ensign; *broadly* **:** INSIGNIA **3 :** PAGEANTRY

herb \ˈərb, *US also & Brit usu* ˈhərb\ *n, often attrib* [ME *herbe,* fr. AF, fr. L *herba*] (14c) **1 :** a seed-producing annual, biennial, or perennial that does not develop persistent woody tissue but dies down at the end of a growing season **2 :** a plant or plant part valued for its medicinal, savory, or aromatic qualities **3** *slang* **:** MARIJUANA 2 — **herb·like** \ˈ(h)ərb-ˌlīk\ *adj* — **herby** \ˈ(h)ər-bē\ *adj*

her·ba·ceous \ˌ(h)ər-ˈbā-shəs\ *adj* (1640) **1 a :** of, relating to, or having the characteristics of an herb **b** *of a stem* **:** having little or no woody tissue and persisting usu. for a single growing season **2 :** having the texture, color, or appearance of a leaf

herb·age \ˈ(h)ər-bij\ *n* (14c) **1 :** herbaceous vegetation (as grass) esp. when used for grazing **2 :** the succulent parts of herbaceous plants

[1]**herb·al** \ˈ(h)ər-bəl\ *n* (1516) **1 :** a book about plants esp. with reference to their medicinal properties **2** *archaic* **:** HERBARIUM 1

[2]**herbal** *adj* (1612) **:** of, relating to, utilizing, or made of herbs

herb·al·ism \ˈ(h)ər-bə-ˌliz-əm\ *n* (1855) **:** HERBAL MEDICINE 1

herb·al·ist \ˈ(h)ər-bə-list\ *n* (1589) **1 :** a person who practices healing by the use of herbs **2 :** a person who collects or grows herbs

herbal medicine *n* (1848) **1 :** the art or practice of using herbs and herbal preparations to maintain health and to prevent, alleviate, or cure disease **2 :** a plant or plant part or an extract or mixture of these used in herbal medicine

her·bar·i·um \ˌ(h)ər-ˈber-ē-əm\ *n, pl* **-ia** \-ē-ə\ (1776) **1 :** a collection of dried plant specimens usu. mounted and systematically arranged for reference **2 :** a place that houses an herbarium

herb doctor *n* (1828) **:** HERBALIST 1

herbed \ˈ(h)ərbd\ *adj* (1950) **:** seasoned with herbs

her·bi·cide \ˈ(h)ər-bə-ˌsīd\ *n* [L *herba* + ISV *-cide*] (1899) **:** an agent used to destroy or inhibit plant growth — **her·bi·cid·al** \ˌ(h)ər-bə-ˈsī-dᵊl\ *adj* — **her·bi·cid·al·ly** \-dᵊl-ē\ *adv*

her·bi·vore \ˈ(h)ər-bə-ˌvȯr\ *n* [NL *Herbivora,* group of mammals, fr. neut. pl. of *herbivorus*] (1854) **:** a herbivorous animal

her·biv·o·rous \ˌ(h)ər-ˈbiv-rəs, -ˈbi-və-\ *adj* [NL *herbivorus,* fr. L *herba* grass + *-vorus* -vorous] (1661) **:** feeding on plants — **her·biv·o·ry** \-ˈbi-və-rē\ *n*

her·bol·o·gy \(h)ər-ˈbä-lə-jē\ *n* (1961) **:** HERBAL MEDICINE 1

herb Rob·ert \ˈ(h)ərb-ˈrä-bərt\ *n* [ML *herba Roberti,* prob. fr. *Robertus* (St. Robert) †1067 Fr. ecclesiastic] (13c) **:** a low annual or biennial geranium (*Geranium robertianum*) with small reddish-purple flowers

Her·cu·le·an \ˌhər-kyə-ˈlē-ən, ˌhər-ˈkyü-lē-\ *adj* (1513) **1 :** of, relating to, or characteristic of Hercules **2** *often not cap* **:** of extraordinary power, extent, intensity, or difficulty ⟨~ tasks⟩ ⟨~ proportions⟩

Her·cu·les \'hər-kyə-ˌlēz\ n [L, fr. Gk *Hēraklēs*] (13c) **1** : a mythical Greek hero renowned for his great strength and esp. for performing 12 labors imposed on him by Hera **2** [L (gen. *Herculis*)] : a northern constellation between Corona Borealis and Lyra

Her·cu·les'–club \'hər-kyə-ˌlēz-ˌkləb\ n (1847) **1** : a small prickly eastern U.S. tree (*Aralia spinosa*) of the ginseng family with large compound leaves — called also *angelica tree* **2** : a small prickly southern U.S. tree (*Zanthoxylum clava-herculis*) of the rue family

¹**herd** \'hərd\ n [ME, fr. OE *heord;* akin to OHG *herta* herd, MW *cordd* troop, Lith *kerdžius* shepherd] (bef. 12c) **1 a** : a number of animals of one kind kept together under human control **b** : a congregation of gregarious wild animals **2 a** (1) : a group of people usu. having a common bond ⟨a ~ of tourists⟩ (2) : a large assemblage of like things **b** : the undistinguished masses : CROWD ⟨isolate the individual prophets from the ~ —Norman Cousins⟩ — **herd·like** \-ˌlīk\ adj

²**herd** vt (13c) **1 a** : to gather, lead, or drive as if in a herd ⟨~ed the children into the car⟩ **b** : to keep or move (animals) together **2** : to place in a group ~ vi **1** : to assemble or move in a herd **2** : to place oneself in a group : ASSOCIATE

herd·er \'hərd-ər\ n (1635) : one that herds; *specif* : HERDSMAN 1

herds·man \'hərdz-mən\ n (1567) **1** : a manager, breeder, or tender of livestock **2** cap : BOÖTES

¹**here** \'hir\ adv [ME, fr. OE *hēr;* akin to OHG *hier* here, OE *hē* he] (bef. 12c) **1 a** : in or at this place ⟨turn ~⟩ — often used interjectionally esp. in answering a roll call **b** : NOW ⟨~ it's morning already⟩ **c** : in an arbitrary location ⟨a book ~, a paper there⟩ **2** : at or in this point, particular, or case ⟨~ we agree⟩ **3** : in the present life or state **4** : HITHER ⟨come ~⟩ **5** — used interjectionally in rebuke or encouragement — **here goes** — used interjectionally to express resolution or resignation esp. at the beginning of a difficult or unpleasant undertaking — **neither here nor there** : having no interest or relevance : of no consequence ⟨comfort is *neither here nor there* to a real sailor⟩

²**here** adj (15c) **1** — used for emphasis esp. after a demonstrative pronoun or after a noun modified by a demonstrative adjective ⟨this book ~⟩ **2** nonstand — used for emphasis after a demonstrative adjective but before the noun modified ⟨this ~ book⟩

³**here** n (1605) : this place

here·abouts \'hir-ə-ˌbauts\ or **here·about** \-ˌbaut\ adv (13c) : in this vicinity

¹**here·af·ter** \hir-'af-tər\ adv (bef. 12c) **1** : after this in sequence or in time **2** : in some future time or state

²**hereafter** n, often cap (1546) **1** : FUTURE **2** : an existence beyond earthly life ⟨belief in the ~⟩

³**hereafter** adj (1591) archaic : FUTURE

here and now n (1829) : the present time — used with *the* ⟨man's obligation is in the *here and now* —W. H. Whyte⟩

here and there adv (14c) **1** : in one place and another **2** : from time to time

here·away \'hir-ə-ˌwā\ or **here·aways** \-ˌwāz\ adv (14c) dial : HEREABOUTS

here·by \hir-'bī, 'hir-ˌ\ adv (13c) : by this means

her·e·dit·a·ment \ˌher-ə-'di-tə-mənt\ n [ME, fr. ML *hereditamentum*, fr. LL *hereditare* to inherit, fr. L *hered-, heres*] (15c) : heritable property

he·red·i·tar·i·an \hə-ˌre-də-'ter-ē-ən\ n (1881) : an advocate of the theory that individual differences in human beings can be accounted for primarily on the basis of genetics — **hereditarian** adj

he·red·i·tary \hə-'re-də-ˌter-ē\ adj [ME *hereditarie*, fr. L *hereditarius*, fr. *hereditas*] (15c) **1 a** : genetically transmitted or transmittable from parent to offspring **b** : characteristic of or fostered by one's predecessors **2 a** : received or passing by inheritance or required to pass by inheritance or by reason of birth **b** : having title or possession through inheritance or by reason of birth **3** : of a kind established by tradition ⟨~ enemies⟩ **4** : of or relating to inheritance or heredity syn see INNATE — **he·red·i·tar·i·ly** \-ˌre-də-'ter-ə-lē\ adv

he·red·i·ty \hə-'re-də-tē\ n [MF *heredité*, fr. L *hereditat-, hereditas*, fr. *hered-, heres* heir — more at HEIR] (ca. 1540) **1 a** : INHERITANCE **b** : TRADITION **2 a** : the sum of the characteristics and potentialities genetically derived from one's ancestors **b** : the transmission of such qualities from ancestor to descendant through the genes

Her·e·ford \'hər-fərd sometimes 'her-ə-\ n [*Hereford* former county in England] (1805) : any of a breed of hardy red-coated beef cattle of English origin with white faces and markings

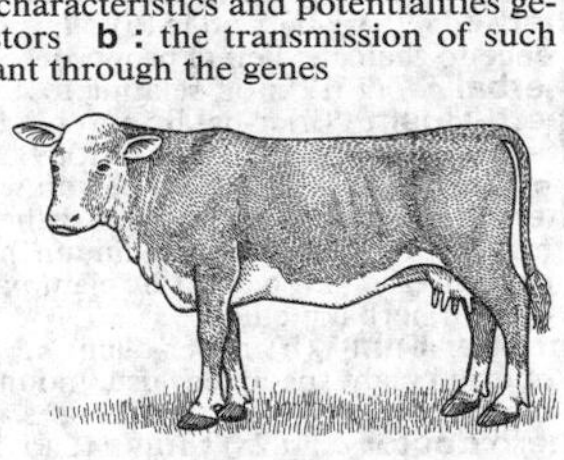

Hereford

here·in \hir-'in\ adv (bef. 12c) : in this

here·in·above \ˌ(ˌ)hir-ˌin-ə-'bəv\ adv (ca. 1812) : at a prior point in this writing or document

here·in·af·ter \ˌhir-ə-'naf-tər\ adv (1590) : in the following part of this writing or document

here·in·be·fore \ˌ(ˌ)hir-ˌin-bi-'for\ adv (1687) : in the preceding part of this writing or document

here·in·be·low \-bi-'lō\ adv (1946) : at a subsequent point in this writing or document

here·of \hir-'əv, -'äv\ adv (bef. 12c) : of this

here·on \-'ȯn, -'än\ adv (12c) : on this

He·re·ro \hə-'rer-(ˌ)ō, 'her-ə-ˌrō\ n, pl **Herero** or **Hereros** (1880) : a member of a Bantu people of central Namibia

her·e·si·arch \hə-'rē-zē-ˌärk, 'her-ə-sē-\ n [LL *haeresiarcha*, fr. LGk *hairesiarchēs*, fr. *hairesis* + Gk *-archēs* -arch] (1624) : an originator or chief advocate of a heresy

her·e·sy \'her-ə-sē, 'he-rə-\ n, pl **-sies** [ME *heresie*, fr. AF, fr. LL *haeresis*, fr. LGk *hairesis*, fr. Gk, action of taking, choice, sect, fr. *hairein* to take] (13c) **1 a** : adherence to a religious opinion contrary to church dogma **b** : denial of a revealed truth by a baptized member of the Roman Catholic Church **c** : an opinion or doctrine contrary to church dogma **2 a** : dissent or deviation from a dominant theory, opinion, or practice **b** : an opinion, doctrine, or practice contrary to the truth or to generally accepted beliefs or standards

her·e·tic \'her-ə-ˌtik, 'he-rə-\ n (14c) **1** : a dissenter from established religious dogma; *esp* : a baptized member of the Roman Catholic Church who disavows a revealed truth **2** : one who dissents from an accepted belief or doctrine : NONCONFORMIST

he·ret·i·cal \hə-'re-ti-kəl\ also **heretic** adj (15c) **1** : of, relating to, or characterized by heresy **2** : of, relating to, or characterized by departure from accepted beliefs or standards : UNORTHODOX — **he·ret·i·cal·ly** \hə-'re-ti-k(ə-)lē\ adv

here·to \hir-'tü\ adv (12c) : to this writing or document

here·to·fore \'hir-tə-ˌfȯr, ˌhir-tə-'\ adv (13c) : up to this time : HITHERTO

here·un·der \hir-'ən-dər\ adv (15c) : under or in accordance with this writing or document

here·un·to \hir-ˌən-(ˌ)tü, ˌhir-(ˌ)ən-'tü\ adv (1509) : to this

here·up·on \'hir-ə-ˌpȯn, -ˌpän, ˌhir-ə-'\ adv (12c) : on this : immediately after this

here·with \hir-'with, -'with\ adv (bef. 12c) **1** : with this communication : enclosed in this **2** : HEREBY

He·rez \he-'rez\ or **He·riz** \-'riz\ n [*Herez, Heriz*, town in Iran] (ca. 1922) : a Persian rug characterized by a large central geometric medallion and by angular floral designs

her·i·ot \'her-ē-ət\ n [ME, fr. OE *heregeatwe*, pl., military equipment, fr. *here* army (akin to OHG *heri* army) + *geatwe* equipment — more at HARRY] (bef. 12c) : a feudal duty or tribute due under English law to a lord on the death of a tenant

her·i·ta·bil·i·ty \ˌher-ə-tə-'bi-lə-tē, ˌhe-rə-\ n (1832) **1** : the quality or state of being heritable **2** : the proportion of observed variation in a particular trait (as height) that can be attributed to inherited genetic factors in contrast to environmental ones

her·i·ta·ble \'her-ə-tə-bəl, 'he-rə-\ adj (14c) **1** : capable of being inherited or of passing by inheritance **2** : HEREDITARY

her·i·tage \'her-ə-tij, 'he-rə-\ n [ME, fr. AF, fr. *heriter* to inherit, fr. LL *hereditare*, fr. L *hered-, heres* heir — more at HEIR] (13c) **1** : property that descends to an heir **2 a** : something transmitted by or acquired from a predecessor : LEGACY, INHERITANCE **b** : TRADITION **3** : something possessed as a result of one's natural situation or birth : BIRTHRIGHT ⟨the nation's ~ of tolerance⟩

her·i·tor \'her-ə-tər\ n (15c) : one that inherits : INHERITOR

herky–jerky \ˌhər-kē-'jər-kē\ adj [redupl. of *jerky*] (1957) : characterized by sudden, irregular, or unpredictable movement or style

herm \'hərm\ n [L *hermes*, fr. Gk *hermēs* statue of Hermes, herm, fr. *Hermēs*] (ca. 1580) : a statue in the form of a square stone pillar surmounted by a bust or head esp. of Hermes

her·ma \'hər-mə\ n, pl **her·mae** \-ˌmē, -ˌmī\ or **her·mai** \-ˌmī\ (1638) : HERM

her·maph·ro·dite \(ˌ)hər-'ma-frə-ˌdīt\ n [ME *hermofrodite*, fr. L *hermaphroditus*, fr. Gk *hermaphroditos*, fr. *Hermaphroditos*] (14c) **1** : an animal or plant having both male and female reproductive organs **2** : something that is a combination of diverse elements — **hermaphrodite** adj — **her·maph·ro·dit·ic** \(ˌ)hər-ˌma-frə-'di-tik\ adj — **her·maph·ro·dit·ism** \-ma-frə-ˌdī-ˌti-zəm\ n

Her·maph·ro·di·tus \(ˌ)hər-ˌma-frə-'dī-təs\ n [L, fr. Gk *Hermaphroditos*, fr. *Hermēs* + *Aphroditē* Aphrodite] (1565) : a son of Hermes and Aphrodite who becomes joined in one body with a nymph while bathing

her·ma·typ·ic \ˌhər-mə-'ti-pik\ adj [Gk *herma* prop, reef + *typtein* to strike, coin + E *-ic* — more at TYPE] (1950) : building reefs ⟨~ corals⟩

her·me·neu·tic \ˌhər-mə-'nü-tik, -'nyü-\ n (1737) **1** pl but sing or pl in constr : the study of the methodological principles of interpretation (as of the Bible) **2** : a method or principle of interpretation

her·me·neu·ti·cal \ˌhər-mə-'nü-ti-kəl, -'nyü-\ or **her·me·neu·tic** \-tik\ adj [Gk *hermēneutikos*, fr. *hermēneuein* to interpret, fr. *hermēneus* interpreter] (1678) : of or relating to hermeneutics : INTERPRETATIVE — **her·me·neu·ti·cal·ly** \-ti-k(ə-)lē\ adv

Her·mes \'hər-(ˌ)mēz\ n [L, fr. Gk *Hermēs*] (14c) : a Greek god of commerce, eloquence, invention, travel, and theft who serves as herald and messenger of the other gods — compare MERCURY

Hermes Tris·me·gis·tus \-ˌtris-mə-'jis-təs\ n [ML, fr. Gk *Hermēs trismegistos*, lit., Hermes thrice greatest] (1583) : a legendary author of works embodying magical, astrological, and alchemical doctrines

her·met·ic \(ˌ)hər-'me-tik\ also **her·met·i·cal** \-ti-kəl\ adj [ML *hermeticus*, fr. *Hermet-, Hermes Trismegistus*] (1605) **1** often cap : of or relating to the mystical and alchemical writings or teachings arising in the first three centuries A.D. and attributed to Hermes Trismegistus **b** : relating to or characterized by occultism or abstruseness : RECONDITE **2** [fr. the belief that Hermes Trismegistus invented a magic seal to keep vessels airtight] **a** : AIRTIGHT ⟨~ seal⟩ **b** : impervious to external influence ⟨trapped inside the ~ military machine —Jack Newfield⟩ **c** : RECLUSE, SOLITARY ⟨leads a ~ life⟩ — **her·met·i·cal·ly** \-ti-k(ə-)lē\ adv

her·met·i·cism \-'me-tə-ˌsi-zəm\ n, often cap (1897) : HERMETISM

her·me·tism \'hər-mə-ˌti-zəm\ n, often cap (1897) **1 a** : a system of ideas based on hermetic teachings **b** : adherence to or practice of hermetic doctrine **2** : the practice of being hermetically mysterious ⟨it is not . . . willful ~, if the message of their art is veiled and indirect —R. J. Goldwater⟩ — **her·me·tist** \-mə-tist\ n

her·mit \'hər-mət\ n [ME *heremite, eremite*, fr. AF, fr. LL *eremita*, fr. LGk *erēmitēs*, fr. Gk, adj., living in the desert, fr. *erēmia* desert, fr. *erēmos* desolate] (12c) **1** : one that retires from society and lives in solitude esp. for religious reasons : RECLUSE **b** obs : BEADSMAN **2 a** : a spiced molasses cookie — **her·mit·ism** \-mə-ˌti-zəm\ n

her·mit·age \'hər-mə-tij\ n (14c) **1 a** : the habitation of a hermit **b** : a secluded residence or private retreat : HIDEAWAY **c** : MONASTERY **2** : the life or condition of a hermit

Her·mi·tage \ˌ(h)er-mi-'täzh\ n [Tain-l'*Ermitage*, commune in France] (1680) : a red or white Rhone valley wine

hermit crab n (1735) : any of numerous chiefly marine small decapod crustaceans (esp. families Diogenidae, Paguridae, and Parapaguridae) having soft asymmetrical abdomens and occupying the empty shells of gastropods

Her·mi·tian matrix \er-'mē-shən-, ˌhər-'mi-shən-\ n [Charles *Hermite* †1901 Fr. mathematician] (1935) : a square matrix having the property that each pair of elements in the ith row and jth column and in the jth row and ith column are conjugate complex numbers

hern \'hern, 'hərn\ dial var of HERON

her·nia \ˈhər-nē-ə\ *n, pl* **-ni·as** *or* **-ni·ae** \-nē-ˌē, -nē-ˌī\ [L — more at YARN] (14c) **:** a protrusion of an organ or part (as the intestine) through connective tissue or through a wall of the cavity (as of the abdomen) in which it is normally enclosed — called also *rupture* — **her·ni·al** \-nē-əl\ *adj*

her·ni·ate \ˈhər-nē-ˌāt\ *vi* **-at·ed; -at·ing** (ca. 1922) **:** to protrude through an abnormal body opening **:** RUPTURE ⟨a *herniated* intervertebral disk⟩ — **her·ni·a·tion** \ˌhər-nē-ˈā-shən\ *n*

he·ro \ˈhir-(ˌ)ō\ *n, pl* **heroes** [L *heros,* fr. Gk *hērōs*] (14c) **1 a :** a mythological or legendary figure often of divine descent endowed with great strength or ability **b :** an illustrious warrior **c :** a man admired for his achievements and noble qualities **d :** one that shows great courage **2 a :** the principal male character in a literary or dramatic work **b :** the central figure in an event, period, or movement **3** *pl usu* **heros :** SUBMARINE 2 **4 :** an object of extreme admiration and devotion **:** IDOL

Hero *n* [L, fr. Gk *Hērō*] (14c) **:** a legendary priestess of Aphrodite loved by Leander

[1]**he·ro·ic** \hi-ˈrō-ik *also* her-ˈō- *or* hē-ˈrō-\ *also* **he·ro·ical** \-i-kəl\ *adj* (1549) **1 :** of, relating to, resembling, or suggesting heroes esp. of antiquity **2 a :** exhibiting or marked by courage and daring **b :** supremely noble or self-sacrificing **3 a :** of impressive size, power, extent, or effect ⟨a ~ voice⟩ **b** (1) **:** of great intensity **:** EXTREME ⟨~ effort⟩ (2) **:** of a kind that is likely only to be undertaken to save a life ⟨~ surgery⟩ **4 :** of, relating to, or constituting drama written during the Restoration in heroic couplets and concerned with a conflict between love and honor — **he·ro·ical·ly** \-i-k(ə-)lē\ *adv*

[2]**heroic** *n* (1596) **1 :** a heroic verse or poem **2** *pl* **a :** flamboyantly heroic language or action **b :** heroic action or behavior **c :** determined effort esp. in the face of difficulty

heroic couplet *n* (1828) **:** a rhyming couplet in iambic pentameter

he·ro·i·cize \hi-ˈrō-ə-ˌsīz *also* her-ˈō- *or* hē-ˈrō-\ *vt* **-ized; -iz·ing** (1897) **:** HEROIZE

he·roi·com·ic \hi-ˌrō-i-ˈkä-mik\ *or* **he·roi·com·i·cal** \-ˈkä-mi-kəl\ *adj* [F *héroïcomique,* fr. *héroïque* heroic + *comique* comic] (1756) **:** comic by being ludicrously noble, bold, or elevated

heroic poem *n* (1693) **:** an epic or a poem in epic style

heroic stanza *n* (ca. 1922) **:** a rhymed quatrain in heroic verse with a rhyme scheme of *abab* — called also *heroic quatrain*

heroic verse *n* (1586) **1 :** dactylic hexameter esp. of epic verse of classical times — called also *heroic meter* **2 :** the iambic pentameter used esp. in English epic poetry during the 17th and 18th centuries — called also *heroic line, heroic meter*

her·o·in \ˈher-ə-wən, ˈhe-rə-\ *n* [fr. *Heroin,* a trademark] (1898) **:** a strongly physiologically addictive narcotic $C_{21}H_{23}NO_5$ that is made by acetylation of but is more potent than morphine and that is prohibited for medical use in the U.S. but is used illicitly for its euphoric effects — **her·o·in·ism** \-wə-ˌni-zəm\ *n*

her·o·ine \ˈher-ə-wən, ˈhir-, ˈhe-rə-\ *n* [L *heroina,* fr. Gk *hērōinē,* fem. of *hērōs*] (1609) **1 a :** a mythological or legendary woman having the qualities of a hero **b :** a woman admired and emulated for her achievements and qualities **2 a :** the principal female character in a literary or dramatic work **b :** the central female figure in an event or period

her·o·ism \ˈher-ə-ˌwi-zəm, ˈhe-rə- *also* ˈhir-\ *n* (1717) **1 :** heroic conduct esp. as exhibited in fulfilling a high purpose or attaining a noble end **2 :** the qualities of a hero

he·ro·ize \ˈhir-(ˌ)ō-ˌīz; ˈher-ə-ˌwīz, ˈhe-rə-\ *vt* **-ized; -iz·ing** (1738) **:** to make heroic

her·on \ˈher-ən, ˈhe-rən\ *n, pl* **herons** *also* **heron** [ME *heiroun, hayroun,* fr. AF *heiron,* of Gmc origin; akin to OHG *heigaro* heron] (14c) **:** any of various long-necked and long-legged wading birds (family Ardeidae) with a long tapering bill, large wings, and soft plumage

her·on·ry \-rē\ *n, pl* **-ries** (1616) **:** a heron rookery

hero–worship *vt* (1884) **:** to feel or express hero worship for — **hero–worshiper** *n*

hero worship *n* (1774) **1 :** veneration of a hero **2 :** foolish or excessive adulation for an individual

her·pes \ˈhər-(ˌ)pēz\ *n* [L, fr. Gk *herpēs,* fr. *herpein* to creep — more at SERPENT] (14c) **:** any of several inflammatory diseases of the skin caused by herpesviruses and characterized by clusters of vesicles; *esp* **:** HERPES SIMPLEX — **her·pet·ic** \(ˌ)hər-ˈpe-tik\ *adj*

herpes sim·plex \-ˈsim-ˌpleks\ *n* [NL, lit., simple herpes] (1907) **:** either of two diseases caused by herpesviruses (species *Human herpesvirus 1* and *Human herpesvirus 2* of the genus *Simplexvirus*) and marked esp. by watery blisters on the skin or mucous membranes of the lips, mouth, face, or genital region

her·pes·vi·rus \-ˈvī-rəs\ *n* (1925) **:** any of a family (*Herpesviridae*) of double-stranded DNA viruses that include the cytomegalovirus and Epstein-Barr virus and the causative agents of chicken pox, herpes simplex, Marek's disease, roseola infantum, and shingles

herpes zoster *n* [NL, lit., girdle herpes] (1807) **:** SHINGLES

her·pe·tol·o·gy \ˌhər-pə-ˈtä-lə-jē\ *n* [Gk *herpeton* quadruped, reptile, fr. neut. of *herpetos* crawling, fr. *herpein*] (1824) **:** a branch of zoology dealing with reptiles and amphibians — **her·pe·to·log·i·cal** \-tə-ˈlä-ji-kəl\ *adj* — **her·pe·tol·o·gist** \ˌhər-pə-ˈtä-lə-jist\ *n*

Herr \(ˌ)her\ *n, pl* **Her·ren** \ˌher-ən, (ˌ)hern\ [G] (1653) — used among German-speaking people as a title equivalent to *Mr.*

her·ren·volk \ˈher-ən-ˌfōk, -ˌfōlk\ *n, often cap* [G] (1940) **:** MASTER RACE

her·ring \ˈher-iŋ, ˈhe-riŋ\ *n, pl* **herring** *or* **herrings** [ME *hering,* fr. OE *hǣring;* akin to OHG *hārinc* herring] (bef. 12c) **1 :** either of two food fishes (genus *Clupeus*): **a :** one (*C. harengus*) that is abundant in the temperate and colder parts of the No. Atlantic and that in the adult state is preserved by smoking or salting and in the young state is extensively canned and sold as sardines **b :** one (*C. pallasi* syn. *C. h. pallasi*) of the No. Pacific harvested esp. for its roe **2 :** any of a large family (Clupeidae) of soft-finned bony fishes (as the herrings, shads, sardines, and menhadens) that have a laterally compressed body and a forked tail and usu. occur in schools

[1]**her·ring·bone** \ˈher-iŋ-ˌbōn, ˈhe-riŋ-\ *n, often attrib* (1659) **1 :** a pattern made up of rows of parallel lines which in any two adjacent rows slope in opposite directions **2 a :** a twilled fabric with a herringbone pattern; *also* **:** a suit made of this fabric **b :** a herringbone arrangement (as of materials or parts) **3 :** a method in skiing of ascending a slope by herringboning

herringbone 1

[2]**herringbone** *vt* (1787) **1 :** to produce a herringbone pattern on **2 :** to arrange in a herringbone pattern ~ *vi* **1 :** to produce a herringbone pattern **2 :** to ascend a slope by toeing out on skis and placing the weight on the inner side

herring gull *n* (1857) **:** a common large gull (*Larus argentatus*) of the northern hemisphere that as an adult is largely white with a gray mantle, dark wing tips, pink feet, and yellow bill

hers \ˈhərz\ *pron, sing or pl in constr* **:** that which belongs to her — used without a following noun as a pronoun equivalent in meaning to the adjective *her*

her·self \(h)ər-ˈself, *Southern also* -ˈsef\ *pron* (bef. 12c) **1 :** that identical female one — used reflexively, for emphasis, in absolute constructions, and in place of *her* esp. when joined to another object ⟨she considers ~ lucky⟩ ⟨she ~ did it⟩ ⟨~ an orphan, she understood the situation⟩ ⟨accepted the award for her colleagues and ~⟩; compare [1]SHE **2 :** her normal, healthy, or sane condition or self **3** *chiefly Irish & Scot* **:** a woman of consequence; *esp* **:** the mistress of the house

her·sto·ry \ˈhər-st(ə-)rē\ *n, pl* **-ries** [blend of *her* and *history*] (1970) **:** HISTORY; *specif* **:** history considered or presented from a feminist viewpoint or with special attention to the experience of women

Herts *abbr* Hertfordshire

hertz \ˈhərts, ˈherts\ *n, pl* **hertz** [Heinrich R. *Hertz*] (ca. 1928) **:** a unit of frequency equal to one cycle per second — abbr. *Hz*

he's \ˈhēz, ēz\ (1588) **:** he is **:** he has

he/she \ˈhē-ˈshē; ˈhē-ər-; ˈhē-ˈslash-\ *pron* (1963) **:** he or she — used as a pronoun of common gender

Hesh·van \ˈkesh-vən\ *n* [Heb *Ḥeshwān*] (1758) **:** the second month of the civil year or the eighth month of the ecclesiastical year in the Jewish calendar — see MONTH table

hes·i·tance \ˈhe-zə-tən(t)s\ *n* (1601) **:** HESITANCY

hes·i·tan·cy \-tən(t)-sē\ *n, pl* **-cies** (1617) **1 :** the quality or state of being hesitant: as **a :** INDECISION **b :** RELUCTANCE ⟨took that drastic step only with the greatest ~⟩ **2 :** HESITATION 1

hes·i·tant \ˈhe-zə-tənt\ *adj* (1647) **:** tending to hesitate **:** slow to act or proceed ***syn*** see DISINCLINED — **hes·i·tant·ly** *adv*

hes·i·tate \ˈhe-zə-ˌtāt\ *vb* **-tat·ed; -tat·ing** [L *haesitatus,* pp. of *haesitare* to stick fast, hesitate, freq. of *haerēre* to stick] *vi* (1598) **1 :** to hold back in doubt or indecision **2 :** to delay momentarily **:** PAUSE **3 :** STAMMER ~ *vt* **:** to hold back from in doubt or uncertainty ⟨wouldn't ~ to commit herself⟩ — **hes·i·tat·er** *n* — **hes·i·tat·ing·ly** \-ˌtā-tiŋ-lē\ *adv*

syn HESITATE, WAVER, VACILLATE, FALTER mean to show irresolution or uncertainty. HESITATE implies a pause before deciding or acting or choosing ⟨*hesitated* before answering the question⟩. WAVER implies hesitation after seeming to decide and so connotes weakness or a retreat ⟨*wavered* in his support of the rebels⟩. VACILLATE implies prolonged hesitation from inability to reach a firm decision ⟨*vacillated* until events were out of control⟩. FALTER implies a wavering or stumbling and often connotes nervousness, lack of courage, or outright fear ⟨never once *faltered* during her testimony⟩.

hes·i·ta·tion \ˌhe-zə-ˈtā-shən\ *n* (14c) **1 :** an act or instance of hesitating **2 :** a pausing or faltering in speech

Hes·pe·ri·an \he-ˈspir-ē-ən\ *adj* [L *Hesperia,* the west, fr. Gk, fr. fem. of *hesperios* of the evening, western, fr. *hesperos* evening — more at WEST] (15c) **:** WESTERN, OCCIDENTAL

Hes·per·i·des \he-ˈsper-ə-ˌdēz\ *n pl* [L, fr. Gk] (1546) **1 :** a legendary garden at the western extremity of the world producing golden apples **2 :** the nymphs in classical mythology who guard with the aid of a dragon a garden in which golden apples grow

hes·per·i·din \he-ˈsper-ə-dən\ *n* [NL *hesperidium* orange, fr. L *Hesperides*] (1838) **:** a crystalline glycoside $C_{28}H_{34}O_{15}$ found in most citrus fruits and esp. in orange peel

hes·per·id·i·um \ˌhes-pə-ˈri-dē-əm\ *n, pl* **-id·ia** \-dē-ə\ [NL] (ca. 1866) **:** a berry (as an orange or lime) having a leathery rind

Hes·per·us \ˈhes-p(ə-)rəs\ *n* [ME, fr. L, fr. Gk *Hesperos*] (14c) **:** EVENING STAR 1

hes·sian \ˈhe-shən\ *n* (1710) **1** *cap* **a :** a native of Hesse **b :** a German mercenary serving in the British forces during the American Revolution; *broadly* **:** a mercenary soldier **2** *chiefly Brit* **:** BURLAP

Hessian boot *n* (1809) **:** a high boot that extends to just below the knee and is commonly ornamented with a tassel and that was introduced into England by the Hessians early in the 19th century

Hessian fly *n* (1786) **:** a small European dipteran fly (*Mayetiola destructor*) introduced into No. America that is destructive to wheat

hes·so·nite \ˈhe-sə-ˌnīt\ *also* **es·so·nite** \ˈe-\ *n* [F, fr. Gk *hēsson* inferior; fr. its being less hard than true hyacinth] (1889) **:** a yellow to brown garnet

hest \ˈhest\ *n* [ME *hest, hes,* fr. OE *hǣs;* akin to OE *hātan* to command — more at HIGHT] (bef. 12c) *archaic* **:** COMMAND, PRECEPT

Hes·tia \ˈhes-tē-ə; ˈhes-chə, ˈhesh-\ *n* [Gk] (1853) **:** the Greek goddess of the hearth and chief goddess of domestic activity — compare VESTA

het \ˈhet\ *n* (ca. 1972) **:** HETEROSEXUAL — **het** *adj*

he·tae·ra \hi-ˈtir-ə\ *or* **he·tai·ra** \-ˈtī-rə\ *n, pl* **he·tae·rae** \-ˈtir-(ˌ)ē\ *or* **hetaeras** *or* **hetairas** *or* **he·tai·rai** \-ˈtī-ˌrī\ [Gk *hetaira,* lit., companion, fem. of *hetairos*] (1820) **1 :** one of a class of highly cultivated courtesans in ancient Greece **2 :** DEMIMONDAINE

heter- *or* **hetero-** *comb form* [LL, fr. Gk, fr. *heteros;* akin to Gk *heis* one — more at SAME] **1 :** other than usual **:** other **:** different ⟨*hetero*phyllous⟩ **2 :** containing atoms of different kinds ⟨*hetero*cyclic⟩

het·ero \ˈhe-tə-ˌrō\ *n, pl* **-er·os** (1933) **:** HETEROSEXUAL — **hetero** *adj*

het·ero·at·om \ˈhe-tə-rō-ˌa-təm\ *n* (1900) **:** an atom other than carbon in the ring of a heterocyclic compound

het·ero·cer·cal \-ˈsər-kəl\ *adj* (1838) **1** *of a fish tail fin* : having the upper lobe larger than the lower with the vertebral column extending into the upper lobe **2** : having or relating to a heterocercal tail fin

het·ero·chro·ma·tin \-ˈkrō-mə-tən\ *n* [G] (1932) : densely staining chromatin that appears as nodules in or along chromosomes and contains relatively few genes — **het·ero·chro·mat·ic** \-krə-ˈma-tik\ *adj*

[1]**het·ero·clite** \ˈhe-tə-rə-ˌklīt\ *n* (1580) **1** : a word irregular in inflection; *esp* : a noun irregular in declension **2** : one that deviates from common forms or rules

[2]**heteroclite** *adj* [MF or LL; MF, fr. LL *heteroclitus,* fr. Gk *heteroklitos,* fr. *heter-* + *klinein* to lean, inflect — more at LEAN] (1598) : deviating from common rules or forms

het·ero·cy·clic \ˌhe-tə-rō-ˈsī-klik, -ˈsi-\ *adj* [ISV] (1899) : relating to, characterized by, or being a ring composed of atoms of more than one kind — **het·ero·cy·cle** \ˈhe-tə-rō-ˌsī-kəl\ *n* — **heterocyclic** *n*

heterocyclic amine *n* (1984) : an amine containing one or more closed rings of carbon and nitrogen; *esp* : any of various carcinogenic amines formed when creatine or creatinine reacts with free amino acids and sugar in meat cooked at high temperatures

het·ero·cyst \ˈhe-tə-rō-ˌsist\ *n* (1872) : a large transparent thick-walled cell that is found in the filaments of some cyanobacteria and is the site of nitrogen fixation — **het·ero·cys·tous** \ˌhe-tə-rō-ˈsis-təs\ *adj*

het·ero·dox \ˈhe-tə-rə-ˌdäks, ˈhe-trə-\ *adj* [LL *heterodoxus,* fr. Gk *heterodoxos,* fr. *heter-* + *doxa* opinion — more at DOXOLOGY] (ca. 1650) **1** : contrary to or different from an acknowledged standard, a traditional form, or an established religion : UNORTHODOX, UNCONVENTIONAL ⟨~ ideas⟩ **2** : holding unorthodox opinions or doctrines

het·ero·doxy \-ˌdäk-sē\ *n, pl* **-dox·ies** (1659) **1** : the quality or state of being heterodox **2** : a heterodox opinion or doctrine

het·ero·du·plex \ˌhe-tə-rō-ˈdü-ˌpleks, -ˈdyü-\ *n* (1962) : a nucleic-acid molecule (as DNA) composed of two chains with each derived from a different parent molecule — **heteroduplex** *adj*

[1]**het·ero·dyne** \ˈhe-tə-rə-ˌdīn, ˈhe-trə-\ *adj* [*heter-* + *-dyne,* modif. of Gk *dynamis* power — more at DYNAMIC] (1908) : of or relating to the production of an electrical beat between two radio frequencies of which one usu. is that of a received signal-carrying current and the other that of an uninterrupted current introduced into the apparatus; *also* : of or relating to the production of a beat between two optical frequencies

[2]**heterodyne** *vt* **-dyned; -dyn·ing** (1923) : to combine (as a radio frequency) with a different frequency so that a beat is produced

het·er·oe·cious \ˌhe-tə-ˈrē-shəs\ *adj* [*heter-* + Gk *oikia* house — more at VICINITY] (1882) : passing through the different stages in the life cycle on alternate and often unrelated hosts ⟨~ aphids⟩ — **het·er·oe·cism** \-ˈrē-ˌsi-zəm\ *n*

het·ero·ga·mete \ˌhe-tə-rō-ˈga-ˌmēt *also* -gə-ˈmēt\ *n* [ISV] (1897) : either of a pair of dissimilar and usu. oogamous gametes

het·ero·ga·met·ic \-gə-ˈme-tik\ *adj* (1910) : forming two kinds of gametes of which one produces male offspring and the other female offspring ⟨the human male is ~⟩ — **het·ero·gam·e·ty** \-ˈga-mə-tē\ *n*

het·er·og·a·mous \ˌhe-tə-ˈrä-gə-məs\ *adj* (1895) : having or marked by fusion of unlike gametes — compare ANISOGAMOUS, ISOGAMOUS

het·er·og·a·my \-mē\ *n* (ca. 1894) **1** : sexual reproduction involving fusion of unlike gametes often differing in size, structure, and physiology **2** : the condition of reproducing by heterogamy

het·ero·ge·ne·i·ty \ˌhe-tə-rō-jə-ˈnē-ə-tē, ˌhe-trō-\ *n* (1641) : the quality or state of being heterogeneous

het·ero·ge·neous \ˌhe-tə-rə-ˈjē-nē-əs, ˌhe-trə-, -nyəs\ *adj* [ML *heterogeneus,* fr. Gk *heterogenēs,* fr. *heter-* + *genos* kind — more at KIN] (1630) : consisting of dissimilar or diverse ingredients or constituents : MIXED — **het·ero·ge·neous·ly** *adv* — **het·ero·ge·neous·ness** *n*

het·er·og·e·nous \ˌhe-tə-ˈrä-jə-nəs\ *adj* (1695) : HETEROGENEOUS

het·er·og·e·ny \-nē\ *n* (1838) : a heterogeneous collection or group

het·ero·glos·sia \ˌhe-tə-rō-ˈglä-sē-ə, -ˈglȯ-\ *n* [NL, fr. *heter-* + Gk *glōssa* tongue, language] (1988) : a diversity of voices, styles of discourse, or points of view in a literary work and esp. a novel

het·er·og·o·ny \ˌhe-tə-ˈrä-gə-nē\ *n* (ca. 1887) **1** : ALTERNATION OF GENERATIONS; *esp* : alternation of a dioecious with a parthenogenetic generation **2** : ALLOMETRY — **het·ero·gon·ic** \ˌhe-tə-rə-ˈgä-nik\ *adj*

het·ero·graft \ˈhe-tə-rō-ˌgraft\ *n* (1923) : XENOGRAFT

het·ero·kary·on \ˌhe-tə-rō-ˈker-ē-ˌän, -ən, -ˈka-rē-\ *n* [NL, fr. *heter-* + *karyon,* nucleus, fr. Gk, nut, kernel] (1941) : a cell (as in the mycelium of a fungus) that contains two or more genetically unlike nuclei

het·ero·kary·o·sis \ˌhe-tə-rō-ˌker-ē-ˈō-səs, -ˌka-rē-\ *n* [NL] (1916) : the condition of having cells that are heterokaryons — **het·ero·kary·ot·ic** \-ē-ˈä-tik\ *adj*

het·er·ol·o·gous \-ˈrä-lə-gəs\ *adj* [*heter-* + *-logous* (as in *homologous*)] (1893) : derived from a different species — **het·er·ol·o·gous·ly** *adv*

het·ero·ly·sis \ˌhe-tə-ˈrä-lə-səs, -ə-rə-ˈlī-səs\ *n* [NL] (1938) : decomposition of a compound into two oppositely charged particles or ions — **het·ero·lyt·ic** \-ə-rə-ˈli-tik\ *adj*

het·ero·mor·phic \ˌhe-tə-rə-ˈmȯr-fik\ *adj* [ISV] (ca. 1859) **1** : deviating from the usual form **2** : exhibiting diversity of form or forms ⟨~ pairs of chromosomes⟩ — **het·ero·mor·phism** \-ˌfi-zəm\ *n*

het·er·on·o·mous \ˌhe-tə-ˈrä-nə-məs\ *adj* (ca. 1871) : subject to external controls and impositions

het·er·on·o·my \-mē\ *n* [*heter-* + *-nomy* (as in *autonomy*)] (1798) : subjection to something else; *esp* : a lack of moral freedom or self-determination

het·ero·nor·ma·tive \ˌhē-tə-rō-ˈnȯr-mə-tiv\ *adj* (1991) : of, relating to, or based on the attitude that heterosexuality is the only normal and natural expression of sexuality — **het·ero·nor·ma·tiv·i·ty** \-ˌnȯr-mə-ˈti-və-tē\ *n*

het·ero·nym \ˈhe-tə-rə-ˌnim\ *n* (ca. 1889) : one of two or more homographs (as a *bass* voice and *bass,* a fish) that differ in pronunciation and meaning

het·ero·phile \ˈhe-tə-rə-ˌfī(-ə)l\ *or* **het·ero·phil** \-ˌfil\ *adj* (1920) : of, relating to, or being an antibody circulating in blood serum that is reactive with antigen originating in a different species

het·er·oph·o·ny \ˌhe-tə-ˈrä-fə-nē\ *n, pl* **-nies** [Gk *heterophōnia* diversity of note, fr. *heter-* + *-phōnia* -phony] (1919) : independent variation on a single melody by two or more voices

het·ero·phyl·lous \ˌhe-tə-rō-ˈfi-ləs\ *adj* (ca. 1828) : having the foliage leaves of more than one form on the same plant or stem — **het·ero·phyl·ly** \ˈhe-tə-rō-ˌfi-lē\ *n*

het·ero·ploid \ˈhe-tə-rə-ˌplȯid\ *adj* [ISV] (1926) : having an abnormal chromosome number that deviates from the normal diploid number of a given species — **heteroploid** *n* — **het·ero·ploi·dy** \-ˌplȯi-dē\ *n*

het·er·op·ter·ous \ˌhe-tə-ˈräp-tə-rəs\ *adj* [ultim. fr. Gk *heter-* + *pteron* wing — more at FEATHER] (1895) : of or relating to an insect order or suborder (Heteroptera) comprising the true bugs

het·ero·sex·ism \ˌhe-tə-rō-ˈsek-si-zəm\ *n* (1972) : discrimination or prejudice by heterosexuals against homosexuals — **het·ero·sex·ist** \-ˈsek-sist\ *adj*

[1]**het·ero·sex·u·al** \ˌhe-tə-rō-ˈsek-sh(ə-)wəl, -ˈsek-shəl\ *adj* [ISV] (1892) **1 a** : of, relating to, or characterized by a tendency to direct sexual desire toward the opposite sex **b** : of, relating to, or involving sexual intercourse between individuals of opposite sex **2** : of or relating to different sexes — **het·ero·sex·u·al·i·ty** \-ˌsek-shə-ˈwa-lə-tē\ *n* — **het·ero·sex·u·al·ly** \-ˈsek-sh(ə-)wə-lē, -ˈsek-shə-lē\ *adv*

[2]**heterosexual** *n* (1920) : a heterosexual person

het·er·o·sis \ˌhe-tə-ˈrō-səs\ *n* [NL] (1914) : the marked vigor or capacity for growth often exhibited by crossbred animals or plants — called also *hybrid vigor* — **het·er·ot·ic** \-ˈrä-tik\ *adj*

het·ero·so·cial \ˌhe-tə-rō-ˈsō-shəl\ *adj* (1965) : of, relating to, or involving social relationships between persons of the opposite sex

het·ero·spo·ry \ˈhe-tə-rə-ˌspȯr-ē, ˌhe-tə-ˈräs-pə-rē\ *n* (1898) : the production of microspores and megaspores (as in seed plants) — **het·ero·spo·rous** \ˌhe-tə-rə-ˈspȯr-əs, -ˈräs-pə-rəs\ *adj*

het·ero·thal·lic \ˌhe-tə-rō-ˈtha-lik\ *adj* [*heter-* + *thallus* + *-ic*] (1904) **1** : having two or more morphologically similar haploid phases or types of which individuals from the same type are mutually sterile but individuals from different types are cross-fertile ⟨~ fungi⟩ ⟨~ spores⟩ **2** : DIOECIOUS — **het·ero·thal·lism** \-ˈtha-ˌli-zəm\ *n*

het·ero·top·ic \-rə-ˈtä-pik\ *adj* [*heter-* + Gk *topos* place] (1878) : occurring in an abnormal place ⟨~ bone formation⟩ ⟨~ liver transplant⟩

het·ero·troph \ˈhe-tə-rə-ˌtrōf, -ˌträf\ *n* (ca. 1900) : a heterotrophic individual

het·ero·tro·phic \ˌhe-tə-rə-ˈtrō-fik\ *adj* (1893) : requiring complex organic compounds of nitrogen and carbon (as that obtained from plant or animal matter) for metabolic synthesis — compare AUTOTROPHIC — **het·ero·tro·phi·cal·ly** \-fi-k(ə-)lē\ *adv* — **het·ero·tro·phy** \ˌhe-tə-ˈrä-trə-fē, ˈhe-tə-rə-ˌtrō-\ *n*

het·ero·typ·ic \ˌhe-tə-rō-ˈti-pik\ *adj* (1876) : different in kind, arrangement, or form

het·ero·zy·go·sis \-(ˌ)zī-ˈgō-səs\ *n* [NL] (1902) : HETEROZYGOSITY

het·ero·zy·gos·i·ty \-ˈgä-sə-tē\ *n* (1912) : the state of being heterozygous

het·ero·zy·gote \-ˈzī-ˌgōt\ *n* (1902) : a heterozygous individual

het·ero·zy·gous \-gəs\ *adj* (1902) : having the two alleles at corresponding loci on homologous chromosomes different for one or more loci

heth \ˈk̲ät, ˈk̲äth, ˈk̲et, ˈk̲eth\ *n* [Heb *ḥēth*] (1823) : the 8th letter of the Hebrew alphabet — see ALPHABET table

het·man \ˈhet-mən\ *n, pl* **hetmans** [Ukrainian *het'man*] (1710) : a Cossack leader

het up \ˈhet-ˈəp\ *adj* [*het,* dial. past of *heat*] (1909) : highly excited : UPSET

heu·land·ite \ˈhyü-lən-ˌdīt\ *n* [Henry *Heuland,* 19th cent. Eng. mineral collector] (1822) : a zeolite consisting of a hydrous aluminosilicate of sodium and calcium

[1]**heu·ris·tic** \hyu̇-ˈris-tik\ *adj* [G *heuristisch,* fr. NL *heuristicus,* fr. Gk *heuriskein* to discover; akin to OIr fo-*fúair* he found] (1821) : involving or serving as an aid to learning, discovery, or problem-solving by experimental and esp. trial-and-error methods ⟨~ techniques⟩ ⟨a ~ assumption⟩; *also* : of or relating to exploratory problem-solving techniques that utilize self-educating techniques (as the evaluation of feedback) to improve performance — **heu·ris·ti·cal·ly** \-ti-k(ə-)lē\ *adv*

[2]**heuristic** *n* (1860) **1** : the study or practice of heuristic procedure **2** : heuristic argument **3** : a heuristic method or procedure

hew \ˈhyü\ *vb* **hewed; hewed** *or* **hewn** \ˈhyün\; **hew·ing** [ME, fr. OE *hēawan;* akin to OHG *houwan* to hew, Lith *kauti* to forge, L *cudere* to beat] *vt* (bef. 12c) **1** : to cut with blows of a heavy cutting instrument **2** : to fell by blows of an ax ⟨~ a tree⟩ **3** : to give form or shape to with or as if with heavy cutting blows ⟨~*ed* their farms from the wilderness —J. T. Shotwell⟩ ~ *vi* **1** : to make cutting blows **2** : CONFORM, ADHERE ⟨~ to tradition⟩ — often used in the phrase *hew to the line* ⟨no pressure . . . on newspapers to ~ to the official line —*N.Y. Times Mag.*⟩ — **hew·er** *n*

HEW *abbr* Department of Health, Education, and Welfare

[1]**hex** \ˈheks\ *vb* [PaG *hexe,* fr. G *hexen,* fr. *Hexe* witch, fr. OHG *hagzissa;* akin to ME *hagge* hag] *vi* (1830) : to practice witchcraft ~ *vt* **1** : to put a hex on **2** : to affect as if by an evil spell : JINX — **hex·er** *n*

[2]**hex** *n* (1856) **1** : a person who practices witchcraft **2** : SPELL, JINX

[3]**hex** *adj* (1924) : HEXAGONAL ⟨a bolt with a ~ head⟩

[4]**hex** *adj or n* (1970) : HEXADECIMAL

[5]**hex** *abbr* hexagon

hexa- *or* **hex-** *comb form* [Gk, fr. *hex* six — more at SIX] **1** : six ⟨*hexa*ploid⟩ **2** : containing six atoms, groups, or equivalents ⟨*hex*ane⟩

hexa·chlo·ro·eth·ane \ˌhek-sə-ˌklȯr-ō-ˈe-ˌthān\ *or* **hexa·chlor·eth·ane** \-ˌklȯr-ˈe-\ *n* [ISV] (1898) : a toxic crystalline compound C_2Cl_6 used esp. in smoke bombs and in the control of liver flukes in ruminants

hexa·chlo·ro·phene \-ˈklȯr-ə-ˌfēn\ *n* [*hexa-* + *chlor-* + *phenol*] (1948) : a powdered phenolic bacteria-inhibiting agent $C_{13}H_6Cl_6O_2$

hexa·chord \ˈhek-sə-ˌkȯrd\ *n* [*hexa-* + Gk *chordē* string — more at YARN] (1730) : a diatonic series of six tones having a semitone between the third and fourth tones

hexa·dec·i·mal \ˌhek-sə-ˈdes-məl, -ˈde-sə-\ *adj* (1954) : of, relating to, or being a number system with a base of 16 — **hexadecimal** *n*

hexa·gon \ˈhek-sə-ˌgän\ *n* [Gk *hexagōnon,* neut. of *hexagōnos* hexagonal, fr. *hexa-* + *gōnia* angle — more at -GON] (1570) : a polygon of six angles and six sides

hex·ag·o·nal \hek-ˈsa-gə-nᵊl\ *adj* (1571) **1** : having six angles and six sides **2** : having a hexagon as section or base **3** : relating to or being a crystal system characterized by three equal lateral axes intersecting at angles of 60 degrees and a vertical axis of variable length at right angles — **hex·ag·o·nal·ly** \-nᵊl-ē\ *adv*

hexa·gram \ˈhek-sə-ˌgram\ *n* [ISV] (1871) **:** a plane figure that has the shape of a 6-pointed star, that consists of two intersecting congruent equilateral triangles having the same point as center and their sides parallel, and that can be formed by constructing external equilateral triangles on the sides of a regular hexagon — compare SOLOMON'S SEAL 2

hexa·he·dron \ˌhek-sə-ˈhē-drən\ *n, pl* **-drons** *also* **-dra** \-drə\ [LL, fr. Gk *hexaedron,* fr. neut. of *hexaedros* of six surfaces, fr. *hexa-* + *hedra* seat — more at SIT] (1571) **:** a polyhedron of six faces (as a cube)

hexa·hy·drate \-ˈhī-ˌdrāt\ *n* (1908) **:** a chemical compound with six molecules of water

hex·am·e·ter \hek-ˈsa-mə-tər\ *n* [L, fr. Gk *hexametron,* fr. neut. of *hexametros* having six measures, fr. *hexa-* + *metron* measure — more at MEASURE] (1546) **:** a line of verse consisting of six metrical feet

hexa·me·tho·ni·um \ˌhek-sə-mə-ˈthō-nē-əm\ *n* [*hexa-* + *meth-* + *-onium*] (1949) **:** either of two compounds $C_{12}H_{30}Br_2N_2$ or $C_{12}H_{30}Cl_2N_2$ used as ganglionic blocking agents in the treatment of hypertension

hexa·meth·y·lene·tet·ra·mine \ˌhek-sə-ˈme-thə-ˌlēn-ˈte-trə-ˌmēn\ *n* [ISV *hexa-* + *methylene* + *tetra-* + *amine*] (1888) **:** a crystalline compound $C_6H_{12}N_4$ used esp. as an accelerator in vulcanizing rubber and as a urinary antiseptic — compare METHENAMINE

hex·ane \ˈhek-ˌsān\ *n* [ISV] (1877) **:** any of several isomeric volatile liquid alkanes C_6H_{14} found in petroleum

hex·a·no·ic acid \ˌhek-sə-ˈnō-ik-\ *n* [ISV *hexane* + *-oic*] (1926) **:** CAPROIC ACID

hexa·ploid \ˈhek-sə-ˌplȯid\ *adj* [ISV] (1912) **:** having or being six times the monoploid chromosome number — **hexaploid** *n* — **hexa·ploi·dy** \-ˌplȯi-dē\ *n*

[1]**hexa·pod** \ˈhek-sə-ˌpäd\ *n* [Gk *hexapod-, hexapous* having six feet, fr. *hexa-* + *pod-, pous* foot — more at FOOT] (1668) **:** INSECT 1b

[2]**hexapod** *adj* (ca. 1847) **1 :** six-footed **2 :** of or relating to insects

Hexa·teuch \ˈhek-sə-ˌtük, -ˌtyük\ *n* [*hexa-* + Gk *teuchos* book — more at PENTATEUCH] (1878) **:** the first six books of the Bible

hex·e·rei \ˌhek-sə-ˈrī\ *n* [PaG, fr. G, fr. *Hexe* witch] (1898) **:** WITCHCRAFT

hexo·bar·bi·tal \ˌhek-sə-ˈbär-bə-ˌtȯl\ *n* [*hexo-* (fr. *hexa-*) + *barbital*] (1941) **:** a barbiturate $C_{12}H_{16}N_2O_3$ used as a sedative and hypnotic and in the form of its soluble sodium salt as an intravenous anesthetic of short duration

hexo·ki·nase \ˌhek-sə-ˈkī-ˌnās, -ˌnāz\ *n* [*hexose* + *kinase*] (1930) **:** any of a group of enzymes that accelerate the phosphorylation of hexoses (as in the formation of glucose-6-phosphate from glucose and ATP) in carbohydrate metabolism

hex·os·a·min·i·dase \ˌhek-ˌsä-sə-ˈmi-nə-ˌdās, -ˌdāz\ *n* [*hexose* + *amino* + *-ide* + *-ase*] (1969) **:** either of two hydrolytic enzymes that catalyze the splitting off of a hexose from a ganglioside and are deficient in some metabolic diseases (as Tay-Sachs disease)

hex·o·san \ˈhek-sə-ˌsan\ *n* (1894) **:** a polysaccharide yielding only hexoses on hydrolysis

hex·ose \ˈhek-ˌsōs, -ˌsōz\ *n* [ISV] (1890) **:** a monosaccharide (as glucose) containing six carbon atoms in a molecule

hex·yl \ˈhek-səl\ *n* [ISV] (1869) **:** any of various isomeric alkyl radicals $C_6H_{13}-$ derived from hexane

hex·yl·res·or·cin·ol \ˌhek-səl-rə-ˈzȯr-sᵊn-ˌȯl, -ˌōl\ *n* (1924) **:** a crystalline phenol $C_{12}H_{18}O_2$ used as an antiseptic and anthelmintic

hey \ˈhā\ *interj* [ME] (13c) — used esp. to call attention or to express interrogation, surprise, or exultation

[1]**hey·day** \ˈhā-ˌdā\ *interj* [irreg. fr. *hey*] (1599) *archaic* — used to express elation or wonder

[2]**heyday** *n* (1590) **1** *archaic* **:** high spirits **2 :** the period of one's greatest popularity, vigor, or prosperity

hey presto \(ˈ)hā-ˈpres-(ˌ)tō\ *interj* (1731) *Brit* **:** suddenly as if by magic

Hez·e·ki·ah \ˌhe-zə-ˈkī-ə\ *n* [Heb *Ḥizqīyāh*] (14c) **:** a king of Judah under whom the kingdom underwent a ruinous Assyrian invasion at the end of the eighth century B.C.

hf *abbr* half

Hf *symbol* hafnium

HF *abbr* high frequency

hg *abbr* **1** hectogram **2** hemoglobin

Hg *symbol* [NL *hydrargyrum* lit., water silver] mercury

HGH *abbr* human growth hormone

hgt *abbr* height

hgwy *abbr* highway

HH *abbr* **1** Her Highness; His Highness **2** His Holiness

HHD *abbr* [NL *humanitatum doctor*] doctor of humanities

H hour *n* [*H,* abbr. for *hour*] (1918) **:** the hour set for launching a specific tactical operation

HHS *abbr* Department of Health and Human Services

hi \ˈhī(-ē)\ *interj* [ME *hy*] (15c) — used esp. as a greeting

HI *abbr* **1** Hawaii **2** high intensity **3** humidity index

hi·a·tal \hī-ˈā-tᵊl\ *adj* (1909) **:** of, relating to, or involving a hiatus

hiatal hernia *n* (ca. 1944) **:** protrusion of part of the stomach upward into the chest cavity through the passage in the diaphragm for the esophagus usu. with movement of the opening of the esophagus into the stomach to a position above the diaphragm — called also *hiatus hernia*

hi·a·tus \hī-ˈā-təs\ *n* [L, fr. *hiare* to yawn — more at YAWN] (1563) **1 a :** a break in or as if in a material object **:** GAP ⟨the ~ between the theory and the practice of the party —J. G. Colton⟩ **b :** a gap or passage in an anatomical part or organ **2 a :** an interruption in time or continuity **:** BREAK; *esp* **:** a period when something (as a program or activity) is suspended or interrupted ⟨after a 5-year ~ from writing⟩ **b :** the occurrence of two vowel sounds without pause or intervening consonantal sound

Hi·a·wa·tha \ˌhī-ə-ˈwȯ-thə, ˌhē-ə-, -ˈwä-\ *n* (1855) **:** the Indian hero of Longfellow's poem *The Song of Hiawatha*

Hib \ˈhib\ *n, often attrib* [*Hi-* (fr. the species name *Haemophilus influenzae*) + type *B*] (1984) **:** a bacterial serotype (*Haemophilus influenzae* type B) that causes bacterial meningitis and pneumonia esp. in children ⟨~ disease⟩ ⟨~ vaccine⟩

hi·ba·chi \hi-ˈbä-chē\ *n* [Jp] (1863) **:** a charcoal brazier

hi·ber·nac·u·lum \ˌhī-bər-ˈna-kyə-ləm\ *n, pl* **-la** \-lə\ [NL, fr. L, winter residence, fr. *hibernare*] (1789) **:** a shelter occupied during the winter by a dormant animal (as an insect or reptile)

hi·ber·nal \hī-ˈbər-nᵊl\ *adj* (1646) **:** of, relating to, or occurring in winter

hi·ber·nate \ˈhī-bər-ˌnāt\ *vi* **-nat·ed; -nat·ing** [L *hibernatus,* pp. of *hibernare* to pass the winter, fr. *hibernus* of winter; akin to L *hiems* winter, Gk *cheimōn*] (ca. 1802) **1 :** to pass the winter in a torpid or resting state **2 :** to be or become inactive or dormant — **hi·ber·na·tion** \ˌhī-bər-ˈnā-shən\ *n* — **hi·ber·na·tor** \ˈhī-bər-ˌnā-tər\ *n*

[1]**Hi·ber·ni·an** \hī-ˈbər-nē-ən\ *adj* [L *Hibernia* Ireland] (1632) **:** of, relating to, or characteristic of Ireland or the Irish

[2]**Hibernian** *n* (1709) **:** a native or inhabitant of Ireland

Hi·ber·no- *comb form* [L *Hibernia*] **1 :** Irish and ⟨*Hiberno*-British⟩ **2 :** Irish ⟨*Hiberno*-English⟩

Hiberno–English *n* (1947) **:** the English language spoken in Ireland

hi·bis·cus \hī-ˈbis-kəs, hə-\ *n* [NL, fr. L, marshmallow] (1706) **:** any of a large genus (*Hibiscus*) of herbs, shrubs, or small trees of the mallow family with large showy flowers and usu. dentate leaves

[1]**hic·cup** *also* **hic·cough** \ˈhi-(ˌ)kəp\ *n* [imit.] (ca. 1580) **1 :** a spasmodic inhalation with closure of the glottis accompanied by a peculiar sound **2 :** an attack of hiccuping — usu. used in pl. but sing. or pl. in constr. **3 a :** a slight irregularity, error, or malfunction ⟨a few ~s in the computer system⟩ **b :** a usu. minor and short-lived interruption or disruption, or change ⟨a ~ in the stock market⟩

[2]**hiccup** *also* **hiccough** *vi* **hic·cuped** *also* **hic·cupped; hic·cup·ing** *also* **hic·cup·ping** (ca. 1580) **:** to make a hiccup; *also* **:** to be affected with hiccups

hic ja·cet \ˈhik-ˈjā-sət, ˈhēk-ˈyä-kət\ *n* [L, lit., here lies] (1654) **:** EPITAPH

[1]**hick** \ˈhik\ *n* [*Hick,* nickname for *Richard*] (1669) **:** an unsophisticated provincial person — **hick·ish** \ˈhi-kish\ *adj*

[2]**hick** *adj* (1913) **:** UNSOPHISTICATED, PROVINCIAL ⟨a ~ town⟩

[1]**hick·ey** \ˈhi-kē\ *n, pl* **hickeys** [origin unknown] (1913) **:** GADGET

[2]**hickey** *n, pl* **hickeys** [origin unknown] (ca. 1918) **1 a :** PIMPLE **b :** a temporary red mark or bruise on the skin (as one produced by biting and sucking) **2** *pl also* **hick·ies :** a small imperfection in printing

hick·o·ry \ˈhi-k(ə-)rē\ *n, pl* **-ries** [short for obs. *pokahickory,* fr. Virginia Algonquian *pawcohiccora* food prepared from pounded nuts] (1670) **1 a :** any of a genus (*Carya*) of No. American hardwood trees of the walnut family that often have sweet edible nuts **b :** the usu. tough wood of a hickory **2 :** a switch or cane (as of hickory wood) used esp. for punishing a child — **hickory** *adj*

hid *adj* (12c) **:** HIDDEN

hi·dal·go \hi-ˈdal-(ˌ)gō, ē-ˈthäl-\ *n, pl* **-gos** *often cap* [Sp, fr. OSp *fijo dalgo,* lit., son of something] (1594) **:** a member of the lower nobility of Spain

Hi·dat·sa \hi-ˈdät-sə\ *n, pl* **Hidatsa** *also* **Hidatsas** [Hidatsa *hiráˑca,* a Hidatsa subgroup] (1873) **1 :** a member of an American Indian people of the Missouri River valley in No. Dakota **2 :** the Siouan language of the Hidatsa

hidden *adj* (13c) **1 :** being out of sight or not readily apparent **:** CONCEALED **2 :** OBSCURE, UNEXPLAINED, UNDISCLOSED — **hid·den·ness** \-nəs\ *n*

hidden agenda *n* (1971) **:** an ulterior motive

hid·den·ite \ˈhi-də-ˌnīt\ *n* [William E. *Hidden* †1918 Am. mineralogist] (1881) **:** a transparent usu. green spodumene valued as a gem

hidden tax *n* (1936) **1 :** a tax that is ultimately paid by someone other than the person on whom it is levied **2 :** an economic inequity that reduces one's real income or buying power

[1]**hide** \ˈhīd\ *n* [ME, fr. OE *hīgid, hīd*] (bef. 12c) **:** any of various old English units of land area; *esp* **:** a unit of 120 acres

[2]**hide** *vb* **hid** \ˈhid\; **hid·den** \ˈhi-dᵊn\ *or* **hid; hid·ing** \ˈhī-diŋ\ [ME *hiden,* fr. OE *hȳdan;* akin to Gk *keuthein* to conceal] *vt* (bef. 12c) **1 a :** to put out of sight **:** SECRETE **b :** to conceal for shelter or protection **:** SHIELD **2 :** to keep secret ⟨~ the truth⟩ **3 :** to screen from or as if from view **:** OBSCURE **4 :** to turn (the eyes or face) away in shame or anger ~ *vi* **1 :** to remain out of sight — often used with *out* **2 :** to seek protection or evade responsibility — **hid·er** \ˈhī-dər\ *n*

syn HIDE, CONCEAL, SCREEN, SECRETE, BURY mean to withhold or withdraw from sight. HIDE may or may not suggest intent ⟨*hide* in the closet⟩ ⟨a house *hidden* in the woods⟩. CONCEAL usu. does imply intent and often specif. implies a refusal to divulge ⟨*concealed* the weapon⟩. SCREEN implies an interposing of something that prevents discovery ⟨a house *screened* by trees⟩. SECRETE suggests a depositing in a place unknown to others ⟨*secreted* the amulet inside his shirt⟩. BURY implies covering up so as to hide completely ⟨*buried* the treasure⟩.

[3]**hide** *n* (14c) *chiefly Brit* **:** BLIND 2

[4]**hide** *n* [ME, fr. OE *hȳd;* akin to OHG *hūt* hide, L *cutis* skin, Gk *kytos* hollow vessel] (bef. 12c) **1 :** the skin of an animal whether raw or dressed — used esp. of large heavy skins **2 :** the life or physical well-being of a person ⟨betrayed his friend to save his own ~⟩ — **hide or hair** *or* **hide nor hair :** a vestige or trace of someone or something ⟨a wife he hadn't seen *hide or hair* of in over 20 years —H. L. Davis⟩

[5]**hide** *vt* **hid·ed; hid·ing** (ca. 1825) **:** to give a beating to **:** FLOG

hide–and–seek \ˌhīd-ᵊn-ˈsēk\ *n* (ca. 1727) **:** a children's game in which one player does not look while others hide and then goes to find them

hide·away \ˈhīd-ə-ˌwā\ *n* (1926) **:** RETREAT, HIDEOUT

hide·bound \ˈhīd-ˌbau̇nd\ *adj* (1603) **1** *of a domestic animal* **:** having a dry skin lacking in pliancy and adhering closely to the underlying flesh **2 :** having an inflexible or ultraconservative character

hid·eous \ˈhi-dē-əs\ *adj* [alter. of ME *hidous,* fr. AF *hidus, hisdos,* fr. OF *hisde, hide* terror] (14c) **1 :** offensive to the senses and esp. to sight **:** exceedingly ugly **2 :** morally offensive **:** SHOCKING — **hid·eos·i·ty** \ˌhi-dē-ˈä-sə-tē\ *n* — **hid·eous·ly** *adv* — **hid·eous·ness** *n*

hide·out \ˈhīd-ˌau̇t\ *n* (1885) **:** a place of refuge, retreat, or concealment

\ə\ **a**but \ᵊ\ kitten, F table \ər\ **fur**ther \a\ **a**sh \ā\ **a**ce \ä\ m**o**p, m**a**r
\au̇\ **ou**t \ch\ **ch**in \e\ b**e**t \ē\ **ea**sy \g\ **g**o \i\ h**i**t \ī\ **i**ce \j\ **j**ob
\ŋ\ si**ng** \ō\ g**o** \ȯ\ l**aw** \ȯi\ b**oy** \th\ **th**in \t͟h\ **th**e \ü\ l**oo**t \u̇\ f**oo**t
\y\ **y**et \zh\ vi**si**on, bei**ge** \k̲, ⁿ, œ, ue, ʸ\ *see* Guide to Pronunciation

hid•ey–hole *or* **hidy–hole** \ˈhī-dē-ˌhōl\ *n* [alter. of earlier *hiding-hole*] (1817) : HIDEAWAY

hie \ˈhī\ *vb* **hied; hy•ing** *or* **hie•ing** [ME, fr. OE *hīgian* to strive, hasten] *vi* (12c) : to go quickly : HASTEN ~ *vt* : to cause (oneself) to go quickly

hi•er•arch \ˈhī-(ə-)ˌrärk\ *n* [ME *ierarchis,* pl., fr. ML *hierarcha,* fr. Gk *hierarchēs,* fr. *hieros* sacred + *-archēs* -arch] (15c) **1 :** a religious leader in a position of authority **2 :** a person high in a hierarchy — **hi•er•ar•chal** \ˌhī-(ə-)ˈrär-kəl\ *adj*

hi•er•ar•chi•cal \ˌhī-(ə-)ˈrär-ki-kəl *also* hir-ˈär-\ *or* **hi•er•ar•chic** \-kik\ *adj* (1561) : of, relating to, or arranged in a hierarchy — **hi•er•ar•chi•cal•ly** \-ki-k(ə-)lē\ *adv*

hi•er•ar•chize \ˈhī-(ə-)ˌrär-ˌkīz\ *vt* **-chized; -chiz•ing** (1884) : to arrange in a hierarchy — **hi•er•ar•chi•za•tion** \ˌhī-(ə-)ˌrär-kə-ˈzā-shən, -ˌkī-ˈzā-\ *n*

hi•er•ar•chy \ˈhī-(ə-)ˌrär-kē *also* ˈhi(-ə)r-ˌär-\ *n, pl* **-chies** [ME *ierarchie* rank or order of holy beings, fr. AF *jerarchie,* fr. ML *hierarchia,* fr. LGk, fr. Gk *hierarchēs*] (14c) **1 :** a division of angels **2 a :** a ruling body of clergy organized into orders or ranks each subordinate to the one above it; *esp* **:** the bishops of a province or nation **b :** church government by a hierarchy **3 :** a body of persons in authority **4 :** the classification of a group of people according to ability or to economic, social, or professional standing; *also* **:** the group so classified **5 :** a graded or ranked series ⟨a ~ of values⟩

hi•er•at•ic \ˌhī-(ə-)ˈra-tik\ *adj* [L *hieraticus* sacerdotal, fr. Gk *hieratikos,* fr. *hierasthai* to perform priestly functions, fr. *hieros* sacred; prob. akin to Skt *iṣara* vigorous] (1669) **1 :** constituting or belonging to a cursive form of ancient Egyptian writing simpler than the hieroglyphic **2 :** SACERDOTAL **3 :** highly stylized or formal ⟨~ poses⟩ — **hi•er•at•i•cal•ly** \-ti-k(ə-)lē\ *adv*

hi•ero•dule \ˈhī-(ə-)rō-ˌdül, hī-ˈer-ə-, -ˌdyül\ *n* [LL *hierodulus,* fr. Gk *hierodoulos,* fr. *hieron* temple + *doulos* slave] (1835) : a slave or prostitute in the service of a temple (as in ancient Greece)

hi•ero•glyph \ˈhī-(ə-)rə-ˌglif\ *n* [F *hiéroglyphe,* fr. MF, back-formation fr. *hieroglyphique*] (1598) **1 :** a character used in a system of hieroglyphic writing **2 :** something that resembles a hieroglyph

[1]**hi•ero•glyph•ic** \ˌhī-(ə-)rə-ˈgli-fik\ *also* **hi•ero•glyph•i•cal** \-fi-kəl\ *adj* [MF *hieroglyphique,* fr. LL *hieroglyphicus,* fr. Gk *hieroglyphikos,* fr. *hieros* + *glyphein* to carve — more at CLEAVE] (1585) **1 :** written in, constituting, or belonging to a system of writing mainly in pictorial characters **2 :** inscribed with hieroglyphic **3 :** resembling hieroglyphic in difficulty of decipherment — **hi•ero•glyph•i•cal•ly** \-fi-k(ə-)lē\ *adv*

[2]**hieroglyphic** *n* (1586) **1 :** HIEROGLYPH **2 :** a system of hieroglyphic writing; *specif* **:** the picture script of the ancient Egyptian priesthood — often used in pl. but sing. or pl. in constr. **3 :** something that resembles a hieroglyph esp. in difficulty of decipherment

hieroglyphic 2

hi•ero•phant \ˈhī-(ə-)rə-ˌfant, hī-ˈer-ə-fənt\ *n* [LL *hierophanta,* fr. Gk *hierophantēs,* fr. *hieros* + *phainein* to show — more at FANCY] (1677) **1 :** a priest in ancient Greece; *specif* **:** the chief priest of the Eleusinian mysteries **2 a :** EXPOSITOR **b :** ADVOCATE 2 — **hi•ero•phan•tic** \ˌhī-(ə-)rə-ˈfan-tik, (ˌ)hī-ˌer-ə-\ *adj*

hifalutin *var of* HIGHFALUTIN

hi–fi \ˈhī-ˈfī\ *n* (1950) **1 :** HIGH FIDELITY **2 :** equipment for reproduction of sound with high fidelity

hig•gle \ˈhi-gəl\ *vi* **hig•gled; hig•gling** \-g(ə-)liŋ\ [prob. alter. of *haggle*] (1633) : HAGGLE — **hig•gler** \-g(ə-)lər\ *n*

hig•gle•dy–pig•gle•dy \ˌhi-gəl-dē-ˈpi-gəl-dē\ *adv* [origin unknown] (1598) : in a confused, disordered, or random manner ⟨tiny hovels piled ~ against each other —Edward Behr⟩ — **higgledy–piggledy** *adj*

Higgs boson \ˈhigz-\ *n* [Peter W. *Higgs* b1929 Brit. physicist] (1974) : a hypothetical elementary particle that has zero spin and large mass and that is required by some gauge theories to account for the masses of other elementary particles

Higgs field *n* (1980) : a hypothetical physical field that endows elementary particles with mass and that is mediated by the Higgs boson

[1]**high** \ˈhī\ *adj* [ME, fr. OE *hēah;* akin to OHG *hōh* high, Lith *kaukaras* hill] (bef. 12c) **1 a :** having large extension upward : taller than average, usual, or expected ⟨a ~ wall⟩ **b :** having a specified elevation : TALL ⟨six feet ~⟩ — often used in combinations ⟨sky-*high*⟩ ⟨waist-*high*⟩ **c :** situated or passing above the normal level, surface, base of measurement, or elevation ⟨the ~ desert⟩ **2 a** (1) **:** advanced toward the acme or culmination ⟨~ summer⟩ (2) **:** advanced toward the most active or culminating period ⟨on the Riviera during ~ season⟩ (3) **:** constituting the late, most fully developed, or most creative stage or period ⟨~ Gothic⟩ (4) **:** advanced in complexity, development, or elaboration ⟨the ~*er* primates including humans⟩ ⟨~*er* mathematics⟩ **b :** verging on lateness — usu. used in the phrase *high time* **c :** long past : REMOTE ⟨~ antiquity⟩ **3 :** elevated in pitch ⟨a ~ note⟩ **4 :** relatively far from the equator ⟨~ latitude⟩ **5 :** rich in quality : LUXURIOUS ⟨~ living⟩ **6 :** slightly tainted ⟨~ game⟩; *also* **:** MALODOROUS ⟨smelled rather ~⟩ **7 :** exalted in character : NOBLE ⟨~ purposes⟩ **8 :** of greater degree, amount, cost, value, or content than average, usual, or expected ⟨~ prices⟩ **9 :** of relatively great importance: as **a :** foremost in rank, dignity, or standing ⟨~ officials⟩ **b :** SERIOUS, GRAVE ⟨~ crimes⟩ **c :** observed with the utmost solemnity ⟨~ religious observances⟩ **d :** CRITICAL, CLIMACTIC ⟨the ~ point of the novel⟩ **e :** intellectually or artistically of the first order ⟨~ culture⟩ **f :** marked by sublime, heroic, or stirring events or subject matter ⟨~ tragedy⟩ ⟨~ adventure⟩ **10 :** FORCIBLE, STRONG ⟨~ winds⟩ **11 :** stressing matters of doctrine and ceremony; *specif* **:** HIGH CHURCH **12 a :** filled with or expressing great joy or excitement ⟨~ spirits⟩ **b :** INTOXICATED; *also* **:** excited or stupefied by or as if by a drug **13 :** articulated with some part of the tongue close to the palate ⟨a ~ vowel⟩ — **high on :** enthusiastically in approval or support of

syn HIGH, TALL, LOFTY mean above the average in height. HIGH implies marked extension upward and is applied chiefly to things which rise from a base or foundation or are placed at a conspicuous height above a lower level ⟨a *high* hill⟩ ⟨a *high* ceiling⟩. TALL applies to what grows or rises high by comparison with others of its kind and usu. implies relative narrowness ⟨a *tall* thin man⟩. LOFTY suggests great or imposing altitude ⟨*lofty* mountain peaks⟩.

[2]**high** *adv* (bef. 12c) **1 :** at or to a high place, altitude, level, or degree ⟨climbed ~*er*⟩ ⟨passions ran ~⟩ **2 :** WELL, LUXURIOUSLY — often used in the phrases *high off the hog* and *high on the hog*

[3]**high** *n* (13c) **1 :** an elevated place or region: as **a :** HILL, KNOLL **b :** the space overhead : SKY — usu. used with *on* **c :** HEAVEN — usu. used with *on* **2 :** a region of high barometric pressure — called also *anticyclone* **3 a :** a high point or level : HEIGHT ⟨sales reached a new ~⟩ **b :** the transmission gear of a vehicle (as an automobile) giving the highest speed of travel **4 a :** an excited, euphoric, or stupefied state produced by or as if by a drug **b :** a state of elation or high spirits

high altar *n* (bef. 12c) : the principal altar in a church

high analysis *adj* (1949) *of a fertilizer* **:** containing more than 20 percent of total plant nutrients

high and dry *adj* (1750) **1 :** being out of reach of the current or tide or out of the water **2 :** being in a helpless or abandoned position

high and low *adv* (14c) : EVERYWHERE

high–and–mighty *adj* (1654) : ARROGANT, IMPERIOUS

[1]**high•ball** \ˈhī-ˌbȯl\ *n* (1895) **1 :** an iced drink containing liquor (as whiskey) and water or a carbonated beverage (as ginger ale) and served in a tall glass **2 :** a railroad signal for a train to proceed at full speed

[2]**highball** *vi* (1912) : to go at full or high speed ⟨a ~*ing* express train⟩

high beam *n* (1939) : a vehicle headlight beam with a long-range focus

high•bind•er \ˈhī-ˌbīn-dər\ *n* [the *Highbinders,* gang of ruffians in New York City *ab*1806] (1876) **1 :** a professional killer operating in the Chinese quarter of an American city **2 :** a corrupt politician

high blood pressure *n* (1899) : abnormally elevated blood pressure esp. of the arteries; *also* **:** HYPERTENSION

high•born \ˈhī-ˈbȯrn\ *adj* (13c) : of noble birth

high•boy \-ˌbȯi\ *n* (1891) : a tall chest of drawers with a legged base

high•bred \-ˈbred\ *adj* (1674) : coming from superior stock

high•brow \-ˌbrau̇\ *n* (ca. 1903) : a person who possesses or has pretensions to superior learning or culture — **highbrow** *adj* — **high•browed** \-ˌbrau̇d\ *adj* — **high•brow•ism** \-ˌbrau̇-ˌi-zəm\ *n*

high•bush \-ˈbu̇sh\ *adj* (1805) : forming a notably tall or erect bush; *also* **:** borne on a highbush plant

highbush blueberry *n* (1913) : a variable moisture-loving No. American shrub (*Vaccinium corymbosum*) that is the source of most cultivated blueberries; *also* **:** its fruit

highbush cranberry *n* (1805) : a shrubby or arborescent viburnum (*Viburnum opulus*) of No. America and Europe with prominently 3-lobed leaves and red fruit — called also *cranberry bush*

high chair *n* (1848) : a child's chair with long legs, a footrest, and usu. a feeding tray

High Church *adj* (1687) : favoring esp. in Anglican worship the sacerdotal, liturgical, ceremonial, and traditional elements in worship

High Churchman *n* (1687) : an Anglican who adheres to High Church elements in worship

high–class \ˈhī-ˈklas\ *adj* (1864) : of superior quality or status

high comedy *n* (1895) : comedy employing subtle characterizations and witty dialogue — compare LOW COMEDY

high command *n* (1917) **1 :** the supreme headquarters of a military force **2 :** the highest leaders in an organization

high commissioner *n* (ca. 1633) : a principal or a high-ranking commissioner; *esp* **:** an ambassadorial representative of the government of one country stationed in another

high–con•cept \ˈhī-ˈkän-ˌsept\ *adj* (1985) : having or exploiting elements (as fast action, glamour, or suspense) that appeal to a wide audience ⟨~ movies⟩

high–count \ˈhī-ˈkau̇nt\ *adj* (1926) : having a large number of warp and weft yarns to the square inch ⟨~ percale sheeting⟩

high court *n* (14c) : SUPREME COURT

high–definition *adj* (1981) : being or relating to an often digital television system that has twice as many scan lines per frame as a conventional system, a proportionally sharper image, and a wide-screen format

high–density lipoprotein *n* (1960) : HDL

high–end \ˈhī-ˈend\ *adj* (1977) **1 :** UPSCALE ⟨~ boutiques⟩ **2 :** of superior quality or sophistication and usu. high in price ⟨~ cameras⟩

high–energy *adj* (1934) **1 a :** having such speed and kinetic energy as to exhibit relativistic departure from classical laws of motion — used esp. of elementary particles whose velocity has been imparted by an accelerator **b :** of or relating to high-energy particles **2 :** yielding a relatively large amount of energy when undergoing hydrolysis

high–energy physics *n* (1964) : PARTICLE PHYSICS

higher criticism *n* (1836) : study of biblical writings to determine their literary history and the purpose and meaning of the authors — compare LOWER CRITICISM — **higher critic** *n*

higher education *n* (1834) : education beyond the secondary level; *esp* **:** education provided by a college or university

higher law *n* (1844) : a principle of divine or moral law that is considered to be superior to constitutions and enacted legislation

higher learning *n* (1926) : education, learning, or scholarship on the collegiate or university level

high•er–up \ˌhī-ər-ˈəp, ˈhī-ər-ˌ\ *n* (1911) : a superior officer or official

high explosive *n* (1877) : an explosive (as TNT) that generates gas with extreme rapidity and has a shattering effect

high•fa•lu•tin *also* **hi•fa•lu•tin** \ˌhī-fə-ˈlü-tᵊn\ *adj* [perh. fr. [2]*high* + alter. of *fluting,* prp. of *flute*] (1839) **1 :** PRETENTIOUS, FANCY **2 :** expressed in or marked by the use of high-flown bombastic language : POMPOUS

high fashion *n* (1804) **1 :** HIGH STYLE **2 :** HAUTE COUTURE

high fidelity *n* (1934) : the reproduction of an effect (as sound or an image) that is very faithful to the original — **high–fidelity** *adj*

high five *n* (1980) : a slapping of upraised right hands by two people (as in celebration) — **high–five** *vb*

high•fli•er *or* **high•fly•er** \ˈhī-ˈflī(-ə)r\ *n* (ca. 1961) **1 :** a stock whose price rises much more rapidly than the market average **2 :** a company whose stock is a highflier **3 :** an ambitiously competitive person with high aspirations

high–flown \ˈhī-ˈflōn\ *adj* (1647) **1 :** exceedingly or excessively high or favorable **2 :** having an excessively embellished or inflated character : PRETENTIOUS ⟨~ language⟩

high–fly·ing \-ˈflī-iŋ\ *adj* (1581) **1 :** marked by extravagance, pretension, or excessive ambition **2 :** rising to considerable height

high frequency *n* (1892) **:** a radio frequency between very high frequency and medium frequency — see RADIO FREQUENCY table

high gear *n* (1896) **1 :** HIGH 3b **2 :** a state of intense or maximum activity — usu. used with *into* or *in* ⟨a project in *high gear*⟩

High German *n* (1673) **1 :** German as natively used in southern and central Germany **2 :** GERMAN 3b

high–grade \ˈhī-ˈgrād\ *adj* (1878) **1 :** of superior grade or quality ⟨~ bonds⟩ **2 a :** being near the upper or most favorable extreme of a specified range **b :** medically serious or life-threatening ⟨a ~ tumor⟩

high–grad·ing \ˈhī-ˈgrā-diŋ\ *n* (1974) **:** the practice of selecting only the most healthy or valuable individuals in harvesting a natural resource (as timber or fish)

high ground *n* (1853) **:** a position of advantage or superiority; *esp* **:** an ethically superior position ⟨took the moral *high ground* during the debate⟩

high–hand·ed \-ˈhan-dəd\ *adj* (1631) **:** having or showing no regard for the rights, concerns, or feelings of others **:** ARBITRARY, OVERBEARING — **high–hand·ed·ly** *adv* — **high–hand·ed·ness** *n*

high–hat \ˈhī-ˈhat\ *adj* (1924) **:** SNOOTY, SNOBBISH — **high–hat** *vt*

high hat *n* (1885) **1 :** 1BEAVER 2 **2** *or* **hi–hat :** a pair of cymbals operated by a foot pedal

high heels *n pl* (1671) **:** shoes with high heels

High Holiday *n* (1918) **:** either of two important Jewish holidays: **a :** ROSH HASHANAH **b :** YOM KIPPUR

high horse *n* (1721) **:** an arrogant and unyielding mood or attitude

highjack *var of* HIJACK

high jinks *also* **hi·jinks** \ˈhī-ˌjiŋks\ *n pl* (1825) **:** boisterous or rambunctious carryings-on **:** carefree antics or horseplay

high jump *n* (1891) **:** a jump for height over a horizontal bar in a track-and-field contest — **high–jump** *vt* — **high jumper** *n*

1high·land \ˈhī-lənd\ *n* (bef. 12c) **:** elevated or mountainous land

2highland *adj* (15c) **1 :** of or relating to a highland **2** *cap* **:** of or relating to the Highlands of Scotland

high·land·er \-lən-dər\ *n* (1610) **1 :** an inhabitant of a highland **2** *cap* **:** an inhabitant of the Highlands of Scotland

Highland fling *n* (1804) **:** a lively Scottish folk dance

high–lev·el \ˈhī-ˈle-vəl\ *adj* (1811) **1 :** occurring, done, or placed at a high level **2 :** being of high importance or rank ⟨~ diplomats⟩ **3 :** of, relating to, or being a computer programming language (as BASIC or Pascal) which is similar to a natural language (as English) and in which each statement is translated by a compiler usu. into several machine language instructions **4 :** relating to or being nuclear waste that contains highly concentrated radioactive components which are environmentally hazardous

high·life \ˈhī-ˌlīf\ *n* (1955) **:** dance music of west African origin that combines syncopated African rhythms with elements of jazz

1high·light \ˈhī-ˌlīt\ *n* (ca. 1889) **1 :** the lightest spot or area (as in a painting) **:** any of several spots in a modeled drawing or painting that receives the greatest amount of illumination **2 :** something (as an event or detail) that is of major significance or special interest

2highlight *vt* **-light·ed; -light·ing** (1927) **1 :** to throw a strong light on **2 a :** to center attention on **b :** to constitute a highlight of **3 a :** to mark (text) with a highlighter **b :** to cause (as text or an icon) to be displayed in a way that stands out on a computer screen

high·light·er \ˈhī-ˌlī-tər\ *n* (1964) **:** a pen with a broad felt tip and brightly colored transparent ink for marking selected passages in a text

high–low–jack \ˌhī-ˌlō-ˈjak\ *n* (1818) **:** an all-fours game in which scores are made by winning the highest trump, the lowest trump, the jack of trumps, and either the ten of trumps or the most points

high·ly \ˈhī-lē\ *adv* (bef. 12c) **1 :** in or to a high place, level, or rank **2 :** in or to a high degree or amount **3 :** with approval **:** FAVORABLY

high mass *n, often cap H&M* (12c) **:** a mass marked by the singing of prescribed parts by the celebrant and the choir or congregation

high–mind·ed \ˈhī-ˈmīn-dəd\ *adj* (1556) **:** marked by elevated principles and feelings; *also* **:** PRETENTIOUS ⟨too ~ to read any fiction —Alfred Kazin⟩ — **high–mind·ed·ly** *adv* — **high–mind·ed·ness** *n*

high–muck–a–muck \ˌhī-ˈmə-ki-ˌmək\ *or* **high–muck·e·ty–muck** \ˌhī-ˈmə-kə-tē-ˌmək\ *n* [by folk etymology fr. Chinook Jargon *hayo makamak* plenty to eat] (1856) **:** MUCKETY-MUCK

high·ness \ˈhī-nəs\ *n* (bef. 12c) **1 :** the quality or state of being high **2** — used as a title for a person of exalted rank (as a king or prince)

high noon *n* (15c) **1 :** precisely noon **2 :** the most advanced, flourishing, or creative stage or period ⟨the *high noon* of her career⟩ **3 :** the time of a decisive confrontation or contest

high–octane *adj* (1932) **1 :** having a high octane number and hence good antiknock properties ⟨~ gasoline⟩ **2 :** very powerful, strong, or effective ⟨~ football⟩ ⟨~ coffee⟩

high–pitched \ˈhī-ˈpicht\ *adj* (1748) **1 :** having a high pitch ⟨a ~ voice⟩ **2 :** marked by or exhibiting strong feeling **:** AGITATED ⟨a ~, almost frantic campaign —Geoffrey Rice⟩

high place *n* (14c) **:** a temple or altar used by the ancient Semites and built usu. on a hill or elevation

high polymer *n* (1942) **:** a substance (as polystyrene) consisting of molecules that are large multiples of units of low molecular weight

high–pow·ered \ˈhī-ˈpau̇(-ə)rd\ *also* **high–pow·er** \-ˈpau̇(-ə)r\ *adj* (1893) **1 :** having great drive, energy, or capacity **:** DYNAMIC ⟨a ~ executive⟩ **2 :** having or conferring great influence ⟨a ~ job⟩

1high–pressure *adj* (1824) **1 a :** having or involving a high or comparatively high pressure esp. greatly exceeding that of the atmosphere **b :** having a high barometric pressure **2 a :** using or involving aggressive and insistent sales techniques **b :** imposing or involving severe strain or tension ⟨~ occupations⟩

2high–pressure *vt* (1926) **:** to sell or influence by high-pressure tactics

high priest *n* (14c) **1 :** a chief priest esp. of the ancient Jewish Levitical priesthood traditionally traced from Aaron **2 :** a priest of the Melchizedek priesthood in the Mormon Church **3 :** the head of a movement or chief exponent of a doctrine or an art — **high priesthood** *n*

high priestess *n* (1645) **:** a chief priestess

high relief *n* (1703) **:** sculptural relief in which at least half of the circumference of the modeled form projects — compare BAS-RELIEF

high–rise \ˈhī-ˈrīz\ *adj* (1954) **1 :** being multistory and equipped with elevators ⟨~ apartments⟩ **2 :** of, relating to, or characterized by high-rise buildings — **high–rise** \ˈhī-ˌ\ *n*

high road *n* (1664) **1 :** HIGHWAY **2 :** the easiest course **3 :** an ethical course

high roller *n* (1881) **1 :** a person who spends freely in luxurious living **2 :** a person who gambles recklessly or for high stakes — **high–rolling** *adj*

1high school *n* (1824) **:** a school esp. in the U.S. usu. including grades 9–12 or 10–12 — **high school·er** \-ˈskü-lər\ *n*

2high school *n* [trans. of F *haute école*] (1884) **:** a system of advanced exercises in horsemanship

high sea *n* (bef. 12c) **:** the open part of a sea or ocean esp. outside territorial waters — usu. used in pl.

high sign *n* (1899) **:** a gesture used as a signal (as of approval or warning) — usu. used in the phrase *give the high sign*

high–sound·ing \ˈhī-ˈsau̇n-diŋ\ *adj* (1711) **:** POMPOUS, IMPOSING

high–speed \ˈhī-ˈspēd\ *adj* (1873) **1 :** operated or adapted for operation at high speed **2 :** relating to the production of short-exposure photographs of rapidly moving objects or events of short duration

high–spir·it·ed \-ˈspir-ə-təd\ *adj* (1603) **:** characterized by a bold or energetic spirit — **high–spir·it·ed·ly** *adv* — **high–spir·it·ed·ness** *n*

high·spot \ˈhī-ˌspät\ *n* (1910) **:** HIGHLIGHT 2

high–stick·ing \-ˌsti-kiŋ\ *n* (1947) **:** the act of carrying the blade of the stick at an illegal height in ice hockey

high street *n* (bef. 12c) *Brit* **:** a main or principal street

high–strung \ˈhī-ˈstrəŋ\ *adj* (1748) **:** having an extremely nervous or sensitive temperament

high style *n* (1933) **:** the newest style in fashion or design usu. adopted by a limited number of people

hight \ˈhīt\ *adj* [ME, pp. (earlier past) of *hoten* to command, call, be called, fr. OE *hātan;* akin to OHG *heizzan* to command, call] (15c) *archaic* **:** being called **:** NAMED

high table *n* (1602) **:** an elevated table in the dining room of a British college for use by the master and fellows and distinguished guests

high·tail \ˈhī-ˌtāl\ *vi* (1919) **:** to move at full speed or rapidly often in making a retreat — usu. used with *it* ⟨~*ed* it out of there⟩

high tea *n* (1831) **:** a fairly substantial late afternoon or early evening meal at which tea is served

high tech *also* **hi–tech** \-ˈtek\ *n* (1969) **1 :** HIGH TECHNOLOGY **2 :** a style of interior design featuring industrial products, materials, or designs — **high–tech** *also* **hi–tech** *adj*

high technology *n* (1964) **:** scientific technology involving the production or use of advanced or sophisticated devices esp. in the fields of electronics and computers

high–tension *adj* (1889) **:** having or using a high voltage

high–test *adj* (1584) **:** meeting a high standard; *also* **:** HIGH-OCTANE

high–tick·et \ˈhī-ˈti-kət\ *adj* (1951) **:** EXPENSIVE 2

high tide *n* (1745) **1 :** the tide when the water is at its greatest elevation **2 :** culminating point **:** CLIMAX ⟨the *hide tide* of the war effort⟩

high–toned \ˈhī-ˈtōnd\ *adj* (1807) **1 :** high in social, moral, or intellectual quality **2 :** PRETENTIOUS, POMPOUS

high–top \ˈhī-ˌtäp\ *adj* (1918) **:** extending up over the ankle ⟨~ sneakers⟩ — **high–tops** *n pl*

high treason *n* (15c) **:** TREASON 2

high–volt·age \ˈhī-ˈvōl-tij\ *adj* (1890) **:** marked by great energy **:** ELECTRIC, DYNAMIC ⟨a ~ performance⟩

high–water *adj* (1856) **:** unusually short ⟨~ pants⟩

high water *n* (15c) **:** a high stage of the water in a river or lake; *also* **:** HIGH TIDE 1

high–water mark *n* (1691) **:** highest point **:** PEAK

high·way \ˈhī-ˌwā\ *n* (bef. 12c) **:** a public way; *esp* **:** a main direct road

high·way·man \-mən\ *n* (1649) **:** a thief who robs travelers on a road

highway robbery *n* (1752) **1 :** robbery committed on or near a public highway usu. against travelers **2 :** excessive profit or advantage derived from a business transaction

high–wire \ˈhī-ˌwī(-ə)r\ *adj* (1956) **1 :** involving great risk ⟨a financial ~ act⟩ **2 :** DARING ⟨~ prose⟩

high–wrought \ˈhī-ˈrȯt\ *adj* (ca. 1580) **:** extremely agitated

high yellow *n* (1923) *often offensive* **:** a black person of light complexion — called also *high yal·ler* \-ˈya-lər\

hi–hat *var of* HIGH HAT 2

hi·jab \hē-ˈjäb, -ˈjab\ *n* [Ar *ḥijāb* cover, screen, veil] (1980) **:** the traditional covering for the hair and neck that is worn by Muslim women

hi·jack *also* **high·jack** \ˈhī-ˌjak\ *vt* [origin unknown] (1923) **1 a :** to steal by stopping a vehicle on the highway **b :** to commandeer (a flying airplane) esp. by coercing the pilot at gunpoint **c :** to stop and steal from (a vehicle in transit) **d :** KIDNAP **2 a :** to steal or rob as if by hijacking **b :** to subject to extortion or swindling — **hijack** *n* — **hi·jack·er** *n*

hijinks *var of* HIGH JINKS

1hike \ˈhīk\ *vb* **hiked; hik·ing** [perh. akin to 1*hitch*] *vi* (1809) **1 a :** to go on a hike **b :** to travel by any means **2 :** to rise up; *esp* **:** to work upward out of place ⟨skirt had *hiked* up in back⟩ ~ *vt* **1 a :** to move, pull, or raise with a sudden motion ⟨*hiked* himself onto the top bunk⟩ **b :** SNAP 6b **c :** to raise in amount sharply or suddenly ⟨~ rents⟩ **2 :** to take on a hike **3 :** to traverse on a hike ⟨~ a trail⟩ — **hik·er** *n*

2hike *n* (1865) **1 :** a long walk esp. for pleasure or exercise **2 :** an increase esp. in quantity or amount ⟨a new wage ~⟩ **3 :** SNAP 11

hi·lar \ˈhī-lər\ *adj* (ca. 1859) **:** of, relating to, or located near a hilum

hi·lar·i·ous \hi-ˈler-ē-əs, hī-\ *adj* [irreg. fr. L *hilarus, hilaris* cheerful, fr. Gk *hilaros*] (ca. 1840) **:** marked by or causing hilarity **:** extremely funny — **hi·lar·i·ous·ly** *adv* — **hi·lar·i·ous·ness** *n*

hi·lar·i·ty \-ə-tē\ *n* (15c) **:** boisterous merriment or laughter

Hil·bert space \ˈhil-bərt-\ *n* [David *Hilbert*] (1911) **:** a vector space for which a scalar product is defined and in which every Cauchy sequence composed of elements in the space converges to a limit in the space

\ə\ **abut** \ə\ **kitten**, F **table** \ər\ **further** \a\ **ash** \ā\ **ace** \ä\ **mop, mar** \au̇\ **out** \ch\ **chin** \e\ **bet** \ē\ **easy** \g\ **go** \i\ **hit** \ī\ **ice** \j\ **job** \ŋ\ **sing** \ō\ **go** \ȯ\ **law** \ȯi\ **boy** \th\ **thin** \t͟h\ **the** \ü\ **loot** \u̇\ **foot** \y\ **yet** \zh\ **vision, beige** \k, ⁿ, œ, ue, ʸ\ *see* Guide to Pronunciation

hil·ding \'hil-diŋ\ *n* [*hilding,* adj., base] (1592) *archaic* **:** a base contemptible person

[1]**hill** \'hil\ *n* [ME, fr. OE *hyll;* akin to L *collis* hill, *culmen* top] (bef. 12c) **1 :** a usu. rounded natural elevation of land lower than a mountain **2 :** an artificial heap or mound (as of earth) **3 :** several seeds or plants planted in a group rather than a row **4 :** SLOPE, INCLINE

[2]**hill** *vt* (1581) **1 :** to form into a heap **2 :** to draw earth around the roots or base of — **hill·er** *n*

hill·bil·ly \'hil-ˌbi-lē\ *n, pl* **-lies** [[1]*hill* + *Billy,* nickname for *William*] (1891) **:** a person from a backwoods area

hillbilly music *n* (1943) **:** COUNTRY MUSIC

hill climb *n* (1905) **:** a road race for automobiles or motorcycles in which competitors are individually timed up a hill

hill·crest \'hil-ˌkrest\ *n* (ca. 1898) **:** the top line of a hill

hill mynah *n* (1872) **:** a largely black Asian mynah (*Gracula religiosa*) often tamed and taught to pronounce words

hill·ock \'hi-lək\ *n* (14c) **:** a small hill — **hill·ocky** \-lə-kē\ *adj*

Hill reaction \'hil-\ *n* [Robert *Hill* †1991 Brit. biochemist] (1950) **:** the light-dependent transfer of electrons by chloroplasts in photosynthesis that results in the cleavage of water molecules and liberation of oxygen

hill·side \-ˌsīd\ *n* (14c) **:** a part of a hill between the top and the foot

hill·slope \-ˌslōp\ *n* (1829) **:** HILLSIDE

hill·top \'hil-ˌtäp\ *n* (15c) **:** the highest part of a hill

hilly \'hi-lē\ *adj* **hill·i·er; -est** (14c) **:** abounding in hills

hilt \'hilt\ *n* [ME, fr. OE; akin to OHG *helza* hilt] (bef. 12c) **:** a handle esp. of a sword or dagger — **to the hilt 1 :** to the very limit **:** COMPLETELY ⟨the farm was mortgaged *to the hilt*⟩ **2 :** with nothing lacking ⟨played the role *to the hilt*⟩

hi·lum \'hī-ləm\ *n, pl* **hi·la** \-lə\ [NL, fr. L, trifle] (ca. 1753) **1 :** a scar on a seed (as a bean) marking the point of attachment of the ovule **2 :** a notch in or opening from a bodily part suggesting the hilum of a bean

him \im, 'him\ *pron, objective case of* HE

[1]**Hi·ma·la·yan** \ˌhi-mə-'lā-ən, hi-'mäl-yən, -'mä-lē-ən\ *adj* (1835) **1 :** of, relating to, or resembling the Himalayas **2 :** enormously large **:** MOUNTAINOUS ⟨a task of ~ proportions⟩

[2]**Himalayan** *n* (1949) **:** any of a breed of domestic cats developed by crossing the Persian and the Siamese and having the stocky build and long thick coat of the former and the blue eyes and coat patterns of the latter

Himalayan

hi·mat·i·on \hi-'ma-tē-ˌän, -ən\ *n* [Gk, dim. of *heimat-, heima* garment; akin to Gk *hennynai* to clothe — more at WEAR] (1850) **:** a rectangular cloth draped over the left shoulder and about the body and worn as a garment in ancient Greece

him·bo \'him-(ˌ)bō\ *n, pl* **himbos** [blend of *him* and *bimbo*] (1988) **:** an attractive but vacuous man

him/her \'him-'hər, 'hi-mər-, 'him-'slash-\ *pron, objective case of* HE/SHE

him·self \(h)im-'self, *Southern also* -'sef\ *pron* (bef. 12c) **1 a :** that identical male one — used reflexively, for emphasis, in absolute constructions, and in place of *him* esp. when joined to another object ⟨he considers ~ lucky⟩ ⟨he ~ did it⟩ ⟨~ unhappy, he understood the situation⟩ ⟨a gift to his wife and ~⟩; compare [1]HE **b —** used reflexively when the sex of the antecedent is unspecified ⟨everyone must fend for ~⟩ **2 :** his normal, healthy, or sane condition or self ⟨hasn't been ~ lately⟩ **3** *chiefly Irish & Scot* **:** a man of consequence; *esp* **:** the master of the house

hin \'hin\ *n* [Heb *hīn,* fr. Egypt *hnw*] (14c) **:** an ancient Hebrew unit of liquid measure equal to about 1.5 U.S. gallons (5.7 liters)

Hi·na·ya·na \ˌhi-nə-'yä-nə, ˌhē-\ *n* [Skt *hīnayāna* lesser vehicle] (1868) **:** THERAVADA — **Hi·na·ya·nist** \-'yä-nist\ *n* — **Hi·na·ya·nis·tic** \-yä-'nis-tik\ *adj*

[1]**hind** \'hīnd\ *n, pl* **hinds** *also* **hind** [ME, fr. OE; akin to OHG *hinta* hind, Gk *kemas* young deer] (bef. 12c) **1 :** the female of the red deer — compare HART **2 :** any of various spotted groupers (esp. genus *Epinephelus*)

[2]**hind** *n* [ME *hine* servant, farmhand, fr. OE *hīna,* gen. of *hīwan,* pl., members of a household; akin to OHG *hīwo* spouse, L *civis* fellow citizen] (1520) **1 :** a British farm assistant **2** *archaic* **:** RUSTIC

[3]**hind** *adj* [ME, prob. back-formation fr. OE *hinder,* adv., behind; akin to OHG *hintar,* prep., behind] (14c) **:** of or forming the part that follows or is behind **:** REAR ⟨the dog's ~ legs⟩

hind·brain \'hīn(d)-ˌbrān\ *n* (1888) **1 :** the posterior of the three primary divisions of the developing vertebrate brain or the corresponding part of the adult brain that includes the cerebellum, the medulla oblongata, and in mammals the pons and that controls autonomic functions and equilibrium — called also *rhombencephalon*; compare METENCEPHALON, MYELENCEPHALON **2 :** the posterior segment of the brain of an invertebrate

[1]**hin·der** \'hin-dər\ *vb* **hin·dered; hin·der·ing** \-d(ə-)riŋ\ [ME *hindren,* fr. OE *hindrian;* akin to OE *hinder* behind] *vt* (bef. 12c) **1 :** to make slow or difficult the progress of **:** HAMPER **2 :** to hold back **:** CHECK ~ *vi* **:** to delay, impede, or prevent action — **hin·der·er** \-dər-ər\ *n*

syn HINDER, IMPEDE, OBSTRUCT, BLOCK mean to interfere with the activity or progress of. HINDER stresses causing harmful or annoying delay or interference with progress ⟨rain *hindered* the climb⟩. IMPEDE implies making forward progress difficult by clogging, hampering, or fettering ⟨tight clothing that *impedes* movement⟩. OBSTRUCT implies interfering with something in motion or in progress by the sometimes intentional placing of obstacles in the way ⟨the view was *obstructed* by billboards⟩. BLOCK implies complete obstruction to passage or progress ⟨a landslide *blocked* the road⟩.

[2]**hind·er** \'hīn-dər\ *adj* [ME, fr. OE *hinder,* adv.] (13c) **:** situated behind or in the rear **:** POSTERIOR

hind·gut \'hīn(d)-ˌgət\ *n* (1878) **:** the posterior part of the alimentary canal; *also* **:** INTESTINE

Hin·di \'hin-(ˌ)dē\ *n* [Hindi & Urdu *hindī,* fr. *Hind* India, fr. Pers] (1801) **1 :** a literary and official language of northern India **2 :** a complex of Indo-Aryan languages and dialects of northern India for which Hindi is the usual literary language — **Hindi** *adj*

hind·most \'hīn(d)-ˌmōst\ *adj* (14c) **:** farthest to the rear **:** LAST

hind·quar·ter \-ˌkwȯ(r)-tər, -ˌkȯ(r)-\ *n* (ca. 1740) **1 :** one side of the back half of the carcass of a quadruped including a leg and usu. one or more ribs **2** *pl* **:** the hind pair of legs of a quadruped; *broadly* **:** all the structures of a quadruped that lie posterior to the attachment of the hind legs to the trunk

hin·drance \'hin-drən(t)s\ *n* (1526) **1 :** the state of being hindered **2 :** IMPEDIMENT **3 :** the action of hindering

hind·sight \'hīn(d)-ˌsīt\ *n* (1866) **:** perception of the nature of an event after it has happened

[1]**Hin·du** *also* **Hin·doo** \'hin-(ˌ)dü\ *n* [Pers *Hindū* inhabitant of India, fr. *Hind* India] (1662) **1 :** an adherent of Hinduism **2 :** a native or inhabitant of India

[2]**Hindu** *also* **Hindoo** *adj* (1698) **:** of, relating to, or characteristic of the Hindus or Hinduism

Hindu–Arabic *adj* (1925) **:** relating to, being, or composed of Arabic numerals ⟨~ numeration system⟩

Hindu calendar *n* (ca. 1909) **:** a lunar calendar usu. dating from 3101 B.C. and used esp. in India

Hin·du·ism \'hin-(ˌ)dü-ˌi-zəm\ *n* (1809) **:** the dominant religion of India that emphasizes dharma with its resulting ritual and social observances and often mystical contemplation and ascetic practices

[1]**Hin·du·stani** \ˌhin-dü-'sta-nē, -'stä-nē\ *n* [Hindi & Urdu *Hindūstānī,* fr. Pers *Hindūstān* India] (1808) **:** a group of Indo-Aryan dialects of northern India of which literary Hindi and Urdu are considered diverse written forms

[2]**Hindustani** *adj* (1800) **:** of or relating to Hindustan or its people or Hindustani

hind wing *n* (1899) **:** either of the posterior wings of a 4-winged insect

[1]**hinge** \'hinj\ *n* [ME *heng;* akin to MD *henge* hook, OE *hangian* to hang] (14c) **1 a :** a jointed or flexible device on which a door, lid, or other swinging part turns **b :** a flexible ligamentous joint **c :** a small piece of thin gummed paper used in fastening a postage stamp in an album **2 :** a determining factor **:** TURNING POINT

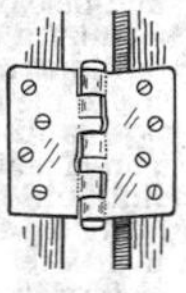

hinge 1a

[2]**hinge** *vb* **hinged; hing·ing** *vi* (1719) **:** to be contingent on a single consideration or point — used with *on* or *upon* ⟨the prosecution's case ~*s* on the DNA evidence⟩ ~ *vt* **:** to attach by or furnish with hinges

hinge joint *n* (1802) **:** a joint between bones (as at the elbow) that permits motion in only one plane

hin·ky \'hiŋ-kē\ *adj* **hin·ki·er; -est** [alter. of argot *hincty* suspicious] (1956) **1** *slang* **:** NERVOUS, JITTERY **2** *slang* **:** SUSPICIOUS

hin·ny \'hi-nē\ *n, pl* **hinnies** [L *hinnus,* fr. Gk *innos*] (1688) **:** a hybrid between a stallion and a female donkey — compare MULE

[1]**hint** \'hint\ *n* [prob. alter. of obs. *hent* act of seizing, fr. *hent,* vb.] (1604) **1** *archaic* **:** OPPORTUNITY, TURN **2 a :** a statement conveying by implication what it is preferred not to say explicitly **b :** an indirect or summary suggestion ⟨helpful ~*s*⟩ **3 :** a slight indication of the existence, approach, or nature of something **:** CLUE **4 :** a very small amount **:** SUGGESTION ⟨with just a ~ of spice⟩

[2]**hint** *vt* (1648) **:** to convey indirectly and by allusion rather than explicitly ⟨a suspicion that she scarcely dared to ~⟩ ~ *vi* **:** to give a hint — usu. used with *at* ⟨~ at the answer⟩ ***syn*** see SUGGEST — **hint·er** *n*

hin·ter·land \'hin-tər-ˌland, -lənd\ *n* [G, fr. *hinter* hinder + *Land*] (1890) **1 :** a region lying inland from a coast **2 a :** a region remote from urban areas **b :** a region lying beyond major metropolitan or cultural centers

[1]**hip** \'hip\ *n* [ME *hipe,* fr. OE *hēope;* akin to OHG *hiafo* hip] (bef. 12c) **:** ROSE HIP

[2]**hip** *n* [ME, fr. OE *hype;* akin to OHG *huf* hip] (bef. 12c) **1 a :** the laterally projecting region of each side of the lower or posterior part of the mammalian trunk formed by the lateral parts of the pelvis and upper part of the femur together with the fleshy parts covering them **b :** HIP JOINT **2 :** the external angle formed by the meeting of two sloping sides of a roof that have their wall plates running in different directions

[3]**hip** *interj* [origin unknown] (1827) — used in a cheer ⟨~ ~ hooray⟩

[4]**hip** *adj* **hip·per; hip·pest** [alter. of [2]*hep*] (1904) **1 a :** having or showing awareness of or involvement in the newest developments or styles **b :** very fashionable **:** TRENDY **2 :** aware or appreciative of something — used with *to* ⟨got ~ to their plan⟩ — **hip·ly** *adv*

[5]**hip** *vt* **hipped; hip·ping** (ca. 1932) **:** to make aware **:** TELL, INFORM

[6]**hip** *n* (1952) **:** HIPNESS

HIPAA *abbr* Health Insurance Portability and Accountability Act

hip and thigh *adv* (1560) **:** in a fierce or ruthless manner

hip bone *n* (12c) **:** the large flaring bone that constitutes a lateral half of the pelvis in mammals and is composed of the ilium, ischium, and pubis which are fused into one bone in the adult

hip boot *n* (1893) **:** a waterproof boot reaching to the hips

hip–hop \'hip-ˌhäp\ *n* [perh. fr. [4]*hip* + [1]*hop*] (1982) **1 :** a subculture esp. of inner-city youths who are typically devotees of rap music **2 :** the stylized rhythmic music that commonly accompanies rap; *also* **:** rap together with this music — **hip–hop** *adj*

hip–hop·per \'hip-ˌhä-pər\ *n* (1983) **:** a devotee of hip-hop music and culture; *also* **:** a performer of hip-hop

hip–hug·gers \'hip-ˌhə-gərz\ *n pl* (ca. 1963) **:** low-slung usu. close-fitting trousers that rest on the hips

hip joint *n* (1794) **:** the articulation between the femur and the innominate bone

hip·line \'hip-ˌlīn\ *n* (1907) **1 :** an arbitrary line encircling the fullest part of the hips **2 :** body circumference at the hips

hip·ness \'hip-nəs\ *n* (1946) **:** the quality or state of being hip

[1]**hipped** \'hipt\ *adj* (1508) **1 :** having hips esp. of a specified kind — often used in combination ⟨a broad-*hipped* person⟩ **2 :** constructed with hips ⟨a ~ roof⟩

[2]**hipped** *adj* [*hip* hypochondria] (ca. 1710) **:** DEPRESSED

[3]**hipped** *adj* [[5]*hip*] (1920) **:** extremely absorbed or interested ⟨~ on astrology⟩

hip·pie *or* **hip·py** \'hi-pē\ *n, pl* **hippies** [[4]*hip* + *-ie*] (1965) **:** a usu. young person who rejects the mores of established society (as by dressing unconventionally or favoring communal living) and advocates a nonviolent ethic; *broadly* **:** a long-haired unconventionally dressed young person — **hip·pie·dom** \-pē-dəm\ *n* — **hip·pie·ish** \-pē-ish\ *adj* — **hip·pie·ness** *or* **hip·pi·ness** \-pē-nəs\ *n*

hip·po \ˈhi-(ˌ)pō\ *n, pl* **hippos** (1872) : HIPPOPOTAMUS

hip·po·cam·pus \ˌhi-pə-ˈkam-pəs\ *n, pl* **-pi** \-ˌpī, -(ˌ)pē\ [NL, fr. Gk *hippokampos* sea horse, fr. *hippos* horse + *kampos* sea monster — more at EQUINE] (1706) : a curved elongated ridge that extends over the floor of the descending horn of each lateral ventricle of the brain, that consists of gray matter covered on the ventricular surface with white matter, and that is involved in forming, storing, and processing memory — **hip·po·cam·pal** \-pəl\ *adj*

hip·po·cras \ˈhi-pə-ˌkras\ *n* [ME *ypocras,* fr. AF *ipocras,* fr. *Ipocras* Hippocrates, to whom its invention was ascribed] (14c) : a mulled wine popular in medieval Europe

Hip·po·crat·ic \ˌhi-pə-ˈkra-tik\ *adj* (ca. 1620) : of or relating to Hippocrates or to the school of medicine that took his name

Hippocratic oath *n* (1747) : an oath embodying a code of medical ethics usu. taken by those about to begin medical practice

Hip·po·crene \ˈhi-pə-ˌkrēn, ˌhi-pə-ˈkrē-nē\ *n* [L, fr. Gk *Hippokrēnē*] (1605) : a fountain on Mount Helicon sacred to the Muses and believed to be a source of poetic inspiration

hip·po·drome \ˈhi-pə-ˌdrōm\ *n* [MF, fr. L *hippodromos,* fr. Gk, fr. *hippos* + *dromos* racecourse — more at DROMEDARY] (1585) **1** : an oval stadium for horse and chariot races in ancient Greece **2** : an arena for equestrian performances

hip·po·griff \-ˌgrif\ *n* [F *hippogriffe,* fr. It *ippogrifo,* fr. *ippo-* (fr. Gk *hippos* horse) + *grifo* griffin, fr. L *gryphus*] (ca. 1656) : a legendary animal having the foreparts of a griffin and the body of a horse

hip pointer *n* (1967) : a deep bruise to the iliac crest or to the attachments of the muscles attached to it that occurs esp. in contact sports (as football)

Hip·pol·y·ta \hi-ˈpä-lə-tə\ *n* [L, fr. Gk *Hippolytē*] (1701) : a queen of the Amazons given in marriage to Theseus by Hercules

Hip·pol·y·tus \-təs\ *n* [L, fr. Gk *Hippolytos*] (1567) : a son of Theseus falsely accused of amorous advances by his stepmother and killed by his father through the agency of Poseidon

Hip·pom·e·nes \hi-ˈpä-mə-nēz\ *n* [L, fr. Gk *Hippomenēs*] (1567) : the successful suitor of Atalanta in Greek mythology

hip·po·pot·a·mus \ˌhi-pə-ˈpä-tə-məs\ *n, pl* **-mus·es** *or* **-mi** \-ˌmī, -(ˌ)mē\ [L, fr. Gk *hippopotamos,* alter. of *hippos potamios,* lit., riverine horse] (1563) : a very large herbivorous 4-toed chiefly aquatic artiodactyl mammal (*Hippopotamus amphibius*) of sub-Saharan Africa with an extremely large head and mouth, bare and very thick grayish skin, and short legs; *also* : a smaller closely related mammal (*Choeropsis liberiensis*) of western Africa

hip·py \ˈhi-pē\ *adj* (1919) : having large hips

hip roof *n* (ca. 1741) : a roof having sloping ends and sloping sides — see ROOF illustration

hip–shoot·ing \ˈhip-ˌshü-tiŋ\ *n* (1951) : action or reaction that is quick and often reckless — **hip shooter** *n*

hip·ster \ˈhip-stər\ *n* [[4]*hip*] (1940) : a person who is unusually aware of and interested in new and unconventional patterns (as in jazz or fashion)

hip·ster·ism \-stə-ˌri-zəm\ *n* (1958) **1** : HIPNESS **2** : the way of life characteristic of hipsters

hi·ra·ga·na \ˌhir-ə-ˈgä-nə\ *n* [Jp, fr. *hira-* ordinary + *kana* syllabary] (1859) : the cursive script that is one of two sets of symbols of Japanese syllabic writing — compare KATAKANA

[1]**hire** \ˈhī(-ə)r\ *n* [ME, fr. OE *hȳr;* akin to OS *hūria* hire] (bef. 12c) **1 a** : payment for the temporary use of something **b** : payment for labor or personal services : WAGES **2 a** : the act or an instance of hiring **b** : the state of being hired : EMPLOYMENT **3** *Brit* : RENTAL — often used attributively **4** : one who is hired ⟨starting wage for the new ~*s*⟩ — **for hire** *also* **on hire** : available for use or service in return for payment

[2]**hire** *vb* **hired; hir·ing** *vt* (bef. 12c) **1 a** : to engage the personal services of for a set sum ⟨~ a crew⟩ **b** : to engage the temporary use of for a fixed sum ⟨~ a hall⟩ **2** : to grant the personal services of or temporary use of for a fixed sum ⟨~ themselves out⟩ **3** : to get done for pay ⟨~ the mowing done⟩ ~ *vi* : to take employment ⟨~ out as a guide during the tourist season⟩ — **hir·er** *n*

syn HIRE, LET, LEASE, RENT, CHARTER mean to engage or grant for use at a price. HIRE and LET, strictly speaking, are complementary terms, HIRE implying the act of engaging or taking for use and LET the granting of use ⟨we *hired* a car for the summer⟩ ⟨decided to *let* the cottage to a young couple⟩. LEASE strictly implies a letting under the terms of a contract but is often applied to hiring on a lease ⟨the diplomat *leased* an apartment for a year⟩. RENT stresses the payment of money for the full use of property and may imply either hiring or letting ⟨instead of buying a house, they decided to *rent*⟩ ⟨will not *rent* to families with children⟩. CHARTER applies to the hiring or letting of a vehicle usu. for exclusive use ⟨*charter* a bus to go to the game⟩.

hired gun *n* (1971) : an expert hired to do a specific and often ethically dubious job

hire·ling \ˈhī(-ə)r-liŋ\ *n* (bef. 12c) : a person who serves for hire esp. for purely mercenary motives

hire purchase *n* (1895) *chiefly Brit* : purchase on the installment plan

hiring hall *n* (1934) : a union-operated placement office where registered applicants are referred in rotation to jobs

hir·sute \ˈhər-ˌsüt, ˈhir-, ˌhər-ˈ, hir-ˈ\ *adj* [L *hirsutus;* akin to L *horrēre* to bristle — more at HORROR] (1621) **1** : HAIRY 1 **2** : covered with coarse stiff hairs ⟨a ~ leaf⟩ — **hir·sute·ness** *n*

hir·sut·ism \ˈhər-sə-ˌti-zəm, ˈhir-\ *n* (1927) : excessive growth of hair of normal or abnormal distribution

hi·ru·din \hi-ˈrü-dᵊn, ˈhir-(y)ə-\ *n* [fr. *Hirudin,* a trademark] (1905) : an anticoagulant extracted from the buccal glands of the medicinal leech

[1]**his** \(h)iz, ˌhiz\ *adj* [ME, fr. OE, gen. of *hē* he] (bef. 12c) : of or relating to him or himself esp. as possessor, agent, or object of an action ⟨~ jobs⟩ ⟨~ writings⟩ ⟨~ confirmation⟩ — compare [1]HE

[2]**his** \ˈhiz\ *pron, sing or pl in constr* (bef. 12c) : that which belongs to him — used without a following noun as a pronoun equivalent in meaning to the adjective *his*

his/her \ˈhiz-ˈhər, ˈhi-zər-ˈhər, ˈhiz-ˈslash-\ *adj* (1952) : his or her — used as an adjective of common gender

His·pan·ic \hi-ˈspa-nik\ *adj* [L *hispanicus,* fr. *Hispania* Iberian Peninsula, Spain] (1584) **1** : of or relating to the people, speech, or culture of Spain or of Spain and Portugal **2** : of, relating to, or being a person of Latin American descent living in the U.S.; *esp* : one of Cuban, Mexican, or Puerto Rican origin — **Hispanic** *n* — **His·pan·i·cism** \-ˈspa-nə-ˌsi-zəm\ *n* — **His·pan·i·cist** \-sist\ *n* — **His·pan·i·cize** \-ˌsīz\ *vt*

his·pa·ni·dad \ˌis-ˌpa-ni-ˈthä(th)\ *n* (1941) : HISPANISM 1

his·pa·nism \ˈhis-pə-ˌni-zəm\ *n, often cap* (1940) **1** : a movement to reassert the cultural unity of Spain and Latin America **2** : a characteristic feature of Spanish occurring in another language

His·pa·nist \-nist\ *n* (1786) : a scholar specially informed in Spanish or Portuguese language, literature, linguistics, or civilization

His·pa·no \hi-ˈspa-(ˌ)nō, ˈhis-pə-ˌnō\ *n, pl* **-nos** [AmerSp *hispano,* prob. short for *hispanoamericano,* lit., Spanish-American] (1946) : a native or resident of the southwestern U.S. descended from Spaniards settled there before annexation; *also* : MEXICAN 1

his·pid \ˈhis-pəd\ *adj* [L *hispidus;* akin to L *horrēre*] (1646) : rough or covered with bristles, stiff hairs, or minute spines ⟨~ leaves⟩

hiss \ˈhis\ *vb* [ME, of imit. origin] *vi* (14c) : to make a sharp sibilant sound ⟨the crowd ~*ed* in disapproval⟩ ⟨~*ing* steam⟩ ~ *vt* **1** : to express disapproval of by hissing ⟨~*ed* the performers off the stage⟩ **2** : to utter or whisper angrily or threateningly and with a hiss — **hiss** *n* — **hiss·er** *n*

his·self \(h)i-ˈself, -ˈsef\ *pron* (12c) *chiefly dial* : HIMSELF 1

hissy \ˈhi-sē\ *n* [perh. by shortening & alter. fr. *hysterical*] (ca. 1934) *chiefly Southern & southern Midland* : TANTRUM

hissy fit *n* (ca. 1970) : TANTRUM

[1]**hist** \s *often prolonged and usu with* p *preceding and* t *following; often read as* ˈhist\ *interj* (1592) — used to attract attention

[2]**hist** \ˈhīst\ *dial var of* HOIST

[3]**hist** *abbr* historian; historical; history

hist- *or* **histo-** *comb form* [F, fr. Gk *histos* mast, loom beam, web, fr. *histanai* to cause to stand — more at STAND] : tissue ⟨*histo*physiology⟩

his·ta·mi·nase \hi-ˈsta-mə-ˌnās, ˈhis-tə-mə-, -ˌnāz\ *n* [ISV] (1930) : a widely occurring flavoprotein enzyme that oxidizes histamine and various diamines

his·ta·mine \ˈhis-tə-ˌmēn, -mən\ *n* [ISV *hist-* + *amine*] (ca. 1913) : a compound $C_5H_9N_3$ esp. of mammalian tissues that causes dilation of capillaries, contraction of smooth muscle, and stimulation of gastric acid secretion, that is released during allergic reactions, and that is formed by decarboxylation of histidine

his·ta·min·er·gic \ˌhis-tə-mə-ˈnər-jik\ *adj* [ISV] (1936) *of autonomic nerve fibers* : liberating or activated by histamine ⟨~ receptors⟩

his·ti·dine \ˈhis-tə-ˌdēn\ *n* [ISV *hist-* + *-idine*] (1896) : a crystalline essential amino acid $C_6H_9N_3O_2$ formed by the hydrolysis of most proteins

his·tio·cyte \ˈhis-tē-ə-ˌsīt\ *n* [Gk *histion* web (dim. of *histos*) + ISV *-cyte*] (1924) : MACROPHAGE; *esp* : a nonmotile macrophage of extravascular tissues and esp. connective tissue — **his·tio·cyt·ic** \ˌhis-tē-ə-ˈsi-tik\ *adj*

his·to·chem·is·try \ˌhis-tō-ˈke-mə-strē\ *n* [ISV] (ca. 1860) : a science that combines the techniques of biochemistry and histology in the study of the chemical constitution of cells and tissues — **his·to·chem·i·cal** \-ˈke-mi-kəl\ *adj* — **his·to·chem·i·cal·ly** \-k(ə-)lē\ *adv*

his·to·com·pat·i·bil·i·ty \ˈhis-(ˌ)tō-kəm-ˌpa-tə-ˈbi-lə-tē\ *n* (1948) : a state of mutual tolerance that allows some tissues to be grafted effectively to others — compare MAJOR HISTOCOMPATIBILITY COMPLEX

his·to·gen·e·sis \ˌhis-tə-ˈje-nə-səs\ *n* [NL] (ca. 1854) : the formation and differentiation of tissues — **his·to·ge·net·ic** \-jə-ˈne-tik\ *adj*

his·to·gram \ˈhis-tə-ˌgram\ *n* [Gk *histos* mast, web + E *-gram*] (1891) : a representation of a frequency distribution by means of rectangles whose widths represent class intervals and whose areas are proportional to the corresponding frequencies

his·tol·o·gy \his-ˈtä-lə-jē\ *n, pl* **-gies** [F *histologie,* fr. *hist-* + *-logie* -logy] (ca. 1847) **1** : a branch of anatomy that deals with the minute structure of animal and plant tissues as discernible with the microscope **2** : tissue structure or organization — **his·to·log·i·cal** \ˌhis-tə-ˈlä-ji-kəl\ *or* **his·to·log·ic** \-ˈlä-jik\ *adj* — **his·to·log·i·cal·ly** \-ji-k(ə-)lē\ *adv* — **his·tol·o·gist** \his-ˈtä-lə-jist\ *n*

his·tol·y·sis \his-ˈtä-lə-səs\ *n* [NL] (ca. 1857) : the breakdown of bodily tissues

his·tone \ˈhis-ˌtōn\ *n* [G *Histon*] (1885) : any of various simple water-soluble proteins that are rich in the basic amino acids lysine and arginine and are complexed with DNA in the nucleosomes of eukaryotic chromatin

his·to·pa·thol·o·gy \ˌhis-tō-pə-ˈthä-lə-jē, -pa-\ *n* [ISV] (1896) **1** : a branch of pathology concerned with the tissue changes characteristic of disease **2** : the tissue changes that affect a part or accompany a disease — **his·to·path·o·log·ic** \-ˌpa-thə-ˈlä-jik\ *or* **his·to·path·o·log·i·cal** \-ji-kəl\ *adj* — **his·to·path·o·log·i·cal·ly** \-ji-k(ə-)lē\ *adv* — **his·to·pa·thol·o·gist** \-pə-ˈthä-lə-jist, -pa-\ *n*

his·to·phys·i·ol·o·gy \-ˌfi-zē-ˈä-lə-jē\ *n* (ca. 1886) **1** : a branch of physiology concerned with the function and activities of tissues **2** : structural and functional tissue organization — **his·to·phys·i·o·log·i·cal** \-ē-ə-ˈlä-ji-kəl\ *or* **his·to·phys·i·o·log·ic** \-jik\ *adj*

his·to·plas·mo·sis \ˌhis-tə-plaz-ˈmō-səs\ *n* [NL, fr. *Histoplasma,* genus of fungi] (1907) : a respiratory disease with symptoms like those of influenza that is caused by a fungus (*Histoplasma capsulatum*) and is marked by benign involvement of lymph nodes of the trachea and bronchi or by severe progressive generalized involvement of the lymph nodes and tissues (as of the liver or spleen) rich in macrophages

his·to·ri·an \hi-ˈstȯr-ē-ən, -ˈstär-\ *n* (15c) **1** : a student or writer of history; *esp* : one who produces a scholarly synthesis **2** : a writer or compiler of a chronicle

his·tor·ic \hi-ˈstȯr-ik, -ˈstär-\ *adj* (1594) : HISTORICAL: as **a** : famous or important in history ⟨~ battlefields⟩ **b** : having great and lasting importance ⟨a ~ occasion⟩ **c** : known or established in the past ⟨~ interest rates⟩ **d** : dating from or preserved from a past time or culture ⟨~ buildings⟩ ⟨~ artifacts⟩

\ə\ **abut** \ᵊ\ **kitten**, F **table** \ər\ **further** \a\ **ash** \ā\ **ace** \ä\ **mop, mar**
\au̇\ **out** \ch\ **chin** \e\ **bet** \ē\ **easy** \g\ **go** \i\ **hit** \ī\ **ice** \j\ **job**
\ŋ\ **sing** \ō\ **go** \ȯ\ **law** \ȯi\ **boy** \th\ **thin** \t͟h\ **the** \ü\ **loot** \u̇\ **foot**
\y\ **yet** \zh\ **vision, beige** \k, ⁿ, œ, ue, ʸ\ *see* Guide to Pronunciation

his·tor·i·cal \-i-kəl\ *adj* (15c) **1 a :** of, relating to, or having the character of history ⟨~ data⟩ **b :** based on history ⟨~ novels⟩ **c :** used in the past and reproduced in historical presentations **2 :** famous in history : HISTORIC a **3 a :** SECONDARY 1c **b :** DIACHRONIC ⟨~ grammar⟩ — **his·tor·i·cal·ness** \-i-kəl-nəs\ *n*

his·tor·i·cal·ly \-i-k(ə-)lē\ *adv* (1550) **1 :** in accordance with or with respect to history ⟨an ~ accurate account⟩ **2 :** in the past ⟨~, stagnant cities seldom have recovered —Jane Jacobs⟩

historical materialism *n* (1925) **:** the Marxist theory of history and society that holds that ideas and social institutions develop only as the superstructure of a material economic base — compare DIALECTICAL MATERIALISM

historical present *n* (1867) **:** the present tense used in relating past events

his·tor·i·cism \hi-ˈstȯr-ə-ˌsi-zəm, -ˈstär-\ *n* (1895) **:** a theory, doctrine, or style that emphasizes the importance of history: as **a :** a theory in which history is seen as a standard of value or as a determinant of events **b :** a style (as in architecture) characterized by the use of traditional forms and elements — **his·tor·i·cist** \-sist\ *adj or n*

his·to·ric·i·ty \ˌhis-tə-ˈri-sə-tē\ *n* (1880) **:** historical actuality

his·tor·i·cize \hi-ˈstȯr-ə-ˌsīz, -ˈstär-\ *vb* **-cized; -ciz·ing** *vt* (1846) **:** to make historical ~ *vi* **:** to use historical material

his·to·ri·og·ra·pher \hi-ˌstȯr-ē-ˈä-grə-fər\ *n* [MF *historiographeur,* fr. LL *historiographus,* fr. Gk *historiographos,* fr. *historia* + *graphein* to write — more at CARVE] (15c) **:** HISTORIAN

his·to·ri·og·ra·phy \-fē\ *n* (1569) **1 a :** the writing of history; *esp* **:** the writing of history based on the critical examination of sources, the selection of particulars from the authentic materials, and the synthesis of particulars into a narrative that will stand the test of critical methods **b :** the principles, theory, and history of historical writing ⟨a course in ~⟩ **2 :** the product of historical writing **:** a body of historical literature — **his·to·rio·graph·i·cal** \-ē-ə-ˈgra-fi-kəl\ *also* **his·to·rio·graph·ic** \-fik\ *adj* — **his·to·rio·graph·i·cal·ly** \-ē-ə-ˈgra-fi-k(ə-)lē\ *adv*

his·to·ry \ˈhis-t(ə-)rē\ *n, pl* **-ries** [ME *histoire, historie,* fr. AF *estoire, histoire,* fr. L *historia,* fr. Gk, inquiry, history, fr. *histōr, istōr* knowing, learned; akin to Gk *eidenai* to know — more at WIT] (14c) **1 :** TALE, STORY **2 a :** a chronological record of significant events (as affecting a nation or institution) often including an explanation of their causes **b :** a treatise presenting systematically related natural phenomena **c :** an account of a patient's medical background **d :** an established record ⟨a prisoner with a ~ of violence⟩ **3 :** a branch of knowledge that records and explains past events ⟨medieval ~⟩ **4 a :** events that form the subject matter of a history **b :** events of the past **c :** one that is finished or done for ⟨the winning streak was ~⟩ ⟨you're ~⟩ **d :** previous treatment, handling, or experience (as of a metal)

his·tri·on·ic \ˌhis-trē-ˈä-nik\ *adj* [LL *histrionicus,* fr. L *histrion-, histrio* actor] (1648) **1 :** deliberately affected **:** THEATRICAL **2 :** of or relating to actors, acting, or the theater ***syn*** see DRAMATIC — **his·tri·on·i·cal·ly** \-ni-k(ə-)lē\ *adv*

his·tri·on·ics \-niks\ *n pl but sing or pl in constr* (1864) **1 :** theatrical performances **2 :** deliberate display of emotion for effect

[1]**hit** \ˈhit\ *vb* **hit; hit·ting** [ME, fr. OE *hyttan,* prob. fr. ON *hitta* to meet with, hit] *vt* (bef. 12c) **1 a :** to reach with or as if with a blow **b :** to come in contact with ⟨the ball ~ the window⟩ **c :** to strike (as a ball) with an object (as a bat, club, or racket) so as to impart or redirect motion **2 a :** to cause to come into contact **b :** to deliver (as a blow) by action **c :** to apply forcefully or suddenly ⟨~ the brakes⟩ **3 :** to affect esp. detrimentally ⟨farmers ~ by drought⟩ **4 :** to make a request of ⟨~ his friend for 10 dollars⟩ — often used with *up* **5 :** to discover or meet esp. by chance **6 a :** to accord with **:** SUIT **b :** REACH, ATTAIN ⟨prices ~ a new high⟩ **c :** to arrive or appear at, in, or on ⟨~ town⟩ ⟨the best time to ~ the stores⟩ **d** *of fish* **:** to bite at or on **e :** to reflect accurately ⟨~ the right note⟩ **f :** to reach or strike (as a target) esp. for a score in a game or contest ⟨couldn't seem to ~ the basket⟩ **g :** BAT 2b **7 :** to indulge in excessively ⟨~ the bottle⟩ **8 :** to deal another card to (as in blackjack) ~ *vi* **1 a :** to strike a blow **b :** to arrive with a forceful effect like that of a blow ⟨the storm ~⟩ **2 a :** to come into contact with something **b :** ATTACK **c** *of a fish* **:** STRIKE 11b **d :** BAT 1 **3 :** to succeed in attaining or coming up with something — often used with *on* or *upon* ⟨~ on a solution⟩ **4** *obs* **:** to be in agreement **:** SUIT **5** *of an internal combustion engine* **:** to fire the charge in the cylinders — **hit·ter** *n* — **hit it big :** to achieve great success — **hit it off :** to get along well **:** become friends ⟨they *hit it off* immediately⟩ — **hit on :** to make esp. sexual overtures to — **hit the books :** to study esp. with intensity — **hit the fan :** to have a major usu. undesirable impact — **hit the ground running :** to begin or proceed quickly, energetically, or effectively — **hit the hay** *or* **hit the sack :** to go to bed — **hit the high points** *or* **hit the high spots :** to touch on or at the most important points or places — **hit the jackpot :** to become notably and unexpectedly successful — **hit the nail on the head :** to be exactly right — **hit the road :** LEAVE, TRAVEL; *also* **:** to set out — **hit the roof** *or* **hit the ceiling :** to give vent to a burst of anger or angry protest — **hit the spot :** to give complete or special satisfaction — used esp. of food or drink — **hit the wall 1 :** to reach the point of physical exhaustion during strenuous activity **2 :** to reach a limiting point or situation at which progress or success ceases

[2]**hit** *n* (15c) **1 :** an act or instance of hitting or being hit ⟨more ~*s* than misses⟩ **2 a :** a stroke of luck **b :** a great success **3 :** a telling or critical remark **4 :** BASE HIT **5 :** a quantity of a drug ingested at one time **6 :** a premeditated murder committed esp. by a member of a crime syndicate **7 :** an instance of connecting to a particular Web site ⟨a million ~*s* per day⟩ **8 :** a successful match in a search (as of a computer database or the Internet) — **hit·less** \ˈhit-ləs\ *adj*

hit–and–miss \ˌhit-ᵊn-ˈmis\ *adj* (1897) **:** sometimes successful and sometimes not **:** not reliably good or successful

[1]**hit–and–run** \-ˈrən\ *adj* (1899) **1 :** being or relating to a hit-and-run in baseball **2 :** being or involving a motor-vehicle driver who does not stop after being involved in an accident **3 :** involving or intended for quick specific action or results ⟨a ~ raid⟩

[2]**hit–and–run** *n* (1904) **:** a baseball play calling for a runner on first to begin running as a pitch is delivered and for the batter to attempt to hit the pitch

[3]**hit–and–run** *vi* (1966) **:** to execute a hit-and-run play in baseball

[1]**hitch** \ˈhich\ *vb* [ME *hytchen*] *vt* (14c) **1 :** to move by jerks or with a tug **2 a :** to catch or fasten by or as if by a hook or knot ⟨~*ed* his horse to the fence post⟩ **b (1) :** to connect (a vehicle or implement) with a source of motive power ⟨~ a rake to a tractor⟩ **(2) :** to attach (a source of motive power) to a vehicle or instrument ⟨~ the horses to the wagon⟩ **c :** to join in marriage ⟨got ~*ed*⟩ **3 :** HITCHHIKE ~ *vi* **1 :** to move with halts and jerks **:** HOBBLE **2 a :** to become entangled, made fast, or linked **b :** to become joined in marriage **3 :** HITCHHIKE — **hitch·er** *n*

[2]**hitch** *n* (1664) **1 :** LIMP **2 :** a sudden movement or pull **:** JERK ⟨gave his trousers a ~⟩ **3 a :** a sudden halt **:** STOPPAGE **b :** a usu. unforeseen difficulty or obstacle ⟨the plan went off without a ~⟩ **4 :** the act or fact of catching hold **5 :** a connection between a vehicle or implement and a detachable source of power (as a tractor or horse) **6 :** a delimited period esp. of military service **7 :** any of various knots used to form a temporary noose in a line or to secure a line temporarily to an object **8 :** LIFT 5b

hitch·hike \ˈhich-ˌhīk\ *vi* (1923) **1 :** to travel by securing free rides from passing vehicles **2 :** to be carried or transported by chance or unintentionally ⟨destructive insects *hitchhiking* on ships⟩ ~ *vt* **:** to solicit and obtain (a free ride) esp. in a passing vehicle — **hitch·hik·er** *n*

hitch up *vi* (1817) **:** to hitch a draft animal or team to a vehicle

hi–tech *var of* HIGH-TECH

[1]**hith·er** \ˈhi-t͟hər\ *adv* [ME *hider, hither,* fr. OE *hider;* akin to Goth *hidre* hither, L *citra* on this side — more at HE] (bef. 12c) **:** to this place

[2]**hither** *adj* (14c) **:** being on the near or adjacent side

hith·er·most \-ˌmōst\ *adj* (1563) **:** nearest on this side

hith·er·to \-ˌtü, ˌhi-t͟hər-ˈtü\ *adv* (13c) **:** up to this or that time

hith·er·ward \ˈhi-t͟hə(r)-wərd\ *adv* (bef. 12c) **:** HITHER

Hit·ler·ism \ˈhit-lə-ˌri-zəm\ *n* (1925) **:** the principles and policies associated with Hitler — **Hit·ler·ite** \-ˌrīt\ *n or adj*

hit list *n* (1972) **:** a list of persons or programs to be opposed or eliminated; *broadly* **:** a list of those targeted for special attention or treatment

hit man *n* (1963) **1 :** a professional assassin who works for a crime syndicate **2 :** HATCHET MAN

hit–or–miss \ˌhit-ər-ˈmis\ *adj* (1848) **:** marked by a lack of care, forethought, system, or plan; *also* **:** HIT-AND-MISS

hit or miss *adv* (1606) **:** in a hit-or-miss manner **:** HAPHAZARDLY

hit parade *n* (1929) **:** a group or listing of the most popular or noteworthy items of a particular kind (as popular songs)

Hit·tite \ˈhi-ˌtīt\ *n* [Heb *Ḥittī,* fr. Hitt *ḫatti*] (1608) **1 :** a member of a conquering people in Asia Minor and Syria with an empire in the second millennium B.C. **2 :** the extinct Indo-European language of the Hittites — see INDO-EUROPEAN LANGUAGES table — **Hittite** *adj*

HIV \ˌāch-ˌī-ˈvē\ *n* (1986) **:** either of two retroviruses that infect and destroy helper T cells of the immune system causing the marked reduction in their numbers that is diagnostic of AIDS — called also *AIDS virus, human immunodeficiency virus*; compare HIV-1, HIV-2

[1]**hive** \ˈhīv\ *n* [ME, fr. OE *hȳf;* perh. akin to ON *hūfr* ship's hull, L *cūpa* tub, Skt *kūpa* cave] (bef. 12c) **1 a :** a container for housing honeybees **b :** the usu. aboveground nest of bees **2 :** a colony of bees **3 :** a place swarming with activity — **hive·less** \-ləs\ *adj*

[2]**hive** *vb* **hived; hiv·ing** *vi* (14c) **1** *of bees* **:** to enter and take possession of a hive **2 :** to reside in close association ~ *vt* **1 :** to collect into a hive **2 :** to store up in or as if in a hive

hive off *vi* (ca. 1856) *chiefly Brit* **:** to break away from or as if from a group **:** become separate ~ *vt, chiefly Brit* **:** to make separate: as **a :** to remove from a group ⟨*hive off* the rookies for special training⟩ **b :** to assign (as assets or responsibilities) to another **c :** SPIN OFF

hives \ˈhīvz\ *n pl but sing or pl in constr* [origin unknown] (ca. 1500) **:** an allergic disorder marked by raised edematous patches of skin or mucous membrane and usu. intense itching and caused by contact with a specific precipitating factor (as a food, drug, or inhalant) either externally or internally — called also *urticaria*

HIV–1 \-ˈwən\ *n* (1986) **:** a lentivirus (species *Human immunodeficiency virus 1*) that is the most prevalent HIV — called also *HTLV-III*

HIV–2 \-ˈtü\ *n* (1986) **:** a lentivirus (species *Human immunodeficiency virus 2*) that causes AIDS esp. in western Africa, is closely related in structure to SIV of monkeys, and is less virulent than HIV-1

hiz·zon·er \ˌhi-ˈzä-nər\ *n, often cap* [alter. of *his honor*] (1882) — used as a title for a man holding the office of mayor

HJ *abbr* [L *hic jacet*] here lies

HJR *abbr* House joint resolution

hl *abbr* hectoliter

HL *abbr* House of Lords

HLA \ˌāch-(ˌ)el-ˈā\ *n* [*h*uman *l*eukocyte *a*ntigen] (1968) **1 :** the major histocompatibility complex in humans **2 :** a genetic locus, gene, or antigen of HLA — often used with one or more letters to designate a locus or with letters and a number to designate an allele at the locus or the antigen corresponding to the locus and allele

HLS *abbr* [L *hoc loco situs*] laid in this place

hm *abbr* hectometer

HM *abbr* Her Majesty; Her Majesty's; His Majesty; His Majesty's

HMAS *abbr* Her Majesty's Australian ship; His Majesty's Australian ship

HMCS *abbr* Her Majesty's Canadian ship; His Majesty's Canadian ship

HMO \ˌāch-(ˌ)em-ˈō\ *n* (1972) **:** an organization that provides comprehensive health care to voluntarily enrolled individuals and families in a particular geographic area by member physicians with limited referral to outside specialists and that is financed by fixed periodic payments determined in advance — called also *health maintenance organization*

Hmong \ˈməŋ\ *n, pl* **Hmong** [Hmong *hmoŋ* (with high level tone), a self-designation] (1977) **1 :** a member of a mountain-dwelling people inhabiting southeastern China and the northern parts of Vietnam, Laos, and Thailand **2 :** the language of the Hmong people

HMS *abbr* Her Majesty's ship; His Majesty's ship

HN *abbr* head nurse

[1]**ho** \ˈhō\ *interj* [ME] (15c) — used esp. to attract attention to something specified ⟨land ~⟩

[2]**ho** *n, pl* **hos** *or* **hoes** [alter. of *whore*] (1965) *slang* **:** WHORE 1

Ho *symbol* holmium

hoa·gie *also* **hoa·gy** \ˈhō-gē\ *n, pl* **hoagies** [origin unknown] (1943) **:** SUBMARINE 2

¹hoar \'hŏr\ *adj* [ME *hor*, fr. OE *hār;* akin to OHG *hēr* hoary] (bef. 12c) : HOARY

²hoar *n* [ME *hor* hoariness, fr. *hor*, adj.] (1567) : FROST 1b

¹hoard \'hŏrd\ *n* [ME *hord*, fr. OE; akin to Goth *huzd* treasure, OE *hȳdan* to hide] (bef. 12c) : a supply or fund stored up and often hidden away

²hoard *vt* (bef. 12c) **1** : to lay up a hoard of **2** : to keep (as one's thoughts) to oneself ∼ *vi* : to lay up a hoard — **hoard·er** *n*

hoard·ing \'hŏr-diŋ\ *n* [*hoard, hoard* hoarding] (ca. 1823) **1** : a temporary board fence put about a building being erected or repaired — called also *hoard* **2** *Brit* : BILLBOARD

hoar·frost \'hŏr-,frŏst\ *n* (14c) : FROST 1b

hoarse \'hŏrs\ *adj* **hoars·er; hoars·est** [ME *hos, hors,* prob. fr. ON *hārs, hāss;* akin to OE *hās* hoarse, OHG *heis*] (bef. 12c) **1** : rough or harsh in sound : GRATING ⟨a ∼ voice⟩ **2** : having a hoarse voice ⟨shouted himself ∼⟩ — **hoarse·ly** *adv* — **hoarse·ness** *n*

hoars·en \'hŏr-sᵊn\ *vb* **hoars·ened; hoars·en·ing** \'hŏrs-niŋ, 'hŏr-sə-\ *vt* (1748) : to make hoarse ∼ *vi* : to become hoarse

hoary \'hŏr-ē\ *adj* **hoar·i·er; -est** (1530) **1** : gray or white with or as if with age **2** : extremely old : ANCIENT ⟨∼ legends⟩ — **hoar·i·ness** *n*

hoa·tzin \hwät'(s)ēn\ *n* [ultim. fr. Nahuatl *huāctzin* the laughing falcon (*Herpetotheres cachinnans*)] (1661) : a crested large So. American bird (*Opisthocomos hoazin*) with blue facial skin, red eyes, brown plumage marked with white above, and claws on the first and second digits of the wing when young

¹hoax \'hŏks\ *vt* [prob. contr. of *hocus*] (ca. 1796) : to trick into believing or accepting as genuine something false and often preposterous — **hoax·er** *n*

²hoax *n* (1808) **1** : an act intended to trick or dupe : IMPOSTURE **2** : something accepted or established by fraud or fabrication

¹hob \'häb\ *n* [ME *hobbe,* fr. *Hobbe,* nickname for *Robert*] (15c) **1** *dial Eng* : HOBGOBLIN, ELF **2** : MISCHIEF, TROUBLE — used with *play* and *raise* ⟨always raising ∼⟩

²hob *n* [origin unknown] (1511) **1** : a projection at the back or side of a fireplace on which something may be kept warm **2** : a cutting tool used for cutting the teeth of worm wheels or gears **3** *Brit* : COOKTOP

³hob *vt* **hobbed; hob·bing** (1799) **1** : to cut with a hob **2** : to furnish with hobnails

Hobbes·ian \'häb-zē-ən\ *adj* (1776) : of or relating to the English philosopher Thomas Hobbes or Hobbism

Hob·bism \'hä-,bi-zəm\ *n* (1691) : the philosophical system of Thomas Hobbes; *esp* : the Hobbesian theory that people have a fundamental right to self-preservation and to pursue selfish aims but will relinquish these rights to an absolute monarch in the interest of common safety and happiness — **Hob·bist** \'hä-bist\ *n or adj*

hob·bit \'hä-bət\ *n* [coined by J.R.R. Tolkien] (1937) : a member of a fictitious peaceful and genial race of small humanlike creatures that dwell underground

¹hob·ble \'hä-bəl\ *vb* **hob·bled; hob·bling** \-b(ə-)liŋ\ [ME *hoblen;* akin to MD *hobbelen* to turn, roll] *vi* (14c) : to move along unsteadily or with difficulty; *esp* : to limp along ∼ *vt* **1** : to cause to limp : make lame : CRIPPLE **2** [prob. alter. of *hopple* to hobble] **a** : to fasten together the legs of (as a horse) to prevent straying : FETTER **b** : to place under handicap : HAMPER, IMPEDE — **hob·bler** \-b(ə-)lər\ *n*

²hobble *n* (1726) **1** : a hobbling movement **2** *archaic* : an awkward situation **3** : something used to hobble an animal

hob·ble·bush \'hä-bəl-,bu̇sh\ *n* (ca. 1818) : a white-flowered shrubby viburnum (*Viburnum alnifolium* syn. *V. lantanoides*) of eastern No. America having serrate rounded leaves and red berries

hob·ble·de·hoy \'hä-bəl-di-,hȯi\ *n* [origin unknown] (1540) : an awkward gawky youth

hobble skirt *n* (1911) : a skirt constricted at the bottom

¹hob·by \'hä-bē\ *n, pl* **hobbies** [ME *hoby,* fr. AF *hobel, hobé*] (15c) : a small Old World falcon (*Falco subbuteo*) that is dark blue above and white below with dark streaking on the breast

²hobby *n, pl* **hobbies** [short for *hobbyhorse*] (1816) : a pursuit outside one's regular occupation engaged in esp. for relaxation — **hob·by·ist** \-bē-ist\ *n*

hob·by·horse \'hä-bē-,hȯrs\ *n* [*hobby* small light horse, fr. ME *hoby, hobyn,* perh. fr. *Hobbin,* nickname for *Robert* or *Robin*] (ca. 1553) **1 a** : a figure of a horse fastened about the waist in the morris dance **b** : a dancer wearing this figure **2** *obs* : BUFFOON **3 a** : a stick having an imitation horse's head at one end that a child pretends to ride **b** : ROCKING HORSE **c** : a toy horse suspended by springs from a frame **4** : a topic to which one constantly reverts **b** : ²HOBBY

hob·gob·lin \'häb-,gäb-lən\ *n* [¹*hob*] (1530) **1** : a mischievous goblin **2** : BOGEY 2, BUGABOO

hob·nail \-,nāl\ *n* [²*hob*] (1592) : a short large-headed nail for studding shoe soles — **hob·nailed** \-,nāld\ *adj*

hob·nob \-,näb\ *vi* **hob·nobbed; hob·nob·bing** [fr. the obs. phrase *drink hobnob* to drink alternately to one another] (1813) **1** *archaic* : to drink sociably **2** : to associate familiarly — **hob·nob·ber** *n*

¹ho·bo \'hō-(,)bō\ *n, pl* **hoboes** *also* **hobos** [origin unknown] (1889) **1** : a migratory worker **2** : a homeless and usu. penniless vagabond

²hobo *vi* (1906) : to live or travel in the manner of a hobo

Hob·son's choice \'häb-sənz-\ *n* [Thomas *Hobson* †1631 Eng. liveryman, who required every customer to take the horse nearest the door] (1649) **1** : an apparently free choice when there is no real alternative **2** : the necessity of accepting one of two or more equally objectionable alternatives

¹hock \'häk\ *n* [ME *hoch, hough,* fr. OE *hōh* heel; akin to ON *hāsin* hock] (1540) **1 a** : the tarsal joint or region in the hind limb of a digitigrade quadruped (as the horse) corresponding to the human ankle but elevated and bending backward — see HORSE illustration **b** : a joint of a fowl's leg that corresponds to the hock of a quadruped **2** : a small cut of meat from a front or hind leg just above the foot ⟨ham ∼s⟩

²hock *n, often cap* [modif. of G *Hochheimer,* fr. *Hochheim,* Germany] (ca. 1625) *chiefly Brit* : RHINE WINE 1

³hock *vt* [⁴*hock*] (1878) : PAWN — **hock·er** *n*

⁴hock *n* [D *hok* pen, prison] (1883) **1 a** : ²PAWN 2 ⟨got his watch out of ∼⟩ **b** : DEBT 3 ⟨in ∼ to the bank⟩ **2** : PRISON

hock·ey \'hä-kē\ *n* [perh. fr. MF *hoquet* shepherd's crook, dim. of *hoc* hook, of Gmc origin; akin to OE *hōc* hook] (1527) **1** : FIELD HOCKEY **2** : ICE HOCKEY

hock·shop \'häk-,shäp\ *n* (1871) : PAWNSHOP

ho·cus \'hō-kəs\ *vt* **ho·cussed** *or* **ho·cused; ho·cus·sing** *or* **ho·cus·ing** [obs. *hocus,* n., short for *hocus-pocus*] (1675) **1** : to perpetrate a trick or hoax on : DECEIVE **2** : to befuddle often with drugged liquor; *also* : DOPE, DRUG ⟨*hocussed* the favorite before the race⟩

¹ho·cus-po·cus \,hō-kəs-'pō-kəs\ *n* [prob. fr. *hocus pocus,* imitation Latin phrase used by jugglers] (1647) **1** : SLEIGHT OF HAND **2** : nonsense or sham used esp. to cloak deception

²hocus-pocus *vt* **-cussed** *or* **-cused; -cus·sing** *or* **-cus·ing** (1774) : to play tricks on

hod \'häd\ *n* [prob. fr. MD *hodde;* akin to MHG *hotte* cradle] (1573) **1** : a tray or trough that has a pole handle and that is borne on the shoulder for carrying loads (as of mortar or brick) **2** : a coal scuttle

hod carrier *n* (1771) : a laborer employed in carrying supplies to bricklayers, stonemasons, cement finishers, or plasterers on the job

hodge·podge \'häj-,päj\ *n* [alter. of *hotchpotch*] (15c) : a heterogeneous mixture : JUMBLE ⟨a ∼ of styles⟩

Hodg·kin's disease \'häj-kinz-\ *n* [Thomas *Hodgkin* †1866 Eng. physician] (1865) : a neoplastic disease that is characterized by progressive enlargement of lymph nodes, spleen, and liver and by progressive anemia — called also *Hodgkin's, Hodgkin's lymphoma*

ho·do·scope \'hä-də-,skōp, 'hō-\ *n* [Gk *hodos* road, path + E *-scope*] (ca. 1933) : an instrument for tracing the paths of ionizing particles by means of ion counters in close array

¹hoe \'hō\ *n* [ME *howe,* fr. AF *houe,* of Gmc origin; akin to OHG *houwa* mattock, *houwan* to hew — more at HEW] (14c) **1** : any of various implements for tilling, mixing, or raking; *esp* : an implement with a thin flat blade on a long handle used esp. for cultivating, weeding, or loosening the earth around plants **2** : BACKHOE

²hoe *vb* **hoed; hoe·ing** *vi* (15c) : to use or work with a hoe ∼ *vt* **1** : to weed, cultivate, or thin (a crop) with a hoe **2** : to remove (weeds) by hoeing **3** : to dress or cultivate (land) by hoeing — **ho·er** \'hō-(ə)r\ *n*

hoe·cake \'hō-,kāk\ *n* (1745) : a small cake made of cornmeal

hoe·down \-,dau̇n\ *n* (1841) **1** : SQUARE DANCE **2** : a gathering featuring hoedowns

¹hog \'hȯg, 'häg\ *n, pl* **hogs** *also* **hog** [ME *hogge,* fr. OE *hogg*] (14c) **1** : a domestic swine esp. when weighing more than 120 pounds (54 kilograms); *broadly* : any of various wild and domestic swine **2** *usu* **hogg,** *Brit* : a young unshorn sheep; *also* : wool from such a sheep **3 a** : a selfish, gluttonous, or filthy person **b** : one that uses something to excess ⟨old cars that are gas ∼s⟩

²hog *vb* **hogged; hog·ging** *vt* (1769) **1** : to cut (a horse's mane) short : ROACH **2** : to cause to arch **3** : to take in excess of one's due ⟨∼ the credit⟩ **4** : to tear up or shred (as waste wood) into bits by machine ∼ *vi* : to become curved upward in the middle — used of a ship's bottom or keel

ho·gan \'hō-,gän\ *n* [Navajo *hooghan*] (1871) : a Navajo Indian dwelling usu. made of logs and mud with a door traditionally facing east

hog·back \'hȯg-,bak, 'häg-\ *n* (1840) : a ridge of land formed by the outcropping edges of tilted strata; *broadly* : a ridge with a sharp summit and steeply sloping sides

hogan

hog cholera *n* (1859) : a highly infectious often fatal disease of swine caused by a flavivirus (species *Classical swine fever virus* of the genus *Pestivirus*) and characterized by fever, loss of appetite, weakness, erythematous lesions esp. in light-skinned animals, and severe leukopenia

hog·fish \'hȯg-,fish, 'häg-\ *n* (1734) : a large West Indian and Florida wrasse (*Lachnolaimus maximus*) often used for food

hog·get \'hä-gət, 'hȯ-\ *n* [ME, fr. ¹*hog* + *-et*] (14c) *chiefly Brit* : HOG 2

hog·gish \'hȯ-gish, 'hä-\ *adj* (15c) : grossly selfish, gluttonous, or filthy — **hog·gish·ly** *adv* — **hog·gish·ness** *n*

hog heaven *n* (1944) : an extremely satisfying state or situation

Hog·ma·nay \,häg-mə-'nā, 'häg-mə-,\ *n* [origin unknown] (ca. 1680) **1** *Scot* : the eve of New Year's Day **2** *Scot* : a gift solicited or given at Hogmanay

hog·nose snake \'hȯg-,nōz-, 'häg-\ *n* (1736) : any of a genus (*Heterodon*) of rather small harmless stout-bodied No. American colubrid snakes with keeled scales and an upturned snout that seldom bite but hiss wildly and often play dead when disturbed — called also *hog-nosed snake, puff adder*

hog score *n* [¹*hog* (curling stone that fails to reach the score)] (1685) : a line which is marked across a curling rink seven yards from the tee and beyond which a stone must pass or be removed from the score — called also *hog line*

hogs·head \'hȯgz-,hed, 'hägz-\ *n* (14c) **1** : a large cask or barrel **2** : any of various units of capacity; *esp* : a U.S. unit equal to 63 gallons (238 liters)

hog sucker *n* (1877) : a No. American sucker (*Hypentelium nigricans*) that is brassy olive marked with brown and is sometimes used for food

hog-tie \'hȯg-,tī, 'häg-\ *vt* (1894) **1** : to tie together the feet of **2** : to make helpless : STYMIE ⟨∼ scientific progress⟩

hog·wash \-,wȯsh, -,wäsh\ *n* (15c) **1** : SWILL 2a, SLOP **2** : NONSENSE, BALDERDASH

hog wild \-'wī(-ə)ld\ *adj* (1904) : lacking in restraint : WILD ⟨would go *hog wild* if unconfined by constitutional limitations —Leo Egan⟩

Ho·hen·stau·fen \'hō-ən-,shtau̇-fən, -,stau̇-\ *adj* (1883) : of or relating to a princely German family that reigned over the Holy Roman Empire from 1138–1254 and over Sicily from 1194–1266 — **Hohenstaufen** *n*

\ə\ abut \ᵊ\ kitten, F table \ər\ **further** \a\ ash \ā\ ace \ä\ mop, mar
\au̇\ **out** \ch\ **chin** \e\ bet \ē\ **easy** \g\ go \i\ hit \ī\ ice \j\ **job**
\ŋ\ **sing** \ō\ go \ȯ\ **law** \ȯi\ **boy** \th\ **thin** \t̲h̲\ **the** \ü\ loot \u̇\ **foot**
\y\ **yet** \zh\ **vision,** beige \k̲, ⁿ, œ, �, ᵻ\ *see* Guide to Pronunciation

Ho·hen·zol·lern \ˌhō-ən-ˈzä-lərn, -ˈzȯ-\ *adj* (1858) **:** of or relating to a princely German family that reigned in Prussia from 1701–1918 and in Germany from 1871–1918 — **Hohenzollern** *n*

Ho·ho·kam \ˌhō-hō-ˈkäm\ *n, pl* **Hohokam** [O'odham (Uto-Aztecan language of southern Arizona) *huhugam,* lit., those who have gone] (1884) **:** a member of a prehistoric desert culture of the southwestern U.S. centering in the Gila Valley of Arizona and characterized esp. by irrigated agriculture — **Hohokam** *adj*

ho–hum \ˈhō-ˈhəm\ *adj* (1969) **1 :** ROUTINE, DULL ⟨a ~ existence⟩ **2 :** BORED, INDIFFERENT ⟨a ~ reaction⟩

ho hum *interj* [imit.] (1924) — used to express weariness, boredom, or disdain

hoick \ˈhȯik\ *vt* [prob. alter. of [1]*hike*] (1898) **:** to move or pull abruptly **:** YANK ⟨was ~*ed* out of my job —Vincent Sheean⟩

hoi pol·loi \ˌhȯi-pə-ˈlȯi\ *n pl* [Gk, the many] (1837) **:** the general populace **:** MASSES

hoise \ˈhȯiz\ *vt* **hoised** \ˈhȯizd\ *or* **hoist** \ˈhȯist\; **hois·ing** \ˈhȯi-ziŋ\ [alter. of *hysse* to hoist, perh. fr. LG *hissen*] (1509) **:** HOIST 1 — **hoist with one's own petard** *or* **hoist by one's own petard :** victimized or hurt by one's own scheme

hoi·sin sauce \ˈhȯi-ˌsin-, ˌhȯi-ˈsin-\ *n* [Chin (Guangdong) *hóisīn-jeung,* lit., seafood sauce] (1968) **:** a thick reddish sauce of soybeans, spices, and garlic used in east Asian cookery

[1]**hoist** \ˈhȯist, *chiefly dial* ˈhīst\ *vb* [alter. of *hoise*] *vt* (15c) **1 :** LIFT, RAISE; *esp* **:** to raise into position by or as if by means of tackle **2 :** DRINK 1 ⟨~ a few beers⟩ ~ *vi* **:** to become hoisted **:** RISE ***syn*** see LIFT — **hoist·er** *n*

[2]**hoist** *n* (1654) **1 :** an act of hoisting **:** LIFT **2 :** an apparatus for hoisting **3 :** the height of a flag when viewed flying

[1]**hoi·ty–toi·ty** \ˌhȯi-tē-ˈtȯi-tē, ˌhī-tē-ˈtī-tē\ *n* [rhyming compound fr. E dial. *hoit* to play the fool] (1668) **:** thoughtless giddy behavior

[2]**hoity–toity** *adj* (1812) **1 :** thoughtlessly silly or frivolous **:** FLIGHTY **2 :** marked by an air of assumed importance **:** HIGHFALUTIN

hoke \ˈhōk\ *vt* **hoked; hok·ing** [*hokum*] (1925) **:** to give a contrived, falsely impressive, or hokey quality to — usu. used with *up* ⟨~ up a movie with lots of action⟩

hok·ey \ˈhō-kē\ *adj* **hok·i·er; -est** (1927) **1 :** [1]CORNY 3 ⟨the usual ~ melodrama⟩ **2 :** obviously contrived **:** PHONY ⟨the plots are tricky but not ~ —Cleveland Amory⟩ — **hok·ey·ness** *or* **hok·i·ness** \ˈhō-kē-nəs\ *n* — **hok·i·ly** \ˈhō-kə-lē\ *adv*

ho·key·po·key \ˌhō-kē-ˈpō-kē\ *n* (ca. 1878) **1 :** HOCUS-POCUS 2 **2 :** ice cream sold by street vendors

hok·ku \ˈhō-(ˌ)kü\ *n, pl* **hokku** [Jp] (1897) **:** HAIKU

ho·kum \ˈhō-kəm\ *n* [prob. blend of *hocus-pocus* and *bunkum*] (1908) **1 :** a device used (as by showmen) to evoke a desired audience response **2 :** pretentious nonsense **:** BUNKUM

hol- *or* **holo-** *comb form* [Gk, fr. *holos* whole — more at SAFE] **1 :** complete **:** total ⟨*holo*hedral⟩ **2 :** completely **:** totally ⟨*hol*andric⟩

hol·an·dric \hō-ˈlan-drik, hä-\ *adj* [ISV, fr. *hol-* + *andr-* + *-ic*] (1930) **:** transmitted by or being a gene in the nonhomologous portion of the Y chromosome ⟨a ~ trait⟩

Hol·arc·tic \hō-ˈlärk-tik, hä-, -ˈlär-tik\ *adj* (1883) **:** of, relating to, or being the biogeographic region including the northern parts of the Old and the New Worlds and comprising the Nearctic and Palearctic regions or subregions

[1]**hold** \ˈhōld\ *vb* **held** \ˈheld\; **hold·ing** [ME, fr. OE *healdan;* akin to OHG *haltan* to hold, and perh. to L *celer* rapid, Gk *klonos* agitation] *vt* (bef. 12c) **1 a :** to have possession or ownership of or have at one's disposal ⟨~*s* property worth millions⟩ ⟨the bank ~*s* the title to the car⟩ **b :** to have as a privilege or position of responsibility ⟨~ a professorship⟩ **c :** to have as a mark of distinction ⟨~*s* the record for the 100-yard dash⟩ ⟨~*s* a PhD⟩ **2 :** to keep under restraint ⟨~ price increases to a minimum⟩: as **a :** to prevent free expression of ⟨~ your temper⟩ **b :** to prevent from some action ⟨ordered the troops to ~ fire⟩ ⟨the only restraining motive which may ~ the hand of a tyrant —Thomas Jefferson⟩ **c :** to keep back from use ⟨ask them to ~ a room for us⟩ ⟨I'll have a hot dog, and ~ the mustard⟩ **d :** to delay temporarily the handling of ⟨please ~ all my calls⟩ **3 :** to make liable or accountable or bound to an obligation ⟨I'll ~ you to your promise⟩ **4 a :** to have or maintain in the grasp ⟨~ my hand⟩ ⟨this is how you ~ the racket⟩; *also* **:** AIM, POINT ⟨*held* a gun on them⟩ **b :** to support in a particular position or keep from falling or moving ⟨~ me up so I can see⟩ ⟨~ the ladder steady⟩ ⟨a clamp ~*s* the whole thing together⟩ ⟨~ your head up⟩ **c :** to bear the pressure of **:** SUPPORT ⟨can the roof ~ all of that weight⟩ **5 :** to prevent from leaving or getting away ⟨~ the train⟩: as **a :** to avoid emitting or letting out ⟨how long can you ~ your breath⟩ **b :** to restrain as or as if a captive ⟨the suspect was *held* without bail⟩ ⟨*held* them at gunpoint⟩; *also* **:** to have strong appeal to ⟨the book *held* my interest throughout⟩ **6 a :** to enclose and keep in a container or within bounds **:** CONTAIN ⟨the jug ~*s* one gallon⟩ ⟨this corral will not ~ all of the horses⟩ **b :** to be able to consume easily or without undue effect ⟨can't ~ any more pie⟩; *esp* **:** to be able to drink (alcoholic beverages) without becoming noticeably drunk ⟨can't ~ your liquor⟩ **c :** ACCOMMODATE ⟨the restaurant ~*s* 400 diners⟩ **d :** to have as a principal or essential feature or attribute ⟨the book ~*s* a number of surprises⟩; *also* **:** to have in store ⟨no one knows what the future ~*s*⟩ **7 a :** to have in the mind or express as a judgment, opinion, or belief ⟨I ~ the view that this is wrong⟩ ⟨~ a grudge⟩ ⟨~*ing* that it is nobody's business but his —Jack Olsen⟩ — often used with *against* ⟨in America they ~ everything you say against you —Paul McCartney⟩ **b :** to think of in a particular way **:** REGARD ⟨were *held* in high esteem⟩ **8 a :** to assemble for and carry on the activity of ⟨*held* a convention⟩ **b :** to cause to be carried on **:** CONDUCT ⟨will ~ a seminar⟩ **c :** to produce or sponsor esp. as a public exhibition ⟨will ~ an art show⟩ **9 a :** to maintain occupation, control, or defense of ⟨the troops *held* the ridge⟩; *also* **:** to resist the offensive efforts or advance of ⟨*held* the opposing team to just two points⟩ **b :** to maintain (a certain condition, situation, or course of action) without change ⟨~ a course due east⟩ **10 :** to cover (a part of the body) esp. for protection ⟨had to ~ their ears because of the cold⟩ ~ *vi* **1 a :** to maintain position **:** refuse to give ground ⟨the defensive line is ~*ing*⟩ **b :** to continue in the same way or to the same degree **:** LAST ⟨hopes the weather will ~⟩ — often used with *up* **2 :** to derive right or title — often used with *of* or *from* **3 :** to be or remain valid **:** APPLY ⟨the rule ~*s* in most cases⟩ — often used in the phrase *hold true* **4 :** to maintain a grasp on something **:** remain fastened to something ⟨the anchor *held* in the rough sea⟩ **5 :** to go ahead as one has been going ⟨*held* south for several miles⟩ **6 :** to bear or carry oneself ⟨asked him to ~ still⟩ **7 :** to forbear an intended or threatened action **:** HALT, PAUSE — often used as a command **8 :** to stop counting during a countdown **9** *slang* **:** to have illicit drug material in one's possession ***syn*** see CONTAIN — **hold a brief for :** ADVOCATE, DEFEND — usu. used in negative constructions ⟨*I hold no brief for* cartels and market allocations —J. D. Upham⟩ — **hold a candle to :** to qualify for comparison with — **hold court :** to be the center of attention among friends or admirers — **hold forth :** to speak at length **:** EXPATIATE — **hold hands :** to engage one's hand with another's esp. as an expression of affection — **hold one's breath 1 :** to prevent oneself from breathing temporarily **2 :** to wait in anxious anticipation — **hold one's horses :** to slow down or stop for a moment — usu. used in the imperative — **hold one's own :** to maintain one's position **:** prove equal to opposition — **hold one's tongue** *or* **hold one's peace :** to keep silent **:** keep one's thoughts to oneself — **hold sway :** to have a dominant influence **:** RULE — **hold the bag 1 :** to be left empty-handed **2 :** to bear alone a responsibility that should have been shared by others — **hold the fort 1 :** to maintain a firm position **2 :** to take care of usual affairs ⟨is *holding the fort* until the manager returns⟩ — **hold the line :** to maintain the current position or situation ⟨*hold the line* on prices⟩ — **hold to :** to give firm assent to **:** adhere to strongly ⟨*holds to* his promise⟩ — **hold to account :** to hold responsible — **hold water :** to stand up under criticism or analysis — **hold with :** to agree with or approve of

[2]**hold** *n* (14c) **1 :** STRONGHOLD 1 **2 a :** CONFINEMENT, CUSTODY **b :** PRISON **3 a** (1) **:** the act or the manner of holding or grasping **:** GRIP ⟨released his ~ on the handle⟩ (2) **:** a manner of grasping an opponent in wrestling **b :** a nonphysical bond that attaches, restrains, or constrains or by which something is affected, controlled, or dominated ⟨has lost its ~ on the broad public —Oscar Cargill⟩ **c :** full comprehension ⟨get ~ of exactly what is happening —J. P. Lyford⟩ **d :** full or immediate control **:** POSSESSION ⟨get ~ of yourself⟩ ⟨wants to get ~ of a road map⟩ **e :** TOUCH 14 — used with *of* ⟨tried to get ~ of me⟩ **4 :** something that may be grasped as a support **5 a :** FERMATA **b :** the time between the onset and the release of a vocal articulation **6 :** a sudden motionless posture at the end of a dance **7 a :** an order or indication that something is to be reserved or delayed **b :** a delay in a countdown (as in launching a spacecraft) — **on hold 1 :** in a state of interruption during a telephone call when one party switches to another line without totally disconnecting the other party **2 :** in a state or period of indefinite suspension ⟨put our plans *on hold*⟩

[3]**hold** *n* [alter. of *hole*] (1591) **1 :** the interior of a ship below decks; *esp* **:** the cargo deck of a ship **2 :** the cargo compartment of a plane

hold·all \ˈhōld-ˌȯl\ *n* (1851) *chiefly Brit* **:** an often cloth traveling case or bag

hold·back \ˈhōl(d)-ˌbak\ *n* (1581) **1 :** something that retains or restrains **2 a :** the act of holding back **b :** something held back

hold back *vt* (1535) **1 a :** to hinder the progress or achievement of **:** RESTRAIN **b :** to keep from advancing to the next stage, grade, or level **2 :** to refrain from revealing or parting with ⟨*held back* important information⟩ ~ *vi* **1 :** to keep oneself in check **2 :** to refrain from revealing or parting with something

hold–down \ˈhōld-ˌdau̇n\ *n* (1888) **1 :** something used to fasten an object in place **2 a :** an act of holding down **b :** LIMIT ⟨agreed to wage-rate ~*s*⟩

hold down *vt* (1533) **1 :** to keep within limits ⟨*hold* the noise *down*⟩ **2 :** to assume or have responsibility for ⟨*holding down* two jobs⟩

hold·en \ˈhōl-dən\ *archaic past part of* HOLD

hold·er \ˈhōl-dər\ *n* (14c) **1 :** a person that holds: as **a** (1) **:** OWNER (2) **:** TENANT **b :** a person in possession of and legally entitled to receive payment of a bill, note, or check **2 :** a device that holds ⟨a cigarette ~⟩

holder in due course (1882) **:** one other than the original recipient who holds a legally effective negotiable instrument (as a promissory note) and who has a right to collect from and no responsibility toward the issuer

hold·fast \ˈhōl(d)-ˌfast\ *n* (1566) **1 :** something to which something else may be firmly secured **2 a :** a part by which a plant clings to a flat surface **b :** an organ by which a parasitic animal attaches itself to its host

[1]**holding** *n* (15c) **1 a :** land held esp. by a vassal or tenant **b :** property (as land or securities) owned — usu. used in pl. **2 :** a ruling of a court esp. on an issue of law raised in a case — compare DICTUM **3 :** something that holds

[2]**holding** *adj* (1568) **1 :** having the effect of holding back or delaying something ⟨the [war] represented a ~ action against the spread of world Communism —Sidney Offit⟩ **2 :** intended for usu. temporary storage or retention ⟨a ~ tank⟩

holding company *n* (1906) **:** a company whose primary business is holding a controlling interest in the securities of other companies — compare INVESTMENT COMPANY

holding pattern *n* (ca. 1952) **1 :** the usu. oval course flown (as over an airport) by aircraft awaiting clearance esp. to land **2 :** a state of waiting or suspended activity or progress

hold off *vt* (15c) **1 :** to block from an objective **:** DELAY **2 :** to defer action on **:** POSTPONE ⟨*hold off* a decision⟩ **3 :** to fight to a standoff **:** WITHSTAND ~ *vi* **:** to defer or temporarily stop doing something

hold on *vi* (13c) **1 a :** to maintain a condition or position **:** PERSIST **b :** to maintain a grasp on something **:** HANG ON **2 :** to await something (as a telephone connection) desired or requested; *broadly* **:** WAIT — **hold on to :** to maintain possession of or adherence to

hold·out \ˈhōld-ˌau̇t\ *n* (1908) **:** one that holds out (as in negotiations); *also* **:** an instance of holding out

hold out *vi* (ca. 1556) **1 :** to remain unsubdued or unyielding ⟨where 30 of the . . . refugees were still *holding out* —Anna Tomforde⟩; *also* **:** to continue to function or be available **:** LAST ⟨prayed that the engine would *hold out*⟩ ⟨as long as our money *holds out*⟩ **2 :** to refuse to go along with others in a concerted action or to come to an agreement ⟨*holding out* for a shorter workweek⟩ ~ *vt* **1 :** to present as something realizable **:** PROFFER **2 :** to represent to be — **hold out on :** to withhold something (as information) from

hold·over \ˈhōld-ˌō-vər\ *n* (1893) **:** one that is held over

hold over *vi* (1647) **:** to continue (as in office) for a prolonged period ~ *vt* **1 a :** POSTPONE, DEFER **b :** to retain in a condition or position from an earlier period **2 :** to prolong the engagement of ‹the film was *held over* another week›

hold·up \ˈhōld-ˌəp\ *n* (1837) **1 :** DELAY **2 :** a robbery carried out at gunpoint

hold up *vt* (1851) **1 :** to rob at gunpoint **2 :** DELAY, IMPEDE **3 :** to call attention to **:** single out ‹his work was *held up* to ridicule› ‹*hold* this *up* as perfection —*Times Lit. Supp.*› ~ *vi* **:** to continue in the same condition without failing or losing effectiveness or force ‹she's *holding up* under the strain› ‹music that *holds up* twenty years later›

1hole \ˈhōl\ *n* [ME, fr. OE *hol* (fr. neut. of *hol,* adj., hollow) & *holh;* akin to OHG *hol,* adj., hollow and perh. to OE *helan* to conceal — more at HELL] (bef. 12c) **1 a :** an opening through something **:** PERFORATION ‹have a ~ in my coat› **b :** an area where something is missing **:** GAP: as **(1) :** a serious discrepancy **:** FLAW, WEAKNESS ‹some ~*s* in your logic› **(2) :** an opening in a defensive formation; *esp* **:** the area of a baseball field between the positions of shortstop and third baseman **(3) :** a defect in a crystal (as of a semiconductor) that is due to an electron's having left its normal position in one of the crystal bonds and that is equivalent in many respects to a positively charged particle **2 :** a hollowed-out place: as **a :** a cave, pit, or well in the ground **b :** BURROW **c :** an unusually deep place in a body of water (as a river) **3 a :** a wretched or dreary place **b :** a prison cell esp. for solitary confinement **4 a :** a shallow cylindrical hole in the putting green of a golf course into which the ball is played **b :** a part of the golf course from tee to putting green ‹just beginning play on the third ~›; *also* **:** the play on such a hole as a unit of scoring ‹won the ~ by two strokes› **5 a :** an awkward position or circumstance **:** FIX ‹got the rebels out of a ~ at the battle —Kenneth Roberts› **b :** a position of owing or losing money ‹$10 million in the ~› ‹raising money to get out of the ~› — **in the hole 1 :** having a score below zero **2 :** at a disadvantage

2hole *vb* **holed; hol·ing** *vt* (bef. 12c) **1 :** to make a hole in **2 :** to drive or hit into a hole ‹~ a putt› ~ *vi* **:** to make a hole in something

hole–and–corner *adj* (1833) **1 :** being or carried on in a place away from public view **:** CLANDESTINE **2 :** INSIGNIFICANT

hole card *n* (1908) **1 :** a card in stud poker that is properly dealt facedown and that the holder need not expose before the showdown **2 :** something (as a reliable advantage) that is held in reserve esp. for use at a strategic moment

hole in one (1925) **:** 1ACE 4

hole–in–the–wall *n, pl* **holes–in–the–wall** (1856) **:** a small and often unpretentious out-of-the-way place (as a restaurant)

hole out *vi* (1857) **:** to play one's ball into the hole in golf

hole up *vi* (1875) **:** to hide out in or as if in a hole or cave ~ *vt* **:** to place in or as if in a refuge or hiding place

hol·ey \ˈhō-lē\ *adj* (13c) **:** having holes

1hol·i·day \ˈhä-lə-ˌdā, *Brit usu* ˈhä-lə-dē\ *n* [ME, fr. OE *hāligdæg,* fr. *hālig* holy + *dæg* day] (bef. 12c) **1 :** HOLY DAY **2 :** a day on which one is exempt from work; *specif* **:** a day marked by a general suspension of work in commemoration of an event **3** *chiefly Brit* **:** VACATION — often used in the phrase *on holiday*; often used in pl. **4 :** a period of exemption or relief ‹corporations enjoying a tax ~›

2holiday *vi* (1869) **:** to take or spend a holiday esp. in travel or at a resort — **hol·i·day·er** *n*

hol·i·day·mak·er \ˈhä-lə-dē-ˌmā-kər, ˈhä-lə-ˌdā-\ *n* (1836) *chiefly Brit* **:** VACATIONER

hol·i·days \-lə-ˌdāz, *Brit usu* -lə-dēz\ *adv* (ca. 1961) **:** on holidays repeatedly **:** on any holiday

ho·li·er–than–thou \ˌhō-lē-ər-t͟hən-ˈt͟hau̇\ *adj* (1859) **:** marked by an air of superior piety or morality

1ho·li·ness \ˈhō-lē-nəs\ *n* (bef. 12c) **1 :** the quality or state of being holy — used as a title for various high religious dignitaries ‹His *Holiness* the Pope› **2 :** SANCTIFICATION 2

2holiness *adj, often cap* (1888) **:** emphasizing the doctrine of the second blessing; *specif* **:** of or relating to a perfectionist movement arising in U.S. Protestantism in the late 19th century

ho·lism \ˈhō-ˌli-zəm\ *n* [*hol-* + *-ism*] (1926) **1 :** a theory that the universe and esp. living nature is correctly seen in terms of interacting wholes (as of living organisms) that are more than the mere sum of elementary particles **2 :** a holistic study or method of treatment — **ho·list** \ˈhō-list\ *n*

ho·lis·tic \hō-ˈlis-tik\ *adj* (1926) **1 :** of or relating to holism **2 :** relating to or concerned with wholes or with complete systems rather than with the analysis of, treatment of, or dissection into parts ‹~ medicine attempts to treat both the mind and the body› ‹~ ecology views humans and the environment as a single system› — **ho·lis·ti·cal·ly** \-ti-k(ə-)lē\ *adv*

hol·land \ˈhä-lənd\ *n, often cap* [ME *holand,* fr. *Holand,* county in the Netherlands, fr. MD *Holland*] (14c) **:** a cotton or linen fabric in plain weave usu. heavily sized or glazed and used for window shades, bookbinding, and clothing

hol·lan·daise \ˌhä-lən-ˈdāz\ *n* [F *sauce hollandaise,* lit., Dutch sauce] (1907) **:** a rich sauce made basically of butter, egg yolks, and lemon juice or vinegar

Hol·lands \ˈhä-lən(d)z\ *n* [D *hollandsch,* fr. *hollandsch genever* Dutch gin] (1788) **:** gin made in the Netherlands — called also *Holland gin*

1hol·ler \ˈhä-lər\ *vb* **hol·lered; hol·ler·ing** \ˈhäl-riŋ, ˈhä-lə-\ [alter. of *hollo*] *vi* (1592) **1 :** to cry out (as to attract attention or in pain) **:** SHOUT **2 :** GRIPE, COMPLAIN ~ *vt* **:** to call out (a word or phrase)

2holler *n* (1825) **1 :** SHOUT, CRY **2 :** COMPLAINT **3 :** a freely improvised work song of black Americans ‹field ~*s*›

3holler *chiefly dial var of* HOLLOW

1hol·lo \ˈhä-(ˌ)lō; hä-ˈlō, hə-\ *or* **hal·loo** \hə-ˈlü, ha-\ *also* **hal·lo** \-ˈlō\ *vi* (14c) **:** to cry hollo **:** HOLLER ~ *vt* **1 :** to call or cry hollo to **2 :** to utter loudly **:** HOLLER

2hollo *or* **halloo** *also* **hallo** *n, pl* **hollos** *or* **halloos** *also* **hallos** (15c) **:** an exclamation or call of hollo

3hollo *or* **halloo** *also* **hallo** *interj* [origin unknown] (1588) **1 —** used to attract attention (as when a fox is spied during a fox hunt) **2 —** used as a call of encouragement or jubilation

1hol·low \ˈhä-(ˌ)lō\ *n* [ME *holw, holh,* fr. OE *holh* hole, hollow — more at HOLE] (bef. 12c) **1 :** an unfilled space **:** CAVITY, HOLE **2 :** a depressed or low part of a surface; *esp* **:** a small valley or basin

2hollow *adj* **hol·low·er** \ˈhä-lə-wər\; **hol·low·est** \-lə-wəst\ [ME *holw, holh,* fr. *holh* hole] (13c) **1 :** having an indentation or inward curve **:** CONCAVE, SUNKEN **2 :** having a cavity within ‹a ~ tree› **3 :** lacking in real value, sincerity, or substance **:** FALSE, MEANINGLESS ‹~ promises› ‹a victory over a weakling is ~ and without triumph —Ernest Beaglehole› **4 :** reverberating like a sound made in or by beating on a large empty enclosure **:** MUFFLED **syn** see VAIN — **hol·low·ly** \ˈhä-lō-lē, -lə-lē\ *adv* — **hol·low·ness** *n*

3hollow *vt* (15c) **1 :** to make hollow **2 :** to form by a hollowing action — usu. used with *out* ‹rain barrels ~*ed* out from trees —Robert Shaplen› ~ *vi* **:** to become hollow

4hollow *adv* (1601) **1 :** so as to have a hollow sound **2 :** COMPLETELY, THOROUGHLY ‹an ongoing story that has the old cowboy-and-Indians genre beat ~ —Barbara Bannon› — often used with *all*

hol·low·ware *or* **hol·lo·ware** \ˈhä-(ˌ)lō-ˌwer\ *n* (1682) **:** vessels (as bowls, cups, or vases) usu. of pottery, glass, or metal that have a significant depth and volume — compare FLATWARE

hol·ly \ˈhä-lē\ *n, pl* **hollies** [ME *holin, holly,* fr. OE *holen;* akin to OHG *hulis* holly, MIr *cuilenn*] (bef. 12c) **1 :** any of a genus (*Ilex* of the family Aquifoliaceae, the holly family) of trees and shrubs; *esp* **:** either of two (*I. opaca* of the eastern U.S. and *I. aquifolium* of Eurasia) with spiny-margined evergreen leaves and usu. red berries often used for Christmas decorations **2 :** the foliage or branches of the holly

hol·ly·hock \ˈhä-lē-ˌhäk, -ˌhȯk\ *n* [ME *holihoc* marshmallow, fr. *holi* holy + *hoc* mallow, fr. OE] (1548) **:** a tall widely cultivated biennial or perennial herb (*Alcea rosea* syn. *Althaea rosea*) of the mallow family that has large coarse rounded leaves and tall spikes of showy flowers and that is prob. of Asian origin

1Hol·ly·wood \ˈhä-lē-ˌwu̇d\ *n* [*Hollywood,* district of Los Angeles, Calif.] (1923) **:** the American motion-picture industry — **Hol·ly·wood·ish** \-ˌwu̇-dish\ *adj*

2Hollywood *adj* (1928) **1 :** of or characteristic of people in the American motion-picture industry ‹the ~ lifestyle› **2 :** of or characteristic of a Hollywood film ‹a story with a ~ happy ending›

Hollywood bed *n* (1947) **:** a mattress on a box spring supported by low legs and often having an upholstered headboard

holm \ˈhō(l)m\ *n* [ME, fr. OE, fr. ON *hōlmr;* akin to OE *hyll* hill] (bef. 12c) *Brit* **:** a small inland or inshore island; *also* **:** BOTTOMS

Holmes·ian \ˈhōm-zē-ən *also* ˈhōlm-\ *adj* [Sherlock *Holmes,* detective in stories by Sir Arthur Conan Doyle] (1929) **:** of, characteristic of, or suggestive of the detective Sherlock Holmes

hol·mi·um \ˈhō(l)-mē-əm\ *n* [NL, fr. *Holmia* Stockholm, Sweden] (1879) **:** a metallic element of the rare-earth group that forms highly magnetic compounds and is obtained esp. from monazite — see ELEMENT table

holm oak *n* (1597) **:** a southern European evergreen oak (*Quercus ilex*)

holo- — see HOL-

ho·lo·blas·tic \ˌhō-lə-ˈblas-tik, ˌhä-\ *adj* [ISV] (1872) **:** characterized by complete cleavage that divides the whole egg into distinct and separate blastomeres — compare MEROBLASTIC

ho·lo·caust \ˈhō-lə-ˌkȯst, ˈhä- *also* -ˌkäst *or* ˈhȯ-lə-kȯst\ *n* [ME, fr. LL *holocaustum,* fr. Gk *holokauston,* fr. neut. of *holokaustos* burnt whole, fr. *hol-* + *kaustos* burnt, fr. *kaiein* to burn — more at CAUSTIC] (13c) **1 :** a sacrifice consumed by fire **2 :** a thorough destruction involving extensive loss of life esp. through fire ‹a nuclear ~› **3 a** *often cap* **:** the mass slaughter of European civilians and esp. Jews by the Nazis during World War II — usu. used with *the* **b :** a mass slaughter of people; *esp* **:** GENOCIDE

Ho·lo·cene \ˈhō-lə-ˌsēn, ˈhä-\ *adj* [ISV] (1897) **:** of, relating to, or being the present or post-Pleistocene geologic epoch — see GEOLOGIC TIME table — **Holocene** *n*

ho·lo·crine \-krən, -ˌkrīn, -ˌkrēn\ *adj* [ISV *hol-* + Gk *krinein* to separate — more at CERTAIN] (ca. 1905) **:** producing or being a secretion resulting from lysis of secretory cells ‹~ sebaceous glands›

ho·lo·en·zyme \ˌhō-lō-ˈen-ˌzīm\ *n* [ISV] (1943) **:** a catalytically active enzyme consisting of an apoenzyme combined with its cofactor

Ho·lo·fer·nes \ˌhä-lə-ˈfər-(ˌ)nēz, ˌhō-\ *n* [LL, fr. Gk *Holophernēs*] (bef. 12c) **:** a general of Nebuchadnezzar's who led an Assyrian army against Israel and was beheaded in his sleep by Judith

ho·lo·gram \ˈhō-lə-ˌgram, ˈhä-\ *n* (1949) **:** a three-dimensional image reproduced from a pattern of interference produced by a split coherent beam of radiation (as a laser); *also* **:** the pattern of interference itself

ho·lo·graph \ˈhō-lə-ˌgraf, ˈhä-\ *n* [LL *holographus,* fr. LGk *holographos,* fr. Gk *hol-* + *graphein* to write — more at CARVE] (ca. 1623) **:** a document wholly in the handwriting of its author; *also* **:** the handwriting itself — **holograph** *or* **ho·lo·graph·ic** \ˌhō-lə-ˈgra-fik, ˌhä-\ *adj*

ho·log·ra·phy \hō-ˈlä-grə-fē\ *n* (1964) **:** the art or process of making or using a hologram — **ho·lo·graph** \ˈhō-lə-ˌgraf, ˈhä-\ *vt* — **ho·log·ra·pher** \hō-ˈlä-grə-fər\ *n* — **ho·lo·graph·ic** \ˌhō-lə-ˈgra-fik, ˌhä-\ *adj* — **ho·lo·graph·i·cal·ly** \-fi-k(ə-)lē\ *adv*

ho·lo·he·dral \ˌhō-lə-ˈhē-drəl, ˌhä-\ *adj* (1837) *of a crystal* **:** having all the faces required by complete symmetry — compare HEMIHEDRAL, TETARTOHEDRAL

ho·lo·me·tab·o·lous \ˌhō-lō-mə-ˈta-bə-ləs, ˌhä-\ *adj* [ultim. fr. Gk *hol-* + *metabolos* changeable, fr. *metabolē* change — more at METABOLISM] (1870) **:** characterized by complete metamorphosis ‹~ insects› — compare HEMIMETABOLOUS — **ho·lo·me·tab·o·lism** \-ˌli-zəm\ *n*

ho·lo·phras·tic \ˌhō-lə-ˈfras-tik, ˌhä-\ *adj* [ISV *hol-* + *-phrastic* (fr. Gk *phrazein* to point out, declare)] (1860) **:** expressing a complex of ideas in a single word or in a fixed phrase

ho·lo·phyt·ic \-ˈfi-tik\ *adj* (1885) **:** obtaining food after the manner of a green plant by photosynthetic activity

ho·lo·thu·ri·an \-ˈthu̇r-ē-ən, -ˈthyu̇r-\ *n* [ultim. fr. Gk *holothourion* water polyp] (ca. 1842) **:** SEA CUCUMBER — **holothurian** *adj*

\ə\ **abut** \ᵊ\ **kitten,** F **table** \ər\ **further** \a\ **ash** \ā\ **ace** \ä\ **mop, mar**
\au̇\ **out** \ch\ **chin** \e\ **bet** \ē\ **easy** \g\ **go** \i\ **hit** \ī\ **ice** \j\ **job**
\ŋ\ **sing** \ō\ **go** \ȯ\ **law** \ȯi\ **boy** \th\ **thin** \t͟h\ **the** \ü\ **loot** \u̇\ **foot**
\y\ **yet** \zh\ **vision, beige** \k̲, ⁿ, œ, ue, ʸ\ *see* Guide to Pronunciation

ho·lo·type \ˈhō-lə-ˌtīp, ˈhä-\ *n* (1897) **1 :** the single specimen designated by an author as the type of a species or lesser taxon at the time of establishing the group **2 :** the type of a species or lesser taxon designated at a date later than that of establishing a group or by a person other than the author of the taxon — **ho·lo·typ·ic** \ˌhō-lə-ˈti-pik, ˌhä-\ *adj*
ho·lo·zo·ic \ˌhō-lə-ˈzō-ik, ˌhä-\ *adj* (1885) **:** characterized by food procurement after the manner of most animals by the ingestion of complex organic matter ⟨~ nutrition⟩
holp \ˈhō(l)p\ *chiefly dial past of* HELP
hol·pen \ˈhō(l)-pən\ *chiefly dial past part of* HELP
hols \ˈhälz\ *n pl* [short for *holidays*] (1905) *Brit* **:** VACATION 2
Hol·stein \ˈhōl-ˌstēn, -ˌstīn\ *n* [short for *Holstein-Friesian*] (1865) **:** any of a breed of large usu. black-and-white dairy cattle orig. from northern Holland and Friesland that produce large quantities of comparatively low-fat milk
Hol·stein–Frie·sian \-ˈfrē-zhən\ *n* [*Holstein,* Germany, its later locality + *Friesian* (var. of *Frisian*)] (1889) **:** HOLSTEIN
hol·ster \ˈhōl-stər\ *n* [D; akin to OE *heolstor* cover, *helan* to conceal — more at HELL] (1663) **:** a leather or fabric case for carrying a firearm on the person (as on the hip or chest), on a saddle, or in a vehicle; *broadly* **:** a case for carrying a usu. small item on the person ⟨a knife ~⟩ ⟨a heart monitor carried in a hip ~⟩
holt \ˈhōlt\ *n* [ME, fr. OE; akin to OHG *holz* wood, Gk *klados* twig] (bef. 12c) *archaic* **:** a small woods **:** COPPICE
ho·lus–bo·lus \ˌhō-ləs-ˈbō-ləs\ *adv* [prob. redupl. of *bolus*] (1857) **:** all at once ⟨she . . . put it back, ~, in her pocket —Wilkie Collins⟩
ho·ly \ˈhō-lē\ *adj* **ho·li·er; -est** [ME, fr. OE *hālig;* akin to OE *hāl* whole — more at WHOLE] (bef. 12c) **1 :** exalted or worthy of complete devotion as one perfect in goodness and righteousness **2 :** DIVINE ⟨for the Lord our God is ~ —Ps 99:9(AV)⟩ **3 :** devoted entirely to the deity or the work of the deity ⟨a ~ temple⟩ ⟨~ prophets⟩ **4 a :** having a divine quality ⟨~ love⟩ **b :** venerated as or as if sacred ⟨~ scripture⟩ ⟨a ~ relic⟩ **5** — used as an intensive ⟨this is a ~ mess⟩ ⟨he was a ~ terror when he drank —Thomas Wolfe⟩; often used in combination as a mild oath ⟨~ smoke⟩ — **ho·li·ly** \-lə-lē\ *adv*
holy city *n* (14c) **:** a city that is the center of religious worship and traditions
Holy Communion *n* (1548) **:** COMMUNION 2a
holy day *n* (bef. 12c) **:** a day set aside for special religious observance
holy day of obligation (1909) **:** a feast on which Roman Catholics are duty-bound to attend mass
Holy Father *n* (15c) **:** POPE 1
Holy Ghost *n* (bef. 12c) **:** the third person of the Trinity **:** HOLY SPIRIT
Holy Grail *n* (15c) **1 :** GRAIL **2** *often not cap* **:** an object or goal that is sought after for its great significance
Holy Joe \ˈhō-lē-ˈjō\ *n* (ca. 1874) *slang* **:** PARSON, CHAPLAIN
Holy Office *n* (ca. 1741) — used formerly as the name of the Roman Catholic congregation of the curia charged with protecting faith and morals that is now called the Congregation for the Doctrine of the Faith
holy of holies [trans. of LL *sanctum sanctorum,* trans. of Heb *qōdhesh haq-qōdhāshīm*] (1641) **:** the innermost and most sacred chamber of the Jewish tabernacle and temple
holy oil *n* (14c) **:** olive oil blessed by a bishop for use in a sacrament or sacramental
holy order *n, often cap H&O* (14c) **1 a :** MAJOR ORDER — usu. used in pl. **b :** one of the orders of the ministry in the Anglican or Episcopal church **2 :** the rite or sacrament of ordination — usu. used in pl.
Holy Roller *n* (1841) *often offensive* **:** a member of one of the Protestant sects whose worship meetings are characterized by spontaneous expressions of emotional excitement
Holy Roman Empire *n* (1728) **:** an empire consisting primarily of a loose confederation of German and Italian territories under the suzerainty of an emperor and existing from the 9th or 10th century to 1806
Holy Saturday *n* (14c) **:** the Saturday before Easter
Holy See *n* (1765) **:** the see of the pope
Holy Spirit *n* (14c) **:** the third person of the Christian Trinity
ho·ly·stone \ˈhō-lē-ˌstōn\ *n* (ca. 1823) **:** a soft sandstone used to scrub a ship's wooden decks — **holystone** *vt*
Holy Synod *n* (1768) **:** the governing body of a national Eastern church
Holy Thursday *n* (13c) **1 :** ASCENSION DAY **2 :** MAUNDY THURSDAY
holy war *n* (1639) **:** a war or violent campaign waged by religious partisans to propagate or defend their faith
holy water *n* (bef. 12c) **:** water blessed by a priest and used as a purifying sacramental
Holy Week *n* (1710) **:** the week before Easter during which the last days of Christ's life are commemorated
holy writ *n, often cap H&W* (bef. 12c) **1 :** BIBLE 1 **2 :** a writing or utterance having unquestionable authority ⟨its financial precepts were not necessarily *Holy Writ* —Herbert Stein⟩
Holy Year *n* (1699) **:** a Roman Catholic jubilee year
hom- *or* **homo-** *comb form* [L, fr. Gk, fr. *homos* — more at SAME] **1 :** one and the same **:** similar **:** alike ⟨*homo*graph⟩ ⟨*homo*sporous⟩ **2 :** homosexual ⟨*homo*phobia⟩
hom·age \ˈä-mij, ˈhä-\ *n* [ME, fr. AF *homage, omage,* fr. *home* man, vassal, fr. L *homin-, homo* human being; akin to OE *guma* human being, L *humus* earth — more at HUMBLE] (14c) **1 a :** a feudal ceremony by which a man acknowledges himself the vassal of a lord **b :** the relationship between a feudal lord and his vassal **c :** an act done or payment made in meeting the obligations of vassalage **2 a :** expression of high regard **:** RESPECT — often used with *pay* **b :** something that shows respect or attests to the worth or influence of another **:** TRIBUTE ⟨his long life filled with international ~s to his unique musical talent —*People*⟩ ***syn*** see HONOR
hom·ag·er \ˈä-mi-jər, ˈhä-\ *n* (15c) **:** VASSAL
hom·bre \ˈäm-brā, ˈəm-, ˈōm-, -ˌbrē\ *n* [Sp, man, fr. L *homin-, homo*] (1846) **:** GUY, FELLOW
hom·burg \ˈhäm-ˌbərg\ *n* [*Bad Homburg,* Germany] (1894) **:** a man's felt hat with a stiff curled brim and a high crown creased lengthwise

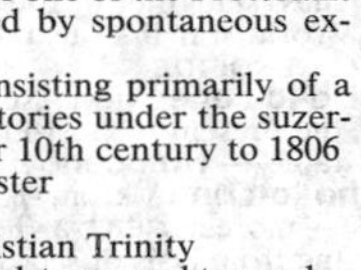
homburg

[1]home \ˈhōm\ *n* [ME *hom,* fr. OE *hām* village, home; akin to OHG *heim* home, Lith *šeima* family, servants, Skt *kṣema* habitable, *kṣeti* he dwells, Gk *ktizein* to inhabit] (bef. 12c) **1 a :** one's place of residence **:** DOMICILE **b :** HOUSE **2 :** the social unit formed by a family living together **3 a :** a familiar or usual setting **:** congenial environment; *also* **:** the focus of one's domestic attention ⟨~ is where the heart is⟩ **b :** HABITAT **4 a :** a place of origin ⟨salmon returning to their ~ to spawn⟩; *also* **:** one's own country ⟨having troubles at ~ and abroad⟩ **b :** HEADQUARTERS 2 ⟨~ of the dance company⟩ **5 :** an establishment providing residence and care for people with special needs ⟨~s for the elderly⟩ **6 :** the objective in various games; *esp* **:** HOME PLATE — **at home 1 :** relaxed and comfortable **:** at ease ⟨felt completely *at home* on the stage⟩ **2 :** in harmony with the surroundings **3 :** on familiar ground **:** KNOWLEDGEABLE ⟨teachers *at home* in their subject fields⟩
[2]home *adv* (bef. 12c) **1 :** to or at one's home ⟨go ~⟩ ⟨stayed ~ all day⟩ **2 a :** to a final, closed, or ultimate position ⟨drive a nail ~⟩ **b :** to or at an ultimate objective (as a goal or finish line) **3 :** to a vital sensitive core ⟨the truth struck ~⟩ — **home free :** out of jeopardy **:** in a comfortable position with respect to some objective
[3]home *adj* (1552) **1 :** of, relating to, or being a home, place of origin, or base of operations ⟨~ office⟩ **2 :** prepared, done, or designed for use in a home ⟨~ remedies⟩ ⟨~ cooking⟩ ⟨a ~ videotape system⟩ **3 :** operating or occurring in a home area ⟨the ~ team⟩ ⟨~ games⟩
[4]home *vb* **homed; hom·ing** *vi* (1765) **1 :** to go or return home **2** *of an animal* **:** to return accurately to one's home or natal area from a distance **3 :** to proceed to or toward a source of radiated energy used as a guide ⟨missiles ~ in on radar⟩ **4 :** to proceed or direct attention toward an objective ⟨science is *homing* in on the mysterious human process —Sam Glucksberg⟩ ~ *vt* **:** to send to or provide with a home
home·body \ˈhōm-ˌbä-dē\ *n* (1821) **:** one whose life centers on home
[1]home·bound \ˈhōm-ˌbau̇nd\ *adj* [*home* + [1]*bound*] (1598) **:** going homeward **:** bound for home ⟨~ travelers⟩
[2]homebound *adj* [*home* + [5]*bound*] (1882) **:** confined to the home
home·boy \ˈhōm-ˌbȯi\ *n* (1927) **1 :** a boy or man from one's neighborhood, hometown, or region **2 :** a fellow member of a youth gang **3 :** an inner-city youth
home·bred \ˈhōm-ˈbred\ *adj* (1587) **:** produced at home **:** INDIGENOUS
home brew *n* (1853) **:** an alcoholic beverage (as beer) made at home
home·built \ˈhōm-ˈbilt\ *adj* (1676) **:** HOMEMADE 1
home·com·ing \ˈhōm-ˌkə-miŋ\ *n* (14c) **1 :** a return home **2 :** the return of a group of people usu. on a special occasion to a place formerly frequented or regarded as home; *esp* **:** an annual celebration for alumni at a college or university
home computer *n* (1976) **:** a personal computer used in the home
home economics *n pl but sing or pl in constr* (1899) **:** the theory and practice of homemaking — called also *home ec* \-ˈek\ — **home economist** *n*
home fries *n pl* (1951) **:** potatoes that have usu. been parboiled, sliced, and then fried — called also *home fried potatoes*
home front *n* (1919) **:** the sphere of civilian activity in war
home·girl \ˈhōm-ˌgərl\ *n* (1934) **1 :** a girl or woman from one's neighborhood, hometown, or region **2 :** a girl or woman who is a member of one's peer group **3 :** an inner-city girl or woman
home·grown \ˈhōm-ˈgrōn\ *adj* (1827) **1 :** grown or produced at home or in a particular local area ⟨~ vegetables⟩ ⟨~ films⟩ **2 :** native to or characteristic of a particular area ⟨the festival will feature ~ artists⟩
home·land \-ˌland *also* -lənd\ *n* (1670) **1 :** native land **:** FATHERLAND **2 :** a state or area set aside to be a state for a people of a particular national, cultural, or racial origin; *esp* **:** BANTUSTAN
home·less \-ləs\ *adj* (1615) **:** having no home or permanent place of residence — **home·less·ness** *n*
home·like \ˈhōm-ˌlīk\ *adj* (1817) **:** characteristic of a home
home·ly \ˈhōm-lē\ *adj* **home·li·er; -est** (14c) **1 :** suggestive or characteristic of a home **2 :** being something familiar with which one is at home ⟨satisfy themselves with houses, furniture, books and clothes that were worn and ~ and friendly to the touch —Brendan Gill⟩ **3 a :** unaffectedly natural **:** SIMPLE **b :** not elaborate or complex ⟨~ virtues⟩ **4 :** plain or unattractive in appearance — **home·li·ness** *n*
home·made \ˈhō(m)-ˈmād\ *adj* (1596) **1 :** made in the home, on the premises, or by one's own efforts **2 :** of domestic manufacture
home·mak·er \ˈhōm-ˌmā-kər\ *n* (1876) **:** one who manages a household esp. as a wife and mother — **home·mak·ing** \-kiŋ\ *n or adj*
homeo- *or* **homoe-** *or* **homoeo-** *also* **homoio-** *comb form* [L & Gk; L *homoeo-,* fr. Gk *homoi-, homoio-,* fr. *homoios,* fr. *homos* same — more at SAME] **1 :** like **:** similar ⟨*homeo*stasis⟩ **2 :** homeotic ⟨*homeo*box⟩
ho·meo·box \ˈhō-mē-ə-ˌbäks\ *n* (1984) **:** a short usu. highly conserved DNA sequence in various eukaryotic genes and esp. homeotic genes that encodes a DNA-binding amino acid domain of some proteins
ho·meo·mor·phism \ˌhō-mē-ə-ˈmȯr-ˌfi-zəm\ *n* [ISV] (1854) **:** a function that is a one-to-one mapping between sets such that both the function and its inverse are continuous and that in topology exists for geometric figures which can be transformed one into the other by an elastic deformation — **ho·meo·mor·phic** \-ˈmȯr-fik\ *adj*
ho·meo·path·ic \ˌhō-mē-ə-ˈpa-thik\ *adj* (1830) **1 :** of or relating to homeopathy **2 :** of a diluted or insipid nature ⟨a ~ abolitionist —W. A. White⟩ — **ho·meo·path·i·cal·ly** \-thi-k(ə-)lē\ *adv*
ho·me·op·a·thy \ˌhō-mē-ˈä-pə-thē, ˌhä-\ *n* [G *Homöopathie,* fr. *homöo-* homeo- + *-pathie* -pathy] (1826) **:** a system of medical practice that treats a disease esp. by the administration of minute doses of a remedy that would in larger amounts produce in healthy persons symptoms similar to those of the disease — **ho·meo·path** \ˈhō-mē-ə-ˌpath\ *n*
ho·meo·sta·sis \ˌhō-mē-ō-ˈstā-səs\ *n* [NL] (1926) **:** a relatively stable state of equilibrium or a tendency toward such a state between the different but interdependent elements or groups of elements of an organism, population, or group — **ho·meo·stat·ic** \-ˈsta-tik\ *adj*
ho·meo·ther·mic \ˌhō-mē-ō-ˈthər-mik\ *also* **ho·moio·ther·mic** \hō-ˌmȯi-ə-\ *adj* (1870) **:** WARM-BLOODED 1 — **ho·meo·therm** \ˈhō-mē-ə-ˌthərm\ *also* **ho·moio·therm** \hō-ˈmȯi-ə-\ *n* — **ho·meo·ther·my** \ˈhō-mē-ə-ˌthər-mē\ *also* **ho·moio·ther·my** \hō-ˈmȯi-ə-\ *n*
ho·me·o·tic \ˌhō-mē-ˈä-tik, ˌhä-\ *adj* [fr. *homeosis, homoeosis* a shift in structural development, fr. Gk *homoiōsis* assimilation, resemblance, fr. *homoioun* to make like, fr. *homoios*] (1894) **:** relating to, caused by, or being a gene producing a usu. major shift in the developmental fate of an organ or body part

home page *n* (1992) **:** the page typically encountered first on a Web site that usu. contains links to the other pages of the site
home plate *n* (1875) **:** a 5-sided rubber slab at one corner of a baseball diamond at which a batter stands when batting and which must be touched by a base runner in order to score
home·port \'hōm-ˌpȯrt\ *vt* (1957) **:** to provide with or assign to a home port
home port *n* (ca. 1891) **:** the port from which a ship hails or from which it is documented
1**ho·mer** \'hō-mər\ *n* [Heb *ḥōmer*] (1535) **:** an ancient Hebrew unit of capacity equal to about 10½ or later 11½ bushels or 100 U.S. gallons (378 liters)
2**hom·er** \'hō-mər\ *n* [1*home*] (1868) **1 :** HOME RUN **2 :** HOMING PIGEON
3**hom·er** *vi* (1940) **:** to hit a home run
home range *n* (1884) **:** the area to which an animal usu. confines its daily activities
Ho·mer·ic \hō-'mer-ik\ *adj* (ca. 1771) **1 :** of, relating to, or characteristic of the Greek poet Homer, his age, or his writings **2 :** of epic proportions **:** HEROIC ⟨~ feats⟩ — **Ho·mer·i·cal·ly** \-i-k(ə-)lē\ *adv*
home·room \'hōm-ˌrüm, -ˌrům\ *n* (1915) **:** a classroom where pupils report esp. at the beginning of each school day
home rule *n* (1860) **:** self-government or limited autonomy in internal affairs by a dependent political unit (as a territory or municipality)
home run *n* (1856) **1 :** a hit in baseball that enables the batter to make a complete circuit of the bases and score a run **2 :** an impressive success ⟨the president's speech was a *home run*⟩
home·school \'hōm-ˌskül\ *vi* (1980) **:** to teach school subjects to one's children at home ~ *vt* **:** to teach (one's children) at home
home·school·er \-ˌskü-lər\ *n* (1981) **1 :** one that homeschools **2 :** a child who is homeschooled
home screen *n* (1968) **:** TELEVISION 2
home·sick \'hōm-ˌsik\ *adj* (1756) **:** longing for home and family while absent from them — **home·sick·ness** *n*
home·site \-ˌsīt\ *n* (1911) **:** a location of or suitable for a home
1**home·spun** \-ˌspən\ *adj* (1591) **1 a :** spun or made at home **b :** made of homespun **2 :** SIMPLE, HOMELY ⟨~ philosophy⟩
2**homespun** *n* (1607) **:** a loosely woven usu. woolen or linen fabric orig. made from homespun yarn
home stand *n* (1965) **:** a series of baseball games played at a team's home field
home·stay \'hōm-ˌstā\ *n* (1956) **:** a stay at a residence by a traveler and esp. by a visiting foreign student who is hosted by a local family
1**home·stead** \'hōm-ˌsted, -stid\ *n* (bef. 12c) **1 a :** the home and adjoining land occupied by a family **b :** an ancestral home **c :** HOUSE **2 :** a tract of land acquired from U.S. public lands by filing a record and living on and cultivating the tract
2**home·stead** \-ˌsted\ *vt* (1872) **:** to acquire or occupy as a homestead ~ *vi* **:** to acquire or settle on land under a homestead law — **home·stead·er** \-ˌste-dər\ *n*
homestead law *n* (1847) **1 :** a law exempting a homestead from attachment or sale under execution for general debts **2 :** any of several legislative acts authorizing the sale of public lands in homesteads
home·stretch \'hōm-'strech\ *n* (1841) **1 :** the part of a racecourse between the last turn and the winning post **2 :** a final stage
home theater *n* (1980) **:** an entertainment system for the home that usu. consists of a large television with video components (as a DVD player and VCR) and an audio system offering surround sound
home·town \-'tau̇n\ *n, often attrib* (1912) **:** the city or town where one was born or grew up; *also* **:** the place of one's principal residence
home truth *n* (1711) **1 :** an unpleasant fact that jars the sensibilities **2 :** a statement of undisputed fact
home video *n* (1968) **1 :** prerecorded videocassettes or videodiscs marketed for home viewing **2 :** a homemade movie usu. filmed with a camcorder
1**home·ward** \'hōm-wərd\ *or* **home·wards** \-wərdz\ *adv* (bef. 12c) **:** toward home ⟨look ~, angel —John Milton⟩
2**homeward** *adj* (1542) **:** being or going in the direction of home
home·work \'hōm-ˌwərk\ *n* (ca. 1683) **1 :** piecework done at home for pay **2 :** an assignment given to a student to be completed outside the regular class period **3 :** preparatory reading or research (as for a discussion or a debate)
1**hom·ey** *also* **homy** \'hō-mē\ *adj* **hom·i·er; -est** (1856) **1 :** HOMELIKE ⟨a ~ atmosphere⟩; *also* **:** evocative of home ⟨a ~ meal⟩ **2 :** HOMELY 3 ⟨~ anecdotes⟩ — **hom·ey·ness** *or* **hom·i·ness** *n*
2**homey** *or* **hom·ie** \'hō-mē\ *n, pl* **homeys** *or* **homies** [by shortening & alter.] (1944) **:** HOMEBOY
ho·mi·cid·al \ˌhä-mə-'sī-dəl, ˌhō-\ *adj* (1725) **:** of, relating to, or tending toward homicide — **ho·mi·cid·al·ly** \-dəl-ē\ *adv*
ho·mi·cide \'hä-mə-ˌsīd, 'hō-\ *n* [in sense 1, fr. ME, fr. AF, fr. L *homicida,* fr. *homo* human being + *-cida* -cide; in sense 2, fr. ME, fr. AF, fr. L *homicidium,* fr. *homo* + *-cidium* -cide] (14c) **1 :** a person who kills another **2 :** a killing of one human being by another
hom·i·let·ic \ˌhä-mə-'le-tik\ *or* **hom·i·let·i·cal** \-ti-kəl\ *adj* [LL *homileticus,* fr. Gk *homilētikos* of conversation, fr. *homilein*] (1644) **1 :** of, relating to, or resembling a homily **2 :** of or relating to homiletics; *also* **:** PREACHY
hom·i·let·ics \-tiks\ *n pl but sing in constr* (1830) **:** the art of preaching
hom·i·ly \'hä-mə-lē\ *n, pl* **-lies** [ME *omelie,* fr. AF, fr. LL *homilia,* fr. LGk, fr. Gk, conversation, discourse, fr. *homilein* to consort with, address, fr. *homilos* crowd, assembly; akin to Gk *homos* same — more at SAME] (14c) **1 :** a usu. short sermon **2 :** a lecture or discourse on or of a moral theme **3 :** an inspirational catchphrase; *also* **:** PLATITUDE
homing pigeon *n* (1886) **:** a racing pigeon trained to return home
hom·i·nid \'hä-mə-nəd, -ˌnid\ *n* [NL *Hominidae,* fr. *Homin-, Homo* + *-idae*] (ca. 1889) **:** any of a family (Hominidae) of erect bipedal primate mammals that includes recent humans together with extinct ancestral and related forms and in some recent classifications the gorilla, chimpanzee, and orangutan — **hominid** *adj*
hom·i·nin \'hä-mə-nən, -ˌnin\ *n* [NL *Hominini,* fr. *Homin-, Homo* + *-ini,* tribe suffix, fr. L *-inus* 1-ine] (1989) **:** any of a taxonomic tribe (Hominini) of hominids that includes recent humans together with extinct ancestral and related forms
hom·i·ni·za·tion \ˌhä-mə-nə-'zā-shən\ *n* [L *homin-, homo* + E *-ization*] (1952) **:** the evolutionary development of human characteristics that differentiate hominids from their primate ancestors
hom·i·noid \'hä-mə-ˌnȯid\ *n* [NL *Hominoidea,* fr. *Homin-, Homo* + *-oidea,* suffix of higher taxa, fr. L *-oïdes* 2-oid] (1949) **:** any of a superfamily (Hominoidea) of primates including recent hominids, gibbons, and pongids together with extinct ancestral and related forms (as of the genera *Proconsul* and *Dryopithecus*) — **hominoid** *adj*
hom·i·ny \'hä-mə-nē\ *n* [Virginia Algonquian *-homen,* lit., that treated (in the way specified)] (1629) **:** kernels of corn that have been soaked in a caustic solution (as of lye) and then washed to remove the hulls
hominy grits *n pl but sing or pl in constr* (1876) **:** GRITS
1**ho·mo** \'hō-(ˌ)mō\ *n, pl* **homos** *often cap* [NL *Homin-, Homo,* fr. L, human being — more at HOMAGE] (1591) **:** any of a genus (*Homo*) of hominids that includes modern humans (*H. sapiens*) and several extinct related species (as *H. erectus* and *H. habilis*)
2**homo** *n, pl* **homos** [by shortening] (1922) *often disparaging* **:** HOMOSEXUAL — **homo** *adj, often disparaging*
homo- — see HOM-
ho·mo·cer·cal \ˌhō-mə-'sər-kəl, ˌhä-\ *adj* (1838) **1** *of a fish tail fin* **:** having the upper and lower lobes approximately symmetrical and the vertebral column ending at or near the middle of the base **2 :** having or relating to a homocercal tail fin
ho·mo·cys·te·ine \ˌhō-mō-'sis-tə-ˌēn, ˌhä-\ *n* [ISV *hom-* + *cysteine*] (1932) **:** an amino acid $C_4H_9NO_2S$ that is produced in animal metabolism by the demethylation of methionine and that appears to be associated with an increased risk of cardiovascular disease when occurring at high levels in the blood
homoe- — see HOMEO-
ho·mo·erot·ic \ˌhō-mō-i-'rä-tik\ *adj* (1916) **:** HOMOSEXUAL; *specif* **:** marked by, revealing, or portraying homosexual desire ⟨~ photographs⟩ — **ho·mo·erot·i·cism** \-'rä-tə-ˌsi-zəm\ *n*
ho·mo·ga·met·ic \ˌhō-mō-gə-'me-tik, ˌhä-\ *adj* (1910) **:** forming gametes which all have the same type of sex chromosome
ho·mog·a·my \hō-'mä-gə-mē\ *n* [G *Homogamie,* fr. *hom-* + *-gamie* -gamy] (1897) **:** the mating of like with like — **ho·mog·a·mous** \-məs\ *adj*
ho·mog·e·nate \hō-'mä-jə-ˌnāt, hə-\ *n* (1941) **:** a product of homogenizing
ho·mo·ge·ne·i·ty \ˌhō-mə-jə-'nē-ə-tē, -'nā- *also* ÷-'nī-; *esp Brit* ˌhä-\ *n* (1625) **1 :** the quality or state of being homogeneous **2 :** the state of having identical cumulative distribution function or values
ho·mo·ge·neous \-'jē-nē-əs, -nyəs\ *adj* [ML *homogeneus, homogenus,* fr. Gk *homogenēs,* fr. *hom-* + *genos* kind — more at KIN] (1641) **1 :** of the same or a similar kind or nature **2 :** of uniform structure or composition throughout ⟨a culturally ~ neighborhood⟩ **3 :** having the property that if each variable is replaced by a constant times that variable the constant can be factored out **:** having each term of the same degree if all variables are considered ⟨a ~ equation⟩ — **ho·mo·ge·neous·ly** *adv* — **ho·mo·ge·neous·ness** *n*
ho·mog·e·ni·sa·tion, ho·mog·e·nise *Brit var of* HOMOGENIZATION, HOMOGENIZE
ho·mog·e·ni·za·tion \hō-ˌmä-jə-nə-'zā-shən, hə-\ *n* (1908) **1 :** the act or process of homogenizing **2 :** the quality or state of being homogenized
ho·mog·e·nize \hō-'mä-jə-ˌnīz, hə-\ *vb* **-nized; -niz·ing** *vt* (1886) **1 a :** to blend (diverse elements) into a uniform mixture **b :** to make homogeneous **2 a :** to reduce to small particles of uniform size and distribute evenly usu. in a liquid **b :** to reduce the particles of so that they are uniformly small and evenly distributed; *specif* **:** to break up the fat globules of (milk) into very fine particles ~ *vi* **:** to become homogenized — **ho·mog·e·niz·er** *n*
ho·mog·e·nous \-nəs\ *adj* (1919) **1 :** HOMOPLASTIC 2 **2 :** HOMOGENEOUS
ho·mo·graft \'hō-mə-ˌgraft, 'hä-\ *n* (1923) **:** a graft of tissue taken from a donor of the same species as the recipient — compare XENOGRAFT
ho·mo·graph \'hä-mə-ˌgraf, 'hō-\ *n* (1873) **:** one of two or more words spelled alike but different in meaning or derivation or pronunciation (as the *bow* of a ship, a *bow* and arrow) — **ho·mo·graph·ic** \ˌhä-mə-'gra-fik, ˌhō-\ *adj*
homoio- — see HOMEO-
homoiotherm, homoiothermic, homoiothermy *var of* HOMEOTHERM, HOMEOTHERMIC, HOMEOTHERMY
ho·moi·ou·si·an \hō-ˌmȯi-'ü-zē-ən, hä-, -'ü-sē-\ *n* [LGk *homoiousios* of like substance, fr. Gk *homoi-* homeo- + *ousia* essence, substance, fr. *ont-, ōn,* prp. of *einai* to be — more at IS] (1732) **:** an adherent of an ecclesiastical party of the fourth century holding that the Son is essentially like the Father but not of the same substance
ho·mol·o·gate \hō-'mä-lə-ˌgāt, hə-\ *vt* **-gat·ed; -gat·ing** [ML *homologatus,* pp. of *homologare* to agree, fr. Gk *homologein,* fr. *homologos*] (1593) **:** SANCTION, ALLOW; *esp* **:** to approve or confirm officially — **ho·mol·o·ga·tion** \-ˌmä-lə-'gā-shən\ *n*
ho·mo·log·i·cal \ˌhō-mə-'lä-ji-kəl, ˌhä-\ *adj* (ca. 1847) **1 :** HOMOLOGOUS **2 :** of or relating to topological homology theory ⟨~ algebra⟩ — **ho·mo·log·i·cal·ly** \-ji-k(ə-)lē\ *adv*
ho·mol·o·gize \hō-'mä-lə-ˌjīz, hə-\ *vt* **-gized; -giz·ing** (1811) **1 :** to make homologous **2 :** to demonstrate the homology of — **ho·mol·o·giz·er** *n*
ho·mol·o·gous \hō-'mä-lə-gəs, hə-\ *adj* [Gk *homologos* agreeing, fr. *hom-* + *legein* to say — more at LEGEND] (1660) **1 a :** having the same relative position, value, or structure: as (1) **:** exhibiting biological homology (2) **:** having the same or allelic genes with genetic loci usu. arranged in the same order ⟨~ chromosomes⟩ **b :** belonging to or consisting of a chemical series whose successive members have a regular difference in composition esp. of one methylene group **2 :** derived from or developed in response to organisms of the same species
ho·mo·logue *or* **ho·mo·log** \'hō-mə-ˌlȯg, 'hä-, -ˌläg\ *n* (1848) **:** something (as a chemical compound or a chromosome) homologous

\ə\ **abut** \ᵊ\ **kitten,** F **table** \ər\ **further** \a\ **ash** \ā\ **ace** \ä\ **mop, mar** \au̇\ **out** \ch\ **chin** \e\ **bet** \ē\ **easy** \g\ **go** \i\ **hit** \ī\ **ice** \j\ **job** \ŋ\ **sing** \ō\ **go** \ȯ\ **law** \ȯi\ **boy** \th\ **thin** \t͟h\ **the** \ü\ **loot** \u̇\ **foot** \y\ **yet** \zh\ **vision, beige** \k, ⁿ, œ, ue, ʸ\ *see* Guide to Pronunciation

ho·mol·o·gy \hō-ˈmä-lə-jē, hə-\ *n, pl* **-gies** (ca. 1656) **1 :** a similarity often attributable to common origin **2 a :** likeness in structure between parts of different organisms (as the wing of a bat and the human arm) due to evolutionary differentiation from a corresponding part in a common ancestor — compare ANALOGY **b :** correspondence in structure between a series of parts (as vertebrae) in the same individual **3 :** similarity of nucleotide or amino acid sequence (as in nucleic acids or proteins) **4 :** a branch of the theory of topology concerned with partitioning space into geometric components (as points, lines, and triangles) and with the study of the number and interrelationships of these components esp. by the use of group theory — called also *homology theory*; compare COHOMOLOGY

ho·mo·lyt·ic \ˌhō-mə-ˈli-tik, ˌhä-\ *adj* (1941) *of a chemical compound* **:** decomposing into two uncharged atoms or radicals — **ho·mol·y·sis** \hō-ˈmä-lə-səs\ *n*

ho·mo·mor·phism \ˌhō-mə-ˈmȯr-ˌfi-zəm, ˌhä-\ *n* [ISV] (1935) **:** a mapping of a mathematical set (as a group, ring, or vector space) into or onto another set or itself in such a way that the result obtained by applying the operations to elements of the first set is mapped onto the result obtained by applying the corresponding operations to their respective images in the second set — **ho·mo·mor·phic** \-fik\ *adj*

ho·mo·nu·cle·ar \ˌhō-mə-ˈnü-klē-ər, ˌhä-, -ˈnyü-, ÷-kyə-lər\ *adj* (1930) **:** of or relating to a molecule composed of identical nuclei

hom·onym \ˈhä-mə-ˌnim, ˈhō-\ *n* [L *homonymum,* fr. Gk *homōnymon,* fr. neut. of *homōnymos*] (1697) **1 a :** HOMOPHONE **b :** HOMOGRAPH **c :** one of two or more words spelled and pronounced alike but different in meaning (as the noun *quail* and the verb *quail*) **2 :** NAMESAKE **3 :** a taxonomic designation rejected as invalid because the identical term has been used to designate another group of the same rank — compare SYNONYM — **hom·onym·ic** \ˌhä-mə-ˈni-mik, ˌhō-\ *adj*

hom·on·y·mous \hō-ˈmä-nə-məs\ *adj* [L *homonymus* having the same name, fr. Gk *homōnymos,* fr. *hom-* + *onyma, onoma* name — more at NAME] (1621) **1 :** AMBIGUOUS **2 :** having the same designation **3 :** of, relating to, or being homonyms — **hom·on·y·mous·ly** *adv*

hom·on·y·my \-mē\ *n* (1597) **:** the quality or state of being homonymous

ho·mo·ou·si·an \hō-ˌmō-ˈü-zē-ən, hä-, -ˈü-sē-\ *n* [LGk *homoousios* of the same substance, fr. Gk *hom-* + *ousia* substance — more at HOMOIOUSIAN] (1565) **:** an adherent of an ecclesiastical party of the fourth century holding to the doctrine of the Nicene Creed that the Son is of the same substance with the Father

ho·mo·phile \ˈhō-mə-ˌfī(-ə)l\ *adj* [*hom-* + [2]*-phil*] (1945) **:** GAY 4b

ho·mo·phobe \-ˌfōb\ *n* (1971) **:** a person characterized by homophobia

ho·mo·pho·bia \ˌhō-mə-ˈfō-bē-ə\ *n* (1969) **:** irrational fear of, aversion to, or discrimination against homosexuality or homosexuals — **ho·mo·pho·bic** \-ˈfō-bik\ *adj*

ho·mo·phone \ˈhä-mə-ˌfōn, ˈhō-\ *n* [ISV] (1843) **1 :** one of two or more words pronounced alike but different in meaning or derivation or spelling (as the words *to, too,* and *two*) **2 :** a character or group of characters pronounced the same as another character or group — **ho·moph·o·nous** \hō-ˈmä-fə-nəs\ *adj*

ho·mo·pho·nic \ˌhä-mə-ˈfä-nik, ˌhō-, -ˈfō-\ *adj* [Gk *homophōnos* being in unison, fr. *hom-* + *phōnē* sound — more at BAN] (ca. 1879) **1 :** CHORDAL **2 :** of or relating to homophones — **ho·moph·o·ny** \hō-ˈmä-fə-nē\ *n*

ho·mo·plas·tic \ˌhō-mə-ˈplas-tik, ˌhä-\ *adj* (1870) **1 :** of or relating to homoplasy **2 :** of, relating to, or derived from another individual of the same species ⟨~ grafts⟩

ho·mo·pla·sy \ˈhō-mə-ˌplā-sē, ˈhä-, -ˌpla-; hō-ˈmä-plə-sē\ *n* (1870) **:** correspondence between parts or organs acquired as the result of parallel evolution or convergence

ho·mo·po·lar \ˌhō-mə-ˈpō-lər, ˌhä-\ *adj* (1896) **1** *of a motor or generator* **:** using or producing direct current without the use of commutators **2 :** of or relating to a union of atoms of like polarity **:** NONIONIC

ho·mo·pol·y·mer \-ˈpä-lə-mər\ *n* (1946) **:** a polymer (as polyethylene) consisting of identical monomer units — **ho·mo·pol·y·mer·ic** \-ˌpä-lə-ˈmer-ik\ *adj*

ho·mop·ter·an \hō-ˈmäp-tə-rən\ *n* [ultim. fr. Gk *hom-* + *pteron* wing — more at FEATHER] (ca. 1842) **:** any of an order or suborder (Homoptera) of insects (as aphids and cicadas) that have sucking mouthparts — **homopteran** *adj* — **ho·mop·ter·ous** \-rəs\ *adj*

homos *pl of* HOMO

Ho·mo sa·pi·ens \ˌhō-(ˌ)mō-ˈsā-pē-ˌenz, -ənz, *esp Brit* -ˈsa-pē-ənz\ *n* [NL, species name, fr. *Homo,* genus name + *sapiens,* specific epithet, fr. L, wise, intelligent — more at HOMO, SAPIENT] (1802) **:** HUMANKIND

ho·mo·sce·das·tic·i·ty \ˌhō-mō-si-ˌdas-ˈti-sə-tē, ˌhä-\ *n* [*hom-* + Gk *skedastikos* able to disperse, fr. *skedannynai* to disperse] (1905) **:** the property of having equal statistical variances — **ho·mo·sce·das·tic** \-ˈdas-tik\ *adj*

[1]**ho·mo·sex·u·al** \ˌhō-mə-ˈsek-sh(ə-)wəl, -ˈsek-shəl\ *adj* (1892) **1 :** of, relating to, or characterized by a tendency to direct sexual desire toward another of the same sex **2 :** of, relating to, or involving sexual intercourse between persons of the same sex — **ho·mo·sex·u·al·ly** *adv*

[2]**homosexual** *n* (1892) **:** a homosexual person and esp. a male

ho·mo·sex·u·al·i·ty \ˌhō-mə-ˌsek-shə-ˈwa-lə-tē\ *n* (1892) **1 :** the quality or state of being homosexual **2 :** erotic activity with another of the same sex

ho·mo·so·cial \-ˈsō-shəl\ *adj* (1968) **:** of, relating to, or involving social relationships between persons of the same sex and esp. between men — **ho·mo·so·ci·al·i·ty** \-ˌsō-shē-ˈa-lə-tē\ *n*

ho·mo·spo·ry \ˈhō-mə-ˌspȯr-ē, ˈhä-; hō-ˈmäs-pə-rē\ *n* (1903) **:** the production by various plants (as the club mosses and horsetails) of asexual spores of only one kind — **ho·mo·spo·rous** \ˌhō-mə-ˈspȯr-əs, ˌhä-; hō-ˈmäs-pə-rəs\ *adj*

ho·mo·thal·lic \ˌhō-mō-ˈtha-lik\ *adj* [*hom-* + Gk *thallein* to sprout, grow — more at THALLUS] (1904) **1 :** having a haploid phase that produces two kinds of gametes capable of fusing to form a zygote — used esp. of algae and fungi **2 :** MONOECIOUS — **ho·mo·thal·lism** \-ˈtha-ˌli-zəm\ *n*

ho·mo·trans·plant \ˌhō-mō-ˈtran(t)s-ˌplant, ˌhä-\ *n* (1927) **:** HOMOGRAFT — **ho·mo·trans·plan·ta·tion** \-ˌtran(t)s-ˌplan-ˈtā-shən\ *n*

ho·mo·zy·go·sis \ˌhō-mə-zi-ˈgō-səs, ˌhä-\ *n* [NL] (1905) **:** HOMOZYGOSITY

ho·mo·zy·gos·i·ty \-ˈgä-sə-tē\ *n* (1916) **:** the state of being homozygous

ho·mo·zy·gote \-ˈzī-ˌgōt\ *n* [ISV] (1902) **:** a homozygous individual

ho·mo·zy·gous \-ˈzī-gəs\ *adj* (1902) **:** having the two genes at corresponding loci on homologous chromosomes identical for one or more loci — **ho·mo·zy·gous·ly** *adv*

ho·mun·cu·lus \hō-ˈməŋ-kyə-ləs\ *n, pl* **-li** \-ˌlī, -ˌlē\ [L, dim. of *homin-, homo* human being — more at HOMAGE] (1656) **1 :** a little man **:** MANIKIN **2 :** a miniature adult that in the theory of preformation is held to inhabit the germ cell and to produce a mature individual merely by an increase in size

homy *var of* HOMEY

[1]**hon** \ˈhən\ *n* (ca. 1906) **:** HONEY 2a

[2]**hon** *abbr* honor; honorable; honorary

hon·cho \ˈhän-(ˌ)chō\ *n, pl* **honchos** [Jp *hanchō* squad leader, fr. *han* squad + *chō* head, chief] (1955) **:** BOSS, BIG SHOT; *also* **:** HOTSHOT

[1]**hone** \ˈhōn\ *n* [ME, fr. OE *hān* stone; akin to ON *hein* whetstone, L *cotcos,* Skt *śiśāti* he whets] (14c) **:** WHETSTONE

[2]**hone** *vt* **honed; hon·ing** (1798) **1 :** to sharpen or smooth with a whetstone **2 :** to make more acute, intense, or effective **:** WHET ⟨helped her ~ her comic timing —Patricia Bosworth⟩ — **hon·er** *n*

[3]**hone** *vi* **honed; hon·ing** [MF *hoigner* to grumble] (1600) **1** *dial* **:** YEARN — often used with *for* or *after* **2** *dial* **:** GRUMBLE, MOAN

hone in *vi* [alter. of *home in*] (1965) **:** to move toward or focus attention on an objective ⟨looking back for the ball *honing in* —George Plimpton⟩ ⟨a missile *honing in* on its target —Bob Greene⟩ ⟨*hones in* on the plights and victories of the common man —Lisa Russell⟩

usage The few commentators who have noticed *hone in* consider it to be a mistake for *home in.* It may have arisen from *home in* by the weakening of the \m\ sound to \n\ or may perhaps simply be due to the influence of *hone.* Though it seems to have established itself in American English (and mention in a British usage book suggests it is used in British English too), your use of it esp. in writing is likely to be called a mistake. *Home in* or in figurative use *zero in* does nicely.

[1]**hon·est** \ˈä-nəst\ *adj* [ME, fr. AF, fr. L *honestus* honorable, fr. *honos, honor* honor] (14c) **1 a :** free from fraud or deception **:** LEGITIMATE, TRUTHFUL ⟨an ~ plea⟩ **b :** GENUINE, REAL ⟨making ~ stops at stop signs —*Christian Science Monitor*⟩ **c :** HUMBLE, PLAIN ⟨good ~ food⟩ **2 a :** REPUTABLE, RESPECTABLE ⟨~ decent people⟩ **b** *chiefly Brit* **:** GOOD, WORTHY **3 :** CREDITABLE, PRAISEWORTHY ⟨an ~ day's work⟩ **4 a :** marked by integrity **b :** marked by free, forthright, and sincere expression **:** FRANK ⟨an ~ appraisal⟩ **c :** INNOCENT, SIMPLE ***syn*** see UPRIGHT

[2]**honest** *adv* (1596) **1 :** in an honest manner **:** HONESTLY ⟨I have ever found thee ~ true —Shak.⟩ **2 :** with all sincerity ⟨I didn't do it, ~⟩

honest broker *n* (ca. 1884) **:** a neutral mediator

hon·est·ly \ˈä-nəst-lē\ *adv* (14c) **1 :** in an honest manner: as **a :** without cheating ⟨counted the ballots ~⟩ **b :** REALLY, GENUINELY ⟨was ~ scared⟩ **c :** without frills ⟨food ~ prepared⟩ **2 :** to be honest **:** to tell the truth ⟨~, I don't know⟩

hon·es·ty \ˈä-nəs-tē\ *n, pl* **-ties** (14c) **1** *obs* **:** CHASTITY **2 a :** fairness and straightforwardness of conduct **b :** adherence to the facts **:** SINCERITY **3 :** any of a genus (*Lunaria*) of European herbs of the mustard family with toothed leaves and flat disk-shaped siliques

syn HONESTY, HONOR, INTEGRITY, PROBITY mean uprightness of character or action. HONESTY implies a refusal to lie, steal, or deceive in any way. HONOR suggests an active or anxious regard for the standards of one's profession, calling, or position. INTEGRITY implies trustworthiness and incorruptibility to a degree that one is incapable of being false to a trust, responsibility, or pledge. PROBITY implies tried and proven honesty or integrity.

[1]**hon·ey** \ˈhə-nē\ *n, pl* **honeys** [ME *hony,* fr. OE *hunig;* akin to OHG *honag* honey, and prob. to Skt *kāñcana* gold, L *canicae* bran] (bef. 12c) **1 a :** a sweet viscid material elaborated out of the nectar of flowers in the honey sac of various bees **b :** a sweet fluid resembling honey that is collected or elaborated by various insects **2 a :** a loved one **:** SWEETHEART, DEAR **b :** a superlative example **3 :** the quality or state of being sweet **:** SWEETNESS **4 :** an attractive woman

[2]**honey** *vb* **hon·eyed** *also* **hon·ied** \ˈhə-nēd\; **hon·ey·ing** *vt* (14c) **1 :** to sweeten with or as if with honey **2 :** to speak ingratiatingly to **:** FLATTER ~ *vi* **:** to use blandishments or cajolery

[3]**honey** *adj* (14c) **1 :** of, relating to, or resembling honey **2 :** much loved **:** DEAR

hon·ey·bee \ˈhə-nē-ˌbē\ *n* (15c) **:** a honey-producing bee (genus *Apis* of the family Apidae); *esp* **:** a European bee (*A. mellifera*) introduced worldwide and kept in hives for the honey it produces

[1]**hon·ey·comb** \-ˌkōm\ *n* (bef. 12c) **1 :** a mass of hexagonal wax cells built by honeybees in their nest to contain their brood and stores of honey **2 :** something that resembles a honeycomb in structure or appearance; *esp* **:** a strong lightweight cellular structural material

[2]**honeycomb** *vt* (1774) **1 a :** to cause to be full of cavities like a honeycomb **b :** to make into a checkered pattern **:** FRET **2 a :** to penetrate into every part **:** FILL **b :** SUBVERT, WEAKEN ~ *vi* **:** to become pitted, checked, or cellular

hon·ey·creep·er \ˈhə-nē-ˌkrē-pər\ *n* (1872) **1 :** any of numerous small bright-colored oscine birds (esp. genera *Cyanerpes* and *Chlorophanes* of the family Coerebidae) of tropical America **2 :** any of a family (Drepanididae) of often colorful oscine birds found only in Hawaii

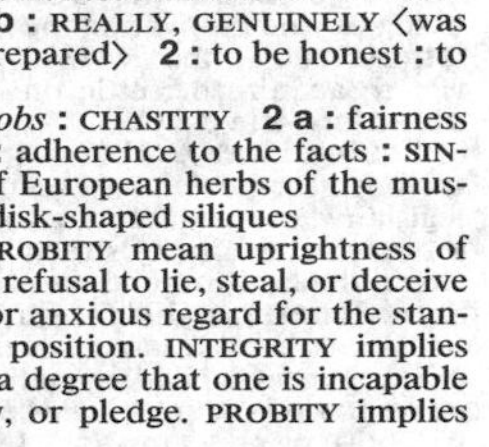

honeycreeper 2

hon·ey·dew \-ˌdü, -ˌdyü\ *n* (1577) **1 :** a saccharine deposit secreted on the leaves of plants usu. by aphids or scale insects or sometimes by a fungus **2 :** HONEYDEW MELON

honeydew melon *n* (1916) **:** a pale smooth-skinned winter melon with sweet greenish flesh

hon·ey·eat·er \-ˌē-tər\ *n* (1822) **:** any of a family (Meliphagidae) of oscine birds chiefly of the So. Pacific that have a long extensible tongue adapted for extracting nectar and small insects from flowers

honeyed *adj* (14c) **1 a :** made with or having honey **b :** resembling honey **2 :** pleasingly sweet ⟨her ~ voice⟩

hon·ey·guide \-ˌgīd\ *n* (1777) **:** any of a family (Indicatoridae) of small plainly colored nonpasserine birds that inhabit Africa, the Himalayas, and the East Indies and that include some which lead people or animals to the nests of bees

honey locust *n* (1736) **:** a tall usu. spiny No. American leguminous tree (*Gleditsia triacanthos*) with very hard wood and long twisted pods containing a sweet edible pulp and seeds that resemble beans

hon·ey·moon \ˈhə-nē-ˌmün\ *n* [fr. the idea that the first month of marriage is the sweetest] (1546) **1 :** a period of harmony immediately following marriage **2 :** a period of unusual harmony esp. following the establishment of a new relationship **3 :** a trip or vacation taken by a newly married couple — **honeymoon** *vi* — **hon·ey·moon·er** *n*

hon·ey·pot \ˈhə-nē-ˌpät\ *n* (1924) **1 :** one that is attractive or desirable **2 :** a substantial source of money

honey sac *n* (1886) **:** a distension of the esophagus of a bee in which honey is elaborated — called also *honey stomach*

hon·ey·suck·le \ˈhə-nē-ˌsə-kəl\ *n* [ME *honysoukel* clover, alter. of *honysouke,* fr. OE *hunisūce,* fr. *hunig* honey + *sūcan* to suck] (1548) **:** any of a genus (*Lonicera* of the family Caprifoliaceae, the honeysuckle family) of shrubs with opposite leaves and fragrant tubular flowers rich in nectar; *broadly* **:** any of various plants (as a columbine or azalea) with tubular flowers rich in nectar

hong \ˈhäŋ, ˈhȯŋ\ *n* [Chin (Guangdong) *hòhng,* lit., row] (1726) **:** a commercial establishment or house of foreign trade in China

[1]**honk** \ˈhäŋk, ˈhȯŋk\ *vb* [imit.] *vi* (ca. 1835) **1 :** to make the characteristic cry of a goose **2 :** to make a sound resembling the cry of a goose ~ *vt* **:** to cause (as a horn) to honk

[2]**honk** *n* (1854) **:** the characteristic cry of a goose; *also* **:** a similar sound

honk·er \ˈhäŋ-kər, ˈhȯŋ-\ *n* (ca. 1889) **1 :** one that honks **2** *slang* **:** a very large nose

hon·ky *or* **hon·kie** *also* **hon·key** \ˈhȯŋ-kē, ˈhäŋ-\ *n, pl* **honkies** *also* **honkeys** [prob. alter. of *Hunky*] (1958) *usu disparaging* **:** a white person

[1]**hon·ky–tonk** \ˈhäŋ-kē-ˌtäŋk, ˈhȯŋ-kē-ˌtȯŋk\ *n* [origin unknown] (1894) **1 :** a usu. tawdry nightclub or dance hall; *esp* **:** one that features country music **2 :** a district marked by places of cheap entertainment **3 :** country music that has a heavy beat and lyrics dealing usu. with vice or misfortune — **hon·ky–tonk·er** \-ˌtäŋ-kər, -ˌtȯŋ-\ *n*

[2]**honky–tonk** *adj* (ca. 1920) **1 :** of, used in, or being a form of ragtime piano playing performed typically on an upright piano **2 :** marked by or characteristic of honky-tonks

[1]**hon·or** \ˈä-nər\ *n* [ME, fr. AF *onur, honur,* fr. L *honos, honor*] (13c) **1 a :** good name or public esteem **:** REPUTATION **b :** a showing of usu. merited respect **:** RECOGNITION ⟨pay ~ to our founder⟩ **2 :** PRIVILEGE ⟨had the ~ of joining the captain for dinner⟩ **3 :** a person of superior standing — now used esp. as a title for a holder of high office ⟨if Your *Honor* please⟩ **4 :** one whose worth brings respect or fame **:** CREDIT ⟨an ~ to the profession⟩ **5 :** the center point of the upper half of an armorial escutcheon **6 :** an evidence or symbol of distinction: as **a :** an exalted title or rank **b** (1) **:** BADGE, DECORATION (2) **:** a ceremonial rite or observance ⟨buried with full military ~*s*⟩ **c :** an award in a contest or field of competition **d** *archaic* **:** a gesture of deference **:** BOW **e** *pl* (1) **:** an academic distinction conferred on a superior student (2) **:** a course of study for superior students supplementing or replacing a regular course **7 :** CHASTITY, PURITY ⟨fought fiercely for her ~ and her life —Barton Black⟩ **8 a :** a keen sense of ethical conduct **:** INTEGRITY ⟨a man of ~⟩ **b :** one's word given as a guarantee of performance ⟨on my ~, I will be there⟩ **9** *pl* **:** social courtesies or civilities extended by a host ⟨asked her to do the ~*s*⟩ **10 a** (1) **:** an ace, king, queen, jack, or ten esp. of the trump suit in bridge (2) **:** the scoring value of honors held in bridge — usu. used in pl. **b :** the privilege of playing first from the tee in golf

syn HONOR, HOMAGE, REVERENCE, DEFERENCE mean respect and esteem shown to another. HONOR may apply to the recognition of one's right to great respect or to any expression of such recognition ⟨the nomination is an *honor*⟩. HOMAGE adds the implication of accompanying praise ⟨paying *homage* to Shakespeare⟩. REVERENCE implies profound respect mingled with love, devotion, or awe ⟨great *reverence* for my father⟩. DEFERENCE implies a yielding or submitting to another's judgment or preference out of respect or reverence ⟨showed no *deference* to their elders⟩. ***syn*** see in addition HONESTY

[2]**honor** *vt* **hon·ored; hon·or·ing** \ˈä-nə-riŋ, ˈän-riŋ\ (13c) **1 a :** to regard or treat with honor or respect **b :** to confer honor on **2 a :** to live up to or fulfill the terms of ⟨~ a commitment⟩ **b :** to accept as payment ⟨~ a credit card⟩ **3 :** to salute with a bow in square dancing — **hon·or·ee** \ˌä-nə-ˈrē\ *n* — **hon·or·er** \ˈä-nər-ər\ *n*

hon·or·able \ˈä-nər-(ə-)bəl, ˈän-rə-\ *adj* (14c) **1 :** deserving of honor **2 a :** of great renown **:** ILLUSTRIOUS **b :** entitled to honor — used as a title for the children of certain British noblemen and for various government officials **3 :** performed or accompanied with marks of honor or respect **4 a :** attesting to creditable conduct **b :** consistent with an untarnished reputation ⟨an ~ withdrawal⟩ **5 :** characterized by integrity **:** guided by a high sense of honor and duty ***syn*** see UPRIGHT — **hon·or·abil·i·ty** \ˌän-rə-ˈbi-lə-tē, ˌä-nə-\ *n* — **hon·or·able·ness** \ˈän-rə-bəl-nəs, ˈä-nə-\ *n* — **hon·or·ably** \-blē\ *adv*

honorable mention *n* (1862) **:** a distinction conferred (as in a contest or exhibition) on works or persons of exceptional merit but not deserving of top honors

hon·o·rar·i·um \ˌä-nə-ˈrer-ē-əm\ *n, pl* **-ia** \-ē-ə\ *also* **-i·ums** [L, fr. neut. of *honorarius*] (1658) **:** a payment for a service (as making a speech) on which custom or propriety forbids a price to be set

hon·or·ary \ˈä-nə-ˌrer-ē\ *adj* [L *honorarius,* fr. *honor*] (1568) **1 a :** having or conferring distinction **b :** COMMEMORATIVE **2 :** dependent on honor for fulfillment **3 a :** conferred or elected in recognition of achievement or service without the usual prerequisites or obligations ⟨an ~ degree⟩ ⟨an ~ member⟩ **b :** UNPAID, VOLUNTARY ⟨an ~ chairman⟩ — **hon·or·ari·ly** \ˌä-nə-ˈrer-ə-lē\ *adv* — **honorary** *n*

honor guard *n* (1925) **:** a guard assigned to a ceremonial duty (as to accompany a casket at a military funeral)

hon·or·if·ic \ˌä-nə-ˈri-fik\ *adj* (1650) **1 :** conferring or conveying honor ⟨~ titles⟩ **2 :** belonging to or constituting a class of grammatical forms used in speaking to or about a social superior — **honorific** *n* — **hon·or·if·i·cal·ly** \-fi-k(ə-)lē\ *adv*

honor killing *n* (1929) **:** the traditional practice in some countries of killing a family member who is believed to have brought shame on the family

honor roll *n* (1909) **:** a roster of names of persons deserving honor; *esp* **:** a list of students achieving academic distinction

honor society *n* (1927) **:** a society for the recognition of scholarly achievement esp. of undergraduates

honor system *n* (1904) **:** a system (as at a college) whereby persons are trusted to abide by the regulations (as for a code of conduct) without supervision or surveillance

hon·our, hon·our·able, hon·our·ary *chiefly Brit var of* HONOR, HONORABLE, HONORARY

[1]**hooch** \ˈhüch\ *n* [short for *hoochinoo,* a distilled liquor made by the Hoochinoo (Hutsnuwu) Indians, a Tlingit tribe] (1897) *slang* **:** alcoholic liquor esp. when inferior or illicitly made or obtained

[2]**hooch** *or* **hootch** \ˈhüch\ *n* [modif. of Jp *uchi* house] (1960) *slang* **:** a usu. thatched hut; *broadly* **:** DWELLING

hooch·ie \ˈhü-chē\ *n* [perh. fr. *hootchy* (as in *hootchy-kootchy* exotic dance)] (1991) *slang* **:** a sexually promiscuous young woman

[1]**hood** \ˈhu̇d\ *n* [ME, fr. OE *hōd;* akin to OHG *huot* head covering, *huota* guard] (bef. 12c) **1 a** (1) **:** a flexible covering for the head and neck (2) **:** a protective covering for the head and face **b :** a covering for a hawk's head and eyes **c :** a covering for a horse's head; *also* **:** BLINDER **2 a :** an ornamental scarf worn over an academic gown that indicates by its color the wearer's college or university **b :** a color marking or crest on the head of an animal or an expansion of the head that suggests a hood **3 a :** something resembling a hood in form or use **b :** a cover for parts of mechanisms; *specif* **:** the movable metal covering over the engine of an automobile **c** *chiefly Brit* **:** a top cover over the passenger section of a vehicle usu. designed to be folded back **d :** an enclosure or canopy provided with a draft for carrying off fumes, sprays, smokes, or dusts **e :** a covering for an opening (as a companion hatch) on a boat — **hood** *vt* — **hood·like** \-ˌlīk\ *adj*

[2]**hood** \ˈhu̇d, ˈhüd\ *n* (1880) **:** HOODLUM — **hoody** \ˈhu̇-dē, ˈhü-\ *adj*

[3]**hood** *or* **'hood** \ˈhu̇d\ *n* [short for *neighborhood*] (1967) **:** a neighborhood and esp. an inner-city neighborhood; *also* **:** INNER CITY

-hood *n suffix* [ME *-hod,* fr. OE *-hād;* akin to OHG *-heit* state, Goth *haidus* way, manner] **1 :** state **:** condition **:** quality **:** character ⟨widower*hood*⟩ ⟨hardi*hood*⟩ **2 :** time **:** period ⟨child*hood*⟩ **3 :** instance of a (specified) state or quality ⟨false*hood*⟩ **4 :** individuals sharing a (specified) state or character ⟨brother*hood*⟩

hood·ed \ˈhu̇-dəd\ *adj* (15c) **1 :** having a hood **2 :** shaped like a hood ⟨~ spathes⟩ **3 a :** having the head conspicuously different in color from the rest of the body ⟨~ bird⟩ **b :** having a crest on the head that suggests a hood ⟨~ seals⟩ **c :** having the skin at each side of the neck capable of expansion by movements of the ribs ⟨a ~ cobra⟩ **4 :** half-closed ⟨~ eyes⟩ — **hood·ed·ness** *n*

hood·ie \ˈhu̇-dē\ *n* [[1]*hood* + *-ie*] (1992) **:** a hooded sweatshirt

hood·lum \ˈhüd-ləm, ˈhu̇d-\ *n* [perh. fr. G dial. (Swabia) *hudelum* disorderly] (1871) **1 :** THUG; *esp* **:** a violent criminal **2 :** a young ruffian — **hood·lum·ish** \-lə-mish\ *adj* — **hood·lum·ism** \-ˌmi-zəm\ *n*

hood·man–blind \ˌhu̇d-mən-ˈblīnd\ *n* (1565) *archaic* **:** BLINDMAN'S BUFF

[1]**hoo·doo** \ˈhü-(ˌ)dü\ *n, pl* **hoodoos** [perh. alter. of *voodoo*] (1875) **1 :** a body of practices of sympathetic magic traditional esp. among blacks in the southern U.S. **2 :** a natural column of rock in western No. America often in fantastic form **3 :** something that brings bad luck **4 :** NONSENSE, HOKUM — **hoo·doo·ism** \-ˌi-zəm\ *n*

[2]**hoodoo** *vt* (1886) **:** to cast a spell on; *broadly* **:** to bring bad luck to

hood·wink \ˈhu̇d-ˌwiŋk\ *vt* [[1]*hood* + *wink*] (1562) **1** *archaic* **:** BLINDFOLD **2** *obs* **:** HIDE **3 :** to deceive by false appearance **:** DUPE — **hood·wink·er** *n*

hoo·ey \ˈhü-ē\ *n* [origin unknown] (1912) **:** NONSENSE

[1]**hoof** \ˈhu̇f, ˈhüf\ *n, pl* **hooves** \ˈhüvz, ˈhu̇vz\ *also* **hoofs** [ME, fr. OE *hōf;* akin to OHG *huof* hoof, Skt *śapha*] (bef. 12c) **1 :** a curved covering of horn that protects the front of or encloses the ends of the digits of an ungulate mammal and that corresponds to a nail or claw **2 :** a hoofed foot esp. of a horse — **on the hoof** *of a meat animal* **:** before butchering **:** LIVING ⟨90¢ a pound *on the hoof*⟩

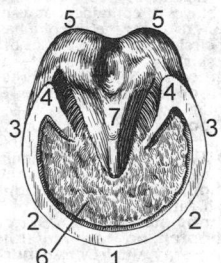

hoof 2: *1, 2, 3, 4* parts of wall (*1* toe, *2* side walls, *3* quarters, *4* buttresses), *5* bulbs, *6* sole, *7* frog

[2]**hoof** *vt* (1641) **1 :** WALK ⟨~*ed* it to the lecture hall⟩ **2 :** KICK, TRAMPLE ~ *vi* **:** to move on the feet; *esp* **:** DANCE

hoof–and–mouth disease *n* (1884) **:** FOOT-AND-MOUTH DISEASE

hoof·beat \ˈhu̇f-ˌbēt, ˈhüf-\ *n* (1847) **:** the sound of a hoof striking a hard surface (as the ground)

hoofed \ˈhu̇ft, ˈhüft, ˈhüvd, ˈhu̇vd\ *or* **hooved** \ˈhüvd, ˈhu̇vd\ *adj* (1513) **:** furnished with hooves **:** UNGULATE

hoof·er \ˈhu̇-fər, ˈhü-\ *n* (1916) **:** a professional dancer

hoof·print \ˈhu̇f-ˌprint, ˈhüf-\ *n* (1804) **:** an impression made by a hoof

hoo–ha *also* **hoo–hah** \ˈhü-ˌhä\ *n* [prob. fr. Yiddish *hu-ha* uproar, exclamation of surprise] (1931) **:** UPROAR

[1]**hook** \ˈhu̇k\ *n* [ME, fr. OE *hōc;* akin to MD *hoec* fishhook, corner, Lith *kengė* hook] (bef. 12c) **1 a :** a curved or bent device for catching, holding, or pulling **b :** something intended to attract and ensnare **c :** ANCHOR 1 **2 :** something curved or bent like a hook; *esp, pl* **:** FINGERS **3 :** a flight or course of a ball that deviates from straight in a direction opposite to the dominant hand of the player propelling it; *also* **:** a ball following such a course — compare SLICE **4 :** a short blow delivered with a circular motion by a boxer while the elbow remains bent and rigid **5 :** HOOK SHOT **6 :** BUTTONHOOK **7 :** quick or summary

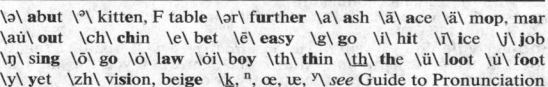

removal — used with *get* or *give* ⟨the pitcher got the ~ after giving up three runs⟩ **8 :** a device esp. in music or writing that catches the attention **9 :** a selling point or marketing scheme **10 :** CRADLE 1b(2) — **by hook or by crook :** by any means — **off the hook 1 :** out of trouble **2 :** free of responsibility or accountability — **on one's own hook :** by oneself : INDEPENDENTLY

[2]**hook** *vt* (13c) **1 :** to form into a hook : CROOK **2 a :** to seize or make fast by or as if by a hook **b :** to connect by or as if by a hook — often used with *up* **3 :** STEAL, PILFER **4 :** to make (as a rug) by drawing loops of yarn, thread, or cloth through a coarse fabric with a hook **5 :** to hit or throw (a ball) so that a hook results ~ *vi* **1 :** to form a hook : CURVE **2 :** to become hooked **3 :** to work as a prostitute

hoo·kah \ˈhu̇-kə, ˈhü-\ *n* [Ar *ḥuqqa* bottle of a water pipe] (1763) **:** WATER PIPE 2

hook and eye *n* (ca. 1626) **:** a 2-part fastening device (as on a garment or a door) consisting of a metal hook that catches over a bar or into a loop

hook and ladder truck *n* (1865) **:** a piece of mobile fire apparatus carrying ladders and usu. other firefighting and rescue equipment — called also *hook and ladder, ladder truck*

hook check *n* (ca. 1939) **:** an act or instance of attempting to knock the puck away from an opponent in ice hockey by hooking it with the stick

hooked \ˈhu̇kt, *1 is also* ˈhu̇-kəd\ *adj* (bef. 12c) **1 :** having the form of a hook **2 :** provided with a hook **3 :** made by hooking ⟨a ~ rug⟩ **4 a :** addicted to narcotics **b :** fascinated by or devoted to something

[1]**hook·er** \ˈhu̇-kər\ *n* (1567) **1 :** one that hooks **2 :** DRINK ⟨a ~ of Scotch⟩ **3 :** PROSTITUTE

[2]**hooker** *n* [D *hoeker,* alter. of MD *hoecboot,* fr. *hoec* fishhook + *boot* boat] (1801) **:** a one-masted fishing boat used on the English and Irish coasts; *also* **:** a small clumsy boat

Hooke's law \ˈhu̇ks-\ *n* [Robert *Hooke*] (1853) **:** a statement in physics: the stress within an elastic solid is proportional to the strain responsible for it

hook·let \ˈhu̇k-lət\ *n* (ca. 1839) **:** a small hook

hook, line and sinker *adv* [fr. analogy with a well-hooked fish] (1838) **:** without hesitation or reservation : COMPLETELY ⟨fell for the story *hook, line and sinker*⟩

hook shot *n* (ca. 1932) **:** a shot in basketball made usu. while standing sideways to the basket by swinging the ball up in an arc with the far hand

hook·up \ˈhu̇k-ˌəp\ *n* (1903) **1 :** a state of cooperation or alliance **2 :** an assemblage (as of circuits) used for a specific purpose (as radio transmission); *also* **:** the plan of such an assemblage **3 :** an arrangement of mechanical parts; *also* **:** CONNECTION ⟨a campsite with electric, water, and sewer ~*s*⟩ **4 :** an act or an instance of hooking up; *esp* **:** a casual sexual encounter

hook up *vi* (1907) **:** to become associated esp. in a working, social, or sexual relationship

hook·worm \ˈhu̇k-ˌwərm\ *n* (1902) **1 :** any of several parasitic nematode worms (family Ancylostomatidae) that have strong buccal hooks or plates for attaching to the host's intestinal lining and that include serious bloodsucking pests **2 :** infestation with or disease caused by hookworms; *esp* **:** a lethargic anemic state in humans due to blood loss from hookworms feeding in the small intestine

hooky *also* **hook·ey** \ˈhu̇-kē\ *n, pl* **hook·ies** *also* **hookeys** [prob. fr. slang *hook, hook it* to make off] (1842) **:** TRUANT — used chiefly in the phrase *play hooky*

hoo·li·gan \ˈhü-li-gən\ *n* [perh. fr. Patrick *Hooligan fl*1896 Irish hoodlum in Southwark, London] (1896) **:** RUFFIAN, HOODLUM

hoo·li·gan·ism \ˈhü-li-gə-ˌni-zəm\ *n* (1898) **:** rowdy, violent, or destructive behavior

[1]**hoop** \ˈhüp *also* ˈhu̇p\ *n, often attrib* [ME, fr. OE *hōp;* akin to MD *hoep* ring, hoop] (12c) **1 :** a circular strip used esp. for holding together the staves of containers or as a plaything **2 a :** a circular figure or object : RING **b :** the rim of a basketball goal; *broadly* **:** the entire goal **3 :** a circle or series of circles of flexible material used to expand a woman's skirt **4 :** BASKETBALL — usu. used in pl. — **hoop·like** \-ˌlīk\ *adj*

[2]**hoop** *vt* (15c) **:** to bind or fasten with or as if with a hoop — **hoop·er** *n*

hoop·la \ˈhü-ˌplä, ˈhu̇-\ *n* [F *houp-là,* interj.] (1877) **:** TO-DO; *also* **:** BALLYHOO

hoo·poe \ˈhü-(ˌ)pü, -(ˌ)pō\ *n* [alter. of obs. *hoop,* fr. MF *huppe,* fr. L *upupa,* of imit. origin] (1668) **:** a crested Old World nonpasserine bird (*Upupa epops* of the family Upupidae) having a slender decurved bill and barred black-and-white wings and tail

hoop·skirt \ˈhüp-ˈskərt *also* ˈhu̇p-\ *n* (1857) **:** a skirt stiffened with or as if with hoops

hoop·ster \ˈhüp-stər\ *n* (ca. 1934) **:** a basketball player

hoorah, hooray *var of* HURRAH

hoo·ray \hu̇-ˈrā\ *also* **hur·rah** \hu̇-ˈrȯ, -ˈrä\ *or* **hur·ray** \-ˈrā\ *interj* [perh. fr. G *hurra*] (1686) — used to express joy, approval, or encouragement

hoose·gow \ˈhüs-ˌgau̇\ *n* [Sp *juzgado* panel of judges, courtroom, fr. pp. of *juzgar* to judge, fr. L *judicare* — more at JUDGE] (1909) **:** JAIL

Hoo·sier \ˈhü-zhər\ *n* [perh. alter. of E dial. *hoozer* anything large of its kind] (1826) **:** a native or resident of Indiana — used as a nickname — **Hoosier** *adj*

[1]**hoot** \ˈhüt\ *vb* [ME *houten,* of imit. origin] *vi* (13c) **1 :** to shout or laugh usu. derisively **2 :** to make the natural throat noise of an owl or a similar cry **3 :** to make a loud clamorous mechanical sound ~ *vt* **1 :** to assail or drive out by hooting ⟨~*ed* down the speaker⟩ **2 :** to express or utter with hoots ⟨~*ed* their disapproval⟩

[2]**hoot** *n* (15c) **1 :** a sound of hooting; *esp* **:** the cry of an owl **2 :** a minimum amount or degree : the least bit ⟨don't give a ~⟩ **3 :** something or someone amusing ⟨the play is a real ~⟩ — **hooty** \ˈhü-tē\ *adj*

[3]**hoot** \ˈhüt\ *or* **hoots** \ˈhüts\ *interj* [origin unknown] (1540) *chiefly Scot* — used to express impatience, dissatisfaction, or objection

hoo·te·nan·ny \ˈhü-tə-ˌna-nē\ *n, pl* **-nies** [origin unknown] (1929) **1** *chiefly dial* **:** GADGET **2 :** a gathering at which folksingers entertain often with the audience joining in

hoot·er \ˈhü-tər\ *n* (1856) **1 :** one that hoots **2** *often vulgar* **:** BREAST — usu. used in pl.

Hoo·ver·ville \ˈhü-vər-ˌvil\ *n* [Herbert *Hoover* + *-ville*] (1930) **:** a shantytown of temporary dwellings during the depression years in the U.S.; *broadly* **:** any similar area of temporary dwellings

[1]**hop** \ˈhäp\ *vb* **hopped; hop·ping** [ME *hoppen,* fr. OE *hoppian*] *vi* (bef. 12c) **1 :** to move by a quick springy leap or in a series of leaps; *also* **:** to move as if by hopping ⟨~ in the car⟩ **2 :** to make a quick trip esp. by air **3 :** to set about doing something — usu. used in the phrase *hop to it* ~ *vt* **1 :** to jump over ⟨~ a fence⟩ **2 :** to ride on ⟨*hopped* a flight⟩; *also* **:** to ride surreptitiously and without authorization ⟨~ a freight train⟩

[2]**hop** *n* (1508) **1 a :** a short brisk leap esp. on one leg **b :** BOUNCE, REBOUND ⟨shortstop scooped it up on the first ~⟩ **2 :** DANCE 3 **3 a :** a flight in an aircraft **b :** a short trip

[3]**hop** *n* [ME *hoppe,* fr. MD; akin to OHG *hopfo* hop] (15c) **1** *pl* **:** the ripe dried pistillate catkins of a perennial north-temperate zone twining vine (*Humulus lupulus*) of the hemp family used esp. to impart a bitter flavor to malt liquors **2 :** the vine from which hops are obtained having 3- to 5-lobed leaves and inconspicuous flowers of which the pistillate ones are in glandular cone-shaped catkins

[3]hop 2

[4]**hop** *vt* **hopped; hop·ping** (1572) **:** to flavor with hops

[1]**hope** \ˈhōp\ *vb* **hoped; hop·ing** [ME, fr. OE *hopian;* akin to MHG *hoffen* to hope] *vi* (bef. 12c) **1 :** to cherish a desire with anticipation ⟨~*s* for a promotion⟩ **2** *archaic* **:** TRUST ~ *vt* **1 :** to desire with expectation of obtainment **2 :** to expect with confidence : TRUST ***syn*** see EXPECT — **hop·er** *n* — **hope against hope :** to hope without any basis for expecting fulfillment

[2]**hope** *n* (bef. 12c) **1** *archaic* **:** TRUST, RELIANCE **2 a :** desire accompanied by expectation of or belief in fulfillment ⟨came in ~*s* of seeing you⟩; *also* **:** expectation of fulfillment or success ⟨no ~ of a cure⟩ **b :** someone or something on which hopes are centered ⟨our only ~ for victory⟩ **c :** something hoped for

HOPE *abbr* Health Opportunity for People Everywhere

hope chest *n* (1911) **:** a young woman's accumulation of clothes and domestic furnishings (as silver and linen) kept in anticipation of her marriage; *also* **:** a chest for such an accumulation

[1]**hope·ful** \ˈhōp-fəl\ *adj* (1568) **1 :** having qualities which inspire hope ⟨~ signs of economic recovery⟩ **2 :** full of hope : inclined to hope — **hope·ful·ness** *n*

[2]**hopeful** *n* (1720) **:** ASPIRANT ⟨Olympic ~*s*⟩

hope·ful·ly \ˈhōp-fə-lē\ *adv* (1593) **1 :** in a hopeful manner **2 :** it is hoped : I hope : we hope ⟨~ the rain will end soon⟩

usage In the 1960s the second sense of *hopefully,* which dates to the early 18th century and had been in fairly widespread use since at least the 1930s, underwent a surge in popularity. A surge of criticism followed in reaction, but the criticism took no account of the grammar of adverbs. *Hopefully* in its second sense is a member of a class of adverbs known as disjuncts. Disjuncts serve as a means by which the author or speaker can comment directly to the reader or hearer usu. on the content of the sentence to which they are attached. Many other adverbs (as *interestingly, frankly, clearly, luckily, unfortunately*) are similarly used; most are so ordinary as to excite no comment or interest whatsoever. The second sense of *hopefully* is entirely standard.

hope·less \ˈhō-pləs\ *adj* (1534) **1 a :** having no expectation of good or success : DESPAIRING **b :** not susceptible to remedy or cure **c :** incapable of redemption or improvement **2 a :** giving no ground for hope : DESPERATE **b :** incapable of solution, management, or accomplishment : IMPOSSIBLE ***syn*** see DESPONDENT — **hope·less·ness** *n*

hope·less·ly \-lē\ *adv* (1616) **:** in a hopeless manner — used esp. as an intensifier ⟨the formerly despised and ~ middle-class game of golf —Ejner Jensen⟩

hop·head \ˈhäp-ˌhed\ *n* (1911) *slang* **:** a drug addict

hop hornbeam *n* (1785) **:** a chiefly eastern No. American tree (*Ostrya virginiana*) of the birch family with fruiting clusters resembling hops

Ho·pi \ˈhō-(ˌ)pē\ *n, pl* **Hopi** *or* **Hopis** [Hopi *hópi,* lit., good, peaceful] (1877) **1 :** a member of an American Indian people of northeastern Arizona **2 :** the Uto-Aztecan language of the Hopi people

hop·lite \ˈhäp-ˌlīt\ *n* [Gk *hoplitēs,* fr. *hoplon* tool, weapon, fr. *hepein* to care for, work at — more at SEPULCHRE] (ca. 1741) **:** a heavily armed infantry soldier of ancient Greece

hop–o'–my–thumb \ˌhä-pə-mə-ˈthəm\ *n* [earlier *hop on my thumb,* imperative issued to one supposedly small enough to be held in the hand] (1530) **:** a very small person

hopped–up \ˈhäpt-ˈəp, -ˌəp\ *adj* (1920) **1 a :** full of enthusiasm or excitement; *also* **:** overly excited **b :** being under the influence of a narcotic **c :** more exciting or attractive than normal or usual **2 :** having more than usual power : being souped up

hop·per \ˈhä-pər\ *n* (13c) **1 a :** one that hops **b :** a leaping insect; *specif* **:** an immature hopping form of an insect (as a grasshopper or locust) **2** [fr. the shaking motion of hoppers used to feed grain into a mill] **a :** a usu. funnel-shaped receptacle for delivering material (as grain or coal); *also* **:** any of various other receptacles for the temporary storage of material **b :** a freight car with a floor sloping to one or more hinged doors for discharging bulk materials — called also *hopper car* **c :** a box in which a bill to be considered by a legislative body is dropped **d :** a tank holding liquid and having a device for releasing its contents through a pipe **e :** a mix of things to be considered or done

[1]**hopping** *adv* (1675) **:** EXTREMELY, VIOLENTLY — used in the phrase *hopping mad*

[2]**hopping** *adj* (1785) **1 :** intensely active : BUSY ⟨they kept us ~⟩ **2 :** extremely angry

[3]**hopping** *n* (1879) **:** a going from one place to another of the same kind — usu. used in combination ⟨gallery-*hopping*⟩

hopping John \ˌhä-pən-ˈjän, -piŋ-\ *or* **hop·pin' John** \ˌhä-pən-\ *n, often cap H* (1838) **:** a dish made essentially of cowpeas, rice, and salt pork or bacon

hop·py \ˈhä-pē\ *adj* **hop·pi·er; -est** (ca. 1889) **:** having the taste or aroma of hops — used esp. of ale or beer

hop·sack \ˈhäp-ˌsak\ *also* **hop·sack·ing** \-ˌsa-kiŋ\ *n* [ME *hopsak* sack for hops, fr. *hoppe* hop + *sak* sack] (1888) **:** a rough-surfaced loosely woven clothing fabric

[1]hop·scotch \ˈhäp-ˌskäch\ *n* [[1]*hop* + [2]*scotch* (line, score)] (1801) **:** a child's game in which a player tosses an object (as a stone) into areas of a figure outlined on the ground and hops through the figure and back to regain the object

[2]hopscotch *vi* (1918) **:** to move as if by hopping ⟨~*ed* across Europe⟩

hop, skip, and jump *n* (1760) **:** a short distance

hop, step, and jump *n* (ca. 1719) **:** TRIPLE JUMP

hor *abbr* horizontal

ho·ra *also* **ho·rah** \ˈhȯr-ə\ *n* [ModHeb *hōrāh,* fr. Rom *horă*] (1853) **:** a circle dance of Romania and Israel

Ho·rae \ˈhȯr-ˌē, -ˌī\ *n pl* [L, fr. Gk *Hōrai*] (1724) **:** the Greek goddesses of the seasons

ho·ra·ry \ˈhȯr-ər-ē, ˈhär-\ *adj* [ML *horarius,* fr. L *hora* hour — more at HOUR] (1632) **:** of or relating to an hour; *also* **:** HOURLY

Ho·ra·tio Al·ger \hə-ˈrā-shō-ˈal-jər\ *adj* (1925) **:** of, relating to, or resembling the fiction of Horatio Alger in which success is achieved through self-reliance and hard work

Ho·ra·tius \hə-ˈrā-sh(ē-)əs\ *n* [L] (1542) **:** a hero in Roman legend noted for his defense of a bridge over the Tiber against the Etruscans

horde \ˈhȯrd\ *n* [MF, G, & Pol; MF & G, fr. Pol *horda,* fr. Ukrainian dial. *gorda,* alter. of Ukrainian *orda,* fr. ORuss, fr. Turkic *orda, ordu* khan's residence] (1555) **1 a :** a political subdivision of central Asian nomads **b :** a people or tribe of nomadic life **2 :** a teeming crowd or throng **:** SWARM ***syn*** see CROWD

hore·hound \ˈhȯr-ˌhau̇nd\ *n* [ME *horhoune,* fr. OE *hārhūne,* fr. *hār* hoary + *hūne* horehound — more at HOAR] (bef. 12c) **1 a :** an Old World bitter perennial mint (*Marrubium vulgare*) with downy leaves **b :** an extract or confection made from the dried leaves and flowering tops of this plant **2 :** any of several mints resembling the horehound

ho·ri·zon \hə-ˈrī-zᵊn\ *n* [ME *orizon,* fr. LL *horizont-, horizon,* fr. Gk *horizont-, horizōn,* fr. prp. of *horizein* to bound, define, fr. *horos* boundary; perh. akin to L *urvum* curved part of a plow] (14c) **1 a :** the apparent junction of earth and sky **b :** the great circle on the celestial sphere formed by the intersection of the celestial sphere with a plane tangent to the earth's surface at an observer's position — see AZIMUTH illustration **c :** range of perception or experience **d :** something that might be attained ⟨new ~*s*⟩ **2 a :** the geological deposit of a particular time usu. identified by distinctive fossils **b :** any of the reasonably distinct layers of soil or its underlying material in a vertical section of land **c :** a cultural area or level of development indicated by separated groups of artifacts — **ho·ri·zon·al** \-ˈrī-zᵊn-əl\ *adj*

ho·ri·zon·less \-ləs\ *adj* (ca. 1839) **1 a :** having no horizon **b :** ENDLESS 1 **2 :** HOPELESS

hor·i·zon·tal \ˌhȯr-ə-ˈzän-tᵊl, ˌhär-\ *adj* (1555) **1 a :** of, relating to, or situated near the horizon **b :** parallel to, in the plane of, or operating in a plane parallel to the horizon or to a baseline **:** LEVEL ⟨~ distance⟩ ⟨a ~ engine⟩ **2 :** relating to, directed toward, or consisting of individuals or entities of similar status or on the same level ⟨~ mergers⟩ ⟨~ hostility⟩ — **horizontal** *n* — **hor·i·zon·tal·i·ty** \-ˌzän-ˈta-lə-tē\ *n* — **hor·i·zon·tal·ly** \-ˈzän-tᵊl-ē\ *adv*

horizontal bar *n* (1827) **1 :** a steel bar supported in a horizontal position approximately eight feet above the floor and used for swinging feats in gymnastics **2 :** an event in gymnastics competition in which the horizontal bar is used

hor·mo·go·ni·um \ˌhȯr-mə-ˈgō-nē-əm\ *n, pl* **-nia** \-nē-ə\ [NL, fr. Gk *hormos* chain, necklace + NL *-gonium* — more at SERIES] (1880) **:** a portion of a filament in many cyanobacteria that becomes detached as a reproductive body

hor·mon·al \hȯr-ˈmō-nᵊl\ *adj* (1926) **:** of, relating to, or effected by hormones — **hor·mon·al·ly** \-nᵊl-ē\ *adv*

hor·mone \ˈhȯr-ˌmōn\ *n* [Gk *hormōn,* prp. of *horman* to stir up, fr. *hormē* impulse, assault; akin to Gk *ornynai* to rouse — more at RISE] (1905) **1 :** a product of living cells that circulates in body fluids (as blood) or sap and produces a specific often stimulatory effect on the activity of cells usu. remote from its point of origin; *also* **:** a synthetic substance that acts like a hormone **2 :** SEX HORMONE — **hor·mone·like** \-ˌlīk\ *adj*

hormone replacement therapy *n* (1966) **:** the administration of estrogen often along with a synthetic progestin esp. to ameliorate the symptoms of menopause and reduce the risk of postmenopausal osteoporosis — abbr. *HRT*

horn \ˈhȯrn\ *n* [ME, fr. OE; akin to OHG *horn,* L *cornu,* Gk *keras*] (bef. 12c) **1 a :** one of the usu. paired bony processes that arise from the head of many ungulates and that are found in some extinct mammals and reptiles: as **(1) :** one of the permanent paired hollow sheaths of keratin usu. present in both sexes of cattle and their relatives that function chiefly for defense and arise from a bony core anchored to the skull — see COW illustration **(2) :** ANTLER **(3) :** a permanent solid horn of keratin that is attached to the nasal bone of a rhinoceros **(4) :** one of a pair of permanent bone protuberances from the skull of a giraffe or okapi that are covered with hairy skin **b :** a part like an animal's horn attributed esp. to the devil **c :** a natural projection or excrescence from an animal resembling or suggestive of a horn **d (1) :** the tough fibrous material consisting chiefly of keratin that covers or forms the horns of cattle and related animals, hooves, or other horny parts (as claws or nails) **(2) :** a manufactured product (as a plastic) resembling horn **e :** a hollow horn used to hold something **2 :** something resembling or suggestive of a horn: as **a :** one of the curved ends of a crescent **b :** a sharp mountain peak **c :** a body of land or water shaped like a horn **d :** a beak-shaped part of an anvil **e :** a high pommel of a saddle **f :** CORNU **3 a :** an animal's horn used as a wind instrument **b :** a brass wind instrument: as **(1) :** HUNTING HORN **(2) :** FRENCH HORN **c :** a wind instrument used in a jazz band; *esp* **:** TRUMPET **d :** a usu. electrical device that makes a noise like that of a horn **4 :** a source of strength **5 :** one of the equally disadvantageous alternatives presented by a dilemma **6** *slang* **:** TELEPHONE — **horn** *adj* — **horned** \ˈhȯrnd *also* ˈhȯr-nəd\ *adj* — **horned·ness** \ˈhȯr-nəd-nəs, ˈhȯrn(d)-nəs\ *n* — **horn·less** \ˈhȯrn-ləs\ *adj* — **horn·less·ness** *n* — **horn·like** \-ˌlīk\ *adj*

horn·beam \ˈhȯrn-ˌbēm\ *n* (14c) **:** any of a genus (*Carpinus*) of trees of the birch family having smooth gray bark and hard white wood

horn·bill \-ˌbil\ *n* (1773) **:** any of a family (Bucerotidae) of large nonpasserine birds of Africa and Eurasia having enormous bills

horn·blende \-ˌblend\ *n* [G] (1770) **:** a mineral that is the common dark green to black variety of aluminous amphibole; *broadly* **:** AMPHIBOLE 2 — **horn·blend·ic** \ˌhȯrn-ˈblen-dik\ *adj*

hornbill

horn·book \ˈhȯrn-ˌbu̇k\ *n* (ca. 1595) **1 :** a child's primer consisting of a sheet of parchment or paper protected by a sheet of transparent horn **2 :** a rudimentary treatise

horn·dog \ˈhȯrn-ˌdȯg, -ˌdäg\ *n* (ca. 1984) *slang* **:** a lustful or sexually aggressive man

horned lark *n* (1888) **:** a brownish chiefly Holarctic lark (*Eremophila alpestris* of the family Alaudidae) that has small tufts of black feathers on top of the head

horned lizard *n* (1806) **:** HORNED TOAD

horned owl *n* (14c) **:** any of various owls having conspicuous tufts of feathers on the head; *esp* **:** GREAT HORNED OWL

horned pout *n* (1837) **:** a bullhead (genus *Ameiurus*); *esp* **:** a common mottled olive to brown bullhead (*A. nebulosus* syn. *Ictalurus nebulosus*) of eastern No. America that has been introduced into western streams

horned toad \ˈhȯrnd-; ˈhȯr-nəd-, -nət-\ *n* (1806) **:** any of several small harmless insectivorous lizards (genus *Phrynosoma*) of the western U.S. and Mexico that resemble toads and have hornlike spines

horned viper *n* (1767) **:** a venomous viper (*Cerastes cerastes* syn. *C. cornutus*) of No. Africa and the Middle East having a horny process over each eye

hor·net \ˈhȯr-nət\ *n* [ME *hernet,* fr. OE *hyrnet;* akin to OHG *hornaz* hornet, L *crabro*] (bef. 12c) **:** any of the larger vespid wasps (as of the genus *Vespa*) — compare YELLOW JACKET

hornet's nest *n* (ca. 1740) **1 :** a troublesome or hazardous situation **2 :** an angry reaction ⟨must have known that his frank comments . . . would stir up a *hornet's nest* —*U.S. Investor*⟩

horn·fels \ˈhȯrn-ˌfelz\ *n* [G, fr. *Horn* horn + *Fels* cliff, rock] (1854) **:** a fine-grained silicate rock produced by metamorphism esp. of slate

horn fly *n* (1708) **:** a small dark gray European dipteran fly (*Haematobia irritans*) that has been introduced into No. America where it is a blood-sucking pest esp. of cattle

horn in *vi* (1911) **:** to participate without invitation or consent **:** INTRUDE

horn·ist \ˈhȯr-nist\ *n* (1836) **:** one who plays a French horn

horn–mad \ˈhȯrn-ˈmad\ *adj* (1579) **:** furiously enraged

horn of plenty (ca. 1586) **:** CORNUCOPIA

horn·pipe \ˈhȯrn-ˌpīp\ *n* (15c) **1 :** a single-reed wind instrument consisting of a wooden or bone pipe with finger holes, a bell, and mouthpiece usu. of horn **2 :** a lively folk dance of the British Isles orig. accompanied by hornpipe playing

horn–rims \-ˌrimz\ *n pl* (1927) **:** glasses with horn rims

horn·stone \ˈhȯrn-ˌstōn\ *n* (1728) **:** a mineral that is a variety of quartz much like flint but more brittle

horn·swog·gle \-ˌswä-gəl\ *vt* **-swog·gled; -swog·gling** \-g(ə-)liŋ\ [origin unknown] (ca. 1829) *slang* **:** BAMBOOZLE, HOAX

horn·tail \-ˌtāl\ *n* (1884) **:** any of various hymenopterous insects (family Siricidae) related to the typical sawflies but having females with a stout hornlike ovipositor and larvae that burrow in woody plants

horn·worm \-ˌwərm\ *n* (1676) **:** a hawk moth caterpillar having a hornlike tail process — compare TOMATO HORNWORM

horn·wort \-ˌwərt, -ˌwȯrt\ *n* (ca. 1805) **:** any of a genus (*Ceratophyllum* of the family Ceratophyllaceae) of rootless thin-stemmed aquatic monoecious herbs with female flowers having a single carpel

horny \ˈhȯr-nē\ *adj* **horn·i·er; -est** (14c) **1 a :** of or made of horn **b :** HARD, CALLOUS ⟨*horny*-handed⟩ **c :** compact and homogeneous with a dull luster — used of a mineral **2 :** having horns **3** [*horn* erect penis + [1]*-y*] **a :** desiring sexual gratification **b :** excited sexually — **horn·i·ness** *n*

hor·o·loge \ˈhȯr-ə-ˌlōj, ˈhär-\ *n* [ME *orloge,* fr. AF *oriloge,* fr. L *horologium,* fr. Gk *hōrologion,* fr. *hōra* hour + *legein* to gather — more at YEAR, LEGEND] (14c) **:** a timekeeping device

hor·o·log·i·cal \ˌhȯr-ə-ˈlä-ji-kəl\ *adj* (15c) **:** of or relating to a horologe or horology

ho·rol·o·gist \hə-ˈrä-lə-jist\ *n* (1798) **1 :** a person skilled in the practice or theory of horology **2 :** a maker of clocks or watches

ho·rol·o·gy \-jē\ *n* [Gk *hōra* + E *-logy*] (1819) **1 :** the science of measuring time **2 :** the art of making instruments for indicating time

horo·scope \ˈhȯr-ə-ˌskōp, ˈhär-\ *n* [ME *horoscopum,* fr. L *horoscopus,* fr. Gk *hōroskopos,* fr. *hōra* + *skopos* watcher; akin to Gk *skopein* to look at — more at SPY] (14c) **1 :** a diagram of the relative positions of planets and signs of the zodiac at a specific time (as at one's birth) for use by astrologers in inferring individual character and personality traits and in foretelling events of a person's life **2 :** an astrological forecast

hor·ren·dous \hȯ-ˈren-dəs, hä-, hə-\ *adj* [L *horrendus,* fr. gerundive of *horrēre*] (1659) **:** HORRIBLE, DREADFUL ⟨the tax rate was ~⟩ ⟨~ crimes⟩ — **hor·ren·dous·ly** *adv*

hor·rent \ˈhȯr-ənt, ˈhär-\ *adj* [L *horrent-, horrens,* prp. of *horrēre*] (1667) **1** *archaic* **:** covered with bristling points **:** BRISTLED **2** *archaic* **:** standing up like bristles **:** BRISTLING

hor·ri·ble \ˈhȯr-ə-bəl, ˈhär-\ *adj* [ME *orrible, horrible,* fr. AF, fr. L *horribilis,* fr. *horrēre*] (14c) **1 :** marked by or arousing horror ⟨a ~ accident⟩ **2 :** extremely bad or unpleasant ⟨a ~ mistake⟩ ⟨~ food⟩ — **horrible** *n* — **hor·ri·ble·ness** *n* — **hor·ri·bly** \-blē\ *adv*

hor·rid \ˈhȯr-əd, ˈhär-\ *adj* [L *horridus,* fr. *horrēre*] (1590) **1** *archaic* **:** ROUGH, BRISTLING **2 :** innately offensive or repulsive: **a :** inspiring horror **:** SHOCKING **b :** inspiring disgust or loathing **:** NASTY ⟨a ~ man⟩ **c :** HORRIBLE 2 ⟨the tenor bell . . . gives out a ~ discordant noise —Robert Graves⟩ — **hor·rid·ly** *adv* — **hor·rid·ness** *n*

\ə\ **abut** \ᵊ\ **kitten, F table** \ər\ **further** \a\ **ash** \ā\ **ace** \ä\ **mop, mar**
\au̇\ **out** \ch\ **chin** \e\ **bet** \ē\ **easy** \g\ **go** \i\ **hit** \ī\ **ice** \j\ **job**
\ŋ\ **sing** \ō\ **go** \ȯ\ **law** \ȯi\ **boy** \th\ **thin** \t͟h\ **the** \ü\ **loot** \u̇\ **foot**
\y\ **yet** \zh\ **vision, beige** \k̲, ⁿ, œ, ue, ʸ\ *see* **Guide to Pronunciation**

hor·rif·ic \hȯ-'ri-fik, hä-\ *adj* (1653) : having the power to horrify ⟨a ~ account of the tragedy⟩ — **hor·rif·i·cal·ly** \-fi-k(ə-)lē\ *adv*

hor·ri·fy \'hȯr-ə-ˌfī, 'här-\ *vt* **-fied; -fy·ing** (1791) **1** : to cause to feel horror **2** : to fill with distaste : SHOCK *syn* see DISMAY — **hor·ri·fy·ing·ly** \-ˌfī-iŋ-lē\ *adv*

¹hor·ror \'hȯr-ər, 'här-\ *n* [ME *horrour*, fr. AF **orur*, fr. L *horror* action of bristling, fr. *horrēre* to bristle, shiver; akin to Skt *harṣate* he is excited] (14c) **1 a** : painful and intense fear, dread, or dismay ⟨astonishment giving place to ~ on the faces of the people about me —H. G. Wells⟩ **b** : intense aversion or repugnance **2 a** : the quality of inspiring horror : repulsive, horrible, or dismal quality or character ⟨contemplating the ~ of their lives —Liam O'Flaherty⟩ **b** : something that inspires horror **3** *pl* : a state of extreme depression or apprehension

²horror *adj* (1936) : calculated to inspire feelings of dread or horror : BLOODCURDLING ⟨a ~ movie⟩

horror show *n* (ca. 1959) : something difficult to deal with or watch ⟨the trial was a *horror show*⟩

horror story *n* (1937) : an account of an unsettling or unfortunate occurrence ⟨heard *horror stories* about recent layoffs⟩; *also* : something unsettling or unfortunate ⟨his childhood was a *horror story*⟩

hor·ror–struck \-ˌstrək\ *adj* (1814) : struck with horror ⟨stood ~ as they watched . . . their own city destroyed —*Nashville Tennessean*⟩

hors de com·bat \ˌȯr-də-kōⁿ-'bä\ *adv or adj* [F] (1757) : out of combat : DISABLED

hors d'oeuvre \ȯr-'dərv\ *n, pl* **hors d'oeuvres** *also* **hors d'oeuvre** \-'dərv(z)\ [F *hors-d'œuvre*, lit., outside of the work] (1714) : any of various savory foods usu. served as appetizers

¹horse \'hȯrs\ *n, pl* **hors·es** *also* **horse** [ME *hors*, fr. OE; akin to OHG *hros* horse] (bef. 12c) **1 a** (1) : a large solid-hoofed herbivorous ungulate mammal (*Equus caballus*, family Equidae, the horse family) domesticated since prehistoric times and used as a beast of burden, a draft animal, or for riding (2) : RACEHORSE ⟨play the ~s⟩ **b** : a male horse; *esp* : STALLION **c** : a recent or extinct animal (as a zebra, ass, or onager) of the horse family **2 a** : JACKSTAY **b** : a frame usu. with legs used for supporting something (as planks or staging) **c** (1) : POMMEL HORSE (2) : VAULTING HORSE **3** *horse pl* : CAVALRY **4** : a mass of the same geological character as the wall rock occurring within a vein **5** : HORSEPOWER **6** *slang* : HEROIN **7** : an athlete whose performance is consistently strong and reliable ⟨a team with the ~s to win the pennant⟩ **8** *or* H-O-R-S-E : a game in which players take turns attempting to duplicate successful basketball shots, a letter of the word "horse" is awarded for each missed attempt, and the first player to receive all five letters loses — **horse·less** \'hȯr-sləs\ *adj* — **horse·like** \'hȯrs-ˌlīk\ *adj* — **from the horse's mouth** : from the original source

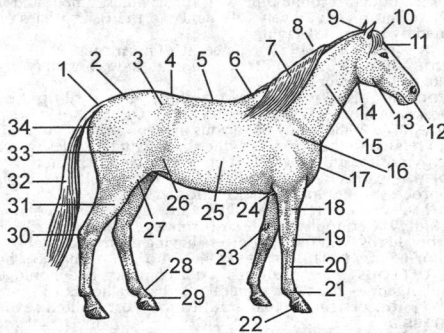

horse 1a(1): *1* dock, *2* croup, *3* point of hip, *4* loin, *5* back, *6* withers, *7* mane, *8* crest, *9* poll, *10* forelock, *11* forehead, *12* muzzle, *13* cheek, *14* throatlatch, *15* neck, *16* shoulder, *17* chest, *18* forearm, *19* knee, *20* cannon, *21* fetlock, *22* hoof, *23* chestnut, *24* elbow, *25* barrel, *26* flank, *27* stifle, *28* pastern, *29* coronet, *30* hock, *31* gaskin, *32* tail, *33* thigh, *34* buttock

²horse *vb* **horsed; hors·ing** *vt* (bef. 12c) **1** : to provide with a horse **2** : to move by brute force ~ *vi, of a mare* : to be in heat

³horse *adj* (15c) **1 a** : of or relating to a horse **b** : hauled or powered by a horse ⟨a ~ barge⟩ **2** : large or coarse of its kind **3** : mounted on horses ⟨~ guards⟩

horse–and–buggy *adj* (ca. 1926) **1** : of or relating to the era before the advent of certain socially revolutionizing inventions (as the automobile) **2** : clinging to outdated attitudes or ideas : OLD-FASHIONED

horse around *vi* (1919) : to engage in horseplay ⟨*horse around* together, joking and laughing and pushing each other —D. K. Shipler⟩; *also* : FOOL AROUND 1

¹horse·back \'hȯrs-ˌbak\ *n* (14c) : the back of a horse

²horseback *adv* (1727) : on horseback

³horseback *adj* (1879) : given without thorough consideration ⟨a ~ opinion⟩

horse·bean \'hȯrs-ˌbēn\ *n* (1684) **1** : BROAD BEAN **2** : JERUSALEM THORN

horse·car \-ˌkär\ *n* (1833) **1** : a streetcar drawn by horses **2** : a car fitted for transporting horses

horse chestnut *n* (1597) **1** : a large tree (*Aesculus hippocastanum* of the family Hippocastanaceae, the horse-chestnut family) of southeastern Europe that has palmate leaves and erect conical clusters of showy flowers and is widely cultivated as an ornamental and shade tree and naturalized as an escape; *also* : BUCKEYE **2** : the large glossy brown seed of a horse chestnut

horse coper *n* (1614) *Brit* : COPER

horse·feath·ers \'hȯrs-ˌfe-thərz\ *n pl* (1927) *slang* : NONSENSE, BALDERDASH

horse·flesh \-ˌflesh\ *n* (15c) : horses considered esp. with reference to riding, driving, or racing

horse·fly \-ˌflī\ *n* (14c) : any of a family (Tabanidae) of swift usu. large dipteran flies with bloodsucking females

horse gentian *n* (1837) : FEVERWORT

horse·hair \'hȯrs-ˌher\ *n* (14c) **1** : the hair of a horse esp. from the mane or tail **2** : cloth made from horsehair

horsehair worm *n* (ca. 1753) : HAIRWORM 1

horse·hide \'hȯrs-ˌhīd\ *n* (14c) **1** : the dressed or raw hide of a horse **2** : the ball used in the game of baseball

horse latitudes *n pl* (1777) : either of two belts or regions in the neighborhood of 30° N and 30° S latitude characterized by high pressure, calms, and light variable winds

horse·laugh \'hȯrs-ˌlaf, -ˌläf\ *n* (1713) : a loud boisterous laugh

horseless carriage *n* (1895) : AUTOMOBILE — used esp. of early models

horse mackerel *n* (ca. 1705) **1** : any of various large carangid food fishes; *esp* : JACK MACKEREL **2** : BLUEFIN TUNA

horse·man \'hȯrs-mən\ *n* (14c) **1** : a rider or driver of horses; *esp* : one whose skill is exceptional **2** : a person skilled in caring for or managing horses **3** : a person who breeds or raises horses — **horse·man·ship** \-ˌship\ *n*

horse·mint \'hȯrs-ˌmint\ *n* (bef. 12c) : any of various coarse mints; *esp* : MONARDA

horse nettle *n* (ca. 1818) : a coarse prickly weed (*Solanum carolinense*) of the nightshade family with bright yellow fruit resembling berries

horse opera *n* (1927) : WESTERN 2

horse·play \'hȯrs-ˌplā\ *n* (1589) : rough or boisterous play

horse·play·er \-ər\ *n* (1947) : one who habitually bets on horse races

horse·pow·er \'hȯrs-ˌpau̇(-ə)r\ *n* (1806) **1** : the power that a horse exerts in pulling **2** : a unit of power equal in the U.S. to 746 watts and nearly equivalent to the English gravitational unit of the same name that equals 550 foot-pounds of work per second **3** : effective power ⟨intellectual ~⟩ ⟨computing ~⟩

horse race *n* (1954) : a close contest (as in politics)

horse·rad·ish \'hȯrs-ˌra-dish, -ˌre-\ *n* (1597) **1** : a tall coarse white-flowered herb (*Armoracia rusticana* syn. *A. lapathifolia*) of the mustard family **2** : a condiment made from ground-up horseradish root

horse's ass \'hȯr-səz-\ *n* (ca. 1865) *often vulgar* : a stupid or incompetent person : BLOCKHEAD

horse sense *n* (1832) : COMMON SENSE

horse·shit \'hȯrs-ˌshit, 'hȯrsh-\ *n* (1923) *usu vulgar* : NONSENSE, BUNK

horse·shoe \'hȯrs-ˌshü, 'hȯrsh-\ *n* (14c) **1** : a usu. U-shaped band of iron fitted and nailed to the rim of a horse's hoof to protect it **2** : something (as a valley) shaped like a horseshoe **3** *pl* : a game like quoits played with horseshoes or with horseshoe-shaped pieces of metal — **horseshoe** *vt* — **horse·sho·er** \-ˌshü-ər\ *n*

horseshoe arch *n* (1797) : an arch having an intrados that widens above the springing before narrowing to a rounded or pointed crown — see ARCH illustration

horseshoe crab *n* (1797) : any of several closely related marine arthropods (order Xiphosura and class Merostomata) with a broad crescentic cephalothorax, six pairs of legs, and a spikelike tail; *esp* : one (*Limulus polyphemus*) of coastal waters from Maine to the Yucatán Peninsula — called also *king crab*

horse show *n* (1813) : an exhibition of horses that usu. includes competition in riding, driving, and jumping

horse·tail \'hȯrs-ˌtāl\ *n* (15c) : any of a genus (*Equisetum* of the order Equisetales) of lower tracheophytes comprising perennial plants that spread by creeping rhizomes and have leaves reduced to nodal sheaths on the hollow jointed ribbed shoots

horse trade *n* (1846) : negotiation accompanied by shrewd bargaining and reciprocal concessions ⟨a political *horse trade*⟩ — **horse–trade** *vi* — **horse trader** *n*

horse·weed \'hȯrs-ˌwēd\ *n* (1790) **1** : a common annual American composite herb (*Conyza canadensis* syn. *Erigeron canadensis*) with an erect usu. hairy stem and small discoid heads of yellow disk flowers **2** : a coarse annual No. American ragweed (*Ambrosia trifida*)

horsetail: *1* vegetative plant, *2* fertile plant

horse·whip \'hȯrs-ˌwip, 'hȯrs-ˌhwip\ *vt* (1751) : to flog with or as if with a whip made to be used on a horse — **horse·whip·per** *n*

horse·wom·an \'hȯrs-ˌwu̇-mən\ *n* (ca. 1578) **1** : a woman who is a rider or a driver of horses; *esp* : one whose skill is exceptional **2** : a woman skilled in caring for or managing horses **3** : a woman who breeds or raises horses

hors·ey *also* **horsy** \'hȯr-sē\ *adj* **hors·i·er; -est** (1591) **1** : of, relating to, or resembling a horse **2** : having to do with horses or horse racing **3** : characteristic of the manners, dress, or tastes of horsemen or horsewomen — **hors·i·ly** \-sə-lē\ *adv* — **hors·i·ness** \-sē-nəs\ *n*

horst \'hȯrst\ *n* [G, lit., thicket] (1893) : a block of the earth's crust separated by faults from adjacent relatively depressed blocks

hort *abbr* horticultural; horticulture

hor·ta·tive \'hȯr-tə-tiv\ *adj* [LL *hortativus*, fr. L *hortatus*, pp. of *hortari* to urge — more at YEARN] (1623) : giving exhortation : ADVISORY — **hor·ta·tive·ly** *adv*

hor·ta·to·ry \'hȯr-tə-ˌtȯr-ē\ *adj* (1576) : HORTATIVE, EXHORTATORY ⟨~ sermons⟩

hor·ti·cul·ture \'hȯr-tə-ˌkəl-chər\ *n* [L *hortus* garden + E *-i-* + *culture* — more at YARD] (1678) : the science and art of growing fruits, vegetables, flowers, or ornamental plants — **hor·ti·cul·tur·al** \ˌhȯr-tə-ˌkəl-chə-rəl\ *adj* — **hor·ti·cul·tur·al·ly** \-rə-lē\ *adv* — **hor·ti·cul·tur·ist** \-rist\ *also* **hor·ti·cul·tur·al·ist** \-ch(ə-)rə-list\ *n*

Ho·rus \'hȯr-əs\ *n* [LL, fr. Gk *Hōros*, fr. Egypt *Ḥr*] (1832) : the falcon-headed Egyptian god of light and the son of Osiris and Isis

Hos *abbr* Hosea

ho·san·na *also* **ho·san·nah** \hō-ˈza-nə *also* -ˈzä-\ *interj* [ME *osanna,* fr. OE, fr. LL, fr. Gk *hōsanna,* fr. Heb *hōshīʽāh-nnā* pray, save (us)!] (bef. 12c) — used as a cry of acclamation and adoration — **hosanna** *n*

HO scale \(ˈ)ā-ˈchō-\ *n* [*half* + *O (gauge)*] (1939) : a scale of 3.5 millimeters to one foot used esp. for model toys (as automobiles or trains)

[1]**hose** \ˈhōz\ *n, pl* **hose** *or* **hos·es** [ME, fr. OE *hosa* stocking, husk; akin to OHG *hosa* leg covering] (bef. 12c) **1** *pl hose* **a** (1) : a cloth leg covering that sometimes covers the foot (2) : STOCKING, SOCK **b** (1) : a close-fitting garment covering the legs and waist that is usu. attached to a doublet by points (2) : short breeches reaching to the knee **2** : a flexible tube for conveying fluids (as from a faucet or hydrant)

[2]**hose** *vt* **hosed; hos·ing** (1889) **1 a** : to spray, water, or wash with a hose — often used with *down* ⟨~ down a stable floor⟩ **b** *slang* : to fire automatic weapons at — usu. used with *down* **2** *slang* : to deprive of something due or expected : TRICK, CHEAT

Ho·sea \hō-ˈzā-ə, -ˈzē-\ *n* [Heb *Hōshēaʽ*] (14c) **1** : a Hebrew prophet of the eighth century B.C. **2** : a prophetic book of canonical Jewish and Christian Scripture — see BIBLE table

ho·sel \ˈhō-zəl\ *n* [dim. of [1]*hose*] (1899) : a socket in the head of a golf club into which the shaft is inserted

hose·pipe \ˈhōz-ˌpīp\ *n* (1825) *chiefly Brit* : HOSE 2

ho·siery \ˈhōzh-rē, ˈhōz-; ˈhō-zhə-rē, -zə-\ *n* (1739) **1** : HOSE 1a **2** *chiefly Brit* : KNITWEAR

hosp *abbr* hospital

hos·pice \ˈhäs-pəs\ *n* [F, fr. OF *hospise,* fr. L *hospitium,* fr. *hospit-, hospes* host — more at HOST] (1818) **1** : a lodging for travelers, young persons, or the underprivileged esp. when maintained by a religious order **2** : a facility or program designed to provide a caring environment for meeting the physical and emotional needs of the terminally ill

hos·pi·ta·ble \hä-ˈspi-tə-bəl, ˈhäs-(ˌ)pi-\ *adj* (ca. 1570) **1 a** : given to generous and cordial reception of guests **b** : promising or suggesting generous and cordial welcome **c** : offering a pleasant or sustaining environment **2** : readily receptive : OPEN ⟨~ to new ideas⟩ — **hos·pi·ta·bly** \-blē\ *adv*

hos·pi·tal \ˈhäs-(ˌ)pi-tᵊl\ *n, often attrib* [ME, fr. AF, fr. ML *hospitale* hospice, guest house, fr. neut. of L *hospitalis* of a guest, fr. *hospit-, hospes*] (14c) **1** : a charitable institution for the needy, aged, infirm, or young **2** : an institution where the sick or injured are given medical or surgical care — usu. used in British English without an article after a preposition **3** : a repair shop for specified small objects ⟨a clock ~⟩

hos·pi·tal·ise *Brit var of* HOSPITALIZE

hos·pi·tal·ist \ˈhäs-(ˌ)pi-tə-list\ *n* (1996) : a physician who specializes in treating hospitalized patients of other physicians in order to minimize the number of hospital visits by other physicians

hos·pi·tal·i·ty \ˌhäs-pə-ˈta-lə-tē\ *n, pl* **-ties** (14c) : hospitable treatment, reception, or disposition

hospitality suite *n* (1963) : a room or suite esp. in a hotel set aside as a place for socializing esp. for business purposes

hos·pi·tal·ize \ˈhäs-ˌpi-tə-ˌlīz\ *vt* **-ized; -iz·ing** (ca. 1899) : to place in a hospital as a patient — **hos·pi·tal·i·za·tion** \ˌhäs-ˌpi-tᵊl-ə-ˈzā-shən\ *n*

Hos·pi·tal·ler *or* **Hos·pi·tal·er** \-tᵊl-ər\ *n* [ME *hospiteler,* fr. AF, fr. ML *hospitalarius,* fr. LL *hospitale*] (14c) : a member of a religious military order established in Jerusalem in the 12th century

[1]**host** \ˈhōst\ *n* [ME, fr. AF *ost,* fr. LL *hostis,* fr. L, stranger, enemy — more at GUEST] (14c) **1** : ARMY **2** : a great number : MULTITUDE

[2]**host** *vi* (15c) : to assemble in a host usu. for a hostile purpose

[3]**host** *n* [ME *hoste* host, guest, fr. AF, fr. L *hospit-, hospes,* prob. fr. *hostis*] (14c) **1 a** : one that receives or entertains guests socially, commercially, or officially **b** : one that provides facilities for an event or function ⟨our college served as ~ for the basketball tournament⟩ **2 a** : a living animal or plant on or in which a parasite lives **b** : the larger, stronger, or dominant member of a commensal or symbiotic pair **c** : an individual into which a tissue, part, or embryo is transplanted from another **3** : a mineral or rock that is older than the minerals or rocks in it; *also* : a substance that contains a usu. small amount of another substance incorporated in its structure **4** : a radio or television emcee **5** : a computer that controls communications in a network or that administers a database; *also* : SERVER 6

[4]**host** *vt* (15c) **1** : to serve as host to, at, or for ⟨~ friends⟩ ⟨~ a dinner⟩ **2** : EMCEE ⟨~*ed* a series of TV programs⟩

[5]**host** *n, often cap* [ME *hoste, oste,* fr. AF *oste, oiste,* fr. LL & L; LL *hostia* Eucharist, fr. L, sacrifice] (14c) : the eucharistic bread

hos·ta \ˈhō-stə, ˈhä-\ *n* [NL, fr. Nicolaus *Host* †1834 Austrian botanist] (1930) : any of a genus (*Hosta*) of Asian perennial herbaceous plants of the lily family with densely growing basal leaves and tall racemes of white or violet flowers — called also *funkia, plantain lily*

hos·tage \ˈhäs-tij\ *n* [ME, fr. AF, fr. *hoste*] (13c) **1 a** : a person held by one party in a conflict as a pledge pending the fulfillment of an agreement **b** : a person taken by force to secure the taker's demands **2** : one that is involuntarily controlled by an outside influence

[1]**hos·tel** \ˈhäs-tᵊl\ *n* [ME, fr. AF, fr. ML *hospitale* hospice] (14c) **1** : INN **2 a** *chiefly Brit* : a supervised institutional residence **b** : a supervised lodging for usu. young travelers — called also *youth hostel*

[2]**hostel** *vi* **-teled** *or* **-telled; -tel·ing** *or* **-tel·ling** (14c) : to stay at hostels overnight in the course of traveling

hos·tel·er *or* **hos·tel·ler** \ˈhäs-tə-lər\ *n* (14c) **1** : one that lodges guests or strangers **2** : a traveler who stops at hostels overnight

hos·tel·ry \ˈhäs-tᵊl-rē\ *n, pl* **-ries** (14c) : INN, HOTEL

[1]**host·ess** \ˈhōs-təs\ *n* (14c) **1** : a woman who entertains socially **2 a** : a woman in charge of a public dining room who seats diners **b** : a female employee on a public conveyance (as an airplane) who manages the provisioning of food and attends passengers **c** : a woman who acts as a partner or companion to male patrons in a dance hall or bar

[2]**hostess** *vi* (1927) : to act as hostess ~ *vt* : to serve as hostess to

hos·tile \ˈhäs-tᵊl, -ˌtī(-ə)l\ *adj* [MF or L; MF, fr. L *hostilis,* fr. *hostis*] (1580) **1 a** : of or relating to an enemy ⟨~ fire⟩ **b** : marked by malevolence ⟨a ~ act⟩ **c** : openly opposed or resisting ⟨a ~ critic⟩ ⟨~ to new ideas⟩ **d** (1) : not hospitable ⟨plants growing in a ~ environment⟩ (2) : having an intimidating, antagonistic, or offensive nature ⟨a ~ workplace⟩ **2 a** : of or relating to the opposing party in a legal controversy ⟨a ~ witness⟩ **b** : adverse to the interests of a property owner or corporation management ⟨a ~ takeover⟩ — **hostile** *n* — **hos·tile·ly** \-tᵊl-(l)ē, -ˌtī(-ə)l-lē\ *adv*

hos·til·i·ty \hä-ˈsti-lə-tē\ *n, pl* **-ties** (15c) **1 a** : deep-seated usu. mutual ill will **b** (1) : hostile action (2) *pl* : overt acts of warfare : WAR **2** : conflict, opposition, or resistance in thought or principle ***syn*** see ENMITY

hos·tler \ˈhäs-lər, ˈäs-\ *also* **os·tler** \ˈäs-\ *n* [ME, innkeeper, hostler, fr. AF *hosteler,* fr. *hostel*] (14c) **1** : one who takes care of horses or mules **2** : one who moves locomotives in and out of a roundhouse; *also* : one who services locomotives

host·ly \ˈhōst-lē\ *adj* (1893) : of or appropriate to a host

[1]**hot** \ˈhät\ *adj* **hot·ter; hot·test** [ME, fr. OE *hāt;* akin to OHG *heiz* hot, Lith *kaisti* to get hot] (bef. 12c) **1 a** : having a relatively high temperature **b** : capable of giving a sensation of heat or of burning, searing, or scalding **c** : having heat in a degree exceeding normal body heat **2 a** : VIOLENT, STORMY ⟨a ~ temper⟩ ⟨a ~ battle⟩; *also* : ANGRY ⟨got ~ about the remark⟩ **b** (1) : sexually excited or receptive (2) : SEXY **c** : EAGER, ZEALOUS ⟨~ for reform⟩ **d** *of jazz* : emotionally exciting and marked by strong rhythms and free melodic improvisations **3** : having or causing the sensation of an uncomfortable degree of body heat ⟨~ and tired⟩ ⟨it's ~ in here⟩ **4 a** : newly made : FRESH ⟨a ~ scent⟩ ⟨~ off the press⟩ **b** : close to something sought ⟨~ on the trail⟩ **5 a** : suggestive of heat or of burning or glowing objects ⟨~ colors⟩ **b** : PUNGENT, PEPPERY **6 a** : of intense and immediate interest ⟨some ~ gossip⟩ **b** : unusually lucky or favorable ⟨on a ~ streak⟩ **c** : temporarily capable of unusual performance (as in a sport) **d** : currently popular or in demand ⟨a ~ commodity⟩ **e** : very good ⟨a ~ idea⟩ ⟨not feeling too ~⟩ **f** : ABSURD, UNBELIEVABLE ⟨wants to fight the champ? that's a ~ one⟩ **7 a** : electrically energized esp. with high voltage **b** : RADIOACTIVE; *also* : dealing with radioactive material **c** *of an atom or molecule* : being in an excited state **8 a** : recently and illegally obtained ⟨~ jewels⟩ **b** : wanted by the police; *also* : unsafe for a fugitive **9** : FAST ⟨a ~ new fighter plane⟩ ⟨a ~ lap around the track⟩ — **hot·ness** *n* — **hot·tish** \ˈhä-tish\ *adj* — **hot under the collar** : extremely exasperated or angry

[2]**hot** *adv* (bef. 12c) **1** : HOTLY **2** : FAST, QUICKLY

[3]**hot** *n* (13c) **1** : HEAT 1d(1) ⟨the ~ of the day⟩ **2** : one that is hot (as a hot meal or a horse just after a workout) **3** *pl* : strong sexual desire — used with *the*

[4]**hot** *vt* **hot·ted; hot·ting** (1561) *chiefly Southern, southern Midland, & Brit* : HEAT, WARM — usu. used with *up*

hot air *n* (1873) : empty talk

hot·bed \ˈhät-ˌbed\ *n* (1626) **1** : a bed of soil enclosed in glass, heated esp. by fermenting manure, and used for forcing or for raising seedlings **2** : an environment that favors rapid growth or development ⟨a ~ of activity⟩

hot·blood \-ˌbləd\ *n* (1798) **1** : one that is hot-blooded; *esp* : one having strong passions or a quick temper **2** : THOROUGHBRED 3

hot–blood·ed \-ˈblə-dəd\ *adj* (1598) **1** : easily excited : PASSIONATE **2** *of a horse* : having Arab or Thoroughbred ancestors — **hot–blood·ed·ness** *n*

hot·box \-ˌbäks\ *n* (1848) : a journal bearing (as of a railroad car) overheated by friction

hot button *n* (1975) : an emotional and usu. controversial issue or concern that triggers immediate intense reaction — **hot–button** *adj*

hot·cake \-ˌkāk\ *n* (1683) : PANCAKE — **like hotcakes** : at a rapid rate ⟨selling *like hotcakes*⟩

hotch \ˈhäch\ *vi* [ME, prob. fr. MF *hocher* to shake, fr. OF *hochier*] (15c) **1** *Scot* : WIGGLE, FIDGET **2** *chiefly Scot* : SWARM

hotch·pot \ˈhäch-ˌpät\ *n* [AF *hochepot*] (1552) : the combining of properties into a common lot to ensure equality of division among heirs

hotch·potch \ˈhäch-ˌpäch\ *n* [ME *hochepot,* fr. AF, fr. *hocher* to shake + *pot* pot] (1583) **1 a** : a thick soup or stew of vegetables, potatoes, and usu. meat **b** : HODGEPODGE **2** : HOTCHPOT

hot comb *n* (1970) : a metal comb usu. electrically heated for straightening or styling the hair — **hot–comb** *vt*

hot corner *n* (1903) : THIRD BASE 2

hot·dog \ˈhät-ˌdȯg\ *vi* [[2]*hot dog*] (1963) : to perform in a conspicuous or often ostentatious manner; *esp* : to perform fancy stunts and maneuvers (as while surfing or skiing) — **hot·dog·ger** \-ˌdȯ-gər\ *n*

[1]**hot dog** \ˈhät-ˌdȯg\ *n* (1895) **1** : FRANKFURTER; *esp* : a frankfurter heated and served in a long split roll **2** [perh. fr. [2]*hot dog*] : one that hotdogs; *also* : SHOW-OFF

[2]**hot dog** \ˈhät-ˈdȯg\ *interj* (ca. 1906) — used to express approval or gratification

ho·tel \hō-ˈtel, ˈhō-ˌ\ *n* [F *hôtel,* fr. OF *hostel* hostel] (1765) : an establishment that provides lodging and usu. meals, entertainment, and various personal services for the public : INN — **ho·tel·dom** \-dəm\ *n*

Hotel (1952) — a communications code word for the letter *h*

ho·te·lier \hō-ˈtel-yər; ˌō-tᵊl-ˈyā, ˌȯ-\ *n* [F *hôtelier,* fr. OF *hostelier,* fr. *hostel*] (1905) : a proprietor or manager of a hotel

ho·tel·man \hō-ˈtel-ˌman, -mən\ *n* (1920) : one who is engaged in the hotel business esp. in a supervisory or managerial capacity

hot flash *n* (1910) : a sudden brief flushing and sensation of heat caused by dilation of skin capillaries usu. associated with menopausal endocrine imbalance — called also *hot flush*

[1]**hot·foot** \ˈhät-ˌfu̇t\ *adv* (14c) : in haste

[2]**hotfoot** *vi* (1896) : to go hotfoot : HURRY — usu. used with *it*

[3]**hotfoot** *n, pl* **hotfoots** (1934) : a practical joke in which a match is surreptitiously inserted between the upper and the sole of a victim's shoe and lighted

hot·head \ˈhät-ˌhed\ *n* (1660) : a hotheaded person

hot·head·ed \-ˈhe-dəd\ *adj* (1641) : easily angered : FIERY, IMPETUOUS — **hot·head·ed·ly** *adv* — **hot·head·ed·ness** *n*

[1]**hot·house** \-ˌhau̇s\ *n* (1511) **1** *obs* : BORDELLO **2** : a greenhouse maintained at a high temperature esp. for the culture of tropical plants **3** : HOTBED 2

[2]**hothouse** *adj* (1838) **1** : grown in a hothouse **2** : suggestive of growth and development in a hothouse ⟨a ~ existence⟩; *also* : suggesting a hothouse ⟨a ~ atmosphere⟩

\ə\ abut \ᵊ\ kitten, F table \ər\ further \a\ ash \ā\ ace \ä\ mop, mar
\au̇\ out \ch\ chin \e\ bet \ē\ easy \g\ go \i\ hit \ī\ ice \j\ job
\ŋ\ sing \ō\ go \ȯ\ law \ȯi\ boy \th\ thin \t͟h\ the \ü\ loot \u̇\ foot
\y\ yet \zh\ vision, beige \k, ⁿ, œ, ue, ʸ\ see Guide to Pronunciation

hot key *n* (1983) : a key or combination of keys on a computer keyboard programmed to perform a specific function when pressed

hot·line \ˈhät-ˌlīn\ *n* (1955) **1 :** a direct telephone line in constant operational readiness so as to facilitate immediate communication **2 :** a usu. toll-free telephone service available to the public for some specific purpose ⟨a consumer ~⟩

hot link *n* (1989) : HYPERLINK — **hot–link** *vb*

hot·ly \ˈhät-lē\ *adv* (15c) : in a hot manner ⟨a ~ contested series⟩

hot–melt \ˈhät-ˌmelt\ *n* (1939) : a fast-drying nonvolatile adhesive applied hot in the molten state

hot metal *n* (1960) : composition in which the type is cast from molten metal

hot money *n* (1936) : investment funds intended for the highest short-term rate of return

hot pants *n pl* (1970) : very short shorts

hot pepper *n* (1945) : any of various small and usu. thin-walled capsicum fruits of marked pungency; *also* : a plant (esp. variants or cultivars of *Capsicum annuum* and *C. frutescens*) bearing hot peppers

hot plate *n* (1845) **1 :** a heated iron plate for cooking **2 :** a simple portable appliance for heating or for cooking in limited spaces

hot pot *n* (1851) **1 :** a stew of meat and vegetables **2 :** FIREPOT 2

hot potato *n* (1950) : a controversial question or issue that involves unpleasant or dangerous consequences for anyone dealing with it

hot pursuit *n* (1743) : close and avid or intense pursuit; *specif* : close continuous pursuit of a fleeing suspected lawbreaker or hostile military force esp. across territorial lines

hot rod *n* (1945) : an automobile rebuilt or modified for high speed and fast acceleration

hot–rod·der \ˈhät-ˌrä-dər\ *n* (1949) : a hot rod driver, builder, or enthusiast — **hot–rod** \ˈhät-ˈräd\ *vb*

hot seat *n* (1925) **1** *slang* : ELECTRIC CHAIR **2 :** a position of uneasiness, embarrassment, or anxiety

hot·shot \ˈhät-ˌshät\ *n, often attrib* (ca. 1925) **1 :** a fast freight **2 :** a person who is conspicuously talented or successful ⟨a ~ lawyer⟩

hot spot *n* (1929) **1 :** a place of more than usual interest, activity, or popularity ⟨birding *hot spots*⟩ **2 :** a place in the upper mantle of the earth at which hot magma from the lower mantle upwells to melt through the crust usu. in the interior of a tectonic plate to form a volcanic feature; *also* : a place in the crust overlying a hot spot **3 :** an area of political, military, or civil unrest usu. considered dangerous ⟨global *hot spots*⟩ **4 :** a place where a wireless Internet connection is available

hot spring *n* (1669) : a spring whose water issues at a temperature higher than that of its surroundings

hot stuff *n* (1889) : someone or something unusually good

Hot·ten·tot \ˈhä-tᵊn-ˌtät\ *n* [Afrik] (1677) *often offensive* : KHOIKHOI

hot ticket *n* (1950) : someone or something very popular : RAGE

hot·tie \ˈhä-tē\ *n* (1913) : a physically attractive person

hot tub *n* (1975) : a large tub of hot water in which bathers soak and usu. socialize; *esp* : such a tub with a whirlpool device — **hot–tub** *vi*

hot up *vi* (1878) *chiefly Brit* : to increase in intensity, pace, or excitement ⟨air raids began to *hot up* about the beginning of February —George Orwell⟩ ~ *vt, chiefly Brit* : to make livelier, speedier, or more intense

hot war *n* (1947) : a conflict involving actual fighting — compare COLD WAR

hot water *n* (1537) : TROUBLE 4, DIFFICULTY ⟨was in *hot water* with the authorities⟩

hot–wire \ˈhät-ˌwī(-ə)r\ *vt* (1954) : to start (as an automobile) by short-circuiting the ignition system

[1]**hound** \ˈhau̇nd\ *n* [ME, fr. OE *hund;* akin to OHG *hunt* dog, L *canis,* Gk *kyōn*] (bef. 12c) **1 a :** DOG **b :** a dog of any of numerous hunting breeds including both scent hounds (as the bloodhound and beagle) and sight hounds (as the greyhound and Afghan hound) **2 :** a mean or despicable person **3 :** DOGFISH **4 :** a person who pursues like a hound; *esp* : one who avidly seeks or collects something ⟨autograph ~*s*⟩

[2]**hound** *vt* (1528) **1 :** to pursue with or as if with hounds **2 :** to drive or affect by persistent harassing ***syn*** see BAIT — **hound·er** *n*

hounds \ˈhau̇n(d)z\ *n pl* [ME *houne,* fr. ON *hūnn* knob at the top of a masthead] (15c) : the framing at the masthead of a ship that supports the heel of the topmast and the upper parts of the lower rigging

hound's–tongue \ˈhau̇n(d)z-ˌtəŋ\ *n* (bef. 12c) : any of various coarse plants (genus *Cynoglossum,* esp. *C. officinale*) of the borage family having tongue-shaped leaves and reddish flowers

hounds·tooth *also* **hound's–tooth** \ˈhau̇n(d)z-ˌtüth\ *n* (1936) : a usu. small broken-check textile pattern; *also* : a fabric woven in this pattern — called also *houndstooth check, hound's-tooth check*

hour \ˈau̇(-ə)r\ *n* [ME, fr. AF *ure, eure,* fr. LL & L; LL *hora* canonical hour, fr. L, hour of the day, fr. Gk *hōra* — more at YEAR] (13c) **1 :** a time or office for daily liturgical devotion; *esp* : CANONICAL HOUR **2 :** the 24th part of a day : 60 minutes **3 a :** the time of day reckoned in two 12-hour periods **b** *pl* : the time reckoned in one 24-hour period from midnight to midnight using a 4-digit number of which the first two digits indicate the hour and the last two digits indicate the minute ⟨in the military 4:30 p.m. is called 1630 ~*s*⟩ **4 a :** a customary or particular time ⟨lunch ~⟩ ⟨in our ~ of need⟩; *also* : MOMENT 1b ⟨hero of the ~⟩ **b** *pl* : time of going to bed ⟨keeps late ~*s*⟩; *also* : time of working ⟨banker's ~*s*⟩ **5 :** an angular unit of right ascension equal to 15 degrees measured along the celestial equator **6 :** the work done or distance traveled at normal rate in an hour ⟨the city was two ~*s* away⟩ **7 a :** a class session **b :** CREDIT HOUR, SEMESTER HOUR — **after hours :** after the regular quitting or closing time

hour angle *n* (ca. 1837) : the angle between the celestial meridian of an observer and the hour circle of a celestial object measured westward from the meridian

hour circle *n* (1690) : a circle on the celestial sphere that passes through both celestial poles

[1]**hour·glass** \ˈau̇(-ə)r-ˌglas\ *n* (ca. 1515) : an instrument for measuring time consisting of a glass vessel having two compartments from the upper of which a quantity of usu. sand runs in an hour into the lower one

[2]**hourglass** *adj* (ca. 1834) : shaped like an hourglass ⟨an ~ figure⟩

hour hand *n* (1669) : the short hand that marks the hours on the face of a watch or clock

hou·ri \ˈhu̇r-ē, ˈhü-rē\ *n* [F, fr. Pers *hūri,* fr. Ar *ḥūrīya*] (1737) **1 :** one of the beautiful maidens that in Muslim belief live with the blessed in paradise **2 :** a voluptuously beautiful young woman

hour–long \ˈau̇(-ə)r-ˈlȯŋ\ *adj* (1803) : lasting an hour

[1]**hour·ly** \ˈau̇(-ə)r-lē\ *adv* (15c) : at or during every hour; *also* : FREQUENTLY, CONTINUALLY

[2]**hourly** *adj* (ca. 1530) **1 a :** occurring hour by hour ⟨~ bus service⟩ **b :** FREQUENT, CONTINUAL ⟨in ~ expectation of the rain's stopping⟩ **2 :** computed in terms of an hour ⟨an ~ wage⟩ **3 :** paid by the hour ⟨~ workers⟩

[1]**house** \ˈhau̇s\ *n, pl* **hous·es** \ˈhau̇-zəz *also* -səz\ *often attrib* [ME *hous,* fr. OE *hūs;* akin to OHG *hūs* house] (bef. 12c) **1 :** a building that serves as living quarters for one or a few families : HOME **2 a** (1) **:** a shelter or refuge (as a nest or den) of a wild animal (2) **:** a natural covering (as a test or shell) that encloses and protects an animal or a colony of zooids **b :** a building in which something is housed ⟨a carriage ~⟩ **3 a :** one of the 12 equal sectors in which the celestial sphere is divided in astrology **b :** a zodiacal sign that is the seat of a planet's greatest influence **4 a :** HOUSEHOLD **b :** a family including ancestors, descendants, and kindred ⟨the ~ of Tudor⟩ **5 a :** a residence for a religious community or for students **b :** the community or students in residence **6 a :** a legislative, deliberative, or consultative assembly; *esp* : one constituting a division of a bicameral body **b :** the building or chamber where such an assembly meets **c :** a quorum of such an assembly **7 a :** a place of business or entertainment ⟨a movie ~⟩ **b** (1) **:** a business organization ⟨a publishing ~⟩ (2) **:** a gambling establishment **c :** the audience in a theater or concert hall ⟨a full ~ on opening night⟩ **8 :** the circular area 12 feet in diameter surrounding the tee and within which a curling stone must rest in order to count **9** [fr. The Ware*house,* Chicago dance club that pioneered the style] **:** a type of dance music mixed by a disc jockey that features overdubbing with a heavy repetitive drumbeat and repeated electronic melody lines — **house·ful** \ˈhau̇s-ˌfu̇l\ *n* — **house·less** \ˈhau̇-sləs\ *adj* — **house·less·ness** *n* — **on the house :** without charge : FREE

[2]**house** \ˈhau̇z\ *vb* **housed; hous·ing** *vt* (bef. 12c) **1 a :** to provide with living quarters or shelter **b :** to store in a house **2 :** to encase, enclose, or shelter as if by putting in a house **3 :** to serve as a shelter or container for : CONTAIN ⟨buildings that ~ government offices⟩ ~ *vi* : to take shelter : LODGE

house arrest *n* (1848) : confinement often under guard to one's house or quarters instead of in prison

house·boat \ˈhau̇s-ˌbōt\ *n* (1790) : a boat fitted for use as a dwelling; *esp* : a pleasure craft with a broad beam, a usu. shallow draft, and a large superstructure resembling a house — **house·boat·er** \-ˌbō-tər\ *n*

house·bound \ˈhau̇s-ˌbau̇nd\ *adj* (1878) : confined to the house

house·boy \-ˌbȯi\ *n* (ca. 1898) : HOUSEMAN

house·break \-ˌbrāk\ *vt* **-broke** \-ˌbrōk\; **-bro·ken** \-ˌbrō-kən\; **-break·ing** [back-formation fr. *housebroken*] (1938) **1 :** to make housebroken **2 a :** to teach acceptable social manners to **b :** TAME, SUBDUE

house·break·ing \ˈhau̇s-ˌbrā-kiŋ\ *n* (1617) : an act of breaking open and entering the dwelling house of another with a felonious purpose — **house·break·er** \-ˌbrā-kər\ *n*

house·bro·ken \-ˌbrō-kən\ *adj* (1900) **1 :** trained to excretory habits acceptable in indoor living — used of a household pet **2 :** made tractable or polite

house call *n* (1960) : a visit (as by a doctor or a repair person) to a home to provide a requested service

house·carl \-ˌkär(-ə)l\ *n* [OE *hūscarl,* fr. ON *hūskarl,* fr. *hūs* house + *karl* man; akin to OE *ceorl* churl] (bef. 12c) : a member of the bodyguard of a Danish or early English king or noble

house cat *n* (1607) : CAT 1a

house·clean \ˈhau̇s-ˌklēn\ *vb* [back-formation fr. *housecleaning*] *vi* (1863) **1 :** to clean a house and its furniture **2 :** to get rid of unwanted or undesirable items or people ~ *vt* **1 :** to clean the surfaces and furnishings of **2 :** to improve or reform by ridding of undesirable people or practices — **house·clean·ing** *n*

house·coat \ˈhau̇s-ˌkōt\ *n* (1913) : a woman's often long-skirted informal garment for wear around the house

house cricket *n* (1774) : a widely distributed cricket (*Acheta domesticus*) usu. living in or about dwellings

house detective *n* (1898) : a person who is employed (as by a hotel) to prevent disorderly or improper conduct of patrons

house·dress \ˈhau̇s-ˌdres\ *n* (1893) : a dress with simple lines that is suitable for housework and is made usu. of a washable fabric

house–dust mite *n* (1967) : either of two widely distributed mites (*Dermatophagoides farinae* and *D. pteronyssinus*) that commonly occur in house dust and often induce allergic responses esp. in children

house·fa·ther \-ˌfä-t͟hər\ *n* (1884) : a man in charge of a dormitory, hall, or hostel

house finch *n* (1869) : a small finch (*Carpodacus mexicanus*) that has a male with a red head, breast, and rump and that is native to Mexico and the western U.S. and has been introduced in the eastern U.S.

house·fly \ˈhau̇s-ˌflī\ *n* (15c) : a cosmopolitan dipteran fly (*Musca domestica*) that is often about human habitations and may act as a mechanical vector of diseases (as typhoid fever); *also* : any of various flies of similar appearance or habitat

house·front \-ˌfrənt\ *n* (1838) : the facade of a house

house girl *n* (1835) : HOUSEMAID

house·guest \ˈhau̇s-ˌgest\ *n* (1917) : GUEST 1a

[1]**house·hold** \ˈhau̇s-ˌhōld, ˈhau̇-ˌsōld\ *n* (14c) : those who dwell under the same roof and compose a family; *also* : a social unit composed of those living together in the same dwelling

[2]**household** *adj* (14c) **1 :** of or relating to a household : DOMESTIC ⟨cooking and other ~ arts⟩ **2 :** FAMILIAR, COMMON ⟨a ~ name⟩

house·hold·er \ˈhau̇s-ˌhōl-dər, ˈhau̇-ˌsōl-\ *n* (14c) : a person who occupies a house or tenement alone or as the head of a household

household troops *n pl* (1711) : troops appointed to attend and guard a sovereign or the residence of a sovereign

house·hus·band \ˈhau̇s-ˌhəz-bənd\ *n* (1955) : a husband who does housekeeping usu. while his wife earns the family income

house·keep \ˈhau̇s-ˌkēp\ *vi* **-kept** \-ˌkept\; **-keep·ing** [back-formation fr. *housekeeper*] (1842) : to perform the routine duties (as cooking and cleaning) of managing a house

house·keep·er \-ˌkē-pər\ *n* (1607) **1 :** one employed to manage the domestic duties involved in maintaining a house **2 :** HOUSEWIFE 1
housekeeping *n* (1550) **1 :** the management of a house and home affairs **2 :** the care and management of property and the provision of equipment and services (as for an industrial organization) **3 :** the routine tasks that must be done in order for a system to function or to function efficiently
[1]**hou·sel** \ˈhau̇-zəl\ *n* [ME, fr. OE *hūsel* sacrifice, Eucharist; akin to Goth *hunsl* sacrifice] (bef. 12c) *archaic* **:** the Eucharist or the act of administering or receiving it
[2]**housel** *vt* (bef. 12c) *archaic* **:** to administer communion to
house·leek \ˈhau̇s-ˌlēk\ *n* (14c) **:** a pink-flowered thick-leaved European plant (*Sempervivum tectorum*) of the orpine family that tends to form clusters of rosettes and is often grown in rock gardens; *broadly* **:** SEMPERVIVUM
house·lights \ˈhau̇s-ˌlīts\ *n pl* (1920) **:** the lights that illuminate the auditorium of a theater
house·maid \ˈhau̇s-ˌmād\ *n* (ca. 1694) **:** a girl or woman who is a servant employed to do housework
housemaid's knee *n* [fr. its occurrence among women who work a great deal on their knees] (1831) **:** a swelling over the knee due to an enlargement of the bursa in the front of the patella
house·man \ˈhau̇s-mən, -ˌman\ *n* (1920) **:** a person who performs general work about a house or hotel
house·mas·ter \-ˌmas-tər\ *n* (1884) **:** a master in charge of a house in a boy's boarding school
house·mate \ˈhau̇s-ˌmāt\ *n* (ca. 1810) **:** a person who lives in the same house with another
house·moth·er \ˈhau̇s-ˌmə-t͟hər\ *n* (1882) **:** a woman acting as hostess, chaperone, and often housekeeper in a group residence
house mouse *n* (1577) **:** a common nearly cosmopolitan grayish-brown mouse (*Mus musculus*) that usu. lives and breeds about buildings, may act as a vector of diseases, and is an important laboratory animal
house of assembly (1653) **:** a legislative body or the lower house of a legislature (as in various British colonies, protectorates, and countries of the Commonwealth of Nations)
House of Burgesses (1658) **:** the colonial representative assembly of Virginia
house of cards (1645) **:** a structure, situation, or institution that is insubstantial, shaky, or in constant danger of collapse
House of Commons (1621) **:** the lower house of the British and Canadian parliaments
house of correction (ca. 1576) **:** a penal institution for persons convicted of a minor offense and considered capable of reformation
house of delegates (1783) **:** HOUSE 6a; *esp* **:** the lower house of the state legislature in Maryland, Virginia, and West Virginia
House of Lords (1643) **:** the upper house of the British Parliament composed of the lords temporal and spiritual
house of representatives (1716) **:** the lower house of a legislative body (as the U.S. Congress)
house of studies (1929) **:** an educational institution serving scholars of a religious order — called also *house of study*
house organ *n* (1907) **:** a periodical distributed by a business concern among its employees, sales personnel, or customers
house·paint·er \ˈhau̇s-ˌpān-tər\ *n* (1688) **:** one whose business or occupation is painting houses
house·par·ent \-ˌper-ənt\ *n* (1944) **:** an adult in charge of a dormitory, hall, hostel, or group residence
house party *n* (1876) **:** a party lasting over one or more nights at a residence (as a home or fraternity house)
house·per·son \ˈhau̇s-ˌpər-sᵊn\ *n* (1974) **:** a person who does housekeeping
house·plant \ˈhau̇s-ˌplant\ *n* (1871) **:** a plant grown or kept indoors
house–proud \ˈhau̇s-ˌprau̇d\ *adj* (1849) *chiefly Brit* **:** proud of one's house or housekeeping
hous·er \ˈhau̇-zər\ *n* (1940) **:** one that promotes or administers housing projects
house–rais·ing \ˈhau̇s-ˌrā-ziŋ\ *n* (1704) **:** the joint erection of a house or its framework by a gathering of neighbors
house·room \-ˌrüm, -ˌru̇m\ *n* (1582) **:** space for accommodation in or as if in a house ⟨given ~ by a family all too eager to have a celebrity in their midst —Walter Kerr⟩
house rule *n* (1947) **:** a rule (as in a game) that applies only among a certain group or in a certain place
house seat *n* (1948) **:** a theater seat reserved by the management for a special guest
house sitter *n* (1966) **:** a person who occupies a dwelling to provide security and maintenance while the tenant is away — **house–sit** \ˈhau̇(s)-ˌsit\ *vi* — **house–sit·ting** \-ˌsi-tiŋ\ *n*
house sparrow *n* (1674) **:** a sparrow (*Passer domesticus*) native to Eurasia that has been introduced worldwide and is found esp. in urban and agricultural areas — called also *English sparrow*
house–to–house \ˌhau̇s-tə-ˈhau̇s\ *adj* (1859) **:** going or done by going from one building to the next ⟨~ fighting⟩
house·top \ˈhau̇s-ˌtäp\ *n* (1526) **:** ROOF; *esp* **:** the level surface of a flat roof — **from the housetops :** for all to hear **:** OPENLY ⟨shouting their grievances *from the housetops*⟩
house trailer *n* (1937) **:** MOBILE HOME
house–train \ˈhau̇s-ˌtrān\ *vt* (1924) *chiefly Brit* **:** HOUSEBREAK
house·wares \ˈhau̇s-ˌwerz\ *n pl* (1898) **:** furnishings for a house; *esp* **:** small articles of household equipment (as cooking utensils)
house·warm·ing \ˈhau̇s-ˌwȯr-miŋ\ *n* (1577) **:** a party to celebrate the taking possession of a house or premises
house·wife \ˈhau̇s-ˌwīf; *esp 2 & in early poetry* ˈhə-zəf *or* -səf\ *n, pl* **house·wives** \ˈhau̇s-ˌwīvz *also* ˈhau̇z-ˌwīvz; ˈhə-zəfs, -zəvz, -səfs, -səvz\ (13c) **1 :** a married woman in charge of a household **2 :** a pocket-size container for small articles (as thread) — **house·wife·li·ness** \-lē-nəs\ *n* — **house·wife·ly** \-lē\ *adj* — **house·wif·ery** \-ˌwī-f(ə-)rē; *Brit* -(ˌ)wi-f(ə-)rē *also* ˈhə-zə-frē\ *n* — **house·wif·ey** \ˈhau̇s-ˌwī-fē\ *adj*
house·work \ˈhau̇s-ˌwərk\ *n* (1835) **:** the work of housekeeping
[1]**housing** *n* (14c) **1 a :** SHELTER, LODGING **b :** dwellings provided for people **2 a :** a niche for a sculpture **b :** the space taken out of a structural member (as a timber) to admit the insertion of part of another **3 :** something that covers or protects: as **a :** a case or enclosure (as for a mechanical part or an instrument) **b :** a casing (as an enclosed bearing) in which a shaft revolves **c :** a support (as a frame) for mechanical parts
[2]**housing** *n* [ME, fr. *house* housing (fr. AF *huce, houce,* of Gmc origin) + *-ing;* akin to MHG *hulft* covering] (15c) **:** CAPARISON 1
housing development *n* (1951) **:** a group of individual dwellings or apartment houses typically of similar design that are usu. built and sold or leased by one management
housing estate *n* (1920) *Brit* **:** HOUSING DEVELOPMENT
housing project *n* (ca. 1937) **:** a publicly supported and administered housing development planned usu. for low-income families
Hou·yhn·hnm \ˈhwi-nəm, hü-ˈi-nəm\ *n* (1726) **:** a member of a race of horses endowed with reason in Swift's *Gulliver's Travels*
HOV *abbr* high-occupancy vehicle
hove *past and past part of* HEAVE
hov·el \ˈhə-vəl, ˈhä-\ *n* [ME] (15c) **1 :** an open shed or shelter **2 :** TABERNACLE **3 :** a small, wretched, and often dirty house **:** HUT
hov·er \ˈhə-vər, ˈhä-\ *vi* **hov·ered; hov·er·ing** \-v(ə-)riŋ\ [ME *hoveren,* freq. of *hoven* to hover] (15c) **1 a :** to hang fluttering in the air or on the wing **b :** to remain suspended over a place or object **2 a :** to move to and fro near a place **:** fluctuate around a given point ⟨unemployment *~ed* around 10 percent⟩ **b :** to be in a state of uncertainty, irresolution, or suspense — **hover** *n* — **hov·er·er** \-vər-ər\ *n*
hov·er·craft \-vər-ˌkraft\ *n* (1959) **:** a vehicle that is supported above the surface of land or water by a cushion of air produced by downwardly directed fans
hov·er·fly \ˈhə-vər-ˌflī, ˈhä-\ *n* (1881) **:** any of a family (Syrphidae) of dipteran flies that are noted for frequenting flowers and hovering at one place in the air and include some whose larvae prey on plant lice — called also *syrphid fly*
[1]**how** \ˈhau̇\ *adv* [ME, fr. OE *hū;* akin to OHG *hwuo* how, OE *hwā* who — more at WHO] (bef. 12c) **1 a :** in what manner or way **b :** for what reason **:** WHY **c :** with what meaning **:** to what effect **d :** by what name or title **2 :** to what degree or extent **3 :** in what state or condition ⟨~ are you⟩ **4 :** at what price ⟨~ a score of ewes now —Shak.⟩ — **how about :** what do you say to or think of ⟨*how about* it, are you going?⟩ — **how come :** how does it happen that **:** WHY
[2]**how** *conj* (bef. 12c) **1 a :** the way or manner in which ⟨remember ~ they fought⟩; *also* **:** the state or condition in which **b :** THAT ⟨told them ~ he had a situation —Charles Dickens⟩ **2 :** HOWEVER, AS ⟨a reader can shift his attention ~ he likes —William Empson⟩
[3]**how** *n* (1533) **1 :** a question about manner or method **2 :** MANNER, METHOD
[1]**how·be·it** \hau̇-ˈbē-ət\ *conj* (14c) **:** ALTHOUGH
[2]**howbeit** *adv* (15c) **:** NEVERTHELESS
how·dah \ˈhau̇-də\ *n* [Hindi & Urdu *hauda,* fr. Ar *hawdaj*] (1774) **:** a seat or covered pavilion on the back of an elephant or camel

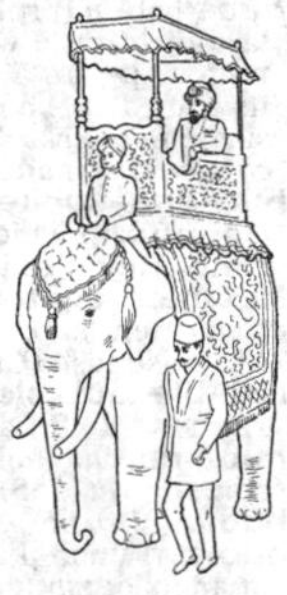
howdah

how·dy \ˈhau̇-dē\ *interj* [alter. of *how do ye*] (1712) — used to express greeting — **howdy** *vb*
howe \ˈhau̇, ˈhō\ *n* [ME (northern) *holl* hollow place, fr. OE *hol,* fr. *hol,* adj., hollow — more at HOLE] (bef. 12c) *Scot* **:** HOLLOW, VALLEY
[1]**how·ev·er** \hau̇-ˈe-vər\ *conj* (14c) **1 :** in whatever manner or way that ⟨will help ~ I can⟩ **2** *archaic* **:** ALTHOUGH
[2]**however** *adv* (14c) **1 a :** in whatever manner or way ⟨shall serve you, sir, truly, ~ else —Shak.⟩ **b :** to whatever degree or extent ⟨has done this for ~ many thousands of years —Emma Hawkridge⟩ **2 :** in spite of that **:** on the other hand ⟨still seems possible, ~, that conditions will improve⟩ ⟨would like to go; ~, I think I'd better not⟩ **3 :** how in the world ⟨~ did you manage to do it⟩
howff *or* **howf** \ˈhau̇f, ˈhōf\ *n* [D *hof* enclosure; akin to OE *hof* enclosure, and perh. to *hufil* hill] (1711) *Scot* **:** HAUNT, RESORT
how·it·zer \ˈhau̇-ət-sər\ *n* [D *houwitser,* ultim. fr. Czech *houfnice* ballista] (1695) **:** a short cannon used to fire projectiles at medium muzzle velocities and with relatively high trajectories
howl \ˈhau̇(-ə)l\ *vb* [ME *houlen;* akin to MHG *hiulen* to howl] *vi* (14c) **1 :** to emit a loud sustained doleful sound characteristic of members of the dog family **2 :** to cry out loudly and without restraint under strong impulse (as pain, grief, or amusement) **3 :** to go on a spree or rampage ~ *vt* **1 :** to utter with unrestrained outcry **2 :** to drown out or cause to fail by adverse outcry — used esp. with *down* — **howl** *n*
howl·er \ˈhau̇-lər\ *n* (1800) **1 a :** HOWLER MONKEY **b :** one that howls **2 :** a humorous and ridiculous blunder
howler monkey *n* (1932) **:** any of a genus (*Alouatta*) of So. and Central American monkeys that have a long prehensile tail and enlargement of the hyoid and laryngeal apparatus enabling them to make loud howling noises
howl·ing \ˈhau̇-liŋ\ *adj* (1599) **1 :** producing or marked by a sound resembling a howl ⟨a ~ storm⟩ **2 :** DESOLATE, WILD ⟨a ~ wilderness⟩ **3 :** very great **:** PRONOUNCED ⟨a ~ success⟩ — **howl·ing·ly** *adv*
how·so·ev·er \ˌhau̇-sə-ˈwe-vər, -sō-ˈe-\ *adv* (14c) **1 :** in whatever manner **2 :** to whatever degree or extent
[1]**how–to** \ˈhau̇-ˈtü\ *adj* (1926) **:** giving practical instruction and advice (as on a craft) ⟨~ books on all sorts of hobbies —Harry Milt⟩
[2]**how–to** *n* (1954) **:** a practical method or instruction ⟨the *~s* of balancing a checkbook⟩; *also* **:** something (as a book) that provides such instruction
[1]**hoy** \ˈhȯi\ *interj* [ME] (14c) — used in attracting attention or in driving animals
[2]**hoy** *n* [ME, fr. MD *hoei*] (15c) **1 :** a small usu. sloop-rigged coasting ship **2 :** a heavy barge for bulky cargo

\ə\ **a**but \ᵊ\ kitten, F table \ər\ f**ur**ther \a\ **a**sh \ā\ **a**ce \ä\ m**o**p, m**a**r
\au̇\ **ou**t \ch\ **ch**in \e\ b**e**t \ē\ **ea**sy \g\ **g**o \i\ h**i**t \ī\ **i**ce \j\ **j**ob
\ŋ\ si**ng** \ō\ g**o** \ȯ\ l**aw** \ȯi\ b**oy** \th\ **th**in \t͟h\ **th**e \ü\ l**oo**t \u̇\ f**oo**t
\y\ **y**et \zh\ vi**si**on, bei**ge** \k, ⁿ, œ, ue, ʸ\ *see* Guide to Pronunciation

hoya \ˈhȯi-ə\ *n* [NL, fr. Thomas *Hoy* †1821 Eng. gardener] (1851) : any of a genus (*Hoya*) of climbing Asian and Australian evergreen shrubs of the milkweed family
hoy·den \ˈhȯi-dᵊn\ *n* [perh. fr. obs D *heiden* country lout, fr. MD, heathen; akin to OE *hǣthen* heathen] (1676) : a girl or woman of saucy, boisterous, or carefree behavior — **hoy·den·ish** \-ish\ *adj*
hoyle \ˈhȯi(-ə)l\ *n, often cap* [Edmond *Hoyle* †1769 Eng. writer on games] (1926) : an encyclopedia of the rules of indoor games and esp. card games
hp *abbr* horsepower
HP *abbr* **1** half play **2** high pressure
HPA *abbr* high-powered amplifier
HPF *abbr* **1** highest possible frequency **2** high power field
HPLC *abbr* high-performance liquid chromatography
HPV *abbr* **1** human papillomavirus **2** human-powered vehicle
HQ *abbr* headquarters
hr *abbr* **1** here **2** hour
HR *abbr* **1** home run **2** House of Representatives **3** House resolution **4** human resources
H Res *abbr* House resolution
HRH *abbr* Her Royal Highness; His Royal Highness
HRT *abbr* hormone replacement therapy
hryv·nia \ˈ(h)riv-nē-ə\ *also* **hryv·na** \ˈ(h)riv-nə\ *n, pl* **hryvnia** *or* **hryvnias** *also* **hryvna** *or* **hryvnas** [Ukrainian *gryvnya* 3-kopeck coin of pre-independence Ukraine, fr. ORuss *grivĭna* necklace, ring, weight, coin, fr. *griva* mane] (1991) — see MONEY table
hrzn *abbr* horizon
hs *abbr* [L *hora somni*] at bedtime
Hs *symbol* hassium
HS *abbr* high school
Hsia \shē-ˈä\ *n* [Chin (Beijing) *Xià*] (ca. 1909) : the legendary first dynasty of Chinese history traditionally dated from about 2200–1766 B.C.
HST *abbr* **1** Hawaiian standard time **2** hypersonic transport
ht *abbr* height
HT *abbr* **1** halftone **2** hardtop **3** Hawaii time **4** high-tension **5** high tide
HTLV \ˌāch-(ˌ)tē-(ˌ)el-ˈvē\ *n* [*h*uman *T*-cell *l*ymphotropic *v*irus] (1980) : any of several retroviruses — often used with a number or Roman numeral to indicate the type
HTLV–III \-(ˌ)vē-ˈthrē\ *n* (1984) : HIV-1
HTML \ˌāch-(ˌ)tē-(ˌ)em-ˈel\ *n* [*h*yper*t*ext *m*arkup *l*anguage] (1992) : a markup language that is used to create documents on the World Wide Web incorporating text, graphics, sound, video, and hyperlinks
http *abbr* hypertext transfer protocol; hypertext transport protocol
HUAC *abbr* House Un-American Activities Committee
hua·ra·che \wə-ˈrä-chē, hə-\ *n* [MexSp, fr. Tarascan *kʷarách*] (1892) : a low-heeled sandal having an upper made of interwoven leather strips
hub \ˈhəb\ *n* [prob. alter. of [2]*hob*] (1649) **1** : the central part of a circular object (as a wheel or propeller) **2 a** : a center of activity : FOCAL POINT **b** : an airport or city through which an airline routes most of its traffic **c** : a central device that connects multiple computers on a single network **3** : a steel punch from which a working die for a coin or medal is made
hub–and–spoke *adj* (1980) : being or relating to a system of routing air traffic in which a major airport serves as a central point for coordinating flights to and from other airports
Hub·bard squash \ˈhə-bərd-\ *n* [prob. fr. the name *Hubbard*] (1868) : an often large variably green squash of any of several cultivars of a winter squash (*Cucurbita maxima*) — called also *Hubbard*
hub·ble–bub·ble \ˈhə-bəl-ˌbə-bəl\ *n* [redupl. of *bubble*] (1634) **1** : WATER PIPE 2 **2** : a flurry of sound or activity : COMMOTION
hub·bub \ˈhə-ˌbəb\ *n* [perh. of Ir origin; akin to ScGael *ub ub*, interj. of contempt] (1555) **1** : NOISE, UPROAR **2** : CONFUSION, TURMOIL
hub·by \ˈhə-bē\ *n, pl* **hubbies** [by alter.] (1688) : HUSBAND
hub·cap \ˈhəb-ˌkap\ *n* (1903) : a removable usu. metal cap over the end of an axle; *esp* : one used on the wheel of a motor vehicle
hu·bris \ˈhyü-brəs\ *n* [Gk *hybris*] (1884) : exaggerated pride or self-confidence — **hu·bris·tic** \hyü-ˈbris-tik\ *adj*
huck \ˈhək\ *n* (1851) : HUCKABACK
huck·a·back \ˈhə-kə-ˌbak\ *n* [origin unknown] (1690) : an absorbent durable fabric of cotton, linen, or both used chiefly for towels
huck·le·ber·ry \ˈhə-kəl-ˌber-ē\ *n* [perh. alter. of *hurtleberry* huckleberry] (1670) **1** : any of a genus (*Gaylussacia*) of American shrubs of the heath family; *also* : the edible dark blue to black usu. acid berry (esp. of *G. baccata*) with 10 nutlets **2** : BLUEBERRY
[1]**huck·ster** \ˈhək-stər\ *n* [ME *hukster*, fr. MD *hokester*, fr. *hoeken* to peddle] (13c) **1** : HAWKER, PEDDLER **2** : one who produces promotional material for commercial clients esp. for radio or television — **huck·ster·ism** \-stə-ˌri-zəm\ *n*
[2]**huckster** *vb* **huck·stered; huck·ster·ing** \-st(ə-)riŋ\ *vi* (1592) : HAGGLE ~ *vt* **1** : to deal in or bargain over **2** : to promote aggressively
HUD *abbr* Department of Housing and Urban Development
[1]**hud·dle** \ˈhə-dᵊl\ *vb* **hud·dled; hud·dling** \ˈhəd-liŋ, ˈhə-dᵊl-iŋ\ [prob. fr. or akin to ME *hoderen* to huddle] *vt* (1579) **1** *Brit* : to arrange carelessly or hurriedly **2 a** : to crowd together **b** : to draw (oneself) together : CROUCH **3** : to wrap closely in (as clothes) ~ *vi* **1 a** : to gather in a close-packed group **b** : to curl up : CROUCH **2 a** : to hold a consultation **b** : to gather in a huddle in football — **hud·dler** \ˈhəd-lər, ˈhə-dᵊl-ər\ *n*
[2]**huddle** *n* (1586) **1** : a close-packed group : BUNCH ⟨~*s* of children⟩ ⟨a ~ of cottages⟩ **2 a** : MEETING, CONFERENCE **b** : a brief gathering of football players away from the line of scrimmage to receive instructions (as from the quarterback) for the next down
Hu·di·bras·tic \ˌhyü-də-ˈbras-tik\ *adj* [irreg. fr. *Hudibras*, satirical poem by Samuel Butler †1680] (1712) **1** : written in humorous octosyllabic couplets **2** : MOCK-HEROIC — **Hudibrastic** *n*
hue \ˈhyü\ *n* [ME *hewe*, fr. OE *hīw*; akin to ON *hȳ* plant down, Goth *hiwi* form] (bef. 12c) **1** : COMPLEXION, ASPECT ⟨political parties of every ~ —Louis Wasserman⟩ **2 a** : COLOR **b** : gradation of color **c** : the attribute of colors that permits them to be classed as red, yellow, green, blue, or an intermediate between any contiguous pair of these colors — compare BRIGHTNESS 2, LIGHTNESS 2, SATURATION 4
hue and cry *n* [*hue* outcry] (15c) **1 a** : a loud outcry formerly used in the pursuit of one who is suspected of a crime **b** : the pursuit of a suspect or a written proclamation for the capture of a suspect **2** : a clamor of alarm or protest **3** : HUBBUB
hued \ˈhyüd\ *adj* (bef. 12c) : COLORED — usu. used in combination ⟨green-*hued*⟩
hue·vos ran·che·ros \ˈwā-vōs-ˌrän-ˈcher-ōs\ *n pl but sing or pl in constr* [MexSp, lit., ranch-style eggs] (1901) : fried or poached eggs served on a tortilla and topped with a usu. tomato-based sauce
[1]**huff** \ˈhəf\ *vb* [imit.] *vi* (1583) **1 a** : to emit puffs (as of breath or steam) **b** : to proceed with labored breathing ⟨~*ed* up to the peak⟩ **2 a** : to make empty threats : BLUSTER **b** : to react or behave indignantly ~ *vt* **1** *archaic* : to treat with contempt **2** : to make angry **3** : to utter with indignation or scorn **4** : to inhale (noxious fumes) through the mouth for the euphoric effect produced by the inhalant
[2]**huff** *n* (1684) : a usu. peevish and transitory spell of anger or resentment ⟨quit in a ~⟩ ***syn*** see OFFENSE
huff·ish \ˈhə-fish\ *adj* (ca. 1755) : ARROGANT, SULKY
huffy \ˈhə-fē\ *adj* **huff·i·er; -est** (1677) **1** : HAUGHTY, ARROGANT **2 a** : roused to indignation : IRRITATED **b** : easily offended : TOUCHY — **huff·i·ly** \ˈhə-fə-lē\ *adv* — **huff·i·ness** \-fē-nəs\ *n*
hug \ˈhəg\ *vt* **hugged; hug·ging** [perh. of Scand origin; akin to ON *hugga* to soothe] (1567) **1** : to press tightly esp. in the arms **2 a** : CONGRATULATE **b** : to hold fast : CHERISH ⟨*hugged* his miseries like a sulky child —John Buchan⟩ **3** : to stay close to ⟨the road ~*s* the river⟩ — **hug** *n* — **hug·ga·ble** \ˈhə-gə-bəl\ *adj* — **hug·ger** *n*
huge \ˈhyüj, ˈyüj\ *adj* **hug·er; hug·est** [ME, fr. OF *ahuge*] (12c) : very large or extensive: as **a** : of great size or area **b** : great in scale or degree ⟨a ~ deficit⟩ **c** : great in scope or character ⟨a dancer of ~ talent⟩ ***syn*** see ENORMOUS — **huge·ly** *adv* — **huge·ness** *n*
huge·ous \ˈhyü-jəs, ˈyü-\ *adj* (1519) : HUGE — **huge·ous·ly** *adv*
[1]**hug·ger–mug·ger** \ˈhə-gər-ˌmə-gər\ *n* [origin unknown] (1529) **1** : SECRECY **2** : CONFUSION, MUDDLE
[2]**hugger–mugger** *adj* (1692) **1** : SECRET **2** : of a confused or disorderly nature : JUMBLED — **hugger–mugger** *adv*
hug–me–tight \ˈhəg-mē-ˌtīt\ *n* (1860) : a woman's short usu. knitted sleeveless close-fitting jacket
Hu·gue·not \ˈhyü-gə-ˌnät\ *n* [MF, alter. of MF dial. (Geneva) *eyguenot*, adherent of a Swiss political movement, fr. G dial. *eidgnosse* confederate] (1565) : a member of the French Reformed communion esp. of the 16th and 17th centuries — **Hu·gue·not·ic** \ˌhyü-gə-ˈnä-tik\ *adj* — **Hu·gue·not·ism** \ˈhyü-gə-ˌnä-ˌti-zəm\ *n*
huh *a grunt articulated as a syllabic* m *or* n *with a voiceless onset, or as the syllable* ˈhə *or* ˈhəⁿ, *often ending in a glottal stop, and uttered with a range of intonations; often read as* ˈhə\ *interj* [imit. of a grunt] (1608) — used to express surprise, disbelief, or confusion, or as an inquiry inviting affirmative reply
Hui·chol \wē-ˈchōl\ *n, pl* **Huichol** *or* **Hui·cho·les** [MexSp] (1900) **1** : a member of an American Indian people of the mountains between Zacatecas and Nayarit, Mexico **2** : the Uto-Aztecan language of the Huichol people — **Huichol** *adj*
hui·sa·che \wē-ˈsä-chē\ *n* [MexSp, fr. Nahuatl *huixachi*, fr. *huitzli* thorn + *ixachi* a great amount, many] (1838) : a widely cultivated thorny shrubby acacia (*Acacia farnesiana*) of the southern U.S. and tropical America with fragrant ball-shaped yellow flowers
hu·la \ˈhü-lə\ *also* **hu·la–hu·la** \ˌhü-lə-ˈhü-lə\ *n* [Hawaiian] (1825) : a sinuous Polynesian dance characterized by rhythmic movement of the hips and mimetic gestures with the hands and often accompanied by chants and rhythmic drumming
Hu·la–Hoop \ˈhü-lə-ˌhüp *also* -ˌhu̇p\ *trademark* — used for a plastic toy hoop that is twirled around the body
[1]**hulk** \ˈhəlk\ *n* [ME *hulke*, fr. OE *hulc*, prob. fr. ML *holcas*, fr. Gk *holkas*, fr. *helkein* to pull — more at SULCUS] (bef. 12c) **1 a** : a heavy clumsy ship **b (1)** : the body of an old ship unfit for service **(2)** : a ship used as a prison — usu. used in pl. ⟨every prisoner sent to the ~*s* —Kenneth Roberts⟩ **c** : an abandoned wreck or shell (as of a building or automobile) **2** : one that is bulky or unwieldy
[2]**hulk** *vi* (ca. 1825) **1** *dial Eng* : to move ponderously **2** : to appear impressively large or massive : LOOM ⟨factories ~*ed* along the river⟩
hulk·ing \ˈhəl-kiŋ\ *adj* (1698) : PONDEROUS, MASSIVE ⟨a ~ wrestler⟩
[1]**hull** \ˈhəl\ *n* [ME, fr. OE *hulu*; akin to OHG *hala* hull, OE *helan* to conceal — more at HELL] (bef. 12c) **1 a** : the outer covering of a fruit or seed **b** : the persistent calyx or involucre that subtends some fruits (as a strawberry) **2 a** : the frame or body of a ship or boat exclusive of masts, yards, sails, and rigging **b** : the main body of a usu. large or heavy craft or vehicle (as an airship or tank) **3** : COVERING, CASING — **hull–less** \ˈhəl-ləs\ *adj*
[2]**hull** *vt* (14c) : to remove the hulls of : SHUCK — **hull·er** *n*
hul·la·ba·loo \ˈhə-lə-bə-ˌlü\ *n, pl* **-loos** [perh. fr. *hallo* + Sc *balloo*, interj. used to hush children] (1762) : DIN; *also* : UPROAR
hull down *adv or adj* (1775) *of a ship* : at such a distance that only the superstructure is visible
hulled corn *n* (1788) : whole grain corn from which the hulls have been removed by soaking or boiling in lye water
hul·lo \(ˌ)hə-ˈlō\ *chiefly Brit var of* HELLO
[1]**hum** \ˈhəm\ *vb* **hummed; hum·ming** [ME *hummen*; akin to MHG *hummen* to hum, MD *hommel* bumblebee] *vi* (14c) **1 a** : to utter a sound like that of the speech sound \m\ prolonged **b** : to make the natural noise of an insect in motion or a similar sound : DRONE **c** : to give forth a low continuous blend of sound **2 a** : to be busily active ⟨the museum *hummed* with visitors⟩ **b** : to run smoothly ⟨the business started to ~⟩ ~ *vt* **1** : to sing with the lips closed and without articulation **2** : to affect or express by humming ⟨*hummed* his displeasure⟩ — **hum** *n* — **hum·ma·ble** \ˈhə-mə-bəl\ *adj*
[2]**hum** *chiefly Brit var of* HEM
[1]**hu·man** \ˈhyü-mən, ˈyü-\ *adj* [ME *humain*, fr. AF, fr. L *humanus*; akin to L *homo* human being — more at HOMAGE] (14c) **1** : of, relating to, or characteristic of humans **2** : consisting of humans **3 a** : having human form or attributes **b** : susceptible to or representative of the sympathies and frailties of human nature ⟨such an inconsistency is very ~ —P. E. More⟩ — **hu·man·ness** \-mən-nəs\ *n*
[2]**human** *n* (ca. 1533) : a bipedal primate mammal (*Homo sapiens*) : MAN; *broadly* : HOMINID — **hu·man·like** \-mən-ˌlīk\ *adj*
human being *n* (1751) : HUMAN
human chorionic gonadotropin *n* (1977) : a glycoprotein hormone similar in structure to luteinizing hormone that is secreted by the pla-

centa during early pregnancy to maintain corpus luteum function and is commonly tested for as an indicator of pregnancy

hu·mane \hyü-ˈmān, yü-\ *adj* [ME *humain*] (1552) **1 :** marked by compassion, sympathy, or consideration for humans or animals **2 :** characterized by or tending to broad humanistic culture : HUMANISTIC ‹~ studies› — **hu·mane·ly** *adv* — **hu·mane·ness** \-ˈmān-nəs\ *n*

human ecology *n* (1907) **1 :** a branch of sociology dealing esp. with the spatial and temporal interrelationships between humans and their economic, social, and political organization **2 :** the ecology of human communities and populations esp. as concerned with preservation of environmental quality (as of air or water) through proper application of conservation and civil engineering practices

human engineering *n* (1920) **1 :** management of humans and their affairs esp. in industry **2 :** ERGONOMICS 1

human factors *n pl but sing in constr* (1964) : ERGONOMICS 1

human growth hormone *n* (1960) : the naturally occurring growth hormone of humans or a genetically engineered form that is used to treat children with growth hormone deficiencies and has been used esp. by athletes to increase muscle mass

human immunodeficiency virus *n* (1986) : HIV

hu·man·ism \ˈhyü-mə-ˌni-zəm, ˈyü-\ *n* (1832) **1 a :** devotion to the humanities : literary culture **b :** the revival of classical letters, individualistic and critical spirit, and emphasis on secular concerns characteristic of the Renaissance **2 :** HUMANITARIANISM **3 :** a doctrine, attitude, or way of life centered on human interests or values; *esp* : a philosophy that usu. rejects supernaturalism and stresses an individual's dignity and worth and capacity for self-realization through reason — **hu·man·ist** \-nist\ *n or adj* — **hu·man·is·tic** \ˌhyü-mə-ˈnis-tik, ˌyü-\ *adj* — **hu·man·is·ti·cal·ly** \-ti-k(ə-)lē\ *adv*

hu·man·i·tar·i·an \hyü-ˌma-nə-ˈter-ē-ən, yü-\ *n* (1844) : a person promoting human welfare and social reform : PHILANTHROPIST — **humanitarian** *adj* — **hu·man·i·tar·i·an·ism** \-ē-ə-ˌni-zəm\ *n*

hu·man·i·ty \hyü-ˈma-nə-tē, yü-\ *n, pl* **-ties** (14c) **1 :** the quality or state of being humane **2 a :** the quality or state of being human **b** *pl* : human attributes or qualities ‹his work has the ripeness of the 18th century, and its rough *humanities* —Pamela H. Johnson› **3** *pl* : the branches of learning (as philosophy, arts, or languages) that investigate human constructs and concerns as opposed to natural processes (as in physics or chemistry) and social relations (as in anthropology or economics) **4 :** the human race : the totality of human beings

hu·man·ize \ˈhyü-mə-ˌnīz, ˈyü-\ *vt* **-ized; -iz·ing** (1603) **1 a :** to represent as human : attribute human qualities to **b :** to adapt to human nature or use **2 :** to make humane — **hu·man·i·za·tion** \ˌhyü-mə-nə-ˈzā-shən, ˌyü-\ *n* — **hu·man·iz·er** *n*

hu·man·kind \ˈhyü-mən-ˌkīnd, ˈyü-\ *n sing but sing or pl in constr* (1594) : the human race

human leukocyte antigen *n* (1978) : any of various proteins that are encoded by genes of the major histocompatibility complex in humans and are found on the surface of many cell types (as white blood cells); *broadly* : HLA 2

hu·man·ly \ˈhyü-mən-lē, ˈyü-\ *adv* (15c) **1 a :** with regard to human needs and emotions ‹provide ~ for those who are not needed in the economy —E. F. Bacon› **b :** with regard to or in keeping with human proneness to error or weakness ‹~ inaccurate› **2 a :** from a human viewpoint ‹~ speaking, the process works . . . like this —Elizabeth Janeway› **b :** within the range of human capacity ‹did everything ~ possible› **c :** by humans ‹~ made›

human nature *n* (1594) : the nature of humans; *esp* : the fundamental dispositions and traits of humans

hu·man·oid \ˈhyü-mə-ˌnȯid, ˈyü-\ *adj* (1918) : having human form or characteristics ‹~ dentition› ‹~ robots› — **humanoid** *n*

human papillomavirus *n* (1963) : any of numerous papillomaviruses (as of the genera *Alphapapillomavirus, Betapapillomavirus,* and *Gammapapillomavirus*) that cause various human papillomas (as genital warts and plantar warts) and include some associated with the production of human cancer — abbr. *HPV*

human relations *n pl but usu sing in constr* (1946) **1 :** a study of human problems arising from organizational and interpersonal relations (as in industry) **2 :** a course, study, or program designed to develop better interpersonal and intergroup adjustments

human resources *n pl* (1961) **1 :** PERSONNEL 1a **2 :** PERSONNEL 2

human rights *n pl* (1766) : rights (as freedom from unlawful imprisonment, torture, and execution) regarded as belonging fundamentally to all persons

human trafficking *n* (1988) : organized criminal activity in which human beings are treated as possessions to be controlled and exploited (as by being forced into prostitution or involuntary labor)

hu·mate \ˈhyü-ˌmāt, ˈyü-\ *n* (1844) : a salt or ester of a humic acid

[1]**hum·ble** \ˈhəm-bəl *also chiefly Southern* ˈəm-\ *adj* **hum·bler** \-b(ə-)lər\; **hum·blest** \-b(ə-)ləst\ [ME, fr. AF, fr. L *humilis* low, humble, fr. *humus* earth; akin to Gk *chthōn* earth, *chamai* on the ground] (13c) **1 :** not proud or haughty : not arrogant or assertive **2 :** reflecting, expressing, or offered in a spirit of deference or submission ‹a ~ apology› **3 a :** ranking low in a hierarchy or scale : INSIGNIFICANT, UNPRETENTIOUS **b :** not costly or luxurious ‹a ~ contraption› — **humble·ness** \-bəl-nəs\ *n* — **hum·bly** \-blē\ *adv*

[2]**humble** *vt* **hum·bled; hum·bling** \-b(ə-)liŋ\ (14c) **1 :** to make humble in spirit or manner **2 :** to destroy the power, independence, or prestige of — **hum·bler** \-b(ə-)lər\ *n* — **hum·bling·ly** \-b(ə-)liŋ-lē\ *adv*

hum·ble–bee \ˈhəm-bəl-ˌbē\ *n* [ME *humbylbee,* fr. *humbyl-* (akin to MD *hommel* bumblebee) + *bee* — more at HUM] (15c) : BUMBLEBEE

humble pie *n* (1830) : a figurative serving of humiliation usu. in the form of a forced submission, apology, or retraction — often used in the phrase *eat humble pie*

[1]**hum·bug** \ˈhəm-ˌbəg\ *n* [origin unknown] (1750) **1 a :** something designed to deceive and mislead **b :** a willfully false, deceptive, or insincere person **2 :** an attitude or spirit of pretense and deception **3 :** NONSENSE, DRIVEL **4** *Brit* : a hard usu. mint-flavored candy ***syn*** see IMPOSTURE — **hum·bug·gery** \-ˌbə-g(ə-)rē\ *n*

[2]**humbug** *vb* **hum·bugged; hum·bug·ging** *vt* (1751) : DECEIVE, HOAX ~ *vi* : to engage in a hoax or deception

hum·ding·er \ˈhəm-ˈdiŋ-ər\ *n* [prob. alter. of *hummer*] (ca. 1904) : a striking or extraordinary person or thing

hum·drum \ˈhəm-ˌdrəm\ *adj* [redupl. of *hum*] (1553) : MONOTONOUS, DULL — **humdrum** *n*

hu·mec·tant \hyü-ˈmek-tənt\ *n* [L *humectant-, humectans,* prp. of *humectare* to moisten, fr. *humectus* moist, fr. *humēre* to be moist — more at HUMOR] (ca. 1867) : a substance that promotes retention of moisture — **humectant** *adj*

hu·mer·al \ˈhyü-mə-rəl\ *adj* (1615) **1 :** of, relating to, or situated in the region of the humerus or shoulder **2 :** of, relating to, or being a body part analogous to the humerus or shoulder — **humeral** *n*

humeral veil *n* (1853) : an oblong vestment worn around the shoulders and over the hands by a priest holding a sacred vessel

hu·mer·us \ˈhyü-mə-rəs\ *n, pl* **hu·meri** \-ˌrī, -ˌrē\ [ME, fr. L *humerus, umerus* upper arm, shoulder; akin to Goth *ams* shoulder, Gk *ōmos*] (15c) : the long bone of the upper arm or forelimb extending from the shoulder to the elbow

hu·mic \ˈhyü-mik, ˈyü-\ *adj* (1842) : of, relating to, or derived at least in part from humus

humic acid *n* (1843) : any of various organic acids obtained from humus

hu·mid \ˈhyü-məd, ˈyü-\ *adj* [F or L; F *humide,* fr. L *humidus,* fr. *humēre*] (15c) : containing or characterized by perceptible moisture esp. to the point of being oppressive ***syn*** see WET — **hu·mid·ly** *adv*

hu·mid·i·fi·er \hyü-ˈmid-ə-ˌfī(-ə)r, yü-\ *n* (1884) : a device for supplying or maintaining humidity

hu·mid·i·fy \-ˌfī\ *vt* **-fied; -fy·ing** (1885) : to make humid — **hu·mid·i·fi·ca·tion** \-ˌmi-də-fə-ˈkā-shən\ *n*

hu·mid·i·stat \hyü-ˈmi-də-ˌstat, yü-\ *n* (ca. 1904) : an instrument for regulating or maintaining the degree of humidity

hu·mid·i·ty \hyü-ˈmi-də-tē, yü-\ *n, pl* **-ties** (15c) : a moderate degree of wetness esp. of the atmosphere — compare RELATIVE HUMIDITY

hu·mi·dor \ˈhyü-mə-ˌdȯr, ˈyü-\ *n* [*humid* + *-or* (as in *cuspidor*)] (1903) : a case or enclosure (as for storing cigars) in which the air is kept properly humidified

hu·mi·fi·ca·tion \ˌhyü-mə-fə-ˈkā-shən, ˌyü-\ *n* (1897) : formation of or conversion into humus

hu·mi·fied \ˈhyü-mə-ˌfīd, ˈyü-\ *adj* (1906) : converted into humus

hu·mil·i·ate \hyü-ˈmi-lē-ˌāt, yü-\ *vt* **-at·ed; -at·ing** [LL *humiliatus,* pp. of *humiliare,* fr. L *humilis* low — more at HUMBLE] (ca. 1534) : to reduce to a lower position in one's own eyes or others' eyes : MORTIFY — **hu·mil·i·a·tion** \-ˌmi-lē-ˈā-shən\ *n*

humiliating *adj* (1757) : extremely destructive to one's self-respect or dignity : HUMBLING — **hu·mil·i·at·ing·ly** \-tiŋ-lē\ *adv*

hu·mil·i·ty \hyü-ˈmi-lə-tē, yü-\ *n* (14c) : the quality or state of being humble

hum·mer \ˈhə-mər\ *n* (1605) **1 :** one that hums **2 :** HUMMINGBIRD **3 :** HUMDINGER **4 :** FASTBALL

hum·ming·bird \ˈhə-miŋ-ˌbərd\ *n* (1637) : any of a family (Trochilidae) of tiny brightly colored nonpasserine American birds related to the swifts that have a very slender bill and an extensible tongue for sipping nectar and that usu. hover rather than perch when feeding

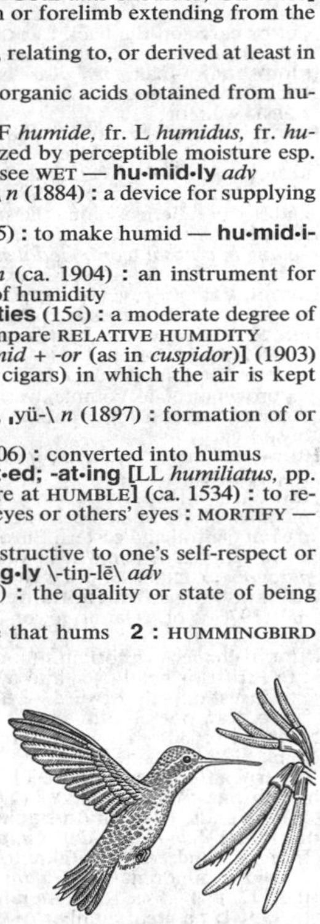

hummingbird

hum·mock \ˈhə-mək\ *n* [alter. of [2]*hammock*] (1555) **1 :** a rounded knoll or hillock **2 :** a ridge of ice **3 :** [2]HAMMOCK 2 — **hummock** *vb* — **hum·mocky** \-mə-kē\ *adj*

hum·mus \ˈhə-məs, ˈhü-\ *n* [Ar *ḥummuṣ* chickpeas] (1949) : a paste of pureed chickpeas usu. mixed with sesame oil or sesame paste and eaten as a dip or sandwich spread

hu·mon·gous \hyü-ˈməŋ-gəs, yü-, -ˈmäŋ-\ *also* **hu·mun·gous** \-ˈməŋ-gəs\ *adj* [perh. alter. of *huge* + *monstrous*] (ca. 1967) : extremely large : HUGE ‹a ~ building› ‹~ amounts of money›

[1]**hu·mor** \ˈhyü-mər, ˈyü-\ *n* [ME *humour,* fr. AF *umor, umour,* fr. ML & L; ML *humor,* fr. L *humor, umor* moisture; akin to ON *vǫkr* damp, L *humēre* to be moist, and perh. to Gk *hygros* wet] (14c) **1 a :** a normal functioning bodily semifluid or fluid (as the blood or lymph) **b :** a secretion (as a hormone) that is an excitant of activity **2 a** *in medieval physiology* : a fluid or juice of an animal or plant; *specif* : one of the four fluids entering into the constitution of the body and determining by their relative proportions a person's health and temperament **b :** characteristic or habitual disposition or bent : TEMPERAMENT ‹of cheerful ~› **c :** an often temporary state of mind imposed esp. by circumstances ‹was in no ~ to listen› **d :** a sudden, unpredictable, or unreasoning inclination : WHIM **3 a :** that quality which appeals to a sense of the ludicrous or absurdly incongruous **b :** the mental faculty of discovering, expressing, or appreciating the ludicrous or absurdly incongruous **c :** something that is or is designed to be comical or amusing ***syn*** see WIT — **out of humor :** out of sorts

[2]**humor** *vt* **hu·mored; hu·mor·ing** \ˈhyüm-riŋ, ˈyüm-, ˈhyü-mə-, ˈyü-\ (1588) **1 :** to soothe or content by indulgence **2 :** to adapt oneself to ***syn*** see INDULGE

hu·mor·al \ˈhyü-mə-rəl, ˈyü-\ *adj* (15c) **1 :** of, relating to, proceeding from, or involving a bodily humor (as a hormone) **2 :** relating to or being the part of immunity or the immune response that involves antibodies secreted by B cells and circulating in bodily fluids

hu·mor·esque \ˌhyü-mə-ˈresk, ˌyü-\ *n* [G *Humoreske,* fr. *Humor,* fr. ML] (1889) : a typically whimsical or fanciful musical composition

hu·mor·ist \ˈhyü-mə-rist, ˈyü-\ *n* (1589) **1** *archaic* : a person subject to whims **2 :** a person specializing in or noted for humor

hu·mor·is·tic \ˌhyü-mə-ˈris-tik, ˌyü-\ *adj* (1818) : HUMOROUS

hu·mor·less \ˈhyü-mər-ləs\ *adj* (ca. 1847) **1 :** lacking a sense of humor **2 :** lacking humorous characteristics — **hu·mor·less·ly** \-lē\ *adv* — **hu·mor·less·ness** *n*

\ə\ **abut** \ᵊ\ **kitten**, F **table** \ər\ **further** \a\ **ash** \ā\ **ace** \ä\ **mop, mar** \au̇\ **out** \ch\ **chin** \e\ **bet** \ē\ **easy** \g\ **go** \i\ **hit** \ī\ **ice** \j\ **job** \ŋ\ **sing** \ō\ **go** \ȯ\ **law** \ȯi\ **boy** \th\ **thin** \t͟h\ **the** \ü\ **loot** \u̇\ **foot** \y\ **yet** \zh\ **vision, beige** \k̟, ⁿ, œ, ue, ʸ\ *see* Guide to Pronunciation

hu·mor·ous \ˈhyüm-rəs, ˈyüm-, ˈhyü-mə-, ˈyü-\ *adj* (15c) **1** *obs* : HUMID **2 a** : full of or characterized by humor : FUNNY **b** : indicating or expressive of a sense of humor ***syn*** see WITTY — **hu·mor·ous·ly** *adv* — **hu·mor·ous·ness** *n*

hu·mour *chiefly Brit var of* HUMOR

1**hump** \ˈhəmp\ *n* [akin to MLG *hump* bump, D *homp* lump, chunk, Fris *homp, himp*] (1681) **1** : a rounded protuberance: as **a** : HUMPBACK 1 **b** : a fleshy protuberance on the back of an animal (as a camel, bison, or whale) **c** (1) : MOUND, HUMMOCK (2) : MOUNTAIN, RANGE ⟨the Himalayan ~⟩ **2** *Brit* : a fit of depression or sulking **3** : a difficult, trying, or critical phase or obstacle — often used in the phrase *over the hump* — **humped** *adj*

2**hump** *vt* (ca. 1785) **1** *often vulgar* : to copulate with **2** : to exert (oneself) vigorously **3** : to make humpbacked : HUNCH **4** *chiefly Brit* : to put or carry on the back : LUG; *also* : TRANSPORT ~ *vi* **1** : to exert oneself : HUSTLE **2** : to move swiftly : RACE

hump·back \-ˌbak, *for 1 also* -ˈbak\ *n* (1697) **1** : a humped or crooked back; *also* : KYPHOSIS **2** : HUNCHBACK 1 **3** : HUMPBACK WHALE **4** : PINK SALMON

hump·backed \-ˈbakt\ *adj* (1681) **1** : having a humped back **2** : convexly curved ⟨a ~ bridge⟩

humpback whale *n* (1725) : a large baleen whale (*Megaptera novaeangliae*) that is black above and white below and has very long flippers, and fleshy tubercles along the snout

1**humph** *a snort articulated as a syllabic* m *or* n *with a voiceless onset and ending in a nasal* h *or a glottal stop; often read as* ˈhəm(p)f\ *interj* [imit. of a grunt] (1803) — used to express doubt or contempt

2**humph** \ˈhəm(p)f\ *vi* (1814) : to utter a humph ~ *vt* : to utter (as a remark) in a tone suggestive of a humph

humpy \ˈhəm-pē\ *adj* **hump·i·er; -est** (1708) **1** : full of humps **2** : covered with humps

hu·mus \ˈhyü-məs, ˈyü-\ *n* [NL, fr. L, earth — more at HUMBLE] (1796) : a brown or black complex variable material resulting from partial decomposition of plant or animal matter and forming the organic portion of soil

Hum·vee \ˌhəm-ˈvē, ˈhəm-ˌ\ *trademark* — used for a military automotive vehicle

Hun \ˈhən\ *n* [ME, fr. OE *Hunas*, pl., fr. LL *Hunni*, pl.] (bef. 12c) **1** : a member of a nomadic central Asian people gaining control of a large part of central and eastern Europe under Attila about A.D. 450 **2 a** *often not cap* : a person who is wantonly destructive : VANDAL **b** *usu disparaging* : GERMAN; *esp* : a German soldier

Hu·nan \ˈhü-ˈnän\ *or* **Hu·na·nese** \ˌhü-nə-ˈnēz, -ˈnēs\ *adj* [*Hunan*, China] (1970) : of, relating to, or being a hot and spicy style of Chinese cooking

1**hunch** \ˈhənch\ *vb* [origin unknown] *vt* (1581) **1** : JOSTLE, SHOVE **2** : to thrust or bend over into a humped or crooked position ~ *vi* **1** : to thrust oneself forward **2 a** : to assume a bent or crooked posture **b** : to draw oneself into a ball : curl up **c** : HUDDLE, SQUAT

2**hunch** *n* (1630) **1** : an act or instance of hunching : PUSH **2 a** : a thick piece : LUMP **b** : HUMP **3** : a strong intuitive feeling concerning esp. a future event or result

hunch·back \ˈhənch-ˌbak\ *n* (1712) **1** : a person with a humpback **2** : HUMPBACK 1 — **hunch·backed** \-ˈbakt\ *adj*

hun·dred \ˈhən-drəd, -dərd\ *n, pl* **hundreds** *or* **hundred** [ME, fr. OE, fr. *hund* hundred + *-red* (akin to Goth *rathjo* account, number); akin to L *centum* hundred, Gk *hekaton*, OE *tien* ten — more at TEN, REASON] (bef. 12c) **1** — see NUMBER table **2** *hundreds pl* **a** : the numbers 100 to 999 **b** : a great number ⟨~*s* of times⟩ **3** : a 100-dollar bill **4** : a subdivision of some English and American counties — **hundred** *adj* — **hun·dred·fold** \-ˌfōld\ *adj or adv* — **hun·dredth** \-drədth, -drətth\ *adj or n*

hun·dred–per·cent·er \-pər-ˈsen-tər\ *n* [*hundred-percent (American)*] (1921) : a thoroughgoing nationalist — **hun·dred–per·cent·ism** \-ˈsen-ˌti-zəm\ *n*

hundreds place *n* (1937) : the place three to the left of the decimal point in a number expressed in the Arabic system of notation

hun·dred·weight \ˈhən-drəd-ˌwāt, -dərd-ˌwāt\ *n, pl* **hundredweight** *or* **hundredweights** (1577) **1** : a unit of weight equal to 100 pounds — called also *short hundredweight*; see WEIGHT table **2** *Brit* : a unit of weight equal to 112 pounds — called also *long hundredweight*

1**hung** *past and past part of* HANG

2**hung** *adj* (1848) : unable to reach a decision or verdict ⟨a ~ jury⟩; *also, Brit* : not having a political party with an overall majority ⟨a ~ parliament⟩

Hung *abbr* Hungary

Hun·gar·i·an \ˌhəŋ-ˈger-ē-ən\ *n* (1553) **1 a** : a native or inhabitant of Hungary : MAGYAR **b** : a person of Hungarian descent **2** : the Finno-Ugric language of the Hungarians — **Hungarian** *adj*

1**hun·ger** \ˈhəŋ-gər\ *n* [ME, fr. OE *hungor;* akin to OHG *hungar* hunger, Lith *kanka* torture] (bef. 12c) **1 a** : a craving or urgent need for food or a specific nutrient **b** : an uneasy sensation occasioned by the lack of food **c** : a weakened condition brought about by prolonged lack of food **2** : a strong desire : CRAVING ⟨a ~ for success⟩ — **from hunger** : very bad or inept ⟨the jokes were *from hunger* —Mordecai Richler⟩

2**hunger** *vb* **hun·gered; hun·ger·ing** \-g(ə-)riŋ\ *vi* (bef. 12c) **1** : to feel or suffer hunger **2** : to have an eager desire ~ *vt* : to make hungry ***syn*** see LONG

hunger strike *n* (1889) : refusal (as by a prisoner) to eat enough to sustain life — **hunger striker** *n*

hung·over \ˈhəŋ-ˈō-vər\ *adj* (1941) : suffering from a hangover

hun·gry \ˈhəŋ-grē\ *adj* **hun·gri·er; -est** [ME, fr. OE *hungrig;* akin to OE *hungor*] (bef. 12c) **1 a** : feeling hunger **b** : characterized by or characteristic of hunger or appetite **2 a** : EAGER, AVID ⟨~ for affection⟩ **b** : strongly motivated (as by ambition) **3** : not rich or fertile : BARREN — **hun·gri·ly** \-grə-lē\ *adv* — **hun·gri·ness** \-grē-nəs\ *n*

hung up *adj* (1878) **1** : delayed or detained for a time **2** : anxiously nervous **3** : having great or excessive interest in or preoccupation with someone or something — usu. used with *on* ⟨they broke up but he's still *hung up* on her⟩ ⟨*hung up* on winning⟩

hunk \ˈhəŋk\ *n* [D dial. *hunke*] (ca. 1813) **1** : a large lump, piece, or portion ⟨a ~ of bread⟩ **2** : an attractive and usu. well-built man

hun·ker \ˈhəŋ-kər\ *vi* **hun·kered; hun·ker·ing** \-k(ə-)riŋ\ [prob. akin to MD *hucken, huken* to squat, MLG *hōken* to squat, peddle, ON *hūka* to squat] (1720) **1** : CROUCH, SQUAT — usu. used with *down* **2** : to settle in or dig in for a sustained period — used with *down* ⟨~ down for a good long wait —*New Yorker*⟩

hun·kers \ˈhəŋ-kərz\ *n pl* (1756) : HAUNCHES

hunks \ˈhəŋ(k)s\ *n pl but sing in constr* [origin unknown] (1602) : a surly ill-natured person; *esp* : MISER

hunky \ˈhəŋ-kē\ *adj* **hunk·i·er; -est** (1972) : being a hunk : attractive and usu. well-built ⟨the film's ~ leading man⟩

Hun·ky *also* **Hun·kie** \ˈhəŋ-kē\ *n, pl* **Hunkies** [alter. of *Hungarian*] (ca. 1896) *usu disparaging* : a person of central or east European birth or descent

hun·ky–do·ry \ˌhəŋ-kē-ˈdȯr-ē\ *adj* [obs. E dial. *hunk* home base + *-dory* (of unknown origin)] (1866) : quite satisfactory : FINE

Hun·nish \ˈhə-nish\ *adj* (1644) : relating to or resembling the Huns

1**hunt** \ˈhənt\ *vb* [ME, fr. OE *huntian;* akin to OE *hentan* to seize] *vt* (bef. 12c) **1 a** : to pursue for food or in sport ⟨~ buffalo⟩ **b** : to manage in the search for game ⟨~*s* a pack of dogs⟩ **2 a** : to pursue with intent to capture ⟨~*ed* the escapees⟩ **b** : to search out : SEEK **3** : to drive or chase esp. by harrying ⟨members . . . were ~*ed* from their homes —J. T. Adams⟩ **4** : to traverse in search of prey ⟨~*s* the woods⟩ ~ *vi* **1** : to take part in a hunt **2** : to attempt to find something **3** : to oscillate alternately to each side (as of a neutral point) or to run alternately faster and slower — used esp. of a device or machine

2**hunt** *n* (14c) **1** : the act, the practice, or an instance of hunting **2** : a group of mounted hunters and their hunting dogs

hunt–and–peck \ˌhənt-ᵊn-ˈpek\ *n* (1939) : a method of typing in which one looks at the keyboard and types using usu. the index fingers

hunt·er \ˈhən-tər\ *n* (13c) **1 a** : a person who hunts game **b** : a dog used or trained for hunting **c** : a horse used or adapted for use in hunting with hounds; *esp* : a fast strong horse trained for cross-country work and jumping **2** : one that searches for something **3** : a pocket watch with a hinged protective cover

hunt·er–gath·er·er \ˈhən-tər-ˈga-t͟hər-ər\ *n* (1974) : a member of a culture in which food is obtained by hunting, fishing, and foraging rather than by agriculture or animal husbandry

hunter green *n* (ca. 1930) : a dark yellowish green

hunt·ing \ˈhən-tiŋ\ *n* (bef. 12c) **1** : the act of one that hunts; *specif* : the pursuit of game **2** : the process of hunting **3 a** : a periodic variation in speed of a synchronous electrical machine **b** : a self-induced and undesirable oscillation of a variable above and below the desired value in an automatic control system **c** : a continuous attempt by an automatically controlled system to find a desired equilibrium condition

hunting horn *n* (1598) : a signal horn used in the chase; *specif* : a coiled circular horn with a flared bell and a cup-shaped mouthpiece

Hun·ting·ton's disease \ˈhən-tiŋ-tənz-\ *n* [George *Huntington* †1916 Am. physician] (1892) : a chorea usu. beginning in middle age that is inherited as an autosomal dominant trait and progresses to dementia — called also *Huntington's chorea*

hunt·ress \ˈhən-trəs\ *n* (14c) : a woman who hunts game; *also* : a female animal that hunts prey

hunts·man \ˈhən(t)-smən\ *n* (1561) **1** : HUNTER 1a **2** : a person who manages a hunt and looks after the hounds

hup \ˈhəp, ˈhət\ *interj* [prob. alter. of 1*hep*] (1951) — used to mark a marching cadence

huppah *var of* CHUPPAH

hur·dies \ˈhər-dēz\ *n pl* [origin unknown] (14c) *dial Brit* : RUMP

1**hur·dle** \ˈhər-dᵊl\ *n* [ME *hurdel,* fr. OE *hyrdel;* akin to OHG *hurt* hurdle, L *cratis* wickerwork, hurdle] (bef. 12c) **1 a** : a portable panel usu. of wattled withes and stakes used esp. for enclosing land or livestock **b** : a frame or sled formerly used in England for dragging traitors to execution **2 a** : an artificial barrier over which racers must leap **b** *pl* : any of various track events in which a series of hurdles must be surmounted **3** : BARRIER, OBSTACLE

2**hurdle** *vt* **hur·dled; hur·dling** \ˈhərd-liŋ, ˈhər-dᵊl-iŋ\ (1896) **1** : to leap over esp. while running (as in a sporting competition) **2** : OVERCOME, SURMOUNT — **hur·dler** \ˈhərd-lər, ˈhər-dᵊl-ər\ *n*

hur·dy–gur·dy \ˌhər-dē-ˈgər-dē, ˈhər-dē-ˌ\ *n, pl* **-gurdies** [prob. imit.] (1749) **1** : a stringed instrument in which sound is produced by the friction of a rosined wheel turned by a crank against the strings and the pitches are varied by keys **2** : any of various mechanical musical instruments (as the barrel organ)

hurl \ˈhər(-ə)l\ *vb* **hurled; hurl·ing** \ˈhər-liŋ\ [ME] *vi* (13c) **1** : RUSH, HURTLE **2** : PITCH 5a, b **3** : VOMIT ~ *vt* **1** : to send or thrust with great vigor ⟨the forces that were to be ~*ed* against the Turks —N. T. Gilroy⟩ **2** : to throw down with violence **3 a** : to throw forcefully : FLING ⟨~*ed* the manuscript into the fire⟩ ⟨~*ed* myself over the fence⟩ **b** : PITCH 2a **4** : to utter with vehemence ⟨~*ed* insults at the police⟩ ***syn*** see THROW — **hurl** *n* — **hurl·er** \ˈhər-lər\ *n*

hurling *n* (1780) : an Irish game resembling field hockey played between two teams of 15 players each

hur·ly \ˈhər-lē\ *n* [prob. short for *hurly-burly*] (1594) : UPROAR, TUMULT

hur·ly–bur·ly \ˌhər-lē-ˈbər-lē\ *n* [prob. alter. & redupl. of *hurling,* gerund of *hurl*] (1539) : UPROAR, TUMULT — **hurly–burly** *adj*

Hu·ron \ˈhyu̇r-ən, -ˌän\ *n, pl* **Hurons** *or* **Huron** [F, lit., boor] (1658) **1** : a member of a confederacy of American Indian peoples formerly occupying the country between Georgian Bay and Lake Ontario **2** : the Iroquoian language of the Hurons

1**hur·rah** \hu̇-ˈrȯ, -ˈrä, ˈhü-,\ *also* **hoo·ray** \hu̇-ˈrā\ *or* **hoo·rah** \-ˈrä, -ˈrȯ\ *n* (1686) **1 a** : EXCITEMENT, FANFARE **b** : CHEER 7 **2** : FUSS

2**hurrah, hurray** *var of* HOORAY

Hur·ri·an \ˈhu̇r-ē-ən\ *n* (1911) **1** : a member of an ancient non-Semitic people of northern Mesopotamia, Syria, and eastern Asia Minor about 1500 B.C. **2** : the language of the Hurrian people

1**hur·ri·cane** \ˈhər-ə-ˌkān, -i-kən, ˈhə-rə-, ˈhə-ri-\ *n* [Sp *huracán,* fr. Taino *hurakán*] (1555) **1** : a tropical cyclone with winds of 74 miles (119 kilometers) per hour or greater that occurs esp. in the western Atlantic, that is usu. accompanied by rain, thunder, and lightning, and that sometimes moves into temperate latitudes — see BEAUFORT SCALE table **2** : something resembling a hurricane esp. in its turmoil

2**hurricane** *adj* (1894) : having or being a glass chimney providing protection from wind ⟨a ~ lamp⟩

hurried *adj* (1667) **1 :** going or working at speed ⟨a ~ waitress⟩ **2 :** done in a hurry : HASTY ⟨a ~ departure⟩ — **hur·ried·ly** \ˈhər-əd-lē, ˈhə-rəd-\ *adv* — **hur·ried·ness** \ˈhər-ēd-nəs, ˈhə-rēd-\ *n*

[1]**hur·ry** \ˈhər-ē, ˈhə-rē\ *vb* **hur·ried; hur·ry·ing** [perh. fr. ME *horyen*] *vt* (1592) **1 a :** to carry or cause to go with haste ⟨~ them to the hospital⟩ **b :** to impel to rash or precipitate action **2 a :** to impel to greater speed : PROD ⟨used spurs to ~ the horse⟩ **b :** EXPEDITE **c :** to perform with undue haste ⟨~ a minuet⟩ ~ *vi* **:** to move or act with haste ⟨please ~ up⟩ — **hur·ri·er** *n*

[2]**hurry** *n* (1600) **1 :** disturbed or disorderly activity : COMMOTION **2 a :** agitated and often bustling or disorderly haste **b :** a state of eagerness or urgency : RUSH ***syn*** see HASTE — **in a hurry :** without delay : as rapidly as possible ⟨the police got there *in a hurry*⟩

hur·ry–scur·ry *or* **hur·ry–skur·ry** \ˌhər-ē-ˈskər-ē, ˌhə-rē-ˈskə-rē\ *n* [redupl. of [2]*hurry*] (1754) **:** a confused rush : TURMOIL — **hurry–scurry** *adj or adv*

hur·ry–up \ˈhər-ē-ˌəp, ˈhə-rē-\ *adj* (1902) **:** speeded up : completed in a hurry ⟨a ~ dinner⟩

[1]**hurt** \ˈhərt\ *vb* **hurt; hurt·ing** [ME, prob. fr. AF *hurter* to strike, prick, collide with, prob. of Gmc origin; akin to ON *hrūtr* male sheep] *vt* (13c) **1 a :** to inflict with physical pain : WOUND **b :** to do substantial or material harm to : DAMAGE ⟨the dry summer has ~ the land⟩ **2 a :** to cause emotional pain or anguish to : OFFEND **b :** to be detrimental to : HAMPER ⟨charges of graft ~ my chances of being elected⟩ ~ *vi* **1 a :** to suffer pain or grief **b :** to be in need — usu. used with *for* ⟨~*ing* for money⟩ **2 :** to cause damage or distress ⟨hit where it ~*s*⟩ ***syn*** see INJURE — **hurt** *adj* — **hurt·er** *n*

[2]**hurt** *n* (13c) **1 :** a cause of injury or damage : BLOW **2 a :** a bodily injury or wound **b :** mental distress or anguish : SUFFERING **3 :** WRONG, HARM

hurt·ful \ˈhərt-fəl\ *adj* (1526) **:** causing injury, detriment, or suffering : DAMAGING — **hurt·ful·ly** \-fə-lē\ *adv* — **hurt·ful·ness** *n*

hur·tle \ˈhər-tᵊl\ *vb* **hur·tled; hur·tling** \ˈhərt-liŋ, ˈhər-tᵊl-iŋ\ [ME *hurtlen* to collide, freq. of *hurten* to cause to strike, hurt] *vi* (14c) **:** to move rapidly or forcefully ~ *vt* **:** HURL, FLING — **hurtle** *n*

hurt·less \ˈhərt-ləs\ *adj* (1549) **:** causing no pain or injury : HARMLESS

[1]**hus·band** \ˈhəz-bənd\ *n* [ME *husbonde,* fr. OE *hūsbonda* master of a house, fr. ON *hūsbōndi,* fr. *hūs* house + *bōndi* householder; akin to ON *būa* to inhabit; akin to OE *būan* to dwell — more at BOWER] (13c) **1 :** a male partner in a marriage **2** *Brit* **:** MANAGER, STEWARD **3 :** a frugal manager — **hus·band·ly** *adj*

[2]**husband** *vt* (15c) **1 a :** to manage prudently and economically **b :** to use sparingly : CONSERVE **2** *archaic* **:** to find a husband for : MATE — **hus·band·er** *n*

hus·band·man \ˈhəz-bən(d)-mən\ *n* (14c) **1 :** one that plows and cultivates land : FARMER **2 :** a specialist in a branch of farm husbandry

hus·band·ry \ˈhəz-bən-drē\ *n* (14c) **1** *archaic* **:** the care of a household **2 :** the control or judicious use of resources : CONSERVATION **3 a :** the cultivation or production of plants or animals : AGRICULTURE **b :** the scientific control and management of a branch of farming and esp. of domestic animals

[1]**hush** \ˈhəsh\ *vb* [back-formation fr. *husht* hushed, fr. ME *hussht,* fr. *huissht,* interj. used to enjoin silence] *vt* (1546) **1 :** CALM, QUIET ⟨~*ed* the children as they entered the library⟩ **2 :** to put at rest : MOLLIFY **3 :** to keep from public knowledge : SUPPRESS ⟨~ the story up⟩ ~ *vi* **:** to become quiet

[2]**hush** *adj* (1602) **1** *archaic* **:** SILENT, STILL **2 :** intended to prevent the dissemination of certain information ⟨~ money⟩

[3]**hush** *n* (1650) **:** a silence or calm esp. following noise : QUIET

hush–hush \ˈhəsh-ˌhəsh\ *adj* (1916) **:** SECRET, CONFIDENTIAL

hush puppy *n* [fr. its occasional use as food for dogs] (ca. 1918) *chiefly Southern & southern Midland* **:** cornmeal dough shaped into small balls and fried in deep fat — usu. used in pl.

[1]**husk** \ˈhəsk\ *n* [ME] (14c) **1 a :** a usu. dry or membranous outer covering (as a pod or one composed of bracts) of various seeds and fruits (as barley and corn) : HULL; *also* **:** one of the constituent parts **b :** a carob pod **2 a :** an outer layer : SHELL **b :** an emptied shell : REMNANT **c :** a supporting framework

[2]**husk** *vt* (1562) **:** to strip the husk from — **husk·er** *n*

husk·ing \ˈhəs-kiŋ\ *n* (1692) **:** CORNHUSKING — called also *husking bee*

husk–to·ma·to \ˈhəsk-tə-ˌmā-(ˌ)tō *also* -ˌmä- *or* -ˌma-\ *n* (1895) **:** GROUND-CHERRY

[1]**husky** \ˈhəs-kē\ *adj* **husk·i·er; -est** (1552) **:** resembling, containing, or full of husks

[2]**hus·ky** \ˈhəs-kē\ *adj* **hus·ki·er; -est** [prob. fr. *husk* huskiness, fr. obs. *husk* to have a dry cough] (ca. 1722) **:** hoarse with or as if with emotion — **hus·ki·ly** \-kə-lē\ *adv* — **hus·ki·ness** \-kē-nəs\ *n*

[3]**hus·ky** *n, pl* **huskies** [shortening of *Huskemaw, Uskemaw* Eskimo, fr. Cree *aškime·w;* akin to Montagnais (Algonquian language of eastern Canada) *aiachkime8* Micmac, Eskimo — more at ESKIMO] (1852) **1 :** a heavy-coated working dog of the New World arctic region **2 :** SIBERIAN HUSKY

[4]**hus·ky** *n, pl* **huskies** (1864) **:** one that is husky

[5]**hus·ky** *adj* **hus·ki·er; -est** [prob. fr. [1]*husk*] (1869) **1 :** BURLY, ROBUST **2 :** LARGE

hus·sar \(ˌ)hə-ˈzär, -ˈsär\ *n* [Hung *huszár* hussar, (obs.) highway robber, fr. Serbian & Croatian *husar* pirate, fr. ML *cursarius* — more at CORSAIR] (1532) **:** a member of any of various European military units orig. modeled on the Hungarian light cavalry of the 15th century

Huss·ite \ˈhə-ˌsīt, ˈhu̇-\ *n* [NL *Hussita,* fr. John Huss] (1532) **:** a member of the Bohemian religious and nationalist movement originating with John Huss — **Hussite** *adj* — **Huss·it·ism** \-ˌsī-ˌti-zəm\ *n*

hus·sy \ˈhə-sē, -zē\ *n, pl* **hussies** [alter. of ME *huswif* housewife, fr. *hus* house + *wif* wife, woman] (1505) **1 :** a lewd or brazen woman **2 :** a saucy or mischievous girl

hus·tings \ˈhəs-tiŋz\ *n pl but sing or pl in constr* [ME, fr. OE *hūsting,* fr. ON *hūsthing,* fr. *hūs* house + *thing* assembly] (bef. 12c) **1 a :** a local court formerly held in various English municipalities and still held infrequently in London **b :** a local court in some cities in Virginia **2 a :** a raised platform used until 1872 for the nomination of candidates for the British Parliament and for election speeches **b :** an election platform : STUMP **c :** the proceedings or locale of an election campaign

hus·tle \ˈhə-səl\ *vb* **hus·tled; hus·tling** \ˈhə-s(ə-)liŋ\ [D *husselen* to shake, fr. MD *hutselen,* freq. of *hutsen*] *vt* (1720) **1 a :** JOSTLE, SHOVE **b :** to convey forcibly or hurriedly **c :** to urge forward precipitately **2 a :** to obtain by energetic activity ⟨~ up new customers⟩ **b :** to sell something to or obtain something from by energetic and esp. underhanded activity ⟨*hustling* the suckers⟩ **c :** to sell or promote energetically and aggressively ⟨*hustling* a new product⟩ **d :** to lure less skillful players into competing against oneself at (a gambling game) ⟨~ pool⟩ ~ *vi* **1 :** SHOVE, PRESS **2 :** HASTEN, HURRY **3 a :** to make strenuous efforts to obtain esp. money or business **b :** to obtain money by fraud or deception **c :** to engage in prostitution **4 :** to play a game or sport in an alert aggressive manner — **hustle** *n* — **hus·tler** \ˈhə-slər\ *n*

[1]**hut** \ˈhət\ *n* [F *hutte,* fr. OF *hute,* fr. OHG *hutta* hut; prob. akin to OE *hȳd* skin, hide] (1655) **1 :** an often small and temporary dwelling of simple construction : SHACK **2 :** a simple shelter from the elements — **hut** *vb*

[2]**hut** \ˈhət, ˈhəp\ *interj* [prob. alter. of [1]*hep*] (1948) — used to mark a marching cadence

hutch \ˈhəch\ *n* [ME *huche,* fr. AF] (13c) **1 a :** a chest or compartment for storage **b :** a cupboard usu. surmounted by open shelves **2 :** a pen or coop for an animal **3 :** SHACK, SHANTY

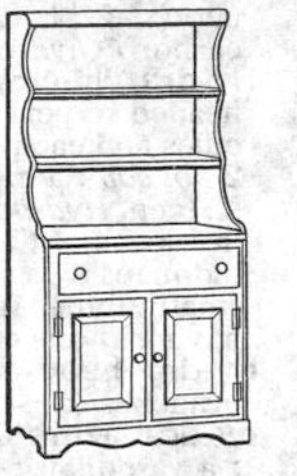

hutch 1b

hut·ment \ˈhət-mənt\ *n* (1889) **1 :** a collection of huts : ENCAMPMENT **2 :** HUT

Hut·ter·ite \ˈhə-tə-ˌrīt, ˈhu̇-\ *n* [Jakob *Hutter* †1536 Moravian Anabaptist] (1910) **:** a member of an Anabaptist sect of northwestern U.S. and Canada living communally and holding property in common — **Hut·te·ri·an** \ˌhə-ˈtir-ē-ən, hu̇-\ *adj*

Hu·tu \ˈhü-(ˌ)tü\ *n, pl* **Hutu** *or* **Hutus** [Kinyarwanda & Kirundi (Bantu languages of East Africa)] (1952) **:** a member of a Bantu-speaking people of Rwanda and Burundi

hutzpah *or* **hutzpa** *var of* CHUTZPAH

huz·zah *or* **huz·za** \(ˌ)hə-ˈzä\ *n* [origin unknown] (1573) **:** an expression or shout of acclaim — often used interjectionally to express joy or approbation

hv *abbr* have

HV *abbr* **1** high velocity **2** high voltage

HVAC *abbr* heating, ventilating, and air-conditioning; heating, ventilation, and air-conditioning

hvy *abbr* heavy

HW *abbr* **1** high water **2** highway **3** hot water

HWM *abbr* high-water mark

hwy *abbr* highway

hy·a·cinth \ˈhī-ə-(ˌ)sin(t)th, -sən(t)th\ *n* [L *hyacinthus,* a precious stone, a flowering plant, fr. Gk *hyakinthos*] (1553) **1 a :** a precious stone of the ancients sometimes held to be the sapphire **b :** a gem zircon or essonite **2 a :** a plant of the ancients held to be a lily, iris, larkspur, or gladiolus **b :** a bulbous perennial herb (*Hyacinthus orientalis*) of the lily family that is native to the Mediterranean region but is widely grown for its dense spikes of fragrant flowers — compare GRAPE HYACINTH, WATER HYACINTH **3 :** a light violet to moderate purple — **hy·a·cin·thine** \ˌhī-ə-ˈsin(t)-thən\ *adj*

Hy·a·cin·thus \ˌhī-ə-ˈsin(t)-thəs\ *n* [L, fr. Gk *Hyakinthos*] (1565) **:** a youth loved and accidentally killed by Apollo who memorializes him with a hyacinth growing from the youth's blood

Hy·a·des \ˈhī-ə-ˌdēz\ *n pl* [L, fr. Gk] (14c) **:** a V-shaped cluster of stars in the head of the constellation Taurus held by the ancients to indicate rainy weather when they rise with the sun

hyal- *or* **hyalo-** *comb form* [LL, glass, fr. Gk, fr. *hyalos*] **:** glass : glassy : hyaline ⟨*hyal*uronic acid⟩

[1]**hy·a·line** \ˈhī-ə-lən, -ˌlīn\ *adj* [LL *hyalinus,* fr. Gk *hyalinos,* fr. *hyalos*] (ca. 1661) **:** transparent or nearly so and usu. homogeneous

[2]**hy·a·line** \ˈhī-ə-lən, -ˌlīn, *in sense 2* -lən *or* -ˌlēn\ *n* (1667) **1 :** something (as the clear atmosphere) that is transparent **2** *or* **hy·a·lin** \-lən\ **:** any of several translucent nitrogenous substances related to chitin, found esp. around cells, and readily stained by eosin

hyaline cartilage *n* (1855) **:** translucent bluish-white cartilage with the cells embedded in an apparently homogeneous matrix present in joints and respiratory passages and forming most of the fetal skeleton

hy·a·lite \ˈhī-ə-ˌlīt\ *n* [G *Hyalit,* fr. Gk *hyalos*] (1794) **:** a colorless opal that is clear as glass or sometimes translucent or whitish

hy·a·loid \-ˌlȯid\ *adj* [Gk *hyaloeidēs,* fr. *hyalos*] (ca. 1836) **:** GLASSY, TRANSPARENT

hy·a·lo·plasm \hī-ˈa-lə-ˌpla-zəm, ˈhī-ə-lō-\ *n* [prob. fr. G *Hyaloplasma,* fr. *hyal-* + *-plasma* -plasm] (1886) **:** CYTOSOL

hy·al·uron·ic acid \ˌhīl-yu̇-ˈrä-nik-, ˌhī-əl-yu̇-\ *n* [ISV] (1934) **:** a viscous glycosaminoglycan chiefly of the matrix of tissues that occurs esp. in the vitreous humor, umbilical cord, synovial fluid, and loose connective tissue and serves esp. as a structural element and lubricant

hy·al·uron·i·dase \-ˈrä-nə-ˌdās, -ˌdāz\ *n* [ISV, fr. *hyaluronic* (*acid*) + *-idase* (as in *glucosidase*)] (1940) **:** a mucolytic enzyme that facilitates the spread of fluids through tissues by lowering the viscosity of hyaluronic acid

hy·brid \ˈhī-brəd\ *n* [L *hybrida*] (1601) **1 :** an offspring of two animals or plants of different races, breeds, varieties, species, or genera **2 :** a person whose background is a blend of two diverse cultures or traditions **3 a :** something heterogeneous in origin or composition : COMPOSITE ⟨~*s* of complementary DNA and RNA strands⟩ ⟨a ~ of medieval and Renaissance styles⟩ **b :** something (as a power plant, vehicle, or electronic circuit) that has two different types of components performing essentially the same function — **hybrid** *adj* — **hy·brid·ism** \-brə-ˌdi-zəm\ *n* — **hy·brid·i·ty** \hī-ˈbri-də-tē\ *n*

hybrid computer *n* (1968) **:** a computer system consisting of a combination of analog and digital computer systems

hy·brid·ize \ˈhī-brə-ˌdīz\ *vb* **-ized; -iz·ing** *vt* (1845) **:** to cause to produce hybrids : INTERBREED ~ *vi* **:** to produce hybrids — **hy·brid·i·za·tion** \ˌhī-brə-də-ˈzā-shən\ *n* — **hy·brid·iz·er** *n*

\ə\ **a**but \ᵊ\ **k**itten, F ta**ble** \ər\ **fur**ther \a\ **a**sh \ā\ **a**ce \ä\ **mo**p, **mar** \au̇\ **ou**t \ch\ **ch**in \e\ **be**t \ē\ **ea**sy \g\ **g**o \i\ **hi**t \ī\ **i**ce \j\ **j**ob \ŋ\ **si**ng \ō\ **go** \ȯ\ **law** \ȯi\ **boy** \th\ **th**in \t͟h\ **th**e \ü\ **loo**t \u̇\ **foo**t \y\ **y**et \zh\ **vi**sion, bei**ge** \k̲, ⁿ, œ,ue, ʸ\ *see* Guide to Pronunciation

hy·brid·oma \ˌhī-brə-ˈdō-mə\ *n* (1978) **:** a hybrid cell produced by the fusion of an antibody-producing lymphocyte with a tumor cell and used to culture continuously a specific monoclonal antibody
hybrid tea rose *n* (1888) **:** any of numerous moderately hardy cultivated hybrid bush roses grown esp. for their strongly recurrent bloom of large usu. scentless flowers — called also *hybrid tea*
hybrid vigor *n* (1918) **:** HETEROSIS
hyd *abbr* 1 hydraulics 2 hydrostatics
hy·da·thode \ˈhī-də-ˌthōd\ *n* [ISV, fr. Gk *hydat-, hydōr* water + *hodos* road] (1895) **:** a specialized pore on the leaves of higher plants that functions in the exudation of water
hy·da·tid \ˈhī-də-təd, -ˌtid\ *n* [Gk *hydatid-, hydatis* watery cyst, fr. *hydat-, hydōr*] (1683) **:** the larval cyst of a tapeworm (genus *Echinococcus*) occurring as a fluid-filled sac containing daughter cysts in which scolices develop
hydr- *or* **hydro-** *comb form* [L *hydr-, hydro-,* fr. Gk, fr. *hydōr* — more at WATER] **1 a :** water ⟨*hydr*ous⟩ ⟨*hydro*electric⟩ **b :** liquid ⟨*hydro*kinetic⟩ **2 :** hydrogen **:** containing or combined with hydrogen ⟨*hydro*carbon⟩ ⟨*hydr*oxyl⟩ **3 :** hydroid ⟨*hydro*medusa⟩
Hy·dra \ˈhī-drə\ *n* [ME *Ydra,* fr. L *Hydra,* fr. Gk] (15c) **1 :** a many-headed serpent or monster in Greek mythology that was slain by Hercules and each head of which when cut off was replaced by two others **2** *not cap* **:** a multifarious evil not to be overcome by a single effort **3** [L (gen. *Hydrae*), fr. Gk] **:** a southern constellation of great length that lies south of Cancer, Sextans, Corvus, and Virgo and is represented on old maps by a serpent **4** *not cap* [NL, fr. L, Hydra] **:** any of numerous small tubular freshwater hydrozoan polyps (*Hydra* and related genera) having at one end a mouth surrounded by tentacles
hy·dra–head·ed \ˌhī-drə-ˈhe-dəd\ *adj* (1599) **:** having many centers or branches ⟨a ~ organization⟩
hy·dral·azine \hī-ˈdra-lə-ˌzēn\ *n* [*hydr-* + phth*al*ic (acid) + *azine*] (1952) **:** a vasodilator $C_8H_8N_4$ used in the form of its hydrochloride to treat hypertension
hy·dran·gea \hī-ˈdrān-jə\ *n* [NL, fr. *hydr-* + Gk *angeion* vessel — more at ANGI-] (ca. 1753) **:** any of a genus (*Hydrangea*) of mostly shrubs having opposite leaves and showy clusters of usu. sterile white, pink, or bluish flowers that is either placed in the saxifrage family or the hydrangea family (Hydrangeaceae)
hy·drant \ˈhī-drənt\ *n* (1806) **1 :** a discharge pipe with a valve and spout at which water may be drawn from a water main (as for fighting fires) — called also *fireplug* **2 :** FAUCET
hy·dranth \ˈhī-ˌdran(t)th\ *n* [ISV *hydr-* + Gk *anthos* flower — more at ANTHOLOGY] (1874) **:** one of the feeding zooids of a hydroid colony
hy·drase \ˈhī-ˌdrās, -ˌdrāz\ *n* (1943) **:** an enzyme that promotes the addition or removal of water to or from its substrate
[1]**hy·drate** \ˈhī-ˌdrāt\ *n* (1802) **:** a compound formed by the union of water with some other substance
[2]**hydrate** *vb* **hy·drat·ed; hy·drat·ing** *vt* (1846) **1 :** to cause to take up or combine with water or the elements of water **2 :** to supply with ample fluid or moisture ⟨~*s* and softens the skin⟩ ~ *vi* **:** to become a hydrate — **hy·dra·tion** \hī-ˈdrā-shən\ *n* — **hy·dra·tor** \ˈhī-ˌdrā-tər\ *n*
hy·drau·lic \hī-ˈdrȯ-lik\ *adj* [L *hydraulicus,* fr. Gk *hydraulikos,* fr. *hydraulis* hydraulic organ, fr. *hydr-* + *aulos* reed instrument — more at ALVEOLUS] (1661) **1 :** operated, moved, or effected by means of water **2 a :** of or relating to hydraulics ⟨~ engineer⟩ **b :** of or relating to water or other liquid in motion ⟨~ erosion⟩ **3 :** operated by the resistance offered or the pressure transmitted when a quantity of liquid (as water or oil) is forced through a comparatively small orifice or through a tube ⟨~ brakes⟩ **4 :** hardening or setting under water ⟨~ cement⟩ — **hy·drau·li·cal·ly** \-li-k(ə-)lē\ *adv*
hy·drau·lics \hī-ˈdrȯ-liks\ *n pl but sing in constr* (1671) **:** a branch of science that deals with practical applications (as the transmission of energy or the effects of flow) of liquid (as water) in motion
hy·dra·zide \ˈhī-drə-ˌzīd\ *n* (1888) **:** any of a class of compounds resulting from the replacement of hydrogen by an acid group in hydrazine or in one of its derivatives
hy·dra·zine \ˈhī-drə-ˌzēn\ *n* [ISV] (1887) **:** a colorless fuming corrosive strongly reducing liquid base N_2H_4 used esp. in fuels for rocket and jet engines; *also* **:** an organic base derived from this compound
hy·dra·zo·ic acid \ˌhī-drə-ˈzō-ik-\ *n* [*hydr-* + *azo-* + [1]*-ic*] (1894) **:** a colorless volatile poisonous explosive liquid HN_3 that has a foul odor and yields explosive salts of heavy metals
hy·dric \ˈhī-drik\ *adj* (1926) **:** characterized by, relating to, or requiring an abundance of moisture ⟨a ~ habitat⟩ ⟨a ~ plant⟩ — compare MESIC, XERIC
-hydric *adj suffix* **:** containing acid hydrogen ⟨mono*hydric*⟩
hy·dride \ˈhī-ˌdrīd\ *n* (1869) **:** a compound of hydrogen with a more electropositive element or group
hy·dril·la \hī-ˈdri-lə\ *n* [NL, prob. fr. L *Hydra* Hydra] (1969) **:** a freshwater aquatic Asian plant (*Hydrilla verticillata* of the Hydrocharitaceae family) that has small narrow leaves growing in whorls of three to eight around stems which become heavily branched near the water surface
hy·dri·od·ic acid \ˌhī-drē-ˈä-dik-\ *n* [ISV *hydr-* + *iodic acid*] (1816) **:** an aqueous solution of hydrogen iodide HI that is a strong acid and a strong reducing agent
[1]**hy·dro** \ˈhī-(ˌ)drō\ *n, pl* **hydros** [short for *hydropathic establishment*] (1882) *Brit* **:** an establishment offering hydropathic treatment (as for weight loss) **:** HEALTH SPA
[2]**hydro** *n, often attrib* [short for *hydropower*] (1916) **:** hydroelectric power
hy·dro·bi·ol·o·gy \ˌhī-drō-bī-ˈä-lə-jē\ *n* (1926) **:** the biology of bodies or units of water; *esp* **:** LIMNOLOGY — **hy·dro·bi·o·log·i·cal** \-ˌbī-ə-ˈlä-ji-kəl\ *adj* — **hy·dro·bi·ol·o·gist** \-bī-ˈä-lə-jist\ *n*
hy·dro·bro·mic acid \ˌhī-drə-ˈbrō-mik-\ *n* [ISV] (1830) **:** an aqueous solution of hydrogen bromide HBr that is a strong acid and a weak reducing agent and that is used esp. for making bromides
hy·dro·car·bon \ˈhī-drō-ˌkär-bən\ *n* (1826) **:** an organic compound (as acetylene or butane) containing only carbon and hydrogen and often occurring in petroleum, natural gas, coal, and bitumens
hy·dro·cele \ˈhī-drə-ˌsēl\ *n* [L, fr. Gk *hydrokēlē,* fr. *hydr-* + *kēlē* tumor — more at -CELE] (1597) **:** an accumulation of serous fluid in a saclike cavity (as the scrotum)
hy·dro·ce·phal·ic \ˌhī-drō-sə-ˈfa-lik\ *adj* (1815) **:** relating to, characterized by, or affected with hydrocephalus — **hydrocephalic** *n*
hy·dro·ceph·a·lus \-ˈse-fə-ləs\ *also* **hy·dro·ceph·a·ly** \-lē\ *n* [NL *hydrocephalus,* fr. LL, hydrocephalic, adj., fr. Gk *hydrokephalos,* fr. *hydr-* + *kephalē* head — more at CEPHALIC] (1670) **:** an abnormal increase in the amount of cerebrospinal fluid within the cranial cavity that is accompanied by expansion of the cerebral ventricles and often increased intracranial pressure, skull enlargement, and cognitive decline
hy·dro·chlo·ric acid \ˌhī-drə-ˈklȯr-ik-\ *n* [ISV] (1819) **:** an aqueous solution of hydrogen chloride HCl that is a strong corrosive irritating acid, is normally present in dilute form in gastric juice, and is widely used in industry and in the laboratory
hy·dro·chlo·ride \-ˈklȯr-ˌīd\ *n* (1826) **:** a chemical complex composed of an organic base (as an alkaloid) in association with hydrogen chloride
hy·dro·chlo·ro·fluo·ro·car·bon \-ˌklȯr-ō-ˌflȯr-ō-ˈkär-bən, -ˌflu̇r-\ *n* (1977) **:** any of several simple gaseous compounds that contain carbon, chlorine, fluorine, and hydrogen
hy·dro·chlo·ro·thi·a·zide \-ˌklȯr-ə-ˈthī-ə-ˌzīd\ *n* [*hydr-* + *chlor-* + *thiazine* + *-ide*] (1958) **:** a diuretic and antihypertensive drug $C_7H_8ClN_3O_4S_2$
hy·dro·col·loid \ˌhī-drō-ˈkä-ˌlȯid\ *n* (1916) **:** a substance that yields a gel with water — **hy·dro·col·loi·dal** \-kə-ˈlȯi-dᵊl, -kä-\ *adj*
hy·dro·cor·ti·sone \-ˈkȯr-tə-ˌsōn, -ˌzōn\ *n* (1951) **:** CORTISOL; *esp* **:** cortisol used pharmaceutically
hy·dro·crack·ing \ˈhī-drə-ˌkra-kiŋ\ *n* (1940) **:** the cracking of hydrocarbons in the presence of hydrogen — **hy·dro·crack** \-ˌkrak\ *vt* — **hy·dro·crack·er** *n*
hy·dro·cy·an·ic acid \ˌhī-drō-sī-ˈa-nik-\ *n* [ISV] (1816) **:** an aqueous solution of hydrogen cyanide HCN that is a poisonous weak acid and is used chiefly in fumigating and in organic synthesis
hy·dro·dy·nam·ic \-dī-ˈna-mik\ *also* **hy·dro·dy·nam·i·cal** \-mi-kəl\ *adj* [NL *hydrodynamicus,* fr. *hydr-* + *dynamicus* dynamic] (ca. 1828) **:** of, relating to, or involving principles of hydrodynamics — **hy·dro·dy·nam·i·cal·ly** \-mi-k(ə-)lē\ *adv*
hy·dro·dy·nam·ics \-miks\ *n pl but sing in constr* (1779) **:** a branch of physics that deals with the motion of fluids and the forces acting on solid bodies immersed in fluids and in motion relative to them — compare HYDROSTATICS — **hy·dro·dy·nam·i·cist** \-ˈna-mə-sist\ *n*
hy·dro·elec·tric \ˌhī-drō-i-ˈlek-trik\ *adj* [ISV] (1884) **:** of or relating to production of electricity by waterpower ⟨constructed a ~ power plant at the dam site⟩ — **hy·dro·elec·tri·cal·ly** \-tri-k(ə-)lē\ *adv* — **hy·dro·elec·tric·i·ty** \-ˌlek-ˈtri-sə-tē, -ˈtris-tē\ *n*
hy·dro·flu·or·ic acid \ˌhī-drō-ˈflȯr-ik, -ˈflu̇r-\ *n* [ISV] (1830) **:** an aqueous solution of hydrogen fluoride HF that is a weak poisonous acid, that attacks silica and silicates, and that is used esp. in finishing and etching glass
hy·dro·fluo·ro·car·bon \-ˌflȯr-ō-ˈkär-bən, -ˌflu̇r-\ *n* (1986) **:** any of several simple gaseous compounds that contain carbon, fluorine, and hydrogen
hy·dro·foil \ˈhī-drə-ˌfȯi(-ə)l\ *n* (1919) **1 :** a body similar to an airfoil but designed for action in or on water **2 :** a motorboat that has metal plates or fins attached by struts fore and aft for lifting the hull clear of the water as speed is attained
hy·dro·gel \ˈhī-drə-ˌjel\ *n* (1864) **:** a gel composed usu. of one or more polymers suspended in water
hy·dro·gen \ˈhī-drə-jən, -dər-\ *n* [F *hydrogène,* fr. *hydr-* + *-gène* -gen; fr. the fact that water is generated by its combustion] (1788) **:** a nonmetallic element that is the simplest and lightest of the elements, is normally a colorless odorless highly flammable diatomic gas, and is used esp. in synthesis — see ELEMENT table; compare DEUTERIUM, TRITIUM — **hy·drog·e·nous** \hī-ˈdrä-jə-nəs\ *adj*
hy·drog·e·nase \hī-ˈdrä-jə-ˌnās, -ˌnāz\ *n* (1900) **:** an enzyme of various microorganisms that promotes the formation and utilization of gaseous hydrogen
hy·dro·ge·nate \hī-ˈdrä-jə-ˌnāt, ˈhī-drə-\ *vt* **-nat·ed; -nat·ing** (1809) **:** to combine or treat with or expose to hydrogen; *esp* **:** to add hydrogen to the molecule of (an unsaturated organic compound) — **hy·dro·ge·na·tion** \hī-ˌdrä-jə-ˈnā-shən, ˌhī-drə-\ *n*
hydrogen bomb *n* (1947) **:** a bomb whose violent explosive power is due to the sudden release of atomic energy resulting from the fusion of light nuclei (as of hydrogen atoms) at very high temperature and pressure to form helium nuclei
hydrogen bond *n* (1923) **:** an electrostatic attraction between a hydrogen atom in one polar molecule (as of water) and a small electronegative atom (as of oxygen, nitrogen, or fluorine) in usu. another molecule of the same or a different polar substance — **hydrogen bonding** *n*
hydrogen bromide *n* (1869) **:** a colorless irritating gas HBr that fumes in moist air and yields hydrobromic acid when dissolved in water
hydrogen chloride *n* (1869) **:** a colorless pungent poisonous gas HCl that fumes in moist air and yields hydrochloric acid when dissolved in water
hydrogen cyanide *n* (1869) **1 :** a poisonous usu. gaseous compound HCN that has the odor of bitter almonds **2 :** HYDROCYANIC ACID
hydrogen fluoride *n* (1869) **:** a colorless corrosive fuming usu. gaseous compound HF that yields hydrofluoric acid when dissolved in water
hydrogen iodide *n* (1869) **:** an acrid colorless gas HI that fumes in moist air and yields hydriodic acid when dissolved in water
hydrogen ion *n* (1896) **1 :** the cation H^+ of acids consisting of a hydrogen atom whose electron has been transferred to the anion of the acid **2 :** HYDRONIUM
hydrogen peroxide *n* (1872) **:** an unstable compound H_2O_2 used esp. as an oxidizing and bleaching agent, an antiseptic, and a propellant
hydrogen sulfide *n* (1869) **:** a flammable poisonous gas H_2S that has an odor suggestive of rotten eggs and is found esp. in many mineral waters and in putrefying matter
hy·dro·ge·ol·o·gy \ˌhī-drō-jē-ˈä-lə-jē\ *n* (1824) **:** a branch of geology concerned with the occurrence, use, and functions of surface water and groundwater; *also* **:** the phenomena dealt with in hydrogeology — **hy·dro·ge·ol·o·gist** \-jist\ *n*
hy·dro·graph·ic \ˌhī-drə-ˈgra-fik\ *adj* [F *hydrographique,* fr. MF, fr. *hydr-* + *-graphique* -graphic] (1665) **1 :** of or relating to the characteristic features (as flow or depth) of bodies of water **2 :** relating to the charting of bodies of water — **hy·drog·ra·pher** \hī-ˈdrä-grə-fər\ *n* — **hy·drog·ra·phy** \-grə-fē\ *n*
[1]**hy·droid** \ˈhī-ˌdrȯid\ *adj* [ultim. fr. NL *Hydra*] (ca. 1864) **:** of or relating to a hydrozoan; *esp* **:** resembling a typical hydra

²**hydroid** *n* (1865) : HYDROZOAN; *esp* : a hydrozoan polyp as distinguished from a hydrozoan jellyfish

hy·dro·ki·net·ic \ˌhī-drō-kə-'ne-tik, -(ˌ)kī-\ *adj* (1876) : of or relating to the motions of fluids or the forces which produce or affect such motions — compare HYDROSTATIC

hy·dro·lase \'hī-drə-ˌlās, -ˌlāz\ *n* [ISV, fr. NL *hydrolysis* + ISV *-ase*] (1910) : a hydrolytic enzyme

hydrologic cycle *n* (1936) : the sequence of conditions through which water passes from vapor in the atmosphere through precipitation upon land and water surfaces and ultimately back into the atmosphere as a result of evaporation and transpiration — called also *hydrological cycle*

hy·drol·o·gy \hī-'drä-lə-jē\ *n* [NL *hydrologia*, fr. L *hydr-* + *-logia* -logy] (1762) : a science dealing with the properties, distribution, and circulation of water on and below the earth's surface and in the atmosphere — **hy·dro·log·ic** \ˌhī-drə-'lä-jik\ *or* **hy·dro·log·i·cal** \-ji-kəl\ *adj* — **hy·dro·log·i·cal·ly** \-ji-k(ə-)lē\ *adv* — **hy·drol·o·gist** \hī-'drä-lə-jist\ *n*

hy·dro·ly·sate \hī-'drä-lə-ˌsāt\ *also* **hy·dro·ly·zate** \-ˌzāt\ *n* (1915) : a product of hydrolysis

hy·dro·ly·sis \hī-'drä-lə-səs\ *n* [NL] (1880) : a chemical process of decomposition involving the splitting of a bond and the addition of the hydrogen cation and the hydroxide anion of water — **hy·dro·lyt·ic** \ˌhī-drə-'li-tik\ *adj* — **hy·dro·lyt·i·cal·ly** \-ti-k(ə-)lē\ *adv*

hy·dro·lyze \'hī-drə-ˌlīz\ *vb* **-lyzed; -lyz·ing** [ISV, fr. NL *hydrolysis*] (1880) : to subject to hydrolysis ∼ *vi* : to undergo hydrolysis — **hy·dro·lyz·able** \-ˌlī-zə-bəl\ *adj*

hy·dro·mag·net·ic \ˌhī-drō-mag-'ne-tik\ *adj* (1943) : MAGNETOHYDRODYNAMIC

hy·dro·man·cy \'hī-drə-ˌman(t)-sē\ *n* [ME *ydromancie*, fr. MF *hydromancie*, fr. L *hydromantia*, fr. *hydr-* + *-mantia* -mancy] (14c) : divination by the appearance or motion of liquids (as water)

hy·dro·mas·sage \ˌhī-drō-mə-'säzh, -'säj\ *n* (1940) 1 : a massage using jets of water 2 : SPA 5

hy·dro·me·chan·i·cal \ˌhī-drō-mi-'ka-ni-kəl\ *adj* (1825) : relating to a branch of mechanics that deals with the equilibrium and motion of fluids and of solid bodies immersed in them — **hy·dro·me·chan·ics** \-'ka-niks\ *n pl but sing in constr*

hy·dro·me·du·sa \ˌhī-drō-mi-'dü-sə, -'dyü-, -zə\ *n, pl* **-sae** \-ˌsē, -ˌzē\ [NL] (ca. 1889) : a jellyfish (as of the orders Anthomedusae and Leptomedusae) produced as a bud from a hydroid

hy·dro·met·al·lur·gy \ˌhī-drō-'me-tə-ˌlər-jē\ *n* [ISV] (ca. 1859) : the treatment of ores by wet processes (as leaching) — **hy·dro·met·al·lur·gi·cal** \-ˌme-tə-'lər-ji-kəl\ *adj* — **hy·dro·met·al·lur·gist** \-'me-tə-ˌlər-jist\ *n*

hy·dro·me·te·or \ˌhī-drō-'mē-tē-ər, -tē-ˌȯr\ *n* [ISV] (1857) : a product (as rain) formed by the condensation of atmospheric water vapor

hy·dro·me·te·o·rol·o·gy \ˌmē-tē-ə-'rä-lə-jē\ *n* (ca. 1859) : a branch of meteorology that deals with water in the atmosphere esp. as precipitation — **hy·dro·me·te·o·ro·log·i·cal** \-tē-ə-rə-'lä-ji-kəl, -ˌär-ə-, -ə-rə-\ *adj* — **hy·dro·me·te·o·rol·o·gist** \-tē-ə-'rä-lə-jist\ *n*

hy·drom·e·ter \hī-'drä-mə-tər\ *n* (1675) : an instrument for determining the specific gravity of a liquid (as battery acid or an alcohol solution) and hence its strength — **hy·dro·met·ric** \ˌhī-drə-'me-trik\ *adj*

hy·dro·mor·phic \ˌhī-drə-'mȯr-fik\ *adj* (1938) *of a soil* : developed in the presence of an excess of moisture which tends to suppress aerobic factors in soil-building

hy·dron·ic \hī-'drä-nik\ *adj* [*hydr-* + *-onic* (as in *electronic*)] (1946) : of, relating to, or being a system of heating or cooling that involves transfer of heat by a circulating fluid (as water or vapor) in a closed system of pipes — **hy·dron·i·cal·ly** \-ni-k(ə-)lē\ *adv*

hy·dro·ni·um \hī-'drō-nē-əm\ *n* [ISV *hydr-* + *-onium*] (1908) : a hydrated hydrogen ion H_3O^+

hy·drop·a·thy \hī-'drä-pə-thē\ *n* [ISV] (1843) : a method of treating disease by copious and frequent use of water both externally and internally — compare HYDROTHERAPY — **hy·dro·path·ic** \ˌhī-drə-'pa-thik\ *adj*

hy·dro·per·ox·ide \ˌhī-drō-pə-'räk-ˌsīd\ *n* (1900) : a compound containing an O_2H group

hy·dro·phane \'hī-drō-ˌfān\ *n* (1784) : a semitranslucent opal that becomes translucent or transparent on immersion in water

hy·dro·phil·ic \ˌhī-drə-'fi-lik\ *adj* [NL *hydrophilus*, fr. Gk *hydr-* + *-philos* -philous] (1901) : of, relating to, or having a strong affinity for water ⟨∼ proteins⟩ — **hy·dro·phi·lic·i·ty** \ˌhī-drə-fi-'li-sə-tē\ *n*

hy·dro·pho·bia \ˌhī-drə-'fō-bē-ə\ *n* [LL, fr. Gk, fr. *hydr-* + *-phobia* -phobia] (1547) 1 : RABIES 2 : a morbid dread of water

hy·dro·pho·bic \-'fō-bik\ *adj* (1807) 1 : of, relating to, or suffering from hydrophobia 2 : lacking affinity for water — **hy·dro·pho·bic·i·ty** \-fō-'bi-sə-tē\ *n*

hy·dro·phone \'hī-drə-ˌfōn\ *n* (1860) : an instrument for listening to sound transmitted through water

hy·dro·phyte \-ˌfīt\ *n* [ISV] (1832) 1 : a plant that grows either partly or totally submerged in water; *also* : a plant growing in waterlogged soil — **hy·dro·phyt·ic** \ˌhī-drə-'fi-tik\ *adj*

¹**hy·dro·plane** \'hī-drə-ˌplān\ *n* (1904) 1 : a powerboat designed for racing that skims the surface of the water 2 : SEAPLANE

²**hydroplane** *vi* (1962) : to skim on water; *esp, of a vehicle* : to skid on a wet surface (as pavement) because a film of water on the surface causes the tires to lose contact with it

hy·dro·pon·ics \ˌhī-drə-'pä-niks\ *n pl but sing in constr* [*hydr-* + *-ponics* (as in *geoponics*) agriculture)] (1937) : the growing of plants in nutrient solutions with or without an inert medium (as soil) to provide mechanical support — **hy·dro·pon·ic** \-nik\ *adj* — **hy·dro·pon·i·cal·ly** \-ni-k(ə-)lē\ *adv*

hy·dro·pow·er \'hī-drə-ˌpau̇(-ə)r\ *n* (1933) : hydroelectric power

hy·dro·qui·none \ˌhī-drō-kwi-'nōn, -'kwi-ˌnōn\ *n* (1872) : a white crystalline strongly reducing phenol $C_6H_6O_2$ used esp. as a photographic developer, as an antioxidant and stabilizer, and in medicine to remove pigmentation from hyperpigmented areas of skin

hy·dro·sere \'hī-drə-ˌsir\ *n* (1920) : an ecological sere originating in an aquatic habitat

hy·dro·sol \'hī-drə-ˌsäl, -ˌsȯl\ *n* [*hydr-* + *-sol* (fr. *solution*)] (1864) : a sol in which the liquid is water — **hy·dro·sol·ic** \ˌhī-drə-'säl-ik\ *adj*

hy·dro·space \-ˌspās\ *n* (1963) : the regions beneath the surface of the ocean

hy·dro·sphere \-ˌsfir\ *n* [ISV] (1887) : the aqueous vapor of the atmosphere; *broadly* : the aqueous envelope of the earth including bodies of water and aqueous vapor in the atmosphere — **hy·dro·spher·ic** \ˌhī-drə-'sfir-ik, -'sfer-\ *adj*

hy·dro·stat·ic \ˌhī-drə-'sta-tik\ *adj* [prob. fr. NL *hydrostaticus*, fr. *hydr-* + *staticus* static] (1666) : of or relating to fluids at rest or to the pressures they exert or transmit — compare HYDROKINETIC — **hy·dro·stat·i·cal·ly** \-ti-k(ə-)lē\ *adv*

hy·dro·stat·ics \-tiks\ *n pl but sing in constr* (1660) : a branch of physics that deals with the characteristics of fluids at rest and esp. with the pressure in a fluid or exerted by a fluid on an immersed body — compare HYDRODYNAMICS

hy·dro·ther·a·py \ˌhī-drō-'ther-ə-pē\ *n* [ISV] (1876) : the therapeutic use of water (as in a whirlpool bath) — compare HYDROPATHY

hy·dro·ther·mal \ˌhī-drə-'thər-məl\ *adj* [ISV] (1849) : of or relating to hot water — used esp. of the formation of minerals by hot solutions rising from a cooling magma — **hy·dro·ther·mal·ly** \-mə-lē\ *adv*

hydrothermal vent *n* (1975) : a fissure in the ocean floor esp. at or near a mid-ocean ridge from which mineral-rich superheated water issues

hy·dro·tho·rax \-'thȯr-ˌaks\ *n* [NL] (1793) : an excess of serous fluid in the pleural cavity; *esp* : an effusion resulting from failing circulation (as in heart disease or from lung infection)

hy·drot·ro·pism \hī-'drä-trə-ˌpi-zəm\ *n* [ISV] (ca. 1882) : a tropism (as in plant roots) in which water or water vapor is the orienting factor — **hy·dro·tro·pic** \ˌhī-drə-'trō-pik, -'trä-\ *adj*

hy·drous \'hī-drəs\ *adj* (1826) : containing water usu. in chemical association (as in hydrates)

hy·drox·ide \hī-'dräk-ˌsīd\ *n* [ISV] (1851) 1 : the monovalent anion OH^- consisting of one atom of hydrogen and one of oxygen — called also *hydroxide ion* 2 : an ionic compound of hydroxide with an element or group

hy·droxy \hī-'dräk-sē\ *adj* [ISV, fr. *hydroxyl*] (1812) : being or containing hydroxyl; *esp* : containing hydroxyl esp. in place of hydrogen — usu. used in combination ⟨*hydroxy*acetic acid⟩

hy·droxy·ap·a·tite \hī-ˌdräk-sē-'a-pə-ˌtīt⟩ *or* **hy·drox·yl·ap·a·tite** \-sə-'la-pə-ˌtīt⟩ *n* (1912) : a complex phosphate of calcium $Ca_5(PO_4)_3OH$ that occurs as a mineral and is the chief structural element of vertebrate bone

hy·droxy·bu·tyr·ic acid \hī-ˌdräk-sē-byü-'tir-ik-\ *n* (1879) : a hydroxy derivative $C_4H_8O_3$ of butyric acid that is excreted in increased quantities in the urine in diabetes

hy·drox·yl \hī-'dräk-səl\ *n* [*hydr-* + *ox-* + *-yl*] (1869) 1 : the chemical group, ion, or radical OH that consists of one atom of hydrogen and one of oxygen and is neutral or negatively charged 2 : HYDROXIDE 1 — **hy·drox·yl·ic** \ˌhī-ˌdräk-'si-lik\ *adj*

hy·drox·yl·amine \hī-ˌdräk-sə-lə-ˌmēn, ˌhī-ˌdräk-'si-lə-ˌmēn\ *n* [ISV] (1869) : a colorless odorless nitrogenous base NH_3O that resembles ammonia in its reactions but is less basic and that is used esp. as a reducing agent

hy·drox·y·lase \hī-'dräk-sə-ˌlās, -ˌlāz\ *n* (1953) : any of a group of enzymes that catalyze oxidation reactions in which one of the two atoms of molecular oxygen is incorporated into the substrate and the other is used to oxidize NADH or NADPH

hy·drox·yl·ate \hī-'dräk-sə-ˌlāt⟩ *vt* **-at·ed; -at·ing** (ca. 1909) : to introduce hydroxyl into — **hy·drox·yl·ation** \-ˌdräk-sə-'lā-shən\ *n*

hy·droxy·pro·line \hī-ˌdräk-sē-'prō-ˌlēn\ *n* (1905) : an amino acid $C_5H_9NO_3$ that occurs naturally as a constituent of collagen

hy·droxy·tryp·ta·mine \-'trip-tə-ˌmēn\ *n* (1949) : SEROTONIN — usu. preceded by the numeral 5 ⟨5-*hydroxytryptamine*⟩

hy·droxy·urea \-yu̇-'rē-ə\ *n* (1949) : a drug $CH_4N_2O_2$ used to treat some forms of leukemia, melanoma, and malignant tumors

hy·droxy·zine \hī-'dräk-sə-ˌzēn\ *n* [*hydroxy-* + *piperazine*] (1956) : a compound $C_{21}H_{27}ClN_2O_2$ used as an antihistamine and tranquilizer

hy·dro·zo·an \ˌhī-drə-'zō-ən\ *n* [ultim. fr. Gk *hydr-* + *zōion* animal — more at ZO-] (1877) : any of a class (Hydrozoa) of coelenterates that includes solitary and colonial polyps and jellyfishes having no stomodeum or gastric tentacles — **hydrozoan** *adj*

hy·e·na \hī-'ē-nə\ *n, pl* **hyenas** *also* **hyena** [ME *hyene*, fr. L *hyaena*, fr. Gk *hyaina*, fr. *hys* hog — more at SOW] (14c) : any of several large strong nocturnal carnivorous Old World mammals (family Hyaenidae) that usu. feed as scavengers — **hy·e·nic** \-'ē-nik, -'e-nik\ *adj*

Hy·ge·ia \hī-'jē-ə\ *n* [L, fr. Gk *Hygieia*] (1615) : the goddess of health in Greek mythology

hy·giene \'hī-ˌjēn *also* hī-'\ *n* [F *hygiène* & NL *hygieina*, fr. Gk, neut. pl. of *hygieinos* healthful, fr. *hygiēs* healthy; akin to Skt *su* well and to L *vivus* living — more at QUICK] (1671) 1 : a science of the establishment and maintenance of health 2 : conditions or practices (as of cleanliness) conducive to health — **hy·gien·ist** \hī-'jē-nist, 'hī-ˌjē-, hī-'je-\ *n*

hy·gien·ic \ˌhī-'jē-nik, -'je- *also* -jē-'e-nik\ *adj* (1833) 1 a : of or relating to hygiene b : having or showing good hygiene ⟨∼ conditions⟩ 2 a : ANTISEPTIC 3c ⟨sweetly ∼ production . . . comic in an entirely innocuous way —J. W. Aldridge⟩ b : ANTISEPTIC 4 ⟨a ∼ view of national realities and moral imperatives —I. L. Horowitz⟩ — **hy·gien·i·cal·ly** \-ni-k(ə-)lē\ *adv*

hy·gien·ics \ˌhī-'jē-niks, -'je- *also* -jē-'e-niks\ *n pl but sing in constr* (1855) : HYGIENE 1

hygr- *also* **hygro-** *comb form* [Gk, fr. *hygros* wet — more at HUMOR] : humidity : moisture ⟨*hygro*phyte⟩

hy·gro·graph \'hī-grə-ˌgraf\ *n* [ISV] (ca. 1864) : an instrument for recording automatically variations in atmospheric humidity

hy·grom·e·ter \hī-'grä-mə-tər\ *n* [prob. fr. F *hygromètre*, fr. *hygr-* + *-mètre* -meter] (1670) : any of several instruments for measuring the humidity of the atmosphere — **hy·gro·met·ric** \ˌhī-grə-'me-trik\ *adj*

hy·groph·i·lous \hī-'grä-fə-ləs\ *adj* (1863) : living or growing in moist places

---

\ə\ abut \ᵊ\ kitten, F table \ər\ further \a\ ash \ā\ ace \ä\ mop, mar \au̇\ out \ch\ chin \e\ bet \ē\ easy \g\ go \i\ hit \ī\ ice \j\ job \ŋ\ sing \ō\ go \ȯ\ law \ȯi\ boy \th\ thin \t͟h\ the \ü\ loot \u̇\ foot \y\ yet \zh\ vision, beige \k, ⁿ, œ, ᵫ, �ᵉ\ see Guide to Pronunciation

hy·gro·scop·ic \ˌhī-grə-ˈskä-pik\ *adj* [*hygroscope,* an instrument showing changes in humidity + [1]*-ic;* fr. the use of such materials in the hygroscope] (1790) **1 :** readily taking up and retaining moisture **2 :** taken up and retained under some conditions of humidity and temperature ⟨~ water in clay⟩ — **hy·gro·scop·ic·i·ty** \-(ˌ)skä-ˈpi-sə-tē\ *n*

hying *pres part of* HIE

Hyk·sos \ˈhik-ˌsäs, -ˌsōs\ *adj* [Gk *Hyksōs,* dynasty ruling Egypt, perh. fr. Egypt *ḥqꜣ* ruler + *ḫꜣst* foreign land] (1602) **:** of or relating to a Semite dynasty that ruled Egypt from about the 18th to the 16th century B.C.

hy·lo·zo·ism \ˌhī-lə-ˈzō-ˌi-zəm\ *n* [Gk *hylē* matter, lit., wood + *zōos* alive, living; akin to Gk *zōē* life — more at QUICK] (1678) **:** a doctrine held esp. by early Greek philosophers that all matter has life — **hy·lo·zo·ist** \-ˈzō-ist\ *n* — **hy·lo·zo·is·tic** \-zō-ˈis-tik\ *adj*

hy·men \ˈhī-mən\ *n* [LL, fr. Gk *hymēn* membrane] (1543) **:** a fold of mucous membrane partly closing the orifice of the vagina — **hy·men·al** \-mə-nᵊl\ *adj*

Hymen *n* [L, fr. Gk *Hymēn*] (1567) **:** the Greek god of marriage

[1]**hy·me·ne·al** \ˌhī-mə-ˈnē-əl\ *adj* [L *hymenaeus* wedding song, wedding, fr. Gk *hymenaios,* fr. *Hymēn*] (1602) **:** NUPTIAL — **hy·me·ne·al·ly** \-ˈnē-ə-lē\ *adv*

[2]**hymeneal** *n* (1655) **1** *pl, archaic* **:** NUPTIALS **2** *archaic* **:** a wedding hymn

hy·me·ni·um \hī-ˈmē-nē-əm\ *n, pl* **-nia** \-nē-ə\ *or* **-niums** [NL, fr. Gk *hymēn*] (1830) **:** a spore-bearing layer in fungi

hy·me·nop·ter·an \ˌhī-mə-ˈnäp-tə-rən\ *n* [NL *Hymenoptera,* fr. Gk, neut. pl. of *hymenopteros* membrane-winged, fr. *hymēn* + *pteron* wing — more at FEATHER] (ca. 1842) **:** any of an order (Hymenoptera) of highly specialized insects with complete metamorphosis that include the bees, wasps, ants, ichneumon flies, sawflies, gall wasps, and related forms, often associate in large colonies with complex social organization, and have usu. four membranous wings and the abdomen generally borne on a slender pedicel — **hymenopteran** *adj* — **hy·me·nop·ter·ous** \-rəs\ *adj*

hy·me·nop·ter·on \-tə-ˌrän, -rən\ *n, pl* **-tera** \-rə\ *also* **-terons** [NL, fr. Gk, neut. of *hymenopteros*] (1877) **:** HYMENOPTERAN

[1]**hymn** \ˈhim\ *n* [ME *ymne,* fr. OE *ymen,* fr. L *hymnus* song of praise, fr. Gk *hymnos*] (bef. 12c) **1 a :** a song of praise to God **b :** a metrical composition adapted for singing in a religious service **2 :** a song of praise or joy **3 :** something resembling a hymn **:** PAEAN — **hymn·like** \-ˌlīk\ *adj*

[2]**hymn** *vb* **hymned** \ˈhimd\; **hymn·ing** \ˈhi-miŋ\ *vt* (1667) **:** to praise or worship in or as if in hymns ⟨the heroes ~*ed* in this book⟩ ~ *vi* **:** to sing a hymn

hym·nal \ˈhim-nəl\ *n* [ME *hymnale,* fr. ML, fr. L *hymnus*] (15c) **:** a collection of church hymns

hym·na·ry \ˈhim-nə-rē\ *n, pl* **-ries** (1888) **:** HYMNAL

hymn·book \ˈhim-ˌbu̇k\ *n* (bef. 12c) **:** HYMNAL

hym·no·dy \ˈhim-nə-dē\ *n* [LL *hymnodia,* fr. Gk *hymnōidia,* fr. *hymnos* + *aeidein* to sing — more at ODE] (1711) **1 :** hymn singing **2 :** hymn writing **3 :** the hymns of a time, place, or church

hym·nol·o·gy \him-ˈnä-lə-jē\ *n* [Gk *hymnologia* singing of hymns, fr. *hymnos* + *-logia* -logy] (ca. 1638) **1 :** HYMNODY **2 :** the study of hymns

hy·oid \ˈhī-ˌȯid\ *adj* [NL *hyoides* hyoid bone] (1842) **:** of or relating to the hyoid bone

hyoid bone *n* [NL *hyoides,* fr. Gk *hyoeidēs* shaped like the letter upsilon (Υ, υ), being the hyoid bone, fr. *y, hy* upsilon] (ca. 1811) **:** a U-shaped bone or complex of bones that is situated between the base of the tongue and the larynx and that supports the tongue, the larynx, and their muscles — called also *hyoid*

hy·o·scine \ˈhī-ə-ˌsēn\ *n* [ISV *hyos*cyamine + *-ine*] (1872) **:** SCOPOLAMINE; *esp* **:** the levorotatory form of scopolamine

hy·o·scy·a·mine \ˌhī-ə-ˈsī-ə-ˌmēn\ *n* [G *Hyoscyamin,* fr. NL *Hyoscyamus,* genus of herbs, fr. L, henbane, fr. Gk *hyoskyamos,* lit., swine's bean, fr. *hyos* (gen. of *hys* swine) + *kyamos* bean — more at SOW] (1858) **:** a poisonous crystalline alkaloid $C_{17}H_{23}NO_3$ of which atropine is a racemic mixture; *esp* **:** its levorotatory form found esp. in the plants belladonna and henbane and used similarly to atropine

hyp *abbr* hypothesis; hypothetical

hyp- — see HYPO-

hyp·abys·sal \ˌhi-pə-ˈbi-səl, ˌhī-\ *adj* [ISV] (1895) **:** of or relating to a fine-grained igneous rock usu. formed at a moderate distance below the surface — **hyp·abys·sal·ly** \-sə-lē\ *adv*

hy·pae·thral \hī-ˈpē-thrəl\ *adj* [L *hypaethrus* exposed to the open air, fr. Gk *hypaithros,* fr. *hypo-* + *aithēr* ether, air — more at ETHER] (1794) **1 :** having a roofless central space ⟨~ temple⟩ **2 :** open to the sky

hy·pal·la·ge \hī-ˈpa-lə-jē, hi-\ *n* [L, fr. Gk *hypallagē,* lit., interchange, fr. *hypallassein* to interchange, fr. *hypo-* + *allassein* to change, fr. *allos* other — more at ELSE] (1586) **:** an interchange of two elements in a phrase or sentence from a more logical to a less logical relationship (as in "a mind is a terrible thing to waste" for "to waste a mind is a terrible thing")

hy·pan·thi·um \hī-ˈpan(t)-thē-əm\ *n, pl* **-thia** \-thē-ə\ [NL, fr. *hypo-* + *anth-* + *-ium*] (ca. 1855) **:** an enlargement of the floral receptacle bearing on its rim the stamens, petals, and sepals and often enlarging and surrounding the fruits (as in the rose hip)

[1]**hype** \ˈhīp\ *n* [by shortening & alter. fr. *hypodermic*] (1924) **1** *slang* **:** a narcotics addict **2** *slang* **:** HYPODERMIC

[2]**hype** *vt* **hyped; hyping** (1938) **1 :** STIMULATE, ENLIVEN — usu. used with *up* ⟨*hyping* herself up for the game⟩ **2 :** INCREASE — **hyped–up** \ˈhīp-ˈdəp\ *adj*

[3]**hype** *vt* **hyped; hyp·ing** [origin unknown] (ca. 1931) **1 :** PUT ON, DECEIVE **2 :** to promote or publicize extravagantly ⟨*hyping* this fall's TV lineup⟩

[4]**hype** *n* (1955) **1 :** DECEPTION, PUT-ON **2 :** PUBLICITY; *esp* **:** promotional publicity of an extravagant or contrived kind ⟨all the ~ before the boxing match⟩

[5]**hype** *adj* (1989) *slang* **:** EXCELLENT, COOL

hy·per \ˈhī-pər\ *adj* [short for *hyperactive*] (ca. 1942) **1 :** HIGH-STRUNG, EXCITABLE; *also* **:** highly excited **2 :** extremely active

hyper- *prefix* [L *hyper-,* fr. Gk, fr. *hyper* — more at OVER] **1 :** above **:** beyond **:** SUPER- ⟨*hyper*market⟩ **2 a :** excessively ⟨*hyper*sensitive⟩ **b :** excessive ⟨*hyper*emia⟩ **3 :** that is or exists in a space of more than three dimensions ⟨*hyper*space⟩ **4 :** bridging points within an entity (as a database or network) nonsequentially ⟨*hyper*text⟩

hy·per·acu·ity
hy·per·acute
hy·per·aes·thet·ic
hy·per·ag·gres·sive
hy·per·ag·gres·sive·ness
hy·per·alert
hy·per·arid
hy·per·arous·al
hy·per·aware
hy·per·aware·ness
hy·per·ca·tab·o·lism
hy·per·cau·tious
hy·per·charged
hy·per·civ·i·lized
hy·per·co·ag·u·la·bil·i·ty
hy·per·co·ag·u·la·ble
hy·per·com·pet·i·tive
hy·per·con·cen·tra·tion
hy·per·con·scious
hy·per·con·scious·ness
hy·per·de·vel·op·ment
hy·per·ef·fi·cient
hy·per·emo·tion·al
hy·per·emo·tion·al·i·ty
hy·per·en·dem·ic
hy·per·en·er·get·ic
hy·per·ex·cit·abil·i·ty
hy·per·ex·cit·able
hy·per·ex·cit·ed
hy·per·ex·cite·ment
hy·per·ex·cre·tion
hy·per·fas·tid·i·ous
hy·per·func·tion
hy·per·func·tion·al
hy·per·func·tion·ing
hy·per·im·mune
hy·per·im·mu·ni·za·tion
hy·per·im·mu·nize
hy·per·in·flat·ed
hy·per·in·ner·va·tion
hy·per·in·tel·lec·tu·al
hy·per·in·tel·li·gent
hy·per·in·tense
hy·per·in·vo·lu·tion
hy·per·ma·nia
hy·per·man·ic
hy·per·mas·cu·line
hy·per·met·a·bol·ic
hy·per·me·tab·o·lism
hy·per·mo·bil·i·ty
hy·per·mod·ern
hy·per·mod·ern·ist
hy·per·mu·ta·bil·i·ty
hy·per·mu·ta·ble
hy·per·na·tion·al·is·tic
hy·per·phys·i·cal
hy·per·pig·men·ta·tion
hy·per·pig·ment·ed
hy·per·pro·duc·er
hy·per·pro·duc·tion
hy·per·pure
hy·per·ra·tio·nal
hy·per·ra·tio·nal·i·ty
hy·per·re·ac·tive
hy·per·re·ac·tiv·i·ty
hy·per·re·ac·tor
hy·per·re·spon·sive
hy·per·ro·man·tic
hy·per·sa·line
hy·per·sa·lin·i·ty
hy·per·sal·i·va·tion
hy·per·se·cre·tion
hy·per·sen·si·ti·za·tion
hy·per·sen·si·tize
hy·per·som·no·lence
hy·per·stat·ic
hy·per·stim·u·late
hy·per·stim·u·la·tion
hy·per·sus·cep·ti·bil·i·ty
hy·per·sus·cep·ti·ble
hy·per·tense
hy·per·typ·i·cal
hy·per·vig·i·lance
hy·per·vig·i·lant
hy·per·vir·u·lent
hy·per·vis·cos·i·ty

hy·per·acid·i·ty \ˌhī-pər-ə-ˈsi-də-tē\ *n* (ca. 1890) **:** the condition of containing more than the normal amount of acid — **hy·per·ac·id** \ˌhī-pər-ˈa-səd\ *adj*

hy·per·ac·tive \ˌhī-pər-ˈak-tiv\ *adj* (1867) **1 :** affected with or exhibiting hyperactivity; *broadly* **:** more active than is usual or desirable **2 :** intricately or elaborately designed or detailed — **hyperactive** *n*

hy·per·ac·tiv·i·ty \-ˌak-ˈti-və-tē\ *n* (1888) **:** the state or condition of being excessively or pathologically active; *esp* **:** ATTENTION DEFICIT DISORDER

hyperaesthesia *var of* HYPERESTHESIA

hy·per·al·i·men·ta·tion \ˌhī-pər-ˌa-lə-mən-ˈtā-shən\ *n* (1962) **:** the administration of nutrients through intravenous feeding esp. to patients who cannot ingest food through the alimentary tract

hy·per·bar·ic \ˌhī-pər-ˈber-ik, -ˈba-rik\ *adj* [*hyper-* + *bar-* + [1]*-ic*] (1962) **:** of, relating to, or utilizing greater than normal pressure esp. of oxygen ⟨a ~ chamber⟩ ⟨~ medicine⟩ — **hy·per·bar·i·cal·ly** \-i-k(ə-)lē\ *adv*

hy·per·bo·la \hī-ˈpər-bə-lə\ *n, pl* **-las** *or* **-lae** \-(ˌ)lē\ [NL, fr. Gk *hyperbolē*] (1668) **:** a plane curve generated by a point so moving that the difference of the distances from two fixed points is a constant **:** a curve formed by the intersection of a double right circular cone with a plane that cuts both halves of the cone

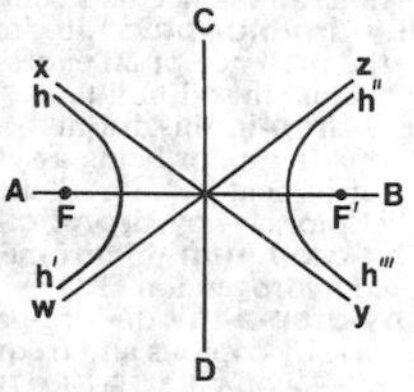

hyperbola: *AB, CD* axes; *F, F'* foci; *xy, zw* asymptotes; *h, h', h'', h'''* hyperbola

hy·per·bo·le \hī-ˈpər-bə-(ˌ)lē\ *n* [L, fr. Gk *hyperbolē* excess, hyperbole, hyperbola, fr. *hyperballein* to exceed, fr. *hyper-* + *ballein* to throw — more at DEVIL] (15c) **:** extravagant exaggeration (as "mile-high ice-cream cones") — **hy·per·bo·list** \-list\ *n*

[1]**hy·per·bol·ic** \ˌhī-pər-ˈbä-lik\ *also* **hy·per·bol·i·cal** \-li-kəl\ *adj* (15c) **:** of, relating to, or marked by hyperbole — **hy·per·bol·i·cal·ly** \-li-k(ə-)lē\ *adv*

[2]**hyperbolic** *adj* (1676) **1 :** of, relating to, or being analogous to a hyperbola **2 :** of, relating to, or being a space in which more than one line parallel to a given line passes through a point ⟨~ geometry⟩

hyperbolic function *n* (ca. 1890) **:** any of a set of six functions analogous to the trigonometric functions but related to the hyperbola in a way similar to that in which the trigonometric functions are related to a circle

hyperbolic paraboloid *n* (1842) **:** a saddle-shaped quadric surface whose sections by planes parallel to one coordinate plane are hyperbolas while those sections by planes parallel to the other two are parabolas if proper orientation of the coordinate axes is assumed

hy·per·bo·lize \hī-ˈpər-bə-ˌlīz\ *vb* **-lized; -liz·ing** *vi* (1599) **:** to indulge in hyperbole ~ *vt* **:** to exaggerate to a hyperbolic degree

hy·per·bo·loid \-ˌlȯid\ *n* (1743) **:** a quadric surface whose sections by planes parallel to one coordinate plane are ellipses while those sections by planes parallel to the other two are hyperbolas if proper orientation of the axes is assumed — **hy·per·bo·loi·dal** \(ˌ)hī-ˌpər-bə-ˈlȯi-dᵊl\ *adj*

[1]**hy·per·bo·re·an** \ˌhī-pər-ˈbȯr-ē-ən, -(ˌ)pər-bə-ˈrē-ən\ *n* [L *Hyperborei* (pl.), fr. Gk *Hyperboreoi,* fr. *hyper-* + *Boreas*] (15c) **1** *often cap* **:** a member of a people held by the ancient Greeks to live beyond the north wind in a region of perpetual sunshine **2 :** an inhabitant of a cool northern climate

[2]**hyperborean** *adj* (1591) **1 :** of or relating to an extreme northern region **:** FROZEN **2 :** of or relating to any of the arctic peoples

hy·per·cal·ce·mia \ˌhī-pər-ˌkal-ˈsē-mē-ə\ *n* [NL] (1925) **:** an excess of calcium in the blood — **hy·per·cal·ce·mic** \-ˈsē-mik\ *adj*

hy·per·cap·nia \-ˈkap-nē-ə\ *n* [NL, fr. *hyper-* + Gk *kapnos* smoke; prob. akin to Lith *kvapas* breath] (1908) **:** the presence of excessive amounts of carbon dioxide in the blood — **hy·per·cap·nic** \-nik\ *adj*

hy·per·cat·a·lex·is \-ˌka-tə-ˈlek-səs\ *n, pl* **-lex·es** \-ˈlek-ˌsēz\ [NL] (ca. 1890) **:** the occurrence of an additional syllable after the final complete foot or dipody in a line of verse — **hy·per·cat·a·lec·tic** \-ˈlek-tik\ *adj*

hy·per·charge \ˈhī-pər-ˌchärj\ *n* [short for *hyperonic charge,* fr. *hyperon*] (1956) **:** a quantum characteristic of a group of subatomic particles governed by the strong force that is related to strangeness and is represented by a number equal to twice the average value of the electric charge of the group

hy·per·cho·les·ter·ol·emia \ˌhī-pər-kə-ˌles-tə-rə-ˈlē-mē-ə\ *n* [NL] (1916) **:** the presence of excess cholesterol in the blood — **hy·per·cho·les·ter·ol·emic** \-mik\ *adj*

hy·per·cor·rect \ˌhī-pər-kə-ˈrekt\ *adj* (1922) **:** of, relating to, or characterized by the production of a nonstandard linguistic form or construction on the basis of a false analogy (as "badly" in "my eyes have gone badly") — **hy·per·cor·rec·tion** \-ˈrek-shən\ *n* — **hy·per·cor·rect·ly** \-ˈrek-(t)lē\ *adv* — **hy·per·cor·rect·ness** \-ˈrek(t)-nəs\ *n*

hy·per·crit·ic \ˌhī-pər-ˈkri-tik\ *n* [NL *hypercriticus,* fr. *hyper-* + L *criticus* critic] (1633) **:** a carping or unduly censorious critic — **hy·per·crit·i·cism** \-ˈkri-tə-ˌsi-zəm\ *n*

hy·per·crit·i·cal \-ˈkri-ti-kəl\ *adj* (1605) **:** meticulously or excessively critical **syn** see CRITICAL — **hy·per·crit·i·cal·ly** \-k(ə-)lē\ *adv*

hy·per·cube \ˈhī-pər-ˌkyüb\ *n* (1909) **1 :** a geometric figure (as a tesseract) in Euclidean space of *n* dimensions that is analogous to a cube in three dimensions **2 :** a computer architecture in which each processor is connected to *n* others based on analogy to a hypercube of *n* dimensions

hy·per·drive \ˈhī-pər-ˌdrīv\ *n* (1977) **:** OVERDRIVE 2

hy·per·emia \ˌhī-pər-ˈē-mē-ə\ *n* [NL] (ca. 1839) **:** excess of blood in a body part **:** CONGESTION — **hy·per·emic** \-mik\ *adj*

hy·per·es·the·sia *also* **hy·per·aes·the·sia** \ˌhī-pər-es-ˈthē-zh(ē-)ə\ *n* [NL, fr. *hyper-* + *-esthesia* (as in *anesthesia*)] (ca. 1852) **:** unusual or pathological sensitivity of the skin or of a particular sense — **hy·per·es·thet·ic** \-ˈthe-tik\ *adj*

hy·per·eu·tec·tic \ˌhī-pər-yu̇-ˈtek-tik\ *adj* (1902) **:** HYPEREUTECTOID

hy·per·eu·tec·toid \-ˌtȯid\ *adj* (1908) **:** containing the minor component in excess of that contained in the eutectoid

hy·per·ex·tend \ˌhī-pər-ik-ˈstend\ *vt* (1883) **:** to extend so that the angle between bones of a joint is greater than normal ⟨a *~ed* elbow⟩; *also* **:** to extend (as a body part) beyond the normal range of motion ⟨*~ed* her neck⟩ — **hy·per·ex·ten·sion** \-ˈsten(t)-shən\ *n*

hy·per·fine \ˈhī-pər-ˌfīn\ *adj* (1926) **:** being or relating to a fine-structure multiplet occurring in an atomic spectrum that is due to interaction between electrons and nuclear spin

hy·per·fo·cal distance \ˌhī-pər-ˈfō-kəl-\ *n* [ISV] (1905) **:** the nearest distance upon which a photographic lens may be focused to produce satisfactory definition at infinity

hy·per·ga·my \hī-ˈpər-gə-mē\ *n, pl* **-mies** (1883) **:** marriage into an equal or higher caste or social group

hy·per·geo·met·ric distribution \ˌhī-pər-ˌjē-ə-ˈme-trik-\ *n* (1936) **:** a probability function *f(x)* that gives the probability of obtaining exactly *x* elements of one kind and *n* – *x* elements of another if *n* elements are chosen at random without replacement from a finite population containing *N* elements of which *M* are of the first kind and *N* – *M* are of the second kind and that has the form

$$f(x) = \frac{\binom{M}{x}\binom{N-M}{n-x}}{\binom{N}{n}} \text{ where } \binom{M}{x} = \frac{M!}{x!(M-x)!}$$

hy·per·gly·ce·mia \ˌhī-pər-glī-ˈsē-mē-ə\ *n* [NL] (1894) **:** excess of sugar in the blood — **hy·per·gly·ce·mic** \-mik\ *adj*

hy·per·gol·ic \ˌhī-pər-ˈgä-lik\ *adj* [G *Hypergol* a hypergolic fuel, prob. fr. *hyper-* + *erg-* + *-ol* (hydrocarbon)] (1947) **1 :** igniting upon contact of components without external aid (as a spark) **2 :** of, relating to, or using hypergolic fuel — **hy·per·gol·i·cal·ly** \-li-k(ə-)lē\ *adv*

hy·per·hi·dro·sis \ˌhī-pər-hī-ˈdrō-səs\ *n* [NL *hidrosis* perspiration, fr. Gk *hidrōsis,* fr. *hidroun* to sweat, fr. *hidrōs* sweat — more at SWEAT] (ca. 1860) **:** generalized or local excessive sweating

hy·per·in·fla·tion \ˌhī-pər-in-ˈflā-shən\ *n* (1930) **:** inflation growing at a very high rate in a very short time; *also* **:** a period of hyperinflation — **hy·per·in·fla·tion·ary** \-shə-ˌner-ē\ *adj*

hy·per·in·su·lin·ism \ˌhī-pər-ˈin(t)-s(ə-)lə-ˌni-zəm\ *n* [ISV] (1924) **:** the presence of excess insulin in the body resulting in hypoglycemia

Hy·pe·ri·on \hī-ˈpir-ē-ən\ *n* [L, fr. Gk *Hyperiōn*] (1567) **:** a Titan and the father of Eos, Selene, and Helios

hy·per·ir·ri·ta·bil·i·ty \ˌhī-pər-ˌir-ə-tə-ˈbi-lə-tē\ *n* (1908) **:** abnormally great or uninhibited response to stimuli — **hy·per·ir·ri·ta·ble** \-ˈir-ə-tə-bəl\ *adj*

hy·per·ker·a·to·sis \ˌhī-pər-ˌker-ə-ˈtō-səs\ *n, pl* **-to·ses** \-ˈtō-ˌsēz\ [NL] (1841) **:** hypertrophy of the corneous layer of the skin — **hy·per·ker·a·tot·ic** \-ˈtä-tik\ *adj*

hy·per·ki·ne·sia \-kə-ˈnē-zh(ē-)ə, -kī-\ *n* [NL, fr. *hyperkinesis*] (ca. 1848) **:** HYPERKINESIS

hy·per·ki·ne·sis \-ˈnē-səs\ *n* [NL] (ca. 1855) **1 :** abnormally increased and sometimes uncontrollable activity or muscular movements **2 :** a condition esp. of childhood characterized by hyperactivity

hy·per·ki·net·ic \-ˈne-tik\ *adj* (1888) **1 :** of, relating to, or affected with hyperkinesis or hyperactivity ⟨the ~ child⟩ **2 :** characterized by fast-paced or frenetic activity ⟨a ~ movie⟩

hy·per·link \ˈhī-pər-ˌliŋk\ *n* (1988) **:** an electronic link providing direct access from one distinctively marked place in a hypertext or hypermedia document to another in the same or a different document — **hyperlink** *vt*

hy·per·li·pe·mia \ˌhī-pər-lī-ˈpē-mē-ə\ *n* [NL] (ca. 1894) **:** HYPERLIPIDEMIA — **hy·per·li·pe·mic** \-mik\ *adj*

hy·per·lip·id·emia \-ˌli-pə-ˈdē-mē-ə\ *n* [NL] (1961) **:** the presence of excess fat or lipids in the blood

hy·per·mar·ket \ˈhī-pər-ˌmär-kət\ *n* (1970) **:** a very large store that carries products found in a supermarket as well as merchandise commonly found in department stores

hy·per·me·dia \-ˌmē-dē-ə\ *n* (1965) **:** a database format similar to hypertext in which text, sound, or video images related to that on a display can be accessed directly from the display

hy·per·me·ter \hī-ˈpər-mə-tər\ *n* [LL *hypermetrus* hypercatalectic, fr. Gk *hypermetros* beyond measure, beyond the meter, fr. *hyper-* + *metron* measure, meter] (ca. 1656) **1 :** a verse marked by hypercatalexis **2 :** a period comprising more than two or three cola — **hy·per·met·ric** \ˌhī-pər-ˈme-trik\ *or* **hy·per·met·ri·cal** \-tri-kəl\ *adj*

hy·per·me·tro·pia \ˌhī-pər-mi-ˈtrō-pē-ə\ *n* [NL, fr. Gk *hypermetros* + NL *-opia*] (1868) **:** HYPEROPIA — **hy·per·me·tro·pic** \-ˈtrō-pik, -ˈträ-\ *adj*

hy·per·mil·ing \ˈhī-pər-ˌmī-liŋ\ *n* (2006) **:** the use of fuel-saving techniques (as lower speeds and frequent coasting) to maximize a vehicle's fuel mileage — **hy·per·mil·er** \-lər\ *n*

hy·perm·ne·sia \ˌhī-(ˌ)pərm-ˈnē-zh(ē-)ə\ *n* [NL, fr. *hyper-* + *-mnesia* (as in *amnesia*)] (1882) **:** abnormally vivid or complete memory or recall of the past — **hy·perm·ne·sic** \-ˈnē-zik, -sik\ *adj*

hy·per·on \ˈhī-pə-ˌrän\ *n* [prob. fr. *hyper-* + [2]*-on*] (1953) **:** an elementary particle of the baryon group having greater mass than a nucleon

hy·per·opia \ˌhī-pə-ˈrō-pē-ə\ *n* [NL] (1884) **:** a condition in which visual images come to a focus behind the retina of the eye and vision is better for distant than for near objects — called also *farsightedness* — **hy·per·opic** \-ˈrō-pik, -ˈrä-\ *adj*

hy·per·os·to·sis \ˌhī-pər-ˌäs-ˈtō-səs\ *n, pl* **-to·ses** \-ˈtō-ˌsēz\ [NL] (ca. 1836) **:** excessive growth or thickening of bone tissue — **hy·per·os·tot·ic** \-ˈtä-tik\ *adj*

hy·per·par·a·site \ˌhī-pər-ˈper-ə-ˌsīt, -ˈpa-rə-\ *n* (1833) **:** a parasite that is parasitic upon another parasite — **hy·per·par·a·sit·ic** \-ˌper-ə-ˈsi-tik, -ˌpa-rə-\ *adj* — **hy·per·par·a·sit·ism** \-ˈper-ə-ˌsī-ˌti-zəm, -ˈpa-rə-, -sə-ˌti-\ *n*

hy·per·para·thy·roid·ism \-ˌper-ə-ˈthī-ˌrȯi-ˌdi-zəm, -ˌpa-rə-\ *n* (1917) **:** the presence of excess parathyroid hormone in the body resulting in disturbance of calcium metabolism with increase in serum calcium and decrease in inorganic phosphorus, loss of calcium from bone, and renal damage with frequent kidney-stone formation

hy·per·pha·gia \-ˈfā-j(ē-)ə\ *n* [NL] (1941) **:** abnormally increased appetite for consumption of food frequently associated with injury to the hypothalamus — **hy·per·phag·ic** \-ˈfa-jik\ *adj*

hy·per·pi·tu·ita·rism \-pə-ˈtü-ə-tə-ˌri-zəm, -ˈtü-ə-ˌtri-, -ˈtyü-\ *n* [ISV] (1909) **:** excessive production of growth hormones by the pituitary gland — **hy·per·pi·tu·itary** \-ˈtü-ə-ˌter-ē, -ˈtyü-\ *adj*

hy·per·plane \ˈhī-pər-ˌplān\ *n* (1903) **:** a figure in hyperspace corresponding to a plane in ordinary space

hy·per·pla·sia \ˌhī-pər-ˈplā-zh(ē-)ə\ *n* [NL] (1861) **:** an abnormal or unusual increase in the elements composing a part (as cells composing a tissue) — compare BENIGN PROSTATIC HYPERPLASIA — **hy·per·plas·tic** \-ˈplas-tik\ *adj*

hy·per·ploid \ˈhī-pər-ˌplȯid\ *adj* [ISV] (1930) **:** having a chromosome number slightly greater than an exact multiple of the monoploid number — **hyperploid** *n* — **hy·per·ploi·dy** \-ˌplȯi-dē\ *n*

hy·per·pnea \ˌhī-pər-ˈnē-ə, -ˌpərp-ˈnē-\ *n* [NL] (ca. 1860) **:** abnormally rapid or deep breathing — **hy·per·pne·ic** \-ˈnē-ik\ *adj*

hy·per·po·lar·ize \ˌhī-pər-ˈpō-lə-ˌrīz\ *vt* (1946) **:** to produce an increase in potential difference across (a biological membrane) ~ *vi* **:** to undergo or produce an increase in potential difference across something — **hy·per·po·lar·i·za·tion** \-ˌpō-lə-rə-ˈzā-shən\ *n*

hy·per·py·rex·ia \-pī-ˈrek-sē-ə\ *n* [NL] (1875) **:** exceptionally high fever (as in a particular disease)

hy·per·re·al·ism \ˌhī-pər-ˈrē-ə-ˌli-zəm, -ˈrēl-ˌi-\ *n* (1937) **:** realism in art characterized by depiction of real life in an unusual or striking manner — compare PHOTO-REALISM — **hy·per·re·al·ist** \-list, -ist\ *adj* — **hy·per·re·al·is·tic** \-ˌrē-ə-ˈlis-tik, -ˌrēl-ˈis-\ *adj*

hy·per·sen·si·tive \ˌhī-pər-ˈsen(t)-s(ə-)tiv\ *adj* (1871) **1 :** excessively or abnormally sensitive **2 :** abnormally susceptible physiologically to a specific agent (as a drug or antigen) — **hy·per·sen·si·tive·ness** *n* — **hy·per·sen·si·tiv·i·ty** \-ˌsen(t)-sə-ˈti-və-tē\ *n*

hy·per·sex·u·al \-ˈsek-sh(ə-)wəl, -ˈsek-shəl\ *adj* (1915) **:** exhibiting unusual or excessive concern with or indulgence in sexual activity — **hy·per·sex·u·al·i·ty** \-ˌsek-shə-ˈwa-lə-tē\ *n*

hy·per·son·ic \-ˈsä-nik\ *adj* [ISV] (1946) **1 :** of or relating to speed five or more times that of sound in air — compare SONIC **2 :** moving, capable of moving, or utilizing air currents that move at hypersonic speed ⟨~ wind tunnel⟩ — **hy·per·son·i·cal·ly** \-ni-k(ə-)lē\ *adv*

hy·per·space \ˈhī-pər-ˌspās\ *n* (1867) **1 :** space of more than three dimensions **2 :** a fictional space in which extraordinary events happen

hy·per·sthene \ˈhī-pərs-ˌthēn\ *n* [F *hypersthène,* fr. Gk *hyper-* + *sthenos* strength] (ca. 1808) **:** an orthorhombic grayish or greenish black or dark brown pyroxene — **hy·per·sthe·nic** \ˌhī-pərs-ˈthe-nik, -ˈthē-\ *adj*

hy·per·sur·face \ˈhī-pər-ˌsər-fəs\ *n* (ca. 1909) **:** a figure that is the analogue in hyperspace of a surface in three-dimensional space

hy·per·ten·sion \ˌhī-pər-ˈten(t)-shən\ *n* [ISV] (1893) **1 :** abnormally high blood pressure and esp. arterial blood pressure **2 :** the systemic condition accompanying high blood pressure

[1]**hy·per·ten·sive** \ˌhī-pər-ˈten(t)-siv\ *adj* (1904) **:** affected with or caused by hypertension

[2]**hypertensive** *n* (1939) **:** an individual affected with hypertension

hy·per·text \ˈhī-pər-ˌtekst\ *n* (1965) **:** a database format in which information related to that on a display can be accessed directly from the display; *also* **:** material (as text) in this format — **hy·per·tex·tu·al** \ˌhī-pər-ˈteks-chə-wəl, -chəl\ *adj*

hypertext markup language *n* (1989) **:** HTML

hypertext transfer protocol *n* (1992) **:** a communications protocol governing the exchange of data (as HTML files) esp. on the World Wide Web — called also *hypertext transport protocol*

hy·per·ther·mia \ˌhī-pər-ˈthər-mē-ə\ *n* [NL, fr. *hyper-* + *therm-* + *-ia*] (1887) **:** exceptionally high fever esp. when induced artificially for therapeutic purposes — **hy·per·ther·mic** \-mik\ *adj*

hy·per·ther·mo·phile \ˌhī-pər-ˈthər-mə-ˌfī(-ə)l\ *n* (1988) **:** an organism that lives in extremely hot environments (as hot springs) with temperatures around the boiling point of water — **hy·per·ther·mo·phil·ic** \-ˌthər-mə-ˈfi-lik\ *adj*

hy·per·thy·roid \-ˈthī-ˌrȯid\ *adj* [back-formation fr. *hyperthyroidism*] (1916) **:** of, relating to, or affected with hyperthyroidism

hy·per·thy·roid·ism \-ˌrȯi-ˌdi-zəm\ *n* [ISV] (ca. 1900) **:** excessive functional activity of the thyroid gland; *also* **:** the resulting condition

\ə\ **abut** \ᵊ\ **kitten,** F **table** \ər\ **further** \a\ **ash** \ā\ **ace** \ä\ **mop, mar** \au̇\ **out** \ch\ **chin** \e\ **bet** \ē\ **easy** \g\ **go** \i\ **hit** \ī\ **ice** \j\ **job** \ŋ\ **sing** \ō\ **go** \ȯ\ **law** \ȯi\ **boy** \th\ **thin** \t͟h\ **the** \ü\ **loot** \u̇\ **foot** \y\ **yet** \zh\ **vision, beige** \k̲, ⁿ, œ, ue, ʸ\ *see* Guide to Pronunciation

marked esp. by increased metabolic rate, enlargement of the thyroid gland, rapid heart rate, and high blood pressure

hy·per·to·nia \ˌhī-pər-ˈtō-nē-ə\ *n* (ca. 1842) **:** the condition of exhibiting excessive muscular tone or tension

hy·per·ton·ic \-ˈtä-nik\ *adj* [ISV] (1855) **1 :** exhibiting excessive tone or tension ⟨a ~ baby⟩ ⟨a ~ bladder⟩ **2 :** having a higher osmotic pressure than a surrounding medium or a fluid under comparison

hy·per·to·nic·i·ty \-tə-ˈni-sə-tē\ *n, pl* **-ties** (1886) **:** the condition of being hypertonic; *esp* **:** HYPERTONIA

1**hy·per·tro·phy** \hī-ˈpər-trə-fē\ *n, pl* **-phies** [prob. fr. NL *hypertrophia,* fr. *hyper-* + *-trophia* -trophy] (1834) **1 :** excessive development of an organ or part; *specif* **:** increase in bulk (as by thickening of muscle fibers) without multiplication of parts **2 :** exaggerated growth or complexity — **hy·per·tro·phic** \ˌhī-pər-ˈtrō-fik\ *adj*

2**hypertrophy** *vi* **-phied; -phy·ing** (1883) **:** to undergo hypertrophy

hy·per·ur·ban·ism \ˌhī-pər-ˈər-bə-ˌni-zəm\ *n* (1925) **:** use of hypercorrect forms in language; *also* **:** such a form

hy·per·uri·ce·mia \ˌhī-pər-ˌyu̇r-ə-ˈsē-mē-ə\ *n* [NL] (ca. 1894) **:** excess uric acid in the blood

hy·per·var·i·able \ˌhī-pər-ˈver-ē-ə-bəl\ *adj* (1970) **:** relating to or being any of the relatively short extremely variable polypeptide chain segments in the light chain or heavy chain of an antibody; *also* **:** relating to, containing, or being a highly variable nucleotide sequence

hy·per·ve·loc·i·ty \-və-ˈlä-sə-tē, -ˈläs-tē\ *n* (1949) **:** a high or relatively high velocity (as thousands of feet or meters per second)

hy·per·ven·ti·late \ˌhī-pər-ˈven-tə-ˌlāt\ *vi* (1931) **:** to breathe rapidly and deeply **:** undergo hyperventilation

hy·per·ven·ti·la·tion \-ˌven-tə-ˈlā-shən\ *n* (1928) **:** excessive rate and depth of respiration leading to abnormal loss of carbon dioxide from the blood

hy·per·vi·ta·min·osis \-ˌvī-tə-mə-ˈnō-səs\ *n, pl* **-oses** \-ˈnō-ˌsēz\ [NL] (1928) **:** an abnormal state resulting from excessive intake of one or more vitamins

hy·pha \ˈhī-fə\ *n, pl* **hy·phae** \-(ˌ)fē\ [NL, fr. Gk *hyphē* web; akin to Gk *hyphos* web — more at WEAVE] (1866) **:** one of the threads that make up the mycelium of a fungus, increase by apical growth, and are transversely septate or nonseptate — **hy·phal** \-fəl\ *adj*

1**hy·phen** \ˈhī-fən\ *n* [LL & Gk; LL, fr. Gk, fr. *hyph' hen* under one, fr. *hypo* under + *hen,* neut. of *heis* one — more at UP, SAME] (ca. 1620) **:** a punctuation mark - used esp. to divide or to compound words, word elements, or numbers — **hy·phen·less** \-ləs\ *adj*

2**hyphen** *vt* (1814) **:** HYPHENATE

1**hy·phen·ate** \ˈhī-fə-ˌnāt\ *vt* **-at·ed; -at·ing** (ca. 1889) **:** to connect (as two words) or divide (as a word at the end of a line of print) with a hyphen — **hy·phen·ation** \ˌhī-fə-ˈnā-shən\ *n*

2**hyphenate** *n* [fr. the hyphens in the titles of such people, as *producer-director*] (1974) **:** a person who performs more than one function (as a producer-director in filmmaking)

hyphenated *adj* [fr. the use of hyphenated words (as German-American) to designate foreign-born citizens of the U.S.] (ca. 1893) **:** of, relating to, or being an individual or unit of mixed or diverse background or composition ⟨~ Americans⟩

hypn- *or* **hypno-** *comb form* [F, fr. LL, fr. Gk, fr. *hypnos* — more at SOMNOLENT] **1 :** sleep ⟨*hypno*pompic⟩ **2 :** hypnotism ⟨*hypno*therapy⟩

hyp·na·go·gic *also* **hyp·no·go·gic** \ˌhip-nə-ˈgä-jik, -ˈgō-\ *adj* [F *hypnagogique,* fr. Gk *hypn-* + *-agōgos* leading, inducing, fr. *agein* to lead — more at AGENT] (1886) **:** of, relating to, or occurring in the period of drowsiness immediately preceding sleep ⟨~ hallucinations⟩

hyp·noid \ˈhip-ˌnȯid\ *or* **hyp·noi·dal** \hip-ˈnȯi-dᵊl\ *adj* (1898) **:** of or relating to sleep or hypnosis

hyp·no·pom·pic \ˌhip-nə-ˈpäm-pik\ *adj* [*hypn-* + Gk *pompē* act of sending — more at POMP] (ca. 1901) **:** associated with the semiconsciousness preceding waking ⟨~ illusions⟩

Hyp·nos \ˈhip-nəs, -ˌnōs\ *n* [Gk] (1892) **:** the Greek god of sleep

hyp·no·sis \hip-ˈnō-səs\ *n, pl* **-no·ses** \-ˌsēz\ [NL] (1876) **1 :** a trancelike state that resembles sleep but is induced by a person whose suggestions are readily accepted by the subject **2 :** any of various conditions that resemble sleep **3 :** HYPNOTISM 1

hyp·no·ther·a·py \ˌhip-nō-ˈther-ə-pē\ *n* (1897) **1 :** treatment by hypnotism **2 :** psychotherapy that facilitates suggestion, reeducation, or analysis by hypnosis — **hyp·no·ther·a·pist** \-pist\ *n*

1**hyp·not·ic** \hip-ˈnä-tik\ *adj* [F or LL; F *hypnotique,* fr. LL *hypnoticus,* fr. Gk *hypnōtikos,* fr. *hypnoun* to put to sleep, fr. *hypnos*] (1625) **1 :** tending to produce sleep **:** SOPORIFIC **2 a :** of or relating to hypnosis or hypnotism **b :** readily holding the attention ⟨a ~ personality⟩ ⟨a simple ~ beat⟩ — **hyp·not·i·cal·ly** \-ti-k(ə-)lē\ *adv*

2**hypnotic** *n* (1681) **1 :** a sleep-inducing agent **:** SOPORIFIC **2 :** one that is or can be hypnotized

hyp·no·tism \ˈhip-nə-ˌti-zəm\ *n* (1842) **1 :** the study or act of inducing hypnosis — compare MESMERISM **2 :** HYPNOSIS 1 — **hyp·no·tist** \-tist\ *n*

hyp·no·tize \-ˌtīz\ *vt* **-tized; -tiz·ing** (1843) **1 :** to induce hypnosis in **2 :** to dazzle or overcome by or as if by suggestion ⟨a voice that ~*s* its hearers⟩ ⟨drivers *hypnotized* by speed⟩ — **hyp·no·tiz·abil·i·ty** \ˌhip-nə-ˌtī-zə-ˈbi-lə-tē\ *n* — **hyp·no·tiz·able** \ˈhip-nə-ˌtī-zə-bəl\ *adj*

1**hy·po** \ˈhī-(ˌ)pō\ *n, pl* **hypos** (1711) **:** HYPOCHONDRIA

2**hypo** *n, pl* **hypos** [short for *hyposulfite* thiosulfate] (1855) **:** SODIUM THIOSULFATE; *also* **:** a solution of sodium thiosulfate

3**hypo** *n, pl* **hypos** (1925) **1 :** HYPODERMIC SYRINGE **2 :** HYPODERMIC INJECTION **3 :** STIMULUS

4**hypo** *vt* (1942) **:** STIMULATE ⟨do everything possible to ~ the economy —Clem Morgello⟩

hypo- *or* **hyp-** *prefix* [LL *hypo-, hyp-,* fr. Gk, fr. *hypo* — more at UP] **1 :** under **:** beneath **:** down ⟨*hypo*blast⟩ ⟨*hypo*dermic⟩ **2 :** less than normal or normally ⟨*hyp*esthesia⟩ ⟨*hypo*tension⟩ **3 :** in a lower state of oxidation **:** in a low and usu. the lowest position in a series of compounds ⟨*hypo*chlorous acid⟩ ⟨*hypo*xanthine⟩

hy·po·al·ler·gen·ic \ˌhī-pō-ˌa-lər-ˈje-nik\ *adj* (1940) **:** having little likelihood of causing an allergic response ⟨~ cosmetics⟩ ⟨~ foods⟩

hy·po·blast \ˈhī-pə-ˌblast\ *n* (1875) **:** the endoderm of an embryo

hy·po·cal·ce·mia \ˌhī-pō-ˌkal-ˈsē-mē-ə\ *n* [NL] (1925) **:** a deficiency of calcium in the blood — **hy·po·cal·ce·mic** \-mik\ *adj*

hy·po·caust \ˈhī-pə-ˌkȯst\ *n* [L *hypocaustum,* fr. Gk *hypokauston,* fr. *hypokaiein* to light a fire under, fr. *hypo-* + *kaiein* to burn] (1678) **:** an ancient Roman central heating system with underground furnace and tile flues to distribute the heat

hy·po·cen·ter \ˈhī-pə-ˌsen-tər\ *n* (1905) **1 :** the focus of an earthquake — compare EPICENTER 1 **2 :** the point on the earth's surface directly below the center of a nuclear bomb explosion — **hy·po·cen·tral** \ˌhī-pə-ˈsen-trəl\ *adj*

hy·po·chlo·rite \ˌhī-pə-ˈklȯr-ˌīt\ *n* (ca. 1849) **:** a salt or ester of hypochlorous acid

hy·po·chlo·rous acid \ˌhī-pə-ˈklȯr-əs-\ *n* [ISV] (1841) **:** an unstable strongly oxidizing but weak acid $HClO$ obtained in solution along with hydrochloric acid by reaction of chlorine with water and used esp. in the form of salts as an oxidizing agent, bleaching agent, disinfectant, and chlorinating agent

hy·po·chon·dria \ˌhī-pə-ˈkän-drē-ə\ *n* [NL, fr. LL, pl., upper abdomen (formerly regarded as the seat of hypochondria), fr. Gk, lit., the parts under the cartilage (of the breastbone), fr. *hypo-* + *chondros* cartilage] (1668) **:** extreme depression of mind or spirits often centered on imaginary physical ailments; *specif* **:** HYPOCHONDRIASIS

1**hy·po·chon·dri·ac** \-drē-ˌak\ *adj* [F *hypochondriaque,* fr. Gk *hypochondriakos,* fr. *hypochondria*] (1599) **1 :** HYPOCHONDRIACAL **2 :** of, relating to, or being the two regions of the abdomen lying on either side of the epigastric region and above the lumbar regions

2**hypochondriac** *n* (1639) **:** one affected by hypochondria

hy·po·chon·dri·a·cal \-kən-ˈdrī-ə-kəl, -ˌkän-\ *adj* (1665) **:** affected or produced by hypochondria — **hy·po·chon·dri·a·cal·ly** \-k(ə-)lē\ *adv*

hy·po·chon·dri·a·sis \-ˈdrī-ə-səs\ *n, pl* **-a·ses** \-ˌsēz\ [NL] (1766) **:** morbid concern about one's health esp. when accompanied by delusions of physical disease

hy·po·chro·mic \ˌhī-pə-ˈkrō-mik\ *adj* (1924) **:** marked by or being red blood cells with deficient hemoglobin ⟨~ anemia⟩

hy·po·co·rism \hī-ˈpä-kə-ˌri-zəm; ˌhī-pə-ˈkȯr-ˌi-\ *n* [LL *hypocorisma,* fr. Gk *hypokorisma,* fr. *hypokorizesthai* to call by pet names, fr. *hypo-* + *korizesthai* to caress, fr. *koros* boy, *korē* girl] (1850) **1 :** a pet name **2 :** the use of pet names — **hy·po·co·ris·tic** \ˌhī-pə-kə-ˈris-tik\ *or* **hy·po·co·ris·ti·cal** \-ti-kəl\ *adj* — **hy·po·co·ris·ti·cal·ly** \-ti-k(ə-)lē\ *adv*

hy·po·cot·yl \ˈhī-pə-ˌkä-tᵊl\ *n* [ISV *hypo-* + *cotyl*edon] (1880) **:** the part of the axis of a plant embryo or seedling below the cotyledon

hy·poc·ri·sy \hi-ˈpä-krə-sē *also* hī-\ *n, pl* **-sies** [ME *ypocrisie,* fr. AF, fr. LL *hypocrisis,* fr. Gk *hypokrisis* act of playing a part on the stage, hypocrisy, fr. *hypokrinesthai* to answer, act on the stage, fr. *hypo-* + *krinein* to decide — more at CERTAIN] (13c) **1 :** a feigning to be what one is not or to believe what one does not; *esp* **:** the false assumption of an appearance of virtue or religion **2 :** an act or instance of hypocrisy

hyp·o·crite \ˈhi-pə-ˌkrit\ *n* [ME *ypocrite,* fr. AF, fr. LL *hypocrita,* fr. Gk *hypokritēs* actor, hypocrite, fr. *hypokrinesthai*] (13c) **1 :** a person who puts on a false appearance of virtue or religion **2 :** a person who acts in contradiction to his or her stated beliefs or feelings — **hypocrite** *adj*

hyp·o·crit·i·cal \ˌhi-pə-ˈkri-ti-kəl\ *adj* (1561) **:** characterized by hypocrisy; *also* **:** being a hypocrite — **hyp·o·crit·i·cal·ly** \-k(ə-)lē\ *adv*

hy·po·cy·cloid \ˌhī-pō-ˈsī-ˌklȯid\ *n* (1843) **:** a curve traced by a point on the circumference of a circle rolling internally on the circumference of a fixed circle

hy·po·der·mal \ˌhī-pə-ˈdər-məl\ *adj* (1854) **1 :** of or relating to a hypodermis **2 :** lying beneath an outer skin or epidermis

1**hy·po·der·mic** \-mik\ *adj* [ISV] (1863) **1 :** adapted for use in or administered by injection beneath the skin **2 :** of or relating to the parts beneath the skin **3 :** resembling a hypodermic injection in effect **:** STIMULATING — **hy·po·der·mi·cal·ly** \-mi-k(ə-)lē\ *adv*

2**hypodermic** *n* (ca. 1889) **1 :** HYPODERMIC INJECTION **2 :** HYPODERMIC SYRINGE

hypodermic injection *n* (1868) **:** an injection made into the subcutaneous tissues

hypodermic needle *n* (ca. 1909) **1 :** NEEDLE 1c(1) **2 :** a hypodermic syringe complete with needle

hypodermic syringe *n* (1893) **:** a small syringe used with a hollow needle for injection of material into or beneath the skin

hy·po·der·mis \ˌhī-pə-ˈdər-məs\ *n* [NL] (ca. 1866) **1 :** the tissue immediately beneath the epidermis of a plant esp. when modified to serve as a supporting and protecting layer **2 :** the cellular layer that underlies and secretes the chitinous cuticle (as of an arthropod) **3 :** SUPERFICIAL FASCIA

hy·po·dip·loid \ˌhī-pō-ˈdi-ˌplȯid\ *adj* (1962) **:** having slightly fewer than the diploid number of chromosomes — **hy·po·dip·loi·dy** \-ˌplȯi-dē\ *n*

hy·po·eu·tec·toid \ˌhī-pō-yu̇-ˈtek-ˌtȯid\ *adj* (1911) **:** containing less of the minor component than is contained in the eutectoid

hy·po·gas·tric \ˌhī-pə-ˈgas-trik\ *adj* [F *hypogastrique,* fr. *hypogastre* hypogastric region, fr. Gk *hypogastrion,* fr. *hypo-* + *gastr-, gastēr* belly — more at GASTRIC] (ca. 1656) **:** of or relating to the lower median region of the abdomen

hy·po·ge·al \ˌhī-pə-ˈjē-əl\ *or* **hy·po·ge·an** \-ˈjē-ən\ *or* **hy·po·ge·ous** \-ˈjē-əs\ *adj* [LL *hypogeus* subterranean, fr. Gk *hypogaios,* fr. *hypo-* + *gaia* earth] (1686) **1 :** growing or living below the surface of the ground **2** *of a cotyledon* **:** remaining below the ground while the epicotyl elongates

hy·po·gene \ˈhī-pə-ˌjēn\ *adj* [*hypo-* + Gk *-genēs* born, produced — more at -GEN] (1831) **:** formed, crystallized, or lying at depths below the earth's surface **:** PLUTONIC — used of various rocks

hy·po·ge·um \ˌhī-pə-ˈjē-əm\ *n, pl* **-gea** \-ˈjē-ə\ [L, fr. Gk *hypogaion,* fr. neut. of *hypogaios*] (ca. 1706) **:** the subterranean part of an ancient building; *also* **:** an ancient underground burial chamber

hy·po·glos·sal \ˌhī-pə-ˈglä-səl\ *adj* (1831) **:** of or relating to the hypoglossal nerves

hypoglossal nerve *n* (1831) **:** either of the 12th and final pair of cranial nerves which are motor nerves arising from the medulla oblongata and supplying muscles of the tongue in higher vertebrates — called also *hypoglossal*

hy·po·gly·ce·mia \ˌhī-pō-glī-ˈsē-mē-ə\ *n* [NL] (ca. 1894) **:** abnormal decrease of sugar in the blood — **hy·po·gly·ce·mic** \-mik\ *adj or n*

hy·pog·y·nous \hī-ˈpä-jə-nəs\ *adj* (1821) **1** *of a floral organ* **:** inserted upon the receptacle or axis below the gynoecium and free from it **2 :** having hypogynous floral organs — **hy·pog·y·ny** \-nē\ *n*

hy·po·ka·le·mia \ˌhī-pō-ˌkā-ˈlē-mē-ə\ *n* [NL, fr. *hypo-* + *kal*ium potassium (fr. *kali* alkali, fr. Ar *qily* saltwort) + *-emia*] (1949) **:** a deficiency of potassium in the blood — **hy·po·ka·le·mic** \-mik\ *adj*

hy·po·lim·ni·on \ˌhī-pō-ˈlim-nē-ˌän, -nē-ən\ *n, pl* **-nia** \-nē-ə\ [NL, fr. *hypo-* + Gk *limnion,* dim. of *limnē* lake — more at LIMNETIC] (1910) **:** the part of a lake below the thermocline made up of water that is stagnant and of essentially uniform temperature except during the period of overturn

hy·po·mag·ne·se·mia \ˌhī-pə-ˌmag-nə-ˈsē-mē-ə\ *n* [NL, fr. *hypo-* + *magnesium* + *-emia*] (1933) **:** deficiency of magnesium in the blood

hy·po·ma·nia \ˌhī-pə-ˈmā-nē-ə, -nyə\ *n* [NL] (1882) **:** a mild mania esp. when part of bipolar disorder — **hy·po·man·ic** \-ˈma-nik\ *adj*

hy·po·para·thy·roid·ism \ˈhī-pō-ˌpa-rə-ˈthī-ˌrȯi-ˌdi-zəm\ *n* (1910) **:** deficiency of parathyroid hormone in the body; *also* **:** the resultant abnormal state marked by low serum calcium and a tendency to chronic tetany

hy·po·phar·ynx \-ˈfer-iŋ(k)s\ *n* [NL] (1826) **1 :** an appendage or thickened fold on the floor of the mouth of many insects that resembles a tongue **2 :** the laryngeal part of the pharynx extending from the hyoid bone to the lower margin of the cricoid cartilage

hy·po·phy·se·al *also* **hy·po·phy·si·al** \(ˌ)hī-ˌpä-fə-ˈsē-əl, ˌhī-pə-, -ˈzē-; ˌhī-pə-ˈfi-zē-əl\ *adj* [irreg. fr. NL *hypophysis*] (1882) **:** of or relating to the hypophysis

hy·poph·y·sec·to·mize \(ˌ)hī-ˌpä-fə-ˈsek-tə-ˌmīz\ *vt* **-mized; -miz·ing** (1910) **:** to remove the pituitary gland from

hy·poph·y·sec·to·my \-mē\ *n, pl* **-mies** (1909) **:** surgical removal of the pituitary gland

hy·poph·y·sis \hī-ˈpä-fə-səs\ *n, pl* **-y·ses** \-ˌsēz\ [NL, fr. Gk, attachment underneath, fr. *hypophyein* to grow beneath, fr. *hypo-* + *phyein* to grow, produce — more at BE] (1825) **:** PITUITARY GLAND

hy·po·pi·tu·ita·rism \ˌhī-pō-pə-ˈtü-ə-tə-ˌri-zəm, -ˈtü-ə-ˌtri-, -ˈtyü-\ *n* [ISV] (1909) **:** deficient production of growth hormones by the pituitary gland — **hy·po·pi·tu·itary** \-ˈtü-ə-ˌter-ē, -ˈtyü-\ *adj*

hy·po·pla·sia \-ˈplā-zh(ē-)ə\ *n* [NL] (1889) **:** a condition of arrested development in which an organ or part remains below the normal size or in an immature state — **hy·po·plas·tic** \-ˈplas-tik\ *adj*

hy·po·ploid \ˈhī-pō-ˌplȯid\ *adj* (1930) **:** having a chromosome number slightly less than an exact multiple of the monoploid number — **hypoploid** *n*

hy·po·sen·si·ti·za·tion \ˌhī-pō-ˌsen(t)-sə-tə-ˈzā-shən, -ˌsen(t)-stə-ˈzā-\ *n* (1922) **:** the state or process of being reduced in sensitivity esp. to an allergen **:** DESENSITIZATION — **hy·po·sen·si·tize** \-ˈsen(t)-sə-ˌtīz\ *vt*

hy·po·spa·di·as \ˌhī-pə-ˈspā-dē-əs\ *n* [NL, fr. Gk, man with hypospadias, fr. *hypo-* + *-spadias,* fr. *-spad-, -spas* something torn, fr. *span* to tear, pluck off] (ca. 1855) **:** an abnormality of the penis in which the urethra opens on the undersurface

hy·pos·ta·sis \hī-ˈpäs-tə-səs\ *n, pl* **-ta·ses** \-ˌsēz\ [LL, substance, sediment, fr. Gk, support, foundation, substance, sediment, fr. *hyphistasthai* to stand under, support, fr. *hypo-* + *histasthai* to be standing — more at STAND] (1590) **1 a :** something that settles at the bottom of a fluid **b :** the settling of blood in the dependent parts of an organ or body **2 :** PERSON 3 **3 a :** the substance or essential nature of an individual **b :** something that is hypostatized **4** [NL, fr. LL] **:** failure of a gene to produce its usual effect when coupled with another gene that is epistatic toward it — **hy·po·stat·ic** \ˌhī-pə-ˈsta-tik\ *adj* — **hy·po·stat·i·cal·ly** \-ti-k(ə-)lē\ *adv*

hy·pos·ta·tize \hī-ˈpäs-tə-ˌtīz\ *vt* **-tized; -tiz·ing** [Gk *hypostatos* substantially existing, fr. *hyphistasthai*] (1829) **:** to attribute real identity to (a concept) — **hy·pos·ta·ti·za·tion** \-ˌpäs-tə-tə-ˈzā-shən\ *n*

hy·po·stome \ˈhī-pə-ˌstōm\ *n* [ISV *hypo-* + *-stome* (fr. Gk *stoma* mouth) — more at STOMACH] (ca. 1862) **:** any of several structures associated with the mouth: as **a :** the manubrium of a hydrozoan **b :** a rodlike organ that arises at the base of the beak in various mites and ticks

hy·po·style \ˈhī-pə-ˌstī(-ə)l\ *adj* [Gk *hypostylos,* fr. *hypo-* + *stylos* pillar — more at STEER] (1831) **:** having the roof resting on rows of columns — **hypostyle** *n*

hy·po·tac·tic \ˌhī-pə-ˈtak-tik\ *adj* [Gk *hypotaktikos,* fr. *hypotassein*] (1896) **:** of or relating to hypotaxis

hy·po·tax·is \-ˈtak-səs\ *n* [NL, fr. Gk, subjection, fr. *hypotassein* to arrange under, fr. *hypo-* + *tassein* to arrange] (1883) **:** syntactic subordination (as by a conjunction)

hy·po·ten·sion \ˌhī-pō-ˈten(t)-shən\ *n* [ISV] (1893) **:** abnormally low blood pressure

[1]**hy·po·ten·sive** \ˌhī-pō-ˈten(t)-siv\ *adj* (1904) **1 :** characterized by or due to hypotension **2 :** causing low blood pressure or a lowering of blood pressure ⟨~ drugs⟩

[2]**hypotensive** *n* (1941) **:** a person with hypotension

hy·pot·e·nuse \hī-ˈpä-tə-ˌnüs, -ˌnyüz\ *also* **hy·poth·e·nuse** \-ˈpä-thə-\ *n* [L *hypotenusa,* fr. Gk *hypoteinousa,* fr. fem. of *hypoteinōn,* prp. of *hypoteinein* to subtend, fr. *hypo-* + *teinein* to stretch — more at THIN] (1594) **1 :** the side of a right-angled triangle that is opposite the right angle **2 :** the length of a hypotenuse

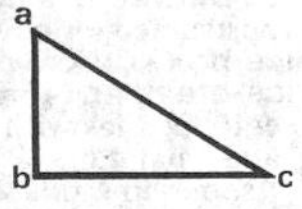

ac hypotenuse

hy·po·tha·lam·ic \ˌhī-pō-thə-ˈla-mik\ *adj* (1899) **:** of or relating to the hypothalamus ⟨~ neurons⟩

hy·po·thal·a·mus \-ˈtha-lə-məs\ *n* [NL] (1896) **:** a basal part of the diencephalon that lies beneath the thalamus on each side, forms the floor of the third ventricle, and includes vital autonomic regulatory centers

[1]**hy·poth·e·cate** \hi-ˈpä-thə-ˌkāt, hī-\ *vt* **-cat·ed; -cat·ing** [ML *hypothecare* to pledge, fr. LL *hypotheca* pledge, fr. Gk *hypothēkē,* fr. *hypotithenai* to put under, deposit as a pledge] (1681) **:** to pledge as security without delivery of title or possession — **hy·poth·e·ca·tion** \-ˌpä-thə-ˈkā-shən\ *n* — **hy·poth·e·ca·tor** \-ˈpä-thə-ˌkā-tər\ *n*

[2]**hy·poth·e·cate** \hī-ˈpä-thə-ˌkāt\ *vt* **-cat·ed; -cat·ing** [Gk *hypothēkē* suggestion, fr. *hypotithenai*] (1906) **:** HYPOTHESIZE

hy·po·ther·mal \ˌhī-pō-ˈthər-məl\ *adj* (1922) **:** of or relating to a hydrothermal metalliferous ore vein deposited at high temperature

hy·po·ther·mia \-ˈthər-mē-ə\ *n* [NL] (ca. 1886) **:** subnormal temperature of the body — **hy·po·ther·mic** \-mik\ *adj*

hy·poth·e·sis \hī-ˈpä-thə-səs\ *n, pl* **-e·ses** \-ˌsēz\ [Gk, fr. *hypotithenai* to put under, suppose, fr. *hypo-* + *tithenai* to put — more at DO] (ca. 1656) **1 a :** an assumption or concession made for the sake of argument **b :** an interpretation of a practical situation or condition taken as the ground for action **2 :** a tentative assumption made in order to draw out and test its logical or empirical consequences **3 :** the antecedent clause of a conditional statement

syn HYPOTHESIS, THEORY, LAW mean a formula derived by inference from scientific data that explains a principle operating in nature. HYPOTHESIS implies insufficient evidence to provide more than a tentative explanation ⟨a *hypothesis* explaining the extinction of the dinosaurs⟩. THEORY implies a greater range of evidence and greater likelihood of truth ⟨the *theory* of evolution⟩. LAW implies a statement of order and relation in nature that has been found to be invariable under the same conditions ⟨the *law* of gravitation⟩.

hy·poth·e·size \-ˌsīz\ *vb* **-sized; -siz·ing** *vi* (1738) **:** to make a hypothesis ~ *vt* **:** to adopt as a hypothesis

hy·po·thet·i·cal \ˌhī-pə-ˈthe-ti-kəl\ *adj* (1588) **:** being or involving a hypothesis **:** CONJECTURAL ⟨~ arguments⟩ ⟨a ~ situation⟩ — **hypothetical** *n* — **hy·po·thet·i·cal·ly** \-ti-k(ə-)lē\ *adv*

hy·po·thet·i·co–de·duc·tive \ˌhī-pə-ˈthe-ti-ˌkō-di-ˈdək-tiv\ *adj* (1912) **:** relating to, being, or making use of the method of proposing hypotheses and testing their acceptability or falsity by determining whether their logical consequences are consistent with observed data

hy·po·thy·roid \ˌhī-pō-ˈthī-ˌrȯid\ *adj* (1909) **:** of, relating to, or affected with hypothyroidism

hy·po·thy·roid·ism \-ˌrȯi-ˌdi-zəm\ *n* [ISV] (1905) **:** deficient activity of the thyroid gland; *also* **:** a resultant bodily condition characterized by lowered metabolic rate and general loss of vigor

hy·po·to·nia \ˌhī-pə-ˈtō-nē-ə, -pō-\ *n* [NL] (ca. 1886) **:** the state of having hypotonic muscle tone

hy·po·ton·ic \ˌhī-pə-ˈtä-nik, -pō-\ *adj* [ISV] (1895) **1 :** having deficient tone or tension ⟨~ children⟩ **2 :** having a lower osmotic pressure than a surrounding medium or a fluid under comparison ⟨~ organisms⟩ — **hy·po·to·nic·i·ty** \-tə-ˈni-sə-tē\ *n*

hy·po·xan·thine \ˌhī-pō-ˈzan-ˌthēn\ *n* [ISV] (ca. 1857) **:** a purine base $C_5H_4N_4O$ found in plant and animal tissues that yields xanthine on oxidation

hyp·ox·emia \ˌhi-ˌpäk-ˈsē-mē-ə, ˌhī-\ *n* [NL] (ca. 1886) **:** deficient oxygenation of the blood — **hyp·ox·emic** \-mik\ *adj*

hyp·ox·ia \hi-ˈpäk-sē-ə, hī-\ *n* [NL] (1941) **:** a deficiency of oxygen reaching the tissues of the body — **hyp·ox·ic** \-sik\ *adj*

hyp·som·e·ter \hip-ˈsä-mə-tər\ *n* [ISV, fr. Gk *hypsos* height (akin to OE *ūp* up) + ISV *-meter* — more at UP] (1927) **:** any of various instruments for determining the height of trees by triangulation

hyp·so·met·ric \ˌhip-sə-ˈme-trik\ *adj* [Gk *hypsos*] (1845) **:** of, relating to, or indicating elevation (as on a map) ⟨~ curve⟩

hy·rax \ˈhī-ˌraks\ *n* [Gk *hyrak-, hyrax* shrew] (1832) **:** any of a family (Procaviidae) of small ungulate mammals of Africa and the Middle East characterized by thickset body with short legs and ears and rudimentary tail, feet with soft pads and broad nails, and teeth of which the molars resemble those of the rhinoceros and the incisors those of rodents — called also *coney, dassie*

hy·son \ˈhī-sᵊn\ *n* [Chin (Guangdong) *héichēun,* lit., bright spring] (1740) **:** a Chinese green tea made from thinly rolled and twisted leaves

hys·sop \ˈhi-səp\ *n* [ME *ysop,* fr. OE *ysope,* fr. L *hyssopus,* fr. Gk *hyssōpos,* of Sem origin; akin to Heb *ēzōbh* hyssop] (bef. 12c) **1 :** a plant used in purificatory sprinkling rites by the ancient Hebrews **2 :** a European mint (*Hyssopus officinalis*) that has highly aromatic and pungent leaves and is sometimes used as a potherb

hyster- *or* **hystero-** *comb form* [F or L; F *hystér-,* fr. L *hyster-,* fr. Gk, fr. *hystera*] **:** womb ⟨*hyster*ectomy⟩

hys·ter·ec·to·my \ˌhis-tə-ˈrek-tə-mē\ *n, pl* **-mies** (ca. 1886) **:** surgical removal of the uterus — **hys·ter·ec·to·mized** \-tə-ˌmīzd\ *adj*

hys·ter·e·sis \ˌhis-tə-ˈrē-səs\ *n, pl* **-e·ses** \-ˌsēz\ [NL, fr. Gk *hysterēsis* shortcoming, fr. *hysterein* to be late, fall short, fr. *hysteros* later — more at OUT] (1881) **:** a retardation of an effect when the forces acting upon a body are changed (as if from viscosity or internal friction); *esp* **:** a lagging in the values of resulting magnetization in a magnetic material (as iron) due to a changing magnetizing force — **hys·ter·et·ic** \-ˈre-tik\ *adj*

hys·te·ria \his-ˈter-ē-ə, -ˈtir-\ *n* [NL, fr. E *hysteric,* adj., fr. L *hystericus,* fr. Gk *hysterikos,* fr. *hystera* womb; fr. the Greek notion that hysteria was peculiar to women and caused by disturbances of the uterus] (1801) **1 :** a psychoneurosis marked by emotional excitability and disturbances of the psychic, sensory, vasomotor, and visceral functions **2 :** behavior exhibiting overwhelming or unmanageable fear or emotional excess ⟨political ~⟩ — **hys·ter·ic** \-ˈter-ik\ *n* — **hys·ter·i·cal** \-ˈter-i-kəl\ *also* **hysteric** *adj* — **hys·ter·i·cal·ly** \-i-k(ə-)lē\ *adv*

hys·ter·ics \-ˈter-iks\ *n pl but sing or pl in constr* (1721) **:** a fit of uncontrollable laughter or crying

hys·ter·oid \ˈhis-tə-ˌrȯid\ *adj* (ca. 1855) **:** resembling or tending toward hysteria

hys·ter·on prot·er·on \ˌhis-tə-ˌrän-ˈprä-tə-ˌrän, -tə-rən-ˈprä-tə-rən, -ˈprō-\ *n* [LL, fr. Gk, lit., (the) later earlier, (the) latter first] (1565) **:** a figure of speech consisting of the reversal of a natural or rational order (as in "then came the thunder and the lightning")

hys·ter·o·sal·pin·go·gram \ˌhis-tə-rō-ˌsal-ˈpiŋ-gə-ˌgram\ *n* (1971) **:** a radiograph made by hysterosalpingography

hys·ter·o·sal·pin·gog·ra·phy \ˌhis-tə-rō-ˌsal-piŋ-ˈgäg-rə-fē\ *n, pl* **-phies** [*hyster-* + L *salping-, salpinx* fallopian tube + E *-graphy* — more at SALPINGITIS] (1941) **:** examination of the uterus and fallopian tubes by radiography after injection of an opaque medium

hys·ter·o·scope \ˈhis-tə-rō-ˌskōp\ *n* (1860) **:** an endoscope used for hysteroscopy

hys·ter·os·co·py \ˌhis-tə-ˈräs-kə-pē\ *n, pl* **-pies** (1928) **:** visual examination of the cervix and interior of the uterus with an endoscope — **hys·ter·o·scop·ic** \ˌhis-tə-rō-ˈskä-pik\ *adj*

hys·ter·ot·o·my \ˌhis-tə-ˈrä-tə-mē\ *n, pl* **-mies** [NL *hysterotomia,* fr. *hyster-* + *-tomia* -tomy] (1801) **:** surgical incision of the uterus; *esp* **:** CESAREAN SECTION

Hz *abbr* hertz

\ə\ **a**but \ᵊ\ kitten, F table \ər\ **f**ur**ther** \a\ **a**sh \ā\ **a**ce \ä\ m**o**p, m**ar**
\au̇\ **ou**t \ch\ **ch**in \e\ b**e**t \ē\ **ea**sy \g\ **g**o \i\ h**i**t \ī\ **i**ce \j\ **j**ob
\ŋ\ si**ng** \ō\ g**o** \ȯ\ l**aw** \ȯi\ b**oy** \th\ **th**in \t͟h\ **th**e \ü\ l**oo**t \u̇\ f**oo**t
\y\ **y**et \zh\ vi**si**on, bei**ge** \k, ⁿ, œ, ue, ʸ\ *see* Guide to Pronunciation

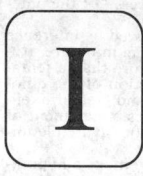

I

[1]**i** \ˈī\ *n, pl* **i's** *or* **is** \ˈīz\ *often cap, often attrib* (bef. 12c) **1 a :** the 9th letter of the English alphabet **b :** a graphic representation of this letter **c :** a speech counterpart of orthographic *i* **2 :** ONE — see NUMBER table **3 :** a graphic device for reproducing the letter *i* **4 :** one designated *i* esp. as the ninth in order or class **5 :** something shaped like the letter I **6 :** a unit vector parallel to the x-axis **7** [abbr. for *incomplete*] **a :** a grade rating a student's work as incomplete **b :** one graded or rated with an I **8 :** I FORMATION

[2]**i** *abbr* **1** industrial **2** initial **3** intelligence **4** intensity **5** interlaced **6** intransitive **7** island; isle

[3]**i** *symbol* imaginary unit

[1]**I** \ˈī, ə\ *pron* [ME, fr. OE *ic;* akin to OHG *ih* I, L *ego,* Gk *egō*] (bef. 12c) **:** the one who is speaking or writing ⟨∼ feel fine⟩ — compare ME, MINE, MY, WE ***usage*** see ME

[2]**I** \ˈī\ *n, pl* **I's** *or* **Is** \ˈīz\ (1539) **:** someone aware of possessing a personal individuality **:** SELF

[3]**I** *abbr* **1** electric current **2** Indian **3** interstate **4** Israeli

[4]**I** *symbol* iodine

-i- [L, thematic vowel of most nouns and adjectives in combination] — used as a connective vowel to join word elements esp. of Latin origin ⟨matr*i*lineal⟩ ⟨rat*i*cide⟩

Ia *or* **IA** *abbr* Iowa

[1]**-ia** *n suffix* [NL, fr. L & Gk, suffix forming feminine nouns] **1 :** pathological condition ⟨hyster*ia*⟩ **2 :** genus of plants or animals ⟨Fuchs*ia*⟩ **3 :** territory **:** world **:** society ⟨suburb*ia*⟩

[2]**-ia** *n pl suffix* [NL, fr. L (neut. pl. of *-ius,* adj. ending) & Gk, neut. pl. of *-ios,* adj. ending] **1 :** higher taxon (as class or order) consisting of (such plants or animals) ⟨Saur*ia*⟩ **2 :** things derived from or relating to (something specified) ⟨militar*ia*⟩

[3]**-ia** *pl of* -IUM

IAA *abbr* indoleacetic acid

IAAF *abbr* International Amateur Athletic Federation

IABA *abbr* International Amateur Boxing Association

IAEA *abbr* International Atomic Energy Agency

Ia·go \ē-ˈä-(ˌ)gō\ *n* (ca. 1605) **:** the villain of Shakespeare's tragedy *Othello*

-ial *adj suffix* [L *-ialis,* fr. *-i-* + *-alis* -al] **:** [1]-AL ⟨manor*ial*⟩

IALC *abbr* instrument approach and landing chart

IAM *abbr* International Association of Machinists and Aerospace Workers

iamb \ˈī-ˌam(b)\ *or* **iam·bus** \ī-ˈam-bəs\ *n, pl* **iambs** \ˈī-ˌamz\ *or* **iam·bus·es** [L *iambus,* fr. Gk *iambos*] (1586) **:** a metrical foot consisting of one short syllable followed by one long syllable or of one unstressed syllable followed by one stressed syllable (as in *above*) — **iam·bic** \ī-ˈam-bik\ *adj or n*

-ian — see -AN

-iana — see -ANA

IAP *abbr* international airport

IAS *abbr* indicated airspeed

-iasis *n suffix, pl* **-iases** [NL, fr. L, fr. Gk, suffix of action, fr. denominative verbs in *-ian, -iazein*] **:** disease having characteristics of or produced by (something specified) ⟨onchocerc*iasis*⟩ ⟨ancylostom*iasis*⟩

IATA *abbr* International Air Transport Association

-iatric *also* **-iatrical** *adj comb form* [NL *-iatria*] **:** of or relating to (such) medical treatment or healing ⟨ped*iatric*⟩

-iatrics *n pl comb form but sing or pl in constr* **:** medical treatment ⟨ped*iatrics*⟩

iat·ro·gen·ic \(ˌ)ī-ˌa-trə-ˈje-nik\ *adj* [Gk *iatros* physician + E *-genic*] (1924) **:** induced inadvertently by a physician or surgeon or by medical treatment or diagnostic procedures ⟨an ∼ rash⟩ — **iat·ro·gen·e·sis** \-trō-ˈje-nə-səs\ *n* — **iat·ro·gen·i·cal·ly** \-trə-ˈje-ni-k(ə-)lē\ *adv*

-iatry *n comb form* [F *-iatrie,* fr. NL *-iatria,* fr. Gk *iatreia* art of healing, fr. *iatros* healer, fr. *iasthai* to heal] **:** medical treatment **:** healing ⟨pod*iatry*⟩

IAU *abbr* **1** International Association of Universities **2** International Astronomical Union

IB *abbr* **1** in bond **2** incendiary bomb

I beam *n* (ca. 1889) **:** an iron or steel beam that is I-shaped in cross section

[1]**Ibe·ri·an** \ī-ˈbir-ē-ən\ *n* [*Iberia,* ancient region of the Caucasus] (1601) **:** a member of one or more peoples anciently inhabiting the Caucasus in Asia between the Black and Caspian seas — **Iberian** *adj*

[2]**Iberian** *n* [*Iberia,* peninsula in Europe] (1611) **1 a :** a member of one or more peoples anciently inhabiting parts of the peninsula comprising Spain and Portugal **b :** a native or inhabitant of Spain or Portugal or the Basque region **2 :** one or more of the languages of the ancient Iberians — **Iberian** *adj*

ibex \ˈī-ˌbeks\ *n, pl* **ibex** *or* **ibex·es** [L] (1607) **:** any of several wild goats (genus *Capra,* esp. *C. ibex*) living chiefly in high mountain areas of the Old World and having large recurved horns transversely ridged in front

ibid *abbr* ibidem

ibi·dem \ˈi-bə-ˌdem; i-ˈbī-dəm, -ˈbē-\ *adv* [L] (ca. 1771) **:** in the same place

-ibility — see -ABILITY

ibis \ˈī-bəs\ *n, pl* **ibis** *or* **ibis·es** [ME, fr. L, fr. Gk, fr. Egypt *hbw*] (14c) **:** any of various chiefly tropical or subtropical wading birds (family Threskiornithidae) related to the herons but distinguished by a long slender downwardly curved bill

Ibi·zan hound \i-ˈbē-zən-, -thən-\ *n* [*Ibiza* Island] (1960) **:** any of a breed of slender medium-sized hunting dogs developed in the Balearic Islands with a short and smooth or a wirehaired coat

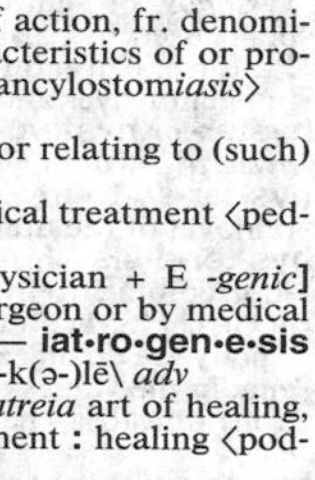

Ibizan hound

-ible — see -ABLE

Ibo \ˈē-(ˌ)bō\ *or* **Ig·bo** \ˈig-(ˌ)bō\ *n, pl* **Ibo** *or* **Ibos** *or* **Igbo** *or* **Igbos** [Ibo *Igbo* the Ibo language] (1732) **1 :** a member of a people of the area around the lower Niger in Africa **2 :** the languages of the Ibo people

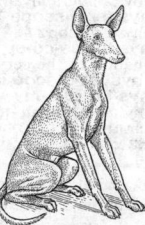

IBRD *abbr* International Bank for Reconstruction and Development

IBS *abbr* irritable bowel syndrome

Ib·sen·ism \ˈib-sə-ˌni-zəm, ˈip-\ *n* (1890) **1 :** dramatic invention or construction characteristic of Ibsen **2 :** championship of Ibsen's plays and ideas — **Ib·sen·ite** \-ˌnīt\ *n or adj*

ibu·pro·fen \ˌī-byü-ˈprō-fən *also* ī-ˈbyü-prə-fən\ *n* [*is-* + *bu*tyl + *pro*pionic acid + *-fen* (alter. of *phenyl*)] (1967) **:** a nonsteroidal anti-inflammatory drug $C_{13}H_{18}O_2$ used to relieve pain and fever

[1]**IC** \ˌī-ˈsē\ *n* (1947) **:** IMMEDIATE CONSTITUENT

[2]**IC** *n* (1966) **:** INTEGRATED CIRCUIT

[1]**-ic** *adj suffix* [ME, fr. AF & L; AF *-ic, -ique,* fr. L *-icus* — more at -Y] **1 :** having the character or form of **:** being ⟨panoram*ic*⟩ **:** consisting of ⟨run*ic*⟩ **2 a :** of or relating to ⟨alderman*ic*⟩ **b :** related to, derived from, or containing ⟨alcohol*ic*⟩ **3 :** in the manner of **:** like that of **:** characteristic of ⟨Byron*ic*⟩ **4 :** associated or dealing with ⟨Ved*ic*⟩ **:** utilizing ⟨electron*ic*⟩ **5 :** characterized by **:** exhibiting ⟨nostalg*ic*⟩ **:** affected with ⟨allerg*ic*⟩ **6 :** caused by ⟨amoeb*ic*⟩ **7 :** tending to produce ⟨analges*ic*⟩ **8 :** having a valence relatively higher than in compounds or ions named with an adjective ending in *-ous* ⟨ferr*ic* iron⟩

[2]**-ic** *n suffix* **:** one having the character or nature of **:** one belonging to or associated with **:** one exhibiting or affected by **:** one that produces

ICA *abbr* International Cooperative Alliance

-ical *adj suffix* [ME, fr. LL *-icalis* (as in *clericalis* clerical, *radicalis* radical)] **:** -IC ⟨symmetr*ical*⟩ ⟨geolog*ical*⟩ — sometimes differing from *-ic* in that adjectives formed with *-ical* have a wider or more transferred semantic range than corresponding adjectives in *-ic*

ICAO *abbr* International Civil Aviation Organization

Ic·a·rus \ˈi-kə-rəs\ *n* [L, fr. Gk *Ikaros*] (14c) **:** the son of Daedalus who to escape imprisonment flies by means of artificial wings but falls into the sea and drowns when the wax of his wings melts as he flies too near the sun — **Icar·i·an** \ī-ˈker-ē-ən, i-\ *adj*

ICBM \ˌī-ˌsē-(ˌ)bē-ˈem\ *n, pl* **ICBM's** *or* **ICBMs** \-ˈemz\ (1955) **:** an intercontinental ballistic missile

ICC *abbr* **1** International Chamber of Commerce **2** Interstate Commerce Commission

[1]**ice** \ˈīs\ *n, often attrib* [ME *is,* fr. OE *īs;* akin to OHG *īs* ice, Av *isu-* icy] (bef. 12c) **1 a :** frozen water **b :** a sheet or stretch of ice **2 :** a substance resembling ice; *esp* **:** the solid state of a substance usu. found as a gas or liquid ⟨ammonia ∼ in the rings of Saturn⟩ **3 :** a state of coldness (as from formality or reserve) **4 a :** a frozen dessert containing a flavoring (as fruit juice); *esp* **:** one containing no milk or cream **b** *Brit* **:** a serving of ice cream **5** *slang* **:** DIAMONDS; *broadly* **:** JEWELRY **6 :** an undercover premium paid to a theater employee for choice theater tickets **7 :** methamphetamine in the form of crystals of its hydrochloride salt $C_{10}H_{15}N{\cdot}HCl$ when used illicitly for smoking — called also *crystal, crystal meth* — **ice·less** \ˈīs-ləs\ *adj* — **on ice 1 :** with every likelihood of being won or accomplished **2 :** in reserve or safekeeping — **on thin ice :** in a precarious or risky situation

[2]**ice** *vb* **iced; ic·ing** *vt* (15c) **1 a :** to coat with or convert into ice **b :** to chill with ice **c :** to supply with ice **2 :** to cover with or as if with icing **3 :** to put on ice **4 :** SECURE 1b ⟨made two free throws . . . to ∼ the win —Jack McCallum⟩ **5 :** to shoot (an ice hockey puck) the length of the rink and beyond the opponents' goal line **6** *slang* **:** KILL 1a ∼ *vi* **1 :** to become ice-cold **2 a :** to become covered with ice — often used with *up* or *over* **b :** to have ice form inside

Ice *abbr* Iceland

ICE *abbr* **1** internal combustion engine **2** International Cultural Exchange

ice age *n* (1855) **1 :** a time of widespread glaciation **2** *cap I&A* **:** the Pleistocene glacial epoch

ice ax *n* (1820) **:** a combination pick and adze with a spiked handle that is used in mountain climbing

ice bag *n* (1857) **:** a waterproof bag to hold ice for local application of cold to the body

ice·berg \ˈīs-ˌbərg\ *n* [prob. part trans. of Dan or Norw *isberg,* fr. *is* ice + *berg* mountain] (1820) **1 :** a large floating mass of ice detached from a glacier **2 :** an emotionally cold person **3 :** ICEBERG LETTUCE

iceberg lettuce *n* (1893) **:** any of various crisp light green lettuces that when mature have the leaves arranged in a compact head

ice·blink \-ˌbliŋk\ *n* (1817) **:** a glare in the sky over an ice field

ice·boat \-ˌbōt\ *n* (1768) **:** a skeleton boat or frame on runners propelled on ice usu. by sails

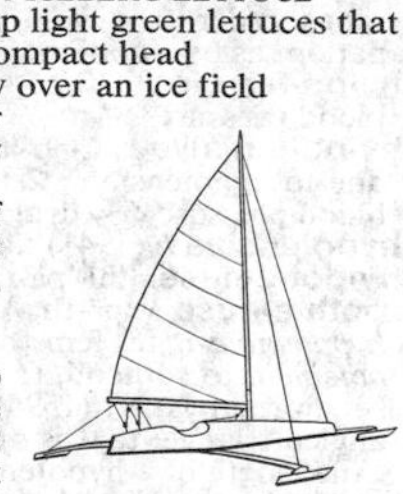

iceboat

ice·boat·ing \-ˌbō-tiŋ\ *n* (1879) **:** the sport of sailing in iceboats — **ice·boat·er** \-ˌbō-tər\ *n*

ice·bound \-ˌbaůnd\ *adj* (1641) **:** surrounded, obstructed, or covered by ice

ice·box \-ˌbäks\ *n* (1846) **:** REFRIGERATOR

ice·break·er \-ˌbrā-kər\ *n* (1853) **1 :** a ship equipped (as with a reinforced bow) to make and maintain a channel through ice **2 :** something that breaks the ice on a project or occasion; *esp* **:** MIXER 1c

ice cap *n* (ca. 1860) **1 :** an ice bag shaped to the head **2 :** a cover of perennial ice and snow; *specif* **:** a glacier forming on an extensive area of relatively level land and flowing outward from its center

ice–cold \ˈīs-ˈkōld\ *adj* (bef. 12c) **:** extremely cold

ice–cream *adj* (1890) **:** of a color similar to that of vanilla ice cream

ice cream \ˌīs-ˈkrēm, ˈīs-ˌ\ *n* (1744) **:** a sweet flavored frozen food containing cream or butterfat and usu. eggs

ice–cream chair *n* [fr. its use in ice cream parlors] (1949) **:** a small armless chair with a circular seat for use at a table (as at a café)

ice–cream cone *n* (1905) **:** a thin crisp edible cone for holding ice cream; *also* **:** one filled with ice cream

ice–cream headache *n* (1964) **:** BRAIN FREEZE

ice dancing *n* (1925) **:** a sport in which ice-skating pairs perform to music routines similar to ballroom dances

ice·fall \ˈīs-ˌfȯl\ *n* (1817) **1 :** a frozen waterfall **2 :** the mass of usu. jagged blocks into which a glacier may break when it moves down a steep declivity

ice field *n* (1694) **1 :** an extensive sheet of sea ice **2 :** ICE CAP 2

ice floe *n* (1819) **:** a usu. large flat free mass of floating sea ice

ice fog *n* (1851) : a fog composed of ice particles
ice hockey *n* (1868) : a game played on an ice rink by two teams of six players on skates whose object is to drive a puck into the opponents' goal with a hockey stick
ice·house \ˈīs-ˌhau̇s, ˈī-ˌsau̇s\ *n* (1666) : a building in which ice is made or stored
[1]**Ice·lan·dic** \īs-ˈlan-dik\ *adj* (1674) : of, relating to, or characteristic of Iceland, the Icelanders, or Icelandic
[2]**Icelandic** *n* (1710) : the North Germanic language of Iceland
Ice·land moss \ˈīs-lən(d)-, -ˌlan(d)-\ *n* (1785) : a lichen (*Cetraria islandica*) of mountainous and arctic regions sometimes used in medicine or as food
Iceland poppy *n* (1870) : a poppy (*Papaver nudicaule*) of holarctic regions often cultivated for its usu. single showy flowers
ice·man \ˈīs-ˌman\ *n* (1827) **1** : a man skilled in traveling on ice **2** : one who sells or delivers ice
ice milk *n* (1942) : a sweetened frozen food made of skim milk
Ice·ni \ī-ˈsē-ˌnī\ *n pl* [L] (1573) : an ancient British people that under their queen Boudicca revolted against the Romans in A.D. 60 — **Ice·ni·an** \-ˈsē-nē-ən\ *or* **Ice·nic** \-ˈsē-nik, -ˈse-\ *adj*
ice–out \ˈīs-ˌau̇t\ *n* (1914) : the disappearance of ice from the surface of a body of water (as a lake) as a result of thawing
ice pack *n* (1835) : an expanse of pack ice
ice pick *n* (1851) : a hand tool ending in a spike for chipping ice
ice plant *n* (1753) : any of various usu. succulent herbs (as of the genera *Carpobrotus, Delosperma,* and *Mesembryanthemum*) of the carpetweed family used esp. as ground covers or for erosion control
ice point *n* (1832) : the freezing point of water of 0° Celsius or 273.15 kelvins at standard atmospheric pressure
ice·scape \ˈī(s)-ˌskāp\ *n* (1839) **1** : an area covered with ice or ice formations **2** : a picture representing an icescape
ice sheet *n* (1831) : ICE CAP 2
ice show *n* (1920) : an entertainment consisting of various exhibitions by ice-skaters usu. with musical accompaniment
ice–skate \ˈī(s)-ˌskāt\ *vi* (1914) : to skate on ice — **ice–skat·er** \-ˌskā-tər\ *n*
ice skate *n* (1786) : a shoe with a metal runner attached for ice-skating
ice storm *n* (1797) : a storm in which falling rain freezes on contact
ice water *n* (1669) : chilled or iced water esp. served as a beverage
ice wine *n* (1953) : EISWEIN
ICF *abbr* intermediate care facility
ICFTU *abbr* International Confederation of Free Trade Unions
ich·neu·mon \ik-ˈnü-mən, -ˈnyü-\ *n* [ME, fr. L, fr. Gk *ichneumōn,* lit., tracker, fr. *ichneuein* to track, fr. *ichnos* footprint] (15c) **1** : a mongoose (*Herpestes ichneumon*) of Africa, southern Europe, and southwestern Asia **2** : ICHNEUMON WASP
ichneumon wasp *n* (1713) : any of a family (Ichneumonidae) of hymenopterous insects whose larvae are usu. internal parasites of other insect larvae and esp. of caterpillars — called also *ichneumon fly*
ichor \ˈī-ˌkȯr, -kər\ *n* [Gk *ichōr*] (15c) **1** : a thin watery or blood-tinged discharge **2** : an ethereal fluid taking the place of blood in the veins of the ancient Greek gods — **ichor·ous** \-kə-rəs\ *adj*
ichthy- *or* **ichthyo-** *comb form* [L, fr. Gk, fr. *ichthys;* akin to Arm *jukn* fish, Lith *žuvis*] : fish ⟨*ichthy*ology⟩
ich·thyo·fau·na \ˌik-thē-ō-ˈfȯ-nə, -ˈfä-\ *n* [NL] (1883) : the fish life of a region — **ich·thyo·fau·nal** \-ˈfȯ-nᵊl, -ˈfä-\ *adj*
ich·thy·ol·o·gy \ˌik-thē-ˈä-lə-jē\ *n* (1646) : a branch of zoology that deals with fishes — **ich·thy·o·log·i·cal** \-thē-ə-ˈlä-ji-kəl\ *adj* — **ich·thy·o·log·i·cal·ly** \-k(ə-)lē\ *adv* — **ich·thy·ol·o·gist** \-thē-ˈä-lə-jist\ *n*
ich·thy·oph·a·gous \ˌik-thē-ˈä-fə-gəs\ *adj* [Gk *ichthyophagos,* fr. *ichthy-* + *-phagos* -phagous] (ca. 1828) : eating or subsisting on fish
ich·thyo·saur \ˈik-thē-ə-ˌsȯr\ *n* [ultim. fr. Gk *ichthy-* + *sauros* lizard] (1830) : any of an order (Ichthyosauria) of extinct marine reptiles of the Mesozoic specialized for aquatic life by a streamlined body with a long snout, limbs reduced to small fins for steering, and a large lunate caudal fin — **ich·thyo·sau·ri·an** \ˌik-thē-ə-ˈsȯr-ē-ən\ *adj or n*
-ician *n suffix* [F *-icien,* fr. OF, fr. L *-ica* (as in *rhetorica* rhetoric) + OF *-ien* -ian] : specialist : practitioner ⟨beaut*ician*⟩
ici·cle \ˈī-ˌsi-kəl\ *n* [ME *isikel,* fr. *is* ice + *ikel* icicle, fr. OE *gicel;* akin to OHG *ihilla* icicle, MIr *aig* ice] (14c) **1** : a pendent mass of ice formed by the freezing of dripping water **2** : an emotionally cold person **3** : a long narrow strip (as of foil) used to decorate a Christmas tree
[1]**ic·ing** \ˈī-siŋ\ *n* (ca. 1740) **1** : a sweet flavored usu. creamy mixture used to coat baked goods (as cupcakes) — called also *frosting* **2** : something that adds to the interest, value, or appeal of an item or event — often used in the phrase *icing on the cake*
[2]**icing** *n* (1948) : an illegal act by an ice-hockey player of shooting a puck from within the defensive zone or defensive half of the rink beyond the opponents' goal line but not into the goal
ICJ *abbr* International Court of Justice
icky \ˈi-kē\ *adj* **ick·i·er; -est** [perh. baby talk alter. of *sticky*] (1929) : offensive to the senses or sensibilities : DISTASTEFUL ⟨put off by her ~ triteness —Renata Adler⟩ — **ick·i·ness** \-nəs\ *n*
icon *also* **ikon** \ˈī-ˌkän\ *n* [L, fr. Gk *eikōn,* fr. *eikenai* to resemble] (1572) **1** : a usu. pictorial representation : IMAGE **2** [LGk *eikōn,* fr. Gk] : a conventional religious image typically painted on a small wooden panel and used in the devotions of Eastern Christians **3** : an object of uncritical devotion : IDOL **4** : EMBLEM, SYMBOL ⟨the house became an ~ of 1960's residential architecture —Paul Goldberger⟩ **5 a** : a sign (as a word or graphic symbol) whose form suggests its meaning **b** : a graphic symbol on a computer display screen that represents an object (as a file) or function (as the command to delete)
icon- *or* **icono-** *comb form* [Gk eikon-, eikono-, fr. *eikon-, eikōn*] : image ⟨*icono*latry⟩
icon·ic \ī-ˈkä-nik\ *adj* (1656) **1** : of, relating to, or having the characteristics of an icon **2 a** : widely recognized and well-established ⟨an ~ brand name⟩ **b** : widely known and acknowledged esp. for distinctive excellence ⟨an ~ writer⟩ ⟨a region's ~ wines⟩ — **icon·i·cal·ly** \-ni-k(ə-)lē\ *adv*
ico·nic·i·ty \ˌī-kə-ˈni-sə-tē\ *n* (1946) : correspondence between form and meaning ⟨the ~ of the Roman numeral III⟩
icon·o·clasm \ī-ˈkä-nə-ˌkla-zəm\ *n* (1797) : the doctrine, practice, or attitude of an iconoclast
icon·o·clast \-ˌklast\ *n* [ML *iconoclastes,* fr. MGk *eikonoklastēs,* lit., image destroyer, fr. Gk *eikono-* + *klan* to break — more at CLAST] (1641) **1** : a person who destroys religious images or opposes their veneration **2** : a person who attacks settled beliefs or institutions — **icon·o·clas·tic** \(ˌ)ī-ˌkä-nə-ˈklas-tik\ *adj* — **icon·o·clas·ti·cal·ly** \-ti-k(ə-)lē\ *adv*
ico·nog·ra·pher \ˌī-kə-ˈnä-grə-fər\ *n* (1888) **1** : a maker of figures or drawings esp. of a conventional type **2** : a student of iconography
icon·o·graph·ic \(ˌ)ī-ˌkä-nə-ˈgra-fik\ *or* **icon·o·graph·i·cal** \-fi-kəl\ *adj* (ca. 1855) **1** : of or relating to iconography **2** : representing something by pictures or diagrams — **icon·o·graph·i·cal·ly** \-fi-k(ə-)lē\ *adv*
ico·nog·ra·phy \ˌī-kə-ˈnä-grə-fē\ *n, pl* **-phies** [ML *iconographia,* fr. Gk *eikonographia* sketch, description, fr. *eikonographein* to describe, fr. *eikon-* + *graphein* to write — more at CARVE] (1678) **1** : pictorial material relating to or illustrating a subject **2** : the traditional or conventional images or symbols associated with a subject and esp. a religious or legendary subject **3** : the imagery or symbolism of a work of art, an artist, or a body of art **4** : ICONOLOGY
ico·nol·a·try \-ˈnä-lə-trē\ *n* (1624) : the worship of images or icons
ico·nol·o·gy \-ˈnä-lə-jē\ *n* [F *iconologie,* fr. *icono-* icon- + *-logie* -logy] (ca. 1736) : the study of icons or artistic symbolism — **icon·o·log·i·cal** \(ˌ)ī-ˌkä-nə-ˈlä-ji-kəl\ *adj*
icon·o·scope \ī-ˈkä-nə-ˌskōp\ *n* [fr. *Iconoscope,* a trademark] (1932) : a camera tube containing an electron gun and a photoemissive mosaic screen of which each cell produces a charge proportional to the varying light intensity of the image focused on the screen
ico·nos·ta·sis \ˌī-kə-ˈnäs-tə-səs, (ˌ)ī-ˈkä-nə-ˌstä-səs\ *n, pl* **-ta·ses** \-ˌsēz\ [modif. of MGk *eikonostasion,* fr. LGk, shrine, fr. Gk *eikono-* + *-stasion* (fr. *histanai* to stand) — more at STAND] (1833) : a screen or partition with doors and tiers of icons that separates the bema from the nave in Eastern churches
ico·sa·he·dral \(ˌ)ī-ˌkō-sə-ˈhē-drəl, -ˌkä-\ *adj* (ca. 1828) : of or having the form of an icosahedron
ico·sa·he·dron \-drən\ *n, pl* **-drons** *or* **-dra** \-drə\ [Gk *eikosaedron,* fr. *eikosi* twenty + *-edron* -hedron — more at VIGESIMAL] (1570) : a polyhedron having 20 faces
ICRC *abbr* International Committee of the Red Cross
-ics *n pl suffix but sing or pl in constr* [[1]-ic + [1]-s; trans. of Gk *-ika,* fr. neut. pl. of *-ikos* -ic] **1** : study : knowledge : skill : practice ⟨linguist*ics*⟩ ⟨electron*ics*⟩ **2** : characteristic actions or activities ⟨acrobat*ics*⟩ **3** : characteristic qualities, operations, or phenomena ⟨mechan*ics*⟩
ic·ter·ic \ik-ˈter-ik\ *adj* (ca. 1600) : of, relating to, or affected with jaundice
ic·ter·us \ˈik-tə-rəs\ *n* [NL, fr. Gk *ikteros*] (ca. 1673) : JAUNDICE
ic·tus \ˈik-təs\ *n* [L, lit., blow, fr. *icere* to strike] (1752) : the recurring stress or beat in a rhythmic or metrical series of sounds
ICU *abbr* intensive care unit
icy \ˈī-sē\ *adj* **ic·i·er; -est** (bef. 12c) **1 a** : covered with, abounding in, or consisting of ice **b** : intensely cold **2** : characterized by coldness : FRIGID ⟨an ~ stare⟩; *also* : STEELY ⟨~ nerves⟩ — **ic·i·ly** \-sə-lē\ *adv* — **ic·i·ness** \-sē-nəs\ *n*
[1]**id** \ˈid\ *n* [NL, fr. L, it] (1924) : the one of the three divisions of the psyche in psychoanalytic theory that is completely unconscious and is the source of psychic energy derived from instinctual needs and drives — compare EGO, SUPEREGO
[2]**id** *abbr* idem
[1]**ID** \ˈī-ˈdē\ *n, pl* **ID's** *or* **IDs** (1941) : a document (as a card) bearing identifying information about and often a photograph of the individual whose name appears on it — called also *ID card, identification card, identity card*
[2]**ID** \ˈī-ˈdē\ *vt* **ID'd** *or* **IDed; ID'ing** *or* **IDing** (1944) : IDENTIFY ⟨*ID'd* the thief⟩
[3]**ID** *abbr* **1** Idaho **2** identification **3** independent distributor **4** industrial design **5** *often not cap* inside diameter; inner diameter; internal diameter **6** *often not cap* inside dimensions **7** intelligence department
[1]**-id** *n suffix* [in sense 1, fr. L *-ides,* masc. patronymic suffix, fr. Gk *-idēs;* in sense 2, fr. It *-ide,* fr. L *-id-, -is,* fem. patronymic suffix, fr. Gk] **1** : one belonging to a (specified) dynastic line ⟨Abbas*id*⟩ **2** : meteor associated with or radiating from a (specified) constellation or comet ⟨Perse*id*⟩
[2]**-id** *n suffix* [prob. fr. L *-id-, -is,* fem. patronymic suffix, fr. Gk] : body : particle ⟨chromat*id*⟩
I'd \ˈīd\ (ca. 1592) : I would : I had : I should
IDA *abbr* International Development Association
-idae *n pl suffix* [NL, fr. L, fr. Gk *-idai,* pl. of *-idēs*] : members of the family of — in names of zoological families ⟨Fel*idae*⟩
IDDM *abbr* insulin-dependent diabetes mellitus
IDE *abbr* integrated drive electronics
-ide *also* **-id** *n suffix* [G & F; G *-id,* fr. F *-ide* (as in *oxide*)] **1** : binary chemical compound — added to the contracted name of the nonmetallic or more electronegative element ⟨hydrogen sulf*ide*⟩ or group ⟨cyan*ide*⟩ **2** : chemical compound derived from or related to another (usu. specified) compound ⟨anhydr*ide*⟩ ⟨glucos*ide*⟩
idea \ī-ˈdē-ə, -ˈdēə *also* ˈī-(ˌ)dē-ə *or* ˈī-dē\ *n* [ME, fr. L, fr. Gk, fr. *idein* to see — more at WIT] (14c) **1 a** : a transcendent entity that is a real pattern of which existing things are imperfect representations **b** : a standard of perfection : IDEAL **c** : a plan for action : DESIGN **2** *archaic* : a visible representation of a conception : a replica of a pattern **3 a** *obs* : an image recalled by memory **b** : an indefinite or unformed conception **c** : an entity (as a thought, concept, sensation, or image) actually or potentially present to consciousness **4** : a formulated thought or opinion **5** : whatever is known or supposed about something ⟨a child's ~ of time⟩ **6** : the central meaning or chief end of a particular action or situation **7** *Christian Science* : an image in Mind — **idea·less** \-ləs\ *adj*
syn IDEA, CONCEPT, CONCEPTION, THOUGHT, NOTION, IMPRESSION mean what exists in the mind as a representation (as of something

comprehended) or as a formulation (as of a plan). IDEA may apply to a mental image or formulation of something seen or known or imagined, to a pure abstraction, or to something assumed or vaguely sensed ⟨innovative *ideas*⟩ ⟨my *idea* of paradise⟩. CONCEPT may apply to the idea formed by consideration of instances of a species or genus or, more broadly, to any idea of what a thing ought to be ⟨a society with no *concept* of private property⟩. CONCEPTION is often interchangeable with CONCEPT; it may stress the process of imagining or formulating rather than the result ⟨our changing *conception* of what constitutes art⟩. THOUGHT is likely to suggest the result of reflecting, reasoning, or meditating rather than of imagining ⟨commit your *thoughts* to paper⟩. NOTION suggests an idea not much resolved by analysis or reflection and may suggest the capricious or accidental ⟨you have the oddest *notions*⟩. IMPRESSION applies to an idea or notion resulting immediately from some stimulation of the senses ⟨the first *impression* is of soaring height⟩.

[1]**ide·al** \ī-ˈdē(-ə)l, ˈī-ˌ\ *adj* [ME *ydeall,* fr. LL *idealis,* fr. L *idea*] (15c) **1** : existing as an archetypal idea **2 a** : existing as a mental image or in fancy or imagination only; *broadly* : lacking practicality **b** : relating to or constituting mental images, ideas, or conceptions **3 a** : of, relating to, or embodying an ideal ⟨~ beauty⟩ **b** : conforming exactly to an ideal, law, or standard : PERFECT ⟨an ~ gas⟩ — compare REAL 2b(3) **4** : of or relating to philosophical idealism

[2]**ideal** *n* (15c) **1** : a standard of perfection, beauty, or excellence **2** : one regarded as exemplifying an ideal and often taken as a model for imitation **3** : an ultimate object or aim of endeavor : GOAL **4** : a subset of a mathematical ring that is closed under addition and subtraction and contains the products of any given element of the subset with each element of the ring ***syn*** see MODEL — **ide·al·less** \ī-ˈdē(-ə)l-ləs\ *adj*

ide·al·ise *Brit var of* IDEALIZE

ide·al·ism \ī-ˈdē-(ə-)ˌliz-əm, ˈī-(ˌ)dē-\ *n* (1773) **1 a (1)** : a theory that ultimate reality lies in a realm transcending phenomena **(2)** : a theory that the essential nature of reality lies in consciousness or reason **b (1)** : a theory that only the perceptible is real **(2)** : a theory that only mental states or entities are knowable **2 a** : the practice of forming ideals or living under their influence **b** : something that is idealized **3** : literary or artistic theory or practice that affirms the preeminent value of imagination as compared with faithful copying of nature — compare REALISM

[1]**ide·al·ist** \-(ə-)list\ *n* (1701) **1 a** : an adherent of a philosophical theory of idealism **b** : an artist or author who advocates or practices idealism in art or writing **2** : one guided by ideals; *esp* : one that places ideals before practical considerations

[2]**idealist** *adj* (1875) : IDEALISTIC

ide·al·is·tic \(ˌ)ī-ˌdē-(ə-)ˈlis-tik, ˌī-dē-\ *adj* (1829) : of or relating to idealists or idealism — **ide·al·is·ti·cal·ly** \-ti-k(ə-)lē\ *adv*

ide·al·i·ty \ˌī-dē-ˈa-lə-tē\ *n, pl* **-ties** (1817) **1 a** : the quality or state of being ideal **b** : existence only in idea **2** : something imaginary or idealized

ide·al·ize \ī-ˈdē-(ə-)ˌlīz\ *vb* **-ized; -iz·ing** *vi* (1786) **1** : to form ideals **2** : to work idealistically ~ *vt* **1 a** : to give an ideal form or value to **b** : to attribute ideal characteristics to ⟨tended to ~ her teachers⟩ **2** : to treat idealistically ⟨portraitists who ~ their subjects⟩ — **ide·al·i·za·tion** \-ˌdē-(ə-)lə-ˈzā-shən\ *n* — **ide·al·iz·er** \-ˈdē-(ə-)ˌlī-zər\ *n*

ide·al·ly \ī-ˈdē-ə-lē, -ˈdē(ə)l-lē\ *adv* (1598) **1** : in idea or imagination : MENTALLY **2** : in relation to an exemplar **3 a** : conformably to or in respect to an ideal : PERFECTLY **b** : for best results ⟨~, the counselor should vary his techniques for each applicant —T. M. Martinez⟩ **c** : in accordance with an ideal or typical standard : CLASSICALLY

ideal point *n* (1879) : a point added to the plane or to space to eliminate special cases; *specif* : the point at infinity added in projective geometry as the assumed intersection of two parallel lines

ide·ate \ˈī-dē-ˌāt\ *vb* **-at·ed; -at·ing** *vt* (1610) : to form an idea or conception of ~ *vi* : to form an idea

ide·a·tion \ˌī-dē-ˈā-shən\ *n* (1818) : the capacity for or the act of forming or entertaining ideas ⟨suicidal ~⟩

ide·a·tion·al \-shnəl, -shə-nᵊl\ *adj* (1853) : of, relating to, or produced by ideation; *broadly* : of or relating to ideas — **ide·a·tion·al·ly** *adv*

idée fixe \(ˌ)ē-ˌdā-ˈfēks\ *n, pl* **idées fixes** *same*\ [F, lit., fixed idea] (1836) : an idea that dominates one's mind esp. for a prolonged period : OBSESSION

idem \ˈī-ˌdem, ˈē-, ˈi-\ *pron* [ME, fr. L, same — more at IDENTITY] (14c) : the same as something previously mentioned — used chiefly in bibliographies

idem·po·tent \ˈī-dəm-ˌpō-tᵊnt\ *adj* [L *idem* same + *potent-, potens* having power — more at POTENT] (1870) : relating to or being a mathematical quantity which when applied to itself under a given binary operation (as multiplication) equals itself; *also* : relating to or being an operation under which a mathematical quantity is idempotent — **idempotent** *n*

iden·tic \ī-ˈden-tik, ə-\ *adj* (1649) : IDENTICAL: as **a** : constituting a diplomatic action or expression in which two or more governments follow precisely the same course or employ an identical form **b** : constituting an action or expression in which a government follows precisely the same course or employs identical forms with reference to two or more other governments

iden·ti·cal \ī-ˈden-ti-kəl, ə-\ *adj* [prob. fr. ML *identicus,* fr. LL *identitas*] (1581) **1** : being the same : SELFSAME ⟨the ~ place we stopped before⟩ **2** : having such close resemblance as to be essentially the same ⟨~ hats⟩ — often used with *to* or *with* **3 a** : having the same cause or origin ⟨~ infections⟩ **b** : MONOZYGOTIC ***syn*** see SAME — **iden·ti·cal·ly** \-k(ə-)lē\ *adv* — **iden·ti·cal·ness** \-kəl-nəs\ *n*

iden·ti·fi·ca·tion \ī-ˌden-tə-fə-ˈkā-shən, ə-\ *n* (1644) **1 a** : an act of identifying : the state of being identified **b** : evidence of identity **2 a** : psychological orientation of the self in regard to something (as a person or group) with a resulting feeling of close emotional association **b** : a largely unconscious process whereby an individual models thoughts, feelings, and actions after those attributed to an object that has been incorporated as a mental image

identification card *n* (1908) : ID

iden·ti·fi·er \ī-ˈden-tə-ˌfī(-ə)r, ə-\ *n* (1889) : one that identifies

iden·ti·fy \ī-ˈden-tə-ˌfī, ə-\ *vb* **-fied; -fy·ing** *vt* (1644) **1 a** : to cause to be or become identical **b** : to conceive as united (as in spirit, outlook, or principle) ⟨groups that are *identified* with conservation⟩ **2 a** : to establish the identity of **b** : to determine the taxonomic position of (a biological specimen) ~ *vi* **1** : to be or become the same **2** : to practice psychological identification ⟨~ with the hero of a novel⟩ — **iden·ti·fi·able** \-ˌden-tə-ˈfī-ə-bəl\ *adj* — **iden·ti·fi·ably** \-blē\ *adv*

iden·ti·ty \ī-ˈden-tə-tē, ə-, -ˈde-nə-\ *n, pl* **-ties** [MF *identité,* fr. LL *identitat-, identitas,* prob. fr. L *identidem* repeatedly, contr. of *idem et idem,* lit., same and same] (1570) **1 a** : sameness of essential or generic character in different instances **b** : sameness in all that constitutes the objective reality of a thing : ONENESS **2 a** : the distinguishing character or personality of an individual : INDIVIDUALITY **b** : the relation established by psychological identification **3** : the condition of being the same with something described or asserted ⟨establish the ~ of stolen goods⟩ **4** : an equation that is satisfied for all values of the symbols **5** : IDENTITY ELEMENT

identity card *n* (1900) : ID

identity crisis *n* (1954) **1** : personal psychosocial conflict esp. in adolescence that involves confusion about one's social role and often a sense of loss of continuity to one's personality **2** : a state of confusion in an institution or organization regarding its nature or direction

identity element *n* (1902) : an element (as 0 in the set of all integers under addition or 1 in the set of positive integers under multiplication) that leaves any element of the set to which it belongs unchanged when combined with it by a specified operation

identity matrix *n* (ca. 1929) : a square matrix that has numeral 1's along the principal diagonal and 0's elsewhere

identity politics *n pl but sing or pl in constr* (1988) : PARTICULARISM 2

identity theft *n* (1991) : the illegal use of someone else's personal information (as a Social Security number) esp. in order to obtain money or credit

ideo- *comb form* [F *idéo-,* fr. Gk *idea*] : idea ⟨*ideo*gram⟩

ideo·gram \ˈi-dē-ə-ˌgram, ˈī-\ *n* (1838) **1** : a picture or symbol used in a system of writing to represent a thing or an idea but not a particular word or phrase for it; *esp* : one that represents not the object pictured but some thing or idea that the object pictured is supposed to suggest **2** : LOGOGRAM — **ideo·gram·ic** *or* **ideo·gram·mic** \ˌi-dē-ə-ˈgra-mik, ˌī-\ *adj* — **ideo·gram·mat·ic** \-dē-ō-grə-ˈma-tik\ *adj*

ideo·graph \ˈi-dē-ə-ˌgraf, ˈī-\ *n* (ca. 1840) : IDEOGRAM — **ideo·graph·ic** \ˌi-dē-ə-ˈgra-fik, ˌī-\ *adj* — **ideo·graph·i·cal·ly** \-fi-k(ə-)lē\ *adv*

ide·og·ra·phy \ˌi-dē-ˈä-grə-fē, ˌī-\ *n* (ca. 1846) **1** : the use of ideograms **2** : the representation of ideas by graphic symbols

ideo·log·i·cal \ˌī-dē-ə-ˈlä-ji-kəl, ˌi-\ *also* **ideo·log·ic** \-ˈlä-jik\ *adj* (1797) **1** : relating to or concerned with ideas **2** : of, relating to, or based on ideology — **ideo·log·i·cal·ly** \-ˈlä-ji-k(ə-)lē\ *adv*

ide·ol·o·gize \ˌī-dē-ˈä-lə-ˌjīz, ˌi-\ *vt* **-gized; -giz·ing** (1860) : to give an ideological character or interpretation to; *esp* : to change or interpret in relation to a sociopolitical ideology often seen as biased or limited

ideo·logue *also* **idea·logue** \ˈī-dē-ə-ˌlȯg, -ˌläg\ *n* [F *idéologue,* back-formation fr. *idéologie*] (1815) **1** : an impractical idealist : THEORIST **2** : an often blindly partisan advocate or adherent of a particular ideology

ide·ol·o·gy \ˌī-dē-ˈä-lə-jē, ˌi-\ *also* **ide·al·o·gy** \-ˈä-lə-jē, -ˈa-\ *n, pl* **-gies** [F *idéologie,* fr. *idéo-* ideo- + *-logie* -logy] (1813) **1** : visionary theorizing **2 a** : a systematic body of concepts esp. about human life or culture **b** : a manner or the content of thinking characteristic of an individual, group, or culture **c** : the integrated assertions, theories and aims that constitute a sociopolitical program — **ide·ol·o·gist** \-jist\ *n*

ideo·mo·tor \ˌī-dē-ə-ˈmō-tər, ˌi-\ *adj* [ISV] (1867) : not reflex but motivated by an idea ⟨~ muscular activity⟩

ides \ˈīdz\ *n pl but sing or pl in constr* [ME, fr. AF, fr. L *idus*] (14c) : the 15th day of March, May, July, or October or the 13th day of any other month in the ancient Roman calendar; *broadly* : this day and the seven days preceding it

-idin *or* **-idine** *n suffix* [ISV *-ide* + *-in, -ine*] : chemical compound related in origin or structure to another compound ⟨tolu*idine*⟩ ⟨guan*idine*⟩

idio- *comb form* [Gk, fr. *idios* — more at IDIOT] : one's own : personal : separate : distinct ⟨*idio*blast⟩

id·i·o·blast \ˈi-dē-ə-ˌblast\ *n* [ISV] (1822) : a plant cell (as a sclereid) that differs markedly from neighboring cells — **id·io·blas·tic** \ˌi-dē-ə-ˈblas-tik\ *adj*

id·i·o·cy \ˈi-dē-ə-sē\ *n, pl* **-cies** (ca. 1529) **1** *usu offensive* : extreme mental retardation **2** : something notably stupid or foolish

id·i·o·graph·ic \ˌi-dē-ə-ˈgra-fik\ *adj* [ISV] (ca. 1890) : relating to or dealing with something concrete, individual, or unique ⟨~ case studies⟩

id·i·o·lect \ˈi-dē-ə-ˌlekt\ *n* [*idio-* + *-lect* (as in *dialect*)] (1948) : the language or speech pattern of one individual at a particular period of life — **id·io·lec·tal** \ˌi-dē-ə-ˈlek-tᵊl\ *adj*

id·i·om \ˈi-dē-əm\ *n* [MF & LL; MF *idiome,* fr. LL *idioma* individual peculiarity of language, fr. Gk *idiōmat-, idiōma,* fr. *idiousthai* to appropriate, fr. *idios*] (1588) **1 a** : the language peculiar to a people or to a district, community, or class : DIALECT **b** : the syntactical, grammatical, or structural form peculiar to a language **2** : an expression in the usage of a language that is peculiar to itself either grammatically (as *no, it wasn't me*) or in having a meaning that cannot be derived from the conjoined meanings of its elements (as *ride herd on* for "supervise") **3** : a style or form of artistic expression that is characteristic of an individual, a period or movement, or a medium or instrument ⟨the modern jazz ~⟩; *broadly* : MANNER, STYLE ⟨a new culinary ~⟩

id·i·o·mat·ic \ˌi-dē-ə-ˈma-tik\ *adj* (1712) **1** : of, relating to, or conforming to idiom **2** : peculiar to a particular group, individual, or style — **id·i·o·mat·i·cal·ly** \-ti-k(ə-)lē\ *adv* — **id·i·o·mat·ic·ness** \-tik-nəs\ *n*

id·i·o·mor·phic \ˌi-dē-ə-ˈmȯr-fik\ *adj* [Gk *idiomorphos,* fr. *idio-* + *-morphos* -morphous] (1887) : having the proper form or shape — used of minerals whose crystalline growth has not been interfered with

id·i·o·path·ic \ˌi-dē-ə-ˈpa-thik\ *adj* (1669) **1** : arising spontaneously or from an obscure or unknown cause : PRIMARY ⟨~ epilepsy⟩ **2** : peculiar to the individual — **id·i·o·path·i·cal·ly** \-ˈpa-thi-k(ə-)lē\ *adv*

id·i·o·syn·cra·sy \ˌi-dē-ə-ˈsiŋ-krə-sē\ *n, pl* **-sies** [Gk *idiosynkrasia,* fr. *idio-* + *synkerannynai* to blend, fr. *syn-* + *kerannynai* to mingle, mix — more at CRATER] (1604) **1 a** : a peculiarity of constitution or temperament : an individualizing characteristic or quality **b** : individual hypersensitiveness (as to a drug or food) **2** : characteristic peculiarity (as of temperament); *broadly* : ECCENTRICITY — **id·i·o·syn·crat·ic**

\ˌi-dē-ō-(ˌ)sin-ˈkra-tik\ *adj* — **id·i·o·syn·crat·i·cal·ly** \-ˈkra-ti-k(ə-)lē\ *adv*

id·i·ot \ˈi-dē-ət\ *n* [ME, fr. AF *ydiote,* fr. L *idiota* ignorant person, fr. Gk *idiōtēs* one in a private station, layman, ignorant person, fr. *idios* one's own, private; akin to L *suus* one's own — more at SUICIDE] (14c) **1** *usu offensive* : a person affected with extreme mental retardation **2** : a foolish or stupid person — **idiot** *adj*

idiot box *n* (ca. 1955) : TELEVISION

id·i·ot·ic \ˌi-dē-ˈä-tik\ *also* **id·i·ot·i·cal** \-ˈä-ti-kəl\ *adj* (1713) **1** : characterized by idiocy **2** : showing complete lack of thought or common sense : FOOLISH — **id·i·ot·i·cal·ly** \-ti-k(ə-)lē\ *adv*

[1]**id·i·o·tism** \ˈi-dē-ə-ˌti-zəm\ *n* [MF *idiotisme,* fr. L *idiotismus* common speech, fr. Gk *idiōtismos,* fr. *idiōtēs*] (1588) **1** *obs* : IDIOM 1 **2** : IDIOM 2

[2]**id·i·ot·ism** \ˈi-dē-ə-(ˌ)ti-zəm\ *n* [*idiot* + *-ism*] (1592) *archaic* : IDIOCY 2

idiot light *n* (1966) : a colored light on an instrument panel (as of an automobile) designed to give a warning (as of low oil pressure)

id·i·ot·proof \ˈi-dē-ət-ˌprüf\ *adj* (1976) : extremely easy to operate or maintain

idiot sa·vant \ˈē-ˌdyō-sä-ˈvänⁿ, *or same as* IDIOT *and* SAVANT *for respective sing and pl forms*\ *n, pl* **idiots savants** \-ˌdyō-sä-ˈväⁿ(z)\ *or* **idiot savants** \-ˈväⁿ(z)\ [F, lit., learned idiot] (1927) **1** : a person affected with a mental disability (as autism or mental retardation) who exhibits exceptional skill or brilliance in some limited field (as mathematics or music) — called also *savant* **2** : a person who is highly knowledgeable about one subject but knows little about anything else

id·io·type \ˈi-dē-ə-ˌtīp\ *n* (1960) : the molecular structure and conformation of an antibody that confers its antigenic specificity — **id·io·typ·ic** \ˌi-dē-ə-ˈti-pik\ *adj*

-idium *n suffix, pl* **-idiums** *or* **-idia** [NL, fr. Gk *-idion,* dim. suffix] : small one ⟨anther*idium*⟩

[1]**idle** \ˈī-dᵊl\ *adj* **idler** \ˈīd-lər, ˈī-dᵊl-ər\; **idlest** \ˈīd-ləst, ˈī-dᵊl-əst\ [ME *idel,* fr. OE *īdel;* akin to OHG *ītal* worthless] (bef. 12c) **1** : lacking worth or basis : VAIN ⟨~ chatter⟩ ⟨~ pleasure⟩ **2** : not occupied or employed: as **a** : having no employment : INACTIVE ⟨~ workers⟩ **b** : not turned to normal or appropriate use ⟨~ farmland⟩ **c** : not scheduled to compete ⟨the team will be ~ tomorrow⟩ **3 a** : SHIFTLESS, LAZY **b** : having no evident lawful means of support ***syn*** see VAIN, INACTIVE — **idle·ness** \ˈī-dᵊl-nəs\ *n* — **idly** \ˈīd-lē, ˈī-dᵊl-ē\ *adv*

[2]**idle** *vb* **idled; idling** \ˈīd-liŋ, ˈī-dᵊl-iŋ\ *vi* (1592) **1 a** : to spend time in idleness **b** : to move idly **2** : to run at low power and often disconnected usu. so that power is not used for useful work ⟨the engine is *idling*⟩ ~ *vt* **1** : to pass in idleness **2** : to make idle ⟨workers *idled* by a strike⟩ **3** : to cause to idle — **idler** \ˈīd-lər, ˈī-dᵊl-ər\ *n*

syn IDLE, LOAF, LOUNGE, LOLL, LAZE mean to spend time doing nothing. IDLE may be used in reference to persons that move lazily or without purpose ⟨*idled* the day away⟩. LOAF suggests either resting or wandering about as though there were nothing to do ⟨she does her work and then *loafs* the rest of the day⟩. LOUNGE, though occasionally used as equal to *idle* or *loaf,* typically conveys an additional implication of resting or reclining against a support or of physical comfort and ease in relaxation ⟨he *lounged* against the wall⟩. LOLL also carries an implication of a posture similar to that of *lounge,* but places greater stress upon an indolent or relaxed attitude ⟨*lolling* on the couch⟩. LAZE usu. implies the relaxation of a busy person enjoying a vacation or moments of leisure ⟨*lazed* about between appointments⟩.

idler pulley *n* (ca. 1890) : a guide or tightening pulley for a belt or chain

idler wheel *n* (1929) **1** : a wheel, gear, or roller used to transfer motion or to guide or support something **2** : IDLER PULLEY

idlesse \ˈīd-ləs, īd-ˈles\ *n* [ME, fr. *idle* + *-esse* (as in *richesse* wealth) — more at RICHES] (15c) : the quality or state of being idle : IDLENESS

ido·crase \ˈī-də-ˌkrās, ˈi-, -ˌkrāz\ *n* [F, fr. Gk *eidos* form + *krasis* mixture, fr. *kerannynai* to mix — more at CRATER] (1804) : a mineral that is a complex silicate esp. of calcium, magnesium, iron, and aluminum

idol \ˈī-dᵊl\ *n* [ME, fr. AF *idle,* fr. LL *idolum,* fr. Gk *eidōlon* image, idol; akin to Gk *eidos* form — more at IDYLL] (13c) **1** : a representation or symbol of an object of worship; *broadly* : a false god **2 a** : a likeness of something **b** *obs* : PRETENDER, IMPOSTOR **3** : a form or appearance visible but without substance ⟨an enchanted phantom, a lifeless ~ —P. B. Shelley⟩ **4** : an object of extreme devotion ⟨a movie ~⟩; *also* : IDEAL 2 **5** : a false conception : FALLACY

idol·a·ter *or* **idol·a·tor** \ī-ˈdä-lə-tər\ *n* (14c) **1** : a worshiper of idols **2** : a person that admires intensely and often blindly one that is not usu. a subject of worship

idol·a·trous \ī-ˈdä-lə-trəs\ *adj* (ca. 1500) **1** : of or relating to idolatry **2** : having the character of idolatry ⟨the religion of ~ nationalism —Aldous Huxley⟩ **3** : given to idolatry — **idol·a·trous·ly** *adv* — **idol·a·trous·ness** *n*

idol·a·try \-trē\ *n, pl* **-tries** [ME *ydolatrie,* fr. AF, fr. ML *idolatria,* alter. of LL *idololatria,* fr. Gk *eidōlolatreia,* fr. *eidōlon* idol + *-latreia* -latry] (13c) **1** : the worship of a physical object as a god **2** : immoderate attachment or devotion to something

idol·ize \ˈī-də-ˌlīz\ *vb* **-ized; -iz·ing** *vt* (1598) : to worship as a god; *broadly* : to love or admire to excess ⟨the common people whom he so *idolized* —*Times Lit. Supp.*⟩ ~ *vi* : to practice idolatry — **idol·i·za·tion** \ˌī-də-lə-ˈzā-shən\ *n* — **idol·iz·er** \ˈī-də-ˌlī-zər\ *n*

IDP *abbr* international driving permit

idyll *also* **idyl** \ˈī-dᵊl, *Brit usu* ˈi-(ˌ)dil\ *n* [L *idyllium,* fr. Gk *eidyllion,* fr. dim. of *eidos* form; akin to Gk *idein* to see — more at WIT] (1586) **1 a** : a simple descriptive work in poetry or prose that deals with rustic life or pastoral scenes or suggests a mood of peace and contentment **b** : a narrative poem (as Tennyson's *Idylls of the King*) treating an epic, romantic, or tragic theme **2 a** : a lighthearted carefree episode that is a fit subject for an idyll **b** : a romantic interlude

idyl·lic \ī-ˈdi-lik, *chiefly Brit* i-\ *adj* (1856) **1** : pleasing or picturesque in natural simplicity **2** : of, relating to, or being an idyll — **idyl·li·cal·ly** \-ˈdi-li-k(ə-)lē\ *adv*

i.e. *abbr* [L *id est*] that is

IE *abbr* industrial engineer

-ie *also* **-y** *n suffix* [ME] **1** : little one : dear little one ⟨bird*ie*⟩ ⟨sonn*y*⟩ **2 a** : one belonging to : one having to do with ⟨town*ie*⟩ **b** : one who is ⟨preem*ie*⟩ **3** : one of (such) a kind or quality ⟨cut*ie*⟩ ⟨tough*ie*⟩

IED *abbr* improvised explosive device

IEEE *abbr* The Institute of Electrical and Electronics Engineers

-ier — see -ER

[1]**if** \ˈif, əf\ *conj* [ME, fr. OE *gif;* akin to OHG *ibu* if] (bef. 12c) **1 a** : in the event that **b** : allowing that **c** : on the assumption that **d** : on condition that **2** : WHETHER ⟨asked ~ the mail had come⟩ ⟨I doubt ~ I'll pass the course⟩ **3** — used as a function word to introduce an exclamation expressing a wish ⟨~ it would only rain⟩ **4** : even though : although perhaps ⟨an interesting ~ untenable argument⟩ **5** : and perhaps not even ⟨few ~ any changes are expected⟩ — often used with *not* ⟨difficult ~ not impossible⟩ — **if anything** : on the contrary even : perhaps even ⟨*if anything,* you ought to apologize⟩

[2]**if** \ˈif\ *n* (1513) **1** : CONDITION, STIPULATION ⟨the question . . . depends on too many ~*s* to allow an answer —*Encounter*⟩ **2** : SUPPOSITION

-iferous *adj comb form* [L *-ifer,* fr. *-i-* + *-fer* -ferous] : -FEROUS

iff \ˈif-ᵊn(d)-ˈōn-lē-ˌif; ˈif, *sometimes read with a prolonged* f\ *conj* [alter. of [1]*if*] (1955) : if and only if ⟨two figures are congruent ~ one can be placed over the other so that they coincide⟩

IFF *abbr* identification, friend or foe

if·fy \ˈi-fē\ *adj* [[1]*if*] (1937) **1** : having many uncertain or unknown qualities or conditions ⟨an ~ proposition⟩ **2** : of inconsistent or unreliable quality — **if·fi·ness** *n*

-ification *n suffix* [L *-ification-, -ificatio,* fr. *-i-* + *-ficatio* -fication] : -FICATION ⟨desert*ification*⟩

IFO *abbr* identified flying object

-iform *adj comb form* [L *-iformis,* fr. *-i-* + *-formis* -form] : -FORM ⟨patel*liform*⟩

I formation *n* (1951) : an offensive football formation in which the running backs line up in a line directly behind the quarterback — compare T FORMATION

-ify *vb suffix* [ME *-ifien,* fr. AF *-ifier,* fr. L *-ificare,* fr. *-i-* + *-ficare* -fy] : -FY

Ig *abbr* immunoglobulin

IG *abbr* inspector general

IgA \ˌī-(ˌ)jē-ˈā\ *n* [*i*mmuno*g*lobulin] (1969) **1** : a class of immunoglobulins including antibodies found in external bodily secretions (as saliva, tears, and sweat) **2** : an antibody of the class IgA

Igbo *var of* IBO

IgE \ˌī-(ˌ)jē-ˈē\ *n* (1969) **1** : a class of immunoglobulins including antibodies that function esp. in allergic reactions **2** : an antibody of the class IgE

IGF *abbr* insulin-like growth factor

IgG \-ˈjē\ *n* (1965) **1** : a class of immunoglobulins including the most common antibodies circulating in the blood that facilitate the phagocytic destruction of microorganisms foreign to the body, that bind to and activate complement, and that are the only immunoglobulins to cross over the placenta from mother to fetus **2** : an antibody of the class IgG

ig·loo \ˈi-(ˌ)glü\ *n, pl* **igloos** [Inuit *iglu* house] (1856) **1** : an Eskimo house usu. made of sod, wood, or stone when permanent or of blocks of snow or ice in the shape of a dome when built for temporary purposes **2** : a building or structure shaped like a dome

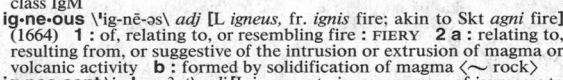

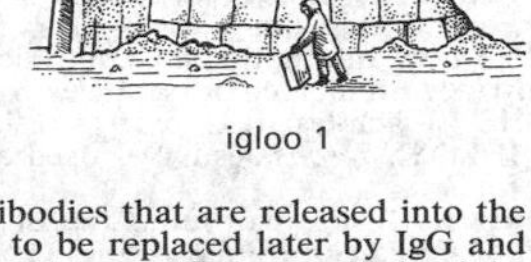
igloo 1

IgM \ˌī-(ˌ)jē-ˈem\ *n* (1969) **1** : a class of immunoglobulins of high molecular weight including the primary antibodies that are released into the blood early in the immune response to be replaced later by IgG and that are highly efficient in binding complement **2** : an antibody of the class IgM

ig·ne·ous \ˈig-nē-əs\ *adj* [L *igneus,* fr. *ignis* fire; akin to Skt *agni* fire] (1664) **1** : of, relating to, or resembling fire : FIERY **2 a** : relating to, resulting from, or suggestive of the intrusion or extrusion of magma or volcanic activity **b** : formed by solidification of magma ⟨~ rock⟩

ig·nes·cent \ig-ˈne-sᵊnt\ *adj* [L *ignescent-, ignescens,* prp. of *ignescere* to catch fire, fr. *ignis*] (ca. 1828) : VOLATILE

ig·nim·brite \ˈig-nəm-ˌbrīt\ *n* [G *Ignimbrit,* fr. L *ignis* + *imbr-* (fr. *imber* rain) + G *-it* [1]-ite — more at IMBRICATE] (1932) : a hard rock formed by solidification of chiefly fine deposits of volcanic ash

ig·nis fat·u·us \ˈig-nəs-ˈfa-chə-wəs, -ˈfach-wəs\ *n, pl* **ig·nes fat·ui** \-ˌnēz-ˈfa-chə-ˌwī\ [ML, lit., foolish fire] (1563) **1** : a light that sometimes appears in the night over marshy ground and is often attributable to the combustion of gas from decomposed organic matter **2** : a deceptive goal or hope

ig·nite \ig-ˈnīt\ *vb* **ig·nit·ed; ig·nit·ing** [L *ignitus,* pp. of *ignire* to ignite, fr. *ignis*] *vt* (1666) **1** : to subject to fire or intense heat; *esp* : to render luminous by heat **2 a** : to set afire; *also* : KINDLE **b** : to cause (a fuel) to burn **3 a** : to heat up : EXCITE ⟨oppression that *ignited* the hatred of the people⟩ **b** : to set in motion : SPARK ⟨~ a debate⟩ ~ *vi* **1** : to catch fire **2** : to begin to glow — **ig·nit·abil·i·ty** \ig-ˌnī-tə-ˈbi-lə-tē\ *n* — **ig·nit·able** *also* **ig·nit·ible** \-ˈnī-tə-bəl\ *adj* — **ig·nit·er** *also* **ig·ni·tor** \-ˈnī-tər\ *n*

ig·ni·tion \ig-ˈni-shən\ *n* (1612) **1** : the act or action of igniting: as **a** : the starting of a fire **b** : the heating of a plasma to a temperature high enough to sustain nuclear fusion **2 a** : the process or means (as an electric spark) of igniting a fuel mixture **b** : a device that activates an ignition system (as in an automobile) ⟨put the key in the ~⟩

ig·ni·tron \ig-ˈnī-ˌträn\ *n* [L *ignis* fire + E *-tron*] (1933) : a mercury-containing rectifier tube in which the arc is struck again at the beginning of each cycle by a special electrode separately energized by an auxiliary circuit

ig·no·ble \ig-ˈnō-bəl\ *adj* [ME, fr. MF, fr. L *ignobilis,* fr. *in-* + OL *gnobilis* noble] (15c) **1** : of low birth or common origin : PLEBEIAN **2** : characterized by baseness, lowness, or meanness ***syn*** see MEAN — **ig·no·bil·i·ty** \ˌig-nō-ˈbi-lə-tē\ *n* — **ig·no·ble·ness** \ig-ˈnō-bəl-nəs\ *n* — **ig·no·bly** \-blē *also* -bə-lē\ *adv*

ig·no·min·i·ous \ˌig-nə-ˈmi-nē-əs\ *adj* (15c) **1 :** marked with or characterized by disgrace or shame **:** DISHONORABLE **2 :** deserving of shame or infamy **:** DESPICABLE **3 :** HUMILIATING, DEGRADING ⟨an ~ defeat⟩ — **ig·no·min·i·ous·ly** *adv* — **ig·no·min·i·ous·ness** *n*

ig·no·mi·ny \ˈig-nə-ˌmi-nē, -mə-nē *also* ig-ˈnä-mə-nē\ *n, pl* **-nies** [MF or L; MF *ignominie,* fr. L *ignominia,* fr. *ig-* (as in *ignorare* to be ignorant of, ignore) + *nomin-, nomen* name, repute — more at NAME] (1540) **1 :** deep personal humiliation and disgrace **2 :** disgraceful or dishonorable conduct, quality, or action ***syn*** see DISGRACE

ig·no·ra·mus \ˌig-nə-ˈrā-məs *also* -ˈra-\ *n, pl* **-mus·es** *also* **-mi** \-mē\ [*Ignoramus,* ignorant lawyer in *Ignoramus* (1615), play by George Ruggle, fr. L, lit., we are ignorant of] (ca. 1616) **:** an utterly ignorant person **:** DUNCE

ig·no·rance \ˈig-n(ə-)rən(t)s\ *n* (13c) **:** the state or fact of being ignorant **:** lack of knowledge, education, or awareness

ig·no·rant \ˈig-n(ə-)rənt\ *adj* (14c) **1 a :** destitute of knowledge or education ⟨an ~ society⟩; *also* **:** lacking knowledge or comprehension of the thing specified ⟨parents ~ of modern mathematics⟩ **b :** resulting from or showing lack of knowledge or intelligence ⟨~ errors⟩ **2 :** UNAWARE, UNINFORMED — **ig·no·rant·ly** *adv* — **ig·no·rant·ness** *n*

syn IGNORANT, ILLITERATE, UNLETTERED, UNTUTORED, UNLEARNED mean not having knowledge. IGNORANT may imply a general condition or it may apply to lack of knowledge or awareness of a particular thing ⟨an *ignorant* fool⟩ ⟨*ignorant* of nuclear physics⟩. ILLITERATE applies to either an absolute or a relative inability to read and write ⟨much of the population is still *illiterate*⟩. UNLETTERED implies ignorance of the knowledge gained by reading ⟨an allusion meaningless to the *unlettered*⟩. UNTUTORED may imply lack of schooling in the arts and ways of civilization ⟨strange monuments built by an *untutored* people⟩. UNLEARNED suggests ignorance of advanced subjects ⟨poetry not for academics but for the *unlearned* masses⟩.

ig·no·ra·tio elen·chi \ˌig-nə-ˈrä-tē-ˌō-i-ˈleŋ-ˌkē\ *n* [L, lit., ignorance of proof] (1588) **:** a fallacy in logic of supposing a point proved or disproved by an argument proving or disproving something not at issue

ig·nore \ig-ˈnȯr\ *vt* **ig·nored; ig·nor·ing** [obs. *ignore* to be ignorant of, fr. F *ignorer,* fr. L *ignorare,* fr. *ignarus* ignorant, unknown, fr. *in-* + *gnoscere, noscere* to know — more at KNOW] (1801) **1 :** to refuse to take notice of **2 :** to reject (a bill of indictment) as ungrounded ***syn*** see NEGLECT — **ig·nor·able** \-ˈnȯr-ə-bəl\ *adj* — **ig·nor·er** *n*

Igo·rot \ˌē-gə-ˈrōt\ *n, pl* **Igorot** *or* **Igorots** (1821) **1 :** a member of any of several related peoples of northwestern Luzon, Philippines **2 :** any of the Austronesian languages of the Igorot

Igraine \i-ˈgrān\ *n* (15c) **:** the wife of Uther and mother of King Arthur

igua·na \i-ˈgwä-nə\ *n* [Sp, fr. Arawak & Carib *iwana*] (1555) **:** any of various large chiefly herbivorous usu. green or brownish tropical American lizards (family Iguanidae, the iguana family) that have a serrated dorsal crest and large dewlap; *broadly* **:** any of various large lizards

iguan·odon \i-ˈgwä-nə-ˌdän\ *n* [NL *Iguanodont-, Iguanodon,* fr. Sp *iguana* + Gk *odōn* tooth, fr. *odont-, odous* — more at TOOTH] (1830) **:** any of a genus (*Iguanodon*) of very large herbivorous dinosaurs of the Early Cretaceous

IGY *abbr* International Geophysical Year

ihp *abbr* indicated horsepower

IHS \ˌī-ˌāch-ˈes\ [LL, part transliteration of Gk IHΣ, abbreviation for IHΣOYΣ *Iēsous* Jesus] — used as a Christian symbol and monogram for *Jesus*

IIE *abbr* Institute of Industrial Engineers

ikat \ˈē-ˌkät\ *n* [Malay, tying] (1927) **:** a fabric in which the yarns have been tie-dyed before weaving

ike·ba·na \ˌi-kā-ˈbä-nə, ˌi-ki-, ˌē-\ *n* [Jp, fr. *ikeru* to keep alive, arrange + *hana* flower] (1901) **:** the Japanese art of flower arranging that emphasizes form and balance

ikon *var of* ICON

IL *abbr* **1** Illinois **2** interleukin — often used with an identifying number ⟨*IL-6*⟩

il- — see IN-

ILA *abbr* International Longshoremen's Association

ilang–ilang *var of* YLANG-YLANG

[1]**-ile** *adj suffix* [L *-ilis*] **:** tending to or capable of ⟨contract*ile*⟩

[2]**-ile** *n suffix* [*-ile* (as in *quartile,* n.)] **:** segment of a (specified) size in a frequency distribution ⟨dec*ile*⟩

il·e·i·tis \ˌi-lē-ˈī-təs\ *n* [NL] (ca. 1855) **:** inflammation of the ileum

il·e·um \ˈi-lē-əm\ *n, pl* **il·ea** \-lē-ə\ [NL, alter. of L *ilia,* pl., groin, viscera] (1682) **:** the last division of the small intestine extending between the jejunum and large intestine — **il·e·al** \-lē-əl\ *adj*

il·e·us \ˈi-lē-əs\ *n* [L, fr. Gk *eileos,* fr. *eilyein* to roll — more at VOLUBLE] (1693) **:** functional obstruction of the gastrointestinal tract and esp. the small intestine that is marked by the absence of peristalsis

ilex \ˈī-ˌleks\ *n* [ME, fr. L] (14c) **1 :** HOLM OAK **2 :** HOLLY 1

ILGWU *abbr* International Ladies' Garment Workers' Union

il·i·ac \ˈi-lē-ˌak\ *also* **il·i·al** \ˈi-lē-əl\ *adj* [LL *iliacus,* fr. L *ilium*] (1541) **:** of, relating to, or located on or near the ilium

Il·i·ad \ˈi-lē-əd, -ˌad\ *n* [*Iliad,* ancient Greek epic poem attributed to Homer, fr. L *Iliad-, Ilias,* fr. Gk, fr. *Ilion* Troy] (1603) **1 a :** a series of miseries or disastrous events **b :** a series of exploits regarded as suitable for an epic **2 :** a long narrative; *esp* **:** an epic in the Homeric tradition — **Il·i·ad·ic** \ˌi-lē-ˈa-dik\ *adj*

il·i·um \ˈi-lē-əm\ *n, pl* **il·ia** \-lē-ə\ [NL, alter. of L *ilia*] (1706) **:** the broad, dorsal, upper, and largest of the three principal bones composing either half of the pelvis

[1]**ilk** \ˈilk\ *pron* [ME, fr. OE *ilca,* fr. *i- that, the same (akin to Goth *is* he, L, he, that) + *lik- form (whence OE *līc* body) — more at ITERATE, LIKE] (bef. 12c) *chiefly Scot* **:** SAME — used with *that* esp. in the names of landed families

[2]**ilk** *n* (1790) **:** SORT, KIND ⟨politicians and their ~⟩

[3]**ilk** *pron* [ME, adj. & pron., fr. OE *ylc, ǣlc* — more at EACH] (bef. 12c) *chiefly Scot* **:** EACH

il·ka \ˈil-kə\ *adj* [ME, fr. *ilk* + *a* (indef. art.)] (13c) *chiefly Scot* **:** EACH, EVERY

[1]**ill** \ˈil\ *adj* **worse** \ˈwərs\; **worst** \ˈwərst\ [ME, fr. ON *illr*] (12c) **1 a** *chiefly Scot* **:** IMMORAL, VICIOUS **b :** resulting from, accompanied by, or indicative of an evil or malevolent intention ⟨~ deeds⟩ **c :** attributing evil or an objectionable quality ⟨held an ~ opinion of his neighbors⟩ **2 a :** causing suffering or distress ⟨~ weather⟩ **b** *comparative also* **ill·er;** *superlative also* **ill·est** (1) **:** not normal or sound ⟨~ health⟩ (2) **:** not in good health; *also* **:** NAUSEATED **3 a :** not suited to circumstances or not to one's advantage **:** UNLUCKY ⟨an ~ omen⟩ **b :** involving difficulty **:** HARD **4 a :** not meeting an accepted standard ⟨~ manners⟩ **b** *archaic* **:** notably unskillful or inefficient **5 :** UNFRIENDLY, HOSTILE ⟨~ feeling⟩

[2]**ill** *adv* **worse; worst** (13c) **1 a :** with displeasure or hostility **b :** in a harsh manner **c :** so as to reflect unfavorably ⟨spoke ~ of the neighbors⟩ **2 :** in a reprehensible manner **3 :** HARDLY, SCARCELY ⟨can ~ afford such extravagances⟩ **4 a :** in an unfortunate manner **:** BADLY, UNLUCKILY ⟨~ fares the land . . . where wealth accumulates, and men decay —Oliver Goldsmith⟩ **b :** in a faulty, inefficient, insufficient, or unpleasant manner — often used in combination ⟨the methods used may be *ill*-adapted to the aims in view —R. M. Hutchins⟩

[3]**ill** *n* (13c) **1 :** the reverse of good **:** EVIL **2 a :** MISFORTUNE, DISTRESS **b** (1) **:** AILMENT, SICKNESS (2) **:** something that disturbs or afflicts **:** TROUBLE ⟨economic and social ~*s*⟩ **3 :** something that reflects unfavorably ⟨spoke no ~ of him⟩

[4]**ill** *abbr* illustrated; illustration; illustrator

Ill *abbr* Illinois

I'll \ˈī(-ə)l, ˈäl\ (1566) **:** I will **:** I shall

ill–ad·vised \ˌil-əd-ˈvīzd\ *adj* (ca. 1593) **:** resulting from or showing lack of wise and sufficient counsel or deliberation ⟨an ~ decision⟩ — **ill–ad·vis·ed·ly** \-ˈvī-zəd-lē\ *adv*

ill at ease *adj* (14c) **:** not feeling easy **:** UNCOMFORTABLE

il·la·tion \i-ˈlā-shən\ *n* [LL *illation-, illatio,* fr. L, action of bringing in, fr. *inferre* (pp. *illatus*) to bring in, fr. *in-* + *ferre* to carry — more at TOLERATE, BEAR] (1533) **1 :** the action of inferring **:** INFERENCE **2 :** a conclusion inferred

[1]**il·la·tive** \ˈi-lə-tiv, i-ˈlā-\ *n* (1591) **1 :** a word (as *therefore*) or phrase (as *as a consequence*) introducing an inference **2 :** ILLATION 2

[2]**illative** *adj* (1611) **:** INFERENTIAL — **il·la·tive·ly** *adv*

il·laud·able \(ˌ)i(l)-ˈlȯ-də-bəl\ *adj* [L *illaudabilis,* fr. *in-* + *laudabilis* laudable] (1589) **:** deserving no praise — **il·laud·ably** \-blē\ *adv*

ill–be·ing \ˈil-ˈbē-iŋ\ *n* (1840) **:** a condition of being deficient in health, happiness, or prosperity

ill–bod·ing \-ˈbō-diŋ\ *adj* (1591) **:** boding evil **:** INAUSPICIOUS

ill–bred \-ˈbred\ *adj* (1604) **:** badly brought up or showing bad upbringing **:** IMPOLITE

[1]**il·le·gal** \(ˌ)i(l)-ˈlē-gəl\ *adj* [MF or ML; MF *illegal,* fr. ML *illegalis,* fr. L *in-* + *legalis* legal] (1538) **:** not according to or authorized by law **:** UNLAWFUL, ILLICIT; *also* **:** not sanctioned by official rules (as of a game) — **il·le·gal·i·ty** \ˌi-li-ˈga-lə-tē\ *n* — **il·le·gal·ly** \(ˌ)i(l)-ˈlē-gə-lē\ *adv*

[2]**illegal** *n* (1939) **:** an illegal immigrant

il·le·gal·ize \(ˌ)i(l)-ˈlē-gə-ˌlīz\ *vt* (ca. 1818) **:** to make or declare illegal — **il·le·gal·i·za·tion** \-ˌlē-gə-lə-ˈzā-shən\ *n*

il·leg·i·ble \(ˌ)i(l)-ˈle-jə-bəl\ *adj* (1580) **:** not legible **:** INDECIPHERABLE ⟨~ writing⟩ — **il·leg·i·bil·i·ty** \-ˌle-jə-ˈbi-lə-tē\ *n* — **il·leg·i·bly** \-ˈle-jə-blē\ *adv*

il·le·git·i·ma·cy \ˌi-li-ˈji-tə-mə-sē\ *n* (1680) **1 :** the quality or state of being illegitimate **2 :** BASTARDY 2

il·le·git·i·mate \-ˈji-tə-mət\ *adj* (1536) **1 :** not recognized as lawful offspring; *specif* **:** born of parents not married to each other **2 :** not rightly deduced or inferred **:** ILLOGICAL **3 :** departing from the regular **:** ERRATIC **4 a :** not sanctioned by law **:** ILLEGAL **b :** not authorized by good usage **c** *of a taxon* **:** published but not in accordance with the rules of the relevant international code — **il·le·git·i·mate·ly** *adv*

ill–fat·ed \ˈil-ˈfā-təd\ *adj* (1710) **1 :** having or destined to a hapless fate **:** UNFORTUNATE ⟨an ~ expedition⟩ **2 :** that causes or marks the beginning of misfortune

ill–fa·vored \-ˈfā-vərd\ *adj* (ca. 1530) **1 :** unattractive in physical appearance; *esp* **:** having an ugly face **2 :** OFFENSIVE, OBJECTIONABLE

ill–got·ten \-ˈgä-tᵊn\ *adj* (1552) **:** acquired by illicit or improper means ⟨~ gains⟩

ill–hu·mored \ˈil-ˈhyü-mərd, -ˈyü-\ *adj* (1687) **:** SURLY, IRRITABLE — **ill–hu·mored·ly** *adv*

il·lib·er·al \(ˌ)i(l)-ˈli-b(ə-)rəl\ *adj* [MF or L; MF, fr. L *illiberalis* ignoble, stingy, fr. L *in-* + *liberalis* liberal] (1535) **:** not liberal: as **a** *archaic* (1) **:** lacking a liberal education (2) **:** lacking culture and refinement **b :** not requiring the background of a liberal arts education ⟨~ occupations⟩ **c** *archaic* **:** not generous **:** STINGY **d :** not broad-minded **:** BIGOTED ⟨~ thinking⟩ **e :** opposed to liberalism ⟨~ tendencies⟩ — **il·lib·er·al·i·ty** \-ˌli-bə-ˈra-lə-tē\ *n* — **il·lib·er·al·ly** \-ˈli-b(ə-)rə-lē\ *adv* — **il·lib·er·al·ness** \-b(ə-)rəl-nəs\ *n*

il·lib·er·al·ism \-b(ə-)rə-ˌli-zəm\ *n* (1839) **:** opposition to or lack of liberalism

il·lic·it \(ˌ)i(l)-ˈli-sət\ *adj* [L *illicitus,* fr. *in-* + *licitus* lawful — more at LICIT] (1506) **:** not permitted **:** UNLAWFUL — **il·lic·it·ly** *adv*

il·lim·it·able \(ˌ)i(l)-ˈli-mə-tə-bəl\ *adj* (1596) **:** incapable of being limited or bounded **:** MEASURELESS ⟨the ~ reaches of space and time⟩ — **il·lim·it·abil·i·ty** \-ˌli-mə-tə-ˈbi-lə-tē\ *n* — **il·lim·it·able·ness** \-ˈli-mə-tə-bəl-nəs\ *n* — **il·lim·it·ably** \-blē\ *adv*

Il·li·nois \ˌi-lə-ˈnȯi *also* -ˈnȯiz\ *n, pl* **Illinois** [F, earlier *Erinioua*i, sing., prob. fr. a word in an Algonquian language derived fr. Proto-Algonquian *elen- ordinary + *-we· make a sound] (1703) **1** *pl* **:** a confederacy of American Indian peoples of Illinois, Iowa, and Wisconsin **2 :** a member of any of the Illinois peoples **3 :** the Algonquian language of the Illinois

il·liq·uid \(ˌ)i(l)-ˈlik-wəd\ *adj* (1913) **1 :** not being cash or readily convertible into cash ⟨~ holdings⟩ **2 :** deficient in liquid assets ⟨an ~ bank⟩ — **il·li·quid·i·ty** \-ˌli-ˈkwi-də-tē\ *n*

il·lite \ˈi-ˌlīt\ *n* [*Ill*inois, state of U.S. + [1]*-ite*] (1937) **:** any of a group of clay minerals having essentially the crystal structure of muscovite — **il·lit·ic** \i-ˈli-tik\ *adj*

il·lit·er·a·cy \(ˌ)i(l)-ˈli-t(ə-)rə-sē\ *n, pl* **-cies** (1660) **1 :** the quality or state of being illiterate; *esp* **:** inability to read or write **2 :** a mistake or crudity (as in speaking) typical of one who is illiterate

il·lit·er·ate \(ˌ)i(l)-ˈli-t(ə-)rət\ *adj* [ME, fr. L *illiteratus,* fr. *in-* + *litteratus* literate] (15c) **1 :** having little or no education; *esp* **:** unable to read or write ⟨an ~ population⟩ **2 a :** showing or marked by a lack of familiarity with language and literature ⟨an ~ magazine⟩ **b :** violating approved patterns of speaking or writing **3 :** showing or marked by a lack of acquaintance with the fundamentals of a particular field of knowledge ⟨musically ∼⟩ **syn** see IGNORANT — **illiterate** n — **il·lit·er·ate·ly** adv — **il·lit·er·ate·ness** n

ill-man·nered \'il-'ma-nərd\ adj (15c) : having bad manners : RUDE

ill-na·tured \-'nā-chərd\ adj (1605) **1** : MALEVOLENT, SPITEFUL **2** : having a bad disposition : CROSS, SURLY — **ill-na·tured·ly** adv

ill·ness \'il-nəs\ n (ca. 1500) **1** obs **a** : WICKEDNESS **b** : UNPLEAS-ANTNESS **2 a** : an unhealthy condition of body or mind **b** : SICKNESS 2

il·lo·cu·tion·ary \i-lə-'kyü-shə-ner-ē, ¡i(l)-lō-\ adj [²in- + locution] (1955) : relating to or being the communicative effect (as commanding or requesting) of an utterance ⟨"There's a snake under you" may have the ∼ force of a warning⟩

il·log·ic \(¡)i(l)-'lä-jik\ n [back-formation fr. illogical] (1856) : the quality or state of being illogical : ILLOGICALITY

il·log·i·cal \-ji-kəl\ adj (1588) **1** : not observing the principles of logic ⟨an ∼ argument⟩ **2** : devoid of logic : SENSELESS ⟨∼ policies⟩ — **il·log·i·cal·i·ty** \-¡lä-jə-'ka-lə-tē\ n — **il·log·i·cal·ly** \-'lä-ji-k(ə-)lē\ adv — **il·log·i·cal·ness** \-kəl-nəs\ n

ill-sort·ed \'il-'sȯr-təd\ adj (1691) **1** : not well matched ⟨he and his wife were an ∼ pair —Lord Byron⟩ **2** Scot : much displeased

ill-starred \-'stärd\ adj (1604) : ILL-FATED, UNLUCKY ⟨an ∼ venture⟩

ill-tem·pered \-'tem-pərd\ adj (1601) : ILL-NATURED, QUARRELSOME — **ill-tem·pered·ly** \-lē\ adv

ill-treat \-'trēt\ vt (1689) : to treat cruelly or improperly : MALTREAT — **ill-treat·ment** \-mənt\ n

il·lume \i-'lüm\ vt **il·lumed; il·lum·ing** (1602) : ILLUMINATE

il·lu·mi·nance \i-'lü-mə-nən(t)s\ n (ca. 1938) : ILLUMINATION 2

il·lu·mi·nant \-nənt\ n (1644) : an illuminating device or substance

¹il·lu·mi·nate \i-'lü-mə-nət\ adj (15c) **1** archaic : brightened with light **2** archaic : intellectually or spiritually enlightened

²il·lu·mi·nate \-¡nāt\ vt **-nat·ed; -nat·ing** [ME, fr. L illuminatus, pp. of illuminare, fr. in- + luminare to light up, fr. lumin-, lumen light — more at LUMINARY] (15c) **1 a** : to enlighten spiritually or intellectually **b** (1) : to supply or brighten with light (2) : to make luminous or shining **c** archaic : to set alight **2 a** : to subject to radiation **2 a** : to make clear : ELUCIDATE **b** : to bring to the fore : HIGHLIGHT ⟨a crisis can ∼ how interdependent we all are⟩ **3** : to make illustrious or resplendent **4** : to decorate (as a manuscript) with gold or silver or brilliant colors or with often elaborate designs or miniature pictures — **il·lu·mi·nat·ing·ly** \-¡nā-tiŋ-lē\ adv — **il·lu·mi·na·tor** \-¡nā-tər\ n

³il·lu·mi·nate \-nət\ n (1600) archaic : one having or claiming unusual enlightenment

il·lu·mi·na·ti \i-¡lü-mə-'nä-tē\ n pl [It & NL; It, fr. NL, fr. L, pl. of illuminatus] (1599) **1** cap : any of various groups claiming special religious enlightenment **2** : persons who are or who claim to be unusually enlightened **3** : ELITE 1d ⟨members of the academic ∼⟩

il·lu·mi·na·tion \i-¡lü-mə-'nā-shən\ n (14c) **1** : the action of illuminating or state of being illuminated: as **a** : spiritual or intellectual enlightenment **b** (1) : a lighting up (2) : decorative lighting or lighting effects **c** : decoration by the art of illuminating **2** : the luminous flux per unit area on an intercepting surface at any given point **3** : one of the decorative features used in the art of illuminating or in decorative lighting

il·lu·mi·na·tive \i-'lü-mə-¡nā-tiv\ adj (1644) : of, relating to, or producing illumination : ILLUMINATING

il·lu·mine \i-'lü-mən\ vt **-mined; -min·ing** (14c) : ILLUMINATE — **il·lu·min·able** \-mə-nə-bəl\ adj

il·lu·mi·nism \-mə-¡ni-zəm\ n (1798) **1** : belief in or claim to a personal enlightenment not accessible to humankind in general **2** cap : beliefs or claims viewed as forming doctrine or principles of Illuminati — **il·lu·mi·nist** \-nist\ n

illus or **illust** abbr illustrated; illustration

ill-us·age \'il-'yü-sij, -zij\ n (1593) : harsh, unkind, or abusive treatment

ill-use \-'yüz\ vt (1841) : to use badly : MALTREAT, ABUSE

il·lu·sion \i-'lü-zhən\ n [ME, fr. AF, fr. LL illusion-, illusio, fr. L, action of mocking, fr. illudere to mock at, fr. in- + ludere to play, mock — more at LUDICROUS] (14c) **1 a** obs : the action of deceiving **b** (1) : the state or fact of being intellectually deceived or misled : MISAPPRE-HENSION (2) : an instance of such deception **2 a** (1) : a misleading image presented to the vision (2) : something that deceives or misleads intellectually **b** (1) : perception of something objectively existing in such a way as to cause misinterpretation of its actual nature (2) : HALLUCINATION 1 (3) : a pattern capable of reversible perspective **3** : a fine plain transparent bobbinet or tulle usu. made of silk and used for veils, trimmings, and dresses **syn** see DELUSION — **il·lu·sion·al** \-'lü-zhə-nᵊl, -'lü-zhə-nᵊl\ adj

il·lu·sion·ary \i-'lü-zhə-¡ner-ē\ adj (1866) : ILLUSORY

il·lu·sion·ism \i-'lü-zhə-¡ni-zəm\ n (1911) : the use of artistic techniques (as perspective or shading) to create the illusion of reality esp. in a work of art

il·lu·sion·ist \i-'lüzh-nist, -'lü-zhə-\ n (1850) : a person who produces illusory effects: as **a** : one (as an artist) whose work is marked by illusionism **b** : a sleight-of-hand performer or a magician — **il·lu·sion·is·tic** \-¡lü-zhə-'nis-tik\ adj — **il·lu·sion·is·ti·cal·ly** \-ti-k(ə-)lē\ adv

il·lu·sive \i-'lü-siv, -ziv\ adj (1606) : ILLUSORY — **il·lu·sive·ly** adv — **il·lu·sive·ness** n

il·lu·so·ry \i-'lüs-rē, -'lüz-; -'lü-sə-, -zə-\ adj (ca. 1631) : based on or producing illusion : DECEPTIVE ⟨∼ hopes⟩ **syn** see APPARENT — **il·lu·so·ri·ly** \-rə-lē\ adv — **il·lu·so·ri·ness** \-rē-nəs\ n

il·lus·trate \'i-ləs-¡trāt also i-'ləs-¡\ vb **-trat·ed; -trat·ing** [L illustratus, pp. of illustrare, fr. in- + lustrare to purify, make bright — more at LUSTER] vt (1526) **1** obs **a** : ENLIGHTEN **b** : to light up **2 a** archaic : to make illustrious **b** obs (1) : to make bright (2) : ADORN **3 a** : to make clear : CLARIFY **b** : to make clear by giving or by serving as an example or instance **c** : to provide with visual features intended to explain or decorate ⟨∼ a book⟩ **4** : to show clearly : DEMONSTRATE ∼ vi : to give an example or instance — **il·lus·tra·tor** \'i-ləs-¡trā-tər also i-'ləs-\ n

il·lus·tra·tion \¡i-ləs-'trā-shən also i-¡ləs-\ n (14c) **1 a** : the action of illustrating : the condition of being illustrated **b** archaic : the action of making illustrious or honored or distinguished **2** : something that serves to illustrate: as **a** : an example or instance that helps make

something clear **b** : a picture or diagram that helps make something clear or attractive **syn** see INSTANCE — **il·lus·tra·tion·al** \-shnᵊl, -shə-nᵊl\ adj

il·lus·tra·tive \i-'ləs-trə-tiv also 'i-lə-¡strā-\ adj (1643) : serving, tending, or designed to illustrate ⟨∼ examples⟩ ⟨art that is ∼ of provincial life⟩ — **il·lus·tra·tive·ly** adv

il·lus·tri·ous \i-'ləs-trē-əs\ adj [L illustris, prob. fr. illustrare] (1588) **1** : notably or brilliantly outstanding because of dignity or achievements or actions : EMINENT **2** archaic **a** : shining brightly with light **b** : clearly evident **syn** see FAMOUS — **il·lus·tri·ous·ly** adv — **il·lus·tri·ous·ness** n

il·lu·vi·a·tion \i-¡lü-vē-'ā-shən\ n [²in- + -luviation (as in eluviation)] (1928) : accumulation of dissolved or suspended soil materials in one area or horizon as a result of eluviation from another — **il·lu·vi·at·ed** \i-'lü-vē-¡ā-təd\ adj

ill will n (14c) : unfriendly feeling **syn** see MALICE

ill-wish·er \'il-¡wi-shər, -'wi-\ n (1607) : one that wishes ill to another

il·ly \'i(l)-lē\ adv (1549) : not wisely or well : BADLY, ILL ⟨his ∼ concealed pride —Della Lutes⟩

Il·lyr·i·an \i-'lir-ē-ən\ n (1549) **1** : a native or inhabitant of ancient Illyria **2** : the poorly attested Indo-European languages of the Illyrians — see INDO-EUROPEAN LANGUAGES table — **Illyrian** adj

il·men·ite \'il-mə-¡nīt\ n [G Ilmenit, fr. Ilmen range, Ural Mts., Russia] (ca. 1827) : a usu. massive iron-black mineral that consists of an oxide of iron and titanium and that is a major titanium ore

ILO abbr International Labor Organization

Ilo·ca·no or **Ilo·ka·no** \¡ē-lə-'kä-(¡)nō, ¡i-\ n, pl **Ilocanos** or **Ilokano** or **Ilokanos** (1898) **1** : a member of a major people of northern Luzon in the Philippines **2** : the Austronesian language of the Ilocano people

ILS abbr instrument landing system

¹IM \'ī-'em\ vb **IM'd; IM'ing** (1994) : to send an instant message to ∼ vi : to communicate by instant message

²IM abbr **1** individual medley **2** instant message **3** intramural

im- — see IN-

I'm \'īm also 'äm, əm\ (1584) : I am

¹im·age \'i-mij\ n [ME, fr. AF, short for imagene, fr. L imagin-, imago; perh. akin to L imitari to imitate] (13c) **1** : a reproduction or imitation of the form of a person or thing; esp : an imitation in solid form : STATUE **2 a** : the optical counterpart of an object produced by an optical device (as a lens or mirror) or an electronic device **b** : a visual representation of something: as (1) : a likeness of an object produced on a photographic material (2) : a picture produced on an electronic display (as a television or computer screen) **3 a** : exact likeness : SEMBLANCE ⟨God created man in his own ∼ —Gen 1:27(RSV)⟩ **b** : a person strikingly like another person ⟨she is the ∼ of her mother⟩ **4 a** : a tangible or visible representation : INCARNATION ⟨the ∼ of filial devotion⟩ **b** archaic : an illusory form : APPARITION **5 a** (1) : a mental picture or impression of something ⟨had a negative body ∼ of herself⟩ (2) : a mental conception held in common by members of a group and symbolic of a basic attitude and orientation ⟨a disorderly courtroom can seriously tarnish a community's ∼ of justice —Herbert Brownell⟩ **b** : IDEA, CONCEPT **6** : a vivid or graphic representation or description **7** : FIGURE OF SPEECH **8** : a popular conception (as of a person, institution, or nation) projected esp. through the mass media ⟨promoting a corporate ∼ of brotherly love and concern —R. C. Buck⟩ **9** : a set of values given by a mathematical function (as a homomorphism) that corresponds to a particular subset of the domain

²image vt **im·aged; im·ag·ing** (14c) **1** : to call up a mental picture of : IMAGINE **2** : to describe or portray in language esp. in a vivid manner **3 a** : to create a representation of; also : to form an image of ⟨imaged Jupiter's rings⟩ ⟨∼ the bone using X-rays⟩ **b** : to represent symbolically **4 a** : REFLECT, MIRROR **b** : to make appear : PROJECT — **im·ag·er** \'i-mi-jər\ n

im·ag·ery \'i-mij-rē, -mi-jə-\ n, pl **-er·ies** (14c) **1 a** : the product of image makers : IMAGES; also : the art of making images **b** : pictures produced by an imaging system **2** : figurative language **3** : mental images; esp : the products of imagination

image tube n (1936) : an electron tube in which incident electromagnetic radiation (as light or infrared) produces a visible image on its fluorescent screen duplicating the original pattern of radiation — called also image converter

imag·in·able \i-'maj-nə-bəl, -'ma-jə-\ adj (14c) : capable of being imagined : CONCEIVABLE ⟨any ∼ location⟩ — **imag·in·able·ness** n — **imag·in·ably** \-blē\ adv

¹imag·i·nal \i-'ma-jə-nᵊl\ adj [imagine + ¹-al] (1647) : of or relating to imagination, images, or imagery

²ima·gi·nal \i-'ma-jə-nᵊl, -'mä-; -'mä-gə-\ adj [NL imagin-, imago] (1877) : of or relating to the insect imago

imag·i·nary \i-'ma-jə-¡ner-ē, -¡ne-rē\ adj (14c) **1 a** : existing only in imagination : lacking factual reality **b** : formed or characterized imaginatively or arbitrarily ⟨his canvases, chiefly ∼, somber landscapes —Current Biog.⟩ **2** : containing or relating to the imaginary unit ⟨∼ roots⟩ — **imag·i·nari·ly** \i-¡ma-jə-'ner-ə-lē\ adv — **imag·i·nari·ness** \-'ma-jə-¡ner-ē-nəs\ n

syn IMAGINARY, FANCIFUL, VISIONARY, FANTASTIC, CHIMERICAL, QUIXOTIC mean unreal or unbelievable. IMAGINARY applies to something which is fictitious and purely the product of one's imagination ⟨an imaginary desert isle⟩. FANCIFUL suggests the free play of the imagination ⟨a teller of fanciful stories⟩. VISIONARY stresses impracticality or incapability of realization ⟨visionary schemes⟩. FANTASTIC implies incredibility or strangeness beyond belief ⟨a fantastic world inhabited by monsters⟩. CHIMERICAL combines the implication of VISIONARY and FANTASTIC ⟨chimerical dreams of future progress⟩. QUIXOTIC implies a devotion to romantic or chivalrous ideals unrestrained by ordinary prudence and common sense ⟨a quixotic crusade⟩.

\ə\ abut \ᵊ\ kitten, F table \ər\ further \a\ ash \ā\ ace \ä\ mop, mar \au̇\ out \ch\ chin \e\ bet \ē\ easy \g\ go \i\ hit \ī\ ice \j\ job \ŋ\ sing \ō\ go \ȯ\ law \ȯi\ boy \th\ thin \t̲h̲\ the \ü\ loot \u̇\ foot \y\ yet \zh\ vision, beige \k̲, ⁿ, œ, ᵫ, �\ see Guide to Pronunciation

imaginary number *n* (ca. 1911) : a complex number (as 2 + 3*i*) in which the coefficient of the imaginary unit is not zero — called also *imaginary*; compare PURE IMAGINARY

imaginary part *n* (1845) : the part of a complex number (as 3*i* in 2 + 3*i*) that has the imaginary unit as a factor

imaginary unit *n* (ca. 1911) : the positive square root of minus 1 denoted by *i* or $+\sqrt{-1}$

imag·i·na·tion \i-ˌma-jə-ˈnā-shən\ *n* [ME, fr. AF, fr. L *imagination-, imaginatio,* fr. *imaginari*] (14c) **1 :** the act or power of forming a mental image of something not present to the senses or never before wholly perceived in reality **2 a :** creative ability **b :** ability to confront and deal with a problem : RESOURCEFULNESS ⟨use your ~ and get us out of here⟩ **c :** the thinking or active mind : INTEREST ⟨stories that fired the ~⟩ **3 a :** a creation of the mind; *esp* : an idealized or poetic creation **b :** fanciful or empty assumption

imag·i·na·tive \i-ˈmaj-nə-tiv; -ˈma-jə-ˌnā-, -nə-\ *adj* (14c) **1 a :** of, relating to, or characterized by imagination **b :** devoid of truth : FALSE **2 :** given to imagining : having a lively imagination **3 :** of or relating to images; *esp* : showing a command of imagery — **imag·i·na·tive·ly** *adv* — **imag·i·na·tive·ness** *n*

imag·ine \i-ˈma-jən\ *vb* **imag·ined; imag·in·ing** \-ˈmaj-niŋ, -ˈma-jə-\ [ME, fr. AF *imaginer,* fr. L *imaginari,* fr. *imagin-, imago* image] *vt* (14c) **1 :** to form a mental image of (something not present) ⟨~ accidents at every turn⟩ **2** *archaic* **:** PLAN, SCHEME **3 :** SUPPOSE, GUESS ⟨I ~ it will rain⟩ **4 :** to form a notion of without sufficient basis : FANCY ⟨~*s* himself to be a charming conversationalist⟩ ~ *vi* **1 :** to use the imagination **2 :** BELIEVE 3 ***syn*** see THINK

imaginings *n pl* (1605) : products of the imagination : THOUGHTS, IMAGES ⟨formless ~ of danger and terror —Jack Shaefer⟩

im·ag·ism \ˈi-mi-ˌji-zəm\ *n, often cap* (1912) : a 20th century movement in poetry advocating free verse and the expression of ideas and emotions through clear precise images — **im·ag·ist** \-mi-jist\ *n or adj, often cap* — **im·ag·is·tic** \ˌi-mi-ˈjis-tik\ *adj* — **im·ag·is·ti·cal·ly** \-ti-k(ə-)lē\ *adv*

ima·go \i-ˈmä-(ˌ)gō, -ˈmā-\ *n, pl* **imagoes** *or* **ima·gi·nes** \-ˈmā-gə-ˌnēz, -ˈmä-; -ˈmā-jə-, -ˈma-\ [NL, fr. L, image] (ca. 1797) **1 :** an insect in its final, adult, sexually mature, and typically winged state **2 :** an idealized mental image of another person or the self

imam \i-ˈmäm, ē-ˈ, -ˈmam\ *n, often cap* [Ar *imām*] (1613) **1 :** the prayer leader of a mosque **2 :** a Muslim leader of the line of Ali held by Shiites to be the divinely appointed, sinless, infallible successors of Muhammad **3 :** any of various rulers that claim descent from Muhammad and exercise spiritual and temporal leadership over a Muslim region

imam·ate \-ˈmä-ˌmāt, -ˈma-\ *n, often cap* (ca. 1741) **1 :** the office of an imam **2 :** the region or country ruled over by an imam

ima·ret \i-ˈmär-ət\ *n* [Turk] (1613) : an inn or hospice in Turkey

Ima·ri \i-ˈmär-ē\ *n* [*Imari,* Japan] (1875) : a multicolored Japanese porcelain usu. characterized by elaborate floral designs — **Imari** *adj*

im·bal·ance \(ˌ)im-ˈba-lən(t)s\ *n* (ca. 1890) : lack of balance : the state of being out of equilibrium or out of proportion ⟨a vitamin ~⟩ ⟨racial ~ in schools⟩ — **im·bal·anced** \-lən(t)st\ *adj*

im·be·cile \ˈim-bə-səl, -ˌsil\ *n* [F *imbécile,* n., fr. adj., weak, weak-minded, fr. L *imbecillus*] (1802) **1** *usu offensive* **:** a person affected with moderate mental retardation **2 :** FOOL, IDIOT — **imbecile** *or* **im·be·cil·ic** \ˌim-bə-ˈsi-lik\ *adj*

im·be·cil·i·ty \ˌim-bə-ˈsi-lə-tē\ *n, pl* **-ties** (ca. 1533) **1 :** the quality or state of being imbecile or an imbecile **2 a :** utter foolishness; *also* : FUTILITY **b :** something that is foolish or nonsensical

imbed *var of* EMBED

im·bibe \im-ˈbīb\ *vb* **im·bibed; im·bib·ing** [ME *enbiben* to absorb, cause to absorb, fr. L *imbibere* to drink in, absorb, fr. *in-* + *bibere* to drink — more at POTABLE] *vt* (14c) **1** *archaic* **:** SOAK, STEEP **2 a :** to receive into the mind and retain ⟨~ moral principles⟩ **b :** to assimilate or take into solution **3 a :** DRINK **b :** to take in or up ⟨a sponge ~*s* moisture⟩ ~ *vi* **1 :** DRINK 2 **2 a :** to take in liquid **b :** to absorb or assimilate moisture, gas, light, or heat — **im·bib·er** *n*

im·bi·bi·tion \ˌim-bə-ˈbi-shən\ *n* (15c) : the act or action of imbibing; *esp* : the taking up of fluid by a colloidal system resulting in swelling — **im·bi·bi·tion·al** \-ˈbish-nəl, -ˈbi-shə-nᵊl\ *adj*

im·bit·ter *archaic var of* EMBITTER

im·bo·som *archaic var of* EMBOSOM

[1]**im·bri·cate** \ˈim-bri-kət\ *adj* [LL *imbricatus,* pp. of *imbricare* to cover with pantiles, fr. L *imbric-, imbrex* pantile, fr. *imbr-, imber* rain; akin to Gk *ombros* rain] (ca. 1610) : lying lapped over each other in regular order ⟨~ scales⟩

[2]**im·bri·cate** \ˈim-brə-ˌkāt\ *vt* **-cat·ed; -cat·ing** (1784) : OVERLAP; *esp* : to overlap like roof tiles

im·bri·ca·tion \ˌim-brə-ˈkā-shən\ *n* (1713) **1 :** an overlapping of edges (as of tiles or scales) **2 :** a decoration or pattern showing imbrication

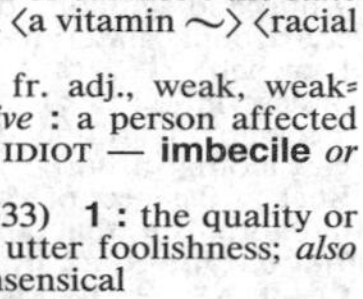

imbrication

im·bro·glio \im-ˈbrōl-(ˌ)yō\ *n, pl* **-glios** [It, fr. *imbrogliare* to entangle, fr. MF *embrouiller* — more at EMBROIL] (1750) **1 :** a confused mass **2 a :** an intricate or complicated situation (as in a drama or novel) **b :** an acutely painful or embarrassing misunderstanding **c :** a violently confused or bitterly complicated altercation : EMBROILMENT **d :** SCANDAL 3a ⟨survived the political ~⟩

im·brown *archaic var of* EMBROWN

im·brue *also* **em·brue** \im-ˈbrü\ *vt* **im·brued** *also* **em·brued; im·bru·ing** *also* **em·bru·ing** [ME *enbrewen, embrowen,* fr. AF *embrower* to soil, prob. alter. of OF *abevrer, abreuver* to water, soak, ultim. fr. L *bibere* to drink — more at POTABLE] (15c) : STAIN

im·brute \im-ˈbrüt\ *vb* **im·brut·ed; im·brut·ing** *vi* (1634) : to sink to the level of a brute ~ *vt* : to degrade to the level of a brute

im·bue \-ˈbyü\ *vt* **im·bued; im·bu·ing** [L *imbuere*] (1555) **1 :** to permeate or influence as if by dyeing ⟨the spirit that ~*s* the new constitution⟩ **2 :** to tinge or dye deeply **3 :** ENDOW 3 ⟨Spanish missions ~ the city with Old World charm —Scott Pendleton⟩ ***syn*** see INFUSE

IMF *abbr* International Monetary Fund

IMHO *abbr* in my humble opinion

im·id·az·ole \ˌi-mə-ˈda-ˌzōl\ *n* [ISV] (1892) : a white crystalline heterocyclic base $C_3H_4N_2$ that is an antimetabolite related to histidine; *broadly* : any of various derivatives of this

im·ide \ˈi-ˌmīd\ *n* [ISV, alter. of *amide*] (1857) : a compound containing the NH group that is derived from ammonia by replacement of two hydrogen atoms by a metal or an equivalent of acid groups — compare AMIDE — **im·id·ic** \i-ˈmi-dik\ *adj*

im·i·do \ˈi-mə-ˌdō\ *adj* (1937) : relating to or containing the NH group or its substituted form NR united to one or two acid groups

im·ine \ˈi-ˌmēn\ *n* [ISV, alter. of *amine*] (1883) : a compound containing the NH group or its substituted form NR that is derived from ammonia by replacement of two hydrogen atoms by a hydrocarbon group or other nonacid organic group

im·i·no \ˈi-mə-ˌnō\ *adj* (1901) : relating to or containing the NH group or its substituted form NR united to a group other than an acid group

imip·ra·mine \i-ˈmi-prə-ˌmēn\ *n* [*imide* + *propyl* + *amine*] (1958) : a tricyclic antidepressant drug $C_{19}H_{24}N_2$

im·i·ta·ble \ˈi-mə-tə-bəl\ *adj* (1550) : capable or worthy of being imitated or copied

im·i·tate \ˈi-mə-ˌtāt\ *vt* **-tat·ed; -tat·ing** [L *imitatus,* pp. of *imitari* — more at IMAGE] (1534) **1 :** to follow as a pattern, model, or example **2 :** to be or appear like : RESEMBLE **3 :** to produce a copy of : REPRODUCE **4 :** MIMIC, COUNTERFEIT ⟨can ~ his father's booming voice⟩ ***syn*** see COPY — **im·i·ta·tor** \-ˌtā-tər\ *n*

[1]**im·i·ta·tion** \ˌi-mə-ˈtā-shən\ *n* (14c) **1 :** an act or instance of imitating **2 :** something produced as a copy : COUNTERFEIT **3 :** a literary work designed to reproduce the style of another author **4 :** the repetition by one voice of a melody, phrase, or motive stated earlier in the composition by a different voice **5 :** the quality of an object in possessing some of the nature or attributes of a transcendent idea **6 :** the assumption of behavior observed in other individuals

[2]**imitation** *adj* (1818) : resembling something else that is usu. genuine and of better quality : not real ⟨~ leather⟩

im·i·ta·tive \ˈi-mə-ˌtā-tiv, *esp Brit* -tə-tiv\ *adj* (1584) **1 a :** marked by imitation ⟨acting is an ~ art⟩ **b :** reproducing or representing a natural sound : ONOMATOPOEIC ⟨"hiss" is an ~ word⟩ **c :** exhibiting mimicry **2 :** inclined to imitate **3 :** imitating something superior : COUNTERFEIT — **im·i·ta·tive·ly** *adv* — **im·i·ta·tive·ness** *n*

im·mac·u·la·cy \i-ˈma-kyə-lə-sē\ *n* (1799) : the quality or state of being immaculate

im·mac·u·late \i-ˈma-kyə-lət\ *adj* [ME *immaculat,* fr. L *immaculatus,* fr. *in-* + *maculatus* stained — more at MACULATE] (15c) **1 :** having no stain or blemish : PURE **2 :** containing no flaw or error **3 a :** spotlessly clean **b :** having no colored spots or marks ⟨petals ~⟩ — **im·mac·u·late·ly** *adv*

Immaculate Conception *n* (1687) **1 :** the conception of the Virgin Mary in which as decreed in Roman Catholic dogma her soul was preserved free from original sin by divine grace **2 :** December 8 observed as a Roman Catholic feast in commemoration of the Immaculate Conception

im·mane \i-ˈmān\ *adj* [L *immanis,* fr. *in-* + *manus* good — more at MATURE] (1602) *archaic* **:** HUGE; *also* : monstrous in character

im·ma·nence \ˈi-mə-nən(t)s\ *n* (1816) : the quality or state of being immanent; *esp* : INHERENCE

im·ma·nen·cy \-nən(t)-sē\ *n* (1659) : IMMANENCE

im·ma·nent \-nənt\ *adj* [LL *immanent-, immanens,* prp. of *immanēre* to remain in place, fr. L *in-* + *manēre* to remain — more at MANSION] (1535) **1 :** INDWELLING, INHERENT ⟨beauty is not something imposed but something ~ —Anthony Burgess⟩ **2 :** being within the limits of possible experience or knowledge — compare TRANSCENDENT — **im·ma·nent·ly** *adv*

im·ma·nent·ism \-nən-ˌti-zəm\ *n* (1907) : any of several theories according to which God or an abstract mind or spirit pervades the world — **im·ma·nent·ist** \-nən-tist, -ˌnen-\ *n or adj* — **im·ma·nent·is·tic** \ˌi-mə-nən-ˈtis-tik\ *adj*

Im·man·u·el *or* **Em·man·u·el** \i-ˈman-yə-wəl, -yəl\ *n* [ME *Emanuel,* fr. LL *Emmanuel,* fr. Gk *Emmanouēl,* fr. Heb *ʿimmānū'ēl,* lit., with us is God] (15c) : MESSIAH 1

im·ma·te·ri·al \ˌi-mə-ˈtir-ē-əl\ *adj* [ME *immaterial,* fr. LL *immaterialis,* fr. L *in-* + LL *materialis* material] (14c) **1 :** not consisting of matter : INCORPOREAL **2 :** of no substantial consequence : UNIMPORTANT

im·ma·te·ri·al·ism \-ē-ə-ˌli-zəm\ *n* (1713) : a philosophical theory that material things have no reality except as mental perceptions — **im·ma·te·ri·al·ist** \-list\ *n*

im·ma·te·ri·al·i·ty \ˌi-mə-ˌtir-ē-ˈa-lə-tē\ *n, pl* **-ties** (1570) **1 :** the quality or state of being immaterial **2 :** something immaterial

im·ma·te·ri·al·ize \-ˈtir-ē-ə-ˌlīz\ *vt* (1661) : to make immaterial or incorporeal

im·ma·ture \ˌi-mə-ˈtu̇r, -ˈtyu̇r, -ˈchu̇r\ *adj* [L *immaturus,* fr. *in-* + *maturus* mature] (1548) **1** *archaic* **:** PREMATURE **2 a :** lacking complete growth, differentiation, or development ⟨~ fruits⟩ ⟨a sexually ~ bird⟩ **b :** having the potential capacity to attain a definitive form or state : CRUDE, UNFINISHED ⟨a vigorous but ~ school of art⟩ **c :** exhibiting less than an expected degree of maturity ⟨emotionally ~ adults⟩ — **immature** *n* — **im·ma·ture·ly** *adv* — **im·ma·tu·ri·ty** \-ˈtu̇r-ə-tē, -ˈtyu̇r-, -ˈchu̇r-\ *n*

im·mea·sur·able \(ˌ)i(m)-ˈmezh-rə-bəl, -ˈmāzh-; -ˈme-zhə-rə-, -ˈmā-, -zhər-bəl\ *adj* (14c) : incapable of being measured; *broadly* : indefinitely extensive — **im·mea·sur·able·ness** *n* — **im·mea·sur·ably** \-blē\ *adv*

immed *abbr* immediate; immediately

im·me·di·a·cy \i-ˈmē-dē-ə-sē, *Brit often* -ˈmē-jə-sē\ *n, pl* **-cies** (1605) **1 :** the quality or state of being immediate **2 :** something that is immediate — usu. used in pl.

im·me·di·ate \i-ˈmē-dē-ət, *Brit often* -ˈmē-jit\ *adj* [ME *immediat,* fr. AF, fr. LL *immediatus,* fr. L *in-* + LL *mediatus* intermediate — more at MEDIATE] (15c) **1 a :** acting or being without the intervention of another object, cause, or agency : DIRECT ⟨the ~ cause of death⟩ **b :** present to the mind independently of other states or factors ⟨~ awareness⟩ **c :** involving or derived from a single premise ⟨an ~ inference⟩ **2 :** being next in line or relation ⟨the ~ family⟩ **3 a :** existing without intervening space or substance ⟨brought into ~ contact⟩ **b :** being near at hand ⟨the ~ neighborhood⟩ **4 a :** occurring, acting, or accomplished without loss or interval of time : INSTANT ⟨an ~

need⟩ **b** (1) **:** near to or related to the present ⟨the ~ past⟩ (2) **:** of or relating to the here and now **:** CURRENT ⟨too busy with ~ concerns to worry about the future⟩ **5 :** directly touching or concerning a person or thing ⟨the child's ~ world is the classroom⟩
immediate constituent *n* (1933) **:** any of the meaningful constituents directly forming a larger linguistic construction (as a phrase or sentence)
1**im·me·di·ate·ly** \i-ˈmē-dē-ət-lē *also* -ˈmē-dit-, *Brit often* -ˈmē-jit-\ *adv* (15c) **1 :** in direct connection or relation **:** DIRECTLY ⟨the parties ~ involved in the case⟩ ⟨the house ~ beyond this one⟩ **2 :** without interval of time **:** STRAIGHTWAY ⟨I'll make that call ~⟩
2**immediately** *conj* (1839) *chiefly Brit* **:** AS SOON AS
im·me·di·ate·ness *n* (1633) **:** IMMEDIACY 1
im·med·i·ca·ble \(ˌ)i(m)-ˈme-di-kə-bəl\ *adj* [L *immedicabilis,* fr. *in-* + *medicabilis* medicable] (1533) **:** INCURABLE ⟨wounds ~ —John Milton⟩ — **im·med·i·ca·bly** \-blē\ *adv*
Im·mel·mann \ˈi-məl-mən\ *n* [Max *Immelmann*] (1917) **:** a maneuver in which an airplane reverses direction by executing half of a loop upwards followed by half of a roll — called also *Immelmann turn*
im·me·mo·ri·al \ˌi-mə-ˈmȯr-ē-əl\ *adj* [prob. fr. F *immémorial,* fr. MF, fr. ML *immemorialis* lacking memory, fr. L *in-* + *memorialis* memorial] (1602) **:** extending or existing since beyond the reach of memory, record, or tradition ⟨existing from time ~⟩ — **im·me·mo·ri·al·ly** \-ē-ə-lē\ *adv*
im·mense \i-ˈmen(t)s\ *adj* [ME, fr. MF, fr. L *immensus* immeasurable, fr. *in-* + *mensus,* pp. of *metiri* to measure — more at MEASURE] (15c) **1 :** marked by greatness esp. in size or degree; *esp* **:** transcending ordinary means of measurement ⟨the ~ universe⟩ **2 :** supremely good ***syn*** see ENORMOUS — **im·mense·ly** *adv* — **im·mense·ness** *n*
im·men·si·ty \i-ˈmen(t)-sə-tē\ *n, pl* **-ties** (15c) **1 :** the quality or state of being immense **2 :** something immense
im·men·su·ra·ble \(ˌ)i(m)-ˈmen(t)s-rə-bəl, -ˈmen(t)sh-; -ˈmen(t)-sə-, -shə-\ *adj* [ME, fr. LL *immensurabilis,* fr. L *in-* + LL *mensurabilis* measurable, fr. *mensurare* to measure, fr. L *mensura* measure — more at MEASURE] (15c) **:** IMMEASURABLE
im·merge \i-ˈmərj\ *vi* **im·merged; im·merg·ing** [L *immergere*] (1706) **:** to plunge into or immerse oneself in something
im·merse \i-ˈmərs\ *vt* **im·mersed; im·mers·ing** [ME, fr. L *immersus,* pp. of *immergere,* fr. *in-* + *mergere* to merge] (15c) **1 :** to plunge into something that surrounds or covers; *esp* **:** to plunge or dip into a fluid **2 :** ENGROSS, ABSORB ⟨completely *immersed* in his work⟩ **3 :** to baptize by immersion
im·mers·ible \i-ˈmər-sə-bəl\ *adj* (ca. 1846) **:** capable of being totally submerged in water without damage (as to the heating element of an electric appliance) ⟨an ~ electric frying pan⟩
im·mer·sion \i-ˈmər-zhən, -shən\ *n* (15c) **:** the act of immersing or the state of being immersed: as **a :** baptism by complete submersion of the person in water **b :** absorbing involvement ⟨~ in politics⟩ **c :** instruction based on extensive exposure to surroundings or conditions that are native or pertinent to the object of study; *esp* **:** foreign language instruction in which only the language being taught is used ⟨learned French through ~⟩
immersion blender *n* (1982) **:** a handheld electric appliance for blending or grinding food with a protected blade that can be submerged in the food being processed — called also *hand blender, stick blender*
immersion heater *n* (1914) **:** a usu. electric unit that heats the liquid in which it is immersed
immesh *var of* ENMESH
im·me·thod·i·cal \ˌi-mə-ˈthä-di-kəl\ *adj* (1605) **:** not methodical — **im·me·thod·i·cal·ly** \-k(ə-)lē\ *adv*
im·mi·grant \ˈi-mə-grənt\ *n* (1789) **:** one that immigrates: as **a :** a person who comes to a country to take up permanent residence **b :** a plant or animal that becomes established in an area where it was previously unknown — **immigrant** *adj*
im·mi·grate \ˈi-mə-ˌgrāt\ *vb* **-grat·ed; -grat·ing** [L *immigratus,* pp. of *immigrare* to remove, go in, fr. *in-* + *migrare* to migrate] *vi* (ca. 1623) **:** to enter and usu. become established; *esp* **:** to come into a country of which one is not a native for permanent residence ~ *vt* **:** to bring in or send as immigrants — **im·mi·gra·tion** \ˌi-mə-ˈgrā-shən\ *n* — **im·mi·gra·tion·al** \-shnəl, -shə-nᵊl\ *adj*
im·mi·nence \ˈi-mə-nən(t)s\ *n* (1606) **1 :** something imminent; *esp* **:** impending evil or danger **2 :** the quality or state of being imminent
im·mi·nen·cy \-nən-sē\ *n* (1665) **:** IMMINENCE 2
im·mi·nent \ˈi-mə-nənt\ *adj* [L *imminent-, imminens,* prp. of *imminēre* to project, threaten, fr. *in-* + *-minēre* (akin to L *mont-, mons* mountain) — more at MOUNT] (1528) **:** ready to take place; *esp* **:** hanging threateningly over one's head ⟨was in ~ danger⟩ — **im·mi·nent·ly** *adv*
im·min·gle \i-ˈmiŋ-gəl\ *vb* (1606) **:** BLEND, INTERMINGLE
im·mis·ci·ble \(ˌ)i(m)-ˈmi-sə-bəl\ *adj* (1671) **:** incapable of mixing or attaining homogeneity — **im·mis·ci·bil·i·ty** \-ˌmi-sə-ˈbi-lə-tē\ *n*
im·mis·er·a·tion \(ˌ)i(m)-ˌmi-zə-ˈrā-shən\ *n* [2*in-* + *miser*able + *-ation*] (1948) **:** the act of making miserable; *esp* **:** IMPOVERISHMENT ⟨the ~ of the working class —C. R. Morris⟩
im·mit·i·ga·ble \(ˌ)i(m)-ˈmi-ti-gə-bəl\ *adj* [LL *immitigabilis,* fr. L *in-* + *mitigare* to mitigate] (1576) **:** not capable of being mitigated — **im·mit·i·ga·bly** \-blē\ *adv*
im·mit·tance \(ˌ)i(m)-ˈmi-tᵊn(t)s\ *n* [*im*pedance + ad*mittance*] (ca. 1948) **:** electrical admittance or impedance
im·mix \i-ˈmiks\ *vt* [back-formation fr. *immixed* mixed in, fr. ME *immixte,* fr. L *immixtus,* pp. of *immiscēre,* fr. *in-* + *miscēre* to mix — more at MIX] (15c) **:** to mix in — **im·mix·ture** \-ˈmiks-chər\ *n*
im·mo·bile \(ˌ)i(m)-ˈmō-bəl, -ˌbī(-ə)l *also* -ˌbēl\ *adj* [ME *in-mobill,* fr. L *immobilis,* fr. *in-* + *mobilis* mobile] (14c) **1 :** incapable of being moved **:** FIXED **2 :** not moving **:** MOTIONLESS ⟨keep the patient ~⟩ — **im·mo·bil·i·ty** \ˌi-(ˌ)mō-ˈbi-lə-tē\ *n*
im·mo·bi·lism \i-ˈmō-bə-ˌli-zəm\ *n* (1949) **:** a policy of extreme conservatism and opposition to change
im·mo·bi·lize \i-ˈmō-bə-ˌlīz\ *vt* (1871) **:** to make immobile: as **a :** to prevent freedom of movement or effective use of ⟨the planes were *immobilized* by bad weather⟩ **b :** to reduce or eliminate motion of (the body or a part) by mechanical means or by strict bed rest **c :** to withhold (money or capital) from circulation — **im·mo·bi·li·za·tion** \-ˌmō-bə-lə-ˈzā-shən\ *n* — **im·mo·bi·liz·er** \-ˈmō-bə-ˌlī-zər\ *n*
im·mod·er·a·cy \(ˌ)i(m)-ˈmä-d(ə-)rə-sē\ *n* (1682) **:** lack of moderation
im·mod·er·ate \-d(ə-)rət\ *adj* [ME *immoderat,* fr. L *immoderatus,* fr. *in-* + *moderatus,* pp. of *moderare* to moderate] (14c) **:** exceeding just, usual, or suitable bounds ⟨~ pride⟩ ⟨an ~ appetite⟩ ***syn*** see EXCESSIVE — **im·mod·er·ate·ly** *adv* — **im·mod·er·ate·ness** *n* — **im·mod·er·a·tion** \(ˌ)i-ˌmä-də-ˈrā-shən\ *n*
im·mod·est \(ˌ)i(m)-ˈmä-dəst\ *adj* [L *immodestus,* fr. *in-* + *modestus* modest] (1550) **:** not modest; *specif* **:** not conforming to the sexual mores of a particular time or place — **im·mod·est·ly** *adv* — **im·mod·es·ty** \-də-stē\ *n*
im·mo·late \ˈi-mə-ˌlāt\ *vt* **-lat·ed; -lat·ing** [L *immolatus,* pp. of *immolare* to sprinkle with meal before sacrificing, sacrifice, fr. *in-* + *mola* sacrificial barley cake, lit., millstone; akin to L *molere* to grind — more at MEAL] (15c) **1 :** to offer in sacrifice; *esp* **:** to kill as a sacrificial victim **2 :** to kill or destroy often by fire — **im·mo·la·tor** \-ˌlā-tər\ *n*
im·mo·la·tion \ˌi-mə-ˈlā-shən\ *n* (15c) **1 :** the act of immolating **:** the state of being immolated **2 :** something that is immolated
im·mor·al \(ˌ)i(m)-ˈmȯr-əl, -ˈmär-\ *adj* (1660) **:** not moral; *broadly* **:** conflicting with generally or traditionally held moral principles — **im·mor·al·ly** \-ə-lē\ *adv*
im·mor·al·ist \-ə-list\ *n* (1697) **:** an advocate of immorality — **im·mor·al·ism** \-ˌli-zəm\ *n*
im·mo·ral·i·ty \ˌi-(ˌ)mȯ-ˈra-lə-tē, ˌi-mə-\ *n* (ca. 1566) **1 :** the quality or state of being immoral; *esp* **:** UNCHASTITY **2 :** an immoral act or practice
1**im·mor·tal** \(ˌ)i-ˈmȯr-tᵊl\ *adj* [ME, fr. L *immortalis,* fr. *in-* + *mortalis* mortal] (14c) **1 :** exempt from death ⟨the ~ gods⟩ **2 :** exempt from oblivion **:** IMPERISHABLE ⟨~ fame⟩ **3 :** connected with or relating to immortality **4 :** able or tending to divide indefinitely ⟨~ cell lines produced in culture⟩ — **im·mor·tal·ly** \-tᵊl-ē\ *adv*
2**immortal** *n* (1616) **1 a :** one exempt from death **b** *pl, often cap* **:** the gods of the Greek and Roman pantheon **2 a :** a person whose fame is lasting **b** *cap* **:** any of the 40 members of the Académie Française
im·mor·tal·ise *Brit var of* IMMORTALIZE
im·mor·tal·i·ty \ˌi-ˌmȯr-ˈta-lə-tē\ *n* (14c) **:** the quality or state of being immortal: **a :** unending existence **b :** lasting fame
im·mor·tal·ize \i-ˈmȯr-tə-ˌlīz\ *vt* **-ized; -iz·ing** (ca. 1566) **:** to make immortal — **im·mor·tal·i·za·tion** \-ˌmȯr-tə-lə-ˈzā-shən\ *n* — **im·mor·tal·iz·er** \-ˈmȯr-tə-ˌlī-zər\ *n*
im·mor·telle \ˌi-ˌmȯr-ˈtel\ *n* [F, fr. fem. of *immortel* immortal, fr. L *immortalis*] (1832) **:** EVERLASTING 3
im·mo·tile \(ˌ)i(m)-ˈmō-tᵊl, -ˌtī(-ə)l\ *adj* (1872) **:** lacking motility
1**im·mov·able** \(ˌ)i(m)-ˈmü-və-bəl\ *adj* (14c) **1 :** incapable of being moved; *broadly* **:** not moving or not intended to be moved **2 a :** STEADFAST, UNYIELDING **b :** not capable of being moved emotionally — **im·mov·abil·i·ty** \-ˌmü-və-ˈbi-lə-tē\ *n* — **im·mov·able·ness** \-ˈmü-və-bəl-nəs\ *n* — **im·mov·ably** \-blē\ *adv*
2**immovable** *n* (1588) **1 :** one that cannot be moved **2** *pl* **:** real property as opposed to movable property
immun *abbr* **1** immunity **2** immunization
im·mune \i-ˈmyün\ *adj* [ME, fr. L *immunis,* fr. *in-* + *munia* services, obligations; akin to L *munus* service — more at MEAN] (15c) **1 a :** FREE, EXEMPT ⟨~ from further taxation⟩ **b :** marked by protection ⟨some criminal leaders are ~ from arrest⟩ **2 :** not susceptible or responsive ⟨~ to all pleas⟩; *esp* **:** having a high degree of resistance to a disease ⟨~ to diphtheria⟩ **3 a :** having or producing antibodies or lymphocytes capable of reacting with a specific antigen ⟨an ~ serum⟩ **b :** produced by, involved in, or concerned with immunity or an immune response ⟨~ agglutinins⟩ ⟨~ globulins⟩ — **immune** *n*
immune response *n* (1953) **:** a bodily response to an antigen that occurs when lymphocytes identify the antigenic molecule as foreign and induce the formation of antibodies and lymphocytes capable of reacting with it and rendering it harmless — called also *immune reaction*
immune system *n* (ca. 1919) **:** the bodily system that protects the body from foreign substances, cells, and tissues by producing the immune response and that includes esp. the thymus, spleen, lymph nodes, special deposits of lymphoid tissue (as in the gastrointestinal tract and bone marrow), macrophages, lymphocytes including the B cells and T cells, and antibodies
im·mu·ni·ty \i-ˈmyü-nə-tē\ *n, pl* **-ties** (14c) **:** the quality or state of being immune; *esp* **:** a condition of being able to resist a particular disease esp. through preventing development of a pathogenic microorganism or by counteracting the effects of its products
im·mu·nize \ˈi-myə-ˌnīz\ *vt* **-nized; -niz·ing** (1892) **:** to make immune — **im·mu·ni·za·tion** \ˌi-myə-nə-ˈzā-shən *also* i-ˌmyü-nə-\ *n*
immuno- *comb form* [ISV, fr. *immune*] **1 :** physiological immunity ⟨*immuno*logy⟩ **2 :** immunologic ⟨*immuno*chemistry⟩ **:** immunologically ⟨*immuno*competent⟩ **:** immunology and ⟨*immuno*genetics⟩
im·mu·no·as·say \ˌi-myə-nō-ˈa-ˌsā, i-ˌmyü-nō-, -a-ˈsā\ *n* (1959) **:** a technique or test used to detect the presence or quantity of a substance (as a protein) based on its capacity to act as an antigen — **im·mu·no·as·say·able** \-a-ˈsā-ə-bəl\ *adj*
im·mu·no·blot \ˈi-myə-nə-ˌblät, i-ˈmyü-(ˌ)nō-\ *n* (1982) **:** a blot (as a Western blot) in which a radioactively labeled antibody is used as the molecular probe — **im·mu·no·blot·ting** \-ˌblä-tiŋ\ *n*
im·mu·no·chem·is·try \ˌi-myə-nō-ˈke-mə-strē, i-ˌmyü-nō-\ *n* [ISV] (1907) **:** a branch of chemistry that deals with the chemical aspects of immunology — **im·mu·no·chem·i·cal** \-ˈke-mi-kəl\ *adj* — **im·mu·no·chem·i·cal·ly** \-k(ə-)lē\ *adv* — **im·mu·no·chem·ist** \-ˈke-mist\ *n*
im·mu·no·com·pe·tence \-ˈkäm-pə-tən(t)s\ *n* (1966) **:** the capacity for a normal immune response — **im·mu·no·com·pe·tent** \-tənt\ *adj*
im·mu·no·com·pro·mised \-ˈkäm-prə-ˌmīzd\ *adj* (1974) **:** having the immune system impaired or weakened (as by drugs or illness)
im·mu·no·cy·to·chem·is·try \-ˌsī-tō-ˈke-mə-strē\ *n* (1960) **:** the application of biochemistry to cellular immunology — **im·mu·no·cy·to·chem·i·cal** \-ˈke-mi-kəl\ *adj* — **im·mu·no·cy·to·chem·i·cal·ly** \-ˈke-mi-k(ə-)lē\ *adv*

\ə\ **abut** \ᵊ\ **kitten,** F **table** \ər\ **further** \a\ **ash** \ā\ **ace** \ä\ **mop, mar** \au̇\ **out** \ch\ **chin** \e\ **bet** \ē\ **easy** \g\ **go** \i\ **hit** \ī\ **ice** \j\ **job** \ŋ\ **sing** \ō\ **go** \ȯ\ **law** \ȯi\ **boy** \th\ **thin** \t͟h\ **the** \ü\ **loot** \u̇\ **foot** \y\ **yet** \zh\ **vision, beige** \k̲, ⁿ, œ, ᵫ, ʸ\ *see* Guide to Pronunciation

im·mu·no·de·fi·cien·cy \-di-ˈfi-shən(t)-sē\ *n* (1969) **:** inability to produce a normal complement of antibodies or immunologically sensitized T cells esp. in response to specific antigens — **im·mu·no·de·fi·cient** \-shənt\ *adj*
im·mu·no·di·ag·nos·tic \-ˌdī-ig-ˈnäs-tik, -əg-\ *adj* (1962) **:** of, relating to, or being analytical methods using antibodies as reagents ⟨an ~ test for cancer⟩ — **im·mu·no·di·ag·no·sis** \-ˈnō-səs\ *n*
im·mu·no·dif·fu·sion \-di-ˈfyü-zhən\ *n* (1959) **:** any of several techniques for obtaining a precipitate between an antibody and its specific antigen by suspending one in a gel and letting the other migrate through it from a well or by letting both antibody and antigen migrate through the gel from separate wells to form an area of precipitation
im·mu·no·elec·tro·pho·re·sis \-ə-ˌlek-trə-fə-ˈrē-səs\ *n, pl* **-re·ses** \-ˌsēz\ (1958) **:** electrophoretic separation of proteins followed by identification by the formation of precipitates through specific immunologic reactions — **im·mu·no·elec·tro·pho·ret·ic** \-ˈre-tik\ *adj* — **im·mu·no·elec·tro·pho·ret·i·cal·ly** \-ti-k(ə-)lē\ *adv*
im·mu·no·flu·o·res·cence \-(ˌ)flȯ-ˈre-sᵊn(t)s, -(ˌ)flü-(-ə)-\ *n* (1960) **:** the labeling of antibodies or antigens with fluorescent dyes esp. for the purpose of demonstrating the presence of a particular antigen or antibody in a tissue preparation or smear — **im·mu·no·flu·o·res·cent** \-sᵊnt\ *adj*
im·mu·no·gen \i-ˈmyü-nə-jən, -ˌjen\ *n* [fr. *Immunogen,* a trademark] (1959) **:** a substance that produces an immune response
im·mu·no·ge·net·ics \ˌi-myə-nō-jə-ˈne-tiks, i-ˌmyü-nō-\ *n pl but sing in constr* (1936) **:** a branch of immunology concerned with the interrelations of heredity, disease, and the immune system and its components — **im·mu·no·ge·net·ic** \-tik\ *adj* — **im·mu·no·ge·net·i·cal·ly** \-ti-k(ə-)lē\ *adv* — **im·mu·no·ge·net·i·cist** \-jə-ˈne-tə-sist\ *n*
im·mu·no·gen·ic \ˌi-myə-nō-ˈje-nik, i-ˌmyü-nō-\ *adj* (ca. 1923) **:** relating to or producing an immune response ⟨~ substances⟩ — **im·mu·no·gen·e·sis** \-ˈje-nə-səs\ *n* — **im·mu·no·ge·nic·i·ty** \-jə-ˈni-sə-tē\ *n*
im·mu·no·glob·u·lin \-ˈglä-byə-lən\ *n* (1953) **:** ANTIBODY — abbr. *Ig*
im·mu·no·he·ma·tol·o·gy \-ˌhē-mə-ˈtä-lə-jē\ *n* (1950) **:** a branch of immunology that deals with the immunologic properties of blood — **im·mu·no·he·ma·to·log·ic** \-ˌhē-mə-tə-ˈlä-jik\ *or* **im·mu·no·he·ma·to·log·i·cal** \-ˈlä-ji-kəl\ *adj* — **im·mu·no·he·ma·tol·o·gist** \-ˌhē-mə-ˈtä-lə-jist\ *n*
im·mu·no·his·to·chem·i·cal \-ˌhis-tō-ˈke-mi-kəl\ *adj* (1960) **:** of or relating to the application of histochemical and immunologic methods to chemical analysis of living cells and tissues — **im·mu·no·his·to·chem·is·try** \-ˈke-mə-strē\ *n*
im·mu·nol·o·gy \ˌi-myə-ˈnä-lə-jē\ *n* [ISV] (1910) **:** a science that deals with the immune system and the cell-mediated and humoral aspects of immunity and immune responses — **im·mu·no·log·ic** \-nə-ˈlä-jik\ *or* **im·mu·no·log·i·cal** \-ˈlä-ji-kəl\ *adj* — **im·mu·no·log·i·cal·ly** \-ji-k(ə-)lē\ *adv* — **im·mu·nol·o·gist** \ˌi-myə-ˈnä-lə-jist\ *n*
im·mu·no·mod·u·la·tor \ˌi-myə-nō-ˈmä-jə-ˌlā-tər, i-ˌmyü-nō-\ *n* (1977) **:** a substance that affects the functioning of the immune system — **im·mu·no·mod·u·la·to·ry** \-ˈmä-jə-lə-ˌtȯr-ē\ *adj*
im·mu·no·pa·thol·o·gy \-pə-ˈthä-lə-jē, -pa-\ *n* (1959) **:** a branch of medicine that deals with immune responses associated with disease — **im·mu·no·path·o·log·ic** \-ˌpa-thə-ˈlä-jik\ *or* **im·mu·no·path·o·log·i·cal** \-ji-kəl\ *adj* — **im·mu·no·pa·thol·o·gist** \-pə-ˈthä-lə-jist, -pa-\ *n*
im·mu·no·pre·cip·i·ta·tion \-pri-ˌsi-pə-ˈtā-shən\ *n* (1962) **:** precipitation of a complex of an antibody and its specific antigen — **im·mu·no·pre·cip·i·tate** \-ˈsi-pə-tət, -pə-ˌtāt\ *n* — **im·mu·no·pre·cip·i·tate** \-pə-ˌtāt\ *vt*
im·mu·no·re·ac·tive \-rē-ˈak-tiv\ *adj* (1966) **:** reacting to particular antigens or haptens ⟨~ lymphocytes⟩ — **im·mu·no·re·ac·tiv·i·ty** \-(ˌ)rē-ˌak-ˈti-və-tē\ *n*
im·mu·no·reg·u·la·to·ry \-ˈre-gyə-lə-ˌtōr-ē, -ˌtȯr-\ *adj* (1971) **:** of or relating to the regulation of the immune system ⟨~ T cells⟩ — **im·mu·no·reg·u·la·tion** \-ˌre-gyə-ˈlā-shən, -gə-\ *n*
im·mu·no·sor·bent \-ˈsȯr-bənt\ *adj* (1966) **:** relating to or using a substrate consisting of a specific antibody or antigen chemically combined with an insoluble substance (as cellulose) to selectively remove the corresponding specific antigen or antibody from solution — **immunosorbent** *n*
im·mu·no·sup·pres·sion \-sə-ˈpre-shən\ *n* (1963) **:** suppression (as by drugs) of natural immune responses — **im·mu·no·sup·press** \-sə-ˈpres\ *vt* — **im·mu·no·sup·pres·sant** \-ˈpre-sᵊnt\ *n or adj* — **im·mu·no·sup·pres·sive** \-ˈpre-siv\ *adj*
im·mu·no·ther·a·py \-ˈther-ə-pē\ *n* [ISV] (ca. 1911) **:** the treatment or prevention of disease by taking measures to increase immune system functioning (as by the administration of antibodies or hyposensitization) — **im·mu·no·ther·a·peu·tic** \-ˌther-ə-ˈpyü-tik\ *adj*
im·mure \i-ˈmyu̇r\ *vt* **im·mured; im·mur·ing** [ML *immurare,* fr. L *in-* + *murus* wall — more at MUNITION] (1583) **1 a :** to enclose within or as if within walls **b :** IMPRISON **2 :** to build into a wall; *esp* **:** to entomb in a wall — **im·mure·ment** \-ˈmyu̇r-mənt\ *n*
im·mu·ta·ble \(ˌ)i(m)-ˈmyü-tə-bəl\ *adj* [ME, fr. L *immutabilis,* fr. *in-* + *mutabilis* mutable] (15c) **:** not capable of or susceptible to change — **im·mu·ta·bil·i·ty** \-ˌmyü-tə-ˈbi-lə-tē\ *n* — **im·mu·ta·ble·ness** \-ˈmyü-tə-bəl-nəs\ *n* — **im·mu·ta·bly** \-blē\ *adv*
IMO *abbr* International Maritime Organization
[1]**imp** \ˈimp\ *n* [ME *impe,* fr. OE *impa,* fr. *impian* to imp] (bef. 12c) **1** *obs* **:** SHOOT, BUD; *also* **:** GRAFT **2 a :** a small demon **:** FIEND **b :** a mischievous child **:** URCHIN
[2]**imp** *vt* [ME, fr. OE *impian* to graft, fr. VL **imputare,* fr. LL *impotus* grafted shoot, fr. Gk *emphytos* implanted, fr. *emphyein* to implant, fr. *em-* [2]en- + *phyein* to bring forth — more at BE] (15c) **1 :** to graft or repair (a wing, tail, or feather) with a feather to improve a falcon's flying capacity **2 :** to equip with wings
[3]**imp** *abbr* **1** imperative **2** imperfect **3** imperial **4** import; imported
[1]**im·pact** \im-ˈpakt\ *vb* [L *impactus,* pp. of *impingere* to push against — more at IMPINGE] *vt* (1601) **1 a :** to fix firmly by or as if by packing or wedging **b :** to press together **2 a :** to have a direct effect or impact on **:** impinge on **b :** to strike forcefully; *also* **:** to cause to strike forcefully ~ *vi* **1 :** to have an impact — often used with *on* **2 :** to impinge or make contact esp. forcefully — **im·pact·ful** \im-ˈpakt-fəl, ˈim-ˌpakt-fəl\ *adj* — **im·pac·tive** \im-ˈpak-tiv\ *adj* — **im·pac·tor** *also* **im·pact·er** \-tər\ *n*
[2]**im·pact** \ˈim-ˌpakt\ *n* (1781) **1 a :** an impinging or striking esp. of one body against another **b :** a forceful contact or onset; *also* **:** the impetus communicated in or as if in such a contact **2 :** the force of impression of one thing on another **:** a significant or major effect ⟨the ~ of science on our society⟩ ⟨an environmental ~ study⟩
syn IMPACT, COLLISION, SHOCK, CONCUSSION mean a forceful, even violent contact between two or more things. IMPACT may be used to imply contact between two things, at least one of which is impelled toward the other ⟨the glass shattered on *impact* with the floor⟩. COLLISION implies the coming together of two or more things with such force that both or all are damaged or their progress is severely impeded ⟨the *collision* damaged the vehicle⟩. SHOCK often denotes the effect produced by a collision and carries the suggestion of something that strikes or hits with force ⟨the *shock* of falling rocks⟩. CONCUSSION when not in technical use, often suggests the shattering, disrupting, or weakening effects of a collision, explosion, or blow ⟨bystanders felt the *concussion* of the blast⟩.
im·pact·ed \im-ˈpak-təd\ *adj* (ca. 1616) **1 a :** packed or wedged in **b :** deeply entrenched **:** not easily changed or removed **2** *of a tooth* **:** wedged between the jawbone and another tooth **3 :** of, relating to, or being an area (as a school district) providing tax-supported services to a population having a large proportion of federal employees and esp. those living or working on tax-exempt federal property ⟨aid to education in ~ areas⟩
im·pac·tion \im-ˈpak-shən\ *n* (1739) **:** the act of becoming or the state of being impacted; *esp* **:** lodgment of something (as feces) in a body passage or cavity
impact printer *n* (1968) **:** a printing device in which a printing element directly strikes a surface (as in a typewriter)
im·paint \im-ˈpānt\ *vt* (1596) *obs* **:** PAINT, DEPICT
im·pair \im-ˈper\ *vt* [ME *empeiren,* fr. AF *empeirer,* fr. VL **impejorare,* fr. L *in-* + LL *pejorare* to make worse — more at PEJORATIVE] (14c) **:** to damage or make worse by or as if by diminishing in some material respect ⟨his health was ~*ed* by overwork⟩ ⟨the strike seriously ~*ed* community services⟩ ***syn*** see INJURE — **im·pair·er** *n* — **im·pair·ment** \-mənt\ *n*
im·paired \-ˈperd\ *adj* (1582) **:** being in a less than perfect or whole condition: as **a :** disabled or functionally defective — often used in combination ⟨hearing-*impaired*⟩ **b :** intoxicated by alcohol or narcotics ⟨driving while ~⟩
im·pa·la \im-ˈpa-lə, -ˈpä-\ *n, pl* **impalas** *or* **impala** [Zulu] (1875) **:** a large brownish antelope (*Aepyceros melampus*) of southeastern Africa that in the male has slender curved horns with ridges

impala

im·pale \im-ˈpāl\ *vt* **im·paled; im·pal·ing** [MF & ML; MF *empaler,* fr. ML *impalare,* fr. L *in-* + *palus* stake — more at POLE] (1605) **1 :** to join (coats of arms) on a heraldic shield divided vertically by a pale **2 a :** to pierce with or as if with something pointed; *esp* **:** to torture or kill by fixing on a sharp stake **b :** to fix in an inescapable or helpless position — **im·pale·ment** \-mənt\ *n* — **im·pal·er** \-ˈpā-lər\ *n*
im·pal·pa·ble \(ˌ)im-ˈpal-pə-bəl\ *adj* (1509) **1 a :** incapable of being felt by touch **:** INTANGIBLE ⟨the ~ aura of power that emanated from him —Osbert Sitwell⟩ **b :** so finely divided that no grains or grit can be felt ⟨rock worn to an ~ powder⟩ **2 :** not readily discerned by the mind ⟨~ evils⟩ — **im·pal·pa·bil·i·ty** \-ˌpal-pə-ˈbi-lə-tē\ *n* — **im·pal·pa·bly** \-ˈpal-pə-blē\ *adv*
im·pan·el *or* **em·pan·el** \im-ˈpa-nᵊl\ *vt* (15c) **:** to enroll in or on a panel ⟨~ a jury⟩
im·par·a·dise \im-ˈper-ə-ˌdīs, -ˌdīz, -ˈpa-rə-\ *vt* **-dised; -dis·ing** (1592) **:** ENRAPTURE
im·par·i·ty \(ˌ)im-ˈper-ə-tē, -ˈpa-rə-\ *n, pl* **-ties** [LL *imparitas,* fr. L *impar* unequal, fr. *in-* + *par* equal] (1563) **:** INEQUALITY, DISPARITY
im·part \im-ˈpärt\ *vt* [ME, fr. AF & L; AF *empartir,* fr. L *impartire,* fr. *in-* + *partire* to divide, part] (15c) **1 :** to give, convey, or grant from or as if from a store ⟨her experience ~*ed* authority to her words⟩ ⟨the flavor ~*ed* by herbs⟩ **2 :** to communicate the knowledge of **:** DISCLOSE ⟨~*ed* my scheme to no one⟩ — **im·par·ta·tion** \ˌim-ˌpär-ˈtā-shən\ *n* — **im·part·ment** \im-ˈpärt-mənt\ *n*
im·par·tial \(ˌ)im-ˈpär-shəl\ *adj* (1587) **:** not partial or biased **:** treating or affecting all equally ***syn*** see FAIR — **im·par·tial·i·ty** \-ˌpär-shē-ˈa-lə-tē, -ˌpär-ˈsha-\ *n* — **im·par·tial·ly** \-ˈpär-sh(ə-)lē\ *adv*
im·par·ti·ble \(ˌ)im-ˈpär-tə-bəl\ *adj* [ME *impartibil,* fr. LL *impartibilis,* fr. L *in-* + LL *partibilis* divisible, fr. L *partire*] (14c) **:** not partible **:** not subject to partition ⟨an ~ inheritance⟩ — **im·par·ti·bly** \-blē\ *adv*
im·pass·able *also* **im·pas·si·ble** \(ˌ)im-ˈpa-sə-bəl\ *adj* (1562) **:** incapable of being passed, traveled, crossed, or surmounted — **im·pass·abil·i·ty** \-ˌpa-sə-ˈbi-lə-tē\ *n* — **im·pass·able·ness** \-ˈpa-sə-bəl-nəs\ *n* — **im·pass·ably** \-blē\ *adv*
im·passe \ˈim-ˌpas, im-ˈ\ *n* [F, fr. *in-* + *passer* to pass] (1851) **1 a :** a predicament affording no obvious escape **b :** DEADLOCK **2 :** an impassable road or way **:** CUL-DE-SAC
[1]**im·pas·si·ble** \(ˌ)im-ˈpa-sə-bəl\ *adj* [ME, fr. MF or LL; MF, fr. LL *impassibilis,* fr. L *in-* + LL *passibilis* passible] (14c) **1 a :** incapable of suffering or of experiencing pain **b :** inaccessible to injury **2 :** incapable of feeling **:** IMPASSIVE — **im·pas·si·bil·i·ty** \-ˌpa-sə-ˈbi-lə-tē\ *n* — **im·pas·si·bly** \-ˈpa-sə-blē\ *adv*
[2]**impassible** *var of* IMPASSABLE
im·pas·sion \im-ˈpa-shən\ *vt* **im·pas·sioned; im·pas·sion·ing** \-sh(ə-)niŋ\ [prob. fr. It *impassionare,* fr. *in-* (fr. L) + *passione* passion, fr. LL *passion-, passio*] (1591) **:** to arouse the feelings or passions of
impassioned *adj* (1603) **:** filled with passion or zeal **:** showing great warmth or intensity of feeling
syn IMPASSIONED, PASSIONATE, ARDENT, FERVENT, FERVID, PERFERVID mean showing intense feeling. IMPASSIONED implies warmth and intensity without violence and suggests fluent verbal expression ⟨an *impassioned* plea for justice⟩. PASSIONATE implies great vehemence

and often violence and wasteful diffusion of emotion ⟨a *passionate* denunciation⟩. ARDENT implies an intense degree of zeal, devotion, or enthusiasm ⟨an *ardent* supporter of human rights⟩. FERVENT stresses sincerity and steadiness of emotional warmth or zeal ⟨*fervent* good wishes⟩. FERVID suggests warmly and spontaneously and often feverishly expressed emotion ⟨*fervid* love letters⟩. PERFERVID implies the expression of exaggerated or overwrought feelings ⟨*perfervid* expressions of patriotism⟩.

im·pas·sive \(ˌ)im-ˈpa-siv\ *adj* (1605) **1 a** *archaic* **:** unsusceptible to pain **b :** unsusceptible to physical feeling **:** INSENSIBLE **c :** unsusceptible to or destitute of emotion **:** APATHETIC **2 :** giving no sign of feeling or emotion **:** EXPRESSIONLESS — **im·pas·sive·ly** *adv* — **im·pas·sive·ness** *n* — **im·pas·siv·i·ty** \ˌim-ˌpa-ˈsi-və-tē\ *n*

syn IMPASSIVE, STOIC, PHLEGMATIC, APATHETIC, STOLID mean unresponsive to something that might normally excite interest or emotion. IMPASSIVE stresses the absence of any external sign of emotion in action or facial expression ⟨met the news with an *impassive* look⟩. STOIC implies an apparent indifference to pleasure or esp. to pain often as a matter of principle or self-discipline ⟨was resolutely *stoic* even in adversity⟩. PHLEGMATIC implies a temperament or constitution hard to arouse ⟨a *phlegmatic* man unmoved by tears⟩. APATHETIC may imply a puzzling or deplorable indifference or inertness ⟨charitable appeals met an *apathetic* response⟩. STOLID implies a habitual absence of interest, responsiveness, or curiosity ⟨*stolid* workers wedded to routine⟩.

im·paste \im-ˈpāst\ *vt* [It *impastare,* fr. *in-* (fr. L) + *pasta* paste, fr. LL] (1576) *obs* **:** to make into a paste or crust

im·pas·to \im-ˈpas-(ˌ)tō, -ˈpäs-\ *n, pl* **-tos** [It, fr. *impastare*] (1784) **1 :** the thick application of a pigment to a canvas or panel in painting; *also* **:** the body of pigment so applied **2 :** raised decoration on ceramic ware usu. of slip or enamel — **im·pas·toed** \-(ˌ)tōd\ *adj*

im·pa·tience \(ˌ)im-ˈpā-shən(t)s\ *n* (13c) **:** the quality or state of being impatient

im·pa·tiens \im-ˈpā-shənz, -shən(t)s\ *n* [NL, fr. L, impatient] (1785) **:** any of a widely distributed genus (*Impatiens* of the family Balsaminaceae) of annual or perennial herbs with irregular spurred or saccate flowers and forcefully dehiscent capsules — compare TOUCH-ME-NOT

im·pa·tient \(ˌ)im-ˈpā-shənt\ *adj* [ME *impacient,* fr. AF *impacient,* fr. L *impatient-, impatiens,* fr. *in-* + *patient-, patiens* patient] (14c) **1 a :** not patient **:** restless or short of temper esp. under irritation, delay, or opposition **b :** INTOLERANT 1 ⟨~ of delay⟩ **2 :** prompted or marked by impatience ⟨an ~ reply⟩ **3 :** eagerly desirous **:** ANXIOUS ⟨~ to get home⟩ — **im·pa·tient·ly** *adv*

im·pawn \im-ˈpȯn, -ˈpän\ *vt* (1567) *archaic* **:** to put in pawn **:** PLEDGE

[1]im·peach \im-ˈpēch\ *vt* [ME *empechen,* fr. AF *empecher, enpechier* to ensnare, impede, prosecute, fr. LL *impedicare* to fetter, fr. L *in-* + *pedica* fetter, fr. *ped-, pes* foot — more at FOOT] (14c) **1 a :** to bring an accusation against **b :** to charge with a crime or misdemeanor; *specif* **:** to charge (a public official) before a competent tribunal with misconduct in office **c :** to remove from office esp. for misconduct **2 :** to cast doubt on; *esp* **:** to challenge the credibility or validity of ⟨~ the testimony of a witness⟩ — **im·peach·able** \-ˈpē-chə-bəl\ *adj* — **im·peach·ment** \-ˈpēch-mənt\ *n*

[2]impeach *n* (1590) *obs* **:** CHARGE, IMPEACHMENT

im·pearl \im-ˈpər(-ə)l\ *vt* [ME *enperlen,* fr. *en-* + *perle* pearl] (15c) **:** to form into pearls; *also* **:** to form of or adorn with pearls

im·pec·ca·ble \(ˌ)im-ˈpek-ə-bəl\ *adj* [L *impeccabilis,* fr. *in-* + *peccare* to sin] (1531) **1 :** not capable of sinning or liable to sin **2 :** free from fault or blame **:** FLAWLESS ⟨spoke ~ French⟩ — **im·pec·ca·bil·i·ty** \-ˌpe-kə-ˈbi-lə-tē\ *n* — **im·pec·ca·bly** \-ˈpe-kə-blē\ *adv*

im·pe·cu·nious \ˌim-pi-ˈkyü-nyəs, -nē-əs\ *adj* [[1]*in-* + obs. E *pecunious* rich, fr. ME, fr. L *pecuniosus,* fr. *pecunia* money — more at FEE] (1596) **:** having very little or no money usu. habitually **:** PENNILESS — **im·pe·cu·ni·os·i·ty** \-ˌkyü-nē-ˈä-sə-tē\ *n* — **im·pe·cu·nious·ly** *adv* — **im·pe·cu·nious·ness** *n*

im·ped·ance \im-ˈpē-dᵊn(t)s\ *n* (1886) **:** something that impedes **:** HINDRANCE: as **a :** the apparent opposition in an electrical circuit to the flow of an alternating current that is analogous to the actual electrical resistance to a direct current and that is the ratio of effective electromotive force to the effective current **b :** the ratio of the pressure to the volume displacement at a given surface in a sound-transmitting medium

im·pede \im-ˈpēd\ *vt* **im·ped·ed; im·ped·ing** [L *impedire,* fr. *in-* + *ped-, pes* foot — more at FOOT] (ca. 1595) **:** to interfere with or slow the progress of ***syn*** see HINDER — **im·ped·er** *n*

im·ped·i·ment \im-ˈpe-də-mənt\ *n* (14c) **1 :** something that impedes; *esp* **:** an impairment (as a stutter or a lisp) that interferes with the proper articulation of speech **2 :** a bar or hindrance (as lack of sufficient age) to a lawful marriage

im·ped·i·men·ta \(ˌ)im-ˌpe-də-ˈmen-tə\ *n pl* [L, pl. of *impedimentum* impediment, fr. *impedire*] (1600) **1 :** APPURTENANCES, EQUIPMENT **2 :** things that impede

im·pel \im-ˈpel\ *vt* **im·pelled; im·pel·ling** [ME *impellen,* fr. L *impellere,* fr. *in-* + *pellere* to drive — more at FELT] (15c) **1 :** to urge or drive forward or on by or as if by the exertion of strong moral pressure **:** FORCE ⟨felt *impelled* to correct the misconception⟩ **2 :** to impart motion to **:** PROPEL ***syn*** see MOVE

im·pel·ler *also* **im·pel·lor** \im-ˈpe-lər\ *n* (1685) **1 :** one that impels **2 a :** a rotor located in a conduit to impart motion to a fluid **b :** a blade of a rotor

im·pend \im-ˈpend\ *vi* [L *impendēre,* fr. *in-* + *pendēre* to hang — more at PENDANT] (1585) **1 a :** to hover threateningly **:** MENACE **b :** to be about to occur ⟨the *impending* trial⟩ **2** *archaic* **:** to hang suspended

im·pen·dent \im-ˈpen-dənt\ *adj* (1590) **:** being near at hand **:** APPROACHING

im·pen·e·tra·bil·i·ty \(ˌ)im-ˌpe-nə-trə-ˈbi-lə-tē\ *n* (1653) **1 :** the inability of two portions of matter to occupy the same space at the same time **2 :** the quality or state of being impenetrable

im·pen·e·tra·ble \(ˌ)im-ˈpe-nə-trə-bəl\ *adj* [ME *impenetrabel,* fr. MF *impenetrable,* fr. L *impenetrabilis,* fr. *in-* + *penetrabilis* penetrable] (15c) **1 a :** incapable of being penetrated or pierced **b :** inaccessible to knowledge, reason, or sympathy **:** IMPERVIOUS **2 :** incapable of being comprehended **:** INSCRUTABLE — **im·pen·e·tra·bly** \-blē\ *adv*

im·pen·i·tence \(ˌ)im-ˈpe-nə-tən(t)s\ *n* (1595) **:** the quality or state of being impenitent

im·pen·i·tent \-tənt\ *adj* [ME, fr. LL *impaenitent-, impaenitens,* fr. L *in-* + *paenitent-, paenitens* penitent] (15c) **:** not penitent — **im·pen·i·tent·ly** *adv*

[1]im·per·a·tive \im-ˈper-ə-tiv, -ˈpe-rə-\ *adj* [ME *imperatyf,* fr. LL *imperativus,* fr. L *imperatus,* pp. of *imperare* to command — more at EMPEROR] (15c) **1 a :** of, relating to, or constituting the grammatical mood that expresses the will to influence the behavior of another **b :** expressive of a command, entreaty, or exhortation **c :** having power to restrain, control, and direct **2 :** not to be avoided or evaded **:** NECESSARY ⟨an ~ duty⟩ ***syn*** see MASTERFUL — **im·per·a·tive·ly** *adv* — **im·per·a·tive·ness** *n*

[2]imperative *n* (1530) **1 :** the imperative mood or a verb form or verbal phrase expressing it **2 :** something that is imperative: as **a :** COMMAND, ORDER **b :** RULE, GUIDE **c :** an obligatory act or duty **d :** an imperative judgment or proposition

im·pe·ra·tor \ˌim-pə-ˈrä-tər, -ˌtȯr\ *n* [L — more at EMPEROR] (ca. 1580) **:** a commander in chief or emperor of the ancient Romans — **im·per·a·to·ri·al** \(ˌ)im-ˌper-ə-ˈtȯr-ē-əl\ *adj*

im·per·ceiv·able \ˌim-pər-ˈsē-və-bəl\ *adj* (ca. 1617) *archaic* **:** IMPERCEPTIBLE

im·per·cep·ti·ble \ˌim-pər-ˈsep-tə-bəl\ *adj* [ME, fr. MF, fr. ML *imperceptibilis,* fr. L *in-* + LL *perceptibilis* perceptible] (15c) **:** not perceptible by a sense or by the mind **:** extremely slight, gradual, or subtle ⟨~ differences⟩ — **im·per·cep·ti·bly** \-ˈsep-tə-blē\ *adv*

im·per·cep·tive \ˌim-pər-ˈsep-tiv\ *adj* (1661) **:** not perceptive ⟨an ~ reader⟩ — **im·per·cep·tive·ness** *n*

im·per·cip·i·ence \-ˈsi-pē-ən(t)s\ *n* (1891) **:** the quality or state of being imperceptive — **im·per·cip·i·ent** \-ənt\ *adj*

imperf *abbr* **1** imperfect **2** imperforate

[1]im·per·fect \(ˌ)im-ˈpər-fikt\ *adj* [alter. of ME *imparfit,* fr. L *imperfectus,* fr. *in-* + *perfectus* perfect] (14c) **1 :** not perfect: as **a :** DEFECTIVE **b** *of a flower* **:** having stamens or pistils but not both **c :** lacking or not involving sexual reproduction ⟨the ~ stage of a fungus⟩ **2 :** of, relating to, or constituting a verb tense used to designate a continuing state or an incomplete action esp. in the past **3 :** not enforceable at law — **im·per·fect·ly** \-fik(t)-lē\ *adv* — **im·per·fect·ness** \-fik(t)-nəs\ *n*

[2]imperfect *n* (1871) **:** an imperfect tense; *also* **:** the verb form expressing it

imperfect fungus *n* (ca. 1895) **:** any of various fungi (order Fungi Imperfecti syn. Deuteromycetes) of which only the conidial stage is known

im·per·fec·tion \ˌim-pər-ˈfek-shən\ *n* (14c) **:** the quality or state of being imperfect; *also* **:** FAULT, BLEMISH

im·per·fec·tive \ˌim-pər-ˈfek-tiv\ *adj* (1887) *of a verb form or aspect* **:** expressing action as incomplete or without reference to completion or as reiterated — compare PERFECTIVE — **imperfective** *n*

im·per·fo·rate \(ˌ)im-ˈpər-f(ə-)rət, -fə-ˌrāt\ *adj* (1673) **1 :** having no opening or aperture; *specif* **:** lacking the usual or normal opening **2** *of a stamp or a sheet of stamps* **:** lacking perforations or roulettes

[1]im·pe·ri·al \im-ˈpir-ē-əl\ *adj* [ME, fr. AF, fr. LL *imperialis,* fr. L *imperium* command, empire] (14c) **1 a :** of, relating to, befitting, or suggestive of an empire or an emperor **b** (1) **:** of or relating to the United Kingdom as distinguished from the constituent parts (2) **:** of or relating to the Commonwealth of Nations and British Empire **2 a :** SOVEREIGN **b :** REGAL, IMPERIOUS **3 :** of superior or unusual size or excellence **4 :** belonging to the official British series of weights and measures — see WEIGHT table — **im·pe·ri·al·ly** \-ə-lē\ *adv*

[2]imperial *n* (ca. 1524) **1** *cap* **:** an adherent or soldier of the Holy Roman emperor **2 :** EMPEROR **3** [F *impériale;* fr. the beard worn by Napoléon III] **:** a pointed beard growing below the lower lip **4 :** something of unusual size or excellence

im·pe·ri·al·ism \im-ˈpir-ē-ə-ˌli-zəm\ *n* (1800) **1 :** imperial government, authority, or system **2 :** the policy, practice, or advocacy of extending the power and dominion of a nation esp. by direct territorial acquisitions or by gaining indirect control over the political or economic life of other areas; *broadly* **:** the extension or imposition of power, authority, or influence ⟨union ~⟩ — **im·pe·ri·al·ist** \-list\ *n or adj* — **im·pe·ri·al·is·tic** \-ˌpir-ē-ə-ˈlis-tik\ *adj* — **im·pe·ri·al·is·ti·cal·ly** \-ti-k(ə-)lē\ *adv*

imperial moth *n* (ca. 1904) **:** a large No. American saturniid moth (*Eacles imperialis*) having yellow wings marked with reddish-brown spots and patches

im·per·il \im-ˈper-əl, -ˈpe-rəl\ *vt* **-iled** *or* **-illed; -il·ing** *or* **-il·ling** (15c) **:** to bring into peril **:** ENDANGER — **im·per·il·ment** \-mənt\ *n*

im·pe·ri·ous \im-ˈpir-ē-əs\ *adj* [L *imperiosus,* fr. *imperium*] (1540) **1 a :** befitting or characteristic of one of eminent rank or attainments **:** COMMANDING, DOMINANT ⟨an ~ manner⟩ **b :** marked by arrogant assurance **:** DOMINEERING **2 :** intensely compelling **:** URGENT ⟨the ~ problems of the new age —J. F. Kennedy⟩ ***syn*** see MASTERFUL — **im·pe·ri·ous·ly** *adv* — **im·pe·ri·ous·ness** *n*

im·per·ish·able \(ˌ)im-ˈper-i-shə-bəl\ *adj* (ca. 1585) **1 :** not perishable or subject to decay **2 :** enduring or occurring forever ⟨~ fame⟩ — **im·per·ish·abil·i·ty** \-ˌper-i-shə-ˈbi-lə-tē\ *n* — **imperishable** *n* — **im·per·ish·able·ness** \-ˈper-i-shə-bəl-nəs\ *n* — **im·per·ish·ably** \-blē\ *adv*

im·pe·ri·um \im-ˈpir-ē-əm\ *n* [L — more at EMPIRE] (1651) **1 a :** supreme power or absolute dominion **:** CONTROL **b :** EMPIRE 1 **c :** EMPIRE 2 **2 :** the right to command or to employ the force of the state **:** SOVEREIGNTY

im·per·ma·nence \(ˌ)im-ˈpərm-nən(t)s, -ˈpər-mə-\ *n* (1796) **:** the quality or state of being impermanent

im·per·ma·nen·cy \-nən(t)-sē\ *n* (1648) **:** IMPERMANENCE

im·per·ma·nent \-nənt\ *adj* (1653) **:** not permanent **:** TRANSIENT — **im·per·ma·nent·ly** *adv*

im·per·me·able \(ˌ)im-ˈpər-mē-ə-bəl\ *adj* [LL *impermeabilis,* fr. L *in-* + LL *permeabilis* permeable] (1697) : not permitting passage (as of a fluid) through its substance; *broadly* : IMPERVIOUS — **im·per·me·abil·i·ty** \-ˌpər-mē-ə-ˈbi-lə-tē\ *n*

im·per·mis·si·ble \ˌim-pər-ˈmi-sə-bəl\ *adj* (1858) : not permissible — **im·per·mis·si·bil·i·ty** \-ˌmi-sə-ˈbi-lə-tē\ *n* — **im·per·mis·si·bly** \-ˈmi-sə-blē\ *adv*

im·per·son·al \(ˌ)im-ˈpərs-nəl, -ˈpər-sə-nəl\ *adj* [ME, fr. LL *impersonalis,* fr. L *in-* + LL *personalis* personal] (15c) **1 a :** denoting the verbal action of an unspecified agent and hence used with no expressed subject (as *methinks*) or with a merely formal subject (as *rained* in *it rained*) **b** *of a pronoun* : INDEFINITE **2 a :** having no personal reference or connection ⟨~ criticism⟩ **b :** not engaging the human personality or emotions ⟨the machine as compared with the hand tool is an ~ agency —John Dewey⟩ **c :** not existing as a person : not having human qualities or characteristics — **im·per·son·al·i·ty** \-ˌpər-sə-ˈna-lə-tē\ *n* — **im·per·son·al·ly** \-ˈpərs-nə-lē, -ˈpər-sə-nə-lē\ *adv*

im·per·son·al·ize \(ˌ)im-ˈpərs-nə-ˌlīz, -ˈpər-sə-nə-\ *vt* (ca. 1899) : to make impersonal ⟨technology that ~*s* the learning process⟩ — **im·per·son·al·i·za·tion** \-ˌpərs-nə-lə-ˈzā-shən, -ˌpər-sə-nə-\ *n*

im·per·son·ate \im-ˈpər-sə-ˌnāt\ *vt* **-at·ed; -at·ing** (1715) : to assume or act the character of : PERSONATE — **im·per·son·a·tion** \-ˌpər-sə-ˈnā-shən\ *n* — **im·per·son·a·tor** \-ˈpər-sə-ˌnā-tər\ *n*

im·per·ti·nence \(ˌ)im-ˈpər-tə-nən(t)s, -ˈpərt-nən(t)s\ *n* (1603) **1 :** the quality or state of being impertinent: as **a :** IRRELEVANCE, INAPPROPRIATENESS **b :** INCIVILITY, INSOLENCE **2 :** an instance of impertinence

im·per·ti·nen·cy \-ən(t)-sē, -nən(t)-\ *n, pl* **-cies** (1589) : IMPERTINENCE

im·per·ti·nent \(ˌ)im-ˈpər-tə-nənt, -ˈpərt-nənt\ *adj* [ME, fr. AF, fr. LL *impertinent-, impertinens,* fr. L *in-* + *pertinent-, pertinens,* prp. of *pertinēre* to pertain] (14c) **1 :** not pertinent : IRRELEVANT **2 a :** not restrained within due or proper bounds esp. of propriety or good taste ⟨~ curiosity⟩ **b :** given to or characterized by insolent rudeness ⟨an ~ answer⟩ — **im·per·ti·nent·ly** *adv*

syn IMPERTINENT, OFFICIOUS, MEDDLESOME, INTRUSIVE, OBTRUSIVE mean given to thrusting oneself into the affairs of others. IMPERTINENT implies exceeding the bounds of propriety in showing interest or curiosity or in offering advice ⟨resented their *impertinent* interference⟩. OFFICIOUS implies the offering of services or attentions that are unwelcome or annoying ⟨*officious* friends made the job harder⟩. MEDDLESOME stresses an annoying and usu. prying interference in others' affairs ⟨a *meddlesome* landlord⟩. INTRUSIVE implies a tactless or otherwise objectionable thrusting into others' affairs ⟨tried to be helpful without being *intrusive*⟩. OBTRUSIVE stresses improper or offensive conspicuousness of interfering actions ⟨expressed an *obtrusive* concern for his safety⟩.

im·per·turb·able \ˌim-pər-ˈtər-bə-bəl\ *adj* [ME, fr. LL *imperturbabilis,* fr. L *in-* + *perturbare* to perturb] (15c) : marked by extreme calm, impassivity, and steadiness : SERENE ***syn*** see COOL — **im·per·turb·abil·i·ty** \-ˌtər-bə-ˈbi-lə-tē\ *n* — **im·per·turb·ably** \-ˈtər-bə-blē\ *adv*

im·per·vi·ous \(ˌ)im-ˈpər-vē-əs\ *adj* [L *impervius,* fr. *in-* + *pervius* pervious] (1640) **1 a :** not allowing entrance or passage : IMPENETRABLE ⟨a coat ~ to rain⟩ **b :** not capable of being damaged or harmed ⟨a carpet ~ to rough treatment⟩ **2 :** not capable of being affected or disturbed ⟨~ to criticism⟩ — **im·per·vi·ous·ly** *adv* — **im·per·vi·ous·ness** *n*

im·pe·ti·go \ˌim-pə-ˈtē-(ˌ)gō, -ˈtī-\ *n* [ME, fr. L, fr. *impetere* to attack — more at IMPETUS] (14c) : an acute contagious staphylococcal or streptococcal skin disease characterized by vesicles, pustules, and yellowish crusts

im·pe·trate \ˈim-pə-ˌtrāt\ *vt* **-trat·ed; -trat·ing** [L *impetratus,* pp. of *impetrare,* fr. *in-* + *patrare* to accomplish — more at PERPETRATE] (ca. 1534) **1 :** to obtain by request or entreaty **2 :** to ask for : ENTREAT — **im·pe·tra·tion** \ˌim-pə-ˈtrā-shən\ *n*

im·pet·u·os·i·ty \im-ˌpe-chə-ˈwä-sə-tē, -chü-ˈä-\ *n, pl* **-ties** (15c) **1 :** the quality or state of being impetuous **2 :** an impetuous action or impulse

im·pet·u·ous \im-ˈpech-wəs; -ˈpe-chə-, -chü-əs\ *adj* [ME, fr. AF, fr. LL *impetuosus,* fr. L *impetus*] (14c) **1 :** marked by impulsive vehemence or passion ⟨an ~ temperament⟩ **2 :** marked by force and violence of movement or action ⟨an ~ wind⟩ ***syn*** see PRECIPITATE — **im·pet·u·ous·ly** *adv* — **im·pet·u·ous·ness** *n*

im·pe·tus \ˈim-pə-təs\ *n* [L, assault, impetus, fr. *impetere* to attack, fr. *in-* + *petere* to go to, seek — more at FEATHER] (1641) **1 a (1) :** a driving force : IMPULSE **(2) :** INCENTIVE, STIMULUS **b :** stimulation or encouragement resulting in increased activity **2 :** the property possessed by a moving body in virtue of its mass and its motion — used of bodies moving suddenly or violently to indicate the origin and intensity of the motion

im·pi·e·ty \(ˌ)im-ˈpī-ə-tē\ *n, pl* **-ties** (14c) **1 :** the quality or state of being impious : IRREVERENCE **2 :** an impious act

im·pinge \im-ˈpinj\ *vi* **im·pinged; im·ping·ing** [L *impingere,* fr. *in-* + *pangere* to fasten, drive in — more at PACT] (1605) **1 :** to strike or dash esp. with a sharp collision ⟨I heard the rain ~ upon the earth —James Joyce⟩ **2 :** to have an effect : make an impression ⟨waiting for the germ of a new idea to ~ upon my mind —Phyllis Bentley⟩ **3 :** ENCROACH, INFRINGE ⟨~ on other people's rights⟩ — **im·pinge·ment** \-ˈpinj-mənt\ *n*

im·pi·ous \ˈim-pē-əs, (ˌ)im-ˈpī-\ *adj* [L *impius,* fr. *in-* + *pius* pious] (1542) : not pious : lacking in reverence or proper respect (as for God or one's parents) : IRREVERENT — **im·pi·ous·ly** *adv*

imp·ish \ˈim-pish\ *adj* (1652) : of, relating to, or befitting an imp; *esp* : MISCHIEVOUS — **imp·ish·ly** *adv* — **imp·ish·ness** *n*

im·pla·ca·ble \(ˌ)im-ˈpla-kə-bəl, -ˈplā-\ *adj* [ME, fr. L *implacabilis,* fr. *in-* + *placabilis* placable] (15c) : not placable : not capable of being appeased, significantly changed, or mitigated ⟨an ~ enemy⟩ — **im·pla·ca·bil·i·ty** \-ˌpla-kə-ˈbi-lə-tē, -ˌplā-\ *n* — **im·pla·ca·bly** \-ˈpla-kə-blē, -ˈplā-\ *adv*

¹im·plant \im-ˈplant\ *vt* (15c) **1 a :** to fix or set securely or deeply ⟨a ruby ~*ed* in the idol's forehead⟩ **b :** to set permanently in the consciousness or habit patterns : INCULCATE **2 :** to insert in living tissue (as for growth, slow release, or formation of an organic union) ⟨subcutaneously ~*ed* hormone pellets⟩ ~ *vi* : to undergo implantation ⟨the failure of embryos to ~⟩ — **im·plant·able** \-ˈplan-tə-bəl\ *adj* — **im·plant·er** \im-ˈplan-tər\ *n*

syn IMPLANT, INCULCATE, INSTILL, INSEMINATE, INFIX mean to introduce into the mind. IMPLANT implies teaching that makes for permanence of what is taught ⟨*implanted* a love of reading in her students⟩. INCULCATE implies persistent or repeated efforts to impress on the mind ⟨tried to *inculcate* in him high moral standards⟩. INSTILL stresses gradual, gentle imparting of knowledge over a long period of time ⟨*instill* traditional values in your children⟩. INSEMINATE applies to a sowing of ideas in many minds so that they spread through a class or nation ⟨*inseminated* an unquestioning faith in technology⟩. INFIX stresses firmly inculcating a habit of thought ⟨*infixed* a chronic cynicism⟩.

²im·plant \ˈim-ˌplant\ *n* (1890) : something (as a graft or device) implanted in tissue — compare COCHLEAR IMPLANT

im·plan·ta·tion \ˌim-ˌplan-ˈtā-shən\ *n* (1578) **1 a :** the act or process of implanting something **b :** the state resulting from being implanted **2** *in placental mammals* : the process of attachment of the early embryo to the maternal uterine wall

im·plau·si·ble \(ˌ)im-ˈplȯ-zə-bəl\ *adj* (ca. 1677) : not plausible : provoking disbelief — **im·plau·si·bil·i·ty** \-ˌplȯ-zə-ˈbi-lə-tē\ *n* — **im·plau·si·bly** \-ˈplȯ-zə-blē\ *adv*

im·plead \im-ˈplēd\ *vt* [ME *empleden,* fr. AF *empleder,* fr. *en-* + *pleder* to plead] (14c) : to sue or prosecute at law

¹im·ple·ment \ˈim-plə-mənt\ *n* [ME, fr. AF, fr. LL *implementum* action of filling up, fr. L *implēre* to fill up, fr. *in-* + *plēre* to fill — more at FULL] (15c) **1 :** an article serving to equip ⟨the ~*s* of religious worship⟩ **2 :** a device used in the performance of a task : TOOL, UTENSIL **3 :** one that serves as an instrument or tool ⟨the partnership agreement does not seem to be a very potent ~ —H. B. Hoffman⟩

syn IMPLEMENT, TOOL, INSTRUMENT, APPLIANCE, UTENSIL mean a relatively simple device for performing work. IMPLEMENT may apply to anything necessary to perform a task ⟨crude stone *implements*⟩ ⟨farm *implements*⟩. TOOL suggests an implement adapted to facilitate a definite kind or stage of work and suggests the need of skill more strongly than IMPLEMENT ⟨a carpenter's *tools*⟩. INSTRUMENT suggests a device capable of delicate or precise work ⟨the dentist's *instruments*⟩. APPLIANCE refers to a tool or instrument utilizing a power source and suggests portability or temporary attachment ⟨household *appliances*⟩. UTENSIL applies to a device used in domestic work or some routine unskilled activity ⟨kitchen *utensils*⟩.

²im·ple·ment \-ˌment\ *vt* (1806) **1 :** CARRY OUT, ACCOMPLISH; *esp* : to give practical effect to and ensure of actual fulfillment by concrete measures **2 :** to provide instruments or means of expression for — **im·ple·men·ta·tion** \ˌim-plə-mən-ˈtā-shən, -ˌmen-\ *n* — **im·ple·men·ter** *or* **im·ple·men·tor** \ˈim-plə-ˌmən-tər\ *n*

im·pli·cate \ˈim-plə-ˌkāt\ *vt* **-cat·ed; -cat·ing** [ME, to convey by implication, fr. ML *implicatus,* pp. of *implicare,* fr. L, to entwine, involve — more at EMPLOY] (15c) **1 :** to involve as a consequence, corollary, or natural inference : IMPLY **2** *archaic* : to fold or twist together : ENTWINE **3 a :** to bring into intimate or incriminating connection ⟨evidence that ~*s* him in the bombing⟩ **b :** to involve in the nature or operation of something

im·pli·ca·tion \ˌim-plə-ˈkā-shən\ *n* (15c) **1 a :** the act of implicating : the state of being implicated **b :** close connection; *esp* : an incriminating involvement **2 a :** the act of implying : the state of being implied **b (1) :** a logical relation between two propositions that fails to hold only if the first is true and the second is false — see TRUTH TABLE table **(2) :** a logical relationship between two propositions in which if the first is true the second is true **(3) :** a statement exhibiting a relation of implication **3 :** something implied: as **a :** SUGGESTION **b :** a possible significance ⟨the book has political ~*s*⟩ — **im·pli·ca·tive** \ˈim-plə-ˌkā-tiv, im-ˈpli-kə-\ *adj* — **im·pli·ca·tive·ly** *adv* — **im·pli·ca·tive·ness** *n*

im·plic·it \im-ˈpli-sət\ *adj* [L *implicitus,* pp. of *implicare*] (1599) **1 a :** capable of being understood from something else though unexpressed : IMPLIED ⟨an ~ assumption⟩ **b :** involved in the nature or essence of something though not revealed, expressed, or developed : POTENTIAL ⟨a sculptor may see different figures ~ in a block of stone —John Dewey⟩ **c** *of a mathematical function* : defined by an expression in which the dependent variable and the one or more independent variables are not separated on opposite sides of an equation — compare EXPLICIT 4 **2 :** being without doubt or reserve : UNQUESTIONING ⟨an ~ trust⟩ — **im·plic·it·ly** *adv* — **im·plic·it·ness** *n*

implicit differentiation *n* (ca. 1889) : the process of finding the derivative of a dependent variable in an implicit function by differentiating each term separately, by expressing the derivative of the dependent variable as a symbol, and by solving the resulting expression for the symbol

im·plode \im-ˈplōd\ *vb* **im·plod·ed; im·plod·ing** [²*in-* + *-plode* (as in *explode*)] *vi* (1881) **1 a :** to burst inward ⟨a blow causing a vacuum tube to ~⟩ **b :** to undergo violent compression ⟨massive stars which ~⟩ **2 :** to collapse inward as if from external pressure; *also* : to become greatly reduced as if from collapsing **3 :** to break down or fall apart from within : SELF-DESTRUCT ⟨the firm . . . *imploded* from greed and factionalism —Jan Hoffman⟩ ~ *vt* : to cause to implode

im·plore \im-ˈplȯr\ *vt* **im·plored; im·plor·ing** [MF or L; MF *implorer,* fr. L *implorare,* fr. *in-* + *plorare* to cry out] (ca. 1540) **1 :** to call upon in supplication : BESEECH **2 :** to call or pray for earnestly : ENTREAT ⟨*implored* the crowd to be quiet⟩ ***syn*** see BEG — **im·plor·ing·ly** *adv*

im·plo·sion \im-ˈplō-zhən\ *n* [²*in-* + *-plosion* (as in *explosion*)] (1877) **1 :** the inrush of air in forming a suction stop **2 :** the action of imploding **3 :** the act or action of bringing to or as if to a center; *also* : INTEGRATION ⟨this ~ of cultures makes realistic for the first time the age-old vision of a world culture —Kenneth Keniston⟩ — **im·plo·sive** \-ˈplō-siv, -ziv\ *adj or n*

im·ply \im-ˈplī\ *vt* **im·plied; im·ply·ing** [ME *emplien,* fr. AF *emplier* to entangle — more at EMPLOY] (14c) **1** *obs* : ENFOLD, ENTWINE **2 :** to involve or indicate by inference, association, or necessary consequence rather than by direct statement ⟨rights ~ obligations⟩ **3 :** to contain potentially **4 :** to express indirectly ⟨his silence *implied* consent⟩ ***syn*** see SUGGEST ***usage*** see INFER

im·po·lite \ˌim-pə-ˈlīt\ *adj* [L *impolitus,* fr. *in-* + *politus* polite] (1739) : not polite : RUDE — **im·po·lite·ly** *adv* — **im·po·lite·ness** *n*

im·pol·i·tic \(ˌ)im-ˈpä-lə-ˌtik\ *adj* (ca. 1600) **:** not politic **:** UNWISE — **im·po·lit·i·cal** \-pə-ˈli-ti-kəl\ *adj* — **im·po·lit·i·cal·ly** \-ˈli-ti-k(ə-)lē\ *adv* — **im·pol·i·tic·ly** \-ˈpä-lə-ˌti-klē\ *adv*

im·pon·der·a·ble \(ˌ)im-ˈpän-d(ə-)rə-bəl\ *adj* [ML *imponderabilis,* fr. L *in-* + LL *ponderabilis* ponderable] (1794) **:** not ponderable **:** incapable of being weighed or evaluated with exactness ⟨the ~ beauties of Beethoven's . . . sonatas —Cecelia Porter⟩ — **im·pon·der·a·bil·i·ty** \-ˌpän-d(ə-)rə-ˈbi-lə-tē\ *n* — **imponderable** *n* — **im·pon·der·a·bly** \-ˈpän-d(ə-)rə-blē\ *adv*

im·pone \im-ˈpōn\ *vt* **im·poned; im·pon·ing** [L *imponere* to put upon, fr. *in-* + *ponere* to put — more at POSITION] (ca. 1623) *obs* **:** WAGER, BET

[1]**im·port** \im-ˈpȯrt, ˈim-ˌ\ *vb* [ME, fr. ML *importare* to bring in, cause, signify, fr. L, to bring in, cause, fr. *in-* + *portare* to carry — more at FARE] *vt* (15c) **1 a :** to bear or convey as meaning or portent **:** SIGNIFY **b** *archaic* **:** EXPRESS, STATE **c :** IMPLY **2 :** to bring from a foreign or external source: as **a :** to bring (as merchandise) into a place or country from another country **b :** to transfer (as files or data) from one format to another usu. within a new file **3** *archaic* **:** to be of importance to **:** CONCERN ~ *vi* **:** to be of consequence **:** MATTER — **im·port·able** \im-ˈpȯr-tə-bəl, ˈim-ˌ\ *adj* — **im·port·er** *n*

[2]**im·port** \ˈim-ˌpȯrt\ *n* (ca. 1568) **1 :** IMPORTANCE; *esp* **:** relative importance ⟨it is hard to judge the ~ of this decision⟩ **2 :** PURPORT, SIGNIFICATION **3 :** something that is imported **4 :** IMPORTATION

im·por·tance \im-ˈpȯr-tᵊn(t)s, *esp Southern & NewEng* -tən(t)s, -dən(t)s\ *n* (1508) **1 a :** the quality or state of being important **:** CONSEQUENCE **b :** an important aspect or bearing **:** SIGNIFICANCE **2** *obs* **:** IMPORT, MEANING **3** *obs* **:** IMPORTUNITY **4** *obs* **:** a weighty matter

syn IMPORTANCE, CONSEQUENCE, MOMENT, WEIGHT, SIGNIFICANCE mean a quality or aspect having great worth or significance. IMPORTANCE implies a value judgment of the superior worth or influence of something or someone ⟨a region with no cities of *importance*⟩. CONSEQUENCE generally implies importance because of probable or possible effects ⟨the style you choose is of little *consequence*⟩. MOMENT implies conspicuous or self-evident consequence ⟨a decision of great *moment*⟩. WEIGHT implies a judgment of the immediate relative importance of something ⟨the argument carried no *weight* with the judge⟩. SIGNIFICANCE implies a quality or character that should mark a thing as important but that is not self-evident and may or may not be recognized ⟨the treaty's *significance*⟩.

im·por·tan·cy \-tᵊn(t)-sē, -tən(t)-, -dən(t)-\ *n* (1540) *archaic* **:** IMPORTANCE

im·por·tant \im-ˈpȯr-tᵊnt, *esp Southern & NewEng* -tənt, -dənt\ *adj* [ME *importante,* fr. ML *important-, importans,* prp. of *importare* to signify — more at IMPORT] (15c) **1 :** marked by or indicative of significant worth or consequence **:** valuable in content or relationship **2** *obs* **:** IMPORTUNATE, URGENT **3 :** giving evidence of a feeling of self-importance ***usage*** see IMPORTANTLY

im·por·tant·ly \-lē\ *adv* (1611) **1 :** in an important way ⟨contributed ~ to the language of the field —Ernst Mayr⟩ ⟨cleared his throat ~ and waited —E. K. Gann⟩ ⟨the real story is ~ different —Alexander Woollcott⟩ **2 :** it is important that ⟨more ~ he stands a chance of having his publication barred —H. L. Mencken⟩

usage A number of commentators have objected to *importantly* as a sentence modifier (sense 2) and have recommended *important* instead. Actually both the adverb and the adjective are in reputable standard use in this function. *Important* is always used with *more* or *most* ⟨had bronze weapons and composite bows; more *important,* they utilized the horse and war chariot —Harry A. Gailey, Jr.⟩ ⟨second and most *important,* the book contains no important woman character —F. Scott Fitzgerald⟩. *Importantly* is somewhat more flexible in not requiring *more* or *most* ⟨sticks and, just as *importantly,* unsticks easily —Phoebe Hawkins⟩ ⟨*importantly,* the leaven in the mixture is quality —George O'Brien⟩.

im·por·ta·tion \ˌim-ˌpȯr-ˈtā-shən, -pər-\ *n* (1601) **1 :** the act or practice of importing **2 :** something imported

imported cabbage worm *n* (1892) **:** a small European white butterfly (*Pieris rapae*) introduced into temperate regions worldwide; *also* **:** its green larva that is a pest of cruciferous plants and esp. cabbage

imported fire ant *n* (ca. 1949) **:** either of two mound-building So. American fire ants (*Solenopsis richteri* and *S. invicta*) introduced into the southeastern U.S. that are agricultural pests and can produce stings requiring medical attention

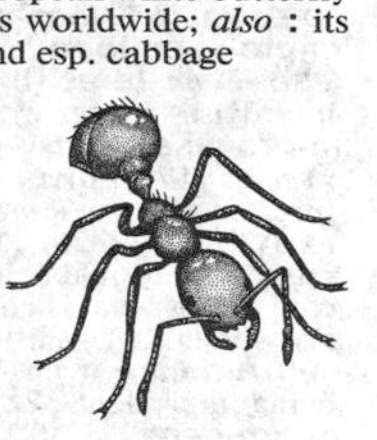
imported fire ant

im·por·tu·nate \im-ˈpȯr-chə-nət, -tyü-nət\ *adj* (1528) **1 :** troublesomely urgent **:** overly persistent in request or demand ⟨~ creditors⟩ **2 :** TROUBLESOME — **im·por·tu·nate·ly** *adv* — **im·por·tu·nate·ness** *n*

[1]**im·por·tune** \ˌim-pər-ˈtün, -ˈtyün; im-ˈpȯr-ˌ, -chən\ *adj* [ME, fr. AF & L; AF *importun,* fr. L *importunus,* fr. *in-* + *-portunus* (as in *opportunus* fit) — more at OPPORTUNE] (15c) **:** IMPORTUNATE — **im·por·tune·ly** *adv*

[2]**importune** *vb* **-tuned; -tun·ing** *vt* (1530) **1 a :** to press or urge with troublesome persistence **b** *archaic* **:** to request or beg for urgently **2 :** ANNOY, TROUBLE ~ *vi* **:** to beg, urge, or solicit persistently or troublesomely ***syn*** see BEG — **im·por·tun·er** *n*

im·por·tu·ni·ty \ˌim-pər-ˈtü-nə-tē, -ˈtyü-\ *n, pl* **-ties** (15c) **1 :** the quality or state of being importunate **2 :** an importunate request or demand

im·pose \im-ˈpōz\ *vb* **im·posed; im·pos·ing** [MF *imposer,* fr. L *imponere,* lit., to put upon (perf. indic. *imposui*), fr. *in-* + *ponere* to put — more at POSITION] *vt* (1581) **1 a :** to establish or apply by authority ⟨~ a tax⟩ ⟨~ new restrictions⟩ ⟨~ penalties⟩ **b :** to establish or bring about as if by force ⟨those limits *imposed* by our own inadequacies —C. H. Plimpton⟩ **2 a :** PLACE, SET **b :** to arrange (as pages) in the proper order for printing **3 :** PASS OFF ⟨~ fake antiques on the public⟩ **4 :** to force into the company or on the attention of another ⟨~ oneself on others⟩ ~ *vi* **:** to take unwarranted advantage of something ⟨*imposed* on his good nature⟩ — **im·pos·er** *n*

imposing *adj* (1786) **:** impressive in size, bearing, dignity, or grandeur ***syn*** see GRAND — **im·pos·ing·ly** \-ziŋ-lē\ *adv*

im·po·si·tion \ˌim-pə-ˈzi-shən\ *n* (14c) **1 :** something imposed: as **a :** LEVY, TAX **b :** an excessive or uncalled-for requirement or burden **2 :** the act of imposing **3 :** DECEPTION **4 :** the order of arrangement of imposed pages

im·pos·si·bil·i·ty \(ˌ)im-ˌpä-sə-ˈbi-lə-tē\ *n* (14c) **1 :** the quality or state of being impossible **2 :** something impossible

im·pos·si·ble \(ˌ)im-ˈpä-sə-bəl\ *adj* [ME, fr. AF & L; AF, fr. L *impossibilis,* fr. *in-* + *possibilis* possible] (14c) **1 a :** incapable of being or of occurring **b :** felt to be incapable of being done, attained, or fulfilled **:** insuperably difficult ⟨an ~ deadline⟩ **2 a :** extremely undesirable **:** UNACCEPTABLE **b :** extremely awkward or difficult to deal with ⟨the actor was ~ on the set⟩ — **im·pos·si·ble·ness** *n*

im·pos·si·bly \-blē\ *adv* (ca. 1580) **1 :** not possibly **2 :** to an improbable degree **:** UNBELIEVABLY ⟨an ~ green lawn⟩

[1]**im·post** \ˈim-ˌpōst\ *n* [MF, fr. ML *impositum,* fr. L, neut. of *impositus,* pp. of *imponere*] (1568) **:** something imposed or levied **:** TAX

[2]**impost** *n* [F *imposte,* ultim. fr. L *impositus*] (1664) **:** a block, capital, or molding from which an arch springs — see ARCH illustration

im·pos·tor *or* **im·pos·ter** \im-ˈpäs-tər\ *n* [LL *impostor,* fr. L *imponere*] (1564) **:** one that assumes false identity or title for the purpose of deception

im·pos·tume \im-ˈpäs-ˌchüm\ *or* **im·pos·thume** \-ˌthüm, -ˌthyüm\ *n* [ME *emposteme,* ultim. fr. Gk *apostēma,* fr. *aphistanai* to remove, fr. *apo-* + *histanai* to cause to stand — more at STAND] (14c) *archaic* **:** ABSCESS

im·pos·ture \im-ˈpäs-chər\ *n* [LL *impostura,* fr. L *impositus, impostus,* pp. of *imponere*] (1537) **1 :** the act or practice of deceiving by means of an assumed character or name **2 :** an instance of imposture

syn IMPOSTURE, FRAUD, SHAM, FAKE, HUMBUG, COUNTERFEIT mean a thing made to seem other than it is. IMPOSTURE applies to any situation in which a spurious object or performance is passed off as genuine ⟨their claim of environmental concern is an *imposture*⟩. FRAUD usu. implies a deliberate perversion of the truth ⟨the diary was exposed as a *fraud*⟩. SHAM applies to fraudulent imitation of a real thing or action ⟨condemned the election as a *sham*⟩. FAKE implies an imitation of or substitution for the genuine but does not necessarily imply dishonesty ⟨these jewels are *fakes;* the real ones are in the vault⟩. HUMBUG suggests elaborate pretense usu. so flagrant as to be transparent ⟨creating publicity by foisting *humbugs* on a gullible public⟩. COUNTERFEIT applies esp. to the close imitation of something valuable ⟨20-dollar bills that were *counterfeits*⟩.

im·po·tence \ˈim-pə-tən(t)s\ *n* (15c) **:** the quality or state of being impotent

im·po·ten·cy \-tən(t)-sē\ *n* (15c) **:** IMPOTENCE

im·po·tent \ˈim-pə-tənt\ *adj* [ME, fr. AF & L; AF, fr. L *impotent-, impotens,* fr. *in-* + *potent-, potens* potent] (14c) **1 a :** not potent **:** lacking in power, strength, or vigor **:** HELPLESS **b :** unable to engage in sexual intercourse because of inability to have and maintain an erection; *broadly* **:** STERILE **2** *obs* **:** incapable of self-restraint **:** UNGOVERNABLE — **impotent** *n* — **im·po·tent·ly** *adv*

im·pound \im-ˈpau̇nd\ *vt* (15c) **1 a :** to shut up in or as if in a pound **:** CONFINE **b :** to seize and hold in the custody of the law **c :** to take possession of ⟨she was dismissed and her manuscript ~*ed* —Jonathan Weiner⟩ **2 :** to collect and confine (water) in or as if in a reservoir

im·pound·ment \-ˈpau̇n(d)-mənt\ *n* (ca. 1665) **1 :** the act of impounding **:** the state of being impounded **2 :** a body of water formed by impounding

im·pov·er·ish \im-ˈpäv-rish, -ˈpä-və-\ *vt* [ME *enpoverisshen,* fr. AF *empoveriss-,* stem of *empoverir,* fr. *en-* + *povre* poor — more at POOR] (15c) **1 :** to make poor **2 :** to deprive of strength, richness, or fertility by depleting or draining of something essential ***syn*** see DEPLETE — **im·pov·er·ish·er** *n* — **im·pov·er·ish·ment** \-mənt\ *n*

impoverished *adj* (1862) *of a fauna or flora* **:** represented by few species or individuals

im·prac·ti·ca·ble \(ˌ)im-ˈprak-ti-kə-bəl\ *adj* (1653) **1 :** IMPASSABLE ⟨an ~ road⟩ **2 :** not practicable **:** incapable of being performed or accomplished by the means employed or at command ⟨an ~ proposal⟩ — **im·prac·ti·ca·bil·i·ty** \-ˌprak-ti-kə-ˈbi-lə-tē\ *n* — **im·prac·ti·ca·bly** \-ˈprak-ti-kə-blē\ *adv*

im·prac·ti·cal \(ˌ)im-ˈprak-ti-kəl\ *adj* (1865) **:** not practical: as **a :** not wise to put into or keep in practice or effect **b :** incapable of dealing sensibly or prudently with practical matters **c :** IMPRACTICABLE **d :** IDEALISTIC — **im·prac·ti·cal·i·ty** \-ˌprak-ti-ˈka-lə-tē\ *n* — **im·prac·ti·cal·ly** \-ˈprak-ti-k(ə-)lē\ *adv*

im·pre·cate \ˈim-pri-ˌkāt\ *vb* **-cat·ed; -cat·ing** [L *imprecatus,* pp. of *imprecari,* fr. *in-* + *precari* to pray — more at PRAY] *vt* (1613) **:** to invoke evil on **:** CURSE ~ *vi* **:** to utter curses

im·pre·ca·tion \ˌim-pri-ˈkā-shən\ *n* (15c) **1 :** CURSE **2 :** the act of imprecating — **im·pre·ca·to·ry** \ˈim-pri-kə-ˌtȯr-ē, im-ˈpre-kə-\ *adj*

im·pre·cise \ˌim-pri-ˈsīs\ *adj* (1805) **:** not precise **:** INEXACT, VAGUE ⟨an ~ estimate⟩ — **im·pre·cise·ly** *adv* — **im·pre·cise·ness** *n* — **im·pre·ci·sion** \-ˈsi-zhən\ *n*

im·preg·na·ble \im-ˈpreg-nə-bəl\ *adj* [ME *imprenable,* fr. MF, fr. *in-* + *prenable* vulnerable to capture, fr. *prendre* to take — more at PRIZE] (15c) **1 :** incapable of being taken by assault **:** UNCONQUERABLE ⟨an ~ fortress⟩ **2 :** UNASSAILABLE; *also* **:** IMPENETRABLE ⟨~ walls⟩ — **im·preg·na·bil·i·ty** \(ˌ)im-ˌpreg-nə-ˈbi-lə-tē\ *n* — **im·preg·na·ble·ness** \im-ˈpreg-nə-bəl-nəs\ *n* — **im·preg·na·bly** \-blē\ *adv*

im·preg·nant \im-ˈpreg-nənt\ *n* (1926) **:** a substance used for impregnating another substance

[1]**im·preg·nate** \im-ˈpreg-ˌnāt, ˈim-ˌ\ *vt* **-nat·ed; -nat·ing** [LL *impraegnatus,* pp. of *impraegnare,* fr. L *in-* + *praegnas* pregnant] (1605) **1 a :** to cause to be filled, imbued, permeated, or saturated ⟨~ wood with varnish⟩ **b :** to permeate thoroughly **2 :** to make pregnant **:** FERTILIZE ***syn*** see SOAK — **im·preg·na·tion** \(ˌ)im-ˌpreg-ˈnā-shən\ *n* — **im·preg·na·tor** \im-ˈpreg-ˌnā-tər, ˈim-ˌ\ *n*

[2]**im·preg·nate** \im-ˈpreg-nət\ *adj* (1646) **:** being filled or saturated

---

\ə\ **abut** \ᵊ\ **kitten,** F table \ər\ **further** \a\ **ash** \ā\ **ace** \ä\ **mop, mar** \au̇\ **out** \ch\ **chin** \e\ **bet** \ē\ **easy** \g\ **go** \i\ **hit** \ī\ **ice** \j\ **job** \ŋ\ **sing** \ō\ **go** \ȯ\ **law** \ȯi\ **boy** \th\ **thin** \t͟h\ **the** \ü\ **loot** \u̇\ **foot** \y\ **yet** \zh\ **vision, beige** \k̟, ⁿ, œ, ue, ʸ\ *see* Guide to Pronunciation

im·pre·sa \im-ˈprā-zə, -sə\ *n* [It, lit., undertaking] (1588) **:** a device with a motto used in the 16th and 17th centuries; *broadly* **:** EMBLEM

im·pre·sa·rio \ˌim-prə-ˈsär-ē-ˌō, -ˈser-, -ˈzär-\ *n, pl* **-ri·os** [It, fr. *impresa* undertaking, fr. *imprendere* to undertake, fr. VL **imprehendere* — more at EMPRISE] (1746) **1 :** the promoter, manager, or conductor of an opera or concert company **2 :** a person who puts on or sponsors an entertainment (as a television show or sports event) **3 :** MANAGER, DIRECTOR

1**im·press** \im-ˈpres\ *vb* [ME, fr. L *impressus,* pp. of *imprimere,* fr. *in-* + *premere* to press — more at PRESS] *vt* (14c) **1 a :** to apply with pressure so as to imprint **b :** to produce (as a mark) by pressure **c :** to mark by or as if by pressure or stamping **2 a :** to produce a vivid impression of **b :** to affect esp. forcibly or deeply **:** gain the admiration or interest of ⟨her honesty ~*ed* us⟩ **3 :** TRANSFER, TRANSMIT **~** *vi* **:** to produce an impression ***syn*** see AFFECT — **im·press·ibil·i·ty** \-ˌpre-sə-ˈbi-lə-tē\ *n* — **im·press·ible** \-ˈpre-sə-bəl\ *adj*

2**im·press** \ˈim-ˌpres *also* im-ˈ\ *n* (1590) **1 :** a characteristic or distinctive mark **:** STAMP ⟨the ~ of a fresh and vital intelligence is stamped . . . in his work —Lytton Strachey⟩ **2 :** IMPRESSION, EFFECT ⟨have an ~ on history⟩ **3 :** the act of impressing **4 a :** a mark made by pressure **:** IMPRINT **b :** an image of something formed by or as if by pressure; *esp* **:** SEAL **c :** a product of pressure or influence

3**im·press** \im-ˈpres\ *vt* [[1]*in-* + [3]*press*] (1596) **1 :** to levy or take by force for public service; *esp* **:** to force into naval service **2 a :** to procure or enlist by forcible persuasion **b :** FORCE ⟨~*ed* him into a white coat for the Christmas festivities —Nancy Hale⟩

4**im·press** \ˈim-ˌpres *also* im-ˈ\ *n* (1602) **:** IMPRESSMENT

im·pres·sion \im-ˈpre-shən\ *n* (14c) **1 a :** a characteristic, trait, or feature resulting from some influence ⟨the ~ on behavior produced by the social milieu⟩ **b :** an effect of alteration or improvement ⟨the settlement left little ~ on the wilderness⟩ **c :** a telling image impressed on the senses or the mind **2 :** the effect produced by impressing: as **a :** a stamp, form, or figure resulting from physical contact **b :** an imprint of the teeth and adjacent portions of the jaw for use in dentistry **c :** an esp. marked and often favorable influence or effect on feeling, sense, or mind **3 :** the act of impressing: as **a :** an affecting by stamping or pressing **b :** a communicating of a mold, trait, or character by an external force or influence **4 a :** the amount of pressure with which an inked printing surface deposits its ink on the paper **b :** one instance of the meeting of a printing surface and the material being printed; *also* **:** a single print or copy so made **c :** all the copies (as of a book) printed in one continuous operation from a single makeready **5 :** an often indistinct or imprecise notion or remembrance **6 a :** the first coat of color in painting **b :** a coat of paint for ornament or preservation **7 :** an imitation or representation of salient features in an artistic or theatrical medium; *esp* **:** an imitation in caricature of a noted personality as a form of theatrical entertainment ***syn*** see IDEA

im·pres·sion·able \im-ˈpre-sh(ə-)nə-bəl\ *adj* (1836) **:** capable of being easily impressed — **im·pres·sion·abil·i·ty** \-ˌpre-sh(ə-)nə-ˈbi-lə-tē\ *n*

im·pres·sion·ism \im-ˈpre-shə-ˌni-zəm\ *n* (1882) **1** *often cap* **:** a theory or practice in painting esp. among French painters of about 1870 of depicting the natural appearances of objects by means of dabs or strokes of primary unmixed colors in order to simulate actual reflected light **2 a :** the depiction (as in literature) of scene, emotion, or character by details intended to achieve a vividness or effectiveness more by evoking subjective and sensory impressions than by recreating an objective reality **b :** a style of musical composition designed to create subtle moods and impressions

im·pres·sion·ist \im-ˈpre-sh(ə-)nist\ *n* (1876) **1** *often cap* **:** one (as a painter) who practices or adheres to the theories of impressionism **2 :** an entertainer who does impressions

im·pres·sion·is·tic \(ˌ)im-ˌpre-shə-ˈnis-tik\ *adj* (1886) **1** *or* **im·pres·sion·ist** \im-ˈpre-sh(ə-)nist\ *often cap* **:** of, relating to, or constituting impressionism **2 :** based on or involving impression as distinct from expertise or fact ⟨intuitions and ~ anecdotal accounts —Sidney Hook⟩ — **im·pres·sion·is·ti·cal·ly** \(ˌ)im-ˌpre-shə-ˈnis-ti-k(ə-)lē\ *adv*

im·pres·sive \im-ˈpre-siv\ *adj* (1598) **:** making or tending to make a marked impression **:** having the power to excite attention, awe, or admiration ⟨an ~ display of skill⟩ ***syn*** see MOVING — **im·pres·sive·ly** *adv* — **im·pres·sive·ness** *n*

im·press·ment \im-ˈpres-mənt\ *n* (1787) **:** the act of seizing for public use or of impressing into public service

im·pres·sure \im-ˈpre-shər\ *n* (1600) *archaic* **:** a mark made by pressure **:** IMPRESSION

im·prest \ˈim-ˌprest\ *n* [obs. *imprest* to lend, prob. fr. It *imprestare*] (1568) **:** a loan or advance of money

im·pri·ma·tur \ˌim-prə-ˈmä-ˌtu̇r, im-ˈpri-mə-ˌtu̇r, -ˌtyu̇r\ *n* [NL, let it be printed, fr. *imprimere* to print, fr. L, to imprint, impress — more at IMPRESS] (1640) **1 a :** a license to print or publish esp. by Roman Catholic episcopal authority **b :** approval of a publication under circumstances of official censorship **2 a :** SANCTION, APPROVAL **b :** IMPRINT **c :** a mark of approval or distinction

im·pri·mis \im-ˈprī-məs, -ˈprē-\ *adv* [ME *imprimis,* fr. L *in primis* among the first (things)] (15c) **:** in the first place — used to introduce a list of items or considerations

1**im·print** \im-ˈprint, ˈim-ˌ\ *vb* [ME *emprenten,* fr. AF *emprient,* 3d sing. of *enpreindre* to impress (fr. L *imprimere*) & *empreinter,* fr. *emprent,* pp. of *enpreindre*] *vt* (14c) **1 :** to mark by or as if by pressure **:** IMPRESS **2 a :** to fix indelibly or permanently (as on the memory) **b :** to subject to or induce by imprinting ⟨an ~*ed* preference⟩ **~** *vi* **:** to undergo imprinting — **im·print·er** \-ˈprin-tər, -ˌprin-\ *n*

2**im·print** \ˈim-ˌprint\ *n* [ME *enpreent,* fr. AF *emprente,* fr. fem. of *emprent,* pp. of *enpreindre*] (15c) **:** something imprinted or printed: as **a :** a mark or depression made by pressure ⟨the fossil ~ of a dinosaur's foot⟩ **b :** an identifying name (as of a publisher) placed conspicuously on a product; *also* **:** the name under which a publisher issues books **c :** an indelible distinguishing effect or influence

im·print·ing \ˈim-ˌprin-tiŋ, im-ˈ\ *n* (1937) **:** a rapid learning process that takes place early in the life of a social animal (as a goose) and establishes a behavior pattern (as recognition of and attraction to its own kind or a substitute)

im·pris·on \im-ˈpri-zᵊn\ *vt* [ME, fr. AF *emprisoner,* fr. *en-* + *prison* prison] (14c) **:** to put in or as if in prison **:** CONFINE — **im·pris·on·ment** \-mənt\ *n*

im·prob·a·ble \(ˌ)im-ˈprä-bə-bəl, -ˈpräb-bəl\ *adj* [MF or L; MF, fr. L *improbabilis,* fr. *in-* + *probabilis* probable] (1598) **:** unlikely to be true or to occur; *also* **:** unlikely but real or true — **im·prob·a·bil·i·ty** \-ˌprä-bə-ˈbi-lə-tē\ *n* — **im·prob·a·bly** \-ˈprä-bə-blē, -ˈpräb-blē\ *adv*

1**im·promp·tu** \im-ˈpräm(p)-(ˌ)tü, -(ˌ)tyü\ *n* [F, fr. *impromptu* extemporaneously, fr. L *in promptu* in readiness] (1683) **1 :** something that is impromptu **2 :** a musical composition suggesting improvisation

2**impromptu** *adj* (1764) **1 :** made, done, or formed on or as if on the spur of the moment **:** IMPROVISED **2 :** composed or uttered without previous preparation **:** EXTEMPORANEOUS — **impromptu** *adv*

im·prop·er \(ˌ)im-ˈprä-pər\ *adj* [ME, fr. MF *impropre,* fr. L *improprius,* fr. *in-* + *proprius* proper] (15c) **:** not proper: as **a :** not in accord with fact, truth, or right procedure **:** INCORRECT ⟨~ inference⟩ **b :** not regularly or normally formed or not properly so called **c :** not suited to the circumstances, design, or end ⟨~ medicine⟩ **d :** not in accord with propriety, modesty, good manners, or good taste ⟨~ language⟩ ***syn*** see INDECOROUS — **im·prop·er·ly** *adv* — **im·prop·er·ness** *n*

improper fraction *n* (1542) **:** a fraction whose numerator is equal to, larger than, or of equal or higher degree than the denominator

improper integral *n* (1939) **:** a definite integral whose region of integration is unbounded or includes a point at which the integrand is undefined or tends to infinity

im·pro·pri·e·ty \ˌim-p(r)ə-ˈprī-ə-tē\ *n, pl* **-ties** [F or LL; F *impropriété,* fr. LL *improprietat-, improprietas,* fr. L *improprius*] (1607) **1 :** an improper or indecorous act or remark; *esp* **:** an unacceptable use of a word or of language **2 :** the quality or state of being improper

im·prov \ˈim-ˌpräv\ *adj* [short for *improvisation*] (1978) **:** of, relating to, or being improvisation and esp. an improvised comedy routine — **improv** *n*

im·prove \im-ˈprüv\ *vb* **im·proved; im·prov·ing** [ME *improuen, emprouen,* fr. AF *emprouer* to make profit from, fr. F *en-* + *pru, prou* advantage, fr. LL *prode* — more at PROUD] *vt* (ca. 1529) **1** *archaic* **:** EMPLOY, USE **2 a :** to enhance in value or quality **:** make better **b :** to increase the value of (land or property) by making it more useful for humans (as by cultivation or the erection of buildings) **c :** to grade and drain (a road) and apply surfacing material other than pavement **3 :** to use to good purpose **~** *vi* **1 :** to advance or make progress in what is desirable **2 :** to make useful additions or amendments — **im·prov·abil·i·ty** \(ˌ)im-ˌprü-və-ˈbi-lə-tē\ *n* — **im·prov·able** \-ˈprü-və-bəl\ *adj* — **im·prov·er** *n*

syn IMPROVE, BETTER, HELP, AMELIORATE mean to make more acceptable or to bring nearer a standard. IMPROVE and BETTER are general and interchangeable and apply to what can be made better whether it is good or bad ⟨measures to further *improve* the quality of medical care⟩ ⟨immigrants hoping to *better* their lot⟩. HELP implies a bettering that still leaves room for improvement ⟨a coat of paint would *help* that house⟩. AMELIORATE implies making more tolerable or acceptable conditions that are hard to endure ⟨tried to *ameliorate* the lives of people in the tenements⟩.

im·prove·ment \im-ˈprüv-mənt\ *n* (ca. 1550) **1 :** the act or process of improving **2 a :** the state of being improved; *esp* **:** enhanced value or excellence **b :** an instance of such improvement **:** something that enhances value or excellence

im·prov·i·dence \(ˌ)im-ˈprä-və-dən(t)s, -ˌden(t)s\ *n* (15c) **:** the quality or state of being improvident

im·prov·i·dent \-dənt, -ˌdent\ *adj* [LL *improvident-, improvidens,* fr. L *in-* + *provident-, providens* provident] (1514) **:** not provident **:** not foreseeing and providing for the future — **im·prov·i·dent·ly** *adv*

im·pro·vi·sa·tion \(ˌ)im-ˌprä-və-ˈzā-shən, ˌim-prə-və- *also* ˌim-prə-(ˌ)vī-\ *n* (1786) **1 :** the act or art of improvising **2 :** something (as a musical or dramatic composition) improvised — **im·pro·vi·sa·tion·al** \-shnəl, -shə-nᵊl\ *adj* — **im·pro·vi·sa·tion·al·ly** *adv*

im·prov·i·sa·tor \im-ˈprä-və-ˌzā-tər\ *n* (1795) **:** one that improvises — **im·prov·i·sa·to·ri·al** \(ˌ)im-ˌprä-və-zə-ˈtȯr-ē-əl\ *adj* — **im·pro·vi·sa·to·ry** \im-ˈprä-və-zə-ˌtȯr-ē, ˌim-prə-ˈvī-zə-\ *adj*

im·pro·vi·sa·to·re \(ˌ)im-ˌprä-və-zə-ˈtȯr-ē, ˌim-prə-ˌvē-zə-\ *n, pl* **-to·ri** \-ˈtȯr-ē\ *or* **-tores** [It *improvvisatore,* fr. *improvvisare*] (1765) **:** one that improvises (as verse) usu. extemporaneously

im·pro·vise \ˈim-prə-ˌvīz *also* ˌim-prə-ˈ\ *vb* **-vised; -vis·ing** [F *improviser,* fr. It *improvvisare,* fr. *improvviso* sudden, fr. L *improvisus,* lit., unforeseen, fr. *in-* + *provisus,* pp. of *providēre* to see ahead — more at PROVIDE] *vt* (1826) **1 :** to compose, recite, play, or sing extemporaneously **2 :** to make, invent, or arrange offhand **3 :** to make or fabricate out of what is conveniently on hand ⟨~ a meal⟩ **~** *vi* **:** to improvise something — **im·pro·vis·er** *or* **im·pro·vi·sor** \-ˌvī-zər, -ˈvī-\ *n*

im·pru·dence \(ˌ)im-ˈprü-dᵊn(t)s\ *n* (15c) **1 :** the quality or state of being imprudent **2 :** an imprudent act

im·pru·dent \-dᵊnt\ *adj* [ME, fr. L *imprudent-, imprudens,* fr. *in-* + *prudent-, prudens* prudent] (14c) **:** not prudent **:** lacking discretion, wisdom, or good judgment ⟨an ~ investor⟩ — **im·pru·dent·ly** *adv*

im·pu·dence \ˈim-pyə-dən(t)s\ *n* (14c) **:** the quality or state of being impudent

im·pu·dent \-dənt\ *adj* [ME, fr. L *impudent-, impudens,* fr. *in-* + *pudent-, pudens,* prp. of *pudēre* to feel shame] (14c) **1** *obs* **:** lacking modesty **2 :** marked by contemptuous or cocky boldness or disregard of others **:** INSOLENT — **im·pu·dent·ly** *adv*

im·pugn \im-ˈpyün\ *vt* [ME, fr. AF *empugner,* fr. L *inpugnare,* fr. *in-* + *pugnare* to fight — more at PUNGENT] (14c) **1 :** to assail by words or arguments **:** oppose or attack as false or lacking integrity ⟨~*ed* the defendant's character⟩ **2** *obs* **a :** ASSAIL **b :** RESIST — **im·pugn·able** \-ˈpyü-nə-bəl\ *adj* — **im·pugn·er** \-nər\ *n*

im·puis·sance \(ˌ)im-ˈpwi-sᵊn(t)s, (ˌ)im-ˈpyü-ə-sən(t)s; ˌim-pyü-ˈi-sᵊn(t)s\ *n* [ME, fr. MF, fr. *in-* + *puissance* puissance, power] (15c) **:** WEAKNESS, POWERLESSNESS

im·puis·sant \-sᵊnt, -sənt\ *adj* [F] (1629) **:** WEAK, POWERLESS

1**im·pulse** \ˈim-ˌpəls, im-ˈ\ *vt* **im·pulsed; im·puls·ing** (1611) **:** to give an impulse to

2**im·pulse** \ˈim-ˌpəls\ *n* [L *impulsus,* fr. *impellere* to impel] (1647) **1 a :** INSPIRATION, MOTIVATION **b :** a force so communicated as to produce motion suddenly **c :** INCENTIVE **2 a :** the act of driving onward with sudden force **:** IMPULSION **b :** motion produced by such an impulsion : IMPETUS **c** : a wave of excitation transmitted through tissues and esp. nerve fibers and muscles that results in physiological activity or inhibition **3 a** : a sudden spontaneous inclination or incitement to some usu. unpremeditated action **b** : a propensity or natural tendency usu. other than rational **4 a** : the product of the average value of a force and the time during which it acts : the change in momentum produced by the force **b** : PULSE 4a ***syn*** see MOTIVE

im·pul·sion \im-ˈpəl-shən\ *n* (15c) **1 a** : the act of impelling : the state of being impelled **b** : an impelling force **c** : an onward tendency derived from an impulsion **2** : IMPULSE 3a **3** : COMPULSION 2

im·pul·sive \im-ˈpəl-siv\ *adj* (15c) **1** : having the power of or actually driving or impelling **2 a** : arising from an impulse ⟨an ~ decision⟩ **b** : prone to act on impulse ⟨an ~ young man⟩ **3** : acting momentarily ***syn*** see SPONTANEOUS — **im·pul·sive·ly** *adv* — **im·pul·sive·ness** *n* — **im·pul·siv·i·ty** \-ˌpəl-ˈsi-və-tē\ *n*

im·pu·ni·ty \im-ˈpyü-nə-tē\ *n* [MF or L; MF *impunité,* fr. L *impunitat-, impunitas,* fr. *impune* without punishment, fr. *in-* + *poena* punishment — more at PAIN] (1532) : exemption or freedom from punishment, harm, or loss ⟨laws were flouted with ~⟩

im·pure \(ˌ)im-ˈpyu̇r\ *adj* [ME, fr. MF & L; MF, fr. L *impurus,* fr. *in-* + *purus* pure] (15c) : not pure: as **a** : LEWD, UNCHASTE **b** : containing something unclean : FOUL ⟨~ water⟩ **c** : ritually unclean **d** : mixed or impregnated with an extraneous and usu. unwanted substance ⟨an ~ chemical⟩ — **im·pure·ly** *adv* — **im·pure·ness** *n*

im·pu·ri·ty \(ˌ)im-ˈpyu̇r-ə-tē\ *n, pl* **-ties** (15c) **1** : something that is impure or makes something else impure ⟨removing *impurities* from water⟩ **2** : the quality or state of being impure

im·pu·ta·tion \ˌim-pyə-ˈtā-shən\ *n* (1581) **1** : the act of imputing: as **a** : ATTRIBUTION, ASCRIPTION **b** : ACCUSATION ⟨denied any ~ of unfairness⟩ **c** : INSINUATION **2** : something imputed — **im·pu·ta·tive** \im-ˈpyü-tə-tiv\ *adj* — **im·pu·ta·tive·ly** *adv*

im·pute \im-ˈpyüt\ *vt* **im·put·ed; im·put·ing** [ME, fr. AF *imputer,* fr. L *imputare,* fr. *in-* + *putare* to consider] (14c) **1** : to lay the responsibility or blame for often falsely or unjustly **2** : to credit to a person or a cause : ATTRIBUTE ⟨our vices as well as our virtues have been *imputed* to bodily derangement —B. N. Cardozo⟩ ***syn*** see ASCRIBE — **im·put·abil·i·ty** \-ˌpyü-tə-ˈbi-lə-tē\ *n* — **im·put·able** \-ˈpyü-tə-bəl\ *adj*

[1]**in** \ˈin, ən, ᵊn\ *prep* [ME, fr. OE; akin to OHG *in* in, L *in,* Gk *en*] (bef. 12c) **1 a** — used as a function word to indicate inclusion, location, or position within limits ⟨~ the lake⟩ ⟨wounded ~ the leg⟩ ⟨~ the summer⟩ **b** : INTO 1 ⟨went ~ the house⟩ **2** — used as a function word to indicate means, medium, or instrumentality ⟨written ~ pencil⟩ ⟨bound ~ leather⟩ **3 a** — used as a function word to indicate limitation, qualification, or circumstance ⟨alike ~ some respects⟩ ⟨left ~ a hurry⟩ **b** : INTO 2a ⟨broke ~ pieces⟩ **4** — used as a function word to indicate purpose ⟨said ~ reply⟩ **5** — used as a function word to indicate the larger member of a ratio ⟨one ~ six is eligible⟩

[2]**in** \ˈin\ *adv* (bef. 12c) **1 a (1)** : to or toward the inside esp. of a house or other building ⟨come ~⟩ **(2)** : to or toward some destination or particular place ⟨flew ~ on the first plane⟩ **(3)** : at close quarters : NEAR ⟨play close ~⟩ **b** : so as to incorporate ⟨mix ~ the flour⟩ — often used in combination ⟨built-*in* bookcases⟩ **c** : to or at an appropriate place ⟨fit a piece ~⟩ **2 a** : within a particular place; *esp* : within the customary place of residence or business ⟨the doctor is ~⟩ **b** : in the position of participant, insider, or officeholder — often used with *on* ⟨~ on the joke⟩ **c (1)** : on good terms **(2)** : in a specified relation ⟨~ bad with the boss⟩ **(3)** : in a position of assured or definitive success **d** : in vogue or season **e** *of an oil well* : in production **f** : in one's presence, possession, or control ⟨after the crops are ~⟩ **g** : from a condition of indistinguishability to one of clarity ⟨fade ~⟩ — **in for** : certain to experience ⟨*in for* a rude awakening⟩

[3]**in** \ˈin\ *adj* (1599) **1 a** : that is located inside or within ⟨the ~ part⟩ **b** : that is in position, operation, or power ⟨the ~ party⟩ **c** : INSIDE 2 **2** : that is directed or bound inward : INCOMING ⟨the ~ train⟩ **3 a** : extremely fashionable ⟨the ~ thing to do⟩ **b** : keenly aware of and responsive to what is new and fashionable ⟨the ~ crowd⟩

[4]**in** \ˈin\ *n* (1764) **1** : one who is in office or power or on the inside ⟨a matter of ~*s* versus outs⟩ **2** : INFLUENCE, PULL ⟨enjoyed some sort of ~ with the commandant —Henriette Roosenburg⟩

[5]**in** *abbr* **1** inch **2** inlet

In *symbol* indium

IN *abbr* Indiana

[1]**in-** *or* **il-** *or* **im-** *or* **ir-** *prefix* [ME, fr. AF, fr. L; akin to OE *un-*] : not : NON-, UN- — usu. *il-* before *l* ⟨*il*logical⟩, *im-* before *b, m,* or *p* ⟨*im*balance⟩ ⟨*im*moral⟩ ⟨*im*practical⟩, *ir-* before *r* ⟨*ir*reducible⟩, and *in-* before other sounds ⟨*in*conclusive⟩

[2]**in-** *or* **il-** *or* **im-** *or* **ir-** *prefix* [ME, fr. AF, fr. L, fr. *in* in, into] **1** : in : within : into : toward : on — usu. *il-* before *l* ⟨*il*luviation⟩, *im-* before *b, m,* or *p* ⟨*im*mingle⟩, *ir-* before *r* ⟨*ir*radiance⟩, and *in-* before other sounds ⟨*in*filtrate⟩ **2** : [1]EN- ⟨*im*brute⟩ ⟨*im*peril⟩ ⟨*in*spirit⟩

[1]**-in** *n suffix* [F *-ine,* fr. L *-īna,* fem. of *-īnus* of or belonging to — more at -EN] **1 a** : neutral chemical compound ⟨insul*in*⟩ **b** : enzyme ⟨pancreat*in*⟩ **c** : antibiotic ⟨penicill*in*⟩ **2** : [2]-INE 1a, b ⟨epinephr*in*⟩ **3** : pharmaceutical product ⟨niac*in*⟩

[2]**-in** *n comb form* [sit-*in*] : organized public protest by means of or in favor of : demonstration ⟨teach-*in*⟩ ⟨love-*in*⟩

in·abil·i·ty \ˌi-nə-ˈbi-lə-tē\ *n* [ME *inhabilite* disqualification, fr. ML *inhabilitas,* fr. L *in-* + *habilitas* ability] (15c) : lack of sufficient power, resources, or capacity ⟨his ~ to do math⟩

in ab·sen·tia \ˌin-ab-ˈsen(t)-sh(ē-)ə\ *adv* [L] (1886) : in absence ⟨gave him the award *in absentia*⟩

in·ac·ces·si·ble \ˌi-nik-ˈse-sə-bəl, (ˌ)i-ˌnak-\ *adj* [ME, fr. MF or LL; MF, fr. LL *inaccessibilis,* fr. L *in-* + LL *accessibilis* accessible] (15c) : not accessible ⟨an ~ area⟩ ⟨an ~ goal⟩ — **in·ac·ces·si·bil·i·ty** \-ˌse-sə-ˈbi-lə-tē\ *n* — **in·ac·ces·si·bly** \-ˈse-sə-blē\ *adv*

in·ac·cu·ra·cy \(ˌ)i-ˈna-kyə-rə-sē, -k(ə-)rə-sē\ *n, pl* **-cies** (ca. 1755) **1** : the quality or state of being inaccurate **2** : MISTAKE, ERROR

in·ac·cu·rate \-ˈa-kyə-rət, -k(ə-)rət\ *adj* (1738) : not accurate : FAULTY ⟨~ information⟩ — **in·ac·cu·rate·ly** \-kyə-rət-lē, -k(ə-)rət-, -kyərt-\ *adv*

in·ac·tion \(ˌ)i-ˈnak-shən\ *n* (1707) : lack of action or activity : IDLENESS

in·ac·ti·vate \(ˌ)i-ˈnak-tə-ˌvāt\ *vt* (1906) : to make inactive ⟨chemicals to ~ viruses⟩ — **in·ac·ti·va·tion** \-ˌnak-tə-ˈvā-shən\ *n*

in·ac·tive \(ˌ)i-ˈnak-tiv\ *adj* (1664) : not active: as **a (1)** : SEDENTARY **(2)** : INDOLENT, SLUGGISH **b (1)** : being out of use **(2)** : relating to or being members of the armed forces who are not performing or available for military duties **(3)** *of a disease* : QUIESCENT **c (1)** : chemically inert **(2)** : optically neutral in polarized light **d** : biologically inert esp. because of the loss of some quality (as infectivity or antigenicity) — **in·ac·tive·ly** *adv* — **in·ac·tiv·i·ty** \-ˌnak-ˈti-və-tē\ *n*

syn INACTIVE, IDLE, INERT, PASSIVE, SUPINE mean not engaged in work or activity. INACTIVE applies to anyone or anything not in action or in operation or at work ⟨on *inactive* status as an astronaut⟩ ⟨*inactive* accounts⟩. IDLE applies to persons that are not busy or occupied or to their powers or their implements ⟨workers were *idle* in the fields⟩. INERT as applied to things implies powerlessness to move or to affect other things; as applied to persons it suggests an inherent or habitual indisposition to activity ⟨*inert* ingredients in drugs⟩ ⟨an *inert* citizenry⟩. PASSIVE implies immobility or lack of normally expected response to an external force or influence and often suggests deliberate submissiveness or self-control ⟨*passive* resistance⟩. SUPINE applies only to persons and commonly implies abjectness or indolence ⟨a *supine* willingness to play the fool⟩.

in·ad·e·qua·cy \(ˌ)i-ˈna-di-kwə-sē\ *n, pl* **-cies** (1787) **1** : the quality or state of being inadequate **2** : INSUFFICIENCY, DEFICIENCY

in·ad·e·quate \-kwət\ *adj* (1671) : not adequate : INSUFFICIENT ⟨~ equipment⟩; *also* : not capable ⟨was ~ as a leader⟩ — **in·ad·e·quate·ly** *adv* — **in·ad·e·quate·ness** *n*

in·ad·mis·si·ble \ˌi-nəd-ˈmi-sə-bəl\ *adj* (1776) : not admissible ⟨~ evidence⟩ — **in·ad·mis·si·bil·i·ty** \-ˌmi-sə-ˈbi-lə-tē\ *n* — **in·ad·mis·si·bly** \-ˈmi-sə-blē\ *adv*

in·ad·ver·tence \ˌi-nəd-ˈvər-tᵊn(t)s\ *n* [ME, fr. ML *inadvertentia,* fr. L *in-* + *advertent-, advertens,* prp. of *advertere* to advert] (15c) **1** : the fact or action of being inadvertent **2** : a result of inattention : OVERSIGHT

in·ad·ver·ten·cy \-tᵊn(t)-sē\ *n, pl* **-cies** (1592) : INADVERTENCE

in·ad·ver·tent \-tᵊnt\ *adj* [back-formation fr. *inadvertence*] (1653) **1** : not focusing the mind on a matter : INATTENTIVE **2** : UNINTENTIONAL ⟨an ~ omission⟩ — **in·ad·ver·tent·ly** *adv*

in·ad·vis·able \ˌi-nəd-ˈvī-zə-bəl\ *adj* (1870) : not advisable : not wise or prudent ⟨~ haste⟩ — **in·ad·vis·abil·i·ty** \-ˌvī-zə-ˈbi-lə-tē\ *n*

-inae *n pl suffix* [NL *-inae,* fr. L, fem. pl. of *-inus*] : members of the subfamily of — in all names of zoological subfamilies in recent classifications ⟨Fel*inae*⟩

in·alien·able \(ˌ)i-ˈnāl-yə-nə-bəl, -ˈnā-lē-ə-nə-\ *adj* [prob. fr. F *inaliénable,* fr. *in-* + *aliénable* alienable] (ca. 1645) : incapable of being alienated, surrendered, or transferred ⟨~ rights⟩ — **in·alien·abil·i·ty** \-ˌnāl-yə-nə-ˈbi-lə-tē, -ˌnā-lē-ə-nə-\ *n* — **in·alien·ably** \-ˈnāl-yə-nə-blē, -ˈnā-lē-ə-nə-\ *adv*

in·al·ter·able \(ˌ)i-ˈnȯl-t(ə-)rə-bəl\ *adj* (1541) : not alterable : UNALTERABLE — **in·al·ter·abil·i·ty** \-ˌnȯl-t(ə-)rə-ˈbi-lə-tē\ *n* — **in·al·ter·able·ness** \-ˈnȯl-t(ə-)rə-bəl-nəs\ *n* — **in·al·ter·ably** \-blē\ *adv*

in·amo·ra·ta \i-ˌna-mə-ˈrä-tə\ *n* [It *innamorata,* fr. fem. of *innamorato,* pp. of *innamorare* to inspire with love, fr. *in-* (fr. L) + *amore* love, fr. L *amor* — more at AMOROUS] (1651) : a woman with whom one is in love or has intimate relations

in–and–in \ˌin-ən(d)-ˈin\ *adv or adj* (1765) : in repeated generations of the same or closely related stock ⟨families . . . of one blood through mating or marrying ~ —F. H. Giddings⟩ ⟨~ breeding⟩

[1]**inane** \i-ˈnān\ *adj* **inan·er; -est** [L *inanis*] (1662) **1** : EMPTY, INSUBSTANTIAL **2** : lacking significance, meaning, or point : SILLY ⟨~ comments⟩ ***syn*** see INSIPID — **inane·ly** *adv* — **inane·ness** \-ˈnān-nəs\ *n*

[2]**inane** *n* (1677) : void or empty space ⟨a voyage into the limitless ~ —V. G. Childe⟩

in·an·i·mate \(ˌ)i-ˈna-nə-mət\ *adj* [ME, fr. LL *inanimatus,* fr. L *in-* + *animatus,* pp. of *animare* to animate] (15c) **1** : not animate: **a** : not endowed with life or spirit ⟨an ~ object⟩ **b** : lacking consciousness or power of motion ⟨an ~ body⟩ **2** : not animated or lively : DULL — **in·an·i·mate·ly** *adv* — **in·an·i·mate·ness** *n*

in·a·ni·tion \ˌi-nə-ˈni-shən\ *n* (14c) : the quality or state of being empty: **a** : the exhausted condition that results from lack of food and water **b** : the absence or loss of social, moral, or intellectual vitality or vigor

inan·i·ty \i-ˈna-nə-tē\ *n, pl* **-ties** (1603) **1** : the quality or state of being inane: as **a** : lack of substance : EMPTINESS **b** : vapid, pointless, or fatuous character : SHALLOWNESS **2** : something that is inane

in·ap·par·ent \ˌi-nə-ˈper-ənt\ *adj* (1626) : not apparent — **in·ap·par·ent·ly** *adv*

in·ap·peas·able \ˌi-nə-ˈpē-zə-bəl\ *adj* (1803) : UNAPPEASABLE

in·ap·pe·tence \(ˌ)i-ˈna-pə-tən(t)s\ *n* (ca. 1691) : loss or lack of appetite

in·ap·pli·ca·ble \(ˌ)i-ˈna-pli-kə-bəl *also* ˌi-nə-ˈpli-kə-\ *adj* (1656) : not applicable : IRRELEVANT — **in·ap·pli·ca·bil·i·ty** \-ˌna-pli-kə-ˈbi-lə-tē *also* ˌi-nə-ˌpli-kə-\ *n* — **in·ap·pli·ca·bly** \(ˌ)i-ˈna-pli-kə-blē *also* ˌi-nə-ˈpli-kə-\ *adv*

in·ap·po·site \(ˌ)i-ˈna-pə-zət\ *adj* (1661) : not apposite : not apt or pertinent — **in·ap·po·site·ly** *adv* — **in·ap·po·site·ness** *n*

in·ap·pre·cia·ble \ˌi-nə-ˈprē-shə-bəl, -ˈpri-sh(ē-)ə-bəl\ *adj* [prob. fr. F *inappréciable,* fr. MF *inappreciable,* fr. *in-* + *appreciable*] (1802) : too small to be perceived ⟨an ~ amount⟩ — **in·ap·pre·cia·bly** \-blē\ *adv*

in·ap·pre·cia·tive \ˌi-nə-ˈprē-shə-tiv, -ˈpri- *also* -ˈprē-shē-ˌā-\ *adj* (1869) : not appreciative ⟨~ of their workers⟩ — **in·ap·pre·cia·tive·ly** *adv* — **in·ap·pre·cia·tive·ness** *n*

in·ap·proach·able \ˌi-nə-ˈprō-chə-bəl\ *adj* (ca. 1828) : not approachable : INACCESSIBLE ⟨her boss came across as ~⟩

in·ap·pro·pri·ate \ˌi-nə-ˈprō-prē-ət\ *adj* (1804) : not appropriate : UNSUITABLE — **in·ap·pro·pri·ate·ly** *adv* — **in·ap·pro·pri·ate·ness** *n*

in·apt \(ˌ)i-ˈnapt\ *adj* (ca. 1670) : not apt: **a** : not suitable ⟨an ~ analogy⟩ **b** : INEPT — **in·apt·ly** \-ˈnap(t)-lē\ *adv* — **in·apt·ness** \-nəs\ *n*

in·ap·ti·tude \(ˌ)i-ˈnap-tə-ˌtüd, -ˌtyüd\ *n* (1620) : lack of aptitude

in·ar·gu·able \(ˌ)i-ˈnär-gyə-wə-bəl\ *adj* (ca. 1875) : not arguable : not open to doubt or debate ⟨her impact was substantial and ~⟩

in·ar·gu·ably \-blē\ *adv* (1925) : it cannot be argued : UNQUESTIONABLY ⟨~, December is the best month for retailers⟩

in·ar·tic·u·la·cy \ˌi-(ˌ)när-ˈti-kyə-lə-sē\ *n* (1921) : the quality or state of being inarticulate

[1]**in·ar·tic·u·late** \-kyə-lət\ *adj* [LL *inarticulatus,* fr. L *in-* + *articulatus,* pp. of *articulare* to utter distinctly — more at ARTICULATE] (1603) **1 a** *of a sound* : uttered or formed without the definite articulations of intelligible speech **b** (1) : incapable of speech esp. under stress of emotion : MUTE (2) : incapable of being expressed by speech ⟨~ fear⟩ (3) : not voiced or expressed : UNSPOKEN ⟨society functions on many ~ premises⟩ **2** : incapable of giving coherent, clear, or effective expression to one's ideas or feelings **3** [NL *inarticulatus,* fr. L *in-* + NL *articulatus* articulate] : relating to, characteristic of, or being an inarticulate or its shell — **in·ar·tic·u·late·ly** *adv* — **in·ar·tic·u·late·ness** *n*

[2]**inarticulate** *n* (1952) : any of a class (Inarticulata) of brachiopods lacking a hinge connecting the two shell valves

in·ar·tis·tic \ˌi-när-ˈtis-tik\ *adj* (1859) **1** : not conforming to the principles of art **2** : not appreciative of art — **in·ar·tis·ti·cal·ly** \-ti-k(ə-)lē\ *adv*

in·as·much as \ˌi-nəz-ˈmə-chəz, -ˈməch-ˌaz\ *conj* (14c) **1** : in the degree that : INSOFAR AS **2** : in view of the fact that : SINCE

in·at·ten·tion \ˌi-nə-ˈten(t)-shən\ *n* (ca. 1670) : failure to pay attention

in·at·ten·tive \-ˈten-tiv\ *adj* (1692) : not attentive : not paying attention — **in·at·ten·tive·ly** *adv* — **in·at·ten·tive·ness** *n*

in·au·di·ble \(ˌ)i-ˈnȯ-də-bəl\ *adj* [LL *inaudibilis,* fr. L *in-* + LL *audibilis* audible] (1601) : not audible ⟨~ comments⟩ — **in·au·di·bil·i·ty** \(ˌ)i-ˌnȯ-də-ˈbi-lə-tē\ *n* — **in·au·di·bly** \(ˌ)i-ˈnȯ-də-blē\ *adv*

[1]**in·au·gu·ral** \i-ˈnȯ-gyə-rəl, -g(ə-)rəl\ *adj* (1689) **1** : of or relating to an inauguration **2** : marking a beginning : first in a projected series

[2]**inaugural** *n* (1832) **1** : an inaugural address **2** : INAUGURATION

in·au·gu·rate \i-ˈnȯ-gyə-ˌrāt, -gə-ˌrāt\ *vt* **-rat·ed; -rat·ing** [L *inauguratus,* pp. of *inaugurare,* lit., to practice augury, fr. *in-* + *augurare* to augur; fr. the rites connected with augury] (1606) **1** : to induct into an office with suitable ceremonies **2 a** : to dedicate ceremoniously : observe formally the beginning of ⟨~ a new school⟩ **b** : to bring about the beginning of ***syn*** see BEGIN — **in·au·gu·ra·tor** \-ˌrā-tər\ *n*

in·au·gu·ra·tion \-ˌnȯ-gyə-ˈrā-shən, -gə-\ *n* (1569) : an act of inaugurating; *esp* : a ceremonial induction into office

Inauguration Day *n* (1829) : January 20 following a presidential election on which the president of the U.S. is inaugurated

in·aus·pi·cious \ˌi-ˌnȯ-ˈspi-shəs\ *adj* (1592) : not auspicious ⟨an ~ start⟩ — **in·aus·pi·cious·ly** *adv* — **in·aus·pi·cious·ness** *n*

in·au·then·tic \ˌi-ˌnȯ-ˈthen-tik\ *adj* (1860) : not authentic — **in·au·then·tic·i·ty** \ˌi-ˌnȯ-ˌthen-ˈti-sə-tē, -thən-\ *n*

in–be·tween \ˌin-bi-ˈtwēn\ *adj or n* (1815) : INTERMEDIATE

in between *adv or prep* (1610) : BETWEEN

[1]**in·board** \ˈin-ˌbȯrd\ *adv* (1830) **1** : inside the line of a ship's bulwarks or hull **2** : toward the center line of a vehicle or craft (as a ship or aircraft)

[2]**inboard** *adj* (1847) **1** : located inboard ⟨an ~ engine⟩ ⟨an ~ spoiler⟩ **2** *of a boat* : having an inboard engine

[3]**inboard** *n* (1939) : a boat with an inboard motor

in·born \ˈin-ˈbȯrn\ *adj* (1513) **1** : present from or as if from birth **2** : HEREDITARY, INHERITED ***syn*** see INNATE

in·bound \ˈin-ˌbau̇nd\ *adj* (1894) : inward bound ⟨~ traffic⟩

in·bounds \ˈin-ˈbau̇n(d)z\ *adj* (1968) : involving putting a basketball in play by passing it onto the court from out of bounds

inbounds line *n* (ca. 1961) : either of two broken lines running the length of a football field at right angles to the yard lines

in–box \ˈin-ˌbäks\ *n* (1969) : a box or tray (as on a desk) for holding incoming interoffice mail; *also* : a computer folder devoted to incoming e-mail

in·breathe \ˈin-ˌbrē*th*\ *vt* (14c) : to breathe (something) in : INHALE

in·bred \ˈin-ˈbred\ *adj* (ca. 1592) **1** : rooted and ingrained in one's nature as deeply as if implanted by heredity ⟨an ~ love of freedom⟩ **2** [fr. pp. of *inbreed*] : subjected to or produced by inbreeding ***syn*** see INNATE — **in·bred** \ˈin-ˌbred\ *n*

in·breed \ˈin-ˈbrēd\ *vb* **-bred** \-ˈbred\; **-breed·ing** *vt* (1599) : to subject to inbreeding ~ *vi* : to engage in inbreeding

inbreeding *n* (ca. 1842) **1** : the interbreeding of closely related individuals esp. to preserve and fix desirable characters of and to eliminate unfavorable characters from a stock **2** : confinement to a narrow range or a local or limited field of choice

in·built \ˈin-ˈbilt\ *adj* (1923) *chiefly Brit* : BUILT-IN

inc *abbr* **1** incomplete **2** *often cap* incorporated **3** increase

In·ca \ˈiŋ-kə\ *n* [Sp, fr. Quechua *inka* ruler of the Inca empire] (1594) **1 a** : a member of the Quechuan peoples of Peru maintaining an empire until the Spanish conquest **b** : a king or noble of the Inca empire **2** : a member of any people under Inca influence — **In·ca·ic** \in-ˈkā-ik\ *adj* — **In·can** \ˈiŋ-kən\ *adj*

in·cal·cu·la·ble \(ˌ)in-ˈkal-kyə-lə-bəl\ *adj* (1795) : not capable of being calculated: as **a** : very great ⟨did ~ damage⟩ **b** : not predictable : UNCERTAIN ⟨an ~ outcome⟩ — **in·cal·cu·la·bil·i·ty** \-ˌkal-kyə-lə-ˈbi-lə-tē\ *n* — **in·cal·cu·la·bly** \-ˈkal-kyə-lə-blē\ *adv*

in·ca·les·cence \ˌin-kə-ˈle-sᵊn(t)s, ˌiŋ-\ *n* [L *incalescere* to become warm, fr. *in-* + *calescere* to become warm, incho. of *calēre* to be warm — more at LEE] (1646) : a growing warm or ardent — **in·ca·les·cent** \-sᵊnt\ *adj*

in camera *adv* [NL, lit., in a chamber] (1872) : in private : SECRETLY

in·can·desce \ˌin-kən-ˈdes *also* -(ˌ)kan-\ *vi* **-desced; -desc·ing** [L *incandescere*] (1874) : to be or become incandescent

in·can·des·cence \ˌin-kən-ˈde-sᵊn(t)s *also* -(ˌ)kan-\ *n* (ca. 1656) : the quality or state of being incandescent; *esp* : emission by a hot body of radiation that makes it visible

[1]**in·can·des·cent** \-sᵊnt\ *adj* [prob. fr. F, fr. L *incandescent-, incandescens,* prp. of *incandescere* to become hot, fr. *in-* + *candescere* to become hot, fr. *candēre* to glow — more at CANDID] (1794) **1 a** : white, glowing, or luminous with intense heat **b** : strikingly bright, radiant, or clear **c** : marked by brilliance esp. of expression ⟨~ wit⟩ **d** : characterized by glowing zeal : ARDENT ⟨~ affection⟩ **2 a** : of, relating to, or being light produced by incandescence **b** : producing light by incandescence — **in·can·des·cent·ly** *adv*

[2]**incandescent** *n* (1900) : LIGHTBULB a

incandescent lamp *n* (1881) : LIGHTBULB a

in·cant \in-ˈkant\ *vi* [L *incantare*] (1945) : RECITE, UTTER

in·can·ta·tion \ˌin-ˌkan-ˈtā-shən\ *n* [ME *incantacioun,* fr. MF *incantation,* fr. LL *incantation-, incantatio,* fr. L *incantare* to enchant — more at ENCHANT] (14c) : a use of spells or verbal charms spoken or sung as a part of a ritual of magic; *also* : a written or recited formula of words designed to produce a particular effect — **in·can·ta·tion·al** \-shnəl, -shə-nᵊl\ *adj* — **in·can·ta·to·ry** \in-ˈkan-tə-ˌtȯr-ē, -ˌtȯr-\ *adj*

in·ca·pa·ble \(ˌ)in-ˈkā-pə-bəl\ *adj* [MF, fr. *in-* + *capable* capable] (1594) **1** : lacking capacity, ability, or qualification for the purpose or end in view: as **a** *archaic* : not able to take in, hold, or keep **b** *archaic* : not receptive **c** : not being in a state or of a kind to admit : INSUSCEPTIBLE **d** : not able or fit for the doing or performance : INCOMPETENT **2** : lacking legal qualification or power (as by reason of mental incompetence) : DISQUALIFIED — **in·ca·pa·bil·i·ty** \-ˌkā-pə-ˈbi-lə-tē\ *n* — **in·ca·pa·ble·ness** \-ˈkā-pə-bəl-nəs\ *n* — **in·ca·pa·bly** \-blē\ *adv*

in·ca·pac·i·tate \ˌin-kə-ˈpa-sə-ˌtāt\ *vt* **-tat·ed; -tat·ing** (1657) **1** : to make legally incapable or ineligible **2** : to deprive of capacity or natural power : DISABLE — **in·ca·pac·i·ta·tion** \-ˌpa-sə-ˈtā-shən\ *n*

in·ca·pac·i·ty \ˌin-kə-ˈpa-sə-tē, -ˈpas-tē\ *n, pl* **-ties** [F *incapacité,* fr. MF, fr. *in-* + *capacité* capacity] (1611) : the quality or state of being incapable; *esp* : lack of physical or intellectual power or of natural or legal qualifications

in·car·cer·ate \in-ˈkär-sə-ˌrāt\ *vt* **-at·ed; -at·ing** [L *incarceratus,* pp. of *incarcerare,* fr. *in-* + *carcer* prison] (1560) **1** : to put in prison **2** : to subject to confinement — **in·car·cer·a·tion** \(ˌ)in-ˌkär-sə-ˈrā-shən\ *n*

in·car·di·na·tion \(ˌ)in-ˌkär-dᵊn-ˈā-shən\ *n* [LL *incardination-, incardinatio,* fr. *incardinare* to ordain as chief priest, fr. L *in-* [2]in- + LL *cardinalis* principal — more at CARDINAL] (1897) : the formal acceptance by a diocese of a clergyman from another diocese

[1]**in·car·na·dine** \in-ˈkär-nə-ˌdīn, -ˌdēn, -dən\ *adj* [MF *incarnadin,* fr. OIt *incarnadino,* fr. *incarnato* flesh-colored, fr. LL *incarnatus*] (1591) **1** : having the pinkish color of flesh **2** : RED; *esp* : BLOODRED

[2]**incarnadine** *vt* **-dined; -din·ing** (1605) : to make incarnadine : REDDEN

[1]**in·car·nate** \in-ˈkär-nət, -ˌnāt\ *adj* [ME *incarnat,* fr. LL *incarnatus,* pp. of *incarnare* to incarnate, fr. L *in-* + *carn-, caro* flesh — more at CARNAL] (14c) **1 a** : invested with bodily and esp. human nature and form **b** : made manifest or comprehensible : EMBODIED ⟨a fiend ~⟩ **2** : INCARNADINE ⟨~ clover⟩

[2]**in·car·nate** \in-ˈkär-ˌnāt, ˈin-ˌ\ *vt* **-nat·ed; -nat·ing** (1533) : to make incarnate: as **a** : to give bodily form and substance to ⟨~*s* the devil as a serpent⟩ **b** (1) : to give a concrete or actual form to : ACTUALIZE (2) : to constitute an embodiment or type of ⟨no one culture ~*s* every important human value —Denis Goulet⟩

in·car·na·tion \ˌin-(ˌ)kär-ˈnā-shən\ *n* (14c) **1 a** (1) : the embodiment of a deity or spirit in some earthly form (2) *cap* : the union of divinity with humanity in Jesus Christ **b** : a concrete or actual form of a quality or concept; *esp* : a person showing a trait or typical character to a marked degree ⟨she is the ~ of goodness⟩ **2** : the act of incarnating : the state of being incarnate **3** : a particular physical form or state : VERSION ⟨in another ~ he might be a first vice-president —Walter Teller⟩ ⟨TV and movie ~*s* of the story⟩ — **in·car·na·tion·al** \-shə-nᵊl, -shnəl\ *adj*

in case *conj* (14c) **1** : IF ⟨*in case* we are surprised, keep by me —Washington Irving⟩ **2** : as a precaution against the event that ⟨carries a gun *in case* he is attacked⟩

in·cau·tion \(ˌ)in-ˈkȯ-shən\ *n* (ca. 1720) : lack of caution : HEEDLESSNESS

in·cau·tious \-shəs\ *adj* (ca. 1703) : lacking in caution : CARELESS ⟨an ~ remark⟩ — **in·cau·tious·ly** *adv* — **in·cau·tious·ness** *n*

in·cen·di·a·rism \in-ˈsen-dē-ə-ˌri-zəm\ *n* (ca. 1710) : incendiary action or behavior

[1]**in·cen·di·ary** \in-ˈsen-dē-ˌer-ē; -ˈsen-də-rē, -dyə-\ *n, pl* **-ar·ies** [ME, fr. L *incendiarius,* fr. *incendium* conflagration, fr. *incendere*] (15c) **1 a** : a person who commits arson : ARSONIST **b** : an incendiary agent (as a bomb) **2** : a person who excites factions, quarrels, or sedition : AGITATOR

[2]**incendiary** *adj* (15c) **1** : of, relating to, or involving arson : ARSONOUS **2** : tending to excite or inflame : INFLAMMATORY ⟨~ speeches⟩ **3 a** : igniting combustible materials spontaneously **b** : of, relating to, or being a weapon (as a bomb) designed to start fires **4** : extremely hot ⟨~ chili peppers⟩

[1]**in·cense** \ˈin-ˌsen(t)s\ *n* [ME *encens,* fr. AF, fr. LL *incensum,* fr. L, neut. of *incensus,* pp. of *incendere* to set on fire, fr. *in-* + *-cendere* to burn; akin to L *candēre* to glow — more at CANDID] (13c) **1** : material used to produce a fragrant odor when burned **2** : the perfume exhaled from some spices and gums when burned; *broadly* : a pleasing scent **3** : pleasing attention : FLATTERY

[2]**incense** *vt* **in·censed; in·cens·ing** (13c) **1** : to apply or offer incense to **2** : to perfume with incense

[3]**in·cense** \in-ˈsen(t)s\ *vt* **in·censed; in·cens·ing** [ME *encensen,* prob. fr. L *incensus,* pp. of *incendere* to set on fire, provoke] (15c) **1** *archaic* : to cause (a passion or emotion) to become aroused **2** : to arouse the extreme anger or indignation of

incense cedar *n* (1877) : a tall tree (*Calocedrus decurrens* syn. *Libocedrus decurrens*) of the cypress family found growing from Oregon to Baja California that has reddish-brown bark, scalelike foliage, and light soft aromatic wood; *also* : its wood

in·cent \in-ˈsent\ *vt* [back-formation fr. *incentive*] (1981) : INCENTIVIZE

in·cen·ter \ˈin-ˌsen-tər\ *n* [*in*scribe + [1]*center*] (ca. 1890) : the single point in which the three bisectors of the interior angles of a triangle intersect and which is the center of the inscribed circle

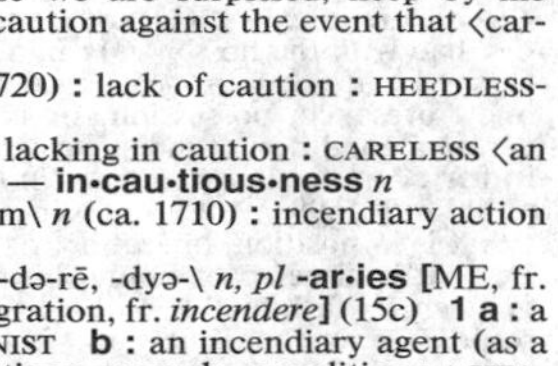

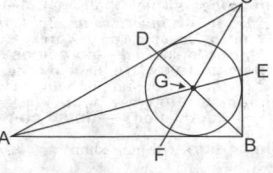

incenter: *ABC* triangle; *AE, BD, CF* bisectors; *G* incenter

in·cen·tive \in-ˈsen-tiv\ *n* [ME, fr. LL *incentivum,* fr. neut. of *incentivus* stimulating, fr. L, setting the tune, fr. *incentus,* pp. of *incinere* to play (a tune), fr. *in-* + *canere* to sing — more at CHANT] (15c)

: something that incites or has a tendency to incite to determination or action ***syn*** see MOTIVE — **incentive** *adj*

in·cen·tiv·ize \in-ˈsen-tə-ˌvīz\ *vt* **-ized; -iz·ing** (1970) : to provide with an incentive ⟨would ~ employees with stock options⟩

in·cep·tion \in-ˈsep-shən\ *n* [ME *incepcion,* fr. L *inception-, inceptio,* fr. *incipere* to begin, fr. *in-* + *capere* to take] (15c) : an act, process, or instance of beginning : COMMENCEMENT ***syn*** see ORIGIN

[1]**in·cep·tive** \in-ˈsep-tiv\ *n* (1612) : an inchoative verb

[2]**inceptive** *adj* (1656) **1** : INCHOATIVE 2 **2** : of or relating to a beginning — **in·cep·tive·ly** *adv*

in·cer·ti·tude \(ˌ)in-ˈsər-tə-ˌtüd, -ˌtyüd\ *n* [ME, fr. MF, fr. LL *incertitudo,* fr. L *in-* + LL *certitudo* certitude] (15c) : UNCERTAINTY: **a** : absence of assurance or confidence : DOUBT **b** : the quality or state of being unstable or insecure

in·ces·san·cy \(ˌ)in-ˈse-sᵊn(t)-sē\ *n* (1615) : the quality or state of being incessant

in·ces·sant \(ˌ)in-ˈse-sᵊnt\ *adj* [ME *incessaunt,* fr. LL *incessant-, incessans,* fr. L *in-* + *cessant-, cessans,* prp. of *cessare* to delay — more at CEASE] (15c) : continuing or following without interruption : UNCEASING ***syn*** see CONTINUAL — **in·ces·sant·ly** *adv*

in·cest \ˈin-ˌsest\ *n* [ME, fr. L *incestus* sexual impurity, fr. *incestus* impure, fr. *in-* + *castus* pure — more at CASTE] (13c) : sexual intercourse between persons so closely related that they are forbidden by law to marry; *also* : the statutory crime of such a relationship

in·ces·tu·ous \in-ˈses-chə-wəs, -ˈsesh-\ *adj* (1532) **1** : constituting or involving incest **2** : guilty of incest **3** : excessively or improperly intimate or exclusive ⟨mainstream fashion magazines have an ~ relationship with advertisers —Guy Trebay⟩ — **in·ces·tu·ous·ly** *adv* — **in·ces·tu·ous·ness** *n*

[1]**inch** \ˈinch\ *n* [ME, fr. OE *ynce,* fr. L *uncia* — more at OUNCE] (bef. 12c) **1** : a unit of length equal to 1/36 yard — see WEIGHT table **2** : a small amount, distance, or degree ⟨is like cutting a dog's tail off by ~*es* —Milton Friedman⟩ **3** *pl* : STATURE, HEIGHT **4 a** : a fall (as of rain or snow) sufficient to cover a surface or to fill a gauge to the depth of one inch **b** : a degree of atmospheric or other pressure sufficient to balance the weight of a column of liquid (as mercury) one inch high in a barometer or manometer **5** : a small advantage esp. from lenient or compassionate treatment — usu. used in the phrase *give an inch* — **every inch** : to the utmost degree ⟨looks *every inch* a winner⟩ — **inch by inch** : very gradually or slowly — **within an inch of** : almost to the point of ⟨came *within an inch of* succeeding⟩

[2]**inch** *vi* (1599) : to move by small degrees : progress slowly ⟨the long line of people ~*ing* up the stairs⟩ ~ *vt* : to cause to move slowly ⟨sooner or later they begin ~*ing* prices back up —*Forbes*⟩

[3]**inch** *n* [ME (Sc), fr. ScGael *innis*] (15c) *chiefly Scot* : ISLAND

inched \ˈincht\ *adj* (1605) : measuring a specified number of inches

-inch·er \ˈin-chər\ *n comb form* : one that has a dimension of a specified number of inches ⟨a four-*incher*⟩

inch·meal \ˈinch-ˌmēl, -ˈmēl\ *adv* [[1]*inch* + *-meal* (as in *piecemeal*)] (1530) : LITTLE BY LITTLE, GRADUALLY

in·cho·ate \in-ˈkō-ət, ˈin-kə-ˌwāt\ *adj* [L *inchoatus,* pp. of *inchoare* to start work on, perh. fr. *in-* + *cohum* part of a yoke to which the beam of a plow is fitted] (1534) : being only partly in existence or operation : INCIPIENT; *esp* : imperfectly formed or formulated : FORMLESS, INCOHERENT ⟨misty, ~ suspicions that all is not well with the nation —J. M. Perry⟩ — **in·cho·ate·ly** *adv* — **in·cho·ate·ness** *n*

in·cho·a·tive \in-ˈkō-ə-tiv\ *adj* (ca. 1631) **1** : INITIAL, FORMATIVE ⟨the ~ stages⟩ **2** : denoting the beginning of an action, state, or occurrence — used of verbs — **inchoative** *n* — **in·cho·a·tive·ly** *adv*

inch·worm \ˈinch-ˌwərm\ *n* (ca. 1861) : LOOPER 1

in·ci·dence \ˈin(t)-sə-dən(t)s, -ˌden(t)s\ *n* (1626) **1 a** : ANGLE OF INCIDENCE **b** : the arrival of something (as a projectile or a ray of light) at a surface **2 a** : an act or the fact or manner of falling upon or affecting : OCCURRENCE **b** : rate of occurrence or influence ⟨a high ~ of crime⟩

[1]**in·ci·dent** \ˈin(t)-sə-dənt, -ˌdent\ *n* [ME, fr. MF, fr. ML *incident-, incidens,* fr. L, prp. of *incidere* to fall into, fr. *in-* + *cadere* to fall — more at CHANCE] (15c) **1** : something dependent on or subordinate to something else of greater or principal importance **2 a** : an occurrence of an action or situation that is a separate unit of experience : HAPPENING **b** : an accompanying minor occurrence or condition : CONCOMITANT **3** : an action likely to lead to grave consequences esp. in diplomatic matters ⟨a serious border ~⟩ ***syn*** see OCCURRENCE

[2]**incident** *adj* (15c) **1** : occurring or likely to occur esp. as a minor consequence or accompaniment ⟨the confusion ~ to moving day⟩ **2** : dependent on or relating to another thing in law **3** : falling or striking on something ⟨~ light rays⟩

[1]**in·ci·den·tal** \ˌin(t)-sə-ˈden-tᵊl\ *adj* (1644) **1 a** : being likely to ensue as a chance or minor consequence ⟨social obligations ~ to the job⟩ **b** : MINOR 1 **2** : occurring merely by chance or without intention or calculation

[2]**incidental** *n* (1707) **1** *pl* : minor items (as of expense) that are not particularized **2** : something that is incidental

in·ci·den·tal·ly \-ˈden-tᵊl-ē, *esp for 2* -ˈdent-lē\ *adv* (1665) **1** : in an incidental manner : not intentionally ⟨the arrant nonsense of some of his statements is ~ hilarious —John Lahr⟩ **2** : by way of interjection or digression : by the way ⟨fortunate in having a good teacher . . . —still living, ~ —John Fischer⟩

incidental music *n* (1864) : descriptive music played during a play to project a mood or to accompany stage action

in·cin·er·ate \in-ˈsi-nə-ˌrāt\ *vt* **-at·ed; -at·ing** [ML *incineratus,* pp. of *incinerare,* fr. L *in-* + *ciner-, cinis* ashes; akin to Gk *konis* dust, ashes] (1555) : to cause to burn to ashes — **in·cin·er·a·tion** \-ˌsi-nə-ˈrā-shən\ *n*

in·cin·er·a·tor \in-ˈsi-nə-ˌrā-tər\ *n* (1883) : one that incinerates; *esp* : a furnace or a container for incinerating waste materials

in·cip·i·ence \in-ˈsi-pē-ən(t)s\ *n* (ca. 1864) : INCIPIENCY

in·cip·i·en·cy \-ən(t)-sē\ *n* (1817) : the state or fact of being incipient : BEGINNING

in·cip·i·ent \-ənt\ *adj* [L *incipient-, incipiens,* prp. of *incipere* to begin — more at INCEPTION] (1669) : beginning to come into being or to become apparent ⟨an ~ solar system⟩ ⟨evidence of ~ racial tension⟩ — **in·cip·i·ent·ly** *adv*

in·ci·pit \ˈin(t)-sə-pət, ˈiŋ-kə-ˌpit; in-ˈsi-pət, -ˈki-\ *n* [L, it begins, fr. *incipere*] (1897) : the first part : BEGINNING; *specif* : the opening words of a text of a medieval manuscript or early printed book

in·ci·sal \in-ˈsī-zəl, -səl\ *adj* (1903) : relating to, involving, or being the cutting edge or surface of a tooth (as an incisor)

in·cise \in-ˈsīz, -ˈsīs\ *vt* **in·cised; in·cis·ing** [MF or L; MF *inciser,* fr. L *incisus,* pp. of *incidere,* fr. *in-* + *caedere* to cut] (1567) **1** : to cut into **2 a** : to carve figures, letters, or devices into : ENGRAVE **b** : to carve (as an inscription) into a surface

incised *adj* (15c) **1** : cut in : ENGRAVED; *esp* : decorated with incised figures **2** : having a margin that is deeply and sharply notched ⟨an ~ leaf⟩

in·ci·sion \in-ˈsi-zhən\ *n* (14c) **1 a** : CUT, GASH; *specif* : a wound made esp. in surgery by incising the body **b** : a marginal notch (as in a leaf) **2** : an act of incising something **3** : the quality or state of being incisive

in·ci·sive \in-ˈsī-siv\ *adj* (ca. 1834) : impressively direct and decisive (as in manner or presentation) ⟨an ~ analysis⟩ ⟨an ~ unsentimental writer⟩ — **in·ci·sive·ly** *adv* — **in·ci·sive·ness** *n*

in·ci·sor \in-ˈsī-zər\ *n* (1666) : a front tooth typically adapted for cutting; *esp* : one of the cutting teeth in mammals located between the canines when canines are present — see TOOTH illustration

in·ci·ta·tion \ˌin-ˌsī-ˈtā-shən, ˌin(t)-sə-\ *n* (15c) **1** : an act of inciting : STIMULATION **2** : something that incites to action : INCENTIVE

in·cite \in-ˈsīt\ *vt* **in·cit·ed; in·cit·ing** [MF *inciter,* fr. L *incitare,* fr. *in-* + *citare* to put in motion — more at CITE] (15c) : to move to action : stir up : spur on : urge on — **in·cit·ant** \-ˈsī-tᵊnt\ *n* — **in·cite·ment** \-ˈsīt-mənt\ *n* — **in·cit·er** *n*

syn INCITE, INSTIGATE, ABET, FOMENT mean to spur to action. INCITE stresses a stirring up and urging on, and may or may not imply initiating ⟨*inciting* a riot⟩. INSTIGATE definitely implies responsibility for initiating another's action and often connotes underhandedness or evil intention ⟨*instigated* a conspiracy⟩. ABET implies both assisting and encouraging ⟨aiding and *abetting* the enemy⟩. FOMENT implies persistence in goading ⟨*fomenting* rebellion⟩.

in·ci·vil·i·ty \ˌin(t)-sə-ˈvi-lə-tē\ *n* [MF *incivilité,* fr. LL *incivilitat-, incivilitas,* fr. *incivilis,* fr. L *in-* + *civilis* civil] (1584) **1** : the quality or state of being uncivil **2** : a rude or discourteous act

incl *abbr* include; included; including; inclusive

in·clem·en·cy \(ˌ)in-ˈkle-mən(t)-sē\ *n* (1559) : the quality or state of being inclement

in·clem·ent \(ˌ)in-ˈkle-mənt, ˈin-klə-\ *adj* [L *inclement-, inclemens,* fr. *in-* + *clement-, clemens* clement] (1621) : lacking mildness: as **a** *archaic* : severe in temper or action : UNMERCIFUL **b** : physically severe : STORMY ⟨~ weather⟩ — **in·clem·ent·ly** *adv*

in·clin·able \in-ˈklī-nə-bəl\ *adj* (15c) **1** : having a tendency or inclination; *also* : disposed to favor or think well of ⟨~ to our pleas⟩ **2** : capable of being inclined ⟨an ~ steering column⟩

in·cli·na·tion \ˌin-klə-ˈnā-shən, ˌiŋ-\ *n* (14c) **1 a** *obs* : natural disposition : CHARACTER **b** : a particular disposition of mind or character : PROPENSITY; *esp* : LIKING ⟨had little ~ for housekeeping⟩ **2** : an act or the action of bending or inclining: as **a** : BOW, NOD **b** : a tilting of something **3 a** : a deviation from the true vertical or horizontal : SLANT; *also* : the degree of such deviation **b** : an inclined surface : SLOPE **c** (1) : the angle determined by two lines or planes (2) : the angle made by a line with the x-axis measured counterclockwise from the positive direction of that axis **4** : a tendency to a particular aspect, state, character, or action ⟨the clutch has an ~ to slip⟩ — **in·cli·na·tion·al** \-shnəl, -shə-nᵊl\ *adj*

[1]**in·cline** \in-ˈklīn\ *vb* **in·clined; in·clin·ing** [ME, fr. AF *incliner, encliner,* fr. L *inclinare,* fr. *in-* + *clinare* to lean — more at LEAN] *vi* (14c) **1** : to bend the head or body forward : BOW **2** : to lean, tend, or become drawn toward an opinion or course of conduct **3** : to deviate from a line, direction, or course; *specif* : to deviate from the vertical or horizontal ~ *vt* **1** : to cause to stoop or bow : BEND **2** : to have influence on : PERSUADE ⟨his love of books *inclined* him toward a literary career⟩ **3** : to give a bend or slant to — **in·clin·er** *n*

syn INCLINE, BIAS, DISPOSE, PREDISPOSE mean to influence one to have or take an attitude toward something. INCLINE implies a tendency to favor one of two or more actions or conclusions ⟨*I incline* to agree⟩. BIAS suggests a settled and predictable leaning in one direction and connotes unfair prejudice ⟨the experience *biased* him against foreigners⟩. DISPOSE suggests an affecting of one's mood or temper so as to incline one toward something ⟨her nature *disposes* her to trust others⟩. PREDISPOSE implies the operation of a disposing influence well in advance of the opportunity to manifest itself ⟨does fictional violence *predispose* them to accept real violence?⟩.

[2]**in·cline** \ˈin-ˌklīn\ *n* (1846) : an inclined plane : GRADE, SLOPE

in·clined \in-ˈklīnd, *2 also* ˈin-ˌ\ *adj* (14c) **1** : having inclination, disposition, or tendency **2 a** : having a leaning or slope **b** : making an angle with a line or plane

inclined plane *n* (1710) : a plane surface that makes an oblique angle with the plane of the horizon

in·clin·ing \in-ˈklī-niŋ\ *n* (14c) **1** : INCLINATION **2** *archaic* : PARTY, FOLLOWING

in·cli·nom·e·ter \ˌin-klə-ˈnä-mə-tər, ˌiŋ-; ˌin-ˌklī-\ *n* (1852) : an instrument for indicating the inclination to the horizontal of an axis (as of an airplane)

in·clip \in-ˈklip\ *vt* (1608) *archaic* : CLASP, ENCLOSE

inclose, inclosure *var of* ENCLOSE, ENCLOSURE

in·clude \in-ˈklüd\ *vt* **in·clud·ed; in·clud·ing** [ME, fr. L *includere,* fr. *in-* + *claudere* to close — more at CLOSE] (15c) **1** : to shut up : ENCLOSE **2** : to take in or comprise as a part of a whole or group **3** : to contain between or within ⟨two sides and the *included* angle⟩ — **in·clud·able** *or* **in·clud·ible** \-ˈklü-də-bəl\ *adj*

syn INCLUDE, COMPREHEND, EMBRACE, INVOLVE mean to contain within as part of the whole. INCLUDE suggests the containment of

\ə\ **abut** \ᵊ\ kitten, F table \ər\ **further** \a\ **ash** \ā\ **ace** \ä\ **mop, mar** \au̇\ **out** \ch\ **chin** \e\ **bet** \ē\ **easy** \g\ **go** \i\ **hit** \ī\ **ice** \j\ **job** \ŋ\ **sing** \ō\ **go** \ȯ\ **law** \ȯi\ **boy** \th\ **thin** \t͟h\ **the** \ü\ **loot** \u̇\ **foot** \y\ **yet** \zh\ **vision, beige** \k̲, ⁿ, œ, ue, ʸ\ *see* Guide to Pronunciation

something as a constituent, component, or subordinate part of a larger whole ⟨the price of dinner *includes* dessert⟩. COMPREHEND implies that something comes within the scope of a statement or definition ⟨his system *comprehends* all history⟩. EMBRACE implies a gathering of separate items within a whole ⟨her faith *embraces* both Christian and non-Christian beliefs⟩. INVOLVE suggests inclusion by virtue of the nature of the whole, whether by being its natural or inevitable consequence ⟨the new job *involves* a lot of detail⟩.

in·clu·sion \in-ˈklü-zhən\ *n* [L *inclusion-, inclusio,* fr. *includere*] (1600) **1 :** the act of including **:** the state of being included **2 :** something that is included: as **a :** a gaseous, liquid, or solid foreign body enclosed in a mass (as of a mineral) **b :** a passive usu. temporary product of cell activity (as a starch grain) within the cytoplasm or nucleus **3 :** a relation between two classes that exists when all members of the first are also members of the second — compare MEMBERSHIP 3 **4 :** the act or practice of including students with disabilities in regular school classes — **in·clu·sion·ary** \in-ˈklü-zhə-ner-ē\ *adj*

inclusion body *n* (1913) **:** an inclusion, abnormal structure, or foreign cell within a cell (as the eosinophilic body formed by a cytomegalovirus or the abnormal filament characteristic of some myopathies)

in·clu·sive \in-ˈklü-siv, -ziv\ *adj* (15c) **1 :** comprehending stated limits or extremes ⟨from Monday to Friday ~⟩ **2 a :** broad in orientation or scope **b :** covering or intended to cover all items, costs, or services — **in·clu·sive·ly** *adv* — **in·clu·sive·ness** *n*

inclusive disjunction *n* (1942) **:** a complex sentence in logic that is true when either or both of its constituent propositions are true — see TRUTH TABLE table

inclusive of *prep* (1709) **:** including or taking into account ⟨the cost of building *inclusive of* materials⟩

in·clu·siv·i·ty \in-(ˌ)klü-ˈsi-və-tē, -ˈzi-\ *n* (1939) **:** the quality or state of being inclusive **:** INCLUSIVENESS

in·co·erc·ible \ˌin-kō-ˈər-sə-bəl\ *adj* (1710) **:** incapable of being controlled, checked, or confined

incog *abbr* incognito

in·cog·i·tant \in-ˈkä-jə-tənt\ *adj* [L *incogitant-, incogitans,* fr. *in-* + *cogitant-, cogitans,* prp. of *cogitare* to cogitate] (1628) **:** THOUGHTLESS, INCONSIDERATE ⟨~ litterbugs⟩

in·cog·ni·ta \ˌin-ˌkäg-ˈnē-tə *also* in-ˈkäg-nə-tə\ *adv or adj* [It, fem. of *incognito*] (1638) **:** INCOGNITO — used only of a woman — **incognita** *n*

¹**in·cog·ni·to** \ˌin-ˌkäg-ˈnē-(ˌ)tō *also* in-ˈkäg-nə-ˌtō\ *adv or adj* [It, fr. L *incognitus* unknown, fr. *in-* + *cognitus,* pp. of *cognoscere* to know — more at COGNITION] (1635) **:** with one's identity concealed

²**incognito** *n, pl* **-tos** (1638) **1 :** one appearing or living incognito **2 :** the state or assumed identity of one living or traveling incognito or incognita

in·cog·ni·zant \(ˌ)in-ˈkäg-nə-zənt\ *adj* (1837) **:** lacking awareness or consciousness ⟨~ of the danger⟩ — **in·cog·ni·zance** \-zən(t)s\ *n*

in·co·her·ence \ˌin-kō-ˈhir-ən(t)s, -ˈher-\ *n* (1611) **1 :** the quality or state of being incoherent **2 :** something that is incoherent

in·co·her·ent \-ənt\ *adj* (1626) **:** lacking coherence: as **a :** lacking cohesion **:** LOOSE **b :** lacking orderly continuity, arrangement, or relevance **:** INCONSISTENT ⟨an ~ essay⟩ **c :** lacking normal clarity or intelligibility in speech or thought ⟨~ with grief⟩ — **in·co·her·ent·ly** *adv*

in·com·bus·ti·ble \ˌin-kəm-ˈbəs-tə-bəl\ *adj* [ME, prob. fr. MF, fr. *in-* + *combustible* combustible] (15c) **:** not combustible **:** incapable of being burned — **in·com·bus·ti·bil·i·ty** \-ˌbəs-tə-ˈbi-lə-tē\ *n* — **incombustible** *n*

in·come \ˈin-ˌkəm *also* ˈin-kəm *or* ˈiŋ-kəm\ *n* (14c) **1 :** a coming in **:** ENTRANCE, INFLUX ⟨fluctuations in the nutrient ~ of a body of water⟩ **2 :** a gain or recurrent benefit usu. measured in money that derives from capital or labor; *also* **:** the amount of such gain received in a period of time ⟨has an ~ of $30,000 a year⟩

income account *n* (1869) **:** a financial statement of a business showing the details of revenues, costs, expenses, losses, and profits for a given period — called also *income statement*

income bond *n* (ca. 1864) **:** a bond that pays interest at a rate based on the issuer's earnings

in·com·er \ˈin-ˌkə-mər\ *n* (1526) *chiefly Brit* **:** one who comes in **:** IMMIGRANT, NEWCOMER

income tax *n* (1799) **:** a tax on the net income of an individual or a business

¹**in·com·ing** \ˈin-ˌkə-miŋ\ *n* (14c) **1 :** the act of coming in **:** ARRIVAL **2 :** INCOME 2 — usu. used in pl.

²**incoming** *adj* (1753) **1 :** coming in **:** ARRIVING ⟨an ~ ship⟩ ⟨~ mail⟩ **2 :** taking a new place or position esp. as part of a succession ⟨the ~ president⟩ **3 :** just starting or beginning ⟨the ~ year⟩

in·com·men·su·ra·ble \ˌin-kə-ˈmen(t)s-rə-bəl, -ˈmen(t)sh-; -ˈmen(t)-sə-, -shə-\ *adj* (1570) **:** not commensurable; *broadly* **:** lacking a basis of comparison in respect to a quality normally subject to comparison — **in·com·men·su·ra·bil·i·ty** \-ˌmen(t)s-rə-ˈbi-lə-tē, -ˌmen(t)sh-; -ˌmen(t)-sə-, -shə-\ *n* — **incommensurable** *n* — **in·com·men·su·ra·bly** \-ˈmen(t)s-rə-blē, -ˈmen(t)sh-; -ˈmen(t)-sə-, -shə-\ *adv*

in·com·men·su·rate \-ˈmen(t)s-rət, -ˈmen(t)sh-; -ˈmen(t)-sə-, -shə-\ *adj* (1650) **:** not commensurate: as **a :** INCOMMENSURABLE **b :** INADEQUATE **c :** DISPROPORTIONATE ⟨a confidence ~ with their ability⟩

in·com·mode \ˌin-kə-ˈmōd\ *vt* **-mod·ed; -mod·ing** [MF *incommoder,* fr. L *incommodare,* fr. *incommodus* inconvenient, fr. *in-* + *commodus* convenient — more at COMMODE] (1598) **:** to give inconvenience or distress to **:** DISTURB

in·com·mo·di·ous \ˌin-kə-ˈmō-dē-əs\ *adj* (1551) **:** not commodious **:** INCONVENIENT ⟨could sleep in the most ~ places⟩ — **in·com·mo·di·ous·ly** *adv* — **in·com·mo·di·ous·ness** *n*

in·com·mod·i·ty \-ˈmä-də-tē\ *n* (15c) **:** a source of inconvenience **:** DISADVANTAGE ⟨the *incommodities* of a single life —Samuel Johnson⟩

in·com·mu·ni·ca·ble \ˌin-kə-ˈmyü-ni-kə-bəl\ *adj* [MF or LL; MF, fr. LL *incommunicabilis,* fr. L *in-* + LL *communicabilis* communicable] (1568) **:** not communicable: as **a :** UNCOMMUNICATIVE **b :** incapable of being communicated or imparted — **in·com·mu·ni·ca·bil·i·ty** \-ˌmyü-ni-kə-ˈbi-lə-tē\ *n* — **in·com·mu·ni·ca·bly** \-ˈmyü-ni-kə-blē\ *adv*

in·com·mu·ni·ca·do \-ˌmyü-nə-ˈkä-(ˌ)dō\ *adv or adj* [Sp *incomunicado,* fr. pp. of *incomunicar* to deprive of communication, fr. *in-* (fr. L) + *comunicar* to communicate, fr. L *communicare*] (1844) **:** without means of communication **:** in a situation or state not allowing communication ⟨a prisoner held ~⟩ ⟨remained ~ while working on her book⟩

in·com·mu·ni·ca·tive \-ˈmyü-nə-ˌkā-tiv, -ni-kə-tiv\ *adj* (1670) **:** UNCOMMUNICATIVE

in·com·mut·able \ˌin-kə-ˈmyü-tə-bəl\ *adj* [ME, fr. L *incommutabilis,* fr. *in-* + *commutabilis* commutable] (15c) **:** not commutable: as **a :** not interchangeable **b :** UNCHANGEABLE — **in·com·mut·ably** \-blē\ *adv*

in·com·pa·ra·ble \(ˌ)in-ˈkäm-p(ə-)rə-bəl *also* ˌin-kəm-ˈpa-rə-, -ˈper-ə-\ *adj* [ME, fr. AF, fr. L *incomparabilis,* fr. *in-* + *comparabilis* comparable] (15c) **1 :** eminent beyond comparison **:** MATCHLESS **2 :** not suitable for comparison — **in·com·pa·ra·bil·i·ty** \(ˌ)in-ˌkäm-p(ə-)rə-ˈbi-lə-tē *also* ˌin-kəm-ˌpa-rə-, -ˌper-ə-\ *n* — **in·com·pa·ra·bly** \(ˌ)in-ˈkäm-p(ə-)rə-blē *also* ˌin-kəm-ˌpa-rə-, -ˌper-ə-\ *adv*

in·com·pat·i·bil·i·ty \ˌin-kəm-ˌpa-tə-ˈbi-lə-tē\ *n, pl* **-ties** (1611) **1 a :** the quality or state of being incompatible **b :** lack of interfertility between two plants **2** *pl* **:** mutually antagonistic things or qualities

in·com·pat·i·ble \ˌin-kəm-ˈpa-tə-bəl\ *adj* [ME, fr. ML *incompatibilis,* fr. L *in-* + ML *compatibilis* compatible] (15c) **1 :** incapable of being held by one person at one time — used of offices that make conflicting demands on the holder **2 :** not compatible: as **a :** incapable of association or harmonious coexistence ⟨~ colors⟩ **b :** unsuitable for use together because of undesirable chemical or physiological effects ⟨~ drugs⟩ **c :** not both true ⟨~ propositions⟩ **d :** incapable of blending into a stable homogeneous mixture — **incompatible** *n* — **in·com·pat·i·bly** \-blē\ *adv*

in·com·pe·tence \(ˌ)in-ˈkäm-pə-tən(t)s\ *n* (1663) **:** the state or fact of being incompetent

in·com·pe·ten·cy \-tən(t)-sē\ *n* (1611) **:** INCOMPETENCE

in·com·pe·tent \(ˌ)in-ˈkäm-pə-tənt\ *adj* [MF *incompétent,* fr. *in-* + *compétent* competent] (1595) **1 :** not legally qualified **2 :** inadequate to or unsuitable for a particular purpose **3 a :** lacking the qualities needed for effective action **b :** unable to function properly ⟨~ heart valves⟩ — **incompetent** *n* — **in·com·pe·tent·ly** *adv*

in·com·plete \ˌin-kəm-ˈplēt\ *adj* [ME *incompleet,* fr. LL *incompletus,* fr. L *in-* + *completus* complete] (14c) **1 :** not complete **:** UNFINISHED: as **a :** lacking a part; *esp* **:** lacking one or more sets of floral organs **b** *of insect metamorphosis* **:** characterized by the absence of a pupal stage between the immature stages and the adult of an insect in which the young usu. resemble the adult — compare COMPLETE 5 **2** *of a football pass* **:** not legally caught — **in·com·plete·ly** *adv* — **in·com·plete·ness** *n*

in·com·pli·ant \ˌin-kəm-ˈplī-ənt\ *adj* (1647) **:** not compliant or pliable

in·com·pre·hen·si·ble \(ˌ)in-ˌkäm-pri-ˈhen(t)-sə-bəl\ *adj* [ME, fr. L *incomprehensibilis,* fr. *in-* + *comprehensibilis* comprehensible] (14c) **1** *archaic* **:** having or subject to no limits **2 :** impossible to comprehend **:** UNINTELLIGIBLE ⟨~ instructions⟩ — **in·com·pre·hen·si·bil·i·ty** \-ˌhen(t)-sə-ˈbi-lə-tē\ *n* — **in·com·pre·hen·si·ble·ness** *n* — **in·com·pre·hen·si·bly** \-ˈhen(t)-sə-blē\ *adv*

in·com·pre·hen·sion \-ˈhen(t)-shən\ *n* (1605) **:** lack of comprehension or understanding

in·com·press·ible \ˌin-kəm-ˈpre-sə-bəl\ *adj* (ca. 1736) **:** incapable of or resistant to compression

in·com·put·able \ˌin-kəm-ˈpyü-tə-bəl\ *adj* (1606) **:** not computable **:** very great — **in·com·put·ably** \-blē\ *adv*

in·con·ceiv·able \ˌin-kən-ˈsē-və-bəl\ *adj* (1624) **:** not conceivable: as **a :** impossible to comprehend **b :** UNBELIEVABLE — **in·con·ceiv·abil·i·ty** \-ˌsē-və-ˈbi-lə-tē\ *n* — **in·con·ceiv·able·ness** \-ˈsē-və-bəl-nəs\ *n* — **in·con·ceiv·ably** \-blē\ *adv*

in·con·cin·ni·ty \ˌin-kən-ˈsi-nə-tē\ *n* [L *inconcinnitas,* fr. *in-* + *concinnitas* concinnity] (ca. 1616) **:** lack of suitability or congruity **:** INELEGANCE

in·con·clu·sive \ˌin-kən-ˈklü-siv, -ziv\ *adj* (1707) **:** leading to no conclusion or definite result ⟨~ evidence⟩ ⟨an ~ argument⟩ — **in·con·clu·sive·ly** *adv* — **in·con·clu·sive·ness** *n*

in·con·dite \in-ˈkän-dət, -ˌdīt\ *adj* [L *inconditus,* fr. *in-* + *conditus,* pp. of *condere* to put together, fr. *com-* + *-dere* to put — more at DO] (1539) **:** badly put together **:** CRUDE ⟨~ prose⟩

in·con·for·mi·ty \ˌin-kən-ˈfȯr-mə-tē\ *n* (1594) **:** NONCONFORMITY

in·con·gru·ence \ˌin-kən-ˈgrü-ən(t)s, (ˌ)in-ˈkäŋ-grə-wən(t)s\ *n* (1610) **:** INCONGRUITY

in·con·gru·ent \-ənt, -wənt\ *adj* [ME, fr. L *incongruent-, incongruens,* fr. *in-* + *congruent-, congruens* congruent] (15c) **:** not congruent ⟨~ triangles⟩ — **in·con·gru·ent·ly** *adv*

in·con·gru·i·ty \ˌin-kən-ˈgrü-ə-tē, -ˌkän-\ *n, pl* **-ties** (ca. 1532) **1 :** the quality or state of being incongruous **2 :** something that is incongruous

in·con·gru·ous \(ˌ)in-ˈkäŋ-grə-wəs\ *adj* [LL *incongruus,* fr. L *in-* + *congruus* congruous] (1611) **:** lacking congruity: as **a :** not harmonious **:** INCOMPATIBLE ⟨~ colors⟩ **b :** not conforming **:** DISAGREEING ⟨conduct ~ with principle⟩ **c :** inconsistent within itself ⟨an ~ story⟩ **d :** lacking propriety **:** UNSUITABLE ⟨~ manners⟩ — **in·con·gru·ous·ly** *adv* — **in·con·gru·ous·ness** *n*

in·con·scient \(ˌ)in-ˈkän(t)-shənt\ *adj* [prob. fr. F, fr. *in-* + *conscient* mindful, fr. L *conscient-, consciens,* prp. of *conscire* to be conscious — more at CONSCIENCE] (1885) **:** UNCONSCIOUS, MINDLESS

in·con·sec·u·tive \ˌin-kən-ˈse-kyə-tiv, -kə-tiv\ *adj* (1831) **:** not consecutive ⟨on ~ days⟩

in·con·se·quence \(ˌ)in-ˈkän(t)-sə-ˌkwen(t)s, -si-kwən(t)s\ *n* (1579) **:** the quality or state of being inconsequent

in·con·se·quent \-ˌkwent, -kwənt\ *adj* [LL *inconsequent-, inconsequens,* fr. L *in-* + *consequent-, consequens* consequent] (1579) **1 a :** lacking reasonable sequence **:** ILLOGICAL **b :** INCONSECUTIVE **2 :** INCONSEQUENTIAL 2 **3 :** IRRELEVANT — **in·con·se·quent·ly** *adv*

in·con·se·quen·tial \(ˌ)in-ˌkän(t)-sə-ˈkwen(t)-shəl\ *adj* (1621) **1 a :** ILLOGICAL **b :** IRRELEVANT **2 :** of no significance **:** UNIMPORTANT — **in·con·se·quen·ti·al·i·ty** \-ˌkwen(t)-shē-ˈa-lə-tē\ *n* — **in·con·se·quen·tial·ly** \-ˈkwen(t)-shlē, -ˈkwen(t)-shə-lē\ *adv*

in·con·sid·er·able \ˌin-kən-ˈsi-dər-(ə-)bəl, -ˈsi-drə-bəl\ *adj* [F, fr. *in-* + *considerable* considerable, fr. ML *considerabilis*] (1637) **:** not considerable **:** SLIGHT, TRIVIAL ⟨the cost was not ~⟩ — **in·con·sid·er·able·ness** *n* — **in·con·sid·er·ably** \-blē\ *adv*

in·con·sid·er·ate \ˌin-kən-ˈsi-d(ə-)rət\ *adj* [ME *inconsyderatt,* fr. L *inconsideratus,* fr. *in-* + *consideratus* considerate] (15c) **1 a :** HEEDLESS, THOUGHTLESS **b :** careless of the rights or feelings of others **2 :** not adequately considered : ILL-ADVISED — **in·con·sid·er·ate·ly** *adv* — **in·con·sid·er·ate·ness** *n* — **in·con·sid·er·ation** \-ˌsi-də-ˈrā-shən\ *n*

in·con·sis·tence \ˌin-kən-ˈsis-tən(t)s\ *n* (1643) : INCONSISTENCY

in·con·sis·ten·cy \-tən(t)s-sē\ *n* (1647) **1** : an instance of being inconsistent **2** : the quality or state of being inconsistent

in·con·sis·tent \-tənt\ *adj* (1620) : lacking consistency: as **a** : not compatible with another fact or claim ⟨~ statements⟩ **b** : containing incompatible elements ⟨an ~ argument⟩ **c** : incoherent or illogical in thought or actions : CHANGEABLE **d** : not satisfiable by the same set of values for the unknowns ⟨~ equations⟩ ⟨~ inequalities⟩ — **in·con·sis·tent·ly** *adv*

in·con·sol·able \ˌin-kən-ˈsō-lə-bəl\ *adj* [L inconsolabilis, fr. in- + consolabilis consolable] (1596) : incapable of being consoled : DISCONSOLATE — **in·con·sol·able·ness** *n* — **in·con·sol·ably** \-blē\ *adv*

in·con·so·nance \(ˌ)in-ˈkän(t)-s(ə-)nən(t)s\ *n* (ca. 1811) : lack of consonance or harmony : DISAGREEMENT

in·con·so·nant \-s(ə-)nənt\ *adj* (1658) : not consonant : DISCORDANT

in·con·spic·u·ous \ˌin-kən-ˈspi-kyə-wəs, -kyü-əs\ *adj* [L inconspicuus, fr. in- + conspicuus conspicuous] (1648) : not readily noticeable — **in·con·spic·u·ous·ly** *adv* — **in·con·spic·u·ous·ness** *n*

in·con·stan·cy \(ˌ)in-ˈkän(t)-stən(t)-sē\ *n* (1526) : the quality or state of being inconstant

in·con·stant \-stənt\ *adj* [ME, fr. MF, fr. L inconstant-, inconstans, fr. in- + constant-, constans constant] (15c) : likely to change frequently without apparent or cogent reason — **in·con·stant·ly** *adv*
syn INCONSTANT, FICKLE, CAPRICIOUS, MERCURIAL, UNSTABLE mean lacking firmness or steadiness (as in purpose or devotion). INCONSTANT implies an incapacity for steadiness and an inherent tendency to change ⟨an *inconstant* friend⟩. FICKLE suggests unreliability because of perverse changeability and incapacity for steadfastness ⟨performers discover how *fickle* fans can be⟩. CAPRICIOUS suggests motivation by sudden whim or fancy and stresses unpredictability ⟨an utterly *capricious* critic⟩. MERCURIAL implies a rapid changeability in mood ⟨made anxious by her boss's *mercurial* temperament⟩. UNSTABLE implies an incapacity for remaining in a fixed position or steady course and applies esp. to a lack of emotional balance ⟨too *unstable* to hold a job⟩.

in·con·sum·able \ˌin-kən-ˈsü-mə-bəl\ *adj* (1646) : not capable of being consumed — **in·con·sum·ably** \-blē\ *adv*

in·con·test·able \ˌin-kən-ˈtes-tə-bəl\ *adj* [F, fr. in- + contestable, fr. contester to contest] (1673) : not contestable : INDISPUTABLE ⟨an ~ fact⟩ ⟨~ talent⟩ — **in·con·test·abil·i·ty** \-ˌtes-tə-ˈbi-lə-tē\ *n* — **in·con·test·ably** \-ˈtes-tə-blē\ *adv*

in·con·ti·nence \(ˌ)in-ˈkän-tə-nən(t)s\ *n* (14c) : the quality or state of being incontinent: as **a** : failure to restrain sexual appetite : UNCHASTITY **b** : inability of the body to control the evacuative functions of urination or defecation

in·con·ti·nen·cy \-nən(t)-sē\ *n* (15c) : INCONTINENCE

¹**in·con·ti·nent** \(ˌ)in-ˈkän-tə-nənt\ *adj* [ME, fr. AF or L; AF, fr. L incontinent-, incontinens, fr. in- + continent-, continens continent] (14c) : not continent: as **a** (1) : lacking self-restraint (2) : not being under control **b** : unable to retain urine or feces voluntarily

²**incontinent** *adv* [ME, fr. AF, fr. LL in continenti] (15c) : ¹INCONTINENTLY

¹**in·con·ti·nent·ly** *adv* (15c) : without delay : IMMEDIATELY

²**incontinently** *adv* (ca. 1552) : in an incontinent or unrestrained manner: as **a** : without moral restraint : LEWDLY **b** : without due or reasonable consideration

in·con·trol·la·ble \ˌin-kən-ˈtrō-lə-bəl\ *adj* (1599) : UNCONTROLLABLE

in·con·tro·vert·ible \(ˌ)in-ˌkän-trə-ˈvər-tə-bəl\ *adj* (1646) : not open to question : INDISPUTABLE ⟨~ facts⟩ — **in·con·tro·vert·ibly** \-blē\ *adv*

¹**in·con·ve·nience** \ˌin-kən-ˈvē-nyən(t)s\ *n* [ME, misfortune, inconsistency, fr. AF, fr. LL inconvenientia, fr. L inconvenient-, inconveniens] (1534) **1** : something that is inconvenient **2** : the quality or state of being inconvenient

²**inconvenience** *vt* **-nienced; -nienc·ing** (ca. 1656) : to subject to inconvenience : put to trouble ⟨sorry to ~ you⟩

in·con·ve·nien·cy \ˌin-kən-ˈvē-nyən(t)-sē\ *n, pl* **-cies** (ca. 1552) : INCONVENIENCE

in·con·ve·nient \ˌin-kən-ˈvē-nyənt\ *adj* [ME, incongruous, harmful, fr. AF, fr. L inconvenient-, inconveniens, fr. in- + convenient-, conveniens convenient] (1651) : not convenient esp. in giving trouble or annoyance : INOPPORTUNE ⟨an ~ time⟩ — **in·con·ve·nient·ly** *adv*

in·con·vert·ible \-ˈvər-tə-bəl\ *adj* [prob. fr. LL inconvertibilis, fr. L in- + convertibilis convertible] (1646) : not convertible: as **a** of paper money : not exchangeable for coin **b** of a currency : not exchangeable for a foreign currency — **in·con·vert·ibil·i·ty** \-ˌvər-tə-ˈbi-lə-tē\ *n* — **in·con·vert·ibly** \-ˈvər-tə-blē\ *adv*

in·con·vin·ci·ble \ˌin-kən-ˈvin(t)-sə-bəl\ *adj* (1674) : incapable of being convinced

in·co·or·di·na·tion \-(ˌ)kō-ˌȯr-də-ˈnā-shən\ *n* (1876) : lack of coordination; *esp* : ATAXIA

¹**in·cor·po·rate** \in-ˈkȯr-pə-ˌrāt\ *vb* **-rat·ed; -rat·ing** [ME, fr. LL incorporatus, pp. of incorporare, fr. L in- + corpor-, corpus body — more at MIDRIFF] *vt* (14c) **1 a** : to unite or work into something already existent so as to form an indistinguishable whole **b** : to blend or combine thoroughly **2 a** : to form into a legal corporation **b** : to admit to membership in a corporate body **3** : to give material form to : EMBODY ~ *vi* **1** : to unite in or as one body **2** : to form or become a corporation — **in·cor·po·ra·ble** \-p(ə-)rə-bəl\ *adj* — **in·cor·po·ra·tion** \-ˌkȯr-pə-ˈrā-shən\ *n* — **in·cor·po·ra·tive** \-ˈkȯr-pə-ˌrā-tiv, -p(ə-)rə-tiv\ *adj* — **in·cor·po·ra·tor** \-pə-ˌrā-tər\ *n*

²**in·cor·po·rate** \in-ˈkȯr-p(ə-)rət\ *adj* (14c) : INCORPORATED

incorporated *adj* (1599) **1** : united in one body **2** : formed into a legal corporation

in·cor·po·re·al \ˌin-(ˌ)kȯr-ˈpȯr-ē-əl\ *adj* [ME incorporealle, fr. AF incorporel, fr. L incorporeus, fr. in- + corporeus corporeal] (15c) **1** : not corporeal : having no material body or form **2** : of, relating to, or constituting a right that is based on property (as bonds or patents) which has no intrinsic value — **in·cor·po·re·al·ly** *adv*

in·cor·po·re·ity \(ˌ)in-ˌkȯr-pə-ˈrē-ə-tē\ *n* (1601) : the quality or state of being incorporeal : IMMATERIALITY

in·cor·rect \ˌin-kə-ˈrekt\ *adj* [ME, fr. MF or L; MF, fr. L incorrectus, fr. in- + correctus correct] (15c) **1** obs : not corrected or chastened **2 a**

: INACCURATE, FAULTY ⟨an ~ transcription⟩ **b** : not true : WRONG ⟨~ answers⟩ **3** : UNBECOMING, IMPROPER ⟨~ behavior⟩ — **in·cor·rect·ly** \-ˈrek(t)-lē\ *adv* — **in·cor·rect·ness** \-nəs\ *n*

in·cor·ri·gi·ble \(ˌ)in-ˈkȯr-ə-jə-bəl, -ˈkär-\ *adj* [ME, fr. LL incorrigibilis, fr. L in- + corrigere to correct — more at CORRECT] (14c) : incapable of being corrected or amended: as **a** (1) : not reformable : DEPRAVED (2) : DELINQUENT **b** : not manageable : UNRULY **c** : UNALTERABLE, INVETERATE — **in·cor·ri·gi·bil·i·ty** \-ˌkȯr-ə-jə-ˈbi-lə-tē, -ˌkär-\ *n* — **in·cor·ri·gi·ble·ness** \-ˈkȯr-ə-jə-bəl-nəs, -ˈkär-\ *n* — **in·cor·ri·gi·bly** \-blē\ *adv*

in·cor·rupt \ˌin-kə-ˈrəpt\ *also* **in·cor·rupt·ed** \-ˈrəp-təd\ *adj* [ME, fr. L incorruptus, fr. in- + corruptus corrupt] (14c) : free from corruption: as **a** obs : not affected with decay **b** : not defiled or depraved : UPRIGHT **c** : free from error — **in·cor·rupt·ly** \-ˈrəp(t)-lē\ *adv* — **in·cor·rupt·ness** \-nəs\ *n*

in·cor·rupt·ible \ˌin-kə-ˈrəp-tə-bəl\ *adj* (14c) : incapable of corruption: as **a** : not subject to decay or dissolution **b** : incapable of being bribed or morally corrupted — **in·cor·rupt·ibil·i·ty** \-ˌrəp-tə-ˈbi-lə-tē\ *n* — **incorruptible** *n* — **in·cor·rupt·ibly** \-ˈrəp-tə-blē\ *adv*

in·cor·rup·tion \ˌin-kə-ˈrəp-shən\ *n* (14c) archaic : the quality or state of being free from physical decay

incr abbr increase; increased

¹**in·crease** \in-ˈkrēs, ˈin-ˌ\ *vb* **in·creased; in·creas·ing** [ME encresen, fr. AF encreistre, fr. L increscere, fr. in- + crescere to grow — more at CRESCENT] *vi* (14c) **1** : to become progressively greater (as in size, amount, number, or intensity) **2** : to multiply by the production of young ~ *vt* **1** : to make greater : AUGMENT **2** obs : ENRICH — **in·creas·able** \-ˈkrē-sə-bəl, -ˌkrē-\ *adj* — **in·creas·er** *n*
syn INCREASE, ENLARGE, AUGMENT, MULTIPLY mean to make or become greater. INCREASE used intransitively implies progressive growth in size, amount, or intensity ⟨his waistline *increased* with age⟩; used transitively it may imply simple not necessarily progressive addition ⟨*increased* her landholdings⟩. ENLARGE implies expansion or extension that makes greater in size or capacity ⟨*enlarged* the kitchen⟩. AUGMENT implies addition to what is already well grown or well developed ⟨the inheritance *augmented* his fortune⟩. MULTIPLY implies increase in number by natural generation or by indefinite repetition of a process ⟨with each attempt the problems *multiplied*⟩.

²**in·crease** \ˈin-ˌkrēs, in-ˈ\ *n* (14c) **1** : the act or process of increasing: as **a** : addition or enlargement in size, extent, or quantity **b** obs : PROPAGATION **2** : something that is added to an original stock or amount by augmentation or growth (as offspring, produce, profit) — **on the increase** : becoming greater (as in size, number, or amount) : INCREASING ⟨crime is on the increase⟩

increased *adj* (1540) : made or become greater : AUGMENTED ⟨at ~ risk for heart disease⟩

in·creas·ing·ly \in-ˈkrē-siŋ-lē, ˈin-ˌkrē-\ *adv* (14c) : to an increasing degree ⟨an ~ dangerous situation⟩

in·cre·ate \ˌin-krē-ˈāt, in-ˈkrē-ət\ *adj* [ME increat, fr. LL increatus, fr. L in- + creatus, pp. of creare to create] (15c) : UNCREATED

in·cred·i·ble \(ˌ)in-ˈkre-də-bəl\ *adj* [ME, fr. L incredibilis, fr. in- + credibilis credible] (15c) **1** : too extraordinary and improbable to be believed ⟨making ~ claims⟩ **2** : AMAZING, EXTRAORDINARY ⟨~ skill⟩ ⟨an ~ appetite⟩ ⟨met an ~ woman⟩ — **in·cred·i·bil·i·ty** \-ˌkre-də-ˈbi-lə-tē\ *n* — **in·cred·i·ble·ness** \-ˈkre-də-bəl-nəs\ *n*

in·cred·i·bly \-blē\ *adv* (ca. 1500) **1** : in an incredible manner **2** : EXTREMELY ⟨~ difficult⟩

in·cre·du·li·ty \ˌin-kri-ˈdü-lə-tē, -ˈdyü-\ *n* (15c) : the quality or state of being incredulous : DISBELIEF

in·cred·u·lous \(ˌ)in-ˈkre-jə-ləs, -dyə-ləs\ *adj* [L incredulus, fr. in- + credulus credulous] (1579) **1** : unwilling to admit or accept what is offered as true : not credulous : SKEPTICAL **2** : INCREDIBLE 1 **3** : expressing incredulity ⟨an ~ stare⟩ — **in·cred·u·lous·ly** *adv*
usage Sense 2 was revived in the 20th century after a couple of centuries of disuse. Although it is a sense with good literary precedent—among others Shakespeare used it—many people think it is a result of confusion with *incredible*, which is still the usual word in this sense.

in·cre·ment \ˈiŋ-krə-mənt, ˈin-\ *n* [ME, fr. AF, fr. L incrementum, fr. in- crescere to increase] (15c) **1** : the action or process of increasing esp. in quantity or value : ENLARGEMENT **2 a** : something gained or added **b** : one of a series of regular consecutive additions **c** : a minute increase in quantity **3** : the amount or degree by which something changes; *esp* : the amount of positive or negative change in the value of one or more of a set of variables

in·cre·men·tal \ˌiŋ-krə-ˈmen-t³l, ˌin-\ *adj* (1696) : of, relating to, being, or occurring in esp. small increments ⟨~ additions⟩ ⟨~ change⟩ — **in·cre·men·tal·ly** \-ˈt³l-ē\ *adv*

in·cre·men·tal·ism \ˌiŋ-krə-ˈmen-tə-ˌli-zəm\ *n* (1966) : a policy or advocacy of a policy of political or social change by degrees : GRADUALISM — **in·cre·men·tal·ist** \-tə-list\ *n*

incremental repetition *n* (1918) : repetition in each stanza (as of a ballad) of part of the preceding stanza usu. with a slight change in wording for dramatic effect

in·cres·cent \in-ˈkre-s³nt\ *adj* [L increscent-, increscens, prp. of increscere to increase — more at INCREASE] (ca. 1658) : becoming gradually greater : WAXING ⟨the ~ moon⟩

in·crim·i·nate \in-ˈkri-mə-ˌnāt\ *vt* **-nat·ed; -nat·ing** [LL incriminatus, pp. of incriminare, fr. L in- + crimin-, crimen crime] (ca. 1736) : to charge with or show evidence or proof of involvement in a crime or fault — **in·crim·i·na·tion** \-ˌkri-mə-ˈnā-shən\ *n* — **in·crim·i·na·to·ry** \-ˈkrim-nə-ˌtȯr-ē, -ˈkri-mə-\ *adj*

incrust var of ENCRUST

in·crus·ta·tion \ˌin-ˌkrəs-ˈtā-shən\ *also* **en·crus·ta·tion** \ˌin-, ˌen-\ *n* [L incrustation-, incrustatio, fr. incrustare to encrust] (1644) **1 a** : a crust or hard coating **b** : a growth or accumulation (as of habits, opinions, or customs) resembling a crust **2** : the act of encrusting **3 a** : OVERLAY a **b** : INLAY

\ə\ abut \ᵊ\ kitten, F table \ər\ further \a\ ash \ā\ ace \ä\ mop, mar
\au̇\ out \ch\ chin \e\ bet \ē\ easy \g\ go \i\ hit \ī\ ice \j\ job
\ŋ\ sing \ō\ go \ȯ\ law \ȯi\ boy \th\ thin \t͟h\ the \ü\ loot \u̇\ foot
\y\ yet \zh\ vision, beige \ḵ, ⁿ, œ, ɶ, �\ see Guide to Pronunciation

in·cu·bate \ˈiŋ-kyə-ˌbāt, ˈin-\ *vb* **-bat·ed; -bat·ing** [L *incubatus,* pp. of *incubare,* fr. *in-* + *cubare* to lie] *vt* (1641) **1 a :** to sit on (eggs) so as to hatch by the warmth of the body **b :** to maintain (as an embryo or a chemically active system) under conditions favorable for hatching, development, or reaction **2 :** to cause or aid the development of ⟨~ an idea⟩ ~ *vi* **1 :** to sit on eggs **2 :** to undergo incubation : DEVELOP — **in·cu·ba·tive** \-ˌbā-tiv\ *adj* — **in·cu·ba·to·ry** \-kyə-bə-ˌtȯr-ē, -ˌbā-tə-rē\ *adj*

in·cu·ba·tion \ˌiŋ-kyə-ˈbā-shən, ˌin-\ *n* (1646) **1 :** the act or process of incubating **2 :** INCUBATION PERIOD

incubation period *n* (1879) **:** the period between the infection of an individual by a pathogen and the manifestation of the illness or disease it causes

in·cu·ba·tor \ˈiŋ-kyə-ˌbā-tər, ˈin-\ *n* (1857) **:** one that incubates: as **a :** an apparatus by which eggs are hatched artificially **b :** an apparatus with a chamber used to provide controlled environmental conditions esp. for the cultivation of microorganisms or the care and protection of premature or sick babies **c :** an organization or place that aids the development of new business ventures esp. by providing low-cost commercial space, management assistance, or shared services

in·cu·bus \ˈiŋ-kyə-bəs, ˈin-\ *n, pl* **-bi** \-ˌbī, -ˌbē\ *also* **-bus·es** [ME, fr. LL, fr. L *incubare*] (13c) **1 :** an evil spirit that lies on persons in their sleep; *esp* **:** one that has sexual intercourse with women while they are sleeping — compare SUCCUBUS **2 :** NIGHTMARE 2 **3 :** one that oppresses or burdens like a nightmare

in·cul·cate \in-ˈkəl-ˌkāt, ˈin-(ˌ)\ *vt* **-cat·ed; -cat·ing** [L *inculcatus,* pp. of *inculcare,* lit., to tread on, fr. *in-* + *calcare* to trample, fr. *calc-, calx* heel] (1539) **:** to teach and impress by frequent repetitions or admonitions ***syn*** see IMPLANT — **in·cul·ca·tion** \ˌin-(ˌ)kəl-ˈkā-shən\ *n* — **in·cul·ca·tor** \in-ˈkəl-ˌkā-tər, ˈin-(ˌ)\ *n*

in·cul·pa·ble \(ˌ)in-ˈkəl-pə-bəl\ *adj* (15c) **:** free from guilt : BLAMELESS

in·cul·pate \in-ˈkəl-ˌpāt, ˈin-(ˌ)\ *vt* **-pat·ed; -pat·ing** [LL *inculpatus,* fr. L *in-* + *culpatus,* pp. of *culpare* to blame, fr. *culpa* guilt] (1799) **:** INCRIMINATE — **in·cul·pa·tion** \ˌin-(ˌ)kəl-ˈpā-shən\ *n* — **in·cul·pa·to·ry** \in-ˈkəl-pə-ˌtȯr-ē\ *adj*

in·cult \in-ˈkəlt\ *adj* [L *incultus,* fr. *in-* + *cultus,* pp. of *colere* to cultivate — more at WHEEL] (1599) **:** COARSE, UNCULTURED

in·cum·ben·cy \in-ˈkəm-bən(t)-sē\ *n, pl* **-cies** (ca. 1608) **1 :** something that is incumbent : DUTY **2 :** the quality or state of being incumbent **3 :** the sphere of action or period of office of an incumbent

[1]**in·cum·bent** \in-ˈkəm-bənt\ *n* [ME, fr. AF, fr. L *incumbent-, incumbens,* prp. of *incumbere* to lie down on, fr. *in-* + *-cumbere* to lie down; akin to *cubare* to lie] (15c) **1 :** the holder of an office or ecclesiastical benefice **2 :** one that occupies a particular position or place

[2]**incumbent** *adj* (1567) **1 :** imposed as a duty : OBLIGATORY ⟨~ on us to take action⟩ **2 :** having the status of an incumbent ⟨the team's ~ third baseman⟩; *esp* **:** occupying a specified office **3 :** lying or resting on something else **4 :** bent over so as to rest on or touch an underlying surface

in·cum·ber *archaic var of* ENCUMBER

in·cu·na·ble \in-ˈkyü-nə-bəl\ *n* [F, fr. NL *incunabulum*] (1886) **:** INCUNABULUM

in·cu·nab·u·lum \ˌin-kyə-ˈna-byə-ləm, ˌiŋ-\ *n, pl* **-la** \-lə\ [NL, fr. L *incunabula,* pl., bands holding the baby in a cradle, fr. *in-* + *cunae* cradle] (1849) **1 :** a book printed before 1501 **2 :** a work of art or of industry of an early period

in·cur \in-ˈkər\ *vt* **in·curred; in·cur·ring** [ME *incurren,* fr. L *incurrere,* lit., to run into, fr. *in-* + *currere* to run — more at CAR] (15c) **:** to become liable or subject to : bring down upon oneself ⟨~ expenses⟩

in·cur·able \(ˌ)in-ˈkyu̇r-ə-bəl\ *adj* [ME, fr. AF or LL; AF, fr. LL *incurabilis,* fr. L *in-* + *curabilis* curable] (14c) **:** not curable ⟨an ~ disease⟩; *broadly* **:** not likely to be changed or corrected ⟨~ optimism⟩ — **incurable** *n* — **in·cur·ably** \-blē\ *adv*

in·cu·ri·ous \(ˌ)in-ˈkyu̇r-ē-əs\ *adj* [L *incuriosus,* fr. *in-* + *curiosus* curious] (ca. 1618) **:** lacking a normal or usual curiosity : UNINTERESTED ⟨a blank ~ stare⟩ ***syn*** see INDIFFERENT — **in·cu·ri·os·i·ty** \-ˌkyu̇r-ē-ˈä-sə-tē\ *n* — **in·cu·ri·ous·ly** \-ˈkyu̇r-ē-əs-lē\ *adv* — **in·cu·ri·ous·ness** *n*

in·cur·rence \in-ˈkər-ən(t)s, -ˈkə-rən(t)s\ *n* (ca. 1656) **:** the act or process of incurring

in·cur·rent \-ənt, -rənt\ *adj* [L *incurrent-, incurrens,* prp. of *incurrere*] (ca. 1856) **:** giving passage to a current that flows inward

in·cur·sion \in-ˈkər-zhən\ *n* [ME, fr. MF or L; MF, fr. L *incursion-, incursio,* fr. *incurrere*] (15c) **1 :** a hostile entrance into a territory : RAID **2 :** an entering in or into (as an activity or undertaking) ⟨his only ~ into the arts⟩

in·cur·vate \ˈin-kər-ˌvāt, (ˌ)in-ˈkər-\ *vt* **-vat·ed; -vat·ing** (1578) **:** to cause to curve inward : BEND — **in·cur·vate** \ˈin-ˌkər-ˌvāt, (ˌ)in-ˈkər-vət\ *adj* — **in·cur·va·tion** \ˌin-ˌkər-ˈvā-shən\ *n* — **in·cur·va·ture** \(ˌ)in-ˈkər-və-ˌchu̇r, -chər, -ˌtyu̇r, -ˌtu̇r\ *n*

in·curve \(ˌ)in-ˈkərv, ˈin-ˌ\ *vt* [L *incurvare,* fr. *in-* + *curvare* to curve, fr. *curvus* curved — more at CURVE] (1610) **:** to bend so as to curve inward

in·cus \ˈiŋ-kəs\ *n, pl* **in·cu·des** \iŋ-ˈkyü-(ˌ)dēz, ˈiŋ-kyə-ˌdēz\ [NL, fr. L, anvil, fr. *incudere*] (1615) **:** the middle bone of a chain of three small bones in the ear of a mammal — called also *anvil;* see EAR illustration

in·cuse \in-ˈkyüz, -ˈkyüs\ *adj* [L *incusus,* pp. of *incudere* to stamp, strike, fr. *in-* + *cudere* to beat — more at HEW] (1818) **:** formed by stamping or punching in — used chiefly of old coins or features of their design

ind *abbr* **1** independent **2** index **3** industrial; industry

[1]**Ind** \ˈind, ˈīnd\ *n* (13c) **1** *archaic* **:** India **2** *obs* **:** Indies

[2]**Ind** *abbr* **1** Indian **2** Indiana

IND *abbr* investigational new drug

ind- *or* **indo-** *comb form* [ISV, fr. L *indicum* — more at INDIGO] **1 :** indigo ⟨*ind*oxyl⟩ **2 :** resembling indigo (as in color) ⟨*indo*phenol⟩

in·da·ba \in-ˈdä-bə\ *n* [Zulu, matter for discussion, affair] (1827) *chiefly SoAfr* **:** CONFERENCE, PARLEY

in·da·gate \ˈin-də-ˌgāt\ *vt* **-gat·ed; -gat·ing** [L *indagatus,* pp. of *indagare,* fr. *indago* ring of hunters encircling game, act of searching, fr. OL *indu* in + L *agere* to drive — more at END-, AGENT] (ca. 1623) **:** to search into : INVESTIGATE — **in·da·ga·tion** \ˌin-də-ˈgā-shən\ *n* — **in·da·ga·tor** \ˈin-də-ˌgā-tər\ *n*

IndE *abbr* industrial engineer

in·debt·ed \in-ˈde-təd\ *adj* [ME *indetted,* fr. AF *endetté,* pp. of *endetter* to run into debt, fr. *en-* + *dette* debt] (13c) **1 :** owing gratitude or recognition to another : BEHOLDEN **2 :** owing money

in·debt·ed·ness *n* (1647) **1 :** the condition of being indebted **2 :** something (as an amount of money) that is owed

in·de·cen·cy \(ˌ)in-ˈdē-sᵊn(t)-sē\ *n* (1589) **1 :** the quality or state of being indecent **2 :** something (as a word or action) that is indecent

in·de·cent \-sᵊnt\ *adj* [MF or L; MF *indécent,* fr. L *indecent-, indecens,* fr. *in-* + *decent-, decens* decent] (ca. 1587) **:** not decent: as **a :** grossly improper or offensive ⟨~ language⟩ **b :** UNSEEMLY, INAPPROPRIATE ⟨he took ~ pleasure in her troubles⟩ — **in·de·cent·ly** *adv*

indecent assault *n* (1855) **:** an offensive sexual act or series of acts exclusive of rape committed against another person without consent

indecent exposure *n* (1828) **:** intentional exposure of part of one's body (as the genitals) in a place where such exposure is likely to be an offense against the generally accepted standards of decency

in·de·ci·pher·able \ˌin-di-ˈsī-f(ə-)rə-bəl\ *adj* (1802) **:** incapable of being deciphered

in·de·ci·sion \ˌin-di-ˈsi-zhən\ *n* [F *indécision,* fr. *indécis* undecided, fr. LL *indecisus,* fr. L *in-* + *decisus,* pp. of *decidere* to decide] (ca. 1763) **:** a wavering between two or more possible courses of action : IRRESOLUTION

in·de·ci·sive \ˌin-di-ˈsī-siv\ *adj* (1726) **1 :** not decisive : INCONCLUSIVE ⟨an ~ battle⟩ **2 :** marked by or prone to indecision : IRRESOLUTE ⟨an ~ state of mind⟩ **3 :** not clearly marked out : INDEFINITE — **in·de·ci·sive·ly** *adv* — **in·de·ci·sive·ness** *n*

in·de·clin·able \ˌin-di-ˈklī-nə-bəl\ *adj* [ME, fr. LL *indeclinabilis,* fr. L *in-* + LL *declinabilis* capable of being inflected, fr. L *declinare* to inflect — more at DECLINE] (14c) **:** having no grammatical inflections

in·de·com·pos·able \ˌin-ˌdē-kəm-ˈpō-zə-bəl\ *adj* (1807) **:** not capable of being separated into component parts or elements

in·de·co·rous \(ˌ)in-ˈde-k(ə-)rəs; ˌin-di-ˈkȯr-əs\ *adj* [L *indecorus,* fr. *in-* + *decorus* decorous] (1668) **:** not decorous : conflicting with accepted standards of good conduct or good taste — **in·de·co·rous·ly** *adv* — **in·de·co·rous·ness** *n*

syn INDECOROUS, IMPROPER, UNSEEMLY, UNBECOMING, INDELICATE mean not conforming to what is accepted as right, fitting, or in good taste. INDECOROUS suggests a violation of accepted standards of good manners ⟨*indecorous* behavior⟩. IMPROPER applies to a broader range of transgressions of rules not only of social behavior but of ethical practice or logical procedure or prescribed method ⟨*improper* use of campaign contributions⟩. UNSEEMLY adds a suggestion of special inappropriateness to a situation or an offensiveness to good taste ⟨remarried with *unseemly* haste⟩. UNBECOMING suggests behavior or language that does not suit one's character or status ⟨conduct *unbecoming* to an officer⟩. INDELICATE implies a lack of modesty or of tact or of refined perception of feeling ⟨*indelicate* expressions for bodily functions⟩.

in·de·co·rum \ˌin-di-ˈkȯr-əm\ *n* [L, neut. of *indecorus*] (1575) **1 :** something that is indecorous **2 :** lack of decorum : IMPROPRIETY

in·deed \in-ˈdēd\ *adv* (14c) **1 :** without any question : TRULY, UNDENIABLY — often used interjectionally to express irony or disbelief or surprise **2 :** in reality **3 :** all things considered : as a matter of fact

in·de·fat·i·ga·ble \ˌin-di-ˈfa-ti-gə-bəl\ *adj* [MF, fr. L *indefatigabilis,* fr. *in-* + *defatigare* to fatigue, fr. *de-* + *fatigare* to fatigue] (1608) **:** incapable of being fatigued : UNTIRING ⟨an ~ worker⟩ — **in·de·fat·i·ga·bil·i·ty** \-ˌfa-ti-gə-ˈbi-lə-tē\ *n* — **in·de·fat·i·ga·ble·ness** \-ˈfa-ti-gə-bəl-nəs\ *n* — **in·de·fat·i·ga·bly** \-blē\ *adv*

in·de·fea·si·ble \-ˈfē-zə-bəl\ *adj* (1548) **:** not capable of being annulled or voided or undone ⟨an ~ right⟩ — **in·de·fea·si·bil·i·ty** \-ˌfē-zə-ˈbi-lə-tē\ *n* — **in·de·fea·si·bly** \-ˈfē-zə-blē\ *adv*

in·de·fec·ti·ble \-ˈfek-tə-bəl\ *adj* (1659) **1 :** not subject to failure or decay : LASTING **2 :** free of faults : FLAWLESS — **in·de·fec·ti·bil·i·ty** \-ˌfek-tə-ˈbi-lə-tē\ *n* — **in·de·fec·ti·bly** \-ˈfek-tə-blē\ *adv*

in·de·fen·si·ble \-ˈfen(t)-sə-bəl\ *adj* (1529) **1 a :** incapable of being maintained as right or valid : UNTENABLE **b :** incapable of being justified or excused : INEXCUSABLE ⟨~ comments⟩ **2 :** incapable of being protected against physical attack — **in·de·fen·si·bil·i·ty** \-ˌfen(t)-sə-ˈbi-lə-tē\ *n* — **in·de·fen·si·bly** \-ˈfen(t)-sə-blē\ *adv*

in·de·fin·able \-ˈfī-nə-bəl\ *adj* (1810) **:** incapable of being precisely described or analyzed ⟨~ feelings⟩ ⟨an ~ concept⟩ — **in·de·fin·abil·i·ty** \-ˌfī-nə-ˈbi-lə-tē\ *n* — **indefinable** *n* — **in·de·fin·able·ness** \-ˈfī-nə-bəl-nəs\ *n* — **in·de·fin·ably** \-blē\ *adv*

in·def·i·nite \(ˌ)in-ˈdef-nət, -ˈde-fə-\ *adj* [L *indefinitus,* fr. *in-* + *definitus* definite] (1530) **:** not definite: as **a :** typically designating an unidentified, generic, or unfamiliar person or thing ⟨the ~ articles *a* and *an*⟩ ⟨~ pronouns⟩ **b :** not precise : VAGUE **c :** having no exact limits — **indefinite** *n* — **in·def·i·nite·ly** *adv* — **in·def·i·nite·ness** *n*

indefinite integral *n* (1831) **:** any function whose derivative is a given function

in·de·his·cent \ˌin-di-ˈhi-sᵊnt\ *adj* (1830) **:** remaining closed at maturity ⟨~ fruits⟩ — **in·de·his·cence** \-sᵊn(t)s\ *n*

in·del·i·ble \in-ˈde-lə-bəl\ *adj* [ME *indelyble,* fr. ML *indelibilis,* alter. of L *indelebilis,* fr. *in-* + *delēre* to delete] (15c) **1 a :** that cannot be removed, washed away, or erased **b :** making marks that cannot easily be removed ⟨an ~ pencil⟩ **2 a :** LASTING ⟨~ memories⟩ **b :** UNFORGETTABLE, MEMORABLE ⟨an ~ performance⟩ — **in·del·i·bil·i·ty** \(ˌ)in-ˌde-lə-ˈbi-lə-tē\ *n* — **in·del·i·bly** \in-ˈde-lə-blē\ *adv*

in·del·i·ca·cy \(ˌ)in-ˈde-li-kə-sē\ *n* (1712) **1 :** the quality or state of being indelicate **2 :** something that is indelicate

in·del·i·cate \-li-kət\ *adj* (1742) **:** not delicate: **a (1) :** lacking in or offending against propriety : IMPROPER **(2) :** verging on the indecent : COARSE **b :** marked by a lack of feeling for the sensibilities of others : TACTLESS ***syn*** see INDECOROUS — **in·del·i·cate·ly** *adv* — **in·del·i·cate·ness** *n*

in·dem·ni·fi·ca·tion \in-ˌdem-nə-fə-ˈkā-shən\ *n* (1732) **1 a :** the action of indemnifying **b :** the condition of being indemnified **2 :** INDEMNITY 2b

in·dem·ni·fy \in-ˈdem-nə-ˌfī\ *vt* **-fied; -fy·ing** [L *indemnis* unharmed, fr. *in-* + *damnum* damage] (1611) **1 :** to secure against hurt, loss, or damage **2 :** to make compensation to for incurred hurt, loss, or damage ***syn*** see PAY — **in·dem·ni·fi·er** \-ˌfī(-ə)r\ *n*

in·dem·ni·ty \in-ˈdem-nə-tē\ *n, pl* **-ties** (15c) **1 a :** security against hurt, loss, or damage **b :** exemption from incurred penalties or liabilities **2 a :** INDEMNIFICATION 1 **b :** something that indemnifies **3 :** FEE-FOR-SERVICE — usu. used attributively ⟨an ~ plan⟩

in·de·mon·stra·ble \ˌin-di-ˈmän(t)-strə-bəl, (ˌ)in-ˈde-mən-strə-\ *adj* (1570) **:** incapable of being demonstrated **:** not subject to proof — **in·de·mon·stra·bly** \-blē\ *adv*

[1]**in·dent** \in-ˈdent\ *vb* [ME, fr. AF *endenter,* fr. *en-* + *dent* tooth, fr. L *dent-, dens* — more at TOOTH] *vt* (14c) **1 a :** to divide (a document) so as to produce sections with irregular edges that can be matched for authentication **b :** to draw up (as a deed) in two or more exactly corresponding copies **2 :** to notch the edge of **:** make jagged **3 :** INDENTURE **4 :** to set (as a line of a paragraph) in from the margin **5** *chiefly Brit* **:** to order by an indent ~ *vi* **1** *obs* **:** to make a formal or express agreement **2 :** to form an indentation **3** *chiefly Brit* **:** to make out an indent for something — **in·dent·er** *n* — **indent on 1** *chiefly Brit* **:** to make a requisition on **2** *chiefly Brit* **:** to draw on

[2]**in·dent** \in-ˈdent, ˈin-ˌ\ *n* (15c) **1 a :** INDENTURE 1 **b :** a certificate issued by the U.S. at the close of the American Revolution for the principal or interest on the public debt **2** *chiefly Brit* **a :** an official requisition **b :** a purchase order for goods esp. when sent from a foreign country **3 :** INDENTION

[3]**in·dent** \in-ˈdent\ *vt* [ME *endenten,* fr. *en-* + *denten* to dent] (15c) **1 :** to force inward so as to form a depression **2 :** to form a dent in — **in·dent·er** *n*

[4]**in·dent** \in-ˈdent, ˈin-ˌ\ *n* (1596) **:** INDENTATION

in·den·ta·tion \ˌin-ˌden-ˈtā-shən\ *n* (ca. 1728) **1 a :** an angular cut in an edge **:** NOTCH **b :** a recess in a surface **2 :** the action of indenting **:** the condition of being indented **3 :** DENT **4 :** INDENTION 2b

in·den·tion \in-ˈden(t)-shən\ *n* (1763) **1** *archaic* **:** INDENTATION 1 **2 a :** the action of indenting **:** the condition of being indented **b :** the blank space produced by indenting

[1]**in·den·ture** \in-ˈden-chər\ *n* [ME *endenture,* fr. AF, fr. *endenter*] (14c) **1 a (1) :** a document or a section of a document that is indented **(2) :** a formal or official document usu. executed in two or more copies **(3) :** a contract binding one person to work for another for a given period of time — often used in pl. **b :** a formal certificate (as an inventory or voucher) prepared for purposes of control **c :** a document stating the terms under which a security (as a bond) is issued **2 :** INDENTATION 1 **3** [[3]*indent*] **:** DENT

[2]**indenture** *vt* **in·den·tured; in·den·tur·ing** \-ˈden-ch(ə-)riŋ\ (1676) **:** to bind (as an apprentice) by or as if by indentures

indentured servant *n* (1723) **:** a person who signs and is bound by indentures to work for another for a specified time esp. in return for payment of travel expenses and maintenance

in·de·pen·dence \ˌin-də-ˈpen-dən(t)s\ *n* (1640) **1 :** the quality or state of being independent **2** *archaic* **:** COMPETENCE 1

Independence Day *n* (1791) **:** a civil holiday for the celebration of the anniversary of the beginnings of national independence; *specif* **:** July 4 observed as a legal holiday in the U.S. in commemoration of the adoption of the Declaration of Independence in 1776

in·de·pen·den·cy \ˌin-də-ˈpen-dən(t)-sē\ *n* (ca. 1611) **1 :** INDEPENDENCE 1 **2** *cap* **:** the Independent polity or movement **3 :** an independent political unit

[1]**in·de·pen·dent** \ˌin-də-ˈpen-dənt\ *adj* (1611) **1 :** not dependent: as **a (1) :** not subject to control by others **:** SELF-GOVERNING **(2) :** not affiliated with a larger controlling unit ⟨an ~ bookstore⟩ **b (1) :** not requiring or relying on something else **:** not contingent ⟨an ~ conclusion⟩ **(2) :** not looking to others for one's opinions or for guidance in conduct **(3) :** not bound by or committed to a political party **c (1) :** not requiring or relying on others (as for care or livelihood) ⟨~ of her parents⟩ **(2) :** being enough to free one from the necessity of working for a living ⟨a person of ~ means⟩ **d :** showing a desire for freedom ⟨an ~ manner⟩ **e (1) :** not determined by or capable of being deduced or derived from or expressed in terms of members (as axioms or equations) of the set under consideration; *esp* **:** having linear independence ⟨an ~ set of vectors⟩ **(2) :** having the property that the joint probability (as of events or samples) or the joint probability density function (as of random variables) equals the product of the probabilities or probability density functions of separate occurrence **2** *cap* **:** of or relating to the Independents **3 a :** MAIN 5 ⟨an ~ clause⟩ **b :** neither deducible from nor incompatible with another statement ⟨~ postulates⟩ ***syn*** see FREE — **in·de·pen·dent·ly** *adv*

[2]**independent** *n* (1644) **1** *cap* **:** a sectarian of an English religious movement for congregational autonomy originating in the late 16th century, giving rise to Congregationalists, Baptists, and Friends, and forming one of the major political groupings of the period of Cromwell **2 :** one that is independent; *esp, often cap* **:** one that is not bound by or definitively committed to a political party

independent assortment *n* (1941) **:** formation of random combinations of chromosomes in meiosis and of genes on different pairs of homologous chromosomes by the passage according to the laws of probability of one of each diploid pair of homologous chromosomes into each gamete independently of each other pair

independent variable *n* (1816) **:** a mathematical variable that is independent of the other variables in an expression or function and whose value determines one or more of the values of the other variables

in–depth \(ˈ)in-ˈdepth\ *adj* (1965) **:** COMPREHENSIVE ⟨an ~ study⟩

in·de·scrib·able \ˌin-di-ˈskrī-bə-bəl\ *adj* (1751) **1 :** that cannot be described ⟨an ~ sensation⟩ **2 :** surpassing description ⟨~ joy⟩ — **in·de·scrib·able·ness** *n* — **in·de·scrib·ably** \-blē\ *adv*

in·de·struc·ti·ble \-ˈstrək-tə-bəl\ *adj* [prob. fr. LL *indestructibilis,* fr. L *in-* + *destructus,* pp. of *destruere* to tear down — more at DESTROY] (1667) **:** incapable of being destroyed, ruined, or rendered ineffective — **in·de·struc·ti·bil·i·ty** \-ˌstrək-tə-ˈbi-lə-tē\ *n* — **in·de·struc·ti·ble·ness** \-ˈstrək-tə-bəl-nəs\ *n* — **in·de·struc·ti·bly** \-blē\ *adv*

in·de·ter·min·able \ˌin-di-ˈtərm-nə-bəl, -ˈtər-mə-\ *adj* (15c) **1 :** incapable of being definitely decided or settled **2 :** incapable of being definitely fixed or ascertained — **in·de·ter·min·ably** \-blē\ *adv*

in·de·ter·mi·na·cy \-nə-sē\ *n* (1649) **:** the quality or state of being indeterminate

indeterminacy principle *n* (ca. 1928) **:** UNCERTAINTY PRINCIPLE

in·de·ter·mi·nate \ˌin-di-ˈtərm-nət, -ˈtər-mə-\ *adj* [ME *indeterminat,* fr. LL *indeterminatus,* fr. L *in-* + *determinatus,* pp. of *determinare* to determine] (14c) **1 a :** not definitely or precisely determined or fixed **:** VAGUE **b :** not known in advance **c :** not leading to a definite end or result **2 :** having an infinite number of solutions ⟨a system of ~ equations⟩ **3 :** being one of the seven undefined mathematical expressions

$$\frac{0}{0}, \frac{\infty}{\infty}, \infty \cdot 0, 1^{\infty}, 0^{0}, \infty^{0}, \infty - \infty$$

4 : characterized by sequential flowering from the lateral or basal buds to the central or uppermost buds; *also* **:** characterized by growth in which the main stem continues to elongate indefinitely without being limited by a terminal inflorescence — compare DETERMINATE 4 — **in·de·ter·mi·nate·ly** *adv* — **in·de·ter·mi·nate·ness** *n* — **in·de·ter·mi·na·tion** \-ˌtər-mə-ˈnā-shən\ *n*

in·de·ter·min·ism \-ˈtər-mə-ˌni-zəm\ *n* (1874) **1 a :** a theory that the will is free and that deliberate choice and actions are not determined by or predictable from antecedent causes **b :** a theory that holds that not every event has a cause **2 :** the quality or state of being indeterminate; *esp* **:** UNPREDICTABILITY — **in·de·ter·min·ist** \-ˈtərm-nist, -ˈtər-mə-\ *n* — **in·de·ter·min·is·tic** \-ˌtər-mə-ˈnis-tik\ *adj*

[1]**in·dex** \ˈin-ˌdeks\ *n, pl* **in·dex·es** *or* **in·di·ces** \-də-ˌsēz\ [L *indic-, index,* fr. *indicare* to indicate] (1561) **1 a :** a device (as the pointer on a scale or the gnomon of a sundial) that serves to indicate a value or quantity **b :** something (as a physical feature or a mode of expression) that leads one to a particular fact or conclusion **:** INDICATION **2 :** a list (as of bibliographical information or citations to a body of literature) arranged usu. in alphabetical order of some specified datum (as author, subject, or keyword): as **a :** a list of items (as topics or names) treated in a printed work that gives for each item the page number where it may be found **b :** THUMB INDEX **c :** a bibliographical analysis of groups of publications that is usu. published periodically **d :** a list of publicly traded companies and their stock prices **3 :** a list of restricted or prohibited material; *specif, cap* **:** a formerly published list of books the reading of which was prohibited or restricted for Roman Catholics by the church authorities **4** *pl usu* ***indices*** **:** a number or symbol or expression (as an exponent) associated with another to indicate a mathematical operation to be performed or to indicate use or position in an arrangement ⟨3 is the ~ of the expression $\sqrt[3]{5}$ to indicate the cube root of 5⟩ **5 :** a character ☞ used to direct attention to a note or paragraph — called also *fist* **6 a :** a number (as a ratio) derived from a series of observations and used as an indicator or measure; *specif* **:** INDEX NUMBER **b :** the ratio of one dimension of a thing (as an anatomical structure) to another dimension

[2]**index** *vt* (1720) **1 a :** to provide with an index **b :** to list in an index ⟨all persons and places mentioned are carefully ~*ed*⟩ **2 :** to serve as an index of **3 :** to regulate (as wages, prices, or interest rates) by indexation ~ *vi* **:** to index something — **in·dex·er** *n*

in·dex·ation \ˌin-dek-ˈsā-shən\ *n* (1960) **:** a system of economic control in which certain variables (as wages and interest) are tied to a cost-of-living index so that both rise or fall at the same rate and the detrimental effect of inflation is theoretically eliminated

index finger *n* (1849) **:** the finger next to the thumb — called also *forefinger*

index fossil *n* (1900) **:** a fossil usu. with a narrow time range and wide spatial distribution that is used in the identification of related geologic formations

[1]**in·dex·i·cal** \(ˌ)in-ˈdek-si-kəl\ *adj* (ca. 1828) **1 :** of or relating to an index **2 a :** varying in reference with the individual speaker ⟨the ~ words *I, here, now*⟩ **b :** associated with or identifying an individual speaker ⟨~ features of speech⟩

[2]**indexical** *n* (1971) **:** an indexical word, sign, or feature

indexing *n* (1974) **:** INDEXATION

index number *n* (1875) **:** a number used to indicate change in magnitude (as of cost or price) as compared with the magnitude at some specified time usu. taken as 100

index of refraction (1829) **:** REFRACTIVE INDEX

In·dia \ˈin-dē-ə\ (1952) — a communications code word for the letter *i*

india ink *n, often cap 1st I* (1665) **1 :** a solid black pigment (as specially prepared lampblack) used in drawing and lettering **2 :** a fluid ink consisting usu. of a fine suspension of india ink in a liquid

In·dia·man \ˈin-dē-ə-mən\ *n* (1709) **:** a merchant ship formerly used in trade with India; *esp* **:** a large sailing ship used in this trade

In·di·an \ˈin-dē-ən, *dial* -jən *or* -din\ *n* (14c) **1 a :** a native or inhabitant of India or of the East Indies **b :** a person of Indian descent **2 a :** AMERICAN INDIAN **b :** one of the native languages of American Indians — **Indian** *adj* — **In·di·an·ness** *n*

Indian agent *n* (1807) **:** an official representative of the U.S. federal government to American Indian tribes esp. on reservations

Indian club *n* (1857) **:** a usu. wooden club shaped like a large bottle or tenpin that is swung for gymnastic exercise

Indian corn *n* (1617) **1 :** a tall widely cultivated American cereal grass (*Zea mays*) bearing seeds on elongated ears **2 :** the ears of Indian corn; *also* **:** its edible seeds **3 :** corn having hard kernels of various colors (as reddish brown, dark purple, and yellow) that is typically used for ornamental purposes

Indian elephant *n* (1555) **:** ELEPHANT 1b

Indian file *n* (1758) **:** SINGLE FILE — **Indian file** *adv*

Indian giver *n* (ca. 1848) *sometimes offensive* **:** a person who gives something to another and then takes it back or expects an equivalent in return — **Indian giving** *n, sometimes offensive*

Indian grass *n* (1764) **:** a tall perennial No. American grass (*Sorghastrum nutans*) with long flat leaves and narrow feathery golden-brown panicles

Indian hemp *n* (1619) **1 :** a No. American dogbane (*Apocynum cannabinum*) with milky juice, tough fibrous bark, and an emetic and cathartic root **2 :** HEMP 1

In·di·an·ism \ˈin-dē-ə-ˌni-zəm\ *n* (1651) **1 :** the qualities or culture distinctive of American Indians **2 :** policy designed to further the interests or culture of American Indians — **In·di·an·ist** \-nist\ *adj or n*

\ə\ **abut** \ᵊ\ **kitten**, F **table** \ər\ **further** \a\ **ash** \ā\ **ace** \ä\ **mop, mar** \au̇\ **out** \ch\ **chin** \e\ **bet** \ē\ **easy** \g\ **go** \i\ **hit** \ī\ **ice** \j\ **job** \ŋ\ **sing** \ō\ **go** \ȯ\ **law** \ȯi\ **boy** \th\ **thin** \t͟h\ **the** \ü\ **loot** \u̇\ **foot** \y\ **yet** \zh\ **vision, beige** \k̲, ⁿ, œ, ue, ʸ\ *see* Guide to Pronunciation

In·di·an·ize \ˈin-dē-ə-ˌnīz\ *vt* **-ized; -iz·ing** (1702) **1 :** to cause to acquire or conform to the characteristics, culture, or usage of American Indians or of India **2 :** to bring (as a region) under the cultural or political influence or control of India — **In·di·an·i·za·tion** \ˌin-dē-ə-(ˌ)nī-ˈzā-shən\ *n*

Indian licorice *n* (ca. 1890) **:** ROSARY PEA 1

Indian meal *n* (1609) **:** CORNMEAL

Indian paintbrush *n* (ca. 1892) **1 :** any of a genus (*Castilleja*) of herbaceous plants of the snapdragon family that have brightly colored bracts — called also *painted cup* **2 :** ORANGE HAWKWEED

Indian pipe *n* (ca. 1818) **:** a waxy white saprophytic herb (*Monotropa uniflora* of the family Monotropaceae, the Indian-pipe family) of Asia and No. America with leaves reduced to scales and that turns black in drying

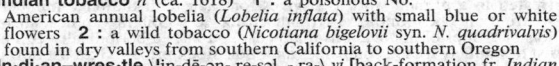

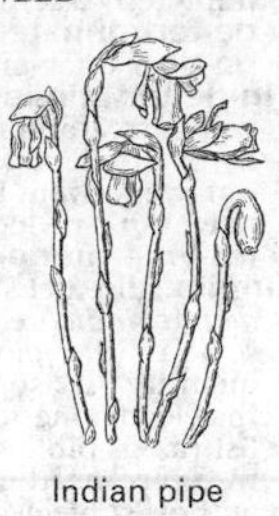
Indian pipe

Indian pudding *n* (1722) **:** a baked pudding made chiefly of cornmeal, milk, and molasses

Indian red *n* (1672) **1 :** any of various usu. dark red pigments consisting chiefly of iron oxide **2 :** a strong or moderate reddish brown

Indian sign *n* (1910) *chiefly Brit* **:** HEX, SPELL

Indian summer *n* (1778) **1 :** a period of warm or mild weather in late autumn or early winter **2 :** a happy or flourishing period occurring toward the end of something ⟨the crowning performance of the *Indian summer* of her career —Octavio Roca⟩

Indian tobacco *n* (ca. 1618) **1 :** a poisonous No. American annual lobelia (*Lobelia inflata*) with small blue or white flowers **2 :** a wild tobacco (*Nicotiana bigelovii* syn. *N. quadrivalvis*) found in dry valleys from southern California to southern Oregon

In·di·an–wres·tle \ˈin-dē-ən-ˌre-səl, -ˌra-\ *vi* [back-formation fr. *Indian wrestling*] (1938) **:** to engage in Indian wrestling

Indian wrestling *n* (1913) **1 :** wrestling in which two people lie side by side on their backs in reversed position locking their near arms and raising and locking the corresponding legs and attempt to force each other's leg down and turn the other wrestler facedown **2 :** wrestling in which two people stand face to face gripping usu. their right hands and setting the outsides of the corresponding feet together and attempt to force each other off balance **3 :** ARM WRESTLING

India paper *n* (1768) **1 :** a thin absorbent paper used esp. for proving inked intaglio surfaces (as steel engravings) **2 :** a thin tough opaque printing paper

india rubber *n, often cap I* (1790) **:** [1]RUBBER 2a

In·dic \ˈin-dik\ *adj* (1877) **1 :** of or relating to the subcontinent of India **:** INDIAN **2 :** of, relating to, or constituting the Indo-Aryan branch of the Indo-European languages — **Indic** *n*

in·di·can \ˈin-də-ˌkan\ *n* [L *indicum* indigo — more at INDIGO] (1859) **1 :** an indigo-forming substance $C_8H_7NO_4S$ found as a salt in urine and other animal fluids; *also* **:** its potassium salt $C_8H_6KNO_4S$ **2 :** a glucoside $C_{14}H_{17}NO_6$ occurring esp. in the indigo plant and being a source of natural indigo

in·di·cant \ˈin-di-kənt\ *n* (1623) **:** something that serves to indicate

in·di·cate \ˈin-də-ˌkāt\ *vt* **-cat·ed; -cat·ing** [L *indicatus,* pp. of *indicare,* fr. *in-* + *dicare* to proclaim, dedicate — more at DICTION] (1541) **1 a :** to point out or point to **b :** to be a sign, symptom, or index of ⟨the high fever ~*s* a serious condition⟩ **c :** to demonstrate or suggest the necessity or advisability of ⟨*indicated* the need for a new school⟩ ⟨the *indicated* treatment⟩ **2 :** to state or express briefly ⟨*indicated* a desire to cooperate⟩

in·di·ca·tion \ˌin-də-ˈkā-shən\ *n* (15c) **1 a :** something that serves to indicate **b :** something that is indicated as advisable or necessary **2 :** the action of indicating — **in·di·ca·tion·al** \-shnəl, -shə-nᵊl\ *adj*

[1]**in·dic·a·tive** \in-ˈdi-kə-tiv\ *adj* (15c) **1 :** of, relating to, or constituting a verb form or set of verb forms that represents the denoted act or state as an objective fact ⟨the ~ mood⟩ **2 :** serving to indicate ⟨actions ~ of fear⟩ — **in·dic·a·tive·ly** *adv*

[2]**indicative** *n* (1530) **1 :** the indicative mood of a language **2 :** a form in the indicative mood

in·di·ca·tor \ˈin-də-ˌkā-tər\ *n* (1666) **1 :** one that indicates: as **a :** an index hand (as on a dial) **:** POINTER **b** (1) **:** GAUGE 2b, DIAL 4a (2) **:** an instrument for automatically making a diagram that indicates the pressure in and volume of the working fluid of an engine throughout the cycle **2 a :** a substance (as litmus) used to show visually (as by change of color) the condition of a solution with respect to the presence of a particular material (as a free acid or alkali) **b :** TRACER 4b **3 :** an organism or ecological community so strictly associated with particular environmental conditions that its presence is indicative of the existence of these conditions **4 :** any of a group of statistical values (as level of employment) that taken together give an indication of the health of the economy — **in·dic·a·to·ry** \in-ˈdi-kə-ˌtȯr-ē\ *adj*

indices *pl of* INDEX

in·di·cia \in-ˈdi-sh(ē-)ə\ *n pl* [L, pl. of *indicium* sign, fr. *indicare*] (ca. 1626) **1 :** distinctive marks **:** INDICATIONS **2 :** postal markings often imprinted on mail or on labels to be affixed to mail

in·dict \in-ˈdīt\ *vt* [alter. of earlier *indite,* fr. ME *inditen,* fr. AF *enditer* to write, point out, indict — more at INDITE] (ca. 1626) **1 :** to charge with a fault or offense **:** CRITICIZE, ACCUSE **2 :** to charge with a crime by the finding or presentment of a jury (as a grand jury) in due form of law — **in·dict·er** *or* **in·dict·or** \-ˈdī-tər\ *n*

in·dict·able \-ˈdī-tə-bəl\ *adj* (ca. 1706) **1 :** subject to being indicted **:** liable to indictment **2 :** making one liable to indictment ⟨an ~ offense⟩

in·dic·tion \in-ˈdik-shən\ *n* [ME *indiccion,* fr. AF, fr. LL *indiction-, indictio,* fr. L, proclamation, fr. *indicere* to proclaim, fr. *in-* + *dicere* to say — more at DICTION] (14c) **:** a 15-year cycle used as a chronological unit in several ancient and medieval systems

in·dict·ment \in-ˈdīt-mənt\ *n* (14c) **1 a :** the action or the legal process of indicting **b :** the state of being indicted **2 :** a formal written statement framed by a prosecuting authority and found by a jury (as a grand jury) charging a person with an offense **3 :** an expression of strong disapproval ⟨an ~ of government policy on immigrants⟩

in·die \ˈin-dē\ *n* [by shortening & alter. fr. *independent*] (1928) **1 :** one that is independent; *esp* **:** an unaffiliated record or motion-picture production company **2 :** something (as a record or film) produced by an indie — **indie** *adj*

in·dif·fer·ence \in-ˈdi-fərn(t)s, -f(ə-)rən(t)s\ *n* (15c) **1 :** the quality, state, or fact of being indifferent **2 a** *archaic* **:** lack of difference or distinction between two or more things **b :** absence of compulsion to or toward one thing or another

in·dif·fer·en·cy \-fərn(t)-sē, -f(ə-)rən(t)-sē\ *n* (15c) *archaic* **:** INDIFFERENCE

in·dif·fer·ent \in-ˈdi-fərnt, -f(ə-)rənt\ *adj* [ME, fr. AF or L; AF, fr. L *indifferent-, indifferens,* fr. *in-* + *different-, differens,* prp. of *differre* to be different — more at DIFFER] (14c) **1 :** marked by impartiality **:** UNBIASED **2 a :** that does not matter one way or the other **b :** of no importance or value one way or the other **3 a :** marked by no special liking for or dislike of something ⟨~ about which task he was given⟩ **b :** marked by a lack of interest, enthusiasm, or concern for something **:** APATHETIC ⟨~ to suffering and poverty⟩ **4 :** being neither excessive nor inadequate **:** MODERATE ⟨hills of ~ size⟩ **5 a :** being neither good nor bad **:** MEDIOCRE ⟨does ~ work⟩ **b :** being neither right nor wrong **6 :** characterized by lack of active quality **:** NEUTRAL ⟨an ~ chemical⟩ **7 a :** not differentiated ⟨~ tissues of the human body⟩ **b :** capable of development in more than one direction; *esp* **:** not yet embryologically determined — **in·dif·fer·ent·ly** *adv*

syn INDIFFERENT, UNCONCERNED, INCURIOUS, ALOOF, DETACHED, DISINTERESTED mean not showing or feeling interest. INDIFFERENT implies neutrality of attitude from lack of inclination, preference, or prejudice ⟨*indifferent* to the dictates of fashion⟩. UNCONCERNED suggests a lack of sensitivity or regard for others' needs or troubles ⟨*unconcerned* about the homeless⟩. INCURIOUS implies an inability to take a normal interest due to dullness of mind or to self-centeredness ⟨*incurious* about the world⟩. ALOOF suggests a cool reserve arising from a sense of superiority or disdain for inferiors or from shyness ⟨*aloof* from his coworkers⟩. DETACHED implies an objective attitude achieved through absence of prejudice or selfishness ⟨observed family gatherings with *detached* amusement⟩. DISINTERESTED implies a circumstantial freedom from concern for personal or esp. financial advantage that enables one to judge or advise without bias ⟨judged by a panel of *disinterested* observers⟩.

in·dif·fer·ent·ism \-fərn-ˌti-zəm, -f(ə-)rən-\ *n* (1827) **:** INDIFFERENCE; *specif* **:** belief that all religions are equally valid — **in·dif·fer·ent·ist** \-fərn-tist, -f(ə-)rən-\ *n*

in·di·gence \ˈin-di-jən(t)s\ *n* (14c) **:** a level of poverty in which real hardship and deprivation are suffered and comforts of life are wholly lacking ***syn*** see POVERTY

in·di·gene \ˈin-də-ˌjēn\ *also* **in·di·gen** \-di-jən, -də-ˌjen\ *n* [L *indigena*] (1598) **:** NATIVE

in·dig·e·nize \in-ˈdi-jə-ˌnīz\ *vt* **-nized; -niz·ing** (1951) **:** to cause to have indigenous characteristics or personnel ⟨the former colony began to ~ its businesses⟩ — **in·dig·e·ni·za·tion** \-ˌdi-jə-nə-ˈzā-shən, -ˌnī-ˈ\ *n*

in·dig·e·nous \in-ˈdi-jə-nəs\ *adj* [LL *indigenus,* fr. L *indigena,* n., native, fr. OL *indu, endo* in, within + L *gignere* to beget — more at END-, KIN] (1646) **1 :** having originated in and being produced, growing, living, or occurring naturally in a particular region or environment ⟨~ plants⟩ ⟨the ~ culture⟩ **2 :** INNATE, INBORN ***syn*** see NATIVE — **in·dig·e·nous·ly** *adv* — **in·dig·e·nous·ness** *n*

in·di·gent \ˈin-di-jənt\ *adj* [ME, fr. MF, fr. OF, fr. L *indigent-, indigens,* prp. of *indigēre* to need, fr. OL *indu* + L *egēre* to need; perh. akin to OHG *echerode* poor] (15c) **1 :** suffering from indigence **:** IMPOVERISHED **2 a** *archaic* **:** DEFICIENT **b** *archaic* **:** totally lacking in something specified — **indigent** *n*

in·di·gest·ed \ˌin-(ˌ)dī-ˈjes-təd, -də-\ *adj* (1587) **:** not carefully thought out or arranged **:** FORMLESS

in·di·gest·ible \-ˈjes-tə-bəl\ *adj* [ME, fr. LL *indigestibilis,* fr. L *in-* + LL *digestibilis* digestible] (15c) **:** not digestible **:** not easily digested — **in·di·gest·ibil·i·ty** \-ˌjes-tə-ˈbi-lə-tē\ *n* — **indigestible** *n*

in·di·ges·tion \-ˈjes-chən, -ˈjesh-\ *n* (14c) **1 :** inability to digest or difficulty in digesting something **2 :** a case or attack of indigestion marked esp. by a burning sensation or discomfort in the upper abdomen

in·dign \in-ˈdīn\ *adj* [ME *indigne,* fr. AF, fr. L *indignus*] (14c) **1** *archaic* **:** UNWORTHY, UNDESERVING **2** *obs* **:** UNBECOMING, DISGRACEFUL

in·dig·nant \in-ˈdig-nənt\ *adj* [L *indignant-, indignans,* prp. of *indignari* to be indignant, fr. *indignus* unworthy, fr. *in-* + *dignus* worthy — more at DECENT] (1590) **:** filled with or marked by indignation ⟨became ~ at the accusation⟩ — **in·dig·nant·ly** *adv*

in·dig·na·tion \ˌin-dig-ˈnā-shən\ *n* (14c) **:** anger aroused by something unjust, unworthy, or mean ***syn*** see ANGER

in·dig·ni·ty \in-ˈdig-nə-tē\ *n, pl* **-ties** [L *indignitat-, indignitas,* fr. *indignus*] (1581) **1 a :** an act that offends against a person's dignity or self-respect **:** INSULT **b :** humiliating treatment **2** *obs* **:** lack or loss of dignity or honor

in·di·go \ˈin-di-ˌgō\ *n, pl* **-gos** *or* **-goes** [It dial., fr. L *indicum,* fr. Gk *indikon,* fr. neut. of *indikos* Indic, fr. *Indos* India] (1555) **1 a :** a blue vat dye obtained from plants (as indigo plants) **b :** the principal coloring matter $C_{16}H_{10}N_2O_2$ of natural indigo usu. synthesized as a blue powder with a coppery luster **2 :** INDIGO PLANT **3 :** a deep reddish blue

indigo bunting *n* (1783) **:** a small finch (*Passerina cyanea* of the family Cardinalidae) chiefly of eastern No. America of which the male is largely deep blue in spring and summer

indigo plant *n* (1712) **:** a plant that yields indigo; *esp* **:** any of a genus (*Indigofera*) of leguminous herbs

indigo snake *n* (ca. 1885) **:** a very large blue-black or brownish colubrid snake (*Drymarchon corais*) of the southeastern U.S. and Texas to Argentina — called also *gopher snake*

in·di·go·tin \in-ˈdi-gə-tən, ˌin-di-ˈgō-tᵊn\ *n* [F *indigotine,* irreg. fr. *indigo* indigo] (1838) **:** INDIGO 1b

in·din·a·vir \(ˌ)in-ˈdi-nə-ˌvir\ *n* [*indina-* (perh. alter. of *indanyl* monovalent radical of the cyclic hydrocarbon indan) + *-vir* (as in *saquinavir*)] (1995) **:** a protease inhibitor $C_{36}H_{47}N_5O_4$ used in the form of its sulfate in combination with antiretroviral drugs (as AZT) to treat HIV infection

in·di·rect \ˌin-də-ˈrekt, -(ˌ)dī-\ *adj* [ME, fr. ML *indirectus,* fr. L *in-* + *directus* direct — more at DRESS] (14c) **:** not direct: as **a** (1) **:** deviating from a direct line or course : ROUNDABOUT (2) : not going straight to the point ⟨an ~ accusation⟩ (3) : being or involving proof of a proposition or theorem by demonstration that its negation leads to an absurdity or contradiction **b** : not straightforward and open : DECEITFUL **c** : not directly aimed at or achieved ⟨~ consequences⟩ **d** : stating what a real or supposed original speaker said with changes in wording that conform the statement grammatically to the sentence in which it is included ⟨~ discourse⟩ ⟨an ~ question⟩ **e** : not effected by the action of the people or the electorate ⟨~ government representation⟩ — **in·di·rect·ly** \-ˈrek(t)-lē\ *adv* — **in·di·rect·ness** \-nəs\ *n*

indirect cost *n* (ca. 1909) : a cost that is not identifiable with a specific product, function, or activity

indirect evidence *n* (1824) : evidence that establishes immediately collateral facts from which the main fact may be inferred : CIRCUMSTANTIAL EVIDENCE

in·di·rec·tion \ˌin-də-ˈrek-shən, -(ˌ)dī-\ *n* (1590) **1 a** : indirect action or procedure **b** : lack of direction : AIMLESSNESS **2 a** : lack of straightforwardness and openness : DECEITFULNESS **b** : something (as an act or statement) marked by lack of straightforwardness ⟨hated diplomatic ~*s* —*Rev. of Reviews*⟩

indirect lighting *n* (1922) : lighting in which the light emitted by a source is diffusely reflected (as by the ceiling)

indirect object *n* (1879) : a grammatical object representing the secondary goal of the action of its verb (as *her* in "I gave her the book")

in·dis·cern·ible \ˌin-di-ˈsər-nə-bəl, -ˈzər-\ *adj* (1635) : incapable of being discerned : not recognizable as distinct

in·dis·ci·plin·able \(ˌ)in-ˌdi-sə-ˈpli-nə-bəl; -ˈdi-sə-plə-\ *adj* (1600) : not subject to or capable of being disciplined

in·dis·ci·pline \(ˌ)in-ˈdi-sə-plən\ *n* (1783) : lack of discipline — **in·disci·plined** \-plənd, -(ˌ)plind\ *adj*

in·dis·cov·er·able \ˌin-dis-ˈkəv-rə-bəl, -ˈkə-və-\ *adj* (1640) : not discoverable

in·dis·creet \ˌin-di-ˈskrēt\ *adj* [ME *indiscrete,* fr. LL *indiscretus,* fr. L, indistinguishable, fr. *in-* + *discretus,* pp. of *discernere* to separate — more at DISCERN] (15c) : not discreet : IMPRUDENT ⟨an ~ comment⟩ — **in·dis·creet·ly** *adv* — **in·dis·creet·ness** *n*

in·dis·cre·tion \ˌin-dis-ˈkre-shən\ *n* (14c) **1** : lack of discretion : IMPRUDENCE ⟨dietary ~⟩ **2 a** : something (as an act or remark) marked by lack of discretion **b** : an act at variance with the accepted morality of a society ⟨resigned because of financial ~*s*⟩

in·dis·crim·i·nate \ˌin-dis-ˈkrim-nət, -ˈkri-mə-\ *adj* (ca. 1598) **1 a** : not marked by careful distinction : deficient in discrimination and discernment ⟨~ reading habits⟩ ⟨~ mass destruction⟩ **b** : HAPHAZARD, RANDOM ⟨~ application of a law⟩ **2 a** : PROMISCUOUS, UNRESTRAINED ⟨~ sexual behavior⟩ **b** : HETEROGENEOUS, MOTLEY ⟨an ~ collection⟩ — **in·dis·crim·i·nate·ly** *adv* — **in·dis·crim·i·nate·ness** *n*

in·dis·crim·i·nat·ing \-ˈkri-mə-ˌnā-tiŋ\ *adj* (ca. 1767) : not discriminating — **in·dis·crim·i·nat·ing·ly** \-tiŋ-lē\ *adv*

in·dis·crim·i·na·tion \-ˌkri-mə-ˈnā-shən\ *n* (1649) : lack of discrimination

in·dis·pens·able \ˌin-di-ˈspen(t)-sə-bəl\ *adj* (1653) **1** : not subject to being set aside or neglected ⟨an ~ obligation⟩ **2** : absolutely necessary : ESSENTIAL ⟨an ~ member of the staff⟩ — **in·dis·pens·abil·i·ty** \-ˌspen(t)-sə-ˈbi-lə-tē\ *n* — **indispensable** *n* — **in·dis·pens·able·ness** \-ˈspen(t)-sə-bəl-nəs\ *n* — **in·dis·pens·ably** \-blē\ *adv*

in·dis·pose \ˌin-di-ˈspōz\ *vt* **-posed; -pos·ing** [prob. back-formation fr. *indisposed*] (1653) **1 a** : to make unfit : DISQUALIFY **b** : to make averse : DISINCLINE **2** *archaic* : to cause to be in poor physical health

in·dis·posed \-ˈspōzd\ *adj* (15c) **1** : slightly ill **2** : AVERSE

in·dis·po·si·tion \(ˌ)in-ˌdis-pə-ˈzi-shən\ *n* (15c) : the condition of being indisposed: **a** : DISINCLINATION **b** : a usu. slight illness

in·dis·put·able \ˌin-di-ˈspyü-tə-bəl, (ˌ)in-ˈdis-pyə-\ *adj* [LL *indisputabilis,* fr. L *in-* + *disputabilis* disputable] (1551) : not disputable : UNQUESTIONABLE ⟨~ proof⟩ — **in·dis·put·able·ness** *n* — **in·dis·put·ably** \-blē\ *adv*

in·dis·so·cia·ble \ˌin-di-ˈsō-sh(ē-)ə-bəl, -sē-ə-\ *adj* (1855) : not dissociated : INSEPARABLE — **in·dis·so·cia·bly** \-blē\ *adv*

in·dis·sol·u·ble \ˌin-di-ˈsäl-yə-bəl\ *adj* (1542) : not dissoluble; *esp* : incapable of being annulled, undone, or broken : PERMANENT ⟨an ~ contract⟩ — **in·dis·sol·u·bil·i·ty** \-ˌsäl-yə-ˈbi-lə-tē\ *n* — **in·dis·sol·u·ble·ness** \-ˈsäl-yə-bəl-nəs\ *n* — **in·dis·sol·u·bly** \-blē\ *adv*

in·dis·tinct \ˌin-di-ˈstiŋ(k)t\ *adj* [L *indistinctus,* fr. *in-* + *distinctus* distinct] (1526) : not distinct: as **a** : not sharply outlined or separable : BLURRED ⟨~ figures in the fog⟩ **b** : FAINT, DIM ⟨an ~ light in the distance⟩ **c** : not clearly recognizable or understandable : UNCERTAIN — **in·dis·tinct·ly** \-ˈstiŋ(k)t-lē, -ˈstiŋ-klē\ *adv* — **in·dis·tinct·ness** \-ˈstiŋ(k)t-nəs, -ˈstiŋk-nəs\ *n*

in·dis·tinc·tive \-ˈstiŋ(k)-tiv\ *adj* (1846) : lacking distinctive qualities

in·dis·tin·guish·able \ˌin-di-ˈstiŋ-gwi-shə-bəl, -ˈstiŋ-wi-\ *adj* (1606) : not distinguishable: as **a** : indeterminate in shape or structure ⟨~ forms in the mist⟩ **b** : not clearly recognizable or understandable ⟨~ differences⟩ **c** : lacking identifying or individualizing qualities ⟨seemingly ~ alternatives⟩ — **in·dis·tin·guish·abil·i·ty** \-ˌstiŋ-gwi-shə-ˈbi-lə-tē, -ˌstiŋ-wi-\ *n* — **in·dis·tin·guish·able·ness** \-ˈstiŋ-gwi-shə-bəl-nəs, -ˈstiŋ-wi-\ *n* — **in·dis·tin·guish·ably** \-blē\ *adv*

in·dite \in-ˈdīt\ *vt* **in·dit·ed; in·dit·ing** [ME *enditen,* fr. AF *enditer* to write, compose, fr. VL **indictare,* freq. of L *indicere* to make known formally, proclaim, fr. *in-* + *dicere* to say — more at DICTION] (14c) **1 a** : MAKE UP, COMPOSE ⟨~ a poem⟩ **b** : to give literary or formal expression to **c** : to put down in writing ⟨~ a message⟩ **2** *obs* : DICTATE — **in·dit·er** *n*

in·di·um \ˈin-dē-əm\ *n* [ISV *ind-* + NL *-ium*] (1864) : a silvery malleable fusible chiefly trivalent metallic element that occurs esp. in sphalerite ores and is used esp. as a plating material, in alloys, and in electronics — see ELEMENT table

indium antimonide *n* (1957) : a synthetic compound InSb of indium and antimony that is a semiconducting and photosensitive material and is used esp. in infrared photodetectors

indiv *abbr* individual

[1]**in·di·vid·u·al** \ˌin-də-ˈvij-wəl, -ˈvi-jə-wəl, -ˈvi-jəl, -ˈvi-jü-əl\ *adj* [ML *individualis,* fr. L *individuus* indivisible, fr. *in-* + *dividuus* divided, fr. *dividere* to divide] (15c) **1** *obs* : INSEPARABLE **2 a** : of, relating to, or distinctively associated with an individual ⟨an ~ effort⟩ **b** : being an individual or existing as an indivisible whole **c** : intended for one person ⟨an ~ serving⟩ **3** : existing as a distinct entity : SEPARATE **4** : having marked individuality ⟨an ~ style⟩ ***syn*** see SPECIAL, CHARACTERISTIC — **in·di·vid·u·al·ly** *adv*

[2]**individual** *n* (1605) **1 a** : a particular being or thing as distinguished from a class, species, or collection: as (1) : a single human being as contrasted with a social group or institution ⟨a teacher who works with ~*s*⟩ (2) : a single organism as distinguished from a group **b** : a particular person ⟨are you the ~ I spoke with on the telephone?⟩ **2** : an indivisible entity **3** : the reference of a name or variable of the lowest logical type in a calculus

in·di·vid·u·al·ise *Brit var of* INDIVIDUALIZE

in·di·vid·u·al·ism \ˌin-də-ˈvij-wə-ˌli-zəm, -ˈvi-jə-wə-, -ˈvi-jə-ˌli-\ *n* (1827) **1 a** (1) : a doctrine that the interests of the individual are or ought to be ethically paramount; *also* : conduct guided by such a doctrine (2) : the conception that all values, rights, and duties originate in individuals **b** : a theory maintaining the political and economic independence of the individual and stressing individual initiative, action, and interests; *also* : conduct or practice guided by such a theory **2 a** : INDIVIDUALITY **b** : an individual peculiarity : IDIOSYNCRASY

in·di·vid·u·al·ist \-list\ *n* (1840) **1** : one that pursues a markedly independent course in thought or action **2** : one that advocates or practices individualism — **individualist** *or* **in·di·vid·u·al·is·tic** \-ˌvij-wə-ˈlis-tik, -ˌvi-jə-wə-, -ˌvi-jə-ˈlis-\ *adj* — **in·di·vid·u·al·is·ti·cal·ly** \-ˈlis-ti-k(ə-)lē\ *adv*

in·di·vid·u·al·i·ty \-ˌvi-jə-ˈwa-lə-tē\ *n, pl* **-ties** (1614) **1 a** : total character peculiar to and distinguishing an individual from others **b** : PERSONALITY **2** *archaic* : the quality or state of being indivisible **3** : separate or distinct existence **4** : INDIVIDUAL, PERSON

in·di·vid·u·al·ize \-ˈvij-wə-ˌlīz, -ˈvi-jə-wə-, -ˈvi-jə-ˌlīz\ *vt* **-ized; -iz·ing** (1637) **1** : to make individual in character **2** : to treat or notice individually : PARTICULARIZE **3** : to adapt to the needs or special circumstances of an individual ⟨~ teaching according to student ability⟩ — **in·di·vid·u·al·i·za·tion** \-ˌvij-wə-lə-ˈzā-shən, -ˌvi-jə-wə-, -ˌvi-jə-lə-\ *n*

individual medley *n* (ca. 1949) : a swimming race in which each contestant swims each part of the course with a different stroke

individual retirement account *n* (1974) : IRA

in·di·vid·u·ate \ˌin-də-ˈvi-jə-ˌwāt\ *vt* **-at·ed; -at·ing** (1614) **1** : to give individuality to **2** : to form into a distinct entity

in·di·vid·u·a·tion \-ˌvi-jə-ˈwā-shən\ *n* (1628) **1** : the act or process of individuating: as **a** (1) : the development of the individual from the universal (2) : the determination of the individual in the general **b** : the process by which individuals in society become differentiated from one another **c** : regional differentiation along a primary embryonic axis **2** : the state of being individuated; *specif* : INDIVIDUALITY

in·di·vis·i·ble \ˌin-də-ˈvi-zə-bəl\ *adj* [ME, fr. LL *indivisibilis,* fr. L *in-* + LL *divisibilis* divisible] (14c) : not divisible — **in·di·vis·i·bil·i·ty** \-ˌvi-zə-ˈbi-lə-tē\ *n* — **indivisible** *n* — **in·di·vis·i·bly** \-ˈvi-zə-blē\ *adv*

indn *abbr* indication

indo- — see IND-

Indo- *comb form* [Gk, fr. *Indos* India] **1** : India or the East Indies ⟨*Indo*-Pakistani⟩ **2** : Indo-European ⟨*Indo*-Hittite⟩

In·do–Ar·y·an \ˌin-dō-ˈer-ē-ən, -ˈär-yən\ *n* (1881) **1** : a member of one of the peoples of the Indian subcontinent speaking an Indo-European language **2** : one of the early Indo-European invaders of southern Asia **3** : a branch of the Indo-European language family that includes Hindi, Bengali, Punjabi, and other languages spoken primarily in India, Pakistan, Bangladesh, and Sri Lanka — see INDO-EUROPEAN LANGUAGES table — **Indo–Aryan** *adj*

In·do–Chi·nese \-ˌchī-ˈnēz, -ˈnēs\ *n* (ca. 1934) **1** : a native or inhabitant of Indochina **2** : SINO-TIBETAN — **Indo–Chinese** *adj*

in·doc·ile \(ˌ)in-ˈdä-səl *also* -ˌsī(-ə)l, *esp Brit* -ˈdō-ˌsīl\ *adj* [MF, fr. L *indocilis,* fr. *in-* + *docilis* docile] (1603) : unwilling or indisposed to be taught or disciplined : INTRACTABLE — **in·do·cil·i·ty** \ˌin-dä-ˈsi-lə-tē, -dō-\ *n*

in·doc·tri·nate \in-ˈdäk-trə-ˌnāt\ *vt* **-nat·ed; -nat·ing** [prob. fr. ME *endoctrinen,* fr. AF *endoctriner,* fr. *en-* + *doctrine* doctrine] (1626) **1** : to instruct esp. in fundamentals or rudiments : TEACH **2** : to imbue with a usu. partisan or sectarian opinion, point of view, or principle — **in·doc·tri·na·tion** \(ˌ)in-ˌdäk-trə-ˈnā-shən\ *n* — **in·doc·tri·na·tor** \in-ˈdäk-trə-ˌnā-tər\ *n*

[1]**In·do–Eu·ro·pe·an** \ˌin-dō-ˌyu̇r-ə-ˈpē-ən\ *adj* (1813) : of, relating to, or constituting the Indo-European languages

[2]**Indo–European** *n* (1832) **1 a** : a member of the people speaking an unrecorded prehistoric language from which the Indo-European languages are descended **b** : this language **2** : INDO-EUROPEAN LANGUAGES

In·do–Eu·ro·pe·an·ist \-ˌyu̇r-ə-ˈpē-ə-nist\ *n* (1926) : a specialist in Indo-European linguistics

Indo–European languages *n pl* (1843) : a family of languages comprising those spoken in most of Europe and in the parts of the world colonized by Europeans since 1500 and also in Persia, the subcontinent of India, and some other parts of Asia

☞ The Indo-European Languages Table is on the following page.

In·do–Ger·man·ic \ˌin-dō-jər-ˈma-nik\ *adj* (1822) : INDO-EUROPEAN — **Indo–Germanic** *n*

In·do–Hit·tite \-ˈhi-ˌtīt\ *n* (1929) **1** : a hypothetical parent language of Indo-European and Anatolian **2** : a language family including Indo-European and Anatolian — **Indo–Hittite** *adj*

In·do–Ira·ni·an \-ir-ˈā-nē-ən\ *adj* (1874) : of, relating to, or constituting a subfamily of the Indo-European languages that consists of the Indo-Aryan and the Iranian branches — see INDO-EUROPEAN LANGUAGES table — **Indo–Iranian** *n*

in·dole \ˈin-ˌdōl\ *n* [ISV *ind-* + *-ole*] (1869) : a crystalline alkaloid compound C_8H_7N that is a decomposition product of proteins containing tryptophan, that can be made synthetically, and that is used in perfumes; *also* : a derivative of indole

\ə\ **abut** \ᵊ\ **kitten, F table** \ər\ **further** \a\ **ash** \ā\ **ace** \ä\ **mop, mar**
\au̇\ **out** \ch\ **chin** \e\ **bet** \ē\ **easy** \g\ **go** \i\ **hit** \ī\ **ice** \j\ **job**
\ŋ\ **sing** \ō\ **go** \ȯ\ **law** \ȯi\ **boy** \th\ **thin** \t͟h\ **the** \ü\ **loot** \u̇\ **foot**
\y\ **yet** \zh\ **vision, beige** \k̲, ⁿ, œ, ue, ʸ\ *see* Guide to Pronunciation

INDO-EUROPEAN LANGUAGES

BRANCH	GROUP	LANGUAGES AND MAJOR DIALECTS[1]			PROVENIENCE
		ANCIENT	MEDIEVAL	MODERN	
	Anatolian	*Hittite, Lydian, Lycian, Luwian, Palaic, Hieroglyphic Luwian*			ancient Asia Minor
INDO-IRANIAN	Nuristani			languages of eastern Afghanistan	Afghanistan
	Indo-Aryan — Sanskritic	Sanskrit, Pali *Prakrits*	*Prakrits*		India
				Shina, Khowar	Upper Indus valley
				Kashmiri	Kashmir
				Lahnda	western Punjab
				Sindhi	Sind
				Panjabi	Punjab
				Rajasthani	Rajasthan
				Gujarati	Gujarat
				Marathi	western India
				Konkani	western India
				Oriya	Orissa
				Bengali	Bangladesh, West Bengal
				Assamese	Assam
				Bhojpuri	Bihar, Uttar Pradesh
				Hindi	northern India
				Urdu	Pakistan, India
				Nepali	Nepal
				Sinhalese	Sri Lanka
				Romany	uncertain
	Iranian — West	*Old Persian*	*Pahlavi* *Persian*		Persia Iran
				Persian	Iran
				Kurdish	Iran, Iraq, Turkey
				Baluchi	Pakistan
				Tajiki	Tajikistan
	Iranian — East	*Avestan*			ancient Persia
			Sogdian, Khotanese		central Asia
				Pashto	Afghanistan, Pakistan
				Ossetic	Caucasus
Armenian			*Armenian*	Armenian	Asia Minor, Caucasus
Greek or Hellenic	Greek	Greek	Greek	Greek	Greece, the eastern Mediterranean
BALTO-SLAVIC	Baltic		*Old Prussian*		East Prussia
				Lithuanian	Lithuania
				Latvian	Latvia
	Slavic — South		*Old Church Slavic*		
				Slovene	Slovenia
				Serbian, Croatian	Croatia, Bosnia and Herzegovina, Serbia, Montenegro
				Macedonian	Macedonia
				Bulgarian	Bulgaria
	Slavic — West			Czech, Slovak	Czech Republic, Slovakia
				Polish, Kashubian	Poland
				Wendish, *Polabian*	Germany
	Slavic — East		*Old Russian*	Russian	Russia
				Ukrainian	Ukraine
				Belarusian	Belarus
Albanian			*Albanian*	Albanian	Albania, Serbia, Macedonia
Scantily recorded and of uncertain affinities within Indo-European		*Ligurian, Messapian Illyrian, Thracian Phrygian*			ancient Italy Balkans Asia Minor
Tocharian			*Tocharian A, Tocharian B*		central Asia
GERMANIC	East	*Gothic*			eastern Europe
	North		*Old Norse*	Icelandic	Iceland
				Faeroese	Faeroe Islands
				Norwegian	Norway
				Swedish	Sweden
				Danish	Denmark
	West		*Old High German, Middle High German*	German	Germany, Switzerland, Austria
				Yiddish	Germany, eastern Europe
			Old Saxon, Middle Low German	Low German	northern Germany
			Middle Dutch	Dutch	Netherlands, Belgium
				Afrikaans	South Africa
			Old Frisian	Frisian	Netherlands, Germany
			Old English, Middle English	English	England
ITALIC		*Venetic, Oscan, Umbrian, Faliscan* *Latin*			ancient Italy
				Portuguese	Portugal
				Spanish	Spain
				Judeo-Spanish	Mediterranean lands
				Catalan	Spain (Catalonia)
			Old Occitan	Occitan	southern France
			Old French, Middle French	French	France, Belgium, Switzerland
				Italian	Italy, Switzerland
				Rhaeto-Romance	Switzerland, Italy
				Sardinian	Sardinia
				Dalmatian	Adriatic coast
				Romanian	Romania, Balkans
CELTIC	Continental	*Gaulish*			Gaul
	Goidelic		*Old Irish, Middle Irish*	Irish	Ireland
				Scottish Gaelic	Scotland
				Manx	Isle of Man
	Brythonic		*Old Welsh, Middle Welsh*	Welsh	Wales
			Old Cornish	Cornish	Cornwall
			Old Breton	Breton	Brittany

[1] Italics denote dead languages. Languages listed in roman type in the ancient or medieval column survive only in some special use, as in literary composition or liturgy.

in·dole·ace·tic acid \ˌin-(ˌ)dō-lə-ˈsē-tik-\ *n* (1937) **:** a crystalline plant hormone $C_{10}H_9NO_2$ that is a naturally occurring auxin promoting growth and rooting of plants
in·dole·bu·tyr·ic acid \ˌin-(ˌ)dōl-byü-ˈtir-ik-\ *n* (1936) **:** a crystalline acid $C_{12}H_{13}NO_2$ similar to indoleacetic acid in its effects on plants
in·do·lence \ˈin-də-lən(t)s\ *n* (1710) **:** inclination to laziness **:** SLOTH
in·do·lent \-lənt\ *adj* [LL *indolent-, indolens* insensitive to pain, fr. L *in-* + *dolent-, dolens,* prp. of *dolēre* to feel pain] (1663) **1 a :** causing little or no pain **b :** slow to develop or heal ⟨~ tumors⟩ ⟨~ ulcers⟩ **2 a :** averse to activity, effort, or movement **:** habitually lazy **b :** conducive to or encouraging laziness ⟨~ heat⟩ **c :** exhibiting indolence ⟨an ~ sigh⟩ ***syn*** see LAZY — **in·do·lent·ly** *adv*
In·dol·o·gy \(ˌ)in-ˈdä-lə-jē\ *n* (1888) **:** the study of India and its people — **In·dol·o·gist** \-jist\ *n*
in·do·meth·a·cin \ˌin-dō-ˈme-thə-sən\ *n* [*indo*le + *meth-* + *a*cetic acid + ¹*-in*] (1963) **:** a nonsteroidal drug $C_{19}H_{16}ClNO_4$ with anti-inflammatory, analgesic, and antipyretic properties used esp. to treat painful inflammatory conditions (as rheumatoid arthritis and osteoarthritis)
in·dom·i·ta·ble \in-ˈdä-mə-tə-bəl\ *adj* [LL *indomitabilis,* fr. L *in-* + *domitare* to tame — more at DAUNT] (1634) **:** incapable of being subdued **:** UNCONQUERABLE ⟨~ courage⟩ — **in·dom·i·ta·bil·i·ty** \(ˌ)in-ˌdä-mə-tə-ˈbi-lə-tē\ *n* — **in·dom·i·ta·ble·ness** \in-ˈdä-mə-tə-bəl-nəs\ *n* — **in·dom·i·ta·bly** \-blē\ *adv*
Indon *abbr* Indonesia; Indonesian
In·do·ne·sian \ˌin-də-ˈnē-zhən, -shən\ *n* (1850) **1 :** a native or inhabitant of the Malay Archipelago **2 a :** a native or inhabitant of the Republic of Indonesia **b :** the language based on Malay that is the national language of the Republic of Indonesia — **Indonesian** *adj*
in·door \ˈin-ˈdȯr\ *adj* (1711) **1 :** of or relating to the interior of a building **2 :** living, located, or carried on within a building ⟨an ~ sport⟩
in·doors \ˈin-ˈdȯrz, (ˌ)in-\ *adv* (1832) **:** in or into a building
in·do·phe·nol \ˌin-dō-ˈfē-ˌnōl, -ˌnȯl, ˌin-(ˌ)dō-fi-ˈ\ *n* [ISV] (ca. 1881) **:** any of various blue or green dyes
indorse, indorsement *var of* ENDORSE, ENDORSEMENT
in·dox·yl \in-ˈdäk-səl\ *n* [ISV *ind-* + hydr*oxyl*] (ca. 1886) **:** a crystalline compound C_8H_7NO found in plants and animals or synthesized as a step in indigo manufacture
in·draft \ˈin-ˌdraft, -ˌdräft\ *n* (1577) **1 :** an inward flow or current (as of air or water) **2 :** a drawing or pulling in
in·drawn \ˈin-ˌdrȯn\ *adj* (1751) **1 :** ALOOF, RESERVED **2 :** drawn in
in·dri \ˈin-drē\ *n, pl* **indris** [F, fr. Malagasy *indry* look!] (1839) **:** a large diurnal black-and-white lemur (*Indri indri*) of Madagascar that is about two feet long with a rudimentary tail

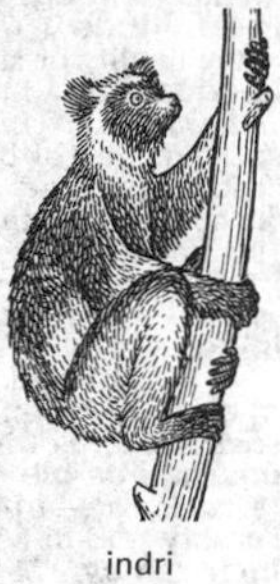
indri

in·du·bi·ta·ble \(ˌ)in-ˈdü-bə-tə-bəl, -ˈdyü-\ *adj* [ME *indubitabyll,* fr. L *indubitabilis,* fr. *in-* + *dubitabilis* dubitable] (15c) **:** too evident to be doubted **:** UNQUESTIONABLE — **in·du·bi·ta·bil·i·ty** \-ˌdü-bə-tə-ˈbi-lə-tē, -ˌdyü-\ *n* — **in·du·bi·ta·ble·ness** \-ˈdü-bə-tə-bəl-nəs, -ˈdyü-\ *n* — **in·du·bi·ta·bly** \-blē\ *adv*
in·duce \in-ˈdüs, -ˈdyüs\ *vt* **in·duced; in·duc·ing** [ME, fr. AF *inducer,* fr. L *inducere,* fr. *in-* + *ducere* to lead — more at TOW] (14c) **1 a :** to move by persuasion or influence **b :** to call forth or bring about by influence or stimulation **2 a :** EFFECT, CAUSE **b :** to cause the formation of **c :** to produce (as an electric current) by induction **3 :** to determine by induction; *specif* **:** to infer from particulars
in·duce·ment \in-ˈdüs-mənt, -ˈdyüs-\ *n* (1594) **1 :** a motive or consideration that leads one to action or to additional or more effective actions **2 :** the act or process of inducing **3 :** matter presented by way of introduction or background to explain the principal allegations of a legal cause, plea, or defense ***syn*** see MOTIVE
in·duc·er \-ˈdü-sər, -ˈdyü-\ *n* (ca. 1538) **:** one that induces; *esp* **:** a substance that is capable of activating the transcription of a gene by combining with and inactivating a genetic repressor
in·duc·ible \in-ˈdü-sə-bəl, -ˈdyü-\ *adj* (ca. 1677) **:** capable of being induced: as **a :** formed by a cell in response to the presence of its substrate ⟨~ enzymes⟩ **b :** activated or undergoing expression only in the presence of a particular molecule ⟨an ~ promoter⟩ — **in·duc·ibil·i·ty** \-ˌdü-sə-ˈbi-lə-tē, -ˌdyü-\ *n*
in·duct \in-ˈdəkt\ *vt* [ME, fr. ML *inductus,* pp. of *inducere,* fr. L] (14c) **1 :** to put in formal possession (as of a benefice or office) **:** INSTALL ⟨was ~*ed* as president of the college⟩ **2 a :** to admit as a member ⟨~*ed* into a scholastic society⟩ **b :** INTRODUCE, INITIATE **c :** to enroll for military training or service (as under a selective service act) **3 :** LEAD, CONDUCT
in·duc·tance \in-ˈdək-tən(t)s\ *n* (1886) **1 a :** a property of an electric circuit by which an electromotive force is induced in it by a variation of current either in the circuit itself or in a neighboring circuit **b :** the measure of this property that is equal to the ratio of the induced electromotive force to the rate of change of the inducing current **2 :** a circuit or a device possessing inductance
in·duct·ee \(ˌ)in-ˌdək-ˈtē, in-ˈdək-ˌ\ *n* (1940) **:** one who is inducted
in·duc·tion \in-ˈdək-shən\ *n* (14c) **1 a :** the act or process of inducting (as into office) **b :** an initial experience **:** INITIATION **c :** the formality by which a civilian is inducted into military service **2 a (1) :** inference of a generalized conclusion from particular instances — compare DEDUCTION 2a **(2) :** a conclusion arrived at by induction **b :** mathematical demonstration of the validity of a law concerning all the positive integers by proving that it holds for the integer 1 and that if it holds for an arbitrarily chosen positive integer *k,* it must hold for the integer *k* + 1 — called also *mathematical induction* **3 :** a preface, prologue, or introductory scene esp. of an early English play **4 a :** the act of bringing forward or adducing (as facts or particulars) **b :** the act of causing or bringing on or about **c :** the process by which an electrical conductor becomes electrified when near a charged body, by which a magnetizable body becomes magnetized when in a magnetic field or in the magnetic flux set up by a magnetomotive force, or by which an electromotive force is produced in a circuit by varying the magnetic field linked with the circuit **d :** the inspiration of the fuel-air charge from the carburetor into the combustion chamber of an internal combustion engine **e :** the process by which the fate of embryonic cells is determined (as by the action of adjacent cells) and morphogenetic differentiation brought about
induction coil *n* (1837) **:** an apparatus for obtaining intermittent high voltage that consists of a primary coil through which the direct current flows, an interrupter, and a secondary coil of a larger number of turns in which the high voltage is induced
induction heating *n* (1919) **:** heating of material by means of an electric current that is caused to flow through the material or its container by electromagnetic induction
induction motor *n* (1897) **:** an alternating-current motor in which torque is produced by the reaction between a varying magnetic field generated in the stator and the current induced in the coils of the rotor
in·duc·tive \in-ˈdək-tiv\ *adj* (15c) **1 :** leading on **:** INDUCING **2 :** of, relating to, or employing mathematical or logical induction ⟨~ reasoning⟩ **3 :** of or relating to inductance or electrical induction **4 :** INTRODUCTORY **5 :** involving the action of an embryological organizer **:** tending to produce induction — **in·duc·tive·ly** *adv*
in·duc·tor \in-ˈdək-tər\ *n* (1652) **1 :** one that inducts **2 a :** a part of an electrical apparatus that acts upon another or is itself acted upon by induction **b :** REACTOR 2 **3 :** ORGANIZER 2
indue *var of* ENDUE
in·dulge \in-ˈdəlj\ *vb* **in·dulged; in·dulg·ing** [L *indulgēre* to be complaisant] *vt* (ca. 1623) **1 a :** to give free rein to **b :** to take unrestrained pleasure in **:** GRATIFY **2 a :** to yield to the desire of **:** HUMOR ⟨please ~ me for a moment⟩ **b :** to treat with excessive leniency, generosity, or consideration ~ *vi* **:** to indulge oneself — **in·dulg·er** *n*
syn INDULGE, PAMPER, HUMOR, SPOIL, BABY, MOLLYCODDLE mean to show undue favor to a person's desires and feelings. INDULGE implies excessive compliance and weakness in gratifying another's or one's own desires ⟨*indulged* myself with food at the slightest excuse⟩. PAMPER implies inordinate gratification of desire for luxury and comfort with consequent enervating effect ⟨*pampered* by the amenities of modern living⟩. HUMOR stresses a yielding to a person's moods or whims ⟨*humored* him by letting him tell the story⟩. SPOIL stresses the injurious effects on character by indulging or pampering ⟨foolish parents *spoil* their children⟩. BABY suggests excessive care, attention, or solicitude ⟨*babying* students by grading too easily⟩. MOLLYCODDLE suggests an excessive degree of care and attention to another's health or welfare ⟨refused to *mollycoddle* her malingering son⟩.
in·dul·gence \in-ˈdəl-jən(t)s\ *n* (14c) **1 :** remission of part or all of the temporal and esp. purgatorial punishment that according to Roman Catholicism is due for sins whose eternal punishment has been remitted and whose guilt has been pardoned (as through the sacrament of reconciliation) **2 :** the act of indulging **:** the state of being indulgent **3 a :** an indulgent act **b :** an extension of time for payment or performance granted as a favor **4 a :** the act of indulging in something; *esp* **:** SELF-INDULGENCE **b :** something indulged in ⟨walk off gastronomic ~*s* —Barbara L. Michaels⟩
in·dul·gent \in-ˈdəl-jənt\ *adj* [L *indulgent-, indulgens,* prp. of *indulgēre*] (1509) **:** indulging or characterized by indulgence; *esp* **:** LENIENT — **in·dul·gent·ly** *adv*
in·dult \ˈin-ˌdəlt, in-ˈ\ *n* [ME (Sc), fr. ML *indultum,* fr. LL, grant, fr. L, neut. of *indultus,* pp. of *indulgēre*] (15c) **:** a special often temporary dispensation granted in the Roman Catholic Church
¹**in·du·rate** \ˈin-də-rət, -dyə-; in-ˈdu̇r-ət, -ˈdyu̇r-\ *adj* (14c) **:** physically or morally hardened
²**in·du·rate** \ˈin-də-ˌrāt, -dyə-\ *vb* **-rat·ed; -rat·ing** [L *induratus,* pp. of *indurare,* fr. *in-* + *durare* to harden, fr. *durus* hard — more at DURING] *vt* (1538) **1 :** to make unfeeling, stubborn, or obdurate **2 :** to make hardy **:** INURE **3 :** to make hard ⟨great heat ~*s* clay⟩ **4 :** to establish firmly **:** CONFIRM ~ *vi* **1 :** to grow hard **:** HARDEN **2 :** to become established
indurated *adj* (1578) **:** having become firm or hard esp. by increase of fibrous elements ⟨~ tissue⟩
in·du·ra·tion \ˌin-də-ˈrā-shən, -dyə-\ *n* (14c) **:** the process of or condition produced by growing hard; *specif* **:** sclerosis esp. when associated with inflammation — **in·du·ra·tive** \ˈin-də-ˌrā-tiv, -dyə-; in-ˈdu̇r-ə-, -ˈdyu̇r-\ *adj*
indus *abbr* industrial; industry
in·du·si·um \in-ˈdü-zē-əm, -ˈdyü-, -zhē-\ *n, pl* **-sia** \-zē-ə, -zhē-\ [NL, fr. L, tunic] (1807) **:** an investing outgrowth or membrane; *esp* **:** an outgrowth of a fern frond that covers the sori
¹**in·dus·tri·al** \in-ˈdəs-trē-əl\ *adj* (15c) **1 :** of or relating to industry **2 :** derived from human industry ⟨~ wealth⟩ **3 :** engaged in industry ⟨the ~ classes⟩ **4 :** used in or developed for use in industry ⟨~ diamonds⟩; *also* **:** HEAVY-DUTY ⟨an ~ zipper⟩ **5 :** characterized by highly developed industries ⟨an ~ nation⟩ — **in·dus·tri·al·ly** \-trē-ə-lē\ *adv*
²**industrial** *n* (1865) **1 a :** one that is employed in industry **b :** a company engaged in industrial production or service **2 :** a stock or bond issued by an industrial corporation or enterprise
industrial action *n* (ca. 1931) *Brit* **:** JOB ACTION
industrial archaeology *n* (1951) **:** the study of the buildings, machinery, and equipment of the industrial revolution — **industrial archaeologist** *n*
industrial arts *n pl but sing in constr* (ca. 1925) **:** a subject taught in elementary and secondary schools that aims at developing manual skill and familiarity with tools and machines
industrial engineering *n* (ca. 1924) **:** engineering that deals with the design, improvement, and installation of integrated systems (as of people, materials, and energy) in industry — **industrial engineer** *n*
in·dus·tri·al·ise *Brit var of* INDUSTRIALIZE
in·dus·tri·al·ism \in-ˈdəs-trē-ə-ˌli-zəm\ *n* (1831) **:** social organization in which industries and esp. large-scale industries are dominant

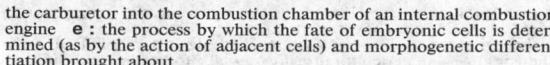

in·dus·tri·al·ist \-list\ *n* (1864) : one owning or engaged in the management of an industry : MANUFACTURER
in·dus·tri·al·ize \in-ˈdəs-trē-ə-ˌlīz\ *vb* **-ized; -iz·ing** *vt* (1886) : to make industrial ⟨~ an agricultural region⟩ ~ *vi* : to become industrial — **in·dus·tri·al·i·za·tion** \-ˌdəs-trē-ə-lə-ˈzā-shən\ *n*
industrial melanism *n* (1943) : genetically determined melanism as a population phenomenon esp. in moths in which the proportion of dark individuals tends to increase due to differential predation esp. by birds which more easily find and eat lighter-colored individuals in habitats darkened by industrial pollution
industrial psychology *n* (1917) : the application of the findings and methods of experimental, clinical, and social psychology to industrial concerns — **industrial psychologist** *n*
industrial relations *n pl* (1904) : the dealings or relationships of a usu. large business or industrial enterprise with its own workers, with labor in general, with governmental agencies, or with the public
industrial revolution *n* (1848) : a rapid major change in an economy (as in England in the late 18th century) marked by the general introduction of power-driven machinery or by an important change in the prevailing types and methods of use of such machines
industrial school *n* (1853) : a school specializing in the teaching of industrial arts; *specif* : one for juvenile delinquents
industrial sociology *n* (1948) : sociological analysis directed at institutions and social relationships within and largely controlled or affected by industry
in·dus·tri·al–strength \in-ˈdəs-trē-əl-ˈstreŋ(k)th, -ˈstren(t)th\ *adj* (1976) **1** : suitable for industrial use **2** : marked by more than usual power, durability, or intensity ⟨~ boots⟩ ⟨an ~ voice⟩
industrial union *n* (1902) : a labor union open to workers in an industry irrespective of their occupation or craft — compare CRAFT UNION
in·dus·tri·ous \in-ˈdəs-trē-əs\ *adj* (15c) **1** *obs* : SKILLFUL, INGENIOUS **2** : constantly, regularly, or habitually active or occupied : DILIGENT ⟨an ~ worker⟩ ***syn*** see BUSY — **in·dus·tri·ous·ly** *adv* — **in·dus·tri·ous·ness** *n*
in·dus·try \ˈin-(ˌ)dəs-trē\ *n, pl* **-tries** [ME (Sc) *industrie,* fr. MF, fr. L *industria,* fr. *industrius* diligent, fr. OL *indostruus,* perh. fr. *indu* in + *-struus* (akin to L *struere* to build) — more at END-, STREW] (15c) **1** : diligence in an employment or pursuit; *esp* : steady or habitual effort **2 a** : systematic labor esp. for some useful purpose or the creation of something of value **b** : a department or branch of a craft, art, business, or manufacture; *esp* : one that employs a large personnel and capital esp. in manufacturing **c** : a distinct group of productive or profit-making enterprises ⟨the banking ~⟩ **d** : manufacturing activity as a whole ⟨the nation's ~⟩ **3** : work devoted to the study of a particular subject or author ⟨the Shakespeare ~⟩ ***syn*** see BUSINESS
in·dwell \in-ˈdwel, ˈin-ˌ\ *vi* (14c) : to exist as an inner activating spirit, force, or principle ~ *vt* : to exist within as an activating spirit, force, or principle — **in·dwell·er** *n*
in·dwell·ing \ˈin-ˌdwe-liŋ\ *adj* (1646) **1** : being an inner activating or guiding force **2** : left within a bodily organ or passage esp. to promote drainage — used of an implanted tube (as a catheter)
In·dy car \ˈin-dē-\ *n* [*indy* by shortening & alter. fr. *Indianapolis,* Indiana] (1964) : a single-seat open-cockpit racing car with the engine in the rear
[1]**-ine** *adj suffix* **1** [F *-in, -ine,* fr. L *-īnus* — more at -EN] : of or relating to ⟨estuar*ine*⟩ **2** [F *-in, -ine,* fr. L *-īnus,* fr. Gk *-inos* — more at -EN] : made of : like ⟨opal*ine*⟩
[2]**-ine** *n suffix* [F *-ine,* fr. L *-īna,* fr. fem. of *-īnus,* adj. suffix] **1** : chemical substance: as **a** : halogen element ⟨chlor*ine*⟩ **b** : basic or base-containing carbon compound that contains nitrogen ⟨quin*ine*⟩ ⟨cyst*ine*⟩ **c** : mixture of compounds (as of hydrocarbons) ⟨gasol*ine*⟩ **d** : hydride ⟨ars*ine*⟩ **2** : -IN 1a **3** : commercial product or material ⟨glass*ine*⟩
in·ebri·ant \i-ˈnē-brē-ənt\ *n* (1819) : INTOXICANT
[1]**in·ebri·ate** \i-ˈnē-brē-ˌāt\ *vt* **-at·ed; -at·ing** [ME *inebryat,* fr. L *inebriatus,* pp. of *inebriare,* fr. *in-* + *ebriare* to intoxicate, fr. *ebrius* drunk] (15c) **1** : to exhilarate or stupefy as if by liquor **2** : to make drunk : INTOXICATE — **in·ebri·a·tion** \-ˌnē-brē-ˈā-shən\ *n*
[2]**in·ebri·ate** \i-ˈnē-brē-ət, -ˌāt\ *adj* (15c) **1** : affected by alcohol : DRUNK **2** : addicted to excessive drinking
[3]**in·ebri·ate** \-ət\ *n* (ca. 1796) : one who is drunk; *esp* : DRUNKARD
in·ebri·at·ed \-brē-ˌā-təd\ *adj* (1609) : exhilarated or confused by or as if by alcohol : INTOXICATED
in·ebri·ety \ˌi-ni-ˈbrī-ə-tē\ *n* [prob. blend of *inebriation* and *ebriety* drunkenness] (1801) : the state of being inebriated : DRUNKENNESS
in·ed·i·ble \(ˌ)i-ˈne-də-bəl\ *adj* (1786) : not fit to be eaten
in·ed·u·ca·ble \(ˌ)i-ˈne-jə-kə-bəl\ *adj* (1884) : incapable of being educated — **in·ed·u·ca·bil·i·ty** \-ˌne-jə-kə-ˈbi-lə-tē\ *n*
in·ef·fa·ble \(ˌ)i-ˈne-fə-bəl\ *adj* [ME, fr. L *ineffabilis,* fr. *in-* + *effabilis* capable of being expressed, fr. *effari* to speak out, fr. *ex-* + *fari* to speak — more at BAN] (14c) **1 a** : incapable of being expressed in words : INDESCRIBABLE ⟨~ joy⟩ **b** : UNSPEAKABLE ⟨~ disgust⟩ **2** : not to be uttered : TABOO ⟨the ~ name of Jehovah⟩ — **in·ef·fa·bil·i·ty** \-ˌne-fə-ˈbi-lə-tē\ *n* — **in·ef·fa·ble·ness** \-ˈne-fə-bəl-nəs\ *n* — **in·ef·fa·bly** \-blē\ *adv*
in·ef·face·able \ˌi-nə-ˈfā-sə-bəl\ *adj* [prob. fr. F *ineffaçable,* fr. MF, fr. *in-* + *effaçable* effaceable] (1804) : not effaceable : INERADICABLE — **in·ef·face·abil·i·ty** \-ˌfā-sə-ˈbi-lə-tē\ *n* — **in·ef·face·ably** \-ˈfā-sə-blē\ *adv*
in·ef·fec·tive \ˌi-nə-ˈfek-tiv\ *adj* (1649) **1** : not producing an intended effect : INEFFECTUAL ⟨~ lighting⟩ **2** : not capable of performing efficiently or as expected : INCAPABLE ⟨an ~ executive⟩ — **in·ef·fec·tive·ly** *adv* — **in·ef·fec·tive·ness** *n*
in·ef·fec·tu·al \ˌi-nə-ˈfek-chə(-wə)l, -ˈfeksh-wəl\ *adj* (15c) **1** : not producing the proper or intended effect : FUTILE **2** : INEFFECTIVE 2 — **in·ef·fec·tu·al·i·ty** \-ˌfek-chə-ˈwa-lə-tē\ *n* — **in·ef·fec·tu·al·ly** \-ˈfek-chə(-wə)-lē, -ˈfek-shwə-\ *adv* — **in·ef·fec·tu·al·ness** *n*
in·ef·fi·ca·cious \(ˌ)i-ˌne-fə-ˈkā-shəs\ *adj* (1658) : lacking the power to produce a desired effect : INEFFECTIVE — **in·ef·fi·ca·cious·ly** *adv* — **in·ef·fi·ca·cious·ness** *n*
in·ef·fi·ca·cy \(ˌ)i-ˈne-fi-kə-sē\ *n* [LL *inefficacia,* fr. L *inefficac-, inefficax* inefficacious, fr. *in-* + *efficac-, efficax* efficacious] (ca. 1615) : lack of power to produce a desired effect
in·ef·fi·cien·cy \ˌi-nə-ˈfi-shən(t)-sē\ *n, pl* **-cies** (1749) **1** : the quality or state of being inefficient **2** : something that is inefficient
in·ef·fi·cient \-ˈfi-shənt\ *adj* (1750) : not efficient: as **a** : not producing the effect intended or desired **b** : wasteful of time or energy ⟨~ operating procedures⟩ **c** : INCAPABLE, INCOMPETENT ⟨an ~ worker⟩ — **inefficient** *n* — **in·ef·fi·cient·ly** *adv*
in·e·gal·i·tar·i·an \ˌi-ni-ˌga-lə-ˈter-ē-ən\ *adj* (1940) : marked by disparity in social and economic standing
in·elas·tic \ˌi-nə-ˈlas-tik\ *adj* (1748) : not elastic: as **a** : slow to react or respond to changing conditions **b** : INFLEXIBLE, UNYIELDING — **in·elas·tic·i·ty** \ˌi-ni-ˌlas-ˈti-s(ə-)tē, (ˌ)i-ˌnē-ˌlas-\ *n*
inelastic collision *n* (1937) : a collision in which part of the kinetic energy of the colliding particles changes into another form of energy (as heat or radiation)
inelastic scattering *n* (1938) : a scattering of particles as the result of inelastic collision in which the total kinetic energy of the colliding particles changes
in·el·e·gance \(ˌ)i-ˈne-li-gən(t)s\ *n* (1726) : lack of elegance
in·el·e·gant \-gənt\ *adj* [MF, fr. L *inelegant-, inelegans,* fr. *in-* + *elegant-, elegans* elegant] (ca. 1570) : lacking in refinement, grace, or good taste — **in·el·e·gant·ly** *adv*
in·el·i·gi·ble \(ˌ)i-ˈne-lə-jə-bəl\ *adj* [F *inéligible,* fr. *in-* + *éligible* eligible] (1770) : not eligible: as **a** : not qualified for an office or position **b** : not permitted under football rules to catch a forward pass ⟨an ~ receiver⟩ — **in·el·i·gi·bil·i·ty** \-ˌne-lə-jə-ˈbi-lə-tē\ *n* — **ineligible** *n*
in·el·o·quent \(ˌ)i-ˈne-lə-kwənt\ *adj* (ca. 1530) : not eloquent : having or showing a lack of eloquence — **in·el·o·quent·ly** *adv*
in·eluc·ta·ble \ˌi-ni-ˈlək-tə-bəl\ *adj* [L *ineluctabilis,* fr. *in-* + *eluctari* to struggle clear of, fr. *ex-* + *luctari* to struggle, wrestle; akin to L *luxus* dislocated — more at LOCK] (ca. 1623) : not to be avoided, changed, or resisted : INEVITABLE ⟨an ~ fate⟩ — **in·eluc·ta·bil·i·ty** \-ˌlək-tə-ˈbi-lə-tē\ *n* — **in·eluc·ta·bly** \-ˈlək-tə-blē\ *adv*
in·elud·ible \ˌi-ni-ˈlü-də-bəl\ *adj* (1662) : INESCAPABLE
in·enar·ra·ble \ˌi-ni-ˈna-rə-bəl\ *adj* [ME, fr. L *inenarrabilis,* fr. *in-* + *enarrare* to explain in detail, fr. *e-* + *narrare* to narrate] (15c) : incapable of being narrated : INDESCRIBABLE
in·ept \i-ˈnept\ *adj* [MF *inepte,* fr. L *ineptus,* fr. *in-* + *aptus* apt] (1542) **1** : lacking in fitness or aptitude : UNFIT ⟨~ at sports⟩ **2** : lacking sense or reason : FOOLISH **3** : not suitable to the time, place, or occasion : inappropriate often to an absurd degree ⟨an ~ metaphor⟩ **4** : generally incompetent : BUNGLING ⟨~ leadership⟩ ***syn*** see AWKWARD — **in·ept·ly** \-ˈnep(t)-lē\ *adv* — **in·ept·ness** \-nəs\ *n*
in·ep·ti·tude \(ˌ)i-ˈnep-tə-ˌtüd, -ˌtyüd\ *n* [L *ineptitudo,* fr. *ineptus*] (1615) : the quality or state of being inept; *esp* : INCOMPETENCE
in·equal·i·ty \ˌi-ni-ˈkwä-lə-tē\ *n* [ME *inequalite,* fr. L *inaequalitat-, inaequalitas,* fr. *inaequalis* unequal, fr. *in-* + *aequalis* equal] (15c) **1** : the quality of being unequal or uneven: as **a** : lack of evenness **b** : social disparity **c** : disparity of distribution or opportunity **d** : the condition of being variable : CHANGEABLENESS **2** : an instance of being unequal **3** : a formal statement of inequality between two quantities usu. separated by a sign of inequality (as <, >, or ≠ signifying respectively *is less than, is greater than,* or *is not equal to*)
in·eq·ui·ta·ble \(ˌ)i-ˈne-kwə-tə-bəl\ *adj* (1667) : not equitable : UNFAIR ⟨an ~ distribution of funds⟩ — **in·eq·ui·ta·bly** \-blē\ *adv*
in·eq·ui·ty \(ˌ)i-ˈne-kwə-tē\ *n* (1556) **1** : INJUSTICE, UNFAIRNESS **2** : an instance of injustice or unfairness
in·erad·i·ca·ble \ˌi-ni-ˈra-di-kə-bəl\ *adj* (1818) : incapable of being eradicated — **in·erad·i·ca·bil·i·ty** \-ˌra-di-kə-ˈbi-lə-tē\ *n* — **in·erad·i·ca·bly** \-ˈra-di-kə-blē\ *adv*
in·er·ran·cy \(ˌ)i-ˈner-ən(t)-sē\ *n* (ca. 1834) : exemption from error : INFALLIBILITY ⟨the question of biblical ~⟩
in·er·rant \-ənt\ *adj* [L *inerrant-, inerrans,* fr. *in-* + *errant-, errans,* prp. of *errare* to err] (1837) : free from error
in·ert \i-ˈnərt\ *adj* [L *inert-, iners* unskilled, idle, fr. *in-* + *art-, ars* skill — more at ARM] (1647) **1** : lacking the power to move **2** : very slow to move or act : SLUGGISH **3** : deficient in active properties; *esp* : lacking a usual or anticipated chemical or biological action ***syn*** see INACTIVE — **inert** *n* — **in·ert·ly** *adv* — **in·ert·ness** *n*
inert gas *n* (1898) : NOBLE GAS
in·er·tia \i-ˈnər-shə, -shē-ə\ *n* [NL, fr. L, lack of skill, fr. *inert-, iners*] (1713) **1 a** : a property of matter by which it remains at rest or in uniform motion in the same straight line unless acted upon by some external force **b** : an analogous property of other physical quantities (as electricity) **2** : indisposition to motion, exertion, or change : INERTNESS — **in·er·tial** \-shəl\ *adj* — **in·er·tial·ly** \-ˈnər-sh(ə-)lē\ *adv*
inertial guidance *n* (ca. 1948) : guidance (as of an aircraft or spacecraft) by means of self-contained automatically controlling devices that respond to inertial forces — called also *inertial navigation*
in·es·cap·able \ˌi-nə-ˈskā-pə-bəl\ *adj* (1792) : incapable of being avoided, ignored, or denied : INEVITABLE — **in·es·cap·ably** \-blē\ *adv*
in·es·sen·tial \ˌi-nə-ˈsen(t)-shəl\ *adj* (1677) **1** : having no essence **2** : not essential : UNESSENTIAL — **inessential** *n*
in·es·ti·ma·ble \(ˌ)i-ˈnes-tə-mə-bəl\ *adj* [ME, fr. MF, fr. L *inaestimabilis,* fr. *in-* + *aestimabilis* estimable] (14c) **1** : incapable of being estimated or computed ⟨storms caused ~ damage⟩ **2** : too valuable or excellent to be measured or appreciated ⟨has performed an ~ service for his country⟩ — **in·es·ti·ma·bly** \-blē\ *adv*
in·ev·i·ta·ble \i-ˈne-və-tə-bəl\ *adj* [ME, fr. L *inevitabilis,* fr. *in-* + *evitabilis* evitable] (14c) : incapable of being avoided or evaded ⟨an ~ outcome⟩ — **in·ev·i·ta·bil·i·ty** \-ˌne-və-tə-ˈbi-lə-tē\ *n* — **in·ev·i·ta·ble·ness** \-ˈne-və-tə-bəl-nəs\ *n*
in·ev·i·ta·bly \-blē\ *adv* (15c) **1** : in an inevitable way **2** : as is to be expected ⟨~, it rained⟩
in·ex·act \ˌi-nig-ˈzakt\ *adj* [F, fr. *in-* + *exact* exact] (ca. 1828) **1** : not precisely correct or true : INACCURATE ⟨an ~ translation⟩ **2** : not rigorous and careful ⟨an ~ thinker⟩ — **in·ex·act·ly** \-ˈzak(t)-lē\ *adv* — **in·ex·act·ness** \-nəs\ *n*
in·ex·ac·ti·tude \(ˌ)i-ˌnig-ˈzak-tə-ˌtüd, -ˌtyüd\ *n* [F, fr. *inexact*] (1782) **1** : lack of exactitude or precision **2** : an instance of inexactness
in ex·cel·sis \ˌin-ik-ˈsel-səs *also* -ˈchel-\ *adv* [LL, on high] (14c) : in the highest degree
in·ex·cus·able \ˌi-nik-ˈskyü-zə-bəl\ *adj* [ME, fr. L *inexcusabilis,* fr. *in-* + *excusabilis* excusable] (15c) : impossible to excuse or justify ⟨~ rudeness⟩ — **in·ex·cus·able·ness** *n* — **in·ex·cus·ably** \-blē\ *adv*

in·ex·haust·ible \ˌi-nig-ˈzȯ-stə-bəl\ *adj* (1601) **:** not exhaustible: as **a :** incapable of being used up ‹~ riches› **b :** incapable of being wearied or worn out ‹an ~ hiker› — **in·ex·haust·ibil·i·ty** \-ˌzȯ-stə-ˈbi-lə-tē\ *n* — **in·ex·haust·ible·ness** \-ˈzȯ-stə-bəl-nəs\ *n* — **in·ex·haust·ibly** \-blē\ *adv*

in·ex·is·tence \ˌi-nig-ˈzis-tən(t)s\ *n* (ca. 1623) **:** absence of existence **:** NONEXISTENCE

in·ex·is·tent \-tənt\ *adj* [LL *inexsistent-, inexsistens,* fr. L *in-* + *exsistent-, exsistens,* prp. of *exsistere* to exist] (1646) **:** not having existence **:** NONEXISTENT

in·ex·o·ra·ble \(ˌ)i-ˈneks-rə-bəl, -ˈnek-sə-, -ˈneg-zə-rə-\ *adj* [L *inexorabilis,* fr. *in-* + *exorabilis* pliant, fr. *exorare* to prevail upon, fr. *ex-* + *orare* to speak — more at ORATION] (1542) **:** not to be persuaded, moved, or stopped **:** RELENTLESS ‹~ progress› — **in·ex·o·ra·bil·i·ty** \(ˌ)i-ˌneks-rə-ˈbi-lə-tē, -ˌnek-sə-, -ˌneg-zə-\ *n* — **in·ex·o·ra·ble·ness** \-ˈneks-rə-bəl-nəs, -ˈnek-sə-, -ˈneg-zə-\ *n* — **in·ex·o·ra·bly** \-blē\ *adv*

in·ex·pe·di·ence \ˌi-nik-ˈspē-dē-ən(t)s\ *n* (1608) **:** INEXPEDIENCY

in·ex·pe·di·en·cy \-ən(t)-sē\ *n* (1641) **:** the quality or fact of being inexpedient

in·ex·pe·di·ent \-ənt\ *adj* (1608) **:** not expedient **:** INADVISABLE — **in·ex·pe·di·ent·ly** *adv*

in·ex·pen·sive \ˌi-nik-ˈspen(t)-siv\ *adj* (ca. 1846) **:** reasonable in price **:** CHEAP — **in·ex·pen·sive·ly** *adv* — **in·ex·pen·sive·ness** *n*

in·ex·pe·ri·ence \ˌi-nik-ˈspir-ē-ən(t)s\ *n* [MF, fr. LL *inexperientia,* fr. L *in-* + *experientia* experience] (1598) **1 :** lack of practical experience **2 :** lack of knowledge of the ways of the world — **in·ex·pe·ri·enced** \-ən(t)st\ *adj*

in·ex·pert \(ˌ)i-ˈnek-ˌspərt, ˌi-nik-ˈ\ *adj* [ME, fr. L *inexpertus,* fr. *in-* + *expertus* expert] (15c) **:** not expert **:** UNSKILLED — **in·ex·pert** \-ˈnek-ˌspərt\ *n* — **in·ex·pert·ly** \-ˈnek-ˌspərt-lē, ˌi-nik-ˈ\ *adv* — **in·ex·pert·ness** *n*

in·ex·pi·a·ble \(ˌ)i-ˈnek-spē-ə-bəl\ *adj* [ME *inexpyable,* fr. L *inexpiabilis,* fr. *in-* + *expiare* to expiate] (15c) **1 :** not capable of being atoned for **2** *obs* **:** IMPLACABLE, UNAPPEASABLE — **in·ex·pi·a·bly** \-blē\ *adv*

in·ex·plain·able \ˌi-nik-ˈsplā-nə-bəl\ *adj* (ca. 1623) **:** INEXPLICABLE

in·ex·pli·ca·ble \ˌi-nik-ˈspli-kə-bəl, (ˌ)i-ˈnek-(ˌ)spli-\ *adj* [ME, fr. L *inexplicabilis,* fr. *in-* + *explicabilis* explicable] (15c) **:** incapable of being explained, interpreted, or accounted for ‹an ~ disappearance› — **in·ex·pli·ca·bil·i·ty** \ˌi-nik-ˌspli-kə-ˈbi-lə-tē, (ˌ)i-ˌnek-(ˌ)spli-\ *n* — **in·ex·pli·ca·ble·ness** \ˌi-nik-ˈspli-kə-bəl-nəs, (ˌ)i-ˈnek-(ˌ)spli-\ *n* — **in·ex·pli·ca·bly** \-blē\ *adv*

in·ex·plic·it \ˌi-nik-ˈspli-sət\ *adj* (ca. 1812) **:** not explicit

in·ex·press·ible \-ˈspre-sə-bəl\ *adj* (1625) **:** not capable of being expressed **:** INDESCRIBABLE ‹~ joy› — **in·ex·press·ibil·i·ty** \-ˌspre-sə-ˈbi-lə-tē\ *n* — **in·ex·press·ible·ness** \-ˈspre-sə-bəl-nəs\ *n* — **in·ex·press·ibly** \-blē\ *adv*

in·ex·pres·sive \-ˈspre-siv\ *adj* (1652) **1** *archaic* **:** INEXPRESSIBLE **2 :** lacking expression or meaning ‹an ~ face› — **in·ex·pres·sive·ly** *adv* — **in·ex·pres·sive·ness** *n*

in·ex·pug·na·ble \ˌi-nik-ˈspəg-nə-bəl, -ˈspyü-nə-\ *adj* [ME *in-expungnabull,* fr. L *inexpugnabilis,* fr. *in-* + *expugnare* to take by storm, fr. *ex-* + *pugnare* to fight — more at PUNGENT] (15c) **1 :** incapable of being subdued or overthrown **:** IMPREGNABLE ‹an ~ position› **2 :** STABLE, FIXED ‹~ hatred› — **in·ex·pug·na·ble·ness** *n* — **in·ex·pug·na·bly** \-blē\ *adv*

in·ex·pung·ible \ˌi-nik-ˈspən-jə-bəl\ *adj* [*in-* + *expunge*] (1888) **:** incapable of being obliterated

in ex·ten·so \ˌin-ik-ˈsten(t)-(ˌ)sō\ *adv* [ML] (1826) **:** at full length ‹the passage was quoted *in extenso*›

in·ex·tin·guish·able \ˌi-nik-ˈstiŋ-gwi-shə-bəl, -ˈstiŋ-wi-\ *adj* (15c) **:** not extinguishable **:** UNQUENCHABLE ‹an ~ flame› ‹an ~ longing› — **in·ex·tin·guish·ably** \-blē\ *adv*

in ex·tre·mis \ˌin-ik-ˈstrē-məs, -ˈstrā-\ *adv* [L] (ca. 1530) **:** in extreme circumstances; *esp* **:** at the point of death

in·ex·tri·ca·ble \ˌi-nik-ˈstri-kə-bəl, (ˌ)i-ˈnek-(ˌ)stri-\ *adj* [ME, fr. MF or L; MF, fr. L *inextricabilis,* fr. *in-* + *extricabilis* extricable] (15c) **1 :** forming a maze or tangle from which it is impossible to get free **2 a :** incapable of being disentangled or untied ‹an ~ knot› **b :** not capable of being solved — **in·ex·tri·ca·bil·i·ty** \ˌi-nik-ˌstri-kə-ˈbi-lə-tē, (ˌ)i-ˌnek-(ˌ)stri-\ *n* — **in·ex·tri·ca·bly** \ˌi-nik-ˈstri-kə-blē, (ˌ)i-ˈnek-(ˌ)stri-\ *adv*

inf *abbr* **1** infantry **2** infinitive

INF *abbr* intermediate range nuclear forces

in·fal·li·ble \(ˌ)in-ˈfa-lə-bəl\ *adj* [ME, fr. ML *infallibilis,* fr. L *in-* + LL *fallibilis* fallible] (15c) **1 :** incapable of error **:** UNERRING ‹an ~ memory› **2 :** not liable to mislead, deceive, or disappoint **:** CERTAIN ‹an ~ remedy› **3 :** incapable of error in defining doctrines touching faith or morals — **in·fal·li·bil·i·ty** \-ˌfa-lə-ˈbi-lə-tē\ *n* — **in·fal·li·bly** \-ˈfa-lə-blē\ *adv*

in·fall·ing \ˈin-ˌfȯ-liŋ\ *adj* (1964) **:** moving under the influence of gravity toward a celestial object (as a black hole) — **in·fall** \-ˌfȯl\ *n*

in·fa·mous \ˈin-fə-məs\ *adj* [ME, fr. L *infamis,* fr. *in-* + *fama* fame] (14c) **1 :** having a reputation of the worst kind **:** notoriously evil ‹an ~ traitor› **2 :** causing or bringing infamy **:** DISGRACEFUL ‹an ~ crime› **3 :** convicted of an offense bringing infamy — **in·fa·mous·ly** *adv*

in·fa·my \-mē\ *n, pl* **-mies** (15c) **1 :** evil reputation brought about by something grossly criminal, shocking, or brutal **2 a :** an extreme and publicly known criminal or evil act **b :** the state of being infamous ***syn*** see DISGRACE

in·fan·cy \ˈin-fən(t)-sē\ *n, pl* **-cies** (14c) **1 :** early childhood **2 :** a beginning or early period of existence **3 :** the legal status of an infant

[1]**in·fant** \ˈin-fənt\ *n* [ME *enfaunt,* fr. AF *enfant,* fr. L *infant-, infans,* fr. *infant-, infans,* adj., incapable of speech, young, fr. *in-* + *fant-, fans,* prp. of *fari* to speak — more at BAN] (14c) **1 :** a child in the first period of life **2 :** a person who is not of full age **:** MINOR

[2]**infant** *adj* (ca. 1586) **1 :** intended for young children **2 :** being in an early stage of development **3 :** of, relating to, or being in infancy

in·fan·ta \in-ˈfan-tə, -ˈfän-\ *n* [Sp & Pg, fem. of *infante*] (1593) **:** a daughter of a Spanish or Portuguese monarch

in·fan·te \in-ˈfan-tē, -ˈfän-(ˌ)tā\ *n* [Sp & Pg, lit., infant, fr. L *infant-, infans*] (1555) **:** a younger son of a Spanish or Portuguese monarch

in·fan·ti·cide \in-ˈfan-tə-ˌsīd\ *n* [LL *infanticidium,* fr. L *infant-, infans* + *-i-* + *-cidium* -cide] (1611) **1 :** the killing of an infant **2** [LL *infanticida,* fr. L *infant-, infans* + *-i-* + *-cida* -cide] **:** one who kills an infant — **in·fan·ti·ci·dal** \-ˌfan-tə-ˈsī-dᵊl\ *adj*

in·fan·tile \ˈin-fən-ˌtī(-ə)l, -tᵊl, -ˌtēl, -(ˌ)til\ *adj* (1696) **1 :** of or relating to infants or infancy **2 :** suitable to or characteristic of an infant; *esp* **:** very immature ‹~ humor› — **in·fan·til·i·ty** \ˌin-fən-ˈti-lə-tē\ *n*

infantile paralysis *n* (1843) **:** POLIOMYELITIS

in·fan·til·ism \ˈin-fən-ˌtī-ˌli-zəm, -tə-ˌli-; in-ˈfan-tə-ˌli-\ *n* (1895) **1 :** retention of childish physical, mental, or emotional qualities in adult life; *esp* **:** failure to attain sexual maturity **2 :** an act or expression that indicates lack of maturity

in·fan·til·ize \ˈin-fən-ˌtī-ˌlīz, -fən-tə-ˌlīz, in-ˈfan-tə-\ *vt* **-ized; -iz·ing** (1943) **1 :** to make or keep infantile **2 :** to treat as if infantile — **in·fan·til·i·za·tion** \ˌin-fən-ˌti-lə-ˈzā-shən, -fən-tə-, in-ˌfan-tə-\ *n*

in·fan·tine \ˈin-fən-ˌtīn, -ˌtēn\ *adj* (1603) **:** INFANTILE, CHILDISH

in·fan·try \ˈin-fən-trē\ *n, pl* **-tries** [MF & OIt; MF *infanterie,* fr. OIt *infanteria,* fr. *infante* boy, foot soldier, fr. L *infant-, infans*] (1579) **1 a :** soldiers trained, armed, and equipped to fight on foot **b :** a branch of an army composed of these soldiers **2 :** an infantry regiment or division

in·fan·try·man \-trē-mən\ *n* (1883) **:** an infantry soldier

infant school *n* (1824) *Brit* **:** a school for children aged five to seven or eight

in·farct \ˈin-ˌfärkt, in-ˈ\ *n* [L *infarctus,* pp. of *infarcire* to stuff, fr. *in-* + *farcire* to stuff] (1873) **:** an area of necrosis in a tissue or organ resulting from obstruction of the local circulation by a thrombus or embolus — **in·farct·ed** \in-ˈfärk-təd\ *adj* — **in·farc·tion** \in-ˈfärk-shən\ *n*

in·fare \ˈin-ˌfer\ *n* [ME, entrance, fr. OE *infær,* fr. *in* + *fær* way, fr. *faran* to go — more at FARE] (1595) *chiefly dial* **:** a reception for a newly married couple

[1]**in·fat·u·ate** \in-ˈfa-chə-wət, -chü-ət\ *adj* (15c) **:** being in an infatuated state or condition

[2]**in·fat·u·ate** \-ˌwāt, -ˌāt\ *vt* **-at·ed; -at·ing** [L *infatuatus,* pp. of *infatuare,* fr. *in-* + *fatuus* fatuous] (1533) **1 :** to cause to be foolish **:** deprive of sound judgment **2 :** to inspire with a foolish or extravagant love or admiration — **in·fat·u·a·tion** \-ˌfa-chə-ˈwā-shən, -chü-ˈā-\ *n*

in·fau·na \ˈin-ˌfȯ-nə, -ˌfä-\ *n* [NL, fr. [2]*in-* + *fauna*] (1914) **:** benthic fauna living in the substrate and esp. in a soft sea bottom — compare EPIFAUNA — **in·fau·nal** \-ˌfȯ-nᵊl, -ˌfä-\ *adj*

in·fea·si·ble \(ˌ)in-ˈfē-zə-bəl\ *adj* (1533) **:** not feasible **:** IMPRACTICABLE — **in·fea·si·bil·i·ty** \-ˌfē-zə-ˈbi-lə-tē\ *n*

in·fect \in-ˈfekt\ *vt* [ME, fr. L *infectus,* pp. of *inficere,* fr. *in-* + *facere* to make, do — more at DO] (14c) **1 :** to contaminate with a disease-producing substance or agent (as bacteria) **2 a :** to communicate a pathogen or a disease to **b** *of a pathogenic organism* **:** to invade (an individual or organ) usu. by penetration **c** *of a computer virus* **:** to become transmitted and copied to (as a computer) **3 a :** CONTAMINATE, CORRUPT ‹the inflated writing that ~s such stories› **b :** to work upon or seize upon so as to induce sympathy, belief, or support ‹trying to ~ their salespeople with their enthusiasm› — **in·fec·tor** \-ˈfek-tər\ *n*

in·fec·tion \in-ˈfek-shən\ *n* (14c) **1 :** the act or result of affecting injuriously **2 :** an infective agent or material contaminated with an infective agent **3 a :** the state produced by the establishment of an infective agent in or on a suitable host **b :** a disease resulting from infection **4 :** an act or process of infecting; *also* **:** the establishment of a pathogen in its host after invasion **5 :** the communication of emotions or qualities through example or contact

in·fec·tious \-shəs\ *adj* (1542) **1 a :** capable of causing infection ‹viruses and other ~ agents› **b :** communicable by infection ‹an ~ disease› — compare CONTAGIOUS **2 :** that corrupts or contaminates **3 :** spreading or capable of spreading rapidly to others ‹their enthusiasm was ~› ‹an ~ grin› — **in·fec·tious·ly** *adv* — **in·fec·tious·ness** *n*

infectious hepatitis *n* (ca. 1941) **:** HEPATITIS A

infectious mononucleosis *n* (1920) **:** an acute infectious disease caused by the Epstein-Barr virus and characterized by fever, swelling of lymph nodes, and lymphocytosis

in·fec·tive \in-ˈfek-tiv\ *adj* (14c) **1 :** producing or capable of producing infection **2 :** affecting others **:** INFECTIOUS — **in·fec·tiv·i·ty** \(ˌ)in-ˌfek-ˈti-və-tē\ *n*

in·fe·lic·i·tous \ˌin-fi-ˈli-sə-təs\ *adj* (1835) **:** not felicitous: as **a :** not appropriate or well-timed ‹an ~ remark› **b :** AWKWARD, UNFORTUNATE ‹an ~ moment› — **in·fe·lic·i·tous·ly** *adv*

in·fe·lic·i·ty \-sə-tē\ *n, pl* **-ties** [ME *infelicite* unhappiness, fr. L *infelicitas,* fr. *infelic-, infelix* unhappy, fr. *in-* + *felic-, felix* fruitful — more at FEMININE] (1617) **1 :** the quality or state of being infelicitous **2 :** something (as a word or phrase) that is infelicitous ‹minor *infelicities*›

in·fer \in-ˈfər\ *vb* **in·ferred; in·fer·ring** [MF or L; MF *inferer,* fr. L *inferre,* lit., to carry or bring into, fr. *in-* + *ferre* to carry — more at BEAR] *vt* (1528) **1 :** to derive as a conclusion from facts or premises ‹we see smoke and ~ fire —L. A. White› — compare IMPLY **2 :** GUESS, SURMISE ‹your letter . . . allows me to ~ that you are as well as ever —O. W. Holmes †1935› **3 a :** to involve as a normal outcome of thought **b :** to point out **:** INDICATE ‹this doth ~ the zeal I had to see him —Shak.› ‹another survey . . . ~s that two-thirds of all present computer installations are not paying for themselves —H. R. Chellman› **4 :** SUGGEST, HINT ‹are you *inferring* I'm incompetent?› ~ *vi* **:** to draw inferences ‹men . . . have observed, *inferred,* and reasoned . . . to all kinds of results —John Dewey› — **in·fer·able** *also* **in·fer·ri·ble** \in-ˈfər-ə-bəl\ *adj* — **in·fer·rer** \-ˈfər-ər\ *n*

syn INFER, DEDUCE, CONCLUDE, JUDGE, GATHER mean to arrive at a mental conclusion. INFER implies arriving at a conclusion by reasoning from evidence; if the evidence is slight, the term comes close to *surmise* ‹from that remark, I *inferred* that they knew each other›. DEDUCE often adds to INFER the special implication of drawing a particular inference from a generalization ‹denied we could *deduce* anything important from human mortality›. CONCLUDE implies arriving at a necessary inference at the end of a chain of reasoning ‹*concluded* that only the accused could be guilty›. JUDGE stresses a weighing of

the evidence on which a conclusion is based ⟨*judge* people by their actions⟩. GATHER suggests an intuitive forming of a conclusion from implications ⟨*gathered* their desire to be alone without a word⟩.
usage Sir Thomas More is the first writer known to have used both *infer* and *imply* in their approved senses (1528). He is also the first to have used *infer* in a sense close in meaning to *imply* (1533). Both of these uses of *infer* coexisted without comment until some time around the end of World War I. Since then, senses 3 and 4 of *infer* have been frequently condemned as an undesirable blurring of a useful distinction. The actual blurring has been done by the commentators. Sense 3, descended from More's use of 1533, does not occur with a personal subject. When objections arose, they were to a use with a personal subject (now sense 4). Since dictionaries did not recognize this use specifically, the objectors assumed that sense 3 was the one they found illogical, even though it had been in respectable use for four centuries. The actual usage condemned was a spoken one never used in logical discourse. At present sense 4 is found in print chiefly in letters to the editor and other informal prose, not in serious intellectual writing. The controversy over sense 4 has apparently reduced the frequency of use of sense 3.

in·fer·ence \ˈin-f(ə-)rən(t)s, -fərn(t)s\ *n* (1594) **1 :** the act or process of inferring: as **a :** the act of passing from one proposition, statement, or judgment considered as true to another whose truth is believed to follow from that of the former **b :** the act of passing from statistical sample data to generalizations (as of the value of population parameters) usu. with calculated degrees of certainty **2 :** something that is inferred; *esp* **:** a proposition arrived at by inference **3 :** the premises and conclusion of a process of inferring

in·fer·en·tial \ˌin-fə-ˈren(t)-shəl\ *adj* [ML *inferentia,* fr. L *inferent-, inferens,* prp. of *inferre*] (1657) **1 :** relating to, involving, or resembling inference **2 :** deduced or deducible by inference

in·fer·en·tial·ly \-ˈren(t)-sh(ə-)lē\ *adv* (1691) **:** by way of inference **:** through inference

in·fe·ri·or \in-ˈfir-ē-ər\ *adj* [ME, fr. L, compar. of *inferus* lower — more at UNDER] (15c) **1 :** situated lower down **:** LOWER **2 a :** of low or lower degree or rank **b :** of poor quality **:** MEDIOCRE **3 :** of little or less importance, value, or merit **4 a :** situated below another and esp. another similar superior part of an upright body **b :** situated in a relatively low posterior or ventral position in a quadrupedal body **c** (1) **:** situated below another plant part or organ (2) **:** ABAXIAL **5 :** relating to or being a subscript — **inferior** *n* — **in·fe·ri·or·i·ty** \(ˌ)in-ˌfir-ē-ˈȯr-ə-tē, -ˈär-\ *n* — **in·fe·ri·or·ly** \in-ˈfir-ē-ər-lē\ *adv*

inferior conjunction *n* (1833) **:** a conjunction of an inferior planet with the sun in which the planet is aligned between the earth and the sun

inferiority complex *n* (1922) **1 :** an acute sense of personal inferiority often resulting either in timidity or through overcompensation in exaggerated aggressiveness **2 :** a collective sense of cultural, regional, or national inferiority

inferior planet *n* (1633) **:** either of the planets Mercury and Venus whose orbits lie within that of the earth

in·fer·nal \in-ˈfər-nᵊl\ *adj* [ME, fr. AF *enfernal,* fr. LL *infernalis,* fr. *infernus* hell, fr. L, lower, fr. *inferus*] (14c) **1 :** of or relating to a nether world of the dead **2 a :** of or relating to hell **b :** HELLISH, DIABOLICAL **3 :** DAMNABLE ⟨an ~ nuisance⟩ — **in·fer·nal·ly** \-nᵊl-ē\ *adv*

infernal machine *n* (1810) **:** a machine or apparatus maliciously designed to explode and destroy life or property; *esp* **:** a concealed or disguised bomb

in·fer·no \in-ˈfər-(ˌ)nō\ *n, pl* **-nos** [It, hell, fr. LL *infernus*] (1834) **:** a place or a state that resembles or suggests hell ⟨the ~ of war⟩; *also* **:** an intense fire **:** CONFLAGRATION ⟨a raging ~⟩

in·fer·tile \(ˈ)in-ˈfər-tᵊl\ *adj* [MF, fr. LL *infertilis,* fr. L *in-* + *fertilis* fertile] (1597) **:** not fertile or productive ⟨~ eggs⟩ ⟨~ fields⟩; *esp* **:** incapable of or unsuccessful in achieving pregnancy ⟨~ couples⟩ — **in·fer·til·i·ty** \ˌin-(ˌ)fər-ˈti-lə-tē\ *n*

in·fest \in-ˈfest\ *vt* [F *infester,* fr. L *infestare,* fr. *infestus* hostile] (1602) **1 :** to spread or swarm in or over in a troublesome manner ⟨a slum *~ed* with crime⟩ ⟨shark-*infested* waters⟩ **2 :** to live in or on as a parasite — **in·fes·tant** \-ˈfes-tənt\ *n* — **in·fes·ta·tion** \ˌin-ˌfes-ˈtā-shən\ *n* — **in·fest·er** \in-ˈfes-tər\ *n*

in·fib·u·la·tion \(ˌ)in-ˌfi-byə-ˈlā-shən\ *n* [L *infibulare* to fasten the labia majora or prepuce with stitches or a clasp, fr. *in-* + *fibula* clasp, fibula] (1798) **:** extreme female genital mutilation involving complete excision of the clitoris, labia minora, and most of the labia majora followed by stitching to close up most of the vagina

in·fi·del \ˈin-fə-dᵊl, -fə-ˌdel\ *n* [ME *infidele,* fr. MF, fr. LL *infidelis* unbelieving, fr. L, unfaithful, fr. *in-* + *fidelis* faithful — more at FIDELITY] (15c) **1 :** one who is not a Christian or who opposes Christianity **2 a :** an unbeliever with respect to a particular religion **b :** one who acknowledges no religious belief **3 :** a disbeliever in something specified or understood — **infidel** *adj*

in·fi·del·i·ty \ˌin-fə-ˈde-lə-tē, -(ˌ)fī-\ *n, pl* **-ties** (15c) **1 :** lack of belief in a religion **2 a :** unfaithfulness to a moral obligation **:** DISLOYALTY **b :** marital unfaithfulness or an instance of it

in·field \ˈin-ˌfēld\ *n* (1606) **1 :** a field near a farmhouse **2 a :** the area of a baseball field enclosed by the three bases and home plate **b :** the defensive positions comprising first base, second base, shortstop, and third base; *also* **:** the players who play these positions **3 :** the area enclosed by a racetrack or running track

in·field·er \-ˌfēl-dər\ *n* (1867) **:** a baseball player who plays in the infield

infield hit *n* (1907) **:** a base hit on a ball that does not leave the infield

infield out *n* (1926) **:** a ground ball on which the batter is put out by an infielder

in·fight·ing \ˈin-ˌfī-tiŋ\ *n* (1816) **1 :** fighting or boxing at close quarters **2 :** rough-and-tumble fighting **3 :** prolonged and often bitter dissension or rivalry among members of a group or organization ⟨bureaucratic ~⟩ — **in·fight** \ˈin-ˌfīt\ *vi* — **in·fight·er** \-ˌfī-tər\ *n*

in·fil·trate \in-ˈfil-ˌtrāt, ˈin-(ˌ)\ *vb* **-trat·ed; -trat·ing** *vt* (1758) **1 :** to cause (as a liquid) to permeate something by penetrating its pores or interstices **2 :** to pass into or through (a substance) by filtering or permeating **3 :** to pass (troops) singly or in small groups through gaps in the enemy line **4 :** to enter or become established in gradually or unobtrusively usu. for subversive purposes ⟨the intelligence staff had been *infiltrated* by spies⟩ ~ *vi* **:** to enter, permeate, or pass through a substance or area by filtering or by insinuating gradually — **infiltrate** *n* — **in·fil·tra·tion** \ˌin-(ˌ)fil-ˈtrā-shən\ *n* — **in·fil·tra·tive** \ˈin-(ˌ)fil-ˌtrā-tiv, in-ˈfil-trə-\ *adj* — **in·fil·tra·tor** \in-ˈfil-ˌtrā-tər, ˈin-(ˌ)\ *n*

¹in·fi·nite \ˈin-fə-nət\ *adj* [ME *infinit,* fr. AF or L; AF, fr. L *infinitus,* fr. *in-* + *finitus* finite] (14c) **1 :** extending indefinitely **:** ENDLESS ⟨~ space⟩ **2 :** immeasurably or inconceivably great or extensive **:** INEXHAUSTIBLE ⟨~ patience⟩ **3 :** subject to no limitation or external determination **4 a :** extending beyond, lying beyond, or being greater than any preassigned finite value however large ⟨~ number of positive numbers⟩ **b :** extending to infinity ⟨~ plane surface⟩ **c :** characterized by an infinite number of elements or terms ⟨an ~ set⟩ ⟨an ~ series⟩ — **in·fi·nite·ly** *adv* — **in·fi·nite·ness** *n*

²infinite *n* (15c) **:** something that is infinite (as in extent, duration, or number)

¹in·fin·i·tes·i·mal \(ˌ)in-ˌfi-nə-ˈte-sə-məl, -zə-məl\ *n* [NL *infinitesimus* infinite in rank, fr. L *infinitus*] (1706) **:** an infinitesimal quantity or variable

²infinitesimal *adj* (1710) **1 :** taking on values arbitrarily close to but greater than zero **2 :** immeasurably or incalculably small ⟨an ~ difference⟩ — **in·fin·i·tes·i·mal·ly** \-mə-lē\ *adv*

infinitesimal calculus *n* (1801) **:** CALCULUS 1b

in·fin·i·ti·val \(ˌ)in-ˌfi-nə-ˈtī-vəl\ *adj* (1869) **:** relating to the infinitive

¹in·fin·i·tive \in-ˈfi-nə-tiv\ *adj* [ME *infinityf,* fr. LL *infinitivus,* fr. L *infinitus*] (15c) **:** formed with the infinitive — **in·fin·i·tive·ly** *adv*

²infinitive *n* (1530) **:** a verb form normally identical in English with the first person singular that performs some functions of a noun and at the same time displays some characteristics of a verb and that is used with *to* (as in "I asked him *to go*") except with auxiliary and various other verbs (as in "no one saw him *leave*")

in·fin·i·tude \in-ˈfi-nə-ˌtüd, -ˌtyüd\ *n* (1641) **1 :** the quality or state of being infinite **:** INFINITENESS **2 :** something that is infinite esp. in extent **3 :** an infinite number or quantity

in·fin·i·ty \in-ˈfi-nə-tē\ *n, pl* **-ties** (14c) **1 a :** the quality of being infinite **b :** unlimited extent of time, space, or quantity **:** BOUNDLESSNESS **2 :** an indefinitely great number or amount ⟨an ~ of stars⟩ **3 a :** the limit of the value of a function or variable when it tends to become numerically larger than any preassigned finite number **b :** a part of a geometric magnitude that lies beyond any part whose distance from a given reference position is finite ⟨do parallel lines ever meet if they extend to ~⟩ **c :** a transfinite number (as aleph-null) **4 :** a distance so great that the rays of light from a point source at that distance may be regarded as parallel

infinity pool *n* (1992) **:** an outdoor swimming pool having an edge over which water flows into a trough but seems to flow to the horizon

in·firm \in-ˈfərm\ *adj* [ME, fr. L *infirmus,* fr. *in-* + *firmus* firm] (14c) **1 :** of poor or deteriorated vitality; *esp* **:** feeble from age **2 :** weak of mind, will, or character **:** IRRESOLUTE, VACILLATING **3 :** not solid or stable **:** INSECURE ***syn*** see WEAK — **in·firm·ly** *adv*

in·fir·ma·ry \in-ˈfərm-rē, -ˈfər-mə-\ *n, pl* **-ries** (15c) **:** a place where the infirm or sick are lodged for care and treatment

in·fir·mi·ty \in-ˈfər-mə-tē\ *n, pl* **-ties** (14c) **1 a :** the quality or state of being infirm **b :** the condition of being feeble **:** FRAILTY **2 :** DISEASE, MALADY **3 :** a personal failing **:** FOIBLE ⟨one of the besetting *infirmities* of living creatures is egotism —A. J. Toynbee⟩

¹in·fix \ˈin-ˌfiks, in-ˈ\ *vt* [L *infixus,* pp. of *infigere,* fr. *in-* + *figere* to fasten — more at FIX] (1502) **1 :** to fasten or fix by piercing or thrusting in **2 :** to impress firmly in the consciousness or disposition **3 :** to insert (as a sound or letter) as an infix ***syn*** see IMPLANT — **in·fix·ation** \ˌin-(ˌ)fik-ˈsā-shən\ *n*

²in·fix \ˈin-ˌfiks\ *n* (1881) **:** a derivational or inflectional affix appearing in the body of a word (as Sanskrit *-n-* in *vindami* "I know" as contrasted with *vid* "to know")

³in·fix *same as* ²\ *adj* (1971) **:** characterized by placement of a binary operator between the operands ⟨$a + b$ is expressed in ~ notation⟩ — compare POSTFIX, PREFIX

infl *abbr* influenced

in fla·gran·te \ˌin-flə-ˌgrän-tē, -ˌgran-\ *adv* (1612) **:** IN FLAGRANTE DELICTO

in flagrante de·lic·to \-di-ˈlik-(ˌ)tō\ *adv* [ML, lit., while the crime is blazing] (1772) **1 :** in the very act of committing a misdeed **:** REDHANDED **2 :** in the midst of sexual activity

in·flame *also* **en·flame** \in-ˈflām\ *vb* **in·flamed** *also* **en·flamed; in·flam·ing** *also* **en·flam·ing** [ME *enflamen,* fr. AF *enflamer,* fr. L *inflammare,* fr. *in-* + *flamma* flame] *vt* (14c) **1 a :** to excite to excessive or uncontrollable action or feeling; *esp* **:** to make angry **b :** to make more heated or violent **:** INTENSIFY ⟨insults served only to ~ the feud⟩ **2 :** to set on fire **:** KINDLE **3 :** to cause to redden or grow hot from anger or excitement ⟨a face *inflamed* with passion⟩ **4 :** to cause inflammation in (bodily tissue) ~ *vi* **1 :** to burst into flame **2 :** to become excited or angered **3 :** to become affected with inflammation — **in·flam·er** *n*

in·flam·ma·ble \in-ˈfla-mə-bəl\ *adj* [F, fr. ML *inflammabilis,* fr. L *inflammare*] (1605) **1 :** FLAMMABLE **2 :** easily inflamed, excited, or angered **:** IRASCIBLE — **in·flam·ma·bil·i·ty** \-ˌfla-mə-ˈbi-lə-tē\ *n* — **inflammable** *n* — **in·flam·ma·ble·ness** \-ˈfla-mə-bəl-nəs\ *n* — **in·flam·ma·bly** \-blē\ *adv*

in·flam·ma·tion \ˌin-flə-ˈmā-shən\ *n* (15c) **1 :** a local response to cellular injury that is marked by capillary dilatation, leukocytic infiltration, redness, heat, and pain and that serves as a mechanism initiating the elimination of noxious agents and of damaged tissue **2 :** the act of inflaming **:** the state of being inflamed

in·flam·ma·to·ry \in-ˈfla-mə-ˌtȯr-ē\ *adj* (ca. 1711) **1 :** tending to excite anger, disorder, or tumult **:** SEDITIOUS **2 :** tending to inflame or excite the senses **3 :** accompanied by or tending to cause inflammation — **in·flam·ma·to·ri·ly** \-ˌfla-mə-ˈtȯr-ə-lē\ *adv*

inflammatory bowel disease *n* (1977) **:** either of two inflammatory diseases of the bowel: **a :** CROHN'S DISEASE **b :** ULCERATIVE COLITIS

in·flat·able \in-ˈflā-tə-bəl\ *adj* (1878) **:** capable of being inflated ⟨an ~ boat⟩ — **inflatable** *n*

in·flate \in-ˈflāt\ *vb* **in·flat·ed; in·flat·ing** [ME, fr. L *inflatus,* pp. of *inflare,* fr. *in-* + *flare* to blow — more at BLOW] *vt* (15c) **1 :** to swell or distend with air or gas **2 :** to puff up **:** ELATE ⟨~ one's ego⟩ **3 :** to expand or increase abnormally or imprudently ~ *vi* **:** to become inflated ***syn*** see EXPAND — **in·fla·tor** *or* **in·flat·er** \-ˈflā-tər\ *n*

inflated *adj* (1652) **1 :** elaborated or heightened by artificial or empty means ⟨an ~ style of writing⟩ **2 :** distended with air or gas **3 :** expanded to an abnormal or unjustifiable volume or level ⟨~ prices⟩ **4 :** being hollow and enlarged or distended

in·fla·tion \in-ˈflā-shən\ *n* (14c) **1 :** an act of inflating **:** a state of being inflated: as **a :** DISTENSION **b :** a hypothetical extremely brief period of very rapid expansion of the universe immediately following the big bang **c :** empty pretentiousness **:** POMPOSITY **2 :** a continuing rise in the general price level usu. attributed to an increase in the volume of money and credit relative to available goods and services

in·fla·tion·ary \-shə-ˌner-ē\ *adj* (1920) **:** of, characterized by, or productive of inflation ⟨~ policies⟩

inflationary spiral *n* (1931) **:** a continuous rise in prices that is sustained by the tendency of wage increases and cost increases to react on each other

in·fla·tion·ism \in-ˈflā-shə-ˌni-zəm\ *n* (1919) **:** the policy of economic inflation — **in·fla·tion·ist** \-sh(ə-)nist\ *n or adj*

in·flect \in-ˈflekt\ *vb* [ME, fr. L *inflectere,* fr. *in-* + *flectere* to bend] *vt* (15c) **1 :** to turn from a direct line or course **:** CURVE **2 :** to vary (a word) by inflection **:** DECLINE, CONJUGATE **3 :** to change or vary the pitch of (as the voice) **4 :** to affect or alter noticeably **:** INFLUENCE ⟨an approach ~*ed* by feminism⟩ ~ *vi* **:** to become modified by inflection — **in·flect·able** \-ˈflek-tə-bəl\ *adj* — **in·flec·tive** \-ˈflek-tiv\ *adj*

in·flec·tion \in-ˈflek-shən\ *n* (1531) **1 :** the act or result of curving or bending **:** BEND **2 :** change in pitch or loudness of the voice **3 a :** the change of form that words undergo to mark such distinctions as those of case, gender, number, tense, person, mood, or voice **b :** a form, suffix, or element involved in such variation **c :** ACCIDENCE **4 a :** change in curvature of an arc or curve from concave to convex or conversely **b :** INFLECTION POINT

in·flec·tion·al \-shnəl, -shə-nᵊl\ *adj* (1832) **:** of, relating to, or characterized by inflection ⟨an ~ suffix⟩ — **in·flec·tion·al·ly** *adv*

inflection point *n* (ca. 1721) **:** a point on a curve that separates an arc concave upward from one concave downward and vice versa

in·flexed \ˈin-ˌflekst\ *adj* [L *inflexus,* pp. of *inflectere*] (1661) **:** bent or turned abruptly inward or downward or toward the axis ⟨~ petals⟩

in·flex·i·ble \(ˌ)in-ˈflek-sə-bəl\ *adj* [ME, fr. L *inflexibilis,* fr. *in-* + *flexibilis* flexible] (14c) **1 :** rigidly firm in will or purpose **:** UNYIELDING **2 :** not readily bent **:** lacking or deficient in suppleness **3 :** incapable of change **:** UNALTERABLE — **in·flex·i·bil·i·ty** \-ˌflek-sə-ˈbi-lə-tē\ *n* — **in·flex·i·ble·ness** \-ˈflek-sə-bəl-nəs\ *n* — **in·flex·i·bly** \-blē\ *adv*

syn INFLEXIBLE, OBDURATE, ADAMANT mean unwilling to alter a predetermined course or purpose. INFLEXIBLE implies rigid adherence or even slavish conformity to principle ⟨*inflexible* in their demands⟩. OBDURATE stresses hardness of heart and insensitivity to appeals for mercy or the influence of divine grace ⟨*obdurate* in his refusal to grant clemency⟩. ADAMANT implies utter immovability in the face of all temptation or entreaty ⟨*adamant* that the work should continue⟩. ***syn*** see in addition STIFF

in·flex·ion *chiefly Brit var of* INFLECTION

in·flict \in-ˈflikt\ *vt* [L *inflictus,* pp. of *infligere,* fr. *in-* + *fligere* to strike — more at PROFLIGATE] (1566) **1 :** AFFLICT **2 a :** to give by or as if by striking ⟨~ pain⟩ **b :** to cause (something unpleasant) to be endured — **in·flict·er** *or* **in·flic·tor** \-ˈflik-tər\ *n* — **in·flic·tive** \-tiv\ *adj*

in·flic·tion \in-ˈflik-shən\ *n* (1534) **1 :** the act of inflicting **2 :** something (as punishment or suffering) that is inflicted

in–flight \ˈin-ˈflīt, (ˌ)in-\ *adj* (1944) **:** made, carried out, or provided for use or enjoyment while in flight ⟨~ movies⟩

in·flo·res·cence \ˌin-flə-ˈre-sᵊn(t)s\ *n* [NL *inflorescentia,* fr. LL *inflorescent-, inflorescens,* prp. of *inflorescere* to begin to bloom, fr. L *in-* + *florescere* to begin to bloom — more at FLORESCENCE] (1760) **1 a :** the mode of development and arrangement of flowers on an axis **b :** a floral axis with its appendages; *also* **:** a flower cluster **2 :** the budding and unfolding of blossoms **:** FLOWERING

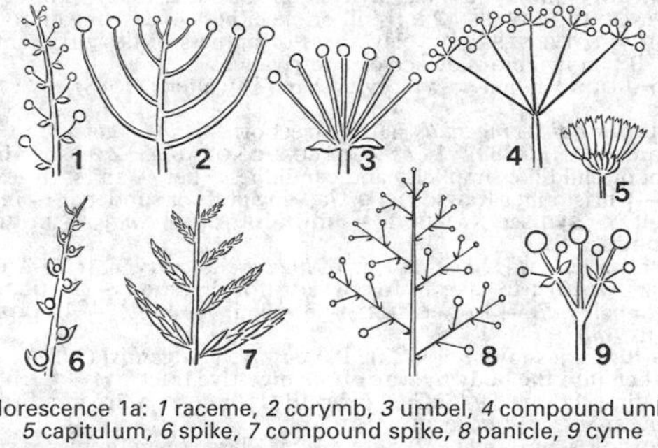

inflorescence 1a: *1* raceme, *2* corymb, *3* umbel, *4* compound umbel, *5* capitulum, *6* spike, *7* compound spike, *8* panicle, *9* cyme

in·flow \ˈin-ˌflō\ *n* (1839) **:** a flowing in ⟨the ~ of air⟩ ⟨an ~ of funds⟩

1in·flu·ence \ˈin-ˌflü-ən(t)s, *esp Southern* in-ˈ\ *n* [ME, fr. OF, fr. ML *influentia,* fr. L *influent-, influens,* prp. of *influere* to flow in, fr. *in-* + *fluere* to flow — more at FLUID] (14c) **1 a :** an ethereal fluid held to flow from the stars and to affect the actions of humans **b :** an emanation of occult power held to derive from stars **2 :** an emanation of spiritual or moral force **3 a :** the act or power of producing an effect without apparent exertion of force or direct exercise of command **b :** corrupt interference with authority for personal gain **4 :** the power or capacity of causing an effect in indirect or intangible ways **:** SWAY **5 :** one that exerts influence — **under the influence :** affected by alcohol **:** DRUNK ⟨was arrested for driving *under the influence*⟩

syn INFLUENCE, AUTHORITY, PRESTIGE, WEIGHT, CREDIT mean power exerted over the minds or behavior of others. INFLUENCE may apply to a force exercised and received consciously or unconsciously ⟨used her *influence* to get the bill passed⟩. AUTHORITY implies the power of winning devotion or allegiance or of compelling acceptance and belief ⟨his opinions lacked *authority*⟩. PRESTIGE implies the ascendancy given by conspicuous excellence or reputation for superiority ⟨the *prestige* of the newspaper⟩. WEIGHT implies measurable or decisive influence in determining acts or choices ⟨their wishes obviously carried much *weight*⟩. CREDIT suggests influence that arises from the confidence of others ⟨his *credit* with the press⟩.

2influence *vt* **-enced; -enc·ing** (1658) **1 :** to affect or alter by indirect or intangible means **2 :** to have an effect on the condition or development of ***syn*** see AFFECT — **in·flu·ence·able** \-ən(t)-sə-bəl\ *adj*

1in·flu·ent \ˈin-ˌflü-ənt, in-ˈ\ *adj* (15c) **:** flowing in

2influent *n* (1859) **1 :** something that flows in: as **a :** a tributary stream **b :** fluid input into a reservoir or process **2 :** a factor modifying the balance and stability of an ecological community

1in·flu·en·tial \ˌin-(ˌ)flü-ˈen(t)-shəl\ *adj* (1570) **:** exerting or possessing influence — **in·flu·en·tial·ly** \-ˈen(t)-sh(ə-)lē\ *adv*

2influential *n* (1831) **:** one who has great influence

in·flu·en·za \ˌin-(ˌ)flü-ˈen-zə\ *n* [It, lit., influence, fr. ML *influentia;* fr. the belief that epidemics were due to the influence of the stars] (1743) **1 a** (1) **:** an acute typically severe respiratory disease caused by an orthomyxovirus (species *Influenza A virus* of the genus *Influenzavirus A*) and marked by sudden onset, fever, prostration, severe aches and pains, and progressive inflammation of the respiratory mucous membranes — called also *influenza A* (2) **:** either of two usu. milder or even subclinical respiratory diseases caused by two other orthomyxoviruses (species *Influenza B virus* of the genus *Influenzavirus B* and species *Influenza C virus* of the genus *Influenzavirus C*) — often used with the letter *B* or *C* to denote the causative species **b :** any of various human respiratory infections of undetermined cause — not used technically **2 :** any of numerous febrile usu. virus diseases of domestic animals marked by respiratory symptoms, inflammation of mucous membranes, and often systemic involvement — **in·flu·en·zal** \-zəl\ *adj*

in·flux \ˈin-ˌfləks\ *n* [ML *influxus,* fr. L *influere*] (1626) **:** a coming in ⟨an ~ of tourists⟩

in·fo \ˈin-(ˌ)fō\ *n* (1907) **:** INFORMATION

in·fold \in-ˈfōld\ *vt* (15c) **:** ENFOLD, ENVELOP ~ *vi* **:** to fold inward or toward one another

in·fo·mer·cial \ˈin-(ˌ)fō-ˌmər-shəl, -fə-\ *n* [*information* + 2*commercial*] (1981) **:** a television program that is an extended advertisement often including a discussion or demonstration

in·form \in-ˈfȯrm\ *vb* [ME, fr. AF *enformer,* fr. L *informare,* fr. *in-* + *forma* form] *vt* (14c) **1** *obs* **:** to give material form to **2 a :** to give character or essence to ⟨the principles which ~ modern teaching⟩ **b :** to be the characteristic quality of **:** ANIMATE ⟨the compassion that ~*s* her work⟩ **3** *obs* **:** GUIDE, DIRECT **4** *obs* **:** to make known **5 :** to communicate knowledge to ⟨~ a prisoner of his rights⟩ ~ *vi* **1 :** to impart information or knowledge **2 :** to give information (as of another's wrongdoing) to an authority ⟨~*ed* on a member of his own gang⟩

syn INFORM, ACQUAINT, APPRISE, NOTIFY mean to make one aware of something. INFORM implies the imparting of knowledge esp. of facts or occurrences ⟨*informed* us of the crisis⟩. ACQUAINT lays stress on introducing to or familiarizing with ⟨*acquaint* yourself with the keyboard⟩. APPRISE implies communicating something of special interest or importance ⟨keep us *apprised* of the situation⟩. NOTIFY implies sending notice of something requiring attention or demanding action ⟨*notified* the witness when to appear⟩.

in·for·mal \(ˌ)in-ˈfȯr-məl\ *adj* (1585) **1 :** marked by the absence of formality or ceremony ⟨an ~ meeting⟩ **2 :** characteristic of or appropriate to ordinary, casual, or familiar use ⟨~ clothes⟩ — **in·for·mal·i·ty** \-(ˌ)fȯr-ˈma-lə-tē, -fər-\ *n* — **in·for·mal·ly** \-ˈfȯr-mə-lē\ *adv*

in·for·mant \in-ˈfȯr-mənt\ *n* (1657) **:** a person who gives information: as **a :** INFORMER **b :** one who supplies cultural or linguistic data in response to interrogation by an investigator

in for·ma pau·pe·ris \ˌin-ˈfȯr-mə-ˈpȯ-pə-rəs, -ˈpau̇-\ *adj or adv* [L, in the form of a pauper] (1592) **:** as a poor person

in·for·mat·ics \ˌin-fər-ˈma-tiks\ *n pl but sing in constr* [ISV *informat*ion + *-ics*] (ca. 1967) **:** INFORMATION SCIENCE

in·for·ma·tion \ˌin-fər-ˈmā-shən\ *n* (14c) **1 :** the communication or reception of knowledge or intelligence **2 a** (1) **:** knowledge obtained from investigation, study, or instruction (2) **:** INTELLIGENCE, NEWS (3) **:** FACTS, DATA **b :** the attribute inherent in and communicated by one of two or more alternative sequences or arrangements of something (as nucleotides in DNA or binary digits in a computer program) that produce specific effects **c** (1) **:** a signal or character (as in a communication system or computer) representing data (2) **:** something (as a message, experimental data, or a picture) which justifies change in a construct (as a plan or theory) that represents physical or mental experience or another construct **d :** a quantitative measure of the content of information; *specif* **:** a numerical quantity that measures the uncertainty in the outcome of an experiment to be performed **3 :** the act of informing against a person **4 :** a formal accusation of a crime made by a prosecuting officer as distinguished from an indictment presented by a grand jury — **in·for·ma·tion·al** \-shnəl, -shə-nᵊl\ *adj* — **in·for·ma·tion·al·ly** *adv*

information retrieval *n* (1950) **:** the techniques of storing and recovering and often disseminating recorded data esp. through the use of a computerized system

information science *n* (1960) **:** the collection, classification, storage, retrieval, and dissemination of recorded knowledge treated both as a pure and as an applied science

information superhighway *n* (1983) **:** a telecommunications infrastructure or system (as of television, telephony, or computer networks) used for widespread and usu. rapid access to information; *esp* **:** INTERNET — called also *infobahn, information highway*

information technology *n* (1978) **:** the technology involving the development, maintenance, and use of computer systems, software, and networks for the processing and distribution of data

information theory *n* (1950) **:** a theory that deals statistically with information, with the measurement of its content in terms of its distinguishing essential characteristics or by the number of alternatives from

\ə\ **abut** \ᵊ\ **kitten**, F **table** \ər\ **further** \a\ **ash** \ā\ **ace** \ä\ **mop**, **mar** \au̇\ **out** \ch\ **chin** \e\ **bet** \ē\ **easy** \g\ **go** \i\ **hit** \ī\ **ice** \j\ **job** \ŋ\ **sing** \ō\ **go** \ȯ\ **law** \ȯi\ **boy** \th\ **thin** \t͟h\ **the** \ü\ **loot** \u̇\ **foot** \y\ **yet** \zh\ **vision**, **beige** \k̲, ^{n}, œ, ue, ^{y}\ *see* Guide to Pronunciation

which it makes a choice possible, and with the efficiency of processes of communication between humans and machines

in·for·ma·tive \in-ˈfȯr-mə-tiv\ *adj* (1655) **:** imparting knowledge **:** INSTRUCTIVE — **in·for·ma·tive·ly** *adv* — **in·for·ma·tive·ness** *n*

in·for·ma·to·ry \-mə-ˌtȯr-ē\ *adj* (ca. 1879) **:** conveying information — **in·for·ma·to·ri·ly** \in-ˌfȯr-mə-ˈtȯr-ə-lē\ *adv*

in·formed \in-ˈfȯrmd\ *adj* (15c) **1 a :** having information ⟨∼ sources⟩ ⟨∼ observers⟩ **b :** based on possession of information ⟨an ∼ opinion⟩ **2 :** EDUCATED, KNOWLEDGEABLE ⟨what the ∼ person should know⟩ — **in·formed·ly** \-ˈfȯrmd-lē, -ˈfȯr-məd-lē\ *adv*

informed consent *n* (ca. 1957) **:** consent to surgery by a patient or to participation in a medical experiment by a subject after achieving an understanding of what is involved

in·form·er \in-ˈfȯr-mər\ *n* (14c) **1 :** one that imparts knowledge or news **2 :** one that informs against another; *specif* **:** one who makes a practice esp. for a financial reward of informing against others for violations of penal laws

in·fo·tain·ment \ˌin-(ˌ)fō-ˈtān-mənt\ *n* [*info*rmation + enter*tainment*] (1980) **:** a television program that presents information (as news) in a manner intended to be entertaining

in·fo·tech \ˈin-fō-ˌtek\ *n* (1981) **:** INFORMATION TECHNOLOGY

in·fra \ˈin-frə *also* -ˌfrä\ *adv* [L] (ca. 1740) **:** later in this writing **:** BELOW ⟨for additional examples see ∼⟩

infra- *prefix* [L *infra* — more at UNDER] **1 :** below ⟨*infra*human⟩ ⟨*infra*sonic⟩ **2 :** within ⟨*infra*specific⟩ **3 :** below in a scale or series ⟨*infra*red⟩

in·frac·tion \in-ˈfrak-shən\ *n* [ME, fr. ML *infraction-, infractio,* fr. L, subduing, fr. *infringere* to break — more at INFRINGE] (15c) **:** the act of infringing **:** VIOLATION — **in·fract** \in-ˈfrakt\ *vt*

in·fra dig \ˈin-frə-ˈdig, -(ˌ)frä-\ *adj* [short for L *infra dignitatem*] (1824) **:** being beneath one's dignity **:** UNDIGNIFIED ⟨while his work . . . was financially profitable, it was just a bit *infra dig* —John McCarten⟩

in·fra·hu·man \ˌin-frə-ˈhyü-mən, -(ˌ)frä-, -ˈyü-\ *adj* (1847) **:** less or lower than human ⟨∼ primates⟩ — **infrahuman** *n*

in·fran·gi·ble \(ˌ)in-ˈfran-jə-bəl\ *adj* [MF, fr. LL *infrangibilis,* fr. L *in-* + *frangere* to break — more at BREAK] (1597) **1 :** not capable of being broken or separated into parts ⟨∼ iron bars⟩ **2 :** not to be infringed or violated ⟨∼ laws⟩ — **in·fran·gi·bil·i·ty** \-ˌfran-jə-ˈbi-lə-tē\ *n* — **in·fran·gi·bly** \-ˈfran-jə-blē\ *adv*

in·fra·or·der \ˈin-frə-ˌȯr-dər\ *n* (1945) **:** a taxonomic category in biological classification ranking above a superfamily and below a suborder

in·fra·red \ˌin-frə-ˈred, -(ˌ)frä-, -fə-\ *adj* (1881) **1 :** situated outside the visible spectrum at its red end — used of radiation having a wavelength between about 700 nanometers and 1 millimeter **2 :** relating to, producing, or employing infrared radiation ⟨∼ therapy⟩ **3 :** sensitive to infrared radiation ⟨∼ sensors that detect body heat⟩ — **infrared** *n*

in·fra·son·ic \ˌin-frə-ˈsä-nik, -(ˌ)frä-\ *adj* (1927) **1 :** having or relating to a frequency below the audibility range of the human ear **2 :** utilizing or produced by infrasonic waves or vibrations

in·fra·spe·cif·ic \-spi-ˈsi-fik\ *adj* (1939) **:** occurring within a species ⟨∼ variability⟩

in·fra·struc·ture \ˈin-frə-ˌstrək-chər, -(ˌ)frä-\ *n* (1927) **1 :** the underlying foundation or basic framework (as of a system or organization) **2 :** the permanent installations required for military purposes **3 :** the system of public works of a country, state, or region; *also* **:** the resources (as personnel, buildings, or equipment) required for an activity — **in·fra·struc·tur·al** \-ˌstrək-chə-rəl, -ˌstrək-shrəl\ *adj*

in·fre·quence \(ˌ)in-ˈfrē-kwən(t)s\ *n* (1611) **:** INFREQUENCY

in·fre·quen·cy \-kwən(t)-sē\ *n* (1677) **:** rarity of occurrence

in·fre·quent \(ˌ)in-ˈfrē-kwənt\ *adj* [L *infrequent-, infrequens,* fr. *in-* + *frequent-, frequens* frequent] (ca. 1615) **1 :** seldom happening or occurring **:** RARE **2 :** placed or occurring at wide intervals in space or time ⟨a slope dotted with ∼ pines⟩ ⟨∼ visits⟩ — **in·fre·quent·ly** *adv*

syn INFREQUENT, UNCOMMON, SCARCE, RARE, SPORADIC mean not common or abundant. INFREQUENT implies occurrence at wide intervals in space or time ⟨*infrequent* family visits⟩. UNCOMMON suggests a frequency below normal expectation ⟨smallpox is now *uncommon* in many countries⟩. SCARCE implies falling short of a standard or required abundance ⟨jobs were *scarce* during the Depression⟩. RARE suggests extreme scarcity or infrequency and often implies consequent high value ⟨*rare* first editions⟩. SPORADIC implies occurrence in scattered instances or isolated outbursts ⟨*sporadic* cases of influenza⟩.

in·fringe \in-ˈfrinj\ *vb* **in·fringed; in·fring·ing** [ML *infringere,* fr. L, to break, crush, fr. *in-* + *frangere* to break — more at BREAK] *vt* (1513) **1 :** to encroach upon in a way that violates law or the rights of another ⟨∼ a patent⟩ **2** *obs* **:** DEFEAT, FRUSTRATE ∼ *vi* **:** ENCROACH — used with *on* or *upon* ⟨∼ on our rights⟩ ***syn*** see TRESPASS — **in·fring·er** *n*

in·fringe·ment \in-ˈfrinj-mənt\ *n* (1628) **1 :** the act of infringing **:** VIOLATION **2 :** an encroachment or trespass on a right or privilege

in·fun·dib·u·lar \ˌin-(ˌ)fən-ˈdi-byə-lər\ *adj* (1795) **:** of, relating to, or having an infundibulum

in·fun·dib·u·lum \ˌin-(ˌ)fən-ˈdi-byə-ləm\ *n, pl* **-la** \-lə\ [NL, fr. L, funnel — more at FUNNEL] (1543) **:** any of various funnel-shaped organs or parts: as **a :** the hollow conical process of gray matter connecting the pituitary gland to the hypothalamus **b :** the calyx of a kidney **c :** the abdominal opening of a fallopian tube

¹**in·fu·ri·ate** \in-ˈfyu̇r-ē-ˌāt\ *vt* **-at·ed; -at·ing** [ML *infuriatus,* pp. of *infuriare,* fr. L *in-* + *furia* fury] (1667) **:** to make furious — **in·fu·ri·at·ing·ly** \-ˌā-tiŋ-lē\ *adv* — **in·fu·ri·a·tion** \-ˌfyu̇r-ē-ˈā-shən\ *n*

²**in·fu·ri·ate** \in-ˈfyu̇r-ē-ət\ *adj* (1667) **:** furiously angry

in·fuse \in-ˈfyüz\ *vt* **in·fused; in·fus·ing** [ME, to pour in, fr. MF & L; MF *infuser,* fr. L *infusus,* pp. of *infundere* to pour in, fr. *in-* + *fundere* to pour — more at FOUND] (1526) **1 a :** to cause to be permeated with something (as a principle or quality) that alters usu. for the better ⟨∼ the team with confidence⟩ **b :** INTRODUCE, INSINUATE ⟨a new spirit was *infused* into American art —*Amer. Guide Series: N.Y.*⟩ **2 :** INSPIRE, ANIMATE ⟨the sense of purpose that *infuses* scientific research⟩ **3 :** to steep in liquid (as water) without boiling so as to extract the soluble constituents or principles **4 :** to administer or inject by infusion ⟨stem cells were ∼*ed* into the patient⟩ — **in·fus·er** *n*

syn INFUSE, SUFFUSE, IMBUE, INGRAIN, INOCULATE, LEAVEN mean to introduce one thing into another so as to affect it throughout. INFUSE implies a pouring in of something that gives new life or significance ⟨new members *infused* enthusiasm into the club⟩. SUFFUSE implies a spreading through of something that gives an unusual color or quality ⟨a room *suffused* with light⟩. IMBUE implies the introduction of a quality that fills and permeates the whole being ⟨*imbue* students with intellectual curiosity⟩. INGRAIN, used only in the passive or past participle, suggests the deep implanting of a quality or trait ⟨clung to *ingrained* habits⟩. INOCULATE implies an imbuing or implanting with a germinal idea and often suggests stealth or subtlety ⟨an electorate *inoculated* with dangerous ideas⟩. LEAVEN implies introducing something that enlivens, tempers, or markedly alters the total quality ⟨a serious play *leavened* with comic moments⟩.

in·fus·ible \(ˌ)in-ˈfyü-zə-bəl\ *adj* (1555) **:** incapable of being fused **:** very difficult to fuse — **in·fus·ibil·i·ty** \-ˌfyü-zə-ˈbi-lə-tē\ *n* — **in·fus·ible·ness** \-ˈfyü-zə-bəl-nəs\ *n*

in·fu·sion \in-ˈfyü-zhən\ *n* (15c) **1 :** the act or process of infusing ⟨an ∼ of new ideas⟩ **2 :** a product obtained by infusing ⟨herbal ∼*s*⟩ **3 :** the continuous slow introduction of a solution esp. into a vein

in·fu·so·ri·al earth \ˈin-fyü-ˈzȯr-ē-əl-, -ˈsȯr-\ *n* (1868) **:** KIESELGUHR

in·fu·so·ri·an \-ē-ən\ *n* [ultim. fr. L *infusus*] (1859) **:** any of a heterogeneous group of minute organisms found esp. in water with decomposing organic matter; *esp* **:** a ciliated protozoan — **infusorian** *adj*

¹**-ing** \iŋ *also* ēŋ; *in some dialects & in other dialects informally* in, ən *also* ēn; *after certain consonants* ᵊn, ᵊm, ᵊŋ\ *n suffix* [ME, fr. OE *-ung, -ing,* suffix forming nouns from verbs; akin to OHG *-ung,* suffix forming nouns from verbs] **1 :** action or process ⟨runn*ing*⟩ ⟨sleep*ing*⟩ **:** instance of an action or process ⟨a meet*ing*⟩ **2 a :** product or result of an action or process ⟨an engrav*ing*⟩ — often in pl. ⟨earn*ings*⟩ **b :** something used in an action or process ⟨a bed cover*ing*⟩ ⟨the lin*ing* of a coat⟩ **3 :** action or process connected with (a specified thing) ⟨boat*ing*⟩ **4 :** something connected with, consisting of, or used in making (a specified thing) ⟨scaffold*ing*⟩ ⟨shirt*ing*⟩ **5 :** something related to (a specified concept) ⟨off*ing*⟩

²**-ing** *n suffix* [ME, fr. OE *-ing, -ung;* akin to OHG *-ing* one of a (specified) kind] **:** one of a (specified) kind ⟨sweet*ing*⟩

³**-ing** *vb suffix or adj suffix* [ME, prob. fr. ¹*-ing*] — used to form the present participle ⟨sail*ing*⟩ and sometimes to form an adjective resembling a present participle but not derived from a verb ⟨swashbuckl*ing*⟩

usage Though the pronunciation of *-ing* with the consonant \n\, misleadingly referred to as "dropping the *g,*" is often deprecated, this pronunciation is frequently heard. It is not known for certain why the Middle English present participle ending *-ende* was replaced by *-ing.* Analogy with the earlier noun suffix *-ing* prob. had something to do with it. In early Modern English, present participles were regularly formed with *-ing* pronounced \iŋg\ (as can still be heard in a few dialects) and later \iŋ\. Evidence also shows that some speakers used \in\ and by the 18th century this pronunciation became widespread. Though teachers (with some success) campaigned against it, \in\ remained a feature of the speech of many of the best speakers in Britain and the U.S. well into the 20th century. It has by now lost its respectability, at least when attention is drawn to it, but throughout the U.S. it persists largely unnoticed and in some dialects it predominates over \iŋ\.

in·gath·er \ˈin-ˌga-t͟hər, -ˌge-\ *vt* (1557) **:** to gather in ∼ *vi* **:** ASSEMBLE — **in·gath·er·ing** \-ˌgath-riŋ, -ˌgeth-; -ˌga-t͟hə-, -ˌge-\ *n*

in·ge·nious \in-ˈjēn-yəs\ *adj* [ME *ingenyous,* fr. MF *ingenieus,* fr. L *ingeniosus,* fr. *ingenium* natural capacity — more at ENGINE] (15c) **1** *obs* **:** showing or calling for intelligence, aptitude, or discernment **2 :** marked by especial aptitude at discovering, inventing, or contriving **3 :** marked by originality, resourcefulness, and cleverness in conception or execution ⟨an ∼ contraption⟩ ***syn*** see CLEVER — **in·ge·nious·ly** *adv* — **in·ge·nious·ness** *n*

in·ge·nue *or* **in·gé·nue** \ˈan-jə-ˌnü, ˈän-; ˈaⁿ-zhə-, ˈäⁿ-\ *n* [F *ingénue,* fem. of *ingénu* ingenuous, fr. L *ingenuus*] (1848) **1 :** a naive girl or young woman **2 :** the stage role of an ingenue; *also* **:** an actress playing such a role

in·ge·nu·i·ty \ˌin-jə-ˈnü-ə-tē, -ˈnyü-\ *n, pl* **-ties** (ca. 1592) **1** *obs* **:** CANDOR, INGENUOUSNESS **2 a :** skill or cleverness in devising or combining **:** INVENTIVENESS **b :** cleverness or aptness of design or contrivance **3 :** an ingenious device or contrivance

¹**in·gen·u·ous** \in-ˈjen-yə-wəs, -yü-əs\ *adj* [by alter.] (1588) *obs* **:** INGENIOUS

²**ingenuous** *adj* [L *ingenuus* native, freeborn, fr. *in-* + *gignere* to beget — more at KIN] (1588) **1** *obs* **:** NOBLE, HONORABLE **2 a :** showing innocent or childlike simplicity and candidness ⟨her ∼ thirst for experience —Christopher Rawson⟩ **b :** lacking craft or subtlety ⟨∼ in their brutality⟩ ***syn*** see NATURAL — **in·gen·u·ous·ly** *adv* — **in·gen·u·ous·ness** *n*

in·gest \in-ˈjest\ *vt* [L *ingestus,* pp. of *ingerere* to carry in, fr. *in-* + *gerere* to bear] (1620) **:** to take in for or as if for digestion — **in·gest·ible** \-ˈjes-tə-bəl\ *adj* — **in·ges·tion** \-ˈjes-chən, -ˈjesh-\ *n* — **in·ges·tive** \-ˈjes-tiv\ *adj*

in·ges·ta \in-ˈjes-tə\ *n pl* [NL, fr. L, neut. pl. of *ingestus*] (1727) **:** material taken into the body by way of the digestive tract

in·gle \ˈiŋ-gəl, ˈiŋ-əl\ *n* [ScGael *aingeal*] (1508) **1 :** a fire in a fireplace **2 :** FIREPLACE **3 :** CORNER, ANGLE

in·gle·nook \-ˌnu̇k\ *n* (1772) **:** a nook by a large open fireplace; *also* **:** a bench or settle occupying this nook

in·glo·ri·ous \(ˌ)in-ˈglȯr-ē-əs\ *adj* [L *inglorius,* fr. *in-* + *gloria* glory] (1573) **1 :** SHAMEFUL, IGNOMINIOUS ⟨an ∼ defeat⟩ **2 :** not glorious **:** lacking fame or honor ⟨made an ∼ comeback⟩ — **in·glo·ri·ous·ly** *adv* — **in·glo·ri·ous·ness** *n*

in·got \ˈiŋ-gət\ *n* [ME, perh. modif. of MF *lingot* ingot of metal, incorrectly divided as *l'ingot,* as if fr. *le* the] (14c) **1 :** a mold in which metal is cast **2 :** a mass of metal cast into a convenient shape for storage or transportation to be later processed

ingot iron *n* (1877) **:** iron containing only small proportions of impurities (as less than 0.05 percent carbon)

¹**in·grain** *also* **en·grain** \(ˌ)in-ˈgrān\ *vt* (ca. 1641) **:** to work indelibly into the natural texture or mental or moral constitution ***syn*** see INFUSE

²**in·grain** \ˈin-ˌgrān\ *adj* (1766) **1 a :** made of fiber that is dyed before being spun into yarn **b :** made of yarn that is dyed before being woven or knitted **2 :** thoroughly worked in **:** INNATE

³**in·grain** \ˈin-ˌgrān\ *n* (1899) **:** innate quality or character

in·grained *also* **en·grained** \ˈin-ˌgrānd, (ˌ)in-ˈ\ *adj* (1599) **1 :** worked into the grain or fiber **2 :** forming a part of the essence or inmost be-

ing : DEEP-SEATED ⟨~ prejudice⟩ — **in·grained·ly** *also* **en·grained·ly** \ˈin-ˌgrā-nəd-lē, ˈin-ˌgrānd-lē, (ˌ)in-ˈ\ *adv*
in·grate \ˈin-ˌgrāt\ *n* [L *ingratus* ungrateful, fr. *in-* + *gratus* grateful — more at GRACE] (1622) : an ungrateful person
in·gra·ti·ate \in-ˈgrā-shē-ˌāt\ *vt* **-at·ed; -at·ing** [[2]*in-* + L *gratia* grace] (1621) : to gain favor or favorable acceptance for by deliberate effort — usu. used with *with* ⟨~ themselves with the community leaders —William Attwood⟩ — **in·gra·ti·a·tion** \-ˌgrā-shē-ˈā-shən\ *n* — **in·gra·tia·to·ry** \-ˈgrā-sh(ē-)ə-ˌtōr-ē\ *adj*
ingratiating *adj* (1655) **1** : capable of winning favor : PLEASING ⟨an ~ smile⟩ **2** : intended or adopted in order to gain favor : FLATTERING — **in·gra·ti·at·ing·ly** \-ˈgrā-shē-ˌā-tiŋ-lē\ *adv*
in·grat·i·tude \(ˌ)in-ˈgra-tə-ˌtüd, -ˌtyüd\ *n* [ME, fr. MF, fr. ML *ingratitudo,* fr. L *in-* + LL *gratitudo* gratitude] (14c) : forgetfulness of or poor return for kindness received : UNGRATEFULNESS
in·gre·di·ent \in-ˈgrē-dē-ənt\ *n* [ME, fr. L *ingredient-, ingrediens,* prp. of *ingredi* to go into, fr. *in-* + *gradi* to go — more at GRADE] (15c) : something that enters into a compound or is a component part of any combination or mixture : CONSTITUENT ***syn*** see ELEMENT — **ingredient** *adj*
in·gress \ˈin-ˌgres\ *n* [ME, fr. L *ingressus,* fr. *ingredi*] (15c) **1** : the act of entering : ENTRANCE ⟨the seal prevents ~ of moisture⟩ **2** : the power or liberty of entrance or access ⟨an area with restricted ~⟩ — **in·gres·sion** \in-ˈgre-shən\ *n*
in·gres·sive \in-ˈgre-siv\ *adj* (1649) **1** : of, relating to, or involving ingress; *esp* : produced by ingress of air into the vocal tract ⟨~ sounds⟩ **2** : INCHOATIVE 2 — **ingressive** *n* — **in·gres·sive·ness** *n*
in·ground \ˈin-ˌgraund\ *adj* (1969) : built into the ground ⟨an ~ pool⟩
in–group \ˈin-ˌgrüp\ *n* (1907) **1** : a group with which one feels a sense of solidarity or community of interests — compare OUT-GROUP **2** : CLIQUE
in·grow·ing \ˈin-ˌgrō-iŋ\ *adj* (1869) : growing or tending inward
in·grown \-ˌgrōn\ *adj* (1670) **1** : grown in; *specif* : having the free tip or edge embedded in the flesh ⟨an ~ toenail⟩ **2** : having the direction of growth or activity or interest inward rather than outward ⟨swarms of ~, infighting bureaucracies —H. R. Cilley⟩ — **in·grown·ness** \(ˌ)in-ˈgrōn-nəs\ *n*
in·growth \ˈin-ˌgrōth\ *n* (1870) **1** : a growing inward (as to fill a void) **2** : something that grows in or into a space
in·gui·nal \ˈiŋ-gwə-nᵊl\ *adj* [ME *inguynale,* fr. L *inguinalis,* fr. *inguin-, inguen* groin — more at ADEN-] (15c) : of, relating to, or situated in the region of the groin or in either of the lowest lateral regions of the abdomen ⟨an ~ hernia⟩
in·gur·gi·tate \in-ˈgər-jə-ˌtāt\ *vt* **-tat·ed; -tat·ing** [L *ingurgitatus,* pp. of *ingurgitare,* fr. *in-* + *gurgit-, gurges* whirlpool — more at VORACIOUS] (ca. 1570) : to swallow greedily or in large quantities : GUZZLE — **in·gur·gi·ta·tion** \(ˌ)in-ˌgər-jə-ˈtā-shən\ *n*
INH *abbr* [iso-nicotinic acid hydrazide] isoniazid
in·hab·it \in-ˈha-bət\ *vb* [ME *enhabiten,* fr. AF & L; AF *inhabiter, enhabiter,* fr. L *inhabitare,* fr. *in-* + *habitare* to dwell, freq. of *habēre* to have — more at GIVE] *vt* (14c) **1** : to occupy as a place of settled residence or habitat : live in ⟨~ a small house⟩ **2** : to be present in or occupy in any manner or form ⟨the human beings who ~ this tale —Al Newman⟩ ~ *vi, archaic* : to have residence in a place : DWELL — **in·hab·it·able** \-bə-tə-bəl\ *adj* — **in·hab·it·er** *n*
in·hab·i·tan·cy \in-ˈha-bə-tən(t)-sē\ *n* (1681) : INHABITATION
in·hab·i·tant \in-ˈha-bə-tənt\ *n* (15c) : one that occupies a particular place regularly, routinely, or for a period of time ⟨~*s* of large cities⟩ ⟨the tapeworm is an ~ of the intestine⟩
in·hab·i·ta·tion \in-ˌha-bə-ˈtā-shən\ *n* (15c) : the act of inhabiting : the state of being inhabited
inhabited *adj* (15c) : having inhabitants
in·hal·ant \in-ˈhā-lənt\ *n* (ca. 1890) : something (as an allergen or medication) that is inhaled — **inhalant** *adj*
in·ha·la·tion \ˌin-hə-ˈlā-shən, ˌi-nə-ˈlā-\ *n* (ca. 1623) **1** : the act or an instance of inhaling **2** : material (as medication) to be taken in by inhaling — **in·ha·la·tion·al** \-shnəl, -shə-nᵊl\ *adj*
in·ha·la·tor \ˈin-hə-ˌlā-tər, ˈi-nə-ˌlā-\ *n* (1925) : a device providing a mixture of oxygen and carbon dioxide for breathing that is used esp. in conjunction with artificial respiration
in·hale \in-ˈhāl\ *vb* **in·haled; in·hal·ing** [*in-* + ex*hale*] *vt* (1725) **1** : to draw in by breathing **2** : to take in eagerly or greedily ⟨*inhaled* about four meals at once —Ring Lardner⟩ ~ *vi* : to breathe in — **in·hale** \in-ˈ, ˈin-ˌ\ *n*
in·hal·er \in-ˈhā-lər\ *n* (1778) **1** : a device by means of which medicinal material is inhaled ⟨an asthma ~⟩ **2** : one that inhales
in·har·mon·ic \ˌin-(ˌ)här-ˈmä-nik\ *adj* (ca. 1828) : not harmonic
in·har·mo·ni·ous \-ˈmō-nē-əs\ *adj* (1662) **1** : not harmonious : DISCORDANT **2** : not fitting or congenial : CONFLICTING ⟨~ personalities⟩ — **in·har·mo·ni·ous·ly** *adv* — **in·har·mo·ni·ous·ness** *n*
in·har·mo·ny \(ˌ)in-ˈhär-mə-nē\ *n* (1799) : DISCORD
in·here \in-ˈhir\ *vi* **in·hered; in·her·ing** [ME *enheren* to be a companion, belong, fr. L *inhaerēre* to be attached, fr. *in-* + *haerēre* to adhere] (15c) : to be inherent ⟨does selfishness ~ in each of us?⟩
in·her·ence \in-ˈhir-ən(t)s, -ˈher-\ *n* (1577) : the quality, state, or fact of inhering
in·her·ent \-ənt\ *adj* [L *inhaerent-, inhaerens,* prp. of *inhaerēre*] (1581) : involved in the constitution or essential character of something : belonging by nature or habit : INTRINSIC ⟨risks ~ in the venture⟩ — **in·her·ent·ly** *adv*
in·her·it \in-ˈher-ət, -ˈhe-rət\ *vb* [ME *enheriten* to give right of inheritance to, fr. AF *enheriter,* fr. LL *inhereditare,* fr. L *in-* + *hereditas* inheritance — more at HEREDITY] *vt* (14c) **1** : to come into possession of or receive esp. as a right or divine portion ⟨and every one who has left houses or brothers or sisters . . . for my name's sake, will receive a hundredfold, and ~ eternal life —Mt 19:29 (RSV)⟩ **2 a** : to receive from an ancestor as a right or title descendible by law at the ancestor's death **b** : to receive as a devise or legacy **3** : to receive from a parent or ancestor by genetic transmission ⟨~ a defective enzyme⟩ **4** : to have in turn or receive as if from an ancestor ⟨~*ed* the problem from his predecessor⟩ ~ *vi* : to take or hold a possession or rights by inheritance — **in·her·i·tor** \-(r)ə-tər\ *n* — **in·her·i·tress** \-(r)ə-trəs\ *or* **in·her·i·trix** \-(r)ə-(ˌ)triks\ *n*
in·her·it·able \in-ˈher-ə-tə-bəl, -ˈhe-rə-\ *adj* (15c) **1** : capable of being inherited : TRANSMISSIBLE ⟨an ~ title⟩ **2** : capable of taking by inheritance ⟨the eldest son is ~ to the crown⟩ — **in·her·it·abil·i·ty** \-ˌher-ə-tə-ˈbi-lə-tē, -ˌhe-rə-\ *n* — **in·her·it·able·ness** \-ˈher-ə-tə-bəl-nəs, -ˈhe-rə-\ *n*
in·her·i·tance \in-ˈher-ə-tən(t)s, -ˈhe-rə-\ *n* (14c) **1 a** : the act of inheriting property **b** : the reception of genetic qualities by transmission from parent to offspring **c** : the acquisition of a possession, condition, or trait from past generations **2** : something that is or may be inherited **3 a** : TRADITION **b** : a valuable possession that is a common heritage from nature **4** *obs* : POSSESSION
inheritance tax *n* (1841) **1** : a tax on a decedent's net estate that is levied after the estate is transmitted to the inheritors **2** : DEATH TAX; *esp* : ESTATE TAX
in·hib·in \in-ˈhi-bən\ *n* [L *inhibēre* to inhibit + E [1]*-in*] (1932) : a glycoprotein hormone that is secreted by the pituitary gland and in the male by the Sertoli cells and in the female by the granulosa cells and that inhibits the secretion of follicle-stimulating hormone
in·hib·it \in-ˈhi-bət\ *vb* [ME, fr. L *inhibitus,* pp. of *inhibēre,* fr. *in-* [2]in- + *habēre* to have — more at HABIT] *vt* (15c) **1** : to prohibit from doing something **2 a** : to hold in check : RESTRAIN **b** : to discourage from free or spontaneous activity esp. through the operation of inner psychological or external social constraints ~ *vi* : to cause inhibition ***syn*** see FORBID — **in·hib·i·tive** \-bə-tiv\ *adj* — **in·hib·i·to·ry** \-bə-ˌtōr-ē\ *adj*
in·hi·bi·tion \ˌin-hə-ˈbi-shən, ˌi-nə-\ *n* (14c) **1 a** : the act of inhibiting : the state of being inhibited **b** : something that forbids, debars, or restricts **2** : an inner impediment to free activity, expression, or functioning: as **a** : a mental process imposing restraint upon behavior or another mental process (as a desire) **b** : a restraining of the function of a bodily organ or an agent (as an enzyme)
in·hib·i·tor \in-ˈhi-bə-tər\ *n* (ca. 1611) : one that inhibits: as **a** : an agent that slows or interferes with a chemical action **b** : a substance that reduces or suppresses the activity of another substance (as an enzyme)
in·hold·ing \ˈin-ˌhōl-diŋ\ *n* (1947) : privately owned land inside the boundary of a national park
in·ho·mo·ge·ne·i·ty \(ˌ)in-ˌhō-mə-jə-ˈnē-ə-tē, -ˈnā- *also* ÷-ˈnī-; *esp Brit* -ˌhä-mə-\ *n, pl* **-ties** (1899) **1** : the condition or an instance of not being homogeneous **2** : a part that is not homogeneous with the larger uniform mass in which it occurs; *esp* : a localized collection of matter in the universe — **in·ho·mo·ge·neous** \-ˈjē-nē-əs, -nyəs\ *adj*
in·hos·pi·ta·ble \ˌin-(ˌ)hä-ˈspi-tə-bəl, (ˌ)in-ˈhäs-(ˌ)pi-\ *adj* (ca. 1570) **1** : not showing hospitality : not friendly or receptive **2** : providing no shelter or sustenance ⟨an ~ environment⟩ — **in·hos·pi·ta·ble·ness** *n* — **in·hos·pi·ta·bly** \-blē\ *adv*
in·hos·pi·tal·i·ty \(ˌ)in-ˌhäs-pə-ˈta-lə-tē\ *n* (ca. 1576) : the quality or state of being inhospitable
in–house \ˈin-ˌhau̇s, -ˈhau̇s\ *adj* (ca. 1956) : existing, originating, or carried on within a group or organization or its facilities : not outside ⟨an ~ publication⟩ ⟨a company's ~ staff⟩ — **in–house** *adv*
in·hu·man \(ˌ)in-ˈhyü-mən, -ˈyü-\ *adj* [ME *inhumayne,* fr. MF & L; MF *inhumain,* fr. L *inhumanus,* fr. *in-* + *humanus* human] (15c) **1 a** : lacking pity, kindness, or mercy : SAVAGE ⟨an ~ tyrant⟩ **b** : COLD, IMPERSONAL ⟨his usual quiet, almost ~ courtesy —F. Tennyson Jesse⟩ **c** : not worthy of or conforming to the needs of human beings ⟨~ living conditions⟩ **2** : of or suggesting a nonhuman class of beings — **in·hu·man·ly** *adv* — **in·hu·man·ness** \-mən-nəs\ *n*
in·hu·mane \ˌin-(ˌ)hyü-ˈmān, -(ˌ)yü-\ *adj* [MF *inhumain* & L *inhumanus*] (1536) : not humane : INHUMAN 1 ⟨the ~ treatment of prisoners⟩ — **in·hu·mane·ly** *adv*
in·hu·man·i·ty \-ˈma-nə-tē\ *n, pl* **-ties** (15c) **1 a** : the quality or state of being cruel or barbarous **b** : a cruel or barbarous act **2** : absence of warmth or geniality : IMPERSONALITY
in·hume \in-ˈhyüm\ *vt* **in·humed; in·hum·ing** [prob. fr. F *inhumer,* fr. ML *inhumare,* fr. L *in-* + *humus* earth — more at HUMBLE] (1604) : BURY, INTER — **in·hu·ma·tion** \ˌin-hyü-ˈmā-shən\ *n*
in·im·i·cal \i-ˈni-mi-kəl\ *adj* [LL *inimicalis,* fr. L *inimicus* enemy — more at ENEMY] (1573) **1** : being adverse often by reason of hostility or malevolence ⟨forces ~ to democracy⟩ **2 a** : having the disposition of an enemy : HOSTILE ⟨~ factions⟩ **b** : reflecting or indicating hostility : UNFRIENDLY ⟨his father's ~ glare⟩ — **in·im·i·cal·ly** \-mi-k(ə-)lē\ *adv*
in·im·i·ta·ble \(ˌ)i-ˈni-mə-tə-bəl\ *adj* [ME, fr. L *inimitabilis,* fr. *in-* + *imitabilis* imitable] (15c) : not capable of being imitated : MATCHLESS ⟨her own ~ style⟩ — **in·im·i·ta·ble·ness** *n* — **in·im·i·ta·bly** \-blē\ *adv*
in·i·on \ˈi-nē-ˌän, -ən\ *n* [NL, fr. Gk, back of the head, dim. of *in-, is* sinew, tendon] (ca. 1811) : the external occipital protuberance of the skull
in·iq·ui·tous \i-ˈni-kwə-təs\ *adj* (1726) : characterized by iniquity ***syn*** see VICIOUS — **in·iq·ui·tous·ly** *adv* — **in·iq·ui·tous·ness** *n*
in·iq·ui·ty \-kwə-tē\ *n, pl* **-ties** [ME *iniquite,* fr. AF *iniquité,* fr. L *iniquitat-, iniquitas,* fr. *iniquus* uneven, fr. *in-* + *aequus* equal] (14c) **1** : gross injustice : WICKEDNESS **2** : a wicked act or thing : SIN
[1]**ini·tial** \i-ˈni-shəl\ *adj* [AF & L; AF *iniciel,* fr. L *initialis,* fr. *initium* beginning, fr. *inire* to go into, fr. *in-* + *ire* to go — more at ISSUE] (1526) **1** : of or relating to the beginning : INCIPIENT ⟨his ~ reaction⟩ **2** : placed at the beginning : FIRST ⟨the ~ word of the verse⟩ — **ini·tial·ly** \i-ˈni-sh(ə-)lē\ *adv* — **ini·tial·ness** \i-ˈni-shəl-nəs\ *n*
[2]**initial** *n* (1627) **1 a** : the first letter of a name **b** *pl* : the first letter of each word in a full name ⟨found that their ~*s* were identical⟩ **2** : a large letter beginning a text or a division or paragraph **3** : ANLAGE, PRECURSOR; *specif* : a meristematic cell
[3]**initial** *vt* **ini·tialed** *or* **ini·tialled; ini·tial·ing** *or* **ini·tial·ling** \i-ˈni-sh(ə-)liŋ\ (ca. 1864) **1** : to affix an initial to **2** : to authenticate or give preliminary approval to by affixing the initials of an authorizing representative

ini·tial·ism \i-ˈni-shə-ˌli-zəm\ *n* (1899) **:** an abbreviation formed from initial letters

ini·tial·ize \-ˌlīz\ *vt* **-ized; -iz·ing** (1957) **:** to set (as a computer program counter) to a starting position, value, or configuration — **ini·tial·i·za·tion** \i-ˌni-sh(ə-)lə-ˈzā-shən\ *n*

initial rhyme *n* (1838) **:** ALLITERATION

initial side *n* (1957) **:** a stationary straight line that contains a point about which another straight line is rotated to form an angle — compare TERMINAL SIDE

[1]**ini·ti·ate** \i-ˈni-shē-ˌāt\ *vt* **-at·ed; -at·ing** [LL *initiatus,* pp. of *initiare,* fr. L, to induct, fr. *initium*] (1533) **1 :** to cause or facilitate the beginning of **:** set going ⟨~ a program of reform⟩ ⟨enzymes that ~ fermentation⟩ **2 :** to induct into membership by or as if by special rites **3 :** to instruct in the rudiments or principles of something **:** INTRODUCE ***syn*** see BEGIN — **ini·ti·a·tor** \-ˌā-tər\ *n*

[2]**ini·tiate** \i-ˈni-sh(ē-)ət\ *adj* (1537) **1 a :** initiated or properly admitted (as to membership or an office) **b :** instructed in some secret knowledge **2** *obs* **:** relating to an initiate

[3]**ini·tiate** \i-ˈni-sh(ē-)ət\ *n* (1811) **1 :** a person who is undergoing or has undergone an initiation **2 :** a person who is instructed or adept in some special field

ini·ti·a·tion \i-ˌni-shē-ˈā-shən\ *n* (1583) **1 a :** the act or an instance of initiating **b :** the process of being initiated **c :** the rites, ceremonies, ordeals, or instructions with which one is made a member of a sect or society or is invested with a particular function or status **2 :** the condition of being initiated into some experience or sphere of activity **:** KNOWLEDGEABLENESS

[1]**ini·tia·tive** \i-ˈni-shə-tiv *also* -shē-ə-tiv\ *adj* (1795) **:** of or relating to initiation **:** INTRODUCTORY, PRELIMINARY

[2]**initiative** *n* (1793) **1 :** an introductory step ⟨took the ~ in attempting to settle the issue⟩ **2 :** energy or aptitude displayed in initiation of action **:** ENTERPRISE ⟨showed great ~⟩ **3 a :** the right to initiate legislative action **b :** a procedure enabling a specified number of voters by petition to propose a law and secure its submission to the electorate or to the legislature for approval — compare REFERENDUM 1 — **on one's own initiative :** at one's own discretion **:** independently of outside influence or control

ini·tia·to·ry \i-ˈni-sh(ē-)ə-ˌtȯr-ē\ *adj* (ca. 1615) **1 :** constituting a beginning ⟨~ proceedings⟩ **2 :** tending or serving to initiate ⟨~ rites⟩

in·ject \in-ˈjekt\ *vt* [L *injectus,* pp. of *inicere,* fr. *in-* + *jacere* to throw — more at JET] (1601) **1 a :** to introduce into something forcefully ⟨~ fuel into an engine⟩ **b :** to force a fluid into (as for medical purposes) ⟨~ a drug into the bloodstream⟩ **2 :** to introduce as an element or factor in or into some situation or subject ⟨condemning any attempt to ~ religious bigotry into the campaign —*Current Biog.*⟩ — **in·ject·able** \-ˈjek-tə-bəl\ *adj or n* — **in·jec·tor** \-ˈjek-tər\ *n*

in·jec·tant \-ˈjek-tənt\ *n* (1950) **:** a substance that is injected into something

in·jec·tion \in-ˈjek-shən\ *n* (15c) **1 a :** an act or instance of injecting **b :** the placing of an artificial satellite or a spacecraft into an orbit or on a trajectory; *also* **:** the time or place at which injection occurs **2 :** something (as a medication) that is injected **3 :** a mathematical function that is a one-to-one mapping — compare BIJECTION, SURJECTION

injection molding *n* (1932) **:** a method of forming articles (as of plastic) by heating the molding material until it can flow and injecting it into a mold — **injection–molded** *adj*

in·jec·tive \in-ˈjek-tiv\ *adj* (1952) **:** being a one-to-one mathematical function

in–joke \ˈin-ˌjōk, -ˈjōk\ *n* (1964) **:** a joke for or about a select group of people

in·ju·di·cious \ˌin-jü-ˈdi-shəs\ *adj* (1649) **:** not judicious **:** INDISCREET, UNWISE ⟨~ outbursts⟩ — **in·ju·di·cious·ly** *adv* — **in·ju·di·cious·ness** *n*

in·junc·tion \in-ˈjəŋ(k)-shən\ *n* [ME *injunccion,* fr. AF & LL; AF *enjunxion,* fr. LL *injunction-, injunctio,* fr. L *injungere* to enjoin — more at ENJOIN] (15c) **1 :** the act or an instance of enjoining **:** ORDER, ADMONITION **2 :** a writ granted by a court of equity whereby one is required to do or to refrain from doing a specified act — **in·junc·tive** \-ˈjəŋ(k)-tiv\ *adj*

in·jure \ˈin-jər\ *vt* **in·jured; in·jur·ing** \ˈinj-riŋ, ˈin-jə-\ [ME *enjuren,* fr. AF **enjurer,* fr. LL *injuriare,* fr. L *injuria* injury] (15c) **1 a :** to do an injustice to **:** WRONG **b :** to harm, impair, or tarnish the standing of ⟨*injured* his reputation⟩ **c :** to give pain to ⟨~ a person's pride⟩ **2 a :** to inflict bodily hurt on **b :** to impair the soundness of ⟨*injured* her health⟩ **c :** to inflict material damage or loss on — **in·jur·er** \ˈin-jər-ər\ *n*

syn INJURE, HARM, HURT, DAMAGE, IMPAIR, MAR mean to affect injuriously. INJURE implies the inflicting of anything detrimental to one's looks, comfort, health, or success ⟨badly *injured* in an accident⟩. HARM often stresses the inflicting of pain, suffering, or loss ⟨careful not to *harm* the animals⟩. HURT implies inflicting a wound to the body or to the feelings ⟨*hurt* by their callous remarks⟩. DAMAGE suggests injury that lowers value or impairs usefulness ⟨a table *damaged* in shipping⟩. IMPAIR suggests a making less complete or efficient by deterioration or diminution ⟨years of smoking had *impaired* his health⟩. MAR applies to injury that spoils perfection (as of a surface) or causes disfigurement ⟨the text is *marred* by many typos⟩.

in·ju·ri·ous \in-ˈju̇r-ē-əs\ *adj* (15c) **1 :** inflicting or tending to inflict injury **:** DETRIMENTAL ⟨~ to health⟩ **2 :** ABUSIVE, DEFAMATORY ⟨speak not ~ words —George Washington⟩ — **in·ju·ri·ous·ly** *adv* — **in·ju·ri·ous·ness** *n*

in·ju·ry \ˈinj-rē, ˈin-jə-\ *n, pl* **-ries** [ME *injurie,* fr. AF, L *injuria,* fr. *injurus* injurious, fr. *in-* + *jur-, jus* right — more at JUST] (14c) **1 a :** an act that damages or hurts **:** WRONG **b :** violation of another's rights for which the law allows an action to recover damages **2 :** hurt, damage, or loss sustained ***syn*** see INJUSTICE

in·jus·tice \(ˌ)in-ˈjəs-təs\ *n* [ME, fr. MF, fr. L *injustitia,* fr. *injustus* unjust, fr. *in-* + *justus* just] (14c) **1 :** absence of justice **:** violation of right or of the rights of another **:** UNFAIRNESS **2 :** an unjust act **:** WRONG

syn INJUSTICE, INJURY, WRONG, GRIEVANCE mean an act that inflicts undeserved hurt. INJUSTICE applies to any act that involves unfairness to another or violation of one's rights ⟨the *injustices* suffered by the lower classes⟩. INJURY applies in law specif. to an injustice for which one may sue to recover compensation ⟨libel constitutes a legal *injury*⟩. WRONG applies also in law to any act punishable according to the criminal code; it may apply more generally to any flagrant injustice ⟨determined to right society's *wrongs*⟩. GRIEVANCE applies to a circumstance or condition that constitutes an injustice to the sufferer and gives just ground for complaint ⟨a list of employee *grievances*⟩.

[1]**ink** \ˈiŋk\ *n, often attrib* [ME *enke,* fr. AF *encre, enke,* fr. LL *encaustum,* fr. neut. of L *encaustus* burned in, fr. Gk *enkaustos,* verbal of *enkaiein* to burn in — more at ENCAUSTIC] (13c) **1 :** a colored usu. liquid material for writing and printing **2 :** the black protective secretion of a cephalopod **3** *slang* **:** PUBLICITY 2d — **ink·i·ness** \ˈiŋ-kē-nəs\ *n* — **inky** \ˈiŋ-kē\ *adj*

[2]**ink** *vt* (1562) **1 :** to put ink on ⟨~ a pen⟩; *also* **:** to draw or write on in ink **2 a :** SIGN 2a ⟨~*ed* a new contract⟩ **b :** SIGN 4

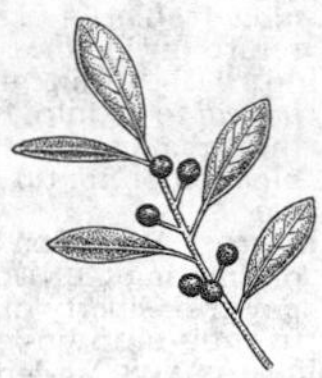

inkberry 1a

ink·ber·ry \ˈiŋk-ˌber-ē\ *n* [fr. the use of the berries for making ink] (1765) **1 a :** a holly (*Ilex glabra*) of eastern No. America with evergreen oblong leathery leaves and small usu. black berries **b :** POKEWEED **2 :** the fruit of an inkberry

ink·blot test \ˈiŋk-ˌblät-\ *n* (1928) **:** any of several psychological tests (as a Rorschach test) based on the interpretation of irregular figures (as blots of ink)

[1]**ink·horn** \ˈiŋk-ˌhȯrn\ *n* (14c) **:** a small portable bottle (as of horn) for holding ink

[2]**inkhorn** *adj* (1543) **:** ostentatiously learned **:** PEDANTIC ⟨~ terms⟩

in–kind \ˈin-ˈkīnd\ *adj* (1973) **:** consisting of something (as goods or commodities) other than money ⟨~ relief for the poor⟩

ink–jet \ˈiŋk-ˈjet\ *adj* (1976) **:** of, relating to, or being a printer in which electrically charged droplets of ink are sprayed onto the paper — **ink–jet** *n*

in·kle \ˈiŋ-kəl\ *n* [origin unknown] (1541) **:** a colored linen tape or braid woven on a very narrow loom and used for trimming; *also* **:** the thread used

in·kling \ˈiŋ-kliŋ\ *n* [ME *yngkiling* whisper, mention, prob. fr. *inclen* to hint at; akin to OE *inca* suspicion] (1513) **1 :** a slight indication or suggestion **:** HINT, CLUE ⟨there was no path—no ~ even of a track —*New Yorker*⟩ **2 :** a slight knowledge or vague notion ⟨had not the faintest ~ of what it was all about —H. W. Carter⟩

ink·stand \ˈiŋk-ˌstand\ *n* (1770) **:** INKWELL; *also* **:** a stand with fittings for holding ink and pens

ink·stone \ˈiŋk-ˌstōn\ *n* (ca. 1889) **:** a stone used in Chinese art and calligraphy on which dry ink and water are mixed

ink·well \ˈiŋk-ˌwel\ *n* (ca. 1875) **:** a container (as in a desk) for ink

inky cap *n* (1923) **:** a mushroom (genus *Coprinus,* esp. *C. atramentarius*) whose pileus deliquesces into an inky fluid after the spores have matured — called also *ink cap*

in·laid \ˈin-ˈlād\ *adj* (1598) **1 a :** set into a surface in a decorative design ⟨tables with ~ marble⟩ **b :** decorated with a design or material set into a surface ⟨a table with an ~ top⟩ **2** *of linoleum* **:** having a design that goes all the way through to the backing

[1]**in·land** \ˈin-ˌland, -lənd\ *adj* (15c) **1 :** of or relating to the interior of a country **2** *chiefly Brit* **:** not foreign **:** DOMESTIC

[2]**inland** *n* (1573) **:** the interior part of a country

[3]**inland** *adv* (1600) **:** into or toward the interior

in·land·er \ˈin-ˌlan-dər, -lən-\ *n* (1610) **:** one who lives inland

in–law \ˈin-ˌlȯ\ *n* [mother-*in-law,* etc.] (1894) **:** a relative by marriage

[1]**in·lay** \(ˌ)in-ˈlā, ˈin-ˌ\ *vt* **in·laid** \-ˈlād, -ˌlād\; **in·lay·ing** (1596) **1 a :** to set into a surface or ground material **b :** to adorn with insertions **c :** to insert (as a color plate) into a mat or other reinforcement **2 :** to rub, beat, or fuse (as wire) into an incision in metal, wood, or stone — **in·lay·er** *n*

[2]**in·lay** \ˈin-ˌlā\ *n* (1667) **1 :** inlaid work or a decorative inlaid pattern **2 :** a tooth filling shaped to fit a cavity and then cemented into place

in·let \ˈin-ˌlet, -lət\ *n* [fr. its letting water in] (ca. 1576) **1 a :** a bay or recess in the shore of a sea, lake, or river; *also* **:** CREEK **b :** a narrow water passage between peninsulas or through a barrier island leading to a bay or lagoon **2 :** a way of entering; *esp* **:** an opening for intake

in·li·er \ˈin-ˌlī(-ə)r\ *n* [[3]*in* + out*lier*] (ca. 1859) **1 :** a mass of rock whose outcrop is surrounded by rock of younger age **2 :** a distinct area or formation completely surrounded by another; *also* **:** ENCLAVE

in–line \ˈin-ˈlīn, ˌin-\ *adj or adv* (1929) **:** having the parts or units arranged in a straight line; *also* **:** being so arranged

in–line engine \(ˌ)in-ˈlīn-, ˈin-ˌ\ *n* (1929) **:** an internal combustion engine in which the cylinders are arranged in one or more straight lines

in–line skate *n* (1987) **:** a roller skate whose wheels are set in-line for greater speed and maneuverability — **in–line skater** *n* — **in–line skating** *n*

[1]**in lo·co pa·ren·tis** \in-ˈlō-kō-pə-ˈren-təs\ *adv* [L] (1818) **:** in the place of a parent ⟨school officials acting *in loco parentis*⟩

[2]**in loco parentis** *n* (1968) **:** regulation or supervision by an administrative body (as at a university) acting in loco parentis

in·ly \ˈin-lē\ *adv* (bef. 12c) **1 :** INWARDLY **2 :** in a manner suggesting great depth of knowledge or understanding **:** THOROUGHLY

in·mate \ˈin-ˌmāt\ *n* (1580) **:** any of a group occupying a single place of residence; *esp* **:** a person confined (as in a prison or hospital)

in me·di·as res \in-ˈme-dē-əs-ˈrās, -ˈmē-dē-əs-ˈrēz\ *adv* [L, lit., into the midst of things] (1786) **:** in or into the middle of a narrative or plot

in me·mo·ri·am \ˌin-mə-ˈmȯr-ē-əm\ *prep* [L] (1850) **:** in memory of — used esp. in epitaphs

in–mi·grant \ˈin-ˌmī-grənt\ *n* (1942) **:** one that in-migrates

in–mi·grate \ˈin-ˌmī-ˌgrāt\ *vi* (1942) **:** to move into or come to live in a region or community esp. as part of a large-scale and continuing movement of population — compare OUT-MIGRATE — **in–mi·gra·tion** \ˌin-mī-ˈgrā-shən\ *n*

in·most \ˈin-ˌmōst\ *adj* [ME, fr. OE *innemest,* superl. of *inne,* adv., in, within, fr. *in,* adv.] (bef. 12c) **:** deepest within **:** farthest from the outside

[1]**inn** \ˈin\ *n* [ME, fr. OE; akin to ON *inni* dwelling, inn, OE *in,* adv.] (12c) **1 a :** an establishment for the lodging and entertaining of travelers **b :** TAVERN **2 :** a residence formerly provided for British students in London and esp. for students of law

[2]**inn** *vi* (14c) **:** to put up at an inn

in·nards \ˈi-nərdz\ *n pl* [alter. of *inwards*] (ca. 1825) **1 :** the internal organs of a human being or animal; *esp* **:** VISCERA **2 :** the internal parts esp. of a structure or mechanism

in·nate \i-ˈnāt, ˈi-ˌ\ *adj* [ME *innat,* fr. L *innatus,* pp. of *innasci* to be born in, fr. *in-* + *nasci* to be born — more at NATION] (15c) **1 :** existing in, belonging to, or determined by factors present in an individual from birth **:** NATIVE, INBORN ⟨~ behavior⟩ **2 :** belonging to the essential nature of something **:** INHERENT **3 :** originating in or derived from the mind or the constitution of the intellect rather than from experience — **in·nate·ly** *adv* — **in·nate·ness** *n*

syn INNATE, INBORN, INBRED, CONGENITAL, HEREDITARY mean not acquired after birth. INNATE applies to qualities or characteristics that are part of one's inner essential nature ⟨an *innate* sense of fair play⟩. INBORN suggests a quality or tendency either actually present at birth or so marked and deep-seated as to seem so ⟨her *inborn* love of nature⟩. INBRED suggests something either acquired from parents by heredity or so deeply rooted and ingrained as to seem acquired in that way ⟨*inbred* political loyalties⟩. CONGENITAL and HEREDITARY refer to what is acquired before or at birth, the former to things acquired during fetal development and the latter to things transmitted from one's ancestors ⟨a *congenital* heart murmur⟩ ⟨eye color is *hereditary*⟩.

in·ner \ˈi-nər\ *adj* [ME, fr. OE *innera,* compar. of *inne* within] (bef. 12c) **1 a :** situated farther in ⟨the ~ bark⟩ **b :** being near a center esp. of influence ⟨the ~ circles of political power⟩ **2 a :** of or relating to the mind or spirit ⟨the ~ life⟩ **b :** existing as an often repressed part of one's psychological makeup ⟨~ child⟩ ⟨~ artist⟩ — **inner** *n* — **in·ner·ly** *adv*

inner city *n* (1961) **:** the usu. older, poorer, and more densely populated central section of a city — **inner–city** *adj*

in·ner–di·rect·ed \ˈi-nər-də-ˈrek-təd, -(ˌ)dī-\ *adj* (1950) **:** directed in thought and action by one's own scale of values as opposed to external norms

inner ear *n* (1855) **:** the essential organ of hearing and equilibrium that is located in the temporal bone, is innervated by the auditory nerve, and includes the vestibule, the semicircular canals, and the cochlea

inner light *n, often cap I&L* (1856) **:** a divine presence held (as in Quaker doctrine) to enlighten and guide the soul

[1]**in·ner·most** \ˈi-nər-ˌmōst\ *adj* (14c) **:** farthest inward **:** INMOST

[2]**innermost** *n* (14c) **:** the inmost part

inner planet *n* (1951) **:** any of the planets Mercury, Venus, Earth, and Mars whose orbits are within the asteroid belt

inner product *n* (ca. 1911) **:** SCALAR PRODUCT

in·ner·sole \ˈi-nər-ˈsōl\ *n* (1830) **:** INSOLE

inner space *n* (1958) **1 :** space at or near the earth's surface and esp. under the sea **2 :** one's inner self

in·ner·spring \ˈi-nər-ˈspriŋ\ *adj* (1928) **:** having coil springs inside a padded casing ⟨~ mattress⟩

inner tube *n* (1894) **:** an inflatable usu. ring-shaped rubber tube designed for use inside a pneumatic tire

in·ner·vate \i-ˈnər-ˌvāt, ˈi-(ˌ)nər-\ *vt* **-vat·ed; -vat·ing** (1870) **:** to supply with nerves — **in·ner·va·tion** \ˌi-(ˌ)nər-ˈvā-shən, i-ˌnər-\ *n*

in·ning \ˈi-niŋ\ *n* [[2]*in* + [1]*-ing*] (1735) **1 a** *pl but sing or pl in constr* **:** a division of a cricket match **b :** a division of a baseball game consisting of a turn at bat for each team; *also* **:** a baseball team's turn at bat ending with the third out **c :** a player's turn (as in horseshoes, pool, or croquet) **2 :** a chance or opportunity for action or accomplishment — usu. used in pl. but sing. or pl. in constr. ⟨that momentous ~*s* which was to project him into world politics —*Times Lit. Supp.*⟩

inn·keep·er \ˈin-ˌkē-pər\ *n* (15c) **1 :** a proprietor of an inn **2 :** HOTELMAN

in·no·cence \ˈi-nə-sən(t)s\ *n* (14c) **1 a :** freedom from guilt or sin through being unacquainted with evil **:** BLAMELESSNESS **b :** CHASTITY **c :** freedom from legal guilt of a particular crime or offense **d** (1) **:** freedom from guile or cunning **:** SIMPLICITY (2) **:** lack of worldly experience or sophistication **e :** lack of knowledge **:** IGNORANCE ⟨written in entire ~ of the Italian language —E. R. Bentley⟩ **2 :** one that is innocent **3 :** BLUET

in·no·cen·cy \-sən(t)-sē\ *n, pl* **-cies** (14c) **:** INNOCENCE; *also* **:** an innocent action or quality

in·no·cent \ˈi-nə-sənt\ *adj* [ME, fr. AF, fr. L *innocent-, innocens,* fr. *in-* + *nocent-, nocens* wicked, fr. prp. of *nocēre* to harm — more at NOXIOUS] (14c) **1 a :** free from guilt or sin esp. through lack of knowledge of evil **:** BLAMELESS ⟨an ~ child⟩ **b :** harmless in effect or intention ⟨searching for a hidden motive in even the most ~ conversation —Leonard Wibberley⟩; *also* **:** CANDID ⟨gave me an ~ gaze⟩ **c :** free from legal guilt or fault; *also* **:** LAWFUL ⟨a wholly ~ transaction⟩ **2 a :** lacking or reflecting a lack of sophistication, guile, or self-consciousness **:** ARTLESS, INGENUOUS **b :** IGNORANT ⟨almost entirely ~ of Latin —C. L. Wrenn⟩; *also* **:** UNAWARE ⟨perfectly ~ of the confusion he had created —B. R. Haydon⟩ **3 :** lacking or deprived of something ⟨her face ~ of cosmetics —Marcia Davenport⟩ — **innocent** *n* — **in·no·cent·ly** *adv*

in·noc·u·ous \i-ˈnä-kyə-wəs\ *adj* [L *innocuus,* fr. *in-* + *nocēre*] (1598) **1 :** producing no injury **:** HARMLESS **2 :** not likely to give offense or to arouse strong feelings or hostility **:** INOFFENSIVE, INSIPID — **in·noc·u·ous·ly** *adv* — **in·noc·u·ous·ness** *n*

in·nom·i·nate \i-ˈnä-mə-nət\ *adj* [LL *innominatus,* fr. L *in-* + *nominatus,* pp. of *nominare* to nominate] (1638) **:** having no name **:** UNNAMED; *also* **:** ANONYMOUS

innominate artery *n* (1870) **:** BRACHIOCEPHALIC ARTERY

innominate bone *n* (1866) **:** HIP BONE

innominate vein *n* (1876) **:** BRACHIOCEPHALIC VEIN

in·no·vate \ˈi-nə-ˌvāt\ *vb* **-vat·ed; -vat·ing** [L *innovatus,* pp. of *innovare,* fr. *in-* + *novus* new — more at NEW] *vt* (1548) **1 :** to introduce as or as if new **2** *archaic* **:** to effect a change in ⟨the dictates of my father were . . . not to be altered, *innovated,* or even discussed —Sir Walter Scott⟩ ~ *vi* **:** to make changes **:** do something in a new way — **in·no·va·tor** \-ˌvā-tər\ *n* — **in·no·va·to·ry** \ˈi-nə-və-ˌtȯr-ē, ˈi-nə-ˌvā-tə-rē\ *adj*

in·no·va·tion \ˌi-nə-ˈvā-shən\ *n* (15c) **1 :** the introduction of something new **2 :** a new idea, method, or device **:** NOVELTY — **in·no·va·tion·al** \-shnəl, -shə-nᵊl\ *adj*

in·no·va·tive \ˈi-nə-ˌvā-tiv\ *adj* (1608) **:** characterized by, tending to, or introducing innovations — **in·no·va·tive·ly** *adv* — **in·no·va·tive·ness** *n*

Inns of Court (15c) **1 :** the four sets of buildings in London belonging to four societies of students and practitioners of the law **2 :** the four societies that alone admit to practice at the English bar

in·nu·en·do \ˌin-yə-ˈwen-(ˌ)dō, -yü-ˈen-\ *n, pl* **-dos** *or* **-does** [L, by nodding, fr. *innuere* to nod to, make a sign to, fr. *in-* + *nuere* to nod; akin to L *nutare* to nod — more at NUMEN] (1678) **1 a :** an oblique allusion **:** HINT, INSINUATION; *esp* **:** a veiled or equivocal reflection on character or reputation **b :** the use of such allusions ⟨resorting to ~⟩ **2 :** a parenthetical explanation introduced into the text of a legal document

Innuit *var of* INUIT

in·nu·mer·a·ble \i-ˈnüm-rə-bəl, -ˈnyüm-; -ˈn(y)ü-mə-\ *adj* [ME, fr. AF, fr. L *innumerabilis,* fr. *in-* + *numerabilis* numerable] (14c) **:** too many to be numbered **:** COUNTLESS; *also* **:** very many — **in·nu·mer·a·bly** \-blē\ *adv*

in·nu·mer·ate \-rət\ *adj* (1959) **:** marked by an ignorance of mathematics and the scientific approach — **in·nu·mer·a·cy** \-rə-sē\ *n* — **innumerate** *n*

in·nu·mer·ous \-rəs\ *adj* [L *innumerus,* fr. *in-* + *numerus* number] (1531) **:** INNUMERABLE

in·ob·ser·vance \ˌin-əb-ˈzər-vən(t)s\ *n* [F & L; F, fr. L *inobservantia,* fr. *in-* + *observantia* observance] (1611) **1 :** lack of attention **:** HEEDLESSNESS **2 :** failure to fulfill **:** NONOBSERVANCE — **in·ob·ser·vant** \-vənt\ *adj*

in·oc·u·lant \i-ˈnä-kyə-lənt\ *n* (1898) **:** INOCULUM

in·oc·u·late \i-ˈnä-kyə-ˌlāt\ *vt* **-lat·ed; -lat·ing** [ME, to insert a bud in a plant, fr. L *inoculatus,* pp. of *inoculare,* fr. *in-* + *oculus* eye, bud — more at EYE] (1721) **1 a :** to introduce a microorganism into ⟨~ mice with anthrax⟩ ⟨beans *inoculated* with nitrogen-fixing bacteria⟩ **b :** to introduce (as a microorganism) into a suitable situation for growth **c :** to introduce immunologically active material (as an antibody or antigen) into esp. in order to treat or prevent a disease ⟨~ children against diphtheria⟩ **2 :** to introduce something into the mind of **3 :** to protect as if by inoculation ***syn*** see INFUSE — **in·oc·u·la·tive** \-ˌlā-tiv\ *adj* — **in·oc·u·la·tor** \-ˌlā-tər\ *n*

in·oc·u·la·tion \i-ˌnä-kyə-ˈlā-shən\ *n* (1714) **1 :** the act or process or an instance of inoculating; *esp* **:** the introduction of a pathogen or antigen into a living organism to stimulate the production of antibodies **2 :** INOCULUM

in·oc·u·lum \i-ˈnä-kyə-ləm\ *n, pl* **-la** \-lə\ [NL, fr. L *inoculare*] (1902) **:** material used for inoculation

in·of·fen·sive \ˌin-ə-ˈfen(t)-siv\ *adj* (1646) **1 :** causing no harm or injury **2 a :** giving no provocation **:** PEACEABLE **b :** not objectionable to the senses — **in·of·fen·sive·ly** *adv* — **in·of·fen·sive·ness** *n*

in·op·er·a·ble \(ˌ)in-ˈä-p(ə-)rə-bəl\ *adj* [prob. fr. F *inopérable*] (1886) **1 :** not treatable or remediable by surgery **2 :** INOPERATIVE

in·op·er·a·tive \-ˈä-p(ə-)rə-tiv, -ˈä-pə-ˌrā-\ *adj* (ca. 1631) **:** not operative: as **a :** not functioning ⟨an ~ clock⟩ **b :** having no effect or force ⟨an ~ law⟩ — **in·op·er·a·tive·ness** *n*

in·op·por·tune \(ˌ)in-ˌä-pər-ˈtün, -ˈtyün\ *adj* [L *inopportunus,* fr. *in-* + *opportunus* opportune] (ca. 1507) **:** INCONVENIENT, UNSEASONABLE — **in·op·por·tune·ly** *adv* — **in·op·por·tune·ness** \-ˈt(y)ün-nəs\ *n*

in order that *conj* (1711) **:** THAT 2a(1)

in·or·di·nate \in-ˈȯr-dᵊn-ət, -ˈȯrd-nət\ *adj* [ME *inordinat,* fr. L *inordinatus,* fr. *in-* + *ordinatus,* pp. of *ordinare* to arrange — more at ORDAIN] (14c) **1** *archaic* **:** DISORDERLY, UNREGULATED **2 :** exceeding reasonable limits **:** IMMODERATE ***syn*** see EXCESSIVE — **in·or·di·nate·ly** *adv* — **in·or·di·nate·ness** *n*

inorg *abbr* inorganic

in·or·gan·ic \ˌin-(ˌ)ȯr-ˈga-nik\ *adj* (1729) **1 a** (1) **:** being or composed of matter other than plant or animal **:** MINERAL (2) **:** forming or belonging to the inanimate world **b :** of, relating to, or dealt with by a branch of chemistry concerned with substances not usu. classed as organic **2 :** not arising from natural growth **:** ARTIFICIAL; *also* **:** lacking structure, character, or vitality ⟨dull ~ things, without individuality or prestige —John Buchan⟩ — **in·or·gan·i·cal·ly** \-ni-k(ə-)lē\ *adv*

in·os·cu·late \i-ˈnäs-kyə-ˌlāt\ *vb* **-lat·ed; -lat·ing** [[2]*in-* + *osculate*] (1671) **:** JOIN, UNITE — **in·os·cu·la·tion** \(ˌ)i-ˌnäs-kyə-ˈlā-shən\ *n*

ino·sine \ˈi-nə-ˌsēn, ˈī-, -sən\ *n* [ISV *inosinic* acid (the acid $C_{10}H_{13}N_4O_8P$; *inosinic,* fr. Gk *in-, is* sinew + ISV [2]*-ose* + [1]*-in* + [1]*-ic*) + [2]*-ine*] (1911) **:** a nucleoside $C_{10}H_{12}N_4O_5$ that is composed of hypoxanthine and ribose, that in the form of its monophosphate is a biosynthetic precursor of both AMP and its guanosine analog, and that binds to adenine, cytosine, or uracil esp. in some transfer RNAs — compare POLY I:C

ino·si·tol \i-ˈnō-sə-ˌtȯl, ī-ˈnō-, -ˌtōl\ *n* [ISV, fr. *inosite* inositol, fr. Gk *in-, is* sinew + ISV [2]*-ose* + [1]*-ite*] (1891) **:** any of several crystalline stereoisomeric cyclic alcohols $C_6H_{12}O_6$; *esp* **:** MYOINOSITOL

ino·trope \ˈī-nə-ˌtrōp\ *n* (1975) **:** an inotropic drug or agent (as epinephrine or a beta-blocker)

ino·tro·pic \ˌē-nə-ˈtrō-pik, ˌī-nə-, -ˈträ-\ *adj* [ISV *ino-* (fr. Gk *in-, is* sinew) + *-tropic*] (1903) **:** increasing or decreasing the force of muscular contractions ⟨an ~ drug⟩

INP *abbr* International News Photo

in·pa·tient \ˈin-ˌpā-shənt\ *n* (1760) **:** a hospital patient who receives lodging and food as well as treatment — compare OUTPATIENT

in per·so·nam \ˌin-pər-ˈsō-ˌnam, -ˌnäm\ *adv or adj* [LL, against a person] (1771) **:** against a person for the purpose of imposing a liability or obligation — used esp. of legal actions, judgments, or jurisdiction; compare IN REM

in pet·to \in-ˈpe-(ˌ)tō\ *adv or adj* [It, lit., in the breast] (ca. 1674) **1 :** in private **:** SECRETLY **2 :** in miniature

in·pour·ing \ˈin-ˌpȯr-iŋ\ *n* (1721) **:** INRUSH

in–print \ˈin-ˈprint\ *adj* (1880) **:** being in print

in–pro·cess \(ˌ)in-ˈprä-ˌses, -ˈprō-, -səs\ *adj* (1925) **:** of, relating to, or being goods in manufacture as distinguished from raw materials or from finished products

\ə\ **abut** \ᵊ\ **kitten**, F **table** \ər\ **further** \a\ **ash** \ā\ **ace** \ä\ **mop, mar**
\au̇\ **out** \ch\ **chin** \e\ **bet** \ē\ **easy** \g\ **go** \i\ **hit** \ī\ **ice** \j\ **job**
\ŋ\ **sing** \ō\ **go** \ȯ\ **law** \ȯi\ **boy** \th\ **thin** \t͟h\ **the** \ü\ **loot** \u̇\ **foot**
\y\ **yet** \zh\ **vision, beige** \k̲, ⁿ, œ, ue, ʸ\ *see* Guide to Pronunciation

in pro·pria per·so·na \in-ˈprō-prē-ə-pər-ˈsō-nə\ *adv* [ML] (1654) **:** in one's own person or character **:** PERSONALLY; *esp* **:** without the assistance of an attorney

[1]**in·put** \ˈin-ˌpu̇t\ *n* (ca. 1888) **1 :** something that is put in: as **a :** an amount put in ⟨increased ~ of fertilizer increases crop yield⟩ **b :** power or energy put into a machine or system for storage, conversion in kind, or conversion of characteristics usu. with the intent of sizable recovery in the form of output **c :** a component of production (as land, labor, or raw materials) **d :** information fed into a data processing system or computer **e :** ADVICE, OPINION, COMMENT **f :** a stimulus that acts on and is integrated into a bodily system ⟨sensory ~⟩ **2 :** the means by which or the point at which an input (as of energy, material, or data) is made **3 :** the act or process of putting in

[2]**input** *vt* **in·put·ted** *or* **input; in·put·ting** (1946) **:** to enter (as data) into a computer or data processing system

inq *abbr* inquire

in·quest \ˈin-ˌkwest\ *n* [ME, fr. AF *enqueste,* fr. VL **inquaesta,* fem. of **inquaestus,* pp. of **inquaerere* to inquire] (13c) **1 a :** a judicial or official inquiry or examination esp. before a jury ⟨a coroner's ~⟩ **b :** a body of people (as a jury) assembled to hold such an inquiry **c :** the finding of the jury upon such inquiry or the document recording it **2 :** INQUIRY, INVESTIGATION

in·qui·etude \(ˌ)in-ˈkwī-ə-ˌtüd, -ˌtyüd\ *n* [ME, fr. LL *inquietudo,* fr. L *inquietus* disturbed, fr. *in-* + *quietus* quiet] (15c) **:** disturbed state **:** DISQUIETUDE

in·qui·line \ˈin-kwə-ˌlīn, ˈiŋ-, -lən\ *n* [L *inquilinus* tenant, lodger, fr. *in-* + *colere* to cultivate, dwell — more at WHEEL] (1879) **:** an animal that lives habitually in the nest or abode of some other species

in·quire \in-ˈkwī(-ə)r\ *vb* **in·quired; in·quir·ing** [ME *enquiren,* fr. AF *enquerre,* fr. VL **inquaerere,* alter. of L *inquirere,* fr. *in-* + *quaerere* to seek] *vt* (13c) **1 :** to ask about ⟨some kindred spirit shall ~ thy fate —Thomas Gray⟩ **2 :** to search into **:** INVESTIGATE ~ *vi* **1 :** to put a question **:** seek for information by questioning ⟨*inquired* about the horses⟩ **2 :** to make investigation or inquiry — often used with *into* ***syn*** see ASK — **in·quir·er** *n* — **in·quir·ing·ly** \-ˈkwī-riŋ-lē\ *adv* — **inquire after :** to ask about the health of

in·qui·ry \in-ˈkwī(-ə)r-ē, ˈin-ˌ; ˈin-kwə-rē, ˈiŋ-; ˈin-ˌkwir-ē\ *n, pl* **-ries** (15c) **1 :** examination into facts or principles **:** RESEARCH **2 :** a request for information **3 :** a systematic investigation often of a matter of public interest

in·qui·si·tion \ˌin-kwə-ˈzi-shən, ˌiŋ-\ *n* [ME *inquisicioun,* fr. AF *inquisition,* fr. L *inquisition-, inquisitio,* fr. *inquirere*] (14c) **1 :** the act of inquiring **:** EXAMINATION **2 :** a judicial or official inquiry or examination usu. before a jury; *also* **:** the finding of the jury **3 a** *cap* **:** a former Roman Catholic tribunal for the discovery and punishment of heresy **b :** an investigation conducted with little regard for individual rights **c :** a severe questioning — **in·qui·si·tion·al** \-ˈzi-sh(ə-)nᵊl\ *adj*

in·quis·i·tive \in-ˈkwi-zə-tiv\ *adj* (14c) **1 :** given to examination or investigation **2 :** inclined to ask questions; *esp* **:** inordinately or improperly curious about the affairs of others ***syn*** see CURIOUS — **in·quis·i·tive·ly** *adv* — **in·quis·i·tive·ness** *n*

in·quis·i·tor \in-ˈkwi-zə-tər\ *n* (1504) **:** one who inquires or makes inquisition; *esp* **:** one who is unduly harsh, severe, or hostile in making an inquiry — **in·quis·i·to·ri·al** \-ˌkwi-zə-ˈtȯr-ē-əl\ *adj* — **in·quis·i·to·ri·al·ly** \-ē-ə-lē\ *adv*

in re \in-ˈrā, -ˈrē\ *prep* [L] (1877) **:** in the matter of **:** CONCERNING, RE — often used in the title or name of a law case

in rem \in-ˈrem\ *adv or adj* [LL] (1761) **:** against a thing (as a right, status, or property) — used esp. of legal actions, judgments, or jurisdiction; compare IN PERSONAM

INRI *abbr* [L *Iesus Nazarenus Rex Iudaeorum*] Jesus of Nazareth, King of the Jews

in·ro \ˈin-(ˌ)rō\ *n, pl* **inro** [Jp *inrō*] (1617) **:** a small compartmented and usu. ornamented container hung from an obi to hold small objects (as medicines)

in·road \ˈin-ˌrōd\ *n* (1548) **1 :** a sudden hostile incursion **:** RAID **2 :** an advance or penetration often at the expense of someone or something — usu. used in pl.

in·run \ˈin-ˌrən\ *n* (1941) **:** the approach ramp of a ski jump

in·rush \ˈin-ˌrəsh\ *n* (1817) **:** a crowding or flooding in

ins *abbr* **1** inches **2** insurance

INS *abbr* **1** Immigration and Naturalization Service **2** inertial navigation system

in·sa·lu·bri·ous \ˌin-sə-ˈlü-brē-əs\ *adj* [L *insalubris,* fr. *in-* + *salubris* healthful — more at SAFE] (1615) **:** not conducive to health **:** UNWHOLESOME ⟨an ~ climate⟩ — **in·sa·lu·bri·ty** \-brə-tē\ *n*

ins and outs \ˌinz-ən(d)-ˈau̇ts\ *n pl* (ca. 1670) **1 :** characteristic peculiarities or technicalities **:** WORKINGS **2 :** RAMIFICATIONS

in·sane \(ˌ)in-ˈsān\ *adj* [L *insanus,* fr. *in-* + *sanus* sane] (ca. 1550) **1 :** mentally disordered **:** exhibiting insanity **2 :** used by, typical of, or intended for insane persons ⟨an ~ asylum⟩ **3 :** ABSURD ⟨an ~ scheme for making money⟩ **4 :** EXTREME 1 — **in·sane·ly** *adv* — **in·sane·ness** \-ˈsān-nəs\ *n*

in·san·i·tary \(ˌ)in-ˈsa-nə-ˌter-ē\ *adj* (1866) **:** unclean enough to endanger health **:** CONTAMINATED — **in·san·i·ta·tion** \in-ˌsa-nə-ˈtā-shən\ *n*

in·san·i·ty \in-ˈsa-nə-tē\ *n, pl* **-ties** (1590) **1 :** a deranged state of the mind usu. occurring as a specific disorder (as schizophrenia) **2 :** such unsoundness of mind or lack of understanding as prevents one from having the mental capacity required by law to enter into a particular relationship, status, or transaction or as removes one from criminal or civil responsibility **3 a :** extreme folly or unreasonableness **b :** something utterly foolish or unreasonable

in·sa·tia·ble \(ˌ)in-ˈsā-shə-bəl\ *adj* [ME *insaciable,* fr. AF, fr. L *insatiabilis,* fr. *in-* + *satiare* to satisfy — more at SATIATE] (15c) **:** incapable of being satisfied **:** QUENCHLESS ⟨had an ~ desire for wealth⟩ — **in·sa·tia·bil·i·ty** \(ˌ)in-ˌsā-shə-ˈbi-lə-tē\ *n* — **in·sa·tia·ble·ness** \(ˌ)in-ˈsā-shə-bəl-nəs\ *n* — **in·sa·tia·bly** \-blē\ *adv*

in·sa·tiate \(ˌ)in-ˈsā-sh(ē-)ət\ *adj* (15c) **:** INSATIABLE — **in·sa·tiate·ly** *adv* — **in·sa·tiate·ness** *n*

in·scribe \in-ˈskrīb\ *vt* [ME, fr. L *inscribere,* fr. *in-* + *scribere* to write — more at SCRIBE] (15c) **1 a :** to write, engrave, or print as a lasting record **b :** to enter on a list **:** ENROLL **2 a :** to write, engrave, or print characters upon **b :** to autograph or address (a book) as a gift **3 :** to dedicate to someone **4 :** to draw within a figure so as to touch in as many places as possible ⟨a regular polygon *inscribed* in a circle⟩ **5** *Brit* **:** to register the name of the holder of (a security) — **in·scrib·er** *n*

in·scrip·tion \in-ˈskrip-shən\ *n* [ME *inscripcioun,* fr. L *inscription-, inscriptio,* fr. *inscribere*] (14c) **1 a :** something that is inscribed; *also* **:** SUPERSCRIPTION **b :** EPIGRAPH 2 **c :** the wording on a coin, medal, seal, or currency note **2 :** the dedication of a book or work of art **3 a :** the act of inscribing **b :** the entering of a name on or as if on a list **:** ENROLLMENT **4** *Brit* **a :** the act of inscribing securities **b** *pl* **:** inscribed securities — **in·scrip·tion·al** \-shnəl, -shə-nᵊl\ *adj*

in·scrip·tive \in-ˈskrip-tiv\ *adj* (1740) **:** relating to or constituting an inscription — **in·scrip·tive·ly** *adv*

in·scroll \in-ˈskrōl\ *vt* (1596) *archaic* **:** to write on a scroll **:** RECORD

in·scru·ta·ble \in-ˈskrü-tə-bəl\ *adj* [ME, fr. LL *inscrutabilis,* fr. L *in-* + *scrutari* to search — more at SCRUTINY] (15c) **:** not readily investigated, interpreted, or understood **:** MYSTERIOUS ⟨an ~ smile⟩ ⟨~ motives⟩ — **in·scru·ta·bil·i·ty** \-ˌskrü-tə-ˈbi-lə-tē\ *n* — **in·scru·ta·ble·ness** \-ˈskrü-tə-bəl-nəs\ *n* — **in·scru·ta·bly** \-blē\ *adv*

in·sculp \in-ˈskəlp\ *vt* [ME, fr. L *insculpere,* fr. *in-* + *scalpere* to scratch, carve] (15c) *archaic* **:** ENGRAVE, SCULPTURE

in·seam \ˈin-ˌsēm\ *n* (1886) **:** the seam on the inside of the leg of a pair of pants; *also* **:** the length of this seam

in·sect \ˈin-ˌsekt\ *n* [L *insectum,* fr. neut. of *insectus,* pp. of *insecare* to cut into, fr. *in-* + *secare* to cut — more at SAW] (1601) **1 a :** any of numerous small invertebrate animals (as spiders or centipedes) that are more or less obviously segmented — not used technically **b :** any of a class (Insecta) of arthropods (as bugs or bees) with well-defined head, thorax, and abdomen, only three pairs of legs, and typically one or two pairs of wings **2 :** a trivial or contemptible person — **insect** *adj*

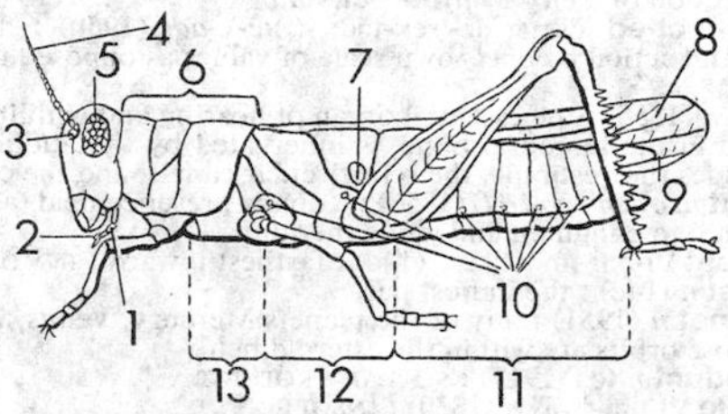

insect 1b: *1* labial palpus, *2* maxillary palpus, *3* simple eye, *4* antenna, *5* compound eye, *6* prothorax, *7* tympanum, *8* wing, *9* ovipositor, *10* spiracles, *11* abdomen, *12* metathorax, *13* mesothorax

in·sec·ta·ry \ˈin-ˌsek-tə-rē, in-ˈ\ *n, pl* **-ries** (1888) **:** a place for the keeping or rearing of living insects

in·sec·ti·cid·al \(ˌ)in-ˌsek-tə-ˈsī-dᵊl\ *adj* (1857) **1 :** destroying or controlling insects **2 :** of or relating to an insecticide — **in·sec·ti·cid·al·ly** \-dᵊl-ē\ *adv*

in·sec·ti·cide \in-ˈsek-tə-ˌsīd\ *n* [ISV] (1865) **:** an agent that destroys insects

in·sec·tile \(ˌ)in-ˈsek-tᵊl, -ˌtī(-ə)l, -(ˌ)til\ *adj* (ca. 1626) **:** being or suggestive of an insect

in·sec·ti·vore \in-ˈsek-tə-ˌvȯr\ *n* [NL *Insectivora,* fr. L *insectum* + *-vorus* -vorous] (1840) **1 :** any of an order (Insectivora) of small usu. nocturnal mammals (as moles, shrews, and hedgehogs) that feed mainly on insects **2 :** an insectivorous plant or animal

in·sec·tiv·o·rous \ˌin-ˌsek-ˈtiv-rəs, -ˈti-və-\ *adj* (1661) **:** feeding on insects

in·se·cure \ˌin-si-ˈkyu̇r\ *adj* [ML *insecurus,* fr. L *in-* + *securus* secure] (1649) **1 :** not confident or sure **:** UNCERTAIN ⟨feeling somewhat ~ of his reception⟩ **2 :** not adequately guarded or sustained **:** UNSAFE ⟨an ~ investment⟩ **3 :** not firmly fastened or fixed **:** SHAKY ⟨the hinge is loose and ~⟩ **4 a :** not highly stable or well-adjusted ⟨an ~ marriage⟩ **b :** deficient in assurance **:** beset by fear and anxiety ⟨always felt ~ in a group of strangers⟩ — **in·se·cure·ly** *adv* — **in·se·cure·ness** *n* — **in·se·cu·ri·ty** \-ˈkyu̇r-ə-tē\ *n*

in·sel·berg \ˈin(t)-səl-ˌbərg, ˈin-zəl-, -ˌberg\ *n, pl* **-bergs** *also* **-ber·ge** \-ˌbər-gə, -ˌber-\ [G, fr. *Insel* island + *Berg* mountain] (1913) **:** an isolated mountain

in·sem·i·nate \in-ˈse-mə-ˌnāt\ *vt* **-nat·ed; -nat·ing** [L *inseminatus,* pp. of *inseminare,* fr. *in-* + *semin-, semen* seed — more at SEMEN] (ca. 1623) **1 :** SOW **2 :** to introduce semen into the genital tract of (a female) ***syn*** see IMPLANT — **in·sem·i·na·tion** \-ˌse-mə-ˈnā-shən\ *n*

in·sem·i·na·tor \-ˈse-mə-ˌnā-tər\ *n* (1944) **:** one that inseminates cattle artificially

in·sen·sate \(ˌ)in-ˈsen-ˌsāt, -sət\ *adj* [LL *insensatus,* fr. L *in-* + LL *sensatus* having sense, fr. L *sensus* sense] (15c) **1 :** lacking sense or understanding; *also* **:** FOOLISH **2 :** lacking animate awareness or sensation **3 :** lacking humane feeling **:** BRUTAL — **in·sen·sate·ly** *adv*

in·sen·si·ble \(ˌ)in-ˈsen(t)-sə-bəl\ *adj* [ME, fr. AF & L; AF, fr. L *insensibilis,* fr. *in-* + *sensibilis* sensible] (14c) **1 :** IMPERCEPTIBLE ⟨dampened by an ~ dew⟩; *broadly* **:** SLIGHT, GRADUAL ⟨~ motion⟩ **2 :** incapable or bereft of feeling or sensation: as **a :** not endowed with life or spirit **:** INSENTIENT ⟨~ earth⟩ **b :** UNCONSCIOUS ⟨knocked ~ by a sudden blow⟩ **c :** lacking sensory perception or ability to react ⟨~ to pain⟩ **3 a :** lacking emotional response **:** APATHETIC, INDIFFERENT ⟨~ to fear⟩ **b :** UNAWARE ⟨~ of their danger⟩ **4** *archaic* **:** STUPID, SENSELESS **5 :** not intelligible **:** MEANINGLESS **6 :** lacking delicacy or refinement — **in·sen·si·bil·i·ty** \(ˌ)in-ˌsen(t)-sə-ˈbi-lə-tē\ *n* — **in·sen·si·ble·ness** \(ˌ)in-ˈsen(t)-sə-bəl-nəs\ *n* — **in·sen·si·bly** \-blē\ *adv*

in·sen·si·tive \(ˌ)in-ˈsen(t)-s(ə-)tiv\ *adj* (1834) **1 a :** not responsive or susceptible ⟨~ to the demands of the public⟩ **b :** lacking feeling or tact ⟨so ~ as to laugh at someone in pain⟩ **2 :** not physically or chemically sensitive — **in·sen·si·tive·ly** *adv* — **in·sen·si·tive·ness** *n* — **in·sen·si·tiv·i·ty** \(ˌ)in-ˌsen(t)-sə-ˈti-və-tē\ *n*

in·sen·tient \(ˌ)in-ˈsen(t)-sh(ē-)ənt\ *adj* (1764) **:** lacking perception, consciousness, or animation — **in·sen·tience** \-sh(ē-)ən(t)s\ *n*

in·sep·a·ra·ble \(ˌ)in-ˈse-p(ə-)rə-bəl\ *adj* [ME, fr. L *inseparabilis,* fr. *in-* + *separabilis* separable] (14c) **1 :** incapable of being separated or disjoined ⟨~ issues⟩ **2 :** seemingly always together **:** very intimate ⟨~

friends〉 — **in·sep·a·ra·bil·i·ty** \(ˌ)in-ˌse-p(ə-)rə-ˈbi-lə-tē\ *n* — **inseparable** *n* — **in·sep·a·ra·ble·ness** \(ˌ)in-ˈse-p(ə-)rə-bəl-nəs\ *n* — **in·sep·a·ra·bly** \-blē\ *adv*

[1]**in·sert** \in-ˈsərt\ *vb* [L *insertus,* pp. of *inserere,* fr. *in-* + *serere* to join — more at SERIES] *vt* (1529) **1 :** to put or thrust in 〈~ the key in the lock〉 **2 :** to put or introduce into the body of something **:** INTERPOLATE 〈~ a change in a manuscript〉 **3 :** to set in and make fast; *esp* **:** to insert by sewing between two cut edges **4 :** to place into action (as in a game) 〈~ a new pitcher〉 ~ *vi, of a muscle* **:** to be in attachment to the part to be moved ***syn*** see INTRODUCE — **in·sert·er** *n*

[2]**in·sert** \ˈin-ˌsərt\ *n* (ca. 1889) **:** something that is inserted; *esp* **:** written or printed material inserted (as between the leaves of a book)

in·ser·tion \in-ˈsər-shən\ *n* (1539) **1 :** something that is inserted: as **a :** the part of a muscle that inserts **b :** the mode or place of attachment of an organ or part **c :** embroidery or needlework inserted as ornament between two pieces of fabric **d :** a section of genetic material that is inserted into an existing gene sequence **2 a :** the act or process of inserting **b :** the mutational process producing a genetic insertion — **in·ser·tion·al** \-shnəl, -shə-n^{ə}l\ *adj*

in–ser·vice \ˈin-ˈsər-vəs\ *adj* (1928) **1 :** going on or continuing while one is fully employed 〈~ teacher education workshops〉 **2 :** of, relating to, or being one that is fully employed 〈~ police officers〉

[1]**in·set** \ˈin-ˌset\ *n* (1559) **1 a :** a place where something flows in **:** CHANNEL **b :** a setting or flowing in **2 :** something that is inset: as **a :** a small graphic representation (as a map or picture) set within a larger one **b :** a piece of cloth set into a garment (as for decoration) **c :** a part or section of a utensil that fits into an outer part

[2]**in·set** \ˈin-ˌset, in-ˈ\ *vt* **inset** *or* **in·set·ted; in·set·ting** (1658) **1 :** SET IN; *esp* **:** to insert within something else in such a way as to be visible **2 :** to provide with an inset

[1]**in·shore** \ˈin-ˈshȯr\ *adj* (1701) **1 :** situated, living, or carried on near shore **2 :** moving toward shore 〈an ~ current〉

[2]**inshore** *adv* (1748) **:** to or toward shore 〈boats driven ~ by the storm〉

[1]**in·side** \(ˌ)in-ˈsīd, ˈin-ˌ\ *n* (14c) **1 a :** an interior or internal part or place **:** the part within **b :** inward nature, thoughts, or feeling **c :** VISCERA, ENTRAILS — usu. used in pl. **2 :** an inner side or surface **3 a :** a position of power, trust, or familiarity 〈only someone on the ~ could have told〉 **b :** confidential information 〈has the ~ on what happened at the convention〉 **4 :** the area nearest a specified or implied point of reference: as **a :** the side of home plate nearest the batter **b :** the middle portion of a playing area **c :** the area near or underneath the basket in basketball

[2]**inside** *adv* (15c) **1 :** on the inner side **2 :** in or into the interior 〈stayed ~ during the storm〉 **3 :** to or on the inside **4 :** in prison

[3]**inside** *adj* (1611) **1 :** of, relating to, or being on or near the inside 〈an ~ pitch〉 **2 a :** relating or known to a select group 〈~ information〉 **b :** BEHIND-THE-SCENES

[4]**inside** *prep* (1791) **1 a :** in or into or as if in or into the interior of 〈waited ~ the church〉 **b :** on the inner side of 〈just ~ the door〉 **2 :** WITHIN 〈~ an hour〉

inside address *n* (ca. 1941) **:** ADDRESS 5c

inside of *prep* (1836) **:** INSIDE

inside out *adv* (ca. 1600) **1 :** in such a manner that the inner surface becomes the outer 〈turned the shirt *inside out*〉 **2 :** to a thorough degree 〈knows the subject *inside out*〉 **3 :** in or into a state of disarray often involving drastic reorganization 〈turned the business *inside out*〉

in·sid·er \(ˌ)in-ˈsī-dər, ˈin-ˌ\ *n* (1848) **:** a person recognized or accepted as a member of a group, category, or organization: as **a :** a person who is in a position of power or has access to confidential information **b :** one (as an officer or director) who is in a position to have special knowledge of the affairs of or to influence the decisions of a company

insider trading *n* (1966) **:** the illegal use of information available only to insiders in order to make a profit in financial trading

inside track *n* (1857) **:** an advantageous competitive position 〈the owner's son has the *inside track* for the job〉

in·sid·i·ous \in-ˈsi-dē-əs\ *adj* [L *insidiosus,* fr. *insidiae* ambush, fr. *insidēre* to sit in, sit on, fr. *in-* + *sedēre* to sit — more at SIT] (1545) **1 a :** awaiting a chance to entrap **:** TREACHEROUS **b :** harmful but enticing **:** SEDUCTIVE 〈~ drugs〉 **2 a :** having a gradual and cumulative effect **:** SUBTLE 〈the ~ pressures of modern life〉 **b** *of a disease* **:** developing so gradually as to be well established before becoming apparent — **in·sid·i·ous·ly** *adv* — **in·sid·i·ous·ness** *n*

in·sight \ˈin-ˌsīt\ *n* (13c) **1 :** the power or act of seeing into a situation **:** PENETRATION **2 :** the act or result of apprehending the inner nature of things or of seeing intuitively ***syn*** see DISCERNMENT

in·sight·ful \ˈin-ˌsīt-fəl, in-ˈ\ *adj* (1907) **:** exhibiting or characterized by insight 〈~ criticism〉 — **in·sight·ful·ly** *adv*

in·sig·nia \in-ˈsig-nē-ə\ *also* **in·sig·ne** \-(ˌ)nē\ *n, pl* **-nia** *or* **-ni·as** [L *insignia,* pl. of *insigne* mark, badge, fr. neut. of *insignis* marked, distinguished, fr. *in-* + *signum* mark — more at SIGN] (1648) **1 :** a badge of authority or honor **2 :** a distinguishing mark or sign

in·sig·nif·i·cance \ˌin(t)-sig-ˈni-fi-kən(t)s\ *n* (1699) **:** the quality or state of being insignificant

in·sig·nif·i·can·cy \-kən(t)-sē\ *n, pl* **-cies** (1651) **1 :** INSIGNIFICANCE **2 :** an insignificant thing or person

in·sig·nif·i·cant \-kənt\ *adj* (1651) **:** not significant: as **a :** lacking meaning or import **b :** not worth considering **:** UNIMPORTANT **c :** lacking weight, position, or influence **:** CONTEMPTIBLE **d :** small in size, quantity, or number — **in·sig·nif·i·cant·ly** *adv*

in sil·i·co \in-ˈsi-li-ˌkō\ *adv or adj* [NL, lit., in silicon] (1992) **:** in or on a computer **:** done or produced by using computer software or simulation 〈*in silico* predictions〉 〈dissect a frog *in silico*〉

in·sin·cere \ˌin-sin-ˈsir, -sən-\ *adj* [L *insincerus,* fr. *in-* + *sincerus* sincere] (1634) **:** not sincere **:** HYPOCRITICAL — **in·sin·cere·ly** *adv* — **in·sin·cer·i·ty** \-ˈser-ə-tē *also* -ˈsir-\ *n*

in·sin·u·ate \in-ˈsin-yə-ˌwāt, -yü-ˌāt\ *vb* **-at·ed; -at·ing** [L *insinuatus,* pp. of *insinuare,* fr. *in-* + *sinuare* to bend, curve, fr. *sinus* curve] *vt* (1529) **1 a :** to introduce (as an idea) gradually or in a subtle, indirect, or covert way 〈~ doubts into a trusting mind〉 **b :** to impart or suggest in an artful or indirect way **:** IMPLY 〈I resent what you're *insinuating*〉 **2 :** to introduce (as oneself) by stealthy, smooth, or artful means ~ *vi* **1** *archaic* **:** to enter gently, slowly, or imperceptibly **:** CREEP **2** *archaic* **:** to ingratiate oneself ***syn*** see INTRODUCE, SUGGEST — **in·sin·u·a·tive** \-ˌwā-tiv, -ˌā-tiv\ *adj* — **in·sin·u·a·tor** \-ˌwā-tər, -ˌā-tər\ *n*

insinuating *adj* (1591) **1 :** winning favor and confidence by imperceptible degrees **:** INGRATIATING **2 :** tending gradually to cause doubt, distrust, or change of outlook often in a slyly subtle manner 〈~ remarks〉 — **in·sin·u·at·ing·ly** *adv*

in·sin·u·a·tion \(ˌ)in-ˌsin-yə-ˈwā-shən, -yü-ˈā-\ *n* (1526) **1 :** the act or process of insinuating **2 :** something that is insinuated; *esp* **:** a sly, subtle, and usu. derogatory utterance

in·sip·id \in-ˈsi-pəd\ *adj* [F & LL; F *insipide,* fr. LL *insipidus,* fr. L *in-* + *sapidus* savory, fr. *sapere* to taste — more at SAGE] (1609) **1 :** lacking taste or savor **:** TASTELESS 〈~ food〉 **2 :** lacking in qualities that interest, stimulate, or challenge **:** DULL, FLAT 〈~ prose〉 — **in·si·pid·i·ty** \ˌin-sə-ˈpi-də-tē\ *n* — **in·sip·id·ly** \in-ˈsi-pəd-lē\ *adv*

syn INSIPID, VAPID, FLAT, JEJUNE, BANAL, INANE mean devoid of qualities that make for spirit and character. INSIPID implies a lack of sufficient taste or savor to please or interest 〈an *insipid* romance with platitudes on every page〉. VAPID suggests a lack of liveliness, force, or spirit 〈an exciting story given a *vapid* treatment〉. FLAT applies to things that have lost their sparkle or zest 〈although well-regarded in its day, the novel now seems *flat*〉. JEJUNE suggests a lack of rewarding or satisfying substance 〈a *jejune* and gassy speech〉. BANAL stresses the complete absence of freshness, novelty, or immediacy 〈a *banal* tale of unrequited love〉. INANE implies a lack of any significant or convincing quality 〈an *inane* interpretation of the play〉.

in·sist \in-ˈsist\ *vb* [MF or L; MF *insister,* fr. L *insistere* to stand upon, persist, fr. *in-* + *sistere* to take a stand; akin to L *stare* to stand — more at STAND] *vi* (1586) **1 :** to be emphatic, firm, or resolute about something intended, demanded, or required 〈they ~ on going〉 **2** *archaic* **:** PERSIST ~ *vt* **:** to maintain in a persistent or positive manner 〈~*ed* that the story was true〉

in·sis·tence \in-ˈsis-tən(t)s\ *n* (15c) **1 :** the act or an instance of insisting **2 :** the quality or state of being insistent **:** URGENCY

in·sis·ten·cy \-tən(t)-sē\ *n, pl* **-cies** (1859) **:** INSISTENCE

in·sis·tent \in-ˈsis-tənt\ *adj* [L *insistent-, insistens,* prp. of *insistere*] (1868) **1 :** disposed to insist **:** PERSISTENT **2 :** compelling attention 〈the ~ pounding of the waves〉 — **in·sis·tent·ly** *adv*

in si·tu \(ˌ)in-ˈsī-(ˌ)tü, -ˈsi-, -(ˌ)tyü *also* -ˈsē-, -(ˌ)chü\ *adv or adj* [L, in position] (1740) **:** in the natural or original position or place 〈an *in situ* cancer confined to the breast duct〉

in·so·bri·ety \ˌin-sə-ˈbrī-ə-tē, -sō-\ *n* (1611) **:** lack of sobriety or moderation; *esp* **:** intemperance in drinking

in·so·cia·ble \(ˌ)in-ˈsō-shə-bəl\ *adj* [L *insociabilis,* fr. *in-* + *sociabilis* sociable] (1588) **:** not sociable — **in·so·cia·bil·i·ty** \-(ˌ)sō-shə-ˈbi-lə-tē\ *n* — **in·so·cia·bly** \-ˈsō-shə-blē\ *adv*

in·so·far \ˌin-sə-ˈfär\ *adv* (1596) **:** to such extent or degree

insofar as *conj* (15c) **:** to the extent or degree that 〈we agree only *insofar as* the budget is concerned〉

insol *abbr* insoluble

in·so·la·tion \ˌin-(ˌ)sō-ˈlā-shən\ *n* [F or L; F, fr. L *insolation-, insolatio,* fr. *insolare* to expose to the sun, fr. *in-* + *sol* sun — more at SOLAR] (1617) **1 :** exposure to the sun's rays **2 :** SUNSTROKE **3 a :** solar radiation that has been received **b :** the rate of delivery of direct solar radiation per unit of horizontal surface; *broadly* **:** that relating to total solar radiation

in·sole \ˈin-ˌsōl\ *n* (ca. 1861) **1 :** an inside sole of a shoe **2 :** a loose thin strip placed inside a shoe for warmth or comfort

in·so·lence \ˈin(t)-s(ə-)lən(t)s\ *n* (14c) **1 :** the quality or state of being insolent **2 :** an instance of insolent conduct or treatment

in·so·lent \-s(ə-)lənt\ *adj* [ME, fr. L *insolent-, insolens* unaccustomed, overbearing, fr. *in-* + *solens,* prp. of *solēre* to be accustomed; perh. akin to L *sodalis* comrade — more at SIB] (14c) **1 :** insultingly contemptuous in speech or conduct **:** OVERBEARING **2 :** exhibiting boldness or effrontery **:** IMPUDENT ***syn*** see PROUD — **insolent** *n* — **in·so·lent·ly** *adv*

in·sol·u·bi·lize \(ˌ)in-ˈsäl-yə-bə-ˌlīz\ *vt* (1897) **:** to make insoluble — **in·sol·u·bi·li·za·tion** \-ˌsäl-yə-bə-lə-ˈzā-shən\ *n*

in·sol·u·ble \(ˌ)in-ˈsäl-yə-bəl\ *adj* [ME *insolible,* fr. L *insolubilis,* fr. *in-* + *solvere* to free, dissolve — more at SOLVE] (14c) **:** not soluble: as **a** *archaic* **:** INDISSOLUBLE **b :** having or admitting of no solution or explanation 〈an ~ problem〉 **c :** incapable of being dissolved in a liquid and esp. water; *also* **:** soluble only with difficulty or to a slight degree — **in·sol·u·bil·i·ty** \-ˌsäl-yə-ˈbi-lə-tē\ *n* — **insoluble** *n* — **in·sol·u·ble·ness** \-ˈsäl-yə-bəl-nəs\ *n* — **in·sol·u·bly** \-blē\ *adv*

in·solv·able \(ˌ)in-ˈsäl-və-bəl, -ˈsȯl-\ *adj* (1693) **:** admitting no solution 〈an apparently ~ problem〉 — **in·solv·ably** \-blē\ *adv*

in·sol·ven·cy \(ˌ)in-ˈsäl-vən(t)-sē, -ˈsȯl-\ *n* (1660) **:** the fact or state of being insolvent **:** inability to pay debts

in·sol·vent \(ˌ)in-ˈsäl-vənt, -ˈsȯl-\ *adj* (1591) **1 a :** unable to pay debts as they fall due in the usual course of business **b :** having liabilities in excess of a reasonable market value of assets held **2 :** insufficient to pay all debts 〈an ~ estate〉 — **insolvent** *n*

in·som·nia \in-ˈsäm-nē-ə\ *n* [L, fr. *insomnis* sleepless, fr. *in-* + *somnus* sleep — more at SOMNOLENT] (ca. 1623) **:** prolonged and usu. abnormal inability to get enough sleep — **in·som·ni·ac** \-nē-ˌak\ *adj or n*

in·so·much as \ˌin(t)-sō-ˈməch-\ *conj* (14c) **:** INASMUCH AS

insomuch that *conj* (14c) **:** SO 1

in·sou·ci·ance \in-ˈsü-sē-ən(t)s, a^{n}-süs-ˈyä^{n}s\ *n* [F, fr. *in-* + *soucier* to trouble, disturb, fr. OF, fr. L *sollicitare* — more at SOLICIT] (1799) **:** lighthearted unconcern **:** NONCHALANCE — **in·sou·ci·ant** \in-ˈsü-sē-ənt, a^{n}-süs-yä^{n}\ *adj* — **in·sou·ci·ant·ly** \in-ˈsü-sē-ənt-lē\ *adv*

in·source \ˈin-ˌsȯrs\ *vt* (1983) **:** to procure (as some goods or services needed by a business or organization) under contract with a domestic or in-house supplier — compare OUTSOURCE

insp *abbr* inspector

in·span \in-ˈspan, ˈin-ˌ\ *vb* [Afrik, fr. D *inspannen*] (ca. 1827) *chiefly SoAfr* **:** YOKE, HARNESS

in·spect \in-ˈspekt\ *vb* [L *inspectus,* pp. of *inspicere,* fr. *in-* + *specere* to look — more at SPY] *vt* (ca. 1623) **1 :** to view closely in critical ap-

\ə\ **a**but \$^{ə}$\ kitt**e**n, F ta**ble** \ər\ f**ur**th**er** \a\ **a**sh \ā\ **a**ce \ä\ m**o**p, m**a**r
\au̇\ **ou**t \ch\ **ch**in \e\ b**e**t \ē\ **ea**sy \g\ **g**o \i\ h**i**t \ī\ **i**ce \j\ **j**ob
\ŋ\ si**ng** \ō\ g**o** \ȯ\ l**aw** \ȯi\ b**oy** \th\ **th**in \t͟h\ **th**e \ü\ l**oo**t \u̇\ f**oo**t
\y\ **y**et \zh\ vi**si**on, bei**ge** \k̟, ^{n}, œ, ue, ^{y}\ *see* Guide to Pronunciation

praisal : look over **2** : to examine officially ⟨~*s* the barracks every Friday⟩ ~ *vi* : to make an inspection ***syn*** see SCRUTINIZE — **in·spec·tive** \-ˈspek-tiv\ *adj*

in·spec·tion \in-ˈspek-shən\ *n* (14c) **1 a** : the act of inspecting **b** : recognition of a familiar pattern leading to immediate solution of a mathematical problem ⟨solve an equation by ~⟩ **2** : a checking or testing of an individual against established standards

inspection arms *n* [fr. the command *inspection arms!*] (ca. 1884) : a position in the manual of arms in which the rifle is held at port arms with the chamber open for inspection; *also* : a command to assume this position

in·spec·tor \in-ˈspek-tər\ *n* (1602) **1** : a person employed to inspect something **2 a** : a police officer who is in charge of usu. several precincts and ranks below a superintendent or deputy superintendent **b** : a person appointed to oversee a polling place — **in·spec·tor·ship** \-ˌship\ *n*

in·spec·tor·ate \in-ˈspek-t(ə-)rət\ *n* (1762) **1** : the office, position, work, or district of an inspector **2** : a body of inspectors

inspector general *n* (1702) : a person who heads an inspectorate or a system of inspection (as of an army)

in·spi·ra·tion \ˌin(t)-spə-ˈrā-shən, -(ˌ)spi-\ *n* (14c) **1 a** : a divine influence or action on a person believed to qualify him or her to receive and communicate sacred revelation **b** : the action or power of moving the intellect or emotions **c** : the act of influencing or suggesting opinions **2** : the act of drawing in; *specif* : the drawing of air into the lungs **3 a** : the quality or state of being inspired **b** : something that is inspired ⟨a scheme that was pure ~⟩ **4** : an inspiring agent or influence — **in·spi·ra·tion·al** \-shnəl, -shə-nᵊl\ *adj* — **in·spi·ra·tion·al·ly** *adv*

in·spi·ra·tor \ˈin(t)-spə-ˌrā-tər, -(ˌ)spi-\ *n* (1624) : one that inspires ⟨teachers who are ~*s* of the young⟩

in·spi·ra·to·ry \in-ˈspī-rə-ˌtȯr-ē, ˈin(t)-sp(ə-)rə-\ *adj* (1773) : of, relating to, used for, or associated with inspiration

in·spire \in-ˈspī(-ə)r\ *vb* **in·spired; in·spir·ing** [ME, fr. AF & L; AF *inspirer,* fr. L *inspirare,* fr. *in-* + *spirare* to breathe] *vt* (14c) **1 a** : to influence, move, or guide by divine or supernatural inspiration **b** : to exert an animating, enlivening, or exalting influence on ⟨was particularly *inspired* by the Romanticists⟩ **c** : to spur on : IMPEL, MOTIVATE ⟨threats don't necessarily ~ people to work⟩ **d** : AFFECT ⟨seeing the old room again *inspired* him with nostalgia⟩ **2 a** *archaic* : to breathe or blow into or upon **b** *archaic* : to infuse (as life) by breathing **3 a** : to communicate to an agent supernaturally **b** : to draw forth or bring out ⟨thoughts *inspired* by a visit to the cathedral⟩ **4** : INHALE 1 **5 a** : BRING ABOUT, OCCASION ⟨the book was *inspired* by his travels in the Far East⟩ **b** : INCITE **6** : to spread (rumor) by indirect means or through the agency of another ~ *vi* : INHALE — **in·spir·er** *n*

inspired *adj* (15c) : outstanding or brilliant in a way or to a degree suggestive of divine inspiration ⟨gave an ~ performance⟩

inspiring *adj* (1717) : having an animating or exalting effect

in·spir·it \in-ˈspir-ət\ *vt* (15c) : to fill with spirit ***syn*** see ENCOURAGE — **in·spir·it·ing·ly** \-ə-tiŋ-lē\ *adv*

in·spis·sate \in-ˈspi-ˌsāt, ˈin(t)-spə-ˌsāt\ *vt* **-sat·ed; -sat·ing** [LL *inspissatus,* pp. of *inspissare,* fr. L *in-* + *spissus* slow, dense; akin to Gk *spidnos* compact, Lith *spisti* to form a swarm] (1626) : to make thick or thicker — **in·spis·sa·tion** \ˌin(t)-spə-ˈsā-shən, (ˌ)in-ˌspi-ˈsā-\ *n* — **in·spis·sa·tor** \in-ˈspi-ˌsā-tər, ˈin(t)-spə-ˌsā-\ *n*

in·spis·sat·ed \in-ˈspi-ˌsā-təd, ˈin(t)-spə-ˌsā-\ *adj* (1655) : thickened in consistency; *broadly* : made or having become thick, heavy, or intense

inst *abbr* **1** instant **2** institute; institution; institutional

in·sta·bil·i·ty \ˌin(t)-stə-ˈbi-lə-tē\ *n* (15c) : the quality or state of being unstable; *esp* : lack of emotional or mental stability

in·sta·ble \(ˌ)in-ˈstā-bəl\ *adj* [ME, fr. MF or L; MF, fr. L *instabilis,* fr. *in-* + *stabilis* stable] (15c) : UNSTABLE

in·stal *chiefly Brit var of* INSTALL

in·stall \in-ˈstȯl\ *vt* [ME, fr. AF *enstaller, installer,* fr. ML *installare,* fr. L *in-* + ML *stallum* stall, fr. OHG *stal*] (15c) **1 a** : to place in an office or dignity by seating in a stall or official seat **b** : to induct into an office, rank, or order ⟨~*ed* the new president⟩ **2** : to establish in an indicated place, condition, or status ⟨~*ing* herself in front of the fireplace⟩ **3** : to set up for use or service ⟨had an exhaust fan ~*ed* in the kitchen⟩ ⟨~ software⟩ — **in·stall·er** *n*

in·stal·la·tion \ˌin(t)-stə-ˈlā-shən\ *n* (15c) **1** : the act of installing : the state of being installed **2** : something that is installed for use **3** : a military camp, fort, or base **4** : a work of art that usu. consists of multiple components often in mixed media and that is exhibited in a usu. large space in an arrangement specified by the artist

[1]**in·stall·ment** *also* **in·stal·ment** \in-ˈstȯl-mənt\ *n* (1589) : INSTALLATION 1

[2]**installment** *also* **instalment** *n* [alter. of earlier *estallment* payment by installment, fr. *estall* to arrange payments by installment, fr. AF *estaler,* fr. *estal* station, stall, division of a stage, of Gmc origin; akin to OHG *stal* place, stall] (1776) **1** : one of the parts into which a debt is divided when payment is made at intervals **2 a** : one of several parts (as of a publication) presented at intervals **b** : one part of a serial story — **in·stall·ment** *adj*

installment plan *n* (1876) : a system of paying for goods by installments

[1]**in·stance** \ˈin(t)-stən(t)s\ *n* (14c) **1 a** *archaic* : urgent or earnest solicitation **b** : INSTIGATION, REQUEST ⟨am writing to you at the ~ of my client⟩ **c** *obs* : an impelling cause or motive **2 a** *archaic* : EXCEPTION **b** : an individual illustrative of a category or brought forward in support or disproof of a generalization **c** *obs* : TOKEN, SIGN **3** : the institution and prosecution of a lawsuit : SUIT **4** : a step, stage, or situation viewed as part of a process or series of events ⟨prefers, in this ~, to remain anonymous —*Times Lit. Supp.*⟩ — **for instance** \fə-ˈrin(t)-stən(t)s, ˈfrin(t)-\ : as an instance or example ⟨older people, like my grandmother, *for instance*⟩

syn INSTANCE, CASE, ILLUSTRATION, EXAMPLE, SAMPLE, SPECIMEN mean something that exhibits distinguishing characteristics in its category. INSTANCE applies to any individual person, act, or thing that may be offered to illustrate or explain ⟨an *instance* of history repeating itself⟩. CASE is used to direct attention to a real or assumed occurrence or situation that is to be considered, studied, or dealt with ⟨a *case* of mistaken identity⟩. ILLUSTRATION applies to an instance offered as a means of clarifying or illuminating a general statement ⟨a telling *illustration* of Murphy's Law⟩. EXAMPLE applies to a typical, representative, or illustrative instance or case ⟨a typical *example* of bureaucratic waste⟩. SAMPLE implies a part or unit taken at random from a larger whole and so presumed to be typical of its qualities ⟨show us a *sample* of your work⟩. SPECIMEN applies to any example or sample whether representative or merely existent and available ⟨one of the finest *specimens* of the jeweler's art⟩.

[2]**instance** *vt* **in·stanced; in·stanc·ing** (1601) **1** : to illustrate or demonstrate by an instance **2** : to mention as a case or example : CITE

in·stan·cy \ˈin(t)-stən(t)-sē\ *n, pl* **-cies** (1515) **1** : URGENCY, INSISTENCE **2** : nearness of approach : IMMINENCE **3** : immediacy of occurrence or action : INSTANTANEOUSNESS

[1]**in·stant** \ˈin(t)-stənt\ *n* [ME, fr. AF, fr. ML *instant-, instans,* fr. *instant-, instans,* adj., instant, fr. L] (14c) **1** : an infinitesimal space of time; *esp* : a point in time separating two states ⟨at the ~ of death⟩ **2** : the present or current month

[2]**instant** *adj* [ME, fr. AF or L; AF, fr. L *instant-, instans,* fr. prp. of *instare* to stand upon, urge, fr. *in-* + *stare* to stand — more at STAND] (15c) **1** : IMPORTUNATE, URGENT **2 a** : PRESENT, CURRENT ⟨previous felonies not related to the ~ crime⟩ **b** : of or occurring in the present month — abbr. *inst* **3** : IMMEDIATE, DIRECT ⟨the play was an ~ success⟩ **4 a (1)** : premixed or precooked for easy final preparation ⟨~ pudding⟩ **(2)** : appearing in or as if in ready-to-use form ⟨~ poetry⟩ **b** : immediately soluble in water ⟨~ coffee⟩ **5** : produced or occurring with or as if with extreme rapidity and ease — **in·stant·ness** *n*

in·stan·ta·neous \ˌin(t)-stən-ˈtā-nē-əs, -nyəs\ *adj* [ML *instantaneus,* fr. *instant-, instans,* n.] (1651) **1** : done, occurring, or acting without any perceptible duration of time ⟨death was ~⟩ **2** : done without any delay being purposely introduced ⟨took ~ corrective action⟩ **3** : occurring or present at a particular instant ⟨~ velocity⟩ — **in·stan·ta·ne·i·ty** \in-ˌstan-tə-ˈnē-ə-tē, ˌin(t)-stən-tə-ˈnē-\ *n* — **in·stan·ta·neous·ly** \ˌin(t)-stən-ˈtā-nē-əs-lē, -nyəs-lē\ *adv* — **in·stan·ta·neous·ness** *n*

in·stan·ter \in-ˈstan-tər\ *adv* [ML, fr. *instant-, instans*] (1688) : at once

in·stan·ti·ate \in-ˈstan(t)-shē-ˌāt\ *vt* **-at·ed; -at·ing** (1949) : to represent (an abstraction) by a concrete instance ⟨heroes ~ ideals —W. J. Bennett⟩ — **in·stan·ti·a·tion** \-ˌstan(t)-shē-ˈā-shən\ *n*

[1]**in·stant·ly** \ˈin(t)-stənt-lē\ *adv* (15c) **1** : with importunity : URGENTLY **2** : without the least delay : IMMEDIATELY

[2]**instantly** *conj* (1793) : as soon as ⟨he ran across the grass ~ he perceived his mother —W. M. Thackeray⟩

instant messaging *n* (1995) : a means or system for transmitting electronic messages instantly — **instant message** *n or vb*

instant replay *n* (1966) : a video recording of an action (as a play in football) that can be played back (as in slow motion) immediately after the action has been completed; *also* : the playing of such a recording

in·star \ˈin-ˌstär\ *n* [NL, fr. L, equivalent] (1895) : a stage in the life of an arthropod (as an insect) between two successive molts; *also* : an individual in a specified instar

in·state \in-ˈstāt\ *vt* (1603) **1** *obs* **a** : INVEST, ENDOW **b** : BESTOW, CONFER **2** : to set or establish in a rank or office : INSTALL

in sta·tu quo \in-ˌstā-(ˌ)tü-ˈkwō, -ˌsta-; -ˌsta-(ˌ)chü-\ *adv* [NL, lit., in the state in which] (1602) : in the former or same state

in·stau·ra·tion \ˌin-ˌstȯ-ˈrā-shən, ˌin(t)-stə-\ *n* [L *instauration-, instauratio,* fr. *instaurare* to renew, restore — more at STORE] (ca. 1603) **1** : restoration after decay, lapse, or dilapidation **2** : an act of instituting or establishing something

in·stead \in-ˈsted\ *adv* (1667) **1** : as a substitute or equivalent ⟨was going to write but called ~⟩ **2** : as an alternative to something expressed or implied : RATHER ⟨longed ~ for a quiet country life⟩

in·stead of \in-ˈste-də(v), -ˈsti-\ *prep* [ME *in sted of*] (13c) : in place of : as a substitute for or alternative to ⟨chose tea *instead of* coffee⟩

in·step \ˈin-ˌstep\ *n* (15c) **1** : the arched middle portion of the human foot in front of the ankle joint; *esp* : its upper surface **2** : the part of a shoe or stocking that fits over the instep

in·sti·gate \ˈin(t)-stə-ˌgāt\ *vt* **-gat·ed; -gat·ing** [L *instigatus,* pp. of *instigare* — more at STICK] (1542) : to goad or urge forward : PROVOKE ***syn*** see INCITE — **in·sti·ga·tion** \ˌin(t)-stə-ˈgā-shən\ *n* — **in·sti·ga·tive** \ˈin(t)-stə-ˌgā-tiv\ *adj* — **in·sti·ga·tor** \-ˌgā-tər\ *n*

in·stil *chiefly Brit var of* INSTILL

in·still \in-ˈstil\ *vt* [ME, fr. L *instillare,* fr. *in-* + *stillare* to drip, fr. *stilla* drop] (15c) **1** : to cause to enter drop by drop ⟨~ medication into the infected eye⟩ **2** : to impart gradually ⟨~*ing* a love of learning in children⟩ ***syn*** see IMPLANT — **in·stil·la·tion** \ˌin(t)-stə-ˈlā-shən, -(ˌ)sti-\ *n* — **in·still·er** \in-ˈsti-lər\ *n* — **in·still·ment** \-mənt\ *n*

[1]**in·stinct** \ˈin-ˌstiŋ(k)t\ *n* [ME, fr. L *instinctus* impulse, fr. *instinguere* to incite; akin to L *instigare* to instigate] (15c) **1** : a natural or inherent aptitude, impulse, or capacity ⟨had an ~ for the right word⟩ **2 a** : a largely inheritable and unalterable tendency of an organism to make a complex and specific response to environmental stimuli without involving reason **b** : behavior that is mediated by reactions below the conscious level — **in·stinc·tu·al** \in-ˈstiŋ(k)-chə-wəl, -chəl, -shwəl, -chü-əl\ *adj* — **in·stinc·tu·al·ly** *adv*

[2]**in·stinct** \in-ˈstiŋ(k)t, ˈin-ˌ\ *adj* (1667) **1** *obs* : impelled by an inner or animating or exciting agency **2** : profoundly imbued : INFUSED ⟨my mood, ~ with romance —S. J. Perelman⟩

in·stinc·tive \in-ˈstiŋ(k)-tiv\ *adj* (15c) **1** : of, relating to, or being instinct **2** : prompted by natural instinct or propensity : arising spontaneously ⟨an ~ fear of innovation —V. L. Parrington⟩ ***syn*** see SPONTANEOUS — **in·stinc·tive·ly** *adv*

[1]**in·sti·tute** \ˈin(t)-stə-ˌtüt, -ˌtyüt\ *vt* **-tut·ed; -tut·ing** [ME, fr. L *institutus,* pp. of *instituere,* fr. *in-* + *statuere* to set up — more at STATUTE] (14c) **1** : to establish in a position or office **2 a** : to originate and get established : ORGANIZE **b** : to set going : INAUGURATE ⟨*instituting* an investigation⟩ — **in·sti·tut·er** *or* **in·sti·tu·tor** \-ˌtü-tər, -ˌtyü-\ *n*

[2]**institute** *n* (1546) : something that is instituted: as **a (1)** : an elementary principle recognized as authoritative **(2)** *pl* : a collection of such principles and precepts; *esp* : a legal compendium **b** : an organization for the promotion of a cause : ASSOCIATION ⟨a research ~⟩ ⟨an ~ for the blind⟩ **c** : an educational institution and esp. one devoted to technical fields **d** : a usu. brief intensive course of instruction on selected topics relating to a particular field ⟨an urban studies ~⟩

in·sti·tu·tion \ˌin(t)-stə-ˈtü-shən, -ˈtyü-\ *n* (14c) **1** : an act of instituting : ESTABLISHMENT **2 a** : a significant practice, relationship, or organization in a society or culture ⟨the ~ of marriage⟩; *also* : something or

someone firmly associated with a place or thing ⟨she has become an ~ in the theater⟩ **b :** an established organization or corporation (as a bank or university) esp. of a public character; *also* **:** ASYLUM 4
in·sti·tu·tion·al \ˌin(t)-stə-ˈt(y)ü-shnəl, -shə-nᵊl\ *adj* (1617) **1 :** of or relating to an institution ⟨~ knowledge⟩ **2 :** characteristic of or appropriate to institutions ⟨bland ~ cooking⟩ ⟨~ green walls⟩ — **in·sti·tu·tion·al·ly** *adv*
in·sti·tu·tion·al·ise *Brit var of* INSTITUTIONALIZE
in·sti·tu·tion·al·ism \-shnə-ˌli-zəm, -shə-nə-ˌli-zəm\ *n* (1862) **1 :** emphasis on organization (as in religion) at the expense of other factors **2 :** public institutional care of disabled, delinquent, or dependent persons **3 :** an economic school of thought that emphasizes the role of social institutions in influencing economic behavior — **in·sti·tu·tion·al·ist** \-shnə-list, -shə-nə-list\ *n*
in·sti·tu·tion·al·ize \-shnə-ˌlīz, -shə-nə-ˌlīz\ *vt* **-ized; -iz·ing** (1865) **1 :** to make into an institution **:** give character of an institution to ⟨*institutionalized* housing⟩; *esp* **:** to incorporate into a structured and often highly formalized system ⟨*institutionalized* values⟩ **2 :** to put in the care of an institution ⟨~ alcoholics⟩ — **in·sti·tu·tion·al·i·za·tion** \-ˌtü-shnə-lə-ˈzā-shən, -shə-nə-lə-ˈzā-\ *n*
in–store \ˈin-ˈstȯr\ *adj* (1961) **:** relating to or being an operation or activity located or taking place inside a store ⟨~ consumer survey⟩
instr *abbr* **1** instructor **2** instrument; instrumental
in·struct \in-ˈstrəkt\ *vt* [ME, fr. L *instructus,* pp. of *instruere,* fr. *in-* + *struere* to build — more at STRUCTURE] (15c) **1 :** to give knowledge to **:** TEACH, TRAIN **2 :** to provide with authoritative information or advice ⟨the judge ~*ed* the jury⟩ **3 :** to give an order or command to **:** DIRECT ***syn*** see TEACH, COMMAND
in·struc·tion \in-ˈstrək-shən\ *n* (15c) **1 a :** PRECEPT ⟨prevailing cultural ~*s*⟩ **b :** a direction calling for compliance **:** ORDER — usu. used in pl. ⟨had ~*s* not to admit strangers⟩ **c** *pl* **:** an outline or manual of technical procedure **:** DIRECTIONS **d :** a code that tells a computer to perform a particular operation **2 :** the action, practice, or profession of teaching — **in·struc·tion·al** \-shnəl, -shə-nᵊl\ *adj*
in·struc·tive \in-ˈstrək-tiv\ *adj* (1611) **:** carrying a lesson **:** ENLIGHTENING — **in·struc·tive·ly** *adv* — **in·struc·tive·ness** *n*
in·struc·tor \in-ˈstrək-tər\ *n* (15c) **:** one that instructs **:** TEACHER; *esp* **:** a college teacher below professorial rank — **in·struc·tor·ship** \-ˌship\ *n*
in·struc·tress \-ˈstrək-trəs\ *n* (1630) **:** a woman who is an instructor
1in·stru·ment \ˈin(t)-strə-mənt\ *n* [ME, fr. AF, fr. L *instrumentum,* fr. *instruere* to arrange, instruct] (14c) **1 :** a device used to produce music; *also* **:** a singing voice **2 a :** a means whereby something is achieved, performed, or furthered **b :** one used by another as a means or aid **:** DUPE, TOOL **3 :** IMPLEMENT; *esp* **:** one designed for precision work **4 :** a formal legal document (as a deed, bond, or agreement) **5 a :** a measuring device for determining the present value of a quantity under observation **b :** an electrical or mechanical device used in navigating an airplane; *esp* **:** such a device used as the sole means of navigating ***syn*** see IMPLEMENT
2in·stru·ment \-ˌment\ *vt* (1752) **1 :** to address a legal instrument to **2 :** to score for musical performance **:** ORCHESTRATE **3 :** to equip with instruments esp. for measuring and recording data
in·stru·men·tal \ˌin(t)-strə-ˈmen-tᵊl\ *adj* (14c) **1 a :** serving as a crucial means, agent, or tool ⟨was ~ in organizing the strike⟩ **b :** of, relating to, or done with an instrument or tool **2 :** relating to, composed for, or performed on a musical instrument **3 :** of, relating to, or being a grammatical case or form expressing means or agency **4 :** of or relating to instrumentalism **5 :** OPERANT 3 ⟨~ learning⟩ ⟨~ conditioning⟩ — **instrumental** *n* — **in·stru·men·tal·ly** \-tᵊl-ē\ *adv*
in·stru·men·tal·ism \-ˌi-zəm\ *n* (1909) **:** a doctrine that ideas are instruments of action and that their usefulness determines their truth
in·stru·men·tal·ist \-ist\ *n* (1823) **1 :** a player on a musical instrument **2 :** an exponent of instrumentalism — **instrumentalist** *adj*
in·stru·men·tal·i·ty \ˌin(t)-strə-mən-ˈta-lə-tē, -ˌmen-\ *n, pl* **-ties** (1651) **1 :** the quality or state of being instrumental **2 :** MEANS, AGENCY
in·stru·men·ta·tion \ˌin(t)-strə-mən-ˈtā-shən, -ˌmen-\ *n* (1845) **1 :** the arrangement or composition of music for instruments esp. for a band or orchestra **2 :** the use or application of instruments (as for observation, measurement, or control) **3 :** instruments for a particular purpose; *also* **:** a selection or arrangement of instruments
instrument flying *n* (1928) **:** navigation of an airplane by instruments only
instrument landing *n* (1938) **:** a landing made with limited visibility by means of instruments and by ground radio direction
instrument panel *n* (1922) **:** a panel on which instruments are mounted; *esp* **:** DASHBOARD 2
in·sub·or·di·nate \ˌin(t)-sə-ˈbȯr-də-nət, -ˈbȯrd-nət\ *adj* (ca. 1828) **:** disobedient to authority — **insubordinate** *n* — **in·sub·or·di·nate·ly** *adv* — **in·sub·or·di·na·tion** \-ˌbȯr-də-ˈnā-shən\ *n*
in·sub·stan·tial \ˌin(t)-səb-ˈstan(t)-shəl\ *adj* [prob. fr. F *insubstantiel,* fr. LL *insubstantialis,* fr. L *in-* + LL *substantialis* substantial] (1607) **:** not substantial: as **a :** lacking substance or material nature **b :** lacking firmness or solidity **:** FLIMSY — **in·sub·stan·ti·al·i·ty** \-ˌstan(t)-shē-ˈa-lə-tē\ *n*
in·suf·fer·able \(ˌ)in-ˈsə-f(ə-)rə-bəl\ *adj* (15c) **:** not to be endured **:** INTOLERABLE ⟨an ~ bore⟩ — **in·suf·fer·able·ness** *n* — **in·suf·fer·ably** \-blē\ *adv*
in·suf·fi·cien·cy \ˌin(t)-sə-ˈfi-shən(t)-sē\ *n, pl* **-cies** (1526) **1 :** the quality or state of being insufficient: as **a :** lack of mental or moral fitness **:** INCOMPETENCE ⟨the ~ of this person for public office⟩ **b :** lack of adequate supply ⟨~ of provisions⟩ **c :** lack of physical power or capacity; *esp* **:** inability of an organ or body part to function normally ⟨renal ~⟩ **2 :** something that is insufficient or falls short of expectations
in·suf·fi·cient \ˌin(t)-sə-ˈfi-shənt\ *adj* [ME, fr. AF, fr. LL *insufficient-, insufficiens,* fr. L *in-* + *sufficient-, sufficiens* sufficient] (14c) **:** not sufficient **:** INADEQUATE ⟨~ funds⟩; *esp* **:** lacking adequate power, capacity, or competence ⟨~ bandwidth⟩ — **in·suf·fi·cient·ly** *adv*
in·suf·fla·tion \ˌin(t)-sə-ˈflā-shən, in-ˌsə-ˈflā-\ *n* [ME *insufflacion,* fr. LL *insufflation-, insufflatio,* fr. *insufflare* to blow upon, fr. L *in-* + *sufflare* to inflate, fr. *sub-* + *flare* to blow — more at BLOW] (15c) **:** an act or the action of blowing on, into, or in: as **a :** a Christian ceremonial rite of exorcism performed by breathing on a person **b :** the act of blowing something (as a gas, powder, or vapor) into a body cavity — **in·suf·flate** \ˈin(t)-sə-ˌflāt, in-ˈsə-ˌflāt\ *vt* — **in·suf·fla·tor** \-ˌflā-tər\ *n*
in·su·lant \ˈin(t)-sə-lənt\ *n* (ca. 1929) *chiefly Brit* **:** INSULATION 2
in·su·lar \ˈin(t)-su̇-lər, -syu̇-, ˈin-shə-lər\ *adj* [LL *insularis,* fr. L *insula* island] (1611) **1 a :** of, relating to, or constituting an island **b :** dwelling or situated on an island ⟨~ residents⟩ **2 :** characteristic of an isolated people; *esp* **:** being, having, or reflecting a narrow provincial viewpoint **3 :** of or relating to an island of cells or tissue — **in·su·lar·ism** \-lə-ˌri-zəm\ *n* — **in·su·lar·i·ty** \ˌin(t)-su̇-ˈla-rə-tē, -syu̇-, ˌin-shə-ˈla-\ *n* — **in·su·lar·ly** \ˈin(t)-su̇-lər-lē, -syu̇-, ˈin-shə-\ *adv*
in·su·late \ˈin(t)-sə-ˌlāt\ *vt* **-lat·ed; -lat·ing** [L *insula*] (ca. 1741) **:** to place in a detached situation **:** ISOLATE; *esp* **:** to separate from conducting bodies by means of nonconductors so as to prevent transfer of electricity, heat, or sound
in·su·la·tion \ˌin(t)-sə-ˈlā-shən\ *n* (1798) **1 a :** the action of insulating **b :** the state of being insulated **2 :** material used in insulating
in·su·la·tor \ˈin(t)-sə-ˌlā-tər\ *n* (1801) **:** one that insulates: as **a :** a material that is a poor conductor (as of electricity or heat) — compare SEMICONDUCTOR **b :** a device made of an electrical insulating material and used for separating or supporting conductors
in·su·lin \ˈin(t)-s(ə-)lən\ *n* [NL *insula* islet (of Langerhans), fr. L, island] (1914) **:** a protein pancreatic hormone secreted by the beta cells of the islets of Langerhans that is essential esp. for the metabolism of carbohydrates and the regulation of glucose levels in the blood and that when insufficiently produced results in diabetes mellitus
insulin–dependent diabetes *n* (1977) **:** TYPE 1 DIABETES
insulin–dependent diabetes mellitus *n* (1980) **:** TYPE 1 DIABETES — abbr. *IDDM*
insulin–like growth factor *n* (1976) **:** either of two polypeptides structurally similar to insulin that are secreted either during fetal development or during childhood and that mediate growth hormone activity
insulin resistance *n* (1965) **:** reduced sensitivity to insulin by the body's insulin-dependent processes (as glucose uptake and lipolysis) that is typical of type 2 diabetes but often occurs in the absence of diabetes
insulin resistance syndrome *n* (1992) **:** METABOLIC SYNDROME
insulin shock *n* (1925) **:** severe hypoglycemia that is associated with the presence of excessive insulin in the system and that if left untreated may result in convulsions and progressive development of coma
1in·sult \in-ˈsəlt\ *vb* [MF or L; MF *insulter,* fr. L *insultare,* lit., to spring upon, fr. *in-* + *saltare* to leap — more at SALTATION] *vi* (1540) *archaic* **:** to behave with pride or arrogance **:** VAUNT ~ *vt* **:** to treat with insolence, indignity, or contempt **:** AFFRONT; *also* **:** to affect offensively or damagingly ⟨doggerel that ~*s* the reader's intelligence⟩ ***syn*** see OFFEND — **in·sult·er** *n* — **in·sult·ing·ly** \in-ˈsəl-tiŋ-lē\ *adv*
2in·sult \ˈin-ˌsəlt\ *n* (1671) **1 :** a gross indignity **2 :** injury to the body or one of its parts; *also* **:** something that causes or has a potential for causing such insult ⟨pollution and other environmental ~*s*⟩
in·su·per·a·ble \(ˌ)in-ˈsü-p(ə-)rə-bəl\ *adj* [ME, fr. L *insuperabilis,* fr. *in-* + *superare* to surmount, fr. *super* over — more at OVER] (14c) **:** incapable of being surmounted, overcome, passed over, or solved ⟨~ difficulties⟩ — **in·su·per·a·bly** \-blē\ *adv*
in·sup·port·able \ˌin(t)-sə-ˈpȯr-tə-bəl\ *adj* [MF or LL; MF, fr. LL *insupportabilis,* fr. L *in-* + *supportare* to support] (ca. 1530) **:** not supportable: **a :** more than can be endured ⟨~ pain⟩ **b :** impossible to justify ⟨~ charges⟩ — **in·sup·port·ably** \-blē\ *adv*
in·sup·press·ible \ˌin(t)-sə-ˈpre-sə-bəl\ *adj* (1610) **:** IRREPRESSIBLE
insur *abbr* insurance
in·sur·able \in-ˈshu̇r-ə-bəl\ *adj* (1810) **:** that may be insured — **in·sur·abil·i·ty** \-ˌshu̇r-ə-ˈbi-lə-tē\ *n*
1in·sur·ance \in-ˈshu̇r-ən(t)s *also* ˈin-ˌ\ *n* (1651) **1 a :** the business of insuring persons or property **b :** coverage by contract whereby one party undertakes to indemnify or guarantee another against loss by a specified contingency or peril **c :** the sum for which something is insured **2 :** a means of guaranteeing protection or safety ⟨the contract is your ~ against price changes⟩
2insurance *adj* (1954) **:** being a score that adds to a team's lead and makes it impossible for the opposing team to tie the game with its next score ⟨an ~ run⟩
in·sure \in-ˈshu̇r\ *vb* **in·sured; in·sur·ing** [ME, to assure, prob. alter. of *assuren*] *vt* (1635) **1 :** to provide or obtain insurance on or for **2 :** to make certain esp. by taking necessary measures and precautions ~ *vi* **:** to contract to give or take insurance ***syn*** see ENSURE
insured *n* (1681) **:** a person whose life or property is insured
in·sur·er \in-ˈshu̇r-ər\ *n* (1654) **:** one that insures; *specif* **:** an insurance underwriter
in·sur·gence \in-ˈsər-jən(t)s\ *n* (1847) **:** an act or the action of being insurgent **:** INSURRECTION
in·sur·gen·cy \-jən(t)-sē\ *n, pl* **-cies** (1803) **1 :** the quality or state of being insurgent; *specif* **:** a condition of revolt against a government that is less than an organized revolution and that is not recognized as belligerency **2 :** INSURGENCE
1in·sur·gent \-jənt\ *n* [L *insurgent-, insurgens,* prp. of *insurgere* to rise up, fr. *in-* + *surgere* to rise — more at SURGE] (1765) **1 :** a person who revolts against civil authority or an established government; *esp* **:** a rebel not recognized as a belligerent **2 :** one who acts contrary to the policies and decisions of one's own political party
2insurgent *adj* (1807) **:** rising in opposition to civil authority or established leadership **:** REBELLIOUS — **in·sur·gent·ly** *adv*
in·sur·mount·able \ˌin(t)-sər-ˈmau̇n-tə-bəl\ *adj* (1690) **:** incapable of being surmounted **:** INSUPERABLE ⟨~ problems⟩ — **in·sur·mount·ably** \-blē\ *adv*
in·sur·rec·tion \ˌin(t)-sə-ˈrek-shən\ *n* [ME *insureccion,* fr. AF, fr. LL *insurrection-, insurrectio,* fr. *insurgere*] (15c) **:** an act or instance of revolting against civil authority or an established government ***syn*** see REBELLION — **in·sur·rec·tion·al** \-shnəl, -shə-nᵊl\ *adj* — **in·sur·rec·tion·ary** \-shə-ˌner-ē\ *adj or n* — **in·sur·rec·tion·ist** \-sh(ə-)nist\ *n*

\ə\ **abut** \ᵊ\ kitten, F table \ər\ **fur**ther \a\ **ash** \ā\ **ace** \ä\ **mop**, **mar** \au̇\ **out** \ch\ **chin** \e\ **bet** \ē\ **easy** \g\ **go** \i\ **hit** \ī\ **ice** \j\ **job** \ŋ\ **sing** \ō\ **go** \ȯ\ **law** \ȯi\ **boy** \th\ **thin** \t͟h\ **the** \ü\ **loot** \u̇\ **foot** \y\ **yet** \zh\ **vision**, **beige** \k̲, ⁿ, œ, ue, ʸ\ *see* Guide to Pronunciation

in·sus·cep·ti·ble \ˌin(t)-sə-ˈsep-tə-bəl\ *adj* (1603) : not susceptible ⟨∼ to flattery⟩ — **in·sus·cep·ti·bil·i·ty** \-ˌsep-tə-ˈbi-lə-tē\ *n* — **in·sus·cep·ti·bly** \ˌin(t)-sə-ˈsep-tə-blē\ *adv*

int *abbr* **1** intelligence **2** intercept **3** interest **4** interim **5** interior **6** interjection **7** intermediate **8** internal **9** international **10** interpreter **11** intersection **12** interval **13** interview **14** intransitive

in·tact \in-ˈtakt\ *adj* [ME *intacte,* fr. L *intactus,* fr. *in-* + *tactus,* pp. of *tangere* to touch — more at TANGENT] (15c) **1** : untouched esp. by anything that harms or diminishes : ENTIRE, UNINJURED **2** *of a living body or its parts* : having no relevant component removed or destroyed: **a** : physically virginal **b** : not castrated ***syn*** see PERFECT — **in·tact·ness** \-ˈtak(t)-nəs\ *n*

in·ta·glio \in-ˈtal-(ˌ)yō, -ˈtäl-; -ˈta-glē-ˌō, -ˈtä-\ *n, pl* **-glios** [It, fr. *intagliare* to engrave, cut, fr. ML *intaliare,* fr. L *in-* + LL *taliare* to cut — more at TAILOR] (1644) **1 a** : an engraving or incised figure in stone or other hard material depressed below the surface so that an impression from the design yields an image in relief **b** : the art or process of executing intaglios **c** : printing (as in die stamping and gravure) done from a plate in which the image is sunk below the surface **2** : something (as a gem) carved in intaglio

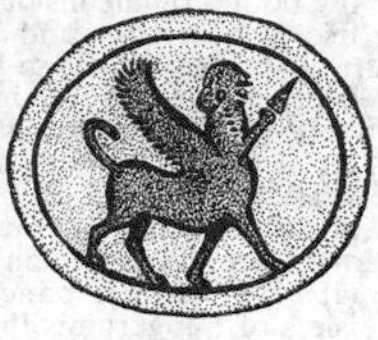
intaglio 1a

in·take \ˈin-ˌtāk\ *n* (15c) **1** : an opening through which fluid enters an enclosure **2 a** : a taking in **b** (1) : the amount taken in (2) : something (as energy) taken in : INPUT

[1]**in·tan·gi·ble** \(ˌ)in-ˈtan-jə-bəl\ *adj* [F or ML; F, fr. ML *intangibilis,* fr. L *in-* + LL *tangibilis* tangible] (1640) : not tangible : IMPALPABLE ⟨education's ∼ benefits⟩ — **in·tan·gi·bil·i·ty** \-ˌtan-jə-ˈbi-lə-tē\ *n* — **in·tan·gi·ble·ness** \-ˈtan-jə-bəl-nəs\ *n* — **in·tan·gi·bly** \-blē\ *adv*

[2]**intangible** *n* (1914) : something intangible: as **a** : an asset (as goodwill) that is not corporeal **b** : an abstract quality or attribute

in·tar·sia \in-ˈtär-sē-ə\ *n* [G, modif. of It *intarsio*] (1867) **1** : a mosaic usu. of wood fitted into a support; *also* : the art or process of making such a mosaic **2** : a colored design knitted on both sides of a fabric

in·te·ger \ˈin-ti-jər\ *n* [L, adj., whole, entire — more at ENTIRE] (1571) **1** : any of the natural numbers, the negatives of these numbers, or zero **2** : a complete entity

in·te·gra·ble \ˈin-ti-grə-bəl\ *adj* (ca. 1741) : capable of being integrated ⟨∼ functions⟩ — **in·te·gra·bil·i·ty** \ˌin-ti-grə-ˈbi-lə-tē\ *n*

[1]**in·te·gral** \ˈin-ti-grəl (*usu so in mathematics*); in-ˈte-grəl *also* -ˈtē- *also* ÷ˈin-trə-gəl\ *adj* (1551) **1 a** : essential to completeness : CONSTITUENT ⟨an ∼ part of the curriculum⟩ **b** (1) : being, containing, or relating to one or more mathematical integers (2) : relating to or concerned with mathematical integrals or integration **c** : formed as a unit with another part ⟨a seat with ∼ headrest⟩ **2** : composed of integral parts **3** : lacking nothing essential : ENTIRE — **in·te·gral·i·ty** \ˌin-tə-ˈgra-lə-tē\ *n* — **in·te·gral·ly** \ˈin-ti-grə-lē; in-ˈte-grə- *also* -ˈtē-\ *adv*

[2]**integral** *n* (ca. 1741) : the result of a mathematical integration — compare DEFINITE INTEGRAL, INDEFINITE INTEGRAL

integral calculus *n* (ca. 1741) : a branch of mathematics concerned with the theory and applications (as in the determination of lengths, areas, and volumes and in the solution of differential equations) of integrals and integration

integral domain *n* (1937) : a mathematical ring in which multiplication is commutative, which has a multiplicative identity element, and which contains no pair of nonzero elements whose product is zero ⟨the integers under the operations of addition and multiplication form an *integral domain*⟩

in·te·grand \ˈin-tə-ˌgrand\ *n* [L *integrandus,* gerundive of *integrare*] (1897) : a mathematical expression to be integrated

in·te·grate \ˈin-tə-ˌgrāt\ *vb* **-grat·ed; -grat·ing** [L *integratus,* pp. of *integrare,* fr. *integr-, integer*] *vt* (ca. 1586) **1** : to form, coordinate, or blend into a functioning or unified whole : UNITE **2** : to find the integral of (as a function or equation) **3 a** : to unite with something else **b** : to incorporate into a larger unit **4 a** : to end the segregation of and bring into equal membership in society or an organization **b** : DESEGREGATE ⟨∼ school districts⟩ ∼ *vi* : to become integrated

integrated *adj* (1922) **1** : marked by the unified control of all aspects of production from raw materials through distribution of finished products **2** : characterized by integration and esp. racial integration

integrated circuit *n* (1959) : a tiny complex of electronic components and their connections that is produced in or on a small slice of material (as silicon) — **integrated circuitry** *n*

integrated pest management *n* (1976) : management of agricultural and horticultural pests that minimizes the use of chemicals and emphasizes natural and low-toxicity methods (as the use of crop rotation and beneficial predatory insects)

in·te·gra·tion \ˌin-tə-ˈgrā-shən\ *n* (1620) **1** : the act or process or an instance of integrating: as **a** : incorporation as equals into society or an organization of individuals of different groups (as races) **b** : coordination of mental processes into a normal effective personality or with the environment **2 a** : the operation of finding a function whose differential is known **b** : the operation of solving a differential equation

in·te·gra·tion·ist \-sh(ə-)nist\ *n* (1951) : a person who believes in, advocates, or practices social integration — **integrationist** *adj*

in·te·gra·tive \ˈin-tə-ˌgrā-tiv\ *adj* (1862) : serving to integrate or favoring integration : directed toward integration ⟨the ∼ powers of the human imagination —J. A. McPherson⟩

in·te·gra·tor \-ˌgrā-tər\ *n* (1876) : one that integrates; *esp* : a device or computer unit that totalizes variable quantities in a manner comparable to mathematical integration

in·teg·ri·ty \in-ˈte-grə-tē\ *n* [ME *integrite,* fr. MF & L; MF *integrité,* fr. L *integritat-, integritas,* fr. *integr-, integer* entire] (14c) **1** : firm adherence to a code of esp. moral or artistic values : INCORRUPTIBILITY **2** : an unimpaired condition : SOUNDNESS **3** : the quality or state of being complete or undivided : COMPLETENESS ***syn*** see HONESTY

in·teg·u·ment \in-ˈte-gyə-mənt\ *n* [L *integumentum,* fr. *integere* to cover, fr. *in-* + *tegere* to cover — more at THATCH] (ca. 1611) : something that covers or encloses; *esp* : an enveloping layer (as a skin, membrane, or cuticle) of an organism or one of its parts — **in·teg·u·men·ta·ry** \-ˈmen-t(ə-)rē\ *adj*

intel *abbr* intelligence

in·tel·lect \ˈin-tə-ˌlekt\ *n* [ME, fr. MF or L; MF, fr. L *intellectus,* fr. *intellegere* to understand — more at INTELLIGENT] (14c) **1 a** : the power of knowing as distinguished from the power to feel and to will : the capacity for knowledge **b** : the capacity for rational or intelligent thought esp. when highly developed **2** : a person with great intellectual powers

in·tel·lec·tion \ˌin-tə-ˈlek-shən\ *n* (1579) **1** : an act of the intellect : THOUGHT **2** : exercise of the intellect : REASONING

in·tel·lec·tive \-ˈlek-tiv\ *adj* (15c) : having, relating to, or belonging to the intellect : RATIONAL — **in·tel·lec·tive·ly** *adv*

[1]**in·tel·lec·tu·al** \ˌin-tə-ˈlek-chə-wəl, -chəl, -shwəl, -chü(-ə)l\ *adj* (14c) **1 a** : of or relating to the intellect or its use **b** : developed or chiefly guided by the intellect rather than by emotion or experience : RATIONAL **c** : requiring use of the intellect ⟨∼ games⟩ **2 a** : given to study, reflection, and speculation **b** : engaged in activity requiring the creative use of the intellect ⟨∼ playwrights⟩ — **in·tel·lec·tu·al·i·ty** \-ˌlek-chə-ˈwa-lə-tē\ *n* — **in·tel·lec·tu·al·ly** \-ˈlek-chə-wə-lē, -chə-lē, -shwə-lē, -chü(-ə)-lē\ *adv* — **in·tel·lec·tu·al·ness** \-ˈlek-chə-wəl-nəs, -chəl-, -shwəl-, -chü(-ə)l-\ *n*

[2]**intellectual** *n* (1615) **1** *pl, archaic* : intellectual powers **2** : an intellectual person

intellectual disability *n* (1809) : significant impairment in intellectual ability accompanied by deficits in skills necessary for independent daily functioning : MENTAL RETARDATION

in·tel·lec·tu·al·ism \ˌin-tə-ˈlek-chə-wə-ˌli-zəm, -chə-ˌli-, -shwə-ˌli-, -chü(-ə)-ˌli-\ *n* (1800) : devotion to the exercise of intellect or to intellectual pursuits — **in·tel·lec·tu·al·ist** \-list\ *n or adj* — **in·tel·lec·tu·al·is·tic** \-ˌlek-chə-wə-ˈlis-tik, -chə-ˈlis-, -shwə-ˈlis-, -chü(-ə)-ˈlis-\ *adj*

in·tel·lec·tu·al·ize \ˌin-tə-ˈlek-chə-wə-ˌlīz, -chə-ˌlīz, -shwə-ˌlīz, -chü(-ə)-ˌlīz\ *vt* **-ized; -iz·ing** (ca. 1819) : to give rational form or content to — **in·tel·lec·tu·al·i·za·tion** \-ˌlek-chə-wə-lə-ˈzā-shən, -chə-lə-, -shwə-lə-, -chü(-ə)-lə-\ *n* — **in·tel·lec·tu·al·iz·er** \-ˈlek-chə-wə-ˌlī-zər, -chə-ˌlī-, -shwə-ˌlī-, -chü(-ə)-ˌlī-\ *n*

intellectual property *n* (ca. 1808) : property (as an idea, invention, or process) that derives from the work of the mind or intellect; *also* : an application, right, or registration relating to this

in·tel·li·gence \in-ˈte-lə-jən(t)s\ *n* [ME, fr. MF, fr. L *intelligentia,* fr. *intelligent-, intelligens* intelligent] (14c) **1 a** (1) : the ability to learn or understand or to deal with new or trying situations : REASON; *also* : the skilled use of reason (2) : the ability to apply knowledge to manipulate one's environment or to think abstractly as measured by objective criteria (as tests) **b** *Christian Science* : the basic eternal quality of divine Mind **c** : mental acuteness : SHREWDNESS **2 a** : an intelligent entity; *esp* : ANGEL **b** : intelligent minds or mind ⟨cosmic ∼⟩ **3** : the act of understanding : COMPREHENSION **4 a** : INFORMATION, NEWS **b** : information concerning an enemy or possible enemy or an area; *also* : an agency engaged in obtaining such information **5** : the ability to perform computer functions

intelligence quotient *n* (1916) : IQ 1

in·tel·li·genc·er \in-ˈte-lə-jən(t)-sər; -ˈte-lə-ˌjen(t)-, -ˌte-lə-ˈ\ *n* (1581) **1** : a secret agent : SPY **2** : a bringer of news : REPORTER

intelligence test *n* (1914) : a test designed to determine the relative mental capacity of a person

in·tel·li·gent \in-ˈte-lə-jənt\ *adj* [L *intelligent-, intelligens,* prp. of *intelligere, intellegere* to understand, fr. *inter-* + *legere* to gather, select — more at LEGEND] (1509) **1 a** : having or indicating a high or satisfactory degree of intelligence and mental capacity **b** : revealing or reflecting good judgment or sound thought : SKILLFUL **2 a** : possessing intelligence **b** : guided or directed by intellect : RATIONAL **3 a** : guided or controlled by a computer; *esp* : using a built-in microprocessor for automatic operation, for processing of data, or for achieving greater versatility — compare DUMB 7 **b** : able to produce printed material from digital signals ⟨an ∼ copier⟩ — **in·tel·li·gen·tial** \-ˌte-lə-ˈjen(t)-shəl\ *adj* — **in·tel·li·gent·ly** \-ˈte-lə-jənt-lē\ *adv*

syn INTELLIGENT, CLEVER, ALERT, QUICK-WITTED mean mentally keen or quick. INTELLIGENT stresses success in coping with new situations and solving problems ⟨an *intelligent* person could assemble it fast⟩. CLEVER implies native ability or aptness and sometimes suggests a lack of more substantial qualities ⟨*clever* with words⟩. ALERT stresses quickness in perceiving and understanding ⟨*alert* to new technology⟩. QUICK-WITTED implies promptness in finding answers in debate or in devising expedients in moments of danger or challenge ⟨no match for his *quick-witted* opponent⟩.

intelligent design *n* (1990) : the theory that matter, the various forms of life, and the world were created by a designing intelligence

in·tel·li·gent·sia \in-ˌte-lə-ˈjen(t)-sē-ə, -ˈgen(t)-\ *n* [Russ *intelligentsiya,* fr. L *intelligentia* intelligence] (1905) : intellectuals who form an artistic, social, or political vanguard or elite

in·tel·li·gi·ble \in-ˈte-lə-jə-bəl\ *adj* [ME, fr. L *intelligibilis,* fr. *intelligere*] (14c) **1** : apprehensible by the intellect only **2** : capable of being understood or comprehended ⟨jargon ∼ only to the initiated⟩ — **in·tel·li·gi·bil·i·ty** \-ˌte-lə-jə-ˈbi-lə-tē\ *n* — **in·tel·li·gi·ble·ness** \-ˈte-lə-jə-bəl-nəs\ *n* — **in·tel·li·gi·bly** \-blē\ *adv*

in·tem·per·ance \(ˌ)in-ˈtem-p(ə-)rən(t)s\ *n* (15c) : lack of moderation; *esp* : habitual or excessive drinking of intoxicants

in·tem·per·ate \-p(ə-)rət\ *adj* [ME *intemperat,* fr. L *intemperatus,* fr. *in-* + *temperatus,* pp. of *temperare* to temper] (14c) : not temperate ⟨∼ criticism⟩; *esp* : given to excessive use of intoxicating liquors — **in·tem·per·ate·ly** *adv* — **in·tem·per·ate·ness** *n*

in·tend \in-ˈtend\ *vb* [ME *entenden, intenden,* fr. AF *entendre,* fr. L *intendere* to stretch out, direct, aim at, fr. *in-* + *tendere* to stretch — more at THIN] *vt* (14c) **1** : to direct the mind on **2** *archaic* : to proceed on (a course) **3 a** : SIGNIFY, MEAN **b** : to refer to **4 a** : to have in mind as a purpose or goal : PLAN **b** : to design for a specified use or future ∼ *vi, archaic* : SET OUT, START — **in·tend·er** *n*

in·ten·dance \in-ˈten-dən(t)s\ *n* (1739) **1** : MANAGEMENT, SUPERINTENDENCE **2** : an administrative department

in·ten·dant \-dənt\ *n* [F, fr. MF, fr. L *intendent-, intendens,* prp. of *intendere* to intend, attend] (1652) : an administrative official (as a governor) esp. under the French, Spanish, or Portuguese monarchies

[1]**intended** *adj* (15c) **1** : expected to be such in the future ⟨an ∼ career⟩ ⟨his ∼ bride⟩ **2** : INTENTIONAL — **in·tend·ed·ly** *adv*

[2]**intended** *n* (1767) : the person to whom another is engaged

intending *adj* (1788) : PROSPECTIVE, ASPIRING ⟨an ∼ teacher⟩

in·tend·ment \in-ˈtend(d)-mənt\ *n* (14c) : the true meaning or intention esp. of a law

in·ten·er·ate \in-ˈte-nə-ˌrāt\ *vt* **-at·ed; -at·ing** [²*in-* + L *tener* soft, tender — more at TENDER] (1576) : to make tender : SOFTEN — **in·ten·er·a·tion** \-ˌte-nə-ˈrā-shən\ *n*

in·tense \in-ˈten(t)s\ *adj* [ME, fr. MF, fr. L *intensus,* fr. pp. of *intendere* to stretch out] (15c) **1 a** : existing in an extreme degree ⟨the excitement was ∼⟩ ⟨∼ pain⟩ **b** : having or showing a characteristic in an extreme degree ⟨∼ colors⟩ **2** : marked by or expressive of great zeal, energy, determination, or concentration ⟨∼ effort⟩ **3 a** : exhibiting strong feeling or earnestness of purpose ⟨an ∼ student⟩ **b** : deeply felt — **in·tense·ly** *adv* — **in·tense·ness** *n*

in·ten·si·fi·er \in-ˈten(t)-sə-ˌfī(-ə)r\ *n* (1835) : one that intensifies; *esp* : INTENSIVE

in·ten·si·fy \in-ˈten(t)-sə-ˌfī\ *vb* **-fied; -fy·ing** *vt* (1817) **1** : to make intense or more intensive : STRENGTHEN **2 a** : to increase the density and contrast of (a photographic image) by chemical treatment **b** : to make more acute : SHARPEN ∼ *vi* : to become intense or more intensive : grow stronger or more acute — **in·ten·si·fi·ca·tion** \-ˌten(t)s-fə-ˈkā-shən, -ˌten(t)-sə-\ *n*

in·ten·sion \in-ˈten(t)-shən\ *n* (1604) **1** : INTENSITY **2** : CONNOTATION 3 — **in·ten·sion·al** \-ˈtench-nəl, -ˈten(t)-shə-nᵊl\ *adj* — **in·ten·sion·al·i·ty** \-ˌten(t)-shə-ˈna-lə-tē\ *n* — **in·ten·sion·al·ly** \-ˈtench-nə-lē, -ˈten(t)-shə-nᵊl-ē\ *adv*

in·ten·si·ty \in-ˈten(t)-sə-tē\ *n, pl* **-ties** (1665) **1** : the quality or state of being intense; *esp* : extreme degree of strength, force, energy, or feeling **2** : the magnitude of a quantity (as force or energy) per unit (as of area, charge, mass, or time) **3** : SATURATION 4a

¹in·ten·sive \in-ˈten(t)-siv\ *adj* (15c) : of, relating to, or marked by intensity or intensification: as **a** : highly concentrated ⟨∼ study⟩ **b** : tending to strengthen or increase; *esp* : tending to give force or emphasis ⟨∼ adverb⟩ **c** : constituting or relating to a method designed to increase productivity by the expenditure of more capital and labor rather than by increase in scope ⟨∼ farming⟩ — **in·ten·sive·ly** *adv* — **in·ten·sive·ness** *n*

²intensive *n* (1813) : an intensive linguistic element

intensive care *n* (1963) **1** : continuous monitoring and treatment of seriously ill patients using special medical equipment and services **2** : a unit in a hospital providing intensive care ⟨heart patients in *intensive care*⟩

¹in·tent \in-ˈtent\ *n* [ME *entente,* fr. AF, fr. LL *intentus,* fr. L, act of stretching out, fr. *intendere*] (13c) **1 a** : the act or fact of intending : PURPOSE; *esp* : the design or purpose to commit a wrongful or criminal act ⟨admitted wounding him with ∼⟩ **b** : the state of mind with which an act is done : VOLITION **2** : a usu. clearly formulated or planned intention : AIM ⟨the director's ∼⟩ **3 a** : MEANING, SIGNIFICANCE **b** : CONNOTATION 3 *syn* see INTENTION

²intent *adj* [L *intentus,* fr. pp. of *intendere*] (14c) **1** : directed with strained or eager attention : CONCENTRATED **2** : having the mind, attention, or will concentrated on something or some end or purpose ⟨∼ on their work⟩ — **in·tent·ly** *adv* — **in·tent·ness** *n*

in·ten·tion \in-ˈten(t)-shən\ *n* (14c) **1** : a determination to act in a certain way : RESOLVE **2** : IMPORT, SIGNIFICANCE **3 a** : what one intends to do or bring about **b** : the object for which a prayer, mass, or pious act is offered **4** : a process or manner of healing of incised wounds **5** : CONCEPT; *esp* : a concept considered as the product of attention directed to an object of knowledge **6** *pl* : purpose with respect to marriage

syn INTENTION, INTENT, PURPOSE, DESIGN, AIM, END, OBJECT, OBJECTIVE, GOAL mean what one intends to accomplish or attain. INTENTION implies little more than what one has in mind to do or bring about ⟨announced his *intention* to marry⟩. INTENT suggests clearer formulation or greater deliberateness ⟨the clear *intent* of the statute⟩. PURPOSE suggests a more settled determination ⟨being successful was her *purpose* in life⟩. DESIGN implies a more carefully calculated plan ⟨the order of events came by accident, not *design*⟩. AIM adds to these implications of effort directed toward attaining or accomplishing ⟨her *aim* was to raise film to an art form⟩. END stresses the intended effect of action often in distinction or contrast to the action or means as such ⟨willing to use any means to achieve his *end*⟩. OBJECT may equal END but more often applies to a more individually determined wish or need ⟨his constant *object* was the achievement of pleasure⟩. OBJECTIVE implies something tangible and immediately attainable ⟨their *objective* is to seize the oil fields⟩. GOAL suggests something attained only by prolonged effort and hardship ⟨worked years to reach her *goals*⟩.

in·ten·tion·al \in-ˈtench-nəl, -ˈten(t)-shə-nᵊl\ *adj* (ca. 1677) **1** : done by intention or design : INTENDED ⟨∼ damage⟩ **2 a** : of or relating to epistemological intention **b** : having external reference *syn* see VOLUNTARY — **in·ten·tion·al·i·ty** \-ˌten(t)-shə-ˈna-lə-tē\ *n* — **in·ten·tion·al·ly** \-ˈtench-nə-lē, -ˈten(t)-shə-nᵊl-ē\ *adv*

in·ter \in-ˈtər\ *vt* **in·terred; in·ter·ring** [ME *enteren,* fr. AF *enterrer,* fr. VL **interrare,* fr. *in-* + L *terra* earth — more at TERRACE] (14c) : to deposit (a dead body) in the earth or in a tomb

inter- *prefix* [ME *inter-, enter-,* fr. AF & L; AF *inter-, entre-,* fr. L *inter-,* fr. *inter;* akin to OHG *untar* among, Gk *enteron* intestine, OE *in* in] **1** : between : among : in the midst ⟨*inter*crop⟩ ⟨*inter*penetrate⟩ ⟨*inter*stellar⟩ **2** : reciprocal ⟨*inter*relation⟩ : reciprocally ⟨*inter*marry⟩ **3** : located between ⟨*inter*station⟩ **4** : carried on between ⟨*inter*national⟩ **5** : occurring between ⟨*inter*borough⟩ : intervening ⟨*inter*glacial⟩ **6** : shared by, involving, or derived from two or more ⟨*inter*faith⟩ **7** : between the limits of : within ⟨*inter*tropical⟩ **8** : existing between ⟨*inter*communal⟩ ⟨*inter*company⟩

in·ter–Af·ri·can	in·ter·bed	in·ter·chro·mo·som·al
in·ter–agen·cy	in·ter·bor·ough	in·ter·church
in·ter–Amer·i·can	in·ter·branch	in·ter·city
in·ter·an·i·ma·tion	in·ter·cal·i·bra·tion	in·ter·clan
in·ter·an·nu·al	in·ter·cam·pus	in·ter·class
in·ter·as·so·ci·a·tion	in·ter·caste	in·ter·club
in·ter·atom·ic	in·ter·cell	in·ter·clus·ter
in·ter·avail·abil·i·ty	in·ter·cel·lu·lar	in·ter·coast·al
in·ter·bank	in·ter·chain	in·ter·co·lo·nial
in·ter·ba·sin	in·ter·chan·nel	in·ter·com·mu·nal

in·ter·com·mu·ni·ty	in·ter·group	in·ter·pop·u·la·tion
in·ter·com·pa·ny	in·ter·hemi·spher·ic	in·ter·pop·u·la·tion·al
in·ter·com·pare	in·ter·hos·pi·tal	in·ter·pro·fes·sion·al
in·ter·com·par·i·son	in·ter·in·di·vid·u·al	in·ter·pro·vin·cial
in·ter·cor·po·rate	in·ter·in·dus·try	in·ter·psy·chic
in·ter·cor·re·late	in·ter·in·flu·ence	in·ter·re·gion·al
in·ter·cor·re·la·tion	in·ter·in·sti·tu·tion·al	in·ter·re·li·gious
in·ter·coun·try	in·ter·ion·ic	in·ter·re·nal
in·ter·coun·ty	in·ter·is·land	in·ter·row
in·ter·cou·ple	in·ter·ju·ris·dic·tion·al	in·ter·school
in·ter·cra·ter	in·ter·la·cus·trine	in·ter·sec·tion·al
in·ter·crys·tal·line	in·ter·lam·i·nar	in·ter·seg·ment
in·ter·cul·tur·al	in·ter·lay	in·ter·seg·men·tal
in·ter·cul·tur·al·ly	in·ter·lay·er	in·ter·sen·so·ry
in·ter·cul·ture	in·ter·league	in·ter·so·ci·etal
in·ter·deal·er	in·ter·lend	in·ter·so·ci·ety
in·ter·de·nom·i·na·tion·al	in·ter·li·brary	in·ter·stage
	in·ter·lin·er	in·ter·sta·tion
in·ter·de·part·men·tal	in·ter·lob·u·lar	in·ter·stim·u·la·tion
in·ter·de·part·men·tal·ly	in·ter·lo·cal	in·ter·stim·u·lus
in·ter·de·pend	in·ter·male	in·ter·strain
in·ter·de·pen·dence	in·ter·mem·brane	in·ter·strand
in·ter·de·pen·den·cy	in·ter·men·stru·al	in·ter·strat·i·fi·ca·tion
in·ter·de·pen·dent	in·ter·min·is·te·ri·al	in·ter·strat·i·fied
in·ter·de·pen·dent·ly	in·ter·mi·tot·ic	in·ter·sys·tem
in·ter·di·a·lec·tal	in·ter·mo·lec·u·lar	in·ter·term
in·ter·dis·trict	in·ter·mo·lec·u·lar·ly	in·ter·ter·mi·nal
in·ter·di·vi·sion·al	in·ter·moun·tain	in·ter·ter·ri·to·ri·al
in·ter·do·min·ion	in·ter·nu·cle·ar	in·ter·trans·lat·able
in·ter·elec·trode	in·ter·nu·cle·on	in·ter·tri·al
in·ter·elec·tron·ic	in·ter·nu·cle·o·tide	in·ter·trib·al
in·ter·ep·i·dem·ic	in·ter·ob·serv·er	in·ter·troop
in·ter·eth·nic	in·ter·ocean	in·ter·union
in·ter·fac·ul·ty	in·ter·oce·an·ic	in·ter·unit
in·ter·fa·mil·ial	in·ter·of·fice	in·ter·uni·ver·si·ty
in·ter·fam·i·ly	in·ter·op·er·ate	in·ter·ur·ban
in·ter·fi·ber	in·ter·op·er·a·tive	in·ter·val·ley
in·ter·firm	in·ter·or·bit·al	in·ter·ven·tric·u·lar
in·ter·flow	in·ter·or·gan	in·ter·ver·te·bral
in·ter·flu·vi·al	in·ter·or·ga·ni·za·tion·al	in·ter·vil·lage
in·ter·fold	in·ter·pan·dem·ic	in·ter·vis·i·bil·i·ty
in·ter·fra·ter·ni·ty	in·ter·par·ish	in·ter·vis·i·ble
in·ter·gang	in·ter·pa·ro·chi·al	in·ter·vis·i·ta·tion
in·ter·gen·er·a·tion	in·ter·par·ti·cle	in·ter·war
in·ter·gen·er·a·tion·al	in·ter·par·ty	in·ter·work
in·ter·ge·ner·ic	in·ter·pha·lan·ge·al	in·ter·work·ing
in·ter·graft	in·ter·plan·e·tary	in·ter·zon·al
in·ter·gran·u·lar	in·ter·point	in·ter·zone

in·ter·act \ˌin-tər-ˈakt\ *vi* (1839) : to act upon one another

in·ter·ac·tant \-ˈak-tənt\ *n* (1949) : one that interacts

in·ter·ac·tion \ˌin-tər-ˈak-shən\ *n* (1832) : mutual or reciprocal action or influence — **in·ter·ac·tion·al** \-shnəl, -shə-nᵊl\ *adj*

in·ter·ac·tive \-ˈak-tiv\ *adj* (1832) **1** : mutually or reciprocally active **2** : involving the actions or input of a user; *esp* : of, relating to, or being a two-way electronic communication system (as a telephone, cable television, or a computer) that involves a user's orders (as for information or merchandise) or responses (as to a poll) — **in·ter·ac·tive·ly** *adv* — **in·ter·ac·tiv·i·ty** \-ˌak-ˈti-və-tē\ *n*

in·ter alia \ˌin-tər-ˈā-lē-ə, -ˈä-\ *adv* [L] (1665) : among other things

in·ter ali·os \-lē-ˌōs\ *adv* [L] (ca. 1670) : among other persons

in·ter·al·lied \ˌin-tər-ˈa-ˌlīd, -ə-ˈlīd\ *adj* (1917) : relating to, composed of, or involving allies

in·ter·breed \ˌin-tər-ˈbrēd\ *vb* **-bred** \-ˈbred\; **-breed·ing** *vi* (1859) : to breed together: as **a** : CROSSBREED **b** : to breed within a closed population ∼ *vt* : to cause to breed together

in·ter·ca·lary \in-ˈtər-kə-ˌler-ē, ˌin-tər-ˈka-lə-rē\ *adj* [L *intercalarius,* fr. *intercalare*] (1614) **1 a** : inserted in a calendar ⟨an ∼ day⟩ **b** *of a year* : containing an intercalary period (as a day or month) **2** : inserted between other things or parts : INTERPOLATED

in·ter·ca·late \in-ˈtər-kə-ˌlāt\ *vt* **-lat·ed; -lat·ing** [L *intercalatus,* pp. of *intercalare,* fr. *inter-* + *calare* to proclaim, call — more at LOW] (1603) **1** : to insert (as a day) in a calendar **2** : to insert between or among existing elements or layers *syn* see INTRODUCE — **in·ter·ca·la·tion** \-ˌtər-kə-ˈlā-shən\ *n*

in·ter·cede \ˌin-tər-ˈsēd\ *vi* **-ced·ed; -ced·ing** [L *intercedere,* fr. *inter-* + *cedere* to go] (1597) : to intervene between parties with a view to reconciling differences : MEDIATE *syn* see INTERPOSE — **in·ter·ced·er** *n*

in·ter·cen·sal \ˌin-tər-ˈsen(t)-səl\ *adj* (1887) : occurring between censuses ⟨∼ estimates⟩ ⟨∼ period⟩

¹in·ter·cept \ˌin-tər-ˈsept\ *vt* [ME, fr. L *interceptus,* pp. of *intercipere,* fr. *inter-* + *capere* to take, seize — more at HEAVE] (15c) **1** *obs* : PREVENT, HINDER **2 a** : to stop, seize, or interrupt in progress or course or before arrival **b** : to receive (a communication or signal directed elsewhere) usu. secretly **3** *obs* : to interrupt communication or connection with **4** : to include (part of a curve, surface, or solid) between two points, curves, or surfaces ⟨the part of a circumference ∼*ed* between two radii⟩ **5 a** : to gain possession of (an opponent's pass) **b** : to intercept a pass thrown by (an opponent)

²in·ter·cept \ˈin-tər-ˌsept\ *n* (1821) **1** : the distance from the origin to a point where a graph crosses a coordinate axis **2** : INTERCEPTION; *esp* : the interception of a missile by an interceptor or of a target by a missile **3** : a message, code, or signal that is intercepted (as by monitoring radio communications)

\ə\ abut \ᵊ\ kitten, F table \ər\ further \a\ ash \ā\ ace \ä\ mop, mar \aù\ out \ch\ chin \e\ bet \ē\ easy \g\ go \i\ hit \ī\ ice \j\ job \ŋ\ sing \ō\ go \ò\ law \òi\ boy \th\ thin \t̲h̲\ the \ü\ loot \ù\ foot \y\ yet \zh\ vision, beige \ḵ, ⁿ, œ, ᵫ, �\ see Guide to Pronunciation

in·ter·cep·tion \ˌin-tər-ˈsep-shən\ *n* (15c) **1 a :** the action of intercepting **b :** the state of being intercepted **2 :** something that is intercepted; *esp* : an intercepted forward pass

in·ter·cep·tor *also* **in·ter·cept·er** \ˌin-tər-ˈsep-tər\ *n* (1598) **:** one that intercepts; *specif* : a light high-speed fast-climbing fighter plane or missile designed for defense against raiding bombers or missiles

in·ter·ces·sion \ˌin-tər-ˈse-shən\ *n* [ME, fr. MF or L; MF, fr. L *intercession-, intercessio,* fr. *intercedere*] (15c) **1 :** the act of interceding **2 :** prayer, petition, or entreaty in favor of another — **in·ter·ces·sion·al** \-ˈsesh-nəl, -ˈse-shə-nᵊl\ *adj* — **in·ter·ces·sor** \-ˈse-sər\ *n* — **in·ter·ces·so·ry** \-ˈses-rē, -ˈse-sə-rē\ *adj*

[1]**in·ter·change** \ˌin-tər-ˈchānj\ *vb* [ME *entrechaungen,* fr. AF **entrechanger,* fr. *entre-* inter- + *changer* to change] *vt* (14c) **1 :** to put each of (two things) in the place of the other **2 :** EXCHANGE ~ *vi* **:** to change places mutually — **in·ter·chang·er** *n*

[2]**in·ter·change** \ˈin-tər-ˌchānj\ *n* (15c) **1 :** the act, process, or an instance of interchanging : EXCHANGE **2 :** a junction of two or more highways by a system of separate levels that permit traffic to pass from one to another without the crossing of traffic streams

in·ter·change·able \ˌin-tər-ˈchān-jə-bəl\ *adj* (14c) **:** capable of being interchanged; *esp* : permitting mutual substitution ⟨~ parts⟩ — **in·ter·change·abil·i·ty** \-ˌchān-jə-ˈbi-lə-tē\ *n* — **in·ter·change·able·ness** \-ˈchān-jə-bəl-nəs\ *n* — **in·ter·change·ably** \-blē\ *adv*

in·ter·col·le·giate \ˌin-tər-kə-ˈlē-jət, -jē-ət\ *adj* (ca. 1874) **:** existing, carried on, or participating in activities between colleges ⟨~ athletics⟩

in·ter·co·lum·ni·a·tion \ˌin-tər-kə-ˌləm-nē-ˈā-shən\ *n* [L *intercolumnium* space between two columns, fr. *inter-* + *columna* column] (1624) **1 :** the clear space between the columns of a series **2 :** the system of spacing of the columns of a colonnade

in·ter·com \ˈin-tər-ˌkäm\ *n* [short for *intercommunication system*] (1940) **:** a two-way communication system with a microphone and loudspeaker at each station for localized use

in·ter·com·mu·ni·cate \ˌin-tər-kə-ˈmyü-nə-ˌkāt\ *vi* (1586) **1 :** to exchange communication with one another **2 :** to afford passage from one to another — **in·ter·com·mu·ni·ca·tion** \-ˌmyü-nə-ˈkā-shən\ *n*

intercommunication system *n* (1911) **:** INTERCOM

in·ter·com·mu·nion \ˌin-tər-kə-ˈmyü-nyən\ *n* (1921) **:** interdenominational participation in communion

in·ter·con·nect \ˌin-tər-kə-ˈnekt\ *vt* (1865) **:** to connect with one another ~ *vi* **:** to be or become mutually connected — **in·ter·con·nec·tion** \-ˈnek-shən\ *n* — **in·ter·con·nec·tiv·i·ty** \-(ˌ)kä-ˌnek-ˈti-və-tē, -kə-\ *n*

interconnected *adj* (1865) **1 :** mutually joined or related ⟨~ highways⟩ ⟨~ political issues⟩ **2 :** having internal connections between the parts or elements — **in·ter·con·nec·ted·ness** *n*

in·ter·con·ti·nen·tal \ˌin-tər-ˌkän-tə-ˈnen-tᵊl\ *adj* (ca. 1855) **1 :** extending among continents or carried on between continents **2 :** capable of traveling between continents ⟨~ ballistic missile⟩

in·ter·con·ver·sion \ˌin-tər-kən-ˈvər-zhən, -shən\ *n* (1865) **:** mutual conversion ⟨~ of chemical compounds⟩ — **in·ter·con·vert** \-ˈvərt\ *vt* — **in·ter·con·vert·ibil·i·ty** \-ˌvər-tə-ˈbi-lə-tē\ *n* — **in·ter·con·vert·ible** \-ˈvər-tə-bəl\ *adj*

in·ter·cool·er \ˌin-tər-ˈkü-lər\ *n* (1899) **:** a device for cooling a fluid (as air) between successive heat-generating processes

in·ter·cos·tal \ˌin-tər-ˈkäs-tᵊl\ *adj* [NL *intercostalis,* fr. L *inter-* + *costa* rib — more at COAST] (1597) **:** situated or extending between the ribs ⟨~ spaces⟩ ⟨~ muscles⟩ — **intercostal** *n*

in·ter·course \ˈin-tər-ˌkȯrs\ *n* [ME *intercurse,* prob. fr. MF *entrecours,* fr. ML *intercursus,* fr. L, act of running between, fr. *intercurrere* to run between, fr. *inter-* + *currere* to run — more at CAR] (15c) **1 :** connection or dealings between persons or groups **2 :** exchange esp. of thoughts or feelings : COMMUNION **3 :** physical sexual contact between individuals that involves the genitalia of at least one person ⟨anal ~⟩ ⟨oral ~⟩; *esp* : SEXUAL INTERCOURSE 1 ⟨heterosexual ~⟩

in·ter·crop \ˌin-tər-ˈkräp, ˈin-tər-ˌ\ *vt* (1898) **:** to grow a crop in between (another) ~ *vi* **:** to grow two or more crops simultaneously (as in alternate rows) on the same plot — **in·ter·crop** \ˈin-tər-ˌkräp\ *n*

[1]**in·ter·cross** \ˌin-tər-ˈkrȯs\ *vt* (1711) **:** CROSS 8 ~ *vi* **:** INTERBREED, HYBRIDIZE

[2]**in·ter·cross** \ˈin-tər-ˌkrȯs\ *n* (1859) **:** an instance or a product of crossbreeding

in·ter·cur·rent \ˌin-tər-ˈkər-ənt, -ˈkə-rənt\ *adj* [L *intercurrent-, intercurrens,* prp. of *intercurrere*] (1611) **:** occurring during and modifying the course of another disease ⟨an ~ infection⟩

in·ter·cut \ˌin-tər-ˈkət\ *vt* (1932) **1 :** to insert (a contrasting camera shot) into a take by cutting **2 :** to insert a contrasting camera shot into (a take) by cutting ~ *vi* **:** to alternate contrasting camera shots by cutting

in·ter·den·tal \ˌin-tər-ˈden-tᵊl\ *adj* (ca. 1874) **1 :** situated or intended for use between the teeth **2 :** formed with the tip of the tongue between the upper and lower front teeth — **in·ter·den·tal·ly** \-tᵊl-ē\ *adv*

[1]**in·ter·dict** \ˈin-tər-ˌdikt\ *n* [ME, alter. of *entredite,* fr. AF, fr. L *interdictum* prohibition, fr. neut. of *interdictus,* pp. of *interdicere* to interpose, forbid, fr. *inter-* + *dicere* to say — more at DICTION] (15c) **1 :** a Roman Catholic ecclesiastical censure withdrawing most sacraments and Christian burial from a person or district **2 :** a prohibitory decree

[2]**in·ter·dict** \ˌin-tər-ˈdikt\ *vt* (15c) **1 :** to lay under or prohibit by an interdict **2 :** to forbid in a usu. formal or authoritative manner **3 a :** to destroy, damage, or cut off (as an enemy line of supply) by firepower to stop or hamper an enemy **b :** INTERCEPT 2a ⟨~ drug shipments⟩ ***syn*** see FORBID — **in·ter·dic·tion** \-ˈdik-shən\ *n* — **in·ter·dic·tive** \-ˈdik-tiv\ *adj* — **in·ter·dic·tor** \-tər\ *n* — **in·ter·dic·to·ry** \-t(ə-)rē\ *adj*

in·ter·dif·fu·sion \-di-ˈfyü-zhən\ *n* (ca. 1872) **:** the process of diffusing and mixing freely so as to approach a homogeneous mixture — **in·ter·dif·fuse** \-ˈfyüz\ *vi*

in·ter·dig·i·tate \-ˈdi-jə-ˌtāt\ *vi* **-tat·ed; -tat·ing** [*inter-* + L *digitus* finger — more at TOE] (ca. 1849) **:** to become interlocked like the fingers of folded hands — **in·ter·dig·i·ta·tion** \-ˌdi-jə-ˈtā-shən\ *n*

in·ter·dis·ci·plin·ary \-ˈdi-sə-plə-ˌner-ē\ *adj* (1926) **:** involving two or more academic, scientific, or artistic disciplines — **in·ter·dis·ci·plin·ar·i·ty** \-ˌdi-sə-plə-ˈner-ə-tē, -ˈna-rə-\ *n*

[1]**in·ter·est** \ˈin-t(ə-)rəst; ˈin-tə-ˌrest, -ˌtrest; ˈin-tərst\ *n* [ME, prob. alter. of earlier *interesse,* fr. AF & ML; AF, fr. ML, fr. L, to be between, make a difference, concern, fr. *inter-* + *esse* to be — more at IS] (15c) **1 a** (1) **:** right, title, or legal share in something (2) **:** participation in advantage and responsibility **b :** BUSINESS, COMPANY **2 a :** a charge for borrowed money generally a percentage of the amount borrowed **b :** the profit in goods or money that is made on invested capital **c :** an excess above what is due or expected ⟨returned the insults with ~⟩ **3 :** ADVANTAGE, BENEFIT; *also* : SELF-INTEREST **4 :** SPECIAL INTEREST **5 a :** a feeling that accompanies or causes special attention to an object or class of objects : CONCERN **b :** something that arouses such attention **c :** a quality in a thing arousing interest

[2]**interest** *vt* (1608) **1 :** to induce or persuade to participate or engage **2 :** to engage the attention or arouse the interest of

in·ter·est·ed \ˈin-t(ə-)rəs-təd; ˈin-tə-ˌres-, ˈin-ˌtres-; ˈin-tərs-\ *adj* (1602) **1 :** having the attention engaged ⟨~ listeners⟩ **2 :** being affected or involved ⟨~ parties⟩ — **in·ter·est·ed·ly** *adv*

interest group *n* (1908) **:** a group of persons having a common identifying interest that often provides a basis for action

in·ter·est·ing \ˈin-t(ə-)rəs-tiŋ; ˈin-tə-ˌres-, ˈin-ˌtres-; ˈin-tərs-\ *adj* (1768) **:** holding the attention : arousing interest — **in·ter·est·ing·ness** *n*

in·ter·est·ing·ly \-lē\ *adv* (1811) **1 :** in an interesting manner **2 :** as a matter of interest

[1]**in·ter·face** \ˈin-tər-ˌfās\ *n* (1882) **1 :** a surface forming a common boundary of two bodies, spaces, or phases ⟨an oil-water ~⟩ **2 a :** the place at which independent and often unrelated systems meet and act on or communicate with each other ⟨the man-machine ~⟩ **b :** the means by which interaction or communication is achieved at an interface — **in·ter·fa·cial** \ˌin-tər-ˈfā-shəl\ *adj*

[2]**interface** *vt* (1962) **1 :** to connect by means of an interface ⟨~ a machine with a computer⟩ **2 :** to serve as an interface for ~ *vi* **1 :** to become interfaced **2 :** to interact or coordinate harmoniously

in·ter·fac·ing \-ˌfā-siŋ\ *n* (1942) **:** fabric sewn between the facing and the outside of a garment (as in a collar or cuff) for stiffening and shape retention

in·ter·faith \ˌin-tər-ˈfāth\ *adj* (1932) **:** involving persons of different religious faiths

in·ter·fere \ˌin-tə(r)-ˈfir\ *vi* **-fered; -fer·ing** [ME *enterferen,* fr. AF *(s')entreferir* to strike one another, fr. *entre-* inter- + *ferir* to strike, fr. L *ferire* — more at BORE] (15c) **1 :** to interpose in a way that hinders or impedes : come into collision or be in opposition **2 :** to strike one foot against the opposite foot or ankle in walking or running — used esp. of horses **3 :** to enter into or take a part in the concerns of others **4 :** to act reciprocally so as to augment, diminish, or otherwise affect one another — used of waves ***syn*** see INTERPOSE — **in·ter·fer·er** *n*

in·ter·fer·ence \-ˈfir-ən(t)s\ *n* (1783) **1 a :** the act or process of interfering **b :** something that interferes : OBSTRUCTION **2 :** the mutual effect on meeting of two wave trains (as of light or sound) that constitutes alternating areas of increased and decreased amplitude (as light and dark lines or louder and softer sound) **3 a :** the legal blocking of an opponent in football to make way for the ballcarrier **b :** the illegal hindering of an opponent in sports **4 :** partial or complete inhibition or sometimes facilitation of other genetic crossovers in the vicinity of a chromosomal locus where a preceding crossover has occurred **5 a :** confusion of a received radio signal due to the presence of noise (as atmospherics) or signals from two or more transmitters on a single frequency **b :** something that produces such confusion **6 :** the disturbing effect of new learning on the performance of previously learned behavior with which it is inconsistent — **in·ter·fer·en·tial** \-fə-ˈren(t)-shəl, -ˌfir-ˈen(t)-\ *adj*

in·ter·fer·o·gram \ˌin-tə(r)-ˈfir-ə-ˌgram\ *n* (1921) **:** a photographic record made by an apparatus for recording optical interference phenomena

in·ter·fer·om·e·ter \ˌin-tə(r)-fə-ˈrä-mə-tər, -ˌfi-ˈrä-\ *n* [ISV] (1897) **:** an apparatus that utilizes the interference of waves (as of light) for precise determinations (as of distance or wavelength) — **in·ter·fer·o·met·ric** \-ˌfir-ə-ˈme-trik\ *adj* — **in·ter·fer·o·met·ri·cal·ly** \-tri-k(ə-)lē\ *adv* — **in·ter·fer·om·e·try** \-fə-ˈrä-mə-trē, -ˌfi-ˈrä-\ *n*

in·ter·fer·on \ˌin-tə(r)-ˈfir-ˌän\ *n* [*interfere* + [2]*-on*] (1957) **:** any of a group of heat-stable soluble basic antiviral glycoprotein cytokines of low molecular weight that are produced by cells exposed usu. to the action of a virus, sometimes to the action of another intracellular parasite (as a bacterium), or experimentally to the action of some chemicals

interferon alpha *n* (1980) **:** ALPHA INTERFERON

interferon beta *n* (1981) **:** BETA INTERFERON

interferon gamma *n* (ca. 1982) **:** GAMMA INTERFERON

in·ter·fer·tile \ˌin-tər-ˈfər-tᵊl\ *adj* (1899) **:** capable of interbreeding — **in·ter·fer·til·i·ty** \-(ˌ)fər-ˈti-lə-tē\ *n*

in·ter·file \ˌin-tər-ˈfī(-ə)l\ *vt* (1950) **:** to arrange in or add to a file : FILE

in·ter·fluve \ˈin-tər-ˌflüv\ *n* [*inter-* + L *fluvius* river — more at FLUVIAL] (1895) **:** the area between adjacent streams flowing in the same direction

in·ter·fuse \ˌin-tər-ˈfyüz\ *vb* [L *interfusus,* pp. of *interfundere* to pour between, fr. *inter-* + *fundere* to pour — more at FOUND] *vt* (1593) **1 :** to combine by fusing : BLEND **2 :** to add as if by fusing : INFUSE ~ *vi* **:** BLEND, FUSE — **in·ter·fu·sion** \-ˈfyü-zhən\ *n*

in·ter·ga·lac·tic \ˌin-tər-gə-ˈlak-tik\ *adj* (1928) **1 :** situated in or relating to the spaces between galaxies **2 :** of, relating to, or occurring in outer space ⟨~ battles⟩

in·ter·gla·cial \-ˈglā-shəl\ *n* (1867) **:** a warm period between glacial epochs — **interglacial** *adj*

in·ter·gov·ern·men·tal \-ˌgə-vər(n)-ˈmen-tᵊl\ *adj* (1927) **:** existing or occurring between two or more governments or levels of government

in·ter·gra·da·tion \-grā-ˈdā-shən, -grə-\ *n* (1874) **:** the condition of an individual or population that intergrades — **in·ter·gra·da·tion·al** \-shnəl, -shə-nᵊl\ *adj*

[1]**in·ter·grade** \ˌin-tər-ˈgrād\ *vi* (1874) **:** to merge gradually one with another through a continuous series of intermediate forms

[2]**in·ter·grade** \ˈin-tər-ˌgrād\ *n* (1888) **:** an intermediate form

in·ter·growth \ˈin-tər-ˌgrōth\ *n* (1844) **:** a growing between or together; *also* : the product of such growth

[1]**in·ter·im** \ˈin-tə-rəm\ *n* [L, adv., meanwhile, fr. *inter* between — more at INTER-] (ca. 1580) **:** an intervening time : INTERVAL

[2]**interim** *adj* (1604) **:** done, made, appointed, or occurring for an interim

[1]**in·te·ri·or** \in-ˈtir-ē-ər\ *adj* [MF & L; MF *interiore,* fr. L, compar. of OL **interus* inward, on the inside; akin to L *inter*] (15c) **1 :** lying, occurring, or functioning within the limiting boundaries : INNER ⟨an ~

point of a triangle〉 **2** : belonging to mental or spiritual life 〈a simple ~ piety〉 **3** : belonging to the inner constitution or concealed nature of something 〈~ meaning of a poem〉 **4** : lying away or remote from the border or shore — **in·te·ri·or·ly** \in-ˈtir-ē-ər-lē\ *adv*

[2]**interior** *n* (1596) **1** : the inner or spiritual nature : CHARACTER **2** : the interior part (as of a country or island) **3** : the internal or inner part of a thing : INSIDE **4** : the internal affairs of a state or nation **5** : a representation (as in a play or movie) of the interior of a building

interior angle *n* (1756) **1** : the inner of the two angles formed where two sides of a polygon come together **2** : any of the four angles formed in the area between a pair of parallel lines when a third line cuts them

interior decoration *n* (1807) : INTERIOR DESIGN

interior decorator *n* (1867) : INTERIOR DESIGNER, DECORATOR

interior design *n* (1927) : the art or practice of planning and supervising the design and execution of architectural interiors and their furnishings

interior designer *n* (1938) : one who specializes in interior design

in·te·ri·or·ise *Brit var of* INTERIORIZE

in·te·ri·or·i·ty \(ˌ)in-ˌtir-ē-ˈȯr-ə-tē, -ˈär-\ *n* (1701) **1** : interior quality or character **2** : inner life or substance : psychological existence

in·te·ri·or·ize \in-ˈtir-ē-ə-ˌrīz\ *vt* **-ized; -iz·ing** (1906) : to make interior; *esp* : to make a part of one's own inner being or mental structure — **in·te·ri·or·i·za·tion** \-ˌtir-ē-ə-rə-ˈzā-shən\ *n*

interior monologue *n* (1922) : a usu. extended representation in monologue of a fictional character's thought and feeling

interj *abbr* interjection

in·ter·ject \ˌin-tər-ˈjekt\ *vt* [L *interjectus,* pp. of *intericere,* fr. *inter-* + *jacere* to throw — more at JET] (1588) : to throw in between or among other things : INTERPOLATE 〈~ a remark〉 ***syn*** see INTRODUCE — **in·ter·jec·tor** \-ˈjek-tər\ *n* — **in·ter·jec·to·ry** \-t(ə-)rē\ *adj*

in·ter·jec·tion \ˌint-ər-ˈjek-shən\ *n* (15c) **1 a** : the act of uttering exclamations : EJACULATION **b** : the act of putting in between : INTERPOSITION **2** : an ejaculatory utterance usu. lacking grammatical connection: as **a** : a word or phrase used in exclamation (as *Heavens! Dear me!*) **b** : a cry or inarticulate utterance (as *Alas! ouch! phooey! ugh!*) expressing an emotion **3** : something that is interjected or that interrupts

in·ter·jec·tion·al \-shnəl, -shə-nᵊl\ *adj* (1761) **1** : of, relating to, or constituting an interjection : EJACULATORY **2** : thrown in between other words : PARENTHETICAL — **in·ter·jec·tion·al·ly** *adv*

in·ter·lace \ˌin-tər-ˈlās\ *vb* [ME *entrelacen,* fr. AF *entrelacer,* fr. *entre-* inter- + *lacer* to lace] *vt* (14c) **1** : to unite by or as if by lacing together : INTERWEAVE **2** : to vary by alternation or intermixture : INTERSPERSE 〈narrative *interlaced* with anecdotes〉 ~ *vi* : to cross one another as if woven together : INTERTWINE — **in·ter·lace·ment** \-mənt\ *n*

in·ter·laced \ˈin-tər-ˌlāst\ *adj* (1935) : of, relating to, or using a method of video scanning (as for television or a computer monitor) in which the odd and even horizontal lines of each frame are drawn on alternating passes — compare PROGRESSIVE

in·ter·lard \ˌin-tər-ˈlärd\ *vt* [MF *entrelarder,* fr. OF, fr. *entre* inter- + *larder* to lard, fr. *lard,* n.] (ca. 1587) : to vary by intermixture : INTERSPERSE, INTERLACE

in·ter·leave \ˌin-tər-ˈlēv\ *vt* **-leaved; -leav·ing** (1668) : to arrange in or as if in alternate layers

in·ter·leu·kin \ˌin-tər-ˈlü-kən\ *n* [*inter-* + *leuk-* + [1]*-in*] (1979) : any of various cytokines of low molecular weight that are produced by lymphocytes, macrophages, and monocytes and that function esp. in regulation of the immune system and esp. cell-mediated immunity

in·ter·leu·kin–1 \-ˈwən\ *n* (1979) : an interleukin produced esp. by monocytes and macrophages that regulates immune responses by activating lymphocytes and mediates other biological processes (as the onset of fever) usu. associated with infection and inflammation

in·ter·leu·kin–2 \-ˈtü\ *n* (1979) : an interleukin produced by antigen-stimulated helper T cells in the presence of interleukin-1 that induces proliferation of immune cells (as T cells and B cells) and is used experimentally esp. in treating certain cancers

[1]**in·ter·line** \ˌin-tər-ˈlīn\ *vt* [ME *enterlinen,* fr. ML *interlineare,* fr. L *inter-* + *linea* line] (15c) : to insert between lines already written or printed — **in·ter·lin·e·a·tion** \-ˌli-nē-ˈā-shən\ *n*

[2]**interline** *vt* [ME, fr. *inter-* + *linen* to line] (15c) : to provide (a garment) with an interlining

[3]**interline** *adj* (1897) : relating to, involving, or carried by two or more transportation lines

[1]**in·ter·lin·ear** \ˌin-tər-ˈli-nē-ər\ *adj* [ME *interliniare,* fr. ML *interlinearis,* fr. L *inter-* + *linea* line] (15c) **1** : inserted between lines already written or printed **2** : written or printed in different languages or texts in alternate lines — **in·ter·lin·ear·ly** *adv*

[2]**interlinear** *n* (1850) : a book having interlinear matter; *esp* : a book in a foreign language with interlinear translation

in·ter·lin·gual \ˌin-tər-ˈliŋ-gwəl *also* -gyə-wəl\ *adj* [*inter-* + L *lingua* tongue, language — more at TONGUE] (1854) : of, relating to, or existing between two or more languages 〈~ dictionaries〉

in·ter·lin·ing \ˈin-tər-ˌlī-niŋ\ *n* (1881) : a lining (as of a coat) sewn between the ordinary lining and the outside fabric

in·ter·link \ˌin-tər-ˈliŋk\ *vt* (1587) : to link together — **in·ter·link** \ˈin-tər-ˌliŋk\ *n*

[1]**in·ter·lock** \ˌin-tər-ˈläk\ *vi* (1632) : to become locked together or interconnected ~ *vt* **1** : to lock together : UNITE **2** : to connect so that the motion or operation of any part is constrained by another

[2]**in·ter·lock** \ˈin-tər-ˌläk\ *n* (1874) **1** : the quality, state, sense, or an instance of being interlocked **2** : an arrangement in which the operation of one part or mechanism automatically brings about or prevents the operation of another 〈a safety ~〉 **3 a** : a stretchable fabric made on a circular knitting machine and consisting of two ribbed fabrics joined by interlocking **b** : a garment made of interlock

in·ter·loc·u·tor \ˌin-tər-ˈlä-kyə-tər\ *n* [L *interloqui* to speak between, issue an interlocutory decree, fr. *inter-* + *loqui* to speak] (1514) **1** : one who takes part in dialogue or conversation **2** : a man in the middle of the line in a minstrel show who questions the end men and acts as leader

in·ter·loc·u·to·ry \-kyə-ˌtȯr-ē\ *adj* (15c) : made during the progress of a legal action and not final or definitive 〈an ~ appeal〉 〈an ~ decree〉

in·ter·lope \ˌin-tər-ˈlōp, ˈin-tər-ˌ\ *vi* **-loped; -lop·ing** [prob. back-formation fr. *interloper,* fr. *inter-* + *-loper* (akin to MD *lopen* to run, OE *hlēapan* to leap) — more at LEAP] (1615) **1** : to encroach on the rights (as in trade) of others **2** : INTRUDE, INTERFERE

in·ter·lop·er \ˌin-tər-ˈlō-pər, ˈin-tər-ˌ\ *n* (ca. 1590) : one that interlopes: as **a** : an illegal or unlicensed trader **b** : one that intrudes in a place or sphere of activity

in·ter·lude \ˈin-tər-ˌlüd\ *n* [ME *enterlude,* fr. ML *interludium,* fr. L *inter-* + *ludus* play — more at LUDICROUS] (14c) **1** : a usu. short simple play or dramatic entertainment **2** : an intervening or interruptive period, space, or event : INTERVAL **3** : a musical composition inserted between the parts of a longer composition, a drama, or a religious service

in·ter·lu·nar \ˌin-tər-ˈlü-nər\ *also* **in·ter·lu·na·ry** \-nə-rē\ *adj* [prob. fr. MF *interlunaire,* fr. L *interlunium* interlunar period, fr. *inter-* + *luna* moon — more at LUNAR] (1598) : relating to the interval between old and new moon when the moon is invisible

in·ter·mar·riage \ˌin-tər-ˈmer-ij, -ˈma-rij\ *n* (1579) **1** : ENDOGAMY **2** : marriage between members of different groups

in·ter·mar·ry \-ˈmer-ē, -ˈma-rē\ *vi* (1574) **1 a** : to marry each other **b** : to marry within a group **2** : to become connected by intermarriage

in·ter·med·dle \ˌin-tər-ˈme-dᵊl\ *vi* [ME *entermedlen,* fr. AF *entremeller, entremedler,* fr. *entre-* inter- + *medler* to mix — more at MEDDLE] (15c) : to meddle impertinently and officiously and usu. so as to interfere — **in·ter·med·dler** \-ˈmed-lər, -ˈme-dᵊl-ər\ *n*

in·ter·me·di·a·cy \ˌin-tər-ˈmē-dē-ə-sē\ *n* (1713) **1** : the act or action of intermediating **2** : the quality or state of being intermediate

[1]**in·ter·me·di·ary** \ˌin-tər-ˈmē-dē-ˌer-ē\ *adj* (1788) **1** : INTERMEDIATE **2** : acting as a mediator 〈an ~ agent〉 〈an ~ particle〉

[2]**intermediary** *n, pl* **-ar·ies** (1791) **1 a** : MEDIATOR, GO-BETWEEN **b** : MEDIUM, MEANS **2** : an intermediate form, product, or stage

[1]**in·ter·me·di·ate** \ˌin-tər-ˈmē-dē-ət\ *adj* [ME, fr. ML *intermediatus,* fr. L *intermedius,* fr. *inter-* + *medius* mid, middle — more at MID] (15c) **1** : being or occurring at the middle place, stage, or degree or between extremes **2** : of or relating to an intermediate school 〈an ~ curriculum〉 — **in·ter·me·di·ate·ly** *adv* — **in·ter·me·di·ate·ness** *n*

[2]**intermediate** *n* (1650) **1** : one that is intermediate **2** : MEDIATOR, GO-BETWEEN **3 a** : a chemical compound synthesized from simpler compounds and usu. intended to be used in later syntheses of more complex products **b** : a usu. short-lived chemical species formed in a reaction as an intermediate step between the starting material and the final product **4** : an automobile larger than a compact but smaller than a full-sized automobile

[3]**in·ter·me·di·ate** \-dē-ˌāt\ *vi* [ML *intermediatus,* pp. of *intermediare,* fr. L *inter-* + LL *mediare* to mediate] (1610) **1** : INTERVENE, INTERPOSE **2** : to act as an intermediate

intermediate host *n* (1878) **1** : a host which is normally used by a parasite in the course of its life cycle and in which it may multiply asexually but not sexually — compare DEFINITIVE HOST **2 a** : RESERVOIR **3 b** : VECTOR

intermediate school *n* (1842) **1** : JUNIOR HIGH SCHOOL **2** : a school usu. comprising grades four to six

intermediate vector boson *n* (1968) : any of three particles that mediate the weak force — called also *intermediate boson*; compare W PARTICLE, Z PARTICLE

in·ter·me·di·a·tion \ˌin-tər-ˌmē-dē-ˈā-shən\ *n* (1602) : the act of coming between : INTERVENTION, MEDIATION

in·ter·me·din \ˌin-tər-ˈmē-dᵊn\ *n* (1932) : MELANOCYTE-STIMULATING HORMONE

in·ter·ment \in-ˈtər-mənt\ *n* (14c) : the act or ceremony of interring

in·ter·mesh \ˌin-tər-ˈmesh\ *vi* (ca. 1903) : INTERLOCK ~ *vt* : to mesh together : INTERLOCK

in·ter·me·tal·lic \ˌin-tər-mə-ˈta-lik\ *adj* (1900) : composed of two or more metals or of a metal and a nonmetal; *esp* : being an alloy having a characteristic crystal structure and usu. a definite composition 〈~ compound〉 — **intermetallic** *n*

in·ter·mez·zo \ˌin-tər-ˈmet-(ˌ)sō, -ˈmed-(ˌ)zō\ *n, pl* **-zi** \-(ˌ)sē, -(ˌ)zē\ *or* **-zos** [It, ultim. fr. L *intermedius* intermediate] (1771) **1** : a short light entr'acte **2 a** : a movement coming between the major sections of an extended musical work (as an opera) **b** : a short independent instrumental composition **3** : a usu. brief interlude or diversion

in·ter·mi·na·ble \(ˌ)in-ˈtərm-nə-bəl, -ˈtər-mə-\ *adj* [ME, fr. LL *interminabilis,* fr. L *in-* + *terminare* to terminate] (15c) : having or seeming to have no end; *esp* : wearisomely protracted 〈an ~ sermon〉 — **in·ter·mi·na·ble·ness** *n* — **in·ter·mi·na·bly** \-blē\ *adv*

in·ter·min·gle \ˌin-tər-ˈmiŋ-gəl\ *vb* (15c) : INTERMIX

in·ter·mis·sion \ˌin-tər-ˈmi-shən\ *n* [ME *intermyssyown,* fr. L *intermission-, intermissio,* fr. *intermittere*] (15c) **1** : the act of intermitting : the state of being intermitted **2** : an interval between the parts of an entertainment (as the acts of a play) — **in·ter·mis·sion·less** *adj*

in·ter·mit \-ˈmit\ *vb* **-mit·ted; -mit·ting** [L *intermittere,* fr. *inter-* + *mittere* to send] *vt* (ca. 1542) : to cause to cease for a time or at intervals : DISCONTINUE ~ *vi* : to be intermittent — **in·ter·mit·ter** *n*

in·ter·mit·tence \-ˈmi-tən(t)s\ *n* (1796) : the quality or state of being intermittent

in·ter·mit·ten·cy \-ˈmi-tən(t)-sē\ *n* (1662) : INTERMITTENCE

in·ter·mit·tent \-ˈmi-tᵊnt\ *adj* [L *intermittent-, intermittens,* prp. of *intermittere*] (1601) : coming and going at intervals : not continuous 〈~ rain〉; *also* : OCCASIONAL 〈~ trips abroad〉 — **in·ter·mit·tent·ly** *adv*

in·ter·mix \ˌin-tər-ˈmiks\ *vb* [back-formation fr. obs. *intermixt* intermingled, fr. L *intermixtus,* pp. of *intermiscēre* to intermix, fr. *inter-* + *miscēre* to mix — more at MIX] *vt* (1542) : to mix together ~ *vi* : to become mixed together — **in·ter·mix·ture** \-ˈmiks-chər\ *n*

in·ter·mod·al \-ˈmō-dəl\ *adj* (1963) **1** : being or involving transportation by more than one form of carrier during a single journey **2** : used for intermodal transport

\ə\ **a**but \ᵊ\ **k**itten, F table \ər\ **fur**ther \a\ **a**sh \ā\ **a**ce \ä\ **m**op, m**ar** \au̇\ **ou**t \ch\ **ch**in \e\ **b**et \ē\ **ea**sy \g\ **g**o \i\ h**i**t \ī\ **i**ce \j\ **j**ob \ŋ\ si**ng** \ō\ g**o** \ȯ\ l**aw** \ȯi\ b**oy** \th\ **th**in \th\ **th**e \ü\ l**oo**t \u̇\ f**oo**t \y\ **y**et \zh\ vi**si**on, beige \k, n, œ, ue, y\ *see* Guide to Pronunciation

in·ter·mod·u·la·tion \-ˌmä-jə-ˈlā-shən\ *n* [ISV] (1931) **:** the production in an electrical device of currents having frequencies equal to the sums and differences of frequencies supplied to the device or of their harmonics

in·ter·mon·tane \ˌin-tər-ˈmän-ˌtān\ *or* **in·ter·mont** \ˈin-tər-ˌmänt\ *adj* [L *mont-, mons* mount] (1807) **:** situated between mountains ⟨an ~ basin⟩

[1]**in·tern** *or* **in·terne** \in-ˈtərn, ˈin-ˌ\ *adj* [MF *interne,* fr. L *internus*] (ca. 1500) *archaic* **:** INTERNAL

[2]**in·tern** \ˈin-ˌtərn, in-ˈ\ *vt* (1866) **:** to confine or impound esp. during a war ⟨~ enemy aliens⟩ — **in·tern·ee** \(ˌ)in-ˌtər-ˈnē\ *n* — **in·tern·ment** \in-ˈtərn-mənt, ˈin-ˌ\ *n*

[3]**in·tern** *also* **in·terne** \ˈin-ˌtərn\ *n* [F *interne,* fr. *interne,* adj.] (ca. 1879) **:** an advanced student or graduate usu. in a professional field (as medicine or teaching) gaining supervised practical experience (as in a hospital or classroom) — **in·tern·ship** \-ˌship\ *n*

[4]**in·tern** \ˈin-ˌtərn\ *vi* (ca. 1928) **:** to work as an intern

in·ter·nal \in-ˈtər-nᵊl, ˈin-ˌ\ *adj* [ME *internalle,* fr. L *internus;* akin to L *inter* between] (15c) **1 :** existing or situated within the limits or surface of something: as **a** (1) **:** situated near the inside of the body (2) **:** situated on the side toward the median plane of the body **b :** of, relating to, or occurring on the inside of an organized structure (as a club, company, or state) ⟨~ affairs⟩ **2 :** relating or belonging to or existing within the mind **3 :** INTRINSIC, INHERENT ⟨~ evidence of forgery in a document⟩ **4 :** present or arising within an organism or one of its parts ⟨~ stimulus⟩ **5 :** applied or intended for application through the stomach by being swallowed ⟨an ~ remedy⟩ — **in·ter·nal·i·ty** \ˌin-ˌtər-ˈna-lə-tē\ *n* — **in·ter·nal·ly** \in-ˈtər-nᵊl-ē\ *adv*

internal combustion engine *n* (1884) **:** a heat engine in which the combustion that generates the heat takes place inside the engine proper instead of in a furnace

in·ter·nal·ise *Brit var of* INTERNALIZE

in·ter·nal·ize \in-ˈtər-nə-ˌlīz\ *vt* **-ized; -iz·ing** (1884) **:** to give a subjective character to; *specif* **:** to incorporate (as values or patterns of culture) within the self as conscious or subconscious guiding principles through learning or socialization — **in·ter·nal·i·za·tion** \-ˌtər-nə-lə-ˈzā-shən\ *n*

internal medicine *n* (ca. 1904) **:** a branch of medicine that deals with the diagnosis and treatment of diseases not requiring surgery

internal respiration *n* (ca. 1890) **:** an exchange of gases between the cells of the body and the blood by way of the fluid bathing the cells — compare EXTERNAL RESPIRATION

internal rhyme *n* (1903) **:** rhyme between a word within a line and another either at the end of the same line or within another line

internal secretion *n* (1895) **:** HORMONE 1

[1]**in·ter·na·tion·al** \ˌin-tər-ˈnash-nəl, -ˈna-shə-nᵊl\ *adj* (1780) **1 :** of, relating to, or affecting two or more nations ⟨~ trade⟩ **2 :** of, relating to, or constituting a group or association having members in two or more nations ⟨~ movement⟩ **3 :** active, known, or reaching beyond national boundaries ⟨an ~ reputation⟩ — **in·ter·na·tion·al·i·ty** \-ˌnashə-ˈna-lə-tē\ *n* — **in·ter·na·tion·al·ly** \-ˈnash-nə-lē, -ˈna-shə-nᵊl-ē\ *adv*

[2]**international** *n* (1870) **:** one that is international; *esp* **:** an organization of international scope

international date line *n* (ca. 1909) **:** an arbitrary line approximately along the 180th meridian designated as the place where each calendar day begins

in·ter·na·tion·al·ise *Brit var of* INTERNATIONALIZE

in·ter·na·tion·al·ism \-ˈnash-nə-ˌli-zəm, -ˈna-shə-nə-ˌli-zəm\ *n* (1851) **1 :** international character, principles, interests, or outlook **2 a :** a policy of cooperation among nations **b :** an attitude or belief favoring such a policy — **in·ter·na·tion·al·ist** \-list, -ist\ *n or adj*

in·ter·na·tion·al·ize \ˌin-tər-ˈnash-nə-ˌlīz, -ˈna-shə-nə-ˌlīz\ *vt* (ca. 1864) **:** to make international; *also* **:** to place under international control ⟨a proposal to ~ the city⟩ — **in·ter·na·tion·al·i·za·tion** \-ˌnash-nə-lə-ˈzā-shən, -ˌna-shə-nə-lə-\ *n*

international law *n* (ca. 1828) **:** a body of rules that control or affect the rights of nations in their relations with each other

International Phonetic Alphabet *n* (1898) **:** IPA

international pitch *n* (1904) **:** a tuning standard of 440 vibrations per second for A above middle C

international relations *n pl but sing in constr* (1880) **:** a branch of political science concerned with relations between nations and primarily with foreign policies

International Scientific Vocabulary *n* (ca. 1959) **:** a part of the vocabulary of the sciences and other specialized studies that consists of words or other linguistic forms current in two or more languages and differing from New Latin in being adapted to the structure of the individual languages in which they appear — abbr. *ISV*

International Style *n* (1932) **1 :** a style in European art of the 14th and early 15th centuries marked by sinuous line, rich color, and decorative surface detail **2 :** a style in architecture developed in the 1920s that uses modern materials (as steel, glass, and reinforced concrete), expresses structure directly, and eliminates nonstructural ornament

International System of Units *n* (1932) **:** a system of units based on the metric system and developed and refined by international convention esp. for scientific work — abbr. *SI*

international unit *n* (1922) **:** a quantity of a biologically active substance (as a vitamin) that produces a particular biological effect agreed upon as an international standard

in·ter·ne·cine \ˌin-tər-ˈne-ˌsēn, -ˈnē-sᵊn, -ˈnē-ˌsīn, -nə-ˈsēn; in-ˈtər-nə-ˌsēn\ *adj* [L *internecinus,* fr. *internecare* to destroy, kill, fr. *inter-* + *necare* to kill, fr. *nec-, nex* violent death — more at NOXIOUS] (1663) **1 :** marked by slaughter **:** DEADLY; *esp* **:** mutually destructive **2 :** of, relating to, or involving conflict within a group ⟨bitter ~ feuds⟩

In·ter·net \ˈin-tər-ˌnet\ *n* (1985) **:** an electronic communications network that connects computer networks and organizational computer facilities around the world

in·ter·neu·ron \ˌin-tər-ˈnu̇r-ˌän, -ˈnyu̇r-\ *n* (1939) **:** a neuron that conveys impulses from one neuron to another — **in·ter·neu·ro·nal** \-ˈnu̇r-ə-nᵊl, -ˈnyu̇r-; -nu̇-ˈrō-, -nyu̇-ˈ\ *adj*

in·ter·nist \ˈin-ˌtər-nist\ *n* (1904) **:** a specialist in internal medicine

in·ter·node \ˈin-tər-ˌnōd\ *n* [L *internodium,* fr. *inter-* + *nodus* knot] (1667) **:** an interval or part between two nodes (as of a stem) — **in·ter·nod·al** \ˌin-tər-ˈnō-dᵊl\ *adj*

in·ter·nun·ci·al \ˌin-tər-ˈnən(t)-sē-əl, -ˈnu̇n(t)-\ *adj* (1845) **1 :** of or relating to an internuncio **2 :** of, relating to, or being interneurons

in·ter·nun·cio \ˌin-tər-ˈnən(t)-sē-ˌō, -ˈnu̇n(t)-\ *n* [It *internunzio,* fr. L *internuntius,* fr. *inter-* + *nuntius* messenger] (1641) **1 :** a messenger between two parties **:** GO-BETWEEN **2 :** a papal legate of lower rank than a nuncio

in·ter·o·cep·tive \ˌin-tə-rō-ˈsep-tiv\ *adj* [*interior* + *-o-* + *-ceptive* (as in *receptive*)] (ca. 1921) **:** of, relating to, or being stimuli arising within the body and esp. in the viscera

in·ter·o·cep·tor \-tər\ *n* (1906) **:** a sensory receptor excited by interoceptive stimuli

in·ter·op·er·a·bil·i·ty \ˌin-tər-ˌä-p(ə-)rə-ˈbi-lə-tē\ *n* (1977) **:** ability of a system (as a weapons system) to work with or use the parts or equipment of another system — **in·ter·op·er·a·ble** \-ˈä-p(ə-)rə-bəl\ *adj*

in·ter·pel·late \ˌin-tər-ˈpe-ˌlāt, in-ˈtər-pə-ˌlāt\ *vt* **-lat·ed; -lat·ing** [L *interpellatus,* pp. of *interpellare* to interrupt, fr. *inter-* + *-pellare* (fr. *pellere* to drive) — more at FELT] (1874) **:** to question (as a foreign minister) formally concerning an official action or policy or personal conduct — **in·ter·pel·la·tion** \ˌin-tər-pə-ˈlā-shən\ *n* — **in·ter·pel·la·tor** \ˌin-tər-ˈpe-ˌlā-tər, in-ˈtər-pə-ˌlā-\ *n*

in·ter·pen·e·trate \ˌin-tər-ˈpe-nə-ˌtrāt\ *vi* (ca. 1810) **:** to penetrate mutually ~ *vt* **:** to penetrate between, within, or throughout **:** PERMEATE — **in·ter·pen·e·tra·tion** \-ˌpe-nə-ˈtrā-shən\ *n*

in·ter·per·son·al \-ˈpərs-nəl, -ˈpər-sə-nəl\ *adj* (1842) **:** being, relating to, or involving relations between persons — **in·ter·per·son·al·ly** *adv*

in·ter·phase \ˈin-tər-ˌfāz\ *n* (1913) **:** the interval between the end of one mitotic or meiotic division and the beginning of another

in·ter·plant \ˌin-tər-ˈplant\ *vt* (1911) **:** to plant a crop between (plants of another kind); *also* **:** to set out young trees among (existing growth)

in·ter·play \ˈin-tər-ˌplā\ *n* (1862) **:** INTERACTION ⟨the ~ of opposing forces⟩ — **in·ter·play** \ˌin-tər-ˈ, ˈin-tər-ˌ\ *vi*

in·ter·plead \ˌin-tər-ˈplēd\ *vi* [AF *enterpleder,* fr. *enter-* inter- + *pleder, plaider* to plead — more at PLEAD] (1567) **:** to go to trial with each other in order to determine a right on which the action of a third party depends

[1]**in·ter·plead·er** \-ˈplē-dər\ *n* [AF *enterpleder,* fr. *enterpleder,* v.] (1567) **:** a proceeding to enable a person to compel parties making the same claim against him to litigate the matter between themselves

[2]**interpleader** *n* (ca. 1846) **:** one that interpleads

Interpol *abbr* International Criminal Police Organization

in·ter·po·late \in-ˈtər-pə-ˌlāt\ *vb* **-lat·ed; -lat·ing** [L *interpolatus,* pp. of *interpolare* to refurbish, alter, interpolate, fr. *inter-* + *-polare* (fr. *polire* to polish)] *vt* (1612) **1 a :** to alter or corrupt (as a text) by inserting new or foreign matter **b :** to insert (words) into a text or into a conversation **2 :** to insert between other things or parts **:** INTERCALATE **3 :** to estimate values of (data or a function) between two known values ~ *vi* **:** to make insertions (as of estimated values) ***syn*** see INTRODUCE — **in·ter·po·la·tion** \-ˌtər-pə-ˈlā-shən\ *n* — **in·ter·po·la·tive** \-ˈtər-pə-ˌlā-tiv\ *adj* — **in·ter·po·la·tor** \-ˌlā-tər\ *n*

in·ter·pose \ˌin-tər-ˈpōz\ *vb* **-posed; -pos·ing** [MF *interposer,* fr. L *interponere* (perf. indic. *interposui*), fr. *inter-* + *ponere* to put — more at POSITION] *vt* (1582) **1 a :** to place in an intervening position **b :** to put (oneself) between **:** INTRUDE **2 :** to put forth by way of interference or intervention **3 :** to introduce or throw in between the parts of a conversation or argument ~ *vi* **1 :** to be or come between **2 :** to step in between parties at variance **:** INTERVENE **3 :** INTERRUPT — **in·ter·pos·er** *n*

syn INTERPOSE, INTERFERE, INTERVENE, MEDIATE, INTERCEDE mean to come or go between. INTERPOSE often implies no more than this ⟨*interposed* herself between him and the door⟩. INTERFERE implies hindering ⟨noise *interfered* with my concentration⟩. INTERVENE may imply an occurring in space or time between two things or a stepping in to stop a conflict ⟨quarreled until the manager *intervened*⟩. MEDIATE implies intervening between hostile factions ⟨*mediated* between the parties⟩. INTERCEDE implies acting for an offender in begging mercy or forgiveness ⟨*interceded* on our behalf⟩. ***syn*** see in addition INTRODUCE

in·ter·po·si·tion \-pə-ˈzi-shən\ *n* (14c) **1 a :** the act of interposing **b :** the action of a state whereby its sovereignty is placed between its citizens and the federal government **2 :** something interposed

in·ter·pret \in-ˈtər-prət, -pət\ *vb* [ME, fr. AF & L; AF *interpreter,* fr. L *interpretari,* fr. *interpret-, interpres* agent, negotiator, interpreter] *vt* (14c) **1 :** to explain or tell the meaning of **:** present in understandable terms ⟨~ dreams⟩ ⟨needed help ~*ing* the results⟩ **2 :** to conceive in the light of individual belief, judgment, or circumstance **:** CONSTRUE ⟨~ a contract⟩ **3 :** to represent by means of art **:** bring to realization by performance or direction ⟨~*s* a role⟩ ~ *vi* **:** to act as an interpreter between speakers of different languages ***syn*** see EXPLAIN — **in·ter·pret·abil·i·ty** \-ˌtər-prə-tə-ˈbi-lə-tē, -pə-tə-\ *n* — **in·ter·pret·able** \-ˈtər-prə-tə-bəl, -pə-tə-\ *adj*

in·ter·pre·ta·tion \in-ˌtər-prə-ˈtā-shən, -pə-\ *n* (14c) **1 :** the act or the result of interpreting **:** EXPLANATION **2 :** a particular adaptation or version of a work, method, or style **3 :** a teaching technique that combines factual with stimulating explanatory information ⟨natural history ~ program⟩ — **in·ter·pre·ta·tion·al** \-shnəl, -shə-nᵊl\ *adj* — **in·ter·pre·ta·tive** \in-ˈtər-prə-ˌtā-tiv *also* -prə-tə-tiv\ *adj* — **in·ter·pre·ta·tive·ly** *adv* — **in·ter·pre·tive** \-ˈtər-prə-tiv, -pə-\ *adj* — **in·ter·pre·tive·ly** *adv*

in·ter·pret·er \in-ˈtər-prə-tər, -pə-\ *n* (14c) **1 :** one that interprets: as **a :** one who translates orally for parties conversing in different languages **b :** one who explains or expounds **2 a :** a machine that prints on punch cards the symbols recorded in them by perforations **b :** a computer program that executes each of a set of high-level instructions before going to the next instruction

in·ter·prox·i·mal \ˌin-tər-ˈpräk-sə-məl\ *adj* (1897) **:** situated or used in the areas between adjoining teeth ⟨~ space⟩

in·ter·pu·pil·lary \ˌin-tər-ˈpyü-pə-ˌler-ē\ *adj* (ca. 1904) **:** extending between the pupils of the eyes; *also* **:** extending between the centers of a pair of spectacle lenses ⟨~ distance⟩

in·ter·ra·cial \-ˈrā-shəl\ *adj* (1888) **:** of, involving, or designed for members of different races — **in·ter·ra·cial·ly** \-shə-lē\ *adv*

interred *past and past part of* INTER

in·ter·reg·num \ˌin-tə-ˈreg-nəm\ *n, pl* **-nums** *or* **-na** \-nə\ [L, fr. *inter-* + *regnum* reign — more at REIGN] (1590) **1 :** the time during which a throne is vacant between two successive reigns or regimes **2 :** a period during which the normal functions of government or control are suspended **3 :** a lapse or pause in a continuous series

in·ter·re·late \ˌin-tə(r)-ri-ˈlāt\ *vt* (1888) **:** to bring into mutual relation ~ *vi* **:** to have mutual relationship — **in·ter·re·la·tion** \-ˈlā-shən\ *n* — **in·ter·re·la·tion·ship** \-ˌship\ *n*

in·ter·re·lat·ed \-ˈlā-təd\ *adj* (1827) **:** having a mutual or reciprocal relation — **in·ter·re·lat·ed·ly** *adv* — **in·ter·re·lat·ed·ness** *n*

interring *pres part of* INTER

in·ter·ro·bang \in-ˈter-ə-ˌbaŋ\ *n* [*interro*gation (point) + *bang* (printers' slang for *exclamation point*)] (1967) **:** a punctuation mark ‽ designed for use esp. at the end of an exclamatory rhetorical question

in·ter·ro·gate \in-ˈter-ə-ˌgāt, -ˈte-rə-\ *vt* **-gat·ed; -gat·ing** [L *interrogatus,* pp. of *interrogare,* fr. *inter-* + *rogare* to ask — more at RIGHT] (15c) **1 :** to question formally and systematically **2 :** to give or send out a signal to (as a transponder) for triggering an appropriate response ***syn*** see ASK — **in·ter·ro·ga·tee** \-ˌter-ə-(ˌ)gā-ˈtē\ *n* — **in·ter·ro·ga·tion** \-ˌter-ə-ˈgā-shən\ *n* — **in·ter·ro·ga·tion·al** \-shnəl, -shə-nᵊl\ *adj*

interrogation point *n* (ca. 1864) **:** QUESTION MARK 2

[1]**in·ter·rog·a·tive** \ˌin-tə-ˈrä-gə-tiv\ *adj* (15c) **1 a :** used in a question **b :** having the form or force of a question **2 :** INQUISITIVE, QUESTIONING — **in·ter·rog·a·tive·ly** *adv*

[2]**interrogative** *n* (1522) **1 :** a word (as *who, what, which*) or a particle (as Latin *-ne*) used in asking questions **2 :** QUESTION 1a

in·ter·ro·ga·tor \in-ˈter-ə-ˌgā-tər, -ˈte-rə-\ *n* (1751) **1 :** one that interrogates **2 :** a radio transmitter and receiver for sending out a signal that triggers a transponder and for receiving and displaying the reply

[1]**in·ter·rog·a·to·ry** \ˌin-tə-ˈrä-gə-ˌtȯr-ē\ *n, pl* **-ries** (1515) **:** a formal question or inquiry; *esp* **:** a written question required to be answered under direction of a court

[2]**interrogatory** *adj* (1576) **:** INTERROGATIVE

in·ter·ro·gee \in-ˌter-ə-ˈgē\ *n* (1919) **:** one who is interrogated

[1]**in·ter·rupt** \ˌin-tə-ˈrəpt\ *vb* [ME, fr. L *interruptus,* pp. of *interrumpere,* fr. *inter-* + *rumpere* to break — more at REAVE] *vt* (15c) **1 :** to stop or hinder by breaking in ⟨~*ed* the speaker with frequent questions⟩ **2 :** to break the uniformity or continuity of ⟨a hot spell occasionally ~*ed* by a period of cool weather⟩ ~ *vi* **:** to break in upon an action; *esp* **:** to break in with questions or remarks while another is speaking — **in·ter·rupt·ible** \-ˈrəp-tə-bəl\ *adj* — **in·ter·rup·tion** \-ˈrəp-shən\ *n* — **in·ter·rup·tive** \-ˈrəp-tiv\ *adv*

[2]**in·ter·rupt** \ˌin-tə-ˈrəpt, ˈin-tə-ˌ\ *n* (1957) **:** a feature of a computer that permits the temporary interruption of one activity (as the execution of a program) in order to perform another; *also* **:** the interruption itself

in·ter·rupt·er *also* **in·ter·rup·tor** \ˌin-tə-ˈrəp-tər\ *n* (ca. 1512) **:** one that interrupts; *esp* **:** a device for interrupting an electric current usu. automatically

in·ter·scho·las·tic \ˌin-tər-skə-ˈlas-tik\ *adj* (1879) **:** existing or carried on between schools ⟨~ athletics⟩

in·ter se \ˌin-tər-ˈsā, -ˈsē\ *adv or adj* [L] (1845) **:** among or between themselves

in·ter·sect \ˌin-tər-ˈsekt\ *vb* [L *intersectus,* pp. of *intersecare,* fr. *inter-* + *secare* to cut — more at SAW] *vt* (1615) **:** to pierce or divide by passing through or across **:** CROSS ⟨a comet ~*ing* earth's orbit⟩ ⟨one line ~*s* another⟩ ~ *vi* **1 :** to meet and cross at a point ⟨lines ~*ing* at right angles⟩ **2 :** to share a common area **:** OVERLAP ⟨where morality and self-interest ~⟩

in·ter·sec·tion \ˌin-tər-ˈsek-shən, *esp in sense 2* ˈin-tər-ˌ\ *n* (1559) **1 :** the act or process of intersecting **2 :** a place or area where two or more things (as streets) intersect **3 a :** the set of elements common to two or more sets; *esp* **:** the set of points common to two geometric configurations **b :** the operation of finding the intersection of two or more sets

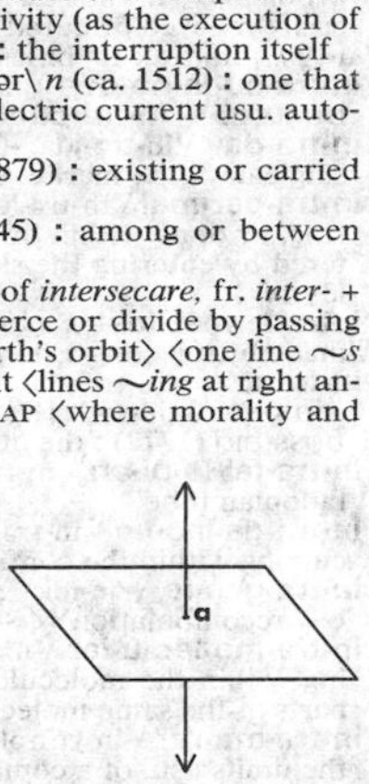

a intersection 3a

in·ter·ser·vice \ˌin-tər-ˈsər-vəs\ *adj* (1946) **:** existing between or relating to two or more of the armed services ⟨~ rivalry⟩

in·ter·ses·sion \ˈin-tər-ˌse-shən\ *n* (1932) **:** a period between two academic sessions or terms sometimes utilized for brief concentrated courses

in·ter·sex \ˈin-tər-ˌseks\ *n* [ISV] (1910) **:** an intersexual individual

in·ter·sex·u·al \ˌin-tər-ˈsek-shə-wəl, -shwəl, -shəl\ *adj* [ISV] (ca. 1866) **1 :** existing between sexes ⟨~ hostility⟩ **2 :** intermediate in sexual characters between a typical male and a typical female — **in·ter·sex·u·al·i·ty** \-ˌsek-shə-ˈwa-lə-tē\ *n* — **in·ter·sex·u·al·ly** \-ˈsek-shə-wə-lē, -shwə-lē, -shə-lē\ *adv*

[1]**in·ter·space** \ˈin-tər-ˌspās\ *n* (15c) **:** an intervening space **:** INTERVAL

[2]**in·ter·space** \ˌin-tər-ˈspās\ *vt* (1685) **:** to occupy or fill the space between

in·ter·spe·cif·ic \ˌin-tər-spi-ˈsi-fik\ *also* **in·ter·spe·cies** \-ˈspē-(ˌ)shēz, -(ˌ)sēz\ *adj* (1889) **:** existing, occurring, or arising between species ⟨~ hybrid⟩

in·ter·sperse \ˌin-tər-ˈspərs\ *vt* **-spersed; -spers·ing** [L *interspersus* interspersed, fr. *inter-* + *sparsus,* pp. of *spargere* to scatter — more at SPARK] (1566) **1 :** to place something at intervals in or among ⟨~ a book with pictures⟩ **2 :** to insert at intervals among other things ⟨*interspersing* drawings throughout the text⟩ — **in·ter·sper·sion** \-ˈspər-zhən, -shən\ *n*

in·ter·sta·di·al \ˌin-tər-ˈstā-dē-əl\ *n* [ISV *inter-* + NL *stadium* stage, phase, fr. L — more at STADIUM] (1914) **:** a subdivision within a glacial stage marking a temporary retreat of the ice

[1]**in·ter·state** \ˌin-tər-ˈstāt\ *adj* (1844) **:** of, connecting, or existing between two or more states esp. of the U.S. ⟨~ commerce⟩

[2]**in·ter·state** \ˈin-tər-ˌstāt\ *n* (1968) **:** any of a system of expressways connecting most major U.S. cities — called also *interstate highway*

in·ter·stel·lar \-ˈste-lər\ *adj* (1626) **:** located, taking place, or traveling among the stars esp. of the Milky Way galaxy

in·ter·stice \in-ˈtər-stəs\ *n, pl* **-stic·es** \-stə-ˌsēz, -stə-səz\ [ME, fr. L *interstitium,* fr. *inter-* + *-stit-, -stes* standing (as in *superstes* standing over) — more at SUPERSTITION] (15c) **1 a :** a space that intervenes between things; *esp* **:** one between closely spaced things ⟨~*s* of a wall⟩ **b :** a gap or break in something generally continuous ⟨the ~*s* of society⟩ ⟨passages of genuine literary merit in the ~*s* of the ludicrous . . . plots —Joyce Carol Oates⟩ **2 :** a short space of time between events

in·ter·sti·tial \ˌin-tər-ˈsti-shəl\ *adj* (1646) **1 :** relating to or situated in the interstices **2 a :** situated within but not restricted to or characteristic of a particular organ or tissue — used esp. of fibrous tissue **b :** affecting the interstitial tissues of an organ or part **3 :** being or relating to a crystalline compound in which usu. small atoms or ions of a nonmetal occupy holes between the larger metal atoms or ions in the crystal lattice — **in·ter·sti·tial·ly** \-shə-lē\ *adv*

in·ter·sub·jec·tive \ˌin-tər-səb-ˈjek-tiv\ *adj* (1899) **1 :** involving or occurring between separate conscious minds ⟨~ communication⟩ **2 :** accessible to or capable of being established for two or more subjects **:** OBJECTIVE ⟨~ reality of the physical world⟩ — **in·ter·sub·jec·tive·ly** *adv* — **in·ter·sub·jec·tiv·i·ty** \-(ˌ)səb-ˌjek-ˈti-və-tē\ *n*

in·ter·tes·ta·men·tal \-ˌtes-tə-ˈmen-tᵊl\ *adj* (1929) **:** of, relating to, or forming the period of two centuries between the composition of the last book of the Old Testament and the first book of the New Testament

in·ter·tex·tu·al·i·ty \-ˌteks-chə-ˈwa-lə-tē\ *n, pl* **-ties** [F *intertextualité,* fr. *inter-* + *textuel* textual + *-ité* -ity] (1975) **:** the complex interrelationship between a text and other texts taken as basic to the creation or interpretation of the text — **in·ter·tex·tu·al** \-ˈteks-chə-wəl\ *adj* — **in·ter·tex·tu·al·ly** *adv*

in·ter·tid·al \-ˈtī-dᵊl\ *adj* (1883) **:** of, relating to, or being the part of the littoral zone above low-tide mark — **in·ter·tid·al·ly** \-dᵊl-ē\ *adv*

in·ter·tie \ˈin-tər-ˌtī\ *n* (1951) **:** an interconnection permitting passage of current between two or more electric utility systems

in·ter·till \ˌin-tər-ˈtil\ *vt* (1912) **:** to cultivate between the rows of (a crop) — **in·ter·till·age** \-ˈti-lij\ *n*

in·ter·trop·i·cal \-ˈträ-pi-kəl\ *adj* (1794) **1 :** situated between or within the tropics **2 :** relating to regions within the tropics **:** TROPICAL

in·ter·twine \-ˈtwīn\ *vt* (1641) **:** to unite by twining one with another ~ *vi* **:** to twine about one another; *also* **:** to become mutually involved — **in·ter·twine·ment** \-mənt\ *n*

in·ter·twist \-ˈtwist\ *vb* (ca. 1659) **:** INTERTWINE — **in·ter·twist** \ˈin-tər-ˌtwist\ *n*

in·ter·val \ˈin-tər-vəl\ *n* [ME *intervalle,* fr. AF & L; AF *entreval,* fr. L *intervallum* space between ramparts, interval, fr. *inter-* + *vallum* rampart — more at WALL] (14c) **1 a :** a space of time between events or states **b** *Brit* **:** INTERMISSION **2 a :** a space between objects, units, points, or states **b :** difference in pitch between tones **3 :** a set of real numbers between two numbers either including or excluding one or both of them **4 :** one of a series of fast-paced exercises interspersed with slower ones or brief rests for training (as of an athlete) — **in·ter·val·lic** \ˌin-tər-ˈva-lik\ *adj*

in·ter·vale \ˈin-tər-vəl, -ˌvāl\ *n* [obs. *intervale* interval] (1647) *chiefly NewEng* **:** BOTTOMLAND

in·ter·val·om·e·ter \ˌin-tər-və-ˈlä-mə-tər\ *n* (1933) **:** a device that operates a control (as for a camera shutter) at regular intervals

in·ter·vene \ˌin-tər-ˈvēn\ *vi* **-vened; -ven·ing** [L *intervenire* to come between, fr. *inter-* + *venire* to come — more at COME] (1587) **1 :** to occur, fall, or come between points of time or events ⟨only six months *intervened* between their marriage and divorce⟩ **2 :** to enter or appear as an irrelevant or extraneous feature or circumstance ⟨it's business as usual until a crisis ~*s*⟩ **3 a :** to come in or between by way of hindrance or modification ⟨~ to stop a fight⟩ **b :** to interfere with the outcome or course esp. of a condition or process (as to prevent harm or improve functioning) **4 :** to occur or lie between two things **5 a :** to become a third party to a legal proceeding begun by others for the protection of an alleged interest **b :** to interfere usu. by force or threat of force in another nation's internal affairs esp. to compel or prevent an action ***syn*** see INTERPOSE — **in·ter·ven·tion** \-ˈven(t)-shən\ *n* — **in·ter·ven·tion·al** \-ˈvench-nəl, ˈven(t)-shə-nᵊl\ *adj*

in·ter·ve·nor \-ˈvē-nər, -ˌnȯr\ *or* **in·ter·ven·er** \-ˈvē-nər\ *n* (1621) **:** one who intervenes; *esp* **:** one who intervenes as a third party in a legal proceeding

in·ter·ven·tion·ism \-ˈven(t)-shə-ˌni-zəm\ *n* (1923) **:** the theory or practice of intervening; *specif* **:** governmental interference in economic affairs at home or in political affairs of another country — **in·ter·ven·tion·ist** \-ˈvench-nist, -ˈven(t)-shə-nist\ *n or adj*

in·ter·ver·te·bral disk \ˌin-tər-ˈvər-tə-brəl-, -(ˌ)vər-ˈtē-\ *n* (ca. 1860) **:** any of the tough elastic disks that are interposed between the centra of adjoining vertebrae and that consist of an outer fibrous ring enclosing an inner pulpy nucleus

in·ter·view \ˈin-tər-ˌvyü\ *n* [AF *entreveue* meeting, fr. (*s'*)*entreveer* to see one another, meet, fr. *entre-* inter- + *veer* to see — more at VIEW] (1514) **1 :** a formal consultation usu. to evaluate qualifications (as of a prospective student or employee) **2 a :** a meeting at which information is obtained (as by a reporter, television commentator, or pollster) from a person **b :** a report or reproduction of information so obtained **3 :** INTERVIEWEE — **interview** *vb* — **in·ter·view·er** *n*

in·ter·view·ee \ˌin-tər-(ˌ)vyü-ˈē\ *n* (1884) **:** one who is interviewed

in·ter vi·vos \ˈin-tər-ˈvē-ˌvōs, -ˈvī-\ *adv or adj* [LL] (1837) **:** between living persons ⟨transaction *inter vivos*⟩; *esp* **:** from one living person to another ⟨*inter vivos* gifts⟩ ⟨property transferred *inter vivos*⟩

inter vivos trust *n* (1949) **:** LIVING TRUST

in·ter·vo·cal·ic \ˌin-tər-vō-ˈka-lik\ *adj* (1887) **:** immediately preceded and immediately followed by a vowel — **in·ter·vo·cal·i·cal·ly** \-lik(ə-)lē\ *adv*

in·ter·weave \ˌin-tər-ˈwēv\ *vb* **-wove** \-ˈwōv\ *also* **-weaved; -wo·ven** \-ˈwō-vən\ *also* **-weaved; -weav·ing** *vt* (1598) **1 :** to weave together **2 :** to mix or blend together ⟨*interweaving* his own insights . . . with letters and memoirs —Phoebe Adams⟩ ~ *vi* **:** INTERTWINE, INTERMINGLE — **in·ter·weave** \ˈin-tər-ˌwēv\ *n* — **in·ter·wo·ven** \ˌin-tər-ˈwō-vən\ *adj*

in·tes·ta·cy \in-ˈtes-tə-sē\ *n* (1767) **:** the quality or state of being or dying intestate

[1]**in·tes·tate** \in-ˈtes-ˌtāt, -tət\ *adj* [ME, fr. L *intestatus,* fr. *in-* + *testatus* testate] (14c) **1 :** having made no valid will ‹died ~› **2 :** not disposed of by will ‹an ~ estate›

[2]**intestate** *n* (1658) : one who dies intestate

in·tes·ti·nal \in-ˈtes-tə-nᵊl, -ˈtes(t)-nəl, -ˈte-sᵊn-əl, *Brit often* ˌin-(ˌ)tes-ˈtī-nᵊl\ *adj* (15c) **1 :** affecting, occurring, or living in the intestine **2 :** of, relating to, or being the intestine — **in·tes·ti·nal·ly** *adv*

intestinal fortitude *n* [euphemism for *guts*] (ca. 1937) : COURAGE, STAMINA

[1]**in·tes·tine** \in-ˈtes-tən\ *adj* [ME, fr. MF or L; MF *intestin,* fr. L *intestinus,* fr. *intus* within — more at ENT-] (15c) : INTERNAL; *specif* : of or relating to the internal affairs of a state or country ‹~ war›

[2]**intestine** *n* [ME, fr. MF *intestin,* fr. L *intestinum,* fr. neut. of *intestinus*] (15c) : the tubular part of the alimentary canal that extends from the stomach to the anus — compare LARGE INTESTINE, SMALL INTESTINE

in·ti \ˈin-tē\ *n* [Quechua, sun] (1985) : the basic monetary unit of Peru from 1985 to 1990

in·ti·fa·da \ˌin-tə-ˈfä-də\ *n* [Ar *intifāḍa,* lit., the act of shaking off] (1985) : UPRISING, REBELLION; *specif* : an armed uprising of Palestinians against Israeli occupation of the West Bank and Gaza Strip

in·ti·ma \ˈin-tə-mə\ *n, pl* **-mae** \-ˌmē, -ˌmī\ *or* **-mas** [NL, fr. L, fem. of *intimus*] (1873) : the innermost coat of an organ (as a blood vessel) consisting usu. of an endothelial layer backed by connective tissue and elastic tissue — **in·ti·mal** \-məl\ *adj*

in·ti·ma·cy \ˈin-tə-mə-sē\ *n, pl* **-cies** (1641) **1 :** the state of being intimate : FAMILIARITY **2 :** something of a personal or private nature

[1]**in·ti·mate** \ˈin-tə-ˌmāt\ *vt* **-mat·ed; -mat·ing** [LL *intimatus,* pp. of *intimare* to put in, announce, fr. L *intimus* innermost, superl. of OL **interus* inward — more at INTERIOR] (1522) **1 :** to make known esp. publicly or formally : ANNOUNCE **2 :** to communicate delicately and indirectly : HINT ***syn*** see SUGGEST — **in·ti·mat·er** *n* — **in·ti·ma·tion** \ˌin-tə-ˈmā-shən\ *n*

[2]**in·ti·mate** \ˈin-tə-mət\ *adj* [alter. of obs. *intime,* fr. L *intimus*] (1632) **1 a :** INTRINSIC, ESSENTIAL **b :** belonging to or characterizing one's deepest nature **2 :** marked by very close association, contact, or familiarity ‹~ knowledge of the law› **3 a :** marked by a warm friendship developing through long association ‹~ friends› **b :** suggesting informal warmth or privacy ‹~ clubs› **4 :** of a very personal or private nature ‹~ secrets› — **in·ti·mate·ly** *adv* — **in·ti·mate·ness** *n*

[3]**in·ti·mate** \ˈin-tə-mət\ *n* (1659) : an intimate friend or confidant

in·tim·i·date \in-ˈti-mə-ˌdāt\ *vt* **-dat·ed; -dat·ing** [ML *intimidatus,* pp. of *intimidare,* fr. L *in-* + *timidus* timid] (1646) : to make timid or fearful : FRIGHTEN; *esp* : to compel or deter by or as if by threats ‹tried to ~ a witness› — **in·tim·i·dat·ing·ly** \-ˌdā-tiŋ-lē\ *adv* — **in·tim·i·da·tion** \-ˌti-mə-ˈdā-shən\ *n* — **in·tim·i·da·tor** \-ˈti-mə-ˌdā-tər\ *n*

syn INTIMIDATE, COW, BULLDOZE, BULLY, BROWBEAT mean to frighten into submission. INTIMIDATE implies inducing fear or a sense of inferiority into another ‹*intimidated* by so many other bright freshmen›. COW implies reduction to a state where the spirit is broken or all courage is lost ‹not at all *cowed* by the odds against making it in show business›. BULLDOZE implies an intimidating or an overcoming of resistance usu. by urgings, demands, or threats ‹*bulldozed* the city council into approving the plan›. BULLY implies intimidation through threats, insults, or aggressive behavior ‹*bullied* into giving up their lunch money›. BROWBEAT implies a cowing through arrogant, scornful, or contemptuous treatment ‹*browbeat* the witness into a contradiction›.

in·tim·i·da·to·ry \-ˈti-mə-də-ˌtȯr-ē\ *adj* (ca. 1846) : tending or intended to intimidate ‹~ propaganda›

in·tinc·tion \in-ˈtiŋ(k)-shən\ *n* [LL *intinction-, intinctio* baptism, fr. L *intingere* to dip in, fr. *in-* + *tingere* to dip, moisten — more at TINGE] (1872) : the administration of the sacrament of Communion by dipping bread in wine and giving both together to the communicant

in·tine \ˈin-ˌtēn\ *n* [prob. fr. G, fr. L *intus* within + NL *in-* fibrous tissue, fr. Gk *in-, is* tendon] (1835) : the inner mostly cellulose wall of some spores and esp. pollen grains

in·ti·tule \in-ˈti-(ˌ)chül\ *vt* **-uled; -ul·ing** [ME *intitulen, entitlen* to give a title to — more at ENTITLE] (15c) *Brit* : to furnish (as a legislative act) with a title or designation

intl *or* **intnl** *abbr* international

in·to \ˈin-(ˌ)tü, -tə\ *prep* [ME, fr. OE *intō,* fr. [2]*in* + *tō* to] (bef. 12c) **1 —** used as a function word to indicate entry, introduction, insertion, superposition, or inclusion ‹came ~ the house› ‹enter ~ an alliance› **2 a :** to the state, condition, or form of ‹got ~ trouble› **b :** to the occupation, action, or possession of ‹go ~ farming› **c :** involved with or interested in ‹~ hard drugs› ‹~ Latin epigrammatists› **3 —** used as a function word to indicate a period of time or an extent of space part of which is passed or occupied ‹far ~ the night› **4 :** in the direction of ‹looking ~ the sun› **5 :** to a position of contact with : AGAINST ‹ran ~ a wall› **6 —** used as a function word to indicate the dividend in division ‹dividing 3 ~ 6 gives 2›

in·tol·er·a·ble \(ˌ)in-ˈtäl-rə-bəl, -ˈtä-lə-rə-, -ˈtä-lər-bəl\ *adj* [ME, fr. AF, fr. L *intolerabilis,* fr. *in-* + *tolerabilis* tolerable] (15c) **1 :** not tolerable : UNBEARABLE ‹~ pain› **2 :** EXCESSIVE — **in·tol·er·a·bil·i·ty** \-ˌtäl-rə-ˈbi-lə-tē, -ˌtä-lə-rə-, -ˌtä-lər-\ *n* — **in·tol·er·a·ble·ness** \-ˈtäl-rə-bəl-nəs, -ˈtä-lə-rə-, -ˈtä-lər-bəl-\ *n* — **in·tol·er·a·bly** \-blē\ *adv*

in·tol·er·ance \(ˌ)in-ˈtäl-rən(t)s, -ˈtä-lə-\ *n* (1765) **1 :** the quality or state of being intolerant **2 :** exceptional sensitivity (as to a drug); *specif* : inability to properly metabolize or absorb a substance

in·tol·er·ant \-rənt\ *adj* (ca. 1735) **1 :** unable or unwilling to endure **2 a :** unwilling to grant equal freedom of expression esp. in religious matters **b :** unwilling to grant or share social, political, or professional rights : BIGOTED **3 :** exhibiting physiological intolerance ‹lactose ~› — **in·tol·er·ant·ly** *adv* — **in·tol·er·ant·ness** *n*

in·to·nate \ˈin-tə-ˌnāt, -(ˌ)tō-\ *vt* **-nat·ed; -nat·ing** (1795) : INTONE, UTTER

in·to·na·tion \ˌin-tə-ˈnā-shən, -(ˌ)tō-\ *n* (1620) **1 :** something that is intoned; *specif* : the opening tones of a Gregorian chant **2 :** the act of intoning and esp. of chanting **3 :** the ability to play or sing notes in tune **4 :** manner of utterance; *specif* : the rise and fall in pitch of the voice in speech — **in·to·na·tion·al** \-shnəl, -shə-nᵊl\ *adj*

in·tone \in-ˈtōn\ *vb* **in·toned; in·ton·ing** [MF *entoner,* fr. ML *intonare,* fr. L *in-* + *tonus* tone] *vt* (1513) : to utter in musical or prolonged tones : recite in singing tones or in a monotone ~ *vi* : to utter something in singing tones or in monotone — **in·ton·er** *n*

in to·to \in-ˈtō-(ˌ)tō\ *adv* [L, on the whole] (1796) : TOTALLY, ENTIRELY

in·tox·i·cant \in-ˈtäk-si-kənt\ *n* (1863) : something that intoxicates; *esp* : an alcoholic drink — **intoxicant** *adj*

[1]**in·tox·i·cate** \-si-kət\ *adj* (15c) *archaic* : INTOXICATED

[2]**in·tox·i·cate** \-sə-ˌkāt\ *vt* **-cat·ed; -cat·ing** [ME, fr. ML *intoxicatus,* pp. of *intoxicare,* fr. L *in-* + *toxicum* poison — more at TOXIC] (15c) **1 :** POISON **2 a :** to excite or stupefy by alcohol or a drug esp. to the point where physical and mental control is markedly diminished **b :** to excite or elate to the point of enthusiasm or frenzy

in·tox·i·cat·ed \-sə-ˌkā-təd\ *adj* (1576) : affected by or as if by alcohol : DRUNK — **in·tox·i·cat·ed·ly** \-ˌkā-təd-lē\ *adv*

in·tox·i·ca·tion \in-ˌtäk-sə-ˈkā-shən\ *n* (15c) **1 :** an abnormal state that is essentially a poisoning ‹carbon monoxide ~› **2 a :** the condition of being drunk : INEBRIATION **b :** a strong excitement or elation

in·tra- \ˈin-trə, -(ˌ)trä\ *prefix* [LL, fr. L *intra,* fr. OL **interus,* adj., inward — more at INTERIOR] **1 a :** within ‹*intra*galactic› **b :** during ‹*intra*day› **c :** between layers of ‹*intra*dermal› **2 :** INTRO- ‹an *intra*muscular injection›

in·tra–ar·te·ri·al \-är-ˈtir-ē-əl\ *adj* (1897) : situated or occurring within, administered into, or involving entry by way of an artery ‹~ chemotherapy› — **in·tra–ar·te·ri·al·ly** \-ē-ə-lē\ *adv*

in·tra–ar·tic·u·lar \-är-ˈti-kyə-lər\ *adj* (ca. 1888) : situated within, occurring within, or administered by entry into a joint ‹~ injection›

in·tra·car·di·ac \-ˈkär-dē-ˌak\ *also* **in·tra·car·di·al** \-dē-əl\ *adj* (1876) : situated or occurring within or introduced or involving entry into the heart ‹an ~ shunt› — **in·tra·car·di·al·ly** \-dē-ə-lē\ *adv*

in·tra·cel·lu·lar \-ˈsel-yə-lər\ *adj* (1876) : existing, occurring, or functioning within a cell ‹~ parasites› — **in·tra·cel·lu·lar·ly** *adv*

in·tra·ce·re·bral \-sə-ˈrē-brəl, -ˈser-ə-\ *adj* (1881) : situated or occurring within or introduced or administered into the cerebrum ‹~ injections› ‹~ bleeding› — **in·tra·ce·re·bral·ly** \-brə-lē\ *adv*

in·tra·com·pa·ny \-ˈkəmp-nē, -ˈkəm-pə-\ *adj* (1926) : occurring within or taking place between branches or employees of a company ‹~ transactions›

in·tra·cra·ni·al \-ˈkrā-nē-əl\ *adj* (ca. 1849) : existing or occurring within the cranium; *also* : affecting or involving intracranial structures — **in·tra·cra·ni·al·ly** \-nē-ə-lē\ *adv*

in·trac·ta·ble \(ˌ)in-ˈtrak-tə-bəl\ *adj* [L *intractabilis,* fr. *in-* + *tractabilis* tractable] (1531) **1 :** not easily governed, managed, or directed ‹~ problems› **2 :** not easily manipulated or wrought ‹~ metal› **3 :** not easily relieved or cured ‹~ pain› ***syn*** see UNRULY — **in·trac·ta·bil·i·ty** \(ˌ)in-ˌtrak-tə-ˈbi-lə-tē\ *n* — **in·trac·ta·bly** \-blē\ *adv*

in·tra·cu·ta·ne·ous \ˌin-trə-kyü-ˈtā-nē-əs, -(ˌ)trä-\ *adj* (1885) : INTRADERMAL — **in·tra·cu·ta·ne·ous·ly** *adv*

in·tra·day \ˈin-trə-ˌdā, -(ˌ)trä-\ *adj* (1950) : occurring in the course of a single day ‹the market showed wide ~ fluctuations›

in·tra·der·mal \ˌin-trə-ˈdər-məl, -(ˌ)trä-\ *adj* (ca. 1900) : situated, occurring, or done within or between the layers of the skin; *also* : administered by entering the skin ‹~ injections› — **in·tra·der·mal·ly** \-mə-lē\ *adv*

intradermal test *n* (1916) : a test for immunity or hypersensitivity made by injecting a minute amount of diluted antigen into the skin

in·tra·dos \ˈin-trə-ˌdäs, -ˌdō; in-ˈtrā-ˌdäs\ *n, pl* **-dos** \-ˌdōz, -ˌdäs\ *or* **-dos·es** \-ˌdä-səz\ [F, fr. L *intra* within + F *dos* back — more at DOSSIER] (1772) : the interior curve of an arch — see ARCH illustration

in·tra·fal·lo·pi·an \ˌin-trə-fə-ˈlō-pē-ən\ *adj* (1976) : occurring within a fallopian tube

in·tra·ga·lac·tic \ˌin-trə-gə-ˈlak-tik, -(ˌ)trä-\ *adj* (1964) : situated or occurring within the confines of a single galaxy

in·tra·gen·ic \-ˈje-nik\ *adj* (1937) : being or occurring within a gene ‹~ recombination› ‹~ mutation›

in·tra·mo·lec·u·lar \-mə-ˈle-kyə-lər\ *adj* [ISV] (1884) : existing or acting within the molecule; *also* : formed by reaction between different parts of the same molecule — **in·tra·mo·lec·u·lar·ly** *adv*

in·tra·mu·ral \-ˈmyu̇r-əl\ *adj* (1846) **1 a :** being or occurring within the limits usu. of a community, organization, or institution ‹~ squabbles› **b :** competed only within the student body ‹~ sports› **2 :** situated or occurring within the substance of the walls of an organ — **in·tra·mu·ral·ly** \-ə-lē\ *adv*

in·tra·mus·cu·lar \-ˈməs-kyə-lər\ *adj* [ISV] (1874) : situated in, occurring in, or administered by entering a muscle ‹an ~ injection› — **in·tra·mus·cu·lar·ly** *adv*

in·tra·na·sal \-ˈnā-zəl\ *adj* (1886) : lying within or administered by way of the nasal structures — **in·tra·na·sal·ly** \-ˈnāz-lē, -ˈnā-zə-\ *adv*

in·tra·net \ˈin-trə-ˌnet\ *n* (1993) : a network operating like the World Wide Web but having access restricted to a limited group of authorized users (as employees of a company)

intrans *abbr* intransitive

in·tran·si·geance \in-ˈtran(t)-sə-jən(t)s, -ˈtran-zə-\ *n* [F] (1899) : INTRANSIGENCE — **in·tran·si·geant** \-jənt\ *adj or n* — **in·tran·si·geant·ly** *adv*

in·tran·si·gence \-jən(t)s\ *n* (1882) : the quality or state of being intransigent

in·tran·si·gent \-jənt\ *adj* [Sp *intransigente,* fr. *in-* + *transigente,* prp. of *transigir* to compromise, fr. L *transigere* to come to an agreement — more at TRANSACT] (ca. 1879) : characterized by refusal to compromise or to abandon an extreme position or attitude : UNCOMPROMISING ‹~ in their opposition› ‹an ~ attitude› — **intransigent** *n* — **in·tran·si·gent·ly** *adv*

in·tran·si·tive \(ˌ)in-ˈtran(t)-sə-tiv, -ˈtran-zə-; -ˈtran(t)s-tiv\ *adj* [LL *intransitivus,* fr. L *in-* + LL *transitivus* transitive] (1612) : not transitive; *esp* : characterized by not having or containing a direct object ‹an ~ verb› — **in·tran·si·tive·ly** *adv* — **in·tran·si·tive·ness** *n* — **in·tran·si·tiv·i·ty** \(ˌ)in-ˌtran(t)-sə-ˈti-və-tē, -ˌtran-zə-\ *n*

in·tra·oc·u·lar \ˌin-trə-ˈä-kyə-lər, -(ˌ)trä-\ *adj* [ISV] (1872) : implanted in, occurring in, or administered by entering the eyeball ‹~ pressure› — **in·tra·oc·u·lar·ly** *adv*

in·tra·per·i·to·ne·al \ˌin-trə-ˌper-ə-tə-ˈnē-əl\ *adj* (ca. 1836) : existing within or administered by entry into the peritoneum ‹~ chemotherapy› — **in·tra·per·i·to·ne·al·ly** \-ˈnē-ə-lē\ *adv*

in·tra·per·son·al \-ˈpərs-nəl, -ˈpər-sə-nəl\ *adj* (1909) : occurring within the individual mind or self ‹~ concerns of the aged›

in·tra·plate \ˈin-trə-ˌplāt, -(ˌ)trä-\ *adj* (1973) **:** relating to or occurring within the interior of a tectonic plate ⟨an ~ earthquake⟩

in·tra·pop·u·la·tion \ˈin-trə-ˌpä-pyə-ˈlā-shən, -(ˌ)trä-\ *adj* (1959) **:** occurring within or taking place between members of a population

in·tra·pre·neur \ˌin-trə-prə-ˈnər, -ˈnu̇r, -ˈnyu̇r\ *n* [*intra-* + *entrepreneur*] (1978) **:** a corporate executive who develops new enterprises within the corporation — **in·tra·pre·neur·ial** \-ˈnər-ē-əl, -ˈn(y)u̇r-\ *adj*

in·tra·psy·chic \ˌin-trə-ˈsī-kik, -(ˌ)trä-\ *adj* (1917) **:** being or occurring within the psyche, mind, or personality — **in·tra·psy·chi·cal·ly** \-ki-k(ə-)lē\ *adv*

in·tra·spe·cies \-ˈspē-(ˌ)shēz, -(ˌ)sēz\ *adj* (1927) **:** INTRASPECIFIC

in·tra·spe·cif·ic \-spi-ˈsi-fik\ *adj* (1919) **:** occurring within a species or involving members of one species ⟨~ competition⟩

in·tra·state \-ˈstāt\ *adj* (1903) **:** existing or occurring within a state

in·tra·the·cal \-ˈthē-kəl\ *adj* (1887) **:** introduced into or occurring in the space under the arachnoid membrane of the brain or spinal cord ⟨~ drugs⟩ — **in·tra·the·cal·ly** \-k(ə-)lē\ *adv*

in·tra·tho·rac·ic \-thə-ˈra-sik\ *adj* [ISV] (1862) **:** situated or occurring within the thorax ⟨~ pressure⟩ — **in·tra·tho·rac·i·cal·ly** *adv*

in·tra·uter·ine \-ˈyü-tə-rən, -ˌrīn\ *adj* [ISV] (ca. 1836) **:** situated, used, or occurring within the uterus ⟨~ insemination⟩; *also* **:** involving the part of development that takes place in the uterus ⟨~ mortality⟩

intrauterine device *n* (1964) **:** a device inserted into and left in the uterus to prevent effective conception — called also *intrauterine contraceptive device, IUD*

in·tra·vas·cu·lar \ˌin-trə-ˈvas-kyə-lər, -(ˌ)trä-\ *adj* (1876) **:** situated in, occurring in, or administered by entry into a blood vessel ⟨~ thrombosis⟩ ⟨an ~ injection⟩ — **in·tra·vas·cu·lar·ly** *adv*

in·tra·ve·nous \ˌin-trə-ˈvē-nəs\ *adj* [ISV] (ca. 1849) **:** situated, performed, or occurring within or entering by way of a vein; *also* **:** used in or using intravenous procedures — **in·tra·ve·nous·ly** *adv*

in·tra·ven·tric·u·lar \ˌin-trə-ven-ˈtri-kyə-lər, -(ˌ)trä-\ *adj* (1875) **:** situated within, occurring within, or administered into a ventricle ⟨~ hemorrhage⟩ — **in·tra·ven·tric·u·lar·ly** *adv*

in·tra·vi·tal \-ˈvī-tᵊl\ *adj* [ISV] (ca. 1890) **1 :** performed upon or found in a living subject **2 :** having or utilizing the property of staining cells within a living body — compare SUPRAVITAL — **in·tra·vi·tal·ly** \-tᵊl-ē\ *adv*

in·tra·vi·tam \-ˈvī-ˌtam, -ˈwē-ˌtäm\ *adj* [NL *intra vitam* during life] (1881) **:** INTRAVITAL

in·tra·zon·al \ˌin-trə-ˈzō-nᵊl, -(ˌ)trä-\ *adj* (1927) **:** of, relating to, or being a soil or a major soil group marked by relatively well-developed characteristics that are determined primarily by essentially local factors (as the parent material) rather than climate and vegetation — compare AZONAL, ZONAL

intreat *archaic var of* ENTREAT

intrench *var of* ENTRENCH

in·trep·id \in-ˈtre-pəd\ *adj* [L *intrepidus,* fr. *in-* + *trepidus* alarmed — more at TREPIDATION] (1680) **:** characterized by resolute fearlessness, fortitude, and endurance ⟨an ~ explorer⟩ — **in·tre·pid·i·ty** \ˌin-trə-ˈpi-də-tē\ *n* — **in·trep·id·ly** \in-ˈtre-pəd-lē\ *adv* — **in·trep·id·ness** *n*

in·tri·ca·cy \ˈin-tri-kə-sē\ *n, pl* **-cies** (1602) **1 :** the quality or state of being intricate **2 :** something intricate ⟨the *intricacies* of a plot⟩

in·tri·cate \ˈin-tri-kət\ *adj* [ME, fr. L *intricatus,* pp. of *intricare* to entangle, fr. *in-* + *tricae* trifles, complications] (15c) **1 :** having many complexly interrelating parts or elements **:** COMPLICATED ⟨~ machinery⟩ ⟨an ~ plot⟩ **2 :** difficult to resolve or analyze ***syn*** see COMPLEX — **in·tri·cate·ly** *adv* — **in·tri·cate·ness** *n*

in·tri·gant *or* **in·tri·guant** \ˌin-trē-ˈgänt, ˌan-, -ˈgä^{n}\ *n* [F *intrigant,* fr. It *intrigante,* prp. of *intrigare*] (1781) **:** one that intrigues

1**in·trigue** \ˈin-ˌtrēg, in-ˈ\ *n* [F intricate affair, fr. It *intrigo,* fr. *intrigare* to entangle, fr. L *intricare*] (1609) **1 a :** a secret scheme **:** MACHINATION **b :** the practice of engaging in intrigues **2 :** a clandestine love affair ***syn*** see PLOT

2**in·trigue** \in-ˈtrēg\ *vb* **in·trigued; in·trigu·ing** *vt* (1612) **1 :** CHEAT, TRICK **2 :** to accomplish by intrigue ⟨*intrigued* myself into the club⟩ **3** *obs* **:** ENTANGLE **4 :** to arouse the interest, desire, or curiosity of ⟨*intrigued* by the tale⟩ ~ *vi* **:** to carry on an intrigue; *esp* **:** PLOT, SCHEME — **in·trigu·er** *n*

intriguing *adj* (1752) **:** engaging the interest to a marked degree **:** FASCINATING ⟨an ~ story⟩

in·trigu·ing·ly \-giŋ-lē\ *adv* (1742) **1 :** in an intriguing manner **2 :** as a matter of marked interest

in·trin·sic \in-ˈtrin-zik, -ˈtrin(t)-sik\ *adj* [F *intrinsèque* internal, fr. LL *intrinsecus,* fr. L, adv., inwardly; akin to L *intra* within — more at INTRA-] (1635) **1 a :** belonging to the essential nature or constitution of a thing ⟨the ~ worth of a gem⟩ ⟨the ~ brightness of a star⟩ **b :** being or relating to a semiconductor in which the concentration of charge carriers is characteristic of the material itself instead of the content of any impurities it contains **2 a :** originating or due to causes within a body, organ, or part ⟨an ~ metabolic disease⟩ **b :** originating and included wholly within an organ or part ⟨~ muscles⟩ — compare EXTRINSIC 1b — **in·trin·si·cal·ly** \-zi-k(ə-)lē, -si-\ *adv*

in·trin·si·cal \-zi-kəl, -si-\ *adj* (ca. 1548) *archaic* **:** INTRINSIC

intrinsic factor *n* (1932) **:** a substance produced by normal gastrointestinal mucosa that facilitates absorption of vitamin B_{12}

in·tro \ˈin-(ˌ)trō\ *n, pl* **intros** (ca. 1899) **:** INTRODUCTION

intro- *prefix* [L, fr. *intro* inside, to the inside, fr. OL **interus,* adj., inward] **1 :** in **:** into ⟨*intro*jection⟩ **2 :** inward **:** within ⟨*intro*vert⟩ — compare EXTRO-

introd *abbr* introduction

in·tro·duce \ˌin-trə-ˈdüs, -ˈdyüs\ *vt* **-duced; -duc·ing** [ME, fr. L *introducere,* fr. *intro-* + *ducere* to lead — more at TOW] (15c) **1 :** to lead or bring in esp. for the first time ⟨~ a nonnative species⟩ **2 a :** to bring into play **b :** to bring into practice or use **:** INSTITUTE **3 :** to lead to or make known by a formal act, announcement, or recommendation: as **a :** to cause to be acquainted **b :** to present formally at court or into society **c :** to present or announce formally or officially or by an official reading ⟨~ legislation⟩ **d :** to make preliminary explanatory or laudatory remarks about **e :** to bring (as an actor or singer) before the public for the first time **4 :** PLACE, INSERT ⟨~ foreign genes into crops⟩ **5 :** to bring to a knowledge of something ⟨*introduced* them to new ideas⟩ — **in·tro·duc·er** *n*

syn INTRODUCE, INSERT, INSINUATE, INTERPOLATE, INTERCALATE, INTERPOSE, INTERJECT mean to put between or among others. INTRODUCE is a general term for bringing or placing a thing or person into a group or body already in existence ⟨*introduced* a new topic into the conversation⟩. INSERT implies putting into a fixed or open space between or among ⟨*inserted* a clause in the contract⟩. INSINUATE implies introducing gradually or by gentle pressure ⟨*insinuated* himself into the group⟩. INTERPOLATE applies to the inserting of something extraneous or spurious ⟨*interpolated* her own comments into the report⟩. INTERCALATE suggests an intrusive inserting of something in an existing series or sequence ⟨new chapters *intercalated* with the old⟩. INTERPOSE suggests inserting an obstruction or cause of delay ⟨*interpose* barriers to communication⟩. INTERJECT implies an abrupt or forced introduction ⟨*interjected* a question⟩.

in·tro·duc·tion \ˌin-trə-ˈdək-shən\ *n* [ME *introduccioun* act of introducing, fr. AF *introduction,* fr. L *introduction-, introductio,* fr. *introducere*] (14c) **1 :** something that introduces: as **a** (1) **:** a part of a book or treatise preliminary to the main portion (2) **:** a preliminary treatise or course of study **b :** a short introductory musical passage **2 :** the act or process of introducing **:** the state of being introduced **3 :** a putting in **:** INSERTION **4 :** something introduced; *specif* **:** a new or exotic plant or animal

in·tro·duc·to·ry \ˌin-trə-ˈdək-t(ə-)rē\ *adj* (1605) **:** of, relating to, or being a first step that sets something going or in proper perspective ⟨an ~ course in calculus⟩ — **in·tro·duc·to·ri·ly** \-t(ə-)rə-lē\ *adv*

in·tro·gres·sion \ˌin-trə-ˈgre-shən\ *n* [*intro-* + *-gression* (as in *regression*)] (1938) **:** the entry or introduction of a gene from one gene complex into another (as by hybridization) — **in·tro·gres·sant** \-ˈgre-sᵊnt\ *adj or n* — **in·tro·gres·sive** \-ˈgre-siv\ *adj*

in·troit \ˈin-ˌtrȯit, -ˌtrō-ət, in-ˈ\ *n* [ME, fr. ML *introitus,* fr. L, entrance, fr. *introire* to go in, fr. *intro-* + *ire* to go — more at ISSUE] (15c) **1** *often cap* **:** the first part of the traditional proper of the Mass consisting of an antiphon, verse from a psalm, and the Gloria Patri **2 :** a piece of music sung or played at the beginning of a worship service

in·tro·ject \ˌin-trə-ˈjekt\ *vt* [back-formation fr. *introjection,* fr. ISV *intro-* + pro*jection*] (1924) **:** to incorporate (attitudes or ideas) into one's personality unconsciously — **in·tro·jec·tion** \-ˈjek-shən\ *n*

in·tro·mis·sion \ˌin-trə-ˈmi-shən\ *n* [F, fr. MF, fr. ML *intromission-, intromissio,* fr. L *intromittere*] (1601) **:** the act or process of intromitting; *esp* **:** the insertion or period of insertion of the penis in the vagina in copulation

in·tro·mit \-ˈmit\ *vt* **-mit·ted; -mit·ting** [L *intromittere,* fr. *intro-* + *mittere* to send] (ca. 1588) **:** to send or put in **:** INSERT — **in·tro·mit·tent** \-ˈmi-tᵊnt\ *adj* — **in·tro·mit·ter** \-tər\ *n*

in·tron \ˈin-ˌträn\ *n* [*inter*vening sequence + 2*-on*] (1978) **:** a polynucleotide sequence in a nucleic acid that does not code information for protein synthesis and is removed before translation of messenger RNA — compare EXON

in·trorse \ˈin-ˌtrȯrs\ *adj* [L *introrsus,* adv., inward, fr. *intro-* + *versus* toward, fr. pp. of *vertere* to turn — more at WORTH] (1842) **:** facing inward or toward the axis of growth ⟨an ~ anther⟩

in·tro·spec·tion \ˌin-trə-ˈspek-shən\ *n* [L *introspectus,* pp. of *introspicere* to look inside, fr. *intro-* + *specere* to look — more at SPY] (ca. 1677) **:** a reflective looking inward **:** an examination of one's own thoughts and feelings — **in·tro·spect** \-ˈspekt\ *vb* — **in·tro·spec·tion·al** \-ˈspek-shnəl, -shə-nᵊl\ *adj* — **in·tro·spec·tive** \-ˈspek-tiv\ *adj* — **in·tro·spec·tive·ly** *adv* — **in·tro·spec·tive·ness** *n*

in·tro·spec·tion·ism \-shə-ˌni-zəm\ *n* (1922) **:** a doctrine that psychology must be based essentially on data derived from introspection — compare BEHAVIORISM — **in·tro·spec·tion·ist** \-sh(ə-)nist\ *or* **in·tro·spec·tion·is·tic** \-ˌspek-shə-ˈnis-tik\ *adj* — **introspectionist** *n*

in·tro·ver·sion \ˌin-trə-ˈvər-zhən, -shən\ *n* [*intro-* + *-version* (as in *diversion*)] (1654) **1 :** the act of introverting **:** the state of being introverted **2 :** the state of or tendency toward being wholly or predominantly concerned with and interested in one's own mental life — **in·tro·ver·sive** \-ˈvər-siv, -ziv\ *adj* — **in·tro·ver·sive·ly** *adv*

1**in·tro·vert** \ˈin-trə-ˌvərt\ *vt* [*intro-* + *-vert* (as in *divert*)] (1669) **:** to turn inward or in upon itself: as **a :** to concentrate or direct upon oneself **b :** to produce psychological introversion in

2**introvert** *n* (1883) **1 :** something (as the retractile proboscis of some worms) that is or can be drawn in esp. by invagination **2 :** one whose personality is characterized by introversion; *broadly* **:** a reserved or shy person

in·trude \in-ˈtrüd\ *vb* **in·trud·ed; in·trud·ing** [ME, fr. L *intrudere* to thrust in, fr. *in-* + *trudere* to thrust — more at THREAT] *vi* (15c) **1 :** to thrust oneself in without invitation, permission, or welcome **2 :** to enter as a geological intrusion ~ *vt* **1 :** to thrust or force in or upon someone or something esp. without permission, welcome, or fitness ⟨*intruded* himself into their lives⟩ **2 :** to cause to enter as if by force — **in·trud·er** *n*

in·tru·sion \in-ˈtrü-zhən\ *n* [ME, fr. AF, fr. ML *intrusion-, intrusio,* fr. L *intrudere*] (15c) **1 :** the act of intruding or the state of being intruded; *esp* **:** the act of wrongfully entering upon, seizing, or taking possession of the property of another **2 :** the forcible entry of molten rock or magma into or between other rock formations; *also* **:** the intruded magma

in·tru·sive \in-ˈtrü-siv, -ziv\ *adj* (15c) **1 a :** characterized by intrusion **b :** intruding where one is not welcome or invited **2 a :** projecting inward ⟨an ~ arm of the sea⟩ **b** (1) *of a rock* **:** having been forced while in a plastic state into cavities or between layers (2) **:** PLUTONIC **3 :** having nothing that corresponds to a sound or letter in orthography or etymon ⟨~ \t\ in \ˈmints\ for *mince*⟩ ***syn*** see IMPERTINENT — **intrusive** *n* — **in·tru·sive·ly** *adv* — **in·tru·sive·ness** *n*

intrust *var of* ENTRUST

in·tu·ba·tion \ˌin-(ˌ)tü-ˈbā-shən, -(ˌ)tyü-, -tə-\ *n* (1887) **:** the introduction of a tube into a hollow organ (as the trachea) — **in·tu·bate** \ˈin-(ˌ)tü-ˌbāt, -(ˌ)tyü-, -tə-\ *vt*

\ə\ **abut** \ᵊ\ **kitten**, F **table** \ər\ **further** \a\ **ash** \ā\ **ace** \ä\ **mop, mar** \au̇\ **out** \ch\ **chin** \e\ **bet** \ē\ **easy** \g\ **go** \i\ **hit** \ī\ **ice** \j\ **job** \ŋ\ **sing** \ō\ **go** \ȯ\ **law** \ȯi\ **boy** \th\ **thin** \t͟h\ **the** \ü\ **loot** \u̇\ **foot** \y\ **yet** \zh\ **vision, beige** \k̲, ^{n}, œ, ue, ʸ\ *see* Guide to Pronunciation

in·tu·it \in-ˈtü-ət, -ˈtyü-\ *vt* (1855) **:** to know, sense, or understand by intuition — **in·tu·it·able** \-ə-tə-bəl\ *adj*

in·tu·i·tion \ˌin-tü-ˈi-shən, -tyü-\ *n* [ME *intuycyon,* fr. LL *intuition-, intuitio* act of contemplating, fr. L *intuēri* to look at, contemplate, fr. *in-* + *tuēri* to look at] (15c) **1 :** quick and ready insight **2 a :** immediate apprehension or cognition **b :** knowledge or conviction gained by intuition **c :** the power or faculty of attaining to direct knowledge or cognition without evident rational thought and inference — **in·tu·i·tion·al** \-ˈish-nəl, -ˈi-shə-n^{ə}l\ *adj*

in·tu·i·tion·ism \ˌin-tü-ˈi-shə-ˌni-zəm\ *n* (1847) **1 a :** a doctrine that objects of perception are intuitively known to be real **b :** a doctrine that there are basic truths intuitively known **2 :** a doctrine that right or wrong or fundamental principles about what is right and wrong can be intuited **3 :** a philosophical thesis that human beings have a direct intuitive understanding of mathematics and that rejects the principle that every mathematical statement must be true or false — **in·tu·i·tion·ist** \-sh(ə-)nist\ *adj or n*

in·tu·i·tive \in-ˈtü-ə-tiv, -ˈtyü-\ *adj* (ca. 1645) **1 a :** known or perceived by intuition **:** directly apprehended ⟨had an ~ awareness of his sister's feelings⟩ **b :** knowable by intuition ⟨~ truths⟩ **c :** based on or agreeing with intuition ⟨~ responses⟩ ⟨makes ~ sense⟩ **d :** readily learned or understood ⟨software with an ~ interface⟩ **2 :** knowing or perceiving by intuition **3 :** possessing or given to intuition or insight ⟨an ~ mind⟩ — **in·tu·i·tive·ly** *adv* — **in·tu·i·tive·ness** *n*

in·tu·mes·cence \ˌin-tü-ˈme-s^{ə}n(t)s, -tyü-\ *n* [F, fr. L *intumescere* to swell up, fr. *in-* + *tumescere* to swell — more at TUMESCENCE] (1650) **:** a swollen or enlarged part of a plant or animal; *also* **:** the process of swelling up or enlarging

in·tu·mes·cent \-s^{ə}nt\ *adj* (1953) *of paint* **:** swelling and charring when exposed to flame

in·tus·sus·cept \ˌin-tə-sə-ˈsept\ *vb* [back-formation fr. *intussusception*] *vt* (1802) **:** to take in by or cause to undergo intussusception; *esp* **:** INVAGINATE ~ *vi* **:** to undergo intussusception

in·tus·sus·cep·tion \-ˈsep-shən\ *n* [L *intus* within + *susception-, susceptio* action of undertaking, fr. *suscipere* to take up — more at SUSCEPTIBLE] (1707) **:** a drawing in of something from without: as **a :** INVAGINATION; *esp* **:** the slipping of a length of intestine into an adjacent portion usu. producing obstruction **b :** the assimilation of new material and its dispersal among preexistent matter — **in·tus·sus·cep·tive** \-ˈsep-tiv\ *adj*

In·u·it *also* **In·nu·it** \ˈi-nü-wət, -nyü-\ *n* [Inuit *inuit,* pl. of *inuk* person] (1765) **1** *pl* **Inuit** *or* **Inuits** *also* **Innuit** *or* **Innuits a** (1) **:** the Eskimo people of No. America and Greenland (2) **:** the Eskimo people of Canada **b :** a member of such people **2 a :** ESKIMO 2 **b :** the group of Eskimo dialects spoken from northwestern Canada to Greenland

Inuk \i-ˈnük\ *n, pl* **Inuit** [Inuit *inuk*] (1951) **:** a member of the Inuit people

Inuk·ti·tut \i-ˈnük-tə-ˌtüt\ *n* [Inuit, fr. *inuk* person + *-titut* like, in the manner of] (1974) **:** the group of Eskimo dialects spoken by the Inuit of central and eastern arctic Canada

in·u·lin \ˈin-yə-lən\ *n* [prob. fr. G *Inulin,* fr. L *inula* elecampane] (1813) **:** a white plant polysaccharide used esp. to improve the flavor and texture of low-fat and low-sugar processed foods

in·unc·tion \i-ˈnəŋ(k)-shən\ *n* [ME, fr. L *inunction-, inunctio,* fr. *inunguere* to anoint — more at ANOINT] (15c) **:** an act of applying oil or ointment **:** ANOINTING

in·un·date \ˈi-(ˌ)nən-ˌdāt\ *vt* **-dat·ed; -dat·ing** [L *inundatus,* pp. of *inundare,* fr. *in-* + *unda* wave — more at WATER] (1590) **1 :** to cover with a flood **:** OVERFLOW **2 :** OVERWHELM ⟨was *inundated* with phone calls⟩ — **in·un·da·tion** \ˌi-(ˌ)nən-ˈdā-shən\ *n* — **in·un·da·tor** \ˈi-(ˌ)nən-ˌdā-tər\ *n* — **in·un·da·to·ry** \i-ˈnən-də-ˌtȯr-ē\ *adj*

Inu·pi·at \i-ˈnü-pē-ˌät, -ˈnyü-\ *also* **Inu·pi·aq** \-ˌäk\ *n* [Inupiat *in^{y}upiaq,* pl. *in^{y}upiat,* lit., real person] (1967) **1** *pl* **Inupiat** *or* **Inupiats** *also* **Inupiaq** *or* **Inupiaqs :** a member of the Eskimo people of northern Alaska **2 :** the language of the Inupiat people

in·ure \i-ˈnu̇r, -ˈnyu̇r\ *vb* **in·ured; in·ur·ing** [ME *enuren,* fr. *in ure* customary, fr. *putten in ure* to use, put into practice, part trans. of AF *mettre en ovre, en uevre*] *vt* (15c) **:** to accustom to accept something undesirable ⟨children *inured* to violence⟩ ~ *vi* **:** to become of advantage ⟨policies that ~ to the benefit of employees⟩ — **in·ure·ment** \-mənt\ *n*

in·urn \i-ˈnərn\ *vt* (1602) **1 :** ENTOMB **2 :** to place (as cremated remains) in an urn — **in·urn·ment** \-mənt\ *n*

in utero \in-ˈyü-tə-ˌrō\ *adv or adj* [L] (1713) **:** in the uterus **:** before birth ⟨a disease acquired *in utero*⟩ ⟨an *in utero* diagnosis⟩

in·utile \(ˌ)in-ˈyü-t^{ə}l, -ˌtī(-ə)l\ *adj* [ME, fr. AF, fr. L *inutilis,* fr. *in-* + *utilis* useful — more at UTILITY] (15c) **:** USELESS, UNUSABLE — **in·util·i·ty** \ˌin-yü-ˈti-lə-tē\ *n*

inv *abbr* **1** inventor **2** invoice

in vac·uo \in-ˈva-kyə-ˌwō\ *adv* [NL] (1660) **:** in a vacuum

in·vade \in-ˈvād\ *vt* **in·vad·ed; in·vad·ing** [ME, fr. L *invadere,* fr. *in-* + *vadere* to go — more at WADE] (15c) **1 :** to enter for conquest or plunder **2 :** to encroach upon **:** INFRINGE **3 a :** to spread over or into as if invading **:** PERMEATE ⟨doubts ~ his mind⟩ **b :** to affect injuriously and progressively ⟨gangrene ~s healthy tissue⟩ ***syn*** see TRESPASS — **in·vad·er** *n*

in·vag·i·nate \in-ˈva-jə-ˌnāt\ *vb* **-nat·ed; -nat·ing** [ML *invaginatus,* pp. of *invaginare,* fr. L *in-* + *vagina* sheath] *vt* (ca. 1656) **1 :** ENCLOSE, SHEATHE **2 :** to fold in so that an outer becomes an inner surface ~ *vi* **:** to undergo invagination

in·vag·i·na·tion \-ˌva-jə-ˈnā-shən\ *n* (ca. 1658) **1 :** an act or process of invaginating; *specif* **:** the formation of a gastrula by an infolding of part of the wall of the blastula **2 :** an invaginated part

[1]**in·val·id** \(ˌ)in-ˈva-ləd\ *adj* [L *invalidus* weak, fr. *in-* + *validus* strong — more at VALID] (1542) **:** not valid: **a :** being without foundation or force in fact, truth, or law ⟨an ~ assumption⟩ ⟨declared the will ~⟩ **b :** logically inconsequent — **in·val·id·ly** \-lē\ *adv*

[2]**in·va·lid** \ˈin-və-ləd, *Brit usu* -ˌlēd\ *adj* [L & F; F *invalide,* fr. L *invalidus*] (1642) **1 :** suffering from disease or disability **:** SICKLY **2 :** of, relating to, or suited to one that is sick ⟨an ~ chair⟩

[3]**invalid** *same as* [2]\ *n* (1701) **:** one who is sickly or disabled

[4]**in·va·lid** \ˈin-və-ləd, -ˌlid, *Brit usu* -ˌlēd *or* ˌin-və-ˈlēd\ *vt* (1787) **1 :** to remove from active duty by reason of sickness or disability **2 :** to make sickly or disabled

in·val·i·date \(ˌ)in-ˈva-lə-ˌdāt\ *vt* (1649) **:** to make invalid; *esp* **:** to weaken or destroy the cogency of ***syn*** see NULLIFY — **in·val·i·da·tion** \-ˌva-lə-ˈdā-shən\ *n* — **in·val·i·da·tor** \in-ˈva-lə-ˌdā-tər\ *n*

in·va·lid·ism \ˈin-və-lə-ˌdi-zəm\ *n* (1794) **:** a chronic condition of being an invalid

in·val·id·i·ty \ˌin-və-ˈli-də-tē, -va-\ *n, pl* **-ties** (ca. 1550) **1 :** lack of validity or cogency **2 :** incapacitating bodily disability; *also* **:** INVALIDISM

in·valu·able \(ˌ)in-ˈval-yə-bəl, -yə-wə-bəl, -yü(-ə)-bəl\ *adj* [[1]*in-* + *value,* v. + *-able*] (1576) **:** valuable beyond estimation **:** PRICELESS ⟨providing ~ assistance⟩ — **in·valu·able·ness** *n* — **in·valu·ably** \-blē\ *adv*

In·var \ˈin-ˌvär\ *trademark* — used for an alloy of iron and nickel that does not expand much when heated

in·vari·able \(ˌ)in-ˈver-ē-ə-bəl\ *adj* (15c) **:** not changing or capable of change **:** CONSTANT ⟨an ~ routine⟩ — **in·vari·abil·i·ty** \-ˌver-ē-ə-ˈbi-lə-tē\ *n* — **invariable** *n*

in·vari·ably \-blē\ *adv* (1646) **:** on every occasion **:** ALWAYS ⟨~ late⟩

in·vari·ance \(ˌ)in-ˈver-ē-ən(t)s\ *n* (1878) **:** the quality or state of being invariant

in·vari·ant \-ənt\ *adj* (1874) **:** CONSTANT, UNCHANGING; *specif* **:** unchanged by specified mathematical or physical operations or transformations ⟨~ factor⟩ — **invariant** *n*

in·va·sion \in-ˈvā-zhən\ *n* [ME *invasioune,* fr. AF *invasion,* fr. LL *invasion-, invasio,* fr. L *invadere* to invade] (15c) **1 :** an act of invading; *esp* **:** incursion of an army for conquest or plunder **2 :** the incoming or spread of something usu. hurtful

in·va·sive \-siv, -ziv\ *adj* (1598) **1 :** of, relating to, or characterized by military aggression **2 :** tending to spread; *esp* **:** tending to invade healthy tissue ⟨~ cancer cells⟩ **3 :** tending to infringe **4 :** involving entry into the living body (as by incision or by insertion of an instrument) ⟨~ diagnostic techniques⟩ — **in·va·sive·ness** *n*

[1]**in·vec·tive** \in-ˈvek-tiv\ *adj* [ME *invectif,* fr. MF, fr. L *invectivus,* fr. *invectus,* pp. of *invehere*] (15c) **:** of, relating to, or characterized by insult or abuse — **in·vec·tive·ly** *adv* — **in·vec·tive·ness** *n*

[2]**invective** *n* (1523) **1 :** an abusive expression or speech **2 :** insulting or abusive language **:** VITUPERATION ***syn*** see ABUSE

in·veigh \in-ˈvā\ *vi* [L *invehi* to attack, inveigh, pass. of *invehere* to carry in, fr. *in-* + *vehere* to carry — more at WAY] (1529) **:** to protest or complain bitterly or vehemently **:** RAIL — **in·veigh·er** *n*

in·vei·gle \in-ˈvā-gəl *sometimes* -ˈvē-\ *vt* **in·vei·gled; in·vei·gling** \-g(ə-)liŋ\ [AF *enveegler, aveogler, avogler* to blind, hoodwink, fr. *avogle, enveugle* blind, fr. ML *ab oculis,* lit., lacking eyes] (1539) **1 :** to win over by wiles **:** ENTICE **2 :** to acquire by ingenuity or flattery **:** WANGLE ⟨*inveigled* her way into a promotion⟩ ***syn*** see LURE — **in·vei·gle·ment** \-gəl-mənt\ *n* — **in·vei·gler** \-g(ə-)lər\ *n*

in·vent \in-ˈvent\ *vt* [ME, fr. L *inventus,* pp. of *invenire* to come upon, find, fr. *in-* + *venire* to come — more at COME] (15c) **1** *archaic* **:** FIND, DISCOVER **2 :** to devise by thinking **:** FABRICATE **3 :** to produce (as something useful) for the first time through the use of the imagination or of ingenious thinking and experiment — **in·ven·tor** \-ˈven-tər\ *n* — **in·ven·tress** \-ˈven-trəs\ *n*

in·ven·tion \in-ˈven(t)-shən\ *n* (14c) **1 :** DISCOVERY, FINDING **2 :** productive imagination **:** INVENTIVENESS **3 a :** something invented: as (1) **:** a product of the imagination; *esp* **:** a false conception (2) **:** a device, contrivance, or process originated after study and experiment **b :** a short keyboard composition featuring two- or three-part counterpoint **4 :** the act or process of inventing

in·ven·tive \in-ˈven-tiv\ *adj* (15c) **1 :** adept or prolific at producing inventions **:** CREATIVE ⟨an ~ mind⟩ **2 :** characterized by invention ⟨an ~ method⟩ — **in·ven·tive·ly** *adv* — **in·ven·tive·ness** *n*

[1]**in·ven·to·ry** \ˈin-vən-ˌtȯr-ē\ *n, pl* **-ries** [ME *inventarie, inventorie,* fr. AF *inventaire, inventorie,* fr. L *inventarium,* fr. *inventum* thing found, topic, neut. of *inventus*] (15c) **1 a :** an itemized list of current assets: as (1) **:** a catalog of the property of an individual or estate (2) **:** a list of goods on hand **b :** a survey of natural resources **c :** a list of traits, preferences, attitudes, interests, or abilities used to evaluate personal characteristics or skills **2 :** SURVEY, SUMMARY **3 :** the quantity of goods or materials on hand **:** STOCK **4 :** the act or process of taking an inventory — **in·ven·to·ri·al** \ˌin-vən-ˈtȯr-ē-əl\ *adj* — **in·ven·to·ri·al·ly** \-ē-ə-lē\ *adv*

[2]**inventory** *vt* **-ried; -ry·ing** (1602) **:** to make an inventory of **:** CATALOG

in·ver·ness \ˌin-vər-ˈnes\ *n* [*Inverness,* Scotland] (1859) **:** a loose belted coat having a cape with a close-fitting round collar

[1]**in·verse** \(ˌ)in-ˈvərs, ˈin-ˌ\ *adj* [ME, turned upside down, fr. L *inversus,* fr. pp. of *invertere*] (15c) **1 :** opposite in order, nature, or effect **2 :** being an inverse function ⟨~ sine⟩

[2]**inverse** *n* (ca. 1681) **1 :** something of a contrary nature or quality **:** OPPOSITE, REVERSE **2 :** a proposition or theorem formed by contradicting both the subject and predicate or both the hypothesis and conclusion of a given proposition or theorem ⟨the ~ of "if A then B" is "if not-A then not-B"⟩ — compare CONTRAPOSITIVE **3 a :** INVERSE FUNCTION; *also* **:** an operation (as subtraction) that undoes the effect of another operation **b :** a set element that is related to another element in such a way that the result of applying a given binary operation to them is an identity element of the set

inverse function *n* (1816) **:** a function that is derived from a given function by interchanging the two variables ⟨$y = \sqrt[3]{x}$ is the *inverse function* of $y = x^3$⟩ — compare LOGARITHMIC FUNCTION

in·verse·ly \ˈin-ˌvərs-lē, (ˌ)in-ˈ\ *adv* (1660) **1 :** in an inverse order or manner **2 :** in the manner of inverse variation ⟨varies ~⟩

inversely proportional *adj* (1864) **:** related by inverse variation — compare DIRECTLY PROPORTIONAL

inverse square law *n* (1921) **:** a statement in physics: a given physical quantity (as illumination) varies with the distance from the source inversely as the square of the distance

inverse variation *n* (1936) **1 :** mathematical relationship between two variables which can be expressed by an equation in which the product of two variables is equal to a constant **2 :** an equation or function expressing inverse variation — compare DIRECT VARIATION

in·ver·sion \in-ˈvər-zhən, -shən\ *n* (1586) **1 :** a reversal of position, order, form, or relationship: as **a** (1) **:** a change in normal word order; *esp* **:** the placement of a verb before its subject (2) **:** the process or result of changing or reversing the relative positions of the notes of a musical interval, chord, or phrase **b :** the condition of being turned inward or inside out **c :** a breaking off of a chromosome section and its subsequent reattachment in inverted position; *also* **:** a chromosomal section that has undergone this process **2 :** the act or process of inverting **3 a :** a change in the order of the terms of a mathematical proportion effected by inverting each ratio **b :** the operation of forming the inverse of a magnitude, a function, an operation, or an element **4 a :** the conversion of dextrorotatory sucrose into a levorotatory mixture of glucose and fructose **b :** a change from one stereochemical figuration at a chiral center in a usu. organic molecule to the opposite configuration that is brought about by a reaction in which a substitution of one group is made for a different group **5 :** HOMOSEXUALITY **6 :** an increase of temperature with height through a layer of air

in·ver·sive \-ˈvər-siv, -ziv\ *adj* (1875) **:** marked by inversion

[1]**in·vert** \in-ˈvərt\ *vt* [L *invertere,* fr. *in-* + *vertere* to turn — more at WORTH] (1533) **1 a :** to reverse in position, order, or relationship **b :** to subject to inversion **2 a :** to turn inside out or upside down **b :** to turn inward **3 :** to find the mathematical reciprocal of ⟨to divide using fractions, ∼ the divisor and multiply⟩ ***syn*** see REVERSE

[2]**in·vert** \ˈin-ˌvərt\ *n* (1838) **:** one characterized by inversion; *esp* **:** HOMOSEXUAL

in·ver·tase \in-ˈvər-ˌtās, -ˌtāz; ˈin-vər-ˌ\ *n* [ISV] (1887) **:** an enzyme that catalyzes the hydrolysis of sucrose

in·ver·te·brate \(ˌ)in-ˈvər-tə-brət, -ˌbrāt\ *adj* [NL *invertebratus,* fr. L *in-* + NL *vertebratus* vertebrate] (1832) **1 :** lacking a spinal column; *also* **:** of, relating to, or concerned with invertebrate animals **2 :** lacking in strength or vitality **:** WEAK — **invertebrate** *n*

inverted comma *n* (1789) *chiefly Brit* **:** QUOTATION MARK

in·vert·er \in-ˈvər-tər\ *n* (1611) **1 :** one that inverts **2 :** a device for converting direct current into alternating current

in·vert·ible \in-ˈvər-tə-bəl\ *adj* (1881) **:** capable of being inverted or subjected to inversion ⟨an ∼ matrix⟩

invert sugar *n* (1880) **:** a mixture of dextrose and levulose found in fruits or produced artificially by the inversion of sucrose

[1]**in·vest** \in-ˈvest\ *vt* [L *investire* to clothe, surround, fr. *in-* + *vestis* garment — more at WEAR] (ca. 1534) **1** [ML *investire,* fr. L, to clothe] **a :** to array in the symbols of office or honor **b :** to furnish with power or authority **c :** to grant someone control or authority over **:** VEST **2 :** to cover completely **:** ENVELOP **3 :** CLOTHE, ADORN **4** [MF *investir,* fr. OIt *investire,* fr. L, to surround] **:** to surround with troops or ships so as to prevent escape or entry **5 :** to endow with a quality **:** INFUSE

[2]**invest** *vb* [It *investire* to clothe, invest money, fr. L, to clothe] *vt* (1613) **1 :** to commit (money) in order to earn a financial return **2 :** to make use of for future benefits or advantages ⟨∼*ed* her time wisely⟩ **3 :** to involve or engage esp. emotionally ⟨were deeply ∼*ed* in their children's lives⟩ ∼ *vi* **:** to make an investment — **in·vest·able** \-ˈves-tə-bəl\ *adj* — **in·ves·tor** \-tər\ *n*

in·ves·ti·gate \in-ˈves-tə-ˌgāt\ *vb* **-gat·ed; -gat·ing** [L *investigatus,* pp. of *investigare* to track, investigate, fr. *in-* + *vestigium* footprint, track] *vt* (ca. 1510) **:** to observe or study by close examination and systematic inquiry ∼ *vi* **:** to make a systematic examination; *esp* **:** to conduct an official inquiry — **in·ves·ti·ga·tion** \-ˌves-tə-ˈgā-shən\ *n* — **in·ves·ti·ga·tive** \-ˈves-tə-ˌgā-tiv\ *adj* — **in·ves·ti·ga·tor** \-ˌgā-tər\ *n* — **in·ves·ti·ga·to·ry** \-ˈves-ti-gə-ˌtȯr-ē\ *adj*

in·ves·ti·ga·tion·al \in-ˌves-tə-ˈgā-shnəl, -shə-nᵊl\ *adj* (1905) **1 :** of or relating to investigation ⟨∼ activities⟩ **2 :** relating to or being a drug or medical procedure that is not approved for general use but is under investigation in clinical trials regarding its safety and efficacy ⟨an ∼ new drug⟩

in·ves·ti·ture \in-ˈves-tə-ˌchu̇r, -chər, -ˌtyu̇r, -ˌtu̇r\ *n* [ME, fr. ML *investitura,* fr. *investitus,* pp. of *investire*] (14c) **1 :** the act of establishing in office or ratifying **2 :** something that covers or adorns

[1]**in·vest·ment** \in-ˈves(t)-mənt\ *n* [[1]*invest*] (1597) **1 a** *archaic* **:** VESTMENT **b :** an outer layer **:** ENVELOPE **2 :** INVESTITURE 1 **3 :** BLOCKADE, SIEGE

[2]**investment** *n* [[2]*invest*] (1615) **:** the outlay of money usu. for income or profit **:** capital outlay; *also* **:** the sum invested or the property purchased

investment company *n* (ca. 1917) **:** a company whose primary business is holding securities of other companies purely for investment purposes — compare HOLDING COMPANY

in·vet·er·a·cy \in-ˈve-t(ə-)rə-sē\ *n* [*inveterate* + *-cy*] (ca. 1719) **:** the quality or state of being obstinate or persistent **:** TENACITY

in·vet·er·ate \in-ˈve-t(ə-)rət\ *adj* [ME, fr. L *inveteratus,* fr. pp. of *inveterare* to age (v.t.), fr. *in-* + *veter-, vetus* old — more at WETHER] (14c) **1 :** firmly established by long persistence ⟨the ∼ tendency to overlook the obvious⟩ **2 :** confirmed in a habit **:** HABITUAL ⟨an ∼ liar⟩ — **in·vet·er·ate·ly** *adv*

syn INVETERATE, CONFIRMED, CHRONIC mean firmly established. INVETERATE applies to a habit, attitude, or feeling of such long existence as to be practically ineradicable or unalterable ⟨an *inveterate* smoker⟩. CONFIRMED implies a growing stronger and firmer with time so as to resist change or reform ⟨a *confirmed* bachelor⟩. CHRONIC suggests something that is persistent or endlessly recurrent and troublesome ⟨a *chronic* complainer⟩.

in·vi·a·ble \(ˌ)in-ˈvī-ə-bəl\ *adj* [ISV] (1918) **:** incapable of surviving esp. because of a deleterious genetic constitution — **in·vi·a·bil·i·ty** \-ˌvī-ə-ˈbi-lə-tē\ *n*

in·vid·i·ous \in-ˈvi-dē-əs\ *adj* [L *invidiosus* envious, invidious, fr. *invidia* envy — more at ENVY] (1606) **1 :** tending to cause discontent, animosity, or envy ⟨the ∼ task of arbitration⟩ **2 :** ENVIOUS **3 a :** of an unpleasant or objectionable nature **:** OBNOXIOUS ⟨∼ remarks⟩ **b :** of a kind to cause harm or resentment ⟨an ∼ comparison⟩ — **in·vid·i·ous·ly** *adv* — **in·vid·i·ous·ness** *n*

in·vig·i·late \in-ˈvi-jə-ˌlāt\ *vb* **-lat·ed; -lat·ing** [L *invigilatus,* pp. of *invigilare* to stay awake, be watchful, fr. *in-* + *vigilare* to stay awake — more at VIGILANT] *vi* (1553) **:** to keep watch; *esp, Brit* **:** to supervise students at an examination ∼ *vt* **:** SUPERVISE, MONITOR — **in·vig·i·la·tion** \-ˌvi-jə-ˈlā-shən\ *n* — **in·vig·i·la·tor** \-ˈvi-jə-ˌlā-tər\ *n*

in·vig·o·rate \in-ˈvi-gə-ˌrāt\ *vt* **-rat·ed; -rat·ing** [prob. fr. *in-* + *vigor*] (1646) **:** to give life and energy to **:** ANIMATE; *also* **:** STIMULATE 1 — **in·vig·o·rat·ing·ly** \-ˌrā-tiŋ-lē\ *adv* — **in·vig·o·ra·tion** \-ˌvi-gə-ˈrā-shən\ *n* — **in·vig·o·ra·tor** \-ˈvi-gə-ˌrā-tər\ *n*

in·vin·ci·ble \(ˌ)in-ˈvin(t)-sə-bəl\ *adj* [ME, fr. MF or LL; MF, fr. LL *invincibilis,* fr. L *in-* + *vincere* to conquer — more at VICTOR] (15c) **:** incapable of being conquered, overcome, or subdued ⟨a seemingly ∼ army⟩ — **in·vin·ci·bil·i·ty** \-ˌvin(t)-sə-ˈbi-lə-tē\ *n* — **in·vin·ci·ble·ness** \-ˈvin(t)-sə-bəl-nəs\ *n* — **in·vin·ci·bly** \-blē\ *adv*

in·vi·o·la·ble \(ˌ)in-ˈvī-ə-lə-bəl\ *adj* [ME, fr. MF or L; MF, fr. L *inviolabilis,* fr. *in-* + *violare* to violate] (15c) **1 :** secure from violation or profanation ⟨an ∼ law⟩ **2 :** secure from assault or trespass **:** UNASSAILABLE ⟨∼ borders⟩ — **in·vi·o·la·bil·i·ty** \-ˌvī-ə-lə-ˈbi-lə-tē\ *n* — **in·vi·o·la·ble·ness** \-ˈvī-ə-lə-bəl-nəs\ *n* — **in·vi·o·la·bly** \-blē\ *adv*

in·vi·o·la·cy \(ˌ)in-ˈvī-ə-lə-sē\ *n* (ca. 1846) **:** the quality or state of being inviolate

in·vi·o·late \-ˈvī-ə-lət\ *adj* (15c) **:** not violated or profaned; *esp* **:** PURE — **in·vi·o·late·ly** *adv* — **in·vi·o·late·ness** *n*

in·vis·cid \(ˌ)in-ˈvi-səd\ *adj* (ca. 1889) **1 :** having zero viscosity **2 :** of or relating to an inviscid fluid ⟨∼ flow⟩

in·vis·i·ble \(ˌ)in-ˈvi-zə-bəl\ *adj* [ME, fr. AF, fr. L *invisibilis,* fr. *in-* + *visibilis* visible] (14c) **1 a :** incapable by nature of being seen **b :** inaccessible to view **:** HIDDEN **2 :** IMPERCEPTIBLE, INCONSPICUOUS **3 a :** not appearing in published financial statements **b :** not reflected in statistics — **in·vis·i·bil·i·ty** \-ˌvi-zə-ˈbi-lə-tē\ *n* — **invisible** *n* — **in·vis·i·ble·ness** \-ˈvi-zə-bəl-nəs\ *n* — **in·vis·i·bly** \-blē\ *adv*

invisible hand *n* (1776) **:** a hypothetical economic force that in a freely competitive market works for the benefit of all

in·vi·ta·tion \ˌin-və-ˈtā-shən\ *n* (15c) **1 a :** the act of inviting **b :** an often formal request to be present or participate **2 :** INCENTIVE, INDUCEMENT

in·vi·ta·tion·al \-shnəl, -shə-nᵊl\ *adj* (1918) **1 :** limited to invited participants ⟨an ∼ tournament⟩ **2 :** prepared or entered in response to a request ⟨an ∼ article⟩ — **invitational** *n*

[1]**in·vi·ta·to·ry** \in-ˈvī-tə-ˌtȯr-ē\ *adj* (14c) **:** containing an invitation

[2]**invitatory** *n, pl* **-ries** (14c) **:** an invitatory psalm or antiphon

[1]**in·vite** \in-ˈvīt\ *vt* **in·vit·ed; in·vit·ing** [MF or L; MF *inviter,* fr. L *invitare*] (1533) **1 a :** to offer an incentive or inducement to **:** ENTICE **b :** to increase the likelihood of ⟨∼ trouble⟩ **2 a :** to request the presence or participation of ⟨*invited* us to dinner⟩ **b :** to request formally **c :** to urge politely **:** WELCOME ⟨∼ comments⟩ — **in·vit·er** *n*

[2]**in·vite** \ˈin-ˌvīt\ *n* (1659) **:** INVITATION 1

in·vi·tee \ˌin-və-ˈtē, -ˌvī-\ *n* (1837) **:** an invited person

inviting *adj* (1604) **:** ATTRACTIVE, TEMPTING — **in·vit·ing·ly** *adv*

in vi·tro \in-ˈvē-(ˌ)trō, -ˈvi-, -ˈwē-\ *adv or adj* [NL, lit., in glass] (ca. 1894) **:** outside the living body and in an artificial environment

in vitro fertilization *n* (1969) **:** fertilization of an egg in a laboratory dish or test tube; *specif* **:** fertilization by mixing sperm with eggs surgically removed from an ovary followed by uterine implantation of one or more of the resulting fertilized eggs — abbr. *IVF*

in vi·vo \in-ˈvē-(ˌ)vō, -ˈwē-(ˌ)wō\ *adv or adj* [NL, lit., in the living] (1901) **:** in the living body of a plant or animal

in·vo·cate \ˈin-və-ˌkāt\ *vt* (1526) *archaic* **:** INVOKE

in·vo·ca·tion \ˌin-və-ˈkā-shən\ *n* [ME *invocacioun,* fr. MF & L; MF *invocation,* fr. L *invocation-, invocatio,* fr. *invocare*] (14c) **1 a :** the act or process of petitioning for help or support; *specif, often cap* **:** a prayer of entreaty (as at the beginning of a service of worship) **b :** a calling upon for authority or justification **2 :** a formula for conjuring **:** INCANTATION **3 :** an act of legal or moral implementation **:** ENFORCEMENT — **in·vo·ca·tion·al** \-shnəl, -shə-nᵊl\ *adj* — **in·voc·a·to·ry** \in-ˈvä-kə-ˌtȯr-ē\ *adj*

[1]**in·voice** \ˈin-ˌvȯis\ *n* [modif. of MF *envois,* pl. of *envoi* message — more at ENVOI] (1560) **1 :** an itemized list of goods shipped usu. specifying the price and the terms of sale **:** BILL **2 :** a consignment of merchandise

[2]**invoice** *vt* **in·voiced; in·voic·ing** (1698) **:** to send an invoice for or to

in·voke \in-ˈvōk\ *vt* **in·voked; in·vok·ing** [ME *envoken,* fr. MF *invoquer,* fr. L *invocare,* fr. *in-* + *vocare* to call, fr. *voc-, vox* voice — more at VOICE] (15c) **1 a :** to petition for help or support **b :** to appeal to or cite as authority **2 :** to call forth by incantation **:** CONJURE **3 :** to make an earnest request for **:** SOLICIT **4 :** to put into effect or operation **:** IMPLEMENT **5 :** BRING ABOUT, CAUSE — **in·vok·er** *n*

in·vo·lu·cre \ˈin-və-ˌlü-kər\ *n* [F, fr. NL *involucrum*] (1785) **:** one or more whorls of bracts situated below and close to a flower, flower cluster, or fruit — **in·vo·lu·cral** \ˌin-və-ˈlü-krəl\ *adj* — **in·vo·lu·crate** \-krət, -ˌkrāt\ *adj*

in·vo·lu·crum \ˌin-və-ˈlü-krəm\ *n, pl* **-cra** \-krə\ [NL, sheath, involucre, fr. L, wrapper, fr. *involvere* to wrap] (1657) **:** a surrounding envelope or sheath

in·vol·un·tary \(ˌ)in-ˈvä-lən-ˌter-ē, -ˌte-rē\ *adj* [ME *involuntari,* fr. LL *involuntarius,* fr. L *in-* + *voluntarius* voluntary] (15c) **1 :** done contrary to or without choice **2 :** COMPULSORY **3 :** not subject to control of the will **:** REFLEX — **in·vol·un·tari·ly** \-ˌvä-lən-ˈter-ə-lē, -ˈte-rə-\ *adv* — **in·vol·un·tari·ness** \-ˈvä-lən-ˌter-ē-nəs, -ˌte-rē-\ *n*

involuntary manslaughter *n* (ca. 1879) **:** manslaughter resulting from the failure to perform a legal duty expressly required to safeguard human life, from the commission of an unlawful act not constituting a felony, or from the commission of a lawful act in a negligent or improper manner

involuntary muscle *n* (1840) **:** muscle governing reflex functions and not under direct voluntary control; *esp* **:** SMOOTH MUSCLE

[1]**in·vo·lute** \ˈin-və-ˌlüt\ *adj* [L *involutus* concealed, fr. pp. of *involvere*] (1661) **1 a :** curled spirally **b (1) :** curled or curved inward **(2) :** having the edges rolled over the upper surface toward the midrib ⟨an ∼ leaf⟩ **c :** having the form of an involute ⟨a gear with ∼ teeth⟩ **2 :** INVOLVED, INTRICATE

[2]**involute** *n* (ca. 1796) **:** a curve traced by a point

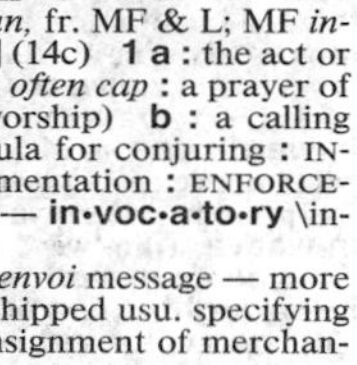

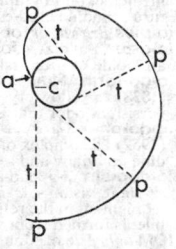

involute *a, p, p, p, p* traced by any point *p* of the thread *t* unwinding from curve *c* on a thread kept taut as it is unwound from another curve ⟨~ of a circle⟩

[3]**in·vo·lute** \ˌin-və-ˈlüt\ *vi* **-lut·ed; -lut·ing** (1816) **1 :** to become involute **2 a :** to return to a former condition **b :** to become cleared up **:** DISAPPEAR

in·vo·lu·tion \ˌin-və-ˈlü-shən\ *n* [L *involution-, involutio,* fr. *involvere*] (ca. 1611) **1 a (1) :** the act or an instance of enfolding or entangling **:** INVOLVEMENT **(2) :** an involved grammatical construction usu. characterized by the insertion of clauses between the subject and predicate **b :** COMPLEXITY, INTRICACY **2 :** EXPONENTIATION **3 a :** an inward curvature or penetration **b :** the formation of a gastrula by ingrowth of cells formed at the dorsal lip **4 :** a shrinking or return to a former size **5 :** the regressive alterations of a body or its parts characteristic of the aging process ⟨skeletal ~ due to loss of estrogens at menopause⟩ — **in·vo·lu·tion·al** \-shnəl, -shə-nᵊl\ *adj*

in·volve \in-ˈvälv, -ˈvȯlv *also* -ˈväv *or* -ˈvȯv\ *vt* **in·volved; in·volv·ing** [ME, to roll up, wrap, fr. L *involvere,* fr. *in-* + *volvere* to roll — more at VOLUBLE] (14c) **1** *archaic* **:** to enfold or envelop so as to encumber **2 a :** to engage as a participant ⟨workers *involved* in building a house⟩ **b :** to oblige to take part ⟨right of Congress to ~ the nation in war⟩ **c :** to occupy (as oneself) absorbingly; *esp* **:** to commit (as oneself) emotionally ⟨was *involved* with a married man⟩ **3 :** to surround as if with a wrapping **:** ENVELOP **4 a** *archaic* **:** to wind, coil, or wreathe about **b :** to relate closely **:** CONNECT **5 a :** to have within or as part of itself **:** INCLUDE **b :** to require as a necessary accompaniment **:** ENTAIL **c :** [3]AFFECT ⟨the cancer *involved* the lymph nodes⟩ ***syn*** see INCLUDE — **in·volve·ment** \-ˈvälv-mənt, -ˈvȯlv-\ *n* — **in·volv·er** *n*

involved *adj* (15c) **1 :** INVOLUTE, TWISTED **2 a :** marked by extreme and often needless or excessive complexity **b :** difficult to deal with because of complexity or disorder **3 :** being affected or implicated ***syn*** see COMPLEX — **in·volv·ed·ly** \-ˈväl-vəd-lē, -ˈvȯl- *also* -ˈvä-vəd- *or* -ˈvȯ-\ *adv*

in·vul·ner·a·ble \(ˌ)in-ˈvəl-n(ə-)rə-bəl, -nər-bəl\ *adj* [L *invulnerabilis,* fr. *in-* + *vulnerare* to wound — more at VULNERABLE] (1595) **1 :** incapable of being wounded, injured, or harmed **2 :** immune to or proof against attack **:** IMPREGNABLE — **in·vul·ner·a·bil·i·ty** \-ˌvəl-n(ə-)rə-ˈbi-lə-tē\ *n* — **in·vul·ner·a·ble·ness** \-ˈvəl-n(ə-)rə-bəl-nəs, -nər-bəl-\ *n* — **in·vul·ner·a·bly** \-blē\ *adv*

[1]**in·ward** \ˈin-wərd\ *adj* [ME, fr. OE *inweard* (akin to OHG *inwert*), fr. *in* + *-weard* [1]-ward] (bef. 12c) **1 :** situated on the inside **:** INNER **2 a :** of or relating to the mind or spirit ⟨~ peace⟩ **b :** absorbed in one's own mental or spiritual life **:** INTROSPECTIVE **3 :** marked by close acquaintance **:** FAMILIAR **4 :** directed toward the interior

[2]**inward** *or* **in·wards** \-wərdz\ *adv* (bef. 12c) **1 :** toward the inside, center, or interior **2 :** toward the inner being

[3]**inward** *n* (bef. 12c) **1 :** something that is inward **2 in·wards** \ˈin-ərdz, -wərdz\ *pl* **:** INNARDS

Inward Light *n* (ca. 1632) **:** INNER LIGHT

in·ward·ly \ˈin-wərd-lē\ *adv* (bef. 12c) **1 :** in the innermost being **:** MENTALLY, SPIRITUALLY **2 a :** beneath the surface **:** INTERNALLY ⟨bled ~⟩ **b :** to oneself **:** PRIVATELY ⟨cursed ~⟩

in·ward·ness *n* (14c) **1 :** internal quality or substance **2 :** close acquaintance **:** FAMILIARITY **3 :** fundamental nature **:** ESSENCE **4 :** absorption in one's own mental or spiritual life

in·weave \(ˌ)in-ˈwēv\ *vt* **-wove** \-ˈwōv\ *also* **-weaved; -wo·ven** \-ˈwō-vən\ *also* **-weaved; -weav·ing** (15c) **:** INTERWEAVE, INTERLACE

in–wrought \(ˌ)in-ˈrȯt, ˈin-ˌ\ *adj* (1637) **1 :** having decoration worked in **:** ORNAMENTED; *esp* **:** decorated with embroidery **2 :** worked in esp. as decoration

in–your–face *adj* (1982) **:** characterized by or expressive of bold and often defiant aggressiveness ⟨~ basketball⟩; *also* **:** aggressively intrusive ⟨~ advertising⟩

Io \ˈī-(ˌ)ō\ *n* [L, fr. Gk *Iō*] (1563) **:** a maiden loved by Zeus and changed by him into a heifer so that she might escape the jealous rage of Hera

I/O *abbr* input/output

IOC *abbr* International Olympic Committee

iod- *or* **iodo-** *comb form* [F *iode*] **:** iodine ⟨*iod*ize⟩ ⟨*iodo*form⟩

io·date \ˈī-ə-ˌdāt, -dət\ *n* [F, fr. *iode*] (1826) **:** a salt containing the IO_3^- ion

io·dide \ˈī-ə-ˌdīd\ *n* [ISV] (1822) **:** a salt of hydriodic acid; *also* **:** the monovalent anion I^- of such a salt

io·din·ate \ˈī-ə-də-ˌnāt\ *vt* **-at·ed; -at·ing** (1908) **:** to treat or cause to combine with iodine or a compound of iodine — **io·din·ation** \ˌī-ə-də-ˈnā-shən\ *n*

io·dine \ˈī-ə-ˌdīn, -dᵊn, -ˌdēn\ *n, often attrib* [F *iode,* fr. Gk *ioeidēs* violet colored, fr. *ion* violet] (1814) **1 :** a nonmetallic halogen element obtained usu. as heavy shining blackish-gray crystals and used esp. in medicine, photography, and analysis — see ELEMENT table **2 :** a tincture of iodine used esp. as a topical antiseptic

io·dise *Brit var of* IODIZE

io·dize \ˈī-ə-ˌdīz\ *vt* **io·dized; io·diz·ing** (1841) **:** to treat with iodine or an iodide ⟨*iodized* salt⟩

io·do·form \ī-ˈō-də-ˌfȯrm, -ˈä-\ *n* [ISV *iod-* + *-form* (as in *chloroform*)] (1838) **:** a yellow crystalline volatile compound CHI_3 with a penetrating persistent odor that is used as an antiseptic dressing

io·do·phor \-ˌfȯr\ *n* [*iod-* + Gk *-phoros* carrier — more at -PHORE] (1952) **:** a complex of iodine and a surface-active agent that releases iodine gradually and serves as a disinfectant

io·dop·sin \ˌī-ə-ˈdäp-sən\ *n* [*iod-* (fr. Gk *ioeidēs* violet colored) + Gk *opsis* sight, vision + E *-in* — more at OPTIC] (1938) **:** a photosensitive violet pigment in the retinal cones that is similar to rhodopsin but more labile, is formed from vitamin A, and is important in daylight vision

IOM *abbr* Isle of Man

Io moth \ˈī-(ˌ)ō-\ *n* [L *Io*] (1870) **:** a chiefly No. American saturniid moth (*Automeris io*) having a large circular eyelike spot on the upper surface of each hind wing and a green larva with stinging spines

ion \ˈī-ən, ˈī-ˌän\ *n* [Gk, neut. of *iōn,* prp. of *ienai* to go — more at ISSUE] (ca. 1834) **1 :** an atom or group of atoms that carries a positive or negative electric charge as a result of having lost or gained one or more electrons **2 :** a charged subatomic particle (as a free electron)

Ion *abbr* Ionic

-ion *n suffix* [F *-ion,* fr. L *-ion-, -io*] **1 a :** act or process ⟨valida*tion*⟩ **b :** result of an act or process ⟨regula*tion*⟩ **2 :** state or condition ⟨hydra*tion*⟩

ion channel *n* (1985) **:** a cell membrane channel that is selectively permeable to certain ions (as of calcium or sodium)

ion engine *n* (1958) **:** a reaction engine deriving thrust from the ejection of a stream of ionized particles

ion exchange *n* (1923) **:** a reversible interchange of one kind of ion present on an insoluble solid with another of like charge present in a solution surrounding the solid with the reaction being used esp. for softening or demineralizing water, the purification of chemicals, or the separation of substances — **ion exchanger** *n*

ion exchange resin *n* (1943) **:** an insoluble material of high molecular weight that contains groups which can be exchanged with ions in a solution with which it is in contact

Io·ni·an \ī-ˈō-nē-ən\ *n* [*Ionia,* Asia Minor] (1550) **1 :** a member of any of the Greek peoples who settled on the islands of the Aegean Sea and the western shore of Asia Minor toward the end of the second millennium B.C. **2 :** a native or inhabitant of Ionia — **Ionian** *adj*

ion·ic \ī-ˈä-nik\ *adj* [ISV] (1890) **1 :** of, relating to, existing as, or characterized by ions ⟨~ gases⟩ ⟨the ~ charge⟩ **2 :** based on or functioning by means of ions ⟨~ conduction⟩ — **ion·ic·i·ty** \ˌī-ə-ˈni-sə-tē\ *n*

[1]**Ion·ic** \ī-ˈä-nik\ *adj* [L & MF; MF *ionique,* fr. L *ionicus,* fr. Gk *iōnikos,* fr. *Iōnia* Ionia] (1585) **1 :** of or relating to the ancient Greek architectural order distinguished esp. by fluted columns on bases and scroll volutes in its capitals — see ORDER illustration **2 :** of or relating to Ionia or the Ionians

[2]**Ionic** *n* (1668) **:** a dialect of ancient Greek spoken esp. in Ionia and the Cyclades

ionic bond *n* (1939) **:** a chemical bond formed between oppositely charged species because of their mutual electrostatic attraction

ion·ise *Brit var of* IONIZE

io·ni·um \ī-ˈō-nē-əm\ *n* [*ion;* fr. its ionizing action] (1907) **:** a natural radioactive isotope of thorium having a mass number of 230

ionization chamber *n* (1904) **:** a partially evacuated tube provided with electrodes so that its conductivity due to the ionization of the residual gas reveals the presence of ionizing radiation

ion·ize \ˈī-ə-ˌnīz\ *vb* **ion·ized; ion·iz·ing** [ISV] *vt* (1898) **:** to convert wholly or partly into ions ~ *vi* **:** to become ionized — **ion·iz·able** \-ˌnī-zə-bəl\ *adj* — **ion·i·za·tion** \ˌī-ə-nə-ˈzā-shən\ *n* — **ion·iz·er** \ˈī-ə-ˌnī-zər\ *n*

ion·o·phore \ī-ˈä-nə-ˌfȯr\ *n* (ca. 1955) **:** a compound that facilitates transmission of an ion (as of calcium) across a lipid barrier (as in a cell membrane) by combining with the ion or by increasing the permeability of the barrier to it

ion·o·sphere \ī-ˈä-nə-ˌsfir\ *n* (1926) **:** the part of the earth's atmosphere in which ionization of atmospheric gases affects the propagation of radio waves, which extends from about 30 miles (50 kilometers) to the exosphere, and which is contiguous with the upper portion of the mesosphere and the thermosphere; *also* **:** a comparable region of charged particles surrounding another celestial body (as Venus) — **ion·o·spher·ic** \ˌī-ˌä-nə-ˈsfir-ik, -ˈsfer-\ *adj* — **ion·o·spher·i·cal·ly** \-i-k(ə-)lē\ *adv*

ion·to·pho·re·sis \(ˌ)ī-ˌän-tə-fə-ˈrē-səs\ *n, pl* **-re·ses** \-ˌsēz\ [NL, fr. *ionto-* ion (fr. Gk *iont-, iōn,* prp. of *ienai*) + *-phoresis*] (1909) **:** the introduction of an ionized substance (as a drug) through intact skin by the application of a direct electric current — **ion·to·pho·ret·ic** \-ˈre-tik\ *adj* — **ion·to·pho·ret·i·cal·ly** \-ti-k(ə-)lē\ *adv*

IOOF *abbr* Independent Order of Odd Fellows

io·ta \ī-ˈō-tə\ *n* [L, fr. Gk *iōta,* of Sem origin; akin to Heb *yōdh* yod] (1542) **1 :** the 9th letter of the Greek alphabet — see ALPHABET table **2 :** an infinitesimal amount **:** JOT ⟨did not show an ~ of interest⟩

IOU \ˌī-(ˌ)ō-ˈyü\ *n* [fr. the pronunciation of *I owe you*] (1795) **1 :** a paper that has on it the letters IOU, a stated sum, and a signature and that is given as an acknowledgment of debt **2 :** DEBT, OBLIGATION

-ious *adj suffix* [ME, partly fr. AF *-ious,* fr. L *-iosus,* fr. *-i-,* penultimate vowel of some noun stems + *-osus* -ous; partly fr. L *-ius,* adj. suffix] **:** -OUS ⟨edac*ious*⟩

IOW *abbr* Isle of Wight

IP *abbr* **1** initial point **2** innings pitched **3** intermediate pressure **4** Internet protocol

[1]**IPA** \ˌī-(ˌ)pē-ˈā\ *n* [*I*nternational *P*honetic *A*lphabet] (1933) **:** an alphabet designed to represent each human speech sound with a unique symbol

[2]**IPA** *abbr* individual practice association

IP address \ˈīˈpē-\ *n* [*I*nternet *p*rotocol] (1985) **:** the numeric address of a computer on the Internet

ip·e·cac \ˈi-pi-ˌkak\ *also* **ipe·ca·cu·a·nha** \ˌi-pi-ˌka-kyə-ˈwä-nə, -nyə\ *n* [Pg *ipecacuanha,* fr. Tupi *ipekakwãnʸa,* fr. *ipéka* duck + *akwãnʸa* penis] (1682) **1 :** the dried rhizome and roots of either of two tropical American plants (*Cephaelis acuminata* and *C. ipecacuanha*) of the madder family used esp. as a source of emetine; *also* **:** either of these plants **2 :** an emetic and expectorant drug that contains emetine and is prepared from ipecac esp. as a syrup for use in treating accidental poisoning

Iph·i·ge·nia \ˌi-fə-jə-ˈnī-ə\ *n* [L, fr. Gk *Iphigeneia*] (1563) **:** a daughter of Agamemnon nearly sacrificed by him to Artemis but saved by her and made a priestess

ipm *abbr* inches per minute

IPM *abbr* integrated pest management

IPO \ˌī-(ˌ)pē-ˈō\ *n, pl* **IPOs** [*i*nitial *p*ublic *o*ffering] (1980) **:** an initial public offering of a company's stock

ipro·ni·a·zid \ˌī-prə-ˈnī-ə-zəd\ *n* [blend of *isoniazid* and *propyl*] (1952) **:** a derivative $C_9H_{13}N_3O$ of isoniazid that is used as a monoamine oxidase inhibitor and was formerly used in treating tuberculosis

ips *abbr* inches per second

ip·se dix·it \ˈip-sē-ˈdik-sət\ *n* [L, he himself said it] (15c) **:** an assertion made but not proved **:** DICTUM

ip·si·lat·er·al \ˌip-si-ˈla-t(ə-)rəl\ *adj* [ISV, fr. L *ipse* self, himself + *later-, latus* side] (1907) **:** situated or appearing on or affecting the same side of the body — **ip·si·lat·er·al·ly** \-t(ə-)rə-lē\ *adv*

ip·sis·si·ma ver·ba \ip-ˈsi-sə-mə-ˈvər-bə\ *n pl* [NL, lit., the selfsame words] (1807) **:** the exact language used by someone quoted

ip·so fac·to \ˈip-(ˌ)sō-ˈfak-(ˌ)tō\ *adv* [NL, lit., by the fact itself] (1548) **:** by that very fact or act **:** as an inevitable result

IPTS *abbr* International Practical Temperature Scale

iq *abbr* [L *idem quod*] the same as

IQ \ˌī-ˈkyü\ *n* [*i*ntelligence *q*uotient] (1920) **1 :** a number used to express the apparent relative intelligence of a person: as **a :** the ratio of the mental age (as reported on a standardized test) to the chronological age multiplied by 100 **b :** a score determined by one's performance on a standardized intelligence test relative to the average performance of others of the same age **2 :** proficiency in or knowledge of a specified subject ⟨nobody questioned his hockey ~⟩

Ir *symbol* iridium

IR *abbr* **1** information retrieval **2** infrared **3** *Brit* inland revenue **4** intelligence ratio **5** internal revenue

ir- — see IN-

[1]**IRA** \ˌī-(ˌ)är-ˈā; ˈī-rə\ *n, pl* **IRAs** [*i*ndividual *r*etirement *a*ccount] (1974) **:** a retirement savings account in which income taxes on certain deposits and on all gains are deferred until withdrawals are made

[2]**IRA** *abbr* Irish Republican Army

irai·mbi·la·nja \ē-ˌrīm-bē-ˈlän(d)-zə\ *n, pl* **iraimbilanja** [Malagasy] (1993) — see MONEY table

Ira·ni·an \i-ˈrā-nē-ən, -ˈra-, -ˈrä-; ī-ˈ\ *n* (1789) **1 :** a native or inhabitant of Iran **2 :** a branch of the Indo-European family of languages that includes Persian — see INDO-EUROPEAN LANGUAGES table — **Iranian** *adj*

iras·ci·ble \i-ˈra-sə-bəl\ *adj* [MF, fr. LL *irascibilis,* fr. L *irasci* to become angry, be angry, fr. *ira*] (ca. 1530) **:** marked by hot temper and easily provoked anger — **iras·ci·bil·i·ty** \-ˌra-sə-ˈbi-lə-tē\ *n* — **iras·ci·ble·ness** \i-ˈra-sə-bəl-nəs\ *n* — **iras·ci·bly** \-blē\ *adv*

irate \ī-ˈrāt, ˈī-ˌ, i-ˈrāt\ *adj* (1838) **1 :** roused to ire ⟨an ~ taxpayer⟩ **2 :** arising from anger ⟨~ words⟩ — **irate·ly** *adv* — **irate·ness** *n*

IRBM *abbr* intermediate range ballistic missile

IRD *abbr* integrated receiver decoder; integrated receiver descrambler

ire \ˈī(-ə)r\ *n* [ME, fr. AF, fr. L *ira;* perh. akin to Gk *oistros* gadfly, frenzy] (14c) **:** intense and usu. openly displayed anger ***syn*** see ANGER — **ire** *vt* — **ire·ful** \-fəl\ *adj*

Ire *abbr* Ireland

ire·nic \ī-ˈre-nik, -ˈrē-\ *adj* [Gk *eirēnikos,* fr. *eirēnē* peace] (ca. 1864) **:** favoring, conducive to, or operating toward peace, moderation, or conciliation — **ire·ni·cal·ly** \-ˈre-ni-k(ə-)lē, -ˈrē-\ *adv*

irid *abbr* iridescent

irid- *or* **irido-** *comb form* **1** [L *irid-, iris*] **:** rainbow ⟨*irid*escent⟩ **2** [NL *irid-, iris*] **:** iris of the eye ⟨*irido*logy⟩

ir·i·des·cence \ˌir-ə-ˈde-s^{ə}n(t)s\ *n* (1804) **1 :** a lustrous rainbowlike play of color caused by differential refraction of light waves (as from an oil slick, soap bubble, or fish scales) that tends to change as the angle of view changes **2 :** a lustrous or attractive quality or effect

ir·i·des·cent \-s^{ə}nt\ *adj* (1796) **:** having or exhibiting iridescence — **ir·i·des·cent·ly** *adv*

irid·ic \i-ˈri-dik, ī-ˈri-dik\ *adj* (ca. 1890) **:** of or relating to the iris of the eye

irid·i·um \i-ˈri-dē-əm\ *n* [NL, fr. L *irid-, iris;* fr. the colors produced by its dissolving in hydrochloric acid] (1804) **:** a rare silver-white hard brittle very heavy metallic element — see ELEMENT table

ir·i·dol·o·gy \ˌi-rə-ˈdä-lə-jē\ *n, pl* **-gies** (1916) **:** the study of the iris of the eye for indications of bodily health and disease — **ir·i·dol·o·gist** \-jist\ *n*

ir·id·os·mine \ˌir-ə-ˈdäz-ˌmēn\ *n* [G, fr. NL *iridium* + *osmium*] (1827) **:** a mineral that is a native iridium osmium alloy usu. containing some rhodium and platinum

[1]**iris** \ˈī-rəs\ *n, pl* **iris·es** *also* **iri·des** \ˈī-rə-ˌdēz, ˈir-ə-\ [ME, fr. L *irid-, iris* rainbow, iris plant, fr. Gk, rainbow, iris plant, iris of the eye — more at WIRE] (15c) **1 :** RAINBOW **2** [NL *irid-, iris,* fr. Gk] **a :** the opaque contractile diaphragm perforated by the pupil and forming the colored portion of the eye — see EYE illustration **b :** IRIS DIAPHRAGM; *also* **:** a similar device with a circular opening that can be varied in size **3** *also pl* **iris** [NL *Irid-, Iris,* genus name, fr. L] **:** any of a large genus (*Iris* of the family Iridaceae, the iris family) of perennial herbaceous plants with linear usu. basal leaves and large showy flowers

iris 3

[2]**iris** *vt* (1816) **:** to make iridescent

Iris \ˈī-rəs\ *n* [L, fr. Gk] (15c) **:** the Greek goddess of the rainbow and a messenger of the gods

iris diaphragm *n* (1867) **:** an adjustable diaphragm of thin opaque plates that can be turned by a ring so as to change the diameter of a central opening usu. to regulate the aperture of a lens

Irish \ˈī-rish\ *n* [ME, fr. OE **Īrisc,* fr. *Īras* Irishmen, of Celt origin; akin to OIr *Ériu* Ireland] (13c) **1** *pl in constr* **:** natives or inhabitants of Ireland or their descendants esp. when of Celtic speech or culture **2 a :** the Celtic language of Ireland esp. as used since the later medieval period **b :** English spoken by the Irish **3 :** IRISH WHISKEY — **Irish** *adj*

Irish bull *n* (1802) **:** an incongruous statement (as "it was hereditary in his family to have no children")

Irish coffee *n* (1948) **:** hot sugared coffee and Irish whiskey topped with whipped cream

Irish confetti *n* (1913) **:** a rock or brick used as a missile

Irish Gaelic *n* (1891) **:** IRISH 2a

Irish·ism \ˈī-ri-ˌshi-zəm\ *n* (1734) **1 :** a word, phrase, or expression characteristic of the Irish **2 :** IRISH BULL

Irish·ly \ˈī-rish-lē\ *adv* (1571) **:** in a manner characteristic of the Irish

Irish mail *n* (1908) **:** a 3- or 4-wheeled toy vehicle activated by a hand lever

Irish·man \ˈī-rish-mən\ *n* (13c) **1 :** a native or inhabitant of Ireland **2 :** a person who is of Irish descent

Irish moss *n* (1837) **1 :** the dried and bleached plants of a red alga (esp. *Chondrus crispus*) used as an agent for thickening or emulsifying or as a demulcent and as a source of carrageenan **2 :** a red alga that is a source of Irish moss — called also *carrageen*

Irish·ness \ˈī-rish-nəs\ *n* (1804) **:** the fact or quality of being Irish

Irish potato *n* (1664) **:** POTATO 2b

Irish·ry \ˈī-rish-rē\ *n, pl* **-ries** (14c) **1 :** IRISH 1 **2 a :** Irish quality or character **b :** an Irish peculiarity or trait

Irish setter *n* (1866) **:** any of a breed of bird dogs resembling English setters but with a glossy mahogany-red coat

Irish stew *n* (1800) **:** a stew having as its principal ingredients meat (as lamb), potatoes, and onions in a thick gravy

Irish terrier *n* (1857) **:** any of a breed of active medium-sized terriers characterized by a dense close usu. reddish wiry coat

Irish water spaniel *n* (1865) **:** any of a breed of medium-sized retrievers characterized by a topknot, a heavy curly coat which is dark liver in color, and a short-haired tail

Irish whiskey *n* (1798) **:** whiskey made in Ireland chiefly of barley

Irish wolfhound *n* (1838) **:** any of a breed of very tall heavily built hounds having a rough wiry coat

Irish·wom·an \ˈī-rish-ˌwu̇-mən\ *n* (15c) **:** a woman born in Ireland or of Irish descent

iri·tis \ī-ˈrī-təs\ *n* [NL, irreg. fr. *iris*] (1818) **:** inflammation of the iris of the eye

[1]**irk** \ˈərk\ *vt* [ME] (15c) **:** to make weary, irritated, or bored ***syn*** see ANNOY

[2]**irk** *n* (ca. 1570) **1 :** the fact of being annoying **2 :** a source of annoyance

irk·some \ˈərk-səm\ *adj* (15c) **:** tending to irk **:** TEDIOUS ⟨an ~ task⟩ — **irk·some·ly** *adv* — **irk·some·ness** *n*

iro·ko \ə-ˈrō-(ˌ)kō\ *n* [Yoruba *ìrokò*] (1890) **:** a large tropical western African tree (*Chlorophora excelsa*) of the mulberry family having strong streaky insect-resistant wood which is often used as a teak substitute; *also* **:** this wood

[1]**iron** \ˈī(-ə)rn\ *n* [ME, fr. OE *īsern, īren;* akin to OHG *īsarn* iron] (bef. 12c) **1 :** a silver-white malleable ductile magnetic heavy metallic element that readily rusts in moist air, occurs native in meteorites and combined in most igneous rocks, is the most used of metals, and is vital to biological processes — see ELEMENT table **2 :** something made of iron: as **a** *pl* **:** shackles for the hands or legs **b :** a heated metal implement used for branding or cauterizing **c :** a household device usu. with a flat metal base that is heated to smooth, finish, or press (as cloth) **d :** STIRRUP — usu. used in pl. **e :** any of a series of numbered golf clubs having relatively thin metal heads — compare WOOD **3 :** great strength, hardness, or determination — **iron in the fire 1 :** a matter requiring close attention **2 :** a prospective course of action

[2]**iron** *adj* (bef. 12c) **1 :** of, relating to, or made of iron **2 :** resembling iron **3 a :** strong and healthy **:** ROBUST ⟨an ~ constitution⟩ **b :** INFLEXIBLE, UNRELENTING ⟨~ determination⟩ **c :** holding or binding fast ⟨an ~ grip⟩ — **iron·ness** \ˈī(-ə)rn-nəs\ *n*

[3]**iron** *vt* (15c) **1 :** to furnish or cover with iron **2 :** to shackle with irons **3 a :** to smooth with or as if with a heated iron ⟨~ a shirt⟩ **b :** to remove (as wrinkles) by ironing ~ *vi* **:** to smooth or press cloth or clothing with a heated iron

Iron Age *n* (1865) **:** the period of human culture characterized by the smelting of iron and its use in industry beginning somewhat before 1000 B.C. in western Asia and Egypt

iron·bark \ˈī(-ə)rn-ˌbärk\ *n* (1799) **:** any of several Australian eucalypti having hard gray bark and heavy hard durable wood used esp. in heavy construction; *also* **:** this wood

iron·bound \-ˈbau̇nd\ *adj* (14c) **:** bound with or as if with iron: as **a :** HARSH, RUGGED ⟨~ coast⟩ **b :** STERN, RIGOROUS ⟨~ traditions⟩

[1]**iron·clad** \-ˈklad\ *adj* (ca. 1847) **1 :** sheathed in iron armor — used esp. of naval vessels **2 :** so firm or secure as to be unbreakable: as **a :** BINDING ⟨an ~ oath⟩ **b :** having no obvious weakness ⟨an ~ case against the defendant⟩

[2]**iron·clad** \-ˌklad\ *n* (1862) **:** an armored naval vessel esp. of the mid to late 19th century

iron curtain *n* (1819) **1 :** an impenetrable barrier ⟨the *iron curtain* between the ego and the unconscious —C. J. Rolo⟩ **2 :** a political, military, and ideological barrier that cuts off and isolates an area; *specif, often cap* **:** one formerly isolating an area under Soviet control

iron·er \ˈī(-ə)r-nər\ *n* (1773) **:** one that irons; *specif* **:** MANGLE

iron·fisted \ˈī(-ə)rn-ˈfis-təd\ *adj* (1599) **1 :** STINGY, MISERLY **2 :** being both harsh and ruthless ⟨~ methods⟩

iron gray *n* (bef. 12c) **:** a slightly greenish dark gray

iron hand *n* (1703) **:** stern or rigorous control ⟨ruled with an *iron hand*⟩ — **iron·hand·ed** \ˈī(-ə)rn-ˈhan-dəd\ *adj*

iron·heart·ed \ˈī(-ə)rn-ˈhär-təd\ *adj* (1600) **:** CRUEL, HARD-HEARTED

iron horse *n* (1840) **:** LOCOMOTIVE 1; *esp* **:** a steam locomotive

iron·ic \ˌī-ˈrä-nik *also* i-ˈrä-\ *also* **iron·i·cal** \-ni-kəl\ *adj* (1576) **1 :** relating to, containing, or constituting irony ⟨an ~ remark⟩ ⟨an ~ coincidence⟩ **2 :** given to irony ⟨an ~ sense of humor⟩ ***syn*** see SARCASTIC — **iron·i·cal·ness** \-ni-kəl-nəs\ *n*

iron·i·cal·ly \-ni-k(ə-)lē\ *adv* (1576) **1 :** in an ironic manner **2 :** it is ironic, curious, or surprising

iron·ing \ˈī(-ə)r-niŋ\ *n* (ca. 1710) **1 :** the action or process of smoothing or pressing with or as if with a heated iron **2 :** clothes ironed or to be ironed

ironing board *n* (1833) **:** a flat padded cloth-covered surface on which clothes are ironed

iro·nist \ˈī-rə-nist\ *n* (1727) **:** one who uses irony esp. in the development of a literary work or theme

iro·nize \-ˌnīz\ *vb* **-nized; -niz·ing** *vt* (1602) **:** to make ironic in appearance or effect ~ *vi* **:** to use irony **:** speak or behave ironically

iron lung *n* (1932) **:** a device for artificial respiration in which rhythmic alternations in the air pressure in a chamber surrounding a patient's chest force air into and out of the lungs

iron maiden *n* (ca. 1895) **:** a supposed medieval torture device consisting of a hollow iron statue or coffin in the shape of a woman that is lined with spikes which impale the enclosed victim

iron man *n* (ca. 1902) **:** a man of unusual physical endurance

iron·mas·ter \ˈī(-ə)rn-ˌmas-tər\ *n* (1664) **:** a manufacturer of iron

iron·mon·ger \-ˌmən-gər, -ˌmäŋ-\ *n* (14c) *Brit* **:** a dealer in iron and hardware

iron·mon·gery \-g(ə-)rē\ *n* (1711) **:** something made of metal; *esp, Brit* **:** HARDWARE 1

\ə\ **abut** \$^{ə}$\ **kitten**, F table \ər\ **further** \a\ **ash** \ā\ **ace** \ä\ **mop, mar**
\au̇\ **out** \ch\ **chin** \e\ **bet** \ē\ **easy** \g\ **go** \i\ **hit** \ī\ **ice** \j\ **job**
\ŋ\ **sing** \ō\ **go** \ȯ\ **law** \ȯi\ **boy** \th\ **thin** \t͟h\ **the** \ü\ **loot** \u̇\ **foot**
\y\ **yet** \zh\ **vision, beige** \k̲, ^{n}, œ, ue, ^{y}\ *see* Guide to Pronunciation

iron out *vt* (1858) **1 :** to make smooth or flat by or as if by pressing **2 :** to resolve or work out a solution to ⟨*ironed out* their differences⟩
iron oxide *n* (1864) **:** any of several oxides of iron: as **a :** FERRIC OXIDE **b :** the monoxide FeO of iron
iron pyrites *n* (ca. 1817) **:** PYRITE — called also *iron pyrite*
iron ration *n* (1876) **:** an emergency ration
iron·side \-ˌsīd\ *n* (13c) **:** a man of great strength or bravery
iron·stone \ˈī(-ə)rn-ˌstōn\ *n* (1522) **1 :** a hard sedimentary rock rich in iron; *esp* **:** a siderite in a coal region **2 :** IRONSTONE CHINA
ironstone china *n* (1825) **:** a hard heavy durable white pottery developed in England early in the 19th century
iron sulfide *n* (1885) **:** any of several sulfides of iron
iron·ware \ˈī(-ə)rn-ˌwer\ *n* (15c) **:** articles made of iron
iron·weed \-ˌwēd\ *n* (1819) **:** any of a genus (*Vernonia*) of mostly weedy composite plants usu. having alternate leaves and perfect red, purple, or white tubular flowers in terminal cymose heads
iron·wood \-ˌwu̇d\ *n* (1657) **1 :** any of numerous trees and shrubs (as a hornbeam or hop hornbeam) with exceptionally tough or hard wood **2 :** the wood of an ironwood
iron·work \-ˌwərk\ *n* (15c) **1 :** work in iron; *also* **:** something made of iron **2** *pl but sing or pl in constr* **:** a mill or building where iron or steel is smelted or heavy iron or steel products are made — **iron·work·er** \-ˌwər-kər\ *n*
iro·ny \ˈī-rə-nē *also* ˈī(-ə)r-nē\ *n, pl* **-nies** [L *ironia,* fr. Gk *eirōnia,* fr. *eirōn* dissembler] (1502) **1 :** a pretense of ignorance and of willingness to learn from another assumed in order to make the other's false conceptions conspicuous by adroit questioning — called also *Socratic irony* **2 a :** the use of words to express something other than and esp. the opposite of the literal meaning **b :** a usu. humorous or sardonic literary style or form characterized by irony **c :** an ironic expression or utterance **3 a (1) :** incongruity between the actual result of a sequence of events and the normal or expected result **(2) :** an event or result marked by such incongruity **b :** incongruity between a situation developed in a drama and the accompanying words or actions that is understood by the audience but not by the characters in the play — called also *dramatic irony, tragic irony* ***syn*** see WIT
Ir·o·quoi·an \ˌir-ə-ˈkwȯi-ən\ *n* (1697) **1 :** a member of any of the peoples constituting the Iroquois **2 :** an American Indian language family of eastern No. America including Cayuga, Cherokee, Mohawk, Onondaga, Oneida, Seneca, and Tuscarora — **Iroquoian** *adj*
Ir·o·quois \ˈir-ə-ˌkwȯi *also* -ˌkwä\ *n, pl* **Iroquois** \-ˌkwȯi(z), -ˌkwä(z)\ [F, prob. of Algonquian origin] (1666) **1** *pl* **:** an American Indian confederacy orig. of New York consisting of the Cayuga, Mohawk, Oneida, Onondaga, and Seneca and later including the Tuscarora **2 :** a member of any of the Iroquois peoples
IRQ *abbr* interrupt request
ir·ra·di·ance \i-ˈrā-dē-ən(t)s\ *n* (1599) **1 :** RADIANCE 1 **2 :** the density of radiation incident on a given surface usu. expressed in watts per square centimeter or square meter
ir·ra·di·ate \i-ˈrā-dē-ˌāt\ *vb* **-at·ed; -at·ing** [L *irradiatus,* pp. of *irradiare,* fr. *in-* + *radius* ray] *vt* (1603) **1 a :** to cast rays of light upon **:** ILLUMINATE **b :** to enlighten intellectually or spiritually **c :** to affect or treat by radiant energy (as heat); *specif* **:** to treat by irradiation **2 :** to emit like rays of light **:** RADIATE ⟨*irradiating* strength and comfort⟩ ~ *vi, archaic* **:** to emit rays **:** SHINE — **ir·ra·di·a·tive** \-ˌā-tiv\ *adj* — **ir·ra·di·a·tor** \-ˌā-tər\ *n*
ir·ra·di·a·tion \i-ˌrā-dē-ˈā-shən\ *n* (1901) **1 :** exposure to radiation (as X rays or alpha particles) **2 :** the application of radiation (as X rays or gamma rays) for therapeutic purposes or for sterilization (as of food); *also* **:** partial or complete sterilization by irradiation
ir·rad·i·ca·ble \i-ˈra-di-kə-bəl, ˌi(r)-\ *adj* [ML *irradicabilis,* fr. L *in-* + *radic-, radix* root — more at ROOT] (1728) **:** impossible to eradicate **:** DEEP-ROOTED ⟨~ hatred⟩ — **ir·rad·i·ca·bly** \-blē\ *adv*
[1]**ir·ra·tio·nal** \i-ˈra-sh(ə-)nəl, ˌi(r)-\ *adj* [ME, fr. L *irrationalis,* fr. *in-* + *rationalis* rational] (14c) **:** not rational: as **a (1) :** not endowed with reason or understanding **(2) :** lacking usual or normal mental clarity or coherence **b :** not governed by or according to reason ⟨~ fears⟩ **c** *Greek & Latin prosody* **(1)** *of a syllable* **:** having a quantity other than that required by the meter **(2)** *of a foot* **:** containing such a syllable **d (1) :** being an irrational number ⟨an ~ root of an equation⟩ **(2) :** having a numerical value that is an irrational number ⟨a length that is ~⟩ — **ir·ra·tio·nal·i·ty** \-ˌra-shə-ˈna-lə-tē\ *n* — **ir·ra·tio·nal·ly** \-ˈra-sh(ə-)nə-lē\ *adv*
[2]**irrational** *n* (1646) **1 :** an irrational being **2 :** IRRATIONAL NUMBER
ir·ra·tio·nal·ism \i-ˈra-sh(ə-)nə-ˌli-zəm\ *n* (1811) **1 :** a system emphasizing intuition, instinct, feeling, or faith rather than reason or holding that the universe is governed by irrational forces **2 :** the quality or state of being irrational — **ir·ra·tio·nal·ist** \-list\ *n or adj* — **ir·ra·tio·nal·is·tic** \-ˌra-sh(ə-)nə-ˈlis-tik\ *adj*
irrational number *n* (1551) **:** a number that can be expressed as an infinite decimal with no set of consecutive digits repeating itself indefinitely and that cannot be expressed as the quotient of two integers
ir·re·al \i-ˈrē(-ə)l, ˌi(r)-\ *adj* (1943) **:** not real
ir·re·al·i·ty \ˌir-ē-ˈa-lə-tē\ *n* (1803) **:** UNREALITY
ir·re·claim·able \ˌir-i-ˈklā-mə-bəl\ *adj* (1662) **:** incapable of being reclaimed — **ir·re·claim·ably** \-blē\ *adv*
[1]**ir·rec·on·cil·able** \i-ˌre-kən-ˈsī-lə-bəl, -ˈre-kən-ˌ, ˌi(r)-\ *adj* (1587) **:** impossible to reconcile ⟨~ differences⟩ — **ir·rec·on·cil·abil·i·ty** \-ˌre-kən-ˌsī-lə-ˈbi-lə-tē\ *n* — **ir·rec·on·cil·able·ness** \-ˌre-kən-ˈsī-lə-bəl-nəs, -ˈre-kən-ˌ\ *n* — **ir·rec·on·cil·ably** \-blē\ *adv*
[2]**irreconcilable** *n* (1748) **:** one that is irreconcilable; *esp* **:** a member of a group (as a political party) opposing compromise or collaboration
ir·re·cov·er·able \ˌir-i-ˈkəv-rə-bəl, -ˈkə-və-\ *adj* (15c) **:** not capable of being recovered or rectified **:** IRREPARABLE ⟨an ~ loss⟩ — **ir·re·cov·er·able·ness** *n* — **ir·re·cov·er·ably** \-blē\ *adv*
ir·re·cu·sa·ble \ˌir-i-ˈkyü-zə-bəl\ *adj* [LL *irrecusabilis,* fr. L *in-* + *recusare* to reject, refuse — more at RECUSANT] (1776) **:** not subject to exception or rejection ⟨~ proof⟩ — **ir·re·cu·sa·bly** \-blē\ *adv*
irred *abbr* irredeemable
ir·re·deem·able \ˌir-i-ˈdē-mə-bəl\ *adj* (1609) **1 :** not redeemable: as **a :** not terminable by payment of the principal ⟨~ bond⟩ **b :** INCONVERTIBLE a **2 :** being beyond remedy **:** HOPELESS ⟨~ mistakes⟩ — **ir·re·deem·ably** \-blē\ *adv*
ir·re·den·ta *also* **ir·ri·den·ta** \ˌir-i-ˈden-tə\ *n* [It *Italia irredenta,* lit., unredeemed Italy, Italian-speaking territory not incorporated in Italy] (1914) **:** a territory historically or ethnically related to one political unit but under the political control of another
ir·re·den·tism \-ˈden-ˌti-zəm\ *n* (1883) **:** a political principle or policy directed toward the incorporation of irredentas within the boundaries of their historically or ethnically related political unit — **ir·re·den·tist** \-ˈden-tist\ *n or adj*
ir·re·duc·ible \ˌir-i-ˈdü-sə-bəl, -ˈdyü-\ *adj* (1633) **1 :** impossible to transform into or restore to a desired or simpler condition ⟨an ~ matrix⟩; *specif* **:** incapable of being factored into polynomials of lower degree with coefficients in some given field (as the rational numbers) or integral domain (as the integers) ⟨an ~ equation⟩ **2 :** impossible to make less or smaller ⟨an ~ minimum⟩ — **ir·re·duc·ibil·i·ty** \-ˌdü-sə-ˈbi-lə-tē, -ˌdyü-\ *n* — **ir·re·duc·ibly** \-ˈdü-sə-blē, -ˈdyü-\ *adv*
ir·re·flex·ive \ˌir-i-ˈflek-siv\ *adj* (ca. 1890) **:** being a relation for which the reflexive property does not hold for any element of a given set
ir·re·form·able \ˌir-i-ˈfȯr-mə-bəl\ *adj* (1609) **1 :** incapable of being reformed **:** INCORRIGIBLE **2 :** not subject to revision or alteration ⟨~ dogma⟩ — **ir·re·form·abil·i·ty** \-ˌfȯr-mə-ˈbi-lə-tē\ *n*
ir·re·fra·ga·ble \i-ˈre-frə-gə-bəl, ˌi(r)-; ˌir-i-ˈfra-gə-\ *adj* [LL *irrefragabilis,* fr. L *in-* + *refragari* to oppose, fr. *re-* + *-fragari* (as in *suffragari* to vote for); akin to L *suffragium* suffrage] (1533) **1 :** impossible to refute ⟨~ arguments⟩ **2 :** impossible to break or alter ⟨~ rules⟩ — **ir·re·fra·ga·bil·i·ty** \i-ˌre-frə-gə-ˈbi-lə-tē, ˌi(r)-; ˌir-i-ˌfra-gə-\ *n* — **ir·ref·ra·ga·bly** \i-ˈre-frə-gə-blē, ˌi(r)-; ˌir-i-ˈfra-gə-\ *adv*
ir·re·fut·able \ˌir-i-ˈfyü-tə-bəl; i-ˈre-fyə-tə-, ˌi(r)-\ *adj* [LL *irrefutabilis,* fr. L *in-* + *refutare* to refute] (1607) **:** impossible to refute **:** INCONTROVERTIBLE ⟨~ proof⟩ — **ir·re·fut·abil·i·ty** \ˌir-i-ˌfyü-tə-ˈbi-lə-tē; i-ˌre-fyə-tə-, ˌi(r)-\ *n* — **ir·re·fut·ably** \ˌir-i-ˈfyü-tə-blē; i-ˈre-fyə-tə-, ˌi(r)-\ *adv*
irreg *abbr* irregular
ir·re·gard·less \ˌir-i-ˈgärd-ləs\ *adv* [prob. blend of *irrespective* and *regardless*] (ca. 1912) *nonstand* **:** REGARDLESS
usage *Irregardless* originated in dialectal American speech in the early 20th century. Its fairly widespread use in speech called it to the attention of usage commentators as early as 1927. The most frequently repeated remark about it is that "there is no such word." There is such a word, however. It is still used primarily in speech, although it can be found from time to time in edited prose. Its reputation has not risen over the years, and it is still a long way from general acceptance. Use *regardless* instead.
[1]**ir·reg·u·lar** \i-ˈre-gyə-lər, ˌi(r)-\ *adj* [ME *irreguler,* fr. AF, fr. LL *irregularis* not in accordance with rule, fr. L *in-* + *regularis* regular] (14c) **1 a :** not being or acting in accord with laws, rules, or established custom ⟨~ conduct⟩ **b :** not conforming to the usual pattern of inflection ⟨~ verbs⟩; *specif* **:** STRONG 16 **c :** not following a usual or prescribed procedure; *esp, Brit* **:** celebrated without either proclamation of the banns or publication of intention to marry ⟨~ marriage⟩ **2 :** not belonging to or a part of a regular organized group; *specif* **:** not belonging to a regular army but raised for a special purpose ⟨~ troops⟩ **3 a :** lacking perfect symmetry or evenness ⟨an ~ coastline⟩ **b :** having one or more floral parts of the same whorl different in size, shape, or arrangement; *specif* **:** ZYGOMORPHIC **4 :** lacking continuity or regularity esp. of occurrence or activity ⟨~ employment⟩ — **ir·reg·u·lar·ly** *adv*
syn IRREGULAR, ANOMALOUS, UNNATURAL mean not conforming to rule, law, or custom. IRREGULAR implies not conforming to a law or regulation imposed for the sake of uniformity in method, practice, or conduct ⟨concerned about his *irregular* behavior⟩. ANOMALOUS implies not conforming to what might be expected because of the class or type to which it belongs or the laws that govern its existence ⟨her drive made her an *anomalous* figure in a sleepy organization⟩. UNNATURAL suggests what is contrary to nature or to principles or standards felt to be essential to the well-being of civilized society ⟨prisoners treated with *unnatural* cruelty⟩.
[2]**irregular** *n* (15c) **:** one that is irregular: as **a :** a soldier who is not a member of a regular military force **b** *pl* **:** merchandise that has minor defects or that falls next below the manufacturer's standard for firsts
ir·reg·u·lar·i·ty \i-ˌre-gyə-ˈla-rə-tē, ˌi(r)-\ *n, pl* **-ties** [ME *irregularite,* fr. ML *irregularitat-, irregularitas,* fr. LL *irregularis*] (14c) **1 :** something that is irregular (as improper or dishonest conduct) ⟨alleged *irregularities* in the city government⟩ **2 :** the quality or state of being irregular **3 :** CONSTIPATION
ir·rel·a·tive \-ˈre-lə-tiv\ *adj* (1640) **:** not relative: **a :** not related **b :** IRRELEVANT — **ir·rel·a·tive·ly** *adv*
ir·rel·e·vance \-ˈre-lə-vən(t)s\ *n* (1843) **1 :** the quality or state of being irrelevant **2 :** something irrelevant
ir·rel·e·van·cy \-vən(t)-sē\ *n, pl* **-cies** (1592) **:** IRRELEVANCE
ir·rel·e·vant \-vənt\ *adj* (1786) **:** not relevant **:** INAPPLICABLE ⟨that statement is ~ to your argument⟩ — **ir·rel·e·vant·ly** *adv*
ir·re·li·gion \ˌir-i-ˈli-jən\ *n* [MF or LL; MF, fr. LL *irreligion-, irreligio,* fr. L *in-* + *religion-, religio* religion] (1598) **:** the quality or state of being irreligious — **ir·re·li·gion·ist** \-ˈlij-nist, -ˈli-jə-\ *n*
ir·re·li·gious \-ˈli-jəs\ *adj* (15c) **1 :** neglectful of religion **:** lacking religious emotions, doctrines, or practices ⟨so ~ that they exploit popular religion for professional purposes —G. B. Shaw⟩ **2 :** indicating lack of religion — **ir·re·li·gious·ly** *adv*
ir·re·me·able \i-ˈre-mē-ə-bəl, ˌi(r)-\ *adj* [L *irremeabilis,* fr. *in-* + *remeare* to go back, fr. *re-* + *meare* to go — more at PERMEATE] (1569) **:** offering no possibility of return ⟨~ losses⟩
ir·re·me·di·a·ble \ˌir-i-ˈmē-dē-ə-bəl\ *adj* [ME, fr. L *irremediabilis,* fr. *in-* + *remediabilis* remediable] (15c) **:** not remediable ⟨an ~ error⟩; *also* **:** INCURABLE — **ir·re·me·di·a·ble·ness** *n* — **ir·re·me·di·a·bly** \-blē\ *adv*
ir·re·mov·able \-ˈmü-və-bəl\ *adj* (1598) **:** not removable — **ir·re·mov·abil·i·ty** \-ˌmü-və-ˈbi-lə-tē\ *n* — **ir·re·mov·ably** \-ˈmü-və-blē\ *adv*
ir·rep·a·ra·ble \i-ˈre-p(ə-)rə-bəl, ˌi(r)- *also* ÷ˌir-(r)ə-ˈper-ə-bəl\ *adj* [ME, fr. MF, fr. L *irreparabilis,* fr. *in-* + *reparabilis* reparable] (15c) **:** not reparable **:** IRREMEDIABLE ⟨~ damage⟩ — **ir·rep·a·ra·ble·ness** *n* — **ir·rep·a·ra·bly** \-blē\ *adv*
ir·re·peal·able \ˌir-i-ˈpē-lə-bəl\ *adj* (1633) **:** not repealable — **ir·re·peal·abil·i·ty** \-ˌpē-lə-ˈbi-lə-tē\ *n*

ir·re·place·able \-ˈplā-sə-bəl\ *adj* (1807) **:** not replaceable ⟨an ~ antique⟩ — **ir·re·place·abil·i·ty** \-ˌplā-sə-ˈbi-lə-tē\ *n* — **ir·re·place·able·ness** \-ˈplā-sə-bəl-nəs\ *n* — **ir·re·place·ably** \-blē\ *adv*

ir·re·press·ible \-ˈpre-sə-bəl\ *adj* (1811) **:** impossible to repress, restrain, or control ⟨~ curiosity⟩ — **ir·re·press·ibil·i·ty** \-ˌpre-sə-ˈbi-lə-tē\ *n* — **ir·re·press·ibly** \-ˈpre-sə-blē\ *adv*

ir·re·proach·able \-ˈprō-chə-bəl\ *adj* (1634) **:** not reproachable **:** BLAMELESS, IMPECCABLE ⟨~ conduct⟩ — **ir·re·proach·abil·i·ty** \-ˌprō-chə-ˈbi-lə-tē\ *n* — **ir·re·proach·able·ness** \-ˈprō-chə-bəl-nəs\ *n* — **ir·re·proach·ably** \-blē\ *adv*

ir·re·pro·duc·ible \i-ˌrē-prə-ˈdü-sə-bəl, ˌi(r)-, -ˈdyü-\ *adj* (1868) **:** not reproducible ⟨~ craftsmanship⟩ — **ir·re·pro·duc·ibil·i·ty** \-ˌdü-sə-ˈbi-lə-tē, -ˌdyü-\ *n*

ir·re·sist·ible *also* **ir·re·sist·able** \ˌir-i-ˈzis-tə-bəl\ *adj* (1597) **:** impossible to resist ⟨an ~ attraction⟩ — **ir·re·sist·ibil·i·ty** *also* **ir·re·sist·abil·i·ty** \-ˌzis-tə-ˈbi-lə-tē\ *n* — **ir·re·sist·ible·ness** *also* **ir·re·sist·able·ness** \-ˈzis-tə-bəl-nəs\ *n* — **ir·re·sist·ibly** *also* **ir·re·sist·ably** \-blē\ *adv*

ir·re·sol·u·ble \-ˈzäl-yə-bəl\ *adj* [L *irresolubilis,* fr. *in-* + *resolvere* to resolve] (1666) **1** *archaic* **:** INDISSOLUBLE **2 :** having or admitting of no solution or explanation ⟨an ~ question⟩

ir·res·o·lute \i-ˈre-zə-ˌlüt, ˌi(r)-, -lət\ *adj* (1579) **:** uncertain how to act or proceed **:** VACILLATING ⟨~ legislators⟩ — **ir·res·o·lute·ly** \-ˌlüt-lē, -lət-; -ˌre-zə-ˈlüt-\ *adv* — **ir·res·o·lute·ness** \-ˌlüt-nəs, -lət-, -ˈlüt-\ *n* — **ir·res·o·lu·tion** \-ˌre-zə-ˈlü-shən\ *n*

ir·re·solv·able \ˌir-i-ˈzäl-və-bəl, -ˈzȯl-\ *adj* (1660) **:** incapable of being resolved ⟨an ~ conflict⟩; *also* **:** not analyzable

ir·re·spec·tive of \ˌir-i-ˈspek-tiv-\ *prep* (1833) **:** REGARDLESS OF ⟨paid *irrespective of* how hard they work —Lee Bowes⟩

[1]**ir·re·spon·si·ble** \ˌir-i-ˈspän(t)-sə-bəl\ *adj* (1648) **:** not responsible: as **a :** not answerable to higher authority ⟨an ~ dictatorship⟩ **b :** said or done with no sense of responsibility ⟨~ accusations⟩ **c :** lacking a sense of responsibility **d :** unable esp. mentally or financially to bear responsibility — **ir·re·spon·si·bil·i·ty** \ˌir-i-ˌspän(t)-sə-ˈbi-lə-tē\ *n* — **ir·re·spon·si·ble·ness** \ˌir-i-ˈspän(t)-sə-bəl-nəs\ *n* — **ir·re·spon·si·bly** \-blē\ *adv*

[2]**irresponsible** *n* (1892) **:** a person who is irresponsible

ir·re·spon·sive \ˌir-i-ˈspän(t)-siv\ *adj* (ca. 1846) **:** not responsive; *esp* **:** not able, ready, or inclined to respond — **ir·re·spon·sive·ness** *n*

ir·re·triev·able \ˌir-i-ˈtrē-və-bəl\ *adj* (1702) **:** not retrievable **:** impossible to regain or recover — **ir·re·triev·abil·i·ty** \-ˌtrē-və-ˈbi-lə-tē\ *n* — **ir·re·triev·ably** \ˌir-i-ˈtrē-və-blē\ *adv*

ir·rev·er·ence \i-ˈrev-rənts, ˌi(r)-, -ˈre-və-; -ˈre-vərn(t)s\ *n* (14c) **1 :** lack of reverence **2 :** an irreverent act or utterance

ir·rev·er·ent \-rənt; -vərnt\ *adj* [ME, fr. L *irreverent-, irreverens,* fr. *in-* + *reverent-, reverens* reverent] (15c) **:** lacking proper respect or seriousness; *also* **:** SATIRIC — **ir·rev·er·ent·ly** *adv*

ir·re·vers·ible \ˌir-i-ˈvər-sə-bəl\ *adj* (1630) **:** not reversible — **ir·re·vers·ibil·i·ty** \-ˌvər-sə-ˈbi-lə-tē\ *n* — **ir·re·vers·ibly** \-ˈvər-sə-blē\ *adv*

ir·rev·o·ca·ble \i-ˈre-və-kə-bəl, ˌi(r)- *sometimes* ˌir-(r)ə-ˈvō-kə-\ *adj* [ME, fr. L *irrevocabilis,* fr. *in-* + *revocabilis* revocable] (14c) **:** not possible to revoke **:** UNALTERABLE ⟨an ~ decision⟩ — **ir·rev·o·ca·bil·i·ty** \-ˌre-və-kə-ˈbi-lə-tē, ˌir-(r)ə-ˌvō-kə-\ *n* — **ir·rev·o·ca·ble·ness** \-ˈre-və-kə-bəl-nəs, ˌir-(r)ə-ˈvō-kə-\ *n* — **ir·rev·o·ca·bly** \-blē\ *adv*

irridenta *var of* IRREDENTA

ir·ri·ga·ble \ˈir-ə-gə-bəl\ *adj* (1844) **:** suitable for irrigation ⟨~ land⟩

ir·ri·gate \ˈir-ə-ˌgāt\ *vb* **-gat·ed; -gat·ing** [L *irrigatus,* pp. of *irrigare,* fr. *in-* + *rigare* to water; perh. akin to OHG *regan* rain — more at RAIN] *vt* (1615) **1 :** WET, MOISTEN: as **a :** to supply (as land or crops) with water by artificial means **b :** to flush (a body part) with a stream of liquid (as in removing a foreign body or medicating) **2 :** to refresh as if by watering ~ *vi* **:** to practice irrigation — **ir·ri·ga·tor** \ˈir-ə-ˌgā-tər\ *n*

ir·ri·ga·tion \ˌir-ə-ˈgā-shən\ *n* (1612) **1 :** the therapeutic flushing of a body part with a stream of liquid **2 :** the watering of land by artificial means to foster plant growth

ir·ri·ta·bil·i·ty \ˌir-ə-tə-ˈbi-lə-tē\ *n, pl* **-ties** (1755) **1 :** the property of protoplasm and of living organisms that permits them to react to stimuli **2 :** the quality or state of being irritable: as **a :** quick excitability to annoyance, impatience, or anger **:** PETULANCE **b :** abnormal or excessive excitability of an organ or part of the body

ir·ri·ta·ble \ˈir-ə-tə-bəl\ *adj* (1662) **:** capable of being irritated: as **a :** easily exasperated or excited ⟨gets ~ when he tires⟩ **b :** responsive to stimuli — **ir·ri·ta·ble·ness** *n* — **ir·ri·ta·bly** \-blē\ *adv*

irritable bowel syndrome *n* (1943) **:** a chronic functional disorder of the colon that is characterized esp. by constipation or diarrhea, cramping abdominal pain, and the passage of mucus in the stool — abbr. *IBS*

[1]**ir·ri·tant** \ˈir-ə-tənt\ *adj* (1636) **:** causing irritation; *specif* **:** tending to produce physical irritation

[2]**irritant** *n* (1802) **:** something that irritates or excites

ir·ri·tate \ˈir-ə-ˌtāt\ *vb* **-tat·ed; -tat·ing** [L *irritatus,* pp. of *irritare*] *vt* (1598) **1 :** to provoke impatience, anger, or displeasure in **:** ANNOY **2 :** to induce irritability in or of ~ *vi* **:** to cause or induce displeasure or irritation — **ir·ri·tat·ing·ly** \-ˌtā-tiŋ-lē\ *adv*

syn IRRITATE, EXASPERATE, NETTLE, PROVOKE, RILE, PEEVE mean to excite a feeling of anger or annoyance. IRRITATE implies an often gradual arousing of angry feelings that may range from mere impatience to rage ⟨constant nagging that *irritated* me greatly⟩. EXASPERATE suggests galling annoyance and the arousing of extreme impatience ⟨his *exasperating* habit of putting off needed decisions⟩. NETTLE suggests a sharp but passing annoyance or stinging ⟨your pompous attitude *nettled* several people⟩. PROVOKE implies an arousing of strong annoyance that may excite to action ⟨remarks made solely to *provoke* her⟩. RILE implies inducing an angry or resentful agitation ⟨the new work schedules *riled* the employees⟩. PEEVE suggests arousing fretful often petty or querulous irritation ⟨a toddler *peeved* at being refused a cookie⟩.

irritated *adj* (1595) **:** subjected to irritation; *esp* **:** roughened, reddened, or inflamed by an irritant ⟨~ eyes⟩

ir·ri·ta·tion \ˌir-ə-ˈtā-shən\ *n* (15c) **1 a :** the act of irritating **b :** something that irritates **c :** the state of being irritated **2 :** a condition of irritability, soreness, roughness, or inflammation of a bodily part

ir·ri·ta·tive \ˈir-ə-ˌtā-tiv\ *adj* (1644) **1 :** serving to excite **:** IRRITATING **2 :** accompanied with or produced by irritation ⟨~ coughing⟩

ir·ro·ta·tion·al \ˌir-(r)ō-ˈtā-shnəl, -shə-nᵊl\ *adj* (1875) **1 :** not rotating or involving rotation **2 :** free of vortices ⟨~ flow⟩

ir·rupt \i-ˈrəpt\ *vi* [L *irruptus,* pp. of *irrumpere,* fr. *in-* + *rumpere* to break — more at REAVE] (1886) **1 :** to rush in forcibly or violently **2** *of a natural population* **:** to undergo a sudden upsurge in numbers esp. when natural ecological balances and checks are disturbed **3 :** ERUPT 1c ⟨the crowd ~*ed* in a fervor of patriotism —*Time*⟩ — **ir·rup·tion** \-ˈrəp-shən\ *n*

ir·rup·tive \-ˈrəp-tiv\ *adj* (1593) **:** irrupting or tending to irrupt ⟨~ passions⟩ — **ir·rup·tive·ly** *adv*

IRS *abbr* Internal Revenue Service

[1]**is** [ME, fr. OE; akin to OHG *ist* is (fr. *sīn* to be), L *est* (fr. *esse* to be), Gk *esti* (fr. *einai* to be)] *pres 3d sing of* BE, *dial pres 1st & 2d sing of* BE, *dial pres pl of* BE

[2]**is** *abbr* island; isle

IS *abbr* information system

is- *or* **iso-** *comb form* [LL, fr. Gk, fr. *isos* equal] **1 :** equal **:** homogeneous **:** uniform ⟨*is*entropic⟩ **2 :** isomeric ⟨*iso*cyanate⟩ **3 :** for or from different individuals of the same species ⟨*iso*agglutinin⟩

Isa *or* **Is** *abbr* Isaiah

ISA *abbr* Industry Standard Architecture

Isaac \ˈī-zik, -zək\ *n* [LL, fr. Heb *Yiṣḥāq*] (bef. 12c) **:** the son of Abraham and father of Jacob according to the account in Genesis

Isa·iah \ī-ˈzā-ə, *chiefly Brit* -ˈzī-\ *n* [Heb *Yĕshaʽyāhū*] (13c) **1 :** a major Hebrew prophet in Judah about 740 to 701 B.C. **2 :** a prophetic book of canonical Jewish and Christian Scripture — see BIBLE table

Isa·ias \-əs\ *n* [LL, fr. Gk *Ēsaias,* fr. Heb *Yĕshaʽyāhū*] (bef. 12c) **:** ISAIAH

is·al·lo·bar \(ˌ)ī-ˈsa-lə-ˌbär\ *n* [ISV *is-* + *all-* + *-bar* (as in *isobar*)] (1910) **:** an imaginary line or a line on a chart connecting the places of equal change of atmospheric pressure within a specified time — **is·al·lo·bar·ic** \ˌī-ˌsa-lə-ˈbär-ik, -ˈber-, -ˈba-rik\ *adj*

ISBN *abbr* International Standard Book Number

ISC *abbr* interstate commerce

is·chae·mia *chiefly Brit var of* ISCHEMIA

is·che·mia \is-ˈkē-mē-ə\ *n* [NL *ischaemia,* fr. *ischaemus* styptic, fr. Gk *ischaimos,* fr. *ischein* to restrain (akin to Gk *echein* to hold) + *haima* blood — more at SCHEME] (1855) **:** deficient supply of blood to a body part (as the heart or brain) that is due to obstruction of the inflow of arterial blood — **is·che·mic** \-mik\ *adj*

is·chi·um \ˈis-kē-əm\ *n, pl* **is·chia** \-ə\ [L, hip joint, fr. Gk *ischion*] (1646) **:** the dorsal and posterior of the three principal bones composing either half of the pelvis — **is·chi·al** \-əl\ *adj*

ISDN *abbr* integrated services digital network

-ise *vb suffix, chiefly Brit* **:** -IZE

is·en·tro·pic \ˌī-sᵊn-ˈtrō-pik, -ˈträ-\ *adj* (1873) **:** of or relating to equal or constant entropy; *esp* **:** taking place without change of entropy — **is·en·tro·pi·cal·ly** \-ˈtrō-pi-k(ə-)lē, -ˈträ-\ *adv*

Iseult \i-ˈsült, -ˈzült\ *n* [OF *Isolt, Iseut*] (1796) **:** ISOLDE

-ish *adj suffix* [ME, fr. OE *-isc;* akin to OHG *-isc,* -ish, Gk *-iskos,* dim. suffix] **1 :** of, relating to, or being — chiefly in adjectives indicating nationality or ethnic group ⟨Finn*ish*⟩ **2 a :** characteristic of ⟨boy*ish*⟩ ⟨Pollyanna*ish*⟩ **b :** inclined or liable to ⟨book*ish*⟩ ⟨qualm*ish*⟩ **3 a :** having a touch or trace of ⟨purpl*ish*⟩ **:** somewhat ⟨dark*ish*⟩ **b :** having the approximate age of ⟨forty*ish*⟩

Ish·ma·el \ˈish-(ˌ)mā-əl, -mē-\ *n* [Heb *Yishmāʽēl*] (bef. 12c) **1 :** the outcast son of Abraham and Hagar according to the account in Genesis and a prophet of Islam according to the Koran **2 :** a social outcast

Ish·ma·el·ite \-ə-ˌlīt\ *n* (14c) **1 :** a descendant of Ishmael **2 :** ISHMAEL 2 — **Ish·ma·el·it·ish** \-ˌlī-tish\ *adj* — **Ish·ma·el·it·ism** \-ˌlī-ˌtizəm\ *n*

isin·glass \ˈī-zᵊn-ˌglas, ˈī-ziŋ-\ *n* [prob. by folk etymology fr. obs. D *huizenblas,* fr. MD *huusblase,* fr. *huus* sturgeon + *blase* bladder] (1535) **1 :** a semitransparent whitish very pure gelatin prepared from the air bladders of fishes (as sturgeons) and used esp. as a clarifying agent and in jellies and glue **2 :** mica esp. when in thin transparent sheets; *esp* **:** MUSCOVITE 2

Isis \ˈī-səs\ *n* [L *Isid-, Isis,* fr. Gk, fr. Egypt *'st*] (14c) **:** an Egyptian nature goddess and wife and sister of Osiris

isl *abbr* island

Is·lam \is-ˈläm, iz-, -ˈlam, ˈis-ˌ, ˈiz-ˌ\ *n* [Ar *islām* submission (to the will of God)] (1817) **1 :** the religious faith of Muslims including belief in Allah as the sole deity and in Muhammad as his prophet **2 a :** the civilization erected upon Islamic faith **b :** the group of modern nations in which Islam is the dominant religion — **Is·lam·ic** \is-ˈlä-mik, iz-, -ˈla-\ *adj* — **Is·lam·ics** \-miks\ *n pl but sing or pl in constr*

Islamic calendar *n* (1974) **:** a lunar calendar reckoned from the Hegira in A.D. 622 and organized in cycles of 30 years — see MONTH table

Islamic era *n* (1969) **:** the era used in Muslim countries for numbering Islamic calendar years since the Hegira

Is·lam·ism \is-ˈlä-ˌmi-zəm, iz-, -ˈla-; ˈiz-lə-\ *n* (1747) **1 :** the faith, doctrine, or cause of Islam **2 :** a popular reform movement advocating the reordering of government and society in accordance with laws prescribed by Islam — **Is·lam·ist** \-mist\ *n*

Is·lam·ize \ˈiz-lə-ˌmīz; is-ˈlä-ˌmīz, iz-, -ˈla-\ *vt* **-ized; -iz·ing** (ca. 1846) **:** to make Islamic; *esp* **:** to convert to Islam — **Is·lam·i·za·tion** \ˌiz-lə-mə-ˈzā-shən; is-ˌlä-mə-, iz-, -ˌla-\ *n*

[1]**is·land** \ˈī-lənd\ *n, often attrib* [alter. (influenced by AF *isle*) of earlier *iland,* fr. ME, fr. OE *īgland* (akin to ON *eyland*), fr. *īg* island (akin to OE *ēa* river, L *aqua* water) + *land* land] (bef. 12c) **1 :** a tract of land surrounded by water and smaller than a continent **2 :** something resembling an island esp. in its isolated or surrounded position: as **a :** a usu. raised area within a thoroughfare, parking lot, or driveway used esp. to separate or direct traffic **b :** a superstructure on the deck of a ship (as an aircraft carrier) **c :** a kitchen counter that is approachable from all sides **3 :** an isolated group or area; *esp* **:** an isolated ethnological group

\ə\ **abut** \ᵊ\ **kitten**, F **table** \ər\ **further** \a\ **ash** \ā\ **ace** \ä\ **mop, mar**
\au̇\ **out** \ch\ **chin** \e\ **bet** \ē\ **easy** \g\ **go** \i\ **hit** \ī\ **ice** \j\ **job**
\ŋ\ **sing** \ō\ **go** \ȯ\ **law** \ȯi\ **boy** \th\ **thin** \t͟h\ **the** \ü\ **loot** \u̇\ **foot**
\y\ **yet** \zh\ **vision, beige** \k̲, ⁿ, œ, ue, ʸ\ *see* Guide to Pronunciation

[2]**island** *vt* (1661) **1 a :** to make into or as if into an island **b :** to dot with or as if with islands **2 :** ISOLATE

is·land·er \ˈī-lən-dər\ *n* (ca. 1550) **:** a native or inhabitant of an island

is·land–hop \ˈī-lənd-ˌhäp\ *vi* (1944) **:** to travel from island to island in a chain

island universe *n* (1867) **:** a galaxy other than the Milky Way

[1]**isle** \ˈī(-ə)l\ *n* [ME, fr. AF *ile, isle,* fr. L *insula*] (13c) **:** ISLAND; *esp* **:** ISLET 1

[2]**isle** *vt* **isled; isl·ing** (ca. 1576) **1 :** to make an isle of **2 :** to place on or as if on an isle

is·let \ˈī-lət\ *n* (1538) **1 :** a little island **2 :** ISLET OF LANGERHANS

islet of Lang·er·hans \-ˈläŋ-ər-ˌhänz, -ˌhän(t)s\ [Paul *Langerhans* †1888 Ger. physician] (1896) **:** any of the groups of small slightly granular endocrine cells that form anastomosing trabeculae among the tubules and alveoli of the pancreas and secrete insulin and glucagon

ism \ˈi-zəm\ *n* [*-ism*] (1680) **1 :** a distinctive doctrine, cause, or theory **2 :** an oppressive and esp. discriminatory attitude or belief ⟨we all have got to come to grips with our ~*s* —Joycelyn Elders⟩

-ism *n suffix* [ME *-isme,* fr. MF & L; MF, partly fr. L *-isma* (fr. Gk) & partly fr. L *-ismus,* fr. Gk *-ismos;* Gk *-isma* & *-ismos,* fr. verbs in *-izein* -ize] **1 a :** act **:** practice **:** process ⟨critic*ism*⟩ ⟨plagiar*ism*⟩ **b :** manner of action or behavior characteristic of a (specified) person or thing ⟨animal*ism*⟩ **c :** prejudice or discrimination on the basis of a (specified) attribute ⟨rac*ism*⟩ ⟨sex*ism*⟩ **2 a :** state **:** condition **:** property ⟨barbarian*ism*⟩ **b :** abnormal state or condition resulting from excess of a (specified) thing ⟨alcohol*ism*⟩ or marked by resemblance to (such) a person or thing ⟨giant*ism*⟩ **3 a :** doctrine **:** theory **:** religion ⟨Buddh*ism*⟩ **b :** adherence to a system or a class of principles ⟨stoic*ism*⟩ **4 :** characteristic or peculiar feature or trait ⟨colloquial*ism*⟩

isn't \ˈi-zᵊnt, -ᵊn, *dial also* ˈi-dᵊn(t) *or* ˈin(t)\ (1608) **:** is not

ISO *abbr* International Organization for Standardization; International Standards Organization

iso- — see IS-

iso·al·lox·a·zine \-ə-ˈläk-sə-ˌzēn\ *n* [*is-* + *all*antoic + *ox*alic + *azine*] (1936) **:** a yellow solid $C_{10}H_6N_4O_2$ that is the precursor of various flavins (as riboflavin)

iso·bar \ˈī-sə-ˌbär\ *n* [ISV *is-* + *-bar* (fr. Gk *baros* weight); akin to Gk *barys* heavy — more at GRIEVE] (ca. 1864) **1 :** an imaginary line or a line on a map or chart connecting or marking places of equal barometric pressure **2 :** one of two or more atoms or elements having the same atomic weights or mass numbers but different atomic numbers

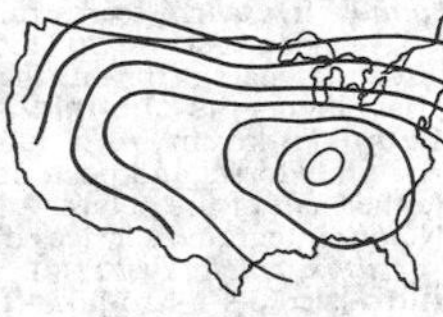

isobar 1

iso·bar·ic \ˌī-sə-ˈbär-ik, -ˈber-, -ˈba-rik\ *adj* [ISV] (1878) **1 :** of or relating to an isobar **2 :** characterized by constant or equal pressure ⟨an ~ process⟩

iso·bu·tane \ˌī-sō-ˈbyü-ˌtān\ *n* [ISV] (1876) **:** a gaseous branched-chain hydrocarbon $(CH_3)_3CH$ isomeric with normal butane that is used esp. as a fuel

iso·bu·tyl·ene \-ˈbyü-tə-ˌlēn\ *n* [ISV] (1872) **:** a gaseous butylene C_4H_8 used esp. in making butyl rubber and gasoline components

iso·ca·lo·ric \-kə-ˈlȯr-ik, -ˈlär-; -ˈka-lə-rik\ *adj* (1922) **:** having similar caloric values ⟨~ diets⟩

iso·car·box·az·id \-ˌkär-ˈbäk-sə-zəd\ *n* [*is-* + *carb-* + *ox-* + hydr*azide*] (1959) **:** an antidepressant drug $C_{12}H_{13}N_3O_2$

iso·chro·mo·some \ˌī-sə-ˈkrō-mə-ˌsōm, -ˌzōm\ *n* (1939) **:** a chromosome produced by transverse splitting of the centromere so that both arms are derived from the dyad on one side of the centromere of the parental chromosome and each arm has identical genes arranged in the same order counting away from the centromere

iso·chron \ˈī-sə-ˌkrän\ *or* **iso·chrone** \-ˌkrōn\ *n* [ISV *is-* + *-chron* (fr. Gk *chronos* time)] (1881) **:** an imaginary line or a line on a chart connecting points at which an event occurs simultaneously or which represents the same time or time difference

iso·chro·nal \ī-ˈsä-krə-nᵊl, ˌī-sə-ˈkrō-\ *adj* [Gk *isochronos,* fr. *is-* + *chronos* time] (1680) **:** uniform in time **:** having equal duration **:** recurring at regular intervals — **iso·chro·nal·ly** \-nᵊl-ē\ *adv* — **iso·chro·nism** \ī-ˈsä-krə-ˌni-zəm, ˌī-sə-ˈkrō-\ *n*

iso·chro·nous \ī-ˈsä-krə-nəs, ˌī-sə-ˈkrō-\ *adj* [Gk *isochronos*] (1706) **:** ISOCHRONAL — **iso·chro·nous·ly** *adv*

iso·cit·ric acid \ˌī-sə-ˈsi-trik-\ *n* (1869) **:** a crystalline isomer of citric acid that occurs esp. as an intermediate stage in the Krebs cycle

iso·cy·a·nate \ˌī-sō-ˈsī-ə-ˌnāt, -nət\ *n* [ISV] (1872) **:** an ester of isomeric cyanic acid used esp. in plastics and adhesives

iso·cy·clic \-ˈsī-klik, -ˈsi-\ *adj* [ISV] (1900) **:** having or being a ring composed of atoms of only one element; *esp* **:** CARBOCYCLIC

iso·di·a·met·ric \-ˌdī-ə-ˈme-trik\ *adj* [ISV] (ca. 1879) **:** having equal diameters

iso·dose \ˈī-sə-ˌdōs\ *adj* [ISV] (1922) **:** of or relating to points or zones in a medium that receive equal doses of radiation

iso·elec·tric \ˌī-sō-i-ˈlek-trik\ *adj* [ISV] (1877) **1 :** having or representing zero difference of electric potential **2 :** being the pH at which the electrolyte will not migrate in an electric field ⟨the ~ point of a protein⟩

isoelectric focusing *n* (1966) **:** an electrophoretic technique for separating proteins by causing them to migrate under the influence of an electric field through a medium (as a gel) having a pH gradient to locations with pH values corresponding to their isoelectric points

iso·elec·tron·ic \-i-ˌlek-ˈträ-nik\ *adj* [ISV] (1926) **:** having the same number of electrons or valence electrons — **iso·elec·tron·i·cal·ly** \-ni-k(ə-)lē\ *adv*

iso·en·zyme \-ˈen-ˌzīm\ *n* (1960) **:** any of two or more chemically distinct but functionally similar enzymes — **iso·en·zy·mat·ic** \-ˌen-zə-ˈma-tik, -zī-\ *adj* — **iso·en·zy·mic** \-en-ˈzī-mik\ *adj*

iso·fla·vone \ˌī-sō-ˈflā-ˌvōn\ *n* (1926) **:** a bioactive ketone $C_{15}H_{10}O_2$ noted for its numerous derivatives that are found in plants (as the soybean) and have antioxidant and estrogenic activity; *also* **:** any of these derivatives (as daidzein or genistein)

iso·form \ˈī-sə-ˌfȯrm\ *n* (1983) **:** any of two or more functionally similar proteins that have a similar but not an identical amino acid sequence

iso·ga·mete \ˌī-sō-ˈga-ˌmēt *also* -gə-ˈmēt\ *n* [ISV] (1891) **:** a gamete indistinguishable in form or size or behavior from another gamete with which it can unite to form a zygote — **iso·ga·met·ic** \-gə-ˈme-tik\ *adj*

isog·a·mous \ī-ˈsä-gə-məs\ *adj* [prob. fr. NL **isogamus,* fr. *is-* + *-gamus* -gamous] (1887) **:** having or involving isogametes — compare HETEROGAMOUS — **isog·a·my** \-mē\ *n*

iso·ge·ne·ic \ˌī-sō-jə-ˈnē-ik, -ˈnā-\ *adj* [alter. of *isogenic*] (1963) **:** SYNGENEIC ⟨an ~ graft⟩

iso·gen·ic \-ˈje-nik\ *adj* [*is-* + *gene* + [1]*-ic*] (ca. 1931) **:** characterized by essentially identical genes ⟨identical twins are ~⟩

iso·gloss \ˈī-sə-ˌgläs, -ˌglȯs\ *n* [ISV *is-* + Gk *glōssa* language — more at GLOSS] (1925) **1 :** a boundary line between places or regions that differ in a particular linguistic feature **2 :** a line on a map representing an isogloss — **iso·gloss·al** \ˌī-sə-ˈglä-səl, -ˈglȯ-\ *adj* — **iso·gloss·ic** \-ˈglä-sik, -ˈglȯ-\ *adj*

iso·gon·ic \ˌī-sə-ˈgä-nik\ *adj* [*isogony,* fr. *is-* + *-gony*] (1924) **:** exhibiting equivalent relative growth of parts such that size relations remain constant — **isog·o·ny** \ī-ˈsä-gə-nē\ *n*

isogonic line *n* (ca. 1859) **:** an imaginary line or a line on a map joining points on the earth's surface at which the magnetic declination is the same — called also *isogonal*

iso·graft \ˈī-sə-ˌgraft\ *n* (1958) **:** a homograft between genetically identical or nearly identical individuals — **isograft** *vt*

iso·gram \ˈī-sə-ˌgram\ *n* (1889) **:** ISOLINE

iso·hy·et \ˌī-sō-ˈhī-ət\ *n* [ISV *is-* + Gk *hyetos* rain, fr. *hyein* to rain; prob. akin to Toch B *swese* rain] (1899) **:** a line on a map or chart connecting areas of equal rainfall — **iso·hy·et·al** \-ə-təl\ *adj*

iso·la·ble \ˈī-sə-lə-bəl *also* ˈi-\ *or* **iso·lat·able** \ˌī-sə-ˈlā-tə-bəl *also* ˌi-\ *adj* (ca. 1855) **:** capable of being isolated

[1]**iso·late** \ˈī-sə-ˌlāt *also* ˈi-\ *vt* **-lat·ed; -lat·ing** [back-formation fr. *isolated* set apart, fr. F *isolé,* fr. It *isolato,* fr. *isola* island, fr. L *insula*] (1799) **1 :** to set apart from others; *also* **:** QUARANTINE **2 :** to select from among others; *esp* **:** to separate from another substance so as to obtain pure or in a free state **3 :** INSULATE — **iso·la·tor** \-ˌlā-tər\ *n*

[2]**iso·late** \-lət, -ˌlāt\ *adj* (1819) **:** being alone **:** SOLITARY, ISOLATED

[3]**iso·late** \-lət, -ˌlāt\ *n* (1890) **1 :** an individual, population, strain, or culture obtained by or resulting from selection or separation **2 :** an individual socially withdrawn or removed from society

isolated *adj* (1763) **1 :** occurring alone or once **:** UNIQUE **2 :** SPORADIC

iso·la·tion \ˌī-sə-ˈlā-shən *also* ˌi-\ *n* (1833) **:** the action of isolating **:** the condition of being isolated ***syn*** see SOLITUDE

iso·la·tion·ism \-shə-ˌni-zəm\ *n* (1922) **:** a policy of national isolation by abstention from alliances and other international political and economic relations — **iso·la·tion·ist** \-sh(ə-)nist\ *n or adj*

Isol·de \i-ˈzōl-də, -ˈsōl-\ *n* [G, fr. OF *Isolt, Iseut*] (1851) **1 :** an Irish princess married to King Mark of Cornwall and loved by Tristram **2 :** the daughter of the King of Brittany and wife of Tristram

iso·leu·cine \ˌī-sō-ˈlü-ˌsēn\ *n* [ISV] (1903) **:** a crystalline essential amino acid $C_6H_{13}NO_2$ isomeric with leucine

iso·line \ˈī-(ˌ)sō-ˌlīn\ *n* (1944) **:** a line on a map or chart along which there is a constant value (as of temperature or rainfall)

iso·mer \ˈī-sə-mər\ *n* [ISV, back-formation fr. *isomeric*] (1855) **1 :** one of two or more compounds, radicals, or ions that contain the same number of atoms of the same elements but differ in structural arrangement and properties **2 :** a nuclide isomeric with one or more others

isom·er·ase \ī-ˈsä-mə-ˌrās, -ˌrāz\ *n* (1927) **:** an enzyme that catalyzes the conversion of its substrate to an isomeric form

iso·mer·ic \ˌī-sə-ˈmer-ik\ *adj* [G *isomerisch,* fr. Gk *isomerēs* equally divided, fr. *is-* + *meros* part — more at MERIT] (1833) **:** of, relating to, or exhibiting isomerism

isom·er·ism \ī-ˈsä-mə-ˌri-zəm\ *n* (1838) **1 :** the relationship of two or more chemical species that are isomers **2 :** the relation of two or more nuclides with the same mass numbers and atomic numbers but different energy states and rates of radioactive decay

isom·er·ize \ī-ˈsä-mə-ˌrīz\ *vb* **-ized; -iz·ing** *vi* (1891) **:** to become changed into an isomeric form ~ *vt* **:** to cause to isomerize — **isom·er·i·za·tion** \-ˌsä-mə-rə-ˈzā-shən\ *n*

iso·met·ric \ˌī-sə-ˈme-trik\ *adj* (ca. 1855) **1 :** of, relating to, or characterized by equality of measure; *esp* **:** relating to or being a crystallographic system characterized by three equal axes at right angles **2 :** of, relating to, involving, or being muscular contraction (as in isometrics) against resistance, without significant shortening of muscle fibers, and with marked increase in muscle tone — compare ISOTONIC — **iso·met·ri·cal·ly** \-tri-k(ə-)lē\ *adv*

isometric line *n* (ca. 1911) **1 :** a line representing changes of pressure or temperature under conditions of constant volume **2 :** a line (as a contour line) drawn on a map and indicating a true constant value throughout its extent

iso·met·rics \ˌī-sə-ˈme-triks\ *n pl but sing or pl in constr* (1962) **:** exercise or a system of exercises in which opposing muscles are so contracted that there is little shortening but a great increase in tone of muscle fibers involved

isom·e·try \ī-ˈsä-mə-trē\ *n, pl* **-tries** (1881) **:** a mapping of a metric space onto another or onto itself so that the distance between any two points in the original space is the same as the distance between their images in the second space ⟨rotation and translation are *isometries* of the plane⟩

iso·mor·phic \ˌī-sə-ˈmȯr-fik\ *adj* (1862) **1 a :** being of identical or similar form, shape, or structure ⟨~ crystals⟩ **b :** having sporophytic and gametophytic generations alike in size and shape **2 :** related by an isomorphism ⟨~ mathematical rings⟩ — **iso·mor·phi·cal·ly** \-fi-k(ə-)lē\ *adv*

iso·mor·phism \ˌī-sə-ˈmȯr-ˌfi-zəm\ *n* [ISV] (ca. 1828) **1 :** the quality or state of being isomorphic: as **a :** similarity in organisms of different ancestry resulting from convergence **b :** similarity of crystalline form between chemical compounds **2 :** a one-to-one correspondence between two mathematical sets; *esp* **:** a homomorphism that is one-to-one — compare ENDOMORPHISM

iso·mor·phous \ˌī-sə-ˈmȯr-fəs\ *adj* (1827) **:** ISOMORPHIC 1a — **iso·morph** \ˈī-sə-ˌmȯrf\ *n*

iso·ni·a·zid \ˌī-sə-ˈnī-ə-zəd\ *n* [*is-* + *ni*cotinic acid + hydr*azide*] (1952) **:** a crystalline compound $C_6H_7N_3O$ used in treating tuberculosis

iso·oc·tane \ˌī-sō-ˈäk-ˌtān\ *n* [ISV] (1909) **:** an octane of branched-chain structure or a mixture of such octanes; *esp* **:** a flammable liquid octane used in determining the octane number of fuels

iso·pach \ˈī-sə-ˌpak\ *n* [*is-* + *-pach* (fr. Gk *pachys* thick) — more at PACHYDERM] (ca. 1918) **:** an isoline that connects points of equal thickness of a geological stratum formation or group of formations

iso·phote \ˈī-sə-ˌfōt\ *n* [ISV *is-* + *-phote* (fr. Gk *phōt-, phōs* light) — more at FANCY] (ca. 1909) **:** a curve on a chart joining points of equal light intensity from a given source — **iso·phot·al** \ˌī-sə-ˈfō-təl\ *adj*

iso·pi·es·tic \ˌī-sō-pē-ˈes-tik, -pī-\ *adj* [*is-* + Gk *piestos,* verbal of *piezein* to press — more at PIEZO-] (1873) **:** of, relating to, or marked by equal pressure

iso·pleth \ˈī-sə-ˌpleth\ *n* [ISV *is-* + Gk *plēthos* quantity; akin to Gk *plēthein* to be full — more at FULL] (1908) **1 :** an isoline on a graph showing the occurrence or frequency of a phenomenon as a function of two variables **2 :** a line on a map connecting points at which a given variable has a specified constant value — **iso·pleth·ic** \ˌī-sə-ˈple-thik\ *adj*

iso·pod \ˈī-sə-ˌpäd\ *n* [ultim. fr. Gk *is-* + *pod-, pous* foot — more at FOOT] (ca. 1835) **:** any of a large order (Isopoda) of small sessile-eyed aquatic or terrestrial crustaceans with the body composed of seven free thoracic segments each bearing a pair of similar legs — **isopod** *adj*

iso·pren·a·line \ˌī-sə-ˈpre-nə-lən\ *n* [prob. fr. *iso*propyl + adre*naline*] (1951) **:** ISOPROTERENOL

iso·prene \ˈī-sə-ˌprēn\ *n* [prob. fr. *is-* + *pr*opyl + *-ene*] (1860) **:** a flammable liquid unsaturated hydrocarbon C_5H_8 used esp. in synthetic rubber

iso·pren·oid \ˌī-sə-ˈprē-ˌnȯid\ *adj* (1940) **:** relating to, containing, or being a branched-chain grouping characteristic of isoprene — **isoprenoid** *n*

iso·pro·pyl \ˌī-sə-ˈprō-pəl\ *n, often attrib* [ISV] (1866) **:** the alkyl radical isomeric with straight-chain propyl — often used in combination

isopropyl alcohol *n* (1872) **:** a volatile flammable alcohol C_3H_8O used esp. as a solvent and rubbing alcohol

iso·pro·ter·e·nol \ˌī-sə-prō-ˈter-ə-ˌnȯl, -ˌnōl\ *n* [*isopro*pyl + *arterenol* norepinephrine, fr. *Arterenol,* a trademark] (1957) **:** a sympathomimetic agent $C_{11}H_{17}NO_3$ used in the treatment of asthma

iso·pyc·nic \ˌī-sō-ˈpik-nik\ *adj* [*is-* + Gk *pyknos* dense] (ca. 1890) **1 :** of, relating to, or marked by equal or constant density **2 :** being or produced by a technique (as centrifugation) in which the components of a mixture are separated on the basis of differences in density

isos·ce·les \ī-ˈsäs-ˌlēz, -ˈsä-sə-\ *adj* [LL *isosceles* having two equal sides, fr. Gk *isoskelēs,* fr. *is-* + *skelos* leg; perh. akin to OE *sceol* wry] (1551) **1** *of a triangle* **:** having two equal sides — see TRIANGLE illustration **2** *of a trapezoid* **:** having the two nonparallel sides equal

is·os·mot·ic \ˌī-ˌsäz-ˈmä-tik, -ˌsäs-\ *adj* [ISV] (1895) **:** of, relating to, or exhibiting equal osmotic pressure ⟨∼ solutions⟩ — **is·os·mot·i·cal·ly** \-ˈmä-ti-k(ə-)lē\ *adv*

iso·spin \ˈī-sə-ˌspin\ *n* (1961) **:** a quantum characteristic of a group of closely related subatomic particles (as a proton and a neutron) handled mathematically like ordinary spin with the possible orientations in a hypothetical space specifying the number of particles of differing electric charge comprising the group — called also *isotopic spin*

isos·ta·sy \ī-ˈsäs-tə-sē\ *n* [ISV *is-* + Gk *-stasia* condition of standing, fr. *histanai* to cause to stand — more at STAND] (1889) **1 :** general equilibrium in the earth's crust maintained by a yielding flow of rock material beneath the surface under gravitative stress **2 :** the quality or state of being subjected to equal pressure from every side — **iso·stat·ic** \ˌī-sə-ˈsta-tik\ *adj* — **iso·stat·i·cal·ly** \-ˈsta-ti-k(ə-)lē\ *adv*

iso·tac·tic \ˌī-sə-ˈtak-tik\ *adj* (1955) **:** having or relating to a stereochemical regularity of structure in the repeating units of a polymer — compare ATACTIC

iso·therm \ˈī-sə-ˌthərm\ *n* [F *isotherme,* adj.] (1859) **1 :** a line on a map or chart of the earth's surface connecting points having the same temperature at a given time or the same mean temperature for a given period **2 :** a line on a chart representing changes of volume or pressure under conditions of constant temperature

iso·ther·mal \ˌī-sə-ˈthər-məl\ *adj* [F *isotherme,* fr. *is-* + *-therme* (fr. Gk *thermos* hot) — more at THERM] (1826) **1 :** of, relating to, or marked by equality of temperature **2 :** of, relating to, or marked by changes of volume or pressure under conditions of constant temperature — **iso·ther·mal·ly** \-mə-lē\ *adv*

iso·thio·cy·a·nate \ˌī-sō-ˌthī-ō-ˈsī-ə-ˌnāt\ *n* (1891) **:** a compound containing the monovalent group –NCS

iso·ton·ic \ˌī-sə-ˈtä-nik\ *adj* [ISV] (1891) **1 :** of, relating to, or being muscular contraction in the absence of significant resistance, with marked shortening of muscle fibers, and without great increase in muscle tone — compare ISOMETRIC **2 :** ISOSMOTIC — used of solutions — **iso·ton·i·cal·ly** \-ni-k(ə-)lē\ *adv* — **iso·to·nic·i·ty** \-tō-ˈni-sə-tē\ *n*

iso·tope \ˈī-sə-ˌtōp\ *n* [*is-* + Gk *topos* place] (1913) **1 :** any of two or more species of atoms of a chemical element with the same atomic number and nearly identical chemical behavior but with differing atomic mass or mass number and different physical properties **2 :** NUCLIDE — **iso·to·pic** \ˌī-sə-ˈtä-pik, -ˈtō-\ *adj* — **iso·to·pi·cal·ly** \-ˈtä-pi-k(ə-)lē, -ˈtō-\ *adv*

isotopic spin *n* (1937) **:** ISOSPIN

iso·tret·i·noin \ˌī-sō-ˈtre-tə-ˌnȯin\ *n* (1980) **:** a cis isomer of retinoic acid that is a synthetic derivative of vitamin A, inhibits sebaceous gland function and keratinization, and is used in the treatment of severe inflammatory acne

iso·tro·pic \ˌī-sə-ˈtrō-pik, -ˈträ-\ *adj* [ISV] (1856) **:** exhibiting properties (as velocity of light transmission) with the same values when measured along axes in all directions ⟨an ∼ crystal⟩ — **isot·ro·py** \ī-ˈsä-trə-pē\ *n*

iso·zyme \ˈī-sə-ˌzīm\ *n* (1959) **:** ISOENZYME — **iso·zy·mic** \ˌī-sə-ˈzī-mik\ *adj*

ISP *abbr* Internet service provider

Isr *abbr* Israel; Israeli

Is·ra·el \ˈiz-rē-əl, -(ˌ)rā- *also* ˈis- *or* ˈiz-rəl\ *n* [ME, fr. OE, fr. LL, fr. Gk *Israēl,* fr. Heb *Yiśrā'ēl*] **1 :** JACOB 2 **2 :** the Jewish people **3 :** a people chosen by God — **Israel** *adj*

[1]**Is·rae·li** \iz-ˈrā-lē *also* ˌiz-rə-ˈā-lē\ *adj* [ModHeb *yiśrĕ'ēlī,* fr. Heb, Israelite, n. & adj., fr. *Yiśrā'ēl*] (1948) **:** of or relating to the people or the republic of Israel

[2]**Israeli** *n, pl* **Israelis** *also* **Israeli** (1948) **:** a native or inhabitant of the republic of Israel

[1]**Is·ra·el·ite** \ˈiz-r(ē-)ə-ˌlīt\ *n* [ME, fr. LL *Israelita,* fr. Gk *Israēlitēs,* fr. *Israēl*] (14c) **:** a descendant of the Hebrew patriarch Jacob; *specif* **:** a native or inhabitant of the ancient northern kingdom of Israel

[2]**Israelite** *adj* (1851) **:** of or relating to Israel or to the Israelites

Is·sa·char \ˈi-sə-ˌkär\ *n* [LL, fr. Gk, fr. Heb *Yiśśākhār*] (bef. 12c) **:** a son of Jacob and the traditional eponymous ancestor of one of the tribes of Israel

is·sei \(ˌ)ē-ˈsā, ˈē-ˌsā\ *n, pl* **issei** *often cap* [Jp, lit., first generation] (1937) **:** a Japanese immigrant esp. to the U.S.

ISSN *abbr* International Standard Serial Number

is·su·able \ˈi-shü-ə-bəl\ *adj* (ca. 1570) **1 :** open to contest, debate, or litigation **2 :** authorized for issue ⟨bonds ∼ under the merger terms⟩ **3 :** possible as a result or consequence — **is·su·ably** \-blē\ *adv*

is·su·ance \ˈi-shə-wən(t)s, -shü-ən(t)s\ *n* (1863) **1 :** ISSUE 2 **2 :** ISSUE 9a

is·su·ant \-wənt, -ənt\ *adj* (1610) **1** *of a heraldic animal* **:** rising with only the upper part visible **2** *archaic* **:** coming forth **:** EMERGING

[1]**is·sue** \ˈi-(ˌ)shü, *chiefly Southern* ˈi-shə, *chiefly Brit* ˈis-(ˌ)yü\ *n* [ME, exit, proceeds, fr. AF, fr. *issir* to come out, go out, fr. L *exire* to go out, fr. *ex-* + *ire* to go; akin to Goth *iddja* he went, Gk *ienai* to go, Skt *eti* he goes] (14c) **1** *pl* **:** proceeds from a source of revenue (as an estate) **2 :** the action of going, coming, or flowing out **:** EGRESS, EMERGENCE **3 :** a means or place of going out **:** EXIT, OUTLET **4 :** OFFSPRING, PROGENY ⟨died without ∼⟩ **5 a :** a final outcome that usu. constitutes a solution (as of a problem) or resolution (as of a difficulty) **b** *obs* **:** a final conclusion or decision about something arrived at after consideration **c** *archaic* **:** TERMINATION, END ⟨hope that his enterprise would have a prosperous ∼ —T. B. Macaulay⟩ **6 a :** a matter that is in dispute between two or more parties **b** (1) **:** a vital or unsettled matter ⟨economic ∼*s*⟩ (2) **:** CONCERN, PROBLEM ⟨I have ∼*s* with his behavior⟩ **c :** the point at which an unsettled matter is ready for a decision ⟨brought the matter to an ∼⟩ **7 :** a discharge (as of blood) from the body **8 a :** something coming forth from a specified source ⟨∼*s* of a disordered imagination⟩ **b** *obs* **:** DEED **9 a :** the act of publishing or officially giving out or making available ⟨the next ∼ of commemorative stamps⟩ ⟨∼ of supplies by the quartermaster⟩ **b :** the thing or the whole quantity of things given out at one time ⟨read the latest ∼⟩ — **is·sue·less** \ˈi-shü-ləs\ *adj* — **at issue 1 :** in a state of controversy **:** in disagreement **2** *also* **in issue :** under discussion or in dispute

[2]**issue** *vb* **is·sued; is·su·ing** *vi* (14c) **1 a :** to go, come, or flow out **b :** to come forth **:** EMERGE **2 :** ACCRUE ⟨profits *issuing* from the sale of the stock⟩ **3** *archaic* **:** to descend from a specified parent or ancestor **4 :** to be a consequence or final outcome **:** EMANATE, RESULT **5 :** to appear or become available through being officially put forth or distributed **6 :** EVENTUATE, TERMINATE ∼ *vt* **1 :** to cause to come forth **:** DISCHARGE, EMIT **2 a :** to put forth or distribute usu. officially ⟨government *issued* a new airmail stamp⟩ ⟨∼ orders⟩ **b :** to send out for sale or circulation **:** PUBLISH **c** *Brit* **:** PROVIDE 2b, SUPPLY ***syn*** see SPRING — **is·su·er** *n*

[1]**-ist** *n suffix* [F *-iste,* fr. L *-ista, -istes,* fr. Gk *-istēs,* fr. verbs in *-izein* -ize] **1 a :** one that performs a (specified) action ⟨cycl*ist*⟩ **:** one that makes or produces a (specified) thing ⟨novel*ist*⟩ **b :** one that plays a (specified) musical instrument ⟨harp*ist*⟩ **c :** one that operates a (specified) mechanical instrument or contrivance ⟨automobil*ist*⟩ **2 :** one that specializes in a (specified) art or science or skill ⟨geolog*ist*⟩ ⟨ventriloqu*ist*⟩ **3 :** one that adheres to or advocates a (specified) doctrine or system or code of behavior ⟨social*ist*⟩ ⟨royal*ist*⟩ ⟨hedon*ist*⟩ or that of a (specified) individual ⟨Calvin*ist*⟩ ⟨Darwin*ist*⟩

[2]**-ist** *adj suffix* **:** of, relating to, or characteristic of ⟨elit*ist*⟩

isth *abbr* isthmus

[1]**isth·mi·an** \ˈis-mē-ən\ *n* (1601) **1 :** a native or inhabitant of an isthmus **2** *cap* **:** a native or inhabitant of the Isthmus of Panama

[2]**isthmian** *adj* (1603) **:** of, relating to, or situated in or near an isthmus: as **a** *often cap* **:** of or relating to the Isthmus of Corinth in Greece or the games held there in ancient times **b** *often cap* **:** of or relating to the Isthmus of Panama connecting the No. American and So. American continents

isth·mic \ˈis-mik\ *adj* (1888) **:** of or relating to an anatomical isthmus

isth·mus \ˈis-məs\ *n* [L, fr. Gk *isthmos*] (1555) **1 :** a narrow strip of land connecting two larger land areas **2 :** a narrow anatomical part or passage connecting two larger structures or cavities

is·tle \ˈist-lē\ *n* [AmerSp *ixtle,* fr. Nahuatl *ichtli*] (1883) **:** a strong fiber (as for cordage or basketwork) obtained from various tropical American plants (as an agave)

ISV *abbr* International Scientific Vocabulary

[1]**it** \ˈit, ət\ *pron* [ME, fr. OE *hit* — more at HE] (bef. 12c) **1 :** that one — used as subject or direct object or indirect object of a verb or object of a preposition usu. in reference to a lifeless thing ⟨took a quick look at the house and noticed ∼ was very old⟩, a plant ⟨there is a rosebush near the fence and ∼ is now blooming⟩, a person or animal whose sex is unknown or disregarded ⟨don't know who ∼ is⟩, a group of individuals or things, or an abstract entity ⟨beauty is everywhere and ∼ is a source of joy⟩; compare HE, ITS, SHE, THEY **2 —** used as subject of an impersonal verb that expresses a condition or action without reference to an agent ⟨∼ is raining⟩ **3 a —** used as anticipatory subject or object of a verb ⟨∼ is necessary to repeat the whole thing⟩; often used to shift emphasis to a part of a statement other than the subject ⟨∼ was in this city that the treaty was signed⟩ **b —** used with many verbs as a direct object with little or no meaning ⟨footed ∼ back to camp⟩ **4 —** used to refer to an explicit or implicit state of affairs or circumstances ⟨how is ∼ going⟩ **5 :** a crucial or climactic point ⟨this is ∼⟩

[2]**it** \ˈit\ *n* (1842) **:** the player in a game who performs the principal action of the game (as trying to find others in hide-and-seek)

It *abbr* Italian; Italy

IT *abbr* information technology

it·a·con·ic acid \ˌi-tə-ˈkä-nik-\ *n* [ISV, anagram of *aconitic acid,* $C_3H_3(COOH)_3$, fr. *aconite*] (ca. 1872) **:** a crystalline dicarboxylic acid $C_5H_6O_4$ obtained usu. by fermentation of sugars with molds (genus *Aspergillus*) and used as a monomer for polymers and polyesters

ital *abbr* italic; italicized

¹Ital·ian \ə-ˈtal-yən, i- *also* ˌī-\ *n* (14c) **1 a :** a native or inhabitant of Italy **b :** a person of Italian descent **2 :** the Romance language of the Italians

²Italian *adj* (15c) **:** of, relating to, or characteristic of Italy, the Italians, or Italian

ital·ian·ate \-yə-ˌnāt\ *vt* **-at·ed; -at·ing** *often cap* (1567) **:** ITALIANIZE

Ital·ian·ate \-nət, -ˌnāt\ *adj* (1572) **:** Italian in quality or characteristics

Italian dressing *n* (ca. 1902) **:** a salad dressing flavored esp. with garlic and oregano

Italian greyhound *n* (1743) **:** any of a breed of toy dogs resembling the standard greyhound in miniature

ital·ian·ise *often cap, Brit var of* ITALIANIZE

Ital·ian·ism \ə-ˈtal-yə-ˌni-zəm, i- *also* ī-\ *n* (1594) **1 a :** a quality characteristic of Italy or the Italian people **b :** a characteristic feature of Italian occurring in another language **2 a :** specialized interest in or emulation of Italian qualities or achievements **b :** promotion or love of Italian policies or ideals

ital·ian·ize \ə-ˈtal-yə-ˌnīz, i- *also* ī-\ *vb* **-ized; -iz·ing** *often cap, vi* (ca. 1611) **:** to act Italian; *specif* **:** to follow the style or technique of recognized Italian painters ~ *vt* **:** to make Italian (as in appearance or behavior) — **Ital·ian·i·za·tion** \-ˌtal-yə-nə-ˈzā-shən\ *n*

Italian parsley *n* (1972) **:** a flat-leaved parsley

Italian sandwich *n* (ca. 1953) **:** SUBMARINE 2

Italian sonnet *n* (1613) **:** a sonnet consisting of an octave rhyming *abba abba* and a sestet rhyming in any of various patterns (as *cde cde* or *cdc dcd*) — called also *Petrarchan sonnet*

¹ital·ic \ə-ˈta-lik, i-, ī-\ *adj* (1598) **1 a :** of or relating to a type style with characters that slant upward to the right (as in "*these words are italic*") — compare ROMAN **b :** of or relating to a style of slanted cursive handwriting developed in the 15th and 16th centuries **2** *cap* **:** of or relating to ancient Italy, its peoples, or their Indo-European languages

²italic *n* (1676) **1 :** an italic character or type **2** *cap* **:** a branch of the Indo-European language family that includes Latin, Oscan, and Umbrian — see INDO-EUROPEAN LANGUAGES table

ital·i·cise *Brit var of* ITALICIZE

ital·i·cize \ə-ˈta-lə-ˌsīz, i-, ī-\ *vt* **-cized; -ciz·ing** (1795) **1 :** to print in italics or underscore with a single line **2 :** EMPHASIZE ⟨the microphone ~*s* every curdled top note —P. G. Davis⟩ — **ital·i·ci·za·tion** \-ˌta-lə-sə-ˈzā-shən\ *n*

Ita·lo- \i-ˈta-lō *also* ˈi-tə-lō\ *comb form* **1 :** Italian ⟨*Italo*phile⟩ **2 :** Italian and ⟨*Italo*-Austrian⟩

Ita·lo·phile \i-ˈta-lə-ˌfī(-ə)l\ *adj* (ca. 1902) **:** friendly to or favoring what is Italian — **Italophile** *n*

¹itch \ˈich\ *vb* [ME *icchen,* fr. OE *giccan;* akin to OHG *jucchen* to itch] *vi* (bef. 12c) **1 a :** to have an itch ⟨her arm ~*ed*⟩ **b :** to produce an itchy sensation ⟨long underwear that ~*es*⟩ **2 :** to have a restless desire or hankering for something ⟨were ~*ing* to go outside⟩ ~ *vt* **1 :** to cause to itch **2 :** VEX, IRRITATE

²itch *n* (bef. 12c) **1 a :** an uneasy irritating sensation in the upper surface of the skin usu. held to result from mild stimulation of pain receptors **b :** a skin disorder accompanied by such a sensation; *esp* **:** a contagious eruption caused by a mite (*Sarcoptes scabiei*) that burrows in the skin and causes intense itching **2 a :** a restless usu. constant often compulsive desire ⟨an ~ to travel⟩ **b :** LUST, PRURIENCE — **itch·i·ness** \ˈi-chē-nəs\ *n* — **itchy** \ˈi-chē\ *adj*

it'd \ˈi-təd, ˌid\ (1859) **:** it had **:** it would

¹-ite *n suffix* [fr. L *-ita, -ites,* fr. Gk *-itēs*] **1 a :** native **:** resident ⟨Brooklyn*ite*⟩ **b :** descendant ⟨Ephraim*ite*⟩ **c :** adherent **:** follower ⟨Jacob*ite*⟩ ⟨Pusey*ite*⟩ **2 a** (1) **:** product ⟨metabol*ite*⟩ (2) **:** commercially manufactured product ⟨ebon*ite*⟩ **b :** -ITOL ⟨mann*ite*⟩ **3** [NL *-ites,* fr. L] **:** fossil ⟨ammon*ite*⟩ **4 :** mineral ⟨erythr*ite*⟩ **:** rock ⟨anorthos*ite*⟩ **5** [F, fr. L *-ita, -ites*] **:** segment or constituent part of a body or of a bodily part ⟨som*ite*⟩ ⟨dendr*ite*⟩

²-ite *n suffix* [F, alter. of *-ate* -ate, fr. NL *-atum*] **:** salt or ester of an acid with a name ending in *-ous* ⟨nitr*ite*⟩

¹item \ˈī-ˌtem, ˈī-təm\ *adv* [ME, fr. L, fr. *ita* thus] (14c) **:** and in addition **:** ALSO — used to introduce each article in a list or enumeration

²item \ˈī-təm\ *n* (1561) **1** *obs* **:** WARNING, HINT **2 :** a distinct part in an enumeration, account, or series **:** ARTICLE **3 :** an object of attention, concern, or interest **4 :** a separate piece of news or information **5 :** a couple in a romantic or sexual relationship

syn ITEM, DETAIL, PARTICULAR mean one of the distinct parts of a whole. ITEM applies to each thing specified separately in a list or in a group of things that might be listed or enumerated ⟨every *item* on the list⟩. DETAIL applies to one of the small component parts of a larger whole such as a task, building, painting, narration, or process ⟨leave the *details* to others⟩. PARTICULAR stresses the smallness, singleness, and esp. the concreteness of a detail or item ⟨a description that included few *particulars*⟩.

³item \ˈī-təm\ *vt* (1601) **1** *archaic* **:** COMPUTE, RECKON **2** *archaic* **:** to set down the particular details of

item·ise *Brit var of* ITEMIZE

item·i·za·tion \ˌī-tə-mə-ˈzā-shən\ *n* (1894) **:** the act of itemizing; *also* **:** an itemized list

item·ize \ˈī-tə-ˌmīz\ *vt* **-ized; -iz·ing** (1857) **:** to set down in detail or by particulars **:** LIST ⟨*itemized* all expenses⟩

it·er·ance \ˈi-tə-rən(t)s\ *n* (1604) **:** REPETITION 1a

it·er·ant \-rənt\ *adj* (1626) **:** marked by repetition, reiteration, or recurrence ⟨~ echoes⟩

it·er·ate \ˈi-tə-ˌrāt\ *vt* **-at·ed; -at·ing** [L *iteratus,* pp. of *iterare,* fr. *iterum* again; akin to L *is* he, that, *ita* thus, Skt *itara* the other, *iti* thus] (1533) **:** to say or do again or again and again **:** REITERATE

it·er·a·tion \ˌi-tə-ˈrā-shən\ *n* (15c) **1 :** the action or a process of iterating or repeating: as **a :** a procedure in which repetition of a sequence of operations yields results successively closer to a desired result **b :** the repetition of a sequence of computer instructions a specified number of times or until a condition is met — compare RECURSION **2 :** one execution of a sequence of operations or instructions in an iteration **3 :** VERSION, INCARNATION ⟨the latest ~ of the operating system⟩

it·er·a·tive \ˈi-tə-ˌrā-tiv, -rə-\ *adj* (15c) **:** involving repetition: as **a :** expressing repetition of a verbal action **b :** relating to or being iteration of an operation or procedure — **it·er·a·tive·ly** *adv*

ithy·phal·lic \ˌi-thi-ˈfa-lik\ *adj* [LL *ithyphallicus,* fr. Gk *ithyphallikos,* fr. *ithyphallos* erect phallus, fr. *ithys* straight + *phallos* phallus] (1795) **1 :** of or relating to the phallus carried in procession in ancient festivals of Bacchus **2 a :** having an erect penis — usu. used of figures in an art representation **b :** OBSCENE, LEWD

itin·er·an·cy \ī-ˈti-nə-rən(t)-sē\ *n* (1789) **1 :** a system (as in the Methodist Church) of rotating ministers who itinerate **2 a :** the act of itinerating **b :** the state of being itinerant

itin·er·ant \-rənt\ *adj* [LL *itinerant-, itinerans,* prp. of *itinerari* to journey, fr. L *itiner-, iter* journey, way; akin to Hitt *itar* way, L *ire* to go — more at ISSUE] (ca. 1576) **:** traveling from place to place; *esp* **:** covering a circuit ⟨~ preacher⟩ — **itinerant** *n* — **itin·er·ant·ly** *adv*

itin·er·ary \ī-ˈti-nə-ˌrer-ē, ə-, *chiefly Brit* ÷-ˈti-nə-rē\ *n, pl* **-ar·ies** (15c) **1 :** the route of a journey or tour or the proposed outline of one **2 :** a travel diary **3 :** a traveler's guidebook — **itinerary** *adj*

itin·er·ate \ī-ˈti-nə-ˌrāt, ə-\ *vi* **-at·ed; -at·ing** (1775) **:** to travel a preaching or judicial circuit — **itin·er·a·tion** \-ˌti-nə-ˈrā-shən\ *n*

-itious *adj suffix* [L *-icius, -itius*] **:** of, relating to, or having the characteristics of ⟨excrement*itious*⟩

-itis *n suffix, pl* **-itises** *also* **-itides** *or* **-ites** [NL, fr. L & Gk; L, fr. Gk, fr. fem. of *-itēs* -ite] **1 :** disease or inflammation ⟨bronch*itis*⟩ **2** *pl usu* *-itises* **:** condition likened to a disease — chiefly in nonce formations ⟨television*itis*⟩

it'll \ˈi-tᵊl\ (1824) **:** it will **:** it shall

ITO *abbr* International Trade Organization

-itol *n suffix* [ISV ¹*-ite* + ¹*-ol*] **:** polyhydroxy alcohol usu. related to a sugar ⟨mann*itol*⟩

its \ˈits, əts\ *adj* (ca. 1507) **:** of or relating to it or itself esp. as possessor, agent, or object of an action ⟨going to ~ kennel⟩ ⟨a child proud of ~ first drawings⟩ ⟨~ final enactment into law⟩

it's \ˈits, əts\ (ca. 1555) **:** it is **:** it has

it·self \it-ˈself, ət-, *Southern also* -ˈsef\ *pron* (bef. 12c) **1 :** that identical one — compare IT 1 — used reflexively ⟨watched the cat giving ~ a bath⟩, for emphasis ⟨the letter ~ was missing⟩, or in absolute constructions ⟨~ a splendid specimen of classic art, it has been exhibited throughout the world⟩ **2 :** its normal, healthy, or sane condition — **in itself :** in its own nature **:** INTRINSICALLY ⟨was not *in itself* bad⟩

it·ty–bit·ty \ˈi-tē-ˈbi-tē\ *or* **it·sy–bit·sy** \ˈit-sē-ˈbit-sē\ *adj* [prob. fr. baby talk for *little bit*] (1938) **:** extremely small **:** TINY

ITU *abbr* **1** International Telecommunication Union **2** International Typographical Union

ITV *abbr* instructional television

-ity *n suffix, pl* **-ities** [MF *-ité,* fr. L *-itat-, -itas,* fr. *-i-* (stem vowel of adjs.) + *-tat-, -tas* -ty; akin to Gk *-tēt-, -tēs* -ity] **:** quality **:** state **:** degree ⟨alkalin*ity*⟩ ⟨theatrical*ity*⟩

IU *abbr* international unit

IUD \ˌī-(ˌ)yü-ˈdē\ *n* (1965) **:** INTRAUTERINE DEVICE

-ium *n suffix* **1** [NL, fr. L, ending of some neut. nouns] **a :** a chemical element ⟨sod*ium*⟩ **b :** cation ⟨tetrazol*ium*⟩ **2** *pl* **-iums** *or* **-ia** [NL, fr. L, fr. Gk *-ion*] **:** small one **:** mass — esp. in botanical terms ⟨pollin*ium*⟩

¹IV \ˌī-ˈvē\ *n, pl* **IVs** [*intravenous*] (ca. 1955) **:** an apparatus used to administer a fluid (as of medication, blood, or nutrients) intravenously; *also* **:** a fluid administered by IV

²IV *abbr* intravenous; intravenously

-ive *adj suffix* [MF *-ive,* fr. L *-ivus*] **:** that performs or tends toward an (indicated) action ⟨amus*ive*⟩

I've \ˈīv, əv\ (1586) **:** I have

iver·mec·tin \ˌī-vər-ˈmek-tən\ *n* [perh. fr. *di-* + NL *avermitilis* (specific epithet of *Streptomyces avermitilis,* bacterium from which it is derived) + E *-ect-* (of unknown origin) + ¹*-in*] (1981) **:** a drug mixture of two structurally similar semisynthetic lactones that is used in veterinary medicine as an anthelmintic, acaricide, and insecticide and in human medicine to treat onchocerciasis

IVF *abbr* in vitro fertilization

ivied \ˈī-vēd\ *adj* (ca. 1771) **1 :** overgrown with ivy **2 :** ACADEMIC

ivo·ry \ˈīv-rē, ˈī-və-rē\ *n, pl* **-ries** [ME *ivorie,* fr. AF *ivoire, ivurie,* fr. L *eboreus* of ivory, fr. *ebor-, ebur* ivory, fr. Egypt *ꜣb, ꜣbw* elephant, ivory] (13c) **1 a :** the hard creamy-white modified dentine that composes the tusks of a tusked mammal (as an elephant, walrus, or narwhal) **b :** a tusk that yields ivory **2 :** a variable color averaging a pale yellow **3** *slang* **:** TOOTH **4 :** something (as a piano key) made of ivory or of a similar substance — **ivory** *adj*

ivo·ry·bill \-ˌbil\ *n* (1787) **:** IVORY-BILLED WOODPECKER

ivo·ry–billed woodpecker \-ˈbild-\ *n* (1811) **:** a very large black-and-white woodpecker (*Campephilus principalis*) of the southeastern U.S. and Cuba that has a showy red crest in the male and is presumed extinct in the U.S.

ivory black *n* (1634) **:** a fine black pigment made by calcining ivory

ivory nut *n* (ca. 1847) **:** the nutlike seed of a So. American palm (*Phytelephas macrocarpa*) containing a very hard endosperm used for carving and turning — compare VEGETABLE IVORY

ivory tower *n* [trans. of F *tour d'ivoire*] (1911) **1 :** an impractical often escapist attitude marked by aloof lack of concern with or interest in practical matters or urgent problems **2 :** a secluded place that affords the means of treating practical issues with an impractical often escapist attitude; *esp* **:** a place of learning — **ivory–tower** *adj* — **ivo·ry–tow·er·ish** \-ˈtau̇-(ə-)rish\ *adj*

ivo·ry–tow·ered \-ˈtau̇(-ə)rd\ *adj* (1937) **:** divorced from reality and practical matters ⟨an ~ recluse⟩

¹ivy \ˈī-vē\ *n, pl* **ivies** [ME, fr. OE *īfig;* akin to OHG *ebah* ivy] (bef. 12c) **1 :** a widely cultivated ornamental climbing or prostrate or sometimes shrubby chiefly Eurasian vine (*Hedera helix*) of the ginseng family with evergreen leaves, small yellowish flowers, and black berries **2 :** POISON IVY **3** *often cap* **:** an Ivy League college

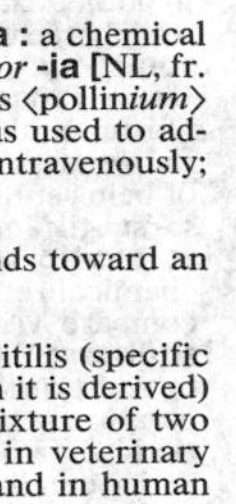

ivy 1

²ivy *adj* [fr. the prevalence of ivy-covered buildings on the campuses of older U.S. colleges] (1933) **1** : ACADEMIC **2** : IVY LEAGUE

Ivy League *adj* (1936) **1** : of, relating to, or characteristic of a group of long-established eastern U.S. colleges and universities widely regarded as high in scholastic and social prestige **2** : of, relating to, or characteristic of the students of Ivy League schools

Ivy Leaguer *n* (1943) : a student at or a graduate of an Ivy League school

IW *abbr* **1** inside width **2** isotopic weight

iwis \ē-ˈwis, ī-\ *adv* [ME, fr. OE *gewis* certain; akin to OHG *giwisso* certainly, OE *witan* to know — more at WIT] (12c) *archaic* : SURELY

IWW *abbr* Industrial Workers of the World

Ix·i·on \ik-ˈsī-ən\ *n* [L, fr. Gk *Ixiōn*] : a Thessalian king bound by Zeus to a burning wheel in Tartarus for attempting to seduce Hera

ix·o·did \ˈik-sə-ˌdid, ik-ˈsō-dəd\ *adj* [ultim. fr. Gk *ixōdēs* sticky, fr. *ixos* birdlime] (ca. 1909) : of or relating to a family (Ixodidae) of ticks (as the deer tick and American dog tick) having a hard outer shell and feeding on usu. three hosts during the life cycle — **ixodid** *n*

Iyar \ˈē-ˌyär\ *n* [Heb *Iyyār*] (1737) : the eighth month of the civil year or the second month of the ecclesiastical year in the Jewish calendar — see MONTH table

-ization *n suffix* : action, process, or result of making ⟨social*ization*⟩

-ize *vb suffix* [MF *-iser*, fr. LL *-izare*, fr. Gk *-izein*] **1 a** (1) : cause to be or conform to or resemble ⟨system*ize*⟩ ⟨American*ize*⟩ : cause to be formed into ⟨union*ize*⟩ (2) : subject to a (specified) action ⟨plagiar*ize*⟩ (3) : impregnate or treat or combine with ⟨alumin*ize*⟩ **b** : treat like ⟨idol*ize*⟩ **c** : treat according to the method of ⟨bowdler*ize*⟩ **2 a** : become : become like ⟨crystall*ize*⟩ **b** : be productive in or of ⟨hypothes*ize*⟩ : engage in a (specified) activity ⟨philosoph*ize*⟩ **c** : adopt or spread the manner of activity or the teaching of ⟨Platon*ize*⟩

usage The suffix *-ize* has been productive in English since the time of Thomas Nashe (1567–1601), who claimed credit for introducing it into English to remedy the surplus of monosyllabic words. Almost any noun or adjective can be made into a verb by adding *-ize* ⟨hospital*ize*⟩ ⟨familiar*ize*⟩; many technical terms are coined this way ⟨oxid*ize*⟩ as well as verbs of ethnic derivation ⟨American*ize*⟩ and verbs derived from proper names ⟨bowdler*ize*⟩ ⟨mesmer*ize*⟩. Nashe noted in 1591 that his *-ize* coinages were being criticized, and to this day new words ending in *-ize* ⟨final*ize*⟩ ⟨prioriti*ze*⟩ are sure to draw critical fire.

iz·zard \ˈi-zərd\ *n* [alter. of earlier *ezod, ezed*, prob. fr. MF *et zede* and Z] (ca. 1726) *chiefly dial* : the letter *z*

---

¹j \ˈjā\ *n, pl* **j's** *or* **js** \ˈjāz\ *often cap, often attrib* (15c) **1 a** : the 10th letter of the English alphabet **b** : a speech counterpart of orthographic *j* **2 a** : a graphic device for reproducing the letter *j* **b** : a unit vector parallel to the y-axis **3** : one designated *j* esp. as the 10th in order or class **4** : something shaped like the letter J

²j *abbr* **1** jack **2** journal **3** judge; justice

J *abbr* **1** joule **2** jumper; jump shot

JA *abbr* **1** joint account **2** judge advocate

¹jab \ˈjab\ *vb* **jabbed; jab·bing** [alter. of *job* to strike] *vt* (1827) **1 a** : to pierce with or as if with a sharp object : STAB **b** : to poke quickly or abruptly : THRUST **2** : to strike with a short straight blow ~ *vi* **1** : to make quick or abrupt thrusts with a sharp object **2** : to strike a person with a short straight blow

²jab *n* (1872) : an act of jabbing; *esp* : a short straight boxing punch delivered with the leading hand

¹jab·ber \ˈja-bər\ *vb* **jab·bered; jab·ber·ing** \ˈja-b(ə-)riŋ\ [ME *jaberen*, of imit. origin] *vi* (15c) : to talk rapidly, indistinctly, or unintelligibly ~ *vt* : to speak rapidly or indistinctly — **jab·ber·er** \ˈja-bər-ər\ *n*

²jabber *n* (1708) : GIBBERISH, CHATTER

jab·ber·wocky \ˈja-bər-ˌwä-kē\ *n* [*Jabberwocky*, nonsense poem by Lewis Carroll] (1902) : meaningless speech or writing

jab·i·ru \ˌzha-bə-ˈrü\ *n* [NL, fr. Pg *jaburu, jabiru*, fr. Tupi *jamburú, jamurú*] (1774) : a large tropical American stork (*Jabiru mycteria*) with a massive black bill

jab·o·ran·di \ˌzha-bə-ˌran-ˈdē, -ˈran-dē\ *n* [Pg, fr. Tupi *jambirandí, jamirandí*] (ca. 1875) : the dried leaves of either of two So. American shrubs (*Pilocarpus jaborandi* and *P. microphyllus*) of the rue family that are a source of pilocarpine

ja·bot \zha-ˈbō, ˈja-ˌbō\ *n* [F] (1823) **1** : a fall of lace or cloth attached to the front of a neckband and worn esp. by men in the 18th century **2** : a pleated frill of cloth or lace attached down the center front of a woman's blouse or dress

ja·bo·ti·ca·ba \ˌzha-ˌbü-ti-ˈkä-ba\ *n* [Pg, fr. Tupi *jaßotikáßa*] (1824) : a Brazilian tree (*Myrciaria cauliflora*) of the myrtle family cultivated in warm regions for its edible usu. purplish fruit

ja·cal \hə-ˈkäl\ *n, pl* **ja·ca·les** \-ˈkä-(ˌ)läs\ *also* **ja·cals** [MexSp, fr. Nahuatl *xahcalli*] (1838) : a hut in Mexico and southwestern U.S. with a thatched roof and walls made of upright poles or sticks covered and chinked with mud or clay

jac·a·mar \ˈzha-kə-ˌmär\ *n* [F, modif. of Pg *jacamacira, jacamarici*, prob. of Tupi-Guarani origin] (1825) : any of a family (Galbulidae) of usu. iridescent green or bronze insectivorous birds of tropical American forests having a long sharp bill

ja·ca·na \ˌjə-ˈkä-nə, ˌzha-sə-ˈnä\ *n* [Pg *jaçanã*, fr. Tupi *jasanã*] (ca. 1753) : any of a family (Jacanidae) of long-legged and long-toed tropical wading birds that frequent coastal freshwater marshes and ponds

jac·a·ran·da \ˌja-kə-ˈran-də\ *n* [NL, fr. Pg *jacarandá* a tree of this genus, fr. Tupi *jakaraná, jakarandá*] (ca. 1753) : any of a genus (*Jacaranda*) of tropical American trees of the bignonia family with bipinnate leaves and panicles of showy usu. blue flowers

jacamar

ja·cinth \ˈjā-sᵊn(t)th, ˈja-\ *n* [ME *iacinct*, fr. AF *jacinte*, fr. L *hyacinthus*, fr. Gk *hyakinthos*] (13c) **1** : HYACINTH **2** : a gem more nearly orange in color than a hyacinth

¹jack \ˈjak\ *n* [ME *Jacke*, familiar term of address to a social inferior, nickname for *Johan* John] (1548) **1 a** : MAN — usu. used as an intensive in such phrases as *every man jack* **b** *often cap* : SAILOR **c** (1) : SERVANT, LABORER (2) : LUMBERJACK **2** : any of various usu. mechanical devices: as **a** : a device for turning a spit **b** : a usu. portable mechanism or device for exerting pressure or lifting a heavy body a short distance **3** : something that supports or holds in position: as **a** : an iron bar at a topgallant masthead to support a royal mast and spread the royal shrouds **b** : a wooden brace fastened behind a scenic unit in a stage set to prop it up **4 a** : any of several fishes; *esp* : any of various carangids **b** : a male donkey **c** : JACKRABBIT **d** : any of several birds (as a jackdaw) **5 a** : a small white target ball in lawn bowling **b** : a small national flag flown by a ship **c** (1) *pl but sing in constr* : a game played with a set of small objects that are tossed, caught, and moved in various figures (2) : a small 6-pointed metal object used in the game of jacks **6 a** : a playing card carrying the figure of a soldier or servant and ranking usu. below the queen **b** : JACKPOT 1a(2) **7** *slang* : MONEY **8** : a female fitting in an electric circuit used with a plug to make a connection with another circuit **9 a** : APPLEJACK **b** : BRANDY **10** : JACKKNIFE 2 **11** : MONTEREY JACK

²jack *vi* (ca. 1841) : to hunt or fish at night with a jacklight ~ *vt* **1** : to hunt or fish for at night with a jacklight **2 a** : to move or lift by or as if by a jack **b** : to raise the level of — usu. used with *up* ⟨~ up the price⟩ **c** : to take to task — **jack·er** *n*

jack·al \ˈja-kəl *also* -ˌkȯl\ *n* [Turk *çakal*, fr. Pers *shaqāl*, of Indo-Aryan origin; akin to Skt *sṛgāla* jackal] (1603) **1** : any of several small omnivorous canids (as *Canis aureus*) of Africa and Asia having large ears, long legs, and bushy tails **2 a** : a person who performs routine or menial tasks for another **b** : a person who serves or collaborates with another esp. in the commission of base acts

Jack-a–Lent \ˈjak-ə-ˌlent\ *n* [¹*jack* + *a* (of) + *Lent*] (1598) **1** : a small stuffed puppet set up to be pelted for fun in Lent **2** : a simple or insignificant person

jack·a·napes \ˈja-kə-ˌnāps\ *n* [ME *Jack Napis*, nickname for William de la Pole †1450 duke of Suffolk] (1526) **1** : MONKEY, APE **2 a** : an impudent or conceited fellow **b** : a saucy or mischievous child

jack·ass \ˈjak-ˌas\ *n* (1727) **1** : DONKEY; *esp* : a male donkey **2** : a stupid person : FOOL

jack bean *n* (1885) : a bushy annual tropical American legume (*Canavalia ensiformis*) grown esp. for forage

jack·boot \ˈjak-ˌbüt\ *n* (1686) **1** : a heavy military boot made of glossy black leather extending above the knee and worn esp. during the 17th and 18th centuries **2** : the spirit or policy of militarism or totalitarianism **3** : a laceless military boot reaching to the calf

jack·boot·ed \-ˌbü-təd\ *adj* (1846) **1** : wearing jackboots **2** : ruthlessly and violently oppressive ⟨~ force⟩

jack cheese *n, often cap J* (1912) : MONTEREY JACK

jack crevalle *n* (1948) : a carangid fish (*Caranx hippos*) that is an important food fish esp. along the west coast of Florida

jack·daw \ˈjak-ˌdȯ\ *n* (1543) **1** : a common black and gray bird (*Corvus monedula*) of Eurasia and northern Africa that is related to but smaller than the carrion crow **2** : GRACKLE 1

¹jack·et \ˈja-kət\ *n* [ME *jaket*, fr. AF *jackés*, pl., dim. of MF *jaque* short jacket, fr. *jacques* peasant, fr. the name *Jacques* James] (15c) **1 a** : a garment for the upper body usu. having a front opening, collar, lapels, sleeves, and pockets **b** : something worn or fastened around the body but not for use as clothing **2 a** (1) : the natural covering of an animal (2) : the fur or wool of a mammal **b** : the skin of a potato **3** : an outer covering or casing: as **a** (1) : a thermally nonconducting cover **b** : a covering that encloses an intermediate space through which a temperature-controlling fluid circulates (3) : a tough cold-worked

---

\ə\ abut \ᵊ\ kitten, F table \ər\ **further** \a\ ash \ā\ ace \ä\ mop, mar
\au̇\ **out** \ch\ **chin** \e\ bet \ē\ **easy** \g\ go \i\ hit \ī\ **ice** \j\ **job**
\ŋ\ **sing** \ō\ **go** \ȯ\ **law** \ȯi\ **boy** \th\ **thin** \t̲h̲\ **the** \ü\ **loot** \u̇\ **foot**
\y\ **yet** \zh\ **vision, beige** \k̲, ⁿ, œ, ɶ, ᵛ\ *see* Guide to Pronunciation

metal casing that forms the outer shell of a built-up bullet **b** (1) **:** a wrapper or open envelope for a document (2) **:** an envelope for enclosing registered mail during delivery from one post office to another **c** (1) **:** a detachable protective cover for a book (2) **:** a paper or cardboard envelope for a phonograph record — **jack·et·less** \-ləs\ *adj*

[2]**jacket** *vt* (1856) **:** to put a jacket on **:** enclose in or with a jacket

Jack Frost *n* (1826) **:** frost or frosty weather personified

jack·fruit \ˈjak-ˌfrüt\ *n* [Pg *jaca* jackfruit, fr. Malayalam *cakka*] (1830) **:** a large tropical Asian tree (*Artocarpus heterophyllus*) related to the breadfruit that yields a fine-grained yellow wood and immense fruits which contain an edible pulp and nutritious seeds; *also* **:** its fruit

jack·ham·mer \ˈjak-ˌha-mər\ *n* (1916) **1 :** a pneumatically operated percussive rock-drilling tool usu. held in the hands **2 :** a device in which a tool (as a chisel for breaking up pavements) is driven percussively by compressed air — **jackhammer** *vb*

jack–in–the–box \ˈjak-ən-t͟hə-ˌbäks\ *n, pl* **jack–in–the–box·es** *or* **jacks–in–the–box** (1702) **:** a toy consisting of a small box out of which a figure (as of a clown's head) springs when the lid is raised

jack–in–the–pul·pit \ˌjak-ən-t͟hə-ˈpu̇l-ˌpit, -pət *also* -ˈpəl-\ *n, pl* **jack–in–the–pulpits** *also* **jacks–in–the–pulpit** (1837) **:** a No. American spring-flowering woodland herb (*Arisaema triphyllum* syn. *A. atrorubens*) of the arum family having an upright club-shaped spadix arched over by a green and purple spathe

[1]**jack·knife** \ˈjak-ˌnīf\ *n* (1711) **1 :** a large strong pocketknife **2 :** a dive executed headfirst in which the diver bends from the waist and touches the ankles while holding the knees unbent and then straightens out

[2]**jackknife** *vt* (1806) **1 :** to cut with a jackknife **2 :** to cause to double up like a jackknife ~ *vi* **1 :** to double up like a jackknife ⟨*jackknifed* into a seat beside me, folding up his six feet eight —Lady Bird Johnson⟩ **2 :** to turn and form an angle of 90 degrees or less with each other — used esp. of a tractor-trailer combination

jack·leg \ˈjak-ˌleg, -ˌläg\ *adj* [[1]*jack* + *-leg* (as in *blackleg*)] (1850) **1 a :** characterized by unscrupulousness, dishonesty, or lack of professional standards ⟨a ~ lawyer⟩ **b :** lacking skill or training **:** AMATEUR ⟨a ~ carpenter⟩ **2 :** designed as a temporary expedient **:** MAKESHIFT — **jackleg** *n*

jack·light \-ˌlīt\ *n* (ca. 1841) **:** a light used esp. in hunting or fishing at night

jack mackerel *n* (1882) **:** a carangid food fish (*Trachurus symmetricus*) of the Pacific coast of America that is iridescent green or bluish above and silvery below

jack–of–all–trades \ˌjak-əv-ˌȯl-ˈtrādz\ *n, pl* **jacks–of–all–trades** (1618) **:** a person who can do passable work at various tasks **:** a handy versatile person

jack off *vb* [prob. alter. of *jerk off*] (ca. 1916) *usu vulgar* **:** MASTURBATE

jack–o'–lan·tern \ˈja-kə-ˌlan-tərn\ *n* (1667) **1 :** IGNIS FATUUS **2 :** a lantern made of a pumpkin cut to look like a human face **3 :** a large orangish gill fungus (*Omphalotus olearius* syn. *Clitocybe illudens*) that is poisonous and luminescent

jack pine *n* (1883) **:** a slender pine (*Pinus banksiana*) of northern No. America that has two stout needles in each fascicle and wood used esp. for pulpwood — see CONE illustration

jack plane *n* (ca. 1816) **:** a medium-sized general-purpose plane used in carpentry and joinery

jack·pot \ˈjak-ˌpät\ *n* (1879) **1 a** (1) **:** a hand or game of draw poker in which a pair of jacks or better is required to open (2) **:** a large pot (as in poker) formed by the accumulation of stakes from previous play **b** (1) **:** a combination on a slot machine that wins a top prize or all the coins available for paying out (2) **:** the sum so won **c :** the top prize in a game or contest (as a lottery) that is typically a large fund of money formed by the accumulation of unwon prizes **2 :** an impressive often unexpected success or reward **3** *chiefly West* **:** a tight spot **:** JAM

jack·rab·bit \-ˌra-bət\ *n* [[1]*jack* (jackass) + *rabbit;* fr. its long ears] (1863) **:** any of several large hares (genus *Lepus*) of western No. America having very long ears and long hind legs

Jack Russell terrier \ˈjak-ˈrə-səl-\ *n* [*Jack* (John) *Russell* †1883 Eng. clergyman & dog breeder] (1961) **:** any of a breed of small terriers having a white coat with brown, black, or brown-and-black markings — called also *Jack Russell*

jack salmon *n* (1871) **1 :** WALLEYE 3 **2 :** GRILSE

jack·screw \ˈjak-ˌskrü\ *n* (1769) **:** SCREW JACK

jack·smelt \-ˌsmelt\ *n* (1949) **:** a large silverside (*Atherinopsis californiensis*) of the Pacific coast of No. America that is the chief commercial smelt of the California markets

Jack·son Day \ˈjak-sən-\ *n* [Andrew *Jackson;* fr. his defense of New Orleans] (1885) **:** January 8 celebrated as a legal holiday in Louisiana to commemorate the successful defense of New Orleans in 1815

jack stand *n* (1968) **:** a stand whose height may be adjusted and which is used to support an automobile that has been raised by a jack

jack·stay \-ˌstā\ *n* (ca. 1840) **1 :** an iron rod, wooden bar, or wire rope along a yard of a ship to which the sails are fastened **2 :** a support of wood, iron, or rope running up a mast on which the parrel of a yard travels

jack·straw \ˈjak-ˌstrȯ\ *n* (1801) **1** *pl but sing in constr* **:** a game in which a set of straws or thin strips is let fall in a heap with each player in turn trying to remove one at a time without disturbing the rest **2 :** one of the pieces used in the game jackstraws

jack–tar \-ˈtär\ *n, often cap* (1781) **:** SAILOR

jack–up \ˈjak-ˌəp\ *n* (1965) **:** a drilling rig used in offshore drilling whose drilling platform is a barge from which legs are lowered to the bottom when over the drill site and which is raised above the water and supported on the legs to conduct drilling operations

Ja·cob \ˈjā-kəb\ *n* [LL, fr. Gk *Iakōb,* fr. Heb *Yaʽăqōbh*] (bef. 12c) **1 :** a son of Isaac and Rebekah, the twin brother of Esau, and heir of God's promise of blessing to Abraham **2 :** the ancient Hebrew nation

Jac·o·be·an \ˌja-kə-ˈbē-ən\ *adj* [NL *Jacobaeus,* fr. *Jacobus* James] (1844) **:** of, relating to, or characteristic of James I of England or his age — **Jacobean** *n*

jacobean lily *n, often cap J* [LL *Jacobus* (St. James)] (ca. 1774) **:** a Mexican bulbous herb (*Sprekelia formosissima*) of the amaryllis family cultivated for its bright red solitary flower

Ja·co·bi·an \jə-ˈkō-bē-ən, yä-\ *n* [K. G. J. *Jacobi* †1851 Ger. mathematician] (1881) **:** a determinant which is defined for a finite number of functions of the same number of variables and in which each row consists of the first partial derivatives of the same function with respect to each of the variables

Jac·o·bin \ˈja-kə-bən\ *n* [ME, fr. AF *jacopin,* fr. ML *Jacobinus,* fr. LL *Jacobus* (St. James); fr. the location of the first Dominican convent in the street of St. James, Paris] (14c) **1 :** DOMINICAN **2** [F, fr. *Jacobin* Dominican; fr. the group's founding in the Dominican convent in Paris] **:** a member of an extremist or radical political group; *esp* **:** a member of such a group advocating egalitarian democracy and engaging in terrorist activities during the French Revolution of 1789 — **Jac·o·bin·ic** \ˌja-kə-ˈbi-nik\ *or* **Jac·o·bin·i·cal** \-ni-kəl\ *adj* — **Jac·o·bin·ism** \ˈja-kə-bə-ˌni-zəm\ *n*

[1]**Jac·o·bite** \ˈja-kə-ˌbīt\ *n* [ME, fr. ML *Jacobita,* fr. *Jacobus* Baradaeus (Jacob Baradai) †578 Syrian monk] (15c) **:** a member of any of various Monophysite Eastern churches; *esp* **:** a member of the Monophysite Syrian church

[2]**Jacobite** *n* [*Jacobus* (James II)] (1689) **:** a partisan of James II of England or of the Stuarts after the revolution of 1688 — **Jac·o·bit·i·cal** \ˌja-kə-ˈbi-ti-kəl\ *adj* — **Jac·o·bit·ism** \ˈja-kə-ˌbī-ˌti-zəm\ *n*

Ja·cob's ladder \ˈjā-kəbz-\ *n* [fr. the ladder seen in a dream by Jacob in Gen 28:12] (1733) **1 :** any of a genus (*Polemonium*) of herbs of the phlox family that have pinnate leaves, a bell-shaped corolla, and a several-seeded capsule; *esp* **:** a perennial herb (*P. caeruleum*) with bright blue or occas. white flowers **2 :** a marine ladder of rope or chain with wooden or iron rungs

Ja·cob·son's organ \ˈjā-kəb-sənz-\ *n* [Ludvig L. *Jacobson* †1843 Dan. anatomist] (1885) **:** VOMERONASAL ORGAN

Ja·co·bus \jə-ˈkō-bəs\ *n* [*Jacobus* (James I), during whose reign unites were coined] (1612) **:** UNITE

jac·o·net \ˈja-kə-ˌnet\ *n* [modif. of Hindi & Urdu *jagannāthī,* fr. *Jagannāth,* seaport in India] (1769) **:** a lightweight cotton cloth used for clothing and bandages

jac·quard \ˈja-ˌkärd\ *n, often cap, often attrib* [Joseph *Jacquard*] (1890) **1 a :** the control mechanism of a Jacquard loom **b :** JACQUARD LOOM **2 :** a fabric of intricate variegated weave or pattern

Jacquard loom *n* (1851) **:** a loom designed to weave fabrics of intricate design whose control mechanism makes use of cards with holes punched in them

jac·que·rie \ˌzhä-kə-ˈrē, ˌzha-\ *n, often cap* [MF, fr. the French peasant revolt in 1358, fr. *jacque* peasant — more at JACKET] (1523) **:** a peasants' revolt

jac·ti·ta·tion \ˌjak-tə-ˈtā-shən\ *n* [LL *jactitation-, jactitatio,* fr. *jactitare,* freq. of L *jactare* to throw — more at JET] (1665) **:** a tossing to and fro or jerking and twitching of the body

Ja·cuz·zi \jə-ˈkü-zē\ *trademark* — used for a whirlpool bath and a recreational bathing tub or pool

[1]**jade** \ˈjād\ *n* [ME] (14c) **1 :** a broken-down, vicious, or worthless horse **2 a :** a disreputable woman **b :** a flirtatious girl

[2]**jade** *vb* **jad·ed; jad·ing** *vt* (1524) **1 a :** to wear out by overwork or abuse **b :** to tire or dull through repetition or excess **2** *obs* **:** to make ridiculous ~ *vi* **:** to become weary or dulled ***syn*** see TIRE

[3]**jade** *n* [F, fr. obs. Sp (*piedra de la*) *ijada,* lit., loin stone, ultim. fr. L *ilia,* pl., flanks; fr. the belief that jade cures renal colic] (ca. 1741) **1 :** either of two tough compact typically green gemstones that take a high polish: **a :** JADEITE **b :** NEPHRITE **2 :** a sculpture or artifact of jade **3 :** JADE GREEN

jaded *adj* (1600) **1 :** fatigued by overwork **:** EXHAUSTED **2 :** made dull, apathetic, or cynical by experience or by surfeit ⟨~ network viewers⟩ ⟨~ voters⟩ — **jad·ed·ly** *adv* — **jad·ed·ness** *n*

jade green *n* (1890) **:** a light bluish green

jade·ite \ˈjā-ˌdīt\ *n* [F] (1865) **:** a usu. green monoclinic mineral of the pyroxene group that is a silicate of sodium and aluminum and is a jade — **ja·dit·ic** \jā-ˈdi-tik\ *adj*

jade plant *n* (1944) **:** any of several succulent plants (genus *Crassula*) of the orpine family cultivated as foliage plants

jae·ger \ˈyā-gər\ *n* [G *Jäger*] (1781) **1 a :** HUNTER, HUNTSMAN **b :** one attending a person of rank or wealth and wearing hunter's costume **2 :** any of several large dark-colored birds (genus *Stercorarius*) of northern seas that are related to the skua, are strong fliers, and tend to harass weaker birds until they drop or disgorge their prey

[1]**jag** \ˈjag\ *vb* **jagged; jag·ging** [ME *jaggen*] *vt* (15c) **1** *chiefly dial* **:** PRICK, STAB **2 :** to cut indentations into; *also* **:** to form teeth on (a saw) by cutting indentations ~ *vi* **1 :** PRICK, THRUST **2 :** to move in jerks — **jag·ger** *n*

[2]**jag** *n* (1578) **:** a sharp projecting part **:** BARB

[3]**jag** *n* [origin unknown] (1597) **1 :** a small load **2 a :** a state or feeling of exhilaration or intoxication usu. induced by liquor **b :** SPREE ⟨a crying ~⟩

JAG *abbr* judge advocate general

jag·ged \ˈja-gəd\ *adj* (1523) **1 :** having a sharply uneven edge or surface ⟨~ peaks⟩ **2 :** having a harsh, rough, or irregular quality ⟨~ rhythms⟩ — **jag·ged·ly** *adv* — **jag·ged·ness** *n*

jag·gery \ˈja-gə-rē\ *n* [Pg *jágara,* prob. fr. Malayalam *chakkara* sugar] (1631) **:** an unrefined brown sugar made from palm sap

jag·gy \ˈja-gē\ *adj* **jag·gi·er; -est** (1717) **:** JAGGED, NOTCHED

jag·uar \ˈja-ˌgwär, -gyə-ˌwär, -gwər; *dial* -gwī(-ə)r, *esp Brit* ˈja-gyə-wər\ *n, pl* **jaguars** *also* **jaguar** [Pg, fr. Tupi *jawára* large carnivore] (1604) **:** a large cat (*Panthera onca*) chiefly of Central and So. America that is larger and stockier than the leopard and is brownish yellow or buff with black spots

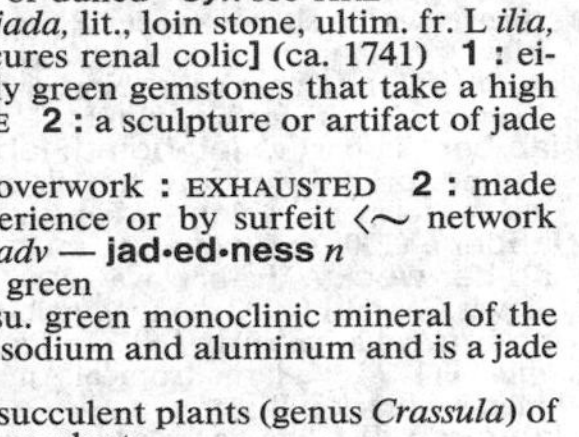

jaguar

jag·ua·run·di \ˌzha-gwə-ˈrən-dē, ˌja-\ *also* **jag·ua·ron·di** \-ˈrän-\ *n* [AmerSp, fr. Old Guarani *yaguarundi;* akin to Tupi *jawarundi* jaguarundi] (ca. 1885) **:** a slender long-tailed short-legged black, gray, or reddish wildcat (*Felis yagouaroundi*) chiefly of Central and So. America

Jah \ˈjä\ *n* [Heb *Yāh*] (1975) **:** the Supreme Being of Rastafarianism

Jahveh *var of* YAHWEH

jai alai \ˈhī-ˌlī, ˌhī-ə-ˈlī\ *n* [Sp, fr. Basque, fr. *jai* festival + *alai* merry] (1903) **:** a court game somewhat like handball played usu. by two or four players with a ball and a long curved wicker basket strapped to the wrist

[1]**jail** \ˈjāl\ *n* [ME *jaiole,* fr. AF *gaiole, jaiole,* fr. LL *caveola,* dim. of L *cavea* cage — more at CAGE] (13c) **1 :** a place of confinement for persons held in lawful custody; *specif* **:** such a place under the jurisdiction of a local government (as a county) for the confinement of persons awaiting trial or those convicted of minor crimes — compare PRISON **2 :** confinement in a jail ⟨sentenced to ~⟩

[2]**jail** *vt* (1604) **:** to confine in or as if in a jail

jail·bait \ˈjāl-ˌbāt\ *n* (1930) **:** a girl under the age of consent with whom sexual intercourse is unlawful and constitutes statutory rape

jail·bird \-ˌbərd\ *n* (1603) **:** a person confined in jail; *esp* **:** a habitual criminal

jail·break \-ˌbrāk\ *n* (1910) **:** a forcible escape from jail

jail·er *also* **jail·or** \ˈjā-lər\ *n* (13c) **1 :** a keeper of a jail **2 :** one that restricts another's liberty as if by imprisonment

jail·house \ˈjāl-ˌhau̇s\ *n* (1812) **:** JAIL 1

jailhouse lawyer *n* (1969) **:** a prison inmate self-taught in the law who tries to gain release through legal maneuvers or who advises fellow inmates on their legal problems

Jain \ˈjīn\ *or* **Jai·na** \ˈjī-nə\ *n* [Hindi & Urdu *Jain,* fr. Skt *Jaina*] (1805) **:** an adherent of Jainism

Jain·ism \ˈjī-ˌni-zəm\ *n* (1858) **:** a religion of India originating in the sixth century B.C. and teaching liberation of the soul by right knowledge, right faith, and right conduct

[1]**jake** \ˈjāk\ *adj* [origin unknown] (1914) *slang* **:** ALL RIGHT, FINE

[2]**jake** *n* [prob. fr. *Jake,* nickname for *Jacob*] (1979) **:** a sexually immature male wild turkey under two years old

jake leg \ˈjāk-ˌleg, -ˌlāg\ *n* [*jake* grain alcohol flavored with an alcoholic extract of ginger] (1932) **:** a paralysis caused by drinking improperly distilled or contaminated liquor

jakes \ˈjāks\ *n pl but sing or pl in constr* [perh. fr. F *Jacques* James] (1538) **:** PRIVY 1

jal·ap \ˈja-ləp, ˈjä-\ *n* [F & Sp; F *jalap,* fr. Sp *jalapa,* fr. *Jalapa,* Mexico] (1644) **1 a :** the dried tuberous root of a Mexican plant (*Ipomoea purga* syn. *Exogonium purga*) of the morning-glory family; *also* **:** a powdered purgative drug prepared from it that contains resinous glycosides **b :** the root or derived drug of plants related to the one supplying jalap **2 :** a plant yielding jalap

ja·la·pe·ño *also* **ja·la·pe·no** \ˌhä-lə-ˈpā-(ˌ)nyō, ˌha-, -ˈpā-(ˌ)nō, -ˈpē-(ˌ)nō\ *n, pl* **-ños** *also* **-nos** [MexSp, fr. *jalapeño,* adj., of Jalapa] (1939) **:** a small plump dark green chili pepper of Mexico and the southern U.S. — called also *jalapeño pepper*

ja·lopy \jə-ˈlä-pē\ *n, pl* **ja·lop·ies** [origin unknown] (1928) **:** a dilapidated old vehicle (as an automobile)

jal·ou·sie \ˈja-lə-sē\ *n* [F, lit., jealousy, fr. OF *gelus* jealous] (1766) **1 :** a blind with adjustable horizontal slats for admitting light and air while excluding direct sun and rain **2 :** a window made of adjustable glass louvers that control ventilation

[1]**jam** \ˈjam\ *vb* **jammed; jam·ming** [origin unknown] *vi* (1706) **1 a :** to become blocked or wedged **b :** to become unworkable through the jamming of a movable part **2 :** to force one's way into a restricted space **3 :** to take part in a jam session **4 :** DUNK 2 ~ *vt* **1 a :** to press into a close or tight position ⟨~ his hat on⟩ **b** (1) **:** to cause to become wedged so as to be unworkable ⟨~ the typewriter keys⟩ (2) **:** to make unworkable by jamming **c :** to block passage of **:** OBSTRUCT **d :** to fill often to excess **:** PACK ⟨the crowd *jammed* the theater⟩ **2 :** to push forcibly; *esp* **:** to apply (brakes) suddenly and forcibly — used with *on* **3 :** CRUSH, BRUISE **4 a :** to make unintelligible by sending out interfering signals or messages **b :** to make (as a radar apparatus) ineffective by jamming signals or by causing reflection of radar waves **5 :** to block, crowd, or bump (a pass receiver) near the line of scrimmage in football **6 :** to pitch inside to (a batter) — **jam·mer** \ˈja-mər\ *n*

[2]**jam** *n* (1805) **1 a :** an act or instance of jamming **b :** a crowded mass that impedes or blocks ⟨a traffic ~⟩ **2 a :** the quality or state of being jammed **b :** the pressure or congestion of a crowd **:** CRUSH **3 :** a difficult state of affairs **:** FIX ⟨got into a ~⟩ **4 :** JAM SESSION **5 :** DUNK SHOT **6** *slang* **:** a musical piece

[3]**jam** *n* [prob. fr. [1]*jam*] (ca. 1736) **:** a food made by boiling fruit and sugar to a thick consistency — **jam·my** \ˈja-mē\ *adj*

Jam *abbr* Jamaica

Jamaica rum *n* (1734) **:** a heavy-bodied rum made by slow fermentation and marked by a pungent bouquet

jamb \ˈjam\ *n* [ME *jambe,* fr. AF *jambe, gambe,* lit., leg, fr. LL *gamba* — more at GAMBIT] (14c) **1 :** an upright piece or surface forming the side of an opening (as for a door, window, or fireplace) **2 :** a projecting columnar part or mass

jam·ba·laya \ˌjəm-bə-ˈlī-ə\ *n* [LaF, fr. Occitan *jambalaia*] (1872) **1 :** rice cooked usu. with ham, sausage, chicken, shrimp, or oysters and seasoned with herbs **2 :** a mixture of diverse elements ⟨curious ~*s* of competing elements —Neil Hickey⟩

jam·beau \ˈjam-(ˌ)bō\ *n, pl* **jam·beaux** \-(ˌ)bōz\ [ME, prob. modif. of AF *jambers,* pl., fr. *jambe*] (14c) **:** a piece of medieval armor for the leg below the knee — see ARMOR illustration

jam·bo·ree \ˌjam-bə-ˈrē\ *n* [origin unknown] (1864) **1 :** a noisy or unrestrained carouse **2 a :** a large festive gathering **b :** a national or international camping assembly of Boy Scouts **3 :** a long mixed program of entertainment

James \ˈjāmz\ *n* [ME, fr. AF, fr. VL **Jacomus,* alter. of LL *Jacobus, Jacob* Jacob] (13c) **1 :** an apostle, son of Zebedee, and brother of the apostle John according to the Gospel accounts **2 :** an apostle and son of Alphaeus according to the Gospel accounts — called also *James the Less* **3 :** a brother of Jesus traditionally held to be the author of the New Testament Epistle of James **4 :** a moral lecture addressed to early Christians and included as a book in the New Testament — see BIBLE table

jam·mies \ˈja-mēz\ *n pl* [by shortening & alter.] (1973) **:** PAJAMAS 2

jam–pack \ˈjam-ˈpak\ *vt* (1924) **:** to pack tightly or to excess

Jams \ˈjamz\ *trademark* — used for knee-length loose-fitting swim trunks

jam session *n* [[2]*jam*] (1933) **:** an often impromptu performance by a group esp. of jazz musicians that is characterized by improvisation

Jam·shid *or* **Jam·shyd** \jam-ˈshēd\ *n* [Pers *Jamshīd*] (1815) **:** an early legendary king of Persia who reigned for 700 years

jam–up \ˈjam-ˌəp\ *n* (1941) **:** JAM 1

Jan *abbr* January

Jane Doe \ˈjān-ˈdō\ *n* (1936) **:** a woman who is a party to legal proceedings and whose true name is unknown or withheld

Jane·ite \ˈjā-ˌnīt\ *n* (1896) **:** an enthusiastic admirer of Jane Austen's writings

[1]**jan·gle** \ˈjaŋ-gəl\ *vb* **jan·gled; jan·gling** \-g(ə-)liŋ\ [ME, fr. AF *jangler,* of Gmc origin; akin to MD *jangelen* to grumble] *vi* (14c) **1 :** to talk idly **2 :** to quarrel verbally **3 :** to make a harsh or discordant often ringing sound ⟨keys *jangling* in my pocket⟩ ~ *vt* **1 :** to utter or sound in a discordant, babbling, or chattering way **2 a :** to cause to sound harshly or inharmoniously **b :** to excite to tense irritation ⟨*jangled* nerves⟩ — **jan·gler** \-g(ə-)lər\ *n*

[2]**jangle** *n* (14c) **1 :** idle talk **2 :** noisy quarreling **3 :** a discordant often ringing sound ⟨the ~ of spurs⟩

jan·gly \ˈjaŋ-g(ə-)lē\ *adj* (1892) **:** marked by jangling **:** having a jangling quality ⟨~ earrings⟩ ⟨~ guitar music⟩

jan·is·sary *also* **jan·i·zary** \ˈja-nə-ˌser-ē, -ˌzer-\ *n, pl* **-sar·ies** *also* **-zar·ies** [It *gianizzero,* fr. Turk *yeniçeri,* fr. *yeni* new + *çeri* soldier] (1529) **1** *often cap* **:** a soldier of an elite corps of Turkish troops organized in the 14th century and abolished in 1826 **2 :** a member of a group of loyal or subservient troops, officials, or supporters

jan·i·tor \ˈja-nə-tər\ *n* [L, fr. *janus* arch, gate] (1629) **1 :** DOORKEEPER **2 :** one who keeps the premises of a building (as an apartment or office) clean, tends the heating system, and makes minor repairs — **jan·i·to·ri·al** \ˌja-nə-ˈtȯr-ē-əl\ *adj*

Jan·sen·ism \ˈjan(t)-sə-ˌni-zəm\ *n* [F *jansénisme,* fr. Cornelis *Jansen*] (ca. 1656) **1 :** a system of doctrine based on moral determinism, defended by various reformist factions among 17th and 18th century western European Roman Catholic clergy, religious, and scholars, and condemned as heretical by papal authority **2 :** a puritanical attitude (as toward sex) — **Jan·sen·ist** \-nist\ *n* — **Jan·sen·is·tic** \ˌjan(t)-sə-ˈnis-tik\ *adj*

Jan·u·ary \ˈjan-yə-ˌwer-ē, -ˌwe-rē\ *n, pl* **-ar·ies** *or* **-ar·ys** [ME *Januarie,* fr. L *Januarius,* 1st month of the ancient Roman year, fr. *Janus*] (14c) **:** the first month of the Gregorian calendar

Ja·nus \ˈjā-nəs\ *n* [L] (1508) **:** a Roman god that is identified with doors, gates, and all beginnings and that is depicted with two opposite faces

Janus–faced \-ˌfāst\ *adj* (1682) **:** having two contrasting aspects; *esp* **:** DUPLICITOUS, TWO-FACED

Janus green *n* [prob. fr. *Janus,* a trademark] (1898) **:** a basic azine dye used esp. as a vital biological stain (as for mitochondria)

Jap \ˈjap\ *n or adj* (1886) *usu disparaging* **:** JAPANESE

JAP \ˈjap\ *n* (ca. 1973) *usu disparaging* **:** JEWISH AMERICAN PRINCESS

[1]**ja·pan** \jə-ˈpan\ *adj* (1673) **:** of, relating to, or originating in Japan **:** of a kind or style characteristic of Japanese workmanship

[2]**japan** *n* (1688) **1 a :** any of several varnishes yielding a hard brilliant finish **b :** a hard dark coating containing asphalt and a drier that is used esp. on metal and fixed by heating — called also *japan black* **2 :** work (as lacquer ware) finished and decorated in the Japanese manner

[3]**japan** *vt* **ja·panned; ja·pan·ning** (1703) **1 :** to cover with or as if with a coat of japan **2 :** to give a high gloss to — **ja·pan·ner** *n*

Jap·a·nese \ˌja-pə-ˈnēz, -ˈnēs\ *n, pl* **Japanese** (1613) **1 a :** a native or inhabitant of Japan **b :** a person of Japanese descent **2 :** the language of the Japanese — **Japanese** *adj*

Japanese an·drom·e·da \-ˌan-ˈdrä-mə-də\ *n* [NL *Andromeda,* genus of plants, fr. L *Andromeda,* Ethiopian princess, fr. Gk *Andromedē*] (1948) **:** a shrubby evergreen heath (*Pieris japonica*) of southeastern Asia with glossy leaves and drooping clusters of usu. whitish flowers

Japanese beetle *n* (1900) **:** a small metallic green and brown scarab beetle (*Popillia japonica*) that has been introduced into eastern No. America from Japan and as a grub feeds on the roots of grasses and decaying vegetation and as an adult eats foliage and fruits

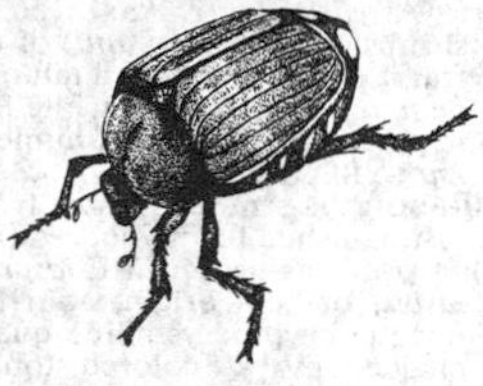

Japanese beetle

Japanese cedar *n* (ca. 1880) **:** a large Chinese and Japanese evergreen tree (*Cryptomeria japonica*) of the cypress family grown as an ornamental and for its valuable soft wood

Japanese eggplant *n* (1981) **:** a long slender eggplant having a dark purple thin skin

Japanese iris *n* (1883) **:** any of various beardless garden irises (esp. *Iris kaempferi*) with very large showy flowers

Japanese lacquer *n* (1876) **:** LACQUER 1b

Japanese maple *n* (1898) **:** a maple (*Acer palmatum*) of Japan, China, and Korea with purple flowers and usu. deeply parted leaves that is widely cultivated as a shrub or small tree

Japanese millet *n* (1900) **:** a coarse annual grass (*Echinochloa frumentacea*) cultivated esp. in Asia for its edible seeds

Japanese plum *n* (1893) **:** a small plum tree (*Prunus salicina*) native to China and cultivated esp. in Japan for its large sweet usu. yellow to light red fruit; *also* **:** its fruit

Japanese quail *n* (1963) **:** a quail (*Coturnix japonica* syn. *C. coturnix japonica*) of eastern Asia that is sometimes raised for its meat or eggs and is used in laboratory research

Japanese quince *n* (1900) **:** either of two ornamental shrubs (*Chaenomeles speciosa* syn. *C. lagenaria* of China and *C. japonica* of Japan) of the rose family with usu. scarlet, pink, or white flowers

\ə\ abut \ᵊ\ kitten, F table \ər\ further \a\ ash \ā\ ace \ä\ mop, mar \au̇\ out \ch\ chin \e\ bet \ē\ easy \g\ go \i\ hit \ī\ ice \j\ job \ŋ\ sing \ō\ go \ȯ\ law \ȯi\ boy \th\ thin \t͟h\ the \ü\ loot \u̇\ foot \y\ yet \zh\ vision, beige \k̲, ⁿ, œ, ue, ʸ\ *see* Guide to Pronunciation

Japanese spurge *n* (1924) : a low Japanese pachysandra (*Pachysandra terminalis*) often used as a ground cover

Jap·a·nize \ˈja-pə-ˌnīz\ *vt* **-nized; -niz·ing** (1890) **1** : to make Japanese **2** : to bring (as an area or industry) under the influence of Japan — **Jap·a·ni·za·tion** \ˌja-pə-nə-ˈzā-shən\ *n*

Japan wax *n* (1859) : a yellowish fat obtained from the berries of several Asian sumacs (as *Rhus verniciflua* and *R. succedanea*) and used chiefly in polishes

[1]**jape** \ˈjāp\ *vb* **japed; jap·ing** [ME] *vi* (14c) : to say or do something jokingly or mockingly ~ *vt* : to make mocking fun of — **jap·er** \ˈjā-pər\ *n* — **jap·ery** \ˈjā-p(ə-)rē\ *n*

[2]**jape** *n* (14c) : something designed to arouse amusement or laughter: as **a** : an amusing literary or dramatic production ⟨a ~ that would be okay as a sophomore class play —John Simon⟩ **b** : GIBE

Ja·pheth \ˈjā-fəth\ *n* [L *Japheth* or Gk *Iapheth,* fr. Heb *Yepheth*] (bef. 12c) : a son of Noah held to be the progenitor of the Medes and Greeks

ja·po·nais·e·rie \zhä-pō-ne-zə-ˈrē, -nez-ˈrē\ *n, often cap* [F, fr. *japonais* Japanese] (1896) : a style in art reflecting Japanese qualities or motifs; *also* : an object or decoration in this style

ja·pon·i·ca \jə-ˈpä-ni-kə\ *n* [NL, fr. fem. of *Japonicus* Japanese, fr. *Japonia* Japan] (1819) : JAPANESE QUINCE

[1]**jar** \ˈjär\ *vb* **jarred; jar·ring** [prob. of imit. origin] *vi* (1526) **1 a** : to make a harsh or discordant sound **b** : to have a harshly disagreeable or disconcerting effect **c** : to be out of harmony; *specif* : BICKER **2** : to undergo severe vibration ~ *vt* : to cause to jar: as **a** : to affect disagreeably : UNSETTLE **b** : to make unstable or loose : SHAKE ⟨~ the ball free⟩ — **jar·ring·ly** \ˈjär-iŋ-lē\ *adv*

[2]**jar** *n* (1537) **1 a** : a state or manifestation of discord or conflict **b** : a harsh grating sound **2 a** : a sudden or unexpected shake **b** : an unsettling shock **c** : an unpleasant break or conflict in rhythm, flow, or transition

[3]**jar** *n* [MF *jarre,* fr. Old Occitan *jarra,* fr. Ar *jarra* earthen water vessel] (1592) **1** : a widemouthed container made typically of earthenware or glass **2** : as much as a jar will hold — **jar·ful** \-ˌfu̇l\ *n*

[4]**jar** *n* [alter. of earlier *char* turn, fr. ME — more at CHARE] (1674) *archaic* : the position of being ajar — usu. used in the phrase *on the jar*

jar·di·niere *or* **jar·di·nière** \ˌjär-də-ˈnir, ˌzhär-dᵊn-ˈyer, -ˈer\ *n* [F *jardinière,* lit., female gardener] (1841) **1 a** : an ornamental stand for plants or flowers **b** : a large usu. ceramic flowerpot holder **2** : a garnish for meat consisting of several cooked vegetables cut into pieces

[1]**jar·gon** \ˈjär-gən, -ˌgän\ *n* [ME, fr. AF *jargun, gargon*] (14c) **1 a** : confused unintelligible language **b** : a strange, outlandish, or barbarous language or dialect **c** : a hybrid language or dialect simplified in vocabulary and grammar and used for communication between peoples of different speech **2** : the technical terminology or characteristic idiom of a special activity or group **3** : obscure and often pretentious language marked by circumlocutions and long words — **jar·gony** \-gə-nē, -ˌgä-nē\ *adj*

[2]**jargon** *vi* (14c) **1** : TWITTER, WARBLE **2** : JARGONIZE

jar·gon·ish \ˈjär-gə-nish\ *adj* (1816) : JARGONISTIC

jar·gon·is·tic \ˌjär-gə-ˈnis-tik\ *adj* (1929) : characterized by the use of jargon : phrased in jargon

jar·gon·ize \ˈjär-gə-ˌnīz\ *vb* **-ized; -iz·ing** *vi* (1803) : to speak or write jargon ~ *vt* **1** : to express in jargon **2** : to make into jargon

jar·goon \jär-ˈgün\ *or* **jar·gon** \-ˈgän\ *n* [F *jargon* — more at ZIRCON] (1769) : a colorless, pale yellow, or smoky zircon

jar·head \ˈjär-ˌhed\ *n* (1943) *slang* : MARINE 2

jarl \ˈyär(-ə)l\ *n* [ON — more at EARL] (1820) : a Scandinavian noble ranking immediately below the king

jar·rah \ˈja-rə\ *n* [Nyungar (Australian aboriginal language of southwest Western Australia) *jarrilʸ*] (ca. 1866) : a tall eucalyptus (*Eucalyptus marginata*) of western Australia with rough bark, alternate leaves, and durable hard wood; *also* : its wood

Jas *abbr* James

jas·mine \ˈjaz-mən\ *also* **jes·sa·mine** \ˈjes-mən, ˈje-sə-\ *n* [MF *jasmin,* fr. Ar *yāsamīn,* fr. Pers] (1562) **1 a** : any of numerous often climbing shrubs (genus *Jasminum*) of the olive family that usu. have extremely fragrant flowers; *esp* : a tall-climbing semievergreen Asian shrub (*J. officinale*) with fragrant white flowers from which oil is extracted for use in perfumes **b** : any of numerous plants having sweet-scented flowers; *esp* : YELLOW JESSAMINE **2** : a light yellow

Ja·son \ˈjā-sᵊn\ *n* [L *Iason,* fr. Gk *Iasōn*] (14c) : a legendary Greek hero distinguished for his successful quest of the Golden Fleece

jas·per \ˈjas-pər\ *n* [ME *jaspre,* fr. AF *jaspre, jaspe,* fr. L *jaspis,* fr. Gk *iaspis,* of Sem origin; akin to Heb *yāshĕpheh* jasper] (14c) **1** : an opaque cryptocrystalline quartz of any of several colors; *esp* : green chalcedony **2** : colored stoneware with raised white decoration **3** : a blackish green — **jas·pery** \-pə-rē\ *adj*

jas·per·ware \ˈjas-pər-ˌwer\ *n* (1857) : JASPER 2

jas·sid \ˈja-səd\ *n* [ultim. fr. Gk *Iasos,* town in Asia Minor] (1892) : any of numerous small leafhoppers that include many economically significant pests of cultivated plants; *broadly* : LEAFHOPPER

Jat \ˈjät\ *n* [Hindi & Urdu *Jāṭ*] (1622) : a member of an Indo-Aryan people of the Punjab and Uttar Pradesh

JATO *abbr* jet-assisted takeoff

jaunce \ˈjȯn(t)s, ˈjän(t)s\ *vi* [origin unknown] (1593) *archaic* : PRANCE

jaun·dice \ˈjȯn-dəs, ˈjän-\ *n* [ME *jawnes, jaundis,* fr. AF *jaunice, galniz,* fr. *jaune, gaune* yellow, fr. L *galbinus* greenish yellow] (14c) **1** : yellowish pigmentation of the skin, tissues, and body fluids caused by the deposition of bile pigments **2** : a disease or abnormal condition characterized by jaundice **3** : a state or attitude characterized by satiety, distaste, or hostility

jaun·diced \-dəst\ *adj* (1640) **1** : affected with or as if with jaundice **2** : exhibiting or influenced by envy, distaste, or hostility ⟨a ~ eye⟩

[1]**jaunt** \ˈjȯnt, ˈjänt\ *vi* [origin unknown] (1575) **1** *archaic* : to trudge about **2** : to make a usu. short journey for pleasure

[2]**jaunt** *n* (1592) **1** *archaic* : a tiring trip **2** : an excursion undertaken esp. for pleasure

jaunting car *n* (1801) : a light 2-wheeled open horse-drawn vehicle used esp. in Ireland with lengthwise seats placed face-to-face or back to back

jaun·ty \ˈjȯn-tē, ˈjän-\ *adj* **jaun·ti·er; -est** [modif. of F *gentil*] (1662) **1** *archaic* **a** : STYLISH **b** : GENTEEL **2** : sprightly in manner or appearance : LIVELY ⟨sporting a ~ red beret⟩ ⟨a ~ stroll⟩ — **jaun·ti·ly** \ˈjȯn-tə-lē, ˈjän-\ *adv* — **jaun·ti·ness** \ˈjȯn-tē-nəs, ˈjän-\ *n*

Jav *abbr* Javanese

ja·va \ˈja-və, ˈjä-, -vē\ *n, often cap* [*Java,* island of Indonesia] (1823) : COFFEE

Ja·va man \ˈjä-və-, ˈja-\ *n* (1911) : a Pleistocene hominid known from fragmentary skeletons found in Trinil and Djetis, Java, and classified with the direct ancestor (*Homo erectus*) of modern humans

Ja·va·nese \ˌja-və-ˈnēz, ˌjä-, -ˈnēs\ *n, pl* **Javanese** [*Java* + *-nese* (as in *Japanese*)] (1704) **1** : a member of an Indonesian people inhabiting the island of Java **2** : an Austronesian language of the Javanese people — **Javanese** *adj*

jav·e·lin \ˈjav-lən, ˈja-və-\ *n* [ME *chafeveleyn,* fr. MF *javeline,* alter. of *javelot,* of Celt origin; akin to OIr *gabul* forked stick] (15c) **1** : a light spear thrown as a weapon of war or in hunting **2** : a slender usu. metal shaft at least 260 centimeters long that is thrown for distance in a field event

ja·ve·li·na \ˌhä-və-ˈlē-nə\ *n* [AmerSp *jabalina,* fr. Sp, fem. of *jabalí* wild boar, fr. Ar *jabalī*] (1822) : PECCARY

Ja·velle water \zha-ˈvel, zhə-\ *n* [*Javel,* former village in France] (1890) : an aqueous solution of sodium hypochlorite used as a disinfectant or a bleaching agent

[1]**jaw** \ˈjȯ\ *n* [ME] (14c) **1 a** : either of two complex cartilaginous or bony structures in most vertebrates that border the mouth, support the soft parts enclosing it, usu. bear teeth on their oral margin, and are an upper that is more or less firmly fused with the skull and a lower that is hinged, movable, and articulated with the temporal bone of either side — compare MANDIBLE, MAXILLA **b** : the parts constituting the walls of the mouth and serving to open and close it — usu. used in pl. **c** : any of various organs of invertebrates that perform the function of the vertebrate jaws **2** : something resembling the jaw of an animal: as **a** : one of the sides of a narrow pass or channel **b** : either of two or more opposable parts that open and close for holding or crushing something between them **3 a** : a space lying between or as if between open jaws ⟨escaped from out of the ~s of the whale⟩ **b** : a position or situation in which one is threatened ⟨rode into the ~s of danger⟩ **4** : a friendly chat

[2]**jaw** *vi* (1748) : to talk esp. abusively, indignantly, or long-windedly ⟨~*ing* with the referee⟩ ~ *vt* : to talk to in a scolding or boring manner

[1]**jaw·bone** \ˈjȯ-ˌbōn\ *n* (15c) : JAW 1a; *esp* : MANDIBLE

[2]**jawbone** *vt* (1965) : to speak forcefully and persuasively to ⟨*jawboned* them into accepting the deal⟩ ~ *vi* : to talk esp. forcefully and persuasively ⟨*jawboning* about the tax cuts⟩

jaw·bon·ing \-ˌbō-niŋ\ *n* (1969) : the use of public appeals (as by a president) to influence the actions esp. of business and labor leaders; *broadly* : the use of spoken persuasion

jaw·break·er \-ˌbrā-kər\ *n* (1839) **1** : a word difficult to pronounce **2** : a round hard candy

jaw–drop·ping \ˈjȯ-ˌdrä-piŋ\ *adj* (1980) : causing great surprise or astonishment — **jaw–drop·per** \-pər\ *n* — **jaw–drop·ping·ly** \-piŋ-lē\ *adv*

jawed \ˈjȯd\ *adj* (ca. 1529) : having jaws ⟨~ fishes⟩ — usu. used in combination ⟨square-*jawed*⟩ ⟨a three-*jawed* chuck⟩

jaw·less fish \ˈjȯ-ləs-\ *n* (ca. 1941) : any of the taxonomic group (Agnatha) of primitive vertebrates without jaws including cyclostomes and extinct related forms — compare BONY FISH, CARTILAGINOUS FISH

jaw·line \ˈjȯ-ˌlīn\ *n* (1924) : the outline of the lower jaw

[1]**jay** \ˈjā\ *n* [ME, fr. AF, fr. LL *gaius*] (14c) **1 a** : a predominantly fawn-colored Old World bird (*Garrulus glandarius*) of the crow family with a black-and-white crest and wings marked with black, white, and blue **b** : any of various usu. crested and largely blue chiefly New World birds that are related to the common Old World jay and have roving habits and harsh voices — compare BLUE JAY **2 a** : an impertinent chatterer **b** : DANDY 1 **c** : GREENHORN **3** : a moderate blue

[2]**jay** *n* (1818) **1** : the letter *j* **2** : JOINT 4

jay·bird \ˈjā-ˌbərd\ *n* (1661) **1** : [1]JAY 1 **2** : [1]JAY 2

Jay·cee \ˌjā-ˈsē\ *n* [fr. the initials of Junior Citizens, former name of the organization] (1938) : a member of a major national and international civic organization

jay·gee \ˈjā-ˈjē\ *n* [*j*unior *g*rade] (1943) : LIEUTENANT JUNIOR GRADE

jay·hawk·er \ˈjā-ˌhȯ-kər\ *n* (1858) **1 a** *often cap* : a member of a band of antislavery guerrillas in Kansas and Missouri before and during the American Civil War **b** : BANDIT **2** *cap* : a native or resident of Kansas — used as a nickname

jay·vee \ˌjā-ˈvē\ *n* [*j*unior *v*arsity] (1937) **1** : JUNIOR VARSITY **2** : a member of a junior varsity team

jay·walk \ˈjā-ˌwȯk\ *vi* (1915) : to cross a street carelessly or in an illegal manner so as to be endangered by traffic — **jay·walk·er** *n*

[1]**jazz** \ˈjaz\ *n, often attrib* [origin unknown] (1913) **1 a** : American music developed esp. from ragtime and blues and characterized by propulsive syncopated rhythms, polyphonic ensemble playing, varying degrees of improvisation, and often deliberate distortions of pitch and timbre **b** : popular dance music influenced by jazz and played in a loud rhythmic manner **2** : empty talk : HUMBUG ⟨spouted all the scientific ~ —Pete Martin⟩ **3** : similar but unspecified things : STUFF ⟨that wind, and the waves, and all that ~ —John Updike⟩ — **jazz·like** \-ˌlīk\ *adj*

[2]**jazz** *vt* (1915) **1** : to play in the manner of jazz **2 a** : ENLIVEN — usu. used with *up* **b** : accelerate ~ *vi* **1** : to go here and there : GAD **2** : to dance to or play jazz

jazz·man \ˈjaz-ˌman, -mən\ *n* (1926) : a jazz musician

jazz–rock \-ˈräk\ *n* (1968) : a blend of jazz and rock music

jazzy \ˈja-zē\ *adj* **jazz·i·er; -est** (1915) **1** : having the characteristics of jazz **2** : marked by unrestraint, animation, or flashiness — **jazz·i·ly** \ˈja-zə-lē\ *adv* — **jazz·i·ness** \ˈja-zē-nəs\ *n*

J–bar lift \ˈjā-ˌbär-\ *n* (1954) : a ski lift having a series of J-shaped bars each of which pulls one skier

JBS *abbr* John Birch Society

JC *abbr* junior college

JCAHO *abbr* Joint Commission on Accreditation of Healthcare Organizations

JCB *abbr* [NL *juris canonici baccalaureus*] bachelor of canon law
JCD *abbr* [NL *juris canonici doctor*] doctor of canon law
JCL *abbr* [NL *juris canonici licentiatus*] licentiate in canon law
JCS *abbr* joint chiefs of staff
jct *abbr* junction
JD *abbr* **1** [NL *juris doctor*] doctor of jurisprudence; doctor of law; [NL *jurum doctor*] doctor of laws **2** justice department **3** juvenile delinquent
jeal·ous \ˈje-ləs\ *adj* [ME *jelous*, fr. AF *gelus*, fr. VL **zelosus*, fr. LL *zelus* zeal — more at ZEAL] (13c) **1 a :** intolerant of rivalry or unfaithfulness **b :** disposed to suspect rivalry or unfaithfulness **2 :** hostile toward a rival or one believed to enjoy an advantage **3 :** vigilant in guarding a possession ⟨new colonies were ~ of their new independence —Scott Buchanan⟩ — **jeal·ous·ly** *adv* — **jeal·ous·ness** *n*
jeal·ou·sy \ˈje-lə-sē\ *n, pl* **-sies** (13c) **1 :** a jealous disposition, attitude, or feeling **2 :** zealous vigilance
jean \ˈjēn\ *n* [short for *jean fustian*, fr. ME *Gene* Genoa, Italy + *fustian*] (1577) **1 :** a durable twilled cotton cloth used esp. for sportswear and work clothes **2 :** pants usu. made of jean or denim — usu. used in pl.
[1]**jeep** \ˈjēp\ *n* [prob. ultim. fr. Eugene the *Jeep*, character in the comic strip *Thimble Theater* by Elzie C. Segar] (1940) **:** a small general-purpose motor vehicle with 80-inch wheelbase, ¼-ton capacity, and four-wheel drive used by the U.S. Army in World War II; *also* **:** a similar but larger and more powerful U.S. army vehicle
[2]**jeep** *vi* (1942) **:** to travel by jeep
Jeep *trademark* — used for a civilian automotive vehicle
jee·pers \ˈjē-pərz\ *interj* [euphemism for *Jesus*] (1927) — used as a mild oath
jeepers cree·pers \-ˈkrē-pərz\ *interj* [euphemism for *Jesus Christ*] (1928) **:** JEEPERS
jeep·ney \ˈjēp-nē\ *n* [*jeep* + *jitney*] (ca. 1949) **:** a Philippine jitney bus converted from a jeep
[1]**jeer** \ˈjir\ *vb* [origin unknown] *vi* (1561) **:** to speak or cry out with derision or mockery ~ *vt* **:** to deride with jeers **:** TAUNT ***syn*** see SCOFF — **jeer·er** *n* — **jeer·ing·ly** \-iŋ-lē\ *adv*
[2]**jeer** *n* (1625) **:** a jeering remark or sound **:** TAUNT
jeez *also* **geez** \ˈjēz\ *interj* [euphemism for *Jesus*] (1923) — used as a mild oath or introductory expletive (as to express surprise)
je·fe \ˈhā-(ˌ)fā, ˈhe-; ˈhe-fē\ *n* [Sp, fr. F *chef*, fr. OF *chief* — more at CHIEF] (1903) **:** CHIEF, LEADER
Jef·fer·son Da·vis's Birthday \ˈje-fər-sən-ˈdā-və-səz-\ *n* (1929) **:** the first Monday in June observed as a legal holiday in many Southern states
Jef·frey pine \ˈje-frē-\ *n* [John *Jeffrey* †1854 Scot. botanical explorer] (1858) **:** a tall pine (*Pinus jeffreyi*) of the western U.S. having elongated cones and long needles in groups of three
jehad *var of* JIHAD
Je·hosh·a·phat \ji-ˈhä-sə-ˌfat, -shə-\ *n* [Heb *Yĕhōshāphāṭ*] (ca. 1500) **:** a king of Judah who brought Judah into an alliance with the northern kingdom of Israel in the ninth century B.C.
Je·ho·vah \ji-ˈhō-və\ *n* [NL, reading (as *Yĕhōwāh*) of Heb *yhwh* Yahweh with the vowel points of *ʾadhōnāy* my lord] (1530) **:** GOD 1a
Jehovah's Witness *n* (1931) **:** a member of a group that witness by distributing literature and by personal evangelism to beliefs in the theocratic rule of God, the sinfulness of organized religions and governments, and an imminent millennium
je·hu \ˈjē-(ˌ)hyü, -(ˌ)hü\ *n* [Heb *Yēhū*] (1560) **1** *cap* **:** a king of Israel in the ninth century B.C. who according to the account in II Kings had Jezebel killed in accordance with Elijah's prophecy **2 :** a driver of a coach or cab
je·ju·nal \ji-ˈjü-nᵊl\ *adj* (ca. 1887) **:** of or relating to the jejunum
je·june \ji-ˈjün\ *adj* [L *jejunus* empty of food, hungry, meager] (1646) **1 :** lacking nutritive value ⟨~ diets⟩ **2 :** devoid of significance or interest **:** DULL ⟨~ lectures⟩ **3 :** JUVENILE, PUERILE ⟨~ reflections on life and art⟩ ***syn*** see INSIPID — **je·june·ly** *adv* — **je·june·ness** \-ˈjün-nəs\ *n*
je·ju·num \ji-ˈjü-nəm\ *n, pl* **je·ju·na** \-nə\ [ME, fr. ML, fr. neut. of L *jejunus*] (14c) **:** the section of the small intestine that comprises the first two fifths beyond the duodenum and that is larger, thicker-walled, and more vascular and has more circular folds than the ileum
Je·kyll and Hyde \ˈje-kəl-ən-ˈhīd *also* ˈjē- *or* ˈjā-\ *n* [Dr. *Jekyll* & Mr. *Hyde*, representing the two-sided personality of the protagonist in *The Strange Case of Dr. Jekyll and Mr. Hyde* (1886) by R. L. Stevenson] (ca. 1922) **:** one having a two-sided personality one side of which is good and the other evil
jell \ˈjel\ *vb* [back-formation fr. *jelly*] *vi* (1869) **1 :** to come to the consistency of jelly **:** CONGEAL, SET **2 :** to take shape and achieve distinctness **:** become cohesive ~ *vt* **:** to cause to jell
jellied gasoline *n* (1944) **:** NAPALM
Jell–O \ˈje-(ˌ)lō\ *trademark* — used for a gelatin dessert usu. with the flavor and color of fruit
[1]**jel·ly** \ˈje-lē\ *n, pl* **jellies** [ME *gelly*, fr. AF *gelee*, fr. fem. of *gelé*, pp. of *geler* to freeze, congeal, fr. L *gelare* — more at COLD] (14c) **1 :** a soft somewhat elastic food product made usu. with gelatin or pectin; *esp* **:** a fruit product made by boiling sugar and the juice of fruit **2 :** a substance resembling jelly in consistency **3 :** a state of fear or irresolution **4 :** a shapeless structureless mass **:** PULP — **jel·ly·like** \-ˌlīk\ *adj*
[2]**jelly** *vb* **jel·lied; jel·ly·ing** *vi* (1590) **1 :** JELL **2 :** to make jelly ~ *vt* **:** to bring to the consistency of jelly
jelly bean *n* (1886) **:** a sugar-glazed bean-shaped candy
jel·ly·fish \ˈje-lē-ˌfish\ *n* (1841) **1 a :** a free-swimming marine coelenterate that is the sexually reproducing form of a hydrozoan or scyphozoan and has a nearly transparent saucer-shaped body and extensible marginal tentacles studded with stinging cells **b :** SIPHONOPHORE **c :** CTENOPHORE **2 :** a person lacking backbone or firmness

jellyfish 1a

jelly roll *n* (1867) **:** a thin sheet of sponge cake spread with jelly and rolled up
jel·u·tong \ˈje-lə-ˌtȯŋ\ *n* [Malay *jĕlutong*] (ca. 1836) **1 :** any of several trees (genus *Dyera*) of the dogbane family **2 :** the resinous rubbery latex of a jelutong (esp. *Dyera costulata*) used esp. as a chicle substitute
jem·my \ˈje-mē\ *n, pl* **jemmies** [fr. the name *Jemmy*] (ca. 1811) *Brit* **:** JIMMY
je ne sais quoi \zhə-nə-ˌsā-ˈkwä\ *n* [F, lit., I know not what] (ca. 1656) **:** something that cannot be adequately described or expressed
jen·net \ˈhe-nā, ˈje-nət\ *n* [ME *genett*, fr. AF *genet*, fr. Catal, Zenete (member of a Berber people), horse] (15c) **1 :** a small Spanish horse **2 a :** a female donkey **b :** HINNY
jen·ny \ˈje-nē\ *n, pl* **jennies** [fr. the name *Jenny*] (1600) **1 a :** a female bird ⟨a ~ wren⟩ **b :** a female donkey **2 :** SPINNING JENNY
je·on \(ˌ)jā-ˈȯn\ *n, pl* **jeon** [Korean *chŏn*] (ca. 1969) **:** the chon of South Korea
jeop·ard \ˈje-pərd\ *vt* [ME, back-formation fr. *jeopardie*] (14c) **:** JEOPARDIZE
jeop·ar·dise *Brit var of* JEOPARDIZE
jeop·ar·dize \ˈje-pər-ˌdīz\ *vt* **-dized; -diz·ing** (1582) **:** to expose to danger or risk **:** IMPERIL
jeop·ar·dy \ˈje-pər-dē\ *n* [ME *jeopardie*, fr. AF *juparti, jeuparti* alternative, lit., divided game] (14c) **1 :** exposure to or imminence of death, loss, or injury **:** DANGER **2 :** the danger that an accused person is subjected to when on trial for a criminal offense
je·quir·i·ty bean \jə-ˈkwir-ə-tē-\ *n* [F *jékwirity*, fr. Pg *jequiriti, juqueriti*, prob. of Tupi-Guarani origin; akin to Tupi *jukirí* rosary pea] (ca. 1889) **1 :** the poisonous scarlet and black seed of the rosary pea often used for beads **2 :** ROSARY PEA 1
Jer *abbr* Jeremiah; Jeremias
jer·boa \jər-ˈbō-ə, jer-\ *n* [NL, fr. Ar *yarbūʿ*] (1662) **:** any of several social nocturnal jumping rodents (family Dipodidae) of arid parts of Asia and northern Africa having a long tail and long hind legs
jer·e·mi·ad \ˌjer-ə-ˈmī-əd, -ˌad\ *n* [F *jérémiade*, fr. *Jérémie* Jeremiah, fr. LL *Jeremias*] (1780) **:** a prolonged lamentation or complaint; *also* **:** a cautionary or angry harangue
Jer·e·mi·ah \-ˈmī-ə\ *n* [LL *Jeremias*, fr. Gk *Hieremias*, fr. Heb *Yirmĕyāh*] (14c) **1 :** a major Hebrew prophet of the seventh and sixth centuries B.C. **2 :** person who is pessimistic about the present and foresees a calamitous future **3 :** a prophetic book of canonical Jewish and Christian Scripture — see BIBLE table
Jer·e·mi·as \-ˈmī-əs\ *n* [LL] (ca. 1534) **:** JEREMIAH
[1]**jerk** \ˈjərk\ *n* [prob. alter. of *yerk*] (1575) **1 :** a single quick motion of short duration **2 a :** jolting, bouncing, or thrusting motions **b :** a tendency to produce spasmodic motions **3 a :** an involuntary spasmodic muscular movement due to reflex action **b** *pl* **:** involuntary twitchings due to nervous excitement **4 a :** an annoyingly stupid or foolish person **b :** an unlikable person; *esp* **:** one who is cruel, rude, or small-minded **5 :** the pushing of a weight from shoulder height to a position overhead in weight lifting
[2]**jerk** *vt* (1589) **1 :** to give a quick suddenly arrested push, pull, or twist to **2 :** to propel or move with or as if with a quick suddenly arrested motion **3 :** to mix and serve (as sodas) behind a soda fountain ~ *vi* **1 :** to make a sudden spasmodic motion **2 :** to move in short abrupt motions or with frequent jolts — **jerk·er** *n*
[3]**jerk** *vt* [back-formation fr. [1]*jerky*] (1707) **:** to preserve (meat) in long sun-dried slices
jerk around *vt* (1932) **:** to treat badly esp. by being underhanded or inconsistent
jer·kin \ˈjər-kən\ *n* [origin unknown] (1519) **:** a close-fitting hip-length usu. sleeveless jacket
jerk off *vb* (ca. 1896) *usu vulgar* **:** MASTURBATE
jerk·wa·ter \ˈjərk-ˌwȯ-tər, -ˌwä-\ *adj* [fr. *jerkwater* rural train] (1888) **1 :** remote and unimportant ⟨~ towns⟩ **2 :** TRIVIAL
[1]**jerky** \ˈjər-kē\ *adj* **jerk·i·er; -est** (1670) **1 a :** moving along with or marked by fits and starts **b :** characterized by abrupt transitions **2 :** INANE, FOOLISH — **jerk·i·ly** \-kə-lē\ *adv* — **jerk·i·ness** \-kē-nəs\ *n*
[2]**jer·ky** \ˈjər-kē\ *n* [Sp *charqui*, fr. Quechua *ch'arki*] (1850) **:** jerked meat
jer·o·bo·am \ˌjer-ə-ˈbō-əm\ *n* [*Jeroboam* I †*ab*912 B.C. king of the northern kingdom of Israel] (1889) **:** an oversize wine bottle holding about three liters
jer·ri·can *or* **jerry can** \ˈjer-ē-ˌkan\ *n* [*Jerry* + *can*; fr. its German design] (1943) **:** a narrow flat-sided container for liquids usu. holding about five U.S. gallons (about 19 liters)
Jer·ry \ˈjer-ē, ˈje-rē\ *n, pl* **Jerries** [by shortening & alter.] (1915) *chiefly Brit* **:** GERMAN
jer·ry–build \ˈjer-ē-ˌbild\ *vt* **-built** \-ˌbilt\; **-build·ing** [back-formation fr. *jerry-built*] (1885) **:** to build cheaply and flimsily — **jer·ry–build·er** *n*
jerry–built *adj* [origin unknown] (1869) **1 :** built cheaply and unsubstantially **2 :** carelessly or hastily put together
jer·ry–rigged \ˈjer-ē-ˌrigd\ *adj* [prob. blend of *jerry-built* and *jury-rigged*] (1959) **:** organized or constructed in a crude or improvised manner ⟨a ~ plan⟩
jer·sey \ˈjər-zē\ *n, pl* **jerseys** [*Jersey*, one of the Channel Islands] (1587) **1 :** a plain weft-knitted fabric made of wool, cotton, nylon, rayon, or silk and used esp. for clothing **2 :** any of various close-fitting usu. circular-knitted garments esp. for the upper body **3** *cap* **:** any of a breed of small short-horned predominantly yellowish brown or fawn dairy cattle noted for their rich milk
Jersey barrier *n* [New *Jersey*, U.S.] (1969) **:** a concrete slab 32 inches high with slanted sides that is used in tandem with others to block or reroute traffic or to divide highways
Jersey pine *n* (1743) **:** VIRGINIA PINE
Je·ru·sa·lem artichoke \jə-ˌrü-s(ə-)ləm-, -ˌrüz-ləm-, -ˈrü-zə-\ *n* [*Jerusalem* by folk etymology fr. It *girasole* girasol] (1639) **:** a perennial sunflower (*Helianthus tuberosus*) of the U.S. and Canada widely cultivated for its tubers that are used as a vegetable and as a livestock feed; *also* **:** its tubers

Jerusalem cherry *n* [*Jerusalem,* Palestine] (1788) **:** either of two plants (*Solanum pseudocapsicum* and *S. capsicastrum*) of the nightshade family cultivated as ornamental houseplants for their orange to red berries
Jerusalem cricket *n* (1947) **:** a large-headed burrowing nocturnal orthopteran insect (*Stenopelmatus fuscus*) of the southwestern U.S.
Jerusalem thorn *n* (1866) **:** a widely cultivated tropical American spiny shrub or small tree (*Parkinsonia aculeata*) of the legume family with pinnate leaves and showy racemose yellow flowers
jess \ˈjes\ *n* [ME *ges,* fr. AF *gez, jettes,* pl. of *get,* lit., throw, fr. *geter, jeter* to throw, release (a hawk) — more at JET] (14c) **:** a short strap secured on the leg of a hawk and usu. provided with a ring for attaching a leash — **jessed** \ˈjest\ *adj*
jessamine *var of* JASMINE
Jes•se \ˈje-sē\ *n* [Heb *Yishay*] (bef. 12c) **:** the father of David, king of Israel, according to the account in I Samuel
jest \ˈjest\ *n* [ME *geste* idle tale, story in verse, fr. AF, deed, action, narrative, fr. L *gesta* deeds, fr. neut. pl. of *gestus,* pp. of *gerere* to bear, wage] (ca. 1548) **1 :** an utterance (as a jeer or quip) intended to be taken as mockery or humor **2 a :** PRANK **b :** a ludicrous circumstance or incident **3 a :** a frivolous mood or manner ⟨spoken in ~⟩ **b :** gaiety and merriment **4 :** LAUGHINGSTOCK ***syn*** see FUN — **jest** *vb*
jest•er \ˈjes-tər\ *n* (14c) **1 :** FOOL 2a **2 :** one given to jests
Je•su•it \ˈje-zü-ət, -zhü- *also* -zyü-\ *n* [NL *Jesuita,* fr. LL *Jesus*] (1548) **1 :** a member of the Roman Catholic Society of Jesus founded by St. Ignatius Loyola in 1534 and devoted to missionary and educational work **2 :** one given to intrigue or equivocation — **je•su•it•i•cal** \ˌje-zü-ˈ(w)i-ti-kəl, -zhü-, -zyü-\ *also* **je•su•it•ic** \-tik\ *adj, often cap* — **je•su•it•i•cal•ly** \-ti-k(ə-)lē\ *adv, often cap* — **je•su•it•ism** \ˈje-zü-ə-ˌti-zəm, -zhü-, -zyü-\ *or* **je•su•it•ry** \-ə-trē\ *n, often cap*
Je•sus \ˈjē-zəs, -zəz *also* -ˌzəs *and* -ˌzəz\ *n* [LL, fr. Gk *Iēsous,* fr. Heb *Yēshūaʿ*] (bef. 12c) **1 :** the Jewish religious teacher whose life, death, and resurrection as reported by the Evangelists are the basis of the Christian message of salvation — called also *Jesus Christ* **2** *Christian Science* **:** the highest human corporeal concept of the divine idea rebuking and destroying error and bringing to light man's immortality
[1]**jet** \ˈjet\ *n* [ME, fr. AF *jaiet,* fr. L *gagates,* fr. Gk *gagatēs,* fr. *Gagas,* town and river in Asia Minor] (14c) **1 :** a compact velvet-black coal that takes a good polish and is often used for jewelry **2 :** an intense black
[2]**jet** *adj* (1658) **:** of the color jet
[3]**jet** *vb* **jet•ted; jet•ting** [F *jeter,* lit., to throw, fr. OF, fr. L *jactare* to throw, freq. of *jacere* to throw; akin to Gk *hienai* to send] *vi* (1692) **:** to spout forth **:** GUSH ~ *vt* **:** to emit in a stream **:** SPOUT
[4]**jet** *n* (ca. 1696) **1 a** (1) **:** a usu. forceful stream of fluid (as water or gas) discharged from a narrow opening or a nozzle (2) **:** a narrow stream of material (as plasma) emanating or appearing to emanate from a celestial object (as a radio galaxy) **b :** a nozzle for a jet of fluid **2 :** something issuing as if in a jet ⟨talk poured from her in a brilliant ~ —*Time*⟩ **3 a :** JET ENGINE **b :** an airplane powered by one or more jet engines **4 :** a long narrow current of high-speed winds (as a jet stream) — **jet•like** \-ˌlīk\ *adj*
[5]**jet** *vi* **jet•ted; jet•ting** (1949) **1 :** to travel by jet airplane **2 :** to move or progress by or as if by jet propulsion
jet•bead \ˈjet-ˌbēd\ *n* (ca. 1930) **:** a deciduous ornamental Asian shrub (*Rhodotypos scandens*) of the rose family that has black shiny fruit
jet–black \-ˈblak\ *adj* (15c) **:** black as jet
je•té \zhə-ˈtā\ *n* [F, fr. pp. of *jeter*] (1830) **:** a springing jump in ballet made from one foot to the other in any direction
jet engine *n* (1943) **:** an engine that produces motion as a result of the rearward discharge of a jet of fluid; *specif* **:** an airplane engine that uses atmospheric oxygen to burn fuel and produces a rearward discharge of heated air and exhaust gases — see AIRPLANE illustration
jet lag *n* (1969) **:** a condition that is characterized by various psychological and physiological effects (as fatigue and irritability), occurs following long flight through several time zones, and prob. results from disruption of circadian rhythms in the human body — **jet–lagged** \ˈjet-ˌlagd\ *adj*
jet•lin•er \ˈjet-ˌlī-nər\ *n* (1949) **:** a jet-propelled airliner
jet•port \ˈjet-ˌpȯrt\ *n* (1961) **:** an airport designed to handle jet airplanes
jet–pro•pelled \ˈjet-prə-ˈpeld\ *adj* (1877) **1 :** moving by jet propulsion **2 :** suggestive of the speed and force of a jet airplane
jet propulsion *n* (1867) **:** propulsion of a body produced by the forwardly directed forces of the reaction resulting from the rearward discharge of a jet of fluid; *esp* **:** propulsion of an airplane by jet engines
jet•sam \ˈjet-səm\ *n* [alter. of *jettison*] (1591) **1 :** the part of a ship, its equipment, or its cargo that is cast overboard to lighten the load in time of distress and that sinks or is washed ashore **2 :** FLOTSAM 2
jet set *n* (1951) **:** an international social group of wealthy individuals who frequent fashionable resorts — **jet–set** *adj* — **jet–set•ter** \-ˌse-tər\ *n* — **jet–set•ting** \-ˌse-tiŋ\ *adj*
Jet Ski *trademark* — used for a small motorized usu. recreational watercraft
jet stream *n* (1947) **:** a long narrow meandering current of high-speed winds near the tropopause blowing from a generally westerly direction and often exceeding a speed of 250 miles (402 kilometers) per hour
[1]**jet•ti•son** \ˈje-tə-sən, -zən\ *n* [ME *jetteson,* fr. AF *geteson,* lit., action of throwing, fr. L *jactation-, jactatio,* fr. *jactare* — more at JET] (15c) **:** a voluntary sacrifice of cargo to lighten a ship's load in time of distress
[2]**jettison** *vt* (1848) **1 :** to make jettison of **2 :** to get rid of as superfluous or encumbering **:** omit or forgo as part of a plan or as the result of some other decision ⟨must be prepared to ~ many romantic notions — Christopher Catling⟩ **3 :** to drop from an aircraft or spacecraft in flight — **jet•ti•son•able** \-sə-nə-bəl, -zə-\ *adj*
[1]**jet•ty** \ˈje-tē\ *n, pl* **jetties** [ME *getee, jette,* fr. AF *geté, getee,* fr. pp. of *geter, jeter* to throw — more at JET] (15c) **1 a :** a structure extended into a sea, lake, or river to influence the current or tide or to protect a harbor **b :** a protecting frame of a pier **2 :** a landing wharf
[2]**jetty** *vi* **jet•tied; jet•ty•ing** (1598) **:** PROJECT, JUT
[3]**jetty** *adj* (1586) **:** black as jet
Jet•way \ˈjet-ˌwā\ *trademark* — used for a telescoping passenger ramp between an aircraft and a terminal building
jeu d'es•prit \zhœ-des-ˈprē\ *n, pl* **jeux d'esprit** *same*\ [F, lit., play of the mind] (1712) **:** a witty comment or composition
jeu•nesse do•rée \zhœ-nes-dȯ-ˈrā\ *n* [F, gilded youth] (1836) **:** young people of wealth and fashion
Jew \ˈjü\ *n* [ME, fr. AF *ju, jeu,* fr. L *Judaeus,* fr. Gk *Ioudaios,* fr. Heb *Yĕhūdhī,* fr. *Yĕhūdhāh* Judah, Jewish kingdom] (13c) **1 a :** a member of the tribe of Judah **b :** ISRAELITE **2 :** a member of a nation existing in Palestine from the sixth century B.C. to the first century A.D. **3 :** a person belonging to a continuation through descent or conversion of the ancient Jewish people **4 :** one whose religion is Judaism
[1]**jew•el** \ˈjü-əl, ˈjül *also* ˈju̇l\ *n, often attrib* [ME *juel,* fr. AF, dim. of *ju, jeu* game, play, fr. L *jocus* game, joke — more at JOKE] (13c) **1 :** an ornament of precious metal often set with stones or decorated with enamel and worn as an accessory of dress **2 :** one that is highly esteemed ⟨regarded the library as the ~ of the campus⟩ **3 :** a precious stone **:** GEM **4 :** a bearing for a pivot (as in a watch) made of crystal, glass, or a gem — **jew•el•like** \-ˌlīk\ *adj*
[2]**jewel** *vt* **-eled** *or* **-elled; -el•ing** *or* **-el•ling** (1601) **1 :** to adorn or equip with jewels **2 :** to give beauty to as if with jewels **:** EMBELLISH
jewel box *n* (1727) **1 :** a small box or case designed to hold jewelry **2 :** something (as a theater) of exquisite or ornate design **3 :** a thin plastic case for a CD or DVD — called also *jewel case*
jew•el•er *or* **jew•el•ler** \ˈjü-ə-lər, ˈjü-lər *also* ˈju̇-lər\ *n* (14c) **1 :** one who makes or repairs jewelry **2 :** one who deals in jewelry, precious stones, watches, and usu. silverware and china
jew•el•lery *chiefly Brit var of* JEWELRY
jew•el•ry \ˈjü-əl-rē, ˈjül-rē, ˈju̇l-; ÷ˈjü-lə-rē\ *n* (14c) **:** JEWELS; *esp* **:** objects of precious metal often set with gems and worn for personal adornment
jewel tone *n* (1939) **:** any of various colors (as amethyst, emerald, and ruby) that resemble those of gemstones
jew•el•weed \-ˌwēd\ *n* (1818) **:** TOUCH-ME-NOT
Jew•ess \ˈjü-əs\ *n* (14c) *sometimes offensive* **:** a Jewish girl or woman
jew•fish \ˈjü-ˌfish\ *n* (1679) **:** any of various large groupers (esp. *Epinephelus itajara*) that are usu. dusky green, brown, or blackish, thickheaded, and rough-scaled; *also* **:** any of various other large fishes (as *Argyrosomus hololepidotus*)
Jew•ish \ˈjü-ish\ *adj* (ca. 1546) **:** of, relating to, or characteristic of the Jews; *also* **:** being a Jew — **Jew•ish•ly** *adv* — **Jew•ish•ness** *n*
Jewish American Princess *n* (ca. 1973) *often disparaging* **:** a stereotypical well-to-do or spoiled American Jewish girl or woman — called also *Jewish Princess*
Jewish calendar *n* (ca. 1888) **:** a calendar in use among Jewish peoples that is reckoned from the year 3761 B.C. and dates in its present form from about A.D. 360 — see MONTH table

JEWISH YEARS 5764–5783

JEWISH YEAR			JEWISH YEAR		
5764	begins	Sept. 27, 2003	5774	begins	Sept. 5, 2013
5765	begins	Sept. 16, 2004	5775	begins	Sept. 25, 2014
5766	begins	Oct. 4, 2005	5776	begins	Sept. 14, 2015
5767	begins	Sept. 23, 2006	5777	begins	Oct. 3, 2016
5768	begins	Sept. 13, 2007	5778	begins	Sept. 21, 2017
5769	begins	Sept. 30, 2008	5779	begins	Sept. 10, 2018
5770	begins	Sept. 19, 2009	5780	begins	Sept. 30, 2019
5771	begins	Sept. 9, 2010	5781	begins	Sept. 19, 2020
5772	begins	Sept. 29, 2011	5782	begins	Sept. 7, 2021
5773	begins	Sept. 17, 2012	5783	begins	Sept. 26, 2022

Jew•ry \ˈju̇(-ə)r-ē, ˈjü-rē\ *n* (14c) **1** *pl* **Jewries :** a community of Jews **2 :** the Jewish people
Jew's harp *or* **Jews' harp** \ˈjüz-ˌhärp, ˈjüs-\ *n* (1595) **:** a small lyre-shaped instrument that when held between the teeth gives tones from a metal tongue struck by the finger

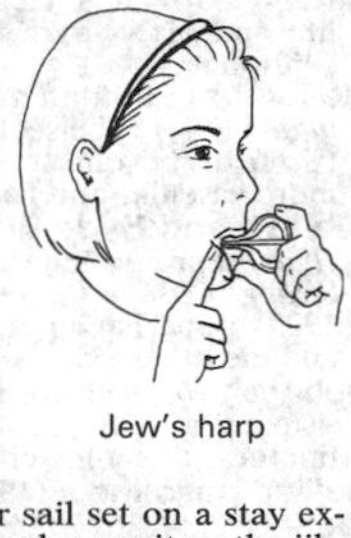
Jew's harp

Jez•e•bel \ˈje-zə-ˌbel\ *n* [Heb *Izebhel*] (14c) **1 :** the Phoenician wife of Ahab who according to the account in I and II Kings pressed the cult of Baal on the Israelite kingdom but was finally killed in accordance with Elijah's prophecy **2** *often not cap* **:** an impudent, shameless, or morally unrestrained woman
jg *abbr* junior grade
JHVH *var of* YHWH
jiao \jē-ˈau̇\ *n, pl* **jiao** [Chin (Beijing) *jiǎo*] (1949) **:** a monetary unit of the People's Republic of China equal to 1/10 yuan
[1]**jib** \ˈjib\ *n* [origin unknown] (1661) **:** a triangular sail set on a stay extending usu. from the head of the foremast to the bowsprit or the jibboom; *also* **:** the small triangular headsail on a sloop — see SAIL illustration
[2]**jib** *n* [prob. by shortening & alter. fr. *gibbet*] (1764) **1 :** the projecting arm of a crane **2 :** a derrick boom
[3]**jib** *vi* **jibbed; jib•bing** [prob. fr. *jib* to shift from one side of a ship to the other, perh. fr. [1]*jib*] (1811) **:** to refuse to proceed further **:** BALK — **jib•ber** *n*
jib•boom \ˈji(b)-ˈbüm\ *n* [[1]*jib* + *boom*] (1748) **:** a spar that forms an extension of the bowsprit
[1]**jibe** *var of* GIBE
[2]**jibe** *also* **gybe** \ˈjīb\ *vb* **jibed** *also* **gybed; jib•ing** *also* **gyb•ing** [perh. modif. of D *gijben*] *vi* (1693) **1 :** to shift suddenly and forcibly from one side to the other — used of a fore-and-aft sail **2 :** to change a vessel's course when sailing with the wind so that as the stern passes through the eye of the wind the boom swings to the opposite side ~ *vt* **:** to cause to jibe — **jibe** *also* **gybe** *n*
[3]**jibe** *vi* **jibed; jib•ing** [origin unknown] (1813) **:** to be in accord **:** AGREE
ji•ca•ma \ˈhē-kə-mə\ *n* [MexSp *jícama,* fr. Nahuatl *xicamatl*] (ca. 1909) **:** an edible starchy tuberous root of a tropical American vine (*Pachyrhizus erosus*) of the legume family that is eaten raw or cooked
Ji•ca•ril•la \ˌhē-kə-ˈrē-yə\ *n, pl* **Jicarilla** *or* **Jicarillas** [AmerSp *apaches de la xicarilla,* lit., gourd-cup Apaches, fr. *Cerro de la Xicarilla,* lit.,

gourd-cup peak, unidentified mountain in Jicarilla territory] (1850) **1** : a member of an Apache people orig. of southeastern Colorado, northern New Mexico, and adjacent areas and now living chiefly in northern New Mexico **2** : the language of the Jicarilla people

jiff \ˈjif\ *n* (1797) : JIFFY

jif·fy \ˈji-fē\ *n, pl* **jiffies** [origin unknown] (1779) : MOMENT, INSTANT ⟨ready in a ~⟩

1jig \ˈjig\ *n* [perh. fr. MF *giguer* to frolic, fr. *gigue* fiddle, of Gmc origin; akin to OHG *gīga* fiddle; akin to ON *geiga* to turn aside] (ca. 1560) **1 a** : any of several lively springy dances in triple rhythm **b** : music to which a jig may be danced **2** : TRICK, GAME — used chiefly in the phrase *the jig is up* **3 a** : any of several fishing devices that are jerked up and down or drawn through the water **b** : a device used to maintain mechanically the correct positional relationship between a piece of work and the tool or between parts of work during assembly **c** : a device in which crushed ore is concentrated or coal is cleaned by agitating in water — **in jig time** : in a short time : QUICKLY

2jig *vb* **jigged; jig·ging** *vi* (1604) **1 a** : to move with rapid jerky motions **b** : to dance a jig **2** : to fish with a jig ~ *vt* **1** : to dance in the rapid lively manner of a jig **2 a** : to give a rapid jerky motion to **b** : to separate (a mineral or ore from waste) with a jig **3** : to catch (a fish) with a jig **4** : to machine by means of a jig-controlled tool operation

3jig *n* [short for *jigaboo* black person] (1927) *usu offensive* : BLACK 4

1jig·ger \ˈji-gər\ *n* (1675) **1** : one that jigs or operates a jig **2** : any of several sails **3** : JIG 3a **4 a (1)** : a mechanical device usu. with a jerky reciprocating motion **(2)** : a mold or a machine incorporating a revolving mold on which ceramic items (as plates) are formed **b** : GADGET, DOODAD **5** : a measure used in mixing drinks that usu. holds 1 to 2 ounces (30 to 60 milliliters)

2jigger *n* [perh. fr. Wolof *jiga* insect] (1781) : CHIGGER

3jigger *vb* [freq. of *2jig*] *vi* (1867) : to jerk up and down ~ *vt* : to alter or rearrange esp. by manipulating ⟨~ an election district⟩

jig·gery–pok·ery \ˈji-gər-ē-ˈpō-kər-ē\ *n* [prob. alter. of Sc *joukery-pawkery,* fr. *jouk* to dodge, cheat + *pawk* trick, wile] (ca. 1892) : underhanded manipulation or dealings : TRICKERY

jig·gle \ˈji-gəl\ *vb* **jig·gled; jig·gling** \-g(ə-)liŋ\ [freq. of *2jig*] *vt* (1836) : to cause to move with quick little jerks or oscillating motions ~ *vi* : to move from or as if from being jiggled — **jiggle** *n* — **jig·gly** \-g(ə-)lē\ *adj*

1jig·saw \ˈjig-ˌsȯ\ *n* (1873) **1** : SCROLL SAW 2 **2** : a light portable electric saw with a vertically reciprocating blade that is used esp. for cutting curves **3** : JIGSAW PUZZLE

2jigsaw *vt* (1873) **1** : to cut or form by or as if by a jigsaw **2** : to arrange or place in an intricate or interlocking way

3jigsaw *adj* (1884) : suggesting a jigsaw puzzle or its separate pieces

jigsaw puzzle *n* (1919) : a puzzle consisting of small irregularly cut pieces that are to be fitted together to form a picture; *also* : something suggesting a jigsaw puzzle

ji·had *also* **je·had** \ji-ˈhäd, *chiefly Brit* -ˈhad\ *n* [Ar *jihād*] (1869) **1** : a holy war waged on behalf of Islam as a religious duty; *also* : a personal struggle in devotion to Islam esp. involving spiritual discipline **2** : a crusade for a principle or belief

ji·had·ist \ji-ˈhä-dist, *chiefly Brit* -ˈha-\ *n* (1989) : a Muslim who advocates or participates in a jihad — **jihadist** *adj*

jil·lion \ˈjil-yən, ˈji-lē-ən\ *n* [*j* + *-illion* (as in *million*)] (ca. 1942) : ZILLION — **jillion** *adj*

1jilt \ˈjilt\ *vt* (1673) : to drop (as a lover) capriciously or unfeelingly — **jilt·er** *n*

2jilt *n* [alter. of *jillet* flirtatious girl] (ca. 1674) : one who jilts a lover

jim crow \ˈjim-ˈkrō\ *n, often cap J&C* [*Jim Crow,* stereotype black man in a 19th cent. song-and-dance act] (1838) **1** *usu offensive* : BLACK 4 **2** : ethnic discrimination esp. against blacks by legal enforcement or traditional sanctions — **jim crow** *adj, often cap J&C* — **jim crow·ism** \-ˌi-zəm\ *n, often cap J&C*

jim–dan·dy \ˈjim-ˈdan-dē\ *n* [fr. the name *Jim*] (1887) : something excellent of its kind — **jim–dandy** *adj*

jim·jams \ˈjim-ˌjamz\ *n pl* [perh. alter. of *delirium tremens*] (1852) : JITTERS

jim·mies \ˈji-mēz\ *n pl* [origin unknown] (ca. 1947) : tiny rod-shaped bits of usu. chocolate-flavored candy often sprinkled on ice cream

1jim·my \ˈji-mē\ *n, pl* **jimmies** [fr. the name *Jimmy*] (1848) : a short crowbar

2jimmy *vt* **jim·mied; jim·my·ing** (1893) : to force open with or as if with a jimmy ⟨the burglar *jimmied* a window⟩

jim·son·weed \ˈjim(p)-sən-ˌwēd\ *n, often cap* [*Jamestown,* Va.] (1832) : a poisonous tall annual weed (*Datura stramonium*) of the nightshade family with rank-smelling foliage, large white or violet trumpet-shaped flowers, and roundish prickly fruits — called also *thorn apple*

1jin·gle \ˈjiŋ-gəl\ *vb* **jin·gled; jin·gling** \-g(ə-)liŋ\ [ME *ginglen,* of imit. origin] *vi* (14c) **1** : to make a light clinking or tinkling sound **2** : to rhyme or sound in a catchy repetitious manner ~ *vt* : to cause to jingle — **jin·gler** \-g(ə-)lər\ *n*

2jingle *n* (1599) **1 a** : a light clinking or tinkling sound **b** : a catchy repetition of sounds in a poem **2 a** : something that jingles **b** : a short verse or song marked by catchy repetition — **jin·gly** \-g(ə-)lē\ *adj*

1jin·go \ˈjiŋ-(ˌ)gō\ *interj* [prob. euphemism for *Jesus*] (1694) — used as a mild oath usu. in the phrase *by jingo*

2jingo *n, pl* **jingoes** [fr. the fact that the phrase *by jingo* appeared in the refrain of a chauvinistic song] (1878) : one characterized by jingoism — **jin·go·ish** \-ish\ *adj*

jin·go·ism \ˈjiŋ-(ˌ)gō-ˌi-zəm\ *n* (1878) : extreme chauvinism or nationalism marked esp. by a belligerent foreign policy — **jin·go·ist** \-ist\ *n or adj* — **jin·go·is·tic** \ˌjiŋ-gō-ˈis-tik\ *adj* — **jin·go·is·ti·cal·ly** \-ti-k(ə-)lē\ *adv*

1jink \ˈjiŋk\ *vi* [origin unknown] (1785) : to move quickly or unexpectedly with sudden turns and shifts (as in dodging)

2jink *n* (1786) **1** : a quick evasive turn : SLIP **2** *pl* : PRANKS, FROLICS; *esp* : HIGH JINKS

jin·ni \ˈjē-nē, ˈji-, jə-ˈnē\ *or* **jinn** \ˈjin\ *also* **djin·ni** \ˈjē-nē, ˈji-, jə-ˈnē\ *or* **djinn** \ˈjin\ *n, pl* **jinn** *or* **jinns** *also* **djinn** *or* **djinns** [Ar *jinnī* demon] (1684) **1** : one of a class of spirits that according to Muslim demonology inhabit the earth, assume various forms, and exercise supernatural power **2** : GENIE 2

jin·rick·sha *or* **jin·rik·i·sha** \jin-ˈrik-ˌshȯ\ *n* [Jp] (1874) : RICKSHAW

1jinx \ˈjiŋ(k)s\ *n* [perh. alter. of *jynx* wryneck; fr. the use of wrynecks in witchcraft] (1911) : one that brings bad luck; *also* : the state or spell of bad luck brought on by a jinx

2jinx *vt* (1917) : to foredoom to failure or misfortune : bring bad luck to

ji·pi·ja·pa \ˌhē-pē-ˈhä-pə\ *n* [Sp, fr. *Jipijapa,* Ecuador] (1858) **1** : a palmlike Central and So. American plant (*Carludovica palmata* of the family Cyclanthaceae) with leaves used esp. to make Panama hats **2** : PANAMA

JIT *abbr* **1** job instruction training **2** just in time

jit·ney \ˈjit-nē\ *n, pl* **jitneys** [origin unknown] (1903) **1** *slang* : NICKEL 2a(1) **2** [fr. the original 5 cent fare] : BUS 1a; *esp* : a small bus that carries passengers over a regular route on a flexible schedule **3** : an unlicensed taxicab

1jit·ter \ˈji-tər\ *n* [origin unknown] (1929) **1** *pl* : a sense of panic or extreme nervousness ⟨had a bad case of the ~*s* before his performance⟩ **2** : the state of mind or the movement of one that jitters **3** : irregular random movement (as of a pointer or an image on a television screen); *also* : vibratory motion

2jitter *vi* (1931) **1** : to be nervous or act in a nervous way **2** : to make continuous fast repetitive movements

1jit·ter·bug \ˈji-tər-ˌbəg\ *n* (1938) **1** : a jazz variation of the two-step in which couples swing, balance, and twirl in standardized patterns and often with vigorous acrobatics **2** : one who dances the jitterbug

2jitterbug *vi* (1939) **1** : to dance the jitterbug **2** : to move around or back and forth with quick often jerky movements esp. to confuse or disconcert an opponent in sports

jit·tery \ˈji-tə-rē\ *adj* (1931) **1** : suffering from the jitters **2** : marked by jittering movements — **jit·ter·i·ness** \-nəs\ *n*

jiujitsu *var of* JUJITSU

1jive \ˈjīv\ *n* [origin unknown] (1928) **1** : swing music or the dancing performed to it **2 a** : glib, deceptive, or foolish talk **b** : the jargon of hipsters **c** : a special jargon of difficult or slang terms — **jivey** \ˈjī-vē\ *adj*

2jive *vb* **jived; jiv·ing** *vt* (1928) **1** : TEASE, CAJOLE **2** : SWING 5 ~ *vi* **1** : to talk jive : kid around **2** : to dance to or play jive

3jive *adj* (1953) *slang* : PHONY

Jn *or* **Jno** *abbr* John

JND *abbr* just noticeable difference

jnr *abbr, Brit* junior

jo \ˈjō\ *n, pl* **joes** [alter. of *joy*] (ca. 1529) *chiefly Scot* : SWEETHEART, DEAR

Jo *abbr* Joel

1job \ˈjäb\ *n* [perh. fr. obs. E *job* lump] (ca. 1627) **1 a** : a piece of work; *esp* : a small miscellaneous piece of work undertaken on order at a stated rate **b** : the object or material on which work is being done **c** : something produced by or as if by work ⟨did a nice ~⟩ **d** : an example of a usu. specified type : ITEM ⟨the limousine was a long white ~⟩ **2 a** : something done for private advantage ⟨the whole incident was a put-up ~⟩ **b** : a criminal enterprise; *specif* : ROBBERY **c** : a damaging or destructive bit of work ⟨did a ~ on him⟩ **3 a (1)** : something that has to be done : TASK **(2)** : an undertaking requiring unusual exertion ⟨it was a real ~ to talk over that noise⟩ **b** : a specific duty, role, or function **c** : a regular remunerative position **d** *chiefly Brit* : state of affairs — usu. used with *bad* or *good* ⟨it was a good ~ you didn't hit the old man —E. L. Thomas⟩ **4** : plastic surgery for cosmetic purposes ⟨a nose ~⟩ ***syn*** see TASK — **on the job** : at work

2job *vb* **jobbed; job·bing** *vi* (1694) **1** : to do odd or occasional pieces of work for hire **2** : to carry on public business for private gain **3** : to carry on the business of a middleman or wholesaler ~ *vt* **1** : to buy and sell (as stock) for profit : SPECULATE **2** : to hire or let by the job or for a period of service **3** : to get, deal with, or effect by jobbery **4** : to do or cause to be done by separate portions or lots : SUBCONTRACT — often used with *out* **5** : to penalize or deprive unfairly

3job *adj* (1710) **1** *Brit* : that is for hire for a given service or period **2** : used in, engaged in, or done as job work ⟨a ~ shop⟩ **3** : of or relating to a job or to employment ⟨a guarantee of ~ security⟩

Job \ˈjōb\ *n* [L, fr. Gk *Iōb,* fr. Heb *Iyyōbh*] (14c) **1** : the hero of the book of Job who endures afflictions with fortitude and faith **2** : a narrative and poetic book of canonical Jewish and Christian Scripture — see BIBLE table

job action *n* (1958) : a temporary action (as a slowdown) by workers as a protest and means of forcing compliance with demands

job·ber \ˈjä-bər\ *n* (1670) : one that jobs: as **a (1)** : WHOLESALER; *specif* : a wholesaler who operates on a small scale or who sells only to retailers and institutions **(2)** : STOCKJOBBER a **b** : a person who works by the job

job·bery \ˈjä-b(ə-)rē\ *n* (1837) : the act or practice of jobbing; *esp* : corruption in public office

jobbing *adj* (1705) *chiefly Brit* : working occasionally at separate short jobs

job·hold·er \ˈjäb-ˌhōl-dər\ *n* (1904) : a person having a regular job

job–hop·ping \-ˌhä-piŋ\ *n* (ca. 1952) : the practice of moving from job to job — **job–hop·per** \-ˌhä-pər\ *n*

job·less \ˈjäb-ləs\ *adj* (1919) **1** : having no job **2** : of or relating to those having no job ⟨~ benefits⟩ — **job·less·ness** *n*

job lot *n* (1851) **1** : a miscellaneous collection of goods for sale as a lot usu. to a retailer **2** : a miscellaneous and usu. inferior collection or group

Job's comforter \ˈjōbz-\ *n* [fr. the tone of the speeches made to Job by his friends] (1738) : a person who discourages or depresses while seemingly giving comfort and consolation

Job's tears *n pl* (1597) **1** : hard usu. pearly white seeds of a tropical southeast Asian grass (*Coix lacryma-jobi*) often used as beads **2** *sing in constr* : the grass producing Job's tears

\ə\ **abut** \ᵊ\ **kitten,** F **table** \ər\ **further** \a\ **ash** \ā\ **ace** \ä\ **mop, mar**
\au̇\ **out** \ch\ **chin** \e\ **bet** \ē\ **easy** \g\ **go** \i\ **hit** \ī\ **ice** \j\ **job**
\ŋ\ **sing** \ō\ **go** \ȯ\ **law** \ȯi\ **boy** \th\ **thin** \t͟h\ **the** \ü\ **loot** \u̇\ **foot**
\y\ **yet** \zh\ **vision, beige** \k̲, ⁿ, œ, ue, ʸ\ *see* Guide to Pronunciation

Jo·cas·ta \jō-ˈkas-tə\ *n* [L, fr. Gk *Iokastē*] (15c) : a queen of Thebes who marries Oedipus not knowing that he is her son

[1]**jock** \ˈjäk\ *n* (1826) **1** : JOCKEY 1 **2** : DISC JOCKEY

[2]**jock** *n* [*jockstrap*] (1922) **1** : ATHLETIC SUPPORTER **2** : ATHLETE; *esp* : a school or college athlete **3** : PILOT; *esp* : a fighter pilot **4** : a person devoted to a single pursuit or interest ⟨computer ~*s*⟩

[1]**jock·ey** \ˈjä-kē\ *n, pl* **jockeys** [*Jockey,* Sc nickname for *John*] (1643) **1** : a person who rides or drives a horse esp. as a professional in a race **2** : a person who operates or works with a specified vehicle, device, object, or material ⟨a bus ~⟩ ⟨pencil ~*s*⟩

[2]**jockey** *vb* **jock·eyed; jock·ey·ing** *vt* (1708) **1** : to deal shrewdly or fraudulently with **2 a** : to ride or drive (a horse) as a jockey **b** : DRIVE, OPERATE **3 a** : to maneuver or manipulate by adroit or devious means ⟨was ~*ed* out of the job⟩ **b** : to change the position of by a series of movements ⟨~ a truck into position⟩ ~ *vi* **1** : to act as a jockey **2** : to maneuver for advantage — often used in the phrase *jockey for position*

jockey club *n* (1775) : an association for the promotion and regulation of horse racing

jock itch *n* [[2]*jock*] (1950) : TINEA CRURIS

jock·strap \ˈjäk-ˌstrap\ *n* [E slang *jock* penis + E *strap*] (1886) : ATHLETIC SUPPORTER

jo·cose \jō-ˈkōs, jə-\ *adj* [L *jocosus,* fr. *jocus* joke] (1673) **1** : given to joking : MERRY **2** : characterized by joking : HUMOROUS ***syn*** see WITTY — **jo·cose·ly** *adv* — **jo·cose·ness** *n* — **jo·cos·i·ty** \jō-ˈkä-sə-tē, jə-\ *n*

joc·u·lar \ˈjä-kyə-lər\ *adj* [L *jocularis,* fr. *joculus,* dim. of *jocus*] (1626) **1** : given to jesting : habitually jolly or jocund **2** : characterized by jesting : PLAYFUL ***syn*** see WITTY — **joc·u·lar·i·ty** \ˌjä-kyə-ˈler-ə-tē, -ˈla-rə-\ *n* — **joc·u·lar·ly** \ˈjä-kyə-lər-lē\ *adv*

jo·cund \ˈjä-kənd *also* ˈjō-(ˌ)kənd\ *adj* [ME, fr. LL *jocundus,* alter. of L *jucundus,* fr. *juvare* to help] (14c) : marked by or suggestive of high spirits and lively mirthfulness ⟨a poet could not but be gay, in such a ~ company —William Wordsworth⟩ ***syn*** see MERRY — **jo·cun·di·ty** \jō-ˈkən-də-tē, jä-\ *n* — **jo·cund·ly** \ˈjä-kənd-lē, ˈjō-(ˌ)\ *adv*

jodh·pur \ˈjäd-(ˌ)pər\ *n* [*Jodhpur,* India] (1899) **1** *pl* : riding breeches cut full through the hips and close-fitting from knee to ankle **2** : an ankle-high boot fastened with a strap that is buckled at the side — called also *jodhpur boot*

[1]**joe** \ˈjō\ *n, often cap* [fr. *Joe,* nickname for *Joseph*] (1846) : FELLOW, GUY ⟨an average ~⟩

[2]**joe** *n* [perh. alter. of *java*] (1927) : COFFEE 1a

Joe Blow *n* (1924) : an average or ordinary man

Jo·el \ˈjō(-ə)l\ *n* [L, fr. Gk *Iōēl,* fr. Heb *Yō'ēl*] (14c) **1** : the traditionally assumed author of the book of Joel **2** : a narrative and apocalyptic book of canonical Jewish and Christian Scripture — see BIBLE table

joe–pye weed \ˈjō-ˈpī-\ *n* [origin unknown] (1818) : any of several tall No. American perennial composite herbs (esp. *Eupatorium maculatum* and *E. purpureum*) with whorled leaves and corymbose heads of typically purplish tubular flowers

Joe Six–Pack *n* [fr. the stereotype of a six-pack of beer as a workingman's drink] (1975) : an ordinary man; *specif* : a blue-collar worker

jo·ey \ˈjō-ē\ *n* [origin unknown] (1839) *Austral* : a baby animal; *esp* : a baby kangaroo

[1]**jog** \ˈjäg, ˈjȯg\ *vb* **jogged; jog·ging** [prob. alter. of *shog*] *vt* (1548) **1** : to give a slight shake or push to : NUDGE **2** : to rouse to alertness ⟨*jogged* his memory⟩ **3** : to cause (as a horse) to go at a jog **4** : to align the edges of (piled sheets of paper) by hitting or shaking against a flat surface ~ *vi* **1** : to move up and down or about with a short heavy motion ⟨his . . . holster *jogging* against his hip —Thomas Williams⟩ **2 a** : to run or ride at a slow trot **b** : to go at a slow, leisurely, or monotonous pace : TRUDGE — **jog·ger** \ˈjä-gər, ˈjȯ-\ *n*

[2]**jog** *n* (1635) **1** : a slight shake : NUDGE **2 a** : a movement, pace, or instance of jogging (as for exercise) **b** : a horse's slow measured trot

[3]**jog** *n* [prob. alter. of [2]*jag*] (1715) **1 a** : a projecting or retreating part (as of a line or surface) **b** : the space in the angle of a jog **2** : a brief abrupt change in direction

[4]**jog** *vi* **jogged; jog·ging** (1953) : to make a jog ⟨the road ~*s* to the right⟩

[1]**jog·gle** \ˈjä-gəl\ *vb* **jog·gled; jog·gling** \-g(ə-)liŋ\ [freq. of [1]*jog*] *vt* (1513) : to shake slightly ~ *vi* : to move shakily or jerkily — **jog·gler** \-g(ə-)lər\ *n*

[2]**joggle** *n* (ca. 1727) : [2]JOG 2a

[3]**joggle** *n* [dim. of [3]*jog*] (1793) **1** : a notch or tooth in a joining surface (as of a piece of building material) to prevent slipping **2** : a dowel for joining two adjacent blocks of masonry

[4]**joggle** *vt* **jog·gled; jog·gling** \ˈjä-g(ə-)liŋ\ (1820) : to join by means of a joggle so as to prevent sliding apart

jog trot *n* (1796) **1** : [2]JOG 2b **2** : a routine habit or course of action

Jo·han·nine \jō-ˈha-ˌnīn, -nən\ *adj* [LL *Johannes* John] (1861) : of, relating to, or characteristic of the apostle John or the New Testament books ascribed to him

Jo·han·nis·berg Riesling \yō-ˈhä-nəs-ˌberg-\ *n* [*Johannisberg,* village in Germany] (1976) : a Riesling produced in the U.S. (as in California)

john \ˈjän\ *n* [fr. the name *John*] (1856) **1** [prob. short for *johnny, johnny house* privy] : TOILET **2** : a prostitute's client

John \ˈjän\ *n* [LL *Johannes,* fr. Gk *Iōannēs,* fr. Heb *Yōhānān*] (12c) **1** : a Jewish prophet who according to Gospel accounts foretold Jesus' messianic ministry and baptized him — called also *John the Baptist* **2** : an apostle who according to various Christian traditions wrote the fourth Gospel, the three Johannine Epistles, and the Book of Revelation **3** : the fourth Gospel in the New Testament — see BIBLE table **4** : any of three short didactic letters addressed to early Christians and included in the New Testament — see BIBLE table

John Barleycorn *n* (ca. 1620) : alcoholic liquor personified

john·boat \ˈjän-ˌbōt\ *n* [fr. the name *John*] (1905) : a narrow flat-bottomed square-ended boat usu. propelled by a pole or paddle and used on inland waterways

John Bull \-ˈbu̇l\ *n* [*John Bull,* character typifying the English nation in *The History of John Bull* (1712) by John Arbuthnot] (1778) **1** : the English nation personified : the English people **2** : a typical Englishman — **John Bull·ish** \-ˈbu̇-lish\ *adj* — **John Bull·ish·ness** *n* — **John Bull·ism** \-ˌli-zəm\ *n*

John Doe \-ˈdō\ *n* (ca. 1659) **1** : a party to legal proceedings whose true name is unknown **2** : an average man

John Do·ry \-ˈdȯr-ē\ *n, pl* **John Dories** [earlier *dory,* fr. ME *dorre,* fr. AF *doree,* lit., gilded one] (1754) : a widely distributed marine food fish (*Zeus faber* of the family Zeidae) that is yellow to olive in color with a dark spot on each side and has an oval compressed body and long dorsal spines

Joh·ne's disease \ˈyō-nəz-\ *n* [Heinrich A. *Johne* †1910 Ger. bacteriologist] (1907) : a chronic often fatal contagious enteritis of ruminants and esp. of cattle that is caused by a bacterium (*Mycobacterium paratuberculosis*) and is characterized by persistent diarrhea and gradual emaciation

John Han·cock \ˈjän-ˈhan-ˌkäk\ *n* [*John Hancock;* fr. the prominence of his signature on the Declaration of Independence] (1903) : an autograph signature

John Hen·ry \-ˈhen-rē\ *n* [fr. the name *John Henry,* fr. confusion with *John Hancock*] (ca. 1914) : an autograph signature

John Mark *n* : MARK 1a

john·ny \ˈjä-nē\ *n, pl* **johnnies** [fr. the name *Johnny*] (1673) **1** *often cap* : FELLOW, GUY **2** : a short-sleeved collarless gown that is open in the back and is worn by persons (as hospital patients) undergoing medical examination or treatment

john·ny·cake \ˈjä-nē-ˌkāk\ *n* [prob. fr. the name *Johnny*] (1739) : a bread made with cornmeal

John·ny–come–late·ly \ˈjä-nē-(ˌ)kəm-ˈlāt-lē\ *n, pl* **Johnny–come–latelies** *or* **Johnnies–come–lately** (1839) **1** : a late or recent arrival : NEWCOMER **2** : UPSTART ⟨established families tend to hold themselves above the *Johnny-come-latelies* —William Zeckendorf †1976⟩

John·ny–jump–up \ˌjä-nē-ˈjəmp-ˌəp\ *n* (1842) **1** : a common cultivated European viola (*Viola tricolor*) which has short-spurred flowers usu. blue or purple mixed with white and yellow and from which most of the garden pansies are derived; *broadly* : any of various small-flowered cultivated pansies **2** : any of various American violets

John·ny–on–the–spot \ˈjä-nē-ˌȯn-t͟hə-ˈspät, -ˌän-\ *n* (1896) : a person who is on hand and ready to perform a service or respond to an emergency

Johnny Reb \-ˈreb\ *n* [fr. the name *Johnny* + *reb* rebel] (1865) : a Confederate soldier

john·son \ˈjän(t)-sən\ *n, often cap* [fr. the surname *Johnson*] (1863) *often vulgar* : PENIS

John·son·ese \ˌjän(t)-sə-ˈnēz, -ˈnēs\ *n* [Samuel *Johnson*] (1843) : a literary style characterized by balanced phraseology and Latinate diction

john·son·grass \ˈjän(t)-sən-ˌgras\ *n, often cap* [William *Johnston* †1859 Am. agriculturist] (1884) : a tall perennial sorghum (*Sorghum halepense*) orig. of the Mediterranean region that is widely used for forage in warm areas and often becomes naturalized as a weed

joie de vi·vre \ˌzhwä-də-ˈvēvrᵊ\ *n* [F, lit., joy of living] (1889) : keen or buoyant enjoyment of life

[1]**join** \ˈjȯin\ *vb* [ME, fr. AF *joindre,* fr. L *jungere* — more at YOKE] *vt* (13c) **1 a** : to put or bring together so as to form a unit ⟨~ two blocks of wood with glue⟩ **b** : to connect (as points) by a line **c** : ADJOIN **2** : to put or bring into close association or relationship ⟨~*ed* in marriage⟩ **3** : to engage in (battle) **4 a** : to come into the company of ⟨~*ed* us for lunch⟩ **b** : to associate oneself with ⟨~*ed* the church⟩ ~ *vi* **1 a** : to come together so as to be connected ⟨nouns ~ to form compounds⟩ **b** : ADJOIN ⟨the two estates ~⟩ **2** : to come into close association or relationship: as **a** : to form an alliance **b** : to become a member of a group **c** : to take part in a collective activity ⟨~ in singing⟩ — **join·able** \ˈjȯi-nə-bəl\ *adj*

syn JOIN, COMBINE, UNITE, CONNECT, LINK, ASSOCIATE, RELATE mean to bring or come together into some manner of union. JOIN implies a bringing into contact or conjunction of any degree of closeness ⟨*joined* forces in an effort to win⟩. COMBINE implies some merging or mingling with corresponding loss of identity of each unit ⟨*combined* jazz and rock to create a new music⟩. UNITE implies somewhat greater loss of separate identity ⟨the colonies *united* to form a republic⟩. CONNECT suggests a loose or external attachment with little or no loss of identity ⟨a mutual defense treaty *connected* the two nations⟩. LINK may imply strong connection or inseparability of elements still retaining identity ⟨a name forever *linked* with liberty⟩. ASSOCIATE stresses the mere fact of frequent occurrence or existence together in space or in logical relation ⟨opera is popularly *associated* with high society⟩. RELATE suggests the existence of a real or presumed logical connection ⟨*related* what he observed to what he already knew⟩.

[2]**join** *n* (1884) **1** : JOINT **2** : UNION 2d

join·der \ˈjȯin-dər\ *n* [AF *joinder, joindre,* fr *joindre* to join] (1601) **1** : CONJUNCTION 1 **2 a (1)** : a joining of parties as plaintiffs or defendants in a suit **(2)** : a joining of causes of action or defense **b** : acceptance of an issue tendered

join·er \ˈjȯi-nər\ *n* (14c) : one that joins: as **a** : a person whose occupation is to construct articles by joining pieces of wood **b** : a gregarious or civic-minded person who joins many organizations

join·ery \ˈjȯi-nə-rē, ˈjȯin-rē\ *n* (1678) **1** : the art or trade of a joiner **2** : work done by a joiner

join·ing \ˈjȯi-niŋ\ *n* (14c) **1** : the act or an instance of joining one thing to another : JUNCTURE **2 a** : the place or manner of being joined together **b** : something that joins two things together

[1]**joint** \ˈjȯint\ *n* [ME *jointe,* fr. AF, fr. *joindre*] (13c) **1 a (1)** : the point of contact between elements of an animal skeleton with the parts that surround and support it **(2)** : NODE 5b **b** : a part or space included between two articulations, knots, or nodes **c** : a large piece of meat for roasting **2 a** : a place where two things or parts are joined **b** : a space between the adjacent surfaces of two bodies joined and held together (as by cement or mortar) **c** : a fracture or crack in rock not accompanied by dislocation **d** : the flexing part of a cover along either spine edge of a book **e** : the junction of two or more members of a framed structure **f** : a union formed by two abutting rails in a track including the elements (as bars and bolts) necessary to hold the abutting rails together **g** : an area at which two ends, surfaces, or edges are attached **3 a** : a shabby or disreputable place of entertainment **b** : PLACE, ESTABLISHMENT **c** *slang* : PRISON 2 **4** : a marijuana cigarette — **joint·ed** \ˈjȯin-təd\ *adj* — **joint·ed·ly** *adv* — **joint·ed·ness** *n* — **out of joint** **1 a** *of a bone* : having the head slipped from its socket

b : at variance **2 a** : DISORDERED 2a **b** : being out of humor : DISSATISFIED ⟨losing put him *out of joint*⟩

[2]**joint** *adj* [ME, fr. AF, fr. pp. of *joindre*] (14c) **1** : UNITED, COMBINED ⟨the ~ influences of culture and climate⟩ **2** : common to two or more: as **a** (1) : involving the united activity of two or more ⟨a ~ effort⟩ (2) : constituting an activity, operation, or organization in which elements of more than one armed service participate ⟨~ maneuvers⟩ (3) : constituting an action or expression of two or more governments ⟨~ peace talks⟩ **b** : shared by or affecting two or more ⟨a ~ fine⟩ **3** : united, joined, or sharing with another (as in a right or status) ⟨~ heirs⟩ **4** : being a function of or involving two or more variables and esp. random variables — **joint·ly** *adv*

[3]**joint** *vb* [ˈjoint] *vt* (1530) **1** : to separate the joints of (as meat) **2 a** : to unite by a joint : fit together **b** : to provide with a joint : ARTICULATE **c** : to prepare (as a board) for joining by planing the edge ~ *vi* **1** : to fit as if by joints ⟨the stones ~ neatly⟩ **2** : to form joints as a stage in growth — used esp. of small grains

Joint Chiefs of Staff (1943) : a military advisory group composed of the chiefs of staff of the army and air force, the chief of naval operations, and sometimes the commandant of the marine corps

joint compound *n* (1954) : a compound made of gypsum, clay, and latex resin that is used to seal wall joints or fill shallow holes

joint·er \ˈjȯin-tər\ *n* (1678) : one that joints; *esp* : any of various tools used in preparing wood (as for a joint)

joint resolution *n* (1838) : a resolution passed by both houses of a legislative body that has the force of law when signed by or passed over the veto of the executive

join·tress \ˈjȯin-trəs\ *n* (1602) : a woman having a legal jointure

joint–stock company *n* (1776) : a company or association consisting of individuals organized to conduct a business for gain and having a joint stock of capital represented by shares owned individually by the members and transferable without the consent of the group

join·ture \ˈjȯin-chər\ *n* (14c) **1 a** : an act of joining : the state of being joined **b** : JOINT **2 a** : an estate settled on a wife to be taken by her in lieu of dower **b** : a settlement on the wife of a freehold estate for her lifetime

joint·worm \ˈjȯint-ˌwərm\ *n* (1851) : the larva of any of several small chalcid wasps (genus *Harmolita*) that attacks the stems of grain and causes swellings like galls at or just above the first joint

joist \ˈjȯist\ *n* [ME *giste, joiste,* fr. AF *giste,* fr. VL **jacitum,* fr. L *jacēre* to lie — more at ADJACENT] (15c) : any of the small timbers or metal beams ranged parallel from wall to wall in a structure to support a floor or ceiling

J joist

jo·jo·ba \hə-ˈhō-bə\ *n* [MexSp, of Uto-Aztecan origin; akin to O'odham *hohowai* jojoba, Yaqui *hohoovam*] (1900) : a shrub or small tree (*Simmondsia chinensis* syn. *S. californica*) of the box family of southwestern No. America with edible seeds that yield a valuable liquid wax used esp. in cosmetics

[1]**joke** \ˈjōk\ *n* [L *jocus;* perh. akin to OHG *gehan* to say, Skt *yācati* he asks] (1670) **1 a** : something said or done to provoke laughter; *esp* : a brief oral narrative with a climactic humorous twist **b** (1) : the humorous or ridiculous element in something (2) : an instance of jesting : KIDDING ⟨can't take a ~⟩ **c** : PRACTICAL JOKE **d** : LAUGHINGSTOCK **2** : something not to be taken seriously : a trifling matter ⟨consider his skiing a ~ —Harold Callender⟩ — often used in negative constructions ⟨it is no ~ to be lost in the desert⟩

[2]**joke** *vb* **joked; jok·ing** *vi* (1670) : to make jokes : JEST ~ *vt* : to make the object of a joke : KID — **jok·ing·ly** \ˈjō-kiŋ-lē\ *adv*

jok·er \ˈjō-kər\ *n* (ca. 1726) **1 a** : a person given to joking : WAG **b** : FELLOW, GUY; *esp* : an insignificant, obnoxious, or incompetent person ⟨a shame to let a ~ like this win —Harold Robbins⟩ **2** : a playing card added to a pack as a wild card or as the highest-ranking card **3 a** (1) : an ambiguous or apparently immaterial clause inserted in a legislative bill to make it inoperative or uncertain in some respect (2) : an unsuspected, misleading, or misunderstood clause, phrase, or word in a document that nullifies or greatly alters it **b** : something (as an expedient or stratagem) held in reserve to gain an end or escape from a predicament **c** : an unsuspected or not readily apparent fact, factor, or condition that thwarts or nullifies a seeming advantage

joke·ster \ˈjōk-stər\ *n* (1877) : JOKER 1

jok·ey *also* **joky** \ˈjō-kē\ *adj* **jok·i·er; -est** (ca. 1825) **1** : given to joking **2** : HUMOROUS, COMICAL **3** : amusingly ridiculous : LAUGHABLE — **jok·i·ly** \-kə-lē\ *adv* — **jok·i·ness** \-kē-nəs\ *n*

jol·li·fi·ca·tion \ˌjä-li-fə-ˈkā-shən\ *n* (1809) : FESTIVITY, MERRYMAKING

jol·li·ty \ˈjä-lə-tē\ *n, pl* **-ties** (14c) **1** : the quality or state of being jolly : MERRIMENT **2** *Brit* : a festive gathering

[1]**jol·ly** \ˈjä-lē\ *adj* **jol·li·er; -est** [ME *joli,* fr. AF *jolif,* fr. *jol-,* prob. fr. ON *jōl* midwinter festival — more at YULE] (14c) **1 a** (1) : full of high spirits : JOYOUS (2) : given to conviviality : JOVIAL **b** : expressing, suggesting, or inspiring gaiety : CHEERFUL **2** : extremely pleasant or agreeable : SPLENDID ***syn*** see MERRY

[2]**jolly** *adv* (1549) : VERY ⟨would . . . do as they were ~ well told —John Stockbridge⟩

[3]**jolly** *vb* **jol·lied; jol·ly·ing** *vi* (1610) : to engage in good-natured banter ~ *vt* : to put or try to put in good humor esp. to gain an end

[4]**jolly** *n, pl* **jollies** (1905) **1** *chiefly Brit* : a good time : JOLLIFICATION **2** *pl* : KICKS ⟨get their *jollies* by reenacting famous murders —H. F. Waters⟩

jol·ly boat \ˈjä-lē-\ *n* [origin unknown] (ca. 1741) : a ship's boat of medium size used for general-purpose work

Jol·ly Rog·er \ˈjä-lē-ˈrä-jər\ *n* [prob. fr. [1]*jolly* + the name *Roger*] (ca. 1785) : a black flag with a white skull and crossbones formerly used by pirates as their ensign

[1]**jolt** \ˈjōlt\ *vb* [prob. blend of obs. *joll* to strike and *jot* to bump] *vt* (1596) **1** : to cause to move with a sudden jerky motion **2** : to give a knock or blow to; *specif* : to jar with a quick or hard blow **3 a** : to disturb the composure of : SHOCK ⟨crudely ~*ed* out of that mood —Virginia Woolf⟩ **b** : to interfere with roughly, abruptly, and disconcertingly ⟨determination to pursue his own course was ~*ed* badly —F. L. Paxson⟩ ~ *vi* : to move with a sudden jerky motion — **jolt·er** *n*

[2]**jolt** *n* (1599) **1** : an abrupt sharp jerky blow or movement **2 a** (1) : a sudden feeling of shock, surprise, or disappointment (2) : an event or development causing such a feeling ⟨the defeat was quite a ~⟩ **b** : a serious check or reverse ⟨a severe financial ~⟩ **3** : a small potent or bracing portion ⟨a ~ of horseradish⟩ — **jolty** \ˈjōl-tē\ *adj*

jolt–wag·on \ˈjōlt-ˌwa-gən\ *n* (1886) *Midland* : a farm wagon

jo·mon \ˈjō-ˌmän\ *adj, often cap* [Jp *jōmon,* lit., straw rope pattern; fr. the decoration on the pottery] (1943) : of, relating to, or typical of a Japanese cultural period from about the fifth or fourth millennium B.C. to about 200 B.C. and characterized by elaborately ornamented hand-formed unglazed pottery

Jon *abbr* Jonah; Jonas

Jo·nah \ˈjō-nə, *3 is also* -nər\ *n* [Heb *Yōnāh*] (14c) **1** : an Israelite prophet who according to the account in the book of Jonah resisted a divine call to preach repentance to the people of Nineveh, was swallowed and vomited by a great fish, and eventually carried out his mission **2** : a narrative book of canonical Jewish and Christian Scripture — see BIBLE table **3** : one believed to bring bad luck

Jo·nas \ˈjō-nəs\ *n* [LL, fr. Heb *Yōnāh*] (14c) : JONAH

Jon·a·than \ˈjä-nə-thən\ *n* [Heb *Yōnāthān*] (14c) **1** : a son of Saul and friend of David according to the account in I Samuel **2** : AMERICAN; *esp* : a New Englander **3** : a medium-sized red-skinned apple

[1]**jones** \ˈjōnz\ *n* [origin unknown] (1965) **1** *slang* : HABIT, ADDICTION; *esp* : addiction to heroin **2** *slang* : HEROIN **3** *slang* : an avid desire or appetite for something : CRAVING

[2]**jones** *vi* (1974) *slang* : to have a strong desire or craving for something ⟨he was ~*ing* for a drink⟩

jon·gleur \zhō^{n}-ˈglər\ *n* [F, fr. OF *jogleour* — more at JUGGLER] (1779) : an itinerant medieval entertainer proficient in juggling, acrobatics, music, and recitation

jon·quil \ˈjän-kwəl, ˈjäŋ-\ *n* [F *jonquille,* fr. Sp *junquillo,* dim. of *junco* reed, fr. L *juncus*] (1664) : a Mediterranean perennial bulbous herb (*Narcissus jonquilla*) of the amaryllis family with long linear leaves that is widely cultivated for its yellow or white fragrant short-tubed clustered flowers — compare DAFFODIL

Jor·dan almond \ˈjȯr-d^{ə}n-\ *n* [ME *jardin almande,* fr. AF *jardin, gardin* garden + ME *almande* almond] (1615) : a large Spanish almond esp. when salted or coated with sugar of various colors

Jor·dan curve \zhȯr-ˈdä^{n}-, ˈjȯr-d^{ə}n-\ *n* [Camille *Jordan* †1922 Fr. mathematician] (1900) : SIMPLE CLOSED CURVE

Jordan curve theorem *n* (1947) : a fundamental theorem of topology: every simple closed curve divides the plane into two regions for which it is the common boundary

jo·rum \ˈjȯr-əm\ *n* [perh. fr. *Joram* in the Bible who "brought with him vessels of silver" (2 Sam 8:10—AV)] (1730) : a large drinking vessel or its contents

jo·seph \ˈjō-zəf *also* -səf\ *n* [L, fr. Gk *Iōsēph,* fr. Heb *Yōsēph*] (14c) **1** *cap* **a** : a son of Jacob who according to the account in Genesis rose to high political office in Egypt after being sold into slavery by his brothers **b** : the husband of Mary the mother of Jesus according to the Gospel accounts **2** : a long cloak worn esp. by women in the 18th century

Jo·seph·ite \ˈjō-zə-ˌfīt, -sə-\ *n* (1890) : a member of St. Joseph's Society of the Sacred Heart founded in 1871 in Baltimore, Md. and devoted to missionary work among black Americans

Joseph of Ar·i·ma·thea \-ˌa-rə-mə-ˈthē-ə\ (14c) : a rich councillor of the Sanhedrin who according to the Gospel accounts placed the body of Jesus in his own tomb and according to medieval legend took the Holy Grail to England

Jo·seph·son junction \ˈjō-zəf-sən- *also* -səf-sən-\ *n* [Brian D. *Josephson*] (1965) : an electronic fast-switching device that consists of two layers of superconducting metal separated by a thin layer of insulator through which low current flows but increased current causes the insulator to block the flow

[1]**josh** \ˈjäsh\ *vb* [origin unknown] *vi* (1845) : to engage in banter : JOKE ~ *vt* : to tease good-naturedly : KID — **josh·er** *n*

[2]**josh** *n* (1878) : a good-humored joke : JEST

Josh *abbr* Joshua

Josh·ua \ˈjä-sh(ə-)wə\ *n* [Heb *Yĕhōshūaʿ*] (bef. 12c) **1** : the divinely commissioned successor of Moses and military leader of the Israelites during the conquest of Canaan according to the account in the book of Joshua **2** : a mainly narrative book of canonical Jewish and Christian Scripture — see BIBLE table

Joshua tree *n* (1884) : a tall branched arborescent yucca (*Yucca brevifolia*) of arid regions of the southwestern U.S. that has clustered greenish-white flowers

joss \ˈjäs, ˈjȯs\ *n* [Chin Pidgin E, fr. Pg *deus* god, fr. L — more at DEITY] (1711) : a Chinese idol or cult image

joss house *n* (1771) : a Chinese temple or shrine

joss stick *n* (1845) : a slender stick of incense burned in front of a joss

[1]**jos·tle** \ˈjä-səl\ *vb* **jos·tled; jos·tling** \-s(ə-)liŋ\ [alter. of *justle,* freq. of [1]*joust*] *vi* (1546) **1 a** : to come in contact or into collision **b** : to make one's way by pushing and shoving ⟨*jostling* toward the exit⟩ **c** : to exist in close proximity **2** : to vie in gaining an objective : CONTEND ⟨*jostled* to get a glimpse of the celebrity⟩ ~ *vt* **1 a** : to come in contact or into collision with **b** : to force by pushing : ELBOW **c** : to stir up : AGITATE ⟨thunder *jostled* us awake⟩ **d** : to exist in close proximity with **2** : to vie with in attaining an objective

[2]**jostle** *n* (1611) **1** : a jostling encounter or experience **2** : the state of being crowded or jostled together

Jos·ue \ˈjä-shü-(ˌ)ē\ *n* [LL, fr. Heb *Yĕhōshūaʿ*] (bef. 12c) : JOSHUA

[1]**jot** \ˈjät\ *n* [L *iota, jota* iota] (1500) : the least bit : IOTA

[2]**jot** *vt* **jot·ted; jot·ting** (1721) : to write briefly or hurriedly : set down in the form of a note ⟨~ this down⟩

jotting *n* (1814) : a brief note : MEMORANDUM

Jo·tun *also* **Jo·tunn** \ˈyō-t^{ə}n, -ˌtün\ *n* [ON *jǫtunn*] (1842) : a member of a race of giants in Norse mythology

\ə\ **abut** \$^{ə}$\ kitten, F table \ər\ **fur**ther \a\ **a**sh \ā\ **a**ce \ä\ m**o**p, m**a**r
\au̇\ **ou**t \ch\ **ch**in \e\ b**e**t \ē\ **ea**sy \g\ **g**o \i\ h**i**t \ī\ **i**ce \j\ **j**ob
\ŋ\ si**ng** \ō\ g**o** \ȯ\ l**aw** \ȯi\ b**oy** \th\ **th**in \t͟h\ **th**e \ü\ l**oo**t \u̇\ f**oo**t
\y\ **y**et \zh\ vi**s**ion, beige \k, ^{n}, œ, ue, ^{y}\ *see* Guide to Pronunciation

Jo·tun·heim *also* **Jo·tunn·heim** \-ˌhīm, -ˌhām\ *n* [ON *Jǫtunheimar*] (1855) : the home of the Jotuns in Norse mythology

jou·al \zhü-ˈal, -ˈäl\ *n* [CanF, rendering of a nonstandard pron. of F *cheval* horse] (1962) : spoken Canadian French; *esp* : the local forms of the spoken French of Quebec that differ the most from prescribed forms

joule \ˈjül *also* ÷ˈjau̇(-ə)l\ *n* [James P. *Joule*] (1882) : a unit of work or energy equal to the work done by a force of one newton acting through a distance of one meter

[1]**jounce** \ˈjau̇n(t)s\ *vb* **jounced; jounc·ing** [ME] *vi* (15c) : to move in an up-and-down manner : BOUNCE ~ *vt* : to cause to jounce

[2]**jounce** *n* (ca. 1787) : JOLT

jouncy \ˈjau̇n(t)-sē\ *adj* **jounc·i·er; -est** (1943) : marked by a jouncing motion or effect

jour *abbr* **1** journal **2** journeyman

jour·nal \ˈjər-nᵊl\ *n* [ME, service book containing the day hours, fr. AF *jurnal,* fr. *jurnal,* adj., daily, fr. L *diurnalis,* fr. *diurnus* of the day, fr. *dies* day — more at DEITY] (15c) **1 a** : a record of current transactions; *esp* : a book of original entry in double-entry bookkeeping **b** : an account of day-to-day events **c** : a record of experiences, ideas, or reflections kept regularly for private use **d** : a record of transactions kept by a deliberative or legislative body **e** : LOG 3 **f** : LOG 4 **2 a** : a daily newspaper **b** : a periodical dealing esp. with matters of current interest **3** : the part of a rotating shaft, axle, roll, or spindle that turns in a bearing

journal box *n* (ca. 1859) : a metal housing used to support and protect a journal bearing

jour·nal·ese \ˌjər-nə-ˈlēz, -ˈlēs\ *n* (1882) : a style of writing held to be characteristic of newspapers

jour·nal·ism \ˈjər-nə-ˌli-zəm\ *n* (1791) **1 a** : the collection and editing of news for presentation through the media **b** : the public press **c** : an academic study concerned with the collection and editing of news or the management of a news medium **2 a** : writing designed for publication in a newspaper or magazine **b** : writing characterized by a direct presentation of facts or description of events without an attempt at interpretation **c** : writing designed to appeal to current popular taste or public interest

jour·nal·ist \-nə-list\ *n* (1693) **1 a** : a person engaged in journalism; *esp* : a writer or editor for a news medium **b** : a writer who aims at a mass audience **2** : a person who keeps a journal

jour·nal·is·tic \ˌjər-nə-ˈlis-tik\ *adj* (1791) : of, relating to, or characteristic of journalism or journalists ⟨~ principles⟩ — **jour·nal·is·ti·cal·ly** \-ti-k(ə-)lē\ *adv*

jour·nal·ize \ˈjər-nə-ˌlīz\ *vb* **-ized; -iz·ing** *vt* (1766) : to record in a journal ~ *vi* **1** : to keep a journal in accounting **2** : to keep a personal journal — **jour·nal·iz·er** *n*

[1]**jour·ney** \ˈjər-nē\ *n, pl* **journeys** [ME, fr. AF *jurnee* day, day's journey, fr. *jur* day, fr. LL *diurnum,* fr. L, neut. of *diurnus*] (13c) **1** : an act or instance of traveling from one place to another : TRIP **2** *chiefly dial* : a day's travel **3** : something suggesting travel or passage from one place to another ⟨the ~ from youth to maturity⟩ ⟨a ~ through time⟩

[2]**journey** *vb* **jour·neyed; jour·ney·ing** *vi* (14c) : to go on a journey : TRAVEL ~ *vt* : to travel over or through — **jour·ney·er** *n*

jour·ney·man \-mən\ *n* [ME, fr. *journey* journey, a day's labor + *man*] (15c) **1** : a worker who has learned a trade and works for another person usu. by the day **2** : an experienced reliable worker, athlete, or performer esp. as distinguished from one who is brilliant or colorful ⟨a good ~ trumpeter —New Yorker⟩ ⟨a ~ outfielder⟩

jour·ney·work \-ˌwərk\ *n* (1601) **1** : work done by a journeyman **2** : HACKWORK

[1]**joust** \ˈjau̇st *sometimes* ˈjəst *or* ˈjüst\ *vi* [ME, fr. AF *juster* to unite, joust, fr. VL **juxtare,* fr. L *juxta* near; akin to L *jungere* to join — more at YOKE] (14c) **1 a** : to fight on horseback as a knight or man-at-arms **b** : to engage in combat with lances on horseback **2** : to engage in combat or competition as if in a joust ⟨~*ing* debaters⟩ ⟨~*ing* bighorn rams⟩ — **joust·er** *n*

[2]**joust** *n* (14c) **1 a** : a combat on horseback between two knights with lances esp. as part of a tournament **b** *pl* : TOURNAMENT **2** : a personal combat or competition : STRUGGLE

Jove \ˈjōv\ *n* [L *Jov-, Juppiter*] (14c) : JUPITER — often used interjectionally to express surprise or agreement esp. in the phrase *by Jove*

jo·vial \ˈjō-vē-əl, -vyəl\ *adj* (1592) **1** *cap* : of or relating to Jove **2** : markedly good-humored esp. as evidenced by jollity and conviviality **syn** see MERRY — **jo·vi·al·i·ty** \ˌjō-vē-ˈa-lə-tē\ *n* — **jo·vial·ly** \ˈjō-vē-ə-lē, -vyə-\ *adv*

Jo·vi·an \ˈjō-vē-ən\ *adj* (1530) : of, relating to, or characteristic of the god or planet Jupiter

jow \ˈjau̇\ *n* [ME *jollen* to knock] (1515) *chiefly Scot* : STROKE, TOLL

jo·war \jə-ˈwär\ *n* [Hindi & Urdu *joār, juvār,* fr. Skt *yavākāra* barley-shaped, fr. *yava* barley + *karoti* he makes] (1800) : DURRA

[1]**jowl** \ˈjau̇(-ə)l *sometimes* ˈjōl\ *n* [alter. of ME *choll*] (15c) : a cut of fish consisting of the head and usu. adjacent parts

[2]**jowl** *n* [alter. of ME *cholle,* prob. fr. OE *ceole* throat — more at GLUTTON] (1591) : usu. slack flesh (as a dewlap, wattle, or the pendulous part of a double chin) associated with the cheeks, lower jaw, or throat

[3]**jowl** *n* [alter. of ME *chavel,* fr. OE *ceafl;* akin to MHG *kivel* jaw, Av *zafar-* mouth] (1598) **1 a** : JAW; *esp* : MANDIBLE **b** : one of the lateral halves of the mandible **2 a** : CHEEK 1 **b** : the cheek meat of a hog

jowly \ˈjau̇-lē *sometimes* ˈjō-\ *adj* **jowl·i·er; -est** (ca. 1873) : having marked jowls : having full or saggy flesh about the lower cheeks and jaw area ⟨elderly man with a disillusioned ~ face —John Dos Passos⟩

[1]**joy** \ˈjȯi\ *n* [ME, fr. AF *joie,* fr. L *gaudia,* pl. of *gaudium,* fr. *gaudēre* to rejoice; prob. akin to Gk *gēthein* to rejoice] (13c) **1 a** : the emotion evoked by well-being, success, or good fortune or by the prospect of possessing what one desires : DELIGHT **b** : the expression or exhibition of such emotion : GAIETY **2** : a state of happiness or felicity : BLISS **3** : a source or cause of delight — **joy·less** \-ləs\ *adj* — **joy·less·ly** *adv* — **joy·less·ness** *n*

[2]**joy** *vi* (14c) : to experience great pleasure or delight : REJOICE ~ *vt* **1** *archaic* : GLADDEN **2** *archaic* : ENJOY

joy·ance \ˈjȯi-ən(t)s\ *n* (1590) *archaic* : DELIGHT, ENJOYMENT

joy·ful \ˈjȯi-fəl\ *adj* (13c) : experiencing, causing, or showing joy : HAPPY — **joy·ful·ly** \-fə-lē\ *adv* — **joy·ful·ness** *n*

joy·ous \ˈjȯi-əs\ *adj* (14c) : JOYFUL — **joy·ous·ly** *adv* — **joy·ous·ness** *n*

joy·pad \ˈjȯi-ˌpad\ *n* (1988) : GAME PAD

joy·pop \ˈjȯi-ˌpäp\ *vi* (1953) : to use habit-forming drugs occasionally or irregularly without becoming addicted — **joy·pop·per** *n*

joy·ride \ˈjȯi-ˌrīd\ *n* (1909) **1** : a ride taken for pleasure (as in a car or aircraft); *esp* : an automobile ride marked by reckless driving (as in a stolen car) **2** : conduct or action resembling a joyride esp. in disregard of cost or consequences — **joyride** *vi* — **joy·rid·er** \-ˌrī-dər\ *n* — **joy·rid·ing** *n*

joy·stick \-ˌstik\ *n* [perh. fr. E slang *joystick* penis] (1910) **1** : a lever in an airplane that operates the elevators by a fore-and-aft motion and the ailerons by a side-to-side motion **2** : a control for any of various devices (as a computer) that resembles an airplane's joystick esp. in being capable of motion in two or more directions

JP *abbr* **1** jet propulsion **2** justice of the peace

JPEG \ˈjā-ˌpeg\ *n* [*J*oint *P*hotographic *E*xperts *G*roup] (1988) : a computer file format for the compression and storage of usu. high-quality photographic digital images

Jpn *abbr* Japan; Japanese

J/psi particle \ˌjā-ˈsī-, -ˈpsī-\ *n* (1977) : an unstable neutral fundamental particle of the meson group that has a mass about 6000 times the mass of an electron — called also *J particle, J/psi, psi particle*

Jr *abbr* junior

JSD *abbr* [NL *juris scientiae doctor*] doctor of science of law

jt *or* **jnt** *abbr* joint

ju·ba \ˈjü-bə\ *n* [origin unknown] (1834) : a dance of Southern plantation blacks accompanied by complexly rhythmic hand clapping and slapping of the knees and thighs

Ju·bal \ˈjü-bəl\ *n* [Heb *Yūbhāl*] (bef. 12c) : a descendant of Cain who according to the account in Genesis is the father of those who play the harp and organ

ju·bi·lance \ˈjü-bə-lən(t)s\ *n* (1864) : JUBILATION 1

ju·bi·lant \ˈjü-bə-lənt\ *adj* (1667) : EXULTANT — **ju·bi·lant·ly** *adv*

ju·bi·lar·i·an \ˌjü-bə-ˈler-ē-ən\ *n* (1782) : one celebrating a jubilee

ju·bi·late \ˈjü-bə-ˌlāt\ *vi* **-lat·ed; -lat·ing** [L *jubilatus,* pp. of *jubilare;* akin to MHG *jū* (exclamation of joy), Gk *iygē* shout] (ca. 1641) : REJOICE ⟨too dispassionate to ~ —Cynthia Ozick⟩

Ju·bi·la·te \ˌyü-bə-ˈlä-ˌtā, ˌjü-\ *n* [L, 2d pers. pl. imper. of *jubilare*] (1549) **1 a** : the 100th Psalm in the Authorized Version **b** *not cap* : a joyous song or outburst **2** : the third Sunday after Easter

ju·bi·la·tion \ˌjü-bə-ˈlā-shən\ *n* (14c) **1** : an act of rejoicing : the state of being jubilant **2** : an expression of great joy

[1]**ju·bi·lee** \ˈjü-bə-(ˌ)lē, ˌjü-bə-ˈlē\ *n* [ME, fr. AF & LL; AF *jubilé,* fr. LL *jubilaeus,* modif. of LGk *iōbēlaios,* fr. Heb *yōbhēl* ram's horn, jubilee] (14c) **1** *often cap* : a year of emancipation and restoration provided by ancient Hebrew law to be kept every 50 years by the emancipation of Hebrew slaves, restoration of alienated lands to their former owners, and omission of all cultivation of the land **2 a** : a special anniversary; *esp* : a 50th anniversary **b** : a celebration of such an anniversary **3 a** : a period of time proclaimed by the Roman Catholic pope ordinarily every 25 years as a time of special solemnity **b** : a special plenary indulgence granted during a year of jubilee to Roman Catholics who perform certain specified works of repentance and piety **4 a** : JUBILATION **b** : a season of celebration **5** : a religious song of black Americans usu. referring to a time of future happiness

[2]**jubilee** *adj, often cap* (1951) : FLAMBÉ ⟨cherries ~⟩

ju·co \ˈjü-ˌkō\ *n, pl* **jucos** [*ju*nior *co*llege] (1939) : JUNIOR COLLEGE; *also* : an athlete at a junior college

Jud *abbr* Judith

Ju·dah \ˈjü-də\ *n* [Heb *Yĕhūdhāh*] (bef. 12c) : a son of Jacob and the traditional eponymous ancestor of one of the tribes of Israel

Ju·da·ic \jü-ˈdā-ik\ *also* **Ju·da·ical** \-ˈdā-ə-kəl\ *adj* [ME *Judeical,* fr. L *judaicus,* fr. Gk *ioudaikos,* fr. *Ioudaios* Jew — more at JEW] (15c) : of, relating to, or characteristic of Jews or Judaism

Ju·da·ica \-ˈdā-ə-kə\ *n pl* [L, neut. pl. of *Judaicus*] (1923) : literary or historical materials relating to Jews or Judaism

Ju·da·ism \ˈjü-dē-ˌi-zəm, ˈjü-də-, ˈjü-(ˌ)dā-, *Brit also* ˈjü-ˌdi-zəm\ *n* (14c) **1** : a religion developed among the ancient Hebrews and characterized by belief in one transcendent God who has revealed himself to Abraham, Moses, and the Hebrew prophets and by a religious life in accordance with Scriptures and rabbinic traditions **2** : conformity to Jewish rites, ceremonies, and practices **3** : the cultural, social, and religious beliefs and practices of the Jews **4** : the whole body of Jews : the Jewish people

Ju·da·ist \ˈjü-dē-ist, ˈjü-də-, jü-ˈdā-\ *n* (ca. 1846) : one that believes in or practices Judaism — **Ju·da·is·tic** \ˌjü-də-ˈis-tik, ˌjü-dē-, ˌjü-(ˌ)dā-\ *adj*

Ju·da·ize \ˈjü-dē-ˌīz, ˈjü-də-, ˈjü-(ˌ)dā-\ *vb* **-ized; -iz·ing** *vi* (1582) : to adopt the customs, beliefs, or character of a Jew ~ *vt* : to make Jewish — **Ju·da·i·za·tion** \ˌjü-dē-ə-ˈzā-shən, ˌjü-də-ə-, ˌjü-(ˌ)dā-ə-\ *n* — **Ju·da·iz·er** \ˈjü-dē-ˌī-zər, ˈjü-də-, ˈjü-(ˌ)dā-\ *n*

Ju·das \ˈjü-dəs\ *n* [LL, fr. Gk *Ioudas,* fr. Heb *Yĕhūdhāh*] (bef. 12c) **1 a** : the apostle who in the Gospel accounts betrayed Jesus **b** : a son of James and one of the twelve apostles **2** : TRAITOR; *esp* : one who betrays under the guise of friendship **3** *not cap* : PEEPHOLE — called also *judas hole, judas window*

Judas Is·car·i·ot \-is-ˈka-rē-ət\ *n* [LL *Judas Iscariotes,* fr. Gk *Ioudas Iskariōtēs*] (ca. 1534) : JUDAS 1a

Judas tree *n* [fr. the belief that Judas Iscariot hanged himself from a tree of this kind] (1668) : any of a genus (*Cercis*) of leguminous trees and shrubs (as a redbud) often cultivated for their showy flowers; *esp* : a Eurasian tree or shrub (*C. siliquastrum*) with purplish pink flowers

[1]**jud·der** \ˈjə-dər\ *vi* [prob. alter. of *shudder*] (1931) *chiefly Brit* : to vibrate with intensity ⟨the engine stalled and kept ~*ing* —Roy Spicer⟩

[2]**judder** *n* (1935) *chiefly Brit* : the action or sound of juddering

Jude \ˈjüd\ *n* [LL *Judas*] (14c) **1** : the author of the New Testament Epistle of Jude **2** : a short hortatory epistle addressed to early Christians and included as a book in the New Testament — see BIBLE table

Ju·deo–Chris·tian \jü-ˌdā-ō-ˈkris-chən, -ˈkrish- *also* ˌjü-dē-ō- *or* jü-ˌdē-ō-\ *adj* [L *Judaeus* Jew — more at JEW] (1847) : having historical roots in both Judaism and Christianity

Ju·deo–Span·ish \-ˈspa-nish\ *n* (1851) : the Romance language of Sephardic Jews esp. in the Balkans and Asia Minor

Judg *abbr* Judges

[1]judge \ˈjəj\ *vb* **judged; judg·ing** [ME *juggen,* fr. AF *juger,* fr. L *judicare,* fr. *judic-, judex* judge, fr. *jus* right, law + *dicere* to decide, say — more at JUST, DICTION] *vt* (13c) **1 :** to form an opinion about through careful weighing of evidence and testing of premises **2 :** to sit in judgment on : TRY **3 :** to determine or pronounce after inquiry and deliberation **4 :** GOVERN, RULE — used of a Hebrew tribal leader **5 :** to form an estimate or evaluation of; *esp* **:** to form a negative opinion about ⟨shouldn't ~ him because of his accent⟩ **6 :** to hold as an opinion : GUESS, THINK ⟨I ~ she knew what she was doing⟩ ~ *vi* **1 :** to form an opinion **2 :** to decide as a judge ***syn*** see INFER — **judg·er** *n*

[2]judge *n* [ME *juge,* fr. AF, fr. L *judex*] (14c) **:** one who judges: as **a :** a public official authorized to decide questions brought before a court **b** *often cap* **:** a tribal hero exercising leadership among the Hebrews after the death of Joshua **c :** one appointed to decide in a contest or competition : UMPIRE **d :** one who gives an authoritative opinion **e :** CRITIC — **judge·ship** \-ˌship\ *n*

judge advocate *n* (1677) **1 :** an officer assigned to the judge advocate general's corps or department **2 :** a staff officer serving as legal adviser to a military commander

judge advocate general *n* (1862) **:** the senior legal officer and chief legal adviser in the army, air force, or navy

Judg·es \ˈjə-jəz\ *n* **:** a narrative and historical book of Jewish and Christian Scripture — see BIBLE table

judg·mat·ic \ˌjəj-ˈma-tik\ *or* **judg·mat·i·cal** \-ti-kəl\ *adj* [prob. irreg. fr. *judgment*] (1826) **:** JUDICIOUS — **judg·mat·i·cal·ly** \-ti-k(ə-)lē\ *adv*

judg·ment *or* **judge·ment** \ˈjəj-mənt\ *n* (13c) **1 a :** a formal utterance of an authoritative opinion **b :** an opinion so pronounced **2 a :** a formal decision given by a court **b (1) :** an obligation (as a debt) created by the decree of a court **(2) :** a certificate evidencing such a decree **3 a** *cap* **:** the final judging of humankind by God **b :** a divine sentence or decision; *specif* **:** a calamity held to be sent by God **4 a :** the process of forming an opinion or evaluation by discerning and comparing **b :** an opinion or estimate so formed **5 a :** the capacity for judging : DISCERNMENT **b :** the exercise of this capacity **6 :** a proposition stating something believed or asserted ***syn*** see SENSE

judg·men·tal \ˌjəj-ˈmen-tᵊl\ *adj* (1909) **1 :** of, relating to, or involving judgment **2 :** characterized by a tendency to judge harshly ⟨~ prigs⟩ — **judg·men·tal·ly** \-ē\ *adv*

judgment call *n* (1847) **:** a subjective decision, ruling, or opinion

judgment day *n* (1591) **1** *cap J&D* **:** the day of God's judgment of humankind at the end of the world according to various theologies **2 :** a day of final judgment

ju·di·ca·to·ry \ˈjü-di-kə-ˌtȯr-ē\ *n, pl* **-ries** (ca. 1575) **1 :** JUDICIARY 1a **2 :** JUDICATURE 2

ju·di·ca·ture \ˈjü-di-kə-ˌchu̇r, -chər, -ˌtyu̇r, -ˌtu̇r\ *n* [MF, fr. ML *judicatura,* fr. L *judicatus,* pp. of *judicare*] (ca. 1530) **1 :** the action of judging : the administration of justice **2 :** a court of justice **3 :** JUDICIARY 1

ju·di·cial \jü-ˈdi-shəl\ *adj* [ME, fr. L *judicialis,* fr. *judicium* judgment, fr. *judex*] (14c) **1 a :** of or relating to a judgment, the function of judging, the administration of justice, or the judiciary ⟨~ processes⟩ **b :** belonging to the branch of government that is charged with trying all cases that involve the government and with the administration of justice within its jurisdiction — compare EXECUTIVE, LEGISLATIVE **2 :** ordered or enforced by a court ⟨a ~ sale⟩ **3 :** of, characterized by, or expressing judgment : CRITICAL 1b **4 :** arising from a judgment of God **5 :** belonging or appropriate to a judge or the judiciary — **ju·di·cial·ly** \-ˈdi-sh(ə-)lē\ *adv*

judicial review *n* (ca. 1924) **1 :** REVIEW 5 **2 :** a constitutional doctrine that gives to a court system the power to annul legislative or executive acts which the judges declare to be unconstitutional

ju·di·cia·ry \jü-ˈdi-shē-ˌer-ē, -ˈdi-shə-rē\ *n* [*judiciary,* adj., fr. L *judiciarius* judicial, fr. *judicium*] (1787) **1 a :** a system of courts of law **b :** the judges of these courts **2 :** a branch of government in which judicial power is vested — **judiciary** *adj*

ju·di·cious \jü-ˈdi-shəs\ *adj* (1591) **:** having, exercising, or characterized by sound judgment : DISCREET ***syn*** see WISE — **ju·di·cious·ly** *adv* — **ju·di·cious·ness** *n*

Ju·dith \ˈjü-dəth\ *n* [LL, fr. Gk *Ioudith,* fr. Heb *Yĕhūdhīth*] (bef. 12c) **1 :** the Jewish heroine who saves the city of Bethulia in the book of Judith **2 :** a book of Scripture included in the Roman Catholic canon of the Old Testament and in the Protestant Apocrypha — see BIBLE table

ju·do \ˈjü-(ˌ)dō\ *n* [Jp *jūdō,* fr. *jū* weakness, gentleness + *dō* art] (1889) **:** a sport developed from jujitsu that emphasizes the use of quick movement and leverage to throw an opponent — **judo·ist** \-ˌō-ist\ *n*

ju·do·ka \ˈjü-dō-ˌkä, ˌjü-dō-ˈkä\ *n, pl* **judoka** *or* **judokas** [Jp *jūdōka,* fr. *jūdō* judo + *-ka* person] (1949) **:** one who participates in judo

[1]jug \ˈjəg\ *n* [perh. fr. *Jug,* nickname for *Joan*] (1538) **1 a** *chiefly Brit* **:** a small pitcher **b (1) :** a large deep usu. earthenware or glass container with a narrow mouth and a handle **(2) :** the contents of such a container : JUGFUL **2 :** JAIL, PRISON

[2]jug *vt* **jugged; jug·ging** (1747) **1 :** to stew (as a hare) in an earthenware vessel **2 :** JAIL, IMPRISON

jug band *n* (ca. 1933) **:** a band that uses primitive or improvised instruments (as jugs, washboards, and kazoos) to play blues, jazz, and folk music

jug–eared \ˈjəg-ˌird\ *adj* (1947) **:** having protuberant ears

jug·ful \ˈjəg-ˌfu̇l\ *n* (1831) **1 :** as much as a jug will hold **2 :** a great deal — used in the phrase *not by a jugful*

jug·ger·naut \ˈjə-gər-ˌnȯt, -ˌnät\ *n* [Hindi *Jagannāth,* lit., lord of the world, title of Vishnu] (1841) **1** *chiefly Brit* **:** a large heavy truck **2 :** a massive inexorable force, campaign, movement, or object that crushes whatever is in its path ⟨an advertising ~⟩ ⟨a political ~⟩

[1]jug·gle \ˈjə-gəl\ *vb* **jug·gled; jug·gling** \-g(ə-)liŋ\ [ME *jogelen,* fr. AF *jugler,* fr. L *joculari* to jest, joke, fr. *joculus,* dim. of *jocus* joke] *vi* (15c) **1 :** to perform the tricks of a juggler **2 :** to engage in manipulation esp. in order to achieve a desired end ~ *vt* **1 a :** to practice deceit or trickery on : BEGUILE **b :** to manipulate or rearrange esp. in order to achieve a desired end ⟨~ an account to hide a loss⟩ **2 a :** to toss in the manner of a juggler **b :** to hold or balance precariously **3 :** to handle or deal with usu. several things (as obligations) at one time so as to satisfy often competing requirements ⟨~ the responsibilities of family life and full-time job —Jane S. Gould⟩

[2]juggle *n* (1664) **:** an act or instance of juggling: **a :** a trick of magic **b :** a show of manual dexterity **c :** an act of manipulation esp. to achieve a desired end

jug·gler \ˈjə-g(ə-)lər\ *n* [ME *jogelour* minstrel, magician, fr. AF *jugleur, jogolur,* fr. L *joculator,* fr. *joculari*] (14c) **1 a :** one who performs tricks or acts of magic or deftness **b :** one skilled in keeping several objects in motion in the air at the same time by alternately tossing and catching them **2 :** one who manipulates esp. in order to achieve a desired end

jug·glery \ˈjə-glə-rē\ *n* (14c) **1 :** the art or practice of a juggler **2 :** manipulation or trickery esp. to achieve a desired end

[1]jug·u·lar \ˈjə-gyə-lər *also* ˈjü- *also* -g(ə-)lər\ *adj* [LL *jugularis,* fr. L *jugulum* collarbone, throat, fr. *jugum* yoke — more at YOKE] (1597) **1 :** of or relating to the throat or neck **2 :** of or relating to the jugular vein

[2]jugular *n* (1615) **1 :** JUGULAR VEIN **2 :** the most vital or vulnerable part of something ⟨showed an instinct for the ~ in competition⟩

jugular vein *n* (1597) **:** any of several veins of each side of the neck that return blood from the head

jug wine *n* (1971) **:** table wine sold in large bottles

[1]juice \ˈjüs\ *n* [ME *jus,* fr. AF, broth, juice, fr. L; akin to ON *ostr* cheese, Gk *zymē* leaven, Skt *yūṣa* broth] (14c) **1 :** the extractable fluid contents of cells or tissues **2 a** *pl* **:** the natural fluids of an animal body **b :** the liquid or moisture contained in something **3 a :** the inherent quality of a thing : ESSENCE **b :** STRENGTH, VIGOR, VITALITY ⟨pioneers . . . full of ~ and jests —Sinclair Lewis⟩ **4 :** a medium (as electricity or gasoline) that supplies power **5** *slang* **:** LIQUOR **6** *slang* **:** exorbitant interest exacted of a borrower under the threat of violence **7** *slang* **:** INFLUENCE, CLOUT **8 :** a motivating, inspiring, or enabling force or factor ⟨creative ~*s*⟩ — **juice·less** \ˈjüs-ləs\ *adj*

[2]juice *vt* **juiced; juic·ing** (1603) **1 :** to add juice to **2 :** to extract the juice of

juiced \ˈjüst\ *adj* (1592) **1 :** containing juice — usu. used in combination ⟨precious-*juiced* flowers —Shak.⟩ **2** *slang* **:** DRUNK 1a **3 :** full of energy and motivation : EXCITED

juice·head \ˈjüs-ˌhed\ *n* (1955) *slang* **:** ALCOHOLIC

juic·er \ˈjü-sər\ *n* (1938) **1 :** an appliance for extracting juice from fruit or vegetables **2** *slang* **:** a heavy or habitual drinker

juice up *vt* (1955) **:** to give life, energy, or spirit to

juicy \ˈjü-sē\ *adj* **juic·i·er; -est** (15c) **1 :** having much juice : SUCCULENT **2 :** rewarding or profitable esp. financially : FAT ⟨~ contract⟩ ⟨a ~ dramatic role⟩ **3 a :** rich in interest : COLORFUL ⟨~ details⟩ **b :** SENSATIONAL, RACY ⟨a ~ scandal⟩ **c :** full of vitality : LUSTY — **juic·i·ly** \-sə-lē\ *adv* — **juic·i·ness** \-sē-nəs\ *n*

ju·jit·su *also* **ju·jut·su** *or* **jiu·jit·su** \jü-ˈjit-(ˌ)sü\ *n* [Jp *jūjutsu,* fr. *jū* weakness, gentleness + *jutsu* art, skill] (1875) **:** an art of weaponless fighting employing holds, throws, and paralyzing blows to subdue or disable an opponent

[1]ju·ju \ˈjü-(ˌ)jü\ *n* [of W. African origin; akin to the source of Hausa *jùju* fetish] (1894) **1 :** a fetish, charm, or amulet of West African peoples **2 :** the magic attributed to or associated with jujus

[2]juju *n* [Yoruba *jújú*] (1982) **:** a style of West African music that is characterized by a rapid beat, the use of percussion instruments, and vocal harmonies

ju·jube \ˈjü-ˌjüb, *esp for 2* ˈjü-jü-ˌbē\ *n* [ME, fr. ML *jujuba,* alter. of L *zizyphum,* fr. Gk *zizyphon*] (14c) **1 a :** an edible drupaceous fruit of any of several trees (genus *Ziziphus*) of the buckthorn family; *esp* **:** one of an Asian tree (*Z. jujuba*) **b :** a tree producing this fruit **2 :** a fruit-flavored gumdrop or lozenge

juke \ˈjük\ *vb* **juked; juk·ing** [prob. alter. of E dial. *jouk* to cheat, deceive] *vt* (1967) **:** to fake out of position (as in football) ~ *vi* **:** to juke someone

juke·box \ˈjük-ˌbäks\ *n* [fr. dial. *jukehouse* brothel, fr. *juke* to have sexual intercourse with, of Atlantic Creole origin; akin to Jamaican E *juk* to poke, stab, Krio *chuk*] (1939) **:** a coin-operated phonograph or compact-disc player that automatically plays recordings selected from its list

jukebox musical *n* (1993) **:** a musical that features popular songs from the past

juke joint *n* (1937) **:** a small inexpensive establishment for eating, drinking, or dancing to the music of a jukebox or a live band

Jul *abbr* July

ju·lep \ˈjü-ləp\ *n* [ME, fr. MF, fr. Ar *julāb,* fr. Pers *gulāb,* fr. *gul* rose + *āb* water] (14c) **1 :** a drink consisting of sweet syrup, flavoring, and water **2 :** a drink consisting of a liquor (as bourbon or brandy) and sugar poured over crushed ice and garnished with mint

Ju·lian calendar \ˈjül-yən-\ *n* [L *julianus,* fr. Gaius *Julius* Caesar] (1696) **:** a calendar introduced in Rome in 46 B.C. establishing the 12-month year of 365 days with each fourth year having 366 days and the months each having 31 or 30 days except for February which has 28 or in leap years 29 days — compare GREGORIAN CALENDAR

[1]ju·li·enne \ˌjü-lē-ˈen, ˌzhü-\ *n* [F, short for *potage à la julienne,* prob. fr. *Julienne* woman's name] (1841) **1 :** a consommé containing julienned vegetables **2 a :** food (as meat or vegetables) that has been julienned **b :** a preparation or garnish of julienned food ⟨a ~ of leeks⟩ — **julienne** *adj*

[2]julienne *vt* **-enned; -en·ning** (ca. 1930) **:** to slice into thin strips about the size of matchsticks ⟨wash and ~ the carrots⟩

Ju·liet \ˈjül-yət; ˌjü-lē-ˈet, ˈjü-lē-ˌ\ *n* **:** the heroine of Shakespeare's tragedy *Romeo and Juliet* who dies for love of Romeo

Ju·li·ett \ˌjü-lē-ˈet\ [prob. irreg. fr. *Juliet*] (1952) — a communications code word for the letter *j*

Ju·ly \ju̇-ˈlī, jə-\ *n* [ME *Julie,* fr. OE *Julius,* fr. L, fr. Gaius *Julius* Caesar] (13c) **:** the seventh month of the Gregorian calendar

Ju·ma·da \ju̇-ˈmä-də\ *n* [Ar *Jumādā*] (1771) **:** either of two months of the Islamic year: **a :** JUMADA AL-AWWAL **b :** JUMADA AL-THANI

Ju·ma·da al–Aw·wal \ju̇-ˈmä-də-äl-ə-ˈwäl\ *n* [Ar *jumādā al-awwal,* lit., first Jumada] (1993) **:** the fifth month of the Islamic year — see MONTH table

\ə\ **abut** \ᵊ\ **kitten,** F **table** \ər\ **further** \a\ **ash** \ā\ **ace** \ä\ **mop, mar** \au̇\ **out** \ch\ **chin** \e\ **bet** \ē\ **easy** \g\ **go** \i\ **hit** \ī\ **ice** \j\ **job** \ŋ\ **sing** \ō\ **go** \ȯ\ **law** \ȯi\ **boy** \th\ **thin** \t͟h\ **the** \ü\ **loot** \u̇\ **foot** \y\ **yet** \zh\ **vision, beige** \k̲, ⁿ, œ, ue, ʸ\ *see* Guide to Pronunciation

Ju·ma·da al–Tha·ni \-äl-tä-ˈnē\ *n* [Ar *jumādā al-thānī*, lit., second Jumada] (1987) : the sixth month of the Islamic year — see MONTH table
[1]**jum·ble** \ˈjəm-bəl\ *vb* **jum·bled; jum·bling** \-b(ə-)liŋ\ [perh. imit.] *vi* (ca. 1529) : to move in a confused or disordered manner ~ *vt* : to mix into a confused or disordered mass — often used with *up*
[2]**jumble** *n* (1657) **1 a :** a mass of things mingled together without order or plan : HODGEPODGE **b :** a state of confusion **2** *Brit* : articles for a rummage sale
[3]**jumble** *n* [origin unknown] (1615) : a small thin usu. ring-shaped sugared cookie or cake
jumble sale *n* (1898) *Brit* : RUMMAGE SALE
jum·bo \ˈjəm-(ˌ)bō\ *n, pl* **jumbos** [*Jumbo,* a huge elephant exhibited by P. T. Barnum] (1883) : a very large specimen of its kind — **jumbo** *adj*
[1]**jump** \ˈjəmp\ *vb* [prob. akin to LG *gumpen* to jump] *vi* (1530) **1 a :** to spring into the air : LEAP; *esp* : to spring free from the ground or other base by the muscular action of feet and legs **b :** to move suddenly or involuntarily : START **c :** to move over a position occupied by an opponent's piece in a board game often thereby capturing the piece **d :** to undergo a vertical or lateral displacement owing to improper alignment of the film on a projector mechanism **e :** to start out or forward : BEGIN — usu. used with *off* ⟨~ off to a big lead⟩ **f :** to move energetically : HUSTLE **g :** to go from one sequence of instructions in a computer program to another **2 :** COINCIDE, AGREE **3 a :** to move haphazardly or irregularly : shift abruptly ⟨~*ed* from job to job⟩ **b :** to change or abandon employment esp. in violation of contract **c :** to rise suddenly in rank or status **d :** to undergo a sudden sharp change in value ⟨prices ~*ed*⟩ **e :** to make a jump in bridge **f :** to make a hurried judgment ⟨~ to conclusions⟩ **g :** to show eagerness ⟨~*ed* at the chance⟩ **h :** to enter eagerly ⟨~ on the bandwagon⟩ **4 :** to make a sudden physical or verbal attack ⟨~*ed* on him for his criticism⟩ **5 :** to bustle with activity ⟨the restaurant was ~*ing*⟩ ~ *vt* **1 a :** to leap over ⟨~ a hurdle⟩ **b :** to move over (a piece) in a board game **c :** to act, move, or begin before (as a signal) ⟨~ the green light⟩ **d :** to leap aboard ⟨~ a freight⟩ **2** *obs* : RISK, HAZARD **3 a :** to escape from : AVOID **b :** to leave hastily or in violation of contract ⟨~ town without paying their bills —Hamilton Basso⟩ **c :** to depart from (a normal course) ⟨~ the track⟩ **4 a :** to make a sudden physical or verbal attack on **b :** to occupy illegally ⟨~ a mining claim⟩ **5 a** (1) **:** to cause to leap (2) **:** to cause (game) to break cover : START, FLUSH **b :** to elevate in rank or status **c :** to raise (a bridge partner's bid) by more than one rank **d :** to increase suddenly and sharply — **jump bail :** to abscond after being released from prison on bail — **jump ship 1 :** to leave the company of a ship without authority **2 :** to desert a cause or party esp. abruptly — **jump the gun 1 :** to start in a race before the starting signal **2 :** to act, move, or begin something before the proper time — **jump the queue** *Brit* : to advance directly to or as if to the head of a line — **jump the shark :** to undergo a significant change for the worse that marks the point at which a period of success ends (as for a TV series)
[2]**jump** *adv* (1539) *obs* : EXACTLY, PAT
[3]**jump** *n* (ca. 1552) **1 a** (1) **:** an act of jumping : LEAP (2) **:** any of several sports competitions featuring a leap, spring, or bound (3) **:** a leap in figure skating in which the skater leaves the ice with both feet and turns in the air (4) **:** a space cleared or covered by a leap (5) **:** an obstacle to be jumped over or from **b :** a sudden involuntary movement : START **c :** a move made in a board game by jumping **d :** a transfer from one sequence of instructions in a computer program to a different sequence **2** *obs* : VENTURE **3 a** (1) **:** a sharp sudden increase (2) **:** a bid in bridge of more tricks than are necessary to overcall the preceding bid — compare SHIFT **b :** an abrupt change or transition **c** (1) **:** a quick short journey (2) **:** one in a series of moves from one place to another **d :** the portion of a published item (as a newspaper article or story) that comprises the continuation of an item that begins on a preceding page **4 :** an advantage at the start ⟨getting the ~ on the competition⟩ **5 :** jazz music with a fast tempo
jump ball *n* (1924) : a method of putting a basketball into play by tossing it into the air between two opponents who jump up and attempt to tap the ball to a teammate; *also* : a ball put into play in this manner
jump boot *n* (1942) : a boot worn esp. by paratroopers
jump cut *n* (1947) : a sudden often jarring cut from one shot or scene to another without intervening devices (as fade-outs); *broadly* : an abrupt transition (as in a narrative) — **jump–cut** \ˈjəmp-ˌkət\ *vb*
jump drive *n* (2002) : a small usu. rectangular device used for storing and transferring computer data : FLASH DRIVE
[1]**jump·er** \ˈjəm-pər\ *n* (1611) **1 :** a person who jumps **2 a :** any of various devices operating with a jumping motion **b :** any of several sleds **c :** a connection used to close a break or cut out part of a circuit **3 :** any of several jumping animals; *esp* : a saddle horse trained to jump obstacles **4 :** JUMP SHOT
[2]**jum·per** \ˈjəm-pər\ *n* [prob. fr. E dial. *jump* jumper] (1850) **1 :** a loose blouse or jacket worn by workmen **2 :** a sleeveless one-piece dress worn usu. with a blouse **3 :** a child's coverall — usu. used in pl. **4** *chiefly Brit* : SWEATER 2a
jumper cables *n pl* (ca. 1926) : a pair of electrical cables with alligator clips used to make a connection for jump-starting a vehicle
jumper's knee *n* (1977) : a painful condition of the knee caused by inflammation or small tears in the tendon of the patella that occurs esp. in sports requiring strenuous jumping
jump hook *n* (1982) : a hook shot in which the player jumps before releasing the ball
jumping bean *n* (ca. 1889) : a seed of any of several Mexican shrubs (genera *Sebastiania* and *Sapium*) of the spurge family that tumbles about because of the movements of the larva of a small tortricid moth (*Cydia saltitans* syn. *Laspeyresia saltitans*) inside it
jumping jack *n* (1883) **1 :** a toy figure of a man jointed and made to jump or dance by means of strings or a sliding stick **2 :** a conditioning exercise performed from a standing position by jumping to a position with legs spread and arms raised and then to the original position
jumping mouse *n* (1826) : any of several small hibernating No. American rodents (family Zapodidae) with long hind legs and tail and no cheek pouches
jumping–off place \ˌjəm-piŋ-ˈȯf-\ *n* (1826) **1 :** a remote or isolated place **2 :** a place or point from which an enterprise, investigation, or discussion is launched — called also *jumping-off point*
jumping plant louse *n* (1881) : any of numerous plant lice (family Psyllidae) with the femurs thickened and adapted for leaping
jumping spider *n* (1736) : any of a family (Salticidae) of small spiders that stalk and leap upon their prey
jump jet *n* (1964) : a military jet aircraft with vertical takeoff and landing capability
jump·mas·ter \ˈjəmp-ˌmas-tər\ *n* (1941) : a person who supervises parachutists
jump–off \ˈjəmp-ˌȯf\ *n* (1917) **1 :** the start of a race or an attack **2 :** a jumping competition to break a tie at the end of regular competition (as in a horse show)
jump pass *n* (ca. 1948) : a pass made by a player (as in football or basketball) while jumping
jump rope *n* (1834) : a rope used for exercises and children's games that involve jumping over the usu. twirling rope each time it reaches its lowest point; *also* : a game played with a jump rope
jump seat *n* (ca. 1864) **1 :** a movable carriage seat **2 :** a folding seat between the front and rear seats of a passenger automobile
jump shooter *n* (1972) : a basketball player who makes jump shots
jump shot *n* (1948) : a shot in basketball made by jumping into the air and releasing the ball with one or both hands at the peak of the jump
jump–start \ˈjəmp-ˈstärt\ *vt* (1973) **1 :** to start (an engine or vehicle) by temporary connection to an external power source (as another vehicle's battery) **2 a :** to start or restart rapidly or forcefully ⟨advertising can ~ a political campaign⟩ **b :** to impart fresh or renewed energy to : ENERGIZE ⟨a plan to ~ the stagnant economy⟩ — **jump start** *n*
jump·suit \ˈjəmp-ˌsüt\ *n* (1944) **1 :** a coverall worn by parachutists for jumping **2 :** a one-piece garment consisting of a blouse or shirt with attached trousers or shorts
jumpy \ˈjəm-pē\ *adj* **jump·i·er; -est** (1869) **1 :** characterized by jumps or sudden variations **2 :** NERVOUS, JITTERY — **jump·i·ness** *n*
[1]**jun** \ˈjən\ *n, pl* **jun** [Korean *chŏn*] (1966) : the chon of North Korea
[2]**jun** *abbr* junior
Jun *abbr* June
junc *abbr* junction
jun·co \ˈjəŋ-(ˌ)kō\ *n, pl* **juncos** *or* **juncoes** [NL, fr. Sp, reed — more at JONQUIL] (1887) : any of a genus (*Junco* of the family Emberizidae) of small widely distributed No. American finches usu. having a pink bill, ashy gray head and back, and conspicuous white lateral tail feathers
junc·tion \ˈjəŋ(k)-shən\ *n* [L *junction-, junctio,* fr. *jungere* to join — more at YOKE] (1711) **1 :** an act of joining : the state of being joined **2 a :** a place or point of meeting **b :** an intersection of roads esp. where one terminates **c :** a point (as in a thermocouple) at which dissimilar metals make contact **d :** an interface in a semiconductor device between regions with different electrical characteristics **3 :** something that joins — **junc·tion·al** \-shnəl, -shə-nᵊl\ *adj*
junc·tur·al \ˈjəŋ(k)-chə-rəl, ˈjəŋ(k)-shrəl\ *adj* (1942) : of or relating to phonetic juncture
junc·ture \ˈjəŋ(k)-chər\ *n* (14c) **1 a :** JOINT, CONNECTION **b :** the manner of transition or mode of relationship between two consecutive sounds in speech **2 :** an instance of joining : JUNCTION **3 :** a point of time; *esp* : one made critical by a concurrence of circumstances
syn JUNCTURE, EXIGENCY, EMERGENCY, CONTINGENCY, PINCH, STRAITS, CRISIS mean a critical or crucial time or state of affairs. JUNCTURE stresses the significant concurrence or convergence of events ⟨an important *juncture* in our country's history⟩. EXIGENCY stresses the pressure of restrictions or urgency of demands created by a special situation ⟨provide for *exigencies*⟩. EMERGENCY applies to a sudden unforeseen situation requiring prompt action to avoid disaster ⟨the presence of mind needed to deal with *emergencies*⟩. CONTINGENCY implies an emergency or exigency that is regarded as possible but uncertain of occurrence ⟨*contingency* plans⟩. PINCH implies urgency or pressure for action to a less intense degree than EXIGENCY or EMERGENCY ⟨come through in a *pinch*⟩. STRAITS applies to a troublesome situation from which escape is extremely difficult ⟨in dire *straits*⟩. CRISIS applies to a juncture whose outcome will make a decisive difference ⟨a *crisis* of confidence⟩.
June \ˈjün\ *n* [ME, fr. AF & L; AF *Juin,* fr. L *Junius*] (14c) : the sixth month of the Gregorian calendar
June·ber·ry \ˈjün-ˌber-ē\ *n* (ca. 1810) : SERVICEBERRY
june bug *n, often cap J* (1829) : any of numerous rather large leaf-eating scarab beetles (subfamily Melolonthinae) that fly chiefly in late spring and have larvae that are white grubs which live in soil and feed chiefly on the roots of grasses and other plants — called also *june beetle*
June·teenth \ˌjün-ˈtēn(t)th\ *n* [blend of *June* and *nineteenth*] (1903) : June 19 celebrated esp. in Texas to commemorate the belated announcement there of the Emancipation Proclamation in 1865
Jung·ian \ˈyu̇ŋ-ē-ən\ *adj* (ca. 1930) : of, relating to, or characteristic of C. G. Jung or his psychological doctrines — **Jungian** *n*
jun·gle \ˈjəŋ-gəl\ *n, often attrib* [Hindi *jaṅgal* & Urdu *jangal* forest, fr. Skt *jaṅgala* desert region] (1776) **1 a :** an impenetrable thicket or tangled mass of tropical vegetation **b :** a tract overgrown with thickets or masses of vegetation **2 :** a hobo camp **3 a** (1) **:** a confused or disordered mass of objects : JUMBLE (2) **:** something that baffles or frustrates by its tangled or complex character : MAZE ⟨the ~ of housing laws —Bernard Taper⟩ **b :** a place of ruthless struggle for survival ⟨the city is a ~ where no one is safe after dark —Stuart Chase⟩ **4 :** electronic dance music that combines elements of techno, reggae, and hip-hop and is marked esp. by an extremely fast beat — **jun·gle·like** \-gə(l)-ˌlīk\ *adj* — **jun·gly** \-g(ə-)lē\ *adj*
jungle cat *n* (1877) : a small grayish to tawny cat (*Felis chaus*) found from northern Africa to Asia and having a black-tipped tail and tufted ears; *broadly* : a wild cat (as a leopard) of tropical regions
jun·gled \-gəld\ *adj* (1842) : abounding in jungle ⟨a ~ island⟩
jungle fowl *n* (ca. 1825) : any of several Asian wild birds (genus *Gallus*) related to the pheasants; *esp* : a bird (*G. gallus*) of southeastern Asia from which domestic chickens have prob. descended
jungle gym *n* [fr. *Junglegym,* a trademark] (1923) : a structure of vertical and horizontal bars for use by children at play
[1]**ju·nior** \ˈjün-yər\ *adj* [ME, fr. L, compar. of *juvenis* young — more at YOUNG] (13c) **1 a :** less advanced in age : YOUNGER — used chiefly to distinguish a son with the same given name as his father **b** (1) **:** YOUTHFUL (2) **:** designed for young people and esp. adolescents **c :** of more recent date and therefore inferior or subordinate ⟨a ~ lien⟩

2 a : lower in standing or rank ⟨~ partners⟩ **b** : duplicating or suggesting on a smaller scale something typically large or powerful ⟨a ~ gale⟩ **3** : of or relating to juniors or the class of juniors at an educational institution ⟨the ~ prom⟩

[2]junior *n* [L, n. & adj.] (1526) **1 a** (1) : a person who is younger than another ⟨a man six years my ~⟩ (2) : a male child : SON (3) : a young person **b** : a clothing size for women and girls with slight figures **2 a** : a person holding a lower position in a hierarchy of ranks **b** : a student in the next-to-the-last year before graduating from an educational institution **3** *cap* : a member of a program of the Girl Scouts for girls in the third through sixth grades in school

ju•nior•ate \ˈjün-yə-ˌrāt, -rət\ *n* (1845) **1** : a course of high school or college study for candidates for the priesthood, brotherhood, or sisterhood; *specif* : one preparatory to the course in philosophy **2** : a seminary for juniorate training

junior college *n* (1899) : an educational institution that offers two years of studies corresponding to those in the first two years of a four-year college and that often offers technical, vocational, and liberal studies to the adults of a community

junior high school *n* (1907) : a school usu. including grades seven to nine — called also *junior high*

Junior Leaguer *n* (1903) : a member of a league of young women organized for volunteer service to civic and social organizations

junior miss *n* (1923) **1** : an adolescent girl **2** : JUNIOR 1b

junior varsity *n* (1902) : a team composed of members lacking the experience or qualification required for the varsity

ju•ni•per \ˈjü-nə-pər\ *n* [ME *junipere,* fr. L *juniperus*] (14c) **1 a** : any of numerous shrubs or trees (genus *Juniperus*) of the cypress family with leaves resembling needles or scales and female cones usu. resembling berries **b** : the berrylike cone or fruit of a juniper; *esp* : the bluish one of a common juniper (*J. communis*) which is used to flavor foods and from which is obtained an acrid essential oil used esp. as a flavoring in gin and liqueurs — called also *juniper berry* **2** : any of several coniferous trees resembling true junipers

juniper tar *n* (ca. 1930) : a tarry liquid used topically in treating skin diseases and obtained by distillation from the wood of a Eurasian juniper (*Juniperus oxycedrus*) — called also *cade oil, juniper tar oil*

[1]junk \ˈjəŋk\ *n* [ME *jonke*] (14c) **1** : pieces of old cable or cordage used esp. to make gaskets, mats, swabs, or oakum **2 a** (1) : old iron, glass, paper, or other waste that may be used again in some form (2) : secondhand, worn, or discarded articles (3) : CLUTTER 1b **b** : something of poor quality : TRASH **c** : something of little meaning, worth, or significance **3** *slang* : NARCOTICS; *esp* : HEROIN **4** : JUNK BOND **5 a** : baseball pitches that break or are off-speed (as curveballs or changeups) **b** *slang* : male genitalia — **junky** \ˈjəŋ-kē\ *adj*

[2]junk *vt* (1916) : to get rid of as worthless : SCRAP ***syn*** see DISCARD

[3]junk *n* [Pg *junco,* fr. Jav *joṅ*] (1609) : any of various ships of Chinese waters with bluff lines, a high poop and overhanging stem, little or no keel, high pole masts, and a deep rudder

[3]junk

junk art *n* (1962) : three-dimensional art made from discarded material (as metal, mortar, glass, or wood) — **junk artist** *n*

junk bond *n* (1974) : a high-risk bond that offers a high yield

junk DNA *n* (1972) : a region of DNA that usu. consists of a repeating DNA sequence, does not code for protein, and has no known function

junk e–mail *n* (1986) : SPAM

junk•er \ˈjəŋ-kər\ *n* [[1]*junk* + [2]*-er*] (1944) : something (as an automobile) of such age and condition as to be ready for scrapping

Jun•ker \ˈyu̇ŋ-kər\ *n* [G, fr. OHG *junchērro,* lit., young lord] (1554) : a member of the Prussian landed aristocracy — **Jun•ker•dom** \-kər-dəm\ *n* — **Jun•ker•ism** \-kə-ˌri-zəm\ *n*

[1]jun•ket \ˈjəŋ-kət\ *n* [ME *ioncate,* ultim. fr. VL **juncata,* fr. L *juncus* rush] (15c) **1** : a dessert of sweetened flavored milk set with rennet **2 a** : a festive social affair **b** : TRIP, JOURNEY: as (1) : a trip made by an official at public expense (2) : a promotional trip made at another's expense ⟨a film's press ~⟩

[2]junket *vi* (1555) **1** : FEAST, BANQUET **2** : to go on a junket — **jun•ke•teer** \ˌjəŋ-kə-ˈtir\ *or* **jun•ket•er** \ˈjəŋ-kə-tər\ *n*

junk food *n* (1960) **1** : food that is high in calories but low in nutritional content **2** : something that is appealing or enjoyable but of little or no real value ⟨video *junk food*⟩

junk•ie *also* **junky** \ˈjəŋ-kē\ *n, pl* **junk•ies** (1923) **1 a** : a narcotics peddler or addict **b** : a person who gets an unusual amount of pleasure from or has an unusual amount of interest in something ⟨television news ~⟩ **2** : a junk dealer

junk mail *n* (1954) : unsolicited mail that consists mainly of promotional materials, catalogs, and requests for donations

junk sculpture *n* (1965) : JUNK ART

junk•yard \ˈjəŋk-ˌyärd\ *n* (1880) : a yard used to store sometimes resalable junk

Ju•no \ˈjü-(ˌ)nō\ *n* (bef. 12c) : the wife of Jupiter, queen of heaven, and goddess of light, birth, women, and marriage — compare HERA

Ju•no•esque \ˌjü-(ˌ)nō-ˈesk\ *adj* (1888) : marked by stately beauty

jun•ta \ˈhu̇n-tə, ˈjən-, ˈhən-\ *n* [Sp, fr. fem. of *junto* joined, fr. L *junctus,* pp. of *jungere* to join — more at YOKE] (1622) **1** : a council or committee for political or governmental purposes; *esp* : a group of persons controlling a government esp. after a revolutionary seizure of power **2** : JUNTO

jun•to \ˈjən-(ˌ)tō\ *n, pl* **juntos** [prob. alter. of *junta*] (1623) : a group of persons joined for a common purpose

Ju•pi•ter \ˈjü-pə-tər\ *n* [L] (13c) **1** : the chief Roman god, husband of Juno, and god of light, of the sky and weather, and of the state and its welfare and its laws — compare ZEUS **2** : the largest of the planets and fifth in order from the sun — see PLANET table

ju•ral \ˈju̇r-əl\ *adj* [L *jur-, jus* law] (1635) **1** : of or relating to law **2** : of or relating to rights or obligations — **ju•ral•ly** \-ə-lē\ *adv*

Ju•ras•sic \ju̇-ˈra-sik\ *adj* [F *jurassique,* fr. *Jura* mountain range] (1831) : of, relating to, or being the period of the Mesozoic era between the Triassic and the Cretaceous or the corresponding system of rocks marked by the presence of dinosaurs and the first appearance of birds — see GEOLOGIC TIME table — **Jurassic** *n*

ju•rat \ˈju̇r-ˌat\ *n* [short for L *juratum* (*est*) it has been sworn, 3d sing. perf. pass. of *jurare* to swear — more at JURY] (1796) : a certificate added to an affidavit stating when, before whom, and where it was made

ju•rel \hü-ˈrel\ *n* [Sp] (ca. 1772) : any of several carangid fishes (as a jack crevalle) of warm seas

ju•rid•i•cal \ju̇-ˈri-di-kəl\ *also* **ju•rid•ic** \-dik\ *adj* [L *juridicus,* fr. *jur-, jus* + *dicere* to say — more at DICTION] (1502) **1** : of or relating to the administration of justice or the office of a judge **2** : of or relating to law or jurisprudence : LEGAL — **ju•rid•i•cal•ly** \-di-k(ə-)lē\ *adv*

ju•ris•con•sult \ˌju̇r-əs-ˈkän-ˌsəlt, -kən-ˈ\ *n* [L *jurisconsultus,* fr. *juris* (gen. of *jus*) + *consultus,* pp. of *consulere* to consult] (1605) : JURIST; *esp* : one learned in international and public law

ju•ris•dic•tion \ˌju̇r-əs-ˈdik-shən\ *n* [ME *jurisdiccioun,* fr. AF & L; AF *jurisdiction,* fr. L *jurisdiction-, jurisdictio,* fr. *juris* + *diction-, dictio* act of saying — more at DICTION] (14c) **1** : the power, right, or authority to interpret and apply the law **2 a** : the authority of a sovereign power to govern or legislate **b** : the power or right to exercise authority : CONTROL **3** : the limits or territory within which authority may be exercised ***syn*** see POWER — **ju•ris•dic•tion•al** \-shnəl, -shə-nᵊl\ *adj* — **ju•ris•dic•tion•al•ly** *adv*

Ju•ris Doctor \ˈju̇r-əs-\ *n* [L, doctor of law] (1969) : a degree conferred by a law school usu. after three years of full-time study

ju•ris•pru•dence \ˌju̇r-əs-ˈprü-dᵊn(t)s\ *n* (1654) **1** : the science or philosophy of law **2 a** : a system or body of law **b** : the course of court decisions **3** : a department of law ⟨medical ~⟩ — **ju•ris•pru•den•tial** \-prü-ˈden(t)-shəl\ *adj* — **ju•ris•pru•den•tial•ly** \-ˈden(t)-sh(ə-)lē\ *adv*

ju•ris•pru•dent \-ˈprü-dᵊnt\ *n* [LL *jurisprudent-, jurisprudens,* fr. L *juris* + *prudent-, prudens* skilled, prudent] (1628) : JURIST

ju•rist \ˈju̇r-ist\ *n* [MF *juriste,* fr. ML *jurista,* fr. L *jur-, jus*] (15c) : one having a thorough knowledge of law; *esp* : JUDGE

ju•ris•tic \ju̇-ˈris-tik\ *adj* (1831) **1** : of or relating to a jurist or jurisprudence ⟨~ thought⟩ **2** : of, relating to, or recognized in law ⟨~ theory⟩ — **ju•ris•ti•cal•ly** \-ti-k(ə-)lē\ *adv*

ju•ror \ˈju̇r-ər, ˈju̇r-ˌȯr\ *n* (14c) **1 a** : a member of a jury **b** : a person summoned to serve on a jury **2** : a person who takes an oath (as of allegiance)

[1]ju•ry \ˈju̇r-ē\ *n, pl* **juries** [ME *jure,* fr. AF *juree,* fr. *jurer* to swear, fr. L *jurare,* fr. *jur-, jus*] (15c) **1** : a body of persons sworn to give a verdict on some matter submitted to them; *esp* : a body of persons legally selected and sworn to inquire into any matter of fact and to give their verdict according to the evidence **2** : a committee for judging and awarding prizes at a contest or exhibition **3** : one (as the public or test results) that will decide — used esp. in the phrase *the jury is still out*

[2]jury *adj* [ME *jory* (in *jory saile* improvised sail)] (15c) : improvised for temporary use esp. in an emergency : MAKESHIFT ⟨a ~ mast⟩ ⟨a ~ rig⟩

[3]jury *vt* **jur•ied; jury•ing** [[1]*jury*] (1947) : to select material as appropriate for exhibition in (as an art show) — used chiefly as a participle ⟨a *juried* show⟩

jury nullification *n* (1982) : the acquitting of a defendant by a jury in disregard of the judge's instructions and contrary to the jury's findings of fact

ju•ry–rig \ˈju̇r-ē-ˌrig, -ˈrig\ *vt* [[2]*jury*] (1788) : to erect, construct, or arrange in a makeshift fashion

jus gen•ti•um \ˈyüs-ˈgen-tē-əm\ *n* [L, law of nations] (ca. 1549) : INTERNATIONAL LAW

jus san•gui•nis \-ˈsäŋ-gwə-nəs\ *n* [L, right of blood] (1902) : a rule that a child's citizenship is determined by its parents' citizenship

jus•sive \ˈjə-siv\ *n* [L *jussus,* pp. of *jubēre* to order; akin to Pol *judzić* to incite, Skt *yudhyati* he fights] (1846) : a word, form, case, or mood expressing command — **jussive** *adj*

jus so•li \ˈyüs-ˈsō-ˌlē\ *n* [L, right of the soil] (1902) : a rule that the citizenship of a child is determined by the place of its birth

[1]just \ˈjəst, ˈjüst\ *archaic var of* JOUST

[2]just \ˈjəst\ *adj* [ME, fr. AF & L; AF *juste,* fr. L *justus,* fr. *jus* right, law; akin to Skt *yos* welfare] (14c) **1 a** : having a basis in or conforming to fact or reason : REASONABLE ⟨a ~ but not a generous decision⟩ **b** *archaic* : faithful to an original **c** : conforming to a standard of correctness : PROPER ⟨~ proportions⟩ **2 a** (1) : acting or being in conformity with what is morally upright or good : RIGHTEOUS ⟨a ~ war⟩ (2) : being what is merited : DESERVED ⟨a ~ punishment⟩ **b** : legally correct : LAWFUL ⟨~ title to an estate⟩ ***syn*** see FAIR, UPRIGHT — **just•ly** *adv* — **just•ness** \ˈjəs(t)-nəs\ *n*

[3]just \ˈjəst, ˈjist, ˈjest *also without* t\ *adv* (15c) **1 a** : EXACTLY, PRECISELY ⟨~ right⟩ **b** : very recently ⟨the bell ~ rang⟩ **2 a** : by a very small margin : BARELY ⟨~ too late⟩ **b** : IMMEDIATELY, DIRECTLY ⟨~ west of here⟩ **3 a** : ONLY, SIMPLY ⟨~ last year⟩ ⟨~ be yourself⟩ **b** : QUITE, VERY ⟨~ wonderful⟩ **4** : PERHAPS, POSSIBLY ⟨it ~ might work⟩ — **just about** : ALMOST ⟨the work is *just about* done⟩

just–folks \ˈjəs(t)-ˈfōks\ *adj* (1952) : marked by the absence of formality or sophistication : UNPRETENTIOUS ⟨her ~ manner⟩

jus•tice \ˈjəs-təs\ *n* [ME, fr. AF *justise,* fr. L *justitia,* fr. *justus*] (12c) **1 a** : the maintenance or administration of what is just esp. by the impartial adjustment of conflicting claims or the assignment of merited rewards or punishments **b** : JUDGE **c** : the administration of law; *esp* : the establishment or determination of rights according to the rules of law or equity **2 a** : the quality of being just, impartial, or fair **b** (1) : the principle or ideal of just dealing or right action (2) : conformity to this principle or ideal : RIGHTEOUSNESS **c** : the quality of conforming to law **3** : conformity to truth, fact, or reason : CORRECTNESS

\ə\ **abut** \ᵊ\ **kitten, F table** \ər\ **further** \a\ **ash** \ā\ **ace** \ä\ **mop, mar** \au̇\ **out** \ch\ **chin** \e\ **bet** \ē\ **easy** \g\ **go** \i\ **hit** \ī\ **ice** \j\ **job** \ŋ\ **sing** \ō\ **go** \ȯ\ **law** \ȯi\ **boy** \th\ **thin** \t͟h\ **the** \ü\ **loot** \u̇\ **foot** \y\ **yet** \zh\ **vision, beige** \k̲, ⁿ, œ, ue, ʸ\ *see* Guide to Pronunciation

justice of the peace (15c) : a local magistrate empowered chiefly to administer summary justice in minor cases, to commit for trial, and to administer oaths and perform marriages

jus·ti·cia·ble \ˌjə-'sti-sh(ē-)ə-bəl\ *adj* (15c) **1** : liable to trial in a court of justice ⟨a ~ offense⟩ **2** : capable of being decided by legal principles or by a court of justice — **jus·ti·cia·bil·i·ty** \ˌjə-ˌsti-sh(ē-)ə-'bi-lə-tē\ *n*

jus·ti·ci·ar \jə-'sti-shē-ər, -ˌär\ *n* [ML *justitiarius,* fr. L *justitia*] (ca. 1580) : the chief political and judicial officer of the Norman and later kings of England until the 13th century

jus·ti·fi·able \'jəs-tə-ˌfī-ə-bəl\ *adj* (1561) : capable of being justified : EXCUSABLE ⟨~ family pride —*Current Biog.*⟩ — **jus·ti·fi·abil·i·ty** \ˌjəs-tə-ˌfī-ə-'bi-lə-tē\ *n* — **jus·ti·fi·ably** \'jəs-tə-ˌfī-ə-blē\ *adv*

jus·ti·fi·ca·tion \ˌjəs-tə-fə-'kā-shən\ *n* (14c) **1** : the act, process, or state of being justified by God **2 a** : the act or an instance of justifying : VINDICATION **b** : something that justifies **3** : the process or result of justifying lines of text

jus·ti·fi·ca·tive \'jəs-tə-fə-ˌkā-tiv\ *adj* (1611) : JUSTIFICATORY

jus·ti·fi·ca·to·ry \ˌjəs-'ti-fi-kə-ˌtōr-ē, 'jəs-tə-fə-ˌkā-tə-rē\ *adj* (1579) : tending or serving to justify : VINDICATORY

jus·ti·fy \'jəs-tə-ˌfī\ *vb* **-fied; -fy·ing** [ME *justifien,* fr. AF or LL; AF *justifier,* fr. LL *justificare,* fr. L *justus*] *vt* (14c) **1 a** : to prove or show to be just, right, or reasonable **b** (1) : to show to have had a sufficient legal reason (2) : to qualify (oneself) as a surety by taking oath to the ownership of sufficient property **2 a** *archaic* : to administer justice to **b** *archaic* : ABSOLVE **c** : to judge, regard, or treat as righteous and worthy of salvation **3 a** : to space (as lines of text) so that the lines come out even at the margin **b** : to make even by justifying ⟨*justified* margins⟩ ~ *vi* **1 a** : to show a sufficient lawful reason for an act done **b** : to qualify as bail or surety **2** : to justify lines of text **syn** *see* MAINTAIN — **jus·ti·fi·er** \-ˌfī(-ə)r\ *n*

just-in-time *n, often attrib* (1977) : a manufacturing strategy wherein parts are produced or delivered only as needed

1jut \'jət\ *vb* **jut·ted; jut·ting** [perh. short for ²*jutty*] *vi* (ca. 1573) : to extend out, up, or forward : PROJECT ⟨mountains *jutting* into the sky⟩ ⟨a *jutting* jaw⟩ ~ *vt* : to cause to project

2jut *n* (1786) : something that juts : PROJECTION

jute \'jüt\ *n* [Bengali *jhuṭo*] (1746) : the glossy fiber of either of two Asian plants (*Corchorus olitorius* and *C. capsularis*) of the linden family used chiefly for sacking, burlap, and twine; *also* : a plant producing jute

Jute \'jüt\ *n* [ME, fr. ML *Jutae* Jutes, of Gmc origin; akin to OE *Eotenas* Jutes] (14c) : a member of a Germanic people invading England from the Continent and settling in Kent in the fifth century — **Jut·ish** \'jü-tish\ *adj*

1jut·ty \'jə-tē\ *n, pl* **jutties** [ME] (15c) **1** *archaic* : JETTY **2** : a projecting part of a building

2jutty *vt* **jut·tied; jut·ty·ing** (1599) *obs* : to project beyond

juv *abbr* juvenile

ju·ve·nes·cence \ˌjü-və-'ne-s°n(t)s\ *n* (1800) : the state of being youthful or of growing young — **ju·ve·nes·cent** \-s°nt\ *adj*

1ju·ve·nile \'jü-və-ˌnī(-ə)l, -n°l\ *adj* [F or L; F *juvénile,* fr. L *juvenilis,* fr. *juvenis* young person — more at YOUNG] (1625) **1 a** : physiologically immature or undeveloped — YOUNG **b** : derived from sources within the earth and coming to the surface for the first time — used esp. of water and gas **2** : of, relating to, characteristic of, or suitable for children or young people ⟨~ books⟩ **3** : reflecting psychological or intellectual immaturity : CHILDISH

2juvenile *n* (1733) **1 a** : a young person : YOUTH **b** : a book for children or young people **2** : a young individual resembling an adult of its kind except in size and reproductive activity: as **a** : a fledged bird not yet in adult plumage **b** : a 2-year-old racehorse **3** : an actor or actress who plays youthful parts

juvenile court *n* (1899) : a court that has special jurisdiction over delinquent and dependent children usu. up to the age of 18

juvenile delinquency *n* (1816) **1** : conduct by a juvenile characterized by antisocial behavior that is beyond parental control and therefore subject to legal action **2** : a violation of the law committed by a juvenile and not punishable by death or life imprisonment — **juvenile delinquent** *n*

juvenile diabetes *n* (1951) : TYPE 1 DIABETES

juvenile hormone *n* (1940) : an insect hormone that is secreted by the corpora allata, inhibits maturation to the imago, and plays a role in reproduction

juvenile officer *n* (1954) : a police officer charged with the detection, prosecution, and care of juvenile delinquents

juvenile–onset diabetes *n* (1975) : TYPE 1 DIABETES

ju·ve·nil·ia \ˌjü-və-'ni-lē-ə\ *n pl* [L, neut. pl. of *juvenilis*] (1622) **1** : compositions produced in the artist's or author's youth **2** : artistic or literary compositions suited to or designed for the young

ju·ve·nil·i·ty \ˌjü-və-'ni-lə-tē\ *n, pl* **-ties** (ca. 1623) **1** : the quality or state of being juvenile : YOUTHFULNESS **2 a** : immaturity of thought or conduct **b** : an instance of being juvenile

jux·ta·pose \'jək-stə-ˌpōz\ *vt* **-posed; -pos·ing** [prob. back-formation fr. *juxtaposition*] (1851) : to place side by side ⟨~ unexpected combinations of colors, shapes and ideas —J. F. T. Bugental⟩

juxtaposed *adj* (1855) : placed side by side : being in juxtaposition **syn** *see* ADJACENT

jux·ta·po·si·tion \ˌjək-stə-pə-'zi-shən\ *n* [L *juxta* near + E *position* — more at JOUST] (1654) : the act or an instance of placing two or more things side by side; *also* : the state of being so placed — **jux·ta·po·si·tion·al** \-'zish-nəl, -ˌzi-shə-n°l\ *adj*

JV *abbr* junior varsity

K

1k \'kā\ *n, pl* **k's** *or* **ks** \'kāz\ *often cap, often attrib* (bef. 12c) **1 a** : the 11th letter of the English alphabet **b** : a graphic representation of this letter **c** : a speech counterpart of orthographic *k* **2 a** : a graphic device for reproducing the letter *k* **3** : one designated *k* esp. as the 11th in order or class **4** : something shaped like the letter K **5** : a unit vector parallel to the z-axis **6** [*kilo-*] : THOUSAND ⟨a salary of $24K⟩ **7** [*kilo-*] : a unit of computer storage capacity equal to 1024 bytes ⟨uses 350K of disk space⟩ **8** *cap* [struck] : STRIKEOUT

2k *abbr* **1** karat **2** kindergarten **3** king **4** kitchen **5** knit **6** knot **7** koruna **8** kosher — often enclosed in a circle **9** kyat

1K *abbr* **1** Kelvin **2** kilometer

2K *symbol* [NL *kalium*] potassium

ka *abbr* [G *kathode*] cathode

Ka·a·ba \'kä-bə\ *n* [Ar *ka'ba,* lit., cubic building] (1734) : a small stone building in the court of the Great Mosque at Mecca that contains a sacred black stone and is the goal of Islamic pilgrimage and the point toward which Muslims turn in praying

kab·ba·lah *also* **kab·ba·la** *or* **ka·ba·la** *or* **cab·ba·la** *or* **cab·ba·lah** \kə-'bä-lə, 'ka-bə-lə\ *n, often cap* [ML *cabbala* — more at CABAL] **1** : a medieval and modern system of Jewish theosophy, mysticism, and thaumaturgy marked by belief in creation through emanation and a cipher method of interpreting Scripture **2 a** : a traditional, esoteric, occult, or secret matter **b** : esoteric doctrine or mysterious art — **kab·ba·lism** \'kä-bə-ˌli-zəm, 'ka-\ *n* — **kab·ba·lis·tic** \ˌkä-bə-'lis-tik, ˌka-\ *adj*

kabob *var of* KEBAB

Ka·bu·ki \kə-'bü-kē, 'kä-bü-(ˌ)kē\ *n* [Jp] (1899) : traditional Japanese popular drama performed with highly stylized singing and dancing

Ka·byle \kə-'bī(-ə)l\ *n* [Ar *qabā'il,* pl. of *qabīla* tribe] (1738) **1** : a member of a Berber people living in the mountainous coastal area east of Algiers **2** : the Berber language of the Kabyles

ka·chi·na *also* **ka·tchi·na** *or* **ka·tci·na** \kə-'chē-nə\ *n* [Hopi *qacína*] (1888) **1** : one of the deified ancestral spirits believed among the Hopi and other Pueblo Indians to visit the pueblos at intervals **2** : one of the elaborately masked kachina impersonators that dance at agricultural ceremonies **3** : a doll representing a kachina

kad·dish \'kä-dish\ *n, pl* **kad·dish·es** *also* **kad·di·shim** \kä-'di-shim, -(ˌ)shēm\ *often cap* [Aram *qaddīsh* holy] (1613) : a Jewish prayer recited in the daily ritual of the synagogue and by mourners at public services after the death of a close relative

kaf·fee·klatsch \'kö-fē-ˌklach, 'kä-fē-, -ˌkläch, -ˌkläch\ *n, often cap* [G, fr. *Kaffee* coffee + *Klatsch* gossip] (1888) : an informal social gathering for coffee and conversation

Kaf·fir *or* **Kaf·ir** \'ka-fər\ *n* [Ar *kāfir* infidel] (1778) **1** *archaic* : a member of a group of southern African Bantu-speaking peoples **2** *often not cap, chiefly So.Afr, usu disparaging* : a black African

Kaffir lime *n* (1978) : a citrus tree (*Citrus hystrix*) of southeastern Asia having aromatic leaves and roundish thick-rinded green fruits used esp. in Thai cooking; *also* : its leaves or fruit

kaf·fi·yeh *also* **kef·fi·yeh** \kə-'fē-ə\ *n* [Ar *kūfīya, kaffīya,* fr. al-*Kufa,* town in Iraq] (ca. 1817) : an Arab headdress consisting of a square of cloth folded to form a triangle and held on by a cord

kachina 3

kaf·ir \'ka-fər\ *n* (ca. 1785) : a grain sorghum with stout short-jointed somewhat juicy stalks and erect heads

Kaf·ir \'ka-fər\ *n* [Ar *kāfir*] (1759) : NURISTANI 1

Kaf·iri \'ka-fə-rē\ *n* (1901) : NURISTANI 2

Kaf·ka·esque \ˌkäf-kə-'esk, ˌkaf-\ *adj* (1946) : of, relating to, or suggestive of Franz Kafka or his writings; *esp* : having a nightmarishly complex, bizarre, or illogical quality ⟨~ bureaucratic delays⟩

kaftan *var of* CAFTAN

ka·hu·na \kə-'hü-nə\ *n* [Hawaiian] (1875) **1** : a Hawaiian shaman **2** : a preeminent person or thing : BIG GUN ⟨the industry's big ~, with . . . 57 percent of the market —A. E. Serwer⟩

kai·nite \'kī-ˌnīt, 'kä-\ *also* **kai·nit** \kī-'nēt\ *n* [G *Kainit,* fr. Gk *kainos* new — more at RECENT] (1868) : a natural salt $KMg(SO_4)Cl \cdot 3H_2O$ consisting of a hydrous sulfate and chloride of magnesium and potassium that is used as a fertilizer and as a source of potassium and magnesium compounds

kai·ro·mone \'kī-rə-ˌmōn, -rō-\ *n* [Gk *kairos* critical time, opportunity + E *-mone* (as in *pheromone*)] (1970) : a chemical substance emitted by one species and esp. an insect or plant that has an adaptive benefit (as a stimulus for oviposition) to another species

kai·ser \ˈkī-zər\ *n* [ME, fr. ON *keisari;* akin to OHG *keisur* emperor; both fr. a prehistoric Gmc word borrowed fr. L *Caesar,* cognomen of the Emperor Augustus] (13c) **:** EMPEROR; *esp* **:** the ruler of Germany from 1871 to 1918 — **kai·ser·dom** \-zər-dəm\ *n* — **kai·ser·ism** \-zə-ˌri-zəm\ *n*

kai·se·rin \ˈkī-zə-rən\ *n* [G, fem. of *Kaiser*] (ca. 1888) **:** the wife of a kaiser

kaiser roll *n* (ca. 1898) **:** a round crusty roll often used for sandwiches

ka·ka \ˈkä-kə\ *n* [Maori] (ca. 1774) **:** an olive-brown New Zealand parrot (*Nestor meridionalis*) with gray and red markings

ka·ka·po \ˌkä-kə-ˈpō\ *n, pl* **-pos** [Maori] (1843) **:** a large chiefly nocturnal burrowing New Zealand parrot (*Strigops habroptilus*) that has green and brown barred plumage and well-developed wings with little power of flight

ka·ke·mo·no \ˌkä-ki-ˈmō-(ˌ)nō\ *n, pl* **-nos** [Jp] (1889) **:** a vertical Japanese ornamental pictorial or calligraphic scroll — compare MAKIMONO

ka·ki·e·mon \ˌkä-kē-ˈā-ˌmän\ *n, often cap* [Sakaida *Kakiemon fl*1650 Japanese potter] (1890) **:** a Japanese porcelain decorated with enamel

ka·la–azar \ˌkä-lə-ə-ˈzär, ˌka-\ *n* [Hindi & Urdu *kālā-āzār,* lit., black disease] (1883) **:** a severe parasitic disease chiefly of tropical areas that is marked by fever, progressive anemia, leukopenia, and enlargement of the spleen and liver and caused by a leishmania (*Leishmania donovani*) transmitted by the bite of sand flies

ka·la·ma·ta *also* **ca·la·ma·ta** \ˌkä-lə-ˈmä-tə, ˌka-\ *n, often cap* [*Kalamata,* port in Greece] (1979) **:** a brine-cured black olive grown in Greece

ka·lan·choe \ˌka-lən-ˈkō-ē *also* kə-ˈlaŋ-kə-(ˌ)wē *or* ˈka-lən-ˌchō\ *n* [NL] (1830) **:** any of a genus (*Kalanchoe*) of chiefly African tropical succulent herbs or shrubs of the orpine family often cultivated as ornamentals — called also *bryophyllum*

Ka·lash·ni·kov \kə-ˈlash-nə-ˌkȯf, -ˈläsh-, -ˌkäf\ *n* [Mikhail Timofeevich *Kalashnikov b*1919 Soviet weapons designer] (1970) **:** a Soviet-designed assault rifle; *esp* **:** AK-47

kale \ˈkāl\ *n* [Sc, fr. ME (northern) *cal,* fr. OE *cāl* — more at COLE] (14c) **1 a :** COLE **b :** a hardy cabbage (*Brassica oleracea acephala*) with curled often finely incised leaves that do not form a dense head; *also* **:** its leaves used as a vegetable **2** *slang* **:** MONEY

ka·lei·do·scope \kə-ˈlī-də-ˌskōp\ *n* [Gk *kalos* beautiful + *eidos* form + E *-scope* — more at IDYLL] (1817) **1 :** an instrument containing loose bits of colored material (as glass or plastic) between two flat plates and two plane mirrors so placed that changes of position of the bits of material are reflected in an endless variety of patterns **2 :** something resembling a kaleidoscope: as **a :** a variegated changing pattern or scene ⟨a ∼ of colors⟩ **b :** a succession of changing phases or actions ⟨a ∼ of changing fashions⟩ **c :** a diverse collection — **ka·lei·do·scop·ic** \-ˌlī-də-ˈskä-pik\ *adj* — **ka·lei·do·scop·i·cal·ly** \-pi-k(ə-)lē\ *adv*

kalends *var of* CALENDS

Ka·li \ˈkä-ˌlē\ *n* [Skt *Kālī*] (1798) **:** the Hindu goddess of death and destruction

kal·li·din \ˈka-lə-dən\ *n* [G, fr. *Kalli*krein + Pepti*d* peptide + *-in*] (1950) **:** either of two vasodilator kinins formed from blood plasma globulin by the action of kallikrein: **a :** BRADYKININ **b :** one with a terminal lysine amino acid residue added to bradykinin

kal·li·kre·in \ˌka-lə-ˈkrē-ən, kə-ˈli-krē-ən\ *n* [G, fr. Gk *kallikreas* sweetbread, pancreas, fr. *kalli-* beautiful (fr. *kallos* beauty) + *kreas* flesh — more at RAW] (1930) **:** a hypotensive protease that liberates kinins from blood plasma proteins and is used therapeutically for vasodilation

Kal·muck *or* **Kal·muk** \ˈkal-ˌmək, kal-ˈ\ *or* **Kal·myk** \kal-ˈmik\ *n* [Russ *kalmyk,* fr. Volga Tatar *kalmık*] (1613) **1 :** a member of a Buddhist Mongol people orig. of Dzungaria living mainly northwest of the Caspian Sea in Russia **2 :** the Mongolian language of the Kalmucks

Ka·ma \ˈkä-mə\ *n* [Skt *Kāma,* fr. *kāma* love] (1861) **:** the Hindu god of love

ka·ma·ai·na \ˌkä-mə-ˈī-nə\ *n* [Hawaiian *kama'āina,* fr. *kama* child + *'āina* land] (1903) **:** one who has lived in Hawaii for a long time

kame \ˈkām\ *n* [Sc, kame, comb, fr. ME (northern) *camb* comb, fr. OE] (1795) **:** a short ridge, hill, or mound of stratified drift deposited by glacial meltwater

Ka·me·ha·me·ha Day \kə-ˌmā-ə-ˈmā-(ˌ)hä-\ *n* (1925) **:** June 11 observed as a holiday in Hawaii in commemoration of the birthday of Kamehameha I

[1]**ka·mi·ka·ze** \ˌkä-mi-ˈkä-zē\ *n* [Jp, lit., divine wind] (1945) **1 :** a member of a Japanese air attack corps in World War II assigned to make a suicidal crash on a target (as a ship) **2 :** an airplane containing explosives to be flown in a suicide crash on a target

[2]**kamikaze** *adj* (1945) **1 :** of, relating to, or resembling a kamikaze **2 :** having or showing reckless disregard for safety or personal welfare

kam·pong \ˈkäm-ˌpȯŋ, ˈkam-\ *n* [Malay] (1844) **:** a hamlet or village in a Malay-speaking country

Kan *or* **Kans** *abbr* Kansas

ka·na \ˈkä-nə\ *n, pl* **kana** *often attrib* [Jp] (1727) **:** a Japanese system of syllabic writing having characters that can be used exclusively for writing foreign words or in combination with kanji (as for indicating pronunciations or grammatical inflections); *also* **:** a single character belonging to the kana system — compare HIRAGANA, KATAKANA

Ka·nak \kə-ˈnäk, -ˈnak\ *n* [F *canaque,* prob. fr. E *Kanaka* South Sea islander, fr. Hawaiian, person] (1910) **:** a native Melanesian inhabitant of New Caledonia

kana·my·cin \ˌka-nə-ˈmī-sᵊn\ *n* [NL *kanamyceticus,* specific epithet of *Streptomyces kanamyceticus*] (1957) **:** a broad-spectrum antibiotic from a Japanese soil streptomyces (*Streptomyces kanamyceticus*)

Kan·a·rese \ˌka-nə-ˈrēz, -ˈrēs\ *n, pl* **Kanarese** [*Kanara,* India] (1847) **1 :** KANNADA **2 :** a member of a Kannada-speaking people of Karnataka, southern India

kan·ban \ˈkän-ˌbän\ *n, often attrib* [Jp, sign, placard; fr. the cards used on assembly lines to signal that parts are needed] (1977) **:** JUST-IN-TIME

kan·ga·roo \ˌkaŋ-gə-ˈrü\ *n, pl* **-roos** [Guugu Yimidhirr (Australian aboriginal language of northern Queensland) *gaŋurru*] (1770) **:** any of various herbivorous leaping marsupial mammals (family Macropodidae) of Australia, New Guinea, and adjacent islands with a small head, large ears, long powerful hind legs, a long thick tail used as a support and in balancing, and rather small forelegs not used in locomotion

kangaroo court *n* (1853) **1 :** a mock court in which the principles of law and justice are disregarded or perverted **2 :** a court characterized by irresponsible, unauthorized, or irregular status or procedures **3 :** judgment or punishment given outside of legal procedure

kangaroo

kangaroo rat *n* (1867) **:** any of a genus (*Dipodomys*) of nocturnal burrowing rodents of arid parts of western No. America that travel by hopping on their long hind legs and have a long tail and fur-lined cheek pouches

kan·ji \ˈkän-(ˌ)jē\ *n, pl* **kanji** *often attrib* [Jp] (1920) **:** a Japanese system of writing that utilizes characters borrowed or adapted from Chinese writing; *also* **:** a single character in the kanji system — compare KANA

Kan·na·da \ˈkä-nə-də *also* ˈka-\ *n* [Kannada *kannaḍa*] (1856) **:** the major Dravidian language of Karnataka, southern India

kan·te·le \ˈkän-tə-lə\ *n* [Finn] (ca. 1903) **:** a traditional Finnish zither orig. having five strings but now having as many as thirty

ka·o·lin \ˈkā-ə-lən\ *n* [F *kaolin,* fr. *Gaoling* hill in China] (ca. 1741) **:** a fine usu. white clay that is used in ceramics and refractories, as a filler or extender, and in medicine esp. as an adsorbent in the treatment of diarrhea

ka·o·lin·ite \-lə-ˌnīt\ *n* (1867) **:** a white mineral consisting of a hydrous silicate of aluminum that constitutes the principal mineral in kaolin — **ka·o·lin·it·ic** \ˌkā-ə-lə-ˈni-tik\ *adj*

ka·on \ˈkā-ˌän\ *n* [ISV *ka* kay (fr. *K-meson,* its earlier name) + [2]*-on*] (1958) **:** an unstable meson that occurs in both charged and neutral forms and is about 970 times more massive than an electron

ka·pell·meis·ter \kə-ˈpel-ˌmīs-tər, kä-\ *n, often cap* [G, fr. *Kapelle* choir + *Meister* master] (1838) **:** the director of a choir or orchestra

ka·pey·ka \kä-ˈpā-kä\ *n, pl* **ka·pe·ek** \kä-ˈpā-ək\ [Belarusian *kapeĭka* (gen. pl. *kapeek*) kopeck] (1992) — see *rubel* at MONEY table

kaph \ˈkäf, ˈkȯf\ *n* [Heb, lit., palm of the hand] (ca. 1823) **:** the 11th letter of the Hebrew alphabet — see ALPHABET table

ka·pok \ˈkā-ˌpäk\ *n* [Malay] (ca. 1750) **:** a mass of silky fibers that invest the seeds of the ceiba tree and are used esp. as a filling for mattresses, life preservers, and sleeping bags and as insulation

Ka·po·si's sarcoma \ˈka-pə-sēz- *also* -shēz-, kə-ˈpō-sēz-\ *n* [Moritz *Kaposi* †1902 Hung. dermatologist] (1916) **:** a neoplastic disease that occurs esp. in individuals coinfected with HIV and a specific herpesvirus (species *Human herpesvirus 8* of the genus *Rhadinovirus*), that affects esp. the skin and mucous membranes, and that is marked usu. by pink to reddish-brown or bluish plaques, macules, papules, or nodules esp. on the lower extremities — abbr. *KS*

kap·pa \ˈka-pə\ *n* [ME, fr. Gk, of Sem origin; akin to Heb *kaph*] (15c) **:** the 10th letter of the Greek alphabet — see ALPHABET table

ka·put *also* **ka·putt** \kə-ˈpu̇t, kä-, -ˈpüt\ *adj* [G *kaputt,* fr. F *capot* not having made a trick at piquet] (1895) **1 :** utterly finished, defeated, or destroyed **2 :** unable to function **3 :** hopelessly outmoded

karabiner *var of* CARABINER

Kara·ism \ˈker-ə-ˌi-zəm, ˈka-rə-\ *n* [LHeb *qĕrāīm* Karaites, fr. Heb *qārā* to read] (ca. 1883) **:** a Jewish doctrine originating in Baghdad in the eighth century that rejects rabbinism and talmudism and bases its tenets on Scripture alone — **Kara·ite** \-ˌīt\ *n*

kar·a·kul \ˈker-ə-kəl, ˈka-rə-\ *n* [*Karakul,* village in Uzbekistan] (1853) **1** *often cap* **:** any of a breed of hardy fat-tailed sheep of central Asian origin with a narrow body and coarse wiry fur **2 :** the usu. curly glossy black coat of a very young karakul lamb valued as fur — compare BROADTAIL 2, PERSIAN LAMB 1

kar·a·o·ke \ˌker-ē-ˈō-kē, ˌka-rē- *also* kə-ˈrō-kē, ˌkä-rä-ˈō-(ˌ)kā\ *n* [Jp, fr. *kara* empty + *ōke,* short for *ōkesutora* orchestra] (1979) **:** a device that plays instrumental accompaniments for a selection of songs to which the user sings along and that records the user's singing with the music; *also* **:** a form of entertainment involving the use of a karaoke machine

kar·at *or* **car·at** \ˈker-ət, ˈka-rət\ *n* [ME *carrat* — more at CARAT] (15c) **:** a unit of fineness for gold equal to $\frac{1}{24}$ part of pure gold in an alloy

ka·ra·te \kə-ˈrä-tē\ *n* [Jp, fr. *kara* empty + *te* hand] (1947) **:** a Japanese art of self-defense employing hand strikes and kicks to disable or subdue an opponent — **ka·ra·te·ist** \-tē-ist\ *n*

ka·ra·ya gum \kə-ˈrī-ə-\ *n* [Hindi *karāyal* resin] (1916) **:** any of several vegetable gums similar to tragacanth and often used as substitutes for it that are obtained from tropical Asian trees (genera *Sterculia* of the family Sterculiaceae and *Cochlospermum* of the family Bixaceae); *esp* **:** one derived from an Indian tree (*S. urens*)

Ka·re·lian \kə-ˈrē-lē-ən, -ˈrēl-yən\ *n* (1854) **1 :** a native or inhabitant of Karelia **2 :** the Finno-Ugric language of the Karelians — **Karelian** *adj*

Ka·ren \kə-ˈren\ *n, pl* **Karen** *or* **Karens** (1833) **1 :** a member of a group of peoples of eastern and southern Myanmar **2 a :** a group of languages spoken by the Karen peoples **b :** a language of this group

kar·ma \ˈkär-mə *also* ˈkər-\ *n* [Skt *karma* fate, work] (1827) **1** *often cap* **:** the force generated by a person's actions held in Hinduism and Buddhism to perpetuate transmigration and in its ethical consequences to determine the nature of the person's next existence **2 :** VIBRATION 4 — **kar·mic** \-mik\ *adj*

ka·roo *or* **kar·roo** \kə-ˈrü\ *n, pl* **karoos** *or* **karroos** [Afrik *karo,* fr. Khoikhoi *karo, karro* hard, dry] (1789) **:** a dry tableland of southern Africa

ka·ross \kə-ˈräs\ *n* [Afrik *karos,* fr. Khoikhoi *karo-s, kro-s*] (ca. 1731) **:** a simple garment or rug of skins used esp. by native tribesmen of southern Africa

karst \ˈkärst\ *n* [G, fr. Slovene dial. or Croatian dial. *kras, kars,* type of rock, region composed of such rock] (1902) **:** an irregular limestone region with sinkholes, underground streams, and caverns — **karst·ic** \ˈkär-stik\ *adj*

\ə\ **abut** \ᵊ\ **kitten,** F **table** \ər\ **further** \a\ **ash** \ā\ **ace** \ä\ **mop, mar** \au̇\ **out** \ch\ **chin** \e\ **bet** \ē\ **easy** \g\ **go** \i\ **hit** \ī\ **ice** \j\ **job** \ŋ\ **sing** \ō\ **go** \ȯ\ **law** \ȯi\ **boy** \th\ **thin** \t͟h\ **the** \ü\ **loot** \u̇\ **foot** \y\ **yet** \zh\ **vision, beige** \ḵ, ⁿ, œ, ue, ʸ\ *see* Guide to Pronunciation

kart \'kärt\ *n* (1961) : GO-KART — **kart•ing** *n*

kary- *or* **karyo-** *also* **cary-** *or* **caryo-** *comb form* [NL, fr. Gk *karyon* nut — more at CAREEN] **1** : nucleus of a cell ⟨*karyo*kinesis⟩ **2** : nut : kernel ⟨*cary*opsis⟩

kar•y•og•a•my \ˌka-rē-'ä-gə-mē\ *n, pl* **-mies** (1891) : the fusion of cell nuclei (as in fertilization)

kar•yo•ki•ne•sis \ˌka-rē-ō-kə-'nē-səs, -kī-\ *n* [NL] (1882) **1** : the nuclear phenomena characteristic of mitosis **2** : the whole process of mitosis — **kar•yo•ki•net•ic** \-'ne-tik\ *adj*

kar•y•ol•o•gy \ˌka-rē-'ä-lə-jē\ *n* [ISV] (1895) **1** : the minute cytological characteristics of the cell nucleus esp. with regard to the chromosomes **2** : a branch of cytology concerned with the karyology of cell nuclei — **kar•y•o•log•i•cal** \-rē-ə-'lä-ji-kəl\ *also* **kar•y•o•log•ic** \-jik\ *adj*

kar•yo•some \'ka-rē-ə-ˌsōm\ *n* [ISV] (1889) : a mass of chromatin in a cell nucleus that resembles a nucleolus

1**kar•yo•type** \'ka-rē-ə-ˌtīp\ *n* [ISV] (1929) : the chromosomal characteristics of a cell; *also* : the chromosomes themselves or a representation of them — **kar•yo•typ•ic** \ˌka-rē-ə-'ti-pik\ *adj* — **kar•yo•typ•i•cal•ly** \-pi-k(ə-)lē\ *adv*

2**karyotype** *vt* (1963) : to determine or analyze the karyotype of

Kasbah *var of* CASBAH

ka•sha \'kä-shə, 'ka-\ *n* [Russ] (1808) **1** : a porridge made usu. from buckwheat groats **2** : kasha grain before cooking

Ka•shan \kə-'shän\ *n* [*Kashan*, Iran] (1905) : an Oriental rug with floral motifs in soft colors

Kash•miri \kash-'mir-ē, kazh-\ *n, pl* **Kashmiris** *or* **Kashmiri** (1880) **1** : an Indo-Aryan language spoken in Kashmir **2** : a native or inhabitant of Kashmir

kash•ruth *or* **kash•rut** \käsh-'rüt, -'shrüth\ *n* [Heb *kashrūth*, lit., fitness] (1907) **1** : the Jewish dietary laws **2** : the state of being kosher

Ka•shu•bi•an \kə-'shü-bē-ən\ *n* [*Kashube* a member of a Slavic people] (1919) : a Slavic language spoken northwest and southwest of Gdansk

kat *var of* KHAT

ka•ta \'kä-(ˌ)tä\ *n, pl* **kata** *or* **katas** [Jp, lit., model, pattern] (1945) : a set combination of positions and movements (as in karate) performed as an exercise

kat•a•bat•ic \ˌka-tə-'ba-tik\ *adj* [Gk *katabatos* descending, verbal of *katabainein* to go down, fr. *kata-* cata- + *bainein* to go — more at COME] (1918) : relating to or being a wind produced by the flow of cold dense air down a slope (as of a mountain or glacier) in an area subject to radiational cooling

ka•ta•ka•na \ˌkä-tə-'kä-nə\ *n* [Jp, fr. *kata* part + *kana* kana] (1727) : the form of Japanese syllabic writing used esp. for scientific terms, official documents, and words adopted from other languages — compare HIRAGANA

katchina *or* **katcina** *var of* KACHINA

Ka•tha•re•vou•sa *or* **Ka•tha•re•vu•sa** \ˌkä-thə-'re-və-ˌsä\ *n* [ModGk *kathareuousa*, fr. Gk, fem. of *kathareuōn*, prp. of *kathareuein* to be pure, fr. *katharos* pure] (1936) : modern Greek conforming to classic Greek usage

ka•thar•sis *archaic var of* CATHARSIS

kat•su•ra tree \'kät-sə-rə-\ *n* [Jp *katsura* katsura tree] (ca. 1924) : a deciduous tree (*Cercidiphyllum japonicum* of the family Cercidiphyllaceae) of Japan and China sometimes grown as an ornamental for its dark blue-green ovate leaves which turn bright yellow or red in autumn — called also *katsura*

ka•ty•did \'kā-tē-ˌdid\ *n* [imit.] (1784) : any of various large green American long-horned grasshoppers usu. having stridulating organs on the forewings of the males that produce a loud shrill sound

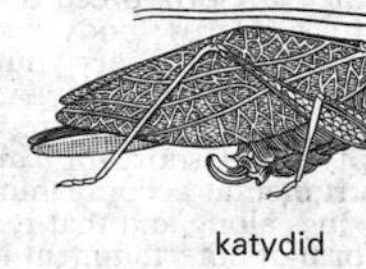

katydid

kat•zen•jam•mer \'kat-sən-ˌja-mər\ *n* [G, fr. *Katze* cat + *Jammer* distress] (1849) **1** : HANGOVER **2** : DISTRESS 2 **3** : a discordant clamor

kau•ri \'kau̇(-ə)r-ē\ *n* [Maori *kawri*] (1823) **1** : any of various trees (genus *Agathis*) of the araucaria family; *esp* : a tall timber tree (*A. australis*) of New Zealand having fine white straight-grained wood — called also *kauri pine* **2** : a light-colored to brown resin from the kauri tree found as a fossil in the ground or collected from living trees and used esp. in varnishes and linoleum — called also *kauri gum, kauri resin*

ka•va \'kä-və\ *n* [Tongan & Marquesan, lit., bitter] (1810) **1** : an Australasian shrubby pepper (*Piper methysticum*) from whose crushed root an intoxicating beverage is made; *also* : the beverage made from kava **2** : the dried rhizome and roots of the kava used esp. as a dietary supplement chiefly to relieve stress and anxiety

kava kava \'kä-və-'kä-və\ *n* (1891) : KAVA

Ka•wa•sa•ki disease \ˌkä-wə-'sä-kē-\ *n* [Tomisaku *Kawasaki* b1925 Jp. pediatrician] (1977) : an acute illness of unknown cause that chiefly affects infants and children and is characterized esp. by fever, rash, conjunctivitis, inflammation of lips and tongue, and swollen lymph nodes of the neck — called also *Kawasaki syndrome*

kay \'kā\ *n* (14c) : the letter *k*

Kay \'kā\ *n* (14c) : a boastful overbearing knight of the Round Table who is foster brother and seneschal of King Arthur

kay•ak \'kī-ˌak\ *n* [Inuit *qayaq*] (1757) **1** : an Eskimo canoe made of a frame covered with skins except for a small opening in the center and propelled by a double-bladed paddle **2** : a portable boat styled like an Eskimo kayak — **kayak** *vi* — **kay•ak•er** \-ˌa-kər\ *n* — **kay•ak•ing** \-kiŋ\ *n*

1**kayo** \(ˌ)kā-'ō, 'kā-(ˌ)ō\ *n* [pronunciation of *KO*, abbr.] (1920) : KNOCKOUT 1

2**kayo** *vt* **kay•oed; kayo•ing** (1921) : KNOCK OUT

Ka•zak \kə-'zak, -'zäk\ *n* [*Kazak* (Kazakh), town in Azerbaijan] (1900) : an Oriental rug in bold colors with geometric designs or stylized plant and animal forms

Ka•zakh *also* **Ka•zak** \kə-'zak, -'zäk\ *n* [Russ *kazakh*, fr. Kazakh *kazak*] (1832) **1** : a member of a Turkic people of Kazakhstan and other countries of central Asia **2** : the language of the Kazakhs

ka•zil•lion \kə-'zil-yən, -'zi-lē-\ *n* [alter. of *zillion*] (1986) : ZILLION — **kazillion** *adj*

1**ka•zoo** \kə-'zü\ *n, pl* **kazoos** [imit.] (1884) : an instrument that imparts a buzzing quality to the human voice and that usu. consists of a small metal or plastic tube with a side hole covered by a thin membrane

2**kazoo** *n, pl* **kazoos** [origin unknown] (1968) *slang* : WAZOO

kb *abbr* **1** kilobar **2** kilobase

KB *abbr* kilobyte

K–band \'kā-\ *n* (ca. 1948) : a segment of the radio spectrum that lies between 10.9 GHz and 36.0 GHz and spans the upper superhigh-frequency and lower extremely-high-frequency bands and that is used esp. for police radars, satellite communication, and astronomical observation

kbar *abbr* kilobar

Kbps *abbr* kilobits per second

kc *abbr* kilocycle

KC *abbr* **1** Kansas City **2** King's Counsel **3** Knights of Columbus

kcal *abbr* kilocalorie

KCB *abbr* knight commander of the Order of the Bath

kc/s *abbr* kilocycles per second

KD *abbr* **1** kiln-dried **2** knockdown; knocked down

kea \'kē-ə\ *n* [Maori] (1862) : a large mostly dull green New Zealand parrot (*Nestor notabilis*) that is normally insectivorous but sometimes destroys sheep by slashing the back to feed on the kidney fat

ke•bab *or* **ke•bob** *also* **ka•bob** \kə-'bäb *also* 'kā-ˌ\ *n* [ultim. fr. Ar or Pers *kabāb*, fr. Turk *kebap*] (1673) : cubes of meat (as lamb or beef) marinated and cooked with vegetables usu. on a skewer

keb•buck *or* **keb•bock** \'ke-bək\ *n* [ME (Sc dial.) *cabok*, fr. ScGael *ceapag*] (15c) *dial Brit* : a whole wheel or ball of cheese

1**kedge** \'kej\ *vb* **kedged; kedg•ing** [ME *caggen*] *vt* (1627) : to move (a ship) by means of a line attached to a small anchor dropped at the distance and in the direction desired ~ *vi* : to move a ship by kedging

2**kedge** *n* (1765) : a small anchor used esp. in kedging

ked•ge•ree \'ke-jə-rē\ *n* [Hindi & Urdu *khicaṛī*, ultim. fr. Skt *khiccā*] (1662) **1** : an Indian dish of seasoned rice, beans, lentils, and sometimes smoked fish **2** : cooked or smoked fish, rice, hard-boiled eggs, and seasoning heated in cream

1**keek** \'kēk\ *vi* [ME *kiken*] (14c) *chiefly Scot* : PEEP, LOOK

2**keek** *n* (1721) *chiefly Scot* : PEEP, LOOK

1**keel** \'kēl\ *vb* [ME *kelen*, fr. OE *cēlan*, fr. *cōl* cool] (bef. 12c) *chiefly dial* : COOL

2**keel** *n* [ME *kele*, fr. MD *kiel*; akin to OE *cēol* ship] (14c) : a flat-bottomed barge used esp. on the Tyne to carry coal

3**keel** *n* [ME *kele*, fr. ON *kjǫlr*; akin to OE *ceole* throat, beak of a ship — more at GLUTTON] (14c) **1 a** : the chief structural member of a boat or ship that extends longitudinally along the center of its bottom and that often projects from the bottom; *also* : this projection **b** : SHIP **2** : a projection suggesting a keel; *esp* : CARINA 1 — **keeled** \'kēld\ *adj* — **keel•less** \'kēl-ləs\ *adj*

4**keel** *vi* (1832) **1** : to fall in or as if in a faint — usu. used with *over* **2** : to heel or lean precariously

5**keel** *n* [ME (Sc) *keyle*] (15c) *chiefly dial* : RED OCHER

keel•boat \'kēl-ˌbōt\ *n* (1695) **1** : a shallow covered keeled riverboat that is usu. rowed, poled, or towed and that is used for freight **2** : a keeled sailboat

keel•haul \-ˌhȯl\ *vt* [D *kielhalen*, fr. *kiel* keel + *halen* to haul] (1666) **1** : to haul under the keel of a ship as punishment or torture **2** : to rebuke severely

keel•son \'kel-sən, 'kēl-\ *n* [ME *kelswayn*, prob. of Scand origin; akin to Sw *kölsvin* keelson] (13c) : a longitudinal structure running above and fastened to the keel of a ship in order to stiffen and strengthen its framework

1**keen** \'kēn\ *adj* [ME *kene* brave, sharp, fr. OE *cēne* brave; akin to OHG *kuoni* brave] (13c) **1 a** : having a fine edge or point : SHARP **b** : affecting one as if by cutting ⟨~ sarcasm⟩ **c** : pungent to the sense ⟨a ~ scent⟩ **2 a (1)** : showing a quick and ardent responsiveness : ENTHUSIASTIC ⟨a ~ swimmer⟩ **(2)** : EAGER ⟨was ~ to begin⟩ **b** *of emotion or feeling* : INTENSE ⟨the ~ delight in the chase —F. W. Maitland⟩ **3 a** : intellectually alert : having or characteristic of a quick penetrating mind ⟨a ~ student⟩ ⟨a ~ awareness of the problem⟩; *also* : shrewdly astute **b** : sharply contested ⟨~ debate⟩ **c** : extremely sensitive in perception ⟨~ eyes⟩ **4** : WONDERFUL, EXCELLENT ***syn*** see SHARP, EAGER — **keen•ly** *adv* — **keen•ness** \'kēn-nəs\ *n* — **keen on** : very enthusiastic or excited about ⟨wasn't *keen on* going⟩

2**keen** *n* (1830) : a lamentation for the dead uttered in a loud wailing voice or sometimes in a wordless cry

3**keen** *vb* [Ir *caoinim* I lament, weep] *vi* (1845) **1 a** : to lament with a keen **b** : to make a sound suggestive of a keen **2** : to lament, mourn, or complain loudly ~ *vt* : to utter by keening — **keen•er** *n*

1**keep** \'kēp\ *vb* **kept** \'kept\; **keep•ing** [ME *kepen*, fr. OE *cēpan*; perh. akin to OHG *chapfēn* to look] *vt* (bef. 12c) **1** : to take notice of by appropriate conduct : FULFILL: as **a** : to be faithful to ⟨~ a promise⟩ **b** : to act fittingly in relation to ⟨~ the Sabbath⟩ **c** : to conform to in habits or conduct ⟨~ late hours⟩ **d** : to stay in accord with (a beat) ⟨~ time⟩ **2** : PRESERVE, MAINTAIN: as **a** : to watch over and defend ⟨~ us from harm⟩ **b (1)** : to take care of : TEND ⟨~ a garden⟩ **(2)** : SUPPORT **(3)** : to maintain in a good, fitting, or orderly condition — usu. used with *up* **c** : to continue to maintain ⟨~ watch⟩ **d (1)** : to cause to remain in a given place, situation, or condition ⟨~ him waiting⟩ **(2)** : to preserve (food) in an unspoiled condition **e (1)** : to have or maintain in an established position or relationship ⟨~ a mistress⟩ — often used with *on* ⟨*kept* the cook on⟩ **(2)** : to lodge or feed for pay ⟨~ boarders⟩ **f (1)** : to maintain a record in ⟨~ a diary⟩ **(2)** : to enter in a book ⟨~ records⟩ **g** : to have customarily in stock for sale **3 a** : to restrain from departure or removal : DETAIN ⟨~ children after school⟩ **b** : HOLD BACK, RESTRAIN ⟨~ them from going⟩ ⟨*kept* him back with difficulty⟩ **c** : SAVE, RESERVE ⟨~ some for later⟩ ⟨*kept* some out for a friend⟩ **d** : to refrain from revealing ⟨~ a secret⟩ **4 a** : to retain in one's possession or power ⟨*kept* the money we found⟩ **b** : to refrain from granting, giving, or allowing ⟨*kept* the news back⟩ **c** : to have in control ⟨~ your temper⟩ **5** : to confine oneself to ⟨~ my room⟩ **6 a** : to stay or continue in ⟨~ the path⟩ ⟨~ your seat⟩ **b** : to stay or remain on or in usu. against opposition : HOLD ⟨*kept* her ground⟩ **7** : CONDUCT, MANAGE ⟨~ a tearoom⟩ ~ *vi* **1** *chiefly Brit* : LIVE, LODGE **2 a** : to maintain a course, direction, or progress ⟨~ to the right⟩ **b** : to continue usu. without interruption ⟨~ talking⟩

⟨~ quiet⟩ ⟨~ on smiling⟩ **c :** to persist in a practice ⟨*kept* bothering them⟩ ⟨*kept* on smoking in spite of warnings⟩ **3 :** STAY, REMAIN ⟨~ out of the way⟩ ⟨~ off the grass⟩: as **a :** to stay even — usu. used with *up* ⟨~ up with the Joneses⟩ **b :** to remain in good condition ⟨meat will ~ in the freezer⟩ **c :** to remain secret ⟨the secret would ~⟩ **d :** to call for no immediate action ⟨the matter will ~ until morning⟩ **4 :** ABSTAIN, REFRAIN ⟨can't ~ from talking⟩ **5 :** to be in session ⟨school will ~ through the winter —W. M. Thayer⟩ **6** *of a quarterback* **:** to retain possession of a football esp. after faking a handoff — **keep an eye on :** WATCH — **keep at :** to persist in doing or concerning oneself with — **keep company :** to go together as frequent companions or in courtship — **keep house :** to manage a household — **keep one's distance** *or* **keep at a distance :** to stay aloof **:** maintain a reserved attitude — **keep one's eyes open** *or* **keep one's eyes peeled :** to be on the alert **:** be watchful — **keep one's hand in :** to keep in practice — **keep one's head down :** to avoid attracting notice — **keep one's nose clean :** to avoid trouble esp. through good behavior — **keep pace :** to stay even; *also* **:** KEEP UP 1 — **keep step :** to keep in step — **keep to 1 a :** to stay in **b :** to limit oneself to **2 :** to abide by — **keep to oneself 1 :** to keep secret ⟨*kept* the facts *to myself*⟩ **2 :** to remain solitary or apart from other people

syn KEEP, OBSERVE, CELEBRATE, COMMEMORATE mean to notice or honor a day, occasion, or deed. KEEP stresses the idea of not neglecting or violating ⟨*kept* the Sabbath by refraining from work⟩. OBSERVE suggests marking the occasion by ceremonious performance ⟨not all holidays are *observed* nationally⟩. CELEBRATE suggests acknowledging an occasion by festivity ⟨traditionally *celebrates* Thanksgiving with a huge dinner⟩. COMMEMORATE suggests that an occasion is marked by observances that remind one of the origin and significance of the event ⟨*commemorate* Memorial Day with the laying of wreaths⟩.

syn KEEP, RETAIN, DETAIN, WITHHOLD, RESERVE mean to hold in one's possession or under one's control. KEEP may suggest a holding securely in one's possession, custody, or control ⟨*keep* this while I'm gone⟩. RETAIN implies continued keeping, esp. against threatened seizure or forced loss ⟨managed to *retain* their dignity even in poverty⟩. DETAIN suggests a delay in letting go ⟨*detained* them for questioning⟩. WITHHOLD implies restraint in letting go or a refusal to let go ⟨*withheld* information from the authorities⟩. RESERVE suggests a keeping in store for future use ⟨*reserve* some of your energy for the last mile⟩.

[2]**keep** *n* (1579) **1 a** *archaic* **:** CUSTODY, CHARGE **b :** MAINTENANCE **2 :** one that keeps or protects: as **a :** FORTRESS, CASTLE; *specif* **:** the strongest and securest part of a medieval castle **b :** one whose job is to keep or tend **c :** PRISON, JAIL **3 :** the means or provisions by which one is kept ⟨earned his ~⟩ **4 :** KEEPER 5 — **for keeps 1 a :** with the provision that one keep what one has won ⟨played marbles *for keeps*⟩ **b :** with deadly seriousness **2 :** for an indefinitely long time **:** PERMANENTLY **3 :** with the result of ending the matter

keep–away \ˈkēp-ə-ˌwā\ *n* (1960) **:** a game in which two or more players try to keep an object (as a ball) from one or more other players

keep down *vt* (1548) **1 :** to keep in control ⟨*keep* expenses *down*⟩ **2 :** to prevent from growing, advancing, or succeeding

keep·er \ˈkē-pər\ *n* (14c) **1 :** one that keeps: as **a :** PROTECTOR **b :** GAMEKEEPER **c :** WARDEN **d :** CUSTODIAN **e** *chiefly Brit* **:** CURATOR **2 :** any of various devices for keeping something in position **3 a :** one suitable for or worth keeping: as (1) **:** a fruit or vegetable that keeps well (2) **:** a fish large enough to be legally caught and kept (3) **:** one having genuine or lasting merit ⟨their new album is a ~⟩ **b :** a domestic animal considered with respect to how easy it is to care for ⟨an easy ~⟩ **4 :** GOALKEEPER **5 :** an offensive football play in which the quarterback runs with the ball

keeping *n* (14c) **1 :** the act of one that keeps: as **a :** CUSTODY, MAINTENANCE **b :** OBSERVANCE **c :** a reserving or preserving for future use **2 a :** the means by which something is kept **:** SUPPORT, PROVISION **b :** the state of being kept or the condition in which something is kept ⟨the house is in good ~⟩ **3 :** CONFORMITY ⟨in ~ with good taste⟩ ⟨out of ~ with the decor⟩

keeping room *n* (1771) **:** a common room (as in a colonial house) usu. used for multiple purposes

keep·sake \ˈkēp-ˌsāk\ *n* [[1]*keep* + *-sake* (as in *namesake*)] (1790) **:** something kept or given to be kept as a memento

keep up *vt* (15c) **:** to persist or persevere in ⟨*kept up* the good work⟩; *also* **:** MAINTAIN, SUSTAIN ⟨*keep* standards *up*⟩ ~ *vi* **1 :** to keep adequately informed or up-to-date ⟨*keep up* on international affairs⟩ **2 :** to continue without interruption ⟨rain *kept up* all night⟩ **3 :** to maintain contact or relations with someone ⟨*keep up* with old friends⟩

kees·hond \ˈkās-ˌhȯnt\ *n, pl* **kees·hon·den** \-ˌhȯn-dən\ [D, prob. fr. *Kees,* nickname for *Cornelis* Cornelius + *hond* dog, fr. MD; akin to OE *hund* hound] (1926) **:** any of a Dutch breed of compact medium-sized dogs that have a dense heavy grayish coat and a foxy head

kef \ˈkēf, ˈkef, ˈkäf\ *or* **kif** \ˈkif, ˈkēf\ *n* [Ar *kayf* pleasure] (1808) **1 :** a state of dreamy tranquillity **2 :** a smoking material (as marijuana) that produces kef

keffiyeh *var of* KAFFIYEH

ke·fir \ke-ˈfir; ˈkē-fər, ˈke-\ *n* [Russ] (1884) **:** a beverage of fermented cow's milk

keg \ˈkeg, *dial* ˈkag, ˈkāg\ *n* [ME *kag,* of Scand origin; akin to ON *kaggi* keg] (ca. 1632) **1 :** a small cask or barrel having a capacity of 30 gallons or less **2 :** the contents of a keg

Ke·gel exercises \ˈkā-gəl-, ˈkē-\ *n pl* [Arnold H. *Kegel* †1976 Am. gynecologist] (1975) **:** repetitive contractions of the pelvic muscles that control the flow in urination in order to strengthen these muscles esp. to control or prevent incontinence or to enhance sexual responsiveness during intercourse — called also *Kegels*

keg·ger \ˈke-gər\ *n* (ca. 1968) **:** a party featuring one or more kegs of beer — called also *keg party*

keg·ler \ˈke-glər, ˈkā-\ *n* [G, fr. *kegeln* to bowl, fr. *Kegel* bowling pin, fr. OHG *kegil* stake, peg] (1932) **:** [1]BOWLER

keg·ling \ˈkā-gliŋ, ˈke-\ *n* (1938) **:** BOWLING

kei·ret·su \kā-ˈret-(ˌ)sü, ke-\ *n, pl* **keiretsu** *also* **keiretsus** [Jp, lit., system, series, fr. *kei* system + *retsu* row, line] (1975) **:** a powerful alliance of Japanese businesses often linked by cross-shareholding

keis·ter \ˈkēs-tər, ˈkīs-\ *also* **kees·ter** \ˈkēs-\ *n* [E slang *keister* satchel] (ca. 1931) *slang* **:** BUTTOCKS

kelim *var of* KILIM

kel·ly green \ˈke-lē-\ *n, often cap K* [fr. the common Irish name *Kelly;* fr. the association of Ireland with the color green] (ca. 1927) **:** a strong yellowish green

ke·loid \ˈkē-ˌlȯid\ *n* [F *kéloïde,* fr. Gk *chēlē* claw] (1854) **:** a thick scar resulting from excessive growth of fibrous tissue — **keloid** *adj* — **ke·loi·dal** \kē-ˈlȯi-dᵊl\ *adj*

kelp \ˈkelp\ *n* [ME *culp*] (14c) **1 a :** any of various large brown seaweeds (order Laminariales) **b :** a mass of large seaweeds **2 :** the ashes of seaweed used esp. as a source of iodine

kelp bass *n* (ca. 1936) **:** a mottled sea bass (*Paralabrax clathratus*) that occurs along the Pacific coast of the U.S. and is an important sport fish

[1]**kel·pie** \ˈkel-pē\ *n* [perh. fr. ScGael *cailpeach, colpach* heifer, colt] (1747) **:** a water sprite of Scottish folklore that delights in or brings about the drowning of wayfarers

[2]**kelpie** *n* [*Kelpie,* name of a dog of this breed] (1903) **:** any of a breed of energetic working dogs developed in Australia from British sheepdogs

kel·vin \ˈkel-vən\ *n* (1968) **:** the base unit of temperature in the International System of Units that is equal to 1/273.16 of the Kelvin scale temperature of the triple point of water

Kelvin *adj* [William Thomson, Lord *Kelvin*] (1908) **:** relating to, conforming to, or having a thermometric scale on which the unit of measurement equals the Celsius degree and according to which absolute zero is 0 K, the equivalent of −273.15°C

kemp \ˈkemp\ *n* [ME *kempe* coarse hair, perh. of Scand origin; akin to ON *kampr* mustache; akin to OE *cenep* mustache] (1641) **:** a coarse fiber esp. of wool that is usu. short, wavy, and white, has little affinity for dye, and is used in mixed wools

Kemp's ridley \ˈkemps-\ *n* [Richard M. *Kemp fl*1873 Am. amateur naturalist] (1979) **:** a small gray sea turtle (*Lepidochelys kempii*) with a wide rounded shell that occurs esp. in the Gulf of Mexico and along the U.S. Atlantic coast — called also *Kemp's ridley turtle*

kempt \ˈkem(p)t\ *adj* [back-formation fr. *unkempt*] (1929) **:** neatly kept

[1]**ken** \ˈken\ *vb* **kenned; ken·ning** [ME *kennen,* fr. OE *cennan* to make known & ON *kenna* to perceive; both akin to OE *can* know — more at CAN] *vt* (13c) **1** *archaic* **:** SEE **2** *chiefly dial* **:** RECOGNIZE **3** *chiefly Scot* **:** KNOW ~ *vi, chiefly Scot* **:** KNOW

[2]**ken** *n* (1590) **1 a :** the range of vision **b :** SIGHT, VIEW ⟨'tis double death to drown in ~ of shore —Shak.⟩ **2 :** the range of perception, understanding, or knowledge ⟨abstract words that are beyond the ~ of young children —Lois M. Rettie⟩

ke·naf \kə-ˈnaf\ *n* [Pers] (1891) **:** an African hibiscus (*Hibiscus cannabinus*) widely cultivated for its fiber; *also* **:** the fiber used esp. for making paper and cordage

Ken·dal green \ˈken-dᵊl-\ *n* [*Kendal,* England] (1514) **:** a green woolen cloth resembling homespun or tweed

ken·do \ˈken-(ˌ)dō\ *n* [Jp *kendō,* fr. *ken* sword + *dō* art] (1921) **:** a Japanese sport of fencing usu. with bamboo swords

[1]**ken·nel** \ˈke-nᵊl\ *n* [ME *kenel,* fr. AF **kenil,* fr. VL **canile,* fr. L *canis* dog — more at HOUND] (14c) **1 a :** a shelter for a dog or cat **b :** an establishment for the breeding or boarding of dogs or cats **2 :** a pack of dogs

[2]**kennel** *vb* **-neled** *or* **-nelled; -nel·ing** *or* **-nel·ling** *vi* (1552) **:** to take shelter in or as if in a kennel ~ *vt* **:** to put or keep in or as if in a kennel

[3]**kennel** *n* [alter. of *cannel* gutter] (15c) **:** a gutter in a street

[1]**ken·ning** \ˈke-niŋ\ *n* [ME, sight, view, fr. gerund of *kennen*] (1786) *chiefly Scot* **:** a perceptible but small amount

[2]**kenning** *n* [ON, fr. *kenna*] (1883) **:** a metaphorical compound word or phrase (as *swan-road* for *ocean*) used esp. in Old English and Old Norse poetry

ke·no \ˈkē-(ˌ)nō\ *n* [F *quine,* set of five winning numbers in a lottery + E *-o* (as in *lotto*)] (1814) **:** a game resembling bingo

ke·no·sis \kə-ˈnō-səs, kē-\ *n* [LGk *kenōsis,* fr. Gk, action of emptying, fr. *kenoun* to purge, empty, fr. *kenos* empty] (1873) **:** the relinquishment of divine attributes by Jesus Christ in becoming human — **ke·not·ic** \-ˈnä-tik\ *adj*

ken·speck·le \ˈken-ˌspe-kəl\ *adj* [prob. of Scand origin; akin to Norw *kjennspak* quick to recognize] (1616) *chiefly Scot* **:** CONSPICUOUS

ken·te cloth \ˈken-ˌtā-\ *n* [Twi *kenté*] (1957) **:** colorfully patterned cloth traditionally woven by hand in Ghana — called also *kente*

kent·ledge \ˈkent-lij\ *n* [origin unknown] (1607) **:** pig iron or scrap metal used as ballast

Ken·tucky bluegrass \kən-ˈtə-kē-\ *n* [*Kentucky,* state of U.S.] (1849) **:** an Old World pasture and meadow grass (*Poa pratensis*) naturalized in No. America and often used in lawns — called also *bluegrass*

Kentucky coffee tree *n* (1785) **:** a tall No. American tree (*Gymnocladus dioica*) of the legume family with bipinnate leaves and large woody brown pods whose seeds have been used as a substitute for coffee

Kentucky rifle *n* (1832) **:** a muzzle-loading long-barreled flintlock rifle developed in the 18th century in Pennsylvania and used extensively on the American frontier

Ke·ogh plan \ˈkē-(ˌ)ō-\ *n* [Eugene James *Keogh* †1989 Am. politician] (1974) **:** an individual retirement account for the self-employed

ke·pi \ˈkā-pē, ˈke-\ *also* **ké·pi** \ˈkā-\ *n* [F *képi,* fr. G dial. (Switzerland) *käppi* cap] (1861) **:** a military cap with a round flat top usu. sloping toward the front and a visor

kept *past and past part of* KEEP

kerat- *or* **kerato-** *comb form* [ISV, fr. Gk *kerato-, keras* horn — more at HORN] **:** cornea ⟨*kerat*itis⟩

ker·a·tec·to·my \ˌker-ə-ˈtek-tə-mē\ *n, pl* **-mies** (1871) **:** surgical excision of part of the cornea — compare PHOTOREFRACTIVE KERATECTOMY

ker·a·tin \ˈker-ə-tən\ *n* [ISV] (ca. 1849) **:** any of various sulfur-containing fibrous proteins that form the chemical basis of horny epidermal tissues (as hair and nails) — **ke·ra·ti·nous** \kə-ˈra-tə-nəs\ *adj*

\ə\ **a**but \ᵊ\ kitt**e**n, F ta**ble** \ər\ f**ur**ther \a\ **a**sh \ā\ **a**ce \ä\ m**o**p, m**ar**
\au̇\ **ou**t \ch\ **ch**in \e\ b**e**t \ē\ **ea**sy \g\ **g**o \i\ h**i**t \ī\ **i**ce \j\ **j**ob
\ŋ\ si**ng** \ō\ g**o** \ȯ\ l**aw** \ȯi\ b**oy** \th\ **th**in \t͟h\ **th**e \ü\ l**oo**t \u̇\ f**oo**t
\y\ **y**et \zh\ vi**si**on, bei**ge** \k͟, ⁿ, œ, ue, ʸ\ *see* Guide to Pronunciation

ke·ra·ti·ni·za·tion \ˌker-ə-tə-nə-ˈzā-shən, kə-ˌra-tə-nə-\ *n* (ca. 1887) : conversion into keratin or keratinous tissue — **ke·ra·ti·nize** \ˈker-ə-tə-ˌnīz, kə-ˈra-tə-ˌnīz\ *vb*

ker·a·ti·tis \ˌker-ə-ˈtī-təs\ *n, pl* **-tit·i·des** \-ˈti-tə-ˌdēz\ [NL] (1858) : inflammation of the cornea of the eye

ker·a·to·con·junc·ti·vi·tis \ˈker-ə-(ˌ)tō-kən-ˌjəŋ(k)-tə-ˈvī-təs\ *n* [NL] (1887) : combined inflammation of the cornea and conjunctiva

ker·at·o·mil·eu·sis \ˌker-ə-tō-mil-ˈ(y)ü-səs\ *n* [NL, irreg. fr. *kerat-* + Gk *smileusis* carving, fr. *smilē* knife, lancet] (1978) : keratoplasty in which a piece of the cornea is removed, frozen, shaped to correct refractive error, and reinserted — compare LASIK

ker·a·to·plas·ty \ˈker-ə-tō-ˌplas-tē\ *n, pl* **-ties** (ca. 1857) : plastic surgery on the cornea; *esp* : corneal grafting

ker·a·to·sis \ˌker-ə-ˈtō-səs\ *n, pl* **-to·ses** \-ˌsēz\ [NL] (1885) : an area of skin marked by overgrowth of horny tissue — **ker·a·tot·ic** \-ˈtä-tik\ *adj*

kerb \ˈkərb\ *n* (1805) *Brit* : CURB 5

ker·chief \ˈkər-chəf, -ˌchēf\ *n, pl* **kerchiefs** \-chəfs, -ˌchēfs\ *also* **kerchieves** \-ˌchēvz\ [ME *courchef*, fr. AF *coverchef, cuerchief*, fr. *coverir* to cover + *chef* head — more at CHIEF] (13c) **1** : a square of cloth used as a head covering or worn as a scarf around the neck **2** : HANDKERCHIEF 1 — **ker·chiefed** \-chəft, -ˌchēft\ *adj*

Ke·res \ˈkā-ˌrās\ *n, pl* **Keres** [AmerSp *Queres, Quires*] (1893) **1** : KERESAN 2 **2** : the group of dialects spoken by the Keresans

Ker·e·san \ˈker-ə-sən\ *n* (1891) **1** : a family of American Indian languages of which the Keres dialects comprise the only member **2** : a member of any of the seven Keres-speaking Pueblo Indian communities of central New Mexico

kerf \ˈkərf\ *n* [ME, action of cutting, fr. OE *cyrf;* akin to OE *ceorfan* to carve — more at CARVE] (1523) **1** : a slit or notch made by a saw or cutting torch **2** : the width of cut made by a saw or cutting torch

ker·floo·ey \kər-ˈflü-ē\ *adj* [*ker-*, echoic prefix + *flooey*] (1918) : AWRY, KAPUT ⟨go ~⟩

ker·fuf·fle \kər-ˈfə-fəl\ *n* [alter. of *carfuffle*, fr. Sc *car-* (prob. fr. ScGael *cearr* wrong, awkward) + *fuffle* to become disheveled] (1946) *chiefly Brit* : DISTURBANCE, FUSS

Kerman *var of* KIRMAN

ker·mes \ˈkər-(ˌ)mēz\ *n* [F *kermès*, fr. Ar *qirmiz*] (1603) : the dried bodies of the females of various scale insects (genus *Kermes*) that are found on a Mediterranean oak (*Quercus coccifera*) and constitute a red dyestuff; *also* : the dye

ker·mis \ˈkər-məs\ *or* **ker·mess** \-məs, -ˌmes\ *or* **ker·messe** \-məs, -ˌmes\ *n* [D *kermis*, fr. MD *kercmisse*, fr. *kerc, kerke* church + *misse* mass, church festival] (1577) **1** : an outdoor festival of the Low Countries **2** : a fair held usu. for charitable purposes

[1]**kern** *or* **kerne** \ˈkərn, ˈkern\ *n* [ME *kerne*, fr. MIr *cethern* band of soldiers] (15c) **1** : a light-armed foot soldier of medieval Ireland or Scotland **2** : YOKEL

[2]**kern** \ˈkərn\ *n* [F *carne* corner, fr. F dial., fr. L *cardin-, cardo* hinge] (1683) : a part of a typeset letter that projects beyond its side bearings

ker·nel \ˈkər-nᵊl\ *n* [ME, fr. OE *cyrnel*, dim. of *corn*] (bef. 12c) **1** *chiefly dial* : a fruit seed **2** : the inner softer part of a seed, fruit stone, or nut **3** : a whole seed of a cereal ⟨a ~ of corn⟩ **4** : a central or essential part : GERM ⟨like many stereotypes . . . this one too contains some ~*s* of truth —S. M. Lyman⟩ **5** : a subset of the elements of one set (as a group) that a function (as a homomorphism) maps onto an identity element of another set

kern·ite \ˈkər-ˌnīt\ *n* [*Kern* Co., Calif.] (1927) : a colorless to white mineral that consists of a hydrous borate of sodium

ker·o·gen \ˈker-ə-jən, ˈke-rə-\ *n* [Gk *kēros* wax + E *-gen* — more at CERUMEN] (1906) : bituminous material occurring in shale and yielding oil when heated

ker·o·sene *also* **ker·o·sine** \ˈker-ə-ˌsēn, ˌker-ə-ˈ\ *n* [Gk *kēros* + E *-ene* (as in *camphene*)] (1854) : a flammable hydrocarbon oil usu. obtained by distillation of petroleum and used as a fuel, solvent, and thinner

ker·ria \ˈker-ē-ə, ˈke-rē-ə\ *n* [NL, fr. William *Kerr* †1814 Eng. gardener] (1823) : a shrub (*Kerria japonica*) of the rose family that is native to China and Japan and has solitary yellow and often double flowers

ker·ry \ˈker-ē, ˈke-rē\ *n, pl* **kerries** *often cap* [County *Kerry*, Ireland] (1829) : any of an Irish breed of small hardy black dairy cattle

Kerry blue terrier *n* (1922) : any of an Irish breed of medium-sized terriers with a long squarish head, deep chest, and silky bluish coat

ker·sey \ˈkər-zē\ *n, pl* **kerseys** [ME, fr. *Kersey*, England] (14c) **1 a** : a coarse ribbed woolen cloth for hose and work clothes **b** : a heavy wool or wool and cotton fabric used esp. for uniforms and coats **2** : a garment of kersey

ker·sey·mere \ˈkər-zē-ˌmir\ *n* [alter. of *cassimere*] (1793) : a fine woolen fabric with a close nap made in fancy twill weaves

ke·ryg·ma \kə-ˈrig-mə\ *n* [Gk *kērygma*, fr. *kēryssein* to proclaim, fr. *kēryx* herald — more at CADUCEUS] (1889) : the apostolic proclamation of salvation through Jesus Christ — **ker·yg·mat·ic** \ˌker-ig-ˈma-tik\ *adj*

kes·trel \ˈkes-trəl\ *n* [ME *castrel*, fr. MF *crecerelle*, fr. *crecelle* rattle; fr. its cry] (15c) : any of various small chiefly Old World falcons (genus *Falco*) that usu. hover in the air while searching for prey: as **a** : a common Eurasian falcon (*F. tinnunculus*) **b** : an American falcon (*F. sparverius*) having a reddish-brown back and tail and bluish-gray wings

ket- *or* **keto-** *comb form* [ISV] : ketone ⟨*ke*tosis⟩

ke·ta·mine \ˈkē-tə-ˌmēn\ *n* [*ket-* + *amine*] (1966) : a general anesthetic administered intravenously and intramuscularly in the form of its hydrochloride $C_{13}H_{16}ClNO \cdot HCl$ — compare SPECIAL K

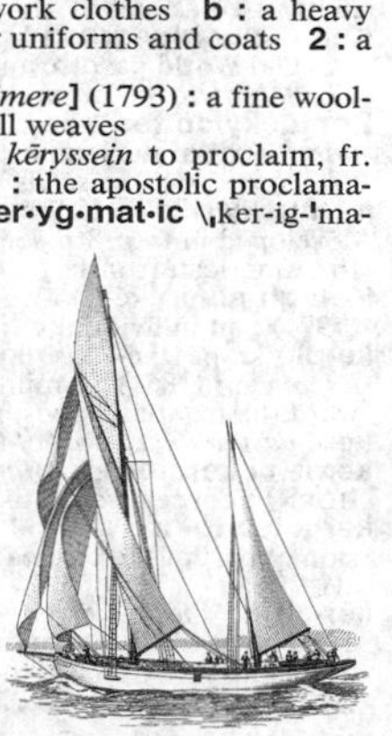
ketch

ketch \ˈkech\ *n* [alter. of *catch*, fr. ME *cache*] (ca. 1649) : a fore-and-aft rigged vessel similar to a yawl but with a larger mizzen sail and with the mizzenmast stepped farther forward

ketch·up *also* **catch·up** \ˈke-chəp, ˈka-\ *or* **cat·sup** \ˈke-chəp, ˈka-; ˈkat-səp\ *n* [Malay *kĕchap* fish sauce] (ca. 1690) : a seasoned pureed condiment usu. made from tomatoes

ke·tene \ˈkē-ˌtēn\ *n* [ISV] (1907) : a colorless poisonous gas C_2H_2O of penetrating odor used esp. as an acetylating agent; *also* : any of various derivatives of this compound

ke·to \ˈkē-(ˌ)tō\ *adj* [*ket-*] (1891) : of or relating to a ketone; *also* : containing a ketone group

ke·to·co·na·zole \ˌkē-tō-ˈkō-nə-ˌzōl\ *n* [*ket-* + *-conazole* (as in *miconazole*)] (1979) : a synthetic broad-spectrum antifungal agent $C_{26}H_{28}Cl_2N_4O_4$ used to treat chronic internal and cutaneous infections

ke·to·gen·e·sis \ˌkē-tō-ˈje-nə-səs\ *n* [NL] (1915) : the production of ketone bodies (as in diabetes) — **ke·to·gen·ic** \-ˈje-nik\ *adj*

ke·to·glu·tar·ic acid \-glü-ˈta-rik-\ *n* (1908) : either of two crystalline keto derivatives $C_5H_6O_5$ of glutaric acid; *esp* : the alpha keto isomer formed in various metabolic processes (as the Krebs cycle)

ke·tone \ˈkē-ˌtōn\ *n* [G *Keton*, alter. of *Aceton* acetone] (1851) : any of a class of organic compounds (as acetone) characterized by a carbonyl group attached to two carbon atoms — **ke·ton·ic** \kē-ˈtä-nik\ *adj*

ketone body *n* (1915) : any of the three compounds acetoacetic acid, acetone, and beta-hydroxybutyric acid which are normal intermediates in lipid metabolism and accumulate in the blood and urine in abnormal amounts in conditions of impaired metabolism (as diabetes mellitus)

ke·tose \ˈkē-ˌtōs, -ˌtōz\ *n* [ISV] (1891) : a sugar (as fructose) containing in its acyclic form one ketone group per molecule

ke·to·sis \kē-ˈtō-səs\ *n* [NL] (1917) : an abnormal increase of ketone bodies in the body — **ke·tot·ic** \-ˈtä-tik\ *adj*

ke·to·ste·roid \ˌkē-tō-ˈstir-ˌȯid *also* -ˈster-\ *n* [ISV] (1939) : a steroid (as cortisone or estrone) containing a ketone group

ket·tle \ˈke-tᵊl\ *n* [ME *ketel*, fr. ON *ketill* (akin to OE *cietel* kettle), both fr. a prehistoric Gmc word borrowed fr. L *catillus*, dim. of *catinus* bowl] (13c) **1** : a metallic vessel usu. used for boiling liquids; *esp* : TEAKETTLE **2** : KETTLEDRUM **3 a** : POTHOLE 1b **b** : a steep-sided hollow without surface drainage esp. in a deposit of glacial drift

ket·tle·bell \ˈke-tᵊl-ˌbel\ *n* [*kettle* + *-bell* (as in *barbell*)] (1928) : a round weight with a flat bottom and thick handle on top that is used for exercise and weight training

kettle chip *n* (1983) : a type of potato chip made so as to be thicker and crunchier than the typical potato chip

ket·tle·drum \-ˌdrəm\ *n* (1602) : a percussion instrument that consists of a hollow brass, copper, or fiberglass hemisphere with a calfskin or plastic head whose tension can be changed to vary the pitch

kettle of fish (1742) **1** : a bad state of affairs : MESS **2** : something to be considered or dealt with : MATTER ⟨a different *kettle of fish*⟩

keV *abbr* kilo-electron-volt

Kew·pie \ˈkyü-pē\ *trademark* — used for a small chubby doll with a topknot of hair

[1]**key** \ˈkē\ *n* [ME, fr. OE *cǣg;* akin to OFris *kēi* key] (bef. 12c) **1 a** : a usu. metal instrument by which the bolt of a lock is turned **b** : any of various devices having the form or function of such a key **2 a** : a means of gaining or preventing entrance, possession, or control **b** : an instrumental or deciding factor **3 a** : something that gives an explanation or identification or provides a solution ⟨the ~ to a riddle⟩ **b** : a list of words or phrases giving an explanation of symbols or abbreviations **c** : an aid to interpretation or identification : CLUE **d** : an arrangement of the salient characters of a group of plants or animals or of taxa designed to facilitate identification **e** : a map legend **4 a** (1) : COTTER PIN (2) : COTTER **b** : a keystone in an arch **c** : a small piece of wood or metal used as a wedge or for preventing motion between parts **5 a** : one of the levers of a keyboard musical instrument that actuates the mechanism and produces the tones **b** : a lever that controls a vent in the side of a woodwind instrument or a valve in a brass instrument **c** : a part to be depressed by a finger that serves as one unit of a keyboard **6** : SAMARA **7** : a system of tones and harmonies generated from a hierarchical scale of seven tones based on a tonic ⟨the ~ of G major⟩ **8 a** : characteristic style or tone **b** : the tone or pitch of a voice **c** : the predominant tone of a photograph with respect to its lightness or darkness **9** : a decoration or charm resembling a key **10** : a small switch for opening or closing an electric circuit ⟨a telegraph ~⟩ **11** : the set of instructions governing the encipherment and decipherment of messages **12** : a free-throw area in basketball — **keyed** \ˈkēd\ *adj* — **key·less** \ˈkē-ləs\ *adj*

[2]**key** *vt* (14c) **1** : to lock with or as if with a key : FASTEN: as **a** : to secure (as a pulley on a shaft) by a key **b** : to finish off (an arch) by inserting a keystone **2** : to regulate the musical pitch of **3** : to bring into harmony or conformity : make appropriate : ATTUNE ⟨remarks ~*ed* to a situation⟩ **4** : to identify (a biological specimen) by a key **5** : to provide with identifying or explanatory cross-references ⟨instructions ~*ed* to accompanying drawings —John Gartner⟩ **6** : to make nervous, tense, or excited — usu. used with *up* **7** : KEYBOARD — often used with *in* **8** : to be essential to : play the most important part in ⟨defense ~*ed* the victory⟩ ~ *vi* **1** : to use a key **2** : to observe the position or movement of an opposing player in football in order to anticipate the play — usu. used with *on* **3** : KEYBOARD

[3]**key** *adj* (1913) : IMPORTANT, FUNDAMENTAL ⟨~ issues⟩

[4]**key** *n* [Sp *cayo*, fr. Taino] (1697) : a low island or reef; *specif* : any of the coral islets off the southern coast of Florida

[5]**key** *n* [by shortening & alter. fr. *kilo*] (1968) *slang* : a kilogram esp. of marijuana or heroin

[1]**key·board** \ˈkē-ˌbȯrd\ *n* (1819) **1 a** : a bank of keys on a musical instrument (as a piano) that usu. consists of seven white and five raised black keys to the octave **b** : a musical instrument that is played by means of a keyboard **2** : an assemblage of systematically arranged keys by which a machine or device is operated ⟨a computer ~⟩ **3** : a board on which keys for locks are hung

[2]**keyboard** *vt* (1961) : to capture or set (as data or text) by means of a keyboard ~ *vi* : to operate a machine (as for typesetting) by means of a keyboard — **key·board·er** *n*

key·board·ist \ˈkē-ˌbȯr-dist\ *n* (1973) : a person who plays a keyboard musical instrument

key·but·ton \ˈkē-ˌbə-tᵊn\ *n* (ca. 1920) : KEY 5c

key club *n* [fr. the key to the premises provided to each member] (1962) : a private club serving liquor and providing entertainment

key deer *n, often cap K* (1950) : a very small rare white-tailed deer (*Odocoileus virginianus clavium*) native to the Florida Keys

key grip \ˌkē-\ *n* (1977) : the technician in charge of moving and setting up camera tracks and scenery in a motion-picture or television production

¹key·hole \ˈkē-ˌhōl\ *n* (ca. 1592) **1** : a hole for receiving a key **2** : KEY 12

²keyhole *adj* (1937) **1** : revealingly intimate ⟨a ~ report⟩ **2** : intent on revealing intimate details ⟨~ columnists⟩

keyhole saw *n* (1777) : a narrow pointed fine-toothed handsaw used esp. for cutting curves of short radius

key light *n* (ca. 1937) : the main light illuminating a photographic subject

key lime *n, often cap K* [Florida *Keys*] (1929) : a small aromatic lime

key lime pie *n, often cap K* (1954) : a usu. meringue-topped lime-custard pie traditionally made from key limes

Keynes·ian·ism \ˈkān-zē-ə-ˌni-zəm\ *n* (1946) : the economic theories and programs ascribed to John M. Keynes and his followers; *specif* : the advocacy of monetary and fiscal programs by government to increase employment and spending — **Keynes·ian** \ˈkān-zē-ən\ *n or adj*

¹key·note \ˈkē-ˌnōt\ *n* (1776) **1** : the first and harmonically fundamental tone of a scale **2** : the fundamental or central fact, idea, or mood ⟨sadness is the ~ of this little collection —*Books Abroad*⟩

²keynote *vt* (1914) **1** : to set the keynote of **2** : to deliver the keynote address at — **key·not·er** *n*

keynote address *n* (ca. 1908) : an address designed to present the issues of primary interest to an assembly (as a political convention) and often to arouse unity and enthusiasm — called also *keynote speech*

keynote speaker *n* (1950) : one who delivers a keynote address

key·pad \ˈkē-ˌpad\ *n* (1975) : a small often handheld keyboard

¹key·punch \ˈkē-ˌpənch\ *n* (1918) : a machine with a keyboard used to cut holes or notches in punch cards

²keypunch *vt* (1959) : to enter (data) on punch cards with a keypunch — **key·punch·er** *n*

key signature *n* (1875) : the sharps or flats placed after a clef in music to indicate the key

key·stone \ˈkē-ˌstōn\ *n* (ca. 1637) **1** : the wedge-shaped piece at the crown of an arch that locks the other pieces in place — see ARCH illustration **2** : something on which associated things depend for support ⟨determination, a ~ of the puritan ethic —L. S. Lewis⟩ **3** : a species of plant or animal that produces a major impact (as by predation) on its ecosystem and is considered essential to maintaining optimum ecosystem function or structure

¹key·stroke \-ˌstrōk\ *n* (ca. 1910) : the act or an instance of depressing a key on a keyboard

²keystroke *vt* (1966) : KEYBOARD

key·way \-ˌwā\ *n* (ca. 1864) **1** : a groove or channel for a key **2** : the aperture for the key in a lock having a flat metal key

key word *n* (1859) : a word that is a key: as **a** : a word exemplifying the meaning or value of a letter or symbol **b** *usu* **key·word** \-ˌwərd\ : a significant word from a title or document used esp. as an index to content

kg *abbr* **1** keg **2** kilogram **3** king

kG *abbr* kilogauss

KG *abbr* knight of the Order of the Garter

KGB *abbr* [Russ *Komitet gosudarstvennoĭ bezopasnosti*] (Soviet) State Security Committee

kgps *abbr* kilograms per second

khad·dar \ˈkä-dər\ *or* **kha·di** \ˈkä-dē\ *n* [Hindi & Urdu *khādar, khādī*] (ca. 1885) : homespun cotton cloth of India

kha·ki \ˈka-kē, ˈkä-, *Canad often* ˈkär-\ *n* [Hindi & Urdu *khākī* dust-colored, fr. *khāk* dust, fr. Pers] (1857) **1 a** : a khaki-colored cloth made usu. of cotton or wool and used esp. for military uniforms **b** : a garment of this cloth; *esp* : a military uniform — usu. used in pl. **2** : a light yellowish brown — **khaki** *adj*

Khal·kha \ˈkal-kə, ˈkal-kə\ *n* (1873) **1** : a member of a Mongol people of Outer Mongolia **2** : the language of the Khalkha people used as the official language of the country of Mongolia

kham·sin \kam-ˈsēn\ *n* [Ar *rīḥ al-khamsīn* the wind of the fifty (days between Easter and Pentecost)] (1685) : a hot southerly Egyptian wind

¹khan \ˈkän *also* ˈkan\ *n* [ME *caan,* fr. MF *kan, kaan,* of Turkic origin; akin to Turk *han* prince] (15c) **1** : a medieval sovereign of China and ruler over the Turkish, Tatar, and Mongol tribes **2** : a local chieftain or man of rank in some countries of central Asia

²khan *n* [Ar *khān*] (1614) : a caravansary or rest house in some Asian countries

khan·ate \ˈkä-ˌnāt *also* ˈka-\ *n* (1799) : the state or jurisdiction of a khan

khap·ra beetle \ˈka-prə-, ˈkä-\ *n* [Hindi & Urdu *khaprā,* lit., destroyer] (1928) : a dermestid beetle (*Trogoderma granarium*) that is native to the Indian subcontinent and is now a serious pest of stored grain in most parts of the world

khat *also* **qat** *or* **kat** \ˈkät\ *n* [Ar *qāt*] (1858) : a shrub (*Catha edulis*) of the staff-tree family cultivated in the Middle East and Africa for its leaves and buds that are the source of a habituating stimulant when chewed or used as a tea; *also* : its leaves and buds

khe·dive \kə-ˈdēv\ *n* [F *khédive,* fr. Turk *hidiv*] (1847) : a ruler of Egypt from 1867 to 1914 governing as a viceroy of the sultan of Turkey — **khe·div·ial** \-ˈdē-vē-əl\ *or* **khe·div·al** \-ˈdē-vəl\ *adj*

Khmer \kə-ˈmer\ *n, pl* **Khmer** *or* **Khmers** [northern or western dial. Khmer *khmeːr,* a self-designation (standard Khmer *khmaε*)] (1876) **1** : a member of an aboriginal people of Cambodia **2** : the Mon-Khmer language of the Khmer people that is the official language of Cambodia — **Khmer** *adj*

Khoi·khoi \ˈkȯi-ˌkȯi\ *n, pl* **Khoikhoi** (1791) **1** : a member of any of a group of Khoisan-speaking pastoral peoples of southern Africa **2** : the group of Khoisan languages spoken by the Khoikhoi

Khoi·san \ˈkȯi-ˌsän, -ˈsän\ *n* [*Khoi*khoi + *San*] (1930) **1** : a group of African peoples speaking Khoisan languages **2** : a family of African languages comprising principally Khoikhoi and the Bushman languages

khoum \ˈküm, ˈküm\ *n* [modif. of Ar *khums,* lit., one fifth] (1973) — see *ouguiya* at MONEY table

Kho·war \ˈkō-ˌwär\ *n* [Khowar *khowàr,* fr. *khów,* people and area of Chitral, Pakistan] (1882) : an Indo-Aryan language of northwest Pakistan

kHz *abbr* kilohertz

ki \ˈkē\ *n* [Jp & Korean] (1967) : CHI

KIA *abbr* killed in action

ki·ang \kē-ˈäŋ\ *n* [Tibetan (Lhasa dial.) *gyå, gyåŋ* (written Tibetan *rgyaŋ*)] (1869) : an Asian wild ass (*Equus kiang* syn. *E. hemionus kiang*) usu. with reddish back and sides and white underparts, muzzle, and legs

kiaugh \ˈkyäk\ *n* [origin unknown] (1786) *Scot* : TROUBLE, ANXIETY

kib·be *or* **kib·beh** *or* **kib·bi** \ˈki-bē\ *n* [Ar dial. (Levant) *kibba*] (1874) : a Near Eastern dish of ground lamb and bulgur that is eaten cooked or raw

¹kib·ble \ˈki-bəl\ *vt* **kib·bled; kib·bling** \-b(ə-)liŋ\ [origin unknown] (ca. 1790) : to grind coarsely ⟨*kibbled* dog biscuit⟩ ⟨*kibbled* grain⟩

²kibble *n* (ca. 1905) : coarsely ground meal or grain (as for animal feed)

kib·butz \ki-ˈbu̇ts, -ˈbüts\ *n, pl* **kib·but·zim** \-ˌbu̇t-ˈsēm, -ˌbüt-\ [ModHeb *qibbūṣ*] (1926) : a communal farm or settlement in Israel

kib·butz·nik \-ˈbu̇t-snik, -ˈbüt-\ *n* [Yiddish *kibutsnik,* fr. *kibuts* kibbutz (fr. ModHeb *qibbūṣ*) + *-nik,* agent suffix] (1947) : a member of a kibbutz

kibe \ˈkīb\ *n* [ME] (14c) : an ulcerated chilblain esp. on the heel; *also* : HEEL

ki·bitz *also* **kib·bitz** \ˈki-bəts, kə-ˈbits\ *vb* [Yiddish *kibetsn*] *vi* (1927) **1** : to act as a kibitzer **2** : to exchange comments : CHAT ~ *vt* : to observe as a kibitzer; *esp* : to be a kibitzer at ⟨~ a card game⟩

ki·bitz·er *also* **kib·bitz·er** \ˈki-bət-sər, kə-ˈbit-\ *n* (1922) : one who looks on and often offers unwanted advice or comment ⟨a ~ at a card game⟩; *broadly* : one who offers opinions

ki·bosh \ˈkī-ˌbäsh, kī-ˈ; ki-ˈbäsh\ *n* [origin unknown] (1836) : something that serves as a check or stop ⟨put the ~ on that⟩ — **kibosh** *vt*

¹kick \ˈkik\ *vb* [ME *kiken*] *vi* (14c) **1 a** : to strike out with the foot or feet **b** : to make a kick in football **2 a** : to show opposition : RESIST, REBEL **b** : to protest strenuously or urgently : express grave discontent; *broadly* : COMPLAIN **3** : to function with vitality and energy ⟨alive and ~*ing*⟩ **4** *of a firearm* : to recoil when fired **5** : to go from one place to another as circumstance or whim dictates **6** : to run at a faster speed during the last part of a race ~ *vt* **1 a** : to strike, thrust, or hit with the foot **b** : to strike suddenly and forcefully as if with the foot **c** : to remove by a kicking motion ⟨~*ed* off her shoes⟩ **d** : to remove from a position or status ⟨~*ed* him off the team⟩ **2** : to score by kicking a ball **3** : to heap reproaches upon (oneself) ⟨~*ed* themselves for not going⟩ **4** : to free oneself of (as a drug habit) — **kick·able** \ˈki-kə-bəl\ *adj* — **kick ass** *often vulgar* : to kick butt — **kick butt** : to use forceful or coercive measures in order to achieve a purpose; *also* : to succeed or win overwhelmingly — **kick over the traces** : to cast off restraint, authority, or control — **kick the bucket** : DIE — **kick up one's heels** **1** : to show sudden delight **2** : to have a lively time — **kick upstairs** : to promote to a higher but less desirable position

²kick *n* (1530) **1 a** : a blow or sudden forceful thrust with the foot; *specif* : a sudden propelling of a ball with the foot **b** : the power to kick **c** : a rhythmic motion of the legs used in swimming **d** : a burst of speed in racing **2** : a sudden forceful jolt or thrust suggesting a kick; *esp* : the recoil of a gun **3** : POCKET, WALLET **4 a** : a feeling or expression of opposition or objection ⟨a ~ against the administration⟩ **b** : the grounds for objection **5 a** : an effect suggestive of a kick ⟨chili with a ~⟩ **b** : a stimulating or pleasurable effect or experience ⟨got a big ~ out of meeting him⟩ **c** : pursuit of an absorbing or obsessive new interest ⟨a skiing ~⟩ **6** : KICKER 2

kick around *vi* (1839) **1** : to wander or pass time aimlessly **2 a** : to lie about mostly unnoticed or forgotten **b** : to undergo consideration usu. intermittently over a period of time ⟨ideas that have been *kicking around* for years⟩ ~ *vt* **1** : to treat in an inconsiderate or high-handed fashion **2** : to consider, examine, or discuss from various angles

kick–ass \ˈkik-ˌas\ *adj* (1970) *often vulgar* : strikingly or overwhelmingly tough, aggressive, powerful, or effective

kick·back \ˈkik-ˌbak\ *n* (1920) **1** : a sharp violent reaction **2** : a return of a part of a sum received often because of confidential agreement or coercion ⟨every city contract had been let with a ten percent ~ to city officials —D. K. Shipler⟩

kick back *vi* (1972) : to assume a relaxed position or attitude; *also* : to spend time relaxing : take it easy ⟨spent the weekend just *kicking back*⟩

kick·board \-ˌbȯrd\ *n* (1949) : a buoyant rectangular board held by a swimmer while developing kicking techniques

kick·box·ing \-ˌbäk-siŋ\ *n* (1971) : boxing in which boxers are permitted to kick with bare feet as in karate — **kick·box** \-ˌbäks\ *vi* — **kick·box·er** \-ˌbäk-sər\ *n*

kick·er \ˈki-kər\ *n* (ca. 1580) **1** : one that kicks or kicks something **2** : an unexpected and surprising remark, revelation, or set of circumstances

kick in *vt* (1906) : CONTRIBUTE ~ *vi* **1** *slang* : DIE **2** : to make a contribution **3** : to begin operating or having an effect : get started ⟨waiting for the heater to *kick in*⟩

kick·off \ˈkik-ˌȯf\ *n* (1856) **1** : a kick that puts the ball into play in a football or soccer game **2** : COMMENCEMENT 1 ⟨the campaign ~⟩

kick off *vi* (1857) **1** : to start or resume play in football by a placekick **2 a** : to initiate proceedings **b** : to start out : BEGIN ⟨the movie *kicks off* with a bank robbery⟩ **3** *slang* : DIE ~ *vt* : to mark the beginning of ⟨*kick off* the campaign⟩

kick out *vt* (1697) : to dismiss or eject forcefully or summarily

kick over *vi* (1951) : to begin to fire — used of an internal combustion engine ~ *vt* : TURN OVER 1b

kick pleat *n* (1926) : a short inverted pleat (as at the bottom of a skirt) used to give breadth

kick·shaw \ˈkik-ˌshȯ\ *n* [by folk etymology fr. F *quelque chose* something] (1597) **1** : a fancy dish : DELICACY **2** : TRINKET, GEWGAW

\ə\ **abut** \ᵊ\ **kitten,** F table \ər\ **further** \a\ **ash** \ā\ **ace** \ä\ **mop, mar** \au̇\ **out** \ch\ **chin** \e\ **bet** \ē\ **easy** \g\ **go** \i\ **hit** \ī\ **ice** \j\ **job** \ŋ\ **sing** \ō\ **go** \ȯ\ **law** \ȯi\ **boy** \th\ **thin** \t͟h\ **the** \ü\ **loot** \u̇\ **foot** \y\ **yet** \zh\ **vision, beige** \k, ⁿ, œ, ue, ʸ\ *see* Guide to Pronunciation

kick·stand \ˈkik-ˌstand\ *n* [fr. its being put in position by a kick] (1947) **:** a swiveling metal bar or rod attached to a 2-wheeled vehicle (as a bicycle) and used to prop up the vehicle when it is not in use

kick–start \ˈkik-ˌstärt\ *vt* (1928) **1 :** to start (as a motorcycle) by means of a kick-starter **2 —** JUMP-START 2 **— kick start** *n*

kick–start·er \ˈkik-ˌstär-tər\ *n* (1916) **:** a motor starter (as on a motorcycle) that is activated by a thrust of the foot

kick turn *n* (1910) **:** a standing half turn in skiing made by swinging one ski high with a jerk and planting it in the desired direction and then lifting the other ski into a parallel position

kick·up \ˈkik-ˌəp\ *n* (ca. 1793) **:** a noisy quarrel **:** ROW

kick up *vt* (1756) **1 :** to cause to rise upward ⟨clouds of dust *kicked up* by passing cars⟩ **2 :** to stir up **:** PROVOKE ⟨*kick up* a fuss⟩ **~** *vi* **:** to give evidence of disorder

kicky \ˈki-kē\ *adj* (1942) **:** providing a kick or thrill **:** EXCITING; *also* **:** excitingly fashionable

[1]**kid** \ˈkid\ *n* [ME *kide,* of Scand origin; akin to ON *kith* kid] (13c) **1 a :** a young goat **b :** a young individual of various animals related to the goat **2 a :** the flesh, fur, or skin of a kid **b :** something made of kid **3 :** a young person; *esp* **:** CHILD — often used as a generalized reference to one esp. younger or less experienced ⟨the ~ on the pro golf tour⟩ ⟨poor ~⟩ **— kid·dish** \ˈki-dish\ *adj*

[2]**kid** *vi* **kid·ded; kid·ding** (15c) **:** to bring forth young — used of a goat or an antelope

[3]**kid** *adj* (1895) **:** YOUNGER ⟨my ~ brother⟩

[4]**kid** *vb* **kid·ded; kid·ding** [prob. fr. [1]*kid*] *vt* (ca. 1873) **1 a :** to deceive as a joke ⟨it's the truth; I wouldn't ~ you⟩ **b :** to fail to admit the truth to ⟨they're *kidding* themselves⟩ **2 :** to make fun of **~** *vi* **:** to engage in good-humored fooling or horseplay — often used with *around* **— kid·der** *n* **— kid·ding·ly** \ˈki-diŋ-lē\ *adv*

Kid·der·min·ster \ˈki-dər-ˌmin(t)-stər\ *n* [*Kidderminster,* England] (1836) **:** an ingrain carpet — called also *Kidderminster carpet*

kid·die *also* **kid·dy** \ˈki-dē\ *n, pl* **kiddies** *often attrib* [[1]*kid*] (1889) **:** a small child ⟨a ~ pool⟩ ⟨~ rides⟩

kid·do \ˈki-(ˌ)dō\ *n, pl* **kiddos** [[1]*kid*] (1905) **1 —** used as a familiar form of address ⟨you'll be okay, ~⟩ **2 :** CHILD, KID

kid·dush \ˈki-dəsh, -dish; ki-ˈdüsh\ *n* [LHeb *qiddūsh* sanctification] (1753) **:** a ceremonial blessing pronounced over wine or bread in a Jewish home or synagogue on a holy day (as the Sabbath)

kid–glove \ˈkid-ˈgləv\ *adj* (1888) **:** marked by extreme care or deference ⟨~ treatment⟩

kid glove *n* (1725) **:** a dress glove made of kid leather **— kid–gloved** \ˈkid-ˈgləvd\ *adj* **— with kid gloves :** with special consideration

kid leather *n* (1687) **1 :** a soft pliable leather made from kidskin **2 :** a glove leather made from lambskin or goatskin

kid·nap \ˈkid-ˌnap\ *vt* **-napped** *also* **-naped** \-ˌnapt\; **-nap·ping** *also* **-nap·ing** [prob. back-formation fr. *kidnapper,* fr. *kid* + obs. *napper* thief] (1682) **:** to seize and detain or carry away by unlawful force or fraud and often with a demand for ransom **— kid·nap·pee** *or* **kid·nap·ee** \ˌkid-ˌna-ˈpē\ *n* **— kid·nap·per** *also* **kid·nap·er** *n*

kid·ney \ˈkid-nē\ *n, pl* **kidneys** [ME] (14c) **1 a :** one of a pair of vertebrate organs situated in the body cavity near the spinal column that excrete waste products of metabolism, in humans are bean-shaped organs about 4½ inches (11½ centimeters) long lying behind the peritoneum in a mass of fatty tissue, and consist chiefly of nephrons by which urine is secreted, collected, and discharged into a main cavity whence it is conveyed by the ureter to the bladder **b :** any of various excretory organs of invertebrate animals **2 :** the kidney of an animal eaten as food **3 :** sort or kind esp. with regard to temperament ⟨a nice helpful guy, of a different ~ entirely from the . . . Secret Police —Paula Lecler⟩

kidney bean *n* (1548) **1 :** an edible and nutritious usu. kidney-shaped seed of any of various cultivated beans of the common species (*Phaseolus vulgaris*); *esp* **:** a large dark red kidney bean **2 :** a plant bearing kidney beans

kidney stone *n* (1874) **:** a calculus (as of calcium salts) in the kidney

kid·skin \ˈkid-ˌskin\ *n* (14c) **:** the skin of a young or sometimes a mature goat; *also* **:** KID LEATHER

kid stuff *n* (1922) **1 :** something befitting or appropriate only to children **2 :** something extremely simple or easy

kiel·ba·sa \kēl-ˈbä-sə, kil- *also* ki-ˈbä-sə\ *n, pl* **-basas** *also* **-ba·sy** \-ˈbä-sē\ [Pol *kiełbasa*] (1910) **:** a smoked sausage of Polish origin

kie·sel·guhr \ˈkē-zəl-ˌgu̇r\ *n* [G *Kieselgur*] (1875) **:** loose or porous diatomite

kie·ser·ite \ˈkē-zə-ˌrīt\ *n* [G *Kieserit,* fr. Dietrich *Kieser* †1862 Ger. physician] (1862) **:** a mineral that is a white hydrous magnesium sulfate

kif *var of* KEF

kike \ˈkīk\ *n* [origin unknown] (1901) *usu offensive* **:** JEW

Ki·kon·go \kē-ˈkäŋ-(ˌ)gō\ *n* (1890) **:** KONGO 2

Ki·ku·yu \kē-ˈkü-(ˌ)yü\ *n, pl* **Kikuyu** *or* **Kikuyus** (1894) **1 :** a member of a Bantu-speaking people of Kenya **2 :** the Bantu language of the Kikuyu people

kil·der·kin \ˈkil-dər-kən\ *n* [ME, fr. MD *kindekijn,* fr. ML *quintale* quintal] (14c) **1 :** an English unit of capacity equal to ½ barrel **2 :** CASK

ki·lim *also* **ke·lim** \kē-ˈlēm\ *n* [Turk, fr. Pers *kilīm*] (1881) **:** a pileless handwoven reversible rug or covering made in Turkey, Kurdistan, the Caucasus, Iran, and western Turkestan

[1]**kill** \ˈkil\ *vb* [ME, perh. fr. OE **cyllan;* akin to OE *cwellan* to kill — more at QUELL] *vt* (14c) **1 a :** to deprive of life **:** cause the death of **b** (1) **:** to slaughter (as a hog) for food (2) **:** to convert a food animal into (a kind of meat) by slaughtering **2 a :** to put an end to ⟨~ competition⟩ **b :** DEFEAT, VETO ⟨~*ed* the amendment⟩ **c :** to mark for omission; *also* **:** DELETE **d :** ANNIHILATE, DESTROY ⟨~ an enemy⟩ **3 a :** to destroy the vital or essential quality of ⟨~*ed* the pain with drugs⟩ **b :** to cause to stop ⟨~ the motor⟩ **c :** to check the flow of current through **4 :** to make a markedly favorable impression on ⟨she ~*ed* the audience⟩ **5 :** to get through uneventfully ⟨~ time⟩; *also* **:** to get through (the time of a penalty) without being scored on ⟨~ a penalty⟩ **6 a :** to cause extreme pain to **b :** to tire almost to the point of collapse **7 :** to hit (a shot) so hard in various games that a return is impossible **8 :** to consume (as a drink) totally **~** *vi* **1 :** to deprive one of life **2 :** to make a markedly favorable impression ⟨was dressed to ~⟩

syn KILL, SLAY, MURDER, ASSASSINATE, DISPATCH, EXECUTE mean to deprive of life. KILL merely states the fact of death caused by an agency in any manner ⟨*killed* in an accident⟩ ⟨frost *killed* the plants⟩. SLAY is a chiefly literary term implying deliberateness and violence but not necessarily motive ⟨*slew* thousands of the Philistines⟩. MURDER specif. implies stealth and motive and premeditation and therefore full moral responsibility ⟨convicted of *murdering* a rival⟩. ASSASSINATE applies to deliberate killing openly or secretly often for political motives ⟨terrorists *assassinated* the Senator⟩. DISPATCH stresses quickness and directness in putting to death ⟨*dispatched* the sentry with one bullet⟩. EXECUTE stresses putting to death as a legal penalty ⟨*executed* by lethal gas⟩.

[2]**kill** *n* (1814) **1 a :** an act or instance of killing **b :** a decisive act that conclusively secures something (as a deal or win) **2 :** something killed: as **a** (1) **:** an animal shot in a hunt (2) **:** animals killed in a hunt, season, or particular period of time **b :** an enemy unit (as an airplane or ship) destroyed by military action **c :** a return shot in any of various games (as badminton, handball, or table tennis) that is too hard for an opponent to handle

[3]**kill** *n, often cap* [D *kil*] (1669) **:** CHANNEL, CREEK — used chiefly in place names in Delaware, Pennsylvania, and New York

kill·deer \ˈkil-ˌdir\ *n, pl* **killdeers** *or* **killdeer** [imit.] (1731) **:** an American plover (*Charadrius vociferus*) characterized by two black breast bands and a plaintive penetrating cry

killed \ˈkild\ *adj* (1919) **:** being or containing a virus that has been inactivated (as by chemicals) so that it is no longer infectious ⟨~ vaccines⟩

[1]**kill·er** \ˈki-lər\ *n* (15c) **1 :** one that kills **2 :** KILLER WHALE **3 a :** one that has a forceful, violent, or striking impact **b :** one that is extremely difficult to deal with

[2]**killer** *adj* (1951) **1 :** strikingly impressive or effective ⟨a ~ smile⟩ ⟨a ~ résumé⟩ **2 :** extremely difficult to deal with ⟨a ~ fastball⟩; *also* **:** causing death or devastation ⟨a ~ tornado⟩

killer app *n* (1988) **:** a computer application of such great value or popularity that it assures the success of the technology with which it is associated; *broadly* **:** a feature or component that in itself makes something worth having or using

killer bee *n* (1976) **:** AFRICANIZED BEE

killer cell *n* (1972) **:** a lymphocyte (as a killer T cell or a natural killer cell) with cytotoxic activity

killer instinct *n* (1931) **:** an aggressive tenacious urge for domination in a struggle to attain a set goal

killer T cell *n* (1975) **:** a T cell that functions in cell-mediated immunity by destroying a cell (as one infected with a virus) having specific antigenic molecules on its surface — called also *cytotoxic T cell*

killer whale *n* (1884) **:** a small gregarious toothed whale (*Orcinus orca* of the family Delphinidae) that is black with a white ventral side and white oval-shaped patches behind the eyes and attains a length of 20 to 30 feet (6.1 to 9.1 meters) — called also *orca*

kil·li·fish \ˈki-li-ˌfish\ *n* [*killie* killifish (perh. fr. [3]*kill*) + *fish*] (1836) **1 :** any of a family (Cyprinodontidae) of numerous small oviparous fishes much used as bait and in mosquito control **2 :** any of various live-bearers (family Poeciliidae)

[1]**kill·ing** \ˈki-liŋ\ *n* (15c) **1 :** the act of one that kills **2 :** KILL 2a **3 :** a sudden notable gain or profit ⟨made a ~ in the stock market⟩

[2]**killing** *adj* (15c) **1 :** that kills or relates to killing **2 :** highly amusing **3 :** extremely difficult to deal with ⟨the suspense is ~⟩; *also* **:** calling for great strength, stamina, or endurance ⟨a ~ schedule⟩ **— kill·ing·ly** \-lē\ *adv*

killing field *n* (1980) **:** a scene of mass killing (as from a battle or massacre)

kill·joy \ˈkil-ˌjȯi\ *n* (1776) **:** one who spoils the pleasure of others

kill off *vt* (1607) **:** to destroy in large numbers or totally

kiln \ˈkiln, ˈkil\ *n* [ME *kilne,* fr. OE *cyln,* fr. L *culina* kitchen, fr. *coquere* to cook — more at COOK] (bef. 12c) **:** an oven, furnace, or heated enclosure used for processing a substance by burning, firing, or drying **— kiln** *vt*

ki·lo \ˈkē-(ˌ)lō *also* ˈki-\ *n, pl* **kilos** (1870) **:** KILOGRAM

Kilo (1952) — a communications code word for the letter *k*

kilo- *comb form* [F, modif. of Gk *chilioi*] **:** thousand ⟨*kilo*ton⟩

ki·lo·bar \ˈkē-lə-ˌbär, ˈki-lə-\ *n* [ISV] (1926) **:** a unit of pressure equal to 1000 bars

ki·lo·base \-ˌbās\ *n* (1975) **:** a unit of measure of the length of a nucleic-acid chain that equals one thousand base pairs

ki·lo·bit \-ˌbit\ *n* [ISV] (1961) **1 :** 1000 bits **2 :** 1024 bits

ki·lo·byte \-ˌbīt\ *n* [fr. the fact that 1024 (2^{10}) is the power of 2 closest to 1000] (1970) **:** 1024 bytes

ki·lo·cal·o·rie \-ˌka-lə-rē, -ˈkal-rē\ *n* [ISV] (1894) **1 :** CALORIE 1b **2 :** CALORIE 2a

kilo·cy·cle \ˈki-lə-ˌsī-kəl\ *n* [ISV] (1921) **:** 1000 cycles; *esp* **:** KILOHERTZ

ki·lo·gauss \ˈkē-lə-ˌgau̇s, ˈki-lə-\ *n* [ISV] (1895) **:** 1000 gauss

ki·lo·gram \-ˌgram\ *n* [F *kilogramme,* fr. *kilo-* + *gramme* gram] (1797) **1 :** the base unit of mass in the International System of Units that is equal to the mass of a prototype agreed upon by international convention and that is nearly equal to the mass of 1000 cubic centimeters of water at the temperature of its maximum density — see METRIC SYSTEM table **2 :** a unit of force or weight equal to the weight of a kilogram mass under a gravitational attraction equal to that of the earth

kilogram–meter *n* (1866) **:** the meter-kilogram-second gravitational unit of work and energy equal to the work done by a kilogram force acting through a distance of one meter in the direction of the force **:** about 7.235 foot-pounds

ki·lo·hertz \ˈki-lə-ˌhərts, ˈkē-lə-, -ˌherts\ *n* [ISV] (1929) **:** 1000 hertz

ki·lo·joule \-ˌjül\ *n* [ISV] (ca. 1889) **:** 1000 joules; *also* **:** a unit in nutrition equivalent to 0.239 calorie

kilo·li·ter \ˈki-lə-ˌlē-tər\ *n* [F *kilolitre,* fr. *kilo-* + *litre* liter] (1810) — see METRIC SYSTEM table

ki·lo·me·ter \kə-ˈlä-mə-tər, ki-; ˈki-lə-ˌmē-tər\ *n* [F *kilomètre,* fr. *kilo-* + *mètre* meter] (1810) **:** a metric unit of length equal to 1000 meters — see METRIC SYSTEM table

usage In No. American speech *kilometer* is most often pronounced with primary stress on the second syllable. This pronunciation is also heard frequently in British speech. Those who object to second syllable stress say that the first syllable should be stressed in accord with the stress patterns of *centimeter, millimeter,* etc. However, the pronunciation of *kilometer* does not parallel that of other metric compounds. From 1828 to 1841 Noah Webster indicated only second syllable stress, and his successor added a first syllable stress variant in the first Merriam-Webster dictionary of 1847. Thus, both pronunciations are venerable. Most scientists use second syllable stress, although first syllable stress seems to occur with a higher rate of frequency among scientists than among nonscientists.

ki·lo·par·sec \ˈki-lə-ˌpär-ˌsek, ˈkē-lə-\ *n* (1922) **:** 1000 parsecs

ki·lo·pas·cal \ˌki-lə-ˌpas-ˈkal\ *n* (1978) **:** 1000 pascals

ki·lo·rad \ˈki-lə-ˌrad\ *n* [ISV] (1965) **:** 1000 rads

ki·lo·ton \-ˌtən *also* -ˌtän\ *n* (1950) **1 :** 1000 tons **2 :** an explosive force equivalent to that of 1000 tons of TNT

ki·lo·volt \-ˌvōlt\ *n* [ISV] (ca. 1898) **:** a unit of potential difference equal to 1000 volts

kilo·watt \ˈki-lə-ˌwät\ *n* [ISV] (1884) **:** 1000 watts

kilowatt–hour *n* (1892) **:** a unit of work or energy equal to that expended by one kilowatt in one hour or to 3.6 million joules

[1]**kilt** \ˈkilt\ *vb* [ME, of Scand origin; akin to ON *kjalta* lap, fold of a gathered skirt] *vt* (14c) **1** *chiefly dial* **:** to tuck up (as a skirt) **2 :** to equip with a kilt ~ *vi* **:** to move nimbly

[2]**kilt** *n* (ca. 1730) **1 :** a knee-length pleated skirt usu. of tartan worn by men in Scotland and by Scottish regiments in the British armies **2 :** a garment that resembles a Scottish kilt

kil·ter \ˈkil-tər\ *n* [origin unknown] (1628) **:** proper or usual state or condition **:** ORDER ⟨out of ~⟩

kilt·ie \ˈkil-tē\ *n* (1842) **1** *or* **kilty :** one who wears a kilt **2 :** a shoe with a long slashed tongue that folds over the instep; *also* **:** such a tongue

kim·ber·lite \ˈkim-bər-ˌlīt\ *n* [*Kimberley*, So. Africa + [1]*-ite*] (1887) **:** an agglomerate biotite-peridotite that occurs in pipes esp. in southern Africa and that often contains diamonds

Kim·bun·du \kim-ˈbu̇n-(ˌ)dü\ *n* (ca. 1895) **:** a Bantu language of northern Angola

kim·chi *also* **kim·chee** \ˈkim-chē\ *n* [Korean *kimch'i*] (1898) **:** a vegetable pickle seasoned with garlic, red pepper, and ginger that is the national dish of Korea

ki·mo·no \kə-ˈmō-(ˌ)nō, -nə\ *n, pl* **-nos** [Jp, clothes, fr. *ki* wearing + *mono* thing] (1886) **1 :** a long robe with wide sleeves traditionally worn with a broad sash as an outer garment by the Japanese **2 :** a loose dressing gown or jacket — **ki·mo·noed** \-(ˌ)nōd, -nəd\ *adj*

kimono 1

[1]**kin** \ˈkin\ *n* [ME, fr. OE *cynn;* akin to OHG *chunni* race, L *genus* birth, race, kind, Gk *genos,* L *gignere* to beget, Gk *gignesthai* to be born] (bef. 12c) **1 :** a group of persons of common ancestry **:** CLAN **2 a :** one's relatives **:** KINDRED **b :** KINSMAN ⟨he wasn't any ~ to you —Jean Stafford⟩ **3** *archaic* **:** KINSHIP

[2]**kin** *adj* (1597) **:** KINDRED, RELATED

-kin \kən\ *also* **-kins** \kənz\ *n suffix* [ME, fr. MD *-kin;* akin to OHG *-chīn,* dim. suffix] **:** little ⟨cat*kin*⟩ ⟨baby*kins*⟩

ki·na \ˈkē-nə\ *n, pl* **kina** [New Guinea Pidgin, lit., gold lip (kind of oyster shell used as currency)] (1974) — see MONEY table

ki·na·ra \kē-ˈnä-rə\ *n* [Swahili, candlestick] (1975) **:** a candelabra with seven candlesticks used in celebrating Kwanzaa

ki·nase \ˈkī-ˌnās, -ˌnāz\ *n* [ISV, fr. *kinetic*] (1947) **:** any of various enzymes that catalyze the transfer of phosphate groups from a high-energy phosphate-containing molecule (as ATP) to a substrate — compare PROTEIN KINASE

[1]**kind** \ˈkīnd\ *n* [ME *kinde,* fr. OE *cynd;* akin to OE *cynn* kin] (bef. 12c) **1 a** *archaic* **:** NATURE **b** *archaic* **:** FAMILY, LINEAGE **2** *archaic* **:** MANNER **3 :** fundamental nature or quality **:** ESSENCE **4 a :** a group united by common traits or interests **:** CATEGORY **b :** a specific or recognized variety ⟨what ~ of car do you drive⟩ **c :** a doubtful or barely admissible member of a category ⟨a ~ of gray⟩ **5 a :** goods or commodities as distinguished from money ⟨payment in ~⟩ **b :** the equivalent of what has been offered or received ***syn*** see TYPE — **all kinds of 1 :** MANY ⟨likes *all kinds of* sports⟩ **2 :** plenty of ⟨has *all kinds of* time⟩

[2]**kind** *adj* (14c) **1** *chiefly dial* **:** AFFECTIONATE, LOVING **2 a :** of a sympathetic or helpful nature **b :** of a forbearing nature **:** GENTLE **c :** arising from or characterized by sympathy or forbearance ⟨a ~ act⟩ **3 :** of a kind to give pleasure or relief

kin·der·gar·ten \ˈkin-də(r)-ˌgär-tᵊn, -dᵊn\ *n* [G, fr. *Kinder* children + *Garten* garden] (1852) **:** a school or class for children usu. from four to six years old

kin·der·gart·ner \-ˌgärt-nər, -ˌgärd-\ *also* **kin·der·gar·ten·er** \-ˌgär-tə-nər, -də-\ *n* (1881) **1 :** a teacher at a kindergarten **2 :** a child attending or of an age to attend kindergarten

kind·heart·ed \ˌkīnd-ˈhär-təd\ *adj* (1535) **:** having or showing a sympathetic nature — **kind·heart·ed·ly** *adv* — **kind·heart·ed·ness** *n*

[1]**kin·dle** \ˈkin-dᵊl\ *vb* **kin·dled; kin·dling** \ˈkin(d)-liŋ, ˈkin-dᵊl-iŋ\ [ME, prob. modif. of ON *kynda;* akin to OHG *cuntesal* fire] *vt* (13c) **1 :** to start (a fire) burning **:** LIGHT **2 a :** to stir up **:** AROUSE ⟨~ interest⟩ **b :** to bring into being **:** START **3 :** to cause to glow **:** ILLUMINATE ~ *vi* **1 :** to catch fire **2 a :** to flare up **b :** to become animated **3 :** to become illuminated — **kin·dler** \ˈkin(d)-lər, ˈkin-dᵊl-ər\ *n*

[2]**kindle** *vb* **kin·dled; kin·dling** [ME, fr. *kindle* young animal, prob. fr. *kinde,* n., kind] *vt* (13c) **:** BEAR 2a — used esp. of a rabbit ~ *vi* **:** to bring forth young — used esp. of a rabbit

kind·less \ˈkīn(d)-ləs\ *adj* (13c) **1** *obs* **:** INHUMAN **2 :** DISAGREEABLE, UNCONGENIAL — **kind·less·ly** *adv*

kind·li·ness \ˈkīn(d)-lē-nəs\ *n* (15c) **1 :** the quality or state of being kindly **2 :** a kindly deed

kin·dling \ˈkin(d)-liŋ, ˈkin-lən\ *n* (1513) **:** easily combustible material for starting a fire

[1]**kind·ly** \ˈkīn(d)-lē\ *adj* **kind·li·er; -est** [ME, fr. OE *cyndelīc,* fr. *cynd*] (bef. 12c) **1 a** *obs* **:** NATURAL **b** *archaic* **:** LAWFUL **2 :** of an agreeable or beneficial nature **:** PLEASANT ⟨a ~ climate⟩ **3 :** of a sympathetic or generous nature

[2]**kindly** *adv* (bef. 12c) **1 a :** in the normal way **:** NATURALLY ⟨old wounds which had healed ~ —*Amer. Mercury*⟩ **b :** READILY ⟨did not take ~ to suggestions⟩ **2 a :** in a kind manner **:** SYMPATHETICALLY **b :** as a gesture of goodwill ⟨would take it ~ if you would put in a good word⟩ **c :** in a gracious manner **:** COURTEOUSLY ⟨they ~ invited us along⟩ **d :** as a matter of courtesy **:** PLEASE ⟨would you ~ order me a cab⟩ **3** *chiefly Southern* **:** SOMEWHAT, KIND OF ⟨it's ~ embarrassing —Walter Davis⟩

kind·ness \ˈkīn(d)-nəs\ *n* (13c) **1 :** a kind deed **:** FAVOR **2 a :** the quality or state of being kind **b** *archaic* **:** AFFECTION

kind of *adv* (1775) **1 :** to a moderate degree **:** SOMEWHAT ⟨it's *kind of* late to begin⟩ **2 :** in a way that approximates **:** MORE OR LESS ⟨*kind of* sneaked up on us⟩

[1]**kin·dred** \ˈkin-drəd\ *n* [ME, fr. *kin* + OE *rǣden* condition, fr. *rǣdan* to advise, read] (12c) **1 a :** a group of related individuals **b :** one's relatives **2 :** family relationship **:** KINSHIP

[2]**kindred** *adj* (14c) **1 :** of a similar nature or character **:** LIKE ⟨a ~ spirit⟩ **2 :** of the same ancestry

kine \ˈkīn\ *archaic pl of* COW

kin·e·ma \ˈki-nə-mə\ *Brit var of* CINEMA

ki·ne·mat·ics \ˌki-nə-ˈma-tiks *also* ˌkī-\ *n pl but sing in constr* [F *cinématique,* fr. Gk *kinēmat-, kinēma* motion, fr. *kinein* to move] (1840) **:** a branch of dynamics that deals with aspects of motion apart from considerations of mass and force — **ki·ne·mat·ic** \-tik\ *or* **ki·ne·mat·i·cal** \-ti-kəl\ *adj* — **ki·ne·mat·i·cal·ly** \-ti-k(ə-)lē\ *adv*

[1]**ki·ne·scope** \ˈki-nə-ˌskōp *also* ˈkī-\ *n* [fr. *Kinescope,* a trademark] (1930) **1 :** PICTURE TUBE **2 :** a motion picture made from an image on a picture tube

[2]**kinescope** *vt* **-scoped; -scop·ing** (1949) **:** to make a kinescope of

ki·ne·sics \kə-ˈnē-siks, kī-, -ziks\ *n pl but sing in constr* [Gk *kinēsis* motion + E *-ics*] (1952) **:** a systematic study of the relationship between nonlinguistic body motions (as blushes, shrugs, or eye movement) and communication

ki·ne·si·ol·o·gy \kə-ˌnē-sē-ˈä-lə-jē, kī-, -zē-\ *n* [Gk *kinēsis*] (1894) **:** the study of the principles of mechanics and anatomy in relation to human movement — **ki·ne·si·ol·o·gist** \-ˈä-lə-jist\ *n*

ki·ne·sis \kə-ˈnē-səs, kī-\ *n, pl* **ki·ne·ses** \-ˌsēz\ [NL, fr. Gk *kinēsis*] (1905) **:** a movement that lacks directional orientation and depends upon the intensity of stimulation

-kinesis *n comb form, pl* **-kineses** [NL, fr. Gk *kinēsis,* fr. *kinein* to move; akin to L *ciēre* to move] **1 :** division ⟨karyo*kinesis*⟩ **2 :** production of motion ⟨tele*kinesis*⟩

kin·es·the·sia \ˌki-nəs-ˈthē-zh(ē-)ə, ˌkī-\ *or* **kin·es·the·sis** \-ˈthē-səs\ *n, pl* **-the·sias** *or* **-the·ses** \-ˌsēz\ [NL, fr. Gk *kinein* + *aisthēsis* perception — more at ANESTHESIA] (1880) **:** a sense mediated by receptors located in muscles, tendons, and joints and stimulated by bodily movements and tensions; *also* **:** sensory experience derived from this sense — **kin·es·thet·ic** \-ˈthe-tik\ *adj* — **kin·es·thet·i·cal·ly** \-ti-k(ə-)lē\ *adv*

kinet- *or* **kineto-** *comb form* [Gk *kinētos* moving] **:** movement **:** motion ⟨*kineto*some⟩

ki·net·ic \kə-ˈne-tik *also* kī-\ *adj* [Gk *kinētikos,* fr. *kinētos,* fr. *kinein*] (1864) **1 :** of or relating to the motion of material bodies and the forces and energy associated therewith **2 a :** ACTIVE, LIVELY **b :** DYNAMIC, ENERGIZING ⟨a ~ performer⟩ **3 :** of or relating to kinetic art — **ki·net·i·cal·ly** \-ti-k(ə-)lē\ *adv*

kinetic art *n* (1961) **:** art (as sculpture or assemblage) having mechanical parts which can be set in motion — **kinetic artist** *n*

kinetic energy *n* (1870) **:** energy associated with motion

ki·net·i·cist \kə-ˈne-tə-sist *also* kī-\ *n* (1960) **1 :** a specialist in kinetics **2 :** a person who works in kinetic art **:** KINETIC ARTIST

ki·net·ics \kə-ˈne-tiks *also* kī-\ *n pl but sing or pl in constr* (ca. 1859) **1 a :** a branch of science that deals with the effects of forces upon the motions of material bodies or with changes in a physical or chemical system **b :** the rate of change in such a system **2 :** the mechanism by which a physical or chemical change is effected

kinetic theory *n* (1864) **:** either of two theories in physics based on the fact that the minute particles of a substance are in vigorous motion: **a :** a theory that the temperature of a substance increases with an increase in either the average kinetic energy of the particles or the average potential energy of separation (as in fusion) of the particles or in both when heat is added — called also *kinetic theory of heat* **b :** a theory that the particles of a gas move in straight lines with high average velocity, continually encounter one another and thus change their individual velocities and directions, and cause pressure by their impact against the walls of a container — called also *kinetic theory of gases*

ki·ne·tin \ˈkī-nə-tən\ *n* (1955) **:** a cytokinin $C_{10}H_9N_5O$ used esp. to stimulate cell division in plant tissue culture

ki·net·o·chore \kə-ˈne-tə-ˌkȯr, kī-\ *n* [*kinet-* + Gk *chōros* place] (1934) **1 :** CENTROMERE **2 :** a specialized structure on the centromere to which the microtubular spindle fibers attach during mitosis and meiosis

ki·net·o·plast \kə-ˈne-tə-ˌplast, kī-\ *n* [ISV] (1925) **:** a DNA-containing organelle esp. of trypanosomes usu. found in an elongated mitochondrian located adjacent to the basal body

ki·net·o·scope \kə-ˈne-tə-ˌskōp, kī-\ *n* [fr. *Kinetoscope,* a trademark] (1894) **:** a device for viewing through a magnifying lens a sequence of pictures on an endless band of film moved continuously over a light source and a rapidly rotating shutter that creates an illusion of motion

ki·net·o·some \-ˌsōm\ *n* (1912) **:** BASAL BODY

kin·folk \ˈkin-ˌfōk\ *or* **kinfolks** *n pl* (1873) **:** RELATIVES

king \ˈkiŋ\ *n* [ME, fr. OE *cyning;* akin to OHG *kuning* king, OE *cynn* kin] (bef. 12c) **1 a :** a male monarch of a major territorial unit; *esp* **:** one whose position is hereditary and who rules for life **b :** a paramount chief **2** *cap* **:** GOD, CHRIST **3 :** one that holds a preeminent position; *esp* **:** a chief among competitors **4 :** the principal piece of each color in chess having the power to move ordinarily one square in any direction and to capture opposing pieces but being obliged never to enter or remain in check **5 :** a playing card marked with a stylized figure of a king **6 :** a checker that has been crowned **7 :** CHINOOK SALMON

king·bird \-ˌbərd\ *n* (1778) **:** any of various American tyrant flycatchers (genus *Tyrannus*) that are gray above and white, gray, or yellow below

king·bolt \-ˌbōlt\ *n* (1825) **:** a vertical bolt by which the forward axle and wheels of a vehicle or the trucks of a railroad car are connected with the other parts

King Charles spaniel \-ˈchär(-ə)lz-\ *n* [*Charles* II of England] (1833) **1** *Brit* **:** ENGLISH TOY SPANIEL **2 :** CAVALIER KING CHARLES SPANIEL — not used technically

king cobra *n* (1894) **:** a large cobra (*Ophiophagus hannah* syn. *Naja hannah*) of southeastern Asia and the Philippines that may attain a length of 18 feet (5.5 meters)

king crab *n* (1698) **1 :** HORSESHOE CRAB **2 :** any of several very large crabs; *esp* **:** one (*Paralithoides camtschaticus*) of the No. Pacific caught commercially for food

king·craft \ˈkiŋ-ˌkraft\ *n* (1643) **:** the art of governing as a king

king·cup \-ˌkəp\ *n* (1538) **:** any of several plants of the buttercup family; *esp* **:** MARSH MARIGOLD

king·dom \ˈkiŋ-dəm\ *n* (bef. 12c) **1** *archaic* **:** KINGSHIP **2 :** a politically organized community or major territorial unit having a monarchical form of government headed by a king or queen **3** *often cap* **a :** the eternal kingship of God **b :** the realm in which God's will is fulfilled **4 a :** a realm or region in which something is dominant **b :** an area or sphere in which one holds a preeminent position **5 a :** one of the three primary divisions into which natural objects are commonly classified — compare ANIMAL KINGDOM, MINERAL KINGDOM, PLANT KINGDOM **b :** a major category (as Plantae or Protista) in biological taxonomy that ranks above the phylum and below the domain

kingdom come *n* [fr. the phrase "Thy *kingdom come*" (Mt 6:10)] (1785) **:** the next world **:** HEAVEN

king·fish \ˈkiŋ-ˌfish\ *n* (1750) **1 :** any of several marine croakers (family Sciaenidae) **a :** any of three fishes (*Menticirrhus americanus, M. littoralis,* and *M. saxatilis*) of shallow coastal waters of the Atlantic Ocean **b :** a small silvery food and sport fish (*Genyonemus lineatus*) of inshore waters esp. of California — called also *white croaker* **2 :** KING MACKEREL **3 :** an undisputed master in an area or group

king·fish·er \-ˌfi-shər\ *n* (15c) **:** any of numerous nonpasserine birds (family Alcedinidae) that are usu. crested and bright-colored with a short tail and a long stout sharp bill

King James Version \-ˈjāmz-\ *n* [*James* I of England] (1884) **:** AUTHORIZED VERSION

king·let \ˈkiŋ-lət\ *n* (1603) **1 :** a weak or petty king **2 :** any of several small birds (genus *Regulus*) that are related to the gnatcatchers

king·ly \ˈkiŋ-lē\ *adj* **king·li·er; -est** (14c) **1 :** having royal rank **2 :** of, relating to, or befitting a king **3 :** MONARCHICAL — **king·li·ness** *n* — **kingly** *adv*

king mackerel *n* (ca. 1930) **:** a mackerel (*Scomberomorus cavalla*) of the western Atlantic Ocean that is noted esp. as a fighting sport fish

king·mak·er \ˈkiŋ-ˌmā-kər\ *n* (1599) **:** one having great influence over the choice of candidates for political office

king of arms (15c) **:** an officer of arms of the highest rank

king penguin *n* (1885) **:** a large penguin (*Aptenodytes patagonicus*) chiefly of subantarctic areas with a yellow patch on the upper breast

king·pin \ˈkiŋ-ˌpin\ *n* (1801) **1 :** any of several bowling pins: as **a :** HEADPIN **b :** the pin that stands in the middle of a triangular arrangement of bowling pins **2 :** the chief person in a group or undertaking **3 a :** KINGBOLT **b :** a pin connecting the two parts of a knuckle joint (as in an automobile steering linkage)

king post *n* (1776) **:** a vertical member connecting the apex of a triangular truss (as of a roof) with the base

Kings \ˈkiŋz\ *n pl but sing in constr* (bef. 12c) **1 :** either of two narrative and historical books of canonical Jewish and Christian Scripture — see BIBLE table **2 :** any of four narrative and historical books in the former Roman Catholic canon of the Old Testament

king salmon *n* (1881) **:** CHINOOK SALMON

King's Bench *n* (14c) **:** a division in the English superior courts system that hears civil and criminal cases

King's Counsel *n* (1678) **:** a barrister selected to serve as counsel to the British crown

King's English *n* (1553) **:** standard, pure, or correct English speech or usage

king's evil *n, often cap K&E* [fr. the former belief that it could be healed by a king's touch] (14c) **:** SCROFULA

king·ship \ˈkiŋ-ˌship\ *n* (14c) **1 :** the position, office, or dignity of a king **2 :** the personality of a king **3 :** government by a king

king·side \-ˌsīd\ *n* (1941) **:** the side of a chessboard containing the file on which the king sits at the beginning of the game

king–size \-ˌsīz\ *or* **king–sized** \-ˌsīzd\ *adj* (1942) **1 :** longer than the regular or standard size ⟨a ~ cigarette⟩ **2 :** unusually large **3 a :** having dimensions of approximately 76 by 80 inches (about 1.9 by 2.0 meters) — used of a bed; compare FULL-SIZE, QUEEN-SIZE, TWIN-SIZE **b :** of a size that fits a king-size bed ⟨~ sheets⟩

king snake *n* (1709) **:** any of numerous brightly marked colubrid snakes (genus *Lampropeltis*) chiefly of No. and Central America

king's ransom *n* (ca. 1590) **:** a very large sum of money

king·wood \-ˌwu̇d\ *n* (ca. 1851) **:** the wood of any of several tropical American leguminous trees (esp. genus *Dalbergia*); *esp* **:** the wood of a Brazilian tree (*D. cearensis*) used esp. for furniture

ki·nin \ˈkī-nən\ *n* [Gk *kinein* to move, stimulate + E [1]*-in* — more at -KINESIS] (1954) **1 :** any of various polypeptide hormones that are formed locally in the tissues and cause dilation of blood vessels and contraction of smooth muscle **2 :** CYTOKININ

[1]**kink** \ˈkiŋk\ *n* [D; akin to MLG *kinke* kink] (1678) **1 :** a short tight twist or curl caused by a doubling or winding of something upon itself **2 a :** a mental or physical peculiarity **:** ECCENTRICITY, QUIRK **b :** WHIM **3 :** a clever unusual way of doing something **4 :** a cramp in some part of the body **5 :** an imperfection likely to cause difficulties in the operation of something **6 :** unconventional sexual taste or behavior

[2]**kink** *vi* (1697) **:** to form a kink ~ *vt* **:** to make a kink in

kin·ka·jou \ˈkiŋ-kə-ˌjü\ *n* [F, alter. of *quincajou* wolverine, of Algonquian origin; akin to Ojibwa *kwi·nkwaʔa·ke·* wolverine] (1796) **:** a nocturnal arboreal omnivorous mammal (*Potos flavus*) found from Mexico to So. America that is related to the raccoon and has a long prehensile tail, large eyes, and yellowish brown fur

kinkajou

kinky \ˈkiŋ-kē\ *adj* **kink·i·er; -est** (1844) **1 :** closely twisted or curled **2 :** relating to, having, or appealing to unconventional tastes esp. in sex; *also* **:** sexually deviant **3 :** OUTLANDISH, FAR-OUT — **kink·i·ly** \ˈkiŋ-kə-lē\ *adv* — **kink·i·ness** \ˈkiŋ-kē-nəs\ *n*

kin·ni·kin·nick \ˌki-ni-kə-ˈnik, ˈki-ni-kə-ˌ\ *n* [of Algonquian origin; akin to Massachusett *kinukkinuk* mixture] (1799) **1 :** a mixture of dried leaves and bark and sometimes tobacco smoked by the Indians and pioneers esp. in the Ohio valley **2 :** a plant (as a sumac or dogwood) used in kinnikinnick; *esp* **:** BEARBERRY

-kins — see -KIN

kin selection *n* (1975) **:** a theory of natural selection which states that a usu. altruistic behavior or attribute that lowers the fitness of a particular individual is selected for if it increases the probability of survival and reproduction of related kin who possess some or all of the same genes as the altruistic individual

kins·folk \ˈkinz-ˌfōk\ *n pl* (15c) **:** RELATIVES

kin·ship \ˈkin-ˌship\ *n* (1833) **:** the quality or state of being kin **:** RELATIONSHIP

kins·man \ˈkinz-mən\ *n* (12c) **:** RELATIVE; *specif* **:** a male relative

kins·wom·an \-ˌwu̇-mən\ *n* (14c) **:** a female relative

ki·osk \ˈkē-ˌäsk\ *n* [Turk *köşk,* fr. Pers *kūshk* portico] (1625) **1 :** an open summerhouse or pavilion **2 :** a small structure with one or more open sides that is used to vend merchandise (as newspapers) or services (as film developing) **3 :** a small stand-alone device providing information and services on a computer screen ⟨a museum with interactive ~*s*⟩

Ki·o·wa \ˈkī-ə-ˌwȯ, -ˌwä, -ˌwā\ *n, pl* **Kiowa** *or* **Kiowas** [ultim. fr. Kiowa *kɔ́ygú,* a self-designation] (1808) **1 :** a member of an American Indian people of what are now Colorado, Kansas, New Mexico, Oklahoma, and Texas **2 :** the language of the Kiowa people

[1]**kip** \ˈkip\ *n* [obs. D; akin to MLG *kip* bundle of hides] (ca. 1525) **:** a bundle of undressed hides of young or small animals; *also* **:** one of the hides

[2]**kip** *n* [perh. fr. Dan *kippe* cheap tavern] (1879) **1 :** BED ⟨ready for the ~ after this screwball day —K. M. Dodson⟩ **2** *chiefly Brit* **:** SLEEP, NAP ⟨roused the . . . family from their ~ —Sylvia Margolis⟩

[3]**kip** *vi* **kipped; kip·ping** (ca. 1889) *Brit* **:** SLEEP — sometimes used with *down* ⟨~ down on a spare bed —Alice Glenday⟩

[4]**kip** *n* [*ki*lo- + *p*ound] (1914) **:** a unit of weight equal to 1000 pounds (454 kilograms) used to express deadweight load

[5]**kip** \ˈkip, ˈgip\ *n, pl* **kip** *or* **kips** [Lao *kì:p,* lit., ingot] (1955) — see MONEY table

[1]**kip·per** \ˈki-pər\ *n* [ME *kypre,* fr. OE *cypera;* akin to OE *coper* copper] (bef. 12c) **1 :** a male salmon or sea trout during or after the spawning season **2 :** a kippered herring or salmon

[2]**kipper** *vt* **kip·pered; kip·per·ing** \-p(ə-)riŋ\ (1773) **:** to cure (split dressed fish) by salting and smoking — **kip·per·er** \-pər-ər\ *n*

Kirghiz *var of* KYRGYZ

kirk \ˈkirk, ˈkərk\ *n* [ME (northern dial.), fr. ON *kirkja,* fr. OE *cirice* — more at CHURCH] (12c) **1** *chiefly Scot* **:** CHURCH **2** *cap* **:** the national church of Scotland as distinguished from the Church of England or the Episcopal Church in Scotland

Kir·li·an photography \ˈkir-lē-ən-\ *n* [Semën D. *Kirlian* †1978 and Valentina Kh. *Kirlian* †1971 Soviet inventors] (1972) **:** a process in which an image is obtained by application of a high-frequency electric field to an object so that it radiates a characteristic pattern of luminescence that is recorded on photographic film — **Kirlian photograph** *n*

Kir·man \kər-ˈmän, kir-\ *also* **Ker·man** \kər-, ker-\ *n* [*Kirman,* province in Iran] (1876) **:** a Persian carpet or rug characterized by elaborate fluid designs and soft colors

kirsch \ˈkirsh\ *n* [G, short for *Kirschwasser,* fr. *Kirsche* cherry + *Wasser* water] (1869) **:** a dry colorless brandy distilled from the fermented juice of the black morello cherry

Kirt·land's warbler \ˈkərt-lən(d)z-\ *n* [Jared P. *Kirtland* †1877 Am. naturalist] (1858) **:** a rare warbler (*Dendroica kirtlandii*) of northeastern No. America that breeds in Michigan and winters in the Bahamas

kir·tle \ˈkər-tᵊl\ *n* [ME *kirtel,* fr. OE *cyrtel,* fr. OE **curt* short, fr. L *curtus* mutilated, curtailed — more at SHEAR] (bef. 12c) **1 :** a tunic or coat worn by men esp. in the Middle Ages **2 :** a long gown or dress worn by women

kish·ke *also* **kish·ka** \ˈkish-kə\ *n* [Yiddish *kishke* gut, sausage, of Slavic origin; akin to Pol *kiszka* gut, sausage] (ca. 1936) **:** beef or fowl casing stuffed (as with meat, flour, and spices) and cooked

Kis·lev \ˈkis-ləf\ *n* [Heb *Kislēw*] (14c) **:** the third month of the civil year or the ninth month of the ecclesiastical year in the Jewish calendar — see MONTH table

kis·met \ˈkiz-ˌmet, -mət\ *n, often cap* [Turk, fr. Ar *qisma* portion, lot] (1834) **1 :** FATE 1 **2 :** FATE 2a

[1]**kiss** \ˈkis\ *vb* [ME, fr. OE *cyssan;* akin to OHG *kussen* to kiss] *vt* (bef. 12c) **1 :** to touch with the lips esp. as a mark of affection or greeting ⟨~*ed* his wife good-bye⟩ **2 :** to touch gently or lightly ⟨wind gently ~*ing* the trees⟩ ~ *vi* **1 :** to salute or caress one another with the lips **2 :** to come in gentle contact — **kiss·able** \ˈki-sə-bəl\ *adj* — **kiss ass** *usu vulgar* **:** to act obsequiously esp. to gain favor — **kiss good–bye** **1 :** LEAVE **2 :** to resign oneself to the loss of — **kiss one's ass** *usu vulgar* **:** to act obsequiously toward one esp. to gain favor — **kiss up to :** to curry favor with

[2]**kiss** *n* (bef. 12c) **1 :** a caress with the lips ⟨a range of ~*es* from a passionate embrace to a friendly peck⟩ **2 :** a gentle touch or contact **3 a :** a small drop cookie made of meringue **b :** a bite-size piece of candy often wrapped in paper or foil **4 :** an expression of affection ⟨sent him ~*es* in her letter⟩

kiss–and–tell \ˈkis-ᵊn(d)-ˈtel\ *adj* (ca. 1948) **:** telling details of private matters ⟨~ autobiographies⟩

kiss·er \ˈki-sər\ *n* (1537) **1 :** one that kisses **2** *slang* **a :** MOUTH **b :** FACE

kissing bug *n* (1899) **:** any of various large bloodsucking bugs and esp. some assassin bugs (genus *Triatoma*) including some capable of inflicting painful bites — called also *conenose*

kissing cousin *n* (1941) **1 :** a person and esp. a relative whom one knows well enough to kiss more or less formally upon meeting **2 :** one that is closely related in kind to something else

kissing disease *n* [fr. the belief that it is frequently transmitted by kissing] (1962) **:** INFECTIOUS MONONUCLEOSIS

kiss of death [fr. the kiss with which Judas betrayed Jesus (Mk 14:44–46)] (1943) **:** something (as an act or association) ultimately causing ruin

kiss off *vt* (ca. 1935) **:** to dismiss usu. lightly ⟨*kisses* the other performers *off* as mere amateurs⟩ — **kiss–off** \ˈki-ˌsȯf\ *n*

kiss of life (1961) *chiefly Brit* **:** artificial respiration by the mouth-to-mouth method

kiss of peace (ca. 1898) **:** a ceremonial kiss, embrace, or handclasp used in Christian liturgies and esp. the Eucharist as a sign of fraternal unity

kist \ˈkist\ *n* [ME *kiste,* fr. ON *kista,* ultim. fr. L *cista* — more at CHEST] (14c) *chiefly Scot & SoAfr* **:** CHEST 1b

1**kit** \ˈkit\ *n* [ME] (14c) **1** *dial Brit* **:** a wooden tub **2 a** (1) **:** a collection of articles usu. for personal use ⟨a travel ~⟩ (2) **:** a set of tools or implements ⟨a carpenter's ~⟩ (3) **:** a set of parts to be assembled or worked up ⟨a model-airplane ~⟩ (4) **:** a packaged collection of related material ⟨a convention ~⟩ (5) *chiefly Brit* **:** GEAR ⟨run over to my billet and get some overnight ~ —Lionel Shapiro⟩ **b :** a container for any of such sets or collections **3 :** a group of persons or things — usu. used in the phrase *the whole kit and caboodle*

2**kit** *vt* **kit·ted; kit·ting** (1919) *chiefly Brit* **:** EQUIP, OUTFIT — often used with *up* or *out*

3**kit** *n* [origin unknown] (1519) **:** a small narrow violin

4**kit** *n* (1562) **1 :** KITTEN **2 :** a young or undersized fur-bearing animal; *also* **:** its pelt

5**kit** *abbr* kitchen

kit bag *n* [1*kit*] (1893) **1 :** KNAPSACK **2 :** a suitcase usu. with sides that fasten at the top or open to the full width of the bag

kitch·en \ˈki-chən\ *n* [ME *kichene,* fr. OE *cycene,* fr. LL *coquina,* fr. L *coquere* to cook — more at COOK] (bef. 12c) **1 :** a place (as a room) with cooking facilities **2 :** the personnel that prepares, cooks, and serves food **3 :** CUISINE

kitchen cabinet *n* (1832) **1 :** an informal group of advisers to one in a position of power (as the head of a government) **2 :** a cupboard with drawers and shelves for use in a kitchen

kitch·en·ette \ˌki-chə-ˈnet\ *n* (1903) **:** a small kitchen or an alcove containing cooking facilities

kitchen garden *n* (1580) **:** a garden in which plants (as vegetables or herbs) for use in the kitchen are cultivated

kitchen midden *n* (1863) **:** a refuse heap; *specif* **:** a mound marking the site of a primitive human habitation

kitchen police *n* (ca. 1917) **1 :** KP **2 :** the work of KPs

kitch·en–sink \-ˈsiŋk\ *adj* (1941) **1** *chiefly Brit* **:** portraying or emphasizing the squalid aspects of modern life ⟨the ~ realism of contemporary British drama —*Current Biog.*⟩ **2 :** being or made up of a hodgepodge of disparate elements or ingredients

kitch·en·ware \-ˌwer\ *n* (1722) **:** utensils and appliances for use in a kitchen

1**kite** \ˈkīt\ *n* [ME, fr. OE *cȳta;* akin to MHG *kūze* owl] (bef. 12c) **1 :** any of various usu. small hawks (family Accipitridae) with long narrow wings and often a notched or forked tail **2 :** a person who preys on others **3 :** a light frame covered with paper, cloth, or plastic, often provided with a stabilizing tail, and designed to be flown in the air at the end of a long string **4 :** a check drawn against uncollected funds in a bank account or fraudulently raised before cashing **5 :** a light sail used in a light breeze usu. in addition to the regular working sails; *esp* **:** SPINNAKER — **kite·like** *adj*

2**kite** *vb* **kit·ed; kit·ing** *vt* (1839) **1 :** to use (a bad check) to get credit or money **2 :** to cause to soar ⟨*kited* the prices they charged wealthy clients⟩ ~ *vi* **1 a :** to go in a rapid, carefree, or flighty manner **b :** to rise rapidly **:** SOAR **2 :** to get money or credit by a kite — **kit·er** *n*

kite·board·ing \ˈkīt-ˌbȯr-diŋ\ *n* (1996) **:** the sport of riding on a small surfboard that is propelled across water by a large kite to which the rider is harnessed — called also *kitesurfing*

kit fox *n* [4*kit*] (1805) **1 a :** SWIFT FOX **b :** a fox (*Vulpes macrotis*) of the southwestern U.S. and Mexico with exceptionally large ears and a black tip on the tail **2 :** the fur or pelt of a kit fox

kith \ˈkith\ *n* [ME, fr. OE *cȳthth;* akin to *cūth* known — more at UNCOUTH] (bef. 12c) **:** familiar friends, neighbors, or relatives ⟨~ and kin⟩

kith·a·ra \ˈki-thə-rə\ *or* **cith·a·ra** \ˈsi-, ˈki-\ *n* [ME *cithara,* fr. L, fr. Gk *kithara*] (14c) **:** an ancient Greek stringed instrument similar to but larger than the lyre and having a box-shaped resonator

kithe \ˈkīth\ *vb* **kithed; kith·ing** [ME, fr. OE *cȳthan,* fr. *cūth*] *vt* (bef. 12c) *chiefly Scot* **:** to make known ~ *vi, chiefly Scot* **:** to become known

kitsch \ˈkich\ *n* [G] (1925) **1 :** something that appeals to popular or lowbrow taste and is often of poor quality **2 :** a tacky or lowbrow quality or condition ⟨teetering on the brink of ~ —Ron Miller⟩ — **kitsch** *adj* — **kitschy** \ˈki-chē\ *adj*

1**kit·ten** \ˈki-tᵊn\ *n* [ME *kitoun,* fr. AF **kiton, chiton,* dim. of *cat, chat* cat, fr. LL *cattus*] (14c) **:** a young cat; *also* **:** an immature or young individual of various other small mammals

2**kitten** *vi* **kit·tened; kit·ten·ing** \ˈkit-niŋ, ˈki-tᵊn-iŋ\ (15c) **:** to give birth to kittens

kitten heel *n* (1956) **:** a short stiletto heel on women's shoes

kit·ten·ish \ˈkit-nish, ˈki-tᵊn-ish\ *adj* (1754) **:** resembling a kitten; *esp* **:** coyly playful — **kit·ten·ish·ly** *adv* — **kit·ten·ish·ness** *n*

kit·ti·wake \ˈki-tē-ˌwāk\ *n* [imit.] (1661) **:** either of two cliff-nesting gulls (*Rissa tridactyla* and *R. brevirostris*) that winter on the open ocean

1**kit·tle** \ˈki-tᵊl\ *vt* **kit·tled; kit·tling** \ˈkit-liŋ, ˈki-tᵊl-iŋ\ [ME (northern dial.) *kytyllen*] (bef. 12c) **1** *chiefly Scot* **:** TICKLE **2** *chiefly Scot* **:** PERPLEX

2**kittle** *adj* (1568) *chiefly Scot* **:** TICKLISH, TOUCHY

1**kit·ty** \ˈki-tē\ *n, pl* **kitties** (1719) **:** CAT 1a; *esp* **:** KITTEN

2**kitty** *n, pl* **kitties** [1*kit*] (ca. 1887) **1 :** a fund in a poker game made up of contributions from each pot **2 :** a sum of money or collection of goods often made up of small contributions **:** POOL

kit·ty–cor·ner *also* **cat·ty–cor·ner** *or* **cat·er·cor·ner** \ˈki-tē-ˌkȯr-nər, ˈka-tē-, ˈka-tə-\ *or* **kit·ty–cor·nered** *or* **cat·ty–cor·nered** *or* **cat·er·cor·nered** \-nərd\ *adv or adj* [*kitty-corner* alter. of *cater-corner,* fr. obs. *cater* four + *corner*] (1838) **:** in a diagonal or oblique position ⟨the house stood ~ across the square⟩

ki·va \ˈkē-və\ *n* [Hopi *kíva*] (1871) **:** a Pueblo Indian ceremonial structure that is usu. round and partly underground

Ki·wa·ni·an \kə-ˈwä-nē-ən\ *n* [*Kiwanis (Club)*] (1921) **:** a member of a major national and international service club

ki·wi \ˈkē-(ˌ)wē\ *n* [Maori] (1835) **1 :** any of a small genus (*Apteryx*) of flightless New Zealand birds with rudimentary wings, stout legs, a long bill, and grayish brown hairlike plumage **2** *cap* **:** a native or resident of New Zealand — used as a nickname **3 :** KIWIFRUIT

ki·wi·fruit \-ˌfrüt\ *n* (1965) **:** the edible fruit of a Chinese gooseberry having a fuzzy brown skin and slightly acidic typically green flesh

kJ *abbr* kilojoule

KJV *abbr* King James Version

KKK *abbr* Ku Klux Klan

kl *abbr* kiloliter

Klam·ath weed \ˈkla-məth-\ *n* [*Klamath (River)*] (1922) **:** a European yellow-flowered perennial Saint-John's-wort (*Hypericum perforatum*) that is naturalized in No. America esp. in rangelands

Klan \ˈklan\ *n* [*(Ku Klux) Klan*] (1867) **:** an organization of Ku Kluxers; *also* **:** a subordinate unit of such an organization — **Klan·ism** \-ˌi-zəm\ *n* — **Klans·man** \ˈklanz-mən\ *n*

klatch *also* **klatsch** \ˈklach, ˈkläch\ *n* [G *Klatsch* gossip] (1941) **1 :** a gathering characterized usu. by informal conversation **2 :** GROUP 2a

klav·ern \ˈkla-vərn\ *n, often cap* [blend of *Klan* and *cavern*] (ca. 1924) **:** a local unit of the Klan

Klax·on \ˈklak-sən\ *trademark* — used for an electrically operated horn or warning signal

kleb·si·el·la \ˌkleb-zē-ˈe-lə\ *n* [NL, fr. Edwin *Klebs* †1913 Ger. pathologist] (1928) **:** any of a genus (*Klebsiella*) of nonmotile enterobacteria that includes causative agents of respiratory and urogenital infections

Klee·nex \ˈklē-ˌneks\ *trademark* — used for a cleansing tissue

Klein bottle \ˈklīn-\ *n* [Felix *Klein* †1925 Ger. mathematician] (1941) **:** a one-sided surface that is formed by passing the narrow end of a tapered tube through the side of the tube and flaring this end out to join the other end

klepht \ˈkleft\ *n, often cap* [ModGk *klephtēs,* lit., robber, fr. Gk *kleptēs,* fr. *kleptein*] (1820) **:** a Greek belonging to any of several independent guerrilla communities formed after the Turkish conquest of Greece — **kleph·tic** \ˈklef-tik\ *adj, often cap*

klep·to \ˈklep-(ˌ)tō\ *n, pl* **kleptos** (1953) **:** KLEPTOMANIAC

klepto- *comb form* [Gk, fr. *kleptein* to steal; akin to Goth *hlifan* to steal, L *clepere*] **:** stealing **:** theft ⟨*klepto*mania⟩

klep·toc·ra·cy \klep-ˈtä-krə-sē\ *n, pl* **-cies** (1819) **:** government by those who seek chiefly status and personal gain at the expense of the governed; *also* **:** a particular government of this kind — **klep·to·crat** \ˈklep-tə-ˌkrat\ *n* — **klep·to·crat·ic** \ˌklep-tə-ˈkra-tik\ *adj*

klep·to·ma·nia \ˌklep-tə-ˈmā-nē-ə, -nyə\ *n* [NL] (1830) **:** a persistent neurotic impulse to steal esp. without economic motive

klep·to·ma·ni·ac \-nē-ˌak\ *n* (1861) **:** a person evidencing kleptomania

klez·mer \ˈklez-mər\ *n, pl* **klez·mo·rim** \(ˌ)klez-ˈmȯr-əm\ [Yiddish, fr. Heb *kĕlēy zemer* musical instruments] (1908) **1 :** a Jewish instrumentalist esp. of traditional eastern European music **2 :** the music played by klezmorim

klieg light *or* **kleig light** \ˈklēg-\ *n* [John H. *Kliegl* †1959 & Anton T. *Kliegl* †1927 German-born Am. lighting experts] (1919) **:** a carbon arc lamp used esp. in making motion pictures

Kline·fel·ter's syndrome \ˈklīn-ˌfel-tərz-\ *n* [Harry F. *Klinefelter* †1990 Am. physician] (1950) **:** an abnormal condition in a male characterized by usu. two X and one Y chromosomes, infertility, smallness of the testicles, sparse facial and body hair, and enlarged breasts — called also *Klinefelter syndrome*

klis·ter \ˈklis-tər\ *n* [Norw, lit., paste, fr. MLG *klīster*] (1936) **:** a soft wax used on skis

kloof \ˈklüf\ *n* [Afrik] (1731) *SoAfr* **:** a deep glen **:** RAVINE

kludge \ˈklüj\ *or* **kluge** \ˈklüj, *US also & Brit esp* ˈkləj; ˈklü-jē\ *n* [origin unknown] (1962) **:** a system and esp. a computer system made up of poorly matched components — **kludgy** *also* **kludgey** \ˈklü-jē, *US also & Brit esp* ˈklə-\ *adj*

klutz \ˈkləts\ *n* [Yiddish *klots,* lit., wooden beam, fr. MHG *kloz* lumpy mass — more at CLOUT] (1960) **:** a clumsy person — **klutz·i·ness** \ˈklət-sē-nəs\ *n* — **klutzy** \ˈklət-sē\ *adj*

kly·stron \ˈklī-ˌsträn\ *n* [fr. *Klystron,* a trademark] (1939) **:** an electron tube in which bunching of electrons is produced by electric fields and which is used for the generation and amplification of ultrahigh-frequency current

km *abbr* kilometer

K–me·son \ˈkā-\ *n* (1951) **:** KAON

kmh *or* **kmph** *abbr* kilometers per hour

kmps *abbr* kilometers per second

kn *abbr* knot

knack \ˈnak\ *n* [ME *knak*] (14c) **1 a :** a clever trick or stratagem **b :** a clever way of doing something **2 :** a special ready capacity that is hard to analyze or teach **3** *archaic* **:** an ingenious device; *broadly* **:** TOY, KNICKKNACK ***syn*** see GIFT

knack·er \ˈna-kər\ *n* [prob. fr. E dial., saddlemaker] (1812) **1** *Brit* **:** a buyer of worn-out domestic animals or their carcasses for use esp. as animal food or fertilizer **2** *Brit* **:** a buyer of old structures for their constituent materials

knack·ered \ˈna-kərd\ *adj* [E slang *knacker* to kill, tire, perh. fr. *knacker,* n.] (1886) *Brit* **:** TIRED, EXHAUSTED

knackwurst *var of* KNOCKWURST

\ə\ **abut** \ᵊ\ **kitten, F table** \ər\ **further** \a\ **ash** \ā\ **ace** \ä\ **mop, mar** \au̇\ **out** \ch\ **chin** \e\ **bet** \ē\ **easy** \g\ **go** \i\ **hit** \ī\ **ice** \j\ **job** \ŋ\ **sing** \ō\ **go** \ȯ\ **law** \ȯi\ **boy** \th\ **thin** \t͟h\ **the** \ü\ **loot** \u̇\ **foot** \y\ **yet** \zh\ **vision, beige** \k͟, ⁿ, œ, ue, ʸ\ *see* Guide to Pronunciation

[1]**knap** \ˈnap\ *n* [ME, fr. OE *cnæp;* akin to OE *cnotta* knot] (bef. 12c) **1** *chiefly dial* : a crest of a hill : SUMMIT **2** *chiefly dial* : a small hill

[2]**knap** *vt* **knapped; knap·ping** [ME *knappen,* of imit. origin] (15c) **1** *dial Brit* : [2]RAP 1 **2** : to break with a quick blow; *esp* : to shape (as flints) by breaking off pieces **3** *dial Brit* : SNAP, CROP **4** *dial Brit* : CHATTER — **knap·per** *n*

knap·sack \ˈnap-ˌsak\ *n* [LG *knappsack* or D *knapzak,* fr. LG & D *knappen* to make a snapping noise, eat + LG *sack* or D *zak* sack] (1603) : a bag (as of canvas or nylon) strapped on the back and used for carrying supplies or personal belongings — **knap·sacked** \-ˌsakt\ *adj*

knap·weed \-ˌwēd\ *n* [ME *knopwed,* fr. *knop* knop + *wed* weed] (15c) : any of various weedy centaureas; *esp* : a widely naturalized European perennial (*Centaurea nigra*) with tough wiry stems and knobby heads of purple flowers

knave \ˈnāv\ *n* [ME, fr. OE *cnafa;* akin to OHG *knabo* boy] (bef. 12c) **1** *archaic* **a** : a boy servant **b** : a male servant **c** : a man of humble birth or position **2** : a tricky deceitful fellow **3** : JACK 6a

knav·ery \ˈnā-və-rē, ˈnāv-rē\ *n, pl* **-er·ies** (1528) **1 a** : RASCALITY **b** : a roguish or mischievous act **2** *obs* : roguish mischief

knav·ish \ˈnā-vish\ *adj* (14c) : of, relating to, or characteristic of a knave; *esp* : DISHONEST — **knav·ish·ly** *adv*

knead \ˈnēd\ *vt* [ME *kneden,* fr. OE *cnedan;* akin to OHG *knetan* to knead] (bef. 12c) **1 a** : to work and press into a mass with or as if with the hands ⟨~*ing* dough⟩ **b** : to manipulate or massage with a kneading motion ⟨~*ed* sore neck muscles⟩ **2** : to form or shape by or as if by kneading — **knead·able** \ˈnē-də-bəl\ *adj* — **knead·er** *n*

[1]**knee** \ˈnē\ *n, often attrib* [ME, fr. OE *cnēow;* akin to OHG *kneo* knee, L *genu,* Gk *gony*] (bef. 12c) **1 a** : a joint in the middle part of the human leg that is the articulation between the femur, tibia, and patella; *also* : the part of the leg that includes this joint **b** (1) : the joint in the hind leg of a four-footed vertebrate that corresponds to the human knee (2) : the carpal joint of the foreleg of a four-footed vertebrate **c** : the tarsal joint of a bird **d** : the joint between the femur and tibia of an insect **2** : something resembling the human knee: as **a** : a piece of timber naturally or artificially bent for use in supporting structures coming together at an angle (as the deck beams of a ship) **b** : a rounded or conical process rising from the roots of various swamp-growing trees ⟨cypress ~⟩ **3** : the part of a garment covering the knee **4** : a blow with the bent knee — **kneed** \ˈnēd\ *adj* — **to one's knees** : into a state of submission or defeat

[2]**knee** *vt* **kneed; knee·ing** (bef. 12c) **1** *archaic* : to bend the knee to **2** : to strike with the knee

knee breeches *n pl* (1833) : BREECH 1a

knee·cap \ˈnē-ˌkap\ *n* (1869) : PATELLA

knee·cap·ping \ˈnē-ˌka-piŋ\ *n* (1974) : the terroristic act or practice of maiming a person's knees (as by gunshot) — **kneecap** *vt*

knee–deep \-ˈdēp\ *adj* (15c) **1 a** : sunk to the knees ⟨~ in mud⟩ **b** : deeply engaged or occupied ⟨~ in work⟩ **2** : KNEE-HIGH

knee–high \-ˈhī\ *adj* (1743) : rising or reaching upward to the knees ⟨~ stockings⟩ — **knee–high** \-ˌhī\ *n*

knee·hole \-ˌhōl\ *n* (1893) : an open space (as under a desk) for the knees

knee–jerk \ˈnē-ˌjərk, -ˈjərk\ *adj* (1951) : readily predictable : AUTOMATIC ⟨~ reactions⟩; *also* : reacting in a readily predictable way ⟨~ liberals⟩

knee jerk *n* (1876) : an involuntary forward kick produced by a light blow on the tendon below the patella

kneel \ˈnēl\ *vi* **knelt** \ˈnelt\ *or* **kneeled; kneel·ing** [ME *knelen,* fr. OE *cnēowlian;* akin to OE *cnēow* knee] (bef. 12c) : to bend the knee : fall or rest on the knees

kneel·er \ˈnē-lər\ *n* (14c) **1** : one that kneels **2** : something (as a cushion or board) to kneel on

knee·pan \ˈnē-ˌpan\ *n* (15c) : PATELLA

knee–slap·per \-ˌsla-pər\ *n* (1966) : an extremely funny joke, line, or story

knee·sock \-ˌsäk\ *n* (1964) : a knee-high sock

[1]**knell** \ˈnel\ *vb* [ME, fr. OE *cnyllan;* akin to MHG *erknellen* to toll] *vt* (bef. 12c) : to summon or announce by or as if by a knell ~ *vi* **1** : to ring esp. for a death, funeral, or disaster : TOLL **2** : to sound in an ominous manner or with an ominous effect

[2]**knell** *n* (bef. 12c) **1** : a stroke or sound of a bell esp. when rung slowly (as for a death, funeral, or disaster) **2** : an indication of the end or the failure of something ⟨sounded the death ~ for our hopes⟩

knew *past of* KNOW

knick·er·bock·er \ˈni-kə(r)-ˌbä-kər\ *n* [Diedrich *Knickerbocker,* fictitious author of *History of New York* (1809) by Washington Irving] (1848) **1** *cap* : a descendant of the early Dutch settlers of New York; *broadly* : a native or resident of the city or state of New York — used as a nickname **2** *pl* : KNICKERS

knick·ers \ˈni-kərz\ *n pl* [short for *knickerbockers*] (1881) **1** : loose-fitting short pants gathered at the knee **2** *chiefly Brit* : UNDERPANTS

knick·knack *also* **nick·nack** \ˈnik-ˌnak\ *n* [redupl. of *knack*] (1682) : a small trivial article usu. intended for ornament

[1]**knife** \ˈnīf\ *n, pl* **knives** \ˈnīvz\ *often attrib* [ME *knif,* fr. OE *cnīf,* perh. fr. ON *knīfr;* akin to MLG *knīf* knife] (bef. 12c) **1 a** : a cutting instrument consisting of a sharp blade fastened to a handle **b** : a weapon resembling a knife **2** : a sharp cutting blade or tool in a machine **3** : SURGERY 4 — usu. used in the phrase *under the knife* — **knife·like** \ˈnīf-ˌlīk\ *adj*

[2]**knife** *vb* **knifed; knif·ing** *vt* (1865) **1** : to use a knife on; *specif* : to stab, slash, or wound with a knife **2** : to cut, mark, or spread with a knife **3** : to try to defeat by underhanded means **4** : to move like a knife in ⟨birds *knifing* the autumn sky⟩ ~ *vi* : to cut a way with or as if with a knife blade ⟨the cruiser *knifed* through the heavy seas⟩

knife–edge \ˈnīf-ˌej\ *n* (1818) **1** : a sharp wedge of steel or other hard material used as a fulcrum for a lever beam in a precision instrument **2** : a sharp narrow knifelike edge

knife·point \-ˌpȯint\ *n* (ca. 1911) : the point of a knife — **at knifepoint** : under a threat of being knifed

[1]**knight** \ˈnīt\ *n* [ME, fr. OE *cniht* man-at-arms, boy, servant; akin to OHG *kneht* youth, military follower] (bef. 12c) **1 a** (1) : a mounted man-at-arms serving a feudal superior; *esp* : a man ceremonially inducted into special military rank usu. after completing service as page and squire (2) : a man honored by a sovereign for merit and in Great Britain ranking below a baronet (3) : a person of antiquity equal to a knight in rank **b** : a man devoted to the service of a lady as her attendant or champion **c** : a member of an order or society **2** : either of two pieces of each color in a set of chessmen having the power to make an L-shaped move of two squares in one row and one square in a perpendicular row over squares that may be occupied

[2]**knight** *vt* (13c) : to make a knight of

knight–er·rant \ˌnīt-ˈer-ənt\ *n, pl* **knights–errant** (14c) : a knight traveling in search of adventures in which to exhibit military skill, prowess, and generosity

knight–er·rant·ry \-ˈer-ən-trē\ *n, pl* **knight–errantries** (1620) **1** : the practice or actions of a knight-errant **2** : quixotic conduct

knight·hood \ˈnīt-ˌhu̇d\ *n* (13c) **1** : the rank, dignity, or profession of a knight **2** : the qualities befitting a knight : CHIVALRY **3** : knights as a class or body

knight·ly \ˈnīt-lē\ *adj* (14c) **1** : of, relating to, or characteristic of a knight ⟨tales of ~ adventures⟩ **2** : made up of knights — **knight·li·ness** *n* — **knightly** *adv*

Knight of Co·lum·bus \-kə-ˈləm-bəs\ *n, pl* **Knights of Columbus** [Christopher *Columbus*] (1882) : a member of a benevolent and fraternal society of Roman Catholic men

Knight of Pyth·i·as \-ˈpi-thē-əs\ *n, pl* **Knights of Pythias** (1869) : a member of a secret benevolent and fraternal order

Knight of the Mac·ca·bees \-ˈma-kə-ˌbēz\ *n, pl* **Knights of the Maccabees** (1922) : a member of a secret benevolent society

Knight Templar *n, pl* **Knights Templars** *or* **Knights Templar** (1610) **1** : TEMPLAR 1 **2** : a member of an order of Freemasonry conferring three orders in the York rite

knish \kə-ˈnish\ *n* [Yiddish, fr. Pol *knysz*] (1916) : a small round or square of dough stuffed with a filling (as potato) and baked or fried

[1]**knit** \ˈnit\ *vb* **knit** *or* **knit·ted; knit·ting** [ME *knitten,* fr. OE *cnyttan;* akin to OE *cnotta* knot] *vt* (bef. 12c) **1** *chiefly dial* : to tie together **2 a** : to link firmly or closely ⟨*knitted* my hands⟩ **b** : to cause to grow together ⟨time and rest will ~ a fractured bone⟩ **c** : to contract into wrinkles ⟨*knitted* her brow⟩ **3** : to form by interlacing yarn or thread in a series of connected loops with needles ~ *vi* **1** : to make knitted fabrics or objects **2 a** : to become compact **b** : to grow together **c** : to become drawn together — **knit·ter** *n*

[2]**knit** *n* (1596) **1** : KNIT STITCH **2 a** : a knit fabric **b** *pl* : KNITWEAR

knit stitch *n* (ca. 1885) : a basic knitting stitch usu. made with the yarn at the back of the work by inserting the right needle into the front part of a loop on the left needle from the left side, catching the yarn with the point of the right needle, and bringing it through the first loop to form a new loop — compare PURL STITCH

knit·ting *n* (15c) **1** : the action or method of one that knits **2** : work done or being done by one that knits

knit·wear \ˈnit-ˌwer\ *n* (1926) : knitted clothing

knob \ˈnäb\ *n* [ME *knobbe;* akin to MLG *knubbe* knob] (14c) **1 a** : a rounded protuberance : LUMP **b** : a small rounded ornament or handle **2** : a rounded usu. isolated hill or mountain — **knobbed** \ˈnäbd\ *adj* — **knob·by** \ˈnä-bē\ *adj*

knob·bly \ˈnä-b(ə-)lē\ *adj* (1859) : having very small knobs ⟨a ~ walking stick⟩

knob·ker·rie \ˈnäb-ˌker-ē\ *n* [Afrik *knopkierie,* fr. *knop* knob + *kierie* club] (1844) : a short wooden club with a knob at one end used as a missile or in close attack esp. by Zulus of southern Africa

[1]**knock** \ˈnäk\ *vb* [ME *knoken,* fr. OE *cnocian;* akin to MHG *knochen* to press] *vi* (bef. 12c) **1** : to strike something with a sharp blow **2** : to collide with something **3 a** : BUSTLE ⟨heard them ~*ing* around in the kitchen⟩ **b** : WANDER ⟨~*ed* about Europe all summer⟩ **4 a** : to make a pounding noise **b** : to have engine knock **5** : to find fault ~ *vt* **1 a** (1) : to strike sharply (2) : to drive, force, or make by or as if by so striking ⟨was ~*ed* out of the campaign⟩ **b** : to set forcibly in motion with a blow **2** : to cause to collide **3** : to find fault with ⟨always ~*ing* those in authority⟩ — **knock cold** : KNOCK OUT 2a(1) — **knock dead** : to move strongly esp. to admiration or applause ⟨a comedian who really *knocks* them *dead*⟩ — **knock for a loop 1 a** : OVERCOME ⟨*knocked* my opponent *for a loop*⟩ **b** : DEMOLISH ⟨*knocked* our idea *for a loop*⟩ **2** : DUMBFOUND, AMAZE ⟨the news *knocked* them *for a loop*⟩ — **knock one's socks off** : to overwhelm or amaze one ⟨a performance that will *knock your socks off*⟩ — **knock on wood** — used interjectionally to ward off misfortune — **knock together** : to make or assemble esp. hurriedly or in a makeshift way ⟨*knocked together* my own bookcase⟩

[2]**knock** *n* (14c) **1 a** : a sharp blow : RAP, HIT ⟨a loud ~ on the door⟩ **b** (1) : a severe misfortune or hardship (2) : SETBACK, REVERSAL **2 a** : a pounding noise **b** : a sharp repetitive metallic noise caused by abnormal ignition in an automobile engine **3** : a harsh and often petty criticism ⟨the ~ on him was that he couldn't handle the pressure⟩

knock·about \ˈnäk-ə-ˌbau̇t\ *adj* (1880) **1** : suitable for rough use ⟨~ clothing⟩ **2 a** : being noisy and rough : BOISTEROUS ⟨~ games⟩ **b** : characterized by boisterous antics and often extravagant burlesque ⟨~ comedy⟩ **3** *of a sailing vessel* : having a simplified rig marked by absence of bowsprit and topmast ⟨a ~ sloop⟩ — **knockabout** *n*

knock back *vt* (ca. 1931) : DRINK, SWALLOW; *specif* : to toss down (an alcoholic beverage)

[1]**knock·down** \ˈnäk-ˌdau̇n\ *adj* (1690) **1** : having such force as to strike down or overwhelm ⟨a bewildering assortment of ~ arguments —J. W. Krutch⟩ **2** : that can easily be assembled or disassembled ⟨a ~ table⟩ **3** *chiefly Brit* : extremely low : REDUCED ⟨~ prices⟩

[2]**knockdown** *n* (1809) **1** : the action of knocking down **2** : something (as a blow) that strikes down or overwhelms **3** : something (as a piece of furniture) that can be easily assembled or disassembled

knock down \-ˈdau̇n\ *vt* (15c) **1** : to strike to the ground with or as if with a sharp blow : FELL **2** : to dispose of (an item) to a bidder at an auction sale **3** : to take apart : DISASSEMBLE **4** : to receive as income or salary : EARN ⟨positions where they were able to *knock down* good money —*Infantry Jour.*⟩ **5** : REDUCE ⟨*knocked* the price *down*⟩

knock–down, drag–out *or* **knock–down–and–drag–out** *adj* (1834) : marked by extreme violence or bitterness and by the showing of no mercy ⟨~ political debates⟩ — **knock–down–drag–out** *n*

knock·er \ˈnä-kər\ *n* (14c) **1** : one that knocks: as **a** : a metal ring, bar, or hammer hinged to a door for use in knocking **b** : a persistently pessimistic critic **2** *often vulgar* : BREAST — usu. used in pl.

knock–knee \ˈnäk-ˈnē, -ˌnē\ *n* (1879) : a condition in which the legs curve inward at the knees — **knock–kneed** \-ˈnēd\ *adj*

knock·off \ˈnäk-ˌȯf\ *n* (1966) : a copy that sells for less than the original; *broadly* : a copy or imitation of someone or something popular

knock off *vi* (1649) : to stop doing something ∼ *vt* **1** : to do hurriedly or routinely ⟨*knocked off* one painting after another⟩ **2** : DISCONTINUE, STOP ⟨*knocked off* work at five⟩ **3** : DEDUCT ⟨*knocked off* a little to make the price more attractive⟩ **4 a** : KILL ⟨*knocked off* two men . . . on mercenary grounds —Lewis Baker⟩ **b** : OVERCOME, DEFEAT ⟨*knocked off* each center of rebellion⟩ **5** : ROB ⟨*knocked off* a couple of banks⟩ **6** : to make a knockoff of : COPY, IMITATE ⟨*knocks off* popular dress designs⟩

knock·out \ˈnäk-ˌau̇t\ *n* (1887) **1 a** : the act of knocking out : the condition of being knocked out **b (1)** : the termination of a boxing match when one boxer has been knocked down and is unable to rise and resume boxing within a specified time **(2)** : TECHNICAL KNOCKOUT **c** : a blow that knocks out an opponent **2** : a sensationally striking, appealing, or attractive person or thing

knockout *adj* (1818) **1** : causing a knockout ⟨a ∼ blow⟩ **2** : sensationally striking, appealing, or attractive ⟨a ∼ dress⟩ **3** : having all or part of a gene eliminated or inactivated by genetic engineering ⟨∼ mice predisposed to diabetes mellitus⟩

knock out *vt* (1856) **1** : to produce roughly or hastily **2 a (1)** : to defeat (a boxing opponent) by a knockout **(2)** : to make unconscious ⟨the drug *knocked* him *out*⟩ **b** : to make inoperative or useless ⟨electricity was *knocked out* by the storm⟩ **c** : to get rid of : ELIMINATE ⟨*knocked out* illegal gambling⟩ **3** : to tire out : EXHAUST ⟨*knocked* themselves *out* with work⟩ **4** : to cause (an opposing pitcher) to be removed from a baseball game by a batting rally

knockout drops *n pl* (1895) : drops of a solution of a drug (as chloral hydrate) put into a drink to produce unconsciousness or stupefaction

knock over *vt* (ca. 1814) **1 a (1)** : to strike to the ground : FELL **(2)** : OVERWHELM ⟨was *knocked over* by the news⟩ **b** : ELIMINATE ⟨*knocked over* every difficulty⟩ **2 a** : STEAL; *esp* : HIJACK ⟨*knocks over* a truckload of merchandise —J. B. Martin⟩ **b** : ROB ⟨*knocking over* a bank⟩

knock up *vt* (1592) **1** *Brit* : ROUSE, SUMMON **2** *sometimes vulgar* : to make pregnant

knock·wurst *also* **knack·wurst** \ˈnäk-(ˌ)wərst *also* -ˌvu̇(r)st, *sometimes* -ˌvu̇sht\ *n* [G *Knackwurst,* fr. *knacken* to crackle (of imit. origin) + *Wurst* wurst] (ca. 1929) : a short thick heavily seasoned sausage

¹knoll \ˈnōl\ *n* [ME *knol,* fr. OE *cnoll;* akin to ON *knollr* mountaintop] (bef. 12c) : a small round hill : MOUND

²knoll *vb* [ME, prob. alter. of *knellen* to knell] (15c) *archaic* : KNELL

knop \ˈnäp\ *n* [ME, fr. OE *-cnoppa* knob] (bef. 12c) : a usu. ornamental knob — **knopped** \ˈnäpt\ *adj*

¹knot \ˈnät\ *n* [ME, fr. OE *cnotta;* akin to OHG *knoto* knot] (bef. 12c) **1 a** : an interlacement of the parts of one or more flexible bodies forming a lump or knob (as for fastening or tying together) **b** : the lump or knob so formed **c** : a tight constriction or the sense of constriction ⟨my stomach was all in ∼*s*⟩ **2** : something hard to solve : PROBLEM ⟨a matter full of legal ∼*s*⟩ **3** : a bond of union; *esp* : the marriage bond **4 a** : a protuberant lump or swelling in tissue ⟨a ∼ in a gland⟩ **b** : the base of a woody branch enclosed in the stem from which it arises; *also* : its section in lumber **5** : a cluster of persons or things : GROUP **6** : an ornamental bow of ribbon : COCKADE **7 a** : a division of the log's line serving to measure a ship's speed **b (1)** : one nautical mile per hour **(2)** : one nautical mile — not used technically **8** : a closed curve in three-dimensional space

²knot *vb* **knot·ted; knot·ting** *vt* (1547) **1** : to tie in or with a knot : form knots in **2** : to unite closely or intricately : ENTANGLE **3** : TIE 4b ⟨*knotted* the score⟩ ∼ *vi* : to form knots — **knot·ter** *n*

³knot *n, pl* **knots** *or* **knot** [ME *knott*] (15c) : either of two sandpipers (*Calidris canutus* and *C. tenuirostris*) that breed in the Arctic and winter in temperate or warm parts of the New and Old World

knot garden *n* (1519) : an elaborately designed garden esp. of flowers or herbs

knot·grass \ˈnät-ˌgras\ *n* (1538) **1** : a cosmopolitan prostrate weed (*Polygonum aviculare*) of the buckwheat family with jointed stems, prominent sheathing stipules, and minute flowers; *broadly* : any of several congeneric plants **2** : any of several grasses (as *Paspalum distichum*) with markedly jointed stems

knot 1b: *1* Blackwall hitch, *2* carrick bend, *3* clove hitch, *4* cat's-paw, *5* figure eight, *6* granny knot, *7* bowline, *8* overhand knot, *9* fisherman's bend, *10* half hitch, *11* square knot, *12* slipknot, *13* stevedore knot, *14* true lover's knot, *15* surgeon's knot, *16* Turk's head, *17* sheet bend, *18* timber hitch, *19* seizing, *20* rolling hitch, *21* sheepshank

knot·hole \-ˌhōl\ *n* (1726) : a hole in a board or tree trunk where a knot or branch has come out

knotted *adj* (12c) **1** : tied in or with a knot **2** : full of knots : GNARLED **3** : KNOTTY **4** : ornamented with knots or knobs

knot theory *n* (1981) : a branch of topology concerned with the properties and classification of mathematical knots — **knot theorist** *n*

knot·ty \ˈnä-tē\ *adj* **knot·ti·er; -est** (13c) : marked by or full of knots; *esp* : so full of difficulties and complications as to be likely to defy solution ⟨a ∼ problem⟩ ***syn*** see COMPLEX — **knot·ti·ness** *n*

knotty pine *n* (ca. 1898) : pine wood that has a decorative distribution of knots and is used esp. for interior finish

knot·weed \ˈnät-ˌwēd\ *n* (1884) : any of several herbs (genus *Polygonum*) of the buckwheat family with leaves and bracts jointed and having a very short petiole; *broadly* : POLYGONUM

knout \ˈnau̇t, *sometimes* ˈnüt\ *n* [Russ *knut,* of Scand origin; akin to ON *knūtr* knot; akin to OE *cnotta*] (1716) : a whip used for flogging — **knout** *vt*

¹know \ˈnō\ *vb* **knew** \ˈnü *also* ˈnyü\; **known** \ˈnōn\; **know·ing** [ME, fr. OE *cnāwan;* akin to OHG bi*chnāan* to recognize, L *gnoscere, noscere* to come to know, Gk *gignōskein*] *vt* (bef. 12c) **1 a (1)** : to perceive directly : have direct cognition of **(2)** : to have understanding of ⟨importance of ∼*ing* oneself⟩ **(3)** : to recognize the nature of : DISCERN **b (1)** : to recognize as being the same as something previously known **(2)** : to be acquainted or familiar with **(3)** : to have experience of **2 a** : to be aware of the truth or factuality of : be convinced or certain of **b** : to have a practical understanding of ⟨∼*s* how to write⟩ **3** *archaic* : to have sexual intercourse with ∼ *vi* **1** : to have knowledge **2** : to be or become cognizant — sometimes used interjectionally with *you* esp. as a filler in informal speech — **know·able** \ˈnō-ə-bəl\ *adj* — **know·er** \ˈnō-ər\ *n* — **know from** : to have knowledge of ⟨didn't *know from* sibling rivalry —Penny Marshall⟩

²know *n* (1592) : KNOWLEDGE — **in the know** : in possession of exclusive knowledge or information; *broadly* : WELL-INFORMED

know–all \ˈnō-ˌȯl\ *n* (ca. 1864) *chiefly Brit* : KNOW-IT-ALL

know–how \ˈnō-ˌhau̇\ *n* (1838) : knowledge of how to do something smoothly and efficiently : EXPERTISE

¹knowing *n* (14c) : ACQUAINTANCE, COGNIZANCE

²knowing *adj* (14c) **1** : having or reflecting knowledge, information, or intelligence **2 a** : shrewdly and keenly alert : ASTUTE ⟨a ∼ observer⟩ **b** : indicating possession of exclusive inside knowledge or information ⟨a ∼ smile⟩ **3** : COGNITIVE **4** : DELIBERATE ⟨∼ interference in the affairs of another⟩ — **know·ing·ly** *adv* — **know·ing·ness** *n*

know–it–all \ˈnō-ət-ˌȯl\ *n* (1895) : one who claims to know everything; *also* : one who disdains advice — **know–it–all** *adj*

knowl·edge \ˈnä-lij\ *n* [ME *knowlege,* fr. *knowlechen* to acknowledge, irreg. fr. *knowen*] (14c) **1** *obs* : COGNIZANCE **2 a (1)** : the fact or condition of knowing something with familiarity gained through experience or association **(2)** : acquaintance with or understanding of a science, art, or technique **b (1)** : the fact or condition of being aware of something **(2)** : the range of one's information or understanding ⟨answered to the best of my ∼⟩ **c** : the circumstance or condition of apprehending truth or fact through reasoning : COGNITION **d** : the fact or condition of having information or of being learned ⟨a person of unusual ∼⟩ **3** *archaic* : SEXUAL INTERCOURSE **4 a** : the sum of what is known : the body of truth, information, and principles acquired by humankind **b** *archaic* : a branch of learning

syn KNOWLEDGE, LEARNING, ERUDITION, SCHOLARSHIP mean what is or can be known by an individual or by humankind. KNOWLEDGE applies to facts or ideas acquired by study, investigation, observation, or experience ⟨rich in the *knowledge* of human nature⟩. LEARNING applies to knowledge acquired esp. through formal, often advanced, schooling ⟨a book that demonstrates vast *learning*⟩. ERUDITION strongly implies the acquiring of profound, recondite, or bookish learning ⟨an *erudition* unusual even in a scholar⟩. SCHOLARSHIP implies the possession of learning characteristic of the advanced scholar in a specialized field of study or investigation ⟨a work of first-rate literary *scholarship*⟩.

knowl·edge·able \ˈnä-lij-ə-bəl\ *adj* (1829) : having or showing knowledge or intelligence — **knowl·edge·abil·i·ty** \ˌnä-li-jə-ˈbi-lə-tē\ *n* — **knowl·edge·able·ness** *n* — **knowl·edge·ably** \-blē\ *adv*

knowledge engineering *n* (1980) : a branch of artificial intelligence that emphasizes the development and use of expert systems — **knowledge engineer** *n*

known *adj* (13c) : generally recognized ⟨a ∼ authority on art⟩

know–noth·ing \ˈnō-ˌnə-thiŋ\ *n* (1827) **1 a** : IGNORAMUS **b** : AGNOSTIC **2** *cap K&N* : a member of a 19th century secret American political organization hostile to the political influence of recent immigrants and Roman Catholics — **know–nothing** *adj*

know–noth·ing·ism \-thiŋ-ˌi-zəm\ *n* (1854) **1** *cap K&N* : the principles and policies of the Know-Nothings **2** : the condition of knowing nothing or desiring to know nothing or the conviction that nothing can be known with certainty esp. in religion or morality **3** *often cap K&N* : a mid-20th century political attitude characterized by anti-intellectualism, exaggerated patriotism, and fear of foreign subversive influences

¹knuck·le \ˈnə-kəl\ *n* [ME *knokel;* akin to MHG *knöchel* knuckle] (14c) **1 a** : the rounded prominence formed by the ends of the two adjacent bones at a joint — used esp. of those at the joints of the fingers **b** : the joint of a knuckle **2** : a cut of meat consisting of the tarsal or carpal joint with the adjoining flesh **3** : something resembling a knuckle: as **a (1)** : one of the joining parts of a hinge through which a pin or rivet passes **(2)** : KNUCKLE JOINT **b** : the meeting of two surfaces at a sharp angle (as in a roof) **c** : a pivotal point **4** *pl* : a set of metal finger rings or guards attached to a transverse piece and worn over the front of the doubled fist for use as a weapon — called also *brass knuckles* — **knuck·led** *adj*

²knuckle *vb* **knuck·led; knuck·ling** \ˈnə-k(ə-)liŋ\ *vi* (1740) : to place the knuckles on the ground in shooting a marble ∼ *vt* : to press or rub with the knuckles

knuck·le·ball \ˈnə-kəl-ˌbȯl\ *n* (1910) : a slow baseball pitch that moves erratically and unpredictably and that is thrown with little spin by gripping the ball with the knuckles or the tips of the fingers pressed against the top — **knuck·le·ball·er** \-ˌbȯ-lər\ *n*

knuck·le·bone \ˈnək-əl-ˌbōn\ *n* (1577) **1 :** a bone (as a metatarsus or metacarpus of a sheep) used in games and formerly in divination **2** *pl but sing in constr* **:** a game played with knucklebones or jacks

knuckle down *vi* (ca. 1864) **:** to apply oneself earnestly

knuck·le–dust·er \ˈnə-kəl-ˌdəs-tər\ *n* (1858) **:** KNUCKLE 4

knuck·le·head \-ˌhed\ *n* (1942) **:** DUMBBELL 2 — **knuck·le·head·ed** \-ˌhed-əd\ *adj*

knuckle joint *n* (ca. 1864) **:** a hinge joint in which a projection with an eye on one piece enters a jaw between two corresponding projections with eyes on another piece and is retained by a pin or rivet

knuck·ler \ˈnə-k(ə-)lər\ *n* (1928) **:** KNUCKLEBALL

knuckle under *vi* (1869) **:** GIVE IN, SUBMIT

knur \ˈnər\ *n* [ME *knorre;* akin to MHG *knorre* burl] (14c) **:** a hard excrescence (as on a tree trunk) **:** GNARL

knurl \ˈnər(-ə)l\ *n* [prob. blend of *knur* and *gnarl*] (1608) **1 :** a small protuberance, excrescence, or knob **2 :** one of a series of small ridges or beads on a metal surface to aid in gripping — **knurled** \ˈnər(-ə)ld\ *adj* — **knurly** \ˈnər-lē\ *adj*

[1]**KO** \(ˌ)kā-ˈō, ˈkā-(ˌ)ō\ *n* [*k*nock *o*ut] (1911) **:** KNOCKOUT

[2]**KO** *vt* **KO'd** \kā-ˈōd, ˈkā-(ˌ)ōd\; **KO'·ing** \-ˈō-iŋ, -(ˌ)ō-\ (1926) **:** to knock out (as in boxing)

koa \ˈkō-ə\ *n* [Hawaiian] (1824) **1 :** a Hawaiian timber tree (*Acacia koa*) with crescent-shaped phyllodes and pale yellow flowers borne in small round heads **2 :** the fine-grained red wood of the koa used esp. for furniture

ko·ala \kə-ˈwä-lə, kō-ˈä-\ *n* [Dharuk (Australian aboriginal language of the Port Jackson area) *gula, gulawan^{y}*] (1803) **:** an Australian arboreal marsupial (*Phascolarctos cinereus*) that has a broad head, large hairy ears, dense gray fur, and sharp claws and feeds on eucalyptus leaves — called also *koala bear*

ko·an \ˈkō-ˌän\ *n* [Jp *kōan,* fr. *kō* public + *an* proposition] (1945) **:** a paradox to be meditated upon that is used to train Zen Buddhist monks to abandon ultimate dependence on reason and to force them into gaining sudden intuitive enlightenment

Ko·be beef \ˈkō-bē-, -ˌbā-\ *n* [*Kobe,* Japan] (1889) **:** highly marbled premium beef from Japanese cattle that is noted for exceptional tenderness and flavor

ko·bo \ˈkō-(ˌ)bō\ *n, pl* **kobo** [alter. of [1]*copper*] (1972) — see *naira* at MONEY table

ko·bold \ˈkō-ˌbȯld\ *n* [G — more at COBALT] (1830) **1 :** a gnome that in German folklore inhabits underground places **2 :** an often mischievous domestic spirit of German folklore

Ko·di·ak bear \ˈkō-dē-ˌak-\ *n* [*Kodiak* Island, Alaska] (1899) **:** a large brown bear of the southern coast of Alaska and adjacent islands

K of C *abbr* Knights of Columbus

kohl \ˈkōl\ *n* [Ar *kuḥl*] (1799) **:** a preparation used esp. in Arabia and Egypt to darken the edges of the eyelids

kohl·ra·bi \kōl-ˈrä-bē *also* -ˈra-\ *n, pl* **-bies** [G, fr. It *cavolo rapa,* fr. *cavolo* cabbage + *rapa* turnip] (1807) **:** a cabbage (*Brassica oleracea gongylodes*) having a greatly enlarged, fleshy, turnip-shaped edible stem; *also* **:** its stem used as a vegetable

koi \ˈkȯi\ *n, pl* **koi** [Jp] (1727) **:** a carp (*Cyprinus carpio*) bred esp. in Japan for large size and a variety of colors and often stocked in ornamental ponds

koi·ne *also* **koi·né** \kȯi-ˈnā, ˈkȯi-ˌ; kē-ˈnē\ *n* [Gk *koinē,* fr. fem. of *koinos* common] (1909) **1** *cap* **:** the Greek language commonly spoken and written in eastern Mediterranean countries in the Hellenistic and Roman periods **2 :** a dialect or language of a region that has become the common or standard language of a larger area

ko·kan·ee \kō-ˈka-nē\ *n* [perh. fr. Shuswap (Salishan language of British Columbia) *kəknǽx^{w}*] (1933) **:** a small landlocked sockeye salmon

kok–sa·ghyz *or* **kok–sa·gyz** \ˌkōk-sə-ˈgēz, ˌkäk-, -ˈgiz\ *n* [Russ *kok-sagyz*] (1932) **:** a perennial Asian dandelion (*Taraxacum kok-saghyz*) cultivated for its fleshy roots that have a high rubber content

ko·la nut *also* **co·la nut** \ˈkō-lə-\ *n* [*kola,* perh. modif. of Malinke *kolo* kola nut] (1868) **:** the bitter caffeine-containing chestnut-sized seed of a kola tree used esp. as a masticatory and in beverages

kola tree *or* **cola tree** *n* (1937) **:** an African tree (genus *Cola,* esp. *C. nitida* and *C. acuminata* of the family Sterculiaceae) cultivated in various tropical areas for its kola nuts

ko·lin·sky \kə-ˈlin(t)-skē\ *n, pl* **-skies** [origin unknown] (1851) **1 :** any of several Asian weasels (esp. *Mustela siberica*) **2 :** the fur or pelt of a kolinsky

kol·khoz \käl-ˈkȯz, -ˈkȯs\ *n, pl* **kol·kho·zy** \-ˈkȯ-zē\ *or* **kol·khoz·es** \-ˈkȯ-zəz\ [Russ, fr. *kol*lektivnoe *khoz*yaĭstvo collective farm] (1921) **:** a collective farm of the former U.S.S.R.

kol·khoz·nik \käl-ˈkȯz-nik\ *n, pl* **-ni·ki** \-ni-kē\ *or* **-niks** [Russ, fr. *kolkhoz* + *-nik,* agent suffix] (1944) **:** a member of a kolkhoz

Kol Ni·dre \kōl-ˈni-(ˌ)drā, kȯl-, -drə; -ni-ˈdrā\ *n* [Aram *kol nidhrē* all the vows; fr. the opening phrase of the prayer] (1881) **:** a formula for the annulment of private vows chanted in the synagogue on the eve of Yom Kippur

ko·lo \ˈkō-(ˌ)lō\ *n, pl* **kolos** [Serbian & Croatian, lit., circle, wheel; akin to Gk *kyklos* circle — more at WHEEL] (1851) **:** a central European folk dance in which dancers form a circle and progress slowly to right or left while one or more dancers perform elaborate steps in the center

ko·mat·ik \kō-ˈma-tik\ *n* [Inuit *qamutik*] (ca. 1824) **:** an Eskimo sledge with wooden runners and crossbars lashed with rawhide

kom·bu \ˈkäm-(ˌ)bü\ *n* [Jp] (1884) **:** a laminarian kelp used esp. in Japanese cooking as a seasoning in soup stock

Ko·mo·do dragon \kə-ˈmō-dō-\ *n* [*Komodo* Island, Indonesia] (1927) **:** an Indonesian monitor lizard (*Varanus komodoensis*) that is the largest of all known lizards and may attain a length of 10 feet (3 meters)

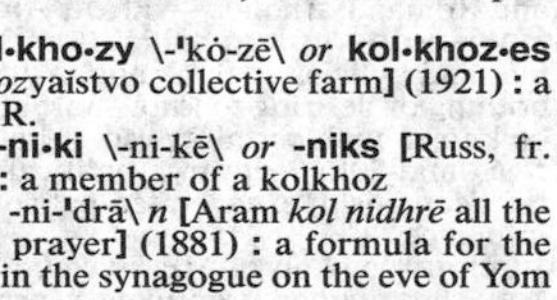

Komodo dragon

ko·mon·dor \ˈkä-mən-ˌdȯr, ˈkō-\ *n, pl* **-dors** *or* **-dor·ok** \-ˌdȯr-ək\ [Hung] (1931) **:** any of a breed of large powerful shaggy-coated white dogs of Hungarian origin that are used to guard sheep

Kom·so·mol \ˈkäm-sə-ˌmȯl, -ˌmōl\ *n* [Russ, fr. *Kom*munisticheskiĭ *So*yuz *Mol*odezhi Communist Union of Youth] (1925) **:** a Russian Communist youth organization

Kon·go \ˈkäŋ-(ˌ)gō\ *n, pl* **Kongo** *or* **Kongos** (ca. 1902) **1 :** a member of a Bantu people of the lower Congo River **2 :** the Bantu language of the Kongo people

Kon·ka·ni \ˈkäŋ-kə-(ˌ)nē\ *n* [Marathi *Koṅkaṇī*] (1873) **:** an Indo-Aryan language of the west coast of India

koodoo *var of* KUDU

kook \ˈkük\ *n* [by shortening & alter. fr. *cuckoo*] (1960) **:** one whose ideas or actions are eccentric, fantastic, or insane **:** SCREWBALL

kook·a·bur·ra \ˈku̇-kə-ˌbər-ə, -ˌbə-rə\ *n* [Wiradhuri (Australian aboriginal language of central New South Wales) *gugubarra*] (1834) **:** a brownish kingfisher (*Dacelo novaeguineae* syn. *D. gigas*) of Australia that is about the size of a crow and has a call resembling loud laughter — called also *laughing jackass*

kooky *also* **kook·ie** \ˈkü-kē\ *adj* **kook·i·er; -est** (1959) **:** having the characteristics of a kook **:** CRAZY, OFFBEAT — **kook·i·ness** *n*

Koo·te·nai *or* **Ku·te·nai** \ˈkü-tə-ˌnā, -ˌnē\ *n, pl* **-nai** *or* **-nais** [ultim. fr. Kootenai *ktunaxa,* a self-designation of some Canadian Kootenai] (1801) **1 :** a member of an American Indian people of the Rocky Mountains in both the U.S. and Canada **2 :** the language of the Kootenai people

ko·peck *or* **ko·pek** *also* **co·peck** \ˈkō-ˌpek\ *n* [Russ *kopeĭka*] (1669) — see *ruble* at MONEY table

koph *var of* QOPH

ko·piy·ka \ˌkō-ˈpē-kä\ *n* [Ukrainian, lit., kopeck] (1996) — see *hryvnia* at MONEY table

kop·je *or* **kop·pie** \ˈkä-pē\ *n* [Afrik *koppie*] (1848) **:** a small usu. rocky hill esp. on the African veld

kor *var of* COR

Kor *abbr* Korea; Korean

ko·ra \ˈkȯr-ə\ *n* [Malinke] (1799) **:** a 21-stringed African musical instrument resembling a lute

Ko·ran \kə-ˈran, -ˈrän; ˈkȯr-ˌan\ *also* **Qur·an** *or* **Qur·'an** \kə-ˈran, -ˈrän; ku̇-\ *n* [Ar *qur'ān*] (ca. 1615) **:** the book composed of sacred writings accepted by Muslims as revelations made to Muhammad by Allah through the angel Gabriel — **Ko·ran·ic** *also* **Qu·ran·ic** *or* **Qur·'an·ic** \kə-ˈra-nik\ *adj*

Ko·rat \kō-ˈrät, kȯ-\ *n* [*Korat* province, Thailand] (1967) **:** any of a breed of short-haired domestic cats originating in Thailand and having a heart-shaped face, a silver-blue coat, and usu. green eyes

ko·re \ˈkȯ-(ˌ)rā, ˈkō-\ *n, pl* **ko·rai** \-ˌrī, -(ˌ)rā\ [Gk *korē* girl; akin to Gk *koros* boy — more at CRESCENT] (1920) **:** an ancient Greek statue of a clothed young woman standing with feet together

Ko·re·an \kə-ˈrē-ən, *esp Southern* (ˌ)kō-\ *n* (1600) **1 :** a native or inhabitant of Korea **2 :** the language of the Korean people — **Korean** *adj*

kor·ma \ˈkȯr-mə\ *n* [Hindi & Urdu *qormā,* of Turkic origin; akin to Turk *kavurma* fried meat, fr. *kavur-* to fry, roast] (1832) **:** an Indian dish of usu. braised meat or vegetables cooked with spices and often yogurt or cream

ko·ru·na \ˈkȯr-ə-ˌnä, ˈkär-\ *n, pl* **ko·ru·ny** \-ə-nē\ *or* **korunas** *or* **korun** \ˈkȯr-ən, ˈkär-\ [Czech, lit., crown, fr. L *corona* — more at CROWN] (1930) **1** — see MONEY table **2** [Slovak] **:** the basic monetary unit of Slovakia from 1992 to 2009

[1]**ko·sher** \ˈkō-shər\ *adj* [Yiddish, fr. Heb *kāshēr* fit, proper] (1851) **1 a :** sanctioned by Jewish law; *esp* **:** ritually fit for use ⟨∼ meat⟩ **b :** selling or serving food ritually fit according to Jewish law ⟨a ∼ restaurant⟩ **2 :** being proper, acceptable, or satisfactory ⟨is the deal ∼?⟩

[2]**kosher** *vt* **ko·shered; ko·sher·ing** \-sh(ə-)riŋ\ (1871) **:** to make kosher

[3]**kosher** *n* (1886) **:** the observance of kosher practices ⟨keep ∼⟩

ko·to \ˈkō-(ˌ)tō\ *n* [Jp] (1795) **:** a long Japanese zither having 13 strings

kou·miss *or* **ku·miss** \kü-ˈmis, ˈkü-məs\ *n* [Russ *kumys,* of Turkic origin; akin to Turk *kımız* koumiss] (1607) **:** a beverage of fermented mare's milk made orig. by the nomadic peoples of central Asia

kou·prey \ˈkü-ˌprā\ *n* [Khmer *ko:prey*] (1940) **:** a rare short-haired ox (*Bos sauveli*) having a large dewlap and found in forests in parts of Cambodia, Thailand, Laos, and Vietnam

kou·ros \ˈkü-ˌrȯs\ *n, pl* **kou·roi** \-(ˌ)rȯi\ [Gk *kouros, koros* boy — more at CRESCENT] (1920) **:** an ancient Greek statue of a nude male youth standing with the left leg forward and arms at the sides

[1]**kow·tow** \(ˌ)kau̇-ˈtau̇, ˈkau̇-ˌ\ *n* [Chin (Beijing) *kòutóu,* fr. *kòu* to knock + *tóu* head] (1804) **:** an act of kowtowing

[2]**kowtow** *vi* (1826) **1 :** to show obsequious deference **:** FAWN ⟨∼*s* to the boss⟩ **2 :** to kneel and touch the forehead to the ground in token of homage, worship, or deep respect

KP \ˌkā-ˈpē\ *n* [*k*itchen *p*olice] (1918) **1 :** an enlisted man detailed to assist the cooks in a military mess **2 :** the work of KPs

kPa *abbr* kilopascal

kpc *abbr* kiloparsec

kph *abbr* kilometers per hour

Kr *symbol* krypton

[1]**kraal** \ˈkrȯl, ˈkräl\ *n* [Afrik, fr. Pg *curral* pen for cattle, enclosure, fr. VL **currale* enclosure for vehicles — more at CORRAL] (1731) **1 a :** a village of southern African natives **b :** the native village community **2 :** an enclosure for animals esp. in southern Africa

[2]**kraal** *vt* (1827) **:** to pen in a kraal

kraft \ˈkraft, ˈkräft\ *n, often attrib* [G, lit., strength, fr. OHG — more at CRAFT] (1906) **:** a strong paper or cardboard made from wood pulp produced from wood chips boiled in an alkaline solution containing sodium sulfate

krait \ˈkrīt\ *n* [Hindi & Urdu *karait*] (1874) **:** any of a genus (*Bungarus*) of brightly banded extremely venomous nocturnal elapid snakes of Pakistan, India, southeastern Asia, and adjacent islands

kra·ken \ˈkrä-kən\ *n, pl* **krakens** *or* **kraken** [Norw dial.] (1755) **:** a fabulous Scandinavian sea monster

kra·ter *also* **cra·ter** \ˈkrā-tər, krä-ˈter\ *n* [Gk *kratēr* — more at CRATER] (ca. 1736) **:** a jar or vase of classical antiquity having a large round body and a wide mouth and used for mixing wine and water

K ration \ˈkā-\ *n* [prob. alter. of *C ration,* but taken as initial of Ancel B. Keys †2004 Am. physiologist] (ca. 1940) **:** a packaged ration of emergency foods developed for the U.S. armed forces in World War II

kraut \ˈkrau̇t\ *n* [G, cabbage, fr. OHG *krūt*] (1855) **1 :** SAUERKRAUT **2** *often cap, usu disparaging* **:** GERMAN

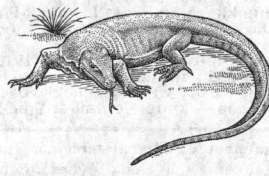

Krebs cycle \ˈkrebz-\ *n* [H. A. *Krebs*] (1941) : a sequence of reactions in the living organism in which oxidation of acetic acid or acetyl equivalent provides energy for storage in phosphate bonds (as in ATP) — called also *citric acid cycle, tricarboxylic acid cycle*

krem·lin \ˈkrem-lən\ *n* [obs. G *Kremelien* the citadel of Moscow, ultim. fr. ORuss *kremlĭ*] (1662) **1** : the citadel of a Russian city **2** *cap* [the *Kremlin,* citadel of Moscow and seat of government of Russia and formerly of the U.S.S.R.] : the Russian government

krem·lin·ol·o·gy \ˌkrem-lə-ˈnä-lə-jē\ *n, often cap* (1958) : the study of the policies and practices of the former Soviet government — **krem·lin·ol·o·gist** \-jist\ *n, often cap*

krep·lach \ˈkrep-lək, -ˌläk\ *n* [Yiddish *kreplekh,* pl. of *krepl* filled dumpling] (ca. 1892) : square or triangular dumplings filled with ground meat or cheese, boiled or fried, and usu. served in soup

kreu·zer \ˈkrȯit-sər\ *n* [G, fr. *Kreuz* cross; fr. its markings] (1547) : a small coin formerly used in Austria and Germany

krewe \ˈkrü\ *n* [alter. of *crew*] (1936) : a private organization staging festivities (as parades) during Mardi Gras in New Orleans

krill \ˈkril\ *n* [Norw *kril* fry of fish] (1907) : planktonic crustaceans and their larvae (order or suborder Euphausiacea and esp. genus *Euphausia*) that constitute the principal food of baleen whales

Krio \ˈkrē-ō\ *n* [Krio, speaker of Krio, Krio language, perh. fr. Yoruba *Kiriyó* Christian, ultim. fr. Pg *crioulo* Creole] (1955) : an English-based creole spoken in Sierra Leone

kris \ˈkrēs\ *n* [Malay *kĕris*] (ca. 1580) : a Malay or Indonesian dagger with a ridged serpentine blade

Krish·na \ˈkrish-nə, ˈkrēsh-\ *n* [Skt *Kṛṣṇa*] (1864) : a deity or deified hero of later Hinduism worshipped as an incarnation of Vishnu

Krish·na·ism \-ˌi-zəm\ *n* (1885) : a widespread form of Hindu religion characterized by the worship of Krishna

Kriss Krin·gle \ˈkris-ˈkriŋ-gəl\ *n* [modif. of G *Christkindl* Christ child, Christmas gift, dim. of *Christkind* Christ child] (1849) : SANTA CLAUS

¹**kro·na** \ˈkrō-nə\ *n, pl* **kro·nor** \-ˌnȯr, -nər\ [Sw, lit., crown] (1875) — see MONEY table

²**kro·na** \ˈkrō-nə\ *n, pl* **kro·nur** \-nər\ [Icel *krōna,* lit., crown] (1886) — see MONEY table

¹**kro·ne** \ˈkrō-nə\ *n, pl* **kro·ner** \-nər\ [Dan, lit., crown] (1885) — see MONEY table

²**kro·ne** \ˈkrō-nə\ *n, pl* **kro·nen** \-nən\ [G, lit., crown] (1895) **1** : the basic monetary unit of Austria from 1892 to 1925 **2** : a coin representing one krone

Kro·neck·er delta \ˈkrō-ˌne-kər-\ *n* [Leopold *Kronecker* †1891 Ger. mathematician] (1926) : a function of two variables that is 1 when the variables have the same value and is 0 when they have different values

kroon \ˈkrōn\ *n, pl* **kroo·ni** \ˈkrō-nē\ *or* **kroons** [Estonian (partitive sing. *krooni*), lit., crown, fr. Sw *krona* or G *Krone*] (1925) : the basic monetary unit of Estonia until 2011

Kru·ger·rand \ˈkrü-gə(r)-ˌrand, -ˌränd, -ˌränt\ *n* [S. J. P. *Kruger* + *rand*] (1967) : a one-ounce gold coin of the Republic of So. Africa

krumm·holz \ˈkrüm-ˌhōlts\ *n, pl* **krummholz** [G, fr. *krumm* crooked + *Holz* wood] (1903) : stunted forest characteristic of timberline

krumm·horn *also* **crum·horn** *or* **krum·horn** \ˈkrəm-ˌhȯrn\ *n* [G *Krummhorn,* fr. *krumm* curved + *Horn* horn] (ca. 1696) : a Renaissance double-reed woodwind instrument consisting of a curved boxwood tube and having a pierced cap covering the reed

kryp·ton \ˈkrip-ˌtän\ *n* [Gk, neut. of *kryptos* hidden — more at CRYPT] (1898) : a colorless relatively inert gaseous element found in air in trace amounts and used esp. in electric lamps — see ELEMENT table

KS *abbr* **1** Kansas **2** Kaposi's sarcoma

Ksha·tri·ya \ˈksha-trē-ə, ˈcha-\ *n* [Skt *kṣatriya,* fr. *kṣatra* dominion — more at CHECK] (1794) : a Hindu of an upper caste traditionally assigned to governing and military occupations

kt *abbr* **1** karat **2** knight **3** knot

KT *abbr* kiloton

K–T \ˈkā-ˈtē\ *adj* (1983) : of, relating to, or occurring at the K-T boundary ⟨~ extinctions⟩

K–T boundary *n* [*K* (alternative for *C* as abbr. for *Cretaceous*) + *T*ertiary] (1983) : the transition between the Cretaceous and Tertiary periods of geologic time characterized by a mass extinction of many forms of life including the dinosaurs; *also* : a geologic stratum marking this boundary

Ku·che·an \kü-ˈchē-ən\ *n* [*Kuche, Kucha* (Kuga), Xinjiang, China] (ca. 1934) : TOCHARIAN B

ku·chen \ˈkü-kən, -k̲ən\ *n, pl* **kuchen** [G, cake, fr. OHG *kuocho* — more at CAKE] (1854) : any of various coffee cakes made from sweet yeast dough

ku·do \ˈkü-(ˌ)dō, ˈkyü-\ *n, pl* **kudos** \-(ˌ)dōz\ [back-formation fr. *kudos* (taken as a pl.)] (1926) **1** : AWARD, HONOR ⟨a score of honorary degrees and ... other ~*s* —*Time*⟩ **2** : COMPLIMENT, PRAISE ⟨rarely hear that kind of ~ to men anymore —Ellen Goodman⟩

usage Some commentators hold that since *kudos* is a singular word it cannot be used as a plural and that the word *kudo* is impossible. But *kudo* does exist; it is simply one of the most recent words created by back-formation from another word misunderstood as a plural. *Kudos* was introduced into English in the 19th century; it was used in contexts where a reader unfamiliar with Greek could not be sure whether it was singular or plural. By the 1920s it began to appear as a plural, and about 25 years later *kudo* began to appear. It may have begun as a misunderstanding, but then so did *cherry* and *pea.*

ku·dos \ˈkü-ˌdäs, ˈkyü-, -ˌdōs\ *n* [Gk *kydos*] (1831) **1** : fame and renown resulting from an act or achievement : PRESTIGE **2** : praise given for achievement

ku·du *also* **koo·doo** \ˈkü-(ˌ)dü\ *n, pl* **kudu** *or* **kudus** *also* **koodoo** *or* **koodoos** [Afrik *koedoe,* fr. Khoikhoi *kudu-b, kudu-s*] (1777) : a large grayish brown African antelope (*Tragelaphus strepsiceros*) with large annulated spirally twisted horns; *also* : a related antelope (*T. imberbis*)

kud·zu \ˈküd-(ˌ)zü, ˈkəd-\ *n* [Jp *kuzu*] (1876) : a fast-growing Asian vine (*Pueraria lobata*) of the legume family that is used for forage and erosion control and is often a serious weed in the southeastern U.S.

ku·fi \ˈkü-fē\ *n* [ultim. fr. Ar *kūfīya* kaffiyeh] (1981) : a close-fitting brimless cylindrical or round hat

ku·gel \ˈkü-gəl\ *n* [Yiddish *kugl,* fr. MHG *kugel* ball — more at CUDGEL] (1846) : a baked pudding (as of potatoes or noodles) usu. served as a side dish

Kui·per Belt \ˈkī-pər-\ *n* [Gerald A. *Kuiper* †1973 U.S. (Dutch-born) astronomer] (1988) : a band of small celestial bodies beyond the orbit of Neptune from which many short-period comets are believed to originate — compare OORT CLOUD

Ku Klux·er \ˈkü-ˈklək-sər *also* ˈkyü- *or* ˈklü-\ *n* (1880) : a member of the Ku Klux Klan — **Ku Klux·ism** \-ˈklək-ˌsi-zəm\ *n*

Ku Klux Klan \ˈkü-ˈklǝks-ˈklan *also* ˈkyü- *or* ˈklü-\ *n* (1867) **1** : an American post-Civil War secret society advocating white supremacy **2** : a 20th century secret fraternal group held to confine its membership to American-born white Christians

Ku Klux Klansman *n* (1868) : KU KLUXER

kuk·ri \ˈku̇-krē\ *n* [Hindi & Urdu *kukṛī*] (1811) : a curved short sword with a broad blade used esp. by Gurkhas

ku·lak \ˈkü-ˌlak, -ˌläk, kü-ˈ\ *n* [Russ, lit., fist] (1877) **1** : a prosperous or wealthy peasant farmer in 19th century Russia **2** : a farmer characterized by Communists as having excessive wealth

kul·tur \ku̇l-ˈtu̇r\ *n, often cap* [G, fr. L *cultura* culture] (1914) **1** : CULTURE 5 **2** : culture emphasizing practical efficiency and individual subordination to the state **3** : German culture held to be superior esp. by militant Nazi and Hohenzollern expansionists

Kul·tur·kampf \-ˌkäm(p)f\ *n* [G, fr. *Kultur* + *Kampf* conflict] (1879) : conflict between civil government and religious authorities esp. over control of education and church appointments; *broadly* : a conflict between cultures or value systems

kumiss *var of* KOUMISS

küm·mel \ˈki-məl\ *n* [G, lit., caraway seed, fr. OHG *kumīn* cumin] (1864) : a colorless liqueur flavored principally with caraway seeds

kum·quat \ˈkəm-ˌkwät\ *n* [Chin (Guangdong) *gām-gwāt,* fr. *gām* gold + *gwāt* citrus fruit] (1699) : any of several small yellow to orange citrus fruits with sweet spongy rind and somewhat acid pulp that are used chiefly for preserves; *also* : a tree or shrub (genus *Fortunella*) of the rue family that bears kumquats

ku·na \ˈkü-ˌnä, -nə\ *n, pl* **kuna** *or* **ku·ne** \-nā\ [Serbian & Croatian (nom. pl. *kune,* gen. pl. *kunā*), lit., marten (the skin of which was used as currency in medieval Slavic cultures)] (1951) — see MONEY table

kun·da·li·ni \ˌku̇n-də-ˈlē-nē, ˌkən-\ *n, often cap* [Skt *kuṇḍalinī,* fr. fem. of *kuṇḍalin* circular, coiled, fr. *kuṇḍala* ring] (1897) : the yogic life force that is held to lie coiled at the base of the spine until it is aroused and sent to the head to trigger enlightenment

Kung \ˈku̇ŋ, ˈküŋ; *in !Kung the initial sound is a type of click*\ *n, pl* **Kung** (1926) **1** : a member of a people of southern Africa — usu. preceded in writing by ! **2** : the Khoisan language of the !Kung people — usu. preceded in writing by !

kung fu \ˌkəŋ-ˈfü, ˌku̇ŋ-\ *n* [Chin (Beijing) *gōngfu* skill, art] (1966) : any of various Chinese martial arts and related disciplines that are practiced esp. for self-defense, exercise, and spiritual growth

kung pao \ˈkəŋ-ˈpau̇, ˈküŋ-, ˈku̇ŋ-\ *adj* [Chin (Beijing) *gōng bǎo,* lit., palace guardian] (1976) : being stir-fried or sometimes deep-fried and served in a spicy hot sauce usu. with peanuts ⟨*kung pao* chicken⟩

kunz·ite \ˈku̇n(t)-ˌsīt\ *n* [G. F. *Kunz* †1932 Am. gem expert] (1903) : a pinkish-lilac variety of spodumene used as a gem

Kurd \ˈku̇rd, ˈkərd\ *n* (1595) : a member of a pastoral and agricultural people who inhabit a plateau region in adjoining parts of Turkey, Iran, Iraq, Syria, Armenia, and Azerbaijan — **Kurd·ish** \ˈku̇r-dish, ˈkər-\ *adj*

Kurdish *n* (1813) : the Iranian language of the Kurds

Kur·di·stan \ˌku̇r-də-ˈstan, ˌkər-\ *n* [*Kurdistan,* Asia] (1904) : an Oriental rug woven by the Kurds and noted for fine colors

kur·gan \ku̇r-ˈgän, -ˈgan\ *n* [Russ, of Turkic origin; akin to Turk *kurgan* fortress, castle] (1889) : a burial mound of eastern Europe or Siberia

kur·ra·jong \ˈkər-ə-ˌjȯŋ, ˈkə-rə-, -ˌjäŋ\ *n* [Dharuk (Australian aboriginal language of the Port Jackson area) *garajuŋ,* lit., fishing line] (1823) : any of several Australian trees or shrubs (family Sterculiaceae, esp. genus *Brachychiton*); *esp* : one (*B. populneum*) often planted as a shade tree or in windbreaks

kur·ta \ˈkər-tə, ˈku̇r-tä\ *n* [Hindi & Urdu *kurtā,* fr. Pers *kurta*] (1913) : a long loose-fitting collarless shirt of a style originating in India

kur·to·sis \(ˌ)kər-ˈtō-səs\ *n* [Gk *kyrtōsis* convexity, fr. *kyrtos* convex — more at CURVE] (1905) : the peakedness or flatness of the graph of a frequency distribution esp. with respect to the concentration of values near the mean as compared with the normal distribution

ku·ru \ˈku̇r-(ˌ)ü\ *n* [Fore (language of eastern highland Papua New Guinea)] (1957) : a rare progressive fatal prion disease that resembles Creutzfeldt-Jakob disease and has occurred among tribespeople in eastern New Guinea who engaged in a form of ritual cannibalism

ku·rush *or* **ku·rus** \kə-ˈrüsh\ *n, pl* **kurush** *or* **kurus** [Turk *kuruş*] (1882) — see *lira* at MONEY table

Kutenai *var of* KOOTENAI

kV *abbr* kilovolt

kvass \ˈkväs, ˈkfäs\ *n* [Russ *kvas*] (ca. 1553) : a slightly alcoholic beverage of eastern Europe made from fermented mixed cereals and often flavored

kvell \ˈkvel\ *vi* [Yiddish *kveln* to be delighted, fr. MHG *quellen* to well, gush, swell] (ca. 1952) : to be extraordinarily proud : REJOICE

¹**kvetch** \ˈkvech, ˈkfech\ *vi* [Yiddish *kvetshn,* lit., to squeeze, pinch, fr. MHG *quetschen*] (ca. 1952) : to complain habitually : GRIPE — **kvetch·er** *n*

²**kvetch** *n* (1964) **1** : a habitual complainer **2** : COMPLAINT 1 — **kvetchy** \ˈkve-chē, ˈkfe-\ *adj*

kW *abbr* kilowatt

Kwa \ˈkwä\ *n* (1857) : a branch of the Niger-Congo language family that is spoken along the African coast and its hinterland from the Ivory Coast to southwestern Nigeria

kwa·cha \ˈkwä-chə\ *n, pl* **kwa·chas** *or* **kwacha** [Bemba or Chichewa (Bantu language of Malawi), lit., it dawns] (1966) — see MONEY table

Kwa·ki·utl \ˌkwä-kē-ˈyü-tᵊl, ˌkwä-ˈkyü-\ *n, pl* **Kwakiutl** [Kwakiutl *kʷágut, kʷágu'ʔt,* a Kwakiutl tribe] (1848) **1** : a member of an Ameri-

\ə\ **abut** \ᵊ\ **kitten**, F **table** \ər\ **further** \a\ **ash** \ā\ **ace** \ä\ **mop, mar**
\au̇\ **out** \ch\ **chin** \e\ **bet** \ē\ **easy** \g\ **go** \i\ **hit** \ī\ **ice** \j\ **job**
\ŋ\ **sing** \ō\ **go** \ȯ\ **law** \ȯi\ **boy** \th\ **thin** \t͟h\ **the** \ü\ **loot** \u̇\ **foot**
\y\ **yet** \zh\ **vision, beige** \k̲, ⁿ, œ, ue, ʸ\ *see* Guide to Pronunciation

can Indian people of the Canadian Pacific coast   **2** : the language of the Kwakiutl people

kwan·za \'kwän-zə\ *n, pl* **kwanzas** *or* **kwanza** [*Kwanza* (Cuanza), river in Angola] (1978) — see MONEY table

Kwan·zaa *also* **Kwan·za** \'kwän-zə\ *n* [Swahili *kwanza* first] (1972) : an African-American cultural festival held from December 26 to January 1

kwash·i·or·kor \ˌkwä-shē-'ôr-kər, -ôr-'kòr\ *n* [Ga (Kwa language of coastal Ghana) *kwàʃiɔkɔ́* influence a child is said to be under when a second child comes] (1935) : severe malnutrition in infants and children esp. of impoverished regions caused by a diet low in protein

kWh *abbr* kilowatt-hour

KWIC \'kwik\ *n* [*keyword in context*] (1959) : a computer-generated index alphabetized on a keyword that appears within a brief context

Ky *or* **KY** *abbr* Kentucky

ky·ack \'kī-ˌak\ *n* [origin unknown] (1901) : a packsack to be swung on either side of a packsaddle

ky·a·nite \'kī-ə-ˌnīt\ *n* [G *Zyanit*, fr. Gk *kyanos* dark blue enamel, lapis lazuli] (1794) : an aluminum silicate mineral Al_2SiO_5 that occurs usu. in blue thin-bladed triclinic crystals and crystalline aggregates

kyat \'chät\ *n, pl* **kyats** *or* **kyat** [Burmese *c³at*] (1952) — see MONEY table

ky·bosh *chiefly Brit var of* KIBOSH

ky·mo·graph \-ˌgraf\ *n* [Gk *kyma* wave + ISV *-graph* — more at CYME] (1872) : a device which graphically records motion or pressure (as of blood) — **ky·mo·graph·ic** \ˌkī-mə-'gra-fik\ *adj* — **ky·mog·ra·phy** \kī-'mä-grə-fē\ *n*

Kymric *var of* CYMRIC

ky·pho·sis \kī-'fō-səs\ *n* [NL, fr. Gk *kyphōsis*, fr. *kyphos* humpbacked] (1847) : exaggerated outward curvature of the thoracic region of the spine resulting in a rounded upper back — compare LORDOSIS — **ky·phot·ic** \-'fä-tik\ *adj*

Kyr·gyz *or* **Kir·ghiz** \ˌkir-'gēz\ *n, pl* **Kyrgyz** *or* **Kirghiz** [Kyrgyz *Kirgiz*] (1991)   **1** : a member of a Turkic people of Kyrgyzstan and adjacent areas of central Asia   **2** : the language of the Kyrgyz — **Kyrgyz** *adj*

ky·rie \'kir-ē-ˌā\ *n, often cap* [ME, fr. ML, fr. LL *kyrie eleison*, transliteration of Gk *kyrie eleēson* Lord, have mercy] (14c) : a short liturgical prayer that begins with or consists of the words "Lord, have mercy"

ky·rie elei·son \'kir-ē-ˌā-ə-'lā-(ə-)ˌsän, -(ə-)sən *also* 'kir-ē-ə-'lā-\ *n, often cap K&E* (13c) : KYRIE

kyte \'kīt\ *n* [prob. fr. LG *küt* bowel] (ca. 1540)   **1** *chiefly Scot* : BELLY 1   **2** *chiefly Scot* : BELLY 2

kythe *var of* KITHE

¹l \'el\ *n, pl* **l's** *or* **ls** \'elz\ *often cap, often attrib* (bef. 12c)   **1 a** : the 12th letter of the English alphabet   **b** : a graphic representation of this letter   **c** : a speech counterpart of orthographic *l*   **2** : FIFTY — see NUMBER table   **3** : a graphic device for reproducing the letter *l*   **4** : one designated *l* esp. as the 12th in order or class   **5** : something shaped like the letter L; *specif* : ²ELL 1   **6** : ²EL

²l *abbr*   **1** lady   **2** lake   **3** lambert   **4** land   **5** large   **6** late   **7** left   **8** length   **9** [L *libra*] pound   **10** line   **11** liquid   **12** lira   **13** liter   **14** little   **15** low

l *abbr*   **1** Lagrangian   **2** long   **3** loss; losses

l- *prefix* [ISV, fr. *lev-*]   **1** \ˌel-(ˌ)vō, ˌel, 'el\ : levorotatory ⟨*l*-tartaric acid⟩   **2** \ˌel, 'el\ : having a similar configuration at a selected carbon atom to the configuration of levorotatory glyceraldehyde — usu. printed as a small capital ⟨L-fructose⟩

¹la \'lò, 'lä\ *interj* [ME (northern dial.), fr. OE *lā*] (bef. 12c) *chiefly dial* — used for emphasis or expressing surprise

²la \'lä\ *n* [ME, fr. ML, fr. the syllable sung to this note in a medieval hymn to St. John the Baptist] (14c) : the sixth tone of the diatonic scale in solmization

¹La *abbr* Louisiana

²La *symbol* lanthanum

LA *abbr*   **1** law agent   **2** legislative assistant   **3** Los Angeles   **4** Louisiana

laa·ger \'lä-gər\ *n* [obs. Afrik *lager* (now *laer*), fr. G *Lager*, fr. OHG *legar* couch — more at LAIR] (1850)   **1** *SoAfr* : CAMP; *esp* : an encampment protected by a circle of wagons or armored vehicles   **2** : a defensive position, policy, or attitude — **laager** *vi*

laa·ri \'lä-(ˌ)rē\ *n, pl* **laari** [prob. fr. Divehi (Indo-Aryan language of the Maldive Islands), fr. Pers *lārī* piece of silver wire used as currency] (1983) — see *rufiyaa* at MONEY table

lab \'lab\ *n* (ca. 1878) : LABORATORY

¹Lab \'lab\ *n* (1957) : LABRADOR RETRIEVER

²Lab *abbr* Labrador

la·ba·no·ta·tion \ˌlä-bə-nō-'tā-shən, ˌla-; lə-ˌbä-(ˌ)nō-\ *n* [Rudolf *Laban* †1958 Hung. dance theorist + E *notation*] (1952) : a method of recording bodily movement (as in dance) on a staff by means of symbols (as of direction) that can be aligned with musical accompaniment

lab·a·rum \'la-bə-rəm\ *n* [LL] (1606) : an imperial standard of the later Roman emperors resembling the vexillum; *esp* : the standard bearing the Chi-Rho adopted by Constantine after he converted to Christianity

lab coat *n* (1960) : a loose usu. white coat with deep pockets that is worn in a laboratory or medical office

lab·da·num \'lab-də-nəm\ *also* **lad·a·num** \'la-də-nəm, 'lad-nəm\ *n* [ML *lapdanum*] (14c) : a soft dark fragrant bitter oleoresin derived from various rockroses (genus *Cistus*) and used in making perfumes

¹la·bel \'lä-bəl\ *n* [ME, fr. AF *labelle*] (14c)   **1** *archaic* : BAND, FILLET; *specif* : one attached to a document to hold an appended seal   **2** : a heraldic charge that consists of a narrow horizontal band with usu. three pendants   **3 a** : a slip (as of paper or cloth) inscribed and affixed to something for identification or description   **b** : written or printed matter accompanying an article to furnish identification or other information   **c** : a descriptive or identifying word or phrase: as   **(1)** : EPITHET   **(2)** : a word or phrase used with a dictionary definition to provide additional information   **d** : a usu. radioactive isotope used in labeling   **4** : an adhesive stamp (as for postage or revenue)   **5 a (1)** : a brand of commercial recordings issued under a usu. trademarked name   **(2)** : a recording so issued   **(3)** : a company issuing such recordings   **b** : the brand name of a retail store selling clothing, a clothing manufacturer, or a fashion designer

²label *vt* **la·beled** *or* **la·belled**; **la·bel·ing** *or* **la·bel·ling** \'lä-b(ə-)liŋ\ (1601)   **1 a** : to affix a label to   **b** : to describe or designate with or as if with a label   **2 a** : to distinguish (an element or atom) by using an isotope distinctive in some manner (as in mass or radioactivity)   **b** : to distinguish (as a compound or cell) by introducing a traceable constituent (as a dye or labeled atom) — **la·bel·able** \'lä-bə-lə-bəl\ *adj* — **la·bel·er** \'lä-b(ə-)lər\ *n*

la·bel·lum \lə-'be-ləm\ *n, pl* **la·bel·la** \-lə\ [NL, fr. L, dim. of *labrum* lip — more at LIP] (1830)   **1** : the median and usu. most morphologically distinct member of the corolla of an orchid   **2** : a terminal part of the labium or labrum of various insects

la·bel·mate \'lä-bəl-ˌmāt\ *n* (1981) : a singer or musician who records for the same company as another

labia *pl of* LABIUM

¹la·bi·al \'lä-bē-əl\ *adj* [ML *labialis*, fr. L *labium* lip] (1594)   **1** : uttered with the participation of one or both lips ⟨the ~ sounds \f\, \p\, and \ü\⟩   **2** : of, relating to, or situated near the lips or labia — **la·bi·al·ly** \-ē-lē\ *adv*

²labial *n* (1668) : a labial consonant

la·bi·al·ize \'lä-bē-ə-ˌlīz\ *vt* **-ized**; **-iz·ing** (1867) : to make labial : ROUND 1b(2) — **la·bi·al·i·za·tion** \ˌlä-bē-ə-lə-'zā-shən, -byə-lə-\ *n*

la·bia ma·jo·ra \'lä-bē-ə-mə-'jòr-ə\ *n pl* [NL, lit., larger lips] (1838) : the outer fatty folds of the vulva bounding the vestibule

labia mi·no·ra \-mə-'nòr-ə\ *n pl* [NL, lit., smaller lips] (1838) : the inner highly vascular largely connective-tissue folds of the vulva bounding the vestibule

¹la·bi·ate \'lä-bē-ət, -bē-ˌāt\ *adj* [NL *labiatus*, fr. L *labium*] (1706)   **1** : having the limb of a tubular corolla or calyx divided into two unequal parts projecting one over the other like lips ⟨mints and the snapdragon are ~⟩   **2** : of or relating to the mint family

²labiate *n* (1845) : a plant of the mint family

la·bile \'lä-ˌbī(-ə)l, -bəl\ *adj* [F, fr. MF, prone to err, fr. LL *labilis*, fr. L *labi* to slip — more at SLEEP] (1603)   **1** : readily or continually undergoing chemical, physical, or biological change or breakdown ⟨UNSTABLE ⟨a ~ mineral⟩   **2** : readily open to change — **la·bil·i·ty** \lä-'bi-lə-tē\ *n*

labio- *comb form* [L *labium*] : labial and ⟨*labio*dental⟩

la·bio·den·tal \ˌlä-bē-ō-'den-t³l\ *adj* (1669) : uttered with the participation of the lip and teeth ⟨the ~ sounds \f\ and \v\⟩ — **labiodental** *n*

la·bio·ve·lar \-'vē-lər\ *adj* [ISV] (1894) : both labial and velar ⟨the ~ sound \w\⟩ — **labiovelar** *n*

la·bi·um \'lä-bē-əm\ *n, pl* **la·bia** \-ə\ [NL, fr. L, lip — more at LIP] (1634)   **1** : any of the folds at the margin of the vulva — compare LABIA MAJORA, LABIA MINORA   **2** : the lower lip of a labiate corolla   **3 a** : a lower mouthpart of an insect that is formed by the second pair of maxillae united in the middle line   **b** : a liplike part of various invertebrates

¹la·bor \'lä-bər\ *n* [ME, fr. AF *labur*, fr. L *labor;* perh. akin to L *labare* to totter, *labi* to slip — more at SLEEP] (14c)   **1 a** : expenditure of physical or mental effort esp. when difficult or compulsory   **b (1)** : human activity that provides the goods or services in an economy   **(2)** : the services performed by workers for wages as distinguished from those rendered by entrepreneurs for profits   **c** : the physical activities (as dilation of the cervix and contraction of the uterus) involved in giving birth; *also* : the period of such labor   **2** : an act or process requiring labor : TASK   **3** : a product of labor   **4 a** : an economic group comprising those who do manual labor or work for wages   **b (1)** : workers employed in an establishment   **(2)** : workers available for employment   **c** : the organizations or officials representing groups of workers   **5** *usu Labour* : the Labour party of the United Kingdom or of another part of the Commonwealth of Nations   *syn* see WORK

²labor *vb* **la·bored; la·bor·ing** \-b(ə-)riŋ\ *vi* (14c)   **1** : to exert one's powers of body or mind esp. with painful or strenuous effort : WORK   **2** : to move with great effort ⟨the truck ~ed up the hill⟩   **3** : to be in the labor of giving birth   **4** : to suffer from some disadvantage or distress ⟨~ under a delusion⟩   **5** *of a ship* : to pitch or roll heavily ~ *vt*   **1** *archaic* **a** : to spend labor on or produce by labor   **b** : to strive to effect or achieve   **2** : to treat or work out in often laborious detail ⟨~ the obvious⟩   **3** : DISTRESS, BURDEN   **4** : to cause to labor

³labor *adj* (1640)   **1** : of or relating to labor   **2** *cap* : of, relating to, or constituting a political party held to represent the interests of workers or made up largely of organized labor groups

lab·o·ra·to·ry \'la-b(ə-)rə-ˌtòr-ē *sometimes* 'la-bə(r)-, *or* lə-'bòr-ə-, *Brit usu* lə-'bär-ə-t(ə-)rē\ *n, pl* **-ries** *often attrib* [ML *laboratorium*, fr. L

laborare to labor, fr. *labor*] (1605) **1 a :** a place equipped for experimental study in a science or for testing and analysis; *broadly* **:** a place providing opportunity for experimentation, observation, or practice in a field of study **b :** a place like a laboratory for testing, experimentation, or practice **2 :** an academic period set aside for laboratory work
labor camp *n* (1900) **1 :** a penal colony where forced labor is performed **2 :** a camp for migratory laborers
Labor Day *n* (1880) **:** a day set aside for special recognition of working people: as **a :** the first Monday in September observed in the U.S. and Canada as a legal holiday **b :** May 1 in many countries
labored *adj* (1608) **:** produced or performed with labor ⟨~ breathing⟩; *also* **:** lacking ease of expression ⟨a ~ speech⟩
la·bor·er \-bər-ər\ *n* (14c) **:** one that labors; *specif* **:** a person who does unskilled physical work for wages
labor force *n* (1863) **:** WORKFORCE
la·bor–in·ten·sive \ˈlā-bər-in-ˌten(t)-siv\ *adj* (1953) **:** having high labor costs per unit of output; *esp* **:** requiring greater expenditure on labor than in capital
la·bo·ri·ous \lə-ˈbȯr-ē-əs\ *adj* (14c) **1 :** devoted to labor **:** INDUSTRIOUS **2 :** involving or characterized by hard or toilsome effort **:** LABORED — **la·bo·ri·ous·ly** *adv* — **la·bo·ri·ous·ness** *n*
la·bor·ite \ˈlā-bə-ˌrīt\ *n* (1889) **1 :** a member of a group favoring the interests of labor **2** *cap* **a :** a member of a political party devoted chiefly to the interests of labor **b** *usu* **La·bour·ite :** a member of the British Labour party
la·bor·sav·ing \ˈlā-bər-ˌsā-viŋ\ *adj* (ca. 1779) **:** adapted to replace or decrease human and esp. manual labor ⟨~ machines⟩
labor union *n* (1866) **:** an organization of workers formed for the purpose of advancing its members' interests in respect to wages, benefits, and working conditions
la·bour *chiefly Brit var of* LABOR
lab·ra·doo·dle \ˈla-brə-ˌdü-dᵊl\ *n, often cap* [*Labrador* (retriever) + *poodle*] (1970) **:** a dog that is a cross between a Labrador retriever and a poodle
lab·ra·dor·ite \ˈla-brə-ˌdȯr-ˌīt\ *n* [*Labrador* Peninsula, Canada] (1814) **:** an iridescent feldspar used esp. in jewelry
Lab·ra·dor retriever \ˈla-brə-ˌdȯr-\ *n* [*Labrador,* Newfoundland] (1910) **:** any of a breed of medium-sized strongly built retrievers largely developed in England from stock originating in Newfoundland and having a short dense black, yellow, or chocolate coat and a thick rounded tail — called also *Lab, Labrador*

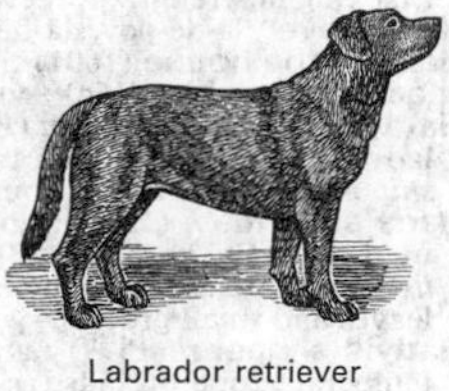
Labrador retriever

Labrador tea *n* (1767) **:** a low-growing ericaceous evergreen shrub (*Ledum groenlandicum*) chiefly of northern No. America with white or creamy bell-shaped flowers and leaves sometimes used in making tea; *also* **:** a related shrub (*L. glandulosum*) of western No. America
la·bret \ˈlā-brət\ *n* [L *labrum*] (1857) **:** an ornament worn in a perforation of the lip
la·brum \ˈlā-brəm\ *n* [NL, fr. L, lip, edge — more at LIP] (1826) **1 :** an upper or anterior mouthpart of an arthropod consisting of a single median piece in front of or above the mandibles **2 :** a ring of fibrous cartilage forming the margin of the shallow cavity of the upper part of the scapula by which the humerus articulates with the pectoral girdle
la·bur·num \lə-ˈbər-nəm\ *n* [NL, fr. L] (1567) **:** any of a small genus (*Laburnum,* esp. *L. anagyroides*) of poisonous leguminous shrubs and trees of Eurasia with pendulous racemes of bright yellow flowers
lab·y·rinth \ˈla-bə-ˌrin(t)th, -rən(t)th\ *n* [ME *laborintus,* fr. L *labyrinthus,* fr. Gk *labyrinthos*] (14c) **1 a :** a place constructed of or full of intricate passageways and blind alleys **b :** a maze (as in a garden) formed by paths separated by high hedges **2 :** something extremely complex or tortuous in structure, arrangement, or character **:** INTRICACY, PERPLEXITY ⟨a ~ of swamps and channels⟩ ⟨guided them through the ~*s* of city life —Paul Blanshard⟩ **3 :** a tortuous anatomical structure; *esp* **:** the internal ear or its bony or membranous part
lab·y·rin·thi·an \ˌla-bə-ˈrin(t)-thē-ən\ *adj* (1588) **:** LABYRINTHINE
lab·y·rin·thine \-ˈrin(t)-thən; -ˈrin-ˌthīn, -ˌthēn\ *adj* (1632) **1 :** of, relating to, or resembling a labyrinth **:** INTRICATE, INVOLVED **2 :** of, relating to, or originating in the internal ear ⟨~ lesions⟩
lab·y·rin·tho·dont \-ˈrin(t)-thə-ˌdänt\ *n* [NL *Labyrinthodontia,* fr. Gk *labyrinthos* + *odont-, odous* tooth — more at TOOTH] (ca. 1852) **:** any of a superorder (Labyrinthodontia) of extinct amphibians of the Late Paleozoic and Early Mesozoic typically having bodies resembling salamanders or crocodiles and considered to be the earliest tetrapod vertebrates — **labyrinthodont** *adj*
lac \ˈlak\ *n* [Pers *lak* & Hindi & Urdu *lākh,* fr. Skt *lākṣā*] (1598) **:** a resinous substance secreted by a scale insect (*Laccifer lacca*) and used chiefly in the form of shellac
lac·co·lith \ˈla-kə-ˌlith\ *n* [Gk *lakkos* pond, reservoir + E *-lith* — more at LAKE] (1879) **:** a mass of igneous rock that is intruded between sedimentary beds and produces a domical bulging of the overlying strata — **lac·co·lith·ic** \ˌla-kə-ˈli-thik\ *adj*
[1]**lace** \ˈlās\ *vb* **laced; lac·ing** [ME, fr. AF *lacer,* fr. L *laqueare* to ensnare, fr. *laqueus*] *vt* (13c) **1 :** to draw together the edges of by or as if by a lace passed through eyelets ⟨~*s* her fingers behind her head⟩ **2 :** to draw or pass (as a lace) through something (as eyelets) **3 :** to confine or compress by tightening laces of a garment **4 a :** to adorn with or as if with lace ⟨the surrounding countryside was *laced* with villages and hamlets —L. C. Heinemann⟩ **b :** to mark with streaks of color **5 :** BEAT, LASH **6 a :** to add a dash of liquor to **b :** to add something to impart pungency, savor, or zest to ⟨a sauce *laced* with garlic⟩ ⟨conversation *laced* with sarcasm⟩ **c :** to adulterate with a substance ⟨*laced* a guard's coffee with a sedative⟩ ~ *vi* **1 :** to admit of being tied or fastened with a lace **2 :** to make a verbal attack — usu. used with *into* ⟨his boss *laced* into him for being late⟩ — **lac·er** *n*
[2]**lace** *n* [ME, fr. AF *lace, laz,* fr. L *laqueus* snare] (14c) **1 :** a cord or string used for drawing together two edges (as of a garment or a shoe) **2 :** an ornamental braid for trimming coats or uniforms **3 :** an openwork usu. figured fabric made of thread or yarn and used for trimmings, household coverings, and entire garments — **laced** \ˈlāst\ *adj* — **lace·less** \ˈlās-ləs\ *adj* — **lace·like** \ˈlās-ˌlīk\ *adj*
lace–curtain *adj* (1934) **:** copying middle-class attributes **:** aspiring to middle-class standing
[1]**lac·er·ate** \ˈla-sə-ˌrāt\ *vt* **-at·ed; -at·ing** [ME, fr. L *laceratus,* pp. of *lacerare* to tear; akin to Gk *lakis* tear] (15c) **1 :** to tear or rend roughly **:** wound jaggedly **2 :** to cause sharp mental or emotional pain to **:** DISTRESS — **lac·er·a·tive** \-ˌrā-tiv\ *adj*
[2]**lac·er·ate** \-rət, -ˌrāt\ *or* **lac·er·at·ed** \-ˌrā-təd\ *adj* (1542) **1 a :** torn jaggedly **:** MANGLED **b :** extremely harrowed or distracted **2 :** having the edges deeply and irregularly cut ⟨a ~ petal⟩
lac·er·a·tion \ˌla-sə-ˈrā-shən\ *n* (1597) **1 :** the act of lacerating **2 :** a torn and ragged wound
lace·wing \ˈlās-ˌwiŋ\ *n* (1854) **:** any of various neuropterous insects (as genera *Chrysopa* and *Hemerobius*) having delicate lacelike wing venation, long antennae, and often brilliant eyes — called also *lacewing fly*
lace·work \ˈlās-ˌwərk\ *n* (1763) **:** objects or patterns consisting of or resembling lace
lacey *var of* LACY
la·ches \ˈla-chəz, ˈlā-\ *n, pl* **laches** [ME *lachesse,* fr. AF *laschesce,* fr. *lasche* lax, ultim. fr. L *laxare* to loosen — more at LEASE] (14c) **:** negligence in the observance of duty or opportunity; *specif* **:** undue delay in asserting a legal right or privilege
lach·ry·mal *or* **lac·ri·mal** \ˈla-krə-məl\ *adj* [ME *lacrimale,* fr. MF or ML; MF *lacrymal,* fr. ML *lacrimalis,* fr. L *lacrima* tear, fr. OL *dacrima,* prob. fr. Gk *dakry* — more at TEAR] (15c) **1** *usu lacrimal* **:** of, relating to, or being glands that produce tears **2 :** of, relating to, or marked by tears
lach·ry·mose \-ˌmōs\ *adj* [L *lacrimosus,* fr. *lacrima*] (ca. 1727) **1 :** given to tears or weeping **:** TEARFUL **2 :** tending to cause tears **:** MOURNFUL — **lach·ry·mose·ly** *adv* — **lach·ry·mos·i·ty** \ˌla-krə-ˈmä-sə-tē\ *n*
lacing *n* (14c) **1 :** the action of one that laces **2 :** something that laces **:** LACE **3 :** a contrasting marginal band of color (as on a feather) **4 a :** a dash of liquor in a food or beverage **b :** a trace or sprinkling that adds spice or flavor **5 :** a decisive defeat
la·cin·i·ate \lə-ˈsi-nē-ət, -ˌāt\ *adj* [L *lacinia* flap; akin to L *lacerare*] (ca. 1760) **:** bordered with a fringe; *esp* **:** cut into deep irregular usu. pointed lobes ⟨~ leaves⟩ — **la·cin·i·a·tion** \-ˌsi-nē-ˈā-shən\ *n*
[1]**lack** \ˈlak\ *vi* (13c) **1 :** to be deficient or missing ⟨time is ~*ing* for a full explanation⟩ **2 :** to be short or have need of something ⟨he will not ~ for advisers⟩ ~ *vt* **:** to stand in need of **:** suffer from the absence or deficiency of ⟨~ the necessities of life⟩
[2]**lack** *n* [ME *lak;* akin to MD *lak* lack, ON *lakr* defective] (14c) **1 :** the fact or state of being wanting or deficient ⟨a ~ of evidence⟩ **2 :** something that is lacking or is needed
lack·a·dai·si·cal \ˌla-kə-ˈdā-zi-kəl\ *adj* [irreg. fr. *lackaday* + *-ical*] (1768) **:** lacking life, spirit, or zest **:** LANGUID ***syn*** see LANGUID — **lack·a·dai·si·cal·ly** \-k(ə-)lē\ *adv*
lack·a·day \ˈla-kə-ˌdā\ *interj* [by alter. & shortening fr. *alack the day*] (1695) *archaic* — used to express regret or deprecation
[1]**lack·ey** \ˈla-kē\ *n, pl* **lackeys** [MF *laquais*] (1523) **1 a :** FOOTMAN 2, SERVANT **b :** someone who does menial tasks or runs errands for another **2 :** a servile follower **:** TOADY
[2]**lackey** *vb* **lack·eyed; lack·ey·ing** *vi* (1568) *archaic* **:** to serve as a lackey **:** TOADY ~ *vt* **:** to wait upon or serve obsequiously
lack·lus·ter \ˈlak-ˌləs-tər\ *adj* (1600) **:** lacking in sheen, brilliance, or vitality **:** DULL, MEDIOCRE — **lackluster** *n*
lack·lus·tre *chiefly Brit var of* LACKLUSTER
la·con·ic \lə-ˈkä-nik\ *adj* [L *laconicus* Spartan, fr. Gk *lakōnikos;* fr. the Spartan reputation for terseness of speech] (1589) **:** using or involving the use of a minimum of words **:** concise to the point of seeming rude or mysterious ***syn*** see CONCISE — **la·con·i·cal·ly** \-ni-k(ə-)lē\ *adv*
lac·o·nism \ˈla-kə-ˌni-zəm\ *n* (1570) **1 :** brevity or terseness of expression or style **2 :** a laconic expression
[1]**lac·quer** \ˈla-kər\ *n* [Pg *lacré* sealing wax, fr. *laca* lac, fr. Ar *lakk,* fr. Pers *lak* — more at LAC] (1592) **1 a :** a spirit varnish (as shellac) **b :** any of various durable natural varnishes; *esp* **:** a varnish obtained from an Asian sumac (*Rhus verniciflua*) — called also *Japanese lacquer* **2 :** any of various clear or colored synthetic organic coatings that typically dry to form a film by evaporation of the solvent; *esp* **:** a solution of a cellulose derivative (as nitrocellulose)
[2]**lacquer** *vt* **lac·quered; lac·quer·ing** \-k(ə-)riŋ\ (1688) **1 :** to coat with or as if with lacquer **2 :** to give a smooth finish or appearance to **:** make glossy ⟨~*ed* her hair⟩ — **lac·quer·er** \-kər-ər\ *n*
lac·quer·ware \-ˌwer\ *n* (1697) **:** a decorative article usu. made of wood and coated with lacquer; *also* **:** such articles or ware collectively
lac·quer·work \-ˌwərk\ *n* (1854) **:** LACQUERWARE
lac·ri·ma·tion \ˌla-krə-ˈmā-shən\ *n* (1572) **:** the secretion of tears esp. when abnormal or excessive
lac·ri·ma·tor *or* **lach·ry·ma·tor** \ˈla-krə-ˌmā-tər\ *n* [L *lacrimare* to weep, fr. *lacrima* tear — more at LACHRYMAL] (1918) **:** a tear-producing substance (as tear gas)
la·crosse \lə-ˈkrȯs\ *n* [CanF *la crosse,* lit., the crooked stick] (1718) **:** a goal game in which players use a long-handled stick that has a triangular head with a mesh pouch to catch, carry, and throw the ball
lact- *or* **lacti-** *or* **lacto-** *comb form* [F & L; F, fr. L, fr. *lact-, lac* — more at GALAXY] **1 :** milk ⟨*lacto*globulin⟩ **2 a :** lactic acid ⟨*lact*ate⟩ **b :** lactose ⟨*lact*ase⟩
lact·al·bu·min \ˌlak-ˌtal-ˈbyü-mən\ *n* [ISV] (ca. 1857) **:** an albumin that is obtained from whey and is similar to serum albumin
lac·tase \ˈlak-ˌtās, -ˌtāz\ *n* [ISV] (1891) **:** an enzyme that hydrolyzes beta-galactosides (as lactose) and occurs esp. in the intestines of young mammals and in yeasts
[1]**lac·tate** \ˈlak-ˌtāt\ *n* (ca. 1794) **:** a salt or ester of lactic acid
[2]**lactate** *vi* **lac·tat·ed; lac·tat·ing** [L *lactatus,* pp. of *lactare,* fr. *lact-, lac*] (ca. 1889) **:** to secrete milk — **lac·ta·tion** \lak-ˈtā-shən\ *n* — **lac·ta·tion·al** \-shnəl, -shə-nᵊl\ *adj*

\ə\ **abut** \ᵊ\ **kitten,** F table \ər\ **further** \a\ **ash** \ā\ **ace** \ä\ **mop, mar** \au̇\ **out** \ch\ **chin** \e\ **bet** \ē\ **easy** \g\ **go** \i\ **hit** \ī\ **ice** \j\ **job** \ŋ\ **sing** \ō\ **go** \ȯ\ **law** \ȯi\ **boy** \th\ **thin** \t͟h\ **the** \ü\ **loot** \u̇\ **foot** \y\ **yet** \zh\ **vision, beige** \k̲, ⁿ, œ, ue, ʸ\ *see* Guide to Pronunciation

lactate dehydrogenase *n* (1966) **:** any of a group of isoenzymes that catalyze reversibly the conversion of pyruvic acid to lactic acid — called also *lactic dehydrogenase*

[1]**lac·te·al** \ˈlak-tē-əl\ *adj* [L *lacteus* of milk, fr. *lact-, lac*] (1633) **1 :** relating to, consisting of, producing, or resembling milk **2 a :** conveying or containing a milky fluid **b :** of or relating to the lacteals

[2]**lacteal** *n* (1680) **:** any of the lymphatic vessels arising from the villi of the small intestine and conveying chyle to the thoracic duct

lac·tic \ˈlak-tik\ *adj* (1790) **1 a :** of or relating to milk **b :** obtained from sour milk or whey **2 :** involving the production of lactic acid

lactic acid *n* (1790) **:** a hygroscopic organic acid $C_3H_6O_3$ present normally esp. in muscle tissue as a product of anaerobic glycolysis, produced in carbohydrate matter usu. by bacterial fermentation, and used esp. in food and medicine and in industry

lac·tif·er·ous \lak-ˈti-f(ə-)rəs\ *adj* [F or LL; F *lactifère,* fr. LL *lactifer,* fr. L *lact-, lac* + *-fer*] (ca. 1674) **1 :** yielding a milky juice ⟨~ plants⟩ **2 :** secreting or conveying milk

lac·to·ba·cil·lus \ˌlak-tō-bə-ˈsi-ləs\ *n* [NL] (1924) **:** any of a genus (*Lactobacillus*) of bacteria that produce lactic acid

lac·to·gen·ic \ˌlak-tə-ˈje-nik\ *adj* (1933) **:** inducing lactation ⟨~ hormones⟩

lac·to·glob·u·lin \-ˈglä-byə-lən\ *n* (1885) **:** a crystalline protein fraction that is obtained from the whey of milk

lac·tone \ˈlak-ˌtōn\ *n* [ISV] (1880) **:** any of various cyclic esters formed from hydroxy acids — **lac·ton·ic** \lak-ˈtä-nik\ *adj*

lac·to–ovo vegetarian \ˈlak-tō-ˈō-vō-\ *n* (1952) **:** a vegetarian whose diet includes dairy products, eggs, vegetables, fruits, grains, and nuts — called also *ovo-lacto vegetarian*; compare LACTO-VEGETARIAN

lac·tose \ˈlak-ˌtōs, -ˌtōz\ *n* [ISV] (1857) **:** a disaccharide sugar $C_{12}H_{22}O_{11}$ that is present in milk and yields glucose and galactose upon hydrolysis and yields esp. lactic acid upon fermentation

lac·to–veg·e·tar·i·an \ˌlak-tō-ˌve-jə-ˈter-ē-ən\ *n* (1971) **:** a vegetarian whose diet includes dairy products, vegetables, fruits, grains, and nuts — compare LACTO-OVO VEGETARIAN

la·cu·na \lə-ˈkü-nə, -ˈkyü-\ *n, pl* **la·cu·nae** \-ˈkyü-(ˌ)nē, -ˈkü-ˌnī\ *also* **la·cu·nas** \-ˈkü-nəz, -ˈkyü-\ [L, pool, pit, gap — more at LAGOON] (1652) **1 :** a blank space or a missing part **:** GAP ⟨the evident *lacunae* in his story —Shirley Hazzard⟩; *also* **:** DEFICIENCY 1 ⟨despite all these *lacunae,* those reforms were a vast improvement —*New Republic*⟩ **2 :** a small cavity, pit, or discontinuity in an anatomical structure — **la·cu·nar** \-ˈkü-nər, -ˈkyü-\ *also* **la·cu·nate** \lə-ˈkü-nət, -ˈkyü-, -ˌnāt; ˈla-kyə-ˌnāt\ *adj*

la·cus·trine \lə-ˈkəs-trən\ *adj* [F or It *lacustre,* fr. L *lacus* lake] (1830) **:** of, relating to, formed in, living in, or growing in lakes ⟨~ deposits⟩ ⟨~ faunas⟩

lacy *also* **lac·ey** \ˈlā-sē\ *adj* **lac·i·er; -est** (1804) **:** resembling or consisting of lace

lad \ˈlad\ *n* [ME *ladde*] (14c) **1 :** a male person of any age between early boyhood and maturity **:** BOY, YOUTH **2 :** FELLOW, CHAP

ladanum *var of* LABDANUM

lad·der \ˈla-dər\ *n, often attrib* [ME, fr. OE *hlǣder;* akin to OHG *leitara* ladder, OE *hlinian* to lean — more at LEAN] (bef. 12c) **1 :** a structure for climbing up or down that consists essentially of two long sidepieces joined at intervals by crosspieces on which one may step **2 :** something that resembles or suggests a ladder in form or use; *esp* **:** RUN 11a **3 :** a series of usu. ascending steps or stages **:** SCALE ⟨climbing up the corporate ~⟩ — **lad·der·like** \-ˌlīk\ *adj*

lad·der–back \-ˌbak\ *adj* (1908) *of furniture* **:** having a back consisting of two upright posts connected by horizontal slats

ladder truck *n* (1889) **:** HOOK AND LADDER TRUCK

lad·die \ˈla-dē\ *n* (1546) **:** a young lad

lade \ˈlād\ *vb* **lad·ed; laded** *or* **lad·en** \ˈlā-dᵊn\; **lad·ing** [ME, fr. OE *hladan;* akin to OHG *hladan* to load, OCS *klasti* to place] *vt* (bef. 12c) **1 a :** to put a load or burden on or in **:** LOAD **b :** to put or place as a load esp. for shipment **:** SHIP **c :** to load heavily or oppressively **2 :** DIP, LADLE ~ *vi* **1 :** to take on cargo **:** LOAD ⟨a place for ships to ~⟩ **2 :** to take up or convey a liquid by dipping

[1]**lad·en** \ˈlā-dᵊn\ *vt* **lad·ened; lad·en·ing** \ˈlād-niŋ, ˈlā-dᵊn-iŋ\ (1514) **:** LADE

[2]**laden** *adj* (bef. 12c) **:** carrying a load or burden

la–di–da *also* **la–de–da** *or* **lah–de–dah** *or* **lah–dee–dah** *or* **lah–di–dah** \ˌlä-dē-ˈdä\ *adj* [perh. alter. of *lardy-dardy* foppish] (1889) **:** affectedly refined in manners or tastes **:** PRETENTIOUS, ELEGANT

la·dies \ˈlā-dēz\ *n pl but sing or pl in constr* (1918) *chiefly Brit* **:** LADIES' ROOM

ladies' man *also* **lady's man** *n* (1784) **:** a man who shows a marked fondness for the company of women or is esp. attentive to women

ladies' room *n* (1870) **:** a room equipped with lavatories and toilets for the use of women

ladies' tresses *n pl but sing or pl in constr* (1548) **:** any of a widely distributed genus (*Spiranthes*) of terrestrial orchids with slender often twisted spikes of white irregular flowers

La·din \lə-ˈdēn\ *n* [Rhaeto-Romance, fr. L *Latinum* Latin] (1837) **1 a :** a Rhaeto-Romance dialect of Alto Adige in northern Italy **b :** the Rhaeto-Romance dialects of the Engadine Valley in Switzerland **2 :** one speaking Ladin as a mother tongue

lading *n* (1500) **1 a :** LOADING 1 **b :** an act of bailing, dipping, or ladling **2 :** CARGO, FREIGHT

la·di·no \lə-ˈdē-(ˌ)nō\ *n, pl* **-nos** [Sp, lit., Latin, fr. L *latinus*] (1877) **1** *often cap* [AmerSp] **:** a westernized Spanish-speaking Latin American; *esp* **:** MESTIZO **2** *cap* [Judeo-Spanish, fr. OSp] **:** JUDEO-SPANISH

la·di·no clover \lə-ˈdī-(ˌ)nō-, -nə-\ *n* [perh. irreg. fr. *Lodi,* Italy + It *-ino,* adj. suffix] (1924) **:** a large nutritious rapidly growing clover that is a variety of white clover and is widely planted esp. for forage — called also *ladino*

[1]**la·dle** \ˈlā-dᵊl\ *n* [ME *ladel,* fr. OE *hlædel,* fr. *hladan*] (bef. 12c) **1 :** a deep-bowled long-handled spoon used esp. for dipping up and conveying liquids **2 :** something resembling a ladle in form or function — **la·dle·ful** \-ˌfu̇l\ *n*

[2]**ladle** *vt* **la·dled; la·dling** \ˈlād-liŋ, ˈlā-dᵊl-iŋ\ (ca. 1532) **:** to take up and convey in or as if in a ladle

la dol·ce vi·ta \(ˌ)lä-ˈdōl-(ˌ)chā-ˈvē-(ˌ)tä\ *n* (1961) **:** DOLCE VITA

la·dy \ˈlā-dē\ *n, pl* **ladies** *often attrib* [ME, fr. OE *hlǣfdige,* fr. *hlāf* bread + *-dige* (akin to *dǣge* kneader of bread) — more at LOAF, DAIRY] (bef. 12c) **1 a :** a woman having proprietary rights or authority esp. as a feudal superior **b :** a woman receiving the homage or devotion of a knight or lover **2** *cap* **:** VIRGIN MARY — usu. used with *Our* **3 a :** a woman of superior social position **b :** a woman of refinement and gentle manners **c :** WOMAN, FEMALE — often used in a courteous reference ⟨show the ~ to a seat⟩ or usu. in the pl. in address ⟨*ladies* and gentlemen⟩ **4 a :** WIFE **b :** GIRLFRIEND, MISTRESS **5 a :** any of various titled women in Great Britain — used as the customary title of (1) a marchioness, countess, viscountess, or baroness or (2) the wife of a knight, baronet, member of the peerage, or one having the courtesy title of *lord* and used as a courtesy title for the daughter of a duke, marquess, or earl **b :** a woman who is a member of an order of knighthood — compare DAME

lady apple *n* (1850) **:** a small red to yellow apple used esp. as a garnish

la·dy·bug \ˈlā-dē-ˌbəg\ *n* [Our *Lady,* the Virgin Mary] (1699) **:** any of numerous small nearly hemispherical often brightly colored often spotted beetles (family Coccinellidae) of temperate and tropical regions that usu. feed both as larvae and adults on other insects (as aphids) — called also *lady beetle, ladybird, ladybird beetle*

lady chapel *n, often cap L&C* (15c) **:** a chapel dedicated to the Virgin Mary

Lady Day *n* (13c) **:** ANNUNCIATION 1

la·dy·fin·ger \ˈlā-dē-ˌfiŋ-gər\ *n* (1820) **:** a small finger-shaped sponge cake

la·dy·fish \-ˌfish\ *n* (1712) **1 :** BONEFISH 1 **2 :** a large silvery bony fish (*Elops saurus*) of the western Atlantic that is related to the tarpon and is often caught for sport

la·dy–in–wait·ing \ˈlā-dē-in-ˈwā-tiŋ\ *n, pl* **ladies–in–waiting** (ca. 1860) **:** a lady of a queen's or a princess's household appointed to wait on her

la·dy–kill·er \ˈlā-dē-ˌki-lər\ *n* (ca. 1810) **:** a man who is extremely attractive to women

la·dy·like \-ˌlīk\ *adj* (1586) **1 :** becoming or suitable to a lady **2 :** resembling a lady in appearance or manners **:** WELL-BRED **3 a :** feeling or showing too much concern about elegance or propriety ⟨~ embarrassment at not being the wife of a real doctor —Lewis Vogler⟩ **b :** lacking in strength, force, or virility

la·dy·love \ˈlā-dē-ˌləv, ˌlā-dē-ˈ\ *n* (1733) **:** SWEETHEART, MISTRESS

lady of the house (1601) **:** the chief female in a household

Lady of the Lake (15c) **:** VIVIAN

la·dy·ship \ˈlā-dē-ˌship\ *n* (13c) **:** the condition of being a lady **:** rank of lady — used as a title for a woman having the rank of lady ⟨her *Ladyship* is not at home⟩ ⟨if your *Ladyship* please⟩

lady's mantle *n* (1548) **:** any of a genus (*Alchemilla*) of widely distributed perennial herbaceous plants of the rose family; *esp* **:** one (*A. mollis*) cultivated as a garden plant for its large circular grayish-green hairy leaves and small greenish-yellow flowers

lady's slipper *n* (1597) **:** any of several No. American temperate-zone orchids (as of the genus *Cypripedium*) having flowers whose shape suggests a slipper — called also *lady slipper*

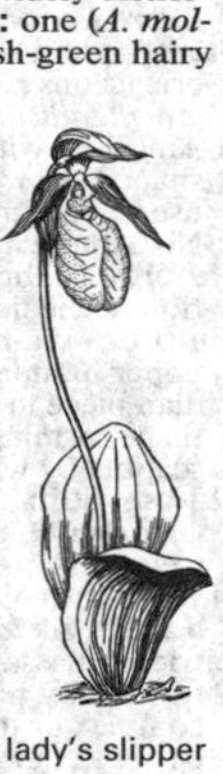
lady's slipper

la·dy's–smock \-ˌsmäk\ *n* (1588) **:** CUCKOOFLOWER 1

lady's thumb *n* (1837) **:** a widely distributed weedy annual herb (*Polygonum persicaria*) of the buckwheat family that has large lanceolate leaves often with a blackish blotch suggesting a thumbprint

La·er·tes \lā-ˈər-tēz, -ˈer-\ *n* [L, fr. Gk *Laertēs*] (ca. 1565) **1 :** the father of Odysseus in Greek mythology **2 :** the son of Polonius and brother of Ophelia in Shakespeare's *Hamlet*

Lae·ta·re Sunday \lā-ˈtär-ē-, -ˈter-\ *n* [L *laetare,* sing. imper. of *laetari* to rejoice] (ca. 1870) **:** the fourth Sunday in Lent

la·e·trile \ˈlā-ə-(ˌ)tril, -trəl\ *n, often cap* [*lae*vorotatory (levorotatory) + ni*trile*] (1953) **:** a drug derived esp. from apricot pits that contains amygdalin and has been used in the treatment of cancer although of unproved effectiveness

[1]**lag** \ˈlag\ *n* [prob. of Scand origin; akin to Norw dial. *lagga* to go slowly] (1514) **1 :** one that lags or is last **2 a :** the act or the condition of lagging **b :** comparative slowness or retardation **c** (1) **:** an amount of lagging or the time during which lagging continues (2) **:** a space of time esp. between related events or phenomena **:** INTERVAL **3 :** the action of lagging for opening shot (as in marbles or billiards) **4 :** a usu. long putt struck with the aim of having the ball stop near the hole

[2]**lag** *vb* **lagged; lag·ging** *vi* (1530) **1 a :** to stay or fall behind **:** LINGER, LOITER **b :** to move, function, or develop with comparative slowness **c :** to become retarded in attaining maximum value **2 :** to slacken or weaken gradually **:** FLAG **3 :** to toss or roll a marble toward a line or a cue ball toward the head cushion to determine order of play **4 :** to hit a lag putt ~ *vt* **1 :** to lag behind ⟨current that ~*s* the voltage⟩ **2 :** to pitch or shoot (as a coin or marble) at a mark **3 :** to hit (a golf ball or putt) with the aim of having the ball stop near the hole ***syn*** see DELAY — **lag·ger** *n*

[3]**lag** *adj* (1552) **:** LAST, HINDMOST

[4]**lag** *n* [prob. of Scand origin; akin to ON *lǫgg* rim of a barrel] (1672) **1 :** a barrel stave **2 :** a stave, slat, or strip (as of wood or asbestos) forming part of a covering for a cylindrical object

[5]**lag** *vt* **lagged; lag·ging** (1870) **:** to cover or provide with lags

[6]**lag** *vt* **lagged; lag·ging** [origin unknown] (ca. 1812) **1** *slang chiefly Brit* **:** to transport or jail for crime **2** *slang chiefly Brit* **:** ARREST

[7]**lag** *n* (ca. 1812) **1** *slang chiefly Brit* **a :** a person transported for crime **b :** CONVICT **c :** an ex-convict **2** *slang chiefly Brit* **:** a jail sentence **:** STRETCH

lag·an \ˈla-gən\ *also* **lag·end** \-gənd\ *n* [MF *lagan* or ML *laganum* debris washed up from the sea] (1641) **:** goods thrown into the sea with a buoy attached so that they may be found again

Lag b'Omer \ˈläg-ˈbō-mər, ˌläg-bə-ˈō-\ *n* [Heb, 33d in Omer] (1874) **:** a Jewish holiday falling on the 33d day of the Omer and commemorating the heroism of Bar Kokhba and Akiba ben Joseph

la·ger \ˈlä-gər\ *n* [G *Lagerbier* beer made for storage, fr. *Lager* storehouse + *Bier* beer] (1852) **:** a beer brewed by slow fermentation and matured under refrigeration

[1]**lag·gard** \ˈla-gərd\ *adj* (1702) **:** lagging or tending to lag **:** DILATORY — **lag·gard·ly** *adv or adj* — **lag·gard·ness** *n*
[2]**laggard** *n* (1705) **:** one that lags or lingers
lagging *n* (1851) **:** a lag or material used for making lags: as **a :** material for thermal insulation esp. around a cylindrical object **b :** planking used esp. for preventing cave-ins in earthwork or for supporting an arch during construction
la·gniappe \ˈlan-ˌyap, lan-ˈ\ *n* [AmerF, fr. AmerSp *la ñapa* the lagniappe, fr. *la* + *ñapa, yapa,* fr. Quechua *yapa* something added] (1844) **:** a small gift given a customer by a merchant at the time of a purchase; *broadly* **:** something given or obtained gratuitously or by way of good measure
lago·morph \ˈla-gə-ˌmȯrf\ *n* [ultim. fr. Gk *lagōs* hare + *morphē* form] (1882) **:** any of an order (Lagomorpha) of gnawing herbivorous mammals having two pairs of incisors in the upper jaw one behind the other and comprising the rabbits, hares, and pikas
la·goon \lə-ˈgün\ *n* [F & It; F *lagune,* fr. It *laguna,* fr. L *lacuna* pit, pool, fr. *lacus* lake] (1673) **1 :** a shallow sound, channel, or pond near or communicating with a larger body of water **2 :** a shallow artificial pool or pond (as for the processing of sewage or storage of a liquid) — **la·goon·al** \-ˈgü-nᵊl\ *adj*
La·grang·ian \lə-ˈgrän-jē-ən, -ˈgräⁿ-zhē-\ *n* [Joseph-Louis *Lagrange*] (1929) **:** a function that describes the state of a dynamic system in terms of position coordinates and their time derivatives and that is equal to the difference between the potential energy and kinetic energy — compare HAMILTONIAN
la·har \ˈlä-ˌhär\ *n* [Jav] (1929) **:** a moving fluid mass composed of volcanic debris and water
lah–de–dah, lah–dee–dah, lah–di–dah *var of* LA-DI-DA
Lahn·da \ˈlän-də\ *n* (1901) **:** an Indo-Aryan dialect group of eastern Pakistan
la·ical \ˈlā-ə-kəl\ *or* **la·ic** \ˈlā-ik\ *adj* [LL *laicus,* fr. LGk *laïkos,* fr. Gk, of the people, fr. *laos* people] (1562) **:** of or relating to the laity **:** SECULAR — **laic** *n* — **la·ical·ly** \ˈlā-ə-k(ə-)lē\ *adv*
la·i·cism \ˈlā-ə-ˌsi-zəm\ *n* (ca. 1909) **:** a political system characterized by the exclusion of ecclesiastical control and influence
la·i·cize \ˈlā-ə-ˌsīz\ *vt* **la·i·cized; la·i·ciz·ing** (1870) **1 :** to reduce to lay status **2 :** to put under the direction of or open to the laity — **la·i·ci·za·tion** \ˌlā-ə-sə-ˈzā-shən\ *n*
laid *past and past part of* LAY
laid–back \ˈlād-ˈbak, ˌlād-\ *adj* (1969) **:** having a relaxed style or character ⟨~ music⟩ — **laid–back·ness** \-nəs\ *n*
laid paper \ˈlād-\ *n* (1839) **:** paper watermarked with fine lines running across the grain — compare WOVE PAPER
lain *past part of* LIE
[1]**lair** \ˈler\ *n* [ME, fr. OE *leger;* akin to OHG *legar* bed, OE *licgan* to lie — more at LIE] (bef. 12c) **1** *dial Brit* **:** a resting or sleeping place **:** BED **2 a :** the resting or living place of a wild animal **:** DEN **b :** a refuge or place for hiding
[2]**lair** *vb* [Sc *lair* mire] *vt* (ca. 1560) *chiefly Scot* **:** to cause to sink in mire ~ *vi, chiefly Scot* **:** WALLOW
laird \ˈlerd\ *n* [ME (northern dial.) *lord, lard* lord] (14c) *chiefly Scot* **:** a landed proprietor — **laird·ly** \-lē\ *adj*
lais·ser–faire *chiefly Brit var of* LAISSEZ-FAIRE
lais·ser–pas·ser *chiefly Brit var of* LAISSEZ-PASSER
lais·sez–faire \ˌle-ˌsā-ˈfer, ˌlā-, -ˌzā-\ *n* [F *laissez faire,* imper. of *laisser faire* to let (people) do (as they choose)] (1825) **1 :** a doctrine opposing governmental interference in economic affairs beyond the minimum necessary for the maintenance of peace and property rights **2 :** a philosophy or practice characterized by a usu. deliberate abstention from direction or interference esp. with individual freedom of choice and action — **laissez–faire** *adj*
lais·sez–pas·ser \-ˌpa-ˈsā\ *n* [F, fr. *laissez passer* let (someone) pass] (1914) **:** PERMIT, PASS
lai·tance \ˈlā-tᵊn(t)s\ *n* [F, fr. *lait* milk, fr. L *lact-, lac* — more at GALAXY] (ca. 1902) **:** an accumulation of fine particles on the surface of fresh concrete due to an upward movement of water (as when excessive mixing water is used)
la·ity \ˈlā-ə-tē\ *n* [[5]*lay*] (15c) **1 :** the people of a religious faith as distinguished from its clergy **2 :** the mass of the people as distinguished from those of a particular profession or those specially skilled
La·ius \ˈlā-əs, ˈlī-əs\ *n* [L, fr. Gk *Laïos*] (1573) **:** a king of Thebes slain by his son Oedipus in fulfillment of an oracle
[1]**lake** \ˈlāk\ *n, often attrib* [ME, fr. OE, AF, & L; OE *lacu* stream, pool, fr. L *lacus* lake, pool, pit & AF *lac* pit, fr. L *lacus;* akin to OE *lagu* sea, Gk *lakkos* pond] (12c) **:** a considerable inland body of standing water; *also* **:** a pool of other liquid (as lava, oil, or pitch) — **lake·like** \-ˌlīk\ *adj*
[2]**lake** *n* [F *laque* lac, fr. Old Occitan *laca,* fr. Ar *lakk* — more at LACQUER] (1598) **1 a :** a purplish red pigment prepared from lac or cochineal **b :** any of numerous usu. bright translucent organic pigments composed essentially of a soluble dye absorbed on or combined with an inorganic carrier **2 :** CARMINE 2 — **laky** \ˈlā-kē\ *adj*
[3]**lake** *vb* **laked; lak·ing** *vt* (1903) **:** to cause (blood) to undergo a physiological change in which the hemoglobin becomes dissolved in the plasma ~ *vi, of blood* **:** to undergo the process by which hemoglobin becomes dissolved in the plasma
lake dwelling *n* (1863) **:** a dwelling built on piles in a lake; *specif* **:** one built in prehistoric times — **lake dweller** *n*
lake effect *n* (1951) **:** a meteorological phenomenon in which warm moist air rising from a body of water mixes with cold dry air overhead resulting in precipitation esp. downwind — usu. hyphenated when used attributively ⟨*lake-effect* snows⟩
lake·front \ˈlāk-ˌfrənt\ *n* (1880) **:** an area fronting on a lake
lake herring *n* (1842) **:** a cisco (*Coregonus artedii*) found from the Mississippi River basin, Great Lakes, and St. Lawrence River northward and important as a commercial food fish
Lake·land terrier \ˈlāk-lənd-, -ˌland-\ *n* [*Lakeland,* England] (1928) **:** any of an English breed of rather small harsh-coated terriers
lak·er \ˈlā-kər\ *n* (1823) **:** one associated with a lake; *esp* **:** a fish (as a lake trout) living in or taken from a lake
lake·shore \ˈlāk-ˌshȯr\ *n* (1798) **:** the shore of a lake; *also* **:** LAKEFRONT
lake·side \-ˌsīd\ *n* (1560) **:** LAKEFRONT
lake trout *n* (1668) **:** any of various trout and salmon found in lakes; *esp* **:** MACKINAW TROUT
lakh \ˈläk, ˈlak\ *n* [Hindi & Urdu *lākh*] (1599) **1 :** one hundred thousand ⟨50 ~*s* of rupees⟩ **2 :** a great number — **lakh** *adj*
La·ko·ta \lə-ˈkō-tə\ *n, pl* **Lakota** *also* **Lakotas** [Lakota *lakʰóta,* a self-designation] (1918) **1 :** a member of a western division of the Dakota peoples **2 :** a dialect of Dakota
la–la land \ˈlä-ˌlä-\ *n* [perh. fr. *la-la* nonsense syllables in the refrains of songs] (1983) **:** a euphoric dreamlike mental state detached from the harsher realities of life
-lalia *n comb form* [NL, fr. Gk *lalia* chatter, fr. *lalein* to chat] **:** speech disorder (of a specified type) ⟨echo*lalia*⟩
lal·lan \ˈla-lən\ *or* **lal·land** \-lən(d)\ *Scot var of* LOWLAND
Lal·lans \ˈla-lənz\ *n* (1785) **:** Scots as spoken and written in the lowlands of Scotland
lal·ly column \ˈlä-lē-\ *n, often cap L* [fr. *Lally,* a trademark] (1926) **:** a concrete-filled cylindrical steel structural column
lallygag *var of* LOLLYGAG
[1]**lam** \ˈlam\ *vb* **lammed; lam·ming** [perh. of Scand origin; akin to ON *lemja* to thrash; akin to OE *lama* lame] *vt* (1595) **:** to beat soundly **:** THRASH ~ *vi* **1 :** STRIKE, THRASH **2 :** to flee hastily **:** SCRAM
[2]**lam** *n* (ca. 1897) **:** sudden or hurried flight esp. from the law ⟨on the ~⟩
Lam *abbr* Lamentations
la·ma \ˈlä-mə\ *n* [Tibetan *blama*] (1654) **:** a Lamaist monk
La·ma·ism \ˈlä-mə-ˌi-zəm\ *n* (1817) **:** TIBETAN BUDDHISM — **La·ma·ist** \-mə-ist\ *n or adj* — **La·ma·is·tic** \ˌlä-mə-ˈis-tik\ *adj*
La·marck·ism \lə-ˈmär-ˌki-zəm\ *n* [J.-B. de Monet de *Lamarck*] (1884) **:** a theory of organic evolution asserting that environmental changes cause structural changes in animals and plants that are transmitted to offspring — **La·marck·ian** \-kē-ən\ *adj*
la·ma·sery \ˈlä-mə-ˌser-ē\ *n, pl* **-ser·ies** [F *lamaserie,* irreg. fr. *lama* + *-erie* -ery] (1849) **:** a monastery of lamas
La·maze \lə-ˈmäz\ *adj* [Fernand *Lamaze* †1957 Fr. obstetrician] (1959) **:** relating to or being a method of childbirth that involves psychological and physical preparation by the mother in order to suppress pain and facilitate delivery without drugs
[1]**lamb** \ˈlam\ *n* [ME, fr. OE; akin to OHG *lamb* lamb] (bef. 12c) **1 a :** a young sheep; *esp* **:** one that is less than one year old or without permanent teeth **b :** the young of various animals (as the smaller antelopes) other than sheep **2 a :** a gentle or weak person **b :** DEAR, PET **c :** a person easily cheated or deceived esp. in trading securities **3 a :** the flesh of a lamb used as food **b :** LAMBSKIN — **lamb·like** \-ˌlīk\ *adj* — **lamby** \ˈla-mē\ *adj*

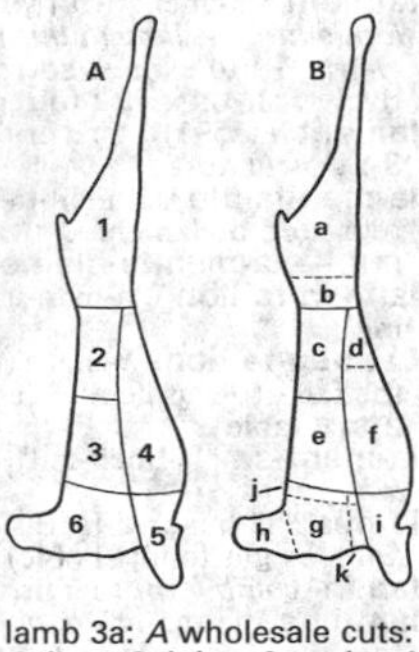

lamb 3a: *A* wholesale cuts: *1* leg, *2* loin, *3* rack, *4* breast, *5* shank, *6* shoulder; *B* retail cuts: *a* leg, *b* sirloin chops and roast, *c* loin chops, rolled loin roast, *d* patties and chopped roast, *e* rib chops, crown roast, *f* riblets, stew, and stuffed or rolled breast, *g* shoulder roast, shoulder chops, *h* neck slices, *i* shanks, *j* blade chops, *k* arm chops

[2]**lamb** *vi* (1611) **:** to bring forth a lamb ~ *vt* **1 :** to bring forth (a lamb) **2 :** to tend (ewes) at lambing time — **lamb·er** \ˈla-mər\ *n*
lam·baste *or* **lam·bast** \(ˌ)lam-ˈbāst, -ˈbast; ˈlam-ˌ\ *vt* [prob. fr. [1]*lam* + *baste*] (1620) **1 :** to assault violently **:** BEAT, WHIP **2 :** to attack verbally **:** CENSURE ⟨critics *lambasted* his performance⟩
lamb·da \ˈlam-də\ *n* [ME, fr. Gk, of Sem origin; akin to Heb *lāmedh* lamed] (15c) **1 :** the 11th letter of the Greek alphabet — see ALPHABET table **2 :** an uncharged unstable elementary particle that has a mass 2183 times that of an electron and that decays typically into a nucleon and a pion
lam·ben·cy \ˈlam-bən(t)-sē\ *n, pl* **-cies** (1817) **:** the quality, state, or an instance of being lambent
lam·bent \ˈlam-bənt\ *adj* [L *lambent-, lambens,* prp. of *lambere* to lick — more at LAP] (1647) **1 :** playing lightly on or over a surface **:** FLICKERING **2 :** softly bright or radiant **3 :** marked by lightness or brilliance esp. of expression — **lam·bent·ly** *adv*
lam·bert \ˈlam-bərt\ *n* [Johann H. *Lambert* †1777 Ger. physicist & philosopher] (1915) **:** the centimeter-gram-second unit of brightness equal to the brightness of a perfectly diffusing surface that radiates or reflects one lumen per square centimeter
lamb·kill \ˈlam-ˌkil\ *n* (1790) **:** SHEEP LAUREL
lam·bre·quin \ˈlam-bər-kən, -bri-kən\ *n* [F] (ca. 1725) **1 :** a scarf used to cover a knight's helmet **2 :** a short decorative drapery for a shelf edge or for the top of a window casing **:** VALANCE
Lam·brus·co \lam-ˈbrü-(ˌ)skō, -ˈbrü-\ *n* [It, fr. L *labruscum* fruit of the wild grape *Vitis labrusca*] (1868) **:** a fruity and fizzy red Italian table wine
lamb's ears *n pl but usu sing in constr* (1930) **:** a widely cultivated perennial southwest Asian herb (*Stachys byzantina* syn. *S. olympica*) of the mint family having leaves covered with densely matted hairs
lamb·skin \ˈlam-ˌskin\ *n* (14c) **:** a lamb's skin or a small fine-grade sheepskin or the leather made from either; *specif* **:** such a skin dressed with the wool on and used esp. for winter clothing
lamb's lettuce *n* (1597) **:** CORN SALAD
lamb's–quar·ter \ˈlamz-ˌkwȯ(r)-tər, -ˌkȯ(r)-\ *n* (1773) **1 :** a goosefoot (*Chenopodium album*) having glaucous foliage that is sometimes used as greens — usu. used in pl. but sing. or pl. in constr. **2 :** any of several oraches — usu. used in pl. but sing. or pl. in constr.
[1]**lame** \ˈlām\ *adj* **lam·er; lam·est** [ME, fr. OE *lama;* akin to OHG *lam* lame, Lith *limti* to break down] (bef. 12c) **1 a :** having a body part and esp. a limb so disabled as to impair freedom of movement **b :** marked by stiffness and soreness ⟨a ~ shoulder⟩ **2 :** lacking needful or desir-

able substance : WEAK, INEFFECTUAL ⟨a ~ excuse⟩ **3** *slang* : not being in the know : SQUARE **4 a** : INFERIOR ⟨a ~ school⟩ **b** : CONTEMPTIBLE, NASTY ⟨~ racist jokes⟩ — **lame·ly** *adv* — **lame·ness** *n*

²**lame** *vt* **lamed; lam·ing** (14c) **1** : to make lame : CRIPPLE **2** : to make weak or ineffective : DISABLE

³**lame** *n* (1959) *slang* : a person who is not in the know : SQUARE

⁴**lame** \ˈlām, ˈlam\ *n* [MF, fr. L *lamina*] (ca. 1586) **1** : a thin plate esp. of metal : LAMINA **2** *pl* : small overlapping steel plates joined to slide on one another (as in medieval armor)

la·mé \lä-ˈmā, la-\ *n* [F] (1922) : a brocaded clothing fabric made from any of various fibers combined with tinsel filling threads

lame·brain \ˈlām-ˌbrān\ *n* (1944) : a dull-witted person : DOLT — **lamebrain** *or* **lame·brained** \-ˈbrānd\ *adj*

la·med \ˈlä-ˌmed\ *n* [Heb *lāmedh*, lit., ox goad] (1665) : the 12th letter of the Hebrew alphabet — see ALPHABET table

lame duck *n* (1761) **1** : one that is weak or that falls behind in ability or achievement; *esp, chiefly Brit* : an ailing company **2** : an elected official or group continuing to hold political office during the period between the election and the inauguration of a successor **3** : one whose position or term of office will soon end — **lame–duck** \ˈlām-ˈdək\ *adj*

la·mel·la \lə-ˈme-lə\ *n, pl* **la·mel·lae** \-ˈme-(ˌ)lē, -ˌlī\ *also* **lamellas** [NL, fr. L, dim. of *lamina* thin plate] (1678) : a thin flat scale, membrane, or layer: as **a** : one of the thin plates composing the gills of a bivalve mollusk **b** : a gill of a mushroom

la·mel·lar \lə-ˈme-lər\ *adj* (1794) **1** : composed of or arranged in lamellae **2** : having the form of a thin plate ⟨~ armor⟩

la·mel·late \lə-ˈme-lət, ˈla-mə-ˌlāt\ *adj* (1826) **1** : composed of or furnished with lamellae **2** : LAMELLAR 2 — **la·mel·late·ly** *adv*

la·mel·li·branch \lə-ˈme-lə-ˌbraŋk\ *n, pl* **-branchs** [NL *Lamellibranchia*, fr. *lamella* + L *branchia* gill] (1855) : any of a class (Lamellibranchia) of bivalve mollusks (as clams, oysters, and mussels) that have the body bilaterally symmetrical, compressed, and enclosed within the mantle and that build up a shell whose right and left parts are connected by a hinge over the animal's back — **lamellibranch** *adj*

¹**la·ment** \lə-ˈment\ *vb* [ME *lementen*, fr. MF & L; MF *lamenter*, fr. L *lamentari*, fr. *lamentum*, n., lament] *vi* (15c) : to mourn aloud : WAIL ~ *vt* **1** : to express sorrow, mourning, or regret for often demonstratively : MOURN **2** : to regret strongly ***syn*** see DEPLORE

²**lament** *n* (1591) **1** : a crying out in grief : WAILING **2** : DIRGE, ELEGY **3** : COMPLAINT

la·men·ta·ble \lə-ˈmen-tə-bəl *also* ˈla-mən-\ *adj* (15c) **1** : that is to be regretted or lamented : DEPLORABLE **2** : expressing grief : MOURNFUL — **la·men·ta·ble·ness** *n* — **la·men·ta·bly** \-blē\ *adv*

lam·en·ta·tion \ˌla-mən-ˈtā-shən\ *n* (14c) : an act or instance of lamenting

Lam·en·ta·tions \-shənz\ *n pl but sing in constr* (14c) : a poetic book on the fall of Jerusalem in canonical Jewish and Christian Scripture — see BIBLE table

la·ment·ed \lə-ˈmen-təd\ *adj* (1611) : mourned for — **la·ment·ed·ly** *adv*

la·mia \ˈlā-mē-ə\ *n* [ME, fr. L, fr. Gk, devouring monster; akin to Gk *lamyros* gluttonous] (14c) : a female demon : VAMPIRE

lamin- *comb form* : lamina ⟨*lamin*ar⟩

lam·i·na \ˈla-mə-nə\ *n, pl* **-nae** \-ˌnē, -ˌnī\ *or* **-nas** [L] (ca. 1656) **1** : a thin plate or scale : LAYER **2** : the expanded part of a foliage leaf **3** : one of the narrow thin parallel plates of soft vascular sensitive tissue that cover the flesh within the wall of a hoof

lam·i·nal \ˈla-mə-nᵊl\ *adj* (1825) **1** : LAMINAR **2** : produced with the blade of the tongue (as \sh\, \zh\, \ch\, \j\, or \y\) — compare APICAL

lamina pro·pria \-ˈprō-prē-ə\ *n, pl* **laminae pro·pri·ae** \-prē-ˌē, -ˌī\ [NL, lit., proper lamina] (1937) : a highly vascular layer of connective tissue under the basement membrane lining a layer of epithelium

lam·i·nar \ˈla-mə-nər\ *adj* (1811) : arranged in, consisting of, or resembling laminae

laminar flow *n* (1935) : uninterrupted flow in a fluid near a solid boundary in which the direction of flow at every point remains constant — compare TURBULENT FLOW

lam·i·nar·ia \ˌla-mə-ˈner-ē-ə\ *n* [NL, fr. L *lamina*] (1848) : any of a genus (*Laminaria*) of large chiefly perennial kelps with an unbranched cylindrical or flattened stipe and a smooth or convoluted blade; *broadly* : any of various related kelps (order Laminariales) — **lam·i·nar·i·an** \-ē-ən\ *adj or n*

lam·i·nar·in \ˌlam-ə-ˈner-ən\ *n* [ISV *laminar-* (fr. NL *Laminaria*) + ¹*-in*] (ca. 1931) : a polysaccharide that is found in various brown algae and yields only glucose on hydrolysis

¹**lam·i·nate** \ˈla-mə-ˌnāt\ *vb* **-nat·ed; -nat·ing** *vt* (1665) **1** : to roll or compress into a thin plate **2** : to separate into laminae **3 a** : to make (as a windshield) by uniting superposed layers of one or more materials **b** : to unite (layers of material) by an adhesive or other means ~ *vi* : to divide into laminae — **lam·i·na·tor** \-ˌnā-tər\ *n*

²**lam·i·nate** \-nət, -ˌnāt\ *adj* (1668) **1** : consisting of laminae **2** : bearing or covered with laminae

³**lam·i·nate** \-nət, -ˌnāt\ *n* (1939) : a product made by laminating

laminated *adj* (1665) **1** : LAMINATE 1 **2 a** : composed of layers of firmly united material **b** : made by bonding or impregnating superposed layers (as of paper, wood, or fabric) with resin and compressing under heat

lam·i·na·tion \ˌla-mə-ˈnā-shən\ *n* (ca. 1676) **1** : the process of laminating **2** : the state of being laminated **3** : a laminated structure **4** : LAMINA

lam·i·nin \ˈla-mə-nən\ *n* [*lamina* + ¹*-in*] (1979) : a glycoprotein component of connective tissue basement membrane that promotes cell adhesion

lam·i·ni·tis \ˌla-mə-ˈnī-təs\ *n* [NL] (1843) : inflammation of the laminae esp. in the hoof of a horse — called also *founder*

Lam·mas \ˈla-məs\ *n* [ME *Lammasse*, fr. OE *hlāfmæsse*, fr. *hlāf* loaf, bread + *mæsse* mass; fr. the fact that formerly loaves from the first ripe grain were consecrated on this day] (bef. 12c) **1** : August 1 orig. celebrated in England as a harvest festival — called also *Lammas Day* **2** : the time of the year around Lammas Day

Lam·mas·tide \-ˌtīd\ *n* (14c) : LAMMAS 2

lam·mer·gei·er *or* **lam·mer·gey·er** \ˈla-mər-ˌgī(-ə)r\ *n* [G *Lämmergeier*, fr. *Lämmer* lambs + *Geier* vulture] (1817) : a large Old World vulture (*Gypaetus barbatus*) that occurs in mountain regions and in flight resembles a huge falcon

lamp \ˈlamp\ *n* [ME, fr. AF *lampe*, fr. L *lampas*, fr. Gk, fr. *lampein* to shine; akin to Hitt *lap-* to burn] (13c) **1 a** : any of various devices for producing light or sometimes heat: as **(1)** : a vessel with a wick for burning an inflammable liquid (as oil) to produce light **(2)** : a glass bulb or tube that emits light produced by electricity (as an incandescent lightbulb or fluorescent lamp) **b** : a decorative appliance housing a lamp that is usu. covered by a shade **2** : a celestial body **3** : a source of intellectual or spiritual illumination **4** : EYE 1a — usu. used in pl.

lamp·black \-ˌblak\ *n* (1598) : a finely powdered black soot deposited in incomplete combustion of carbonaceous materials and used chiefly as a pigment (as in paints, enamels, and printing inks)

lamp·brush chromosome \ˈlamp-ˌbrəsh-\ *n* (1911) : a greatly enlarged diplotene chromosome that has apparently filamentous granular loops extending from the chromomeres and is characteristic of some animal oocytes

lamp·light \ˈlamp-ˌlīt\ *n* (14c) : the light of a lamp

lamp·light·er \-ˌlī-tər\ *n* (1750) : one that lights a lamp

¹**lam·poon** \lam-ˈpün\ *n* [F *lampon*] (1645) : SATIRE 1; *specif* : a harsh satire usu. directed against an individual

²**lampoon** *vt* (ca. 1657) : to make the subject of a lampoon : RIDICULE — **lam·poon·er** *n* — **lam·poon·ery** \-ˈpü-nə-rē, -ˈpün-rē\ *n*

lamp·post \ˈlam(p)-ˌpōst\ *n* (1790) : a post supporting a usu. outdoor lamp or lantern

lam·prey \ˈlam-prē, -ˌprā\ *n, pl* **lampreys** [ME, fr. AF *lampreie*, fr. ML *lampreda*] (14c) : any of a family (Petromyzontidae) of eel-shaped freshwater or anadromous jawless fishes that include those cyclostomes having well-developed eyes and a large disk-shaped suctorial mouth armed with horny teeth — called also *lamprey eel*

lamp·shell \ˈlamp-ˌshel\ *n* [fr. the resemblance of the shell and its protruding peduncle to an ancient oil lamp with the wick protruding] (1854) : BRACHIOPOD

lam·ster \ˈlam(p)-stər\ *n* [²*lam* + *-ster*] (1904) : a fugitive esp. from the law

LAN \ˈlan, ˌel-(ˌ)ā-ˈen\ *n* (1981) : LOCAL AREA NETWORK

la·nai \lə-ˈnī, lä-\ *n* [Hawaiian *lānai*] (1823) : PORCH, VERANDA

Lan·ca·shire \ˈlaŋ-kə-ˌshir, -shər\ *n* [*Lancashire*, England] (1896) : a moist crumbly white English cheese that is used esp. in cooking

Lan·cas·tri·an \lan-ˈkas-trē-ən, laŋ-\ *adj* [John of Gaunt, duke of *Lancaster*] (1612) : of or relating to the English royal house that ruled from 1399 to 1461

¹**lance** \ˈlan(t)s\ *n* [ME, fr. AF, fr. L *lancea*] (14c) **1** : a steel-tipped spear carried by mounted knights or light cavalry **2** : any of various sharp objects suggestive of a lance: as **a** : LANCET **b** : a spear used for killing whales or fish **3** : LANCER 1b

²**lance** *vb* **lanced; lanc·ing** [ME *launcen*, fr. AF *lancer*, fr. LL *lanceare*, fr. L *lancea*] *vt* (14c) **1 a** : to pierce with or as if with a lance **b** : to open with or as if with a lancet ⟨~ a boil⟩ **2** : to throw forward : HURL ~ *vi* : to move forward quickly

lance corporal *n* [*lance* (as in obs. *lancepesade* lance corporal, fr. MF *lancepessade*)] (1786) : an enlisted man in the marine corps ranking above a private first class and below a corporal

lance·let \ˈlan(t)-slət\ *n* (ca. 1836) : any of a subphylum (Cephalochordata) of small translucent marine primitive chordate animals that are fishlike in appearance and usu. live partially buried on the ocean floor — called also *amphioxus*

Lan·ce·lot \ˈlan(t)-sə-ˌlät, ˈlän(t)-, -s(ə-)lət\ *n* (15c) : a knight of the Round Table and lover of Queen Guinevere

lan·ce·o·late \ˈlan(t)-sē-ə-ˌlāt\ *adj* [LL *lanceolatus*, fr. L *lanceola*, dim. of *lancea*] (ca. 1760) : shaped like a lance head; *specif* : tapering to a point at the apex and sometimes at the base ⟨~ leaves⟩ ⟨~ prisms⟩ — see LEAF illustration

lanc·er \ˈlan(t)-sər\ *n* (1590) **1 a** : one who carries a lance **b** : a member of a military unit formerly composed of light cavalry armed with lances **2** *pl but sing in constr* **a** : a set of five quadrilles each in a different meter **b** : the music for such dances

lan·cet \ˈlan(t)-sət\ *n* (15c) **1** : a sharp-pointed and commonly 2-edged surgical instrument used to make small incisions **2 a** : LANCET WINDOW **b** : LANCET ARCH

lancet arch *n* (ca. 1823) : an acutely pointed arch — see ARCH illustration

lan·cet·ed \ˈlan(t)-sə-təd\ *adj* (1855) : having a lancet arch or lancet windows

lancet window *n* (1781) : a high narrow window with an acutely pointed head and without tracery

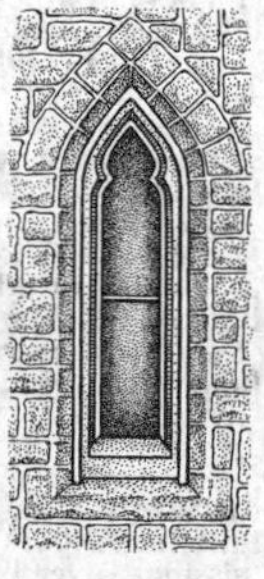
lancet window

lance·wood \ˈlan(t)s-ˌwu̇d\ *n* (1697) : a tough elastic wood used esp. for shafts, fishing rods, and bows; *also* : a tropical American tree (*Oxandra lanceolata*) of the custard-apple family yielding this wood

lan·ci·nat·ing \ˈlan(t)-sə-ˌnā-tiŋ\ *adj* [*lancinate* to pierce, fr. L *lancinatus*, pp. of *lancinare*; akin to L *lacerare* to rend — more at LACERATE] (1762) : characterized by piercing or stabbing sensations ⟨~ pain⟩

Lancs *abbr* Lancashire

¹**land** \ˈland\ *n, often attrib* [ME, fr. OE; akin to OHG *lant* land, MIr *lann*] (bef. 12c) **1 a** : the solid part of the surface of the earth; *also* : a corresponding part of a celestial body (as the moon) **b** : ground or soil of a specified situation, nature, or quality ⟨dry ~⟩ **c** : the surface of the earth and all its natural resources **2** : a portion of the earth's solid surface distinguishable by boundaries or ownership ⟨bought ~ in the country⟩: as **a** : COUNTRY ⟨the finest cheese in all the ~⟩ **b** : a rural area characterized by farming or ranching; *also* : farming or ranching as a way of life ⟨wanted to move back to the ~⟩ **3** : REALM, DOMAIN ⟨in the ~ of dreams⟩ — sometimes used in combination ⟨TV-*land*⟩ **4** : the people of a country ⟨the ~ rose in rebellion⟩ **5** : an area of a partly machined surface (as the inside of a gun barrel) that is left without machining — **land·less** \ˈland-ləs\ *adj* — **land·less·ness** \-nəs\ *n*

[2]**land** *vt* (13c) **1 :** to set or put on shore from a ship : DISEMBARK **2 a :** to set down after conveying **b :** to cause to reach or come to rest in a particular place ⟨never ~*ed* a punch⟩ **c :** to bring to a specified condition ⟨his wit ~*ed* him in trouble⟩ **d :** to bring (as an airplane) to a landing **e :** to complete successfully by landing ⟨the skater ~*ed* all her jumps⟩ **3 a :** to catch and bring in (as a fish) **b :** GAIN, SECURE ⟨~ a job⟩ ⟨~*ed* the leading role⟩ ~ *vi* **1 a :** to go ashore from a ship : DISEMBARK **b** *of a ship or boat* **:** to touch at a place on shore **2 a :** to come to the end of a course or to a stage in a journey : ARRIVE ⟨took a wrong turn and ~*ed* on a dead-end street⟩ **b :** to come to be in a condition or situation ⟨~*ed* in jail⟩ **c :** to strike or meet a surface (as after a fall) ⟨~*ed* on my head⟩ **d :** to alight on a surface

lan·dau \ˈlan-ˌdau̇, -ˌdȯ\ *n* [*Landau,* Bavaria, Germany] (1743) **:** a four-wheel carriage with a top divided into two sections that can be folded away or removed and with a raised seat outside for the driver

lan·dau·let \ˌlan-də-ˈlet\ *n* (1794) **:** a small landau

land bank *n* (1696) **:** a bank that provides financing for land development and for farm mortgages

land·ed \ˈlan-dəd\ *adj* (15c) **1 :** having an estate in land ⟨~ proprietors⟩ **2 :** consisting in or derived from land or real estate ⟨~ wealth⟩

land·er \ˈlan-dər\ *n* (1859) **:** one that lands; *esp* **:** a space vehicle that is designed to land on a celestial body (as the moon or a planet)

land·fall \ˈlan(d)-ˌfȯl\ *n* (1627) **1 :** a sighting of land after a voyage or flight **2 :** a reaching of land (as by a traveler, craft, or storm) **3 :** the land first sighted on a voyage or flight

land·fill \-ˌfil\ *n* (1903) **1 :** an area built up by landfill **2 :** a system of trash and garbage disposal in which the waste is buried between layers of earth to build up low-lying land — called also *sanitary landfill* — **landfill** *vt*

land·form \-ˌfȯrm\ *n* (1893) **:** a natural feature of a land surface

land·grab \-ˌgrab\ *n* (1860) **:** a usu. swift acquisition of property (as land or patent rights) often by fraud or force — **land–grab·ber** \-ˌgra-bər\ *n*

land grant *n* (1862) **:** a grant of land made by the government esp. for roads, railroads, or agricultural colleges

land·hold·er \ˈland-ˌhōl-dər\ *n* (15c) **:** a holder or owner of land

land·hold·ing \-ˌhōl-diŋ\ *n* (ca. 1890) **1 :** the state or fact of holding or owning land **2 :** property in land — **landholding** *adj*

land·ing \ˈlan-diŋ\ *n* (15c) **1 :** an act or process of one that lands; *esp* **:** a going or bringing to a surface (as land or shore) after a voyage or flight **2 :** a place for discharging and taking on passengers and cargo **3 :** a level part of a staircase (as at the end of a flight of stairs) **4** *pl* **:** the amount of fish or shellfish landed annually in a particular area

landing craft *n* (1940) **:** any of numerous naval craft designed for conveying troops and equipment from a transport to a beach in an amphibious assault

landing field *n* (ca. 1920) **:** a field where aircraft may land and take off

landing gear *n* (1911) **:** the part that supports the weight of an airplane or spacecraft when in contact with the land or water

landing strip *n* (1930) **:** AIRSTRIP

land·la·dy \ˈland-ˌlā-dē\ *n* (ca. 1536) **:** a woman who is a landlord

land·line \-ˌlīn\ *n* (1865) **:** a line of communication (as by telephone cable) on land

land·locked \-ˌläkt\ *adj* (1622) **1 :** enclosed or nearly enclosed by land ⟨a ~ country⟩ **2 :** confined to freshwater by some barrier ⟨~ salmon⟩ **3 :** living or located away from the ocean ⟨a ~ sailor⟩

land·lord \-ˌlȯrd\ *n* (bef. 12c) **1 :** the owner of property (as land, houses, or apartments) that is leased or rented to another **2 :** the master of an inn or lodging house : INNKEEPER

land·lord·ism \-ˌlȯr-ˌdi-zəm\ *n* (1844) **:** an economic system or practice by which ownership of land is vested in one who leases it to cultivators

land·lub·ber \-ˌlə-bər\ *n* (ca. 1700) **:** LANDSMAN 2 ⟨clumsy ~*s* learning to sail⟩ — **land·lub·ber·li·ness** \-bər-lē-nəs\ *n* — **land·lub·ber·ly** \-bər-lē\ *adj* — **land·lub·bing** \-biŋ\ *adj*

land·mark \-ˌmärk\ *n* (bef. 12c) **1 :** an object (as a stone or tree) that marks the boundary of land **2 a :** a conspicuous object on land that marks a locality **b :** an anatomical structure used as a point of orientation in locating other structures **3 :** an event or development that marks a turning point or a stage **4 :** a structure (as a building) of unusual historical and usu. aesthetic interest; *esp* **:** one that is officially designated and set aside for preservation

land·mass \-ˌmas\ *n* (1856) **:** a large area of land ⟨continental ~*es*⟩

land mine *n* (1890) **1 :** a mine usu. placed just below the surface of the ground and designed to be exploded usu. by the weight of vehicles or troops passing over it **2 :** BOOBY TRAP 1

land office *n* (1681) **:** a government office in which entries upon and sales of public land are registered

land–office business *n* (1839) **:** extensive and rapid business ⟨money changers . . . did a *land-office business* on payday —F. J. Haskin⟩

land·own·er \ˈland-ˌō-nər\ *n* (ca. 1733) **:** an owner of land — **land·own·er·ship** \-ˌship\ *n* — **land·own·ing** \-ˌō-niŋ\ *adj or n*

land–poor \ˈlan(d)-ˌpu̇r\ *adj* (1873) **:** owning so much unprofitable or encumbered land as to lack funds to develop the land or pay the charges due on it

Land·ra·ce \ˈlän(d)-ˌrä-sə\ *n* [Dan, fr. *land* + *race*] (1935) **:** a swine of any of several breeds locally developed in northern Europe

land reform *n* (1846) **:** measures designed to effect a more equitable distribution of agricultural land esp. by governmental action; *also* **:** the resulting redistribution

[1]**land·scape** \ˈlan(d)-ˌskāp\ *n, often attrib* [D *landschap,* fr. *land* + *-schap* -ship] (1598) **1 a :** a picture representing a view of natural inland scenery **b :** the art of depicting such scenery **2 a :** the landforms of a region in the aggregate **b :** a portion of territory that can be viewed at one time from one place **c :** a particular area of activity : SCENE ⟨the political ~⟩ **3** *obs* **:** VISTA, PROSPECT

[2]**landscape** *vb* **land·scaped; land·scap·ing** *vt* (1914) **:** to modify or ornament (a natural landscape) by altering the plant cover ~ *vi* **:** to engage in landscape gardening — **land·scap·er** *n*

[3]**landscape** *adj* (1932) **:** of, relating to, or being a document having the horizontal dimension longer than the vertical dimension

landscape architect *n* (1863) **:** a person who develops land for human use and enjoyment through effective placement of structures, vehicular and pedestrian ways, and plantings — **landscape architecture** *n*

landscape gardener *n* (ca. 1763) **:** a person who is engaged in the development and decorative planting of gardens and grounds — **landscape gardening** *n*

land·scap·ist \ˈlan(d)-ˌskā-pist\ *n* (1843) **:** a painter of landscapes

[1]**land·slide** \ˈlan(d)-ˌslīd\ *n* (1822) **1 :** the usu. rapid downward movement of a mass of rock, earth, or artificial fill on a slope; *also* **:** the mass that moves down **2 a :** a great majority of votes for one side **b :** an overwhelming victory

[2]**landslide** *vi* **-slid** \-ˌslid\; **-slid·ing** \-ˌslī-diŋ\ (1926) **1 :** to produce a landslide **2 :** to win an election by a heavy majority

land·slip \-ˌslip\ *n* (1679) **:** LANDSLIDE 1

Lands·mål *or* **Lands·maal** \ˈlän(t)s-ˌmȯl\ *n* [Norw, fr. *land* country + *mål* speech] (1886) **:** NYNORSK

lands·man \ˈlan(d)z-mən\ *n* (1598) **1 :** a fellow countryman **2 :** a person who lives on the land; *esp* **:** one who knows little or nothing of the sea or seamanship

land·ward \ˈland-wərd\ *adv or adj* (15c) **:** to or toward the land

land yacht *n* (1967) **1 :** a 3-wheel wind-driven recreation vehicle consisting usu. of a bare-frame structure and a single sail and used esp. on areas of firmly packed sand **2 :** a large motor vehicle

[1]**lane** \ˈlān\ *n* [ME, fr. OE *lanu;* akin to MD *lane* lane] (bef. 12c) **1 :** a narrow passageway between fences or hedges **2 :** a relatively narrow way or track: as **a :** an ocean route used by or prescribed for ships **b :** a strip of roadway for a single line of vehicles **c :** AIR LANE **d :** any of several parallel courses on a track or swimming pool in which a competitor must stay during a race **e :** an unmarked lengthwise division of a playing area which defines the playing zone of a particular player **f :** a narrow hardwood surface having pins at one end and a gutter along each side that is used in bowling **g :** FREE THROW LANE

[2]**lane** *Scot var of* LONE

lane·way \ˈlān-ˌwā\ *n* (1882) *Brit* **:** LANE

lang *abbr* language

lang·bein·ite \ˈlaŋ-ˌbī-ˌnīt\ *n* [G *Langbeinit,* fr. A. *Langbein,* 19th cent. Ger. industrialist] (ca. 1897) **:** a mineral that is a sulfate of potassium and magnesium used in the fertilizer industry

Lang·er·hans cell \ˈläŋ-ər-ˌhän(t)s-\ *n* [Paul *Langerhans* †1888 Ger. physician] (1890) **:** a cell found in the epidermis that functions as an antigen-presenting cell which binds antigen entering through the skin

lang·lauf \ˈläŋ-ˌlau̇f\ *n* [G, fr. *lang* long + *Lauf* race] (1927) **:** cross-country running or racing on skis — **lang·lauf·er** \-ˌlau̇-fər\ *n*

lang·ley \ˈlaŋ-lē\ *n, pl* **langleys** [Samuel P. *Langley*] (1947) **:** a unit of solar radiation equivalent to one gram calorie per square centimeter of irradiated surface

Lan·go·bard \ˈlaŋ-gə-ˌbärd\ *n* [L *Langobardus*] (1788) **:** LOMBARD 1a — **Lan·go·bar·dic** \ˌlaŋ-gə-ˈbär-dik\ *adj*

lan·gos·ti·no \ˌlaŋ-gə-ˈstē-(ˌ)nō\ *n, pl* **-ti·nos** [Sp, dim. of *langosta* spiny lobster, locust, fr. VL **lacusta,* alter. of L *locusta*] (1915) **:** any of several edible crustaceans (as of the genus *Pleuroncodes*) that are or resemble small lobsters or large shrimp; *specif* **:** LANGOUSTINE

lan·gouste \läⁿ-ˈgüst\ *n* [F, grasshopper, lobster, fr. OF *languste,* fr. Old Occitan *langosta,* fr. VL **lacusta*] (1832) **:** SPINY LOBSTER

lan·gous·tine \ˌlaŋ-gə-ˈstēn\ *n* [F, dim. of *langouste*] (1946) **:** a small edible lobster (*Nephrops norvegicus*) of European seas having long slender claws — called also *Dublin Bay prawn, Norway lobster*

[1]**lang syne** \(ˌ)laŋ-ˈzīn, -ˈsīn\ *adv* [ME (Sc), fr. *lang* long + *syne* since] (15c) *chiefly Scot* **:** at a distant time in the past

[2]**lang syne** *n* (1694) *chiefly Scot* **:** times past ⟨should auld acquaintance be forgot, and days o' auld *lang syne* —Robert Burns⟩

lan·guage \ˈlaŋ-gwij, -wij\ *n* [ME, fr. AF *langage,* fr. *lange, langue* tongue, language, fr. L *lingua* — more at TONGUE] (14c) **1 a :** the words, their pronunciation, and the methods of combining them used and understood by a community **b** (1) **:** audible, articulate, meaningful sound as produced by the action of the vocal organs (2) **:** a systematic means of communicating ideas or feelings by the use of conventionalized signs, sounds, gestures, or marks having understood meanings (3) **:** the suggestion by objects, actions, or conditions of associated ideas or feelings ⟨~ in their very gesture —Shak.⟩ (4) **:** the means by which animals communicate (5) **:** a formal system of signs and symbols (as FORTRAN or a calculus in logic) including rules for the formation and transformation of admissible expressions (6) **:** MACHINE LANGUAGE 1 **2 a :** form or manner of verbal expression; *specif* **:** STYLE **b :** the vocabulary and phraseology belonging to an art or a department of knowledge **c :** PROFANITY **3 :** the study of language esp. as a school subject **4 :** specific words esp. in a law or regulation

language arts *n pl* (1948) **:** the subjects (as reading, spelling, literature, and composition) that aim at developing the student's comprehension and capacity for use of written and oral language

langue \ˈläⁿg\ *n* [F, lit., language] (1924) **:** language viewed abstractly as a system of forms and conventions used for communication in a community; *also* **:** COMPETENCE 3 — compare PAROLE

langue d'oc \läŋ-ˈdȯk, läⁿg-ˈdȯk\ *n* [F, fr. OF, lit., language of *oc;* fr. the Occitan use of the word *oc* for "yes"] (1703) **:** OCCITAN

langue d'oïl \läŋ-ˈdȯi(-ə)l, -ˈdȯi; läⁿg-dȯ-ˈēl, -ˈdȯi\ *n* [F, fr. OF, lit., language of *oïl;* fr. the French use of the word *oïl* for "yes"] (1703) **:** FRENCH 1

lan·guet \ˈlaŋ-gwət, laŋ-ˈgwet\ *n* [ME, fr. MF *languete,* dim. of *langue*] (15c) **:** something resembling the tongue in form or function

lan·guid \ˈlaŋ-gwəd\ *adj* [MF *languide,* fr. L *languidus,* fr. *languēre* to languish — more at SLACK] (1597) **1 :** drooping or flagging from or as if from exhaustion : WEAK **2 :** sluggish in character or disposition : LISTLESS **3 :** lacking force or quickness of movement : SLOW — **lan·guid·ly** *adv* — **lan·guid·ness** *n*

syn LANGUID, LANGUOROUS, LACKADAISICAL, LISTLESS, SPIRITLESS mean lacking energy or enthusiasm. LANGUID refers to an unwillingness or inability to exert oneself due to fatigue or physical weakness ⟨was depressed and *languid* for weeks after surgery⟩. LANGUOROUS suggests a dreamy boredom and delicacy that avoids unnecessary activity ⟨*languorous* cats lying in the sun⟩. LACKADAISICAL implies a carefree indifference marked by halfhearted efforts ⟨*lackadaisical* college seniors pretending to study⟩. LISTLESS suggests a lack of interest caused by physical weakness or dissatisfied boredom ⟨*listless* hospital patients⟩ ⟨*listless* children flipping through picture books on a rainy day⟩. SPIRITLESS refers to a lack of animation or vigor that gives one's actions and words life ⟨a *spiritless* recital of the poem⟩.

lan·guish \ˈlaŋ-gwish\ *vi* [ME, fr. AF *languiss-*, stem of *languir*, fr. VL **languire*, fr. L *languēre*] (14c) **1 a :** to be or become feeble, weak, or enervated **b :** to be or live in a state of depression or decreasing vitality **2 a :** to become dispirited **b :** to suffer neglect ⟨the bill ~*ed* in the Senate for eight months⟩ **3 :** to assume an expression of grief or emotion appealing for sympathy — **lan·guish·er** *n* — **lan·guish·ing·ly** \-gwi-shiŋ-lē\ *adv* — **lan·guish·ment** \-gwish-mənt\ *n*

lan·guor \ˈlaŋ-gər *also* -ər\ *n* [ME, fr. AF *langur*, fr. L *languor*, fr. *languēre*] (14c) **1 :** weakness or weariness of body or mind **2 :** listless indolence or inertia ***syn*** see LETHARGY

lan·guor·ous \ˈlaŋ-gə-rəs, -grəs *also* -ə-rəs\ *adj* (15c) **1 :** producing or tending to produce languor ⟨a ~ climate⟩ **2 :** full of or characterized by languor ***syn*** see LANGUID — **lan·guor·ous·ly** *adv*

lan·gur \läŋ-ˈgu̇r\ *n* [Hindi *lāgūr* & Urdu *langūr*] (1825) **:** any of several slender long-tailed Asian monkeys (subfamily Colobinae)

La Ni·ña \lä-ˈnē-nyə, -nyä\ *n, pl* **La Niñas** [Sp, the (female) child] (1988) **:** an irregularly recurring upwelling of unusually cold water to the ocean surface along the western coast of South America that often occurs following an El Niño and that disrupts typical regional and global weather patterns esp. in a manner opposite to that of El Niño

lank \ˈlaŋk\ *adj* [ME, fr. OE *hlanc;* akin to OHG *hlanca* loin] (bef. 12c) **1 :** not well filled out **:** SLENDER, THIN ⟨~ cattle⟩ **2 :** insufficient in quantity, degree, or extent **3 :** hanging straight and limp without spring or curl ***syn*** see LEAN — **lank·ly** *adv* — **lank·ness** *n*

lanky \ˈlaŋ-kē\ *adj* **lank·i·er; -est** (ca. 1818) **:** ungracefully tall and thin ***syn*** see LEAN — **lank·i·ly** \-kə-lē\ *adv* — **lank·i·ness** \-kē-nəs\ *n*

lan·ner \ˈla-nər\ *n* [ME *laner*, fr. AF *laner, lanier*] (14c) **:** a falcon (*Falco biarmicus*) of southern Europe, southwestern Asia, and Africa; *specif* **:** a female lanner

lan·ner·et \ˌla-nə-ˈret\ *n* (15c) **:** a male lanner

lan·o·lin \ˈla-nə-lən\ *n* [L *lana* wool + ISV ³*-ol* + ¹*-in*] (1885) **:** wool grease esp. when refined for use in ointments and cosmetics

lan·ta·na \lan-ˈtä-nə\ *n* [NL, fr. It dial., viburnum] (1791) **:** any of a genus (*Lantana*) of tropical shrubs or perennial herbs of the vervain family with showy heads of small bright flowers

lan·tern \ˈlan-tərn\ *n, often attrib* [ME *lanterne*, fr. AF, fr. L *lanterna*, fr. Gk *lamptēr*, fr. *lampein* to shine — more at LAMP] (13c) **1 :** a usu. portable protective case for a light with transparent openings — compare CHINESE LANTERN **2 a** *obs* **:** LIGHTHOUSE **b :** the chamber in a lighthouse containing the light **c :** a structure with glazed or open sides above an opening in a roof for light or ventilation **d :** a small tower or cupola or one stage of a cupola **3 :** PROJECTOR 2b

lantern fish *n* (ca. 1753) **:** any of a family (Myctophidae) of small deep-sea bony fishes that have a large mouth, large eyes, and usu. numerous photophores

lantern fly *n* (ca. 1753) **:** any of several large brightly marked homopterous insects (family Fulgoridae) having the front of the head prolonged into a hollow structure

lantern jaw *n* (1711) **:** an undershot jaw — **lan·tern–jawed** \ˈlan-tərn-ˌjȯd\ *adj*

lan·tha·nide \ˈlan(t)-thə-ˌnīd\ *also* **lan·tha·noid** \-ˌnȯid\ *n* [ISV] (1926) **:** any of the series of elements with increasing atomic numbers that begins with lanthanum or cerium and ends with lutetium — see PERIODIC TABLE table

lan·tha·num \-nəm\ *n* [NL, fr. Gk *lanthanein* to escape notice — more at LATENT] (1841) **:** a white soft malleable metallic element that occurs in rare-earth minerals — see ELEMENT table

lant·horn \ˈlan-tərn\ *n* (1587) *chiefly Brit* **:** LANTERN

la·nu·gi·nous \lə-ˈnü-jə-nəs, -ˈnyü-\ *adj* [L *lanuginosus*, fr. *lanugin-, lanugo*] (1575) **:** covered with down or fine soft hair **:** DOWNY

la·nu·go \lə-ˈnü-(ˌ)gō, -ˈnyü-\ *n* [L, down, fr. *lana* wool — more at WOOL] (15c) **:** a dense cottony or downy growth of hair; *specif* **:** the soft woolly hair that covers the fetus of some mammals

lan·yard \ˈlan-yərd\ *n* [ME *lanyer* thong, lanyard, fr. AF *lanier*] (15c) **1 :** a piece of rope or line for fastening something in a ship; *esp* **:** one of the pieces passing through deadeyes to extend shrouds or stays **2 a :** a cord or strap to hold something (as a knife or a whistle) and usu. worn around the neck **b :** a cord worn as a symbol of a military citation **3 :** a strong line used to activate a system (as in firing a cannon)

Lao \ˈlau̇\ *n, pl* **Lao** *or* **Laos** \ˈlau̇z\ (1808) **1 :** a member of a Buddhist people living in Laos and adjacent parts of northeastern Thailand **2 :** the Thai language of the Lao people — **Lao** *adj*

La·oc·o·ön \lā-ˈä-kə-ˌwän\ *n* [L, fr. Gk *Laokoōn*] (1582) **:** a Trojan priest killed with his sons by two sea serpents after warning the Trojans against the wooden horse

La·od·i·ce·an \lā-ˌä-də-ˈsē-ən, ˌlā-ō-də-\ *adj* [fr. the reproach to the church of the Laodiceans in Rev 3:15–16] (1633) **:** lukewarm or indifferent in religion or politics — **Laodicean** *n*

lao·gai \ˈlau̇-ˈgī\ *n, pl* **laogai** [Chin (Beijing) *láogǎi* reform through labor, short for *láodòng gǎizào*, fr. *láodòng* work, labor + *gǎizào* transform, reform] (1983) **:** the penal system of China consisting of a network of labor camps; *also* **:** such a labor camp

Lao·tian \lā-ˈō-shən, ˈlau̇-shən\ *n* [prob. fr. F *laotien*, adj. & n., fr. *Lao*] (1847) **1 :** a native or inhabitant of Laos; *also* **:** LAO 1 **2 :** LAO 2 — **Laotian** *adj*

¹lap \ˈlap\ *n* [ME *lappe*, fr. OE *læppa;* akin to OHG *lappa* flap] (bef. 12c) **1 a :** a loose overlapping or hanging panel or flap esp. of a garment **b** *archaic* **:** the skirt of a coat or dress **2 a :** the clothing that lies on the knees, thighs, and lower part of the trunk when one sits **b :** the front part of the lower trunk and thighs of a seated person **3 :** responsible custody **:** CONTROL ⟨going to drop the whole thing in your ~ —Hamilton Basso⟩ — **lap·ful** \ˈlap-ˌfu̇l\ *n* — **the lap of luxury :** an environment of great ease, comfort, and wealth

²lap *vb* **lapped; lap·ping** *vt* (14c) **1 a :** to fold over or around something **:** WIND **b :** to envelop entirely **:** SWATHE **2 :** to fold over esp. into layers **3 :** to hold protectively in or as if in the lap **:** CUDDLE **4 a :** to place over and cover a part of **:** OVERLAP ⟨~ shingles on a roof⟩ **b :** to join (as two boards) by a lap joint **5 a :** to dress, smooth, or polish (as a metal surface) to a high degree of refinement or accuracy **b :** to shape or fit by working two surfaces together with or without abrasives until a very close fit is produced **6 a :** to overtake and thereby lead or increase the lead over (another contestant) by a full circuit of a racecourse **b :** to complete the circuit of (a racecourse) ~ *vi* **1 :** FOLD, WIND **2 a :** to project beyond or spread over something **b :** to lie partly over or alongside of something or of one another **:** OVERLAP **3 :** to traverse a course — **lap·per** *n*

³lap *n* (1800) **1 a :** the amount by which one object overlaps or projects beyond another **b :** the part of an object that overlaps another **2 :** a smoothing and polishing tool usu. consisting of a piece of wood, leather, felt, or soft metal in a special shape used with or without an embedded abrasive **3 :** a doubling or layering of a flexible substance (as fibers or paper) **4 a :** the act or an instance of traversing a course (as a racing track or swimming pool); *also* **:** the distance covered **b :** one segment of a larger unit (as a journey) **c :** one complete turn (as of a rope around a drum)

⁴lap *vb* **lapped; lap·ping** [ME, fr. OE *lapian;* akin to OHG *laffan* to lick, L *lambere*, Gk *laphyssein* to devour] *vi* (bef. 12c) **1 :** to take in food or drink with the tongue **2 a :** to make a gentle intermittent splashing sound **b :** to move in little waves **:** WASH ~ *vt* **1 a :** to take in (food or drink) with the tongue **b :** to take in or absorb eagerly or quickly — used with *up* ⟨the crowd *lapped* up every word he said⟩ **2 :** to flow or splash against in little waves — **lap·per** *n*

⁵lap *n* (14c) **1 a :** an act or instance of lapping **b :** the amount that can be carried to the mouth by one lick or scoop of the tongue **2 :** a thin or weak beverage or food **3 :** a gentle splashing sound

laparo- *comb form* [Gk *lapara* flank, fr. *laparos* slack] **:** abdominal wall ⟨*laparo*tomy⟩

lap·a·ro·scope \ˈla-p(ə-)rə-ˌskōp\ *n* [ISV] (ca. 1923) **:** a fiberoptic instrument inserted through an incision in the abdominal wall and used to examine visually the interior of the peritoneal cavity

lap·a·ros·co·py \ˌla-pə-ˈräs-kə-pē\ *n, pl* **-pies** (1916) **1 :** visual examination of the abdomen by means of a laparoscope **2 :** an operation (as tubal ligation or gall bladder removal) involving laparoscopy — **lap·a·ro·scop·ic** \-rə-ˈskä-pik\ *adj* — **lap·a·ros·co·pist** \ˌla-pə-ˈräs-kə-pist\ *n*

lap·a·rot·o·my \ˌla-pə-ˈrä-tə-mē\ *n, pl* **-mies** (1878) **:** surgical incision of the abdominal wall

lap belt *n* (1952) **:** a seat belt that fastens across the lap

lap·board \ˈlap-ˌbȯrd\ *n* (1804) **:** a board used on the lap as a table or desk

lap dancing *n* (1988) **:** an activity in which a usu. seminude performer sits and gyrates on the lap of a customer — **lap dance** *n* — **lap dancer** *n*

lap·dog \-ˌdȯg\ *n* (1645) **1 :** a small dog that may be held in the lap **2 :** a servile dependent or follower

la·pel \lə-ˈpel\ *n* [dim. of ¹*lap*] (1789) **:** the part of a garment that is turned back; *specif* **:** the fold of the front of a coat that is usu. a continuation of the collar — **la·pelled** *or* **la·peled** *adj*

lap·i·dar·i·an \ˌla-pə-ˈder-ē-ən\ *adj* (1864) **:** LAPIDARY 1

¹lap·i·dary \ˈla-pə-ˌder-ē\ *n, pl* **-dar·ies** (14c) **1 :** a cutter, polisher, or engraver of precious stones usu. other than diamonds **2 :** the art of cutting gems

²lapidary *adj* [L *lapidarius* of stone, fr. *lapid-, lapis* stone] (1724) **1 :** having the elegance and precision associated with inscriptions on monumental stone ⟨a stanza that has a ~ dignity⟩ **2 a :** sculptured in or engraved on stone **b :** of, relating to, or suggestive of precious stones or the art of cutting them

la·pil·lus \lə-ˈpi-ləs\ *n, pl* **-li** \-ˌlī, -(ˌ)lē\ [L, dim. of *lapis*] (1747) **:** a small stony or glassy fragment of lava ejected in a volcanic eruption

lap·in \ˈla-pən\ *n* [F] (1905) **1 :** RABBIT; *specif* **:** a castrated male rabbit **2 :** rabbit fur usu. sheared and dyed

la·pis la·zu·li \ˌla-pəs-ˈla-zə-lē, -ˈla-zhə-\ *n* [ME, fr. ML, fr. L *lapis* + ML *lazuli*, gen. of *lazulum* lapis lazuli, fr. Ar *lāzaward* — more at AZURE] (15c) **:** a semiprecious stone that is usu. rich azure blue and is essentially a complex silicate often with spangles of pyrites — called also *lapis*

lap joint *n* (1823) **:** a joint made by overlapping two ends or edges and fastening them together — **lap–joint·ed** \ˈlap-ˌjȯin-təd\ *adj*

La·place transform \lə-ˈpläs-, -ˈplas-\ *n* [Pierre Simon, Marquis de *Laplace*] (1942) **:** a transformation of a function $f(x)$ into the function

$$g(t) = \int_0^\infty e^{-xt} f(x)dx$$

that is useful esp. in reducing the solution of an ordinary linear differential equation with constant coefficients to the solution of a polynomial equation

Lapp \ˈlap\ *n* [Sw] (1641) *sometimes offensive* **:** SAMI — **Lapp·ish** *adj or n*

lap·pet \ˈla-pət\ *n* (1573) **1 :** a fold or flap on a garment or headdress **2 :** a flat overlapping or hanging piece

lap robe *n* (ca. 1866) **:** a covering (as a blanket) for the legs, lap, and feet esp. of a passenger in a car or carriage

Lap·sang souchong \ˈläp-ˌsäŋ-, ˈlap-ˌsaŋ-\ *n* [origin unknown] (ca. 1878) **:** a souchong tea having a pronounced smoky flavor and aroma

¹lapse \ˈlaps\ *n* [L *lapsus*, fr. *labi* to slip — more at SLEEP] (1526) **1 a :** a slight error typically due to forgetfulness or inattention ⟨a ~ in table manners⟩ **b :** a temporary deviation or fall esp. from a higher to a lower state ⟨a ~ from grace⟩ **2 :** a becoming less **:** DECLINE **3 a (1) :** the termination of a right or privilege through neglect to exercise it within some limit of time **(2) :** termination of coverage for nonpayment of premiums **b :** INTERRUPTION, DISCONTINUANCE ⟨returned to college after a ~ of several years⟩ **4 :** an abandonment of religious faith **5 :** a passage of time; *also* **:** INTERVAL ***syn*** see ERROR

²lapse *vb* **lapsed; laps·ing** *vi* (1611) **1 a :** to fall from an attained and usu. high level (as of morals or manners) to one much lower; *also* **:** to depart from an accepted pattern or standard **b :** SINK, SLIP ⟨*lapsed* into unconsciousness⟩ **2 :** to go out of existence **:** CEASE ⟨after a few polite exchanges, the conversation *lapsed*⟩ **3 :** to pass from one proprietor to another or from an original owner by omission or negligence ⟨allowed the insurance policy to ~⟩ **4 :** to glide along **:** PASS ⟨time ~*s*⟩ ~ *vt* **:** to let slip **:** FORFEIT ⟨all of those who have *lapsed* their membership —*AAUP Bull.*⟩ — **laps·er** *n*

lapsed *adj* (1638) **:** having ceased to be active in practice, membership, or belief ⟨a ~ Catholic⟩
lapse rate *n* (1918) **:** the adiabatic rate of decrease of atmospheric temperature with increasing altitude
lap·strake \ˈlap-ˌstrāk\ *adj* (1771) **:** CLINKER-BUILT
[1]**lap·top** \ˈlap-ˌtäp\ *adj* (1984) **:** of a size and design that makes operation and use on one's lap convenient — compare DESKTOP
[2]**laptop** *n* (1984) **:** a portable microcomputer having its main components (as processor, keyboard, and display screen) integrated into a single unit capable of battery-powered operation
La·pu·tan \lə-ˈpyü-tᵊn\ *n* (1726) **:** an inhabitant of a flying island in Swift's *Gulliver's Travels* characterized by a neglect of useful occupations and a devotion to visionary projects — **Laputan** *adj*
lap·wing \ˈlap-ˌwiŋ\ *n* [ME, by folk etymology fr. OE *hlēapewince;* akin to OE *hlēapan* to leap and to OE *wincian* to wink] (14c) **:** a crested Old World plover (*Vanellus vanellus*) noted for its slow irregular flapping flight and shrill wailing cry; *also* **:** any of several related plovers
Lar \ˈlär\ *n, pl* **Lar·es** \ˈler-(ˌ)ēz\ [L — more at LARVA] (1586) **:** a tutelary god or spirit associated with Vesta and the Penates as a guardian of the household by the ancient Romans
lar·board \ˈlär-bərd\ *n* [ME *ladeborde*] (14c) **:** [5]PORT — **larboard** *adj*
lar·ce·ner \ˈlärs-nər, ˈlär-sə-nər\ *n* (ca. 1635) **:** LARCENIST
lar·ce·nist \-nist, -sə-nist\ *n* (1803) **:** a person who commits larceny
lar·ce·nous \-nəs, -sə-nəs\ *adj* (1742) **1 :** having the character of or constituting larceny **2 :** committing larceny — **lar·ce·nous·ly** *adv*
lar·ce·ny \-nē, -sə-nē\ *n, pl* **-nies** [ME, fr. AF *larecin* theft, fr. L *latrocinium* robbery, fr. *latron-, latro* mercenary soldier, prob. fr. Gk **latrōn,* fr. *latron* pay] (15c) **:** the unlawful taking of personal property with intent to deprive the rightful owner of it permanently
larch \ˈlärch\ *n* [prob. fr. G *Lärche,* fr. MHG *lerche,* fr. L *laric-, larix*] (1548) **:** any of a genus (*Larix*) of northern hemisphere trees of the pine family with short fascicled deciduous leaves; *also* **:** the wood of a larch
[1]**lard** \ˈlärd\ *vt* (14c) **1 a :** to dress (meat) for cooking by inserting or covering with something (as strips of fat) **b :** to cover or soil with grease **2 :** to augment or intersperse esp. with something superfluous or excessive ⟨the book is ~*ed* with subplots⟩ **3** *obs* **:** to make rich with or as if with fat
[2]**lard** *n* [ME, fr. AF, fr. L *lardum, laridum;* perh. akin to Gk *larinos* fat] (14c) **:** a soft white solid or semisolid fat obtained by rendering fatty pork — **lardy** \ˈlär-dē\ *adj*
lar·der \ˈlär-dər\ *n* [ME, fr. AF, fr. *lard*] (14c) **1 :** a place where food is stored **:** PANTRY **2 :** a supply of food
lar·doon \lär-ˈdün\ *or* **lar·don** \ˈlär-ˌdän\ *n* [ME, fr. AF *lardun* piece of fat pork, fr. *lard*] (14c) **:** a strip (as of salt pork) with which meat is larded
lares and penates *see* LAR, PENATES\ *n pl* (1775) **1 :** household gods **2 :** personal or household effects
[1]**large** \ˈlärj\ *adj* **larg·er; larg·est** [ME, fr. AF, broad, wide, generous, fr. L *largus* generous, plentiful] (12c) **1** *obs* **:** LAVISH **2** *obs* **a :** AMPLE, ABUNDANT **b :** EXTENSIVE, BROAD **3 a :** having more than usual capacity or scope **:** COMPREHENSIVE ⟨take the ~ view⟩ ⟨will take a *larger* role in the negotiations⟩ **b :** POWERFUL, FORCEFUL **c :** very successful or popular ⟨a ~ rock band⟩ **4 a :** exceeding most other things of like kind esp. in quantity or size **:** BIG **b :** dealing in great numbers or quantities ⟨a ~ and highly profitable business⟩ **5** *obs* **a** *of language or expression* **:** COARSE, VULGAR **b :** lax in conduct **:** LOOSE **6** *of a wind* **:** FAVORABLE **7 :** EXTRAVAGANT, BOASTFUL ⟨~ talk⟩ — **large·ness** *n* — **larg·ish** \ˈlär-jish\ *adj*
[2]**large** *adv* (14c) **1** *obs* **:** in abundance **:** AMPLY, LIBERALLY **2 :** with the wind abaft the beam **3 :** in a large manner **:** EXTRAVAGANTLY ⟨living ~⟩
[3]**large** *n* (14c) **1** *obs* **:** LIBERALITY, GENEROSITY **2** *slang* **:** a thousand dollars — **at large 1 a :** free of restraint or confinement ⟨the escaped prisoner is still *at large*⟩ **b :** without a specific subject or assignment ⟨critic *at large*⟩ **2 :** at length **3 :** in a general way **4 :** as a whole ⟨society *at large*⟩ **5 :** as the political representative of or to a whole area rather than of one of its subdivisions — used in combination with a preceding noun ⟨a congressman-*at-large*⟩ — **in the large :** on a large scale **:** in general
large calorie *n* (ca. 1909) **:** CALORIE 1b
large·heart·ed \ˌlärj-ˈhär-təd\ *adj* (1645) **:** having a generous disposition **:** SYMPATHETIC — **large·heart·ed·ness** *n*
large intestine *n* (1823) **:** the more terminal division of the vertebrate intestine that is wider and shorter than the small intestine, typically divided into cecum, colon, and rectum, and concerned esp. with the resorption of water and the formation of feces
large·ly \ˈlärj-lē\ *adv* (13c) **1 :** in a large manner; *esp* **:** to a large extent **:** MOSTLY, PRIMARILY ⟨words ~ unknown a decade ago⟩
large–mind·ed \ˌlärj-ˈmīn-dəd\ *adj* (1725) **:** generous and comprehensive in outlook, range, or capacity — **large–mind·ed·ly** *adv* — **large–mind·ed·ness** *n*
large·mouth bass \ˈlärj-ˌmau̇th-\ *n* (1941) **:** a large No. American black bass (*Micropterus salmoides*) that is blackish green above and lighter below and has the maxillary bones of the upper jaw extending to behind the eyes — called also *largemouth, largemouth black bass*
large–print \-ˈprint\ *adj* (1968) **:** being set in a large size of type (as 14 point or larger) esp. for use by the partially sighted ⟨~ books⟩
larger–than–life *adj* (1950) **:** of the sort legends are made of ⟨~ heroes⟩; *broadly* **:** EXTRAORDINARY
large–scale integration *n* (1966) **:** the process of placing a large number of circuits on a small chip
lar·gesse *also* **lar·gess** \lär-ˈzhes, lär-ˈjes *also* ˈlär-ˌjes\ *n* [ME *largesse,* fr. AF, fr. *large*] (13c) **1 :** liberal giving (as of money) to or as if to an inferior; *also* **:** something so given **2 :** GENEROSITY
[1]**lar·ghet·to** \lär-ˈge-(ˌ)tō\ *n, pl* **-tos** (ca. 1724) **:** a movement played larghetto
[2]**larghetto** *adv or adj* [It, somewhat slow, fr. *largo*] (ca. 1801) **:** slower than andante but not so slow as largo — used as a direction in music
[1]**lar·go** \ˈlär-(ˌ)gō\ *adv or adj* [It, slow, broad, fr. L *largus* abundant] (1683) **:** at a very slow tempo — used as a direction in music
[2]**largo** *n, pl* **largos** (ca. 1753) **:** a largo movement
lari \ˈlä-rē\ *n, pl* **lari** [Georgian, lit., treasury, valuables] (1995) — see MONEY table
lar·i·at \ˈler-ē-ət\ *n* [AmerSp *la reata* the lasso, fr. Sp *la* the + AmerSp *reata* lasso, fr. Sp *reatar* to tie again, fr. *re-* + *atar* to tie, fr. L *aptare* to fit — more at ADAPT] (1832) **:** a long light rope (as of hemp or leather) used with a running noose to catch livestock or with or without the noose to tether grazing animals **:** LASSO
[1]**lark** \ˈlärk\ *n* [ME *laveroc, laverke,* fr. OE *lāwerce;* akin to OHG *lērihha* lark] (bef. 12c) **:** any of a family (Alaudidae) of chiefly Old World ground-dwelling songbirds that are usu. brownish in color; *esp* **:** SKYLARK — compare MEADOWLARK
[2]**lark** *n* [[3]*lark*] (ca. 1811) **:** a source of or quest for amusement or adventure ⟨thought life was a ~⟩ ⟨entered the race on a ~⟩
[3]**lark** *vi* [prob. alter. of *lake* to frolic] (1813) **:** to engage in harmless fun or mischief — often used with *about* — **lark·er** *n*
lark·spur \ˈlärk-ˌspər\ *n* (1578) **1 :** DELPHINIUM **2 :** any of the delphiniums that are annuals, have the upper two petals of the corolla united and the bottom two missing, are now often placed in a separate genus (*Consolida*), and include several widely cultivated forms
larky \ˈlär-kē\ *adj* **lark·i·er; -est** (1841) **1 :** given to or ready for larking **:** SPORTIVE **2 :** resulting from a lark — **lark·i·ness** \-nəs\ *n*
lar·ri·gan \ˈla-ri-gən\ *n* [origin unknown] (1886) **:** an oil-tanned moccasin with a leg often reaching the knee
lar·ri·kin \ˈla-ri-kən\ *n* [origin unknown] (1868) *chiefly Austral* **:** HOODLUM, ROWDY — **larrikin** *adj*
[1]**lar·rup** \ˈla-rəp\ *n* [origin unknown] (ca. 1820) *dial* **:** [5]BLOW
[2]**larrup** *vt* (ca. 1823) **1** *dial* **:** to flog soundly **:** WHIP **2** *dial* **:** to defeat decisively **:** TROUNCE ~ *vi, dial* **:** to move indolently or clumsily
la·rum \ˈlär-əm, ˈler-\ *n* [short for *alarum*] (15c) *archaic* **:** ALARM
lar·va \ˈlär-və\ *n, pl* **lar·vae** \-(ˌ)vē, -ˌvī\ *also* **larvas** [NL, fr. L, specter, mask; akin to L *lar* Lar] (1768) **1 :** the immature, wingless, and often wormlike feeding form that hatches from the egg of many insects, alters chiefly in size while passing through several molts, and is finally transformed into a pupa or chrysalis from which the adult emerges **2 :** the early form of an animal (as a frog or sea urchin) that at birth or hatching is fundamentally unlike its parent and must metamorphose before assuming the adult characters — **lar·val** \-vəl\ *adj*
lar·vi·cide \ˈlär-və-ˌsīd\ *n* (ca. 1888) **:** an agent for killing larval pests — **lar·vi·cid·al** \ˌlär-və-ˈsī-dᵊl\ *adj*
laryng- *or* **laryngo-** *comb form* [NL, fr. Gk, fr. *laryng-, larynx*] **:** larynx ⟨*laryng*itis⟩
[1]**la·ryn·geal** \lə-ˈrin-jəl *also* -jē-əl; ˌla-rən-ˈjē-əl\ *adj* (1795) **1 :** of, relating to, or used on the larynx ⟨a ~ obstruction⟩ **2 :** produced by or with constriction of the larynx ⟨~ articulation of sounds⟩
[2]**laryngeal** *n* (ca. 1902) **1 :** an anatomical part (as a nerve or artery) that supplies or is associated with the larynx **2 a :** a laryngeal sound **b :** any of a set of several conjectured phonemes reconstructed for Proto-Indo-European chiefly on indirect evidence
lar·yn·gec·to·mee \ˌla-rən-ˌjek-tə-ˈmē\ *n* (1956) **:** a person who has undergone laryngectomy
lar·yn·gec·to·my \-ˈjek-tə-mē\ *n, pl* **-mies** (ca. 1888) **:** surgical removal of all or part of the larynx — **lar·yn·gec·to·mized** \-tə-ˌmīzd\ *adj*
lar·yn·gi·tis \ˌla-rən-ˈjī-təs\ *n* [NL] (ca. 1834) **:** inflammation of the larynx — **lar·yn·git·ic** \-ˈji-tik\ *adj*
lar·yn·gol·o·gy \ˌla-rən-ˈgä-lə-jē\ *n* [ISV] (ca. 1842) **:** a branch of medicine dealing with diseases of the larynx and nasopharynx
la·ryn·go·scope \lə-ˈriŋ-gə-ˌskōp, -ˈrin-jə-\ *n* [ISV] (1860) **:** an endoscope for examining the interior of the larynx — **lar·yn·gos·co·py** \ˌla-rən-ˈgäs-kə-pē\ *n*
lar·ynx \ˈler-iŋ(k)s, ˈla-riŋ(k)s\ *n, pl* **la·ryn·ges** \lə-ˈrin-(ˌ)jēz\ *or* **lar·ynx·es** [NL *laryng-, larynx,* fr. Gk] (1578) **:** the modified upper part of the trachea of air-breathing vertebrates that in humans, most other mammals, and some amphibians and reptiles contains the vocal cords
la·sa·gna \lə-ˈzän-yə\ *n* [It *lasagna,* fr. VL **lasania* cooking pot, its contents, fr. L *lasanum* chamber pot, fr. Gk *lasanon*] (1846) **1** *also* **la·sa·gne** \-yə\ **:** pasta in the form of broad often ruffled ribbons **2 :** a baked dish containing layers of boiled lasagna, and usu. cheese, a seasoned sauce of tomatoes, and meat or vegetables
las·car \ˈlas-kər\ *n* [Hindi & Urdu *lashkar* army] (1615) **:** an Indian sailor, army servant, or artilleryman
las·civ·i·ous \lə-ˈsi-vē-əs\ *adj* [ME, fr. LL *lasciviosus,* fr. L *lascivia* wantonness, fr. *lascivus* wanton — more at LUST] (15c) **:** LEWD, LUSTFUL — **las·civ·i·ous·ly** *adv* — **las·civ·i·ous·ness** *n*
lase \ˈlāz\ *vi* **lased; las·ing** [back-formation fr. *laser*] (1962) **:** to emit coherent light
[1]**la·ser** \ˈlā-zər\ *n, often attrib* [*l*ight *a*mplification by *s*timulated *e*mission of *r*adiation] (1957) **1 :** a device that utilizes the natural oscillations of atoms or molecules between energy levels for generating a beam of coherent electromagnetic radiation usu. in the ultraviolet, visible, or infrared regions of the spectrum **2 :** something resembling a laser beam in accuracy, speed, or intensity ⟨threw a ~ into the end zone⟩ ⟨a ~ stare⟩
[2]**laser** *vt* (1978) **:** to subject to the action of a laser **:** treat with a laser
laser disc *n* (1979) **:** OPTICAL DISK; *esp* **:** one containing a video recording (as of a motion picture)
laser printer *n* (1979) **:** a high-resolution printer for computer output that xerographically prints an image formed by a laser
[1]**lash** \ˈlash\ *vb* [ME] *vi* (14c) **1 :** to move violently or suddenly **:** DASH **2 :** to thrash or beat violently ⟨rain ~*ed* at the windowpanes⟩ **3 :** to make a verbal attack or retort — usu. used with *out* ~ *vt* **1 a :** to whip or fling about violently ⟨the big cat ~*ed* its tail about threateningly⟩ **b :** to strike or beat with or as if with a whip ⟨waves ~*ed* the shore⟩ **2 a :** to assail with stinging words **b :** DRIVE, WHIP ⟨~*ed* them into a fury with his fiery speech⟩ — **lash·er** *n*
[2]**lash** *n* (14c) **1 a (1) :** a stroke with or as if with a whip **(2) :** the flexible part of a whip; *also* **:** WHIP **b :** punishment by whipping **2 :** a beating, whipping, or driving force **3 :** a stinging rebuke **4 :** EYELASH **5 :** the clearance or play between adjacent movable mechanical parts

---

\ə\ abut \ᵊ\ kitten, F table \ər\ further \a\ ash \ā\ ace \ä\ mop, mar
\au̇\ out \ch\ chin \e\ bet \ē\ easy \g\ go \i\ hit \ī\ ice \j\ job
\ŋ\ sing \ō\ go \ȯ\ law \ȯi\ boy \th\ thin \t͟h\ the \ü\ loot \u̇\ foot
\y\ yet \zh\ vision, beige \k, ⁿ, œ, ue, ʸ\ *see* Guide to Pronunciation

[3]**lash** *vt* [ME *lasschyn* to lace, fr. AF *lacer, lasser* — more at LACE] (1624) : to bind with or as if with a line — **lash·er** *n*

lash·ing \ˈla-shiŋ\ *n* (1669) : something used for binding, wrapping, or fastening

lash·ings \ˈla-shiŋz, -shənz\ *also* **lash·ins** \-shənz\ *n pl* [fr. gerund of [1]*lash*] (1829) *chiefly Brit* : a great plenty : ABUNDANCE ⟨piles of bread and butter and ∼ of tea —Molly Weir⟩

lash–up \ˈlash-ˌəp\ *n* [[3]*lash*] (1898) **1 :** something hastily put together or improvised **2 :** OUTFIT 3

LA·SIK \ˈlā-sik\ *n* [*la*ser-assisted *i*n situ *k*eratomileusis] (1994) : a surgical operation to reshape the cornea for correction of myopia, farsightedness, or astigmatism in which the surface layer of the cornea is separated to create a hinged flap providing access to the inner cornea where varying amounts of tissue are removed by an excimer laser

L–as·par·a·gi·nase \ˈel-as-ˈpa-rə-jə-ˌnās, -ˌnāz\ *n* (1962) : an enzyme that breaks down the physiologically commoner form of asparagine, is obtained esp. from bacteria, and is used esp. to treat leukemia

lass \ˈlas\ *n* [ME *las*] (14c) **1 :** a young woman : GIRL **2 :** SWEETHEART

Las·sa fever \ˈla-sə-\ *n* [*Lassa,* village in Nigeria] (1970) : a disease esp. of Africa that is caused by an arenavirus (species *Lassa virus* of the genus *Arenavirus*) and is characterized by a high fever, headaches, mouth ulcers, muscle aches, small hemorrhages under the skin, heart and kidney failure, and a high mortality rate

lass·ie \ˈla-sē\ *n* (1725) : LASS 1

las·si·tude \ˈla-sə-ˌtüd, -ˌtyüd\ *n* [ME, fr. L *lassitudo,* fr. *lassus* weary; prob. akin to OE *læt* late — more at LATE] (15c) **1 :** a condition of weariness or debility : FATIGUE **2 :** a condition of listlessness : LANGUOR ***syn*** see LETHARGY

[1]**las·so** \ˈla-(ˌ)sō, la-ˈsü\ *vt* (1807) : to capture with or as if with a lasso : ROPE — **las·so·er** *n*

[2]**lasso** *n, pl* **lassos** *or* **lassoes** [Sp *lazo,* fr. L *laqueus* snare] (1808) : a rope or long thong of leather with a noose used esp. for catching horses and cattle : LARIAT

[1]**last** \ˈlast\ *vb* [ME, fr. OE *lǣstan* to last, follow; akin to OE *lāst* footprint] *vi* (bef. 12c) **1 :** to continue in time **2 a :** to remain fresh or unimpaired : ENDURE **b :** to manage to continue (as in a course of action) **c :** to continue to live ∼ *vt* **1 :** to continue in existence or action as long as or longer than — often used with *out* ⟨couldn't ∼ out the training program⟩ **2 :** to be enough for the needs of ⟨the supplies will ∼ them a week⟩ ***syn*** see CONTINUE — **last·er** *n*

[2]**last** *n* [ME, fr. OE *lǣste,* fr. *lāst* footprint; akin to OHG *leist* shoemaker's last, L *lira* furrow — more at LEARN] (bef. 12c) : a form (as of metal or plastic) which is shaped like the human foot and over which a shoe is shaped or repaired

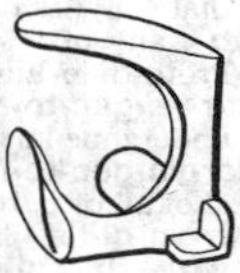

[2]last

[3]**last** *vt* (ca. 1859) : to shape with a last — **last·er** *n*

[4]**last** *adv* [ME, fr. OE *latost,* superl. of *læt* late] (bef. 12c) **1 :** after all others : at the end ⟨came ∼ and left first⟩ **2 :** most lately ⟨saw him ∼ in Rome⟩ **3 :** in conclusion ⟨∼, let's consider the social aspect⟩

[5]**last** *adj* (13c) **1 a :** following all the rest ⟨he was the ∼ one out⟩ **b :** being the only remaining ⟨our ∼ dollar⟩ **2 :** belonging to the final stage (as of life) ⟨his ∼ hours on earth⟩ **3 a :** next before the present : most recent ⟨∼ week⟩ ⟨his ∼ book was a failure⟩ **b :** most up-to-date : LATEST ⟨it's the ∼ thing in fashion⟩ **4 a :** lowest in rank or standing; *also* : WORST **b :** farthest from a specified quality, attitude, or likelihood ⟨would be the ∼ person to fall for flattery⟩ **5 a :** CONCLUSIVE ⟨there is no ∼ answer to the problem⟩ **b :** highest in degree : SUPREME, ULTIMATE **c :** DISTINCT, SEPARATE — used as an intensive ⟨ate every ∼ piece of food⟩ — **last·ly** *adv*

syn LAST, FINAL, TERMINAL, ULTIMATE mean following all others (as in time, order, or importance). LAST applies to something that comes at the end of a series but does not always imply that the series is completed or stopped ⟨*last* page of a book⟩ ⟨*last* news we had of him⟩. FINAL applies to that which definitely closes a series, process, or progress ⟨*final* day of school⟩. TERMINAL may indicate a limit of extension, growth, or development ⟨*terminal* phase of a disease⟩. ULTIMATE implies the last degree or stage of a long process beyond which further progress or change is impossible ⟨the *ultimate* collapse of the system⟩.

[6]**last** *n* (13c) : something that is last — **at last** *or* **at long last :** at the end of a period of time : FINALLY ⟨*at last* you've come home⟩

last–ditch \ˈlas(t)-ˌdich, -ˈdich\ *adj* (1937) **1 :** fought or conducted from the last ditch : waged with desperation or unyielding defiance ⟨put up a ∼ resistance⟩ **2 :** made as a final effort esp. to avert disaster ⟨a ∼ attempt to raise the money⟩

last ditch *n* (ca. 1715) : a place of final defense or resort

last–gasp \ˈlas(t)-ˈgasp\ *adj* (1921) : done or coming at the very end ⟨a ∼ attempt to score⟩ — **last gasp** *n*

last hurrah *n* [fr. *The Last Hurrah* (1956) by Edwin O'Connor †1968 Am. novelist] (1966) : a final often valedictory effort, production, or appearance ⟨his unsuccessful Senate run was his *last hurrah* —R. W. Daly⟩

last–in first–out *adj* (1934) : of, relating to, or being a method of inventory accounting that values stock on hand according to costs at the time of acquisition and not according to the cost of replacement

[1]**last·ing** \ˈlas-tiŋ\ *adj* (12c) : existing or continuing a long while : ENDURING — **last·ing·ly** \ˈlas-tiŋ-lē\ *adv* — **last·ing·ness** *n*

syn LASTING, PERMANENT, DURABLE, STABLE mean enduring for so long as to seem fixed or established. LASTING implies a capacity to continue indefinitely ⟨a book that left a *lasting* impression on me⟩. PERMANENT adds usu. the implication of being designed or planned to stand or continue indefinitely ⟨*permanent* living arrangements⟩. DURABLE implies power to resist destructive agencies ⟨*durable* fabrics⟩. STABLE implies lastingness because of resistance to being overturned or displaced ⟨a *stable* government⟩.

[2]**lasting** *n* (15c) **1** *archaic* : long life **2 :** a sturdy cotton or worsted cloth used esp. in shoes and luggage

Last Judgment *n* (14c) : the judgment of humankind before God at the end of the world

last laugh *n* (1872) : the satisfaction of ultimate triumph or success esp. after being scorned or regarded as a failure ⟨he got the *last laugh* on his early critics⟩

last minute *n* (1920) : the moment just before some climactic, decisive, or disastrous event — **last–minute** *adj*

last name *n* (1897) : SURNAME 2

last rites *n* (1922) : EXTREME UNCTION

last straw *n* [fr. the fable of the last straw that broke the camel's back when added to its burden] (1848) : the last of a series (as of events or indignities) that brings one beyond the point of endurance

Last Supper *n* (14c) : the supper eaten by Jesus and his disciples on the night of his betrayal

last word *n* (1563) **1 :** the final remark in a verbal exchange **2 a :** the power of final decision **b :** a definitive statement or treatment ⟨this study will surely be the *last word* on the subject for many years⟩ **3 :** the most advanced, up-to-date, or fashionable exemplar of its kind ⟨the *last word* in sports cars⟩

[1]**lat** \ˈlat\ *n* (1939) : LATISSIMUS DORSI — usu. used in pl.

[2]**lat** *abbr* latitude

LAT *abbr* local apparent time

lat·a·kia \ˌla-tə-ˈkē-ə\ *n* [*Latakia,* seaport in Syria] (1833) : a highly aromatic Turkish smoking tobacco

[1]**latch** \ˈlach\ *vi* [ME *lachen,* fr. OE *læccan;* perh. akin to Gk *lambanein* to take, seize] (13c) **1 :** to lay hold with or as if with the hands or arms — used with *on* or *onto* **2 :** to associate oneself intimately and often artfully — used with *on* or *onto* ⟨∼*ed* onto a rich widow⟩

[2]**latch** *n* (13c) : any of various devices in which mating mechanical parts engage to fasten but usu. not to lock something: **a :** a fastener (as for a door) consisting essentially of a pivoted bar that falls into a notch **b :** a fastener (as for a door) in which a spring slides a bolt into a hole; *also* : NIGHT LATCH

[3]**latch** *vt* (15c) : to make fast with or as if with a latch

latch·et \ˈla-chət\ *n* [ME *lachet,* fr. AF **lachet, lacete* noose, fr. *lace, laz* snare, lace — more at LACE] (15c) : a narrow leather strap, thong, or lace that fastens a shoe or sandal on the foot

latch·key \ˈlach-ˌkē\ *n* (1825) : a key to an outside and esp. a front door

latchkey child *n* (1944) : a school-aged child of working parents who must spend part of the day unsupervised (as at home) — called also *latchkey kid*

latch·string \-ˌstriŋ\ *n* (1791) : a string on a latch that may be left hanging outside the door to permit the raising of the latch from the outside or drawn inside to prevent intrusion

[1]**late** \ˈlāt\ *adj* **lat·er; lat·est** [ME, late, slow, fr. OE *læt;* akin to OHG *laz* slow, OE *lǣtan* to let] (bef. 12c) **1 a (1) :** coming or remaining after the due, usual, or proper time ⟨a ∼ spring⟩ **(2) :** of, relating to, or imposed because of tardiness **b :** of or relating to an advanced stage in point of time or development ⟨the ∼ Middle Ages⟩; *esp* : far advanced toward the close of the day or night ⟨∼ hours⟩ **2 a :** living comparatively recently : now deceased — used of persons ⟨the ∼ John Doe⟩ and often with reference to a specific relationship or status ⟨his ∼ wife⟩ **b :** being something or holding some position or relationship recently but not now ⟨the ∼ belligerents⟩ **c :** made, appearing, or happening just previous to the present time esp. as the most recent of a succession ⟨our ∼ quarrel⟩ ***syn*** see DEAD — **late·ness** *n*

[2]**late** *adv* **lat·er; lat·est** (bef. 12c) **1 a :** after the usual or proper time ⟨got to work ∼⟩ **b :** at or to an advanced point of time **2 :** not long ago : RECENTLY ⟨a writer ∼ of Chicago⟩ — **of late :** in the period shortly or immediately preceding : RECENTLY ⟨has been sick *of late*⟩

late blight *n* (1900) : a disease of solanaceous plants (as the potato and tomato) that is caused by a fungus (*Phytophthora infestans*) and is characterized by decay of stems, leaves, and in the potato also of tubers

late·com·er \ˈlāt-ˌkə-mər\ *n* (1892) : one that arrives late; *also* : a recent arrival

lat·ed \ˈlā-təd\ *adj* (ca. 1592) : BELATED

[1]**la·teen** \lə-ˈtēn\ *adj* [F *(voile) latine,* lit., Latin (Mediterranean) sail] (ca. 1741) : being or relating to a rig used esp. on the north coast of Africa and characterized by a triangular sail extended by a long spar slung to a low mast

[2]**lateen** *n* (ca. 1775) **1** *also* **la·teen·er** \-ˈtē-nər\ : a lateen-rigged ship **2 :** a lateen sail

Late Greek *n* (ca. 1889) : the Greek language as used in the third to sixth centuries

Late Hebrew *n* (1951) : the Hebrew language used by writers from about the second century B.C. to the early Middle Ages

Late Latin *n* (1888) : the Latin language used by writers in the third to sixth centuries

late·ly \ˈlāt-lē\ *adv* (15c) : of late : RECENTLY ⟨has been friendlier ∼⟩

lat·en \ˈlā-tᵊn\ *vb* **lat·ened; lat·en·ing** \ˈlāt-niŋ, ˈlā-tᵊn-iŋ\ *vi* (1880) : to grow late ∼ *vt* : to cause to grow late

la·ten·cy \ˈlā-tᵊn(t)-sē\ *n, pl* **-cies** (ca. 1638) **1 :** the quality or state of being latent : DORMANCY **2 :** something latent **3 :** a stage of psychosexual development following the phallic stage that extends from about the age of five or six to the beginning of puberty and during which sexual urges often appear to lie dormant **4 :** LATENT PERIOD 2

latency period *n* (1910) **1 :** LATENCY 3 **2 :** LATENT PERIOD

La Tène \lä-ˈten, -ˈtān\ *adj* [*La Tène,* shallows of the Lake of Neuchâtel, Switzerland] (1901) : of or relating to the later period of the Iron Age in Europe assumed to date from 500 B.C. to A.D. 1

la·ten·si·fi·ca·tion \lā-ˌten(t)-sə-fə-ˈkā-shən, lə-\ *n* [blend of [1]*latent* and *intensification*] (1940) : intensification of a latent photographic image by chemical treatment or exposure to light of low intensity

[1]**la·tent** \ˈlā-tᵊnt\ *adj* [ME, fr. L *latent-, latens,* fr. prp. of *latēre* to lie hidden; akin to Gk *lanthanein* to escape notice] (15c) : present and capable of becoming though not now visible, obvious, active, or symptomatic ⟨a ∼ infection⟩ — **la·tent·ly** *adv*

syn LATENT, DORMANT, QUIESCENT, POTENTIAL mean not now showing signs of activity or existence. LATENT applies to a power or quality that has not yet come forth but may emerge and develop ⟨a *latent* desire for success⟩. DORMANT suggests the inactivity of something (as a feeling or power) as though sleeping ⟨their passion had lain *dormant*⟩. QUIESCENT suggests a usu. temporary cessation of activity ⟨the disease was *quiescent*⟩. POTENTIAL applies to what does not yet have existence or effect but is likely soon to have ⟨a *potential* disaster⟩.

[2]**latent** *n* (1923) **:** a fingerprint (as at the scene of a crime) that is scarcely visible but can be developed for study — called also *latent fingerprint, latent print*

latent heat *n* (ca. 1757) **:** heat given off or absorbed in a process (as fusion or vaporization) other than a change of temperature

latent period *n* (1837) **1 :** the incubation period of a disease **2 :** the interval between stimulation and response

latent root *n* (1883) **:** an eigenvalue of a matrix

later *adv* (13c) **:** at some time subsequent to a given time **:** SUBSEQUENTLY, AFTERWARD ⟨one week ~⟩ ⟨they ~ regretted the decision⟩ — often used with *on* ⟨experience that will be useful ~ *on*⟩

-later *n comb form* [F *-lâtre,* fr. LL *-latres,* fr. Gk *-latrēs;* akin to Gk *latron* pay] **:** worshiper ⟨biblio*later*⟩

lat·er·ad \ˈla-tə-ˌrad\ *adv* [L *later-, latus*] (1814) **:** toward the side

[1]**lat·er·al** \ˈla-tə-rəl *also* ˈla-trəl\ *adj* [ME *laterale,* fr. L *lateralis,* fr. *later-, latus* side] (15c) **1 :** of or relating to the side **2 :** situated on, directed toward, or coming from the side **3 :** extending from side to side ⟨the ~ axis of an airplane⟩ **4 :** produced with passage of breath around the side of a constriction formed with the tongue ⟨\l\ is ~⟩ — **lat·er·al·ly** *adv*

[2]**lateral** *n* (1851) **1 :** a branch from the main part (as in an irrigation or electrical system) **2 :** a pass in football thrown parallel to the line of scrimmage or in a direction away from the opponent's goal **3 :** a lateral speech sound

[3]**lateral** *vi* (1944) **:** to throw a lateral

lateral bud *n* (1875) **:** a bud that develops in the axil between a petiole and a stem

lat·er·al·i·za·tion \ˌla-tə-rə-lə-ˈzā-shən, ˌla-trə-\ *n* (ca. 1899) **:** localization of function or activity on one side of the body in preference to the other — **lat·er·al·ize** \ˈla-tə-rə-ˌlīz, ˈla-trə-\ *vt*

lateral line *n* (1752) **:** a canal along the side of a fish containing pores that open into tubes supplied with sense organs sensitive to low vibrations; *also* **:** one of these tubes or sense organs

lat·er·ite \ˈla-tə-ˌrīt\ *n* [L *later* brick] (1807) **:** a residual product of rock decay that is red in color and has a high content in the oxides of iron and hydroxide of aluminum — **lat·er·it·ic** \ˌla-tə-ˈri-tik\ *adj*

lat·er·i·za·tion \ˌla-tə-rə-ˈzā-shən\ *n* (ca. 1882) **:** the process of conversion of rock to laterite

[1]**latest** *adj* (1588) **1** *archaic* **:** LAST **2 :** most recent

[2]**latest** *n* (1801) **1 :** the latest acceptable time — usu. used in the phrase *at the latest* **2 :** something that is the most recent or currently fashionable ⟨the ~ in diving techniques⟩

late·wood \ˈlāt-ˌwu̇d\ *n* (1929) **:** SUMMERWOOD

la·tex \ˈlā-ˌteks\ *n, pl* **la·ti·ces** \ˈlā-tə-ˌsēz, ˈla-\ *or* **la·tex·es** [NL *latic-, latex,* fr. L, fluid] (1835) **1 :** a milky usu. white fluid that is produced by cells of various seed plants (as of the milkweed, spurge, and poppy families) and is the source of rubber, gutta-percha, chicle, and balata **2 :** a water emulsion of a synthetic rubber or plastic obtained by polymerization and used esp. in coatings (as paint) and adhesives

lath \ˈlath *also* ˈla*th*\ *n, pl* **laths** *or* **lath** [ME, fr. OE **lætth-;* akin to OHG *latta* lath, W *llath* yard] (13c) **1 :** a thin narrow strip of wood nailed to rafters, joists, or studding as a groundwork for slates, tiles, or plaster **2 :** a building material in sheets used as a base for plaster **3 :** a quantity of laths — **lath** *vt*

[1]**lathe** \ˈlā*th*\ *n* [prob. fr. ME *lath* supporting stand] (1611) **:** a machine in which work is rotated about a horizontal axis and shaped by a fixed tool

[2]**lathe** *vt* **lathed; lath·ing** (ca. 1903) **:** to cut or shape with a lathe

[1]**lath·er** \ˈla-*th*ər\ *n* [ME **lather,* fr. OE *lēathor;* akin to L *lavere* to wash — more at LYE] (bef. 12c) **1 a :** a foam or froth formed when a detergent (as soap) is agitated in water **b :** foam or froth from profuse sweating (as on a horse) **2 :** an agitated or overwrought state **:** DITHER ⟨worked himself into a ~⟩ — **lath·ery** \-*th*(ə-)rē\ *adj*

[2]**lather** *vb* **lath·ered; lath·er·ing** \-*th*(ə-)riŋ\ *vt* (bef. 12c) **1 :** to spread lather over **2 :** to beat severely **:** FLOG ~ *vi* **:** to form a lather or a froth like lather — **lath·er·er** \-*th*ər-ər\ *n*

lath·y·rism \ˈla-thə-ˌri-zəm\ *n* [NL *Lathyrus,* fr. Gk *lathyros,* a type of pea] (ca. 1888) **:** a diseased condition of humans, domestic animals, and esp. horses that results from poisoning by an amino acid found in some legumes (genus *Lathyrus* and esp. *L. sativus*) and is characterized esp. by spastic paralysis of the hind or lower limbs — **lath·y·rit·ic** \ˌla-thə-ˈri-tik\ *adj*

lati *pl of* LATS

latices *pl of* LATEX

la·tic·i·fer \lā-ˈti-sə-fər\ *n* [ISV *latici-* (fr. NL *latic-, latex*) + *-fer*] (ca. 1928) **:** a plant cell or vessel that contains latex

la·ti·fun·dio \ˌlä-tə-ˈfün-dē-ˌō\ *n, pl* **-di·os** [Sp, fr. L *latifundium*] (ca. 1924) **:** a latifundium in Spain or Latin America

lat·i·fun·di·um \ˌla-tə-ˈfən-dē-əm\ *n, pl* **-dia** \-dē-ə\ [L, fr. *latus* wide + *fundus* piece of landed property, foundation, bottom — more at BOTTOM] (1869) **:** a great landed estate with primitive agriculture and labor often in a state of partial servitude

lat·i·go \ˈla-ti-ˌgō\ *n, pl* **-gos** *also* **-goes** [Sp *látigo*] (1873) *chiefly West* **:** a long strap on a saddletree of a western saddle to adjust the cinch

[1]**Lat·in** \ˈla-tᵊn\ *adj* [ME, fr. OE, fr. L *Latinus,* fr. *Latium,* ancient country of Italy] (bef. 12c) **1 a :** of, relating to, or composed in Latin **b :** ROMANCE **2 :** of or relating to Latium or the Latins **3 :** of or relating to the part of the Catholic Church that until recently used a Latin rite and forms the patriarchate of the pope **4 :** of or relating to the peoples or countries using Romance languages; *specif* **:** of or relating to the peoples or countries of Latin America

[2]**Latin** *n* (bef. 12c) **1 :** the Italic language of ancient Latium and of Rome and until modern times the dominant language of school, church, and state in western Europe — see INDO-EUROPEAN LANGUAGES table **2 :** a member of the people of ancient Latium **3 :** a Catholic of the Latin rite **4 :** a member of one of the Latin peoples; *specif* **:** a native or inhabitant of Latin America **5 :** LATIN ALPHABET

La·ti·na \lə-ˈtē-nə\ *n* [AmerSp, fem. of *latino* Latino] (1983) **1 :** a woman or girl who is a native or inhabitant of Latin America **2 :** a woman or girl of Latin-American origin living in the U.S. — **Latina** *adj*

Latin alphabet *n* (1823) **:** an alphabet that was used for writing Latin and that has been modified for writing many modern languages

Latin Americanist *n* (1972) **:** a specialist in Latin American civilization

Lat·in·ate \ˈla-tə-ˌnāt\ *adj* (1904) **:** of, relating to, resembling, or derived from Latin

Latin cross *n* (1797) **:** a figure of a cross having a long upright shaft and a shorter crossbar traversing it above the middle — see CROSS illustration

Lat·in·ism \ˈla-tə-ˌni-zəm\ *n* (ca. 1570) **1 a :** a characteristic feature of Latin occurring in another language **b :** a word or phrase derived from Latin **2 :** Latin quality or character

Lat·in·ist \ˈla-tə-nist, ˈlat-nist\ *n* (15c) **:** a specialist in the Latin language or Roman culture

la·tin·i·ty \la-ˈti-nə-tē, lə-\ *n, often cap* (1540) **1 :** a manner of speaking or writing Latin **2 :** LATINISM 2

lat·in·ize \ˈla-tə-ˌnīz\ *vb* **-ized; -iz·ing** *often cap, vt* (1589) **1 a** *obs* **:** to translate into Latin **b :** to give a Latin form to **c :** to introduce Latinisms into **d :** ROMANIZE 2 **2 :** to make Latin or Italian in doctrine, ideas, or traits; *specif* **:** to cause to resemble the Roman Catholic Church ~ *vi* **1 :** to use Latinisms **2 :** to exhibit the influence of the Romans or of the Roman Catholic Church — **lat·in·i·za·tion** \ˌla-tə-nə-ˈzā-shən, ˌlat-nə-\ *n, often cap*

La·ti·no \lə-ˈtē-(ˌ)nō\ *n, pl* **-nos** [AmerSp, prob. short for *latinoamericano* Latin American] (1946) **1 :** a native or inhabitant of Latin America **2 :** a person of Latin-American origin living in the U.S. — **Latino** *adj*

Latin square *n* (1890) **:** a square array which contains *n* different elements with each element occurring *n* times but with no element occurring twice in the same column or row and which is used esp. in the statistical design of experiments (as in agriculture)

lat·ish \ˈlā-tish\ *adj* (1611) **:** somewhat late

la·tis·si·mus dor·si \lə-ˈti-sə-məs-ˈdȯr-sī\ *n, pl* **la·tis·si·mi dorsi** \-ˌmī-\ [NL, lit., broadest (muscle) of the back] (1684) **:** a broad flat superficial muscle chiefly of the middle and lower back that extends, adducts, and rotates the arm medially and draws the shoulder downward and backward

lat·i·tude \ˈla-tə-ˌtüd, -ˌtyüd\ *n* [ME, fr. L *latitudin-, latitudo,* fr. *latus* wide; akin to OCS *postĭlati* to spread] (14c) **1** *archaic* **:** extent or distance from side to side **:** WIDTH **2 :** angular distance from some specified circle or plane of reference: as **a :** angular distance north or south from the earth's equator measured through 90 degrees **b :** angular distance of a celestial body from the ecliptic **c :** a region or locality as marked by its latitude **3 a :** SCOPE, RANGE **b :** the range of exposures within which a film or plate will produce a negative or positive of satisfactory quality **4 :** freedom of action or choice ⟨students are allowed considerable ~ in choosing courses⟩ — **lat·i·tu·di·nal** \ˌla-tə-ˈtüd-nəl, -ˈtyüd-; -ˈtü-də-nəl, -ˈtyü-\ *adj* — **lat·i·tu·di·nal·ly** *adv*

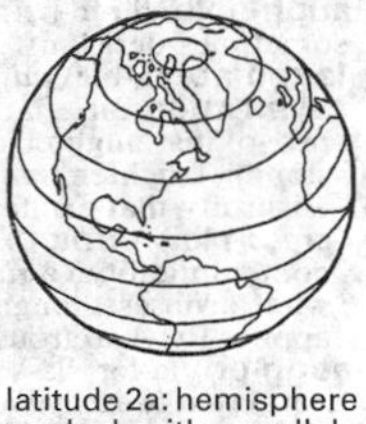

latitude 2a: hemisphere marked with parallels of latitude

lat·i·tu·di·nar·i·an \ˌla-tə-ˌtü-də-ˈner-ē-ən, -ˌtyü-\ *adj* (1697) **:** not insisting on strict conformity to a particular doctrine or standard **:** TOLERANT; *specif* **:** tolerant of variations in religious opinion or doctrine — **latitudinarian** *n* — **lat·i·tu·di·nar·i·an·ism** \-ē-ə-ˌni-zəm\ *n*

lat·ke \ˈlät-kə\ *n* [Yiddish, pancake, fr. Ukrainian *oladka*] (1927) **:** POTATO PANCAKE

lat·o·sol \ˈla-tə-ˌsȯl\ *n* [irreg. fr. L *later* brick + E *-sol* (as in *podsol,* var. of *podzol*)] (1949) **:** a leached red and yellow tropical soil — **lat·o·sol·ic** \ˌla-tə-ˈsȯ-lik\ *adj*

la·trine \lə-ˈtrēn\ *n* [F, fr. L *latrina,* contr. of *lavatrina,* fr. *lavare* to wash — more at LYE] (1642) **1 :** a receptacle (as a pit in the earth) for use as a toilet **2 :** TOILET 3

-latry *n comb form* [F *-latrie,* fr. LL *-latria,* fr. Gk, fr. *latreia;* akin to Gk *latron* pay] **:** worship ⟨helio*latry*⟩

lats \ˈläts\ *n, pl* **la·ti** \ˈlä-tē\ *or* **la·tu** \ˈlä-tü\ [Latvian (nom. pl. *lati,* gen. pl. *latu*), fr. *Latvija* Latvia] (1923) — see MONEY table

lat·te \ˈlä-(ˌ)tā\ *n* (1991) **:** CAFFE LATTE

lat·ten \ˈla-tᵊn\ *n* [ME *laton,* fr. AF] (14c) **:** a yellow alloy identical to or resembling brass typically hammered into thin sheets and formerly much used for church utensils

lat·ter \ˈla-tər\ *adj* [ME, fr. OE *lætra,* compar. of *læt* late] (bef. 12c) **1 a :** belonging to a subsequent time or period **:** more recent ⟨the ~ stages of growth⟩ **b :** of or relating to the end ⟨in their ~ days⟩ **c :** RECENT, PRESENT ⟨affected by ~ calamities⟩ **2 :** of, relating to, or being the second of two groups or things or the last of several groups or things referred to ⟨of ham and beef the ~ meat is cheaper today⟩ ⟨of ham and beef the ~ is cheaper today⟩

lat·ter–day \ˈla-tər-ˌdā\ *adj* (1832) **1 :** of present or recent times ⟨~ prophets⟩ **2 :** of a later or subsequent time

Latter–day Saint *n, often cap D* (1834) **:** a member of any of several religious bodies tracing their origin to Joseph Smith in 1830 and accepting the Book of Mormon as divine revelation **:** MORMON

lat·ter·ly \ˈla-tər-lē\ *adv* (1678) **1 :** LATER **2 :** of late **:** RECENTLY

lat·tice \ˈla-təs\ *n* [ME *latis,* fr. AF *latiz*] (14c) **1 a :** a framework or structure of crossed wood or metal strips **b :** a window, door, or gate having a lattice **c :** a network or design resembling a lattice **2 :** a regular geometrical arrangement of points or objects over an area or in space; *specif* **:** the arrangement of atoms in a crystal **3 :** a mathematical set that has some elements ordered and that is such that for any two elements there exists a greatest element in the subset of all elements less than or equal to both and a least element in the subset of all elements greater than or equal to both — **lattice** *vt* — **lat·ticed** \-tist\ *adj*

lattice girder *n* (1852) **:** a girder with top and bottom flanges connected by a latticework web

lat·tice·work \ˈla-təs-ˌwərk\ *n* (15c) **:** a lattice or work made of lattices

\ə\ **abut** \ᵊ\ **kitten,** F **table** \ər\ **further** \a\ **ash** \ā\ **ace** \ä\ **mop, mar**
\au̇\ **out** \ch\ **chin** \e\ **bet** \ē\ **easy** \g\ **go** \i\ **hit** \ī\ **ice** \j\ **job**
\ŋ\ **sing** \ō\ **go** \ȯ\ **law** \ȯi\ **boy** \th\ **thin** *th*\ **the** \ü\ **loot** \u̇\ **foot**
\y\ **yet** \zh\ **vision, beige** \k, ⁿ, œ, ue, ʸ\ *see* Guide to Pronunciation

la·tus rec·tum \ˈla-təs-ˈrek-təm\ *n* [NL, lit., straight side] (1702) : a chord of a conic section (as an ellipse) that passes through a focus and is parallel to the directrix

Lat·vi·an \ˈlat-vē-ən\ *n* (1924) **1** : the Baltic language of the Latvian people **2** : a native or inhabitant of Latvia — **Latvian** *adj*

lau·an \ˈlü-ˌän, lü-ˈ; lau̇-ˈän\ *n* [Tag *lawaan*] (1894) : the light yellow to reddish-brown or brown wood of any of various tropical southeast Asian trees (as of the genera *Shorea* and *Parashorea*) which sometimes enters commerce as Philippine mahogany

[1]**laud** \ˈlȯd\ *n* [ME *laudes* (pl.), fr. ML, fr. L, pl. of *laud-, laus* praise] (14c) **1** *pl but sing or pl in constr, often cap* : an office of solemn praise to God forming with matins the first of the canonical hours **2** : PRAISE, ACCLAIM

[2]**laud** *vt* [L *laudare,* fr. *laud-, laus*] (14c) : PRAISE, EXTOL

laud·able \ˈlȯ-də-bəl\ *adj* (15c) : worthy of praise : COMMENDABLE — **laud·able·ness** \ˈlȯ-də-bəl-nəs\ *n* — **laud·ably** \-blē\ *adv*

lau·da·num \ˈlȯd-nəm, ˈlȯ-də-nəm\ *n* [NL] (ca. 1603) **1** : any of various formerly used preparations of opium **2** : a tincture of opium

lau·da·tion \lȯ-ˈdā-shən\ *n* (15c) : the act of praising : EULOGY

lau·da·tive \ˈlȯ-də-tiv\ *adj* (15c) : LAUDATORY

lau·da·to·ry \ˈlȯ-də-ˌtȯr-ē\ *adj* (1555) : of, relating to, or expressing praise ⟨~ reviews⟩

[1]**laugh** \ˈlaf, ˈläf\ *vb* [ME, fr. OE *hliehhan;* akin to OHG *lachēn* to laugh] *vi* (bef. 12c) **1 a** : to show emotion (as mirth, joy, or scorn) with a chuckle or explosive vocal sound **b** : to find amusement or pleasure in something ⟨~*ed* at his own clumsiness⟩ **c** : to become amused or derisive ⟨a very skeptical public ~*ed* at our early efforts —Graenum Berger⟩ **2 a** : to produce the sound or appearance of laughter ⟨a ~*ing* brook⟩ **b** : to be of a kind that inspires joy ~ *vt* **1** : to influence or move by laughter ⟨~*ed* the bad singer off the stage⟩ **2** : to utter with a laugh — **laugh·ing·ly** \ˈla-fiŋ-lē, ˈlä-\ *adv*

[2]**laugh** *n* (1690) **1** : the act of laughing **2 a** : a cause for derision or merriment : JOKE **b** : an expression of scorn or mockery : JEER **3** *pl* : DIVERSION, SPORT ⟨play baseball just for ~*s*⟩

laugh·able \ˈla-fə-bəl, ˈlä-\ *adj* (1596) : of a kind to provoke laughter or sometimes derision : amusingly ridiculous — **laugh·able·ness** *n* — **laugh·ably** \-blē\ *adv*

syn LAUGHABLE, LUDICROUS, RIDICULOUS, COMIC, COMICAL mean provoking laughter or mirth. LAUGHABLE applies to anything occasioning laughter ⟨*laughable* attempts at skating⟩. LUDICROUS suggests absurdity that excites both laughter and scorn ⟨a thriller with a *ludicrous* plot⟩. RIDICULOUS suggests extreme absurdity, foolishness, or contemptibility ⟨a *ridiculous* display of anger⟩. COMIC applies esp. to what arouses thoughtful amusement ⟨a *comic* character⟩. COMICAL applies to what arouses spontaneous hilarity ⟨a *comical* hat⟩.

laugh·er \ˈla-fər, ˈlä-\ *n* (15c) **1** : one that laughs **2** : something (as a game) that is easily won or handled

laughing gas *n* (1842) : NITROUS OXIDE

laughing gull *n* (1789) : an American gull (*Larus atricilla*) having a black head in breeding plumage and black wing tips blending into the gray upper side of the wings

laughing jackass *n* (1798) : KOOKABURRA

laughing matter *n* (ca. 1583) : something not to be taken seriously — usu. used in the phrase *no laughing matter*

laugh·ing·stock \ˈla-fiŋ-ˌstäk, ˈlä-\ *n* (1533) : an object of ridicule

laugh off *vt* (1676) : to minimize by treating as amusingly or absurdly trivial

laugh·ter \ˈlaf-tər, ˈläf-\ *n* [ME, fr. OE *hleahtor;* akin to OE *hliehhan*] (bef. 12c) **1** : a sound of or as if of laughing **2** *archaic* : a cause of merriment

laugh track *n* (1962) : recorded laughter that accompanies dialogue or action (as of a television program)

launce \ˈlȯn(t)s, ˈlän(t)s\ *n* [prob. fr. [1]*lance*] (1623) : SAND LANCE

[1]**launch** \ˈlȯnch, ˈlänch\ *vb* [ME, fr. AF **lancher, lancer,* fr. LL *lanceare* to wield a lance — more at LANCE] *vt* (14c) **1 a** : to throw forward : HURL **b** : to release, catapult, or send off (a self-propelled object) ⟨~ a rocket⟩ **2 a** : to set (a boat or ship) afloat **b** : to give (a person) a start ⟨~*ed* her on a new career⟩ **c** (1) : to put into operation or set in motion : INITIATE, INTRODUCE (2) : to get off to a good start **d** : to load into a computer's memory and run ⟨~ a program⟩ ~ *vi* **1 a** : to spring forward : TAKE OFF **b** : to enter energetically ⟨~*ed* into an impromptu speech —Tim Tucker⟩ **2 a** *archaic* : to slide down the ways **b** : to make a start

[2]**launch** *n* (1749) : an act or instance of launching

[3]**launch** *n* [Sp or Pg; Sp *lancha,* fr. Pg] (1697) **1** : a large boat that operates from a ship **2** : a small motorboat that is open or that has the forepart of the hull covered

launch·er \ˈlȯn-chər, ˈlän-\ *n* (1911) : one that launches: as **a** : a device for firing grenades **b** : a device for launching a missile **c** : LAUNCH VEHICLE

launching pad *n* (1951) **1** : LAUNCHPAD **2** : SPRINGBOARD 2

launch·pad \ˈlȯnch-ˌpad, ˈlänch-\ *n* (1958) : a nonflammable platform from which a rocket, launch vehicle, or guided missile can be launched

launch vehicle *n* (ca. 1960) : a rocket used to launch a satellite or spacecraft

launch window *n* (1962) : WINDOW 8

[1]**laun·der** \ˈlȯn-dər, ˈlän-\ *vb* **laun·dered; laun·der·ing** \-d(ə-)riŋ\ [ME *launder,* n.] *vt* (1664) **1** : to wash (as clothes) in water **2** : to make ready for use by washing and ironing ⟨a freshly ~*ed* shirt⟩ **3** : to transfer (as illegally obtained money or investments) through an outside party to conceal the true source **4** : SANITIZE 2 ⟨~*ed* language⟩ ~ *vi* : to wash or wash and iron clothing or household linens — **laun·der·er** \-dər-ər\ *n*

[2]**launder** *n* [ME, launderer, fr. AF *lavandere,* fr. ML *lavandarius,* fr. L *lavandus,* gerundive of *lavare* to wash — more at LYE] (1667) : TROUGH; *esp* : a box conduit conveying particulate material suspended in water in ore dressing

laun·der·ette \ˌlȯn-də-ˈret, ˌlän-\ *also* **laun·drette** \-ˈdret\ *n* [fr. *Launderette,* a service mark] (ca. 1948) : a self-service laundry

laun·dress \ˈlȯn-drəs, ˈlän-\ *n* (1550) : a woman who is a laundry worker

Laun·dro·mat \ˈlȯn-drə-ˌmat, ˈlän-\ *service mark* — used for a self-service laundry

laun·dry \ˈlȯn-drē, ˈlän-\ *n, pl* **laundries** (14c) **1 a** : a room for doing the family wash **b** : a commercial laundering establishment **2** : clothes or linens that have been or are to be laundered

laundry list *n* (1958) : a usu. long list of items ⟨the *laundry list* of new consumer-protection bills —N. C. Miller⟩

laun·dry·man \-mən\ *n* (1708) : a man who is a laundry worker

Laun·fal \ˈlȯn-fəl, ˈlän-\ *n* (15c) : a knight of the Round Table in late Arthurian legend

lau·ra \ˈläv-rə\ *n* [LGk, fr. Gk, lane] (ca. 1752) : a monastery of an Eastern church

[1]**lau·re·ate** \ˈlȯr-ē-ət, ˈlär-\ *n* [ME, crowned with laurel as a distinction, fr. L *laureatus,* fr. *laurea* laurel wreath, fr. fem. of *laureus* of laurel, fr. *laurus*] (ca. 1529) : the recipient of honor or recognition for achievement in an art or science; *specif* : POET LAUREATE — **laureate** *adj* — **lau·re·ate·ship** \-ˌship\ *n*

[2]**lau·re·ate** \ˈlȯr-ē-ˌāt, ˈlär-\ *vt* **-at·ed; -at·ing** (ca. 1610) **1** : to crown with or as if with a laurel wreath for excellence or achievement **2** : to appoint to the office of poet laureate — **lau·re·ation** \ˌlȯr-ē-ˈā-shən, ˌlär-\ *n*

[1]**lau·rel** \ˈlȯr-əl, ˈlär-\ *n* [ME *lorel,* in part fr. ML *laureola* spurge laurel (fr. L, laurel sprig), in part modif. of AF *lorer,* fr. OF *lor* laurel, fr. L *laurus*] (14c) **1** : an evergreen shrub or tree (*Laurus nobilis* of the family Lauraceae, the laurel family) of southern Europe with small yellow flowers, fruits that are ovoid blackish berries, and evergreen foliage once used by the ancient Greeks to crown victors in the Pythian games — called also *bay, sweet bay* **2** : a tree or shrub that resembles the true laurel; *esp* : MOUNTAIN LAUREL **3 a** : a crown of laurel awarded as an honor **b** : a recognition of achievement : HONOR — usu. used in pl.

[2]**laurel** *vt* **-reled** *or* **-relled; -rel·ing** *or* **-rel·ling** (1631) : to deck or crown with laurel

lau·ric acid \ˈlȯr-ik-, ˈlär-\ *n* [ISV, fr. L *laurus*] (1865) : a crystalline fatty acid $C_{12}H_{24}O_2$ found esp. in coconut oil and used chiefly in making soaps and esters

lau·ryl alcohol \ˈlȯr-əl-, ˈlär-\ *n* (1922) : a solid alcohol $C_{12}H_{26}O$

lav *n* (1913) : LAVATORY

la·va \ˈlä-və, ˈla-\ *n* [It, ultim. fr. L *labes* fall; akin to L *labi* to slide — more at SLEEP] (1759) : molten rock that issues from a volcano or from a fissure in the surface of a planet (as earth) or moon; *also* : such rock that has cooled and hardened — **la·va·like** \-ˌlīk\ *adj*

la·va·bo \lə-ˈvä-(ˌ)bō\ *n, pl* **-bos** [L, I shall wash, fr. *lavare*] (ca. 1858) **1** *often cap* : a ceremony at Mass in which the celebrant washes his hands after offering the oblations and says Psalm 25:6–12 (DV) **2 a** : a washbasin and a tank with a spigot that are fastened to a wall **b** : this combination used as a planter

la·vage \lə-ˈväzh, *Brit usu* ˈla-vij\ *n* [F, fr. MF, fr. *laver* to wash, fr. L *lavare*] (ca. 1895) : WASHING; *esp* : the therapeutic washing out of an organ or part

la·va·la·va \ˌlä-və-ˈlä-və\ *n* [Samoan, clothing] (1891) : a rectangular cloth of cotton print worn like a kilt or skirt in Polynesia and esp. in Samoa

la·va·liere *also* **la·val·liere** \ˌlä-və-ˈlir, ˌla-\ *n* [F *lavallière* necktie with a large knot] (1906) : a pendant on a fine chain that is worn as a necklace

la·va·lier microphone \ˌlä-və-ˈlir-, ˌla-\ *also* **lavaliere microphone** *same*\ *n* (ca. 1962) : a small microphone hung around the neck of the user

la·va·tion \lā-ˈvā-shən\ *n* [ME *lavacioun,* fr. L *lavation-, lavatio,* fr. *lavare*] (15c) : the act or an instance of washing or cleansing

lav·a·to·ry \ˈla-və-ˌtȯr-ē, *Brit* -və-t(ə-)rē\ *n, pl* **-ries** [ME *lavatorie,* fr. ML *lavatorium,* fr. L *lavare* to wash — more at LYE] (14c) **1** : a vessel (as a basin) for washing; *esp* : a fixed bowl or basin with running water and drainpipe for washing **2** : a room with conveniences for washing and usu. with one or more toilets **3** : TOILET 3b — **lavatory** *adj*

[1]**lave** \ˈlāv\ *n* [ME (northern dial.), fr. OE *lāf;* akin to OE *belīfan* to remain — more at LEAVE] (bef. 12c) *chiefly dial* : something that is left : RESIDUE

[2]**lave** *vb* **laved; lav·ing** [ME, fr. OE *lafian,* fr. L *lavare*] *vt* (bef. 12c) **1 a** : WASH, BATHE **b** : to flow along or against **2** : POUR ~ *vi, archaic* : to wash oneself : BATHE

[1]**lav·en·der** \ˈla-vən-dər\ *n* [ME *lavendre,* fr. AF, fr. ML *lavandula*] (13c) **1 a** : a Mediterranean mint (*Lavandula angustifolia* syn. *L. officinalis*) widely cultivated for its narrow aromatic leaves and spikes of lilac-purple flowers which are dried and used in sachets and from which is extracted an aromatic oil used chiefly in perfumery **b** : any of several plants congeneric with true lavender and used similarly but often considered inferior **2** : a pale purple

[2]**lavender** *vt* **lav·en·dered; lav·en·der·ing** \-d(ə-)riŋ\ (1820) : to sprinkle or perfume with lavender

[1]**la·ver** \ˈlā-vər\ *n* [ME *lavour,* fr. AF *lavour, lavere,* fr. ML *lavatorium*] (1535) : a large basin used for ceremonial ablutions in the ancient Jewish Tabernacle and Temple worship

[2]**la·ver** \ˈlā-vər, ˈlä-\ *n* [NL, fr. L, a water plant] (1611) : any of several common red algae (genus *Porphyra*) with fronds used esp. for stewing or pickling — compare NORI

La·vin·ia \lə-ˈvi-nē-ə\ *n* [L] (1513) : a daughter of King Latinus in Virgil's *Aeneid* who is betrothed to Turnus but marries Aeneas

[1]**lav·ish** \ˈla-vish\ *adj* [ME *laves, lavage,* prob. fr. MF *lavasse, lavache* downpour of rain, fr. *laver* to wash — more at LAVAGE] (15c) **1** : expending or bestowing profusely : PRODIGAL **2 a** : expended or produced in abundance **b** : marked by profusion or excess ***syn*** see PROFUSE — **lav·ish·ly** *adv* — **lav·ish·ness** *n*

[2]**lavish** *vt* (1542) : to expend or bestow with profusion : SQUANDER

lav·rock \ˈläv-rək, ˈlav-\ *or* **la·ver·ock** \ˈla-və-\ *n* [ME *laverok,* fr. OE *lāwerce*] (14c) *chiefly Scot* : LARK

[1]**law** \ˈlȯ\ *n* [ME, fr. OE *lagu,* of Scand origin; akin to ON *lǫg* law; akin to OE *licgan* to lie — more at LIE] (bef. 12c) **1 a** (1) : a binding custom or practice of a community : a rule of conduct or action prescribed or formally recognized as binding or enforced by a controlling authority (2) : the whole body of such customs, practices, or rules (3) : COMMON LAW **b** (1) : the control brought about by the existence or enforcement of such law (2) : the action of laws considered as a means of redressing wrongs; *also* : LITIGATION (3) : the agency of or an agent of established law **c** : a rule or order that it is advisable or obligatory to observe **d** : something compatible with or enforceable by established law **e** : CONTROL, AUTHORITY **2 a** *often cap* : the revelation of

the will of God set forth in the Old Testament **b** *cap* : the first part of the Jewish scriptures : PENTATEUCH, TORAH — see BIBLE table **3** : a rule of construction or procedure ⟨the ~s of poetry⟩ **4** : the whole body of laws relating to one subject **5 a** : the legal profession **b** : law as a department of knowledge : JURISPRUDENCE **c** : legal knowledge **6 a** : a statement of an order or relation of phenomena that so far as is known is invariable under the given conditions **b** : a general relation proved or assumed to hold between mathematical or logical expressions — **at law** : under or within the provisions of the law ⟨enforceable *at law*⟩

syn LAW, RULE, REGULATION, PRECEPT, STATUTE, ORDINANCE, CANON mean a principle governing action or procedure. LAW implies imposition by a sovereign authority and the obligation of obedience on the part of all subject to that authority ⟨obey the *law*⟩. RULE applies to more restricted or specific situations ⟨the *rules* of the game⟩. REGULATION implies prescription by authority in order to control an organization or system ⟨*regulations* affecting nuclear power plants⟩. PRECEPT commonly suggests something advisory and not obligatory communicated typically through teaching ⟨the *precepts* of effective writing⟩. STATUTE implies a law enacted by a legislative body ⟨a *statute* requiring the use of seat belts⟩. ORDINANCE applies to an order governing some detail of procedure or conduct enforced by a limited authority such as a municipality ⟨a city *ordinance*⟩. CANON suggests in nonreligious use a principle or rule of behavior or procedure commonly accepted as a valid guide ⟨the *canons* of good taste⟩. *syn* see in addition HYPOTHESIS

²**law** *vi* (ca. 1550) : LITIGATE ~ *vt, chiefly dial* : to sue or prosecute at law

law-abid-ing \'lȯ-ə-ˌbī-diŋ\ *adj* (1834) : abiding by or obedient to the law ⟨~ citizens⟩ — **law-abid-ing-ness** *n*

law-and-order *adj* (1844) : relating to, characterized by, or advocating strict laws and their enforcement ⟨a ~ candidate⟩

law-break-er \'lȯ-ˌbrā-kər\ *n* (15c) : a person who violates the law — **law-break-ing** \-kiŋ\ *adj or n*

law-ful \'lȯ-fəl\ *adj* (14c) **1 a** : being in harmony with the law ⟨a ~ judgment⟩ **b** : constituted, authorized, or established by law : RIGHTFUL ⟨~ institutions⟩ **2** : LAW-ABIDING ⟨~ citizens⟩ — **law-ful-ly** \-f(ə-)lē\ *adv* — **law-ful-ness** \-fəl-nəs\ *n*

syn LAWFUL, LEGAL, LEGITIMATE, LICIT mean being in accordance with law. LAWFUL may apply to conformity with law of any sort (as natural, divine, common, or canon) ⟨the *lawful* sovereign⟩. LEGAL applies to what is sanctioned by law or in conformity with the law, esp. as it is written or administered by the courts ⟨*legal* residents of the state⟩. LEGITIMATE may apply to a legal right or status but also, in extended use, to a right or status supported by tradition, custom, or accepted standards ⟨a perfectly *legitimate* question about taxes⟩. LICIT applies to a strict conformity to the provisions of the law and applies esp. to what is regulated by law ⟨the *licit* use of drugs by doctors⟩.

law-giv-er \'lȯ-ˌgi-vər\ *n* (14c) **1** : one who gives a code of laws to a people **2** : LEGISLATOR

law-less \'lȯ-ləs\ *adj* (12c) **1** : not regulated by or based on law **2 a** : not restrained or controlled by law : UNRULY **b** : ILLEGAL — **law-less-ly** *adv* — **law-less-ness** *n*

law-mak-er \'lȯ-ˌmā-kər\ *n* (14c) : one who makes laws : LEGISLATOR — **law-mak-ing** \-kiŋ\ *n*

law-man \'lȯ-mən\ *n* (1944) : a law-enforcement officer (as a sheriff or marshal)

law merchant *n, pl* **laws merchant** (15c) : the legal rules formerly applied to cases arising in commercial transactions

¹**lawn** \'lȯn, 'län\ *n* [ME *launde*, fr. AF *land, launde* wood, unwooded field, of Celt origin; akin to MIr *lann* land — more at LAND] (14c) **1** *archaic* : an open space between woods : GLADE **2** : ground (as around a house or in a garden or park) that is covered with grass and is kept mowed **3** : a relatively even layer of bacteria covering the surface of a culture medium — **lawn** *or* **lawny** \'lȯ-nē, 'lä-\ *adj*

²**lawn** *n* [ME *lawne, laund,* prob. fr. *Laon,* France] (15c) : a fine sheer linen or cotton fabric of plain weave that is thinner than cambric — **lawny** *adj*

lawn bowling *n* (ca. 1929) : a bowling game played on a green with wooden balls which are rolled at a jack

lawn mower *n* (1869) : a machine for cutting grass on lawns

lawn tennis *n* (1874) : TENNIS 2

law of averages (1874) : the commonsense observation that probability influences everyday life so that over the long term the possible outcomes of a repeated event occur with specific frequencies

law of definite proportions (1830) : a statement in chemistry: every definite compound always contains the same elements in the same proportions by weight

law of dominance (1942) : MENDEL'S LAW 3

law of independent assortment (1943) : MENDEL'S LAW 2

law of large numbers (1911) : a theorem in mathematical statistics: the probability that the absolute value of the difference between the mean of a population sample and the mean of the population from which it is drawn is greater than an arbitrarily small amount approaches zero as the size of the sample approaches infinity

Law of Moses (14c) : PENTATEUCH, TORAH

law of nations (ca. 1548) : INTERNATIONAL LAW

law of parsimony (1837) : OCCAM'S RAZOR

law of segregation (1902) : MENDEL'S LAW 1

law of war (1709) : the code that governs or one of the rules that govern the rights and duties of belligerents in international war

law-ren-ci-um \lȯ-'ren(t)-sē-əm\ *n* [NL, fr. Ernest O. *Lawrence*] (1961) : a short-lived radioactive element produced artificially — see ELEMENT table

law-suit \'lȯ-ˌsüt\ *n* (1624) : a suit in law : a case before a court

law-yer \'lȯ-yər, 'lȯi-ər\ *n* (14c) : one whose profession is to conduct lawsuits for clients or to advise as to legal rights and obligations in other matters — **law-yer-like** \-ˌlīk\ *adj* — **law-yer-ly** \-lē\ *adj*

law-yer-ing \'lȯ-yə-riŋ, 'lȯi-ə-\ *n* (1676) : the profession or work of a lawyer

¹**lax** \'laks\ *adj* [ME, fr. L *laxus* loose — more at SLACK] (14c) **1 a** *of the bowels* : LOOSE, OPEN **b** : having loose bowels **2** : deficient in firmness : not stringent ⟨~ control⟩ ⟨a ~ foreman⟩ **3 a** : not tense, firm, or rigid : SLACK ⟨a ~ rope⟩ **b** : having an open or loose texture **c**

: having the constituents spread apart ⟨a ~ flower cluster⟩ **4** : articulated with the muscles involved in a relatively relaxed state (as the vowel \i\ in contrast with the vowel \ē\) *syn* see NEGLIGENT — **lax-a-tion** \lak-'sā-shən\ *n* — **lax-ly** \'laks-lē\ *adv* — **lax-ness** *n*

²**lax** *n* [by shortening & alter. (*x* as symbol for *-crosse*)] (1951) : LACROSSE

¹**lax-a-tive** \'lak-sə-tiv\ *adj* [ME *laxatif,* fr. ML *laxativus,* fr. L *laxatus,* pp. of *laxare* to loosen, fr. *laxus*] (14c) : having a tendency to loosen or relax; *specif* : producing bowel movements and relieving constipation

²**laxative** *n* (14c) : a usu. mild laxative drug

lax-i-ty \'lak-sə-tē\ *n* (1528) : the quality or state of being lax

¹**lay** \'lā\ *vb* **laid** \'lād\; **lay-ing** [ME *leyen,* fr. OE *lecgan;* akin to OE *licgan* to lie — more at LIE] *vt* (bef. 12c) **1** : to beat or strike down with force **2 a** : to put or set down ⟨~ your books on the table⟩ **b** : to place for rest or sleep; *esp* : BURY **3** : to bring forth and deposit (an egg) **4** : CALM, ALLAY ⟨~ the dust⟩ **5** : BET, WAGER **6** : to press down giving a smooth and even surface **7 a** : to dispose or spread over or on a surface ⟨~ track⟩ ⟨~ plaster⟩ **b** : to set in order or position ⟨~ a table for dinner⟩ ⟨~ brick⟩ **c** : to put (strands) in place and twist to form a rope, hawser, or cable; *also* : to make by so doing ⟨~ up rope⟩ **8 a** : to impose as a duty, burden, or punishment ⟨~ a tax⟩ **b** : to put as a burden of reproach ⟨*laid* the blame on her⟩ **c** : to advance as an accusation : IMPUTE ⟨the disaster was *laid* to faulty inspection⟩ **9** : to place (something immaterial) on something ⟨~ stress on grammar⟩ **10** : PREPARE, CONTRIVE ⟨a well-*laid* plan⟩ **11 a** : to bring against or into contact with something : APPLY ⟨*laid* the watch to his ear⟩ **b** : to prepare or position for action or operation ⟨~ a fire in the fireplace⟩; *also* : to adjust (a gun) to the proper direction and elevation **12** : to bring to a specified condition ⟨~ waste the land⟩ **13 a** : ASSERT, ALLEGE ⟨~ claim to an estate⟩ **b** : to submit for examination and judgment ⟨*laid* her case before the commission⟩ **14** *often vulgar* : to copulate with ~ *vi* **1** : to produce and deposit eggs **2** *nonstand* : ¹LIE **3** : WAGER, BET **4** *dial* : PLAN, PREPARE **5 a** : to apply oneself vigorously ⟨*laid* to his oars⟩ **b** : to proceed to a specified place or position on a ship ⟨~ aloft⟩ — **lay an egg** : to fail or blunder esp. embarrassingly — **lay eyes on** : SEE, BEHOLD — **lay into** : to attack esp. verbally ⟨*laid into* the referee⟩ — **lay on the table** **1** : to remove (a parliamentary motion) from consideration indefinitely **2** *Brit* : to put (as legislation) on the agenda

usage LAY has been used intransitively in the sense of "lie" since the 14th century. The practice was unremarked until around 1770; attempts to correct it have been a fixture of schoolbooks ever since. Generations of teachers and critics have succeeded in taming most literary and learned writing, but intransitive *lay* persists in familiar speech and is a bit more common in general prose than one might suspect. Much of the problem lies in the confusing similarity of the principal parts of the two words. Another influence may be a folk belief that *lie* is for people and *lay* is for things. Some commentators are ready to abandon the distinction, suggesting that *lay* is on the rise socially. But if it does rise to respectability, it is sure to do so slowly: many people have invested effort in learning to keep *lie* and *lay* distinct. Remember that even though many people do use *lay* for *lie,* others will judge you unfavorably if you do.

²**lay** *n* (1590) **1** : COVERT, LAIR **2** : something (as a layer) that lies or is laid **3 a** : line of action : PLAN **b** : line of work : OCCUPATION **4 a** : terms of sale or employment : PRICE **b** : share of profit (as on a whaling voyage) paid in lieu of wages **5 a** : the amount of advance of any point in a rope strand for one turn **b** : the nature of a fiber rope as determined by the amount of twist, the angle of the strands, and the angle of the threads in the strands **6** : the way in which a thing lies or is laid in relation to something else ⟨the ~ of the land⟩ **7** : the state of one that lays eggs ⟨hens coming into ~⟩ **8 a** *usu vulgar* : a partner in sexual intercourse **b** *usu vulgar* : SEXUAL INTERCOURSE

³**lay** *past of* LIE

⁴**lay** *n* [ME, fr. AF *lai*] (13c) **1** : a simple narrative poem : BALLAD **2** : MELODY, SONG

⁵**lay** *adj* [ME, fr. AF *lai,* fr. LL *laicus,* fr. Gk *laikos* of the people, fr. *laos* people] (15c) **1** : of or relating to the laity : not ecclesiastical **2** : of or relating to members of a religious house occupied with domestic or manual work ⟨a ~ brother⟩ **3** : not of a particular profession ⟨the ~ public⟩; *also* : lacking extensive knowledge of a particular subject

lay-about \'lā-ə-ˌbaút\ *n* (1932) : a lazy shiftless person : IDLER

lay-away \'lā-ə-ˌwā\ *n* (1944) : a purchasing agreement by which a retailer agrees to hold merchandise secured by a deposit until the price is paid in full by the customer

lay away *vt* (ca. 1928) : to put aside for future use or delivery

lay-by \'lā-ˌbī\ *n* (1939) **1** *Brit* : TURNOUT 4b **2** : the final operation (as a last cultivating) in the growing of a field crop

lay by *vt* (15c) **1** : to lay aside : DISCARD **2** : to store for future use : SAVE **3** : to cultivate (as corn) for the last time

lay day *n* (1845) **1** : one of the days allowed by the charter for loading or unloading a vessel **2** : a day of delay in port

lay down *vt* (13c) **1** : to give up : SURRENDER ⟨*lay down* your arms⟩ **2 a** : ESTABLISH, PRESCRIBE ⟨*lay down* a scale for a map⟩ **b** : to assert or command dogmatically ⟨*lay down* the law⟩ **3 a** : STORE, PRESERVE ⟨*laid down* a young wine⟩ **b** : RECORD ⟨*laying down* songs for their new album⟩ **4 a** : to direct toward a target ⟨*lay down* a barrage⟩ **b** : to hit along the ground ⟨*laid down* a sacrifice bunt⟩ ~ *vi, nonstand* : to lie down

¹**lay-er** \'lā-ər, 'ler\ *n* (13c) **1** : one that lays (as a worker who lays brick or a hen that lays eggs) **2 a** : one thickness, course, or fold laid or lying over or under another **b** : STRATUM **c** : HORIZON 2 **3 a** : a branch or shoot of a plant that roots while still attached to the parent plant **b** : a plant developed by layering — **lay-ered** \'lā-ərd, 'lerd\ *adj*

²**layer** *vt* (1832) **1** : to propagate (a plant) by means of layers **2 a** : to place as a layer **b** : to place a layer on top of ⟨pancakes ~ed with butter and syrup⟩ **c** : to form or arrange in layers ~ *vi* **1 a** : to separate

---

\ə\ abut \ᵊ\ kitten, F table \ər\ further \a\ ash \ā\ ace \ä\ mop, mar
\aú\ out \ch\ chin \e\ bet \ē\ easy \g\ go \i\ hit \ī\ ice \j\ job
\ŋ\ sing \ō\ go \ȯ\ law \ȯi\ boy \th\ thin \th\ the \ü\ loot \ú\ foot
\y\ yet \zh\ vision, beige \k, ⁿ, œ, �, ᵕ\ see Guide to Pronunciation

into layers **b** : to form out of superimposed layers **2** *of a plant* : to form roots where a stem comes in contact with the ground

lay·er·age \ˈlā-ə-rij, ˈler-ij\ *n* (1902) : the practice, art, or process of rooting plants by layering

lay·ette \lā-ˈet\ *n* [F, fr. MF, dim. of *laye* box, fr. MD *lade;* akin to OE *hladan* to load — more at LADE] (1839) : a complete outfit of clothing and equipment for a newborn infant

lay figure *n* [obs. E *layman* lay figure, fr. D *leeman*] (1795) **1** : a jointed model of the human body used by artists to show the disposition of drapery **2** : a person so compliant as to be likened to a puppet

lay·in \ˈlā-ˌin\ *n* (1951) : LAYUP 2

lay in *vt* (1579) : LAY BY, SAVE ⟨*lays in* food for the winter⟩

laying on of hands (15c) : the act of laying hands usu. on a person's head to confer a spiritual blessing (as in Christian ordination, confirmation, or faith healing)

lay·man \ˈlā-mən\ *n* (15c) **1** : a person who is not a member of the clergy **2** : a person who does not belong to a particular profession or who is not expert in some field

lay·off \ˈlā-ˌȯf\ *n* (1889) **1** : a period of inactivity or idleness **2** : the act of laying off an employee or a workforce; *also* : SHUTDOWN

lay off *vt* (1748) **1** : to mark or measure off **2** : to cease to employ (a worker) often temporarily **3** *of a bookie* : to place all or part of (an accepted bet) with another bookie to reduce the risk **4 a** : to leave undisturbed **b** : AVOID, QUIT ⟨was advised to *lay off* smoking and alcohol⟩ **c** : to refrain from swinging at (a pitch) ~ *vi* **1** : to stop doing or taking something **2** : to leave one alone ⟨wish you'd just *lay off*⟩

lay on *vt* (1600) **1 a** : to apply by or as if by spreading on a surface ⟨*laying* it *on* thick⟩ **b** : PROVIDE, ARRANGE ⟨food *laid on* in abundance⟩ **c** : HAND OUT ⟨*laid on* awards⟩ **2** *chiefly Brit* : HIRE ~ *vi* : ATTACK, BEAT

lay·out \ˈlā-ˌau̇t\ *n* (1852) **1** : the plan or design or arrangement of something laid out: as **a** : DUMMY 5b **b** : final arrangement of matter to be reproduced esp. by printing **2** : the act or process of planning or laying out in detail **3 a** : something that is laid out ⟨a model train ~⟩ **b** : land or structures or rooms used for a particular purpose ⟨a cattle-ranching ~⟩; *also* : PLACE **c** : a set or outfit esp. of tools

lay out *vt* (15c) **1** : DISPLAY, EXHIBIT **2** : SPEND **3 a** : to prepare (a corpse) for viewing **b** : to knock flat or unconscious **4** : to plan in detail ⟨*lay out* a campaign⟩ **5** : ARRANGE, DESIGN **6** : to mark (work) for drilling, machining, or filing

lay·over \ˈlā-ˌō-vər\ *n* (1873) : STOPOVER

lay over *vt* (1838) : POSTPONE ~ *vi* : to make a stopover

lay·peo·ple \ˈlā-ˌpē-pəl\ *n pl* (15c) : LAYPERSONS

lay·per·son \-ˌpər-sᵊn\ *n* (1972) : a member of the laity

lay reader *n* (1751) **1** : a layperson authorized to conduct parts of the church services not requiring a priest or minister **2** : LAYMAN 2

lay to *vi* (1796) : LIE TO ~ *vt* : to bring (a ship) into the wind and hold stationary

lay·up \ˈlā-ˌəp\ *n* (1925) **1** : the action of laying up or the condition of being laid up **2** : a shot in basketball made from near the basket usu. by playing the ball off the backboard

lay up *vt* (14c) **1** : to store up : LAY BY **2** : to disable or confine with illness or injury ⟨a knee injury *laid* him *up* for a week⟩ **3** : to take out of active service

lay·wom·an \ˈlā-ˌwu̇-mən\ *n* (1529) : a woman who is a member of the laity

la·zar \ˈla-zər, ˈlā-\ *n* [ME, fr. ML *lazarus,* fr. LL *Lazarus*] (14c) : a person afflicted with a repulsive disease; *specif* : LEPER

laz·a·ret·to \ˌla-zə-ˈre-(ˌ)tō\ *or* **laz·a·ret** \-ˈret\ *also* **laz·a·rette** \-ˈret\ *n, pl* **-rettos** *or* **-rets** *also* **-rettes** [It *lazzaretto,* alter. of *Nazaretto,* quarantine station in Venice, fr. *Santa Maria di Nazareth,* church on the island where it was located] (1549) **1** *usu lazaretto* : an institution (as a hospital) for those with contagious diseases **2** : a building or a ship used for detention in quarantine **3** *usu lazaret or lazarette* : a space in a ship between decks used as a storeroom

La·za·rist \ˈla-zə-rist, lə-ˈzär-ist\ *n* [College of St. *Lazare,* Paris, former home of the congregation] (1747) : VINCENTIAN 1

Laz·a·rus \ˈlaz-rəs, ˈla-zə-\ *n* [LL, fr. Gk *Lazaros,* fr. Heb *Elʿāzār*] (bef. 12c) **1** : a brother of Mary and Martha raised by Jesus from the dead according to the account in John 11 **2** : the diseased beggar in the parable of the rich man and the beggar found in Luke 16

laze \ˈlāz\ *vb* **lazed; laz·ing** [back-formation fr. *lazy*] *vi* (ca. 1592) : to act or lie lazily : IDLE ~ *vt* : to pass (time) in idleness or relaxation *syn* see IDLE — **laze** *n*

la·zu·lite \ˈla-zyü-ˌlīt, -zhə-\ *n* [G *Lazulith,* fr. ML *lazulum* lapis lazuli] (1807) : an often crystalline azure-blue mineral that is a hydrous phosphate of aluminum, iron, and magnesium

[1]**la·zy** \ˈlā-zē\ *adj* **la·zi·er; -est** [perh. fr. MLG *lasich* feeble; akin to MHG er*leswen* to become weak] (1549) **1 a** : disinclined to activity or exertion : not energetic or vigorous **b** : encouraging inactivity or indolence ⟨a ~ summer day⟩ **2** : moving slowly : SLUGGISH **3** : DROOPY, LAX ⟨a rabbit with ~ ears⟩ **4** : placed on its side ⟨~ E livestock brand⟩ **5** : not rigorous or strict ⟨~ scholarship⟩ — **la·zi·ly** \-zə-lē\ *adv* — **la·zi·ness** \-zē-nəs\ *n* — **la·zy·ish** \-zē-ish\ *adj*

syn LAZY, INDOLENT, SLOTHFUL mean not easily aroused to activity. LAZY suggests a disinclination to work or to take trouble ⟨take-out foods for *lazy* cooks⟩. INDOLENT suggests a love of ease and a dislike of movement or activity ⟨the heat made us *indolent*⟩. SLOTHFUL implies a temperamental inability to act promptly or speedily when action or speed is called for ⟨fired for being *slothful* about filling orders⟩.

[2]**lazy** *vi* **la·zied; la·zy·ing** (1612) : to move or lie lazily : LAZE

la·zy·bones \ˈlā-zē-ˌbōnz\ *n pl but sing or pl in constr* (1592) : a lazy person

lazy eye *n* (1939) : AMBLYOPIA; *also* : an eye affected with amblyopia

lazy Su·san \-ˈsü-zᵊn\ *n* (1912) : a revolving tray used for serving food, condiments, or relishes

lazy tongs *n pl* (1836) : a series of jointed and pivoted bars capable of great extension used to pick up or handle something at a distance

lb *abbr* [L *libra*] pound

LB *abbr* Labrador

LBO *abbr* leveraged buyout

lc *abbr* lowercase

LC *abbr* **1** landing craft **2** left center **3** letter of credit **4** Library of Congress

[1]**LCD** \ˌel-(ˌ)sē-ˈdē\ *n* [*l*iquid *c*rystal *d*isplay] (1973) : an electronic display (as of the time in a digital watch) that consists of segments of a liquid crystal whose reflectivity varies according to the voltage applied to them

[2]**LCD** *abbr* least common denominator; lowest common denominator

LCDR *abbr* lieutenant commander

LCL *abbr* less-than-carload lot

LCM *abbr* **1** least common multiple; lowest common multiple **2** [NL *legis comparativae magister*] master of comparative law

LCpl *abbr* lance corporal

LCS *abbr* League Championship Series

ld *abbr* **1** load **2** lord

LD *abbr* **1** laser disc **2** learning disabled; learning disability **3** lethal dose **4** line of departure

LDC *abbr* least developed country; less developed country

LD_{50} \ˌel-ˌdē-ˈfif-tē\ *n* [*l*ethal *d*ose] (1942) : the amount of a toxic agent (as a poison, virus, or radiation) that is sufficient to kill 50 percent of a population of animals usu. within a certain time

ldg *abbr* **1** landing **2** loading

LDH *abbr* lactate dehydrogenase; lactic dehydrogenase

LDL \ˌel-(ˌ)dē-ˈel\ *n* [*l*ow-*d*ensity *l*ipoprotein] (1962) : a lipoprotein of blood plasma that is composed of a moderate proportion of protein with little triglyceride and a high proportion of cholesterol and that is associated with increased probability of developing atherosclerosis — called also *bad cholesterol*; compare HDL

L–do·pa \ˈel-ˈdō-pə\ *n* (1939) : the levorotatory form of dopa that is obtained esp. from broad beans or prepared synthetically, is converted to dopamine in the brain, and is used in treating Parkinson's disease — called also *levodopa*

LDPE *abbr* low-density polyethylene

ldr *abbr* leader

LDS *abbr* Latter-day Saints

LE *abbr* leading edge

[1]**lea** *or* **ley** \ˈlē, ˈlā\ *n* [ME *leye,* fr. OE *lēah;* akin to OHG *lōh* thicket, L *lucus* grove, *lux* light — more at LIGHT] (bef. 12c) **1** : GRASSLAND, PASTURE **2** *usu ley* : arable land used temporarily for hay or grazing

[2]**lea** *abbr* leather

[1]**leach** *var of* LEECH

[2]**leach** \ˈlēch\ *vb* [*leach* vessel through which water is passed to extract lye] *vt* (1796) **1** : to dissolve out by the action of a percolating liquid ⟨~ out alkali from ashes⟩ **2** : to subject to the action of percolating liquid (as water) in order to separate the soluble components **3 a** : to remove (nutritive or harmful elements) from soil by percolation **b** : to draw out or remove as if by percolation ⟨all meaning has been ~*ed* from my life⟩ ~ *vi* : to pass out or through by percolation — **leach·abil·i·ty** \ˌlē-chə-ˈbi-lə-tē\ *n* — **leach·able** \ˈlē-chə-bəl\ *adj* — **leach·er** *n*

leach·ate \ˈlē-ˌchāt\ *n* (1934) : a solution or product obtained by leaching

[1]**lead** \ˈlēd\ *vb* **led** \ˈled\; **lead·ing** [ME *leden,* fr. OE *lǣdan;* akin to OHG *leiten* to lead, OE *līthan* to go] *vt* (bef. 12c) **1 a** : to guide on a way esp. by going in advance **b** : to direct on a course or in a direction **c** : to serve as a channel for ⟨a pipe ~*s* water to the house⟩ **2** : to go through : LIVE ⟨~ a quiet life⟩ **3 a** (1) : to direct the operations, activity, or performance of ⟨~ an orchestra⟩ (2) : to have charge of ⟨~ a campaign⟩ (3) : to suggest to (a witness) the answer desired by asking leading questions **b** (1) : to go at the head of ⟨~ a parade⟩ (2) : to be first in or among ⟨~ the league⟩ (3) : to have a margin over ⟨*led* his opponent⟩ **4** : to bring to some conclusion or condition ⟨*led* to believe otherwise⟩ **5** : to begin play with ⟨~ trumps⟩ **6 a** : to aim in front of (a moving object) ⟨~ a duck⟩ **b** : to pass a ball or puck just in front of (a moving teammate) ~ *vi* **1 a** : to guide someone or something along a way **b** : to lie, run, or open in a specified place or direction ⟨path ~*s* uphill⟩ **c** : to guide a dance partner through the steps of a dance **2 a** : to be first **b** (1) : BEGIN, OPEN (2) : to play the first card of a trick, round, or game **3** : to tend toward or have a result ⟨study ~*ing* to a degree⟩ **4** : to direct the first of a series of blows at an opponent in boxing *syn* see GUIDE — **lead one down the garden path** *also* **lead one up the garden path** : HOODWINK, DECEIVE

[2]**lead** *n* (15c) **1 a** (1) : LEADERSHIP (2) : EXAMPLE, PRECEDENT **b** (1) : position at the front : VANGUARD (2) : INITIATIVE (3) : the act or privilege of leading in cards; *also* : the card or suit led **c** : a margin or measure of advantage or superiority or position in advance **2** : one that leads: as **a** : LODE 2 **b** : a channel of water esp. through a field of ice **c** : INDICATION, CLUE **d** : a principal role in a dramatic production; *also* : one who plays such a role **e** : LEASH 1 **f** (1) : an introductory section of a news story (2) : a news story of chief importance **3** : an insulated electrical conductor connected to an electrical device **4** : the course of a rope from end to end **5** : the amount of axial advance of a point accompanying a complete turn of a thread (as of a screw or worm) **6** : a position taken by a base runner off a base toward the next **7** : the first punch of a series or an exchange of punches in boxing — **lead·less** \-ləs\ *adj*

[3]**lead** *adj* (1828) : acting or serving as a lead or leader ⟨a ~ article⟩

[4]**lead** \ˈled\ *n, often attrib* [ME *leed,* fr. OE *lēad;* akin to MHG *lōt* lead] (bef. 12c) **1** : a bluish-white soft malleable ductile plastic but inelastic heavy metallic element found mostly in combination and used esp. in pipes, cable sheaths, batteries, solder, and shields against radioactivity — see ELEMENT table **2 a** : a plummet for sounding at sea **b** *pl, Brit* : a usu. flat lead roof **c** *pl* : lead framing for panes in windows **d** : a thin strip of metal used to separate lines of type in printing **3 a** : a thin stick of marking substance (as graphite) in or for a pencil **b** : WHITE LEAD **4** : BULLETS, PROJECTILES **5** : TETRAETHYL LEAD — **lead·less** \-ləs\ *adj*

[5]**lead** \ˈled\ *vt* (14c) **1** : to cover, line, or weight with lead **2** : to fix (window glass) in position with leads **3** : to put space between the lines of (typeset matter) **4** : to treat or mix with lead or a lead compound ⟨~*ed* gasoline⟩

lead acetate *n* (1866) : an acetate of lead; *esp* : a poisonous soluble salt $PbC_4H_6O_4 \cdot 3H_2O$

lead arsenate *n* (ca. 1903) **:** an arsenate of lead: as **a :** an acid salt $PbHAsO_4$ used esp. as an insecticide **b :** a neutral salt $Pb_3(AsO_4)_2$ used esp. as an insecticide
lead azide *n* (1918) **:** a crystalline explosive compound $Pb(N_3)_2$ used as a detonating agent
lead carbonate *n* (1869) **:** a carbonate of lead; *esp* **:** a poisonous basic salt $Pb_3(OH)_2(CO_3)_2$ used esp. as a white pigment
lead chromate *n* (1866) **:** a chromate of lead; *esp* **:** CHROME YELLOW
lead dioxide *n* (1863) **:** a poisonous compound PbO_2 used esp. as an oxidizing agent and as an electrode in batteries
lead·en \ˈle-dᵊn\ *adj* (bef. 12c) **1 a :** made of lead **b :** of the color of lead **:** dull gray **2 a :** oppressively heavy **b :** SLUGGISH **c :** lacking spirit or animation — **lead·en·ly** *adv* — **lead·en·ness** \-dᵊn-(n)əs\ *n*
lead·er \ˈlē-dər\ *n* (14c) **1 :** something that leads: as **a :** a primary or terminal shoot of a plant **b :** TENDON, SINEW **c** *pl* **:** dots or hyphens (as in an index) used to lead the eye horizontally **:** ELLIPSIS 2 **d** *chiefly Brit* **:** a newspaper editorial **e** (1) **:** something for guiding fish into a trap (2) **:** a short length of material for attaching the end of a fishing line to a lure or hook **f :** LOSS LEADER **g :** something that ranks first **h :** a blank section at the beginning or end of a reel of film or recorded tape **2 :** a person who leads: as **a :** GUIDE, CONDUCTOR **b** (1) **:** a person who directs a military force or unit (2) **:** a person who has commanding authority or influence **c** (1) **:** the principal officer of a British political party (2) **:** a party member chosen to manage party activities in a legislative body (3) **:** such a party member presiding over the whole legislative body when the party constitutes a majority **d** (1) **:** CONDUCTOR c (2) **:** a first or principal performer of a group **3 :** a horse placed in advance of the other horses of a team — **lead·er·less** \-ləs\ *adj*
lead·er·board \-ˌbȯrd\ *n* (1963) **:** a large board for displaying the ranking of the leaders in a competitive event (as a golf tournament)
leader of the opposition (1771) **:** the principal member of the opposition party in a British legislative body who is given the status of a salaried government official and an important role in organizing the business of the house
lead·er·ship \ˈlē-dər-ˌship\ *n* (1821) **1 :** the office or position of a leader **2 :** capacity to lead **3 :** the act or an instance of leading **4 :** LEADERS ⟨the party ~⟩
lead glass *n* (1849) **:** glass containing a high proportion of lead oxide and having extraordinary clarity and brilliance
lead–in \ˈlēd-ˌin\ *n* (1913) **:** something (as a television show or segment) that leads into something else ⟨a ~ to the commercial⟩ — **lead–in** *adj*
lead·ing \ˈlē-diŋ\ *adj* (1597) **1 :** coming or ranking first **:** FOREMOST **2 :** exercising leadership **3 :** providing direction or guidance ⟨a ~ question⟩ **4 :** given most prominent display ⟨the ~ story⟩
leading edge \ˈlē-diŋ-\ *n* (1877) **1 :** the forward part of something that moves or seems to move **2 :** the foremost edge of an airfoil **3 :** CUTTING EDGE — **leading–edge** *adj*
leading lady *n* (1860) **:** an actress who plays the leading female role
leading light *n* (1655) **:** a prominent and influential member (as of a community or church)
leading man *n* (1827) **:** an actor who plays the leading male role
leading tone *n* (ca. 1889) **:** the seventh tone of a major or minor scale — called also *leading note*
lead line \ˈled-\ *n* (15c) **:** SOUNDING LINE
lead·man \ˈlēd-ˌman, -mən\ *n* (1939) **:** a worker in charge of other workers
lead monoxide *n* (1869) **:** a yellow to brownish-red poisonous compound PbO used in rubber manufacture and glassmaking
lead·off \ˈlēd-ˌȯf\ *n* (ca. 1886) **1 :** a beginning or leading action **2 :** one that leads off — **leadoff** *adj*
lead off \ˈlēd-\ *vi* (1806) **:** BEGIN; *also* **:** to come on or perform first ~ *vt* **1 :** to make a start on **:** OPEN **2 :** to bat first for a baseball team in (an inning)
lead on *vt* (1598) **:** to entice or induce to adopt or continue in a course or belief esp. when unwise or mistaken
lead oxide *n* (1868) **:** any of several oxides of lead; *esp* **:** LEAD MONOXIDE
lead pencil \ˈled-\ *n* (1688) **:** a pencil using graphite as the marking material
lead–pipe \ˈled-ˈpīp\ *adj* (1894) **:** CERTAIN, GUARANTEED ⟨a ~ cinch⟩
lead·plant \ˈled-ˌplant\ *n* (ca. 1833) **:** a leguminous shrub (*Amorpha canescens*) of the western U.S. that has hoary pinnate leaves and bears dull-colored racemose flowers
lead poisoning *n* (ca. 1842) **:** chronic intoxication that is produced by the absorption of lead into the system and is characterized esp. by fatigue, abdominal pain, nausea, diarrhea, loss of appetite, anemia, a dark line along the gums, and muscular paralysis or weakness of limbs
lead·screw \ˈlēd-ˌskrü\ *n* (1875) **:** a threaded rod on which a mechanism travels and can be positioned precisely
leads·man \ˈledz-mən\ *n* (ca. 1841) **:** a man who uses a sounding lead to determine depth of water
lead sulfide *n* (1869) **:** an insoluble black compound PbS that occurs naturally as galena and is used in photoconductive cells
lead time \ˈlēd-\ *n* (1944) **:** the time between the beginning of a process or project and the appearance of its results
lead–up \ˈlēd-ˌəp\ *n* (1942) **:** something that leads up to or prepares the way for something else
lead up \ˈlēd-\ *vi* (1861) **1 :** to prepare the way **2 :** to make a gradual or indirect approach to a topic
lead·work \ˈled-ˌwərk\ *n* (1641) **:** articles made of or work done in lead
leady \ˈle-dē\ *adj* **lead·i·er; -est** (14c) **:** containing or resembling lead
[1]**leaf** \ˈlēf\ *n, pl* **leaves** \ˈlēvz\ *also* **leafs** \ˈlēfs\ *often attrib* [ME *leef,* fr. OE *lēaf;* akin to OHG *loub* leaf] (bef. 12c) **1 a** (1) **:** a lateral outgrowth from a plant stem that is typically a flattened expanded variably shaped greenish organ, constitutes a unit of the foliage, and functions primarily in food manufacture by photosynthesis (2) **:** a modified leaf (as a bract or sepal) primarily engaged in functions other than food manufacture **b** (1) **:** FOLIAGE ⟨trees in full ~⟩ (2) **:** the leaves of a plant as an article of commerce **2 :** something suggestive of a leaf: as **a :** a part of a book or folded sheet containing a page on each side **b** (1) **:** a part (as of window shutters, folding doors, or gates) that slides or is hinged (2) **:** the movable parts of a table top **c** (1) **:** a thin sheet or plate of any substance **:** LAMINA (2) **:** metal (as gold or silver) in sheets usu. thinner than foil (3) **:** one of the plates of a leaf spring — **leaf·less** \ˈlēf-ləs\ *adj* — **leaf·like** \ˈlēf-ˌlīk\ *adj*
[2]**leaf** *vi* (1611) **1 :** to shoot out or produce leaves ⟨will ~ out in spring⟩ **2 :** to turn over pages esp. to browse or skim ⟨~ through a book⟩ ~ *vt* **:** to turn over the pages of
leaf·age \ˈlē-fij\ *n* (1599) **1 :** FOLIAGE 2 **2 :** the representation of leafage (as in architecture)
leaf bud *n* (1664) **:** a bud that develops into a leafy shoot and does not produce flowers
leaf butterfly *n* (1882) **:** any of a genus (*Kallima*) of nymphalid butterflies of southern Asia with wings resembling dried or dead leaves
leaf curl *n* (1899) **:** any of numerous plant diseases caused by ascomycetous fungi (genus *Taphrina* of the family Taphrinaceae) or viruses (esp. genus *Begomovirus* of the family *Geminiviridae*) and characterized by curling of leaves; *esp* **:** PEACH LEAF CURL
leaf–cut·ter \ˈlēf-ˌkə-tər\ *n* (1870) **:** any of various chiefly tropical American ants (genus *Atta*) that cut and carry off the leaves of plants which they use in culturing fungi for food — called also *leaf-cutting ant*
leafed \ˈlēft\ *adj* (1552) **:** LEAVED
leaf fat *n* (ca. 1725) **:** the fat that lines the abdominal cavity and encloses the kidneys; *esp* **:** that of a hog used in the manufacture of lard
leaf·hop·per \ˈlēf-ˌhä-pər\ *n* (1841) **:** any of a family (Cicadellidae) of small leaping homopterous insects that suck the juices of plants

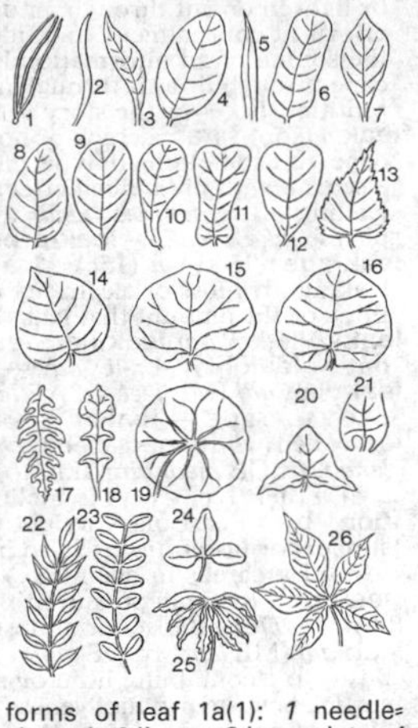

forms of leaf 1a(1): *1* needle-shaped, *2* linear, *3* lanceolate, *4* elliptical, *5* ensiform, *6* oblong, *7* oblanceolate with acuminate tip, *8* ovate with acute tip, *9* obovate, *10* spatulate, *11* fiddle-shaped, *12* cuneate, *13* deltoid, *14* cordate, *15* reniform, *16* orbiculate, *17* runcinate, *18* lyrate, *19* peltate, *20* hastate, *21* sagittate, *22* odd-pinnate, *23* abruptly pinnate, *24* trifoliolate, *25, 26* palmate

leaf lard *n* (ca. 1847) **:** high-quality lard made from leaf fat
[1]**leaf·let** \ˈlēf-lət\ *n* (1785) **1 a :** one of the divisions of a compound leaf **b :** a small or young foliage leaf **2 :** a leaflike organ or part **3 :** a usu. folded printed sheet intended for free distribution
[2]**leaflet** *vb* **-let·ed** *or* **-let·ted; -let·ing** *or* **-let·ting** *vi* (1962) **:** to hand out leaflets ~ *vt* **:** to hand out leaflets to
leaf miner *n* (1830) **:** any of various small insects (as moths or dipteran flies) that in the larval stages burrow in and eat the parenchyma of leaves
leaf mold *n* (1842) **1 :** a compost or layer composed chiefly of decayed leaves **2 :** a mold or mildew that affects foliage
leaf roll *n* (1916) **:** any of various plant diseases characterized esp. by an upward rolling of the leaf margins; *esp* **:** a disease of the potato caused by a single-stranded RNA virus (species *Potato leafroll virus* of the genus *Polerovirus,* family *Luteoviridae*) transmitted by aphids
leaf roller *n* (1830) **:** any of various lepidopterans whose larvae make a nest by rolling up plant leaves
leaf rust *n* (1865) **:** a rust disease of plants and esp. of wheat that affects primarily the leaves
leaf scar *n* (1835) **:** the mark left on a stem after a leaf falls
leaf scorch *n* (1906) **:** any of various plant diseases or conditions characterized by a burned or scorched appearance of the foliage
leaf spot *n* (ca. 1895) **:** any of various plant diseases characterized by discolored often circular spots on the leaves
leaf spring *n* (ca. 1893) **:** a spring made of superposed strips or leaves
leaf·stalk \ˈlēf-ˌstȯk\ *n* (ca. 1776) **:** PETIOLE
leaf trace *n* [[3]*trace*] (1875) **:** a trace associated with a leaf
leafy \ˈlē-fē\ *adj* **leaf·i·er; -est** (15c) **1 a :** furnished with or abounding in leaves ⟨~ woodlands⟩ **b :** having broad-bladed leaves ⟨mosses, grasses, and ~ plants⟩ **c :** consisting chiefly of leaves ⟨~ vegetables⟩ **2 :** resembling a leaf; *specif* **:** LAMINATE
leafy liverwort *n* (1922) **:** any of an order (Jungermanniales) of usu. epiphytic liverworts with a leafy gametophyte that has one ventral and two dorsal rows of leaves on the stem
leafy spurge *n* (ca. 1889) **:** a tall perennial Eurasian herb (*Euphorbia esula*) naturalized as a weed in the northern U.S. and Canada
[1]**league** \ˈlēg\ *n* [ME *leuge, lege,* fr. LL *leuga*] (14c) **1 :** any of various units of distance from about 2.4 to 4.6 statute miles (3.9 to 7.4 kilometers) **2 :** a square league
[2]**league** *n* [ME (Sc) *ligg,* fr. MF *ligue,* fr. OIt *liga,* fr. *ligare* to bind, fr. L — more at LIGATURE] (15c) **1 a :** an association of nations or other political entities for a common purpose **b** (1) **:** an association of persons or groups united by common interests or goals (2) **:** a group of sports teams that regularly play one another **c :** an informal alliance ⟨in ~ with her sister⟩ **2 :** CLASS, CATEGORY
[3]**league** *vb* **leagued; leagu·ing** *vt* (1604) **:** to unite in a league ~ *vi* **:** to form a league
[1]**lea·guer** \ˈlē-gər\ *n* [D *leger;* akin to OHG *legar* bed — more at LAIR] (1537) **1 :** a military camp **2 :** SIEGE
[2]**leaguer** *vt* (ca. 1720) *archaic* **:** BESIEGE, BELEAGUER
[3]**leagu·er** \ˈlē-gər\ *n* [[2]*league*] (1591) **:** a member of a league
[1]**leak** \ˈlēk\ *vb* [ME *leken, liken,* fr. or akin to MD *leken;* akin to OE *hlec* leaky, OHG *zelehhan,* ON *leka* to leak and prob. to OE *leccan* to moisten, MIr *legaid* it melts] *vi* (14c) **1 a :** to enter or escape through an opening usu. by a fault or mistake ⟨fumes ~ in⟩ **b :** to let a substance

or light in or out through an opening **2 a :** to become known despite efforts at concealment ⟨confidential information ~*ed* out⟩ **b :** to be the source of an information leak ~ *vt* **1 :** to permit to enter or escape through or as if through a leak **2 :** to give out (information) surreptitiously ⟨~*ed* the story to the press⟩ — **leak·er** \ˈlē-kər\ *n*

[2]**leak** *n* (15c) **1 a :** a crack or hole that usu. by mistake admits or lets escape **b :** something that permits the admission or escape of something else usu. with prejudicial effect **2 :** the act, process, or an instance of leaking **3** *sometimes vulgar* **:** an act of urinating — used esp. in the phrase *take a leak* — **leak·proof** \ˈlēk-ˌprüf\ *adj*

leak·age \ˈlē-kij\ *n* (15c) **1 a :** the act or process or an instance of leaking **b :** loss of electricity esp. due to faulty insulation **2 :** something or the amount that leaks

leaky \ˈlē-kē\ *adj* **leak·i·er; -est** (15c) **:** permitting fluid to leak in or out — **leak·i·ly** \-kə-lē\ *adv* — **leak·i·ness** \-kē-nəs\ *n*

leal \ˈlēl\ *adj* [ME *leel,* fr. AF *leal* — more at LOYAL] (14c) *chiefly Scot* **:** LOYAL, TRUE — **leal·ly** \ˈlē-ə(l)-lē, ˈlēl-lē\ *adv*

[1]**lean** \ˈlēn\ *vb* **leaned** \ˈlēnd, *chiefly Brit* ˈlent\; **lean·ing** \ˈlē-niŋ\ [ME *lenen,* fr. OE *hleonian;* akin to OHG *hlinēn* to lean, Gk *klinein,* L *clinare*] *vi* (bef. 12c) **1 a :** to incline, deviate, or bend from a vertical position **b :** to cast one's weight to one side for support **2 :** to rely for support or inspiration **3 :** to incline in opinion, taste, or desire ⟨~*ing* toward a career in chemistry⟩ ~ *vt* **:** to cause to lean **:** INCLINE — **lean on :** to apply pressure to

[2]**lean** *n* (1776) **:** the act or an instance of leaning **:** INCLINATION

[3]**lean** *adj* [ME *lene,* fr. OE *hlǣne*] (bef. 12c) **1 a :** lacking or deficient in flesh **b :** containing little or no fat ⟨~ meat⟩ **2 :** lacking richness, sufficiency, or productiveness ⟨~ profits⟩ ⟨the ~ years⟩ **3 :** deficient in an essential or important quality or ingredient: as **a** *of ore* **:** containing little valuable mineral **b :** low in combustible component — used esp. of fuel mixtures **4 :** characterized by economy (as of style, expression, or operation) — **lean·ly** *adv* — **lean·ness** \ˈlēn-nəs\ *n*

syn LEAN, SPARE, LANK, LANKY, GAUNT, RAWBONED, SCRAWNY, SKINNY mean thin because of an absence of excess flesh. LEAN stresses lack of fat and of curving contours ⟨a *lean* racehorse⟩. SPARE suggests leanness from abstemious living or constant exercise ⟨the gymnast's *spare* figure⟩. LANK implies tallness as well as leanness ⟨the *lank* legs of the heron⟩. LANKY suggests awkwardness and loose-jointedness as well as thinness ⟨a *lanky* youth, all arms and legs⟩. GAUNT implies marked thinness or emaciation as from overwork or suffering ⟨a prisoner's *gaunt* face⟩. RAWBONED suggests a large ungainly build without implying undernourishment ⟨a *rawboned* farmer⟩. SCRAWNY and SKINNY imply an extreme leanness that suggests deficient strength and vitality ⟨a *scrawny* chicken⟩ ⟨*skinny* street urchins⟩.

[4]**lean** *vt* (bef. 12c) **:** to make lean

[5]**lean** *n* (15c) **:** the part of meat that consists principally of lean muscle

Le·an·der \lē-ˈan-dər\ *n* [L, fr. Gk *Leandros*] (1513) **:** a youth in Greek mythology who swims the Hellespont nightly to visit Hero and who ultimately drowns in one of the crossings

leaning *n* (15c) **:** a definite but not decisive attraction or tendency — often used in pl. ⟨radical ~*s*⟩

syn LEANING, PROPENSITY, PROCLIVITY, PENCHANT mean a strong instinct or liking for something. LEANING suggests a liking or attraction not strong enough to be decisive or uncontrollable ⟨a student with artistic *leanings*⟩. PROPENSITY implies a deeply ingrained and usu. irresistible inclination ⟨a *propensity* to offer advice⟩. PROCLIVITY suggests a strong natural proneness usu. to something objectionable or evil ⟨a *proclivity* for violence⟩. PENCHANT implies a strongly marked taste in the person or an irresistible attraction in the object ⟨a *penchant* for taking risks⟩.

leant \ˈlent\ *chiefly Brit past of* LEAN

[1]**lean–to** \ˈlēn-ˌtü\ *n, pl* **lean–tos** \-ˌtüz\ (15c) **1 :** a wing or extension of a building having a lean-to roof **2 :** a rough shed or shelter with a lean-to roof

[2]**lean–to** *adj* (1649) **:** having only one slope or pitch ⟨a ~ roof⟩ — see ROOF illustration

[1]**leap** \ˈlēp\ *vb* **leaped** *or* **leapt** \ˈlēpt *also* ˈlept\; **leap·ing** \ˈlē-piŋ\ [ME *lepen,* fr. OE *hlēapan;* akin to OHG *hlouffan* to run] *vi* (bef. 12c) **1 :** to spring free from or as if from the ground **:** JUMP ⟨~ over a fence⟩ ⟨a fish ~*s* out of the water⟩ **2 a :** to pass abruptly from one state or topic to another **b :** to act precipitately ⟨~*ed* at the chance⟩ ~ *vt* **:** to pass over by leaping ⟨~*ed* the wall⟩ — **leap·er** \ˈlē-pər\ *n*

[2]**leap** *n* (bef. 12c) **1 a :** an act of leaping **:** SPRING, BOUND **b** (1) **:** a place leaped over or from (2) **:** the distance covered by a leap **2 a :** a sudden passage or transition ⟨a great ~ forward⟩ **b :** a choice made in an area of ultimate concern ⟨a ~ of faith⟩ — **by leaps and bounds :** with extraordinary rapidity ⟨a town growing *by leaps and bounds*⟩

[1]**leap·frog** \ˈlēp-ˌfrȯg, -ˌfräg\ *n* (1599) **:** a game in which one player bends down and is vaulted over by another player

[2]**leapfrog** *vb* **leap·frogged; leap·frog·ging** *vi* (1872) **:** to leap or progress in or as if in leapfrog ~ *vt* **1 :** to go ahead of (each other) in turn; *specif* **:** to advance (two military units) by keeping one unit in action while moving the other unit past it to a position farther in front **2 :** to evade by or as if by a bypass

leap second *n* (1971) **:** an intercalary second added to Coordinated Universal Time to compensate for the slowing of the earth's rotation and keep Coordinated Universal Time in synchrony with solar time

leap year *n* (14c) **1 :** a year in the Gregorian calendar containing 366 days with February 29 as the extra day **2 :** an intercalary year in any calendar

Lear \ˈlir\ *n* (13c) **:** a legendary king of Britain and hero of Shakespeare's tragedy *King Lear*

learn \ˈlərn\ *vb* **learned** \ˈlərnd, ˈlərnt\; **learn·ing** [ME *lernen,* fr. OE *leornian;* akin to OHG *lernēn* to learn, OE *last* footprint, L *lira* furrow, track] *vt* (bef. 12c) **1 a** (1) **:** to gain knowledge or understanding of or skill in by study, instruction, or experience ⟨~ a trade⟩ (2) **:** MEMORIZE ⟨~ the lines of a play⟩ **b :** to come to be able ⟨~ to dance⟩ **c :** to come to realize ⟨~*ed* that honesty paid⟩ **2 a** *nonstand* **:** TEACH **b** *obs* **:** to inform of something **3 :** to come to know **:** HEAR ⟨we just ~*ed* that he was ill⟩ ~ *vi* **:** to acquire knowledge or skill or a behavioral tendency ***syn*** see DISCOVER — **learn·able** \ˈlər-nə-bəl\ *adj* — **learn·er** *n*

usage *Learn* in the sense of "teach" dates from the 13th century and was standard until at least the early 19th ⟨made them drunk with true Hollands—and then *learned* them the art of making bargains —Washington Irving⟩. But by Mark Twain's time it was receding to a speech form associated chiefly with the less educated ⟨never done nothing for three months but set in his back yard and *learn* that frog to jump —Mark Twain⟩. The present-day status of *learn* has not risen. This use persists in speech, but in writing it appears mainly in the representation of such speech or its deliberate imitation for effect.

learned *adj* (14c) **1** \ˈlər-nəd\ **:** characterized by or associated with learning **:** ERUDITE ⟨a ~ scholar⟩ **2** \ˈlərnd, ˈlərnt\ **:** acquired by learning ⟨~ behavior⟩ — **learn·ed·ly** \ˈlər-nəd-lē\ *adv* — **learn·ed·ness** \-nəd-nəs\ *n*

learning *n* (bef. 12c) **1 :** the act or experience of one that learns **2 :** knowledge or skill acquired by instruction or study **3 :** modification of a behavioral tendency by experience (as exposure to conditioning) ***syn*** see KNOWLEDGE

learning curve *n* (1922) **1 :** a curve plotting performance against practice; *esp* **:** one graphing decline in unit costs with cumulative output **2 :** the course of progress made in learning something

learning disability *n* (1936) **:** any of various conditions (as dyslexia) that interfere with an individual's ability to learn and so result in impaired functioning in language, reasoning, or academic skills and that are thought to be caused by difficulties in processing and integrating information — called also *learning difference* — **learning disabled** *adj*

learnt \ˈlərnt\ *chiefly Brit past and past part of* LEARN

leary *var of* LEERY

[1]**lease** \ˈlēs\ *n* [ME *les,* fr. AF, fr. *lesser*] (14c) **1 :** a contract by which one conveys real estate, equipment, or facilities for a specified term and for a specified rent; *also* **:** the act of such conveyance or the term for which it is made **2 :** a piece of land or property that is leased **3 :** a continuance or opportunity for continuance ⟨a new ~ on life⟩

[2]**lease** *vt* **leased; leas·ing** [AF *lesser, laisser, lescher* to leave, hand over, lease, fr. L *laxare* to loosen, fr. *laxus* slack — more at SLACK] (ca. 1570) **1 :** to grant by lease **2 :** to hold under a lease ***syn*** see HIRE — **leas·able** \ˈlē-sə-bəl\ *adj*

lease·back \ˈlēs-ˌbak\ *n* (1947) **:** the sale of property with the understanding that the seller can lease it from the new owner

lease·hold \ˈlēs-ˌhōld\ *n* (1710) **1 :** a tenure by lease **2 :** property held by lease — **lease·hold·er** *n*

leash \ˈlēsh\ *n* [ME *lees, leshe,* fr. AF **lesche, lesse,* prob. fr. *lesser* to leave, let go] (14c) **1 a :** a line for leading or restraining an animal **b :** something that restrains **:** the state of being restrained ⟨keeping spending on a tight ~⟩ **2 a :** a set of three animals (as greyhounds, foxes, bucks, or hares) **b :** a set of three — **leash** *vt*

leash law *n* (1966) **:** an ordinance requiring dogs to be restrained when not confined to their owner's property

leas·ing \ˈlē-siŋ, -ziŋ\ *n* [ME *lesing,* fr. OE *lēasung,* fr. *lēasian* to lie, fr. *lēas* false] (bef. 12c) *archaic* **:** the act of lying; *also* **:** LIE, FALSEHOOD

[1]**least** \ˈlēst\ *adj, superlative of* [1]LITTLE [ME *leest,* fr. OE *lǣst,* superl. of *lǣssa* less] (bef. 12c) **1 :** lowest in importance or position **2 a :** smallest in size or degree **b :** being a member of a kind distinguished by diminutive size ⟨the ~ bittern⟩ **c :** smallest possible **:** SLIGHTEST

[2]**least** *n* (12c) **:** one that is least — **at least 1 :** at the minimum ⟨*at least* once a week⟩ **2 :** in any case ⟨*at least* you have a choice⟩

[3]**least** *adv, superlative of* [2]LITTLE (13c) **:** in the smallest or lowest degree — **least of all :** especially not ⟨no one, *least of all* the children, paid attention⟩

least common denominator *n* (1851) **:** the least common multiple of two or more denominators

least common multiple *n* (1823) **1 :** the smallest common multiple of two or more numbers **2 :** the common multiple of lowest degree of two or more polynomials

least squares *n pl* (1825) **:** a method of fitting a curve to a set of points representing statistical data in such a way that the sum of the squares of the distances of the points from the curve is a minimum

least tern *n* (ca. 1860) **:** a very small black-capped tern (*Sterna antillarum*) with a white body and forehead that is found chiefly in coastal areas of eastern No. America and California

least·ways \ˈlēst-ˌwāz\ *adv* (14c) *dial* **:** at least

least·wise \-ˌwīz\ *adv* (15c) **:** at least ⟨~, that's what I heard⟩

[1]**leath·er** \ˈle-t͟hər\ *n* [ME *lether,* fr. OE *lether-;* akin to OHG *leder* leather, OIr *lethar*] (13c) **1 :** animal skin dressed for use **2 :** the flap of the ear of a dog — see DOG illustration **3 :** something wholly or partly made of leather — **leather** *adj* — **leath·er·like** \-ˌlīk\ *adj*

[2]**leather** *vt* **leath·ered; leath·er·ing** \ˈle-t͟hə-riŋ, ˈlet͟h-riŋ\ (13c) **1 :** to cover with leather **2 :** to beat with a strap **:** THRASH

leath·er·back \ˈle-t͟hər-ˌbak\ *n* (ca. 1855) **:** the largest existing sea turtle (*Dermochelys coriacea*) distinguished by its flexible carapace composed of a mosaic of small bones embedded in a thick leathery skin

leath·er·ette \ˌle-t͟hə-ˈret\ *n, often attrib* [fr. *Leatherette,* a trademark] (ca. 1879) **:** imitation leather

leath·er·leaf \ˈle-t͟hər-ˌlēf\ *n* (ca. 1818) **:** a temperate-zone bog shrub (*Chamaedaphne calyculata*) of the heath family with leathery evergreen leaves and small white cylindrical flowers

leath·er–lunged \ˈle-t͟hər-ˌləŋd\ *adj* (1846) **:** having an inordinately loud voice ⟨~ singers⟩

leath·ern \ˈle-t͟hərn\ *adj* (bef. 12c) **:** made of, consisting of, or resembling leather

leath·er·neck \-t͟hər-ˌnek\ *n* [fr. the leather collar formerly part of the uniform] (1891) **:** a member of the U.S. Marine Corps

leath·er·wood \ˈle-t͟hər-ˌwu̇d\ *n* (1737) **1 :** a small eastern No. American tree (*Dirca palustris*) of the mezereon family with pliant stems and yellow flowers **2 :** a small tree or shrub (*Cyrilla racemiflora* of the family Cyrillaceae) of the southeastern U.S.

leath·er·work \ˈle-t͟hər-ˌwərk\ *n* (1855) **:** articles made of leather

leath·ery \ˈle-t͟hə-rē, ˈlet͟h-rē\ *adj* (ca. 1552) **:** resembling, characteristic of, or suggestive of leather ⟨a ~ face⟩ ⟨a ~ aroma⟩

[1]**leave** \ˈlēv\ *vb* **left** \ˈleft\; **leav·ing** [ME *leven,* fr. OE *lǣfan;* akin to OHG *verleiben* to leave, OE *belīfan* to be left over, and perh. to Lith *lipti* to adhere, Gk *lipos* grease, fat] *vt* (bef. 12c) **1 a** (1) **:** BEQUEATH,

DEVISE ⟨*left* a fortune to his son⟩ (2) **:** to have remaining after one's death ⟨~*s* a widow and two children⟩ **b :** to cause to remain as a trace or aftereffect ⟨oil ~*s* a stain⟩ ⟨the wound *left* an ugly scar⟩ **2 a :** to cause or allow to be or remain in a specified condition ⟨~ the door open⟩ ⟨his manner *left* me cold⟩ **b :** to fail to include or take along ⟨*left* the notes at home⟩ ⟨the movie ~*s* a lot out⟩ **c :** to have as a remainder ⟨4 from 7 ~*s* 3⟩ **d :** to permit to be or remain subject to another's action or control ⟨just ~ everything to me⟩ **e :** LET **f :** to cause or allow to be or remain available ⟨~ room for expansion⟩ ⟨*left* myself an out⟩ **3 a :** to go away from **:** DEPART ⟨~ the room⟩ **b :** DESERT, ABANDON ⟨*left* his wife⟩ **c :** to terminate association with **:** withdraw from ⟨*left* school before graduation⟩ **4 :** to put, deposit, or deliver before or in the process of departing ⟨I *left* a package for you⟩ ⟨~ a message⟩ ~ *vi* **:** SET OUT, DEPART — **leav·er** *n* — **leave alone :** to refrain from bothering, disturbing, or using

usage *Leave* (sense 2e) with the infinitive but without *to* ⟨*leave* it be⟩ is a mostly spoken idiom used in writing esp. for humorous effect. It is not often criticized in British English, but American commentators, adhering to an opinion first expressed in 1881, still dislike it.

[2]**leave** *n* [ME *leve*, fr. OE *lēaf;* akin to MHG *loube* permission, OE *alȳfan* to allow — more at BELIEVE] (bef. 12c) **1 a :** permission to do something **b :** authorized esp. extended absence from duty or employment **2 :** an act of leaving **:** DEPARTURE

[3]**leave** *vi* **leaved; leav·ing** [ME *leven*, fr. *leef* leaf] (14c) **:** LEAF

leaved *adj* (13c) **:** having leaves — usu. used in combination ⟨palmate-*leaved*⟩ ⟨a four-*leaved* clover⟩

[1]**leav·en** \ˈle-vən\ *n* [ME *levain*, fr. AF *levein*, fr. VL **levamen*, fr. L *levare* to raise — more at LEVER] (14c) **1 a :** a substance (as yeast) used to produce fermentation in dough or a liquid; *esp* **:** SOURDOUGH **b :** a material (as baking powder) used to produce a gas that lightens dough or batter **2 :** something that modifies or lightens

[2]**leaven** *vt* **leav·ened; leav·en·ing** \ˈlev-niŋ, ˈle-və-\ (15c) **1 :** to raise (as bread) with a leaven **2 :** to mingle or permeate with some modifying, alleviating, or vivifying element; *esp* **:** LIGHTEN ⟨a sermon ~*ed* with humor⟩ ***syn*** see INFUSE

leavening *n* (ca. 1626) **:** a leavening agent **:** LEAVEN

leave of absence (1756) **1 :** permission to be absent from duty or employment **2 :** LEAVE 1b

leave off *vb* (14c) **:** STOP, CEASE ⟨picked up where he had *left off*⟩

leaves *pl of* LEAF

leave–tak·ing \ˈlēv-ˌtā-kiŋ\ *n* (14c) **:** DEPARTURE, FAREWELL

leav·ings \ˈlē-viŋz\ *n pl* (14c) **:** REMNANTS, RESIDUE

Leb *abbr* Lebanese; Lebanon

le·bens·raum \ˈlā-bənz-ˌrau̇m, -bən(t)s-\ *n, often cap* [G, fr. *Leben* living, life + *Raum* space] (1905) **1 :** territory believed esp. by Nazis to be necessary for national existence or economic self-sufficiency **2 :** space required for life, growth, or activity

[1]**lech** \ˈlech\ *n* (ca. 1830) **1 :** LETCH, LUST **2 :** LECHER

[2]**lech** *vi* (1911) **:** LUST

lech·er \ˈle-chər\ *n* [ME *lechour*, fr. AF *lechur*, fr. *lecher* to lick, live in debauchery, of Gmc origin; akin to OHG *leckōn* to lick — more at LICK] (13c) **:** a man who engages in lechery

lech·er·ous \ˈle-chə-rəs, ˈlech-rəs\ *adj* (14c) **:** given to or suggestive of lechery — **lech·er·ous·ly** *adv* — **lech·er·ous·ness** *n*

lech·ery \-rē\ *n* (13c) **:** inordinate indulgence in sexual activity **:** LASCIVIOUSNESS

le·chwe \ˈlēch-wē\ *n, pl* **lechwe** *or* **lechwes** [prob. fr. Sesotho *lets'a*] (1857) **:** an antelope (*Kobus leche*) that inhabits wetlands of southern Africa; *also* **:** a related antelope (*K. megaceros*) of the Nile Valley in Sudan and Ethiopia

lec·i·thin \ˈle-sə-thən\ *n* [ISV, fr. Gk *lekithos* yolk of an egg] (1861) **:** any of several waxy hygroscopic phospholipids that are widely distributed in animals and plants, form colloidal solutions in water, and have emulsifying, wetting, and antioxidant properties; *also* **:** a mixture of or substance rich in lecithins

lec·i·thin·ase \-thə-ˌnās, -ˌnāz\ *n* (1910) **:** PHOSPHOLIPASE

lec·tern \ˈlek-tərn\ *n* [ME *lettorne*, fr. AF *leitrun*, fr. ML *lectrinum*, fr. LL *lectrum*, fr. L *legere* to read — more at LEGEND] (14c) **:** a stand used to support a book or script in a convenient position for a standing reader or speaker; *esp* **:** one from which scripture lessons are read in a church service

lec·tin \ˈlek-tən\ *n* [L *lectus* (pp. of *legere* to pick, select) + [1]*-in* — more at LEGEND] (1954) **:** any of a group of proteins esp. of plants that are not antibodies and do not originate in an immune system but bind specif. to carbohydrate-containing receptors on cell surfaces (as of red blood cells)

lec·tion \ˈlek-shən\ *n* [LL *lection-, lectio*, fr. L, act of reading — more at LESSON] (1608) **1 :** a liturgical reading for a particular day **2** [NL *lection-, lectio*, fr. L] **:** a variant reading of a text

lec·tion·ary \ˈlek-shə-ˌner-ē\ *n, pl* **-ar·ies** (1780) **:** a book or list of lections for the church year

lec·tor \ˈlek-tər, -ˌtȯr\ *n* [ME, fr. LL, reader of the lessons in a church service, fr. L, reader, fr. *legere*] (14c) **:** a person who assists at a worship service chiefly by reading the lection

lec·to·type \ˈlek-tə-ˌtīp\ *n* [Gk *lektos* chosen (fr. *legein* to gather, choose) + E *type* — more at LEGEND] (ca. 1905) **:** a specimen chosen as the type of a species or subspecies if the author of the name fails to designate a type

[1]**lec·ture** \ˈlek-chər, -shər\ *n* [ME, act of reading, fr. LL *lectura*, fr. L *lectus*, pp. of *legere*] (15c) **1 :** a discourse given before an audience or class esp. for instruction **2 :** a formal reproof — **lec·ture·ship** \-ˌship\ *n*

[2]**lecture** *vb* **lec·tured; lec·tur·ing** \ˈlek-chə-riŋ, ˈlek-shriŋ\ *vi* (ca. 1590) **:** to deliver a lecture or a course of lectures ~ *vt* **1 :** to deliver a lecture to **2 :** to reprove formally — **lec·tur·er** \-chər-ər, -shrər\ *n*

led *past and past part of* LEAD

LED \ˌel-(ˌ)ē-ˈdē\ *n* [*l*ight-*e*mitting *d*iode] (1968) **:** a semiconductor diode that emits light when a voltage is applied to it and that is used esp. in electronic devices (as for an indicator light)

Le·da \ˈlē-də\ *n* [L, fr. Gk *Lēda*] (ca. 1527) **:** the mother of Clytemnestra and Castor by her husband Tyndareus and of Helen and Pollux by Zeus who comes to her in the form of a swan

lede \ˈlēd\ *n* [alter. of [2]*lead*] (1976) **:** the introductory section of a news story that is intended to entice the reader to read the full story

le·der·ho·sen \ˈlā-dər-ˌhō-zᵊn\ *n pl* [G, fr. MHG *lederhose*, fr. *leder* leather + *hose* trousers] (1936) **:** leather shorts often with suspenders worn esp. in Bavaria

ledge \ˈlej\ *n* [ME *legge* bar of a gate] (1535) **1 :** a raised or projecting edge or molding intended to protect or check ⟨a window ~⟩ **2 :** an underwater ridge or reef esp. near the shore **3 a :** a narrow flat surface or shelf; *esp* **:** one that projects from a wall of rock **b :** rock that is solid or continuous enough to form ledges **:** BEDROCK ⟨the field was full of ~⟩ **4 :** LODE, VEIN — **ledgy** \ˈle-jē\ *adj*

led·ger \ˈle-jər\ *n* [ME *lygger, leger* large breviary, beam, prob. fr. *leyen, leggen* to lay] (1588) **1 :** a book containing accounts to which debits and credits are posted from books of original entry **2 :** a horizontal board used for vertical support (as in scaffolding)

ledger line *also* **leg·er line** \ˈle-jər-\ *n* (1700) **:** a short line added above or below a musical staff to extend its range

[1]**lee** \ˈlē\ *n* [ME, fr. OE *hlēo;* perh. akin to OHG *lāo* lukewarm, L *calēre* to be warm] (bef. 12c) **1 :** protecting shelter **2 :** the side (as of a ship) or area that is sheltered from the wind

[2]**lee** *adj* (15c) **1 :** of, relating to, or being the side sheltered from the wind — compare WEATHER **2 :** facing in the direction of motion of an overriding glacier — used esp. of a hillside

lee·board \ˈlē-ˌbȯrd\ *n* (1691) **:** either of the wood or metal planes attached outside the hull of a sailboat to prevent leeway

[1]**leech** \ˈlēch\ *n* [ME *leche*, fr. OE *lǣce;* akin to OHG *lāhhi* physician] (bef. 12c) **1** *archaic* **:** PHYSICIAN, SURGEON **2** [fr. its former use by physicians for bleeding patients] **:** any of numerous carnivorous or bloodsucking usu. freshwater annelid worms (class Hirudinea) that have typically a flattened lanceolate segmented body with a sucker at each end **3 :** a hanger-on who seeks advantage or gain ***syn*** see PARASITE — **leech·like** \-ˌlīk\ *adj*

[2]**leech** *vt* (1641) **1 :** to bleed by the use of leeches **2 :** to drain the substance of **:** EXHAUST ~ *vi* **:** to attach oneself to a person as a leech

[3]**leech** *also* **leach** \ˈlēch\ *n* [ME *leche*; akin to MLG *līk* boltrope] (15c) **1 :** either vertical edge of a square sail **2 :** the after edge of a fore-and-aft sail

leek \ˈlēk\ *n* [ME, fr. OE *lēac;* akin to OHG *louh* leek] (bef. 12c) **:** a biennial garden herb (*Allium ampeloprasum porrum*) of the lily family grown for its mildly pungent succulent linear leaves and esp. for its thick cylindrical stalk

[1]**leer** \ˈlir\ *vi* [prob. fr. obs. *leer* cheek] (1530) **:** to cast a sidelong glance; *esp* **:** to give a leer — **leer·ing·ly** \-iŋ-lē\ *adv*

[2]**leer** *n* (1598) **:** a lascivious, knowing, or wanton look

leery *also* **leary** \ˈlir-ē\ *adj* (1896) **:** SUSPICIOUS, WARY — often used with *of* ⟨~ of strangers⟩

lees \ˈlēz\ *n pl* [ME *lie*, fr. AF, fr. ML *lia*] (14c) **:** the sediment of a liquor (as wine) during fermentation and aging **:** DREGS

Lee's Birthday \ˈlēz-\ *n* [Robert E. *Lee*] (1910) **:** January 19 or the third Monday in January observed as a legal holiday in many southern states

lee shore *n* (ca. 1580) **:** a shore lying off a ship's leeward side and constituting a severe danger in storm

[1]**lee·ward** \ˈlē-wərd, *esp naut* ˈlü-ərd\ *n* (1549) **:** the lee side

[2]**leeward** *adj* (1630) **:** being in or facing the direction toward which the wind is blowing; *also* **:** being the side opposite the windward

lee·way \ˈlē-ˌwā\ *n* (1669) **1 a :** off-course lateral movement of a ship when under way **b :** the angle between the heading and the track of an airplane **2 :** an allowable margin of freedom or variation **:** TOLERANCE

[1]**left** \ˈleft\ *adj* [ME, fr. OE, weak; akin to MLG *lucht* left; fr. the left hand's being the weaker in most individuals] (13c) **1 a :** of, relating to, situated on, or being the side of the body in which the heart is mostly located **b :** done with the left hand ⟨a ~ hook to the jaw⟩ **c :** located nearer to the left hand than to the right **d** (1) **:** located on the left of an observer facing in the same direction as the object specified ⟨stage ~⟩ (2) **:** located on the left when facing downstream ⟨the ~ bank of a river⟩ **2** *often cap* **:** of, adhering to, or constituted by the left esp. in politics — **left** *adv*

[2]**left** *n* (13c) **1 a :** the left hand **b :** the location or direction of the left side **c :** the part on the left side **d :** a turn to the left ⟨take a ~ at the intersection⟩ **2 a :** LEFT FIELD **b :** a blow struck with the left fist **3** *often cap* **a :** the part of a legislative chamber located to the left of the presiding officer **b :** the members of a continental European legislative body occupying the left as a result of holding more radical political views than other members **4** *often cap* **a :** those professing views usu. characterized by desire to reform or overthrow the established order esp. in politics and usu. advocating change in the name of the greater freedom or well-being of the common man **b :** a radical as distinguished from a conservative position — **left·most** \ˈleft-ˌmōst\ *adj*

[3]**left** *past and past part of* LEAVE

left–bank *adj, often cap L&B* (1929) **:** of, relating to, situated in, or characteristic of the bohemian district of Paris on the left bank of the Seine River

left brain *n* (1976) **:** the left cerebral hemisphere of the human brain esp. when viewed in terms of its predominant thought processes (as analytic and logical thinking) — **left–brained** \ˈleft-ˈbrānd\ *adj*

left field *n* (1857) **1 :** the position of the player defending left field **2 :** the part of the baseball outfield to the left looking out from the plate **3 a :** a state or position far from the mainstream (as of prevailing opinion) ⟨they were really out in *left field* with that idea⟩ **b :** a source of the unexpected or illogical ⟨that question came out of *left field*⟩ — **left fielder** *n*

left–hand \ˈleft-ˈhand, ˈlef-ˈtand\ *adj* (1567) **1 :** situated on the left **2 :** LEFT-HANDED

left–hand·ed \-ˈhan-dəd, -ˈtan-\ *adj* (14c) **1 :** using the left hand habitually or more easily than the right; *also* **:** swinging from left to right ⟨a ~ batter⟩ **2 :** relating to, designed for, or done with the left hand **3 :** MORGANATIC **4 a :** CLUMSY, AWKWARD **b :** INSINCERE, BACK-

\ə\ **abut** \ᵊ\ **kitten**, F table \ər\ **further** \a\ **ash** \ā\ **ace** \ä\ **mop, mar** \au̇\ **out** \ch\ **chin** \e\ **bet** \ē\ **easy** \g\ **go** \i\ **hit** \ī\ **ice** \j\ **job** \ŋ\ **sing** \ō\ **go** \ȯ\ **law** \ȯi\ **boy** \th\ **thin** \t͟h\ **the** \ü\ **loot** \u̇\ **foot** \y\ **yet** \zh\ **vision, beige** \k, ⁿ, œ, ue, ʸ\ *see* Guide to Pronunciation

HANDED, DUBIOUS ⟨a ~ compliment⟩ **5 a :** having a direction contrary to that of the hands of a watch viewed from in front : COUNTERCLOCKWISE **b :** having a spiral structure or form that ascends or advances to the left ⟨a ~ rope⟩ **6 :** having or being the L-form molecular structure — **left–handed** *adv* — **left–hand·ed·ly** *adv* — **left–hand·ed·ness** *n*
left–hand·er \-ˈhan-dər, -ˈtan-\ *n* (1881) **:** a left-handed person
left·ish \ˈlef-tish\ *adj* (1934) **:** showing leftist tendencies or a moderately leftist character
left·ism \ˈlef-ˌti-zəm\ *n* (1920) **1 :** the principles and views of the left; *also* **:** the movement embodying these principles **2 :** advocacy of or adherence to the doctrines of the left — **left·ist** \-tist\ *n or adj*
[1]**left·over** \ˈleft-ˌō-vər\ *n* (1891) **1 :** something that remains unused or unconsumed; *esp* **:** leftover food served at a later meal — usu. used in pl. **2 :** an anachronistic survival **:** VESTIGE
[2]**left·over** *adj* (1897) **:** not consumed or used ⟨~ food⟩ ⟨~ space⟩
left shoulder arms *n* [fr. the command *left shoulder arms!*] (ca. 1918) **:** a position in the manual of arms in which the butt of the rifle is held in the left hand with the barrel resting on the left shoulder; *also* **:** a command to assume this position
left·ward \ˈleft-wərd\ *adj or adv* (15c) **:** being at, toward, or to the left
left wing *n* (1884) **1 :** the leftist division of a group (as a political party) **2 :** LEFT 4a — **left–wing** *adj* — **left–wing·er** \ˈleft-ˈwiŋ-ər\ *n*
lefty \ˈlef-tē\ *n, pl* **left·ies** (1886) **1 :** LEFT-HANDER **2 :** an advocate of leftism — **lefty** *adj*
[1]**leg** \ˈleg *also* ˈlāg\ *n* [ME, fr. ON *leggr*] (14c) **1 :** a limb of an animal used esp. for supporting the body and for walking: as **a (1) :** one of the paired vertebrate limbs that in bipeds extend from the top of the thigh to the foot **(2) :** the part of such a limb between the knee and foot **b :** the back half of a hindquarter of a meat animal **c :** one of the rather generalized segmental appendages of an arthropod used in walking and crawling **2 a :** a pole or bar serving as a support or prop ⟨the ~*s* of a tripod⟩ **b :** a branch of a forked or jointed object ⟨the ~*s* of a compass⟩ **3 a :** the part of an article of clothing that covers the leg **b :** the part of the upper (as of a boot) that extends above the ankle **4 :** OBEISANCE, BOW — used chiefly in the phrase *to make a leg* **5 :** a side of a right triangle that is not the hypotenuse; *also* **:** a side of an isosceles triangle that is not the base **6 a :** the course and distance sailed by a boat on a single tack **b :** a portion of a trip **:** STAGE **c :** one section of a relay race **d :** one of several events or games necessary to be won to decide a competition ⟨won the first two ~*s* of horse racing's Triple Crown⟩ **7 :** a branch or part of an object or system **8** *pl* **:** long-term appeal or interest ⟨a news story with ~*s*⟩ — **leg·less** \-ləs\ *adj* — **a leg to stand on :** SUPPORT; *esp* **:** a basis for one's position in a controversy — **on one's last legs :** at or near the end of one's resources **:** on the verge of failure, exhaustion, or ruin
[2]**leg** *vi* **legged; leg·ging** (1601) **:** to use the legs in walking; *esp* **:** RUN
[3]**leg** *abbr* **1** legal **2** legato **3** legislative; legislature
[1]**leg·a·cy** \ˈle-gə-sē\ *n, pl* **-cies** [ME *legacie* office of a legate, bequest, fr. AF or ML; AF, office of a legate, fr. ML *legatia,* fr. L *legatus*] (15c) **1 :** a gift by will esp. of money or other personal property **:** BEQUEST **2 :** something transmitted by or received from an ancestor or predecessor or from the past ⟨the ~ of the ancient philosophers⟩
[2]**legacy** *adj* (1990) **:** of, relating to, or being a previous or outdated computer system ⟨transfer the ~ data⟩ ⟨a ~ system⟩
[1]**le·gal** \ˈlē-gəl\ *adj* [AF, fr. L *legalis,* fr. *leg-, lex* law] (ca. 1500) **1 :** of or relating to law **2 a :** deriving authority from or founded on law **:** DE JURE **b :** having a formal status derived from law often without a basis in actual fact **:** TITULAR ⟨a corporation is a ~ but not a real person⟩ **c :** established by law; *esp* **:** STATUTORY **3 :** conforming to or permitted by law or established rules **4 :** recognized or made effective by a court of law as distinguished from a court of equity **5 :** of, relating to, or having the characteristics of the profession of law or of one of its members **6 :** created by the constructions of the law ⟨a ~ fiction⟩ ***syn*** see LAWFUL — **le·gal·ly** \-gə-lē\ *adv*
[2]**legal** *n* (1526) **:** one that conforms to rules or the law
legal age *n* (1762) **:** the age at which a person enters into full adult legal rights and responsibilities (as of making contracts or wills)
legal aid *n* (1890) **:** aid provided by an organization established esp. to serve the legal needs of the poor
legal eagle *n* (1942) **:** LAWYER
le·gal·ese \ˌlē-gə-ˈlēz, -ˈlēs\ *n* (1914) **:** the specialized language of the legal profession ⟨replaced ~ with plain talk —Steve Weinberg⟩
legal holiday *n* (1867) **:** a holiday established by legal authority and marked by restrictions on work and transaction of official business
le·gal·ise *Brit var of* LEGALIZE
le·gal·ism \ˈlē-gə-ˌli-zəm\ *n* (1928) **1 :** strict, literal, or excessive conformity to the law or to a religious or moral code ⟨the institutionalized ~ that restricts free choice⟩ **2 :** a legal term or rule
le·gal·ist \-list\ *n* (1646) **1 :** an advocate or adherent of moral legalism **2 :** one that views things from a legal standpoint; *esp* **:** one that places primary emphasis on legal principles or on the formal structure of governmental institutions — **le·gal·is·tic** \ˌlē-gə-ˈlis-tik\ *adj* — **le·gal·is·ti·cal·ly** \-ti-k(ə-)lē\ *adv*
le·gal·i·ty \li-ˈga-lə-tē\ *n, pl* **-ties** (15c) **1 :** attachment to or observance of law **2 :** the quality or state of being legal **:** LAWFULNESS **3** *pl* **:** obligations imposed by law
le·gal·ize \ˈlē-gə-ˌlīz\ *vt* **-ized; -iz·ing** (ca. 1716) **:** to make legal; *esp* **:** to give legal validity or sanction to — **le·gal·i·za·tion** \ˌlē-gə-lə-ˈzā-shən\ *n* — **le·gal·iz·er** \ˈlē-gə-ˌlī-zər\ *n*
legal pad *n* (1967) **:** a writing tablet of ruled yellow paper that is usu. 8.5 by 14 inches (about 22 by 36 centimeters)
legal reserve *n* (ca. 1902) **:** the minimum amount of bank deposits or life insurance company assets required by law to be kept as reserves
legal tender *n* (1739) **:** money that is legally valid for the payment of debts and that must be accepted for that purpose when offered
[1]**leg·ate** \ˈle-gət\ *n* [ME, fr. AF & L; AF *legat,* fr. L *legatus* deputy, emissary, fr. pp. of *legare* to depute, send as emissary, bequeath, fr. *leg-, lex*] (12c) **:** a usu. official emissary — **leg·ate·ship** \-ˌship\ *n*
[2]**le·gate** \li-ˈgāt\ *vt* **le·gat·ed; le·gat·ing** [*legatus,* pp. of *legare* to bequeath] (15c) **:** BEQUEATH 1 — **le·ga·tor** \-ˈgā-tər\ *n*
leg·a·tee \ˌle-gə-ˈtē\ *n* (ca. 1688) **:** one to whom a legacy is bequeathed or a devise is given
leg·a·tine \ˈle-gə-ˌtēn, -ˌtīn\ *adj* (1611) **:** of, headed by, or enacted under the authority of a legate
le·ga·tion \li-ˈgā-shən\ *n* (14c) **1 :** the sending forth of a legate **2 :** a body of deputies sent on a mission; *specif* **:** a diplomatic mission in a foreign country headed by a minister **3 :** the official residence and office of a diplomatic minister in a foreign country
[1]**le·ga·to** \li-ˈgä-(ˌ)tō\ *adv or adj* [It, lit., tied] (1801) **:** in a manner that is smooth and connected (as between successive tones) — used esp. as a direction in music
[2]**legato** *n* (1885) **:** a smooth and connected manner of performance (as of music); *also* **:** a passage of music so performed
leg·end \ˈle-jənd\ *n* [ME *legende,* fr. AF & ML; AF *legende,* fr. ML *legenda,* fr. L, fem. of *legendus,* gerundive of *legere* to gather, select, read; akin to Gk *legein* to gather, say, *logos* speech, word, reason] (14c) **1 a :** a story coming down from the past; *esp* **:** one popularly regarded as historical although not verifiable **b :** a body of such stories ⟨a place in the ~ of the frontier⟩ **c :** a popular myth of recent origin **d :** a person or thing that inspires legends **e :** the subject of a legend ⟨its violence was ~ even in its own time —William Broyles Jr.⟩ **2 a :** an inscription or title on an object (as a coin) **b :** CAPTION 2b **c :** an explanatory list of the symbols on a map or chart
leg·end·ary \ˈle-jən-ˌder-ē, -ˌde-rē\ *adj* (ca. 1587) **1 :** of, relating to, or characteristic of legend or a legend **2 :** WELL-KNOWN, FAMOUS ***syn*** see FICTITIOUS — **leg·en·dari·ly** \ˌle-jən-ˈder-ə-lē, -ˈde-rə-\ *adv*
leg·end·ry \ˈle-jən-drē\ *n* (1849) **:** a body of legends
le·ger·de·main \ˌle-jər-də-ˈmān\ *n* [ME, fr. MF *leger de main* light of hand] (15c) **1 :** SLEIGHT OF HAND **2 :** a display of skill or adroitness
le·ger·i·ty \lə-ˈjer-ə-tē, le-, -ˈje-rə-\ *n* [MF *legereté,* fr. OF, lightness, fr. *leger* light, fr. VL **leviarius,* fr. L *levis* — more at LIGHT] (1561) **:** alert facile quickness of mind or body
leger line *var of* LEDGER LINE
leges *pl of* LEX
leg·ged \ˈle-gəd *also* ˈlā-, *Brit usu* ˈlegd\ *adj* (15c) **:** having a leg or legs esp. of a specified kind or number — often used in combination ⟨a four-*legged* animal⟩
leg·ging *or* **leg·gin** \ˈle-gən *also* ˈlā-, -giŋ\ *n* (1751) **:** a covering (as of leather or cloth) for the leg — usu. used in pl.; *also* **:** TIGHTS
leg·gy \ˈle-gē *also* ˈlā-\ *adj* **leg·gi·er; -est** (1787) **1 :** having disproportionately long legs **2 :** having long and attractive legs **3 :** SPINDLY — used of a plant — **leg·gi·ness** \-nəs\ *n*
leg·hold trap \ˈleg-ˌhōld-\ *n* (1973) **:** a jawed usu. steel trap that is used to hold a wild mammal and operates by springing closed and clamping onto the leg of the animal that steps on it
leg·horn \ˈleg-ˌhȯrn; ˈle-ˌgȯrn, -gərn\ *n* [*Leghorn,* Italy] (1740) **1 a :** a fine plaited straw made from an Italian wheat **b :** a hat of this straw **2 :** any of a Mediterranean breed of small hardy domestic chickens noted for their large production of white eggs

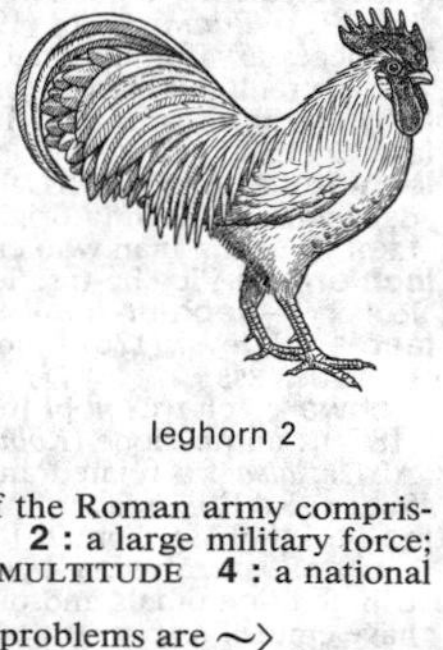
leghorn 2

leg·i·ble \ˈle-jə-bəl\ *adj* [ME, fr. LL *legibilis,* fr. L *legere* to read] (14c) **1 :** capable of being read or deciphered **:** PLAIN ⟨~ handwriting⟩ **2 :** capable of being discovered or understood — **leg·i·bil·i·ty** \ˌle-jə-ˈbi-lə-tē\ *n* — **leg·i·bly** \ˈle-jə-blē\ *adv*
[1]**le·gion** \ˈlē-jən\ *n* [ME, fr. AF, fr. L *legion-, legio,* fr. *legere* to gather — more at LEGEND] (13c) **1 :** the principal unit of the Roman army comprising 3000 to 6000 foot soldiers with cavalry **2 :** a large military force; *esp* **:** ARMY 1a **3 :** a very large number **:** MULTITUDE **4 :** a national association of ex-servicemen
[2]**legion** *adj* (1678) **:** MANY, NUMEROUS ⟨the problems are ~⟩
[1]**le·gion·ary** \ˈlē-jə-ˌner-ē, -ˌne-rē\ *adj* [ME *legyonary,* fr. L *legionarius,* fr. *legion-, legio*] (15c) **:** of, relating to, or constituting a legion
[2]**legionary** *n, pl* **-ar·ies** (1598) **:** LEGIONNAIRE
le·gion·naire \ˌlē-jə-ˈner\ *n* [F *légionnaire,* fr. L *legionarius*] (1818) **:** a member of a legion
Legionnaires' disease \-ˈnerz-\ *also* **Legionnaire's disease** *n* [fr. its first recognized occurrence at an American Legion convention in 1976] (1976) **:** a lobar pneumonia caused by a bacterium (*Legionella pneumophila*)
Legion of Honor (1827) **:** a French order conferred as a reward for civil or military merit
Legion of Merit (1943) **:** a U.S. military decoration awarded for exceptionally meritorious conduct in the performance of outstanding services
legis *abbr* legislation; legislative; legislature
leg·is·late \ˈle-jəs-ˌlāt\ *vb* **-lat·ed; -lat·ing** [back-formation fr. *legislator*] *vi* (1805) **:** to perform the function of legislation; *specif* **:** to make or enact laws ~ *vt* **:** to mandate, establish, or regulate by or as if by legislation
leg·is·la·tion \ˌle-jəs-ˈlā-shən\ *n* (1644) **1 :** the action of legislating; *specif* **:** the exercise of the power and function of making rules (as laws) that have the force of authority by virtue of their promulgation by an official organ of a state or other organization **2 :** the enactments of a legislator or a legislative body **3 :** a matter of business for or under consideration by a legislative body
[1]**leg·is·la·tive** \ˈle-jəs-ˌlā-tiv, -lə-\ *adj* (1640) **1 a :** having the power or performing the function of legislating **b :** belonging to the branch of government that is charged with such powers as making laws, levying and collecting taxes, and making financial appropriations — compare EXECUTIVE, JUDICIAL **2 a :** of or relating to a legislature ⟨~ committees⟩ **b :** composed of members of a legislature ⟨~ caucus⟩ **c :** created by a legislature esp. as distinguished from an executive or judicial body **d :** designed to assist a legislature or its members ⟨a ~ research agency⟩ **3 :** of, concerned with, or created by legislation ⟨~ courts⟩ — **leg·is·la·tive·ly** *adv*
[2]**legislative** *n* (1642) **:** the body or department exercising the power and function of legislating **:** LEGISLATURE
legislative assembly *n, often cap L&A* (1817) **1 :** a bicameral legislature (as in an American state) **2 :** the lower house of a bicameral legislature **3 :** a unicameral legislature; *esp* **:** one in a Canadian province

legislative council *n, often cap L&C* (1787) **1 :** a permanent committee chosen from both houses that meets between sessions of a state legislature to study state problems and plan a legislative program **2 :** a unicameral legislature (as in a British colony) **3 :** the upper house of a British bicameral legislature

leg·is·la·tor \ˈle-jəs-ˌlā-ˌtȯr, -ˌlā-tər *also* ˌle-jəs-ˈlā-ˌtȯr\ *n* [L *legis lator,* lit., proposer of a law, fr. *legis* (gen. of *lex* law) + *lator* proposer, fr. *ferre* (pp. *latus*) to carry, propose — more at TOLERATE, BEAR] (1603) **:** one that makes laws esp. for a political unit; *esp* **:** a member of a legislative body — **leg·is·la·to·ri·al** \ˌle-jəs-lə-ˈtȯr-ē-əl\ *adj* — **leg·is·la·tor·ship** \ˈle-jəs-ˌlā-tər-ˌship\ *n*

leg·is·la·ture \ˈle-jəs-ˌlā-chər *also* ˌle-jəs-ˈ, *Brit often* ˈle-jəs-lə-\ *n* (1654) **:** a body of persons having the power to legislate; *specif* **:** an organized body having the authority to make laws for a political unit

le·gist \ˈlē-jist\ *n* [ME, fr. MF *legiste,* fr. ML *legista,* fr. L *leg-, lex*] (15c) **:** a specialist in law; *esp* **:** one learned in Roman or civil law

le·git \li-ˈjit\ *adj* (1908) *slang* **:** LEGITIMATE

le·git·i·ma·cy \li-ˈji-tə-mə-sē\ *n* (1691) **:** the quality or state of being legitimate

[1]**le·git·i·mate** \li-ˈji-tə-mət\ *adj* [ME *legitimat,* fr. ML *legitimatus,* pp. of *legitimare* to legitimate, fr. L *legitimus* legitimate, fr. *leg-, lex* law] (15c) **1 a :** lawfully begotten; *specif* **:** born in wedlock **b :** having full filial rights and obligations by birth ⟨a ~ child⟩ **2 :** being exactly as purposed **:** neither spurious nor false ⟨a ~ grievance⟩ ⟨a ~ practitioner⟩ **3 a :** accordant with law or with established legal forms and requirements ⟨a ~ government⟩ **b :** ruling by or based on the strict principle of hereditary right ⟨a ~ king⟩ **4 :** conforming to recognized principles or accepted rules and standards ⟨a ~ advertising expenditure⟩ ⟨a ~ inference⟩ **5 :** relating to plays acted by professional actors but not including revues, burlesque, or some forms of musical comedy ⟨the ~ theater⟩ ***syn*** see LAWFUL — **le·git·i·mate·ly** *adv*

[2]**le·git·i·mate** \-ˌmāt\ *vt* **-mat·ed; -mat·ing** (1531) **:** to make legitimate: **a** (1) **:** to give legal status or authorization to (2) **:** to show or affirm to be justified (3) **:** to lend authority or respectability to **b :** to put (a bastard) in the state of a legitimate child before the law by legal means — **le·git·i·ma·tion** \-ˌji-tə-ˈmā-shən\ *n* — **le·git·i·mat·or** \-ˈji-tə-ˌmā-tər\ *n*

le·git·i·ma·tize \li-ˈji-tə-mə-ˌtīz\ *vt* **-tized; -tiz·ing** (1791) **:** LEGITIMATE

le·git·i·mise *Brit var of* LEGITIMIZE

le·git·i·mism \li-ˈji-tə-ˌmi-zəm\ *n, often cap* (1877) **:** adherence to the principles of political legitimacy or to a person claiming legitimacy — **le·git·i·mist** \-mist\ *n, often cap* — **legitimist** *adj*

le·git·i·mize \-ˌmīz\ *vt* **-mized; -miz·ing** (1848) **:** to make legitimate **:** LEGITIMATE — **le·git·i·mi·za·tion** \-ˌji-tə-mə-ˈzā-shən\ *n* — **le·git·i·miz·er** \-ˈji-tə-ˌmī-zər\ *n*

leg·man \ˈleg-ˌman *also* ˈlāg-\ *n* (1923) **1 :** a reporter assigned usu. to gather information **2 :** an assistant who performs various subordinate tasks (as gathering information or running errands)

leg–of–mut·ton *or* **leg–o'–mut·ton** \ˌle-gə(v)-ˈmə-tᵊn *also* ˌlāg-\ *adj* (1840) **:** having the approximately triangular shape or outline of a leg of mutton ⟨a ~ sleeve⟩ ⟨a ~ sail⟩

leg out *vt* (1965) **:** to make (as a base hit) by fast running

leg–pull \ˈleg-ˌpu̇l *also* ˈlāg-\ *n* [fr. the phrase *to pull one's leg*] (1915) **:** a humorous deception or hoax

leg·room \-ˌrüm, -ˌru̇m\ *n* (1926) **:** space in which to extend the legs while seated

le·gume \ˈle-ˌgyüm, li-ˈgyüm\ *n* [F *légume,* fr. L *legumin-, legumen* leguminous plant, fr. *legere* to gather — more at LEGEND] (1676) **1 a :** the fruit or seed of plants of the legume family (as peas or beans) used for food **b :** a vegetable used for food **2 :** any of a large family (Leguminosae syn. Fabaceae, the legume family) of dicotyledonous herbs, shrubs, and trees having fruits that are legumes (sense 3) or loments, bearing nodules on the roots that contain nitrogen-fixing bacteria, and including important food and forage plants (as peas, beans, or clovers) **3 :** a dry dehiscent one-celled fruit developed from a simple superior ovary and usu. dehiscing into two valves with the seeds attached to the ventral suture **:** POD

le·gu·mi·nous \li-ˈgyü-mə-nəs, le-\ *adj* (15c) **1 :** of, resembling, or consisting of legumes (as peas) **2 :** of or relating to the legume family

leg up *n* (1837) **1 :** a helping hand **:** BOOST **2 :** HEAD START

leg warmer *n* (1974) **:** a usu. knitted covering for the leg

leg·work \ˈleg-ˌwərk *also* ˈlāg-\ *n* (1891) **:** active physical work (as in gathering information) that forms the basis of more creative or mentally exacting work (as writing a book)

le·hua \lā-ˈhü-ə\ *n* [Hawaiian] (1888) **:** a common very showy chiefly Polynesian tree (*Metrosideros collinus*) of the myrtle family having bright red flowers and a hard wood; *also* **:** its flower

[1]**lei** \ˈlā, ˈlā-ˌē\ *n* [Hawaiian] (1843) **:** a wreath or necklace usu. of flowers or leaves

[2]**lei** \ˈlā\ *pl of* LEU

Leices·ter \ˈles-tər\ *n* [*Leicester,* county in England] (1798) **1 :** an individual of a breed of white-faced long wool sheep having a massive body and heavy fleece that was orig. developed in England and extensively used in the development of numerous modern sheep breeds **2 :** a hard usu. orange-colored cheese similar to cheddar

Leics *abbr* Leicestershire

leish·man·ia \lēsh-ˈma-nē-ə\ *n* [NL, fr. Sir W. B. *Leishman* †1926 Brit. medical officer] (1914) **:** any of a genus (*Leishmania*) of flagellate protozoans that are parasitic in the tissues of vertebrates; *broadly* **:** an organism resembling the leishmanias that is included in the family (Trypanosomatidae) to which they belong — **leish·man·ial** \-nē-əl\ *adj*

leish·man·i·a·sis \ˌlēsh-mə-ˈnī-ə-səs\ *n, pl* **-ses** \-ˌsēz\ [NL] (1912) **:** infection with or disease caused by leishmanias

leis·ter \ˈlēs-tər\ *n* [of Scand origin; akin to ON *ljóstr* leister] (ca. 1534) **:** a spear armed with three or more barbed prongs for catching fish

lei·sure \ˈlē-zhər, ˈle-, ˈlā-\ *n* [ME *leiser,* fr. AF *leisir,* fr. *leisir* to be permitted, fr. L *licēre*] (14c) **1 :** freedom provided by the cessation of activities; *esp* **:** time free from work or duties **2 :** EASE, LEISURELINESS — **leisure** *adj* — **at leisure** *or* **at one's leisure :** in one's leisure time **:** at one's convenience ⟨read the book *at her leisure*⟩

lei·sured \-zhərd\ *adj* (1631) **:** having leisure **:** LEISURELY

[1]**lei·sure·ly** \-zhər-lē\ *adv* (1576) **:** without haste **:** DELIBERATELY

[2]**leisurely** *adj* (1604) **:** characterized by leisure **:** UNHURRIED ⟨a ~ pace⟩ — **lei·sure·li·ness** *n*

leisure suit *n* (1975) **:** a suit consisting of a shirt jacket and matching trousers for informal wear

leit·mo·tif *also* **leit·mo·tiv** \ˈlīt-mō-ˌtēf\ *n* [G *Leitmotiv,* fr. *leiten* to lead + *Motiv* motive] (ca. 1876) **1 :** an associated melodic phrase or figure that accompanies the reappearance of an idea, person, or situation esp. in a Wagnerian music drama **2 :** a dominant recurring theme

[1]**lek** \ˈlek\ *n* [Sw, short for *lekställe* mating ground, fr. *lek* mating, sport + *ställe* place] (1871) **:** an assembly area where animals (as the prairie chicken) carry on display and courtship behavior; *also* **:** an aggregation of animals assembled on a lek for courtship

[2]**lek** *n, pl* **leks** *or* **le·ke** *or* **lekë** \ˈle-kə\ [Alb] (1927) — see MONEY table

lek·var \ˈlek-ˌvär\ *n* [Hung *lekvár* jam] (ca. 1958) **:** a prune butter used as a pastry filling

LEM *abbr* lunar excursion module; lunar module

le·man \ˈle-mən, ˈlē-\ *n* [ME *lefman, leman,* fr. *lef* lief] (13c) *archaic* **:** SWEETHEART, LOVER; *esp* **:** MISTRESS

[1]**lem·ma** \ˈle-mə\ *n, pl* **lemmas** *or* **lem·ma·ta** \-mə-tə\ [L, fr. Gk *lēmma* thing taken, assumption, fr. *lambanein* to take — more at LATCH] (1570) **1 :** an auxiliary proposition used in the demonstration of another proposition **2 :** the argument or theme of a composition prefixed as a title or introduction; *also* **:** the heading or theme of a comment or note on a text **3 :** a glossed word or phrase

[2]**lemma** *n* [Gk, husk, fr. *lepein* to peel — more at LEPER] (1906) **:** the lower of the two bracts enclosing the flower in the spikelet of grasses

lem·ming \ˈle-miŋ\ *n* [Norw] (1713) **:** any of various small short-tailed furry-footed rodents (as genera *Lemmus* and *Dicrostonyx*) of circumpolar distribution that are notable for population fluctuations and recurrent mass migrations — **lem·ming·like** \-ˌlīk\ *adj*

lem·nis·cate \lem-ˈnis-kət\ *n* [NL *lemniscata,* fr. fem. of L *lemniscatus* with hanging ribbons, fr. *lemniscus*] (ca. 1781) **:** a figure-eight shaped curve whose equation in polar coordinates is $\rho^2=a^2 \cos 2\theta$ or $\rho^2=a^2 \sin 2\theta$

lem·nis·cus \lem-ˈnis-kəs\ *n, pl* **-nis·ci** \-ˈnis-ˌkī, -ˌkē; -ˈni-ˌsī\ [NL, fr. L, ribbon, fr. Gk *lēmniskos*] (ca. 1905) **:** a band of fibers and esp. nerve fibers — **lem·nis·cal** \-kəl\ *adj*

[1]**lem·on** \ˈle-mən\ *n* [ME *lymon,* fr. MF *limon,* fr. ML *limon-, limo,* fr. Ar *laymūn, līmūn,* fr. Pers *līmū, līmun*] (15c) **1 a :** an acid fruit that is botanically a many-seeded pale yellow oblong berry produced by a small thorny citrus tree (*Citrus limon*) and that has a rind from which an aromatic oil is extracted **b :** a tree that bears lemons **2 :** one (as an automobile) that is unsatisfactory or defective

[2]**lemon** *adj* (1598) **1 :** of the color lemon yellow **2 a :** containing lemon **b :** having the flavor or scent of lemon

lem·on·ade \ˌle-mə-ˈnād\ *n* (1604) **:** a beverage of sweetened lemon juice mixed with water

lemon balm *n* (1864) **:** a bushy perennial European mint (*Melissa officinalis*) often cultivated for its lemon-scented leaves; *also* **:** its leaves

lemon curd *n* (1895) **:** a custard made with lemon juice, butter, sugar, and eggs and used as a spread or filling

lem·on·grass \ˈle-mən-ˌgras\ *n* (1801) **:** a grass (*Cymbopogon citratus*) of robust habit native to southern India and Ceylon that is grown in tropical regions for its lemon-scented foliage used as a seasoning and that is the source of an aromatic essential oil; *also* **:** its foliage

lemon law *n* (1981) **:** a law offering car buyers relief (as by repair, replacement, or refund) for defects detected during a specified period after purchase

lemon shark *n* (1942) **:** a medium-sized requiem shark (*Negaprion brevirostris*) of warm waters that is yellowish brown to gray above with yellow or greenish sides

lemon sole *n* (1876) **:** any of several flatfishes and esp. flounders: as **a :** a bottom-dwelling flounder (*Microstomus kitt*) of the northeastern Atlantic that is an important food fish **b :** WINTER FLOUNDER

lemon thyme *n* (1629) **:** a thyme (*Thymus citriodorus*) having lemon-scented leaves used as a seasoning; *also* **:** its leaves

lemon verbena *n* (1869) **:** a small shrub (*Aloysia triphylla*) of Chile and Argentina that has narrow lemon-scented leaves

lem·ony \ˈle-mə-nē\ *adj* (1859) **:** resembling or suggestive of a lemon

lemon yellow *n* (1807) **:** a brilliant greenish yellow color

lem·pi·ra \lem-ˈpir-ə\ *n* [AmerSp, fr. *Lempira,* 16th cent. Honduran Indian cacique] (1931) — see MONEY table

le·mur \ˈlē-mər\ *n* [NL, fr. L *lemures,* pl., ghosts] (1795) **:** any of various arboreal chiefly nocturnal prosimian primates (superfamily Lemuroidea) that were formerly widespread but are now largely confined to Madagascar and that usu. have a longish muzzle, large eyes, very soft woolly fur, and a long furry tail

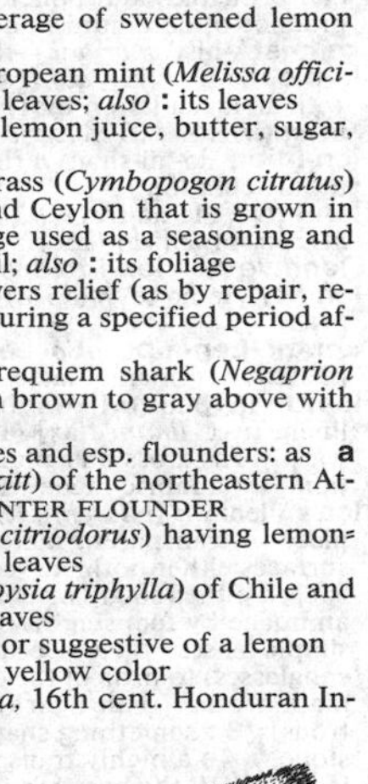

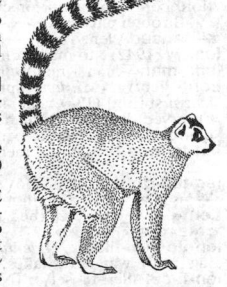

lemur

le·mu·res \ˈle-mə-ˌrās, ˈlem-yə-ˌrēz\ *n pl* [L] (1555) **:** spirits of the unburied dead exorcised from homes in early Roman religious rites

Len·a·pe \ˈle-nə-pē, lə-ˈnä-pē\ *n, pl* **Lenape** *or* **Lenapes** [Delaware (Unami dialects) *lənā·pe·*] (1728) **:** DELAWARE 1

lend \ˈlend\ *vb* **lent** \ˈlent\; **lend·ing** [ME *lenen, lenden,* fr. OE *lǣnan,* fr. *lǣn* loan — more at LOAN] *vt* (bef. 12c) **1 a** (1) **:** to give for temporary use on condition that the same or its equivalent be returned ⟨~ me your pen⟩ (2) **:** to put at another's temporary disposal ⟨*lent* us their services⟩ **b :** to let out (money) for temporary use on condition of repayment with interest **2 a :** to give the assistance or support of **:** AFFORD, FURNISH ⟨a dispassionate and scholarly manner which ~*s* great force to his criticisms —*Times Lit. Supp.*⟩ **b :** to adapt or apply (oneself) readily **:** ACCOMMODATE ⟨a topic that ~*s* itself ad-

mirably to class discussion〉 ~ *vi* : to make a loan ***usage*** see LOAN — **lend·able** \ˈlen-də-bəl\ *adj* — **lend·er** *n*

lending library *n* (1708) : a library from which materials are lent; *esp* : RENTAL LIBRARY

lend–lease \ˈlend-ˈlēs\ *n* [U.S. *Lend-Lease* Act (1941)] (1941) : the transfer of goods and services to an ally to aid in a common cause with payment made by a return of the original items or their use in the cause or by a similar transfer of other goods and services — **lend–lease** *vt*

length \ˈleŋ(k)th, ˈlen(t)th\ *n, pl* **lengths** \ˈleŋ(k)ths, ˈlen(t)ths, ˈleŋ(k)s\ [ME *lengthe,* fr. OE *lengthu,* fr. *lang* long] (bef. 12c) **1 a :** the longer or longest dimension of an object **b :** a measured distance or dimension 〈10 feet in ~〉 — see METRIC SYSTEM table, WEIGHT table **c :** the quality or state of being long **2 a :** duration or extent in time **b :** relative duration or stress of a sound **3 a :** distance or extent in space **b :** the length of something taken as a unit of measure 〈his horse led by a ~〉 **4 :** the degree to which something (as a course of action or a line of thought) is carried — often used in pl. 〈went to great ~*s* to learn the truth〉 **5 a :** a long expanse or stretch **b :** a piece constituting or usable as part of a whole or of a connected series : SECTION 〈a ~ of pipe〉 **6 :** the longer or vertical dimension of a piece of clothing — often used in combination 〈elbow-*length* sleeves〉 — **at length 1 :** FULLY, COMPREHENSIVELY **2 :** at last : FINALLY

length·en \ˈleŋ(k)-thən, ˈlen(t)-\ *vb* **length·ened; length·en·ing** \ˈleŋ(k)th-niŋ, ˈlen(t)th-; ˈleŋ(k)-thə-, ˈlen(t)-\ *vt* (14c) : to make longer ~ *vi* : to grow longer ***syn*** see EXTEND — **length·en·er** \ˈleŋ(k)th-nər, ˈlen(t)th-; ˈleŋ(k)-thə-, ˈlen(t)-\ *n*

length·ways \ˈleŋ(k)th-ˌwāz, ˈlen(t)th-\ *adv* (1599) : LENGTHWISE

length·wise \-ˌwīz\ *adv* (ca. 1580) : in the direction of the length : LONGITUDINALLY — **lengthwise** *adj*

lengthy \ˈleŋ(k)-thē, ˈlen(t)-\ *adj* **length·i·er; -est** (1689) **1 :** protracted excessively : OVERLONG **2 :** EXTENDED, LONG — **length·i·ly** \-thə-lē\ *adv* — **length·i·ness** \-thē-nəs\ *n*

le·nience \ˈlē-nyən(t)s, -nē-ən(t)s\ *n* (1796) : LENIENCY

le·nien·cy \ˈlē-nē-ən(t)-sē, -nyən(t)-sē\ *n, pl* **-cies** (1753) **1 :** the quality or state of being lenient **2 :** a lenient disposition or practice ***syn*** see MERCY

le·nient \ˈlē-nē-ənt, -nyənt\ *adj* [L *lenient-, leniens,* prp. of *lenire* to soften, soothe, fr. *lenis* soft, mild; prob. akin to Lith *lė̃nas* tranquil — more at LET] (1652) **1 :** exerting a soothing or easing influence : relieving pain or stress **2 :** of mild and tolerant disposition; *esp* : INDULGENT — **le·nient·ly** *adv*

Le·nin·ism \ˈle-nə-ˌni-zəm\ *n* (1917) : the political, economic, and social principles and policies advocated by Lenin; *esp* : the theory and practice of communism developed by or associated with Lenin — **Le·nin·ist** \-nist\ *n or adj* — **Le·nin·ite** \-ˌnīt\ *n or adj*

le·nis \ˈlē-nəs, ˈlā-\ *adj* [NL, fr. L, mild, smooth] (ca. 1897) : produced with an articulation that is lax in relation to another speech sound 〈\t\ in *gutter* is ~, \t\ in *toe* is fortis〉

len·i·tion \lə-ˈni-shən\ *n* [L *lenire*] (1912) : the change from fortis to lenis articulation

len·i·tive \ˈle-nə-tiv\ *adj* [ME *lenitif,* fr. MF, fr. ML *lenitivus,* fr. L *lenitus,* pp. of *lenire*] (15c) : alleviating pain or harshness : SOOTHING — **lenitive** *n* — **len·i·tive·ly** *adv*

len·i·ty \ˈle-nə-tē\ *n* (1548) : the quality or state of being lenient : CLEMENCY

Len·ni–Len·a·pe *also* **Leni–Len·a·pe** \ˌle-nē-ˈle-nə-pē, -lə-ˈnä-pē\ *n* [Delaware (Unami dialects) *lə̀ni-lənáˑpˑe*] (ca. 1782) : DELAWARE 1

le·no \ˈlē-(ˌ)nō\ *n* [perh. fr. F *linon* linen fabric, lawn, fr. MF *lin* flax, linen, fr. L *linum* flax] (1821) **1 :** an open weave in which pairs of warp yarns cross one another and thereby lock the filling yarn in position **2 :** a fabric made with a leno weave

[1]**lens** \ˈlenz\ *n* [NL *lent-, lens,* fr. L, lentil; fr. its shape] (1673) **1 a :** a piece of transparent material (as glass) that has two opposite regular surfaces either both curved or one curved and the other plane and that is used either singly or combined in an optical instrument for forming an image by focusing rays of light **b :** a combination of two or more simple lenses **c :** a piece of glass or plastic used (as in safety goggles or sunglasses) to protect the eye **2 :** a device for directing or focusing radiation other than light (as sound waves, radio microwaves, or electrons) **3 :** something shaped like a biconvex optical lens 〈~ of sandstone〉 **4 :** a highly transparent biconvex lens-shaped or nearly spherical body in the eye that focuses light rays (as upon the retina) — see EYE illustration **5 :** something that facilitates and influences perception, comprehension, or evaluation 〈viewing the current legal battle . . . through partisan ~*es* —*New Republic*〉 **6 :** GRAVITATIONAL LENS — **lensed** \ˈlenzd\ *adj* — **lens·less** \ˈlenz-ləs\ *adj*

[2]**lens** *vt* (1942) : to make a motion picture of : FILM

lens·man \-mən, -ˌman\ *n* (1938) : PHOTOGRAPHER

Lent \ˈlent\ *n* [ME *lente* springtime, Lent, fr. OE *lencten;* akin to OHG *lenzin* spring] (13c) : the 40 weekdays from Ash Wednesday to Easter observed by the Roman Catholic, Eastern, and some Protestant churches as a period of penitence and fasting

len·ta·men·te \ˌlen-tə-ˈmen-(ˌ)tā\ *adv or adj* [It, fr. *lento* slow] (1724) : LENTO

len·tan·do \len-ˈtän-(ˌ)dō\ *adv or adj* [It] (ca. 1847) : becoming slower — used as a direction in music

Lent·en \ˈlen-tᵊn\ *adj* (bef. 12c) : of, relating to, or suitable for Lent; *esp* : MEAGER 〈~ fare〉

len·tic \ˈlen-tik\ *adj* [L *lentus* sluggish] (ca. 1935) : of, relating to, or living in still waters (as lakes, ponds, or swamps) — compare LOTIC

len·ti·cel \ˈlen-tə-ˌsel\ *n* [NL *lenticella,* dim. of L *lent-, lens* lentil] (ca. 1864) : a loose aggregation of cells which penetrates the surface (as of a stem) of a woody plant and through which gases are exchanged between the atmosphere and the underlying tissues

len·tic·u·lar \len-ˈti-kyə-lər\ *adj* [ME, fr. L *lenticularis* lentil-shaped, fr. *lenticula* lentil] (15c) **1 :** having the shape of a double-convex lens **2 :** of or relating to a lens **3 :** provided with or utilizing lenticules 〈a ~ screen〉

len·ti·cule \ˈlen-tə-ˌkyül\ *n* [L *lenticula*] (1942) **1 :** any of the minute lenses on the base side of a film used in stereoscopic or color photography **2 :** any of the tiny corrugations or grooves molded or embossed into the surface of a projection screen

len·til \ˈlen-tᵊl\ *n* [ME, fr. AF *lentille,* fr. L *lenticula,* dim. of *lent-, lens*] (13c) **1 :** a widely cultivated Eurasian annual leguminous plant (*Lens culinaris*) with flattened edible seeds and leafy stalks used as fodder **2 :** the seed of the lentil

len·tis·si·mo \len-ˈti-sə-ˌmō\ *adv or adj* [It, superl. of *lento*] (ca. 1903) : at a very slow tempo — used as a direction in music

len·ti·vi·rus \ˌlen-tə-ˈvī-rəs\ *n* [NL, fr. L *lentus* slow + NL *virus*] (1979) : any of a genus (*Lentivirus*) of retroviruses (as the HIVs and SIV) that cause slowly progressive often fatal human and animal diseases (as AIDS)

len·to \ˈlen-(ˌ)tō\ *adv or adj* [It, fr. *lento,* adj., slow, fr. L *lentus* pliant, sluggish, slow — more at LITHE] (ca. 1724) : at a slow tempo — used esp. as a direction in music

Leo \ˈlē-(ˌ)ō\ *n* [L (gen. *Leonis*), lit., lion — more at LION] (bef. 12c) **1 :** a northern constellation east of Cancer **2 a :** the fifth sign of the zodiac in astrology — see ZODIAC table **b :** one born under this sign — **Le·o·nine** \ˈlē-ə-ˌnīn\ *adj*

le·one \lē-ˈōn\ *n, pl* **leones** *or* **leone** [*Sierra Leone*] (1964) — see MONEY table

Le·o·nid \ˈlē-ə-nid\ *n, pl* **Leonids** *or* **Le·on·i·des** \lē-ˈä-nə-ˌdēz\ [L *Leon-, Leo;* fr. their appearing to radiate from a point in Leo] (1876) : any of the meteors in a meteor shower occurring every year about November 14

le·o·nine \ˈlē-ə-ˌnīn\ *adj* [ME, fr. L *leoninus,* fr. *leon-, leo*] (14c) : of, relating to, suggestive of, or resembling a lion

leop·ard \ˈle-pərd\ *n* [ME, fr. AF *lepart, leupart,* fr. LL *leopardus,* fr. Gk *leopardos,* fr. *leōn* lion + *pardos* leopard] (13c) **1 :** a large strong cat (*Panthera pardus*) of southern Asia and Africa that is adept at climbing and is usu. tawny or buff with black spots arranged in rosettes — called also *panther* **2 :** a heraldic representation of a lion passant guardant — **leop·ard·ess** \-pər-dəs\ *n*

leopard cat *n* (1866) : a small spotted cat (*Felis bengalensis*) chiefly of southeastern Asia

leopard frog *n* (1839) : a common frog (*Rana pipiens*) of northern No. America that is bright green or brown with large black white-margined blotches on the back; *also* : a similar frog (*R. sphenocephala*) chiefly of the southeastern U.S.

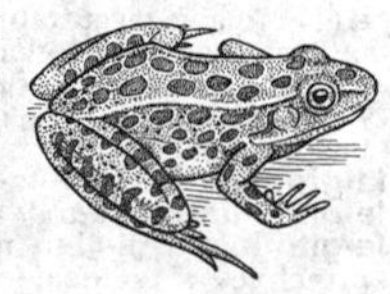

leopard frog

leopard seal *n* (1893) : a spotted slate gray seal (*Hydrurga leptonyx*) esp. of antarctic and subantarctic waters that feeds chiefly on krill, other seals, penguins, and fish

le·o·tard \ˈlē-ə-ˌtärd\ *n* [Jules *Léotard,* †1870 Fr. aerial gymnast] (1886) : a close-fitting one-piece garment worn esp. by dancers, acrobats, and aerialists; *also* : TIGHTS — often used in pl. — **le·o·tard·ed** \-ˌtär-dəd\ *adj*

LEP *abbr* limited English proficiency; limited English proficient

Lep·cha \ˈlep-chə\ *n, pl* **Lepcha** *or* **Lepchas** (1819) **1 :** a member of a people of Sikkim, India **2 :** the Tibeto-Burman language of the Lepcha people

lep·er \ˈle-pər\ *n* [ME, fr. AF, fr. *lepre* leprosy, fr. LL *lepra,* fr. Gk, fr. *lepein* to peel; perh. akin to Lith *lopas* piece, scrap] (14c) **1 :** a person affected with leprosy **2 :** a person shunned for moral or social reasons

lepid- *or* **lepido-** *comb form* [NL, fr. Gk, fr. *lepid-, lepis* scale, fr. *lepein*] : flake : scale 〈*Lepido*ptera〉

le·pid·o·lite \li-ˈpi-də-ˌlīt\ *n* [G *Lepidolith,* fr. *lepid-* + *-lith*] (ca. 1796) : a variable form of mica used esp. in glazes and enamels and as a source of lithium

lep·i·dop·tera \ˌle-pə-ˈdäp-tə-rə\ *n pl* (ca. 1773) : insects that are lepidopterans

lep·i·dop·ter·an \-rən\ *n* [NL *Lepidoptera,* fr. *lepid-* + Gk *pteron* wing — more at FEATHER] (ca. 1901) : any of a large order (Lepidoptera) of insects comprising the butterflies, moths, and skippers that as adults have four broad or lanceolate wings usu. covered with minute overlapping and often brightly colored scales and that as larvae are caterpillars — **lepidopteran** *adj* — **lep·i·dop·ter·ous** \-tə-rəs\ *adj*

lep·i·dop·ter·ist \-tə-rist\ *n* (1826) : a specialist in lepidopterology

lep·i·dop·ter·ol·o·gy \-ˌdäp-tə-ˈrä-lə-jē\ *n* (1898) : a branch of entomology concerned with lepidopterans — **lep·i·dop·ter·o·log·i·cal** \-tə-rə-ˈlä-ji-kəl\ *adj* — **lep·i·dop·ter·ol·o·gist** \-tə-ˈrä-lə-jist\ *n*

lep·i·dote \ˈle-pə-ˌdōt\ *n* [Gk *lepidōtos* scaly, fr. *lepid-, lepis*] (ca. 1836) : a rhododendron with tiny scales on the undersurface of the leaves

lep·re·chaun \ˈle-prə-ˌkän, -ˌkȯn\ *n* [Ir *leipreachán*] (1604) : a mischievous elf of Irish folklore usu. believed to reveal the hiding place of treasure if caught — **lep·re·chaun·ish** \-ˌkä-nish, -ˌkȯ-\ *adj*

le·pro·ma·tous \lə-ˈprä-mə-təs, -ˈprō-\ *adj* [NL *lepromat-, leproma* leprous lesion, fr. LL *lepra*] (1898) : characterized by, exhibiting, or being leprosy with infective superficial granulomatous nodules

lep·ro·sar·i·um \ˌle-prə-ˈser-ē-əm\ *n, pl* **-i·ums** *or* **-ia** \-ē-ə\ [ML, fr. LL *leprosus*] (ca. 1846) : a hospital for leprosy patients

lep·ro·sy \ˈle-prə-sē\ *n* [ME *lepruse,* fr. *leprous*] (15c) **1 :** a chronic infectious disease caused by a mycobacterium (*Mycobacterium leprae*) affecting esp. the skin and peripheral nerves and characterized by the formation of nodules or macules that enlarge and spread accompanied by loss of sensation with eventual paralysis, wasting of muscle, and production of deformities — called also *Hansen's disease* **2 :** a morally or spiritually harmful influence — **lep·rot·ic** \le-ˈprä-tik\ *adj*

lep·rous \ˈle-prəs\ *adj* [ME, fr. AF *leprus,* fr. LL *leprosus,* fr. *lepra* leprosy — more at LEPER] (13c) **1 a :** infected with leprosy **b :** of, relating to, or resembling leprosy or a leper **2 :** SCALY, SCURFY — **lep·rous·ly** *adv*

-lepsy *n comb form* [F *-lepsie,* fr. LL *-lepsia,* fr. Gk *-lēpsia,* fr. *lēpsis,* fr. *lambanein* to take, seize — more at LATCH] : taking : seizure 〈narco*lepsy*〉

lep·tin \ˈlep-tən\ *n* [Gk *leptos* slender + E [1]*-in*] (1995) : a peptide hormone that is produced by fat cells and plays a role in body weight regulation by acting on the hypothalamus to suppress appetite and burn fat stored in adipose tissue

lep·to·ceph·a·lus \ˌlep-tə-ˈse-fə-ləs\ *n, pl* **-li** \-ˌlī, -ˌlē\ [NL, fr. Gk *leptos* + *kephalē* head — more at CEPHALIC] (1769) : a long thin small-headed transparent pelagic first larva of various eels

[1]**lep·ton** \lep-ˈtän\ *n, pl* **lep·ta** \-ˈtä\ [ModGk, fr. Gk, a small coin, fr. neut. of *leptos* peeled, slender, small, fr. *lepein* to peel — more at LEPER] (ca. 1741) : a former monetary unit equal to 1/100 drachma

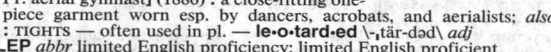

2**lep·ton** \ˈlep-ˌtän\ *n* [Gk *leptos* + E 2*-on*] (ca. 1929) **:** any of a family of particles (as electrons, muons, and neutrinos) that have spin quantum number ½ and that experience no strong forces — **lep·ton·ic** \lep-ˈtä-nik\ *adj*

lep·to·spire \-ˌspī(-ə)r\ *n* [NL *Leptospira,* fr. Gk *leptos* + L *spira* coil — more at SPIRE] (1952) **:** any of a genus (*Leptospira*) of slender aerobic spiral-shaped spirochetes that are free-living or parasitic in mammals — **lep·to·spir·al** \ˌlep-tə-ˈspī-rəl\ *adj*

lep·to·spi·ro·sis \ˌlep-tə-spī-ˈrō-səs\ *n, pl* **-ro·ses** \-ˌsēz\ [NL] (ca. 1926) **:** any of several diseases of humans and domestic animals that are caused by infection with leptospires

lep·to·tene \ˈlep-tə-ˌtēn\ *n* [ISV] (1912) **:** a stage of meiotic prophase immediately preceding synapsis in which the chromosomes appear as fine discrete threads — **leptotene** *adj*

1**les·bi·an** \ˈlez-bē-ən\ *adj* (1567) **1** *often cap* **:** of or relating to Lesbos **2** [fr. the reputed homosexual band associated with Sappho of Lesbos] **:** of or relating to homosexuality between females

2**lesbian** *n* (ca. 1890) **:** a woman who is a homosexual

les·bi·an·ism \ˈlez-bē-ə-ˌni-zəm\ *n* (1870) **:** female homosexuality

lèse–ma·jes·té *or* **lese maj·es·ty** \ˌlāz-ˈma-jə-stē, ˌlez-, ˌlēz-\ *n* [MF *lese majesté,* fr. L *laesa majestas,* lit., injured majesty] (1536) **1 a :** a crime (as treason) committed against a sovereign power **b :** an offense violating the dignity of a ruler as the representative of a sovereign power **2 :** a detraction from or affront to dignity or importance

le·sion \ˈlē-zhən\ *n* [ME, fr. AF, fr. L *laesion-, laesio,* fr. *laedere* to injure] (15c) **1 :** INJURY, HARM **2 :** an abnormal change in structure of an organ or part due to injury or disease; *esp* **:** one that is circumscribed and well defined — **le·sioned** \-zhənd\ *adj*

les·pe·de·za \ˌles-pə-ˈdē-zə\ *n* [NL, irreg. fr. V. M. de *Zespedes fl*1785 Span. governor of East Florida] (1884) **:** any of a genus (*Lespedeza*) of herbaceous or shrubby plants of the legume family including some widely used for forage, soil improvement, and hay

1**less** \ˈles\ *adj, comparative of* 1LITTLE [ME, partly fr. OE *lǣs,* adv. & n.; partly fr. *lǣssa,* adj.; akin to OFris *lēs* less] (bef. 12c) **1 :** constituting a more limited number or amount ⟨～ than three⟩ ⟨～ than half done⟩ **2 :** of lower rank, degree, or importance ⟨no ～ a person than the president himself⟩ **3 a :** of reduced size, extent, or degree **b :** more limited in quantity ⟨in ～ time⟩ — **no less** —used to emphasize that something is regarded as impressive or surprising ⟨wants to be driven to the airport, in a limousine *no less*⟩

usage The traditional view is that *less* applies to matters of degree, value, or amount and modifies collective nouns, mass nouns, or nouns denoting an abstract whole while *fewer* applies to matters of number and modifies plural nouns. *Less* has been used to modify plural nouns since the days of King Alfred and the usage, though roundly decried, appears to be increasing. *Less* is more likely than *fewer* to modify plural nouns when distances, sums of money, and a few fixed phrases are involved ⟨*less* than 100 miles⟩ ⟨an investment of *less* than $2000⟩ ⟨in 25 words or *less*⟩ and as likely as *fewer* to modify periods of time ⟨in *less* (or *fewer*) than four hours⟩.

2**less** *adv, comparative of* 2LITTLE (bef. 12c) **:** to a lesser extent or degree — **less and less :** to a progressively smaller size or extent — **less than :** by no means **:** not at all ⟨*less than* honest in his replies⟩

3**less** *n, pl* **less** (bef. 12c) **1 :** a smaller portion or quantity **2 :** something of less importance

4**less** *prep* (15c) **:** diminished by **:** MINUS

-less *adj suffix* [ME *-les, -lesse,* fr. OE *-lēas,* fr. *lēas* devoid, false; akin to OHG *lōs* loose, OE *losian* to get lost — more at LOSE] **1 :** destitute of **:** not having ⟨wit*less*⟩ ⟨child*less*⟩ **2 :** unable to be acted on or to act (in a specified way) ⟨daunt*less*⟩ ⟨fade*less*⟩

les·see \le-ˈsē\ *n* [ME, fr. AF, fr. *lessé,* pp. of *lesser* to lease — more at LEASE] (15c) **:** one that holds real or personal property under a lease

less·en \ˈle-sᵊn\ *vb* **less·ened; less·en·ing** \ˈles-niŋ, ˈle-sᵊn-iŋ\ *vi* (13c) **:** to shrink in size, number, or degree **:** DECREASE ～ *vt* **1 :** to reduce in size, extent, or degree **2 a** *archaic* **:** to represent as of little value **b :** to lower in status or dignity **:** DEGRADE ***syn*** see DECREASE

1**less·er** \ˈle-sər\ *adj, comparative of* 1LITTLE (13c) **:** of less size, quality, degree, or significance **:** of lower status

2**lesser** *adv* (1539) **:** LESS ⟨*lesser*-known⟩

lesser celandine *n* (ca. 1890) **:** a yellow-flowered Eurasian perennial herb (*Ranunculus ficaria*) of the buttercup family naturalized in No. America

lesser cornstalk borer *n* (ca. 1925) **:** a pyralid moth (*Elasmopalpus lignosellus*) having slender greenish larvae that burrow in the stalk esp. of Indian corn near ground level

lesser panda *n* (1943) **:** RED PANDA

lesser peach tree borer *n* (ca. 1924) **:** a clearwing moth (*Synanthedon pictipes*) whose larva bores into the wood of stone-fruit trees and esp. the peach

lesser yellowlegs *n pl but sing or pl in constr* (ca. 1903) **:** a common American marsh and shore bird (*Tringa flavipes*) that closely resembles the greater yellowlegs in color and markings but is smaller with a shorter more slender bill

1**les·son** \ˈle-sᵊn\ *n* [ME, fr. AF *leçon,* fr. LL *lection-, lectio,* fr. L, act of reading, fr. *legere* to read — more at LEGEND] (13c) **1 :** a passage from sacred writings read in a service of worship **2 a :** a piece of instruction **b :** a reading or exercise to be studied by a pupil **c :** a division of a course of instruction **3 a :** something learned by study or experience ⟨his years of travel had taught him valuable ～*s*⟩ **b :** an instructive example ⟨the ～*s* of history⟩ **c :** REPRIMAND

2**lesson** *vt* **les·soned; les·son·ing** \ˈle-sə-niŋ, ˈles-niŋ\ (1555) **1 :** to give a lesson to **:** INSTRUCT **2 :** LECTURE, REBUKE

les·sor \ˈle-ˌsȯr, le-ˈsȯr\ *n* [ME *lessour,* fr. AF, fr. *lesser* to lease] (14c) **:** one that conveys property by lease

lest \ˈlest\ *conj* [ME *les the, leste,* fr. OE *thȳ lǣs the,* fr. *thȳ* (instrumental of *thæt* that) + *lǣs* + *the,* relative particle] (bef. 12c) **:** for fear that — often used after an expression denoting fear or apprehension ⟨worried ～ she should be late⟩ ⟨hesitant to speak out ～ he be fired⟩

1**let** \ˈlet\ *vt* **let·ted; letted** *or* **let; let·ting** [ME *letten,* fr. OE *lettan* to delay, hinder; akin to OHG *lezzen* to delay, hurt, OE *lǣt* late] (bef. 12c) *archaic* **:** HINDER, PREVENT

2**let** *n* (12c) **1 :** something that impedes **:** OBSTRUCTION ⟨ruled his little world without hindrance or ～ —B. F. Reilly⟩ **2 :** a shot or point in racket games that does not count and must be replayed

3**let** *vb* **let; let·ting** [ME *leten,* fr. OE *lǣtan;* akin to OHG *lāzzan* to permit, and perh. to Lith *lėnas* tranquil] *vt* (bef. 12c) **1 :** to cause to **:** MAKE ⟨～ me know⟩ **2 a** *chiefly Brit* **:** to offer or grant for rent or lease ⟨～ rooms⟩ **b :** to assign esp. after bids ⟨～ a contract⟩ **3 a :** to give opportunity to or fail to prevent ⟨live and ～ live⟩ ⟨a break in the clouds ～ us see the summit⟩ ⟨～ the opportunity slip⟩ **b** — used in the imperative to introduce a request or proposal ⟨～ us pray⟩ **c** — used as an auxiliary to express a warning ⟨～ him try⟩ **4 :** to free from or as if from confinement ⟨～ out a scream⟩ ⟨～ blood⟩ **5 :** to permit to enter, pass, or leave ⟨～ them through⟩ ⟨～ them off with a warning⟩ **6 :** to make an adjustment to ⟨～ out the waist⟩ ～ *vi* **1** *chiefly Brit* **:** to become rented or leased **2 :** to become awarded to a contractor ***syn*** see HIRE — **let alone :** to leave undisturbed ⟨*let* the flowers *alone*⟩; *also* **:** to leave to oneself ⟨wanted to be *let alone*⟩ — **let fly 1 :** to hurl an object **2 :** to give unrestrained expression to an emotion or utterance ⟨*let fly* with some sharp rebukes —Janice Castro⟩ — **let go 1 :** to dismiss from employment ⟨the firm *let* him *go* at the end of the month⟩ **2 :** to abandon self-restraint **:** let fly ⟨spoke in clipped sentences, as if fearful of *letting go* —David Kline⟩ ⟨there just to party, just to *let go* —Philippe Vergne⟩ **3 :** to relax or release one's hold — used with *of* ⟨*let go* of stress —Kathy McCoy⟩ ⟨*let go* of my arm⟩ **4 :** to fail to take care of **:** NEGLECT ⟨*let* himself *go* and got real fat —Bill Parcells⟩ — **let it all hang out :** to reveal one's true feelings **:** act without dissimulation — **let one have it :** to subject to vigorous assault — **let one's hair down :** to act without pretense or self-restraint — **let rip 1 :** to utter or release without restraint ⟨*let* 'er *rip*⟩ **2 :** to do or utter something without restraint ⟨*let rip* at the press⟩ — **let the cat out of the bag :** to give away a secret

-let *n suffix* [ME, fr. MF *-elet,* fr. *-el,* dim. suffix (fr. L *-ellus*) + *-et*] **1 :** small one ⟨book*let*⟩ **2 :** article worn on ⟨wrist*let*⟩

let alone *conj* (1765) **:** to say nothing of **:** not to mention — used esp. to emphasize the improbability of a contrasting example ⟨he would never walk again *let alone* play golf —*Sports Illus.*⟩ ⟨how many ever see an Ambassador or Minister, *let alone* a President —Robert Lacville⟩

letch \ˈlech\ *n* [back-formation fr. *letcher,* alter. of *lecher*] (1757) **1 :** CRAVING; *specif* **:** sexual desire **2** [by shortening & alter.] **:** LECHER

let·down \ˈlet-ˌdau̇n\ *n* (1768) **1 a :** DISCOURAGEMENT, DISAPPOINTMENT ⟨his latest novel is a ～⟩ **b :** a slackening of effort **:** RELAXATION **2 :** the descent of an aircraft or spacecraft to the point at which a landing approach is begun **3 :** a physiological response of a lactating mammal to suckling and allied stimuli whereby previously secreted milk from the acini is expelled into ducts and drawn through the nipple

let down *vt* (12c) **1 :** to allow to descend gradually **2 a :** to fail to support ⟨felt her parents had *let* her *down*⟩ **b :** DISAPPOINT ⟨the plot *lets* you *down* at the end⟩ ⟨afraid of *letting* his father *down*⟩

1**le·thal** \ˈlē-thəl\ *adj* [L *letalis, lethalis,* fr. *letum* death] (ca. 1604) **1 a :** of, relating to, or causing death ⟨death by ～ injection⟩ **b :** capable of causing death ⟨～ chemicals⟩ **2 :** gravely damaging or destructive **:** DEVASTATING ⟨a ～ attack on his reputation⟩ **3 :** very potent or effective ⟨a ～ fastball⟩; *also* **:** having a high alcohol content ⟨a ～ rum punch⟩ ***syn*** see DEADLY — **le·thal·i·ty** \lē-ˈtha-lə-tē\ *n* — **le·thal·ly** \ˈlē-thə-lē\ *adv*

2**lethal** *n* (1917) **1 :** an abnormality of genetic origin causing the death of the organism possessing it **2 :** LETHAL GENE

lethal gene *n* (1939) **:** a gene that in some (as homozygous) conditions may prevent development or cause the death of an organism or its germ cells — called also *lethal factor, lethal mutant, lethal mutation*

le·thar·gic \lə-ˈthär-jik, le-\ *adj* (14c) **1 :** of, relating to, or characterized by lethargy **:** SLUGGISH **2 :** INDIFFERENT, APATHETIC — **le·thar·gi·cal·ly** \-ji-k(ə-)lē\ *adv*

leth·ar·gy \ˈle-thər-jē\ *n* [ME *litargie,* fr. ML *litargia,* fr. LL *lethargia,* fr. Gk *lēthargia,* fr. *lēthargos* forgetful, lethargic, irreg. fr. *lēthē*] (14c) **1 :** abnormal drowsiness **2 :** the quality or state of being lazy, sluggish, or indifferent

syn LETHARGY, LANGUOR, LASSITUDE, STUPOR, TORPOR mean physical or mental inertness. LETHARGY implies such drowsiness or aversion to activity as is induced by disease, injury, or drugs ⟨months of *lethargy* followed my accident⟩. LANGUOR suggests inertia induced by an enervating climate or illness or love ⟨*languor* induced by a tropical vacation⟩. LASSITUDE stresses listlessness or indifference resulting from fatigue or poor health ⟨a depression marked by *lassitude*⟩. STUPOR implies a deadening of the mind and senses by shock, narcotics, or intoxicants ⟨lapsed into an alcoholic *stupor*⟩. TORPOR implies a state of suspended animation as of hibernating animals but may suggest merely extreme sluggishness ⟨a once alert mind now in a *torpor*⟩.

le·the \ˈlē-thē\ *n* [L, fr. Gk *Lēthē,* fr. *lēthē* forgetfulness; akin to Gk *lanthanein* to escape notice, *lanthanesthai* to forget — more at LATENT] (14c) **1** *cap* **:** a river in Hades whose waters cause drinkers to forget their past **2 :** OBLIVION, FORGETFULNESS — **le·the·an** \ˈlē-thē-ən, li-ˈthē-\ *adj, often cap*

let on *vi* (1725) **1 :** to make acknowledgment **:** ADMIT ⟨knows more than he *lets on*⟩ **2 :** to reveal a secret ⟨nobody *let on* about the surprise party⟩ **3 :** PRETEND ⟨*let on* to being a stranger⟩

let out *vi* (1888) **:** to conclude a session or performance ⟨school *let out* in June⟩

let's \ˈlets, *in rapid speech* ˈles\ (1567) **:** let us

Lett \ˈlet\ *n* [G *Lette,* ultim. fr. Latvian *latvis*] (1589) **:** LATVIAN 2

1**let·ter** \ˈle-tər\ *n* [ME, fr. AF *lettre,* fr. L *littera* letter of the alphabet, *litterae,* pl., epistle, literature] (13c) **1 :** a symbol usu. written or printed representing a speech sound and constituting a unit of an alphabet **2 a :** a direct or personal written or printed message addressed to a person or organization **b :** a written communication containing a grant — usu. used in pl. **3** *pl but sing or pl in constr* **a :** LITERATURE, BELLES LETTRES **b :** LEARNING **4 :** the strict or outward sense or significance ⟨the ～ of the law⟩ **5 a :** a single piece of type **b :** a style of

type 6 : the initial of a school awarded to a student for achievement usu. in athletics
[2]**letter** *vt* (1668) **1 :** to set down in letters : PRINT **2 :** to mark with letters ~ *vi* : to win an athletic letter — **let·ter·er** \-tər-ər\ *n*
[3]**let·ter** \ˈle-tər\ *n* (1552) : one that rents or leases
letter bomb *n* (1973) : an explosive device concealed in an envelope and mailed to the intended victim
letter box *n* (1772) *Brit* : MAILBOX 1
let·ter·boxed \ˈle-tər-ˌbäkst\ *also* **let·ter·box** \-ˌbäks\ *adj* [perh. fr. the resemblance of the picture on the TV screen or the bands above and below the picture to slots in a mailbox] (1989) *of a video recording* : formatted so as to display the full rectangular frame of a wide-screen motion picture — **let·ter·box·ing** \-ˌbäk-siŋ\ *n*
letter carrier *n* (ca. 1552) : a person who delivers mail
let·tered \ˈle-tərd\ *adj* (14c) **1 a :** LEARNED, EDUCATED **b :** of, relating to, or characterized by learning : CULTURED **2 :** inscribed with or as if with letters
let·ter·form \ˈle-tər-ˌfȯrm\ *n* (1908) : the shape of a letter of an alphabet esp. from the standpoint of design or development
let·ter·head \-ˌhed\ *n* (ca. 1887) **1 :** stationery printed or engraved usu. with the name and address of an organization; *also* : a sheet of such stationery **2 :** the heading at the top of a letterhead
let·ter·ing \ˈle-tə-riŋ\ *n* (1789) : letters used in an inscription
let·ter·man \ˈle-tər-mən\ *n* (1926) : an athlete who has earned a letter in a school sport
letter of credence (14c) : a formal document attesting to the power of a diplomatic agent to act for the issuing government — called also *letters of credence*
letter of credit (1645) **1 :** a letter addressed by a banker to a correspondent certifying that a person named therein is entitled to draw on the writer's credit up to a certain sum **2 :** a letter addressed by a banker to a person to whom credit is given authorizing drafts on the issuing bank or on a bank in the person's country up to a certain sum and guaranteeing to accept the drafts if duly made
letter of intent (ca. 1942) : a written statement of the intention to enter into a formal agreement
let·ter–per·fect \ˈle-tər-ˈpər-fikt\ *adj* (1845) : correct to the smallest detail; *esp* : VERBATIM
let·ter·press \ˈle-tər-ˌpres\ *n* (ca. 1765) **1 :** the process of printing from an inked raised surface esp. when the paper is impressed directly upon the surface **2** *chiefly Brit* : text (as of a book) distinct from pictorial illustrations
letters close \-ˈklōs\ *n pl* (1891) : letters issued by a government or sovereign to a private person in a private matter
letter sheet *n* (1845) : a sheet of stationery that can be folded and sealed with the message inside to form its own envelope
letters of administration (15c) : a letter evidencing the right of an administrator to administer the goods or estate of a deceased person
letters of marque \-ˈmärk\ (15c) : written authority granted to a private person by a government to seize the subjects of a foreign state or their goods; *specif* : a license granted to a private person to fit out an armed ship to plunder the enemy
let·ter·spac·ing \ˈle-tər-ˌspā-siŋ\ *n* (1917) : insertion of space between the letters of a word
letters patent *n pl* (14c) : a writing (as from a sovereign) that confers on a designated person a grant in a form open for public inspection
[1]**Lett·ish** \ˈle-tish\ *adj* (1831) : of or relating to the Latvians or their language
[2]**Lettish** *n* (1841) : LATVIAN 1
let·tre de ca·chet \ˈle-trə-də-ˌka-ˈshā\ *n, pl* **lettres de cachet** \-trə(z)-\ [F, lit., letter with a seal] (1718) : a letter bearing an official seal and usu. authorizing imprisonment without trial of a named person
let·tuce \ˈle-təs\ *n* [ME *letuse,* fr. AF *letuse,* prob. fr. pl. of *letue* lettuce plant, fr. L *lactuca,* fr. *lact-, lac* milk; fr. its milky juice — more at GALAXY] (14c) : any of a genus (*Lactuca*) of composite plants; *esp* : a common garden vegetable (*L. sativa*) whose succulent leaves are used esp. in salads
let·up \ˈlet-ˌəp\ *n* (1837) : a lessening of effort, activity, or intensity
let up *vi* (1787) **1 a :** to diminish or slow down : SLACKEN **b :** CEASE, STOP **2 :** to become less severe — used with *on*
leu \ˈlā-ü\ *n, pl* **lei** \ˈlā\ [Rom, lit., lion, fr. L *leo* — more at LION] (1879) — see MONEY table
leuc- *or* **leuco-** *chiefly Brit var of* LEUK-
leu·cine \ˈlü-ˌsēn\ *n* [F, fr. *leuc-* leuk-] (1826) : a white crystalline essential amino acid $C_6H_{13}NO_2$ obtained by the hydrolysis of most dietary proteins
leu·cite \ˈlü-ˌsīt\ *n* [G *Leuzit,* fr. *leuz-* leuk-] (1799) : a white or gray mineral consisting of a silicate of potassium and aluminum and occurring in igneous rocks — **leu·cit·ic** \lü-ˈsi-tik\ *adj*
leu·co·ci·din \ˌlü-kə-ˈsī-dᵊn\ *n* [ISV *leuc-* + *-cide* + [1]*-in*] (1894) : a bacterial substance that destroys white blood cells
leu·co·plast \ˈlü-kə-ˌplast\ *n* [ISV] (1886) : a colorless plastid esp. in the cytoplasm of interior plant tissues that is potentially capable of developing into a chloroplast
leuk- *or* **leuko-** *comb form* [NL *leuc-, leuco-,* fr. Gk *leuk-, leuko-,* fr. *leukos* — more at LIGHT] **1 :** white : colorless : weakly colored ⟨*leuko*cyte⟩ ⟨*leuko*rrhea⟩ **2 :** leukocyte ⟨*leuk*emia⟩ **3 :** white matter of the brain ⟨*leuko*tomy⟩
leu·kae·mia *chiefly Brit var of* LEUKEMIA
leu·kae·mo·gen·e·sis *chiefly Brit var of* LEUKEMOGENESIS
leu·ke·mia \lü-ˈkē-mē-ə\ *n* [NL] (ca. 1855) : an acute or chronic disease in humans and other warm-blooded animals characterized by an abnormal increase in the number of white blood cells in the tissues and often in the blood — **leu·ke·mic** \-mik\ *adj or n*
leu·ke·mo·gen·e·sis \lü-ˌkē-mə-ˈje-nə-səs\ *n* [NL] (1942) : induction or production of leukemia — **leu·ke·mo·gen·ic** \-ˈje-nik\ *adj*
leu·ke·moid \-ˌmȯid\ *adj* (1926) : resembling leukemia but not involving the same changes in the blood-forming organs
leu·ko·cyte \ˈlü-kə-ˌsīt\ *n* [ISV] (1870) : WHITE BLOOD CELL — **leu·ko·cyt·ic** \ˌlü-kə-ˈsi-tik\ *adj*
leu·ko·cy·to·sis \ˌlü-kə-sī-ˈtō-səs, -kə-sə-\ *n* [NL] (1866) : an increase in the number of white blood cells in the circulating blood
leu·ko·dys·tro·phy \ˌlü-kō-ˈdis-trə-fē\ *n, pl* **-phies** (1960) : any of several genetically determined diseases characterized by progressive degeneration of myelin in the brain, spinal cord, and peripheral nerves
leu·ko·pe·nia \ˌlü-kə-ˈpē-nē-ə\ *n* [NL] (1898) : a condition in which the number of white blood cells circulating in the blood is abnormally low — **leu·ko·pe·nic** \-nik\ *adj*
leu·ko·pla·kia \ˌlü-kō-ˈplā-kē-ə\ *n* [NL, fr. *leuk-* + Gk *plak-, plax* flat surface — more at FLUKE] (ca. 1888) : an abnormal condition in which thickened white patches of epithelium occur on the mucous membranes (as of the mouth or vulva); *also* : a lesion or lesioned area of leukoplakia — **leu·ko·pla·kic** \-ˈplā-kik\ *adj*
leu·ko·poi·e·sis \-pȯi-ˈē-səs\ *n* [NL] (ca. 1913) : the formation of white blood cells — **leu·ko·poi·et·ic** \-ˈe-tik\ *adj*
leu·kor·rhea \ˌlü-kə-ˈrē-ə\ *n* [NL] (ca. 1797) : a whitish viscid discharge from the vagina resulting from inflammation or congestion of the mucous membrane — **leu·kor·rhe·al** \-ˈrē-əl\ *adj*
leu·ko·sis \lü-ˈkō-səs\ *n, pl* **-ko·ses** \-ˌsēz\ [NL] (1922) : LEUKEMIA; *esp* : any of various leukemic diseases of poultry
leu·kot·o·my \lü-ˈkä-tə-mē\ *n, pl* **-mies** (1937) : LOBOTOMY
leu·ko·tri·ene \ˌlü-kō-ˈtrī-ˌēn\ *n* (1979) : any of a group of eicosanoids that participate in allergic responses (as bronchial constriction)
lev \ˈlef\ *n, pl* **le·va** \ˈle-və\ [Bulg, lit., lion] (ca. 1900) — see MONEY table
Lev *or* **Levit** *abbr* Leviticus
lev- *or* **levo-** *comb form* [F *lévo-,* fr. L *laevus* left; akin to Gk *laios* left] **1 :** levorotatory ⟨*lev*ulose⟩ **2 :** to the left ⟨*levo*rotatory⟩
Le·val·loi·si·an \ˌle-və-ˈlȯi-zē-ən, lə-ˌval-ˈwä-zē-\ *adj* [*Levallois*-Perret, suburb of Paris, France] (1932) : of or relating to a Middle Paleolithic culture characterized by a technique of manufacturing tools by striking flakes from a flint nodule
le·vam·i·sole \lə-ˈva-mə-ˌsōl\ *n* [perh. fr. *lev-* + *-amisole* (alter. of *imidazole*)] (1969) : an anthelmintic drug $C_{11}H_{12}N_2S$ administered in the form of its hydrochloride that also possesses immunomodulatory properties and is used esp. in the treatment of colon cancer
le·vant \lə-ˈvant\ *vi* [perh. fr. Sp *levantar* to break camp, ultim. fr. L *levare*] (1797) *chiefly Brit* : to run away from a debt
le·vant·er \lə-ˈvan-tər\ *n* (1668) **1** *cap* : a native or inhabitant of the Levant **2 :** a strong easterly Mediterranean wind
Le·vant storax \lə-ˈvant-\ *n* (1937) : STORAX 1a
le·va·tor \li-ˈvā-tər\ *n, pl* **lev·a·to·res** \ˌle-və-ˈtȯr-(ˌ)ēz\ *or* **levators** [NL, fr. L *levare* to raise — more at LEVER] (1615) : a muscle that serves to raise a body part — compare DEPRESSOR
[1]**le·vee** \ˈle-vē; lə-ˈvē, -ˈvā\ *n* [F *lever,* fr. MF, act of arising, fr. (*se*) *lever* to rise] (1672) **1 :** a reception held by a person of distinction on rising from bed **2 :** an afternoon assembly at which the British sovereign or his or her representative receives only men **3 :** a reception usu. in honor of a particular person
[2]**lev·ee** \ˈle-vē\ *n* [F *levée,* fr. OF, act of raising, fr. *lever* to raise — more at LEVER] (ca. 1720) **1 a :** an embankment for preventing flooding **b :** a river landing place : PIER **2 :** a continuous dike or ridge (as of earth) for confining the irrigation areas of land to be flooded
[3]**lev·ee** \ˈle-vē\ *vt* **lev·eed; lev·ee·ing** (1832) : to provide with a levee
[1]**lev·el** \ˈle-vəl\ *n* [ME, plumb line, fr. AF *livel,* fr. VL **libellum,* alter. of L *libella,* fr. dim. of *libra* weight, balance] (14c) **1 :** a device for establishing a horizontal line or plane by means of a bubble in a liquid that shows adjustment to the horizontal by movement to the center of a slightly bowed glass tube **2 :** a measurement of the difference of altitude of two points by means of a level **3 :** horizontal condition; *esp* : equilibrium of a fluid marked by a horizontal surface of even altitude ⟨water seeks its own ~⟩ **4 a :** an approximately horizontal line or surface taken as an index of altitude **b :** a practically horizontal surface or area (as of land) **5 :** a position in a scale or rank (as of achievement, significance, or value) ⟨funded at the national ~⟩ ⟨the job appeals to me on many ~*s*⟩ **6 a :** a line or surface that cuts perpendicularly all plumb lines that it meets and hence would everywhere coincide with a surface of still water **b :** the plane of the horizon or a line in it **7 :** a horizontal passage in a mine intended for regular working and transportation **8 :** a concentration of a constituent esp. of a body fluid (as blood) **9 :** the magnitude of a quantity considered in relation to an arbitrary reference value; *broadly* : MAGNITUDE, INTENSITY ⟨a high ~ of hostility⟩ — **on the level :** BONA FIDE, HONEST
[2]**level** *vb* **-eled** *or* **-elled; -el·ing** *or* **-el·ling** \ˈle-və-liŋ, ˈlev-liŋ\ *vt* (15c) **1 :** to make (a line or surface) horizontal : make flat or level ⟨~ a field⟩ ⟨~ off a house lot⟩ **2 a :** to bring to a horizontal aiming position **b :** AIM, DIRECT ⟨~*ed* a charge of fraud⟩ **3 :** to bring to a common level or plane : EQUALIZE ⟨love ~*s* all ranks —W. S. Gilbert⟩ **4 a :** to lay level with or as if with the ground : RAZE **b :** to knock down ⟨~*ed* him with one punch⟩ **5 :** to make (as color) even or uniform **6 :** to find the heights of different points in (a piece of land) esp. with a surveyor's level ~ *vi* **1 :** to attain or come to a level ⟨the plane ~*ed* off at 10,000 feet⟩ **2 :** to aim a gun or other weapon horizontally **3 :** to bring persons or things to a level **4 :** to deal frankly and openly
[3]**level** *adj* (15c) **1 a :** having no part higher than another : conforming to the curvature of the liquid parts of the earth's surface **b :** parallel with the plane of the horizon : HORIZONTAL **2 a :** even or unvarying in height **b :** equal in advantage, progression, or standing **c :** proceeding monotonously or uneventfully **d** (1) : STEADY, UNWAVERING ⟨gave him a ~ look⟩ (2) : CALM, UNEXCITED ⟨spoke in ~ tones⟩ **3 :** REASONABLE, BALANCED ⟨arrive at a justly proportional and ~ judgment on this affair —Sir Winston Churchill⟩ **4 :** distributed evenly ⟨~ stress⟩ **5 :** being a surface perpendicular to all lines of force in a field of force : EQUIPOTENTIAL **6 :** suited to a particular rank or plane of ability or achievement ⟨top-*level* thinking⟩ **7 :** of or relating to the spreading out of a cost or charge in even payments over a period of time — **lev·el·ly** \ˈle-və(l)-lē\ *adv* — **lev·el·ness** \-vəl-nəs\ *n* — **level best :** very best
syn LEVEL, FLAT, PLANE, EVEN, SMOOTH mean having a surface without bends, curves, or irregularities. LEVEL applies to a horizontal surface that lies on a line parallel with the horizon ⟨the vast prairies are nearly *level*⟩. FLAT applies to a surface devoid of noticeable curvatures, prominences, or depressions ⟨the work surface must be *flat*⟩. PLANE applies to any real or imaginary flat surface in which a straight line between any two points on it lies wholly within that surface ⟨the *plane* sides of a crystal⟩. EVEN applies to a surface that is noticeably

flat or level or to a line that is observably straight ‹trim the hedge so it is *even*›. SMOOTH applies esp. to a polished surface free of irregularities ‹a *smooth* skating rink›.

level crossing *n* (ca. 1841) *Brit* : GRADE CROSSING

lev•el•er *or* **lev•el•ler** \ˈle-və-lər, ˈlev-lər\ *n* (1598) **1** : one that levels **2 a** *cap* : one of a group of radicals arising during the English Civil War and advocating equality before the law and religious toleration **b** : one favoring the removal of political, social, or economic inequalities **c** : something that tends to reduce or eliminate differences among individuals

lev•el•head•ed \ˌle-vəl-ˈhe-dəd\ *adj* (1879) : having or showing sound judgment : SENSIBLE — **lev•el•head•ed•ness** *n*

leveling rod *n* (1855) : a graduated rod used in measuring the vertical distance between a point on the ground and the line of sight of a surveyor's level

level off *vi* (1917) : to approach or reach a steady rate, volume, or amount : STABILIZE ‹expect prices to *level off*›

level of significance (1925) : the probability of rejecting the null hypothesis in a statistical test when it is true — called also *significance level*

[1]**le•ver** \ˈle-vər, ˈlē-\ *n* [ME, fr. AF *levier, lever,* fr. *lever* to raise, fr. L *levare,* fr. *levis* light in weight — more at LIGHT] (14c) **1 a** : a bar used for prying or dislodging something **b** : an inducing or compelling force : TOOL ‹use food as a political ~ —*Time*› **2 a** : a rigid piece that transmits and modifies force or motion when forces are applied at two points and it turns about a third; *specif* : a rigid bar used to exert a pressure or sustain a weight at one point of its length by the application of a force at a second and turning at a third on a fulcrum **b** : a projecting piece by which a mechanism is operated or adjusted

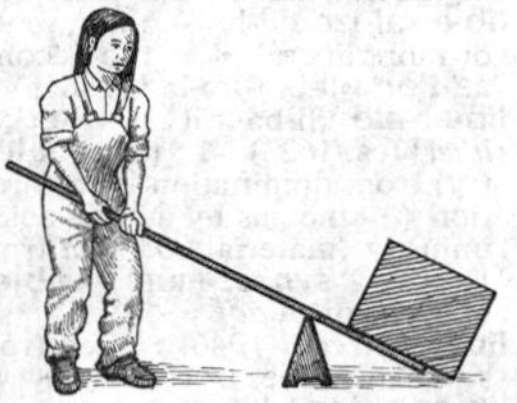
lever 2a

[2]**lever** *vt* **le•vered; le•ver•ing** \ˈle-və-riŋ, ˈlē-; ˈlev-riŋ, ˈlēv-\ (1876) **1** : to pry, raise, or move with or as if with a lever **2** : to operate (a device) in the manner of a lever

[1]**le•ver•age** \ˈle-və-rij, ˈlē-; ˈlev-rij, ˈlēv-\ *n* (1830) **1** : the action of a lever or the mechanical advantage gained by it **2** : POWER, EFFECTIVENESS ‹trying to gain more political ~› **3** : the use of credit to enhance one's speculative capacity

[2]**leverage** *vt* **-aged; -ag•ing** (1957) **1** : to provide (as a corporation) or supplement (as money) with leverage; *also* : to enhance as if by supplying with financial leverage **2** : to use for gain : EXPLOIT ‹shamelessly ~ the system to their advantage —Alexander Wolff›

lev•er•aged \ˈle-və-rijd, ˈlē-; ˈlev-rijd, ˈlēv-\ *adj* (1953) **1** : having a high proportion of debt relative to equity **2** *of the purchase of a company* : made with borrowed money that is secured by the assets of the company bought ‹a ~ buyout›

lev•er•et \ˈle-və-rət, ˈlev-rət\ *n* [ME, fr. AF, hare skin, fr. *levere, levre* hare, fr. L *lepor-, lepus*] (15c) : a hare in its first year

Le•vi \ˈlē-ˌvī\ *n* [LL, from Heb *Lēwī*] (bef. 12c) : a son of Jacob and the traditional eponymous ancestor of the priestly tribe of Levi

levi•able \ˈle-vē-ə-bəl\ *adj* (15c) : capable of being levied or levied upon

le•vi•a•than \li-ˈvī-ə-thən\ *n* [ME, fr. LL, fr. Heb *liwyāthān*] (14c) **1 a** *often cap* : a sea monster defeated by Yahweh in various scriptural accounts **b** : a large sea animal **2** *cap* : the political state; *esp* : a totalitarian state having a vast bureaucracy **3** : something large or formidable — **leviathan** *adj*

lev•i•gate \ˈle-və-ˌgāt\ *vt* **-gat•ed; -gat•ing** [L *levigatus,* pp. of *levigare* to make smooth, fr. *levis* smooth (akin to Gk *leios* smooth and perh. to L *linere* to smear) + *-igare* (akin to *agere* to drive) — more at LIME, AGENT] (1612) **1** : POLISH, SMOOTH **2 a** : to grind to a fine smooth powder while in moist condition **b** : to separate (fine powder) from coarser material by suspending in a liquid — **lev•i•ga•tion** \ˌle-və-ˈgā-shən\ *n*

lev•in \ˈle-vən\ *n* [ME *levene*] (13c) *archaic* : LIGHTNING

le•vi•rate \ˈle-və-rət, ˈlē-, -ˌrāt\ *n* [L *levir* husband's brother; akin to OE *tācor* husband's brother, Gk *daēr*] (1725) : the sometimes compulsory marriage of a widow to a brother of her deceased husband — **le•vi•rat•ic** \ˌle-və-ˈra-tik, ˌlē-\ *adj*

Le•vi's \ˈlē-ˌvīz\ *trademark* — used esp. for blue denim jeans

lev•i•tate \ˈle-və-ˌtāt\ *vb* **-tat•ed; -tat•ing** [*levity*] *vi* (1673) : to rise or float in or as if in the air esp. in seeming defiance of gravitation ~ *vt* : to cause to levitate

lev•i•ta•tion \ˌle-və-ˈtā-shən\ *n* (1668) : the act or process of levitating; *esp* : the rising or lifting of a person or thing by means held to be supernatural — **lev•i•ta•tion•al** \-shnəl, -shə-nᵊl\ *adj*

Le•vite \ˈlē-ˌvīt\ *n* (14c) : a member of the priestly Hebrew tribe of Levi; *specif* : a Levite of non-Aaronic descent assigned to lesser ceremonial offices under the Levitical priests of the family of Aaron

Le•vit•i•cal \li-ˈvi-ti-kəl\ *adj* [LL *Leviticus*] (1535) : of or relating to the Levites or to Leviticus

Le•vit•i•cus \-kəs\ *n* [LL, lit., of the Levites] (bef. 12c) : the third book of canonical Jewish and Christian Scripture consisting mainly of priestly legislation — see BIBLE table

lev•i•ty \ˈle-və-tē\ *n* [L *levitat-, levitas,* fr. *levis* light in weight — more at LIGHT] (1564) **1** : excessive or unseemly frivolity **2** : lack of steadiness : CHANGEABLENESS

le•vo \ˈlē-(ˌ)vō\ *adj* (1906) : LEVOROTATORY

levo- — see LEV-

levo•do•pa \ˌle-və-ˈdō-pə\ *n* (1969) : L-DOPA

le•vo•nor•ges•trel \ˌlē-və-nȯr-ˈjes-trəl\ *n* [lev- + *norgestrel,* a progestin] (1977) : the levorotatory form of a synthetic progestin $C_{21}H_{28}O_2$ used esp. in oral contraceptives

le•vo•ro•ta•to•ry \-ˈrō-tə-ˌtȯr-ē\ *adj* (1864) : turning toward the left or counterclockwise; *specif* : rotating the plane of polarization of light to the left — compare DEXTROROTATORY

lev•u•lose \ˈlev-yə-ˌlōs, -ˌlōz\ *n* [ISV, irreg. fr. *lev-* + [2]*-ose*] (1871) : FRUCTOSE 2

[1]**levy** \ˈle-vē\ *n, pl* **lev•ies** [ME, fr. AF *levé,* lit., raising, fr. *lever* to raise — more at LEVER] (13c) **1 a** : the imposition or collection of an assessment **b** : an amount levied **2 a** : the enlistment or conscription of men for military service **b** : troops raised by levy

[2]**levy** *vb* **lev•ied; levy•ing** *vt* (14c) **1 a** : to impose or collect by legal authority ‹~ a tax› **b** : to require by authority **2** : to enlist or conscript for military service **3** : to carry on (war) : WAGE ~ *vi* : to seize property — **levi•er** *n*

lewd \ˈlüd\ *adj* [ME *lewed* vulgar, fr. OE *lǣwede* laical, ignorant] (14c) **1** *obs* : EVIL, WICKED **2 a** : sexually unchaste or licentious **b** : OBSCENE, VULGAR — **lewd•ly** *adv* — **lewd•ness** *n*

lew•is \ˈlü-əs\ *n* [prob. fr. the name *Lewis*] (1743) : an iron dovetailed tenon that is made in sections, can be fitted into a dovetail mortise, and is used in hoisting large stones

Lew•is acid \ˈlü-əs-\ *n* [Gilbert N. *Lewis* †1946 Am. chemist] (1944) : a substance that is capable of accepting an unshared pair of electrons from a base to form a covalent bond

lew•is•ite \ˈlü-ə-ˌsīt\ *n* [Winford L. *Lewis* †1943 Am. chemist] (1895) : a colorless or brown vesicant liquid $C_2H_2AsCl_3$ developed as a poison gas for war use

lex \ˈleks\ *n, pl* **le•ges** \ˈlā-(ˌ)gās\ [L *leg-, lex*] (ca. 1775) : LAW

lex•eme \ˈlek-ˌsēm\ *n* [Gk *lexis* word, speech + E *-eme* — more at LEXICON] (1938) : a meaningful linguistic unit that is an item in the vocabulary of a language — **lex•em•ic** \lek-ˈsē-mik\ *adj*

lex•i•cal \ˈlek-si-kəl\ *adj* (1836) **1** : of or relating to words or the vocabulary of a language as distinguished from its grammar and construction **2** : of or relating to a lexicon or to lexicography — **lex•i•cal•i•ty** \ˌlek-sə-ˈka-lə-tē\ *n* — **lex•i•cal•ly** \ˈlek-si-k(ə-)lē\ *adv*

lex•i•cal•i•sa•tion *Brit var of* LEXICALIZATION

lex•i•cal•i•za•tion \ˌlek-si-kə-lə-ˈzā-shən\ *n* (1949) **1** : the realization of a meaning in a single word or morpheme rather than in a grammatical construction **2** : the treatment of a formerly freely composed, grammatically regular, and semantically transparent phrase or inflected form as a formally or semantically idiomatic expression — **lex•i•cal•ize** \ˈlek-si-kə-ˌlīz\ *vt*

lexical meaning *n* (1933) : the meaning of the base (as the word *play*) in a paradigm (as *plays, played, playing*) — compare GRAMMATICAL MEANING

lex•i•cog•ra•pher \ˌlek-sə-ˈkä-grə-fər\ *n* [LGk *lexikographos,* fr. *lexikon* + Gk *-graphos* writer, fr. *graphein* to write] (1658) : an author or editor of a dictionary

lex•i•cog•ra•phy \ˌlek-sə-ˈkä-grə-fē\ *n* (1680) **1** : the editing or making of a dictionary **2** : the principles and practices of dictionary making — **lex•i•co•graph•i•cal** \ˌlek-si-kō-ˈgra-fi-kəl\ *or* **lex•i•co•graph•ic** \-fik\ *adj* — **lex•i•co•graph•i•cal•ly** \-fi-k(ə-)lē\ *adv*

lex•i•col•o•gy \ˌlek-sə-ˈkä-lə-jē\ *n* [F *lexicologie,* fr. *lexico-* (fr. LGk *lexiko-,* fr. *lexikon*) + *-logie* -logy] (ca. 1828) : a branch of linguistics concerned with the signification and application of words — **lex•i•co•log•i•cal** \-kō-ˈlä-ji-kəl, -kə-ˈlä-\ *adj* — **lex•i•col•o•gist** \-jist\ *n*

lex•i•con \ˈlek-sə-ˌkän *also* -kən\ *n, pl* **lex•i•ca** \-kə\ *or* **lexicons** [LGk *lexikon,* fr. neut. of *lexikos* of words, fr. Gk *lexis* word, speech, fr. *legein* to say — more at LEGEND] (1580) **1** : a book containing an alphabetical arrangement of the words in a language and their definitions : DICTIONARY **2 a** : the vocabulary of a language, an individual speaker or group of speakers, or a subject **b** : the total stock of morphemes in a language **3** : REPERTOIRE, INVENTORY

lex•is \ˈlek-səs\ *n, pl* **lex•es** \-ˌsēz\ [Gk, speech, word] (1960) : LEXICON 2a

ley *var of* LEA

Ley•den jar \ˈlī-dᵊn-\ *n* [*Leiden, Leyden,* Netherlands] (1825) : an electrical capacitor consisting of a glass jar coated inside and outside with metal foil and having the inner coating connected to a conducting rod passed through an insulating stopper

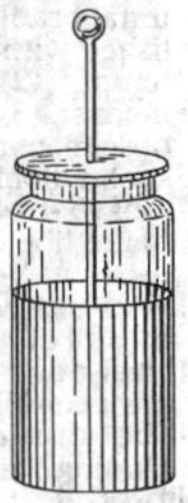
Leyden jar

lf *abbr* lightface

LF *abbr* low frequency

L–form \ˈel-ˌfȯrm\ *n* [*L*ister Institute, London, where it was first isolated] (1948) : a variant bacterium formed esp. under stressful conditions and usu. lacking a cell wall

lg *abbr* **1** large **2** long

LGBT *abbr* lesbian, gay, bisexual, and transgender

LH *abbr* **1** left hand **2** luteinizing hormone

Lha•sa ap•so \ˈlä-sə-ˈäp-(ˌ)sō, ˈla-sə-ˈap-\ *n, pl* **Lhasa apsos** *often cap A* [*Lhasa,* Tibet + Tibetan (Lhasa dial.) *ǝbsɔɔ̀* (written Tibetan *absog*) small hairy dog, Lhasa apso] (1935) : any of a Tibetan breed of small dogs that have a dense coat of long hard straight hair, a heavy fall over the eyes, heavy whiskers and beard, and a well-feathered tail curled over the back — called also *Lhasa*

LHD *abbr* [NL *litterarum humaniorum doctor*] doctor of humane letters; doctor of humanities

L'Ho•pi•tal's rule *or* **L'Hos•pi•tal's rule** \ˌlō-pē-ˈtälz-\ *n* [Guillaume de *l'Hôpital* †1704 Fr. mathematician] (1944) : a theorem in calculus: if at a given point two functions have an infinite limit or zero as a limit and are both differentiable in a neighborhood of this point then the limit of the quotient of the functions is equal to the limit of the quotient of their derivatives provided that this limit exists

Li *symbol* lithium

LI *abbr* Long Island

li•a•bil•i•ty \ˌlī-ə-ˈbi-lə-tē\ *n, pl* **-ties** (1705) **1 a** : the quality or state of being liable **b** : PROBABILITY **2** : something for which one is liable; *esp* : pecuniary obligation : DEBT — usu. used in pl. **3** : one that acts as a disadvantage : DRAWBACK

li•a•ble \ˈlī-ə-bəl, *esp in sense 2 often* ˈlī-bəl\ *adj* [ME *lyable,* fr. AF **liable,* fr. *lier* to bind, fr. L *ligare* — more at LIGATURE] (15c) **1 a** : obligated according to law or equity : RESPONSIBLE **b** : subject to appropriation or attachment **2 a** : being in a position to incur — used with

\ə\ **abut** \ᵊ\ kitten, F table \ər\ **further** \a\ **ash** \ā\ **ace** \ä\ mop, mar \au̇\ **out** \ch\ **chin** \e\ **bet** \ē\ **easy** \g\ **go** \i\ **hit** \ī\ **ice** \j\ **job** \ŋ\ **sing** \ō\ **go** \ȯ\ **law** \ȯi\ **boy** \th\ **thin** \t͟h\ **the** \ü\ **loot** \u̇\ **foot** \y\ **yet** \zh\ **vision, beige** \k̲, ⁿ, œ, ue, ʸ\ *see* Guide to Pronunciation

to ⟨~ to a fine⟩ **b :** exposed or subject to some usu. adverse contingency or action ⟨watch out or you're ~ to fall⟩
syn LIABLE, OPEN, EXPOSED, SUBJECT, PRONE, SUSCEPTIBLE, SENSITIVE mean being by nature or through circumstances likely to experience something adverse. LIABLE implies a possibility or probability of incurring something because of position, nature, or particular situation ⟨*liable* to get lost⟩. OPEN stresses a lack of barriers preventing incurrence ⟨a claim *open* to question⟩. EXPOSED suggests lack of protection or powers of resistance against something actually present or threatening ⟨*exposed* to infection⟩. SUBJECT implies an openness for any reason to something that must be suffered or undergone ⟨all reports are *subject* to review⟩. PRONE stresses natural tendency or propensity to incur something ⟨*prone* to delay⟩. SUSCEPTIBLE implies conditions existing in one's nature or individual constitution that make incurrence probable ⟨very *susceptible* to flattery⟩. SENSITIVE implies a readiness to respond to or be influenced by forces or stimuli ⟨unduly *sensitive* to criticism⟩. ***syn*** see in addition RESPONSIBLE
usage Both *liable* and *apt* when followed by an infinitive are used nearly interchangeably with *likely.* Although conflicting advice has been given over the years, most current commentators accept *apt* when so used. They generally recommend limiting *liable* to situations having an undesirable outcome, and our evidence shows that in edited writing it is more often so used than not.

li·aise \lē-ˈāz\ *vi* **li·aised; li·ais·ing** [back-formation fr. *liaison*] (1928) *chiefly Brit* **1 :** to establish liaison **2 :** to act as a liaison officer

li·ai·son \ˈlē-ə-ˌzän, lē-ˈā-, ÷ˈlā-ə-\ *n* [F, fr. MF, fr. *lier,* fr. OF] (ca. 1648) **1 :** a binding or thickening agent used in cooking **2 a :** a close bond or connection **:** INTERRELATIONSHIP **b :** an illicit sexual relationship **:** AFFAIR 3a **3 a :** communication for establishing and maintaining mutual understanding and cooperation (as between parts of an armed force) **b :** one that establishes and maintains liaison **4 :** the pronunciation of an otherwise absent consonant sound at the end of the first of two consecutive words the second of which begins with a vowel sound and follows without pause

li·a·na \lē-ˈä-nə, -ˈa-\ *also* **li·ane** \-ˈän, -ˈan\ *n* [F *liane*] (1796) **:** any of various usu. woody vines esp. of tropical rain forests that root in the ground

li·ar \ˈlī(-ə)r\ *n* [ME, fr. OE *lēogere,* fr. *lēogan* to lie — more at LIE] (bef. 12c) **:** a person who tells lies

Li·as \ˈlī-əs\ *adj* [*Lias,* division of the European Jurassic, fr. F, fr. E, a limestone rock] (1813) *chiefly Brit* **:** LIASSIC

Li·as·sic \lī-ˈa-sik\ *adj* [modif. of F *liasique,* fr. *Lias*] (1833) **:** of, relating to, or being a subdivision of the European Jurassic

[1]**lib** \ˈlib\ *n* (1970) **:** LIBERATION 2

[2]**lib** *abbr* **1** liberal **2** librarian, library

li·ba·tion \lī-ˈbā-shən\ *n* [ME *libacioun,* fr. L *libation-, libatio,* fr. *libare* to pour as an offering; akin to Gk *leibein* to pour] (14c) **1 a :** an act of pouring a liquid as a sacrifice (as to a deity) **b :** a liquid (as wine) used in a libation **2 a :** an act or instance of drinking often ceremoniously **b :** BEVERAGE; *esp* **:** a drink containing alcohol — **li·ba·tion·ary** \-shə-ˌner-ē\ *adj*

lib·ber \ˈli-bər\ *n* [*lib*] (1971) *often disparaging* **:** a person who supports a liberation movement esp. for women

li·bec·cio \li-ˈbe-chē-ˌō, -ˈbe-chō\ *or* **li·bec·chio** \-ˈbe-kē-ˌō\ *n* [It *libeccio*] (1667) **:** a southwest wind in Italy

[1]**li·bel** \ˈlī-bəl\ *n* [ME, written declaration, fr. AF, fr. L *libellus,* dim. of *liber* book] (14c) **1 a :** a written statement in which a plaintiff in certain courts sets forth the cause of action or the relief sought **b** *archaic* **:** a handbill esp. attacking or defaming someone **2 a :** a written or oral defamatory statement or representation that conveys an unjustly unfavorable impression **b** (1) **:** a statement or representation published without just cause and tending to expose another to public contempt (2) **:** defamation of a person by written or representational means (3) **:** the publication of blasphemous, treasonable, seditious, or obscene writings or pictures (4) **:** the act, tort, or crime of publishing such a libel

[2]**libel** *vb* **-beled** *or* **-belled; -bel·ing** *or* **-bel·ling** \-b(ə-)liŋ\ *vi* (1588) **:** to make libelous statements ~ *vt* **:** to make or publish a libel against — **li·bel·er** \-b(ə-)lər\ *n* — **li·bel·ist** \-bə-list\ *n*

li·bel·ant *or* **li·bel·lant** \ˈlī-bə-lənt\ *n* (1596) **:** one that institutes a suit by a libel

li·bel·ee *or* **li·bel·lee** \ˌlī-bə-ˈlē\ *n* (ca. 1856) **:** one against whom a libel has been filed in a court

li·bel·ous *or* **li·bel·lous** \ˈlī-b(ə-)ləs\ *adj* (1619) **:** constituting or including a libel **:** DEFAMATORY ⟨a ~ statement⟩

[1]**lib·er·al** \ˈli-b(ə-)rəl\ *adj* [ME, fr. AF, fr. L *liberalis* suitable for a freeman, generous, fr. *liber* free; perh. akin to OE *lēodan* to grow, Gk *eleutheros* free] (14c) **1 a :** of, relating to, or based on the liberal arts ⟨~ education⟩ **b** *archaic* **:** of or befitting a man of free birth **2 a :** marked by generosity **:** OPENHANDED ⟨a ~ giver⟩ **b :** given or provided in a generous and openhanded way ⟨a ~ meal⟩ **c :** AMPLE, FULL **3** *obs* **:** lacking moral restraint **:** LICENTIOUS **4 :** not literal or strict **:** LOOSE ⟨a ~ translation⟩ **5 :** BROAD-MINDED; *esp* **:** not bound by authoritarianism, orthodoxy, or traditional forms **6 a :** of, favoring, or based upon the principles of liberalism **b** *cap* **:** of or constituting a political party advocating or associated with the principles of political liberalism; *esp* **:** of or constituting a political party in the United Kingdom associated with ideals of individual esp. economic freedom, greater individual participation in government, and constitutional, political, and administrative reforms designed to secure these objectives — **lib·er·al·ly** \-b(ə-)rə-lē\ *adv* — **lib·er·al·ness** *n*
syn LIBERAL, GENEROUS, BOUNTIFUL, MUNIFICENT mean giving or given freely and unstintingly. LIBERAL suggests openhandedness in the giver and largeness in the thing or amount given ⟨a teacher *liberal* with her praise⟩. GENEROUS stresses warmhearted readiness to give more than size or importance of the gift ⟨a *generous* offer of help⟩. BOUNTIFUL suggests lavish, unremitting giving or providing ⟨children spoiled by *bountiful* presents⟩. MUNIFICENT suggests a scale of giving appropriate to lords or princes ⟨a *munificent* foundation grant⟩.

[2]**liberal** *n* (1820) **:** a person who is liberal: as **a :** one who is open-minded or not strict in the observance of orthodox, traditional, or established forms or ways **b** *cap* **:** a member or supporter of a liberal political party **c :** an advocate or adherent of liberalism esp. in individual rights

liberal arts *n pl* (14c) **1 :** the medieval studies comprising the trivium and quadrivium **2 :** college or university studies (as language, philosophy, literature, abstract science) intended to provide chiefly general knowledge and to develop general intellectual capacities (as reason and judgment) as opposed to professional or vocational skills

lib·er·al·ise *Brit var of* LIBERALIZE

lib·er·al·ism \ˈli-b(ə-)rə-ˌli-zəm\ *n* (1817) **1 :** the quality or state of being liberal **2 a** *often cap* **:** a movement in modern Protestantism emphasizing intellectual liberty and the spiritual and ethical content of Christianity **b :** a theory in economics emphasizing individual freedom from restraint and usu. based on free competition, the self-regulating market, and the gold standard **c :** a political philosophy based on belief in progress, the essential goodness of the human race, and the autonomy of the individual and standing for the protection of political and civil liberties; *specif* **:** such a philosophy that considers government as a crucial instrument for amelioration of social inequities (as those involving race, gender, or class) **d** *cap* **:** the principles and policies of a Liberal party — **lib·er·al·ist** \-b(ə-)rə-list\ *n or adj* — **lib·er·al·is·tic** \ˌli-b(ə-)rə-ˈlis-tik\ *adj*

lib·er·al·i·ty \ˌli-bə-ˈra-lə-tē\ *n, pl* **-ties** (14c) **:** the quality or state of being liberal; *also* **:** an instance of this

lib·er·al·ize \ˈli-b(ə-)rə-ˌlīz\ *vb* **-ized; -iz·ing** *vt* (1774) **:** to make liberal or more liberal ~ *vi* **:** to become liberal or more liberal — **lib·er·al·i·za·tion** \ˌli-b(ə-)rə-lə-ˈzā-shən\ *n* — **lib·er·al·iz·er** \ˈli-b(ə-)rə-ˌlī-zər\ *n*

lib·er·ate \ˈli-bə-ˌrāt\ *vt* **-at·ed; -at·ing** [L *liberatus,* pp. of *liberare,* fr. *liber*] (ca. 1623) **1 :** to set at liberty **:** FREE; *specif* **:** to free (as a country) from domination by a foreign power **2 :** to free from combination ⟨~ the gas by adding acid⟩ **3 :** to take or take over illegally or unjustly ⟨material *liberated* from a nearby construction site —Thorne Dreyer⟩ ***syn*** see FREE — **lib·er·a·tor** \-ˌā-tər\ *n* — **lib·er·a·to·ry** \ˈli-b(ə-)rə-ˌtȯr-ē\ *adj*

liberated *adj* (1946) **:** freed from or opposed to traditional social and sexual attitudes or roles ⟨a ~ woman⟩ ⟨a ~ marriage⟩

lib·er·a·tion \ˌli-bə-ˈrā-shən\ *n* (15c) **1 :** the act of liberating **:** the state of being liberated **2 :** a movement seeking equal rights and status for a group ⟨women's ~⟩ — **lib·er·a·tion·ist** \-sh(ə-)nist\ *n*

liberation theology *n* (1972) **:** a religious movement esp. among Roman Catholic clergy in Latin America that combines political philosophy usu. of a Marxist orientation with a theology of salvation as liberation from injustice — **liberation theologian** *n*

lib·er·tar·i·an \ˌli-bər-ˈter-ē-ən, -ˈte-rē-\ *n* (1789) **1 :** an advocate of the doctrine of free will **2 a :** a person who upholds the principles of individual liberty esp. of thought and action **b** *cap* **:** a member of a political party advocating libertarian principles — **libertarian** *adj* — **lib·er·tar·i·an·ism** \-ē-ə-ˌni-zəm\ *n*

lib·er·tin·age \ˈli-bər-ˌtē-nij\ *n* (1611) **:** LIBERTINISM

lib·er·tine \ˈli-bər-ˌtēn\ *n* [ME *libertyn* freedman, fr. L *libertinus,* fr. *libertinus,* adj., of a freedman, fr. *libertus* freedman, fr. *liber*] (1577) **1** *usu disparaging* **:** a freethinker esp. in religious matters **2 :** a person who is unrestrained by convention or morality; *specif* **:** one leading a dissolute life — **libertine** *adj*

lib·er·tin·ism \ˈli-bər-ˌtē-ˌni-zəm, -tə-\ *n* (1611) **:** the quality or state of being libertine **:** the behavior of a libertine

lib·er·ty \ˈli-bər-tē\ *n, pl* **-ties** [ME, fr. AF *liberté,* fr. L *libertat-, libertas,* fr. *liber* free — more at LIBERAL] (14c) **1 :** the quality or state of being free: **a :** the power to do as one pleases **b :** freedom from physical restraint **c :** freedom from arbitrary or despotic control **d :** the positive enjoyment of various social, political, or economic rights and privileges **e :** the power of choice **2 a :** a right or immunity enjoyed by prescription or by grant **:** PRIVILEGE **b :** permission esp. to go freely within specified limits **3 :** an action going beyond normal limits: as **a :** a breach of etiquette or propriety **:** FAMILIARITY **b :** RISK, CHANCE ⟨took foolish *liberties* with his health⟩ **c :** a violation of rules or a deviation from standard practice **d :** a distortion of fact **4 :** a short authorized absence from naval duty usu. for less than 48 hours ***syn*** see FREEDOM — **at liberty 1 :** FREE **2 :** at leisure **:** UNOCCUPIED

liberty cap *n* (1803) **:** a close-fitting conical cap used as a symbol of liberty by the French revolutionists and in the U.S. before 1800

liberty pole *n* (1770) **:** a tall flagstaff surmounted by a liberty cap or the flag of a republic and set up as a symbol of liberty

li·bid·i·nal \lə-ˈbi-də-nəl, -ˈbid-nᵊl\ *adj* (1922) **:** of or relating to the libido ⟨~ impulses⟩ — **li·bid·i·nal·ly** *adv*

li·bid·i·nous \-də-nəs, -ˈbid-nəs\ *adj* [ME, fr. L *libidinosus,* fr. *libidin-, libido*] (15c) **1 :** having or marked by lustful desires **:** LASCIVIOUS **2 :** LIBIDINAL — **li·bid·i·nous·ly** *adv* — **li·bid·i·nous·ness** *n*

li·bi·do \lə-ˈbē-(ˌ)dō *also* ˈli-bə-ˌdō\ *n, pl* **-dos** [NL *libidin-, libido,* fr. L, desire, lust, fr. *libēre* to please — more at LOVE] (1909) **1 :** instinctual psychic energy that in psychoanalytic theory is derived from primitive biological urges (as for sexual pleasure or self-preservation) and that is expressed in conscious activity **2 :** sexual drive

li·bra *for 1 & 2a* ˈlē-brə, *sometimes* ˈlī-brə, *for 2b* ˈlē-brə *or* ˈlēv-rə\ *n* [ME, fr. L (gen. *Librae*), lit., scales, pound] (bef. 12c) **1** *cap* **a :** a southern zodiacal constellation between Virgo and Scorpio represented by a pair of scales **b** (1) **:** the seventh sign of the zodiac in astrology — see ZODIAC table (2) **:** one born under the sign of Libra **2 a** *pl* **li·brae** \ˈlī-ˌbrē, ˈlē-ˌbrī\ [L] **:** an ancient Roman unit of weight equal to 327.45 grams **b** [Sp & Pg, fr. L] **:** any of various Spanish, Portuguese, Colombian, or Venezuelan units of weight

Li·bran \ˈlē-brən, ˈlī-\ *n* (1911) **:** LIBRA 1b(2)

li·brar·i·an \lī-ˈbrer-ē-ən, -ˈbre-rē-\ *n* (1671) **:** a specialist in the care or management of a library — **li·brar·i·an·ship** \-ˌship\ *n*

li·brary \ˈlī-ˌbrer-ē, -ˌbre-rē; *Brit usu & US sometimes* -brər-ē; *US sometimes* -brē, ÷-ˌber-ē, -ˌbe-rē\ *n, pl* **-brar·ies** [ME, fr. AF *librarie,* ML *librarium,* fr. L, neut. of *librarius* of books, fr. *libr-, liber* inner bark, rind, book] (14c) **1 a :** a place in which literary, musical, artistic, or reference materials (as books, manuscripts, recordings, or films) are kept for use but not for sale **b :** a collection of such materials **2 a :** a collection resembling or suggesting a library **b :** MORGUE 2 **3 a :** a series of related books issued by a publisher **b :** a collection of publications on the same subject **4 :** a collection of cloned DNA fragments that are maintained in a suitable cellular environment and that usu. represent the genetic material of a particular organism or tissue
usage While the pronunciation \ˈlī-ˌbrer-ē\ is the most frequent variant in the U.S., the other variants are not uncommon. The contraction

\ˈlī-brē\ and the dissimilated form \ˈlī-ˌber-ē\ result from the relative difficulty of repeating \r\ in the same syllable or successive syllables; our files contain citations for these variants from educated speakers, including college presidents and professors, as well as with somewhat greater frequency from less educated speakers.

library paste *n* (1953) **:** a thick white adhesive made from starch

library science *n* (ca. 1904) **:** the study or the principles and practices of library care and administration

li·bra·tion \lī-ˈbrā-shən\ *n* [L *libration-, libratio,* fr. *librare* to balance, fr. *libra* scales] (1667) **:** an oscillation in the apparent aspect of a secondary body (as a planet or a satellite) as seen from the primary object around which it revolves — **li·bra·tion·al** \-shnəl, -shə-nᵊl\ *adj* — **li·bra·to·ry** \ˈlī-brə-ˌtȯr-ē\ *adj*

libration point *n* (1962) **:** any of five positions in the plane of a celestial system consisting of one massive body orbiting another at which the gravitational influences of the two bodies are approximately equal

li·bret·tist \lə-ˈbre-tist\ *n* (1862) **:** the writer of a libretto

li·bret·to \lə-ˈbre-(ˌ)tō\ *n, pl* **-tos** *or* **-ti** \-(ˌ)tē\ [It, dim. of *libro* book, fr. L *libr-, liber*] (1742) **1 :** the text of a work (as an opera) for the musical theater **2 :** the book containing a libretto

li·bri·form \ˈlī-brə-ˌfȯrm\ *adj* [L *libr-, liber* + ISV *-iform*] (1877) **:** resembling phloem fibers

Lib·ri·um \ˈli-brē-əm\ *trademark* — used for a preparation of chlordiazepoxide

Lib·y·an \ˈli-bē-ən\ *n* (15c) **1 :** a native or inhabitant of Libya **2 :** a language of ancient No. Africa probably ancestral to Berber dialects — **Libyan** *adj*

lic *abbr* license

lice *pl of* LOUSE

[1]**li·cense** *or* **li·cence** \ˈlī-sᵊn(t)s\ *n* [ME, fr. AF *licence,* fr. L *licentia,* fr. *licent-, licens,* prp. of *licēre* to be permitted] (14c) **1 a :** permission to act **b :** freedom of action **2 a :** a permission granted by competent authority to engage in a business or occupation or in an activity otherwise unlawful **b :** a document, plate, or tag evidencing a license granted **c :** a grant by the holder of a copyright or patent to another of any of the rights embodied in the copyright or patent short of an assignment of all rights **3 a :** freedom that allows or is used with irresponsibility **b :** disregard for standards of personal conduct **:** LICENTIOUSNESS **4 :** deviation from fact, form, or rule by an artist or writer for the sake of the effect gained ***syn*** see FREEDOM — **licensed** *adj*

[2]**license** *also* **licence** *vt* **li·censed** *also* **li·cenced; li·cens·ing** *also* **li·cenc·ing** (15c) **1 a :** to issue a license to **b :** to permit or authorize esp. by formal license **2 :** to give permission or consent to **:** ALLOW — **li·cens·able** \-sᵊn(t)-sə-bəl\ *adj* — **li·cen·sor** \-sər, ˌlī-sᵊn-ˈsȯr\ *also* **li·cens·er** \-sər\ *n*

licensed practical nurse *n* (1951) **:** a person who has undergone training and obtained a license (as from a state) conferring authorization to provide routine care for the sick

licensed vocational nurse *n* (1953) **:** a licensed practical nurse authorized to practice in the states of California or Texas

li·cens·ee \ˌlī-sᵊn(t)-ˈsē\ *n* (ca. 1864) **:** one that is licensed

license plate *n* (ca. 1924) **:** a plate or tag (as of metal) attesting that a license has been secured and usu. bearing a registration number

li·cen·sure \ˈlī-sᵊn-shər, -ˌshu̇r\ *n* (ca. 1846) **:** the granting of licenses esp. to practice a profession; *also* **:** the state of being licensed

licente *pl of* SENTE

li·cen·ti·ate \lī-ˈsen(t)-shē-ət, *esp in sense 2* li-\ *n* [ML *licentiatus,* fr. pp. of *licentiare* to allow, fr. L *licentia*] (1555) **1 :** a person who has a license granted esp. by a university to practice a profession **2 :** an academic degree ranking below that of doctor given by some European universities

li·cen·tious \lī-ˈsen(t)-shəs\ *adj* [L *licentiosus,* fr. *licentia*] (1535) **1 :** lacking legal or moral restraints; *esp* **:** disregarding sexual restraints **2 :** marked by disregard for strict rules of correctness — **li·cen·tious·ly** *adv* — **li·cen·tious·ness** *n*

lichee *var of* LYCHEE

li·chen \ˈlī-kən, *Brit also* ˈli-chən\ *n* [L, fr. Gk *leichēn, lichēn,* fr. *leichein* to lick] (ca. 1657) **1 :** any of several skin diseases characterized by a papular eruption **2 :** any of numerous complex plantlike organisms made up of an alga and a fungus growing in symbiotic association on a solid surface (as a rock) — **li·chened** \-kənd\ *adj* — **li·chen·ous** \-kə-nəs\ *adj*

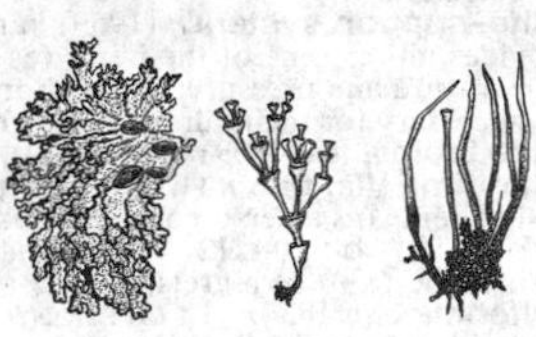

lichen 2

li·chen·ol·o·gy \ˌlī-kə-ˈnä-lə-jē\ *n* [ISV] (1855) **:** the study of lichens — **li·chen·o·log·i·cal** \ˌlī-kə-nə-ˈlä-ji-kəl\ *adj* — **li·chen·ol·o·gist** \ˌlī-kə-ˈnä-lə-jist\ *n*

lich–gate *var of* LYCH-GATE

licht \ˈlikt\ *Scot var of* LIGHT

lic·it \ˈli-sət\ *adj* [MF *licite,* fr. L *licitus,* fr. pp. of *licēre* to be permitted — more at LICENSE] (15c) **:** conforming to the requirements of the law **:** not forbidden by law **:** PERMISSIBLE ***syn*** see LAWFUL — **lic·it·ly** *adv*

[1]**lick** \ˈlik\ *vb* [ME, fr. OE *liccian;* akin to OHG *leckōn* to lick, L *lingere,* Gk *leichein*] *vt* (bef. 12c) **1 a** (1) **:** to draw the tongue over (2) **:** to flicker over like a tongue **b :** to take into the mouth with the tongue **:** LAP **2 a :** to strike repeatedly **:** THRASH **b :** to get the better of **:** OVERCOME, DEFEAT ~ *vi* **1 :** to lap with or as if with the tongue **2 :** to dart like a tongue — **lick into shape :** to put into proper form or condition — **lick one's chops :** to feel or show eager anticipation — **lick one's wounds :** to recover from defeat or disappointment

[2]**lick** *n* (1603) **1 a :** an act or instance of licking **b :** a small amount **:** BIT ⟨couldn't swim a ~⟩ **c :** a hasty careless effort **2 a :** a sharp hit **:** BLOW **b :** a directed effort **:** CRACK — usu. used in pl.; usu. used in the phrase *get in one's licks* **3 a :** a natural salt deposit (as a salt spring) that animals lick **b :** a block of often medicated saline preparation given to livestock to lick **4 :** a musical figure; *specif* **:** an interpolated and usu. improvised figure or flourish **5 :** a critical thrust **:** DIG, BARB — **lick and a promise :** a perfunctory performance of a task

lick·er·ish \ˈli-k(ə-)rish\ *adj* [alter. of *lickerous,* fr. ME *likerous,* prob. modif. of AF **likerous, lecherus* lecherous, fr. *lechur* lecher] (14c) **1 :** GREEDY, DESIROUS **2** *obs* **:** tempting to the appetite **3 :** LECHEROUS — **lick·er·ish·ly** *adv* — **lick·er·ish·ness** *n*

lick·e·ty–split \ˌli-kə-tē-ˈsplit\ *adv* [prob. irreg. fr. [1]*lick* + *split*] (ca. 1859) **:** at great speed

lick·ing *n* (1756) **1 :** a sound thrashing **:** DRUBBING **2 :** DEFEAT

lick·spit·tle \ˈlik-ˌspi-tᵊl\ *n* (1825) **:** a fawning subordinate **:** TOADY

lic·o·rice \ˈli-k(ə-)rish, -k(ə-)rəs\ *n* [ME *licorice,* fr. AF *licoris,* fr. LL *liquiritia,* alter. of L *glycyrrhiza,* fr. Gk *glykyrrhiza,* fr. *glykys* sweet + *rhiza* root — more at DULCET, ROOT] (13c) **1 a :** the dried root of a European leguminous plant (*Glycyrrhiza glabra*) with pinnate leaves and spikes of blue flowers; *also* **:** an extract of this used esp. in medicine, liquors, and confectionery **b :** a candy flavored with licorice or a substitute (as anise) **2 :** a plant yielding licorice; *also* **:** a related plant

lic·tor \ˈlik-tər\ *n* [ME *littour,* fr. L *lictor*] (14c) **:** an ancient Roman officer who bore the fasces as the insignia of his office and whose duties included accompanying the chief magistrates in public appearances

[1]**lid** \ˈlid\ *n* [ME, fr. OE *hlid;* akin to OHG *hlit* cover, and prob. to OE *hlinian* to lean — more at LEAN] (bef. 12c) **1 :** a movable cover for the opening of a hollow container (as a vessel or box) **2 :** EYELID **3 :** the operculum in mosses **4** *slang* **:** HAT **5 :** something that confines, limits, or suppresses **:** CHECK, RESTRAINT **6 :** an ounce of marijuana

[2]**lid** *vt* **lid·ded; lid·ding** (13c) **:** to cover or supply with a lid

li·dar \ˈlī-ˌdär\ *n* [*light* + *radar*] (1963) **:** a device that is similar in operation to radar but emits pulsed laser light instead of microwaves

lidded *adj* (bef. 12c) **1 :** having or covered with a lid ⟨a ~ tureen⟩ **2 :** having lids esp. of a specified kind — usu. used in combination ⟨heavy-*lidded* eyes⟩

lid·less \ˈlid-ləs\ *adj* (14c) **1 :** having no lid **2** *archaic* **:** WATCHFUL

li·do \ˈlē-(ˌ)dō\ *n, pl* **lidos** [*Lido,* Italy] (1860) **:** a fashionable beach resort

li·do·caine \ˈlī-də-ˌkān\ *n* [acetani*lid* + *-o-* + *-caine*] (ca. 1949) **:** a crystalline compound $C_{14}H_{22}N_2O$ that is used in the form of its hydrochloride as a local anesthetic and as an antiarrhythmic agent

[1]**lie** \ˈlī\ *vi* **lay** \ˈlā\; **lain** \ˈlān\; **ly·ing** \ˈlī-iŋ\ [ME, fr. OE *licgan;* akin to OHG *ligen* to lie, L *lectus* bed, Gk *lechos*] (bef. 12c) **1 a :** to be or to stay at rest in a horizontal position **:** be prostrate **:** REST, RECLINE ⟨~ motionless⟩ ⟨~ asleep⟩ **b :** to assume a horizontal position — often used with *down* **c** *archaic* **:** to reside temporarily **:** stay for the night **:** LODGE **d :** to have sexual intercourse — used with *with* **e :** to remain inactive (as in concealment) ⟨~ in wait⟩ **2 :** to be in a helpless or defenseless state ⟨the town *lay* at the mercy of the invaders⟩ **3** *of an inanimate thing* **:** to be or remain in a flat or horizontal position upon a broad support ⟨books *lying* on the table⟩ **4 :** to have direction **:** EXTEND ⟨the route *lay* to the west⟩ **5 a :** to occupy a certain relative place or position ⟨hills ~ behind us⟩ **b :** to have a place in relation to something else ⟨the real reason ~*s* deeper⟩ **c :** to have an effect through mere presence, weight, or relative position ⟨remorse *lay* heavily on him⟩ **d :** to be sustainable or admissible **6 :** to remain at anchor or becalmed **7 a :** to have place **:** EXIST ⟨the choice *lay* between fighting or surrendering⟩ **b :** CONSIST, BELONG ⟨the success of the book ~*s* in its direct style⟩ ⟨responsibility *lay* with the adults⟩ **8 :** REMAIN; *esp* **:** to remain unused, unsought, or uncared for ***usage*** see LAY — **li·er** \ˈlī(-ə)r\ *n* — **lie low 1 :** to lie prostrate, defeated, or disgraced **2 :** to stay in hiding **:** strive to avoid notice **3 :** to bide one's time **:** remain secretly ready for action

[2]**lie** *n* (1697) **1** *chiefly Brit* **:** LAY 6 **2 :** the position or situation in which something lies ⟨a golf ball in a difficult ~⟩ **3 :** the haunt of an animal (as a fish) **:** COVERT **4** *Brit* **:** an act or instance of lying or resting

[3]**lie** *vb* **lied; ly·ing** \ˈlī-iŋ\ [ME, fr. OE *lēogan;* akin to OHG *liogan* to lie, OCS *lŭgati*] *vi* (bef. 12c) **1 :** to make an untrue statement with intent to deceive **2 :** to create a false or misleading impression ~ *vt* **:** to bring about by telling lies ⟨*lied* his way out of trouble⟩

syn LIE, PREVARICATE, EQUIVOCATE, PALTER, FIB mean to tell an untruth. LIE is the blunt term, imputing dishonesty ⟨*lied* about where he had been⟩. PREVARICATE softens the bluntness of LIE by implying quibbling or confusing the issue ⟨during the hearings the witness did his best to *prevaricate*⟩. EQUIVOCATE implies using words having more than one sense so as to seem to say one thing but intend another ⟨*equivocated* endlessly in an attempt to mislead her inquisitors⟩. PALTER implies making unreliable statements of fact or intention or insincere promises ⟨a swindler *paltering* with his investors⟩. FIB applies to a telling of a trivial untruth ⟨*fibbed* about the price of the new suit⟩.

[4]**lie** *n* [ME *lige, lie,* fr. OE *lyge;* akin to OHG *lugī,* OE *lēogan* to lie] (bef. 12c) **1 a :** an assertion of something known or believed by the speaker to be untrue with intent to deceive **b :** an untrue or inaccurate statement that may or may not be believed true by the speaker **2 :** something that misleads or deceives **3 :** a charge of lying

lieb·frau·milch \ˈlēp-ˌfrau̇-ˌmilk, ˈlēb-, -ˌmilk, -ˌmilsh\ *n* [G, alter. of *Liebfrauenmilch,* fr. *Liebfrauenstift,* religious foundation in Worms, Germany + *Milch* milk] (1833) **:** a fruity white Rhine wine

lie by *vi* (1613) **:** to remain inactive **:** REST

lied \ˈlēt\ *n, pl* **lie·der** \ˈlē-dər\ [G, song, fr. OHG *liod*] (1852) **:** a German art song esp. of the 19th century

lie detector *n* (1909) **:** a polygraph for detecting physiological evidence (as change in heart rate) of the tension that accompanies lying

lie down *vi* (1888) **1 :** to submit meekly or abjectly to defeat, disappointment, or insult ⟨won't take that criticism *lying down*⟩ **2 :** to fail to perform or to neglect one's part deliberately ⟨*lying down* on the job⟩

[1]**lief** \ˈlēf, ˈlēv\ *adj* [ME *lief, lef,* fr. OE *lēof;* akin to OE *lufu* love] (bef. 12c) **1** *archaic* **:** DEAR, BELOVED **2** *archaic* **:** WILLING, GLAD

[2]**lief** \ˈlēv, ˈlēf\ *adv* (13c) **:** SOON, GLADLY ⟨I'd as ~ go as not⟩

[1]**liege** \ˈlēj\ *adj* [ME, fr. AF *lige,* fr. LL *laeticus,* fr. *laetus* serf, of Gmc origin; akin to OFris *let* serf] (14c) **1 a :** having the right to feudal allegiance or service ⟨his ~ lord⟩ **b :** obligated to render feudal allegiance and service **2 :** FAITHFUL, LOYAL

[2]**liege** *n* (14c) **1 a :** a vassal bound to feudal service and allegiance **b :** a loyal subject **2 :** a feudal superior to whom allegiance and service are due

liege man *n* (14c) **1 :** VASSAL **2 :** a devoted follower

lie–in \ˈlī-ˌin\ *n* (1963) **:** an act of lying down (as in a public place) in organized protest or as a means of forcing compliance with demands

lien \ˈlēn, ˈlē-ən\ *n* [AF *lien, loyen* bond, restraint, fr. L *ligamen,* fr. *ligare* to bind — more at LIGATURE] (1531) **1 :** a charge upon real or personal property for the satisfaction of some debt or duty ordinarily arising by operation of law **2 :** the security interest created by a mortgage

lie off *vi* (1573) **1 :** to hold back in the early part of a race **2 :** to keep a little away from the shore or another ship **3 :** to cease work for a time

lie over *vi* (ca. 1847) **:** to await disposal or attention at a later time

li•erne \lē-ˈərn, -ˈern\ *n* [F, fr. MF, prob. fr. *lier* to bind, fr. L *ligare*] (1842) **:** a rib in Gothic vaulting that passes from one intersection of the principal ribs to another

lie to *vi* (1711) *of a ship* **:** to stay stationary with head to windward

lieu \ˈlü\ *n* [ME *liue,* fr. AF *liu, lieu,* fr. L *locus* — more at STALL] (14c) *archaic* **:** PLACE, STEAD — **in lieu :** INSTEAD — **in lieu of :** in the place of **:** instead of

lie up *vi* (1699) **1 :** to go into or remain in a dock **2 :** to stay in bed or at rest

lieut *abbr* lieutenant

lieu•ten•an•cy \lü-ˈte-nən(t)-sē, *Brit* le(f)-\ *n* (15c) **:** the office, rank, or commission of a lieutenant

lieu•ten•ant \-ˈte-nənt\ *n* [ME, fr. AF *lieu tenant,* fr. *liu* + *tenant* holding, fr. *tenir* to hold, fr. L *tenēre* — more at THIN] (14c) **1 a :** an official empowered to act for a higher official **b :** an aide or representative of another in the performance of duty **:** ASSISTANT **2 a (1) :** FIRST LIEUTENANT **(2) :** SECOND LIEUTENANT **b :** a commissioned officer in the navy or coast guard ranking above a lieutenant junior grade and below a lieutenant commander **c :** a fire or police department officer ranking below a captain

lieutenant colonel *n* (1598) **:** a commissioned officer in the army, air force, or marine corps ranking above a major and below a colonel

lieutenant commander *n* (1839) **:** a commissioned officer in the navy or coast guard ranking above a lieutenant and below a commander

lieutenant general *n* (1589) **:** a commissioned officer in the army, air force, or marine corps who ranks above a major general and whose insignia is three stars

lieutenant governor *n* (1595) **:** a deputy or subordinate governor: as **a :** an elected official serving as deputy to the governor of an American state **b :** the formal head of the government of a Canadian province appointed by the federal government as the representative of the crown — **lieutenant governorship** *n*

lieutenant junior grade *n, pl* **lieutenants junior grade** (ca. 1909) **:** a commissioned officer in the navy or coast guard ranking above an ensign and below a lieutenant

[1]**life** \ˈlīf\ *n, pl* **lives** \ˈlīvz\ [ME *lif,* fr. OE *līf;* akin to OE *libban* to live — more at LIVE] (bef. 12c) **1 a :** the quality that distinguishes a vital and functional being from a dead body **b :** a principle or force that is considered to underlie the distinctive quality of animate beings **c :** an organismic state characterized by capacity for metabolism, growth, reaction to stimuli, and reproduction **2 a :** the sequence of physical and mental experiences that make up the existence of an individual **b :** one or more aspects of the process of living ⟨sex ~ of the frog⟩ **3 :** BIOGRAPHY 1 **4 :** spiritual existence transcending physical death **5 a :** the period from birth to death **b :** a specific phase of earthly existence ⟨adult ~⟩ **c :** the period from an event until death ⟨a judge appointed for ~⟩ **d :** a sentence of imprisonment for the remainder of a convict's life **6 :** a way or manner of living **7 :** LIVELIHOOD **8 :** a vital or living being; *specif* **:** PERSON ⟨many *lives* were lost in the disaster⟩ **9 :** an animating and shaping force or principle **10 :** SPIRIT, ANIMATION ⟨saw no ~ in her dancing⟩ **11 :** the form or pattern of something existing in reality ⟨painted from ~⟩ **12 :** the period of duration, usefulness, or popularity of something ⟨the expected ~ of the batteries⟩ **13 :** the period of existence (as of a subatomic particle) — compare HALF-LIFE **14 :** a property (as resilience or elasticity) of an inanimate substance or object resembling the animate quality of a living being **15 :** living beings (as of a particular kind or environment) ⟨forest ~⟩ **16 a :** human activities **b :** animate activity and movement ⟨stirrings of ~⟩ **c :** the activities of a given sphere, area, or time ⟨the political ~ of the country⟩ **17 :** one providing interest and vigor ⟨~ of the party⟩ **18 :** an opportunity for continued viability ⟨gave the patient a new ~⟩ **19** *cap, Christian Science* **:** GOD 1b **20 :** something resembling animate life ⟨a grant saved the project's ~⟩

[2]**life** *adj* (13c) **1 :** of or relating to animate being **2 :** LIFELONG ⟨a ~ member⟩ **3 :** using a living model ⟨a ~ class⟩ **4 :** of, relating to, or provided by life insurance ⟨a ~ policy⟩

life–and–death *also* **life–or–death** *adj* (1822) **:** involving or culminating in life or death **:** vitally important as if involving life or death

life belt *n* (ca. 1858) **1** *chiefly Brit* **:** a life preserver in the form of a buoyant belt **2 :** SAFETY BELT

life•blood \ˈlīf-ˈbləd, -ˌbləd\ *n* (1579) **1 :** blood regarded as the seat of vitality **2 :** a vital or life-giving force or component ⟨freedom of inquiry is the ~ of a university⟩

life•boat \-ˌbōt\ *n* (1801) **:** a sturdy buoyant boat (as one carried by a ship) for use in an emergency and esp. in saving lives at sea

life buoy *n* (1801) **:** a ring-shaped life preserver

life–care \ˈlīf-ˌker\ *adj* (1960) **:** of, relating to, or being a residential complex for elderly people that provides an apartment, personal and social services, and health care for life

life coach *n* (1986) **:** an advisor who helps people make decisions, set and reach goals, or deal with problems

life cycle *n* (1873) **1 :** the series of stages in form and functional activity through which an organism passes between successive recurrences of a specified primary stage **2 :** LIFE HISTORY 2 **3 :** a series of stages through which something (as an individual, culture, or manufactured product) passes during its lifetime

life expectancy *n* (1935) **:** the average life span of an individual

life force *n* (1896) **:** ÉLAN VITAL

life–form \ˈlīf-ˈfȯrm, -ˌfȯrm\ *n* (1861) **:** the body form that characterizes a kind of organism (as a species) at maturity; *also* **:** a kind of organism

life•ful \ˈlīf-fəl\ *adj* (13c) *archaic* **:** full of or giving vitality

life–giv•ing \-ˌgi-viŋ\ *adj* (1596) **:** giving or having power to give life and spirit **:** INVIGORATING

life•guard \-ˌgärd\ *n* (1896) **:** a usu. expert swimmer employed (as at a beach or a pool) to safeguard other swimmers — **lifeguard** *vi*

life history *n* (1864) **1 :** a history of the changes through which an organism passes in its development from the primary stage to its natural death **2 :** the history of an individual or thing

life insurance *n* (1809) **:** insurance providing for payment of a stipulated sum to a designated beneficiary upon death of the insured

life jacket *n* (1883) **:** a life preserver in the form of a buoyant vest

life•less \ˈlīf-ləs\ *adj* (bef. 12c) **:** having no life: **a :** DEAD **b :** INANIMATE **c :** lacking qualities expressive of life and vigor **:** INSIPID **d :** destitute of living beings — **life•less•ly** *adv* — **life•less•ness** *n*

life•like \ˈlīf-ˌlīk\ *adj* (14c) **:** accurately representing or imitating real life ⟨a ~ portrait⟩ — **life•like•ness** *n*

life•line \ˈlīf-ˌlīn\ *n* (1700) **1 :** a line (as a rope) used for saving or preserving life: as **a :** a line along the outer edge of the deck of a boat or ship **b :** a line used to keep contact with a person (as a diver or astronaut) in a dangerous or potentially dangerous situation **2 :** something regarded as indispensable for the maintaining or protection of life

life list *n* (1960) **:** a record kept of all birds sighted and identified by a birder

life•long \ˈlīf-ˌlȯŋ\ *adj* (1855) **1 :** lasting or continuing through life **2 :** LONG-STANDING

life•man•ship \ˈlīf-mən-ˌship\ *n* (1949) **:** the skill or practice of achieving superiority or an appearance of superiority over others (as in conversation) by perplexing and demoralizing them

life net *n* (1904) **:** a strong net or sheet (as of canvas) used (as by firefighters) to catch a person jumping from a burning building

life of Ri•ley *also* **life of Reil•ly** \-ˈrī-lē\ [fr. the name *Riley* or *Reilly*] (1911) **:** a carefree comfortable way of living

life peer *n* (1869) **:** a British peer whose title is not hereditary — **life peerage** *n*

life preserver *n* (1804) **1 :** a device (as a life jacket or life buoy) designed to save a person from drowning by providing buoyancy in water **2** *chiefly Brit* **:** BLACKJACK 3

lif•er \ˈlī-fər\ *n* (1827) **1 :** a person sentenced to imprisonment for life **2 :** a person who makes a career of one of the armed forces **3 :** a person who has made a lifelong commitment (as to a way of life)

life raft *n* (1819) **:** a raft usu. made of wood or an inflatable material and designed for use by people forced into the water

life ring *n* (ca. 1909) **:** LIFE BUOY

life•sav•er \ˈlīf-ˌsā-vər\ *n* (1887) **1 :** one trained to save lives of drowning persons **2 :** one that is at once timely and effective in time of distress or need

[1]**life•sav•ing** \-viŋ\ *adj* (1858) **:** designed for or used in saving lives

[2]**lifesaving** *n* (1919) **:** the skill or practice of saving or protecting the lives esp. of drowning persons

life science *n* (1941) **:** a branch of science (as biology, medicine, and sometimes anthropology or sociology) that deals with living organisms and life processes — usu. used in pl. — **life scientist** *n*

life–size \ˈlīf-ˈsīz\ *or* **life–sized** \-ˈsīzd\ *adj* (1841) **:** of natural size **:** of the size of the original ⟨a ~ statue⟩

life span *n* (1898) **1 :** the average length of life of a kind of organism or of a material object esp. in a particular environment or under specified circumstances **2 :** the duration of existence of an individual

[1]**life•style** \ˈlīf-ˈstī(-ə)l, -ˌstī(-ə)l\ *n* (1939) **:** the typical way of life of an individual, group, or culture

[2]**lifestyle** *adj* (1976) **:** associated with, reflecting, or promoting an enhanced or more desirable lifestyle ⟨~ magazines⟩

life–support \-sə-ˈpȯrt\ *adj* (1965) **:** providing support necessary to sustain life; *esp* **:** of or relating to a system providing such support

life support *n* (1959) **:** medical life-support equipment ⟨the patient was placed on ~⟩

life–support system *n* (1959) **:** an artificial or natural system that provides all or some of the items (as oxygen, food, water, control of temperature and pressure, disposition of carbon dioxide and body wastes) necessary for maintaining life or health

life table *n* (ca. 1859) **:** MORTALITY TABLE

[1]**life•time** \ˈlīf-ˌtīm\ *n* (13c) **1 a :** the duration of the existence of a living being (as a person or an animal) or a thing (as a star or a subatomic particle) **b :** LIFE 12 **2 :** an amount accumulated or experienced in a lifetime ⟨a ~ of regrets⟩

[2]**lifetime** *adj* (1834) **1 :** LIFELONG **2 :** of long duration or continuance ⟨~ legislation⟩ **3 :** measured or achieved over the span of a career ⟨a baseball player's ~ batting average⟩

life vest *n* (1939) **:** LIFE JACKET

life•way \-ˌwā\ *n* (1948) **:** LIFE 6

life•work \-ˈwərk\ *n* (1871) **:** the entire or principal work of one's lifetime; *also* **:** a work extending over a lifetime

life•world \ˈlīf-ˌwər(-ə)ld\ *n* (1940) **:** the sum total of physical surroundings and everyday experiences that make up an individual's world

life zone *n* (1893) **:** a region characterized by specific plants and animals

LIFO *abbr* last in, first out

[1]**lift** \ˈlift\ *n* [ME, fr. OE *lyft*] (bef. 12c) *chiefly Scot* **:** HEAVENS, SKY

[2]**lift** *vb* [ME, fr. ON *lypta;* akin to OE *lyft* air — more at LOFT] *vt* (14c) **1 a :** to raise from a lower to a higher position **:** ELEVATE **b :** to raise in rank or condition **c :** to raise in rate or amount **2 :** to put an end to (a blockade or siege) by withdrawing or causing the withdrawal of investing forces **3 :** REVOKE, RESCIND ⟨~ an embargo⟩ **4 a :** STEAL ⟨had her purse ~*ed*⟩ **b :** PLAGIARIZE **c :** to take out of normal setting ⟨~ a word out of context⟩ **5 :** to take up (as a root crop or transplants) from the ground **6 :** to pay off (an obligation) ⟨~ a mortgage⟩ **7 :** to move from one place to another (as by aircraft) **:** TRANSPORT **8 :** to take up (a fingerprint) from a surface ~ *vi* **1 a :** ASCEND, RISE ⟨the rocket ~*ed* off⟩ **b :** to appear elevated (as above surrounding objects) **2** *of inclement weather* **:** to dissipate and clear — **lift•able** \ˈlif-tə-bəl\ *adj* — **lift•er** *n*

syn LIFT, RAISE, REAR, ELEVATE, HOIST, HEAVE, BOOST mean to move from a lower to a higher place or position. LIFT usu. implies exerting effort to overcome resistance of weight ⟨*lift* the chair while I vacuum⟩. RAISE carries a stronger implication of bringing up to the vertical or to a high position ⟨scouts *raising* a flagpole⟩. REAR may add an element of suddenness to RAISE ⟨suddenly *reared* itself up on its hind legs⟩. ELEVATE may replace LIFT or RAISE esp. when exalting or enhancing is implied ⟨*elevated* the taste of the public⟩. HOIST implies lifting something heavy esp. by mechanical means ⟨*hoisted* the cargo on board⟩. HEAVE implies lifting and throwing with great effort or strain ⟨*heaved* the heavy crate inside⟩. BOOST suggests assisting to climb or advance by a push ⟨*boosted* his brother over the fence⟩.

[3]lift *n* (14c) **1 :** the amount that may be lifted at one time **:** LOAD **2 a :** the action or an instance of lifting **b :** the action or an instance of rising **c :** elevated carriage (as of a body part) **d :** the lifting up (as of a dancer) usu. by a partner **3 :** a device (as a handle or latch) for lifting **4 :** an act of stealing **:** THEFT **5 a :** ASSISTANCE, HELP **b :** a ride esp. along one's way **6 :** a layer in the heel of a shoe **7 :** a rise or advance in position or condition **8 :** a slight rise or elevation **9 :** the distance or extent to which something rises **10 :** an apparatus or machine used for hoisting: as **a :** a set of pumps used in a mine **b** *chiefly Brit* **:** ELEVATOR 1b **c :** an apparatus for raising an automobile (as for repair) **d :** SKI LIFT **11 a :** an elevating influence **b :** an elevation of the spirit **12 a :** the component of the total aerodynamic force acting on an airplane or airfoil that is perpendicular to the relative wind and that for an airplane constitutes the upward force that opposes the pull of gravity **b :** an updraft that can be used to increase altitude (as of a sailplane) **13 :** an organized movement of people, equipment, or supplies by some form of transportation; *esp* **:** AIRLIFT **14 :** plastic surgery on a part of the body typically to improve a drooping or sagging appearance esp. by reducing excess skin and fat ⟨a neck *lift*⟩

lift•gate \ˈlift-ˌgāt\ *n* (1953) **:** a rear panel (as on a station wagon) that opens upward

lift•off \-ˌȯf\ *n* (ca. 1956) **:** a vertical takeoff by an aircraft or a rocket vehicle or missile

lig•a•ment \ˈli-gə-mənt\ *n* [ME, fr. ML & L; ML *ligamentum,* fr. L, band, tie, fr. *ligare*] (14c) **1 :** a tough fibrous band of tissue connecting the articular extremities of bones or supporting an organ in place **2 :** a connecting or unifying bond ⟨the law of nations, the great ~ of mankind —Edmund Burke⟩ — **lig•a•men•tous** \-ˈmen-təs\ *adj*

li•gand \ˈli-gənd, ˈlī-\ *n* [L *ligandus,* gerundive of *ligare*] (1949) **:** a group, ion, or molecule coordinated to a central atom or molecule in a complex

li•gase \ˈlī-ˌgās, -ˌgāz\ *n* [ISV *lig-* (fr. L *ligare*) + *-ase*] (1961) **:** SYNTHETASE

li•gate \ˈlī-ˌgāt, lī-ˈ\ *vt* **li•gat•ed; li•gat•ing** [L *ligatus*] (1599) **1 :** to tie with a ligature **2 :** to join together (as DNA or protein chains) by a chemical process

li•ga•tion \lī-ˈgā-shən\ *n* (1597) **1 :** an act of ligating **2 :** something that binds **:** LIGATURE

lig•a•ture \ˈli-gə-ˌchu̇r, -chər, -ˌtu̇r, -ˌtyu̇r\ *n* [ME, fr. LL *ligatura,* fr. L *ligatus,* pp. of *ligare* to bind, tie; akin to Alb *lidh* I tie] (14c) **1 a :** something that is used to bind; *specif* **:** a filament (as a thread) used in surgery **b :** something that unites or connects **:** BOND **2 :** the action of binding or tying **3 :** a compound note in mensural notation indicating a group of musical notes to be sung to one syllable **4 :** a printed or written character (as æ or *ff*) consisting of two or more letters or characters joined together

li•ger \ˈlī-gər\ *n* [blend of *lion* and *tiger*] (1924) **:** a hybrid between a male lion and a female tiger

[1]light \ˈlīt\ *n* [ME, fr. OE *lēoht;* akin to OHG *lioht* light, L *luc-, lux* light, *lucēre* to shine, Gk *leukos* white] (bef. 12c) **1 a :** something that makes vision possible **b :** the sensation aroused by stimulation of the visual receptors **c :** electromagnetic radiation of any wavelength that travels in a vacuum with a speed of about 186,281 miles (300,000 kilometers) per second; *specif* **:** such radiation that is visible to the human eye **2 a :** DAYLIGHT **b :** DAWN **3 :** a source of light: as **a :** a celestial body **b :** CANDLE **c :** an electric light **4** *archaic* **:** SIGHT 4a **5 a :** spiritual illumination **b :** INNER LIGHT **c :** ENLIGHTENMENT **d :** TRUTH **6 a :** public knowledge ⟨facts brought to ~⟩ **b :** a particular aspect or appearance presented to view ⟨saw the matter in a different ~⟩ **7 :** a particular illumination **8 :** something that enlightens or informs ⟨shed some ~ on the problem⟩ **9 :** a medium (as a window) through which light is admitted **10** *pl* **:** a set of principles, standards, or opinions ⟨worship according to one's ~*s* —Adrienne Koch⟩ **11 :** a noteworthy person in a particular place or field ⟨a leading ~ among current writers⟩ **12 :** a particular expression of the eye **13 a :** LIGHTHOUSE, BEACON **b :** TRAFFIC LIGHT **14 :** the representation of light in art **15 :** a flame for lighting something (as a cigarette) — **in the light of 1 :** from the point of view of **2** *or* **in light of :** in view of ⟨*in light of* their findings, new procedures were established⟩

[2]light *adj* (bef. 12c) **1 :** having light **:** BRIGHT ⟨a ~ airy room⟩ **2 a :** not dark, intense, or swarthy in color or coloring **:** PALE **b** *of colors* **:** medium in saturation and high in lightness ⟨~ blue⟩ **3** *of coffee* **:** served with extra milk or cream

[3]light *vb* **lit** \ˈlit\ *or* **light•ed; light•ing** *vi* (bef. 12c) **1 :** to become light **:** BRIGHTEN — usu. used with *up* ⟨her face *lit* up⟩ **2 :** to take fire **3 :** to ignite something (as a cigarette) — often used with *up* ~ *vt* **1 :** to set fire to **2 a :** to conduct with a light **:** GUIDE **b :** ILLUMINATE ⟨rockets ~ up the sky⟩ **c :** ANIMATE, BRIGHTEN ⟨a smile *lit* up her face⟩

[4]light *adj* [ME, fr. OE *lēoht;* akin to OHG *līhti* light, L *levis,* Gk *elachys* small] (bef. 12c) **1 a :** having little weight **:** not heavy **b :** designed to carry a comparatively small load ⟨a ~ truck⟩ **c :** having relatively little weight in proportion to bulk ⟨aluminum is a ~ metal⟩ **d :** containing less than the legal, standard, or usual weight ⟨a ~ coin⟩ **2 a :** of little importance **:** TRIVIAL **b :** not abundant ⟨~ rain⟩ ⟨a ~ lunch⟩ **3 a :** easily disturbed ⟨a ~ sleeper⟩ **b :** exerting a minimum of force or pressure **:** GENTLE ⟨a ~ touch⟩ **c :** resulting from a very slight pressure **:** FAINT ⟨~ print⟩ **4 a :** easily endurable ⟨a ~ illness⟩ **b :** requiring little effort ⟨~ work⟩ **5 :** capable of moving swiftly or nimbly ⟨~ on his feet⟩ **6 a :** FRIVOLOUS 1a ⟨~ conduct⟩ **b :** lacking in stability **:** CHANGEABLE ⟨~ opinions⟩ **c :** sexually promiscuous **7 :** free from care **:** CHEERFUL **8 :** less powerful but usu. more mobile than usual for its kind ⟨~ cavalry⟩ ⟨a ~ cruiser⟩ **9 a :** made with a lower calorie content or with less of some ingredient (as salt, fat, or alcohol) than usual **b :** having a relatively mild flavor **10 a :** easily digested ⟨a ~ soup⟩ **b :** well leavened ⟨a ~ crust⟩ **11 :** coarse and sandy or easily pulverized ⟨~ soil⟩ **12 :** DIZZY, GIDDY ⟨felt ~ in the head⟩ **13 :** intended chiefly to entertain ⟨~ verse⟩ ⟨~ comedy⟩ **14 a :** carrying little or no cargo ⟨the ship returned ~⟩ **b :** producing goods for direct consumption by the consumer ⟨~ industry⟩ **15 :** not bearing a stress or accent ⟨a ~ syllable⟩ **16 :** having a clear soft quality ⟨a ~ voice⟩ **17 :** being in debt to the pot in a poker game ⟨three chips ~⟩ **18 :** SHORT 5d ⟨~ on experience⟩ **19 :** CASUAL, OCCASIONAL ⟨a ~ smoker⟩ ***syn*** see EASY — **light•ish** \ˈlī-tish\ *adj*

[5]light *adv* (bef. 12c) **1 :** LIGHTLY **2 :** with little baggage ⟨travel ~⟩

[6]light *vi* **lit** \ˈlit\ *or* **light•ed; light•ing** [ME, fr. OE *līhtan;* akin to OE *lēoht* light in weight] (bef. 12c) **1 :** DISMOUNT **2 :** SETTLE, ALIGHT ⟨a bird *lit* on the lawn⟩ **3 :** to fall unexpectedly — usu. used with *on* or *upon* **4 :** to arrive by chance **:** HAPPEN — usu. used with *on* or *upon* ⟨*lit* upon a solution⟩ — **light into :** to attack forcefully ⟨I *lit into* that food until I'd finished off the heel of the loaf —Helen Eustis⟩

light adaptation *n* (1900) **:** the process including contraction of the pupil and decrease in rhodopsin by which the eye adapts to conditions of increased illumination — **light–adapt•ed** \ˈlīt-ə-ˌdap-təd\ *adj*

light air *n* (1769) **:** wind having a speed of 1 to 3 miles (about 1 to 5 kilometers) per hour — see BEAUFORT SCALE table

light bread \ˈlīt-ˌbred\ *n* [[2]*light*] (1821) *chiefly Southern & Midland* **:** bread in loaves made from white flour leavened with yeast

light breeze *n* (1742) **:** wind having a speed of 4 to 7 miles (about 6 to 11 kilometers) per hour — see BEAUFORT SCALE table

light•bulb \ˈlīt-ˌbəlb\ *or* **light bulb** *n* (1884) **:** an electric lamp: as **a :** one in which a filament gives off light when heated to incandescence by an electric current — called also *incandescent, incandescent lamp* **b :** FLUORESCENT LAMP

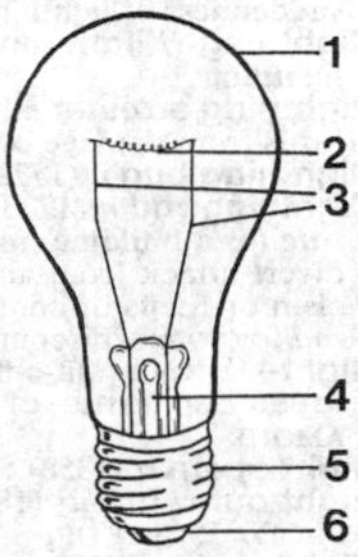

lightbulb (incandescent): *1* bulb containing gas, *2* filament, *3* connecting and supporting wires, *4* exhaust tube, *5* screw base, *6* base contact

light chain *n* (1964) **:** either of the two smaller of the four polypeptide chains comprising antibodies — compare HEAVY CHAIN

light curve *n* (1890) **:** a graph showing the variation in brightness of a celestial object (as a variable star) over a period of time

light–emitting diode *n* (1968) **:** LED

[1]light•en \ˈlī-tᵊn\ *vb* **light•ened; light•en•ing** \ˈlīt-niŋ, ˈlī-tᵊn-iŋ\ [ME *lightenen,* fr. *light*] *vt* (14c) **1 :** to make light or clear **:** ILLUMINATE **2** *archaic* **:** ENLIGHTEN **3 :** to make (as a color) lighter ~ *vi* **1 a** *archaic* **:** to shine brightly **b :** to grow lighter **:** BRIGHTEN **2 :** to give out flashes of lightning — **light•en•er** \ˈlīt-nər, ˈlī-tᵊn-ər\ *n*

[2]lighten *vb* **light•ened; light•en•ing** \ˈlīt-niŋ, ˈlī-tᵊn-iŋ\ *vt* (14c) **1 a :** to relieve of a burden in whole or in part ⟨the news ~*ed* his mind⟩ **b :** to reduce in weight or quantity **:** LESSEN **c :** to make less wearisome **:** ALLEVIATE ⟨~ our sorrow⟩ **2 :** CHEER, GLADDEN ~ *vi* **1 :** to become lighter or less burdensome **2 :** to become more cheerful ***syn*** see RELIEVE — **light•en•er** \ˈlīt-nər, ˈlī-tᵊn-ər\ *n*

lighten up *vi* (1911) **:** to take things less seriously

[1]ligh•ter \ˈlī-tər\ *n* [ME, fr. MD *lichter, fr. *lichten* to unload; akin to OE *lēoht* light in weight] (14c) **:** a large usu. flat-bottomed barge used esp. in unloading or loading ships

[2]lighter *vt* (1840) **:** to convey by a lighter

[3]lighter *n* (1553) **1 :** one that lights or sets a fire **2 :** a device for lighting a fire; *esp* **:** a mechanical or electrical device used for lighting cigarettes, cigars, or pipes

ligh•ter•age \ˈlī-tə-rij\ *n* (15c) **1 :** the loading, unloading, or transportation of goods by means of a lighter **2 :** a price paid for lightering

lighter–than–air *adj* (1903) **:** of less weight than the air displaced

light•face \ˈlīt-ˌfās\ *n* (ca. 1871) **:** a typeface having comparatively light thin lines; *also* **:** printing in lightface — **light•faced** \-ˌfāst\ *adj*

light•fast \-ˌfast\ *adj* (1950) **:** resistant to light and esp. to sunlight; *esp* **:** colorfast to light — **light•fast•ness** \-ˌfas(t)-nəs\ *n*

light–fin•gered \-ˌfiŋ-gərd\ *adj* (1547) **1 :** showing adroitness in stealing or a tendency to steal esp. by picking pockets or shoplifting **2 :** having a light and dexterous touch — **light–fin•gered•ness** *n*

light–foot•ed \-ˌfu̇-təd\ *also* **light–foot** \-ˌfu̇t\ *adj* (15c) **1 :** having a light and springy step **2 :** moving gracefully and nimbly ⟨~ prose⟩

light guide *n* (1951) **:** an optical fiber used esp. for telecommunication

light–hand•ed \ˈlīt-ˌhan-dəd\ *adj* (15c) **:** having a light or delicate touch **:** FACILE ⟨a ~ translation⟩ — **light–hand•ed•ness** *n*

light–head•ed \-ˌhe-dəd\ *adj* (1537) **1 :** mentally disoriented **:** DIZZY **2 :** lacking in maturity or seriousness **:** FRIVOLOUS — **light–head•ed•ly** *adv* — **light–head•ed•ness** *n*

light•heart•ed \-ˌhär-təd\ *adj* (15c) **1 :** free from care, anxiety, or seriousness **:** HAPPY-GO-LUCKY **2 :** cheerfully optimistic and hopeful **:** EASYGOING — **light•heart•ed•ly** *adv* — **light•heart•ed•ness** *n*

light heavyweight *n* (1903) **:** a boxer in a weight division having a maximum limit of 175 pounds for professionals and 178 pounds for amateurs — compare HEAVYWEIGHT, MIDDLEWEIGHT

light•house \ˈlīt-ˌhau̇s\ *n* (1622) **1 :** a structure (as a tower) with a powerful light that gives a continuous or intermittent signal to navigators **2 :** BEACON 3

light housekeeping *n* (1872) **1 :** domestic work restricted to the less laborious duties **2 :** housekeeping in quarters with limited facilities for cooking

lighting *n* (bef. 12c) **1 a :** ILLUMINATION **b :** IGNITION **2 :** an artificial supply of light or the apparatus providing it

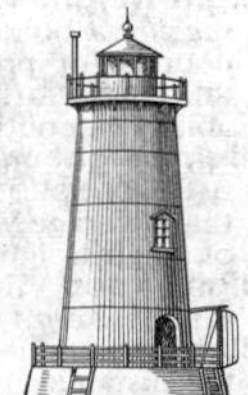
lighthouse 1

light·less \ˈlīt-ləs\ *adj* (bef. 12c) **1 :** receiving no light : DARK **2 :** giving no light
light·ly \ˈlīt-lē\ *adv* (bef. 12c) **:** in a light manner: as **a :** with little weight or force : GENTLY **b :** with indifference or carelessness : UNCONCERNEDLY ⟨the problem should not be passed over ~ —Shelly Halpern⟩ **c :** with little difficulty : EASILY **d :** GAILY, CHEERFULLY **e :** in an agile manner : NIMBLY, SWIFTLY ⟨the cat leapt ~ onto the table⟩ **f :** in a small degree or amount ⟨~ salted food⟩
light meter *n* (1921) **:** a small and often portable device for measuring illumination; *esp* : EXPOSURE METER
light–mind·ed \ˈlīt-ˌmīn-dəd\ *adj* (1575) **:** lacking in seriousness : FRIVOLOUS — **light–mind·ed·ly** *adv* — **light–mind·ed·ness** *n*
[1]**light·ness** \-nəs\ *n* (bef. 12c) **1 :** the quality or state of being illuminated : ILLUMINATION **2 :** the attribute of object colors by which the object appears to reflect or transmit more or less of the incident light — compare BRIGHTNESS 2, HUE 2c, SATURATION 4
[2]**lightness** *n* (12c) **1 :** the quality or state of being light esp. in weight **2 :** lack of seriousness and stability of character often accompanied by casual heedlessness **3 a :** the quality or state of being nimble **b :** an ease and gaiety of style or manner **4 :** a lack of weightiness or force : DELICACY
[1]**light·ning** \ˈlīt-niŋ\ *n* [ME, fr. gerund of *lightenen* to lighten] (13c) **1 :** the flashing of light produced by a discharge of atmospheric electricity; *also* : the discharge itself **2 :** a sudden stroke of fortune
[2]**lightning** *adj* (1576) **:** having or moving with or as if with the speed and suddenness of lightning ⟨a ~ assault⟩
[3]**lightning** *vi* **light·ninged; lightning** (1903) **:** to discharge a flash of lightning
lightning arrester *n* (1860) **:** a device for protecting an electrical apparatus from damage by lightning
lightning bug *n* (1778) **:** FIREFLY
lightning rod *n* (1773) **1 :** a grounded metallic rod set up on a structure (as a building) to protect it from lightning **2 :** one that serves to divert attack from another **3 :** one that is a frequent target of criticism or focus of controversy ⟨she has become a convenient *lightning rod* for voters' discontent with law-and-order issues —Aric Press *et al.*⟩
light–o'–love \ˌlīt-ə-ˈləv\ *also* **light–of–love** \-əv-ˈ\ *n, pl* **light–o'–loves** *also* **lights–of–love** (1589) **1 :** PROSTITUTE **2 :** LOVER, PARAMOUR
light opera *n* (1858) **:** OPERETTA
light out *vi* [[6]*light*] (1866) **1 :** to leave in a hurry ⟨*lit out* for home at once⟩ **2 :** SET OFF
light pen *n* (1958) **:** a pen-shaped device for direct interaction with a computer through a cathode-ray tube display
light pipe *n* (1950) **:** an optical fiber or a solid transparent plastic rod for transmitting light lengthwise
light·plane \ˈlīt-ˈplān\ *n* (1923) **:** a small and comparatively lightweight airplane; *esp* : a privately owned passenger airplane
light pollution *n* (1971) **:** artificial skylight (as from city lights) that interferes esp. with astronomical observations
light·proof \ˈlīt-ˌprüf\ *adj* (1923) **:** impenetrable by light
light quantum *n* (1910) **:** PHOTON; *esp* : one of luminous radiation
light–rail \ˈlīt-ˌrāl\ *n, often attrib* (1975) **:** a means of urban railway transportation using trolley cars
light reaction *n* (ca. 1929) **:** the phase of photosynthesis that requires the presence of light and that involves photophosphorylation
lights \ˈlīts\ *n pl* [ME *lightes,* fr. *light* light in weight] (12c) **:** the lungs esp. of a slaughtered animal
light·ship \ˈlīt-ˌship\ *n* (1837) **:** a ship equipped with a brilliant light and moored at a place dangerous to navigation
light show *n* (1966) **:** a kaleidoscopic display of colored lights, slides, and film loops
[1]**light·some** \ˈlīt-səm\ *adj* (14c) **1 :** free from care : LIGHTHEARTED **2 :** AIRY, NIMBLE — **light·some·ly** *adv* — **light·some·ness** *n*
[2]**lightsome** *adj* (15c) **1 :** well lighted : BRIGHT **2 :** giving light
lights–out \ˈlīts-ˈau̇t\ *n* (1868) **1 :** a command or signal for putting out lights **2 :** a prescribed bedtime for persons living under discipline
light table *n* (ca. 1948) **:** a device that projects even light through a flat translucent surface over which films or tracings may be spread out and viewed
light therapy *n* (1936) **:** the treatment of medical or psychiatric conditions (as seasonal affective disorder) by the controlled application of light — called also *light treatment, phototherapy*
light·tight \ˈlīt-ˌtīt\ *adj* (1884) **:** LIGHTPROOF
light trap *n* (1906) **1 :** a device that allows movement of a sliding part or passage of a person (as into a darkroom) but excludes light **2 :** a device for collecting or destroying insects that consists of a bright light in association with a trapping or killing medium
light water *n* (1933) **:** WATER 1a — compare HEAVY WATER
[1]**light·weight** \ˈlīt-ˌwāt\ *n* (1773) **1 :** one of less than average weight; *specif* : a boxer in a weight division having a maximum limit of 135 pounds for professionals and 132 pounds for amateurs — compare FEATHERWEIGHT, WELTERWEIGHT **2 :** one of little consequence or ability ⟨a political ~⟩
[2]**lightweight** *adj* (1809) **1 :** lacking in earnestness, ability, or profundity : INCONSEQUENTIAL ⟨a ~ painter⟩ ⟨a ~ TV series⟩ **2 :** having less than average weight ⟨~ fabrics⟩ **3 :** of, relating to, or characteristic of a lightweight ⟨the ~ championship⟩
light·wood \ˈlīt-ˌwu̇d, ˈlī-təd\ *n* (1685) *chiefly Southern* **:** wood used for kindling; *esp* : coniferous wood abounding in pitch
light–year \ˈlīt-ˌyir\ *n* (1888) **1 :** a unit of length in astronomy equal to the distance that light travels in one year in a vacuum or about 5.88 trillion miles (9.46 trillion kilometers) **2 :** an extremely large measure of comparison (as of distance, time, or quality) ⟨seems like ~*s* ago⟩ ⟨has ~*s* more talent⟩ ⟨two minutes and yet ~*s* away from the crowded village —Suzanne Patterson⟩
lign– *or* **ligni–** *or* **ligno–** *comb form* [L *lign-, ligni-,* fr. *lignum*] **:** wood ⟨*lign*in⟩ ⟨*ligno*cellulose⟩
lig·nan \ˈlig-ˌnan\ *n* [ISV *lign-* + [3]*-an*] (1944) **:** any of a class of propyl phenolic dimers including many found in plants and noted for having antioxidant and estrogenic activity
lig·ne·ous \ˈlig-nē-əs\ *adj* [L *ligneus,* fr. *lignum* wood, prob. fr. *legere* to gather — more at LEGEND] (1626) **:** of or resembling wood
lig·ni·fy \ˈlig-nə-ˌfī\ *vb* **-fied; -fy·ing** [F *lignifier,* fr. L *lignum*] *vt* (ca. 1828) **:** to convert into wood or woody tissue ~ *vi* **:** to become wood or woody — **lig·ni·fi·ca·tion** \ˌlig-nə-fə-ˈkā-shən\ *n*
lig·nin \ˈlig-nən\ *n* (1822) **:** an amorphous polymer related to cellulose that provides rigidity and together with cellulose forms the woody cell walls of plants and the cementing material between them
lig·nite \ˈlig-ˌnīt\ *n* [F, fr. L *lignum*] (ca. 1808) **:** a usu. brownish black coal intermediate between peat and bituminous coal; *esp* : one in which the texture of the original wood is distinct — called also *brown coal* — **lig·nit·ic** \lig-ˈni-tik\ *adj*
lig·no·cel·lu·lose \ˌlig-nō-ˈsel-yə-ˌlōs, -ˌlōz\ *n* [ISV] (1900) **:** any of several closely related substances constituting the essential part of woody cell walls of plants and consisting of cellulose intimately associated with lignin — **lig·no·cel·lu·los·ic** \-ˌsel-yə-ˈlō-sik, -zik\ *adj*
lig·no·sul·fo·nate \-ˈsəl-fə-ˌnāt\ *n* (1908) **:** any of various compounds produced from the spent sulfite liquor in the pulping of softwood in papermaking and used esp. for binders and dispersing agents
lig·num vi·tae \ˌlig-nəm-ˈvī-tē\ *n, pl* **lignum vitaes** [NL, lit., wood of life] (1594) **1 :** the very hard heavy wood of any of several tropical American guaiacums **2 :** a tree yielding lignum vitae
lig·u·la \ˈli-gyə-lə\ *n, pl* **-lae** \-ˌlē, -ˌlī\ *also* **-las** [NL] (ca. 1760) **1 :** LIGULE **2 :** the distal lobed part of the labium of an insect
lig·u·late \ˈli-gyə-lət, -ˌlāt\ *adj* (1760) **1 :** furnished with ligules, ligulae, or ligulate corollas **2** [L *ligula*] **:** shaped like a strap ⟨~ corolla of a ray flower⟩
lig·ule \ˈli-(ˌ)gyül\ *n* [NL *ligula,* fr. L, small tongue, strap, fr. *lingere* to lick — more at LICK] (ca. 1847) **:** a scalelike projection esp. on a plant: as **a :** a thin appendage of a foliage leaf and esp. of the sheath of a blade of grass **b :** a ligulate corolla of a ray floret in a composite head
lig·ure \ˈli-ˌgyu̇r, -gyər\ *n* [ME *lygire,* fr. LL *ligurius,* fr. Gk *ligyrion*] (13c) **:** a traditional precious stone that is prob. the jacinth
lik·able *or* **like·able** \ˈlī-kə-bəl\ *adj* (1730) **:** having qualities that bring about a favorable regard : PLEASANT, AGREEABLE — **lik·abil·i·ty** \ˌlī-kə-ˈbi-lə-tē\ *n* — **lik·able·ness** *n*
[1]**like** \ˈlīk\ *vb* **liked; lik·ing** [ME, fr. OE *līcian;* akin to OE *gelīc* alike] *vt* (bef. 12c) **1** *chiefly dial* **:** to be suitable or agreeable to ⟨I like onions but they don't ~ me⟩ **2 a :** to feel attraction toward or take pleasure in : ENJOY ⟨~*s* baseball⟩ **b :** to feel toward : REGARD ⟨how would you ~ a change⟩ **3 :** to wish to have : WANT ⟨would ~ a drink⟩ **4 :** to do well in ⟨this plant ~*s* dry soil⟩ ⟨my car does not ~ cold weather⟩ ~ *vi* **1** *dial* : APPROVE **2 :** to feel inclined : CHOOSE, PREFER ⟨leave any time you ~⟩
[2]**like** *n* (1851) **1 :** LIKING, PREFERENCE **2 :** something that one likes
[3]**like** *adj* [ME, alter. of *ilich,* fr. OE *gelīc* like, alike, fr. *ge-,* associative prefix + *līc* body; akin to OHG *gilīh* like, alike, Lith *lygus* like — more at CO-] (13c) **1 a :** the same or nearly the same (as in appearance, character, or quantity) ⟨suits of ~ design⟩ — formerly used with *as, unto, of* ⟨it behoved him to be made ~ unto his brethren —Heb 2:17(AV)⟩ **b** *chiefly Brit* **:** closely resembling the subject or original ⟨the portrait is very ~⟩ **2 :** LIKELY ⟨the importance of statistics as the one discipline ~ to give accuracy of mind —H. J. Laski⟩
[4]**like** *prep* (13c) **1 a :** having the characteristics of : similar to ⟨his house is ~ a barn⟩ ⟨it's ~ when we were kids⟩ **b :** typical of ⟨was ~ him to do that⟩ **c :** comparable to : APPROXIMATING ⟨costs something ~ fifty cents⟩ **2 :** in the manner of : similarly to ⟨acts ~ a fool⟩ **3 :** as though there would be ⟨looks ~ rain⟩ **4 :** such as ⟨a subject ~ physics⟩ **5** — used to form intensive or ironic phrases ⟨fought ~ hell⟩ ⟨~ fun he did⟩ ⟨laughed ~ anything⟩
[5]**like** *n* (13c) **1 a :** one that is similar : COUNTERPART, EQUAL ⟨have . . . never seen the ~ before —Sir Winston Churchill⟩ **b :** KIND 4a — usu. used with a preceding possessive ⟨put him and his ~ to some job —J. R. R. Tolkien⟩ **2 :** one of many that are similar to each other — used chiefly in proverbial expressions ⟨~ breeds like⟩ — **and the like :** ET CETERA — **the likes of** *also* **the like of 1 :** such people as : such things as ⟨reads *the likes of* Austen and Browning⟩ **2 :** such a one as and perhaps others similar to — usu. used with disparaging overtones ⟨have no use for *the likes of* you⟩ **3 :** the kind or sort of ⟨a fantastic celebration *the likes of* which had never been seen before —Joseph Heller⟩
[6]**like** *adv* (14c) **1** *archaic* : EQUALLY **2 :** LIKELY, PROBABLY ⟨you'll try it, some day, ~ enough —Mark Twain⟩ **3 a :** to some extent : RATHER, ALTOGETHER ⟨saunter over nonchalantly ~ —Walter Karig⟩ **b** — used interjectionally in informal speech often to emphasize a word or phrase (as in "He was, like, gorgeous") or for an apologetic, vague, or unassertive effect (as in "I need to, like, borrow some money") **4 :** NEARLY : APPROXIMATELY ⟨the actual interest is more ~ 18 percent⟩ — used interjectionally in informal speech with expressions of measurement ⟨it was, ~, five feet long⟩ ⟨goes there every day, ~⟩ — **as like as not** *or* **like as not :** PROBABLY
[7]**like** *conj* (14c) **1 a :** AS IF ⟨middle-aged men who looked ~ they might be out for their one night of the year —Norman Mailer⟩ **b** — used in intensive phrases ⟨drove ~ mad⟩ ⟨hurts ~ crazy⟩ **2 :** in the same way that : AS ⟨they raven down scenery ~ children do sweetmeats —John Keats⟩ **3 a :** in the way or manner that ⟨the violin sounds ~ an old masterpiece should⟩ ⟨did it ~ you told me⟩ **b** — used interjectionally in informal speech often with the verb *be* to introduce a quotation, paraphrase, or thought expressed by or imputed to the subject of the verb, or with *it's* to report a generally held opinion ⟨so I'm ~, "Give me a break"⟩ ⟨it's ~, "Who cares what he thinks?"⟩ **4 :** such as ⟨a bag ~ a doctor carries⟩ ⟨when your car has trouble — ~ when it won't start⟩ — used interjectionally in informal speech ⟨often stays up late, until ~ three in the morning⟩
usage *Like* has been used as a conjunction since the 14th century. In the 14th, 15th, and 16th centuries it was used in serious literature, but not often; in the 17th and 18th centuries it grew more frequent but less literary. It became markedly more frequent in literary use again in the 19th century. By mid-century it was coming under critical fire, but not from grammarians, oddly enough, who were wrangling over whether it could be called a preposition or not. There is no doubt that, after 600 years of use, conjunctive *like* is firmly established. It has been used by many prestigious literary figures of the past, though perhaps not in their most elevated works; in modern use it may be found in literature, journalism, and scholarly writing. While the present objection to it is perhaps more heated than rational, someone writing in

a formal prose style may well prefer to use *as, as if, such as,* or an entirely different construction instead.

[8]like *or* **liked** \ˈlīkt\ *verbal auxiliary* (15c) *chiefly dial* **:** came near **:** was near ⟨so loud I ~ to fell out of bed —Helen Eustis⟩

-like *adj comb form* **:** resembling or characteristic of ⟨bell-*like*⟩ ⟨lady-*like*⟩

like·li·hood \ˈlī-klē-ˌhu̇d\ *n* (14c) **:** PROBABILITY ⟨a strong ~ that he is correct —T. D. Anderson⟩

[1]like·ly \ˈlī-klē\ *adj* **like·li·er; -est** [ME, fr. OE *gelīclic* fitting (fr. *gelīc* like) and ON *glīkligr, līkligr,* fr. *glīkr* like; akin to OE *gelīc*] (14c) **1 :** having a high probability of occurring or being true **:** very probable ⟨rain is ~ today⟩ **2 :** apparently qualified **:** SUITABLE ⟨a ~ place⟩ **3 :** RELIABLE, CREDIBLE ⟨a ~ enough story⟩ **4 :** PROMISING ⟨a ~ candidate⟩ **5 :** ATTRACTIVE ⟨a ~ child⟩

[2]likely *adv* (14c) **:** in all probability **:** PROBABLY ⟨those who seek power will most ~ wind up exercising it —Halton Arp⟩

like–mind·ed \ˈlīk-ˈmīn-dəd\ *adj* (1526) **:** having a like disposition or purpose **:** of the same mind or habit of thought — **like–mind·ed·ly** *adv* — **like–mind·ed·ness** *n*

lik·en \ˈlī-kən\ *vt* **lik·ened; lik·en·ing** \ˈlī-kə-niŋ, ˈlīk-niŋ\ (14c) **:** COMPARE

like·ness \ˈlīk-nəs\ *n* (bef. 12c) **1 :** COPY, PORTRAIT **2 :** APPEARANCE, SEMBLANCE **3 :** the quality or state of being like **:** RESEMBLANCE

syn LIKENESS, SIMILARITY, RESEMBLANCE, SIMILITUDE, ANALOGY mean agreement or correspondence in details. LIKENESS implies a closer correspondence than SIMILARITY which often implies that things are merely somewhat alike ⟨a remarkable *likeness* to his late father⟩ ⟨some *similarity* between the two cases⟩. RESEMBLANCE implies similarity chiefly in appearance or external qualities ⟨statements that bear little *resemblance* to the truth⟩. SIMILITUDE applies chiefly to correspondence between abstractions ⟨two schools of social thought showing points of *similitude*⟩. ANALOGY implies likeness or parallelism in relations rather than in appearance or qualities ⟨pointed out *analogies* to past wars⟩.

like·wise \ˈlīk-ˌwīz\ *adv* (15c) **1 :** in like manner **:** SIMILARLY ⟨go and do ~⟩ **2 :** in addition **3 :** similarly so with me ⟨answered "~" to "Pleased to meet you"⟩

liking *n* (14c) **:** favorable regard **:** FONDNESS, TASTE ⟨had a greater ~ for law —E. M. Coulter⟩ ⟨took a ~ to the newcomer⟩

li·ku·ta \li-ˈkü-tə\ *n, pl* **ma·ku·ta** \mä-\ [ultim. fr. Kongo *dikuta* (pl. *makuta*) palm-leaf cloth bundle used as currency, fr. *-kuta* to gather, bundle] (1967) **:** a former monetary unit equal to 1/100 zaire

li·lac \ˈlī-ˌläk, -ˌlak, -lək\ *n* [obs. F (now *lilas*), fr. Ar *līlak,* fr. Pers *nīlak* bluish, fr. *nīl* blue, fr. Skt *nīla* dark blue] (1625) **1 a :** a widely cultivated European shrub (*Syringa vulgaris*) of the olive family that has cordate ovate leaves and large panicles of fragrant pinkish-purple or white flowers **b :** a tree or shrub congeneric with the lilac **2 :** a variable color averaging a moderate purple

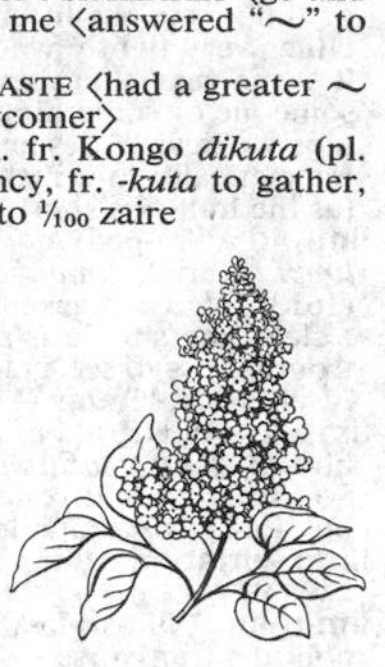

lilac 1a

lil·an·ge·ni \ˌli-lən-ˈge-nē\ *n, pl* **em·a·lan·ge·ni** \ˌe-mə-lən-ˈge-nē\ [Siswati, prob. fr. *ema-Langeni* lineage of the Swazi royal family] (1974) — see MONEY table

lil·ied \ˈli-lēd\ *adj* (1614) **1** *archaic* **:** resembling a lily in fairness **2 :** full of or covered with lilies

Lil·ith \ˈli-ləth\ *n* [LHeb *līlīth,* fr. Heb, a female demon] (1614) **1 :** a woman who in rabbinic legend is Adam's first wife, is supplanted by Eve, and becomes an evil spirit **2 :** a famous witch in medieval demonology

Lil·li·put \ˈli-li-(ˌ)pət\ *n* (1726) **:** an island in Swift's *Gulliver's Travels* where the inhabitants are six inches tall

[1]Lil·li·pu·tian \ˌli-lə-ˈpyü-shən\ *adj* (1726) **1 :** of, relating to, or characteristic of the Lilliputians or the island of Lilliput **2** *often not cap* **a :** SMALL, MINIATURE ⟨a ~ camera⟩ **b :** PETTY

[2]Lilliputian *n* (1726) **1 :** an inhabitant of Lilliput **2** *often not cap* **:** one resembling a Lilliputian; *esp* **:** an undersized individual

[1]lilt \ˈlilt\ *n* (ca. 1680) **1 :** a spirited and usu. cheerful song or tune **2 :** a rhythmical swing, flow, or cadence **3 :** a springy buoyant movement

[2]lilt *vb* [ME *lulten* to sound an alarm] *vt* (1722) **:** to sing or play in a lively cheerful manner ~ *vi* **1 :** to sing or speak rhythmically and with fluctuating pitch **2 :** to move in a lively springy manner

lilt·ing \ˈlil-tiŋ\ *adj* (1800) **1 :** characterized by a rhythmical swing or cadence ⟨a ~ stride⟩ **2 :** CHEERFUL, BUOYANT ⟨a ~ comedy⟩ — **lilt·ing·ly** \-lē\ *adv* — **lilt·ing·ness** *n*

[1]lily \ˈli-lē\ *n, pl* **lil·ies** [ME *lilie,* fr. OE, fr. L *lilium*] (bef. 12c) **1 :** any of a genus (*Lilium* of the family Liliaceae, the lily family) of erect perennial leafy-stemmed bulbous herbs that are native to the temperate northern hemisphere and are widely cultivated for their showy flowers; *broadly* **:** any of various plants of the lily family or of the related amaryllis or iris families **2 :** any of various plants with showy flowers: as **a :** a scarlet anemone (*Anemone coronaria*) of the Mediterranean region **b :** WATER LILY **c :** CALLA LILY **3 :** FLEUR-DE-LIS 2

[2]lily *adj* (15c) **:** resembling a lily in fairness, purity, or fragility ⟨my lady's ~ hand —John Keats⟩

lily–liv·ered \ˈli-lē-ˈli-vərd\ *adj* (1605) **:** lacking courage **:** COWARDLY

lily of the valley (1563) **:** a low perennial herb (*Convallaria majalis*) of the lily family that has usu. two large oblong lanceolate leaves and a raceme of fragrant nodding bell-shaped white flowers

lily pad *n* (1814) **:** a floating leaf of a water lily

[1]lily–white \ˈli-lē-ˈhwīt, -ˈwīt\ *adj* (14c) **1 :** white as a lily **2 :** characterized by or favoring the exclusion of blacks esp. from politics **3 :** IRREPROACHABLE, PURE

[2]lily–white *n* (ca. 1903) **:** a member of a lily-white political organization

Li·ma \ˈlē-mə\ (1952) — a communications code word for the letter *l*

li·ma bean \ˈlī-mə-\ *n* [*Lima,* Peru] (1756) **1 a :** a bushy or tall-growing tropical American bean (*Phaseolus limensis*) that is widely cultivated for its flat edible usu. pale green or whitish seeds **b :** SIEVA BEAN **2 :** the seed of a lima bean

li·ma·çon \ˌlē-mə-ˈsōⁿ\ *n* [F, lit., snail, fr. OF, dim. of *limaz* slug, snail, fr. L *limax;* akin to Russ *slimak* snail and prob. to OE *līm* birdlime — more at LIME] (1873) **:** a plane curve whose equation in polar coordinates has one of the forms $\rho = a \cos \theta \pm b$ or $\rho = a \sin \theta \pm b$ and which reduces to a cardioid when $a = b$

[1]limb \ˈlim\ *n* [ME *lim,* fr. OE; akin to ON *limr* limb and perh. to OE *lith* limb] (bef. 12c) **1 a :** one of the projecting paired appendages (as wings) of an animal body used esp. for movement and grasping but sometimes modified into sensory or sexual organs **b :** a leg or arm of a human being **2 :** a large primary branch of a tree **3 :** an active member or agent **4 :** EXTENSION, BRANCH **5 :** a mischievous child — **limb·less** \ˈlim-ləs\ *adj* — **limby** \ˈli-mē\ *adj* — **out on a limb :** in an exposed or dangerous position with little chance of retreat

[2]limb *vt* (1674) **1 :** DISMEMBER **2 :** to cut off the limbs of (a felled tree)

[3]limb *n* [L *limbus* border] (ca. 1677) **1 :** the outer edge of the apparent disk of a celestial body **2 :** the expanded portion of an organ or structure; *esp* **:** the upper spreading portion of a corolla (as of the phlox) whose lower part consists of a tube of fused petals

lim·ba \ˈlim-bə\ *n* [origin unknown] (1943) **1 :** a tall whitish-trunked West African tree (*Terminalia superba*) with straight-grained wood **2 :** the wood of a limba

lim·beck \ˈlim-ˌbek\ *n* [ME *lembike,* fr. ML *alembicum*] (14c) **:** ALEMBIC

limbed \ˈlimd\ *adj* (14c) **:** having limbs esp. of a specified kind or number — usu. used in combination ⟨strong-*limbed*⟩

[1]lim·ber \ˈlim-bər\ *n* [ME *lymour*] (15c) **:** a two-wheeled vehicle to which a gun or caisson may be attached

[2]limber *adj* [origin unknown] (1565) **1 :** capable of being shaped **:** FLEXIBLE **2 :** having a supple and resilient quality (as of mind or body) **:** AGILE, NIMBLE — **lim·ber·ly** *adv* — **lim·ber·ness** *n*

[3]limber *vb* **lim·bered; lim·ber·ing** \-b(ə-)riŋ\ *vt* (1748) **:** to cause to become limber ⟨~ up his fingers⟩ ~ *vi* **:** to become limber ⟨~ up by running⟩

limber pine *n* (1897) **:** a pine (*Pinus flexilis*) of the western U.S. and Canada that has flexible branches and needles in bundles of five

lim·bic \ˈlim-bik\ *adj* [NL *limbicus* of a border or margin, fr. L *limbus*] (1882) **:** of, relating to, or being the limbic system of the brain

limbic system *n* (1952) **:** a group of subcortical structures (as the hypothalamus, the hippocampus, and the amygdala) of the brain that are concerned esp. with emotion and motivation

[1]lim·bo \ˈlim-(ˌ)bō\ *n, pl* **limbos** [ME, fr. ML, abl. of *limbus* limbo, fr. L, border] (14c) **1** *often cap* **:** an abode of souls that are according to Roman Catholic theology barred from heaven because of not having received Christian baptism **2 a :** a place or state of restraint or confinement **b :** a place or state of neglect or oblivion ⟨proposals kept in ~⟩ **c :** an intermediate or transitional place or state **d :** a state of uncertainty

[2]limbo *n, pl* **limbos** [E of Trinidad & Barbados; akin to Jamaican E *limba* to bend, fr. E [3]*limber*] (ca. 1950) **:** a dance or contest that involves bending over backwards and passing under a horizontal pole lowered slightly for each successive pass

Lim·burg·er \ˈlim-ˌbər-gər\ *n* [D, one from Limburg, fr. *Limburg,* Belgium] (ca. 1870) **:** a pungent semisoft surface-ripened cheese

lim·bus \ˈlim-bəs\ *n* [L, border] (1877) **:** the marginal region of the cornea of the eye by which it is continuous with the sclera

[1]lime \ˈlīm\ *n* [ME, fr. OE *līm;* akin to OHG *līm* birdlime, L *limus* mud, slime, and perh. to L *linere* to smear] (bef. 12c) **1 :** BIRDLIME **2 a :** a caustic highly infusible solid that consists of calcium oxide often together with magnesium oxide, that is obtained by calcining forms of calcium carbonate (as shells or limestone), and that is used in building (as in mortar and plaster) and in agriculture — called also *quicklime* **b :** a dry white powder consisting essentially of calcium hydroxide that is made by treating quicklime with water **c :** CALCIUM ⟨carbonate of ~⟩

[2]lime *vt* **limed; lim·ing** (13c) **1 :** to smear with a sticky substance (as birdlime) **2 :** to entangle with or as if with birdlime **3 :** to treat or cover with lime ⟨~ the lawn in the spring⟩

[3]lime *adj* (15c) **:** of, relating to, or containing lime or limestone

[4]lime *n* [alter. of ME *lind,* fr. OE; akin to OHG *linta* linden] (1625) **:** a linden tree; *esp* **:** LINDEN 1a

[5]lime *n* [MF, fr. Sp *lima,* fr. Ar *līma, līm*] (1583) **1 :** the small globose yellowish green fruit of a widely cultivated spiny tropical Asian citrus tree (*Citrus aurantifolia*) with a usu. acid juicy pulp used as a flavoring agent and as a source of vitamin C **2 :** a tree that bears limes

lime·ade \ˌlīm-ˈād, ˈlī-ˌmād\ *n* (1892) **:** a beverage of sweetened lime juice mixed with plain or carbonated water

lime glass *n* (ca. 1909) **:** glass containing a substantial proportion of lime

lime–juic·er \ˈlīm-ˌjü-sər\ *n* [fr. the use of lime juice on British ships as a beverage to prevent scurvy] (1859) **1** *slang* **:** ENGLISHMAN **2** *slang* **a :** a British ship **b :** a British sailor

lime·kiln \-ˌkil, -ˌkiln\ *n* (13c) **:** a kiln or furnace for reducing limestone or shells to lime by burning

[1]lime·light \-ˌlīt\ *n* (1826) **1 a :** a stage lighting instrument producing illumination by means of an oxyhydrogen flame directed on a cylinder of lime and usu. equipped with a lens to concentrate the light in a beam **b :** the white light produced by such an instrument **c** *Brit* **:** SPOTLIGHT **2 :** the center of public attention

[2]limelight *vt* (1909) **:** to center attention on **:** SPOTLIGHT

li·men \ˈlī-mən\ *n* [L *limin-, limen* transverse beam in a door frame, threshold; prob. akin to L *limus* transverse] (1895) **:** THRESHOLD 3a

lim·er·ick \ˈli-mə-rik, ˈlim-rik\ *n* [*Limerick,* Ireland] (1896) **:** a light or humorous verse form of five chiefly anapestic verses of which lines 1, 2, and 5 are of three feet and lines 3 and 4 are of two feet with a rhyme scheme of *aabba*

lime·stone \ˈlīm-ˌstōn\ *n* (14c) **:** a rock that is formed chiefly by accumulation of organic remains (as shells or coral), consists mainly of calcium carbonate, is extensively used in building, and yields lime when burned

\ə\ **abut** \ᵊ\ **kitten**, F **table** \ər\ **further** \a\ **ash** \ā\ **ace** \ä\ **mop, mar** \au̇\ **out** \ch\ **chin** \e\ **bet** \ē\ **easy** \g\ **go** \i\ **hit** \ī\ **ice** \j\ **job** \ŋ\ **sing** \ō\ **go** \ȯ\ **law** \ȯi\ **boy** \th\ **thin** \t͟h\ **the** \ü\ **loot** \u̇\ **foot** \y\ **yet** \zh\ **vision, beige** \k̲, ⁿ, œ, ue, ʸ\ *see* Guide to Pronunciation

lime–twig \ˈlīm-ˌtwig\ *n* (15c) **1 :** a twig covered with birdlime to catch birds **2 :** SNARE

lime·wa·ter \-ˌwȯ-tər, -ˌwä-\ *n* (ca. 1500) **:** an alkaline water solution of calcium hydroxide used as an antacid

1lim·ey \ˈlī-mē\ *n, pl* **limeys** *often cap* [*lime*-juicer + 4-*y*] (1918) **1** *slang* **:** a British sailor **2** *slang* **:** ENGLISHMAN

2limey *var of* LIMY

lim·i·nal \ˈli-mə-nᵊl\ *adj* [L *limin-, limen* threshold] (1884) **1 :** of or relating to a sensory threshold **2 :** barely perceptible **3 :** of, relating to, or being an intermediate state, phase, or condition **:** IN-BETWEEN, TRANSITIONAL ‹in the ~ state between life and death —Deborah Jowitt›

1lim·it \ˈli-mət\ *n* [ME, fr. AF *limite,* fr. L *limit-, limes* boundary] (14c) **1 a :** something that bounds, restrains, or confines **b :** the utmost extent **2 a :** a geographic or political boundary **b** *pl* **:** the place enclosed within a boundary **:** BOUNDS **3 :** LIMITATION **4 :** a determining feature or differentia in logic **5 :** a prescribed maximum or minimum amount, quantity, or number: as **a :** the maximum quantity of game or fish that may be taken legally in a specified period **b :** a maximum established for a gambling bet, raise, or payoff **6 a :** a number whose numerical difference from a mathematical function is arbitrarily small for all values of the independent variables that are sufficiently close to but not equal to given prescribed numbers or that are sufficiently large positively or negatively **b :** a number that for an infinite sequence of numbers is such that ultimately each of the remaining terms of the sequence differs from this number by less than any given positive amount **7 :** something that is exasperating or intolerable — **lim·it·less** \-ləs\ *adj* — **lim·it·less·ly** *adv* — **lim·it·less·ness** *n*

2limit *vt* (14c) **1 :** to assign certain limits to **:** PRESCRIBE ‹reserved the right to ~ use of the land› **2 a :** to restrict the bounds or limits of ‹the specialist can no longer ~ himself to his specialty› **b :** to curtail or reduce in quantity or extent ‹we must ~ the power of aggressors› — **lim·it·able** \-mə-tə-bəl\ *adj* — **lim·it·er** *n*

syn LIMIT, RESTRICT, CIRCUMSCRIBE, CONFINE mean to set bounds for. LIMIT implies setting a point or line (as in time, space, speed, or degree) beyond which something cannot or is not permitted to go ‹visits are *limited* to 30 minutes›. RESTRICT suggests a narrowing or tightening or restraining within or as if within an encircling boundary ‹laws intended to *restrict* the freedom of the press›. CIRCUMSCRIBE stresses a restriction on all sides and by clearly defined boundaries ‹the work of the investigating committee was carefully *circumscribed*›. CONFINE suggests severe restraint and a resulting cramping, fettering, or hampering ‹our choices were *confined* by finances›.

lim·i·tary \ˈli-mə-ˌter-ē\ *adj* (1620) **1** *archaic* **:** subject to limits **2 a** *archaic* **:** of or relating to a boundary **b :** LIMITING, ENCLOSING

lim·i·ta·tion \ˌli-mə-ˈtā-shən\ *n* (14c) **1 :** an act or instance of limiting **2 :** the quality or state of being limited **3 :** something that limits **:** RESTRAINT **4 :** a certain period limited by statute after which actions, suits, or prosecutions cannot be brought in the courts — **lim·i·ta·tion·al** \-shnəl, -shə-nᵊl\ *adj*

lim·i·ta·tive \ˈli-mə-ˌtā-tiv\ *adj* (1530) **:** LIMITING, RESTRICTIVE

lim·it·ed \ˈli-mə-təd\ *adj* (1597) **1 a :** confined within limits **:** RESTRICTED ‹~ success› **b** *of a train* **:** offering faster service esp. by making a limited number of stops **2 :** characterized by enforceable limitations prescribed (as by a constitution) upon the scope or exercise of powers ‹a ~ monarchy› **3 :** lacking breadth and originality ‹a bit ~; a bit thick in the head —Virginia Woolf› — **lim·it·ed·ly** *adv* — **lim·it·ed·ness** *n*

limited–access *adj* (1944) *of a road* **:** having access restricted to a relatively small number of points

limited edition *n* (1890) **:** an issue of something collectible (as books, prints, or medals) that is advertised to be limited to a relatively small number of copies

limited liability *n* (1848) **:** liability (as of a stockholder or shipowner) limited by statute or treaty

limited liability partnership *n* (1980) **:** a partnership in which the partnership is liable as an entity for debts and obligations and the partners are not liable personally

limited partner *n* (1907) **:** a partner in a venture who has no management authority and whose liability is restricted to the amount of his or her investment — compare GENERAL PARTNER

limited partnership *n* (1846) **:** a partnership having one or more general partners and one or more limited partners

limited war *n* (1939) **:** a war whose objective is less than the total defeat of the enemy

lim·it·ing \ˈli-mə-tiŋ\ *adj* (1644) **1 a :** functioning as a limit **:** RESTRICTIVE ‹~ value› **b :** being an environmental factor (as a nutrient) that limits the population size of an organism **2 :** serving to specify the application of the modified noun ‹*this* in "this book" is a ~ word› — **lim·it·ing·ly** *adv*

limit point *n* (1905) **:** a point that is related to a set of points in such a way that every neighborhood of the point no matter how small contains another point belonging to the set — called also *point of accumulation*

lim·i·trophe \ˈli-mə-ˌtrōf, -ˌtrȯf\ *adj* [F, fr. LL *limitrophus* bordering upon, lit., providing subsistence for frontier troops, irreg. fr. L *limit-, limes* boundary + Gk *trophos* feeder, fr. *trephein* to nourish] (1763) **:** situated on a border or frontier **:** ADJACENT ‹the area ~ to the river›

lim·mer \ˈli-mər\ *n* [ME (Sc)] (15c) **1** *chiefly Scot* **:** SCOUNDREL **2** *chiefly Scot* **:** PROSTITUTE

limn \ˈlim\ *vt* **limned; limn·ing** \ˈli-miŋ, ˈlim-niŋ\ [ME *limnen* to illuminate (a manuscript), prob. back-formation from *lymnour* illuminator, alter. of *lumenur,* fr. AF *aluminer, enluminer* to illuminate, ultim. fr. L *illuminare*] (1592) **1 :** to draw or paint on a surface **2 :** to outline in clear sharp detail **:** DELINEATE **3 :** DESCRIBE ‹the novel ~*s* the frontier life of the settlers› — **limn·er** \ˈli-mər, ˈlim-nər\ *n*

lim·net·ic \lim-ˈne-tik\ *adj* [ISV, fr. Gk *limnē* pool, marshy lake; perh. akin to L *limus* mud — more at LIME] (1899) **:** of, relating to, or inhabiting the open water of a body of freshwater ‹~ environment›

lim·nol·o·gy \lim-ˈnä-lə-jē\ *n* [Gk *limnē* + ISV *-logy*] (ca. 1888) **:** the scientific study of bodies of freshwater (as lakes) — **lim·no·log·i·cal** \ˌlim-nə-ˈlä-ji-kəl\ *also* **lim·no·log·ic** \-ˈlä-jik\ *adj* — **lim·nol·o·gist** \lim-ˈnä-lə-jist\ *n*

limo \ˈli-(ˌ)mō\ *n, pl* **lim·os** (1968) **:** LIMOUSINE

Li·moges \li-ˈmōzh\ *n* [*Limoges,* France] (1844) **:** enamelware or porcelain made at Limoges

lim·o·nene \ˈli-mə-ˌnēn\ *n* [ISV, fr. F *limon* lemon, fr. MF] (1845) **:** a widely distributed terpene hydrocarbon $C_{10}H_{16}$ that occurs in essential oils (as of oranges or lemons) and has a lemon odor

li·mo·nite \ˈlī-mə-ˌnīt\ *n* [G *Limonit,* fr. Gk *leimōn* wet meadow; akin to Gk *limnē* pool] (1823) **:** a native hydrous ferric oxide of variable composition that is an ore of iron — **li·mo·nit·ic** \ˌlī-mə-ˈni-tik\ *adj*

Lim·ou·sin \li-ˈmü-sin, ˈli-mə-ˌzēn, lē-mü-ˈzaⁿ\ *n* [*Limousin,* France] (1920) **:** any of a French breed of medium-sized yellowish-red cattle bred esp. for meat

lim·ou·sine \ˈli-mə-ˌzēn, ˌli-mə-ˈ\ *n* [F, lit., cloak, fr. *Limousin,* France] (1902) **1 :** a large luxurious often chauffeur-driven sedan that usu. has a glass partition separating the driver's seat from the passenger compartment **2 :** a large vehicle for transporting passengers to and from an airport

limousine liberal *n* (1969) **:** a wealthy political liberal

1limp \ˈlimp\ *vi* [prob. fr. ME *lympen* to fall short; akin to OE *limpan* to happen, *lemp*healt lame] (ca. 1570) **1 a :** to walk lamely; *esp* **:** to walk favoring one leg **b :** to go unsteadily **:** FALTER **2 :** to proceed slowly or with difficulty ‹the ship ~*ed* back to port› — **limp·er** *n*

2limp *n* (1818) **:** a limping movement or gait

3limp *adj* [akin to 1*limp*] (ca. 1706) **1 a :** lacking firm texture, substance, or structure ‹~ curtains› ‹her hair hung ~ about her shoulders› **b :** not stiff or rigid ‹a book in a ~ binding› **2 a :** WEARY, EXHAUSTED ‹~ with fatigue› **b :** lacking in strength, vigor, or firmness **:** SPIRITLESS — **limp·ly** *adv* — **limp·ness** *n*

lim·pa \ˈlim-pə\ *n* [Sw] (1948) **:** rye bread made with molasses or brown sugar

lim·pet \ˈlim-pət\ *n* [ME *lempet,* fr. OE *lempedu,* fr. ML *lampreda* lamprey] (bef. 12c) **1 :** a marine gastropod mollusk (esp. families Acmaeidae and Patellidae) that has a low conical shell broadly open beneath, browses over rocks or timbers in the littoral area, and clings very tightly when disturbed **2 :** one that clings tenaciously to someone or something **3 :** an explosive device designed to cling magnetically to a metallic surface (as the hull of a ship)

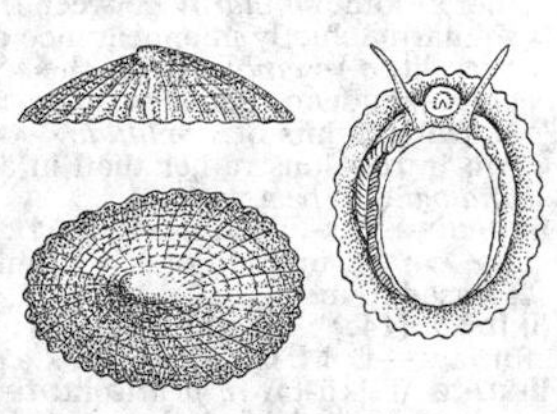

limpet 1

lim·pid \ˈlim-pəd\ *adj* [F or L; F *limpide,* fr. L *limpidus,* perh. fr. *lympha* water — more at LYMPH] (1613) **1 a :** marked by transparency **:** PELLUCID ‹~ streams› **b :** clear and simple in style ‹~ prose› **2 :** absolutely serene and untroubled ***syn*** see CLEAR — **lim·pid·i·ty** \lim-ˈpi-də-tē\ *n* — **lim·pid·ly** \ˈlim-pəd-lē\ *adv* — **lim·pid·ness** *n*

limp·kin \ˈlim(p)-kən\ *n* [perh. fr. 1*limp*] (1871) **:** a large brown wading bird (*Aramus guarauna*) of southern Georgia, Florida, and Central and So. America that resembles a bittern but has a longer slightly curved bill, longer neck and legs, and white stripes on head and neck

limp–wrist·ed \ˈlimp-ˌris-təd\ *adj* (ca. 1960) **1 :** EFFEMINATE **2 :** WEAK

lim·u·lus \ˈlim-yə-ləs\ *n, pl* **-li** \-ˌlī, -ˌlē\ [NL, genus name, fr. L *limus* oblique, transverse — more at LIMEN] (1837) **:** HORSESHOE CRAB

limy *or* **lim·ey** \ˈlī-mē\ *adj* **lim·i·er; -est** (ca. 1552) **1 :** smeared with or consisting of lime **:** VISCOUS **2 :** containing lime or limestone **3 :** resembling or having the qualities of lime

lin *abbr* lineal; linear

lin·ac \ˈli-ˌnak\ *n* (1950) **:** LINEAR ACCELERATOR

lin·age *also* **line·age** \ˈlī-nij\ *n* (1884) **:** the number of lines of printed or written matter

lin·al·o·ol \lə-ˈna-lə-ˌwȯl, lī-, -ˌwōl\ *n* [ISV, fr. MexSp *lindruloe,* tree yielding perfume, fr. ML *lignum aloes,* lit., wood of the aloe] (1891) **:** a fragrant liquid alcohol $C_{10}H_{18}O$ that occurs both free and in the form of esters in many essential oils and is used in perfumes, soaps, and flavoring materials

linch·pin *also* **lynch·pin** \ˈlinch-ˌpin\ *n* [ME *lynspin,* fr. *lyns* linchpin (fr. OE *lynis*) + *pin;* akin to MHG *luns* linchpin] (13c) **1 :** a locking pin inserted crosswise (as through the end of an axle or shaft) **2 :** one that serves to hold together parts or elements that exist or function as a unit ‹the ~ in the defense's case›

Lin·coln \ˈliŋ-kən\ *n* [*Lincoln*shire, England] (1837) **:** any of an English breed of long-wooled mutton-type sheep

Lin·coln·i·a·na \(ˌ)liŋ-ˌkō-nē-ˈa-nə, -ˈa-nə, -ˈä-nə\ *n pl* (1921) **:** materials relating to Abraham Lincoln

Lincoln's Birthday \ˈliŋ-kənz-\ *n* (1898) **1 :** February 12 observed as a legal holiday in many states of the U.S. **2 :** the first Monday in February observed as a legal holiday by some states of the U.S.

lin·co·my·cin \ˌliŋ-kə-ˈmī-sᵊn\ *n* [NL *linco*lnensis (specific epithet of *Streptomyces lincolnensis*) + E *-mycin*] (1963) **:** an antibiotic $C_{18}H_{34}N_2O_6S$ obtained from an actinomycete (*Streptomyces lincolnensis*) and effective esp. against gram-positive bacteria

Lincs *abbr* Lincolnshire

lin·dane \ˈlin-ˌdān\ *n* [T. van der *Linden,* 20th cent. Belgian chemist] (ca. 1949) **:** a persistent organochlorine insecticide that consists chiefly of the gamma isomer of BHC

lin·den \ˈlin-dən\ *n* [ME, made of linden wood, fr. OE, fr. *lind* linden tree; prob. akin to OE *līthe* gentle — more at LITHE] (1577) **1 :** any of a genus (*Tilia* of the family Tiliaceae, the linden family) of deciduous trees of temperate regions that have cordate leaves and a winglike bract attached to the peduncle of the flower and fruit and that are often planted as ornamental and shade trees: as **a :** a commonly cultivated European tree (*T. europaea* syn. *T. vulgaris*) much used for ornamental planting **b :** a tree (*T. americana*) chiefly of the central and eastern U.S. — called also *basswood* **2 :** the light fine-grained white wood of a linden; *esp* **:** BASSWOOD 2

Lin·dy \ˈlin-dē\ *n* [prob. fr. *Lindy,* nickname of Charles A. Lindbergh] (1931) **:** a jitterbug dance originating in Harlem and later developing many local variants — called also *Lindy Hop*

1line \ˈlīn\ *n, often attrib* [ME; partly fr. AF *lingne,* fr. L *linea,* fr. fem. of *lineus* made of flax, fr. *linum* flax; partly fr. OE *līne;* akin to OE *līn* flax

— more at LINEN] (bef. 12c) **1 a :** a length of cord or cord-like material: as (1) **:** a comparatively strong slender cord (2) **:** CLOTHESLINE (3) **:** a rope used on shipboard **b** (1) **:** a device for catching fish consisting of a cord with hooks and other fishing gear (2) **:** scope for activity **:** ROPE **c :** a length of material used in measuring and leveling **d** (1) **:** piping for conveying a fluid (as steam) (2) **:** a narrow short synthetic tube that is inserted approximately one inch into a vein (as of the arm) to provide temporary intravenous access for the administration of fluid, medication, or nutrients **e** (1) **:** a wire or pair of wires connecting one telegraph or telephone station with another or a whole system of such wires; *also* **:** any circuit in an electronic communication system (2) **:** a telephone connection ⟨tried to get a ~⟩; *also* **:** an individual telephone extension ⟨a call on ~ 2⟩ (3) **:** the principal circuits of an electric power system **2 a** (1) **:** a horizontal row of written or printed characters; *also* **:** a blank row in lieu of such characters (2) **:** a unit in the rhythmic structure of verse formed by the grouping of a number of the smallest units of the rhythm (as metrical feet) (3) **:** a distinct segment of a computer program containing a single command or a small number of commands **b :** a short letter **:** NOTE **c** *pl* **:** a certificate of marriage **d :** the words making up a part in a drama — usu. used in pl. **e :** any of the successive horizontal rows of picture elements on the screen of a cathode-ray tube (as a television screen) **3 a :** something (as a ridge or seam) that is distinct, elongated, and narrow **b :** a narrow crease (as on the face) **:** WRINKLE **c :** the course or direction of something in motion **:** ROUTE **d** (1) **:** a state of agreement or conformity **:** ACCORDANCE (2) **:** a state of order, control, or obedience ⟨wouldn't let them get out of ~⟩ **e** (1) **:** a boundary of an area ⟨the state ~⟩ (2) **:** DISTINCTION 2 ⟨the fine ~ between love and hate⟩ **f :** the track and roadbed of a railway **g :** an amount of cocaine that is arranged in a line to be inhaled through the nose **4 a :** a course of conduct, action, or thought; *esp* **:** an official or public position ⟨the party ~⟩ **b :** a field of activity or interest **c :** a glib often persuasive way of talking **5 a :** LIMIT, RESTRAINT **b** *archaic* **:** position in life **:** LOT **6 a** (1) **:** FAMILY, LINEAGE (2) **:** a strain produced and maintained esp. by selective breeding or biological culture (3) **:** a chronological series **b :** dispositions made to cover extended military positions and presenting a front to the enemy — usu. used in pl. **c :** a military formation in which the different elements are abreast of each other **d :** naval ships arranged in a regular order **e** (1) **:** the combatant forces of an army distinguished from the staff corps and supply services (2) **:** the force of a regular navy **f** (1) **:** officers of the navy eligible for command at sea distinguished from officers of the staff (2) **:** officers of the army belonging to a combatant branch **g :** an arrangement or placement of persons or objects of one kind in an orderly series ⟨a ~ of trees⟩ ⟨stand on ~⟩ ⟨waiting in ~⟩; *also* **:** the persons or objects so positioned ⟨the ~ moved slowly at the bank⟩ **h** (1) **:** a group of public conveyances plying regularly under one management over a route (2) **:** a system of transportation together with its equipment, routes, and appurtenances; *also* **:** the company owning or operating it **i :** a succession of musical notes esp. considered in melodic phrases **j** (1) **:** an arrangement of operations in manufacturing permitting sequential occurrence on various stages of production (2) **:** the personnel of an organization that are responsible for its stated objective **k** (1) **:** the seven players including center, two guards, two tackles, and two ends who in offensive football play line up on or within one foot of the line of scrimmage (2) **:** the players who in defensive play line up within one yard of the line of scrimmage **l :** a group of three players including a left winger, center, and right winger who play together as a unit in hockey **7 :** a narrow elongated mark drawn or projected: as **a** (1) **:** a circle of latitude or longitude on a map (2) **:** EQUATOR **b :** a mark (as on a map) recording a boundary, division, or contour **c :** any of the horizontal parallel strokes on a music staff on or between which notes are placed — compare SPACE **d :** a mark (as by pencil) that forms part of the formal design of a picture distinguished from the shading or color **e :** a division on a bridge score dividing the score for bonuses from that for tricks **f** (1) **:** a demarcation of a limit with reference to which the playing of some game or sport is regulated — usu. used in combination (2) **:** a marked or imaginary line across a playing area (as a football field) parallel to the end line (3) **:** LINE OF SCRIMMAGE **8 :** a straight or curved geometric element that is generated by a moving point and that has extension only along the path of the point **:** CURVE **9 a :** a defining outline **:** CONTOUR **b :** a general plan **:** MODEL — usu. used in pl. **10 a** *chiefly Brit* **:** PICA — used to indicate the size of large type **b :** the unit of fineness of halftones expressed as the number of screen lines to the linear inch **11 :** merchandise or services of the same general class for sale or regularly available **12 a :** a source of information **:** INSIGHT **b :** betting odds offered by a bookmaker esp. on a sporting event **13 :** a complete game of 10 frames in bowling — called also *string* **14 :** LINE DRIVE — **liny** *also* **lin·ey** \ˈlī-nē\ *adj* — **between the lines 1 :** by implication **:** in an indirect way **2 :** by way of inference — **down the line 1 :** all the way **:** FULLY **2 :** in the future — **in line for :** due or in a position to receive — **on line :** in or into operation — **on the line 1 :** at great risk ⟨puts his future *on the line* by backing that policy⟩ **2 :** on the border between two categories

[2]**line** *vb* **lined; lin·ing** *vt* (1530) **1 :** to mark or cover with a line or lines ⟨*lined* paper⟩ **2 :** to depict with lines **:** DRAW **3 :** to place or form a line along ⟨pedestrians ~ the walks⟩ **4 :** to form into a line or lines **:** ALIGN ⟨~ up troops⟩ **5 :** to hit (as a baseball) hard and in a usu. straight line ~ *vi* **1 :** to hit a line drive in baseball **2 :** to come into the correct relative position **:** ALIGN

[3]**line** *vt* **lined; lin·ing** [ME, fr. *line* flax, fr. OE *līn*] (14c) **1 :** to cover the inner surface of ⟨~ a cloak with silk⟩ **2 :** to put something in the inside of **:** FILL **3 :** to serve as the lining of ⟨tapestries *lined* the walls⟩ **4** *obs* **:** FORTIFY — **line one's pockets :** to take money freely and esp. dishonestly

[1]**lin·e·age** \ˈli-nē-ij *also* ˈli-nij\ *n* (14c) **1 a :** descent in a line from a common progenitor **b :** DERIVATION **2 :** a group of individuals tracing descent from a common ancestor; *esp* **:** such a group of persons whose common ancestor is regarded as its founder

[2]**lineage** *var of* LINAGE

lin·e·al \ˈli-nē-əl\ *adj* (14c) **1 :** LINEAR **2 :** composed of or arranged in lines **3 a :** consisting of or being in a direct male or female line of ancestry — compare COLLATERAL 2 **b :** relating to or derived from ancestors **:** HEREDITARY **c :** descended in a direct line **4 a :** belonging to one lineage ⟨~ relatives⟩ **b :** of, relating to, or dealing with a lineage — **lin·e·al·i·ty** \ˌli-nē-ˈa-lə-tē\ *n* — **lin·e·al·ly** \ˈli-nē-ə-lē\ *adv*

lin·e·a·ment \ˈli-nē-ə-mənt\ *n* [ME, fr. L *lineamentum,* fr. *lineare* to draw a line, fr. *linea*] (15c) **1 a :** an outline, feature, or contour of a body or figure and esp. of a face — usu. used in pl. **b :** a linear topographic feature (as of the earth) that reveals a characteristic (as a fault or the subsurface structure) **2 :** a distinguishing or characteristic feature — usu. used in pl. — **lin·e·a·men·tal** \ˌli-nē-ə-ˈmen-tᵊl\ *adj*

lin·e·ar \ˈli-nē-ər\ *adj* (ca. 1656) **1 a** (1) **:** of, relating to, resembling, or having a graph that is a line and esp. a straight line **:** STRAIGHT (2) **:** involving a single dimension **b** (1) **:** of the first degree with respect to one or more variables (2) **:** of, relating to, based on, or being linear equations, linear differential equations, linear functions, linear transformations, or linear algebra **c** (1) **:** characterized by an emphasis on line ⟨~ art⟩ (2) **:** composed of simply drawn lines with little attempt at pictorial representation ⟨~ script⟩ **d :** consisting of a straight chain of atoms **2 :** elongated with nearly parallel sides ⟨~ leaf⟩ — see LEAF illustration **3 :** having or being a response or output that is directly proportional to the input **4 :** of, relating to, or based or depending on sequential development ⟨~ thinking⟩ ⟨a ~ narrative⟩ — **lin·e·ar·i·ty** \ˌli-nē-ˈer-ə-tē, -ˈa-rə-\ *n* — **lin·e·ar·ly** \ˈli-nē-ər-lē\ *adv*

Linear A \-ˈā\ *n* (1948) **:** a linear form of writing used in Crete from the 18th to the 15th centuries B.C.

linear accelerator *n* (1945) **:** a device in which charged particles are accelerated in a straight line by successive impulses from a series of electric fields

linear algebra *n* (1870) **:** a branch of mathematics that is concerned with mathematical structures closed under the operations of addition and scalar multiplication and that includes the theory of systems of linear equations, matrices, determinants, vector spaces, and linear transformations

Linear B \-ˈbē\ *n* (1950) **:** a linear form of writing employing syllabic characters and used at Knossos on Crete and on the Greek mainland from the 15th to the 12th centuries B.C. for documents in Mycenaean Greek

linear combination *n* (1960) **:** a mathematical entity (as $4x + 5y + 6z$) which is composed of sums and differences of elements (as variables, matrices, or functions) esp. when the coefficients are not all zero

linear dependence *n* (1907) **:** the property of one set (as of matrices or vectors) having at least one linear combination of its elements equal to zero when the coefficients are taken from another given set and at least one of its coefficients is not equal to zero — **linearly dependent** *adj*

linear equation *n* (1816) **:** an equation of the first degree in any number of variables

linear function *n* (1853) **1 :** a mathematical function in which the variables appear only in the first degree, are multiplied by constants, and are combined only by addition and subtraction **2 :** LINEAR TRANSFORMATION

linear independence *n* (1907) **:** the property of a set (as of matrices or vectors) having no linear combination of all its elements equal to zero when coefficients are taken from a given set unless the coefficient of each element is zero — **linearly independent** *adj*

linear interpolation *n* (1965) **:** estimation of a function (as a logarithm) by assuming that it is a straight line between known values

lin·e·ar·ise *Brit var of* LINEARIZE

lin·e·ar·ize \ˈli-nē-ə-ˌrīz\ *vt* **-ized; -iz·ing** (1895) **:** to give a linear form to; *also* **:** to project in linear form — **lin·e·ar·i·za·tion** \ˌli-nē-ə-rə-ˈzā-shən\ *n*

linear measure *n* (ca. 1890) **1 :** a measure of length **2 :** a system of measures of length

linear motor *n* (1957) **:** a motor that produces thrust in a straight line by direct induction rather than with the use of gears — called also *linear induction motor*

linear perspective *n* (ca. 1656) **:** PERSPECTIVE 1a

linear programming *n* (1949) **:** a mathematical method of solving practical problems (as the allocation of resources) by means of linear functions where the variables involved are subject to constraints

linear regression *n* (1958) **:** the process of finding a straight line (as by least squares) that best approximates a set of points on a graph

linear space *n* (ca. 1884) **:** VECTOR SPACE

linear transformation *n* (ca. 1846) **1 :** a transformation in which the new variables are linear functions of the old variables **2 :** a function that maps the vectors of one vector space onto the vectors of the same or another vector space with the same field of scalars in such a way that the image of the sum of two vectors equals the sum of their images and the image of the product of a scalar and a vector equals the product of the scalar and the image of the vector

lin·e·a·tion \ˌli-nē-ˈā-shən\ *n* [ME *lineacion* outline, fr. L *lineation-, lineatio,* fr. *lineare* to mark with lines, fr. *linea*] (14c) **1 a :** the action of marking with lines **:** DELINEATION **b :** OUTLINE **2 :** an arrangement of lines

line·back·er \ˈlīn-ˌba-kər\ *n* (1949) **:** a defensive football player who lines up immediately behind the line of scrimmage to make tackles on running plays through the line or defend against short passes

line·back·ing \-ˌba-kiŋ\ *n* (1953) **:** the action or art of playing linebacker

line·breed·ing \-ˌbrē-diŋ\ *n* (ca. 1879) **:** the interbreeding of individuals within a particular line of descent usu. to perpetuate desirable characters — **line·bred** \-ˌbred\ *adj*

line·cast·er \-ˌkas-tər\ *n* (1964) **:** a machine that casts metal type in lines — **line·cast·ing** \-tiŋ\ *n*

line·cut \ˈlīn-ˌkət\ *n* (ca. 1909) **:** a photoengraving of a line drawing

line dance *n* (1948) **1 :** CONTREDANSE 1 **2 :** a dance performed by a group usu. in single file **3 :** a dance in which the dancers stand in ranks while performing a particular set of steps in unison — **line dancer** *n* — **line dancing** *n*

\ə\ **a**but \ᵊ\ kitten, F table \ər\ **f**urther \a\ **a**sh \ā\ **a**ce \ä\ m**o**p, m**a**r
\au̇\ **ou**t \ch\ **ch**in \e\ b**e**t \ē\ **ea**sy \g\ **g**o \i\ h**i**t \ī\ **i**ce \j\ **j**ob
\ŋ\ si**ng** \ō\ g**o** \ȯ\ l**aw** \ȯi\ b**oy** \th\ **th**in \t͟h\ **th**e \ü\ l**oo**t \u̇\ f**oo**t
\y\ **y**et \zh\ vi**s**ion, beige \k̲, ⁿ, œ, ue, ʸ\ *see* Guide to Pronunciation

line drawing *n* (1891) : a drawing made in solid lines
line drive *n* (1903) : a batted baseball hit in a nearly straight line usu. not far above the ground
line engraving *n* (1802) : an engraving cut by hand directly in the plate
line graph *n* (ca. 1924) : a graph in which points representing values of a variable for suitable values of an independent variable are connected by a broken line
line–haul \ˈlīn-ˌhȯl\ *n* (ca. 1923) : the transporting of items or persons between terminals
line item *n* (1962) : an appropriation that is itemized on a separate line in a budget — **line–item** \ˈlīn-ˈī-təm\ *adj*
line–item veto *n* (1979) : the power of a government executive to veto specific items in an appropriations bill without vetoing the bill altogether
line judge *n* (1970) : a football linesman whose duties include keeping track of the official time for the game
line•man \ˈlīn-mən\ *n* (1876) **1** : one who sets up or repairs electric wire communication or power lines — called also *linesman* **2** : a player in the forward line of a team; *specif* : a football player in the line
[1]**lin•en** \ˈli-nən\ *adj* [ME, fr. OE *līnen,* fr. *līn* flax, fr. L *linum* flax; akin to Gk *linon* flax, thread] (bef. 12c) **1** : made of flax **2** : made of or resembling linen
[2]**linen** *n* (14c) **1 a** : cloth made of flax and noted for its strength, coolness, and luster **b** : thread or yarn spun from flax **2** : clothing or household articles made of linen cloth or similar fabric **3** : paper made from linen fibers or with a linen finish
line of credit (1917) : the maximum credit allowed a buyer or borrower; *also* : an agreement providing credit up to a certain amount
line of duty (ca. 1918) : all that is authorized, required, or normally associated with some field of responsibility
line officer *n* (1850) : a commissioned officer assigned to the line of the army or navy — compare STAFF OFFICER
line of force (1837) : a line in a field of force (as a magnetic or electric field) whose tangent at any point gives the direction of the field at that point
line of scrimmage (ca. 1909) : an imaginary line in football that is parallel to the goal lines and tangent to the nose of the ball laid on the ground and marks the position of the ball at the start of each down
line of sight (1559) **1** : a line from an observer's eye to a distant point **2** : the line between two points; *specif* : the straight path between a transmitting antenna (as for radio or television signals) and a receiving antenna when unobstructed by the horizon
line out *vt* (1613) **1** : to indicate with or as if with lines : OUTLINE ⟨*line out* a route⟩ **2** : to arrange in an extended line **3** : BELT 4 ⟨*line out* a song⟩ ~ *vi* **1** : to move rapidly ⟨*lined out* for home⟩ **2** : to make an out by hitting a baseball in a line drive that is caught
line printer *n* (1955) : a high-speed printing device (as for a computer) that prints each line as a unit rather than character by character
[1]**lin•er** \ˈlī-nər\ *n* (15c) **1** : one that makes, draws, or uses lines **2 a** : a ship belonging to a regular line **b** : an airplane belonging to an airline **3** : LINE DRIVE **4** : something with which lines are made
[2]**liner** *n* (1611) **1** : one that lines or is used to line or back something **2** : JACKET 3c(2) — **lin•er•less** \-ləs\ *adj*
li•ner•board \ˈlī-nər-ˌbȯrd\ *n* (1948) : a thin cardboard used for the flat facings of corrugated containerboard
liner notes *n pl* (1955) : comments or explanatory notes about a recording printed on the jacket or an insert
line score *n* (1946) : a score of a baseball game giving the runs, hits, and errors made by each team — compare BOX SCORE
lines•man \ˈlīnz-mən\ *n* (1883) **1** : LINEMAN 1 **2** : an official who assists a referee (as in football or hockey) esp. in determining if a ball, puck, or player is out-of-bounds or offside
line squall *n* (1887) : a squall or thunderstorm occurring along a cold front
line storm *n* (1850) : an equinoctial storm
line•up \ˈlī-ˌnəp\ *n* (1889) **1 a** : a list of players taking part in a game (as of baseball) **b** : the players on such a list **2 a** : an alignment (as in entertainment or politics) of persons or things having a common purpose, distinction, or bond ⟨the show's star-studded ~⟩ **b** : LINE 11 **c** : a television programming schedule **3** : a line of persons arranged esp. for inspection or for identification by police
line up *vi* (1864) **1** : to assume an orderly linear arrangement ⟨*line up* for inspection⟩ **2** : to align oneself ⟨he *lined up* with the liberals against the bill⟩ ~ *vt* **1** : to put into alignment **2** : to arrange for ⟨*line up* support for a candidate⟩
[1]**ling** \ˈliŋ\ *n* [ME; akin to D *leng* ling, OE *lang* long] (13c) **1** : any of various fishes (as a hake or burbot) of the cod family **2** : LINGCOD
[2]**ling** *n* [ME, fr. ON *lyng*] (13c) : a heath plant; *esp* : a common Old World heather (*Calluna vulgaris*)
[1]**-ling** *n suffix* [ME, fr. OE; akin to OE *-ing*] **1** : one connected with or having the quality of ⟨hire*ling*⟩ **2** : young, small, or inferior one ⟨duck*ling*⟩
[2]**-ling** *or* **-lings** *adv suffix* [ME *-ling* (fr. OE), *-linges* (fr. *-ling* + *-es* -s); akin to OHG *-lingūn* -ling, OE *lang* long] : in (such) a direction or manner ⟨side*ling*⟩ ⟨flat*ling*⟩
Lin•ga•la \liŋ-ˈgä-lə\ *n* (1922) : a Bantu language widely used in trade and public affairs in the Congo River area
lin•gam \ˈliŋ-gəm\ *or* **lin•ga** \-gə\ *n* [Skt *liṅga* (nom. *liṅgam*), lit., characteristic] (1719) : a stylized phallic symbol that is worshipped in Hinduism as a sign of generative power and that represents the god Shiva — compare YONI
Lin•ga•yat \liŋ-ˈgä-yət\ *n* [Kannada *liṅgāyata*] (1901) : a member of a Saiva sect of southern India marked by wearing of the lingam and characterized by denial of caste distinctions
ling•cod \ˈliŋ-ˌkäd\ *n* (1940) : a large often greenish-fleshed fish (*Ophiodon elongatus*) of the Pacific coast of No. America that is an important food and sport fish and belongs to the same family as the greenlings
lin•ger \ˈliŋ-gər\ *vb* **lin•gered; lin•ger•ing** \-g(ə-)riŋ\ [ME (northern dial.) *lengeren* to dwell, freq. of *lengen* to prolong, fr. OE *lengan;* akin to OE *lang* long] *vi* (14c) **1** : to be slow in parting or in quitting something : TARRY ⟨fans *~ed* outside the door⟩ **2 a** : to remain alive although gradually dying **b** : to remain existent although often waning in strength, importance, or influence ⟨*~ing* doubts⟩ ⟨*~ing* odors⟩ **3** : to be slow to act : PROCRASTINATE **4** : to move slowly : SAUNTER ~ *vt* **1** *obs* : DELAY **2** : to pass (as a period of time) slowly — **lin•ger•er** \-gər-ər\ *n* — **lin•ger•ing•ly** \-g(ə-)riŋ-lē\ *adv*
lin•ge•rie \ˌlän-jə-ˈrā, ˌlän-zhə-, -ˈrē; ˈlan-zhə-(ˌ)rē, ˈlän-jə-, ˈlän-zhə-, -ˌrā\ *n* [F, fr. MF, fr. *linge* linen, fr. L *lineus* made of linen — more at LINE] (1835) **1** *archaic* : linen articles or garments **2** : women's intimate apparel — **lingerie** *adj*
lin•go \ˈliŋ-(ˌ)gō\ *n, pl* **lingos** *or* **lingoes** [prob. fr. Lingua Franca, language, tongue, fr. Occitan, fr. L *lingua* — more at TONGUE] (1660) : strange or incomprehensible language or speech: as **a** : a foreign language **b** : the special vocabulary of a particular field of interest **c** : language characteristic of an individual
ling•on•ber•ry \ˈliŋ-ən-ˌber-ē\ *n* [Sw *lingon* mountain cranberry; akin to ON *lyng* ling] (1920) : the fruit of the mountain cranberry; *also* : MOUNTAIN CRANBERRY
lin•gua \ˈliŋ-gwə\ *n, pl* **lin•guae** \-ˌgwē, -ˌgwī\ [L — more at TONGUE] (ca. 1826) : a tongue or an organ resembling a tongue
lin•gua fran•ca \ˈliŋ-gwə-ˈfraŋ-kə\ *n, pl* **lingua francas** *or* **lin•guae fran•cae** \-gwē-ˈfraŋ-(ˌ)kē\ [It, lit., Frankish language] (1619) **1** *often cap* : a common language consisting of Italian mixed with French, Spanish, Greek, and Arabic that was formerly spoken in Mediterranean ports **2** : any of various languages used as common or commercial tongues among peoples of diverse speech **3** : something resembling a common language ⟨movies are the *lingua franca* of the twentieth century —Gore Vidal⟩
lin•gual \ˈliŋ-gwəl *also* ˈliŋ-gyə-wəl\ *adj* [L *lingua*] (1650) **1 a** : of, relating to, or resembling the tongue **b** : lying near or next to the tongue; *esp* : relating to or being the surface of tooth next to the tongue **c** : produced by the tongue **2** : LINGUISTIC — **lin•gual•ly** *adv*
lin•gui•ca *or* **lin•gui•ça** *also* **lin•gui•sa** \liŋ-ˈgwē-sə\ *n* [Pg *linguiça*] (1953) : a spicy Portuguese sausage
lin•gui•ne *or* **lin•gui•ni** \liŋ-ˈgwē-nē\ *n* [It, pl. of *linguina,* dim. of *lingua* tongue, fr. L] (ca. 1948) : narrow flat pasta
lin•guist \ˈliŋ-gwist\ *n* [L *lingua* language, tongue] (1591) **1** : a person accomplished in languages; *esp* : one who speaks several languages **2** : a person who specializes in linguistics
lin•guis•tic \liŋ-ˈgwis-tik\ *also* **lin•guis•ti•cal** \-ti-kəl\ *adj* (1827) : of or relating to language or linguistics — **lin•guis•ti•cal•ly** \-ti-k(ə-)lē\ *adv*
linguistic atlas *n* (1917) : a publication containing a set of maps on which speech variations are recorded — called also *dialect atlas*
linguistic form *n* (1921) : a meaningful unit of speech (as a morpheme, word, or sentence) — called also *speech form*
linguistic geography *n* (1926) : local or regional variations of a language or dialect studied as a field of knowledge — called also *dialect geography* — **linguistic geographer** *n*
lin•guis•ti•cian \ˌliŋ-gwə-ˈsti-shən\ *n* (1895) : LINGUIST 2
lin•guis•tics \liŋ-ˈgwis-tiks\ *n pl but sing in constr* (ca. 1837) : the study of human speech including the units, nature, structure, and modification of language
lin•i•ment \ˈli-nə-mənt\ *n* [ME, fr. LL *linimentum,* fr. L *linere* to smear — more at LIME] (15c) : a liquid or semiliquid preparation that is applied to the skin as an anodyne or a counterirritant
lin•ing \ˈlī-niŋ\ *n* (14c) **1** : material that lines or that is used to line esp. the inner surface of something (as a garment) **2** : the act or process of providing something with a lining
[1]**link** \ˈliŋk\ *n* [ME, of Scand origin; akin to ON *hlekkr* chain; akin to OE *hlanc* lank] (15c) **1** : a connecting structure: as **a (1)** : a single ring or division of a chain **(2)** : one of the standardized divisions of a surveyor's chain that is 7.92 inches (20.1 centimeters) long and serves as a measure of length **b** : CUFF LINK **c** : BOND 3c **d** : an intermediate rod or piece for transmitting force or motion; *esp* : a short connecting rod with a hole or pin at each end **e** : the fusible member of an electrical fuse **2** : something analogous to a link of chain: as **a** : a segment of sausage in a chain **b** : a connecting element or factor ⟨found a ~ between smoking and cancer⟩ **c** : a unit in a communication system **d** : an identifier attached to an element (as an index term) in a system in order to indicate or permit connection with other similarly identified elements; *esp* : one (as a hyperlink) in a computer file
[2]**link** *vt* (15c) : to couple or connect by or as if by a link ~ *vi* : to become connected by or as if by a link — often used with *up* ⟨the band *~ed* up with a new record label⟩ *syn* see JOIN — **link•er** *n*
[3]**link** *n* [perh. modif. of ML *linchinus* candle, alter. of L *lychnus,* fr. Gk *lychnos;* akin to Gk *leukos* white — more at LIGHT] (1526) : a torch formerly used to light a person's way through the streets
[4]**link** *vi* [origin unknown] (1715) *Scot* : to skip smartly along
link•age \ˈliŋ-kij\ *n* (1874) **1** : the manner or style of being united: as **a** : the manner in which atoms or radicals are linked in a molecule **b** : BOND 3c **2** : the quality or state of being linked; *esp* : the relationship between genes on the same chromosome that causes them to be inherited together — compare MENDEL'S LAW 2 **3** : a system of links; *esp* : a system of links or bars which are jointed together and more or less constrained by having a link or links fixed and by means of which straight or nearly straight lines or other point paths may be traced **4** : LINK 2b **5** : the tactic in diplomatic negotiations of linking often unrelated issues so that progress in one area is dependent on agreement in another
linkage group *n* (1921) : a set of linked genes at different loci on the same chromosome
link•boy \ˈliŋk-ˌbȯi\ *n* (1652) : an attendant formerly employed to bear a light for a person on the streets at night
linked \ˈliŋ(k)t\ *adj* (15c) **1** : marked by linkage and esp. genetic linkage ⟨~ genes⟩ **2** : having or provided with links ⟨a ~ list⟩
linking verb *n* (1923) : a word or expression (as a form of *be, become, feel,* or *seem*) that links a subject with its predicate
link•man \ˈliŋk-mən\ *n* (1716) **1** : LINKBOY **2** *Brit* : a broadcasting moderator or anchorman
links \ˈliŋ(k)s\ *n pl* [ME, fr. OE *hlincas,* pl. of *hlinc* ridge; akin to OE *hlanc* lank] (15c) **1** *Scot* : sand hills esp. along the seashore **2** : GOLF COURSE; *specif* : a golf course on linksland
links•land \ˈliŋ(k)s-ˌland\ *n* (1926) : seaside terrain that is characterized by rolling hills of sand and is often used as the site of golf courses
links•man \ˈliŋ(k)s-mən\ *n* (1937) : one who plays golf
link•up \ˈliŋ-ˌkəp\ *n* (1945) **1** : establishment of contact : MEETING ⟨the ~ of two spacecraft⟩ **2 a** : something that serves as a linking de-

vice or factor **b** : a functional whole resulting from the linking up of separate elements ⟨an instructional TV ~⟩

linn \ˈlin\ *n* [ScGael *linne* pool] (1513) **1** *chiefly Scot* : WATERFALL **2** *chiefly Scot* : a steep ravine

Lin·nae·an *or* **Lin·ne·an** \lə-ˈnē-ən, -ˈnā-; ˈli-nē-\ *adj* [Carolus *Linnaeus*] (1744) : of, relating to, or following the systematic methods of the Swedish botanist Linnaeus who established the system of binomial nomenclature

lin·net \ˈli-nət\ *n* [MF *linette,* fr. *lin* flax, fr. L *linum;* fr. its feeding on flax seeds] (ca. 1530) : a common small brownish Old World finch (*Acanthis cannabina*) of which the male has red on the breast and crown during breeding season

li·no \ˈlī-(ˌ)nō\ *n, pl* **linos** (1907) *chiefly Brit* : LINOLEUM

li·no·cut \ˈlī-nō-ˌkət\ *n* (1907) : a print made from a design cut into a mounted piece of linoleum

li·no·le·ate \lə-ˈnō-lē-ˌāt\ *n* (ca. 1865) : a salt or ester of linoleic acid

lin·o·le·ic acid \ˌli-nə-ˈlē-ik-, -ˈlā-\ *n* [Gk *linon* flax + ISV *oleic* (*acid*)] (1857) : a liquid unsaturated fatty acid $C_{18}H_{32}O_2$ found esp. in semidrying oils (as corn oil) and essential for the nutrition of some animals

lin·o·le·nic acid \-ˈlē-nik-, -ˈlā-\ *n* [ISV, irreg. fr. *linoleic*] (1887) : a liquid unsaturated fatty acid $C_{18}H_{30}O_2$ found esp. in drying oils (as linseed oil) and essential for the nutrition of some animals

li·no·leum \lə-ˈnō-lē-əm, -ˈnōl-yəm\ *n, often attrib* [L *linum* flax + *oleum* oil — more at OIL] (1878) **1** : a floor covering made by laying on a burlap or canvas backing a mixture of solidified linseed oil with gums, cork dust or wood flour or both, and usu. pigments **2** : a material similar to linoleum

Li·no·type \ˈlī-nə-ˌtīp\ *trademark* — used for a typesetting machine that produces each line of type in the form of a solid metal slug

lin·sang \ˈlin-ˌsaŋ\ *n* [Jav *lingsang*] (1821) : either of two small nocturnal chiefly forest-dwelling viverrid Asian mammals (*Prionodon pardicolor* and *P. linsang*) having an elongated slender muzzle and long tail; *also* : a related mammal (*Poiana richardsoni*) of Africa

lin·seed \ˈlin-ˌsēd\ *n* [ME, fr. OE *līnsǣd,* fr. *līn* flax + *sǣd* seed — more at LINEN] (bef. 12c) : FLAXSEED

linseed oil *n* (15c) : a yellowish drying oil obtained from flaxseed and used esp. in paint, varnish, printing ink, and linoleum

lin·sey–wool·sey \ˌlin-zē-ˈwu̇l-zē\ *n* [ME *lynsy wolsye*] (15c) : a coarse sturdy fabric of wool and linen or cotton

lin·stock \ˈlin-ˌstäk\ *n* [D *lontstok,* fr. *lont* match + *stok* stick] (1575) : a staff having a pointed foot (as for sticking into the ground) and a forked tip and formerly used to hold a lighted match for firing cannon

lint \ˈlint\ *n* [ME] (14c) **1 a** : a soft fleecy material made from linen usu. by scraping **b** : fuzz consisting esp. of fine ravelings and short fibers of yarn and fabric **2** : a fibrous coat of thick convoluted hairs borne by cotton seeds that yields the cotton staple — **lint·less** \-ləs\ *adj* — **linty** \ˈlin-tē\ *adj*

lin·tel \ˈlin-tᵊl\ *n* [ME, fr. AF **lintel,* alter. of *linter* threshold, fr. LL *limitaris,* fr. L, constituting a boundary, fr. *limit-, limes* boundary] (14c) : a horizontal architectural member spanning and usu. carrying the load above an opening

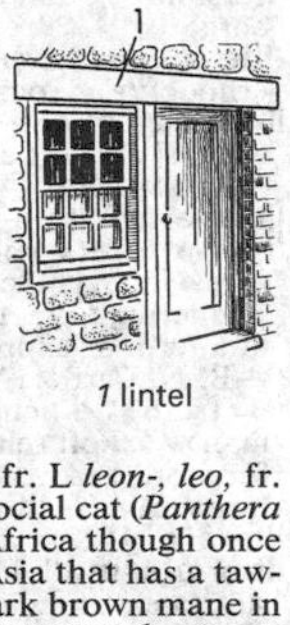

1 lintel

lint·er \ˈlin-tər\ *n* (ca. 1889) **1** : a machine for removing linters **2** *pl* : the fuzz of short fibers that adheres to cottonseed after ginning

lint·white \ˈlint-ˌhwīt, -ˌwīt\ *n* [alter. of ME *lynkwhyt,* by folk etymology fr. OE *līnetwige*] (1513) : LINNET

linz·er torte \ˈlin(t)-sər-, ˈlin-zər-\ *n, often cap L* [G, lit., Linz torte] (1906) : a baked buttery torte made with chopped almonds, sugar, and spices and filled with jam or preserves

li·on \ˈlī-ən\ *n, pl* **lions** [ME *lioun,* fr. AF *leun, lion,* fr. L *leon-, leo,* fr. Gk *leōn*] (12c) **1 a** *or pl* **lion** : a large heavily built social cat (*Panthera leo*) of open or rocky areas chiefly of sub-Saharan Africa though once widely distributed throughout Africa and southern Asia that has a tawny body with a tufted tail and a shaggy blackish or dark brown mane in the male **b** : any of several large wildcats; *esp* : COUGAR 1 **c** *cap* : LEO **2 a** : a person felt to resemble a lion (as in courage or ferocity) **b** : a person of outstanding interest or importance ⟨a literary ~⟩ **3** *cap* [*Lions* (*club*)] : a member of a major national and international service club — **li·on·like** \-ˌlīk\ *adj*

li·on·ess \ˈlī-ə-nəs\ *n* (14c) : a female lion

li·on·fish \ˈlī-ən-ˌfish\ *n* (ca. 1907) : any of several scorpaenid fishes (genus *Pterois*) of the Indian Ocean and the tropical Pacific that are brilliantly striped and barred with elongated fins and venomous dorsal spines

li·on·heart·ed \ˈlī-ən-ˌhär-təd\ *adj* (1616) : COURAGEOUS, BRAVE

li·on·ise *Brit var of* LIONIZE

li·on·ize \ˈlī-ə-ˌnīz\ *vt* **-ized; -iz·ing** (1809) : to treat as an object of great interest or importance — **li·on·i·za·tion** \ˌlī-ə-nə-ˈzā-shən\ *n* — **li·on·iz·er** \ˈlī-ə-ˌnī-zər\ *n*

lion's den *n* (1680) : a place or state of extreme disadvantage, antagonism, or hostility ⟨a young reporter thrown into the *lion's den*⟩

lion's share *n* (1742) : the largest portion ⟨received the *lion's share* of the research money⟩

[1]**lip** \ˈlip\ *n* [ME, fr. OE *lippa;* akin to OHG *leffur* lip and prob. to L *labium, labrum* lip] (bef. 12c) **1** : either of two fleshy folds that surround the mouth in humans and many other vertebrates and are organs of human speech essential to certain articulations; *also* : the red or pinkish margin of the human lip **2** *slang* : BACK TALK **3 a** : a fleshy edge or margin (as of a wound) **b** : LABIUM **c** : LABELLUM 1 **d** : a limb of a labiate corolla **4 a** : the edge of a hollow vessel or cavity **b** : a projecting edge: as (1) : the beveled upper edge of the mouth of an organ flue pipe (2) : the sharp cutting edge on the end of a tool (as an auger) (3) : a short spout (as on a pitcher) **c** : EDGE 2 **5** : EMBOUCHURE — **lip·less** \-ləs\ *adj* — **lip·like** \-ˌlīk\ *adj*

[2]**lip** *adj* (1558) **1** : INSINCERE ⟨~ praise⟩ **2** : produced with the participation of the lips : LABIAL ⟨~ consonants⟩

[3]**lip** *vb* **lipped; lip·ping** *vt* (1589) **1** : to touch with the lips; *esp* : KISS **2** : UTTER **3** : to lap against : LICK **4** : to hit (a putt) so that the ball hits the edge of the cup but fails to drop in — usu. used with *out* ~ *vi* : to hit the edge of the cup without dropping in — used with *out* ⟨the putt *lipped* out⟩

lip- *or* **lipo-** *comb form* [NL, fr. Gk, fr. *lipos* — more at LEAVE] : fat : fatty tissue : fatty ⟨*lip*oid⟩ ⟨*lipo*protein⟩

li·pa \ˈlē-ˌpä, -pə\ *n, pl* **lipa** *also* **lipe** \-ˌpā\ [Serbo-Croatian (nom. pl. *lipe,* gen. pl. *lipā*), lit., linden tree] (1993) — see *kuna* at MONEY table

li·pase \ˈlī-ˌpās, -ˌpāz\ *n* [ISV] (1897) : an enzyme that hydrolyzes glycerides

lip·id \ˈli-pəd\ *also* **lip·ide** \-ˌpīd\ *n* [ISV] (1912) : any of various substances that are soluble in nonpolar organic solvents (as chloroform and ether), that are usu. insoluble in water, that with proteins and carbohydrates constitute the principal structural components of living cells, and that include fats, waxes, phosphatides, cerebrosides, and related and derived compounds — **li·pid·ic** \li-ˈpi-dik\ *adj*

Lip·i·tor \ˈli-pə-ˌtȯr\ *trademark* — used for a preparation of atorvastatin

Lip·iz·zan \ˌli-pət-ˈsän\ *or* **Lip·iz·zan·er** \-ˈsä-nər\ *also* **Lip·pi·zan** \-ˈsän\ *or* **Lip·pi·zan·er** \-ˈsä-nər\ *n* [G *Lipizzaner, Lippizaner,* fr. *Lipizza, Lippiza,* former site of the Austrian Imperial Stud near Trieste, Italy] (1928) : any of a breed of spirited horses developed from Spanish, Italian, Danish, and Arab stock that are usu. born with a dark coat that lightens to white with age

lip–lock \ˈlip-ˌläk\ *n* (1979) : a long amorous kiss

li·po·gen·e·sis \ˌlī-pə-ˈje-nə-səs\ *n* [NL] (1882) : the formation of fat; *specif* : the formation of fatty acids from acetyl coenzyme A in the living body and esp. in adipose tissue and the liver

li·po·ic acid \lī-ˈpō-ik-, li-\ *n* [*lip-, lipo-*] (ca. 1951) : any of several microbial growth factors; *esp* : a fatty acid $C_8H_{14}O_2S_2$ that is essential for the oxidation of alpha-keto acids (as pyruvic acid) in metabolism

[1]**li·poid** \ˈlī-ˌpȯid, ˈli-\ *or* **li·poi·dal** \lī-ˈpȯi-dᵊl, li-\ *adj* [ISV] (1876) : resembling fat

[2]**lipoid** *n* [ISV] (1906) : LIPID

li·pol·y·sis \lī-ˈpä-lə-səs, li-\ *n* [NL] (ca. 1903) : the hydrolysis of fat — **li·po·lyt·ic** \ˌlī-pə-ˈli-tik, ˌli-\ *adj*

li·po·ma \lī-ˈpō-mə, li-\ *n, pl* **-mas** *also* **-ma·ta** \-mə-tə\ [NL] (1830) : a tumor of fatty tissue — **li·po·ma·tous** \-mə-təs\ *adj*

li·po·phil·ic \ˌlī-pə-ˈfi-lik, ˌli-\ *adj* (1939) : having an affinity for lipids (as fats) ⟨a ~ metabolite⟩

li·po·poly·sac·cha·ride \ˌlī-pō-ˌpä-li-ˈsa-kə-ˌrīd, ˌli-\ *n* (1950) : a large molecule consisting of lipids and sugars joined by chemical bonds

li·po·pro·tein \-ˈprō-ˌtēn, -ˈprō-tē-ən\ *n* (1909) : a conjugated protein that is a complex of protein and lipid — compare HDL, LDL, VLDL

li·po·some \ˈlī-pə-ˌsōm, ˈli-\ *n* (1968) : an artificial vesicle composed of one or more concentric phospholipid bilayers and used esp. to deliver microscopic substances (as drugs or DNA) to body cells — **li·po·so·mal** \ˌlī-pə-ˈsō-məl, ˌli-\ *adj*

li·po·suc·tion \ˈli-pə-ˌsək-shən, ˈlī-\ *n* (1983) : surgical removal of local fat deposits (as in the thighs) esp. for cosmetic purposes

li·po·tro·pic \ˌlī-pō-ˈtrō-pik, ˌli-, -ˈträ-\ *adj* [ISV] (1903) : promoting the physiological utilization of fat ⟨~ dietary factors⟩

li·po·tro·pin \-ˈtrō-pən\ *n* (1964) : either of two protein hormones of the pituitary gland that function in the mobilization of fat reserves

lipped \ˈlipt\ *adj* (14c) : having a lip or lips esp. of a specified kind or number — often used in combination ⟨tight-*lipped*⟩

lip·pen \ˈli-pən\ *vb* [ME *lipnien*] *vi* (12c) *chiefly Scot* : TRUST, RELY ~ *vt, chiefly Scot* : ENTRUST

Lippes loop \ˈli-pəs-, -pēz-\ *n* [Jack *Lippes* b1924 Am. gynecologist] (1964) : an S-shaped plastic intrauterine device

lipping *n* (1894) **1** : outgrowth of bone in liplike form at a joint margin **2** : a piece of wood set in an archer's bow where a flaw has been cut out **3** : EMBOUCHURE 1

lip·py \ˈli-pē\ *adj* **lip·pi·er; -est** (ca. 1875) : given to back talk

lip–read \ˈlip-ˌrēd\ *vb* **-read** \-ˌred\; **-read·ing** \-ˌrē-diŋ\ *vt* (1874) : to understand by lipreading ~ *vi* : to use lipreading — **lip–read·er** \-ˌrē-dər\ *n*

lipreading *n* (1874) : the interpreting of speech by watching the speaker's lip and facial movements without hearing the voice

lip service *n* (1644) : an avowal of advocacy, adherence, or allegiance expressed in words but not backed by deeds — usu. used with *pay*

lip·stick \ˈlip-ˌstik\ *n* (1880) : a waxy solid usu. colored cosmetic in stick form for the lips; *also* : a stick of such cosmetic with its case — **lip·sticked** *adj*

lip–synch *or* **lip–sync** \ˈlip-ˌsiŋk\ *vt* (ca. 1961) : to pretend to sing or say in synchronization with recorded sound ~ *vi* : to lip-synch something — **lip sync** *n* — **lip–synch·er** *or* **lip–sync·er** *n*

liq *abbr* **1** liquid **2** liquor

li·quate \ˈlī-ˌkwāt\ *vt* **li·quat·ed; li·quat·ing** [L *liquatus,* pp. of *liquare* to make liquid; akin to L *liquēre*] (ca. 1859) : to cause (a more fusible substance) to separate out of a combination or mixture by the application of heat ⟨~ lead from its ore⟩ — **li·qua·tion** \lī-ˈkwā-shən\ *n*

liq·ue·fac·tion \ˌli-kwə-ˈfak-shən\ *n* [ME, fr. LL *liquefaction-, liquefactio,* fr. L *liquefacere,* fr. *liquēre* to be fluid + *facere* to make — more at DO] (15c) **1** : the process of making or becoming liquid **2** : the state of being liquid **3** : conversion of soil into a fluidlike mass during an earthquake or other seismic event

liquefied petroleum gas *n* (1925) : a compressed gas that consists of flammable hydrocarbons (as propane and butane) and is used esp. as fuel or as raw material for chemical synthesis

liq·ue·fy *also* **liq·ui·fy** \ˈli-kwə-ˌfī\ *vb* **-fied; -fy·ing** [ME *liquefien,* fr. AF *liquefier,* fr. L *liquefacere*] *vt* (15c) : to reduce to a liquid state ~ *vi* : to become liquid — **liq·ue·fi·er** \-ˌfī(-ə)r\ *n*

li·ques·cent \li-ˈkwe-sᵊnt\ *adj* [L *liquescent-, liquescens,* prp. of *liquescere* to become fluid, incho. of *liquēre*] (ca. 1727) : being or tending to become liquid : MELTING

li·queur \li-ˈkər, -ˈku̇r, -ˈkyu̇r\ *n* [F, fr. OF *licour* liquid — more at LIQUOR] (1729) : a usu. sweetened alcoholic liquor (as brandy) flavored with fruit, spices, nuts, herbs, or seeds

[1]**liq·uid** \ˈli-kwəd\ *adj* [ME, fr. MF *liquide,* fr. L *liquidus,* fr. *liquēre* to be fluid; akin to L *lixa* water, lye, and perh. to OIr *fliuch* damp] (14c) **1**

: flowing freely like water **2** : having the properties of a liquid : being neither solid nor gaseous **3 a** : shining and clear ⟨large ~ eyes⟩ **b** : being musical and free of harshness in sound **c** : smooth and unconstrained in movement **d** : articulated without friction and capable of being prolonged like a vowel ⟨a ~ consonant⟩ **4 a** : consisting of or capable of ready conversion into cash ⟨~ assets⟩ **b** : capable of covering current liabilities quickly with current assets — **li·quid·i·ty** \li-ˈkwi-də-tē\ *n* — **liq·uid·ly** \ˈli-kwəd-lē\ *adv* — **liq·uid·ness** *n*

[2]**liquid** *n* (1530) **1** : a liquid consonant **2** : a fluid (as water) that has no independent shape but has a definite volume and does not expand indefinitely and that is only slightly compressible

liq·uid·am·bar \ˌli-kwə-ˈdam-bər\ *n* [NL, fr. L *liquidus* + ML *ambar, ambra* amber] (ca. 1577) **1** : STORAX 1b **2** : any of a genus (*Liquidambar*) of deciduous No. American and Asian trees (as the sweet gum) of the witch-hazel family with monoecious flowers and a spiny globose fruit composed of many woody capsules each having two carpels

liq·ui·date \ˈli-kwə-ˌdāt\ *vb* **-dat·ed; -dat·ing** [LL *liquidatus,* pp. of *liquidare* to melt, fr. L *liquidus*] *vt* (ca. 1575) **1 a** (1) : to determine by agreement or by litigation the precise amount of (indebtedness, damages, or accounts) (2) : to determine the liabilities and apportion assets toward discharging the indebtedness of **b** : to settle (a debt) by payment or other settlement **2** *archaic* : to make clear **3** : to do away with **4** : to convert (assets) into cash ~ *vi* **1** : to liquidate debts, damages, or accounts **2** : to determine liabilities and apportion assets toward discharging indebtedness — **liq·ui·da·tion** \ˌli-kwə-ˈdā-shən\ *n*

liq·ui·da·tor \ˈli-kwə-ˌdā-tər\ *n* (ca. 1828) : one that liquidates; *esp* : an individual appointed by law to liquidate assets

liquid crystal *n* (1891) : an organic liquid whose physical properties resemble those of a crystal in the formation of loosely ordered molecular arrays similar to a regular crystalline lattice and the anisotropic refraction of light

liquid crystal display *n* (1968) : LCD

liq·uid·ize \ˈli-kwə-ˌdīz\ *vt* **-ized; -iz·ing** (1837) : to cause to be liquid

liquid measure *n* (ca. 1678) : a unit or series of units for measuring liquid capacity — see METRIC SYSTEM table, WEIGHT table

[1]**li·quor** \ˈli-kər\ *n* [ME *licour,* fr. AF, fr. L *liquor,* fr. *liquēre*] (13c) : a liquid substance: as **a** : a usu. distilled rather than fermented alcoholic beverage **b** : a watery solution of a drug **c** : BATH 2b(1)

[2]**liquor** *vb* **li·quored; li·quor·ing** \ˈli-k(ə-)riŋ\ *vt* (1502) **1** : to dress (as leather) with oil or grease **2** : to make drunk with alcoholic liquor — usu. used with *up* ~ *vi* : to drink alcoholic liquor esp. to excess — usu. used with *up*

li·quo·rice *chiefly Brit var of* LICORICE

[1]**li·ra** \ˈlir-ə, ˈlē-rə\ *n, pl* **li·re** \ˈlē-(ˌ)rā\ *also* **liras** [It, fr. L *libra,* a unit of weight] (1617) : the basic monetary unit of Italy until 2002

[2]**lira** *n, pl* **liras** [Turk, fr. It] (1871) — see MONEY table

[3]**lira** *n, pl* **li·roth** *or* **li·rot** \lē-ˌrōt, -ˌrōth\ [ModHeb, fr. It] (ca. 1946) : the former Israeli pound

[4]**lira** *n, pl* **li·ri** \ˈlē-(ˌ)rē\ [Maltese, fr. It] (ca. 1985) : the basic monetary unit of Malta until 2008

li·ri·ope \lə-ˈrī-ə-(ˌ)pē\ *n* [NL, fr. *Liriope,* a nymph in Roman mythology] (1946) : any of a genus (*Liriope*) of stemless Asian herbs of the lily family that are widely cultivated as ground cover for their grasslike leaves and small white, blue, or violet flowers

lir·i·pipe \ˈlir-ə-ˌpīp\ *n* [ML *liripipium*] (1594) : a pendent part of a tippet; *also* : TIPPET, SCARF

lisente *pl of* SENTE

lisle \ˈlī(-ə)l\ *n, often attrib* [*Lisle* Lille, France] (1858) : a smooth tightly twisted thread usu. made of long-staple cotton

[1]**lisp** \ˈlisp\ *vb* [ME, fr. OE *-wlyspian;* akin to OHG *lispen* to lisp] *vi* (bef. 12c) **1** : to pronounce the sibilants \s\ and \z\ imperfectly esp. by turning them into \th\ and \t͟h\ **2** : to speak falteringly, childishly, or with a lisp ~ *vt* : to utter falteringly or with a lisp — **lisp·er** *n*

[2]**lisp** *n* (ca. 1625) **1** : a speech defect or affectation characterized by lisping **2** : a sound resembling a lisp

LISP \ˈlisp\ *n* [*list processing*] (1959) : a computer programming language that is designed for easy manipulation of data strings and is used extensively for work in artificial intelligence

lis·some *also* **lis·som** \ˈli-səm\ *adj* [alter. of *lithesome*] (1763) **1 a** : easily flexed **b** : LITHE 2 **2** : NIMBLE — **lis·some·ly** *adv* — **lis·some·ness** *n*

[1]**list** \ˈlist\ *vb* [ME *lysten,* fr. OE *lystan;* akin to OE *lust* desire, lust] *vt* (bef. 12c) *archaic* : PLEASE, SUIT ~ *vi, archaic* : WISH, CHOOSE

[2]**list** *n* [ME, prob. fr. *lysten*] (13c) *archaic* : INCLINATION, CRAVING

[3]**list** *vb* [ME, fr. OE *hlystan,* fr. *hlyst* hearing; akin to OE *hlysnan* to listen] *vi* (bef. 12c) *archaic* : LISTEN ~ *vt, archaic* : to listen to : HEAR

[4]**list** *n* [ME, fr. OE *līste;* akin to OHG *līsta* edge, Alb *leth*] (bef. 12c) **1** : a band or strip of material: as **a** : LISTEL **b** : SELVAGE **c** : a narrow strip of wood cut from the edge of a board **2** *pl but sing or pl in constr* **a** : an arena for combat (as jousting) **b** : a field of competition or controversy **3** *obs* : LIMIT, BOUNDARY **4** : STRIPE

[5]**list** *vt* (1635) **1** : to cut away a narrow strip from the edge of **2** : to prepare or plant (land) in ridges and furrows with a lister

[6]**list** *n* [origin unknown] (1582) : a deviation from the vertical : TILT; *also* : the extent of such a deviation

[7]**list** *vi* (1626) : to tilt to one side; *esp, of a boat or ship* : to tilt to one side in a state of equilibrium (as from an unbalanced load) — compare HEEL ~ *vt* : to cause to list

[8]**list** *n* [F *liste,* fr. It *lista,* of Gmc origin; akin to OHG *līsta* edge] (1602) **1 a** : a simple series of words or numerals (as the names of persons or objects) ⟨a guest ~⟩ **b** : an official roster : ROLL **2** : CATALOG, CHECKLIST **3** : the total number to be considered or included

[9]**list** *vt* (1614) **1 a** : to make a list of : ENUMERATE **b** : to include on a list : REGISTER **2** : to place (oneself) in a specified category ⟨~*s* himself as a political liberal⟩ **3** *archaic* : RECRUIT ~ *vi* **1** *archaic* : ENLIST **2** : to become entered in a catalog with a selling price ⟨a car that ~*s* for $12,000⟩ — **list·ee** \li-ˈstē\ *n*

lis·tel \ˈlis-tᵊl, lis-ˈtel\ *n* [F, fr. It *listello,* dim. of *lista* fillet, roster] (1598) : a narrow band in architecture : FILLET

[1]**lis·ten** \ˈli-sᵊn\ *vb* **lis·tened; lis·ten·ing** \ˈlis-niŋ, ˈli-sᵊn-iŋ\ [ME *listnen,* fr. OE *hlysnan;* akin to Skt *śroṣati* he hears, OE *hlūd* loud] *vt* (bef. 12c) *archaic* : to give ear to : HEAR ~ *vi* **1** : to pay attention to sound ⟨~ to music⟩ **2** : to hear something with thoughtful attention : give consideration ⟨~ to a plea⟩ **3** : to be alert to catch an expected sound ⟨~ for his step⟩ — **lis·ten·er** \ˈlis-nər, ˈli-sᵊn-ər\ *n*

[2]**listen** *n* (1788) : an act of listening

lis·ten·able \ˈlis-nə-bəl, ˈli-sᵊn-ə-\ *adj* (1942) : agreeable to listen to

lis·ten·er·ship \ˈlis-nər-ˌship, ˈli-sᵊn-ər-\ *n* (1943) : the audience for a radio program or recording; *also* : the number or kind of that audience

listen in *vi* (1905) **1** : to tune in to or monitor a broadcast **2** : to listen to a conversation without participating in it; *esp* : EAVESDROP — **lis·ten·er–in** \ˌlis-nər-ˈin, ˌli-sᵊn-ər-\ *n*

listening post *n* (1942) : a center for monitoring electronic communications (as of an enemy)

[1]**list·er** \ˈlis-tər\ *n* (1682) : one that lists or catalogs

[2]**lister** *n* [[5]*list*] (1887) : a double-moldboard plow often equipped with a subsoiling attachment and used mainly where rainfall is limited

lis·te·ri·o·sis \lis-ˌtir-ē-ˈō-səs\ *n, pl* **-o·ses** \-ˌsēz\ [NL, fr. *Listeria,* fr. Joseph *Lister*] (1941) : a serious encephalitic disease of a wide variety of animals that is caused by a bacterium (*Listeria monocytogenes*) and that in animals is often fatal but in humans is usu. not fatal

list·ing \ˈlis-tiŋ\ *n* (1641) **1** : an act or instance of making or including in a list **2** : something that is listed

list·less \ˈlist-ləs\ *adj* [ME *listles,* fr. [2]*list*] (15c) : characterized by lack of interest, energy, or spirit ⟨a ~ melancholy attitude⟩ ***syn*** see LANGUID — **list·less·ly** *adv* — **list·less·ness** *n*

list price *n* (1871) : the basic price of an item as published in a catalog, price list, or advertisement before any discounts are taken

LIST·SERV \ˈlist-ˌsərv\ *trademark* — used for software for managing e-mail transmissions to and from a list of subscribers

[1]**lit** \ˈlit\ *past and past part of* LIGHT

[2]**lit** *n* [by shortening] (1850) : LITERATURE — **lit** *adj*

[3]**lit** *adj* [pp. of [3]*light*] (1904) : affected by alcohol : DRUNK

[4]**lit** *abbr* **1** liter **2** literal; literally

lit·a·ny \ˈli-tə-nē, ˈlit-nē\ *n, pl* **-nies** [ME *letanie,* fr. AF & LL; AF, fr. LL *litania,* fr. LGk *litaneia,* fr. Gk, entreaty, fr. *litanos* supplicant] (13c) **1** : a prayer consisting of a series of invocations and supplications by the leader with alternate responses by the congregation **2 a** : a resonant or repetitive chant ⟨a ~ of cheering phrases —Herman Wouk⟩ **b** : a usu. lengthy recitation or enumeration ⟨a familiar ~ of complaints⟩ **c** : a sizable series or set ⟨a ~ of problems⟩

li·tas \ˈlē-ˌtäs\ *n, pl* **li·tai** \-ˌtī\ *or* **li·tu** \-ˌtü\ [Lith (nom. pl. *litai,* gen. pl. *litų*), fr. initial letters of NL *Lituania,* F *Lituanie,* etc.] (1923) — see MONEY table

Lit B *var of* LITT B

litchi *var of* LYCHEE

lit crit \ˈlit-ˌkrit\ *n* (1963) : literary criticism

Lit D *var of* LITT D

lite \ˈlīt\ *adj* **1** : [4]LIGHT 9a **2** : diminished or lacking in substance or seriousness ⟨~ news⟩; *specif* : being an innocuous or unthreatening version — often used postpositively ⟨it is film noir ~ —James Greenberg⟩

-lite *n comb form* [F, alter. of *-lithe,* fr. Gk *lithos* stone] : mineral ⟨rhodo*lite*⟩ : rock ⟨aero*lite*⟩ : fossil ⟨stromato*lite*⟩

li·ter \ˈlē-tər\ *or* **li·tre** \ˈlē-tər\ *n* [F *litre,* fr. ML *litra,* a measure, fr. Gk, a weight] (1797) : a metric unit of capacity equal to one cubic decimeter — see METRIC SYSTEM table

lit·er·a·cy \ˈli-t(ə-)rə-sē\ *n* (1883) : the quality or state of being literate

[1]**lit·er·al** \ˈli-t(ə-)rəl\ *adj* [ME, fr. MF, fr. ML *litteralis,* fr. L, of a letter, fr. *littera* letter] (14c) **1 a** : according with the letter of the scriptures **b** : adhering to fact or to the ordinary construction or primary meaning of a term or expression : ACTUAL ⟨liberty in the ~ sense is impossible —B. N. Cardozo⟩ **c** : free from exaggeration or embellishment ⟨the ~ truth⟩ **d** : characterized by a concern mainly with facts ⟨a very ~ man⟩ **2** : of, relating to, or expressed in letters **3** : reproduced word for word : EXACT, VERBATIM ⟨a ~ translation⟩ — **lit·er·al·i·ty** \ˌli-tə-ˈra-lə-tē\ *n* — **lit·er·al·ness** \ˈli-t(ə-)rəl-nəs\ *n*

[2]**literal** *n* (1622) : a small error usu. of a single letter (as in writing)

lit·er·al·ism \ˈli-t(ə-)rə-ˌli-zəm\ *n* (1644) **1** : adherence to the explicit substance of an idea or expression ⟨biblical ~⟩ **2** : fidelity to observable fact : REALISM — **lit·er·al·ist** \-list\ *n* — **lit·er·al·is·tic** \ˌli-t(ə-)rə-ˈlis-tik\ *adj*

lit·er·al·ize \ˈli-t(ə-)rə-ˌlīz\ *vt* **-ized; -iz·ing** (1826) : to make literal — **lit·er·al·i·za·tion** \ˌli-t(ə-)rə-lə-ˈzā-shən\ *n*

lit·er·al·ly \ˈli-tə-rə-lē, ˈli-trə-lē, ˈli-tər-lē\ *adv* (1533) **1** : in a literal sense or manner : ACTUALLY ⟨took the remark ~⟩ ⟨was ~ insane⟩ **2** : in effect : VIRTUALLY ⟨will ~ turn the world upside down to combat cruelty or injustice —Norman Cousins⟩

usage Since some people take sense 2 to be the opposite of sense 1, it has been frequently criticized as a misuse. Instead, the use is pure hyperbole intended to gain emphasis, but it often appears in contexts where no additional emphasis is necessary.

lit·er·ary \ˈli-tə-ˌrer-ē\ *adj* (1605) **1 a** : of, relating to, or having the characteristics of humane learning or literature **b** : BOOKISH 2 **c** : of or relating to books **2 a** : WELL-READ **b** : of or relating to authors or scholars or to their professions — **lit·er·ar·i·ly** \ˌli-tə-ˈrer-ə-lē\ *adv* — **lit·er·ar·i·ness** \ˈli-tə-ˌrer-ē-nəs\ *n*

literary executor *n* (1849) : a person entrusted with the management of the papers and unpublished works of a deceased author

[1]**lit·er·ate** \ˈli-tə-rət *also* ˈli-trət\ *adj* [ME *literat,* fr. L *litteratus* marked with letters, literate, fr. *litterae* letters, literature, fr. pl. of *littera*] (15c) **1 a** : EDUCATED, CULTURED **b** : able to read and write **2 a** : versed in literature or creative writing : LITERARY **b** : LUCID, POLISHED ⟨a ~ essay⟩ **c** : having knowledge or competence ⟨computer-*literate*⟩ ⟨politically ~⟩ — **lit·er·ate·ly** *adv* — **lit·er·ate·ness** *n*

[2]**literate** *n* (ca. 1550) **1** : an educated person **2** : a person who can read and write

li·te·ra·ti \ˌli-tə-ˈrä-(ˌ)tē\ *n pl* [obs. It *litterati,* fr. L, pl. of *litteratus*] (1621) **1** : the educated class; *also* : INTELLIGENTSIA **2** : persons interested in literature or the arts

lit·er·a·tim \ˌli-tə-ˈrā-təm, -ˈrä-\ *adv or adj* [ML, fr. L *littera*] (1643) : letter for letter ⟨printed ~ from the manuscript —I. A. Gordon⟩

lit·er·a·tion \ˌli-tə-ˈrā-shən\ *n* [L *littera* + E *-ation*] (ca. 1889) : the representation of sound or words by letters

lit·er·a·tor \ˈli-tə-ˌrā-tər, ˌli-tə-ˈrä-ˌtȯr\ *n* (1791) : LITTERATEUR

lit·er·a·ture \ˈli-tə-rə-ˌchu̇r, ˈli-trə-ˌchu̇r, ˈli-tə(r)-ˌchu̇r, -chər, -ˌtyu̇r, -ˌtu̇r\ *n* [ME, fr. AF, fr. L *litteratura* writing, grammar, learning, fr. *lit-*

teratus] (14c) 1 *archaic* : literary culture 2 : the production of literary work esp. as an occupation 3 **a** (1) : writings in prose or verse; *esp* : writings having excellence of form or expression and expressing ideas of permanent or universal interest (2) : an example of such writings ⟨what came out, though rarely ~, was always a roaring good story —*People*⟩ **b** : the body of written works produced in a particular language, country, or age **c** : the body of writings on a particular subject ⟨scientific ~⟩ **d** : printed matter (as leaflets or circulars) ⟨campaign ~⟩ 4 : the aggregate of a usu. specified type of musical compositions

lit·er·a·tus \ˌli-tə-ˈrä-təs\ *n* [NL, back-formation fr. E *literati* (taken as L)] (1704) : a member of the literati

lith *abbr* lithographic; lithography

lith- *or* **litho-** *comb form* [L, fr. Gk, fr. *lithos*] : stone ⟨*litho*logy⟩

-lith *n comb form* [NL *-lithus* & F *-lithe*, fr. Gk *lithos*] 1 : structure or implement of stone ⟨mega*lith*⟩ ⟨eo*lith*⟩ 2 : calculus ⟨uro*lith*⟩ 3 : -LITE ⟨lacco*lith*⟩

li·tharge \ˈli-ˌthärj, li-ˈ\ *n* [ME, fr. AF *litarge*, fr. L *lithargyrus*, fr. Gk *lithargyros*, fr. *lithos* + *argyros* silver — more at ARGENT] (14c) : a fused lead monoxide; *broadly* : LEAD MONOXIDE

lithe \ˈlīth, ˈlīth\ *adj* [ME, fr. OE *līthe* gentle; akin to OHG *lindi* gentle, L *lentus* slow] (14c) 1 : easily bent or flexed ⟨~ steel⟩ ⟨a ~ vine⟩ 2 : characterized by easy flexibility and grace ⟨a ~ dancer⟩ ⟨treading with a ~ silent step⟩; *also* : athletically slim ⟨the most ~ and graspable of waists —R. P. Warren⟩ — **lithe·ly** *adv* — **lithe·ness** *n*

lithe·some \ˈlīth-səm, ˈlīth-\ *adj* (ca. 1774) : LISSOME

li·thi·a·sis \li-ˈthī-ə-səs\ *n, pl* **-a·ses** \-ˌsēz\ [NL, fr. Gk, fr. *lithos*] (ca. 1657) : the formation of stony concretions in the body (as in the gallbladder)

lith·ic \ˈli-thik\ *adj* [Gk *lithikos*, fr. *lithos*] (1797) 1 : STONY 1 2 : of, relating to, or being a stone tool

-lithic *adj comb form* [*lithic*] : relating to or characteristic of a (specified) stage in humankind's use of stone as a cultural tool ⟨Neo*lithic*⟩

lith·i·fy \ˈli-thə-ˌfī\ *vb* **-fied; -fy·ing** *vt* (1877) : to change to stone : PETRIFY; *esp* : to convert (unconsolidated sediment) into solid rock ~ *vi* : to become changed into stone — **lith·i·fi·ca·tion** \ˌli-thə-fə-ˈkā-shən\ *n*

lith·i·um \ˈli-thē-əm\ *n* [NL, fr. *lithia* oxide of lithium, fr. Gk *lithos*] (1818) 1 : a soft silver-white element of the alkali metal group that is the lightest metal known and that is used esp. in alloys and glass, in chemical synthesis, and in storage batteries — see ELEMENT table 2 : a salt of lithium (as lithium carbonate) used in psychiatric medicine

lithium carbonate *n* (1869) : a crystalline salt Li_2CO_3 used in the glass and ceramic industries and in medicine esp. in the treatment of bipolar disorder

lithium fluoride *n* (1944) : a crystalline salt LiF used esp. in making prisms and ceramics and as a flux

lithium ni·o·bate \-ˈnī-ə-ˌbāt\ *n* [*niob*ium + 1*-ate*] (1966) : a crystalline material $LiNbO_3$ whose physical properties change in response to pressure or the presence of an electric field and which is used in fiber optics and as a synthetic gemstone

litho \ˈlī-(ˌ)thō\ *n, pl* **lith·os** (1889) 1 : LITHOGRAPH 2 : LITHOGRAPHY 1

1**lith·o·graph** \ˈli-thə-ˌgraf\ *vt* (1825) : to produce, copy, or portray by lithography — **li·thog·ra·pher** \li-ˈthä-grə-fər, ˈli-thə-ˌgra-fər\ *n*

2**lithograph** *n* (1828) : a print made by lithography — **lith·o·graph·ic** \ˌli-thə-ˈgra-fik\ *adj* — **lith·o·graph·i·cal·ly** \-fi-k(ə-)lē\ *adv*

li·thog·ra·phy \li-ˈthä-grə-fē\ *n* [G *Lithographie*, fr. *lith-* + *-graphie* -graphy] (1813) 1 : the process of printing from a plane surface (as a smooth stone or metal plate) on which the image to be printed is ink-receptive and the blank area ink-repellent 2 : the process of producing patterns on semiconductor crystals for use as integrated circuits

li·thol·o·gy \li-ˈthä-lə-jē\ *n, pl* **-gies** (1716) 1 : the study of rocks 2 : the character of a rock formation; *also* : a rock formation having a particular set of characteristics — **lith·o·log·ic** \ˌli-thə-ˈlä-jik\ *or* **lith·o·log·i·cal** \-ji-kəl\ *adj* — **lith·o·log·i·cal·ly** \-ji-k(ə-)lē\ *adv*

lith·o·phane \ˈli-thə-ˌfān\ *n* [prob. fr. G *Lithophan*, fr. Gk *lithos* + G *diaphan* diaphanous] (ca. 1889) : porcelain impressed with figures that are made distinct by transmitted light; *also* : an object of this material

lith·o·phyte \ˈli-thə-ˌfīt\ *n* [ISV] (1895) : a plant that grows on rock

lith·o·pone \ˈli-thə-ˌpōn\ *n* [ISV *lith-* + Gk *ponos* work] (ca. 1884) : a white pigment consisting essentially of zinc sulfide and barium sulfate

lith·o·sol \ˈli-thə-ˌsäl, -ˌsȯl\ *n* [*lith-* + L *solum* soil] (ca. 1938) : any of a group of shallow azonal soils consisting of imperfectly weathered rock fragments

lith·o·sphere \ˈli-thə-ˌsfir\ *n* [ISV] (1887) : the solid part of a celestial body (as the earth); *specif* : the outer part of the solid earth composed of rock essentially like that exposed at the surface, consisting of the crust and outermost layer of the mantle, and usu. considered to be about 60 miles (100 kilometers) in thickness — **lith·o·spher·ic** \ˌli-thə-ˈsfir-ik, -ˈsfer-\ *adj*

li·thot·o·my \li-ˈthä-tə-mē\ *n, pl* **-mies** [LL *lithotomia*, fr. Gk, fr. *lithotomein* to perform a lithotomy, fr. *lith-* + *temnein* to cut — more at TOME] (1721) : surgical incision of the urinary bladder for removal of a stone

lith·o·trip·sy \ˈli-thə-ˌtrip-sē\ *n, pl* **-sies** [*lith-* + Gk *tripsis* a rubbing, fr. *tribein* to rub — more at THROW] (1834) : the breaking (as by shock waves or crushing with a surgical instrument) of a calculus in the urinary system into pieces small enough to be voided or washed out

lith·o·trip·ter *also* **lith·o·trip·tor** \ˈli-thə-ˌtrip-tər\ *n* [alter. of *lithontriptor*, fr. *lithontriptic* breaking up bladder stones, modif. of Gk (*pharmaka tōn*) *lithōn thryptika* (drugs) capable of pulverizing stones] (1825) : a device for performing lithotripsy; *esp* : a noninvasive device that pulverizes stones by focusing shock waves on a patient immersed in a water bath

Lith·u·a·nian \ˌli-thə-ˈwā-nē-ən, -nyən, *chiefly Brit* ˌlith-yü-\ *n* (1607) 1 : a native or inhabitant of Lithuania 2 : the Baltic language of the Lithuanian people — **Lithuanian** *adj*

lit·i·gant \ˈli-ti-gənt\ *n* (1659) : one engaged in a lawsuit — **litigant** *adj*

lit·i·gate \ˈli-tə-ˌgāt\ *vb* **-gat·ed; -gat·ing** [L *litigatus*, pp. of *litigare*, fr. *lit-, lis* lawsuit + *agere* to drive — more at AGENT] *vi* (1615) : to carry on a legal contest by judicial process ~ *vt* 1 *archaic* : DISPUTE 2 : to contest at law ⟨~ a claim⟩ — **lit·i·ga·ble** \ˈli-ti-gə-bəl\ *adj* — **lit·i·ga·tion** \ˌli-tə-ˈgā-shən\ *n* — **lit·i·ga·tor** \ˈli-tə-ˌgā-tər\ *n*

li·ti·gious \lə-ˈti-jəs, li-\ *adj* [ME, fr. AF, fr. L *litigiosus*, fr. *litigium* dispute, fr. *litigare*] (14c) 1 **a** : DISPUTATIOUS, CONTENTIOUS **b** : prone to engage in lawsuits 2 : subject to litigation 3 : of, relating to, or marked by litigation — **li·ti·gious·ly** *adv* — **li·ti·gious·ness** *n*

lit·mus \ˈlit-məs\ *n* [ME *litmose*, of Scand origin; akin to ON *litmosi* herbs used in dyeing, fr. *litr* color (akin to OE *wlite* brightness, appearance) + *mosi* moss; akin to OE *mōs* moss] (14c) 1 : a coloring matter from lichens that turns red in acid solutions and blue in alkaline solutions and is used as an acid-base indicator 2 : the critical factor in a litmus test; *also* : LITMUS TEST

litmus paper *n* (1803) : unsized paper colored with litmus and used as an indicator

litmus test *n* (1952) : a test in which a single factor (as an attitude, event, or fact) is decisive

li·to·tes \ˈlī-tə-ˌtēz, ˈli-, lī-ˈtō-ˌtēz\ *n, pl* **litotes** [Gk *litotēs*, fr. *litos* simple, perh. fr. *lit-, lis* linen cloth] (1589) : understatement in which an affirmative is expressed by the negative of the contrary (as in "not a bad singer" or "not unhappy")

litre *var of* LITER

Litt B *or* **Lit B** *abbr* [ML *litterarum baccalaureus*] bachelor of letters; bachelor of literature

Litt D *or* **Lit D** *abbr* [ML *litterarum doctor*] doctor of letters; doctor of literature

lit·ten \ˈli-tᵊn\ *adj* [alter. of *lit*, pp. of *light*] (1845) *archaic* : being lighted

1**lit·ter** \ˈli-tər\ *n* [ME, fr. AF *litere*, fr. *lit* bed, fr. L *lectus* — more at LIE] (14c) 1 **a** : a covered and curtained couch provided with shafts and used for carrying a single passenger **b** : a device (as a stretcher) for carrying a sick or injured person 2 **a** (1) : material used as bedding for animals (2) : material used to absorb the urine and feces of animals **b** : the uppermost slightly decayed layer of organic matter on the forest floor 3 : the offspring at one birth of a multiparous animal ⟨a ~ of puppies⟩ 4 **a** : trash, wastepaper, or garbage lying scattered about ⟨trying to clean up the roadside ~⟩ **b** : an untidy accumulation of objects ⟨a shabby writing-desk covered with a ~ of yellowish dusty documents —Joseph Conrad⟩ — **lit·tery** \-tə-rē\ *adj*

2**litter** *vt* (14c) 1 : BED 1a 2 : to give birth to a litter of (young) 3 **a** : to strew with scattered articles **b** : to scatter about in disorder **c** : to lie about in disorder ⟨their upside-down hats ~*ed* the top of the bar —Michael Chabon⟩ **d** : to mark with objects scattered at random ⟨a book ~*ed* with misprints⟩ ~ *vi* 1 : to give birth to a litter 2 : to strew litter

lit·te·rae hu·ma·ni·o·res \ˈli-tə-ˌrī-hü-ˌmä-nē-ˈȯr-ˌās\ *n pl* [ML, lit., more humane letters] (1747) : HUMANITIES

lit·ter·a·teur *or* **lit·té·ra·teur** \ˌli-tə-rə-ˈtər, ˌli-trə-, -ˈtu̇r\ *n* [F *littérateur*, fr. L *litterator* critic, fr. *litterae* letters, literature] (1806) : a literary person; *esp* : a professional writer

lit·ter·bag \ˈli-tər-ˌbag\ *n* (1955) : a bag used (as in an automobile) for temporary refuse disposal

lit·ter·bug \-ˌbəg\ *n* (1947) : one who litters a public area

lit·ter·er \ˈli-tər-ər\ *n* (1928) : LITTERBUG

lit·ter·mate \ˈli-tər-ˌmāt\ *n* (1921) : one of the offspring in a litter in relation to the others

1**lit·tle** \ˈli-tᵊl\ *adj* **lit·tler** \ˈli-tᵊl-ər, ˈlit-lər\ *or* **less** \ˈles\ *or* **less·er** \ˈle-sər\; **lit·tlest** \ˈli-tᵊl-əst, ˈlit-ləst\ *or* **least** \ˈlēst\ [ME *littel*, fr. OE *lȳtel*; akin to OHG *luzzil* little] (bef. 12c) 1 : not big: as **a** : small in size or extent : TINY ⟨has ~ feet⟩ **b** : YOUNG ⟨was too ~ to remember⟩ **c** *of a plant or animal* : small in comparison with related forms — used in vernacular names **d** : having few members or inhabitants ⟨a ~ group⟩ ⟨~ towns⟩ **e** : small in condition, distinction, or scope ⟨big business trampling on the ~ fellow⟩ **f** : NARROW, MEAN ⟨the pettiness of ~ minds⟩ **g** : pleasingly small ⟨a cute ~ thing⟩ **h** — used as an intensive ⟨why, you ~ devil!⟩ 2 : not much: as **a** : existing only in a small amount or to a slight degree ⟨has ~ money⟩ **b** : short in duration : BRIEF **c** : existing to an appreciable though not extensive degree or amount — used with *a* ⟨had a ~ money in the bank⟩ 3 : small in importance or interest : TRIVIAL ***syn*** see SMALL — **lit·tle·ness** \ˈli-tᵊl-nəs\ *n*

2**little** *adv* **less** \ˈles\; **least** \ˈlēst\ (bef. 12c) 1 **a** : in only a small quantity or degree : SLIGHTLY ⟨facts that were ~ known at the time⟩ **b** : not at all ⟨cared ~ for their neighbors⟩ 2 : RARELY, INFREQUENTLY

3**little** *n* (bef. 12c) 1 : a small amount, quantity, or degree; *also* : practically nothing ⟨~ has changed⟩ 2 **a** : a short time **b** : a short distance — **a little** : SOMEWHAT, RATHER ⟨found the play *a little* dull⟩ — **in little** : on a small scale; *esp* : in miniature

Little Bear *n* (1681) : URSA MINOR

little bitty *adj* (1905) : SMALL, TINY

little bluestem *n* (ca. 1898) : a forage grass (*Schizachyrium scoparium* syn. *Andropogon scoparius*) of eastern and central No. America

little brown bat *n* (1842) : a small widely distributed insectivorous No. American bat (*Myotis lucifugus*) with brown fur

little by little *adv* (15c) : by small degrees or amounts : GRADUALLY

Little Dipper *n* (1842) : the seven principal stars in Ursa Minor

little finger *n* (bef. 12c) : the fourth and smallest finger of the hand counting the index finger as the first

little guy *n* (1863) : LITTLE MAN

Little Hours *n pl* (ca. 1872) : the offices of prime, terce, sext, and none forming part of the canonical hours

Little Ice Age *n* (1951) : an episode of glacial expansion whose maximum extension occurred in the 17th and 18th centuries

little leaf *n* (1916) : any of various plant disorders characterized by small and often chlorotic and distorted foliage

Little League *n* (1952) : a commercially sponsored baseball league for boys and girls from 8 to 12 years old — **Little Leaguer** *n*

little magazine *n* (1900) : a literary usu. noncommercial magazine that features works esp. of writers who are not well-known

little man *n* (1933) : the ordinary individual

\ə\ **a**but \ᵊ\ kitten, F table \ər\ f**ur**ther \a\ **a**sh \ā\ **a**ce \ä\ m**o**p, m**a**r
\au̇\ **ou**t \ch\ **ch**in \e\ b**e**t \ē\ **ea**sy \g\ **g**o \i\ h**i**t \ī\ **i**ce \j\ **j**ob
\ŋ\ si**ng** \ō\ g**o** \ȯ\ l**aw** \ȯi\ b**oy** \th\ **th**in \t͟h\ **th**e \ü\ l**oo**t \u̇\ f**oo**t
\y\ **y**et \zh\ vi**si**on, beige \k, ⁿ, œ, ue, ʸ\ *see* Guide to Pronunciation

lit·tle·neck \ˈli-tᵊl-ˌnek\ *n* [*Littleneck* Bay, Long Island, N.Y.] (1883) **:** a young quahog suitable to be eaten raw — called also *littleneck clam*
Little Office *n* (ca. 1872) **:** an office in honor of the Virgin Mary like but shorter than the Divine Office
little people *n pl* (ca. 1731) **1 :** tiny imaginary beings (as fairies, elves, and leprechauns) of folklore **2 :** CHILDREN **3 :** people of unusually small size **4 :** common people
little slam *n* (ca. 1897) **:** the winning of all tricks except one in bridge
little theater *n* (1912) **:** a small theater for low-cost dramatic productions designed for a relatively limited audience
little toe *n* (bef. 12c) **:** the outermost and smallest digit of the foot
little woman *n* (1795) **:** WIFE
[1]**lit·to·ral** \ˈli-tə-rəl; ˌli-tə-ˈral, -ˈräl\ *adj* [L *litoralis,* fr. *litor-, litus* seashore] (ca. 1656) **:** of, relating to, or situated or growing on or near a shore esp. of the sea
[2]**littoral** *n* (1828) **:** a coastal region; *esp* **:** the shore zone between high tide and low tide points
litu *pl of* LITAS
lit up *adj* (1907) **:** DRUNK 1a
li·tur·gi·cal \lə-ˈtər-ji-kəl, li-\ *adj* (1641) **1 :** of, relating to, or having the characteristics of liturgy **2 :** using or favoring the use of liturgy ⟨~ churches⟩ — **li·tur·gi·cal·ly** \-k(ə-)lē\ *adv*
li·tur·gics \-jiks\ *n pl but sing or pl in constr* (ca. 1855) **:** the practice or study of formal public worship
li·tur·gi·ol·o·gist \-ˌtər-jē-ˈä-lə-jist\ *n* (1866) **:** LITURGIST 2
li·tur·gi·ol·o·gy \-jē\ *n* (1863) **:** LITURGICS
lit·ur·gist \ˈli-tər-jist\ *n* (1649) **1 :** one who adheres to, compiles, or leads a liturgy **2 :** a specialist in liturgics
lit·ur·gy \ˈli-tər-jē\ *n, pl* **-gies** [LL *liturgia,* fr. Gk *leitourgia* public service, fr. Gk (Attic) *leïton* public building (fr. Gk *laos* — Attic *leōs* — people) + *-ourgia* -urgy] (1560) **1** *often cap* **:** a eucharistic rite **2 :** a rite or body of rites prescribed for public worship **3 :** a customary repertoire of ideas, phrases, or observances
liv·abil·i·ty *also* **live·abil·i·ty** \ˌli-və-ˈbi-lə-tē\ *n* (1914) **1 :** survival expectancy **:** VIABILITY — used esp. of poultry and livestock **2 :** suitability for human living
liv·able *also* **live·able** \ˈli-və-bəl\ *adj* (1814) **1 :** suitable for living in, on, or with ⟨a ~ house⟩ ⟨~ wages⟩ **2 :** ENDURABLE — **liv·able·ness** *n*
[1]**live** \ˈliv\ *vb* **lived; liv·ing** [ME, fr. OE *libban;* akin to OHG *lebēn* to live] *vi* (bef. 12c) **1 :** to be alive **:** have the life of an animal or plant **2 :** to continue alive **3 :** to maintain oneself **:** SUBSIST ⟨*lived* on rice and peas⟩ **4 a :** to occupy a home **:** DWELL ⟨*living* in a shabby room⟩ ⟨they had always *lived* in the country⟩ **b :** to be located or stored ⟨the silverware ~*s* here⟩ **5 :** to attain eternal life ⟨though he die, yet shall he ~ —Jn 11:25(RSV)⟩ **6 :** to conduct or pass one's life ⟨*lived* only for his work⟩ **7 :** to remain in human memory or record ⟨the past ~*s* in us all —W. R. Inge⟩ **8 :** to have a life rich in experience **9 :** COHABIT ~ *vt* **1 :** to pass through or spend the duration of ⟨*lived* their lives alone⟩ **2 :** ACT OUT, PRACTICE — often used with *out* ⟨to ~ out their fantasies⟩ **3 :** to exhibit vigor, gusto, or enthusiasm in ⟨*lived* life to the fullest⟩ **4 a :** to experience firsthand ⟨*living* a dream⟩ **b :** to be thoroughly absorbed by or involved with ⟨she ~*s* her work⟩ — **live it up :** to live with gusto and usu. fast and loose ⟨*lived it up* with wine and song —*Newsweek*⟩ — **live up to :** to act or be in accordance with ⟨had no intention of *living up to* his promise⟩ — **live with :** to put up with **:** ACCEPT, TOLERATE ⟨had to *live with* their decision⟩
[2]**live** \ˈlīv\ *adj* [short for *alive*] (1542) **1 a :** having life **:** LIVING ⟨a ~ lobster⟩ **b :** existing in fact or reality **:** ACTUAL ⟨spoke to a real ~ celebrity⟩ **2 :** exerting force or containing energy: as **a :** AFIRE, GLOWING ⟨~ coals⟩ **b :** connected to electric power **c :** charged with explosives and containing shot or a bullet ⟨~ ammunition⟩; *also* **:** armed but not exploded ⟨a ~ bomb⟩ **d :** imparting or driven by power ⟨a ~ axle⟩ **e :** being in operation ⟨a ~ microphone⟩ **3 :** abounding with life **:** VIVID **4 :** being in a pure native state **5 :** of bright vivid color **6 :** of continuing or current interest ⟨~ issues⟩ **7 a :** not yet printed from or plated ⟨~ type⟩ **b :** not yet typeset ⟨~ copy⟩ **8 a :** of or involving a presentation (as a play or concert) in which both the performers and an audience are physically present ⟨a ~ record album⟩ ⟨a nightclub with ~ entertainment⟩ **b :** broadcast directly at the time of production ⟨a ~ radio program⟩ **9 :** being in play ⟨a ~ ball⟩
[3]**live** \ˈlīv\ *adv* (1946) **:** at the actual time of occurrence **:** during, from, or at a live production ⟨the program was broadcast ~⟩
live–ac·tion \ˈlīv-ˈak-shən\ *adj* (1945) **:** of, relating to, or featuring cinematography that is not produced by animation ⟨a ~ film⟩
live–bear·er \ˈlīv-ˌber-ər\ *n* (1934) **:** a fish that brings forth living young rather than eggs; *esp* **:** any of a family (Poeciliidae) of numerous small surface-feeding fishes (as a molly or swordtail)
live–box \-ˌbäks\ *n* (1862) **:** a box or pen suspended in water to keep aquatic animals alive
-lived \ˈlīvd, ˈlivd\ *adj comb form* [ME, fr. *lif* life] **:** having a life of a specified kind or length ⟨long-*lived*⟩
lived–in \ˈlivd-ˌin\ *adj* (1873) **:** of or suggesting long-term human habitation or use ⟨a comfortable ~ room⟩; *also* **:** showing the effects of age or experience ⟨a ~ voice⟩
live down *vt* (1842) **:** to live so as to wipe out the memory or effects of ⟨made a mistake and couldn't *live it down*⟩
live–for·ev·er \ˈliv-fə-ˌre-vər\ *n* (1597) **:** SEDUM
live–in \ˈliv-ˌin\ *adj* (1953) **1 :** living in one's place of employment ⟨a ~ maid⟩ **2 :** involving or involved with cohabitation ⟨a ~ relationship⟩ ⟨a ~ partner⟩ — **live–in** *n*
live in *vi* (1890) **:** to live in one's place of employment **:** live in another's home
live·li·hood \ˈlīv-lē-ˌhu̇d\ *n* [alter. of ME *livelode* course of life, fr. OE *līflād,* fr. *līf* + *lād* course — more at LODE] (15c) **1 :** means of support or subsistence **2** *obs* **:** the quality or state of being lively
live load *n* (1866) **:** the load to which a structure is subjected in addition to its own weight
live·long \ˈliv-ˌlȯŋ\ *adj* [ME *lef long,* fr. *lef* dear + *long* — more at LIEF] (15c) **:** WHOLE, ENTIRE ⟨the ~ day⟩
live·ly \ˈlīv-lē\ *adj* **live·li·er; -est** [ME, fr. OE *līflic,* fr. *līf* life] (bef. 12c) **1** *obs* **:** LIVING **2 :** briskly alert and energetic **:** VIGOROUS, ANIMATED ⟨a ~ discussion⟩ ⟨~ children racing for home⟩ **3 :** ACTIVE, INTENSE ⟨takes a ~ interest in politics⟩ **4 :** BRILLIANT, FRESH ⟨a ~ wit⟩ **5 :** imparting spirit or vivacity **:** STIMULATING ⟨many a peer of England brews *livelier* liquor than the Muse —A. E. Housman⟩ **6 :** quick to rebound **:** RESILIENT **7 :** responding readily to the helm ⟨a ~ boat⟩ **8 :** full of life, movement, or incident ⟨~ streets at carnival time⟩ — **live·li·ly** \ˈlīv-lə-lē\ *adv* — **live·li·ness** \ˈlīv-lē-nəs\ *n* — **lively** *adv*
syn LIVELY, ANIMATED, VIVACIOUS, SPRIGHTLY, GAY mean keenly alive and spirited. LIVELY suggests briskness, alertness, or energy ⟨a *lively* debate on the issues⟩. ANIMATED applies to what is spirited and active ⟨an *animated* discussion of current events⟩. VIVACIOUS suggests an activeness of gesture and wit, often playful or alluring ⟨a *vivacious* party host⟩. SPRIGHTLY suggests lightness and spirited vigor of manner or wit ⟨a tuneful, *sprightly* musical⟩. GAY stresses complete freedom from care and overflowing spirits ⟨the *gay* spirit of Paris in the 1920s⟩.
liv·en \ˈlī-vən\ *vb* **liv·ened; liv·en·ing** \ˈlī-və-niŋ, ˈlīv-niŋ\ *vt* (1884) **:** ENLIVEN — often used with *up* ⟨he . . . ~*ed* up the editorial page —*Current Biog.*⟩ ~ *vi* **:** to become lively
live oak \ˈlīv-\ *n* (1610) **:** any of several American evergreen oaks: as **a :** a medium-sized oak (*Quercus virginiana*) of southeastern No. America often cultivated as a shelter and shade tree and noted for its extremely hard tough durable wood **b :** any of several oaks of the western U.S. with evergreen foliage and hard durable wood

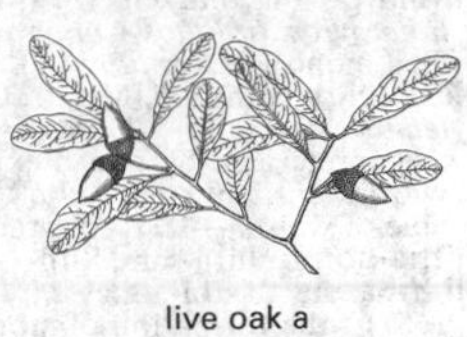
live oak a

[1]**liv·er** \ˈli-vər\ *n* [ME, fr. OE *lifer;* akin to OHG *lebra* liver] (bef. 12c) **1 a :** a large very vascular glandular organ of vertebrates that secretes bile and causes important changes in many of the substances contained in the blood (as by converting sugars into glycogen which it stores up until required and by forming urea) **b :** any of various large compound glands associated with the digestive tract of invertebrate animals and prob. concerned with the secretion of digestive enzymes **2** *archaic* **:** a determinant of the quality or temper of a man **3 :** the liver of an animal (as a calf or chicken) eaten as food **4 :** a grayish reddish brown — called also *liver brown, liver maroon*
[2]**liv·er** \ˈli-vər\ *n* (14c) **1 :** one that lives esp. in a specified way ⟨a fast ~⟩ **2 :** RESIDENT
-livered *adj comb form* **:** expressing vigor or courage considered suggestive of one with (such) a liver ⟨chicken-*livered*⟩ ⟨lily-*livered*⟩
liver fluke *n* (ca. 1798) **:** any of various trematode worms (as *Fasciola hepatica*) that invade the mammalian liver
liv·er·ied \ˈli-və-rēd, ˈliv-rēd\ *adj* (1634) **:** wearing a livery ⟨a ~ chauffeur⟩
liv·er·ish \ˈli-və-rish, ˈliv-rish\ *adj* (1740) **1 :** resembling liver esp. in color **2 a :** suffering from liver disorder **:** BILIOUS **b :** PEEVISH, IRASCIBLE — **liv·er·ish·ness** *n*
liver sausage *n* (1855) **:** a sausage containing cooked ground liver and pork trimmings — called also *liver pudding*
liver spots *n pl* (ca. 1859) **:** AGE SPOTS
liv·er·wort \ˈli-vər-ˌwərt, -ˌwȯrt\ *n* (bef. 12c) **1 :** any of a class (Hepaticae) of bryophytic plants characterized by a thalloid gametophyte or sometimes an upright leafy gametophyte that resembles a moss **2 :** HEPATICA
liv·er·wurst \ˈli-və(r)-ˌwərst *also* -ˌvu̇(r)st; *sometimes* -ˌvu̇sht\ *n* [part trans. of G *Leberwurst,* fr. *Leber* liver + *Wurst* sausage] (1869) **:** LIVER SAUSAGE
[1]**liv·ery** \ˈli-və-rē, ˈliv-rē\ *n, pl* **-er·ies** [ME, fr. AF *liveree, livree,* lit., delivery, fr. *liverer* to deliver, fr. L *liberare* to free — more at LIBERATE] (14c) **1** *archaic* **:** the apportioning of provisions esp. to servants **:** ALLOWANCE **2 a :** the distinctive clothing or badge formerly worn by the retainers of a person of rank **b :** a servant's uniform **c :** distinctive dress **:** GARB **d** *chiefly Brit* **:** an identifying design (as on a vehicle) that designates ownership **3** *archaic* **a :** one's retainers or retinue **b :** the members of a British livery company **4 :** the act of delivering legal possession of property **5 a :** the feeding, stabling, and care of horses for pay **b :** LIVERY STABLE **c :** a concern offering vehicles (as boats) for rent
[2]**livery** *adj* (1778) **1 :** resembling liver **2 :** suggesting liver disorder
livery company *n* (1766) **:** any of various London craft or trade associations that are descended from medieval guilds
liv·ery·man \ˈli-və-rē-mən, ˈliv-rē-\ *n* (1682) **1 :** a freeman of the City of London entitled to wear the livery of the company to which he belongs **2** *archaic* **:** a liveried retainer **3 :** the keeper of a vehicle-rental service
livery stable *n* (1705) **:** a stable where horses and vehicles are kept for hire and where stabling is provided — called also *livery barn*
lives *pl of* LIFE
live steam *n* (ca. 1875) **:** steam direct from a boiler and under full pressure
live·stock \ˈlīv-ˌstäk\ *n* (1742) **:** animals kept or raised for use or pleasure; *esp* **:** farm animals kept for use and profit
live·trap \-ˌtrap\ *vt* (1944) **:** to capture (an animal) in a live trap
live trap *n* (ca. 1875) **:** a trap for catching an animal alive and uninjured
live wire *n* (1903) **:** an alert, active, or aggressive person — **live–wire** *adj*
liv·id \ˈli-vəd\ *adj* [F *livide,* fr. L *lividus,* fr. *livēre* to be blue; akin to W *lliw* color and prob. to Russ *sliva* plum] (1622) **1 :** discolored by bruising **:** BLACK-AND-BLUE ⟨the ~ traces of the sharp scourges —Abraham Cowley⟩ **2 :** ASHEN, PALLID ⟨this cross, thy ~ face, thy pierced hands and feet —Walt Whitman⟩ **3 :** REDDISH ⟨a fan of gladiolas blushed ~ under the electric letters —Truman Capote⟩ **4 :** very angry **:** ENRAGED ⟨was ~ at his son's disobedience⟩ — **li·vid·i·ty** \li-ˈvi-də-tē\ *n* — **liv·id·ness** \ˈli-vəd-nəs\ *n*
[1]**living** *adj* (bef. 12c) **1 a :** having life **b :** ACTIVE, FUNCTIONING ⟨~ languages⟩ **2 a :** exhibiting the life or motion of nature **:** NATURAL ⟨the wilderness is a ~ museum . . . of natural history —*NEA Jour.*⟩ **b :** [2]LIVE 2a **3 a :** full of life or vigor **b :** true to life **:** VIVID ⟨televised in ~ color⟩ **c :** suited for living ⟨the ~ area⟩ **4 :** involving living persons **5 :** VERY — used as an intensive ⟨scared the ~ daylights out of me⟩ — **liv·ing·ness** *n*
[2]**living** *n* (14c) **1 :** the condition of being alive **2 a :** means of subsistence **:** LIVELIHOOD ⟨earning a ~⟩ **b** *archaic* **:** ESTATE, PROPERTY **c**

Brit : BENEFICE 1 **3 :** conduct or manner of life ⟨the collegiate way of ~ —J. B. Conant⟩

living death *n* (1597) : life emptied of joys and satisfactions

living fossil *n* (1922) : an organism (as a horseshoe crab or a ginkgo tree) that has remained essentially unchanged from earlier geologic times and whose close relatives are usu. extinct

living room *n* (1857) **1 :** a room in a residence used for the common social activities of the occupants **2 :** LEBENSRAUM — called also *living space*

living standard *n* (1939) : STANDARD OF LIVING

living trust *n* (1873) : a trust that becomes effective during the lifetime of the settlor — called also *inter vivos trust*

living unit *n* (ca. 1937) : an apartment or house for use by one family

living wage *n* (1860) **1 :** a subsistence wage **2 :** a wage sufficient to provide the necessities and comforts essential to an acceptable standard of living

living will *n* (1972) : a document in which the signer requests to be allowed to die rather than be kept alive by artificial means if disabled beyond a reasonable expectation of recovery — compare ADVANCE DIRECTIVE

livre \ˈlēvrᵊ\ *n* [F, fr. OF, fr. L *libra,* a unit of weight] (1553) **1 :** an old French monetary unit equal to 20 sols **2 :** a coin representing one livre **3 :** the pound of Lebanon

lix·iv·i·ate \lik-ˈsi-vē-ˌāt\ *vt* **-at·ed; -at·ing** [L *lixivium* lye, fr. *lixivius* made of lye, fr. *lixa* lye — more at LIQUID] (1758) : to extract a soluble constituent from (a solid mixture) by washing or percolation — **lix·iv·i·a·tion** \(ˌ)lik-ˌsi-vē-ˈā-shən\ *n*

liz·ard \ˈli-zərd\ *n* [ME *liserd,* fr. AF *lesarde,* fr. L *lacerta*] (14c) **1 :** any of a suborder (Lacertilia) of reptiles distinguished from the snakes by a fused inseparable lower jaw, a single temporal opening, two pairs of well differentiated functional limbs which may be lacking in burrowing forms, external ears, and eyes with movable lids; *broadly* : any relatively long-bodied reptile (as a crocodile or dinosaur) with legs and tapering tail **2 :** leather made from lizard skin

lizard's tail *n* (1737) : a perennial herb (*Saururus cernuus* of the family Saururaceae) of eastern No. American wetlands having spikes of tiny white flowers

Lk *abbr* Luke

'll \l, əl, ᵊl\ *vb* (1578) : WILL ⟨you*'ll* be late⟩

ll *abbr* lines

LL *abbr* **1** limited liability **2** lower left

lla·ma \ˈlä-mə, ˈyä-mə\ *n* [Sp, fr. Quechua] (1600) : any of a genus (*Lama*) of wild or domesticated long-necked So. American ruminants related to the camels but smaller and without a hump; *esp* : a domesticated llama (*L. glama*) descended from the guanaco and used esp. in the Andes as a pack animal and a source of wool

lla·no \ˈlä-(ˌ)nō, ˈla-\ *n, pl* **llanos** [Sp, plain, fr. L *planum* — more at PLAIN] (1604) : an open grassy plain in Spanish America or the southwestern U.S.

LLB *abbr* [NL *legum baccalaureus*] bachelor of laws

LLC *abbr* limited liability company

LLD *abbr* [NL *legum doctor*] doctor of laws

LLM *abbr* [NL *legum magister*] master of laws

LLP *abbr* limited liability partnership

lm *abbr* lumen

LM *abbr* **1** Legion of Merit **2** lunar apparatus module

LMAO *abbr* laughing my ass off

LMG *abbr* light machine gun

LMT *abbr* local mean time

ln *abbr* **1** lane **2** natural logarithm

lndg *abbr* landing

LNG *abbr* liquefied natural gas

lo \ˈlō\ *interj* [ME, fr. OE *lā*] (bef. 12c) — used to call attention or to express wonder or surprise ⟨~ these many years⟩

LO *abbr* liaison officer

LOA *abbr* length overall

loach \ˈlōch\ *n* [ME *loche,* fr. AF] (14c) : any of a family (Cobitidae) of small Old World freshwater fishes related to the carps

[1]**load** \ˈlōd\ *n* [ME *lod,* fr. OE *lād* support, carrying — more at LODE] (12c) **1 a :** the quantity that can be carried at one time by a specified means; *esp* : a measured quantity of a commodity fixed for each type of carrier — often used in combination ⟨a boat*load* of tourists⟩ **b :** whatever is put on a person or pack animal to be carried : PACK **c :** whatever is put in a ship or vehicle or airplane for conveyance : CARGO; *esp* : a quantity of material assembled or packed as a shipping unit **2 a :** a mass or weight supported by something ⟨branches bent low by their ~ of fruit⟩ **b :** the forces to which a structure is subjected due to superposed weight or to wind pressure on the vertical surfaces; *broadly* : the forces to which a given object is subjected **3 a :** something that weighs down the mind or spirits ⟨took a ~ off her mind⟩ **b :** a burdensome or laborious responsibility ⟨always carried his share of the ~⟩ **4** *slang* : an intoxicating amount of liquor drunk **5 :** a large quantity : LOT — usu. used in pl. **6 a :** a charge for a firearm **b :** the quantity of material loaded into a device at one time **7 :** external resistance overcome by a machine or prime mover **8 a :** power output (as of a power plant) or power consumption (as by a device) **b :** a device to which power is delivered **9 a** (1) **:** the amount of work that a person carries or is expected to carry (2) **:** the amount of authorized work to be performed by a machine, a group, a department, or a factory **b :** the demand on the operating resources of a system (as a telephone exchange or a refrigerating apparatus) **10** *slang* : EYEFUL — used in the phrase *get a load of* **11 :** the amount of a deleterious microorganism, parasite, growth, or substance present in a human or animal body ⟨measure viral ~ in the blood⟩ ⟨the worm ~ in rats⟩ — called also *burden* **12 :** an amount added (as to the price of a security or the net premium in insurance) to represent selling expense and profit to the distributor **13 :** GENETIC LOAD

[2]**load** *vt* (15c) **1 a :** to put a load in or on ⟨~ a truck⟩ **b :** to place in or on a means of conveyance ⟨~ freight⟩ **2 a :** to encumber or oppress with something heavy, laborious, or disheartening : BURDEN ⟨a company ~*ed* down with debts⟩ **b :** to place as a burden or obligation ⟨~ more work on him⟩ **3 a :** to increase the weight of by adding something heavy **b :** to add a conditioning substance (as a mineral salt) to for body **c :** to weight or shape (dice) to fall unfairly **d :** to pack with one-sided or prejudicial influences : BIAS **e :** to charge with multiple meanings (as emotional associations or hidden implications) **f :** to weight (as a test) with factors influencing validity or outcome **4 a :** to supply in abundance or excess : HEAP, PACK **b :** to put runners on (first, second, and third bases) in baseball **5 a :** to put a load or charge in (a device or piece of equipment) ⟨~ a gun⟩ **b :** to place or insert esp. as a load in a device or piece of equipment ⟨~ film in a camera⟩ **c :** to copy or transfer (as a program or data) into a computer's memory esp. from an external source (as a disk drive or the Internet) **6 :** to alter (as an alcoholic drink) by adding an adulterant or drug **7 a :** to add a load to (an insurance premium) **b :** to add a sum to after profits and expenses are accounted for ⟨~*ed* prices⟩ ~ *vi* **1 :** to receive a load **2 :** to put a load on or in a carrier, device, or container; *esp* : to insert the charge or cartridge in the chamber of a firearm **3 :** to go or go in as a load ⟨tourists ~*ing* onto a bus⟩ **4 :** to become loaded into a computer's memory ⟨the program ~*s* quickly⟩ — **load·er** *n* — **load up on 1 :** to ingest in usu. large amounts ⟨senators *loading up on* fried chicken and champagne —H. L. Mencken⟩ **2 :** to acquire in usu. large amounts ⟨*loaded up on* hot stocks⟩

load·ed \ˈlō-dəd\ *adj* (1886) **1** *slang* : HIGH 12b **2 :** having a large amount of money **3 a :** equipped with an abundance of options ⟨bought a fully ~ car⟩ **b :** staffed with excellent players ⟨a ~ basketball team⟩

load factor *n* (1943) : the percentage of available seats paid for and occupied in an aircraft

load·ing \ˈlō-diŋ\ *n* (15c) **1 :** a cargo, weight, or stress placed on something **2 :** LOAD 12 **3 :** material used to load something : FILLER

load line *n* (ca. 1859) : the line on a ship indicating the depth to which it sinks in the water when properly loaded — see PLIMSOLL MARK illustration

load·mas·ter \ˈlōd-ˌmas-tər\ *n* (1961) : a crew member of a transport aircraft who is in charge of the cargo

loadstar *var of* LODESTAR

loadstone *var of* LODESTONE

[1]**loaf** \ˈlōf\ *n, pl* **loaves** \ˈlōvz\ [ME *lof,* fr. OE *hlāf;* akin to OHG *hleib* loaf] (bef. 12c) **1 :** a shaped or molded mass of bread **2 :** a shaped or molded often symmetrical mass of food **3** *slang Brit* : HEAD, MIND

[2]**loaf** *vi* [prob. back-formation fr. *loafer*] (1835) : to spend time in idleness ***syn*** see IDLE

loaf·er \ˈlō-fər\ *n* [perh. short for *landloafer,* fr. G *Landläufer* tramp, fr. *Land* + *Läufer* runner] (1830) **1 :** one that loafs : IDLER **2 :** a low step-in shoe

loam \ˈlōm, *chiefly Northern & Midland* ˈlüm, *NewEng also* ˈlu̇m\ *n* [ME *lom,* fr. OE *lām* clay, mud; akin to OE *līm* lime] (12c) **1 a :** a mixture (as for plastering) composed chiefly of moistened clay **b :** a coarse molding sand used in founding **2 :** SOIL; *specif* : a soil consisting of a friable mixture of varying proportions of clay, silt, and sand — **loamy** \ˈlō-mē, ˈlü-, ˈlu̇-\ *adj*

[1]**loan** \ˈlōn\ *n* [ME *lon,* fr. ON *lān;* akin to OE *lǣn* loan, *lēon* to lend, L *linquere* to leave, Gk *leipein*] (12c) **1 a :** money lent at interest **b :** something lent usu. for the borrower's temporary use **2 a :** the grant of temporary use **b :** the temporary duty of a person transferred to another job for a limited time **3 :** LOANWORD

[2]**loan** *vt* (13c) : LEND — **loan·able** \ˈlō-nə-bəl\ *adj*

usage The verb *loan* is one of the words English settlers brought to America and continued to use after it had died out in Britain. Its use was soon noticed by British visitors and somewhat later by the New England literati, who considered it a bit provincial. It was flatly declared wrong in 1870 by a popular commentator, who based his objection on etymology. A later scholar showed that the commentator was ignorant of Old English and thus unsound in his objection, but by then it was too late, as the condemnation had been picked up by many other commentators. Although a surprising number of critics still voice objections, *loan* is entirely standard as a verb. You should note that it is used only literally; *lend* is the verb used for figurative expressions, such as "lending a hand" or "lending enchantment."

lo and behold *interj* (1808) — used to express wonder or surprise

loan·er \ˈlō-nər\ *n* (1926) : one (as a car or a watch) that is lent esp. as a replacement for something being repaired

loan·ing \ˈlō-niŋ\ *n* [ME *loning,* fr. *lone,* alter. of *lane*] (14c) **1** *dial Brit* : LANE **2** *dial Brit* : a milking yard

loan shark *n* (1905) : one who lends money to individuals at exorbitant rates of interest

loan–shark·ing \-ˌshär-kiŋ\ *n* (1914) : the practice of lending money at exorbitant rates of interest

loan translation *n* (1917) : a compound, derivative, or phrase that is introduced into a language through translation of the constituents of a term in another language (as *superman* from German *Übermensch*)

loan·word \ˈlōn-ˌwərd\ *n* (1869) : a word taken from another language and at least partly naturalized

loath *also* **loth** \ˈlōth, ˈlō<u>th</u>\ *or* **loathe** \ˈlō<u>th</u>, ˈlōth\ *adj* [ME *loth* loathsome, fr. OE *lāth;* akin to OHG *leid* loathsome, OIr *lius* loathing] (12c) : unwilling to do something contrary to one's ways of thinking : RELUCTANT ***syn*** see DISINCLINED — **loath·ness** *n*

loathe \ˈlō<u>th</u>\ *vt* **loathed; loath·ing** [ME *lothen,* fr. OE *lāthian* to dislike, be hateful, fr. *lāth*] (12c) : to dislike greatly and often with disgust or intolerance : DETEST ***syn*** see HATE — **loath·er** *n*

loathing *n* (14c) : extreme disgust : DETESTATION

[1]**loath·ly** \ˈlōth-lē, ˈlō<u>th</u>-\ *adj* (bef. 12c) : LOATHSOME, REPULSIVE

[2]**loath·ly** \ˈlōth-lē, ˈlō<u>th</u>-\ *adv* (15c) : not willingly : RELUCTANTLY

loath·some \ˈlōth-səm, ˈlō<u>th</u>-\ *adj* [ME *lothsum,* fr. *loth* evil, fr. OE *lāth,* fr. *lāth,* adj.] (14c) : giving rise to loathing : DISGUSTING — **loath·some·ly** *adv* — **loath·some·ness** *n*

[1]**lob** \ˈläb\ *n* [prob. of LG origin; akin to LG *lubbe* coarse person] (1508) *dial Brit* : a dull heavy person : LOUT

[2]**lob** *vb* **lobbed; lob·bing** [*lob* a loosely hanging object] *vt* (1599) **1 :** to let hang heavily : DROOP **2 :** to throw, hit, or propel easily or in a high

\ə\ **abut** \ᵊ\ kitten, F table \ər\ **fur**ther \a\ **ash** \ā\ **ace** \ä\ **mop, mar**
\au̇\ **out** \ch\ **chin** \e\ **bet** \ē\ **easy** \g\ **go** \i\ **hit** \ī\ **ice** \j\ **job**
\ŋ\ **sing** \ō\ **go** \ȯ\ **law** \ȯi\ **boy** \th\ **thin** \<u>th</u>\ **the** \ü\ **loot** \u̇\ **foot**
\y\ **yet** \zh\ **vi**sion, **beige** \k̲, ⁿ, œ, ue, ʸ\ *see* Guide to Pronunciation

arc **3 :** to direct (as a question or comment) so as to elicit a response ~ *vi* **1 a :** to move slowly and heavily **b :** to move in an arc **2 :** to hit a tennis ball easily in a high arc

[3]**lob** *n* (1851) **:** a soft high-arching shot, throw, or kick

lob- *or* **lobo-** *comb form* [*lobe*] **:** lobe ⟨*lob*ar⟩ ⟨*lobo*tomy⟩

lo·bar \ˈlō-bər, -ˌbär\ *adj* (ca. 1856) **:** of or relating to a lobe

lo·bate \ˈlō-ˌbāt\ *also* **lo·bat·ed** \-ˌbā-təd\ *adj* [NL *lobatus,* fr. LL *lobus*] (ca. 1760) **1 :** LOBED **2 :** resembling a lobe — **lo·ba·tion** \lō-ˈbā-shən\ *n*

[1]**lob·by** \ˈlä-bē\ *n, pl* **lobbies** [ML *lobium* gallery, of Gmc origin; akin to OHG *louba* porch] (1593) **1 :** a corridor or hall connected with a larger room or series of rooms and used as a passageway or waiting room: as **a :** an anteroom of a legislative chamber; *esp* **:** one of two anterooms of a British parliamentary chamber to which members go to vote during a division **b :** a large hall serving as a foyer (as of a hotel or theater) **2 :** a group of persons engaged in lobbying esp. as representatives of a particular interest group

[2]**lobby** *vb* **lob·bied; lob·by·ing** *vi* (1837) **:** to conduct activities aimed at influencing public officials and esp. members of a legislative body on legislation ~ *vt* **1 :** to promote (as a project) or secure the passage of (as legislation) by influencing public officials **2 :** to attempt to influence or sway (as a public official) toward a desired action — **lob·by·er** *n* — **lob·by·ism** \-ˌi-zəm\ *n* — **lob·by·ist** \-ist\ *n*

lob·by·gow \ˈlä-bē-ˌgau̇\ *n* [origin unknown] (1899) **:** an errand boy

lobe \ˈlōb\ *n* [MF, fr. LL *lobus,* fr. Gk *lobos*] (1541) **:** a curved or rounded projection or division; *specif* **:** a usu. somewhat rounded projection or division of a bodily organ or part

lo·bec·to·my \lō-ˈbek-tə-mē\ *n, pl* **-mies** [ISV] (ca. 1911) **:** surgical removal of a lobe of an organ (as a lung) or gland (as the thyroid)

lobed \ˈlōbd\ *adj* (1756) **:** having lobes ⟨palmately ~ leaves⟩

lobe–fin \ˈlōb-ˌfin\ *n* (1941) **:** CROSSOPTERYGIAN — **lobe–finned** \-ˈfind\ *adj*

lo·be·lia \lō-ˈbēl-yə, -ˈbē-lē-ə\ *n* [NL, fr. Matthias de *Lobel* †1616 Flem. botanist] (1739) **1 :** any of a genus (*Lobelia* of the family Lobeliaceae, the lobelia family) of widely cultivated plants having terminal clusters of showy lipped flowers **2 :** the leaves and tops of Indian tobacco

lo·be·line \ˈlō-bə-ˌlēn\ *n* [NL *Lobelia* + E [2]*-ine*] (1852) **:** a crystalline alkaloid $C_{22}H_{27}NO_2$ that is obtained from Indian tobacco and is used chiefly as a respiratory stimulant and as a smoking deterrent

lob·lol·ly \ˈläb-ˌlä-lē\ *n, pl* **-lies** [prob. fr. E dial. *lob* to boil + obs. E dial. *lolly* broth] (1597) **1** *dial* **a :** a thick gruel **b :** MIRE, MUDHOLE **2** *dial* **:** LOUT **3 :** LOBLOLLY PINE

loblolly pine *n* (1760) **:** a pine (*Pinus taeda*) of the southeastern U.S. with flaky bark, long needles in groups of three, and cones having spine-tipped scales; *also* **:** its coarse-grained wood

lo·bo \ˈlō-(ˌ)bō\ *n, pl* **lobos** [Sp, wolf, fr. L *lupus* — more at WOLF] (1839) **:** GRAY WOLF

lo·bot·o·mise *Brit var of* LOBOTOMIZE

lo·bot·o·mize \lō-ˈbä-tə-ˌmīz\ *vt* **-mized; -miz·ing** (1943) **1 :** to perform a lobotomy on **2 :** to deprive of sensitivity, intelligence, or vitality ⟨fear of prosecution was causing the press to ~ itself —Tony Eprile⟩

lo·bot·o·my \lō-ˈbä-tə-mē\ *n, pl* **-mies** [ISV] (1936) **:** surgical severance of nerve fibers connecting the frontal lobes to the thalamus performed esp. formerly for the relief of some mental disorders

lob·scouse \ˈläb-ˌskau̇s\ *n* [origin unknown] (1706) **:** a sailor's dish of stewed or baked meat with vegetables and hardtack

lob·ster \ˈläb-stər\ *n, often attrib* [ME, fr. OE *loppestre,* fr. *loppe* spider] (bef. 12c) **1 :** any of a family (Nephropidae and esp. *Homarus americanus*) of large edible marine decapod crustaceans that have stalked eyes, a pair of large claws, and a long abdomen and that include species from coasts on both sides of the No. Atlantic and from the Cape of Good Hope **2 :** SPINY LOBSTER — **lob·ster·like** \-ˌlīk\ *adj*

lob·ster·ing \ˈläb-st(ə-)riŋ\ *n* (1881) **:** the activity or business of catching lobsters

lob·ster·man \-mən\ *n* (1881) **:** one whose business is lobstering

lobster pot *n* (1764) **:** an oblong case with slat sides and a funnel-shaped net used to trap lobsters — called also *lobster trap*

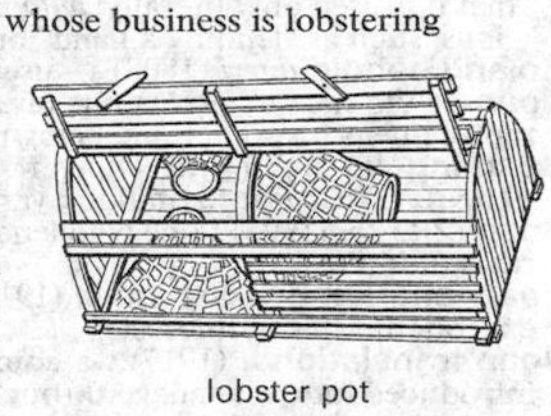

lobster pot

lobster shift *n* (ca. 1933) **:** a work shift (as on a newspaper) that covers the late evening and early morning hours — called also *lobster trick*

lobster ther·mi·dor \-ˈthər-mə-ˌdȯr\ *n* [*thermidor,* fr. F, fr. *Thermidor,* drama (1891) by Victorien Sardou] (1894) **:** cooked lobster meat in a rich wine sauce stuffed into a lobster shell and browned

lob·u·lar \ˈlä-byə-lər\ *adj* (1826) **:** of, relating to, affecting, or resembling a lobule

lob·u·lat·ed \ˈlä-byə-ˌlā-təd\ *also* **lob·u·late** \-ˌlāt\ *adj* (1783) **:** made up of or having lobules ⟨the pancreas is a ~ organ⟩ — **lob·u·la·tion** \ˌlä-byə-ˈlā-shən\ *n*

lob·ule \ˈlä-(ˌ)byül\ *n* (1682) **:** a small lobe; *also* **:** a subdivision of a lobe

[1]**lo·cal** \ˈlō-kəl\ *adj* [ME *localle,* fr. LL *localis,* fr. L *locus* place — more at STALL] (15c) **1 :** characterized by or relating to position in space **:** having a definite spatial form or location **2 a :** of, relating to, or characteristic of a particular place **:** not general or widespread **b :** of, relating to, or applicable to part of a whole **3 a :** primarily serving the needs of a particular limited district **b** *of a public conveyance* **:** making all the stops on a route **4 :** involving or affecting only a restricted part of the organism **:** TOPICAL ⟨a ~ anesthetic⟩ **5 :** of or relating to telephone communication within a specified area

[2]**local** *n* (ca. 1824) **:** a local person or thing: as **a :** a local public conveyance (as a train or an elevator) **b :** a local or particular branch, lodge, or chapter of an organization (as a labor union) **c** *Brit* **:** a nearby or neighborhood pub

local area network *n* (1977) **:** a network of personal computers in a small area (as an office) for sharing resources (as a printer) or exchanging data

local color *n* (1868) **:** the presentation of the features and peculiarities of a particular locality and its inhabitants in writing

lo·cale \lō-ˈkal\ *n* [modif. of F *local,* fr. *local,* adj.] (1772) **1 :** a place or locality esp. when viewed in relation to a particular event or characteristic **2 :** SITE, SCENE ⟨the ~ of a story⟩

local government *n* (1817) **:** the government of a specific local area constituting a subdivision of a major political unit (as a nation or state); *also* **:** the body of persons constituting such a government

lo·cal·ise *Brit var of* LOCALIZE

lo·cal·ism \ˈlō-kə-ˌli-zəm\ *n* (1823) **1 a :** a local idiom **b :** a local peculiarity of speaking or acting **2 :** affection or partiality for a particular place **:** SECTIONALISM

lo·cal·ite \ˈlō-kə-ˌlīt\ *n* (1951) **:** a native or resident of the locality under consideration **:** LOCAL

lo·cal·i·ty \lō-ˈka-lə-tē\ *n, pl* **-ties** (1628) **1 :** the fact or condition of having a location in space or time **2 :** a particular place, situation, or location

lo·cal·ize \ˈlō-kə-ˌlīz\ *vb* **-ized; -iz·ing** *vt* (1792) **1 :** to make local **:** orient locally **2 :** to assign to or keep within a definite locality ~ *vi* **:** to accumulate in or be restricted to a specific or limited area ⟨an infection that ~*s* in the ear⟩ — **lo·cal·iz·abil·i·ty** \ˌlō-kə-ˌlī-zə-ˈbi-lə-tē\ *n* — **lo·cal·iz·able** \ˈlō-kə-ˌlī-zə-bəl\ *adj* — **lo·cal·i·za·tion** \ˌlō-kə-lə-ˈzā-shən\ *n*

lo·cal·ly \ˈlō-k(ə-)lē\ *adv* (15c) **1 :** with respect to a particular place or situation **2 :** NEARBY **3 :** in the region of origin

local option *n* (1878) **:** the power granted by a legislature to a political subdivision to determine by popular vote the local applicability of a law on a controversial issue (as the sale of liquor)

local time *n* (1833) **:** time based on the meridian through a particular place as contrasted with that of a time zone

lo·cate \ˈlō-ˌkāt, lō-ˈ\ *vb* **lo·cat·ed; lo·cat·ing** [L *locatus,* pp. of *locare* to place, fr. *locus*] *vi* (1652) **:** to establish oneself or one's business **:** SETTLE ~ *vt* **1 :** to determine or indicate the place, site, or limits of **2 :** to set or establish in a particular spot **:** STATION **3 :** to seek out and determine the location of **4 :** to find or fix the place of esp. in a sequence **:** CLASSIFY — **lo·cat·able** \-ˌkā-tə-bəl, -ˈkā-\ *adj*

lo·ca·tion \lō-ˈkā-shən\ *n* (1597) **1 a :** a position or site occupied or available for occupancy or marked by some distinguishing feature **:** SITUATION **b** (1) **:** a tract of land designated for a purpose (2) *Austral* **:** FARM, STATION **c :** a place outside a motion-picture studio where a picture or part of it is filmed — usu. used in the phrase *on location* **2 :** the act or process of locating **3 :** the placement of baseball pitches in a particular area of the strike zone; *also* **:** the ability to control the placement of pitches — **lo·ca·tion·al** \-shnəl, -shə-nᵊl\ *adj* — **lo·ca·tion·al·ly** *adv*

[1]**loc·a·tive** \ˈlä-kə-tiv\ *n* [L *locus* + E *-ative* (as in *vocative*)] (1804) **:** the locative case; *also* **:** a word in that case

[2]**locative** *adj* (1841) **:** of or being a grammatical case that denotes place or the place where or wherein

lo·ca·tor *also* **lo·cat·er** \ˈlō-ˌkā-tər, lō-ˈ\ *n* (1784) **:** one that locates something (as a mining claim or the course of a road)

lo·ca·vore \ˈlō-kə-ˌvȯr\ *n* [*local* + *-vore* (as in *carnivore*)] (2005) **:** one who eats foods grown locally whenever possible

loc cit *abbr* [L *loco citato*] in the place cited

loch \ˈläk, ˈläk̲\ *n* [ME (Sc) *louch,* fr. ScGael *loch;* akin to L *lacus* lake — more at LAKE] (14c) **1** *Scot* **:** LAKE **2** *Scot* **:** a bay or arm of the sea esp. when nearly landlocked

loch·an \ˈlä-k̲ən\ *n* [ScGael, dim. of *loch*] (1670) *Scot* **:** a small lake

loci *pl of* LOCUS

[1]**lock** \ˈläk\ *n* [ME *lok,* fr. OE *locc;* akin to OHG *loc* lock, Gk *lygos* withe, L *luxus* dislocated] (bef. 12c) **1 a :** a tuft, tress, or ringlet of hair **b** *pl* **:** the hair of the head **2 :** a cohering bunch (as of wool, cotton, or flax) **:** TUFT **3** *pl* **:** DREADLOCK 2

[2]**lock** *n* [ME *lok,* fr. OE *loc;* akin to OHG *loh* enclosure and perh. to OE *locc* lock of hair] (bef. 12c) **1 a :** a fastening (as for a door) operated by a key or a combination **b :** the mechanism for exploding the charge or cartridge of a firearm **2 a :** an enclosure (as in a canal) with gates at each end used in raising or lowering boats as they pass from level to level **b :** AIR LOCK **3 a :** a locking or fastening together **b :** an intricate mass of objects impeding each other (as in a traffic jam) **c :** a hold in wrestling secured on one part of the body; *broadly* **:** a controlling hold ⟨his paper . . . had a ~ on a large part of the state —John Corry⟩ **4 :** one that is assured of success or favorable outcome

[3]**lock** *vt* (14c) **1 a :** to fasten the lock of **b :** to make fast with or as if with a lock ⟨~ up the house⟩ **2 a :** to fasten in or out or to make secure or inaccessible by or as if by means of locks ⟨~*ed* himself away from the curious world⟩ **b :** to fix in a particular situation or method of operation ⟨a team firmly ~*ed* in last place⟩ **3 a :** to make fast, motionless, or inflexible esp. by the interlacing or interlocking of parts ⟨~ wheels⟩ ⟨~ a knee⟩ **b :** to hold in a close embrace **c :** to grapple in combat; *also* **:** to bind closely ⟨administration and students were ~*ed* in conflict⟩ **4 :** to invest (capital) without assurance of easy convertibility into money **5 :** to move or permit to pass (as a ship) by raising or lowering in a lock ~ *vi* **1 a :** to become locked **b :** to be capable of being locked **2 :** INTERLACE, INTERLOCK **3 :** to go or pass by means of a lock (as in a canal) — **lock·able** \ˈlä-kə-bəl\ *adj* — **lock horns :** to come into conflict — **lock on** *or* **lock onto :** to acquire (as a target or signal) automatically using a sensor (as radar)

lock·box \ˈläk-ˌbäks\ *n* (1872) **:** a box (as a post-office box) that locks

lock·down \-ˌdau̇n\ *n* (1977) **:** the confinement of prisoners to their cells for all or most of the day as a temporary security measure

locked–in \ˈläkt-ˈin\ *adj* (1952) **1 :** not subject to adjustment **:** FIXED ⟨~ interest rates⟩ **2 :** unable or unwilling to shift invested funds because of the tax effect of realizing capital gains

lock·er \ˈlä-kər\ *n* (14c) **1 a :** a drawer, cupboard, or compartment that may be closed with a lock; *esp* **:** one for individual storage use **b :** a chest or compartment on shipboard for compact stowage of articles **c :** a refrigerated compartment or room for the storage of fresh or frozen foods ⟨a meat ~⟩ **2 :** one that locks

lock·er–room \ˈlä-kə(r)-ˌrüm\ *adj* (1946) **:** of, relating to, or suitable for use in a locker room; *esp* **:** of a coarse or sexual nature ⟨~ talk⟩

locker room *n* (ca. 1896) **:** a room for changing clothes and for storing clothing and equipment in lockers; *esp* **:** one for use by sports players

lock·et \ˈlä-kət\ *n* [MF *loquet* latch, fr. MD *loke;* akin to OE *loc*] (1679) **:** a small case usu. of precious metal that has space for a memento and that is worn typically suspended from a chain or necklace

lock·jaw \ˈläk-ˌjȯ\ *n* (1803) **:** an early symptom of tetanus characterized by spasm of the jaw muscles and inability to open the jaws; *also* **:** TETANUS
lock·keep·er \ˈläk-ˌkē-pər\ *n* (1794) **:** a person in charge of a lock (as on a canal)
lock·nut \-ˌnət\ *n* (ca. 1864) **1 :** a nut screwed down hard on another to prevent it from slacking back **2 :** a nut so constructed that it locks itself when screwed tight against another part
lock·out \ˈläk-ˌau̇t\ *n* (1854) **:** the withholding of employment by an employer and the whole or partial closing of the business establishment in order to gain concessions from or resist demands of employees
lock out *vt* (1860) **:** to subject (a body of employees) to a lockout
lock·ram \ˈlä-krəm\ *n* [ME *lokerham,* fr. *Locronan,* town in Brittany] (14c) **:** a coarse plain-woven linen formerly used in England
lock·smith \ˈläk-ˌsmith\ *n* (13c) **:** a person who makes or repairs locks
lock·smith·ing \-ˌsmi-thiŋ\ *n* (1874) **:** the work or business of a locksmith
lock·step \ˈläk-ˌstep\ *n, often attrib* (ca. 1802) **1 :** a mode of marching in step by a body of persons going one after another as closely as possible **2 :** a standard method or procedure that is mindlessly adhered to or that minimizes individuality — **in lockstep :** in perfect or rigid often mindless conformity or unison ⟨politicians marching *in lockstep* with the party line⟩
lock·stitch \ˈläk-ˌstich\ *n* (ca. 1859) **:** a sewing machine stitch formed by the looping together of two threads one on each side of the material being sewn — **lockstitch** *vb*
lock, stock, and barrel *adv* [fr. the principal parts of a flintlock] (1842) **:** WHOLLY, COMPLETELY ⟨the only thing which had not been sold *lock, stock, and barrel* with the . . . house was this piano —Marcia Davenport⟩
lock·up \ˈläk-ˌəp\ *n* (1824) **1 :** JAIL; *esp* **:** a local jail where persons are detained prior to court hearing **2 :** an act of locking **:** the state of being locked
[1]**lo·co** \ˈlō-(ˌ)kō\ *adv or adj* [It dial., there, fr. L *in loco* in the place] (ca. 1801) **:** in the register as written — used as a direction in music
[2]**loco** *n, pl* **locos** *or* **locoes** [MexSp, fr. Sp, crazy] (1844) **1 :** LOCOWEED **2 :** LOCOISM
[3]**loco** *vt* (1884) **1 :** to poison with locoweed **2 :** to make frenzied or crazy
[4]**loco** *adj* [Sp] (1887) *slang* **:** mentally disordered **:** CRAZY, FRENZIED
Lo·co·fo·co \ˌlō-kə-ˈfō-(ˌ)kō\ *n, pl* **-focos** [*locofoco,* a kind of friction match, prob. fr. [1]*locomotive* + It *fuoco, foco* fire, fr. L *focus* hearth] (1835) **1 :** a member of a radical group of New York Democrats organized in 1835 in opposition to the regular party organization **2 :** DEMOCRAT 2
lo·co·ism \ˈlō-(ˌ)kō-ˌi-zəm\ *n* (1900) **:** a disease usu. of horses, cattle, and sheep that is caused by chronic poisoning with locoweeds
lo·co·mote \ˈlō-kə-ˌmōt\ *vi* **-mot·ed; -mot·ing** [back-formation fr. *locomotion*] (1834) **:** to move about
lo·co·mo·tion \ˌlō-kə-ˈmō-shən\ *n* [L *locus* + E *motion*] (1646) **1 :** an act or the power of moving from place to place **2 :** TRAVEL ⟨interest in free ~ and choice of occupation —Zechariah Chafee Jr.⟩
[1]**lo·co·mo·tive** \ˌlō-kə-ˈmō-tiv\ *adj* (1612) **1 :** LOCOMOTORY **2 :** of or relating to travel **3 :** of, relating to, or being a machine that moves about by operation of its own mechanism
[2]**locomotive** *n* (1829) **1 :** a self-propelled vehicle that runs on rails and is used for moving railroad cars **2 :** a school or college cheer characterized by a slow beginning and a progressive increase in speed
lo·co·mo·tor \ˌlō-kə-ˈmō-tər\ *adj* (1870) **1 :** of, relating to, or functioning in locomotion **2 :** affecting or involving the locomotor organs
locomotor ataxia *n* (1875) **:** TABES DORSALIS
lo·co·mo·to·ry \ˌlō-kə-ˈmō-tə-rē\ *adj* (ca. 1836) **1 :** LOCOMOTOR ⟨~ appendages⟩ **2 :** capable of moving independently from place to place ⟨~ animals⟩
lo·co·weed \ˈlō-(ˌ)kō-ˌwēd\ *n* (1879) **:** any of several leguminous plants (genera *Astragalus* and *Oxytropis*) of western No. America that cause locoism esp. in livestock
loc·u·lar \ˈlä-kyə-lər\ *adj* (1783) **:** having or composed of loculi — often used in combination ⟨uni*locular*⟩
loc·ule \ˈlä-(ˌ)kyül\ *n* [F, fr. L *loculus*] (ca. 1888) **:** LOCULUS; *esp* **:** any of the cells of a compound ovary of a plant — **loc·uled** \-(ˌ)kyüld\ *adj*
loc·u·li·ci·dal \ˌlä-kyə-lə-ˈsī-dᵊl\ *adj* [NL *loculus* + L *-cidere* to cut, fr. *caedere*] (ca. 1819) **:** dehiscing longitudinally so as to bisect each loculus ⟨~ fruit⟩
loc·u·lus \ˈlä-kyə-ləs\ *n, pl* **-li** \-ˌlī, -ˌlē\ [NL, fr. L, dim. of *locus*] (1846) **:** a small chamber or cavity esp. in a plant or animal body
lo·cum \ˈlō-kəm\ *n* (1901) *chiefly Brit* **:** LOCUM TENENS
locum te·nens \-ˈtē-ˌnenz, -ˈte-, -nənz\ *n, pl* **locum te·nen·tes** \-ti-ˈnen-ˌtēz\ [ML, lit., (one) holding a place] (1641) **:** one filling an office for a time or temporarily taking the place of another — used esp. of a doctor or clergyman
lo·cus \ˈlō-kəs\ *n, pl* **lo·ci** \ˈlō-ˌsī, -ˌkī, -ˌkē\ [L — more at STALL] (1715) **1 a :** the place where something is situated or occurs **:** SITE, LOCATION ⟨was the culture of medicine in the beginning dispersed from a single focus or did it arise in several *loci*? —S. C. Harvey⟩ **b :** a center of activity, attention, or concentration ⟨in democracy the ~ of power is in the people —H. G. Rickover⟩ **2 :** the set of all points whose location is determined by stated conditions **3 :** the position in a chromosome of a particular gene or allele
locus clas·si·cus \-ˈkla-si-kəs\ *n, pl* **loci clas·si·ci** \-ˈkla-sə-ˌsī, -ˌkī, -ˌkē\ [NL] (1853) **1 :** a passage that has become a standard for the elucidation of a word or subject **2 :** a classic case or example
locus coe·ru·le·us *also* **locus ce·ru·le·us** \-si-ˈrü-lē-əs\ *n* [NL, lit., dark blue place] (1858) **:** a bluish area of the brain stem with many norepinephrine-containing neurons
lo·cust \ˈlō-kəst\ *n* [ME, fr. AF *locuste,* fr. L *locusta*] (14c) **1 :** SHORT-HORNED GRASSHOPPER; *esp* **:** a migratory grasshopper often traveling in vast swarms and stripping the areas passed of all vegetation **2 :** CICADA **3 a :** any of various leguminous trees: as (1) **:** CAROB 1 (2) **:** BLACK LOCUST (3) **:** HONEY LOCUST **b :** the wood of a locust tree
locust bean *n* (1847) **:** CAROB
lo·cu·tion \lō-ˈkyü-shən\ *n* [ME *locucion,* fr. AF, fr. L *locution-, locutio,* fr. *loqui* to speak] (15c) **1 :** a particular form of expression or a peculiarity of phrasing; *esp* **:** a word or expression characteristic of a region, group, or cultural level **2 :** style of discourse **:** PHRASEOLOGY
lode \ˈlōd\ *n* [ME, fr. OE *lād* course, support; akin to OE *līthan* to go — more at LEAD] (bef. 12c) **1** *dial Eng* **:** WATERWAY **2 :** an ore deposit **3 :** something that resembles a lode **:** an abundant store
lo·den \ˈlō-dᵊn\ *n* [G, fr. OHG *lodo* coarse cloth; akin to OE *lotha* mantle] (1911) **1 :** a thick woolen cloth used for outer clothing **2 :** a variable color averaging a dull grayish green
lode·star *also* **load·star** \ˈlōd-ˌstär\ *n* [ME *lode sterre,* fr. *lode* course, fr. OE *lād*] (14c) **1** *archaic* **:** a star that leads or guides; *esp* **:** NORTH STAR **2 :** one that serves as an inspiration, model, or guide
lode·stone *also* **load·stone** \-ˌstōn\ *n* [obs. *lode* course, fr. ME] (ca. 1515) **1 :** magnetite possessing polarity **2 :** something that strongly attracts
[1]**lodge** \ˈläj\ *vb* **lodged; lodg·ing** *vt* (13c) **1 a** (1) **:** to provide temporary quarters for (2) **:** to rent lodgings to **b :** to establish or settle in a place **2 :** to serve as a receptacle for **:** CONTAIN **3 :** to beat (as a crop) flat to the ground **4 :** to bring to an intended or a fixed position (as by throwing or thrusting) **5 :** to deposit for safeguard or preservation **6 :** to place or vest esp. in a source, means, or agent **7 :** to lay (as a complaint) before a proper authority **:** FILE ~ *vi* **1 a :** to occupy a place temporarily **:** SLEEP **b** (1) **:** to have a residence **:** DWELL (2) **:** to be a lodger **2 :** to come to a rest **3 :** to fall or lie down — used esp. of hay or grain crops
[2]**lodge** *n* [ME *loge,* fr. AF, of Gmc origin; akin to OHG *louba* porch] (13c) **1** *chiefly dial* **:** a rude shelter or abode **2 a :** a house set apart for residence in a particular season (as the hunting season) **b :** a resort hotel **:** INN **3 a :** a house on an estate orig. for the use of a gamekeeper, caretaker, or porter **b :** a shelter for an employee (as a gatekeeper) **4 :** a den or lair esp. of gregarious animals (as beavers) **5 a :** the meeting place of a branch of an organization and esp. a fraternal organization **b :** the body of members of such a branch **6 a :** WIGWAM **b :** a family of No. American Indians
lodge·pole pine \ˈläj-ˌpōl-\ *n* (1859) **:** any of several pines of western No. America with needles in pairs and short ovoid usu. asymmetric cones: as **a :** a small chiefly coastal pine (*Pinus contorta* var. *contorta*) with thick deeply furrowed bark and hard strong coarse-grained medium-light wood **b :** a tall straight pine (*P. contorta* var. *latifolia*) with thin and little furrowed bark and soft weak fine-grained light-weight wood
lodg·er \ˈlä-jər\ *n* (1596) **:** ROOMER
lodging *n* (14c) **1 a :** a place to live **:** DWELLING **b :** LODGMENT 3b **2 a** (1) **:** sleeping accommodations ⟨found ~ in the barn⟩ (2) **:** a temporary place to stay ⟨a ~ for the night⟩ **b :** a room in the house of another used as a residence — usu. used in pl. **3 :** the act of lodging
lodging house *n* (1765) **:** ROOMING HOUSE
lodg·ment *or* **lodge·ment** \ˈläj-mənt\ *n* (1598) **1 a :** a lodging place **:** SHELTER **b :** ACCOMMODATIONS, LODGINGS ⟨found ~ in the city⟩ **2 a :** the act, fact, or manner of lodging ⟨a hut for temporary ~ of cattlemen⟩ **b :** a placing, depositing, or coming to rest **3 a :** an accumulation or collection deposited in a place or remaining at rest **b :** a place of rest or deposit
lod·i·cule \ˈlä-di-ˌkyül\ *n* [L *lodicula,* dim. of *lodic-, lodix* cover] (1864) **:** one of usu. two delicate membranous hyaline scales at the base of the ovary of a grass that by their swelling assist in anthesis
loess \ˈles, ˈləs, ˈlō-əs, ˈlərs\ *n* [G *Löss*] (1833) **:** an unstratified usu. buff to yellowish brown loamy deposit found in No. America, Europe, and Asia and believed to be chiefly deposited by the wind — **loess·ial** \ˈle-sē-əl, ˈlə-, lō-ˈe-, ˈlər-\ *adj*
lo–fi \ˈlō-ˈfī\ *n* [*low fidelity*] (1958) **:** the production or reproduction of audio characterized by an unpolished or rough sound quality — **lo–fi** *adj*
[1]**loft** \ˈlȯft\ *n* [ME, fr. OE, air, sky, fr. ON *lopt;* akin to OHG *luft* air] (13c) **1 :** an upper room or floor **:** ATTIC **2 a :** a gallery in a church or hall **b :** one of the upper floors of a warehouse or business building esp. when not partitioned ⟨living in a converted ~⟩ **c :** HAYLOFT **3 a :** the backward slant of the face of a golf-club head **b :** the act of lofting **4 :** the thickness of a fabric or insulating material (as goose down) — **loft·like** \-ˌlīk\ *adj*
[2]**loft** *vt* (1518) **1 :** to place, house, or store in a loft **2 :** to propel through the air or into space ⟨~*ed* a long hit to center⟩ ⟨instruments ~*ed* by a powerful rocket⟩ **3 :** to lay out a full-sized working drawing of the lines and contours of (as a ship's hull) ~ *vi* **1 :** to propel a ball high into the air **2 :** to rise high
lofty \ˈlȯf-tē\ *adj* **loft·i·er; -est** (15c) **1 a :** elevated in character and spirit **:** NOBLE ⟨~ ideals⟩ **b :** elevated in status **:** SUPERIOR **2 :** having a haughty overbearing manner **:** SUPERCILIOUS **3 a :** rising to a great height **:** impressively high ⟨~ mountains⟩ **b :** REMOTE, ESOTERIC **4 :** having full-bodied, firm, and resilient textile fibers ⟨~ flannel⟩ ***syn*** see HIGH — **loft·i·ly** \-tə-lē\ *adv* — **loft·i·ness** \-tē-nəs\ *n*
[1]**log** \ˈlȯg, ˈläg\ *n, often attrib* [ME *logge*] (14c) **1 :** a usu. bulky piece or length of a cut or fallen tree; *esp* **:** a length of a tree trunk ready for sawing and over six feet (1.8 meters) long **2 :** an apparatus for measuring the rate of a ship's motion through the water that consists of a block fastened to a line and run out from a reel **3 a :** the record of the rate of a ship's speed or of her daily progress; *also* **:** the full nautical record of a ship's voyage **b :** the full record of a flight by an aircraft **4 :** a record of performance, events, or day-to-day activities
[2]**log** *vb* **logged; log·ging** *vt* (1699) **1 a :** to cut (trees) for lumber **b :** to clear (land) of trees in lumbering — often used with *off* **2 :** to make a note or record of **:** enter details of or about in a log **3 a :** to move (an indicated distance) or attain (an indicated speed) as noted in a log **b** (1) **:** to sail a ship or fly an airplane for (an indicated distance or period of time) (2) **:** to have (an indicated record) to one's credit **:** ACHIEVE ~ *vi* **:** [3]LUMBER 1
[3]**log** *n, often attrib* [by shortening] (1631) **:** LOGARITHM
[4]**log** *abbr* logic

\ə\ **abut** \ᵊ\ **kitten,** F **table** \ər\ **further** \a\ **ash** \ā\ **ace** \ä\ **mop, mar**
\au̇\ **out** \ch\ **chin** \e\ **bet** \ē\ **easy** \g\ **go** \i\ **hit** \ī\ **ice** \j\ **job**
\ŋ\ **sing** \ō\ **go** \ȯ\ **law** \ȯi\ **boy** \th\ **thin** \t͟h\ **the** \ü\ **loot** \u̇\ **foot**
\y\ **yet** \zh\ **vision, beige** \k̟, ⁿ, œ, ue, ʸ\ *see* Guide to Pronunciation

log- *or* **logo-** *comb form* [Gk, fr. *logos* — more at LEGEND] : word : thought : speech : discourse ⟨*logo*gram⟩ ⟨*log*orrhea⟩
-log — see -LOGUE
lo·gan·ber·ry \ˈlō-gən-ˌber-ē\ *n* [James H. *Logan* †1928 Am. lawyer + E *berry*] (1893) : a red-fruited upright-growing dewberry (*Rubus loganobaccus*) usu. regarded as a hybrid of a western dewberry and a red raspberry or sometimes as a variety (*R. ursinus loganobaccus*) of a western dewberry; *also* : its berry
log·a·oe·dic \ˌlä-gə-ˈē-dik\ *adj* [LL *logaoedicus,* fr. LGk *logaoidikos,* fr. Gk *log-* + *aeidein* to sing; fr. the resemblance of such rhythm to prose — more at ODE] (1844) : marked by the mixture of several meters; *specif* : having a rhythm that uses both dactyls and trochees or anapests and iambs — **logaoedic** *n*
log·a·rithm \ˈlȯ-gə-ˌri-t͟həm, ˈlä-\ *n* [NL *logarithmus,* fr. *log-* + Gk *arithmos* number — more at ARITHMETIC] (ca. 1616) : the exponent that indicates the power to which a base number is raised to produce a given number ⟨the ~ of 100 to the base 10 is 2⟩ — **log·a·rith·mic** \ˌlȯ-gə-ˈrit͟h-mik, ˌlä-\ *adj* — **log·a·rith·mi·cal·ly** \-mi-k(ə-)lē\ *adv*
logarithmic function *n* (1836) : a function (as $y = \log_a x$ or $y = \ln x$) that is the inverse of an exponential function (as $y = a^x$ or $y = e^x$) so that the independent variable appears in a logarithm
logarithmic scale *n* (1740) : a scale on which the actual distance of a point from the scale's zero is proportional to the logarithm of the corresponding scale number rather than to the number itself — compare ARITHMETIC SCALE
log·book \ˈlȯg-ˌbu̇k, ˈläg-\ *n* (ca. 1679) **1** : LOG 3 **2** : LOG 4
loge \ˈlōzh\ *n* [F, fr. OF, a shelter — more at LODGE] (1749) **1 a** : a small compartment : BOOTH **b** : a box in a theater **2 a** : a small partitioned area **b** : a separate forward section of a theater mezzanine or balcony **c** : a raised section or level of seats in a sports stadium
logged \ˈlȯgd, ˈlägd\ *adj* (ca. 1820) **1** : HEAVY, SLUGGISH **2** : sodden esp. with water
log·ger \ˈlȯ-gər, ˈlä-\ *n* (1732) : one engaged in logging
log·ger·head \ˈlȯ-gər-ˌhed, ˈlä-\ *n* [prob. fr. E dial. *logger* block of wood + E *head*] (1588) **1** *chiefly dial* **a** : BLOCKHEAD **b** : HEAD; *esp* : a disproportionately large head **2 a** : a very large chiefly carnivorous sea turtle (*Caretta caretta*) of subtropical and temperate waters **b** : ALLIGATOR SNAPPING TURTLE **3** : an iron tool consisting of a long handle terminating in a ball or bulb that is heated and used to melt tar or to heat liquids — **at loggerheads** : in or into a state of quarrelsome disagreement

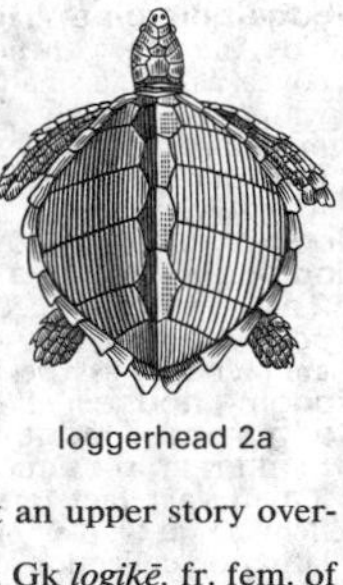
loggerhead 2a

loggerhead shrike *n* (1811) : a large-headed gray shrike (*Lanius ludovicianus*) of No. America with a black mask around the eyes
log·gia \ˈlō-jə, ˈlȯ-(ˌ)jä\ *n, pl* **loggias** \ˈlō-jəz, ˈlȯ-(ˌ)jäz\ *also* **log·gie** \ˈlȯ-(ˌ)jā\ [It, fr. OF *loge* lodge] (1742) : a roofed open gallery esp. at an upper story overlooking an open court
log·ic \ˈlä-jik\ *n* [ME *logik,* fr. AF, fr. L *logica,* fr. Gk *logikē,* fr. fem. of *logikos* of reason, fr. *logos* reason — more at LEGEND] (12c) **1 a** (1) : a science that deals with the principles and criteria of validity of inference and demonstration : the science of the formal principles of reasoning (2) : a branch or variety of logic ⟨modal ~⟩ ⟨Boolean ~⟩ (3) : a branch of semiotics; *esp* : SYNTACTICS (4) : the formal principles of a branch of knowledge **b** (1) : a particular mode of reasoning viewed as valid or faulty (2) : RELEVANCE, PROPRIETY **c** : interrelation or sequence of facts or events when seen as inevitable or predictable **d** : the arrangement of circuit elements (as in a computer) needed for computation; *also* : the circuits themselves **2** : something that forces a decision apart from or in opposition to reason ⟨the ~ of war⟩ — **lo·gi·cian** \lō-ˈji-shən\ *n*
log·i·cal \ˈlä-ji-kəl\ *adj* (15c) **1 a** (1) : of, relating to, involving, or being in accordance with logic (2) : skilled in logic **b** : formally true or valid : ANALYTIC, DEDUCTIVE **2** : capable of reasoning or of using reason in an orderly cogent fashion ⟨a ~ thinker⟩ — **log·i·cal·i·ty** \ˌlä-jə-ˈka-lə-tē\ *n* — **log·i·cal·ly** \ˈlä-ji-k(ə-)lē\ *adv* — **log·i·cal·ness** \-kəl-nəs\ *n*
logical positivism *n* (1931) : a 20th century philosophical movement holding that all meaningful statements are either analytic or conclusively verifiable or at least confirmable by observation and experiment and that metaphysical theories are therefore strictly meaningless — called also *logical empiricism* — **logical positivist** *n*
logic bomb *n* (1978) : a computer program often hidden within another seemingly innocuous program that is designed to perform usu. malicious actions (as deleting files) when certain conditions have been met
log in *vi* (1962) : LOG ON — **log–in** \ˈlȯg-ˌin, ˈläg-\ *n*
lo·gi·on \ˈlō-gē-ˌän\ *n, pl* **lo·gia** \-gē-ˌä\ *or* **logions** [Gk, dim. of *logos*] (1864) : SAYING; *esp* : a saying attributed to Jesus
[1]**lo·gis·tic** \lō-ˈjis-tik, lə-\ *or* **lo·gis·ti·cal** \-ti-kəl\ *adj* (1918) **1 a** : of or relating to symbolic logic **b** : of or relating to the philosophical attempt to reduce mathematics to logic **2** : of or relating to logistics **3** *logistic* : of, represented by, or relating to a logistic curve ⟨a ~ process⟩ — **lo·gis·ti·cal·ly** \-ti-k(ə-)lē\ *adv*
[2]**logistic** *n* (1905) : SYMBOLIC LOGIC
logistic curve *n* (1928) : an S-shaped curve that represents an exponential function and is used in mathematical models of growth processes
lo·gis·ti·cian \ˌlō-jəs-ˈti-shən\ *n* (1932) : a specialist in logistics
lo·gis·tics \lō-ˈjis-tiks, lə-\ *n pl but sing or pl in constr* [F *logistique* art of calculating, logistics, fr. Gk *logistikē* art of calculating, fr. fem. of *logistikos* of calculation, fr. *logizein* to calculate, fr. *logos* reason] (ca. 1861) **1** : the aspect of military science dealing with the procurement, maintenance, and transportation of military matériel, facilities, and personnel **2** : the handling of the details of an operation
log·jam \ˈlȯg-ˌjam, ˈläg-\ *n* (1885) **1** : a jumble of logs jammed together in a watercourse **2 a** : DEADLOCK, IMPASSE ⟨trying to break the ~ in negotiations⟩ **b** : BLOCKAGE **c** : JAM, CROWD — **logjam** *vt*
log·nor·mal \ˌlȯg-ˈnȯr-məl, ˌläg-\ *adj* (1945) : relating to or being a normal distribution that is the distribution of the logarithm of a random variable; *also* : relating to or being such a random variable — **log·nor·mal·i·ty** \-nȯr-ˈma-lə-tē\ *n* — **log·nor·mal·ly** \-ˈnȯr-mə-lē\ *adv*
logo \ˈlō-(ˌ)gō *also* ˈlä-\ *n, pl* **log·os** \-(ˌ)gōz\ (1937) **1** : LOGOTYPE **2** : an identifying statement : MOTTO
Lo·go \ˈlō-(ˌ)gō\ *n* [modif. of Gk *logos* word] (1972) : a computer programming language that employs simple English commands and is used esp. for introducing school children to computers
logo- — see LOG-
logo·cen·trism \ˌlō-gə-ˈsen-tri-zəm, -gō-, ˌlä-\ *n* [ISV] (1968) **1** : a philosophy holding that all forms of thought are based on an external point of reference which is held to exist and given a certain degree of authority **2** : a philosophy that privileges speech over writing as a form of communication because the former is closer to an originating transcendental source — **logo·cen·tric** \-ˈsen-trik\ *adj*
log off *vi* (1979) : to terminate a connection with a time-shared computer or network
logo·gram \ˈlȯ-gə-ˌgram, ˈlä-\ *n* (1840) : a letter, symbol, or sign used to represent an entire word ⟨the ampersand and dollar sign are ~*s*⟩ — **logo·gram·mat·ic** \ˌlȯ-gə-grə-ˈma-tik, ˌlä-\ *adj*
logo·graph \ˈlȯ-gə-ˌgraf, ˈlä-\ *n* (ca. 1888) : LOGOGRAM
logo·graph·ic \ˌlȯ-gə-ˈgra-fik, ˌlä-\ *adj* (1801) : of, relating to, or marked by the use of logographs : consisting of logographs — **logo·graph·i·cal·ly** \-fi-k(ə-)lē\ *adv*
logo·griph \ˈlȯ-gə-ˌgrif, ˈlä-\ *n* [*log-* + Gk *griphos* reed basket, riddle — more at CRIB] (ca. 1598) : a word puzzle (as an anagram)
lo·gom·a·chy \lō-ˈgä-mə-kē\ *n, pl* **-chies** [Gk *logomachia,* fr. *log-* + *machesthai* to fight] (1569) **1** : a dispute over or about words **2** : a controversy marked by verbiage
log on *vi* (1977) : to establish communication and initiate interaction with a time-shared computer or network — often used with *to* — **log–on** \ˈlȯg-ˌȯn, ˈläg-ˌän\ *n*
logo·phile \ˈlȯ-gə-ˌfī(-ə)l, ˈlä-\ *n* (1923) : a lover of words
log·or·rhea \ˌlȯ-gə-ˈrē-ə, ˌlä-\ *n* [NL] (ca. 1892) : excessive and often incoherent talkativeness or wordiness — **log·or·rhe·ic** \-ˈrē-ik\ *adj*
Lo·gos \ˈlō-ˌgäs, -ˌgōs\ *n, pl* **Lo·goi** \-ˌgȯi\ [Gk, speech, word, reason — more at LEGEND] (1587) **1** : the divine wisdom manifest in the creation, government, and redemption of the world and often identified with the second person of the Trinity **2** : reason that in ancient Greek philosophy is the controlling principle in the universe
logo·type \ˈlȯ-gə-ˌtīp, ˈlä-\ *n* (ca. 1816) **1** : a single piece of type or a single plate faced with a term (as the name of a newspaper or a trademark) **2** : an identifying symbol (as for use in advertising)
log·roll \ˈlȯg-ˌrōl, ˈläg-\ *vb* [back-formation fr. *logrolling*] *vi* (1835) : to take part in logrolling ~ *vt* : to promote passage of by logrolling — **log·roll·er** *n*
log·roll·ing \-ˌrō-liŋ\ *n* (1812) **1** [fr. a former American custom of neighbors assisting one another in rolling logs into a pile for burning] : the exchanging of assistance or favors; *specif* : the trading of votes by legislators to secure favorable action on projects of interest to each one **2** : the rolling of logs in water by treading; *also* : a sport in which contestants treading logs try to dislodge one another
-logue *or* **-log** *n comb form* [F *-logue,* fr. L *-logus,* fr. Gk *-logos,* fr. *legein* to speak — more at LEGEND] **1** : discourse : talk ⟨duo*logue*⟩ **2** : student : specialist ⟨sino*logue*⟩
log·wood \ˈlȯg-ˌwu̇d, ˈläg-\ *n* (1581) **1 a** : a leguminous tree (*Haematoxylon campechianum*) of Mexico and the West Indies **b** : the very hard brown or brownish-red heartwood of logwood **2** : a dye extracted from the heartwood of logwood — compare HEMATOXYLIN
lo·gy \ˈlō-gē\ *also* **log·gy** \ˈlȯ-gē, ˈlä-\ *adj* **lo·gi·er; -est** [perh. fr. D *log* heavy; akin to MLG *luggich* lazy] (1847) : SLUGGISH, GROGGY
-logy *n comb form* [F *-logie,* fr. L *-logia,* fr. Gk, fr. *logos* word] **1** : oral or written expression ⟨phraseo*logy*⟩ **2** : doctrine : theory : science ⟨ethno*logy*⟩
Lo·hen·grin \ˈlō-ən-ˌgrin\ *n* [G] (1850) : a son of Parsifal and knight of the Holy Grail in Germanic legend
loin \ˈlȯin\ *n* [ME *loyne,* fr. AF *loigne,* fr. VL **lumbea,* fr. L *lumbus;* akin to OE *lendenu* loins, OCS *lędvije*] (14c) **1 a** : the part of a human being or quadruped on each side of the spinal column between the hipbone and the false ribs **b** : a cut of meat comprising this part of one or both sides of a carcass with the adjoining half of the vertebrae included but without the flank **2** *pl* **a** : the upper and lower abdominal regions and the region about the hips **b** (1) : the pubic region (2) : the reproductive organs
loin·cloth \-ˌklȯth\ *n* (1856) : a cloth worn about the loins often as the sole article of clothing in warm climates
loi·ter \ˈlȯi-tər\ *vi* [ME] (14c) **1** : to delay an activity with idle stops and pauses : DAWDLE **2 a** : to remain in an area for no obvious reason **b** : to lag behind ***syn*** see DELAY — **loiter** *n* — **loi·ter·er** \-tər-ər\ *n*
Lo·ki \ˈlō-kē\ *n* [ON] (1844) : a Norse god who contrives evil and mischief for his fellow gods
LOL *or* **lol** *abbr* laugh out loud; laughing out loud
Lo·li·ta \lō-ˈlē-tə\ *n* [fr. *Lolita,* character in the novel *Lolita* (1955) by Vladimir Nabokov] (1959) : a precociously seductive girl
loll \ˈläl\ *vb* [ME] *vi* (14c) **1** : to hang loosely or laxly : DROOP **2** : to act or move in a lax, lazy, or indolent manner : LOUNGE ~ *vt* : to let droop or dangle ***syn*** see IDLE — **loll·er** \ˈlä-lər\ *n*
lol·la·pa·loo·za \ˌlä-lə-pə-ˈlü-zə\ *n* [origin unknown] (1896) : one that is extraordinarily impressive; *also* : an outstanding example
Lol·lard \ˈlä-lərd\ *n* [ME, fr. MD *lollaert,* fr. *lollen* to mutter] (14c) : one of the followers of Wycliffe who traveled in the 14th and 15th centuries as lay preachers throughout England and Scotland — **Lol·lard·ism** \-lər-ˌdi-zəm\ *n* — **Lol·lardy** \-lər-dē\ *n*
lol·li·pop *or* **lol·ly·pop** \ˈlä-li-ˌpäp\ *n* [perh. fr. E dial. *lolly* tongue + [2]*pop*] (1784) **1** : a piece of hard candy on the end of a stick **2** *Brit* : a round stop sign on a pole used to stop traffic (as at a school crossing)
lol·lop \ˈlä-ləp\ *vi* [*loll* + *-op* (as in *gallop*)] (1745) **1** *dial Eng* : LOLL **2** : to proceed with a bounding or bobbing motion
lol·ly \ˈlä-lē\ *n, pl* **lollies** [short for *lollipop*] (1854) **1** *Brit* : a piece of candy; *esp* : HARD CANDY **2** *Brit* : MONEY
lol·ly·gag *also* **lal·ly·gag** \ˈlä-lē-ˌgag\ *vi* **-gagged; -gag·ging** [origin unknown] (1868) : FOOL AROUND 1 : DAWDLE
Lom·bard \ˈläm-ˌbärd, -bərd\ *n* [ME *Lumbarde,* fr. AF *lombart,* fr. OIt *lombardo,* fr. L *Langobardus*] (14c) **1 a** : a member of a Germanic people that invaded Italy in A.D. 568 and established a kingdom in the Po valley **b** : a native or inhabitant of Lombardy **2** [fr. the prominence of Lombards as moneylenders] : BANKER, MONEYLENDER —

Lom·bar·di·an \läm-ˈbär-dē-ən\ *adj* — **Lom·bar·dic** \läm-ˈbär-dik\ *adj*

Lom·bar·dy poplar \ˈläm-ˌbär-dē-, -bər-\ *n* [*Lombardy*, Italy] (1766) : a poplar of a staminate variety (*Populus nigra italica*) of a European poplar having a columnar shape and strongly ascending branches

lo mein \ˈlō-ˈmān, ˌlō-\ *n* [Chin (Guangdong) *lòu-mihn* stirred noodles] (1970) : a Chinese dish consisting of sliced vegetables, soft noodles, and usu. meat or shrimp in bite-size pieces stir-fried in a seasoned sauce

lo·ment \ˈlō-ˌment, -mənt\ *n* [NL *lomentum*, fr. L, wash made fr. bean meal, fr. *lavere* to wash — more at LYE] (ca. 1830) : a dry indehiscent fruit (as of tick trefoil) that is a modified legume having constrictions between the seeds and that breaks into one-seeded segments at maturity

Lond *abbr* London

Lon·don broil \ˈlən-dən-\ *n* [*London*, England] (1902) : a boneless cut of beef (as from the shoulder or flank) usu. served sliced diagonally across the grain

London plane *n* (1860) : a large pollution-resistant plane (*Platanus acerifolia*) often planted as a street tree that is a hybrid between an Eurasian plane (*P. orientalis*) and the American sycamore (*P. occidentalis*) — called also *London plane tree*

lone \ˈlōn\ *adj* [ME, short for *alone*] (14c) **1 a** : having no company : SOLITARY **b** : preferring solitude **2** : ONLY, SOLE **3** : situated by itself : ISOLATED ***syn*** see ALONE — **lone·ness** \ˈlōn-nəs\ *n*

lone·ly \ˈlōn-lē\ *adj* **lone·li·er; -est** (ca. 1598) **1 a** : being without company : LONE **b** : cut off from others : SOLITARY **2** : not frequented by human beings : DESOLATE **3** : sad from being alone : LONESOME **4** : producing a feeling of bleakness or desolation ***syn*** see ALONE — **lone·li·ness** \ˈlōn-lē-nəs\ *n*

lonely hearts *adj* (1949) : of or relating to lonely persons who are seeking companions or spouses

lon·er \ˈlō-nər\ *n* (1947) : one that avoids others; *esp* : INDIVIDUALIST

lone ranger *n, often cap L&R* [*Lone Ranger*, hero of an Am. radio and television western] (1969) : one who acts alone and without consultation or the approval of others; *broadly* : LONER

[1]**lone·some** \ˈlōn(t)-səm\ *adj* (1647) **1 a** : sad or dejected as a result of lack of companionship or separation from others ⟨don't be ~ while we are gone⟩ **b** : causing a feeling of loneliness ⟨the empty house seemed so ~⟩ **2 a** : REMOTE, UNFREQUENTED ⟨look down, look down that ~ road —Gene Austin⟩ **b** : LONE ***syn*** see ALONE — **lone·some·ly** *adv* — **lone·some·ness** *n*

[2]**lonesome** *n* (1899) : SELF ⟨sat all by his ~⟩

lone star tick *n* (1896) : an ixodid tick (*Amblyomma americanum*) of the southern, central, and eastern U.S. that attacks mammals and birds, is a vector of several diseases (as Rocky Mountain spotted fever and ehrlichiosis), and in which the adult female has a single white spot on the back

lone wolf *n* (1909) : a person who prefers to work, act, or live alone — **lone–wolf** *adj*

[1]**long** \ˈlȯŋ\ *adj* **lon·ger** \ˈlȯŋ-gər *also* -ər\; **lon·gest** \ˈlȯŋ-gəst *also* -əst\ [ME *long, lang*, fr. OE; akin to OHG *lang* long, L *longus*] (bef. 12c) **1 a** : extending for a considerable distance **b** : having greater length than usual ⟨a ~ corridor⟩ **c** : having greater height than usual : TALL **d** : having a greater length than breadth : ELONGATED **e** : having a greater length than desirable or necessary ⟨the column is one line too ~⟩ **f** : FULL-LENGTH ⟨~ pants⟩ **2 a** : having a specified length ⟨six feet ~⟩ **b** : forming the chief linear dimension ⟨the ~ side of the room⟩ **3 a** : extending over a considerable time ⟨a ~ friendship⟩ **b** : having a specified duration ⟨two hours ~⟩ **c** : prolonged beyond the usual time ⟨a ~ look⟩ **d** : lasting too long : TEDIOUS ⟨a ~ explanation⟩ **4 a** : containing many items in a series ⟨a ~ list⟩ **b** : having a specified number of units ⟨300 pages ~⟩ **c** : consisting of a greater number or amount than usual : LARGE **5 a** *of a speech sound* : having a relatively long duration **b** : being the member of a pair of similarly spelled vowel or vowel-containing sounds that is descended from a vowel long in duration ⟨~ *a* in *fate*⟩ ⟨~ *i* in *sign*⟩ **c** *of a syllable in prosody* (1) : of relatively extended duration (2) : bearing a stress or accent **6** : having the capacity to reach, extend, or travel a considerable distance ⟨a ~ left jab⟩ ⟨tried to hit the ~ ball⟩ **7** : larger or longer than the standard ⟨a ~ count by the referee⟩ **8 a** : extending far into the future ⟨the thoughts of youth are ~, ~ thoughts —H. W. Longfellow⟩ **b** : extending beyond what is known ⟨a ~ guess⟩ **c** : payable after a considerable period ⟨a ~ note⟩ **9** : possessing a high degree or a great deal of something specified : STRONG ⟨~ on common sense⟩ **10 a** : of an unusual degree of difference between the amounts wagered on each side ⟨~ odds⟩ **b** : of or relating to the larger amount wagered ⟨take the ~ end of the bet⟩ **11** : subject to great odds **12** : owning or accumulating securities or goods esp. in anticipation of an advance in prices ⟨they are now ~ on wheat⟩ ⟨take a ~ position in steel⟩ — **long·ness** \ˈlȯŋ-nəs\ *n* — **long in the tooth** : past one's best days : OLD — **not long for** : having little time left to do or enjoy something

[2]**long** *adv* (bef. 12c) **1** : for or during a long time ⟨~ a popular hangout⟩ **2** : at or to a long distance : FAR ⟨*long*-traveled⟩ **3** : for the duration of a specified period ⟨month-*long*⟩ ⟨all summer ~⟩ **4** : at a point of time far before or after a specified moment or event ⟨was excited ~ before the big day⟩ **5** : after or beyond a specified or implied time ⟨didn't stay ~*er* than midnight⟩ **6** : for a considerable distance ⟨threw the ball ~⟩ **7** : in or into a long position (as on a market)

[3]**long** *n* (bef. 12c) **1** : a long period of time **2** : a long syllable **3** : one taking a long position esp. in a security or commodity market **4 a** *pl* : long trousers **b** : a size in clothing for tall men — **the long and short** *or* **the long and the short** : GIST

[4]**long** *vi* **longed; long·ing** \ˈlȯŋ-iŋ\ [ME, fr. OE *langian*; akin to OHG *langēn* to long, OE *lang* long] (bef. 12c) : to feel a strong desire or craving esp. for something not likely to be attained ⟨they ~ for peace⟩ ⟨~*ing* to return home⟩ — **long·er** \ˈlȯŋ-ər\ *n*

syn LONG, YEARN, HANKER, PINE, HUNGER, THIRST mean to have a strong desire for something. LONG implies a wishing with one's whole heart and often a striving to attain ⟨*longed* for some rest⟩. YEARN suggests an eager, restless, or painful longing ⟨*yearned* for a stage career⟩. HANKER suggests the uneasy promptings of unsatisfied appetite or desire ⟨always *hankering* for money⟩. PINE implies a languishing or a fruitless longing for what is impossible ⟨*pined* for a lost love⟩. HUNGER and THIRST imply an insistent or impatient craving or a compelling need ⟨*hungered* for a business of his own⟩ ⟨*thirsted* for power⟩.

[5]**long** *vi* [ME, fr. *along* (*on*) because (of)] (13c) *archaic* : to be suitable or fitting

[6]**long** *abbr* longitude

long–ago \ˈlȯŋ-ə-ˈgō\ *adj* (ca. 1834) : of or relating to the past ⟨~ leaders⟩

long ago *n* (1851) : the distant past

lon·gan \ˈlȯŋ-gən, -ən\ *n* [Chin (Beijing) *lóngyǎn*, lit., dragon's eye] (1732) **1** : a pulpy fruit related to the lychee and produced by a southeast Asian evergreen tree (*Euphoria longan* syn. *Dimocarpus longan*) of the soapberry family **2** : a tree that bears the longan

lon·ga·nim·i·ty \ˌlȯŋ-gə-ˈni-mə-tē\ *n* [ME *longanymyte*, fr. LL *longanimitat-, longanimitas*, fr. *longanimis* patient, fr. L *longus* long + *animus* soul — more at ANIMATE] (15c) : a disposition to bear injuries patiently : FORBEARANCE

long ball *n* (1938) : HOME RUN

long·boat \ˈlȯŋ-ˌbōt\ *n* (15c) : a large oared boat usu. carried by a merchant sailing ship

long bone *n* (ca. 1860) : any of the elongated bones supporting a vertebrate limb and consisting of an essentially cylindrical shaft that contains bone marrow and ends in enlarged heads for articulation with other bones — compare DIAPHYSIS, EPIPHYSIS

long·bow \ˈlȯŋ-ˌbō\ *n* (14c) : a hand-drawn wooden bow held vertically and used esp. by medieval English archers

long·bow·man \-mən\ *n* (1925) : an archer who uses a longbow

long·case clock \ˈlȯŋ-ˌkās-\ *n* (1884) : GRANDFATHER CLOCK

long–chain *adj* (1930) : having a relatively long chain of atoms and esp. carbon atoms in the molecule ⟨~ hydrocarbons⟩

long–day *adj* (1920) : responding to or relating to a long photoperiod — used esp. of a plant; compare DAY-NEUTRAL, SHORT-DAY

[1]**long–distance** *adj* (1884) **1** : of or relating to telephone communication with a distant point esp. outside a specified area **2 a** : situated a long distance away **b** : going or covering a long distance ⟨~ roads⟩ ⟨a ~ runner⟩ **c** : conducted or effective over long distance ⟨a ~ relationship⟩ ⟨~ listening devices⟩

[2]**long–distance** *adv* (ca. 1961) **1** : by long-distance telephone ⟨called her ~⟩ **2** : over or from a long distance

long distance *n* (1904) **1** : communication by long-distance telephone **2** : a telephone operator or exchange that gives long-distance connections

long division *n* (1827) : arithmetical division in which the several steps involved in the division are indicated in detail

long–drawn–out *or* **long–drawn** *adj* (1632) : extended to a great length

lon·ge·ron \ˈlän-jə-ˌrän\ *n* [F] (1912) : a fore-and-aft framing member of an airplane fuselage

lon·gev·i·ty \län-ˈje-və-tē, lȯn-\ *n* [LL *longaevitas*, fr. L *longaevus* long-lived, fr. *longus* long + *aevum* age — more at AYE] (1615) **1 a** : a long duration of individual life **b** : length of life ⟨a study of ~⟩ **2** : long continuance : PERMANENCE, DURABILITY

lon·ge·vous \-ˈjē-vəs\ *adj* (1680) : LONG-LIVED

long face *n* (1786) : a facial expression of sadness or melancholy

long green *n* (ca. 1889) *slang* : MONEY

long·hair \ˈlȯŋ-ˌher\ *n* (1920) **1** : an impractical intellectual **2** : a person of artistic gifts or interests; *esp* : a lover of classical music **3** : a person with long hair; *esp* : HIPPIE **4** : a domestic cat having long outer fur — **long–haired** \-ˈherd\ *or* **longhair** *adj*

long·hand \-ˌhand\ *n* (1666) : HANDWRITING: as **a** : characters or words written out fully by hand **b** : cursive writing

long haul *n* (1936) **1** : a long distance **2** : a considerable period of time; *esp* : LONG RUN — **long–haul** *adj*

long·head·ed \-ˌhe-dəd\ *adj* (ca. 1700) **1** : having unusual foresight **2** : DOLICHOCEPHALIC — **long·head·ed·ness** *n*

long·horn \-ˌhȯrn\ *n* (1834) **1 a** : any of the long-horned cattle of Spanish derivation formerly common in southwestern U.S. **b** : TEXAS LONGHORN 2 **2** : a firm-textured usu. mild cheese (as cheddar or Colby)

long–horned beetle \-ˌhȯrn(d)-\ *n* (1840) : any of a family (Cerambycidae syn. Longicornia) of beetles usu. distinguished by their very long antennae — called also *longhorn beetle*

long–horned grasshopper *n* (1893) : any of various grasshoppers (family Tettigoniidae) distinguished by their very long antennae

long horse *n* (ca. 1934) : VAULTING HORSE

long·house \ˈlȯŋ-ˌhau̇s, -ˈhau̇s\ *n* (1643) : a long communal dwelling of some No. American Indians (as the Iroquois)

long hundredweight *n* (ca. 1934) *Brit* : HUNDREDWEIGHT 2

lon·gi·corn \ˈlän-jə-ˌkȯrn\ *adj* [ultim. fr. L *longus* long + *cornu* horn — more at HORN] (ca. 1848) **1** : of, relating to, or being long-horned beetles **2** : having long antennae — **longicorn** *n*

long·ing \ˈlȯŋ-iŋ\ *n* (bef. 12c) : a strong desire esp. for something unattainable : CRAVING — **long·ing·ly** \-iŋ-lē\ *adv*

long·ish \ˈlȯŋ-ish\ *adj* (1611) : somewhat long : moderately long

lon·gi·tude \ˈlän-jə-ˌtüd, -ˌtyüd, *Brit also* ˈläŋ-gə-\ *n* [ME, fr. L *longitudin-, longitudo*, fr. *longus*] (14c) **1 a** : angular distance measured on a great circle of reference from the intersection of the adopted zero meridian with this reference circle to the similar intersection of the meridian passing through the object **b** : the arc or portion of the earth's equator intersected between the meridian of a given place and the prime meridian and expressed either in degrees or in time **2** *archaic* : long duration

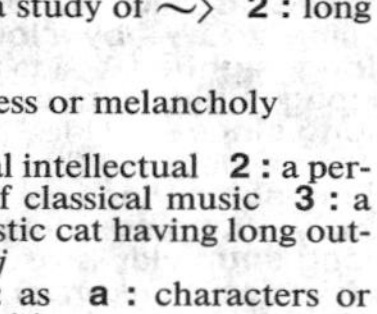

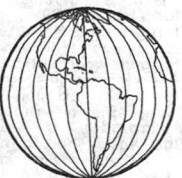

longitude 1a: hemisphere marked with meridians of longitude

lon·gi·tu·di·nal \ˌlän-jə-ˈtüd-nəl, -ˈtyüd-, -ˈt(y)ü-dᵊn-əl, *Brit also* ˌläŋ-gə-\ *adj* (15c) **1 :** placed or running lengthwise **2 :** of or relating to length or the lengthwise dimension **3 :** involving the repeated observation or examination of a set of subjects over time with respect to one or more study variables — **lon·gi·tu·di·nal·ly** *adv*

longitudinal wave *n* (ca. 1931) **:** a wave (as a sound wave) in which the particles of the medium vibrate in the direction of the line of advance of the wave

long johns \ˈlȯŋ-ˌjänz\ *n pl* (1943) **:** long underwear

long jump *n* (1882) **:** a track-and-field event in which a jump for distance is made usu. from a running start — **long jumper** *n*

long·leaf pine \ˈlȯŋ-ˌlēf-\ *n* (1796) **:** a tall timber pine (*Pinus palustris*) of the southeastern U.S. with long needles in bundles of three and long cones; *also* **:** its tough coarse-grained reddish-orange wood consisting mostly of heartwood and used esp. for flooring and joinery

long–leaved pine \-ˌlēv(d)-\ *n* (1765) **:** LONGLEAF PINE

long·line \ˈlȯŋ-ˌlīn, -ˈlīn\ *n* (1876) **:** a heavy fishing line that may be many miles long and that has baited hooks in series

long–lin·er \-ˌlī-nər\ *n* (1909) **:** one that fishes with a longline; *also* **:** a fishing vessel used in long-lining

long–lin·ing \-ˌlī-niŋ\ *n* (1877) **:** fishing with a longline

long–lived \ˈlȯŋ-ˈlivd *also* -ˈlīvd\ *adj* (14c) **1 :** having a long life **:** characterized by long life ⟨a ~ family⟩ **2 :** lasting a long time **:** ENDURING

long meter *n* (1718) **:** a quatrain in iambic tetrameter in which the second and fourth lines and often the first and third lines rhyme — called also *long measure*

long·neck \ˈlȯŋ-ˌnek\ *n* (1978) **:** beer served in a bottle that has a long neck

Lon·go·bard \ˈlȯŋ-gə-ˌbärd, ˈläŋ-\ *n, pl* **Longobards** *also* **Lon·go·bar·di** \ˌlȯŋ-gə-ˈbär-ˌdī, ˌläŋ-, -dē\ [ME *Longobardes,* pl., fr. L *Langobardi, Longobardi*] (14c) **:** LOMBARD 1a — **Lon·go·bar·dic** \ˌlȯŋ-gə-ˈbär-dik, ˌläŋ-\ *adj*

long–play·ing \ˈlȯŋ-ˈplā-iŋ\ *adj* (1929) **:** designed to be played at 33⅓ revolutions per minute — used of a microgroove record

long–range \-ˈrānj\ *adj* (1854) **1 :** relating to or fit for long distances ⟨~ rockets⟩ **2 :** involving or taking into account a long period of time ⟨~ planning⟩

long run *n* (1627) **:** a relatively long period of time — usu. used in the phrase *in the long run* — **long–run** \ˈlȯŋ-ˈrən\ *adj*

long·ship \ˈlȯŋ-ˌship\ *n* (1568) **:** a long sail and oar ship used by the Vikings

long·shore·man \ˈlȯŋ-ˌshȯr-mən, ˌlȯŋ-ˈ\ *n* [*longshore,* short for *alongshore*] (1811) **:** a person who loads and unloads ships at a seaport

long·shor·ing \ˈlȯŋ-ˌshȯr-iŋ, ˌlȯŋ-ˈ\ *n* (1926) **:** the act or occupation of working as a longshoreman

long shot \ˈlȯŋ-ˌshät\ *n* (1867) **1 :** a venture involving great risk but promising a great reward if successful; *also* **:** a venture unlikely to succeed **2 :** an entry (as in a horse race) given little chance of winning **3 :** a bet in which the chances of winning are slight but the possible winnings great — **by a long shot :** by a great deal

long–sight·ed \-ˈsī-təd\ *adj* (ca. 1790) *chiefly Brit* **:** FARSIGHTED — **long–sight·ed·ness** *n, chiefly Brit*

long since *adv* (14c) **1 :** long ago ⟨promises *long since* forgotten⟩ **2 :** for a long time ⟨has *long since* been a devoted friend⟩

long·some \ˈlȯŋ-səm\ *adj* (bef. 12c) **:** tediously long — **long·some·ly** *adv* — **long·some·ness** *n*

long·spur \ˈlȯŋ-ˌspər\ *n* (1831) **:** any of several long-clawed finches (esp. genus *Calcarius*) of the arctic regions and the Great Plains of No. America

long–stand·ing \-ˈstan-diŋ\ *adj* (1814) **:** of long duration ⟨a ~ dispute⟩

long–suf·fer·ing \-ˌsə-f(ə-)riŋ, -ˈsə-\ *adj* (1535) **:** patiently enduring lasting offense or hardship — **long–suffering** *n* — **long–suf·fer·ing·ly** \-lē\ *adv*

long suit *n* (ca. 1876) **1 :** a holding of more than the average number of cards in a suit **2 :** STRONG SUIT, FORTE

long–tailed duck *n* (1766) **:** OLD-SQUAW

long–term \ˈlȯŋ-ˈtərm\ *adj* (1904) **1 :** occurring over or involving a relatively long period of time ⟨seeking ~ solutions⟩ **2 a :** of, relating to, or constituting a financial operation or obligation based on a considerable term and esp. one of more than 10 years ⟨~ bonds⟩ **b :** generated by assets held for longer than six months ⟨a ~ capital gain⟩

long–term potentiation *n* (1984) **:** a long-lasting strengthening of the response of a postsynaptic nerve cell to stimulation across the synapse that occurs with repeated stimulation and is thought to be related to learning and long-term memory — abbr. *LTP*

long·time \ˈlȯŋ-ˈtīm\ *adj* (1584) **:** having been so for a long time **:** LONG-STANDING ⟨a ~ friend⟩ ⟨a ~ friendship⟩

Long Tom \ˈlȯŋ-ˈtäm\ *n* [fr. the name *Tom*] (1832) **1 :** a large land gun having a long range **2 :** a trough for washing gold-bearing earth

long ton *n* (1829) — see WEIGHT table

lon·gueur \lōⁿ-ˈgœr\ *n, pl* **longueurs** \-ˈgœr(z)\ [F, lit., length] (1791) **:** a dull and tedious portion (as of a book) — usu. used in pl.

long view *n* (1912) **:** an approach to a problem or situation that emphasizes long-range factors

long–wind·ed \ˌlȯŋ-ˈwin-dəd, ˈlȯŋ-ˌwin-\ *adj* (1589) **1 :** tediously long in speaking or writing **2 :** not easily subject to loss of breath — **long–wind·ed·ly** *adv* — **long–wind·ed·ness** *n*

[1]**loo** \ˈlü\ *n* [short for obs. E *lanterloo,* fr. F *lanturelu* twaddle] (1675) **1 :** an old card game in which the winner of each trick or a majority of tricks takes a portion of the pool while losing players are obligated to contribute to the next pool **2 :** money staked at loo

[2]**loo** *vt* (1680) **:** to obligate to contribute to a new pool at loo for failing to win a trick

[3]**loo** *n* [origin unknown] (1940) *chiefly Brit* **:** TOILET 3

loo·by \ˈlü-bē\ *n, pl* **loobies** [ME *loby*] (14c) **:** an awkward clumsy fellow **:** LUBBER

loo·fah *also* **luf·fa** \ˈlü-fə\ *n* [NL *luffa,* fr. Ar *lūf*] (1887) **1 :** any of a genus (*Luffa*) of Old World tropical plants of the gourd family with large fruits; *also* **:** its fruit **2 :** a sponge consisting of the fibrous skeleton of the fruit of a loofah (esp. *Luffa aegyptiaca*)

[1]**look** \ˈlu̇k\ *vb* [ME, fr. OE *lōcian;* akin to OS *lōcōn* to look] *vt* (bef. 12c) **1 :** to make sure or take care (that something is done) **2 :** to ascertain by the use of one's eyes ⟨~ what I brought you⟩ **3 a :** to exercise the power of vision upon **:** EXAMINE **b** *archaic* **:** to search for **4 a :** EXPECT, ANTICIPATE ⟨we ~ to have a good year⟩ **b :** to have in mind as an end ⟨~*ing* to win back some lost profits⟩ **5** *archaic* **:** to bring into a place or condition by the exercise of the power of vision **6 :** to express by the eyes or facial expression **7 :** to have an appearance that befits or accords with ⟨~*s* her age⟩ ~ *vi* **1 a :** to exercise the power of vision **:** SEE **b :** to direct one's attention ⟨~ upon the future with hope⟩ ⟨~ at the map⟩ **c :** to direct the eyes ⟨~*ed* up from the newspaper⟩ **2 :** to have the appearance or likelihood of being **:** SEEM ⟨it ~*s* unlikely⟩ ⟨~*s* to be hard work⟩ **3 :** to have a specified outlook ⟨the house ~*ed* east⟩ **4 :** to gaze in wonder or surprise **:** STARE **5 :** to show a tendency ⟨the evidence ~*s* to acquittal⟩ ***syn*** see EXPECT — **look after :** to take care of — **look at 1 :** CONSIDER 1 ⟨*looking at* the possibility of relocating⟩ **2 :** CONFRONT, FACE ⟨*looking at* a mandatory fine —Cindy Kilass⟩ — **look down one's nose :** to view something with arrogance, disdain, or disapproval — **look for 1 :** to await with hope or anticipation **2 :** to search for **:** SEEK ⟨*looking for* a new car⟩ — **look forward :** to anticipate with pleasure or satisfaction ⟨*looking forward* to your visit⟩ — **look into :** EXPLORE 1a — **look the other way :** to direct one's attention away from something unpleasant or troublesome — **look to 1 :** to direct one's attention to ⟨*looking to* the future⟩ **2 :** to rely upon ⟨*looks to* reading for relaxation⟩

[2]**look** *n* (13c) **1 a :** the act of looking **b :** GLANCE **2 a :** the expression of the countenance **b :** physical appearance; *esp* **:** attractive physical appearance — usu. used in pl. **c :** a combination of design features giving a unified appearance ⟨a new ~ in women's fashions⟩ **3 :** the state or form in which something appears

look–alike \ˈlu̇k-ə-ˌlīk\ *n* (1947) **:** one that looks like another **:** DOUBLE — **look–alike** *adj*

look·down \ˈlu̇k-ˌdau̇n\ *n* (ca. 1882) **:** a silvery carangid fish (*Selene vomer*) chiefly of the Atlantic having a laterally compressed deep body and steeply sloping facial profile

look down *vi* (14c) **1 :** to be in a position that affords a downward view **2 :** to regard with contempt **:** DESPISE — used with *on* or *upon*

look·er \ˈlu̇-kər\ *n* (14c) **1 :** one that looks **2 a :** one having an appearance of a specified kind **b :** one that has an attractive appearance

look·er–on \ˌlu̇-kər-ˈȯn, -ˈän\ *n, pl* **lookers–on** (1539) **:** ONLOOKER

look–in \ˈlu̇k-ˌin\ *n* (1870) **1 :** a chance of success **2 :** a quick pass in football to a receiver running diagonally toward the center of the field

looking glass *n* (1562) **:** MIRROR

look·ism \ˈlu̇-ki-zəm\ *also* **looks·ism** \ˈlu̇k-si-\ *n* (1978) **:** prejudice or discrimination based on physical appearance and esp. physical appearance believed to fall short of societal notions of beauty

look on *vi* (ca. 1540) **:** WATCH 3b ⟨*looked on* anxiously from the sidelines⟩

look·out \ˈlu̇k-ˌau̇t\ *n* (1699) **1 :** one engaged in keeping watch **:** WATCHMAN **2 :** an elevated place or structure affording a wide view for observation **3 :** a careful looking or watching ⟨on the ~⟩ **4 :** VIEW, OUTLOOK **5 :** a matter of care or concern

look out *vi* (1602) **:** to take care or concern oneself — used with *for* ⟨*looking out* for number one⟩

look over *vt* (14c) **:** to inspect or examine esp. in a cursory way

look–see \ˈlu̇k-ˈsē, -ˌsē\ *n* (1883) **:** a general survey **:** EVALUATION, INSPECTION

look·up \ˈlu̇k-ˌəp\ *n* (1936) **:** the process or an instance of looking something up; *esp* **:** the process of matching by computer the words of a text with material stored in memory

look up *vi* (14c) **1 :** to cheer up ⟨*look up*—things are not all bad⟩ **2 :** to improve in prospects or conditions ⟨business is *looking up*⟩ ~ *vt* **1 :** to search for in or as if in a reference work ⟨*look up* an address⟩ **2 :** to seek out esp. for a brief visit ⟨*look* me *up* when you're here⟩

[1]**loom** \ˈlüm\ *n* [ME *lome* tool, loom, fr. OE *gelōma* tool; akin to MD *allame* tool] (15c) **:** a frame or machine for interlacing at right angles two or more sets of threads or yarns to form a cloth

[2]**loom** *vi* [origin unknown] (ca. 1541) **1 :** to come into sight in enlarged or distorted and indistinct form often as a result of atmospheric conditions **2 a :** to appear in an impressively great or exaggerated form ⟨deficits ~*ed* large⟩ **b :** to take shape as an impending occurrence

[3]**loom** *n* (1836) **:** the indistinct and exaggerated appearance of something seen on the horizon or through fog or darkness; *also* **:** a looming shadow or reflection

[1]**loon** \ˈlün\ *n* [ME *loun*] (15c) **1 :** LOUT, IDLER **2** *chiefly Scot* **:** BOY **3 a :** a crazy person **b :** SIMPLETON

[2]**loon** *n* [of Scand origin; akin to ON *lōmr* loon] (1634) **:** any of several large birds (genus *Gavia* of the family Gaviidae) of Holarctic regions that feed on fish by diving and have their legs placed far back under the body for optimal locomotion underwater

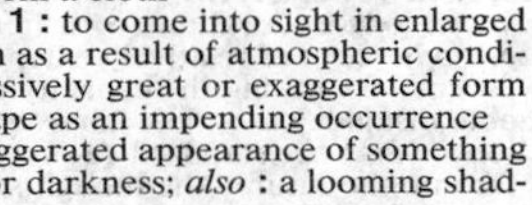

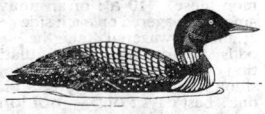

loon

loon·ie \ˈlü-nē\ *n* [fr. the image of a loon on the obverse of the coin] (1987) *Canad* **:** a coin worth one Canadian dollar

loo·ny *also* **loo·ney** \ˈlü-nē\ *adj* **loo·ni·er; -est** [by shortening & alter. fr. *lunatic*] (1872) **:** CRAZY, FOOLISH — **loo·ni·ness** *n* — **loony** *n*

loony bin *n* (1919) **:** a psychiatric hospital **:** MADHOUSE

loony tunes *or* **looney tunes** *adj* (1971) **:** LOONY

[1]**loop** \ˈlüp\ *n* [ME *loupe;* perh. akin to MD *lupen* to watch, peer] (14c) *archaic* **:** LOOPHOLE 1a

[2]**loop** *n* [ME *loupe,* of unknown origin] (14c) **1 a :** a curving or doubling of a line so as to form a closed or partly open curve within itself through which another line can be passed or into which a hook may be hooked **b :** such a fold of cord or ribbon serving as an ornament **2 a :** something shaped like or suggestive of a loop **b :** a circular airplane maneuver executed in the vertical plane **3 :** a ring or curved piece used to form a fastening, handle, or catch **4 :** a closed electric circuit **5 a :** a piece of film or magnetic tape whose ends are spliced together so as to project or play back the same material continuously **b :** a continuously repeated segment of music, dialogue, or images ⟨a drum ~⟩ **6 :** a series of instructions (as for a computer) that is repeated until a terminating condition is reached **7 :** a sports league **8 :** a select well-informed inner circle that is influential in decision making ⟨out of

the policy ~) — **for a loop** : into a state of amazement, confusion, or distress ⟨the news threw us *for a loop*⟩

[3]**loop** *vi* (1832) **1** : to make or form a loop **2** : to execute a loop in an airplane **3** : to move in loops or in an arc ~ *vt* **1 a** : to make a loop in, on, or about **b** : to fasten with a loop **2** : to join (two courses of loops) in knitting **3** : to connect (electric conductors) so as to complete a loop **4** : to cause to move in an arc

looped \ˈlüpt\ *adj* (1513) **1** : having, formed in, or characterized by loops ⟨~ fabrics⟩ **2** : DRUNK 1a

loop·er \ˈlü-pər\ *n* (1731) **1** : any of the usu. rather small hairless caterpillars that are mostly larvae of moths (families Geometridae and Noctuidae) and move with a looping motion in which the hind prolegs draw the posterior body toward the front followed by forward extension by the anterior legs — called also *inchworm* **2** : one that loops

[1]**loop·hole** \ˈlüp-ˌhōl\ *n* [[1]*loop*] (1591) **1 a** : a small opening through which small arms may be fired **b** : a similar opening to admit light and air or to permit observation **2** : a means of escape; *esp* : an ambiguity or omission in the text through which the intent of a statute, contract, or obligation may be evaded

[2]**loophole** *vt* (1664) : to make loopholes in

loop of Hen·le \-ˈhen-lē\ [F. G. J. *Henle* †1885 Ger. pathologist] (1890) : a U-shaped part of the nephron of birds and mammals that lies between and is continuous with the proximal and distal convoluted tubules and that functions in water resorption

loopy \ˈlü-pē\ *adj* **loop·i·er; -est** (1856) **1** : having or characterized by loops **2** : CRAZY, BIZARRE — **loop·i·ly** \-pə-lē\ *adv* — **loop·i·ness** \-pē-nəs\ *n*

[1]**loose** \ˈlüs\ *adj* **loos·er; loos·est** [ME *lous,* fr. ON *lauss;* akin to OHG *lōs* loose — more at -LESS] (13c) **1 a** : not rigidly fastened or securely attached **b (1)** : having worked partly free from attachments ⟨a ~ tooth⟩ **(2)** : having relative freedom of movement **c** : produced freely and accompanied by raising of mucus ⟨a ~ cough⟩ **d** : not tight-fitting **2 a** : free from a state of confinement, restraint, or obligation ⟨a lion ~ in the streets⟩ ⟨spend ~ funds wisely⟩ **b** : not brought together in a bundle, container, or binding **c** *archaic* : DISCONNECTED, DETACHED **3 a** : not dense, close, or compact in structure or arrangement **b** : not solid : WATERY ⟨~ stools⟩ **4 a** : lacking in restraint or power of restraint ⟨a ~ tongue⟩ **b** : lacking moral restraint : UNCHASTE **c** : OVERACTIVE; *specif* : marked by frequent voiding esp. of watery stools ⟨~ bowels⟩ **5 a** : not tightly drawn or stretched : SLACK **b** : being flexible or relaxed ⟨stay ~⟩ **6 a** : lacking in precision, exactness, or care ⟨~ brushwork⟩ ⟨~ usage⟩ **b** : permitting freedom of interpretation **7** : not in the possession of either of two competing teams ⟨a ~ ball⟩ ⟨a ~ puck⟩ — **loose·ly** *adv* — **loose·ness** *n*

[2]**loose** *vb* **loosed; loos·ing** *vt* (13c) **1 a** : to let loose : RELEASE **b** : to free from restraint **2** : to make loose : UNTIE ⟨~ a knot⟩ **3** : to cast loose : DETACH **4** : to let fly : DISCHARGE **5** : to make less rigid, tight, or strict : RELAX ~ *vi* : to let fly a missile (as an arrow) : FIRE

[3]**loose** *adv* (15c) : in a loose manner : LOOSELY

loose box *n* (1849) *Brit* : BOX STALL

loose cannon *n* (1973) : a dangerously uncontrollable person or thing

loose end *n* (1546) **1** : something left hanging loose **2** : a fragment of unfinished business — usu. used in pl. ⟨tying up *loose ends*⟩

loose–joint·ed \ˈlüs-ˈjȯin-təd\ *adj* (1859) **1** : having joints apparently not closely articulated **2** : characterized by unusually free movements — **loose–joint·ed·ness** *n*

loose–leaf \ˈlüs-ˈlēf\ *adj* (1902) **1** : having leaves secured in book form in a cover whose spine may be opened for adding, arranging, or removing leaves ⟨~ notebook⟩ **2** : of, relating to, or used with a loose-leaf binding ⟨~ paper⟩

loos·en \ˈlü-sᵊn\ *vb* **loos·ened; loos·en·ing** \ˈlüs-niŋ, ˈlü-sᵊn-iŋ\ *vt* (14c) **1** : to release from restraint **2** : to make looser ⟨~*ed* his tie⟩ ⟨~ a screw⟩ **3** : to relieve (the bowels) of constipation **4** : to cause or permit to become less strict — often used with *up* ⟨~*ed* the rules⟩ ~ *vi* : to become loose or looser

loosen up *vi* (1922) : to become less tense : RELAX

loose sentence *n* (ca. 1890) : a sentence in which the principal clause comes first and subordinate modifiers or trailing elements follow

loose smut *n* (1890) : a smut disease of grains in which the entire head is transformed into a dusty mass of spores

loose·strife \ˈlü(s)-ˌstrīf\ *n* [intended as trans. of Gk *lysimacheios* loosestrife (as if fr. *lysis* act of loosing + *machesthai* to fight) — more at LYSIS] (1548) **1** : any of a genus (*Lysimachia*) of plants of the primrose family with leafy stems and usu. yellow or white flowers **2** : any of a genus (*Lythrum,* family Lythraceae, the loosestrife family) of herbs having entire leaves and including some with showy spikes of purple flowers; *esp* : PURPLE LOOSESTRIFE

loos·ey–goos·ey \ˌlü-sē-ˈgü-sē\ *adj* (1964) : notably loose or relaxed : not tense ⟨a ~ attitude⟩

[1]**loot** \ˈlüt\ *n* [Hindi & Urdu *lūṭ;* akin to Skt *luṇṭati* he plunders] (ca. 1788) **1** : goods usu. of considerable value taken in war : SPOILS **2** : something held to resemble goods of value seized in war: as **a** : something appropriated illegally often by force or violence **b** : illicit gains by public officials **c** : MONEY **3** : the action of looting *syn* see SPOIL

[2]**loot** *vt* (1845) **1 a** : to plunder or sack in war **b** : to rob esp. on a large scale and usu. by violence or corruption **2** : to seize and carry away by force esp. in war ~ *vi* : to engage in robbing or plundering esp. in war — **loot·er** *n*

[1]**lop** \ˈläp\ *n* [ME *loppe*] (14c) : material cut away from a tree; *esp* : parts discarded in lumbering

[2]**lop** *vt* **lopped; lop·ping** (1519) **1 a (1)** : to cut off branches or twigs from **(2)** : to sever from a woody plant **b (1)** *archaic* : to cut off the head or limbs of **(2)** : to cut from a person **2 a** : to remove superfluous parts from **b** : to eliminate as unnecessary or undesirable — usu. used with *off*

[3]**lop** *vi* **lopped; lop·ping** [perh. imit.] (1578) : to hang downward : DROOP

[1]**lope** \ˈlōp\ *n* [ME *loup, lope* leap, prob. fr. ON *hlaup;* akin to OE *hlēapan* to leap — more at LEAP] (1809) **1** : an easy natural gait of a horse resembling a canter **2** : an easy usu. bounding gait capable of being sustained for a long time

[2]**lope** *vi* **loped; lop·ing** (ca. 1825) : to move or ride at a lope — **lop·er** *n*

lop–eared \ˈläp-ˌird\ *adj* (1687) : having ears that droop

loph·o·phore \ˈlä-fə-ˌfōr\ *n* [Gk *lophos* crest + E *-phore*] (1850) : a circular or horseshoe-shaped organ about the mouth esp. of a brachiopod or bryozoan that bears tentacles and functions esp. in food-getting

lop·per \ˈlä-pər\ *n* (1953) : pruning shears with long handles — usu. used in pl.

lop·sid·ed \ˈläp-ˌsī-dəd\ *adj* (1711) **1** : leaning to one side **2** : lacking in balance, symmetry, or proportion : disproportionately heavy on one side ⟨a ~ vote of 99–1⟩ — **lop·sid·ed·ly** *adv* — **lop·sid·ed·ness** *n*

loq *abbr* [L *loquitur*] he speaks; she speaks

lo·qua·cious \lō-ˈkwā-shəs\ *adj* [L *loquac-, loquax,* fr. *loqui* to speak] (1663) **1** : full of excessive talk : WORDY **2** : given to fluent or excessive talk : GARRULOUS *syn* see TALKATIVE — **lo·qua·cious·ly** *adv* — **lo·qua·cious·ness** *n*

lo·quac·i·ty \-ˈkwa-sə-tē\ *n* (13c) : the quality or state of being very talkative

lo·quat \ˈlō-ˌkwät\ *n* [Chin (Guangdong) *làuh-gwāt*] (1820) : an Asian evergreen tree (*Eriobotrya japonica*) of the rose family often cultivated for its fruit; *also* : its small yellow edible fruit used esp. for preserves

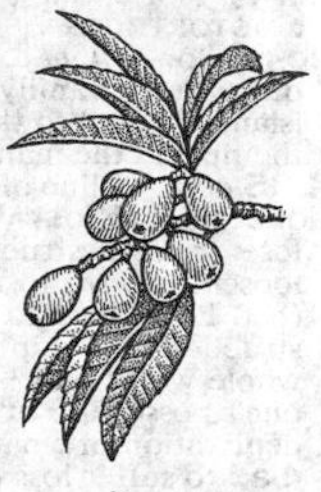
loquat

lo·ran \ˈlōr-ˌan\ *n* [*lo*ng-*ra*nge *n*avigation] (1932) : a system of long-range navigation in which pulsed signals sent out by two pairs of radio stations are used to determine the location of a ship or airplane

lor·az·e·pam \lȯr-ˈa-zə-ˌpam\ *n* [prob. fr. ch*lor-* + *-azepam* (as in *diazepam*)] (1969) : benzodiazepine $C_{15}H_{10}Cl_2N_2O_2$ used esp. to relieve anxiety

[1]**lord** \ˈlȯrd\ *n* [ME *loverd, lord,* fr. OE *hlāford,* fr. *hlāf* loaf + *weard* keeper — more at LOAF, WARD] (bef. 12c) **1** : one having power and authority over others: **a** : a ruler by hereditary right or preeminence to whom service and obedience are due **b** : one of whom a fee or estate is held in feudal tenure **c** : an owner of land or other real property **d** *obs* : the male head of a household **e** : HUSBAND **f** : one that has achieved mastery or that exercises leadership or great power in some area ⟨a drug ~⟩ **2** *cap* **a** : GOD 1 **b** : JESUS **3** : a man of rank or high position: as **a** : a feudal tenant whose right or title comes directly from the king **b** : a British nobleman: as **(1)** : BARON 2a **(2)** : a hereditary peer of the rank of marquess, earl, or viscount **(3)** : the son of a duke or a marquess or the eldest son of an earl **(4)** : a bishop of the Church of England **c** *pl, cap* : HOUSE OF LORDS **4** — used as a British title: as **a** — used as part of an official title ⟨*Lord* Advocate⟩ ⟨*Lord* Mayor⟩ **b** — used informally in place of the full title for a marquess, earl, or viscount **c** — used for a baron **d** — used by courtesy before the name and surname of a younger son of a duke or a marquess **5** : a person chosen to preside over a festival

[2]**lord** *vi* (14c) : to act like a lord; *esp* : to put on airs — usu. used with *it* ⟨~*s* it over his friends⟩

lord chancellor *n, pl* **lords chancellor** (15c) : a British officer of state who presides over the House of Lords in both its legislative and judicial capacities, serves as the head of the British judiciary, and is usu. a leading member of the cabinet

lord·ing \ˈlȯr-diŋ\ *n* (13c) **1** *archaic* : LORD **2** *obs* : LORDLING

lord·ling \ˈlȯrd-liŋ\ *n* (13c) : a little or insignificant lord

lord·ly \-lē\ *adj* **lord·li·er; -est** (bef. 12c) **1 a** : of, relating to, or having the characteristics of a lord : DIGNIFIED **b** : GRAND, NOBLE **2** : exhibiting the pride and assurance associated with one of the highest birth or rank *syn* see PROUD — **lord·li·ness** *n* — **lordly** *adv*

lord of misrule (15c) : a master of Christmas revels in England esp. in the 15th and 16th centuries

lor·do·sis \lȯr-ˈdō-səs\ *n, pl* **-do·ses** \-ˈdō-ˌsēz\ [NL, fr. Gk *lordōsis,* fr. *lordos* curving forward; akin to OE *belyrtan* to deceive] (1704) **1** : abnormally increased inward curvature of the lower region of the spine resulting in a concave back as viewed from the side — compare KYPHOSIS **2** : a mating posture of some sexually receptive female mammals (as rats) in which the head and rump are raised and the back is arched downward — **lor·dot·ic** \-ˈdä-tik\ *adj*

Lord Protector of the Commonwealth (ca. 1653) : PROTECTOR 2b

Lord's day *n, often cap D* (12c) : SUNDAY

lord·ship \ˈlȯrd-ˌship\ *n* (bef. 12c) **1 a** : the rank or dignity of a lord — used as a title **b** : the authority or power of a lord : DOMINION **2** : the territory under the jurisdiction of a lord : SEIGNIORY

Lord's Prayer *n* (ca. 1549) : the prayer with variant versions in Matthew and Luke that according to the Lucan account Christ taught his disciples

Lord's Supper *n* (14c) : COMMUNION 2a

Lord's table *n, often cap T* (1526) : ALTAR 2

Lordy \ˈlȯr-dē\ *interj* [[1]*lord* (God) + [4]*-y*] (1853) — used to express surprise or strength of feeling

[1]**lore** \ˈlȯr\ *n* [ME, fr. OE *lār;* akin to OHG *lēra* doctrine, OE *leornian* to learn] (bef. 12c) **1** *archaic* : something that is taught : LESSON **2** : something that is learned: **a** : knowledge gained through study or experience **b** : traditional knowledge or belief **3** : a particular body of knowledge or tradition

[2]**lore** *n* [NL *lorum,* fr. L, thong, rein; akin to Gk *eulēra* reins] (1828) : the space between the eye and bill in a bird or the corresponding region in a reptile or fish — **lo·re·al** \ˈlȯr-ē-əl\ *adj*

Lo·re·lei \ˈlȯr-ə-ˌlī\ *n* [G] (1865) : a siren of Germanic legend whose singing lures Rhine River boatmen to destruction on a reef

lor·gnette \lȯrn-ˈyet\ *n* [F, fr. *lorgner* to take a sidelong look at, fr. MF, fr. *lorgne* squinting] (1803) : a pair of eyeglasses or opera glasses with a handle

lor·gnon \lȯrn-ˈyōⁿ\ *n* [F, fr. *lorgner*] (1846) : LORGNETTE

lo·ri·ca \lə-ˈrī-kə\ *n, pl* **-cae** \-kē, -ˌsē\ [L] (ca. 1706) **1 :** a Roman cuirass of leather or metal **2** [NL, fr. L] **:** a hard protective case or shell (as of a rotifer)
lor·i·keet \ˈlȯr-ə-ˌkēt, ˈlär-\ *n* [*lory* + *-keet* (as in *parakeet*)] (1770) **:** any of numerous small arboreal chiefly Australasian parrots (family Loriidae) that usu. have long slender tongue papillae which form an organ resembling a brush
lo·ris \ˈlȯr-əs\ *n* [F, prob. fr. obs. D *loeris* simpleton] (1774) **:** any of several nocturnal slow-moving tailless arboreal primates (family Lorisidae): as **a :** a slim-bodied primate (*Loris tardigradus*) of southern India and Sri Lanka **b :** either of two larger related primates (*Nycticebus pygmaeus* or *N. coucang*) of southeastern Asia that are heavier limbed and slower moving
lorn \ˈlȯrn\ *adj* [ME, fr. *loren,* pp. of *lesen* to lose, fr. OE *lēosan* — more at LOSE] (14c) **:** DESOLATE, FORSAKEN
Lor·raine cross \lə-ˈrān-, lȯ-\ *n* (1898) **:** CROSS OF LORRAINE
lor·ry \ˈlȯr-ē, ˈlär-\ *n, pl* **lorries** [origin unknown] (1900) *chiefly Brit* **:** MOTORTRUCK
lo·ry \ˈlȯr-ē\ *n, pl* **lories** [D, fr. Malay *nuri, luri*] (1682) **:** any of numerous parrots (family Loriidae) of Australia, New Guinea, and adjacent islands related to the lorikeets and usu. having the tongue papillose at the tip and the mandibles less toothed than in other parrots
LOS *abbr* **1** line of scrimmage **2** line of sight
lose \ˈlüz\ *vb* **lost** \ˈlȯst\; **los·ing** \ˈlü-ziŋ\ [ME, fr. OE *losian* to perish, lose, fr. *los* destruction; akin to OE *lēosan* to lose; akin to ON *losa* to loosen, L *luere* to atone for, Gk *lyein* to loosen, dissolve, destroy] *vt* (bef. 12c) **1 a :** to bring to destruction — used chiefly in passive construction ⟨the ship was *lost* on the reef⟩ **b :** DAMN ⟨if he shall gain the whole world and ~ his own soul —Mt 16:26(AV)⟩ **2 :** to miss from one's possession or from a customary or supposed place **3 :** to suffer deprivation of **:** part with esp. in an unforeseen or accidental manner **4 a :** to suffer loss through the death or removal of or final separation from (a person) **b :** to fail to keep control of or allegiance of ⟨~ votes⟩ ⟨*lost* his temper⟩ **5 a :** to fail to use **:** let slip by **:** WASTE ⟨no time to ~⟩ **b** (1) **:** to fail to win, gain, or obtain ⟨~ a prize⟩ ⟨~ a contest⟩ (2) **:** to undergo defeat in ⟨*lost* every battle⟩ **c :** to fail to catch with the senses or the mind ⟨*lost* what she said⟩ **6 :** to cause the loss of **7 :** to fail to keep, sustain, or maintain ⟨*lost* my balance⟩ **8 a :** to cause to miss one's way or bearings ⟨*lost* himself in the maze of streets⟩ **b :** to make (oneself) withdrawn from immediate reality ⟨*lost* herself in daydreaming⟩ **9 a :** to wander or go astray from ⟨*lost* his way⟩ **b :** to draw away from **:** OUTSTRIP ⟨*lost* his pursuers⟩ **10 :** to fail to keep in sight or in mind **11 :** to free oneself from **:** get rid of ⟨dieting to ~ weight⟩ **12** *slang* **:** REGURGITATE, VOMIT — often used in such phrases as *lose one's lunch* ~ *vi* **1 :** to undergo deprivation of something of value **2 :** to undergo defeat ⟨~ with good grace⟩ **3** *of a timepiece* **:** to run slow — **los·able** \ˈlü-zə-bəl\ *adj* — **los·able·ness** *n* — **lose ground :** to suffer loss or disadvantage **:** fail to advance or improve — **lose it 1 :** to lose touch with reality; *also* **:** to go crazy **2 :** to become overwhelmed with strong emotion **:** lose one's composure ⟨so angry I almost *lost it*⟩ — **lose one's heart :** to fall in love
lo·sel \ˈlō-zəl\ *n* [ME, fr. *losen* (pp. of *lesen* to lose), alter. of *loren* — more at LORN] (14c) **:** a worthless person
lose–lose \ˈlüz-ˈlüz\ *adj* (1978) **:** presenting two options both of which put one at a disadvantage ⟨a ~ proposition⟩
lose out *vi* (ca. 1858) **:** to fail to win in competition **:** fail to receive an expected reward or gain
los·er \ˈlü-zər\ *n* (1548) **1 :** a person or thing that loses esp. consistently **2 :** a person who is incompetent or unable to succeed; *also* **:** something doomed to fail or disappoint
losing *adj* (1519) **1 :** resulting in or likely to result in defeat ⟨a ~ battle⟩ ⟨a ~ poker hand⟩ **2 :** marked by many losses or more losses than wins ⟨a ~ streak⟩ ⟨a ~ record⟩
loss \ˈlȯs\ *n* [ME *los,* prob. back-formation fr. *lost,* pp. of *losen* to lose] (13c) **1 :** DESTRUCTION, RUIN **2 a :** the act of losing possession **:** DEPRIVATION ⟨~ of sight⟩ **b :** the harm or privation resulting from loss or separation **c :** an instance of losing **3 :** a person or thing or an amount that is lost: as **a** *pl* **:** killed, wounded, or captured soldiers **b :** the power diminution of a circuit or circuit element corresponding to conversion of electrical energy into heat by resistance **4 a :** failure to gain, win, obtain, or utilize **b :** an amount by which the cost of something exceeds its selling price **5 :** decrease in amount, magnitude, or degree **6 :** the amount of an insured's financial detriment by death or damage that the insurer is liable for — **at a loss 1 :** uncertain as to how to proceed ⟨was *at a loss* to explain the discrepancy⟩ **2 :** unable to produce what is needed ⟨*at a loss* for words⟩ — **for a loss :** into a state of distress ⟨events had thrown him *for a loss*⟩
loss leader *n* (1917) **:** something (as merchandise) sold at a loss in order to draw customers — **loss–leader** *adj*
loss·less \ˈlȯs-ləs\ *adj* (ca. 1934) **:** done or being without loss (as of power or data) ⟨~ data compression⟩ ⟨~ power transmission⟩
loss ratio *n* (1926) **:** the ratio between insurance losses incurred and premiums earned during a given period
lossy \ˈlȯ-sē\ *adj* (1946) **:** causing attenuation or dissipation of electrical energy ⟨a ~ transmission line⟩ ⟨a ~ dielectric⟩
lost \ˈlȯst\ *adj* [pp. of *lose*] (15c) **1 :** not made use of, won, or claimed **2 a :** no longer possessed **b :** no longer known **3 :** ruined or destroyed physically or morally **:** DESPERATE **4 a :** taken away or beyond reach or attainment **:** DENIED ⟨regions ~ to the faith⟩ **b :** INSENSIBLE, HARDENED ⟨~ to shame⟩ **5 a :** unable to find the way **b :** no longer visible **c :** lacking assurance or self-confidence **:** HELPLESS **6 :** RAPT, ABSORBED ⟨~ in reverie⟩ **7 :** not appreciated or understood **:** WASTED ⟨their jokes were ~ on me⟩ **8 :** obscured or overlooked during a process or activity ⟨~ in translation⟩ **9 :** hopelessly unattainable **:** FUTILE ⟨a ~ cause⟩ — **lost·ness** \ˈlȯs(t)-nəs\ *n*
lost wax *n* (1909) **:** a process used in metal casting that consists of making a wax model, coating it with a refractory to form a mold, heating until the wax melts and runs out of the mold, and then pouring metal into the vacant mold
¹lot \ˈlät\ *n* [ME, fr. OE *hlot;* akin to OHG *hlōz*] (bef. 12c) **1 :** an object used as a counter in determining a question by chance **2 a :** the use of lots as a means of deciding something **b :** the resulting choice **3 a :** something that comes to one upon whom a lot has fallen **:** SHARE **b :** one's way of life or worldly fate **:** FORTUNE **4 a :** a portion of land **b :** a measured parcel of land having fixed boundaries and designated on a plot or survey **c :** a motion-picture studio and its adjoining property **d :** an establishment for the storage or sale of motor vehicles ⟨a used car ~⟩ **5 a :** a number of units of an article, a single article, or a parcel of articles offered as one item (as in an auction sale) **b :** all the members of a present group, kind, or quantity — usu. used with *the* ⟨sampled the whole ~ of desserts⟩ **6 a :** a number of associated persons **:** SET ⟨fell in with a rough ~⟩ **b :** KIND, SORT **7 :** a considerable quantity or extent ⟨a ~ of money⟩ ⟨~*s* of friends⟩ ***syn*** see FATE — **all over the lot :** covering a wide or varied range ⟨received bids *all over the lot*⟩ — **a lot 1 :** to a considerable degree or extent ⟨this is *a lot* nicer⟩ **2 :** OFTEN, FREQUENTLY ⟨runs *a lot* every day⟩ **3 :** LOTS
²lot *vt* **lot·ted; lot·ting** (15c) **1 :** ALLOT, APPORTION **2 :** to form or divide into lots
Lot \ˈlät\ *n* [Heb *Lōṭ*] (ca. 1534) **:** a nephew of Abraham who according to the account in Genesis escaped from the doomed city of Sodom with his wife who turned into a pillar of salt when she looked back
lo·ta *also* **lo·tah** \ˈlō-tə\ *n* [Hindi & Urdu *loṭā*] (1809) **:** a small usu. spherical water vessel of brass or copper used in India
loth *var of* LOATH
lo·thar·io \lō-ˈther-ē-ˌō, -ˈthär-\ *n, pl* **-i·os** *often cap* [*Lothario,* seducer in the play *The Fair Penitent* (1703) by Nicholas Rowe] (1756) **:** a man whose chief interest is seducing women
lo·ti \ˈlō-tē\ *n, pl* **ma·lo·ti** \mə-ˈlō-tē\ [Sesotho, lit., mountain, prob. fr. the *Maloti* Mountains, Lesotho] (1980) — see MONEY table
lo·tic \ˈlō-tik\ *adj* [L *lotus,* pp. of *lavere*] (1916) **:** of, relating to, or living in actively moving water ⟨a ~ habitat⟩ — compare LENTIC
lo·tion \ˈlō-shən\ *n* [ME *loscion,* fr. L *lotion-, lotio* act of washing, fr. *lavere* to wash — more at LYE] (14c) **:** a liquid preparation for cosmetic or external medicinal use
lots \ˈläts\ *adv* [pl. of ¹*lot*] (1891) **:** MUCH ⟨feeling ~ better⟩
lotte \ˈlät, ˈlȯt\ *n* [F, fr. MF] (1977) **:** MONKFISH
lot·tery \ˈlä-tə-rē *also* ˈlä-trē\ *n, pl* **-ter·ies** *often attrib* [MF *loterie,* fr. MD, fr. *lot* lot; akin to OE *hlot* lot] (1567) **1 a :** a drawing of lots in which prizes are distributed to the winners among persons buying a chance **b :** a drawing of lots used to decide something **2 :** an event or affair whose outcome is or seems to be determined by chance
lot·to \ˈlä-(ˌ)tō\ *n* [It, lottery, lotto, fr. F *lot* lot, of Gmc origin; akin to OE *hlot* lot] (1778) **:** a game of chance resembling bingo
lo·tus \ˈlō-təs\ *n* [L & Gk; L *lotus,* fr. Gk *lōtos*] (ca. 1541) **1** *also* **lo·tos** \ˈlō-təs\ **:** a fruit eaten by the lotus-eaters and considered to cause indolence and dreamy contentment; *also* **:** a tree (as *Zizyphus lotus* of the buckthorn family) reputed to bear this fruit **2 :** any of various water lilies including several represented in ancient Egyptian and Hindu art and religious symbolism **3** [NL, fr. L] **a :** any of a genus (*Lotus*) of widely distributed upright herbs or subshrubs of the legume family **b :** SWEET CLOVER
lo·tus–eat·er \-ˌē-tər\ *n* (1832) **1 :** any of a people in Homer's Odyssey subsisting on the lotus and living in the dreamy indolence it induces **2 :** an indolent person
lo·tus·land \-ˌland\ *n* [fr. the Homeric land of lotus-eaters] (1842) **1 :** a place inducing contentment esp. through offering an idyllic living situation **2 :** a state or an ideal marked by contentment often achieved through self-indulgence
lotus position *n* [fr. the supposed resemblance of the position to a lotus blossom] (1953) **:** a cross-legged sitting position used in yoga in which each foot is on the thigh of the opposite leg
louche \ˈlüsh\ *adj* [F, lit., cross-eyed, squint-eyed, fr. L *luscus* blind in one eye] (1819) **:** not reputable or decent
loud \ˈlau̇d\ *adj* [ME, fr. OE *hlūd;* akin to OHG *hlūt* loud, L *inclutus* famous, Gk *klytos,* Skt *śṛṇoti* he hears] (bef. 12c) **1 a :** marked by intensity or volume of sound **b :** producing a loud sound **2 :** CLAMOROUS, NOISY **3 :** obtrusive or offensive in appearance or smell **:** OBNOXIOUS — **loud** *adv* — **loud·ly** *adv*
syn LOUD, STENTORIAN, EARSPLITTING, RAUCOUS, STRIDENT mean marked by intensity or volume of sound. LOUD applies to any volume above normal and may suggest undue vehemence or obtrusiveness ⟨*loud* shouts of protest⟩. STENTORIAN implies great power and range ⟨an actor with a *stentorian* voice⟩. EARSPLITTING implies loudness that is physically discomforting ⟨the *earsplitting* sound of a siren⟩. RAUCOUS implies a loud harsh grating tone, esp. of voice, and may suggest rowdiness ⟨the *raucous* shouts of drunken revelers⟩. STRIDENT implies a rasping discordant but insistent quality, esp. of voice ⟨the *strident* voices of hecklers⟩.
loud·en \ˈlau̇-dᵊn\ *vb* **loud·ened; loud·en·ing** \ˈlau̇d-niŋ, ˈlau̇-dᵊn-iŋ\ *vi* (ca. 1848) **:** to become loud ~ *vt* **:** to make loud
loud–hail·er \ˌlau̇d-ˈhā-lər\ *n* (1941) *chiefly Brit* **:** BULLHORN
loud·mouth \ˈlau̇d-ˌmau̇th\ *n* (1914) **:** a loudmouthed person
loud·mouthed \-ˌmau̇thd, -ˌmau̇tht\ *adj* (1628) **:** given to loud offensive talk
loud·ness *n* (bef. 12c) **:** the attribute of a sound that determines the magnitude of the auditory sensation produced and that primarily depends on the amplitude of the sound wave involved
loud·speak·er \ˈlau̇d-ˌspē-kər\ *n* (1920) **:** a device that changes electrical signals into sounds loud enough to be heard at a distance
Lou Geh·rig's disease \ˌlü-ˈger-igz-\ *n* [*Lou Gehrig* †1941 Am. baseball player who suffered from the disease] (1958) **:** AMYOTROPHIC LATERAL SCLEROSIS
lough \ˈläk, ˈläk\ *n* [ME, of Celt origin; akin to OIr *loch* lake; akin to L *lacus* lake — more at LAKE] (14c) **1** *chiefly Irish* **:** LAKE **2** *chiefly Irish* **:** a bay or inlet of the sea
lou·is d'or \ˌlü-ē-ˈdȯr\ *n, pl* **louis d'or** [F, fr. *Louis* XIII of France + *d'or* of gold] (1665) **1 :** a French gold coin first struck in 1640 and issued up to the French Revolution **2 :** the French 20-franc gold piece issued after the French Revolution
Lou·is Qua·torze \ˌlü-ē-kə-ˈtȯrz\ *adj* [F, Louis XIV] (1848) **:** of, relating to, or characteristic of the architecture or furniture of the reign of Louis XIV of France
Louis Quinze \-ˈkaⁿz\ *adj* [F, Louis XV] (1855) **:** of, relating to, or characteristic of the architecture or furniture of the reign of Louis XV of France
Louis Seize \-ˈsāz, -ˈsez\ *adj* [F, Louis XVI] (1882) **:** of, relating to, or characteristic of the architecture or furniture of the reign of Louis XVI of France

Louis Treize \-ˈtrāz, -ˈtrez\ *adj* [F, Louis XIII] (1883) : of, relating to, or characteristic of the architecture or furniture of the reign of Louis XIII of France

louma *var of* LUMA

[1]**lounge** \ˈlau̇nj\ *vb* **lounged; loung•ing** [origin unknown] *vi* (1508) : to act or move idly or lazily : LOAF ***syn*** see IDLE ~ *vt* : to pass (time) idly

[2]**lounge** *n* (1775) **1 :** a place for lounging: as **a :** a room in a private home or public building for leisure activities : LIVING ROOM; *also* : LOBBY **b :** a room in a usu. public building or vehicle often combining lounging, smoking, and toilet facilities **2 :** a long couch

lounge car *n* (1947) : CLUB CAR

lounge lizard *n* (1917) **1 :** LADIES' MAN **2 :** FOP **3 :** a social parasite

loung•er \ˈlau̇n-jər\ *n* (1508) **1 :** one that lounges; *esp* : IDLER **2 :** an article of clothing or furniture designed for comfort and leisure use

lounge suit *n* (1901) *chiefly Brit* : BUSINESS SUIT

lounge•wear \ˈlau̇nj-ˌwer\ *n* (ca. 1957) : informal clothing usu. designed to be worn at home

loup \ˈlau̇p, ˈlōp\ *vb* [ME, fr. ON *hlaupa;* akin to OE *hlēapan* to leap — more at LEAP] (14c) *chiefly Scot* : LEAP — **loup** *n*

loupe \ˈlüp\ *n* [F] (ca. 1775) : a small magnifier used esp. by jewelers and watchmakers

loup–ga•rou \ˌlü-gə-ˈrü\ *n, pl* **loups–garous** \ˌlü-gə-ˈrü(z)\ [MF, fr. OF *leu garoul,* fr. *leu* wolf + *garoul* werewolf] (ca. 1580) : WEREWOLF

lour, loury *var of* LOWER, LOWERY

[1]**louse** \ˈlau̇s\ *n* [ME *lous,* fr. OE *lūs;* akin to OHG *lūs* louse, W *llau* lice] (bef. 12c) **1** *pl* **lice** \ˈlīs\ **a :** any of various small wingless usu. flattened insects (orders Anoplura and Mallophaga) parasitic on warm-blooded animals **b :** a small usu. sluggish arthropod (as a biting louse) that lives on other animals or on plants and sucks their blood or juices **c :** any of several small arthropods (as a book louse) that are not parasitic **2** *pl* **lous•es** \ˈlau̇-səz\ : a contemptible person : HEEL

[2]**louse** \ˈlau̇s, ˈlau̇z\ *vt* **loused; lous•ing** (14c) : to remove lice from

louse up *vt* (1934) : FOUL UP, SNARL ~ *vi* : to make a mess

louse•wort \ˈlau̇s-ˌwərt, -ˌwȯrt\ *n* (1597) : any of a genus (*Pedicularis*) of semiparasitic herbs of the snapdragon family typically having pinnatifid leaves and bilabiate flowers in terminal spikes

lousy \ˈlau̇-zē\ *adj* **lous•i•er; -est** (14c) **1 :** infested with lice **2 a :** totally repulsive : CONTEMPTIBLE **b :** miserably poor or inferior ⟨got ~ grades⟩ **c :** somewhat ill ⟨felt ~ after dinner⟩ **d :** amply supplied : REPLETE ⟨~ with money⟩ **3** *of silk* : fuzzy and specked because of splitting of the fiber — **lous•i•ly** \-zə-lē\ *adv* — **lous•i•ness** \-zē-nəs\ *n*

[1]**lout** \ˈlau̇t\ *vi* [ME, fr. OE *lūtan;* akin to ON *lūta* to bow down] (bef. 12c) **1 :** to bow in respect **2 :** SUBMIT, YIELD

[2]**lout** *n* [perh. fr. [1]*lout*] (1542) : an awkward brutish person

[3]**lout** *vt* (ca. 1530) : to treat as a lout : SCORN

lout•ish \ˈlau̇-tish\ *adj* (1542) : resembling or befitting a lout ***syn*** see BOORISH — **lout•ish•ly** *adv* — **lout•ish•ness** *n*

lou•ver *or* **lou•vre** \ˈlü-vər\ *n* [ME *lover,* fr. AF] (14c) **1 :** a roof lantern or turret often with slatted apertures for escape of smoke or admission of light in a medieval building **2 a :** an opening provided with one or more slanted fixed or movable fins to allow flow of air but to exclude rain or sun or to provide privacy **b :** a finned or vaned device for controlling a flow of air or the radiation of light **c :** a fin or shutter of a louver — **lou•vered** *also* **lou•vred** \-vərd\ *adj*

lov•able *also* **love•able** \ˈlə-və-bəl\ *adj* (14c) : having qualities that attract affection — **lov•abil•i•ty** \ˌlə-və-ˈbi-lə-tē\ *n* — **lov•able•ness** *n* — **lov•ably** \-blē\ *adv*

lov•age \ˈlə-vij\ *n* [ME *lovache,* fr. AF *luvasche, lovasche,* fr. LL *levisticum,* alter. of L *ligusticum,* fr. neut. of *ligusticus* Ligurian, fr. *Ligur-, Ligus,* n., Ligurian] (14c) : any of several aromatic perennial herbs of the carrot family; *esp* : a European herb (*Levisticum officinale*) sometimes cultivated for use in medicine esp. as a diuretic and in cookery usu. as a flavoring agent

lov•a•stat•in \ˈlō-və-ˌsta-tᵊn, ˈlə-; ˌlō-və-ˈ, ˌlə-\ *n* [prob. fr. ISV meva*lo*nic acid, a carboxylic acid, $C_6H_{12}O_4$ (fr. *me*thyl + *val*eric + *-onic* — as in *gluconic acid*) + me*vastatin,* a fungal metabolite structurally similar to lovastatin, fr. *meva*lonic + *-stat* + [1]*-in*] (1987) : a drug $C_{24}H_{36}O_8$ that decreases the level of cholesterol in the bloodstream

lov•at \ˈlə-vət\ *n* [prob. fr. T. A. Fraser, Lord *Lovat* †1875 Scot. nobleman who popularized muted tweeds] (1907) : a predominantly dusty color mixture (as of green) in fabrics

[1]**love** \ˈləv\ *n* [ME, fr. OE *lufu;* akin to OHG *luba* love, OE *lēof* dear, L *lubēre, libēre* to please] (bef. 12c) **1 a (1) :** strong affection for another arising out of kinship or personal ties ⟨maternal ~ for a child⟩ **(2) :** attraction based on sexual desire : affection and tenderness felt by lovers **(3) :** affection based on admiration, benevolence, or common interests ⟨~ for his old schoolmates⟩ **b :** an assurance of love ⟨give her my ~⟩ **2 :** warm attachment, enthusiasm, or devotion ⟨~ of the sea⟩ **3 a :** the object of attachment, devotion, or admiration ⟨baseball was his first ~⟩ **b (1) :** a beloved person : DARLING — often used as a term of endearment **(2)** *Brit* — used as an informal term of address **4 a :** unselfish loyal and benevolent concern for the good of another: as **(1) :** the fatherly concern of God for humankind **(2) :** brotherly concern for others **b :** a person's adoration of God **5 :** a god or personification of love **6 :** an amorous episode : LOVE AFFAIR **7 :** the sexual embrace : COPULATION **8 :** a score of zero (as in tennis) **9** *cap, Christian Science* : GOD — **at love :** holding one's opponent scoreless in tennis — **in love :** inspired by affection

[2]**love** *vb* **loved; lov•ing** *vt* (bef. 12c) **1 :** to hold dear : CHERISH **2 a :** to feel a lover's passion, devotion, or tenderness for **b (1) :** CARESS **(2) :** to fondle amorously **(3) :** to copulate with **3 :** to like or desire actively : take pleasure in ⟨*loved* to play the violin⟩ **4 :** to thrive in ⟨the rose *~s* sunlight⟩ ~ *vi* : to feel affection or experience desire

love affair *n* (1591) **1 :** a romantic attachment or episode between lovers **2 :** a lively enthusiasm ⟨America's *love affair* with baseball⟩

love apple *n* [prob. trans. of F *pomme d'amour*] (1578) : TOMATO

love beads *n pl* (1968) : beads worn as a symbol of love and peace

love•bird \ˈləv-ˌbərd\ *n* (1595) : any of various small usu. gray or green parrots (esp. genus *Agapornis* of Africa) that show great affection for their mates

love•bug \-ˌbəg\ *n* [fr. the fact that it is usu. seen copulating] (ca. 1966) : a small black fly (*Plecia nearctica*) with a red thorax that swarms along highways in the Gulf states of the U.S.

love child *n* (1805) : an illegitimate child

love feast *n* (1580) **1 :** a meal eaten in common by a Christian congregation in token of brotherly love **2 :** a gathering held to promote reconciliation and good feeling or show someone affectionate honor

love•fest \ˈləv-ˌfest\ *n* (1972) : LOVE FEAST 2; *broadly* : an expression or exchange of goodwill, praise, or affection

love grass *n* (1702) : any of a genus (*Eragrostis*) of grasses that resemble the bluegrasses but have flattened spikelets and deciduous lemmas

love handles *n pl* (1970) : fatty bulges along the sides of the body at the waist

love–in \ˈləv-ˌin\ *n* (1967) : a gathering of people esp. for the expression of their mutual love

love–in–a–mist \ˈləv-ə-nə-ˌmist\ *n* (ca. 1760) : an Old World annual herb (*Nigella damascena*) of the buttercup family having usu. blue or white flowers enveloped in numerous finely dissected bracts

love knot *n* (14c) : a stylized knot sometimes used as an emblem of love

love•less \ˈləv-ləs\ *adj* (14c) **1 :** having no love ⟨a ~ relationship⟩ **2 :** not loved — **love•less•ly** *adv* — **love•less•ness** *n*

love•lock \-ˌläk\ *n* (1592) : a long lock of hair variously worn (as over the front of the shoulder) esp. by men in the 17th and 18th centuries

love•lorn \-ˌlȯrn\ *adj* (1634) : bereft of love or of a lover ⟨letters from ~ soldiers⟩ — **love•lorn•ness** \-ˌlȯrn-nəs\ *n*

[1]**love•ly** \ˈləv-lē\ *adj* **love•li•er; -est** (bef. 12c) **1** *obs* : LOVABLE **2 :** delightful for beauty, harmony, or grace : ATTRACTIVE **3 :** GRAND, SWELL ⟨what a ~ morning⟩ **4 :** eliciting love by moral or ideal worth ***syn*** see BEAUTIFUL — **love•li•ly** \ˈləv-lə-lē\ *adv* — **love•li•ness** \ˈləv-lē-nəs\ *n* — **lovely** *adv*

[2]**lovely** *n, pl* **lovelies** (1652) **1 :** a beautiful woman **2 :** a lovely object

love•mak•ing \ˈləv-ˌmā-kiŋ\ *n* (15c) **1 :** COURTSHIP **2 :** sexual activity; *esp* : COPULATION — **love•mak•er** \-kər\ *n*

love nest *n* (1919) : a place (as an apartment) used for amorous and often illicit rendezvous

lov•er \ˈlə-vər\ *n* (13c) **1 a :** a person in love; *esp* : a man in love with a woman **b** *pl* : two persons in love with each other **2 :** an affectionate or benevolent friend **3 :** DEVOTEE **4 a :** PARAMOUR **b :** a person with whom one has sexual relations

lov•er•ly \-lē\ *adj* (1875) : resembling or befitting a lover

love seat *n* (1904) : a double chair, sofa, or settee for two persons

love•sick \ˈləv-ˌsik\ *adj* (15c) **1 :** languishing with love : YEARNING ⟨a ~ suitor⟩ **2 :** expressing a lover's longing — **love•sick•ness** *n*

love•some \-səm\ *adj* (bef. 12c) **1 :** WINSOME, LOVELY **2 :** AFFECTIONATE, AMOROUS

love tap *n* (1809) : a gentle blow

lovey–dovey \ˌlə-vē-ˈdə-vē\ *adj* (1886) : expressing much love or sentimentality; *also* : MUSHY — **lovey–dovey•ness** \-nəs\ *n*

loving *adj* (bef. 12c) **1 :** AFFECTIONATE **2 :** PAINSTAKING — **lov•ing•ly** \-viŋ-lē\ *adv* — **lov•ing•ness** *n*

loving cup *n* [fr. its former use in ceremonial drinking] (1812) **1 :** a large ornamental drinking vessel with two or more handles **2 :** a loving cup given as a token or trophy

lov•ing–kind•ness \ˌlə-viŋ-ˈkīn(d)-nəs\ *n* (1535) : tender and benevolent affection

[1]**low** \ˈlō\ *vi* [ME *loowen,* fr. OE *hlōwan;* akin to OHG *hluoen* to moo, L *calare* to call, summon, Gk *kalein*] (bef. 12c) : MOO

[2]**low** *n* (1549) : the deep sustained sound characteristic esp. of a cow

[3]**low** *adj* **low•er** \ˈlō-ər\; **low•est** \ˈlō-əst\ [ME *lah, low,* fr. ON *lāgr;* akin to MHG *læge* low, flat; prob. akin to OE *licgan* to lie] (12c) **1 a :** having a small upward extension or elevation ⟨a ~ wall⟩ **b :** situated or passing little above a reference line, point, or plane ⟨~ bridges⟩ **c (1) :** having a low-cut neckline **(2) :** not extending as high as the ankle ⟨~ oxfords⟩ **2 a :** situated or passing below the normal level, surface, or base of measurement, or the mean elevation ⟨~ ground⟩ **b :** marking a nadir or bottom ⟨the ~ point of his career⟩ **3 :** DEAD — used as a predicate adjective with *lay* ⟨laid the enemy ~⟩ **4 a :** not loud : SOFT **b :** FLAT 8a **c :** characterized by being toward the bottom of the range of pitch attainable (as by an instrument) **5 a :** being near the equator ⟨~ northern latitudes⟩ **b :** being near the horizon **6 :** socially or economically humble in character or status ⟨a person of ~ birth⟩ **7 a :** lacking strength, health, or vitality : WEAK, PROSTRATE ⟨very ~ with pneumonia⟩ **b :** lacking spirit or vivacity : DEPRESSED ⟨a ~ frame of mind⟩ **8 a :** of lesser degree, size, or amount than average or ordinary ⟨~ energy⟩ **b (1) :** small in number or amount **(2) :** SUBSTANDARD, INADEQUATE ⟨a ~ level of employment⟩ ⟨a ~ income group⟩ **(3) :** CHEAP ⟨~ prices⟩ **(4) :** SHORT, DEPLETED ⟨oil is in ~ supply⟩ **c :** of lesser position, rank, or order **9 :** falling short of some standard: as **a :** lacking dignity or elevation ⟨a ~ style of writing⟩ **b :** morally reprehensible : BASE ⟨a ~ trick⟩ **c :** COARSE, VULGAR ⟨~ language⟩ **10 a :** not advanced in complexity, development, or elaboration ⟨~ organisms⟩ **b** *often cap* : LOW CHURCH **11 :** UNFAVORABLE, DISPARAGING ⟨had a ~ opinion of him⟩ **12 :** designed for slow and usu. the slowest speed ⟨~ gear⟩ **13 :** articulated with a wide opening between the relatively flat tongue and the palate : OPEN ⟨\ä\ is a ~ vowel⟩ **14 :** intended to attract little attention ⟨kept a ~ profile⟩ **15 :** being near the basket or net ⟨a player in the ~ post⟩ ***syn*** see BASE — **low** *adv* — **low•ness** *n*

[4]**low** *n* (12c) **1 :** something that is low: as **a :** DEPTH ⟨a new ~ in advertising⟩ **b :** a region of low barometric pressure **2 :** the transmission gear of an automotive vehicle giving the lowest ratio of driveshaft to crankshaft speed

[5]**low** *or* **lowe** \ˈlō\ *n* [ME, fr. ON *logi, log;* akin to OE *lēoht* light — more at LIGHT] (13c) *chiefly Scot* : FLAME, BLAZE

[6]**low** *or* **lowe** *vb* **lowed; low•ing** (14c) *Scot* : FLAME, BLAZE

\ə\ **abut** \ᵊ\ kitten, F table \ər\ **fur**ther \a\ **ash** \ā\ **ace** \ä\ mop, mar
\au̇\ **out** \ch\ **chin** \e\ bet \ē\ **easy** \g\ **go** \i\ **hit** \ī\ **ice** \j\ **job**
\ŋ\ sing \ō\ go \ȯ\ **law** \ȯi\ **boy** \th\ **thin** \t͟h\ **the** \ü\ **loot** \u̇\ **foot**
\y\ yet \zh\ vi**sion**, beige \k̟, ⁿ, œ, ue, ʸ\ *see* Guide to Pronunciation

low·ball \ˈlō-ˌbȯl\ *vt* (1957) **1** : to give (a customer) a deceptively low price or cost estimate **2** : to give a markedly or unfairly low offer ⟨~*ed* him in contract negotiations⟩ — **lowball** *n*

low beam *n* (ca. 1952) : a vehicle headlight beam with a short-range focus

low blood pressure *n* (1924) : HYPOTENSION

low blow *n* (1952) : an unprincipled attack ⟨gossip column that landed one *low blow* after another —James Fallows⟩

low·born \ˈlō-ˈbȯrn\ *adj* (13c) : born in a low condition or rank

low·boy \-ˌbȯi\ *n* (ca. 1891) : a chest or side table about three feet (one meter) high with drawers and usu. with cabriole legs

low·bred \-ˈbred\ *adj* (ca. 1605) : RUDE, VULGAR

low·brow \-ˌbrau̇\ *adj* (1913) : of, relating to, or suitable for a person with little taste or intellectual interest ⟨a ~ horror movie⟩ — **lowbrow** *n*

Low Church *adj* (1703) : tending esp. in Anglican worship to minimize emphasis on the priesthood, sacraments, and ceremonial in worship and often to emphasize evangelical principles

Low Churchman *n* (1702) : a person holding or advocating Low Church views

low comedy *n* (1608) : comedy employing burlesque, horseplay, or the representation of low life — compare HIGH COMEDY

low country *n, often cap L&C* (15c) : a low-lying country or region; *esp* : the part of a southern state extending from the seacoast inland to the fall line — **low–country** *adj, often cap L&C*

low–density lipoprotein *n* (1951) : LDL

low·down \ˈlō-ˌdau̇n\ *n* (1915) : the inside facts : DOPE ⟨gave us the ~ on the situation⟩

low–down \ˈlō-(ˌ)dau̇n\ *adj* (1850) **1** : CONTEMPTIBLE, BASE ⟨a ~ dirty liar⟩ **2** : deeply emotional ⟨~ blues⟩

low earth orbit *n* (1963) : a usu. circular orbit from about 90 to 600 miles (about 140 to 970 kilometers) above the earth

low–end \ˈlō-ˌend\ *adj* (1926) : of, relating to, or being the lowest priced merchandise in a manufacturer's line; *broadly* : INEXPENSIVE

[1]**low·er** \ˈlau̇(-ə)r, ˈlō-ər\ *also* **lour** \ˈlau̇(-ə)r\ *vi* [ME *louren;* akin to MHG *lūren* to lie in wait] (13c) **1** : to look sullen : FROWN **2** : to be or become dark, gloomy, and threatening ⟨an overcast sky ~*ed* over the village⟩

[2]**lower** *also* **lour** *n* (14c) : FROWN

[3]**low·er** \ˈlō-ər\ *adj* [³*low*] (13c) **1** : relatively low in position, rank, or order **2** : SOUTHERN ⟨~ New York State⟩ **3** : less advanced in the scale of evolutionary development **4 a** : situated or held to be situated beneath the earth's surface **b** *cap* : being an earlier epoch or series of the period or system named ⟨*Lower* Cretaceous⟩ ⟨*Lower* Paleolithic⟩ **5** : constituting the popular and often the larger and more representative branch of a bicameral legislative body ⟨~ house⟩

[4]**low·er** \ˈlō-ər\ *vi* (1606) : to move down : DROP; *also* : DIMINISH ~ *vt* **1 a** : to let descend : LET DOWN **b** : to depress as to direction ⟨~ your aim⟩ **c** : to reduce the height of **2 a** : to reduce in value, number, or amount **b (1)** : to bring down in quality or character : DEGRADE **(2)** : ABASE, HUMBLE **c** : to reduce the objective of — **lower the boom** : to deal a crushing blow or punishment

[1]**low·er·case** \ˌlō-ər-ˈkās\ *adj* [fr. the compositor's practice of keeping such types in the lower of a pair of type cases] (1683) *of a letter* : having as its typical form a f g or *b n i* rather than A F G or *B N I* — **lowercase** *n*

[2]**lowercase** *vt* **-cased; -cas·ing** (1908) : to print or set in lowercase letters

low·er–class \ˌlō-ər-ˈklas\ *adj* (1890) **1** : of, relating to, or characteristic of the lower class **2** : being an inferior or low-ranking specimen of its kind ⟨a ~ theater⟩

lower class *n* (1637) : a social class occupying a position below the middle class and having the lowest status in a society

lower criticism *n* (1885) : criticism concerned with the recovery of original texts esp. of Scripture through collation of extant manuscripts — compare HIGHER CRITICISM

lower fungus *n* (1900) : a fungus with hyphae absent or rudimentary and nonseptate

low·er·ing \ˈlau̇-(ə-)riŋ, ˈlō-\ *adj* (15c) : dark and threatening : GLOOMY ⟨rain pouring down from a ~ sky⟩

low·er·most \ˈlō-ər-ˌmōst\ *adj* (1547) : LOWEST

low·ery \ˈlau̇-(ə-)rē, ˈlō-\ *also* **loury** \ˈlau̇-(ə-)rē\ *adj* (15c) : GLOOMY, LOWERING

lowest common denominator *n* (1854) **1** : LEAST COMMON DENOMINATOR **2** : something of small intellectual content designed to appeal to a lowbrow audience; *also* : such an audience

lowest common multiple *n* (1873) : LEAST COMMON MULTIPLE

lowest terms *n pl* (ca. 1675) : the form of a fraction in which the numerator and denominator have no factor in common except 1 ⟨reduce a fraction to *lowest terms*⟩

low frequency *n* (ca. 1898) : a radio frequency between medium frequency and very low frequency — see RADIO FREQUENCY table

Low German *n* (1838) **1** : the German dialects of northern Germany esp. as used since the end of the medieval period : PLATTDEUTSCH **2** : the West Germanic languages other than High German

low–grade \ˈlō-ˈgrād\ *adj* (1878) **1** : of inferior grade or quality **2** : being near that extreme of a specified range which is lowest, least intense, least serious, or least competent ⟨a ~ fever⟩ ⟨a ~ infection⟩

low–key \-ˈkē\ *also* **low–keyed** \-ˈkēd\ *adj* (1907) **1** : having or producing dark tones only with little contrast **2** : of low intensity : RESTRAINED

[1]**low·land** \ˈlō-lənd, -ˌland\ *n* (15c) : low or level country

[2]**lowland** *adj* (1508) **1** *cap* : of or relating to the Lowlands of Scotland **2** : of or relating to a lowland

low·land·er \-lən-dər, -ˌlan-\ *n* (1692) **1** *cap* : an inhabitant of the Lowlands of Scotland **2** : a native or inhabitant of a lowland region

lowland gorilla *n* (1942) : either of two gorillas (*Gorilla gorilla gorilla* or *G. gorilla graueri*) that inhabit lowland rainforests of west central Africa

Low Latin *n* (1872) : postclassical Latin in its later stages

low–lev·el \ˈlō-ˈle-vəl\ *adj* (1881) **1** : occurring, done, or placed at a low level **2** : being of low importance or rank **3** : being or relating to nuclear waste containing low concentrations of radioactive components

low·life \ˈlō-ˌlīf\ *n, pl* **low·lifes** \-ˌlīfs\ *also* **low·lives** \-ˌlīvz\ (1911) **1** : a person of low social status **2** : a person of low moral character — **low–life** *adj*

low·light \ˈlō-ˌlīt\ *n* (1941) : a particularly bad or unpleasant event, detail, or part

low·li·head \ˈlō-lē-ˌhed\ *n* [ME *lowliheed,* fr. *lowly* + *-hed* -hood; akin to ME *-hod* -hood] (15c) *archaic* : lowly state

[1]**low·ly** \ˈlō-lē\ *adv* (14c) **1** : in a humble or meek manner **2** : in a low position, manner, or degree **3** : not loudly

[2]**lowly** *adj* **low·li·er; -est** (14c) **1** : humble in manner or spirit : free from self-assertive pride **2** : not lofty or sublime : PROSAIC **3** : ranking low in some hierarchy **4** : of or relating to a low social or economic rank **5** : low in the scale of biological or cultural evolution — **low·li·ness** *n*

low–ly·ing \ˈlō-ˈlī-iŋ\ *adj* (1856) **1** : rising relatively little above the base of measurement ⟨~ hills⟩ **2** : lying below the normal level, surface, or the base of measurement or mean elevation ⟨~ clouds⟩

low mass *n, often cap L&M* (1568) : a mass that is recited without singing by the celebrant, without a deacon, subdeacon, or choir assisting the celebrant, and without the use of incense

low–mind·ed \ˈlō-ˈmīn-dəd\ *adj* (ca. 1746) : inclined to vulgar or unworthy things — **low–mind·ed·ly** *adv* — **low–mind·ed·ness** *n*

lown \ˈlau̇n, ˈlün\ *adj* [ME (Sc) *lowne*] (15c) *dial* : CALM, QUIET

low–pres·sure \ˈlō-ˈpre-shər\ *adj* (1827) **1** : having, exerting, or operating under a relatively small pressure **2** : EASYGOING

low relief *n* (1711) : BAS-RELIEF

low–rent \ˈlō-ˈrent\ *adj* (1957) : low in character, cost, or prestige ⟨~ thugs⟩ ⟨a ~ movie⟩ ⟨a ~ literary form⟩

low·rid·er \ˈlō-ˌrī-dər\ *n* (ca. 1972) : a customized car with a chassis that has been lowered so that it narrowly clears the ground

low–rise \ˈlō-ˈrīz\ *adj* (1957) **1** : having few stories and not equipped with elevators ⟨a ~ classroom building⟩ **2** : of, relating to, or characterized by low-rise buildings ⟨a ~ housing development⟩

low–slung \ˈlō-ˈsləŋ\ *adj* (1931) : relatively low to the ground or floor ⟨a ~ convertible⟩ ⟨a ~ modern building⟩ ⟨a ~ sofa⟩

low–spir·it·ed \ˈlō-ˈspir-ə-təd\ *adj* (1693) : DEJECTED, DEPRESSED — **low–spir·it·ed·ly** *adv* — **low–spir·it·ed·ness** *n*

Low Sunday *n* (15c) : the Sunday following Easter

low–tech \ˈlō-ˈtek\ *adj* (1981) : technologically simple or unsophisticated ⟨~ industries⟩

low tide *n* (1843) : the farthest ebb of the tide

low water *n* (15c) : a low stage of the water in a river or lake; *also* : LOW TIDE

[1]**lox** \ˈläks\ *n* [*l*iquid *ox*ygen] (1923) : liquid oxygen

[2]**lox** *n, pl* **lox** *or* **lox·es** [Yiddish *laks,* fr. MHG *lahs* salmon, fr. OHG; akin to OE *leax* salmon] (1939) : salmon that has been cured in brine and sometimes smoked

lox·o·drome \ˈläk-sə-ˌdrōm\ *n* [back-formation fr. *loxodromic* of a rhumb line, fr. F *loxodromique,* fr. Gk *loxos* oblique + *dromos* course — more at DROMEDARY] (1880) : RHUMB LINE

loy·al \ˈlȯi(-ə)l\ *adj* [MF, fr. OF *leial, leel,* fr. L *legalis* legal] (1531) **1** : unswerving in allegiance: as **a** : faithful in allegiance to one's lawful sovereign or government **b** : faithful to a private person to whom fidelity is due **c** : faithful to a cause, ideal, custom, institution, or product **2** : showing loyalty **3** *obs* : LAWFUL, LEGITIMATE ***syn*** see FAITHFUL — **loy·al·ly** \ˈlȯi-ə-lē\ *adv*

loy·al·ist \ˈlȯi-ə-list\ *n* (1647) : one who is or remains loyal esp. to a political cause, party, government, or sovereign

loy·al·ty \ˈlȯi(-ə)l-tē\ *n, pl* **-ties** [alter. of ME *leawte, lewte,* fr. AF *lealté, leauté,* fr. *leal, leial* loyal] (15c) : the quality or state or an instance of being loyal ***syn*** see FIDELITY

loz·enge \ˈlä-zᵊnj *also* -sᵊnj\ *n* [ME *losenge,* fr. AF] (14c) **1** : a figure with four equal sides and two acute and two obtuse angles : DIAMOND **2** : something shaped like a lozenge **3** : a small usu. sweetened and flavored medicated material that is designed to be held in the mouth for slow dissolution; *esp* : one that contains a demulcent ⟨sore throat ~*s*⟩ — called also *pastille, troche*

[1]**LP** \ˌel-ˈpē\ *n* [*l*ong-*p*laying] (1948) : a microgroove phonograph record designed to be played at 33⅓ revolutions per minute

[2]**LP** *abbr* low pressure

LPG *abbr* liquefied petroleum gas

LPGA *abbr* Ladies Professional Golf Association

LPN \ˌel-(ˌ)pē-ˈen\ *n* (1948) : LICENSED PRACTICAL NURSE

Lr *symbol* lawrencium

LR *abbr* **1** living room **2** lower right

LRT *abbr* light-rail transit

LRV *abbr* light-rail vehicle

LS *abbr* **1** left side **2** letter signed **3** library science **4** [L *locus sigilli*] place of the seal

LSD \ˌel-(ˌ)es-ˈdē\ *n* [G *Lysergsäure-Diäthylamid* lysergic acid diethylamide] (1950) : a semisynthetic illicit organic compound $C_{20}H_{25}N_3O$ derived from ergot that induces extreme sensory distortions, altered perceptions of reality, and intense emotional states, that may also produce delusions or paranoia, and that may sometimes cause panic reactions in response to the effects experienced — called also *lysergic acid diethylamide*

LSI *abbr* large-scale integrated circuit; large-scale integration

LSM *abbr* letter-sorting machine

LSO *abbr* landing signal officer

LSS *abbr* **1** lifesaving service; lifesaving station **2** life-support system

LST *abbr* **1** landing ship, tank **2** local sidereal time

lt *abbr* light

Lt *abbr* lieutenant

LT *abbr* long ton

LTC *abbr* **1** lieutenant colonel **2** long-term care

Lt Col *abbr* lieutenant colonel

Lt Comdr *abbr* lieutenant commander

ltd *abbr* limited

LTG *or* **Lt Gen** *abbr* lieutenant general

lt gov *abbr* lieutenant governor

LTh *abbr* licentiate in theology

LTJG *abbr* lieutenant junior grade

LTL *abbr* less than truckload

LTP *abbr* long-term potentiation

ltr *abbr* **1** letter **2** lighter
L–tryp·to·phan \ˈel-ˈtrip-tə-ˌfan\ *n* (1949) **:** the levorotatory form of tryptophan that is a precursor of serotonin and was used formerly as a dietary supplement esp. to promote sleep and relieve depression
LTS *abbr* launch telemetry station; launch tracking system
Lu *symbol* lutetium
lu·au \ˈlü-ˌau̇\ *n* [Hawaiian *lūʻau*] (1853) **:** a Hawaiian feast
Lu·ba·vitch·er \ˈlü-bə-ˌvi-chər, lü-ˈbä-\ *n* [Yiddish *lyubavitsher,* fr. *Lyubavitsh,* town in Belarus] (1954) **:** a member of a Hasidic sect founded by Schneour Zalman of Lyady in the late 18th century — **Lubavitcher** *adj*
lub·ber \ˈlə-bər\ *n* [ME *lobre, lobur*] (14c) **1 :** a big clumsy fellow **2 :** a clumsy seaman — **lub·ber·li·ness** \-lē-nəs\ *n* — **lub·ber·ly** \-lē\ *adj or adv*
lubber line *n* (1858) **:** a fixed line on the compass of a ship or airplane that is aligned with the longitudinal axis of the vehicle
lubber's hole *n* (ca. 1784) **:** a hole in a square-rigger's top near the mast through which one may go farther aloft without going over the rim by the futtock shrouds
lube \ˈlüb\ *n* [short for *lubricating oil*] (1926) **1 :** LUBRICANT **2 :** an application of a lubricant **:** LUBRICATION
lu·bric \ˈlü-brik\ *adj* [MF *lubrique,* fr. ML *lubricus*] (15c) *archaic* **:** LUBRICIOUS — **lu·bri·cal** \-bri-kəl\ *adj*
lu·bri·cant \ˈlü-bri-kənt\ *n* (ca. 1828) **1 :** a substance (as grease) capable of reducing friction, heat, and wear when introduced as a film between solid surfaces **2 :** something that lessens or prevents friction or difficulty ⟨a social ~⟩ — **lubricant** *adj*
lu·bri·cate \ˈlü-brə-ˌkāt\ *vb* **-cat·ed; -cat·ing** [L *lubricatus,* pp. of *lubricare,* fr. *lubricus* slippery — more at SLEEVE] *vt* (ca. 1623) **1 :** to make smooth or slippery **2 :** to apply a lubricant to ~ *vi* **:** to act as a lubricant — **lu·bri·ca·tion** \ˌlü-brə-ˈkā-shən\ *n* — **lu·bri·ca·tive** \ˈlü-brə-ˌkā-tiv\ *adj* — **lu·bri·ca·tor** \-ˌkā-tər\ *n*
lu·bri·cious \lü-ˈbri-shəs\ *or* **lu·bri·cous** \ˈlü-bri-kəs\ *adj* [ML *lubricus,* fr. L, slippery, easily led astray] (1535) **1 :** marked by wantonness **:** LECHEROUS; *also* **:** SALACIOUS **2** [L *lubricus*] **:** having a smooth or slippery quality ⟨a ~ skin⟩ — **lu·bri·cious·ly** *adv*
lu·bric·i·ty \lü-ˈbri-sə-tē\ *n, pl* **-ties** (15c) **:** the property or state of being lubricious; *also* **:** the capacity for reducing friction
Lu·can \ˈlü-kən\ *or* **Luk·an** *adj* [LL *lucanus,* fr. *Lucas* Luke, fr. Gk *Loukas*] (1890) **:** of or relating to Luke or the Gospel ascribed to him
lu·carne \lü-ˈkärn\ *n* [F] (ca. 1825) **:** DORMER
Lu·ca·yo \lü-ˈkī-(ˌ)ō\ *also* **Lu·ca·yan** \-ˈkī-ən\ *n* (1929) **:** a member of an Arawakan people of the Bahamas
lu·cen·cy \ˈlü-sᵊn(t)-sē\ *n* (1656) **:** the quality or state of being lucent
lu·cent \ˈlü-sᵊnt\ *adj* [ME, fr. L *lucent-, lucens,* prp. of *lucēre* to shine — more at LIGHT] (15c) **1 :** glowing with light **:** LUMINOUS **2 :** marked by clarity or translucence **:** CLEAR — **lu·cent·ly** *adv*
lu·cern *n* [prob. modif. of G *lüchsern* of a lynx, fr. *Luchs* lynx] (ca. 1533) *obs* **:** LYNX
lu·cerne *also* **lu·cern** \lü-ˈsərn\ *n* [F *luzerne,* fr. Occitan *luserno*] (1626) *chiefly Brit* **:** ALFALFA
lu·cid \ˈlü-səd\ *adj* [L *lucidus,* fr. *lucēre*] (1591) **1 a :** suffused with light **:** LUMINOUS **b :** TRANSLUCENT ⟨snorkeling in the ~ sea⟩ **2 :** having full use of one's faculties **:** SANE **3 :** clear to the understanding **:** INTELLIGIBLE ***syn*** see CLEAR — **lu·cid·ly** *adv* — **lu·cid·ness** *n*
lu·cid·i·ty \lü-ˈsi-də-tē\ *n* (1810) **1 :** clearness of thought or style **2 :** a presumed capacity to perceive the truth directly and instantaneously **:** CLAIRVOYANCE
Lu·ci·fer \ˈlü-sə-fər\ *n* [ME, the morning star, a fallen rebel archangel, the Devil, fr. OE, fr. L, the morning star, fr. *lucifer* light-bearing, fr. *luc-, lux* light + *-fer* -ferous — more at LIGHT] (bef. 12c) **1 —** used as a name of the devil **2 :** the planet Venus when appearing as the morning star **3** *not cap* **:** a friction match having as active substances antimony sulfide and potassium chlorate — **Lu·ci·fe·ri·an** \ˌlü-sə-ˈfir-ē-ən\ *adj*
lu·cif·er·ase \lü-ˈsi-fə-ˌrās, -ˌrāz\ *n* [ISV, fr. *luciferin*] (1888) **:** an enzyme that catalyzes the oxidation of luciferin
lu·cif·er·in \-f(ə-)rən\ *n* [ISV, fr. L *lucifer* light-bearing] (1888) **:** any of various organic substances in luminescent organisms (as fireflies) that upon oxidation produce a virtually heatless light
lu·cif·er·ous \lü-ˈsi-f(ə-)rəs\ *adj* [L *lucifer*] (1648) **:** bringing light or insight **:** ILLUMINATING ⟨a ~ performance of the opera⟩
Lu·ci·na \lü-ˈsī-nə\ *n* [L, Roman goddess of childbirth] (1615) *archaic* **:** MIDWIFE
Lu·cite \ˈlü-ˌsīt\ *trademark* — used for an acrylic resin or plastic consisting essentially of polymerized methyl methacrylate
[1]**luck** \ˈlək\ *n* [ME *lucke,* fr. MD *luc;* akin to MHG *gelücke* luck] (15c) **1 a :** a force that brings good fortune or adversity **b :** the events or circumstances that operate for or against an individual **2 :** favoring chance; *also* **:** SUCCESS ⟨had great ~ growing orchids⟩ — **luck·less** \-ləs\ *adj*
[2]**luck** *vi* (ca. 1584) **1 :** to prosper or succeed esp. through chance or good fortune — usu. used with *out* ⟨the hero ~*s* out and is able to escape⟩ **2 :** to come upon something desirable by chance — usu. used with *out, on, onto,* or *into* ⟨~*ed* into a wonderful opportunity⟩
luck·i·ly \ˈlə-kə-lē\ *adv* (1530) **1 :** in a lucky manner **2 :** FORTUNATELY 2 ⟨~, we were on time⟩ ***usage*** see HOPEFULLY
lucky \ˈlə-kē\ *adj* **luck·i·er; -est** (15c) **1 :** having good luck **2 :** happening by chance **:** FORTUITOUS **3 :** producing or resulting in good by chance **:** FAVORABLE **4 :** seeming to bring good luck ⟨a ~ rabbit's foot⟩ — **luck·i·ness** \ˈlə-kē-nəs\ *n*
syn LUCKY, FORTUNATE, HAPPY, PROVIDENTIAL mean meeting with unforeseen success. LUCKY stresses the agency of chance in bringing about a favorable result ⟨won because of a *lucky* bounce⟩. FORTUNATE suggests being rewarded beyond one's deserts ⟨*fortunate* in my investments⟩. HAPPY combines the implications of LUCKY and FORTUNATE with stress on being blessed ⟨a series of *happy* accidents⟩. PROVIDENTIAL more definitely implies the help or intervention of a higher power ⟨a *providential* change in the weather⟩.
lucky dip *n* (1925) *Brit* **:** GRAB BAG
lu·cra·tive \ˈlü-krə-tiv\ *adj* [ME *lucratif,* fr. MF, fr. L *lucrativus,* fr. *lucratus,* pp. of *lucrari* to gain, fr. *lucrum*] (15c) **:** producing wealth **:** PROFITABLE — **lu·cra·tive·ly** *adv* — **lu·cra·tive·ness** *n*
lu·cre \ˈlü-kər\ *n* [ME, fr. AF, fr. L *lucrum;* prob. akin to OE *lēan* reward, OHG *lōn,* Gk *apolauein* to enjoy] (14c) **:** monetary gain **:** PROFIT ⟨wrote almost entirely for ~⟩; *also* **:** MONEY
lu·cu·bra·tion \ˌlü-kyə-ˈbrā-shən, ˌlü-kə-\ *n* [L *lucubration-, lucubratio* study by night, work produced at night, fr. *lucubrare* to work by lamplight; akin to L *luc-, lux*] (1595) **:** laborious or intensive study; *also* **:** the product of such study — usu. used in pl.
lu·cu·lent \ˈlü-kyə-lənt\ *adj* [L *luculentus,* fr. *luc-, lux* light] (ca. 1548) **:** clear in thought or expression **:** LUCID ⟨the interviewee was ~ and personable⟩ — **lu·cu·lent·ly** *adv*
Lu·cul·lan \lü-ˈkə-lən\ *also* **Lu·cul·li·an** \-ˈkə-lē-ən\ *adj* [L *lucullanus* of Licinius *Lucullus;* fr. his reputation for luxurious banquets] (1861) **:** LAVISH, LUXURIOUS ⟨a ~ feast⟩
Ludd·ite \ˈlə-ˌdīt\ *n* [perh. fr. Ned *Ludd,* 18th cent. Leicestershire workman who destroyed a knitting frame] (1811) **:** one of a group of early 19th century English workmen destroying laborsaving machinery as a protest; *broadly* **:** one who is opposed to esp. technological change — **Luddite** *adj*
lude \ˈlüd\ *n* [short for *Quaalude,* a proprietary name for methaqualone] (1973) **:** a pill of methaqualone — usu. used in pl.
lu·dic \ˈlü-dik\ *adj* [F *ludique,* fr. L *ludus*] (1940) **:** of, relating to, or characterized by play **:** PLAYFUL ⟨~ behavior⟩ ⟨a ~ novel⟩
lu·di·crous \ˈlü-də-krəs\ *adj* [L *ludicrus,* fr. *ludus* play, sport; perh. akin to Gk *loidoros* abusive] (1712) **1 :** amusing or laughable through obvious absurdity, incongruity, exaggeration, or eccentricity **2 :** meriting derisive laughter or scorn as absurdly inept, false, or foolish ***syn*** see LAUGHABLE — **lu·di·crous·ly** *adv* — **lu·di·crous·ness** *n*
lu·es \ˈlü-(ˌ)ēz\ *n, pl* **lues** [NL, fr. L, plague; akin to Gk *lyein* to loosen, destroy — more at LOSE] (1634) **:** SYPHILIS — **lu·et·ic** \lü-ˈe-tik\ *adj*
[1]**luff** \ˈləf\ *n* [ME *lof* spar holding out the windward tack of a sail, weather side of a ship, fr. AF] (14c) **1 :** the act of sailing a ship nearer the wind **2 :** the forward edge of a fore-and-aft sail
[2]**luff** *vi* (14c) **:** to turn the head of a ship toward the wind
luffa *var of* LOOFAH
luft·mensch \ˈlu̇ft-ˌmen(t)sh\ *n, pl* **luft·mensch·en** \-ˌmen(t)-shən\ [Yiddish *luftmentsh,* fr. *luft* air + *mentsh* human being] (1907) **:** an impractical contemplative person having no definite business or income
[1]**lug** \ˈləg\ *vb* **lugged; lug·ging** [ME *luggen* to pull by the hair or ear, drag, prob. of Scand origin; akin to Norw *lugga* to pull by the hair] *vt* (14c) **1 :** DRAG, PULL **2 :** to carry laboriously ⟨*lugged* the bags to the car⟩ **3 :** to introduce in a forced manner ⟨~*s* my name into the argument⟩ ~ *vi* **1 :** to pull with effort **:** TUG **2 :** to move heavily or by jerks ⟨the car ~*s* on hills⟩ **3** *of a racehorse* **:** to swerve from the course toward or away from the inside rail
[2]**lug** *n* (1616) **1** *archaic* **a :** an act of lugging **b :** something that is lugged **c :** a shipping container for produce **2 :** LUGSAIL **3** *pl* **:** superior airs or affectations ⟨put on ~*s*⟩ **4** *slang* **:** an exaction of money — used in the phrase *put the lug on*
[3]**lug** *n* [ME (Sc) *lugge,* perh. fr. ME *luggen*] (15c) **1 :** something (as a handle) that projects like an ear: as **a :** a leather loop on a harness saddle through which the shaft passes **b :** a metal fitting to which electrical wires are soldered or connected **2** *chiefly Brit* **:** EAR **3 :** a ridge (as on the bottom of a shoe) to increase traction **4 :** a nut used to secure a wheel on an automotive vehicle — called also *lug nut* **5 a :** a big clumsy fellow **b :** an ordinary commonplace person
Lu·gan·da \lü-ˈgän-də, -ˈgan-\ *n* (1889) **:** the Bantu language of the Ganda people
luge \ˈlüzh\ *n* [F] (1905) **:** a small sled that is ridden in a supine position and used esp. in competition; *also* **:** the competition itself — **luge** *vi* — **lug·er** \ˈlü-zhər\ *n*
lug·gage \ˈlə-gij\ *n* (1595) **:** something that is lugged; *esp* **:** suitcases for a traveler's belongings **:** BAGGAGE
lug·ger \ˈlə-gər\ *n* [*lugsail*] (1757) **:** a small fishing or coasting boat that carries one or more lugsails
lug·sail \ˈləg-ˌsāl, -səl\ *n* [perh. fr. [3]*lug*] (1677) **:** a 4-sided sail bent to an obliquely hanging yard that is hoisted and lowered with the sail
lu·gu·bri·ous \lu̇-ˈgü-brē-əs *also* -ˈgyü-\ *adj* [L *lugubris,* fr. *lugēre* to mourn; akin to Gk *lygros* mournful] (1585) **1 :** MOURNFUL; *esp* **:** exaggeratedly or affectedly mournful ⟨dark, dramatic and ~ brooding —V. S. Pritchett⟩ **2 :** DISMAL ⟨a ~ landscape⟩ — **lu·gu·bri·ous·ly** *adv* — **lu·gu·bri·ous·ness** *n*

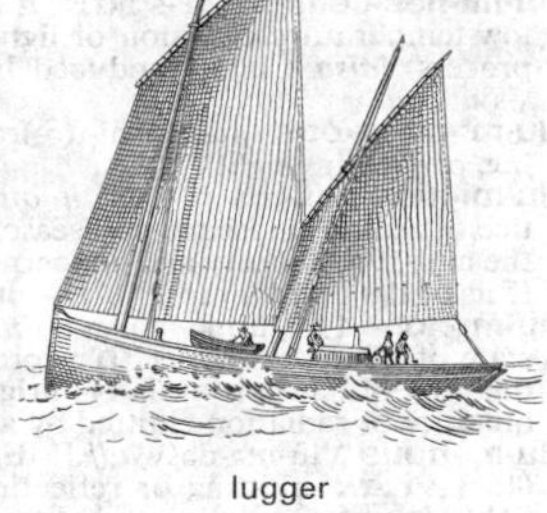
lugger

lug·worm \ˈləg-ˌwərm\ *n* [origin unknown] (1802) **:** any of a genus (*Arenicola*) of marine polychaete worms that have a row of tufted gills along each side of the back and are used for bait
Lukan *var of* LUCAN
Luke \ˈlük\ *n* [L *Lucas,* fr. Gk *Loukas*] (bef. 12c) **1 :** a Gentile physician and companion of the apostle Paul traditionally identified as the author of the third Gospel in the New Testament and of the book of Acts **2 :** the third Gospel in the New Testament — see BIBLE table
luke·warm \ˈlük-ˈwȯrm\ *adj* [ME, fr. *luke* lukewarm + *warm;* prob. akin to OHG *lāo* lukewarm — more at LEE] (14c) **1 :** moderately warm **:** TEPID **2 :** lacking conviction **:** HALFHEARTED ⟨gave them only ~ support⟩ — **luke·warm·ly** *adv* — **luke·warm·ness** *n*
[1]**lull** \ˈləl\ *vt* [ME; prob. of imit. origin] (14c) **1 :** to cause to sleep or rest **:** SOOTHE **2 :** to cause to relax vigilance ⟨were ~*ed* into a false sense of security⟩

\ə\ **abut** \ᵊ\ kitten, F table \ər\ **further** \a\ **ash** \ā\ **ace** \ä\ **mop, mar**
\au̇\ **out** \ch\ **chin** \e\ **bet** \ē\ **easy** \g\ **go** \i\ **hit** \ī\ **ice** \j\ **job**
\ŋ\ **sing** \ō\ **go** \ȯ\ **law** \ȯi\ **boy** \th\ **thin** \t͟h\ **the** \ü\ **loot** \u̇\ **foot**
\y\ **yet** \zh\ **vision, beige** \k̲, ⁿ, œ, ue, ʸ\ *see* Guide to Pronunciation

[2]**lull** *n* (1719) **1** *archaic* : something that lulls; *esp* : LULLABY **2** : a temporary pause or decline in activity ⟨the early-morning ~ in urban noise⟩: as **a** : a temporary calm before or during a storm **b** : a temporary drop in business activity

[1]**lul·la·by** \ˈlə-lə-ˌbī\ *n, pl* **-bies** [obs. E *lulla,* interj. used to lull a child (fr. ME) + *bye,* interj. used to lull a child, fr. ME *by*] (1573) : a soothing refrain; *specif* : a song to quiet children or lull them to sleep

[2]**lullaby** *vt* **-bied; -by·ing** (1576) : to quiet with or as if with a lullaby

lu·lu \ˈlü-(ˌ)lü\ *n* [prob. fr. *Lulu,* nickname fr. *Louise*] (1886) *slang* : one that is remarkable or wonderful ⟨a ~ of a performance⟩

lum \ˈləm\ *n* [origin unknown] (ca. 1628) *chiefly Scot* : CHIMNEY

lu·ma *or* **lou·ma** \ˌlü-ˈmä\ *n, pl* **luma** [Arm *luma, lumay,* lit., small coin, mite, fr. Syriac *lūmā*] (1999) — see *dram* at MONEY table

lum·ba·go \ˌləm-ˈbā-(ˌ)gō\ *n* [L, fr. *lumbus*] (ca. 1693) : acute or chronic pain (as that caused by muscle strain) in the lower back

lum·bar \ˈləm-bər, -ˌbär\ *adj* [NL *lumbaris,* fr. L *lumbus* loin — more at LOIN] (ca. 1656) : of, relating to, or constituting the loins or the vertebrae between the thoracic vertebrae and sacrum ⟨~ region⟩

lumbar puncture *n* (1895) : puncture of the subarachnoid space in the lumbar region of the spinal cord to withdraw cerebrospinal fluid or inject anesthetic drugs

[1]**lum·ber** \ˈləm-bər\ *vi* **lum·bered; lum·ber·ing** \-b(ə-)riŋ\ [ME *lomeren*] (14c) **1** : to move ponderously **2** : RUMBLE

[2]**lumber** *n* [perh. fr. *Lombard;* fr. the use of pawnshops as storehouses of disused property] (1552) **1** : surplus or disused articles (as furniture) that are stored away **2 a** : timber or logs esp. when dressed for use **b** : any of various structural materials prepared in a form similar to lumber — **lumber** *adj*

[3]**lumber** *vb* **lum·bered; lum·ber·ing** \-b(ə-)riŋ\ *vt* (1642) **1** : to clutter with or as if with lumber : ENCUMBER ⟨plan to ~ the tiny town with a giant ski resort —Marilyn Stasio⟩ **2** : to heap together in disorder **3** : to log and saw the timber of ~ *vi* **1** : to cut logs for lumber **2** : to saw logs into lumber for the market — **lum·ber·er** \-bər-ər\ *n*

lum·ber·jack \ˈləm-bər-ˌjak\ *n* (1831) : LOGGER

lum·ber·man \-mən\ *n* (1761) : a person who is engaged in or oversees the business of cutting, processing, and marketing lumber

lumber room *n* (1741) : STOREROOM 1

lum·ber·yard \-ˌyärd\ *n* (1753) : a yard where a stock of lumber is kept for sale

lum·bo·sa·cral \ˌləm-bō-ˈsa-krəl, -ˈsā-\ *adj* (1840) : relating to the lumbar and sacral regions or parts

lu·men \ˈlü-mən\ *n, pl* **lumens** *also* **lu·mi·na** \-mə-nə\ [NL *lumin-, lumen,* fr. L, light, air shaft, opening] (1873) **1** : the cavity of a tubular organ or part ⟨the ~ of a blood vessel⟩ **2** : the bore of a tube (as of a hollow needle or catheter) **3** : a unit of luminous flux equal to the light emitted in a unit solid angle by a uniform point source of one candle intensity — **lu·mi·nal** *also* **lu·men·al** \-mə-nᵊl\ *adj*

lumin- *or* **lumini-** *comb form* [ME *lumin-,* fr. L *lumin-, lumen*] : light ⟨*lumini*ferous⟩

lu·mi·naire \ˌlü-mə-ˈner\ *n* [F, lamp, lighting] (1921) : a complete lighting unit

lu·mi·nance \ˈlü-mə-nən(t)s\ *n* (1867) **1** : the quality or state of being luminous **2** : the luminous intensity of a surface in a given direction per unit of projected area

lu·mi·nar·ia \ˌlü-mə-ˈner-ē-ə\ *n, pl* **-nar·i·as** [Sp, decorative light, fr. LL] (1949) : a traditional Mexican Christmas lantern orig. consisting of a candle set in sand inside a paper bag

lu·mi·nary \ˈlü-mə-ˌner-ē\ *n, pl* **-nar·ies** [ME *luminarye,* fr. AF & LL; AF *luminaire* light, luminary, fr. LL *luminaria,* pl. of *luminare* lamp, heavenly body, fr. L, window, fr. *lumin-, lumen* light; akin to L *lucēre* to shine — more at LIGHT] (15c) **1** : a person of prominence or brilliant achievement **2** : a body that gives light; *esp* : one of the celestial bodies — **luminary** *adj*

lu·mi·nesce \ˌlü-mə-ˈnes\ *vi* **-nesced; -nesc·ing** [back-formation fr. *luminescent*] (1896) : to exhibit luminescence

lu·mi·nes·cence \-ˈne-sᵊn(t)s\ *n* [ISV *lumin-* + *-escence*] (1889) : the low-temperature emission of light (as by a chemical or physiological process); *also* : light produced by luminescence — **lu·mi·nes·cent** \-sᵊnt\ *adj*

lu·mi·nif·er·ous \ˌlü-mə-ˈni-f(ə-)rəs\ *adj* (1801) : transmitting, producing, or yielding light

lu·mi·nism \ˈlü-mə-ˌni-zəm\ *n, often cap* (ca. 1974) : a theory or practice of realist landscape and seascape painting developed in the U.S. in the mid-19th century and concerned with the study and depiction of effects of light and atmosphere — **lu·mi·nist** \-nist\ *n or adj, often cap*

lu·mi·nos·i·ty \ˌlü-mə-ˈnä-sə-tē\ *n, pl* **-ties** (1634) **1 a** : the quality or state of being luminous **b** : something luminous **2 a** : the relative quantity of light **b** : relative brightness of something **3** : the relative quantity of radiation emitted by a celestial source (as a star)

lu·mi·nous \ˈlü-mə-nəs\ *adj* [ME, fr. L *luminosus,* fr. *lumin-, lumen*] (15c) **1 a** : emitting or reflecting usu. steady, suffused, or glowing light **b** : of or relating to light or to luminous flux **2** : bathed in or exposed to steady light ⟨~ with sunlight⟩ **3** : CLEAR, ENLIGHTENING **4** : SHINING, ILLUSTRIOUS ⟨a ~ film star⟩ ⟨a ~ performance⟩ **syn** see BRIGHT — **lu·mi·nous·ly** *adv* — **lu·mi·nous·ness** *n*

luminous energy *n* (1898) : energy transferred in the form of visible radiation

luminous flux *n* (1911) : radiant flux in the visible-wavelength range usu. expressed in lumens instead of watts

luminous paint *n* (1884) : a paint containing a phosphor (as zinc sulfide activated with copper) and so able to glow in the dark

lum·mox \ˈlə-məks, -miks\ *n* [origin unknown] (ca. 1825) : a clumsy person

[1]**lump** \ˈləmp\ *n* [ME] (14c) **1** : a piece or mass of indefinite size and shape **2 a** : AGGREGATE, TOTALITY ⟨taken in the ~⟩ **b** : MAJORITY **3** : PROTUBERANCE; *esp* : an abnormal swelling **4** : a person who is heavy and awkward; *also* : one who is stupid or dull **5** *pl* **a** : BEATINGS, BRUISES ⟨had taken a lot of ~*s* growing up in the city⟩ **b** : DEFEAT, LOSS ⟨can cheerfully take his ~*s* on losers, because the payout is big on the winners —Martin Mayer⟩ — **lump in one's throat** : a constriction of the throat caused by emotion

[2]**lump** *vt* (1624) **1** : to group indiscriminately **2** : to make into lumps; *also* : to make lumps on or in **3** : to move noisily and clumsily ~ *vi* **1** : to become formed into lumps **2** : to move oneself noisily and clumsily

[3]**lump** *adj* (ca. 1700) : not divided into parts : ENTIRE ⟨a ~ sum⟩

[4]**lump** *vt* [origin unknown] (1791) : to put up with ⟨like it or ~ it⟩

lump·ec·to·my \ˌləm-ˈpek-tə-mē\ *n, pl* **-mies** (1972) : excision of a breast tumor with a limited amount of associated tissue

[1]**lum·pen** \ˈlu̇m-pən, ˈləm-\ *adj* [G *Lumpenproletariat* degraded section of the proletariat, fr. *Lump* contemptible person (fr. *Lumpen* rags) + *Proletariat*] (1936) **1** : of or relating to dispossessed and uprooted individuals cut off from the economic and social class with which they might normally be identified ⟨~ proletariat⟩ ⟨~ intellectuals⟩ **2** : PLEBEIAN 2

[2]**lumpen** *n, pl* **lumpen** *also* **lumpens** (1941) : a member of the crude and uneducated lowest class of society

lump·er \ˈləm-pər\ *n* (ca. 1785) **1** : a laborer who handles freight or cargo **2** : one who classifies organisms into large often variable taxonomic groups based on major characters — compare SPLITTER

lump·fish \ˈləmp-ˌfish\ *n* [obs. E *lump* lumpfish (prob. fr. D *lomp* blenny, loach) + E *fish*] (ca. 1620) : a northern Atlantic usu. greenish fish (*Cyclopterus lumpus* of the family Cyclopteridae) having rows of nodules on the body and eggs used as a caviar

lump·ish \ˈləm-pish\ *adj* (1528) **1** : DULL, SLUGGISH **2** *obs* : low in spirits **3** : HEAVY, AWKWARD **4** : LUMPY 1a **5** : tediously slow or dull : BORING; *also* : LUMPY 3 — **lump·ish·ly** *adv* — **lump·ish·ness** *n*

lumpy \ˈləm-pē\ *adj* **lump·i·er; -est** (ca. 1706) **1 a** : filled or covered with lumps **b** : characterized by choppy waves **2** : having a heavy clumsy appearance **3** : uneven and often crude in style — **lump·i·ly** \-pə-lē\ *adv* — **lump·i·ness** \-pē-nəs\ *n*

lumpy jaw *n* (1890) : ACTINOMYCOSIS; *esp* : actinomycosis of the head in cattle

lu·na·cy \ˈlü-nə-sē\ *n, pl* **-cies** [*lunatic*] (1541) **1 a** : INSANITY **b** : intermittent insanity once believed to be related to phases of the moon **2** : wild foolishness : extravagant folly **3** : a foolish act

lu·na moth \ˈlü-nə-\ *n* [NL *luna* (specific epithet of *Actias luna*), fr. L, moon] (1869) : a large mostly pale green American saturniid moth (*Actias luna*) with long tails on the hind wings

lu·nar \ˈlü-nər *also* -ˌnär\ *adj* [ME, fr. L *lunaris,* fr. *luna* moon; akin to L *lucēre* to shine — more at LIGHT] (15c) **1** : CRESCENT, LUNATE **2 a** : of, relating to, or resembling the moon ⟨~ craters⟩ ⟨a ~ landscape⟩ **b** : designed for use on the moon ⟨~ vehicles⟩ **3** : measured by the moon's revolution ⟨~ month⟩

lunar caustic *n* [obs. *luna* silver, fr. ML, fr. L, moon] (1751) : silver nitrate esp. when fused and molded into sticks for use as a caustic

lunar eclipse *n* (1667) : an eclipse in which the full moon passes partially or wholly through the umbra of the earth's shadow

lunar module *n* (1967) : a space vehicle module designed to carry astronauts from the command module to the surface of the moon and back — called also *lunar excursion module*

lu·nate \ˈlü-ˌnāt\ *adj* [L *lunatus,* pp. of *lunare* to bend in a crescent, fr. *luna*] (ca. 1777) : shaped like a crescent

lu·na·tic \ˈlü-nə-ˌtik\ *adj* [ME *lunatik,* fr. AF or LL; AF *lunatic,* fr. LL *lunaticus,* fr. L *luna;* fr. the belief that lunacy fluctuated with the phases of the moon] (14c) **1 a** : affected with lunacy : INSANE **b** : designed for the care of insane persons ⟨~ asylum⟩ **2** : wildly foolish ⟨a ~ idea⟩ — **lunatic** *n*

lunatic fringe *n* (1913) : the members of a usu. political or social movement espousing extreme, eccentric, or fanatical views

lu·na·tion \lü-ˈnā-shən\ *n* [ME *lunacioun,* fr. AF *lunaison,* fr. ML *lunation-, lunatio,* fr. L *luna*] (14c) : the period of time averaging 29 days, 12 hours, 44 minutes, and 2.8 seconds elapsing between two successive new moons

[1]**lunch** \ˈlənch\ *n* [prob. short for *luncheon*] (1812) **1** : a usu. light meal; *esp* : one taken in the middle of the day **2** : the food prepared for a lunch — **out to lunch** *slang* : out of touch with reality

[2]**lunch** *vi* (1811) : to eat lunch ~ *vt* : to treat to lunch — **lunch·er** *n*

lunch–buck·et \ˈlənch-ˌbə-kət\ *adj* (1956) : of, relating to, or possessing working-class values : BLUE-COLLAR ⟨~ issues⟩ ⟨a ~ athlete⟩

lunch counter *n* (1869) **1** : a long counter at which lunches are sold **2** : LUNCHEONETTE

lun·cheon \ˈlən-chən\ *n* [perh. alter. of *nuncheon* light snack, alter. of ME *nonshench* midday refreshment, fr. *non* noon + *schench* drink] (ca. 1652) : LUNCH; *esp* : a formal usu. midday meal as part of a meeting or for entertaining a guest

lun·cheon·ette \ˌlən-chə-ˈnet\ *n* (1913) : a small restaurant serving light lunches

lunch·room \ˈlənch-ˌrüm, -ˌru̇m\ *n* (1830) **1** : LUNCHEONETTE **2** : a room (as in a school) where lunches supplied on the premises or brought from home may be eaten

lunch·time \-ˌtīm\ *n* (1859) : the time at which lunch is usu. eaten : NOON

lune \ˈlün\ *n* [L *luna* moon — more at LUNAR] (ca. 1704) : the part of a plane surface bounded by two intersecting arcs or of a spherical surface bounded by two great circles

lunes \ˈlünz\ *n pl* [F, pl. of *lune* crazy whim, fr. MF, moon, crazy whim, fr. L *luna*] (1601) : fits of lunacy

lu·nette \lü-ˈnet\ *n* [F, fr. OF *lunete* small object shaped like the moon, fr. *lune* moon] (ca. 1639) **1** : something that has the shape of a crescent or half-moon: as **a** : an opening in a vault esp. for a window **b** : the surface at the upper part of a wall that is partly surrounded by a vault which the wall intersects and that is often filled by windows or by mural painting **c** : a low crescentic mound (as of sand) formed by the wind **2** : the figure or shape of a crescent moon

lung \ˈləŋ\ *n* [ME *lunge,* fr. OE *lungen;* akin to OHG *lungun* lung, *līhti* light in weight — more at LIGHT] (bef. 12c) **1 a** : one of the usu. paired compound saccular thoracic organs that constitute the basic respiratory organ of air-breathing vertebrates **b** : any of various respiratory organs of invertebrates **2 a** : a device enabling individuals abandoning a submarine to rise to the surface **b** : a mechanical device for regularly introducing fresh air into and withdrawing stale air from the lung : RESPIRATOR — compare IRON LUNG — **lung·ful** \-ˌfu̇l\ *n*

[1]**lunge** \ˈlənj\ *n* [modif. of F *allonge* extension, reach, fr. OF *alonge,* fr. *alongier* to lengthen, fr. VL *allongare, fr. L *ad-* ad- + LL *longare,* fr. L *longus* long] (1748) **1** : a quick thrust or jab (as of a sword) usu. made

by leaning or striding forward   **2 :** a sudden forward rush or reach ⟨made a ~ to catch the ball⟩

²**lunge** *vb* **lunged; lung·ing** *vi* (1772) **:** to make a lunge **:** move with or as if with a lunge ~ *vt* **:** to thrust or propel (as a blow) in a lunge

lunged \'ləŋd\ *adj* (1693) **1 :** having lungs **:** PULMONATE   **2 :** having a lung or lungs of a specified kind or number — used in combination ⟨one-*lunged*⟩

¹**lung·er** \'ləŋ-jər\ *n* (1842) **:** one that lunges

²**lung·er** \'ləŋ-ər\ *n* (1893) **:** a person suffering from a chronic disease of the lungs; *esp* **:** one who is tubercular

lung·fish \'ləŋ-ˌfish\ *n* (1883) **:** any of an order (Dipnoi) of bony fishes that breathe by a modified swim bladder as well as gills

lungfish

lung·worm \-ˌwərm\ *n* (1882) **:** any of various nematodes that infest the lungs and air passages of mammals

lung·wort \-ˌwərt, -ˌwȯrt\ *n* (bef. 12c) **:** any of several plants (as a mullein) formerly used in the treatment of respiratory disorders; *esp* **:** a European herb (*Pulmonaria officinalis*) of the borage family with hispid leaves and usu. bluish flowers

lu·ni·so·lar \ˌlü-ni-'sō-lər *also* -ˌlär\ *adj* [L *luna* moon + E *-i-* + *solar*] (1691) **:** relating or attributed to the moon and the sun

lun·ker \'ləŋ-kər\ *n* [origin unknown] (1867) **:** something large of its kind — used *esp.* of a game fish

lunk·head \'ləŋk-ˌhed\ *n* [prob. alter. of *lump* + *head*] (1868) **:** a stupid person **:** DOLT — **lunk·head·ed** \-ˌhed-əd\ *adj*

lu·nule \'lü-(ˌ)nyül\ *n* [NL *lunula*, fr. L crescent-shaped ornament, fr. dim. of *luna* moon] (1828) **:** a crescent-shaped body part or marking (as the whitish mark at the base of a fingernail)

lu·pa·nar \lü-'pä-nər, -'pä-\ *n* [L, fr. *lupa* prostitute, lit., she-wolf, fem. of *lupus*] (1864) **:** BORDELLO

Lu·per·ca·lia \ˌlü-pər-'kā-lē-ə, -'käl-yə\ *n* [L, pl., fr. *Lupercus*, god of flocks] (ca. 1580) **:** an ancient Roman festival celebrated February 15 to ensure fertility for the people, fields, and flocks — **Lu·per·ca·lian** \-'kā-lē-ən, -'käl-yən\ *adj*

¹**lu·pine** *also* **lu·pin** \'lü-pən\ *n* [ME, fr. AF, fr. L *lupinus, lupinum*, fr. *lupinus*, adj.] (14c) **:** any of a genus (*Lupinus*) of leguminous herbs including some poisonous forms and others cultivated for their long showy racemes of usu. blue, purple, white, or yellow flowers or for green manure, fodder, or their edible seeds; *also* **:** an edible lupine seed

²**lu·pine** \-ˌpīn\ *adj* [L *lupinus*, fr. *lupus* wolf — more at WOLF] (1660) **:** WOLFISH

lu·pus \'lü-pəs\ *n* [ME, fr. ML, fr. L, wolf] (14c) **:** any of several diseases characterized by skin lesions; *esp* **:** SYSTEMIC LUPUS ERYTHEMATOSUS

lupus er·y·the·ma·to·sus \-ˌer-ə-ˌthē-mə-'tō-səs\ *n* [NL, lit., erythematous lupus] (1860) **:** a disorder characterized by skin inflammation; *esp* **:** SYSTEMIC LUPUS ERYTHEMATOSUS

¹**lurch** \'lərch\ *vb* [ME *lorchen*, prob. alter. of *lurken* to lurk] *vi* (15c) *dial chiefly Eng* **:** to loiter about a place furtively **:** PROWL ~ *vt* **1** *obs* **:** STEAL   **2** *archaic* **:** CHEAT

²**lurch** *n* [MF *lourche*, adj., defeated by a lurch, deceived] (1598) **:** a decisive defeat in which an opponent wins a game by more than double the defeated player's score esp. in cribbage — **in the lurch :** in a vulnerable and unsupported position

³**lurch** *vt* (ca. 1651) **1** *archaic* **:** to leave in the lurch   **2 :** to defeat by a lurch (as in cribbage)

⁴**lurch** *n* [origin unknown] (1805) **1 :** a sudden roll of a ship to one side   **2 :** an abrupt jerking, swaying, or tipping movement ⟨the car moved forward with a ~⟩; *also* **:** STAGGER 2

⁵**lurch** *vi* (ca. 1828) **1 :** to roll or tip abruptly **:** PITCH   **2 :** to move with a lurch ⟨suddenly ~*ed* forward⟩; *also* **:** STAGGER ⟨has ~*ed* from crisis to crisis —Jere Longman⟩

lurch·er \'lər-chər\ *n* [¹*lurch*] (1528) **1** *archaic* **:** a petty thief **:** PILFERER   **2** *Brit* **:** a crossbred dog; *esp* **:** one that resembles a greyhound   **3** *archaic* **:** one who lurks; *also* **:** SPY

lur·dane \'lər-dᵊn\ *n* [ME *lurdan*, fr. AF **lurdin*, fr. *lurd* dull, stupid, fr. L *luridus* lurid] (14c) *archaic* **:** a lazy stupid person — **lurdane** *adj*

¹**lure** \'lu̇r\ *n* [ME, fr. AF *lure, leure*, of Gmc origin; akin to MHG *luoder* bait; perh. akin to OE *lathian* to invite, OHG *ladōn*] (14c) **1 :** an object usu. of leather or feathers attached to a long cord and used by a falconer to recall or exercise a hawk   **2 a :** an inducement to pleasure or gain **:** ENTICEMENT   **b :** APPEAL, ATTRACTION   **3 :** a decoy for attracting animals to capture: as   **a :** artificial bait used for catching fish   **b :** an often luminous structure on the head of pediculate fishes that is used to attract prey

²**lure** *vt* **lured; lur·ing** (14c) **1 :** to recall or exercise (a hawk) by means of a lure   **2 :** to draw with a hint of pleasure or gain **:** attract actively and strongly

syn LURE, ENTICE, INVEIGLE, DECOY, TEMPT, SEDUCE mean to lead astray from one's true course. LURE implies a drawing into danger, evil, or difficulty through attracting and deceiving ⟨*lured* naive investors with get-rich-quick schemes⟩. ENTICE suggests drawing by artful or adroit means ⟨advertising designed to *entice* new customers⟩. INVEIGLE implies enticing by cajoling or flattering ⟨fund-raisers *inveigling* wealthy alumni⟩. DECOY implies a luring into entrapment by artifice ⟨attempting to *decoy* the enemy into an ambush⟩. TEMPT implies the presenting of an attraction so strong that it overcomes the restraints of conscience or better judgment ⟨*tempted* by the offer of money⟩. SEDUCE implies a leading astray by persuasion or false promises ⟨*seduced* by assurances of assistance⟩.

Lur·ex \'lu̇r-eks\ *trademark* — used for metallic yarn or thread

lu·rid \'lu̇r-əd\ *adj* [L *luridus* pale yellow, sallow] (1603) **1 a :** causing horror or revulsion **:** GRUESOME   **b :** MELODRAMATIC, SENSATIONAL; *also* **:** SHOCKING ⟨paperbacks in the usual ~ covers —T. R. Fyvel⟩   **2 a :** wan and ghastly pale in appearance   **b :** of any of several light or medium grayish colors ranging in hue from yellow to orange   **3 :** shining with the red glow of fire seen through smoke or cloud *syn* see GHASTLY — **lu·rid·ly** *adv* — **lu·rid·ness** *n*

lurk \'lərk\ *vi* [ME; akin to MHG *lüren* to lie in wait — more at LOWER] (14c) **1 a :** to lie in wait in a place of concealment esp. for an evil purpose   **b :** to move furtively or inconspicuously   **c :** to persist in staying   **2 a :** to be concealed but capable of being discovered; *specif* **:** to constitute a latent threat   **b :** to lie hidden   **3 :** to read messages on an Internet discussion forum (as a newsgroup or chat room) without contributing — **lurk·er** *n*

syn LURK, SKULK, SLINK, SNEAK mean to behave so as to escape attention. LURK implies a lying in wait in a place of concealment and often suggests an evil intent ⟨suspicious men *lurking* in alleyways⟩. SKULK suggests more strongly cowardice or fear or sinister intent ⟨something *skulking* in the shadows⟩. SLINK implies moving stealthily often merely to escape attention ⟨*slunk* around the corner⟩. SNEAK may add an implication of entering or leaving a place or evading a difficulty by furtive or underhanded methods ⟨*sneaked* out early⟩.

lus·cious \'lə-shəs\ *adj* [ME *lucius*, perh. alter. of *licius*, short for *delicious*] (15c) **1 a :** having a delicious taste or smell **:** SWEET   **b** *archaic* **:** excessively sweet **:** CLOYING   **2 :** sexually attractive **:** SEDUCTIVE, SEXY   **3 a :** richly luxurious or appealing to the senses   **b :** excessively ornate — **lus·cious·ly** *adv* — **lus·cious·ness** *n*

¹**lush** \'ləsh\ *adj* [ME *lusch* soft, tender] (1610) **1 a :** growing vigorously esp. with luxuriant foliage ⟨~ grass⟩   **b :** lavishly productive: as   (1) **:** FERTILE   (2) **:** THRIVING   (3) **:** characterized by abundance **:** PLENTIFUL   (4) **:** PROSPEROUS, PROFITABLE   **2 a :** SAVORY, DELICIOUS   **b :** appealing to the senses ⟨the ~ sounds of the orchestra⟩   **c :** OPULENT, SUMPTUOUS ⟨~ accommodations⟩ *syn* see PROFUSE — **lush·ly** *adv* — **lush·ness** *n*

²**lush** *n* [origin unknown] (ca. 1790) **1** *slang* **:** intoxicating liquor **:** DRINK   **2 :** a habitual heavy drinker **:** DRUNKARD

³**lush** *vb* (ca. 1811) *slang* **:** DRINK

Lu·so- \'lü-(ˌ)sō\ *comb form* [Pg, fr. *lusitano* Portuguese, fr. L *Lusitanus* of Lusitania (ancient region corresponding approximately to modern Portugal)] **:** Portuguese and ⟨*Luso*-Brazilian⟩

¹**lust** \'ləst\ *n* [ME, fr. OE; akin to OHG *lust* pleasure and perh. to L *lascivus* wanton] (bef. 12c) **1 a :** PLEASURE, DELIGHT   **b :** personal inclination **:** WISH   **2 :** usu. intense or unbridled sexual desire **:** LASCIVIOUSNESS   **3 a :** an intense longing **:** CRAVING ⟨a ~ to succeed⟩   **b :** ENTHUSIASM, EAGERNESS ⟨admired his ~ for life⟩

²**lust** *vi* (12c) **:** to have an intense desire or need **:** CRAVE; *specif* **:** to have a sexual urge

¹**lus·ter** *or* **lus·tre** \'ləs-tər\ *n* [ME *lustre*, fr. L *lustrum*] (14c) **:** a period of five years **:** LUSTRUM 2

²**luster** *or* **lustre** *n* [MF *lustre*, fr. OIt *lustro*, fr. *lustrare* to brighten, fr. L, to purify ceremonially, fr. *lustrum*] (ca. 1522) **1 a :** a glow of reflected light **:** SHEEN; *specif* **:** the appearance of the surface of a mineral dependent upon its reflecting qualities   **2 a :** a glow of light from within **:** LUMINOSITY   **b :** an inner beauty **:** RADIANCE   **3 :** a superficial attractiveness or appearance of excellence   **4 a :** a glass pendant used esp. to ornament a candlestick or chandelier   **b :** a decorative object (as a chandelier) hung with glass pendants   **5** *chiefly Brit* **:** a fabric with cotton warp and a filling of wool, mohair, or alpaca   **6 :** LUSTERWARE — **lus·ter·less** \-tər-ləs\ *adj*

³**luster** *or* **lustre** *vb* **lus·tered** *or* **lus·tred; lus·ter·ing** *or* **lus·tring** \-t(ə-)riŋ\ *vi* (1528) **:** to have luster **:** GLEAM ~ *vt* **1 :** to give luster or distinction to   **2 :** to coat or treat with a substance that imparts luster

lus·ter·ware \'ləs-tər-ˌwer\ *n* (1825) **:** pottery with an iridescent metallic sheen in the glaze

lust·ful \'ləst-fəl\ *adj* (14c) **:** excited by lust **:** LECHEROUS — **lust·ful·ly** \-fə-lē\ *adv* — **lust·ful·ness** *n*

lust·i·hood \'ləs-tē-ˌhu̇d\ *n* (1599) **1 :** vigor of body or spirit **:** ROBUSTNESS   **2 :** sexual inclination or capacity

lus·tral \'ləs-trəl\ *adj* [L *lustralis*, fr. *lustrum*] (1533) **:** PURIFICATORY

lus·trate \'ləs-ˌtrāt\ *vt* **lus·trat·ed; lus·trat·ing** [L *lustratus*, pp. of *lustrare*] (1653) **:** to purify ceremonially — **lus·tra·tion** \ˌləs-'trā-shən\ *n*

¹**lus·tring** \'ləs-triŋ\ *n* [modif. of It *lustrino*] (1697) *archaic* **:** LUTESTRING

²**lus·tring** \'ləs-t(ə-)riŋ\ *n* [*lustring*, gerund of ³*luster*] (ca. 1889) **:** a finishing process (as calendering) for giving a gloss to yarns and cloth

lus·trous \'ləs-trəs\ *adj* (1601) **1 :** reflecting light evenly and efficiently without glitter or sparkle ⟨a ~ satin⟩ ⟨the ~ glow of an opal⟩   **2 :** radiant in character or reputation **:** ILLUSTRIOUS *syn* see BRIGHT — **lus·trous·ly** *adv* — **lus·trous·ness** *n*

lus·trum \'ləs-trəm\ *n, pl* **lustrums** *or* **lus·tra** \-trə\ [L] (1590) **1 :** a period of five years   **2 a :** a purification of the whole Roman people made in ancient times after the census every five years   **b :** the Roman census

lusty \'ləs-tē\ *adj* **lust·i·er; -est** (13c) **1** *archaic* **:** MERRY, JOYOUS   **2 :** LUSTFUL ⟨~ passion⟩   **3 a :** full of strength and vitality **:** HEALTHY, VIGOROUS ⟨a young, ~ growing country —Helen Harris⟩   **b :** HEARTY, ROBUST ⟨a ~ beef stew⟩   **c :** ENTHUSIASTIC, ROUSING ⟨a ~ rendition of the song⟩ *syn* see VIGOROUS — **lust·i·ly** \-tə-lē\ *adv* — **lust·i·ness** \-tē-nəs\ *n*

¹**lute** \'lüt\ *n* [ME, fr. MF *lut*, fr. Old Occitan *laut*, fr. Ar *al-'ūd*, lit., the wood] (13c) **:** a stringed instrument having a large pear-shaped body, a vaulted back, a fretted fingerboard, and a head with tuning pegs which is often angled backward from the neck

²**lute** *vt* **lut·ed; lut·ing** [ME, fr. L *lutare*, fr. *lutum* mud — more at POLLUTE] (14c) **:** to seal or cover (as a joint or surface) with lute

³**lute** *n* (15c) **:** a substance (as cement or clay) for packing a joint or coating a porous surface to make it impervious to gas or liquid

lute- *or* **luteo-** *comb form* [NL (*corpus*) *luteum*] **:** corpus luteum ⟨*lute*al⟩

lu·te·al \'lü-tē-əl\ *adj* (1920) **:** of, relating to, or involving the corpus luteum or its formation ⟨the ~ phase of the menstrual cycle⟩

lute·fisk \'lüt-ˌfisk, 'lüt-ə-\ *n* [Norw, fr. *lute* to wash in lye solution + *fisk* fish] (1924) **:** dried codfish that has been soaked in a water and lye solution before cooking

\ə\ abut \ᵊ\ kitten, F table \ər\ further \a\ ash \ā\ ace \ä\ mop, mar
\au̇\ out \ch\ chin \e\ bet \ē\ easy \g\ go \i\ hit \ī\ ice \j\ job
\ŋ\ sing \ō\ go \ȯ\ law \ȯi\ boy \th\ thin \th\ the \ü\ loot \u̇\ foot
\y\ yet \zh\ vision, beige \k, ⁿ, œ, ᵫ, �\ *see* Guide to Pronunciation

lu·tein \ˈlü-tē-ən, ˈlü-ˌtēn\ *n* (1869) : an orange xanthophyll $C_{40}H_{56}O_2$ occurring in plants, animal fat, egg yolk, and the corpus luteum

lu·tein·i·za·tion \ˌlü-tē-ə-nə-ˈzā-shən, ˌlü-ˌtē-nə-\ *n* (1929) : the process of forming corpora lutea — **lu·tein·ize** \ˈlü-tē-ə-ˌnīz, ˈlü-ˌtē-ˌnīz\ *vb*

luteinizing hormone *n* (1931) : a hormone secreted by the anterior lobe of the pituitary gland that in the female stimulates ovulation and the development of corpora lutea and in the male the development of interstitial tissue in the testis

luteinizing hormone–releasing factor *n* (1964) : GONADOTROPIN-RELEASING HORMONE

luteinizing hormone–releasing hormone *n* (1970) : GONADOTROPIN-RELEASING HORMONE

lu·te·nist *or* **lu·ta·nist** \ˈlü-tə-nist, ˈlüt-nist\ *n* [ML *lutanista,* fr. *lutana* lute, prob. fr. MF *lut* lute] (1600) : a lute player

lu·teo·tro·pic \ˌlü-tē-ə-ˈtrō-pik, -ˈträ-\ *or* **lu·teo·tro·phic** \-ˈtrō-fik, -ˈträ-\ *adj* (1941) : acting on the corpora lutea

luteotropic hormone *or* **luteotrophic hormone** *n* (1949) : PROLACTIN

lu·teo·tro·pin \ˌlü-tē-ə-ˈtrō-pən\ *or* **lu·teo·tro·phin** \-fən\ *n* (1941) : PROLACTIN

lu·te·ous \ˈlü-tē-əs\ *adj* [L *luteus* yellow, fr. *lutum,* a plant (*Reseda luteola*) used for dyeing yellow] (1657) : yellow tinged with green or brown

lute·string \ˈlüt-(ˌ)striŋ\ *n* [by folk etymology fr. It *lustrino* glossy fabric, fr. *lustro* luster] (1661) : a plain glossy silk formerly much used for women's dresses and ribbons

lu·te·tium \lü-ˈtē-sh(ē-)əm\ *n* [NL, fr. L *Lutetia,* ancient name of Paris] (1907) : a metallic element of the rare-earth group — see ELEMENT table

[1]**Lu·ther·an** \ˈlü-th(ə-)rən\ *n* (1521) : a member of a Lutheran church

[2]**Lutheran** *adj* (1530) **1 :** of or relating to religious doctrines (as justification by faith alone) developed by Martin Luther or his followers **2 :** of or relating to the Protestant churches adhering to Lutheran doctrines, liturgy, and polity — **Lu·ther·an·ism** \-rə-ˌni-zəm\ *n*

lu·thi·er \ˈlü-tē-ər, -thē-ər\ *n* [F, fr. *luth* lute (fr. MF *lut*)] (1879) : one who makes stringed musical instruments (as violins or guitars)

lutz \ˈləts\ *n* [prob. irreg. fr. Gustave *Lussi* †1993 Am. (Swiss-born) figure skating coach] (1938) : a backward figure-skating jump with a takeoff from the outside edge of one skate followed by a full turn in the air and a landing on the outside edge of the other skate

Lu·wi·an \ˈlü-ē-ən\ *n* [*Luwi,* an ancient people of the southern coast of Asia Minor] (1924) : an Anatolian language of the Indo-European language family — see INDO-EUROPEAN LANGUAGES table — **Luwian** *adj*

lux \ˈləks\ *n, pl* **lux** *or* **lux·es** [L, light — more at LIGHT] (1889) : a unit of illumination equal to the direct illumination on a surface that is everywhere one meter from a uniform point source of one candle intensity or equal to one lumen per square meter

lux·a·tion \ˌlək-ˈsā-shən\ *n* [LL *luxation-, luxatio,* fr. L *luxare* to dislocate, fr. *luxus* dislocated — more at LOCK] (1552) : dislocation of an anatomical part (as a bone at a joint or the lens of the eye)

luxe \ˈlüks, ˈləks, ˈlüks\ *adj* [F, fr. L *luxus* — more at LUXURY] (1888) : LUXURIOUS, SUMPTUOUS — **luxe** *n*

lux·u·ri·ance \(ˌ)ləg-ˈzhu̇r-ē-ən(t)s, (ˌ)lək-ˈshu̇r-\ *n* (1654) : the quality or state of being luxuriant

lux·u·ri·ant \-ē-ənt\ *adj* (ca. 1540) **1 a :** yielding abundantly : FERTILE, FRUITFUL **b :** characterized by abundant growth : LUSH ⟨~ vegetation⟩ **2 :** abundantly and often extravagantly rich and varied : PROLIFIC **3 :** characterized by luxury : LUXURIOUS ⟨a ~ fabric⟩ *syn* see PROFUSE — **lux·u·ri·ant·ly** *adv*

lux·u·ri·ate \-ē-ˌāt\ *vi* **-at·ed; -at·ing** [L *luxuriatus,* pp. of *luxuriare,* fr. *luxuria*] (1604) **1 a :** to grow profusely : THRIVE **b :** to develop extensively **2 :** to indulge oneself luxuriously : REVEL

lux·u·ri·ous \(ˌ)ləg-ˈzhu̇r-ē-əs, (ˌ)lək-ˈshu̇r-\ *adj* (14c) **1 :** LECHEROUS **2 :** marked by or given to self-indulgence ⟨~ tastes⟩ ⟨~ feeling⟩ **3 :** of, relating to, or marked by luxury ⟨~ accommodations⟩ **4 :** of the finest and richest kind ⟨~ cashmeres⟩ ⟨a ~ chocolate sauce⟩ *syn* see SENSUOUS — **lux·u·ri·ous·ly** *adv* — **lux·u·ri·ous·ness** *n*

lux·u·ry \ˈlək-sh(ə-)rē, -zh(ə-)rē\ *n, pl* **-ries** [ME *luxurie,* fr. AF *luxorie,* fr. L *luxuria* rankness, luxury, excess; akin to L *luxus* luxury, excess] (14c) **1** *archaic* : LECHERY, LUST **2 :** a condition of abundance or great ease and comfort : sumptuous environment ⟨lived in ~⟩ **3 a :** something adding to pleasure or comfort but not absolutely necessary ⟨one of life's *luxuries*⟩ **b :** an indulgence in something that provides pleasure, satisfaction, or ease ⟨had the ~ of rejecting a handful of job offers —Terri Minsky⟩ — **luxury** *adj*

luxury box *n* (1980) : SKYBOX

lv *abbr* leave

LVN *abbr* licensed vocational nurse

LVT *abbr* landing vehicle, tracked

LW *abbr* low water

lwei \lə-ˈwā\ *n, pl* **lwei** *also* **lweis** [prob. fr. *Lwei* (Lué), name of several rivers in Angola] (ca. 1977) — see *kwanza* at MONEY table

LWM *abbr* low-water mark

LWV *abbr* League of Women Voters

lx *abbr* lux

ly- *or* **lyo-** *comb form* [ISV, fr. Gk *lyein* to loosen, dissolve — more at LOSE] **1 :** degrading : reduction ⟨*ly*ase⟩ **2 :** dispersed state : dispersion ⟨*lyo*philic⟩

[1]**-ly** \lē; *in some dialects, esp Brit, Southern, NewEng, often* li *but not shown at individual entries*\ *adj suffix* [ME, fr. OE *-līc, -lic;* akin to OHG *-līh, -lic,* OE *līc* body — more at LIKE] **1 :** like in appearance, manner, or nature : having the characteristics of ⟨queen*ly*⟩ ⟨father*ly*⟩ **2 :** characterized by regular recurrence in (specified) units of time : every ⟨hour*ly*⟩ ⟨week*ly*⟩

[2]**-ly** *adv suffix* [ME, fr. OE *-līce, -lice,* fr. *-līc,* adj. suffix] **1 a :** in a (specified) manner ⟨slow*ly*⟩ **b :** at a (specified) time interval ⟨annual*ly*⟩ **2 :** from a (specified) point of view ⟨eschatological*ly*⟩ **3 :** with respect to ⟨part*ly*⟩ **4 :** to a (specified) degree ⟨relative*ly*⟩ **5 :** in a (specified) place in a series ⟨second*ly*⟩

ly·am–hound \ˈlī-əm-ˌhau̇nd\ *or* **lyme–hound** \ˈlīm-ˌhau̇nd\ *n* [obs. *lyam* leash] (1527) *archaic* : BLOODHOUND

ly·art \ˈlī-ərt\ *adj* [ME, fr. AF *liart*] (14c) *chiefly Scot* : streaked with gray : GRAY

ly·ase \ˈlī-ˌās, -ˌāz\ *n* (1961) : an enzyme (as a decarboxylase) that forms double bonds by removing groups from a substrate other than by hydrolysis or that adds groups to double bonds

ly·can·thro·py \lī-ˈkan(t)-thrə-pē\ *n* [NL *lycanthropia,* fr. Gk *lykanthrōpia,* fr. *lykanthrōpos* werewolf, fr. *lykos* wolf + *anthrōpos* human being — more at WOLF] (1594) **1 :** a delusion that one has become a wolf **2 :** the assumption of the form and characteristics of a wolf held to be possible by witchcraft or magic — **ly·can·throp·ic** \ˌlī-kən-ˈthrä-pik\ *adj*

ly·cée \lē-ˈsā\ *n* [F, fr. MF, lyceum, fr. L *Lyceum*] (1865) : a French public secondary school that prepares students for the university

ly·ce·um \lī-ˈsē-əm, ˈlī-sē-\ *n* [L *Lyceum,* gymnasium near Athens where Aristotle taught, fr. Gk *Lykeion,* fr. neut. of *lykeios,* epithet of Apollo] (1786) **1 :** a hall for public lectures or discussions **2 :** an association providing public lectures, concerts, and entertainments **3 :** LYCÉE

ly·chee *or* **li·tchi** *also* **li·chee** \ˈlē-(ˌ)chē, ˈlī-\ *n* [Chin (Beijing) *lìzhī*] (1588) **1 :** the oval fruit of a Chinese tree (*Litchi chinensis*) of the soapberry family having a hard scaly reddish outer covering and sweet whitish edible flesh that surrounds a single large seed — called also *lychee nut* **2 :** a tree bearing lychees

lych–gate *also* **lich–gate** \ˈlich-ˌgāt\ *n* [ME *lycheyate,* fr. *lich* body, corpse (fr. OE *līc*) + *gate, yate* gate] (15c) : a roofed gate in a churchyard under which a bier rests during the initial part of the burial service

lych·nis \ˈlik-nəs\ *n* [NL, fr. L, a red flower, fr. Gk; akin to Gk *lychnos* lamp, L *lux* light — more at LIGHT] (1601) : any of a genus (*Lychnis*) of north-temperate zone herbs of the pink family with terminal cymes of showy mostly red or white flowers having five or rarely four styles

Ly·cian \ˈli-sh(ē-)ən\ *n* (1583) **1 :** a native or inhabitant of Lycia **2 :** an Anatolian language of the Indo-European language family — see INDO-EUROPEAN LANGUAGES table — **Lycian** *adj*

ly·co·pene \ˈlī-kə-ˌpēn\ *n* [ISV *lycop-* (fr. NL *Lycopersicon,* genus of herbs) + *-ene*] (ca. 1929) : a carotenoid pigment $C_{40}H_{56}$ that is the red coloring matter of the tomato

ly·co·pod \ˈlī-kə-ˌpäd\ *n* [NL *Lycopodium*] (1861) : LYCOPODIUM 1; *broadly* : CLUB MOSS

ly·co·po·di·um \ˌlī-kə-ˈpō-dē-əm\ *n* [NL, fr. Gk *lykos* wolf + *podion,* dim. of *pod-, pous* foot — more at FOOT] (ca. 1706) **1 :** any of a large genus (*Lycopodium*) of erect or creeping club mosses with reduced or scalelike evergreen leaves **2 :** a fine yellowish flammable powder composed of lycopodium spores and used esp. in pharmacy

Ly·cra \ˈlī-krə\ *trademark* — used for a spandex synthetic fiber

lydd·ite \ˈli-ˌdīt\ *n* [*Lydd,* England] (1888) : a high explosive composed chiefly of picric acid

Lyd·i·an \ˈli-dē-ən\ *n* (15c) **1 :** a native or inhabitant of Lydia **2 :** an Anatolian language of the Indo-European language family — see INDO-EUROPEAN LANGUAGES table — **Lydian** *adj*

lye \ˈlī\ *n* [ME, fr. OE *lēag;* akin to OHG *louga* lye, L *lavare, lavere* to wash, Gk *louein*] (bef. 12c) **1 :** a strong alkaline liquor rich in potassium carbonate leached from wood ashes and used esp. in making soap and for washing; *broadly* : a strong alkaline solution (as of sodium hydroxide or potassium hydroxide) **2 :** a solid caustic (as sodium hydroxide)

ly·gus bug \ˈlī-gəs-\ *n* [NL *Lygus*] (1936) : any of various small sucking bugs (genus *Lygus*) including some pests of cultivated plants

[1]**lying** *pres part of* LIE

[2]**lying** *adj* [ME *leghynge,* prp. of *lien* to lie] (14c) : marked by or containing falsehoods : FALSE ⟨a ~ account of the accident⟩

ly·ing–in \ˌlī-iŋ-ˈin\ *n, pl* **lyings–in** *or* **lying–ins** (15c) : the state attending and consequent to childbirth : CONFINEMENT

Lyme disease \ˈlīm-\ *n* [*Lyme,* Connecticut, where it was first reported] (1979) : an acute inflammatory disease that is caused by a spirochete (*Borrelia burgdorferi*) transmitted by ticks (genus *Ixodes* and esp. *I. dammini*), that is usu. characterized initially by a spreading red annular erythematous skin lesion and by fatigue, fever, and chills, and that if left untreated may later manifest itself in joint pain, arthritis, and cardiac and neurological disorders — called also *Lyme*

lymph \ˈlim(p)f\ *n* [L *lympha,* water goddess, water, perh. modif. of Gk *nymphē* nymph — more at NUPTIAL] (ca. 1673) **1** *archaic* : the sap of plants **2** [NL *lympha,* fr. L, water] : a usu. clear coagulable fluid that passes from intercellular spaces of body tissue into the lymphatic vessels, is discharged into the blood by way of the thoracic duct, and resembles blood plasma in containing white blood cells and esp. lymphocytes but normally few red blood cells and no platelets

lymph- *or* **lympho-** *comb form* [NL *lympha*] : lymph : lymphatic tissue ⟨*lympho*granuloma⟩

lymph·ad·e·ni·tis \ˌlim-ˌfa-də-ˈnī-təs\ *n* [NL, fr. *lymphaden* lymph gland, fr. *lymph-* + Gk *adēn* gland — more at ADEN-] (1860) : inflammation of lymph nodes

lymph·ade·nop·a·thy \ˌlim-ˌfa-də-ˈnä-pə-thē\ *n, pl* **-thies** (1920) : abnormal enlargement of the lymph nodes

lymph·an·gi·og·ra·phy \ˌlim-ˌfan-jē-ˈä-grə-fē\ *n* (ca. 1941) : X-ray depiction of lymph vessels and nodes after use of a radiopaque material — called also *lymphography* — **lymph·an·gio·gram** \(ˌ)lim-ˈfan-jē-ə-ˌgram\ *n* — **lymph·an·gio·graph·ic** \ˌlim-ˌfan-jē-ə-ˈgra-fik\ *adj*

[1]**lym·phat·ic** \lim-ˈfa-tik\ *adj* (1649) **1 a :** of, relating to, or produced by lymph, lymphoid tissue, or lymphocytes **b :** conveying lymph **2 :** lacking physical or mental energy : SLUGGISH — **lym·phat·i·cal·ly** \-ti-k(ə-)lē\ *adv*

[2]**lymphatic** *n* (1667) : a vessel that contains or conveys lymph — called also *lymph vessel*

lymphatic system *n* (1830) : the part of the circulatory system that is concerned esp. with scavenging fluids and proteins which have escaped from cells and tissues and returning them to the blood, with the phagocytic removal of cellular debris and foreign material, and with the immune response and that consists esp. of lymphoid tissue, lymph, and lymph-transporting vessels — called also *lymph system*

lymph·ede·ma \ˌlim(p)-fi-ˈdē-mə\ *n* [NL] (1889) : edema due to faulty lymphatic drainage

lymph gland *n* (ca. 1858) : LYMPH NODE

lymph node *n* (1892) : any of the rounded masses of lymphoid tissue that are surrounded by a capsule of connective tissue, are distributed along the lymphatic vessels, and contain numerous lymphocytes which filter the flow of lymph passing through the node

lym·pho·blast \'lim(p)-fə-,blast\ *n* [ISV] (ca. 1909) : a lymphocyte that has enlarged following stimulation by an antigen, has the capacity to recognize the stimulating antigen, and is undergoing proliferation and differentiation either to an effector state in which it functions to eliminate the antigen or to a memory state in which it functions to recognize the future reappearance of the antigen — **lym·pho·blas·tic** \,lim(p)-fə-'blas-tik\ *adj*

lym·pho·cyte \'lim(p)-fə-,sīt\ *n* [ISV] (1890) : any of the colorless weakly motile cells originating from stem cells and differentiating in lymphoid tissue (as of the thymus or bone marrow) that are the typical cellular elements of lymph, include the cellular mediators of immunity, and constitute 20 to 30 percent of the white blood cells of normal human blood — compare B CELL, T CELL — **lym·pho·cyt·ic** \,lim(p)-fə-'si-tik\ *adj*

lymphocytic cho·rio·men·in·gi·tis \-,kòr-ē-ō-,me-nən-'jī-təs\ *n* [NL *choriomeningitis* cerebral meningitis, fr. *chorio-* of a membrane resembling the chorion] (1934) : an acute disease that is caused by an arenavirus (species *Lymphocytic choriomeningitis virus* of the genus *Arenavirus*), that is characterized by fever, nausea and vomiting, headache, stiff neck, and slow pulse, that is marked by the presence of numerous lymphocytes in the cerebrospinal fluid, and that is transmitted esp. by rodents

lymphocytic leukemia *n* (1956) : leukemia of either of two types marked by an abnormal increase in the number of white blood cells (as lymphocytes) which accumulate esp. in bone marrow, lymphoid tissue, and circulating blood — called also *lymphatic leukemia*

lym·pho·cy·to·sis \,lim(p)-fə-,sī-'tō-səs, -fə-sə-\ *n* [NL, fr. ISV *lymphocyte*] (1896) : an increase in the number of lymphocytes in the blood usu. associated with chronic infections or inflammations

lym·pho·gran·u·lo·ma \'lim(p)-fō-,gran-yə-'lō-mə\ *n* [NL] (1924) : LYMPHOGRANULOMA VENEREUM

lymphogranuloma in·gui·na·le \-,in-gwə-'nä-lē, -'na-, -'nā-\ *n* [NL, inguinal lymphogranuloma] (1932) : LYMPHOGRANULOMA VENEREUM

lym·pho·gran·u·lo·ma·to·sis \-,lō-mə-'tō-səs\ *n, pl* **-to·ses** \-,sēz\ [NL *lymphogranulomat-, lymphogranuloma* + *-osis*] (1911) : the development of benign or malignant nodular swellings of lymph nodes in various parts of the body; *also* : a condition characterized by these

lymphogranuloma ve·ne·re·um \-,və-'nir-ē-əm\ *n* [NL, venereal lymphogranuloma] (1938) : a contagious venereal disease caused by various strains of a chlamydia (*Chlamydia trachomatis*) that is marked by painful swelling and inflammation of the lymph nodes esp. in the region of the groin

lym·phog·ra·phy \lim-'fä-grə-fē\ *n* (ca. 1935) : LYMPHANGIOGRAPHY — **lym·pho·gram** \'lim(p)-fə-,gram\ *n* — **lym·pho·graph·ic** \,lim-fə-'gra-fik\ *adj*

lym·phoid \'lim-,fòid\ *adj* (1867) **1** : of, relating to, or being tissue (as of the lymph nodes or thymus) containing lymphocytes **2** : of, relating to, or resembling lymph

lym·pho·kine \'lim(p)-fə-,kīn\ *n* [*lymph-* + *-kine*, fr. Gk *kinein* to move about — more at KINESIS] (1969) : any of various substances (as interleukin-2) of low molecular weight that are not antibodies, are secreted by T cells in response to stimulation by antigens, and have a role (as the activation of macrophages or the enhancement or inhibition of antibody production) in cell-mediated immunity

lym·pho·ma \lim-'fō-mə\ *n, pl* **-mas** *also* **-ma·ta** \-mə-tə\ [NL] (1873) : a usu. malignant tumor of lymphoid tissue — **lym·pho·ma·tous** \-mə-təs\ *adj*

lym·pho·ma·to·sis \(,)lim-,fō-mə-'tō-səs\ *n, pl* **-to·ses** \-,sēz\ [NL *lymphomat-, lymphoma* + *-osis*] (ca. 1900) : the presence of multiple lymphomas in the body

lym·pho·sar·co·ma \,lim(p)-fə-sär-'kō-mə\ *n* [NL] (1874) : a malignant lymphoma that tends to metastasize freely

lynch \'linch\ *vt* [*lynch law*] (1836) : to put to death (as by hanging) by mob action without legal sanction — **lynch·er** *n*

lynch law *n* [William *Lynch* †1820 Am. vigilante] (1811) : the punishment of presumed crimes or offenses usu. by death without due process of law

lynchpin *var of* LINCHPIN

lynx \'liŋ(k)s\ *n, pl* **lynx** *or* **lynx·es** [ME, fr. L, fr. Gk; akin to OE *lox* lynx and prob. to Gk *leukos* white — more at LIGHT] (14c) : any of several wildcats with relatively long legs, a short stubby tail, mottled coat, and often tufted ears that are thought to comprise a distinct genus (*Lynx*) of the cat family or to be part of a genus (*Felis*) that includes the domestic cat and cougar as **a** : a lynx (*L. lynx*) of northern Europe and Asia **b** : BOBCAT **c** : a No. American lynx (*L. canadensis*) distinguished from the bobcat by its larger size, longer tufted ears, and wholly black tail tip — called also *Canadian lynx*

lynx–eyed \'liŋ(k)s-,īd\ *adj* (1597) : SHARP-SIGHTED

lyo- — see LY-

ly·on·naise \,lī-ə-'näz\ *adj* [F (*à la*) *lyonnaise* in the manner of Lyons, France] (1846) : prepared with onions ⟨~ potatoes⟩

Ly·on·nesse \,lī-ə-'nes\ *n* (15c) : a country that according to Arthurian legend was contiguous to Cornwall before sinking beneath the sea

lyo·phile \'lī-ə-,fīl\ *adj* [ISV] (1934) **1** : of or relating to freeze-drying **2** *or* **lyo·philed** \-,fīld\ : obtained by freeze-drying

lynx

lyo·phil·ic \,lī-ə-'fi-lik\ *adj* (1911) : marked by strong affinity between a dispersed phase and the liquid in which it is dispersed ⟨a ~ colloid⟩

ly·oph·i·lise *Brit var of* LYOPHILIZE

ly·oph·i·lize \lī-'ä-fə-,līz\ *vt* **-lized; -liz·ing** (1938) : FREEZE-DRY — **ly·oph·i·li·za·tion** \-,ä-fə-lə-'zā-shən\ *n* — **ly·oph·i·liz·er** \-'ä-fə-,lī-zər\ *n*

Ly·ra \'lī-rə\ *n* [L (gen. *Lyrae*), lit., lyre] (1551) : a northern constellation representing the lyre of Orpheus or Mercury and containing Vega

ly·rate \'lī-,rāt\ *adj* (ca. 1760) : having or suggesting the shape of a lyre ⟨the ~ horns of the impala⟩

lyre \'lī(-ə)r\ *n* [ME *lire*, fr. AF, fr. L *lyra*, fr. Gk] (13c) **1** : a stringed instrument of the harp class having an approximately U-shaped frame and used by the ancient Greeks esp. to accompany song and recitation **2** *cap* : LYRA

lyre·bird \-,bərd\ *n* (1834) : either of two Australian passerine birds (genus *Menura*) distinguished in the male by very long tail feathers displayed in the shape of a lyre during courtship

¹lyr·ic \'lir-ik\ *n* (1581) **1** : a lyric composition; *specif* : a lyric poem **2** : the words of a song — often used in pl.

²lyric *adj* [MF or L; MF *lyrique*, fr. L *lyricus*, fr. Gk *lyrikos*, fr. *lyra*] (1567) **1 a** : suitable for singing to the lyre or for being set to music and sung **b** : of, relating to, or being drama set to music; *esp* : OPERATIC ⟨~ stage⟩ **2 a** : expressing direct usu. intense personal emotion esp. in a manner suggestive of song ⟨~ poetry⟩ **b** : EXUBERANT, RHAPSODIC **3** *of an opera singer* : having a light voice and a melodic style — compare DRAMATIC

lyr·i·cal \'lir-i-kəl\ *adj* (1581) : LYRIC — **lyr·i·cal·ly** \-i-k(ə-)lē\ *adv* — **lyr·i·cal·ness** \-kəl-nəs\ *n*

lyr·i·cism \'lir-ə-,si-zəm\ *n* (1760) **1** : the quality or state of being lyric : SONGFULNESS **2 a** : an intense personal quality expressive of feeling or emotion in an art (as poetry or music) **b** : EXUBERANCE ⟨the sort of author who inspires ~ or invective, not judicious interpretation —*Time*⟩

lyr·i·cist \-sist\ *n* (1881) : a writer of lyrics

lyr·ism \'lir-,i-zəm\ *n* (1859) : LYRICISM

lyr·ist *n* (ca. 1656) **1** \'lī(-ə)r-ist\ : a player on the lyre **2** \'lir-ist\ : LYRICIST

lys- *or* **lysi-** *or* **lyso-** *comb form* [NL, fr. Gk *lys-, lysi-* loosening, fr. *lysis*] : lysis ⟨*lysin*⟩

ly·sate \'lī-,sāt\ *n* (1922) : a product of lysis

lyse \'līs, 'līz\ *vb* **lysed; lys·ing** [back-formation fr. NL *lysis*] *vt* (1924) : to cause to undergo lysis ~ *vi* : to undergo lysis

-lyse *chiefly Brit var of* -LYZE

Ly·sen·ko·ism \lə-'seŋ-kō-,i-zəm\ *n* [Trofim *Lysenko*] (1948) : a biological doctrine asserting the fundamental influence of somatic and environmental factors on heredity in contradiction of orthodox genetics

ly·ser·gic acid \lə-'sər-jik-, (,)lī-\ *n* [ISV *lys-* + *ergot* + *¹-ic*] (1934) : a crystalline acid $C_{16}H_{16}N_2O_2$ from ergotic alkaloids; *also* : LSD

lysergic acid di·eth·yl·am·ide \-,dī-,e-thə-'la-,mīd\ *n* (1944) : LSD

ly·sim·e·ter \lī-'si-mə-tər\ *n* (1879) : a device for measuring the percolation of water through soils and for determining the soluble constituents removed in the drainage — **ly·si·met·ric** \,lī-sə-'me-trik\ *adj*

ly·sin \'lī-s⁰n\ *n* (1900) : a substance (as an antibody) capable of causing lysis

ly·sine \'lī-,sēn\ *n* (1892) : a crystalline essential amino acid $C_6H_{14}N_2O_2$ obtained from the hydrolysis of various proteins

ly·sis \'lī-səs\ *n, pl* **ly·ses** \-,sēz\ [NL, fr. Gk, act of loosening, dissolution, remission of fever, fr. *lyein* to loosen — more at LOSE] (1543) **1** : the gradual decline of a disease process (as fever) **2** : a process of disintegration or dissolution (as of cells)

-lysis *n comb form, pl* **-lyses** [NL, fr. L & Gk; L, loosening, fr. Gk, fr. *lysis*] **1** : decomposition ⟨electro*lysis*⟩ **2** : disintegration : breaking down ⟨auto*lysis*⟩

ly·so·gen \'lī-sə-jən\ *n* (ca. 1934) : a lysogenic bacterium or bacterial strain

ly·so·gen·ic \,lī-sə-'je-nik\ *adj* [fr. the capacity of the prophage to lyse other bacteria] (1899) **1** : harboring a prophage as hereditary material ⟨~ bacteria⟩ **2** : TEMPERATE 3 ⟨~ viruses⟩ — **ly·so·ge·nic·i·ty** \-jə-'ni-sə-tē\ *n*

ly·sog·e·nise *Brit var of* LYSOGENIZE

ly·sog·e·nize \lī-'sä-jə-,nīz\ *vt* **-nized; -niz·ing** (1953) : to render lysogenic — **ly·sog·e·ni·za·tion** \-,sä-jə-nə-'zā-shən\ *n*

ly·sog·e·ny \lī-'sä-jə-nē\ *n* (1956) : the state of being lysogenic

ly·so·lec·i·thin \,lī-sə-'le-sə-thən\ *n* (1923) : a hydrolytic substance formed by the enzymatic hydrolysis (as by some snake venoms) of a lecithin

ly·so·some \'lī-sə-,sōm\ *n* [ISV *lys-* + *³-some*] (1955) : a saclike cellular organelle that contains various hydrolytic enzymes — see CELL illustration — **ly·so·som·al** \,lī-sə-'sō-məl\ *adj*

ly·so·zyme \'lī-sə-,zīm\ *n* (1922) : a basic bacteriolytic protein that hydrolyzes peptidoglycan and is present in egg white and in human tears and saliva

-lyte *n comb form* [Gk *lytos* that may be untied, soluble, fr. *lyein*] : substance capable of undergoing (such) decomposition ⟨electro*lyte*⟩

lyt·ic \'li-tik\ *adj* [Gk *lytikos* able to loose, fr. *lyein*] (1889) : of or relating to lysis or a lysin; *also* : productive of or effecting lysis (as of cells) — **lyt·i·cal·ly** \-ti-k(ə-)lē\ *adv*

-lytic *adj suffix* [Gk *lytikos*] : of, relating to, or effecting (such) decomposition ⟨hydro*lytic*⟩

-lyze *vb comb form* **-lyzed; -lyzing** [ISV, prob. irreg. fr. NL *-lysis*] : produce or undergo lytic disintegration or dissolution ⟨electro*lyze*⟩

LZ *abbr* landing zone

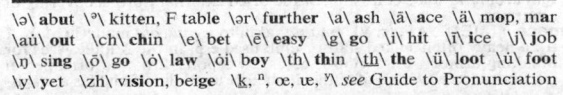

\ə\ abut \ᵊ\ kitten, F table \ər\ further \a\ ash \ā\ ace \ä\ mop, mar
\aù\ out \ch\ chin \e\ bet \ē\ easy \g\ go \i\ hit \ī\ ice \j\ job
\ŋ\ sing \ō\ go \ò\ law \òi\ boy \th\ thin \t͟h\ the \ü\ loot \ù\ foot
\y\ yet \zh\ vision, beige \k, ⁿ, œ, ɶ, ᵜ\ *see* Guide to Pronunciation

M

[1]m \ˈem\ *n, pl* **m's** *or* **ms** \ˈemz\ *often cap, often attrib* (bef. 12c) **1 a** : the 13th letter of the English alphabet **b** : a graphic representation of this letter **c** : a speech counterpart of orthographic *m* **2** : one thousand — see NUMBER table **3** : a graphic device for reproducing the letter *m* **4** : one designated *m* esp. as the 13th in order or class **5** : something shaped like the letter M **6 a** : EM 2 **b** : PICA 2

[2]m *abbr* **1** male **2** manual **3** married **4** martyr **5** masculine **6** mass **7** measure **8** meridian **9** [L *meridies*] noon **10** meter **11** middle **12** mile **13** [L *mille*] thousand **14** milli- **15** minute **16** molal; molality **17** mole **18** month **19** moon **20** morning **21** muscle

M *abbr* **1** Mach **2** magnitude **3** March **4** May **5** medium **6** mega- **7** million **8** molar; molarity **9** monsieur

m- *abbr* meta-

'm \m\ *vb* (1584) : AM ⟨I'm going⟩

ma \ˈmä, ˈmȯ\ *n* [short for *mama*] (1829) : MOTHER

mA *abbr* milliampere

Ma *abbr* million years ago

MA *abbr* **1** [ML *magister artium*] master of arts **2** Massachusetts **3** mental age **4** Middle Ages

MAA *abbr* master of applied arts

ma'am \ˈmam, *after "yes" often* əm\ *n* (1668) : MADAM

ma–and–pa \ˌmä-ən-ˈpä, ˌmȯ-ən-ˈpȯ\ *adj* (1671) : MOM-AND-POP

Mab \ˈmab\ *n* (ca. 1595) : a queen of fairies in English literature

mabe pearl \ˈmä-ˌbā-\ *n* [*mabe* prob. fr. Ryukyuan Jp (Amami dial.), the pearl oyster *Pteria penguin*] (1951) : a cultured pearl essentially hemispherical in form — called also *mabe*

mac *or* **mack** \ˈmak\ *n* (1901) *Brit* : MACKINTOSH

[1]Mac \ˈmak\ *n* [*Mac-, Mc-,* patronymic prefix in Scottish and Irish surnames] (ca. 1918) : FELLOW — used informally to address a man whose name is not known

[2]Mac *abbr* Machabees

[3]Mac *or* **Macc** *abbr* Maccabees

MAC *abbr* military airlift command

ma·ca·bre \mə-ˈkäb; -ˈkä-brə, -bər; -ˈkäbrᵊ\ *adj* [F, fr. (*danse*) *macabre* dance of death, fr. MF (*danse de*) *Macabré*] (1889) **1** : having death as a subject : comprising or including a personalized representation of death **2** : dwelling on the gruesome **3** : tending to produce horror in a beholder ***syn*** see GHASTLY

mac·ad·am \mə-ˈka-dəm\ *n* [John L. *McAdam* †1836 Brit. engineer] (1824) : macadamized roadway or pavement esp. with a bituminous binder

mac·a·da·mia nut \ˌma-kə-ˈdā-mē-ə-\ *n* [NL *Macadamia,* fr. John *Macadam* †1865 Australian chemist] (1929) : a hard-shelled nut of an Australian evergreen tree (genus *Macadamia,* esp. *M. integrifolia* or *M. tetraphylla*) of the protea family that somewhat resembles the filbert and is cultivated extensively in Hawaii — called also *macadamia*

mac·ad·am·ize \mə-ˈka-də-ˌmīz\ *vt* **-ized; -iz·ing** (1824) : to construct or finish (a road) by compacting into a solid mass a layer of small broken stone on a convex well-drained roadbed and using a binder (as cement or asphalt) for the mass

ma·caque \mə-ˈkak, -ˈkäk\ *n* [F, fr. Pg *macaco,* fr. *kaku* mangabey, pl. *makaku,* in one or more Bantu languages of Gabon and Congo] (1757) : any of a genus (*Macaca*) of chiefly Asian monkeys typically having a sturdy build and including some short-tailed or tailless forms; *esp* : RHESUS MONKEY

macaque

mac·a·ro·ni \ˌma-kə-ˈrō-nē\ *n* [It *maccheroni,* pl. of *maccherone,* fr. It dial. *maccarone* dumpling, macaroni] (1599) **1** : pasta made from semolina and shaped in the form of slender tubes **2** *pl* **macaronis** *or* **macaronies** [*Macaroni* Club, a group of such Englishmen] **a** : a member of a class of traveled young Englishmen of the late 18th and early 19th centuries who affected foreign ways **b** : an affected young man : FOP **3** : MACARONI PENGUIN

mac·a·ron·ic \-ˈrä-nik\ *adj* [NL *macaronicus,* fr. It dial. *maccarone* macaroni] (1638) **1** : characterized by a mixture of vernacular words with Latin words or with non-Latin words having Latin endings **2** : characterized by a mixture of two languages — **macaronic** *n*

macaroni penguin *n* [prob. fr. the resemblance of the penguin's crest to headgear supposedly worn by macaronis] (1832) : a small penguin (*Eudyptes chrysolophus*) that has an orange, yellow, and black crest on the head and a black chin and that breeds on subantarctic islands

mac·a·roon \ˌma-kə-ˈrün\ *n* [F *macaron,* fr. It dial. *maccarone*] (ca. 1611) : a small cookie composed chiefly of egg whites, sugar, and ground almonds or coconut

ma·caw \mə-ˈkȯ\ *n* [Pg (now obs.) *macao*] (1625) : any of numerous parrots (esp. genus *Ara*) of South and Central America including some of the largest and showiest of parrots

Mac·beth \mək-ˈbeth, mak-\ *n* (ca. 1606) : a Scottish general who is the protagonist of Shakespeare's tragedy *Macbeth*

Mac·ca·bees \ˈma-kə-(ˌ)bēz\ *n pl* [Gk *Makkabaioi,* fr. pl. of *Makkabaios,* surname of Judas Maccabaeus 2d cent. B.C. Jewish patriot] (15c) **1** : a priestly family leading a Jewish revolt begun in 168 B.C. against Hellenism and Syrian rule and reigning over Palestine from 142 B.C. to 63 B.C. **2** *sing in constr* : either of two narrative and historical books included in the Roman Catholic canon of the Old Testament and in the Protestant Apocrypha — see BIBLE table — **Mac·ca·be·an** \ˌma-kə-ˈbē-ən\ *adj*

mac·chi·a·to \ˌmä-kē-ˈä-(ˌ)tō\ *n* [It, short for *caffè macchiato* lit., coffee with a spot (of milk)] (1987) : espresso topped with a thin layer of foamed milk

[1]mace \ˈmās\ *n* [ME, fr. AF, fr. OF *mascie, macis,* fr. ML *macis*] (13c) : an aromatic spice consisting of the dried external fibrous covering of a nutmeg

[2]mace *n* [ME, fr. AF, fr. VL **mattia;* akin to L *mateola* mallet] (14c) **1 a** : a heavy often spiked staff or club used esp. in the Middle Ages for breaking armor **b** : a club used as a weapon **2 a** : an ornamental staff borne as a symbol of authority before a public official (as a magistrate) or a legislative body **b** : one who carries a mace

[3]mace *vt* **maced; mac·ing** (1968) : to attack with the liquid Mace

Mace \ˈmās\ *trademark* — used for a temporarily disabling liquid usu. used as a spray

ma·cé·doine \ˌma-sə-ˈdwän\ *n* [F, fr. *Macédoine* Macedonia; perh. fr. the mixture of ethnic groups in Macedonia] (1820) **1** : a confused mixture : MEDLEY **2** : a mixture of fruits or vegetables served as a salad or cocktail or in a jellied dessert or used in a sauce or as a garnish

Mac·e·do·nian \ˌma-sə-ˈdō-nyən, -nē-ən\ *n* (1556) **1** : the language of ancient Macedonia of uncertain affinity but generally assumed to be Indo-European **2** : a native or inhabitant of Macedonia **3** : the Slavic language of modern Macedonia

mac·er·ate \ˈma-sə-ˌrāt\ *vb* **-at·ed; -at·ing** [L *maceratus,* pp. of *macerare* to soften, steep] *vt* (1547) **1** : to cause to waste away by or as if by excessive fasting **2** : to cause to become soft or separated into constituent elements by or as if by steeping in fluid; *broadly* : STEEP, SOAK ~ *vi* : to soften and wear away esp. as a result of being wetted or steeped — **mac·er·a·tion** \ˌma-sə-ˈrā-shən\ *n* — **mac·er·a·tor** \ˈma-sə-ˌrā-tər\ *n*

Mac·Guf·fin *or* **Mc·Guf·fin** \mə-ˈgə-fən\ *n* [coined by Alfred Hitchcock] (ca. 1939) : an object, event, or character in a film or story that serves to set and keep the plot in motion despite usu. lacking intrinsic importance

mach *abbr* machine; machinery; machinist

Mach \ˈmäk\ *n* [*Mach number*] (1946) : a usu. high speed expressed by a Mach number ⟨an airplane flying at ~ 2⟩

Mach·a·bees \ˈma-kə-(ˌ)bēz\ *n pl but sing in constr* [ME, fr. LL *Machabaei,* modif. of Gk *Makkabaioi*] (14c) : MACCABEES

mâche \ˈmäsh\ *n* [F, perh. alter. of F dial. *pomache,* fr. VL **pomasca,* fr. L *pomum* fruit] (1961) : CORN SALAD

ma·chete \mə-ˈshe-tē, -ˈche-; -ˈshet\ *n* [Sp] (ca. 1575) : a large heavy knife used for cutting sugarcane and underbrush and as a weapon

Ma·chi·a·vel·lian \ˌma-kē-ə-ˈve-lē-ən, -ˈvel-yən\ *adj* [Niccolo *Machiavelli*] (1572) **1** : of or relating to Machiavelli or Machiavellianism **2** : suggesting the principles of conduct laid down by Machiavelli; *specif* : marked by cunning, duplicity, or bad faith — **Machiavellian** *n*

Ma·chi·a·vel·lian·ism \-ˈve-lē-ə-ˌni-zəm, -ˈvel-yə-ˌni-zəm\ *n* (1607) : the political theory of Machiavelli; *esp* : the view that politics is amoral and that any means however unscrupulous can justifiably be used in achieving political power

ma·chic·o·la·tion \mə-ˌchi-kə-ˈlā-shən\ *n* [ML *machicolare* to furnish with machicolations, fr. MF *machicoller,* fr. *machicoleis* machicolation, fr. *macher* to crush + *col* neck, fr. L *collum* — more at COLLAR] (1787) **1 a** : an opening between the corbels of a projecting parapet or in the floor of a gallery or roof of a portal for discharging missiles upon assailants below — see BATTLEMENT illustration **b** : a gallery or parapet containing such openings **2** : construction imitating medieval machicolation — **ma·chic·o·lat·ed** \mə-ˈchi-kə-ˌlā-təd\ *adj*

mach·i·nate \ˈma-kə-ˌnāt, ˈma-shə-\ *vb* **-nat·ed; -nat·ing** [L *machinatus,* pp. of *machinari,* fr. *machina* machine, contrivance] *vi* (1537) : to plan or plot esp. to do harm ~ *vt* : to scheme or contrive to bring about : PLOT — **mach·i·na·tor** \-ˌnā-tər\ *n*

mach·i·na·tion \ˌma-kə-ˈnā-shən, ˌma-shə-\ *n* (15c) **1** : an act of machinating **2** : a scheming or crafty action or artful design intended to accomplish some usu. evil end ⟨backstage ~*s* . . . that have dominated the film industry —Peter Bogdanovich⟩ ***syn*** see PLOT

[1]ma·chine \mə-ˈshēn\ *n, often attrib* [MF, fr. L *machina,* fr. Gk *mēchanē* (Dor dial. *machana*), fr. *mēchos* means, expedient — more at MAY] (ca. 1545) **1 a** *archaic* : a constructed thing whether material or immaterial **b** : CONVEYANCE, VEHICLE; *esp* : AUTOMOBILE **c** *archaic* : a military engine **d** : any of various apparatuses formerly used to produce stage effects **e** (1) : an assemblage of parts that transmit forces, motion, and energy one to another in a predetermined manner (2) : an instrument (as a lever) designed to transmit or modify the application of power, force, or motion **f** : a mechanically, electrically, or electronically operated device for performing a task **g** : a coin-operated device ⟨a cigarette ~⟩ **h** : MACHINERY — used with *the* or in pl. **2 a** : a living organism or one of its functional systems **b** : one that resembles a machine (as in being methodical, tireless, or consistently productive) ⟨a gifted publicist and quote ~ —John Lancaster⟩ **c** (1) : a combination of persons acting together for a common end along with the agencies they use (2) : a highly organized political group under the leadership of a boss or small clique **3** : a literary device or contrivance introduced for dramatic effect

[2]machine *vt* **ma·chined; ma·chin·ing** (1853) : to process by or as if by machine; *esp* : to reduce or finish by or as if by turning, shaping, planing, or milling by machine-operated tools — **ma·chin·abil·i·ty** *also* **ma·chine·abil·i·ty** \-ˌshē-nə-ˈbi-lə-tē\ *n* — **ma·chin·able** *also* **ma·chine·able** \-ˈshē-nə-bəl\ *adj*

ma·chine–gun \mə-ˈshēn-ˌgən\ *adj* (1906) : characterized by rapidity and sharpness : RAPID-FIRE ⟨a comic's ~ delivery⟩

machine gun *n* (1867) : a gun for sustained rapid fire that uses bullets; *broadly* : an automatic weapon — **machine–gun** *vb* — **machine gun·ner** *n*

machine language *n* (1947) **1** : the set of symbolic instruction codes usu. in binary form that is used to represent operations and data in a machine (as a computer) — called also *machine code* **2** : ASSEMBLY LANGUAGE

ma·chine·like \mə-ˈshēn-ˌlīk\ *adj* (ca. 1713) : resembling or suggesting a machine esp. in regularity of action or stereotyped uniformity of product

machine pistol *n* (1940) : a small submachine gun with a pistol grip

machine–readable *adj* (1961) : directly usable by a computer ⟨~ text⟩

ma·chin·ery \mə-ˈshē-nə-rē, -ˈshēn-rē\ *n, pl* **-er·ies** (1687) **1 a** : machines in general or as a functioning unit **b** : the working parts of a machine **2** : the means or system by which something is kept in action or a desired result is obtained ⟨the ~ of government⟩

machine shop *n* (1827) : a workshop in which work is machined to size and assembled

machine tool *n* (1852) : a machine designed for shaping solid work

ma·chin·ist \mə-ˈshē-nist\ *n* (ca. 1706) **1 a** : a worker who fabricates, assembles, or repairs machinery **b** : a craftsman skilled in the use of machine tools **c** : one who operates a machine **2** *archaic* : a person

in charge of the mechanical aspects of a theatrical production **3 :** a warrant officer who supervises machinery and engine operation
ma·chis·mo \mä-ˈchēz-(ˌ)mō, mə-, -ˈkēz-, -ˈkiz-, -ˈchiz-\ *n* [Sp, fr. *macho*] (ca. 1948) **1 :** a strong sense of masculine pride : an exaggerated masculinity **2 :** an exaggerated or exhilarating sense of power or strength
Mach number \ˈmäk-\ *n* [Ernst *Mach* †1916 Austrian physicist] (1937) **:** a number representing the ratio of the speed of a body (as an aircraft) to the speed of sound in a surrounding medium (as air)
[1]**ma·cho** \ˈmä-(ˌ)chō\ *adj* [Sp, lit., male, fr. L *masculus* — more at MASCULINE] (1928) **:** characterized by machismo : aggressively virile
[2]**macho** *n, pl* **machos** (1951) **1 :** one who exhibits machismo **2 :** MACHISMO
mack *var of* MAC
mack daddy \ˈmak-\ *n* [argot *mac, mack* pimp, prob. short for obs. argot *mackerel,* fr. ME *makerel,* fr. AF *makerelle* procuress, ultim. fr. MD *mākelaer* broker] (1989) **1** *slang* **:** a conspicuously successful pimp **2** *slang* **:** a slick womanizer **3** *slang* **:** one that is the best
mack·er·el \ˈma-k(ə-)rəl\ *n, pl* **mackerel** *or* **mackerels** [ME *makerel,* fr. AF] (14c) **1 :** a scombroid fish (*Scomber scombrus* of the family Scombridae) of the No. Atlantic that is green above with dark blue bars and silvery below and is a commercially important food fish **2 :** any of various fishes (as the wahoo and king mackerel) in the same family as the mackerel esp. when distinguished from the related bonito or tuna by a comparatively smaller size
mackerel shark *n* (1819) **:** any of a family (Lamnidae) of large pelagic sharks including the great white shark and mako sharks; *esp* **:** PORBEAGLE
mackerel sky *n* (1667) **:** a sky covered with rows of altocumulus or cirrocumulus clouds resembling the patterns on a mackerel's back
mack·i·naw \ˈma-kə-ˌnȯ\ *n* [*Mackinaw* (Mackinac), trading post at site of Mackinaw City, Michigan] (1833) **1 :** a heavy woolen blanket formerly distributed by the U.S. government to the Indians **2 a :** a heavy cloth of wool or wool and other fibers often with a plaid design and usu. heavily napped and felted **b :** a short coat of mackinaw or similar heavy fabric **3 :** MACKINAW TROUT
mackinaw trout *n, often cap M* (1840) **:** a large dark No. American char (*Salvelinus namaycush*) that is an important commercial food fish in northern lakes — called also *lake trout, mackinaw*
mack·in·tosh *also* **mac·in·tosh** \ˈma-kən-ˌtäsh\ *n* [Charles *Macintosh* †1843 Scot. chemist & inventor] (1836) **1** *chiefly Brit* **:** RAINCOAT **2 :** a lightweight waterproof fabric orig. of rubberized cotton
Mac·lau·rin series \mə-ˈklȯr-ən(z)-\ *n* [Colin *Maclaurin* †1746 Scot. mathematician] (1902) **:** a Taylor's series that is expanded about the reference point zero and that takes the form

$$f(x) = f(0) + \frac{f'(0)}{1!}x + \frac{f''(0)}{2!}x^2 + \ldots + \frac{f^{[n]}(0)}{n!}x^n + \ldots$$

subject to the conditions holding for a Taylor's series — called also *Maclaurin's series*
ma·cle \ˈma-kəl\ *n* [F, wide-meshed net, lozenge voided, macle, fr. OF, mesh, lozenge voided, of Gmc origin; akin to OHG *masca* mesh — more at MESH] (1801) **1 :** a twin crystal **2 :** a flat often triangular diamond that is usu. a twin crystal — **ma·cled** \ˈma-kəld\ *adj*
ma·con *also* **mâ·con** \ma-ˈkōⁿ\ *n, often cap* [F *mâcon,* fr. *Mâcon,* France] (1863) **:** a dry red or white wine produced in the area around Mâcon, France
Mac·Pher·son strut \mək-ˈfir-sᵊn-, -ˈfər-\ *n* [Earle S. *MacPherson* †1960 Am. engineer] (1960) **:** a component of an automobile suspension consisting of a shock absorber mounted within a coil spring
macr- *or* **macro-** *comb form* [F & L, fr. Gk *makr-, makro-* long, fr. *makros* — more at MEAGER] **1 :** long ⟨*macro*biotic⟩ **2 :** large ⟨*macro*molecule⟩
mac·ra·mé *also* **mac·ra·me** \ˈma-krə-ˌmā\ *n* [F or It; F *macramé,* fr. It *macramè,* fr. Turk *makrama* napkin, towel, fr. Ar *miqrama* coverlet] (1865) **:** a coarse lace or fringe made by knotting threads or cords in a geometrical pattern; *also* **:** the art of tying knots in patterns
[1]**mac·ro** \ˈma-(ˌ)krō\ *adj* [*macr-*] (1923) **1 :** being large, thick, or exceptionally prominent **2 a :** of, involving, or intended for use with relatively large quantities or on a large scale **b :** of or relating to macroeconomics **3 :** GROSS 1c **4 :** of or relating to a macro lens or to close-up photography
[2]**macro** *n, pl* **macros** [short for *macroinstruction*] (1959) **:** a single computer instruction that stands for a sequence of operations
mac·ro·ag·gre·gate \ˌma-krō-ˈa-gri-gət\ *n* (1926) **:** a relatively large particle (as of soil) — **mac·ro·ag·gre·gat·ed** \-ˌgā-təd\ *adj*
mac·ro·bi·ot·ic \-bī-ˈä-tik, -bē-\ *adj* (1965) **:** of, relating to, or being a diet based on the Chinese cosmological principles of yin and yang that consists of whole cereals and grains supplemented esp. with beans and vegetables and that in its esp. former more restrictive forms has been linked to nutritional deficiencies — **macrobiotics** *n pl but sing in constr*
mac·ro·cosm \ˈma-krə-ˌkä-zəm\ *n* [F *macrocosme,* fr. ML *macrocosmos,* fr. L *macr-* + Gk *kosmos* order, universe] (1600) **1 :** the great world : UNIVERSE **2 :** a complex that is a large-scale reproduction of one of its constituents — **mac·ro·cos·mic** \ˌma-krə-ˈkäz-mik\ *adj* — **mac·ro·cos·mi·cal·ly** \-mi-k(ə-)lē\ *adv*
mac·ro·cy·clic \ˌma-krō-ˈsī-klik, -ˈsi-\ *adj* (1936) **:** containing or being a chemical ring that consists usu. of 15 or more atoms
mac·ro·cyte \ˈma-krə-ˌsīt\ *n* [ISV] (ca. 1889) **:** an exceptionally large red blood cell occurring chiefly in anemias — **mac·ro·cyt·ic** \ˌma-krə-ˈsi-tik\ *adj*
mac·ro·cy·to·sis \ˌma-krə-sī-ˈtō-səs, -krə-sə-\ *n, pl* **-to·ses** \-ˌsēz\ [NL] (ca. 1893) **:** the occurrence of macrocytes in the blood
mac·ro·eco·nom·ics \ˈma-krō-ˌe-kə-ˈnä-miks, -ˌē-kə-\ *n pl but usu sing in constr* (1948) **:** a study of economics in terms of whole systems esp. with reference to general levels of output and income and to the interrelations among sectors of the economy — compare MICROECONOMICS — **mac·ro·eco·nom·ic** \-mik\ *adj*
mac·ro·evo·lu·tion \ˈma-krō-ˌe-və-ˈlü-shən *also* -ˌē-və-\ *n* (1939) **:** evolution that results in relatively large and complex changes (as in species formation) — **mac·ro·evo·lu·tion·ary** \-shə-ˌner-ē\ *adj*
mac·ro·fos·sil \ˈma-krō-ˌfä-səl\ *n* (1937) **:** a fossil large enough to be observed by direct inspection
mac·ro·ga·mete \ˌma-krō-ˈga-ˌmēt *also* -gə-ˈmēt\ *n* [ISV] (1899) **:** the larger and usu. female gamete of a heterogamous organism
mac·ro·glob·u·lin \-ˈglä-byə-lən\ *n* [ISV] (1952) **:** a highly polymerized globulin (as IgM) of high molecular weight
mac·ro·glob·u·li·ne·mia \-ˌglä-byə-lə-ˈnē-mē-ə\ *n* [NL] (1949) **:** a disorder characterized by increased blood serum viscosity and the presence of macroglobulins in the serum — **mac·ro·glob·u·li·ne·mic** \-mik\ *adj*
mac·ro·in·struc·tion \ˌma-krō-in-ˈstrək-shən\ *n* (1959) **:** MACRO
macro lens *n* [*macr-,* fr. the fact that the focal length is greater than normal] (1961) **:** a camera lens designed to focus at very short distances with up to life-size magnification of the image
mac·ro·lep·i·dop·tera \ˈma-krō-ˌle-pə-ˈdäp-tə-rə\ *n pl* [NL] (1882) **:** lepidoptera (as butterflies, skippers, saturniids, and noctuids) that include most of the large forms and none of the minute ones
mac·ro·mere \ˈma-krə-ˌmir\ *n* (1877) **:** a large blastomere — see BLASTULA illustration
mac·ro·mol·e·cule \ˌma-krō-ˈmä-li-ˌkyü(ə)l\ *n* [ISV] (ca. 1929) **:** a very large molecule (as of a protein or rubber) — **mac·ro·mo·lec·u·lar** \-mə-ˈle-kyə-lər\ *adj*
ma·cron \ˈmā-ˌkrän, ˈma-, -krən\ *n* [Gk *makron,* neut. of *makros* long] (1851) **:** a mark ¯ placed over a vowel to indicate that the vowel is long or placed over a syllable or used alone to indicate a stressed or long syllable in a metrical foot
mac·ro·nu·cle·us \ˌma-krō-ˈnü-klē-əs, -ˈnyü-\ *n* [NL] (1892) **:** a relatively large densely staining nucleus of most ciliate protozoans that is derived from micronuclei and controls various nonreproductive functions — **mac·ro·nu·cle·ar** \ˌmak-rō-ˈnü-klē-ər, -ˈnyü-, ÷-kyə-lər\ *adj*
mac·ro·nu·tri·ent \-ˈnü-trē-ənt, -ˈnyü-\ *n* (1942) **1 :** a chemical element (as nitrogen, phosphorus, or potassium) of which relatively large quantities are essential to the growth and health of a plant **2 :** a substance (as protein or carbohydrate) essential in large amounts to the growth and health of an animal — compare MICRONUTRIENT 2
mac·ro·phage \ˈma-krə-ˌfāj\ *n* [ISV] (1890) **:** a phagocytic tissue cell of the immune system that may be fixed or freely motile, is derived from a monocyte, functions in the destruction of foreign antigens (as bacteria and viruses), and serves as an antigen-presenting cell — compare HISTIOCYTE — **mac·ro·phag·ic** \ˌma-krə-ˈfa-jik\ *adj*
mac·ro·pho·tog·ra·phy \ˌma-krō-fə-ˈtä-grə-fē\ *n* (1889) **:** the making of photographs in which the object is either unmagnified or slightly magnified up to a limit often of about 10 diameters — **mac·ro·pho·to·graph** \-ˈfō-tə-ˌgraf\ *n*
mac·ro·phyte \ˈma-krə-ˌfīt\ *n* (1903) **:** a member of the macroscopic plant life esp. of a body of water — **mac·ro·phyt·ic** \ˌma-krə-ˈfi-tik\ *adj*
mac·rop·ter·ous \ma-ˈkräp-tə-rəs\ *adj* [Gk *makropteros,* fr. *makr-* + *pteron* wing — more at FEATHER] (ca. 1836) **:** having long or large wings ⟨∼ insects⟩
mac·ro·scale \ˈma-krō-ˌskāl\ *n* (1931) **:** a large often macroscopic scale
mac·ro·scop·ic \ˌma-krə-ˈskä-pik\ *adj* [ISV *macr-* + *-scopic* (as in *microscopic*)] (1872) **1 :** observable by the naked eye **2 :** involving large units or elements — **mac·ro·scop·i·cal·ly** \-pi-k(ə-)lē\ *adv*
mac·ro·struc·ture \ˈma-krō-ˌstrək-chər\ *n* (ca. 1899) **:** the structure (as of metal, a body part, or the soil) revealed by visual examination with little or no magnification — **mac·ro·struc·tur·al** \ˌma-krō-ˈstrək-chə-rəl, -ˈstrək-shə-rəl\ *adj*
mac·u·la \ˈma-kyə-lə\ *n, pl* **-lae** \-ˌlē, -ˌlī\ *also* **-las** [ME, fr. L] (14c) **1 :** SPOT, BLOTCH; *esp* **:** MACULE **2 :** an anatomical structure having the form of a spot differentiated from surrounding tissues; *esp* **:** MACULA LUTEA — **mac·u·lar** \-lər\ *adj*
macula lu·tea \-ˈlü-tē-ə\ *n, pl* **maculae lu·te·ae** \-tē-ˌē, -tē-ˌī\ [NL, lit., yellow spot] (1848) **:** a small yellowish area lying slightly lateral to the center of the retina that constitutes the region of maximum visual acuity — called also *yellow spot*
macular degeneration *n* (1918) **:** a gradual loss of the central part of the field of vision usu. affecting both eyes that occurs esp. in the elderly and that in a slowly progressing form is marked esp. by accumulation of yellow deposits in and thinning of the macula lutea and in a rapidly progressing form by scarring produced by bleeding and fluid leakage below the macula lutea
mac·u·late \ˈma-kyə-lət\ *or* **mac·u·lat·ed** \-ˌlā-təd\ *adj* [L *maculatus,* pp. of *maculare* to stain, fr. *macula*] (15c) **1 :** marked with spots : BLOTCHED **2 :** IMPURE, BESMIRCHED
mac·u·la·tion \ˌma-kyə-ˈlā-shən\ *n* (15c) **1** *archaic* **:** the state of being spotted **2 a :** a blemish in the form of a discrete spot ⟨acne scars and ∼*s*⟩ **b :** the arrangement of spots and markings on an animal or plant
mac·ule \ˈma-(ˌ)kyü(ə)l\ *n* [F, fr. L *macula*] (1863) **:** a patch of skin that is altered in color but usu. not elevated and that is a characteristic feature of various diseases (as smallpox)
ma·cum·ba \mə-ˈküm-bə\ *n* [BrazPg] (1939) **:** a polytheistic religion of African origin involving syncretistic elements and practiced mainly by Brazilian blacks in urban areas
[1]**mad** \ˈmad\ *adj* **mad·der; mad·dest** [ME *medd, madd,* fr. OE *gemǣd,* pp. of **gemǣdan* to madden, fr. *gemād* silly, mad; akin to OHG *gimeit* foolish, crazy] (bef. 12c) **1 :** disordered in mind : INSANE **2 a :** completely unrestrained by reason and judgment ⟨driven ∼ by the pain⟩ **b :** incapable of being explained or accounted for ⟨a ∼ decision⟩ **3 :** carried away by intense anger : FURIOUS ⟨∼ about the delay⟩ **4 :** carried away by enthusiasm or desire ⟨∼ about horses⟩ **5 :** affected with rabies : RABID **6 :** marked by wild gaiety and merriment : HILARIOUS **7 :** intensely excited : FRANTIC **8 :** marked by intense and often chaotic activity : WILD ⟨a ∼ scramble⟩ — **mad·dish** \ˈma-dish\ *adj* — **like mad :** to an extreme degree ⟨spending *like mad*⟩
[2]**mad** *vb* **mad·ded; mad·ding** (14c) **:** MADDEN
[3]**mad** *n* (1834) **1 :** a fit or mood of bad temper **2 :** ANGER, FURY

MAD *abbr* mutual assured destruction; mutually assured destruction
Mad·a·gas·car periwinkle \ˌma-də-ˈgas-kər-\ *n* [*Madagascar,* Africa] (1821) : ROSY PERIWINKLE
mad·am \ˈma-dəm\ *n, pl* **madams** [ME, fr. AF *ma dame,* lit., my lady] (14c) **1** *pl* **mes·dames** \mā-ˈdäm, -ˈdam\ : LADY — used without a name as a form of respectful or polite address to a woman **2** : MISTRESS 1 — used as a title formerly with the given name but now with the surname or esp. with a designation of rank or office ⟨*Madam* Chairman⟩ ⟨*Madam* President⟩ **3** : the female head of a house of prostitution **4** : the female head of a household : WIFE
ma·dame \mə-ˈdam, ma-ˈ, *before a surname also* ˈma-dəm\ *n* [F, fr. OF *ma dame*] (ca. 1674) **1** *pl* **mes·dames** \mā-ˈdäm, -ˈdam\ — used as a title equivalent to *Mrs.* for a married woman not of English-speaking nationality **2** *pl* **madames** : MADAM 3
mad–brained \ˈmad-ˈbrānd\ *adj* (1562) : RASH, HOTHEADED
mad·cap \ˈmad-ˌkap\ *adj* (1588) : marked by capriciousness, recklessness, or foolishness — **madcap** *n*
mad cow disease *n* (1988) : BOVINE SPONGIFORM ENCEPHALOPATHY
mad·den \ˈma-dᵊn\ *vb* **mad·dened; mad·den·ing** \ˈmad-niŋ, ˈma-dᵊn-iŋ\ *vi* (1735) : to become or act as if mad ~ *vt* **1** : to drive mad : CRAZE **2** : to make intensely angry : ENRAGE
maddening *adj* (1822) **1** : tending to craze **2 a** : tending to infuriate **b** : tending to vex : IRRITATING — **mad·den·ing·ly** \-lē\ *adv*
mad·der \ˈma-dər\ *n* [ME, fr. OE *mædere;* akin to OHG *matara* madder] (bef. 12c) **1** : a Eurasian herb (*Rubia tinctorum* of the family Rubiaceae, the madder family) with whorled leaves and small yellowish panicled flowers succeeded by dark berries; *broadly* : any of several related herbs (genus *Rubia*) **2 a** : the root of the Eurasian madder used formerly in dyeing; *also* : an alizarin dye prepared from it **b** : a moderate to strong red

madder 1

madding *adj* (1579) : acting in a frenzied manner — usu. used in the phrase *madding crowd* to denote esp. the crowded world of human activity and strife ⟨built his home far from the *madding crowd*⟩
made \ˈmād\ *adj* [ME, fr. pp. of *maken* to make] (14c) **1 a** : FICTITIOUS, INVENTED ⟨a ~ excuse⟩ **b** : artificially produced **c** : put together of various ingredients ⟨a ~ dish⟩ **2** : assured of success ⟨a ~ man⟩ — usu. used in the phrase *have it made*
Ma·dei·ra \mə-ˈdir-ə, -ˈder-\ *n* [Pg, fr. *Madeira* Islands] (1596) : an amber-colored fortified wine from Madeira; *also* : a similar wine made elsewhere
mad·e·leine \ˈma-də-lən, ˌma-də-ˈlān\ *n* [F, perh. fr. *Madeleine* Paumier, 19th cent. Fr. pastry cook] (1845) **1** : a small rich shell-shaped cake **2** : one that evokes a memory
ma·de·moi·selle \ˌmad-mwə-ˈzel, ˌma-də-, -mə-ˈzel, *sometimes* mam-ˈzel\ *n, pl* **ma·de·moi·selles** \-ˈzelz\ *or* **mes·de·moi·selles** \ˌmād-mwə-ˈzel, ˌmā-də-, -mə-ˈzel\ [ME *madamoiselle,* fr. MF, fr. OF *ma damoisele,* lit., my (young) lady] (15c) **1** : an unmarried French girl or woman — used as a title equivalent to *Miss* for an unmarried woman not of English-speaking nationality **2** : a French governess **3** : SILVER PERCH a
made–to–measure *adj* (1900) : fashioned to measurements specifically required : CUSTOM-MADE ⟨a ~ suit⟩
made–to–order *adj* (ca. 1908) **1** : produced to supply a special or an individual demand : CUSTOM-MADE **2** : ideally suited (as to a particular purpose) ⟨started the double play on a ~ grounder⟩
made–up \ˈmād-ˈəp\ *adj* (1607) **1** : fully manufactured **2** : marked by the use of makeup **3** : fancifully conceived or falsely devised
mad·house \ˈmad-ˌhau̇s\ *n* (1687) **1** : a place where insane persons are detained and treated **2** : a place of uproar or confusion
Mad·i·son Avenue \ˈma-də-sən-\ *n* [*Madison Avenue,* New York City, former center of the American advertising business] (1952) : the American advertising industry
mad·ly \ˈmad-lē\ *adv* (13c) **1** : in a mad manner **2** : to an extreme or excessive degree ⟨~ in love⟩
mad·man \ˈmad-ˌman, -mən\ *n* (14c) : a man who is or acts as if insane
mad money *n* (1922) : money that a woman carries to pay her fare home in case a date ends in a quarrel; *also* : money set aside for an emergency or personal use
mad·ness \ˈmad-nəs\ *n* (14c) **1** : the quality or state of being mad: as **a** : RAGE **b** : INSANITY **c** : extreme folly **d** : ECSTASY, ENTHUSIASM **2** : any of several ailments of animals marked by frenzied behavior; *specif* : RABIES
Ma·don·na \mə-ˈdä-nə\ *n* [It, fr. OIt *ma donna,* lit., my lady] (1584) **1** *archaic* : LADY — used as a form of respectful address **2** *obs* : an Italian lady **3 a** : VIRGIN MARY **b** : an artistic depiction (as a painting or statue) of the Virgin Mary **4** : a morally pure and chaste woman
Madonna lily *n* (1877) : a widely cultivated Eurasian lily (*Lilium candidum*) with bell-shaped to broad funnel-shaped white flowers
ma·dras \ˈma-drəs; mə-ˈdras, -ˈdräs\ *n* [*Madras,* India] (ca. 1830) **1** : a large silk or cotton kerchief usu. of bright colors that is often worn as a turban **2 a** : a fine plain-woven shirting and dress fabric usu. of cotton with varied designs (as plaid) in bright colors or in white **b** : a light open usu. cotton fabric with a heavy design used for curtains
ma·dras·sa *or* **ma·dra·sa** *also* **ma·dras·sah** *or* **ma·dra·sah** \mə-ˈdra-sə, -ˈdrä-\ *n* [Ar *madrasa*] (1662) : a Muslim school, college, or university that is often part of a mosque
mad·re·pore \ˈma-drə-ˌpȯr\ *n* [F *madrépore,* fr. It *madrepora,* fr. *madre* mother (fr. L *mater*) + *poro* pore (fr. L *porus*) — more at MOTHER] (1751) : any of various stony reef-building corals (order Madreporaria) of tropical seas that assume a variety of branching, encrusting, or massive forms — **mad·re·po·ri·an** \ˌma-drə-ˈpȯr-ē-ən\ *adj or n* — **mad·re·por·ic** \-ˈpȯr-ik\ *adj*
mad·re·por·ite \ˈma-drə-ˌpȯr-ˌīt\ *n* [ISV *madrepore* + [1]*-ite* (segment); fr. the resemblances of the perforations to those of a madrepore] (1877) : a perforated or porous body that is situated at the distal end of the stone canal in echinoderms
mad·ri·gal \ˈma-dri-gəl\ *n* [It *madrigale,* prob. fr. ML *matricale,* fr. neut. of **matricalis* simple, fr. LL, of the womb, fr. L *matric-, matrix* womb, fr. *mater* mother] (1588) **1** : a medieval short lyrical poem in a strict poetic form **2 a** : a complex polyphonic unaccompanied vocal piece on a secular text developed esp. in the 16th and 17th centuries **b** : PART-SONG; *esp* : GLEE — **mad·ri·gal·ian** \ˌma-drə-ˈga-lē-ən, -ˈgā-\ *adj* — **mad·ri·gal·ist** \ˈma-dri-gə-list\ *n*
ma·dri·lene \ˌma-drə-ˈlen, -ˈlān\ *n* [F (*consommé*) *madrilène,* lit., Madrid consommé] (1907) : a consommé flavored with tomato
ma·dro·ne *or* **ma·dro·na** *also* **ma·dro·no** \mə-ˈdrō-nə\ *n* [Sp *madroño*] (1841) : any of several evergreen trees (genus *Arbutus*) of the heath family; *esp* : one (*A. menziesii*) of the Pacific coast of No. America with smooth red bark, thick shining leaves, and edible red berries
ma·du·ro \mə-ˈdu̇r-(ˌ)ō\ *n, pl* **-ros** [Sp, fr. *maduro* ripe, fr. L *maturus* — more at MATURE] (1850) : a dark-colored relatively strong cigar
mad·wom·an \ˈmad-ˌwu̇-mən\ *n* (15c) : a woman who is or acts as if insane
mad·wort \-ˌwərt, -ˌwȯrt\ *n* (1597) **1** : ALYSSUM 1 **2** : a low hairy annual European herb (*Asperugo procumbens*) of the borage family with blue flowers and a root used as a substitute for madder
MAE *or* **MA Ed** *abbr* master of arts in education
Mae·ce·nas \mi-ˈsē-nəs\ *n* [L, fr. Gaius *Maecenas* †8 B.C. Roman statesman & patron of literature] (1542) : a generous patron esp. of literature or art
mael·strom \ˈmāl-strəm, -ˌsträm\ *n* [obs. D (now *maalstroom*), fr. *malen* to grind + *strom* stream] (1682) **1** : a powerful often violent whirlpool sucking in objects within a given radius **2** : something resembling a maelstrom in turbulence
mae·nad \ˈmē-ˌnad\ *n* [L *maenad-, maenas,* fr. Gk *mainad-, mainas,* fr. *mainesthai* to be mad; akin to Gk *menos* spirit — more at MIND] (1579) **1** : BACCHANTE **2** : an unnaturally excited or distraught woman — **mae·nad·ic** \mē-ˈna-dik\ *adj*
mae·sto·so \mī-ˈstō-(ˌ)sō, -(ˌ)zō\ *adj or adv* [It, fr. L *majestosus,* fr. *majestas* majesty] (ca. 1724) : majestic and stately — used as a direction in music
mae·stro \ˈmī-(ˌ)strō\ *n, pl* **maestros** *or* **mae·stri** \-ˌstrē\ [It, lit., master, fr. L *magister* — more at MASTER] (1724) : a master usu. in an art; *esp* : an eminent composer, conductor, or teacher of music
Mae West \ˈmā-ˈwest\ *n* [*Mae West* †1980 Am. actress noted for her full figure] (1940) : an inflatable life jacket in the form of a collar extending down the chest that was worn by fliers in World War II
maf·fick \ˈma-fik\ *vi* [back-formation fr. *Mafeking Night,* English celebration of the lifting of the siege of Mafeking, So. Africa, May 17, 1900] (1900) : to celebrate with boisterous rejoicing and hilarious behavior
Ma·fia \ˈmä-fē-ə, ˈma-\ *n* [*Mafia, Maffia,* a Sicilian secret criminal society, fr. It dial. (Sicily), prob. fr. *mafiusu*] (1875) **1 a** : a secret criminal society of Sicily or Italy **b** : a similarly conceived criminal organization in the U.S.; *also* : a similar organization elsewhere ⟨the Japanese ~⟩ **c** : a criminal organization associated with a particular traffic ⟨the cocaine ~⟩ **2** *often not cap* : a group of people likened to the Mafia; *esp* : a group of people of similar interests or backgrounds prominent in a particular field or enterprise : CLIQUE
maf·ic \ˈma-fik\ *adj* [NL *magnesium* + L *ferrum* iron + E *-ic*] (1912) : of, relating to, or being a group of usu. dark-colored minerals rich in magnesium and iron
ma·fi·o·so \ˌmä-fē-ˈō-(ˌ)sō, ˌma-, -(ˌ)zō\ *n, pl* **-si** \-(ˌ)sē, -(ˌ)zē\ [It, fr. It dial. (Sicily) *mafiusu* gallant, swaggerer, perh. alter. of *marfusu* scoundrel] (1875) : a member of the Mafia or a mafia
[1]**mag** \ˈmag\ *n* (1796) : MAGAZINE
[2]**mag** *abbr* **1** magnesium **2** magnetism **3** magneto **4** magnitude
mag·a·zine \ˈma-gə-ˌzēn, ˌma-gə-ˈ\ *n* [MF, fr. Old Occitan, fr. Ar *makhāzin,* pl. of *makhzan* storehouse] (1583) **1** : a place where goods or supplies are stored : WAREHOUSE **2** : a room in which powder and other explosives are kept in a fort or a ship **3** : the contents of a magazine: as **a** : an accumulation of munitions of war **b** : a stock of provisions or goods **4 a** : a periodical containing miscellaneous pieces (as articles, stories, poems) and often illustrated; *also* : such a periodical published online **b** : a similar section of a newspaper usu. appearing on Sunday **c** : a radio or television program presenting usu. several short segments on a variety of topics **5** : a supply chamber: as **a** : a holder in or on a gun for cartridges to be fed into the gun chamber **b** : a lightproof chamber for films or plates on a camera or for film on a motion-picture projector
mag·a·zin·ist \-ˌzē-nist, -ˈzē-\ *n* (1821) : a person who writes for or edits a magazine
mag·da·len \ˈmag-də-lən\ *or* **mag·da·lene** \-ˌlēn\ *n, often cap* [Mary *Magdalen* or *Magdalene* woman healed by Jesus of evil spirits (Lk 8:2), considered identical with a reformed prostitute (Lk 7:36–50)] (1697) **1** : a reformed prostitute **2** : a house of refuge or reformatory for prostitutes
Mag·da·le·ni·an \ˌmag-də-ˈlē-nē-ən\ *adj* [F *magdalénien,* fr. *La Madeleine,* rock shelter in southwest France] (1885) : of or relating to an Upper Paleolithic culture characterized by flint, bone, and ivory implements, carving, and paintings
mage \ˈmāj\ *n* [ME, fr. L *magus*] (14c) : MAGUS
Mag·el·lan·ic Cloud \ˌma-jə-ˈla-nik-, *chiefly Brit* ˌma-gə-\ *n* [Ferdinand *Magellan*] (ca. 1686) : either of the two small galaxies that appear as conspicuous patches of light near the south celestial pole and are companions to the Milky Way galaxy
Magellanic penguin *n* (1826) : a penguin (*Spheniscus magellanicus*) of the southern tip of So. America and surrounding islands that has a pink mark above the eyes and two broad black bands on the neck and upper chest
Ma·gen Da·vid *or* **Mo·gen David** \ˈmȯ-gən-ˈdȯ-vid, -ˈdə-; ˈmō-gən-ˈdā-vəd\ *n* [Heb *māghēn Dāwīdh,* lit., shield of David] (ca. 1904) : a hexagram used as a symbol of Judaism
ma·gen·ta \mə-ˈjen-tə\ *n* [*Magenta,* Italy] (1860) **1** : FUCHSIN **2** : a deep purplish red
mag·got \ˈma-gət\ *n* [ME *magot,* prob. alter. of *mathek, maddok;* akin to MLG *mēdeke* maggot, ON *mathkr,* OE *matha*] (14c) **1** : a soft-bodied legless grub that is the larva of a dipterous insect (as the housefly) **2** : a fantastic or eccentric idea : WHIM — **mag·goty** \-gə-tē\ *adj*
magi *pl of* MAGUS
[1]**Ma·gi·an** \ˈmā-jē-ən\ *n* (1578) : MAGUS
[2]**Ma·gi·an** \-jē-ən, -ˌjī-\ *adj* (1716) : of or relating to the Magi — **Ma·gi·an·ism** \-ə-ˌni-zəm\ *n*

[1]**mag·ic** \ˈma-jik\ *n* [ME *magique,* fr. MF, fr. L *magice,* fr. Gk *magikē,* fem. of *magikos* Magian, magical, fr. *magos* magus, sorcerer, of Iranian origin; akin to OPers *maguš* sorcerer] (14c) **1 a :** the use of means (as charms or spells) believed to have supernatural power over natural forces **b :** magic rites or incantations **2 a :** an extraordinary power or influence seemingly from a supernatural source **b :** something that seems to cast a spell : ENCHANTMENT **3 :** the art of producing illusions by sleight of hand

[2]**magic** *adj* (14c) **1 :** of or relating to magic **2 a :** having seemingly supernatural qualities or powers **b :** giving a feeling of enchantment — **mag·i·cal** \ˈma-ji-kəl\ *adj* — **mag·i·cal·ly** \-ji-k(ə-)lē\ *adv*

[3]**magic** *vt* **mag·icked; mag·ick·ing** (1906) **:** to produce, remove, or influence by magic

magic bullet *n* (1940) **1 :** a substance or therapy capable of destroying pathogens (as bacteria or cancer cells) or providing an effective remedy for a disease or condition without deleterious side effects **2 :** something providing an effective solution to a difficult or previously unsolvable problem ⟨a *magic bullet* to stem voter apathy⟩

ma·gi·cian \mə-ˈji-shən\ *n* (14c) **1 :** one skilled in magic; *esp* **:** SORCERER **2 :** one who performs tricks of illusion and sleight of hand

magic lantern *n* (1696) **:** an early form of optical projector of still pictures using a transparent slide

Magic Marker *trademark* — used for a felt-tipped pen

magic mushroom *n* (1966) **:** a fungus (as genus *Psilocybe*) containing hallucinogenic alkaloids (as psilocybin)

magic realism *n* (1933) **1 :** painting in a meticulously realistic style of imaginary or fantastic scenes or images **2 :** a literary genre or style associated esp. with Latin America that incorporates fantastic or mythical elements into otherwise realistic fiction — called also *magical realism* — **magic realist** *n*

magic square *n* (ca. 1704) **:** a square containing a number of integers arranged so that the sum of the numbers is the same in each row, column, and main diagonal and often in some or all of the other diagonals

4	9	2
3	5	7
8	1	6

6	3	10	15
9	16	5	4
7	2	11	14
12	13	8	1

magic squares

Ma·gi·not Line \ˈma-zhə-ˌnō-, ˈma-jə-\ *n* [André *Maginot* †1932 Fr. minister of war] (1936) **1 :** a line of defensive fortifications built before World War II to protect the eastern border of France but easily outflanked by German invaders **2 :** a defensive barrier or strategy that inspires a false sense of security

mag·is·te·ri·al \ˌma-jə-ˈstir-ē-əl\ *adj* [LL *magisterialis* of authority, fr. *magisterium* office of a master, fr. *magister*] (1632) **1 a** (1) **:** of, relating to, or having the characteristics of a master or teacher : AUTHORITATIVE (2) **:** marked by an overbearingly dignified or assured manner or aspect **b :** of, relating to, or required for a master's degree **2 :** of or relating to a magistrate or a magistrate's office or duties ***syn*** see DICTATORIAL — **mag·is·te·ri·al·ly** \-ē-ə-lē\ *adv*

mag·is·te·ri·um \ˌma-jə-ˈstir-ē-əm\ *n* [L] (1866) **:** teaching authority esp. of the Roman Catholic Church

mag·is·tra·cy \ˈma-jə-strə-sē\ *n, pl* **-cies** (ca. 1585) **1 :** the state of being a magistrate **2 :** the office, power, or dignity of a magistrate **3 :** a body of magistrates **4 :** the district under a magistrate

ma·gis·tral \ˈma-jə-strəl, mə-ˈjis-trəl\ *adj* [LL *magistralis,* fr. L *magistr-, magister*] (1605) **:** MAGISTERIAL 1a — **ma·gis·tral·ly** \-ē\ *adv*

mag·is·trate \ˈma-jə-ˌstrāt, -strət\ *n* [ME *magestrat,* fr. L *magistratus* magistracy, magistrate, fr. *magistr-, magister* master, political superior — more at MASTER] (14c) **:** an official entrusted with administration of the laws: as **a :** a principal official exercising governmental powers over a major political unit (as a nation) **b :** a local official exercising administrative and often judicial functions **c :** a local judiciary official having limited original jurisdiction esp. in criminal cases — **mag·is·trat·i·cal** \ˌma-jə-ˈstra-ti-kəl\ *adj*

magistrate's court *n* (1867) **1 :** POLICE COURT **2 :** a court that has minor civil and criminal jurisdiction

mag·is·tra·ture \ˈma-jə-ˌstrā-chər, -strə-ˌchu̇r\ *n* (1672) **:** MAGISTRACY

mag·lev \ˈmag-ˌlev\ *n, often attrib* [*mag*netic *lev*itation] (1969) **1 :** the use of the physical properties of magnetic fields generated by superconducting magnets to cause an object (as a vehicle) to float above a solid surface **2 :** a train utilizing maglev technology

mag·ma \ˈmag-mə\ *n* [ME, fr. L *magmat-, magma,* fr. Gk, thick unguent, fr. *massein* to knead — more at MINGLE] (15c) **1** *archaic* **:** DREGS, SEDIMENT **2 :** a thin pasty suspension (as of a precipitate in water) **3 :** molten rock material within the earth from which igneous rock results by cooling — **mag·mat·ic** \mag-ˈma-tik\ *adj*

Mag·na Car·ta *also* **Mag·na Char·ta** \ˌmag-nə-ˈkär-tə\ *n* [ME, fr. ML, lit., great charter] (15c) **1 :** a charter of liberties to which the English barons forced King John to give his assent in June 1215 at Runnymede **2 :** a document constituting a fundamental guarantee of rights and privileges

mag·na cum lau·de \ˈmäg-nə-(ˌ)ku̇m-ˈlau̇-də, -ˈlau̇-dē; ˈmag-nə-ˌkəm-ˈlȯ-dē\ *adv or adj* [L] (1900) **:** with great distinction ⟨graduated *magna cum laude*⟩ — compare CUM LAUDE, SUMMA CUM LAUDE

mag·na·nim·i·ty \ˌmag-nə-ˈni-mə-tē\ *n, pl* **-ties** (14c) **1 :** the quality of being magnanimous : loftiness of spirit enabling one to bear trouble calmly, to disdain meanness and pettiness, and to display a noble generosity **2 :** a magnanimous act

mag·nan·i·mous \mag-ˈna-nə-məs\ *adj* [L *magnanimus,* fr. *magnus* great + *animus* spirit — more at MUCH, ANIMATE] (1567) **1 :** showing or suggesting a lofty and courageous spirit ⟨the irreproachable lives and ~ sufferings of their followers —Joseph Addison⟩ **2 :** showing or suggesting nobility of feeling and generosity of mind ⟨too sincere for dissimulation, too ~ for resentment —Ellen Glasgow⟩ — **mag·nan·i·mous·ly** *adv* — **mag·nan·i·mous·ness** *n*

mag·nate \ˈmag-ˌnāt, -nət\ *n* [ME *magnates,* pl., fr. LL, fr. L *magnus*] (15c) **:** a person of rank, power, influence, or distinction often in a specified area

mag·ne·sia \mag-ˈnē-shə, -zhə\ *n* [NL, fr. *magnes carneus,* a white earth, lit., flesh magnet] (1755) **:** MAGNESIUM OXIDE — compare MILK OF MAGNESIA — **mag·ne·sian** \-shən, -zhən\ *adj*

mag·ne·site \ˈmag-nə-ˌsīt\ *n* (1815) **:** native magnesium carbonate used esp. in making refractories and magnesium oxide

mag·ne·sium \mag-ˈnē-zē-əm, -zhəm\ *n* [NL, fr. *magnesia*] (1812) **:** a silver-white malleable ductile light metallic element that occurs abundantly in nature and is used in metallurgical and chemical processes, in photography, signaling, and pyrotechnics because of the intense white light it produces on burning, and in construction esp. in the form of light alloys — see ELEMENT table

magnesium carbonate *n* (1869) **:** a carbonate of magnesium; *esp* **:** a white crystalline salt $MgCO_3$ that occurs naturally as dolomite and magnesite

magnesium chloride *n* (1866) **:** a bitter deliquescent salt $MgCl_2$ used esp. as a source of magnesium metal

magnesium hydroxide *n* (ca. 1909) **:** a slightly alkaline crystalline compound $Mg(OH)_2$ used esp. as a laxative and gastric antacid

magnesium oxide *n* (1866) **:** a white highly infusible compound MgO used esp. in refractories, cements, insulation, and fertilizers, in rubber manufacture, and in medicine as an antacid and mild laxative

magnesium sulfate *n* (1869) **:** a sulfate of magnesium: as **a :** a white salt $MgSO_4$ used in medicine and in industry **b :** EPSOM SALTS

mag·net \ˈmag-nət\ *n* [ME *magnete,* fr. AF, fr. L *magnet-, magnes,* fr. Gk *magnēs* (*lithos*), lit., stone of Magnesia, ancient city in Asia Minor] (15c) **1 a :** LODESTONE **b :** a body having the property of attracting iron and producing a magnetic field external to itself; *specif* **:** a mass of iron, steel, or alloy that has this property artificially imparted **2 :** something that attracts ⟨a box-office ~⟩

magnet- *or* **magneto-** *comb form* [L *magnet-, magnes*] **1 :** magnetic force ⟨*magneto*meter⟩ **2 :** magnetism : magnetic ⟨*magneto*electric⟩ ⟨*magnet*on⟩ **3 :** magnetoelectric ⟨*magneto*resistance⟩ **4 :** magnetosphere ⟨*magneto*pause⟩

[1]**mag·net·ic** \mag-ˈne-tik\ *adj* (1611) **1 :** possessing an extraordinary power or ability to attract ⟨a ~ personality⟩ **2 a :** of or relating to a magnet or to magnetism **b :** of, relating to, or characterized by the earth's magnetism **c :** magnetized or capable of being magnetized **d :** actuated by magnetic attraction — **mag·net·i·cal·ly** \-ti-k(ə-)lē\ *adv*

[2]**magnetic** *n* (1654) **:** a magnetic substance

magnetic bubble *n* (1969) **:** a tiny movable magnetized cylindrical volume in a thin magnetic material that along with other like volumes can be used to represent a bit of information (as in a computer)

magnetic disk *n* (ca. 1960) **:** DISK 4b

magnetic equator *n* (1832) **:** an imaginary line roughly parallel to the geographical equator and passing through those points where a magnetic needle has no dip

magnetic field *n* (1845) **:** the portion of space near a magnetic body or a current-carrying body in which the magnetic forces due to the body or current can be detected

magnetic flux *n* (1896) **:** a measure of magnetic induction represented by lines of force

magnetic levitation *n* (1966) **:** MAGLEV 1

magnetic mirror *n* (1952) **:** a magnetic field that confines a plasma by reflecting ions back toward the main plasma concentration

magnetic moment *n* (1865) **:** a vector quantity that is a measure of the torque exerted on a magnetic system (as a bar magnet or dipole) when placed in a magnetic field and that for a magnet is the product of the distance between its poles and the strength of either pole

magnetic north *n* (1812) **:** the northerly direction in the earth's magnetic field indicated by the north-seeking pole of a compass needle

magnetic pole *n* (1701) **1 :** either of two small regions which are located respectively in the polar areas of the northern and southern hemispheres and toward which a compass needle points from any direction throughout adjacent regions; *also* **:** either of two comparable regions on a celestial body **2 :** either of the poles of a magnet

magnetic quantum number *n* (1923) **:** an integer that expresses the component of the quantized angular momentum of an electron, atom, or molecule in the direction of an externally applied magnetic field

magnetic recording *n* (1945) **:** the process of recording sound, data (as for a computer), or a television program by producing varying local magnetization of a moving tape or disc — **magnetic recorder** *n*

magnetic resonance *n* (1903) **:** the excitation of particles (as atomic nuclei or electrons) in a magnetic field by exposure to electromagnetic radiation of a specific frequency

magnetic resonance imaging *n* (1977) **:** a noninvasive diagnostic technique that produces computerized images of internal body tissues and is based on nuclear magnetic resonance of atoms within the body induced by the application of radio waves — abbr. *MRI*

magnetic storm *n* (ca. 1855) **:** a marked temporary disturbance of the earth's magnetic field held to be related to sunspots

magnetic tape *n* (1937) **:** a thin ribbon (as of plastic) coated with a magnetic material on which information (as sound or television images) may be stored

mag·ne·tise *Brit var of* MAGNETIZE

mag·ne·tism \ˈmag-nə-ˌti-zəm\ *n* (1616) **1 a :** a class of physical phenomena that include the attraction for iron observed in lodestone and a magnet, are inseparably associated with moving electricity, are exhibited by both magnets and electric currents, and are characterized by fields of force **b :** a science that deals with magnetic phenomena **2 :** an ability to attract or charm

mag·ne·tite \ˈmag-nə-ˌtīt\ *n* (1851) **:** a black isometric mineral of the spinel group that is an oxide of iron and an important iron ore

mag·ne·ti·za·tion \ˌmag-nə-tə-ˈzā-shən\ *n* (1801) **:** an instance of magnetizing or the state of being magnetized; *also* **:** the degree to which a body is magnetized

mag·ne·tize \ˈmag-nə-ˌtīz\ *vt* **-tized; -tiz·ing** (1801) **1 :** to induce magnetic properties in **2 :** to attract like a magnet : CHARM — **mag·ne·tiz·able** \-ˌtī-zə-bəl\ *adj* — **mag·ne·tiz·er** *n*

\ə\ **abut** \ᵊ\ **kitten**, F table \ər\ **further** \a\ **ash** \ā\ **ace** \ä\ **mop, mar** \au̇\ **out** \ch\ **chin** \e\ **bet** \ē\ **easy** \g\ **go** \i\ **hit** \ī\ **ice** \j\ **job** \ŋ\ **sing** \ō\ **go** \ȯ\ **law** \ȯi\ **boy** \th\ **thin** \t͟h\ **the** \ü\ **loot** \u̇\ **foot** \y\ **yet** \zh\ **vision, beige** \k̲, ^{n}, œ, ue, ^{y}\ *see* Guide to Pronunciation

mag·ne·to \mag-ˈnē-(ˌ)tō\ *n, pl* **-tos** (1882) **:** a magnetoelectric machine; *esp* **:** an alternator with permanent magnets used to generate current for the ignition in an internal combustion engine
mag·ne·to·elec·tric \-ˌnē-tō-ə-ˈlek-trik, -ˌne-\ *adj* (1831) **:** relating to or characterized by electromotive forces developed by magnetic means
mag·ne·to·en·ceph·a·log·ra·phy \mag-ˌnē-tō-in-ˌse-fə-ˈlä-grə-fē, -ˌne-\ *n* (1968) **:** a noninvasive technique that detects and records the magnetic field associated with electrical activity in the brain
mag·ne·to·flu·id·dy·nam·ics \-ˌnē-tō-ˌflü-ə-dī-ˈna-miks, -ˌne-, -də-ˈ\ *n pl but sing or pl in constr* (1962) **:** the study of magnetohydrodynamic phenomena **:** MAGNETOHYDRODYNAMICS
mag·ne·to·graph \-ˌgraf\ *n* (1847) **:** an automatic instrument for recording measurements of a magnetic field (as of the earth or the sun)
mag·ne·to·hy·dro·dy·nam·ic \mag-ˌnē-tō-ˌhī-drə-dī-ˈna-mik, -ˈne-, -də-ˈ\ *adj* (1943) **:** of, relating to, or being phenomena arising from the motion of electrically conducting fluids (as plasmas) in the presence of electric and magnetic fields — **mag·ne·to·hy·dro·dy·nam·ics** \-miks\ *n pl but sing or pl in constr*
mag·ne·tom·e·ter \ˌmag-nə-ˈtä-mə-tər\ *n* (1827) **:** an instrument used to detect the presence of a metallic object or to measure the intensity of a magnetic field — **mag·ne·to·met·ric** \mag-ˌnē-tə-ˈme-trik, -ˌne-\ *adj* — **mag·ne·tom·e·try** \ˌmag-nə-ˈtä-mə-trē\ *n*
mag·ne·to·mo·tive force \mag-ˌnē-tə-ˈmō-tiv-, -ˌne-\ *n* (1883) **:** a force that is the cause of a flux of magnetic induction
mag·ne·ton \ˈmag-nə-ˌtän\ *n* [ISV *magnet-* + ²*-on*] (1911) **:** a unit of the quantized magnetic moment of a particle (as an atom)
mag·ne·to–op·tic \mag-ˌnē-tō-ˈäp-tik, -ˌne-\ *also* **mag·ne·to–op·ti·cal** \-ti-kəl\ *adj* (1848) **:** of, relating to, or utilizing the influence of a magnetic field upon light ⟨a ~ disk drive⟩ — **mag·ne·to–op·tics** \-tiks\ *n pl but sing or pl in constr*
mag·ne·to·pause \mag-ˈnē-tə-ˌpȯz, -ˈne-\ *n* (1962) **:** the outer boundary of a magnetosphere
mag·ne·to·re·sis·tance \-ˌnē-tō-ri-ˈzis-tən(t)s, -ˌne-\ *n* (1927) **:** a change in electrical resistance due to the presence of a magnetic field — **mag·ne·to·re·sis·tive** \-ˈzis-tiv\ *adj*
mag·ne·to·sphere \mag-ˈnē-tə-ˌsfir, -ˈne-\ *n* (1959) **:** a region of space surrounding a celestial object (as a planet or star) that is dominated by the object's magnetic field so that charged particles are trapped in it — **mag·ne·to·spher·ic** \-ˌnē-tə-ˈsfir-ik, -ˈsfer-\ *adj*
mag·ne·to·stat·ic \mag-ˌnē-tō-ˈsta-tik, -ˌne-\ *adj* (1893) **:** of, relating to, or being a stationary magnetic field
mag·ne·to·stric·tion \-ˈstrik-shən\ *n* [ISV *magnet-* + *-striction* (as in *constriction*)] (1896) **:** the change in the dimensions of a ferromagnetic body caused by a change in its state of magnetization — **mag·ne·to·stric·tive** \-ˈstrik-tiv\ *adj* — **mag·ne·to·stric·tive·ly** *adv*
mag·ne·tron \ˈmag-nə-ˌträn\ *n* [blend of *magnet* and *-tron*] (1921) **:** a vacuum tube in which the flow of electrons is controlled by an applied magnetic field to generate power at microwave frequencies
magnet school *n* (1968) **:** a school with superior facilities and staff and often a specialized curriculum designed to attract pupils from throughout a city or school district
mag·nif·ic \mag-ˈni-fik\ *adj* [MF *magnifique,* fr. L *magnificus*] (15c) **1 :** MAGNIFICENT 2 **2 :** imposing in size or dignity ⟨a ~ temple⟩ **3 a :** SUBLIME, EXALTED **b :** characterized by grandiloquence **:** POMPOUS ⟨commenced the conversation in the most ~ style —S. T. Coleridge⟩ — **mag·nif·i·cal** \-fi-kəl\ *adj* — **mag·nif·i·cal·ly** \-k(ə-)lē\ *adv*
mag·nif·i·cat \mag-ˈni-fi-ˌkat, -ˌkät; män-ˈyi-fi-ˌkät\ *n* [ME, fr. L, magnifies, fr. *magnificare* to magnify; fr. the first word of the canticle] (13c) **1** *cap* **a :** the canticle of the Virgin Mary in Luke 1:46–55 **b :** a musical setting for the Magnificat **2 :** an utterance of praise
mag·ni·fi·ca·tion \ˌmag-nə-fə-ˈkā-shən\ *n* (15c) **1 :** the act of magnifying **2 a :** the state of being magnified **b :** the apparent enlargement of an object by an optical instrument — called also *power*
mag·nif·i·cence \mag-ˈni-fə-sən(t)s, məg-\ *n* [ME, fr. AF, fr. L *magnificentia,* fr. *magnificus* noble in character, magnificent, fr. *magnus* great + *-ficus* -fic — more at MUCH] (14c) **1 :** the quality or state of being magnificent **2 :** splendor of surroundings
mag·nif·i·cent \-sənt\ *adj* (15c) **1 :** great in deed or exalted in place — used only of former famous rulers ⟨Lorenzo the *Magnificent*⟩ **2 :** marked by stately grandeur and lavishness ⟨a ~ way of life⟩ **3 :** sumptuous in structure and adornment ⟨a ~ cathedral⟩; *broadly* **:** strikingly beautiful or impressive ⟨a ~ physique⟩ **4 :** impressive to the mind or spirit **:** SUBLIME ⟨~ prose⟩ **5 :** exceptionally fine ⟨a ~ day⟩ ***syn*** see GRAND — **mag·nif·i·cent·ly** *adv*
mag·nif·i·co \mag-ˈni-fi-ˌkō\ *n, pl* **-coes** *or* **-cos** [It, fr. *magnifico,* adj., magnificent, fr. L *magnificus*] (1573) **1 :** a nobleman of Venice **2 :** a person of high position
mag·ni·fi·er \ˈmag-nə-ˌfī(-ə)r\ *n* (1550) **:** one that magnifies; *esp* **:** a lens or combination of lenses that makes something appear larger
mag·ni·fy \ˈmag-nə-ˌfī\ *vb* **-fied; -fy·ing** [ME *magnifien,* fr. AF *magnifier,* fr. L *magnificare,* fr. *magnificus*] *vt* (14c) **1 a :** EXTOL, LAUD **b :** to cause to be held in greater esteem or respect **2 a :** to increase in significance **:** INTENSIFY **b :** EXAGGERATE ⟨*magnifies* every minor issue to crisis proportions⟩ **3 :** to enlarge in fact or in appearance ~ *vi* **:** to have the power of causing objects to appear larger than they are
mag·nil·o·quence \mag-ˈni-lə-kwən(t)s\ *n* [L *magniloquentia,* fr. *magniloquus* magniloquent, fr. *magnus* + *loqui* to speak] (ca. 1623) **:** the quality or state of being magniloquent
mag·nil·o·quent \-kwənt\ *adj* [back-formation fr. *magniloquence*] (1640) **:** speaking in or characterized by a high-flown often bombastic style or manner ⟨~ boasts⟩ — **mag·nil·o·quent·ly** *adv*
mag·ni·tude \ˈmag-nə-ˌtüd, -ˌtyüd\ *n* [ME, fr. AF, fr. L *magnitudo,* fr. *magnus*] (15c) **1 a :** great size or extent **b (1) :** spatial quality **:** SIZE **(2) :** QUANTITY, NUMBER **2 :** the importance, quality, or caliber of something **3 :** a number representing the intrinsic or apparent brightness of a celestial body on a logarithmic scale in which an increase of one unit corresponds to a reduction in the brightness of light by a factor of 2.512 **4 :** a numerical quantitative measure expressed usu. as a multiple of a standard unit **5 :** the intensity of an earthquake represented by a number on an arbitrary scale ⟨a ~ six earthquake⟩
mag·no·lia \mag-ˈnōl-yə\ *n* [NL, fr. Pierre *Magnol* †1715 Fr. botanist] (1748) **:** any of a genus (*Magnolia* of the family Magnoliaceae, the magnolia family) of American and Asian shrubs and trees with entire evergreen or deciduous leaves and usu. showy white, yellow, rose, or purple flowers usu. appearing in early spring
mag·num \ˈmag-nəm\ *n* [L, neut. of *magnus* great] (1788) **:** a large wine bottle holding about 1.5 liters
Magnum *trademark* — used for revolvers
mag·num opus \ˈmag-nəm-ˈō-pəs\ *n* [L] (1791) **:** a great work; *esp* **:** the greatest achievement of an artist or writer

magpie 1

¹**mag·pie** \ˈmag-ˌpī\ *n* [*Mag* (nickname for *Margaret*) + ¹*pie*] (1598) **1 :** any of various birds (esp. *Pica pica*) related to the jays but having a long graduated tail and black-and-white or brightly colored plumage **2 :** a person who chatters noisily **3 :** one who collects indiscriminately
²**magpie** *adj* (1796) **1 :** collected indiscriminately **:** MISCELLANEOUS ⟨~ compilations of unrelated tidbits —Helen R. Cross⟩ **2 :** given to indiscriminate collecting **:** ACQUISITIVE ⟨what possible ~ instinct had impelled me to retain them —S. J. Perelman⟩
mag tape \ˈmag-\ *n* (1960) **:** MAGNETIC TAPE
ma·guey \mə-ˈgā\ *n* [Sp, fr. Taino] (1555) **1 :** any of various fleshy-leaved agaves (as the century plant) **2 :** any of several hard fibers derived from magueys; *esp* **:** CANTALA
ma·gus \ˈmā-gəs\ *n, pl* **ma·gi** \ˈmā-ˌjī, ˈma-\ [L, fr. Gk *magos* — more at MAGIC] (1555) **1 a :** a member of a hereditary priestly class among the ancient Medes and Persians **b** *often cap* **:** one of the traditionally three wise men from the East paying homage to the infant Jesus **2 :** MAGICIAN, SORCERER
Mag·yar \ˈmag-ˌyär, ˈmäg-; ˈmä-ˌjär\ *n* [Hung] (1797) **1 :** a member of the dominant people of Hungary **2 :** HUNGARIAN 2 — **Magyar** *adj*
ma·ha·ra·ja *or* **ma·ha·ra·jah** \ˌmä-hə-ˈrä-jə, -ˈrä-zhə\ *n* [Hindi & Urdu *mahārājā,* fr. Skt, fr. *mahat* great + *rājan* raja; akin to L *rex* king — more at MUCH, ROYAL] (1698) **:** a Hindu prince ranking above a raja
ma·ha·ra·ni *or* **ma·ha·ra·nee** \-ˈrä-nē\ *n* [Hindi & Urdu *mahārānī,* fr. *mahā* great (fr. Skt *mahat*) + *rānī* rani] (ca. 1855) **1 :** the wife of a maharaja **2 :** a Hindu princess ranking above a rani
ma·ha·ri·shi \ˌmä-hə-ˈrē-shē, -hä-, -ˈri-\ *n* [Skt *maharṣi,* fr. *mahat* + *ṛṣi* sage and poet] (1785) **:** a Hindu teacher of mystical knowledge
ma·hat·ma \mə-ˈhät-mə, -ˈhat-\ *n* [Skt *mahātman,* fr. *mahātman* great-souled, fr. *mahat* + *ātman* soul — more at ATMAN] (1923) **1 :** a person to be revered for high-mindedness, wisdom, and selflessness **2 :** a person of great prestige in a field of endeavor
Ma·ha·ya·na \ˌmä-hə-ˈyä-nə\ *n* [Skt *mahāyāna,* lit., great vehicle] (1855) **:** a liberal and theistic branch of Buddhism comprising sects chiefly in China and Japan, recognizing a large body of scripture in addition to the Pali canon, and teaching social concern and universal salvation — compare THERAVADA — **Ma·ha·ya·nist** \-ˈyä-nist\ *n or adj* — **Ma·ha·ya·nis·tic** \-yä-ˈnis-tik\ *adj*
Mah·di \ˈmä-dē\ *n* [Ar *mahdī,* lit., one rightly guided] (1626) **1 :** the expected messiah of Muslim tradition **2 :** a Muslim leader who assumes a messianic role — **Mah·dism** \ˈmä-ˌdi-zəm\ *n* — **Mah·dist** \ˈmä-dist\ *n*
Ma·hi·can \mə-ˈhē-kən\ *or* **Mo·hi·can** \mō-, mə-\ *n, pl* **-can** *or* **-cans** [Mahican] (ca. 1614) **1 :** a member of an American Indian people of the upper Hudson River valley **2 :** the extinct Algonquian language of the Mahican people
ma·hi·ma·hi \ˌmä-hē-ˈmä-(ˌ)hē\ *n* [Hawaiian, Tahitian, & Marquesan] (1905) **:** the flesh of a dolphinfish (*Coryphaena hippurus*) used for food; *also* **:** the fish
mah–jongg *or* **mah·jong** \ˌmä-ˈzhäŋ, -ˈjäŋ, -ˈzhȯŋ, -ˈjȯŋ, ˈmä-ˌ\ *n* [fr. *Mah-Jongg,* a trademark] (1920) **:** a game of Chinese origin usu. played by four persons with 144 tiles that are drawn and discarded until one player secures a winning hand
mahlstick *var of* MAULSTICK
ma·hoe \mə-ˈhō, ˈmä-ˌ\ *n* [F *maho,* fr. Taino] (1756) **:** either of two tropical hibiscus trees (*Hibiscus elatus* and *H. tiliaceus*)
ma·hog·a·ny \mə-ˈhä-gə-nē\ *n, pl* **-nies** [origin unknown] (1660) **1 :** the wood of any of various chiefly tropical trees (family Meliaceae, the mahogany family): **a (1) :** the durable yellowish-brown to reddish-brown usu. moderately hard and heavy wood of a West Indian tree (*Swietenia mahagoni*) that is widely used for cabinetwork and fine finish work **(2) :** a wood similar to mahogany from a congeneric tropical American tree (esp. *S. macrophylla*) **b (1) :** the rather hard heavy usu. odorless wood of any of several African trees (genus *Khaya*) **(2) :** the rather lightweight cedar-scented wood of any of several African trees (genus *Entandrophragma*) that varies in color from pinkish to deep reddish brown **2 :** any of various woods resembling or substituted for mahogany obtained from trees of the mahogany family **3 :** a tree that yields mahogany **4 :** a moderate reddish brown
ma·ho·nia \mə-ˈhō-nē-ə\ *n* [NL, fr. Bernard Mc*Mahon* †1816 Am. botanist] (1818) **:** any of a genus (*Mahonia*) of American and Asian shrubs (as the Oregon grape) of the barberry family
ma·hout \mə-ˈhau̇t\ *n* [Hindi & Urdu *mahāwat, mahāut*] (1662) **:** a keeper and driver of an elephant
Mahratta *var of* MARATHA
ma huang \ˈmä-ˈhwäŋ\ *n* [Chin (Beijing) *máhuáng*] (1926) **1 :** any of several eastern Asian ephedras (esp. *Ephedra sinica*) having stems and roots yielding ephedrine **2 :** EPHEDRA 2
maid \ˈmād\ *n* [ME *maide,* short for *maiden*] (13c) **1 :** an unmarried girl or woman esp. when young **:** VIRGIN **2 a :** MAIDSERVANT **b :** a woman or girl employed to do domestic work
¹**maid·en** \ˈmā-dᵊn\ *n* [ME, fr. OE *mægden, mǣden,* dim. of *mægeth;* akin to OHG *magad* maiden, OIr *mug* serf] (bef. 12c) **1 :** an unmarried girl or woman **:** MAID **2 :** a former Scottish beheading device resembling the guillotine **3 :** a horse that has never won a race
²**maiden** *adj* (14c) **1 a (1) :** not married ⟨a ~ aunt⟩ **(2) :** VIRGIN **b** *of a female animal* **(1) :** never yet mated **(2) :** never having borne young **2 :** of, relating to, or befitting a maiden **3 :** FIRST, EARLIEST ⟨a ship's ~ voyage⟩ ⟨the ~ flight of a spacecraft⟩
maid·en·hair fern \-ˌher-\ *n* (1833) **:** any of a genus (*Adiantum*) of ferns with delicate palmately branched fronds — called also *maidenhair*

maidenhair tree *n* (1773) : GINKGO

maid·en·head \ˈmā-dᵊn-ˌhed\ *n* [ME *maidenhed,* fr. *maiden* + *-hed* -hood; akin to ME *-hod* -hood] (13c) **1** : the quality or state of being a maiden : VIRGINITY **2** : HYMEN

maid·en·hood \-ˌhu̇d\ *n* (bef. 12c) : the quality, state, or time of being a maiden

maid·en·li·ness \-lē-nəs\ *n* (1555) : conduct or traits befitting a maiden

maid·en·ly \-lē\ *adj* (15c) : of, resembling, or suitable to a maiden

maiden name *n* (1689) : the surname of a woman before she marries

maid·hood \ˈmād-ˌhu̇d\ *n* (bef. 12c) : MAIDENHOOD

maid–in–wait·ing \ˈmād-ᵊn-ˈwā-tiŋ\ *n, pl* **maids–in–wait·ing** \ˈmādz-ᵊn-\ (1953) : a young woman of a queen's or princess's household appointed to attend her

Maid Mar·i·an \-ˈmer-ē-ən\ *n* (ca. 1525) : a companion of Robin Hood in some forms of his legend

maid of honor (ca. 1586) **1** : an unmarried lady usu. of noble birth whose duty it is to attend a queen or a princess **2** : a bride's principal unmarried wedding attendant — compare MATRON OF HONOR

maid·ser·vant \ˈmād-ˌsər-vənt\ *n* (14c) : a female servant

ma·ieu·tic \mā-ˈyü-tik, mī-\ *adj* [Gk *maieutikos* of midwifery] (1655) : relating to or resembling the Socratic method of eliciting new ideas from another

[1]**mail** \ˈmāl\ *n* [ME *male, maille,* fr. OE *māl* agreement, pay, fr. ON *māl* speech, agreement; akin to OE *mǣl* speech] (bef. 12c) *chiefly Scot* : PAYMENT, RENT

[2]**mail** *n, often attrib* [ME *male,* fr. AF, of Gmc origin; akin to OHG *malaha* bag] (13c) **1** *chiefly Scot* : BAG, WALLET **2 a** : material sent or carried in the postal system **b** : a conveyance that transports mail **c** : E-MAIL 2a **3** : a nation's postal system — often used in pl.

[3]**mail** *vt* (1827) : to send by mail : POST — **mail·abil·i·ty** \ˌmā-lə-ˈbi-lə-tē\ *n* — **mail·able** \ˈmā-lə-bəl\ *adj*

[4]**mail** *n* [ME *maille* metal link, mail, fr. AF, fr. L *macula* spot, mesh] (14c) **1** : armor made of metal links or sometimes plates **2** : a hard enclosing covering of an animal (as a tortoise) — **mailed** \ˈmā(ə)ld\ *adj*

mail·bag \ˈmāl-ˌbag\ *n* (1812) **1** : a letter carrier's shoulder bag **2** : a pouch used in the shipment of mail

mail·box \-ˌbäks\ *n* (1868) **1** : a box at or near a dwelling for the occupant's mail **2** : a public box for deposit of outgoing mail **3** : a computer file in which e-mail is collected

mail carrier *n* (1788) : LETTER CARRIER

mail drop *n* (1945) **1** : an address used in transmitting secret communications **2** : a receptacle or a slot for deposit of mail

mai·le \ˈmī-lē\ *n* [Hawaiian] (1825) : a Pacific island vine (*Alyxia olivi-formis*) of the dogbane family with fragrant leaves and bark that are used for decoration and in Hawaii for leis

mailed fist *n* (1897) : a threat of armed or overbearing force

mail·er \ˈmā-lər\ *n* (1884) **1** : one that mails **2** : a container for mailing something **3** : something (as an advertisement) sent by mail

Mail·gram \ˈmāl-ˌgram\ *service mark* — used for a message sent by wire to a post office that delivers it to the addressee

mail·ing \ˈmā-liŋ\ *n* (1928) : mail sent at one time to multiple addressees by a sender (as for promotional purposes)

Mail·lard reaction \mə-ˈlärd-, -ˈyär-\ *n* [Louis-Camille *Maillard* †1936 Fr. biochemist] (1929) : a nonenzymatic reaction between sugars and proteins that occurs upon heating and that produces browning of some foods (as meat and bread)

mail·lot \mī-ˈō, mä-ˈyō\ *n* [F] (1876) **1** : tights for dancers or gymnasts **2** : JERSEY 2 **3** : a woman's one-piece bathing suit

mail·man \ˈmāl-ˌman\ *n* (1786) : a man who delivers mail — called also *postman*

mail order *n* (1867) : an order for goods that is received and filled by mail — **mail–or·der** \-ˌȯr-dər\ *adj*

[1]**maim** \ˈmām\ *vt* [ME *maymen, mahaymen,* fr. AF *maheimer, mahaigner* — more at MAYHEM] (14c) **1** : to commit the felony of mayhem upon **2** : to mutilate, disfigure, or wound seriously — **maim·er** *n*

syn MAIM, CRIPPLE, MUTILATE, BATTER, MANGLE mean to injure so severely as to cause lasting damage. MAIM implies the loss or injury of a bodily member through violence ⟨*maimed* by a shark⟩. CRIPPLE implies the loss or serious impairment of an arm or leg ⟨*crippled* for life in an accident⟩. MUTILATE implies the cutting off or removal of an essential part of a person or thing thereby impairing its completeness, beauty, or function ⟨a tree *mutilated* by inept pruning⟩. BATTER implies a series of blows that bruise deeply, deform, or mutilate ⟨an old ship *battered* by fierce storms⟩. MANGLE implies a tearing or crushing that leaves deep wounds ⟨a soldier's leg *mangled* by shrapnel⟩.

[2]**maim** *n* (14c) **1** *obs* : serious physical injury; *esp* : loss of a member of the body **2** *obs* : a serious loss

[1]**main** \ˈmān\ *n* [in sense 1, fr. ME, fr. OE *mægen;* akin to OHG *magan* strength, OE *magan* to be able; in other senses, fr. [2]*main* or by shortening — more at MAY] (bef. 12c) **1** : physical strength : FORCE — used in the phrase *with might and main* **2 a** : MAINLAND **b** : HIGH SEA **3** : the chief part : essential point ⟨they are in the ~ well-trained⟩ **4** : a pipe, duct, or circuit which carries the combined flow of tributary branches of a utility system **5 a** : MAINMAST **b** : MAINSAIL

[2]**main** *adj* [ME, fr. OE *mægen-,* fr. *mægen* strength] (15c) **1** : CHIEF, PRINCIPAL ⟨the ~ idea⟩ **2** : fully exerted : SHEER ⟨~ force⟩ ⟨by ~ strength⟩ **3** *obs* : of or relating to a broad expanse (as of sea) **4** : connected with or located near the mainmast or mainsail **5** : expressing the chief predication in a complex sentence ⟨the ~ clause⟩

main chance *n* (1584) : the best chance for personal or financial gain ⟨kept an eye on the *main chance*⟩

Maine coon *n* (1935) : any of a breed of large long-haired domestic cats that have a very full tapered tail — called also *coon cat, Maine cat*

main·frame \ˈmān-ˌfrām\ *n* (ca. 1964) : a computer with its cabinet and internal circuits; *also* : a large fast computer that can handle multiple tasks concurrently

main·land \ˈmān-ˌland, -lənd\ *n* (14c) : a continent or the main part of a continent as distinguished from an offshore island or sometimes from a cape or peninsula — **main·land·er** \-ˌlan-dər, -lən-\ *n*

[1]**main·line** \ˈmān-ˌlīn\ *vt* (1938) *slang* : to take by or as if by injecting into a principal vein ~ *vi, slang* : to mainline a narcotic drug

[2]**mainline** *adj* (1941) : being part of an established group; *also* : being in the mainstream

main line *n* (1841) **1** : a principal highway or railroad line **2** *slang* : a principal vein of the circulatory system

main·ly \ˈmān-lē\ *adv* (13c) **1** *obs* : in a forceful manner **2** : for the most part : CHIEFLY

main man *n* (1953) **1** : best male friend **2** : a man whose character or work is most admired **3** : most significant or important person; *also* : CHIEF 2

main·mast \ˈmān-ˌmast, -məst\ *n* (15c) : a sailing ship's principal mast

mains \ˈmānz\ *adj* (1906) *Brit* : of or relating to utility distribution mains ⟨~ voltage⟩ ⟨~ water⟩

main·sail \ˈmān-ˌsāl, ˈmān(t)-səl\ *n* (15c) : the principal sail on the mainmast — see SAIL illustration

main sequence *n* (1925) : the group of stars that on a graph of spectrum versus luminosity forms a band comprising 90 percent of stellar types and that includes stars representative of the stages a normal star passes through during the majority of its lifetime

main·sheet \ˈmān-ˌshēt\ *n* (15c) : a line by which the mainsail is trimmed and secured

main·spring \ˈmān-ˌspriŋ\ *n* (1591) **1** : the chief spring in a mechanism esp. of a watch or clock **2** : the chief or most powerful motive, agent, or cause

main·stay \ˈmān-ˌstā\ *n* (15c) **1** : a ship's stay extending from the maintop forward usu. to the foot of the foremast **2** : a chief support

main stem *n* (1671) : a main trunk or channel: as **a** : the main course of a river or stream **b** : the main street of a city or town

[1]**main·stream** \ˈmān-ˌstrēm\ *n* (1599) : a prevailing current or direction of activity or influence — **mainstream** *adj*

[2]**main·stream** \ˈmān-ˈstrēm\ *vt* (1973) **1** : to place (as a disabled child) in regular school classes **2** : to incorporate in the mainstream

Main Street *n* (1745) **1** : the principal street of a small town **2 a** : the sections of a country centering about its small towns **b** : a place or environment characterized by materialistic self-complacent provincialism **c** : MIDDLE AMERICA 3 — **Main Street·er** \ˈmān-ˌstrē-tər\ *n*

main·tain \mān-ˈtān, mən-\ *vt* [ME *mainteinen,* fr. AF *maintenir, mayn-teiner,* fr. ML *manutenēre,* fr. L *manu tenēre* to hold in the hand] (14c) **1** : to keep in an existing state (as of repair, efficiency, or validity) : preserve from failure or decline ⟨~ machinery⟩ **2** : to sustain against opposition or danger : uphold and defend ⟨~ a position⟩ **3** : to continue or persevere in : CARRY ON, KEEP UP ⟨couldn't ~ his composure⟩ **4 a** : to support or provide for ⟨has a family to ~⟩ **b** : SUSTAIN ⟨enough food to ~ life⟩ **5** : to affirm in or as if in argument : ASSERT ⟨~*ed* that the earth is flat⟩ — **main·tain·abil·i·ty** \-ˌtā-nə-ˈbi-lə-tē\ *n* — **main·tain·able** \-ˈtā-nə-bəl\ *adj* — **main·tain·er** *n*

syn MAINTAIN, ASSERT, DEFEND, VINDICATE, JUSTIFY mean to uphold as true, right, just, or reasonable. MAINTAIN stresses firmness of conviction ⟨steadfastly *maintained* his innocence⟩. ASSERT suggests determination to make others accept one's claim ⟨*asserted* her rights⟩. DEFEND implies maintaining in the face of attack or criticism ⟨*defended* his voting record⟩. VINDICATE implies successfully defending ⟨his success *vindicated* our faith in him⟩. JUSTIFY implies showing to be true, just, or valid by appeal to a standard or to precedent ⟨the action was used to *justify* military intervention⟩.

main·te·nance \ˈmānt-nən(t)s, ˈmān-tə-nən(t)s\ *n* [ME, fr. AF, fr. *maintenir*] (14c) **1** : the act of maintaining : the state of being maintained : SUPPORT **2** : something that maintains **3** : the upkeep of property or equipment **4** : an officious or unlawful intermeddling in a legal suit by assisting either party with means to carry it on

main·top \ˈmān-ˌtäp\ *n* (15c) : a platform about the head of the mainmast of a square-rigged ship

main–top·mast \mān-ˈtäp-ˌmast, -məst\ *n* (15c) : a mast next above the mainmast

main yard *n* (15c) : the yard of a mainsail

mair \ˈmār\ *chiefly Scot var of* MORE

mai·son·ette \ˌmā-zə-ˈnet, -sə-\ *n* [F *maisonnette,* fr. OF, dim. of *maison* house, fr. L *mansion-, mansio* dwelling place — more at MANSION] (1785) **1** : a small house **2** : an apartment often on two floors

mai tai \ˈmī-ˌtī\ *n, pl* **mai tais** [Tahitian *maitai* good] (1961) : a cocktail made with rum, curaçao, orgeat, lime, and fruit juices

maî·tre d' *or* **mai·tre d'** \ˌmā-trə-ˈdē, ˌme-, -tər-\ *n, pl* **maître d's** *or* **maitre d's** \-ˈdēz\ (1950) : MAÎTRE D'HÔTEL, HEADWAITER

maî·tre d'hô·tel \ˌmā-trə-(ˌ)dō-ˈtel, ˌme-; ˌmāt-dō-, ˌmet-\ *n, pl* **maîtres d'hôtel** *same*\ [F, lit., master of house] (1538) **1 a** : MAJORDOMO **b** : HEADWAITER **2** : a sauce of butter, parsley, salt, pepper, and lemon juice — called also *maître d'hôtel butter*

maize \ˈmāz\ *n* [Sp *maíz,* fr. Taino *mahiz*] (1555) : INDIAN CORN

Maj *abbr* major

ma·jes·tic \mə-ˈjes-tik\ *adj* (1601) : having or exhibiting majesty : STATELY ***syn*** see GRAND — **ma·jes·ti·cal·ly** \-ti-k(ə-)lē\ *adv*

maj·es·ty \ˈma-jə-stē\ *n, pl* **-ties** [ME *maieste,* fr. AF *majesté,* fr. L *majestat-, majestas;* akin to L *major* greater] (14c) **1** : sovereign power, authority, or dignity **2** — used in addressing or referring to reigning sovereigns and their consorts ⟨Your *Majesty*⟩ ⟨Her *Majesty's* Government⟩ **3 a** : royal bearing or aspect : GRANDEUR **b** : greatness or splendor of quality or character

Maj Gen *abbr* major general

ma·jol·i·ca \mə-ˈjä-li-kə\ *also* **ma·iol·i·ca** \-ˈyä-\ *n* [It *maiolica,* fr. OIt *Maiolica, Maiorica* Majorca] (1851) **1** : earthenware covered with an opaque tin glaze and decorated on the glaze before firing; *esp* : an Italian ware of this kind **2** : a 19th century earthenware modeled in naturalistic shapes and glazed in lively colors

[1]**ma·jor** \ˈmā-jər\ *adj* [ME *maiour,* fr. L *major,* compar. of *magnus* great, large — more at MUCH] (15c) **1** : greater in dignity, rank, importance, or interest ⟨one of the ~ poets⟩ **2** : greater in number, quantity, or extent ⟨the ~ part of his work⟩ **3** : having attained majority **4 a** : notable or conspicuous in effect or scope : CONSIDERABLE ⟨a ~ im-

provement⟩ **b** : prominent or significant in size, amount, or degree ⟨earned some ~ cash⟩ **5** : involving grave risk : SERIOUS ⟨a ~ illness⟩ **6** : of or relating to a subject of academic study chosen as a field of specialization **7 a** : having half steps between the third and fourth and the seventh and eighth degrees ⟨~ scale⟩ **b** : based on a major scale ⟨~ key⟩ **c** : equivalent to the distance between the keynote and another tone (except the fourth and fifth) of a major scale ⟨~ third⟩ **d** : having a major third above the root ⟨~ triad⟩

[2]**major** *n* (1616) **1** : a person who has attained majority **2 a** : one that is superior in rank, importance, size, or performance ⟨economic power of the oil ~*s*⟩ **b** : a major musical interval, scale, key, or mode **3** : a commissioned officer in the army, air force, or marine corps ranking above a captain and below a lieutenant colonel **4 a** : an academic subject chosen as a field of specialization **b** : a student specializing in such a field ⟨a history ~⟩ **5** *pl* : major league baseball — used with *the* **6** : any of several high-level tournaments in professional golf

[3]**major** *vi* (1913) : to pursue an academic major ⟨~*ed* in English⟩

major axis *n* (1879) : the axis passing through the foci of an ellipse

major depression *n* (1979) **1** : MAJOR DEPRESSIVE DISORDER **2** : an episode of depression characteristic of major depressive disorder

major depressive disorder *n* (1978) : a mood disorder having a clinical course involving one or more episodes of serious psychological depression lasting two or more weeks each with no intervening episodes of mania

ma·jor·do·mo \ˌmā-jər-ˈdō-(ˌ)mō\ *n, pl* **-mos** [Sp *mayordomo* or obs. It *maiordomo,* fr. ML *major domus,* lit., chief of the house] (1589) **1** : a head steward of a large household (as a palace) **2** : BUTLER, STEWARD **3** : a person who speaks, makes arrangements, or takes charge for another; *broadly* : the person who runs an enterprise ⟨the ~ of the fair⟩

ma·jor·ette \ˌmā-jə-ˈret\ *n* (1940) : DRUM MAJORETTE 2

major general *n* [F *major général,* fr. *major,* n. + *général,* adj., general] (1633) : a commissioned officer in the army, air force, or marine corps who ranks above a brigadier general and whose insignia is two stars

major histocompatibility complex *n* (1972) : a group of genes in mammals that code for cell-surface polymorphic glycoprotein molecules which display antigenic peptide fragments for T cell recognition and aid in the ability of the immune system to determine self from nonself

ma·jor·i·tar·i·an \mə-ˌjȯr-ə-ˈter-ē-ən, -ˌjär-\ *n* (1942) : a person who believes in or advocates majoritarianism — **majoritarian** *adj*

ma·jor·i·tar·i·an·ism \-ē-ə-ˌni-zəm\ *n* (1942) : the philosophy or practice according to which decisions of an organized group should be made by a numerical majority of its members

ma·jor·i·ty \mə-ˈjȯr-ə-tē, -ˈjär-\ *n, pl* **-ties** (1552) **1** *obs* : the quality or state of being greater **2 a** : the age at which full civil rights are accorded **b** : the status of one who has attained this age **3 a** : a number or percentage equaling more than half of a total ⟨a ~ of voters⟩ ⟨a two-thirds ~⟩ **b** : the excess of a majority over the remainder of the total : MARGIN ⟨won by a ~ of 10 votes⟩ **c** : the greater quantity or share ⟨the ~ of the time⟩ **4** : the group or political party having the greater number of votes (as in a legislature) **5** : the military office, rank, or commission of a major — **majority** *adj*

majority leader *n* (1909) : a leader of the majority party in a legislative body (as the U.S. Senate)

majority rule *n* (1848) : a political principle providing that a majority usu. constituted by fifty percent plus one of an organized group will have the power to make decisions binding upon the whole

major league *n* (1890) **1** : a league of highest classification in U.S. professional baseball; *broadly* : a league of major importance in any of various sports **2** : BIG TIME 2 — **major–league** *adj* — **major leaguer** *n*

ma·jor·ly \ˈmā-jər-lē\ *adv* (1956) : in a major way **a** : PRIMARILY 1 ⟨was ~ a poet⟩ **b** : EXTREMELY 1 ⟨was ~ annoyed⟩

major–medical *adj* (ca. 1955) : of, relating to, or being a form of insurance designed to pay all or part of the medical bills of major illnesses usu. after deduction of a fixed initial sum

major order *n* (ca. 1741) : one of the Roman Catholic or Eastern clerical orders that are sacramentally conferred and have a sacred character that implies major religious obligations (as clerical celibacy) — usu. used in pl.; compare MINOR ORDER

major party *n* (1950) : a political party having electoral strength sufficient to permit it to win control of a government usu. with comparative regularity and when defeated to constitute the principal opposition to the party in power

major penalty *n* (1925) : a 5-minute suspension of a player in ice hockey or lacrosse

major premise *n* (1821) : the premise of a syllogism containing the major term

major seminary *n* (1945) : a Roman Catholic seminary giving usu. the entire six years of senior college and theological training required for major orders

major suit *n* (1916) : either of the suits hearts or spades having superior scoring value in bridge

major term *n* (1847) : the term of a syllogism constituting the predicate of the conclusion

ma·jus·cule \ˈma-jəs-ˌkyül, mə-ˈjəs-\ *n* [F, fr. L *majusculus* rather large, dim. of *major*] (ca. 1825) : a large letter (as a capital) — **ma·jus·cu·lar** \mə-ˈjəs-kyə-lər\ *adj* — **majuscule** *adj*

makable *var of* MAKEABLE

Ma·kah \ˈmä-(ˌ)kä\ *n, pl* **Makah** *or* **Makahs** [Clallam (Salishan language of the northern Olympic Peninsula) *màqâʔa*] (1855) **1** : a member of an American Indian people of the Pacific Northwest **2** : the Wakashan language of the Makah people

mak·ar \ˈmä-kər, ˈmā-\ *n* [ME *maker*] (14c) *chiefly Scot* : POET

[1]**make** \ˈmāk\ *vb* **made** \ˈmād\; **mak·ing** [ME, fr. OE *macian;* akin to OHG *mahhōn* to prepare, make, Gk *magēnai* to be kneaded, OCS *mazati* to anoint, smear] *vt* (bef. 12c) **1 a** *obs* : BEHAVE, ACT **b** : to begin or seem to begin (an action) ⟨*made* to go⟩ **2 a** : to cause to happen to or be experienced by someone ⟨*made* trouble for us⟩ **b** : to cause to exist, occur, or appear : CREATE ⟨~ a disturbance⟩ **c** : to favor the growth or occurrence of ⟨haste ~*s* waste⟩ **d** : to fit, intend, or destine by or as if by creating ⟨was *made* to be an actor⟩ **3 a** : to bring into being by forming, shaping, or altering material : FASHION ⟨~ a dress⟩ **b** : COMPOSE, WRITE ⟨~ verses⟩ **c** : to lay out and construct ⟨~ a road⟩ **4** : to frame or formulate in the mind ⟨~ plans⟩ **5** : to put together from components : CONSTITUTE ⟨houses *made* of stone⟩ **6 a** : to compute or estimate to be **b** : to form and hold in the mind ⟨~ no doubt of it⟩ **7 a** : to assemble and set alight the materials for (a fire) **b** : to set in order ⟨~ beds⟩ **c** : PREPARE, FIX ⟨~ dinner⟩ **d** : to shuffle (a deck of cards) in preparation for dealing **8** : to prepare (hay) by cutting, drying, and storing **9 a** : to cause to be or become ⟨*made* them happy⟩ ⟨~*s* it possible⟩ **b** : APPOINT ⟨*made* him bishop⟩ **10 a** : ENACT, ESTABLISH ⟨~ laws⟩ **b** : to execute in an appropriate manner ⟨~ a will⟩ **c** : SET, NAME ⟨~ a price⟩ **11 a** *chiefly dial* : SHUT ⟨the doors are *made* against you —Shak.⟩ **b** : to cause (an electric circuit) to be completed **12 a** : to conclude as to the nature or meaning of something ⟨what do you ~ of this development?⟩ **b** : to regard as being ⟨not the fool some ~ him⟩ **13 a** : to carry out (an action indicated or implied by the object) ⟨~ war⟩ ⟨~ a speech⟩ ⟨~ a detour⟩ **b** : to perform with a bodily movement ⟨~ a sweeping gesture⟩ **14 a** : to produce as a result of action, effort, or behavior with respect to something ⟨~ a mess of the job⟩ ⟨tried to ~ a thorough job of it⟩ **b** *archaic* : to turn into another language by translation **15** : to cause to act in a certain way : COMPEL ⟨~ her give it back⟩ **16** : to cause or assure the success or prosperity of ⟨can either ~ you or break you⟩ **17 a** : to amount to in significance ⟨~*s* a great difference⟩ **b** : to form the essential being of ⟨clothes ~ the man⟩ **c** : to form by an assembling of individuals ⟨~ a quorum⟩ **d** : to count as ⟨that ~*s* the third time you've said it⟩ **18 a** : to be or be capable of being changed or fashioned into ⟨rags ~ the best paper⟩ **b** : to develop into ⟨she will ~ a fine judge⟩ **c** : FORM 6b **19 a** : REACH, ATTAIN ⟨*made* port before the storm⟩ — often used with *it* ⟨you'll never ~ it that far⟩ **b** : to gain the rank of ⟨~ major⟩ **c** : to gain a place on or in ⟨~ the team⟩ ⟨the story *made* the papers⟩ **d** : to succeed in providing or obtaining ⟨~ bail⟩ **20** : to gain (as money) by working, trading, or dealing ⟨~ a living⟩ **21 a** : to act so as to earn or acquire ⟨~*s* friends easily⟩ ⟨~*s* poor grades⟩ **b** : to score in a game or sport ⟨~ a field goal⟩ ⟨~ a birdie⟩ **c** : to convert (a split) into a spare in bowling **d** : to succeed in holing ⟨~ a putt⟩ **22 a** : to fulfill (a contract) in a card game **b** : to win a trick with (a card) **23 a** : to include in a route or itinerary ⟨~ New York on the return trip⟩ — often used with *it* ⟨~ it to the party⟩ **b** : CATCH 6b ⟨*made* the bus just in time⟩ **24** : to persuade to consent to sexual intercourse : SEDUCE **25** : to provide the most enjoyable or satisfying experience of ⟨meeting the star of the show really *made* our day⟩ ~ *vi* **1** *archaic* : to compose poetry **2 a** : BEHAVE, ACT **b** : to begin or seem to begin a certain action ⟨*made* as though to hand it to me⟩ **c** : to act so as to be or to seem to be ⟨~ merry⟩ **d** *slang* : to play a part — usu. used with *like* **3** : SET OUT, HEAD ⟨*made* after the fox⟩ ⟨*made* straight for home⟩ **4** : to increase in height or size ⟨the tide is *making* now⟩ **5** : to reach or extend in a certain direction **6** : to have considerable effect ⟨courtesy ~*s* for safer driving⟩ **7** : to undergo manufacture or processing ⟨the silk ~*s* up beautifully⟩ — **make a face** *or* **make faces** : to distort one's features : GRIMACE — **make a mountain out of a molehill** : to treat a trifling matter as of great importance — **make away with 1** : to carry off : STEAL **2** : KILL — **make believe** : PRETEND, FEIGN — **make bold** : VENTURE, DARE — **make book** : to accept bets at calculated odds on all the entrants in a race or contest — **make common cause** : to unite to achieve a shared goal — **make do** : to get along or manage with the means at hand — **make ends meet** : to make one's means adequate to one's needs — **make eyes** : OGLE — **make friends with** : to establish a friendship or friendly relations with — **make fun of** : to make an object of amusement or laughter : RIDICULE, MOCK — **make good 1** *or* **make good on** : to make valid or complete: as **a** : to make up for (a deficiency) **b** : INDEMNIFY ⟨*make good* the loss⟩ **c** : to carry out successfully ⟨*made good* their escape⟩ ⟨*made good on* his promise⟩ **d** : PROVE ⟨*made good* a charge⟩ **2** : to prove to be capable; *also* : SUCCEED — **make hay** : to make use of a situation or circumstance esp. in order to gain an advantage — **make head 1** : to make progress esp. against resistance **2** : to rise in armed revolt — **make it 1 a** : to be successful ⟨trying to *make it* in the big time as a fashion photographer —Joe Kane⟩ **b** : to be satisfactory or pleasing ⟨if it isn't danceable, it doesn't *make it* for me —Judy Hyman⟩ **2** : to have sexual intercourse **3** : SURVIVE, LIVE ⟨half the cubs won't *make it* through their first year⟩ — **make light of** : to treat as of little account — **make love 1** : WOO, COURT **2 a** : NECK, PET **b** : to engage in sexual intercourse — **make much of 1** : to treat as of importance **2** : to treat with obvious affection or special consideration — **make nice** : to be deliberately and often insincerely polite and agreeable ⟨must *make nice* to politicians they cannot stand —Ken Auletta⟩ — **make no bones** : to be straightforward, unhesitating, or sure ⟨*makes no bones* about the seriousness of the matter⟩ — **make one's mark** : to achieve success or fame — **make public** : DISCLOSE — **make sail 1** : to raise or spread sail **2** : to set out on a voyage — **make shift** : to manage with difficulty — **make sport of** : RIDICULE, MOCK — **make the grade** : to measure up to some standard : be successful — **make the most of** : to show or use to the best advantage — **make the scene** : to be present at or participate in a usu. specified activity or event — **make time 1** : to travel fast **2** : to gain time **3** : to make progress toward winning favor ⟨trying to *make time* with the waitress⟩ — **make tracks 1** : to proceed at a walk or run **2** : to go in a hurry : RUN AWAY, FLEE — **make use of** : to put to use : EMPLOY — **make water 1** *of a boat* : LEAK **2** : URINATE — **make waves** : to create a stir or disturbance — **make way 1** : to give room for passing, entering, or occupying **2** : to make progress — **make with** *slang* : PRODUCE, PERFORM — usu. used with *the*

[2]**make** *n* (14c) **1 a** : the manner or style in which a thing is constructed **b** : BRAND 4a **2** : the physical, mental, or moral constitution of a person ⟨men of his ~ are rare⟩ **3 a** : the action of producing or manufacturing **b** : the actual yield or amount produced over a specified period : OUTPUT **4** : the act of shuffling cards; *also* : turn to shuffle — **on the make 1** : in the process of forming, growing, or improving **2** : in quest of a higher social or financial status **3** : in search of sexual adventure

make·able *or* **mak·able** \ˈmā-kə-bəl\ *adj* (15c) : capable of being made; *also* : reasonably likely to be made ⟨a ~ putt⟩

make·bate \ˈmāk-ˌbāt\ *n* [ˈ*make* + obs. *bate* strife] (1529) *archaic* : one that excites contention and quarrels

[1]**make–be·lieve** \ˈmāk-bə-ˌlēv\ *also* **make–be·lief** \-ˌlēf\ *n* (1811) **:** a pretending that what is not real is real ⟨a fiction writer's childish willingness to immerse himself in ~ —John Updike⟩
[2]**make–believe** *adj* (1824) **:** IMAGINARY, PRETENDED
make–do \ˈmāk-ˈdü\ *adj* (1923) **:** MAKESHIFT — **make–do** *n*
make·fast \-ˌfast\ *n* (1898) **:** something (as a post or buoy) to which a boat can be fastened
make off *vi* (1709) **:** to leave in haste — **make off with :** to take away; *esp* **:** GRAB, STEAL
make–or–break \ˈmāk-ər-ˈbrāk\ *adj* (1919) **:** allowing no middle ground between success and failure
make out *vt* (15c) **1 :** to complete (as a printed form) by supplying required information ⟨*make out* a check⟩ **2 :** to find or grasp the meaning of ⟨tried to *make out* what had really happened⟩ **3 :** to form an opinion or idea about **:** CONCLUDE ⟨how do you *make* that *out*⟩ **4 a :** to represent as being ⟨*made* them *out* to be losers⟩ **b :** to pretend to be true ⟨*made out* that he had never heard of me⟩ **5 :** to represent or delineate in detail **6 :** to see and identify with difficulty or effort **:** DISCERN ⟨*make out* a ship through the fog⟩ ~ *vi* **1 :** GET ALONG, FARE ⟨how are you *making out* with the new job⟩ **2 a :** to engage in sexual intercourse **b :** NECK 1
make·over \ˈmāk-ˌō-vər\ *n* (1927) **:** an act or instance of making over ⟨a ~ of the tax system⟩; *esp* **:** a changing of a person's appearance (as by the use of cosmetics or a different hairdo)
make over *vt* (1546) **1 :** to transfer the title of (property) **2 a :** REMAKE, REMODEL, REDESIGN ⟨*made* the whole house *over*⟩ **b :** REFORM 1
mak·er \ˈmā-kər\ *n* (14c) **:** one that makes: as **a** *cap* **:** GOD 1 **b** *archaic* **:** POET **c :** a person who borrows money on a promissory note **d :** MANUFACTURER
make·ready \ˈmāk-ˌre-dē\ *n, pl* **-read·ies** (1887) **:** final preparation (as of a form on a printing press) for running
make·shift \ˈmāk-ˌshift\ *n* (1766) **:** a usu. crude and temporary expedient **:** SUBSTITUTE ***syn*** see RESOURCE — **makeshift** *adj*
make·up \ˈmā-ˌkəp\ *n* (1821) **1 a :** the way in which the parts or ingredients of something are put together **:** COMPOSITION **b :** physical, mental, and moral constitution **2 a :** the operation of making up esp. pages for printing **b :** design or layout of printed matter **3 a (1) :** cosmetics used to color and beautify the face **(2) :** a cosmetic applied to other parts of the body **b :** materials (as wigs and cosmetics) used in making up or in special costuming (as for a play) **4 :** REPLACEMENT; *specif* **:** material added (as in a manufacturing process) to replace material that has been used up ⟨~ water⟩ **5 :** something that makes up for a previous postponement, omission, failure, or deficiency ⟨a ~ exam⟩
make up *vt* (14c) **1 a :** to form by fitting together or assembling ⟨*make up* a train of cars⟩ **b :** to arrange typeset matter in (as pages) for printing **2 a :** to combine to produce (a sum or whole) **b :** CONSTITUTE, COMPOSE ⟨10 chapters *make up* this volume⟩ **3 a :** to compensate for (as a deficiency or omission) ⟨*make up* the difference in lost pay⟩ **b :** to do or take in order to correct an omission ⟨*make up* a history exam⟩ **4 :** SETTLE, DECIDE ⟨*made up* my mind to depart⟩ **5 :** to wrap or fasten up ⟨*make* the books *up* into a parcel⟩ **6 a :** to prepare in physical appearance for a role **b :** to apply cosmetics to **7 a :** INVENT, IMPROVISE ⟨*make up* a story⟩ **b :** to set in order ⟨rooms are *made up* daily⟩ ~ *vi* **1 :** to become reconciled ⟨quarreled but later *made up*⟩ **2 a :** to act ingratiatingly and flatteringly ⟨*made up* to his aunt for a new bicycle⟩ **b :** to make advances **:** COURT **3 :** COMPENSATE ⟨*make up* for lost time⟩ **4 a :** to put on costumes or makeup (as for a play) **b :** to apply cosmetics
make·weight \ˈmāk-ˌwāt\ *n* (1695) **1 a :** something thrown into a scale to bring the weight to a desired value **b :** something of little independent value thrown in to fill a gap **2 :** COUNTERWEIGHT, COUNTERPOISE
make–work \ˈmāk-ˌwərk\ *n* (1923) **:** work assigned or done chiefly to keep one busy
ma·ki·mo·no \ˌmä-ki-ˈmō-(ˌ)nō\ *n, pl* **-nos** [Jp, scroll, fr. *maki* roll, scroll + *mono* thing] (1882) **:** a horizontal Japanese ornamental pictorial or calligraphic scroll — compare KAKEMONO
making *n* [ME, fr. OE *macung,* fr. *macian* to make] (12c) **1 :** the act or process of forming, causing, doing, or coming into being ⟨spots problems in the ~⟩ **2 :** a process or means of advancement or success **3 :** something made; *esp* **:** a quantity produced at one time **:** BATCH **4 a :** POTENTIALITY — often used in pl. ⟨had the ~*s* of a great artist⟩ **b** *pl* **:** the material from which something is to be made; *esp \usu* ˈmā-kənz\ **:** paper and tobacco for rolling cigarettes by hand
ma·ko shark \ˈmā-(ˌ)kō-, ˈmä-\ *n* [Maori *mako* mako shark] (1926) **:** either of two relatively slender mackerel sharks (*Isurus paucus* and *I. oxyrinchus*) that are dark blue above and white below with long pointed snouts and that are notable sport fish — called also *mako*; see SHARK illustration
makuta *pl of* LIKUTA
Mal *abbr* Malachi
mal- *comb form* [ME, fr. AF, fr. *mal* bad (fr. L *malus*) & *mal* badly, fr. L *male,* fr. *malus*] **1 a :** bad ⟨*mal*practice⟩ **b :** badly ⟨*mal*odorous⟩ **2 a :** abnormal ⟨*mal*formation⟩ **b :** abnormally ⟨*mal*formed⟩ **3 a :** inadequate ⟨*mal*adjustment⟩ **b :** inadequately ⟨*mal*nourished⟩
mal·ab·sorp·tion \ˌma-ləb-ˈsȯrp-shən, -ˈzȯrp-\ *n* (ca. 1929) **:** faulty absorption esp. of nutrient materials from the gastrointestinal tract
ma·lac·ca \mə-ˈla-kə\ *adj* [*Malacca,* Malaya] (1844) **:** made or consisting of the cane of an Asian rattan palm (*Calamus rotang*) ⟨an umbrella with a ~ handle⟩ — **malacca** *n*
Mal·a·chi \ˈma-lə-ˌkī\ *n* [Heb *Mal'ākhī*] (14c) **1 :** a prophetic book of canonical Jewish and Christian Scripture — see BIBLE table **2 —** used as the conventional name for the unidentified fifth century B.C. writer of the book of Malachi
Mal·a·chi·as \ˌma-lə-ˈkī-əs\ *n* [LL, fr. Gk, fr. Heb *Mal'ākhī*] (1568) **:** MALACHI
mal·a·chite \ˈma-lə-ˌkīt\ *n* [alter. of ME *melochites,* fr. L *molochites,* fr. Gk *molochitēs,* fr. *molochē, malachē* mallow] (1656) **:** a green mineral that is a basic carbonate of copper used esp. for making ornamental objects
mal·a·col·o·gy \ˌma-lə-ˈkä-lə-jē\ *n* [F *malacologie,* contr. of *malacozoologie,* fr. NL *Malacozoa,* zoological group including soft-bodied animals (fr. Gk *malakos* soft + NL *-zoa*) + F *-logie* -logy] (1836) **:** a branch of zoology dealing with mollusks — **mal·a·co·log·i·cal** \ˌma-lə-kə-ˈlä-ji-kəl\ *adj* — **mal·a·col·o·gist** \ˌma-lə-ˈkä-lə-jist\ *n*
mal·a·cos·tra·can \ˌma-lə-ˈkäs-tri-kən\ *n* [ultim. fr. Gk *malakostrakos* soft-shelled, fr. *malakos* soft + *ostrakon* shell — more at MOLLIFY, OYSTER] (1835) **:** any of a large subclass (Malacostraca) of crustaceans having a thorax consisting of eight segments usu. covered by a carapace and including the decapods and isopods — **malacostracan** *adj*
mal·ad·ap·ta·tion \ˌma-ˌla-ˌdap-ˈtā-shən\ *n* (1877) **:** poor or inadequate adaptation
mal·adapt·ed \ˌma-lə-ˈdap-təd\ *adj* (1918) **:** unsuited or poorly suited (as to a particular use, purpose, or situation)
mal·adap·tive \-tiv\ *adj* (1931) **1 :** marked by poor or inadequate adaptation **2 :** not conducive to adaptation
mal·ad·just·ed \ˌma-lə-ˈjəs-təd\ *adj* (1886) **:** poorly or inadequately adjusted; *specif* **:** lacking harmony with one's environment from failure to adjust one's desires to the conditions of one's life
mal·ad·jus·tive \-ˈjəs-tiv\ *adj* (1928) **:** not conducive to adjustment
mal·ad·just·ment \-ˈjəs(t)-mənt\ *n* (1833) **:** poor, faulty, or inadequate adjustment
mal·ad·min·is·tra·tion \ˌma-ləd-ˌmi-nə-ˈstrā-shən\ *n* (1644) **1 :** corrupt or incompetent administration (as of a public office) **2 :** incorrect administration (as of a drug) — **mal·ad·min·is·ter** \-ˈmi-nə-stər\ *vt*
mal·adroit \ˌma-lə-ˈdrȯit\ *adj* [F, fr. MF, fr. *mal-* + *adroit*] (1685) **:** lacking adroitness **:** INEPT ***syn*** see AWKWARD — **mal·adroit·ly** *adv* — **mal·adroit·ness** *n*
mal·a·dy \ˈma-lə-dē\ *n, pl* **-dies** [ME *maladie,* fr. AF, fr. *malade* sick, fr. L *male habitus* in bad condition] (13c) **1 :** a disease or disorder of the animal body **2 :** an unwholesome or disordered condition
ma·la fi·de \ˌma-lə-ˈfī-dē, -də\ *adv or adj* [LL] (1561) **:** with or in bad faith ⟨claimed the government acted *mala fide*⟩
Ma·la·ga \ˈma-lə-gə\ *n* (1608) **:** a sweet brown fortified wine from Málaga, Spain; *also* **:** a similar wine made elsewhere
Mal·a·gasy \ˌma-lə-ˈga-sē; ˌmä-lə-ˈgä-sē, -shē\ *n, pl* **Malagasy** *also* **Mal·a·gas·ies** (1839) **1 :** a member of a people of Indonesian and African origin who inhabit Madagascar **2 :** the Austronesian language of the Malagasy people — **Malagasy** *adj*
ma·la·gue·na \ˌma-lə-ˈgān-yə, ˌmä-\ *n* [Sp *malagueña,* fr. fem. of *malagueño* of Málaga, fr. *Málaga*] (ca. 1883) **1 :** a folk tune native to Málaga that is similar to a fandango **2 :** a Spanish folk dance for couples that is similar to a fandango
mal·aise \mə-ˈlāz, ma-, -ˈlez\ *n* [F *malaise,* fr. OF, fr. *mal-* + *aise* comfort — more at EASE] (ca. 1768) **1 :** an indefinite feeling of debility or lack of health often indicative of or accompanying the onset of an illness **2 :** a vague sense of mental or moral ill-being ⟨a ~ of cynicism and despair —Malcolm Boyd⟩
mal·a·mute *also* **mal·e·mute** \ˈma-lə-ˌmyüt, -ˌmüt\ *n* [*Malemute,* an Inupiat of the Kotzebue Sound area, Alaska, fr. Inupiat *malimiut*] (1898) **:** a sled dog of northern No. America; *esp* **:** ALASKAN MALAMUTE
ma·lan·ga \mə-ˈläŋ-gə\ *n* [AmerSp] (1853) **1 :** TARO **2 :** YAUTIA
mal·a·pert \ˌma-lə-ˈpərt\ *adj* [ME, fr. *mal-* + *apert* open, frank — more at PERT] (14c) **:** impudently bold **:** SAUCY
mal·ap·por·tioned \ˌma-lə-ˈpȯr-shənd\ *adj* (1964) **:** characterized by an inequitable or unsuitable apportioning of representatives to a legislative body — **mal·ap·por·tion·ment** \-shən-mənt\ *n*
[1]**mal·a·prop** \ˈma-lə-ˌpräp\ *n* [Mrs. *Malaprop*] (1823) **:** an example of malapropism ⟨was famed for ~*s:* he always said "polo bears" and "Remember Pearl Island" and "neon stockings" —*Time*⟩
[2]**malaprop** *or* **mal·a·prop·ian** \ˌma-lə-ˈprä-pē-ən\ *adj* (1840) **:** using or marked by the use of malapropisms
mal·a·prop·ism \ˈma-lə-ˌprä-ˌpi-zəm\ *n* [Mrs. *Malaprop,* character noted for her misuse of words in R. B. Sheridan's comedy *The Rivals* (1775)] (1849) **1 :** the usu. unintentionally humorous misuse or distortion of a word or phrase; *esp* **:** the use of a word sounding somewhat like the one intended but ludicrously wrong in the context **2 :** MALAPROP — **mal·a·prop·ist** \-ˌprä-pist\ *n*
mal·ap·ro·pos \ˌma-ˌla-prə-ˈpō\ *adv* [F *mal à propos*] (1668) **:** in an inappropriate or inopportune way — **malapropos** *adj*
[1]**ma·lar** \ˈmā-lər, -ˌlär\ *adj* [NL *malaris,* fr. L *mala* jawbone, cheek] (1782) **:** of or relating to the cheek or the side of the head
[2]**malar** *n* (ca. 1828) **:** ZYGOMATIC BONE — called also *malar bone*
ma·lar·ia \mə-ˈler-ē-ə\ *n* [It, fr. *mala aria* bad air] (1740) **1** *archaic* **:** air infected with a noxious substance capable of causing disease; *esp* **:** MIASMA **2 a :** a human disease that is caused by sporozoan parasites (genus *Plasmodium*) in the red blood cells, is transmitted by the bite of anopheline mosquitoes, and is characterized by periodic attacks of chills and fever **b :** any of various diseases of birds and mammals caused by blood protozoans — **ma·lar·i·al** \-əl\ *adj* — **ma·lar·i·ous** \-əs\ *adj*
ma·lar·i·ol·o·gy \-ˌler-ē-ˈä-lə-jē\ *n* (ca. 1923) **:** the scientific study of malaria — **ma·lar·i·ol·o·gist** \-jist\ *n*
ma·lar·key *also* **ma·lar·ky** \mə-ˈlär-kē\ *n* [origin unknown] (1929) **:** insincere or foolish talk **:** BUNKUM
ma·late \ˈma-ˌlāt, ˈmā-\ *n* (1794) **:** a salt or ester of malic acid
mal·a·thi·on \ˌma-lə-ˈthī-ən, -ˌän\ *n* [fr. *Malathion,* a trademark] (1953) **:** an organophosphate broad-spectrum insecticide $C_{10}H_{19}O_6PS_2$ that is considerably less toxic to mammals than parathion
Ma·lay \mə-ˈlā, ˈmā-(ˌ)lā\ *n* [obs. D *Malayo* (now *Maleier*), fr. Malay *Mĕlayu*] (1598) **1 :** a member of a people of the Malay Peninsula, eastern Sumatra, parts of Borneo, and some adjacent islands **2 :** the Austronesian language of the Malays — **Malay** *adj* — **Ma·lay·an** \mə-ˈlā-ən, mā-; ˈmā-ˌlā-\ *n or adj*
Mal·a·ya·lam \ˌma-lə-ˈyä-ləm, ˌmä-\ *n* (1837) **:** the Dravidian language of Kerala, southwest India, closely related to Tamil

---

\ə\ **abut** \ᵊ\ kitten, F table \ər\ **further** \a\ **ash** \ā\ **ace** \ä\ **mop, mar** \au̇\ **out** \ch\ **chin** \e\ **bet** \ē\ **easy** \g\ **go** \i\ **hit** \ī\ **ice** \j\ **job** \ŋ\ **sing** \ō\ **go** \ȯ\ **law** \ȯi\ **boy** \th\ **thin** \t͟h\ **the** \ü\ **loot** \u̇\ **foot** \y\ **yet** \zh\ **vision, beige** \k̲, ⁿ, œ, ue, ʸ\ *see* Guide to Pronunciation

¹**mal·con·tent** \ˌmal-kən-ˈtent\ n (1581) : a discontented person: **a** : one who bears a grudge from a sense of grievance or thwarted ambition **b** : one who is in active opposition to an established order or government : REBEL

²**malcontent** adj [MF, fr. mal- + content content] (1586) : dissatisfied with the existing state of affairs : DISCONTENTED

mal·con·tent·ed \-ˈten-təd\ adj (1586) : MALCONTENT — **mal·con·tent·ed·ly** adv — **mal·con·tent·ed·ness** n

mal de mer \ˌmal-də-ˈmer\ n [F] (1796) : SEASICKNESS

mal·dis·tri·bu·tion \ˌmal-ˌdis-trə-ˈbyü-shən\ n (1895) : bad or faulty distribution : undesirable inequality or unevenness of placement or apportionment (as of population, resources, or wealth) over an area or among members of a group

¹**male** \ˈmāl\ n [ME, fr. AF masle, male, adj. & n., fr. L masculus — more at MASCULINE] (14c) **1 a** : a male person : a man or a boy **b** : an individual that produces small usu. motile gametes (as spermatozoa or spermatozoids) which fertilize the eggs of a female **2** : a staminate plant

²**male** adj (14c) **1 a** (1) : of, relating to, or being the sex that produces gametes which fertilize the eggs of a female (2) : STAMINATE; esp : having only staminate flowers and not producing fruit or seeds ⟨a holly⟩ **b** (1) : of, relating to, or characteristic of the male sex ⟨a deep ∼ voice⟩ (2) : made up of usu. adult male individuals ⟨a ∼ choir⟩ **2** : MASCULINE 3a **3** : designed with a projecting part for fitting into a corresponding female part ⟨∼ hose coupling⟩ — **male·ness** \-nəs\ n

male alto n (ca. 1890) : COUNTERTENOR

ma·le·ate \ˈmā-lē-ˌāt, -lē-ət\ n (1853) : a salt or ester of maleic acid

¹**mal·e·dict** \ˌma-lə-ˈdikt\ adj [LL maledictus, pp. of maledicere] (1867) archaic : ACCURSED

²**maledict** vt (1623) : CURSE, EXECRATE

mal·e·dic·tion \ˌma-lə-ˈdik-shən\ n [ME malediccioun, fr. LL malediction-, maledictio, fr. maledicere to curse, fr. L, to speak evil of, fr. male badly + dicere to say — more at MAL-, DICTION] (14c) : CURSE, EXECRATION — **mal·e·dic·to·ry** \-ˈdik-t(ə-)rē\ adj

mal·e·fac·tion \ˌma-lə-ˈfak-shən\ n (15c) : an evil deed : CRIME

mal·e·fac·tor \ˈma-lə-ˌfak-tər\ n [ME malefactour, fr. L malefactor, fr. malefacere to do evil, fr. male + facere to do — more at DO] (15c) **1** : one who commits an offense against the law; esp : FELON **2** : one who does ill toward another

male fern n (1562) : a fern (Dryopteris filix-mas) producing an oleoresin used in expelling tapeworms

ma·lef·ic \mə-ˈle-fik\ adj [L maleficus wicked, mischievous, fr. male + -ficus -fic] (1652) **1** : having malignant influence : BALEFUL **2** : MALICIOUS

ma·lef·i·cence \mə-ˈle-fə-sən(t)s\ n [It maleficenza, fr. L maleficentia, fr. maleficus] (1598) **1 a** : the act of committing harm or evil **b** : a harmful or evil act **2** : the quality or state of being maleficent

ma·lef·i·cent \-sənt\ adj [back-formation fr. maleficence] (1678) : working or productive of harm or evil : BALEFUL

ma·le·ic acid \mə-ˈlē-ik-, -ˈlā-\ n [F acide maléique, alter. of acide malique malic acid; fr. its formation by dehydration of malic acid] (1857) : a crystalline dicarboxylic acid C₄H₄O₄ that is isomeric with fumaric acid and is used esp. in organic synthesis

maleic anhydride n (1857) : a caustic crystalline cyclic anhydride C₄H₂O₃ used esp. in making resins

maleic hydrazide n (1949) : a crystalline cyclic hydrazide C₄H₄N₂O₂ used to retard plant growth

male menopause n (1949) : ANDROPAUSE

malemute var of MALAMUTE

male–pattern baldness n (1966) : typical hereditary baldness in the male characterized by loss of hair on the crown and temples

male–ster·ile \ˈmāl-ˈster-əl\ adj (1921) : having male gametes lacking or nonfunctional ⟨∼ plants⟩

ma·lev·o·lence \mə-ˈle-və-lən(t)s\ n (15c) **1** : the quality or state of being malevolent **2** : malevolent behavior syn see MALICE

ma·lev·o·lent \-lənt\ adj [L malevolent-, malevolens, fr. male badly + volent-, volens, prp. of velle to wish — more at MAL-, WILL] (1509) **1** : having, showing, or arising from intense often vicious ill will, spite, or hatred **2** : productive of harm or evil — **ma·lev·o·lent·ly** adv

mal·fea·sance \ˌmal-ˈfē-zᵊn(t)s\ n [mal- + obs. feasance doing, execution] (1696) : wrongdoing or misconduct esp. by a public official

mal·for·ma·tion \ˌmal-fȯr-ˈmā-shən, -fər-\ n (1800) : irregular, anomalous, abnormal, or faulty formation or structure

mal·formed \ˌmal-ˈfȯrmd\ adj (1817) : characterized by malformation : badly or imperfectly formed : MISSHAPEN

mal·func·tion \ˌmal-ˈfəŋ(k)-shən\ vi (1958) : to function imperfectly or badly : fail to operate normally — **malfunction** n

mal·gré \mal-ˈgrā, ˈmal-ˌ\ prep [F, fr. OF maugré — more at MAUGRE] (1608) : DESPITE

ma·lic \ˈma-lik, ˈmā-\ adj (ca. 1909) : involved in and esp. catalyzing a reaction in which malic acid participates ⟨∼ dehydrogenase⟩

malic acid n [F acide malique, ultim. fr. L malum apple, fr. Gk mēlon, malon] (1790) : a crystalline dicarboxylic acid C₄H₆O₅; esp : the levorotatory isomer of malic acid that is found in various fruits (as apples) and is formed as an intermediate in the Krebs cycle

mal·ice \ˈma-ləs\ n [ME, fr. AF, fr. L malitia, fr. malus bad] (14c) **1** : desire to cause pain, injury, or distress to another **2** : intent to commit an unlawful act or cause harm without legal justification or excuse
syn MALICE, MALEVOLENCE, ILL WILL, SPITE, MALIGNITY, SPLEEN, GRUDGE mean the desire to see another experience pain, injury, or distress. MALICE implies a deep-seated often unexplainable desire to see another suffer ⟨felt no malice toward their former enemies⟩. MALEVOLENCE suggests a bitter persistent hatred that is likely to be expressed in malicious conduct ⟨a look of dark malevolence⟩. ILL WILL implies a feeling of antipathy of limited duration ⟨ill will provoked by a careless remark⟩. SPITE implies petty feelings of envy and resentment that are often expressed in small harassments ⟨petty insults inspired by spite⟩. MALIGNITY implies deep passion and relentlessness ⟨a life consumed by motiveless malignity⟩. SPLEEN suggests the wrathful release of latent spite or persistent malice ⟨venting his spleen against politicians⟩. GRUDGE implies a harbored feeling of resentment or ill will that seeks satisfaction ⟨never one to harbor a grudge⟩.

ma·li·cious \mə-ˈli-shəs\ adj (13c) : given to, marked by, or arising from malice ⟨∼ gossip⟩ — **ma·li·cious·ly** adv — **ma·li·cious·ness** n

malicious mischief n (1769) : willful, wanton, or reckless damage to or destruction of another's property

¹**ma·lign** \mə-ˈlīn\ adj [ME maligne, fr. AF, fr. L malignus, fr. male badly + gignere to beget — more at MAL-, KIN] (14c) **1 a** : evil in nature, influence, or effect : INJURIOUS ⟨the ∼ effects of illicit drugs⟩ **b** : MALIGNANT, VIRULENT **2** : having or showing intense often vicious ill will : MALEVOLENT syn see SINISTER — **ma·lign·ly** adv

²**malign** vt [ME, fr. AF maligner to act maliciously, fr. LL malignari, fr. L malignus] (15c) : to utter injuriously misleading or false reports about : speak evil of
syn MALIGN, TRADUCE, ASPERSE, VILIFY, CALUMNIATE, DEFAME, SLANDER mean to injure by speaking ill of. MALIGN suggests specific and often subtle misrepresentation but may not always imply deliberate lying ⟨the most maligned monarch in British history⟩. TRADUCE stresses the resulting ignominy and distress to the victim ⟨so traduced the governor that he was driven from office⟩. ASPERSE implies continued attack on a reputation often by indirect or insinuated detraction ⟨both candidates aspersed the other's motives⟩. VILIFY implies attempting to destroy a reputation by open and direct abuse ⟨no criminal was more vilified in the press⟩. CALUMNIATE imputes malice to the speaker and falsity to the assertions ⟨falsely calumniated as a traitor⟩. DEFAME stresses the actual loss of or injury to one's good name ⟨sued them for defaming her reputation⟩. SLANDER stresses the suffering of the victim ⟨town gossips slandered their good name⟩.

ma·lig·nance \mə-ˈlig-nən(t)s\ n (ca. 1604) : MALIGNANCY

ma·lig·nan·cy \-nən(t)-sē\ n, pl -cies (1601) **1** : the quality or state of being malignant **2 a** : exhibition (as by a tumor) of malignant qualities : VIRULENCE **b** : a malignant tumor

ma·lig·nant \mə-ˈlig-nənt\ adj [LL malignant-, malignans, prp. of malignari] (ca. 1545) **1 a** obs : MALCONTENT, DISAFFECTED **b** : evil in nature, influence, or effect : INJURIOUS **c** : passionately and relentlessly malevolent : aggressively malicious **2** : tending to produce death or deterioration ⟨∼ malaria⟩; esp : tending to infiltrate, metastasize, and terminate fatally ⟨a ∼ tumor⟩ — **ma·lig·nant·ly** adv

malignant melanoma n (1951) : MELANOMA 2

ma·lig·ni·ty \mə-ˈlig-nə-tē\ n (14c) **1** : MALIGNANCY, MALEVOLENCE **2** : an instance of malignant or malicious behavior or nature syn see MALICE

ma·li·hi·ni \ˌmä-li-ˈhē-nē\ n [Hawaiian] (1914) : a newcomer or stranger among the people of Hawaii

ma·lines \mə-ˈlēn\ n, pl ma·lines \-ˈlēn(z)\ [F, fr. Malines (Mechelen), Belgium] (1833) **1** : MECHLIN **2** also ma·line : a fine stiff net with a hexagonal mesh that is usu. made of silk or rayon and that is often used for veils

ma·lin·ger \mə-ˈliŋ-gər\ vi ma·lin·gered; ma·lin·ger·ing \-g(ə-)riŋ\ [F malingre sickly] (1820) : to pretend or exaggerate incapacity or illness (as to avoid duty or work) — **ma·lin·ger·er** \-gər-ər\ n

Ma·lin·ke \mə-ˈliŋ-kē\ n, pl Malinke or Malinkes (1883) **1** : a member of a people of Mandingo affiliation widespread in the western part of Africa **2** : the language of the Malinke people

Ma·li·nois \ˌma-lən-ˈwä\ n, pl Malinois [F, fr. Malines, fr. Malines (Mechelen), Belgium] (1929) : BELGIAN MALINOIS

mal·i·son \ˈma-lə-sən, -zən\ n [ME, fr. AF maleiçun, fr. LL malediction-, maledictio] (13c) : CURSE, MALEDICTION

mal·kin \ˈmȯ(l)-kən, ˈmal-\ n [ME malkyn servant woman, fr. Malkyn, dim. of the name Maud] (1586) **1** dial chiefly Brit : an untidy woman : SLATTERN **2** dial chiefly Brit **a** : CAT **b** : HARE

mall \ˈmȯl, esp Brit & for 1 ˈmal\ n [short for obs. pall-mall mallet used in pall-mall] (1644) **1** : an alley used for pall-mall **2** [The Mall, promenade in London, orig. a pall-mall alley] **a** : a usu. public area often set with shade trees and designed as a promenade or as a pedestrian walk **b** : a usu. paved or grassy strip between two roadways **3 a** : an urban shopping area featuring a variety of shops surrounding a usu. open-air concourse reserved for pedestrian traffic **b** : a usu. large suburban building or group of buildings containing various shops with associated passageways

mal·lard \ˈma-lərd\ n, pl mallard or mallards [ME, fr. AF mallart] (14c) : a common and widely distributed wild duck (Anas platyrhynchos) of the northern hemisphere the males of which have a green head and white-ringed neck and which is the source of the domestic ducks

mal·lea·ble \ˈma-lē-ə-bəl, ˈmal-yə-bəl, ˈma-lə-bəl\ adj [ME malliable, fr. ML malleabilis, fr. malleare to hammer, fr. L malleus hammer — more at MAUL] (14c) **1** : capable of being extended or shaped by beating with a hammer or by the pressure of rollers **2 a** : capable of being altered or controlled by outside forces or influences **b** : having a capacity for adaptive change syn see PLASTIC — **mal·lea·bil·i·ty** \ˌma-lē-ə-ˈbi-lə-tē, ˌmal-yə-\ n, -ˈbil-\ — **mal·lea·ble·ness** \ˈma-lē-ə-bəl-nəs, ˈmal-yə-\ n — **mal·lea·bly** \-blē\ adv

mal·lee \ˈma-lē\ n [prob. fr. Wemba-Wemba (Australian aboriginal language of western Victoria) mali] (1845) **1** : any of various low-growing shrubby Australian eucalypts (as Eucalyptus dumosa and E. oleosa) **2** : a dense thicket or growth of mallees; also : land covered by such growth

mal·let \ˈma-lət\ n [ME maillet, fr. AF, dim. of mail hammer — more at MAUL] (15c) : a hammer with a typically barrel-shaped head: as **a** : a tool with a large head for driving another tool or for striking a surface without marring it **b** : a long-handled wooden implement used for striking a ball (as in polo or croquet) **c** : a light hammer with a small rounded or spherical usu. padded head used in playing certain musical instruments (as a vibraphone)

mal·le·us \ˈma-lē-əs\ n, pl mal·lei \-lē-ˌī, -lē-ˌē\ [NL, fr. L hammer] (1669) : the outermost of a chain of three small bones of the mammalian middle ear — called also hammer; see EAR illustration

mal·low \ˈma-(ˌ)lō\ n [ME malwe, fr. OE mealwe, fr. L malva] (bef. 12c) : any of a genus

mallow

(*Malva* of the family Malvaceae, the mallow family) of herbs with palmately lobed or dissected leaves, usu. showy flowers, and a disk-shaped fruit

malm·sey \ˈmäm-zē, ˈmälm-\ *n, often cap* [ME *malmesey,* fr. ML *Malmasia* Monemvasia, village in Greece where a sweet wine was produced] (15c) **:** the sweetest variety of Madeira wine

mal·nour·ished \ˌmal-ˈnər-isht, -ˈnə-risht\ *adj* (1927) **:** UNDERNOURISHED

mal·nu·tri·tion \ˌmal-nu̇-ˈtri-shən, -nyu̇-\ *n* (1862) **:** faulty nutrition due to inadequate or unbalanced intake of nutrients or their impaired assimilation or utilization

mal·oc·clu·sion \ˌma-lə-ˈklü-zhən\ *n* (1888) **:** improper occlusion; *esp* **:** abnormality in the coming together of teeth

mal·odor \ˌmal-ˈō-dər\ *n* (1825) **:** an offensive odor

mal·odor·ous \-ˈō-də-rəs\ *adj* (1850) **1 :** having a bad odor **2 :** highly improper ⟨~ practices and chicanery in high financial places —*New Republic*⟩ — **mal·odor·ous·ly** *adv* — **mal·odor·ous·ness** *n*

syn MALODOROUS, STINKING, FETID, NOISOME, PUTRID, RANK, FUSTY, MUSTY mean bad-smelling. MALODOROUS may range from the unpleasant to the strongly offensive ⟨*malodorous* fertilizers⟩. STINKING and FETID suggest the foul or disgusting ⟨prisoners were held in *stinking* cells⟩ ⟨the *fetid* odor of skunk cabbage⟩. NOISOME adds a suggestion of being harmful or unwholesome as well as offensive ⟨a stagnant, *noisome* sewer⟩. PUTRID implies particularly the sickening odor of decaying organic matter ⟨the *putrid* smell of rotting fish⟩. RANK suggests a strong unpleasant smell ⟨*rank* cigar smoke⟩. FUSTY and MUSTY suggest lack of fresh air and sunlight, FUSTY also implying prolonged uncleanliness, MUSTY stressing the effects of dampness, mildew, or age ⟨a *fusty* attic⟩ ⟨the *musty* odor of a damp cellar⟩.

ma·lo·lac·tic \ˌma-lō-ˈlak-tik, ˌmā-\ *adj* [*mal*ic + *-o-* + *lactic*] (1908) **:** relating to or involved in the bacterial conversion of malic acid to lactic acid in wine ⟨~ fermentation⟩

maloti *pl of* LOTI

Mal·pi·ghi·an corpuscle \mal-ˈpi-gē-ən-, -ˈpē-\ *n* [Marcello *Malpighi*] (1848) **:** the part of a nephron that consists of a glomerulus and Bowman's capsule — called also *Malpighian body*

Malpighian layer *n* (1878) **:** the deeper part of the epidermis consisting of cells whose protoplasm has not yet changed into horny material

Malpighian tubule *n* (1877) **:** any of a group of long blind vessels opening into the posterior part of the alimentary canal in most insects and some other arthropods and functioning primarily as excretory organs — called also *Malpighian tube*

mal·po·si·tion \ˌmal-pə-ˈzi-shən\ *n* (ca. 1839) **:** wrong or faulty position

mal·prac·tice \ˌmal-ˈprak-təs\ *n* (1671) **1 :** a dereliction of professional duty or a failure to exercise an ordinary degree of professional skill or learning by one (as a physician) rendering professional services which results in injury, loss, or damage **2 :** an injurious, negligent, or improper practice **:** MALFEASANCE

mal·prac·ti·tio·ner \ˌmal-prak-ˈti-sh(ə-)nər\ *n* (1800) **:** one who engages in or commits malpractice

MALS *abbr* **1** master of arts in liberal studies **2** master of arts in library science

[1]**malt** \ˈmȯlt\ *n* [ME, fr. OE *mealt;* akin to OHG *malz* malt, OE *meltan* to melt] (bef. 12c) **1 :** grain (as barley) softened by steeping in water, allowed to germinate, and used esp. in brewing and distilling **2 :** MALT LIQUOR **3 :** MALTED MILK — **malty** \ˈmȯl-tē\ *adj*

[2]**malt** *vt* (15c) **1 :** to convert into malt **2 :** to make or treat with malt or malt extract ~ *vi* **1 :** to become malt **2 :** to make grain into malt

malt·ase \ˈmȯl-ˌtās, -ˌtāz\ *n* (1890) **:** an enzyme that catalyzes the hydrolysis of maltose to glucose

malted milk *n* (1887) **1 :** a soluble powder prepared from dried milk and malted cereals **2 :** a beverage made by dissolving malted milk in milk and usu. adding ice cream and flavoring — called also *malted*

Mal·tese \mȯl-ˈtēz, -ˈtēs\ *n, pl* **Maltese** (1615) **1 :** a native or inhabitant of Malta **2 :** the Semitic language of the Maltese people **3 :** any of a breed of toy dogs with a long silky white coat, a black nose, and very dark eyes — **Maltese** *adj*

Maltese cross *n* (1877) **1 a :** a cross formée **b :** a cross that resembles the cross formée but has the outer face of each arm indented in a V — see CROSS illustration **2 :** a Eurasian herb (*Lychnis chalcedonica*) of the pink family cultivated for its usu. scarlet flowers

Mal·thu·sian \mal-ˈthü-zhən, mȯl-, -ˈthyü-\ *adj* [Thomas R. *Malthus*] (1821) **:** of or relating to Malthus or to his theory that population tends to increase at a faster rate than its means of subsistence and that unless it is checked by moral restraint or disaster (as disease, famine, or war) widespread poverty and degradation inevitably result — **Malthusian** *n* — **Mal·thu·sian·ism** \-zhə-ˌni-zəm\ *n*

malt liquor *n* (1693) **:** a fermented liquor (as beer) made with malt

malto·dex·trin \ˌmȯl-tō-ˈdek-strən\ *n* [*malt*ose + *-o-* + *dextrin*] (1885) **:** any of various carbohydrates derived from the partial hydrolysis of starch (as of corn or potatoes) and used in prepared foods esp. as a filler and to enhance texture and flavor

malt·ose \ˈmȯl-ˌtōs, -ˌtōz\ *n* [F, fr. E [1]*malt*] (1862) **:** a crystalline dextrorotatory fermentable sugar $C_{12}H_{22}O_{11}$ formed esp. from starch by amylase

mal·treat \ˌmal-ˈtrēt\ *vt* [part trans. of F *maltraiter,* fr. MF, fr. *mal-* + *traiter* to treat, fr. OF *traitier* — more at TREAT] (1708) **:** to treat cruelly or roughly **:** ABUSE — **mal·treat·er** \-ˈtrē-tər\ *n* — **mal·treat·ment** \-ˈtrēt-mənt\ *n*

malt·ster \ˈmȯlt-stər\ *n* (14c) **:** a maker of malt

malt sugar *n* (1862) **:** MALTOSE

malt whiskey *n* (1839) **:** SCOTCH 3

mal·va·sia \ˌmal-və-ˈzē-ə, -ˈsē-\ *n, often cap* [It, a sweet wine, fr. Mod Gk *Monobasia* Monemvasia, village in Greece] (1882) **:** a medium to large cultivated grape of Mediterranean regions that is often blended with other grape varieties to produce aromatic dry or sweet wines

mal·ver·sa·tion \ˌmal-vər-ˈsā-shən\ *n* [MF, fr. *malverser* to be corrupt, fr. *mal* + *verser* to turn, handle, fr. L *versare,* freq. of *vertere* to turn — more at WORTH] (1549) **1 :** misbehavior and esp. corruption in an office, trust, or commission **2 :** corrupt administration

mal·ware \ˈmal-ˌwer\ *n* [*mal*icious + *-ware* (as in *software*)] (1990) **:** software designed to interfere with a computer's normal functioning

ma·ma *also* **mam·ma** *or* **mom·ma** \ˈmä-mə, *chiefly Brit* mə-ˈmä\ *n* [baby talk] (1579) **1 :** MOTHER **2** *slang* **:** WIFE, WOMAN

mama's boy *n* (1850) **:** a usu. polite or timid boy or man who is extremely or excessively close to and solicitous of his mother

mam·ba \ˈmäm-bə, ˈmam-\ *n* [Zulu *imamba*] (1862) **:** any of several chiefly arboreal venomous green or black elapid snakes (genus *Dendroaspis*) of sub-Saharan Africa

mam·bo \ˈmäm-(ˌ)bō\ *n, pl* **mambos** [AmerSp] (1948) **:** a ballroom dance of Cuban origin that resembles the rumba and the cha-cha; *also* **:** the music for this dance — **mambo** *vi*

ma·mey \ma-ˈmē\ *n* [Sp, fr. Taino] (1604) **:** an evergreen tree (*Mammea americana* of the family Guttiferae) native to the West Indies and tropical America that has an ovoid fruit with thick russet leathery rind and yellow or reddish juicy sweet flesh; *also* **:** the fruit

Mam·luk \ˈmam-ˌlük\ *or* **Mam·e·luke** \ˈma-mə-ˌlük\ *n* [Ar *mamlūk,* lit., slave] (ca. 1506) **1 :** a member of a politically powerful Egyptian military class occupying the sultanate from 1250 to 1517 **2** *often not cap* **:** a white or east Asian slave in Muslim countries

mam·ma \ˈma-mə\ *n, pl* **mam·mae** \ˈma-ˌmē, -ˌmī\ [L, mother, breast, of baby-talk origin] (ca. 1693) **:** a mammary gland and its accessory parts

mam·mal \ˈma-məl\ *n* [NL *Mammalia,* fr. LL, neut. pl. of *mammalis* of the breast, fr. L *mamma* breast] (1826) **:** any of a class (Mammalia) of warm-blooded higher vertebrates (as placentals, marsupials, or monotremes) that nourish their young with milk secreted by mammary glands, have the skin usu. more or less covered with hair, and include humans — **mam·ma·li·an** \mə-ˈmā-lē-ən, ma-\ *adj or n*

mam·mal·o·gy \mə-ˈma-lə-jē, ma-ˈma-, -ˈmä-\ *n* [ISV, blend of *mammal* and *-logy*] (1835) **:** a branch of zoology dealing with mammals — **mam·mal·o·gist** \-jist\ *n*

mam·ma·ry \ˈma-mə-rē\ *adj* (1682) **:** of, relating to, lying near, or affecting the mammae

mammary gland *n* (1826) **:** any of the large compound modified sebaceous glands that in female mammals are modified to secrete milk, are situated ventrally in pairs, and usu. terminate in a nipple

mam·mer *vi* [ME *mameren* to stammer, of imit. origin] (ca. 1555) *obs* **:** WAVER, HESITATE

mam·mil·la·ry \ˈma-mə-ˌler-ē, ma-ˈmi-lə-rē\ *adj* [L *mammilla* breast, nipple, dim. of *mamma*] (1669) **1 :** of, relating to, or resembling the breasts **2 :** studded with breast-shaped protuberances

mam·mil·lat·ed \ˈma-mə-ˌlā-təd\ *adj* [LL *mammillatus,* fr. L *mammilla*] (1741) **1 :** having nipples or small protuberances **2 :** having the form of a bluntly rounded protuberance

[1]**mam·mock** \ˈma-mək\ *n* [origin unknown] (ca. 1529) *chiefly dial* **:** a broken piece **:** SCRAP

[2]**mammock** *vt* (1607) *chiefly dial* **:** to tear into fragments **:** MANGLE

mam·mo·gram \ˈma-mə-ˌgram\ *n* [L *mamma* + E *-o-* + *-gram*] (1937) **:** a photograph of the breasts made by X-rays; *also* **:** the procedure for producing a mammogram

mam·mog·ra·phy \ma-ˈmä-grə-fē\ *n* (1937) **:** X-ray examination of the breasts (as for early detection of cancer) — **mam·mo·graph·ic** \ˌma-mə-ˈgra-fik\ *adj*

mam·mon \ˈma-mən\ *n, often cap* [ME, fr. LL *mammona,* fr. Gk *mamōna,* fr. Aram *māmōnā* riches] (15c) **:** material wealth or possessions esp. as having a debasing influence ⟨you cannot serve God and ~ —Mt 6:24 (RSV)⟩ — **mam·mon·ism** \-mə-ˌni-zəm\ *n*

mam·mon·ist \-mə-nist\ *n* (1550) *archaic* **:** one devoted to the ideal or pursuit of wealth

[1]**mam·moth** \ˈma-məth\ *n* [Russ *mamont, mamot*] (1706) **1 :** any of a genus (*Mammuthus*) of extinct Pleistocene mammals of the elephant family distinguished from recent elephants by highly ridged molars, usu. large size, very long tusks that curve upward, and well-developed body hair **2 :** something immense of its kind ⟨a ~ company⟩

[2]**mammoth** *adj* (1802) **:** of very great size ***syn*** see ENORMOUS

mam·my \ˈma-mē\ *n, pl* **mammies** [alter. of *mamma*] (1523) **1 :** MAMA **2 :** a black woman serving as a nurse to white children esp. formerly in the southern U.S.

[1]**man** \ˈman, *in compounds* ˌman *or* mən\ *n, pl* **men** \ˈmen, *in compounds* ˌmen *or* mən\ [ME, fr. OE *man, mon* human being, male human; akin to OHG *man* human being, Skt *manu*] (bef. 12c) **1 a (1) :** an individual human; *esp* **:** an adult male human **(2) :** a man belonging to a particular category (as by birth, residence, membership, or occupation) — usu. used in combination ⟨council*man*⟩ **(3) :** HUSBAND **(4) :** LOVER **b :** the human race **:** HUMANKIND **c :** a bipedal primate mammal (*Homo sapiens*) that is anatomically related to the great apes but distinguished esp. by notable development of the brain with a resultant capacity for articulate speech and abstract reasoning, is usu. considered to form a variable number of freely interbreeding races, and is the sole living representative of the hominid family; *broadly* **:** any living or extinct hominid **d (1) :** one possessing in high degree the qualities considered distinctive of manhood **(2)** *obs* **:** the quality or state of being manly **:** MANLINESS **e :** FELLOW, CHAP — used as mode of familiar address **f** — used interjectionally to express intensity of feeling ⟨~, what a game⟩ **2 a :** INDIVIDUAL, PERSON ⟨a ~ could get killed there⟩ **b :** the individual who can fulfill or who has been chosen to fulfill one's requirements ⟨she's your ~⟩ **3 a :** a feudal tenant **:** VASSAL **b :** an adult male servant **c** *pl* **:** the working force as distinguished from the employer and usu. the management **4 a :** one of the distinctive objects moved by each player in various board games **b :** one of the players on a team **5 :** an alumnus of or student at a college or university ⟨a Bowdoin ~⟩ **6** *Christian Science* **:** the compound idea of infinite Spirit **:** the spiritual image and likeness of God **:** the full representation of Mind **7** *often cap* **:** POLICE ⟨when I heard the siren, I knew it was the *Man* —*Amer. Speech*⟩ **8** *often cap* **:** the white establishment **:** white society ⟨surprise that any black . . . should take on so about The *Man* —Peter Goldman⟩ **9 :** one extremely fond of or devoted to something specified ⟨strictly a vanilla ice cream ~⟩ — **man·less** \ˈman-ləs\ *adj* — **man·like** \-ˌlīk\ *adj* — **as one man :** with the agreement and consent of all **:** UNANIMOUSLY — **one's own man :** free

\ə\ **abut** \ᵊ\ **kitten**, F table \ər\ **further** \a\ **ash** \ā\ **ace** \ä\ **mop, mar**
\au̇\ **out** \ch\ **chin** \e\ **bet** \ē\ **easy** \g\ **go** \i\ **hit** \ī\ **ice** \j\ **job**
\ŋ\ **sing** \ō\ **go** \ȯ\ **law** \ȯi\ **boy** \th\ **thin** \t͟h\ **the** \ü\ **loot** \u̇\ **foot**
\y\ **yet** \zh\ **vision, beige** \k̲, ⁿ, œ, ue, ʸ\ *see* Guide to Pronunciation

from interference or control — **to a man :** without exception
[2]**man** *vt* **manned; man·ning** (12c) **1 a :** to supply with people (as for service) ⟨~ a fleet⟩ **b :** to station members of a ship's crew at ⟨~ the capstan⟩ **c :** to serve in the force or complement of ⟨~ the ticket booth⟩ **2 :** to accustom (as a hawk) to humans and the human environment **3 :** to furnish with strength or powers of resistance : BRACE
[3]**man** *abbr* manual
Man *abbr* Manitoba
ma·na \ˈmä-nə\ *n* [of Polynesian origin; akin to Hawaiian & Maori *mana* mana] (ca. 1843) **1 :** the power of the elemental forces of nature embodied in an object or person **2 :** moral authority : PRESTIGE
man–about–town \ˌman-ə-ˌbau̇t-ˈtau̇n\ *n, pl* **men–about–town** \ˌmen-\ (1734) **:** a worldly and socially active man
[1]**man·a·cle** \ˈma-ni-kəl\ *n* [ME *manicle,* fr. AF, fr. L *manicula* handle, dim. of *manicae* shackles, armor for the hand, fr. *manus* hand — more at MANUAL] (14c) **1 :** a shackle for the hand or wrist : HANDCUFF — usu. used in pl. **2 :** something used as a restraint
[2]**manacle** *vt* **man·a·cled; man·a·cling** \-k(ə-)liŋ\ (14c) **1 :** to confine (the hands) with manacles **2 :** to make fast or secure : BIND; *broadly* **:** to restrain from movement, progress, or action ***syn*** see HAMPER
[1]**man·age** \ˈma-nij\ *vb* **man·aged; man·ag·ing** [It *maneggiare,* fr. *mano* hand, fr. L *manus*] *vt* (1579) **1 :** to handle or direct with a degree of skill: as **a :** to make and keep compliant ⟨can't ~ their child⟩ **b :** to treat with care : HUSBAND ⟨*managed* his resources carefully⟩ **c :** to exercise executive, administrative, and supervisory direction of ⟨~ a business⟩ **2 :** to work upon or try to alter for a purpose ⟨~ the press⟩ ⟨~ stress⟩ **3 :** to succeed in accomplishing : CONTRIVE ⟨*managed* to escape from prison⟩ **4 :** to direct the professional career of ⟨an agency that ~*s* entertainers⟩ ~ *vi* **1 a :** to direct or carry on business or affairs; *also* **:** to direct a baseball team **b :** to admit of being carried on **2 :** to achieve one's purpose ***syn*** see CONDUCT
[2]**manage** *n* [It *maneggio* management, training of a horse, fr. *maneggiare*] (ca. 1587) **1 a** *archaic* **:** the action and paces of a trained riding horse **b :** the schooling or handling of a horse **c :** a riding school **2** *obs* **:** MANAGEMENT
man·age·able \ˈma-ni-jə-bəl\ *adj* (1598) **:** capable of being managed — **man·age·abil·i·ty** \ˌma-ni-jə-ˈbi-lə-tē\ *n* — **man·age·able·ness** \ˈma-ni-jə-bəl-nəs\ *n* — **man·age·ably** \-blē\ *adv*
managed care *n* (1982) **:** a system of health care (as by an HMO or PPO) that controls costs by placing limits on physicians' fees and by restricting the patient's choice of physicians
man·age·ment \ˈma-nij-mənt\ *n* (1598) **1 :** the act or art of managing **:** the conducting or supervising of something (as a business) **2 :** judicious use of means to accomplish an end **3 :** the collective body of those who manage or direct an enterprise — **man·age·men·tal** \ˌma-nij-ˈmen-tᵊl\ *adj*
man·ag·er \ˈma-ni-jər\ *n* (1588) **:** one that manages: as **a :** a person who conducts business or household affairs **b :** a person whose work or profession is management **c** (1) **:** a person who directs a team or athlete (2) **:** a student who in scholastic or collegiate sports supervises equipment and records under the direction of a coach — **man·a·ge·ri·al** \ˌma-nə-ˈjir-ē-əl\ *adj* — **man·a·ge·ri·al·ly** \-ē-ə-lē\ *adv* — **man·ag·er·ship** \ˈma-ni-jər-ˌship\ *n*
man·ag·er·ess \ˈma-ni-jə-rəs\ *n* (1797) **:** a woman who is a manager
managing editor *n* (1837) **:** an editor in executive and supervisory charge of all editorial activities of a publication (as a newspaper)
[1]**ma·ña·na** \mən-ˈyä-nə\ *n* [Sp, lit., tomorrow, fr. VL **maneana,* fr. fem. of **maneanus* early, fr. L *mane* early in the morning] (1845) **:** an indefinite time in the future
[2]**mañana** *adv* (1938) **:** at an indefinite time in the future
man ape *n* (ca. 1864) **1 :** GREAT APE **2 :** any of various fossil primates intermediate in characters between humans and the great apes
Ma·nas·seh \mə-ˈna-sə\ *n* [Heb *Mĕnashsheh*] (1578) **1 :** a son of Joseph and the traditional eponymous ancestor of one of the tribes of Israel **2 :** a king of Judah reigning in the seventh century B.C. and noted for his attempt to establish polytheism
ma·nat \mä-ˈnät\ *n, pl* **manat** *or* **manats** [Azerbaijani, ruble, fr. Pers *munāt,* fr. Russ *moneta, monet* coin, silver ruble coin, fr. Pol *moneta* coin, fr. L — more at MINT] (1990) — see MONEY table
man–at–arms \ˌman-ət-ˈärmz\ *n, pl* **men–at–arms** \ˌmen-\ (1581) **:** SOLDIER; *esp* **:** a heavily armed and usu. mounted soldier
man·a·tee \ˈma-nə-ˌtē\ *n* [Sp *manatí,* prob. of Carib origin; akin to Antillean Carib *manattoüi* manatee] (1555) **:** any of a genus (*Trichechus* of the family Trichechidae) of chiefly tropical aquatic sirenian mammals that differ from the related dugong esp. in having the tail rounded

manatee

man cave *n* (1992) **:** a room or space (as in a basement) designed according to the taste of the man of the house to be used as his personal area for hobbies and leisure activities
Man·ches·ter terrier \ˈman-ˌches-tər-, -chə-stər-\ *n* [*Manchester,* England] (1891) **:** any of a breed of small short-haired black-and-tan terriers developed in England
man–child \ˈman-ˌchī(-ə)ld\ *n, pl* **men–chil·dren** \ˈmen-ˌchil-drən, -dərn\ (14c) **:** a male child : SON
man·chi·neel \ˌman-chə-ˈnēl\ *n* [F *mancenille,* fr. Sp *manzanilla,* fr. dim. of *manzana* apple] (1630) **:** a poisonous tropical American tree (*Hippomane mancinella*) of the spurge family having a blistering milky juice and apple-shaped fruit
Man·chu \ˈman-(ˌ)chü, man-ˈ\ *n, pl* **Manchu** *or* **Manchus** [ultim. fr. Manchu *manju,* a self-designation] (1697) **1 :** a member of an indigenous people of Manchuria who conquered China and established a dynasty there in 1644 **2 :** the Tungusic language of the Manchu people — **Manchu** *adj*
man·ci·ple \ˈman(t)-sə-pəl\ *n* [ME, fr. AF, fr. ML *mancipium* office of steward, fr. L, act of purchase, fr. *mancip-, manceps* purchaser — more at EMANCIPATE] (13c) **:** a steward or purveyor esp. for a college or monastery
-mancy *n comb form* [MF *-mancie,* fr. L *-mantia,* fr. Gk *-manteia,* fr. *manteia,* fr. *mantis* diviner, prophet — more at MANTIS] **:** divination ⟨oneiro*mancy*⟩
M&A *abbr* mergers and acquisitions
Man·dae·an \man-ˈdē-ən\ *n* [ultim. fr. Mandaean *mandayyā* having knowledge] (1767) **1 :** a member of a Gnostic sect of the lower Tigris and Euphrates regions **2 :** a form of Aramaic found in documents written by Mandaeans — **Mandaean** *adj*
man·da·la \ˈmən-də-lə\ *n* [Skt *maṇḍala* circle] (1859) **1 :** a Hindu or Buddhist graphic symbol of the universe; *specif* **:** a circle enclosing a square with a deity on each side that is used chiefly as an aid to meditation **2 :** a graphic and often symbolic pattern usu. in the form of a circle divided into four separate sections or bearing a multiple projection of an image — **man·dal·ic** \ˌmən-ˈda-lik\ *adj*
man·da·mus \man-ˈdā-məs\ *n* [L, we enjoin, fr. *mandare*] (1760) **:** a writ issued by a superior court commanding the performance of a specified official act or duty
Man·dan \ˈman-ˌdan, -dən\ *n, pl* **Mandan** *or* **Mandans** [F *Mantanne, Mendanne,* fr. Dakota (Santee dial.) *mawátąna* or a cognate Sioux form] (1790) **1 :** a member of an American Indian people of the Missouri River valley in No. Dakota **2 :** the Siouan language of the Mandans
[1]**man·da·rin** \ˈman-d(ə-)rən\ *n* [Pg *mandarim,* fr. Malay *mĕntĕri,* fr. Skt *mantrin* counselor, fr. *mantra* counsel — more at MANTRA] (1589) **1 a :** a public official in the Chinese Empire of any of nine superior grades **b** (1) **:** a pedantic official (2) **:** BUREAUCRAT **c :** a person of position and influence often in intellectual or literary circles; *esp* **:** an elder and often traditionalist or reactionary member of such a circle **2** *cap* **a :** a form of spoken Chinese used by the court and the official classes of the Empire **b :** the group of closely related Chinese dialects that are spoken in about four fifths of the country and have a standard variety centering about Beijing **3** [Sw *mandarin* (*apelsin*) mandarin (orange), ultim. fr. Pg *mandarim* mandarin; perh. fr. the color of a mandarin's robes] **a :** a small spiny orange tree (*Citrus reticulata*) of southeastern Asia with yellow to reddish-orange loose-rinded fruits; *also* **:** a tree (as the satsuma) developed in cultivation from the mandarin by artificial selection or hybridization **b :** the fruit of a mandarin — **man·da·rin·ic** \ˌman-də-ˈri-nik\ *adj* — **man·da·rin·ism** \ˈman-d(ə-)rə-ˌni-zəm\ *n*
[2]**mandarin** *adj* (1604) **1 :** of, relating to, or typical of a mandarin ⟨~ graces⟩ **2 :** marked by polished ornate complexity of language ⟨~ prose⟩
man·da·rin·ate \ˈman-d(ə-)rə-ˌnāt\ *n* [prob. fr. F *mandarinat,* fr. *mandarin* mandarin, fr. Pg *mandarim*] (1728) **1 :** the office or status of a mandarin **2 :** a body of mandarins **3 :** rule by mandarins
mandarin collar *n* (1947) **:** a narrow stand-up collar usu. open in front
mandarin orange *n* (1771) **:** MANDARIN 3
man·da·tary \ˈman-də-ˌter-ē\ *n, pl* **-tar·ies** (15c) **:** MANDATORY
[1]**man·date** \ˈman-ˌdāt\ *n* [MF & L; MF *mandat,* fr. L *mandatum,* fr. neut. of *mandatus,* pp. of *mandare* to entrust, enjoin, prob. irreg. fr. *manus* hand + *-dere* to put — more at MANUAL, DO] (1501) **1 :** an authoritative command; *esp* **:** a formal order from a superior court or official to an inferior one **2 :** an authorization to act given to a representative ⟨accepted the ~ of the people⟩ **3 a :** an order or commission granted by the League of Nations to a member nation for the establishment of a responsible government over a former German colony or other conquered territory **b :** a mandated territory
[2]**mandate** *vt* **man·dat·ed; man·dat·ing** (1919) **1 :** to administer or assign (as a territory) under a mandate **2 :** to make mandatory : ORDER; *also* **:** DIRECT, REQUIRE
man·da·tor \ˈman-ˌdā-tər\ *n* (1681) **:** one that gives a mandate
[1]**man·da·to·ry** \ˈman-də-ˌtȯr-ē\ *adj* (15c) **1 :** required by a law or rule **:** OBLIGATORY ⟨the ~ retirement age⟩ **2 :** of, by, relating to, or holding a League of Nations mandate — **man·da·tor·i·ly** \-ˌtȯr-ə-lē\ *adv*
[2]**mandatory** *n, pl* **-ries** (1661) **:** one given a mandate; *esp* **:** a nation holding a mandate from the League of Nations
man–day \ˈman-ˈdā\ *n* (1925) **:** a unit of one day's work by one person
Man·de \ˈmän-ˌdā, män-ˈ\ *n* (1883) **1 :** MANDINGO **2 :** a branch of the Niger-Congo language family spoken primarily in Sierra Leone, Liberia, Guinea, Ivory Coast, Mali, and Burkina Faso
Man·del·brot set \ˈman-dəl-ˌbrät-, -ˌbrȯt-\ *n* [Benoit *Mandelbrot*] (1984) **:** a fractal that when plotted on a computer screen roughly resembles a series of heart-shaped disks to which smaller disks are attached and that consists of a connected set of all points c in the complex plane for which the recursive expression $z_{n+1} = z_n^2 + c$ for $n = 0, 1, 2, 3, \ldots$ with the starting value $z_0 = 0$ remains bounded as n approaches infinity
man·di·ble \ˈman-də-bəl\ *n* [ME, fr. LL *mandibula,* fr. L *mandere* to chew; prob. akin to Gk *masasthai* to chew] (15c) **1 a :** JAW 1a; *esp* **:** a lower jaw consisting of a single bone or of completely fused bones **b :** the lower jaw with its investing soft parts **c :** either the upper or lower segment of the bill of a bird **2 :** any of various invertebrate mouthparts serving to hold or bite food materials; *esp* **:** either member of the anterior pair of mouth appendages of an arthropod often forming strong biting jaws — **man·dib·u·lar** \man-ˈdi-byə-lər\ *adj* — **man·dib·u·late** \-lət\ *adj*
Man·din·go \man-ˈdiŋ-(ˌ)gō\ *n, pl* **Mandingo** *or* **Mandingoes** *or* **Mandingos** (1623) **1 :** a member of a people of western Africa in or near the upper Niger valley **2 :** the language of the Mandingo
Man·din·ka \man-ˈdiŋ-kə\ *n, pl* **Mandinka** *or* **Mandinkas** (1934) **:** MALINKE
mandioca *var of* MANIOC
man·do·la \man-ˈdō-lə\ *n* [It, fr. F *mandore,* modif. of LL *pandura* 3-stringed lute — more at BANDORE] (1758) **:** a 16th and 17th century lute that is the ancestor of the smaller mandolin
man·do·lin \ˌman-də-ˈlin, ˈman-də-lən\ *also* **man·do·line** \ˌman-də-ˈlēn, ˈman-də-lən\ *n* [It *mandolino,* dim. of *mandola*] (1707) **1 :** a musical instrument of the lute family that has a usu. pear-shaped body and fretted neck and four to six pairs of strings **2** *usu* *mandoline* [F, fr. It *mandolino* mandolin] **:** a kitchen utensil with a blade for slicing and shredding — **man·do·lin·ist** \ˌman-də-ˈli-nist\ *n*
man·drag·o·ra \man-ˈdra-gə-rə\ *n* [ME, fr. OE, fr. L *mandragoras,* fr. Gk] (bef. 12c) **:** MANDRAKE 1

mandolin 1

man·drake \ˈman-ˌdrāk\ *n* [ME, prob. alter. of *mandragora*] (14c) **1 a** : a Mediterranean herb (*Mandragora officinarum*) of the nightshade family with large ovate leaves, greenish-yellow or purple flowers, and a large usu. forked root resembling a human in form and formerly credited with magical properties **b** : the root of a mandrake formerly used esp. to promote conception, as a cathartic, or as a narcotic and soporific **2** : MAYAPPLE

man·drel *also* **man·dril** \ˈman-drəl\ *n* [ML *maundrellus,* prob. ultim. fr. Old Occitan *mandre* kingpin] (1554) **1 a** : a usu. tapered or cylindrical axle, spindle, or arbor inserted into a hole in a piece of work to support it during machining **b** : a metal bar that serves as a core around which material (as metal) may be cast, molded, forged, bent, or otherwise shaped **2** : the shaft and bearings on which a tool (as a circular saw) is mounted

man·drill \ˈman-drəl\ *n* [prob. fr. [1]*man* + [3]*drill*] (1774) : a large baboon (*Mandrillus sphinx* syn. *Papio sphinx*) of central Africa west of the Congo River with the male having a bright red and blue muzzle

mane \ˈmān\ *n* [ME, fr. OE *manu;* akin to OHG *mana* mane, L *monile* necklace] (bef. 12c) **1** : long and heavy hair growing about the neck and head of some mammals (as horses and lions) **2** : long heavy hair on a person's head — **maned** \ˈmānd\ *adj*

man–eat·er \ˈman-ˌē-tər\ *n* (1600) : one that has or is thought to have an appetite for human flesh: as **a** : CANNIBAL **b** : MACKEREL SHARK; *esp* : GREAT WHITE SHARK — called also *man-eater shark, man-eating shark* **c** : a large feline (as a lion or tiger) that has acquired the habit of feeding on human flesh — **man–eat·ing** \-ˌē-tiŋ\ *adj*

maned wolf *n* (1902) : a yellowish-red wild canid (*Chrysocyon brachyurus*) of So. American grasslands having black coloration on the nape and lower legs

ma·nège *also* **ma·nege** \ma-ˈnezh, mə-, -ˈnāzh\ *n* [F *manège,* fr. It *maneggio* training of a horse — more at MANAGE] (1644) **1** : a school for teaching horsemanship and for training horses **2** : the art of horsemanship or of training horses **3** : the movements or paces of a trained horse

ma·nes \ˈmä-ˌnās, ˈmā-ˌnēz\ *n pl* [L] (14c) **1** *often cap* : the deified spirits of the ancient Roman dead honored with graveside sacrifices **2** : the venerated or appeased spirit of a dead person

[1]**ma·neu·ver** \mə-ˈnü-vər, -ˈnyü-\ *n* [F *manœuvre,* fr. OF *maneuvre* work done by hand, fr. ML *manuopera,* fr. *manu operare* to perform manual labor — more at MANURE] (1758) **1 a** : a military or naval movement **b** : an armed forces training exercise; *esp* : an extended and large-scale training exercise involving military and naval units separately or in combination — often used in pl. **2** : a procedure or method of working usu. involving expert physical movement **3 a** : evasive movement or shift of tactics **b** : an intended and controlled variation from a straight and level flight path in the operation of an airplane **4 a** : an action taken to gain a tactical end **b** : an adroit and clever management of affairs often using trickery and deception ***syn*** see TRICK

[2]**maneuver** *vb* **ma·neu·vered; ma·neu·ver·ing** \-ˈnü-və-riŋ, -ˈnyü-; -ˈn(y)üv-riŋ\ *vi* (1777) **1 a** : to perform a movement in military or naval tactics in order to secure an advantage **b** : to make a series of changes in direction and position for a specific purpose **2** : to use stratagems : SCHEME ~ *vt* **1** : to cause to execute tactical movements **2** : to manage into or out of a position or condition : MANIPULATE **3 a** : to guide with adroitness and design **b** : to bring about or secure as a result of skillful management — **ma·neu·ver·abil·i·ty** \-ˌnü-və-rə-ˈbi-lə-tē, -ˌnyü-; -ˌn(y)üv-rə-\ *n* — **ma·neu·ver·able** \-ˈnü-və-rə-bəl, -ˈnyü-; -ˈn(y)üv-rə-\ *adj* — **ma·neu·ver·er** \-ˈnü-vər-ər, -ˈnyü-\ *n*

man–for–man \ˌman-fər-ˈman\ *adj* (1923) : MAN-TO-MAN 2

man Friday *n* [*Friday,* servant in *Robinson Crusoe* (1719), novel by Daniel Defoe] (ca. 1809) : an efficient and devoted aide or employee : a right-hand man

man·ful \ˈman-fəl\ *adj* (14c) : having or showing courage and resolution — **man·ful·ly** \-fə-lē\ *adv* — **man·ful·ness** *n*

man·ga \ˈmäŋ-gə\ *n* [Jp, comic, cartoon, fr. *man-* involuntary, aimless + *-ga* picture] (ca. 1951) : a Japanese comic book or graphic novel

man·ga·bey \ˈmaŋ-gə-(ˌ)bē\ *n, pl* **-beys** [F, fr. *Mangabe,* town in eastern Madagascar] (1774) : any of a genus (*Cercocebus*) of slender long-tailed African monkeys

mangan- *comb form* [G *Mangan,* fr. F *manganèse*] : manganese ⟨*manganate*⟩

man·ga·nate \ˈmaŋ-gə-ˌnāt\ *n* (1839) **1** : a salt containing manganese in the anion MnO_4 **2** : MANGANITE

man·ga·nese \ˈmaŋ-gə-ˌnēz, -ˌnēs\ *n* [F *manganèse,* fr. It *manganese* manganese dioxide] (1783) : a grayish-white usu. hard and brittle metallic element that resembles iron but is not magnetic and is used esp. in alloys, batteries, and plant fertilizers — see ELEMENT table — **man·ga·ne·sian** \ˌmaŋ-gə-ˈnē-zhən, -shən\ *adj*

manganese dioxide *n* (1866) : a dark insoluble compound MnO_2 used esp. as an oxidizing agent, as a depolarizer of dry cells, and in making glass and ceramics

man·gan·ic \man-ˈga-nik, maŋ-\ *adj* (1790) : of, relating to, or derived from manganese; *esp* : containing this element with a valence of three or six

man·ga·nite \ˈmaŋ-gə-ˌnīt\ *n* (1827) **1** : a metallic gray to black mineral MnO(OH) that is a hydroxide and minor ore of manganese **2** : any of various unstable salts made by reaction of manganese dioxide with a base

man·ga·nous \-nəs\ *adj* (1842) : of, relating to, or derived from manganese; *esp* : containing this element with a valence of two

mange \ˈmānj\ *n* [alter. of ME *manjewe,* fr. AF *manjue,* fr. *manger* to eat] (1540) : any of various persistent contagious skin diseases marked esp. by eczematous inflammation and loss of hair, affecting domestic animals or sometimes humans, and caused by a minute parasitic mite — compare SARCOPTIC MANGE

man·gel \ˈmaŋ-gəl\ *n* [short for *mangel-wurzel*] (1860) : a large coarse yellow- to reddish-orange beet grown chiefly as food for cattle

man·gel–wur·zel \-ˌwər-zəl\ *n* [G, alter. of *Mangoldwurzel,* fr. *Mangold* beet + *Wurzel* root] (1767) : MANGEL

man·ger \ˈmān-jər\ *n* [ME *mangeour, manger,* fr. AF *mangure,* fr. *manger* to eat, fr. L *manducare* to chew, devour, fr. *manducus* glutton, fr. *mandere* to chew — more at MANDIBLE] (14c) : a trough or open box in a stable designed to hold feed or fodder for livestock

[1]**man·gle** \ˈmaŋ-gəl\ *vt* **man·gled; man·gling** \-g(ə-)liŋ\ [ME, fr. AF *mangler, mahangler,* perh. fr. *mahaigner* to maim — more at MAYHEM] (15c) **1** : to injure with deep disfiguring wounds by cutting, tearing, or crushing ⟨people . . . *mangled* by sharks —V. G. Heiser⟩ **2** : to spoil, injure, or make incoherent esp. through ineptitude ⟨a story *mangled* beyond recognition⟩ ***syn*** see MAIM — **man·gler** \-g(ə-)lər\ *n*

[2]**mangle** *n* [D *mangel,* fr. G, fr. MHG, dim. of *mange* mangonel, mangle, fr. L *manganum*] (1696) : a machine for ironing laundry by passing it between heated rollers

[3]**mangle** *vt* **man·gled; man·gling** \-g(ə-)liŋ\ (ca. 1775) : to press or smooth (as damp linen) with a mangle — **man·gler** \-g(ə-)lər\ *n*

man·go \ˈmaŋ-(ˌ)gō\ *n, pl* **mangoes** *also* **mangos** [Pg *manga,* prob. fr. Malayalam *māṅṅa*] (1582) **1** : a tropical usu. large ovoid or oblong fruit with a firm yellowish-red skin, hard central stone, and juicy aromatic pulp; *also* : an evergreen tree (*Mangifera indica*) of the cashew family that bears mangoes **2** : SWEET PEPPER

man·go·nel \ˈmaŋ-gə-ˌnel\ *n* [ME, fr. AF, prob. fr. ML *manganellus,* dim. of LL *manganum* philter, mangonel, fr. Gk *manganon*] (13c) : a military engine formerly used to throw missiles

man·go·steen \ˈmaŋ-gə-ˌstēn\ *n* [modif. of Malay *manggisutan*] (1598) : a dark reddish-purple fruit of southeastern Asia with a thick rind and juicy flesh having a flavor suggestive of both peach and pineapple; *also* : a tree (*Garcinia mangostana*) of the Saint-John's-wort family that bears mangosteens

man·grove \ˈman-ˌgrōv, ˈmaŋ-\ *n* [prob. fr. Pg *mangue* mangrove (fr. Sp *mangle,* prob. fr. Taino) + E *grove*] (1613) **1** : any of a genus (*Rhizophora,* esp. *R. mangle* of the family Rhizophoraceae) of tropical maritime trees or shrubs that send out many prop roots and form dense masses important in coastal land building and as foundations of unique ecosystems **2** : any of numerous trees (as of the genera *Avicennia* of the vervain family or *Sonneratia* of the family Sonneratiaceae) with growth habits like those of the true mangroves

mangy \ˈmān-jē\ *adj* **mang·i·er; -est** (1515) **1** : affected with or resulting from mange **2 a** : having many worn or bare spots ⟨a ~ rug⟩ **b** : SEEDY, SHABBY ⟨a ~ office⟩ — **man·gi·ness** \-jē-nəs\ *n*

man·han·dle \ˈman-ˌhan-dᵊl\ *vt* (1851) **1** : to handle roughly **2** : to move or manage by human force ⟨*manhandled* the posts into place⟩

man·hat·tan \man-ˈha-tᵊn, mən-\ *n, often cap* [*Manhattan,* borough of New York City] (1884) : a cocktail consisting of vermouth, whiskey, and sometimes a dash of bitters

Manhattan clam chowder *n* (1910) : chowder made with chopped clams, tomatoes, vegetables, and seasonings

man·hole \ˈman-ˌhōl\ *n* (1793) : a hole through which one may go esp. to gain access to an underground or enclosed structure

man·hood \ˈman-ˌhu̇d\ *n* (13c) **1** : the condition of being a human being **2** : qualities associated with men : MANLINESS **3** : the condition of being an adult male as distinguished from a child or female **4** : adult males : MEN **5** : PENIS

man–hour \ˈman-ˈau̇(-ə)r\ *n* (1912) : a unit of one hour's work by one person that is used esp. as a basis for cost accounting and wages

man·hunt \ˈman-ˌhənt\ *n* (1833) : an organized and usu. intensive hunt for a person and esp. for one charged with a crime

ma·nia \ˈmā-nē-ə, -nyə\ *n* [ME, fr. LL, fr. Gk, fr. *mainesthai* to be mad; akin to Gk *menos* spirit — more at MIND] (14c) **1** : excitement manifested by mental and physical hyperactivity, disorganization of behavior, and elevation of mood; *specif* : the manic phase of bipolar disorder **2 a** : excessive or unreasonable enthusiasm ⟨a ~ for saving things⟩ — often used in combination **b** : the object of such enthusiasm

ma·ni·ac \ˈmā-nē-ˌak\ *n* [LL *maniacus* maniacal, fr. Gk *maniakos,* fr. *mania*] (ca. 1763) **1** : MADMAN, LUNATIC **2** : a person characterized by an inordinate or ungovernable enthusiasm for something

ma·ni·a·cal \mə-ˈnī-ə-kəl\ *also* **ma·ni·ac** \ˈmā-nē-ˌak\ *adj* (1526) **1** : affected with or suggestive of madness ⟨~ laughter⟩ **2** : characterized by ungovernable excitement or frenzy : FRANTIC ⟨a ~ mob⟩ — **ma·ni·a·cal·ly** \mə-ˈnī-ə-k(ə-)lē\ *adv*

man·ic \ˈma-nik\ *adj* (ca. 1824) : affected with, relating to, characterized by, or resulting from mania — **manic** *n* — **man·i·cal·ly** \-ni-k(ə-)lē\ *adv*

manic depression *n* (1911) : BIPOLAR DISORDER

man·ic–de·pres·sive \ˌma-nik-di-ˈpre-siv\ *adj* (1902) : characterized by or affected with either mania or depression or alternating mania and depression (as in bipolar disorder) — **manic–depressive** *n*

manic–depressive illness *n* (1951) : BIPOLAR DISORDER

Man·i·chae·an *or* **Man·i·che·an** \ˌma-nə-ˈkē-ən\ *or* **Man·i·chee** \ˈma-nə-ˌkē\ *n* [LL *manichaeus,* fr. LGk *manichaios,* fr. *Manichaios* Manes †*ab* A.D. 276 Pers. founder of the sect] (1556) **1** : a believer in a syncretistic religious dualism originating in Persia in the third century A.D. and teaching the release of the spirit from matter through asceticism **2** : a believer in religious or philosophical dualism — **Manichaean** *or* **Manichean** *adj* — **Man·i·chae·an·ism** *or* **Man·i·che·an·ism** \ˌma-nə-ˈkē-ə-ˌni-zəm\ *n* — **Man·i·chae·ism** *or* **Man·i·che·ism** \ˈma-nə-(ˌ)kē-ˌi-zəm\ *n*

man·i·cot·ti \ˌma-nə-ˈkä-tē\ *n, pl* **manicotti** [It, pl. of *manicotto* muff, fr. *manica* sleeve, fr. L, fr. *manus* hand] (1947) : tubular pasta shells that may be stuffed with ricotta or a meat mixture; *also* : a dish of stuffed manicotti usu. with tomato sauce

[1]**man·i·cure** \ˈma-nə-ˌkyu̇r\ *n* [F, fr. L *manus* hand + F *-icure* (as in *pédicure* pedicure) — more at MANUAL] (1880) **1** : MANICURIST **2** : a treatment for the care of the hands and fingernails

[2]**manicure** *vt* **-cured; -cur·ing** (ca. 1890) **1** : to do manicure work on; *esp* : to trim and polish the fingernails of **2 a** : to trim closely and evenly ⟨*manicured* lawns⟩ **b** : GROOM 2 ⟨*manicured* flower beds⟩

man·i·cur·ist \-ˌkyu̇r-ist\ *n* (1889) : a person who gives manicures

[1]**man·i·fest** \ˈma-nə-ˌfest\ *adj* [ME, fr. AF or L; AF *manifeste,* fr. L *manifestus* caught in the act, flagrant, obvious, perh. fr. *manus* + *-festus* (akin to L in*festus* hostile)] (14c) **1** : readily perceived by the senses and esp. by the sense of sight **2** : easily understood or recognized by the mind : OBVIOUS ***syn*** see EVIDENT — **man·i·fest·ly** *adv*

[2]**manifest** *vt* (14c) : to make evident or certain by showing or displaying *syn* see SHOW — **man·i·fest·er** *n*

[3]**manifest** *n* (1561) **1** : MANIFESTATION, INDICATION **2** : MANIFESTO **3** : a list of passengers or an invoice of cargo for a vehicle (as a ship or plane)

man·i·fes·tant \ˌma-nə-ˈfes-tənt\ *n* (1880) : a person who makes or participates in a manifestation

man·i·fes·ta·tion \ˌma-nə-fə-ˈstā-shən, -ˌfe-ˈstā-\ *n* (15c) **1 a** : the act, process, or an instance of manifesting **b** (1) : something that manifests or is manifest (2) : a perceptible, outward, or visible expression **c** : one of the forms in which an individual is manifested **d** : an occult phenomenon; *specif* : MATERIALIZATION **2** : a public demonstration of power and purpose

manifest destiny *n, often cap M&D* (1845) : a future event accepted as inevitable ⟨in the mid-19th century expansion to the Pacific was regarded as the *Manifest Destiny* of the United States⟩; *broadly* : an ostensibly benevolent or necessary policy of imperialistic expansion

[1]**man·i·fes·to** \ˌma-nə-ˈfes-(ˌ)tō\ *n, pl* **-tos** *or* **-toes** [It, denunciation, manifest, fr. *manifestare* to manifest, fr. L, fr. *manifestus*] (1620) : a written statement declaring publicly the intentions, motives, or views of its issuer

[2]**manifesto** *vi* (1748) : to issue a manifesto

[1]**man·i·fold** \ˈma-nə-ˌfōld\ *adj* [ME, fr. OE *manigfeald,* fr. *manig* many + *-feald* -fold] (bef. 12c) **1 a** : marked by diversity or variety **b** : MANY **2** : comprehending or uniting various features : MULTIFARIOUS **3** : rightfully so-called for many reasons ⟨a ~ liar⟩ **4** : consisting of or operating many of one kind combined ⟨a ~ bellpull⟩ — **man·i·fold·ly** \-ˌfōl(d)-lē\ *adv* — **man·i·fold·ness** \-ˌfōl(d)-nəs\ *n*

[2]**manifold** *adv* (bef. 12c) : many times : a great deal ⟨will increase your blessings ~⟩

[3]**manifold** *vt* (bef. 12c) **1** : to make manifold : MULTIPLY **2** : to make several or many copies of ~ *vi* : to make several or many copies

[4]**manifold** *n* (13c) : something that is manifold: as **a** : a whole that unites or consists of many diverse elements ⟨the ~ of aspirations, passions, frustrations —Harry Slochower⟩ **b** : a pipe fitting with several lateral outlets for connecting one pipe with others; *also* : a fitting on an internal combustion engine that directs a fuel and air mixture to or receives the exhaust gases from several cylinders **c** : SET 21 **d** : a topological space in which every point has a neighborhood that is homeomorphic to the interior of a sphere in Euclidean space of the same number of dimensions

man·i·kin *also* **man·ni·kin** \ˈma-ni-kən\ *n* [D *mannekijn* little man, fr. MD, dim. of *man;* akin to OE *man*] (ca. 1536) **1** : MANNEQUIN **2** : a little man : DWARF, PYGMY

ma·nila *also* **ma·nil·la** \mə-ˈni-lə\ *adj* (1820) **1** *cap* : made from Manila hemp **2** : made of manila paper — **manila** *n*

Manila hemp *n* [*Manila,* Philippine Islands] (1814) : ABACA

manila paper *n, often cap M* (1866) : a strong and durable paper of a brownish or buff color and smooth finish made orig. from Manila hemp

ma·nille \mə-ˈnil\ *n* [modif. of Sp *malilla*] (1674) : the second highest trump in various card games (as ombre)

man in the street (1831) : an average or ordinary person

man·i·oc \ˈma-nē-ˌäk\ *also* **man·di·o·ca** \ˌman-dē-ˈō-kə\ *n* [F *manioc* & Sp & Pg *mandioca,* all ultim. fr. Tupi *maniʔóka, mandiʔóka*] (1544) : CASSAVA

man·i·ple \ˈma-nə-pəl\ *n* [ME, fr. ML *manipulus,* fr. L, handful, fr. *manus* hand + *-pulus* (perh. akin to L *plēre* to fill); fr. its having been orig. held in the hand — more at MANUAL, FULL] (15c) **1** : a long narrow strip of silk formerly worn at mass over the left arm by clerics of or above the order of subdeacon **2** [L *manipulus,* fr. *manipulus* handful] : a subdivision of the Roman legion consisting of either 120 or 60 men

ma·nip·u·la·ble \mə-ˈni-pyə-lə-bəl\ *adj* (1881) : capable of being manipulated — **ma·nip·u·la·bil·i·ty** \-ˌni-pyə-lə-ˈbi-lə-tē\ *n*

ma·nip·u·lar \mə-ˈni-pyə-lər\ *adj* (1623) **1** : of or relating to the ancient Roman maniple **2** : of, relating to, or performed by manipulation : MANIPULATIVE

ma·nip·u·late \mə-ˈni-pyə-ˌlāt\ *vt* **-lat·ed; -lat·ing** [back-formation fr. *manipulation,* fr. F, fr. *manipuler* to handle an apparatus in chemistry, ultim. fr. L *manipulus*] (1834) **1** : to treat or operate with or as if with the hands or by mechanical means esp. in a skillful manner **2 a** : to manage or utilize skillfully **b** : to control or play upon by artful, unfair, or insidious means esp. to one's own advantage **3** : to change by artful or unfair means so as to serve one's purpose : DOCTOR — **ma·nip·u·lat·able** \-ˌlā-tə-bəl\ *adj* — **ma·nip·u·la·tion** \-ˌni-pyə-ˈlā-shən\ *n* — **ma·nip·u·la·tive** \-ˈni-pyə-ˌlā-tiv, -lə-\ *adj* — **ma·nip·u·la·tive·ly** *adv* — **ma·nip·u·la·tive·ness** *n* — **ma·nip·u·la·tor** \-ˌlā-tər\ *n* — **ma·nip·u·la·to·ry** \-lə-ˌtȯr-ē, -ˌtȯr-\ *adj*

ma·nip·u·la·tives \mə-ˈni-pyə-ˌlā-tivz, -lə-\ *n pl* (1965) : objects (as blocks) that a student is instructed to use in a way that teaches or reinforces a lesson

man·i·tou *or* **man·i·tu** \ˈma-nə-ˌtü\ *also* **man·i·to** \-ˌtō\ *n* [Ojibwa *manito·*] (1643) : a supernatural force that according to an Algonquian conception pervades the natural world

man jack \ˈman-ˈjak\ *n* (1807) : individual man ⟨every *man jack*⟩

man·kind *n sing but sing or pl in constr* (13c) **1** \ˈman-ˈkīnd, -ˌkīnd\ : the human race : the totality of human beings **2** \-ˌkīnd\ : men esp. as distinguished from women

[1]**man·ly** \ˈman-lē\ *adv* (bef. 12c) : in a manly manner

[2]**manly** *adj* **man·li·er; -est** (13c) **1** : having qualities generally associated with a man : STRONG, VIRILE **2** : appropriate in character to a man ⟨~ sports⟩ — **man·li·ness** *n*

man–made \ˈman-ˈmād, -ˌmād\ *adj* (1615) : manufactured, created, or constructed by human beings; *specif* : SYNTHETIC ⟨~ fibers⟩

man·na \ˈma-nə\ *n* [ME, fr. OE, fr. LL, fr. Gk, fr. Heb *mān*] (bef. 12c) **1 a** : food miraculously supplied to the Israelites in their journey through the wilderness **b** : divinely supplied spiritual nourishment **c** : a usu. sudden and unexpected source of gratification, pleasure, or gain **2 a** : the sweetish dried exudate of a Eurasian ash (esp. *Fraxinus ornus*) that contains mannitol and has been used as a laxative and demulcent **b** : a similar product excreted by a scale insect (*Trabutina mannipara*) feeding on the tamarisk

manna grass *n* (1759) : any of a genus (*Glyceria*) of chiefly No. American perennial grasses of wetland or aquatic habitats

man·nan \ˈma-ˌnan, -nən\ *n* [ISV *mannose* + [3]*-an*] (1895) : any of several polysaccharides that are polymers of mannose and occur esp. in plant cell walls

manned *adj* (1617) : carrying or performed by a human being ⟨~ spaceflight⟩

man·ne·quin \ˈma-ni-kən\ *n* [F, fr. D *mannekijn* little man — more at MANIKIN] (1730) **1** : an artist's, tailor's, or dressmaker's lay figure; *also* : a form representing the human figure used esp. for displaying clothes **2** : one employed to model clothing

man·ner \ˈma-nər\ *n* [ME *manere,* fr. AF, fr. VL **manuaria,* fr. L, fem. of *manuarius* of the hand, fr. *manus* hand — more at MANUAL] (12c) **1 a** : KIND, SORT ⟨what ~ of man is he⟩ **b** : KINDS, SORTS ⟨all ~ of problems⟩ **2 a** (1) : a characteristic or customary mode of acting : CUSTOM (2) : a mode of procedure or way of acting : FASHION (3) : method of artistic execution or mode of presentation : STYLE **b** *pl* : social conduct or rules of conduct as shown in the prevalent customs ⟨Victorian ~*s*⟩ **c** : characteristic or distinctive bearing, air, or deportment ⟨his poised gracious ~⟩ **d** *pl* (1) : habitual conduct or deportment : BEHAVIOR ⟨mind your ~*s*⟩ (2) : good manners **e** : a distinguished or stylish air *syn* see BEARING, METHOD — **man·ner·less** \-ləs\ *adj* — **to the manner born** : fitted by or as if by birth or rearing to a particular position, role, or status

man·nered \ˈma-nərd\ *adj* (14c) **1** : having manners of a specified kind ⟨well-*mannered*⟩ **2 a** : having or displaying a particular manner **b** : having an artificial or stilted character ⟨passages . . . so ~ as to be unintelligible —R. G. G. Price⟩

man·ner·ism \ˈma-nə-ˌri-zəm\ *n* (1800) **1 a** : exaggerated or affected adherence to a particular style or manner : ARTIFICIALITY, PRECIOSITY ⟨refined almost to the point of ~ —Winthrop Sargeant⟩ **b** *often cap* : an art style in late 16th century Europe characterized by spatial incongruity and excessive elongation of the human figures **2** : a characteristic and often unconscious mode or peculiarity of action, bearing, or treatment *syn* see POSE — **man·ner·ist** \-rist\ *n or adj* — **man·ner·is·tic** \ˌma-nə-ˈris-tik\ *adj*

man·ner·ly \ˈma-nər-lē\ *adj* (ca. 1529) : showing good manners — **man·ner·li·ness** *n* — **mannerly** *adv*

man·nish \ˈma-nish\ *adj* (14c) **1** : resembling or suggesting a man rather than a woman **2** : generally associated with or characteristic of a man rather than a woman ⟨her ~ clothes⟩ — **man·nish·ly** *adv* — **man·nish·ness** *n*

man·nite \ˈma-ˌnīt\ *n* [F, fr. *manna,* fr. LL] (1827) : MANNITOL

man·ni·tol \ˈma-nə-ˌtȯl, -ˌtōl\ *n* [ISV] (1879) : a slightly sweet crystalline alcohol $C_6H_{14}O_6$ found in many plants and used esp. as a diuretic and in testing kidney function

man·nose \ˈma-ˌnōs, -ˌnōz\ *n* [ISV *mannite* + [2]*-ose*] (1888) : an aldose $C_6H_{12}O_6$ whose dextrorotatory enantiomer occurs esp. as a structural unit of mannans from which it can be recovered by hydrolysis

ma·no \ˈmä-(ˌ)nō\ *n, pl* **manos** [Sp, lit., hand, fr. L *manus* — more at MANUAL] (ca. 1892) : a stone used as the upper millstone for grinding foods (as corn) by hand in a metate

ma·no a ma·no \ˌmä-nō-ä-ˈmä-nō\ *adv or adj* [Sp, lit., hand to hand] (1950) : in direct competition or conflict esp. between two people

ma·noeu·vre *chiefly Brit var of* MANEUVER

man of God (1670) : CLERGYMAN

man of letters (1645) **1** : SCHOLAR **2** : AUTHOR

man of straw (1624) : STRAW MAN

man of the house (1535) : the chief male in a household

man of the world (15c) : a practical or worldly-wise man of wide experience

man–of–war \ˌma-nə(v)-ˈwȯr\ *also* **man–o'–war** \-nə-\ *n, pl* **men–of–war** \ˌme-nə(v)-\ *also* **men–o'–war** \-nə-\ (15c) : a combatant warship of a recognized navy

ma·nom·e·ter \mə-ˈnä-mə-tər\ *n* [F *manomètre,* fr. Gk *manos* sparse, loose, rare (akin to Arm *manr* small) + F *-mètre*] (ca. 1730) **1** : an instrument (as a pressure gauge) for measuring the pressure of gases and vapors **2** : SPHYGMOMANOMETER — **man·o·met·ric** \ˌma-nə-ˈme-trik\ *adj* — **man·o·met·ri·cal·ly** \-tri-k(ə-)lē\ *adv* — **ma·nom·e·try** \mə-ˈnä-mə-trē\ *n*

man on horseback (1860) **1** : a usu. military figure whose ambitions and popularity mark him as a potential dictator **2** : DICTATOR

man on the street (1926) : MAN IN THE STREET

man·or \ˈma-nər\ *n* [ME *maner,* fr. OF *manoir,* fr. *manoir* to sojourn, dwell, fr. L *manēre* — more at MANSION] (14c) **1 a** : the house or hall of an estate : MANSION **b** : a landed estate **2 a** : a unit of English rural territorial organization; *esp* : such a unit in the Middle Ages consisting of an estate under a lord enjoying a variety of rights over land and tenants including the right to hold court **b** : a tract of land in No. America occupied by tenants who pay a fixed rent in money or kind to the proprietor — **ma·no·ri·al** \mə-ˈnōr-ē-əl, -ˈnȯr-\ *adj* — **ma·no·ri·al·ism** \-ə-ˌli-zəm\ *n* — **to the manor born** : born into circumstances of wealth and privilege

manor house *n* (1575) : the house of the lord of a manor

man–o'–war bird *n* (1707) : FRIGATE BIRD

man·pack \ˈman-ˌpak\ *adj* (1965) : designed to be carried by one person ⟨a ~ communication system⟩

man power *n* (1859) **1** : power available from or supplied by the physical effort of human beings **2** *usu* **man·pow·er** : the total supply of persons available and fitted for service

man·qué \mäⁿ-ˈkā\ *adj* [F, fr. pp. of *manquer* to lack, fail, fr. It *mancare,* fr. *manco* lacking, left-handed, fr. L, having a crippled hand, prob. fr. *manus*] (1773) : short of or frustrated in the fulfillment of one's aspirations or talents — used postpositively ⟨a poet ~⟩

man·sard \ˈman-ˌsärd, -sərd\ *n* [F *mansarde,* fr. François *Mansart* †1666 Fr. architect] (ca. 1734) : a roof having two slopes on all sides with the lower slope steeper than the upper one — see ROOF illustration — **man·sard·ed** \-ˌsär-dəd, -sər-\ *adj*

man·scap·ing \ˈman-ˌskā-piŋ\ *n* [blend of [1]*man* and *landscaping,* gerund of [2]*landscape*] (2003) : the trimming or shaving of a man's body hair so as to enhance his appearance — **man·scape** \-ˌskāp\ *vb*

manse \ˈman(t)s\ *n* [ME *manss,* fr. ML *mansa, mansus, mansum,* fr. L *mansus* lodging, fr. *manēre*] (15c) **1** *archaic* : the dwelling of a householder **2** : the residence of a minister; *esp* : the house of a Presbyterian minister **3** : a large imposing residence

man·ser·vant \'man-ˌsər-vənt\ *n, pl* **men·ser·vants** \'men-ˌsər-vən(t)s\ (14c) : a male servant

-manship *n suffix* [-*man* + -*ship* (as in *horsemanship*)] **1** : art or practice of a competitive nature ⟨brink*manship*⟩ **2** : skilled engagement in a competitive activity ⟨grants*manship*⟩

man·sion \'man(t)-shən\ *n* [ME, fr. AF, fr. L *mansion-, mansio*, fr. *manēre* to remain, dwell; akin to Gk *menein* to remain] (14c) **1** *obs* : the act of remaining or dwelling : STAY **b** *archaic* : DWELLING, ABODE **2 a** (1) : MANOR HOUSE (2) : a large imposing residence **b** : a separate apartment or lodging in a large structure **3 a** : HOUSE 3b **b** : one of the 28 parts into which the moon's monthly course through the heavens is divided

man–size \'man-ˌsīz\ *or* **man–sized** \-ˌsīzd\ *adj* (1913) **1** : suitable for or requiring a man ⟨a ~ job⟩ **2** : larger than others of its kind ⟨constructed a ~ model⟩

man·slaugh·ter \'man-ˌslȯ-tər\ *n* (14c) : the unlawful killing of a human being without express or implied malice

man·slay·er \-ˌslā-ər\ *n* (14c) : one who commits homicide

man's man (1897) : a man noted or admired for traditionally masculine interests and activities

man·sue·tude \'man(t)-swi-ˌtüd, man-'sü-ə-, -ˌtyüd\ *n* [ME, fr. L *mansuetudo*, fr. *mansuescere* to tame, fr. *manus* hand + *suescere* to accustom; akin to Gk *ēthos* custom — more at MANUAL, SIB] (14c) : the quality or state of being gentle : MEEKNESS, TAMENESS

man·ta \'man-tə\ *n* [Sp, alter. of *manto* cloak, fr. LL *mantus*, prob. back-formation fr. L *mantellum* mantle] (1697) **1** : a square piece of cloth or blanket used in southwestern U.S. and Latin America usu. as a cloak or shawl **2** [AmerSp, fr. Sp; fr. its shape] : MANTA RAY

man–tai·lored \'man-ˌtā-lərd\ *adj* (1915) : made with the severe simplicity associated with men's coats and suits

manta ray *n* (1951) : any of several extremely large rays (genera *Manta* and *Mobula*) that are widely distributed in warm seas and have enlarged pectoral fins resembling wings

man·teau \man-'tō, 'man-ˌ\ *n* [F, fr. OF *mantel*] (1671) : a loose cloak, coat, or robe

man·tel \'man-t⁾l\ *n* [ME, fr. AF, mantle] (15c) **1 a** : a beam, stone, or arch serving as a lintel to support the masonry above a fireplace **b** : the finish around a fireplace **2** : a shelf above a fireplace

man·tel·et \'mant-lət, 'man-t⁾l-ət, ˌman-tə-'let\ *n* [ME, fr. AF, dim. of *mantel*] (14c) **1** : a very short cape or cloak **2** *or* **mant·let** \'mant-lət\ : a movable shelter formerly used by besiegers as a protection when attacking

man·tel·piece \'man-t⁾l-ˌpēs\ *n* (1686) **1** : a mantel with its side elements **2** : MANTEL 2

man·tel·shelf \-ˌshelf\ *n* (ca. 1828) : MANTEL 2

man·tic \'man-tik\ *adj* [Gk *mantikos*, fr. *mantis*] (1839) : of or relating to the faculty of divination : PROPHETIC

man·ti·core \'man-ti-ˌkȯr\ *n* [ME, fr. L *mantichora*, fr. Gk *mantichōras*] (14c) : a legendary animal with the head of a man, the body of a lion, and the tail of a dragon or scorpion

man·tid \'man-təd\ *n* [NL *Mantida*, group name, fr. *Mantis*, genus name] (1895) : MANTIS

man·til·la \man-'tē-yə, -'ti-lə\ *n* [Sp, dim. of *manta*] (1717) **1** : a light scarf worn over the head and shoulders esp. by Spanish and Latin-American women **2** : a short light cape or cloak

man·tis \'man-təs\ *n, pl* **man·tis·es** *also* **man·tes** \'man-ˌtēz\ [NL, fr. Gk, lit., diviner, prophet; akin to Gk *mainesthai* to be mad — more at MANIA] (1646) : any of an order or suborder (Mantodea and esp. family Mantidae) of large usu. green insects that feed on other insects and clasp their prey in forelimbs held up as if in prayer

man·tis·sa \man-'ti-sə\ *n* [L *mantissa, mantissa* makeweight, fr. Etruscan] (1846) : the part of a logarithm to the right of the decimal point

mantis shrimp *n* (1871) : STOMATOPOD

¹**man·tle** \'man-t⁾l\ *n* [ME *mantel*, fr. AF, fr. L *mantellum*] (13c) **1 a** : a loose sleeveless garment worn over other clothes : CLOAK **b** : a figurative cloak symbolizing preeminence or authority ⟨accepted the ~ of leadership⟩ **2 a** : something that covers, enfolds, or envelops **b** (1) : a fold or lobe or pair of lobes of the body wall of a mollusk or brachiopod that in shell-bearing forms lines the shell and bears shell-secreting glands (2) : the soft external body wall that lines the test or shell of a tunicate or barnacle **c** : the outer wall and casing of a blast furnace above the hearth; *broadly* : an insulated support or casing in which something is heated **3** : the upper back of a bird **4** : a lacy hood or sheath of some refractory material that gives light by incandescence when placed over a flame **5 a** : REGOLITH **b** : the part of the interior of a terrestrial planet and esp. the earth that lies beneath the crust and above the central core **6** : MANTEL

²**mantle** *vb* **man·tled; man·tling** \'mant-liŋ, 'man-t⁾l-iŋ\ *vt* (13c) **1** : to cover with or as if with a mantle : CLOAK ⟨the encroaching jungle growth that *mantled* the building —Sanka Knox⟩ ~ *vi* **1** : to become covered with a coating **2** : to spread over a surface : BLUSH ⟨her rich face *mantling* with emotion —Benjamin Disraeli⟩

man–to–man \'man-tə-'man\ *adj* (1902) **1** : characterized by frankness and honesty ⟨a ~ talk⟩ **2** : of, relating to, or being a system of defense (as in football or basketball) in which each defensive player guards a specified opponent — **man–to–man** *adv* — **man–to–man** *n*

Man·toux test \man-'tü-, mä²-\ *n* [Charles Mantoux †1947 Fr. physician] (ca. 1923) : an intradermal test for hypersensitivity to tuberculin that indicates past or present infection with tubercle bacilli

man·tra \'män-trə *also* 'man- *or* 'mən-\ *n* [Skt, sacred counsel, formula, fr. *manyate* he thinks; akin to L *mens* mind — more at MIND] (1795) : a mystical formula of invocation or incantation (as in Hinduism); *also* : WATCHWORD **2** — **man·tric** \-trik\ *adj*

man·trap \'man-ˌtrap\ *n* (1775) : a trap for catching humans : SNARE

man·tua \'man(t)-sh(ə-)wə, 'man-tə-wə\ *n* [modif. of F *manteau* mantle] (1678) : a usu. loose-fitting gown worn esp. in the 17th and 18th centuries

Manu \'ma-(ˌ)nü\ *n* [Skt] (1839) : the progenitor of the human race and giver of the religious laws of Manu according to Hindu mythology

¹**man·u·al** \'man-yə-wəl, -yəl, -yü-əl\ *adj* [ME *manuel*, fr. AF, fr. L *manualis*, fr. *manus* hand; akin to OE *mund* hand and perh. to Gk *marē* hand] (15c) **1 a** : of, relating to, or involving the hands ⟨~ dexterity⟩ **b** : worked or done by hand and not by machine ⟨a ~ transmission⟩

⟨~ computation⟩ ⟨~ indexing⟩ **2** : requiring or using physical skill and energy ⟨~ labor⟩ ⟨~ workers⟩ — **man·u·al·ly** *adv*

²**manual** *n* (15c) **1 a** : a book that is conveniently handled; *esp* : HANDBOOK ⟨an instruction ~⟩ **2** : the prescribed movements in the handling of a weapon or other military item during a drill or ceremony ⟨the ~ of arms⟩ **3 a** : a keyboard for the hands; *specif* : one of the several keyboards of an organ or harpsichord that controls a separate division of the instrument **b** : a device or apparatus intended for manual operation

manual alphabet *n* (ca. 1864) : an alphabet esp. for the deaf in which the letters are represented by finger positions

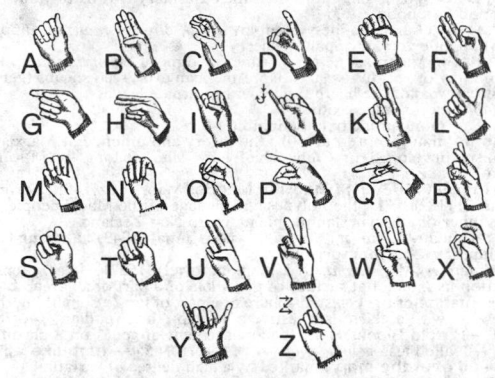

manual alphabet

ma·nu·bri·um \mə-'nü-brē-əm, -'nyü-\ *n, pl* **-bria** \-brē-ə\ *also* **-bri·ums** [NL, fr. L, handle, fr. *manus*] (1705) : an anatomical process or part shaped like a handle: as **a** : the uppermost segment of the sternum of humans and many other mammals **b** : the process that bears the mouth of a hydrozoan : HYPOSTOME

man·u·fac·to·ry \ˌman-yə-'fak-t(ə-)rē, ˌma-nə-\ *n* (1641) : FACTORY 2a

¹**man·u·fac·ture** \ˌman-yə-'fak-chər, ˌma-nə-\ *n* [MF, fr. ML *manufactura*, fr. L *manu factus*, lit., made by hand] (1567) **1** : something made from raw materials by hand or by machinery **2 a** : the process of making wares by hand or by machinery esp. when carried on systematically with division of labor **b** : a productive industry using mechanical power and machinery **3** : the act or process of producing something

²**manufacture** *vb* **-tured; -tur·ing** \-'fak-chə-riŋ, -'fak-shriŋ\ *vt* (1648) **1** : to make into a product suitable for use **2 a** : to make from raw materials by hand or by machinery **b** : to produce according to an organized plan and with division of labor **c** : PREFABRICATE ⟨a *manufactured* home⟩ **3** : INVENT, FABRICATE ⟨known to ~ evidence⟩ **4** : to produce as if by manufacturing : CREATE ⟨writers who ~ stories for television⟩ ~ *vi* : to engage in manufacture — **man·u·fac·tur·abil·i·ty** \-ˌfak-chə-rə-'bi-lə-tē, -ˌfak-shrə-'bi-\ *n* — **man·u·fac·tur·able** \-'fak-chə-rə-bəl, -'fak-shrə-bəl\ *adj* — **manufacturing** *n*

man·u·fac·tur·er \-'fak-chər-ər, -'fak-shrər\ *n* (ca. 1687) : one that manufactures; *esp* : an employer of workers in manufacturing

man·u·mis·sion \ˌman-yə-'mi-shən\ *n* [ME, fr. AF, fr. L *manumission-, manumissio*, fr. *manumittere*] (15c) : the act or process of manumitting; *esp* : formal emancipation from slavery

man·u·mit \ˌman-yə-'mit\ *vt* **-mit·ted; -mit·ting** [ME *manumitten*, fr. AF *manumettre*, fr. L *manumittere*, fr. *manus* hand + *mittere* to let go, send] (15c) : to release from slavery **syn** see FREE

¹**ma·nure** \mə-'nu̇r, -'nyu̇r\ *vt* **ma·nured; ma·nur·ing** [ME *manouren*, fr. AF *mainouverer, meinourer* to till (land), construct, create, fr. ML *manu operare* to perform manual labor, fr. L *manu* by hand + *operari* to work — more at OPERATE] (15c) **1** : CULTIVATE **2** : to enrich (land) by the application of manure — **ma·nur·er** *n*

²**manure** *n* (1532) : material that fertilizes land; *esp* : refuse of stables and barnyards consisting of livestock excreta with or without litter — **ma·nu·ri·al** \-'n(y)u̇r-ē-əl\ *adj*

ma·nus \'mā-nəs, 'mä-\ *n, pl* **ma·nus** \-nəs, -ˌnüs\ [NL, fr. L, hand] (1867) : the distal segment of the vertebrate forelimb from carpus to terminus

man·u·script \'man-yə-ˌskript\ *adj* [L *manu scriptus*] (1597) : written by hand or typed ⟨~ letters⟩

²**manuscript** *n* (1571) **1** : a written or typewritten composition or document as distinguished from a printed copy; *also* : a document submitted for publication **2** : writing as opposed to print

¹**Manx** \'man(k)s\ *adj* [alter. of *Maniske*, fr. ON **manskr*, fr. *Mana* Isle of Man] (ca. 1563) : of, relating to, or characteristic of the Isle of Man, its people, or the Manx language

²**Manx** *n* (1656) **1** : the Celtic language of the Manx people **2** *pl in constr* : the people of the Isle of Man **3** : MANX CAT

Manx cat *n* (1854) : any of a breed of short-haired or long-haired tailless domestic cats

¹**many** \'me-nē\ *adj* **more** \'mȯr\; **most** \'mōst\ [ME, fr. OE *manig*; akin to OHG *manag* many, OCS *mŭnogŭ* much] (bef. 12c) **1** : consisting of or amounting to a large but indefinite number ⟨worked for ~ years⟩ **2** : being one of a large but indefinite number ⟨~ a man⟩ ⟨~ another student⟩ — **as many** : the same in number ⟨saw three plays in *as many* days⟩

\ə\ abut \ᵊ\ kitten, F table \ər\ further \a\ ash \ā\ ace \ä\ mop, mar
\au̇\ out \ch\ chin \e\ bet \ē\ easy \g\ go \i\ hit \ī\ ice \j\ job
\ŋ\ sing \ō\ go \ȯ\ law \ȯi\ boy \th\ thin \t͟h\ the \ü\ loot \u̇\ foot
\y\ yet \zh\ vision, beige \ḵ, ⁿ, œ, ɶ, ᵸ\ *see* Guide to Pronunciation

[2]**many** *pron, pl in constr* (bef. 12c) **:** a large number of persons or things ⟨~ are called⟩
[3]**many** *n, pl in constr* (12c) **1 :** a large but indefinite number ⟨a good ~ of them⟩ **2 :** the great majority of people ⟨the ~⟩
man–year \ˈman-ˈyir\ *n* (1916) **:** a unit of the work done by one person in a year composed of a standard number of working days
many·fold \ˌme-nē-ˈfōld\ *adv* (14c) **:** by many times ⟨aid to research has increased ~⟩
many–sid·ed \ˌme-nē-ˈsī-dəd\ *adj* (1570) **1 :** having many sides or aspects **2 :** having many interests or aptitudes — **many–sid·ed·ness** *n*
many–val·ued \ˌme-nē-ˈval-(ˌ)yüd, -yəd\ *adj* (1893) **1 :** MULTIPLE-VALUED **2 :** possessing more than the customary two truth-values of truth and falsehood
Man·za·nil·la \ˌman-zə-ˈnē-yə, -ˈni-lə\ *n* [Sp, dim. of *manzana* apple] (1843) **:** a pale very dry Spanish sherry
man·za·ni·ta \ˌman-zə-ˈnē-tə\ *n* [AmerSp, dim. of Sp *manzana* apple] (1846) **:** any of various western No. American evergreen shrubs (genus *Arctostaphylos*) of the heath family with alternate leaves
MAO *abbr* monoamine oxidase
MAOI *abbr* monoamine oxidase inhibitor
Mao·ism \ˈmau̇-ˌi-zəm\ *n* (1950) **:** the theory and practice of Marxism-Leninism developed in China chiefly by Mao Zedong — **Mao·ist** \ˈmau̇-ist\ *n or adj*
Mao·ri \ˈmau̇(-ə)r-ē\ *n, pl* **Maori** *or* **Maoris** [Maori *māori,* lit., normal, ordinary] (1828) **1 :** the Polynesian language of the Maori people **2 :** a member of a Polynesian people native to New Zealand
mao–tai \ˈmau̇-ˈtī, -ˈdī\ *n* [*Maotai,* town in China] (1943) **:** a strong Chinese liquor made from sorghum
[1]**map** \ˈmap\ *n* [ML *mappa,* fr. L, napkin, towel] (1527) **1 a :** a representation usu. on a flat surface of the whole or a part of an area **b :** a representation of the celestial sphere or a part of it **2 :** something that represents with a clarity suggestive of a map ⟨the Freudian ~ of the mind —Harold Bloom⟩ **3 :** the arrangement of genes on a chromosome — called also *genetic map* **4 :** FUNCTION 5a — **map·like** \-ˌlīk\ *adj* — **all over the map :** marked by a high degree of variation — **on the map :** in a position of prominence or fame ⟨had put the fledgling university *on the map* —Lon Tinkle⟩
[2]**map** *vb* **mapped; map·ping** *vt* (1586) **1 a :** to make a map of ⟨~ the surface of the moon⟩ **b :** to delineate as if on a map ⟨sorrow was *mapped* on her face⟩ **c :** to make a survey of for or as if for the purpose of making a map **d :** to assign (as a set or element) in a mathematical or exact correspondence ⟨~ picture elements to video memory⟩ **2 :** to plan in detail — often used with *out* ⟨~ out a program⟩ **3 :** to locate (a gene) on a chromosome ~ *vi* **1** *of a gene* **:** to be located **2 :** to be assigned in a relation or connection ⟨the major problems confronting humankind . . . do not ~ well onto the traditional disciplines —P. W. Porter⟩ — **map·pa·ble** \ˈma-pə-bəl\ *adj* — **map·per** *n*
MAP *abbr* modified American plan
ma·ple \ˈmā-pəl\ *n* [ME, fr. OE *mapul-;* akin to ON *mǫpurr* maple] (14c) **:** any of a genus (*Acer* of the family Aceraceae, the maple family) of chiefly deciduous trees or shrubs with opposite leaves and a fruit of two united samaras; *also* **:** the hard light-colored close-grained wood of a maple used esp. for flooring and furniture
maple sugar *n* (1720) **:** sugar made by boiling maple syrup
maple syrup *n* (1792) **:** syrup made by concentrating the sap of maple trees esp. the sugar maple
map·mak·er \ˈmap-ˌmā-kər\ *n* (1639) **:** CARTOGRAPHER — **map·mak·ing** \-kiŋ\ *n*
mapping *n* (ca. 1752) **1 :** the act or process of making a map **2 :** FUNCTION 5a ⟨a one-to-one continuous ~⟩
Ma·pu·che \mə-ˈpü-chē\ *n, pl* **Mapuche** *or* **Mapuches** [Mapuche *mapuče,* a self-designation, fr. *mapu* land + *če* people] (1855) **1 :** an American Indian people of southern Chile; *also* **:** a member of this people **2 :** the Araucanian language of the Mapuche
ma·quette \ma-ˈket\ *n* [F, fr. It *macchietta* sketch, dim. of *macchia,* ultim. fr. L *macula* spot] (1880) **:** a usu. small preliminary model (as of a sculpture or a building)
ma·qui·la·do·ra \mə-ˌkē-lə-ˈdȯr-ə, -ˈt͟hȯr-\ *n* [MexSp (*planta, empresa*) *maquiladora,* fr. *maquilar* to process (material) for a fee, fr. *maquila* processing fee, multure, fr. Sp, multure, fr. Ar. dial. *makīla* measure of grain] (1976) **:** a foreign-owned factory in Mexico at which imported parts are assembled by lower-paid workers into products for export
ma·quil·lage \ˌma-kē-ˈyäzh\ *n* [F] (1892) **:** MAKEUP 3
ma·quis \ma-ˈkē, mä-\ *n, pl* **ma·quis** \-ˈkē(z)\ [F, fr. It *macchie,* pl. of *macchia* thicket, sketch, spot] (1829) **1 :** thick scrubby evergreen underbrush of Mediterranean shores; *also* **:** an area of such underbrush **2** *often cap* **a :** a guerrilla fighter in the French underground during World War II **b :** a band of maquis
[1]**mar** \ˈmär\ *vt* **marred; mar·ring** [ME *marren,* fr. OE *mierran* to obstruct, waste; akin to OHG *merren* to obstruct] (bef. 12c) **1 :** to detract from the perfection or wholeness of **:** SPOIL **2** *archaic* **a :** to inflict serious bodily harm on **b :** DESTROY ***syn*** see INJURE
[2]**mar** *n* (1551) **:** something that mars **:** BLEMISH
[3]**mar** *abbr* maritime
Mar *abbr* March
mar·a·bou *also* **mar·a·bout** \ˈma-rə-ˌbü\ *n* [F *marabout,* lit., marabout] (1819) **1 a :** a soft feathery fluffy material prepared from turkey feathers or the coverts of marabous and used esp. for trimming women's hats or clothes **b** *marabou* **:** a large dark gray African stork (*Leptoptilos crumeniferus*) that has a distensible pouch of pink skin at the front of the neck and feeds esp. on carrion — called also *marabou stork* **2 a :** silk composed of several twisted threads that is dyed before the sericin has been removed **b :** a fabric made of this silk
mar·a·bout \ˈma-rə-bü\ *n, often cap* [F, fr. Pg *marabuto,* fr. Ar *murābiṭ*] (1600) **:** a dervish in Muslim Africa believed to have supernatural power
ma·ra·ca \mə-ˈrä-kə, -ˈra-\ *n* [Pg *maracá,* fr. Tupi *maraká*] (1598) **:** a rattle usu. made from a gourd that is used as a percussion instrument
mar·ag·ing steel \ˈmär-ˌā-jiŋ-\ *n* [*mar*tensite + *aging*] (1962) **:** a strong tough low-carbon martensitic steel which contains up to 25 percent nickel and in which hardening precipitates are formed by aging
maraka *pl of* [3]MARK 2e
mar·a·schi·no \ˌmer-ə-ˈskē-(ˌ)nō, -ˈshē-, ˌma-rə-\ *n, pl* **-nos** *often cap* [It, fr. *marasca* bitter wild cherry, alter. of *amarasca,* fr. *amaro* bitter — more at AMARETTO] (1770) **1 :** a sweet liqueur distilled from the fermented juice of a bitter wild cherry **2 :** a usu. large cherry preserved in true or imitation maraschino
ma·ras·mus \mə-ˈraz-məs\ *n* [LL, fr. Gk *marasmos,* fr. *marainein* to waste away] (1574) **:** a condition of chronic undernourishment occurring esp. in children and usu. caused by a diet deficient in calories and proteins — **ma·ras·mic** \-ˈraz-mik\ *adj*
Ma·ra·tha *also* **Mah·rat·ta** \mə-ˈrä-tə\ *n* [Marathi *Marāṭhā* & Hindi *Marhaṭṭā,* fr. Skt *Mahārāṣṭra* Maharashtra] (1744) **:** a member of a people of the south central part of the subcontinent of India
Ma·ra·thi \mə-ˈrä-tē\ *n* [Marathi *marāṭhī*] (1698) **:** the chief Indo-Aryan language of the state of Maharashtra in India
mar·a·thon \ˈmer-ə-ˌthän, ˈma-rə-\ *n, often attrib* [*Marathon,* Greece, site of a victory of Greeks over Persians in 490 B.C., the news of which was carried to Athens by a long-distance runner] (1896) **1 :** a footrace run on an open course usu. of 26 miles 385 yards (42.2 kilometers); *broadly* **:** a long-distance race **2 a :** an endurance contest **b :** something (as an event, activity, or session) characterized by great length or concentrated effort
mar·a·thon·er \-ˌthä-nər\ *n* (1923) **:** one (as a runner) who takes part in a marathon — **mar·a·thon·ing** \-niŋ\ *n*
ma·raud \mə-ˈrȯd\ *vb* [F *marauder*] *vi* (1684) **:** to roam about and raid in search of plunder ~ *vt* **:** RAID, PILLAGE — **ma·raud·er** *n*
[1]**mar·ble** \ˈmär-bəl\ *n* [ME, fr. AF *marbre,* fr. L *marmor,* fr. Gk *marmaros*] (12c) **1 a :** limestone that is more or less crystallized by metamorphism, that ranges from granular to compact in texture, that is capable of taking a high polish, and that is used esp. in architecture and sculpture **b :** something (as a piece of sculpture) composed of or made from marble **c :** something suggesting marble (as in hardness, coldness, or smoothness) ⟨a heart of ~⟩ **2 a :** a little ball made of a hard substance (as glass) and used in various games **b** *pl but sing in constr* **:** any of several games played with these little balls **c** *pl* **:** the rewards to be won in competition esp. for a championship — used in the phrase *all the marbles* ⟨a game being played for all the ~*s*⟩ **3 :** MARBLING **4** *pl* **:** elements of common sense; *esp* **:** SANITY ⟨persons who are born without all their ~*s* —Arthur Miller⟩ — **marble** *adj*
[2]**marble** *vt* **mar·bled; mar·bling** \-b(ə-)liŋ\ (1675) **:** to give a veined or mottled appearance to ⟨~ the edges of a book⟩
marble cake *n* (1865) **:** a cake made with light and dark batter so as to have a mottled appearance
mar·bled \ˈmär-bəld\ *adj* (1598) **1** [[1]*marble*] **a :** made of or covered with marble or marbling **b :** marked by an extensive use of marble as an architectural or decorative feature ⟨ancient ~ cities⟩ **2 :** having markings or coloration suggestive of marble **3** [[2]*marble*] **:** marked by an intermixture of fat and lean ⟨well-*marbled* beef⟩
mar·ble·ise *Brit var of* MARBLEIZE
mar·ble·ize \ˈmär-bə-ˌlīz\ *vt* **-ized; -iz·ing** (1854) **:** MARBLE
marbling *n* (1686) **1 :** the action or process of making like marble esp. in coloration **2 :** coloration or markings resembling or suggestive of marble **3 :** an intermixture of fat and lean esp. when evenly distributed in a cut of meat
mar·bly \-b(ə-)lē\ *adj* (15c) **:** resembling or suggestive of marble
Mar·burg virus \ˈmär-bərg-\ *n* [*Marburg,* Germany] (1968) **:** a filovirus (species *Lake Victoria marburgvirus* of the genus *Marburgvirus*) that causes an often fatal hemorrhagic fever and was orig. transmitted to humans from green monkeys
marc \ˈmärk\ *n* [F, fr. MF, fr. *marchier* to trample, march] (1601) **1 :** the residue remaining after a fruit has been pressed; *broadly* **:** the organic residue from an extraction process ⟨the protein-rich cottonseed ~⟩ **2 :** brandy made from the residue of wine grapes after pressing
MARC *abbr* machine-readable cataloging
mar·ca·site \ˈmär-kə-ˌsīt, -ˌzīt; ˌmär-kə-ˈzēt\ *n* [ME *marchasite,* fr. ML *marcasita*] (15c) **1 a :** crystallized pyrite **b :** a pale yellow to white mineral of the same composition and appearance as pyrite but of different crystalline organization and lower specific gravity **2 :** a piece of marcasite used in jewelry
mar·ca·to \mär-ˈkä-(ˌ)tō\ *adv or adj* [It, pp. of *marcare* to mark, accent, of Gmc origin; akin to OHG *marcōn* to mark] (ca. 1840) **:** with strong accentuation — used as a direction in music
[1]**mar·cel** \mär-ˈsel\ *n* [*Marcel* Grateau †1936 Fr. hairdresser] (1895) **:** a deep soft wave made in the hair by the use of a heated curling iron
[2]**marcel** *vb* **mar·celled; mar·cel·ling** *vt* (1906) **:** to make a marcel in ~ *vi* **:** to make a marcel
[1]**march** \ˈmärch\ *n* [ME *marche,* fr. AF, of Gmc origin; akin to OHG *marha* boundary — more at MARK] (14c) **:** a border region **:** FRONTIER; *esp* **:** a district orig. set up to defend a boundary — usu. used in pl. ⟨the Welsh ~*es*⟩
[2]**march** *vi* (14c) **:** to have common borders or frontiers ⟨a region that ~*es* with Canada in the north and the Pacific in the west⟩
[3]**march** \ˈmärch, *imperatively often* ˈhärch *in the military*\ *vb* [ME, fr. MF *marchier* to trample, march, fr. OF, to trample, prob. of Gmc origin; akin to OHG *marcōn* to mark] *vi* (15c) **1 :** to move along steadily usu. with a rhythmic stride and in step with others **2 a :** to move in a direct purposeful manner **:** PROCEED **b :** to make steady progress **:** ADVANCE ⟨time ~*es* on⟩ **3 :** to stand in orderly array suggestive of marching ~ *vt* **1 :** to cause to march ⟨~*ed* the children off to bed⟩ **2 :** to cover by marching **:** TRAVERSE ⟨~*ed* 10 miles⟩
[4]**march** \ˈmärch\ *n* (ca. 1572) **1 :** a musical composition that is usu. in duple or quadruple time with a strongly accentuated beat and that is designed or suitable to accompany marching **2 a (1) :** the action of marching **(2) :** the distance covered within a specific period of time by marching **(3) :** a regular measured stride or rhythmic step used in marching **b :** forward movement **:** PROGRESS ⟨the ~ of a movie toward the climax⟩ **3 :** an organized procession of demonstrators who are supporting or protesting something — **march·like** \-ˌlīk\ *adj* — **on the march :** moving steadily **:** ADVANCING
March \ˈmärch\ *n* [ME, fr. AF, fr. L *martius,* fr. *martius* of Mars, fr. *Mart-, Mars*] (13c) **:** the third month of the Gregorian calendar
mär·chen \ˈmer-k̲ən\ *n, pl* **märchen** [G] (1871) **:** TALE; *esp* **:** FOLKTALE
[1]**march·er** \ˈmär-chər\ *n* (14c) **:** one who inhabits a border region
[2]**marcher** *n* (1589) **:** one that marches; *esp* **:** one that marches for a specific cause ⟨a peace ~⟩
mar·che·sa \mär-ˈkā-zə\ *n, pl* **-se** \-(ˌ)zā\ [It, fem. of *marchese*] (1754) **:** an Italian woman holding the rank of a marchese **:** MARCHIONESS

mar·che·se \-(ˌ)zā\ *n, pl* **-si** \-(ˌ)zē\ [It, fr. ML *marcensis,* fr. *marca* border region, of Gmc origin; akin to OHG *marha*] (1517) **:** an Italian nobleman next in rank above a count **:** MARQUESS
marching orders *n pl* (1714) **:** authoritative orders or instructions esp. to set out on or as if on a march
mar·chio·ness \ˈmär-sh(ə-)nəs\ *n* [ML *marchionissa,* fr. *marchion-, marchio* marquess, fr. *marca*] (1570) **1 :** the wife or widow of a marquess **2 :** a woman who holds the rank of marquess in her own right
march·pane \ˈmärch-ˌpān\ *n* [MF *marcepain,* fr. It *marzapane*] (ca. 1556) **:** MARZIPAN
march–past \ˈmärch-ˌpast\ *n* (1863) **:** a filing by **:** PROCESSION
Mar·cion·ism \ˈmär-shə-ˌni-zəm, -sē-ə-, -shē-ə-\ *n* [*Marcion* 2d cent. A.D. Christian Gnostic] (1868) **:** the doctrinal system of a sect of the second and third centuries A.D. accepting some parts of the New Testament but denying Christ's corporality and humanity and condemning the Creator God of the Old Testament — **Mar·cion·ite** \-ˌnīt\ *n*
Marconi rig \mär-ˈkō-nē-\ *n* [prob. fr. the resemblance of the complex arrangement of stays and struts to that used to support the antennae used in wireless telegraphy, invented by Guglielmo *Marconi*] (1916) **:** a fore-and-aft rig in which the sails are triangular and are not supported by gaffs
Mar·di Gras \ˈmär-dē-ˌgrä, *in New Orleans commonly* -ˌgrȯ\ *n* [F, lit., fat Tuesday] (1699) **1 a :** Shrove Tuesday often observed (as in New Orleans) with parades and festivities **b :** a carnival period climaxing on Shrove Tuesday **2 :** a festive occasion resembling a pre-Lenten Mardi Gras
[1]**mare** *n* [ME, fr. OE; akin to OHG *mara* incubus, Serbo-Croatian *mora* nightmare] (bef. 12c) *obs* **:** an evil preternatural being causing nightmares
[2]**mare** \ˈmer\ *n* [ME, fr. OE *mere;* akin to OHG *merha* mare, OE *mearh* horse, W *march*] (bef. 12c) **:** a female horse or other equine animal esp. when fully mature or of breeding age
[3]**ma·re** \ˈmär-(ˌ)ā\ *n, pl* **ma·ria** \ˈmär-ē-ə\ *also* **ma·res** \ˈmär-(ˌ)āz\ [NL, fr. L, sea — more at MARINE] (1860) **:** any of several mostly flat dark areas of considerable extent on the surface of the moon or Mars
ma·re clau·sum \ˈmär-(ˌ)ā-ˈklau̇-səm, -ˈklȯ-\ *n* [NL, lit., closed sea] (1652) **:** a navigable body of water (as a sea) that is under the jurisdiction of one nation and is closed to other nations
Mar·ek's disease \ˈmer-iks-\ *n* [József *Marek* †1952 Hung. veterinarian] (1947) **:** a highly contagious virus disease of poultry that is marked esp. by proliferation of lymphoid cells and is caused by either of two herpesviruses (species *Gallid herpesvirus 2* and *Gallid herpesvirus 3* of the genus *Mardivirus*)
ma·re li·be·rum \ˈmär-(ˌ)ā-ˈlē-bə-ˌru̇m\ *n* [NL, lit., free sea] (1652) **1 :** a navigable body of water (as a sea) that is open to all nations **2 :** FREEDOM OF THE SEAS
ma·ren·go \mə-ˈreŋ-(ˌ)gō\ *adj, often cap* [F, fr. *Marengo,* village in northwest Italy] (ca. 1924) **:** of, consisting of, or served with a sauce of mushrooms, tomatoes, olives, oil, and wine ⟨veal ∼⟩
ma·re no·strum \ˈmär-(ˌ)ā-ˈnōs-trəm\ *n* [NL, lit., our sea] (1921) **:** a navigable body of water (as a sea) that belongs to a single nation or is mutually shared by two or more nations
mare's nest *n, pl* **mare's nests** *or* **mares' nests** (1576) **1 :** a false discovery, illusion, or deliberate hoax **2 :** a place, condition, or situation of great disorder or confusion ⟨a *mare's nest* of intrigue and troubles with the money men —William Cole⟩
mare's tail *n, pl* **mare's tails** *or* **mares' tails** (15c) **1 a :** a common aquatic plant (*Hippuris vulgaris* of the family Hippuridaceae) with elongated shoots having dense whorls of narrow finely tapered leaves **b :** HORSEWEED 1 **2 :** a cirrus cloud that has a long slender flowing appearance
Mar·fan syndrome \ˈmär-ˌfan-\ *n* [Antonin Bernard Jean *Marfan* †1942 Fr. pediatrician] (ca. 1923) **:** a disorder of connective tissue that is inherited as a dominant trait and is characterized by abnormal elongation of the long bones and often by ocular and circulatory defects — called also *Mar·fan's syndrome* \ˈmär-ˌfanz-\
mar·ga·rine \ˈmär-jə-rən, -ˌrēn; ˈmärj-rən\ *n* [F, ultim. fr. Gk *margaron* pearl, prob. back-formation fr. *margaritēs*] (1836) **:** a food product made usu. from vegetable oils churned with ripened skim milk to a smooth emulsion and used like butter
mar·ga·ri·ta \ˌmär-gə-ˈrē-tə\ *n* [fr. the Sp feminine name *Margarita*] (1956) **:** a cocktail consisting of tequila, lime or lemon juice, and an orange-flavored liqueur
mar·ga·rite \ˈmär-gə-ˌrīt\ *n* [ME, fr. AF, fr. L *margarita,* fr. Gk *margaritēs*] (13c) *archaic* **:** PEARL
mar·gay \ˈmär-ˌgā, mär-ˈ\ *n* [F, ultim. fr. Tupi *marakajá*] (1781) **:** a small American spotted cat (*Felis wiedii*) resembling the ocelot and ranging from northern Mexico to Argentina

margay

[1]**marge** \ˈmärj\ *n* [MF, fr. L *margo*] (1548) *archaic* **:** MARGIN
[2]**marge** *n* (1922) *Brit* **:** MARGARINE
mar·gent \ˈmär-jənt\ *n* (15c) *archaic* **:** MARGIN
[1]**mar·gin** \ˈmär-jən\ *n* [ME, fr. AF, fr. L *margin-, margo* border — more at MARK] (14c) **1 :** the part of a page or sheet outside the main body of printed or written matter **2 :** the outside limit and adjoining surface of something **:** EDGE ⟨at the ∼ of the woods⟩ ⟨continental ∼⟩ **3 a :** a spare amount or measure or degree allowed or given for contingencies or special situations ⟨left no ∼ for error⟩ **b** (1) **:** a bare minimum below which or an extreme limit beyond which something becomes impossible or is no longer desirable ⟨on the ∼ of good taste⟩ (2) **:** the limit below which economic activity cannot be continued under normal conditions **c :** an area, state, or condition excluded from or existing outside the mainstream ⟨the ∼*s* of critical discourse —Barbara L. Packer⟩ ⟨living in society's ∼*s*⟩ **4 a :** the difference which exists between net sales and the cost of merchandise sold and from which expenses are usu. met or profit derived **b :** the excess market value of collateral over the face of a loan **c** (1) **:** cash or collateral that is deposited by a client with a commodity or securities broker to protect the broker from loss on a contract (2) **:** the client's equity in securities bought with the aid of credit obtained specif. (as from a broker) for that purpose **d :** a range about a specified figure within which a purchase is to be made **5 :** measure or degree of difference ⟨the bill passed by a one-vote ∼⟩ — **mar·gined** \-jənd\ *adj*
[2]**margin** *vt* (1715) **1 a :** to provide with an edging or border **b :** to form a margin to **:** BORDER **2 a :** to add margin to ⟨∼ up an account⟩ **b** (1) **:** to use as margin ⟨∼ bonds to buy stock⟩ (2) **:** to provide margin for ⟨∼ a transaction⟩ **c :** to buy (securities) on margin
mar·gin·al \ˈmärj-nəl, ˈmär-jə-nᵊl\ *adj* [ML *marginalis,* fr. L *margin-, margo*] (1573) **1 :** written or printed in the margin of a page or sheet ⟨∼ notes⟩ **2 a :** of, relating to, or situated at a margin or border **b :** not of central importance ⟨regards violence as a ∼ rather than a central problem⟩; *also* **:** limited in extent, significance, or stature ⟨had only ∼ success with the business⟩ **c** (1) **:** occupying the borderland of a relatively stable territorial or cultural area ⟨∼ tribes⟩ (2) **:** characterized by the incorporation of habits and values from two divergent cultures and by incomplete assimilation in either ⟨the ∼ cultural habits of new immigrant groups⟩ (3) **:** excluded from or existing outside the mainstream of society, a group, or a school of thought ⟨∼ voters⟩ **3 :** located at the fringe of consciousness ⟨∼ sensations⟩ **4 a :** close to the lower limit of qualification, acceptability, or function **:** barely exceeding the minimum requirements ⟨a semiliterate person of ∼ ability⟩ **b** (1) **:** having a character or capacity fitted to yield a supply of goods which when marketed at existing price levels will barely cover the cost of production ⟨∼ land⟩ (2) **:** of, relating to, or derived from goods produced and marketed with such result ⟨∼ profits⟩ **5 :** relating to or being a function of a random variable that is obtained from a function of several random variables by integrating or summing over all possible values of the other variables ⟨a ∼ probability function⟩ — **mar·gin·al·i·ty** \ˌmär-jə-ˈna-lə-tē\ *n* — **mar·gin·al·ly** \ˈmärj-nə-lē, ˈmär-jə-nᵊl-ē\ *adv*
mar·gi·na·lia \ˌmär-jə-ˈnā-lē-ə\ *n pl* [NL, fr. ML, neut. pl. of *marginalis*] (1832) **1 :** marginal notes or embellishments (as in a book) **2 :** nonessential items ⟨the meat and ∼ of American politics —*Saturday Rev.*⟩
mar·gin·al·ize \ˈmärj-nə-ˌlīz, ˈmär-jə-nᵊl-ˌīz\ *vt* **-ized; -iz·ing** (1970) **:** to relegate to an unimportant or powerless position within a society or group — **mar·gin·al·i·za·tion** \ˌmärj-nə-lə-ˈzā-shən, ˌmär-jə-nᵊl-ə-\ *n*
marginal utility *n* (1890) **:** the amount of additional utility provided by an additional unit of an economic good or service
mar·gin·ate \ˈmär-jə-ˌnāt\ *vt* **-at·ed; -at·ing** (1611) **1 a :** MARGIN 1 **b :** MARGIN 2a **2 :** MARGINALIZE — **mar·gin·ation** \ˌmär-jə-ˈnā-shən\ *n*
mar·gin·at·ed \-ˌnā-təd\ *adj* (ca. 1727) **:** having a distinct margin
mar·gra·vate \ˈmär-grə-ˌvāt\ *or* **mar·gra·vi·ate** \mär-ˈgrā-vē-ət, -ˌāt\ *n* (1788) **:** the territory of a margrave
mar·grave \ˈmär-ˌgrāv\ *n* [D *markgraaf,* fr. MD *marcgrave;* akin to OHG *marha* boundary and to OHG *grāvo* count — more at MARK] (1551) **1 :** the military governor esp. of a German border province **2 :** a member of the German nobility corresponding in rank to a British marquess — **mar·gra·vi·al** \mär-ˈgrā-vē-əl\ *adj*
mar·gra·vine \ˈmär-grə-ˌvēn, ˌmär-grə-ˈ\ *n* (1692) **:** the wife of a margrave
mar·gue·rite \ˌmär-gə-ˈrēt, -gyə-\ *n* [F, fr. MF *margarite* pearl, daisy — more at MARGARITE] (1611) **1 :** DAISY 1b **2 :** any of various single-flowered chrysanthemums; *esp* **:** one (*Chrysanthemum frutescens* syn. *Argyranthemum frutescens*) of the Canary Islands
maria *pl of* MARE
ma·ri·a·chi \ˌmär-ē-ˈä-chē, ˌmer-\ *n* [MexSp, perh. modif. of F *mariage* marriage] (1927) **1 :** a Mexican street band; *also* **:** a musician belonging to such a band **2 :** the music performed by a mariachi
Mar·i·an \ˈmer-ē-ən, ˈmā-rē-\ *adj* (1608) **1 :** of or relating to Mary Tudor or her reign **2 :** of or relating to the Virgin Mary
Mar·i·an·ist \-ə-nist\ *n* (ca. 1899) **:** a member of the Roman Catholic Society of Mary of Paris founded by William Joseph Chaminade in France in 1817 and devoted esp. to education
Ma·ria The·re·sa dollar \mə-ˈrē-ə-tə-ˈrā-sə-, -ˈrā-zə-\ *n* (ca. 1883) **:** a 1780 silver trade coin used in the Middle East
mari·cul·ture \ˈmer-ə-ˌkəl-chər, ˈma-rə-\ *n* [L *mare* sea + E *-culture* (as in *agriculture*)] (ca. 1909) **:** the cultivation of marine organisms in their natural environment — **mari·cul·tur·ist** \ˌmer-ə-ˈkəl-chə-rist, -ˈkəlch-rist, ˌma-rə-\ *n*
mari·gold \ˈmer-ə-ˌgōld\ *n* [ME, fr. *Mary,* mother of Jesus + ME *gold*] (14c) **1 :** POT MARIGOLD **2 :** any of a genus (*Tagetes*) of composite herbs with showy usu. yellow, orange, or maroon flower heads
mar·i·jua·na *also* **mar·i·hua·na** \ˌmer-ə-ˈwä-nə, ˌma-rə- *also* -ˈhwä-\ *n* [MexSp *mariguana, marihuana*] (1894) **1 :** HEMP 1a, c **2 :** the dried leaves and flowering tops of the pistillate hemp plant that yield THC and are smoked in cigarettes for their intoxicating effect — compare BHANG, CANNABIS, HASHISH
ma·rim·ba \mə-ˈrim-bə\ *n* [of Bantu origin; akin to Kimbundu *marimba* xylophone] (1704) **:** a xylophone of southern Africa and Central America with resonators beneath each bar; *also* **:** a modern form of this instrument — **ma·rim·bist** \-bist\ *n*
ma·ri·na \mə-ˈrē-nə\ *n* [It & Sp, seashore, fr. fem. of *marino,* adj., marine, fr. L *marinus*] (1924) **:** a dock or basin providing secure moorings for pleasure boats and often offering supply, repair, and other facilities
[1]**mar·i·nade** \ˌmer-ə-ˈnād, ˌma-rə-\ *n* [F, fr. *mariner* to pickle, marinate, prob. fr. It *marinare*] (1725) **:** a savory usu. acidic sauce in which meat, fish, or a vegetable is soaked to enrich its flavor or to tenderize it
[2]**marinade** *vt* **-nad·ed; -nad·ing** (ca. 1682) **:** MARINATE
mar·i·na·ra \ˌmer-ə-ˈner-ə, -ˈnär-\ *adj* [It (*alla*) *marinara,* lit., in sailor style] (1948) **:** made with tomatoes, onions, garlic, and spices ⟨∼ sauce⟩; *also* **:** served with marinara sauce ⟨spaghetti ∼⟩
mar·i·nate \ˈmer-ə-ˌnāt, ˈma-rə-\ *vb* **-nat·ed; -nat·ing** [prob. fr. It *marinato,* pp. of *marinare* to marinate, fr. *marino*] *vt* (ca. 1645) **:** to

steep (meat, fish, or vegetables) in a marinade ~ *vi* : to become marinated — **mar·i·na·tion** \ˌmer-ə-ˈnā-shən, ˌma-rə-\ *n*

[1]**ma·rine** \mə-ˈrēn\ *adj* [ME, fr. L *marinus,* fr. *mare* sea; akin to OE *mere* sea, pool, OHG *meri* sea, OCS *morje*] (15c) **1 a** : of or relating to the sea ⟨~ life⟩ ⟨~ biology⟩ **b** : of or relating to the navigation of the sea : NAUTICAL ⟨a ~ chart⟩ **c** : of or relating to the commerce of the sea : MARITIME ⟨~ law⟩ **d** : depicting the sea, seashore, or ships ⟨a ~ painter⟩ **2** : of or relating to marines ⟨~ barracks⟩

[2]**marine** *n* (1669) **1 a** : the mercantile and naval shipping of a country **b** : seagoing ships esp. in relation to nationality or class **2** : one of a class of armed services personnel serving on shipboard or in close association with a naval force; *specif* : a member of the U.S. Marine Corps **3** : an executive department (as in France) having charge of naval affairs **4** : a marine picture : SEASCAPE

marine architect *n* (1929) : NAVAL ARCHITECT — **marine architecture** *n*

marine iguana *n* (1924) : a shore-dwelling seaweed-eating iguana (*Amblyrhynchus cristatus*) of the Galápagos Islands that often feeds in the sea

mar·i·ner \ˈmer-ə-nər, ˈma-rə-\ *n* [ME, fr. AF, fr. ML *marinarius,* fr. *marinus*] (14c) : a person who navigates or assists in navigating a ship : SEAMAN, SAILOR

mariner's compass *n* (1594) : a compass used in navigation that consists of parallel magnetic needles or bundles of needles permanently attached to a card marked to indicate direction and degrees of a circle

Mar·i·ol·a·try \ˌmer-ē-ˈä-lə-trē, ˌmā-rē-\ *n* (1612) : excessive veneration of the Virgin Mary — **Mar·i·ol·a·ter** \-ˈä-lə-tər\ *n*

Mar·i·ol·o·gy \-ˈä-lə-jē\ *n* (1857) : study or doctrine relating to the Virgin Mary — **Mar·i·o·log·i·cal** \-ə-ˈlä-ji-kəl\ *adj*

mar·i·on·ber·ry \ˈmer-ē-ən-ˌber-ē\ *n* [*Marion* Co., Oregon] (1982) : the large black juicy fruit of a cultivar of a hybrid blackberry that originated in Oregon and is grown chiefly in the northwestern U.S.; *also* : a bramble bearing marionberries

mar·i·o·nette \ˌmer-ē-ə-ˈnet\ *n* [F *marionnette,* fr. MF *maryonete,* fr. *Marion,* dim. of *Marie* Mary] (ca. 1620) : a small-scale usu. wooden figure (as of a person) with jointed limbs that is moved from above by manipulation of the attached strings or wires

mar·i·po·sa lily \ˌma-rə-ˈpō-zə-, -sə-\ *n* [prob. fr. AmerSp *mariposa,* fr. Sp, butterfly] (1882) : any of a genus (*Calochortus*) of western No. American plants of the lily family with showy flowers having three petals and three sepals — called also *mariposa tulip*; compare SEGO LILY

mar·ish \ˈma-rish\ *n* (15c) *archaic* : MARSH

Mar·ist \ˈmer-ist\ *n* [F *mariste,* fr. *Marie* Mary] (ca. 1872) : a member of the Roman Catholic Society of Mary founded by Jean Claude Colin in France in 1816 and devoted to education

mar·i·tal \ˈmer-ə-tᵊl, ˈma-rə-\ *adj* [L *maritalis,* fr. *maritus* married] (1603) **1** : of or relating to marriage or the married state ⟨~ vows⟩ **2** : of or relating to a husband and his role in marriage — **mar·i·tal·ly** \-tᵊl-ē\ *adv*

mar·i·time \ˈmer-ə-ˌtīm, ˈma-rə-\ *adj* [L *maritimus,* fr. *mare*] (ca. 1550) **1** : of, relating to, or bordering on the sea ⟨a ~ province⟩ **2** : of or relating to navigation or commerce on the sea **3** : having the characteristics of a mariner

mar·jo·ram \ˈmär-jə-rəm, ˈmärj-rəm\ *n* [ME *mageram, marjolane,* fr. MF *majorane, marjolaine,* fr. ML *majorana*] (15c) : any of various usu. fragrant and aromatic Old World mints (genus *Origanum*) often used as seasoning

[1]**mark** \ˈmärk\ *n* [ME, fr. OE *mearc* boundary, march, sign; akin to OHG *marha* boundary, L *margo*] (bef. 12c) **1** : a boundary land **2 a (1)** : a conspicuous object serving as a guide for travelers **(2)** : something (as a line, notch, or fixed object) designed to record position **b** : one of the bits of leather or colored bunting placed on a sounding line at intervals **c** : TARGET **d** : the starting line or position in a track event **e (1)** : GOAL, OBJECT **(2)** : an object of attack, ridicule, or abuse; *specif* : a victim or prospective victim of a swindle **(3)** : the point under discussion **(4)** : condition of being correct or accurate ⟨her observations are on the ~⟩ **f** : a standard of performance, quality, or condition : NORM ⟨not feeling up to the ~ lately⟩ **3 a (1)** : SIGN, INDICATION ⟨a ~ of his esteem⟩ **(2)** : an impression (as a scratch, scar, or stain) made on something **(3)** : a distinguishing trait or quality : CHARACTERISTIC ⟨the ~*s* of an educated person⟩ **b** : a symbol used for identification or indication of ownership **c** : a cross made in place of a signature **d (1)** : TRADEMARK **(2)** *cap* — used with a numeral to designate a particular model of a product ⟨*Mark* II⟩ **e** : a written or printed symbol (as a comma or colon) **f** : POSTMARK **g** : a symbol used to represent a teacher's estimate of a student's work or conduct; *esp* : GRADE **h** : a figure registering a point or level reached or achieved ⟨the halfway ~ in the game⟩; *esp* : RECORD **4 a** : ATTENTION, NOTICE ⟨nothing worthy of ~⟩ **b** : IMPORTANCE, DISTINCTION ⟨a person of ~⟩ **c** : a lasting or strong impression **d** : an assessment of merits : RATING ⟨high ~*s* for honesty⟩ ***syn*** see SIGN

[2]**mark** *vb* [ME, fr. OE *mearcian;* akin to OHG *marcōn* to mark, determine the boundaries of, OE *mearc* boundary] *vt* (bef. 12c) **1 a (1)** : to fix or trace out the bounds or limits of **(2)** : to plot the course of : CHART **b** : to set apart by or as if by a line or boundary — usu. used with *off* **2 a (1)** : to designate as if by a mark **(2)** : to make or leave a mark on **(3)** : to furnish with natural marks ⟨wings ~*ed* with white⟩ **(4)** : to label so as to indicate price or quality **(5)** : to make notations in or on **b (1)** : to make note of in writing : JOT ⟨~*ing* the date in his journal⟩ **(2)** : to indicate by a mark or symbol ⟨~ an accent⟩ **(3)** : REGISTER, RECORD **(4)** : to determine the value of by means of marks or symbols : GRADE ⟨~ term papers⟩ **c (1)** : CHARACTERIZE, DISTINGUISH ⟨the flamboyance that ~*s* her style⟩ **(2)** : SIGNALIZE ⟨this year ~*s* our 50th anniversary⟩ **3** : to take notice of : OBSERVE ⟨~ my words⟩ **4** : to pick up (one's golf ball) from a putting green and substitute a marker ~ *vi* : to take careful notice — **mark time 1** : to keep the time of a marching step by moving the feet alternately without advancing **2** : to maintain a static state of readiness

[3]**mark** *n* [ME, fr. OE *marc,* prob. of Scand origin; akin to ON *mǫrk* mark; akin to OE *mearc* sign] (bef. 12c) **1** : any of various old European units of weight used esp. for gold and silver; *esp* : a unit equal to about eight ounces (248 grams) **2** : a unit of value: **a** : an old English unit equal to 13*s* 4*d* **b** : any one of various old Scandinavian or German units of value; *specif* : a unit and corresponding silver coin of the 16th century worth ½ taler **c (1)** : DEUTSCHE MARK **(2)** : the basic monetary unit of East Germany replaced in 1990 by the West German deutsche mark **d** : MARKKA

Mark \ˈmärk\ *n* [L *Marcus*] (13c) **1 a** : an early Jewish Christian traditionally identified as the writer of the Gospel of Mark — called also *John Mark* **b** : the second Gospel in the New Testament — see BIBLE table **2** : a king of Cornwall, uncle of Tristram, and husband of Isolde

mar·ka \ˈmär-kə\ *or* **mark** *n, pl* **mar·a·ka** \ˈmär-ə-kə\ *or* **mar·kas** *or* **marks** [Bosnian, Croatian & Serbian *marka* (gen. pl. *marākā*) stamp, mark (fr. G *Marke* [1]mark), mark as currency (fr. G *Mark* [3]mark)] (1997) — see MONEY table

mark·down \ˈmärk-ˌdau̇n\ *n* (1880) **1** : a lowering of price **2** : the amount by which an original selling price is reduced

mark down *vt* (1859) : to put a lower price on

marked \ˈmärkt\ *adj* (bef. 12c) **1** : having an identifying mark **2** *or* ˈmär-kəd\ : having a distinctive or emphasized character ⟨has a ~ drawl⟩ **3 a** : enjoying fame or notoriety **b** : being an object of attack, suspicion, or vengeance **4** : overtly signaled by a linguistic feature ⟨with most English nouns the plural is the ~ number⟩ — **mark·ed·ly** \ˈmär-kəd-lē\ *adv* — **mark·ed·ness** \ˈmär-kəd-nəs\ *n*

mark·er \ˈmär-kər\ *n* (15c) **1** : one that marks **2** : something used for marking **3** : SCORE 7; *specif* : RUN **4** : PROMISSORY NOTE, IOU **5** : something that serves to identify, predict, or characterize: as **a** : BIOMARKER **b** : GENETIC MARKER

[1]**mar·ket** \ˈmär-kət\ *n, often attrib* [ME, prob. fr. Continental Gmc; akin to OS *markat* marketplace, OHG *marcāt,* both ultim. fr. L *mercatus* trade, marketplace, fr. *mercari* to trade, fr. *merc-, merx* merchandise] (12c) **1 a (1)** : a meeting together of people for the purpose of trade by private purchase and sale and usu. not by auction **(2)** : the people assembled at such a meeting **b (1)** : a public place where a market is held; *esp* : a place where provisions are sold at wholesale ⟨a farmers' ~⟩ **(2)** : a retail establishment usu. of a specified kind ⟨a fish ~⟩ **2** *archaic* : the act or an instance of buying and selling **3** : the rate or price offered for a commodity or security **4 a (1)** : a geographic area of demand for commodities or services **(2)** : a specified category of potential buyers ⟨the youth ~⟩ **b** : the course of commercial activity by which the exchange of commodities is effected : extent of demand ⟨the ~ is dull⟩ **c (1)** : an opportunity for selling ⟨a good ~ for used cars⟩ **(2)** : the available supply of or potential demand for specified goods or services ⟨the labor ~⟩ **d** : the area of economic activity in which buyers and sellers come together and the forces of supply and demand affect prices ⟨producing goods for ~ rather than for consumption⟩ — **in the market** : in the position of being a potential buyer ⟨*in the market* for a house⟩ — **on the market** : available for purchase; *also* : up for sale ⟨put their house *on the market*⟩

[2]**market** *vt* (15c) **1** : to expose for sale in a market **2** : SELL ~ *vi* : to deal in a market

mar·ket·able \ˈmär-kə-tə-bəl\ *adj* (1600) **1 a** : fit to be offered for sale in a market ⟨food that is not ~⟩ **b** : wanted by purchasers or employers : SALABLE ⟨~ securities⟩ ⟨~ skills⟩ **2** : of or relating to buying or selling — **mar·ket·abil·i·ty** \ˌmär-kə-tə-ˈbi-lə-tē\ *n*

market basket *n* (1943) : a variety of consumer goods and services used to calculate a consumer price index

market capitalization *n* (1975) : CAPITALIZATION 1d

market economy *n* (1929) : an economy in which most goods and services are produced and distributed through free markets

mar·ke·teer \ˌmär-kə-ˈtir\ *n* (1665) : a specialist in promoting or selling a product or service

mar·ket·er \ˈmär-kə-tər\ *n* (1787) : one that deals in a market; *specif* : one that promotes or sells a product or service

market garden *n* (1727) *Brit* : TRUCK FARM — **market gardener** *n, Brit* — **market gardening** *n, Brit*

mar·ket·ing \ˈmär-kə-tiŋ\ *n* (1561) **1 a** : the act or process of selling or purchasing in a market **b** : the process or technique of promoting, selling, and distributing a product or service **2** : an aggregate of functions involved in moving goods from producer to consumer

marketing research *n* (1920) : research into the means of promoting, selling, and distributing a product or service

mar·ket·i·za·tion \ˌmär-kə-tə-ˈzā-shən\ *n* (1961) : the act or process of entering into, participating in, or introducing a free market economy

market maker *n* (1962) : an intermediary in a stock exchange who controls buy and sell orders (as by purchase and resale) for a particular stock or group of stocks

market order *n* (1909) : an order to buy or sell securities or commodities immediately at the best price obtainable in the market

mar·ket·place \ˈmär-kət-ˌplās\ *n* (14c) **1 a** : an open square or place in a town where markets or public sales are held **b** : MARKET ⟨the ~ is the interpreter of supply and demand⟩ **2** : the world of trade or economic activity : the everyday world **3** : a sphere in which intangible values compete for acceptance ⟨the ~ of ideas⟩

market price *n* (15c) : a price actually given in current market dealings

market research *n* (1926) : research into the size, location, and makeup of a product market — **market researcher** *n*

market share *n* (1954) : the percentage of the market for a product or service that a company supplies

mark·ing \ˈmär-kiŋ\ *n* (bef. 12c) **1** : the act, process, or an instance of making or giving a mark **2 a** : a mark made **b** : arrangement, pattern, or disposition of marks

mark·ka \ˈmär-ˌkä\ *n, pl* **mark·kaa** \ˈmär-ˌkä\ *also* **mark·kas** \-ˌkäz\ [Finn, fr. Sw *mark,* a unit of value; akin to ON *mǫrk* mark] (1894) : the basic monetary unit of Finland from 1917 to 2001

Markov chain *n* [A. A. *Markov* †1922 Russ. mathematician] (1938) : a usu. discrete stochastic process (as a random walk) in which the probabilities of occurrence of various future states depend only on the present state of the system or on the immediately preceding state and not on the path by which the present state was achieved — called also *Markoff chain*

Mar·kov·ian \mär-ˈkō-vē-ən, -ˈkȯ-\ *or* **Mar·kov** \ˈmär-ˌkȯf, -ˌkȯv\ *also* **Mar·koff** \ˈmär-ˌkȯf\ *adj* (1944) : of, relating to, or resembling a Markov process or Markov chain esp. by having probabilities defined in terms of transition from the possible existing states to other states

Markov process *n* (1938) : a stochastic process (as Brownian motion) that resembles a Markov chain except that the states are continuous; *also* : MARKOV CHAIN — called also *Markoff process*

marks·man \ˈmärks-mən\ *n* (1644) **:** a person skilled in shooting at a mark or target — **marks·man·ship** \-ˌship\ *n*
marks·wom·an \ˈmärks-ˌwu̇-mən\ *n* (1802) **:** a woman skilled in shooting at a mark or target
mark·up \ˈmärk-ˌəp\ *n* (1916) **1 :** an amount added to the cost price to determine the selling price; *broadly* **:** PROFIT **2 :** a U.S. Congressional committee session at which a bill is put into final form before it is reported out
mark up *vt* (1868) **:** to put a markup on
markup language *n* (1980) **:** a system (as HTML or SGML) for marking or tagging a document that indicates its logical structure (as paragraphs) and gives instructions for its layout on the page esp. for electronic transmission and display
marl \ˈmär(-ə)l\ *n* [ME, fr. AF *marle,* fr. ML *margila,* dim. of L *marga* marl, fr. Gaulish] (14c) **:** a loose or crumbling earthy deposit (as of sand, silt, or clay) that contains a substantial amount of calcium carbonate — **marly** \ˈmär-lē\ *adj*
mar·lin \ˈmär-lən\ *n* [short for *marlinspike;* fr. the appearance of its beak] (1917) **:** any of several large marine billfishes (genera *Makaira* and *Tetrapturus*) that are notable sport fishes
mar·line *also* **mar·lin** \ˈmär-lən\ *n* [ME *merlyn,* prob. fr. MLG *marlinc, merlinc,* fr. *mēren* to tie, moor] (15c) **:** a small usu. tarred line of two strands twisted loosely left-handed that is used esp. for seizing and as a covering for wire rope
mar·line·spike *also* **mar·lin·spike** \ˈmär-lən-ˌspīk\ *n* (1539) **:** a tool (as of wood or iron) that tapers to a point and is used to separate strands of rope or wire (as in splicing)
marl·stone \ˈmär(-ə)l-ˌstōn\ *n* (1756) **:** a rock that consists of a mixture of clay materials and calcium carbonate and often contains kerogen
mar·ma·lade \ˈmär-mə-ˌlād\ *n* [ME *marmelat* quince conserve, Pg *marmelada,* fr. *marmelo* quince, fr. L *melimelum,* a sweet apple, fr. Gk *melimēlon,* fr. *meli* honey + *mēlon* apple — more at MELLIFLUOUS] (ca. 1676) **:** a clear sweetened jelly in which pieces of fruit and fruit rind are suspended
mar·mite \ˈmär-ˌmīt, mär-ˈmēt\ *n* [MF] (1581) **:** a usu. tall covered cooking pot
Mar·mite \ˈmär-ˌmīt\ *trademark* — used for an edible yeast extract
mar·mo·re·al \mär-ˈmȯr-ē-əl\ *also* **mar·mo·re·an** \-ē-ən\ *adj* [L *marmoreus,* fr. *marmor* marble] (1656) **:** of, relating to, or suggestive of marble or a marble statue esp. in coldness or aloofness — **mar·mo·re·al·ly** \-ē-ə-lē\ *adv*
mar·mo·set \ˈmär-mə-ˌset, -ˌzet\ *n* [ME *marmusette* kind of monkey, fr. MF *marmoset* grotesque figure, fr. *marmouser* to mumble, of imit. origin] (1679) **:** any of numerous small soft-furred So. and Central American monkeys (family Callithricidae) with claws instead of nails on all the digits except the big toe
mar·mot \ˈmär-mət\ *n* [F *marmotte*] (1607) **:** any of a genus (*Marmota*) of stout-bodied short-legged chiefly herbivorous burrowing rodents of the squirrel family that have coarse fur, a short bushy tail, and very small ears and that hibernate during the winter — compare WOODCHUCK
mar·o·cain \ˈma-rə-ˌkān\ *n* [F (*crêpe*) *marocain,* lit., Moroccan crepe] (1922) **:** a ribbed crepe fabric used in women's clothing
Mar·o·nite \ˈma-rə-ˌnīt\ *n* [ML *maronita,* fr. *Maron-, Maro* 5th cent. A.D. Syrian monk] (1511) **:** a member of a Uniate church chiefly in Lebanon having a Syriac liturgy and married clergy
[1]**ma·roon** \mə-ˈrün\ *n* [prob. fr. F *maron, marron* feral, fugitive, modif. of AmerSp *cimarrón* wild, savage] (1666) **1** *cap* **:** a fugitive black slave of the West Indies and Guiana in the 17th and 18th centuries; *also* **:** a descendant of such a slave **2 :** a person who is marooned
[2]**maroon** *vt* (ca. 1709) **1 :** to put ashore on a desolate island or coast and leave to one's fate **2 :** to place or leave in isolation or without hope of ready escape
[3]**maroon** *n* [F *marron* Spanish chestnut] (1779) **:** a dark red
mar·plot \ˈmär-ˌplät\ *n* (1764) **:** one who frustrates or ruins a plan or undertaking by meddling
[1]**marque** \ˈmärk\ *n* [ME, fr. AF, fr. Old Occitan *marca,* fr. *marcar* to mark, seize as pledge, of Gmc origin; akin to OHG *marcōn* to mark] (15c) **1** *obs* **:** REPRISAL, RETALIATION **2 :** LETTERS OF MARQUE
[2]**marque** *n* [F, mark, brand, fr. MF, fr. *marquer* to mark, of Gmc origin; akin to OHG *marcōn* to mark] (1906) **:** a brand or make of a product (as a sports car)
[1]**mar·quee** \mär-ˈkē\ *n* [modif. of F *marquise,* lit., marchioness] (1690) **1** *chiefly Brit* **:** a large tent set up for an outdoor party, reception, or exhibition **2 a :** a permanent canopy often of metal and glass projecting over an entrance (as of a hotel or theater) **b :** a sign usu. over the entrance of a theater or arena that displays the names of featured attractions and principal performers
[2]**marquee** *adj* (1946) **:** having or associated with the name recognition and attraction of one whose name appears on a marquee **:** BIG-NAME, STAR ⟨∼ athletes⟩ ⟨∼ events⟩
Mar·que·san \mär-ˈkā-zᵊn, -sᵊn\ *n* (1799) **1 :** a native or inhabitant of the Marquesas Islands **2 :** the Polynesian language of the Marquesans — **Marquesan** *adj*
mar·quess \ˈmär-kwəs\ *or* **mar·quis** \ˈmär-kwəs, mär-ˈkē\ *n, pl* **mar·quess·es** *or* **mar·quis·es** \-kwə-səz\ *or* **mar·quis** \-ˈkē(z)\ [ME *marquis, markis,* fr. AF *marquys, markys,* fr. *marche* march] (14c) **1 :** a nobleman of hereditary rank in Europe and Japan **2 :** a member of the British peerage ranking below a duke and above an earl — **mar·quess·ate** \ˈmär-kwə-sət\ *or* **mar·quis·ate** \ˈmär-kwə-zət, -sət\ *n*
mar·que·try *also* **mar·que·terie** \ˈmär-kə-trē\ *n* [MF *marqueterie,* fr. *marqueter* to checker, inlay, fr. *marque* mark] (1563) **:** decorative work in which elaborate patterns are formed by the insertion of pieces of material (as wood, shell, or ivory) into a wood veneer that is then applied to a surface (as of a piece of furniture)

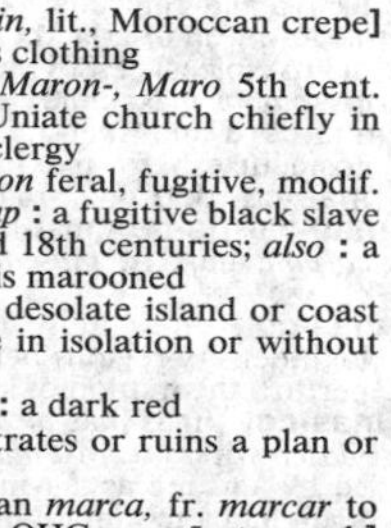

M marquetry

mar·quise \mär-ˈkēz\ *n, pl* **mar·quises** \-ˈkēz, -ˈkē-zəz\ [F, fem. of *marquis*] (1503) **1 :** MARCHIONESS **2 :** MARQUEE **3 :** a gem or a ring setting or bezel usu. elliptical in shape but with pointed ends
mar·qui·sette \ˌmär-kwə-ˈzet, -kə-\ *n* [*marquise* + *-ette*] (1908) **:** a sheer meshed fabric used for clothing, curtains, and mosquito nets
mar·ram grass \ˈma-rəm-\ *n* [of Scand origin; akin to ON *maralmr,* a beach grass] (1834) **:** any of several beach grasses (genus *Ammophila* and esp. *A. arenaria*)
Mar·ra·no \mə-ˈrä-(ˌ)nō\ *n, pl* **-nos** [Sp, lit., pig] (1561) **:** a Christianized Jew of medieval Spain
mar·riage \ˈmer-ij, ˈma-rij\ *n* [ME *mariage,* fr. AF, fr. *marier* to marry] (14c) **1 a** (1) **:** the state of being united to a person of the opposite sex as husband or wife in a consensual and contractual relationship recognized by law (2) **:** the state of being united to a person of the same sex in a relationship like that of a traditional marriage ⟨same-sex ∼⟩ **b :** the mutual relation of married persons **:** WEDLOCK **c :** the institution whereby individuals are joined in a marriage **2 :** an act of marrying or the rite by which the married status is effected; *esp* **:** the wedding ceremony and attendant festivities or formalities **3 :** an intimate or close union ⟨the ∼ of painting and poetry —J. T. Shawcross⟩
mar·riage·able \ˈmer-i-jə-bəl, ˈma-ri-\ *adj* (ca. 1575) **:** fit for or capable of marriage ⟨not yet of ∼ age⟩ — **mar·riage·abil·i·ty** \ˌmer-i-jə-ˈbi-lə-tē, ˌma-ri-\ *n*
marriage of convenience (1711) **:** a marriage contracted for social, political, or economic advantage rather than for mutual affection; *broadly* **:** a union or cooperation formed solely for pragmatic reasons
[1]**married** *adj* (14c) **1 a :** being in the state of matrimony **:** WEDDED **b :** of or relating to marriage **:** CONNUBIAL **2 :** UNITED, JOINED
[2]**married** *n, pl* **marrieds** *or* **married** (1897) **:** a married person ⟨young ∼*s* are paid undue . . . attention —Paul Goodman⟩
married name *n* (1903) **:** a surname acquired by a woman through marriage
mar·ron \ma-ˈrōⁿ\ *n* [F] (1594) **1 :** SPANISH CHESTNUT 1 **2 mar·rons** \-ˈrōⁿ(z)\ *pl* **:** chestnuts and esp. Spanish chestnuts preserved in vanilla-flavored syrup
mar·rons gla·cés \ma-ˈrōⁿ-gla-ˈsā\ *n pl* [F, lit., glazed marrons] (1871) **:** MARRON 2
[1]**mar·row** \ˈmer-(ˌ)ō, ˈma-(ˌ)rō\ *n* [ME *marowe,* fr. OE *mearg;* akin to OHG *marag* marrow, Skt *majjan*] (bef. 12c) **1 a :** BONE MARROW **b :** the substance of the spinal cord **2 a :** the choicest of food **b :** the seat of animal vigor **c :** the inmost, best, or essential part **:** CORE ⟨personal liberty is the ∼ of the American tradition —Clinton Rossiter⟩ **3** *chiefly Brit* **:** VEGETABLE MARROW — **mar·rowy** \ˈmar-ə-wē\ *adj*
[2]**marrow** *n* [ME *marwe, marrow*] (1516) *chiefly Scot* **:** one of a pair
mar·row·bone \ˈmer-ə-ˌbōn, -ō-ˌbōn\ *n* (14c) **1 :** a bone (as a shinbone) rich in marrow **2** *pl* **:** KNEES
mar·row·fat \-ə-ˌfat, -ō-ˌfat\ *n* (1731) **:** any of several wrinkled-seeded garden peas
[1]**mar·ry** \ˈmer-ē, ˈma-rē\ *vb* **mar·ried; mar·ry·ing** [ME *marien,* fr. AF *marier,* fr. L *maritare,* fr. *maritus* married] *vt* (14c) **1 a :** to join in marriage according to law or custom **b :** to give in marriage ⟨*married* his daughter to his partner's son⟩ **c :** to take as spouse **:** WED ⟨*married* the girl next door⟩ **d :** to perform the ceremony of marriage for ⟨a priest will ∼ them⟩ **e :** to obtain by marriage ⟨∼ wealth⟩ **2 :** to unite in close and usu. permanent relation ∼ *vi* **1 :** to take a spouse **:** WED **2 :** COMBINE, UNITE ⟨seafood *marries* with other flavors⟩ — **marry into :** to become a member of by marriage ⟨*married into* a prominent family⟩
[2]**marry** *interj* [ME *marie,* fr. *Marie,* the Virgin Mary] (14c) *archaic* — used for emphasis and esp. to express amused or surprised agreement
Mars \ˈmärz\ *n* [L *Mart-, Mars*] (14c) **1 :** the Roman god of war — compare ARES **2 :** the planet fourth in order from the sun and conspicuous for its red color — see PLANET table
mar·sa·la \mär-ˈsä-lə\ *n, often cap* [*Marsala,* town in Sicily] (1806) **:** a fortified Sicilian wine that varies from dry to sweet and is often used in cooking
marse \ˈmärs\ *n* [by shortening & alter.] (1841) *Southern* **:** MASTER
Mar·seilles \mär-ˈsālz\ *n* [*Marseilles,* France] (1762) **:** a firm cotton fabric that is similar to piqué
marsh \ˈmärsh\ *n, often attrib* [ME *mersh,* fr. OE *merisc, mersc;* akin to MD *mersch* marsh, OE *mere* sea, pool — more at MARINE] (bef. 12c) **:** a tract of soft wet land usu. characterized by monocotyledons (as grasses or cattails)
[1]**mar·shal** *also* **mar·shall** \ˈmär-shəl\ *n* [ME, fr. AF *mareschal,* of Gmc origin; akin to OHG *marahscalc* marshal, fr. *marah* horse + *scalc* servant] (13c) **1 a :** a high official in the household of a medieval king, prince, or noble orig. having charge of the cavalry but later usu. in command of the military forces **b :** a person who arranges and directs the ceremonial aspects of a gathering **2 a :** FIELD MARSHAL **b :** a general officer of the highest military rank **3 a :** an officer having charge of prisoners **b** (1) **:** a ministerial officer appointed for a judicial district (as of the U.S.) to execute the process of the courts and perform various duties similar to those of a sheriff (2) **:** a city law officer entrusted with particular duties **c :** the administrative head of a city police department or fire department — **mar·shal·cy** \-sē\ *n* — **mar·shal·ship** \-ˌship\ *n*
[2]**marshal** *also* **marshall** *vb* **-shaled** *or* **-shalled; -shal·ing** *or* **-shal·ling** \ˈmärsh-(ə-)liŋ\ *vt* (15c) **1 :** to place in proper rank or position ⟨∼*ing* the troops⟩ **2 :** to bring together and order in an appropriate or effective way ⟨∼ arguments⟩ **3 :** to lead ceremoniously or solicitously **:** USHER ⟨∼*ing* her little group of children down the street⟩ ∼ *vi* **:** to take form or order ⟨ideas ∼*ing* neatly⟩ ***syn*** see ORDER
marshal of the Royal Air Force (1947) **:** the highest ranking officer in the British air force
marsh elder *n* (1611) **:** any of a genus (*Iva*) of coarse shrubby composite plants of moist areas in eastern and central No. America
marsh gas *n* (1848) **:** METHANE
marsh hawk *n* (1772) **:** NORTHERN HARRIER

\ə\ **abut** \ᵊ\ **kitten,** F **table** \ər\ **further** \a\ **ash** \ā\ **ace** \ä\ **mop, mar**
\au̇\ **out** \ch\ **chin** \e\ **bet** \ē\ **easy** \g\ **go** \i\ **hit** \ī\ **ice** \j\ **job**
\ŋ\ **sing** \ō\ **go** \ȯ\ **law** \ȯi\ **boy** \th\ **thin** \t͟h\ **the** \ü\ **loot** \u̇\ **foot**
\y\ **yet** \zh\ **vision, beige** \k̟, ⁿ, œ, ue, ʸ\ *see* Guide to Pronunciation

marsh hen *n* (1709) **1 :** any of various American rails **2 :** BITTERN
marsh·land \ˈmärsh-ˌland\ *n* (12c) **:** a marshy tract or area **:** MARSH
marsh·mal·low \ˈmärsh-ˌme-lō, -ˌma-\ *n* (bef. 12c) **1 :** a pink-flowered European perennial herb (*Althaea officinalis*) of the mallow family that is naturalized in the eastern U.S. and has flowers, leaves, and roots used in herbal remedies **2 :** a sweet white confection usu. in the form of a spread or small spongy cylindrical pieces now usu. made from corn syrup, sugar, albumen, and gelatin but formerly from the marshmallow's root; *also* **:** one of these spongy pieces ⟨toasted ~*s* on sticks over a campfire⟩ — **marsh·mal·lowy** \-ˌme-lə-wē, -ˌma-\ *adj*
marsh marigold *n* (1578) **:** a swamp herb (*Caltha palustris*) of the buttercup family that occurs in Europe and No. America and has bright yellow flowers — called also *cowslip, kingcup*
marshy \ˈmär-shē\ *adj* **marsh·i·er; -est** (14c) **1 :** resembling or constituting a marsh ⟨~ ground⟩ **2 :** relating to or occurring in marshes ⟨~ vegetation⟩ — **marsh·i·ness** *n*
1**mar·su·pi·al** \mär-ˈsü-pē-əl\ *adj* (1819) **1 :** of, relating to, or being a marsupial **2 :** of, relating to, or forming a marsupium
2**marsupial** *n* [NL *Marsupialia*, fr. *marsupium*] (ca. 1835) **:** any of an order (Marsupialia) of mammals comprising kangaroos, wombats, bandicoots, opossums, and related animals that do not develop a true placenta and that usu. have a pouch on the abdomen of the female which covers the teats and serves to carry the young
mar·su·pi·um \mär-ˈsü-pē-əm\ *n, pl* **-pia** \-pē-ə\ [NL, fr. L, purse, pouch, fr. Gk *marsypion*] (1698) **1 :** an abdominal pouch that is formed of a fold of the skin and encloses the mammary glands of most marsupials **2 :** any of several structures in various invertebrates (as a bryozoan or mollusk) for enclosing or carrying eggs or young
1**mart** \ˈmärt\ *n* [ME, fr. MD *marct, mart,* ultim. fr. L. *mercatus* market — more at MARKET] (15c) **1** *archaic* **:** a coming together of people to buy and sell **:** 5FAIR 1 **2** *obs* **:** the activity of buying and selling; *also* **:** BARGAIN **3 :** MARKET
2**mart** *vt* (1589) **:** to deal in **:** SELL
mar·tel·lo tower \mär-ˈte-lō-\ *n, often cap M* [Cape *Mortella*, Corsica] (1803) **:** a circular masonry fort or blockhouse
mar·ten \ˈmär-tᵊn\ *n, pl* **marten** *or* **martens** [ME *martryn*, fr. AF *martrine* marten fur, fr. OF *martre* marten, of Gmc origin; akin to OE *mearth* marten] (13c) **1 :** any of several semiarboreal slender-bodied carnivorous mammals (genus *Martes*) of the weasel family that occur in the northern hemisphere **2 :** the fur or pelt of a marten
mar·tens·ite \ˈmär-tᵊn-ˌzīt\ *n* [Adolf *Martens* †1914 Ger. metallurgist] (1898) **:** the hard constituent that is the chief component of quenched steel — **mar·tens·it·ic** \ˌmar-tᵊn-ˈzi-tik, -ˈsi-\ *adj* — **mar·tens·it·i·cal·ly** \-ti-k(ə-)lē\ *adv*
Mar·tha \ˈmär-thə\ *n* [LL, fr. Gk] (bef. 12c) **:** a sister of Lazarus and Mary and friend of Jesus
mar·tial \ˈmär-shəl\ *adj* [ME, fr. L *martialis* of Mars, fr. *Mart-, Mars*] (14c) **1 :** of, relating to, or suited for war or a warrior **2 :** relating to an army or to military life **3 :** experienced in or inclined to war **:** WARLIKE — **mar·tial·ly** \-shə-lē\ *adv*
martial art *n* (1928) **:** any of several arts of combat and self defense (as karate and judo) that are widely practiced as sport — **martial artist** *n*
martial law *n* (1933) **1 :** the law applied in occupied territory by the military authority of the occupying power **2 :** the law administered by military forces that is invoked by a government in an emergency when the civilian law enforcement agencies are unable to maintain public order and safety
mar·tian \ˈmär-shən\ *adj, often cap* (1880) **:** of or relating to the planet Mars or its hypothetical inhabitants — **martian** *n, often cap*
mar·tin \ˈmär-tᵊn\ *n* [prob. fr. St. *Martin*] (1589) **1 :** a small Eurasian bird (*Delichon urbica*) of the swallow family with a forked tail, bluish-black head and back, and white rump and underparts **2 :** any of various birds (esp. genus *Progne*) of the swallow family other than the Eurasian martin — compare PURPLE MARTIN
mar·ti·net \ˌmär-tə-ˈnet\ *n* [Jean *Martinet*, 17th cent. Fr. army officer] (1737) **1 :** a strict disciplinarian **2 :** a person who stresses a rigid adherence to the details of forms and methods
mar·tin·gale \ˈmär-tᵊn-ˌgāl, -tiŋ-\ *n* [MF] (1584) **1 :** a device for steadying a horse's head or checking its upward movement that typically consists of a strap fastened to the girth, passing between the forelegs, and bifurcating to end in two rings through which the reins pass **2 a :** a lower stay of rope or chain for the jibboom used to sustain the strain of the forestays and fastened to or rove through the dolphin striker **b :** DOLPHIN STRIKER **3 :** any of several systems of betting in which a player increases the stake usu. by doubling each time a bet is lost

martingale 1

mar·ti·ni \mär-ˈtē-nē\ *n* [prob. alter. of *Martinez* (*cocktail*), fr. the name *Martinez*] (1894) **:** a cocktail made of gin and dry vermouth; *also* **:** VODKA MARTINI
Mar·tin Lu·ther King Day \ˈmär-tᵊn-ˈlü-thər-ˈkiŋ-\ *n* (1969) **:** the third Monday in January observed as a legal holiday in some states of the U.S.
Mar·tin·mas \ˈmär-tᵊn-məs, -ˌmas\ *n* [ME *martinmasse*, fr. St. *Martin* + ME *masse* mass] (14c) **:** November 11 celebrated as the feast of Saint Martin
mart·let \ˈmärt-lət\ *n* [alter. of *martinet*, fr. MF, prob. fr. St. *Martin*] (15c) **:** MARTIN 1
1**mar·tyr** \ˈmär-tər\ *n* [ME, fr. OE, fr. LL, fr. Gk *martyr-, martys* witness] (bef. 12c) **1 :** a person who voluntarily suffers death as the penalty of witnessing to and refusing to renounce a religion **2 :** a person who sacrifices something of great value and esp. life itself for the sake of principle **3 :** VICTIM; *esp* **:** a great or constant sufferer ⟨a ~ to asthma all his life —A. J. Cronin⟩ — **mar·tyr·i·za·tion** \ˌmär-tə-rə-ˈzā-shən\ *n* — **mar·tyr·ize** \ˈmär-tə-ˌrīz\ *vt*
2**martyr** *vt* (bef. 12c) **1 :** to put to death for adhering to a belief, faith, or profession **2 :** to inflict agonizing pain on **:** TORTURE
mar·tyr·dom \ˈmär-tər-dəm\ *n* (bef. 12c) **1 :** the suffering of death on account of adherence to a cause and esp. to one's religious faith **2 :** AFFLICTION, TORTURE
mar·tyr·ol·o·gist \ˌmär-tə-ˈrä-lə-jist\ *n* (1676) **:** a writer of or a specialist in martyrology
mar·tyr·ol·o·gy \-jē\ *n* (1599) **1 :** a catalog of Roman Catholic martyrs and saints arranged by the dates of their feasts **2 :** ecclesiastical history treating the lives and sufferings of martyrs
mar·tyry \ˈmär-tə-rē\ *n, pl* **-tyr·ies** [LL *martyrium*, fr. LGk *martyrion*, fr. Gk *martyr-, martys*] (1711) **:** a shrine erected in honor of a martyr
1**mar·vel** \ˈmär-vəl\ *n* [ME *mervel*, fr. AF *merveille*, fr. LL *mirabilia* marvels, fr. L, neut. pl. of *mirabilis* wonderful, fr. *mirari* to wonder] (14c) **1 :** one that causes wonder or astonishment ⟨her talent is a ~ to behold⟩ **2 :** intense surprise or interest **:** ASTONISHMENT
2**marvel** *vb* **mar·veled** *or* **mar·velled; mar·vel·ing** *or* **mar·vel·ling** \ˈmärv-liŋ, ˈmär-və-\ *vi* (14c) **:** to become filled with surprise, wonder, or amazed curiosity ⟨~*ed* at the magician's skill⟩ ~ *vt* **:** to feel astonishment or perplexity at or about ⟨~*ed* that they had escaped⟩
mar·vel·ous *or* **mar·vel·lous** \ˈmärv-(ə-)ləs\ *adj* (14c) **1 :** causing wonder **:** ASTONISHING **2 :** MIRACULOUS, SUPERNATURAL ⟨Gothic tales of ~ and bizarre happenings⟩ **3 :** of the highest kind or quality **:** notably superior ⟨has a ~ way with children⟩ — **mar·vel·ous·ly** *adv* — **mar·vel·ous·ness** *n*
Marx·ian \ˈmärk-sē-ən\ *adj* (1887) **:** of, developed by, or influenced by the doctrines of Marx ⟨~ socialism⟩
Marx·ism \ˈmärk-ˌsi-zəm\ *n* (1887) **:** the political, economic, and social principles and policies advocated by Marx; *esp* **:** a theory and practice of socialism including the labor theory of value, dialectical materialism, the class struggle, and dictatorship of the proletariat until the establishment of a classless society — **Marx·ist** \-sist\ *n or adj*
Marx·ism–Le·nin·ism \ˈmärk-ˌsi-zəm-ˈle-nə-ˌni-zəm\ *n* (1929) **:** a theory and practice of communism developed by Lenin from doctrines of Marx — **Marx·ist–Len·in·ist** \ˈmärk-sist-ˈle-nə-nist\ *n or adj*
Mary \ˈmer-ē, ˈma-rē, ˈmā-rē\ *n* [LL *Maria*, fr. Gk *Mariam, Maria*, fr. Heb *Miryām* Miriam] (bef. 12c) **1 :** the mother of Jesus **2 :** a sister of Lazarus and Martha and a friend of Jesus
Mary Jane \-ˈjān\ *n* [by folk etymology (influenced by Sp *Juana* Jane)] (1928) *slang* **:** MARIJUANA
Mary·knoll·er \-ˌnō-lər\ *n* (1923) **:** a member of the Catholic Foreign Mission Society of America founded by T. F. Price and J. A. Walsh at Maryknoll, N.Y. in 1911
Mary Mag·da·lene \-ˈmag-də-lən, -ˌlēn; -ˌmag-də-ˈlē-nē\ *n* [LL *Magdalene*, fr. Gk *Magdalēnē*] **:** a woman who was healed of evil spirits by Jesus and who saw the risen Christ near his sepulchre
mar·zi·pan \ˈmärt-sə-ˌpän, -ˌpan; ˈmär-zə-ˌpan\ *n* [G, fr. It *marzapane*] (1542) **:** a confection of crushed almonds or almond paste, sugar, and egg whites that is often shaped into various forms
ma·sa \ˈmä-sə\ *n* [Sp, mash, dough] (ca. 1896) **:** a dough used in Mexican cuisine (as for tortillas and tamales) that is made from ground corn soaked in a lime and water solution; *also* **:** MASA HARINA
masa ha·ri·na \-ä-ˈrē-nä, -nə\ *n* [MexSp, prob. lit., flour masa (masa in the form of flour)] (1972) **:** a flour made from dried masa
Ma·sai \mä-ˈsī, ˈmä-ˌ\ *n, pl* **Masai** *or* **Masais** [Masai *il-máásài*, a self-designation] (1857) **1 :** a member of a pastoral and hunting people of Kenya and Tanzania **2 :** the Nilotic language of the Masai people
ma·sa·la \mä-ˈsä-lä, -lə, mə-\ *n* [Hindi & Urdu *masālā* materials, ingredients, spices] (1780) **:** a varying blend of spices used in Indian cooking
masc *abbr* masculine
mas·cara \ma-ˈsker-ə, -ˈska-rə\ *n* [prob. fr. It *maschera* mask] (1886) **:** a cosmetic esp. for making the eyelashes darker and more prominent — **mas·ca·raed** \-əd, -rəd\ *adj*
mas·car·po·ne \ˌmas-kär-ˈpō-(ˌ)nā\ *n* [It, fr. It dial. (Lombardy) *mascarpón*, aug. of *mascarpa* cream cheese] (1932) **:** an Italian cream cheese
mas·con \ˈmas-ˌkän\ *n* [2*mass* + *con*centration] (1968) **:** any of the high-density regions below the surface of lunar maria that are held to perturb the motion of spacecraft in lunar orbit
mas·cot \ˈmas-ˌkät *also* -kət\ *n* [F *mascotte*, fr. Occitan *mascoto*, fr. *masco* witch, fr. ML *masca*] (1881) **:** a person, animal, or object adopted by a group as a symbolic figure esp. to bring them good luck ⟨the team had a mountain lion as their ~⟩
1**mas·cu·line** \ˈmas-kyə-lən\ *adj* [ME *masculin*, fr. L *masculinus*, fr. *masculus*, n., male, dim. of *mas* male] (14c) **1 a :** MALE **b :** having qualities appropriate to or usu. associated with a man **2 :** of, relating to, or constituting the gender that ordinarily includes most words or grammatical forms referring to males ⟨~ nouns⟩ **3 a :** having or occurring in a stressed final syllable ⟨~ rhyme⟩ **b :** having the final chord occurring on a strong beat ⟨~ cadence⟩ — **mas·cu·line·ly** *adv* — **mas·cu·lin·i·ty** \ˌmas-kyə-ˈli-nə-tē\ *n*
2**masculine** *n* (14c) **1 :** the masculine gender **2 :** a noun, pronoun, adjective, or inflectional form or class of the masculine gender **3 :** a male person
mas·cu·lin·ise *Brit var of* MASCULINIZE
mas·cu·lin·ist \ˈmas-kyə-lə-(ˌ)nist\ *n* (1918) **:** an advocate of male superiority or dominance — **masculinist** *adj*
mas·cu·lin·ize \ˈmas-kyə-lə-ˌnīz\ *vt* **-ized; -iz·ing** (1858) **:** to give a chiefly masculine character to; *esp* **:** to cause (a female) to take on male characteristics — **mas·cu·lin·i·za·tion** \ˌmas-kyə-lə-nə-ˈzā-shən\ *n*
ma·ser \ˈmā-zər\ *n* [*m*icrowave *a*mplification by *s*timulated *e*mission of *r*adiation] (1955) **:** a device or object that emits coherent microwave radiation produced by the natural oscillations of atoms or molecules between energy levels
1**mash** \ˈmash\ *vt* (13c) **1 a :** to reduce to a soft pulpy state by beating or pressure **b :** CRUSH, SMASH ⟨~ a finger⟩ **2 :** to subject (as crushed malt) to the action of water with heating and stirring in preparing wort
2**mash** *n* [ME *mash-*, fr. OE *māx-;* akin to MHG *meisch* mash] (1577) **1 :** a mixture of ground feeds for livestock **2 :** crushed malt or grain meal steeped and stirred in hot water to produce wort **3 :** a soft pulpy mass **4** *Brit* **:** mashed potatoes
3**mash** *n* [perh. fr. 1*mash*] (1870) **:** CRUSH 4
4**mash** *vt* (1877) **:** to flirt with or seek the affection of
MASH *abbr* mobile army surgical hospital
1**mash·er** \ˈma-shər\ *n* (1591) **:** one that mashes ⟨a potato ~⟩
2**masher** *n* (1875) **:** a man who makes passes at women
mash note *n* (1890) **:** a usu. sentimental or effusive note or letter expressing affection for the recipient

mash–up \ˈmash-ˌəp\ *n* (1859) **:** something created by combining elements from two or more sources: as **a :** a piece of music created by digitally overlaying an instrumental track with a vocal track from a different recording **b :** a movie or video having characters or situations from other sources **c :** a Web service or application that integrates data and functionalities from various online sources

[1]**mask** \ˈmask\ *n* [MF *masque,* fr. OIt *maschera*] (1534) **1 a** (1) **:** a cover or partial cover for the face used for disguise (2) **:** a person wearing a mask **:** MASKER **b** (1) **:** a figure of a head worn on the stage in antiquity to identify the character and project the voice (2) **:** a grotesque false face worn at carnivals or in rituals **c :** an often grotesque carved head or face used as an ornament (as on a keystone) **d :** a sculptured face or a copy of a face made by means of a mold **2 a :** something that serves to conceal or disguise **:** PRETENSE, CLOAK ⟨aware of the ~*s,* facades and defenses people erect to protect themselves —Kenneth Keniston⟩ **b :** something that conceals from view **c :** a translucent or opaque screen to cover part of the sensitive surface in taking or printing a photograph **d :** a pattern of opaque material used to shield selected areas of a surface (as of a semiconductor) in deposition or etching (as in producing an integrated circuit) **3 a :** a protective covering for the face **b :** GAS MASK **c :** a device covering the mouth and nose to facilitate inhalation **d :** a comparable device to prevent exhalation of infective material **e :** a cosmetic preparation for the skin of the face that produces a tightening effect as it dries **4 a :** the head or face of an animal (as a fox or dog) **b :** an area (as the one around the eyes) of an animal's face that is distinguished by usu. darker coloring

[2]**mask** *vi* (ca. 1562) **1 :** to take part in a masquerade **2 a :** to assume a mask **b :** to disguise one's true character or intentions ~ *vt* **1 :** to provide or conceal with a mask: as **a :** to conceal from view ⟨~ a gun battery⟩ **b :** to make indistinct or imperceptible ⟨~*s* undesirable flavors⟩ **c :** to cover up ⟨~*ed* his real purpose⟩ **2 :** to cover for protection **3 :** to modify the size or shape of (as a photograph) by means of an opaque border ***syn*** see DISGUISE — **mask·like** \-ˌlīk\ *adj*

masked \ˈmaskt\ *adj* (1599) **1 :** marked by the use of masks ⟨a ~ ball⟩ **2 :** failing to present or produce the usual symptoms **:** LATENT ⟨a ~ infection⟩ ⟨a ~ virus⟩

mask·er \ˈmas-kər\ *n* (ca. 1548) **:** a person who wears a mask; *esp* **:** a participant in a masquerade

mask·ing tape \ˈmas-kiŋ-\ *n* (1936) **:** a tape with adhesive on one side that has a variety of uses (as to cover a surface when painting near it)

mas·och·ism \ˈma-sə-ˌki-zəm, ˈma-zə- *also* ˈmā-\ *n* [ISV, fr. Leopold von Sacher-*Masoch* †1895 Ger. novelist] (1892) **1 :** a sexual perversion characterized by pleasure in being subjected to pain or humiliation esp. by a love object — compare SADISM **2 :** pleasure in being abused or dominated **:** a taste for suffering — **mas·och·ist** \-kist\ *n* — **mas·och·is·tic** \ˌma-sə-ˈkis-tik, ˌma-zə- *also* ˌmā-\ *adj* — **mas·och·is·ti·cal·ly** \-ˈkis-ti-k(ə-)lē\ *adv*

ma·son \ˈmā-sᵊn\ *n* [ME, fr. AF, of Gmc origin; akin to OE *macian* to make] (13c) **1 :** a skilled worker who builds by laying units of substantial material (as stone or brick) **2** *cap* **:** FREEMASON

Ma·son·ic \mə-ˈsä-nik\ *adj* (1786) **:** of, relating to, or characteristic of Freemasons or Freemasonry

Ma·son·ite \ˈmā-sə-ˌnīt\ *trademark* — used for fiberboard

mason jar *n, often cap M* [John L. *Mason,* †1902 Am. metalsmith] (1888) **:** a widemouthed jar used esp. for home canning

ma·son·ry \ˈmā-sᵊn-rē\ *n, pl* **-ries** (13c) **1 a :** something constructed of materials used by masons **b :** the art, trade, or occupation of a mason **c :** work done by a mason **2** *cap* **:** FREEMASONRY

mason wasp *n* (1815) **:** any of various solitary vespid wasps (subfamily Eumeninae) that construct nests of hardened mud

Ma·so·ra *or* **Ma·so·rah** \mə-ˈsȯr-ə\ *n* [ModHeb *mĕsōrāh,* fr. LHeb *māsōreth* tradition, fr. Heb, bond] (1659) **:** a body of notes on the textual traditions of the Hebrew Scripture compiled by scribes during the first millennium of the Christian era

Mas·o·rete *or* **Mas·so·rete** \ˈma-sə-ˌrēt\ *n* [F *massoreth,* fr. LHeb *māsōreth*] (1653) **:** one of the scribes who compiled the Masora — **Mas·o·ret·ic** \ˌma-sə-ˈre-tik\ *adj*

masque *also* **mask** \ˈmask\ *n* [MF *masque* — more at MASK] (1526) **1 :** MASQUERADE **2 :** a short allegorical dramatic entertainment of the 16th and 17th centuries performed by masked actors

masquer *var of* MASKER

[1]**mas·quer·ade** \ˌmas-kə-ˈrād\ *n* [MF, fr. OIt dial. *mascarada,* fr. OIt *maschera* mask] (1587) **1 a :** a social gathering of persons wearing masks and often fantastic costumes **b :** a costume for wear at such a gathering **2 :** an action or appearance that is mere disguise or show

[2]**masquerade** *vi* **-ad·ed; -ad·ing** (1677) **1 a :** to disguise oneself; *also* **:** to go about disguised **b :** to take part in a masquerade **2 :** to assume the appearance of something one is not — **mas·quer·ad·er** *n*

[1]**mass** \ˈmas\ *n* [ME, fr. OE *mæsse,* modif. of VL **messa,* lit., dismissal at the end of a religious service, fr. LL *missa,* fr. L, fem. of *missus,* pp. of *mittere* to send] (bef. 12c) **1** *cap* **:** the liturgy of the Eucharist esp. in accordance with the traditional Latin rite **2** *often cap* **:** a celebration of the Eucharist ⟨Sunday ~*es* held at three different hours⟩ **3 :** a musical setting for the ordinary of the Mass

[2]**mass** *n* [ME *masse,* fr. AF, fr. L *massa,* fr. Gk *maza;* akin to Gk *massein* to knead — more at MINGLE] (15c) **1 a :** a quantity or aggregate of matter usu. of considerable size **b** (1) **:** EXPANSE, BULK (2) **:** massive quality or effect (3) **:** the main part or body ⟨the great ~ of the continent is buried under an ice cap —Walter Sullivan⟩ (4) **:** AGGREGATE, WHOLE ⟨men in the ~⟩ **c :** the property of a body that is a measure of its inertia and that is commonly taken as a measure of the amount of material it contains and causes it to have weight in a gravitational field **2 :** a large quantity, amount, or number ⟨a ~ of material⟩ **3 a :** a large body of persons in a group ⟨a ~ of spectators⟩ **b :** the great body of the people as contrasted with the elite — often used in pl. ⟨the underprivileged and disadvantaged ~*es* —C. A. Buss⟩ ***syn*** see BULK

[3]**mass** *vt* (14c) **:** to form or collect into a mass ~ *vi* **:** to assemble in a mass ⟨three thousand students had ~*ed* in the plaza —A. E. Neville⟩

[4]**mass** *adj* (1733) **1 a :** of or relating to the mass of the people ⟨~ market⟩; *also* **:** being one of or at one with the mass **:** AVERAGE ⟨~ man⟩ **b :** participated in by or affecting a large number of individuals ⟨~ destruction⟩ **c :** having a large-scale character ⟨~ plantings of tulips⟩ **2 :** viewed as a whole **:** TOTAL ⟨the ~ effect of a design⟩

Mass *abbr* Massachusetts

mas·sa \ˈma-sə\ *n* [by alter.] (1766) *Southern* **:** MASTER

Mas·sa·chu·sett *or* **Mas·sa·chu·set** \ˌma-sə-ˈchü-sət, -zət *also* ˌmas-ˈchü-\ *n, pl* **Massachusetts** *or* **Massachusett** *or* **Massachusets** *or* **Massachuset** [Massachusett, a locality, lit., at the big hill] (1616) **1 :** a member of an American Indian people of Massachusetts **2 :** the extinct Algonquian language of the Massachusett people

[1]**mas·sa·cre** \ˈma-si-kər\ *n* [MF] (ca. 1578) **1 :** the act or an instance of killing a number of usu. helpless or unresisting human beings under circumstances of atrocity or cruelty **2 :** a cruel or wanton murder **3 :** a wholesale slaughter of animals **4 :** an act of complete destruction ⟨the author's ~ of traditional federalist presuppositions —R. G. McCloskey⟩

[2]**massacre** *vt* **mas·sa·cred; mas·sa·cring** \-k(ə-)riŋ\ (1581) **1 :** to kill by massacre **2 :** MANGLE 2 ⟨words were misspelled and syntax *massacred* —Bice Clemow⟩ — **mas·sa·crer** \-kər-ər, -krər\ *n*

[1]**mas·sage** \mə-ˈsäzh, -ˈsäj\ *n* [F, fr. *masser* to massage, fr. Ar *massa* to stroke] (ca. 1860) **:** manipulation of tissues (as by rubbing, kneading, or tapping) with the hand or an instrument for therapeutic purposes

[2]**massage** *vt* **mas·saged; mas·sag·ing** (1887) **1 :** to subject to massage **2 a :** to treat flatteringly **:** BLANDISH **b :** MANIPULATE, DOCTOR ⟨*massaged* the data to help his cause⟩ — **mas·sag·er** *n*

massage parlor *n* (1906) **:** an establishment that provides massage treatments; *also* **:** one offering sexual services in addition to or in lieu of massage

mas·sa·sau·ga \ˌma-sə-ˈsȯ-gə\ *n* [*Missisauga* River, Ontario, Canada] (1835) **:** a small No. American rattlesnake (*Sistrurus catenatus*)

mass card *n* (1930) **:** a card notifying the recipient (as a bereaved family) that a mass is to be offered for the repose of the soul of a specified deceased person

mass driver *n* (1975) **:** a large electromagnetic catapult designed to hurl material (as from an asteroid) into space

mas·sé \ma-ˈsā\ *n* [F, fr. pp. of *masser* to make a massé shot, fr. *masse* sledgehammer, fr. MF *mace* mace] (1873) **:** a shot in billiards or pool made by hitting the cue ball vertically or nearly vertically on the side to drive it around one ball in order to strike another

mas·se·ter \mə-ˈsē-tər, ma-\ *n* [NL, fr. Gk *masētēr,* fr. *masasthai* to chew — more at MANDIBLE] (1578) **:** a large muscle that raises the lower jaw and assists in mastication — **mas·se·ter·ic** \ˌma-sə-ˈter-ik\ *adj*

mas·seur \ma-ˈsər, mə-\ *n* [F, fr. *masser*] (1876) **:** a man who practices massage

mas·seuse \-ˈsə(r)z, -ˈsüz\ *n* [F, fem. of *masseur*] (1879) **:** a woman who practices massage

mas·sif \ma-ˈsēf\ *n* [F, fr. *massif,* adj., fr. MF, alter. of OF *massiz*] (1873) **1 :** a principal mountain mass **2 :** a block of the earth's crust bounded by faults or flexures and displaced as a unit without internal change

mas·sive \ˈma-siv\ *adj* [ME *massiffe,* fr. AF *mascif,* alter. of *massiz,* fr. VL **massicius,* fr. L *massa* mass] (15c) **1 :** forming or consisting of a large mass: **a :** BULKY **b :** WEIGHTY, HEAVY ⟨~ walls⟩ ⟨a ~ volume⟩ **c :** impressively large or ponderous **d :** having no regular form but not necessarily lacking crystalline structure ⟨~ sandstone⟩ **2 a :** large, solid, or heavy in structure ⟨~ jaw⟩ **b :** large in scope or degree ⟨the feeling of frustration, of being ineffectual, is ~ —David Halberstam⟩ **c** (1) **:** large in comparison to what is typical ⟨a ~ dose of penicillin⟩ (2) **:** being extensive and severe ⟨~ hemorrhage⟩ (3) **:** imposing in excellence or grandeur ⟨~ simplicity⟩ **3 :** having mass ⟨a ~ boson⟩ — **mas·sive·ly** *adv* — **mas·sive·ness** *n*

massively parallel *adj* (1977) **:** of, relating to, or being a computer system that uses a large number of separate processors simultaneously to increase power and speed

mass·less \ˈmas-ləs\ *adj* (1879) **:** having no mass ⟨a ~ particle⟩

mass–mar·ket \ˈmas-ˈmär-kət\ *adj* (1952) **1 :** sold through such retail outlets as supermarkets and drugstores as well as through bookstores ⟨a ~ paperback⟩; *also* **:** of, relating to, or publishing mass-market materials **2 :** appealing or sold to a general audience

mass medium *n, pl* **mass media** (1923) **:** a medium of communication (as newspapers, radio, or television) that is designed to reach the mass of the people — usu. used in pl.

mass noun *n* (1933) **:** a noun that denotes a homogeneous substance or a concept without subdivisions and that in English is preceded in indefinite singular constructions by *some* rather than *a* or *an* ⟨"sand" and "water" are *mass nouns*⟩ — compare COUNT NOUN

mass number *n* (1923) **:** an integer that approximates the mass of an isotope and designates the number of nucleons in the nucleus

mass–pro·duce \ˌmas-prə-ˈdüs, -ˈdyüs\ *vt* [back-formation fr. *mass production*] (1923) **:** to produce in quantity usu. by machinery — **mass production** *n*

mass spectrograph *n* (1920) **:** an instrument used to separate and often to determine the masses of isotopes

mass spectrometry *n* (1943) **:** an instrumental method for identifying the chemical constitution of a substance by means of the separation of gaseous ions according to their differing mass and charge — called also *mass spectroscopy* — **mass spectrometric** *adj* — **mass spectrometer** *n*

mass spectrum *n* (1920) **:** the spectrum of a stream of gaseous ions separated according to their differing mass and charge

massy \ˈma-sē\ *adj* (14c) **:** MASSIVE, WEIGHTY

[1]**mast** \ˈmast\ *n* [ME, fr. OE *mæst;* akin to OHG *mast* mast, L *malus*] (bef. 12c) **1 :** a long pole or spar rising from the keel or deck of a ship and supporting the yards, booms, and rigging **2 :** a slender vertical or nearly vertical structure (as an upright post in various cranes) **3 :** a disciplinary proceeding at which the commanding officer of a naval unit hears and disposes of cases against enlisted men — called also *captain's mast* — **mast·ed** \ˈmas-təd\ *adj* — **before the mast 1 :** forward of the foremast **2 :** as a common sailor

[2]**mast** *vt* (ca. 1513) **:** to furnish with a mast

\ə\ **a**but \ᵊ\ kitten, F table \ər\ **fur**ther \a\ **a**sh \ā\ **a**ce \ä\ m**o**p, m**ar** \au̇\ **ou**t \ch\ **ch**in \e\ b**e**t \ē\ **ea**sy \g\ **g**o \i\ h**i**t \ī\ **i**ce \j\ **j**ob \ŋ\ si**ng** \ō\ g**o** \ȯ\ l**aw** \ȯi\ b**oy** \th\ **th**in \th\ **th**e \ü\ l**oo**t \u̇\ f**oo**t \y\ **y**et \zh\ vi**si**on, beige \k, ⁿ, œ, ue, ʸ\ *see* Guide to Pronunciation

3**mast** *n* [ME, fr. OE *mæst;* akin to OHG *mast* food, mast, and prob. to OE *mete* food — more at MEAT] (bef. 12c) **:** nuts (as acorns) accumulated on the forest floor and often serving as food for animals

mas·ta·ba \ˈmas-tə-bə\ *n* [Ar *maṣṭaba* stone bench] (1882) **:** an Egyptian tomb of the time of the Memphite dynasties that is oblong in shape with sloping sides and a flat roof

mast cell \ˈmast-\ *n* [part trans. of G *Mastzelle,* fr. *Mast* food, mast (fr. OHG) + *Zelle* cell] (ca. 1890) **:** a granulocyte that occurs esp. in connective tissue and has basophilic granules containing substances (as histamine and heparin) which mediate allergic reactions

mas·tec·to·my \ma-ˈstek-tə-mē\ *n, pl* **-mies** [Gk *mastos* breast + E *-ectomy*] (ca. 1923) **:** surgical removal of all or part of the breast and sometimes associated lymph nodes and muscles

1**mas·ter** \ˈmas-tər\ *n* [ME, fr. OE *magister* & AF *meistre,* both fr. L *magister;* akin to L *magnus* large — more at MUCH] (bef. 12c) **1 a** (1) **:** a male teacher (2) **:** a person holding an academic degree higher than a bachelor's but lower than a doctor's **b** *often cap* **:** a revered religious leader **c :** a worker or artisan qualified to teach apprentices **d** (1) **:** an artist, performer, or player of consummate skill (2) **:** a great figure of the past (as in science or art) whose work serves as a model or ideal **2 a :** one having authority over another **:** RULER, GOVERNOR **b :** one that conquers or masters **:** VICTOR, SUPERIOR ⟨in the new challenger the champion found his ~⟩ **c :** a person licensed to command a merchant ship **d** (1) **:** one having control (2) **:** an owner esp. of a slave or animal **e :** the employer esp. of a servant **f** (1) *dial* **:** HUSBAND (2) **:** the male head of a household **3 a** (1) *archaic* **:** MR. (2) **:** a youth or boy too young to be called *mister* — used as a title **b :** the eldest son of a Scottish viscount or baron **4 a :** a presiding officer in an institution or society (as a college) **b :** any of several officers of court appointed to assist (as by hearing and reporting) a judge **5 a :** a master mechanism or device **b :** an original from which copies can be made; *esp* **:** a master recording (as a magnetic tape) — **mas·ter·ship** \-ˌship\ *n*

2**master** *adj* (12c) **:** being or relating to a master: as **a :** having chief authority **:** DOMINANT **b :** SKILLED, PROFICIENT ⟨a prosperous ~ builder —*Current Biog.*⟩ **c :** PRINCIPAL, PREDOMINANT **d :** SUPERLATIVE — often used in combination ⟨a *master*-liar⟩ **e :** being a device or mechanism that controls the operation of another mechanism or that establishes a standard (as a dimension or weight) **f :** being or relating to a master from which duplicates are made

3**master** *vt* **mas·tered; mas·ter·ing** \-t(ə-)riŋ\ (13c) **1 :** to become master of **:** OVERCOME ⟨~*ed* his fears⟩ **2 a :** to become skilled or proficient in the use of ⟨~ a foreign language⟩ **b :** to gain a thorough understanding of ⟨had ~*ed* every aspect of publishing —*Current Biog.*⟩ **3 :** to produce a master recording of (as a musical rendition)

master–at–arms *n, pl* **masters–at–arms** (1732) **:** a petty officer charged with maintaining discipline aboard ship

master bedroom *n* (1925) **:** a large or principal bedroom

master chief petty officer *n* (1958) **:** an enlisted man in the navy or coast guard ranking above a senior chief petty officer

master chief petty officer of the coast guard (1966) **:** the ranking petty officer in the coast guard serving as adviser to the commandant

master chief petty officer of the navy (1966) **:** the ranking petty officer in the navy serving as adviser to the chief of naval operations

master class *n* (1952) **:** a seminar for advanced music students conducted by a master musician

mas·ter·ful \ˈmas-tər-fəl\ *adj* (15c) **1 a :** inclined and usu. competent to act as master **b :** suggestive of a domineering nature **2 :** having or reflecting the power and skill of a master — **mas·ter·ful·ly** \-fə-lē\ *adv* — **mas·ter·ful·ness** *n*

syn MASTERFUL, DOMINEERING, IMPERIOUS, PEREMPTORY, IMPERATIVE mean tending to impose one's will on others. MASTERFUL implies a strong personality and ability to act authoritatively ⟨her *masterful* personality soon dominated the movement⟩. DOMINEERING suggests an overbearing or arbitrary manner and an obstinate determination to enforce one's will ⟨children controlled by *domineering* parents⟩. IMPERIOUS implies a commanding nature or manner and often suggests arrogant assurance ⟨an *imperious* executive used to getting his own way⟩. PEREMPTORY implies an abrupt dictatorial manner coupled with an unwillingness to brook disobedience or dissent ⟨given a *peremptory* dismissal⟩. IMPERATIVE implies peremptoriness arising more from the urgency of the situation than from an inherent will to dominate ⟨an *imperative* appeal for assistance⟩.

usage Some commentators insist that use of *masterful* should be limited to sense 1 in order to preserve a distinction between it and *masterly.* The distinction is a modern one, excogitated by a 20th century pundit in disregard of the history of the word. Both words developed in a parallel manner but the earlier sense of *masterly,* equivalent to *masterful* 1, dropped out of use. Since *masterly* had but one sense, the pundit opined that it would be tidy if *masterful* were likewise limited to one sense and he forthwith condemned use of *masterful* 2 as an error. Sense 2 of *masterful,* which is slightly older than the sense of *masterly* intended to replace it, has continued in reputable use all along; it cannot rationally be called an error.

master gunnery sergeant *n* (1958) **:** a noncommissioned officer in the marine corps ranking above a master sergeant

master key *n* (1577) **:** a key designed to open several different locks

mas·ter·ly \ˈmas-tər-lē\ *adj* (15c) **1 :** suitable to or resembling that of a master; *esp* **:** indicating thorough knowledge or superior skill and power ⟨a ~ performance⟩ **2 :** having the power and skill of a master ⟨she's ~ at description —Caroline Knapp⟩ ***usage*** see MASTERFUL — **mas·ter·li·ness** *n* — **masterly** *adv*

1**mas·ter·mind** \ˈmas-tər-ˌmīnd, ˌmas-tər-ˈ\ *n* (1872) **:** a person who supplies the directing or creative intelligence for a project

2**mastermind** *vt* (1940) **:** to be the mastermind of

master of arts *often cap M&A* (15c) **1 :** the recipient of a master's degree that usu. signifies that the recipient has passed an integrated course of study in one or more of the humanities and sometimes has completed a thesis involving research or a creative project and that typically requires two years of work beyond a bachelor's degree **2 :** the degree making one a master of arts — abbr. *MA, AM*

master of ceremonies (ca. 1610) **1 :** a person who determines the forms to be observed on a public occasion **2 :** a person who acts as host at a formal event **3 :** a person who acts as host for a program of entertainment (as on television)

master of science *often cap M&S* (1898) **1 :** the recipient of a master's degree that usu. signifies that the recipient has passed an integrated course of study in one or more of the sciences and sometimes has completed a thesis involving research and that typically requires two years of work beyond a bachelor's degree **2 :** the degree making one a master of science — abbr. *MS, MSc*

mas·ter·piece \ˈmas-tər-ˌpēs\ *n* (1600) **1 :** a work done with extraordinary skill; *esp* **:** a supreme intellectual or artistic achievement **2 :** a piece of work presented to a medieval guild as evidence of qualification for the rank of master

master plan *n* (1914) **:** a plan giving overall guidance

master race *n* (1856) **:** a people held to be racially preeminent and hence fitted to rule or enslave other peoples

mas·ters \ˈmas-tərz\ *adj* (1971) **:** competing in, relating to, or being a competition for athletes over a specified age (as 40) ⟨a ~ runner⟩

master's *n* (1939) **:** a master's degree

master sergeant *n* (1920) **:** a noncommissioned officer ranking in the army above a sergeant first class and below a staff sergeant major, in the air force above a technical sergeant and below a senior master sergeant, and in the marine corps above a gunnery sergeant and below a master gunnery sergeant

mas·ter·sing·er \ˈmas-tər-ˌsiŋ-ər\ *n* (1810) **:** MEISTERSINGER

mas·ter·stroke \-ˌstrōk\ *n* (1679) **:** a masterly performance or move

mas·ter·work \-ˌwərk\ *n* (1617) **:** MASTERPIECE

mas·tery \ˈmas-t(ə-)rē\ *n* [ME *maistrie,* fr. AF *mestrie, maistrie,* fr. *meistre* master] (13c) **1 a :** the authority of a master **:** DOMINION **b :** the upper hand in a contest or competition **:** SUPERIORITY, ASCENDANCY **2 a :** possession or display of great skill or technique **b :** skill or knowledge that makes one master of a subject **:** COMMAND

mast·head \ˈmast-ˌhed\ *n* (15c) **1 :** the top of a mast **2 a :** the printed matter in a newspaper or periodical that gives the title and details of ownership, advertising rates, and subscription rates **b :** the name of a publication (as a newspaper) displayed on the top of the first page

mas·tic \ˈmas-tik\ *n* [ME *mastik,* fr. L *mastiche,* fr. Gk *mastichē,* prob. back-formation fr. *mastichan*] (14c) **1 :** an aromatic resinous exudate from mastic trees used chiefly in varnishes **2 :** any of various pasty materials used as protective coatings or cements

mas·ti·cate \ˈmas-tə-ˌkāt\ *vb* **-cat·ed; -cat·ing** [LL *masticatus,* pp. of *masticare,* fr. Gk *mastichan* to gnash the teeth; akin to Gk *masasthai* to chew — more at MANDIBLE] *vt* (1562) **1 :** to grind or crush (food) with or as if with the teeth **:** CHEW **2 :** to soften or reduce to pulp by crushing or kneading ~ *vi* **:** CHEW — **mas·ti·ca·tion** \ˌmas-tə-ˈkā-shən\ *n* — **mas·ti·ca·tor** \ˈmas-tə-ˌkā-tər\ *n*

1**mas·ti·ca·to·ry** \ˈmas-ti-kə-ˌtȯr-ē\ *n, pl* **-ries** (1583) **:** a substance chewed to increase saliva

2**masticatory** *adj* (1611) **1 :** used for or adapted to chewing ⟨~ limbs of an arthropod⟩ **2 :** of, relating to, or involving the organs of mastication ⟨~ paralysis⟩

mastic tree *n* (15c) **:** a small Mediterranean evergreen tree (*Pistacia lentiscus*) of the cashew family that yields mastic

mas·tiff \ˈmas-təf\ *n* [ME *mastif,* fr. ML *mastivus,* fr. VL **masuetivus,* fr. L *mansuetus* tame — more at MANSUETUDE] (14c) **:** any of a breed of very large massive powerful smooth-coated dogs that are apricot, fawn, or brindle and are often used as guard dogs

mas·ti·goph·o·ran \ˌmas-tə-ˈgä-fə-rən\ *n* [ultim. fr Gk *mastig-, mastix* whip + *pherein* to carry — more at BEAR] (ca. 1911) **:** any of a subphylum (Mastigophora) of protozoans comprising forms with flagella and including many often treated as algae — **mastigophoran** *adj*

mas·ti·tis \ma-ˈstī-təs\ *n, pl* **-tit·i·des** \-ˈsti-tə-ˌdēz\ [NL, fr. Gk *mastos* breast] (ca. 1842) **:** inflammation of the breast or udder usu. caused by infection — **mas·tit·ic** \-ˈsti-tik\ *adj*

mas·to·don \ˈmas-tə-ˌdän, -dən\ *n* [NL *mastodont-, mastodon,* fr. Gk *mastos* + *odont-, odōn, odous* tooth — more at TOOTH] (1811) **1 :** any of various extinct mammals (genus *Mammut* syn. *Mastodon*) of the elephant family existing from the Miocene through the Pleistocene that are distinguished from the related mammoths chiefly by molar teeth with cone-shaped cusps **2 :** one that is unusually large — **mas·to·don·ic** \ˌmas-tə-ˈdä-nik\ *adj* — **mas·to·dont** \ˈmas-tə-ˌdänt\ *adj or n*

1**mas·toid** \ˈmas-ˌtȯid\ *adj* [NL *mastoides* resembling a nipple, mastoid, fr. Gk *mastoeidēs,* fr. *mastos* breast] (1732) **1 :** being the process of the temporal bone behind the ear; *also* **:** being any of several bony elements that occupy a similar position in the skull of lower vertebrates **2 :** of, relating to, or occurring in the region of the mastoid process

2**mastoid** *n* (1840) **:** a mastoid bone or process

mastoid cell *n* (1800) **:** one of the small cavities in the mastoid process that develop after birth and are filled with air

mas·toid·ec·to·my \ˌmas-ˌtȯi-ˈdek-tə-mē\ *n, pl* **-mies** [ISV] (1898) **:** surgical removal of part of the mastoid process of the temporal bone

mas·toid·itis \ˌmas-ˌtȯi-ˈdī-təs\ *n* [NL] (1881) **:** inflammation of the mastoid and esp. of the mastoid cells

mas·tur·bate \ˈmas-tər-ˌbāt\ *vb* **-bat·ed; -bat·ing** [L *masturbatus,* pp. of *masturbari*] *vi* (1839) **:** to practice masturbation ~ *vt* **:** to practice masturbation on — **mas·tur·ba·tor** \-ˌbā-tər\ *n*

mas·tur·ba·tion \ˌmas-tər-ˈbā-shən\ *n* (1603) **:** erotic stimulation esp. of one's own genital organs commonly resulting in orgasm and achieved by manual or other bodily contact exclusive of sexual intercourse, by instrumental manipulation, occas. by sexual fantasies, or by various combinations of these agencies

mas·tur·ba·to·ry \ˈmas-tər-bə-ˌtȯr-ē\ *adj* (1864) **1 :** of, relating to, or involving masturbation ⟨~ fantasies⟩ **2 :** excessively self-absorbed or self-indulgent ⟨write tedious, ~ books . . . about themselves for people to read . . . with envy —D. R. Katz⟩

1**mat** \ˈmat\ *n* [ME, fr. OE *meatte,* fr. LL *matta,* of Sem origin; akin to Heb *miṭṭāh* bed] (bef. 12c) **1 a** (1) **:** a piece of coarse, woven, plaited, or felted fabric used esp. as a floor covering or a support (2) **:** a piece of material placed at a door for wiping soiled shoe soles **b :** a decorative piece of material used under a small item (as a dish) esp. for support or protection **c :** a large thick pad or cushion used as a surface for wrestling, tumbling, and gymnastics **2 :** something made up of densely tangled or adhering filaments or strands esp. of organic matter ⟨an algal ~⟩ ⟨a ~ of unkempt hair⟩ **3 :** a large slab usu. of reinforced concrete used as the supporting base of a building

2**mat** *vb* **mat·ted; mat·ting** *vt* (1549) **1 :** to provide with a mat or matting **2 a :** to form into a tangled mass ⟨dirt and filth *matted* her hair⟩ **b :** to pack down so as to form a dense mass ~ *vi* **:** to become matted
3**mat** \ˈmat\ *vt* **mat·ted; mat·ting** (1602) **1** *also* **matte** *or* **matt :** to make (as a metal, glass, or color) matte **2 :** to provide (a picture) with a mat
4**mat** *var of* 1MATTE
5**mat** *n* [F *mat* dull color, unpolished surface, fr. *mat,* adj. — more at MATTE] (1845) **:** a border going around a picture between picture and frame or serving as the frame
6**mat** *n* (1904) **:** MATRIX 2a
mat·a·dor \ˈma-tə-ˌdȯr\ *n* [Sp, fr. *matar* to kill] (1681) **:** a bullfighter who has the principal role and who kills the bull in a bullfight
1**match** \ˈmach\ *n* [ME *macche,* fr. OE *gemæcca* mate, equal; akin to OE *macian* to make — more at MAKE] (bef. 12c) **1 a :** a person or thing equal or similar to another **b :** one able to cope with another **c :** an exact counterpart **2 :** a pair suitably associated ⟨carpet and curtains are a ~⟩ **3 a :** a contest between two or more parties ⟨a golf ~⟩ ⟨a soccer ~⟩ ⟨a shouting ~⟩ **b :** a contest (as in tennis or volleyball) completed when one player or side wins a specified number of sets or games **4 a :** a marriage union **b :** a prospective partner in marriage
2**match** *vt* (14c) **1 a :** to encounter successfully as an antagonist **b** (1) **:** to set in competition or opposition (2) **:** to provide with a worthy competitor **c :** to set in comparison **2 :** to join or give in marriage **3 a** (1) **:** to put in a set possessing equal or harmonizing attributes (2) **:** to cause to correspond **:** SUIT ⟨~*ed* programs to local needs⟩ **b** (1) **:** to be the counterpart of; *also* **:** to compare favorably with (2) **:** to harmonize with ⟨the jacket ~*ed* the pants⟩ **c :** to provide with a counterpart **d :** to provide funds complementary to ⟨employers may ~ the employee contribution —D. J. Miller⟩ **4 :** to fit together or make suitable for fitting together **5 a :** to flip or toss (coins) and compare exposed faces **b :** to toss coins with ~ *vi* **:** to be a counterpart — **match·able** \ˈma-chə-bəl\ *adj* — **match·er** *n*
3**match** *n* [ME *macche, mecche* candlewick, fr. AF *meche*] (1549) **1 :** a chemically prepared wick or cord formerly used in firing firearms or powder **2 :** a short slender piece of flammable material (as wood) tipped with a combustible mixture that bursts into flame when slightly heated through friction (as by being scratched against a rough surface)
match·board \ˈmach-ˌbȯrd\ *n* (ca. 1858) **:** a board with a groove cut along one edge and a tongue along the other so as to fit snugly with the edges of similarly cut boards

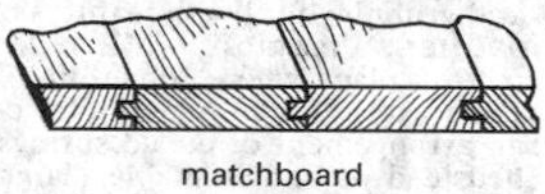

matchboard

match·book \-ˌbu̇k\ *n* (1937) **:** a small folder containing rows of paper matches
match·box \-ˌbäks\ *n* (1786) **:** a box for matches
match·less \-ləs\ *adj* (ca. 1530) **:** having no equal **:** PEERLESS ⟨a ~ view of the valley⟩ — **match·less·ly** *adv*
match·lock \-ˌläk\ *n* (ca. 1637) **1 :** a musket equipped with a matchlock **2 :** a slow-burning match lowered over a hole in the breech of a musket to ignite the charge
match·mak·er \-ˌmā-kər\ *n* (1638) **:** one that arranges a match; *esp* **:** one who tries to bring two unmarried individuals together in an attempt to promote a marriage — **match·mak·ing** \-kiŋ\ *n*
match play *n* (1893) **:** golf competition in which the winner is the person or team winning the greater number of holes — compare STROKE PLAY
match point *n* (1921) **:** a situation (as in tennis) in which one player or side will win the match by winning the next point; *also* **:** the point itself
match·stick \ˈmach-ˌstik\ *n* (1791) **1 :** a slender piece esp. of wood from which a match is made **2 :** something resembling a matchstick esp. in slenderness ⟨cut a carrot into ~*s*⟩
match·up \-ˌəp\ *n* (1959) **:** 1MATCH
match·wood \-ˌwu̇d\ *n* (1786) **:** small pieces of wood **:** SPLINTERS
1**mate** \ˈmāt\ *vt* **mat·ed; mat·ing** [ME, fr. AF *mater,* fr. *mat,* n., checkmate, ultim. fr. Ar *māt* (in *shāh māt*)] (14c) **:** CHECKMATE 2
2**mate** *n* (14c) **:** CHECKMATE 1
3**mate** *n* [ME, prob. fr. MLG *māt;* akin to OE *gemetta* guest at one's table, *mete* food — more at MEAT] (14c) **1 a** (1) **:** ASSOCIATE, COMPANION (2) *chiefly Brit* **:** an assistant to a more skilled worker **:** HELPER (3) *chiefly Brit* **:** FRIEND, BUDDY — often used as a familiar form of address **b** *archaic* **:** MATCH, PEER **2 :** a deck officer on a merchant ship ranking below the captain **3 :** one of a pair: as **a :** either member of a couple and esp. a married couple **b :** either member of a breeding pair of animals **c :** either of two matched objects
4**mate** *vb* **mat·ed; mat·ing** *vt* (1509) **1** *archaic* **:** EQUAL, MATCH **2 :** to join or fit together **:** COUPLE **3 a :** to join together as mates **b :** to provide a mate for ~ *vi* **1 :** to become mated ⟨gears that ~ well⟩ **2 :** COPULATE
ma·té *or* **ma·te** \ˈmä-ˌtā\ *n* [F & AmerSp; F *maté,* fr. AmerSp *mate* maté, vessel for drinking it, fr. Quechua *mati* vessel] (1758) **1 :** a tealike beverage drunk esp. in So. America **2 :** a So. American shrub or tree (*Ilex paraguariensis*) of the holly family whose leaves and shoots are used in making maté; *also* **:** these leaves and shoots
mate·lot \ˈmat-ˌlō, ˈma-tə-\ *n* [F, fr. MF, fr. MD *mattenoot,* lit., bedmate] (ca. 1847) *Brit* **:** SAILOR
ma·te·lote \ˌma-tə-ˈlōt, mat-ˈlōt\ *n* [F, lit., sailor's wife, fr. *matelot*] (ca. 1723) **:** a stew made usu. of fish in a seasoned wine sauce
ma·ter \ˈmā-tər\ *n* [L — more at MOTHER] (ca. 1859) *chiefly Brit* **:** MOTHER
ma·ter·fa·mil·i·as \ˌmā-tər-fə-ˈmi-lē-əs, ˌmä-\ *n* [L, fr. *mater* + *familias,* archaic gen. of *familia* household — more at FAMILY] (1756) **:** a woman who is head of a household
1**ma·te·ri·al** \mə-ˈtir-ē-əl\ *adj* [ME *materiel,* fr. MF & LL; MF, fr. LL *materialis,* fr. L *materia* matter — more at MATTER] (14c) **1 a** (1) **:** relating to, derived from, or consisting of matter; *esp* **:** PHYSICAL ⟨the ~ world⟩ (2) **:** BODILY ⟨~ needs⟩ **b** (1) **:** of or relating to matter rather than form ⟨~ cause⟩ (2) **:** of or relating to the subject matter of reasoning; *esp* **:** EMPIRICAL ⟨~ knowledge⟩ **2 :** having real importance or great consequences ⟨facts ~ to the investigation⟩ **3 a :** being of a physical or worldly nature **b :** relating to or concerned with physical rather than spiritual or intellectual things ⟨~ progress⟩ — **ma·te·ri·al·ly** \-ē-ə-lē\ *adv* — **ma·te·ri·al·ness** *n*

syn MATERIAL, PHYSICAL, CORPOREAL, PHENOMENAL, SENSIBLE, OBJECTIVE mean of or belonging to actuality. MATERIAL implies formation out of tangible matter; used in contrast with *spiritual* or *ideal* it may connote the mundane, crass, or grasping ⟨*material* values⟩. PHYSICAL applies to what is perceived directly by the senses and may contrast with *mental, spiritual,* or *imaginary* ⟨the *physical* benefits of exercise⟩. CORPOREAL implies having the tangible qualities of a body such as shape, size, or resistance to force ⟨artists have portrayed angels as *corporeal* beings⟩. PHENOMENAL applies to what is known or perceived through the senses rather than by intuition or rational deduction ⟨scientists concerned with the *phenomenal* world⟩. SENSIBLE stresses the capability of readily or forcibly impressing the senses ⟨the earth's rotation is not *sensible* to us⟩. OBJECTIVE may stress material or independent existence apart from a subject perceiving it ⟨no *objective* evidence of damage⟩. ***syn*** see in addition RELEVANT

2**material** *n* (1556) **1 a** (1) **:** the elements, constituents, or substances of which something is composed or can be made (2) **:** matter that has qualities which give it individuality and by which it may be categorized ⟨sticky ~⟩ ⟨explosive ~*s*⟩ **b** (1) **:** something (as data) that may be worked into a more finished form ⟨~ for a biography⟩ (2) **:** something used for or made the object of study ⟨~ for the next semester⟩ (3) **:** a performer's repertoire ⟨a comedian's ~⟩ **c :** MATTER 3b **d :** CLOTH **e :** a person potentially suited to some pursuit ⟨varsity ~⟩ ⟨leadership ~⟩ **2 a :** apparatus necessary for doing or making something ⟨writing ~*s*⟩ **b :** MATÉRIEL
ma·te·ri·al·ise *Brit var of* MATERIALIZE
ma·te·ri·al·ism \mə-ˈtir-ē-ə-ˌli-zəm\ *n* (1733) **1 a :** a theory that physical matter is the only or fundamental reality and that all being and processes and phenomena can be explained as manifestations or results of matter **b :** a doctrine that the only or the highest values or objectives lie in material well-being and in the furtherance of material progress **c :** a doctrine that economic or social change is materially caused — compare HISTORICAL MATERIALISM **2 :** a preoccupation with or stress upon material rather than intellectual or spiritual things — **ma·te·ri·al·ist** \-list\ *n or adj* — **ma·te·ri·al·is·tic** \-ˌtir-ē-ə-ˈlis-tik\ *adj* — **ma·te·ri·al·is·ti·cal·ly** \-ti-k(ə-)lē\ *adv*
ma·te·ri·al·i·ty \mə-ˌtir-ē-ˈa-lə-tē\ *n, pl* **-ties** (1570) **1 :** the quality or state of being material **2 :** something that is material
ma·te·ri·al·i·za·tion \mə-ˌtir-ē-ə-lə-ˈzā-shən\ *n* (1843) **1 :** the action of materializing or becoming materialized **2 :** something that has been materialized; *esp* **:** APPARITION
ma·te·ri·al·ize \mə-ˈtir-ē-ə-ˌlīz\ *vb* **-ized; -iz·ing** *vt* (1710) **1 a :** to make material **:** OBJECTIFY **b :** to cause to appear in bodily form ⟨~ the spirits of the dead⟩ **2 :** to cause to be materialistic ~ *vi* **1 :** to assume bodily form **2 a :** to appear esp. suddenly **b :** to come into existence — **ma·te·ri·al·iz·er** *n*
materials science *n* (1956) **:** the scientific study of the properties and applications of materials of construction or manufacture (as ceramics, metals, polymers, and composites) — **materials scientist** *n*
ma·te·ria med·i·ca \mə-ˈtir-ē-ə-ˈme-di-kə\ *n* [NL, lit., medical matter] (1663) **1 :** substances used in the composition of medical remedies **:** DRUGS, MEDICINE **2 a :** a branch of medical science that deals with the sources, nature, properties, and preparation of drugs **b :** a treatise on materia medica
ma·té·ri·el *or* **ma·te·ri·el** \mə-ˌtir-ē-ˈel\ *n* [F *matériel,* fr. *matériel,* adj.] (1819) **:** equipment, apparatus, and supplies used by an organization or institution
ma·ter·nal \mə-ˈtər-nᵊl\ *adj* [ME, fr. MF & ML; MF *maternel,* fr. ML *maternalis,* fr. L *maternus,* fr. *mater* mother — more at MOTHER] (15c) **1 :** of, relating to, belonging to, or characteristic of a mother **:** MOTHERLY **2 a :** related through a mother ⟨his ~ aunt⟩ **b :** inherited or derived from the female parent ⟨~ genes⟩ — **ma·ter·nal·ly** \-nᵊl-ē\ *adv*
1**ma·ter·ni·ty** \mə-ˈtər-nə-tē\ *n, pl* **-ties** (1611) **1 a :** the quality or state of being a mother **:** MOTHERHOOD **b :** the qualities of a mother **:** MOTHERLINESS **2 :** a hospital facility designed for the care of women before and during childbirth and for the care of newborn babies
2**maternity** *adj* (1893) **1 :** designed for wear during pregnancy ⟨a ~ dress⟩ **2 :** effective for the period close to and including childbirth ⟨~ leave⟩
mat·ey \ˈmā-tē\ *adj* (1915) *chiefly Brit* **:** COMPANIONABLE — **mat·ey·ness** \-nəs\ *n, chiefly Brit*
1**math** \ˈmath\ *n* (ca. 1847) **:** MATHEMATICS
2**math** *abbr* mathematical; mathematician
math·e·mat·i·cal \ˌmath-ˈma-ti-kəl, ˌma-thə-\ *also* **math·e·mat·ic** \-tik\ *adj* [ME *mathematicalle,* fr. L *mathematicus,* fr. Gk *mathēmatikos,* fr. *mathēmat-, mathēma* learning, mathematics, fr. *manthanein* to learn; prob. akin to Goth *mundon* to pay attention] (15c) **1 :** of, relating to, or according with mathematics **2 a :** rigorously exact **:** PRECISE **b :** CERTAIN **3 :** possible but highly improbable ⟨only a ~ chance⟩ — **math·e·mat·i·cal·ly** \-ti-k(ə-)lē\ *adv*
mathematical expectation *n* (1838) **:** EXPECTED VALUE
mathematical induction *n* (1838) **:** INDUCTION 2b
mathematical logic *n* (1853) **:** SYMBOLIC LOGIC
math·e·ma·ti·cian \ˌmath-mə-ˈti-shən, ˌma-thə-\ *n* (15c) **:** a specialist or expert in mathematics
math·e·mat·ics \ˌmath-ˈma-tiks, ˌma-thə-\ *n pl but usu sing in constr* (1573) **1 :** the science of numbers and their operations, interrelations, combinations, generalizations, and abstractions and of space configurations and their structure, measurement, transformations, and generalizations **2 :** a branch of, operation in, or use of mathematics ⟨the ~ of physical chemistry⟩
math·e·ma·ti·za·tion \ˌmath-mə-tə-ˈzā-shən, ˌma-thə-\ *n* (1908) **:** reduction to mathematical form — **math·e·ma·tize** \ˈmath-mə-ˌtīz, ˈma-thə-\ *vb*
maths \ˈmaths\ *n pl* (1911) *chiefly Brit* **:** MATHEMATICS

\ə\ **abut** \ᵊ\ **kitten, F table** \ər\ **further** \a\ **ash** \ā\ **ace** \ä\ **mop, mar**
\au̇\ **out** \ch\ **chin** \e\ **bet** \ē\ **easy** \g\ **go** \i\ **hit** \ī\ **ice** \j\ **job**
\ŋ\ **sing** \ō\ **go** \ȯ\ **law** \ȯi\ **boy** \th\ **thin** \th\ **the** \ü\ **loot** \u̇\ **foot**
\y\ **yet** \zh\ **vision, beige** \k, ⁿ, œ, ue, ʸ\ *see* Guide to Pronunciation

mat·in \ˈma-tᵊn\ *adj* [ME, fr. AF] (14c) : of or relating to matins or to early morning

mat·in·al \ˈma-tə-nəl\ *adj* (1803) **1** : of or relating to matins **2** : EARLY

mat·i·nee *or* **mat·i·née** \ˌma-tə-ˈnā\ *n* [F *matinée,* lit., morning, fr. OF, fr. *matin* morning, fr. L *matutinum,* fr. neut. of *matutinus* of the morning, fr. *Matuta,* goddess of morning; akin to L *maturus* ripe — more at MATURE] (1848) : a musical or dramatic performance or social or public event held in the daytime and esp. the afternoon

matinee idol *n* (1897) : a handsome male performer

mat·ins \ˈma-tᵊnz\ *n pl but sing or pl in constr, often cap* [ME *matines,* fr. AF, fr. LL *matutinae,* fr. L, fem. pl. of *matutinus*] (14c) **1** : the night office forming with lauds the first of the canonical hours **2** : MORNING PRAYER

matr- *or* **matri-** *or* **matro-** *comb form* [L *matr-, matri-,* fr. *matr-, mater*] : mother ⟨*matri*arch⟩ ⟨*matro*nymic⟩

ma·tri·arch \ˈmā-trē-ˌärk\ *n* (1606) : a woman who rules or dominates a family, group, or state; *specif* : a mother who is head and ruler of her family and descendants — **ma·tri·ar·chal** \ˌmā-trē-ˈär-kəl\ *adj*

ma·tri·ar·chate \ˈmā-trē-ˌär-kət, -ˌkāt\ *n* (1884) : MATRIARCHY 1

ma·tri·ar·chy \ˈmā-trē-ˌär-kē\ *n, pl* **-chies** (1885) **1** : a family, group, or state governed by a matriarch **2** : a system of social organization in which descent and inheritance are traced through the female line

ma·tri·cide \ˈma-trə-ˌsīd, ˈmā-\ *n* (1594) **1** [L *matricidium,* fr. *matr-* + *-cidium* -cide] : murder of a mother by her son or daughter **2** [L *matricida,* fr. *matr-* + *-cida* -cide] : one that murders his or her mother — **ma·tri·cid·al** \ˌma-trə-ˈsī-dᵊl, ˌmā-\ *adj*

ma·tric·u·late \mə-ˈtri-kyə-ˌlāt\ *vb* **-lat·ed; -lat·ing** [ML *matriculatus,* pp. of *matriculare,* fr. LL *matricula* public roll, dim. of *matric-, matrix* list, fr. L, breeding female] *vt* (1577) : to enroll as a member of a body and esp. of a college or university ~ *vi* : to become matriculated — **ma·tric·u·lant** \-lənt\ *n* — **ma·tric·u·la·tion** \-ˌtri-kyə-ˈlā-shən\ *n*

ma·tri·lin·eal \ˌma-trə-ˈli-nē-əl, ˌmā-\ *adj* (1904) : relating to, based on, or tracing descent through the maternal line ⟨~ society⟩ — **ma·tri·lin·eal·ly** \-nē-ə-lē\ *adv*

mat·ri·mo·nial \ˌma-trə-ˈmō-nē-əl, -nyəl\ *adj* (15c) : of or relating to marriage, the married state, or married persons — **mat·ri·mo·nial·ly** *adv*

mat·ri·mo·ny \ˈma-trə-ˌmō-nē\ *n* [ME, fr. AF *matrimoignie,* fr. L *matrimonium,* fr. *matr-, mater* mother, matron — more at MOTHER] (14c) : the state of being married : MARRIAGE

matrimony vine *n* (ca. 1818) : a shrub or vine (genus *Lycium*) of the nightshade family with often showy flowers and usu. red berries

ma·trix \ˈmā-triks\ *n, pl* **ma·tri·ces** \ˈmā-trə-ˌsēz, ˈma-\ *or* **ma·trix·es** \ˈmā-trik-səz\ [L, female animal used for breeding, parent plant, fr. *matr-, mater*] (1555) **1** : something within or from which something else originates, develops, or takes form **2 a** : a mold from which a relief surface (as a piece of type) is made **b** : DIE 3a(1) **c** : an engraved or inscribed die or stamp **d** : an electroformed impression of a phonograph record used for mass-producing duplicates of the original **3 a** : the natural material (as soil or rock) in which something (as a fossil or crystal) is embedded **b** : material in which something is enclosed or embedded (as for protection or study) **4 a** : the extracellular substance in which tissue cells (as of connective tissue) are embedded **b** : the thickened epithelium at the base of a fingernail or toenail from which new nail substance develops **5 a** : a rectangular array of mathematical elements (as the coefficients of simultaneous linear equations) that can be combined to form sums and products with similar arrays having an appropriate number of rows and columns **b** : something resembling a mathematical matrix esp. in rectangular arrangement of elements into rows and columns **c** : an array of circuit elements (as diodes and transistors) for performing a specific function **6** : a main clause that contains a subordinate clause

ma·tron \ˈmā-trən\ *n* [ME *matrone,* fr. AF, fr. L *matrona,* fr. *matr-, mater*] (14c) **1 a** : a married woman usu. marked by dignified maturity or social distinction **b** : a woman who supervises women or children (as in a school or police station) **c** : the chief officer in a women's organization **2** : a female animal kept for breeding

ma·tron·ly \ˈmā-trən-lē\ *adj* (1630) : having the character of or suitable to a matron

matron of honor (1903) : a bride's principal married wedding attendant — compare MAID OF HONOR

mat·ro·nym·ic \ˌma-trə-ˈni-mik\ *n* [*matr-* + *-onymic* (as in *patronymic*)] (1794) : a name derived from that of the mother or a maternal ancestor

mat·su·ta·ke \ˌmät-sü-ˈtä-kē, -kā\ *n, pl* **matsutake** *also* **matsutakes** [Jp *matsu-take, matsudake,* fr. *matsu* pine tree + *take* mushroom] (1883) : a large brownish edible Japanese mushroom (*Tricholoma matsutake*) having firm flesh and a spicy aroma; *also* : a large whitish mushroom (*Tricholoma magnivelere* syn. *Armillaria ponderosa*) of northern No. America that is similar to the Japanese matsutake

Matt *abbr* Matthew

[1]**matte** *or* **matt** *var of* [3]MAT 1

[2]**matte** *also* **mat** *or* **matt** \ˈmat\ *adj* [F *mat,* fr. OF, faded, defeated] (ca. 1648) : lacking or deprived of luster or gloss: as **a** : having a usu. smooth even surface free from shine or highlights ⟨~ metals⟩ ⟨a ~ finish⟩ **b** : having a rough or granular surface

[3]**matte** \ˈmat\ *n* [F, fr. MF, crude metal, curdled milk, fr. fem. of *mat* thick, dull, matte] (1839) **1** : a crude mixture of sulfides formed in smelting sulfide ores of metals (as copper, lead, or nickel) **2** : a motion-picture effect in which part of a scene is blocked out and later replaced by footage containing other material (as a background painting)

[1]**mat·ter** \ˈma-tər\ *n* [ME *matere,* fr. AF, fr. L *materia* matter, physical substance, fr. *mater*] (13c) **1 a** : a subject under consideration **b** : a subject of disagreement or litigation **c** *pl* : the events or circumstances of a particular situation **d** : the subject or substance of a discourse or writing **e** : something of an indicated kind or having to do with an indicated field or situation ⟨this is a serious ~⟩ ⟨as a ~ of policy⟩ ⟨~*s* of faith⟩ **f** : something to be proved in law **g** *obs* : sensible or serious material as distinguished from nonsense or drollery **h** (1) *obs* : REASON, CAUSE (2) : a source esp. of feeling or emotion **i** : PROBLEM, DIFFICULTY **2 a** : the substance of which a physical object is composed **b** : material substance that occupies space, has mass, and is composed predominantly of atoms consisting of protons, neutrons, and electrons, that constitutes the observable universe, and that is interconvertible with energy **c** : a material substance of a particular kind or for a particular purpose ⟨vegetable ~⟩ **d** (1) : material (as feces or urine) discharged from the living body (2) : material discharged by suppuration : PUS **3 a** : the indeterminate subject of reality; *esp* : the element in the universe that undergoes formation and alteration **b** : the formless substratum of all things which exists only potentially and upon which form acts to produce realities **4** : a more or less definite amount or quantity ⟨cooks in a ~ of minutes⟩ **5** : something written or printed **6** : MAIL **7** *Christian Science* : the illusion that the objects perceived by the physical senses have the reality of substance — **as a matter of fact** : in fact : ACTUALLY — **for that matter** : so far as that is concerned — **no matter** : without regard to : irrespective of ⟨points in the same direction *no matter* how it is tilted⟩ — **no matter what** : regardless of the costs, consequences, or results ⟨wants to win, *no matter what*⟩ — **the matter** : WRONG ⟨nothing's *the matter* with me⟩

[2]**matter** *vi* (1530) **1** : to form or discharge pus : SUPPURATE ⟨~*ing* wound⟩ **2** : to be of importance : SIGNIFY

matter of course (1739) : something that is to be expected as a natural or logical consequence

mat·ter–of–fact \ˌma-tər-ə(v)-ˈfakt\ *adj* (1712) : adhering to the unembellished facts; *also* : being plain, straightforward, or unemotional — **mat·ter–of–fact·ly** \-ˈfak(t)-lē\ *adv* — **mat·ter–of–fact·ness** \-ˈfak(t)-nəs\ *n*

mat·tery \ˈma-tə-rē\ *adj* (14c) : producing or containing pus or material resembling pus ⟨eyes all ~⟩

Mat·the·an *or* **Mat·thae·an** \ma-ˈthē-ən, mə-\ *adj* [LL *Matthaeus*] (1897) : of, relating to, or characteristic of the evangelist Matthew or the gospel ascribed to him

Mat·thew \ˈma-(ˌ)thyü *also* -(ˌ)thü\ *n* [F *Mathieu,* fr. LL *Matthaeus,* fr. Gk *Matthaios,* fr. Heb *Mattithyāh*] (13c) **1** : an apostle traditionally identified as the author of the first Gospel in the New Testament **2** : the first Gospel in the New Testament — see BIBLE table

[1]**matting** *n* (ca. 1847) **1** : material for mats **2** : MATS

[2]**matting** *n* [fr. gerund of [4]*mat*] (1854) : a dull lusterless surface (as on gilding, metalwork, or satin)

mat·tins *often cap, chiefly Brit var of* MATINS

mat·tock \ˈma-tək\ *n* [ME *mattok,* fr. OE *mattuc*] (bef. 12c) : a digging and grubbing tool with features of an adze and an ax or pick

mat·tress \ˈma-trəs\ *n* [ME *materas,* fr. AF, fr. ML *materacium,* fr. Ar *maṭraḥ* place where something is thrown] (14c) **1 a** : a fabric case filled with resilient material (as cotton, hair, feathers, foam rubber, or an arrangement of coiled springs) used either alone as a bed or on a bedstead **b** : an inflatable airtight sack for use as a mattress **2** : a device (as of interwoven brush and poles) used to protect a shoreline, bank, or streambed from erosion

mat·u·rate \ˈma-chə-ˌrāt\ *vb* **-rat·ed; -rat·ing** (1622) : MATURE

mat·u·ra·tion \ˌma-chə-ˈrā-shən\ *n* (1541) **1 a** : the process of becoming mature **b** : the emergence of personal and behavioral characteristics through growth processes **c** : the final stages of differentiation of cells, tissues, or organs **2 a** : the entire process by which diploid gamete-producing cells are transformed into haploid gametes that includes both meiosis and physiological and structural changes **b** : SPERMIOGENESIS — **mat·u·ra·tion·al** \-shnəl, -shə-nᵊl\ *adj*

[1]**ma·ture** \mə-ˈtu̇r, -ˈtyu̇r *also* -ˈchu̇r\ *adj* **ma·tur·er; -est** [ME, fr. L *maturus* ripe; akin to L *mane* in the morning, *manus* good] (15c) **1** : based on slow careful consideration ⟨a ~ judgment⟩ **2 a** (1) : having completed natural growth and development : RIPE (2) : having undergone maturation **b** : having attained a final or desired state ⟨~ wine⟩ **c** : having achieved a low but stable growth rate ⟨paper is a ~ industry⟩ **d** : of, relating to, or being an older adult : ELDERLY ⟨airline discounts for ~ travelers⟩ **3 a** : of or relating to a condition of full development **b** : characteristic of or suitable to a mature individual ⟨~ outlook⟩ ⟨a show with ~ content⟩ **4** : due for payment ⟨a ~ loan⟩ **5** : belonging to the middle portion of a cycle of erosion — **mature·ly** *adv*

[2]**mature** *vb* **ma·tured; ma·tur·ing** *vt* (15c) : to bring to maturity or completion ~ *vi* **1** : to become fully developed or ripe **2** : to become due

ma·tu·ri·ty \mə-ˈtu̇r-ə-tē, -ˈtyu̇r- *also* -ˈchu̇r-\ *n* (15c) **1** : the quality or state of being mature; *esp* : full development ⟨lacks the wisdom and ~ needed to run the company⟩ **2** : termination of the period that an obligation has to run

ma·tu·ti·nal \ˌma-chu̇-ˈtī-nᵊl; mə-ˈtüt-nəl, -ˈtyüt-, -ˈtü-tə-nəl, -ˈtyü-\ *adj* [LL *matutinalis,* fr. L *matutinus* — more at MATINEE] (1567) : of, relating to, or occurring in the morning : EARLY — **ma·tu·ti·nal·ly** *adv*

MATV *abbr* master antenna television

mat·zo *or* **mat·zoh** \ˈmät-sə *also* -(ˌ)sō\ *n, pl* **mat·zoth** \-ˌsōt, -ˌsōth, -sōs\ *or* **mat·zos** *or* **mat·zohs** \-səz, -səs *also* -ˌsōz\ [Yiddish *matse,* fr. Heb *maṣṣāh*] (1650) **1** : unleavened bread eaten esp. at the Passover **2** : a wafer of matzo

matzo ball *n* (1917) : a small ball-shaped dumpling made from matzo meal

maud·lin \ˈmȯd-lən\ *adj* [alter. of Mary *Magdalene;* fr. her depiction as a weeping penitent] (1509) **1** : drunk enough to be emotionally silly ⟨would crack open another beer and become ~ —Patrick Moore⟩ **2** : weakly and effusively sentimental

mau·gre \ˈmȯ-gər\ *prep* [ME, fr. AF *malgré,* fr. *malgré* ill will, fr. *mal, mau* evil + *gré* grace, favor] (13c) *archaic* : in spite of

[1]**maul** \ˈmȯl\ *n* [ME *malle* mace, maul, fr. AF *mail,* fr. L *malleus;* akin to OCS *mlatŭ* hammer, L *molere* to grind — more at MEAL] (13c) : a heavy often wooden-headed hammer used esp. for driving wedges; *also* : a tool like a sledgehammer with one wedge-shaped end that is used to split wood

[2]**maul** *vt* (13c) **1** : BEAT, BRUISE **2** : MANGLE 1 **3** : to handle roughly — **maul·er** *n*

maul·stick *also* **mahl·stick** \ˈmȯl-stik\ *n* [part trans. of D *maalstok,* fr. obs. D *malen* to paint + D *stok* stick, stock] (ca. 1658) : a stick used by painters as a rest for the hand while working

mau–mau \ˈmau̇-ˌmau̇\ *vb* **mau–maued; mau–mau·ing** *often cap both Ms* [*Mau Mau,* anti-European secret society in colonial Kenya] *vt* (1970) : to intimidate (as an official) by hostile confrontation or threats ~ *vi* : to engage in mau-mauing someone

maun \ˈmȯn, ˈmän, mən\ *verbal auxiliary* [ME *man,* fr. ON, pres. of *munu* shall, will; akin to OE *gemynd* mind — more at MIND] (13c) *chiefly Scot* : MUST

maun·der \ˈmȯn-dər, ˈmän-\ *vi* **maun·dered; maun·der·ing** \-d(ə-)riŋ\ [prob. imit.] (1621) **1** *chiefly Brit* : GRUMBLE **2** : to wander slowly and idly **3** : to speak indistinctly or disconnectedly — **maun·der·er** \-dər-ər\ *n*

Maun·dy Thursday \ˈmȯn-dē-, ˈmän-\ *n* [ME *maunde* ceremony of washing the feet of the poor on Maundy Thursday, fr. AF *mandet,* fr. L *mandatum* command; fr. Jesus' words in John 13:34 — more at MANDATE] (15c) : the Thursday before Easter observed in commemoration of the institution of the Eucharist

mau·so·le·um \ˌmȯ-sə-ˈlē-əm, ˌmȯ-zə-\ *n, pl* **-leums** *or* **-lea** \-ˈlē-ə\ [ME, fr. L, fr. Gk *mausōleion,* fr. *Mausōlos* Mausolus †*ab* 353 B.C., ruler of Caria] (15c) **1** : a large tomb; *esp* : a usu. stone building with places for entombment of the dead above ground **2** : a large gloomy building or room

mauve \ˈmȯv, ˈmōv\ *n* [F, lit., mallow, fr. OF, fr. L *malva*] (1859) **1 a** : a moderate purple, violet, or lilac color **b** : a strong purple **2** : a dyestuff that produces a mauve color — **mauve** *adj*

ma·ven *also* **ma·vin** \ˈmā-vən\ *n* [Yiddish *meyvn,* fr. LHeb *mēbhīn*] (1950) : one who is experienced or knowledgeable : EXPERT; *also* : FREAK 4a

[1]**mav·er·ick** \ˈmav-rik, ˈma-və-\ *n* [Samuel A. *Maverick* †1870 Am. pioneer who did not brand his calves] (1867) **1** : an unbranded range animal; *esp* : a motherless calf **2** : an independent individual who does not go along with a group or party

[2]**maverick** *adj* (1886) : characteristic of, suggestive of, or inclined to be a maverick

ma·vis \ˈmā-vəs\ *n* [ME, fr. AF *mauviz*] (14c) : SONG THRUSH

ma·vour·neen \mə-ˈvu̇r-ˌnēn\ *n* [Ir *mo mhuirnín*] (1800) *Irish* : my darling

maw \ˈmȯ\ *n* [ME, fr. OE *maga;* akin to OHG *mago* stomach, Lith *makas* purse] (bef. 12c) **1** : the receptacle into which food is taken by swallowing: **a** : STOMACH **b** : CROP **2 a** : the throat, gullet, or jaws esp. of a voracious animal **b** : something suggestive of a gaping maw

mawk·ish \ˈmȯ-kish\ *adj* [ME *mawke* maggot, prob. fr. ON *mathkr* — more at MAGGOT] (ca. 1697) **1** : having an insipid often unpleasant taste **2** : sickly or puerilely sentimental — **mawk·ish·ly** *adv* — **mawk·ish·ness** *n*

max \ˈmaks\ *n* (1851) **1** : MAXIMUM 1 **2** : MAXIMUM 2 — **max** *adj* — **to the max** : to the greatest extent possible

maxi \ˈmak-sē\ *n, pl* **max·is** [*maxi-*] (1967) : a long skirt, dress, or coat

maxi- *comb form* [*maximum*] **1** : extra long ⟨*maxi*skirt⟩ **2** : extra large ⟨*maxi*-problems⟩

max·il·la \mak-ˈsi-lə\ *n, pl* **max·il·lae** \-ˈsi-(ˌ)lē, -ˌlī\ *or* **maxillas** [L, dim. of *mala* jaw] (1676) **1 a** : JAW 1a **b (1)** : an upper jaw esp. of humans and other mammals in which the bony elements are closely fused **(2)** : either of the two bones that lie with one on each side of the upper jaw lateral to the premaxilla and that in higher vertebrates bear most of the teeth **2** : one of the first or second pair of mouthparts posterior to the mandibles in many arthropods (as insects or crustaceans) — **max·il·lary** \ˈmak-sə-ˌler-ē, *chiefly Brit* mak-ˈsi-lə-rē\ *adj or n*

max·il·li·ped \mak-ˈsi-lə-ˌped\ *n* [ISV *maxilli-* (fr. L *maxilla*) + *-ped*] (1846) : any of the crustacean appendages that comprise the first pair or first three pairs situated next behind the maxillae

max·il·lo·fa·cial \mak-ˌsi-(ˌ)lō-ˈfā-shəl, ˌmak-sə-(ˌ)lō-\ *adj* (ca. 1923) : of, relating to, or treating the maxilla and the face ⟨~ surgeons⟩

max·im \ˈmak-səm\ *n* [ME *maxime,* fr. AF, fr. ML *maxima,* fr. L, fem. of *maximus,* superl. of *magnus* large — more at MUCH] (1567) **1** : a general truth, fundamental principle, or rule of conduct **2** : a proverbial saying

max·i·mal \ˈmak-s(ə-)məl\ *adj* (1882) **1** : being an upper limit : HIGHEST **2** : most comprehensive : COMPLETE — **max·i·mal·ly** *adv*

max·i·mal·ist \-s(ə-)mə-list\ *n* (1907) : one who advocates immediate and direct action to secure the whole of a program or set of goals — **maximalist** *adj*

maxi·min \ˈmak-sə-ˌmin\ *n* [*maxi*mum + *min*imum] (1951) : the maximum of a set of minima; *esp* : the largest of a set of minimum possible gains each of which occurs in the least advantageous outcome of a strategy followed by a participant in a situation governed by game theory — compare MINIMAX

max·i·mise *Brit var of* MAXIMIZE

max·i·mize \ˈmak-sə-ˌmīz\ *vt* **-mized; -miz·ing** (1802) **1** : to increase to a maximum **2** : to make the most of **3** : to find a maximum value of **4** : to increase the size of (a window) to fill an entire computer screen — **max·i·mi·za·tion** \ˌmak-sə-mə-ˈzā-shən\ *n* — **max·i·miz·er** \ˈmak-sə-ˌmī-zər\ *n*

max·i·mum \ˈmak-s(ə-)məm\ *n, pl* **max·i·ma** \-sə-mə\ *or* **maximums** \-s(ə-)məmz\ [L, neut. of *maximus* biggest — more at MAXIM] (1740) **1 a** : the greatest quantity or value attainable or attained **b** : the period of highest, greatest, or utmost development **2** : an upper limit allowed (as by a legal authority) or allowable (as by the circumstances of a particular case) **3** : the largest of a set of numbers; *specif* : the largest value assumed by a real-valued continuous function defined on a closed interval — **maximum** *adj*

maximum likelihood *n* (1922) : a statistical method for estimating population parameters (as the mean and variance) from sample data that selects as estimates those parameter values maximizing the probability of obtaining the observed data

ma·xixe \mə-ˈshēsh, -ˈshē-shə\ *n, pl* **ma·xi·xes** \-ˈshē-shəz\ [BrazPg] (1914) : a ballroom dance of Brazilian origin that resembles the two-step

max out *vi* (1967) : to reach an upper limit or a peak ⟨the car *maxed out* at 85 mph⟩ ~ *vt* : to push to a limit or an extreme; *also* : to use up all available credit on ⟨*maxed out* the credit cards⟩

max·well \ˈmaks-ˌwel, -wəl\ *n* [James Clerk *Maxwell*] (1900) : the centimeter-gram-second electromagnetic unit of magnetic flux equal to the flux per square centimeter of normal cross section in a region where the magnetic induction is one gauss : 10^{-8} weber

[1]**may** \ˈmā\ *verbal auxiliary, past* **might** \ˈmīt\ *pres sing & pl* **may** [ME (1st & 3d sing. pres. indic.), fr. OE *mæg;* akin to OHG *mag* (1st & 3d sing. pres. indic.) have power, am able (infin. *magan*), and perh. to Gk *mēchos* means, expedient] (bef. 12c) **1 a** *archaic* : have the ability to **b** : have permission to ⟨you ~ go now⟩ : be free to ⟨a rug on which children ~ sprawl —C. E. Silberman⟩ — used nearly interchangeably with *can* **c** — used to indicate possibility or probability ⟨you ~ be right⟩ ⟨things you ~ need⟩; sometimes used interchangeably with *can* ⟨one of those slipups that ~ happen from time to time —Jessica Mitford⟩; sometimes used where *might* would be expected ⟨you ~ think from a little distance that the country was solid woods —Robert Frost⟩ **2** — used in auxiliary function to express a wish or desire esp. in prayer, imprecation, or benediction ⟨~ the best man win⟩ **3** — used in auxiliary function expressing purpose or expectation ⟨I laugh that I ~ not weep⟩ or contingency ⟨she'll do her duty come what ~⟩ or concession ⟨he ~ be slow but he is thorough⟩ or choice ⟨the angler ~ catch them with a dip net, or he ~ cast a large, bare treble hook —Nelson Bryant⟩ **4** : SHALL, MUST — used in law where the sense, purpose, or policy requires this interpretation ***usage*** see CAN

[2]**may** \ˈmā\ *n* [ME, fr. OE *mǣg* kinsman, kinswoman, maiden] (bef. 12c) *archaic* : MAIDEN

May \ˈmā\ *n* [ME, fr. AF & L; AF *mai,* fr. L *Maius,* fr. *Maia,* Roman goddess] (12c) **1** : the fifth month of the Gregorian calendar **2** *often not cap* : the early vigorous blooming part of human life : PRIME **3** : the festivities of May Day **4** *not cap* **a** : green or flowering branches used for May Day decorations **b** : a plant that yields may: as **(1)** : HAWTHORN **(2)** : a spring-flowering spirea

ma·ya \ˈmä-yə, ˈmī-ə\ *n* [Skt *māyā*] (1788) : the sense-world of manifold phenomena held in Vedanta to conceal the unity of absolute being; *broadly* : ILLUSION

Ma·ya \ˈmī-ə\ *n, pl* **Maya** *or* **Mayas** [Sp] (1825) **1 a** : a Mayan language of the ancient Maya peoples recorded in inscriptions **b** : YUCATEC; *esp* : the older form of that language known from documents of the Spanish period **2** : a member of a group of Indian peoples chiefly of Yucatán, Belize, and Guatemala whose languages are Mayan

Ma·yan \ˈmī-ən\ *n* (1900) **1** : a member of the peoples speaking Mayan languages **2** : an extensive language family of Central America and Mexico — **Mayan** *adj*

Mayanist \ˈmī-ə-nist\ *n* (1950) : a specialist in Mayan civilization and often languages

may·ap·ple \ˈmā-ˌa-pəl\ *n* [*May*] (ca. 1733) : a No. American herb (*Podophyllum peltatum*) of the barberry family with a poisonous rootstock, one or two large-lobed peltate leaves, and a single large white flower followed by a yellow egg-shaped edible fruit; *also* : its fruit

[1]**may·be** \ˈmā-bē *also* ˈme-\ *adv* (15c) : PERHAPS

[2]**maybe** *n* (ca. 1586) : UNCERTAINTY

May·day \ˈmā-ˌdā\ [F *m'aider* help me] (1927) — an international radio-telephone signal word used as a distress call

May Day \ˈmā-ˌdā\ *n* (13c) : May 1 celebrated as a springtime festival and in some countries as Labor Day

may·est *or* **mayst** \ˈmā-əst, ˈmāst\ *archaic pres 2d sing of* MAY

may·flow·er \ˈmā-ˌflau̇(-ə)r\ *n* (1594) : any of various spring-blooming plants; *esp* : ARBUTUS 2

may·fly \ˈmā-ˌflī\ *n* (ca. 1653) : any of an order (Ephemeroptera) of insects with an aquatic nymph and a short-lived fragile adult having membranous wings and two or three long caudal styles — called also *ephemerid*

may·hap \ˈmā-ˌhap, mā-ˈ\ *adv* [fr. the phrase *may hap*] (ca. 1531) : PERHAPS

may·hem \ˈmā-ˌhem, ˈmā-əm\ *n* [ME *mayme, mahaime,* fr. AF *mahaim* mutilation, mayhem, fr. *maheimer, mahaigner* to maim, prob. of Gmc origin; akin to MHG *meiden* gelding, ON *meitha* to injure] (15c) **1 a** : willful and permanent deprivation of a bodily member resulting in the impairment of a person's fighting ability **b** : willful and permanent crippling, mutilation, or disfigurement of any part of the body **2** : needless or willful damage or violence

may·ing \ˈmā-iŋ\ *n, often cap* (14c) : the celebrating of May Day

mayn't \ˈmā-ənt, ˈmānt\ (ca. 1631) : may not

mayo \ˈmā-(ˌ)ō\ *n* (ca. 1960) : MAYONNAISE

may·on·naise \ˈmā-ə-ˌnāz, ˌmā-ə-ˈ\ *n* [F] (1841) : a dressing made chiefly of egg yolks, vegetable oils, and vinegar or lemon juice

may·or \ˈmā-ər, ˈmer, *esp before names* (ˌ)mer\ *n* [ME *maire,* fr. AF, fr. L *major* greater — more at MAJOR] (14c) : an official elected or appointed to act as chief executive or nominal head of a city, town, or borough — **may·or·al** \ˈmā-ə-rəl, ˈmer-əl; ˌmā-ˈȯr-əl\ *adj*

may·or·al·ty \ˈmā-ə-rəl-tē, ˈmer-əl-\ *n* [ME *mairaltee,* fr. AF *mairalté,* fr. *maire*] (14c) : the office or term of office of a mayor

may·or·ess \ˈmā-ə-rəs, ˈmer-əs\ *n* (15c) *chiefly Brit* **1** : the wife or official hostess of a mayor **2** : a woman holding the office of mayor

may·pole \ˈmā-ˌpōl\ *n, often cap* (1554) : a tall flower-wreathed pole forming a center for May Day sports and dances

may·pop \ˈmā-ˌpäp\ *n* [alter. of *maracock,* perh. fr. Virginia Algonquian] (1851) : a climbing perennial passionflower (*Passiflora incarnata*) of the southern U.S. with a large ovoid yellow edible but insipid berry; *also* : its fruit

May·time \ˈmā-ˌtīm\ *n* (14c) : the month of May

maz·ard *or* **mazzard** \ˈma-zərd\ *n* [obs. E *mazard* mazer, alter. of E *mazer*] (1602) *chiefly dial* : HEAD, FACE

[1]**maze** \ˈmāz\ *vt* **mazed; maz·ing** [ME] (13c) **1** *chiefly dial* : STUPEFY, DAZE **2** : BEWILDER, PERPLEX

[2]**maze** *n* (14c) **1 a** : a confusing intricate network of passages **b** : something confusingly elaborate or complicated ⟨a ~ of regulations⟩ **2** *chiefly dial* : a state of bewilderment — **maze·like** \-ˌlīk\ *adj*

ma·zel tov \ˈmä-zəl-ˌtȯv, -ˌtȯf\ *interj* [Late Heb *mazzāl ṭōbh,* lit., good luck] (1862) — used to express congratulations

ma·zer \ˈmā-zər\ *n* [ME, fr. AF, of Gmc origin; akin to OHG *masar* gnarled excrescence on a tree] (14c) : a large drinking bowl orig. of a hard wood

ma·zur·ka \mə-ˈzər-kə, -ˈzu̇r-\ *also* **ma·zour·ka** \-ˈzu̇r-\ *n* [Russ, fr. Pol *mazurek,* fr. *Mazury* Masuria, region of NE Poland] (1818) **1** : a Polish

\ə\ **a**but \ᵊ\ **k**itten, F ta**ble** \ər\ **fur**ther \a\ **a**sh \ā\ **a**ce \ä\ m**o**p, m**a**r
\au̇\ **ou**t \ch\ **ch**in \e\ b**e**t \ē\ **ea**sy \g\ **g**o \i\ h**i**t \ī\ **i**ce \j\ **j**ob
\ŋ\ si**ng** \ō\ g**o** \ȯ\ l**aw** \ȯi\ b**oy** \th\ **th**in \t͟h\ **th**e \ü\ l**oo**t \u̇\ f**oo**t
\y\ **y**et \zh\ vi**s**ion, bei**g**e \k, ⁿ, œ, ue, ʸ\ *see* Guide to Pronunciation

folk dance in moderate triple measure **2 :** music for the mazurka or in its rhythm usu. in moderate ¾ or ⅜ time
mazy \ˈmā-zē\ *adj* (1579) **:** resembling a maze
[1]**maz·zard** \ˈma-zərd\ *n* [origin unknown] (1578) **:** SWEET CHERRY; *esp* **:** wild or seedling sweet cherry used as a rootstock for grafting
[2]**mazzard** *var of* MAZARD
mb *abbr* millibar
Mb *abbr* megabit
MB *abbr* **1** bachelor of medicine **2** Manitoba **3** megabyte **4** municipal borough
MBA *abbr* master of business administration
mba·qan·ga \ˌu̇m-bä-ˈkäŋ-gä\ *n* [Zulu *umbaqanga,* lit., steamed cornmeal bread] (1987) **:** a South African dance music that combines traditional elements (as chanting and drumming) with elements of modern music (as jazz)
mbd *abbr* million barrels per day
MBD *abbr* minimal brain dysfunction
MBE *abbr* member of the Order of the British Empire
mbi·ra \em-ˈbir-ə\ *n* [Shona] (ca. 1911) **:** an African musical instrument that consists of a wooden or gourd resonator and a varying number of tuned metal or wooden strips that vibrate when plucked

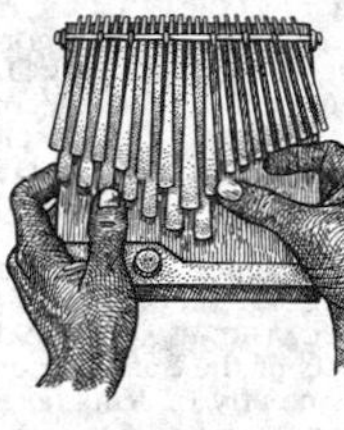
mbira

MBO *abbr* management by objective
Mbps *abbr* megabits per second
MBS *abbr* Mutual Broadcasting System
mc *abbr* **1** megacycle **2** millicurie
[1]**MC** \ˌem-ˈsē\ *n* (1790) **:** MASTER OF CEREMONIES
[2]**MC** *abbr* member of Congress
Mc- \mək; mə *before forms beginning with* k *or* g\ *prefix* [*McDonald's,* chain of fast food restaurants] — used to indicate an inexpensive, convenient, or easy but usu. low-quality or commercialized version of something specified ⟨*Mc*Book⟩
MCAT \ˈem-ˌkat\ *service mark* — used for a standardized test designed to evaluate qualification for admission to medical schools
MCC *abbr* mission control center
Mc·Car·thy·ism \mə-ˈkär-thē-ˌi-zəm *also* -ˈkär-tē-\ *n* [Joseph R. *McCarthy*] (1950) **:** a mid-20th century political attitude characterized chiefly by opposition to elements held to be subversive and by the use of tactics involving personal attacks on individuals by means of widely publicized indiscriminate allegations esp. on the basis of unsubstantiated charges; *broadly* **:** defamation of character or reputation through such tactics — **McCarthyist** *adj* — **Mc·Car·thy·ite** \-ˌīt\ *n or adj*
Mc·Coy \mə-ˈkȯi\ *n* [alter. of *Mackay* (in the phrase *the real Mackay*), of unknown origin] (1922) **:** something that is neither imitation nor substitute — often used in the phrase *the real McCoy*
mcg *abbr* microgram
McGuffin *var of* MACGUFFIN
Mc·In·tosh \ˈma-kən-ˌtäsh\ *n* [John *McIntosh fl*1796 Canad. settler] (1878) **:** a juicy bright red eating apple with a thin skin, white flesh, and aromatic slightly tart flavor
Mc·Job \mək-ˈjäb\ *n* (1986) **:** a low-paying job that requires little skill and provides little opportunity for advancement
[1]**MCL** *abbr* Marine Corps League
[2]**MCL** \ˌem-ˌsē-ˈel\ *n* (1988) **:** MEDIAL COLLATERAL LIGAMENT
Mc·Man·sion \mək-ˈman(t)-shən\ *n* (1990) **:** a very large house built in usu. a suburban neighborhood or development; *esp* **:** one regarded critically as oversized and ostentatious
m–com·merce \ˈem-ˌkä-(ˌ)mərs\ *n* [*m*obile] (1997) **:** business transactions conducted by using a mobile electronic device (as a cell phone)
MCP *abbr* male chauvinist pig
MCPO *abbr* master chief petty officer
MCS *abbr* multiple chemical sensitivity
[1]**Md** *abbr* Maryland
[2]**Md** *symbol* mendelevium
MD *abbr* **1** [NL *medicinae doctor*] doctor of medicine **2** [It *mano destra*] right hand **3** Maryland **4** medical department **5** minidisc **6** months after date **7** muscular dystrophy
M–day \ˈem-ˌdā\ *n* [*m*obilization *day*] (1924) **:** a day on which a military mobilization is to begin
MDC *abbr* more developed country
MDiv *abbr* master of divinity
MDMA \ˌem-(ˌ)dē-(ˌ)em-ˈā\ *n* [*m*ethylene + *d*i- + *m*eth*a*mphetamine] (1978) **:** ECSTASY 4
mdse *abbr* merchandise
MDT *abbr* mountain daylight time
me \ˈmē\ *pron, objective case of* I [ME, fr. OE *mē;* akin to OHG *mīh* me, L *me,* Gk *me,* Skt *mā*]
usage *Me* is used in many constructions where strict grammarians prescribe *I.* This usage is not so much ungrammatical as indicative of the shrinking range of the nominative form: *me* began to replace *I* sometime around the 16th century largely because of the pressure of word order. *I* is now chiefly used as the subject of an immediately following verb. *Me* occurs in every other position: absolute ⟨who, *me*?⟩, emphatically ⟨*me* too⟩, and after prepositions, conjunctions, and verbs, including *be* ⟨come with *me*⟩ ⟨you're as big as *me*⟩ ⟨it's *me*⟩. Almost all usage books recognize the legitimacy of *me* in these positions, esp. in speech; some recommend *I* in formal and esp. written contexts after *be* and after *as* and *than* when the first term of the comparison is the subject of a verb.
Me *abbr* methyl
ME *abbr* **1** *or* **Me** Maine **2** managing editor **3** mechanical engineer **4** medical examiner
mea cul·pa \ˌmā-ə-ˈku̇l-pə, ˌmā-ä-, -ˈku̇l-(ˌ)pä\ *n* [L, through my fault] (1602) **:** a formal acknowledgment of personal fault or error
[1]**mead** \ˈmēd\ *n* [ME *mede,* fr. OE *medu;* akin to OHG *metu* mead, Gk *methy* wine] (bef. 12c) **:** a fermented beverage made of water and honey, malt, and yeast
[2]**mead** *n* [ME *mede,* fr. OE *mǣd*] (bef. 12c) *archaic* **:** MEADOW
mead·ow \ˈme-(ˌ)dō\ *n, often attrib* [ME *medwe,* fr. OE *mǣdwe,* oblique case form of *mǣd;* akin to OE *māwan* to mow — more at MOW] (bef. 12c) **:** land that is covered or mostly covered with grass; *esp* **:** a tract of moist low-lying usu. level grassland — **mead·owy** \ˈme-də-wē\ *adj*
meadow beauty *n* (1840) **:** any of a genus (*Rhexia* of the family Melastomaceae, the meadow-beauty family) of perennial No. American herbs with showy solitary or cymose flowers
meadow fescue *n* (1794) **:** a tall vigorous broad-leaved European fescue grass (*Festuca pratensis*) cultivated for forage and hay
mead·ow·foam \ˈme-(ˌ)dō-ˌfōm\ *n* (1897) **:** any of a genus (*Limnanthes* of the family Limnanthaceae) of annual herbs of the Pacific coast of No. America having white or yellow flowers and including some (as *L. alba*) grown for their seeds which yield an oil used chiefly as an industrial lubricant and in cosmetics
meadow grass *n* (13c) **:** any of various grasses (as of the genus *Poa*) that thrive in the presence of abundant moisture; *esp* **:** KENTUCKY BLUEGRASS
mead·ow·land \ˈme-dō-ˌland, -də-\ *n* (1530) **:** land that is or is used for meadow
mead·ow·lark \ˈme-dō-ˌlärk, -də-\ *n* (1611) **:** any of several American songbirds (genus *Sturnella* of the family Icteridae) that are streaked brown above and in northernmost forms have a yellow breast marked with a black crescent
meadow mushroom *n* (1884) **:** a common edible whitish agaric mushroom (*Agaricus campestris*) that has gills which change from pink to brown and usually grows in moist open areas (as fields or lawns)
meadow nematode *n* (1946) **:** any of numerous plant-parasitic nematodes (esp. genus *Pratylenchus*) that are destructive to plant roots
meadow rue *n* (1668) **:** any of a genus (*Thalictrum*) of widely distributed perennial herbs of the buttercup family growing in typically damp areas
meadow saffron *n* (1578) **:** AUTUMN CROCUS
meadow spittlebug *n* (1942) **:** a widely distributed spittlebug (*Philaenus spumarius*) that does severe damage esp. to grasses
mead·ow·sweet \ˈme-dō-ˌswēt, -də-\ *n* (1530) **1 :** any of several spireas; *esp* **:** a No. American native or naturalized spirea (as *Spiraea alba* and *S. latifolia*) **2 :** any of a genus (*Filipendula*) of herbs closely related to the spireas
meadow vole *n* (1801) **:** any of various voles (genus *Microtus*) that frequent open fields; *esp* **:** one (*M. pennsylvanicus*) that is widespread in No. America — called also *meadow mouse*
mea·ger *or* **mea·gre** \ˈmē-gər\ *adj* [ME *megre,* fr. AF *megre, meigre,* fr. L *macr-, macer* lean; akin to OE *mæger* lean, Gk *makros* long] (14c) **1 :** having little flesh **:** THIN **2 a :** lacking desirable qualities (as richness or strength) ⟨leading a ~ life⟩ **b :** deficient in quality or quantity ⟨a ~ diet⟩ — **mea·ger·ly** *adv* — **mea·ger·ness** *n*
syn MEAGER, SCANTY, SCANT, SKIMPY, SPARE, SPARSE mean falling short of what is normal, necessary, or desirable. MEAGER implies the absence of elements, qualities, or numbers necessary to a thing's richness, substance, or potency ⟨a *meager* portion of meat⟩. SCANTY stresses insufficiency in amount, quantity, or extent ⟨supplies too *scanty* to last the winter⟩. SCANT suggests a falling short of what is desired or desirable rather than of what is essential ⟨in January the daylight hours are *scant*⟩. SKIMPY usu. suggests niggardliness or penury as the cause of the deficiency ⟨tacky housing developments on *skimpy* lots⟩. SPARE may suggest a slight falling short of adequacy or merely an absence of superfluity ⟨a *spare,* concise style of writing⟩. SPARSE implies a thin scattering of units ⟨a *sparse* population⟩.
[1]**meal** \ˈmēl\ *n* [ME *meel* appointed time, meal, fr. OE *mǣl;* akin to OHG *māl* time, L *metiri* to measure — more at MEASURE] (bef. 12c) **1 :** an act or the time of eating a portion of food to satisfy appetite **2 :** the portion of food eaten at a meal
[2]**meal** *n* [ME *mele,* fr. OE *melu;* akin to OHG *melo* meal, L *molere* to grind, Gk *mylē* mill] (bef. 12c) **1 :** the usu. coarsely ground and unbolted seeds of a cereal grass or pulse; *esp* **:** CORNMEAL **2 :** a product resembling seed meal esp. in particle size or texture
-meal *adv comb form* [ME *-mele,* fr. OE *-mǣlum,* fr. *mǣlum,* dat. pl. of *mǣl*] **:** by a (specified) portion or measure at a time ⟨piecemeal⟩
mea·lie \ˈmē-lē\ *n* [Afrik *mielie,* fr. obs. D *milie* millet, maize, fr. MF *mil* millet — more at MILLET] (1855) *SoAfr* **:** [1]CORN 4
meals–on–wheels *n pl but sing in constr* (1961) **:** a service that delivers daily hot meals to the homes of elderly or disabled people
meal ticket *n* (ca. 1899) **:** one that serves as the ultimate source of one's income ⟨an advanced degree was his *meal ticket*⟩
meal·time \ˈmēl-ˌtīm\ *n* (12c) **:** the usual time for serving a meal
meal·worm \-ˌwərm\ *n* (1658) **:** the larva of a darkling beetle (esp. genus *Tenebrio*) that infests grain products but is often raised as food for insectivorous animals, for laboratory use, or as fishing bait
mealy \ˈmē-lē\ *adj* **meal·i·er; -est** (1591) **1 :** containing meal **:** FARINACEOUS **2 :** soft, dry, and friable **3 a :** covered with meal or with fine granules **b :** flecked with another color **c :** SPOTTY, UNEVEN **d :** PALLID, BLANCHED ⟨a ~ complexion⟩ **4 :** MEALYMOUTHED
mealy·bug \ˈmē-lē-ˌbəg\ *n* (1824) **:** any of a family (Pseudococcidae) of scale insects that have a white cottony or waxy covering and are destructive pests esp. of fruit trees
mealy·mouthed \ˈmē-lē-ˌmau̇thd, -ˌmau̇tht\ *adj* (ca. 1572) **:** not plain and straightforward **:** DEVIOUS ⟨a ~ politician⟩
[1]**mean** \ˈmēn\ *vb* **meant** \ˈment\; **mean·ing** \ˈmē-niŋ\ [ME *menen,* fr. OE *mǣnan;* akin to OHG *meinen* to have in mind, OCS *mĕniti* to mention] *vt* (bef. 12c) **1 a :** to have in the mind as a purpose **:** INTEND ⟨she ~*s* to win⟩ — sometimes used interjectionally with *I,* chiefly in informal speech for emphasis ⟨he throws, I ~, hard⟩ or to introduce a phrase restating the point of a preceding phrase ⟨we try to answer what we can, but I ~ we're not God —Bobbie Ann Mason⟩ **b :** to design for or destine to a specified purpose or future ⟨I was *meant* to teach⟩ **2 :** to serve or intend to convey, show, or indicate **:** SIGNIFY ⟨a red sky ~*s* rain⟩ **3 :** to have importance to the degree of ⟨health ~*s* everything⟩ **4 :** to direct to a particular individual ~ *vi* **:** to have an intended purpose ⟨he ~*s* well⟩ — **mean·er** \ˈmē-nər\ *n* — **mean business :** to be in earnest
[2]**mean** \ˈmēn\ *adj* [ME *mene,* fr. *imene* common, shared, fr. OE *gemǣne;* akin to OHG *gimeini* common, L *communis* common, *munus* service, gift, Skt *mayate* he exchanges] (14c) **1 :** lacking distinction or eminence **:** HUMBLE **2 :** lacking in mental discrimination **:** DULL **3 a :** of poor shabby inferior quality or status ⟨~ city streets⟩ **b :** worthy of little regard **:** CONTEMPTIBLE — often used in negative constructions as a term of praise ⟨no ~ feat⟩ **4 :** lacking dignity or honor **:** BASE **5**

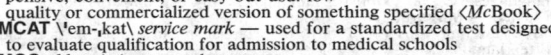

a : PENURIOUS, STINGY **b** : characterized by petty selfishness or malice **c** : causing trouble or bother : VEXATIOUS **d** : EXCELLENT, EFFECTIVE ⟨plays a ~ trumpet⟩ ⟨a lean, ~ athlete⟩ **6** : ASHAMED 1b — **mean·ness** \ˈmēn-nəs\ *n*

syn MEAN, IGNOBLE, ABJECT, SORDID mean being below the normal standards of human decency and dignity. MEAN suggests small-mindedness, ill temper, or cupidity ⟨*mean* and petty satire⟩. IGNOBLE suggests a loss or lack of some essential high quality of mind or spirit ⟨an *ignoble* scramble after material possessions⟩. ABJECT may imply degradation, debasement, or servility ⟨*abject* poverty⟩. SORDID is stronger than all of these in stressing physical or spiritual degradation and abjectness ⟨a *sordid* story of murder and revenge⟩.

[3]**mean** *adj* [ME *mene,* fr. AF *mene, meiene,* fr. L *medianus* — more at MEDIAN] (14c) **1** : occupying a middle position : intermediate in space, order, time, kind, or degree **2** : occupying a position about midway between extremes; *esp* : being the mean of a set of values : AVERAGE ⟨the ~ temperature⟩ **3** : serving as a means : INTERMEDIARY ***syn*** see AVERAGE

[4]**mean** *n* (14c) **1 a** (1) : something intervening or intermediate (2) : a middle point between extremes **b** : a value that lies within a range of values and is computed according to a prescribed law: as (1) : ARITHMETIC MEAN (2) : EXPECTED VALUE **c** : either of the middle two terms of a proportion **2** *pl but sing or pl in constr* : something useful or helpful to a desired end **3** *pl* : resources available for disposal; *esp* : material resources affording a secure life — **by all means** : most assuredly : CERTAINLY — **by means of** : through the use of — **by no means** : in no way : not at all

[1]**me·an·der** \mē-ˈan-dər\ *n* [L *maeander,* fr. Gk *maiandros,* fr. *Maiandros* (now *Menderes*), river in Asia Minor] (1576) **1** : a winding path or course; *esp* : LABYRINTH **2** : a turn or winding of a stream — **me·an·drous** \-drəs\ *adj*

[2]**meander** *vi* **-dered; -der·ing** \-d(ə-)riŋ\ (ca. 1612) **1** : to follow a winding or intricate course **2** : to wander aimlessly or casually without urgent destination : RAMBLE ***syn*** see WANDER

mean deviation *n* (1858) : the mean of the absolute values of the numerical differences between the numbers of a set (as statistical data) and their mean or median

mean distance *n* (1830) : the arithmetical mean of the maximum and minimum distances of an orbiting celestial object from its primary

mean free path *n* (1879) : the average distance traversed between collisions by particles (as molecules of a gas or free electrons in metal) in a system of agitated particles

mean·ie *also* **meany** \ˈmē-nē\ *n, pl* **meanies** (1910) : a mean person

mean·ing \ˈmē-niŋ\ *n* (14c) **1 a** : the thing one intends to convey esp. by language : PURPORT **b** : the thing that is conveyed esp. by language : IMPORT **2** : something meant or intended : AIM ⟨a mischievous ~ was apparent⟩ **3** : significant quality; *esp* : implication of a hidden or special significance ⟨a glance full of ~⟩ **4 a** : the logical connotation of a word or phrase **b** : the logical denotation or extension of a word or phrase — **meaning** *adj* — **mean·ing·ly** \-niŋ-lē\ *adv*

mean·ing·ful \-fəl\ *adj* (1852) **1 a** : having a meaning or purpose **b** : full of meaning : SIGNIFICANT ⟨a ~ life⟩ **2** : having an assigned function in a language system ⟨~ propositions⟩ — **mean·ing·ful·ly** \-fə-lē\ *adv* — **mean·ing·ful·ness** *n*

mean·ing·less \ˈmē-niŋ-ləs\ *adj* (1797) **1** : having no meaning; *esp* : lacking any significance **2** : having no assigned function in a language system — **mean·ing·less·ly** *adv* — **mean·ing·less·ness** *n*

[1]**mean·ly** \ˈmēn-lē\ *adv* (14c) *obs* : fairly well : MODERATELY

[2]**meanly** *adv* (15c) : in a mean manner: as **a** : in a lowly manner : HUMBLY **b** : in an inferior manner **c** : in a base or ungenerous manner

mean proportional *n* (1571) : GEOMETRIC MEAN; *esp* : the square root (as *x*) of the product of two numbers (as *a* and *b*) when expressed as the means of a proportion (as $a/x = x/b$)

mean solar day *n* (1816) : the interval between successive transits of a given meridian by the mean sun

mean–spir·it·ed \ˈmēn-ˈspir-ə-təd, ˌmēn-\ *adj* (1694) : exhibiting or characterized by meanness of spirit — **mean–spir·it·ed·ness** \-nəs\ *n*

mean square *n* (1845) : the mean of the squares of a set of values

mean square deviation *n* (1920) **1** : VARIANCE 5 **2** : STANDARD DEVIATION

means test \ˈmēnz-\ *n* (1930) : an examination into the financial state of a person to determine eligibility for public assistance — **means–test·ed** \-ˌtes-təd\ *adj*

mean sun *n* (1765) : a fictitious sun used for timekeeping that moves uniformly along the celestial equator and maintains a constant rate of apparent motion equal to the average rate of apparent motion of the real sun

[1]**mean·time** \ˈmēn-ˌtīm\ *n* (14c) : the intervening time

[2]**meantime** *adv* (1588) : MEANWHILE

mean time *n* (1751) : time that is based on the motion of the mean sun — called also *mean solar time*

mean value theorem *n* (1900) **1** : a theorem in differential calculus: if a function of one variable is continuous on a closed interval and differentiable on the interval minus its endpoints there is at least one point where the derivative of the function is equal to the slope of the line joining the endpoints of the curve representing the function on the interval **2** : a theorem in integral calculus: if a function of one variable is continuous on a closed interval and differentiable on the interval minus its endpoints, there is at least one point in the interval where the product of the value of the function and the length of the interval is equal to the integral of the function over the interval

[1]**mean·while** \ˈmēn-ˌhwī(-ə)l, -ˌwī(-ə)l\ *n* (14c) : MEANTIME

[2]**meanwhile** *adv* (14c) **1** : during the intervening time **2** : at the same time

meas *abbr* measure

mea·sle \ˈmē-zəl\ *n* [sing. of *measles*] (1863) : a cysticercus tapeworm larva; *specif* : one found in the muscles of a domesticated mammal

mea·sles \ˈmē-zəlz\ *n pl but sing or pl in constr* [ME *meseles,* pl. of *mesel* measles, spot characteristic of measles; akin to MD *masel* spot characteristic of measles] (14c) **1 a** : an acute contagious disease that is caused by a morbillivirus (species *Measles virus*) and is marked esp. by an eruption of distinct red circular spots — called also *rubeola* **b** : any of various eruptive diseases (as German measles) **2** [ME *mesel* infested with tapeworms, lit., leprous, fr. AF, fr. ML *misellus* leper, fr. L, wretch, fr. *misellus,* dim. of *miser* miserable] : infestation with or disease caused by larval tapeworms in the muscles and tissues

mea·sly \ˈmēz-lē, ˈmē-zə-\ *adj* **mea·sli·er; -est** (1687) **1** : infected with measles **2 a** : containing larval tapeworms **b** : infested with trichinae **3** : contemptibly small

[1]**mea·sure** \ˈme-zhər, ˈmā-\ *n* [ME *mesure,* fr. AF, fr. L *mensura,* fr. *mensus,* pp. of *metiri* to measure; akin to OE *mǣth* measure, Gk *metron*] (13c) **1 a** (1) : an adequate or due portion (2) : a moderate degree; *also* : MODERATION, TEMPERANCE (3) : a fixed or suitable limit : BOUNDS ⟨rich beyond ~⟩ **b** : the dimensions, capacity, or amount of something ascertained by measuring **c** : an estimate of what is to be expected (as of a person or situation) **d** (1) : a measured quantity (2) : AMOUNT, DEGREE **2 a** : an instrument or utensil for measuring **b** (1) : a standard or unit of measurement — see WEIGHT table (2) : a system of standard units of measure ⟨metric ~⟩ **3** : the act or process of measuring **4 a** (1) : MELODY, TUNE (2) : DANCE; *esp* : a slow and stately dance **b** : rhythmic structure or movement : CADENCE: as (1) : poetic rhythm measured by temporal quantity or accent; *specif* : METER (2) : musical time **c** (1) : a grouping of a specified number of musical beats located between two consecutive vertical lines on a staff (2) : a metrical unit : FOOT **5** : an exact divisor of a number **6** : a basis or standard of comparison ⟨wealth is not a ~ of happiness⟩ **7** : a step planned or taken as a means to an end; *specif* : a proposed legislative act — **for good measure** : in addition to the minimum required : as an extra

[2]**measure** *vb* **mea·sured; mea·sur·ing** \ˈme-zhə-riŋ, ˈmā-; ˈmezh-riŋ, ˈmāzh-\ *vt* (14c) **1 a** : to choose or control with cautious restraint : REGULATE ⟨~ his acts⟩ **b** : to regulate by a standard : GOVERN **2** : to allot or apportion in measured amounts ⟨~ out three cups⟩ **3** : to lay off by making measurements **4** : to ascertain the measurements of **5** : to estimate or appraise by a criterion ⟨~*s* his skill against his rival⟩ **6** *archaic* : to travel over : TRAVERSE **7** : to serve as a means of measuring ⟨a thermometer ~*s* temperature⟩ ~ *vi* **1** : to take or make a measurement **2** : to have a specified measurement — **mea·sur·abil·i·ty** \ˌme-zhə-rə-ˈbi-lə-tē, ˌmā-; ˌmezh-rə-, ˌmāzh-\ *n* — **mea·sur·able** \ˈme-zhə-rə-bəl, ˈmā-; ˈmezh-rə-, ˈmāzh-\ *adj* — **mea·sur·ably** \-blē\ *adv* — **mea·sur·er** \-zhər-ər\ *n*

measured *adj* (14c) **1** : marked by due proportion **2 a** : marked by rhythm : regularly recurrent ⟨a ~ gait⟩ **b** : METRICAL **3** : DELIBERATE, CALCULATED ⟨a ~ response⟩ — **mea·sured·ly** *adv*

mea·sure·less \-zhər-ləs\ *adj* (14c) **1** : having no observable limit : IMMEASURABLE ⟨the ~ universe⟩ **2** : very great ⟨had ~ energy⟩

mea·sure·ment \ˈme-zhər-mənt, ˈmā-\ *n* (1751) **1** : the act or process of measuring **2** : a figure, extent, or amount obtained by measuring : DIMENSION **3** : MEASURE 2b

measurement ton *n* (ca. 1934) : TON 1c

measure up *vi* (1854) **1** : to have necessary or fitting qualifications — often used with *to* **2** : to be the equal (as in ability) — used with *to*

measuring worm *n* (1843) : LOOPER 1

meat \ˈmēt\ *n* [ME *mete,* fr. OE; akin to OHG *maz* food] (bef. 12c) **1 a** : FOOD; *esp* : solid food as distinguished from drink **b** : the edible part of something as distinguished from its covering (as a husk or shell) **2** : animal tissue considered esp. as food: **a** : FLESH 2b; *also* : flesh of a mammal as opposed to fowl or fish **b** : FLESH 1a; *specif* : flesh of domesticated animals **3** *archaic* : [1]MEAL 1; *esp* : DINNER **4 a** : the core of something : HEART **b** : PITH 2b ⟨a novel with ~⟩ **5** : favorite pursuit or interest — **meat·ed** \ˈmē-təd\ *adj* — **meat·less** *adj*

meat–and–potatoes *adj* (1949) **1** : of fundamental importance : BASIC; *also* : concerned with or emphasizing the basic aspects of something **2** : UNPRETENTIOUS, SIMPLE ⟨a real ~ guy⟩ **3** : providing or preferring simple food (as meat and potatoes)

meat and potatoes *n pl but sing or pl in constr* (1951) : the most interesting or fundamental part : MEAT 4

meat–ax \ˈmēt-ˌaks\ *n* (1831) **1** : CLEAVER 1 **2** : an extreme or heavy-handed method of cutting or altering something

meat·ball \-ˌbȯl\ *n* (1877) : a small ball of chopped or ground meat often mixed with bread crumbs and spices

meat·head \-ˌhed\ *n* (1863) : a stupid or bungling person

meat loaf *n* (1892) : a dish of ground meat seasoned and baked in the form of a loaf

meat market *n* (1896) : a depersonalizing environment in which people are treated as sexual or economic resources

meat·pack·ing \ˈmēt-ˌpa-kiŋ\ *n* (1857) : the wholesale meat industry

me·a·tus \mē-ˈā-təs\ *n, pl* **me·a·tus·es** \-tə-səz\ *or* **me·a·tus** \-ˈā-təs, -ˌtüs\ [LL, fr. L, going, passage, fr. *meare* to go — more at PERMEATE] (1580) : a natural body passage

meaty \ˈmē-tē\ *adj* **meat·i·er; -est** (ca. 1787) **1 a** : full of meat **b** : having the character of meat **2** : rich esp. in matter for thought : SUBSTANTIAL ⟨actors looking for ~ roles⟩ — **meat·i·ness** *n*

mec·a·myl·amine \ˌme-kə-ˈmi-lə-ˌmēn\ *n* [fr. *Mecamylamine,* a trademark] (1955) : a drug that is used orally in the form of its hydrochloride $C_{11}H_{21}N \cdot HCl$ as a ganglionic blocking agent to effect a rapid lowering of severely elevated blood pressure

mec·ca \ˈme-kə\ *n, often cap* [*Mecca,* Saudi Arabia, a destination of pilgrims in the Islamic world] (1843) : a place regarded as a center for a specified group, activity, or interest ⟨a ~ for shoppers⟩

mech *abbr* mechanic; mechanical

mechan- *or* **mechano-** *comb form* [Gk, fr. *mēchanē* machine — more at MACHINE] : mechanical ⟨*mechano*receptor⟩

[1]**me·chan·ic** \mi-ˈka-nik\ *adj* [ME, prob. fr. MF *mecanique,* adj. & n., fr. L *mechanicus,* fr. Gk *mēchanikos,* fr. *mēchanē*] (14c) **1** : of or relating to manual work or skill **2** : MECHANICAL 3a

[2]**mechanic** *n* (1509) **1** : a manual worker : ARTISAN **2** : MACHINIST; *esp* : one who repairs machines

[1]**me·chan·i·cal** \mi-ˈka-ni-kəl\ *adj* (15c) **1 a** (1) : of or relating to machinery or tools ⟨~ applications of science⟩ ⟨a ~ genius⟩ ⟨~ aptitude⟩ (2) : produced or operated by a machine or tool ⟨~ power⟩ ⟨a

\ə\ abut \ᵊ\ kitten, F table \ər\ further \a\ ash \ā\ ace \ä\ mop, mar \au̇\ out \ch\ chin \e\ bet \ē\ easy \g\ go \i\ hit \ī\ ice \j\ job \ŋ\ sing \ō\ go \ȯ\ law \ȯi\ boy \th\ thin \t͟h\ the \ü\ loot \u̇\ foot \y\ yet \zh\ vision, beige \k̲, ⁿ, œ, ue, ʸ\ *see* Guide to Pronunciation

~ refrigerator⟩ ⟨a ~ saw⟩ **b :** of or relating to manual operations **2 :** of or relating to artisans or machinists ⟨the ~ trades⟩ **3 a :** done as if by machine : seemingly uninfluenced by the mind or emotions : AUTOMATIC **b :** of or relating to technicalities or petty matters **4 a :** relating to, governed by, or in accordance with the principles of mechanics ⟨~ energy⟩ **b :** relating to the quantitative relations of force and matter ⟨~ pressure of wind on a tower⟩ **5 :** caused by, resulting from, or relating to a process that involves a purely physical as opposed to a chemical or biological change or process ⟨~ erosion of rock⟩ ***syn*** see SPONTANEOUS — **me·chan·i·cal·ly** \-ni-k(ə-)lē\ *adv*

[2]mechanical *n* (1600) **1** *obs* **:** MECHANIC 1 **2 :** a piece of finished copy consisting typically of type proofs and artwork positioned and mounted for photomechanical reproduction

mechanical advantage *n* (1852) **:** the advantage gained by the use of a mechanism in transmitting force; *specif* **:** the ratio of the force that performs the useful work of a machine to the force that is applied to the machine

mechanical drawing *n* (1811) **1 :** drawing done with the aid of instruments **2 :** a drawing made with instruments

mechanical engineering *n* (ca. 1890) **:** a branch of engineering concerned primarily with the industrial application of mechanics and with the production of tools, machinery, and their products — **mechanical engineer** *n*

mech·a·ni·cian \ˌme-kə-ˈni-shən\ *n* (1570) **:** MECHANIC, MACHINIST

me·chan·ics \mi-ˈka-niks\ *n pl but sing or pl in constr* (1612) **1 :** a branch of physical science that deals with energy and forces and their effect on bodies **2 :** the practical application of mechanics to the design, construction, or operation of machines or tools **3 :** mechanical or functional details or procedure ⟨the ~ of the brain⟩

mech·a·nism \ˈme-kə-ˌni-zəm\ *n* (1662) **1 a :** a piece of machinery **b :** a process, technique, or system for achieving a result **2 :** mechanical operation or action **:** WORKING 2 **3 :** a doctrine that holds natural processes (as of life) to be mechanically determined and capable of complete explanation by the laws of physics and chemistry **4 :** the fundamental processes involved in or responsible for an action, reaction, or other natural phenomenon — compare DEFENSE MECHANISM

mech·a·nist \-nist\ *n* (1606) **1** *archaic* **:** MECHANIC **2 :** an adherent of the doctrine of mechanism

mech·a·nis·tic \ˌme-kə-ˈnis-tik\ *adj* (1884) **1 :** mechanically determined **2 :** of or relating to a mechanism or the doctrine of mechanism **3 :** MECHANICAL — **mech·a·nis·ti·cal·ly** \-ti-k(ə-)lē\ *adv*

mech·a·nize \ˈme-kə-ˌnīz\ *vt* **-nized; -niz·ing** (1678) **1 :** to make mechanical; *esp* **:** to make automatic or routine **2 a :** to equip with machinery esp. to replace human or animal labor **b :** to equip with armed and armored motor vehicles **c :** to provide with mechanical power **3 :** to produce by or as if by machine — **mech·a·niz·able** \-ˌnī-zə-bəl\ *adj* — **mech·a·ni·za·tion** \ˌme-kə-nə-ˈzā-shən\ *n* — **mech·a·niz·er** \ˈme-kə-ˌnī-zər\ *n*

mech·a·no·chem·is·try \ˌme-kə-nō-ˈke-mə-strē\ *n* (1928) **:** chemistry that deals with the conversion of chemical energy into mechanical work (as in the contraction of a muscle) — **mech·a·no·chem·i·cal** \-ˈke-mi-kəl\ *adj*

mech·a·no·re·cep·tor \-ri-ˈsep-tər\ *n* (1927) **:** a neural end organ (as a tactile receptor) that responds to a mechanical stimulus (as a change in pressure) — **mech·a·no·re·cep·tion** \-ˈsep-shən\ *n* — **mech·a·no·re·cep·tive** \-ˈsep-tiv\ *adj*

Mech·lin \ˈme-klən\ *n* [*Mechlin,* Belgium] (1701) **:** a delicate bobbin lace used for dresses and millinery

mec·li·zine \ˈme-klə-ˌzēn\ *n* [*me*thyl + *ch*l*or-* + *-izine* (alter. of *azine*)] (1954) **:** a drug $C_{25}H_{27}ClN_2$ used usu. in the form of its hydrochloride to treat vertigo and nausea (as in motion sickness)

me·co·ni·um \mi-ˈkō-nē-əm\ *n* [L, lit., poppy juice, fr. Gk *mēkōnion,* fr. *mēkōn* poppy; akin to OHG *mago* poppy] (ca. 1706) **:** a dark greenish mass that accumulates in the bowel during fetal life and is discharged shortly after birth

[1]med \ˈmed\ *adj* (ca. 1933) **:** MEDICAL ⟨~ school⟩

[2]med *n* (1942) **:** MEDICATION 2 — usu. used in pl. ⟨took pain ~*s*⟩

[3]med *abbr* **1** medicine **2** medieval **3** medium

Med *abbr* Mediterranean

MEd *abbr* master of education

me·da·ka \mə-ˈdä-kə\ *n* [Jp] (1933) **:** a small Japanese freshwater fish (*Oryzias latipes*) usu. silvery brown in the wild but from pale yellow to deep red in aquarium strains

[1]med·al \ˈme-dᵊl\ *n* [MF *medaille,* fr. OIt *medaglia* coin worth half a denarius, medal, fr. VL **medalis* half, alter. of LL *medialis* middle, fr. L *medius* — more at MID] (ca. 1578) **1 :** a small usu. metal object bearing a religious emblem or picture **2 :** a piece of metal often resembling a coin and having a stamped design that is issued to commemorate a person or event or awarded for excellence or achievement

[2]medal *vi* **med·aled** *also* **med·alled; med·al·ing** *also* **med·al·ling** \ˈmed-liŋ, ˈme-dᵊl-iŋ\ (1979) **:** to win a medal ⟨~*ed* in figure skating⟩

Medal for Merit (1942) **:** a U.S. decoration awarded to civilians for highly meritorious conduct in the performance of outstanding services

med·al·ist *or* **med·al·list** \ˈme-dᵊl-ist\ *n* (1685) **1 :** a designer, engraver, or maker of medals **2 :** a recipient of a medal as an award

me·dal·lic \mə-ˈda-lik\ *adj* (1702) **:** of, relating to, or shown on a medal

me·dal·lion \mə-ˈdal-yən\ *n* [F *médaillon,* fr. It *medaglione,* aug. of *medaglia*] (1658) **1 :** a large medal **2 :** something resembling a large medal; *esp* **:** a tablet or panel in a wall or window bearing a figure in relief, a portrait, or an ornament **3** *also* **me·dail·lon** \mā-dä-ˈyō^n\ **:** a small round or oval serving (as of meat)

Medal of Freedom (1945) **:** a U.S. decoration awarded to civilians for meritorious achievement in any of various fields

Medal of Honor (1861) **:** a U.S. military decoration awarded in the name of the Congress for conspicuous intrepidity at the risk of life in action with an enemy

medal play *n* (1816) **:** STROKE PLAY

med·dle \ˈme-dᵊl\ *vi* **med·dled; med·dling** \ˈmed-liŋ, ˈme-dᵊl-iŋ\ [ME *medlen,* fr. AF *mesler, medler,* fr. VL **misculare,* fr. L *miscēre* to mix — more at MIX] (14c) **:** to interest oneself in what is not one's concern **:** interfere without right or propriety — **med·dler** \ˈmed-lər, ˈme-dᵊl-ər\ *n*

med·dle·some \ˈme-dᵊl-səm\ *adj* (1615) **:** given to meddling ***syn*** see IMPERTINENT — **med·dle·some·ness** *n*

Mede \ˈmēd\ *n* [ME, fr. L *Medus,* fr. Gk *Mēdos*] (14c) **:** a native or inhabitant of ancient Media in Persia

Me·dea \mə-ˈdē-ə\ *n* [L, fr. Gk *Mēdeia*] (14c) **:** an enchantress noted in Greek mythology for helping Jason gain the Golden Fleece and for repeatedly resorting to murder to gain her ends

[1]med·e·vac *also* **med·i·vac** \ˈme-də-ˌvak, -dē-\ *n* [*med*ical *evac*uation] (1966) **1 :** emergency evacuation of the sick or wounded (as from a combat area) **2 :** a helicopter used for medevac

[2]medevac *also* **medivac** *vt* **med·e·vaced** *also* **med·i·vaced** *or* **med·e·vacked** *or* **med·i·vacked; med·e·vac·ing** *also* **med·i·vac·ing** *or* **med·e·vack·ing** *or* **med·i·vack·ing** (1969) **:** to transport in a medevac helicopter

med·fly \ˈmed-ˌflī\ *n, often cap* (1935) **:** MEDITERRANEAN FRUIT FLY

[1]me·dia \ˈmē-dē-ə\ *n, pl* **me·di·ae** \-dē-ˌē\ (1841) **1** [LL, fr. L, fem. of *medius;* fr. the voiced stops' being regarded as intermediate between the tenues and the aspirates] **:** a voiced stop **2** [NL, fr. L] **:** the middle coat of the wall of a blood or lymph vessel consisting chiefly of circular muscle fibers

[2]media *n, pl* **me·di·as** *often attrib* [pl. of *medium*] (1923) **1 :** a medium of cultivation, conveyance, or expression; *esp* **:** MEDIUM 2b **2 a** *sing or pl in constr* **:** MASS MEDIA **b** *pl* **:** members of the mass media

usage The singular *media* and its plural *medias* seem to have originated in the field of advertising over 70 years ago; they are still so used without stigma in that specialized field. In most other applications *media* is used as a plural of *medium.* The popularity of the word in references to the agencies of mass communication is leading to the formation of a mass noun, construed as a singular ⟨there's no basis for it. You know, the news *media* gets on to something —Edwin Meese 3d⟩ ⟨the *media* is less interested in the party's policies —James Lewis, *Guardian Weekly*⟩. This use is not as well established as the mass-noun use of *data* and is likely to incur criticism esp. in writing.

me·di·ad \ˈmē-dē-ˌad\ *adv* (1878) **:** toward the median line or plane of a body or part

media event *n* (1972) **:** a publicity event staged for coverage by the news media

me·dia·gen·ic \ˌmē-dē-ə-ˈje-nik\ *adj* (1971) **:** attractive or well-suited to the communications media

me·di·al \ˈmē-dē-əl\ *adj* [LL *medialis,* fr. L *medius*] (1570) **1 :** MEAN, AVERAGE **2 a :** being or occurring in the middle **b :** extending toward the middle; *esp* **:** lying or extending toward the median axis of the body **3 :** situated between the extremes of initial and final in a word or morpheme — **medial** *n* — **me·di·al·ly** \-ə-lē\ *adv*

medial collateral ligament *n* (1950) **:** a ligament of the inner knee that connects medial parts of the femur and tibia and helps to stabilize the knee joint — called also *MCL*

[1]me·di·an \ˈmē-dē-ən\ *n* [ME *mediane,* fr. LL *mediana* (*vena*) median (vein), fr. fem. of L *medianus* in the middle, central, fr. *medius* middle — more at MID] (15c) **1 :** a medial part (as a vein or nerve) **2 a :** a value in an ordered set of values below and above which there is an equal number of values or which is the arithmetic mean of the two middle values if there is no one middle number **b :** a vertical line that divides the histogram of a frequency distribution into two parts of equal area **c :** a value of a random variable for which all greater values make the cumulative distribution function greater than one half and all lesser values make it less than one half **3 a :** a line from a vertex of a triangle to the midpoint of the opposite side **b :** a line joining the midpoints of the nonparallel sides of a trapezoid **4 :** MEDIAN STRIP ***syn*** see AVERAGE

[2]median *adj* [L *medianus*] (1592) **1 :** being in the middle or in an intermediate position **:** MEDIAL **2 :** lying in the plane dividing a bilateral animal into right and left halves **3 :** relating to or constituting a statistical median **4 :** produced without occlusion along the lengthwise middle line of the tongue — **me·di·an·ly** *adv*

median nerve *n* (1807) **:** a nerve that arises by two roots from the brachial plexus and passes down the middle of the front of the arm

median strip *n* (1948) **:** a paved or planted strip dividing a highway into lanes according to direction of travel

me·di·ant \ˈmē-dē-ənt\ *n* [It *mediante,* fr. LL *mediant-, medians,* prp. of *mediare* to be in the middle] (1822) **:** the third tone of a major or minor scale

me·dia·scape \ˈmē-dē-ə-ˌskāp\ *n* (1968) **1 :** the mélange of mass media within an area **2 :** the various images, sounds, and programs presented by the mass media

me·di·as·ti·num \ˌmē-dē-ə-ˈstī-nəm\ *n, pl* **-na** \-nə\ [NL, fr. ML, neut. of *mediastinus* medial, fr. L *medius*] (1541) **:** the space in the chest between the pleural sacs of the lungs that contains all the tissues and organs of the chest except the lungs and pleurae; *also* **:** this space with its contents — **me·di·as·ti·nal** \-ˈstī-nᵊl\ *adj*

[1]me·di·ate \ˈmē-dē-ət\ *adj* [ME, fr. LL *mediatus* intermediate, fr. pp. of *mediare*] (15c) **1 :** occupying a middle position **2 a :** acting through an intervening agency **b :** exhibiting indirect causation, connection, or relation — **me·di·a·cy** \-dē-ə-sē\ *n* — **me·di·ate·ly** *adv*

[2]me·di·ate \ˈmē-dē-ˌāt\ *vb* **-at·ed; -at·ing** [ML *mediatus,* pp. of *mediare,* fr. LL, to be in the middle, fr. L *medius* middle] *vt* (1568) **1 a :** to bring accord out of by action as an intermediary **b :** to effect by action as an intermediary **2 a :** to act as intermediary agent in bringing, effecting, or communicating **:** CONVEY **b :** to transmit as intermediate mechanism or agency ~ *vi* **1 :** to interpose between parties in order to reconcile them **2 :** to reconcile differences ***syn*** see INTERPOSE — **me·di·a·tive** \-ˌā-tiv\ *adj* — **me·di·a·to·ry** \-ə-ˌtȯr-ē\ *adj*

me·di·a·tion \ˌmē-dē-ˈā-shən\ *n* (14c) **:** the act or process of mediating; *esp* **:** intervention between conflicting parties to promote reconciliation, settlement, or compromise — **me·di·a·tion·al** \-shnəl, -shə-nᵊl\ *adj*

me·di·a·tor \ˈmē-dē-ˌā-tər\ *n* (14c) **1 :** one that mediates; *esp* **:** one that mediates between parties at variance **2 :** a mediating agent in a physical, chemical, or biological process

me·di·a·trix \-ˈā-triks\ *n* (15c) **:** a woman who is a mediator

[1]med·ic \ˈme-dik\ *n* [ME *medike,* fr. L *medica,* fr. Gk *mēdikē,* fr. fem. of *mēdikos* of Media, fr. *Mēdia* Media] (15c) **:** any of a genus (*Medicago*) of leguminous herbs (as alfalfa)

[2]medic *n* [L *medicus*] (1625) **:** one engaged in medical work or study; *esp* **:** CORPSMAN

med·i·ca·ble \ˈme-di-kə-bəl\ *adj* (ca. 1616) **:** CURABLE, REMEDIABLE

Med·ic·aid \ˈme-di-ˌkād\ *n* [*medical aid*] (1966) : a program of medical aid designed for those unable to afford regular medical service and financed by the state and federal governments

med·i·cal \ˈme-di-kəl\ *adj* [F or LL; F *médical,* fr. LL *medicalis,* fr. L *medicus* physician, fr. *mederi* to remedy, heal; akin to Av vī-*mad*- healer, Gk *medesthai* to be mindful of — more at METE] (1646) **1** : of, relating to, or concerned with physicians or the practice of medicine **2** : requiring or devoted to medical treatment — **med·i·cal·ly** \-k(ə-)lē\ *adv*

medical examiner *n* (1877) : a public officer who conducts autopsies on bodies to find the cause of death

med·i·cal·ize \ˈme-di-kə-ˌlīz\ *vt* **-ized; -iz·ing** (1970) : to view or treat as a medical concern, problem, or disorder ⟨those who seek to dispose of social problems by *medicalizing* them —Liam Hudson⟩ — **med·i·cal·i·za·tion** \ˌme-di-kə-lə-ˈzā-shən\ *n*

me·di·ca·ment \mi-ˈdi-kə-mənt, ˈme-di-kə-\ *n* [ME, fr. MF, fr. L *medicamentum,* fr. *medicare*] (15c) : a substance used in therapy — **me·di·ca·men·tous** \mi-ˌdi-kə-ˈmen-təs, ˌme-di-kə-\ *adj*

Medi·care \ˈme-di-ˌker\ *n* [blend of *medical* and *care*] (1955) : a government program of medical care esp. for the aged

med·i·cate \ˈme-də-ˌkāt\ *vt* **-cat·ed; -cat·ing** [L *medicatus,* pp. of *medicare* to heal, fr. *medicus*] (ca. 1623) **1** : to treat medicinally **2** : to impregnate with a medicinal substance ⟨*medicated* soap⟩

med·i·ca·tion \ˌme-də-ˈkā-shən\ *n* (15c) **1** : the act or process of medicating **2** : a medicinal substance : MEDICAMENT

me·dic·i·na·ble \mi-ˈdis-nə-bəl, -ˈdi-sə-nə-; *in Shak* ˈmed-sə-nə-\ *adj* (14c) : MEDICINAL

me·dic·i·nal \mə-ˈdis-nəl, -ˈdi-sᵊn-əl; *in Shak & Milton* ˌme-di-ˈsī-nᵊl & ˈmed-sə-nəl\ *adj* (14c) **1** : tending or used to cure disease or relieve pain **2** : SALUTARY — **medicinal** *n* — **me·dic·i·nal·ly** *adv*

medicinal leech *n* (1804) : a large European freshwater leech (*Hirudo medicinalis*) that is a source of hirudin, is sometimes used to drain blood (as from newly grafted tissue), and was formerly used to bleed patients thought to have excess blood

med·i·cine \ˈme-də-sən, *Brit usu* ˈmed-sən\ *n* [ME, fr. AF, fr. L *medicina,* fr. fem. of *medicinus* of a physician, fr. *medicus*] (13c) **1 a** : a substance or preparation used in treating disease **b** : something that affects well-being **2 a** : the science and art dealing with the maintenance of health and the prevention, alleviation, or cure of disease **b** : the branch of medicine concerned with the nonsurgical treatment of disease **3** : a substance (as a drug or potion) used to treat something other than disease **4** : an object held in traditional American Indian belief to give control over natural or magical forces; *also* : magical power or a magical rite — **medicine** *vt*

medicine ball *n* (1895) : a heavy usu. large ball used esp. in conditioning and strengthening exercises

medicine dropper *n* (1868) : DROPPER 2

medicine man *n* (1801) : a priestly healer or sorcerer esp. among the American Indians : SHAMAN

medicine show *n* (1887) : a traveling show using entertainers to attract a crowd among which remedies or nostrums are sold

med·i·co \ˈme-di-ˌkō\ *n, pl* **-cos** [It *medico* or Sp *médico,* both fr. L *medicus*] (1689) : PHYSICIAN 1; *also* : a medical student

med·i·co·le·gal \ˌme-di-kō-ˈlē-gəl\ *adj* [NL *medicolegalis,* fr. L *medicus* medical + *-o-* + *legalis* legal] (1835) : of or relating to both medicine and law

¹me·di·e·val *also* **me·di·ae·val** \ˌmē-ˈdē-vəl, mi-, ˌme-, -dē-ˈē-vəl\ *adj* [NL *medium aevum* Middle Ages] (1827) **1** : of, relating to, or characteristic of the Middle Ages **2** : having a quality (as cruelty) associated with the Middle Ages **3** : extremely outmoded or antiquated — **me·di·e·val·ly** *adv*

²medieval *also* **mediaeval** *n* (1856) : a person of the Middle Ages

me·di·e·val·ism \-və-ˌli-zəm\ *n* (1853) **1** : medieval quality, character, or state **2** : devotion to the institutions, arts, and practices of the Middle Ages

me·di·e·val·ist \-ˈdē-vist, -ˈdē-və-, -dē-ˈēv-, -dē-ˈē-və-\ *n* (1855) **1** : a specialist in medieval history and culture **2** : a connoisseur or devotee of medieval arts and culture

Medieval Latin *n* (1855) : the Latin used esp. for liturgical and literary purposes from the 7th to the 15th centuries inclusive

med·i·gap \ˈme-də-ˌgap\ *n, often cap, often attrib* [*Medicare* + *gap*] (1975) : supplemental health insurance that covers costs (as of medical care or a hospital stay) not covered by Medicare

me·di·na \mə-ˈdē-nə\ *n* [Ar *madīna* city] (1906) : the non-European part of a northern African city

me·di·o·cre \ˌmē-dē-ˈō-kər\ *adj* [MF, fr. L *mediocris,* fr. *medius* middle + OL *ocris* stony mountain; akin to L *acer* sharp — more at EDGE] (ca. 1586) : of moderate or low quality, value, ability, or performance : ORDINARY, SO-SO

me·di·oc·ri·ty \ˌmē-dē-ˈä-krə-tē\ *n, pl* **-ties** (1588) **1 a** : the quality or state of being mediocre **b** : moderate ability or value **2** : a mediocre person

med·i·tate \ˈme-də-ˌtāt\ *vb* **-tat·ed; -tat·ing** [L *meditatus,* pp. of *meditari,* freq. of *mederi* to remedy — more at MEDICAL] *vi* (1560) **1** : to engage in contemplation or reflection **2** : to engage in mental exercise (as concentration on one's breathing or repetition of a mantra) for the purpose of reaching a heightened level of spiritual awareness ~ *vt* **1** : to focus one's thoughts on : reflect on or ponder over **2** : to plan or project in the mind : INTEND, PURPOSE ***syn*** see PONDER — **med·i·ta·tor** \-ˌtā-tər\ *n*

med·i·ta·tion \ˌme-də-ˈtā-shən\ *n* (13c) **1** : a discourse intended to express its author's reflections or to guide others in contemplation **2** : the act or process of meditating

med·i·ta·tive \ˈme-də-ˌtā-tiv\ *adj* (1611) **1** : marked by or conducive to meditation **2** : disposed or given to meditation — **med·i·ta·tive·ly** *adv* — **med·i·ta·tive·ness** *n*

Med·i·ter·ra·nean \ˌme-də-tə-ˈrā-nē-ən, -nyən\ *adj* (15c) **1 a** : of, relating to, or characteristic of the Mediterranean Sea **b** : of, relating to, or characteristic of the peoples, lands, or cultures bordering the Mediterranean Sea **2** *not cap* [L *mediterraneus,* fr. *medius* middle + *terra* land — more at TERRACE] : enclosed or nearly enclosed with land **3** : of or relating to a group or physical type of the Caucasian race characterized by medium or short stature, slender build, dolichocephaly, and dark complexion

Mediterranean flour moth *n* (1895) : a small largely gray and black nearly cosmopolitan pyralid moth (*Anagasta kuehniella*) whose larva destroys processed grain products

Mediterranean fruit fly *n* (1899) : a small widely distributed yellowish-brown dipteran fly (*Ceratitis capitata*) with a banded abdomen whose larva lives and feeds in ripening fruit — called also *medfly*

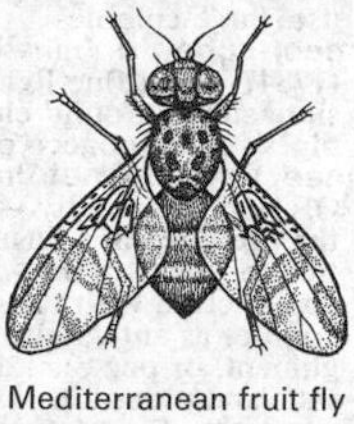
Mediterranean fruit fly

¹me·di·um \ˈmē-dē-əm\ *n, pl* **mediums** *or* **me·dia** \-dē-ə\ [L, fr. neuter of *medius* middle — more at MID] (1589) **1 a** : something in a middle position **b** : a middle condition or degree : MEAN **2** : a means of effecting or conveying something: as **a** (1) : a substance regarded as the means of transmission of a force or effect (2) : a surrounding or enveloping substance (3) : the tenuous material (as gas and dust) in space that exists outside large agglomerations of matter (as stars) ⟨interstellar ~⟩ **b** *pl usu* **media** (1) : a channel or system of communication, information, or entertainment — compare MASS MEDIUM (2) : a publication or broadcast that carries advertising (3) : a mode of artistic expression or communication (4) : something (as a magnetic disk) on which information may be stored **c** : GO-BETWEEN, INTERMEDIARY **d** *pl* **mediums** : an individual held to be a channel of communication between the earthly world and a world of spirits **e** : material or technical means of artistic expression **3 a** : a condition or environment in which something may function or flourish **b** *pl* **media** (1) : a nutrient system for the artificial cultivation of cells or organisms and esp. bacteria (2) : a fluid or solid in which organic structures are placed (as for preservation or mounting) **c** : a liquid with which pigment is mixed by a painter ***usage*** see MEDIA

²medium *adj* (1711) : intermediate in quantity, quality, position, size, or degree

medium frequency *n* (1920) : a radio frequency between high frequency and low frequency — see RADIO FREQUENCY table

me·di·um·is·tic \ˌmē-dē-ə-ˈmis-tik\ *adj* (1860) : of, relating to, or having the qualities of a spiritualistic medium

medium of exchange (1714) : something commonly accepted in exchange for goods and services and recognized as representing a standard of value

me·di·um·ship \ˈmē-dē-əm-ˌship\ *n* (1856) : the capacity, function, or profession of a spiritualistic medium

medivac *var of* MEDEVAC

med·lar \ˈmed-lər\ *n* [ME *medeler,* fr. AF *medler,* fr. *medle* medlar fruit, fr. L *mespilum,* fr. Gk *mespilon*] (14c) : a small deciduous Eurasian tree (*Mespilus germanica*) of the rose family whose fruit resembles a crab apple and is used in preserves; *also* : its fruit

¹med·ley \ˈmed-lē\ *n, pl* **medleys** [ME *medle,* fr. AF *medlee,* fr. fem. of *medlé,* pp. of *medler* to mix — more at MEDDLE] (14c) **1** *archaic* : MELEE **2** : a diverse assortment or mixture; *esp* : HODGEPODGE **3** : a musical composition made up of a series of songs or short pieces

²medley *adj* (14c) : MIXED, MOTLEY

medley relay *n* (1928) : a relay race in swimming in which each member of a team uses a different stroke

Mé·doc \mā-ˈdäk, -ˈdȯk\ *n* [F, fr. *Médoc*] (1783) : a Bordeaux wine made in the Médoc district of France

me·dul·la \mə-ˈdə-lə\ *n, pl* **-las** *or* **-lae** \-(ˌ)lē, -ˌlī\ [ME, fr. L] (15c) **1** *pl* **medullae a** : BONE MARROW **b** : MEDULLA OBLONGATA **2 a** : the inner or deep part of an animal or plant structure ⟨the adrenal ~⟩ **b** : MYELIN SHEATH

medulla ob·lon·ga·ta \-ˌä-ˌblȯŋ-ˈgä-tə\ *n, pl* **medulla oblongatas** *or* **medullae ob·lon·ga·tae** \-ˈgä-tē, -ˌtī\ [NL, lit., oblong medulla] (1668) : the part of the vertebrate brain that is continuous posteriorly with the spinal cord and that contains the centers controlling involuntary vital functions — see BRAIN illustration

med·ul·lary \ˈme-də-ˌler-ē, ˈme-jə-; mə-ˈdə-lə-rē\ *adj* (1830) **1** : of or relating to the pith of a plant **2** : of or relating to a medulla and esp. the medulla oblongata

medullary ray *n* (1830) **1** : a primary tissue composed of radiating bands of parenchyma cells extending between the vascular bundles of herbaceous dicotyledonous stems and connecting the pith with the cortex **2** : VASCULAR RAY

medullary sheath *n* (ca. 1846) : MYELIN SHEATH

med·ul·lat·ed \ˈme-də-ˌlā-təd, ˈme-jə-\ *adj* (1867) **1** : MYELINATED **2** : having a medulla — used of fibers other than nerve fibers

me·dul·lo·blas·to·ma \mə-ˌdə-lō-ˌblas-ˈtō-mə\ *n, pl* **-mas** *also* **-ma·ta** \-mə-tə\ [NL, fr. *medulla* + *-o-* + *blast-* + *-oma*] (1925) : a malignant tumor of the central nervous system arising in the cerebellum esp. in children

me·du·sa \mi-ˈdü-sə, -ˈdyü-, -zə\ *n* (14c) **1** *cap* [L, fr. Gk *Medousa*] : a mortal Gorgon who is slain when decapitated by Perseus **2** *pl* **me·du·sae** \-ˌsē, -ˌzē, -ˌsī, -ˌzī\ *also* **medusas** [NL, fr. L] : JELLYFISH 1a — **me·du·san** \-sᵊn, -zᵊn\ *adj or n* — **me·du·soid** \-ˌsȯid, -ˌzȯid\ *adj or n*

meed \ˈmēd\ *n* [ME, fr. OE *mēd*; akin to OHG *miata* reward, Gk *misthos*] (bef. 12c) **1** *archaic* : an earned reward or wage **2** : a fitting return or recompense

meek \ˈmēk\ *adj* [ME, of Scand origin; akin to ON *mjūkr* gentle; akin to W *esmwyth* soft] (13c) **1** : enduring injury with patience and without resentment : MILD **2** : deficient in spirit and courage : SUBMISSIVE **3** : not violent or strong : MODERATE — **meek·ly** *adv* — **meek·ness** *n*

meer·kat \ˈmir-ˌkat\ *n* [Afrik, fr. D, a kind of monkey, fr. MD *meercatte* monkey, fr. *meer* sea + *catte*

meerkat

cat] (1801) : any of several African mongooses; *esp* : a burrowing highly social primarily insectivorous mammal (*Suricata suricatta*) of southern Africa that is chiefly grayish with faint black markings and lives in usu. large colonies

meer·schaum \ˈmir-shəm, -ˌshȯm\ *n* [G, fr. *Meer* sea + *Schaum* foam] (1784) **1** : a fine light white clayey mineral that is a hydrous magnesium silicate found chiefly in Asia Minor and is used esp. for tobacco pipes **2** : a tobacco pipe of meerschaum

1**meet** \ˈmēt\ *vb* **met** \ˈmet\; **meet·ing** [ME *meten,* fr. OE *mētan;* akin to OE *gemōt* assembly — more at MOOT] *vt* (bef. 12c) **1 a** : to come into the presence of : FIND **b** : to come together with esp. at a particular time or place ⟨I'll ~ you at the station⟩ **c** : to come into contact or conjunction with : JOIN **d** : to appear to the perception of **2** : to encounter as antagonist or foe : OPPOSE **3** : to enter into conference, argument, or personal dealings with **4** : to conform to esp. with exactitude and precision ⟨a concept to ~ all requirements⟩ **5** : to pay fully : SETTLE **6** : to cope with ⟨was able to ~ every social situation⟩ **7** : to provide for ⟨enough money to ~ our needs⟩ **8** : to become acquainted with **9** : ENCOUNTER, EXPERIENCE **10** : to receive or greet in an official capacity ~ *vi* **1 a** : to come face-to-face **b** : to come together for a common purpose : ASSEMBLE **c** : to come together as contestants, opponents, or enemies **2** : to form a junction or confluence ⟨the lines ~ in a point⟩ **3** : to occur together — **meet·er** *n* — **meet halfway** : to compromise with — **meet with** : to be subjected to : ENCOUNTER ⟨the proposal *met with* opposition⟩

2**meet** *n* (1804) **1** : the act of assembling for a hunt or for competitive sports **2** : a competition in which individuals match skills

3**meet** *adj* [ME *mete,* fr. OE *gemǣte;* akin to OE *metan* to mete] (14c) : precisely adapted to a particular situation, need, or circumstance : very proper ***syn*** see FIT — **meet·ly** *adv*

meet and greet *n* (1986) : a reception at which a public figure (as a politician or rock star) socializes with press members and other guests

meeting *n* (14c) **1** : an act or process of coming together: as **a** : an assembly for a common purpose (as worship) **b** : a session of horse or dog racing **2** : a permanent organizational unit of the Society of Friends **3** : INTERSECTION, JUNCTION

meet·ing·house \-ˌhau̇s\ *n* (1632) : a building used for public assembly and esp. for Protestant worship

meeting of minds (1883) : AGREEMENT, CONCORD

mef·lo·quine \ˈmef-lə-ˌkwīn\ *n* [*meth-* + *fluor-* + *quino*line] (1974) : an antimalarial drug $C_{17}H_{16}F_6N_2O$ similar to quinine that is administered in the form of its hydrochloride

1**meg** \ˈmeg\ *n* (1975) : MEGABYTE

2**meg** *abbr* megohm

MEG *abbr* magnetoencephalography

mega \ˈme-gə\ *adj* [*mega-*] (1968) **1** : VAST ⟨a ~ electronics store⟩ **2** : of the highest level of rank, excellence, or importance ⟨a number one hit made her ~⟩

mega- *or* **meg-** *comb form* [Gk, fr. *megas* large — more at MUCH] **1 a** : great : large ⟨*mega*spore⟩ **b** : greatly surpassing others of its kind ⟨*mega*hit⟩ **2** : million (10^6) ⟨*meg*ohm⟩ ⟨*mega*cycle⟩

mega·bar \ˈme-gə-ˌbär\ *n* [ISV] (1903) : a unit of pressure equal to one million bars

mega·bit \-ˌbit\ *n* (1956) : one million bits

mega·buck \-ˌbək\ *n* (1946) : one million dollars; *also* : an indeterminately large sum of money — usu. used in pl.

mega·byte \-ˌbīt\ *n* [fr. the fact that 1,048,576 (2^{20}) is the power of 2 closest to one million] (1965) : 1024 kilobytes or 1,048,576 bytes; *also* : one million bytes

mega·city \-ˌsi-tē\ *n* (1967) : MEGALOPOLIS 1

mega·cor·po·ra·tion \ˌme-gə-ˌkȯr-pə-ˈrā-shən\ *n* (1971) : a huge and powerful corporation

mega·cy·cle \ˈme-gə-ˌsī-kəl\ *n* (1926) : one million cycles; *esp* : MEGAHERTZ

mega·deal \-ˌdēl\ *n* (1978) : a business deal involving a lot of money

mega·death \-ˌdeth\ *n* (1953) : one million deaths — usu. used as a unit in reference to nuclear warfare

mega·dose \-ˌdōs\ *n* (1971) : a large dose (as of a vitamin)

mega·fau·na \-ˌfȯ-nə, -ˌfä-\ *n* (1927) **1** : animals (as bears, bison, or mammoths) of particularly large size **2** : fauna consisting of individuals large enough to be visible to the naked eye — **mega·fau·nal** \-nᵊl\ *adj*

mega·ga·mete \ˌme-gə-ˈga-ˌmēt *also* -gə-ˈmēt\ *n* (1891) : MACROGAMETE

mega·ga·me·to·phyte \-gə-ˈmē-tə-ˌfīt\ *n* (1915) : the female gametophyte produced by a megaspore

mega·hertz \ˈme-gə-ˌhərts, -ˌherts\ *n* [ISV] (1941) : a unit of frequency equal to one million hertz — abbr. *MHz*

mega·hit \-ˌhit\ *n* (1977) : something (as a motion picture) that is extremely successful

mega·kar·yo·cyte \ˌme-gə-ˈka-rē-ō-ˌsīt\ *n* (1890) : a large cell that has a lobulated nucleus, is found esp. in the bone marrow, and is the source of blood platelets — **mega·kar·yo·cyt·ic** \-ˌka-rē-ō-ˈsi-tik\ *adj*

megal- *or* **megalo-** *comb form* [NL, fr. Gk, fr. *megal-, megas* — more at MUCH] : large : of giant size ⟨*megalo*polis⟩ : grandiose ⟨*megalo*mania⟩

mega·lith \ˈme-gə-ˌlith\ *n* (1853) : a very large usu. rough stone used in prehistoric cultures as a monument or building block — **mega·lith·ic** \ˌme-gə-ˈli-thik\ *adj*

meg·a·lo·blast \ˈme-gə-lō-ˌblast\ *n* (1890) : a large erythroblast that appears in the blood esp. in pernicious anemia — **meg·a·lo·blas·tic** \ˌme-gə-lō-ˈblas-tik\ *adj*

meg·a·lo·ma·nia \ˌme-gə-lō-ˈmā-nē-ə, -nyə\ *n* [NL] (1885) **1** : a mania for great or grandiose performance **2** : a delusional mental disorder that is marked by feelings of personal omnipotence and grandeur — **meg·a·lo·ma·ni·ac** \-ˈmā-nē-ˌak\ *adj or n* — **meg·a·lo·ma·ni·a·cal** \-mə-ˈnī-ə-kəl\ *also* **meg·a·lo·man·ic** \-ˈma-nik\ *adj* — **meg·a·lo·ma·ni·a·cal·ly** \-mə-ˈnī-ə-k(ə-)lē\ *adv*

meg·a·lop·o·lis \ˌme-gə-ˈlä-pə-ləs\ *n* (ca. 1828) **1** : a very large city **2** : a thickly populated region centering in a metropolis or embracing several metropolises — **meg·a·lo·pol·i·tan** \-lō-ˈpä-lə-tən\ *n or adj*

-megaly *n comb form* [NL *-megalia,* fr. Gk *megal-, megas*] : abnormal enlargement ⟨hepato*megaly*⟩

mega·merg·er \ˈme-gə-ˌmər-jər\ *n* (1980) : a merger of megacorporations

mega·par·sec \ˌme-gə-ˈpär-ˌsek\ *n* [ISV] (1920) : a unit of measure for distances in intergalactic space equal to one million parsecs

1**mega·phone** \ˈme-gə-ˌfōn\ *n* (1878) : a cone-shaped device used to intensify or direct the voice — **mega·phon·ic** \ˌme-gə-ˈfä-nik\ *adj*

2**megaphone** *vt* (1901) : to transmit or address through or as if through a megaphone ~ *vi* : to speak through or as if through a megaphone

mega·pix·el \ˈme-gə-ˌpik-səl, -ˌsel\ *n* (1983) : one million pixels

mega·plex \-ˌpleks\ *n* (1986) : a large multiplex typically housing 16 or more movie theaters

mega·proj·ect \-ˌprä-ˌjekt, -jikt *also* -ˌprō-\ *n* (1976) : a major project or undertaking (as in business or construction)

Me·gar·i·an \mə-ˈga-rē-ən, me-\ *adj* (1603) : of or relating to a Socratic school of philosophy founded by Euclid of Megara and noted for its subtle attention to logic — **Megarian** *n*

Me·gar·ic \-ˈga-rik\ *adj* (1656) : MEGARIAN — **Megaric** *n*

mega·scop·ic \ˌme-gə-ˈskä-pik\ *adj* [*mega-* + *-scopic* (as in *microscopic*)] (1879) **1** : MACROSCOPIC 1 **2** : based on or relating to observations made with the unaided eye — **mega·scop·i·cal·ly** \-pi-k(ə-)lē\ *adv*

mega·spo·ran·gi·um \ˌme-gə-spə-ˈran-jē-əm\ *n* [NL] (1886) : a sporangium that develops only megaspores

mega·spore \ˈme-gə-ˌspȯr\ *n* [ISV] (1857) : a spore in heterosporous plants giving rise to female gametophytes and usu. larger than a microspore — **mega·spor·ic** \ˌme-gə-ˈspȯr-ik\ *adj*

mega·spo·ro·gen·e·sis \ˌme-gə-ˌspȯr-ə-ˈje-nə-səs\ *n* [NL] (1909) : the formation and maturation of a megaspore

mega·spo·ro·phyll \-ˈspȯr-ə-ˌfil\ *n* (ca. 1899) : a sporophyll that develops only megasporangia

mega·star \ˈme-gə-ˌstär\ *n* (1969) : SUPERSTAR — **mega·star·dom** \-dəm\ *n*

mega·ton \ˈme-gə-ˌtən\ *n* (1952) : an explosive force equivalent to that of one million tons of TNT

mega·ton·nage \-ˌtə-nij\ *n* (1955) : the destructive capability esp. of a collection of nuclear weapons that is expressed in megatons

mega·vi·ta·min \ˌme-gə-ˈvī-tə-mən, *Brit usu* -ˈvi-\ *adj* (1968) : relating to or consisting of very large doses of vitamins ⟨~ therapy⟩

mega·vi·ta·mins \-mənz\ *n pl* (1974) : a large quantity of vitamins

mega·watt \ˈme-gə-ˌwät\ *n* [ISV] (ca. 1900) : one million watts

me·gil·lah \mə-ˈgi-lə\ *n* [Yiddish *megile,* fr. Heb *mĕgillāh* scroll, volume (used esp. of the Book of Esther, read aloud at the Purim celebration)] (1943) *slang* : a long involved story or account ⟨the whole ~⟩

me·gilp \mə-ˈgilp\ *n* [origin unknown] (1768) : a gelatinous preparation commonly of linseed oil and mastic varnish that is used by artists as a vehicle for oil colors

MEGO *abbr* my eyes glaze over

meg·ohm \ˈmeg-ˌōm\ *n* [ISV] (1867) : one million ohms

me·grim \ˈmē-grəm\ *n* [ME *migreime,* fr. MF *migraine* — more at MIGRAINE] (15c) **1 a** : MIGRAINE **b** : VERTIGO, DIZZINESS **2 a** : FANCY, WHIM **b** *pl* : low spirits

1**meh** \ˈme\ *interj* (1994) — used to express indifference or mild disappointment

2**meh** *adj* (2003) **1** : not impressive : SO-SO ⟨a ~ documentary⟩ **2** : APATHETIC, INDIFFERENT ⟨the movie left me feeling ~⟩

Mei·ji \ˈmā-(ˌ)jē\ *n, often attrib* [Jp, lit., enlightened rule] (1873) : the period of the reign (1868–1912) of Emperor Mutsuhito of Japan

meikle *var of* MICKLE

mei·ny *n, pl* **meinies** [ME *meynie,* fr. AF *mesnee* — more at MENIAL] (13c) **1** \ˈmā-nē\ *archaic* : RETINUE, COMPANY **2** \ˈmen-yē\ *chiefly Scot* : MULTITUDE

mei·o·sis \mī-ˈō-səs\ *n* [NL, fr. Gk *meiōsis* diminution, fr. *meioun* to diminish, fr. *meiōn* less; akin to Skt *mīyate* he diminishes] (1550) **1** : the presentation of a thing with underemphasis esp. in order to achieve a greater effect : UNDERSTATEMENT **2** : the cellular process that results in the number of chromosomes in gamete-producing cells being reduced to one half and that involves a reduction division in which one of each pair of homologous chromosomes passes to each daughter cell and a mitotic division — compare MITOSIS — **mei·ot·ic** \mī-ˈä-tik\ *adj* — **mei·ot·i·cal·ly** \-ti-k(ə-)lē\ *adv*

Meis·sen \ˈmī-sᵊn\ *n* [*Meissen,* Saxony, Germany] (1863) : a ceramic ware made at Meissen near Dresden; *esp* : a European porcelain developed under the patronage of the king of Saxony about 1715 and used for both ornamental and table wares — called also *Meissen china, Meissen ware*

meis·ter \ˈmīs-tər\ *n* [Yiddish *mayster* & G *Meister* master, fr. MHG *meister,* fr. OHG *meistar,* fr. L *magister* — more at MASTER] (1979) : one who is knowledgeable about something specified — often used in combination ⟨puzzle-*meister*⟩

Meis·ter·sing·er \ˈmīs-tər-ˌsiŋ-ər, -ˌziŋ-\ *n, pl* **Meistersinger** *or* **Meistersingers** [G, fr. MHG, *meister* master + *singer* singer] (1818) : a member of any of various German guilds formed chiefly in the 15th and 16th centuries by workingmen and craftsmen for the cultivation of poetry and music

meit·ner·i·um \mīt-ˈnir-ē-əm, -ˈner-\ *n* [NL, fr. Lise *Meitner*] (1992) : a short-lived radioactive element produced artificially — see ELEMENT table

MEK *abbr* methyl ethyl ketone

mel·a·leu·ca \ˌme-lə-ˈl(y)ü-kə\ *n* [NL, fr. Gk *melas* black + *leuka,* fem. of *leukos* white — more at LIGHT] (1790) : any of a genus (*Melaleuca*) of Australian and southeast Asian trees and shrubs of the myrtle family; *esp* : CAJEPUT

mel·a·mine \ˈme-lə-ˌmēn\ *n* [G *Melamin*] (ca. 1835) **1** : a white crystalline organic base $C_3H_6N_6$ with a high melting point that is used esp. in melamine resins **2** : a melamine resin or a plastic made from such a resin

melamine resin *n* (1939) : a thermosetting resin made from melamine and an aldehyde and used esp. in molded or laminated products, adhesives, and coatings

melan- *or* **melano-** *comb form* [Gk, fr. *melan-, melas;* perh. akin to Lith *mėlynas* blue, Skt *malina* dirty] **1** : black : dark ⟨*melan*ic⟩ ⟨*melan*in⟩ **2** : melanin ⟨*melano*phore⟩

mel·an·cho·lia \ˌme-lən-ˈkō-lē-ə\ *n* [NL, fr. LL, melancholy] (1607) : a mental condition and esp. a manic-depressive condition characterized by extreme depression, bodily complaints, and often hallucinations and delusions — **mel·an·cho·li·ac** \-lē-ˌak\ *n*

mel·an·chol·ic \ˌme-lən-ˈkä-lik\ *adj* (14c) **1 :** of, relating to, or subject to melancholy : DEPRESSED **2 :** of or relating to melancholia **3 :** tending to depress the spirits : SADDENING — **melancholic** *n*

[1]**mel·an·choly** \ˈme-lən-ˌkä-lē\ *n, pl* **-chol·ies** [ME *malencolie,* fr. AF, fr. LL *melancholia,* fr. Gk, fr. *melan-* + *cholē* bile — more at GALL] (14c) **1 a :** an abnormal state attributed to an excess of black bile and characterized by irascibility or depression **b :** BLACK BILE **c :** MELANCHOLIA **2 a :** depression of spirits : DEJECTION **b :** a pensive mood

[2]**melancholy** *adj* (14c) **1 a :** suggestive or expressive of melancholy ⟨sang in a ~ voice⟩ **b :** causing or tending to cause sadness or depression of mind or spirit : DISMAL ⟨a ~ thought⟩ **2 a :** depressed in spirits : DEJECTED, SAD **b :** PENSIVE

Mel·a·ne·sian \ˌme-lə-ˈnē-zhən, -shən\ *n* (1845) **1 :** a member of the dominant native group of Melanesia **2 :** a language group consisting of the Austronesian languages of Melanesia — **Melanesian** *adj*

mé·lange \mā-ˈläⁿzh, -ˈlänj\ *n* [F, fr. MF, fr. *mesler, meler* to mix — more at MEDDLE] (1653) : a mixture often of incongruous elements

[1]**me·lan·ic** \mə-ˈla-nik\ *adj* (1826) **1 :** MELANOTIC **2 :** affected with, causing, or characterized by melanism

[2]**melanic** *n* (1920) : a melanic individual

mel·a·nin \ˈme-lə-nən\ *n* (1843) : any of various black, dark brown, reddish-brown, or yellow pigments of animal or plant structures (as skin or hair)

mel·a·nism \ˈme-lə-ˌni-zəm\ *n* (1843) **1 :** an increased amount of black or nearly black pigmentation (as of skin, feathers, or hair) of an individual or kind of organism — compare INDUSTRIAL MELANISM **2 :** intense human pigmentation of the skin, eyes, and hair — **mel·a·nis·tic** \ˌme-lə-ˈnis-tik\ *adj*

mel·a·nite \ˈme-lə-ˌnīt\ *n* [G *Melanit,* fr. *melan-*] (ca. 1807) : a black andradite garnet — **mel·a·nit·ic** \ˌme-lə-ˈni-tik\ *adj*

mel·a·nize \ˈme-lə-ˌnīz\ *vt* **-nized; -niz·ing** (1978) **1 :** to convert into or infiltrate with melanin **2 :** to make dark or black — **mel·a·ni·za·tion** \ˌme-lə-nə-ˈzā-shən\ *n*

me·la·no·blast \mə-ˈla-nə-ˌblast, ˈme-lə-nō-\ *n* [ISV] (1901) : a cell that is a precursor of a melanocyte or melanophore

me·la·no·cyte \mə-ˈla-nə-ˌsīt, ˈme-lə-nō-\ *n* [ISV] (ca. 1890) : an epidermal cell that produces melanin

melanocyte–stimulating hormone *n* (1953) : any of several vertebrate hormones of the pituitary gland that darken the skin by stimulating melanin dispersion in pigment-containing cells

me·la·no·gen·e·sis \mə-ˌla-nə-ˈje-nə-səs, ˌme-lə-nō-\ *n* [NL] (1909) : the formation of melanin

mel·a·no·ma \ˌme-lə-ˈnō-mə\ *n, pl* **-mas** *also* **-ma·ta** \-mə-tə\ [NL] (1838) **1 :** a tumor containing dark pigment **2 :** a highly malignant tumor that starts in melanocytes of normal skin or moles and metastasizes rapidly and widely

me·la·no·phore \mə-ˈla-nə-ˌfȯr, ˈme-lə-nə-\ *n* (1903) : a melanin-containing cell esp. of fishes, amphibians, and reptiles

me·la·no·some \-ˌsōm\ *n* (1940) : a melanin-producing granule in a melanocyte

mel·a·not·ic \ˌme-lə-ˈnä-tik\ *adj* (1829) : having or characterized by black pigmentation

mel·a·to·nin \ˌme-lə-ˈtō-nən\ *n* [Gk *melas* black + *-tonin* (as in *serotonin*)] (1958) : a vertebrate hormone that is derived from serotonin, is secreted by the pineal gland esp. in response to darkness, and has been linked to the regulation of circadian rhythms

mel·ba toast \ˈmel-bə-\ *n* [Nellie *Melba*] (1925) : very thin crisp toast

Mel·chite *or* **Mel·kite** \ˈmel-ˌkīt\ *n* [NL *Melchita,* fr. MGk *Melchitēs,* fr. Syriac *malkāyā,* fr. *malkā* king] (1615) **1 :** an Eastern Christian chiefly of Syria and Egypt adhering to Chalcedonian orthodoxy in preference to Monophysitism **2 :** a member of a Uniate body derived from the Melchites

[1]**Mel·chiz·e·dek** \mel-ˈki-zə-ˌdek\ *n* [Gk *Melchisedek,* fr. Heb *Malkīṣedheq*] (14c) : a priest-king of Jerusalem who prepared a ritual meal for Abraham and received tithes from him

[2]**Melchizedek** *adj* (1842) : of or relating to the higher order of the Mormon priesthood

[1]**meld** \ˈmeld\ *vb* [G *melden* to announce, fr. OHG *meldōn;* akin to OE *meldian* to announce, Lith *malda* prayer] *vt* (1887) : to declare or announce (a card or combination of cards) for a score in a card game esp. by placing face up on the table ~ *vi* : to declare a card or combination of cards as a meld

[2]**meld** *n* (1887) : a card or combination of cards that is or can be melded in a card game

[3]**meld** *vb* [blend of *melt* and *weld*] (1936) : MERGE, BLEND

[4]**meld** *n* (1954) : BLEND, MIXTURE

me·lee *also* **mê·lée** \ˈmā-ˌlā, mā-ˈ\ *n* [F *mêlée,* fr. OF *meslee,* fr. *mesler* to mix — more at MEDDLE] (ca. 1648) : a confused struggle; *esp* : a hand-to-hand fight among several people

mel·ic \ˈme-lik\ *adj* [L *melicus,* fr. Gk *melikos,* fr. *melos* song — more at MELODY] (1699) : of or relating to song : LYRIC; *esp* : of or relating to Greek lyric poetry of the seventh and sixth centuries B.C.

mel·i·lot \ˈme-lə-ˌlät\ *n* [ME *mellilot,* fr. OF *melilot,* fr. L *melilotos,* fr. Gk *melilōtos,* fr. *meli* honey + *lōtos* clover, lotus — more at MELLIFLUOUS] (14c) : SWEET CLOVER; *esp* : a yellow-flowered sweet clover (*Melilotus officinalis*)

me·lio·rate \ˈmēl-yə-ˌrāt, ˈmē-lē-ə-\ *vb* **-rat·ed; -rat·ing** [LL *melioratus,* pp. of *meliorare,* fr. L *melior* better; akin to L *multus* much, Gk *mala* very] (1542) : AMELIORATE — **me·lio·ra·tion** \ˌmēl-yə-ˈrā-shən, ˌmē-lē-ə-\ *n* — **me·lio·ra·tive** \ˈmēl-yə-ˌrā-tiv, ˈmē-lē-ə-\ *adj* — **me·lio·ra·tor** \-ˌrā-tər\ *n*

me·lio·rism \ˈmēl-yə-ˌri-zəm, ˈmē-lē-ə-\ *n* (1877) : the belief that the world tends to improve and that humans can aid its betterment — **me·lio·rist** \-rist\ *adj or n* — **me·lio·ris·tic** \ˌmēl-yə-ˈris-tik, ˌmē-lē-ə-\ *adj*

me·lis·ma \mi-ˈliz-mə\ *n, pl* **-ma·ta** \-mə-tə\ [NL, fr. Gk, song, melody, fr. *melizein* to sing, fr. *melos* song] (ca. 1880) **1 :** a group of notes or tones sung on one syllable in plainsong **2 :** melodic embellishment **3 :** CADENZA — **mel·is·mat·ic** \ˌme-ləz-ˈma-tik\ *adj*

mell \ˈmel\ *vb* [ME, fr. MF *mesler*] (14c) : MIX

mel·lif·lu·ent \me-ˈli-flə-wənt\ *adj* [LL *mellifluent-, mellifluens,* fr. L *mell-, mel* + *fluent-, fluens,* prp. of *fluere*] (1601) : MELLIFLUOUS — **mel·lif·lu·ent·ly** *adv*

mel·lif·lu·ous \me-ˈli-flə-wəs, mə-\ *adj* [ME *mellyfluous,* fr. LL *mellifluus,* fr. L *mell-, mel* honey + *fluere* to flow; akin to Goth *milith* honey, Gk *melit-, meli*] (15c) **1 :** having a smooth rich flow ⟨a ~ voice⟩ **2 :** filled with something (as honey) that sweetens — **mel·lif·lu·ous·ly** *adv* — **mel·lif·lu·ous·ness** *n*

mel·lo·phone \ˈme-lə-ˌfōn\ *n* [[1]*mellow* + *-phone*] (1913) : a valved brass instrument similar in form and range to the French horn

mel·lo·tron \ˈme-lə-ˌträn\ *n* [fr. *Mellotron,* a trademark] (1963) : an electronic keyboard instrument programmed to produce the tape-recorded sounds usu. of orchestral instruments

[1]**mel·low** \ˈme-(ˌ)lō\ *adj* [ME *melowe*] (15c) **1 a** *of a fruit* : tender and sweet because of ripeness **b** *of a wine* : well aged and pleasingly mild **2 a :** made gentle by age or experience **b :** rich and full but free from garishness or stridency **c :** warmed and relaxed by or as if by liquor **d :** PLEASANT, AGREEABLE **e :** LAID-BACK **3** *of soil* : having a soft and loamy consistency — **mel·low·ly** *adv* — **mel·low·ness** *n*

[2]**mellow** *vt* (1575) : to make mellow ~ *vi* : to become mellow — often used with *out*

me·lo·de·on \mə-ˈlō-dē-ən\ *n* [G *Melodion,* fr. *Melodie* melody, ultim. fr. LL *melodia*] (1844) : a small reed organ in which a suction bellows draws air inward through the reeds

me·lo·di·ous \mə-ˈlō-dē-əs\ *adj* (14c) **1 :** having a pleasing melody **2 :** of, relating to, or producing melody — **me·lo·di·ous·ly** *adv* — **me·lo·di·ous·ness** *n*

mel·o·dist \ˈme-lə-dist\ *n* (1789) **1 :** SINGER **2 :** a composer of melodies

mel·o·dize \ˈme-lə-ˌdīz\ *vb* **-dized; -diz·ing** *vi* (1662) : to compose a melody ~ *vt* : to make melodious : set to melody — **mel·o·diz·er** *n*

melo·dra·ma \ˈme-lə-ˌdrä-mə, -ˌdra-\ *n* [modif. of F *mélodrame,* fr. Gk *melos* song + F *drame* drama, fr. LL *drama*] (1802) **1 a :** a work (as a movie or play) characterized by extravagant theatricality and by the predominance of plot and physical action over characterization **b :** the genre of dramatic literature constituted by such works **2 :** something resembling a melodrama esp. in having a sensational or theatrical quality — **melo·dra·ma·tist** \ˌme-lə-ˈdra-mə-tist, -ˈdrä-\ *n*

melo·dra·mat·ic \ˌme-lə-drə-ˈma-tik\ *adj* (1808) **1 :** of, relating to, or characteristic of melodrama **2 :** appealing to the emotions : SENSATIONAL ***syn*** see DRAMATIC — **melo·dra·mat·i·cal·ly** \-ti-k(ə-)lē\ *adv*

melo·dra·mat·ics \-tiks\ *n pl but sing or pl in constr* (1879) : melodramatic conduct or writing

melo·dra·ma·tise *Brit var of* MELODRAMATIZE

melo·dra·ma·tize \ˌme-lə-ˈdra-mə-ˌtīz, -ˈdrä-\ *vt* (1820) **1 :** to make melodramatic ⟨~ a situation⟩ **2 :** to make a melodrama of (as a novel) — **melo·dra·ma·ti·za·tion** \-ˌdra-mə-tə-ˈzā-shən, -ˌdrä-\ *n*

mel·o·dy \ˈme-lə-dē\ *n, pl* **-dies** [ME *melodie,* fr. AF, fr. LL *melodia,* fr. Gk *melōidia* chanting, music, fr. *melos* limb, musical phrase, song (prob. akin to Bret *mell* joint) + *aeidein* to sing — more at ODE] (13c) **1 :** a sweet or agreeable succession or arrangement of sounds : TUNEFULNESS **2 :** a rhythmic succession of single tones organized as an aesthetic whole — **me·lod·ic** \mə-ˈlä-dik\ *adj* — **me·lod·i·cal·ly** \-dik(ə-)lē\ *adv*

mel·on \ˈme-lən\ *n, often attrib* [ME, fr. MF, fr. LL *melon-, melo,* short for L *melopepon-, melopepo,* fr. Gk *mēlopepōn,* fr. *mēlon* apple + *pepōn,* an edible gourd — more at PUMPKIN] (14c) **1 :** any of various typically sweet gourds (as a muskmelon or watermelon) usu. eaten raw as fruits **2 :** something rounded like a melon: as **a :** the rounded organ in the front of the head of some cetaceans **b** *pl, slang* : large breasts **3 a :** a surplus of profits available for distribution to stockholders **b :** a financial windfall

melon baller *n* (1950) : a spoonlike utensil with a sharp edge used esp. for cutting ball-shaped pieces from the pulp of a fruit

mel·pha·lan \ˈmel-fə-ˌlan\ *n* [prob. fr. *methanol* + *phenylalanine*] (1960) : an antineoplastic drug $C_{13}H_{18}Cl_2N_2O_2$

Mel·pom·e·ne \mel-ˈpä-mə-(ˌ)nē\ *n* [L, fr. Gk *Melpomenē*] (ca. 1548) : the Greek Muse of tragedy

[1]**melt** \ˈmelt\ *vb* [ME, fr. OE *meltan;* akin to ON *melta* to digest, Gk *meldein* to melt — more at MOLLIFY] *vi* (bef. 12c) **1 :** to become altered from a solid to a liquid state usu. by heat **2 a :** DISSOLVE, DISINTEGRATE ⟨the sugar ~*ed* in the coffee⟩ **b :** to disappear as if by dissolving ⟨her anger ~*ed* at his kind words⟩ **3** *obs* : to become subdued or crushed (as by sorrow) **4 :** to become mild, tender, or gentle **5 :** to lose outline or distinctness : BLEND ~ *vt* **1 :** to reduce from a solid to a liquid state usu. by heat **2 :** to cause to disappear or disperse **3 :** to make tender or gentle : SOFTEN — **melt·abil·i·ty** \ˌmel-tə-ˈbi-lə-tē\ *n* — **melt·able** \ˈmel-tə-bəl\ *adj* — **melt·er** *n*

[2]**melt** *n* (1847) **1 a :** material in the molten state **b :** the mass melted at a single operation or the quantity melted during a specified period **2 a :** the action or process of melting or the period during which it occurs ⟨the spring ~⟩ **b :** the condition of being melted **3 :** a sandwich with melted cheese ⟨a tuna ~⟩

[3]**melt** *n* [ME *milte,* fr. OE; akin to OHG *miltzi* spleen] (bef. 12c) : SPLEEN; *esp* : spleen of slaughtered animals for use as feed or food

melt·down \ˈmelt-ˌdau̇n\ *n* (1956) **1 :** the accidental melting of the core of a nuclear reactor **2 :** a rapid or disastrous decline or collapse **3 :** a breakdown of self-control (as from fatigue or overstimulation)

melt down *vi* (1956) : to suffer a meltdown : COLLAPSE

melt·ing \ˈmel-tiŋ\ *adj* (1565) : TENDER, DELICATE ⟨a love song's ~ lyric⟩ — **melt·ing·ly** *adv*

melting point *n* (1823) : the temperature at which a solid melts

melting pot *n* (1887) **1 a :** a place where a variety of races, cultures, or individuals assimilate into a cohesive whole **b :** the population of such a place **2 :** a process of blending that often results in invigoration or novelty — **melting–pot** *adj*

mel·ton \ˈmel-tᵊn\ *n* [*Melton* Mowbray, town in England] (ca. 1858) : a heavy smooth woolen fabric with short nap

melt·wa·ter \ˈmelt-ˌwȯ-tər, -ˌwä-\ *n* (1923) : water derived from the melting of ice and snow

\ə\ **abut** \ᵊ\ **kit**ten, F table \ər\ **fur**ther \a\ **ash** \ā\ **ace** \ä\ **mop, mar** \au̇\ **out** \ch\ **chin** \e\ **bet** \ē\ **easy** \g\ **go** \i\ **hit** \ī\ **ice** \j\ **job** \ŋ\ **sing** \ō\ **go** \ȯ\ **law** \ȯi\ **boy** \th\ **thin** \th̲\ **the** \ü\ **loot** \u̇\ **foot** \y\ **yet** \zh\ **vi**sion, beige \k̲, ⁿ, œ, ue, ʸ\ *see* Guide to Pronunciation

[1]**mem** \'mem\ *n* [Heb *mēm,* lit., water] (ca. 1567) **:** the 13th letter of the Hebrew alphabet — see ALPHABET table

[2]**mem** *abbr* **1** member **2** memoir **3** memorial

mem•ber \'mem-bər\ *n, often attrib* [ME *membre,* fr. AF, fr. L *membrum;* akin to Goth *mimz* flesh, Gk *mēros* thigh] (14c) **1 :** a body part or organ: as **a :** LIMB **b :** PENIS **c :** a unit of structure in a plant body **2 :** one of the individuals composing a group **3 :** a person baptized or enrolled in a church **4 :** a part of a whole: as **a :** a syntactic or rhythmic unit of a sentence **:** CLAUSE **b :** one of the propositions of a syllogism **c :** one of the elements of a set or class **d :** either of the equated elements in a mathematical equation ***syn*** see PART

mem•bered \'mem-bərd\ *adj* (14c) **:** made up of or divided into members

mem•ber•ship \'mem-bər-ˌship\ *n* (1643) **1 :** the state or status of being a member **2 :** the body of members ⟨an organization with a large ~⟩ **3 :** the relation between an element of a set or class and the set or class — compare INCLUSION 3a

mem•brane \'mem-ˌbrān\ *n* [ME, fr. L *membrana* skin, parchment, fr. *membrum*] (15c) **1 :** a thin soft pliable sheet or layer esp. of animal or plant origin **2 :** a piece of parchment forming part of a roll — **mem•braned** \'mem-ˌbrānd\ *adj*

mem•bra•nous \'mem-brə-nəs\ *adj* (1597) **1 :** of, relating to, or resembling membrane **2 :** thin, pliable, and often somewhat transparent ⟨~ leaves⟩ **3 :** characterized or accompanied by the formation of a usu. abnormal membrane or membranous layer ⟨~ croup⟩ — **mem•bra•nous•ly** *adv*

membranous labyrinth *n* (1840) **:** the sensory structures of the inner ear

meme \'mēm\ *n* [alter. of *mimeme,* fr. *mim-* (as in *mimesis*) + *-eme*] (1976) **:** an idea, behavior, style, or usage that spreads from person to person within a culture

me•men•to \mə-'men-(ˌ)tō, ÷mō-\ *n, pl* **-tos** *or* **-toes** [ME, fr. L, remember, imper. of *meminisse* to remember; akin to L *ment-, mens* mind — more at MIND] (1580) **:** something that serves to warn or remind; *also* **:** SOUVENIR

me•men•to mo•ri \mə-'men-tō-'mȯr-ē\ *n, pl* **memento mori** [L, remember that you must die] (1598) **:** a reminder of mortality; *esp* **:** DEATH'S-HEAD

Mem•non \'mem-ˌnän\ *n* [Gk *Memnōn*] (1567) **:** an Ethiopian king slain by Achilles at a late stage of the Trojan War

memo \'me-(ˌ)mō\ *n, pl* **mem•os** (1705) **:** MEMORANDUM

mem•oir \'mem-ˌwär, -ˌwȯr\ *n* [MF *memoire,* fr. *memoire* memory, fr. L *memoria*] (1571) **1 :** an official note or report **:** MEMORANDUM **2 a :** a narrative composed from personal experience **b :** AUTOBIOGRAPHY — usu. used in pl. **c :** BIOGRAPHY **3 a :** an account of something noteworthy **:** REPORT **b** *pl* **:** the record of the proceedings of a learned society — **mem•oir•ist** \-ist\ *n*

mem•o•ra•bil•ia \ˌme-mə-rə-'bi-lē-ə, -'bē-lē-ə, -'bil-yə\ *n pl* [L, fr. neut. pl. of *memorabilis*] (1785) **1 :** things that are remarkable and worthy of remembrance **2 :** things that stir recollection or are valued or collected for their association with a particular field or interest **:** MEMENTOS ⟨baseball ~⟩

mem•o•ra•bil•i•ty \-'bi-lə-tē\ *n* (ca. 1661) **:** the quality or state of being easy to remember or worth remembering

mem•o•ra•ble \'mem-rə-bəl, 'mə-mə-rə-, 'me-mər-\ *adj* [ME, fr. L *memorabilis,* fr. *memorare* to remind, mention, fr. *memor* mindful] (15c) **:** worth remembering **:** NOTABLE ⟨a ~ occasion⟩ — **mem•o•ra•ble•ness** *n* — **mem•o•ra•bly** \-blē\ *adv*

mem•o•ran•dum \ˌme-mə-'ran-dəm\ *n, pl* **-dums** *or* **-da** \-də\ [ME, to be remembered, fr. L, neut. of *memorandus,* gerundive of *memorare*] (15c) **1 :** an informal record; *also* **:** a written reminder **2 :** an informal written note of a transaction or proposed instrument **3 a :** an informal diplomatic communication **b :** a usu. brief communication written for interoffice circulation **c :** a communication that contains directive, advisory, or informative matter

usage Although some commentators warn against the use of *memoranda* as a singular and condemn the plural *memorandas,* our evidence indicates that these forms are rarely encountered in print. We have a little evidence of the confusion of forms, including use of *memorandum* as a plural, in speech (as at congressional hearings). As plurals *memoranda* and *memorandums* are about equally frequent.

[1]**me•mo•ri•al** \mə-'mȯr-ē-əl\ *adj* [ME, fr. L *memorialis,* fr. *memoria* memory] (14c) **1 :** serving to preserve remembrance **:** COMMEMORATIVE **2 :** of or relating to memory — **me•mo•ri•al•ly** \-ə-lē\ *adv*

[2]**memorial** *n* (14c) **1 :** something that keeps remembrance alive: as **a :** MONUMENT **b :** something (as a speech or ceremony) that commemorates **c :** KEEPSAKE, MEMENTO **2 a :** RECORD, MEMOIR ⟨language and literature . . . the ~*s* of another age —J. H. Fisher⟩ **b :** MEMORANDUM, NOTE; *specif* **:** a legal abstract **c :** a statement of facts addressed to a government and often accompanied by a petition or remonstrance

Memorial Day *n* (1868) **1 :** May 30 formerly observed as a legal holiday in most states of the U.S. in remembrance of war dead **2 :** the last Monday in May observed as a legal holiday in most states of the U.S. **3 :** CONFEDERATE MEMORIAL DAY

me•mo•ri•al•ise *Brit var of* MEMORIALIZE

me•mo•ri•al•ist \mə-'mȯr-ē-ə-list\ *n* (1706) **1 :** a person who writes or signs a memorial **2 :** a person who writes a memoir

me•mo•ri•al•ize \-ˌlīz\ *vt* **-ized; -iz•ing** (1798) **1 :** to address or petition by a memorial **2 :** COMMEMORATE — **me•mo•ri•al•i•za•tion** \mə-ˌmȯr-ē-ə-lə-'zā-shən, -ˌlī-'zā-\ *n*

memorial park *n* (ca. 1928) **:** CEMETERY

mem•o•rise *Brit var of* MEMORIZE

me•mo•ri•ter \mə-'mȯr-ə-ˌter, -'mär-\ *adj* [L, adv., by memory, fr. *memor*] (1827) **:** marked by emphasis on memorization

mem•o•rize \'me-mə-ˌrīz\ *vt* **-rized; -riz•ing** (1834) **:** to commit to memory **:** learn by heart — **mem•o•riz•able** \ˌme-mə-'rī-zə-bəl\ *adj* — **mem•o•ri•za•tion** \ˌme-mə-rə-'zā-shən, ˌme-mə-(ˌ)rī-, ˌmem-rə-\ *n* — **mem•o•riz•er** *n*

mem•o•ry \'mem-rē, 'me-mə-\ *n, pl* **-ries** [ME *memorie,* fr. AF *memoire, memorie,* fr. L *memoria,* fr. *memor* mindful; akin to OE *gemimor* well-known, Gk *mermēra* care, Skt *smarati* he remembers] (14c) **1 a :** the power or process of reproducing or recalling what has been learned and retained esp. through associative mechanisms **b :** the store of things learned and retained from an organism's activity or experience as evidenced by modification of structure or behavior or by recall and recognition **2 a :** commemorative remembrance ⟨erected a statue in ~ of the hero⟩ **b :** the fact or condition of being remembered ⟨days of recent ~⟩ **3 a :** a particular act of recall or recollection **b :** an image or impression of one that is remembered ⟨fond *memories* of her youth⟩ **c :** the time within which past events can be or are remembered **4 a :** a device (as a chip) or a component of a device in which information esp. for a computer can be inserted and stored and from which it may be extracted when wanted; *esp* **:** RAM **b :** capacity for storing information ⟨512 megabytes of ~⟩ **5 :** a capacity for showing effects as the result of past treatment or for returning to a former condition — used esp. of a material (as metal or plastic)

syn MEMORY, REMEMBRANCE, RECOLLECTION, REMINISCENCE mean the capacity for or the act of remembering, or the thing remembered. MEMORY applies both to the power of remembering and to what is remembered ⟨gifted with a remarkable *memory*⟩ ⟨that incident was now just a distant *memory*⟩. REMEMBRANCE applies to the act of remembering or the fact of being remembered ⟨any *remembrance* of his deceased wife was painful⟩. RECOLLECTION adds an implication of consciously bringing back to mind often with some effort ⟨after a moment's *recollection* he produced the name⟩. REMINISCENCE suggests the recalling of usu. pleasant incidents, experiences, or feelings from a remote past ⟨my grandmother's *reminiscences* of her Iowa girlhood⟩.

memory foam *n* (1987) **:** a dense polyurethane foam that becomes more pliable when in contact with heat

memory lane *n* (1903) **:** an imaginary path through the nostalgically remembered past — usu. used in such phrases as *a walk down memory lane*

memory trace *n* (1901) **:** ENGRAM

mem•sa•hib \'mem-ˌsä-(h)ib, -ˌsäb\ *n* [Hindi, fr. E *ma'am* + Hindi & Urdu *sahib* sahib] (1852) **:** a white foreign woman of high social status living in India; *esp* **:** the wife of a British official

men *pl of* MAN

men- *or* **meno-** *comb form* [NL, fr. Gk *mēn* month — more at MOON] **:** menstruation ⟨*meno*rrhagia⟩

[1]**men•ace** \'me-nəs\ *n* [ME *manace,* fr. AF *manace, menace,* fr. L *minacia,* fr. *minac-, minax* threatening, fr. *minari* to threaten — more at MOUNT] (14c) **1 :** a show of intention to inflict harm **:** THREAT **2 a :** one that represents a threat **:** DANGER **b :** an annoying person

[2]**menace** *vb* **men•aced; men•ac•ing** *vt* (14c) **1 :** to make a show of intention to harm **2 :** to represent or pose a threat to **:** ENDANGER ~ *vi* **:** to act in a threatening manner — **men•ac•ing•ly** \-nə-siŋ-lē\ *adv*

men•a•di•one \ˌme-nə-'dī-ˌōn, -dī-'\ *n* [*me*thyl + *na*pthalene + *di-* + ketone] (1941) **:** a yellow crystalline compound $C_{11}H_8O_2$ with the biological activity of natural vitamin K

mé•nage \mā-'näzh, mə-\ *n* [F, fr. OF *mesnage* dwelling, fr. VL **mansionaticum,* fr. L *mansion-, mansio* mansion] (1698) **:** a domestic establishment **:** HOUSEHOLD; *also* **:** HOUSEKEEPING

mé•nage à trois \-ä-'t(r)wä\ *n* [F, lit., household for three] (1856) **:** an arrangement in which three persons (as a married pair and the lover of one of the pair) share sexual relations esp. while living together

me•nag•er•ie \mə-'naj-rē, -'na-jə- *also* -'nazh-rē, -'na-zhə-\ *n* [F *ménagerie,* fr. MF, management of a household or farm, fr. *menage*] (1676) **1 a :** a place where animals are kept and trained esp. for exhibition **b :** a collection of wild or foreign animals kept esp. for exhibition **2 :** a varied mixture ⟨a ~ of comedians —*TV Guide*⟩

men•ar•che \'me-ˌnär-kē\ *n* [NL, fr. *men-* + Gk *archē* beginning] (ca. 1900) **:** the beginning of the menstrual function; *esp* **:** the first menstrual period of an individual — **men•ar•che•al** \ˌme-när-'kē-əl\ *adj*

[1]**mend** \'mend\ *vb* [ME, short for *amenden* — more at AMEND] *vt* (13c) **1 :** to free from faults or defects: as **a :** to improve in manners or morals **:** REFORM **b :** to set right **:** CORRECT **c :** to put into good shape or working order again **:** patch up **:** REPAIR **d :** to improve or strengthen (as a relationship) by negotiation or conciliation — used chiefly in the phrase *mend fences* ⟨spends the weekend ~*ing* political fences —E. O. Hauser⟩ **e :** to restore to health **:** CURE **2 :** to make amends or atonement for ⟨least said, soonest ~*ed*⟩ ~ *vi* **1 :** to improve morally **:** REFORM **2 :** to become corrected or improved **3 :** to improve in health; *also* **:** HEAL — **mend•able** \'men-də-bəl\ *adj* — **mend•er** *n*

syn MEND, REPAIR, PATCH, REBUILD mean to put into good order something that is injured, damaged, or defective. MEND implies making whole or sound something broken, torn, or injured ⟨*mended* the torn dress⟩. REPAIR applies to the fixing of more extensive damage or dilapidation ⟨*repaired* the back steps⟩. PATCH implies an often temporary fixing of a hole or break with new material ⟨*patch* worn jeans⟩. REBUILD suggests making like new without completely replacing ⟨a *rebuilt* automobile engine⟩.

[2]**mend** *n* (14c) **1 :** an act of mending **:** REPAIR **2 :** a mended place — **on the mend :** getting better **:** IMPROVING

men•da•cious \men-'dā-shəs\ *adj* [L *mendac-, mendax* — more at AMEND] (1616) **:** given to or characterized by deception or falsehood or divergence from absolute truth ⟨~ tales of his adventures⟩ ***syn*** see DISHONEST — **men•da•cious•ly** *adv* — **men•da•cious•ness** *n*

men•dac•i•ty \men-'da-sə-tē\ *n, pl* **-ties** (1646) **1 :** the quality or state of being mendacious **2 :** LIE

Men•de \'men-dē, -dā\ *n, pl* **Mende** *or* **Mendes** (1732) **1 :** a Mande language of southern Sierra Leone and eastern Liberia **2 :** a member of a people speaking Mende

men•de•le•vi•um \ˌmen-də-'lē-vē-əm, -'lā-\ *n* [NL, fr. Dmitry *Mendeleyev*] (1955) **:** a radioactive metallic element produced artificially — see ELEMENT table

Men•de•lian \men-'dē-lē-ən, -'dēl-yən\ *adj* (1902) **:** of, relating to, or according with Mendel's laws or Mendelism — **Mendelian** *n*

Mendelian factor *n* (1918) **:** GENE

Mendelian inheritance *n* (ca. 1910) **:** inheritance of characters specif. transmitted by genes in accord with Mendel's laws — called also *particulate inheritance*

Men•del•ism \'men-dᵊl-ˌi-zəm\ *n* (1903) **:** the principles or the operations of Mendel's laws; *also* **:** MENDELIAN INHERITANCE — **Men•del•ist** \-dᵊl-ist\ *adj or n*

Men•del's law \'men-dᵊlz-\ *n* [Gregor *Mendel*] (1903) **1 :** a principle in genetics: hereditary units occur in pairs that separate during gamete formation so that every gamete receives but one member of a pair — called also *law of segregation* **2** : a principle in genetics limited and modified by the subsequent discovery of the phenomenon of linkage: the different pairs of hereditary units are distributed to the gametes independently of each other, the gametes combine at random, and the various combinations of hereditary units occur in the zygotes according to the laws of chance — called also *law of independent assortment* **3** : a principle in genetics proved subsequently to be subject to many limitations: because one of each pair of hereditary units dominates the other in expression, characters are inherited alternatively on an all-or-nothing basis — called also *law of dominance*

men·di·can·cy \'men-di-kən(t)-sē\ *n* (1711) **1** : the condition of being a beggar **2** : the practice of begging

men·di·cant \'men-di-kənt\ *n* [ME, fr. AF, fr. L *mendicant-, mendicans*, prp. of *mendicare* to beg, fr. *mendicus* beggar — more at AMEND] (14c) **1** : BEGGAR 1 **2** *often cap* : a member of a religious order (as the Franciscans) combining monastic life and outside religious activity and orig. owning neither personal nor community property : FRIAR — **mendicant** *adj*

men·dic·i·ty \men-'di-sə-tē\ *n* [ME *mendicite*, fr. MF *mendicité*, fr. L *mendicitat-, mendicitas*, fr. *mendicus*] (15c) : MENDICANCY

Men·e·la·us \ˌme-nə-'lā-əs\ *n* [L, fr. Gk *Menelaos*] (13c) : a king of Sparta, brother of Agamemnon, and husband of the abducted Helen of Troy

men·folk \'men-ˌfōk\ *or* **men·folks** \-ˌfōks\ *n pl* (1749) **1** : men in general **2** : the men of a family or community

MEng *abbr* master of engineering

men·ha·den \men-'hā-dᵊn, mən-\ *n, pl* **-den** *also* **-dens** [of Algonquian origin; akin to Narragansett *munnawhatteaûg* menhaden] (1765) : a marine fish (*Brevoortia tyrannus*) of the herring family abundant along the Atlantic coast of the U.S. where it is used for bait or converted into oil and fertilizer; *also* : any of several congeneric fishes

men·hir \'men-ˌhir\ *n* [F, fr. Bret. fr. *men* stone + *hir* long] (1840) : a single upright rough monolith usu. of prehistoric origin

[1]**me·nial** \'mē-nē-əl, -nyəl\ *n* (14c) : a person doing menial work; *specif* : a domestic servant or retainer

[2]**menial** *adj* [ME *meynial*, fr. AF *meignal*, fr. *mesnee, mayné* household, retinue, fr. VL *mansionata, fr. L *mansion-, mansio* dwelling — more at MANSION] (15c) **1** : of or relating to servants ⟨LOWLY ∼ task⟩ **2** : appropriate to a servant : HUMBLE, SERVILE ⟨answered in ∼ tones⟩ **b** : lacking interest or dignity ⟨a ∼ task⟩ — **me·nial·ly** *adv*

Mé·nière's disease \mən-'yerz-, 'men-yərz-\ *n* [Prosper *Ménière* †1862 Fr. physician] (1871) : a disorder of the membranous labyrinth of the inner ear that is marked by recurrent attacks of dizziness, tinnitus, and hearing loss — called also *Ménière's syndrome*

mening- *or* **meningo-** *also* **meningi-** *comb form* [NL, fr. *mening-, meninx*] **1** : meninges ⟨*meningo*coccus⟩ ⟨*mening*itis⟩ **2** : meninges and ⟨*meningo*encephalitis⟩

men·in·ge·al \ˌme-nən-'jē-əl\ *adj* (1797) : of, relating to, or affecting the meninges

meninges *pl of* MENINX

me·nin·gi·o·ma \mə-ˌnin-jē-'ō-mə\ *n, pl* **-mas** *also* **-ma·ta** \-'ō-mə-tə\ [NL] (1922) : a slow-growing encapsulated typically benign tumor arising from the meninges and often causing damage by pressing upon the brain and adjacent parts

men·in·gi·tis \ˌme-nən-'jī-təs\ *n, pl* **-git·i·des** \-'ji-tə-ˌdēz\ [NL] (1824) **1** : inflammation of the meninges and esp. of the pia mater and the arachnoid **2** : a disease marked by inflammation of the meninges that is either a relatively mild illness caused by a virus (as various Coxsackie viruses) or a more severe life-threatening illness caused by a bacterium (as the meningococcus) — **men·in·git·ic** \-'ji-tik\ *adj*

me·nin·go·coc·cus \mə-ˌniŋ-gə-'kä-kəs, -ˌnin-jə-\ *n, pl* **-coc·ci** \-'käk-ˌsī, -ˌsē; -'kä-ˌkī, -ˌkē\ [NL] (ca. 1893) : the bacterium (*Neisseria meningitidis*) that causes cerebrospinal meningitis — **me·nin·go·coc·cal** \-'käk-əl\ *also* **me·nin·go·coc·cic** \-'käk-sik, -'kä-kik\ *adj*

me·nin·go·en·ceph·a·li·tis \-ˌgō-ən-ˌse-fə-'lī-təs, -jō-\ *n, pl* **-lit·i·des** \-'li-tə-ˌdēz\ [NL] (ca. 1860) : inflammation of the brain and meninges — **me·nin·go·en·ceph·a·lit·ic** \-'li-tik\ *adj*

me·ninx \'mē-niŋ(k)s, 'me-\ *n, pl* **me·nin·ges** \mə-'nin-(ˌ)jēz\ [NL, fr. Gk *mēning-, mēninx* membrane] (1543) : any of the three membranes that envelop the brain and spinal cord

me·nis·cus \mə-'nis-kəs\ *n, pl* **me·nis·ci** \-'ni-ˌskī, -ˌskē, -ˌsī\ *also* **me·nis·cus·es** [NL, fr. Gk *mēniskos*, fr. dim. of *mēnē* moon, crescent — more at MOON] (1685) **1** : a crescent or crescent-shaped body **2** : a concavo-convex lens **3** : the curved upper surface of a column of liquid **4** : a fibrous cartilage within a joint esp. of the knee

Men·no·nite \'me-nə-ˌnīt\ *n* [G *Mennonit*, fr. Menno Simons] (1565) : a member of any of various Protestant groups derived from the Anabaptist movement in Holland and characterized by congregational autonomy and rejection of military service

meno- — see MEN-

me·no mos·so \ˌmā-nō-'mȯ(s)-(ˌ)sō\ *adv* [It] (ca. 1854) : less rapid — used as a direction in music

men·o·pause \'me-nə-ˌpȯz, 'mē-\ *n* [F *ménopause*, fr. *méno-* men- + *pause* stop, pause] (1872) **1** : the natural cessation of menstruation that usu. occurs between the ages of 45 and 55; *also* : the period during which such cessation occurs — called also *climacteric*; compare PERI-MENOPAUSE **2** : cessation of menstruation from other than natural causes — **men·o·paus·al** \ˌme-nə-'pȯ-zəl, ˌmē-\ *adj*

me·no·rah \mə-'nȯr-ə\ *n* [Heb *mĕnōrāh* candlestick] (1886) : a candelabra with seven or nine lights that is used in Jewish worship

men·or·rha·gia \ˌme-nə-'rā-j(ē-)ə, -'rä-zhə; -'rä-jə, -zhə\ *n* [NL] (1779) : abnormally profuse menstrual flow

men·sal \'men(t)-səl\ *adj* [ME, fr. LL *mensalis*, fr. L *mensa* table] (15c) : of, relating to, or done at the table

mensch \'men(t)sh\ *n* [Yiddish *mentsh* human being, fr. MHG *mensch*, fr. OHG *mennisco*; akin to OE *man* human being, man] (1856) : a person of integrity and honor — **menschy** \'men(t)-shē\ *adj*

mense \'men(t)s\ *n* [ME *menske* honor, fr. ON *mennska* humanity;

akin to OE *man*] (ca. 1500) *chiefly Scot* : PROPRIETY — **mense·less** \-ləs\ *adj, chiefly Scot*

men·ses \'men-(ˌ)sēz\ *n pl but sing or pl in constr* [L, lit., months, pl. of *mensis* month — more at MOON] (1597) : the menstrual flow

Men·she·vik \'men(t)-shə-ˌvik, -ˌvēk\ *n, pl* **Mensheviks** *or* **Men·she·vi·ki** \ˌmen(t)-shə-'vi-kē, -'vē-kē\ [Russ *men'shevik*, fr. *men'she* less; fr. their forming the minority group of the party] (1907) : a member of a wing of the Russian Social Democratic party before and during the Russian Revolution believing in the gradual achievement of socialism by parliamentary methods in opposition to the Bolsheviks — **Men·she·vism** \'men(t)-shə-ˌvi-zəm\ *n* — **Men·she·vist** \-vist\ *n or adj*

mens rea \ˌmenz-'rē-ə, -'rā-ə\ *n* [NL, lit., guilty mind] (1861) : criminal intent

men's room *n* (1929) : a room equipped with one or more sinks, toilets, and usu. urinals for the use of men and boys

men·stru·al \'men(t)-strü-əl, -strəl\ *adj* (14c) : of or relating to menstruation — **men·stru·al·ly** *adv*

menstrual cycle *n* (1912) : the cycle of physiological changes from the beginning of one menstrual period to the beginning of the next

men·stru·ate \'men(t)-strü-ˌwāt, 'men-ˌstrāt\ *vi* **-at·ed; -at·ing** [LL *menstruatus*, pp. of *menstruari*, fr. L *menstrua* menses, fr. neut. pl. of *menstruus* monthly, fr. *mensis*] (1713) : to undergo menstruation

men·stru·a·tion \ˌmen(t)-strü-'wā-shən, men-'strā-\ *n* (1686) : a discharging of blood, secretions, and tissue debris from the uterus that recurs in nonpregnant breeding-age primate females at approximately monthly intervals and that is considered to represent a readjustment of the uterus to the nonpregnant state following proliferative changes accompanying the preceding ovulation; *also* : PERIOD 6c

men·stru·um \'men(t)-strü-əm, -strəm\ *n, pl* **-stru·ums** *or* **-strua** \-strü-ə, -strə\ [ML, lit., menses, alter. of L *menstrua*] (1559) : a substance that dissolves a solid or holds it in suspension : SOLVENT

men·su·ra·ble \'men(t)s-rə-bəl, 'men(t)sh-; 'men(t)-sə-rə-, -shə-\ *adj* [LL *mensurabilis*, fr. *mensurare* to measure, fr. L *mensura* measure — more at MEASURE] (1604) **1** : capable of being measured : MEASURABLE **2** : MENSURAL 1 — **men·sur·abil·i·ty** \ˌmen(t)s-rə-'bi-lə-tē, ˌmen(t)sh-; ˌmen(t)-sə-rə-, -shə-\ *n*

men·su·ral \'men(t)s-rəl, 'men(t)sh-; 'men(t)-sə-rəl, -shə-\ *adj* [LL *mensuralis* measurable, fr. L *mensura*] (ca. 1580) **1** : of, relating to, or being polyphonic music originating in the 13th century with each note having a definite and exact time value **2** : of or relating to measure

men·su·ra·tion \ˌmen(t)-sə-'rā-shən, -shə-\ *n* (1571) **1** : the act of measuring : MEASUREMENT **2** : geometry applied to the computation of lengths, areas, or volumes from given dimensions or angles

mens·wear \'menz-ˌwer\ *n* (1854) : clothing for men

-ment *n suffix* [ME, fr. AF, fr. L *-mentum*; akin to L *-men*, suffix denoting concrete result, Gk *-mat-, -ma*] **1 a** : concrete result, object, or agent of a (specified) action ⟨embank*ment*⟩ **b** : concrete means or instrument of a (specified) action ⟨entertain*ment*⟩ **2 a** : action : process ⟨develop*ment*⟩ **b** : place of a (specified) action ⟨encamp*ment*⟩ **3** : state or condition resulting from a (specified) action ⟨amaze*ment*⟩

[1]**men·tal** \'men-tᵊl\ *adj* [ME, fr. LL *mentalis*, fr. L *ment-, mens* mind — more at MIND] (15c) **1 a** : of or relating to the mind; *specif* : of or relating to the total emotional and intellectual response of an individual to external reality ⟨∼ health⟩ **b** : of or relating to intellectual as contrasted with emotional activity **c** : of, relating to, or being intellectual as contrasted with overt physical activity **d** : occurring or experienced in the mind : INNER ⟨∼ anguish⟩ **e** : relating to the mind, its activity, or its products as an object of study : IDEOLOGICAL **f** : relating to spirit or idea as opposed to matter **2 a** (1) : of, relating to, or affected by a psychiatric disorder ⟨∼ patient⟩ (2) : mentally disordered : MAD, CRAZY **b** : intended for the care or treatment of persons affected by psychiatric disorders ⟨∼ hospitals⟩ **3** : of or relating to telepathic or mind-reading powers — **men·tal·ly** \'men-tᵊl-ē\ *adv*

[2]**mental** *adj* [L *mentum* chin — more at MOUTH] (ca. 1727) : of or relating to the chin : GENIAL

mental age *n* (1910) : a measure used in psychological testing that expresses an individual's mental attainment in terms of the number of years it takes an average child to reach the same level

mental deficiency *n* (1856) : MENTAL RETARDATION

mental health day *n* (1971) : a day that an employee takes off from work in order to relieve stress or renew vitality

men·tal·ist \'men-tə-list\ *n* (1909) : MIND READER

men·tal·is·tic \ˌmen-tə-'lis-tik\ *adj* (1882) **1** : of or relating to any school of psychology or psychiatry that in contrast to behaviorism values subjective data (as those gained by introspection) in the study and explanation of behavior **2** : of or relating to mental phenomena — **men·tal·ism** \'men-tə-ˌli-zəm\ *n*

men·tal·i·ty \men-'ta-lə-tē\ *n, pl* **-ties** (1691) **1** : mental power or capacity : INTELLIGENCE **2** : mode or way of thought : OUTLOOK ⟨the imperialist ∼ of the nineteenth century —John Davies⟩

mental retardation *n* (1914) : subaverage intellectual ability equivalent to or less than an IQ of 70 that is accompanied by significant deficits in abilities (as in communication or self-care) necessary for independent daily functioning, is present from birth or infancy, and is manifested esp. by delayed or abnormal development, by learning difficulties, and by problems in social adjustment — **mentally retarded** *adj*

men·ta·tion \men-'tā-shən\ *n* [L *ment-, mens* + E *-ation*] (1850) : mental activity

men·tee \men-'tē\ *n* [*mentor* + *-ee*] (1965) : one who is being mentored : PROTÉGÉ

men·thol \'men-ˌthȯl, -ˌthōl\ *n* [G, ultim. fr. L *mentha* mint] (1876) **1** : a crystalline alcohol $C_{10}H_{20}O$ that occurs esp. in mint oils and has the odor and cooling properties of peppermint **2** *pl* : mentholated cigarettes

men·tho·lat·ed \'men(t)-thə-ˌlā-təd\ *adj* (1922) : containing or impregnated with menthol ⟨a ∼ salve⟩

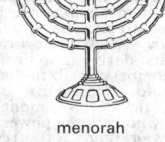

menorah

\ə\ **abut** \ᵊ\ **kitten**, F **table** \ər\ **further** \a\ **ash** \ā\ **ace** \ä\ **mop, mar** \au̇\ **out** \ch\ **chin** \e\ **bet** \ē\ **easy** \g\ **go** \i\ **hit** \ī\ **ice** \j\ **job** \ŋ\ **sing** \ō\ **go** \ȯ\ **law** \ȯi\ **boy** \th\ **thin** \t͟h\ **the** \ü\ **loot** \u̇\ **foot** \y\ **yet** \zh\ **vision, beige** \ḵ, ⁿ, œ, ᵫ, �\ *see* Guide to Pronunciation

[1]**men·tion** \ˈmen(t)-shən\ *n* [ME *mencioun,* fr. AF *mencion,* fr. L *mention-, mentio;* akin to L *meminisse* to remember, *ment-, mens* mind] (14c) **1 :** the act or an instance of citing or calling attention to someone or something esp. in a casual or incidental manner **2 :** formal citation for outstanding achievement

[2]**mention** *vt* **men·tioned; men·tion·ing** \ˈmen(t)-sh(ə-)niŋ\ (1530) **:** to make mention of **:** refer to; *also* **:** to cite for outstanding achievement — **men·tion·able** \ˈmen(t)-sh(ə-)nə-bəl\ *adj* — **men·tion·er** \-sh(ə-)nər\ *n* — **not to mention :** not even yet counting or considering **:** and notably in addition ⟨a proposal that's risky and expensive, *not to mention* unethical⟩

[1]**men·tor** \ˈmen-ˌtȯr, -tər\ *n* [L, fr. Gk *Mentōr*] (1616) **1** *cap* **:** a friend of Odysseus entrusted with the education of Odysseus' son Telemachus **2 a :** a trusted counselor or guide **b :** TUTOR, COACH — **men·tor·ship** \-ˌship\ *n*

[2]**mentor** *vt* (1976) **:** to serve as a mentor for **:** TUTOR

men·tum \ˈmen-təm\ *n, pl* **men·ta** \-tə\ [L, chin — more at MOUTH] (1826) **:** a median plate of the labium of an insect

menu \ˈmen-(ˌ)yü, ˈmān-\ *n, pl* **menus** [F, fr. *menu* small, detailed, fr. OF — more at MINUET] (1837) **1 a :** a list of the dishes that may be ordered (as in a restaurant) or that are to be served (as at a banquet) **b** (1) **:** a comparable list or assortment of offerings ⟨a ~ of television programs⟩ (2) **:** a list shown on the display of a computer from which a user can select the operation the computer is to perform **2 :** the dishes available for or served at a meal; *also* **:** the meal itself

me·nu·do \mə-ˈnü-dō, me-ˈnü-t͟hō\ *n, pl* **-dos** [MexSp, fr. Sp *menudos* innards, giblets] (1929) **:** a tripe stew seasoned with chili peppers

menu–driv·en \-ˌdri-vən\ *adj* (1977) **:** relating to or being a computer program in which options are offered to the user via menus

me·ow *also* **mi·aow** \mē-ˈau̇\ *n* [imit.] (1582) **1 :** the cry of a cat **2 :** a spiteful or malicious remark — **meow** *vi*

MEP *abbr* member of the European Parliament

me·per·i·dine \mə-ˈper-ə-ˌdēn\ *n* [*methyl* + *piperidine*] (1947) **:** a synthetic narcotic drug $C_{15}H_{21}NO_2$ used in the form of its hydrochloride as an analgesic, sedative, and antispasmodic

Meph·is·toph·e·les \ˌme-fə-ˈstä-fə-ˌlēz\ *n* [G] (ca. 1590) **:** a chief devil in the Faust legend — **Me·phis·to·phe·lian** \ˌme-fə-stə-ˈfēl-yən, mə-ˌfis-tə-\ *or* **Me·phis·to·phe·lean** *same, or* ˌme-fə-ˌstä-fə-ˈlē-ən\ *adj*

me·phit·ic \mə-ˈfi-tik\ *adj* (ca. 1623) **:** of, relating to, or resembling mephitis **:** foul-smelling ⟨~ vapors⟩

me·phi·tis \mə-ˈfī-təs\ *n* [L] (1683) **:** a noxious, pestilential, or foul exhalation from the earth; *also* **:** STENCH

mep·ro·bam·ate \ˌme-prō-ˈba-ˌmāt\ *n* [*methyl* + *propyl* + dicar*bamate*] (1955) **:** a bitter carbamate $C_9H_{18}N_2O_4$ used as a tranquilizer

mer *abbr* meridian

-mer *n comb form* [ISV, fr. Gk *meros* part — more at MERIT] **:** member of a (specified) class ⟨mono*mer*⟩

mer·bro·min \ˌmər-ˈbrō-mən\ *n* [*mer*curic + *brom-* + fluoresce*in*] (1941) **:** a green crystalline mercurial compound $C_{20}H_8Br_2HgNa_2O_6$ used as a topical antiseptic and germicide in the form of its red solution

merc \ˈmərk, ˈmərs\ *n* (1967) **:** MERCENARY

Mer·cal·li scale \mer-ˈkä-lē-, (ˌ)mər-\ *n* [Giuseppe *Mercalli* †1914 Ital. priest and geologist] (1921) **:** a scale of earthquake intensity ranging from I for an earthquake detected only by seismographs to XII for one causing total destruction of all buildings

mer·can·tile \ˈmər-kən-ˌtēl, -ˌtī(-ə)l\ *adj* [F, fr. It, fr. *mercante* merchant, fr. L *mercant-, mercans,* fr. prp. of *mercari* to trade — more at MARKET] (1642) **1 :** of or relating to merchants or trading **2 :** of, relating to, or having the characteristics of mercantilism ⟨~ system⟩

mer·can·til·ism \-ˌtē-ˌli-zəm, -ˌtī-, -tə-\ *n* (1838) **1 :** the theory or practice of mercantile pursuits **:** COMMERCIALISM **2 :** an economic system developing during the decay of feudalism to unify and increase the power and esp. the monetary wealth of a nation by a strict governmental regulation of the entire national economy usu. through policies designed to secure an accumulation of bullion, a favorable balance of trade, the development of agriculture and manufactures, and the establishment of foreign trading monopolies — **mer·can·til·ist** \-list\ *n or adj* — **mer·can·til·is·tic** \ˌmər-kən-ˌtē-ˈlis-tik, -ˌtī-, -tə-\ *adj*

mer·cap·tan \(ˌ)mər-ˈkap-ˌtan\ *n* [G, fr. Dan, fr. ML *mercurium captans,* lit., seizing mercury] (1835) **:** THIOL 1

mer·cap·to·pu·rine \(ˌ)mər-ˌkap-tə-ˈpyu̇r-ˌēn\ *n* [*mercaptan* + *-o-* + *purine*] (ca. 1952) **:** an antimetabolite $C_5H_4N_4S$ that interferes esp. with the metabolism of purine bases and the biosynthesis of nucleic acids and that is sometimes used in the treatment of acute leukemia

Mer·ca·tor \(ˌ)mər-ˈkā-tər\ *adj* (1758) **:** of, relating to, or drawn on the Mercator projection

Mercator projection *n* [Gerardus *Mercator*] (ca. 1881) **:** a conformal map projection of which the meridians are usu. drawn parallel to each other and the parallels of latitude are straight lines whose distance from each other increases with their distance from the equator

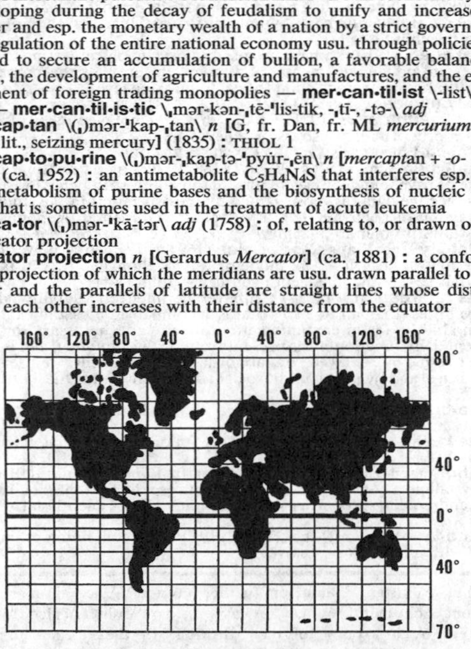

Mercator projection

[1]**mer·ce·nary** \ˈmər-sə-ˌner-ē, -ne-rē\ *n, pl* **-nar·ies** [ME, fr. L *mercenarius,* irreg. fr. *merced-, merces* wages — more at MERCY] (14c) **:** one that serves merely for wages; *esp* **:** a soldier hired into foreign service

[2]**mercenary** *adj* (1532) **1 :** serving merely for pay or sordid advantage **:** VENAL; *also* **:** GREEDY **2 :** hired for service in the army of a foreign country — **mer·ce·nar·i·ly** \ˌmər-sə-ˈner-ə-lē, -ˈne-rə-\ *adv* — **mer·ce·nar·i·ness** \ˈmər-sə-ˌner-ē-nəs, -ˌne-rē-\ *n*

mer·cer \ˈmər-sər\ *n* [ME, fr. AF, fr. *merz* merchandise, fr. L *merc-, merx*] (13c) *Brit* **:** a dealer in usu. expensive fabrics

mer·cer·ise *Brit var of* MERCERIZE

mer·cer·ize \ˈmər-sə-ˌrīz\ *vt* **-ized; -iz·ing** [John *Mercer* †1866 Eng. calico printer] (1852) **:** to give (as cotton yarn) luster, strength, and receptiveness to dyes by treatment under tension with caustic soda — **mer·cer·i·za·tion** \ˌmərs-rə-ˈzā-shən, ˌmər-sə-\ *n*

mer·cery \ˈmərs-rē, ˈmər-sə-\ *n, pl* **-cer·ies** (14c) *Brit* **:** a mercer's wares, shop, or occupation

merch \ˈmərch\ *n* (1982) **:** MERCHANDISE 2

[1]**mer·chan·dise** \ˈmər-chən-ˌdīz, -ˌdīs\ *n* [ME *marchaundise,* fr. AF *marchandise,* fr. *marcheant*] (13c) **1** *archaic* **:** the occupation of a merchant **:** TRADE **2 :** the commodities or goods that are bought and sold in business **:** WARES

[2]**mer·chan·dise** *also* **mer·chan·dize** \-ˌdīz\ *vb* **-dised** *also* **-dized; -dis·ing** *also* **-diz·ing** *vi* (14c) *archaic* **:** to carry on commerce **:** TRADE ~ *vt* **1 :** to buy and sell in business **2 :** to promote for or as if for sale ⟨~ a movie star⟩ — **mer·chan·dis·er** *n*

merchandising *also* **merchandizing** *n* (1917) **:** sales promotion as a comprehensive function including market research, development of new products, coordination of manufacture and marketing, and effective advertising and selling

[1]**mer·chant** \ˈmər-chənt\ *n* [ME *marchant,* fr. AF, fr. VL **mercatant-, mercatans,* fr. prp. of *mercatare* to trade, freq. of L *mercari* — more at MARKET] (13c) **1 a :** a buyer and seller of commodities for profit **:** TRADER **2 :** the operator of a retail business **:** STOREKEEPER **3 :** one that is noted for a particular quality or activity **:** SPECIALIST ⟨a speed ~ on the base paths⟩ — **merchant** *adj*

[2]**merchant** *vi* (14c) *archaic* **:** to deal or trade as a merchant ~ *vt* **:** to deal or trade in

mer·chant·able \ˈmər-chən-tə-bəl\ *adj* (15c) **:** of commercially acceptable quality **:** SALABLE — **mer·chant·abil·i·ty** \ˌmər-chən-tə-ˈbi-lə-tē\ *n*

merchant bank *n* (1904) *chiefly Brit* **:** a bank that specializes in bankers' acceptances and in underwriting or syndicating equity or bond issues — **merchant banker** *n* — **merchant banking** *n*

mer·chant·man \ˈmər-chənt-mən\ *n* (15c) **1** *archaic* **:** MERCHANT **2 :** a ship used in commerce

merchant marine *n* (1839) **1 :** the privately or publicly owned commercial ships of a nation **2 :** the personnel of a merchant marine; *specif* **:** a member of a merchant marine — **merchant mariner** *n*

merchant ship *n* (15c) **:** MERCHANTMAN 2

Mer·cian \ˈmər-sh(ē-)ən\ *n* (1513) **1 :** a native or inhabitant of Mercia **2 :** the Old English dialect of Mercia — **Mercian** *adj*

mer·ci·ful \ˈmər-si-fəl\ *adj* (14c) **:** full of mercy **:** COMPASSIONATE ⟨a ~ ruler⟩; *also* **:** providing relief ⟨a ~ end⟩ — **mer·ci·ful·ness** \-fəl-nəs\ *n*

mer·ci·ful·ly \-f(ə-)lē\ *adv* (14c) **1 :** in a merciful manner **2 :** FORTUNATELY 2 ⟨~ we didn't have to attend the meeting⟩

mer·ci·less \ˈmər-si-ləs\ *adj* (14c) **:** having or showing no mercy **:** PITILESS — **mer·ci·less·ly** *adv* — **mer·ci·less·ness** *n*

[1]**mer·cu·ri·al** \(ˌ)mər-ˈkyu̇r-ē-əl\ *adj* (14c) **1 :** of, relating to, or born under the planet Mercury **2 :** having qualities of eloquence, ingenuity, or thievishness attributed to the god Mercury or to the influence of the planet Mercury **3 :** characterized by rapid and unpredictable changeableness of mood ⟨a ~ temper⟩ **4 :** of, relating to, containing, or caused by mercury ***syn*** see INCONSTANT — **mer·cu·ri·al·ly** \-ē-ə-lē\ *adv* — **mer·cu·ri·al·ness** *n*

[2]**mercurial** *n* (1676) **:** a pharmaceutical or chemical containing mercury

mer·cu·ric \(ˌ)mər-ˈkyu̇r-ik\ *adj* (ca. 1828) **:** of, relating to, or containing mercury; *esp* **:** containing mercury with a valence of two

mercuric chloride *n* (1869) **:** a heavy crystalline poisonous compound $HgCl_2$ used as a disinfectant and fungicide and in photography

Mer·cu·ro·chrome \(ˌ)mər-ˈkyu̇r-ə-ˌkrōm\ *trademark* — used for merbromin

mer·cu·rous \(ˌ)mər-ˈkyu̇r-əs, ˈmər-kyə-rəs\ *adj* (1858) **:** of, relating to, or containing mercury; *esp* **:** containing mercury with a valence of one

mercurous chloride *n* (1859) **:** CALOMEL

mer·cu·ry \ˈmər-kyə-rē, -k(ə-)rē\ *n, pl* **-ries** [L *Mercurius,* Roman god and the planet] (14c) **1 a** *cap* **:** a Roman god of commerce, eloquence, travel, cunning, and theft who serves as messenger to the other gods — compare HERMES **b** *often cap, archaic* **:** a bearer of messages or news or a conductor of travelers **2** [ME *mercurie,* fr. ML *mercurius,* fr. L, the god] **a :** a silver-white poisonous heavy metallic element that is liquid at ordinary temperatures and is used esp. in batteries, in dental amalgam, and in scientific instruments — called also *quicksilver;* see ELEMENT table **b :** the column of mercury in a thermometer or barometer; *also* **:** TEMPERATURE ⟨the ~ rose above 70 degrees⟩ **3** *cap* **:** the planet nearest the sun — see PLANET table

mercury chloride *n* (ca. 1885) **:** a chloride of mercury: as **a :** CALOMEL **b :** MERCURIC CHLORIDE

mercury–vapor lamp *n* (1904) **:** an electric lamp in which the discharge takes place through mercury vapor — called also *mercury lamp*

mer·cy \ˈmər-sē\ *n, pl* **mercies** [ME, fr. AF *merci,* fr. ML *merced-, merces,* fr. L, price paid, wages, fr. *merc-, merx* merchandise] (13c) **1 a :** compassion or forbearance shown esp. to an offender or to one subject to one's power; *also* **:** lenient or compassionate treatment ⟨begged for ~⟩ **b :** imprisonment rather than death imposed as penalty for first-degree murder **2 a :** a blessing that is an act of divine favor or compassion **b :** a fortunate circumstance ⟨it was a ~ they found her before she froze⟩ **3 :** compassionate treatment of those in distress ⟨works of ~ among the poor⟩ — **mercy** *adj* — **at the mercy of :** wholly in the power of **:** with no way to protect oneself against

syn MERCY, CHARITY, CLEMENCY, GRACE, LENIENCY mean a disposition to show kindness or compassion. MERCY implies compassion that forbears punishing even when justice demands it ⟨threw himself on the *mercy* of the court⟩. CHARITY stresses benevolence and goodwill shown in broad understanding and tolerance of others ⟨show a little *charity* for the less fortunate⟩. CLEMENCY implies a mild or merciful disposition in one having the power or duty of punishing ⟨the judge refused to show *clemency*⟩. GRACE implies a benign attitude and a willingness to grant favors or make concessions ⟨by the *grace* of God⟩. LENIENCY implies lack of severity in punishing ⟨criticized the courts for excessive *leniency*⟩.

mercy killing *n* (1935) : EUTHANASIA

merde \ˈmerd\ *n* [F, fr. OF, fr. L *merda;* perh. akin to Lith *smirdėti* to stink] (1907) *sometimes vulgar* : ²CRAP 1a, 2

¹**mere** \ˈmir\ *n* [ME, fr. OE — more at MARINE] (bef. 12c) *chiefly Brit* : an expanse of standing water : LAKE, POOL

²**mere** *n* [ME, fr. OE *mǣre;* akin to ON land*mæri* borderland] (bef. 12c) : BOUNDARY; *also* : LANDMARK

³**mere** *adj, superlative* **mer·est** [ME, fr. L *merus;* akin to OE *āmerian* to purify and perh. to Gk *marmairein* to sparkle — more at MORN] (15c) **1** : having no admixture : PURE **2** *obs* : being nothing less than : ABSOLUTE **3** : being nothing more than ⟨a ~ mortal⟩ ⟨a ~ hint of spice⟩ — **mere·ly** *adv*

-mere *n comb form* [F *-mère,* fr. Gk *meros* part — more at MERIT] : part : segment ⟨meta*mere*⟩

me·ren·gue \mə-ˈreŋ-(ˌ)gā\ *n* [AmerSp] (1936) : a ballroom dance of Haitian and Dominican origin in 2/4 time in which one foot is dragged on every step; *also* : the music for a merengue

mer·e·tri·cious \ˌmer-ə-ˈtri-shəs\ *adj* [L *meretricius,* fr. *meretric-, meretrix* prostitute, fr. *merēre* to earn — more at MERIT] (1626) **1** : of or relating to a prostitute : having the nature of prostitution ⟨~ relationships⟩ **2 a** : tawdrily and falsely attractive ⟨the paradise they found was a piece of ~ trash —Carolyn See⟩ **b** : superficially significant : PRETENTIOUS ⟨scholarly names to provide fig-leaves of respectability for ~ but stylish books —*Times Lit. Supp.*⟩ ***syn*** see GAUDY — **mer·e·tri·cious·ly** *adv* — **mer·e·tri·cious·ness** *n*

mer·gan·ser \(ˌ)mər-ˈgan(t)-sər\ *n* [NL, fr. L *mergus,* a waterfowl (fr. *mergere*) + *anser* goose — more at GOOSE] (1668) : any of various fish-eating diving ducks (esp. genus *Mergus*) with a slender bill hooked at the end and serrated along the margins and usu. a crested head

merge \ˈmərj\ *vb* **merged; merg·ing** [L *mergere;* akin to Skt *majjati* he dives] *vt* (1636) **1** *archaic* : to plunge or engulf in something : IMMERSE **2** : to cause to combine, unite, or coalesce **3** : to blend gradually by stages that blur distinctions ~ *vi* **1** : to become combined into one **2** : to blend or come together without abrupt change ⟨*merging* traffic⟩ ***syn*** see MIX — **mer·gence** \ˈmər-jən(t)s\ *n*

merg·er \ˈmər-jər\ *n* [*merge* + *-er* (as in *waiver*)] (1728) **1** *law* : the absorption of an estate, a contract, or an interest in another, of a minor offense in a greater, or of a cause of action into a judgment **2 a** : the act or process of merging **b** : absorption by a corporation of one or more others; *also* : any of various methods of combining two or more organizations (as business concerns)

me·rid·i·an \mə-ˈri-dē-ən\ *n* [ME, fr. AF *meridien,* fr. *meridien* of noon, fr. L *meridianus,* fr. *meridies* noon, south, irreg. fr. *medius* mid + *dies* day — more at MID, DEITY] (14c) **1** *archaic* : the hour of noon : MIDDAY **2** : a great circle of the celestial sphere passing through its poles and the zenith of a given place — see AZIMUTH illustration **3** : a high point **4 a** (1) : a great circle on the surface of the earth passing through the poles (2) : the half of such a circle included between the poles **b** : a representation of such a circle or half circle numbered for longitude on a map or globe — see LONGITUDE illustration **5** : any of the pathways along which the body's vital energy flows according to the theory behind acupuncture — **meridian** *adj*

¹**me·rid·i·o·nal** \mə-ˈri-dē-ə-nᵊl\ *adj* [ME, fr. MF *meridionel,* fr. LL *meridionalis,* fr. L *meridies*] (14c) **1** : of, relating to, or situated in the south : SOUTHERN **2** : of, relating to, or characteristic of people living in the south esp. of France **3** : of, relating to, or situated on or along a meridian — **me·rid·i·o·nal·ly** \-nᵊl-ē\ *adv*

²**meridional** *n* (1878) : a native or inhabitant of southern Europe and esp. southern France

me·ringue \mə-ˈraŋ\ *n* [F] (1706) **1** : a dessert topping consisting of a baked mixture of stiffly beaten egg whites and sugar **2** : a shell made of meringue and filled with fruit or ice cream

me·ri·no \mə-ˈrē-(ˌ)nō\ *n, pl* **-nos** [Sp] (1804) **1** : any of a breed of fine-wooled white sheep originating in Spain and producing a heavy fleece of exceptional quality **2** : a soft wool or wool and cotton clothing fabric resembling cashmere **3** : a fine wool and cotton yarn used for hosiery and knitwear — **merino** *adj*

-merism *n comb form* [ISV, fr. Gk *meros* part — more at MERIT] : possession of (such) an arrangement of or relation among constituent chemical units ⟨tauto*merism*⟩

mer·i·stem \ˈmer-ə-ˌstem\ *n* [Gk *meristos* divided (fr. *merizein* to divide, fr. *meros*) + E *-em* (as in *system*)] (1872) : a formative plant tissue usu. made up of small cells capable of dividing indefinitely and giving rise to similar cells or to cells that differentiate to produce the definitive tissues and organs — **mer·i·ste·mat·ic** \ˌmer-əs-tə-ˈma-tik\ *adj* — **mer·i·ste·mat·i·cal·ly** \-ti-k(ə-)lē\ *adv*

me·ris·tic \mə-ˈris-tik\ *adj* [Gk *meristos*] (1894) **1** : SEGMENTAL **2** : involving modification in number or in geometrical relation of body parts ⟨~ variation in petals⟩ — **me·ris·ti·cal·ly** \-ti-k(ə-)lē\ *adv*

¹**mer·it** \ˈmer-ət, ˈme-rət\ *n* [ME, fr. AF *merite,* fr. L *meritum,* fr. neut. of *meritus,* pp. of *merēre* to deserve, earn; akin to Gk *meiresthai* to receive as one's portion, *meros* part] (14c) **1 a** *obs* : reward or punishment due **b** : the qualities or actions that constitute the basis of one's deserts **c** : a praiseworthy quality : VIRTUE **d** : character or conduct deserving reward, honor, or esteem; *also* : ACHIEVEMENT **2** : spiritual credit held to be earned by performance of righteous acts and to ensure future benefits **3 a** *pl* : the substance of a legal case apart from matters of jurisdiction, procedure, or form **b** : individual significance or justification — **mer·it·less** \-ləs\ *adj*

²**merit** *vt* (1526) : to be worthy of or entitled or liable to : EARN ~ *vi* **1** *obs* : to be entitled to reward or honor **2** : DESERVE

mer·i·toc·ra·cy \ˌmer-ə-ˈtä-krə-sē\ *n, pl* **-cies** [¹*merit* + *-o-* + *-cracy*] (1958) **1** : a system in which the talented are chosen and moved ahead on the basis of their achievement **2** : leadership selected on the basis of intellectual criteria — **mer·it·o·crat·ic** \ˌmer-ə-tə-ˈkra-tik\ *adj*

mer·it·o·crat \ˈmer-ə-tə-ˌkrat\ *n* (1960) *chiefly Brit* : a person who advances through a meritocratic system

mer·i·to·ri·ous \ˌmer-ə-ˈtȯr-ē-əs\ *adj* (15c) : deserving of honor or esteem — **mer·i·to·ri·ous·ly** *adv* — **mer·i·to·ri·ous·ness** *n*

merit system *n* (1879) : a system by which appointments and promotions in the civil service are based on competence rather than political favoritism

¹**merle** *also* **merl** \ˈmər(-ə)l\ *n* [ME, fr. AF, fr. L *merulus;* akin to OE *ōsle* blackbird, OHG *amsla*] (15c) : BLACKBIRD 1a

²**merle** *n* [origin unknown] (1911) : a bluish or reddish gray mixed with splotches of black that is the color of the coats of some dogs

mer·lin \ˈmər-lən\ *n* [ME *merlioun,* fr. AF *merilun,* alter. of *esmerilun,* aug. of OF *esmeril,* of Gmc origin; akin to OHG *smiril* merlin] (14c) : a small compact falcon (*Falco columbarius*) of the northern hemisphere having a broad dark terminal band on the tail and upperparts that are slate blue in males and brown in females

Mer·lin \ˈmər-lən\ *n* [ML *Merlinus,* fr. MW *Myrddin*] (13c) : a prophet and magician in Arthurian legend

mer·lon \ˈmər-lən\ *n* [F, fr. It *merlone,* aug. of *merlo* battlement, fr. ML *merulus,* fr. L, merle] (ca. 1704) : any of the solid intervals between crenellations of a battlement — see BATTLEMENT illustration

mer·lot \mer-ˈlō, mər-\ *n, often cap* [F] (ca. 1941) : a dry red wine made from a widely grown grape orig. used in the Bordeaux region of France for blending; *also* : the grape itself

mer·maid \ˈmər-ˌmād\ *n* [ME *mermayde,* fr. *mere* sea (fr. OE) + *mayde* maid — more at MARINE] (14c) : a fabled marine creature with the head and upper body of a woman and the tail of a fish

mer·man \-ˌman, -mən\ *n* (1601) : a fabled marine creature with the head and upper body of a man and the tail of a fish

mero- *comb form* [ISV, fr. Gk, fr. *meros* part — more at MERIT] : part : partial ⟨*mero*blastic⟩

mer·o·blas·tic \ˌmer-ə-ˈblas-tik\ *adj* [ISV] (1870) : characterized by incomplete cleavage as a result of the presence of a mass of yolk material — compare HOLOBLASTIC — **mer·o·blas·ti·cal·ly** \-ti-k(ə-)lē\ *adv*

mer·o·crine \ˈmer-ə-krən, -ˌkrīn, -ˌkrēn\ *adj* [ISV, fr *mero-* + Gk *krinein* to separate — more at CERTAIN] (ca. 1905) : producing a secretion that is discharged without major damage to the secretory cells; *also* : produced by a merocrine gland

mer·o·mor·phic \ˌmer-ə-ˈmȯr-fik\ *adj* (ca. 1890) : relating to or being a function of a complex variable that is analytic everywhere in a region except for singularities at each of which infinity is the limit and each of which is contained in a neighborhood where the function is analytic except for the singular point itself

mer·o·my·o·sin \ˌmer-ə-ˈmī-ə-sən\ *n* (1952) : either of two structural subunits of myosin that are obtained esp. by tryptic digestion

-merous *adj comb form* [NL *-merus,* fr. Gk *-merēs,* fr. *meros* — more at MERIT] : having (such or so many) parts ⟨di*merous*⟩

Mer·o·vin·gian \ˌmer-ə-ˈvin-j(ē-)ən\ *adj* [F *mérovingien,* fr. ML *Merovingi* Merovingians, fr. *Merovaeus* Merowig †458 Frankish founder of the dynasty] (1687) : of or relating to the first Frankish dynasty reigning from about A.D. 500 to 751 — **Merovingian** *n*

mer·o·zo·ite \ˌmer-ə-ˈzō-ˌīt\ *n* [ISV, fr. *mero-* + *zo-* + *-ite*] (1900) : a sporozoan trophozoite produced by schizogony that is capable of initiating a new sexual or asexual cycle of development

mer·ri·ment \ˈmer-i-mənt, ˈme-ri-\ *n* (1574) **1** : lighthearted gaiety or fun-making : HILARITY **2** : a lively celebration or party : FESTIVITY

mer·ry \ˈmer-ē, ˈme-rē\ *adj* **mer·ri·er; -est** [ME *mery,* fr. OE *myrge, merge;* akin to OHG *murg* short — more at BRIEF] (bef. 12c) **1** *archaic* : giving pleasure : DELIGHTFUL **2** : full of gaiety or high spirits : MIRTHFUL **3** : marked by festivity or gaiety **4** : QUICK, BRISK ⟨a ~ pace⟩ — **mer·ri·ly** \ˈmer-ə-lē, ˈme-rə-\ *adv* — **mer·ri·ness** \ˈmer-ē-nəs, ˈme-rē-\ *n*

syn MERRY, BLITHE, JOCUND, JOVIAL, JOLLY mean showing high spirits or lightheartedness. MERRY suggests cheerful, joyous, uninhibited enjoyment of frolic or festivity ⟨a *merry* group of revelers⟩. BLITHE suggests carefree, innocent, or even heedless gaiety ⟨arrived late in his usual *blithe* way⟩. JOCUND stresses elation and exhilaration of spirits ⟨singing, dancing, and *jocund* feasting⟩. JOVIAL suggests the stimulation of conviviality and good fellowship ⟨dinner put them in a *jovial* mood⟩. JOLLY suggests high spirits expressed in laughing, bantering, and jesting ⟨our *jolly* host enlivened the party⟩.

mer·ry–an·drew \ˌmer-ē-ˈan-(ˌ)drü\ *n, often cap M&A* [*merry* + *Andrew,* proper name] (1677) : a person who clowns publicly

mer·ry–go–round \ˈmer-ē-gō-ˌrau̇nd, -gə-\ *n* (1729) **1** : an amusement park ride with seats often in the form of animals (as horses) revolving about a fixed center **2** : a cycle of activity that is complex, fast-paced, or difficult to break out of ⟨the corporate ~⟩

mer·ry·mak·er \ˈmer-ē-ˌmā-kər\ *n* (1797) : REVELER

mer·ry·mak·ing \-kiŋ\ *n* (1618) **1** : gay or festive activity : CONVIVIALITY **2** : a convivial occasion : FESTIVITY

mer·ry·thought \ˈmer-ē-ˌthȯt\ *n* (1607) *chiefly Brit* : WISHBONE

merry widow *n, often cap M&W* [*The Merry Widow,* operetta (1905) by Franz Lehár] (1952) : a strapless corset or bustier usu. having garters attached

Mer·thi·o·late \(ˌ)mər-ˈthī-ə-ˌlāt, -lət\ *trademark* — used for thimerosal

mes- *or* **meso-** *comb form* [L, fr. Gk, fr. *mesos* — more at MID] **1** : mid : in the middle ⟨*meso*carp⟩ **2** : intermediate (as in size or type) ⟨*meso*morph⟩ ⟨*meson*⟩

me·sa \ˈmā-sə\ *n* [Sp, lit., table, fr. L *mensa*] (1840) : an isolated relatively flat-topped natural elevation usu. more extensive than a butte and less extensive than a plateau; *also* : a broad terrace with an abrupt slope on one side : BENCH

més·al·liance \ˌmā-ˌzal-ˈyäⁿs, ˌmā-zə-ˈlī-ən(t)s\ *n, pl* **mésalliances** \-ˈyäⁿs(-əz), -ˈlī-ən(t)-səz\ [F, fr. *més-* mis- + *alliance*] (1782) : a marriage with a person of inferior social position

mes·arch \ˈme-ˌzärk, ˈmē-, -ˌsärk\ *adj* (1891) : having metaxylem developed both internal and external to the protoxylem

mes·cal \me-ˈskal, mə-\ *n* [AmerSp *mezcal, mescal,* fr. Nahuatl *mexcalli* liquor made from the maguey plant] (1887) **1** : PEYOTE 2 **2 a** : a

\ə\ **abut** \ᵊ\ kitten, F table \ər\ **further** \a\ **ash** \ā\ **ace** \ä\ **mop, mar** \au̇\ **out** \ch\ **chin** \e\ **bet** \ē\ **easy** \g\ **go** \i\ **hit** \ī\ **ice** \j\ **job** \ŋ\ **sing** \ō\ **go** \ȯ\ **law** \ȯi\ **boy** \th\ **thin** \t͟h\ **the** \ü\ **loot** \u̇\ **foot** \y\ **yet** \zh\ **vision, beige** \k̲, ⁿ, œ, ue, ʸ\ *see* Guide to Pronunciation

usu. colorless Mexican liquor distilled esp. from the central leaves of maguey plants **b** : a plant from which mescal is produced; *esp* : MAGUEY

mescal button *n* (1887) : PEYOTE BUTTON

Mes·ca·le·ro \ˌmes-kə-ˈler-(ˌ)ō\ *n, pl* **Mescalero** *or* **Mescaleros** [AmerSp, fr. *mezcal, mescal* maguey, mescal liquor] (1831) : a member of an Apache people of Texas and New Mexico

mes·ca·line \ˈmes-kə-lən, -ˌlēn\ *n* (1896) : a hallucinatory crystalline alkaloid $C_{11}H_{17}NO_3$ that is the chief active principle in peyote buttons

mes·clun \ˈmes-klən\ *n* [F, fr. Occitan, lit., mixture, fr. *mescla* to mix, fr. Old Occitan *mesclar,* fr. VL **misculare* — more at MEDDLE] (1976) : a mixture of young tender greens (as lettuces, arugula, and chicory); *also* : a salad made with mesclun

mesdames *pl of* MADAM *or of* MADAME *or of* MRS.

mesdemoiselles *pl of* MADEMOISELLE

me·seems \mi-ˈsēmz\ *vb impersonal, past* **me·seemed** \-ˈsēmd\ (15c) *archaic* : it seems to me

me·sem·bry·an·the·mum \mə-ˌzem-brē-ˈan(t)-thə-məm\ *n* [NL, irreg. fr. Gk *mesēmbria* midday (fr. *mes-* + *hēmera* day) + *anthemon* flower, fr. *anthos* — more at ANTHOLOGY] (1753) : any of a genus (*Mesembryanthemum*) of chiefly southern African fleshy-leaved herbs or subshrubs of the carpetweed family

mes·en·ceph·a·lon \ˌme-ˌzen-ˈse-fə-ˌlän, ˌmē-, -zᵊn-, -ˌsen-, -sᵊn-, -lən\ *n* [NL] (1846) : MIDBRAIN — **mes·en·ce·phal·ic** \-ˌzen(t)-sə-ˈfa-lik, -zᵊn(t)-, -ˌsen(t)-, -sᵊn(t)-\ *adj*

mes·en·chy·mal \mə-ˈzeŋ-kə-məl, -ˈseŋ-; ˌme-zᵊn-ˈkī-məl, ˌmē-, -sᵊn-\ *adj* [ISV] (1886) : of, resembling, or being mesenchyme

mes·en·chyme \ˈme-zᵊn-ˌkīm, ˈmē-, -sᵊn-\ *n* [G *Mesenchym,* fr. *mes-* + NL *-enchyma*] (1888) : loosely organized undifferentiated mostly mesodermal cells that give rise to such structures as connective tissues, blood, lymphatics, bone, and cartilage

mes·en·ter·on \(ˌ)me-ˈzen-tə-ˌrän, ˌmē-, -ˈsen-, -rən\ *n, pl* **-tera** \-tə-rə\ [NL] (1877) : the part of the alimentary canal that is developed from the archenteron and is lined with hypoblast

mes·en·tery \ˈme-zᵊn-ˌter-ē, -sᵊn-\ *n, pl* **-ter·ies** [ME *mesenterie,* fr. ML *mesenterion,* fr. Gk, fr. *mes-* + *enteron* intestine — more at INTER-] (15c) **1 a** : one or more vertebrate membranes that consist of a double fold of the peritoneum and invest the intestines and their appendages and connect them with the dorsal wall of the abdominal cavity **b** : a fold of membrane comparable to a mesentery and supporting a viscus (as the heart) that is not a part of the digestive tract **2** : a support or partition in an invertebrate like the vertebrate mesentery — **mes·en·ter·ic** \ˌme-zᵊn-ˈter-ik, -sᵊn-\ *adj*

[1]**mesh** \ˈmesh\ *n* [ME, prob. fr. MD *maesche;* akin to OHG *masca* mesh, Lith *mazgos* knot] (14c) **1** : one of the openings between the threads or cords of a net; *also* : one of the similar spaces in a network — often used to designate screen size as the number of openings per linear inch **2 a** : the fabric of a net **b** : a woven, knit, or knotted material of open texture with evenly spaced holes **c** : an arrangement of interlocking metal links used esp. for jewelry **3 a** : a weblike pattern or construction **b** : WEB, SNARE — usu. used in pl. **4** : working contact (as of the teeth of gears) ⟨in ∼⟩ — **meshed** \ˈmesht\ *adj*

[2]**mesh** *vt* (1532) **1 a** : ENMESH, ENTANGLE **b** : to catch in the openings of a net **2** : to cause to resemble network **3 a** : to cause (as gears) to engage **b** : to coordinate closely : INTERLOCK ∼ *vi* **1** : to become entangled in or as if in meshes **2** : to be in or come into mesh — used esp. of gears **3** : to fit or work together properly

me·shuga *or* **me·shug·ge** *also* **me·shug·ah** *or* **me·shug·gah** \mə-ˈshu̇-gə\ *adj* [Yiddish *meshuge,* fr. Heb *mĕshuggāʿ*] (1885) : CRAZY, FOOLISH

me·shug·gen·er \-ˈshu̇-gə-nər\ *n* [Yiddish *meshugener,* fr. *meshuge*] (1900) : a foolish or crazy person

mesh·work \ˈmesh-ˌwərk\ *n* (1830) : NETWORK 2 ⟨a vascular ∼⟩

me·si·al \ˈmē-zē-əl, -sē-\ *adj* (1803) **1** : MIDDLE, MEDIAN **2** : of, relating to, or being the surface of a tooth that is next to the tooth in front of it or that is closest to the middle of the front of the jaw — compare DISTAL 2 — **me·si·al·ly** \-ə-lē\ *adv*

[1]**me·sic** \ˈme-zik, ˈmē-, -sik\ *adj* [*mes-* + *-ic*] (1926) : characterized by, relating to, or requiring a moderate amount of moisture ⟨a ∼ habitat⟩ ⟨a ∼ plant⟩ — compare HYDRIC, XERIC

[2]**mesic** *adj* [*meson* + *-ic*] (1939) : of or relating to a meson

mes·mer·ic \mez-ˈmer-ik *also* mes-\ *adj* (1829) **1** : of, relating to, or induced by mesmerism **2** : FASCINATING, IRRESISTIBLE — **mes·mer·i·cal·ly** \-i-k(ə-)lē\ *adv*

mes·mer·ise *Brit var of* MESMERIZE

mes·mer·ism \ˈmez-mə-ˌri-zəm *also* ˈmes-\ *n* [F. A. *Mesmer*] (1784) **1** : hypnotic induction held to involve animal magnetism; *broadly* : HYPNOTISM **2** : hypnotic appeal — **mes·mer·ist** \-rist\ *n*

mes·mer·ize \-mə-ˌrīz\ *vt* **-ized; -iz·ing** (1829) **1** : to subject to mesmerism; *also* : HYPNOTIZE **2** : SPELLBIND — **mes·mer·iz·er** *n*

mesne \ˈmēn\ *adj* [AF *mesne, meiene* — more at MEAN] (ca. 1558) : INTERMEDIATE, INTERVENING — used in law

mesne lord *n* (1611) : a feudal lord who holds land as tenant of a superior (as a king) but who is lord to his own tenant

meso- — see MES-

me·so·carp \ˈme-zə-ˌkärp, ˈmē-, -sə-\ *n* (1829) : the middle layer of a pericarp — see ENDOCARP illustration

me·so·cy·clone \ˌme-zə-ˈsī-ˌklōn, ˌmē-, -sə-ˈsī-\ *n* (1963) : a rapidly rotating air mass within a thunderstorm that often gives rise to a tornado

me·so·derm \ˈme-zə-ˌdərm, ˈmē-, -sə-\ *n* [ISV] (1873) : the middle of the three primary germ layers of an embryo that is the source of many bodily tissues and structures (as bone, muscle, connective tissue, and dermis); *broadly* : tissue derived from this germ layer — **me·so·der·mal** \ˌme-zə-ˈdər-məl, ˌmē-, -sə-\ *adj*

me·so·glea *also* **me·so·gloea** \ˌme-zə-ˈglē-ə, ˌmē-, -sə-\ *n* [NL, fr. *mes-* + LGk *gloia, glia* glue — more at CLAY] (1886) : a gelatinous substance between the endoderm and ectoderm of sponges or coelenterates

Me·so·lith·ic \ˌme-zə-ˈli-thik\ *adj* [ISV] (1866) : of, relating to, or being a transitional period of the Stone Age between the Paleolithic and the Neolithic

me·so·mere \ˈme-zə-ˌmir, ˈmē-, -sə-\ *n* (ca. 1900) : a blastomere of medium size; *also* : an intermediate part of the mesoderm

me·so·morph \ˈme-zə-ˌmȯrf, ˈmē-, -sə-\ *n* [*meso*derm + *-morph*] (1940) : a mesomorphic body or person

me·so·mor·phic \ˌme-zə-ˈmȯr-fik, ˌmē-, -sə-\ *adj* [*meso*derm + *-morphic;* fr. the predominance in such types of structures developed from the mesoderm] (1940) **1** : of or relating to the component in W. H. Sheldon's classification of body types that measures esp. the degree of muscularity and bone development **2** : having a husky muscular body build — **me·so·mor·phy** \ˈme-zə-ˌmȯr-fē, -sə-\ *n*

me·son \ˈme-ˌzän, ˈmā-, ˈmē-, -ˌsän\ *n* [ISV *mes-* + [2]*-on*] (1939) : any of a group of fundamental particles (as the pion and kaon) made up of a quark and an antiquark that are subject to the strong force and have zero or an integer number of quantum units of spin — **me·son·ic** \me-ˈzä-nik, mā-, mē-, -ˈsä-\ *adj*

me·so·neph·ros \ˌme-zə-ˈne-frəs, ˌmē-, -sə-, -ˌfräs\ *n, pl* **-neph·roi** \-ˌfrȯi\ [NL, fr. *mes-* + Gk *nephros* kidney — more at NEPHRITIS] (1887) : either member of the second and midmost of the three paired vertebrate renal organs that functions in adult fishes and amphibians but functions only in the embryo of reptiles, birds, and mammals in which it is replaced by a metanephros in the adult — compare METANEPHROS, PRONEPHROS — **me·so·neph·ric** \-frik\ *adj*

me·so·pause \ˈme-zə-ˌpȯz, ˈmē-, -sə-\ *n* [*meso*sphere + *pause*] (1950) : the upper boundary of the mesosphere where the temperature of the atmosphere reaches its lowest point

me·so·pe·lag·ic \ˌme-zə-pə-ˈla-jik, ˌmē-, -sə-\ *adj* (1947) : of or relating to oceanic depths from about 600 feet to 3000 feet (200 to 1000 meters)

me·so·phyll \ˈme-zə-ˌfil, ˈmē-, -sə-\ *n* [NL *mesophyllum,* fr. *mes-* + Gk *phyllon* leaf — more at BLADE] (1848) : the parenchyma between the epidermal layers of a foliage leaf — **me·so·phyl·lic** \ˌme-zə-ˈfi-lik, ˌmē-, -sə-\ *or* **me·so·phyl·lous** \-ləs\ *adj*

me·so·phyte \ˈme-zə-ˌfīt, ˈmē-, -sə-\ *n* [ISV] (1896) : a plant that grows under medium conditions of moisture — **me·so·phyt·ic** \ˌme-zə-ˈfi-tik, ˌmē-, -sə-\ *adj*

me·so·scale \ˈme-zə-ˌskāl, ˈmē-, -sə-\ *adj* (1956) : of intermediate size; *esp* : of or relating to a meteorological phenomenon approximately 10 to 1000 kilometers in horizontal extent ⟨∼ cloud pattern⟩

me·so·some \-ˌsōm\ *n* (1960) : an organelle of bacteria that appears as an invagination of the plasma membrane and functions either in DNA replication and cell division or excretion of exoenzymes

me·so·sphere \-ˌsfir\ *n* (1950) : the part of the earth's atmosphere between the stratosphere and the thermosphere in which temperature decreases with altitude to the atmosphere's absolute minimum — **me·so·spher·ic** \ˌme-zə-ˈsfir-ik, ˌmē-, -sə-, -ˈsfer-\ *adj*

me·so·the·li·o·ma \ˌme-zə-ˌthē-lē-ˈō-mə, ˌmē-, -sə-\ *n, pl* **-mas** *also* **-ma·ta** \-mə-tə\ [NL] (ca. 1899) : a usu. malignant tumor derived from mesothelial tissue (as that lining the peritoneum or pleura)

me·so·the·li·um \-ˈthē-lē-əm\ *n, pl* **-lia** \-lē-ə\ [NL, fr. *mes-* + *epithelium*] (1886) : epithelium derived from mesoderm that lines the body cavity of a vertebrate embryo and gives rise to epithelia (as of the peritoneum, pericardium, and pleura), striated muscle, heart muscle, and several minor structures — **me·so·the·li·al** \-lē-əl\ *adj*

me·so·tho·rac·ic \-thə-ˈra-sik\ *adj* (1839) : of or relating to the mesothorax

me·so·tho·rax \-ˈthȯr-ˌaks\ *n* [NL] (ca. 1826) : the middle of the three segments of the thorax of an insect — see INSECT illustration

me·so·tro·phic \ˌme-zə-ˈtrō-fik, ˌmē-, -sə-, -ˈträ-fik\ *adj* (1911) *of a body of water* : having a moderate amount of dissolved nutrients — compare EUTROPHIC, OLIGOTROPHIC

Me·so·zo·ic \-ˈzō-ik\ *adj* (1840) : of, relating to, or being an era of geological history comprising the interval between the Permian and the Tertiary or the corresponding system of rocks that was marked by the presence of dinosaurs, marine and flying reptiles, ammonites, ferns, and gymnosperms and the appearance of angiosperms, mammals, and birds — see GEOLOGIC TIME table — **Mesozoic** *n*

mes·quite \mə-ˈskēt, me-\ *n* [AmerSp, fr. Nahuatl *mizquitl*] (1759) : any of several spiny leguminous trees or shrubs (genus *Prosopis* and esp. *P. glandulosa*) chiefly of the southwestern U.S. that often form extensive thickets and have sweet pods eaten by livestock; *also* : the wood of the mesquite used esp. in grilling food

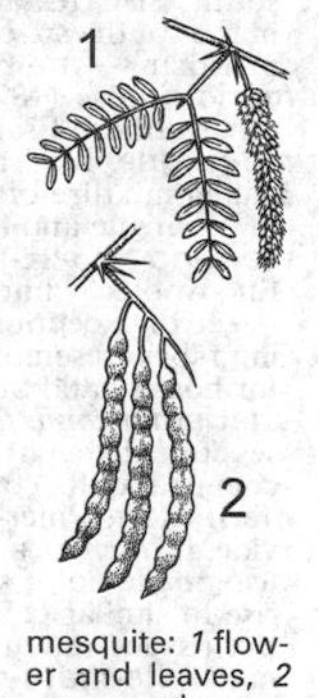

mesquite: *1* flower and leaves, *2* pod

[1]**mess** \ˈmes\ *n* [ME *mes,* fr. AF, fr. LL *missus* course at a meal, fr. *missus,* pp. of *mittere* to put, fr. L, to send — more at SMITE] (14c) **1** : a quantity of food: **a** *archaic* : food set on a table at one time **b** : a prepared dish of soft food; *also* : a mixture of ingredients cooked or eaten together **c** : enough food of a specified kind for a dish or a meal ⟨picked a ∼ of peas for dinner⟩ **2 a** : a group of persons who regularly take their meals together; *also* : a meal so taken **b** : a place where meals are regularly served to a group : MESS HALL **3 a** : a disordered, untidy, offensive, or unpleasant state or condition ⟨your room is in a ∼⟩ **b** : one that is disordered, untidy, offensive, or unpleasant usu. because of blundering, laxity, or misconduct ⟨[the movie] is a ∼, as sloppy in concept as it is in execution —Judith Crist⟩ **4** : a large quantity or number

[2]**mess** *vt* (14c) **1** : to provide with meals at a mess **2 a** : to make dirty or untidy : DISARRANGE — often used with *up* ⟨don't ∼ up your room⟩ **b** : to mix up : BUNGLE — often used with *up* ⟨really ∼*ed* up my life⟩ **3** : to interfere with — often used with *up* ⟨magnetic storms that ∼ up communications —*Time*⟩ **4** : to rough up : MANHANDLE — often used with *up* ⟨∼ him up good so he won't cheat us again⟩ ∼ *vi* **1** : to take meals with a mess **2** : to make a mess **3 a** : PUTTER, TRIFLE ⟨children like to ∼ around with paints⟩ **b** : to handle or play with something esp. carelessly ⟨don't ∼ with my camera⟩ — often used with *around* **c** : to take an active interest in something or someone ⟨∼*ing* around with new video techniques⟩; *also* : INTERFERE, MEDDLE ⟨∼*ing* in other people's affairs⟩ ⟨you'd better not ∼ with me⟩ **4** : to become confused or make an error — usu. used with *up*

[1]**mes·sage** \ˈme-sij\ *n* [ME, fr. AF, fr. ML *missaticum,* fr. L *missus,* pp. of *mittere*] (14c) **1** : a communication in writing, in speech, or by signals **2** : a messenger's mission **3** : an underlying theme or idea

[2]**message** *vb* **mes·saged; mes·sag·ing** *vt* (1583) **1** : to send as a message or by messenger **2** : to send a message to ∼ *vi* : to communicate by message

message board *n* (1973) : BULLETIN BOARD 2
mes·sa·line \ˌme-sə-ˈlēn\ *n* [F] (ca. 1890) : a soft lightweight silk dress fabric with a satin weave
mes·san \ˈme-sᵊn\ *n* [ME (Sc), fr. ScGael *measan*] (15c) *chiefly Scot* : LAPDOG 1
mess around *vi* (1918) **1** : to waste time : DAWDLE, IDLE **2 a** : ASSOCIATE ⟨didn't *mess around* with gangs⟩ **b** : FLIRT, PHILANDER
messeigneurs *pl of* MONSEIGNEUR
mes·sen·ger \ˈme-sᵊn-jər\ *n* [ME *messangere,* fr. AF *messager, messanger,* fr. *message*] (14c) **1** : one who bears a message or does an errand: as **a** *archaic* : FORERUNNER, HERALD **b** : a dispatch bearer in government or military service **c** : an employee who carries messages **2** : a light line used in hauling a heavier line (as between ships) **3** : a substance (as a hormone) that mediates a biological effect **4** : MESSENGER RNA
messenger RNA *n* (1961) : an RNA produced by transcription that carries the code for a particular protein from the nuclear DNA to a ribosome in the cytoplasm and acts as a template for the formation of that protein — compare TRANSFER RNA
mess hall *n* (1843) : a hall or building (as on an army post) in which mess is served
mes·si·ah \mə-ˈsī-ə\ *n* [Heb *māshīaḥ* & Aram *mĕshīḥā,* lit., anointed] (1560) **1** *cap* **a** : the expected king and deliverer of the Jews **b** : JESUS 1 **2** : a professed or accepted leader of some hope or cause — **mes·si·ah·ship** \-ˌship\ *n*
mes·si·an·ic \ˌme-sē-ˈa-nik\ *adj* [prob. fr. F *messianique,* fr. *messianisme*] (ca. 1834) **1** : of or relating to a messiah **2** : marked by idealism and an aggressive crusading spirit ⟨~ zeal⟩
mes·si·a·nism \ˈme-sē-ə-ˌni-zəm; mə-ˈsī-ə-, me-\ *n* [F *messianisme,* fr. *messie* messiah + *-anisme* (as in *christianisme* Christianity)] (1867) **1** : belief in a messiah as the savior of humankind **2** : religious devotion to an ideal or cause
Mes·si·as \mə-ˈsī-əs\ *n* [ME, fr. OE, fr. LL, fr. Gk, fr. Aram *mĕshīḥā*] (bef. 12c) : MESSIAH 1
messieurs *pl of* MONSIEUR
mess jacket *n* (1878) : a fitted waist-length man's jacket worn esp. as part of a dress uniform
mess kit *n* (1855) : a compact kit of nested cooking and eating utensils for use by soldiers and campers
mess·mate \ˈmes-ˌmāt\ *n* (1664) : a person with whom one regularly takes mess (as on a ship)
mess over *vt* (1963) *slang* : to treat harshly or unfairly : ABUSE
Messrs. \ˈme-sərz\ *pl of* MR. ⟨~ Jones, Brown, and Robinson⟩
mes·suage \ˈmes-wij\ *n* [ME, fr. AF, fr. ML *messuagium*] (14c) : PREMISE 3b
messy \ˈme-sē\ *adj* **mess·i·er; -est** (1843) **1** : marked by confusion, disorder, or dirt : UNTIDY ⟨a ~ room⟩ **2** : lacking neatness or precision : CARELESS, SLOVENLY **3** : extremely unpleasant or trying ⟨~ lawsuits⟩ — **mess·i·ly** \ˈme-sə-lē\ *adv* — **mess·i·ness** \ˈme-sē-nəs\ *n*
mes·ti·za \me-ˈstē-zə\ *n* [Sp, fem. of *mestizo*] (ca. 1589) : a woman who is a mestizo
mes·ti·zo \-(ˌ)zō\ *n, pl* **-zos** [Sp, fr. *mestizo,* adj., mixed, fr. LL *mixticius,* fr. L *mixtus,* pp. of *miscēre* to mix — more at MIX] (1582) : a person of mixed blood; *specif* : a person of mixed European and American Indian ancestry
mes·tra·nol \ˈmes-trə-ˌnȯl, -ˌnōl\ *n* [*meth-* + *estr*ogen + pregn*ane* ($C_{21}H_{36}$) + *¹-ol*] (1962) : a synthetic estrogen $C_{21}H_{26}O_2$ used in oral contraceptives
[1]**met** *past and past part of* MEET
[2]**met** *abbr* **1** meteorological; meteorology **2** metropolitan
meta- *or* **met-** *prefix* [NL & ML, fr. L or Gk; L, fr. Gk, among, with, after, fr. *meta* among, with, after; akin to OE *mid, mith* with, OHG *mit*] **1 a** : occurring later than or in succession to : after ⟨*met*estrus⟩ **b** : situated behind or beyond ⟨*met*encephalon⟩ ⟨*meta*carpus⟩ **c** : later or more highly organized or specialized form of ⟨*meta*xylem⟩ **2** : change : transformation ⟨*meta*plasia⟩ **3** [*metaphysics*] : more comprehensive : transcending ⟨*meta*psychological⟩ — usu. used with the name of a discipline to designate a new but related discipline designed to deal critically with the original one ⟨*meta*mathematics⟩ **4 a** : involving substitution at or characterized by two positions in the benzene ring that are separated by one carbon atom ⟨*meta*-xylene⟩ **b** : derived from by loss of water ⟨*meta*phosphoric acid⟩
meta–anal·y·sis \ˌme-tə-ə-ˈna-lə-səs\ *n* (1976) : a quantitative statistical analysis of several separate but similar experiments or studies in order to test the pooled data for statistical significance
met·a·bol·ic \ˌme-tə-ˈbä-lik\ *adj* (1841) : of, relating to, or based on metabolism — **met·a·bol·i·cal·ly** \-li-k(ə-)lē\ *adv*
metabolic syndrome *n* (1991) : a syndrome marked by the presence of usu. three or more of a group of factors (as high blood pressure, abdominal obesity, high triglyceride levels, low HDL levels, and insulin resistance) that are linked to increased risk of cardiovascular disease and type 2 diabetes — called also *insulin resistance syndrome*
me·tab·o·lism \mə-ˈta-bə-ˌli-zəm\ *n* [ISV, fr. Gk *metabolē* change, fr. *metaballein* to change, fr. *meta-* + *ballein* to throw — more at DEVIL] (1878) **1 a** : the sum of the processes in the buildup and destruction of protoplasm; *specif* : the chemical changes in living cells by which energy is provided for vital processes and activities and new material is assimilated **b** : the sum of the processes by which a particular substance is handled in the living body **c** : the sum of the metabolic activities taking place in a particular environment ⟨the ~ of a lake⟩ **2** : METAMORPHOSIS 2 — usu. used in combination ⟨holo*metabolism*⟩
me·tab·o·lite \-ˌlīt\ *n* (1877) **1** : a product of metabolism **2** : a substance essential to the metabolism of a particular organism or to a particular metabolic process
me·tab·o·lize \-ˌlīz\ *vb* **-lized; -liz·ing** *vt* (1877) : to subject to metabolism ~ *vi* : to perform metabolism — **me·tab·o·liz·able** \mə-ˌta-bə-ˈlī-zə-bəl\ *adj*
[1]**meta·car·pal** \ˌme-tə-ˈkär-pəl\ *adj* (1739) : of, relating to, or being the metacarpus or a metacarpal
[2]**metacarpal** *n* (1831) : a bone of the part of the hand or forefoot between the carpus and the phalanges that typically contains five more or less elongated bones when all the digits are present
meta·car·pus \ˌme-tə-ˈkär-pəs\ *n* [NL] (1676) : the part of the hand or forefoot that contains the metacarpals
meta·cen·ter \ˈme-tə-ˌsen-tər\ *n* [F *métacentre,* fr. *méta-* meta- + *centre* center] (1765) : the point of intersection of the vertical through the center of buoyancy of a floating body with the vertical through the new center of buoyancy when the body is displaced

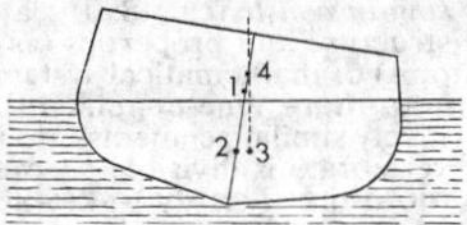

metacenter: *1* center of gravity, *2* center of buoyancy, *3* new center of buoyancy when floating body is displaced, *4* point of intersection

meta·cen·tric \ˌme-tə-ˈsen-trik\ *adj* (1798) **1** : of or relating to a metacenter **2** : having the centromere medially situated so that the two chromosomal arms are of roughly equal length — **metacentric** *n*
meta·cer·car·ia \ˌme-tə-(ˌ)sər-ˈker-ē-ə\ *n* [NL] (1925) : a tailless encysted late larva of a digenetic trematode that is usu. the form which is infective for the definitive host — **meta·cer·car·i·al** \-ē-əl\ *adj*
meta·chro·mat·ic \-krō-ˈma-tik\ *adj* (1876) **1** : staining or characterized by staining in a different color or shade from what is typical ⟨~ granules in a bacterium⟩ **2** : having the capacity to stain different elements of a cell or tissue in different colors or shades ⟨~ stains⟩
meta·cog·ni·tion \-käg-ˈni-shən\ *n* (1977) : awareness or analysis of one's own learning or thinking processes
meta·da·ta \-ˈdā-tə, -ˈda- *also* -ˈdä-\ *n pl but sing or pl in constr* (1983) : data that provides information about other data
meta·eth·ics \-ˈe-thiks\ *n pl but usu sing in constr* (1938) : the study of the meanings of ethical terms, the nature of ethical judgments, and the types of ethical arguments — **meta·eth·i·cal** \-thi-kəl\ *adj*
meta·fic·tion \-ˈfik-shən\ *n* (1960) : fiction which refers to or takes as its subject fictional writing and its conventions — **meta·fic·tion·al** \-shnəl, -shə-nᵊl\ *adj* — **meta·fic·tion·ist** \-sh(ə-)nist\ *n*
meta·gal·axy \-ˈga-lək-sē\ *n* [ISV] (1930) : the entire system of galaxies : UNIVERSE — **meta·ga·lac·tic** \-gə-ˈlak-tik\ *adj*
meta·gen·e·sis \-ˈje-nə-səs\ *n* [NL] (1849) : alternation of generations in animals; *esp* : regular alternation of a sexual and an asexual generation — **meta·ge·net·ic** \-jə-ˈne-tik\ *adj*
[1]**met·al** \ˈme-tᵊl\ *n, often attrib* [ME, fr. AF, fr. L *metallum* mine, metal, fr. Gk *metallon*] (14c) **1** : any of various opaque, fusible, ductile, and typically lustrous substances that are good conductors of electricity and heat, form cations by loss of electrons, and yield basic oxides and hydroxides; *esp* : one that is a chemical element as distinguished from an alloy **2 a** : METTLE 1a **b** : the substance out of which a person or thing is made **3** : glass in its molten state **4 a** : printing type metal **b** : matter set in metal type **5** : ROAD METAL **6** : HEAVY METAL
[2]**metal** *vt* **-aled** *or* **-alled; -al·ing** *or* **-al·ling** (1617) : to cover or furnish with metal
meta·lan·guage \ˈme-tə-ˌlaŋ-gwij\ *n* (1936) : a language used to talk about language
met·al·de·hyde \met-ˈal-də-ˌhīd\ *n* [prob. fr. *meta-* + *aldehyde*] (1841) : a crystalline compound $(CH_3CH0)_4$ that is a polymer of acetaldehyde and is used as a lure and poison for snails and slugs
met·al·head \ˈme-tᵊl-ˌhed\ *n* (1982) : a fan or performer of heavy metal
meta·lin·guis·tic \ˈme-tə-liŋ-ˌgwis-tik\ *adj* (1941) : of or relating to a metalanguage or to metalinguistics
meta·lin·guis·tics \-tiks\ *n pl but sing in constr* (1949) : a branch of linguistics that deals with the relation between language and other cultural factors in a society
metall- *or* **metallo-** *comb form* [NL, fr. L *metallum*] : metal ⟨*metallo*phone⟩
me·tal·lic \mə-ˈta-lik\ *adj* (15c) **1 a** : of, relating to, or being a metal **b** : made of or containing a metal **c** : having properties of a metal **2** : yielding metal **3** : resembling metal: as **a** : having iridescent and reflective properties ⟨~ paint⟩ **b** : having an acrid quality like that of metal ⟨the tea has a ~ taste⟩ **4 a** : having a harsh resonance : GRATING ⟨a ~ voice⟩ **b** : having an impersonal or mechanical quality ⟨a ~ smile⟩ — **me·tal·li·cal·ly** \-li-k(ə-)lē\ *adv*
met·al·lif·er·ous \ˌme-tᵊl-ˈi-f(ə-)rəs\ *adj* [L *metallifer,* fr. *metallum* + *-fer* -ferous] (ca. 1656) : yielding or containing metal
met·al·lize *also* **met·al·ize** \ˈme-tᵊl-ˌīz\ *vt* **met·al·lized** *also* **met·al·ized; met·al·liz·ing** *also* **met·al·iz·ing** (1594) : to coat, treat, or combine with a metal — **met·al·li·za·tion** \ˌme-tᵊl-ə-ˈzā-shən\ *n*
met·al·log·ra·phy \ˌme-tᵊl-ˈä-grə-fē\ *n* [ISV] (1871) : a study of the structure of metals esp. with the microscope — **met·al·log·ra·pher** \ˌme-tᵊl-ˈä-grə-fər\ *n* — **me·tal·lo·graph·ic** \mə-ˌta-lə-ˈgra-fik\ *adj* — **me·tal·lo·graph·i·cal·ly** \-ˈgra-fi-k(ə-)lē\ *adv*
[1]**met·al·loid** \ˈme-tᵊl-ˌȯid\ *n* (1813) **1** : an element intermediate in properties between the typical metals and nonmetals **2** : a nonmetal that can combine with a metal to form an alloy
[2]**metalloid** *also* **met·al·loi·dal** \ˌme-tᵊl-ˈȯi-dᵊl\ *adj* (1836) **1** : resembling a metal **2** : of, relating to, or being a metalloid
me·tal·lo·phone \mə-ˈta-lə-ˌfōn\ *n* (ca. 1883) : a percussion musical instrument consisting of a series of metal bars of varying pitch struck with hammers
met·al·lur·gy \ˈme-tᵊl-ˌər-jē, *esp Brit* mə-ˈta-lər-\ *n* [NL *metallurgia,* fr. *metall-* + *-urgia* -urgy] (1665) : the science and technology of metals — **met·al·lur·gi·cal** \ˌme-tᵊl-ˈər-ji-kəl\ *adj* — **met·al·lur·gi·cal·ly** \-k(ə-)lē\ *adv* — **met·al·lur·gist** \ˈme-tᵊl-ˌər-jist, *esp Brit* mə-ˈta-lər-\ *n*
met·al·mark \ˈme-tᵊl-ˌmärk\ *n* (1889) : any of a family (Riodinidae) of small or medium-sized usu. brightly colored chiefly tropical butterflies that often have metallic coloration on the wings
met·al·smith \-ˌsmith\ *n* (14c) : a person skilled in metalworking
met·al·ware \-ˌwer\ *n* (1791) : ware made of metal; *esp* : metal utensils
met·al·work \-ˌwərk\ *n* (ca. 1845) : the product of metalworking; *esp* : a metal object of artistic merit — **met·al·work·er** \-ˌwər-kər\ *n*
met·al·work·ing \-ˌwər-kiŋ\ *n* (1855) : the act or process of shaping things out of metal
meta·math·e·mat·ics \ˈme-tə-ˌmath-ˈma-tiks, -ma-thə-\ *n pl but usu*

sing in constr (ca. 1890) : a field of study concerned with the formal structure and properties (as the consistency and completeness of axioms) of mathematical systems — **meta·math·e·mat·i·cal** \-ti-kəl\ *adj*
meta·mere \ˈme-tə-ˌmir\ *n* [ISV] (1876) : any of a linear series of primitively similar segments into which the body of a higher invertebrate or vertebrate is divisible — **meta·mer·ic** \ˌme-tə-ˈmer-ik, -ˈmir-\ *adj* — **meta·mer·i·cal·ly** \-i-k(ə-)lē\ *adv*
me·tam·er·ism \mə-ˈta-mə-ˌri-zəm\ *n* (1833) : the condition of having or the stage of evolutionary development characterized by a body made up of metameres
meta·mor·phic \ˌme-tə-ˈmȯr-fik\ *adj* (1816) **1** : of or relating to metamorphosis **2** *of a rock* : of, relating to, or produced by metamorphism — **meta·mor·phi·cal·ly** \-fi-k(ə-)lē\ *adv*
meta·mor·phism \-ˈmȯr-ˌfi-zəm\ *n* (1845) : a change in the constitution of rock; *specif* : a pronounced change effected by pressure, heat, and water that results in a more compact and more highly crystalline condition
meta·mor·phose \-ˌfōz, -ˌfōs\ *vb* **-phosed; -phos·ing** [prob. fr. MF *metamorphoser,* fr. *metamorphose* metamorphosis, fr. L *metamorphosis*] *vt* (1576) **1 a** : to change into a different physical form esp. by supernatural means **b** : to change strikingly the appearance or character of : TRANSFORM **2** : to cause (rock) to undergo metamorphism ~ *vi* **1** : to undergo metamorphosis **2** : to become transformed ***syn*** see TRANSFORM
meta·mor·pho·sis \ˌme-tə-ˈmȯr-fə-səs\ *n, pl* **-pho·ses** \-ˌsēz\ [L, fr. Gk *metamorphōsis,* fr. *metamorphoun* to transform, fr. *meta-* + *morphē* form] (1533) **1 a** : change of physical form, structure, or substance esp. by supernatural means **b** : a striking alteration in appearance, character, or circumstances **2** : a typically marked and more or less abrupt developmental change in the form or structure of an animal (as a butterfly or a frog) occurring subsequent to birth or hatching
met·anal·y·sis \ˌme-tə-ˈna-lə-səs\ *n* (1914) : a reanalysis of the division between sounds or words resulting in different constituents (as in the development of *an apron* from *a napron*)
meta·neph·ros \-ˈne-frəs, -ˌfräs\ *n, pl* **-roi** \-ˌfrȯi\ [NL, fr. *meta-* + Gk *nephros* kidney — more at NEPHRITIS] (1884) : either member of the final and most caudal pair of the three successive pairs of vertebrate renal organs that functions as a permanent adult kidney in reptiles, birds, and mammals but is not present at all in lower forms — compare MESONEPHROS, PRONEPHROS — **meta·neph·ric** \-frik\ *adj*
meta·noia \ˌme-tə-ˈnȯi-ə\ *n* [Gk, fr. *metanoiein* to change one's mind, repent, fr. *meta-* + *noein* to think, fr. *nous* mind] (1577) : a transformative change of heart; *esp* : a spiritual conversion
meta·phase \ˈme-tə-ˌfāz\ *n* [ISV] (1887) : the stage of mitosis and meiosis in which the chromosomes become arranged in the equatorial plane of the spindle
metaphase plate *n* (1937) : a section in the equatorial plane of the metaphase spindle having the chromosomes oriented upon it
met·a·phor \ˈme-tə-ˌfȯr *also* -fər\ *n* [ME *methaphor,* fr. MF or L; MF *metaphore,* fr. L *metaphora,* fr. Gk, fr. *metapherein* to transfer, fr. *meta-* + *pherein* to bear — more at BEAR] (15c) **1** : a figure of speech in which a word or phrase literally denoting one kind of object or idea is used in place of another to suggest a likeness or analogy between them (as in *drowning in money*); *broadly* : figurative language — compare SIMILE **2** : an object, activity, or idea treated as a metaphor : SYMBOL 2 — **met·a·phor·ic** \ˌme-tə-ˈfȯr-ik, -ˈfär-\ *or* **met·a·phor·i·cal** \-i-kəl\ *adj* — **met·a·phor·i·cal·ly** \-i-k(ə-)lē\ *adv*
meta·phos·phate \ˌme-tə-ˈfäs-ˌfāt\ *n* [ISV] (1833) : a salt or ester of a metaphosphoric acid
meta·phos·pho·ric acid \-ˌfäs-ˈfȯr-ik-, -ˈfär-; -ˈfäs-f(ə-)rik-\ *n* (1833) : a glassy solid acid HPO_3 or $(HPO_3)_n$ formed by heating orthophosphoric acid
meta·phrase \ˈme-tə-ˌfrāz\ *n* (1609) : a literal translation
meta·phys·ic \ˌme-tə-ˈfi-zik\ *n* [ME *metaphesyk,* fr. ML *metaphysica*] (14c) **1 a** : METAPHYSICS **b** : a particular system of metaphysics **2** : the system of principles underlying a particular study or subject : PHILOSOPHY 3b — **metaphysic** *adj*
meta·phys·i·cal \-ˈfi-zi-kəl\ *adj* (15c) **1** : of or relating to metaphysics **2 a** : of or relating to the transcendent or to a reality beyond what is perceptible to the senses **b** : SUPERNATURAL **3** : highly abstract or abstruse; *also* : THEORETICAL **4** *often cap* : of or relating to poetry esp. of the early 17th century that is highly intellectual and philosophical and marked by unconventional imagery — **meta·phys·i·cal·ly** \-k(ə-)lē\ *adv*
Metaphysical *n* (1887) : a metaphysical poet of the 17th century
meta·phy·si·cian \ˌme-tə-fə-ˈzi-shən\ *n* (15c) : a student of or specialist in metaphysics
meta·phys·ics \-ˈfi-ziks\ *n pl but sing in constr* [ML *Metaphysica,* title of Aristotle's treatise on the subject, fr. Gk (*ta*) *meta* (*ta*) *physika,* lit., the (works) after the physical (works); fr. its position in his collected works] (1569) **1 a** (1) : a division of philosophy that is concerned with the fundamental nature of reality and being and that includes ontology, cosmology, and often epistemology (2) : ONTOLOGY 2 **b** : abstract philosophical studies : a study of what is outside objective experience **2** : METAPHYSIC 2
meta·pla·sia \-ˈplā-zh(ē-)ə\ *n* [NL] (1883) **1** : transformation of one tissue into another **2** : abnormal replacement of cells of one type by cells of another — **meta·plas·tic** \-ˈplas-tik\ *adj*
meta·psy·chol·o·gy \-sī-ˈkä-lə-jē\ *n* [ISV] (1868) : speculative psychology concerned with postulating the structure (as the ego and id) and processes (as cathexis) of the mind which usu. cannot be demonstrated objectively — **meta·psy·cho·log·i·cal** \-ˌsī-kə-ˈlä-ji-kəl\ *adj*
meta·se·quoia \-si-ˈkwȯi-ə\ *n* [NL] (1948) : any of a genus (*Metasequoia*) of deciduous coniferous trees of the bald cypress family comprising one extant and various fossil forms having leaves, buds, and branches arranged oppositely and flat leaves resembling needles
meta·so·ma·tism \-ˈsō-mə-ˌti-zəm\ *n* [*metasomatic* fr. G *metasomatisch,* fr. Gk *meta-* + *sōmat-, sōma* body] (1886) : metamorphism that involves changes in the chemical composition as well as in the texture of rock — **meta·so·mat·ic** \-sō-ˈma-tik\ *adj*
meta·sta·ble \-ˈstā-bəl\ *adj* [ISV] (1897) : having or characterized by only a slight margin of stability ⟨a ~ compound⟩ — **meta·sta·bil·i·ty** \-stə-ˈbi-lə-tē\ *n* — **meta·sta·bly** \-ˈstā-b(ə-)lē\ *adv*
me·tas·ta·sis \mə-ˈtas-tə-səs\ *n, pl* **-ta·ses** \-ˌsēz\ [NL, fr. LL, transition, fr. Gk, fr. *methistanai* to change, fr. *meta-* + *histanai* to set — more at STAND] (1663) **1 a** : change of position, state, or form **b** : the spread of a disease-producing agency (as cancer cells) from the initial or primary site of disease to another part of the body; *also* : the process by which such spreading occurs **2** : a secondary malignant tumor resulting from metastasis — **met·a·stat·ic** \ˌme-tə-ˈsta-tik\ *adj* — **met·a·stat·i·cal·ly** \-ti-k(ə-)lē\ *adv*
me·tas·ta·size \mə-ˈtas-tə-ˌsīz\ *vi* **-sized; -siz·ing** (1907) : to spread or grow by or as if by metastasis
[1]**meta·tar·sal** \ˌme-tə-ˈtär-səl\ *adj* (1703) : of, relating to, or being the part of the human foot or of the hind foot in quadrupeds between the tarsus and the phalanges that in humans comprises five elongated bones which form the front of the instep and ball of the foot
[2]**metatarsal** *n* (ca. 1839) : a metatarsal bone
meta·tar·sus \ˌme-tə-ˈtär-səs\ *n* [NL] (1676) : the metatarsal part of a human foot or of a hind foot in quadrupeds
me·ta·te \mə-ˈtä-tē\ *n* [Sp, fr. Nahuatl *metatl*] (1625) : a stone with a concave upper surface used as the lower millstone for grinding grains and esp. Indian corn
me·tath·e·sis \mə-ˈta-thə-səs\ *n, pl* **-e·ses** \-ˌsēz\ [LL, fr. Gk, fr. *metatithenai* to transpose, fr. *meta-* + *tithenai* to place — more at DO] (ca. 1538) : a change of place or condition: as **a** : transposition of two phonemes in a word (as in the development of *crud* from *curd* or the pronunciation \ˈpər-tē\ for *pretty*) **b** : a chemical reaction in which different kinds of molecules exchange parts to form other kinds of molecules — **met·a·thet·i·cal** \ˌme-tə-ˈthe-ti-kəl\ *or* **met·a·thet·ic** \-tik\ *adj* — **met·a·thet·i·cal·ly** \-ti-k(ə-)lē\ *adv*
meta·tho·rax \ˌme-tə-ˈthȯr-ˌaks\ *n* [NL] (1817) : the posterior segment of the thorax of an insect — see INSECT illustration — **meta·tho·rac·ic** \ˌme-tə-thə-ˈra-sik\ *adj*
meta·xy·lem \-ˈzī-ləm, -ˌlem\ *n* (1902) : the part of the primary xylem that differentiates after the protoxylem and that is distinguished typically by broader tracheids and vessels with pitted or reticulate walls
meta·zo·al \-ˈzō-əl\ *adj* [NL *Metazoa*] (1928) : of or relating to the metazoans
meta·zo·an \-ˈzō-ən\ *n* [NL *Metazoa,* fr. *meta-* + *-zoa*] (1879) : any of a group (*Metazoa*) that comprises all animals having the body composed of cells differentiated into tissues and organs and usu. a digestive cavity lined with specialized cells — **metazoan** *adj*
[1]**mete** \ˈmēt\ *vt* **met·ed; met·ing** [ME, fr. OE *metan;* akin to OHG *mezzan* to measure, L *modus* measure, Gk *medesthai* to be mindful of] (bef. 12c) **1** *archaic* : MEASURE **2** : to give out by measure : DOLE — usu. used with *out* ⟨~ out punishment⟩
[2]**mete** *n* [ME, fr. AF, fr. L *meta*] (15c) : BOUNDARY ⟨~*s* and bounds⟩
me·tem·psy·cho·sis \mə-ˌtem(p)-si-ˈkō-səs, ˌme-təm-ˌsī-\ *n* [LL, fr. Gk *metempsychōsis,* fr. *metempsychousthai* to undergo metempsychosis, fr. *meta-* + *empsychos* animate, fr. *en-* + *psychē* soul — more at PSYCH-] (1591) : the passing of the soul at death into another body either human or animal
met·en·ceph·a·lon \ˌmet-ˌen-ˈse-fə-ˌlän, -lən\ *n* [NL] (1867) : the anterior segment of the developing vertebrate hindbrain or the corresponding part of the adult brain composed of the cerebellum and pons — **met·en·ce·phal·ic** \-ˌen(t)-sə-ˈfa-lik\ *adj*
me·te·or \ˈmē-tē-ər, -ˌȯr\ *n* [ME *metheour,* fr. MF *meteore,* fr. ML *meteorum,* fr. Gk *meteōron,* fr. neut. of *meteōros* high in air, fr. *meta-* + *-eōros,* fr. *aeirein* to lift] (15c) **1** : an atmospheric phenomenon (as lightning or a snowfall) **2 a** : any of the small particles of matter in the solar system that are directly observable only by their incandescence from frictional heating on entry into the atmosphere **b** : the streak of light produced by the passage of a meteor
me·te·or·ic \ˌmē-tē-ˈȯr-ik, -ˈär-\ *adj* (1785) **1 a** : of or relating to a meteor **b** : resembling a meteor in speed or in sudden and temporary brilliance ⟨a ~ rise to fame⟩ **2** : of, relating to, or derived from the earth's atmosphere ⟨~ water⟩ — **me·te·or·i·cal·ly** \-i-k(ə-)lē\ *adv*
me·te·or·ite \ˈmē-tē-ə-ˌrīt\ *n* (1824) : a meteor that reaches the surface of the earth without being completely vaporized — **me·te·or·it·ic** \ˌmē-tē-ə-ˈri-tik\ *also* **me·te·or·it·i·cal** \-ti-kəl\ *adj*
me·te·or·it·ics \ˌmē-tē-ə-ˈri-tiks\ *n pl but sing in constr* (1915) : a science that deals with meteors — **me·te·or·it·i·cist** \-ˈri-tə-sist\ *n*
me·te·or·oid \ˈmē-tē-ə-ˌrȯid\ *n* (1865) **1** : a meteor particle itself without relation to the phenomena it produces when entering the earth's atmosphere **2** : a meteor in orbit around the sun — **me·te·or·oi·dal** \ˌmē-tē-ə-ˈrȯi-dᵊl\ *adj*
me·te·o·rol·o·gy \ˌmē-tē-ə-ˈrä-lə-jē\ *n* [F or Gk; F *météorologie,* fr. MF, fr. Gk *meteōrologia,* fr. *meteōron* + *-logia* -logy] (1620) **1** : a science that deals with the atmosphere and its phenomena and esp. with weather and weather forecasting **2** : the atmospheric phenomena and weather of a region — **me·te·o·ro·log·ic** \-rə-ˈlä-jik\ *or* **me·te·o·ro·log·i·cal** \-ji-kəl\ *adj* — **me·te·o·ro·log·i·cal·ly** \-ji-k(ə-)lē\ *adv* — **me·te·o·rol·o·gist** \-ˈrä-lə-jist\ *n*
[1]**me·ter** \ˈmē-tər\ *n* [ME, fr. OE & AF; OE *mēter,* fr. L *metrum,* fr. Gk *metron* measure, meter; AF *metre,* fr. L *metrum* — more at MEASURE] (bef. 12c) **1 a** : systematically arranged and measured rhythm in verse: (1) : rhythm that continuously repeats a single basic pattern ⟨iambic ~⟩ (2) : rhythm characterized by regular recurrence of a systematic arrangement of basic patterns in larger figures ⟨ballad ~⟩ **b** : a measure or unit of metrical verse — usu. used in combination ⟨penta*meter*⟩; compare FOOT 4 **c** : a fixed metrical pattern : verse form **2** : the basic recurrent rhythmical pattern of note values, accents, and beats per measure in music
[2]**met·er** \ˈmē-tər\ *n* [ME, fr. *meten* to mete] (14c) : one that measures; *esp* : an official measurer of commodities
[3]**me·ter** *n* [F *mètre,* fr. Gk *metron* measure] (1797) : the base unit of length in the International System of Units that is equal to the distance traveled by light in a vacuum in 1/299,792,458 second or to about 39.37 inches — see METRIC SYSTEM table
[4]**me·ter** *n* [*-meter*] (1815) **1** : an instrument for measuring and sometimes recording the time or amount of something ⟨a parking ~⟩ ⟨a gas ~⟩ **2** : POSTAGE METER; *also* : a marking printed by a postage meter
[5]**me·ter** *vt* (1878) **1** : to measure by means of a meter **2** : to supply in a measured or regulated amount **3** : to print postal indicia on by means of a postage meter
-meter *n comb form* [F *-mètre,* fr. Gk *metron* measure] : instrument or means for measuring ⟨baro*meter*⟩

meter–kilogram–second *adj* (1888) : of, relating to, or being a system of units using the meter, kilogram, and second as its base units — abbr. *mks*

meter maid *n* (1957) : a woman assigned by a police or traffic department to write tickets for parking violations

me·ter·stick \ˈmē-tər-ˌstik\ *n* (1931) : a measuring stick one meter long that is marked off in centimeters and usu. millimeters

met·es·trus \ˌmet-ˈes-trəs\ *n* [NL] (1923) : the period of regression that follows estrus

met·for·min \met-ˈfȯr-mən\ *n* [*meth*yl + *-formin* (as in *phenformin*, an earlier antidiabetic drug)] (1961) : a drug $C_4C_{11}N_5$ used in the form of its hydrochloride to treat type 2 diabetes

meth \ˈmeth\ *n* (1966) : METHAMPHETAMINE

meth- *or* **metho-** *comb form* [ISV, fr. *methyl*] : methyl ⟨*meth*acrylic⟩

meth·ac·ry·late \ˌme-ˈtha-krə-ˌlāt\ *n* [ISV] (1865) **1** : a salt or ester of methacrylic acid **2** : an acrylic resin or plastic made from a derivative of methacrylic acid

meth·acryl·ic acid \ˌme-thə-ˈkri-lik-\ *n* [ISV] (1865) : an acid $C_4H_6O_2$ used esp. in making acrylic resins or plastics

meth·a·done \ˈme-thə-ˌdōn\ *also* **meth·a·don** \-ˌdän\ *n* [*meth*yl + *a*mino + *d*iphenyl + *-one*] (1947) : a synthetic addictive narcotic drug $C_{21}H_{27}NO$ used esp. in the form of its hydrochloride for the relief of pain and as a substitute narcotic in the treatment of heroin addiction

meth·am·phet·amine \ˌme-tham-ˈfe-tə-ˌmēn, -thəm-, -mən\ *n* (1949) : an amine $C_{10}H_{15}N$ used medically in the form of its crystalline hydrochloride esp. in the treatment of obesity and often used illicitly as a stimulant — called also *methedrine*; compare ICE 7

metha·na·tion \ˌme-thə-ˈnā-shən\ *n* (1926) : the production of methane esp. from carbon monoxide and hydrogen

meth·ane \ˈme-ˌthān, *Brit usu* ˈmē-\ *n* [ISV] (1867) : a colorless odorless flammable gaseous hydrocarbon CH_4 that is a product of decomposition of organic matter and of the carbonization of coal, is used as a fuel and as a starting material in chemical synthesis, and is the simplest of the alkanes

meth·a·nol \ˈme-thə-ˌnȯl, -ˌnōl\ *n* [ISV] (1894) : a light volatile flammable poisonous liquid alcohol CH_3OH used esp. as a solvent, antifreeze, or denaturant for ethyl alcohol and in the synthesis of other chemicals

meth·aqua·lone \me-ˈtha-kwə-ˌlōn\ *n* [*meth-* + *-a-* (of unknown origin) + *qu*inoline + *azole* + *-one*] (1961) : a sedative and hypnotic nonbarbiturate drug $C_{16}H_{14}N_2O$ that is habit-forming — compare QUAALUDE

meth·e·drine \ˈme-thə-ˌdrēn, -drən\ *n* [fr. *Methedrine*, a trademark] (1939) : METHAMPHETAMINE

me·theg·lin \mə-ˈthe-glən\ *n* [W *meddyglyn*] (15c) : [1]MEAD

met·he·mo·glo·bin \ˌmet-ˈhē-mə-ˌglō-bən\ *n* [ISV] (1870) : a soluble brown crystalline basic blood pigment that differs from hemoglobin in containing ferric iron and in being unable to combine reversibly with molecular oxygen

met·he·mo·glo·bi·ne·mia \ˌmet-ˌhē-mə-ˌglō-bə-ˈnē-mē-ə\ *n* [NL] (1888) : the presence of methemoglobin in the blood

me·the·na·mine \mə-ˈthē-nə-ˌmēn, -mən\ *n* [*methene* (methylene) + *amine*] (1926) : hexamethylenetetramine esp. when used in the form of an organic salt to treat urinary tract infections

meth·i·cil·lin \ˌme-thə-ˈsi-lən\ *n* [*meth-* + *penicillin*] (1961) : a semisynthetic penicillin $C_{17}H_{19}N_2O_6NaS$ used esp. in the form of its sodium salt against beta-lactamase-producing staphylococci

me·thinks \mi-ˈthiŋ(k)s\ *vb impersonal, past* **me·thought** \-ˈthȯt\ [ME *me thinketh*, fr. OE *mē thincth*, fr. *mē* (dat. of *ic* I) + *thincth* seems, fr. *thyncan* to seem — more at I, THINK] (bef. 12c) *archaic* : it seems to me

me·thi·o·nine \mə-ˈthī-ə-ˌnēn\ *n* [ISV, fr. *methyl* + *thion-* + [2]*-ine*] (1928) : a crystalline sulfur-containing essential amino acid $C_5H_{11}NO_2S$ that occurs in the levorotatory form as a constituent of many proteins

meth·od \ˈme-thəd\ *n* [ME, prescribed treatment, fr. L *methodus*, fr. Gk *methodos*, fr. *meta-* + *hodos* way] (15c) **1** : a procedure or process for attaining an object: as **a** (1) : a systematic procedure, technique, or mode of inquiry employed by or proper to a particular discipline or art (2) : a systematic plan followed in presenting material for instruction **b** (1) : a way, technique, or process of or for doing something (2) : a body of skills or techniques **2** : a discipline that deals with the principles and techniques of scientific inquiry **3 a** : orderly arrangement, development, or classification : PLAN **b** : the habitual practice of orderliness and regularity **4** *cap* : a dramatic technique by which an actor seeks to gain complete identification with the inner personality of the character being portrayed

syn METHOD, MODE, MANNER, WAY, FASHION, SYSTEM mean the means taken or procedure followed in achieving an end. METHOD implies an orderly logical arrangement usu. in steps ⟨effective teaching *methods*⟩. MODE implies an order or course followed by custom, tradition, or personal preference ⟨the preferred *mode* of transportation⟩. MANNER is close to MODE but may imply a procedure or method that is individual or distinctive ⟨an odd *manner* of conducting⟩. WAY is very general and may be used for any of the preceding words ⟨has her own *way* of doing things⟩. FASHION may suggest a peculiar or characteristic way of doing something ⟨rushing about in his typical *fashion*⟩. SYSTEM suggests a fully developed or carefully formulated method often emphasizing rational orderliness ⟨a filing *system*⟩.

me·thod·i·cal \mə-ˈthä-di-kəl\ *also* **me·thod·ic** \-dik\ *adj* (1570) **1** : arranged, characterized by, or performed with method or order ⟨a ~ treatment of the subject⟩ **2** : habitually proceeding according to method : SYSTEMATIC ⟨~ in his daily routine⟩ — **me·thod·i·cal·ly** \-di-k(ə-)lē\ *adv* — **me·thod·i·cal·ness** \-di-kəl-nəs\ *n*

meth·od·ise *Brit var of* METHODIZE

meth·od·ism \ˈme-thə-ˌdi-zəm\ *n* (1739) **1** *cap* **a** : the doctrines and practice of Methodists **b** : the Methodist churches **2** : methodical procedure

meth·od·ist \-dist\ *n* (1593) **1** : a person devoted to or laying great stress on method **2** *cap* : a member of one of the denominations deriving from the Wesleyan revival in the Church of England, having Arminian doctrine and in the U.S. modified episcopal polity, and stressing personal and social morality — **methodist** *adj, often cap* — **meth·od·is·tic** \ˌme-thə-ˈdis-tik\ *adj*

meth·od·ize \ˈme-thə-ˌdīz\ *vt* **-ized; -iz·ing** (ca. 1586) : to reduce to method : SYSTEMATIZE ***syn*** see ORDER

method of fluxions (ca. 1719) : DIFFERENTIAL CALCULUS

meth·od·o·log·i·cal \ˌme-thə-də-ˈlä-ji-kəl\ *adj* (1849) : of or relating to method or methodology — **meth·od·o·log·i·cal·ly** \-k(ə-)lē\ *adv*

meth·od·ol·o·gist \-thə-ˈdä-lə-jist\ *n* (1865) : a student of methodology

meth·od·ol·o·gy \ˌme-thə-ˈdä-lə-jē\ *n, pl* **-gies** [NL *methodologia*, fr. L *methodus* + *-logia* -logy] (1800) **1** : a body of methods, rules, and postulates employed by a discipline : a particular procedure or set of procedures **2** : the analysis of the principles or procedures of inquiry in a particular field

meth·o·trex·ate \ˌme-thə-ˈtrek-ˌsāt\ *n* [*meth-* + *-trexate*, of unknown origin] (1955) : a toxic folic acid analog $C_{20}H_{22}N_8O_5$ that is used to treat certain cancers, severe psoriasis, and rheumatoid arthritis

me·thoxy·chlor \me-ˈthäk-si-ˌklȯr\ *n* [*meth-* + *oxy-* + *chlor-*] (1947) : relatively nontoxic organochlorine insecticide $C_{16}H_{15}Cl_3O_2$

me·thoxy·flu·rane \me-ˌthäk-sē-ˈflu̇r-ˌān\ *n* [*meth-* + *oxy-* + *fluor-* + eth*ane*] (1962) : a potent nonexplosive inhalational general anesthetic $C_3H_4Cl_2F_2O$ administered as a vapor

Me·thu·se·lah \mə-ˈthü-zə-lə, -ˈthyü-; -ˈth(y)üz-lə\ *n* [Heb *Mĕthūshelaḥ*] (14c) **1** : an ancestor of Noah held to have lived 969 years **2** : an oversize wine bottle holding about six liters

meth·yl \ˈme-thəl\ *n* [ISV, back-formation fr. *methylene*] (ca. 1844) : an alkyl radical CH_3 derived from methane — **me·thyl·ic** \mə-ˈthi-lik\ *adj*

methyl acetate *n* (1885) : a flammable fragrant liquid $C_3H_6O_2$ used as a solvent and paint remover and in organic synthesis

methyl alcohol *n* (ca. 1847) : METHANOL

me·thyl·amine \ˌme-thə-lə-ˈmēn, -ˈla-mən; mə-ˈthi-lə-ˌmēn\ *n* [ISV] (ca. 1850) : a flammable explosive gas CH_3NH_2 with a strong ammoniacal odor used esp. in organic synthesis (as of dyes and insecticides)

meth·yl·ase \ˈme-thə-ˌlās, -ˌlāz\ *n* (ca. 1952) : an enzyme that catalyzes methylation (as of RNA or DNA)

meth·yl·ate \ˈme-thə-ˌlāt\ *vt* **-at·ed; -at·ing** (1852) : to introduce the methyl radical into — **meth·yl·a·tion** \ˌme-thə-ˈlā-shən\ *n* — **meth·yl·a·tor** \ˈme-thə-ˌlā-tər\ *n*

methyl bromide *n* (1871) : a poisonous gaseous compound CH_3Br used chiefly as a fumigant against rodents, worms, and insects

meth·yl·cel·lu·lose \ˌme-thəl-ˈsel-yə-ˌlōs, -ˌlōz\ *n* (1921) : any of various gummy products of cellulose methylation that swell in water and are used esp. as emulsifiers, adhesives, thickeners, and bulk laxatives

methyl chloroform *n* (1888) : a methylated derivative CH_3CCl_3 of chloroform used esp. as an industrial solvent

meth·yl·cho·lan·threne \-kə-ˈlan-ˌthrēn\ *n* [*methyl* + *cho*lic acid + *anthracene*] (1933) : a potent carcinogenic hydrocarbon $C_{21}H_{16}$

meth·yl·do·pa \ˌme-thəl-ˈdō-pə\ *n* (1954) : a drug $C_{10}H_{13}NO_4$ used to lower blood pressure

meth·y·lene \ˈme-thə-ˌlēn, -lən\ *n* [F *méthylène*, fr. Gk *methy* wine + *hylē* wood — more at MEAD] (1835) : a divalent hydrocarbon group CH_2 derived from methane

methylene blue *n* (ca. 1890) : a basic thiazine dye $C_{16}H_{18}ClN_3S{\cdot}3H_2O$ used esp. as a biological stain, an antidote in cyanide poisoning, and an oxidation-reduction indicator

methylene chloride *n* (1880) : a toxic nonflammable liquid CH_2Cl_2 used esp. as a solvent, paint remover, and aerosol propellant

methyl ethyl ketone *n* (1876) : a flammable liquid compound C_4H_8O similar to acetone and used chiefly as a solvent — abbr. *MEK*

methyl isocyanate *n* (1889) : an extremely toxic chemical CH_3NCO used esp. in the manufacture of pesticides — abbr. *MIC*

meth·yl·mer·cury \ˌme-thəl-ˈmər-kyə-rē, -ˈmər-k(ə-)rē\ *n* (1915) : any of various toxic compounds of mercury containing the complex CH_3Hg– that often occur as pollutants which accumulate in living organisms (as fish) esp. in higher levels of a food chain

methyl methacrylate *n* (1933) : a volatile flammable liquid $C_5H_8O_2$ that polymerizes readily and is used esp. as a monomer for resins

meth·yl·naph·tha·lene \ˌme-thəl-ˈnaf-thə-ˌlēn, -ˈnap-\ *n* (ca. 1885) : either of two isomeric hydrocarbons $C_{11}H_{10}$; *esp* : an oily liquid used in determining cetane numbers

methyl orange *n* (1881) : an alkaline dye used as a chemical indicator

methyl parathion *n* (1957) : a potent synthetic organophosphate insecticide $C_8H_{10}NO_5PS$ that is more toxic than parathion

meth·yl·phe·ni·date \ˌme-thəl-ˈfe-nə-ˌdāt, -ˈfē-\ *n* [*methyl* + *phen*yl + piper*idine* + acet*ate*] (1956) : a mild stimulant $C_{14}H_{19}NO_2$ of the central nervous system used in the form of its hydrochloride to treat narcolepsy and hyperactivity disorders (as attention deficit disorder) in children

meth·yl·pred·nis·o·lone \-pred-ˈni-sə-ˌlōn\ *n* (1957) : a glucocorticoid $C_{22}H_{30}O_5$ that is a derivative of prednisolone and is used as an anti-inflammatory agent; *also* : any of several of its salts (as an acetate) used similarly

meth·yl·xan·thine \-ˈzan-ˌthēn\ *n* (1949) : a methylated xanthine derivative (as caffeine, theobromine, or theophylline)

meth·y·ser·gide \ˌme-thə-ˈsər-ˌjīd\ *n* [*methyl* + *ly*sergic acid + am*ide*] (1962) : a serotonin antagonist $C_{21}H_{27}N_3O_2$ used in the form of its maleate esp. in the treatment and prevention of migraine headaches

met·i·cal \ˈme-ti-kəl\ *n, pl* **met·i·cais** \-(ˌ)kī\ *also* **meticals** [Pg, miskal (a unit of weight in Muslim countries), fr. Ar *mithqāl*] (1980) — see MONEY table

me·tic·u·lous \mə-ˈti-kyə-ləs\ *adj* [L *meticulosus* fearful, irreg. fr. *metus* fear] (1827) : marked by extreme or excessive care in the consideration or treatment of details ⟨a ~ researcher⟩ ***syn*** see CAREFUL — **me·tic·u·los·i·ty** \-ˌti-kyə-ˈlä-sə-tē\ *n* — **me·tic·u·lous·ly** \-ˈti-kyə-ləs-lē\ *adv* — **me·tic·u·lous·ness** \-nəs\ *n*

mé·tier *also* **me·tier** \ˈme-ˌtyā, me-ˈ\ *n* [F, fr. OF *mestier*, fr. VL **misterium*, alter. of L *ministerium* work, ministry] (1792) **1** : VOCATION, TRADE **2** : an area of activity in which one excels : FORTE ***syn*** see WORK

mé·tis \mā-ˈtē(s)\ *n, pl* **mé·tis** \-ˈtē(s), -ˈtēz\ [F, fr. LL *mixticius* mixed — more at MESTIZO] (1816) : a person of mixed blood; *esp, often cap*

\ə\ **abut** \ᵊ\ kitten, F table \ər\ **fur**ther \a\ **ash** \ā\ **ace** \ä\ **mop, mar** \au̇\ **out** \ch\ **chin** \e\ **bet** \ē\ **easy** \g\ **go** \i\ **hit** \ī\ **ice** \j\ **job** \ŋ\ **sing** \ō\ **go** \ȯ\ **law** \ȯi\ **boy** \th\ **thin** \t͟h\ **the** \ü\ **loot** \u̇\ **foot** \y\ **yet** \zh\ **vi**sion, beige \k̲, ⁿ, œ, ue, ʸ\ *see* Guide to Pronunciation

: the offspring of an American Indian and a person of European ancestry

met·o·nym \'me-tə-ˌnim\ *n* [back-formation fr. *metonymy*] (1862) : a word used in metonymy

me·ton·y·my \mə-'tä-nə-mē\ *n, pl* **-mies** [L *metonymia*, fr. Gk *metōnymia*, fr. *meta-* + *-ōnymon* -onym] (1547) : a figure of speech consisting of the use of the name of one thing for that of another of which it is an attribute or with which it is associated (as "crown" in "lands belonging to the crown") — **met·o·nym·ic** \ˌme-tə-'ni-mik\ *or* **met·o·nym·i·cal** \-mi-kəl\ *adj*

me–too \'mē-'tü\ *adj* (1926) **1** : marked by similarity to or by adoption of successful or persuasive policies or practices used or promoted by someone else **2** : similar or identical to an established product (as a drug) with no significant advantage over it — **me–too·er** \-ər\ *n* — **me–too·ism** \-ˌi-zəm\ *n*

met·o·pe \'me-tə-(ˌ)pē\ *n* [Gk *metopē*, fr. *meta-* + *opē* opening; akin to Gk *ōps* eye, face — more at EYE] (1563) : the space between two triglyphs of a Doric frieze often adorned with carved work

met·o·pro·lol \me-'tō-prə-ˌlȯl, -ˌlōl\ *n* [perh. fr. *methyl* + *-o-* + *propranolol*] (1974) : a beta-blocker $C_{15}H_{25}NO_3$ used in the form of its succinate and tartrate esp. to treat hypertension and angina pectoris

me·tre \'mē-tər\ *chiefly Brit var of* METER

¹**met·ric** \'me-trik\ *n* [Gk *metrikē*, fr. fem. of *metrikos* in meter, by measure, fr. *metron* measure — more at MEASURE] (1760) **1** *pl* : a part of prosody that deals with metrical structure **2** : a standard of measurement ⟨no ~ exists that can be applied directly to happiness —*Scientific Monthly*⟩ **3** : a mathematical function that associates a real nonnegative number analogous to distance with each pair of elements in a set such that the number is zero only if the two elements are identical, the number is the same regardless of the order in which the two elements are taken, and the number associated with one pair of elements plus that associated with one member of the pair and a third element is equal to or greater than the number associated with the other member of the pair and the third element

²**metric** *adj* [F *métrique*, fr. *mètre* meter] (1864) : of, relating to, or using the metric system ⟨a ~ study⟩ — **met·ri·cal·ly** \-tri-k(ə-)lē\ *adv*

-metric *or* **-metrical** *adj comb form* **1** : of, employing, or obtained by (such) a meter ⟨galvano*metric*⟩ **2** : of or relating to (such) an art, process, or science of measuring ⟨geo*metrical*⟩

met·ri·cal \'me-tri-kəl\ *or* **met·ric** \-trik\ *adj* (15c) **1** : of, relating to, or composed in meter **2** : of or relating to measurement — **met·ri·cal·ly** \-tri-k(ə-)lē\ *adv*

met·ri·ca·tion \ˌme-tri-'kā-shən\ *n* (1965) : the act or process of metricizing; *specif* : conversion of an existent system of units into the metric system

met·ri·cize \'me-trə-ˌsīz\ *vt* **-cized; -ciz·ing** (1873) : to change into or express in the metric system

metric space *n* (1927) : a mathematical set for which a metric is defined for any pair of elements

metric system *n* (1864) : a decimal system of weights and measures based on the meter and on the kilogram

metric ton *n* (ca. 1890) — see METRIC SYSTEM table

me·trist \'me-trist, 'mē-\ *n* (1535) **1** : a maker of verses **2** : one skillful in handling meter **3** : a student of meter or metrics

¹**met·ro** \'me-(ˌ)trō, *in French context also* mā-'\ *n, pl* **metros** [F *métro*, short for *(chemin de fer) métropolitain* metropolitan railroad] (1904) : SUBWAY b

²**met·ro** \'me-(ˌ)trō\ *adj* (1953) : METROPOLITAN 2

me·trol·o·gy \me-'trä-lə-jē\ *n* [F *métrologie*, fr. Gk *metrologia* theory of ratios, fr. *metron* measure — more at MEASURE] (1816) **1** : the science of weights and measures or of measurement **2** : a system of weights and measures — **met·ro·log·i·cal** \ˌme-trə-'lä-ji-kəl\ *adj* — **me·trol·o·gist** \me-'trä-lə-jist\ *n*

met·ro·ni·da·zole \ˌme-trə-'nī-də-ˌzōl\ *n* [*methyl* + *-tron-* (prob. alter. of *nitro-*) + *imide* + *azole*] (1960) : a drug $C_6H_9N_3O_3$ used esp. to treat vaginal trichomoniasis, amebiasis, and infections by anaerobic bacteria

met·ro·nome \'me-trə-ˌnōm\ *n* [Gk *metron* + *-nomos* controlling, fr. *nomos* law — more at NIMBLE] (1816) : an instrument designed to mark exact time by a regularly repeated tick

met·ro·nom·ic \ˌme-trə-'nä-mik\ *also* **met·ro·nom·i·cal** \-mi-kəl\ *adj* (1866) : mechanically regular (as in action or tempo) — **met·ro·nom·i·cal·ly** \-mik(ə-)lē\ *adv*

me·trop·o·lis \mə-'trä-p(ə-)ləs\ *n* [ME, fr. LL, fr. Gk *mētropolis*, fr. *mētr-, mētēr* mother + *polis* city — more at MOTHER, POLICE] (14c) **1** : the chief or capital city of a country, state, or region **2** : the city or state of origin of a colony (as of ancient Greece) **3 a** : a city regarded as a center of a specified activity **b** : a large important city

¹**met·ro·pol·i·tan** \ˌme-trə-'pä-lə-tən\ *n* (14c) **1** : the primate of an ecclesiastical province **2** : one who lives in a metropolis or displays metropolitan manners or customs

²**metropolitan** *adj* [ME, fr. LL *metropolitanus* of the see of a metropolitan, fr. *metropolita*, n., metropolitan, fr. LGk *mētropolitēs*, fr. *mētropolis* see of a metropolitan, fr. Gk, capital] (15c) **1** : of or constituting a metropolitan or his see **2** : of, relating to, or characteristic of a metropolis and sometimes including its suburbs **3** : of, relating to, or constituting a mother country as distinguished from a colony

me·tror·rha·gia \ˌmē-trə-'rä-j(ē-)ə, -'rä-zhə; -'rä-jə, -zhə\ *n* [NL, fr. *metro-* womb (fr. Gk *mētra*, fr. *mētr-, mētēr* mother) + *-rrhagia* — more at MOTHER] (1879) : irregular uterine bleeding esp. between menstrual periods

met·ro·sex·u·al \ˌme-trə-'sek-sh(ə-)wəl, -'sek-shəl\ *n* [²*metropolitan* + *-sexual* (as in ²*heterosexual*)] (1994) : a usu. urban heterosexual male given to enhancing his personal appearance by fastidious grooming, beauty treatments, and fashionable clothes — **metrosexual** *adj*

-metry *n comb form* [F *-metrie*, fr. L *-metria*, fr. Gk, fr. *metrein* to measure, fr. *metron* — more at MEASURE] : art, process, or science of measuring ⟨chrono*metry*⟩ ⟨photo*metry*⟩

met·tle \'me-t³l\ *n* [alter. of *metal*] (1581) **1 a** : vigor and strength of

METRIC SYSTEM¹

UNIT	ABBREVIATION	EQUIVALENT IN BASE UNIT	APPROXIMATE U.S. EQUIVALENT
LENGTH			
kilometer	km	1,000 meters	0.62 mile
hectometer	hm	100 meters	328.08 feet
dekameter	dam	10 meters	32.81 feet
meter	m		39.37 inches
decimeter	dm	0.1 meter	3.94 inches
centimeter	cm	0.01 meter	0.39 inch
millimeter	mm	0.001 meter	0.039 inch
micrometer	μm	0.000001 meter	0.000039 inch
AREA			
square kilometer	sq km *or* km²	1,000,000 square meters	0.39 square mile
hectare	ha	10,000 square meters	2.47 acres
are	a	100 square meters	119.60 square yards
square centimeter	sq cm *or* cm²	0.0001 square meter	0.16 square inch
VOLUME			
cubic meter	m³		1.31 cubic yards
cubic decimeter	dm³	0.001 cubic meter	61.02 cubic inches
cubic centimeter	cu cm *or* cm³ *also* cc	0.000001 cubic meter	0.061 cubic inch

UNIT	ABBREVIATION	EQUIVALENT IN BASE UNIT	cubic	dry	liquid
CAPACITY					
kiloliter	kl	1,000 liters	1.31 cubic yards	28.38 bushels	264.17 gallons
hectoliter	hl	100 liters	3.53 cubic feet	2.84 bushels	26.42 gallons
dekaliter	dal	10 liters	0.35 cubic foot	1.14 pecks	2.64 gallons
liter	l		61.02 cubic inches	0.91 quart	1.06 quarts
cubic decimeter	dm³		61.02 cubic inches	0.91 quart	1.06 quarts
deciliter	dl	0.1 liter	6.10 cubic inches	0.18 pint	0.21 pint
centiliter	cl	0.01 liter	0.61 cubic inch		0.34 fluid ounce
milliliter	ml	0.001 liter	0.061 cubic inch		0.27 fluid dram
microliter	μl	0.000001 liter	0.000061 cubic inch		0.00027 fluid dram

UNIT	ABBREVIATION	EQUIVALENT IN BASE UNIT	APPROXIMATE U.S. EQUIVALENT
MASS AND WEIGHT			
metric ton	t	1,000,000 grams	1.10 short tons
kilogram	kg	1,000 grams	2.20 pounds
hectogram	hg	100 grams	3.53 ounces
dekagram	dag	10 grams	0.35 ounce
gram	g		0.035 ounce
decigram	dg	0.1 gram	1.54 grains
centigram	cg	0.01 gram	0.15 grain
milligram	mg	0.001 gram	0.015 grain
microgram	μg *or* mcg	0.000001 gram	0.000015 grain

¹For metric equivalents of U.S. units, see Weights and Measures table.

spirit or temperament **b :** staying quality : STAMINA ⟨equipment that proved its ~⟩ **2 :** quality of temperament or disposition ⟨gentlemen of brave ~ —Shak.⟩ ***syn*** see COURAGE — **met·tled** \-tᵊld\ *adj* — **on one's mettle :** aroused to do one's best

met·tle·some \ˈme-tᵊl-səm\ *adj* (1662) **:** full of mettle : SPIRITED

meu·nière \(ˌ)mə(r)n-ˈyer, mœn-\ *adj* [F (*à la*) *meunière,* lit., in the manner of a miller's wife] (1903) **:** rolled lightly in flour and sautéed in butter ⟨sole ~⟩

Meur·sault \mə(r)-ˈsō, mœ-\ *n* [F, fr. *Meursault,* commune in France] (1833) **:** a dry white burgundy wine

MeV *abbr* million electron volts

[1]mew \ˈmyü\ *n* [ME, fr. OE *mǣw;* akin to ON *mār* gull] (bef. 12c) **:** GULL; *esp* **:** a small gull (*Larus canus*) of Eurasia and western No. America

[2]mew *vb* [ME *mewen,* of imit. origin] *vi* (14c) **:** to utter a mew or similar sound ⟨gulls ~*ed* over the bay⟩ ~ *vt* **:** to utter by mewing : MEOW

[3]mew *n* (1596) **:** MEOW

[4]mew *n* [ME *mewe,* fr. AF *mue, muwe,* fr. *muer* to change, molt, fr. L *mutare* to change — more at MUTABLE] (14c) **1 :** an enclosure for trained hawks — usu. used in pl. **2 :** a place for hiding or retirement **3** *pl but sing or pl in constr, chiefly Brit* **a** (1) **:** stables usu. with living quarters built around a court (2) **:** living quarters adapted from such stables **b :** back street : ALLEY

[5]mew *vt* (15c) **:** to shut up : CONFINE — often used with *up*

mewl \ˈmyül\ *vi* [imit.] (1600) **:** to cry weakly : WHIMPER

Mex·i·can \ˈmek-si-kən\ *n* (1604) **1 a :** a native or inhabitant of Mexico **b :** a person of Mexican descent **c** *Southwest* **:** a person of mixed Spanish and Indian descent **2 :** NAHUATL — **Mexican** *adj*

Mexican bean beetle *n* (1920) **:** a spotted ladybug (*Epilachna varivestis*) that feeds on the leaves of beans

Mexican jumping bean *n* (1922) **:** JUMPING BEAN

Mexican Spanish *n* (1851) **:** the Spanish used in Mexico

Mexican standoff *n* (1891) **:** a situation in which no one emerges a clear winner; *also* **:** DEADLOCK

me·ze \me-ˈzā, ˈmā-(ˌ)zā\ *n, pl* **mezes** *also* **meze** [ModGk & Turk; ModGk *mezes,* fr. Turk *meze,* fr. Pers *maze* taste, snack] (1926) **:** an appetizer in Greek or Middle Eastern cuisine often served with an aperitif

me·ze·re·on \mə-ˈzir-ē-ən\ *n* [ME *mizerion,* fr. ML *mezereon,* fr. Ar *māzariyūn,* perh. fr. Pers *māzaryūn*] (15c) **:** a small Eurasian shrub (*Daphne mezereum* of the family Thymelaeaceae, the mezereon family) with purple flowers and poisonous emetic leaves, fruit, and bark

me·zu·zah *or* **me·zu·za** \mə-ˈzu̇-zə\ *n, pl* **-zahs** *or* **-zas** *or* **-zot** \-ˈzu̇-ˌzōt\ [Heb *mĕzūzāh* doorpost] (1650) **:** a small parchment scroll inscribed with Deut 6:4–9 and 11:13–21 and the name Shaddai and placed in a case fixed to the doorpost by some Jewish families as a sign and reminder of their faith; *also* **:** such a scroll and its case

mez·za·nine \ˈme-zə-ˌnēn, ˌme-zə-ˈ\ *n* [F, fr. It *mezzanino,* fr. *mezzano* middle, fr. L *medianus* middle, median] (1711) **1 :** a low-ceilinged story between two main stories of a building; *esp* **:** an intermediate story that projects in the form of a balcony **2 a :** the lowest balcony in a theater **b :** the first few rows of such a balcony

mez·za vo·ce \ˌmet-sä-ˈvō-(ˌ)chā, ˌmed-zä-\ *adv or adj* [It, half voice] (1775) **:** with medium or half volume — used as a direction in music

mez·zo \ˈmet-(ˌ)sō, ˈmed-(ˌ)zō\ *n, pl* **mezzos** [It, lit., middle, moderate, half, fr. L *medius* — more at MID] (1832) **:** MEZZO-SOPRANO

mez·zo for·te \ˌmet-(ˌ)sō-ˈfȯr-ˌtā, ˌmed-(ˌ)zō-, -ˈfȯr-tē\ *adj or adv* [It] (1811) **:** moderately loud — used as a direction in music

mez·zo pia·no \-pē-ˈä-(ˌ)nō\ *adj or adv* [It] (1811) **:** moderately soft — used as a direction in music

mez·zo–re·lie·vo *or* **mez·zo–ri·lie·vo** \-ri-ˈlē-(ˌ)vō, -rēl-ˈyā-(ˌ)vō\ *n, pl* **-vos** [It *mezzorilievo,* fr. *mezzo* + *rilievo* relief] (1598) **:** sculptural relief intermediate between bas-relief and high relief

mez·zo–so·pra·no \-sə-ˈpra-(ˌ)nō, -ˈprä-\ *n* [It *mezzosoprano,* fr. *mezzo* + *soprano* soprano] (ca. 1753) **:** a woman's voice with a range between soprano and contralto; *also* **:** a singer having this voice

mez·zo·tint \ˈmet-sō-ˌtint, ˈmed-zō-\ *n* [modif. of It *mezzatinta,* fr. *mezza* (fem. of *mezzo*) + *tinta* tint] (1800) **1 :** a manner of engraving on copper or steel by scraping or burnishing a roughened surface to produce light and shade **2 :** an engraving produced by mezzotint

mf *abbr* mezzo forte

MF *abbr* **1** medium frequency **2** microfiche

MFA *abbr* master of fine arts

mfd *abbr* manufactured

mfg *abbr* manufacturing

MFH *abbr* master of foxhounds

MFN *abbr* most favored nation

mfr *abbr* manufacture; manufacturer

mg *abbr* milligram

mG *abbr* milligauss

Mg *symbol* magnesium

MG *abbr* **1** machine gun **2** major general **3** military government

mgal *abbr* milligal

mgd *abbr* million gallons per day

mgmt *or* **mgt** *abbr* management

mgr *abbr* **1** manager **2** monseigneur **3** monsignor

MGy Sgt *abbr* master gunnery sergeant

MH *abbr* **1** medal of honor **2** mental health

MHC *abbr* major histocompatibility complex

MHD *abbr* magnetohydrodynamic; magnetohydrodynamics

mho \ˈmō\ *n, pl* **mhos** [backward spelling of *ohm*] (1883) **:** a unit of conductance equal to the reciprocal of the ohm : SIEMENS

MHW *abbr* mean high water

MHz *abbr* megahertz

[1]mi \ˈmē\ *n* [ML, fr. the syllable sung to this note in a medieval hymn to St. John the Baptist] (15c) **:** the 3d tone of the diatonic scale in solmization

[2]mi *abbr* **1** mile; miles **2** mill

MI *abbr* **1** Michigan **2** military intelligence **3** myocardial infarction

MIA \ˌem-(ˌ)ī-ˈā\ *n* [*m*issing *i*n *a*ction] (1944) **:** a member of the armed forces whose whereabouts following a combat mission are unknown and whose death cannot be established beyond reasonable doubt

Mi·ami \mī-ˈa-mē, -mə\ *n, pl* **Mi·ami** *or* **Mi·am·is** [alter. of F *miamioua,* fr. a Miami self-designation] (1698) **:** a member of an American Indian people orig. of Wisconsin, Illinois, and Indiana

mi·aow *Brit var of* MEOW

mi·as·ma \mī-ˈaz-mə, mē-\ *n, pl* **-mas** *also* **-ma·ta** \-mə-tə\ [NL, fr. Gk, defilement, fr. *miainein* to pollute] (1665) **1 :** a vaporous exhalation formerly believed to cause disease; *also* **:** a heavy vaporous emanation or atmosphere ⟨a ~ of tobacco smoke⟩ **2 :** an influence or atmosphere that tends to deplete or corrupt ⟨freed from the ~ of poverty —Sir Arthur Bryant⟩; *also* **:** an atmosphere that obscures : FOG — **mi·as·mal** \-məl\ *adj* — **mi·as·mat·ic** \ˌmī-əz-ˈma-tik\ *adj* — **mi·as·mic** \mī-ˈaz-mik, mē-\ *adj* — **mi·as·mi·cal·ly** \-mi-k(ə-)lē\ *adv*

mic \ˈmīk\ *n* (1961) **:** MICROPHONE

Mic *abbr* Micah

MIC *abbr* methyl isocyanate

mi·ca \ˈmī-kə\ *n* [NL, fr. L, grain, crumb; perh. akin to Gk *mikros* small] (1777) **:** any of various colored or transparent mineral silicates crystallizing in monoclinic forms that readily separate into very thin leaves — **mi·ca·ceous** \mī-ˈkā-shəs\ *adj*

Mi·cah \ˈmī-kə\ *n* [Heb *Mīkhāh,* short for *Mīkhāyāh*] (1587) **1 :** a prophetic book of canonical Jewish and Christian Scripture — see BIBLE table **2 :** a Hebrew prophet of the eighth century B.C.

Mi·caw·ber \mi-ˈkȯ-bər, -ˈkä-\ *n* [Wilkins *Micawber,* character in the novel *David Copperfield* (1849–50) by Charles Dickens] (1852) **:** one who is poor but lives in optimistic expectation of better fortune — **Mi·caw·ber·ish** \-bə-rish\ *adj*

mice *pl of* MOUSE

mi·celle \mī-ˈsel\ *n* [NL *micella,* fr. L *mica*] (1881) **:** a unit of structure built up from polymeric molecules or ions: as **a :** an ordered region in a fiber (as of cellulose or rayon) **b :** a molecular aggregate that constitutes a colloidal particle — **mi·cel·lar** \-ˈse-lər\ *adj*

Mich *abbr* Michigan

Mi·chael \ˈmī-kəl\ *n* [Heb *Mīkhā'ēl*] (bef. 12c) **:** one of the four archangels named in Hebrew tradition

Mi·chae·lis constant \mī-ˈkā-ləs-, mə-\ *n* [Leonor *Michaelis* †1949 Am. biochemist] (1930) **:** a constant that is a measure of the kinetics of an enzyme reaction and that is equivalent to the concentration of substrate at which the reaction takes place at one half its maximum rate

Mich·ael·mas \ˈmi-kəl-məs\ *n* [ME *mychelmesse,* fr. OE *Michaeles mæsse* Michael's mass] (bef. 12c) **:** September 29 celebrated as the feast of St. Michael the Archangel

Michaelmas daisy *n* (1785) **:** a wild aster; *esp* **:** one blooming about Michaelmas

Mi·che·as \ˈmī-kē-əs, mī-ˈ\ *n* [LL *Michaeas,* fr. Gk *Michaias,* fr. Heb *Mīkhāyāh*] (14c) **:** MICAH

mick \ˈmik\ *n, often cap* [*Mick,* nickname for *Michael,* common Irish given name] (1856) *often offensive* **:** IRISHMAN

Mick·ey Finn \ˌmi-kē-ˈfin\ *n* [prob. fr. *Mickey* (Michael) *Finn fl*1903 Am. saloon keeper who allegedly drugged his customers] (1928) **:** a drink of liquor doctored with a purgative or a drug

Mickey Mouse \ˈmi-kē-ˈmau̇s\ *adj* [*Mickey Mouse,* cartoon character created by Walt Disney] (1930) **1 :** too easy, small, ineffective, or unimportant to be taken seriously ⟨*Mickey Mouse* courses⟩ ⟨a *Mickey Mouse* operation⟩ **2 :** being or performing insipid or corny popular music **3 :** annoyingly petty ⟨*Mickey Mouse* regulations⟩

mick·le \ˈmi-kəl\ *also* **mei·kle** \ˈmē-kəl\ *adj* [ME *mikel,* fr. OE *micel* — more at MUCH] (bef. 12c) *chiefly Scot* **:** GREAT, MUCH — **mickle** *adv, chiefly Scot*

Mic·mac \ˈmik-ˌmak\ *n, pl* **Micmac** *or* **Micmacs** [Micmac *mi·kəmaw*] (1830) **1 :** a member of an American Indian people of eastern Canada **2 :** the Algonquian language of the Micmac people

mi·con·a·zole \mī-ˈkä-nə-ˌzōl\ *n* [*micon-* (perh. part blend, part alter. of *myc-* and NL *Monilia,* a genus of fungi) + imid*azole*] (1970) **:** an antifungal agent $C_{18}H_{14}Cl_4N_2O$ used esp. in the form of its nitrate

MICR *abbr* magnetic ink character recognition

micr- *or* **micro-** *comb form* [ME *micro-,* fr. L, fr. Gk *mikr-, mikro-,* fr. *mikros, smikros* small, short; perh. akin to OE *smēalīc* careful, exquisite] **1 a :** small : minute ⟨*micro*chip⟩ **b :** used for or involving minute quantities or variations ⟨*micro*barograph⟩ **2 :** one millionth (10^{-6}) part of ⟨*micro*gram⟩ **3 a :** using microscopy ⟨*micro*dissection⟩ **:** used in microscopy **b :** revealed by or discernible only by microscopic examination ⟨*micro*organism⟩ **4 :** abnormally small ⟨*micro*cyte⟩ **5 :** of or relating to a small area ⟨*micro*climate⟩ **6 :** employed in or connected with microphotographing or microfilming ⟨*micro*dot⟩

[1]mi·cro \ˈmī-(ˌ)krō\ *adj* [*micr-*] (1923) **1 :** very small; *esp* **:** MICROSCOPIC **2 :** involving minute quantities or variations

[2]micro *n, pl* **micros** (1971) **1 :** MICROCOMPUTER **2 :** MICROPROCESSOR

mi·cro·am·pere \ˌmī-krō-ˈam-ˌpir\ *n* (ca. 1890) **:** a unit of current equal to one millionth of an ampere

mi·cro·anal·y·sis \-ə-ˈna-lə-səs\ *n* (1856) **:** chemical analysis on a small or minute scale that usu. requires special, very sensitive, or small-scale apparatus — **mi·cro·an·a·lyst** \-ˈa-nə-list\ *n* — **mi·cro·an·a·lyt·i·cal** \-ˈli-ti-kəl\ *also* **mi·cro·an·a·lyt·ic** \-ˌa-nə-ˈli-tik\ *adj*

mi·cro·anat·o·my \-ə-ˈna-tə-mē\ *n* (1880) **:** HISTOLOGY — **mi·cro·an·a·tom·i·cal** \-ˌa-nə-ˈtä-mi-kəl\ *adj*

mi·cro·ar·ray \ˌmī-krō-ə-ˈrā\ *n* (1995) **:** a supporting material (as a glass or plastic slide) onto which numerous molecules or fragments usu. of DNA or protein are attached in a regular pattern for use in biochemical or genetic analysis

mi·cro·bal·ance \ˈmī-krō-ˌba-lən(t)s\ *n* (1903) **:** a balance designed to measure very small weights

mi·cro·baro·graph \ˌmī-krō-ˈba-rə-ˌgraf\ *n* [ISV] (1904) **:** a barograph for recording small and rapid changes

mi·crobe \ˈmī-ˌkrōb\ *n* [ISV *micr-* + Gk *bios* life — more at QUICK] (1881) **:** MICROORGANISM, GERM — **mi·cro·bi·al** \mī-ˈkrō-bē-əl\ *also* **mi·cro·bic** \-bik\ *adj*

mi·cro·beam \ˈmī-krō-ˌbēm\ *n* (1950) **:** a beam of radiation of small cross section ⟨a focused laser ~⟩ ⟨a ~ of electrons⟩

mi·cro·bi·cide \mī-ˈkrō-bə-ˌsīd\ *n* (1887) **:** an agent that destroys mi-

crobes (as bacteria) — **mi·cro·bi·ci·dal** \mī-ˌkrō-bə-ˈsī-dᵊl\ *adj*
mi·cro·bi·ol·o·gy \ˌmī-krō-bī-ˈä-lə-jē\ *n* [ISV] (1880) **:** a branch of biology dealing with microscopic forms of life — **mi·cro·bi·o·log·i·cal** \-ˌbī-ə-ˈlä-ji-kəl\ *also* **mi·cro·bi·o·log·ic** \-ˈlä-jik\ *adj* — **mi·cro·bi·o·log·i·cal·ly** \-ji-k(ə-)lē\ *adv* — **mi·cro·bi·ol·o·gist** \-bī-ˈä-lə-jist\ *n*
mi·cro·blog·ging \ˈmī-krō-ˌblȯ-giŋ, -ˌblä-\ *n* (2005) **:** blogging done with severe space or size constraints typically by posting frequent brief messages about personal activities — **mi·cro·blog** \-ˌblȯg, -ˌbläg\ *n*
mi·cro·brew \ˈmī-krō-ˌbrü\ *n* (1985) **:** a beer produced by a microbrewery — **mi·cro·brewed** \-ˌbrüd\ *adj* — **mi·cro·brew·ing** \-ˌbrü-iŋ\ *n*
mi·cro·brew·ery \ˌmī-krō-ˈbrü-ə-rē, -ˈbru̇r-ē\ *n* (1982) **:** a small brewery making specialty beer in limited quantities — **mi·cro·brew·er** \ˈmī-krō-ˌbrü-ər, -ˌbru̇r\ *n*
mi·cro·burst \ˈmī-krō-ˌbərst\ *n* (1981) **:** a violent short-lived localized downdraft that creates extreme wind shears at low altitudes and is usu. associated with thunderstorms
mi·cro·bus \-ˌbəs\ *n* (1945) **:** a station wagon shaped like a bus
mi·cro·cal·o·rim·e·ter \-ˌka-lə-ˈri-mə-tər\ *n* (1911) **:** an instrument for measuring very small quantities of heat — **mi·cro·ca·lo·ri·met·ric** \-ˌka-lə-rə-ˈme-trik; -kə-ˌlȯr-ə-, -ˌlär-\ *adj* — **mi·cro·cal·o·rim·e·try** \-ˌka-lə-ˈri-mə-trē\ *n*
mi·cro·cap·sule \ˈmī-krō-ˌkap-səl, -(ˌ)sül *also* -ˌsyül\ *n* (1961) **:** a tiny capsule containing material (as an adhesive or a medicine) that is released when the capsule is broken, melted, or dissolved
mi·cro·cas·sette \ˌmī-krō-kə-ˈset, -ka-\ *n* (1976) **:** a small cassette of magnetic tape
¹**mi·cro·ce·phal·ic** \-sə-ˈfa-lik\ *adj* (ca. 1856) **:** having a small head; *specif* **:** having an abnormally small head
²**microcephalic** *n* (ca. 1873) **:** one that is microcephalic
mi·cro·ceph·a·ly \-ˈse-fə-lē\ *n* [NL *microcephalia,* fr. *microcephalus* microcephalic, fr. *micr-* + Gk *kephalē* head — more at CEPHALIC] (1863) **:** a condition of abnormal smallness of the head usu. associated with mental defects
mi·cro·chip \ˈmī-krō-ˌchip\ *n* (1969) **:** INTEGRATED CIRCUIT
mi·cro·cir·cuit \-ˌsər-kət\ *n* (1959) **:** a compact electronic circuit **:** INTEGRATED CIRCUIT — **mi·cro·cir·cuit·ry** \ˌmī-krō-ˈsər-kə-trē\ *n*
mi·cro·cir·cu·la·tion \ˌmī-krō-ˌsər-kyə-ˈlā-shən\ *n* (1955) **:** blood circulation in the microvascular system; *also* **:** the microvascular system itself — **mi·cro·cir·cu·la·to·ry** \-ˈsər-kyə-lə-ˌtȯr-ē\ *adj*
mi·cro·cli·mate \ˈmī-krō-ˌklī-mət\ *n* [ISV] (1925) **:** the essentially uniform local climate of a usu. small site or habitat — **mi·cro·cli·mat·ic** \ˌmī-krō-klī-ˈma-tik\ *adj*
mi·cro·cline \ˈmī-krō-ˌklīn\ *n* [G *Mikroklin,* fr. *mikr-* micr- + Gk *klinein* to lean — more at LEAN] (1849) **:** a triclinic mineral of the feldspar group that is like orthoclase in composition
mi·cro·coc·cus \ˌmī-krō-ˈkä-kəs\ *n, pl* **-coc·ci** \-ˈkäk-(ˌ)sī, -(ˌ)sē; -ˈkä-(ˌ)kī, -(ˌ)kē\ [NL] (1870) **:** a small spherical bacterium; *esp* **:** any of a genus (*Micrococcus*) of gram-positive chiefly harmless bacteria that typically occur in irregular clusters — **mi·cro·coc·cal** \-ˈkä-kəl\ *adj*
mi·cro·code \ˈmī-krə-ˌkōd\ *n* (1958) **:** the microinstructions esp. of a microprocessor
mi·cro·com·put·er \ˈmī-krō-kəm-ˌpyü-tər\ *n* (1963) **1 :** a small computer usu. equipped with a microprocessor; *esp* **:** PERSONAL COMPUTER **2 :** MICROPROCESSOR
mi·cro·con·trol·ler \-kən-ˌtrō-lər\ *n* (1971) **:** a microprocessor that controls some or all of the functions of an electronic device (as a home appliance) or system
mi·cro·cosm \ˈmī-krə-ˌkä-zəm\ *n* [ME, fr. ML *microcosmus,* modif. of Gk *mikros kosmos*] (15c) **1 :** a little world; *esp* **:** the human race or human nature seen as an epitome of the world or the universe **2 :** a community or other unity that is an epitome of a larger unity — **mi·cro·cos·mic** \ˌmī-krə-ˈkäz-mik\ *adj* — **mi·cro·cos·mi·cal·ly** \-mi-k(ə-)lē\ *adv* — **in microcosm :** in a greatly diminished size, form, or scale
mi·cro·cos·mos \ˈmī-krə-ˌkäz-məs, -ˌmōs, -ˌmäs\ *n* [ME *mycrocossmos,* fr. ML *microcosmus*] (13c) **1 :** MICROCOSM **2 :** the microscopic or submicroscopic world
mi·cro·crys·tal \ˈmī-krō-ˌkris-tᵊl\ *n* (1886) **:** a microscopic crystal — **mi·cro·crys·tal·line** \ˌmī-krō-ˈkris-tə-lən *also* -ˌlīn *or* -ˌlēn\ *adj* — **mi·cro·crys·tal·lin·i·ty** \-ˌkris-tə-ˈli-nə-tē\ *n*
mi·cro·cul·ture \ˈmī-krō-ˌkəl-chər\ *n* (1892) **1 :** a microscopic culture of cells or organisms **2 :** the culture of a small group of human beings with limited perspective — **mi·cro·cul·tur·al** \ˌmī-krō-ˈkəlch-rəl, -ˈkəl-chə-\ *adj*
mi·cro·cu·rie \ˈmī-krō-ˌkyu̇r-ē, ˌmī-krō-kyu̇-ˈrē\ *n* (1911) **:** a unit of quantity or of radioactivity equal to one millionth of a curie
mi·cro·cyte \ˈmī-krə-ˌsīt\ *n* [ISV] (1876) **:** a small red blood cell present esp. in some anemias — **mi·cro·cyt·ic** \ˌmī-krə-ˈsi-tik\ *adj*
mi·cro·den·si·tom·e·ter \ˈmī-krō-ˌden(t)-sə-ˈtä-mə-tər\ *n* (1935) **:** a densitometer for measuring the densities of microscopic areas — **mi·cro·den·si·to·met·ric** \-sə-tə-ˈme-trik\ *adj* — **mi·cro·den·si·tom·e·try** \-sə-ˈtä-mə-trē\ *n*
mi·cro·dis·sec·tion \ˌmī-krō-di-ˈsek-shən, -dī-\ *n* (1914) **:** dissection under the microscope; *specif* **:** dissection of cells and tissues by means of fine needles that are precisely manipulated by levers
mi·cro·dot \ˈmī-krə-ˌdät, -krō-\ *n* (1946) **:** a photographic reproduction of printed matter reduced to the size of a dot for ease or security of transmittal
mi·cro·earth·quake \ˌmī-krō-ˈərth-ˌkwāk\ *n* (1965) **:** an earthquake of low intensity
mi·cro·eco·nom·ics \-ˌe-kə-ˈnä-miks, -ˌē-kə-\ *n pl but usu sing in constr* (1943) **:** a study of economics in terms of individual areas of activity (as a firm) — compare MACROECONOMICS — **mi·cro·eco·nom·ic** \-ˈnä-mik\ *adj* — **mi·cro·econ·o·mist** \-i-ˈkä-nə-mist\ *n*
mi·cro·elec·trode \ˌmī-krō-i-ˈlek-ˌtrōd\ *n* (1917) **:** a minute electrode; *esp* **:** one that is inserted in a living biological cell or tissue in studying its electrical characteristics
mi·cro·elec·tron·ics \-i-ˌlek-ˈträ-niks\ *n pl* (1958) **1** *sing in constr* **:** a branch of electronics that deals with the miniaturization of electronic circuits and components **2 :** devices, equipment, or circuits produced using the methods of microelectronics — **mi·cro·elec·tron·ic** \-nik\ *adj* — **mi·cro·elec·tron·i·cal·ly** \-ni-k(ə-)lē\ *adv*
mi·cro·elec·tro·pho·re·sis \-i-ˌlek-trə-fə-ˈrē-səs\ *n* [NL] (1930) **:** electrophoresis in which the movement of single particles is observed in a microscope; *also* **:** electrophoresis in which micromethods are used — **mi·cro·elec·tro·pho·ret·ic** \-ˈre-tik\ *adj* — **mi·cro·elec·tro·pho·ret·i·cal·ly** \-ti-k(ə-)lē\ *adv*
mi·cro·el·e·ment \-ˈe-lə-mənt\ *n* (1936) **:** TRACE ELEMENT
mi·cro·en·cap·su·late \-in-ˈkap-sə-ˌlāt\ *vt* (1963) **:** to enclose in a microcapsule — **mi·cro·en·cap·su·la·tion** \-in-ˌkap-sə-ˈlā-shən\ *n*
mi·cro·en·ter·prise \-ˈen-tə(r)-ˌprīz\ *n* (1980) **:** a very small business
mi·cro·en·vi·ron·ment \-in-ˈvī-rən-mənt, -ˈvī(-ə)rn-\ *n* (1931) **:** a small or relatively small usu. distinctly specialized and effectively isolated habitat (as a forest canopy) or environment (as of a neuron) — **mi·cro·en·vi·ron·men·tal** \-ˌvī-rən-ˈmen-tᵊl\ *adj*
mi·cro·evo·lu·tion \-ˌe-və-ˈlü-shən *also* -ˌē-və-\ *n* (1911) **:** comparatively minor evolutionary change involving the accumulation of variations in populations usu. below the species level — **mi·cro·evo·lu·tion·ary** \-shə-ˌner-ē\ *adj*
mi·cro·far·ad \ˈmī-krō-ˌfa-ˌrad, -ˌfa-rəd\ *n* (1871) **:** a unit of capacitance equal to one millionth of a farad
mi·cro·fau·na \ˌmī-krō-ˈfȯ-nə, -ˈfä-\ *n* [NL] (1895) **1 :** minute animals; *esp* **:** those invisible to the naked eye ⟨the soil ~⟩ **2 :** a small or strictly localized fauna (as of a microenvironment) — **mi·cro·fau·nal** \-ˈfȯ-nᵊl, -ˈfä-\ *adj*
mi·cro·fi·ber \ˈmī-krō-ˌfī-bər\ *n* (1966) **:** a fine usu. soft polyester fiber; *also* **:** a fabric made from such fibers
mi·cro·fi·bril \ˌmī-krō-ˈfī-brəl, -ˈfi-\ *n* (1938) **:** a fine fibril; *esp* **:** one of the submicroscopic elongated bundles of cellulose of a plant cell wall — **mi·cro·fi·bril·lar** \-brə-lər\ *adj*
mi·cro·fiche \ˈmī-krō-ˌfēsh, -ˌfish\ *n, pl* **-fiche** *or* **-fiches** \-ˌfē-shəz, -ˌfēsh, -ˌfi-shəz, -ˌfish\ [F, fr. *micr-* micr- + *fiche* peg, marker in a game, index card, slip, from *ficher* to stick in — more at FICHU] (1943) **:** a sheet of microfilm containing rows of images of printed pages
mi·cro·fil·a·ment \ˌmī-krō-ˈfi-lə-mənt\ *n* (1963) **:** any of the minute actin-containing protein filaments of eukaryotic cytoplasm that function in maintaining structure and in intracellular movement
mi·cro·fi·lar·ia \-fə-ˈler-ē-ə\ *n* [NL] (1878) **:** a minute larval filaria — **mi·cro·fi·lar·i·al** \-ē-əl\ *adj*
¹**mi·cro·film** \ˈmī-krə-ˌfilm\ *n* [ISV] (1906) **:** a film bearing a photographic record on a reduced scale of printed or other graphic matter
²**microfilm** *vt* (1937) **:** to reproduce on microfilm ~ *vi* **:** to make microfilms — **mi·cro·film·able** \ˌmī-krə-ˈfil-mə-bəl\ *adj* — **mi·cro·film·er** \ˈmī-krə-ˌfil-mər\ *n*
mi·cro·flo·ra \ˌmī-krə-ˈflȯr-ə\ *n* [NL] (1904) **1 :** microscopic flora **2 :** a small or strictly localized flora (as of a microenvironment) — **mi·cro·flo·ral** \-əl\ *adj*
mi·cro·form \ˈmī-krə-ˌfȯrm\ *n* (1944) **1 :** a process for reproducing printed matter in a much reduced size ⟨documents in ~⟩ **2 :** matter reproduced by microform
mi·cro·fos·sil \ˌmī-krō-ˈfä-səl\ *n* (1924) **:** a small fossil that typically can be studied only microscopically and that may be either a fragment of a larger organism or an entire minute organism
mi·cro·fun·gus \-ˈfəŋ-gəs\ *n* [NL] (1874) **:** a fungus (as a mold) with a microscopic fruiting body
mi·cro·ga·mete \-ˈga-ˌmēt *also* -gə-ˈmēt\ *n* [ISV] (1888) **:** the smaller and usu. male gamete of a heterogamous organism
mi·cro·ga·me·to·cyte \-gə-ˈmē-tə-ˌsīt\ *n* [ISV] (1900) **:** a gametocyte producing microgametes
mi·cro·gram \ˈmī-krə-ˌgram\ *n* [ISV] (ca. 1890) **:** one millionth of a gram — see METRIC SYSTEM table
mi·cro·graph \-ˌgraf\ *n* [ISV] (1869) **:** a graphic reproduction of the image of an object formed by a microscope — **micrograph** *vt*
mi·cro·graph·ics \ˌmī-krə-ˈgra-fiks\ *n pl but sing in constr* (1968) **:** the industry concerned with the manufacture and sale of graphic material in microform; *also* **:** the production of such material — **mi·cro·graph·ic** \-fik\ *adj* — **mi·cro·graph·i·cal·ly** \-fi-k(ə-)lē\ *adv*
mi·cro·grav·i·ty \-ˈgra-və-tē\ *n* (1974) **:** a condition in space in which only minuscule forces are experienced **:** virtual absence of gravity; *broadly* **:** a condition of weightlessness
mi·cro·green \ˈmī-krō-ˌgrēn\ *n* (1998) **:** a shoot of a standard salad plant (as celery or arugula)
mi·cro·groove \ˈmī-krō-ˌgrüv\ *n* (1948) **:** a narrow continuous V-shaped spiral track that has closely spaced turns and that is used on long-playing records
mi·cro·hab·i·tat \ˌmī-krō-ˈha-bə-ˌtat\ *n* (1931) **:** the microenvironment in which an organism lives ⟨decaying wood creates a ~ for insects⟩
mi·cro·im·age \-ˈi-mij\ *n* (1950) **:** an image (as on a microfilm) that is greatly reduced in size
mi·cro·inch \-ˈinch\ *n* (1941) **:** one millionth of an inch
mi·cro·in·jec·tion \ˌmī-krō-in-ˈjek-shən\ *n* (1921) **:** injection under the microscope; *specif* **:** injection by means of a micropipette into a tissue or a single cell — **mi·cro·in·ject** \-ˈjekt\ *vt*
mi·cro·in·struc·tion \-ˈstrək-shən\ *n* (1959) **:** a computer instruction that activates the circuits necessary to perform a single machine operation usu. as part of the execution of a machine-language instruction
mi·cro·lep·i·dop·tera \ˌmī-krō-ˌle-pə-ˈdäp-tə-rə\ *n pl* [NL] (1852) **:** lepidopterous insects (as tortricids) that belong to families of minute or medium-sized moths — **mi·cro·lep·i·dop·ter·ous** \-tə-rəs\ *adj*
mi·cro·li·ter \ˈmī-krō-ˌlē-tər\ *n* [ISV] (ca. 1890) **:** a unit of capacity equal to one millionth of a liter — see METRIC SYSTEM table
mi·cro·lith \ˈmī-krə-ˌlith\ *n* [ISV] (1908) **:** a tiny blade tool esp. of the Mesolithic usu. in a geometric shape (as that of a triangle) and often set in a bone or wooden haft — **mi·cro·lith·ic** \ˌmī-krə-ˈli-thik\ *adj*
mi·cro·man·age \ˌmī-krō-ˈma-nij\ *vt* (1976) **:** to manage esp. with excessive control or attention to details ~ *vi* **:** to direct or conduct the activities of a group or an enterprise by micromanaging them — **mi·cro·man·age·ment** \-mənt\ *n* — **mi·cro·man·ag·er** \-ˈma-ni-jər\ *n*
mi·cro·ma·nip·u·la·tion \ˌmī-krō-mə-ˌni-pyə-ˈlā-shən\ *n* (1921) **:** the technique or practice of manipulating cells or tissues
mi·cro·ma·nip·u·la·tor \-ˈni-pyə-ˌlā-tər\ *n* (1921) **:** an instrument for micromanipulation
mi·cro·mere \ˈmī-krō-ˌmir\ *n* [ISV] (1877) **:** a small blastomere — see BLASTULA illustration
mi·cro·me·te·or·ite \ˌmī-krō-ˈmē-tē-ə-ˌrīt\ *n* (1949) **1 :** a meteorite so small that it can pass through the earth's atmosphere without becoming intensely heated **2 :** a very small particle in interplanetary space — **mi·cro·me·te·or·it·ic** \-ˌmē-tē-ə-ˈri-tik\ *adj*
mi·cro·me·te·or·oid \-ˈmē-tē-ə-ˌrȯid\ *n* (1961) **:** MICROMETEORITE 2

mi·cro·me·te·o·rol·o·gy \-ˌmē-tē-ə-ˈrä-lə-jē\ *n* (1930) **:** meteorology that deals with small-scale weather systems ranging up to several kilometers in diameter and confined to the lower troposphere — **mi·cro·me·te·o·ro·log·i·cal** \-ˌmē-tē-ˌȯr-ə-ˈlä-ji-kəl, -ˌär-ə-, -ə-rə-\ *adj* — **mi·cro·me·te·o·rol·o·gist** \-ˌmē-tē-ə-ˈrä-lə-jist\ *n*

[1]**mi·crom·e·ter** \mī-ˈkrä-mə-tər\ *n* [F *micromètre,* fr. *micr-* + *-mètre* -meter] (1670) **1 :** an instrument used with a telescope or microscope for measuring minute distances **2 :** a caliper for making precise measurements that has a spindle moved by a finely threaded screw

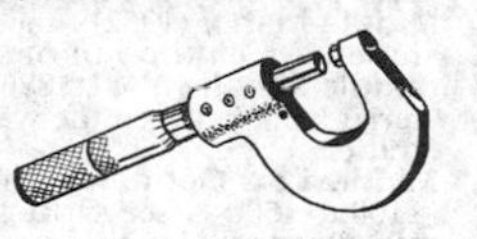
micrometer 2

[2]**mi·cro·me·ter** \ˈmī-krō-ˌmē-tər\ *n* [ISV *micr-* + [3]*meter*] (1880) **:** a unit of length equal to one millionth of a meter — called also *micron;* see METRIC SYSTEM table

mi·cro·meth·od \ˈmī-krō-ˌme-thəd\ *n* (1919) **:** a method (as of microanalysis) that requires only very small quantities of material or that involves the use of the microscope

mi·cro·mini \ˌmī-krō-ˈmi-nē\ *n* (1966) **:** a very short miniskirt

mi·cro·min·i·a·ture \-ˈmi-nē-ə-ˌchu̇r, -ˈmi-ni-ˌchu̇r, -ˈmin-yə-, -chər, -ˌtyu̇r, -ˌtu̇r\ *adj* (1958) **1 :** MICROMINIATURIZED **2 :** suitable for use with microminiaturized parts

mi·cro·min·i·a·tur·i·za·tion \-ˌmi-nē-ə-ˌchu̇r-ə-ˈzā-shən, -ˌmi-ni-ˌchu̇r-, -ˌmin-yə-ˌchu̇r-, -chər-, -ˌtyu̇r-, -ˌtu̇r-\ *n* (1955) **:** the process of producing microminiaturized things

mi·cro·min·i·a·tur·ized \-ˈmi-nē-ə-chə-ˌrīzd, -ˈmi-ni-chə-, -ˈmin-yə-chə-, -ˌtyu̇-, -ˌtu̇-\ *adj* (1959) **:** reduced to or produced in a very small size and esp. in a size smaller than one considered miniature

mi·cro·mole \ˈmī-krə-ˌmōl\ *n* [ISV] (1936) **:** one millionth of a mole — **mi·cro·mo·lar** \ˌmī-krə-ˈmō-lər\ *adj*

mi·cro·mor·phol·o·gy \ˌmī-krō-mȯr-ˈfä-lə-jē\ *n* (1879) **:** MICROSTRUCTURE — **mi·cro·mor·pho·log·i·cal** \-fə-ˈlä-ji-kəl\ *adj*

mi·cron \ˈmī-ˌkrän\ *n* [NL, fr. Gk *mikron,* neut. of *mikros* small — more at MICR-] (1885) **:** [2]MICROMETER

Mi·cro·ne·sian \ˌmī-krə-ˈnē-zhən, -shən\ *n* (1847) **1 :** a native or inhabitant of Micronesia **2 :** a group of Austronesian languages spoken in the Micronesian islands — **Micronesian** *adj*

mi·cron·ize \ˈmī-krə-ˌnīz\ *vt* **-ized; -iz·ing** [*micron*] (1940) **:** to pulverize esp. into particles a few micrometers in diameter

mi·cro·nu·cle·us \ˌmī-krō-ˈnü-klē-əs, -ˈnyü-\ *n* [NL] (1887) **:** a minute nucleus; *specif* **:** one that is primarily concerned with reproductive and genetic functions in most ciliated protozoans

mi·cro·nu·tri·ent \-ˈnü-trē-ənt, -ˈnyü-\ *n* (1939) **1 :** TRACE ELEMENT **2 :** an organic compound (as a vitamin) essential in minute amounts to the growth and health of an animal

mi·cro·or·gan·ism \-ˈȯr-gə-ˌni-zəm\ *n* [ISV] (1880) **:** an organism (as a bacterium or protozoan) of microscopic or ultramicroscopic size

mi·cro·pa·le·on·tol·o·gy \-ˌpā-lē-ˌän-ˈtä-lə-jē, -lē-ən-, *esp Brit* -ˌpa-\ *n* [ISV] (1883) **:** the study of microscopic fossils — **mi·cro·pa·le·on·to·log·i·cal** \-ˌän-tə-ˈlä-ji-kəl\ *also* **mi·cro·pa·le·on·to·log·ic** \-jik\ *adj* — **mi·cro·pa·le·on·tol·o·gist** \-ˌän-ˈtä-lə-jist, -ən-\ *n*

mi·cro·par·ti·cle \-ˈpär-ti-kəl\ *n* (1929) **:** a very small particle; *esp* **:** one that is microscopic in size

mi·cro·phage \ˈmī-krə-ˌfāj *also* -ˌfäzh\ *n* [ISV] (1887) **:** a small phagocyte

mi·cro·phone \ˈmī-krə-ˌfōn\ *n* [ISV] (1878) **:** an instrument whereby sound waves are caused to generate or modulate an electric current usu. for the purpose of transmitting or recording sound (as speech or music) — **mi·cro·phon·ic** \ˌmī-krə-ˈfä-nik\ *adj*

mi·cro·phon·ics \ˌmī-krə-ˈfä-niks\ *n pl* (1929) **:** noises in a loudspeaker caused by mechanical shock or vibration of the electronic components

mi·cro·pho·to·graph \-ˈfō-tə-ˌgraf\ *n* [ISV] (1858) **1 :** a small photograph that is normally magnified for viewing **2 :** PHOTOMICROGRAPH — **microphotograph** *vt* — **mi·cro·pho·tog·ra·pher** \-fə-ˈtä-grə-fər\ *n* — **mi·cro·pho·to·graph·ic** \-ˌfō-tə-ˈgra-fik\ *adj* — **mi·cro·pho·tog·ra·phy** \-fə-ˈtä-grə-fē\ *n*

mi·cro·pho·tom·e·ter \-fō-ˈtä-mə-tər\ *n* [ISV] (1899) **:** an instrument for measuring the amount of light transmitted or reflected by small areas or for measuring the relative densities of spectral lines on a photographic film or plate — **mi·cro·pho·to·met·ric** \-ˌfō-tə-ˈme-trik\ *adj* — **mi·cro·pho·to·met·ri·cal·ly** \-tri-k(ə-)lē\ *adv* — **mi·cro·pho·tom·e·try** \-fō-ˈtä-mə-trē\ *n*

mi·cro·phyll \ˈmī-krə-ˌfil\ *n* [ISV] (1908) **1 :** a leaf (as of a club moss) with single unbranched veins and no demonstrable gap around the leaf trace **2 :** a small leaf — **mi·cro·phyl·lous** \ˌmī-krə-ˈfi-ləs\ *adj*

mi·cro·phys·ics \ˌmī-krō-ˈfi-ziks\ *n* (1885) **:** the physics of molecules, atoms, and elementary particles — **mi·cro·phys·i·cal** \-ˈfi-zi-kəl\ *adj* — **mi·cro·phys·i·cal·ly** \-k(ə-)lē\ *adv*

mi·cro·pi·pette *or* **mi·cro·pi·pet** \-pī-ˈpet\ *n* (1918) **1 :** a pipette for the measurement of minute volumes **2 :** a small and extremely fine-pointed pipette used in making microinjections

mi·cro·plank·ton \-ˈplaŋ(k)-tən, -ˌtän\ *n* [ISV] (1903) **:** microscopic plankton

mi·cro·pol·i·tan \ˌmī-krō-ˈpä-lə-tən\ *adj* [*micr-* + [2]metro*politan*] (1982) **:** of, relating to, or being a population area that includes a city with 10,000 to 50,000 residents and its surrounding communities

mi·cro·pore \ˈmī-krə-ˌpȯr\ *n* [ISV] (1884) **:** a very fine pore — **mi·cro·po·ros·i·ty** \-pə-ˈrä-sə-tē, -pȯ-\ *n* — **mi·cro·po·rous** \ˌmī-krə-ˈpȯr-əs\ *adj*

mi·cro·prism \ˈmī-krə-ˌpri-zəm\ *n* (1962) **:** a usu. circular area on the focusing screen of a camera that is made up of tiny prisms and that causes the image in the viewfinder to blur if the subject is not in focus

mi·cro·probe \-ˌprōb\ *n* (1944) **:** a device for microanalysis that operates by exciting radiation in a minute area of material so that the composition may be determined from the emission spectrum

mi·cro·pro·ces·sor \ˌmī-krō-ˈprä-ˌse-sər, -ˈprō-\ *n* (1969) **:** a computer processor contained on an integrated-circuit chip; *also* **:** such a processor with memory and associated circuits

mi·cro·pro·gram \-ˈprō-ˌgram, -grəm\ *n* (1953) **:** a routine composed of microinstructions used in microprogramming

mi·cro·pro·gram·ming \-ˌgra-miŋ\ *n* (1953) **:** the use of routines stored in memory rather than specialized circuits to control a device (as a computer)

mi·cro·pro·jec·tor \-prə-ˈjek-tər\ *n* (1921) **:** a projector utilizing a compound microscope for projecting on a screen a greatly enlarged image of a microscopic object — **mi·cro·pro·jec·tion** \-ˈjek-shən\ *n*

mi·cro·pub·lish·ing \-ˈpə-bli-shiŋ\ *n* (1959) **:** publishing in microform — **mi·cro·pub·lish·er** \-bli-shər\ *n*

mi·cro·pul·sa·tion \-ˌpəl-ˈsā-shən\ *n* (1949) **:** a pulsation having a short period ⟨a ~ of the earth's magnetic field with a period in the range from a fraction of a second to several hundred seconds⟩

mi·cro·punc·ture \-ˈpəŋ(k)-chər\ *n* (1948) **:** an extremely small puncture (as of a nephron); *also* **:** an act of making a micropuncture

mi·cro·pyle \ˈmī-krə-ˌpī(-ə)l\ *n* [F, fr. *micr-* + Gk *pylē* gate] (1821) **1 :** a minute opening in the integument of an ovule of a seed plant **2 :** a differentiated area of surface in an egg through which a sperm enters — **mi·cro·py·lar** \ˌmī-krə-ˈpī-lər\ *adj*

mi·cro·quake \ˈmī-krō-ˌkwāk\ *n* (1967) **:** MICROEARTHQUAKE

mi·cro·ra·di·og·ra·phy \ˌmī-krō-ˌrā-dē-ˈä-grə-fē\ *n* (1913) **:** radiography in which an X-ray photograph is prepared showing minute internal structure — **mi·cro·ra·dio·graph** \-ˈrā-dē-ə-ˌgraf\ *n* — **mi·cro·ra·dio·graph·ic** \-ˌrā-dē-ə-ˈgra-fik\ *adj*

mi·cro·sat·el·lite \ˌmī-krō-ˈsa-tə-ˌlīt\ *n* (1989) **:** any of numerous short segments of DNA that are distributed throughout the genome, that consist of repeated sequences of usu. two to five nucleotides, and that tend to vary from one individual to another

mi·cro·scale \ˈmī-krō-ˌskāl\ *n* (1929) **:** a very small scale

mi·cro·scope \ˈmī-krə-ˌskōp\ *n* [NL *microscopium,* fr. *micr-* + *-scopium* -scope] (1651) **1 :** an optical instrument consisting of a lens or combination of lenses for making enlarged images of minute objects; *esp* **:** COMPOUND MICROSCOPE **2 :** a non-optical instrument (as one using radiations other than light or using vibrations) for making enlarged images of minute objects ⟨an acoustic ~⟩

mi·cro·scop·ic \ˌmī-krə-ˈskä-pik\ *also* **mi·cro·scop·i·cal** \-pi-kəl\ *adj* (ca. 1672) **1 :** resembling a microscope esp. in perception **2 a :** invisible or indistinguishable without the use of a microscope **b :** very small or fine or precise **3 :** of, relating to, or conducted with the microscope or microscopy — **mi·cro·scop·i·cal·ly** \-pi-k(ə-)lē\ *adv*

mi·cros·co·py \mī-ˈkräs-kə-pē\ *n* (ca. 1665) **:** the use of or investigation with a microscope — **mi·cros·co·pist** \-pist\ *n*

mi·cro·sec·ond \ˈmī-krō-ˌse-kənd, -kənt\ *n* [ISV] (1906) **:** one millionth of a second

mi·cro·seism \ˈmī-krə-ˌsī-zəm\ *n* [ISV *micr-* + Gk *seismos* earthquake — more at SEISMIC] (1887) **:** a feeble rhythmically and persistently recurring earth tremor — **mi·cro·seis·mic** \ˌmī-krə-ˈsīz-mik, -ˈsīs-\ *adj* — **mi·cro·seis·mic·i·ty** \-sīz-ˈmi-sə-tē, -sīs-\ *n*

mi·cro·sen·sor \ˈmī-krō-ˌsen-ˌsȯr, -ˌsen(t)-sər\ *n* (1962) **:** a miniature sensor

mi·cro·some \ˈmī-krə-ˌsōm\ *n* [ISV] (1885) **1 :** any of various minute cellular structures **2 :** a particle in a particulate fraction that is obtained by heavy centrifugation of broken cells and consists of various amounts of ribosomes, fragmented endoplasmic reticulum, and mitochondrial cristae — **mi·cro·som·al** \ˌmī-krə-ˈsō-məl\ *adj*

mi·cro·spec·tro·pho·tom·e·ter \ˌmī-krə-ˌspek-trə-fō-ˈtä-mə-tər\ *n* (1949) **:** a spectrophotometer adapted to the examination of light transmitted by a very small specimen (as a single biological cell) — **mi·cro·spec·tro·pho·to·met·ric** \-ˌfō-tə-ˈme-trik\ *adj* — **mi·cro·spec·tro·pho·tom·e·try** \-fō-ˈtä-mə-trē\ *n*

mi·cro·sphere \ˈmī-krə-ˌsfir\ *n* (1894) **:** a minute sphere — **mi·cro·spher·i·cal** \ˌmī-krə-ˈsfir-i-kəl, -ˈsfer-\ *adj*

mi·cro·spo·ran·gi·um \ˌmī-krō-spə-ˈran-jē-əm\ *n* [NL] (1862) **:** a sporangium that develops only microspores — **mi·cro·spo·ran·gi·ate** \-jē-ət\ *adj*

mi·cro·spore \ˈmī-krə-ˌspȯr\ *n* [ISV] (1847) **:** any of the spores in heterosporous plants that give rise to male gametophytes and are generally smaller than the megaspore — **mi·cro·spo·rous** \ˌmī-krə-ˈspȯr-əs, mī-ˈkräs-pə-rəs\ *adj*

mi·cro·spo·ro·cyte \-ˈspȯr-ə-ˌsīt\ *n* (1906) **:** a microspore mother cell

mi·cro·spo·ro·gen·e·sis \ˌmī-krə-ˌspȯr-ə-ˈje-nə-səs\ *n* [NL] (1904) **:** the formation and maturation of microspores

mi·cro·spo·ro·phyll \-ˌfil\ *n* (1888) **:** a sporophyll that develops only microsporangia

mi·cro·state \ˈmī-krō-ˌstāt\ *n* (1962) **:** a nation that is extremely small in area and population

mi·cro·struc·ture \ˈmī-krō-ˌstrək-chər\ *n* [ISV] (1881) **:** the microscopic structure of a material (as a mineral or a biological cell) — **mi·cro·struc·tur·al** \ˌmī-krō-ˈstrək-chə-rəl, -ˈstrək-shrəl\ *adj*

mi·cro·sur·gery \ˌmī-krō-ˈsərj-rē, -ˈsər-jə-\ *n* (1926) **:** minute dissection or manipulation (as by a micromanipulator or laser beam) of living structures or tissue — **mi·cro·sur·gi·cal** \-ˈsər-ji-kəl\ *adj*

mi·cro·switch \-ˌswich\ *n* (1940) **:** a very small switch that is sensitive to minute motions and is used esp. in automatic devices

mi·cro·tech·nique \ˌmī-krō-tek-ˈnēk\ *also* **mi·cro·tech·nic** \-ˈtek-nik, -tek-ˈnēk\ *n* [ISV] (1892) **:** any of various methods of handling and preparing material for microscopic observation and study

mi·cro·tech·nol·o·gy \-tek-ˈnä-lə-jē\ *n* (1970) **:** technology on a small or microscopic scale

mi·cro·ti·ter \ˈmī-krō-ˌtī-tər\ *n* (1961) **:** a titer determined by microanalytical titration — usu. used attributively ⟨a ~ assay⟩

mi·cro·tome \ˈmī-krə-ˌtōm\ *n* [ISV] (1856) **:** an instrument for cutting sections (as of biological tissues) for microscopic examination

mi·cro·tone \ˈmī-krə-ˌtōn\ *n* (1920) **:** a musical interval smaller than a halftone — **mi·cro·ton·al** \ˌmī-krə-ˈtō-nᵊl\ *adj* — **mi·cro·to·nal·i·ty** \-tō-ˈna-lə-tē\ *n* — **mi·cro·ton·al·ly** \-ˈtō-nᵊl-ē\ *adv*

mi·cro·tu·bule \ˌmī-krō-ˈtü-(ˌ)byül, -ˈtyü-\ *n* (1961) **:** any of the minute tubules in eukaryotic cytoplasm that are composed of the protein tubulin and form an important component of the cytoskeleton, mitotic spindle, cilia, and flagella — **mi·cro·tu·bu·lar** \-byə-lər\ *adj*

mi·cro·vas·cu·lar \-ˈvas-kyə-lər\ *adj* (1959) **:** of, relating to, or constituting the part of the circulatory system made up of minute vessels (as

\ə\ **abut** \ᵊ\ **kitten,** F **table** \ər\ **further** \a\ **ash** \ā\ **ace** \ä\ **mop, mar**
\au̇\ **out** \ch\ **chin** \e\ **bet** \ē\ **easy** \g\ **go** \i\ **hit** \ī\ **ice** \j\ **job**
\ŋ\ **sing** \ō\ **go** \ȯ\ **law** \ȯi\ **boy** \th\ **thin** \t͟h\ **the** \ü\ **loot** \u̇\ **foot**
\y\ **yet** \zh\ **vision, beige** \k, ⁿ, œ, ue, ʸ\ *see* Guide to Pronunciation

venules or capillaries) that average less than 0.3 millimeters in diameter — **mi·cro·vas·cu·la·ture** \-lə-ˌchu̇r, -ˌtyu̇r, -ˌtu̇r\ *n*
mi·cro·vil·lus \-ˈvi-ləs\ *n, pl* **-vil·li** \-ˈvi-ˌlī, -(ˌ)lē\ [NL] (1953) **:** a microscopic projection of a tissue, cell, or cell organelle; *esp* **:** any of the fingerlike outward projections of some cell surfaces — **mi·cro·vil·lar** \-ˈvi-lər\ *adj* — **mi·cro·vil·lous** \-ˈvi-ləs\ *adj*
mi·cro·volt \ˈmī-krə-ˌvōlt\ *n* (1868) **:** one millionth of a volt
mi·cro·watt \-ˌwät\ *n* (ca. 1909) **:** one millionth of a watt
[1]**mi·cro·wave** \-ˌwāv\ *n, often attrib* (1931) **1 :** a comparatively short electromagnetic wave; *esp* **:** one between about one millimeter and one meter in wavelength **2 :** MICROWAVE OVEN
[2]**microwave** *vt* (1973) **:** to cook or heat in a microwave oven — **mi·cro·wav·able** *or* **mi·cro·wave·able** \ˌmī-krə-ˈwā-və-bəl\ *adj*
microwave oven *n* (1955) **:** an oven in which food is cooked by the heat produced by the absorption of microwave energy by water molecules in the food
mi·cro·world \-ˌwər(-ə)ld\ *n* (1923) **:** a small universe; *specif* **:** the natural universe observed at the microscopic or submicroscopic level
mic·tu·rate \ˈmik-chə-ˌrāt, ˈmik-tə-\ *vi* **-rat·ed; -rat·ing** [L *micturire* to desire to urinate, fr. *meiere* to urinate; akin to OE *mīgan* to urinate, Gk *omeichein*] (1842) **:** URINATE — **mic·tu·ri·tion** \ˌmik-chə-ˈri-shən, ˌmik-tə-\ *n*
[1]**mid** \ˈmid\ *adj* [ME, fr. OE *midde;* akin to OHG *mitti* middle, L *medius,* Gk *mesos*] (bef. 12c) **1 :** being the part in the middle or midst ⟨in ~ ocean⟩ — often used in combination ⟨*mid*-August⟩ **2 :** occupying a middle position **3** *of a vowel* **:** articulated with the arch of the tongue midway between its highest and its lowest elevation — **mid** *adv*
[2]**mid** *prep* (15c) **:** AMID
mid·air \ˈmid-ˈer\ *n* (1605) **:** a point or region in the air not immediately adjacent to the ground ⟨the planes collided in ~⟩
Mi·das \ˈmī-dəs\ *n* [L, fr. Gk] (1548) **:** a legendary Phrygian king who is given the power of turning everything he touches to gold
Midas touch *n* (1813) **:** an uncanny ability for making money in every venture
mid·brain \ˈmid-ˌbrān\ *n* (1864) **:** the middle of the three primary divisions of the developing vertebrate brain or the corresponding part of the adult brain between the forebrain and hindbrain that includes the tectum, tegmentum, and substantia nigra — called also *mesencephalon;* see BRAIN illustration
mid·course \-ˈkȯrs\ *adj* (ca. 1951) **:** being or occurring in the middle part of a course (as of a spacecraft) ⟨a ~ correction⟩
mid·day \ˈmid-ˌdā, -ˈdā\ *n, often attrib* (bef. 12c) **:** the middle of the day
mid·den \ˈmi-dᵊn\ *n* [ME *midding,* fr. ON **mykdyngja,* fr. *myki* dung + *dyngja* manure pile — more at DUNG] (14c) **1 :** DUNGHILL **2 a :** a refuse heap; *esp* **:** KITCHEN MIDDEN **b :** a small pile (as of seeds, bones, or leaves) gathered by a rodent (as a pack rat)
[1]**mid·dle** \ˈmi-dᵊl\ *adj* [ME *middel,* fr. OE; akin to OE *midde*] (bef. 12c) **1 :** equally distant from the extremes **:** MEDIAL, CENTRAL ⟨the ~ house in the row⟩ **2 :** being at neither extreme **:** INTERMEDIATE **3** *cap* **a :** constituting a division intermediate between those prior and later or upper and lower ⟨*Middle* Paleozoic⟩ **b :** constituting a period of a language or literature intermediate between one called *Old* and one called *New* or *Modern* ⟨*Middle* Dutch⟩ **4** *of a verb form or voice* **:** typically asserting that a person or thing both performs and is affected by the action represented
[2]**middle** *n* (bef. 12c) **1 :** a middle part, point, or position **2 :** the central portion of the human body **:** WAIST **3 :** the position of being among or in the midst of something ⟨in the ~ of the crowd⟩ **4 :** something intermediate between extremes **:** MEAN **5 :** the center of an offensive or defensive formation; *esp* **:** the area between the second baseman and the shortstop — **middle of nowhere :** an extremely remote and isolated place ⟨ran out of gas in the *middle of nowhere*⟩
middle age *n* (14c) **:** the period of life from about 45 to about 64 — **mid·dle–aged** \ˌmi-dᵊl-ˈājd\ *adj* — **mid·dle–ag·er** \-ˈā-jər\ *n*
Middle Ages *n pl* (1616) **:** the period of European history from about A.D. 500 to about 1500
Middle America *n* (1841) **1 :** the region of the western hemisphere including Mexico, Central America, often the West Indies, and sometimes Colombia and Venezuela **2 :** the midwestern section of the U.S. **3 :** the middle-class segment of the U.S. population; *esp* **:** the traditional or conservative element of the middle class — **middle–American** *adj* — **Middle American** *n*
mid·dle·brow \ˈmi-dᵊl-ˌbrau̇\ *n* (1925) **:** a person who is moderately but not highly cultivated — **middlebrow** *adj*
middle C *n* (1660) **:** the note designated by the first ledger line below the treble staff and the first above the bass staff
mid·dle–class \ˌmi-dᵊl-ˈklas\ *adj* (1836) **:** of or relating to the middle class; *esp* **:** characterized by a high material standard of living, sexual morality, and respect for property — **mid·dle–class·ness** \-nəs\ *n*
middle class *n* (1745) **:** a class occupying a position between the upper class and the lower class; *esp* **:** a fluid heterogeneous socioeconomic grouping composed principally of business and professional people, bureaucrats, and some farmers and skilled workers sharing common social characteristics and values
middle distance *n* (1803) **1 :** a part of a pictorial representation or scene between the foreground and the background **2 :** any footrace distance usu. from 800 to 1500 meters or from 880 yards to one mile
Middle Dutch *n* (1870) **:** the Dutch language in use from about 1100 to about 1500 — see INDO-EUROPEAN LANGUAGES table
middle ear *n* (1808) **:** a small membrane-lined cavity that is separated from the outer ear by the tympanic membrane and that transmits sound waves from the tympanic membrane to the partition between the middle and inner ears through a chain of tiny bones
Middle English *n* (1830) **:** the English in use from the 12th to 15th centuries — see INDO-EUROPEAN LANGUAGES table
middle finger *n* (bef. 12c) **:** the midmost of the five digits of the hand
Middle French *n* (1889) **:** the French in use from the 14th to 16th centuries — see INDO-EUROPEAN LANGUAGES table
middle game *n* (1894) **:** the middle phase of a board game; *specif* **:** the part of a chess game after the pieces have been developed when players attempt to gain and exploit positional and material superiority — compare ENDGAME, OPENING
Middle Greek *n* (1889) **:** the Greek language used in the 7th to 15th centuries
middle ground *n* (1752) **1 :** a standpoint or area midway between extreme or opposing positions, options, or objectives **2 :** MIDDLE DISTANCE 1
Middle High German *n* (1851) **:** the High German in use from about 1100 to 1500 — see INDO-EUROPEAN LANGUAGES table
Middle Irish *n* (1952) **:** the Irish in use between the 10th and 13th centuries — see INDO-EUROPEAN LANGUAGES table
middle lamella *n* (ca. 1886) **:** a layer of pectinaceous intercellular material lying between the walls of adjacent plant cells — see CELL illustration
Middle Low German *n* (ca. 1889) **:** the Low German in use from about 1100 to 1500 — see INDO-EUROPEAN LANGUAGES table
mid·dle·man \ˈmi-dᵊl-ˌman\ *n* (1677) **:** an intermediary or agent between two parties; *esp* **:** a dealer, agent, or company intermediate between the producer of goods and the retailer or consumer
middle management *n* (1941) **:** management personnel intermediate between operational supervisors and policy-making administrators — **middle manager** *n*
middle name *n* (1835) **1 :** a name between one's first name and surname **2 :** a term that is particularly apt to denote a person's qualities or affinities ⟨patience is her *middle name*⟩
middle–of–the–road *adj* (1894) **:** standing for or following a course of action midway between extremes; *esp* **:** being neither liberal nor conservative in politics — **mid·dle–of–the–road·er** \-ˈrō-dər\ *n* — **mid·dle–of–the–road·ism** \-ˈrō-ˌdi-zəm\ *n*
middle of the road (1891) **:** a course of action or a standpoint midway between extremes
Middle Passage *n* (1788) **:** the forced voyage of enslaved Africans across the Atlantic Ocean to the Americas
Middle Persian *n* (1890) **:** any of the varieties of Persian in use from about 200 B.C. to about A.D. 1000
mid·dler \ˈmid-lər, ˈmi-dᵊl-ər\ *n* (1882) **:** one belonging to an intermediate group, division, or class: as **a :** a student in the second-year class of a three-year program (as at a seminary or law school) **b :** a student in the second- or third-year class in some private secondary schools having a four-year course **c :** a student in a division in some private schools that corresponds approximately to junior high school
middle school *n* (1870) **:** a school usu. including grades five to eight or six to eight — **middle school·er** \-ˌskü-lər\ *n*
Middle Scots *n* (1902) **:** the Scots language in use between the latter half of the 15th and the early decades of the 17th centuries
middle term *n* (1605) **:** the term of a syllogism that occurs in both premises
mid·dle·weight \ˈmi-dᵊl-ˌwāt\ *n* (1847) **:** one of average weight; *specif* **:** a boxer in a weight division having a maximum limit of 160 pounds for professionals and 165 pounds for amateurs — compare LIGHT HEAVYWEIGHT, WELTERWEIGHT
Middle Welsh *n* (ca. 1922) **:** the Welsh in use from about 1150 to 1500 — see INDO-EUROPEAN LANGUAGES table
[1]**mid·dling** \ˈmid-liŋ, -lən\ *adj* (15c) **1 :** of middle, medium, or moderate size, degree, or quality **2 :** MEDIOCRE, SECOND-RATE **3 :** of, relating to, or being a middle class — **middling** *adv* — **mid·dling·ly** \-lē\ *adv*
[2]**middling** *n* (1543) **1 :** any of various commodities of intermediate size, quality, or position **2** *pl but sing or pl in constr* **:** a granular product of grain milling; *esp* **:** a wheat milling by-product used in animal feeds
mid·dor·sal \ˈmid-ˈdȯr-səl\ *adj* (1866) **:** of, relating to, or situated in the middle part or median line of the back
mid·dy \ˈmi-dē\ *n, pl* **middies** [by shortening & alter.] (1818) **1 :** MIDSHIPMAN **2 :** a loosely fitting blouse with a sailor collar worn by women and children
mid·field \ˈmid-ˌfēld, ˌmid-ˈ\ *n* (15c) **1 :** the middle portion of a field; *esp* **:** the portion of a playing field (as in football) that is midway between goals **2 :** the players on a team (as in lacrosse or soccer) that normally play in the midfield
mid·field·er \-ˌfēl-dər, -ˈfēl-\ *n* (1938) **:** a member of a midfield
Mid·gard \ˈmid-ˌgärd\ *n* [ON *mithgarthr*] (1770) **:** the abode of human beings in Norse mythology
midge \ˈmij\ *n* [ME *migge,* fr. OE *mycg;* akin to OHG *mucka* midge, Gk *myia* fly, L *musca*] (bef. 12c) **:** a tiny dipteran fly (as a chironomid)
midg·et \ˈmi-jət\ *n, often attrib* [*midge*] (1816) **1 :** something (as an animal) much smaller than usual **2** *sometimes offensive* **:** a very small person; *specif* **:** a person of unusually small size who is physically well-proportioned **3 :** a front-engine, single-seat, open-wheel racing car smaller and of less engine displacement than standard cars of the type
mid·gut \ˈmid-ˌgət\ *n* (1875) **:** the middle part of an alimentary canal
midi \ˈmi-dē\ *n* [[1]*mid* + *-i* (as in *mini*)] (1967) **:** a dress, skirt, or coat that usu. extends to the mid-calf
MIDI \ˈmi-dē\ *n* [*m*usical *i*nstrument *d*igital *i*nterface] (1983) **:** an electronic standard used for the transmission of digitally encoded music
Mid·i·an·ite \ˈmi-dē-ə-ˌnīt\ *n* [*Midian,* son of Abraham] (1560) **:** a member of an ancient northern Arabian people
mid·land \ˈmid-lənd, -ˌland\ *n* (15c) **1 :** the interior or central region of a country **2** *cap* **a :** the dialect of English spoken in the midland counties of England **b :** the dialect of English spoken in an area of the east central U.S. often divided into north Midland extending westward from an area including southern New Jersey; northern Delaware and Maryland; central and southern Pennsylvania; and central Ohio, Indiana, and Illinois and south Midland extending westward and southwestward from an area including the Appalachian regions of Virginia, No. Carolina, So. Carolina, and Georgia; Tennessee, Kentucky, West Virginia; and southern Ohio, Indiana, and Illinois — **midland** *adj, often cap* — **Mid·land·er** \-lən-dər, -ˌlan-\ *n*
mid·lat·i·tudes \ˈmid-ˈla-tə-ˌtüdz, ˌmid-, -ˌtyüdz\ *n pl* (1872) **:** latitudes of the temperate zones or from about 30 to 60 degrees north or south of the equator — **mid·lat·i·tude** \-ˌtüd, -ˌtyüd\ *adj*
mid·life \ˈmid-ˈlīf\ *n* (1807) **:** MIDDLE AGE — **midlife** *adj*
midlife crisis *n* (1965) **:** a period of emotional turmoil in middle age characterized esp. by a strong desire for change
mid·line \ˈmid-ˌlīn, -ˈlīn\ *n* (14c) **:** a median line; *esp* **:** the median line or median plane of the body or some part of the body
mid·most \-ˌmōst\ *adj* (bef. 12c) **1 :** being in or near the exact middle **2 :** most intimate **:** INNERMOST — **midmost** *adv or n*

Midn *abbr* midshipman

mid·night \ˈmid-ˌnīt\ *n* (bef. 12c) **1 :** the middle of the night; *specif* **:** 12 o'clock at night **2 :** deep or extended darkness or gloom — **mid·night** *adj* — **mid·night·ly** *adv or adj*

midnight blue *n* (1810) **:** a deep blackish blue

midnight sun *n* (1787) **:** the sun above the horizon at midnight in the arctic or antarctic summer

mid–ocean ridge \ˈmid-ˈō-shən-\ *n* (1961) **:** an elevated region with a central valley on an ocean floor at the boundary between two diverging tectonic plates where new crust forms from upwelling magma

mid·point \ˈmid-ˌpȯint, -ˈpȯint\ *n* (14c) **:** a point at or near the center or middle

mid·rash \ˈmi-ˌdräsh\ *n, pl* **mid·rash·im** \mi-ˈdrä-shəm\ [Heb *midhrāsh* exposition, explanation] (1613) **1 :** a haggadic or halachic exposition of the underlying significance of a Bible text **2 :** a collection of midrashim **3** *cap* **:** the midrashic literature written during the first Christian millennium — **mid·rash·ic** \mi-ˈdrä-shik\ *adj, often cap*

mid·rib \ˈmid-ˌrib\ *n* (ca. 1793) **:** the central vein of a leaf

mid·riff \ˈmi-ˌdrif\ *n* [ME *midrif,* fr. OE *midhrif,* fr. *midde* mid + *hrif* belly; akin to OHG *href* womb, and prob. to L *corpus* body] (bef. 12c) **1 :** DIAPHRAGM 1 **2 :** the mid-region of the human torso **3 a :** a section of a woman's garment that covers the midriff **b :** a woman's garment that exposes the midriff

mid–rise \ˈmid-ˌrīz, -ˈrīz\ *adj* (1967) **:** being approximately 5 to 10 stories high ⟨~ condominiums⟩

mid·sag·it·tal \ˈmid-ˈsa-jə-tᵊl\ *adj* (1898) **:** median and sagittal

mid·sec·tion \-ˌsek-shən\ *n* (1890) **:** a section midway between the extremes; *esp* **:** MIDRIFF 2

mid·ship·man \ˈmid-ˌship-mən, ˌmid-ˈ\ *n* (1662) **:** a person in training for a naval commission; *esp* **:** a student in a naval academy

mid·ships \ˈmid-ˌships\ *adv* (1779) **:** AMIDSHIPS

mid·size \-ˌsīz\ *also* **mid·sized** \-ˌsīzd\ *adj* (1967) **:** of intermediate size ⟨a ~ car⟩

mid·sole \-ˌsōl\ *n* (1926) **:** a layer (as of leather or rubber) between the insole and the outsole of a shoe

midst \ˈmidst, ˈmitst\ *n* [ME *middest,* alter. of *middes,* short for *amiddes* amid] (15c) **1 :** the interior or central part or point **:** MIDDLE ⟨in the ~ of the forest⟩ **2 :** a position of proximity to the members of a group ⟨a traitor in our ~⟩ **3 :** the condition of being surrounded or beset ⟨in the ~ of his troubles⟩ **4 :** a period of time about the middle of a continuing act or condition ⟨in the ~ of a meal⟩ — **midst** *prep*

mid·stream \ˈmid-ˈstrēm, -ˌstrēm\ *n* (1670) **1 :** the middle of a stream **2 :** an intermediate stage in an act or process ⟨the tone changes in ~⟩

mid·sum·mer \-ˈsə-mər, -ˌsəm-\ *n* (bef. 12c) **1 :** the middle of summer **2 :** the summer solstice — **midsummer** *adj*

Midsummer Day *n* (bef. 12c) **:** June 24 celebrated as the feast of the nativity of John the Baptist

mid·term \ˈmid-ˌtərm (*usual for 1b*), -ˈtərm\ *n* (1906) **1 a :** the middle of an academic term **b :** an examination at midterm **2 :** the approximate middle of a term of office

mid·town \ˈmid-ˌtau̇n, -ˈtau̇n\ *n* (1926) **:** a central section of a city; *esp* **:** one situated between sections conventionally called *downtown* and *uptown* — **midtown** *adj*

[1]**mid·way** \ˈmid-ˌwā, -ˈwā\ *adv* (13c) **:** in the middle of the way or distance **:** HALFWAY

[2]**mid·way** \-ˌwā\ *n* [*Midway (Plaisance),* Chicago, site of the amusement section of the Columbian Exposition 1893] (1893) **:** an avenue at a fair, carnival, or amusement park for concessions and amusements

mid·week \-ˌwēk\ *n* (1706) **:** the middle of the week — **midweek** *adj or adv* — **mid·week·ly** \-ˌwē-klē, -ˈwē-\ *adj or adv*

[1]**mid·wife** \ˈmid-ˌwīf\ *n* [ME *midwif,* fr. *mid* with (fr. OE) + *wif* woman] (14c) **1 :** a person who assists women in childbirth — compare NURSE-MIDWIFE **2 :** one that helps to produce or bring forth something

[2]**midwife** *vt* **mid·wifed** \-ˌwīft\ *or* **mid·wived** \-ˌwīvd\; **mid·wif·ing** \-ˌwī-fiŋ\ *or* **mid·wiv·ing** \-ˌwī-viŋ\ (1638) **:** to assist in producing, bringing forth, or bringing about

mid·wife·ry \ˌmid-ˈwi-f(ə-)rē, -ˈwī-; ˈmid-ˌwī-\ *n* (15c) **1 :** the art or act of assisting at childbirth; *also* **:** OBSTETRICS **2 :** the art, act, or process of producing, bringing forth, or bringing about

mid·win·ter \ˈmid-ˈwin-tər, -ˌwin-\ *n* (bef. 12c) **1 :** the winter solstice **2 :** the middle of winter — **midwinter** *adj*

mid·year \-ˌyir\ *n* (1896) **1 a :** an examination at the middle of an academic year **b** *pl* **:** the set of examinations at the middle of an academic year; *also* **:** the period of such examinations **2 a :** the middle or middle portion of a calendar year **b :** the middle of an academic year — **midyear** *adj*

mien \ˈmēn\ *n* [by shortening & alter. fr. [1]*demean*] (1522) **1 :** air or bearing esp. as expressive of attitude or personality **:** DEMEANOR ⟨of aristocratic ~⟩ **2 :** APPEARANCE, ASPECT ⟨dresses of formal ~⟩ *syn* see BEARING

mi·fep·ris·tone \ˌmi-fə-ˈpris-ˌtōn, mi-ˈfe-pri-ˌstōn\ *n* [perh. fr. ISV *amino* + *fe-* (alter. of *phen-*) + *pri-* (alter. of *prop-*) + estradiol + *-one*] (1985) **:** RU-486

[1]**miff** \ˈmif\ *n* [origin unknown] (1623) **1 :** a fit of ill humor **2 :** a trivial quarrel

[2]**miff** *vt* (1811) **:** to put into an ill humor **:** OFFEND

[1]**might** \ˈmīt\ *verbal auxiliary, past of* MAY [ME, fr. OE *meahte, mihte;* akin to OHG *mahta, mohta* could] (bef. 12c) — used in auxiliary function to express permission, liberty, probability, possibility in the past ⟨the president ~ do nothing without the board's consent⟩ or a present condition contrary to fact ⟨if you were older you ~ understand⟩ or less probability or possibility than *may* ⟨~ get there before it rains⟩ or as a polite alternative to *may* ⟨~ I ask who is calling⟩ or to *ought* or *should* ⟨you ~ at least apologize⟩

[2]**might** *n* [ME, fr. OE *miht;* akin to OHG *maht* might, *magan* to be able — more at MAY] (bef. 12c) **1 a :** the power, authority, or resources wielded (as by an individual or group) **b (1) :** bodily strength **(2) :** the power, energy, or intensity of which one is capable ⟨striving with ~ and main⟩ **2** *dial* **:** a great deal *syn* see POWER

might·i·ly \ˈmī-tə-lē\ *adv* (bef. 12c) **1 :** in a mighty manner **:** VIGOROUSLY ⟨applauded ~⟩ **2 :** very much ⟨depressed me ~⟩

might·i·ness \ˈmī-tē-nəs\ *n* (14c) **:** the quality or state of being mighty

mightn't \ˈmī-tᵊnt\ (1781) **:** might not

[1]**mighty** \ˈmī-tē\ *adj* **might·i·er; -est** (bef. 12c) **1 :** possessing might **:** POWERFUL **2 :** accomplished or characterized by might ⟨a ~ thrust⟩ **3 :** great or imposing in size or extent **:** EXTRAORDINARY

[2]**mighty** *adv* (14c) **:** EXTREMELY, VERY ⟨a ~ handy gadget⟩

usage *Mighty* used as an intensive usu. conveys a folksy down-home feeling ⟨plain and simple fare . . . but *mighty* filling and *mighty* satisfying —*Asheville (N.C.) Citizen-Times*⟩. It is used esp. to create a chatty style ⟨turnip greens, corn bread and biscuits. That sounds *mighty* good to me —Julia Child⟩ or to stress a rural atmosphere ⟨a man must be *mighty* serious about his squirrel hunting —Stuart Williams, *Field & Stream*⟩. In a more formal context, *mighty* is used to create emphasis by drawing attention to itself ⟨the chairman made sure that there were *mighty* few of them —Mollie Panter-Downes⟩.

mi·gnon \mēn-ˈyō^{n}, min-ˈyȯn\ *n* (ca. 1919) **:** FILET MIGNON

mi·gnon·ette \ˌmin-yə-ˈnet\ *n* [F *mignonnette,* fr. obs. F, fem. of *mignonnet* dainty, fr. MF, fr. *mignon* darling] (1785) **1 :** any of a genus (*Reseda* of the family Resedaceae, the mignonette family) of herbs; *esp* **:** a garden annual (*R. odorata*) bearing racemes of fragrant whitish flowers **2 :** a sauce made typically with vinegar, pepper, and herbs and served esp. with oysters

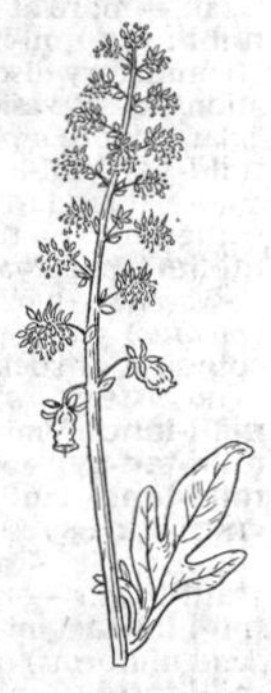

mignonette 1

mi·graine \ˈmī-ˌgrān, *Brit often* ˈmē-\ *n* [ME *mygreyn,* fr. MF *migraine,* modif. of LL *hemicrania* pain in one side of the head, fr. Gk *hēmikrania,* fr. *hēmi-* hemi- + *kranion* cranium] (15c) **1 :** a condition marked by recurrent severe headache often with nausea and vomiting **2 :** an episode or attack of migraine — **mi·grain·ous** \-ˌgrā-nəs\ *adj*

mi·grain·eur \ˌmē-gre-ˈnər\ *n* [prob. fr. *migraine* + *-eur* (as in *entrepreneur*)] (1970) **:** an individual who experiences migraines

mi·grant \ˈmī-grənt\ *n* [L *migrant-, migrans,* prp. of *migrare*] (1760) **:** one that migrates: as **a :** a person who moves regularly in order to find work esp. in harvesting crops **b :** an animal that shifts from one habitat to another — **migrant** *adj*

mi·grate \ˈmī-ˌgrāt, mī-ˈ\ *vi* **mi·grat·ed; mi·grat·ing** [L *migratus,* pp. of *migrare;* perh. akin to Gk *ameibein* to change] (1697) **1 :** to move from one country, place, or locality to another **2 :** to pass usu. periodically from one region or climate to another for feeding or breeding **3 :** to change position in an organism or substance ⟨filarial worms ~ within the human body⟩ — **mi·gra·tion** \mī-ˈgrā-shən\ *n* — **mi·gra·tion·al** \-shnəl, -shə-nᵊl\ *adj* — **mi·gra·tor** \ˈmī-ˌgrā-tər, mī-ˈ\ *n*

mi·gra·to·ry \ˈmī-grə-ˌtȯr-ē\ *adj* (1708) **1 :** of, relating to, or characterized by migration **2 :** WANDERING, ROVING

mih·rab \ˈmē-rəb\ *n* [Ar *miḥrāb*] (1673) **:** a niche or chamber in a mosque indicating the direction of Mecca

mi·ka·do \mə-ˈkä-(ˌ)dō\ *n, pl* **-dos** [Jp] (1727) **:** an emperor of Japan

[1]**mike** \ˈmīk\ *n* [by shortening & alter.] (1924) **:** MICROPHONE

[2]**mike** *vt* **miked; mik·ing** (1939) **:** to supply with a microphone

Mike \ˈmīk\ (1942) — a communications code word for the letter *m*

[1]**mil** \ˈmil\ *n* [L *mille* thousand] (1721) **1 :** THOUSAND ⟨found a salinity of 38.4 per ~⟩ **2 :** a monetary unit formerly used in Cyprus equal to 1/1000 pound **3 :** a unit of length equal to 1/1000 inch used esp. in measuring thickness (as of plastic films) **4 :** a unit of angular measurement equal to 1/6400 of 360 degrees and used esp. in artillery

[2]**mil** *or* **mill** *n, pl* **mil** *or* **mill** [short for *million*] (ca. 1942) *slang* **:** a million dollars

[3]**mil** *abbr* military

mi·la·dy \mi-ˈlā-dē, *US also* mī-\ *n* [F, fr. E *my lady*] (1778) **1 :** an Englishwoman of noble or gentle birth **2 :** a woman of fashion

milch \ˈmilk, ˈmilch, ˈmilks\ *adj* [ME *milche,* fr. OE *-milce;* akin to OE *melcan* to milk — more at EMULSION] (14c) **:** MILK

mil·chig \ˈmil-kik\ *adj* [Yiddish *milkhik,* fr. *milkh* milk, fr. MHG *milch,* fr. OHG *miluh* — more at MILK] (ca. 1928) **:** made of or derived from milk or dairy products — compare FLEISHIG, PAREVE

mild \ˈmī(-ə)ld\ *adj* [ME, fr. OE *milde;* akin to Gk *malthakos* soft, L *mollis* — more at MELT] (bef. 12c) **1 :** gentle in nature or behavior ⟨has a ~ disposition⟩ **2 a (1) :** moderate in action or effect ⟨a ~ sedative⟩ **(2) :** not sharp, spicy, or bitter ⟨~ cheese⟩ ⟨~ ale⟩ **b :** not being or involving what is extreme ⟨an analysis under ~ conditions⟩ **3 :** not severe **:** TEMPERATE ⟨a ~ climate⟩ ⟨~ symptoms of disease⟩ — **mild·ly** \ˈmī(-ə)l(d)-lē\ *adv* — **mild·ness** \ˈmī(-ə)l(d)-nəs\ *n*

[1]**mil·dew** \ˈmil-ˌdü, -ˌdyü\ *n* [ME, fr. OE *meledēaw* honeydew; akin to OHG *militou* honeydew] (14c) **1 a :** a superficial usu. whitish growth produced esp. on organic matter or living plants by fungi (as of the families Erysiphaceae and Peronosporaceae) **b :** a fungus producing mildew **2 :** a discoloration caused by fungi — **mil·dewy** \-ē\ *adj*

[2]**mildew** *vt* (1606) **:** to affect with or as if with mildew ~ *vi* **:** to become affected with mildew

mil·dew·cide \ˈmil-ˌd(y)ü-ˌsīd\ *n* (1945) **:** an agent that destroys mildew

mild steel *n* (1850) **:** a low-carbon structural steel that is easily worked

mile \ˈmī(-ə)l\ *n* [ME, fr. OE *mīl,* fr. L *milia* miles, fr. *milia passuum,* lit., thousands of paces, fr. *milia,* pl. of *mille* thousand] (bef. 12c) **1 :** any of various units of distance: as **a :** a unit equal to 5280 feet — see WEIGHT table **b :** NAUTICAL MILE **2 :** a race of a mile **3 :** a relatively great distance, degree, or interval — used chiefly adverbially in pl. ⟨was **~s** ahead of them in education⟩ — **a mile a minute :** with great speed ⟨talking *a mile a minute*⟩

mile·age \ˈmī-lij\ *n* (1754) **1 :** an allowance for traveling expenses at a certain rate per mile **2 :** aggregate length or distance in miles: as **a :** the total miles traveled esp. in a given period of time **b :** the amount of service that something will yield esp. as expressed in terms of miles of travel **c :** the average number of miles a motor vehicle will travel on a gallon of gasoline that is used as a measure of fuel economy ⟨gets

good ~⟩ **3 a** : USEFULNESS ⟨got a lot of ~ left in it⟩ **b** : benefit derived from something ⟨got good political ~ from the debates⟩
mile·post \ˈmī(-ə)l-ˌpōst\ *n* (1768) **1** : a post indicating the distance in miles from or to a given point; *also* : a post placed a mile from a similar post **2** : MILESTONE 2
mil·er \ˈmī-lər\ *n* (1819) **1** : one that is a specified number of miles in length — used in combination ⟨a 15-*miler*⟩ **2** : one that competes in mile races — often qualified in combination ⟨a quarter-*miler*⟩
mi·les glo·ri·o·sus \ˈmē-ˌlās-ˌglȯr-ə-ˈō-səs\ *n, pl* **mi·li·tes glo·ri·o·si** \ˈmē-lə-ˌtās-ˌglȯr-ē-ˈō-(ˌ)sē\ [L] (ca. 1576) : a boastful soldier; *esp* : a stock character of this type in comedy
mile·stone \ˈmī(-ə)l-ˌstōn\ *n* (1662) **1** : a stone serving as a milepost **2** : a significant point in development
mil·foil \ˈmil-ˌfȯi(-ə)l\ *n* [ME, fr. AF, fr. L *millefolium,* fr. *mille* + *folium* leaf — more at BLADE] (13c) **1** : YARROW **2** : WATER MILFOIL
mil·i·ar·ia \ˌmi-lē-ˈer-ē-ə\ *n* [NL, fr. L, fem. of *miliarius*] (1807) : an inflammatory disorder of the skin that is characterized by redness, eruptions (as of vesicles), and burning or itching due to blockage of sweat gland ducts; *esp* : PRICKLY HEAT — **mil·i·ar·i·al** \-əl\ *adj*
mil·i·ary \ˈmi-lē-ˌer-ē\ *adj* [L *miliarius* of millet, fr. *milium* millet — more at MILLET] (1685) : having or made up of many small projections or lesions ⟨~ tubercles⟩
mi·lieu \mēl-ˈyə(r), -ˈyü, -ˈyœ; ˈmēl-ˌyü\ *n, pl* **milieus** *or* **mi·lieux** \-ˈyə(r)(z), -ˈyüz, -ˈyœ(z); -ˌyü(z)\ [F, fr. OF, midst, fr. *mi* middle (fr. L *medius*) + *lieu* place, fr. L *locus* — more at MID, STALL] (1854) : the physical or social setting in which something occurs or develops : ENVIRONMENT ***syn*** see BACKGROUND
mil·i·tance \ˈmi-lə-tən(t)s\ *n* (1941) : MILITANCY
mil·i·tan·cy \-tən(t)-sē\ *n* (1648) : the quality or state of being militant
mil·i·tant \-tənt\ *adj* (15c) **1** : engaged in warfare or combat : FIGHTING **2** : aggressively active (as in a cause) : COMBATIVE ⟨~ conservationists⟩ ⟨a ~ attitude⟩ ***syn*** see AGGRESSIVE — **militant** *n* — **mil·i·tant·ly** *adv* — **mil·i·tant·ness** *n*
mil·i·tar·ia \ˌmi-lə-ˈter-ē-ə\ *n pl* (1964) : military objects (as firearms and uniforms) of historical value or interest
mil·i·tari·ly \ˌmi-lə-ˈter-ə-lē\ *adv* (1660) **1** : in a military manner **2** : from a military standpoint
mil·i·ta·rise *Brit var of* MILITARIZE
mil·i·ta·rism \ˈmi-lə-tə-ˌri-zəm\ *n* (1864) **1 a** : predominance of the military class or its ideals **b** : exaltation of military virtues and ideals **2** : a policy of aggressive military preparedness — **mil·i·ta·rist** \-rist\ *n or adj* — **mil·i·ta·ris·tic** \ˌmi-lə-tə-ˈris-tik\ *adj* — **mil·i·ta·ris·ti·cal·ly** \-ti-k(ə-)lē\ *adv*
mil·i·ta·rize \ˈmi-lə-tə-ˌrīz\ *vt* **-rized; -riz·ing** (1856) **1** : to give a military character to **2** : to equip with military forces and defenses **3** : to adapt for military use — **mil·i·ta·ri·za·tion** \ˌmi-lə-t(ə-)rə-ˈzā-shən\ *n*
[1]**mil·i·tary** \ˈmi-lə-ˌter-ē\ *adj* [ME, fr. L *militaris,* fr. *milit-, miles* soldier] (15c) **1 a** : of or relating to soldiers, arms, or war **b** : of or relating to armed forces; *esp* : of or relating to ground or sometimes ground and air forces as opposed to naval forces **2 a** : performed or made by armed forces **b** : supported by armed force **3** : of or relating to the army
[2]**military** *n, pl* **military** *also* **mil·i·tar·ies** (1709) **1** : military persons; *esp* : army officers **2** : ARMED FORCES
military–industrial complex *n* (1961) : an informal alliance of the military and related government departments with defense industries that is held to influence government policy
military police *n* (1815) : a branch of an army that exercises guard and police functions
military press *n* (1912) : [1]PRESS 9
military science *n* (ca. 1830) : the principles of military conflict
military time *n* (1955) : time measured in hours numbered to twenty-four (as 0100 or 2300) from one midnight to the next
mil·i·tate \ˈmi-lə-ˌtāt\ *vi* **-tat·ed; -tat·ing** [L *militatus,* pp. of *militare* to engage in warfare, fr. *milit-, miles*] (ca. 1600) : to have weight or effect ⟨his boyish appearance *militated* against his getting an early promotion⟩ ***usage*** see MITIGATE
mi·li·tia \mə-ˈli-shə\ *n* [L, military service, fr. *milit-, miles*] (1625) **1 a** : a part of the organized armed forces of a country liable to call only in emergency **b** : a body of citizens organized for military service **2** : the whole body of able-bodied male citizens declared by law as being subject to call to military service
mi·li·tia·man \-mən\ *n* (1668) : a member of a militia
mil·i·um \ˈmi-lē-əm\ *n, pl* **mil·ia** \-lē-ə\ [NL, fr. L, millet — more at MILLET] (1807) : WHITEHEAD
[1]**milk** \ˈmilk\ *n* [ME, fr. OE *meolc, milc;* akin to OHG *miluh* milk, OE *melcan* to milk — more at EMULSION] (bef. 12c) **1 a** : a fluid secreted by the mammary glands of females for the nourishment of their young; *esp* : cow's milk used as a food by humans **b** : LACTATION ⟨cows in ~⟩ **2** : a liquid resembling milk in appearance: as **a** : the latex of a plant **b** : the juice of a coconut composed of liquid endosperm **c** : the contents of an unripe kernel of grain
[2]**milk** *vt* (bef. 12c) **1 a (1)** : to draw milk from the breasts or udder of **(2)** *obs* : SUCKLE 2 **b** : to draw (milk) from the breast or udder **c** : SUCKLE 1 — used of domestic animals **2** : to draw something from as if by milking: as **a** : to induce (a snake) to eject venom **b** : to draw or coerce profit or advantage from illicitly or to an extreme degree : EXPLOIT ⟨~ the joke for all it's worth⟩ ~ *vi* : to draw or yield milk
[3]**milk** *adj* (14c) : giving milk; *specif* : bred or suitable primarily for milk production ⟨~ cows⟩
milk–and–water *adj* (1753) : WEAK, INSIPID
milk chocolate *n* (1900) : chocolate made with milk solids
milk·er \ˈmil-kər\ *n* (15c) **1** : one that milks an animal **2** : one that yields milk
milk fat *n* (1874) : BUTTERFAT
milk fever *n* (1753) **1** : a febrile disorder following parturition **2** : a disease of fresh cows, sheep, or goats that is caused by excessive drain on the body mineral reserves during the establishment of the milk flow
milk·fish \ˈmilk-ˌfish\ *n* (ca. 1890) : a large fork-tailed silvery herbivorous food fish (*Chanos chanos*) of warm parts of the Pacific and Indian oceans that is the sole living representative of its family (Chanidae)
milk glass *n* (1869) : an opaque and typically milky white glass used esp. for novelty and ornamental objects
milk house *n* (1583) : a building for the cooling, handling, or bottling of milk
milk leg *n* (ca. 1860) : a painful swelling of the leg caused by inflammation and clotting in the veins and affecting some postpartum women
milk–liv·ered \ˈmilk-ˌli-vərd\ *adj* (1606) *archaic* : COWARDLY, TIMOROUS
milk·maid \-ˌmād\ *n* (1552) : DAIRYMAID
milk·man \-ˌman, -mən\ *n* (1589) : a person who sells or delivers milk and milk products
milk of magnesia (1880) : a milky white suspension of magnesium hydroxide in water used as an antacid and laxative
milk punch *n* (1702) : a mixed drink of alcoholic liquor, milk, and sugar
milk run *n* [fr. the resemblance in regularity and uneventfulness to the morning delivery of milk] (1925) : a short, routine, or uneventful flight
milk shake *n* (1889) : a thoroughly shaken or blended drink made of milk, a flavoring syrup, and often ice cream
milk sickness *n* (1823) **1** : an acute disease characterized by weakness, vomiting, and constipation and caused by eating dairy products or meat from cattle poisoned by various plants **2** : TREMBLE 2
milk snake *n* (1800) : a common harmless grayish or tan American colubrid snake (*Lampropeltis triangulum*) having an arrow-shaped occipital marking and brown blotches on the body bordered with black or rings usu. of black, red, and yellow; *broadly* : KING SNAKE
milk·sop \ˈmilk-ˌsäp\ *n* [ME, lit., bread soaked in milk] (14c) : an unmanly man : MOLLYCODDLE
milk sugar *n* (1846) : LACTOSE
milk thistle *n* (1562) : a tall thistle (*Silybum marianum*) having white-veined dark green leaves and large purple flower heads that is native to the Mediterranean region but has become naturalized elsewhere including the U.S.; *also* : an extract of milk thistle and esp. its seeds that is held to protect the liver from damage or disease
milk tooth *n* (1738) : a temporary tooth of a young mammal; *esp* : one of the human dentition including four incisors, two canines, and four molars in each jaw — called also *baby tooth, deciduous tooth*
milk vein *n* (1743) : a large subcutaneous vein that extends along the lower side of the abdomen of a cow and returns blood from the udder — see COW illustration
milk vetch *n* [fr. the popular belief that it increases the milk yield of goats] (1597) : any of a genus (*Astragalus*) of annual or perennial leguminous herbs of north temperate regions
milk·weed \ˈmilk-ˌwēd\ *n* (ca. 1592) : any of various plants that secrete latex; *esp* : any of a genus (*Asclepias* of the family Asclepiadaceae, the milkweed family) of erect chiefly perennial herbs with milky juice and umbellate flowers

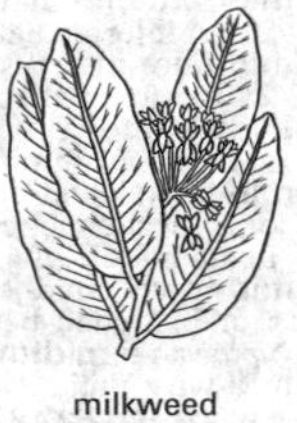
milkweed

milkweed bug *n* (1905) : a large black and reddish-orange bug (*Oncopeltus fasciatus*) that feeds chiefly on milkweed
milkweed butterfly *n* (1880) : any of a family (Danaidae) or nymphalid subfamily (Danaine) of large butterflies feeding on plants of the milkweed family as larvae; *esp* : MONARCH BUTTERFLY
milk·wort \ˈmilk-ˌwərt, -ˌwȯrt\ *n* (1578) : any of a genus (*Polygala* of the family Polygalaceae, the milkwort family) of herbs and shrubs often having showy flowers with three sometimes crested petals united below into a tube and an irregular calyx with two petaloid sepals
milky \ˈmil-kē\ *adj* **milk·i·er; -est** (14c) **1** : resembling milk in color or consistency **2** : MILD, TIMOROUS **3 a** : consisting of, containing, or abounding in milk **b** : yielding milk; *specif* : having the characteristics of a good milk producer — **milk·i·ness** *n*
milky disease *n* (ca. 1940) : a destructive disease of scarab beetle grubs and esp. Japanese beetle larvae that is caused by a bacterium (*Bacillus popilliae*) and is sometimes used in biological control — called also *milky spore disease*
Milky Way *n* (14c) **1** : a broad luminous irregular band of light that stretches completely around the celestial sphere and is caused by the light of myriads of faint stars **2** : MILKY WAY GALAXY
Milky Way galaxy *n* (1948) : the galaxy of which the sun and the solar system are a part and which contains the myriads of stars that create the light of the Milky Way
[1]**mill** \ˈmil\ *n* [ME *mille,* fr. OE *mylen,* fr. LL *molina, molinum,* fr. fem. and neut. of *molinus* of a mill, of a millstone, fr. L *mola* mill, millstone; akin to L *molere* to grind — more at MEAL] (bef. 12c) **1** : a building provided with machinery for grinding grain into flour **2 a** : a machine or apparatus (as a quern) for grinding grain **b** : a machine for crushing or comminuting **3** : a machine that manufactures by the continuous repetition of some simple action **4** : a building or collection of buildings with machinery for manufacturing **5 a** : a machine formerly used for stamping coins **b** : a machine for expelling juice from vegetable tissues by pressure or grinding **6** : MILLING MACHINE, MILLING CUTTER **7 a** : a slow, laborious, or mechanical process or routine **b** : one that produces or processes people or things mechanically or in large numbers ⟨a diploma ~⟩ ⟨a rumor ~⟩ **8** : a difficult and often educational experience — used in the phrase *through the mill* **9** : the engine of an automobile or boat
[2]**mill** *vt* (1511) **1** : to subject to an operation or process in a mill: as **a** : to grind into flour, meal, or powder **b** : to shape or dress by means of a rotary cutter **c** : to mix and condition (as rubber) by passing between rotating rolls **2** : to give a raised rim or a ridged or corrugated edge to (a coin) **3** : to cut grooves in the metal surface of (as a knob) ~ *vi* **1** : to hit out with the fists **2** : to move in a circle or in an eddying mass; *also* : WANDER **3** : to undergo milling
[3]**mill** *n* [L *mille* thousand] (1786) : a money of account equal to 1/10 cent
[4]**mill** *var of* [2]MIL
mill·age \ˈmi-lij\ *n* (1891) : a rate (as of taxation) expressed in mills per dollar
mill·dam \ˈmil-ˌdam\ *n* (12c) : a dam to make a millpond; *also* : MILLPOND
mille \ˈmil\ *n* [L] (bef. 12c) : THOUSAND
mille–feuille \mēl-ˈfwē, mēl-ˈfœ-ē\ *n* [F, fr. *mille feuilles* a thousand leaves] (1895) : a dish composed of puff pastry layered with a filling (as salmon or cream)

mil·le·fi·o·ri \ˌmi-lə-fē-ˈȯr-ē\ *n* [It, fr. *mille fiori* a thousand flowers] (1849) **:** ornamental glass produced by cutting cross sections of fused bundles of glass rods of various colors and sizes

mille·fleur *or* **mille·fleurs** \(ˌ)mēl-ˈflər, -ˈflu̇r\ *adj* [F *mille-fleurs,* fr. *mille fleurs* a thousand flowers] (1908) **:** having an allover pattern of small flowers and plants ⟨~ tapestry⟩

[1]**mil·le·nar·i·an** \ˌmi-lə-ˈner-ē-ən\ *adj* (1626) **1 a :** of or relating to belief in a millennium **b :** APOCALYPTIC 2 **2 :** of or relating to 1000 years

[2]**millenarian** *n* (1661) **:** one that believes in a millennium

mil·le·nar·i·an·ism \-ē-ə-ˌni-zəm\ *n* (1829) **1 :** belief in the millennium of Christian prophecy **2 :** belief in a coming ideal society and esp. one created by revolutionary action

[1]**mil·le·na·ry** \ˈmi-lə-ˌner-ē, mə-ˈle-nə-rē\ *n, pl* **-ries** [LL *millenarium,* fr. neut. of *millenarius* of a thousand, fr. L *milleni* one thousand each, fr. *mille*] (1550) **1 a :** a group of 1000 units or things **b :** 1000 years **:** MILLENNIUM **2 :** MILLENARIAN

[2]**millenary** *adj* [L *millenarius*] (1577) **1 :** suggesting a millennium **2 :** relating to or consisting of 1000

[1]**mil·len·ni·al** \mə-ˈle-nē-əl\ *adj* (1664) **:** of or relating to a millennium

[2]**millennial** *n* (1991) **:** a person born in the 1980s or 1990s — usu. pl.

mil·len·ni·al·ism \-ē-ə-ˌli-zəm\ *n* (1906) **:** MILLENARIANISM

mil·len·ni·al·ist \-list\ *n* (ca. 1841) **:** MILLENARIAN

mil·len·ni·um \mə-ˈle-nē-əm\ *n, pl* **-nia** \-nē-ə\ *or* **-niums** [NL, fr. L *mille* thousand + NL *-ennium* (as in *biennium*)] (ca. 1638) **1 a :** the thousand years mentioned in Revelation 20 during which holiness is to prevail and Christ is to reign on earth **b :** a period of great happiness or human perfection **2 a :** a period of 1000 years; *esp* **:** one reckoned from the beginning of the Christian era ⟨at the start of the third ~⟩ **b :** a 1000th anniversary or its celebration

mill·er \ˈmi-lər\ *n* (14c) **1 :** one that operates a mill; *specif* **:** one that grinds grain into flour **2 :** any of various moths having powdery wings **3 a :** MILLING MACHINE **b :** a tool for use in a milling machine

mil·ler·ite \ˈmi-lə-ˌrīt\ *n* [G *Millerit,* fr. William H. *Miller* †1880 Eng. mineralogist] (1854) **:** sulfide of nickel NiS usu. occurring as a mineral in capillary yellow crystals

mill·er's–thumb \ˌmi-lərz-ˈthəm\ *n* (15c) **:** any of several small freshwater spiny-finned sculpins (genus *Cottus*) of Europe and No. America

mil·les·i·mal \mə-ˈle-sə-məl\ *n* [L *millesimus,* adj., thousandth, fr. *mille*] (1719) **:** the quotient of a unit divided by 1000 **:** one of 1000 equal parts — **millesimal** *adj* — **mil·les·i·mal·ly** \-mə-lē\ *adv*

mil·let \ˈmi-lət\ *n* [ME *milet,* fr. MF, fr. OF, dim. of *mil,* fr. L *milium;* akin to Gk *melinē* millet] (15c) **1 :** any of various small-seeded annual cereal and forage grasses: **a :** a Eurasian grass (*Panicum miliaceum*) cultivated for its grain which is used for food **b :** any of several grasses related to common millet **2 :** the seed of a millet

milli- *comb form* [F, fr. L *milli-* thousand, fr. *mille*] **:** one thousandth part of ⟨*milli*ampere⟩

mil·li·am·pere \ˌmi-lē-ˈam-ˌpir\ *n* [ISV] (1885) **:** one thousandth of an ampere — called also *mil·li·amp* \ˈmi-lē-ˌamp\

mil·liard \ˈmil-ˌyärd, ˈmi-lē-ˌärd\ *n* [F, fr. MF *miliart,* fr. *mili-* (fr. *milion* million)] (1789) *Brit* **:** a thousand millions — see NUMBER table

mil·li·ary \ˈmi-lē-ˌer-ē\ *adj* [L *milliarius, miliarius* consisting of a thousand, one mile long, fr. *mille* thousand, mile] (ca. 1660) **:** marking the distance of a Roman mile

mil·li·bar \ˈmi-lə-ˌbär\ *n* [ISV] (1910) **:** a unit of atmospheric pressure equal to 1/1000 bar or 100 pascals

mil·li·cu·rie \ˌmi-lə-ˈkyu̇r-(ˌ)ē, -kyu̇-ˈrē\ *n* [ISV] (1910) **:** one thousandth of a curie

mil·li·de·gree \-di-ˈgrē\ *n* (1942) **:** one thousandth of a degree

mil·lieme \mē(l)-ˈyem\ *n, pl* **milliemes** \-ˈyem(z)\ [F *millième* thousandth, fr. MF, fr. *mille* thousand, fr. L] (1902) **:** a unit of value of Egypt and Sudan equal to 1/1000 pound

mil·li·gal \ˈmi-lə-ˌgal\ *n* [ISV] (1914) **:** a unit of acceleration equivalent to 1/1000 gal

mil·li·gauss \ˈmi-lə-ˌgau̇s\ *n* (1960) **:** one thousandth of a gauss

mil·li·gram \-ˌgram\ *n* [F *milligramme,* fr. *milli-* + *gramme* gram] (1797) — see METRIC SYSTEM table

mil·li·hen·ry \-ˌhen-rē\ *n* [ISV] (1890) **:** one thousandth of a henry

mil·li·lam·bert \-ˌlam-bərt\ *n* (1916) **:** one thousandth of a lambert

mil·li·li·ter \ˈmi-lə-ˌlē-tər\ *n* [F *millilitre,* fr. *milli-* + *litre* liter] (ca. 1810) — see METRIC SYSTEM table

mil·lime \mə-ˈlēm\ *n* [modif. of Ar *mallim,* fr. F *millième*] (1959) — see *dinar* at MONEY table

mil·li·me·ter \ˈmi-lə-ˌmē-tər\ *n* [F *millimètre,* fr. *milli-* + *mètre* meter] (1797) — see METRIC SYSTEM table

mil·li·mi·cron \ˌmi-lə-ˈmī-ˌkrän\ *n* [ISV] (1904) **:** NANOMETER

mil·li·mole \ˈmi-lə-ˌmōl\ *n* [ISV *milli-* + [5]*mole*] (1904) **:** one thousandth of a mole (as of a substance) — **mil·li·mo·lar** \-ˌmō-lər\ *adj*

mil·li·ner \ˈmi-lə-nər\ *n* [irreg. fr. *Milan,* Italy; fr. the importation of women's finery from Italy in the 16th century] (1530) **:** a person who designs, makes, trims, or sells women's hats

mil·li·nery \ˈmi-lə-ˌner-ē\ *n* (1676) **1 :** women's apparel for the head **2 :** the business or work of a milliner

mill·ing \ˈmi-liŋ\ *n* (ca. 1641) **:** a corrugated edge on a coin

milling cutter *n* (1864) **:** a rotary tool-steel cutter used in a milling machine for shaping and dressing metal surfaces

milling machine *n* (1849) **:** a machine tool on which work usu. of metal secured to a carriage is shaped by rotating milling cutters

mil·lion \ˈmil(l)-yən\ *n, pl* **millions** *or* **million** [ME *milioun,* fr. MF *milion,* fr. OIt *milione,* aug. of *mille* thousand, fr. L] (14c) **1** — see NUMBER table **2 :** a very large number ⟨~*s* of cars on the road⟩ **3 :** the mass of common people — used with *the* — **million** *adj* — **mil·lion·fold** \-ˌfōld\ *adv or adj* — **mil·lionth** \ˈmi(l)-yən(t)th\ *adj or n*

mil·lion·aire \ˌmi(l)-yə-ˈner, ˈmi(l)-yə-ˌ\ *n* [F *millionnaire, fr. million,* fr. MF *milion*] (1786) **:** a person whose wealth is estimated at a million or more (as of dollars or pounds)

mil·lion·air·ess \-ˈer-əs, -ˌer-\ *n* (1871) **1 :** a woman who is a millionaire **2 :** the wife of a millionaire

mil·li·os·mol \ˌmi-lē-ˈäz-ˌmōl, -ˈäs-\ *n* (1939) **:** one thousandth of an osmol

mil·li·pede \ˈmi-lə-ˌpēd\ *n* [L *millepeda,* a small crawling animal, fr. *mille* thousand + *ped-, pes* foot — more at FOOT] (1601) **:** any of a class (Diplopoda) of myriapod arthropods having usu. a cylindrical segmented body covered with hard integument, two pairs of legs on most apparent segments, and unlike centipedes no poison fangs

mil·li·ra·di·an \ˌmi-lə-ˈrā-dē-ən\ *n* [ISV] (1946) **:** one thousandth of a radian

mil·li·rem \ˈmi-lə-ˌrem\ *n* (1947) **:** one thousandth of a rem

mil·li·roent·gen \ˌmi-lə-ˈrent-gən, -ˈrənt-, -jən, -shən\ *n* [ISV] (1947) **:** one thousandth of a roentgen

mil·li·sec·ond \ˈmi-lə-ˌse-kənd, -kənt\ *n* [ISV] (1909) **:** one thousandth of a second

mil·li·volt \-ˌvōlt\ *n* [ISV] (1861) **:** one thousandth of a volt

mil·li·watt \-ˌwät\ *n* [ISV] (ca. 1914) **:** one thousandth of a watt

mill·pond \ˈmil-ˌpänd\ *n* (14c) **:** a pond created by damming a stream to produce a head of water for operating a mill

mill·race \-ˌrās\ *n* (15c) **:** a canal in which water flows to and from a mill wheel; *also* **:** the current that drives the wheel

mill·stone \ˈmil-ˌstōn\ *n* (bef. 12c) **1 :** either of two circular stones used for grinding (as grain) **2 a :** something that grinds or crushes **b :** a heavy burden

mill·stream \-ˌstrēm\ *n* (bef. 12c) **1 :** a stream whose flow is utilized to run a mill **2 :** MILLRACE

mill wheel *n* (bef. 12c) **:** a waterwheel that drives a mill

mill·work \ˈmil-ˌwərk\ *n* (1865) **:** woodwork (as doors, sashes, or trim) manufactured at a mill

mill·wright \-ˌrīt\ *n* (14c) **1 :** a person whose occupation is planning and building mills or setting up their machinery **2 :** a person who maintains and cares for mechanical equipment (as of a mill or factory)

mi·lo \ˈmī-(ˌ)lō\ *n, pl* **milos** [perh. fr. Sesotho *maili*] (1882) **:** a small usu. early and drought-resistant grain sorghum with compact bearded heads of large yellow or whitish seeds

mi·lord \mi-ˈlȯr(d)\ *n* [F, fr. E *my lord*] (1607) **:** an Englishman of noble or gentle birth

mil·pa \ˈmil-pə\ *n* [MexSp, fr. Nahuatl *mīlpan*] (1648) **1 a :** a small field in Mexico or Central America that is cleared from the forest, cropped for a few seasons, and abandoned for a fresh clearing **b :** a corn field in Mexico or Central America **2 :** the corn plant

milque·toast \ˈmilk-ˌtōst\ *n* [Caspar *Milquetoast,* comic strip character created by H. T. Webster †1952 Am. cartoonist] (1935) **:** a timid, meek, or unassertive person

mil·reis \mil-ˈrāsh, -ˈrās\ *n, pl* **mil·reis** *same or* -ˈrāz, -ˈrāzh\ [Pg *mil-réis*] (1589) **1 :** a Portuguese unit of value equal before 1911 to 1000 reis **2 :** the basic monetary unit of Brazil until 1942 **3 :** a coin representing one milreis

milt \ˈmilt\ *n* [prob. fr. MD *milte* milt of fish, spleen; akin to OE *milte* spleen — more at MELT] (15c) **:** the sperm-containing fluid of a male fish

mim \ˈmim\ *adj* [imit. of the act of pursing the lips] (ca. 1586) *dial* **:** affectedly shy or modest

[1]**mime** \ˈmīm *also* ˈmēm\ *n* [L *mimus,* fr. Gk *mimos*] (1616) **1 :** an ancient dramatic entertainment representing scenes from life usu. in a ridiculous manner **2 a :** an actor in a mime **b :** one that practices mime **3 :** MIMIC 2 **4 :** PANTOMIME 3

[2]**mime** *vb* **mimed; mim·ing** *vi* (1728) **:** to act a part with mimic gesture and action usu. without words ~ *vt* **1 :** MIMIC **2 :** to act out in the manner of a mime — **mim·er** *n*

MIME *abbr* multipurpose Internet mail extensions

mim·eo·graph \ˈmi-mē-ə-ˌgraf\ *n* [fr. *Mimeograph,* a trademark] (1889) **:** a duplicator for making many copies that utilizes a stencil through which ink is pressed — **mimeograph** *vt*

mi·me·sis \mə-ˈmē-səs, mī-\ *n* [LL, fr. Gk *mimēsis,* fr. *mimeisthai*] (1550) **:** IMITATION, MIMICRY

mi·met·ic \-ˈme-tik\ *adj* [LL *mimeticus,* fr. Gk *mimētikos,* fr. *mimeisthai* to imitate, fr. *mimos* mime] (1637) **1 :** IMITATIVE **2 :** relating to, characterized by, or exhibiting mimicry ⟨~ coloring of a butterfly⟩ — **mi·met·i·cal·ly** \-ti-k(ə-)lē\ *adv*

[1]**mim·ic** \ˈmi-mik\ *n* (1596) **1 :** MIME 2 **2 :** one that mimics

[2]**mimic** *adj* [L *mimicus,* fr. Gk *mimikos,* fr. *mimos* mime] (1625) **1 a :** IMITATIVE **b :** IMITATION, MOCK ⟨a ~ battle⟩ **2 :** of or relating to mime or mimicry

[3]**mimic** *vt* **mim·icked** \-mikt\; **mim·ick·ing** (1671) **1 :** to imitate closely **:** APE **2 :** to ridicule by imitation **3 :** SIMULATE **4 :** to resemble by biological mimicry ***syn*** see COPY

mim·ic·ry \ˈmi-mi-krē\ *n, pl* **-ries** (1671) **1 a :** an instance of mimicking **b :** the action, practice, or art of mimicking **2 :** a superficial resemblance of one organism to another or to natural objects among which it lives that secures it a selective advantage (as protection from predation)

mi·mo·sa \mə-ˈmō-sə, mī-, -zə\ *n* [NL, fr. L *mimus* mime] (ca. 1731) **1 :** any of a genus (*Mimosa*) of trees, shrubs, and herbs of the legume family that occur in tropical and warm regions and have usu. bipinnate often prickly leaves and globular heads of small white or pink flowers **2 :** SILK TREE **3 :** a mixed drink consisting of champagne and orange juice

min *abbr* **1** minim **2** minimum **3** mining **4** minister **5** minor **6** minute; minutes

mi·na \ˈmī-nə\ *n* [L, fr. Gk *mna,* of Sem origin; akin to Heb *māneh* mina] (15c) **:** an ancient unit of weight and value equal to 1/60 talent

min·able *or* **mine·able** \ˈmī-nə-bəl\ *adj* (ca. 1570) **:** capable of being mined

min·a·ret \ˌmi-nə-ˈret, ˈmi-nə-ˌ\ *n* [F, fr. Turk *minare,* fr. Ar *manāra* lighthouse] (1682) **:** a tall slender tower of a mosque having one or

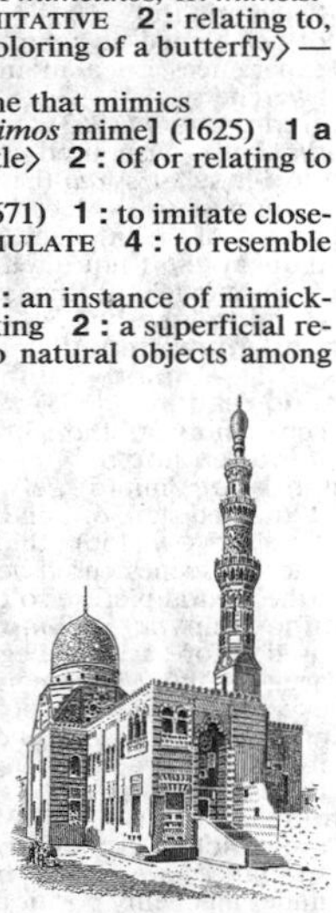

minaret

more balconies from which the summons to prayer is cried by the muezzin

mi·na·to·ry \ˈmi-nə-ˌtȯr-ē, ˈmī-\ *adj* [LL *minatorius,* fr. L *minari* to threaten — more at MOUNT] (1532) : having a menacing quality

min·au·dière \ˌmē-nōd-ˈyer\ *n* [F, fem. of *minaudier* affected, coquettish, fr. *minauder* to mince] (1940) : a small decorative case for carrying small articles (as cosmetics or jewelry)

[1]**mince** \ˈmin(t)s\ *vb* **minced; minc·ing** [ME, fr. AF *mincer,* fr. VL **minutiare,* fr. L *minutia* smallness — more at MINUTIA] *vt* (14c) **1 a :** to cut or chop into very small pieces **b :** to subdivide minutely; *esp* **:** to damage by cutting up **2 :** to utter or pronounce with affectation **3 a** *archaic* **:** MINIMIZE **b :** to restrain (words) within the bounds of decorum ∼ *vi* **:** to walk with short steps in a prim affected manner — **minc·er** *n*

[2]**mince** *n* (1600) **1 :** small chopped bits (as of food); *specif* **:** MINCEMEAT **2** *Brit* **:** HAMBURGER 1a

mince·meat \ˈmin(t)s-ˌmēt\ *n* (1630) **1 :** minced meat **2 :** a finely chopped mixture (as of raisins, apples, and spices) sometimes with meat that is often used as pie filling **3 :** a state of destruction or annihilation — used in the phrase *make mincemeat of*

mincing *adj* (1530) **:** affectedly dainty or delicate ⟨taking ∼ steps⟩ — **minc·ing·ly** \ˈmin(t)-siŋ-lē\ *adv*

[1]**mind** \ˈmīnd\ *n* [ME, fr. OE *gemynd;* akin to OHG *gimunt* memory, L *ment-, mens* mind, *monēre* to remind, warn, Gk *menos* spirit, *mnasthai, mimnēskesthai* to remember] (bef. 12c) **1 :** RECOLLECTION, MEMORY ⟨keep that in ∼⟩ ⟨time out of ∼⟩ **2 a :** the element or complex of elements in an individual that feels, perceives, thinks, wills, and esp. reasons **b :** the conscious mental events and capabilities in an organism **c :** the organized conscious and unconscious adaptive mental activity of an organism **3 :** INTENTION, DESIRE ⟨I changed my ∼⟩ **4 :** the normal or healthy condition of the mental faculties **5 :** OPINION, VIEW **6 :** DISPOSITION, MOOD **7 a :** a person or group embodying mental qualities ⟨the public ∼⟩ **b :** intellectual ability **8** *cap, Christian Science* **:** GOD 1b **9 :** a conscious substratum or factor in the universe **10 :** ATTENTION ⟨pay him no ∼⟩

[2]**mind** *vt* (14c) **1** *chiefly dial* **:** REMIND **2** *chiefly dial* **:** REMEMBER **3 :** to attend to closely **4 a** (1) **:** to become aware of **:** NOTICE (2) **:** to regard with attention **:** consider important — often used in the imperative with following *you* for emphasis ⟨I'm not against inspiration, ∼ you; I simply refuse to sit and stare at a blank page waiting for it —Dennis Whitcomb⟩ **b** *chiefly dial* **:** INTEND, PURPOSE **5 a :** to give heed to attentively in order to obey **b :** to follow the orders or instructions of **6 a :** to be concerned about **b :** DISLIKE ⟨I don't ∼ going⟩ **7 a :** to be careful **:** SEE ⟨∼ you finish it⟩ **b :** to be cautious about ⟨∼ the broken rung⟩ **8 :** to give protective care to **:** TEND ∼ *vi* **1 :** to be attentive or wary **2 :** to become concerned **:** CARE **3 :** to pay obedient heed or attention — **mind·er** *n*

mind–al·ter·ing \ˈmīn(d)-ˌȯl-t(ə-)riŋ\ *adj* (1961) **:** PSYCHOACTIVE

mind–bend·ing \ˈmīn(d)-ˌben-diŋ\ *adj* (1952) **:** MIND-BLOWING — **mind–bend·ing·ly** *adv*

mind–blow·ing \-ˌblō-iŋ\ *adj* (1966) **1 :** PSYCHEDELIC 1a **2 :** MIND-BOGGLING — **mind·blow·er** \-ˌblō-ər\ *n* — **mind–blow·ing·ly** *adv*

mind–bog·gling \-ˌbä-g(ə-)liŋ\ *adj* (1955) **:** mentally or emotionally exciting or overwhelming — **mind–bog·gling·ly** \-lē\ *adv*

mind·ed \ˈmīn-dəd\ *adj* (15c) **1 :** INCLINED, DISPOSED **2 :** having a mind esp. of a specified kind or concerned with a specified thing — usu. used in combination ⟨narrow-*minded*⟩ ⟨health-*minded*⟩ — **mind·ed·ness** \-dəd-nəs\ *n*

mind–ex·pand·ing \ˈmīnd-ik-ˌspan-diŋ\ *adj* (1963) **:** PSYCHEDELIC 1a

mind·ful \ˈmīn(d)-fəl\ *adj* (14c) **1 :** bearing in mind **:** AWARE **2 :** inclined to be aware — **mind·ful·ly** \-fə-lē\ *adv*

mind·ful·ness \ˈmīn(d)-fəl-nəs\ *n* (ca. 1530) **1 :** the quality or state of being mindful **2 :** the practice of maintaining a nonjudgmental state of heightened or complete awareness of one's thoughts, emotions, or experiences on a moment-to-moment basis; *also* **:** such a state of awareness

mind game *n* (1963) **:** a psychological tactic used to manipulate or intimidate — usu. used in pl. ⟨played *mind games* with his opponent⟩

mind·less \-ləs\ *adj* (bef. 12c) **1 a :** marked by a lack of mind or consciousness ⟨a ∼ sleep⟩ **b** (1) **:** marked by or displaying no use of the powers of the intellect ⟨∼ violence⟩ (2) **:** requiring little attention or thought; *esp* **:** not intellectually challenging or stimulating ⟨∼ work⟩ ⟨a ∼ movie⟩ **2 :** not mindful **:** HEEDLESS ⟨∼ of the consequences⟩ — **mind·less·ly** *adv* — **mind·less·ness** *n*

mind–numb·ing \ˈmīn(d)-ˌnə-miŋ\ *adj* (1898) **:** relentlessly tedious **:** DULL — **mind–numb·ing·ly** *adv*

mind reader *n* (1875) **:** one that professes or is held to be able to perceive another's thought without normal means of communication — **mind reading** *n*

mind–set \ˈmīn(d)-ˌset\ *n* (1909) **1 :** a mental attitude or inclination **2 :** a fixed state of mind

mind's eye *n* (15c) **:** the mental faculty of conceiving imaginary or recollected scenes ⟨used her *mind's eye* to create the story's setting⟩; *also* **:** the mental picture so conceived

[1]**mine** \ˈmīn\ *adj* [ME *min,* fr. OE *mīn* — more at MY] (bef. 12c) **:** MY — used before a word beginning with a vowel or *h* ⟨this treasure in ∼ arms —Shak.⟩ or sometimes as a modifier of a preceding noun; archaic except in an elevated style

[2]**mine** *pron, sing or pl in constr* (bef. 12c) **:** that which belongs to me — used without a following noun as a pronoun equivalent in meaning to the adjective *my*

[3]**mine** *n* [ME, fr. AF, fr. VL **mina,* prob. of Celt origin; akin to W *mwyn* ore] (14c) **1 a :** a pit or excavation in the earth from which mineral substances are taken **b :** an ore deposit **2 :** a subterranean passage under an enemy position **3 :** an encased explosive that is placed in the ground or in water and set to explode when disturbed **4 :** a rich source of supply

[4]**mine** *vb* **mined; min·ing** *vt* (14c) **1 a :** to dig under to gain access or cause the collapse of (an enemy position) **b :** UNDERMINE **2 a :** to get (as ore) from the earth **b :** to extract from a source ⟨information *mined* from the files⟩ **3 :** to burrow beneath the surface of ⟨larva that ∼*s* leaves⟩ **4 :** to place military mines in, on, or under ⟨∼ a harbor⟩ **5 a :** to dig into for ore or metal **b :** to process for obtaining a natural constituent ⟨∼ the air for nitrogen⟩ **c :** to seek valuable material in ⟨∼ old records for more details⟩ ∼ *vi* **:** to dig a mine — **min·er** *n*

mine·field \ˈmīn-ˌfēld\ *n* (1884) **1 :** an area (as of water or land) set with mines **2 :** something resembling a minefield esp. in having many dangers or requiring extreme caution ⟨a political ∼⟩

mine·lay·er \-ˌlā-ər, -ˌler\ *n* (1886) **:** a naval vessel for laying underwater mines

[1]**min·er·al** \ˈmin-rəl, ˈmi-nə-\ *n* [ME, fr. ML *minerale,* fr. neut. of *mineralis*] (15c) **1 :** ORE **2 :** an inorganic substance (as in the ash of calcined tissue) **3** *obs* **:** MINE **4 :** something neither animal nor vegetable **5 a :** a solid homogeneous crystalline chemical element or compound that results from the inorganic processes of nature; *broadly* **:** any of various naturally occurring homogeneous substances (as stone, coal, salt, sulfur, sand, petroleum, water, or natural gas) obtained usu. from the ground **b :** a synthetic substance having the chemical composition and crystalline form and properties of a naturally occurring mineral **6** *pl, Brit* **:** MINERAL WATER

[2]**mineral** *adj* [ME, fr. ML *mineralis,* fr. *minera* mine, ore, fr. OF *minere, miniere,* fr. *mine*] (15c) **1 :** of or relating to minerals; *also* **:** INORGANIC **2 :** impregnated with mineral substances

min·er·al·ise *Brit var of* MINERALIZE

min·er·al·ize \ˈmin-rə-ˌlīz, ˈmi-nə-\ *vt* **-ized; -iz·ing** (1655) **1 :** to transform (a metal) into an ore **2 a :** to impregnate or supply with minerals or an inorganic compound **b :** to convert into mineral or inorganic form **3 :** PETRIFY — **min·er·al·iz·able** \ˌmin-rə-ˈlī-zə-bəl, ˌmi-nə-\ *adj* — **min·er·al·i·za·tion** \-rə-lə-ˈzā-shən\ *n* — **min·er·al·iz·er** \ˈmin-rə-ˌlī-zər, ˈmi-nə-\ *n*

mineral kingdom *n* (ca. 1691) **:** a basic group of natural objects that includes inorganic objects — compare ANIMAL KINGDOM, PLANT KINGDOM

min·er·al·o·cor·ti·coid \ˌmin-rə-lō-ˈkȯr-tə-ˌkȯid, ˌmi-nə-\ *n* (1946) **:** a corticosteroid (as aldosterone) that affects chiefly the electrolyte and fluid balance in the body — compare GLUCOCORTICOID

min·er·al·o·gy \ˌmi-nə-ˈrä-lə-jē, -ˈra-\ *n* [prob. fr. NL **mineralogia,* irreg. fr. ML *minerale* + L *-logia* -logy] (1690) **1 :** a science dealing with minerals, their crystallography, properties, classification, and the ways of distinguishing them **2 :** the mineralogical characteristics of an area, a rock, or a rock formation — **min·er·al·og·i·cal** \ˌmi-nə-rə-ˈlä-ji-kəl, ˌmin-rə-\ *also* **min·er·al·og·ic** \-ˈlä-jik\ *adj* — **min·er·al·og·i·cal·ly** \-ˈlä-ji-k(ə-)lē\ *adv* — **min·er·al·o·gist** \ˌmi-nə-ˈrä-lə-jist, -ˈra-\ *n*

mineral oil *n* (1771) **:** an oil of mineral origin; *esp* **:** a refined petroleum oil used esp. as a laxative

mineral spirits *n pl but sing or pl in constr* (1875) **:** a petroleum distillate that is used esp. as a paint or varnish thinner

mineral water *n* (15c) **:** water naturally or artificially infused with mineral salts or gases (as carbon dioxide)

mineral wax *n* (ca. 1864) **:** a wax of mineral origin; *esp* **:** OZOKERITE

mineral wool *n* (1870) **:** any of various lightweight vitreous fibrous materials used esp. in heat and sound insulation

miner's lettuce *n* (1897) **:** a glossy green herb (*Montia perfoliata* syn. *Claytonia perfoliata*) of the purslane family esp. of western No. America that produces racemes of pink to white flowers subtended by a disk of two leaves united around the stem and is used as a salad green

Mi·ner·va \mə-ˈnər-və\ *n* [L] (14c) **:** the Roman goddess of wisdom — compare ATHENA

min·e·stro·ne \ˌmi-nə-ˈstrō-nē, -ˈstrōn\ *n* [It, aug. of *minestra,* fr. *minestrare* to serve, dish up, fr. L *ministrare,* fr. *minister* servant — more at MINISTER] (1871) **:** a rich thick vegetable soup usu. with dried beans and pasta (as macaroni or vermicelli)

mine·sweep·er \ˈmīn-ˌswē-pər\ *n* (1904) **:** a warship for removing or neutralizing mines by dragging — **mine·sweep·ing** \-piŋ\ *n*

Ming \ˈmiŋ\ *n* [Chin (Beijing) *míng* luminous] (1795) **:** a Chinese dynasty dated 1368–1644 and marked by restoration of earlier traditions and in the arts by perfection of established techniques

min·gle \ˈmiŋ-gəl\ *vb* **min·gled; min·gling** \-g(ə-)liŋ\ [ME *menglen,* freq. of *mengen* to mix, fr. OE *mengan;* akin to MHG *mengen* to mix, Gk *massein* to knead] *vt* (15c) **1 :** to bring or mix together or with something else usu. without fundamental loss of identity **:** INTERMIX **2** *archaic* **:** to prepare by mixing **:** CONCOCT ∼ *vi* **1 :** to become mingled **2 a :** to come into contact **:** ASSOCIATE **b :** to move about (as in a group) ⟨*mingled* with the guests⟩ ***syn*** see MIX

ming tree \ˈmiŋ-\ *n* [perh. fr. *Ming*] (1948) **:** a dwarfed evergreen conifer grown as bonsai; *also* **:** an artificial plant resembling this

min·gy \ˈmin-jē\ *adj* **min·gi·er; -est** [perh. blend of [1]*mean* and *stingy*] (1911) **:** MEAN, STINGY

[1]**mini** \ˈmi-nē\ *n, pl* **min·is** [*mini-*] (1960) **:** something small of its kind: as **a :** MINICAR **b :** MINISKIRT **c :** MINICOMPUTER

[2]**mini** *adj* (1963) **1 :** small in relation to others of the same kind **2 :** of short length or duration **:** BRIEF

mini- *comb form* [*miniature*] **:** smaller or briefer than usual, normal, or standard ⟨*mini*course⟩ ⟨*mini*bus⟩

[1]**min·i·a·ture** \ˈmi-nē-ə-ˌchu̇r, ˈmi-ni-ˌchu̇r, ˈmin-yə-, -chər, -ˌtyu̇r, -ˌtu̇r\ *n* [It *miniatura* art of illuminating a manuscript, fr. ML, fr. L *miniatus,* pp. of *miniare* to color with minium, fr. *minium* red lead] (ca. 1586) **1 a :** a copy on a much reduced scale **b :** something small of its kind **2 :** a painting in an illuminated book or manuscript **3 :** the art of painting miniatures **4 :** a very small portrait or other painting (as on ivory or metal) — **min·i·a·tur·ist** \-ˌchu̇r-ist, -chər-, -ˌtyu̇r-, -ˌtu̇r-\ *n* — **min·i·a·tur·is·tic** \ˌmi-nē-ə-chə-ˈris-tik, ˌmi-ni-, ˌmin-yə-, -ˌtyu̇-, -ˌtu̇-\ *adj* — **in miniature :** in a greatly diminished size, form, or scale

[2]**miniature** *adj* (1714) **:** being or represented on a small scale ***syn*** see SMALL

miniature golf *n* (1907) **:** a novelty golf game played with a putter on a miniature course usu. having tunnels, bridges, sharp corners, and obstacles

miniature pin·scher \-ˈpin(t)-shər\ *n* (1929) **:** any of a breed of toy dogs that suggest a small Doberman pinscher and are 10 to 12½ inches (25 to 32 centimeters) in height at the withers

miniature schnauzer *n* (ca. 1929) **:** any of a breed of schnauzers that are 12 to 14 inches (30 to 36 centimeters) in height at the withers and are classified as terriers

min·i·a·tur·ize \ˈmi-nē-ə-chə-ˌrīz, ˈmi-ni-chə-, ˈmin-yə-chə-, -ˌtyu̇-, -ˌtu̇-\ *vt* **-ized; -iz·ing** (1946) **:** to design or construct in small size — **min·i·a·tur·i·za·tion** \ˌmi-nē-ə-ˌchu̇r-ə-ˈzā-shən, ˌmi-ni-, ˌmin-yə-, -chər-, -ˌtyu̇r-, -ˌtu̇r-\ *n*

mini·bar \ˈmi-nē-ˌbär\ *n* (1976) : a small refrigerator in a hotel room that is stocked with esp. alcoholic beverages and snacks for guests
mini·bike \ˈmi-nē-ˌbīk\ *n* (1962) : a small one-passenger motorcycle with a low frame and raised handlebars — **mini·bik·er** *n*
mini·bus \-ˌbəs\ *n* (1958) : a small bus or van
Mini·cam \-ˌkam\ *trademark* — used for a portable television camera
mini·camp \-ˌkamp\ *n* (1977) : a special abbreviated training camp for football players held usu. in the spring or early summer
mini·car \-ˌkär\ *n* (1948) : a very small automobile; *esp* : SUBCOMPACT
mini·com·put·er \ˌmi-nē-kəm-ˈpyü-tər\ *n* (1967) : a small computer that is intermediate between a microcomputer and a mainframe in size, speed, and capacity, that can support time-sharing, and that is often dedicated to a single application
mini·course \ˈmi-nē-ˌkȯrs\ *n* (1970) : a brief course of study usu. lasting less than a semester
mini·disc \ˈmi-nē-ˌdisk\ *n* (1989) : a miniature optical disk
mini·dress \ˈmi-nē-ˌdres\ *n* (1965) : a short close-fitting dress
min·ié ball \ˈmi-nē-, ˌmi-nē-ˈā-\ *n* [Claude Étienne *Minié* †1879 Fr. army officer] (1852) : a rifle bullet with a conical head used in muzzle-loading firearms
min·i·fy \ˈmi-nə-ˌfī\ *vt* **-fied; -fy·ing** [L *min*us less + E *-ify*] (1676) : LESSEN
min·i·kin \ˈmi-ni-kən\ *n* [obs. D *minneken* darling, ultim. fr. MD *minne* love, beloved; akin to OE *gemynd* mind, memory — more at MIND] (1761) : a small or dainty creature — **minikin** *adj*
mini·lab \ˈmi-nē-ˌlab\ *n* (1982) : a retail outlet offering rapid on-site film development and printing
min·im \ˈmi-nəm\ *n* [L *minimus* least] (15c) **1** : HALF NOTE **2** : something very minute **3** — see WEIGHT table — **minim** *adj*
min·i·mal \ˈmi-nə-məl\ *adj* (1666) **1** : relating to or being a minimum: as **a** : the least possible ⟨a victory won with ~ loss of life⟩ **b** : barely adequate ⟨a ~ standard of living⟩ **c** : very small or slight ⟨a ~ interest in art⟩ **2** *often cap* : of, relating to, or being minimal art or minimalism — **min·i·mal·ly** \-mə-lē\ *adv*
minimal art *n* (1965) : abstract art consisting primarily of simple geometric forms executed in an impersonal style
minimal brain dysfunction *n* (1966) : ATTENTION DEFICIT DISORDER
min·i·mal·ism \ˈmi-nə-mə-ˌli-zəm\ *n* (1927) **1** : a style or technique (as in music, literature, or design) that is characterized by extreme spareness and simplicity **2** : MINIMAL ART
[1]**min·i·mal·ist** \-list\ *n* (1907) **1** : one who favors restricting the functions and powers of a political organization or the achievement of a set of goals to a minimum **2 a** : a minimal artist **b** : an adherent of minimalism
[2]**minimalist** *adj* (1929) : of, relating to, or done in the style of minimalism
minimal pair *n* (1942) : two linguistic units that differ in a single distinctive feature or constituent (as voice in the initial consonants of *bat* and *pat*)
mini–mart \ˈmi-nē-ˌmärt\ *n* (1981) : CONVENIENCE STORE
mini·max \ˈmi-ni-ˌmaks\ *n* [*mini*mum + *max*imum] (1917) : the minimum of a set of maxima; *esp* : the smallest of a set of maximum possible losses each of which occurs in the most unfavorable outcome of a strategy followed by a participant in a situation governed by game theory — compare MAXIMIN
mini·mill \ˈmi-nē-ˌmil\ *n* (1969) : a relatively small-scale steel mill that uses scrap metal as starting material
min·i·mise *Brit var of* MINIMIZE
min·i·mize \ˈmi-nə-ˌmīz\ *vt* **-mized; -miz·ing** (1825) **1** : to reduce or keep to a minimum **2** : to underestimate intentionally : PLAY DOWN, SOFT-PEDAL ⟨*minimizing* losses in our own forces while maximizing those of the enemy⟩ **3** : to replace (a window) on a computer display with a small button or icon which will restore the window when selected — **min·i·mi·za·tion** \ˌmi-nə-mə-ˈzā-shən\ *n* — **min·i·miz·er** \ˈmi-nə-ˌmī-zər\ *n*
min·i·mum \ˈmi-nə-məm\ *n, pl* **-i·ma** \-nə-mə\ *or* **-i·mums** [L, neut. of *minimus* smallest; akin to L *minor* smaller — more at MINOR] (1674) **1** : the least quantity assignable, admissible, or possible **2** : the least of a set of numbers; *specif* : the smallest value assumed by a continuous function defined on a closed interval **3 a** : the lowest degree or amount of variation (as of temperature) reached or recorded **b** : the lowest speed allowed on a highway — **minimum** *adj*
minimum wage *n* (1860) **1** : LIVING WAGE **2** : the lowest wage paid or permitted to be paid; *specif* : a wage fixed by legal authority or by contract as the least that may be paid either to employed persons generally or to a particular category of employed persons
mining *n* (14c) : the process or business of working mines
min·ion \ˈmin-yən\ *n* [MF *mignon* darling] (ca. 1500) **1** : a servile dependent, follower, or underling **2** : one highly favored : IDOL **3** : a subordinate or petty official
mini·park \ˈmi-nē-ˌpärk\ *n* (1967) : a small city park
mini·pill \ˈmi-nē-ˌpil\ *n* (1968) : a birth control pill that contains a very low dose of progesterone but no estrogen, is taken daily, and is intended to minimize side effects
mini·school \-ˌskül\ *n* (1968) : an experimental school offering specialized or individual instruction to its students
min·is·cule \ˈmi-nəs-ˌkyül\ *var of* MINUSCULE
usage The adjective *minuscule* is etymologically related to *minus,* but associations with *mini-* have produced the spelling variant *miniscule.* This variant dates to the end of the 19th century, and it now occurs commonly in published writing, but it continues to be widely regarded as an error.
mini·se·ries \ˈmi-nē-ˌsir-(ˌ)ēz\ *n* (1972) : a television production of a story presented in sequential episodes
mini·skirt \ˈmi-nē-ˌskərt\ *n* (1965) : a woman's short skirt with the hemline several inches above the knee — **mini·skirt·ed** *adj*
mini·state \-ˌstāt\ *n* (1966) : a small independent nation
[1]**min·is·ter** \ˈmi-nə-stər\ *n* [ME *ministre,* fr. AF, fr. L *minister* servant; akin to L *minor* smaller] (14c) **1** : AGENT **2 a** : one officiating or assisting the officiant in church worship **b** : a clergyman esp. of a Protestant communion **3 a** : the superior of one of several religious orders — called also *minister-general* **b** : the assistant to the rector or the bursar of a Jesuit house **4** : a high officer of state entrusted with the management of a division of governmental activities **5 a** : a diplomatic representative (as an ambassador) accredited to the court or seat of government of a foreign state **b** : a diplomatic representative ranking below an ambassador
[2]**minister** *vi* **-tered; -ter·ing** \-st(ə-)riŋ\ (14c) **1** : to function as a minister of religion **2** : to give aid or service ⟨~ to the sick⟩
min·is·te·ri·al \ˌmi-nə-ˈstir-ē-əl\ *adj* (1561) **1** : of, relating to, or characteristic of a minister or the ministry **2 a** : being or having the characteristics of an act or duty prescribed by law as part of the duties of an administrative office **b** : relating to or being an act done after ascertaining the existence of a specified state of facts in obedience to a legal order without exercise of personal judgment or discretion **3** : acting or active as an agent — **min·is·te·ri·al·ly** \-ē-ə-lē\ *adv*
minister plenipotentiary *n, pl* **ministers plenipotentiary** (1783) : a diplomatic agent ranking below an ambassador but possessing full power and authority
minister resident *n, pl* **ministers resident** (1794) : a diplomatic agent resident at a foreign court or seat of government and ranking below a minister plenipotentiary
[1]**min·is·trant** \ˈmi-nə-strənt\ *adj* (ca. 1559) *archaic* : performing service in attendance on someone
[2]**ministrant** *n* (1818) : one that ministers
min·is·tra·tion \ˌmi-nə-ˈstrā-shən\ *n* (14c) : the act or process of ministering
ministroke \ˈmi-nē-ˌstrōk\ *n* (1980) : TRANSIENT ISCHEMIC ATTACK
min·is·try \ˈmi-nə-strē\ *n, pl* **-tries** (14c) **1** : MINISTRATION **2** : the office, duties, or functions of a minister **3** : the body of ministers of religion : CLERGY **4** : a person or thing through which something is accomplished : AGENCY, INSTRUMENTALITY **5** : the period of service or office of a minister or ministry **6** *often cap* **a** : the body of ministers governing a nation or state from which a smaller cabinet is sometimes selected **b** : the group of ministers constituting a cabinet **7 a** : a government department presided over by a minister **b** : the building in which the business of a ministry is transacted
mini·tow·er \ˈmi-nē-ˌtau̇(-ə)r\ *n* (1987) : a midsize personal computer case that usu. stands upright
mini·van \ˈmi-nē-ˌvan\ *n* (1960) : a small passenger van
min·i·ver \ˈmi-nə-vər\ *n* [ME *meniver,* fr. AF *menever,* fr. *menu* small + *ver, vair* vair] (13c) : a white fur worn orig. by medieval nobles and used chiefly for robes of state
mink \ˈmiŋk\ *n, pl* **mink** *or* **minks** [ME] (15c) **1** : soft fur or pelt of the mink varying in color from white to dark brown **2** : either of two slender-bodied semiaquatic carnivorous mammals (*Mustela vison* of No. America and *M. lutreola* of Eurasia) of the weasel family that have partially webbed feet, a rather short bushy tail, and a soft thick coat
min·ke whale \ˈmiŋ-kə-\ *n* [part trans. of Norw *minkehval,* fr. *minke-* (perh. fr. *Meincke,* a crewman of Svend Foyn †1894 Norw. whaler) + *hval* whale] (1939) : a small grayish baleen whale (*Balaenoptera acutorostrata*) with a whitish underside — called also *minke*

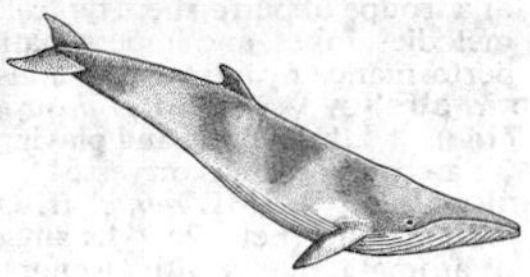
minke whale

Minn *abbr* Minnesota
min·ne·sing·er \ˈmi-nə-ˌsiŋ-ər, -ˌziŋ-\ *n* [G, fr. MHG, fr. *minne* love + *singer* singer] (1825) : any of a class of German poets and musicians of the 12th to the 14th centuries
Min·ne·so·ta Multiphasic Personality Inventory \ˌmi-nə-ˈsō-tə-ˌməl-ti-ˈfā-zik-, -ˌməl-ˌtī-\ *n* [University of *Minnesota*] (1943) : a test of personal and social adjustment based on a complex scaling of the answers to an elaborate true or false test
min·now \ˈmi-(ˌ)nō\ *n, pl* **minnows** *also* **minnow** [ME *menawe;* akin to OE *myne* minnow, OHG *munewa,* a kind of fish] (15c) **1 a** : a small cyprinid, killifish, or topminnow **b** : any of various small fish that are less than a designated size and are not game fish **2** : a live or artificial minnow used as bait
[1]**Mi·no·an** \mə-ˈnō-ən, mī-\ *adj* [L *minous* of Minos, fr. Gk *minōios,* fr. *Minōs* Minos] (1894) : of or relating to a Bronze Age culture of Crete that flourished about 3000 B.C.–1100 B.C.
[2]**Minoan** *n* (1902) : a native or inhabitant of ancient Crete
[1]**mi·nor** \ˈmī-nər\ *adj* [L, smaller, inferior; akin to OHG *minniro* smaller, L *minuere* to lessen] (1526) **1** : inferior in importance, size, or degree : comparatively unimportant **2** : not having reached majority **3 a** : having half steps between the second and third, the fifth and sixth, and sometimes the seventh and eighth degrees ⟨~ scale⟩ **b** : based on a minor scale ⟨~ key⟩ **c** : less by a semitone than the corresponding major interval ⟨~ third⟩ **d** : having a minor third above the root ⟨~ triad⟩ **4** : not serious or involving risk to life ⟨~ illness⟩ **5** : of or relating to an academic subject requiring fewer courses than a major
[2]**minor** *n* (1612) **1** : a person who is not yet old enough to have the rights of an adult **2** : a minor musical interval, scale, key, or mode **3 a** : a minor academic subject **b** : a student taking a specified minor **4** : a determinant or matrix obtained from a given determinant or matrix by eliminating the row and column in which a given element lies **5** *pl* : minor league baseball — used with *the*
[3]**minor** *vi* (1926) : to take courses in a minor subject
minor axis *n* (1862) : the chord of an ellipse passing through the center and perpendicular to the major axis
minor element *n* (1941) : TRACE ELEMENT
Mi·nor·ite \ˈmī-nə-ˌrīt\ *n* [fr. *Friar Minor* Franciscan] (1537) : FRANCISCAN
mi·nor·i·ty \mə-ˈnȯr-ə-tē, mī-, -ˈnär-\ *n, pl* **-ties** *often attrib* (15c) **1 a** : the period before attainment of majority **b** : the state of being a legal minor **2** : the smaller in number of two groups constituting a whole; *specif* : a group having less than the number of votes necessary for control **3 a** : a part of a population differing from others in some

characteristics and often subjected to differential treatment **b** : a member of a minority group ⟨an effort to hire more *minorities*⟩
minority leader *n* (1909) : the leader of the minority party in a legislative body
minor league *n* (1885) : a league of professional clubs in a sport other than the recognized major leagues — **minor–league** *adj*
minor order *n* (ca. 1741) : one of the Roman Catholic or Eastern clerical orders that are lower in rank and less sacred in character than major orders — usu. used in pl.
minor party *n* (1949) : a political party whose electoral strength is so small as to prevent its gaining control of a government except in rare and exceptional circumstances
minor penalty *n* (1925) : a 2-minute suspension of a player in ice hockey with no substitute allowed
minor planet *n* (1823) : ASTEROID
minor premise *n* (ca. 1741) : the premise of a syllogism that contains the minor term
minor seminary *n* (ca. 1948) : a Roman Catholic seminary giving all or part of high school and junior college training with emphasis on preparing candidates for a major seminary
minor suit *n* (1916) : either of the suits diamonds or clubs having inferior scoring value in bridge
minor term *n* (1599) : the term of a syllogism that forms the subject of the conclusion
Mi·nos \ˈmī-nəs\ *n* [L, fr. Gk *Minōs*] (14c) : a son of Zeus and Europa and king of Crete who for his just rule is made supreme judge in the underworld after his death
Mi·no·taur \ˈmi-nə-ˌtȯr, ˈmī-\ *n* [ME, fr. L *Minotaurus,* fr. Gk *Minōtauros,* fr. *Minōs* + *tauros* bull] (14c) : a monster shaped half like a man and half like a bull, confined in the labyrinth built by Daedalus for Minos, and given a periodic tribute of youths and maidens as food until slain by Theseus
mi·nox·i·dil \mə-ˈnäk-sə-ˌdil\ *n* [perh. fr. *amino* + *oxi-* (alter. of *oxy-*) + piper*idine* + *-yl*] (1970) : a peripheral vasodilator $C_9H_{15}N_5O$ used orally to treat hypertension and topically in a propylene glycol solution to promote hair regrowth in male-pattern baldness
min·ster \ˈmin(t)-stər\ *n* [ME, monastery, church attached to a monastery, fr. OE *mynster,* fr. LL *monasterium* monastery] (bef. 12c) : a large or important church often having cathedral status
min·strel \ˈmin(t)-strəl\ *n* [ME *menestrel,* fr. AF *menestral* official, servant, minstrel, fr. LL *ministerialis* imperial household officer, fr. L *ministerium* service, fr. *minister* servant — more at MINISTER] (14c) **1** : one of a class of medieval musical entertainers; *esp* : a singer of verses to the accompaniment of a harp **2 a** : MUSICIAN **b** : POET **3 a** : any of a troupe of performers typically giving a program of black American melodies, jokes, and impersonations and usu. wearing blackface **b** : a performance by a troupe of minstrels
min·strel·sy \-sē\ *n* [ME *minstralcie,* fr. AF *menestralsie,* fr. *menestral*] (14c) **1** : the singing and playing of a minstrel **2** : a body of minstrels **3** : a group of songs or verse
¹**mint** \ˈmint\ *n* [ME *minte,* fr. OE, fr. L *mentha, menta;* akin to Gk *minthē* mint] (bef. 12c) **1** : any of a family (Labiatae, the mint family) of aromatic plants with a square stem and a 4-lobed ovary which produces four one-seeded nutlets in fruit; *esp* : any of a genus (*Mentha*) of mints that have white, purple, or pink verticillate flowers with a nearly regular corolla and four equal stamens and that include some used in flavoring and cookery **2** : a confection flavored with mint — **minty** \ˈmin-tē\ *adj*
²**mint** *n* [ME *mynt* coin, money, fr. OE *mynet,* fr. L *moneta* mint, coin, fr. *Moneta,* epithet of Juno; fr. the fact that the Romans coined money in the temple of Juno Moneta] (15c) **1** : a place where coins, medals, or tokens are made **2** : a place where something is manufactured **3** : a vast sum or amount ⟨worth a ~⟩
³**mint** *vt* (ca. 1520) **1** : to make (as coins) out of metal : COIN **2** : CREATE, PRODUCE **3** : to cause to attain an indicated status ⟨newly ~*ed* doctors⟩ — **mint·er** *n*
⁴**mint** *adj* (1902) : unmarred as if fresh from a mint ⟨in ~ condition⟩
mint·age \ˈmin-tij\ *n* (ca. 1570) **1** : the action or process of minting coins **2** : an impression placed upon a coin **3** : coins produced by minting or in a single period of minting
mint julep *n* (1809) : JULEP 2
min·u·end \ˈmin-yə-ˌwend\ *n* [L *minuendum,* neut. of *minuendus,* gerundive of *minuere* to lessen — more at MINOR] (1706) : a number from which the subtrahend is to be subtracted
min·u·et \ˌmin-yə-ˈwet\ *n* [F *menuet,* fr. obs. F, tiny, fr. OF, fr. *menu* small, fr. L *minutus*] (1672) **1** : a slow graceful dance in ¾ time characterized by forward balancing, bowing, and toe pointing **2** : music for or in the rhythm of a minuet
¹**mi·nus** \ˈmī-nəs\ *prep* [ME, fr. L *minus,* adv., less, fr. neut. of *minor* smaller — more at MINOR] (15c) **1** : diminished by : LESS ⟨seven ~ four is three⟩ **2** : deprived of : WITHOUT ⟨~ his hat⟩
²**minus** *n* (1708) **1** : a negative quantity **2** : a negative quality; *esp* : DRAWBACK
³**minus** *adj* (1776) **1** : algebraically negative ⟨a ~ quantity⟩ ⟨~ ten degrees⟩ **2** : having a negative quality **3** : relating to or being a particular one of the two mating types that are required for successful fertilization in sexual reproduction in some lower plants (as a fungus) **4** : falling low in a specified range ⟨B ~⟩
¹**mi·nus·cule** \ˈmi-nəs-ˌkyül *also* mi-ˈnəs-\ *n* [F, fr. L *minusculus* rather small, dim. of *minor* smaller] (1701) **1** : a lowercase letter **2 a** : one of several ancient and medieval writing styles developed from cursive and having simplified and small forms **b** : a letter in this style
²**minuscule** \ˈmi-nəs-ˌkyül\ *adj* (1703) **1** : written in or in the size or style of minuscules **2** : very small ⟨~ amounts⟩
minus sign *n* (1851) : a sign – used in mathematics to indicate subtraction (as in 8–6=2) or a negative quantity (as in –10°)
¹**min·ute** \ˈmi-nət\ *n* [ME, fr. MF, fr. LL *minuta,* fr. L *minutus* small, fr. pp. of *minuere* to lessen — more at MINOR] (14c) **1 a** : the 60th part of an hour of time : 60 seconds **b** : the 60th part of a degree of angular measure **2** : the distance one can traverse in a minute **3** : a short space of time : MOMENT **4 a** : a brief note (as of summary or recommendation) **b** : MEMORANDUM, DRAFT **c** *pl* : the official record of the proceedings of a meeting
²**minute** *vt* **min·ut·ed; min·ut·ing** (1601) : to make notes or a brief summary of
³**mi·nute** \mī-ˈnüt, mə-, -ˈnyüt\ *adj* **mi·nut·er; -est** [L *minutus*] (1606) **1** : very small : INFINITESIMAL **2** : of small importance : TRIFLING **3** : marked by close attention to details *syn* see SMALL, CIRCUMSTANTIAL — **mi·nute·ness** *n*
minute hand *n* (1720) : the long hand that marks the minutes on the face of a watch or clock
¹**mi·nute·ly** \mī-ˈnüt-lē, mə-, -ˈnyüt-\ *adv* (1599) **1** : into very small pieces **2** : in a minute manner or degree ⟨a ~ detailed analysis⟩
²**min·ute·ly** \ˈmi-nət-lē\ *adj* (ca. 1616) *archaic* : minute by minute
min·ute·man \ˈmi-nət-ˌman\ *n* (1774) : a member of a group of men pledged to take up arms at a minute's notice during and immediately before the American Revolution
min·ute steak \ˈmi-nət-\ *n* (1921) : a small thin steak that can be quickly cooked
mi·nu·tia \mə-ˈnü-sh(ē-)ə, mī-, -ˈnyü-\ *n, pl* **-ti·ae** \-shē-ˌē, -ˌī\ [L *minutiae* trifles, details, fr. pl. of *minutia* smallness, fr. *minutus*] (1782) : a minute or minor detail — usu. used in pl.
minx \ˈmiŋ(k)s\ *n* [origin unknown] (1576) **1** : a pert girl **2** : a wanton woman
min·yan \ˈmin-yən\ *n, pl* **-ya·nim** \ˌmin-yə-ˈnēm\ *or* **-yans** [Heb *minyān,* lit., number, count] (1753) : the quorum required for Jewish communal worship that consists of ten male adults in Orthodox Judaism and usu. ten adults of either sex in Conservative and Reform Judaism
Mio·cene \ˈmī-ə-ˌsēn\ *adj* [*mio-* (fr. Gk *meiōn* less) + *-cene* — more at MEIOSIS] (1831) : of, relating to, or being an epoch of the Tertiary between the Pliocene and the Oligocene or the corresponding series of rocks — see GEOLOGIC TIME table — **Miocene** *n*
mi·o·sis *also* **my·o·sis** \mī-ˈō-səs, mē-\ *n, pl* **mi·o·ses** *also* **my·o·ses** \-ˌsēz\ [NL, fr. Gk *myein* to be closed (of the eyes) + NL *-osis*] (1807) : excessive smallness or contraction of the pupil of the eye
¹**mi·ot·ic** *also* **my·ot·ic** \-ˈä-tik\ *n* (1864) : an agent that causes miosis
²**miotic** *also* **myotic** *adj* (1864) : relating to or characterized by miosis
MIPS *also* **mips** *abbr* million instructions per second
mi·que·let \ˌmi-kə-ˈlet, ˌmē-\ *n* [Sp *miquelete*] (1827) : a Spanish or French irregular soldier during the Peninsular War
mir \ˈmir\ *n* [Russ] (1856) : a village community in czarist Russia in which land was owned jointly but cultivated by individual families
mi·ra·bi·le dic·tu \mə-ˌrä-bə-lē-ˈdik-(ˌ)tü\ [L] (1804) : wonderful to relate
mi·ra·cid·i·um \ˌmir-ə-ˈsi-dē-əm, ˌmī-rə-\ *n, pl* **-cid·ia** \-dē-ə\ [NL, fr. Gk *meirak-, meirax* youth, stripling + NL *-idium*] (1898) : the free-swimming ciliated first larva of a digenetic trematode that seeks out and penetrates a suitable snail intermediate host in which it develops into a sporocyst — **mi·ra·cid·i·al** \-dē-əl\ *adj*
mir·a·cle \ˈmir-i-kəl\ *n* [ME, fr. AF, fr. LL *miraculum,* fr. L, a wonder, marvel, fr. *mirari* to wonder at] (12c) **1** : an extraordinary event manifesting divine intervention in human affairs **2** : an extremely outstanding or unusual event, thing, or accomplishment **3** *Christian Science* : a divinely natural phenomenon experienced humanly as the fulfillment of spiritual law
miracle drug *n* (1944) : a drug usu. newly discovered that elicits a dramatic response in a patient's condition — called also *wonder drug*
miracle fruit *n* (1964) : a tropical African shrub (*Synsepalum dulcificum*) of the sapodilla family whose small red fruit contains a glycoprotein that when applied to the tongue causes sour substances to taste sweet; *also* : its fruit
miracle play *n* (1602) **1** : a medieval drama based on episodes from the life of a saint or martyr **2** : MYSTERY PLAY
mi·rac·u·lous \mə-ˈra-kyə-ləs\ *adj* [ME, fr. MF *miraculos,* fr. ML *miraculosus,* fr. L *miraculum*] (15c) **1** : of the nature of a miracle : SUPERNATURAL ⟨a ~ event⟩ **2** : suggesting a miracle : MARVELOUS ⟨proof of a ~ memory —*Time*⟩ **3** : working or able to work miracles ⟨~ power⟩ — **mi·rac·u·lous·ly** *adv* — **mi·rac·u·lous·ness** *n*
mir·a·dor \ˈmir-ə-ˌdȯr, ˌmir-ə-ˈ\ *n* [Sp, fr. Catal, fr. *mirar* to look at, fr. L *mirari*] (1797) : a turret, window, or balcony designed to command an extensive outlook
mi·rage \mə-ˈräzh\ *n* [F, fr. *mirer* to look at, fr. L *mirari*] (1803) **1** : an optical effect that is sometimes seen at sea, in the desert, or over a hot pavement, that may have the appearance of a pool of water or a mirror in which distant objects are seen inverted, and that is caused by the bending or reflection of rays of light by a layer of heated air of varying density **2** : something illusory and unattainable like a mirage *syn* see DELUSION
Mi·ran·da \mə-ˈran-də\ *adj* [fr. *Miranda v. Arizona,* the U.S. Supreme Court ruling establishing such rights] (1972) : of, relating to, or being the legal rights of an arrested person to have an attorney and to remain silent so as to avoid self-incrimination ⟨~ warnings⟩
Mi·ran·dize \mə-ˈran-ˌdīz\ *vt* **-dized; -diz·ing** (1984) : to recite the Miranda warnings to (a person under arrest)
¹**mire** \ˈmī(-ə)r\ *n* [ME, fr. ON *mýrr;* akin to OE *mōs* marsh — more at MOSS] (14c) **1** : wet spongy earth (as of a bog or marsh) **2** : heavy often deep mud or slush **3** : a troublesome or intractable situation ⟨found themselves in a ~ of debt⟩ — **miry** \ˈmīr-ē\ *adj*
²**mire** *vb* **mired; mir·ing** *vt* (15c) **1 a** : to cause to stick fast in or as if in mire **b** : to hamper or hold back as if by mire : ENTANGLE **2** : to cover or soil with mire ~ *vi* : to stick or sink in mire
mire·poix \mir-ˈpwä\ *n, pl* **mirepoix** [F, prob. fr. Charles de Lévis, duc de *Mirepoix* †1757 Fr. general, or one of his successors] (1877) : a sautéed mixture of diced vegetables (as carrots, celery, and onions), herbs, and sometimes ham or bacon used esp. as a basis for soups, stews, and sauces
mi·rex \ˈmī-ˌreks\ *n* [origin unknown] (1962) : an organochlorine insecticide $C_{10}Cl_{12}$ formerly used esp. against ants
mir·in \ˈmir-in\ *n* [Jp] (1880) : a sweet Japanese cooking wine made from fermented rice
mir·li·ton \ˌmir-lə-ˈtōⁿ\ *n* [LaF] (ca. 1909) : CHAYOTE
¹**mir·ror** \ˈmir-ər, mi-rər\ *n* [ME *mirour,* fr. AF *mirur,* fr. *mirer* to look at, fr. L *mirari* to wonder at] (13c) **1** : a polished or smooth surface (as of glass) that forms images by reflection **2 a** : something that gives a true representation **b** : an exemplary model — **mir·rored** \-(r)ə(r)d\ *adj* — **mir·ror·like** \-ˌlīk\ *adj*

[2]**mirror** *vt* (1593) **1 :** to reflect in or as if in a mirror **2 :** RESEMBLE
mirror image *n* (1885) **1 a :** something that has its parts reversely arranged in comparison with another similar thing or that is reversed with reference to an intervening axis or plane **b :** the direct opposite **2 :** IMAGE 3
mirth \ˈmərth\ *n* [ME, fr. OE *myrgth,* fr. *myrge* merry — more at MERRY] (bef. 12c) **:** gladness or gaiety as shown by or accompanied with laughter — **mirth·ful** \-fəl\ *adj* — **mirth·ful·ly** \-fə-lē\ *adv* — **mirth·ful·ness** *n* — **mirth·less** \-ləs\ *adj* — **mirth·less·ly** \-le\ *adv*
[1]**MIRV** \ˈmərv\ *n* [*m*ultiple *i*ndependently targeted *r*eentry *v*ehicle] (1967) **:** a missile with two or more warheads designed to strike separate enemy targets; *also* **:** any of the warheads of such a missile
[2]**MIRV** *vb* **MIRVed; MIRV·ing** *vt* (1968) **:** to equip with MIRV warheads ~ *vi* **:** to arm one's forces with MIRVs
MIS *abbr* management information systems
mis- *prefix* [partly fr. ME, fr. OE; partly fr. ME *mes-, mis-,* fr. AF *mes-,* of Gmc origin; akin to OE *mis-;* akin to OE *missan* to miss] **1 a :** badly **:** wrongly ⟨*mis*judge⟩ **b :** unfavorably ⟨*mis*esteem⟩ **c :** in a suspicious manner ⟨*mis*doubt⟩ **2 :** bad **:** wrong ⟨*mis*deed⟩ **3 :** opposite or lack of ⟨*mis*trust⟩ **4 :** not ⟨*mis*know⟩

mis·act
mis·ad·dress
mis·ad·just
mis·ad·min·is·tra·tion
mis·ad·vise
mis·aim
mis·align
mis·align·ment
mis·al·lo·cate
mis·al·lo·ca·tion
mis·anal·y·sis
mis·ap·pli·ca·tion
mis·ap·ply
mis·ap·prais·al
mis·ar·tic·u·late
mis·as·sem·ble
mis·as·sump·tion
mis·at·trib·ute
mis·at·tri·bu·tion
mis·bal·ance
mis·be·have
mis·be·hav·er
mis·be·hav·ior
mis·bound
mis·but·ton
mis·cal·cu·late
mis·cal·cu·la·tion
mis·cap·tion
mis·cat·a·log
mis·chan·nel
mis·char·ac·ter·i·za·tion
mis·char·ac·ter·ize
mis·charge
mis·choice
mis·ci·ta·tion
mis·clas·si·fi·ca·tion
mis·clas·si·fy
mis·code
mis·com·pre·hen·sion
mis·com·pu·ta·tion
mis·com·pute
mis·con·ceive
mis·con·ceiv·er
mis·con·cep·tion
mis·con·nect
mis·con·nec·tion
mis·con·struc·tion
mis·con·strue
mis·copy
mis·cor·re·la·tion
mis·count
mis·cre·ate
mis·cre·a·tion
mis·cut
mis·date
mis·deem
mis·de·fine
mis·de·scribe
mis·de·scrip·tion
mis·de·vel·op
mis·di·ag·nose
mis·di·ag·no·sis
mis·dial
mis·dis·tri·bu·tion
mis·di·vi·sion
mis·draw
mis·ed·u·cate
mis·ed·u·ca·tion
mis·em·pha·sis
mis·em·pha·size
mis·em·ploy
mis·em·ploy·ment
mis·es·ti·mate
mis·es·ti·ma·tion
mis·eval·u·ate
mis·eval·u·a·tion
mis·feed
mis·field
mis·file
mis·fo·cus
mis·func·tion
mis·gauge
mis·gov·ern
mis·gov·ern·ment
mis·grade
mis·iden·ti·fi·ca·tion
mis·iden·ti·fy
mis·in·form
mis·in·for·ma·tion
mis·kick
mis·la·bel
mis·learn
mis·lo·cate
mis·lo·ca·tion
mis·man·age
mis·man·age·ment
mis·mark
mis·mar·riage
mis·match
mis·mate
mis·mea·sure
mis·mea·sure·ment
mis·or·der
mis·ori·ent
mis·ori·en·ta·tion
mis·pack·age
mis·per·ceive
mis·per·cep·tion
mis·plan
mis·po·si·tion
mis·print
mis·pro·gram
mis·quo·ta·tion
mis·quote
mis·reck·on
mis·rec·ol·lec·tion
mis·re·cord
mis·ref·er·ence
mis·reg·is·ter
mis·reg·is·tra·tion
mis·re·late
mis·re·mem·ber
mis·ren·der
mis·re·port
mis·route
mis·set
mis·shape
mis·shap·en
mis·shap·en·ly
mis·sort
mis·strike
mis·throw
mis·time
mis·ti·tle
mis·train
mis·tran·scribe
mis·tran·scrip·tion
mis·trans·late
mis·trans·la·tion
mis·truth
mis·tune
mis·type
mis·uti·li·za·tion
mis·vo·cal·i·za·tion
mis·write

mis·ad·ven·ture \ˌmi-səd-ˈven-chər\ *n* [ME *mesaventure,* fr. AF, fr. *mesavenir* to turn out badly, fr. *mes-* mis- + *avenir* to happen, fr. L *advenire* — more at ADVENTURE] (14c) **:** MISFORTUNE, MISHAP
mis·al·li·ance \ˌmi-sə-ˈlī-ən(t)s\ *n* [modif. of F *mésalliance*] (1738) **1 :** an improper alliance **2 a :** MÉSALLIANCE **b :** a marriage between persons unsuited to each other
mis·an·dry \ˈmi-ˌsan-drē\ *n* [*mis-* (as in *misanthropy*) + *andr-* + [2]*-y*] (ca. 1909) **:** a hatred of men — **mis·an·drist** \-drist\ *n or adj*
mis·an·thrope \ˈmi-sᵊn-ˌthrōp\ *n* [Gk *misanthrōpos* hating humankind, fr. *misein* to hate + *anthrōpos* human being] (1683) **:** a person who hates or distrusts humankind
mis·an·throp·ic \ˌmi-sᵊn-ˈthrä-pik\ *adj* (1762) **1 :** of, relating to, or characteristic of a misanthrope **2 :** marked by a hatred or contempt for humankind ***syn*** see CYNICAL — **mis·an·throp·i·cal·ly** \-pi-k(ə-)lē\ *adv*
mis·an·thro·py \mi-ˈsan(t)-thrə-pē\ *n* (1625) **:** a hatred or distrust of humankind
mis·ap·pre·hend \(ˌ)mis-ˌa-pri-ˈhend\ *vt* (1628) **:** to apprehend wrongly **:** MISUNDERSTAND — **mis·ap·pre·hen·sion** \-ˈhen(t)-shən\ *n*
mis·ap·pro·pri·ate \ˌmi-sə-ˈprō-prē-ˌāt\ *vt* (1825) **:** to appropriate wrongly (as by theft or embezzlement) — **mis·ap·pro·pri·a·tion** \-ˌprō-prē-ˈā-shən\ *n*
mis·be·come \ˌmis-bi-ˈkəm\ *vt* **-came** \-ˈkām\; **-come; -com·ing** (1530) **:** to be inappropriate or unbecoming to
mis·be·got·ten \-bi-ˈgä-tᵊn\ *adj* (1554) **1 :** unlawfully conceived **:** ILLEGITIMATE ⟨a ~ child⟩ **2 a :** having a disreputable or improper origin **:** ill-conceived ⟨antiquated and ~ tax laws —R. M. Blough⟩ **b :** CONTEMPTIBLE, DEFORMED ⟨a ~ scoundrel⟩
mis·be·lief \ˌmis-bə-ˈlēf\ *n* (13c) **:** erroneous or false belief **:** HERESY
mis·be·lieve \-ˈlēv\ *vi* (14c) *obs* **:** to hold a false or unorthodox belief
mis·be·liev·er \-ˈlē-vər\ *n* (15c) **:** HERETIC, INFIDEL
mis·brand \ˌmis-ˈbrand\ *vt* (1892) **:** to brand falsely or in a misleading way; *specif* **:** to label in violation of statutory requirements

misc *abbr* miscellaneous
mis·call \ˌmis-ˈkȯl\ *vt* (14c) **:** to call by a wrong name **:** MISNAME
mis·car·riage \ˌmis-ˈker-ij, -ˈka-rij, ˈmis-ˌ\ *n* (ca. 1652) **1 :** corrupt or incompetent management; *esp* **:** a failure in the administration of justice **2 :** spontaneous expulsion of a human fetus before it is viable and esp. between the 12th and 28th weeks of gestation
mis·car·ry \ˌmis-ˈker-ē, -ˈka-rē, ˈmis-ˌ\ *vi* (14c) **1** *obs* **:** to come to harm **2 :** to suffer miscarriage of a fetus **3 :** to fail to achieve the intended purpose **:** go wrong or amiss ⟨the plan *miscarried*⟩ **4 :** to fail to reach the intended destination ⟨the letter has *miscarried*⟩
mis·cast \ˌmis-ˈkast\ *vt* **-cast; -cast·ing** (1925) **:** to cast in an unsuitable role ⟨life had ~ her in the role of wife and mother —Edna Ferber⟩
mis·ce·ge·na·tion \(ˌ)mi-ˌse-jə-ˈnā-shən, ˌmi-si-jə-ˈnā-\ *n* [irreg. fr. L *miscēre* to mix + *genus* race — more at MIX, KIN] (1863) **:** a mixture of races; *esp* **:** marriage, cohabitation, or sexual intercourse between a white person and a member of another race — **mis·ce·ge·na·tion·al** \-shnəl, -shə-nᵊl\ *adj*
mis·cel·la·nea \ˌmi-sə-ˈlā-nē-ə, -nyə\ *n pl* [L, fr. neut. pl. of *miscellaneus*] (1571) **:** a collection of miscellaneous objects or writings
mis·cel·la·neous \ˌmi-sə-ˈlā-nē-əs, -nyəs\ *adj* [L *miscellaneus,* fr. *miscellus* mixed] (1637) **1 :** consisting of diverse things or members **:** HETEROGENEOUS **2 a :** having various traits **b :** dealing with or interested in diverse subjects ⟨as a writer I was too ~ —George Santayana⟩ — **mis·cel·la·neous·ly** *adv* — **mis·cel·la·neous·ness** *n*
mis·cel·la·ny \ˈmi-sə-ˌlā-nē, *chiefly Brit* mi-ˈse-lə-nē\ *n, pl* **-nies** [prob. modif. of F *miscellanées,* pl., fr. L *miscellanea*] (1615) **1 a** *pl* **:** separate writings collected in one volume **b :** a collection of writings on various subjects **2 :** a mixture of various things
mis·chance \ˌmis-ˈchan(t)s\ *n* [ME *mischaunce,* fr. AF *meschance,* fr. *mes-* mis- + *chance* chance] (14c) **1 :** bad luck **2 :** a piece of bad luck **:** MISHAP ***syn*** see MISFORTUNE
mis·chief \ˈmis-chəf, ˈmish-\ *n* [ME *meschief,* fr. AF, misfortune, hardship, fr. OF *meschever* to come out badly, *mes-* + *chief* head, end — more at CHIEF] (14c) **1 :** a specific injury or damage attributed to a particular agent **2 :** a cause or source of harm, evil, or irritation; *esp* **:** a person who causes mischief **3 a :** action that annoys or irritates **b :** the quality or state of being mischievous **:** MISCHIEVOUSNESS ⟨had ~ in his eyes⟩
mis·chie·vous \ˈmis-chə-vəs, ˈmish-; ÷mis-ˈchē-vē-əs, mish-\ *adj* (14c) **1 :** HARMFUL, INJURIOUS ⟨~ gossip⟩ **2 a :** able or tending to cause annoyance, trouble, or minor injury **b :** irresponsibly playful ⟨~ behavior⟩ — **mis·chie·vous·ly** *adv* — **mis·chie·vous·ness** *n*
usage A pronunciation \mis-ˈchē-vē-əs\ and a consequent spelling *mischievious* are of long standing: evidence for the spelling goes back to the 16th century. Our pronunciation files contain modern attestations ranging from dialect speakers to Herbert Hoover. But both the pronunciation and the spelling are still considered nonstandard.
misch metal \ˈmish-\ *n* [G *Mischmetall,* fr. *mischen* to mix + *Metall* metal] (1915) **:** a complex alloy of rare earth metals used esp. in tracer bullets and as a flint in lighters
mis·ci·ble \ˈmi-sə-bəl\ *adj* [ML *miscibilis,* fr. L *miscēre* to mix — more at MIX] (1570) **:** capable of being mixed; *specif* **:** capable of mixing in any ratio without separation of two phases ⟨~ liquids⟩ — **mis·ci·bil·i·ty** \ˌmi-sə-ˈbi-lə-tē\ *n*
mis·com·mu·ni·ca·tion \ˌmis-kə-ˌmyü-nə-ˈkā-shən\ *n* (1964) **:** failure to communicate clearly
mis·con·duct \-ˈkän-(ˌ)dəkt\ *n* (1705) **1 :** mismanagement esp. of governmental or military responsibilities **2 :** intentional wrongdoing; *specif* **:** deliberate violation of a law or standard esp. by a government official **:** MALFEASANCE **3 a :** improper behavior **b :** ADULTERY **4 :** a penalty (as in ice hockey) for improper behavior or abusive language (as toward an official) — **mis·con·duct** \-kən-ˈdəkt\ *vt*
[1]**mis·cre·ant** \ˈmis-krē-ənt\ *adj* [ME *miscreaunt,* fr. AF *mescreant,* prp. of *mescreire* to disbelieve, fr. *mes-* + *creire* to believe, fr. L *credere* — more at CREED] (14c) **1 :** UNBELIEVING, HERETICAL **2 :** DEPRAVED, VILLAINOUS ⟨~ behavior⟩
[2]**miscreant** *n* (14c) **1 :** INFIDEL, HERETIC **2 :** one who behaves criminally or viciously
[1]**mis·cue** \ˌmis-ˈkyü, ˈmis-ˌkyü\ *n* (1838) **1 :** a faulty stroke in billiards in which the cue slips **2 :** MISTAKE, SLIP
[2]**miscue** *vi* (1894) **:** to make a miscue
mis·deal \ˌmis-ˈdēl\ *vb* **-dealt** \-ˈdelt\; **-deal·ing** *vi* (1834) **:** to deal cards incorrectly ~ *vt* **:** to deal incorrectly — **misdeal** *n*
mis·deed \-ˈdēd\ *n* (bef. 12c) **:** a wrong deed **:** OFFENSE
mis·de·mean·ant \-di-ˈmē-nənt\ *n* (1819) **:** a person convicted of a misdemeanor
mis·de·mean·or \-di-ˈmē-nər\ *n* (15c) **1 :** a crime less serious than a felony **2 :** MISDEED
mis·de·mean·our *chiefly Brit var of* MISDEMEANOR
mis·di·rect \-də-ˈrekt, -(ˌ)dī-\ *vt* (1603) **1 :** to give a wrong direction to **2 :** to direct wrongly ⟨~*ed* their energies⟩
mis·di·rec·tion \-ˈrek-shən\ *n* (1749) **1 :** a wrong direction **2 a :** the act or an instance of misdirecting or diverting **b :** the state of being misdirected
mis·do \ˌmis-ˈdü\ *vb* **-did** \-ˈdid\; **-done** \-ˈdən\; **-do·ing** \-ˈdü-iŋ\; **-does** \-ˈdəz\ *vi* (bef. 12c) *obs* **:** to act wrongly **:** transgress the laws of God ⟨the erring soul not wilfully ~*ing* —John Milton⟩ ~ *vt* **:** to do (something) incorrectly or poorly — **mis·do·er** \-ˈdü-ər\ *n*
misdoing *n* (15c) **:** the act or an instance of misbehaving **:** MISCONDUCT
mis·doubt \ˌmis-ˈdau̇t\ *vt* (ca. 1540) **1 :** DOUBT **2 :** SUSPECT, FEAR — **misdoubt** *n*
mise–en–scène \ˌmē-ˌzäⁿ-ˈsen, -ˈsān\ *n, pl* **mise–en–scènes** \-ˈsen(z), -ˈsān(z)\ [F *mise en scène*] (1833) **1 a :** the arrangement of actors and scenery on a stage for a theatrical production **b :** stage setting **2 a :** the physical setting of an action (as of a narrative or a mo-

\ə\ **abut** \ᵊ\ kitten, F table \ər\ **further** \a\ **ash** \ā\ **ace** \ä\ mop, mar
\au̇\ **out** \ch\ **chin** \e\ **bet** \ē\ **easy** \g\ **go** \i\ **hit** \ī\ **ice** \j\ **job**
\ŋ\ **sing** \ō\ **go** \ȯ\ **law** \ȯi\ **boy** \th\ **thin** \t͟h\ **the** \ü\ **loot** \u̇\ **foot**
\y\ **yet** \zh\ **vision, beige** \k̲, ⁿ, œ, ue, ʸ\ *see* Guide to Pronunciation

tion picture) : CONTEXT **b** : ENVIRONMENT, MILIEU *syn* see BACKGROUND

mi·ser \ˈmī-zər\ *n* [L *miser* miserable] (ca. 1560) : a mean grasping person; *esp* : one who is extremely stingy with money

mis·er·a·ble \ˈmi-zər-bəl, ˈmiz-rə-, ˈmi-zə-rə-\ *adj* [ME, fr. MF, fr. L *miserabilis* wretched, pitiable, fr. *miserari* to pity, fr. *miser*] (15c) **1** : being in a pitiable state of distress or unhappiness (as from want or shame) ⟨~ refugees⟩ **2 a** : wretchedly inadequate or meager ⟨a ~ hovel⟩ **b** : causing extreme discomfort or unhappiness ⟨a ~ situation⟩ **3** : being likely to discredit or shame ⟨his ~ neglect of his wife⟩ — **miserable** *n* — **mis·er·a·ble·ness** *n* — **mis·er·a·bly** \-blē\ *adv*

mi·se·re·re \ˌmi-zə-ˈrir-ē, -ˈrer-; ˌmē-zə-ˈrā-(ˌ)rā\ *n* [ME, fr. L, be merciful, fr. *misereri* to be merciful, fr. *miser* wretched; fr. the first word of the Psalm] (13c) **1** *cap* : the 50th Psalm in the Vulgate **2** : MISERICORD **3** : a vocal complaint or lament

mi·ser·i·cord *also* **mi·ser·i·corde** \mə-ˈzer-ə-ˌkȯrd, -ˈser-\ *n* [ML *misericordia* seat in church, fr. L, mercy, fr. *misericord-, misericors* merciful, fr. *misereri* + *cord-, cor* heart — more at HEART] (ca. 1515) : a small projection on the bottom of a hinged church seat that gives support to a standing worshiper when the seat is turned up

mi·ser·ly \ˈmī-zər-lē\ *adj* (1593) : of, relating to, or characteristic of a miser; *esp* : marked by grasping meanness and penuriousness *syn* see STINGY — **mi·ser·li·ness** *n*

mis·ery \ˈmi-zə-rē, ˈmiz-rē\ *n, pl* **-er·ies** (14c) **1** : a state of suffering and want that is the result of poverty or affliction **2** : a circumstance, thing, or place that causes suffering or discomfort **3** : a state of great unhappiness and emotional distress *syn* see DISTRESS

misery index *n* (1975) : the sum of the rate of unemployment and the rate of inflation used as an economic indicator

mis·es·teem \ˌmi-sə-ˈstēm\ *vt* (1611) : to esteem wrongly; *esp* : to hold in too little regard

mis·fea·sance \mis-ˈfē-zᵊn(t)s\ *n* [MF *mesfaisance,* fr. *mesfaire* to do wrong, fr. *mes-* mis- + *faire* to make, do, fr. L *facere* — more at DO] (1596) : TRESPASS; *specif* : the performance of a lawful action in an illegal or improper manner — **mis·fea·sor** \-ˈfē-zər, -ˌzȯr\ *n*

¹**mis·fire** \ˌmis-ˈfī(-ə)r\ *vi* (1752) **1** : to have the explosive or propulsive charge fail to ignite at the proper time ⟨the engine *misfired*⟩ **2** : to fail to fire ⟨the gun *misfired*⟩ **3** : to miss an intended effect or objective ⟨the new ad campaign *misfired*⟩

²**mis·fire** \ˌmis-ˈfī(-ə)r, ˈmis-ˌ\ *n* (1839) **1** : a failure (as of a cartridge or firearm) to fire **2** : something that misfires

mis·fit \ˈmis-ˌfit *also* ˌmis-ˈfit\ *n* (ca. 1823) **1** : something that fits badly **2** : a person who is poorly adapted to a situation or environment ⟨social ~*s*⟩

mis·for·tune \ˌmis-ˈfȯr-chən\ *n* (15c) **1 a** : an event or conjunction of events that causes an unfortunate or distressing result : bad luck ⟨by ~ he fell into bad company⟩ ⟨had the ~ to break his leg⟩ **b** : an unhappy situation ⟨always ready to help people in ~⟩ **2** : a distressing or unfortunate incident or event ⟨~*s* never come singly⟩

syn MISFORTUNE, MISCHANCE, ADVERSITY, MISHAP mean adverse fortune or an instance of this. MISFORTUNE may apply to either the incident or conjunction of events that is the cause of an unhappy change of fortune or to the ensuing state of distress ⟨never lost hope even in the depths of *misfortune*⟩. MISCHANCE applies esp. to a situation involving no more than slight inconvenience or minor annoyance ⟨took the wrong road by *mischance*⟩. ADVERSITY applies to a state of grave or persistent misfortune ⟨had never experienced great *adversity*⟩. MISHAP applies to an often trivial instance of bad luck ⟨the usual *mishaps* of a family vacation⟩.

mis·give \ˌmis-ˈgiv\ *vb* **-gave** \-ˈgāv\; **-giv·en** \-ˈgi-vən\; **-giv·ing** *vt* (1513) : to suggest doubt or fear to ~ *vi* : to be fearful or apprehensive

mis·giv·ing \-ˈgi-viŋ\ *n* (1582) : a feeling of doubt or suspicion esp. concerning a future event

mis·guid·ance \ˌmis-ˈgī-dᵊn(t)s\ *n* (1606) : MISDIRECTION

mis·guide \-ˈgīd\ *vt* (14c) : to lead astray : MISDIRECT ⟨prejudice ~*s* our minds⟩ — **mis·guid·er** *n*

mis·guid·ed \(ˌ)mis-ˈgī-dəd\ *adj* (1500) : led or prompted by wrong or inappropriate motives or ideals ⟨well-meaning but ~ do-gooders⟩ — **mis·guid·ed·ly** \-lē\ *adv* — **mis·guid·ed·ness** \-nəs\ *n*

mis·han·dle \ˌmis-ˈhan-dᵊl\ *vt* (1530) **1** : to treat roughly : MALTREAT **2** : to deal with or manage wrongly or ignorantly

mis·hap \ˈmis-ˌhap, mis-ˈ\ *n* (14c) **1** : an unfortunate accident **2** : bad luck : MISFORTUNE *syn* see MISFORTUNE

mis·hear \ˌmis-ˈhir\ *vb* **-heard** \-ˈhərd\; **-hear·ing** \-ˈhir-iŋ\ *vt* (bef. 12c) : to hear wrongly ~ *vi* : to misunderstand what is heard

mis·hit \ˌmis-ˈhit\ *vt* **-hit; -hit·ting** (1903) : to hit in a faulty manner — **mis·hit** \ˌmis-ˈhit, ˈmis-ˌ\ *n*

mish·mash \ˈmish-ˌmash, -ˌmäsh\ *n* [ME & Yiddish; ME *mysse masche,* perh. redupl. of *mash* mash; Yiddish *mish-mash,* perh. redupl. of *mishn* to mix] (15c) : HODGEPODGE, JUMBLE

Mish·nah *or* **Mish·na** \ˈmish-nə\ *n* [Heb *mishnāh* instruction, oral law] (1610) : the collection of mostly halachic Jewish traditions compiled about A.D. 200 and made the basic part of the Talmud — **Mish·na·ic** \mish-ˈnā-ik\ *adj*

mis·im·pres·sion \ˌmi-sim-ˈpre-shən\ *n* (1670) : a mistaken impression

mis·in·ter·pret \ˌmi-sᵊn-ˈtər-prət, -pət\ *vt* (1547) **1** : to explain wrongly **2** : to understand wrongly — **mis·in·ter·pre·ta·tion** \-ˌtər-prə-ˈtā-shən, -pə-\ *n*

mis·join·der \ˌmis-ˈjȯin-dər\ *n* (1789) : an improper union of parties or of causes of action in a single legal proceeding

mis·judge \ˌmis-ˈjəj\ *vi* (15c) : to be mistaken in judgment ~ *vt* **1** : to estimate wrongly **2** : to have an unjust opinion of — **mis·judg·ment** \-ˈjəj-mənt\ *n*

Mi·ski·to \mis-ˈkē-(ˌ)tō\ *n, pl* **Miskito** *or* **Miskitos** [earlier *Musketa, Moskita,* fr. Sp *Mosquito,* fr. Miskito *miskito,* prob. a self-designation] (1688) **1** : a member of an American Indian people of the Atlantic coast of Nicaragua and Honduras **2** : the language of the Miskito people

mis·know \ˌmis-ˈnō\ *vt* **-knew** \-ˈnü, -ˈnyü\; **-known** \-ˈnōn\; **-know·ing** (15c) : MISUNDERSTAND — **mis·knowl·edge** \-ˈnä-lij\ *n*

mis·lay \ˌmis-ˈlā\ *vt* **-laid** \-ˈlād\; **-lay·ing** (1614) : to put in an unremembered place : LOSE ⟨he *mislaid* his car keys⟩

mis·lead \ˌmis-ˈlēd\ *vb* **-led** \-ˈled\; **-lead·ing** *vt* (bef. 12c) : to lead in a wrong direction or into a mistaken action or belief often by deliberate deceit ~ *vi* : to lead astray : give a wrong impression *syn* see DECEIVE — **mis·lead·er** *n* — **mis·lead·ing·ly** \-ˈlē-diŋ-lē\ *adv*

mis·leared \-ˈlird, -ˈlerd\ *adj* [¹*mis-* + *lear* to learn] (1560) *chiefly Scot* : UNMANNERLY, ILL-BRED

mis·like \-ˈlīk\ *vt* (bef. 12c) **1** *archaic* : DISPLEASE **2** : DISLIKE — **mislike** *n*

mis·name \-ˈnām\ *vt* (1537) : to name incorrectly : MISCALL

mis·no·mer \ˌmis-ˈnō-mər\ *n* [ME *misnoumer,* fr. AF *mesnomer,* fr. *mes-* mis- + *nomer* to name, fr. L *nominare* — more at NOMINATE] (15c) **1** : the misnaming of a person in a legal instrument **2 a** : a use of a wrong or inappropriate name **b** : a wrong name or inappropriate designation — **mis·no·mered** \-mərd\ *adj*

mi·so \ˈmē-(ˌ)sō\ *n* [Jp] (1615) : a high-protein fermented food paste consisting chiefly of soybeans, salt, and usu. grain (as barley or rice) and ranging in taste from very salty to very sweet

mi·sog·a·my \mi-ˈsä-gə-mē, mī-\ *n* [Gk *misein* to hate + E *-gamy*] (ca. 1656) : a hatred of marriage — **mi·sog·a·mist** \-mist\ *n*

mi·sog·y·ny \mə-ˈsä-jə-nē\ *n* [Gk *misogynia,* fr. *misein* to hate + *gynē* woman — more at QUEEN] (ca. 1656) : a hatred of women — **mi·sog·y·nic** \ˌmi-sə-ˈji-nik, -ˈgī-\ *adj* — **mi·sog·y·nist** \mə-ˈsä-jə-nist\ *n or adj* — **mi·sog·y·nis·tic** \mə-ˌsä-jə-ˈnis-tik\ *adj*

mi·sol·o·gy \mə-ˈsä-lə-jē\ *n* [Gk *misologia,* fr. *misein* + *-logia* -logy] (1833) : a hatred of argument, reasoning, or enlightenment

miso·ne·ism \ˌmi-sə-ˈnē-ˌi-zəm\ *n* [It *misoneismo,* fr. Gk *misein* + *neos* new + It *-ismo* -ism — more at NEW] (1886) : a hatred, fear, or intolerance of innovation or change

mi·so·pros·tol \ˌmī-sō-ˈpräs-ˌtōl, -ˌtȯl\ *n* [*miso-* (perh. fr. methyl + *iso-*) + *prost*aglandin + ¹*-ol*] (1982) : a synthetic prostaglandin analog $C_{22}H_{38}O_5$ used to prevent stomach ulcers associated with NSAID use and to induce abortion in conjunction with RU-486

mis·place \ˌmis-ˈplās\ *vt* (1555) **1 a** : to put in a wrong or inappropriate place ⟨~ a comma⟩ **b** : MISLAY ⟨*misplaced* the keys⟩ **2** : to set on a wrong object or eventuality ⟨his trust had been *misplaced*⟩ — **mis·place·ment** \-ˈplās-mənt\ *n*

mis·play \ˈmis-ˌplā\ *n* (1867) : a wrong or unskillful play : ERROR — **mis·play** \ˌmis-ˈplā, ˈmis-ˌ\ *vt*

¹**mis·pri·sion** \(ˌ)mis-ˈpri-zhən\ *n* [ME, fr. AF *mesprisun* error, wrongdoing, fr. *mesprendre* to take by mistake, fr. *mes-* mis- + *prendre* to take, fr. L *prehendere* to seize — more at GET] (15c) **1 a** : neglect or wrong performance of official duty **b** : concealment of treason or felony by one who is not a participant in the treason or felony **c** : seditious conduct against the government or the courts **2** : MISUNDERSTANDING, MISINTERPRETATION

²**misprision** *n* [*misprize*] (1586) : CONTEMPT, SCORN

mis·prize \ˌmis-ˈprīz\ *vt* [AF *mespriser,* fr. *mes-* mis- + *priser, preiser* to appraise — more at PRIZE] (15c) **1** : to hold in contempt : DESPISE **2** : UNDERVALUE

mis·pro·nounce \ˌmis-prə-ˈnau̇n(t)s\ *vt* (1593) : to pronounce incorrectly or in a way regarded as incorrect

mis·pro·nun·ci·a·tion \-ˌnən(t)-sē-ˈā-shən *also* -ˌnau̇n(t)-\ *n* (1530) : the act or an instance of mispronouncing

mis·read \ˌmis-ˈrēd\ *vt* **-read** \-ˈred\; **-read·ing** \-ˈrē-diŋ\ (1658) **1** : to read incorrectly **2** : to misinterpret in or as if in reading ⟨totally ~ the lesson of history —Christopher Hollis⟩

mis·rep·re·sent \(ˌ)mis-ˌre-pri-ˈzent\ *vt* (1647) **1** : to give a false or misleading representation of usu. with an intent to deceive or be unfair ⟨~*ed* the facts⟩ **2** : to serve badly or improperly as a representative of — **mis·rep·re·sen·ta·tion** \(ˌ)mis-ˌre-pri-ˌzen-ˈtā-shən, -zən-\ *n* — **mis·rep·re·sen·ta·tive** \-ˈzen-tə-tiv\ *adj*

¹**mis·rule** \ˌmis-ˈrül\ *vt* (14c) : to rule incompetently : MISGOVERN

²**misrule** *n* (14c) **1** : the action of misruling : the condition of being misruled **2** : DISORDER, ANARCHY

¹**miss** \ˈmis\ *vb* [ME, fr. OE *missan;* akin to OHG *missan* to miss] *vt* (bef. 12c) **1** : to fail to hit, reach, or contact ⟨~ the target⟩ **2** : to discover or feel the absence of **3** : to fail to obtain **4** : ESCAPE, AVOID ⟨just ~*ed* hitting the other car⟩ **5** : to leave out : OMIT **6** : to fail to comprehend, sense, or experience ⟨~*ed* the point of the speech⟩ **7** : to fail to perform or attend ⟨had to ~ school for a week⟩ ~ *vi* **1** *archaic* : to fail to get, reach, or do something **2** : to fail to hit something **3 a** : to be unsuccessful **b** : MISFIRE ⟨the engine ~*ed*⟩ — **miss·able** \ˈmi-sə-bəl\ *adj* — **miss a beat** : to deviate from regular smooth performance ⟨the company changed ownership without *missing a beat*⟩ — **miss out on** : to lose a good opportunity for ⟨*missed out on* a better job⟩ — **miss the boat** : to fail to take advantage of an opportunity

²**miss** *n* (12c) **1** *chiefly dial* : disadvantage or regret resulting from loss ⟨we know the ~ of you, and even hunger . . . to see you —Samuel Richardson⟩ **2 a** : a failure to hit **b** : a failure to attain a desired result **3** : MISFIRE

³**miss** *n* [short for *mistress*] (1667) **1** *cap* **a** — used as a title prefixed to the name of an unmarried woman or girl **b** — used before the name of a place or of a line of activity or before some epithet to form a title for a usu. young unmarried female who is representative of the thing indicated ⟨*Miss* America⟩ **2** : young lady — used without a name as a conventional term of address to a young woman **3** : a young unmarried woman or girl **4** *pl* : a clothing size for women of average height and build

Miss *abbr* Mississippi

mis·sa can·ta·ta \ˌmi-sə-kən-ˈtä-tə\ *n* [NL, sung mass] (ca. 1903) : HIGH MASS

mis·sal \ˈmi-səl\ *n* [ME *messel,* fr. AF & ML; AF *missal, messel,* fr. ML *missale,* fr. neut. of *missalis* of the mass, fr. LL *missa* mass — more at MASS] (14c) : a book containing all that is said or sung at mass during the entire year

mis·sal·ette \ˌmis-sə-ˈlet\ *n* (1973) : a shortened form of a missal published periodically for congregational use

mis·send \ˌmis-ˈsend\ *vt* **-sent** \-ˈsent\; **-send·ing** (15c) : to send incorrectly (as to a wrong destination) ⟨*missent* mail⟩

mis·sense \ˈmis-ˌsen(t)s\ *adj* [¹*mis-* + *-sense* (as in *nonsense*)] (1961) : relating to or being a genetic mutation involving alteration of one or more codons so that different amino acids are determined — compare ANTISENSE, NONSENSE

¹**mis·sile** \ˈmi-səl, *chiefly Brit* -ˌsīl\ *adj* [L *missilis,* fr. *mittere* to throw, send] (1611) **1** : capable of being thrown or projected to strike a distant object **2** : adapted for throwing or hurling missiles

²**missile** *n* (ca. 1656) **:** an object (as a weapon) thrown or projected usu. so as to strike something at a distance ⟨stones, artillery shells, bullets, and rockets are ∼*s*⟩: as **a :** GUIDED MISSILE **b :** BALLISTIC MISSILE
mis·sil·eer \ˌmi-sə-ˈlir\ *n* (1958) **:** MISSILEMAN
mis·sile·man \ˈmi-səl-mən\ *n* (1951) **:** one engaged in designing, building, or operating guided missiles
mis·sile·ry \ˈmi-səl-rē\ *n* (1866) **:** MISSILES; *esp* **:** GUIDED MISSILES
miss·ing \ˈmi-siŋ\ *adj* (ca. 1530) **:** ABSENT; *also* **:** LOST ⟨∼ in action⟩
missing link *n* (1851) **1 :** an absent member needed to complete a series or resolve a problem **2 a :** a hypothetical intermediate evolutionary form between humans and their presumed simian progenitors **b :** a hypothetical intermediate evolutionary form between one animal species or group and its presumed ancestors ⟨a *missing link* between reptiles and birds⟩
mis·si·ol·o·gy \ˌmi-sē-ˈä-lə-jē\ *n* [*mission* + *-logy*] (1924) **:** the study of the church's mission esp. with respect to missionary activity
¹**mis·sion** \ˈmi-shən\ *n* [NL, ML, & L; NL *mission-, missio* religious mission, fr. ML, task assigned, fr. L, act of sending, fr. *mittere* to send] (1530) **1** *obs* **:** the act or an instance of sending **2 a :** a ministry commissioned by a religious organization to propagate its faith or carry on humanitarian work **b :** assignment to or work in a field of missionary enterprise **c** (1) **:** a mission establishment (2) **:** a local church or parish dependent on a larger religious organization for direction or financial support **d** *pl* **:** organized missionary work **e :** a course of sermons and services given to convert the unchurched or quicken Christian faith **3 :** a body of persons sent to perform a service or carry on an activity: as **a :** a group sent to a foreign country to conduct diplomatic or political negotiations **b :** a permanent embassy or legation **c :** a team of specialists or cultural leaders sent to a foreign country **4 a :** a specific task with which a person or a group is charged **b** (1) **:** a definite military, naval, or aerospace task ⟨a bombing ∼⟩ ⟨a space ∼⟩ (2) **:** a flight operation of an aircraft or spacecraft in the performance of a mission ⟨a ∼ to Mars⟩ **c :** a preestablished and often self-imposed objective or purpose ⟨statement of the company's ∼⟩ **5 :** CALLING, VOCATION
²**mission** *vt* **mis·sioned; mis·sion·ing** \ˈmi-sh(ə-)niŋ\ (1692) **1 :** to send on or entrust with a mission **2 :** to carry on a religious mission among or in
³**mission** *adj* (1900) **1 :** of or relating to a style used in the early Spanish missions of the southwestern U.S. ⟨∼ architecture⟩ **2 :** of, relating to, or having the characteristic of a style of plain heavy usu. oak furniture originating in the U.S. in the early part of the 20th century
¹**mis·sion·ary** \ˈmi-shə-ˌner-ē\ *n, pl* **-ar·ies** (1625) **:** a person undertaking a mission and esp. a religious mission
²**missionary** *adj* (1644) **1 :** relating to, engaged in, or devoted to missions **2 :** characteristic of a missionary
missionary position *n* [fr. the name given to the position by Trobriand islanders] (1948) **:** a coital position in which the female lies on her back with the male on top and with his face opposite hers
mission creep *n* (1991) **:** the gradual broadening of the original objectives of a mission or organization
mis·sion·er \ˈmi-sh(ə-)nər\ *n* (1654) **:** MISSIONARY
mis·sion·ize \ˈmi-shə-ˌnīz\ *vb* **-ized; -iz·ing** *vi* (1826) **:** to carry on missionary work ∼ *vt* **:** to do missionary work among — **mis·sion·i·za·tion** \ˌmi-shə-nə-ˈzā-shən\ *n* — **mis·sion·iz·er** \ˈmi-shə-ˌnī-zər\ *n*
Mis·sis·sip·pi·an \ˌmi-sə-ˈsi-pē-ən, (ˌ)mis-ˈsi-\ *adj* [*Mississippi* River] (1835) **1 :** of or relating to Mississippi, its people, or the Mississippi River **2 :** of, relating to, or being the period of the Paleozoic era in No. America following the Devonian and preceding the Pennsylvanian or the corresponding system of rocks — see GEOLOGIC TIME table — **Mississippian** *n*
mis·sive \ˈmi-siv\ *n* [MF *lettre missive,* lit., letter intended to be sent] (1501) **:** a written communication **:** LETTER
miss·out \ˈmis-ˌau̇t\ *n* (1945) **:** a throw of dice that loses the main bet
miss out *vt* (1855) *Brit* **:** to leave out **:** OMIT
mis·speak \ˌmis-ˈspēk\ *vb* **-spoke** \-ˈspōk\; **-spo·ken** \-ˈspō-kən\; **-speak·ing** *vt* (14c) **1 :** to speak (as a word) incorrectly **2 :** to express (oneself) imperfectly or incorrectly ⟨claims now that he *misspoke* himself⟩ ∼ *vi* **:** to speak incorrectly **:** misspeak oneself
mis·spell \ˌmis-ˈspel\ *vt* (1655) **:** to spell incorrectly
mis·spell·ing \-ˈspe-liŋ\ *n* (1807) **:** an incorrect spelling
mis·spend \ˌmis-ˈspend\ *vt* **-spent** \-ˈspent\; **-spend·ing** (14c) **:** to spend wrongly **:** SQUANDER ⟨a *misspent* life⟩
mis·state \ˌmis-ˈstāt\ *vt* (1650) **:** to state incorrectly **:** give a false account of — **mis·state·ment** \-mənt\ *n*
mis·step \-ˈstep\ *n* (1788) **1 :** a mistake in judgment or action **:** BLUNDER **2 :** a wrong step
mis·sus *or* **mis·sis** \ˈmi-səz, -səs, *esp Southern* -zəz\ *n* [alter. of *mistress*] (1790) **1** *dial* **:** MISTRESS 1a **2 :** WIFE ⟨men spend money on themselves, but argue over every dime the ∼ wants —W. A. Lydgate⟩
missy \ˈmi-sē\ *n* (1676) **:** a young girl **:** MISS
¹**mist** \ˈmist\ *n* [ME, fr. OE; akin to MD *mist* mist, Gk *omichlē*] (bef. 12c) **1 :** water in the form of particles floating or falling in the atmosphere at or near the surface of the earth and approaching the form of rain **2 :** something that obscures understanding ⟨∼*s* of antiquity⟩ **3 :** a film before the eyes **4 a :** a cloud of small particles or objects suggestive of a mist **b :** a suspension of a finely divided liquid in a gas **c :** a fine spray **5 :** a drink of liquor served over cracked ice
²**mist** *vi* (bef. 12c) **1 :** to be or become misty **2 :** to become moist or blurred ∼ *vt* **:** to cover or spray with or convert to mist
mis·tak·able \mə-ˈstā-kə-bəl\ *adj* (1646) **:** capable of being misunderstood or mistaken
¹**mis·take** \mə-ˈstāk\ *vb* **mis·took** \-ˈstu̇k\; **mis·tak·en** \-ˈstā-kən\; **mis·tak·ing** [ME] *vt* (14c) **1 :** to blunder in the choice of ⟨*mistook* her way in the dark⟩ **2 a :** to misunderstand the meaning or intention of **:** MISINTERPRET ⟨don't ∼ me, I mean exactly what I said⟩ **b :** to make a wrong judgment of the character or ability of **3 :** to identify wrongly **:** confuse with another ⟨I *mistook* him for his brother⟩ ∼ *vi* **:** to be wrong ⟨you *mistook* when you thought I laughed at you —Thomas Hardy⟩ — **mis·tak·en·ly** *adv* — **mis·tak·er** *n*
²**mistake** *n* (1600) **1 :** a wrong judgment **:** MISUNDERSTANDING **2 :** a wrong action or statement proceeding from faulty judgment, inadequate knowledge, or inattention ***syn*** see ERROR
¹**mis·ter** \ˈmis-tər, *for 1* ˌmis-tər *or in rapid speech* (ˌ)mis(t)\ *n* [alter. of ¹*master*] (1551) **1** *cap* **:** MR. — used sometimes in writing instead of *Mr.* **2 :** SIR — used without a name as a generalized term of direct address of a man who is a stranger ⟨hey, ∼, do you want to buy a paper⟩ **3 :** HUSBAND
²**mist·er** \ˈmis-tər\ *n* [²*mist* + ²*-er*] (1973) **:** a device for spraying a mist
mis·think \ˌmis-ˈthiŋk\ *vb* **-thought** \-ˈthȯt\; **-think·ing** *vi* (ca. 1530) *archaic* **:** to think mistakenly or unfavorably ∼ *vt, archaic* **:** to think badly or unfavorably of
mis·tle·toe \ˈmi-səl-ˌtō, *chiefly Brit* ˈmi-zəl-\ *n* [ME *mistilto,* fr. OE *misteltān,* fr. *mistel* mistletoe + *tān* twig; akin to OHG & OS *mistil* mistletoe and to OHG *zein* twig] (bef. 12c) **:** a European semiparasitic green shrub (*Viscum album* of the family Loranthaceae, the mistletoe family) with thick leaves, small yellowish flowers, and waxy-white glutinous berries; *broadly* **:** any of various plants of the mistletoe family (as of an American genus *Phoradendron*) resembling the true mistletoe

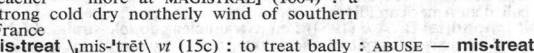

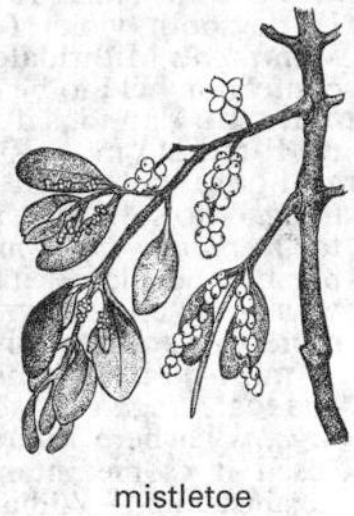
mistletoe

mist net *n* (1955) **:** a finely woven large mesh net erected to entangle and capture birds or bats in flight
mis·tral \ˈmis-trəl, mi-ˈsträl\ *n* [F, fr. Occitan, fr. *mistral* masterful, fr. LL *magistralis* of a teacher — more at MAGISTRAL] (1604) **:** a strong cold dry northerly wind of southern France
mis·treat \ˌmis-ˈtrēt\ *vt* (15c) **:** to treat badly **:** ABUSE — **mis·treat·ment** \-mənt\ *n*
mis·tress \ˈmis-trəs\ *n* [ME *maistresse,* fr. AF *mestresse,* fem. of *mestre* master — more at MASTER] (14c) **1 :** a woman who has power, authority, or ownership: as **a :** the female head of a household **b :** a woman who employs or supervises servants **c :** a woman who is in charge of a school or other establishment **d :** a woman of the Scottish nobility having a status comparable to that of a master **2 a** *chiefly Brit* **:** a female teacher or tutor **b :** a woman who has achieved mastery in some field **3 :** something personified as female that rules, directs, or dominates ⟨when Rome was ∼ of the world⟩ **4 a :** a woman other than his wife with whom a married man has a continuing sexual relationship **b** *archaic* **:** SWEETHEART **5 a —** used archaically as a title prefixed to the name of a married or unmarried woman **b** *chiefly Southern & Midland* **:** MRS. 1a
mistress of ceremonies (1952) **:** a woman who presides at a public ceremony or who acts as hostess of a stage, radio, or television show
mis·tri·al \ˈmis-ˌtrī(-ə)l\ *n* (1628) **:** a trial that has no legal effect by reason of some error or serious prejudicial misconduct in the proceedings
¹**mis·trust** \ˌmis-ˈtrəst\ *n* (14c) **:** a lack of confidence **:** DISTRUST ***syn*** see UNCERTAINTY — **mis·trust·ful** \-fəl\ *adj* — **mis·trust·ful·ly** \-fə-lē\ *adv* — **mis·trust·ful·ness** *n*
²**mistrust** *vt* (14c) **1 :** to have no trust or confidence in **:** SUSPECT ⟨∼*ed* his neighbors⟩ **2 :** to doubt the truth, validity, or effectiveness of ⟨∼*ed* his own judgment⟩ **3 :** SURMISE ⟨your mind ∼*ed* there was something wrong —Robert Frost⟩ ∼ *vi* **:** to be suspicious
misty \ˈmis-tē\ *adj* **mist·i·er; -est** (bef. 12c) **1 a :** obscured by mist **b :** consisting of or marked by mist **2 a :** INDISTINCT ⟨a ∼ recollection of the event⟩ **b :** VAGUE, CONFUSED ⟨avoided the large, vague, ∼ issues —Reuben Abel⟩ **3 :** TEARFUL — **mist·i·ly** \-tə-lē\ *adv* — **mist·i·ness** \-tē-nəs\ *n*
misty–eyed \ˈmis-tē-ˌīd\ *adj* (1895) **1 :** having tearful eyes **2 :** DREAMY, SENTIMENTAL ⟨∼ recollections⟩
mis·un·der·stand \(ˌ)mi-ˌsən-dər-ˈstand\ *vt* **-stood** \-ˈstu̇d\; **-stand·ing** (13c) **1 :** to fail to understand **2 :** to interpret incorrectly
mis·un·der·stand·ing *n* (15c) **1 :** a failure to understand **:** MISINTERPRETATION **2 :** QUARREL, DISAGREEMENT
mis·us·age \ˌmis-ˈyü-sij, ˌmish-, -zij\ *n* (1555) **1 :** bad treatment **:** ABUSE **2 :** wrong or improper use (as of words)
¹**mis·use** \-ˈyüz\ *vt* [ME, partly fr. *mis-* + *usen* to use; partly fr. MF *mesuser* to abuse, fr. OF, fr. *mes-* + *user* to use] (14c) **1 :** to use incorrectly **:** MISAPPLY ⟨*misused* his talents⟩ **2 :** ABUSE, MISTREAT ⟨*misused* his servants⟩ — **mis·us·er** *n*
²**mis·use** \-ˈyüs\ *n* (14c) **:** incorrect or improper use **:** MISAPPLICATION
¹**mite** \ˈmīt\ *n* [ME, fr. OE *mīte;* akin to MD *mite* mite, small copper coin] (bef. 12c) **:** any of numerous small acarid arachnids that often infest animals, plants, and stored foods and include important disease vectors
²**mite** *n* [ME, fr. MF or MD; MF, small Flemish copper coin, fr. MD] (14c) **1 :** a small coin or sum of money **2 a :** a very little **:** BIT **b :** a very small object or creature — **a mite :** SOMEWHAT, RATHER ⟨could be that I am *a mite* prejudiced —John Fischer⟩
¹**mi·ter** *or* **mi·tre** \ˈmī-tər\ *n* [ME *mitre,* fr. AF, fr. L *mitra* headband, turban, fr. Gk] (14c) **1 :** a liturgical headdress worn by bishops and abbots **2** [perh. fr. *miter* headdress] **a :** a surface forming the beveled end or edge of a piece where a joint is made by cutting two pieces at an angle and fitting them together **b :** MITER JOINT
²**miter** *or* **mitre** *vt* **mi·tered** *or* **mi·tred; mi·ter·ing** *or* **mi·tring** \ˈmī-tə-riŋ\ (14c) **1 :** to confer a miter on **2 a :** to match or fit together in a miter joint **b :** to bevel the ends of for making a miter joint — **mi·ter·er** \ˈmī-tər-ər\ *n*
miter box *n* (1678) **:** a device for guiding a handsaw at the proper angle in making a miter joint in wood
miter joint *n* (1688) **:** a usu. perpendicular joint made by fastening together parts with the ends cut at an angle

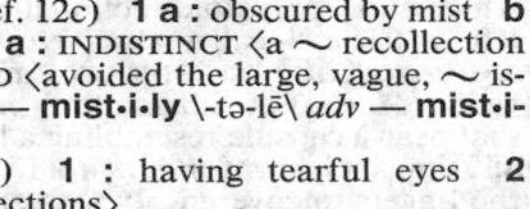

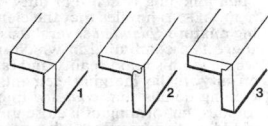

miter joint: *1* plain, *2* milled, *3* rabbeted

miter square *n* (1676) : a bevel with an immovable arm at an angle of 45 degrees for striking marking lines; *also* : a square with an arm adjustable to any angle

Mith·ra·ic \mi-ˈthrā-ik\ *adj* [LGk *mithraikos* of Mithras, ancient Persian god of light, fr. Gk *Mithras,* fr. OPers *Mithra*] (1678) : of or relating to a mystery cult for men of Iranian origin that flourished in the late Roman empire — **Mith·ra·ism** \ˈmith-rə-ˌi-zəm, -(ˌ)rā-\ *n* — **Mith·ra·ist** \mi-ˈthrā-ist\ *n or adj*

mith·ri·date \ˈmith-rə-ˌdāt\ *n* [ML *mithridatum,* fr. LL *mithridatium,* fr. L, dogtooth violet (used as an antidote), fr. Gk *mithridation,* fr. *Mithridatēs* Mithridates VI] (1528) : an antidote against poison; *esp* : a confection held to be effective against poison

mi·ti·cide \ˈmī-tə-ˌsīd\ *n* [ˡmite] (1946) : an agent used to kill mites — **mi·ti·cid·al** \ˌmī-tə-ˈsī-dᵊl\ *adj*

mit·i·gate \ˈmi-tə-ˌgāt\ *vt* **-gat·ed; -gat·ing** [ME, fr. L *mitigatus,* pp. of *mitigare* to soften, fr. *mitis* soft + *-igare* (akin to L *agere* to drive); akin to OIr *moíth* soft — more at AGENT] (15c) **1** : to cause to become less harsh or hostile : MOLLIFY **2 a** : to make less severe or painful : ALLEVIATE **b** : EXTENUATE *syn* see RELIEVE — **mit·i·ga·tion** \ˌmi-tə-ˈgā-shən\ *n* — **mit·i·ga·tive** \ˈmi-tə-ˌgā-tiv\ *adj* — **mit·i·ga·tor** \-ˌgā-tər\ *n* — **mit·i·ga·to·ry** \ˈmi-ti-gə-ˌtȯr-ē\ *adj*

usage Mitigate is sometimes used as an intransitive (followed by *against*) where *militate* might be expected. Even though Faulkner used it ⟨some intangible and invisible social force that *mitigates* against him —William Faulkner⟩ and one critic thinks it should be called an American idiom, it is usu. considered a mistake.

mitochondrial DNA *n* (1964) : an extranuclear double-stranded DNA found exclusively in mitochondria that in most eukaryotes is a circular molecule and is maternally inherited — abbr. *mtDNA*

mi·to·chon·dri·on \ˌmī-tə-ˈkän-drē-ən\ *n, pl* **-dria** \-drē-ə\ [NL, fr. Gk *mitos* thread + *chondrion,* dim. of *chondros* grain] (1901) : any of various round or long cellular organelles of most eukaryotes that are found outside the nucleus, produce energy for the cell through cellular respiration, and are rich in fats, proteins, and enzymes — see CELL illustration — **mi·to·chon·dri·al** \-drē-əl\ *adj*

mi·to·gen \ˈmī-tə-jən\ *n* [*mitosis* + *-gen*] (1946) : a substance that induces mitosis — **mi·to·gen·ic** \ˌmi-tə-ˈje-nik\ *adj* — **mi·to·ge·nic·i·ty** \-jə-ˈni-sə-tē\ *n*

mi·to·my·cin \ˌmī-tə-ˈmī-sᵊn\ *n* [ISV *mito-* (prob. fr. NL *mitosis*) + *-mycin*] (1956) : a complex of antibiotic substances that is produced by a Japanese streptomyces (*Streptomyces caespitosus*); *esp* : one form $C_{15}H_{18}N_4O_5$ that inhibits DNA synthesis and is used as an antineoplastic agent

mi·to·sis \mī-ˈtō-səs\ *n, pl* **-to·ses** \-ˌsēz\ [NL, fr. Gk *mitos* thread] (1887) **1** : a process that takes place in the nucleus of a dividing cell, involves typically a series of steps consisting of prophase, metaphase, anaphase, and telophase, and results in the formation of two new nuclei each having the same number of chromosomes as the parent nucleus — compare MEIOSIS **2** : cell division in which mitosis occurs — **mi·tot·ic** \-ˈtä-tik\ *adj* — **mi·tot·i·cal·ly** \-ti-k(ə-)lē\ *adv*

mi·tral \ˈmī-trəl\ *adj* (1610) **1** : resembling a miter **2** : of, relating to, being, or adjoining a mitral valve or orifice

mitral valve *n* (1696) : a cardiac valve consisting of two triangular flaps which allow only unidirectional blood flow from the left atrium to the left ventricle — called also *bicuspid valve*

mi·tre·wort *also* **mi·ter·wort** \ˈmī-tər-ˌwərt, -ˌwȯrt\ *n* (1771) : any of a genus (*Mitella*) of rhizomatous perennial herbs of the saxifrage family that bear a capsule resembling a bishop's miter

mitt \ˈmit\ *n* [short for *mitten*] (1757) **1 a** : a woman's glove that leaves the fingers uncovered **b** : MITTEN 1 **c** : a baseball catcher's or first baseman's glove made in the style of a mitten **2** *slang* : HAND

mit·ten \ˈmi-tᵊn\ *n* [ME *mitain,* fr. AF, prob. fr. OF *mite,* name for a cat] (14c) **1** : a covering for the hand and wrist having a separate section for the thumb only **2** : MITT 1a — **mit·tened** \-tᵊnd\ *adj*

mit·ti·mus \ˈmi-tə-məs\ *n* [L, we send, fr. *mittere* to send] (1591) : a warrant of commitment to prison

mitz·vah \ˈmits-və\ *n, pl* **mitz·voth** \-ˌvōt, -ˌvōth, -ˌvōs\ *or* **mitz·vahs** [Heb *miṣwāh*] (1723) **1** : a commandment of the Jewish law **2** : a meritorious or charitable act

ˡ**mix** \ˈmiks\ *vb* [ME, back-formation fr. *mixte* mixed, fr. AF, fr. L *mixtus,* pp. of *miscēre* to mix; akin to Gk *mignynai* to mix] *vt* (15c) **1 a (1)** : to combine or blend into one mass **(2)** : to combine with another **b** : to bring into close association ⟨~ business with pleasure⟩ **2 a** : to form by mixing components ⟨~ a drink at the bar⟩ **b** : to produce (a sound recording) by electronically combining or adjusting sounds from more than one source **3** : CONFUSE — often used with *up* ⟨~*es* things up in his eagerness to speak out —Irving Howe⟩ ~ *vi* **1 a** : to become mixed **b** : to be capable of mixing **2** : to enter into relations : ASSOCIATE **3** : CROSSBREED **4** : to become involved : PARTICIPATE ⟨decided not to ~ in politics⟩ — **mix·able** \ˈmik-sə-bəl\ *adj* — **mix it up** : to engage in a fight, contest, or dispute

syn MIX, MINGLE, COMMINGLE, BLEND, MERGE, COALESCE, AMALGAMATE, FUSE mean to combine into a more or less uniform whole. MIX may or may not imply loss of each element's identity ⟨*mix* the salad greens⟩ ⟨*mix* a drink⟩. MINGLE usu. suggests that the elements are still somewhat distinguishable or separately active ⟨fear *mingled* with anticipation in my mind⟩. COMMINGLE implies a closer or more thorough mingling ⟨a sense of duty *commingled* with a fierce pride drove her⟩. BLEND implies that the elements as such disappear in the resulting mixture ⟨*blended* several teas to create a balanced flavor⟩. MERGE suggests a combining in which one or more elements are lost in the whole ⟨in his mind reality and fantasy *merged*⟩. COALESCE implies an affinity in the merging elements and usu. a resulting organic unity ⟨telling details that *coalesce* into a striking portrait⟩. AMALGAMATE implies the forming of a close union without complete loss of individual identities ⟨refugees who were readily *amalgamated* into the community⟩. FUSE stresses oneness and indissolubility of the resulting product ⟨a building in which modernism and classicism are *fused*⟩.

²**mix** *n* (ca. 1595) **1** : an act or process of mixing **2** : a product of mixing: as **a** : a commercially prepared mixture of food ingredients ⟨a cake ~⟩ **b** : a combination of different kinds ⟨the right ~ of jobs, people and amenities —*London Times*⟩ **3** : MIXER 2b

mixed \ˈmikst\ *adj* [ME *mixte*] (15c) **1** : combining characteristics of more than one kind; *specif* : combining features of two or more systems of government ⟨a ~ constitution⟩ **2** : made up of or involving individuals or items of more than one kind: as **a** : made up of or involving persons differing in race, national origin, religion, or class **b** : made up of or involving individuals of both sexes ⟨~ company⟩ **3** : including or accompanied by inconsistent, incompatible, or contrary elements ⟨~ emotions⟩ ⟨received ~ reviews⟩ ⟨a ~ blessing⟩ **4** : deriving from two or more races or breeds ⟨a stallion of ~ blood⟩

mixed alphabet *n* (1931) : an alphabet (as in a cryptographic system) that has been rearranged or disordered systematically or randomly

mixed bag *n* (1919) **1** : a miscellaneous collection : ASSORTMENT **2** : one having both positive and negative qualities or aspects ⟨his performance was a *mixed bag*⟩

mixed bud *n* (1900) : a bud that produces a branch and leaves as well as flowers

mixed drink *n* (1703) : an alcoholic beverage prepared from two or more ingredients

mixed farming *n* (1872) : the growing of food or cash crops, feed crops, and livestock on the same farm

mixed grill *n* (1910) : meats (as lamb chop, kidney, and bacon) and vegetables broiled together and served on one plate

mixed marriage *n* (1649) : a marriage between persons of different races or religions

mixed martial arts *n* (1990) : a contact sport that allows a wide range of fighting techniques including striking, kicking, and grappling

mixed–media *adj* (1962) : MULTIMEDIA

mixed metaphor *n* (ca. 1748) : a figure of speech combining inconsistent or incongruous metaphors

mixed nerve *n* (1861) : a nerve containing both sensory and motor fibers

mixed number *n* (1542) : a number (as 5⅔) composed of an integer and a fraction

mixed–up \ˈmikst-ˈəp\ *adj* (1862) : marked by bewilderment, perplexity, or disorder : CONFUSED

mixed–use \ˈmikst-ˈyüs\ *adj* (1972) : used or suitable for several different functions ⟨a ~ building⟩

mix·er \ˈmik-sər\ *n* (1598) **1** : one that mixes: as **a (1)** : one whose work is mixing the ingredients of a product **(2)** : one who balances and controls the dialogue, music, and sound effects to be recorded for or with a motion picture or television **b** : a container, device, or machine for mixing **c** : a game, stunt, or dance used at a get-together to give members of the group an opportunity to meet one another in a friendly and informal atmosphere; *also* : the get-together itself **2** : one that mixes with others: as **a** : a person considered in regard to casual sociability ⟨was shy and a poor ~⟩ **b** : a nonalcoholic beverage (as ginger ale) used in a mixed drink

mix·ol·o·gy \mik-ˈsä-lə-jē\ *n* (1872) : the art or skill of preparing mixed drinks — **mix·ol·o·gist** \-jist\ *n*

mix·tape \ˈmiks-ˌtāp\ *n* (1991) : a compilation of songs recorded (as onto a cassette tape or a CD) from various sources

Mix·tec \mēs-ˈtek, mis-, mēsh-, mish-\ *n, pl* **Mixtec** *or* **Mixtecs** [AmerSp *mixteco,* fr. Nahuatl *mixtēcatl,* lit., inhabitant of *Mixtlan* (mountainous area of western Oaxaca), fr. *mix-* cloud + *-tēcatl* person (from)] (1850) **1** : the language of the Mixtec people **2** : a member of an American Indian people of the state of Oaxaca, Mexico

mix·ture \ˈmiks-chər\ *n* [ME, fr. AF & L; AF, fr. L *mixtura,* fr. *mixtus*] (15c) **1 a** : the act, the process, or an instance of mixing **b (1)** : the state of being mixed **(2)** : the relative proportions of constituents; *esp* : the proportion of fuel to air produced in a carburetor **2** : a product of mixing : COMBINATION: as **a** : a portion of matter consisting of two or more components in varying proportions that retain their own properties **b** : a fabric woven of variously colored threads **c** : a combination of several different kinds

mix–up \ˈmiks-ˌəp\ *n* (1841) **1** : a state or instance of confusion **2** : MIXTURE **3** : CONFLICT, FIGHT

mi·zu·na \mi-ˈzü-nə\ *n* [Jp, fr. *mizu* water + *na* greens] (1976) : a Japanese mustard (*Brassica rapa nipposinica* syn. *B. rapa japonica*) having mild tasting deeply dissected leaves used esp. in salads; *also* : its leaves

ˡ**miz·zen** *also* **miz·en** \ˈmi-zᵊn\ *n* [ME *mesan,* prob. fr. OSp *mesana* sail set amidships, fr. Catal *mitjana,* fr. fem. of *mitjan* of the middle, fr. L *medianus* — more at MEDIAN] (15c) **1** : a fore-and-aft sail set on the mizzenmast **2** : MIZZENMAST

²**mizzen** *also* **mizen** *adj* (15c) : of or relating to the mizzenmast

miz·zen·mast \-ˌmast, -məst\ *n* (15c) : the mast aft or next aft of the mainmast in a ship

ˡ**miz·zle** \ˈmi-zəl\ *vi* **miz·zled; miz·zling** \ˈmi-zə-liŋ, ˈmiz-liŋ\ [ME *misellen;* akin to D dial. *mizzelen* to drizzle, MD *mist* fog, mist] (15c) : to rain in very fine drops : DRIZZLE — **mizzle** *n* — **miz·zly** \ˈmi-zə-lē, ˈmiz-lē\ *adj*

²**mizzle** *vi* **miz·zled; miz·zling** \ˈmi-zə-liŋ, ˈmiz-liŋ\ [origin unknown] (1781) *chiefly Brit* : to depart suddenly

Mk *abbr* Mark

MKS *abbr* meter-kilogram-second

mkt *abbr* market

mktg *abbr* marketing

ml *abbr* milliliter

mL *abbr* **1** millilambert **2** milliliter

MLA *abbr* **1** Member of the Legislative Assembly **2** Modern Language Association

MLB *abbr* Major League Baseball

MLD *abbr* minimum lethal dose

MLF *abbr* multilateral force

Mlle *abbr* [F] mademoiselle

Mlles *abbr* [F] mesdemoiselles

MLS *abbr* **1** Major League Soccer **2** master of library science

MLW *abbr* mean low water

mm *abbr* **1** measures **2** millimeter

MM *abbr* [F] messieurs

MMA *abbr* mixed martial arts

Mme *abbr* [F] madame

Mmes *abbr* [F] mesdames

mmf *abbr* magnetomotive force

MMORPG *abbr* massively multiplayer online role-playing game

MMPI *abbr* Minnesota Multiphasic Personality Inventory

MMR *abbr* measles-mumps-rubella (vaccine)

Mn *symbol* manganese
MN *abbr* **1** magnetic north **2** Minnesota
MNC *abbr* multinational company; multinational corporation
1**mne·mon·ic** \ni-ˈmä-nik\ *adj* [Gk *mnēmonikos,* fr. *mnēmōn* mindful, fr. *mimnēskesthai* to remember — more at MIND] (1672) **1 :** assisting or intended to assist memory; *also* **:** of or relating to mnemonics **2 :** of or relating to memory — **mne·mon·i·cal·ly** \-ni-k(ə-)lē\ *adv*
2**mnemonic** *n* (1842) **:** a mnemonic device or code
mne·mon·ics \ni-ˈmä-niks\ *n pl but sing in constr* (ca. 1721) **:** a technique of improving the memory
Mne·mos·y·ne \ni-ˈmä-sə-nē, -zə-\ *n* [L, fr. Gk *Mnēmosynē*] (1582) **:** the Greek goddess of memory and mother of the Muses by Zeus
mo *abbr* month
1**Mo** *abbr* **1** Missouri **2** Monday
2**Mo** *symbol* molybdenum
1**MO** \ˈem-ˈō\ *n, often not cap* (1940) **:** MODUS OPERANDI
2**MO** *abbr* **1** mail order **2** medical officer **3** Missouri **4** money order
-mo *n suffix* [duodecimo] — after numerals or their names to indicate the number of leaves made by folding a sheet of paper ⟨sixteen*mo*⟩ ⟨16*mo*⟩
moa \ˈmō-ə\ *n* [Maori] (1839) **:** any of various usu. very large extinct flightless birds of New Zealand of a ratite order (Dinornithiformes) including one (*Dinornis giganteus* of the family Dinornithidae) nearly 12 feet (3.7 meters) in height
Mo·ab·ite \ˈmō-ə-ˌbīt\ *n* [ME, fr. LL *Moabita, Moabites,* fr. Gk *Mōabitēs,* fr. *Mōab* Moab, ancient kingdom in Syria] (14c) **:** a member of an ancient Semitic people related to the Hebrews — **Moabite** *or* **Mo·ab·it·ish** \-ˌbī-tish\ *adj*
1**moan** \ˈmōn\ *n* [ME *mone,* fr. OE **mān*] (13c) **1 :** LAMENTATION, COMPLAINT **2 :** a low prolonged sound of pain or of grief
2**moan** *vt* (14c) **1 :** to bewail audibly **:** LAMENT **2 :** to utter with moans ~ *vi* **1 :** LAMENT, COMPLAIN **2 a :** to make a moan **:** GROAN **b :** to emit a sound resembling a moan — **moan·er** \ˈmō-nər\ *n*
moat \ˈmōt\ *n* [ME *mote,* fr. AF *mote, motte* mound, moat] (14c) **1 :** a deep and wide trench around the rampart of a fortified place (as a castle) that is usu. filled with water **2 :** a channel resembling a moat (as about a seamount or for confinement of animals in a zoo) — **moat·ed** \ˈmō-təd\ *adj* — **moat·like** \-ˌlīk\ *adj*
1**mob** \ˈmäb\ *n* [L *mobile vulgus* vacillating crowd] (1688) **1 :** a large or disorderly crowd; *esp* **:** one bent on riotous or destructive action **2 :** the lower classes of a community **:** MASSES, RABBLE **3** *chiefly Austral* **:** a flock, drove, or herd of animals **4 :** a criminal set **:** GANG; *esp, often cap* **:** MAFIA 1 **5** *chiefly Brit* **:** a group of people **:** CROWD ***syn*** see CROWD — **mob·bish** \ˈmä-bish\ *adj*
2**mob** *vt* **mobbed; mob·bing** (1696) **1 :** to crowd about and attack or annoy ⟨*mobbed* by autograph hunters⟩ **2 :** to crowd into or around
mob·cap \ˈmäb-ˌkap\ *n* [*mob* woman's cap + *cap*] (1785) **:** a woman's indoor cap made with a high full crown and often tied under the chin
mo·be pearl *or* **mo·bé pearl** \ˈmō-ˌbā-, ˌmō-ˈ\ *n, often cap M* [alter. of *mabe*] (1955) **:** MABE
1**mo·bile** \ˈmō-bəl, -ˌbī-əl *also* -ˌbēl\ *adj* [ME *mobyll,* fr. AF *moble,* fr. L *mobilis,* fr. *movēre* to move] (15c) **1 :** capable of moving or being moved **:** MOVABLE ⟨a ~ missile launcher⟩ **2 a :** changeable in appearance, mood, or purpose ⟨~ face⟩ **b :** ADAPTABLE, VERSATILE **3 :** MIGRATORY **4 a :** characterized by the mixing of social groups **b :** having the opportunity for or undergoing a shift in status within the levels of a society ⟨socially ~ workers⟩ **5 :** marked by the use of vehicles for transportation ⟨~ warfare⟩ **6 :** of or relating to a mobile **7 :** CELLULAR 3 ⟨a ~ phone⟩ — **mo·bil·i·ty** \mō-ˈbi-lə-tē\ *n*
2**mo·bile** \ˈmō-ˌbēl\ *n* (1937) **1 :** a construction or sculpture frequently of wire and sheet metal shapes with parts that can be set in motion by air currents; *also* **:** a similar structure (as of paper or plastic) suspended so that it moves in a current of air **2** *Brit* **:** CELL PHONE, MOBILE PHONE
-mobile *n comb form* [*automobile*] **1 :** motorized vehicle ⟨snow*mobile*⟩ **2 :** automotive vehicle bringing services to the public ⟨blood*mobile*⟩ ⟨book*mobile*⟩
mobile home *n* (1934) **:** a dwelling structure built on a steel chassis and fitted with wheels that is intended to be hauled to a usu. permanent site — compare MOTOR HOME
mobile phone *n* (1975) **:** CELL PHONE
mo·bi·lise *chiefly Brit var of* MOBILIZE
mo·bi·li·za·tion \ˌmō-bə-lə-ˈzā-shən\ *n* (1799) **1 :** the act of mobilizing **2 :** the state of being mobilized
mo·bi·lize \ˈmō-bə-ˌlīz\ *vb* **-lized; -liz·ing** *vt* (1838) **1 :** to put into movement or circulation ⟨~ financial assets⟩ **b :** to release (something stored in the organism) for bodily use **2 a :** to assemble and make ready for war duty **b :** to marshal (as resources) for action ⟨~ support for a proposal⟩ ~ *vi* **:** to undergo mobilization
Mö·bi·us strip \ˈmœ-bē-əs-, ˈmə(r)-, ˈmō-\ *n* [August F. *Möbius* †1868 Ger. mathematician] (1904) **:** a one-sided surface that is constructed from a rectangle by holding one end fixed, rotating the opposite end through 180 degrees, and joining it to the first end

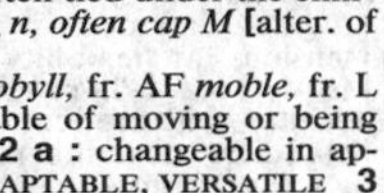

Möbius strip

mo·bled \ˈmä-bəld\ *adj* [pp. of *moble* to muffle, prob. freq. of *mob* to muffle, of unknown origin] (ca. 1601) **:** being wrapped or muffled in or as if in a hood
mob·oc·ra·cy \mä-ˈbä-krə-sē\ *n* (1754) **1 :** rule by the mob **2 :** the mob as a ruling class — **mob·o·crat·ic** \ˌmä-bə-ˈkra-tik\ *adj*
mob·ster \ˈmäb-stər\ *n* (1917) **:** a member of a criminal gang
moc \ˈmäk\ *n* (1913) **:** MOCCASIN 1
moc·ca·sin \ˈmä-kə-sən\ *n* [Virginia Algonquian *mockasin*] (ca. 1612) **1 a :** a soft leather heelless shoe or boot with the sole brought up the sides of the foot and over the toes where it is joined with a puckered seam to a U-shaped piece lying on top of the foot **b :** a regular shoe having a seam on the forepart of the vamp imitating the seam of a moccasin **2 a :** WATER MOCCASIN **b :** a snake (as of the genus *Natrix*) resembling a water moccasin — **moc·ca·sined** \-sənd\ *adj*
moccasin flower *n* (1680) **:** any of several lady's slippers (genus *Cypripedium*); *esp* **:** a once common woodland orchid (*C. acaule*) of eastern No. America with pink or white moccasin-shaped flowers
mo·cha \ˈmō-kə\ *n* [*Mocha,* Yemen] (1773) **1 a** (1) **:** a superior Arabian coffee consisting of small green or yellowish beans (2) **:** a coffee of superior quality **b :** a flavoring made of a strong coffee infusion or of a mixture of cocoa or chocolate with coffee **2 :** a pliable suede-finished glove leather from African sheepskins **3 :** a dark chocolate-brown color
mo·chi \ˈmō-chē\ *n* [Jp] (1970) **:** a doughlike mass made from cooked and pounded glutinous rice used in Japan as an unbaked pastry
1**mock** \ˈmäk, ˈmȯk\ *vb* [ME, fr. *moker*] *vt* (15c) **1 :** to treat with contempt or ridicule **:** DERIDE **2 :** to disappoint the hopes of **3 :** DEFY, CHALLENGE **4 a :** to imitate (as a mannerism) closely **:** MIMIC **b :** to mimic in sport or derision ~ *vi* **:** JEER, SCOFF ***syn*** see RIDICULE, COPY — **mock·er** *n* — **mock·ing·ly** \ˈmä-kiŋ-lē, ˈmȯ-\ *adv*
2**mock** *n* (15c) **1 :** an act of ridicule or derision **:** JEER **2 :** one that is an object of derision or scorn **3 :** MOCKERY **4 a :** an act of imitation **b :** something made as an imitation
3**mock** *adj* (1548) **:** of, relating to, or having the character of an imitation **:** SIMULATED, FEIGNED ⟨the ~ solemnity of the parody⟩
4**mock** *adv* (ca. 1625) **:** in an insincere or counterfeit manner — usu. used in combination ⟨*mock*-serious⟩
mock·ery \ˈmä-k(ə-)rē, ˈmȯ-\ *n, pl* **-er·ies** (15c) **1 :** insulting or contemptuous action or speech **:** DERISION **2 :** a subject of laughter, derision, or sport **3 a :** a counterfeit appearance **:** IMITATION **b :** an insincere, contemptible, or impertinent imitation ⟨makes a ~ of justice⟩ **4 :** something ridiculously or impudently unsuitable
1**mock–he·ro·ic** \ˌmäk-hi-ˈrō-ik, ˌmȯk-\ *n* (ca. 1668) **:** a mock-heroic composition — called also *mock-epic*
2**mock–heroic** *adj* (1708) **:** ridiculing or burlesquing heroic style, character, or action ⟨a ~ poem⟩ — **mock–he·ro·i·cal·ly** \-i-k(ə-)lē\ *adv*
mock·ing·bird \ˈmä-kiŋ-ˌbərd, ˈmȯ-\ *n* (1676) **:** a common grayish No. American bird (*Mimus polyglottos*) related to the thrashers that is remarkable for its exact imitations of the notes of other birds
mock orange *n* (1731) **1 :** any of a genus (*Philadelphus*) of ornamental shrubs of which several are widely grown for their showy white flowers and that is either placed in the saxifrage or hydrangea families or in a family (Philadelphaceae) of its own — called also *philadelphus, syringa* **2 :** any of several usu. shrubby plants considered to resemble the orange
mock turtleneck *n* (1953) **1 :** a collar that is lower and usu. looser than a turtleneck and is not turned over **2 :** a garment with a mock turtleneck
mock turtle soup *n* (1783) **:** a soup made of meat (as calf's head or veal), wine, and spices in imitation of green turtle soup
mock·u·men·ta·ry \ˌmä-kyə-ˈmen-tə-rē, -ˈmen-trē\ *n, pl* **-ries** [blend of *mock* and *documentary*] (1965) **:** a facetious or satirical work (as a film) presented in the style of a documentary
mock–up \ˈmäk-ˌəp, ˈmȯk-\ *n* (1920) **1 :** a full-sized structural model built to scale chiefly for study, testing, or display **2 :** a working sample (as of a magazine) for reviewing format, layout, or content
1**mod** \ˈmäd\ *n* [prob. fr. 2*mod*] (1960) **:** one who wears mod clothes
2**mod** *adj* [short for *modern*] (1964) **1 :** of, relating to, or being the characteristic style of 1960s British youth culture **2 :** HIP, TRENDY
3**mod** *abbr* **1** moderate **2** modification; modified **3** modulo; modulus
mod·acryl·ic fiber \ˌmä-də-ˈkri-lik-\ *n* [*mod*ified *acrylic*] (1960) **:** any of various synthetic textile fibers that are long-chain polymers composed of 35 to 85 percent by weight of acrylonitrile units
mod·al \ˈmō-dᵊl\ *adj* [ML *modalis,* fr. L *modus*] (1569) **1 :** of or relating to modality in logic **2 :** containing provisions as to the mode of procedure or the manner of taking effect — used of a contract or legacy **3 :** of or relating to a musical mode **4 :** of or relating to structure as opposed to substance **5 :** of, relating to, or constituting a grammatical form or category characteristically indicating predication of an action or state in some manner other than as a simple fact **6 :** of or relating to a statistical mode — **mod·al·ly** \-dᵊl-ē\ *adv*
modal auxiliary *n* (ca. 1904) **:** an auxiliary verb (as *can, must, might, may*) that is characteristically used with a verb of predication and expresses a modal modification and that in English differs formally from other verbs in lacking *-s* and *-ing* forms
mo·dal·i·ty \mō-ˈda-lə-tē\ *n, pl* **-ties** (1545) **1 a :** the quality or state of being modal **b :** a modal quality or attribute **:** FORM **2 :** the classification of logical propositions according to their asserting or denying the possibility, impossibility, contingency, or necessity of their content **3 :** one of the main avenues of sensation (as vision) **4 :** a usu. physical therapeutic agency
mod con \ˌmäd-ˈkän\ *n* [fr. *mod. con.,* abbr. for *modern convenience*] (1934) *chiefly Brit* **:** a modern convenience — usu. used in pl.
1**mode** \ˈmōd\ *n* [ME *moede,* fr. L *modus* measure, manner, musical mode — more at METE] (14c) **1 a :** an arrangement of the eight diatonic notes or tones of an octave according to one of several fixed schemes of their intervals **b :** a rhythmical scheme (as in 13th and 14th century music) **2 :** 2MOOD 2 **3** [LL *modus,* fr. L] **a :** 2MOOD 1 **b :** the modal form of the assertion or denial of a logical proposition **4 a :** a particular form or variety of something ⟨flying and other ~s of transport⟩ **b :** a form or manner of expression **:** STYLE **5 :** a possible, customary, or preferred way of doing something ⟨explained in the usual solemn ~⟩ **6 a :** a manifestation, form, or arrangement of being; *specif* **:** a particular form or manifestation of an underlying substance **b :** a particular functioning arrangement or condition **:** STATUS ⟨a computer operating in parallel ~⟩ **7 a :** the most frequent value of a set of data **b :** a value of a random variable for which a function of probabilities defined on it achieves a relative maximum **8 :** any of various stationary vibration patterns of which an elastic body or oscillatory system is capable ⟨the vibration ~ of an airplane propeller blade⟩ ⟨the vibrational ~s of a molecule⟩ ***syn*** see METHOD
2**mode** *n* [F, fr. L *modus*] (1642) **:** a prevailing fashion or style (as of dress or behavior) ***syn*** see FASHION

\ə\ **abut** \ᵊ\ **kitten, F table** \ər\ **further** \a\ **ash** \ā\ **ace** \ä\ **mop, mar** \au̇\ **out** \ch\ **chin** \e\ **bet** \ē\ **easy** \g\ **go** \i\ **hit** \ī\ **ice** \j\ **job** \ŋ\ **sing** \ō\ **go** \ȯ\ **law** \ȯi\ **boy** \th\ **thin** \t͟h\ **the** \ü\ **loot** \u̇\ **foot** \y\ **yet** \zh\ **vision, beige** \k̲, ⁿ, œ, ue, ʸ\ *see* Guide to Pronunciation

1mod·el \ˈmä-dᵊl\ *n* [MF *modelle,* fr. OIt *modello,* fr. VL **modellus,* fr. L *modulus* small measure, fr. *modus*] (1575) **1** *obs* **:** a set of plans for a building **2** *dial Brit* **:** COPY, IMAGE **3 :** structural design ⟨a home on the ~ of an old farmhouse⟩ **4 :** a usu. miniature representation of something; *also* **:** a pattern of something to be made **5 :** an example for imitation or emulation **6 :** a person or thing that serves as a pattern for an artist; *esp* **:** one who poses for an artist **7 :** ARCHETYPE **8 :** an organism whose appearance a mimic imitates **9 :** one who is employed to display clothes or other merchandise **10 a :** a type or design of clothing **b :** a type or design of product (as a car) **11 :** a description or analogy used to help visualize something (as an atom) that cannot be directly observed **12 :** a system of postulates, data, and inferences presented as a mathematical description of an entity or state of affairs; *also* **:** a computer simulation based on such a system ⟨climate ~*s*⟩ **13 :** VERSION 3 **14 :** ANIMAL MODEL

syn MODEL, EXAMPLE, PATTERN, EXEMPLAR, IDEAL mean someone or something set before one for guidance or imitation. MODEL applies to something taken or proposed as worthy of imitation ⟨a decor that is a *model* of good taste⟩. EXAMPLE applies to a person to be imitated or in some contexts on no account to be imitated but to be regarded as a warning ⟨children tend to follow the *example* of their parents⟩. PATTERN suggests a clear and detailed archetype or prototype ⟨American industry set a *pattern* for others to follow⟩. EXEMPLAR suggests either a faultless example to be emulated or a perfect typification ⟨cited Joan of Arc as the *exemplar* of courage⟩. IDEAL implies the best possible exemplification either in reality or in conception ⟨never found a job that matched his *ideal*⟩.

2model *vb* **-eled** *or* **-elled; -el·ing** *or* **-el·ling** \ˈmäd-liŋ, ˈmä-dᵊl-iŋ\ *vt* (1625) **1 :** to plan or form after a pattern **:** SHAPE **2** *archaic* **:** to make into an organization (as an army, government, or parish) **3 a :** to shape or fashion in a plastic material **b :** to produce a representation or simulation of ⟨using a computer to ~ a problem⟩ **4 :** to construct or fashion in imitation of a particular model ⟨~*ed* its constitution on that of the U.S.⟩ **5 :** to display by wearing, using, or posing with ⟨~*ed* gowns⟩ ~ *vi* **1 :** to design or imitate forms **:** make a pattern ⟨enjoys ~*ing* in clay⟩ **2 :** to work or act as a fashion or art model — **mod·el·er** *also* **mod·el·ler** \ˈmäd-lər, ˈmä-dᵊl-ər\ *n*

3model *adj* (1844) **1 :** serving as or capable of serving as a pattern ⟨a ~ student⟩ **2 :** being a usu. miniature representation of something ⟨a ~ airplane⟩

1mo·dem \ˈmō-dəm *also* -ˌdem\ *n* [*mo*dulator + *dem*odulator] (ca. 1952) **:** a device that converts signals produced by one type of device (as a computer) to a form compatible with another (as a telephone)

2modem *vt* (1984) **:** to send (as data) via a modem

1mod·er·ate \ˈmä-d(ə-)rət\ *adj* [ME, fr. L *moderatus,* fr. pp. of *moderare* to moderate; akin to L *modus* measure] (15c) **1 a :** avoiding extremes of behavior or expression **:** observing reasonable limits ⟨a ~ drinker⟩ **b :** CALM, TEMPERATE **2 a :** tending toward the mean or average amount or dimension **b :** having average or less than average quality **:** MEDIOCRE **3 :** professing or characterized by political or social beliefs that are not extreme **4 :** limited in scope or effect **5 :** not expensive **:** reasonable or low in price **6** *of a color* **:** of medium lightness and medium chroma — **mod·er·ate·ly** *adv* — **mod·er·ate·ness** *n*

2mod·er·ate \ˈmä-də-ˌrāt\ *vb* **-at·ed; -at·ing** *vt* (15c) **1 :** to lessen the intensity or extremeness of ⟨the sun *moderated* the chill⟩ **2 :** to preside over or act as chairman of ~ *vi* **1 :** to act as a moderator **2 :** to become less violent, severe, or intense ⟨the wind began to ~⟩ — **mod·er·a·tion** \ˌmä-də-ˈrā-shən\ *n*

3mod·er·ate \ˈmä-d(ə-)rət\ *n* (1794) **:** one who holds moderate views or who belongs to a group favoring a moderate course or program

moderate breeze *n* (ca. 1881) **:** wind having a speed of about 13 to 18 miles (20 to 29 kilometers) per hour — see BEAUFORT SCALE table

moderate gale *n* (1703) **:** wind having a speed of 32 to 38 miles (51 to 61 kilometers) per hour — see BEAUFORT SCALE table

mo·der·a·to \ˌmä-də-ˈrä-(ˌ)tō\ *adv or adj* [It, fr. L *moderatus*] (ca. 1724) **:** MODERATE — used as a direction in music to indicate tempo

mod·er·a·tor \ˈmä-də-ˌrā-tər\ *n* (ca. 1560) **1 :** one who arbitrates **:** MEDIATOR **2 :** one who presides over an assembly, meeting, or discussion: as **a :** the presiding officer of a Presbyterian governing body **b :** the nonpartisan presiding officer of a town meeting **c :** the chairman of a discussion group **3 :** a substance (as graphite) used for slowing neutrons in a nuclear reactor — **mod·er·a·tor·ship** \-ˌship\ *n*

1mod·ern \ˈmä-dərn, ÷ˈmä-d(ə-)rən\ *adj* [LL *modernus,* fr. L *modo* just now, fr. *modus* measure — more at METE] (1585) **1 a :** of, relating to, or characteristic of the present or the immediate past **:** CONTEMPORARY **b :** of, relating to, or characteristic of a period extending from a relevant remote past to the present time **2 :** involving recent techniques, methods, or ideas **:** UP-TO-DATE **3** *cap* **:** of, relating to, or having the characteristics of the present or most recent period of development of a language **4 :** of or relating to modernism **:** MODERNIST — **mo·der·ni·ty** \mə-ˈdər-nə-tē, mä-, -ˈder-\ *n* — **mod·ern·ly** \ˈmä-dərn-lē\ *adv* — **mod·ern·ness** \-dərn-nəs\ *n*

2modern *n* (1585) **1 a :** a person of modern times or views **b :** an adherent of modernism **:** MODERNIST **2 :** a style of printing type distinguished by regularity of shape, precise curves, straight hairline serifs, and heavy downstrokes

mo·derne \mō-ˈdern, mə-\ *n, often cap* [F, modern] (1955) **:** ART DECO — **moderne** *adj*

Modern Greek *n* (1699) **:** Greek as used by the Greeks since the end of the medieval period

Modern Hebrew *n* (1949) **:** the Hebrew language in use in present-day Israel

mod·ern·i·sa·tion, mod·ern·ise *Brit var of* MODERNIZATION, MODERNIZE

mod·ern·ism \ˈmä-dər-ˌni-zəm\ *n* (1737) **1 :** a practice, usage, or expression peculiar to modern times **2** *often cap* **:** a tendency in theology to accommodate traditional religious teaching to contemporary thought and esp. to devalue supernatural elements **3 :** modern artistic or literary philosophy and practice; *esp* **:** a self-conscious break with the past and a search for new forms of expression — **mod·ern·ist** \-nist\ *n or adj* — **mod·ern·is·tic** \ˌmä-dər-ˈnis-tik\ *adj*

mod·ern·i·za·tion \ˌmä-dər-nə-ˈzā-shən\ *n* (1770) **1 :** the act of modernizing **:** the state of being modernized **2 :** something modernized **:** a modernized version

mod·ern·ize \ˈmä-dər-ˌnīz\ *vb* **-ized; -iz·ing** *vt* (1748) **:** to make modern (as in taste, style, or usage) ~ *vi* **:** to adopt modern ways — **mod·ern·iz·er** *n*

modern pentathlon *n* (ca. 1912) **:** a composite contest in which all contestants compete in a 300-meter freestyle swim, a 4000-meter cross-country run, a 5000-meter 30-jump equestrian steeplechase, épée fencing, and target shooting at 25 meters

mod·est \ˈmä-dəst\ *adj* [L *modestus* moderate; akin to L *modus* measure] (1565) **1 a :** placing a moderate estimate on one's abilities or worth **b :** neither bold nor self-assertive **:** tending toward diffidence **2 :** arising from or characteristic of a modest nature **3 :** observing the proprieties of dress and behavior **:** DECENT **4 a :** limited in size, amount, or scope ⟨a family of ~ means⟩ **b :** UNPRETENTIOUS ⟨a ~ home⟩ ***syn*** see SHY, CHASTE — **mod·est·ly** *adv*

mod·es·ty \ˈmä-də-stē\ *n* (1531) **1 :** freedom from conceit or vanity **2 :** propriety in dress, speech, or conduct

mo·di·cum \ˈmä-di-kəm *also* ˈmō-\ *n* [ME, fr. L, neut. of *modicus* moderate, fr. *modus* measure] (15c) **:** a small portion **:** a limited quantity

mod·i·fi·ca·tion \ˌmä-də-fə-ˈkā-shən\ *n* (1603) **1 :** the limiting of a statement **:** QUALIFICATION **2 :** 1MODE 6a **3 a :** the making of a limited change in something; *also* **:** the result of such a change **b :** a change in an organism caused by environmental factors **4 :** a limitation or qualification of the meaning of a word by another word, by an affix, or by internal change

mod·i·fi·er \ˈmä-də-ˌfī(-ə)r\ *n* (1583) **1 :** one that modifies **2 :** a word or phrase that makes specific the meaning of another word or phrase **3 :** a gene that modifies the effect of another

mod·i·fy \ˈmä-də-ˌfī\ *vb* **-fied; -fy·ing** [ME *modifien,* fr. AF *modifier,* fr. L *modificare* to measure, moderate, fr. *modus*] *vt* (14c) **1 :** to make less extreme **:** MODERATE **2 a :** to limit or restrict the meaning of esp. in a grammatical construction **b :** to change (a vowel) by umlaut **3 a :** to make minor changes in **b :** to make basic or fundamental changes in often to give a new orientation to or to serve a new end ⟨the wing of a bird is an arm *modified* for flying⟩ ~ *vi* **:** to undergo change ***syn*** see CHANGE — **mod·i·fi·abil·i·ty** \ˌmä-də-ˌfī-ə-ˈbi-lə-tē\ *n* — **mod·i·fi·able** \ˈmä-də-ˌfī-ə-bəl\ *adj*

mo·dil·lion \mō-ˈdil-yən\ *n* [It *modiglione*] (1563) **:** an ornamental block or bracket under the corona of the cornice (as in the Corinthian order)

mod·ish \ˈmō-dish\ *adj* (1660) **:** FASHIONABLE, STYLISH ⟨a ~ hat⟩ ⟨a ~ writer⟩ — **mod·ish·ly** *adv* — **mod·ish·ness** *n*

mo·diste \mō-ˈdēst\ *n* [F, fr. *mode* style, mode] (ca. 1840) **:** one who makes and sells fashionable dresses and hats for women

Mo·dred \ˈmō-dred\ *n* (13c) **:** a knight of the Round Table and nephew of King Arthur

mod·u·la·bil·i·ty \ˌmä-jə-lə-ˈbi-lə-tē\ *n* (1928) **:** the capability of being modulated

mod·u·lar \ˈmä-jə-lər\ *adj* (1798) **1 :** of, relating to, or based on a module or a modulus **2 :** constructed with standardized units or dimensions for flexibility and variety in use ⟨~ furniture⟩ — **mod·u·lar·i·ty** \ˌmä-jə-ˈla-rə-tē\ *n* — **mod·u·lar·ly** \ˈmä-jə-lər-lē\ *adv*

modular arithmetic *n* (1959) **:** arithmetic that deals with whole numbers where the numbers are replaced by their remainders after division by a fixed number ⟨in a *modular arithmetic* with modulus 5, 3 multiplied by 4 is 2⟩

mod·u·lar·ized \ˈmä-jə-lə-ˌrīzd\ *adj* (1959) **1 :** containing or consisting of modules **2 :** produced in the form of modules

mod·u·late \ˈmä-jə-ˌlāt\ *vb* **-lat·ed; -lat·ing** [L *modulatus,* pp. of *modulari* to play, sing, fr. *modulus* small measure, rhythm, dim. of *modus* measure — more at METE] *vt* (1615) **1 :** to tune to a key or pitch **2 :** to adjust to or keep in proper measure or proportion **:** TEMPER **3 :** to vary the amplitude, frequency, or phase of (a carrier wave or a light wave) for the transmission of information (as by radio); *also* **:** to vary the velocity of electrons in an electron beam ~ *vi* **1 :** to play or sing with modulation **2 :** to pass from one musical key into another by means of intermediary chords or notes that have some relation to both keys **3 :** to pass gradually from one state to another — **mod·u·la·tor** \-ˌlā-tər\ *n* — **mod·u·la·to·ry** \-lə-ˌtōr-ē, -ˌtȯr-\ *adj*

mod·u·la·tion \ˌmä-jə-ˈlā-shən\ *n* (1501) **1 :** an inflection of the tone or pitch of the voice; *specif* **:** the use of stress or pitch to convey meaning **2 :** a regulating according to measure or proportion **:** TEMPERING **3 :** a change from one musical key to another by modulating **4 :** the process of modulating a carrier or signal (as in radio); *also* **:** the result of this process

mod·ule \ˈmä-(ˌ)jül\ *n* [L *modulus*] (ca. 1628) **1 :** a standard or unit of measurement **2 :** the size of some one part taken as a unit of measure by which the proportions of an architectural composition are regulated **3 a :** any in a series of standardized units for use together: as (1) **:** a unit of furniture or architecture (2) **:** an educational unit which covers a single subject or topic **b :** a usu. packaged functional assembly of electronic components for use with other such assemblies **4 :** an independently operable unit that is a part of the total structure of a space vehicle **5 a :** a subset of an additive group that is also a group under addition **b :** a mathematical set that is a commutative group under addition and that is closed under multiplication which is distributive from the left or right or both by elements of a ring and for which $a(bx) = (ab)x$ or $(xb)a = x(ba)$ or both where a and b are elements of the ring and x belongs to the set

mod·u·lo \ˈmä-jə-ˌlō\ *prep* [NL, abl. of *modulus*] (1897) **:** with respect to a modulus of ⟨19 and 54 are congruent ~ 7⟩

mod·u·lus \ˈmä-jə-ləs\ *n, pl* **-li** \-ˌlī, -ˌlē\ [NL, fr. L, small measure] (1753) **1 a :** the factor by which a logarithm of a number to one base is multiplied to obtain the logarithm of the number to a new base **b :** ABSOLUTE VALUE 2 **c** (1) **:** the number (as a positive integer) or other mathematical entity (as a polynomial) in a congruence that divides the difference of the two congruent members without leaving a remainder — compare RESIDUE b (2) **:** the number of different numbers used in a system of modular arithmetic **2 :** a constant or coefficient that expresses usu. numerically the degree to which a body or substance possesses a particular property (as elasticity)

mo·dus ope·ran·di \ˌmō-dəs-ˌä-pə-ˈran-dē, -ˌdī\ *n, pl* **mo·di operandi** \ˈmō-ˌdē-, ˈmō-ˌdī-\ [NL] (1654) **:** a method of procedure; *esp* **:** a distinct pattern or method of operation that indicates or suggests the work of a single criminal in more than one crime

mo·dus vi·ven·di \ˌmō-dəs-vi-ˈven-dē, -ˌdī\ *n, pl* **mo·di vivendi** \ˈmō-ˌdē-, ˈmō-ˌdī-\ [NL, manner of living] (ca. 1878) **1** : a feasible arrangement or practical compromise; *esp* : one that bypasses difficulties **2** : a manner of living : a way of life

Mogen David *var of* MAGEN DAVID

mog·gy *also* **mog·gie** \ˈmä-gē\ *n, pl* **mog·gies** [prob. fr. *Moggy,* fr. *Mog,* nickname fr. the name *Margaret*] (ca. 1911) *Brit* : CAT

Mo·go·llon \ˌmə-gə-ˈyōn, ˌmō-\ *n, often attrib* [*Mogollon,* mountain range and plateau in New Mexico] (1946) : a prehistoric American Indian people inhabiting the mountains of eastern Arizona and western New Mexico

[1]**mo·gul** \ˈmō-(ˌ)gəl\ *n* [Pers *Mughul,* fr. Mongolian *mongyol* Mongol] (1588) **1** *also* **mo·ghul** *or* **mu·ghal** \ˈmü-\ *cap* : an Indian Muslim of or descended from one of several conquering groups of Mongol, Turkish, and Persian origin; *esp* : GREAT MOGUL **2** : a great personage : MAGNATE — **mogul** *also* **moghul** *or* **mughal** *adj, often cap*

[2]**mo·gul** \ˈmō-gəl\ *n* [G dial.; akin to G dial. (Viennese) *mugl* small hill] (1959) : a bump in a ski run

mo·hair \ˈmō-ˌher\ *n* [modif. of obs. It *mocaiarro,* fr. Ar *mukhayyar,* lit., choice] (1619) : a fabric or yarn made wholly or in part of the long silky hair of the Angora goat; *also* : this hair

Mo·ham·med·an *also* **Mu·ham·mad·an** \mō-ˈha-mə-dən, -ˈhä- *also* mü-\ *adj* (1681) : of or relating to Muhammad or Islam — **Mohammedan** *also* **Muhammadan** *n* — **Mo·ham·med·an·ism** *also* **Mu·ham·mad·an·ism** \-də-ˌni-zəm\ *n*

Mo·hawk \ˈmō-ˌhȯk\ *n, pl* **Mohawk** *or* **Mohawks** [of Algonquian origin; akin to Narragansett or Massachusett *Mohowawog* Mohawk, lit., cannibal] (1634) **1** : a member of an American Indian people of the Mohawk River valley, New York **2** : the Iroquoian language of the Mohawk people **3** : a hairstyle with a narrow center strip of usu. upright hair and the sides of the head shaved

Mo·he·gan \mō-ˈhē-gən, mə-\ *or* **Mo·hi·can** \-ˈhē-kən\ *n, pl* **Mohegan** *or* **Mohegans** *or* **Mohican** *or* **Mohicans** [of southern New England Algonquian origin; akin to Narragansett *Monahiganeuck* Mohegans] (1660) : a member of an American Indian people of southeastern Connecticut

mo·hel \ˈmō-(h)el, ˈmȯi(-ə)l\ *n, pl* **mohels** *also* **mo·hal·im** \ˌmō-hä-ˈlēm\ *or* **mo·hel·im** \-(h)e-ˈlēm\ [Heb *mōhēl*] (1650) : a person who performs ritual Jewish circumcisions

Mohican *var of* MAHICAN

Mo·ho \ˈmō-ˌhō\ *n* [short for *Mohorovicic discontinuity,* fr. Andrija *Mohorovičić* †1936 Yugoslavian geologist] (1952) : the boundary layer between the earth's crust and mantle whose depth varies from about 3 miles (5 kilometers) beneath the ocean floor to about 25 miles (40 kilometers) beneath the continents

Mo·hock \ˈmō-ˌhäk\ *n* [alter. of *Mohawk*] (ca. 1712) : one of a gang of aristocratic ruffians who assaulted people in London streets in the early 18th century — **Mo·hock·ism** \-ˌhä-ˌki-zəm\ *n*

Mo·ho·ro·vi·cic discontinuity \ˌmō-hə-ˈrō-və-ˌchich-\ *n* (1936) : MOHO

Mohs' scale \ˈmōz-, ˈmōs-, ˈmō-səz-\ *n* [Friedrich *Mohs* †1839 Ger. mineralogist] (1879) : a scale of hardness for minerals that ranges from a value of 1 for talc to 10 for diamond

mo·hur \ˈmō-ər, mə-ˈhu̇r\ *n* [Hindi & Urdu *muhr* gold coin, seal, fr. Pers, fr. MPers; akin to Skt *mudrā* seal] (1690) : a former gold coin of India and Persia equal to 15 rupees

moi·e·ty \ˈmȯi-ə-tē\ *n, pl* **-ties** [ME *moite,* fr. AF *meité, moité,* fr. LL *medietat-, medietas,* fr. L *medius* middle — more at MID] (15c) **1 a** : one of two equal parts : HALF **b** : one of two approximately equal parts **2** : one of the portions into which something is divided : COMPONENT, PART ⟨an ether molecule with a benzene ~⟩ **3** : one of two basic complementary tribal subdivisions

[1]**moil** \ˈmȯi(-ə)l\ *vb* [ME *mollen, moillen,* fr. AF *moiller,* fr. VL **molliare,* fr. L *mollis* soft — more at MOLLIFY] *vt* (15c) *chiefly dial* : to make wet or dirty ~ *vi* **1** : to work hard : DRUDGE **2** : to be in continuous agitation : CHURN, SWIRL — **moil·er** *n*

[2]**moil** *n* (1612) **1** : hard work : DRUDGERY **2** : CONFUSION, TURMOIL

moil·ing \ˈmȯi-liŋ\ *adj* (1603) **1 a** : requiring hard work **b** : INDUSTRIOUS **2** : violently agitated : TURBULENT — **moil·ing·ly** \-lē\ *adv*

Moi·rai \ˈmȯi-ˌrī\ *n pl* [Gk, fr. pl. of *moira* lot, fate; akin to Gk *meros* part — more at MERIT] (1892) : FATE 4

moire \ˈmȯi(-ə)r, ˈmȯr, ˈmwär\ *n* [F, fr. E *mohair*] (1660) *archaic* : a watered mohair

moi·ré \mȯ-ˈrā, mwä-\ *or* **moire** *same or* ˈmȯi(-ə)r, ˈmȯr, ˈmwär\ *n* [F *moiré,* fr. *moiré* like moire, fr. *moire*] (1818) **1 a** : an irregular wavy finish on a fabric **b** : a ripple pattern on a stamp **2** : a fabric having a wavy watered appearance **3** : an independent usu. shimmering pattern seen when two geometrically regular patterns (as two sets of parallel lines or two halftone screens) are superimposed esp. at an acute angle — **moiré** *or* **moire** *adj*

moist \ˈmȯist\ *adj* [ME *moiste,* fr. AF, perh. fr. VL **muscidus,* alter. of L *mucidus* slimy, fr. *mucus* nasal mucus] (14c) **1** : slightly or moderately wet : DAMP **2** : TEARFUL **3** : characterized by high humidity ***syn*** see WET — **moist·ly** *adv* — **moist·ness** \ˈmȯis(t)-nəs\ *n*

moist·en \ˈmȯi-sᵊn\ *vb* **moist·ened; moist·en·ing** \ˈmȯis-niŋ, ˈmȯi-sᵊn-iŋ\ *vt* (1580) : to make moist ~ *vi* : to become moist — **moist·en·er** \ˈmȯis-nər, ˈmȯi-sᵊn-ər\ *n*

mois·ture \ˈmȯis-chər, ˈmȯish-\ *n* [ME, fr. AF, fr. *moiste*] (14c) : liquid diffused or condensed in relatively small quantity

mois·tur·ise *Brit var of* MOISTURIZE

mois·tur·ize \-chə-ˌrīz\ *vt* **-ized; -iz·ing** (1945) : to add moisture to ⟨~ the air⟩ ⟨a cream that ~s the skin⟩ — **mois·tur·iz·er** *n*

mo·ji·to \mō-ˈhē-tō\ *n, pl* **-tos** [AmerSp, dim. of *moje, mojo* citrus marinade, fr. Sp *mojar* to moisten, fr. VL **molliare* — more at MOIL] (1934) : a cocktail made of rum, sugar, mint, lime juice, and soda water

mo·jo \ˈmō-(ˌ)jō\ *n, pl* **mojoes** *or* **mojos** [prob. of African origin; akin to Fulani *moco'o* medicine man] (1926) : a magic spell, hex, or charm; *broadly* : magical power ⟨works his ~ on the tennis court⟩

moke \ˈmōk\ *n* [origin unknown] (ca. 1839) **1** *slang Brit* : DONKEY **2** *slang Austral* : [1]NAG

[1]**mol** *var of* [5]MOLE

[2]**mol** *abbr* molecular; molecule

MOL *abbr* manned orbiting (*or* orbital) laboratory

mol·al \ˈmō-ləl\ *adj* [[5]*mole*] (1905) : of, relating to, or containing a mole of solute per 1000 grams of solvent — **mo·lal·i·ty** \mō-ˈla-lə-tē\ *n*

[1]**mo·lar** \ˈmō-lər\ *n* [ME *molares,* pl., fr. L *molaris,* fr. *molaris* of a mill, fr. *mola* millstone — more at MILL] (14c) : a tooth with a rounded or flattened surface adapted for grinding; *specif* : one of the cheek teeth in mammals behind the incisors and canines — see TOOTH illustration

[2]**molar** *adj* (1626) **1** : pulverizing by friction : GRINDING **2** : of, relating to, or located near the molar teeth

[3]**molar** *adj* [[5]*mole*] (1902) **1** : of or relating to a mole of a substance ⟨the ~ volume of a gas⟩ **2** : containing one mole of solute in one liter of solution — **mo·lar·i·ty** \mō-ˈla-rə-tē\ *n*

mo·las·ses \mə-ˈla-səz\ *n* [modif. of Pg *melaço,* fr. LL *mellaceum* grape juice, fr. L *mell-, mel* honey — more at MELLIFLUOUS] (1582) **1** : the thick dark to light brown syrup that is separated from raw sugar in sugar manufacture **2** : a syrup made from boiling down sweet vegetable or fruit juice ⟨citrus ~⟩

[1]**mold** \ˈmōld\ *n* [ME, fr. OE *molde;* akin to OHG *molta* soil, L *molere* to grind — more at MEAL] (bef. 12c) **1** : crumbling soft friable earth suited to plant growth : SOIL; *esp* : soil rich in humus — compare LEAF MOLD **2** *dial Brit* **a** : the surface of the earth : GROUND **b** : the earth of the burying ground **3** *archaic* : earth that is the substance of the human body ⟨be merciful great Duke to men of ~ —Shak.⟩

[2]**mold** *n* [ME, fr. AF *molde,* alter. of OF *modle,* fr. L *modulus,* dim. of *modus* measure — more at METE] (13c) **1** : distinctive nature or character : TYPE **2** : the frame on or around which an object is constructed **3 a** : a cavity in which a substance is shaped: as (1) : a matrix for casting metal ⟨a bullet ~⟩ (2) : a form in which food is given a decorative shape **b** : a molded object **4** : MOLDING **5 a** *obs* : an example to be followed **b** : PROTOTYPE **c** : a fixed pattern : DESIGN

[3]**mold** *vt* (14c) **1** *archaic* : to knead (dough) into a desired consistency or shape **2** : to give shape to ⟨the wind ~s the waves⟩ **3** : to form in a mold ⟨~ candles⟩ **4** : to determine or influence the quality or nature of ⟨~ public opinion⟩ **5** : to fit the contours of ⟨fitted skirts that ~ the hips⟩ **6** : to ornament with molding or carving ⟨~*ed* picture frames⟩ — **mold·able** \ˈmōl-də-bəl\ *adj* — **mold·er** *n*

[4]**mold** *n* [ME *mowlde,* perh. alter. of *mowle,* fr. *moulen* to grow moldy, of Scand origin; akin to ODan *mul* mold] (14c) **1** : a superficial often woolly growth produced esp. on damp or decaying organic matter or on living organisms by a fungus (as of the order Mucorales) **2** : a fungus that produces mold

[5]**mold** *vi* (1530) : to become moldy

mold·board \ˈmōl(d)-ˌbȯrd\ *n* (1508) **1** : a curved iron plate attached above a plowshare to lift and turn the soil **2** : a blade on a machine (as a bulldozer) that pushes material to one side as the machine advances

mold·er \ˈmōl-dər\ *vi* **mold·ered; mold·er·ing** \-d(ə-)riŋ\ [freq. of [5]*mold*] (1531) : to crumble into particles : DISINTEGRATE, DECAY

mold·ing \ˈmōl-diŋ\ *n* (14c) **1** : an object produced by molding **2 a** : a decorative recessed or relieved surface **b** : a decorative plane or curved strip used for ornamentation or finishing

moldy \ˈmōl-dē\ *adj* **mold·i·er; -est** (14c) **1** : of, resembling, or covered with mold **2 a** : being old and moldering : CRUMBLING **b** : ANTIQUATED, FUSTY ⟨~ tradition⟩ — **mold·i·ness** *n*

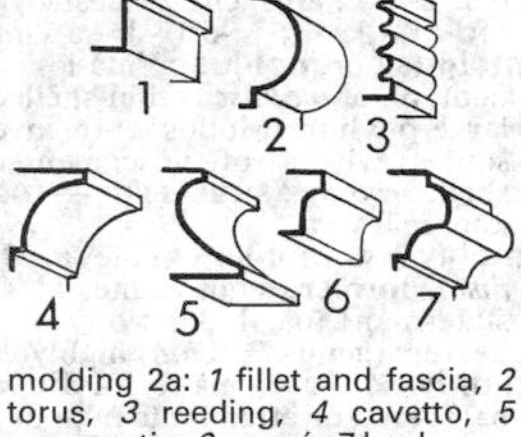

molding 2a: *1* fillet and fascia, *2* torus, *3* reeding, *4* cavetto, *5* scotia, *6* congé, *7* beak

[1]**mole** \ˈmōl\ *n* [ME, fr. OE *māl;* akin to OHG *meil* spot] (14c) : a pigmented spot, mark, or small permanent protuberance on the human body; *esp* : NEVUS

[2]**mole** *n* [ME; akin to MLG *mol*] (14c) **1** : any of numerous burrowing insectivores (esp. family Talpidae) with tiny eyes, concealed ears, and soft fur **2** : one who works in the dark **3** : a machine for tunneling **4** : a spy (as a double agent) who establishes a cover long before beginning espionage; *broadly* : one within an organization who passes on information

[3]**mole** *n* [ME, fr. L *mola* mole, lit., mill, millstone — more at MILL] (15c) : an abnormal mass in the uterus esp. when containing fetal tissues

[4]**mole** *n* [MF, fr. OIt *molo,* fr. LGk *mōlos,* fr. L *moles,* lit., mass, exertion; akin to Gk *mōlos* exertion] (ca. 1548) **1** : a massive work formed of masonry and large stones or earth laid in the sea as a pier or breakwater **2** : the harbor formed by a mole

[5]**mole** *also* **mol** \ˈmōl\ *n* [G *Mol,* short for *Molekulargewicht* molecular weight, fr. *molekular* molecular + *Gewicht* weight] (1902) : the base unit of amount of pure substance in the International System of Units that contains the same number of elementary entities as there are atoms in exactly 12 grams of the isotope carbon 12

[6]**mo·le** \ˈmō-lā\ *n* [MexSp, fr. Nahuatl *mōlli* sauce] (1901) : a spicy sauce made with chilies and usu. chocolate and served with meat

mole cricket *n* (1714) : any of a family (Gryllotalpidae) of widely distributed orthopteran insects that have broad front legs adapted for digging in moist soil and that feed largely on the roots of plants

mo·lec·u·lar \mə-ˈle-kyə-lər\ *adj* (1823) **1** : of, relating to, consisting of, or produced by molecules ⟨~ oxygen⟩ **2** : of or relating to individual or small components ⟨a ~ view of the American Civil War⟩ — **mo·lec·u·lar·ly** \-lē\ *adv*

molecular biology *n* (1938) : a branch of biology dealing with the ultimate physicochemical organization of living matter and esp. with the molecular basis of inheritance and protein synthesis — **molecular biologist** *n*

molecular chaperone *n* (1989) : CHAPERONE 3

molecular formula *n* (1869) : a chemical formula that gives the total number of atoms of each element in each molecule of a substance — compare STRUCTURAL FORMULA

molecular genetics *n pl but sing in constr* (1963) : a branch of genetics dealing with the structure and activity of genetic material at the molecular level

molecular mass *n* (1873) : the mass of a molecule that is equal to the sum of the masses of all the atoms contained in the molecule

molecular orbital *n* (1932) : a solution of the Schrödinger equation that describes the probable location of an electron relative to the nuclei in a molecule and so indicates the nature of any bond in which the electron is involved

molecular sieve *n* (1869) : a crystalline substance (as a zeolite) characterized by uniformly sized pores of molecular dimension that can adsorb small molecules and is used esp. in separations

molecular weight *n* (1869) : the average mass of a molecule of a compound compared to $\frac{1}{12}$ the mass of carbon 12 and calculated as the sum of the atomic weights of the constituent atoms

mol·e·cule \'mä-li-ˌkyül\ *n* [F *molécule,* fr. NL *molecula,* dim. of L *moles* mass] (1794) **1** : the smallest particle of a substance that retains all the properties of the substance and is composed of one or more atoms **2** : a tiny bit : PARTICLE

mole·hill \'mōl-ˌhil\ *n* (15c) : a little mound or ridge of earth pushed up by a mole

mole rat *n* (1781) : any of various burrowing Old World rodents (as of the families Bathyergidae and Muridae) that generally resemble moles in appearance and have large often protruding incisors used for digging — compare NAKED MOLE RAT

mole·skin \-ˌskin\ *n* (1668) **1** : the skin of the mole used as fur **2 a** : a heavy durable cotton fabric with a short thick velvety nap on one side **b** : a garment made of moleskin — usu. used in pl. **c** : adhesive padding (as for blisters) made of moleskin

mo·lest \mə-'lest\ *vt* [ME, fr. AF *molester,* fr. L *molestare,* fr. *molestus* burdensome, annoying; akin to L *moles* mass] (14c) **1** : to annoy, disturb, or persecute esp. with hostile intent or injurious effect **2** : to make annoying sexual advances to; *esp* : to force physical and usu. sexual contact on — **mo·les·ta·tion** \ˌmō-ˌles-'tā-shən, ˌmä-, -ləs-\ *n* — **mo·lest·er** \mə-'les-tər\ *n*

mo·line \mə-'lēn, -'līn\ *adj* [AF **moliné,* fr. *molin* mill, fr. LL *molinum* — more at MILL] (1562) *of a heraldic cross* : having the end of each arm forked and recurved — see CROSS illustration

moll \'mäl, 'mȯl\ *n* [prob. fr. *Moll,* nickname for *Mary*] (1557) **1** : PROSTITUTE **2 a** : DOLL 2 **b** : a gangster's girlfriend

mol·li·fy \'mä-lə-ˌfī\ *vb* **-fied; -fy·ing** [ME *mollifien,* fr. MF *mollifier,* fr. LL *mollificare,* fr. L *mollis* soft; akin to Gk *amaldynein* to soften, Skt *mṛdu* soft, and prob. to Gk *malakos* soft, *amblys* dull, OE *meltan* to melt] *vt* (15c) **1** : to soothe in temper or disposition : APPEASE ⟨*mollified* the staff with a raise⟩ **2** : to reduce the rigidity of : SOFTEN **3** : to reduce in intensity : ASSUAGE, TEMPER ~ *vi, archaic* : SOFTEN, RELENT **syn** see PACIFY — **mol·li·fi·ca·tion** \ˌmä-lə-fə-'kā-shən\ *n*

mol·lus·ci·cide \mə-'ləs-kə-ˌsīd, -'lə-sə-\ *n* [NL *Mollusca* + E *-i-* + *-cide*] (ca. 1947) : an agent for destroying mollusks (as snails) — **mol·lus·ci·cid·al** \-ˌləs-kə-'sī-dᵊl, -ˌlə-sə-\ *adj*

mol·lusk *or* **mol·lusc** \'mä-ləsk\ *n* [F *mollusque,* fr. NL *Mollusca,* fr. L, neut. pl. of *molluscus* thin-shelled (of a nut), fr. *mollis*] (1783) : any of a large phylum (Mollusca) of invertebrate animals (as snails, clams, or squids) with a soft unsegmented body usu. enclosed in a calcareous shell; *broadly* : SHELLFISH — **mol·lus·can** *also* **mol·lus·kan** \mə-'ləs-kən, mä-\ *adj*

mol·ly *also* **mol·lie** \'mä-lē\ *n, pl* **mollies** [by shortening fr. NL *Mollienisia,* former genus name, fr. Comte François N. *Mollien* †1850 Fr. statesman] (ca. 1933) : any of several brightly colored tropical live-bearers (genus *Poecilia*) highly valued as aquarium fishes

[1]**mol·ly·cod·dle** \'mä-lē-ˌkä-dᵊl\ *n* [*Molly,* nickname for *Mary*] (1833) : a pampered or effeminate man or boy

[2]**mollycoddle** *vt* **-cod·dled; -cod·dling** \-ˌkäd-liŋ, -ˌkä-dᵊl-iŋ\ (1864) : to treat with an excessive or absurd degree of indulgence and attention **syn** see INDULGE — **mol·ly·cod·dler** \-ˌkäd-lər, -ˌkä-dᵊl-ər\ *n*

Mo·loch \'mä-lək, 'mō-ˌläk\ *n* [LL, fr. Gk, fr. Heb *Mōlekh*] (14c) : a Semitic god to whom children were sacrificed

Mo·lo·tov cocktail \'mä-lə-ˌtȯf-, 'mȯ-, 'mō-, -ˌtȯv-\ *n* [Vyacheslav M. *Molotov*] (1940) : a crude bomb made of a bottle filled with a flammable liquid (as gasoline) and usu. fitted with a wick (as a saturated rag) that is ignited just before the bottle is hurled

[1]**molt** \'mōlt\ *vb* [alter. of ME *mouten,* fr. OE *-mūtian* to change, fr. L *mutare* — more at MUTABLE] *vi* (15c) : to shed hair, feathers, shell, horns, or an outer layer periodically ~ *vt* : to cast off (an outer covering) periodically; *specif* : to throw off (the old cuticle) — used of arthropods — **molt·er** *n*

[2]**molt** *n* (1815) : the act or process of molting; *specif* : ECDYSIS

mol·ten \'mōl-tᵊn\ *adj* [ME, fr. pp. of *melten* to melt] (14c) **1** *obs* : made by melting and casting **2** : fused or liquefied by heat : MELTED ⟨~ lava⟩ **3** : having warmth or brilliance : GLOWING

mol·to \'mōl-(ˌ)tō, 'mȯl-\ *adv* [It, fr. L *multum,* fr. neut. of *multus* much] (ca. 1801) : MUCH, VERY — used in music directions

mol wt *abbr* molecular weight

mo·ly \'mō-lē\ *n* [L, fr. Gk *mōly*] (1567) : a mythical herb with a black root, white blossoms, and magical powers

mo·lyb·date \mə-'lib-ˌdāt\ *n* (1794) : a salt of molybdenum containing the group MoO_4 or Mo_2O_7

mo·lyb·de·nite \mə-'lib-də-ˌnīt\ *n* [NL *molybdena*] (1837) : a metallic gray usu. foliated mineral consisting of molybdenum disulfide that is a major ore of molybdenum

mo·lyb·de·num \-nəm\ *n* [NL, fr. *molybdena,* a lead ore, molybdenite, molybdenum, fr. L *molybdaena* galena, fr. Gk *molybdaina,* fr. *molybdos* lead] (1814) : a metallic element that resembles chromium and tungsten in many properties, is used esp. in strengthening and hardening steel, and is a trace element in plant and animal metabolism — see ELEMENT table

molybdenum disulfide *n* (ca. 1931) : a compound MoS_2 used esp. as a lubricant in grease

mom \'mäm, 'məm\ *n* [short for *momma*] (ca. 1894) : MOTHER 1a

MOM *abbr* middle of month

mom–and–pop \'mäm-ən(d)-'päp\ *adj* (1951) **1** : being or relating to a small owner-operated business ⟨a ~ grocery⟩ **2** : SMALL-SCALE

mome \'mōm\ *n* [origin unknown] (1553) *archaic* : BLOCKHEAD, FOOL

mo·ment \'mō-mənt\ *n* [ME, fr. AF, fr. L *momentum* movement, particle sufficient to turn the scales, moment, fr. *movēre* to move] (14c) **1 a** : a minute portion or point of time : INSTANT **b** : a comparatively brief period of time **2 a** : present time **b** : a time of excellence or conspicuousness **3** : importance in influence or effect **4** *obs* : a cause or motive of action **5** : a stage in historical or logical development **6 a** : tendency or measure of tendency to produce motion esp. about a point or axis **b** : the product of quantity (as a force) and the distance to a particular axis or point **7 a** : the mean of the *n*th powers of the deviations of the observed values in a set of statistical data from a fixed value **b** : the expected value of a power of the deviation of a random variable from a fixed value **syn** see IMPORTANCE

mo·men·tar·i·ly \ˌmō-mən-'ter-ə-lē\ *adv* (ca. 1666) **1** : for a moment **2** *archaic* : INSTANTLY **3** : at any moment : in a moment

mo·men·tary \'mō-mən-ˌter-ē\ *adj* (15c) **1 a** : continuing only a moment : FLEETING **b** : having a very brief life **2** : operative or recurring at every moment **syn** see TRANSIENT — **mo·men·tar·i·ness** *n*

mo·ment·ly \'mō-mənt-lē\ *adv* (1676) **1** : from moment to moment **2** : at any moment **3** : for a moment

moment of inertia (1830) : a measure of the resistance of a body to angular acceleration about a given axis that is equal to the sum of the products of each element of mass in the body and the square of the element's distance from the axis

moment of truth (1932) **1** : the final sword thrust in a bullfight **2** : a moment of crisis on whose outcome much or everything depends

mo·men·tous \mō-'men-təs, mə-\ *adj* (1656) : IMPORTANT, CONSEQUENTIAL — **mo·men·tous·ly** *adv* — **mo·men·tous·ness** *n*

mo·men·tum \mō-'men-təm, mə-\ *n, pl* **mo·men·ta** \-'men-tə\ *or* **mo·mentums** [NL, fr. L, movement] (1610) **1** : a property of a moving body that the body has by virtue of its mass and motion and that is equal to the product of the body's mass and velocity; *broadly* : a property of a moving body that determines the length of time required to bring it to rest when under the action of a constant force or moment **2** : strength or force gained by motion or by a series of events

momma *var of* MAMA

mom·my \'mä-mē, 'mə-mē\ *n, pl* **mom·mies** [alter. of *mammy*] (1899) : MOTHER 1a

mommy track *n* (1988) : a career path that allows a mother flexible or reduced work hours but tends to slow or block advancement

Mo·mus \'mō-məs\ *n* [L, fr. Gk *Mōmos*] (1561) : the Greek god of censure and mockery

[1]**mon** \'män\ *dial chiefly Brit var of* MAN

[2]**mon** *abbr* monetary

[1]**Mon** \'mōn\ *n, pl* **Mon** *or* **Mons** (1798) **1** : a member of the dominant native people of Pegu division, Myanmar (Burma) **2** : the Mon-Khmer language of the Mon people

[2]**Mon** *abbr* Monday

mon- *or* **mono-** *comb form* [Gk, fr. *monos* alone, single — more at MONK] **1** : one : single : alone ⟨*mono*plane⟩ ⟨*mono*drama⟩ **2 a** : containing one (usu. specified) atom, radical, or group ⟨*mono*hydroxy⟩ **b** : monomolecular ⟨*mono*layer⟩

mon·a·chal \'mä-ni-kəl\ *adj* [MF or LL; MF, fr. LL *monachalis,* fr. *monachus* monk — more at MONK] (1587) : MONASTIC — **mon·a·chism** \'mä-nə-ˌki-zəm\ *n*

mo·nad \'mō-ˌnad\ *n* [LL *monad-, monas,* fr. Gk, fr. *monos*] (1615) **1 a** : UNIT, ONE **b** : ATOM 1 **c** : an elementary individual substance which reflects the order of the world and from which material properties are derived **2** : a flagellated protozoan (as of the genus *Monas*) — **mo·nad·ic** \mō-'na-dik, mə-\ *adj* — **mo·nad·ism** \'mō-ˌna-ˌdi-zəm\ *n*

mon·adel·phous \ˌmä-nə-'del-fəs\ *adj* (1806) *of stamens* : united by the filaments into one group usu. forming a tube around the gynoecium

mo·nad·nock \mə-'nad-ˌnäk\ *n* [Mt. *Monadnock,* N.H.] (1893) : INSELBERG

mon·an·dry \'mä-ˌnan-drē\ *n, pl* **-dries** [*mon-* + *-andry* (as in *polyandry*)] (1855) : a marriage form or custom in which a woman has only one husband at a time

mon·arch \'mä-nərk, -ˌnärk\ *n* [LL *monarcha,* fr. Gk *monarchos,* fr. *mon-* + *-archos* -arch] (15c) **1** : a person who reigns over a kingdom or empire: as **a** : a sovereign ruler **b** : a constitutional king or queen **2** : one that holds preeminent position or power **3** : MONARCH BUTTERFLY — **mo·nar·chal** \mə-'när-kəl, mä-\ *or* **mo·nar·chi·al** \-kē-əl\ *adj*

monarch butterfly *n* (1890) : a large migratory American butterfly (*Danaus plexippus*) that has orange-brown wings with black veins and borders and a larva that feeds on milkweed

monarch butterfly

Mo·nar·chi·an \mə-'när-kē-ən, mä-\ *n* (1765) : an adherent of one of two anti-Trinitarian groups of the second and third centuries A.D. teaching that God is one person as well as one being — **Mo·nar·chi·an·ism** \-kē-ə-ˌni-zəm\ *n*

mo·nar·chi·cal \mə-'när-ki-kəl, mä-\ *also* **mo·nar·chic** \-kik\ *adj* (1793) : of, relating to, suggestive of, or characteristic of a monarch or monarchy — **mo·nar·chi·cal·ly** \-ki-k(ə-)lē\ *adv*

mon·ar·chism \'mä-nər-ˌki-zəm, -ˌnär-\ *n* (1742) : monarchical government or principles — **mon·ar·chist** \-kist\ *n or adj*

mon·ar·chy \'mä-nər-kē *also* -ˌnär-\ *n, pl* **-chies** (14c) **1** : undivided rule or absolute sovereignty by a single person **2** : a nation or state having a monarchical government **3** : a government having a hereditary chief of state with life tenure and powers varying from nominal to absolute

mo·nar·da \mə-'när-də\ *n* [NL, fr. Nicolás *Monardes* †1588 Span. botanist] (1789) : any of a genus (*Monarda*) of coarse annual or perennial No. American mints with a tubular calyx and whorls of showy flowers

mon·as·tery \'mä-nə-ˌster-ē\ *n, pl* **-ter·ies** [ME *monasterie,* fr. LL *monasterium,* fr. LGk *monastērion,* fr. Gk, hermit's cell, fr. *monazein* to live alone, fr. *monos* single — more at MONK] (15c) : a house for persons under religious vows; *esp* : an establishment for monks

mo·nas·tic \mə-'nas-tik\ *adj* (ca. 1563) **1** : of or relating to monasteries or to monks or nuns **2** : resembling (as in seclusion or ascetic simplicity) life in a monastery — **monastic** *n* — **mo·nas·ti·cal·ly** \-ti-k(ə-)lē\ *adv* — **mo·nas·ti·cism** \-tə-ˌsi-zəm\ *n*

mon·atom·ic \ˌmä-nə-ˈtä-mik\ *adj* (1848) **:** consisting of one atom; *esp* **:** having but one atom in the molecule
mon·au·ral \(ˌ)mä-ˈnȯr-əl\ *adj* (1931) **:** MONOPHONIC 2 — **mon·au·ral·ly** \-ə-lē\ *adv*
mon·a·zite \ˈmä-nə-ˌzīt\ *n* [G *Monazit,* fr. Gk *monazein*] (1836) **:** a yellow to red or brown mineral that is a phosphate of thorium and various rare earth elements and occurs esp. in sand and gravel deposits
Mon·day \ˈmən-(ˌ)dā, -dē\ *n* [ME, fr. OE *mōnandæg;* akin to OHG *mānatag* Monday; akin to OE *mōna* moon and to OE *dæg* day] (bef. 12c) **:** the second day of the week — **Mon·days** \-(ˌ)dāz, -dēz\ *adv*
Monday–morning quarterback *n* [fr. a fan's usu. critical rehashing of the weekend football game strategy] (1932) **:** one who second-guesses — **Monday–morning quarterbacking** *n*
mon·de·green \ˈmän-də-ˌgrēn\ *n* [fr. the mishearing in a Scottish ballad of "laid him on the green" as "Lady Mondegreen"] (1954) **:** a word or phrase that results from a mishearing of something said or sung
[1]**mon·do** \ˈmän-(ˌ)dō\ *adv* [fr. reanalysis of *mondo* in title of the Amer. film *Mondo Bizarro* (1966), after the Ital. film *Mondo cane* (1962)] (1968) *slang* **:** EXTREMELY
[2]**mondo** *adj* (1968) *slang* **:** very large or great in amount or number
monecious *var of* MONOECIOUS
mo·ner·an \mō-ˈnir-ən, mə-\ *n* [NL *Monera,* kingdom comprising prokaryotes, ultim. fr. Gk *monērēs* single, fr. *monos*] (1876) **:** PROKARYOTE — **moneran** *adj*
M1 rifle \ˈem-ˈwən-\ *n* (1938) **:** a .30 caliber gas-operated clip-fed semiautomatic rifle used by U.S. troops in World War II
mon·es·trous \(ˌ)mä-ˈnes-trəs\ *adj* (1900) **:** experiencing estrus once each year or breeding season
mon·e·tar·ism \ˈmä-nə-tə-ˌri-zəm *also* ˈmən-\ *n* (1969) **:** a theory in economics that stable economic growth can be assured only by control of the rate of increase of the money supply to match the capacity for growth of real productivity — **mon·e·tar·ist** \-rist\ *n or adj*
mon·e·tary \ˈmä-nə-ˌter-ē *also* ˈmə-\ *adj* [LL *monetarius* of a mint, of money, fr. L *moneta*] (1810) **:** of or relating to money or to the mechanisms by which it is supplied to and circulates in the economy — **mon·e·tar·i·ly** \ˌmä-nə-ˈter-ə-lē *also* ˌmə-\ *adv*
monetary aggregate *n* (1979) **:** one of the formal categories of money (as cash and demand deposits or bank credits) in a national economy that is used as a measure in predictions of economic growth
monetary unit *n* (1810) **:** the standard unit of value of a currency
mon·e·tize \ˈmä-nə-ˌtīz *also* ˈmə-\ *vt* **-tized; -tiz·ing** [L *moneta*] (ca. 1879) **1 :** to coin into money; *also* **:** to establish as legal tender **2 :** to purchase (public or private debt) and thereby free for other uses moneys that would have been devoted to debt service **3 :** to utilize (something of value) as a source of profit — **mon·e·tiz·able** \-ˌtī-zə-bəl\ *adj* — **mon·e·ti·za·tion** \ˌmä-nə-tə-ˈzā-shən *also* ˌmə-\ *n*
[1]**mon·ey** \ˈmə-nē\ *n, pl* **moneys** *or* **mon·ies** \ˈmə-nēz\ *often attrib* [ME *moneye,* fr. AF *moneie,* fr. L *moneta* mint, money — more at MINT] (14c) **1 :** something generally accepted as a medium of exchange, a measure of value, or a means of payment: as **a :** officially coined or stamped metal currency **b :** MONEY OF ACCOUNT **c :** PAPER MONEY **2 a :** wealth reckoned in terms of money **b :** an amount of money **c** *pl* **:** sums of money **:** FUNDS **3 :** a form or denomination of coin or paper money **4 a :** the first, second, and third place winners (as in a horse or dog race) — usu. used in the phrases *in the money* or *out of the money* **b :** prize money ⟨his horse took third ~⟩ **5 a :** persons or interests possessing or controlling great wealth **b :** a position of wealth ⟨born into ~⟩ — **for one's money :** according to one's preference or opinion — **on the money :** exactly right or accurate
☞ The Money Table is on the following page.
[2]**money** *adj* (ca. 1934) **:** involving or reliable in a crucial situation ⟨a ~ player⟩ ⟨a ~ pitch⟩
mon·ey–back \-ˈbak\ *adj* (1922) **:** providing that the purchaser is entitled to a refund if the product is unsatisfactory ⟨a ~ guarantee⟩
mon·ey·bags \ˈmə-nē-ˌbagz\ *n pl but sing or pl in constr* (1596) **1 :** WEALTH **2 :** a wealthy person
money changer *n* (15c) **1 :** one whose business is the exchanging of kinds or denominations of currency **2 :** a device for holding and dispensing sorted change
mon·eyed *also* **mon·ied** \ˈmə-nēd\ *adj* (15c) **1 :** having money **:** WEALTHY **2 :** consisting in or derived from money
mon·ey·er \ˈmə-nē-ər\ *n* [ME, fr. AF *moneour,* fr. *moneer* to mint, fr. *moneie*] (15c) **:** an authorized coiner of money **:** MINTER
mon·ey–grub·ber \ˈmə-nē-ˌgrə-bər\ *n* (1840) **:** a person bent on accumulating money — **mon·ey–grub·bing** \-biŋ\ *adj or n*
mon·ey·lend·er \-ˌlen-dər\ *n* (1673) **:** one whose business is lending money; *specif* **:** PAWNBROKER
mon·ey·mak·er \-ˌmā-kər\ *n* (1834) **1 :** one that accumulates wealth **2 :** one (as a plan or product) that produces profit — **mon·ey·mak·ing** \-kiŋ\ *adj or n*
mon·ey·man \-ˌman\ *n* (ca. 1585) **:** FINANCIER
money market *n* (1950) **:** the trade in short-term negotiable instruments (as certificates of deposit or U.S. Treasury securities)
money of account (1691) **:** a denominator of value or basis of exchange which is used in keeping accounts and for which there may or may not be an equivalent coin or denomination of paper money
money order *n* (1802) **:** an order issued by a post office, bank, or telegraph office for payment of a specified sum of money usu. at any branch of the organization
money plant *n* (1866) **:** HONESTY 3; *esp* **:** a biennial herb (*Lunaria annua*) grown esp. for its seed pods that are silvery white when dried
money shot *n* (1977) **1 :** the scene in a pornographic movie in which a male actor ejaculates **2 :** a very important, impressive, or memorable picture or scene
mon·ey–spin·ner \ˈmə-nē-ˌspi-nər\ *n* (1859) *chiefly Brit* **:** MONEYMAKER — **mon·ey–spin·ning** \-niŋ\ *adj or n, chiefly Brit*
money supply *n* (1878) **:** the total amount of money available in an economy for spending as calculated by any of various methods (as by adding total currency to funds available in private checking accounts)
mon·ey·wort \-ˌwərt, -ˌwȯrt\ *n* (1578) **:** a trailing perennial herb (*Lysimachia nummularia*) of the primrose family with rounded opposite leaves and solitary yellow flowers in their axils
[1]**mon·ger** \ˈmən-gər, ˈmäŋ-\ *n* [ME *mongere,* fr. OE *mangere,* fr. L *mangon-, mango,* of Gk origin; akin to Gk *manganon* charm, philter] (bef. 12c) **1 :** BROKER, DEALER — usu. used in combination ⟨ale*monger*⟩ **2 :** a person who attempts to stir up or spread something that is usu. petty or discreditable — usu. used in combination ⟨war*monger*⟩
[2]**monger** *vt* **mon·gered; mon·ger·ing** \-g(ə-)riŋ\ (ca. 1864) **:** PEDDLE
mon·go \ˈmäŋ-(ˌ)gō\ *n, pl* **mongo** [Mongolian *möngö*] (1935) — see *tugrik* at MONEY table
Mon·gol \ˈmäŋ-gəl; ˈmän-ˌgōl, ˈmäŋ-\ *n* [Mongolian *mongγol*] (ca. 1662) **1 :** a member of any of a group of traditionally pastoral peoples of Mongolia **2 :** MONGOLIAN 1 **3 :** a person of Mongoloid racial stock **4** *often not cap, usu offensive* **:** one affected with Down syndrome — **Mongol** *adj*
[1]**Mon·go·lian** \män-ˈgōl-yən, mäŋ-, -ˈgō-lē-ən\ *adj* (1706) **1 :** of, relating to, or constituting Mongolia, the Mongolian People's Republic, the Mongols, or Mongolian **2** *usu offensive* **:** of, relating to, or affected with Down syndrome
[2]**Mongolian** *n* (1846) **1 a :** the language of the Mongol people **b :** a family of Altaic languages that includes the languages of the Mongols and the Kalmucks **2 a :** MONGOL 1 **b :** a person of Mongoloid racial stock **c :** a native or inhabitant of Mongolia
Mongolian gerbil *n* (1948) **:** a gerbil (*Meriones unguiculatus*) of Mongolia and northern China that has a high capacity for temperature regulation and is often kept as a pet or used as a laboratory animal
Mon·gol·ic \män-ˈgä-lik, mäŋ-\ *adj* (1834) **:** MONGOLOID 1
mon·gol·ism \ˈmäŋ-gə-ˌli-zəm\ *n* (1900) *usu offensive* **:** DOWN SYNDROME
Mon·gol·oid \ˈmäŋ-gə-ˌlȯid\ *adj* (1868) **1 :** of, constituting, or characteristic of a race of humankind native to Asia and classified according to physical features (as the presence of an epicanthic fold) **2** *often not cap, usu offensive* **:** of, relating to, or affected with Down syndrome — **Mongoloid** *n*
mon·goose \ˈmän-ˌgüs, ˈmäŋ-\ *n, pl* **mon·goos·es** *also* **mon·geese** \-ˌgēs\ [Hindi & Marathi *māgūs,* fr. Prakrit *maṁgūsa*] (1698) **:** any of numerous carnivorous mammals (family Herpestidae) that are agile usu. ferret-sized mammals sometimes with bands or stripes, feed chiefly on small animals and fruits, and are sometimes grouped with the viverrids in two subfamilies (Herpestinae and Galidiinae)
mon·grel \ˈmäŋ-grəl, ˈməŋ-\ *n* [ME, prob. fr. *mong* mixture, short for *ymong,* fr. OE *gemong* crowd — more at AMONG] (15c) **1 :** an individual resulting from the interbreeding of diverse breeds or strains; *esp* **:** one of unknown ancestry **2 :** a cross between types of persons or things — **mongrel** *adj* — **mon·grel·i·za·tion** \ˌmäŋ-grə-lə-ˈzā-shən, ˌməŋ-\ *n* — **mon·grel·ize** \ˈmäŋ-grə-ˌlīz, ˈməŋ-\ *vt*
monied *var of* MONEYED
monies *pl of* MONEY
mon·i·ker *also* **mon·ick·er** \ˈmä-ni-kər\ *n* [prob. fr. Shelta (language of Irish itinerants) *mŭnnik,* modif. of Ir *ainm*] (1851) **:** NAME, NICKNAME
mo·nil·i·a·sis \ˌmō-nə-ˈlī-ə-səs, ˌmä-\ *n, pl* **-a·ses** \-ˌsēz\ [NL, fr. *Monilia,* genus of fungi, fr. L *monile* necklace] (1920) **:** CANDIDIASIS
mo·nil·i·form \mə-ˈni-lə-ˌfȯrm\ *adj* [L *monile* necklace — more at MANE] (ca. 1803) **:** jointed or constricted at regular intervals so as to resemble a string of beads ⟨a ~ root⟩ ⟨~ insect antennae⟩
mon·ish \ˈmä-nish\ *vt* [ME *monesen,* alter. of *monesten,* fr. AF *monester,* fr. VL **monestare,* fr. L *monēre* to warn] (14c) *archaic* **:** WARN
mo·nism \ˈmō-ni-zəm, ˈmä-\ *n* [G *Monismus,* fr. *mon-* + *-ismus* -ism] (1862) **1 a :** a view that there is only one kind of ultimate substance **b :** the view that reality is one unitary organic whole with no independent parts **2 :** MONOGENESIS **3 :** a viewpoint or theory that reduces all phenomena to one principle — **mo·nist** \ˈmō-nist, ˈmä-\ *n* — **mo·nis·tic** \mō-ˈnis-tik, mä-\ *adj*
mo·ni·tion \mō-ˈni-shən, mə-\ *n* [ME *monicioun,* fr. AF *monicion,* fr. L *monition-, monitio,* fr. *monēre*] (14c) **1 :** WARNING, CAUTION **2 :** an intimation of danger
[1]**mon·i·tor** \ˈmä-nə-tər\ *n* [L, one that warns, overseer, fr. *monēre* to warn — more at MIND] (1546) **1 a :** a student appointed to assist a teacher **b :** one that warns or instructs **c :** one that monitors or is used in monitoring: as **(1) :** a cathode-ray tube used for display (as of television pictures or computer information) **(2) :** a device for observing a biological condition or function **2 :** MONITOR LIZARD **3** [*Monitor,* first ship of the type] **a :** a heavily armored warship formerly used in coastal operations having a very low freeboard and one or more revolving gun turrets **b :** a small modern warship with shallow draft for coastal bombardment **4 :** a raised central portion of a roof having low windows or louvers for providing light and air — **mon·i·to·ri·al** \ˌmä-nə-ˈtȯr-ē-əl\ *adj* — **mon·i·tor·ship** \ˈmä-nə-tər-ˌship\ *n*
[2]**monitor** *vt* **mon·i·tored; mon·i·tor·ing** \ˈmä-nə-t(ə-)riŋ\ (1924) **:** to watch, keep track of, or check usu. for a special purpose
monitor lizard *n* (1856) **:** any of various tropical carnivorous lizards (genus *Varanus* of the family Varanidae) of Australia, Asia, and Africa
[1]**mon·i·to·ry** \ˈmä-nə-ˌtȯr-ē\ *adj* [ME, fr. L *monitorius,* fr. *monēre*] (15c) **:** giving admonition **:** WARNING
[2]**monitory** *n, pl* **-ries** (15c) **:** a letter giving admonition or warning
[1]**monk** \ˈməŋk\ *n* [ME, fr. OE *munuc,* fr. LL *monachus,* fr. LGk *monachos,* fr. Gk, adj., single, fr. *monos* single, alone] (bef. 12c) **:** a man who is a member of a religious order and lives in a monastery; *also* **:** FRIAR
[2]**monk** *n* (1843) **:** MONKEY
monk·ery \ˈməŋ-kə-rē\ *n, pl* **-er·ies** (ca. 1536) **1 :** monastic life or practice **:** MONASTICISM **2 :** a monastic house **:** MONASTERY
[1]**mon·key** \ˈməŋ-kē\ *n, pl* **monkeys** [prob. of LG origin; akin to *Moneke,* name of an ape, prob. of Romance origin; akin to OSp *mona* monkey] (ca. 1530) **1 :** a nonhuman primate mammal with the exception usu. of the lemurs and tarsiers; *esp* **:** any of the smaller longer-tailed catarrhine or platyrrhine primates as contrasted with the apes **2 a :** a person resembling a monkey **b :** a ludicrous figure **:** DUPE **3 :** any of various machines, implements, or vessels; *esp* **:** the falling weight of a pile driver **4 :** a desperate desire for or addiction to drugs — often used in the phrase *monkey on one's back*; *broadly* **:** a persistent or annoying encumbrance or problem

\ə\ **abut** \ᵊ\ **kitten, F table** \ər\ **further** \a\ **ash** \ā\ **ace** \ä\ **mop, mar**
\au̇\ **out** \ch\ **chin** \e\ **bet** \ē\ **easy** \g\ **go** \i\ **hit** \ī\ **ice** \j\ **job**
\ŋ\ **sing** \ō\ **go** \ȯ\ **law** \ȯi\ **boy** \th\ **thin** \t͟h\ **the** \ü\ **loot** \u̇\ **foot**
\y\ **yet** \zh\ **vision, beige** \k̲, ⁿ, œ, ue, ʸ\ *see* **Guide to Pronunciation**

MONEY

NAME	SYMBOL	SUBDIVISION	COUNTRY
afghani	Af	100 puls	Afghanistan
ariary		5 iraimbilanja	Madagascar
baht or tical	B	100 satang	Thailand
balboa[1]		100 centesimos	Panama
birr	Br	100 cents	Ethiopia
bolivar	B	100 centimos	Venezuela
boliviano	$b	100 centavos	Bolivia
cedi	₵	100 pesewas	Ghana
colón	C or ₡	100 centimos	Costa Rica
córdoba	C$	100 centavos	Nicaragua
dalasi		100 bututs	Gambia
denar		100 deni[2]	Macedonia
dinar	DA	100 centimes	Algeria
dinar	BD	1000 fils	Bahrain
dinar	ID	1000 fils	Iraq
dinar	JD	1000 fils	Jordan
dinar	KD	1000 fils	Kuwait
dinar	LD	1000 dirhams	Libya
dinar		100 paras	Serbia
dinar	D	1000 millimes	Tunisia
dirham	DH	100 centimes	Morocco
dirham		100 fils	United Arab Emirates
dobra	Db	100 centimos	São Tomé and Príncipe
dollar	EC$[3] or $	100 cents	Antigua and Barbuda, Dominica, Grenada, St. Kitts and Nevis, St. Lucia, St. Vincent and the Grenadines
dollar	$A or A$	100 cents	Australia
dollar	$ or B$	100 cents	Bahamas
dollar	$ or Bds$	100 cents	Barbados
dollar	$	100 cents	Belize
dollar	$	100 cents	Bermuda
dollar	B$	100 sen or cents	Brunei
dollar	$	100 cents	Canada
dollar	$ or F$	100 cents	Fiji
dollar	$ or G$	100 cents	Guyana
dollar	$ or HK$	100 cents	Hong Kong
dollar	$ or J$	100 cents	Jamaica
dollar	L$	100 cents	Liberia
dollar	N$	100 cents	Namibia
dollar	NZ$	100 cents	New Zealand
dollar	$ or S$	100 cents	Singapore
dollar	SI$	100 cents	Solomon Islands
dollar	$	100 cents	Suriname
dollar or yuan	NT$	100 cents	Taiwan
dollar	$ or TT$	100 cents	Trinidad and Tobago
dollar	$	100 cents	United States
dollar[4]	$ or Z$	100 cents	Zimbabwe
dollar—see RINGGIT, below			
dong	D	100 xu	Vietnam
dram		100 luma	Armenia
escudo		100 centavos	Cape Verde
euro[5]	€	100 cents	Austria, Belgium, Cyprus, Estonia, Finland, France, Germany, Greece, Ireland, Italy, Luxembourg, Malta, Netherlands, Portugal, Slovakia, Slovenia, Spain
forint	Ft	100 filler[2]	Hungary
franc	F or fr or Fr or FR	100 centimes	Cameroon, Central African Republic, Chad, Republic of the Congo, Equatorial Guinea[6], Gabon
franc	FR or F	100 centimes	Benin, Burkina Faso, Guinea-Bissau, Ivory Coast, Mali, Niger, Senegal, Togo
franc	F or FBu	100 centimes	Burundi
franc	CFr or CF	100 centimes	Comoros
franc		100 centimes	Democratic Republic of the Congo
franc	DFr or DF	100 centimes	Djibouti
franc	GF	100 centimes	Guinea
franc	FR or RF	100 centimes[2]	Rwanda
franc	SFr or SFR	100 centimes or rappen	Switzerland
gourde	G	100 centimes	Haiti
guarani	G or ₲	100 centimes	Paraguay
hryvnia		100 kopiykas	Ukraine
kina	K	100 toea	Papua New Guinea
kip	K	100 at	Laos
koruna	Kčs	100 haleru	Czech Republic
krona	KR	100 aurar (sing eyrir)	Iceland
krona	SKr or KR	100 ore	Sweden
krone	DKr	100 ore	Denmark
krone	KR or NKr	100 ore	Norway
kuna		100 lipa	Croatia
kwacha	K	100 tambala	Malawi
kwacha	K	100 ngwee	Zambia

NAME	SYMBOL	SUBDIVISION	COUNTRY
kwanza		100 lwei	Angola
kyat	K	100 pyas	Myanmar
lari		100 tetri	Republic of Georgia
lats (pl lati or latu)		100 santimi or santimu (sing santims)	Latvia
lek		100 qindarka	Albania
lempira	L	100 centavos	Honduras
leone	Le	100 cents	Sierra Leone
leu		100 bani (sing ban)	Moldova
leu		100 bani (sing ban)	Romania
lev		100 stotinki	Bulgaria
lilangeni (pl emalangeni)	E	100 cents	Swaziland
lira or pound	TL	100 kurus	Turkey
litas		100 centai or centu (sing centas)	Lithuania
livre—see POUND, below			
loti (pl maloti)		100 licente or lisente (sing sente)	Lesotho
manat		100 gopik	Azerbaijan
manat		100 tennesi	Turkmenistan
marka		100 feninga or mark (sing fening)	Bosnia and Herzegovina
metical		100 centavos	Mozambique
naira	₦	100 kobo	Nigeria
nakfa	nfa	100 cents	Eritrea
ngultrum	Nu	100 chetrums	Bhutan
ouguiya		5 khoums	Mauritania
pa'anga	T$	100 seniti	Tonga
pataca		100 avos	Macao
peso		100 centavos	Argentina
peso		100 centavos	Chile
peso	Col$	100 centavos	Colombia
peso		100 centavos	Cuba
peso	RD$	100 centavos	Dominican Republic
peso	$	100 centavos	Mexico
peso or piso	P	100 sentimos or centavos	Philippines
peso	$	100 centesimos	Uruguay
pound	£E	100 piastres	Egypt
pound or livre	£L	100 piastres	Lebanon
pound		100 piastres	South Sudan
pound		100 piastres	Sudan
pound		100 piastres	Syria
pound	£	100 pence (sing penny)	United Kingdom
pound—see LIRA, above			
pula	P	100 thebe	Botswana
quetzal	Q	100 centavos	Guatemala
rand	R	100 cents	South Africa
real	R$	100 centavos	Brazil
rial	R or Rl	100 dinars	Iran
rial	RO	1000 baisa	Oman
rial also riyal	YR or R	100 fils	Yemen
rial—see RIYAL, below			
riel		100 sen	Cambodia
ringgit or dollar	$ or RM	100 sen	Malaysia
riyal also rial	QR	100 dirhams	Qatar
riyal also rial	SR	100 halala	Saudi Arabia
riyal—see RIAL, above			
rubel		100 kapeek (sing kapeyka)	Belarus
ruble	R	100 kopecks	Russia
rufiyaa	Rf	100 laari	Maldives
rupee	Re (pl Rs)	100 paise	India
rupee	Re (pl Rs)	100 cents	Mauritius
rupee	NR	100 paisa	Nepal
rupee	Re (pl Rs)	100 paisa	Pakistan
rupee	SR	100 cents	Seychelles
rupee	Re (pl Rs)	100 cents	Sri Lanka
rupiah	Rp	100 sen	Indonesia
shekel or sheqel	NIS	100 agorot	Israel
shilling	S or KSh	100 cents	Kenya
shilling		100 cents	Somalia
shilling	TSh	100 cents	Tanzania
shilling	USh	100 cents	Uganda
sol	S/	100 centimos	Peru
som		100 tyiyn	Kyrgyzstan
somoni		100 dirams	Tajikistan
sum or som		100 tiyin	Uzbekistan
taka	Tk	100 paisa or poisha	Bangladesh
tala	$	100 sene	Samoa
tenge		100 tyin	Kazakhstan
tical—see BAHT, above			
tugrik	Tug	100 mongo	Mongolia
vatu	VT		Vanuatu
won		100 chon	North Korea
won		100 chon	South Korea
yen	¥	100 sen[2]	Japan
yuan	Y	100 fen	China (mainland)
yuan—see DOLLAR, above			
zloty	Zl	100 groszy	Poland

[1] A monetary unit in name only, replaced by the U.S. dollar.
[2] Now a subdivision in name only.
[3] Dollars issued by the *Eastern Caribbean Central Bank*, established to promote economic cooperation among the member nations.
[4] A monetary unit in name only, replaced by foreign currencies.
[5] Replaced the individual monetary units of participating European Union countries.
[6] The franc of Equatorial Guinea is also called the *franco*.

[2]**monkey** *vb* **mon·keyed; mon·key·ing** *vt* (ca. 1568) **:** MIMIC, MOCK ~ *vi* **1 :** to act in a grotesque or mischievous manner **2 a :** FOOL, TRIFLE — often used with *around* ⟨he likes to ~ around with engines⟩ **b :** TAMPER — usu. used with *with* ⟨don't ~ with the settings⟩

monkey bars *n pl* (1955) **:** a three-dimensional framework of horizontal and vertical bars from which children can hang and swing

monkey business *n* (1835) **:** SHENANIGAN 2 ⟨didn't try any *monkey business* when the boss was away⟩

monkey jacket *n* (ca. 1822) **:** MESS JACKET

mon·key·pod \ˈməŋ-kē-ˌpäd\ *n* (1868) **1 :** an ornamental tropical leguminous tree (*Samanea saman* syn. *Albizia saman*) that has bipinnate leaves, globose clusters of flowers with crimson stamens, sweet-pulp pods eaten by cattle, and wood used in carving — called also *rain tree* **2 :** the wood of a monkeypod

mon·key·pox \ˈməŋ-kē-ˌpäks\ *n* (1959) **:** a rare virus disease esp. of central and western Africa that is caused by a poxvirus (species *Monkeypox virus* of the genus *Orthopoxvirus*), occurs chiefly in wild rodents and primates, and when transmitted to humans resembles smallpox but is milder

monkey puzzle *n* (1856) **:** a tall araucaria (*Araucaria araucana*) that is native to Chile and western Argentina but widely grown elsewhere — called also *monkey puzzle tree*

mon·key·shine \ˈməŋ-kē-ˌshīn\ *n* (ca. 1832) **:** mischievous or playful activity **:** PRANK — usu. used in pl. ⟨grew tired of all the ~*s* in his classroom⟩

monkey wrench *n* (ca. 1807) **1 :** a wrench with one fixed and one adjustable jaw at right angles to a straight handle **2 :** something that disrupts ⟨threw a *monkey wrench* into the peace negotiations⟩

monk·fish \ˈməŋk-ˌfish\ *n* (1666) **:** either of two goosefishes (*Lophius americanus* of America and *L. piscatorius* of Europe) used for food

Mon–Khmer \ˌmōn-kə-ˈmer\ *n* (1887) **:** a language family containing Mon, Khmer, and a number of other languages of southeast Asia

monk·hood \ˈməŋk-ˌhu̇d\ *n* (bef. 12c) **1 :** the character, condition, or profession of a monk **:** MONASTICISM **2 :** monks as a class

monk·ish \ˈməŋ-kish\ *adj* (1537) **1 :** of, relating to, or resembling a monk; *also* **:** resembling that of a monk **2 :** inclined to disciplinary self-denial

monk parakeet *n* (ca. 1925) **:** a So. American green and gray parakeet (*Myiopsitta monachus*) that is kept as a cage bird and has become established in several wild breeding populations in the U.S. from escaped stock

monk's cloth *n* (15c) **:** a coarse heavy fabric in basket weave made orig. of worsted and used for monk's habits but now chiefly of cotton or linen and used for draperies

monk seal *n* (1841) **:** any of a genus (*Monachus*) of hair seals of Hawaii, the Mediterranean Sea, and formerly the Caribbean Sea

monks·hood \ˈməŋ(k)s-ˌhu̇d\ *n* (1577) **:** any of a genus (*Aconitum*) of usu. bluish flowered poisonous herbs of the buttercup family; *esp* **:** a poisonous Eurasian herb (*A. napellus*) often cultivated for its showy terminal racemes of white or purplish flowers — compare WOLFSBANE

[1]**mono** \ˈmä-(ˌ)nō\ *n, pl* **mon·os** [[2]*mono*] (1959) **:** monophonic reproduction

[2]**mono** *adj* (1960) **:** MONOPHONIC 2

[3]**mono** *n* (1962) **:** INFECTIOUS MONONUCLEOSIS

mono- — see MON-

mono·amine \ˌmä-nō-ə-ˈmēn\ *n* [ISV] (1951) **:** an amine RNH_2 that has one organic substituent attached to the nitrogen atom; *esp* **:** one (as serotonin) that is functionally important in neural transmission

monoamine oxidase *n* (1951) **:** an enzyme that deaminates monoamines oxidatively and that functions in the nervous system by breaking down monoamine neurotransmitters

mono·am·in·er·gic \ˌmä-nō-ˌa-mə-ˈnər-jik\ *adj* (1966) **:** liberating or involving monoamines (as serotonin or norepinephrine) in neural transmission ⟨~ neurons⟩ ⟨~ mechanisms⟩

mono·ba·sic \ˌmä-nə-ˈbā-sik\ *adj* [ISV] (1842) *of an acid* **:** having only one replaceable hydrogen atom

mono·car·box·yl·ic \-ˌkär-(ˌ)bäk-ˈsi-lik\ *adj* (1883) **:** containing one carboxyl group ⟨acetic acid is a ~ acid⟩

mono·car·pic \-ˈkär-pik\ *adj* [prob. fr. NL **monocarpicus,* fr. *mon-* + *-carpicus* -carpic] (1849) **:** bearing fruit but once and then dying

mono·cha·si·um \-ˈkā-zē-əm, -zhē-\ *n, pl* **-sia** \-zē-ə, -zhē-\ [NL, fr. *mon-* + *-chasium* (as in *dichasium*)] (ca. 1890) **:** a cymose inflorescence that produces only one main axis — **mono·cha·sial** \-zē-əl, -zhē-\ *adj*

mono·chord \ˈmä-nə-ˌkȯrd\ *n* [ME *monocorde,* fr. MF, fr. ML *monochordum,* fr. Gk *monochordon,* fr. *mon-* + *chordē* string — more at YARN] (15c) **:** an instrument of ancient origin for measuring and demonstrating the mathematical relations of musical tones and that consists of a single string stretched over a sound box and a movable bridge set on a graduated scale

mono·chro·mat \ˈmä-nə-krō-ˌmat, ˌmä-nə-ˈ\ *n* [*mon-* + Gk *chrōmat-, chrōma*] (1893) **:** a completely color-blind individual

mono·chro·mat·ic \ˌmä-nə-krō-ˈma-tik\ *adj* [L *monochromatos,* fr. Gk *monochrōmatos,* fr. *mon-* + *chrōmat-, chrōma* color] (1822) **1 a :** having or consisting of one color or hue **b :** MONOCHROME 2 **2 :** consisting of radiation of a single wavelength or of a very small range of wavelengths **3 :** of, relating to, or exhibiting monochromatism **4 :** lacking variety, creativity, or excitement **:** COLORLESS — **mono·chro·mat·i·cal·ly** \-ti-k(ə-)lē\ *adv* — **mono·chro·ma·tic·i·ty** \-ˌkrō-mə-ˈti-sə-tē\ *n*

mono·chro·ma·tism \-ˈkrō-mə-ˌti-zəm\ *n* (1893) **:** complete color blindness in which all colors appear as shades of gray

mono·chro·ma·tor \ˌmä-nə-ˈkrō-ˌmā-tər\ *n* [*monochromatic* + *illuminator*] (1909) **:** a device for isolating a narrow portion of a spectrum

[1]**mono·chrome** \ˈmä-nə-ˌkrōm\ *n* [ML *monochroma,* fr. L, fem. of *monochromos* of one color, fr. Gk *monochrōmos,* fr. *mon-* + *-chrōmos* -chrome] (1662) **:** a painting, drawing, or photograph in a single hue — **mono·chro·mic** \ˌmä-nə-ˈkrō-mik\ *adj* — **mono·chrom·ist** \ˈmä-nə-ˌkrō-mist\ *n*

[2]**monochrome** *adj* (1839) **1 :** of, relating to, or made with a single color or hue **2 :** involving or producing visual images in a single color or in varying tones of a single color (as gray) ⟨~ film⟩

mon·o·cle \ˈmä-ni-kəl\ *n* [F, fr. LL *monoculus* having one eye, fr. L *mon-* + *oculus* eye — more at EYE] (ca. 1858) **:** an eyeglass for one eye — **mon·o·cled** \-kəld\ *adj*

mono·cline \ˈmä-nə-ˌklīn\ *n* (1879) **:** an oblique geologic fold

mono·clin·ic \ˌmä-nə-ˈkli-nik\ *adj* [ISV] (1856) **:** of, relating to, or constituting a system of crystallization characterized by three unequal axes with one oblique intersection

mono·clo·nal \ˌmä-nə-ˈklō-nᵊl\ *adj* (1914) **:** produced by, being, or composed of cells derived from a single cell — **monoclonal** *n*

mono·coque \ˈmä-nə-ˌkōk, -ˌkäk\ *n* [F, fr. *mon-* + *coque* shell, prob. fr. L *coccum* kermes — more at COCOON] (1913) **1 :** a type of construction (as of a fuselage) in which the outer skin carries all or a major part of the stresses **2 :** a type of vehicle construction (as of an automobile) in which the body is integral with the chassis

mono·cot \-ˌkät\ *n* (1854) **:** MONOCOTYLEDON

mono·cot·y·le·don \ˌmä-nə-ˌkä-tə-ˈlē-dᵊn\ *n* [ultim. fr. NL *mon-* + *cotyledon* cotyledon] (ca. 1727) **:** any of a class or subclass (Liliopsida or Monocotyledoneae) of chiefly herbaceous angiospermous plants having an embryo with a single cotyledon, usu. parallel-veined leaves, and floral organs arranged in cycles of three — compare DICOTYLEDON — **mono·cot·y·le·don·ous** \-dᵊn-əs\ *adj*

mo·noc·ra·cy \mä-ˈnä-krə-sē, mə-\ *n* (1606) **:** government by a single person — **mono·crat** \ˈmä-nə-ˌkrat\ *n* — **mono·crat·ic** \ˌmä-nə-ˈkra-tik\ *adj*

mono·crys·tal \ˈmä-nə-ˌkris-tᵊl\ *n* (1926) **:** a single crystal — **mono·crystal** *adj* — **mono·crys·tal·line** \ˌmä-nə-ˈkris-tə-lən *also* -ˌlīn, -ˌlēn\ *adj*

[1]**mon·oc·u·lar** \mä-ˈnä-kyə-lər, mə-\ *adj* [LL *monoculus* having one eye] (1640) **1 :** of, involving, or affecting a single eye **2 :** suitable for use with only one eye — **mon·oc·u·lar·ly** *adv*

[2]**monocular** *n* (1936) **:** a monocular device

mono·cul·ture \ˈmä-nə-ˌkəl-chər\ *n* (1901) **1 :** the cultivation or growth of a single crop or organism esp. on agricultural or forest land **2 :** a crop or a population of a single kind of organism grown on land in monoculture **3 :** a culture dominated by a single element **:** a prevailing culture marked by homogeneity — **mono·cul·tur·al** \ˌmä-nə-ˈkəlch-rəl, -ˈkəl-chə-\ *adj*

mono·cy·clic \ˌmä-nə-ˈsī-klik, -ˈsi-\ *adj* [ISV] (1910) **:** containing one ring in the molecular structure

mono·cyte \ˈmä-nə-ˌsīt\ *n* [ISV] (ca. 1913) **:** a large white blood cell with finely granulated chromatin dispersed throughout the nucleus that is formed in the bone marrow, enters the blood, and migrates into the connective tissue where it differentiates into a macrophage — **mono·cyt·ic** \ˌmä-nə-ˈsi-tik\ *adj*

mono·dis·perse \ˌmä-nō-dis-ˈpərs\ *adj* [*mon-* + *disperse,* adj., fr. *disperse,* v.] (1925) **:** characterized by particles of uniform size in a dispersed phase

mon·o·dist \ˈmä-nə-dist\ *n* (1751) **:** a writer, singer, or composer of monody

mono·dra·ma \ˈmä-nə-ˌdrä-mə, -ˌdra-\ *n* (1793) **:** a drama acted or designed to be acted by a single person — **mono·dra·mat·ic** \ˌmä-nə-drə-ˈma-tik\ *adj*

mon·o·dy \ˈmä-nə-dē\ *n, pl* **-dies** [ML *monodia,* fr. Gk *monōidia,* fr. *monōidos* singing alone, fr. *mon-* + *aeidein* to sing — more at ODE] (ca. 1623) **1 :** an ode sung by one voice (as in a Greek tragedy) **2 :** an elegy or dirge performed by one person **3 a :** a monophonic vocal piece **b :** the monophonic style of 17th century opera — **mo·nod·ic** \mə-ˈnä-dik\ *or* **mo·nod·i·cal** \-di-kəl\ *adj*

mon·oe·cious *also* **mon·e·cious** \mə-ˈnē-shəs, mä-\ *adj* [ultim. fr. Gk *mon-* + *oikos* house — more at VICINITY] (1761) **1 :** having pistillate and staminate flowers on the same plant **2 :** having male and female sex organs in the same individual **:** HERMAPHRODITIC

mon·oe·cism \-ˈnē-ˌsi-zəm\ *n* (ca. 1875) **:** the condition of being monoecious

mono·es·ter \ˈmä-nō-ˌes-tər\ *n* (1927) **:** an ester (as of a dibasic acid) that contains only one ester group

mono·fil·a·ment \ˌmä-nə-ˈfi-lə-mənt\ *n* (1940) **:** a single untwisted synthetic filament (as of nylon)

mo·nog·a·mist \mə-ˈnä-gə-mist\ *n* (ca. 1721) **:** one who practices or upholds monogamy

mo·nog·a·my \-mē\ *n* [F *monogamie,* fr. LL *monogamia,* fr. Gk, fr. *monogamos* monogamous, fr. *mon-* + *gamos* marriage, fr. *gamein* to marry] (1612) **1** *archaic* **:** the practice of marrying only once during a lifetime **2 :** the state or custom of being married to one person at a time **3 :** the condition or practice of having a single mate during a period of time — **mo·nog·a·mous** \mə-ˈnä-gə-məs\ *also* **mono·gam·ic** \ˌmä-nə-ˈga-mik\ *adj* — **mo·nog·a·mous·ly** *adv*

mono·gas·tric \ˌmä-nə-ˈgas-trik\ *adj* (1814) **:** having a stomach with only a single compartment ⟨swine, chicks, and human beings are ~⟩

mono·ge·ne·an \-ˈjē-nē-ən\ *n* [NL *Monogenea,* group name] (1899) **:** a monogenetic flatworm — **monogenean** *adj*

mono·gen·e·sis \-ˈje-nə-səs\ *n* [NL] (1857) **:** origin of diverse individuals or kinds (as of language) by descent from a single ancestral individual or kind

mono·ge·net·ic \-jə-ˈne-tik\ *adj* (1921) **1 :** relating to or involving monogenesis **2 :** of, relating to, or being any of a class (Monogenea) of flatworms that ordinarily live as ectoparasites on a single host (as a fish or amphibian) throughout their entire life cycle

mono·gen·ic \-ˈje-nik\ *adj* [ISV] (1939) **:** of, relating to, or controlled by a single gene and esp. by either of an allelic pair — **mono·gen·i·cal·ly** \-ni-k(ə-)lē\ *adv*

mono·germ \ˈmä-nə-ˌjərm\ *adj* [*mon-* + *germinate*] (1950) **:** producing or being a fruit that gives rise to a single plant ⟨a ~ sugar beet⟩

mono·glot \-ˌglät\ *adj* [*mono-* + *-glot* (as in *polyglot*)] (1830) **:** MONOLINGUAL — **monoglot** *n*

mono·glyc·er·ide \ˌmä-nə-ˈgli-sə-ˌrīd\ *n* (1860) **:** any of various esters of glycerol in which only one of the three hydroxyl groups is esterified and which are often used as emulsifiers

[1]**mono·gram** \ˈmä-nə-ˌgram\ *n* [LL *monogramma,* fr. Gk *mon-* + *gramma* letter — more at GRAM] (ca. 1696) **:** a sign of identity usu.

\ə\ **abut** \ᵊ\ **kitten,** F **table** \ər\ **further** \a\ **ash** \ā\ **ace** \ä\ **mop, mar**
\au̇\ **out** \ch\ **chin** \e\ **bet** \ē\ **easy** \g\ **go** \i\ **hit** \ī\ **ice** \j\ **job**
\ŋ\ **sing** \ō\ **go** \ȯ\ **law** \ȯi\ **boy** \th\ **thin** \t͟h\ **the** \ü\ **loot** \u̇\ **foot**
\y\ **yet** \zh\ **vision, beige** \ḵ, ⁿ, œ, ue, ʸ\ *see* Guide to Pronunciation

formed of the combined initials of a name — **mono·gram·mat·ic** \ˌmä-nə-grə-ˈma-tik\ *adj*

[2]**monogram** *vt* **-grammed; -gram·ming** (1868) **:** to mark with a monogram — **mono·gram·mer** \-ˌgra-mər\ *n*

[1]**mono·graph** \ˈmä-nə-ˌgraf\ *n* (1821) **:** a learned treatise on a small area of learning; *also* **:** a written account of a single thing — **mono·graph·ic** \ˌmä-nə-ˈgra-fik\ *adj*

[2]**monograph** *vt* (1856) **:** to write a monograph on

mo·nog·y·nous \mə-ˈnä-jə-nəs, mä-\ *adj* (ca. 1890) **:** of, relating to, or living in monogyny

mo·nog·y·ny \-nē\ *n* [ISV] (1876) **:** the state or custom of having only one wife at a time

mono·hull \ˈmä-nə-ˌhəl\ *n* (1967) **:** a vessel (as a sailboat) with a single hull — compare MULTIHULL — **mono·hulled** \-ˌhəld\ *adj*

mono·hy·brid \ˌmä-nō-ˈhī-brəd\ *n* (1903) **:** an individual or strain heterozygous for one specified gene — **monohybrid** *adj*

mono·hy·dric \-ˈhī-drik\ *adj* (1869) **:** MONOHYDROXY

mono·hy·droxy \-(ˌ)hī-ˈdräk-sē\ *adj* [ISV *monohydroxy-*, fr. *mon-* + *hydroxy-*] (ca. 1934) **:** containing one hydroxyl group in the molecule

mono·lay·er \ˈmä-nō-ˌlā-ər, -ˌler\ *n* (1926) **:** a single continuous layer or film that is one cell, molecule, or atom in thickness

mono·lin·gual \ˌmä-nə-ˈliŋ-gwəl, ˌmō-, -ˈliŋ-gyə-wəl\ *adj* (1926) **:** having or using only one language — **monolingual** *n*

mono·lith \ˈmä-nə-ˌlith\ *n* [F *monolithe,* fr. *monolithe* consisting of a single stone, fr. L *monolithus,* fr. Gk *monolithos,* fr. *mon-* + *lithos* stone] (1844) **1 :** a single great stone often in the form of an obelisk or column **2 :** a massive structure **3 :** an organized whole that acts as a single unified powerful or influential force

mono·lith·ic \ˌmä-nə-ˈli-thik\ *adj* (1825) **1 a :** of, relating to, or resembling a monolith **:** HUGE, MASSIVE **b** (1) **:** formed from a single crystal ⟨a ~ silicon chip⟩ (2) **:** produced in or on a monolithic chip ⟨a ~ circuit⟩ **2 a :** cast as a single piece ⟨a ~ concrete wall⟩ **b :** formed or composed of material without joints or seams ⟨a ~ floor covering⟩ **c :** consisting of or constituting a single unit **3 a :** constituting a massive undifferentiated and often rigid whole ⟨a ~ society⟩ **b :** exhibiting or characterized by often rigidly fixed uniformity ⟨~ party unity⟩ — **mono·lith·i·cal·ly** \-thi-k(ə-)lē\ *adv*

mono·logue *also* **mono·log** \ˈmä-nə-ˌlȯg, -ˌläg\ *n* [MF *monologue,* fr. *mon-* + *-logue*] (1549) **1 a :** SOLILOQUY 2 **b :** a dramatic sketch performed by one actor **c :** the routine of a stand-up comic **2 :** a literary composition written in the form of a soliloquy **3 :** a long speech monopolizing conversation — **mono·logu·ist** \-ˌlȯ-gist, -ˌlä-\ *or* **mo·no·lo·gist** *same or* mə-ˈnä-lə-jist, -gist\ *n*

mono·ma·nia \ˌmä-nə-ˈmā-nē-ə, -nyə\ *n* [NL] (1823) **1 :** mental illness esp. when limited in expression to one idea or area of thought **2 :** excessive concentration on a single object or idea — **mono·ma·ni·ac** \-nē-ˌak\ *n or adj* — **mono·ma·ni·a·cal** \-mə-ˈnī-ə-kəl\ *adj* — **mono·ma·ni·a·cal·ly** \-k(ə-)lē\ *adv*

mono·mer \ˈmä-nə-mər\ *n* [ISV] (1914) **:** a chemical compound that can undergo polymerization — **mo·no·mer·ic** \ˌmä-nə-ˈmer-ik, ˌmō-\ *adj*

mono·me·tal·lic \ˌmä-nō-mə-ˈta-lik\ *adj* (1861) **1 :** of or relating to monometallism **2 :** consisting of or employing one metal

mono·met·al·lism \-ˈme-tᵊl-ˌi-zəm\ *n* [ISV *mon-* + *-metallism* (as in *bimetallism*)] (1879) **:** the adoption of one metal only in a currency — **mono·met·al·list** \-tᵊl-ist\ *n*

mo·nom·e·ter \mə-ˈnä-mə-tər, mä-\ *n* [LL, fr. Gk *monometros,* fr. *mon-* + *metron* measure — more at MEASURE] (ca. 1846) **:** a line of verse consisting of a single metrical foot or dipody

mo·no·mi·al \mä-ˈnō-mē-əl, mə-\ *n* [blend of *mon-* and *-nomial* (as in *binomial*)] (ca. 1706) **1 :** a mathematical expression consisting of a single term **2 :** a taxonomic name consisting of a single word or term — **monomial** *adj*

mono·mo·lec·u·lar \ˌmä-nə-mə-ˈle-kyə-lər\ *adj* (1917) **:** being only one molecule thick ⟨a ~ film⟩ — **mono·mo·lec·u·lar·ly** *adv*

mono·mor·phe·mic \-mȯr-ˈfē-mik\ *adj* (1936) **:** consisting of only one morpheme ⟨the word *talk* is ~ but *talked* is not⟩

mono·mor·phic \-ˈmȯr-fik\ *adj* (ca. 1879) **:** having but a single form, structural pattern, or genotype ⟨a ~ species of insect⟩ — **mono·mor·phism** \-ˌfi-zəm\ *n*

mono·nu·cle·ar \-ˈnü-klē-ər, -ˈnyü-, ÷-kyə-lər\ *adj* [ISV] (1886) **:** having only one nucleus ⟨a ~ cell⟩ — **mononuclear** *n*

mononuclear phagocyte system *n* (1983) **:** a system of cells comprising all free and fixed phagocytes together with their ancestral cells including monocytes and their precursors in the bone marrow — called also *reticuloendothelial system*

mono·nu·cle·at·ed \-ˈnü-klē-ˌā-təd, -ˈnyü-\ *also* **mono·nu·cle·ate** \-klē-ət, -ˌāt\ *adj* (1890) **:** MONONUCLEAR

mono·nu·cle·o·sis \-ˌnü-klē-ˈō-səs, -ˌnyü-\ *n* [NL, fr. ISV *mononuclear* + NL *-osis*] (1920) **:** an abnormal increase of mononuclear white blood cells in the blood; *specif* **:** INFECTIOUS MONONUCLEOSIS

mono·nu·cle·o·tide \-ˈnü-klē-ə-ˌtīd, -ˈnyü-\ *n* (1908) **:** a nucleotide that is derived from one molecule each of a nitrogenous base, a sugar, and a phosphoric acid

mo·noph·a·gous \mə-ˈnä-fə-gəs, mä-\ *adj* (ca. 1868) **:** feeding on or utilizing a single kind of food; *esp* **:** feeding on a single kind of plant or animal — **mo·noph·a·gy** \-fə-jē\ *n*

mono·pho·nic \ˌmä-nə-ˈfä-nik, -ˈfō-\ *adj* (ca. 1864) **1 :** having a single unaccompanied melodic line **2 :** of or relating to sound transmission, recording, or reproduction involving a single transmission path — **mono·pho·ni·cal·ly** \-ni-k(ə-)lē\ *adv*

mo·noph·o·ny \mə-ˈnä-fə-nē, mä-\ *n* (ca. 1890) **:** monophonic music

mon·oph·thong \ˈmä-nə(f)-ˌthȯŋ\ *n* [LGk *monophthongos* single vowel, fr. Gk *mon-* + *phthongos* sound] (1616) **:** a vowel sound that throughout its duration has a single constant articulatory position — **mon·oph·thon·gal** \ˌmä-nə(f)-ˈthȯŋ-(g)əl\ *adj*

mono·phy·let·ic \ˌmä-nō-fī-ˈle-tik\ *adj* [ISV] (1874) **:** of or relating to a single stock; *specif* **:** developed from a single common ancestral form — **mono·phy·ly** \ˈmä-nə-ˌfī-lē\ *n*

Mo·noph·y·site \mə-ˈnä-fə-ˌsīt\ *n* [ML *Monophysita,* fr. MGk *Monophysitēs,* fr. Gk *mon-* + *physis* nature — more at PHYSICS] (1698) **:** one holding the doctrine that Christ has a single inseparable nature that is at once divine and human rather than having two distinct but unified natures — **Monophysite** *or* **Mo·noph·y·sit·ic** \-ˌnä-fə-ˈsi-tik\ *adj* — **Mo·noph·y·sit·ism** \-ˈnä-fə-ˌsī-ˌti-zəm\ *n*

mono·plane \ˈmä-nə-ˌplān\ *n* (1907) **:** an airplane with only one main supporting surface

[1]**mono·ploid** \ˈmä-nə-ˌplȯid\ *adj* (1928) **1 :** HAPLOID **2 :** having or being the basic haploid number of chromosomes in a polyploid series of organisms

[2]**monoploid** *n* [ISV] (1944) **:** a monoploid individual or organism

mono·pod \ˈmä-nə-ˌpäd\ *n* [*mon-* + *-pod* (as in *tripod*)] (1970) **:** a one-legged support (as for a camera)

mono·po·di·al \ˌmä-nə-ˈpō-dē-əl\ *adj* [NL *monopodium* main axis, fr. *mon-* + *-podium*] (1876) **:** growing upward with a single main stem or axis that produces leaves and flowers ⟨~ orchids⟩

mono·pole \ˈmä-nə-ˌpōl\ *n* (1937) **1 :** a single positive or negative electric charge; *also* **:** a hypothetical north or south magnetic pole existing alone **2 :** a radio antenna consisting of a single often straight element

mo·nop·o·lise *Brit var of* MONOPOLIZE

mo·nop·o·list \mə-ˈnä-pə-list\ *n* (1601) **:** a person who monopolizes — **mo·nop·o·lis·tic** \-ˌnä-pə-ˈlis-tik\ *adj* — **mo·nop·o·lis·ti·cal·ly** \-ti-k(ə-)lē\ *adv*

mo·nop·o·lize \mə-ˈnä-pə-ˌlīz\ *vt* **-lized; -liz·ing** (1611) **:** to get a monopoly of **:** assume complete possession or control of ⟨~ a conversation⟩ — **mo·nop·o·li·za·tion** \-ˌnä-pə-lə-ˈzā-shən\ *n* — **mo·nop·o·liz·er** \-ˈnä-pə-ˌlī-zər\ *n*

mo·nop·o·ly \mə-ˈnä-p(ə-)lē\ *n, pl* **-lies** [L *monopolium,* fr. Gk *monopōlion,* fr. *mon-* + *pōlein* to sell] (1534) **1 :** exclusive ownership through legal privilege, command of supply, or concerted action **2 :** exclusive possession or control **3 :** a commodity controlled by one party **4 :** one that has a monopoly

mono·pro·pel·lant \ˌmä-nō-prə-ˈpe-lənt\ *n* (ca. 1945) **:** a rocket propellant containing both the fuel and the oxidizer in a single substance

mo·nop·so·ny \mə-ˈnäp-sə-nē\ *n, pl* **-nies** [*mon-* + *-opsony* (as in *oligopsony*)] (1933) **:** an oligopsony limited to one buyer — **mo·nop·so·nis·tic** \-ˌnäp-sə-ˈnis-tik\ *adj*

mono·rail \ˈmä-nə-ˌrāl\ *n* (1897) **:** a single rail serving as a track for a wheeled vehicle; *also* **:** a vehicle traveling on such a track

monorail

mon·or·chid \mä-ˈnȯr-kəd\ *n* [irreg. fr. Gk *monorchis,* fr. *mon-* + *orchis* testicle — more at ORCHIS] (1874) **:** an individual who has only one testis or only one descended into the scrotum — **monorchid** *adj* — **mon·or·chi·dism** \-kə-ˌdi-zəm\ *n*

mono·rhyme \ˈmä-nə-ˌrīm\ *n* (1731) **:** a strophe or poem in which all the lines have the same end rhyme — **mono·rhymed** \-ˌrīmd\ *adj*

mono·sac·cha·ride \ˌmä-nə-ˈsa-kə-ˌrīd\ *n* [ISV] (1896) **:** a sugar that is not decomposable into simpler sugars by hydrolysis, is classed as either an aldose or ketose, and contains one or more hydroxyl groups per molecule — called also *simple sugar*

mono·so·di·um glu·ta·mate \ˌmä-nə-ˌsō-dē-əm-ˈglü-tə-ˌmāt\ *n* (1929) **:** a crystalline sodium salt $C_5H_8NO_4Na$ derived from glutamic acid and used to enhance the flavor of food — abbr. *MSG*

mono·some \ˈmä-nə-ˌsōm\ *n* (ca. 1909) **1 :** a chromosome lacking a synaptic mate; *esp* **:** an unpaired X chromosome **2 :** a single ribosome

mono·so·mic \ˌmä-nə-ˈsō-mik\ *adj* (1926) **:** having one less than the diploid number of chromosomes — **monosomic** *n* — **mono·so·my** \ˈmä-nə-ˌsō-mē\ *n*

mono·spe·cif·ic \ˌmä-nō-spə-ˈsi-fik\ *adj* (1947) **:** specific for a single antigen or receptor site on an antigen — **mono·spec·i·fic·i·ty** \-ˌspe-sə-ˈfi-sə-tē\ *n*

mono·syl·lab·ic \ˌmä-nə-sə-ˈla-bik\ *adj* [prob. fr. F *monosyllabique,* fr. *monosyllabe*] (1766) **1 :** consisting of one syllable or of monosyllables **2 :** using or speaking only monosyllables **3 :** conspicuously brief in answering or commenting **:** TERSE — **mono·syl·lab·i·cal·ly** \-bi-k(ə-)lē\ *adv* — **mono·syl·la·bic·i·ty** \-ˌsi-lə-ˈbi-sə-tē\ *n*

mono·syl·la·ble \ˈmä-nə-ˌsi-lə-bəl, ˌmä-nə-ˈ\ *n* [modif. of MF or LL; MF *monosyllabe,* fr. LL *monosyllabon,* fr. Gk, fr. neut. of *monosyllabos* having one syllable, fr. *mon-* + *syllabē* syllable] (1533) **:** a word of one syllable

mono·syn·ap·tic \ˌmä-nō-sə-ˈnap-tik\ *adj* (1942) **:** having or involving a single neural synapse — **mono·syn·ap·ti·cal·ly** \-ti-k(ə-)lē\ *adv*

mono·ter·pene \ˌmä-nə-ˈtər-ˌpēn\ *n* (ca. 1959) **:** any of a class of terpenes $C_{10}H_{16}$ containing two isoprene units per molecule; *also* **:** a derivative of a monoterpene

mono·the·ism \ˈmä-nə-(ˌ)thē-ˌi-zəm\ *n* (1660) **:** the doctrine or belief that there is but one God — **mono·the·ist** \-ˌthē-ist\ *n* — **mono·the·is·tic** \ˌmä-nə-thē-ˈis-tik\ *also* **mono·the·is·ti·cal** \-ti-kəl\ *adj* — **mono·the·is·ti·cal·ly** \-ti-k(ə-)lē\ *adv*

[1]**mono·tone** \ˈmä-nə-ˌtōn\ *n* [Gk *monotonos* monotonous] (1644) **1 :** a succession of syllables, words, or sentences in one unvaried key or pitch **2 :** a single unvaried musical tone **3 :** a tedious sameness or reiteration **4 :** a person unable to produce or to distinguish between musical intervals

[2]**monotone** *adj* (1760) **1 :** MONOTONIC 2 **2 :** having a uniform color

mono·ton·ic \ˌmä-nə-ˈtä-nik\ *adj* (1797) **1 :** characterized by the use of or uttered in a monotone **2 :** having the property either of never increasing or of never decreasing as the values of the independent variable or the subscripts of the terms increase — **mono·ton·i·cal·ly** \-ni-k(ə-)lē\ *adv* — **mono·to·nic·i·ty** \ˌmä-nə-tō-ˈni-sə-tē\ *n*

mo·not·o·nous \mə-ˈnä-tə-nəs, -ˈnät-nəs\ *adj* [Gk *monotonos,* fr. *mon-* + *tonos* tone] (1776) **1 :** uttered or sounded in one unvarying tone **:** marked by a sameness of pitch and intensity **2 :** tediously uniform or unvarying — **mo·not·o·nous·ly** *adv* — **mo·not·o·nous·ness** *n*

mo·not·o·ny \mə-ˈnä-tə-nē, -ˈnät-nē\ *n* (1706) **1 :** tedious sameness **2 :** sameness of tone or sound

mono·treme \ˈmä-nə-ˌtrēm\ *n* [NL *Monotremata,* fr. Gk *mon-* + *trēmat-, trēma* hole — more at TREMATODE] (1835) **:** any of an order

(Monotremata) of egg-laying mammals comprising the platypuses and echidnas

mono·type \'mä-nə-ˌtīp\ *n* (1882) : an impression on paper of a design painted usu. with the finger or a brush on a surface (as glass)

Monotype *trademark* — used for a keyboard typesetting machine that casts and sets type in separate characters

mono·typ·ic \ˌmä-nə-'ti-pik\ *adj* [*mon-* + *type* + *-ic*] (ca. 1859) : including a single representative — used esp. of a genus with only one species

mono·un·sat·u·rat·ed \ˌmä-nō-ˌən-'sa-chə-ˌrā-təd\ *adj* (ca. 1939) : containing one double or triple bond per molecule — used esp. of an oil, fat, or fatty acid; compare POLYUNSATURATED — **mono·un·sat·u·rate** \-rət\ *n*

mono·va·lent \ˌmä-nə-'vā-lənt\ *adj* [ISV] (1869) **1** : having a valence of one **2** : having specific immunologic activity against a single antigen, microorganism, or disease ⟨a ∼ vaccine⟩

mon·ovu·lar \(ˌ)mä-'näv-yə-lər, -'nōv-\ *adj* (1929) : MONOZYGOTIC

mon·ox·ide \mə-'näk-ˌsīd\ *n* [ISV] (1868) : an oxide containing one atom of oxygen in a molecule

mono·zy·got·ic \ˌmä-nə-zī-'gä-tik\ *adj* (1916) : derived from a single egg ⟨∼ twins⟩

Mon·roe Doctrine \mən-'rō- *also* 'mən- *or* 'män-\ *n* [James *Monroe*] (1853) : a statement of U.S. foreign policy expressing opposition to extension of European control or influence in the western hemisphere

mon·sei·gneur \ˌmōⁿ-ˌsān-'yər\ *n, pl* **mes·sei·gneurs** \ˌmā-ˌsān-'yər(z)\ [F, lit., my lord] (1602) : a French dignitary (as a prince or prelate) — used as a title preceding a title of office or rank

mon·sieur \məs-'yə(r), məsh-; mə-'sir\ *n, pl* **mes·sieurs** \məs-'yə(r)(z), məsh-, mäs-; mə-'sir(z)\ [MF, lit., my lord] (1512) : a Frenchman of high rank or station — used as a title equivalent to *Mister* and prefixed to the name of a Frenchman

mon·si·gnor \män-'sē-nyər, mən-\ *n, pl* **monsignors** *or* **mon·si·gno·ri** \ˌmän-ˌsēn-'yór-ē\ [It *monsignore*, fr. F *monseigneur*] (1607) : a Roman Catholic prelate having a dignity or titular distinction (as of domestic prelate or protonotary apostolic) usu. conferred by the pope — used as a title prefixed to the surname or to the given name and surname — **mon·si·gno·ri·al** \ˌmän-ˌsēn-'yór-ē-əl\ *adj*

mon·soon \män-'sün, 'män-\ *n* [obs. D *monssoen*, fr. Pg *monção*, fr. Ar *mawsim* time, season] (1584) **1** : a periodic wind esp. in the Indian Ocean and southern Asia **2** : the season of the southwest monsoon in India and adjacent areas that is characterized by very heavy rainfall **3** : rainfall that is associated with the monsoon — **mon·soon·al** \-'sü-nᵊl, -ˌsü-\ *adj*

mons pu·bis \ˈmänz-'pyü-bəs\ *n, pl* **mon·tes pubis** \ˈmän-ˌtēz-\ [NL, pubic eminence] (ca. 1903) : a rounded eminence of fatty tissue on the pubic symphysis esp. of the human female

¹mon·ster \'män(t)-stər\ *n* [ME *monstre*, fr. AF, fr. L *monstrum* omen, monster, fr. *monēre* to warn — more at MIND] (14c) **1 a** : an animal or plant of abnormal form or structure **b** : one who deviates from normal or acceptable behavior or character **2** : a threatening force **3 a** : an animal of strange or terrifying shape **b** : one unusually large for its kind **4** : something monstrous; *esp* : a person of unnatural or extreme ugliness, deformity, wickedness, or cruelty **5** : one that is highly successful

²monster *adj* (1837) : enormous or impressive esp. in size, extent, or numbers

mon·strance \'män(t)-strən(t)s\ *n* [ME *mustraunce, monstrans* demonstration, monstrance, fr. AF *mustrance* show, sign, fr. ML *monstrantia*, fr. L *monstrare* to show, fr. *monstrum*] (15c) : a vessel in which the consecrated Host is exposed for the adoration of the faithful

mon·stros·i·ty \män-'strä-sə-tē\ *n, pl* **-ties** (15c) **1 a** : a malformation of a plant or animal **b** : something deviating from the normal : FREAK **2** : the quality or state of being monstrous **3 a** : an object of great and often frightening size, force, or complexity **b** : an excessively bad or shocking example

¹mon·strous \'män(t)-strəs\ *adj* (15c) **1** *obs* : STRANGE, UNNATURAL **2** : having extraordinary often overwhelming size : GIGANTIC **3 a** : having the qualities or appearance of a monster **b** *obs* : teeming with monsters **4 a** : extraordinarily ugly or vicious : HORRIBLE **b** : shockingly wrong or ridiculous **5** : deviating greatly from the natural form

or character : ABNORMAL **6** : very great — used as an intensive — **mon·strous·ly** *adv* — **mon·strous·ness** *n*
syn MONSTROUS, PRODIGIOUS, TREMENDOUS, STUPENDOUS mean extremely impressive. MONSTROUS implies a departure from the normal (as in size, form, or character) and often carries suggestions of deformity, ugliness, or fabulousness ⟨the *monstrous* waste of the project⟩. PRODIGIOUS suggests a marvelousness exceeding belief, usu. in something felt as going far beyond a previous maximum (as of goodness, greatness, intensity, or size) ⟨made a *prodigious* effort and rolled the stone aside⟩. TREMENDOUS may imply a power to terrify or inspire awe ⟨the *tremendous* roar of the cataract⟩. STUPENDOUS implies a power to stun or astound, usu. because of size, numbers, complexity, or greatness beyond description ⟨a *stupendous* volcanic eruption⟩.

²monstrous *adv* (1590) *chiefly dial* : VERY, EXTREMELY ⟨a ∼ long raft —Mark Twain⟩

mons ve·ne·ris \'mänz-'ve-nə-rəs\ *n, pl* **mon·tes veneris** \'män-ˌtēz-\ [NL, lit., eminence of Venus or of venery] (1621) : MONS PUBIS

Mont *abbr* Montana

mon·ta·dale \ˈmän-tə-ˌdāl\ *n* [*Montana* state + *dale*] (1949) : any of an American breed of white-faced hornless sheep noted for heavy fleece and good meat conformation

¹mon·tage \män-'täzh, mōⁿ(n)-\ *n* [F, fr. *monter* to mount] (1929) **1** : the production of a rapid succession of images in a motion picture to illustrate an association of ideas **2 a** : a literary, musical, or artistic composite of juxtaposed more or less heterogeneous elements **b** : a composite picture made by combining several separate pictures **3 a** : heterogeneous mixture : JUMBLE ⟨a ∼ of emotions⟩

²montage *vt* **mon·taged; mon·tag·ing** (1944) : to combine into or depict in a montage

mon·ta·gnard \ˌmōⁿ-ˌtän-'yär(d)\ *n, often cap* [F, mountaineer, fr. *montagne* mountain, fr. OF *montaigne*] (1842) : a member of any of various peoples inhabiting the highlands of central and southern Vietnam — **montagnard** *adj, often cap*

Mon·ta·gue \'män-tə-ˌgyü\ *n* (1592) : the family of Romeo in Shakespeare's *Romeo and Juliet*

mon·tane \ˈmän-'tān, 'män-ˌ\ *adj* [L *montanus* of a mountain — more at MOUNTAIN] (1863) **1** : of, relating to, growing in, or being the biogeographic zone of relatively moist cool upland slopes below timberline dominated by large coniferous trees **2** : of, relating to, or made up of montane plants or animals

Mon·ta·nist \'män-tə-nist\ *n* [*Montanus*, 2d cent. A.D. Phrygian schismatic] (1577) : an adherent of a Christian sect arising in the late second century and stressing apocalyptic expectations, the continuing prophetic gifts of the Spirit, and strict ascetic discipline — **Mon·ta·nism** \-tə-ˌni-zəm\ *n*

mon·tan wax \'män-tᵊn-\ *n* [L *montanus* of a mountain] (1908) : a hard brittle mineral wax obtained usu. from lignites by extraction and used esp. in polishes, carbon paper, and insulating compositions

mon·te \'män-tē\ *n* [Sp, bank, mountain, heap, fr. It, fr. L *mont-, mons* mountain] (1824) **1** : a card game in which players select any two or four cards turned face up in a layout and bet that one of them will be matched before the other as cards are dealt one at a time from the pack — called also *monte bank* **2** : THREE-CARD MONTE

Mon·te Car·lo \ˌmän-tē-'kär-(ˌ)lō\ *adj* [*Monte Carlo*, Monaco, famous for its gambling casino] (1949) : of, relating to, or involving the use of random sampling techniques and often the use of computer simulation to obtain approximate solutions to mathematical or physical problems esp. in terms of a range of values each of which has a calculated probability of being the solution ⟨*Monte Carlo* calculations⟩

mon·teith \män-'tēth\ *n* [*Monteith*, 17th cent. Scot. eccentric who wore a cloak with a scalloped hem] (1683) : a large silver punch bowl with scalloped rim

Mon·te·rey cypress \'män-tə-ˌrā-\ *n* [*Monterey*, California] (1873) : a California cypress (*Cupressus macrocarpa*) that is endemic to the Monterey and Carmel seacoast and is often planted for ornament

Monterey Jack *n* [David *Jack* or *Jacks* †1907 Calif. landowner] (1940) : a semisoft whole-milk cheese with high moisture content

Monterey pine *n* (1834) : a pine (*Pinus radiata*) native to coastal California but widely grown esp. in the southern hemisphere for its wood

MONTHS OF THE PRINCIPAL CALENDARS

GREGORIAN[1]		JEWISH		ISLAMIC	
Name	Days	Name	Days	Name	Days
January begins about 10 days after the winter solstice	31	Tishri in year 5764 begins Sept. 27, 2003	30	Muharram[4] in A.H. 1424 begins Mar. 4, 2003	30
February in leap years	28 29	Heshvan	29 *or* 30	Safar	29
March	31	Kislev	29 *or* 30	Rabi al-Awwal	30
April	30	Tebet	29	Rabi al-Thani	29
May	31	Shebat	30	Jumada al-Awwal	30
June	30	Adar[2]	29	Jumada al-Thani	29
July	31	Nisan[3]	30	Rajab	30
August	31	Iyar	29	Sha'ban	29
September	30	Sivan	30	Ramadan	30
October	31	Tammuz	29	Shawwal	29
November	30	Ab	30	Dhu'l-Qa'dah	30
December	31	Elul	29	Dhu'l-Hijja in leap years	29 30

[1]The equinoxes occur about March 21 and September 23, the solstices about June 22 and December 22.

[2]In leap years, an additional 30-day month called Adar Rishon ("first Adar") precedes the month of Adar Sheni ("second Adar"), which replaces the normal Adar. Adar Sheni, which is also called Veadar, retains the holidays and scriptural readings of a normal Adar.

[3]The first month of the ecclesiastical year; anciently called Abib.

[4]Retrogresses through the seasons; the Islamic year is lunar and each month begins at the approximate new moon; the year 1 A.H. began on Friday, July 16, A.D. 622.

mon·te·ro \män-ˈter-(ˌ)ō\ *n, pl* **-ros** [Sp, hunter, fr. *monte* mountain] (1611) **:** a round hunter's cap with ear flaps

Mon·te·zu·ma's revenge \ˌmän-tə-ˈzü-məz-\ *n* [*Montezuma* II] (1960) **:** traveler's diarrhea esp. when contracted in Mexico

month \ˈmən(t)th\ *n, pl* **months** \ˈmən(t)s, ˈmən(t)ths\ [ME, fr. OE *mōnath;* akin to OHG *mānōd* month, OE *mōna* moon] (bef. 12c) **1 :** a measure of time corresponding nearly to the period of the moon's revolution and amounting to approximately 4 weeks or 30 days or 1/12 of a year **2** *pl* **:** an indefinite usu. extended period of time ⟨he has been gone for ~*s*⟩ **3 :** one ninth of the typical duration of human pregnancy ⟨she was in her eighth ~⟩

month·long \ˈmən(t)th-ˈlȯŋ\ *adj* (1843) **:** lasting a month

1**month·ly** \-lē\ *n, pl* **monthlies** (bef. 12c) **1 :** a monthly periodical **2** *pl* **:** a menstrual period

2**monthly** *adv* (15c) **:** once a month **:** by the month

3**monthly** *adj* (1543) **1 :** lasting a month **2 a :** of or relating to a month **b :** payable or reckoned by the month **3 :** occurring or appearing every month

Monthly Meeting *n* (1664) **:** a local unit of organization of Friends

month's mind *n* (15c) **:** a Roman Catholic requiem mass held a month after a person's death

Mont·mo·ren·cy \ˌmänt-mə-ˈren(t)-sē\ *n* [F, fr. *Montmorency,* France] (1924) **:** a cherry that is grown commercially for its bright red sour fruit; *also* **:** the fruit

mont·mo·ril·lon·ite \ˌmänt-mə-ˈri-lə-ˌnīt, -ˈrē-ə-ˌnīt\ *n* [F, fr. *Montmorillon,* commune in western France] (1854) **:** a soft clayey water-absorbent mineral that is a hydrous aluminum silicate — **mont·mo·ril·lon·it·ic** \-ˌri-lə-ˈni-tik, -ˌrē-ə-ˈni-\ *adj*

Mon·tra·chet \ˌmōⁿ-trä-ˈshe\ *n* [F, fr. *Montrachet,* vineyard in Burgundy, France] (1789) **1 :** a dry white burgundy wine **2 :** a soft goat cheese from the Burgundy region of France

mon·u·ment \ˈmän-yə-mənt\ *n* [ME, fr. AF, fr. L *monumentum,* lit., memorial, fr. *monēre* to remind — more at MIND] (13c) **1** *obs* **:** a burial vault **:** SEPULCHRE **2 :** a written legal document or record **:** TREATISE **3 a** (1) **:** a lasting evidence, reminder, or example of someone or something notable or great (2) **:** a distinguished person **b :** a memorial stone or a building erected in remembrance of a person or event **4** *archaic* **:** an identifying mark **:** EVIDENCE; *also* **:** PORTENT, SIGN **5** *obs* **:** a carved statue **:** EFFIGY **6 :** a boundary or position marker (as a stone) **7 :** NATIONAL MONUMENT **8 :** a written tribute

mon·u·men·tal \ˌmän-yə-ˈmen-tᵊl\ *adj* (1596) **1 :** serving as or resembling a monument **:** MASSIVE; *also* **:** highly significant **:** OUTSTANDING **2 :** of or relating to a monument **3 :** very great ⟨a ~ misunderstanding⟩ — **mon·u·men·tal·i·ty** \-mən-ˈta-lə-tē, -ˌmen-\ *n* — **mon·u·men·tal·ly** \-tᵊl-ē\ *adv*

mon·u·men·tal·ize \-ˈmen-tᵊl-ˌīz\ *vt* **-ized; -iz·ing** (1857) **:** to record or memorialize lastingly by a monument

mon·u·ron \ˈmän-yə-ˌrän\ *n* [*mon-* + *urea* + 1*-on*] (ca. 1957) **:** a persistent herbicide $C_9H_{11}ClN_2O$ used esp. to control broad-leaved weeds

mon·zo·nite \män-ˈzō-ˌnīt, ˈmän-zə-\ *n* [F, fr. Mt. *Monzoni,* Italy] (1895) **:** a granular igneous rock composed of plagioclase and orthoclase in about equal quantities usu. together with augite and biotite

moo \ˈmü\ *vi* [imit.] (1549) **:** to make the throat noise of a cow — **moo** *n*

MOOC \ˈmük\ *abbr* massive open online course

mooch \ˈmüch\ *vb* [prob. fr. F dial. *muchier* to hide, lurk] *vi* (1851) **1 :** to wander aimlessly **:** AMBLE; *also* **:** SNEAK **2 :** BEG, SPONGE ~ *vt* **1 :** to take surreptitiously **:** STEAL **2 :** BEG, SPONGE — **mooch·er** *n*

1**mood** \ˈmüd\ *n* [ME, fr. OE *mōd;* akin to OHG *muot* mood] (bef. 12c) **1 :** a conscious state of mind or predominant emotion **:** FEELING; *also* **:** the expression of mood esp. in art or literature **2** *archaic* **:** a fit of anger **3 a :** a prevailing attitude **b :** a receptive state of mind predisposing to action **c :** a distinctive atmosphere or context **:** AURA

2**mood** *n* [alter. of 1*mode*] (1569) **1 :** the form of a syllogism as determined by the quantity and quality of its constituent propositions **2 :** distinction of form or a particular set of inflectional forms of a verb to express whether the action or state it denotes is conceived as fact or in some other manner (as command, possibility, or wish) **3 :** MODE 1b

mood disorder *n* (1969) **:** any of several psychological disorders (as major depressive disorder or bipolar disorder) characterized by abnormalities of emotional state — called also *affective disorder*

moody \ˈmü-dē\ *adj* **mood·i·er; -est** (1593) **1 :** subject to depression **:** GLOOMY **2 :** subject to moods **:** TEMPERAMENTAL **3 :** expressive of a mood — **mood·i·ly** \ˈmü-də-lē\ *adv* — **mood·i·ness** \ˈmü-dē-nəs\ *n*

mook \ˈmük\ *n* [perh. alter. of *moke*] (1930) *slang* **:** a foolish, insignificant, or contemptible person

moo·la *or* **moo·lah** \ˈmü-(ˌ)lä, -lə\ *n* [origin unknown] (1937) *slang* **:** MONEY

1**moon** \ˈmün\ *n* [ME *mone,* fr. OE *mōna;* akin to OHG *māno* moon, L *mensis* month, Gk *mēn* month, *mēnē* moon] (bef. 12c) **1 a** *often cap* **:** the earth's natural satellite that shines by the sun's reflected light, revolves about the earth from west to east in about 29½ days with reference to the sun or about 27⅓ days with reference to the stars, and has a diameter of 2160 miles (3475 kilometers), a mean distance from the earth of about 238,900 miles (384,400 kilometers), and a mass about one eightieth that of the earth — usu. used with *the* **b :** one complete moon cycle consisting of four phases **c :** SATELLITE 2; *specif* **:** a natural satellite of a planet **2 :** an indefinite usu. extended period of time ⟨a labor of many ~*s*⟩ **3 :** MOONLIGHT **4 :** something that resembles a moon: as **a :** a highly translucent spot on old porcelain **b :** LUNULE **c** *slang* **:** naked buttocks **5 :** something impossible or inaccessible ⟨reach for the ~⟩ — **moon·like** \-ˌlīk\ *adj* — **over the moon :** very pleased **:** in high spirits

2**moon** *vt* (1836) **1 :** to spend in idle reverie **:** DREAM — used with *away* **2** *slang* **:** to expose one's naked buttocks to ~ *vi* **:** to spend time in idle reverie **:** behave abstractedly

moon·beam \ˈmün-ˌbēm\ *n* (1535) **:** a ray of light from the moon

moon blindness *n* (ca. 1720) **:** a recurrent inflammation of the eye of the horse

moon·calf \ˈmün-ˌkaf, -ˌkäf\ *n* (1614) **:** a foolish or absentminded person **:** SIMPLETON

moon·dust \-ˌdəst\ *n* (ca. 1959) **:** fine dry particles of the moon's soil

moon·eye \-ˌī\ *n* (1842) **:** a silvery No. American freshwater bony fish (*Hiodon tergisus* of the family Hiodontidae)

moon–eyed \-ˈīd\ *adj* (1790) **:** having the eyes wide open

moon·faced \-ˌfāst\ *adj* (1619) **:** having a round face

moon·fish \-ˌfish\ *n, pl* **moonfish** *or* **moon·fish·es** (1646) **:** any of various compressed often short deep-bodied silvery or yellowish marine fishes: as **a :** OPAH **b :** PLATY

moon·flow·er \-ˌflau̇(-ə)r\ *n* (ca. 1909) **:** a tropical American morning glory (*Ipomoea alba* syn. *Calonyction aculeatum*) with fragrant flowers; *also* **:** any of several related plants

Moon·ie \ˈmü-nē\ *n* [Sun Myung *Moon b*1920 Korean evangelist] (1974) **:** a member of the Unification Church founded by Sun Myung Moon

moon·ish \ˈmü-nish\ *adj* (15c) **:** influenced by the moon; *also* **:** CAPRICIOUS — **moon·ish·ly** *adv*

moon·less \ˈmün-ləs\ *adj* (1506) **:** lacking the light of the moon

moon·let \-lət\ *n* (1832) **:** a small natural or artificial satellite

1**moon·light** \-ˌlīt\ *n* (14c) **:** the light of the moon

2**moonlight** *vi* **moon·light·ed; moon·light·ing** [back-formation fr. *moonlighter*] (1957) **:** to hold a second job in addition to a regular one — **moon·light·er** *n*

moon·lit \-ˌlit\ *adj* (1817) **:** lighted by the moon

moon·quake \-ˌkwāk\ *n* (1946) **:** a seismic event on the moon

moon·rise \-ˌrīz\ *n* (1728) **1 :** the rising of the moon above the horizon **2 :** the time of the moon's rising

moon·roof \ˈmün-ˌrüf, -ˌru̇f\ *n* (1973) **:** a glass sunroof

moon·scape \-ˌskāp\ *n* (1907) **:** the surface of the moon as seen or as depicted; *also* **:** a landscape resembling this surface

moon·seed \-ˌsēd\ *n* (1739) **:** a twining plant (*Menispermum canadense* of the family Menispermaceae, the moonseed family) of eastern No. America that has crescent-shaped seeds and black fruits

moon·set \-ˌset\ *n* (1818) **1 :** the descent of the moon below the horizon **2 :** the time of the moon's setting

moon shell *n* (1923) **:** MOON SNAIL

moon·shine \ˈmün-ˌshīn\ *n* (15c) **1 :** MOONLIGHT **2 :** empty talk **:** NONSENSE **3 :** intoxicating liquor; *esp* **:** illegally distilled corn whiskey

moon·shin·er \-ˌshī-nər\ *n* (1860) **:** a maker or seller of illicit whiskey

moon shot *n* (1949) **1 :** a spacecraft mission to the moon **2 :** a hit or thrown ball with a very high trajectory

moon snail *n* (1892) **:** any of a cosmopolitan family (Naticidae) of carnivorous marine snails having smooth globular shells

moon·stone \-ˌstōn\ *n* (15c) **:** a transparent or translucent feldspar of pearly or opaline luster used as a gem

moon·struck \-ˌstrək\ *adj* (1674) **:** affected by or as if by the moon: as **a :** mentally unbalanced **b :** romantically sentimental **c :** lost in fantasy or reverie

moon suit *n* (1980) **:** a sealed garment worn esp. for protection from hazardous material (as toxic waste or infectious disease)

moon·walk \ˈmün-ˌwȯk\ *vi* (1984) **:** to dance by gliding backwards while appearing to make forward walking motions — **moonwalk** *n*

moon·ward \-wərd\ *adv* (1834) **:** toward the moon

moony \ˈmü-nē\ *adj* (ca. 1586) **1 :** of or relating to the moon **2 a :** crescent-shaped **b :** resembling the full moon **:** ROUND **3 :** MOONLIT **4 :** DREAMY, MOONSTRUCK

1**moor** \ˈmu̇r\ *n* [ME *mor,* fr. OE *mōr;* akin to OHG *muor* moor] (bef. 12c) **1** *chiefly Brit* **:** an expanse of open rolling infertile land **2 :** a boggy area; *esp* **:** one that is peaty and dominated by grasses and sedges

2**moor** *vb* [ME *moren;* akin to MD *meren, maren* to tie, moor] *vt* (15c) **:** to make fast with or as if with cables, lines, or anchors **:** ANCHOR ~ *vi* **1 :** to secure a boat by mooring **:** ANCHOR **2 :** to be made fast

Moor \ˈmu̇r\ *n* [ME *More,* fr. AF, fr. L *Maurus* inhabitant of Mauretania] (14c) **1 :** one of the Arab and Berber conquerors of Spain **2 :** BERBER — **Moor·ish** \-ish\ *adj*

moor·age \ˈmu̇r-ij\ *n* (1641) **1 :** an act of mooring **2 :** a place to moor

Moore's law \ˈmȯrz-, ˈmu̇rz-\ *n, often cap L* [Gordon E. *Moore b*1929 Am. computer industry executive] (1977) **:** an axiom of microprocessor development usu. holding that processing power doubles about every 18 months esp. relative to cost or size

moor·hen \ˈmu̇r-ˌhen\ *n* (14c) **:** an aquatic bird (*Gallinula chloropus*) of the rail family that is widespread in the New World, Eurasia, and Africa and that has a red bill, red frontal area on the head, and a white band on the flanks — called also *gallinule*

moor·ing \-iŋ\ *n* (15c) **1 :** an act of making fast a boat or aircraft with lines or anchors **2 a :** a place where or an object to which something (as a craft) can be moored **b :** a device (as a line or chain) by which an object is secured in place **3 :** an established practice or stabilizing influence **:** ANCHORAGE 2 — usu. used in pl.

moor·land \-lənd, -ˌland\ *n* (bef. 12c) **:** land consisting of moors **:** a stretch of moor

moose \ˈmüs\ *n, pl* **moose** [of Algonquian origin; akin to Massachusett *moos* moose] (1603) **1 :** a ruminant mammal (*Alces alces*) with humped shoulders, long legs, and broadly palmated antlers that is the largest existing member of the deer family and inhabits forested areas of Canada, the northern U.S., Europe, and Asia **2** *cap* [Loyal Order of *Moose*] **:** a member of a major benevolent and fraternal order

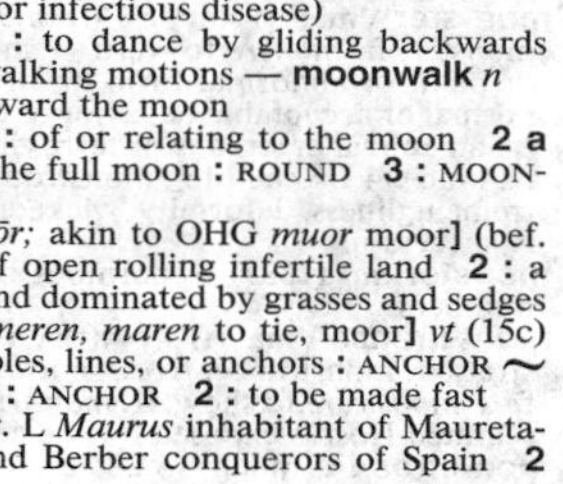

moose 1

1**moot** \ˈmüt\ *n* [ME, fr. OE *mōt, gemōt;* akin to MHG *muoze* meeting] (bef. 12c) **1 :** a deliberative assembly primarily for the administration of justice; *esp* **:** one held by the freemen of an Anglo-Saxon community **2** *obs* **:** ARGUMENT, DISCUSSION

2**moot** *vt* (15c) **1** *archaic* **:** to discuss from a legal standpoint **:** ARGUE **2 a :** to bring up for discussion **:** BROACH **b :** DEBATE

3**moot** *adj* (1563) **1 a :** open to question **:** DEBATABLE **b :** subjected to discussion **:** DISPUTED **2 :** deprived of practical significance **:** made abstract or purely academic

moot court *n* (1788) **:** a mock court in which law students argue hypothetical cases for practice

1**mop** \ˈmäp\ *n* [ME *mappe*] (15c) **1 :** an implement made of absorbent material fastened to a handle and used esp. for cleaning floors **2 :** something that resembles a mop; *esp* **:** a thick mass of hair

2**mop** *vb* **mopped; mop·ping** *vt* (1709) **1 :** to use a mop on; *specif* **:** to clean or clear away by mopping ⟨~ the floors⟩ — often used with *up* ⟨~ up the spillage⟩ **2 :** to wipe as if with a mop ⟨*mopped* his brow with a handkerchief⟩ ~ *vi* **:** to clean a surface (as a floor) with a mop — **mop·per** *n*

mop·board \ˈmäp-ˌbȯrd\ *n* (1853) **:** BASEBOARD

1**mope** \ˈmōp\ *vi* **moped; mop·ing** [prob. fr. obs. *mop, mope* fool] (1568) **1** *archaic* **:** to act in a dazed or stupid manner **2 :** to give oneself up to brooding **:** become listless or dejected **3 :** to move slowly or aimlessly **:** DAWDLE — **mop·er** *n* — **mop·ey** \ˈmō-pē\ *adj*

2**mope** *n* (1693) **1 :** one that mopes **2** *pl* **:** BLUES 1

mo·ped \ˈmō-ˌped\ *n* [Sw, fr. *mo*tor motor + *ped*al pedal] (1955) **:** a lightweight low-powered motorbike that can be pedaled

mop·pet \ˈmä-pət\ *n* [obs. E *mop* fool, child] (1601) **1** *archaic* **:** BABY, DARLING **2 :** CHILD

mop–up \ˈmäp-ˌəp\ *n, often attrib* (1900) **:** a concluding action or phase

mop up *vt* (ca. 1811) **1** *Brit* **:** to consume eagerly **2 :** to gather as if by absorbing; *also* **:** GARNER ⟨*mopped up* all the awards⟩ **3 :** to overcome decisively **:** TROUNCE **4 :** to clear (an area) of remaining pockets of resistance in the wake of a military offensive ~ *vi* **:** to complete a project, transaction, or task

mo·quette \mō-ˈket\ *n* [F] (1762) **:** a carpet or upholstery fabric having a velvety pile

mor \ˈmȯr\ *n* [Dan, lit., humus] (1931) **:** forest humus that forms a layer of largely organic matter distinct from the mineral soil beneath

MOR *abbr* middle of the road

mo·ra \ˈmȯr-ə\ *n, pl* **mo·rae** \ˈmȯr-(ˌ)ē, -ˌī\ *or* **mo·ras** [L, delay; akin to OIr *maraid* it lasts] (1832) **:** the minimal unit of measure in quantitative verse equivalent to the time of an average short syllable

mo·raine \mə-ˈrān\ *n* [F, fr. F dial. (Savoy) *morêna*] (1789) **:** an accumulation of earth and stones carried and finally deposited by a glacier — **mo·rain·al** \-ˈrā-nᵊl\ *adj* — **mo·rain·ic** \-ˈrā-nik\ *adj*

1**mor·al** \ˈmȯr-əl, ˈmär-\ *adj* [ME, fr. AF, fr. L *moralis,* fr. *mor-, mos* custom] (14c) **1 a :** of or relating to principles of right and wrong in behavior **:** ETHICAL ⟨~ judgments⟩ **b :** expressing or teaching a conception of right behavior ⟨a ~ poem⟩ **c :** conforming to a standard of right behavior **d :** sanctioned by or operative on one's conscience or ethical judgment ⟨a ~ obligation⟩ **e :** capable of right and wrong action ⟨a ~ agent⟩ **2 :** probable though not proved **:** VIRTUAL ⟨a ~ certainty⟩ **3 :** perceptual or psychological rather than tangible or practical in nature or effect ⟨a ~ victory⟩ ⟨~ support⟩ — **mor·al·ly** \-ə-lē\ *adv*

syn MORAL, ETHICAL, VIRTUOUS, RIGHTEOUS, NOBLE mean conforming to a standard of what is right and good. MORAL implies conformity to established sanctioned codes or accepted notions of right and wrong ⟨the basic *moral* values of a community⟩. ETHICAL may suggest the involvement of more difficult or subtle questions of rightness, fairness, or equity ⟨committed to the highest *ethical* principles⟩. VIRTUOUS implies moral excellence in character ⟨not a religious person, but *virtuous* nevertheless⟩. RIGHTEOUS stresses guiltlessness or blamelessness and often suggests the sanctimonious ⟨wished to be *righteous* before God and the world⟩. NOBLE implies moral eminence and freedom from anything petty, mean, or dubious in conduct and character ⟨had the *noblest* of reasons for seeking office⟩.

2**mor·al** \ˈmȯr-əl, ˈmär-; *3 is* mə-ˈral\ *n* (15c) **1 a :** the moral significance or practical lesson (as of a story) **b :** a passage pointing out usu. in conclusion the lesson to be drawn from a story **2** *pl* **a :** moral practices or teachings **:** modes of conduct **b :** ETHICS **3 :** MORALE

mo·rale \mə-ˈral\ *n* [in sense 1, fr. F, fr. fem. of *moral,* adj.; in other senses, modif. of F *moral* morale, fr. *moral,* adj.] (1752) **1 :** moral principles, teachings, or conduct **2 a :** the mental and emotional condition (as of enthusiasm, confidence, or loyalty) of an individual or group with regard to the function or tasks at hand **b :** a sense of common purpose with respect to a group **:** ESPRIT DE CORPS **3 :** the level of individual psychological well-being based on such factors as a sense of purpose and confidence in the future

moral hazard *n* (ca. 1917) **:** the possibility of loss to an insurance company arising from the character or circumstances of the insured

mor·al·ise *Brit var of* MORALIZE

mor·al·ism \ˈmȯr-ə-ˌli-zəm, ˈmär-\ *n* (1828) **1 a :** the habit or practice of moralizing **b :** a conventional moral attitude or saying **2 :** an often exaggerated emphasis on morality (as in politics)

mor·al·ist \-list\ *n* (1621) **1 :** one who leads a moral life **2 :** a philosopher or writer concerned with moral principles and problems **3 :** one concerned with regulating the morals of others

mor·al·is·tic \ˌmȯr-ə-ˈlis-tik, ˌmär-\ *adj* (1865) **1 :** characterized by or expressive of a concern with morality **2 :** characterized by or expressive of a narrow moral attitude — **mor·al·is·ti·cal·ly** \-ti-k(ə-)lē\ *adv*

mo·ral·i·ty \mə-ˈra-lə-tē, mȯ-\ *n, pl* **-ties** (14c) **1 a :** a moral discourse, statement, or lesson **b :** a literary or other imaginative work teaching a moral lesson **2 a :** a doctrine or system of moral conduct **b** *pl* **:** particular moral principles or rules of conduct **3 :** conformity to ideals of right human conduct **4 :** moral conduct **:** VIRTUE

morality play *n* (1879) **1 :** an allegorical play popular esp. in the 15th and 16th centuries in which the characters personify abstract qualities or concepts (as virtues, vices, or death) **2 :** something (as a court trial) which involves a direct conflict between right and wrong or good and evil and from which a moral lesson may be drawn

mor·al·ize \ˈmȯr-ə-ˌlīz, ˈmär-\ *vb* **-ized; -iz·ing** *vt* (15c) **1 :** to explain or interpret morally **2 a :** to give a moral quality or direction to **b :** to improve the morals of ~ *vi* **:** to make moral reflections — **mor·al·i·za·tion** \ˌmȯr-ə-lə-ˈzā-shən, ˌmär-\ *n* — **mor·al·iz·er** \ˈmȯr-ə-ˌlī-zər, ˈmär-\ *n*

moral philosophy *n* (1606) **:** ETHICS; *also* **:** the study of human conduct and values

mo·rass \mə-ˈras, mȯ-\ *n* [D *moeras,* modif. of OF *maresc,* of Gmc origin; akin to OE *mersc* marsh — more at MARSH] (1655) **1 :** MARSH, SWAMP **2 a :** a situation that traps, confuses, or impedes ⟨a legal ~⟩ **b :** an overwhelming or confusing mass or mixture ⟨a ~ of traffic jams —Mary Roach⟩ — **mo·rassy** \-ˈra-sē\ *adj*

mor·a·to·ri·um \ˌmȯr-ə-ˈtȯr-ē-əm, ˌmär-\ *n, pl* **-riums** *also* **-ria** \-ē-ə\ [NL, fr. LL, neut. of *moratorius* dilatory, fr. L *morari* to delay, fr. *mora* delay] (1875) **1 a :** a legally authorized period of delay in the performance of a legal obligation or the payment of a debt **b :** a waiting period set by an authority **2 :** a suspension of activity

Mo·ra·vi·an \mə-ˈrā-vē-ən\ *n* (1555) **1 a :** a native or inhabitant of Moravia **b :** the group of Czech dialects spoken in Moravia **2 :** a member of a Protestant denomination arising from a 15th century religious reform movement in Bohemia and Moravia — **Moravian** *adj*

mo·ray eel \mə-ˈrā-, ˈmȯr-(ˌ)ā-\ *n* [Pg *moréia,* fr. L *muraena,* fr. Gk *myraina*] (1926) **:** any of numerous often brightly colored eels (family Muraenidae) that have sharp teeth capable of inflicting a severe bite, that occur in warm seas, and that include a chiefly Mediterranean eel (*Muraena helena*) sometimes used for food — called also *moray*

mor·bid \ˈmȯr-bəd\ *adj* [L *morbidus* diseased, fr. *morbus* disease] (1656) **1 a :** of, relating to, or characteristic of disease ⟨~ anatomy⟩ **b :** affected with or induced by disease ⟨a ~ condition⟩ **c :** productive of disease ⟨~ substances⟩ **2 :** abnormally susceptible to or characterized by gloomy or unwholesome feelings **3 :** GRISLY, GRUESOME ⟨~ details⟩ ⟨~ curiosity⟩ — **mor·bid·ly** *adv* — **mor·bid·ness** *n*

mor·bid·i·ty \mȯr-ˈbi-də-tē\ *n* (ca. 1721) **1 :** the quality or state of being morbid **2 :** the relative incidence of disease

mor·bil·li·vi·rus \mȯr-ˈbi-lə-ˌvī-rəs\ *n* [NL, fr. *morbillus* spot on the skin, pustule (fr. ML, dim. of L *morbus*) + *virus*] (1977) **:** any of a genus (*Morbillivirus*) of paramyxoviruses that include the causative agents of canine distemper, measles, and rinderpest

mor·ceau \mȯr-ˈsō\ *n, pl* **mor·ceaux** \-ˈsō(z)\ [F, fr. OF *morsel* morsel] (1751) **:** a short literary or musical piece

mor·dan·cy \ˈmȯr-dᵊn(t)-sē\ *n* (ca. 1656) **1 :** a biting and caustic quality of style **:** INCISIVENESS **2 :** a sharply critical or bitter quality of thought or feeling **:** HARSHNESS

1**mor·dant** \ˈmȯr-dᵊnt\ *adj* [MF, prp. of *mordre* to bite, fr. L *mordēre;* perh. akin to Skt *mṛdnāti* he presses, rubs] (15c) **1 :** biting and caustic in thought, manner, or style **:** INCISIVE ⟨a ~ wit⟩ **2 :** acting as a mordant **3 :** BURNING, PUNGENT ***syn*** see CAUSTIC — **mor·dant·ly** *adv*

2**mordant** *n* (1791) **1 :** a chemical that fixes a dye in or on a substance by combining with the dye to form an insoluble compound **2 :** a corroding substance used in etching

3**mordant** *vt* (1836) **:** to treat with a mordant

Mor·de·cai \ˈmȯr-di-ˌkī\ *n* [Heb *Mordĕkhai*] (1587) **:** a relative of Esther who gave advice on saving the Jews from the destruction planned by Haman

mor·dent \ˈmȯr-dᵊnt, mȯr-ˈdent\ *n* [It *mordente,* lit., biting, pungent, fr. L *mordent-, mordens,* prp. of *mordēre*] (1806) **:** a musical ornament made by a quick alternation of a principal tone with the tone immediately below it

1**more** \ˈmȯr\ *adj* [ME, fr. OE *māra;* akin to OE *mā,* adv., more, OHG *mēr,* OIr *mó* more] (bef. 12c) **1 :** GREATER ⟨something ~ than she expected⟩ **2 :** ADDITIONAL, FURTHER ⟨~ guests arrived⟩

2**more** *adv* (bef. 12c) **1 a :** in addition ⟨a couple of times ~⟩ **b :** MOREOVER **2 :** to a greater or higher degree — often used with an adjective or adverb to form the comparative ⟨~ evenly matched⟩

3**more** *n* (bef. 12c) **1 :** a greater quantity, number, or amount ⟨liked the idea better the ~ I thought about it⟩ **2 :** something additional **:** an additional amount **3** *obs* **:** persons of higher rank

4**more** *pron, sing or pl in constr* (13c) **:** additional persons or things or a greater amount ⟨~ will arrive shortly⟩ ⟨~ was spilled⟩

more and more *adv* (13c) **:** to a progressively increasing extent

mo·reen \mə-ˈrēn, mȯ-\ *n* [prob. irreg. fr. *moire*] (ca. 1691) **:** a strong fabric of wool, wool and cotton, or cotton with a plain glossy or moiré finish

mo·rel \mə-ˈrel, mȯ-\ *n* [F *morille,* prob. fr. VL **mauricula,* fr. *maurus* brown, fr. L *Maurus* inhabitant of Mauretania] (1672) **:** any of several edible fungi (genus *Morchella,* esp. *M. esculenta*) having a conical cap with a highly pitted surface — called also *morel mushroom*

mo·rel·lo \mə-ˈre-(ˌ)lō\ *n, pl* **-los** [prob. modif. of D dial. *amarelle, marelle,* fr. ML *amarellum,* a sour cherry, fr. L *amarus* bitter, sour] (1598) **:** a cultivated sour cherry (as the Montmorency) having a dark-colored skin and juice — called also *morello cherry*

more or less *adv* (13c) **1 :** to a varying or undetermined extent or degree **:** SOMEWHAT ⟨they were *more or less* willing to help⟩ **2 :** with small variations **:** APPROXIMATELY ⟨contains 16 acres *more or less*⟩

more·over \mȯr-ˈō-vər, ˈmȯr-ˌ\ *adv* (14c) **:** in addition to what has been said **:** BESIDES

mo·res \ˈmȯr-ˌāz *also* -(ˌ)ēz\ *n pl* [L, pl. of *mor-, mos* custom] (ca. 1899) **1 :** the fixed morally binding customs of a particular group **2 :** moral attitudes **3 :** HABITS, MANNERS

1**mo·resque** \mȯ-ˈresk, mə-\ *adj, often cap* [F, fr. Sp *morisco,* fr. *moro* Moor, fr. L *Maurus*] (ca. 1611) **:** having the characteristics of Moorish art or architecture

2**moresque** *n, often cap* (ca. 1752) **:** an ornament or decorative motif in Moorish style

mor·gan \ˈmȯr-gən\ *n* [Thomas Hunt *Morgan*] (1919) **1 :** a unit of inferred distance between genes on a chromosome that is used in constructing genetic maps and is equal to the distance for which the frequency of crossing over between specific pairs of genes is 100 percent **2 :** CENTIMORGAN

Mor·gan \ˈmȯr-gən\ *n* [Justin *Morgan* †1798 Am. teacher] (1841) **:** any of an American breed of light strong horses originated in Vermont from the progeny of one prepotent stallion of uncertain ancestry

mor·ga·nat·ic \ˌmȯr-gə-ˈna-tik\ *adj* [NL *matrimonium ad morganaticam,* lit., marriage with morning gift] (ca. 1741) **:** of, relating to, or being a marriage between a member of a royal or noble family and a person of inferior rank in which the rank of the inferior partner remains unchanged and the children of the marriage do not succeed to the titles, fiefs, or entailed property of the parent of higher rank — **mor·ga·nat·i·cal·ly** \-ti-k(ə-)lē\ *adv*

\ə\ **abut** \ᵊ\ kitten, F table \ər\ **further** \a\ **ash** \ā\ **ace** \ä\ **mop, mar**
\au̇\ **out** \ch\ **chin** \e\ **bet** \ē\ **easy** \g\ **go** \i\ **hit** \ī\ **ice** \j\ **job**
\ŋ\ **sing** \ō\ **go** \ȯ\ **law** \ȯi\ **boy** \th\ **thin** \th\ **the** \ü\ **loot** \u̇\ **foot**
\y\ **yet** \zh\ **vision, beige** \k, ⁿ, œ,ue, ʸ\ *see* Guide to Pronunciation

mor·gan·ite \ˈmȯr-gə-ˌnīt\ *n* [J. P. *Morgan* †1913] (1911) **:** a rose-colored gem variety of beryl

Morgan le Fay \-lə-ˈfā\ *n* [OF *Morgain la fee* Morgan the fairy] (15c) **:** a sorceress and sister of King Arthur

mor·gen \ˈmȯr-gə(n)\ *n, pl* **morgen** [D, lit., morning] (1626) **:** a Dutch and southern African unit of land area equal to 2.116 acres (0.856 hectare)

morgue \ˈmȯrg\ *n* [F] (1821) **1 :** a place where the bodies of dead persons are kept temporarily pending identification or release for burial or autopsy **2 :** a collection of reference works and files of reference material in a newspaper or news periodical office

mor·i·bund \ˈmȯr-ə-(ˌ)bənd, ˈmär-\ *adj* [L *moribundus,* fr. *mori* to die — more at MURDER] (ca. 1721) **1 :** being in the state of dying **:** approaching death **2 :** being in a state of inactivity or obsolescence — **mor·i·bun·di·ty** \ˌmȯr-ə-ˈbən-də-tē, ˌmär-\ *n*

1**mo·ri·on** \ˈmȯr-ē-ˌän\ *n* [MF] (1563) **:** a high-crested helmet with no visor

2**morion** *n* [modif. of L *mormorion*] (1748) **:** a nearly black variety of smoky quartz

Mo·ris·co \mə-ˈris-(ˌ)kō, mȯ-\ *n, pl* **-cos** *or* **-coes** [Sp, fr. *morisco,* adj., fr. *moro* Moor] (1625) **:** MOOR; *esp* **:** a Spanish Moor converted to Christianity — **Morisco** *adj*

Mor·mon \ˈmȯr-mən\ *n* (1830) **1 :** the ancient redactor and compiler of the Book of Mormon presented as divine revelation by Joseph Smith **2 :** LATTER-DAY SAINT; *esp* **:** a member of the Church of Jesus Christ of Latter-day Saints — **Mor·mon·ism** \-mə-ˌni-zəm\ *n*

Mormon cricket *n* (1896) **:** a large dark wingless migratory katydid (*Anabrus simplex*) that resembles a cricket and is found in the western U.S. where it is occas. an abundant pest of crops and forage plants

Mormon tea *n* (1910) **:** any of various ephedras of the arid southwestern U.S. having jointed stems used esp. formerly to make a tea

morn \ˈmȯrn\ *n* [ME, fr. OE *morgen;* akin to OHG *morgan* morning and perh. to Gk *marmairein* to sparkle] (bef. 12c) **1 :** DAWN **2 :** MORNING

Mor·nay sauce \mȯr-ˈnā-\ *n* [Philippe de *Mornay*] (ca. 1924) **:** a cheese-flavored cream sauce

morn·ing \ˈmȯr-niŋ\ *n* [ME, fr. *morn* + *-ing* (as in *evening*)] (13c) **1 a :** DAWN **b :** the time from sunrise to noon **c :** the time from midnight to noon **2 :** a period of first development **:** BEGINNING

morn·ing–after pill \ˌmȯr-niŋ-ˈaf-tər-\ *n* (1957) **:** an oral drug usu. containing high doses of estrogen taken up to usu. three days after unprotected sexual intercourse that interferes with pregnancy by inhibiting ovulation or by blocking implantation of a fertilized egg in the human uterus

morning breath *n* (1986) **:** halitosis upon awakening from sleep that is caused by the buildup of bacteria in the mouth from decreased saliva production

morning coat *n* **:** CUTAWAY 1

morning glory *n* (1814) **:** any of various usu. twining plants (genus *Ipomoea* of the family Convolvulaceae, the morning-glory family) with showy trumpet-shaped flowers; *broadly* **:** an herb, shrub, or tree of the morning-glory family

morning line *n* (ca. 1935) **:** a bookmaker's list of entries for a race meet and the probable odds on each that is printed or posted before the betting begins

Morning Prayer *n* (1552) **:** a service of liturgical prayer used for regular morning worship in churches of the Anglican communion

morn·ings \ˈmȯr-niŋz\ *adv* (14c) **:** in the morning repeatedly **:** on any morning

morning sickness *n* (1879) **:** nausea and vomiting that occurs typically in the morning esp. during the earlier months of pregnancy

morning star *n* (1535) **:** a bright planet (as Venus) seen in the eastern sky before or at sunrise

Mo·ro \ˈmȯr-(ˌ)ō\ *n, pl* **Moros** [Sp, lit., Moor, fr. L *Maurus*] (1886) **1 :** a member of any of several Muslim peoples of the southern Philippines **2 :** any of the Austronesian languages of the Moros

mo·roc·co \mə-ˈrä-(ˌ)kō\ *n* [*Morocco,* Africa] (1634) **:** a fine leather from goatskin tanned with sumac

mo·ron \ˈmȯr-ˌän\ *n* [irreg. fr. Gk *mōros* foolish, stupid] (1910) **1** *usu offensive* **:** a person affected with mild mental retardation **2 :** a very stupid person — **mo·ron·ic** \mə-ˈrä-nik, mȯ-\ *adj* — **mo·ron·i·cal·ly** \-ni-k(ə-)lē\ *adv* — **mo·ron·ism** \ˈmȯr-ˌä-ˌni-zəm\ *n* — **mo·ron·i·ty** \mə-ˈrä-nə-tē, mȯ-\ *n*

mo·rose \mə-ˈrōs, mȯ-\ *adj* [L *morosus,* lit., capricious, fr. *mor-, mos* will] (1565) **1 :** having a sullen and gloomy disposition **2 :** marked by or expressive of gloom ***syn*** see SULLEN — **mo·rose·ly** *adv* — **mo·rose·ness** *n* — **mo·ros·i·ty** \-ˈrä-sə-tē\ *n*

1**morph** \ˈmȯrf\ *n* [back-formation fr. *morpheme*] (1947) **1 a :** ALLOMORPH **b :** a distinctive collocation of phones (as a portmanteau form) that serves as the realization of more than one morpheme in a context (as the French *du* for the sequence of *de* and *le*) **2 a :** a local population of a species that consists of interbreeding organisms and is distinguishable from other populations by morphology or behavior though capable of interbreeding with them **b :** a phenotypic variant of a species

2**morph** *vb* [short for *metamorphose*] *vt* (1982) **:** to change the form or character of **:** TRANSFORM ~ *vi* **:** to undergo transformation; *esp* **:** to undergo transformation from an image of one object into that of another esp. by means of computer-generated animation

3**morph** *abbr* morphology

morph- *or* **morpho-** *comb form* [G, fr. Gk, fr. *morphē*] **1 :** form ⟨*morphogenesis*⟩ **2 :** morpheme ⟨*morphophonemics*⟩

-morph *n comb form* [ISV, fr. *-morphous*] **:** one having (such) a form ⟨iso*morph*⟩

mor·phac·tin \mȯr-ˈfak-tən\ *n* [prob. fr. *morph-* + *active* + 1*-in*] (1966) **:** any of several synthetic fluorine-containing compounds that tend to produce morphological changes and suppress growth in plants

mor·phal·lax·is \ˌmȯr-fə-ˈlak-səs\ *n, pl* **-lax·es** \-ˌsēz\ [NL, fr. *morph-* + Gk *allaxis* exchange, fr. *allassein* to change, exchange, fr. *allos* other — more at ELSE] (1901) **:** regeneration of a part or organism from a fragment by reorganization without cell proliferation

mor·pheme \ˈmȯr-ˌfēm\ *n* [F *morphème,* fr. Gk *morphē* form] (1926) **:** a distinctive collocation of phonemes (as the free form *pin* or the bound form *-s* of *pins*) having no smaller meaningful parts — **mor·phe·mic** \mȯr-ˈfē-mik\ *adj* — **mor·phe·mi·cal·ly** \-mi-k(ə-)lē\ *adv*

mor·phe·mics \mȯr-ˈfē-miks\ *n pl but sing in constr* (1947) **1 :** a branch of linguistic analysis that consists of the study of morphemes **2 :** the structure of a language in terms of morphemes

Mor·pheus \ˈmȯr-fē-əs, -ˌfyüs, -ˌfüs\ *n* [L, fr. Gk] (14c) **:** the Greek god of dreams

mor·phia \ˈmȯr-fē-ə\ *n* [NL, fr. *Morpheus*] (1818) **:** MORPHINE

-morphic *adj comb form* [prob. fr. F *-morphique,* fr. Gk *morphē*] **:** having (such) a form ⟨endo*morphic*⟩

mor·phine \ˈmȯr-ˌfēn\ *n* [F, fr. *Morpheus*] (1828) **:** a bitter crystalline addictive narcotic base $C_{17}H_{19}NO_3$ that is the principal alkaloid of opium and is used in the form of a soluble salt (as a hydrochloride or a sulfate) as an analgesic and sedative

mor·phin·ism \ˈmȯr-ˌfē-ˌni-zəm, -fə-\ *n* (1882) **:** a disordered condition of health produced by habitual use of morphine

-morphism *n comb form* [LL *-morphus* -morphous, fr. Gk *-morphos*] **:** quality or state of having (such) a form ⟨hetero*morphism*⟩

mor·pho \ˈmȯr-(ˌ)fō\ *n, pl* **morphos** [NL, fr. Gk *Morphō,* epithet of Aphrodite] (1853) **:** any of a genus (*Morpho* of the family Morphoidae) of large showy tropical American butterflies that typically have a brilliant blue metallic luster on the upper surface of the wings

mor·pho·gen \ˈmȯr-fə-jən, -ˌjen\ *n* (1950) **:** a diffusible chemical substance that exerts control over morphogenesis esp. by forming a gradient in concentration

mor·pho·gen·e·sis \ˌmȯr-fə-ˈje-nə-səs\ *n* [NL] (ca. 1890) **:** the formation and differentiation of tissues and organs — compare ORGANOGENESIS

mor·pho·ge·net·ic \-jə-ˈne-tik\ *adj* (1884) **:** relating to or concerned with the development of normal organic form ⟨~ movements of early embryonic cells⟩ — **mor·pho·ge·net·i·cal·ly** \-ti-k(ə-)lē\ *adv*

mor·pho·gen·ic \-ˈje-nik\ *adj* (ca. 1890) **:** MORPHOGENETIC

mor·phol·o·gy \mȯr-ˈfä-lə-jē\ *n* [G *Morphologie,* fr. *morph-* + *-logie* -logy] (1830) **1 a :** a branch of biology that deals with the form and structure of animals and plants **b :** the form and structure of an organism or any of its parts **2 a :** a study and description of word formation (as inflection, derivation, and compounding) in language **b :** the system of word-forming elements and processes in a language **3 a :** a study of structure or form **b :** STRUCTURE, FORM **4 :** the external structure of rocks in relation to the development of erosional forms or topographic features — **mor·pho·log·i·cal** \ˌmȯr-fə-ˈlä-ji-kəl\ *also* **mor·pho·log·ic** \-ˈlä-jik\ *adj* — **mor·pho·log·i·cal·ly** \-k(ə-)lē\ *adv* — **mor·phol·o·gist** \mȯr-ˈfä-lə-jist\ *n*

mor·phom·e·try \mȯr-ˈfä-mə-trē\ *n* (ca. 1856) **:** measurement of external form — **mor·pho·met·ric** \ˌmȯr-fə-ˈme-trik\ *adj* — **mor·pho·met·ri·cal·ly** \-tri-k(ə-)lē\ *adv*

mor·pho·pho·ne·mics \ˌmȯr-fō-fə-ˈnē-miks\ *n pl but sing in constr* (1938) **1 :** a study of the phonemic differences between allomorphs of the same morpheme **2 :** the distribution of allomorphs in one morpheme **3 :** the structure of a language in terms of morphophonemics

-morphous *adj comb form* [Gk *-morphos,* fr. *morphē*] **:** having (such) a form ⟨iso*morphous*⟩

-morphy *n comb form* [ISV, fr. *-morphous*] **:** quality or state of having (such) a form ⟨endo*morphy*⟩

mor·ris \ˈmȯr-əs, ˈmär-\ *n* [ME *moreys daunce,* fr. *moreys* Moorish (fr. *More* Moor) + *daunce* dance] (1512) **:** a vigorous English dance traditionally performed by men wearing costumes and bells

morris chair *n* [William *Morris*] (1900) **:** an easy chair with an adjustable back and removable cushions

mor·row \ˈmär-(ˌ)ō, ˈmȯr-\ *n* [ME *morn, morwen* morn] (13c) **1** *archaic* **:** MORNING **2 :** the next day **3 :** the time immediately after a specified event

Morse code \ˈmȯrs-\ *n* [Samuel F. B. *Morse*] (1867) **:** either of two codes consisting of variously spaced dots and dashes or long and short sounds used for transmitting messages by audible or visual signals

INTERNATIONAL MORSE CODE

a	·–	n	–·	á	·––·–	8	–––··
b	–···	o	–––	ä	·–·–	9	––––·
c	–·–·	p	·––·	é	··–··	0	–––––
d	–··	q	––·–	ñ	––·––	,	––··–– (comma)
e	·	r	·–·	ö	–––·	.	·–·–·– (period)
f	··–·	s	···	ü	··––	?	··––·· (question mark)
g	––·	t	–	1	·––––	"	·–··–· (quotation marks)
h	····	u	··–	2	··–––	:	–––··· (colon)
i	··	v	···–	3	···––	'	·––––· (apostrophe)
j	·–––	w	·––	4	····–	-	–····– (hyphen)
k	–·–	x	–··–	5	·····	/	–··–· (slash)
l	·–··	y	–·––	6	–····	(	–·––· (left parenthesis)
m	––	z	––··	7	––···	)	–·––·– (right parenthesis)

1**mor·sel** \ˈmȯr-səl\ *n* [ME, fr. AF, dim. of *mors* bite, fr. L *morsus,* fr. *mordēre* to bite — more at MORDANT] (14c) **1 :** a small piece of food **:** BITE **2 :** a small quantity **:** FRAGMENT **3 a :** a tasty dish **b :** something delectable and pleasing **4 :** a negligible person

2**morsel** *vt* **-seled** *or* **-selled; -sel·ing** *or* **-sel·ling** (1598) **:** to divide into or distribute in small pieces

1**mort** \ˈmȯrt\ *n* [prob. alter. of ME *mot* horn note, fr. AF, word, horn note — more at MOT] (ca. 1500) **1 :** a note sounded on a hunting horn when a deer is killed **2 :** KILLING 1

2**mort** *n* [perh. back-formation fr. 1*mortal*] (1694) **:** a great quantity or number

mor·ta·del·la \ˌmȯr-tə-ˈde-lə\ *n* [It, fr. L *murtatum* sausage seasoned with myrtle berries, fr. *murtus* myrtle] (1613) **:** a large smoked sausage made of beef, pork, and pork fat and seasoned with pepper and garlic

1**mor·tal** \ˈmȯr-tᵊl\ *adj* [ME, fr. AF *mortel, mortal,* fr. L *mortalis,* fr. *mort-, mors* death — more at MURDER] (14c) **1 :** causing or having caused death **:** FATAL ⟨a ~ injury⟩ **2 a :** subject to death ⟨~ man⟩ **b :** POSSIBLE, CONCEIVABLE ⟨have done every ~ thing⟩ **c :** DEADLY 3

⟨waited three ~ hours⟩ **3 :** marked by unrelenting hostility ⟨a ~ enemy⟩ **4 :** marked by great intensity or severity ⟨~ fear⟩ **5 :** HUMAN ⟨~ limits⟩ **6 :** of, relating to, or connected with death ⟨~ agony⟩ ***syn*** see DEADLY

[2]**mortal** *adv* (15c) *chiefly dial* **:** MORTALLY

[3]**mortal** *n* (1567) **:** a human being

mor·tal·i·ty \mȯr-ˈta-lə-tē\ *n* (14c) **1 :** the quality or state of being mortal **2 :** the death of large numbers (as of people or animals) **3** *archaic* **:** DEATH **4 :** the human race **5 a :** the number of deaths in a given time or place **b :** the proportion of deaths to population **c :** the number lost or the rate of loss or failure

mortality table *n* (1880) **:** an actuarial table based on mortality statistics over a number of years

mor·tal·ly \ˈmȯr-tᵊl-ē\ *adv* (14c) **1 :** in a deadly or fatal manner **:** to death ⟨~ wounded⟩ **2 :** to an extreme degree **:** INTENSELY ⟨~ afraid⟩

mortal mind *n* (1875) *Christian Science* **:** a belief that life, substance, and intelligence are in and of matter **:** ILLUSION

mortal sin *n* (15c) **:** a sin (as murder) that is deliberately committed and is of such serious consequence according to Thomist theology that it deprives the soul of sanctifying grace — compare VENIAL SIN 1

[1]**mor·tar** \ˈmȯr-tər\ *n* [ME *morter,* fr. OE *mortere* & AF *mortier,* fr. L *mortarium*] (bef. 12c) **1 :** a sturdy vessel in which material is pounded or rubbed with a pestle **2** [MF *mortier*] **a :** a muzzle-loading cannon having a tube short in relation to its caliber that is used to throw projectiles at high angles **b :** any of several similar firing devices

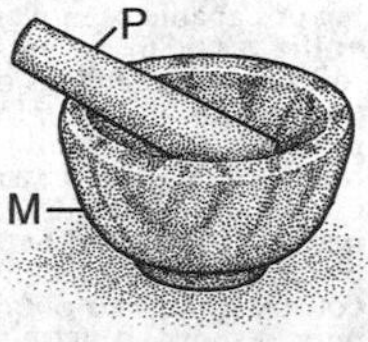

M mortar, *P* pestle

[2]**mortar** *n* [ME *morter,* fr. AF *morter, mortier,* fr. L *mortarium*] (14c) **:** a plastic building material (as a mixture of cement, lime, or gypsum plaster with sand and water) that hardens and is used in masonry or plastering — **mor·tar·less** *adj*

[3]**mortar** *vt* (14c) **:** to plaster or make fast with mortar

mor·tar·board \ˈmȯr-tər-ˌbȯrd\ *n* (1854) **1 :** an academic cap consisting of a closely fitting headpiece with a broad flat projecting square top **2 a :** HAWK 2 **b :** a board or platform about three feet (one meter) square for holding mortar

mor·tar·man \ˈmȯr-tər-mən\ *n* (1862) **:** a soldier who operates a mortar

[1]**mort·gage** \ˈmȯr-gij\ *n* [ME *morgage,* fr. AF *mortgage,* fr. *mort* dead (fr. L *mortuus*) + *gage* gage — more at MURDER] (15c) **1 :** a conveyance of or lien against property (as for securing a loan) that becomes void upon payment or performance according to stipulated terms **2 a :** the instrument evidencing the mortgage **b :** the state of the property so mortgaged **c :** the interest of the mortgagee in such property

[2]**mortgage** *vt* **mort·gaged; mort·gag·ing** (15c) **1 :** to grant or convey by a mortgage **2 :** to subject to a claim or obligation **:** PLEDGE

mort·gag·ee \ˌmȯr-gi-ˈjē\ *n* (1584) **:** a person to whom property is mortgaged

mort·gag·or \ˌmȯr-gi-ˈjȯr\ *also* **mort·gag·er** \ˈmȯr-gi-jər\ *n* (1584) **:** a person who mortgages property

mor·ti·cian \mȯr-ˈti-shən\ *n* [L *mort-, mors* death] (1895) **:** UNDERTAKER 2

mor·ti·fi·ca·tion \ˌmȯr-tə-fə-ˈkā-shən\ *n* (14c) **1 :** the subjection and denial of bodily passions and appetites by abstinence or self-inflicted pain or discomfort **2 :** NECROSIS, GANGRENE **3 a :** a sense of humiliation and shame caused by something that wounds one's pride or self-respect **b :** the cause of such humiliation or shame

mor·ti·fy \ˈmȯr-tə-ˌfī\ *vb* **-fied; -fy·ing** [ME *mortifien,* fr. AF *mortifier,* fr. LL *mortificare,* fr. L *mort-, mors*] *vt* (14c) **1** *obs* **:** to destroy the strength, vitality, or functioning of **2 :** to subdue or deaden (as the body or bodily appetites) esp. by abstinence or self-inflicted pain or discomfort **3 :** to subject to severe and vexing embarrassment **:** SHAME ~ *vi* **1 :** to practice mortification **2 :** to become necrotic or gangrenous

[1]**mor·tise** *also* **mor·tice** \ˈmȯr-təs\ *n* [ME *mortays,* fr. AF *mortais*] (15c) **:** a hole, groove, or slot into or through which some other part of an arrangement of parts fits or passes; *esp* **:** a cavity cut into a piece of material (as timber) to receive a tenon — see DOVETAIL illustration

[2]**mortise** *also* **mortice** *vt* **mor·tised** *also* **mor·ticed; mor·tis·ing** *also* **mor·tic·ing** (15c) **1 :** to join or fasten securely; *specif* **:** to join or fasten by a tenon and mortise **2 :** to cut or make a mortise in

mort·main \ˈmȯrt-ˌmān\ *n* [ME *morte-mayne,* fr. AF *mortmain,* fr. *morte* (fem. of *mort* dead) + *main* hand, fr. L *manus* — more at MANUAL] (15c) **1 a :** an inalienable possession of lands or buildings by an ecclesiastical or other corporation **b :** the condition of property or other gifts left to a corporation in perpetuity esp. for religious, charitable, or public purposes **2 :** the influence of the past regarded as controlling the present

[1]**mor·tu·ary** \ˈmȯr-chə-ˌwer-ē, -chü-ˌer-\ *adj* [L *mortuarius* of the dead, fr. *mortuus* dead] (1514) **1 :** of or relating to the burial of the dead **2 :** of, relating to, or characteristic of death

[2]**mortuary** *n, pl* **-ar·ies** (1865) **:** a place in which dead bodies are kept until burial; *esp* **:** FUNERAL HOME

mor·u·la \ˈmȯr-(y)ə-lə, ˈmär-\ *n, pl* **-lae** \-ˌlē, -ˌlī\ [NL, fr. L *morum* mulberry, fr. Gk *moron*] (1874) **:** a globular solid mass of blastomeres formed by cleavage of a zygote that typically precedes the blastula — **mor·u·lar** \-lər\ *adj* — **mor·u·la·tion** \ˌmȯr-(y)ə-ˈlā-shən, ˌmär-\ *n*

mos *abbr* months

MOS *abbr* **1** metal-oxide semiconductor **2** military occupational specialty

[1]**mo·sa·ic** \mō-ˈzā-ik\ *n* [ME *musycke,* fr. ML *musaicum,* alter. of LL *musivum,* fr. L *museum, musaeum*] (15c) **1 :** a surface decoration made by inlaying small pieces of variously colored material to form pictures or patterns; *also* **:** the process of making it **2 :** a picture or design made in mosaic **3 :** something resembling a mosaic ⟨a ~ of visions and daydreams and memories —Lawrence Shainberg⟩ **4 :** an organism or one of its parts composed of cells of more than one genotype **:** CHIMERA 3 **5 :** any of numerous virus diseases of plants characterized by diffuse light and dark green or yellow and green mottling of the foliage — compare TOBACCO MOSAIC VIRUS **6 :** a composite map made of photographs taken by an aircraft or spacecraft **7 :** the part of a television camera tube consisting of many minute photoelectric particles that convert light to an electric charge — **mo·sa·ic·like** \-ˈzā-ik-ˌlīk\ *adj*

[2]**mosaic** *adj* (1585) **1 :** of, relating to, produced by, or resembling a mosaic **2 :** exhibiting mosaicism **3 :** DETERMINATE 5 — **mo·sa·i·cal·ly** \-ˈzā-ə-k(ə-)lē\ *adv*

[3]**mosaic** *vt* **-icked; -ick·ing** (1839) **1 :** to decorate with mosaics **2 :** to form into a mosaic

Mo·sa·ic \mō-ˈzā-ik\ *adj* [NL *Mosaicus,* fr. *Moses* Moses] (1662) **:** of or relating to Moses or the institutions or writings attributed to him

mo·sa·i·cism \mō-ˈzā-ə-ˌsi-zəm\ *n* (1926) **:** the condition of possessing cells of two or more different genetic constitutions

mo·sa·i·cist \-sist\ *n* (1847) **1 a :** a designer of mosaics **b :** a worker who makes mosaics **2 :** a dealer in mosaics

mo·sa·saur \ˈmō-zə-ˌsȯr\ *n* [NL *Mosasaurus,* fr. L *Mosa* the river Meuse + Gk *sauros* lizard] (1841) **:** any of a family (Mosasauridae) of very large extinct marine fish-eating lizards of the Upper Cretaceous with limbs modified into paddles that are related to the recent monitor lizards

Mo·selle \mō-ˈzel\ *n* [G *Moselwein,* fr. *Mosel* Moselle, river in Germany + G *Wein* wine] (1681) **:** a white wine from the Moselle valley

Mo·ses \ˈmō-zəz *also* -zəs\ *n* [L, fr. Gk *Mōsēs,* fr. Heb *Mōsheh*] (bef. 12c) **:** a Hebrew prophet who led the Israelites out of Egyptian slavery and at Mt. Sinai delivered the Law establishing God's covenant with them

mo·sey \ˈmō-zē\ *vi* **mo·seyed; mo·sey·ing** [origin unknown] (1829) **1 :** to hurry away **2 :** to move in a leisurely or aimless manner **:** SAUNTER ⟨~*ed* around the general store —Eric Sevareid⟩

MOSFET *abbr* metal-oxide-semiconductor field-effect transistor

mosh \ˈmäsh\ *vi* [perh. alter. of *mash* or *mush*] (1983) **:** to engage in uninhibited often frenzied activities (as intentional collision) with others near the stage at a rock concert — **mosh·er** *n*

mo·shav \mō-ˈshäv\ *n, pl* **mo·sha·vim** \ˌmō-shə-ˈvēm\ [ModHeb *mōshābh,* fr. Heb, dwelling] (1928) **:** a cooperative settlement of small individual farms in Israel — compare KIBBUTZ

mosh pit *n* (1988) **:** an area in front of a stage where very physical and rough dancing takes place at a rock concert

Mos·lem \ˈmäz-ləm *also* ˈmäs-\ *var of* MUSLIM

Mo·so·tho \mō-ˈsō-(ˌ)tō, -ˈsü-(ˌ)tü\ *n, pl* **Ba·so·tho** \bä-\ [Sotho — more at BASOTHO] (1952) **:** a member of the Basotho people

mosque \ˈmäsk\ *n* [earlier *mosquee,* fr. MF, fr. OIt *moschea,* fr. OSp *mezquita,* fr. Ar *masjid* temple, fr. *sajada* to prostrate oneself, worship] (1717) **:** a building used for public worship by Muslims

mos·qui·to \mə-ˈskē-(ˌ)tō\ *n, pl* **-toes** *also* **-tos** [Sp, dim. of *mosca* fly, fr. L *musca* — more at MIDGE] (ca. 1583) **:** any of a family (Culicidae) of dipteran flies with females that have a set of slender organs in the proboscis adapted to puncture the skin of animals and to suck their blood and that are in some cases vectors of serious diseases — **mos·qui·to·ey** \-ˈskē-tə-wē\ *adj*

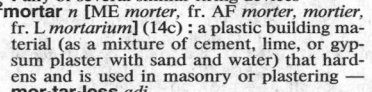

mosquito

mosquito fish *n* (1928) **:** any of three No. American live-bearers (*Gambusia affinis, G. holbrooki,* and *Heterandria formosa* of the family Poeciliidae) used esp. to control mosquito larvae

mosquito hawk *n* (1737) **1** *chiefly Southern* **:** DRAGONFLY **2** *dial* **:** CRANE FLY

mosquito net *n* (1745) **:** a net or screen for keeping out mosquitoes

[1]**moss** \ˈmȯs\ *n* [ME, fr. OE *mos;* akin to OHG *mos* moss, L *muscus*] (bef. 12c) **1** *chiefly Scot* **:** BOG, SWAMP; *esp* **:** a peat bog **2 a :** any of a class (Musci) of bryophytic plants characterized by a gametophyte having a small leafy often tufted stem bearing sex organs at its tip; *also* **:** a clump or sward of these plants **b :** any of various plants resembling moss in appearance or habit of growth **3 :** a mossy covering — **moss·like** \-ˌlīk\ *adj*

[2]**moss** *vt* (15c) **:** to cover or overgrow with moss

moss agate *n* (1798) **:** an agate mineral containing brown, black, or green mosslike or dendritic markings

moss animal *n* (1881) **:** BRYOZOAN

moss·back \ˈmȯs-ˌbak\ *n* (1872) **1 :** a large sluggish fish (as a largemouth bass) **2 :** an extremely old-fashioned or reactionary person **:** FOGY — **moss·backed** \-ˌbakt\ *adj*

moss green *n* (1879) **:** a variable color averaging a moderate yellow-green

moss–grown \ˈmȯs-ˌgrōn\ *adj* (14c) **1 :** overgrown with moss **2 :** ANTIQUATED

moss pink *n* (ca. 1856) **:** a low-growing perennial phlox (*Phlox subulata*) widely cultivated for its abundant usu. pink or white flowers

moss rose *n* (1776) **1 :** an old-fashioned garden rose (*Rosa centifolia mucosa*) that has a glandular mossy calyx and flower stalk **2 :** a So. American portulaca (*Portulaca grandiflora*) grown for its showy flowers

moss–troop·er \ˈmȯs-ˌtrü-pər\ *n* (1645) **1 :** one of a class of 17th century raiders in the marshy border country between England and Scotland **2 :** PIRATE — **moss–troop·ing** \-piŋ\ *adj*

mossy \ˈmȯ-sē\ *adj* **moss·i·er; -est** (15c) **1 :** resembling moss **2 :** covered with moss or something like moss **3 :** ANTIQUATED ⟨the ~ precepts of the . . . prescriptive grammarians —Thomas Pyles⟩

mossy zinc *n* (1910) **:** a granulated form of zinc made by pouring melted zinc into water

[1]**most** \ˈmōst\ *adj* [ME, fr. OE *mǣst;* akin to OHG *meist* most, OE *māra* more — more at MORE] (bef. 12c) **1 :** greatest in quantity, extent, or degree ⟨the ~ ability⟩ **2 :** the majority of ⟨~ people⟩

\ə\ **abut** \ᵊ\ kitten, F table \ər\ **further** \a\ **ash** \ā\ **ace** \ä\ mop, mar \au̇\ **out** \ch\ **chin** \e\ bet \ē\ **easy** \g\ **go** \i\ **hit** \ī\ **ice** \j\ **job** \ŋ\ sing \ō\ go \ȯ\ **law** \ȯi\ **boy** \th\ **thin** \t͟h\ **the** \ü\ **loot** \u̇\ **foot** \y\ yet \zh\ vision, beige \k͟, ⁿ, œ, ue, ʸ\ *see* Guide to Pronunciation

^{2}**most** *adv* (bef. 12c) **1** : to the greatest or highest degree — often used with an adjective or adverb to form the superlative ⟨the ~ challenging job he ever had⟩ **2** : to a very great degree ⟨was ~ persuasive⟩
^{3}**most** *n* (12c) : the greatest amount ⟨it's the ~ I can do⟩ — **at most** *or* **at the most** : as an extreme limit ⟨took him an hour *at most*⟩
^{4}**most** *pron, sing or pl in constr* (13c) : the greatest number or part ⟨~ become discouraged and quit⟩
^{5}**most** *adv* [by shortening] (ca. 1538) : ALMOST ⟨we'll be crossing the river ~ any time now —Hamilton Basso⟩
usage Although considered by some to be unacceptable in all cases, *most* is often used to mean "almost" in both spoken and, to a lesser extent, written English to modify the adjectives *all, every,* and *any;* the pronouns *all, everyone, everything, everybody, anyone, anything,* and *anybody;* and the adverbs *everywhere, anywhere,* and *always.* Other uses of this sense of *most* are dialectal.
-most *adj suffix* [ME, alter. of *-mest* (as in *formest* foremost)] : most ⟨inner*most*⟩ : most toward ⟨head*most*⟩
most·ly \ˈmōst-lē\ *adv* (1563) : for the greatest part : MAINLY
Most Reverend (15c) — used as a title for an archbishop or a Roman Catholic bishop
mot \ˈmō\ *n, pl* **mots** \ˈmō(z)\ [F, word, saying, fr. OF, fr. LL *muttum* grunt — more at MOTTO] (1813) : a pithy or witty saying
^{1}**mote** \ˈmōt\ *verbal auxiliary* [ME, fr. OE *mōtan* to be allowed to — more at MUST] (bef. 12c) *archaic* : MAY, MIGHT
^{2}**mote** \ˈmōt\ *n* [ME *mot,* fr. OE; akin to MD & Fris *mot* sand] (bef. 12c) : a small particle : SPECK
mo·tel \mō-ˈtel\ *n* [blend of *motor* and *hotel*] (1925) : an establishment which provides lodging and parking and in which the rooms are usu. accessible from an outdoor parking area
mo·tet \mō-ˈtet\ *n* [ME, fr. MF, dim. of *mot*] (14c) : a polyphonic choral composition on a sacred text usu. without instrumental accompaniment
moth \ˈmȯth\ *n, pl* **moths** \ˈmȯthz, ˈmȯths\ [ME *mothe,* fr. OE *moththe;* akin to MHG *motte* moth] (bef. 12c) **1** : CLOTHES MOTH **2** : any of various usu. nocturnal lepidopteran insects with antennae that are often feathery, with a stouter body, duller coloring, and proportionately smaller wings than the butterflies, and with larvae that are plant-eating caterpillars — **moth·like** \-ˌlīk\ *adj* — **mothy** \ˈmȯ-thē\ *adj*
^{1}**moth·ball** \ˈmȯth-ˌbȯl\ *n* (1892) **1** : a ball made formerly of camphor but now often of naphthalene and paradichlorobenzene and used to keep moths from clothing **2** *pl* : a condition of protective storage ⟨put the ships in ~*s* after the war⟩; *also* : a state of having been rejected for further use or dismissed from further consideration
^{2}**mothball** *vt* (1926) **1** : to deactivate (as a ship) and prevent deterioration chiefly by dehumidification **2** : to withdraw from use or service and keep in reserve : put aside
moth bean *n* [prob. by folk etymology fr. Marathi *maṭh* moth bean] (1884) : a legume (*Vigna acontifolia* syn. *Phaseolus aconitifolius*) cultivated esp. in India for its edible cylindrical pods and small seeds
moth–eat·en \ˈmȯth-ˌē-tᵊn\ *adj* (14c) **1** : eaten into by moth larvae ⟨~ clothes⟩ **2 a** : DILAPIDATED **b** : ANTIQUATED, OUTMODED
^{1}**moth·er** \ˈmə-thər\ *n* [ME *moder,* fr. OE *mōdor;* akin to OHG *muoter* mother, L *mater,* Gk *mētēr,* Skt *mātṛ*] (bef. 12c) **1 a** : a female parent **b** (1) : a woman in authority; *specif* : the superior of a religious community of women (2) : an old or elderly woman **2** : SOURCE, ORIGIN ⟨necessity is the ~ of invention⟩ **3** : maternal tenderness or affection **4** [short for *motherfucker*] *sometimes vulgar* : MOTHERFUCKER **5** : something that is an extreme or ultimate example of its kind esp. in terms of scale ⟨the ~ of all construction projects⟩ — **moth·er·hood** \-ˌhu̇d\ *n* — **moth·er·less** \-ləs\ *adj* — **moth·er·less·ness** *n*
^{2}**mother** *adj* (13c) **1 a** : of, relating to, or being a mother **b** : bearing the relation of a mother **2** : derived from or as if from one's mother **3** : acting as or providing parental stock — used without reference to sex
^{3}**mother** *vt* **moth·ered; moth·er·ing** \ˈmə-thə-riŋ, ˈməth-riŋ\ (15c) **1 a** : to give birth to **b** : to give rise to : PRODUCE **2** : to care for or protect like a mother
^{4}**mother** *n* [archaic *mother* dregs, lees; akin to MD *moeder* dregs] (1682) : MOTHER OF VINEGAR
moth·er·board \-ˌbȯrd\ *n* (1971) : the main circuit board esp. of a microcomputer
Mother Car·ey's chicken \-ˈker-ēz-\ *n* [origin unknown] (1767) : STORM PETREL
mother cell *n* (1840) : a cell that gives rise to other cells usu. of a different sort
mother country *n* (1567) **1** : the country of one's parents or ancestors; *also* : FATHERLAND **2** : the country from which the people of a colony or former colony derive their origin **3** : a country that is the origin of something
moth·er·fuck·er \ˈmə-thər-ˌfə-kər\ *n* (1918) **1** *usu obscene* : one that is formidable, contemptible, or offensive — usu. used as a generalized term of abuse **2** *usu obscene* : PERSON, FELLOW — **moth·er·fuck·ing** \-kiŋ\ *adj, usu obscene*
Mother Goose *n* (1807) : the legendary author of a collection of nursery rhymes first published in London about 1760
mother hen *n* (1952) : a person who assumes an overly protective maternal attitude
moth·er·house \-ˌhau̇s\ *n* (1661) **1** : the convent in which the superior of a religious community resides **2** : the original convent of a religious community
Mother Hub·bard \-ˈhə-bərd\ *n* [prob. fr. *Mother Hubbard,* character in a nursery rhyme] (1885) : a loose usu. shapeless dress
moth·er–in–law \ˈmə-thər-ən-ˌlȯ, ˈməth-rən-, ˈmə-thərn-\ *n, pl* **moth·ers–in–law** \ˈmə-thər-zən-\ (14c) **1** : the mother of one's spouse **2** *archaic* : STEPMOTHER
moth·er·land \ˈmə-thər-ˌland\ *n* (1565) **1** : MOTHER COUNTRY 1 **2** : a country regarded as a place of origin (as of an idea or a movement)
mother lode *n* (1863) **1** : the principal vein or lode of a region **2** : a principal source or supply
moth·er·ly \-lē\ *adj* (bef. 12c) **1** : of, relating to, or characteristic of a mother ⟨~ advice⟩ **2** : resembling a mother : MATERNAL — **moth·er·li·ness** *n*
moth·er–na·ked \ˌmə-thər-ˈnā-kəd, *esp Southern* -ˈne-kəd\ *adj* (14c) : stark naked
Mother Nature *n* (1601) : nature personified as a woman considered as the source and guiding force of creation
moth·er–of–pearl \ˌmə-thə-rə(v)-ˈpər(-ə)l\ *n* (ca. 1510) : the hard pearly iridescent substance forming the inner layer of a mollusk shell
mother of vinegar (1601) : a slimy membrane composed of yeast and bacterial cells that develops on the surface of alcoholic liquids undergoing acetous fermentation and is added to wine or cider to produce vinegar — called also *mother*
Mother's Day *n* (1890) : the second Sunday in May appointed for the honoring of mothers
mother ship *n* (1867) : a ship serving smaller craft
mother tongue *n* (14c) **1** : one's native language **2** : a language from which another language derives
mother wit *n* (15c) : natural wit or intelligence
^{1}**moth·proof** \ˈmȯth-ˌprüf\ *adj* (1847) : impervious to penetration by moths ⟨~ wool⟩
^{2}**mothproof** *vt* (1888) : to make mothproof — **moth·proof·er** *n*
mo·tif \mō-ˈtēf\ *n* [F, motive, motif, fr. MF — more at MOTIVE] (1848) **1** : a usu. recurring salient thematic element (as in the arts); *esp* : a dominant idea or central theme **2** : a single or repeated design or color — **mo·tif·ic** \-ˈtē-fik, -ˈti-\ *adj*
^{1}**mo·tile** \ˈmō-tᵊl, -ˌtīl(-ə)l\ *adj* [L *motus,* pp. of *movēre*] (1857) : exhibiting or capable of movement — **mo·til·i·ty** \mō-ˈti-lə-tē\ *n*
^{2}**motile** *n* (1886) : a person whose prevailing mental imagery takes the form of inner feelings of action
^{1}**mo·tion** \ˈmō-shən\ *n* [ME *mocioun,* fr. AF *motion,* fr. L *motion-, motio* movement, fr. *movēre* to move] (14c) **1 a** : an act, process, or instance of changing place : MOVEMENT **b** : an active or functioning state or condition ⟨set the divorce proceedings in ~⟩ **2** : an impulse or inclination of the mind or will **3 a** : a proposal for action; *esp* : a formal proposal made in a deliberative assembly **b** : an application made to a court or judge to obtain an order, ruling, or direction **4** *obs* **a** : a puppet show **b** : PUPPET **5** : MECHANISM **6 a** : an act or instance of moving the body or its parts : GESTURE **b** *pl* : ACTIVITIES, MOVEMENTS **7** : melodic change of pitch — **mo·tion·al** \ˈmō-shnəl, -shə-nᵊl\ *adj* — **mo·tion·less** \ˈmō-shən-ləs\ *adj* — **mo·tion·less·ly** *adv* — **mo·tion·less·ness** *n* — **in motion** *of an offensive football player* : running parallel to the line of scrimmage before the snap
^{2}**motion** *vb* **mo·tioned; mo·tion·ing** \ˈmō-sh(ə-)niŋ\ *vi* (1747) : to signal by a movement or gesture ⟨the pitcher ~*ed* to the catcher⟩ ~ *vt* : to direct by a motion ⟨~*ed* me to the seat⟩
motion capture *n* (1992) : a technology for digitally recording specific movements of a person (as an actor) and translating them into computer-animated images
motion picture *n* (1891) **1** : a series of pictures projected on a screen in rapid succession with objects shown in successive positions slightly changed so as to produce the optical effect of a continuous picture in which the objects move **2** : a representation (as of a story) by means of motion pictures : MOVIE
motion sickness *n* (1881) : sickness induced by motion (as in travel by air, car, or ship) and characterized by nausea
mo·ti·vate \ˈmō-tə-ˌvāt\ *vt* **-vat·ed; -vat·ing** (1836) : to provide with a motive : IMPEL ⟨questions that excite and ~ youth⟩ — **mo·ti·va·tive** \-ˌvā-tiv\ *adj* — **mo·ti·va·tor** \-ˌvā-tər\ *n*
mo·ti·va·tion \ˌmō-tə-ˈvā-shən\ *n* (1873) **1 a** : the act or process of motivating **b** : the condition of being motivated **2** : a motivating force, stimulus, or influence : INCENTIVE, DRIVE — **mo·ti·va·tion·al** \-shnəl, -shə-nᵊl\ *adj* — **mo·ti·va·tion·al·ly** *adv*
^{1}**mo·tive** \ˈmō-tiv, *2 is also* mō-ˈtēv\ *n* [ME, fr. AF *motif, motive,* fr. *motif,* adj., moving, fr. ML *motivus,* fr. L *motus,* pp. of *movēre* to move] (15c) **1** : something (as a need or desire) that causes a person to act **2** : a recurrent phrase or figure that is developed through the course of a musical composition **3** : MOTIF — **mo·tive·less** \-ləs\ *adj* — **mo·tive·less·ly** *adv* — **mo·ti·vic** \mō-ˈtē-vik\ *adj*
syn MOTIVE, IMPULSE, INCENTIVE, INDUCEMENT, SPUR, GOAD mean a stimulus to action. MOTIVE implies an emotion or desire operating on the will and causing it to act ⟨a *motive* for the crime⟩. IMPULSE suggests a driving power arising from personal temperament or constitution ⟨buying on *impulse*⟩. INCENTIVE applies to an external influence (as an expected reward) inciting to action ⟨a bonus was offered as an *incentive*⟩. INDUCEMENT suggests a motive prompted by the deliberate enticements or allurements of another ⟨offered a watch as an *inducement* to subscribe⟩. SPUR applies to a motive that stimulates the faculties or increases energy or ardor ⟨fear was a *spur* to action⟩. GOAD suggests a motive that keeps one going against one's will or desire ⟨thought insecurity a *goad* to worker efficiency⟩.
^{2}**mo·tive** \ˈmō-tiv\ *adj* [MF or ML; MF *motif,* fr. ML *motivus*] (14c) **1** : of or relating to motion or the causing of motion ⟨~ energy⟩ **2** : moving or tending to move to action
^{3}**mo·tive** \ˈmō-tiv\ *vt* **mo·tived; mo·tiv·ing** (1657) : MOTIVATE
motive power *n* (1702) **1** : an agency (as water or steam) used to impart motion esp. to machinery **2** : something (as a locomotive or a motor) that provides motive power to a system
mo·tiv·i·ty \mō-ˈti-və-tē\ *n* (ca. 1687) : the power of moving or producing motion
mot juste \mō-ˈzhuest\ *n, pl* **mots justes** *same*\ [F] (1896) : the exactly right word or phrasing
^{1}**mot·ley** \ˈmät-lē\ *adj* [ME, perh. fr. *mot* mote, speck] (14c) **1** : variegated in color ⟨a ~ coat⟩ **2** : composed of diverse often incongruous elements ⟨a ~ crowd⟩
^{2}**motley** *n* [ME, prob. fr. ^{1}*motley*] (14c) **1** : a woolen fabric of mixed colors made in England between the 14th and 17th centuries **2** : a garment made of motley; *esp* : the characteristic dress of the professional fool **3** : JESTER, FOOL **4** : a mixture esp. of incongruous elements
mot·mot \ˈmät-ˌmät\ *n* [NL *momot, motmot*] (1822) : any of a family (Momotidae) of long-tailed mostly green nonpasserine birds of Central and So. American tropical forests
mo·to·cross \ˈmō-tō-ˌkrȯs\ *n* [F, fr. *moto* motorcycle (short for *motocyclette*) + *cross*-country, fr. E] (1951) : a closed-course motorcycle race over natural or simulated rough terrain (as with steep inclines, hairpin turns, and mud); *also* : the sport of engaging in motocross races
mo·to·neu·ron \ˌmō-tə-ˈnü-ˌrän, -ˈnyü-; -ˈnu̇r-ˌän, -ˈnyu̇r-\ *n* [*motor* + *neuron*] (1908) : MOTOR NEURON — **mo·to·neu·ro·nal** \-ˈnu̇r-ə-nᵊl, -ˈnyu̇r-; -nu̇-ˈrō-nᵊl, -nyu̇-\ *adj*

[1]**mo·tor** \ˈmō-tər\ *n* [L, fr. *movēre* to move] (1586) **1 :** one that imparts motion; *specif* **:** PRIME MOVER **2 :** any of various power units that develop energy or impart motion: as **a :** a small compact engine **b :** INTERNAL COMBUSTION ENGINE; *esp* **:** a gasoline engine **c :** a rotating machine that transforms electrical energy into mechanical energy **3 :** MOTOR VEHICLE; *esp* **:** AUTOMOBILE — **mo·tor·dom** \-dəm\ *n* — **mo·tor·less** \-ləs\ *adj*

[2]**motor** *adj* (1824) **1 a :** causing or imparting motion **b :** of, relating to, or being a motor neuron or a nerve containing motor neurons ⟨~ fiber⟩ **c :** of, relating to, concerned with, or involving muscular movement ⟨~ areas of the brain⟩ **2 a :** equipped with or driven by a motor **b :** of, relating to, or involving an automobile **c :** designed for motor vehicles or motorists

[3]**motor** *vi* (1896) **1 :** to travel by automobile **:** DRIVE **2 :** to move or proceed at a vigorous steady pace ⟨~*ed* down the field for a touchdown⟩ ~ *vt* **:** to transport by automobile

mo·tor·bike \ˈmō-tər-ˌbīk\ *n* (1903) **:** a small usu. lightweight motorcycle — **motorbike** *vi*

mo·tor·boat \-ˌbōt\ *n* (1902) **:** a boat propelled usu. by an internal combustion engine — **mo·tor·boat·er** \-ˌbō-tər\ *n* — **mo·tor·boat·ing** \-tiŋ\ *n*

motor bus *n* (1901) **:** BUS 1a — called also *motor coach*

mo·tor·cade \ˈmō-tər-ˌkād\ *n* (1913) **:** a procession of motor vehicles — **motorcade** *vi*

mo·tor·car \-ˌkär\ *n* (ca. 1890) **1 :** AUTOMOBILE **2** *usu* **motor car :** a railroad car containing motors for propulsion

motor court *n* (1936) **:** MOTEL

mo·tor·cy·cle \ˈmō-tər-ˌsī-kəl\ *n* [*motor* bi*cycle*] (1894) **:** an automotive vehicle with two in-line wheels — **motorcycle** *vi* — **mo·tor·cy·clist** \-k(ə-)list\ *n*

motor home *n* (1965) **:** a large motor vehicle equipped as living quarters — compare MOBILE HOME

mo·tor·ic \mō-ˈtȯr-ik, -ˈtär-\ *adj* (1930) **:** MOTOR 1c — **mo·tor·i·cal·ly** \-i-k(ə-)lē\ *adv*

motor inn *n* (1951) **:** MOTEL; *esp* **:** a large multistory motel — called also *motor hotel*

mo·tor·ise *Brit var of* MOTORIZE

mo·tor·ist \ˈmō-tə-rist\ *n* (1896) **:** a person who travels by automobile

mo·tor·ize \ˈmō-tə-ˌrīz\ *vt* **-ized; -iz·ing** (ca. 1913) **1 :** to equip with a motor **2 :** to equip with motor vehicles — **mo·tor·i·za·tion** \ˌmō-tə-rə-ˈzā-shən\ *n*

motor lodge *n* (1949) **:** MOTEL

mo·tor·man \ˈmō-tər-mən\ *n* (1890) **:** an operator of a motor-driven vehicle (as a streetcar or subway train)

mo·tor·mouth \-ˌmau̇th\ *n* (1955) **:** a person who talks excessively — **mo·tor·mouthed** \-ˌmau̇t͟hd, -ˌmau̇tht\ *adj*

motor neuron *n* (1898) **:** a neuron that passes from the central nervous system or a ganglion toward a muscle and conducts an impulse that causes movement — called also *motoneuron*

motor pool *n* (1942) **:** a group of motor vehicles centrally controlled (as by a governmental agency) and dispatched for use as needed

motor sailer *n* (ca. 1923) **:** a motorboat with sailing equipment

motor scooter *n* (1919) **:** a low 2- or 3-wheeled automotive vehicle resembling a child's scooter and having a seat so that the rider does not straddle the engine

motor ship *n* (1915) **:** a seagoing ship propelled by an internal combustion engine

motor torpedo boat *n* (1940) **:** PT BOAT

mo·tor·truck \ˈmō-tər-ˌtrək\ *n* (1916) **:** an automotive truck used esp. for transporting freight

motor unit *n* (1925) **:** a motor neuron together with the muscle fibers on which it acts

motor vehicle *n* (1890) **:** an automotive vehicle not operated on rails; *esp* **:** one with rubber tires for use on highways

mo·tor·way \ˈmō-tər-ˌwā\ *n* (1903) *chiefly Brit* **:** SUPERHIGHWAY 1

motte \ˈmät\ *n* [F, fr. OF *mote, motte*] (1884) **:** MOUND, HILL; *esp* **:** a hill serving as a site for a Norman castle in Britain

motte and bailey *n* (1900) **:** a medieval Norman castle consisting of two connecting ditched stockaded mounds with the higher mound surmounted by the keep and the lower one containing barracks and other buildings

[1]**mot·tle** \ˈmä-tᵊl\ *n* [prob. back-formation fr. *motley*] (1676) **1 :** a colored spot **2 a :** a surface having colored spots or blotches **b :** the arrangement of such spots or blotches on a surface **3 :** MOSAIC 5 — **mot·tled** \-tᵊld\ *adj*

[2]**mottle** *vt* **mot·tled; mot·tling** \ˈmät-liŋ, ˈmä-tᵊl-iŋ\ (1676) **:** to mark with spots or blotches of different color or shades of color as if stained — **mot·tler** \ˈmät-lər, ˈmä-tᵊl-ər\ *n*

mottled enamel *n* (1928) **:** spotted tooth enamel caused by drinking water containing excessive fluorides during the time the teeth are calcifying

mot·to \ˈmä-(ˌ)tō\ *n, pl* **mottoes** *also* **mottos** [It, fr. LL *muttum* grunt, fr. L *muttire* to mutter] (15c) **1 :** a sentence, phrase, or word inscribed on something as appropriate to or indicative of its character or use **2 :** a short expression of a guiding principle

moue \ˈmü\ *n* [F, fr. MF — more at MOW] (1850) **:** a little grimace **:** POUT

mou·flon *also* **mouf·flon** \mü-ˈflō^{n}\ *n* [F *mouflon*, fr. It dial. *muvrone*, fr. LL *mufron-, mufro*] (1774) **:** either of two wild sheep (*Ovis orientalis* and *O. musimon*) of the mountains of Sardinia, Corsica and western Asia that have large curling horns in the males and are sometimes included in a single species

moujik *var of* MUZHIK

mou·lage \mü-ˈläzh\ *n* [F, molding, fr. MF, fr. *mouler* to mold, fr. OF *modle* mold — more at MOLD] (1902) **1 :** an impression or cast made for use esp. as evidence in a criminal investigation **2 :** the taking of an impression for use as evidence in a criminal investigation

mould *chiefly Brit var of* MOLD

mould·ing *chiefly Brit var of* MOLDING

moult *chiefly Brit var of* MOLT

[1]**mound** \ˈmau̇nd\ *vt* [origin unknown] (1515) **1** *archaic* **:** to enclose or fortify with a fence or a ridge of earth **2 :** to form into a mound

[2]**mound** *n, often attrib* [origin unknown] (1551) **1** *archaic* **:** HEDGE, FENCE **2 a** (1) **:** an artificial bank or hill of earth or stones; *esp* **:** one constructed over a burial or ceremonial site (2) **:** the slightly elevated ground on which a baseball pitcher stands **b :** a rounded hill or natural formation **3 a :** HEAP, PILE ⟨~*s* of work⟩ **b :** a small rounded mass ⟨a ~ of mashed potatoes⟩

Mound Builder *n* (1838) **:** a member of a prehistoric American Indian people whose extensive earthworks are found from the Great Lakes down the Mississippi River valley to the Gulf of Mexico

[1]**mount** \ˈmau̇nt\ *n* [ME, fr. OE *munt* & AF *munt, mont,* both fr. L *mont-, mons;* akin to W *mynydd* mountain, L *minari* to project, threaten] (bef. 12c) **1 :** a high hill **:** MOUNTAIN — used esp. before an identifying name ⟨*Mount* Everest⟩ **2** *archaic* **:** EARTHWORK 1 **3 :** MOUND 2a(1)

[2]**mount** *vb* [ME, fr. AF *munter, monter,* fr. VL **montare,* fr. L *mont-, mons*] *vi* (14c) **1 :** RISE, ASCEND **2 :** to increase in amount or extent ⟨expenses began to ~⟩ **3 :** to get up on something above the level of the ground; *esp* **:** to seat oneself (as on a horse) for riding ~ *vt* **1 a :** to go up **:** CLIMB **b** (1) **:** to seat or place oneself on (2) **:** to climb on top of for copulation **2 a :** to lift up **:** RAISE **b** (1) **:** to put or have (as artillery) in position (2) **:** to have as equipment **c** (1) **:** to organize and equip (an attacking force) ⟨~ an army⟩ (2) **:** to launch and carry out (as an assault or a campaign) **3 :** to set on something that elevates **4 a :** to cause to get on a means of conveyance **b :** to furnish with animals for riding **5 :** to post or set up for defense or observation ⟨~*ed* some guards⟩ **6 a :** to attach to a support **b :** to arrange or assemble for use or display **7 a :** to prepare (as a specimen) for examination or display **b :** to prepare and supply with materials needed for performance or execution ⟨~ an opera⟩ — **mount·able** \ˈmau̇n-tə-bəl\ *adj* — **mount·er** *n*

[3]**mount** *n* (15c) **1 :** an act or instance of mounting; *specif* **:** an opportunity to ride a horse in a race **2 :** FRAME, SUPPORT: as **a :** the material (as cardboard) on which a picture is mounted **b :** a jewelry setting **c** (1) **:** an undercarriage or part on which a device (as a motor or an artillery piece) rests in service (2) **:** an attachment for an accessory **d :** a hinge, card, or acetate envelope for mounting a stamp **e :** a glass slide with its accessories on which objects are placed for examination with a microscope **3 :** a means of conveyance; *esp* **:** SADDLE HORSE

moun·tain \ˈmau̇n-tᵊn\ *n, often attrib* [ME, fr. AF *muntaine,* fr. VL **montanea,* fr. fem. of **montaneus* of a mountain, alter. of L *montanus,* fr. *mont-, mons*] (13c) **1 a :** a landmass that projects conspicuously above its surroundings and is higher than a hill **b :** an elongated ridge **2 a :** a great mass **b :** a vast number or quantity

mountain ash *n* (1597) **:** any of various trees or shrubs (genus *Sorbus*) of the rose family with pinnate leaves and red or orange-red fruits

mountain bike *n* (1980) **:** an all-terrain bicycle with wide knobby tires, straight handlebars, and typically 18 to 21 gears — **mountain bike** *vi* — **mountain biker** *n*

mountain bluebird *n* (1861) **:** a bluebird (*Sialia currucoides*) of western No. America having a blue-breasted rather than red-breasted male

mountain cranberry *n* (1848) **:** a low evergreen shrub (*Vaccinium vitis-idaea*) of the heath family that is native to north temperate uplands and has red edible berries — called also *lingonberry*

mountain dew *n* (1816) **:** MOONSHINE 3

moun·tain·eer \ˌmau̇n-tə-ˈnir\ *n* (1610) **1 :** a native or inhabitant of a mountainous region **2 :** a person who climbs mountains for sport

moun·tain·eer·ing \ˌmau̇n-tə-ˈnir-iŋ\ *n* (1803) **:** the sport or technique of scaling mountains

mountain goat *n* (1833) **:** a ruminant mammal (*Oreamnos americanus*) of mountainous northwestern No. America that has a thick yellowish-white coat and slightly curved horns and resembles a goat

mountain goat

mountain gorilla *n* (1939) **:** a gorilla (*Gorilla gorilla beringei*) inhabiting the Virunga mountain range

mountain laurel *n* (1739) **:** a No. American evergreen shrub or small tree (*Kalmia latifolia*) of the heath family with glossy leaves and umbels of rose-colored or white flowers

mountain lion *n* (1859) **:** COUGAR 1

mountain mahogany *n* (1810) **:** any of a genus (*Cercocarpus*) of western No. American evergreen shrubs or small trees of the rose family

mountain man *n* (1839) **:** an American frontiersman (as a trapper) at home in the wilderness

moun·tain·ous \ˈmau̇n-tə-nəs, ˈmau̇nt-nəs\ *adj* (14c) **1 :** containing many mountains **2 :** resembling a mountain **:** HUGE — **moun·tain·ous·ly** *adv* — **moun·tain·ous·ness** *n*

mountain sheep *n* (ca. 1779) **:** any of various wild sheep (as bighorn, argali, or Dall sheep) inhabiting high mountains

mountain sickness *n* (1848) **:** altitude sickness experienced esp. above 10,000 feet (about 3000 meters) and caused by insufficient oxygen in the air

moun·tain·side \ˈmau̇n-tᵊn-ˌsīd\ *n* (14c) **:** the side of a mountain

mountain time *n, often cap M* (1883) **:** the time of the seventh time zone west of Greenwich that includes the Rocky Mountain states of the U.S. — see TIME ZONE illustration

moun·tain·top \ˈmau̇n-tᵊn-ˌtäp\ *n* (ca. 1558) **:** the summit of a mountain

moun·tainy \ˈmau̇n-tᵊn-ē, ˈmau̇nt-nē\ *adj* (1613) **1 :** MOUNTAINOUS **2 :** of, relating to, or living in mountains

[1]**moun·te·bank** \ˈmau̇n-ti-ˌbaŋk\ *n* [It *montimbanco,* fr. *montare* to mount + *in* in, on + *banco, banca* bench] (1577) **1 :** a person who sells quack medicines from a platform **2 :** a boastful unscrupulous pretender **:** CHARLATAN — **moun·te·bank·ery** \-ˌbaŋ-k(ə-)rē\ *n*

[2]**mountebank** *vt* (1607) *obs* **:** to beguile or transform by trickery ⟨I'll ~ their loves —Shak.⟩ ~ *vi* **:** to play the mountebank

Mount·ie \'mau̇n-tē\ *n* [*mounted* policeman] (1914) **:** a member of the Royal Canadian Mounted Police

mount·ing \'mau̇n-tiŋ\ *n* (ca. 1618) **:** [3]MOUNT 2

mourn \'mȯrn\ *vb* [ME, fr. OE *murnan;* akin to OHG *mornēn* to mourn, Gk *mermēra* care — more at MEMORY] *vi* (bef. 12c) **1 :** to feel or express grief or sorrow **2 :** to show the customary signs of grief for a death; *esp* **:** to wear mourning **3 :** to murmur mournfully — used esp. of doves ~ *vt* **1 :** to feel or express grief or sorrow for **2 :** to utter mournfully — **mourn·er** *n* — **mourn·ing·ly** \'mȯr-niŋ-lē\ *adv*

mourn·ful \'mȯrn-fəl\ *adj* (15c) **1 :** expressing sorrow **:** SORROWFUL **2 :** full of sorrow **:** SAD **3 :** causing sorrow or melancholy **:** GLOOMY — **mourn·ful·ly** \-fə-lē\ *adv* — **mourn·ful·ness** *n*

mourn·ing \'mȯr-niŋ\ *n* (13c) **1 :** the act of sorrowing **2 a :** an outward sign (as black clothes or an armband) of grief for a person's death **b :** a period of time during which signs of grief are shown

mourning cloak *n* (1898) **:** a blackish-brown nymphalid butterfly (*Nymphalis antiopa*) that has a broad yellow border on the wings and is found in temperate parts of Europe, Asia, and No. America

mourning dove *n* (1833) **:** an American dove (*Zenaida macroura*) with a pointed tail and a plaintive coo

[1]**mouse** \'mau̇s\ *n, pl* **mice** \'mīs\ [ME, fr. OE *mūs;* akin to OHG *mūs* mouse, L *mus,* Gk *mys* mouse, muscle] (bef. 12c) **1 :** any of numerous small rodents (as of the genus *Mus*) with pointed snout, rather small ears, elongated body, and slender tail **2 :** a timid person **3 :** a dark-colored swelling caused by a blow; *specif* **:** BLACK EYE **4** *pl also* **mous·es :** a small mobile manual device that controls movement of the cursor and selection of functions on a computer display

[2]**mouse** \'mau̇z\ *vb* **moused; mous·ing** *vi* (13c) **1 :** to hunt for mice **2 :** to search or move stealthily or slowly ~ *vt* **1** *obs* **a :** BITE, GNAW **b :** to toy with roughly **2 :** to search for carefully — usu. used with *out*

mouse–ear \'mau̇s-ˌir\ *n* (13c) **1 :** a Eurasian hawkweed (*Hieracium pilosella*) introduced into No. America that has soft hairy leaves and yellow flowers **2 :** any of several plants other than mouse-ear that have soft hairy leaves

mouse–ear chickweed *n* (1731) **:** any of several hairy chickweeds (genus *Cerastium* and esp. *C. fontanum*)

mouse pad *n* (1983) **:** a thin flat pad (as of rubber) on which a computer mouse is used

mouse potato *n* [after *couch potato*] (1993) *slang* **:** a person who spends a great deal of time using a computer

mous·er \'mau̇-sər, *US also & chiefly Brit* -zər\ *n* (15c) **:** a catcher of mice and rats; *esp* **:** a cat proficient at mousing

[1]**mouse·trap** \'mau̇s-ˌtrap\ *n* (15c) **1 :** a trap for mice **2 :** a stratagem that lures one to defeat or destruction **3 :** TRAP 2b

[2]**mousetrap** *vt* (ca. 1864) **:** to snare in or as if in a mousetrap

Mous·que·taire \ˌmü-skə-'ter\ *n* [F — more at MUSKETEER] (1705) **:** a French musketeer; *esp* **:** one of the royal musketeers of the 17th and 18th centuries conspicuous for their daring and their flamboyant dress

mous·sa·ka *also* **mou·sa·ka** \mü-'sä-kə, ˌmü-sä-'kä\ *n* [ModGk *mousakas,* fr. Turk *musakka,* fr. dial. Ar (Egypt) *musaqqa'a,* lit., chilled] (1862) **:** a Middle Eastern dish of ground meat (as lamb or beef) and sliced eggplant often topped with a seasoned sauce

[1]**mousse** \'müs\ *n* [F, lit., froth, moss, fr. OF *mosse,* of Gmc origin; akin to OHG *mos* moss — more at MOSS] (1892) **1 :** a light spongy food usu. containing cream or gelatin **2 :** a molded chilled dessert made with sweetened and flavored whipped cream or egg whites and gelatin ⟨chocolate ~⟩ **3 :** a foamy preparation used in styling hair

[2]**mousse** *vt* **moussed; mouss·ing** (1984) **:** to style (hair) with mousse

mous·se·line \ˌmü-sə-'lēn, ˌmüs-'lēn\ *n* [F, lit., muslin — more at MUSLIN] (1696) **1 :** a fine sheer fabric (as of rayon) that resembles muslin **2 a :** a sauce (as hollandaise) to which whipped cream or beaten egg whites have been added **b :** MOUSSE 1 ⟨salmon ~⟩

mousseline de soie \-də-'swä\ *n, pl* **mousselines de soie** *same*\ [F, lit., silk muslin] (1835) **:** a silk muslin having a crisp finish

moustache *var of* MUSTACHE

moustachio *var of* MUSTACHIO

Mous·te·ri·an \mü-'stir-ē-ən\ *adj* [F *moustérien,* fr. Le *Moustier,* cave in Dordogne, France] (1890) **:** of or relating to a Middle Paleolithic culture that is characterized by well-made flake tools often considered the work of Neanderthal man

mousy *or* **mous·ey** \'mau̇-sē, -zē\ *adj* **mous·i·er; -est** (1853) **:** of, relating to, or resembling a mouse: as **a :** QUIET, STEALTHY **b :** TIMID, RETIRING **c :** grayish brown — **mous·i·ly** \-sə-lē, -zə-\ *adv* — **mous·i·ness** \-sē-nəs, -zē-\ *n*

[1]**mouth** \'mau̇th\ *n, pl* **mouths** \'mau̇t͟hz *also* 'mau̇z, 'mau̇ths; *in synecdochic compounds like "blabbermouths"* ths *more frequently*\ *often attrib* [ME, fr. OE *mūth;* akin to OHG *mund* mouth and perh. to L *mentum* chin] (bef. 12c) **1 a :** the natural opening through which food passes into the body of an animal and which in vertebrates is typically bounded externally by the lips and internally by the pharynx and encloses the tongue, gums, and teeth **b :** GRIMACE ⟨made a ~⟩ **c :** an individual requiring food ⟨had too many ~*s* to feed⟩ **2 a :** VOICE, SPEECH ⟨finally gave ~ to her feelings⟩ **b :** MOUTHPIECE 3a **c** (1) **:** a tendency to excessive talk (2) **:** saucy or disrespectful language **:** IMPUDENCE **3 :** something that resembles a mouth esp. in affording entrance or exit: as **a :** the place where a stream enters a larger body of water **b :** the surface opening of an underground cavity **c :** the opening of a container **d :** an opening in the side of an organ flue pipe — **mouth·like** \'mau̇th-ˌlīk\ *adj* — **down in the mouth :** DEJECTED, SULKY

[2]**mouth** \'mau̇t͟h *also* 'mau̇th\ *vt* (14c) **1 a :** SPEAK, PRONOUNCE **b :** to utter bombastically **:** DECLAIM **c :** to repeat without comprehension or sincerity ⟨always ~*ing* platitudes⟩ **d :** to form soundlessly with the lips ⟨the librarian ~*ed* the word "quiet"⟩ **e :** to utter indistinctly **:** MUMBLE ⟨~*ed* his words⟩ **2 :** to take into the mouth; *esp* **:** EAT ~ *vi* **1 a :** to talk pompously **:** RANT — often used with *off* **b :** to talk insolently or impudently — usu. used with *off* **2 :** to move the mouth esp. so as to make faces — **mouth·er** *n*

mouth·breed·er \'mau̇th-ˌbrē-dər\ *n* (1927) **:** any of several fishes that carry their eggs and young in the mouth; *esp* **:** a No. African cichlid fish (*Haplochromis multicolor*) often kept in aquariums

mouthed \'mau̇t͟hd, 'mau̇tht\ *adj* (14c) **:** having a mouth esp. of a specified kind — often used in combination ⟨a soft-*mouthed* fish⟩

mouth·feel \'mau̇th-ˌfēl\ *n* (1951) **:** the sensation created by food or drink in the mouth

mouth·ful \'mau̇th-ˌfu̇l\ *n* (15c) **1 a :** as much as a mouth will hold **b :** the quantity usu. taken into the mouth at one time **2 :** a small quantity **3 a :** a very long word or phrase **b :** a comment or a statement rich in meaning or substance

mouth harp *n* (1892) **:** HARMONICA 2

mouth hook *n* (1937) **:** one of a pair of hooked larval mouthparts of some dipteran flies that function as jaws

mouth organ *n* (1866) **:** HARMONICA 2

mouth·part \'mau̇th-ˌpärt\ *n* (1799) **:** a structure or appendage near the mouth (as of an insect) esp. when used in gathering or eating food

mouth·piece \-ˌpēs\ *n* (1678) **1 :** something placed at or forming a mouth **2 :** a part (as of an instrument) that goes in the mouth or to which the mouth is applied **3 a :** one that expresses or interprets another's views **:** SPOKESMAN **b** *slang* **:** a criminal lawyer

mouth–to–mouth *adj* (1941) **:** of, relating to, or being a method of artificial respiration in which the rescuer's mouth is placed tightly over the victim's mouth in order to force air into the victim's lungs by blowing forcefully enough every few seconds to inflate them

mouth·wash \'mau̇th-ˌwȯsh, -ˌwäsh\ *n* (1840) **:** a usu. antiseptic liquid preparation for cleaning the mouth and teeth or freshening the breath

mouth·wa·ter·ing \-ˌwȯ-tə-riŋ, -ˌwä-\ *adj* (1900) **:** arousing the appetite **:** tantalizingly delicious or appealing ⟨a ~ aroma⟩ — **mouth·wa·ter·ing·ly** \-lē\ *adv*

mouthy \'mau̇-thē, -t͟hē\ *adj* **mouth·i·er; -est** (1589) **1 :** marked by bombast or back talk **2 :** excessively talkative **:** GARRULOUS

mou·ton \'mü-ˌtän, mü-'\ *n* [F, sheep, sheepskin, fr. MF, ram — more at MUTTON] (1944) **:** processed sheepskin that has been sheared and dyed to resemble beaver or seal

[1]**mov·able** *or* **move·able** \'mü-və-bəl\ *adj* (14c) **1 :** capable of being moved **2 :** changing date from year to year ⟨~ holidays⟩ — **mov·abil·i·ty** \ˌmü-və-'bi-lə-tē\ *n* — **mov·able·ness** \'mü-və-bəl-nəs\ *n* — **mov·ably** \-blē\ *adv*

[2]**movable** *or* **moveable** *n* (15c) **:** something (as an article of furniture) that can be removed or displaced

[1]**move** \'müv\ *vb* **moved; mov·ing** [ME, fr. AF *mover, moveir,* fr. L *movēre;* prob. akin to Skt *mīvati* he moves, pushes] *vi* (13c) **1 a** (1) **:** to go or pass to another place or in a certain direction with a continuous motion ⟨*moved* into the shade⟩ (2) **:** to proceed toward a certain state or condition ⟨*moving* up the executive ladder⟩ (3) **:** to become transferred during play ⟨checkers ~ along diagonally adjacent squares⟩ (4) **:** to keep pace ⟨*moving* with the times⟩ **b :** to start away from some point or place **:** DEPART **c :** to change one's residence or location **2 :** to carry on one's life or activities in a specified environment ⟨~*s* in the best circles⟩ **3 :** to change position or posture **:** STIR ⟨ordered him not to ~⟩ **4 :** to take action **:** ACT **5 a :** to begin operating or functioning or working in a usual way **b :** to show marked activity ⟨after a lull things really began to ~⟩ **c :** to move a piece (as in chess or checkers) during one's turn **6 :** to make a formal request, application, or appeal **7 :** to change hands by being sold or rented ⟨goods that *moved* slowly⟩ **8** *of the bowels* **:** EVACUATE ~ *vt* **1 a** (1) **:** to change the place or position of (2) **:** to dislodge or displace from a fixed position **:** BUDGE **b :** to transfer (as a piece in chess) from one position to another **2 a** (1) **:** to cause to go or pass from one place to another with a continuous motion ⟨~ the flag slowly up and down⟩ (2) **:** to cause to advance **b :** to cause to operate or function **:** ACTUATE ⟨this button ~*s* the whole machine⟩ **c :** to put into activity or rouse up from inactivity **3 :** to cause to change position or posture **4 :** to prompt or rouse to the doing of something **:** PERSUADE ⟨the report *moved* us to take action⟩ **5 a :** to stir the emotions, feelings, or passions of ⟨deeply *moved* by such kindness⟩ **b :** to affect in such a way as to lead to an indicated show of emotion ⟨the story *moved* her to tears⟩ **6 a** *obs* **:** BEG **b :** to make a formal application to **7 :** to propose formally in a deliberative assembly ⟨*moved* the adjournment motion⟩ **8 :** to cause (the bowels) to void **9 :** to cause to change hands through sale or rent — **move house** *Brit* **:** to change one's residence

syn MOVE, ACTUATE, DRIVE, IMPEL mean to set or keep in motion. MOVE is very general and implies no more than the fact of changing position ⟨*moved* the furniture⟩. ACTUATE stresses transmission of power so as to work or set in motion ⟨turbines *actuated* by waterpower⟩. DRIVE implies imparting forward and continuous motion and often stresses the effect rather than the impetus ⟨a ship *driven* aground by hurricane winds⟩. IMPEL is usu. figurative and suggests a great motivating impetus ⟨a candidate *impelled* by ambition⟩.

[2]**move** *n* (1656) **1 a :** the act of moving a piece (as in chess) **b :** the turn of a player to move **2 a :** a step taken esp. to gain an objective **:** MANEUVER ⟨a ~ to end the dispute⟩ ⟨retiring early was a smart ~⟩ **b :** the action of moving from a motionless position **c :** one of a pattern of dance steps **d :** a change of residence or location **e :** an agile or deceptive action esp. in sports — **on the move 1 :** in a state of moving about from place to place **2 :** in a state of moving ahead or making progress ⟨said that civilization is always *on the move*⟩

move in *vi* (1898) **:** to occupy a dwelling or place of work — **move in on :** to make advances or aggressive movements toward

move·less \'müv-ləs\ *adj* (1578) **:** being without movement **:** FIXED, IMMOBILE — **move·less·ly** *adv* — **move·less·ness** *n*

move·ment \'müv-mənt\ *n* (14c) **1 a** (1) **:** the act or process of moving; *esp* **:** change of place or position or posture (2) **:** a particular instance or manner of moving **b** (1) **:** a tactical or strategic shifting of a military unit **:** MANEUVER (2) **:** the advance of a military unit **c :** ACTION, ACTIVITY — usu. used in pl. **2 a :** TENDENCY, TREND ⟨detected a ~ toward fairer pricing⟩ **b :** a series of organized activities working toward an objective; *also* **:** an organized effort to promote or attain an end ⟨the civil rights ~⟩ **3 :** the moving parts of a mechanism that transmit a definite motion **4 a :** MOTION 7 **b :** the rhythmic character or quality of a musical composition **c :** a distinct structural unit or division having its own key, rhythmic structure, and themes and forming part of an extended musical composition **d :** particular rhythmic flow of language **:** CADENCE **5 a :** the quality (as in a painting or sculpture) of representing or suggesting motion **b :** the vibrant quality in literature that comes from elements that constantly hold a reader's interest (as a quickly moving action-filled plot) **6 a :** an act of voiding the bowels **b :** matter expelled from the bowels at one passage

mov·er \ˈmü-vər\ *n* (14c) : one that moves or sets something in motion; *esp* : one whose business or occupation is the moving of household goods from one residence to another
mover and shaker *n, pl* **movers and shakers** (1951) : a person who is active or influential in some field of endeavor
mov·ie \ˈmü-vē\ *n* [*moving picture*] (1911) **1** : MOTION PICTURE **2** *pl* : a showing of a motion picture **3** *pl* : the motion-picture medium or industry
mov·ie·dom \ˈmü-vē-dəm\ *n* (1916) : FILMDOM
mov·ie·go·er \-ˌgō-ər\ *n* (1923) : FILMGOER — **mov·ie·going** \-ˌgō-iŋ, -ˌgȯ(-)iŋ\ *n, often attrib*
mov·ie·mak·er \-ˌmā-kər\ *n* (1915) : one who makes movies — **mov·ie·mak·ing** \-ˌmā-kiŋ\ *n*
moving *adj* (14c) **1 a** : marked by or capable of movement **b** : of or relating to a change of residence ⟨~ expenses⟩ **c** : used for transferring furnishings from one residence to another ⟨a ~ van⟩ **d** : involving a motor vehicle that is in motion ⟨a ~ violation⟩ **2 a** : producing or transferring motion or action **b** : stirring deeply in a way that evokes a strong emotional response — **mov·ing·ly** \ˈmü-viŋ-lē\ *adv*
syn MOVING, IMPRESSIVE, POIGNANT, AFFECTING, TOUCHING, PATHETIC mean having the power to produce deep emotion. MOVING may apply to any strong emotional effect including thrilling, agitating, saddening, or calling forth pity or sympathy ⟨a *moving* appeal for contributions⟩. IMPRESSIVE implies compelling attention, admiration, wonder, or conviction ⟨an *impressive* list of achievements⟩. POIGNANT applies to what keenly or sharply affects one's sensitivities ⟨a *poignant* documentary on the homeless⟩. AFFECTING is close to MOVING but most often suggests pathos ⟨an *affecting* deathbed reunion⟩. TOUCHING implies arousing tenderness or compassion ⟨the *touching* innocence in a child's eyes⟩. PATHETIC implies moving to pity or sometimes contempt ⟨*pathetic* attempts to justify misconduct⟩.
moving picture *n* (1896) : MOTION PICTURE
Mov·i·ola \ˌmü-vē-ˈō-lə\ *trademark* — used for a device for editing motion-picture film and synchronizing the sound
[1]**mow** \ˈmau̇\ *n* [ME, heap, stack, fr. OE *mūga;* akin to ON *mūgi* heap] (bef. 12c) **1** : a piled-up stack (as of hay or fodder); *also* : a pile of hay or grain in a barn **2** : the part of a barn where hay or straw is stored
[2]**mow** \ˈmō\ *vb* **mowed; mowed** *or* **mown** \ˈmōn\; **mow·ing** [ME, fr. OE *māwan;* akin to OHG *māen* to mow, L *metere* to reap, mow, Gk *aman*] *vt* (bef. 12c) **1 a** : to cut down with a scythe or sickle or machine **b** : to cut the standing herbage (as grass) of **2 a (1)** : to kill or destroy in great numbers or mercilessly ⟨machine guns ~*ed* down the enemy⟩ **(2)** : to cause to fall : KNOCK DOWN **b** : to overcome swiftly and decisively : ROUT ⟨~*ed* down the opposing team⟩ ~ *vi* : to cut down standing herbage (as grass) — **mow·er** \ˈmō(-ə)r\ *n*
[3]**mow** \ˈmau̇, ˈmō\ *n* [ME *mowe,* fr. AF *mouwe,* of Gmc origin; akin to MD *mouwe* protruding lip] (14c) : GRIMACE
[4]**mow** \ˈmau̇, ˈmō\ *vi* (15c) : to make grimaces
moxa \ˈmäk-sə\ *n* [NL, fr. Jp *mogusa*] (1675) : a soft woolly mass prepared from the ground young leaves of a Eurasian artemisia (esp. *Artemisia vulgaris*) that is used in traditional Chinese and Japanese medicine typically in the form of sticks or cones which are ignited and placed on or close to the skin or used to heat acupuncture needles
mox·i·bus·tion \ˌmäk-si-ˈbəs-chən\ *n* [*moxa* + *-i-* + *-bustion* (as in *combustion*)] (1910) : the therapeutic use of moxa
mox·ie \ˈmäk-sē\ *n* [fr. *Moxie,* a trademark for a soft drink] (1930) **1** : ENERGY, PEP **2** : COURAGE, DETERMINATION **3** : KNOW-HOW
moyen–âge \mwä-ye-ˈnäzh\ *adj* [F *moyen âge* Middle Ages] (1849) : of or relating to medieval times
moz·za·rel·la \ˌmät-sə-ˈre-lə\ *n* [It, dim. of *mozza,* a kind of cheese, fr. *mozzare* to cut off, fr. *mozzo* cut off, docked, fr. VL **mutius,* alter. of L *mutilus*] (1911) : a moist white unsalted unripened cheese of mild flavor and a smooth rubbery texture
moz·zet·ta \mōt-ˈse-tə\ *n* [It, prob. fr. *mozzo* cut off] (1774) : a short cape with a small ornamental hood worn over the rochet by Roman Catholic prelates
[1]**MP** \ˈem-ˈpē\ *n* (1921) **1** [*military police*] : a member of the military police **2** [*member of Parliament*] : an elected member of a parliament
[2]**MP** *abbr* **1** melting point **2** metropolitan police **3** milepost
MPA *abbr* master of public administration
MPAA *abbr* Motion Picture Association of America
MPEG \ˈem-ˌpeg\ *n* [*Moving Pictures Experts Group*] (1988) **1** : any of a group of computer file formats for the compression and storage of digital video and audio data **2** : a computer file (as of a movie) in an MPEG format
mpg *abbr* miles per gallon
mph *abbr* miles per hour
MPH *abbr* master of public health
M phase *n* [*mitosis*] (1945) : the period in the cell cycle during which cell division takes place — compare G_1 PHASE, G_2 PHASE, S PHASE
MPhil *abbr* master of philosophy
mps *abbr* meters per second
MP3 \ˌem-(ˌ)pē-ˈthrē\ *n* [fr. the file extension *.mp3* used for such files, short for *MPEG Audio Layer 3*] (1996) **1** : a computer file format for the compression and storage of digital audio data **2** : a computer file (as of a song) in the MP3 format
MPV *abbr* multipurpose vehicle
MPX *abbr* multiplex
mR *abbr* milliroentgen
Mr. \ˈmis-tər, *in rapid speech esp in sense 2* (ˌ)mis(t)\ *n, pl* **Messrs.** \ˈme-sərz\ [*Mr.* fr. ME, abbr. of *maister* master; *Messrs.* abbr. of *Messieurs,* fr. F, pl. of *Monsieur*] (15c) **1** — used as a conventional title of courtesy except when usage requires the substitution of a title of rank or an honorific or professional title before a man's surname ⟨spoke to *Mr.* Doe⟩ **2** — used in direct address as a conventional title of respect before a man's title of office ⟨may I ask one more question, *Mr.* President⟩ **3** — used before the name of a place, profession, or activity or before an epithet (as *clever*) to form a title applied to a male viewed as representative of the thing indicated ⟨*Mr.* Baseball⟩
Mr. Charlie \-ˈchär-lē\ *n* [*Charlie,* fr. *Charles,* proper name] (ca. 1941) *usu disparaging* : a white man : white people
MRE *abbr* meals ready to eat
MRI \ˌem-(ˌ)är-ˈī\ *n* (1982) : MAGNETIC RESONANCE IMAGING; *also* : the procedure in which magnetic resonance imaging is used
mri·dan·ga \mri-ˈdäŋ-gə, ˌmər-i-\ *or* **mri·dan·gam** \-gəm\ *n* [Skt *mṛdaṅga*] (1887) : a drum of India that is shaped like an elongated barrel and has tuned heads of different diameters
mRNA *abbr* messenger RNA
Mr. Right *n* (1860) : a man who would make the perfect husband
Mrs. \ˈmi-səz, -səs, *esp Southern* ˈmi-zəz, -zəs, *or in rapid speech in sense 1* (ˌ)miz, *or before given names* (ˌ)mis\ *n, pl* **Mes·dames** \mā-ˈdäm, -ˈdam\ [*Mrs.* abbr. of *mistress; Mesdames* fr. F, pl. of *Madame*] (ca. 1578) **1 a** — used as a conventional title of courtesy except when usage requires the substitution of a title of rank or an honorific or professional title before a married woman's surname ⟨spoke to *Mrs.* Doe⟩ **b** — used before the name of a place (as a country or city) or of a profession or activity (as a sport) or before some epithet (as *clever*) to form a title applied to a married woman viewed or recognized as representative of the thing indicated ⟨*Mrs.* Golf⟩ **2** : WIFE ⟨left with the *Mrs.*⟩
MRSA \ˌem-ˌär-ˌes-ˈā, ˈmər-sə\ *n* [*methicillin-resistant Staphylococcus aureus*] (1980) : any of several strains of a bacterium (*Staphylococcus aureus*) that are resistant to methicillin and related antibiotics (as penicillin) and may cause usu. mild infections of the skin or sometimes more severe infections (as of the blood or lungs) esp. in hospitalized or immunocompromised individuals
Mrs. Grun·dy \-ˈgrən-dē\ *n* [fr. a character alluded to in Thomas Morton's *Speed the Plough* (1798)] (1813) : one marked by prudish conventionality in personal conduct
ms *abbr* millisecond
Ms. \ˈmiz\ *n, pl* **Mss.** *or* **Mses.** \ˈmi-zəz\ [prob. blend of *Miss* and *Mrs.*] (1901) — used instead of *Miss* or *Mrs.* (as when the marital status of a woman is unknown or irrelevant) ⟨*Ms.* Mary Smith⟩
MS *abbr* **1** [It *mano sinistra*] left hand **2** manuscript **3** master of science **4** military science **5** Mississippi **6** motor ship **7** multiple sclerosis
MSc *abbr* master of science
msec *abbr* millisecond
msg *abbr* message
MSG *abbr* **1** master sergeant **2** monosodium glutamate
Msgr *abbr* monsignor
MSgt *abbr* master sergeant
MSH *abbr* melanocyte-stimulating hormone
M16 \ˌem-(ˌ)sik-ˈstēn\ *n* [*model 16*] (1968) : a .223 caliber (5.56 millimeter) gas-operated magazine-fed rifle for semiautomatic or automatic operation used by U.S. troops since the mid 1960s
MSL *abbr* mean sea level
MSN *abbr* master of science in nursing
MSS *abbr* manuscripts
MST *abbr* mountain standard time
MSW *abbr* master of social welfare; master of social work
mt *abbr* mount; mountain
[1]**Mt** *abbr* Matthew
[2]**Mt** *symbol* meitnerium
MT *abbr* **1** machine translation **2** metric ton **3** Montana **4** mountain time
mtDNA *abbr* mitochondrial DNA
mtg *abbr* meeting
mtge *abbr* mortgage
mtn *abbr* mountain
MTO *abbr* Mediterranean theater of operations
mu \ˈmyü, ˈmü\ *n* [Gk *my*] (1638) : the 12th letter of the Greek alphabet — see ALPHABET table
muc- *or* **muci-** *or* **muco-** *comb form* [L *muc-,* fr. *mucus*] **1** : mucus ⟨*muco*protein⟩ **2** : mucous and ⟨*muco*cutaneous⟩
[1]**much** \ˈməch\ *adj* **more** \ˈmȯr\; **most** \ˈmōst\ [ME *muche* large, much, fr. *michel, muchel,* fr. OE *micel, mycel;* akin to OHG *mihhil* great, large, L *magnus,* Gk *megas,* Skt *mahat*] (13c) **1 a** : great in quantity, amount, extent, or degree ⟨there is ~ truth in what you say⟩ ⟨taken too ~ time⟩ **b** : great in importance or significance ⟨nothing ~ happened⟩ **2** *obs* : many in number **3** : more than is expected or acceptable : more than enough ⟨the large pizza is a bit ~ for one person⟩ — **too much 1** : WONDERFUL, EXCITING **2** : TERRIBLE, AWFUL
[2]**much** *adv* **more; most** (13c) **1 a (1)** : to a great degree or extent : CONSIDERABLY ⟨~ happier⟩ **(2)** : VERY ⟨~ gratified⟩ **b (1)** : FREQUENTLY, OFTEN **(2)** : by or for a long time ⟨didn't get to work ~ before noon⟩ **c** : by far ⟨was ~ the brightest student⟩ **2** : NEARLY, APPROXIMATELY ⟨looks ~ the way his father did⟩ — **as much 1** : the same in quantity ⟨not quite *as much* money⟩ **2** : to the same degree
[3]**much** *n* (13c) **1** : a great quantity, amount, extent, or degree ⟨gave away ~⟩ **2** : something considerable or impressive
mu·cha·cho \mü-ˈchä-(ˌ)chō\ *n, pl* **-chos** [Sp, prob. fr. *mocho* cropped, shorn] (1591) **1** *chiefly Southwest* : a male servant **2** *chiefly Southwest* : a young man
much as *conj* (ca. 1699) : however much : even though
much less *conj* (1615) : not to mention — used esp. in negative contexts to add to one item another denoting something less likely ⟨had trouble paying for a car, *much less* a high-definition TV⟩
much·ness \ˈməch-nəs\ *n* (14c) : the quality or state of being great in quantity, extent, or degree — **much of a muchness** : very much the same
mu·ci·lage \ˈmyü-s(ə-)lij\ *n* [ME *muscilage,* fr. LL *mucilago* mucus, musty juice, fr. L *mucus*] (15c) **1** : a gelatinous substance of various plants (as legumes or seaweeds) that contains protein and polysaccharides and is similar to plant gums **2** : an aqueous usu. viscid solution (as of a gum) used esp. as an adhesive
mu·ci·lag·i·nous \ˌmyü-sə-ˈla-jə-nəs\ *adj* [ME *muscilaginous,* fr. LL *mucilaginosus,* fr. *mucilagin-, mucilago*] (15c) **1** : STICKY, VISCID **2** : of, relating to, full of, or secreting mucilage — **mu·ci·lag·i·nous·ly** *adv*
mu·cin \ˈmyü-sᵊn\ *n* [ISV *muc-*] (1838) : any of various mucoproteins that occur esp. in secretions of mucous membranes — **mu·cin·ous** \-sᵊn-əs, ˈmyüs-nəs\ *adj*

\ə\ **abut** \ᵊ\ **kitten, F table** \ər\ **further** \a\ **ash** \ā\ **ace** \ä\ **mop, mar**
\au̇\ **out** \ch\ **chin** \e\ **bet** \ē\ **easy** \g\ **go** \i\ **hit** \ī\ **ice** \j\ **job**
\ŋ\ **sing** \ō\ **go** \ȯ\ **law** \ȯi\ **boy** \th\ **thin** \t͟h\ **the** \ü\ **loot** \u̇\ **foot**
\y\ **yet** \zh\ **vision, beige** \k, ⁿ, œ, ue, ʸ\ *see* Guide to Pronunciation

[1]**muck** \ˈmək\ *n* [ME *muk,* perh. fr. OE *-moc;* akin to ON *myki* dung] (13c) **1 :** soft moist farmyard manure **2 :** slimy dirt or filth **3 a :** defamatory remarks or writings **b :** RUBBISH, NONSENSE ⟨mindless ~⟩ **4 a** (1) **:** dark highly organic soil (2) **:** MIRE, MUD **b :** something resembling muck **:** GUNK **5 :** material removed in the process of excavating or mining — **mucky** \ˈmə-kē\ *adj*

[2]**muck** *vt* (14c) **1 a :** to clean up; *esp* **:** to clear of manure or filth — usu. used with *out* **b :** to clear of muck **2 :** to dress (as soil) with muck **3 :** to dirty with or as if with muck **:** SOIL ~ *vi* **1 :** to move or load muck (as in a mine) **2 a :** to engage in aimless activity — usu. used with *about* or *around* **b :** PUTTER, TINKER — usu. used with *about* or *around* ⟨~*ing* around with his computer⟩ **c :** INTERFERE, MEDDLE — usu. used with *about* or *around* — **muck•er** *n*

muck•ety–muck \ˈmə-kə-tē-ˌmək\ *also* **muck–a–muck** \ˈmə-kə-ˌmək\ *or* **mucky–muck** \ˈmə-kē-\ *n* [short for *high-muck-a-muck*] (1883) **:** an important and often arrogant person

muck•rake \ˈmək-ˌrāk\ *vi* [obs. *muckrake,* n., rake for dung] (1879) **:** to search out and publicly expose real or apparent misconduct of a prominent individual or business — **muck•rak•er** *n*

muck up *vt* (1896) **:** to make a mess of **:** BUNGLE, SPOIL

mu•co•cu•ta•ne•ous \ˌmyü-kō-kyü-ˈtā-nē-əs\ *adj* (1898) **:** made up of or involving both typical skin and mucous membrane

[1]**mu•coid** \ˈmyü-ˌkȯid\ *adj* [ISV *muc-*] (1849) **:** resembling mucus

[2]**mucoid** *n* [ISV] (1898) **:** MUCOPROTEIN

mu•co•lyt•ic \ˌmyü-kə-ˈli-tik\ *adj* (ca. 1923) **:** hydrolyzing glycosaminoglycans **:** tending to break down or lower the viscosity of mucin-containing body secretions or components ⟨~ enzymes⟩

mu•co•pep•tide \ˌmyü-kō-ˈpep-ˌtīd\ *n* (1959) **:** PEPTIDOGLYCAN

mu•co•poly•sac•cha•ride \ˈmyü-kō-ˌpä-li-ˈsa-kə-ˌrīd\ *n* [ISV] (1938) **:** GLYCOSAMINOGLYCAN

mu•co•pro•tein \ˌmyü-kə-ˈprō-ˌtēn *also* -ˈprō-tē-ən\ *n* (1925) **:** any of various complex conjugated proteins (as mucins) that contain polysaccharides and occur in body fluids and tissues

mu•co•sa \myü-ˈkō-zə\ *n, pl* **-sae** \-(ˌ)zē, -ˌzī\ *or* **-sas** [NL, fr. L, fem. of *mucosus* mucous] (1867) **:** MUCOUS MEMBRANE — **mu•co•sal** \-zəl\ *adj*

mu•cous \ˈmyü-kəs\ *adj* [L *mucosus,* fr. *mucus*] (1578) **1 :** of, relating to, or resembling mucus **2 :** secreting or containing mucus **3 :** covered with or as if with mucus **:** SLIMY

mucous membrane *n* (1801) **:** a membrane rich in mucous glands; *specif* **:** one that lines body passages and cavities which communicate directly or indirectly with the exterior

mu•cro \ˈmyü-ˌkrō\ *n, pl* **mu•cro•nes** \myü-ˈkrō-(ˌ)nēz\ [NL *mucron-, mucro,* fr. L, point, edge] (1646) **:** an abrupt sharp terminal point or tip or process (as of a leaf) — **mu•cro•nate** \ˈmyü-krə-ˌnāt\ *adj*

mu•cus \ˈmyü-kəs\ *n* [L, nasal mucus; akin to Gk *myxa* mucus] (1597) **:** a viscid slippery secretion that is usu. rich in mucins and is produced by mucous membranes which it moistens and protects

[1]**mud** \ˈməd\ *n* [ME *mudde,* prob. fr. MLG] (14c) **1 :** a slimy sticky mixture of solid material with a liquid and esp. water; *esp* **:** soft wet earth **2 :** abusive and malicious remarks or charges ⟨political campaigners slinging ~ at each other⟩ **3 :** ANATHEMA 1b — usu. used in the phrase *one's name is mud* **4 :** a mixture of water, clay, and chemicals used in oil-well drilling and having various functions (as lubrication and cooling of the bit and flushing of rock particles to the surface)

[2]**mud** *vt* **mud•ded; mud•ding** (1593) **1 :** to make muddy or turbid **2 :** to treat or plaster with mud

mud•bug \ˈməd-ˌbəg\ *n* (1955) **:** CRAYFISH 1

mud dauber *n* (1856) **:** any of various wasps (esp. family Sphecidae) that construct mud cells in which the female places an egg with spiders or insects paralyzed by a sting to serve as food for the larva

[1]**mud•dle** \ˈmə-dᵊl\ *vb* **mud•dled; mud•dling** \ˈməd-liŋ, ˈmə-dᵊl-iŋ\ [prob. fr. obs. D *moddelen,* fr. MD, fr. *modde* mud; akin to MLG *mudde*] *vt* (1676) **1 :** to make turbid or muddy **2 :** to befog or stupefy esp. with liquor **3 :** to mix confusedly **4 :** to make a mess of **:** BUNGLE ~ *vi* **:** to think or act in a confused aimless way — **mud•dler** \ˈməd-lər, ˈmə-dᵊl-ər\ *n*

[2]**muddle** *n* (1808) **1 :** a state of esp. mental confusion **2 :** a confused mess — **mud•dly** \ˈməd-lē, ˈmə-dᵊl-ē\ *adj*

mud•dle•head•ed \ˌmə-dᵊl-ˈhe-dəd\ *adj* (1760) **1 :** mentally confused **2 :** INEPT, BUNGLING — **mud•dle•head•ed•ly** *adv* — **mud•dle•head•ed•ness** *n*

muddle through *vi* (ca. 1864) **:** to achieve a degree of success without much planning or effort

[1]**mud•dy** \ˈmə-dē\ *adj* **mud•di•er; -est** (15c) **1 :** morally impure **:** BASE **2 a :** full of or covered with mud **b :** characteristic or suggestive of mud ⟨a ~ flavor⟩ ⟨~ colors⟩ **c :** turbid with sediment **3 a :** lacking in clarity or brightness **:** CLOUDY, DULL ⟨a ~ recording⟩ ⟨eyes ~ with sleep⟩ **b :** obscure in meaning **:** MUDDLED, CONFUSED ⟨~ thinking⟩ — **mud•di•ly** \ˈmə-də-lē\ *adv* — **mud•di•ness** \ˈmə-dē-nəs\ *n*

[2]**muddy** *vt* **mud•died; mud•dy•ing** (1604) **1 :** CONFUSE **2 :** to soil or stain with or as if with mud **3 :** to make turbid **4 :** to make cloudy or dull — **muddy the waters :** to make a situation more confusing or difficult

Mu•de•jar \mü-ˈt͟he-ˌhär, -ˌkär\ *n, pl* **-ja•res** \-ˈt͟he-hä-ˌrās, -kä-\ [Sp *mudéjar,* modif. of Ar *mudajjan,* lit., allowed to remain] (1829) **:** a Muslim living under a Christian king esp. during the 8th to 11th centuries — **Mudejar** *adj*

mud flap *n* (1944) **:** SPLASH GUARD

mud•flat \ˈməd-ˌflat\ *n* (1795) **:** a level tract lying at little depth below the surface of water or alternately covered and left bare by the tide

mud•flow \-ˌflō\ *n* (1869) **:** a moving mass of soil made fluid by rain or melting snow; *also* **:** LAHAR

mud•guard \-ˌgärd\ *n* (1886) **1 a :** FENDER d **b :** SPLASH GUARD **2 :** a strip of material applied to a shoe upper just above the sole for protection against dampness or as an ornament

mud•hole \ˈməd-ˌhōl\ *n* (1721) **:** a hole or hollow place containing much mud

mud puppy *n* (1877) **:** a large No. American salamander (*Necturus maculosus*) that has external gills and is gray to rusty brown usu. with bluish-black spots

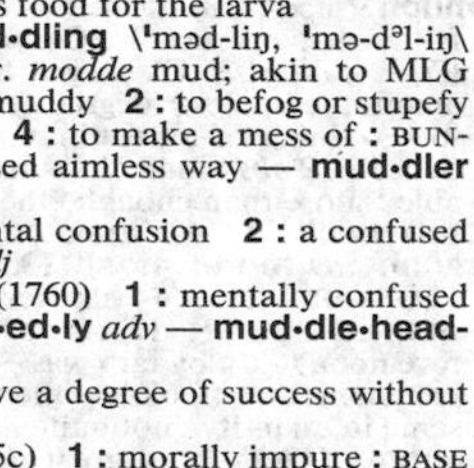

mud puppy

mu•dra \mə-ˈdrä\ *n* [Skt *mudrā*] (1811) **:** one of the symbolic hand gestures used in religious ceremonies and dances of India and in yoga

mud•room \ˈməd-ˌrüm, -ˌru̇m\ *n* (ca. 1950) **:** a room in a house designed esp. for the shedding of dirty or wet footwear and clothing and located typically off the kitchen or in the basement

mud•sill \-ˌsil\ *n* (1685) **1 :** a supporting sill (as of a building or bridge) resting directly on a base and esp. the earth **2 :** a person of the lowest social level

mud•skip•per \-ˌski-pər\ *n* (1860) **:** any of several Asian and African gobies (genera *Periophthalmus* and *Boleophthalmus*) that are able to skip about actively over wet mud and sand

mud•slide \ˈməd-ˌslīd\ *n* (1874) **1 :** MUDFLOW **2 :** a cocktail made with coffee liqueur, vodka, and cream

mud•sling•er \-ˌsliŋ-ər\ *n* (1876) **:** one that makes malicious attacks esp. against a political opponent — **mud•sling•ing** \-ˌsliŋ-iŋ\ *n*

mud•stone \-ˌstōn\ *n* (ca. 1736) **:** an indurated shale produced by the consolidation of mud

mud turtle *n* (1756) **:** any of a genus (*Kinosternon*) of American bottom-dwelling freshwater turtles with two transverse hinges on the plastron

Muen•ster \ˈmən(t)-stər, ˈmün(t)-, ˈmu̇n(t)-, ˈmin(t)-\ *n* [*Münster, Munster,* France] (1858) **:** a semisoft cheese that may be bland or sharp in flavor

mues•li \ˈmyüs-lē, ˈmyüz-\ *n* [G dial. (Swiss) *Müsli,* dim. of G *Mus* soft food, mush, fr. OHG *muos;* akin to OE *mōs* food and prob. to OE *mete* food — more at MEAT] (1939) **:** a breakfast cereal of Swiss origin consisting of rolled oats, nuts, and fruit

mu•ez•zin \mü-ˈe-zᵊn, myü-; ˈmwe-zᵊn\ *n* [ultim. fr. Ar *mu'adhdhin*] (1585) **:** a Muslim crier who calls the hour of daily prayers

[1]**muff** \ˈməf\ *n* [D *mof,* fr. MF *moufle* mitten, fr. ML *muffula*] (1599) **:** a warm tubular covering for the hands

[2]**muff** *vb* [prob. fr. [1]*muff*] *vt* (1846) **1 :** to handle awkwardly **2 :** to fail to hold (a ball) when attempting a catch ~ *vi* **1 :** to act or do something stupidly or clumsily **2 :** to muff a ball — compare FUMBLE

[3]**muff** *n* (1867) **1 :** a bungling performance **2 :** a failure to hold a ball in attempting a catch

muf•fin \ˈmə-fən\ *n* [prob. fr. LG *muffen,* pl. of *muffe* cake] (1703) **:** a quick bread made of batter containing egg and baked in a pan having cuplike molds

muffin top *n* (2003) *slang* **:** the fatty flesh that hangs over tightly worn pants

muf•fle \ˈmə-fəl\ *vt* **muf•fled; muf•fling** \ˈmə-f(ə-)liŋ\ [ME *muflen*] (15c) **1 :** to wrap up so as to conceal or protect **:** ENVELOP **2** *obs* **:** BLINDFOLD **3 a :** to wrap or pad with something to dull the sound ⟨~ the oarlocks⟩ **b :** to deaden the sound of **4 :** KEEP DOWN, SUPPRESS ⟨*muffled* her anger⟩

muf•fler \ˈmə-flər\ *n* (ca. 1536) **1 a :** a scarf worn around the neck **b :** something that hides or disguises **2 :** a device to deaden noise; *esp* **:** one forming part of the exhaust system of an automotive vehicle — **muf•flered** *adj*

muf•fu•let•ta *also* **muf•fa•let•ta** \ˌmə-fə-ˈle-tə\ *n* [prob. fr. It dial., fr. It *muffoletta* little muff, dim. of *muffola* muff, fr. F *moufle,* fr. MF] (1967) **:** a sandwich made with round Italian bread and filled usu. with cold cuts, cheese, and olive salad

[1]**muf•ti** \ˈməf-tē, ˈmu̇f-\ *n* [Ar *muftī*] (1586) **:** a professional jurist who interprets Muslim law

[2]**muf•ti** \ˈməf-tē\ *n* [prob. fr. [1]*mufti*] (1816) **:** ordinary dress as distinguished from that denoting an occupation or station ⟨a priest in ~⟩; *esp* **:** civilian clothes when worn by a person in the armed forces

[1]**mug** \ˈməg\ *n* [origin unknown] (1664) **1 :** a cylindrical drinking cup **2 a :** the face or mouth of a person **b :** GRIMACE **c :** MUG SHOT **3 a** *chiefly Brit* (1) **:** FOOL, BLOCKHEAD (2) **:** a person easily deceived **b :** PUNK, THUG — **mug•ful** *n*

[2]**mug** *vb* **mugged; mug•ging** *vi* (1855) **:** to pose or make faces esp. to attract attention or for a camera ~ *vt* **:** PHOTOGRAPH

[3]**mug** *vt* **mugged; mug•ging** [prob. fr. earlier *mug* to strike in the face, perh. fr. [1]*mug*] (ca. 1864) **1 :** to assault usu. with intent to rob **2 :** to attack suddenly ⟨got *mugged* in the press⟩ — **mug•gee** \ˌmə-ˈgē\ *n*

[1]**mug•ger** \ˈmə-gər\ *n* [Hindi & Urdu *magar,* fr. Skt *makara* water monster] (1844) **:** a usu. harmless freshwater crocodile (*Crocodylus palustris*) of the Indian subcontinent with a broad heavy snout

[2]**mugger** *n* [[3]*mug*] (1863) **:** one who attacks with intent to rob

[3]**mugger** *n* [[2]*mug*] (1892) **:** one that grimaces esp. before an audience

mug•gy \ˈmə-gē\ *adj* **mug•gi•er; -est** [E dial. *mug* drizzle] (1728) **:** being warm, damp, and close — **mug•gi•ness** \ˈmə-gē-nəs\ *n*

Mughal *var of* MOGUL

mu•gho pine \ˈmü-(ˌ)gō-, ˈmyü-\ *n* [prob. fr. F *mugho* mugho pine, fr. It *mugo*] (ca. 1756) **:** a shrubby spreading European pine (*Pinus mugo*) widely cultivated as an ornamental — called also *mugo pine*

mug's game \ˈməgz-\ *n* (1900) **:** a profitless or futile activity

mug shot *n* (1950) **:** a photograph of usu. a person's head and esp. face; *specif* **:** a police photograph of a suspect's face or profile

mug up *vi* (ca. 1860) *Brit* **:** to study intensively (as for an examination) ~ *vt* **:** to work up by study

mug•wort \ˈməg-ˌwərt, -ˌwȯrt\ *n* [ME, fr. OE *mucgwyrt,* fr. *mucg-* (perh. akin to OE *mycg* midge) + *wyrt* wort] (bef. 12c) **1 :** any of several artemisias; *esp* **:** a Eurasian perennial herb (*Artemisia vulgaris*) that is naturalized in No. America and has aromatic leaves used in folk medicine and to flavor beverages **2 :** the leaves of a mugwort — compare *moxa*

mug•wump \ˈməg-ˌwəmp\ *n* [obs. slang *mugwump* kingpin, fr. Massachusett *mugquomp, muggumquomp* war leader] (1884) **1 :** a bolter from the Republican party in 1884 **2 :** a person who is independent (as in politics) or who remains undecided or neutral

Muhammadan *var of* MOHAMMEDAN

Muhammadan calendar *n* (ca. 1889) **:** ISLAMIC CALENDAR

Muhammadan era *n* (ca. 1889) **:** ISLAMIC ERA

Mu•har•ram \mü-ˈha-rəm\ *n* [Ar *Muḥarram*] (ca. 1615) **1 :** the first month of the Islamic year — see MONTH table **2 :** a Muslim festival held during Muharram

mu•ja•hid•een *or* **mu•ja•hed•in** *also* **mu•ja•hed•een** \mü-ˌja-hi-ˈdēn, mu̇-, -ˌjä-\ *n pl* [Ar *mujāhidīn,* pl. of *mujāhid,* lit., person who wages jihad] (1887) **:** Islamic guerrilla fighters esp. in the Middle East

mujik *var of* MUZHIK

muk·luk \'mək-ˌlək\ *n* [Yupik *maklak* bearded seal] (1868) **1** : a seal-skin or reindeer-skin boot worn by Eskimos **2** : a boot often of duck with a soft leather sole and worn over several pairs of socks

muk·tuk \'mək-ˌtək\ *n* [Inuit *maktak*] (1835) : whale skin used for food

mu·lat·to \mə-'la-(ˌ)tō, mü-, myù-, -'lä-\ *n, pl* **-toes** *or* **-tos** [Sp *mulato*, fr. *mulo* mule, fr. L *mulus*] (1593) **1** : the first-generation offspring of a black person and a white person **2** : a person of mixed white and black ancestry

mul·ber·ry \'məl-ˌber-ē, -b(ə-)rē\ *n* [ME *murberie, mulberie*, fr. AF *mure, moure* mulberry (fr. L *morum*, fr. Gk *moron*) + ME *berie* berry] (14c) **1** : any of a genus (*Morus* of the family Moraceae, the mulberry family) of trees with an edible usu. purple multiple fruit that is an aggregate of juicy one-seeded drupes; *also* : the fruit **2** : a dark purple or purplish black

mulch \'məlch\ *n* [perh. irreg. fr. E dial. *melch* soft, mild] (1657) : a protective covering (as of sawdust, compost, or paper) spread or left on the ground to reduce evaporation, maintain even soil temperature, prevent erosion, control weeds, enrich the soil, or keep fruit (as strawberries) clean — **mulch** *vt*

¹**mulct** \'məlkt\ *n* [L *multa, mulcta*] (1591) : FINE, PENALTY

²**mulct** *vt* (1611) **1** : to punish by a fine **2 a** : to defraud esp. of money : SWINDLE **b** : to obtain by fraud, duress, or theft

¹**mule** \'myül\ *n* [ME, fr. AF *mul*, fr. L *mulus*] (13c) **1 a** : a hybrid between a horse and a donkey; *esp* : the offspring of a male donkey and a mare **b** : a self-sterile plant whether hybrid or not **c** : a usu. sterile hybrid **2** : a very stubborn person **3** : a machine for simultaneously drawing and twisting fiber into yarn or thread and winding it into cops **4** *slang* : a person who smuggles or delivers illicit substances (as drugs)

²**mule** *n* [MF, a kind of slipper, fr. L *mulleus* shoe worn by magistrates] (1562) : a shoe or slipper without quarter or heel strap — compare SCUFF

mule deer *n* (1805) : a long-eared deer (*Odocoileus hemionus*) of western No. America that is larger and more heavily built than the white-tailed deer

mule skinner *n* (1870) : MULETEER

mu·le·ta \mü-'lā-tə, myü-\ *n* [Sp, crutch, muleta, dim. of *mula* she-mule, fr. L, fem. of *mulus* mule] (1838) : a small cloth attached to a short tapered stick and used by a matador in place of the large cape during the final stage of a bullfight

mu·le·teer \ˌmyü-lə-'tir\ *n* [F *muletier*, fr. *mulet*, mule, fr. OF, dim. of *mul* mule] (1538) : one who drives mules

mu·ley \'myü-lē, 'mü-, 'mù-\ *adj* [of Celtic origin; akin to Ir & ScGael *maol* bald, hornless, W *moel*] (1840) : POLLED, HORNLESS; *esp* : naturally hornless

mu·li·eb·ri·ty \ˌmyü-lē-'e-brə-tē\ *n* [LL *muliebritat-, muliebritas,* fr. L *muliebris* of a woman, fr. *mulier* woman] (1592) : FEMININITY

mul·ish \'myü-lish\ *adj* [¹*mule*] (1751) : unreasonably and inflexibly obstinate *syn* see OBSTINATE — **mul·ish·ly** *adv* — **mul·ish·ness** *n*

¹**mull** \'məl\ *vb* [ME, fr. *mul, mol* dust, prob. fr. MD; akin to OE *melu* meal — more at MEAL] *vt* (15c) **1** : to grind or mix thoroughly : PULVERIZE **2** : to consider at length : PONDER — often used with *over* ~ *vi* : MEDITATE, PONDER

²**mull** *vt* [origin unknown] (1618) : to heat, sweeten, and flavor (as wine or cider) with spices

³**mull** *n* [by shortening & alter. fr. *mulmul* muslin, fr. Hindi *malmal*] (1798) : a soft fine sheer fabric of cotton, silk, or rayon

⁴**mull** *n* [Dan *muld*, fr. ON *mold* dust, soil; akin to OHG *molta* dust, soil — more at MOLD] (1928) **1** : friable forest humus that forms a layer of mixed organic matter and mineral soil and merges gradually into the mineral soil beneath **2** : a finely powdered solid esp. in a suspension

mul·lah \'mə-lə, 'mù-\ *n* [Turk *molla* & Pers & Urdu *mulla*, fr. Ar *mawlā*] (1613) : an educated Muslim trained in religious law and doctrine and usu. holding an official post — **mul·lah·ism** \-lə-ˌi-zəm\ *n*

mul·lein *also* **mul·len** \'mə-lən\ *n* [ME *moleyne*, fr. AF *moleine*] (14c) : any of a genus (*Verbascum*) of usu. woolly-leaved Eurasian herbs of the snapdragon family including some that are naturalized in No. America

mullein pink *n* (ca. 1850) : an Old World herb (*Lychnis coronaria*) of the pink family cultivated chiefly for its herbage and crimson flowers

mull·er \'mə-lər\ *n* [alter. of ME *molour*, prob. fr. *mullen* to grind] (1612) : a stone or piece of wood, metal, or glass used as a pestle for pounding or grinding

Mül·le·ri·an \myü-'lir-ē-ən, mi-, mə-\ *adj* [Fritz *Müller* †1897 Ger. zoologist] (1898) : of, relating to, or being mimicry that exists between two or more inedible or dangerous species (as of butterflies) and that is considered in evolutionary theory to be a mechanism reducing loss to predation by simplification of the recognition process by predators

mul·let \'mə-lət\ *n, pl* **mullet** *or* **mullets** [ME *molet*, fr. AF *mulet*, fr. L *mullus* red mullet, fr. Gk *myllos*] (14c) **1** : any of a family (Mugilidae) of chiefly marine bony fishes with an elongate rather stout body — compare GOATFISH, RED MULLET **2** [perh. short for *mullet-head* blockhead] : a hairstyle in which the hair is short on the sides and top and long at the back

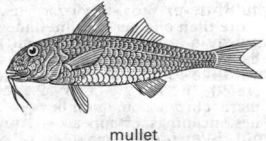

mullet

mul·li·gan \'mə-li-gən\ *n* [prob. fr. the name *Mulligan*] (ca. 1949) : a free shot sometimes given a golfer in informal play when the previous shot was poorly played

mulligan stew *n* [prob. fr. the name *Mulligan*] (1903) : a stew made from whatever ingredients are available

mul·li·ga·taw·ny \ˌmə-li-gə-'tò-nē, -'tä-\ *n* [Tamil *miḷakutaṇṇi*, fr. *miḷaku* pepper + *taṇṇi* water] (1784) : a rich soup usu. of chicken stock seasoned with curry

mul·lion \'məl-yən\ *n* [prob. alter. of *monial* mullion] (1567) : a slender vertical member that forms a division between units of a window, door, or screen or is used decoratively — **mullion** *vt*

mull·ite \'mə-ˌlīt\ *n* [*Mull*, island of the Inner Hebrides] (1924) : a mineral that is an orthorhombic silicate of aluminum which is resistant to corrosion and heat and is used as a refractory

multi- *comb form* [L, fr. *multus* much, many — more at MELIORATE] **1 a** : many : multiple : much ⟨*multi*valent⟩ **b** : more than two ⟨*multi*lateral⟩ **c** : more than one ⟨*multi*parous⟩ ⟨*multi*billion⟩ **2** : many times over ⟨*multi*millionaire⟩

mul·ti·age	mul·ti·drug	mul·ti·par·ty
mul·ti·agen·cy	mul·ti·elec·trode	mul·ti·path
mul·ti·armed	mul·ti·el·e·ment	mul·ti·phase
mul·ti·at·om	mul·ti·em·ploy·er	mul·ti·phasic
mul·ti·au·thor	mul·ti·en·gine	mul·ti·pho·ton
mul·ti·au·thored	mul·ti·fam·i·ly	mul·ti·pic·ture
mul·ti·ax·i·al	mul·ti·fea·tured	mul·ti·piece
mul·ti·band	mul·ti·fil·a·ment	mul·ti·plant
mul·ti·bank	mul·ti·flash	mul·ti·play·er
mul·ti·bar·rel	mul·ti·fo·cal	mul·ti·pole
mul·ti·bar·reled	mul·ti·fre·quen·cy	mul·ti·pow·er
mul·ti·bil·lion	mul·ti·front	mul·ti·prob·lem
mul·ti·bil·lion·aire	mul·ti·func·tion	mul·ti·prod·uct
mul·ti·blad·ed	mul·ti·func·tion·al	mul·ti·pur·pose
mul·ti·branched	mul·ti·gen·er·a·tion·al	mul·ti·range
mul·ti·build·ing	mul·ti·gen·ic	mul·ti·re·gion·al
mul·ti·but·ton	mul·ti·grade	mul·ti·re·li·gious
mul·ti·cam·pus	mul·ti·grain	mul·ti·room
mul·ti·can·di·date	mul·ti·grid	mul·ti·screen
mul·ti·car	mul·ti·group	mul·ti·ser·vice
mul·ti·car·bon	mul·ti·hand·i·capped	mul·ti·sid·ed
mul·ti·caus·al	mul·ti·head·ed	mul·ti·site
mul·ti·cell	mul·ti·hom·er	mul·ti·size
mul·ti·celled	mul·ti·hos·pi·tal	mul·ti·skilled
mul·ti·cel·lu·lar	mul·ti·hued	mul·ti·source
mul·ti·cel·lu·lar·i·ty	mul·ti–in·dus·try	mul·ti·spe·cies
mul·ti·chain	mul·ti–in·sti·tu·tion·al	mul·ti·speed
mul·ti·cham·bered	mul·ti·lane	mul·ti·sport
mul·ti·chan·nel	mul·ti·lev·el	mul·ti·stemmed
mul·ti·char·ac·ter	mul·ti·lev·eled	mul·ti·step
mul·ti·city	mul·ti·line	mul·ti·sto·ried
mul·ti·cli·ent	mul·ti·lobed	mul·ti·sto·ry
mul·ti·coat·ed	mul·ti·lo·ca·tion	mul·ti·strand·ed
mul·ti·col·or	mul·ti·mega·ton	mul·ti·syl·lab·ic
mul·ti·col·ored	mul·ti·mega·watt	mul·ti·sys·tem
mul·ti·col·umn	mul·ti·mem·ber	mul·ti·tal·ent·ed
mul·ti·com·po·nent	mul·ti·me·tal·lic	mul·ti·ter·mi·nal
mul·ti·con·duc·tor	mul·ti·mil·len·ni·al	mul·ti·tiered
mul·ti·coun·ty	mul·ti·mil·lion	mul·ti·ton
mul·ti·course	mul·ti·mil·lion·aire	mul·ti·tone
mul·ti·cur·ren·cy	mul·ti·mil·lion·air·ess	mul·ti·tow·ered
mul·ti·day	mul·ti·mode	mul·ti·track
mul·ti·de·nom·i·na·tion·al	mul·ti·mo·lec·u·lar	mul·ti·tril·lion
	mul·ti·na·tion	mul·ti·union
mul·ti·di·a·lec·tal	mul·ti·nu·cle·ar	mul·ti·unit
mul·ti·di·men·sion·al	mul·ti·nu·cle·ate	mul·ti·use
mul·ti·di·men·sion·al·i·ty	mul·ti·nu·cle·at·ed	mul·ti·valve
	mul·ti·or·gas·mic	mul·ti·voiced
mul·ti·di·rec·tion·al	mul·ti·page	mul·ti·vol·ume
mul·ti·disc	mul·ti·paned	mul·ti·wall
mul·ti·dis·ci·plin·ary	mul·ti·pa·ram·e·ter	mul·ti·war·head
mul·ti·dis·ci·pline	mul·ti·part	mul·ti·wave·length
mul·ti·di·vi·sion·al	mul·ti·par·ti·cle	mul·ti·year

mul·ti·cen·ter \'məl-tē-ˌsen-tər, 'məl-ˌtē-\ *adj* (1979) : involving more than one medical or research institution ⟨a ~ clinical study⟩ — **mul·ti·cen·tered** \-tərd\ *adj*

mul·ti·cul·ti \ˌməl-tē-'kəl-tē\ *adj* (1991) : MULTICULTURAL

mul·ti·cul·tur·al \ˌməl-tē-'kəlch-rəl, -ˌtī-, -'kəl-chə-\ *adj* (1941) : of, relating to, reflecting, or adapted to diverse cultures ⟨a ~ society⟩ ⟨~ education⟩ ⟨a ~ menu⟩ — **mul·ti·cul·tur·al·ism** \-rə-ˌli-zəm\ *n* — **mul·ti·cul·tur·al·ist** \-rə-list\ *n or adj* — **mul·ti·cul·tur·al·ly** \-rə-lē\ *adv*

mul·ti·en·zyme \-'en-ˌzīm\ *adj* (1961) : composed of or involving two or more enzymes that function in a biosynthetic pathway ⟨~ complex⟩

mul·ti·eth·nic \-'eth-nik\ *adj* (1941) : made up of people of various ethnicities ⟨a ~ country⟩; *also* : of, relating to, reflecting, or adapted to diverse ethnicities ⟨~ literature⟩ — **mul·ti·eth·nic·i·ty** \-ˌeth-'ni-sə-tē\ *n*

mul·ti·fac·et·ed \-'fa-sə-təd\ *adj* (1870) : having many facets or aspects

mul·ti·fac·to·ri·al \-fak-'tòr-ē-əl\ *adj* (1920) **1** : having characters or a mode of inheritance dependent on a number of genes at different loci **2** *or* **mul·ti·fac·tor** \-'fak-tər\ : having, involving, or produced by a variety of elements or causes — **mul·ti·fac·to·ri·al·ly** \-fak-'tòr-ē-ə-lē\ *adv*

mul·ti·far·i·ous \ˌməl-tə-'fer-ē-əs\ *adj* [ML *multifarius*, fr. L *multifariam* in many places] (1593) : having or occurring in great variety : DIVERSE — **mul·ti·far·i·ous·ness** *n*

mul·ti·flo·ra rose \ˌməl-tə-'flòr-ə-\ *n* [NL *multiflora*, specific epithet, lit., having many flowers] (1829) : a vigorous thorny rose (*Rosa multiflora*) with clusters of small flowers

mul·ti·fold \'məl-ti-ˌfōld\ *adj* (1806) : MANY, NUMEROUS

mul·ti·form \'məl-ti-ˌfòrm\ *adj* [F *multiforme*, fr. L *multiformis*, fr. *multi-* + *-formis* -form] (1603) : having many forms or appearances — **mul·ti·for·mi·ty** \ˌməl-ti-'fòr-mə-tē\ *n*

mul·ti·germ \ˌməl-tē-'jərm, -ˌtī-\ *adj* [prob. fr. *multi-* + *germ*inate] (1950) : producing or being a fruit cluster capable of giving rise to several plants ⟨a ~ variety of sugar beet⟩

mul·ti·hull \'məl-tē-ˌhəl, -ˌtī-\ *n* (1960) : a vessel (as a catamaran or trimaran) with multiple side-by-side hulls — compare MONOHULL — **mul·ti·hulled** \-ˌhəld\ *adj*

mul·ti–in·stru·men·tal·ist \ˌməl-tē-ˌin(t)-strə-ˈmen-tə-list, -ˌtī-\ *n* (1969) : a musician who plays two or more instruments
mul·ti·lat·er·al \ˌməl-tē-ˈla-t(ə-)rəl, -ˌtī-\ *adj* (ca. 1696) **1** : having many sides **2** : involving or participated in by more than two nations or parties ⟨~ agreements⟩ — **mul·ti·lat·er·al·ism** \-ˈla-t(ə-)rə-ˌli-zəm\ *n* — **mul·ti·lat·er·al·ist** \-list\ *n* — **mul·ti·lat·er·al·ly** *adv*
mul·ti·lay·ered \-ˈlā-ərd, -ˈlerd\ *or* **mul·ti·lay·er** \-ˈlā-ər, -ˈler\ *adj* (1923) : having or involving several distinct layers, strata, or levels
mul·ti·lin·gual \-ˈliŋ-gwəl, -ˈliŋ-gyə-wəl\ *adj* (1838) **1** : of, having, or expressed in several languages ⟨a ~ sign⟩ ⟨~ dictionaries⟩ **2** : using or able to use several languages esp. with equal fluency ⟨~ translators⟩ — **mul·ti·lin·gual·ism** \-gwə-ˌli-zəm, -gyə-wə-\ *n* — **mul·ti·lin·gual·ly** \-gwə-lē, -gyə-wə-lē\ *adv*
1**mul·ti·me·dia** \-ˈmē-dē-ə\ *adj* (1962) : using, involving, or encompassing several media ⟨a ~ approach to learning⟩
2**multimedia** *n pl but sing or pl in constr* (1950) : a technique (as the combining of sound, video, and text) for expressing ideas (as in communication, entertainment, or art) in which several media are employed; *also* : something (as software) using or facilitating such a technique
mul·tim·e·ter \ˌməl-ˈti-mə-tər\ *n* (1910) : an instrument for measuring the properties of an electrical circuit (as resistance, voltage, or current)
mul·ti·mod·al \-ˈmō-dᵊl\ *adj* (1902) : having or involving several modes, modalities, or maxima ⟨~ distributions⟩ ⟨~ therapy⟩
mul·ti·na·tion·al \-ˈnash-nəl, -ˈna-shə-nᵊl\ *adj* (1854) **1** : of or relating to more than two nationalities ⟨a ~ society⟩ **2 a** : of, relating to, or involving more than two nations ⟨a ~ alliance⟩ **b** : having divisions in more than two countries ⟨a ~ corporation⟩ — **multinational** *n*
mul·ti·no·mi·al \-ˈnō-mē-əl\ *n* [*multi-* + *-nomial* (as in *binomial*)] (1674) : a mathematical expression that consists of the sum of several terms : POLYNOMIAL — **multinomial** *adj*
mul·ti·pack \ˈməl-tē-ˌpak\ *n, often attrib* (1965) : a package of several individually packed items sold as a unit
mul·tip·a·rous \ˌməl-ˈti-pə-rəs\ *adj* [NL *multiparus,* fr. *multi-* + L *-parus* -parous] (1646) **1** : producing many or more than one at a birth **2** : having experienced one or more previous parturitions
mul·ti·par·tite \ˌməl-ti-ˈpär-ˌtīt\ *adj* [L *multipartitus,* fr. *multi-* + *partitus,* pp. of *partire* to divide, fr. *part-, pars* part] (1656) **1** : divided into several or many parts **2** : having numerous members or signatories
mul·ti·plat·i·num \ˌməl-tē-ˈplat-nəm, -ˈpla-tə-nəm, -ˌtī-\ *adj* (1983) : having sold two million or more copies of an album
1**mul·ti·ple** \ˈməl-tə-pəl\ *adj* [F, fr. L *multiplex,* fr. *multi-* + *-plex* -fold — more at -FOLD] (1647) **1** : consisting of, including, or involving more than one ⟨~ births⟩ **2** : MANY, MANIFOLD ⟨~ achievements⟩ **3** : shared by many ⟨~ ownership⟩ **4** : having numerous aspects or functions : VARIOUS **5** : being a group of terminals which make a circuit available at a number of points **6** : formed by coalescence of the ripening ovaries of several flowers ⟨a ~ fruit⟩
2**multiple** *n* (1660) **1 a** : the product of a quantity by an integer ⟨35 is a ~ of 7⟩ **b** : something in units of more than one or two **2** : PARALLEL 4b **3** *chiefly Brit* : CHAIN STORE
multiple allele *n* (1938) : an allele of a genetic locus having more than two allelic forms within a population
multiple chemical sensitivity *n* (1988) : a variable group of symptoms (as tachycardia, sweating, fatigue, nausea, trembling, and difficulty concentrating) that typically occur in susceptible individuals upon exposure to low concentrations of usu. harmless chemicals — called also *multiple chemical sensitivity syndrome*; compare SICK BUILDING SYNDROME
multiple–choice *adj* (1926) **1** : having several answers from which one is to be chosen ⟨a ~ question⟩ **2** : composed of multiple-choice questions ⟨a ~ test⟩
multiple factor *n* (1915) : one of a group of nonallelic genes that according to the multiple-factor hypothesis control various quantitative hereditary characters
multiple myeloma *n* (1897) : a disease of bone marrow that is characterized by the presence of numerous myelomas in various bones of the body
multiple personality disorder *n* (1901) : a disorder that is characterized by the presence of two or more distinct and complex identities or personality states each of which becomes dominant and controls behavior from time to time to the exclusion of the others and results from disruption in the integrated functions of consciousness, memory, and identity — called also *multiple personality, dissociative identity disorder*
multiple regression *n* (1924) : regression in which one variable is estimated by the use of more than one other variable
multiple sclerosis *n* (1885) : a demyelinating disease marked by patches of hardened tissue in the brain or the spinal cord and associated esp. with partial or complete paralysis and jerking muscle tremor
multiple star *n* (ca. 1850) : several stars in close proximity that appear to form a single system
multiple store *n* (1929) *chiefly Brit* : CHAIN STORE
mul·ti·plet \ˈməl-tə-plət\ *n* (1922) **1** : a spectrum line having several components **2** : a group of elementary particles that are different in charge but similar in other properties (as mass)
multiple–valued *adj* (1882) : having at least one and sometimes more of the values of the range associated with each value of the domain ⟨a ~ function⟩ — compare SINGLE-VALUED
1**mul·ti·plex** \ˈməl-tə-ˌpleks\ *adj* [L] (1557) **1** : MANY, MULTIPLE **2** : being or relating to a system of transmitting several messages or signals simultaneously on the same circuit or channel
2**multiplex** *vt* (1907) : to send (messages or signals) by a multiplex system ~ *vi* : to multiplex messages or signals — **mul·ti·plex·er** *also* **mul·ti·plex·or** \-ˌplek-sər\ *n*
3**multiplex** *n* (1985) : a complex that houses several movie theaters
mul·ti·pli·cand \ˌməl-tə-plə-ˈkand\ *n* [L *multiplicandus,* gerundive of *multiplicare*] (1594) : the number that is to be multiplied by another
mul·ti·pli·ca·tion \ˌməl-tə-plə-ˈkā-shən\ *n* [ME *multiplicacioun,* fr. AF *multiplicacion,* fr. L *multiplication-, multiplicatio,* fr. *multiplicare* to multiply] (14c) **1** : the act or process of multiplying : the state of being multiplied **2 a** : a mathematical operation that at its simplest is an abbreviated process of adding an integer to itself a specified number of times and that is extended to other numbers in accordance with laws that are valid for integers **b** : any of various mathematical operations that are analogous in some way to multiplication of the real numbers but are defined for other or larger sets of elements (as complex numbers, vectors, matrices, or functions)
multiplication sign *n* (1907) : a symbol used to indicate multiplication: **a** : TIMES SIGN **b** : DOT 2b
mul·ti·pli·ca·tive \ˌməl-tə-ˈpli-kə-tiv, ˈməl-tə-plə-ˌkā-tiv\ *adj* (1653) **1** : tending or having the power to multiply **2** : of, relating to, or associated with a mathematical operation of multiplication ⟨the ~ property of 0 requires that $a \times 0 = 0$ and $0 \times a = 0$⟩ — **mul·ti·pli·ca·tive·ly** *adv*
multiplicative identity *n* (1958) : an identity element (as 1 in the group of rational numbers without 0) that in a given mathematical system leaves unchanged any element by which it is multiplied
multiplicative inverse *n* (1958) : an element of a mathematical set that when multiplied by a given element yields the identity element — called also *reciprocal*
mul·ti·plic·i·ty \ˌməl-tə-ˈpli-sə-tē\ *n, pl* **-ties** [ME, fr. MF *multiplicité,* fr. LL *multiplicitat-, multiplicitas,* fr. L *multiplic-, multiplex*] (15c) **1 a** : the quality or state of being multiple or various **b** : the number of components in a system (as a multiplet or a group of energy levels) **2** : a great number **3** : the number of times a root of an equation or zero of a function occurs when there is more than one root or zero ⟨the ~ of $x = 2$ for the equation $(x - 2)^3 = 0$ is 3⟩
mul·ti·pli·er \ˈməl-tə-ˌplī(-ə)r\ *n* (15c) : one that multiplies: as **a** : a number by which another number is multiplied **b** : an instrument or device for multiplying or intensifying some effect **c** : a machine, mechanism, or circuit that multiplies figures
1**mul·ti·ply** \ˈməl-tə-ˌplī\ *vb* **-plied; -ply·ing** [ME *multiplien,* fr. AF *multiplier,* fr. L *multiplicare,* fr. *multiplic-, multiplex* multiple] *vt* (13c) **1** : to increase in number esp. greatly or in multiples : AUGMENT **2 a** : to find the product of by multiplication ⟨~ 7 and 8⟩ **b** : to use as a multiplicand in multiplication with another number ⟨~ 7 by 8⟩ ~ *vi* **1 a** : to become greater in number : SPREAD **b** : BREED, PROPAGATE **2** : to perform multiplication ***syn*** see INCREASE
2**mul·ti·ply** \-plē\ *adv* (1881) : in a multiple manner : in several ways ⟨~ talented children⟩
mul·ti–ply \ˌməl-tē-ˈplī, -ˌtī-\ *adj* (1926) : composed of several plies
mul·ti·po·lar \-ˈpō-lər\ *adj* [ISV] (1859) **1** : having several poles ⟨a ~ generator⟩ ⟨~ mitoses⟩ **2** : having several dendrites ⟨~ neurons⟩ **3** : characterized by more than two centers of power or interest ⟨a ~ world⟩ — **mul·ti·po·lar·i·ty** \-pō-ˈla-rə-tē\ *n*
mul·ti·po·ten·tial \-pə-ˈten(t)-shəl\ *adj* (1913) : having the potential of becoming any of several mature cell types ⟨~ stem cell⟩
mul·ti·pro·cess·ing \-ˈprä-ˌse-siŋ, -ˈprō-, -sə-siŋ\ *n* (1961) : the processing of several computer programs at the same time esp. by a computer system with two or more processors sharing a single memory — **mul·ti·pro·ces·sor** \-sər\ *n*
mul·ti·pro·gram·ming \-ˈprō-ˌgra-miŋ, -grə-\ *n* (1959) : the technique of utilizing several interleaved programs concurrently in a single computer system
mul·ti·pronged \-ˈprȯŋd\ *adj* (1953) **1** : having several distinct aspects or elements ⟨a ~ attack⟩ **2** : having several prongs
mul·ti·ra·cial \-ˈrā-shəl\ *adj* (1923) : composed of, involving, or representing various races — **mul·ti·ra·cial·ism** \-shə-ˌli-zəm\ *n*
mul·ti·sense \ˈməl-tē-ˌsen(t)s\ *adj* (1957) : having several meanings
mul·ti·sen·so·ry \ˌməl-tē-ˈsen(t)-sə-rē, -ˈsen(t)s-rē\ *adj* (1912) : relating to or involving several physiological senses ⟨~ experiences⟩
mul·ti·spec·tral \-ˈspek-trəl\ *adj* (1965) : of or relating to two or more ranges of frequencies or wavelengths in the electromagnetic spectrum
mul·ti·stage \ˈməl-tē-ˌstāj, -ˌtī-\ *adj* (1904) **1** : having successive operating stages; *esp* : having propulsion units that operate in turn ⟨~ rockets⟩ **2** : conducted by or occurring in stages ⟨a ~ investigation⟩
mul·ti·state \-ˌstāt\ *adj* (1944) **1** : having divisions in several states ⟨~ enterprises⟩ **2** : of, relating to, or involving several states
mul·ti·task·ing \-ˌtas-kiŋ\ *n, often attrib* (1966) **1** : the concurrent performance of several jobs by a computer **2** : the performance of multiple tasks at one time — **mul·ti·task** \-ˌtask\ *vi* — **mul·ti·task·er** \-ˌtas-kər\ *n*
mul·ti·tu·ber·cu·late \ˌməl-tē-ˌtü-ˈbər-kyə-lət\ *n* [NL *Multituberculata,* ultim. fr. L *multi-* + NL *tuberculatus* tuberculate] (1884) : any of an order (Multituberculata) of relatively small extinct mammals of the Mesozoic and early Cenozoic that typically resembled rodents, had many-cusped molars, and have no known living descendants
mul·ti·tude \ˈməl-tə-ˌtüd, -ˌtyüd\ *n* [ME, fr. AF or L; AF, fr. L *multitudin-, multitudo,* fr. *multus* much — more at MELIORATE] (14c) **1** : the state of being many **2** : a great number : HOST **3** : a great number of people **4** : POPULACE, PUBLIC
mul·ti·tu·di·nous \ˌməl-tə-ˈtüd-nəs, -ˈtyüd-; -ˈtü-dᵊn-əs, -ˈtyü-\ *adj* (1604) **1** : including a multitude of individuals : POPULOUS ⟨the ~ city⟩ **2** : existing in a great multitude ⟨~ opportunities⟩ **3** : existing in or consisting of innumerable elements or aspects ⟨~ applause⟩ — **mul·ti·tu·di·nous·ly** *adv* — **mul·ti·tu·di·nous·ness** *n*
mul·ti·us·er \ˌməl-tē-ˈyü-zər, -tē-, -ti-\ *adj* (1964) : able to be used by more than one person simultaneously
mul·tiv·a·lence \ˌməl-ˈti-və-lən(t)s\ *n* (ca. 1882) : the quality or state of having many values, meanings, or appeals
mul·ti·va·lent \ˌməl-tē-ˈvā-lənt, -ˌtī-, *esp in sense 3* ˌməl-ˈti-və-\ *adj* [ISV] (1869) **1** : POLYVALENT **2** : represented more than twice in the somatic chromosome number ⟨~ chromosomes⟩ **3** : having many values, meanings, or appeals — **multivalent** *n*
mul·ti·var·i·able \ˌməl-tē-ˈver-ē-ə-bəl, -ˌtī-\ *adj* (1963) : MULTIVARIATE
mul·ti·var·i·ate \-ˈver-ē-ət, -ˌāt\ *adj* [*multi-* + *variable* + 3*-ate*] (1928) : having or involving a number of independent mathematical or statistical variables ⟨~ calculus⟩ ⟨~ data analysis⟩
mul·ti·verse \ˈməl-tē-ˌvərs\ *n* [*multi-* + *universe*] (1963) *cosmology* : a theoretical reality that includes a possibly infinite number of parallel universes
mul·ti·ver·si·ty \ˌməl-tē-ˈvər-sə-tē, -stē\ *n, pl* **-ties** [*multi-* + *-versity* (as in *university*)] (1926) : a very large university with many component schools, colleges, or divisions and widely diverse functions
1**mul·ti·vi·ta·min** \-ˈvī-tə-mən, *Brit usu* -ˈvi-\ *adj* (1941) : containing several vitamins and esp. all known to be essential to health ⟨a ~ pill⟩
2**multivitamin** *n* (1947) : a multivitamin preparation
mul·ti·vol·tine \-ˈvōl-ˌtēn, -ˈvōl-\ *adj* [*multi-* + *-voltine* having a given number of broods (fr. F, fr. It *volta* time, turn) — more at VOLT] (1874) : having several broods in a season ⟨~ insects⟩

mul·ture \ˈməl-chər, *Scot usu* ˈmü-tər\ *n* [ME *multyr,* fr. AF *multure, molture,* lit., grinding, fr. VL **molitura,* fr. L *molitus,* pp. of *molere* to grind — more at MEAL] (14c) *chiefly Scot* : a fee for grinding grain at a mill

[1]**mum** \ˈməm\ *adj* [ME *mom, momme,* prob. imit. of a sound made with closed lips] (14c) : SILENT ⟨keep ~⟩

[2]**mum** *vi* **mummed; mum·ming** [ME *mommen,* to mumble, perform (a mummer's play), prob. in part fr. *mom,* in part fr. MF *momer* to go masked] (1530) **1** : to perform in a pantomime **2** : to go about merrymaking in disguise during festivals

[3]**mum** *n* [G *Mumme*] (1640) : a strong ale or beer

[4]**mum** *chiefly Brit var of* MOM

[5]**mum** *n* (1917) : CHRYSANTHEMUM

mum·ble \ˈməm-bəl\ *vb* **mum·bled; mum·bling** \-b(ə-)liŋ\ [ME *momelen,* of imit. origin] *vi* (14c) : to utter words in a low confused indistinct manner : MUTTER ~ *vt* **1** : to utter with a low inarticulate voice **2** : to chew or bite with or as if with toothless gums — **mumble** *n* — **mum·bler** \-b(ə-)lər\ *n* — **mum·bly** \-b(ə-)lē\ *adj*

mum·ble·ty–peg \ˈməm-bəl-(tē-)ˌpeg, -blē-ˌpeg\ *also* **mum·ble–the–peg** \-bəl-(t͟hə-)ˌpeg, -blē-ˌpeg\ *or* **mumble peg** \-bəl-ˌpeg, -blē-\ *n* [fr. the phrase *mumble the peg;* fr. the loser's orig. having to pull out with his teeth a peg driven into the ground] (1627) : a game in which the players try to flip a knife from various positions so that the blade will stick into the ground

mum·bo jum·bo \ˌməm-bō-ˈjəm-(ˌ)bō\ *n* [*Mumbo Jumbo,* a masked figure among Mandingo peoples of western Africa] (1738) **1** : an object of superstitious homage and fear **2 a** : a complicated often ritualistic observance with elaborate trappings **b** : complicated activity or language usu. intended to obscure and confuse **3** : unnecessarily involved and incomprehensible language : GIBBERISH **4** : language, behavior, or beliefs based on superstition

mum·mer \ˈmə-mər\ *n* (1502) **1** : a performer in a pantomime; *broadly* : ACTOR **2** : one who goes merrymaking in disguise during festivals

mum·mery \ˈmə-mə-rē\ *n, pl* **-mer·ies** [MF *momerie,* fr. *momer*] (ca. 1530) **1** : a performance by mummers **2** : a ridiculous, hypocritical, or pretentious ceremony or performance

mum·mi·chog \ˈmə-mi-ˌchȯg, -ˌchäg\ *n* [Narragansett *moamitteaúg*] (1787) : a common killifish (*Fundulus heteroclitus* of the family Cyprinodontidae) of eastern No. America

mum·mi·fy \ˈmə-mi-ˌfī\ *vb* **-fied; -fy·ing** *vt* (1628) **1** : to embalm and dry as or as if a mummy **2 a** : to make into or like a mummy **b** : to cause to dry up and shrivel ~ *vi* : to dry up and shrivel like a mummy — **mum·mi·fi·ca·tion** \ˌmə-mi-fə-ˈkā-shən\ *n*

[1]**mum·my** \ˈmə-mē\ *n, pl* **mummies** [ME *mummie* powdered parts of a mummified body used as a drug, fr. AF *mumie,* fr. ML *mumia* mummy, powdered mummy, fr. Ar *mūmiya* bitumen, mummy, fr. Pers *mūm* wax] (1615) **1 a** : a body embalmed or treated for burial with preservatives in the manner of the ancient Egyptians **b** : a body unusually well preserved **2** : one resembling a mummy

[2]**mummy** *chiefly Brit var of* MOMMY

mumps \ˈməmps\ *n pl but sing or pl in constr* [fr. pl. of obs. *mump* grimace] (1598) : an acute contagious virus disease caused by a paramyxovirus (species *Mumps virus* of the genus *Rubulavirus*) and marked by fever and by swelling esp. of the parotid gland

mun *abbr* municipal

munch \ˈmənch\ *vb* [ME *monchen,* prob. of imit. origin] *vt* (14c) : to eat with a chewing action ⟨many a mouthful is ~*ed* in private —Washington Irving⟩; *also* : to snack on ⟨drank coffee and ~*ed* homemade cookies —Lady Bird Johnson⟩ ~ *vi* : to eat or chew something; *also* : SNACK — usu. used with *on* — **munch·er** *n*

Mun·chau·sen syndrome \ˈmən-ˌchau̇-zən-, ˌmən-ˈchau̇-\ *n* [Baron K. F. H. von *Münchhausen* †1797 Ger. soldier and proverbial teller of exaggerated tales] (1951) : a psychological disorder characterized by the feigning of the symptoms of a disease or injury in order to undergo diagnostic tests, hospitalization, or medical or surgical treatment — called also *Munchausen's syndrome*

Munchausen syndrome by proxy *n* (1977) : a psychological disorder in which a parent and typically a mother harms her child (as by poisoning), falsifies the child's medical history, or tampers with the child's medical specimens in order to create a situation that requires or seems to require medical attention — called also *Munchausen's syndrome by proxy*

munch·ies \ˈmən-chēz\ *n pl* (1959) **1** : hunger pangs **2** : light snack foods

munch·kin \ˈmənch-ˌkin\ *n* [the *Munchkins,* diminutive creatures in *The Wonderful Wizard of Oz* (1900) by L. Frank Baum] (1972) : a person who is notably small and often endearing

Mun·da \ˈmu̇n-də\ *n* (1877) : a branch of the Austroasiatic language family spoken by tribal peoples of central and eastern India

mun·dane \ˌmən-ˈdān, ˈmən-ˌ\ *adj* [ME *mondeyne,* fr. AF *mundain,* fr. LL *mundanus,* fr. L *mundus* world] (15c) **1** : of, relating to, or characteristic of the world **2** : characterized by the practical, transitory, and ordinary : COMMONPLACE ⟨the ~ concerns of day-to-day life⟩ ***syn*** see EARTHLY — **mun·dane·ly** *adv* — **mun·dane·ness** \-ˈdān-nəs, -ˌdān-\ *n* — **mun·dan·i·ty** \ˌmən-ˈdā-nə-tē\ *n*

mun·dun·gus \ˌmən-ˈdəŋ-gəs\ *n* [modif. of Sp *mondongo* tripe] (1641) *archaic* : foul-smelling tobacco

mung bean \ˈməŋ-\ *n* [Hindi & Urdu *mūg,* fr. Skt *mudga*] (1910) : an erect bushy annual bean (*Vigna radiata* syn. *Phaseolus aureus*) that is widely cultivated in warm regions for its edible usu. green or yellow seeds, for forage, and as the chief source of bean sprouts; *also* : its seed

mun·go \ˈməŋ-(ˌ)gō\ *n, pl* **mungos** [origin unknown] (1857) : reclaimed wool of poor quality and very short staple

mu·ni \ˈmyü-nē\ *n* (1973) : MUNICIPAL

[1]**mu·nic·i·pal** \myu̇-ˈni-s(ə-)pəl *also* myə-, mə-, -ˈni-sə-bəl, ÷ˌmyü-nə-ˈsi-pəl\ *adj* [L *municipalis* of a municipality, fr. *municip-, municeps* inhabitant of a municipality, fr. *munus* duty, service + *capere* to take — more at MEAN, HEAVE] (ca. 1540) **1** : of or relating to the internal affairs of a major political unit (as a nation) **2 a** : of, relating to, or characteristic of a municipality **b** : having local self-government **3** : restricted to one locality

[2]**municipal** *n* (1925) : a security issued by a state or local government or by an authority set up by such a government — usu. used in pl.

municipal court *n* (1828) **1** : a court that sits in some cities and larger towns and that usu. has civil and criminal jurisdiction over cases arising within the municipality **2** : POLICE COURT

mu·nic·i·pal·i·ty \myu̇-ˌni-sə-ˈpa-lə-tē\ *n, pl* **-ties** (1790) **1** : a primarily urban political unit having corporate status and usu. powers of self-government **2** : the governing body of a municipality

mu·nic·i·pal·ize \myu̇-ˈni-sə-pə-ˌlīz\ *vt* **-ized; -iz·ing** (1880) : to bring under municipal ownership or supervision ⟨a plan to ~ utilities⟩ — **mu·nic·i·pal·i·za·tion** \-ˌni-s(ə-)pə-lə-ˈzā-shən\ *n*

mu·nic·i·pal·ly \myu̇-ˈni-sə-p(ə-)lē\ *adv* (ca. 1842) : by or in terms of a municipality ⟨~ owned property⟩

mu·nif·i·cent \myu̇-ˈni-fə-sənt\ *adj* [back-formation fr. *munificence,* fr. L *munificentia,* fr. *munificus* generous, fr. *munus* service, gift — more at MEAN] (1581) **1** : very liberal in giving or bestowing : LAVISH **2** : characterized by great liberality or generosity ***syn*** see LIBERAL — **mu·nif·i·cence** \-sən(t)s\ *n* — **mu·nif·i·cent·ly** *adv*

mu·ni·ment \ˈmyü-nə-mənt\ *n* [ME, fr. AF, fr. ML *munimentum,* fr. L, defense, safeguard, fr. *munire* to fortify] (15c) **1** : the evidence (as documents) that enables one to defend the title to an estate or a claim to rights and privileges — usu. used in pl. **2** *archaic* : a means of defense

mu·ni·tion \myu̇-ˈni-shən\ *n* [MF, fr. L *munition-, munitio,* fr. *munire* to fortify, fr. *moenia* walls; akin to L *murus* wall and perh. to Skt *minoti* he builds, fastens] (1508) **1** *archaic* : RAMPART, DEFENSE **2** : ARMAMENT, AMMUNITION — **munition** *vt*

Munster *var of* MUENSTER

mun·tin \ˈmən-tᵊn\ *n* [alter. of *montant* vertical dividing bar, fr. F, fr. prp. of *monter* to rise — more at MOUNT] (1774) : a strip separating panes of glass in a sash

munt·jac \ˈmən(t)-ˌjak, ˈmən-ˌchak\ *n* [Sundanese (Austronesian language of western Java) *mənyčək*] (ca. 1798) : any of a genus (*Muntiacus*) of small deer of southeastern Asia with a cry similar to the bark of a dog and having in the male upper canine teeth elongated into small tusks — called also *barking deer*

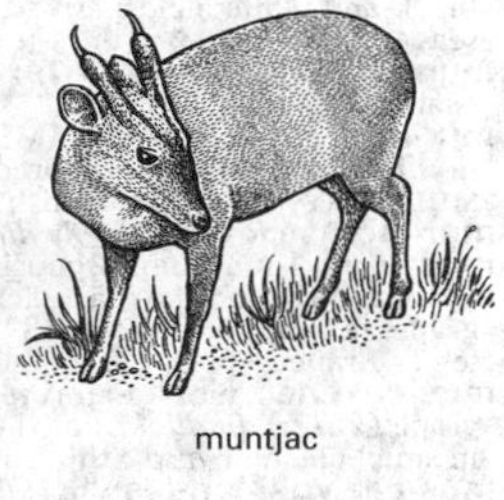
muntjac

mu·on \ˈmyü-ˌän\ *n* [contr. of earlier *mu-meson,* fr. *mu*] (1952) : an unstable lepton that is common in the cosmic radiation near the earth's surface, has a mass about 207 times the mass of the electron, and exists in negative and positive forms — **mu·on·ic** \myü-ˈä-nik\ *adj*

mu·on·ium \myü-ˈō-nē-əm, -ˈä-\ *n* [NL] (1957) : a short-lived quasi-atom consisting of an electron and a positive muon

[1]**mu·ral** \ˈmyu̇r-əl\ *adj* [L *muralis,* fr. *murus* wall — more at MUNITION] (1586) **1** : of, relating to, or resembling a wall **2** : applied to and made integral with a wall or ceiling surface

[2]**mural** *n* (1916) : a mural work of art (as a painting) — **mu·ral·ist** \-ə-list\ *n*

mu·ram·ic acid \myu̇-ˈra-mik-\ *n* [L *mur*us wall + E + gluco*samine* + [1]*-ic*] (1957) : an amino sugar $C_9H_{17}NO_7$ that is a lactic acid derivative of glucosamine and is found esp. in bacterial cell walls

[1]**mur·der** \ˈmər-dər\ *n* [partly fr. ME *murther,* fr. OE *morthor;* partly fr. ME *murdre,* fr. AF, of Gmc origin; akin to OE *morthor;* akin to OHG *mord* murder, L *mort-, mors* death, *mori* to die, *mortuus* dead, Gk *brotos* mortal] (bef. 12c) **1** : the crime of unlawfully killing a person esp. with malice aforethought **2 a** : something very difficult or dangerous ⟨the traffic was ~⟩ **b** : something outrageous or blameworthy ⟨getting away with ~⟩

[2]**murder** *vb* **mur·dered; mur·der·ing** \ˈmər-d(ə-)riŋ\ *vt* (13c) **1** : to kill (a human being) unlawfully and with premeditated malice **2** : to slaughter wantonly : SLAY **3 a** : to put an end to **b** : TEASE, TORMENT **c** : MUTILATE, MANGLE ⟨~*s* French⟩ **d** : to defeat badly ~ *vi* : to commit murder ***syn*** see KILL

mur·der·ee \ˌmər-də-ˈrē\ *n* (1920) : an actual or potential victim of a murder

mur·der·er \ˈmər-dər-ər\ *n* (14c) : one who murders; *esp* : one who commits the crime of murder

mur·der·ess \ˈmər-də-rəs\ *n* (14c) : a woman who murders

mur·der·ous \ˈmər-d(ə-)rəs\ *adj* (1535) **1 a** : having the purpose or capability of murder **b** : characterized by or causing murder or bloodshed **2** : having the ability or power to overwhelm : DEVASTATING ⟨~ heat⟩ — **mur·der·ous·ly** *adv* — **mur·der·ous·ness** *n*

mu·rein \ˈmyu̇r-ē-ən, ˈmyu̇r-ˌēn\ *n* [*mur*amic acid + *-ein,* alter. of [2]*-ine*] (1964) : PEPTIDOGLYCAN

mu·rex \ˈmyu̇r-ˌeks\ *n, pl* **mu·ri·ces** \ˈmyu̇r-ə-ˌsēz\ *or* **mu·rex·es** [NL, fr. L, mollusk yielding a purple dye; akin to Gk *myak-, myax* mussel] (1589) : any of a genus (*Murex* of the family Muricidae) of marine gastropod mollusks having a rough and often spiny shell, abounding in tropical seas, and yielding a purple dye

mu·ri·ate \ˈmyu̇r-ē-ˌāt\ *n* [F, back-formation fr. (*acide*) *muriatique* muriatic acid] (1790) : CHLORIDE

mu·ri·at·ic acid \ˌmyu̇r-ē-ˈa-tik-\ *n* [F *muriatique,* fr. L *muriaticus* pickled in brine, fr. *muria* brine] (1756) : HYDROCHLORIC ACID

mu·rid \ˈmyu̇r-əd\ *adj* [ultim. fr. L *mur-, mus* mouse — more at MOUSE] (ca. 1909) : of or relating to a family (Muridae) comprising the typical mice and rats and often those rodents classified as cricetids — **murid** *n*

mu·rine \ˈmyu̇r-ˌīn\ *adj* [ultim. fr. L *mur-, mus*] (ca. 1729) : of or relating to a murid genus (*Mus*) or its subfamily (Murinae) which includes the common household rats and mice; *also* : of, relating to, or involving these rodents and esp. the house mouse — **murine** *n*

murine typhus *n* (1933) : a mild disease that is marked esp. by fever, headache, and rash, is caused by a rickettsia (*Rickettsia typhi* syn. *R.*

mooseri), is widespread in nature in rodents, and is transmitted to humans by a flea

murk \ˈmərk\ *n* [ME *mirke,* prob. fr. ON *myrkr* darkness; akin to OE *mirce* gloom] (bef. 12c) **:** GLOOM, DARKNESS; *also* **:** FOG — **murk** *adj, archaic*

murky \ˈmər-kē\ *adj* **murk·i·er; -est** (14c) **1 :** characterized by a heavy dimness or obscurity caused by or like that caused by overhanging fog or smoke **2 :** characterized by thickness and heaviness of air **:** FOGGY, MISTY **3 :** darkly vague or obscure ⟨~ official rhetoric⟩ — **murk·i·ly** \-kə-lē\ *adv* — **murk·i·ness** \-kē-nəs\ *n*

[1]**mur·mur** \ˈmər-mər\ *n* [ME *murmure,* fr. AF disturbance, fr. L *murmur* murmur, roar, of imit. origin] (14c) **1 :** a half-suppressed or muttered complaint **:** GRUMBLING **2 a :** a low indistinct but often continuous sound **b :** a soft or gentle utterance **3 :** an atypical sound of the heart typically indicating a functional or structural abnormality

[2]**murmur** *vi* (14c) **1 :** to make a murmur ⟨the breeze ~*ed* in the pines⟩ **2 :** COMPLAIN, GRUMBLE ~ *vt* **:** to say in a murmur — **mur·mur·er** *n*

mur·mur·ous \ˈmər-mə-rəs, ˈmərm-rəs\ *adj* (1582) **:** filled with or characterized by murmurs **:** low and indistinct — **mur·mur·ous·ly** *adv*

Mur·phy \ˈmər-fē\ *n* [Miss *Murphy,* nonexistent prostitute used to lure victims] (1954) **:** any of various confidence games; *esp* **:** one in which the victim believes he is paying for sex

Murphy bed *n* [William L. *Murphy* †1959 Am. inventor] (1913) **:** a bed that may be folded or swung into a closet

Murphy's Law *n* [prob. fr. Edward A. Murphy †1990 Am. engineer] (1951) **:** an observation: anything that can go wrong will go wrong

mur·rain \ˈmər-ən, ˈmə-rən\ *n* [ME *moreyne,* fr. AF *morine,* fr. *morir* to die, fr. L *mori* — more at MURDER] (14c) **:** a pestilence or plague esp. affecting domestic animals

murre \ˈmər\ *n* [origin unknown] (1602) **:** any of a genus (*Uria*) of black-and-white alcids; *esp* **:** a common seabird (*U. aalge*) of northern seas

murre·let \ˈmər-lət\ *n* (1862) **:** any of several small alcids of No. Pacific islands and coasts

mur·rey \ˈmər-ē, ˈmə-rē\ *n* [ME, fr. AF *muré,* fr. ML *moratum,* fr. neut. of *moratus* mulberry colored, fr. L *morum* mulberry — more at MULBERRY] (15c) **:** a purplish black **:** MULBERRY

mur·ther \ˈmər-t͟hər\ *chiefly dial var of* MURDER

mus *abbr* **1** museum **2** music; musical; musician

mus·ca·det \ˌməs-kə-ˈdā, -ˈde\ *n, often cap* [F, fr. Occitan, muscadet grape, fr. *musc* musk] (ca. 1899) **:** a dry white wine from the Loire valley of France

mus·ca·dine \ˈməs-kə-ˌdīn\ *n* [prob. alter. of *muscatel*] (ca. 1785) **:** a grape (*Vitis rotundifolia*) of the southern U.S. with musky fruits borne in small clusters; *also* **:** the fruit

mus·cae vo·li·tan·tes \ˈməs-ˌkē-ˌvä-lə-ˈtan-ˌtēz, ˈmə-ˌsē-\ *n pl* [NL, lit., flying flies] (1797) **:** FLOATER 6

mus·ca·rine \ˈməs-kə-ˌrēn\ *n* [G *Muskarin,* fr. NL (*Amanita*) *muscaria* fly agaric] (1872) **:** a toxic alkaloid base $[C_9H_{20}NO_2]^+$ that is biochemically related to acetylcholine, is found esp. in fly agaric, and acts directly on smooth muscle

mus·ca·rin·ic \ˌməs-kə-ˈri-nik\ *adj* (1936) **:** of, relating to, resembling, producing, or mediating the parasympathetic effects (as a slowed heart rate and increased activity of smooth muscle) produced by muscarine ⟨~ receptors⟩ — compare NICOTINIC

mus·cat \ˈməs-ˌkat, -kət\ *n* [MF, fr. Old Occitan, fr. *muscat* musky, fr. *musc* musk, fr. LL *muscus* — more at MUSK] (1548) **1 :** MUSCATEL **2 :** any of several cultivated grapes used in making wine and raisins

mus·ca·tel \ˌməs-kə-ˈtel\ *n* [ME *muskadell,* fr. ML *muscadellum,* fr. Old Occitan *muscadel,* fr. *muscadel* resembling musk, fr. *muscat*] (15c) **1 :** a sweet fortified wine from muscat grapes **2 :** a raisin from muscat grapes

[1]**mus·cle** \ˈmə-səl\ *n, often attrib* [ME, fr. L *musculus,* fr. dim. of *mus* mouse — more at MOUSE] (14c) **1 a :** a body tissue consisting of long cells that contract when stimulated and produce motion **b :** an organ that is essentially a mass of muscle tissue attached at either end to a fixed point and that by contracting moves or checks the movement of a body part **2 a :** muscular strength **:** BRAWN **b :** effective strength **:** POWER ⟨political ~⟩

[2]**muscle** *vb* **mus·cled; mus·cling** \ˈmə-s(ə-)liŋ\ *vt* (1913) **:** to move or force by or as if by muscular effort ⟨*muscled* him out of office⟩ ~ *vi* **:** to make one's way by brute strength or by force

mus·cle–bound \ˈmə-səl-ˌbau̇nd\ *adj* (1879) **1 :** having some of the muscles tense and enlarged and of impaired elasticity sometimes as a result of excessive exercise **2 :** lacking in flexibility **:** RIGID

muscle car \-ˌkär\ *n* (1969) **:** any of a group of American-made 2-door sports coupes with powerful engines designed for high-performance driving

mus·cled \ˈmə-səld\ *adj* (1644) **:** having muscles esp. of a specified kind — often used in combination ⟨hard-*muscled* arms⟩

mus·cle·man \ˈmə-səl-ˌman\ *n* (1861) **1 :** a man with a muscular physique **2 :** BULLY 3

muscle shirt *n* (1955) **:** a close-fitting usu. sleeveless T-shirt

muscle spindle *n* (1894) **:** a sensory end organ in a muscle that is sensitive to stretch in the muscle, consists of small striated muscle fibers richly supplied with nerve fibers, and is enclosed in a connective tissue sheath — called also *stretch receptor*

mus·co·vite \ˈməs-kə-ˌvīt\ *n* [ML or NL *Muscovia, Moscovia* Moscow] (1535) **1** *cap* **a :** a native or resident of the ancient principality of Moscow or of the city of Moscow **b :** RUSSIAN **2** [*muscovy* (*glass*)] **:** a colorless to pale brown form of mica consisting of a silicate of aluminum and potassium — **Muscovite** *adj*

Mus·co·vy duck \ˈməs-ˌkō-vē-\ *n* [*Muscovy,* principality of Moscow, Russia] (1657) **:** a large dark crested duck (*Cairina moschata*) of Central and So. America that is widely kept in domestication

muscul- *or* **musculo-** *comb form* [LL *muscul-,* fr. L *musculus*] **1 :** muscle ⟨*muscul*ar⟩ **2 :** muscular and ⟨*musculo*skeletal⟩

mus·cu·lar \ˈməs-kyə-lər\ *adj* (1678) **1 a :** of, relating to, or constituting muscle **b :** of, relating to, or performed by the muscles **2 :** having well-developed musculature **3 a :** of or relating to physical strength **:** BRAWNY **b :** having strength of expression or character **:** VIGOROUS ⟨~ prose⟩ **c :** characterized by forcefulness or resolve ⟨~ foreign policy⟩ **d :** FULL-BODIED ⟨~ wines⟩ — **mus·cu·lar·i·ty** \ˌməs-kyə-ˈla-rə-tē\ *n* — **mus·cu·lar·ly** \ˈməs-kyə-lər-lē\ *adv*

muscular dystrophy *n* (1886) **:** any of a group of hereditary diseases characterized by progressive wasting of muscles — compare BECKER MUSCULAR DYSTROPHY, DUCHENNE MUSCULAR DYSTROPHY

mus·cu·la·ture \ˈməs-kyə-lə-ˌchu̇r, -chər, -ˌtyu̇r, -ˌtu̇r\ *n* [F, fr. L *musculus*] (1875) **:** the muscles of all or a part of the animal body

mus·cu·lo·skel·e·tal \ˌməs-kyə-lō-ˈske-lə-tᵊl\ *adj* (ca. 1944) **:** of, relating to, or involving both musculature and skeleton

[1]**muse** \ˈmyüz\ *vb* **mused; mus·ing** [ME, fr. AF *muser* to gape, idle, muse, fr. OF **mus* mouth of an animal, fr. ML *musus*] *vi* (14c) **1 :** to become absorbed in thought; *esp* **:** to turn something over in the mind meditatively and often inconclusively **2** *archaic* **:** WONDER, MARVEL ~ *vt* **:** to think or say reflectively ***syn*** see PONDER — **mus·er** *n*

[2]**muse** *n* (15c) **:** a state of deep thought or dreamy abstraction

[3]**muse** *n* [ME, fr. MF, fr. L *Musa,* fr. Gk *Mousa*] (14c) **1** *cap* **:** any of the nine sister goddesses in Greek mythology presiding over song and poetry and the arts and sciences **2 :** a source of inspiration; *esp* **:** a guiding genius **3 :** POET

mu·se·ol·o·gy \ˌmyü-zē-ˈä-lə-jē\ *n* [*museum* + *-logy*] (1885) **:** the science or profession of museum organization and management — **mu·seo·log·i·cal** \-ə-ˈlä-ji-kəl\ *adj* — **mu·se·ol·o·gist** \-ˈä-lə-jist\ *n*

mu·sette \myu̇-ˈzet\ *n* [ME, fr. MF, dim. of *muse* bagpipe, fr. *muser* to muse, play the bagpipe] (14c) **1 :** a bellows-blown bagpipe popular in France in the 17th and 18th centuries **2 :** a small knapsack; *also* **:** a similar bag with one shoulder strap — called also *musette bag*

mu·se·um \myu̇-ˈzē-əm\ *n* [L *Museum* place for learned occupation, fr. Gk *Mouseion,* fr. neut. of *Mouseios* of the Muses, fr. *Mousa*] (1672) **:** an institution devoted to the procurement, care, study, and display of objects of lasting interest or value; *also* **:** a place where objects are exhibited

mu·se·um·go·er \myu̇-ˈzē-əm-ˌgō-ər\ *n* (1930) **:** a person who frequently goes to museums

museum piece *n* (1901) **1 :** something preserved in or suitable for a museum **2 :** one that is out-of-date **:** a thing of the past

[1]**mush** \ˈməsh, *esp 3 also* ˈmu̇sh\ *n* [prob. alter. of *mash*] (1671) **1 :** a thick porridge made with cornmeal boiled in water or milk **2 :** something soft and spongy or shapeless **3 a :** weak sentimentality **:** DRIVEL **b :** mawkish amorousness

[2]**mush** *vt* (ca. 1781) *chiefly dial* **:** to reduce to a crumbly mass ~ *vi, of an airplane* **:** to fly in a partly or nearly stalled condition — **mush·er** *n*

[3]**mush** *vi* [prob. fr. F *marchons,* 1st pl. imper. of *marcher* to move, march, fr. MF *marchier* — more at MARCH] (1897) **:** to travel esp. over snow with a sled drawn by dogs — often used as a command to a dog team — **mush·er** *n*

[4]**mush** *n* (1902) **:** a trip esp. across snow with a dog team

[1]**mush·room** \ˈməsh-ˌrüm, -ˌru̇m; *chiefly Northern & Midland* -ˌrün; *dial* ˈmə-shə-ˌrüm, -ˌru̇m, -ˌrün\ *n* [ME *musheron,* fr. AF *musherum, musseron,* fr. LL *mussirion-, mussirio*] (15c) **1 a :** an enlarged complex aboveground fleshy fruiting body of a fungus (as a basidiomycete) that consists typically of a stem bearing a pileus; *esp* **:** one that is edible **b :** FUNGUS **2 :** UPSTART **3 :** something resembling a mushroom

[2]**mushroom** *vi* (1893) **1 a :** to well up and spread out laterally from a central source **b :** to become enlarged or extended **:** GROW **2 :** to collect wild mushrooms **3 :** to spring up suddenly or multiply rapidly

mushroom cloud *n* (ca. 1909) **:** a mushroom-shaped cloud; *specif* **:** one caused by the explosion of a nuclear weapon

mushy \ˈmə-shē, *esp 2 also* ˈmu̇-\ *adj* **mush·i·er; -est** (1839) **1 a :** having the consistency of mush **:** SOFT **b :** lacking in definition or precision **2 :** excessively tender or emotional; *esp* **:** mawkishly amorous — **mush·i·ly** \ˈmə-shə-lē, ˈmu̇-\ *adv* — **mush·i·ness** \ˈmə-shē-nəs, ˈmu̇-\ *n*

mu·sic \ˈmyü-zik\ *n, often attrib* [ME *musik,* fr. AF *musike,* fr. L *musica,* fr. Gk *mousikē* any art presided over by the Muses, esp. music, fr. fem. of *mousikos* of the Muses, fr. *Mousa* Muse] (13c) **1 a :** the science or art of ordering tones or sounds in succession, in combination, and in temporal relationships to produce a composition having unity and continuity **b :** vocal, instrumental, or mechanical sounds having rhythm, melody, or harmony **2 a :** an agreeable sound **:** EUPHONY ⟨her voice was ~ to my ears⟩ **b :** musical quality ⟨the ~ of verse⟩ **3 :** a musical accompaniment ⟨a play set to ~⟩ **4 :** the score of a musical composition set down on paper **5 :** a distinctive type or category of music ⟨there is a ~ for everybody —Eric Salzman⟩

[1]**mu·si·cal** \ˈmyü-zi-kəl\ *adj* [ME, fr. ML *musicalis,* fr. *musica*] (15c) **1 a :** of or relating to music **b :** having the pleasing harmonious qualities of music **:** MELODIOUS **2 :** having an interest in or talent for music **3 :** set to or accompanied by music **4 :** of or relating to musicians or music lovers — **mu·si·cal·ly** \-k(ə-)lē\ *adv*

[2]**musical** *n* (1823) **1** *archaic* **:** MUSICALE **2 :** a film or theatrical production typically of a sentimental or humorous nature that consists of musical numbers and dialogue based on a unifying plot

musical box *n* (1829) *chiefly Brit* **:** MUSIC BOX

musical chairs *n pl but sing in constr* (1877) **:** a game in which players march to music around a row of chairs numbering one less than the players and scramble for seats when the music stops; *also* **:** a situation or series of events suggesting the game of musical chairs (as in rapid change or confusing activity)

musical comedy *n* (1765) **:** MUSICAL 2

mu·si·cale \ˌmyü-zi-ˈkal\ *n* [F *soirée musicale,* lit., musical evening] (1872) **:** a social entertainment with music as the leading feature

mu·si·cal·ise *Brit var of* MUSICALIZE

mu·si·cal·i·ty \ˌmyü-zi-ˈka-lə-tē\ *n* (1853) **1 :** sensitivity to, knowledge of, or talent for music **2 :** the quality or state of being musical **:** MELODIOUSNESS

mu·si·cal·ize \ˈmyü-zi-kə-ˌlīz\ *vt* **-ized; -iz·ing** (1919) **:** to set to music — **mu·si·cal·i·za·tion** \ˌmyü-zi-kə-lə-ˈzā-shən\ *n*

musical saw *n* (1927) **:** a handsaw made to produce melody by bending the blade while sounding it with a hammer or violin bow

music box *n* (1844) **:** a container enclosing an apparatus that reproduces music mechanically when activated by a clockwork

music drama *n* (1877) **:** an opera in which the action is not interrupted by formal song divisions (as recitatives or arias) and the music is determined solely by dramatic appropriateness

music hall *n* (1842) **:** a vaudeville theater; *also* **:** VAUDEVILLE

mu·si·cian \myü-ˈzi-shən\ *n* (14c) **:** a composer, conductor, or performer of music; *esp* **:** INSTRUMENTALIST — **mu·si·cian·ly** \-lē\ *adj* — **mu·si·cian·ship** \-ˌship\ *n*

music of the spheres (1609) **:** an ethereal harmony thought by the Pythagoreans to be produced by the vibration of the celestial spheres

mu·si·col·o·gy \ˌmyü-zi-ˈkä-lə-jē\ *n* [It *musicologia,* fr. L *musica* music + *-logia* -logy] (1909) **:** the study of music as a branch of knowledge or field of research as distinct from composition or performance — **mu·si·co·log·i·cal** \-kə-ˈlä-ji-kəl\ *adj* — **mu·si·col·o·gist** \-ˈkä-lə-jist\ *n*

[1]**musing** *n* (14c) **:** MEDITATION

[2]**musing** *adj* (15c) **:** thoughtfully abstracted **:** MEDITATIVE — **mus·ing·ly** \-lē\ *adv*

mu·sique con·crète \myü-ˈzēk-kōⁿ-ˈkret, mue-\ *n* [F, lit., concrete music] (1952) **:** a recorded montage of natural sounds often electronically modified and presented as a musical composition

musk \ˈməsk\ *n* [ME *muske,* fr. MF *musc,* fr. LL *muscus,* fr. LGk *moschos,* fr. MPers **mušk-,* fr. Skt *muṣka* testicle, fr. dim. of *mūṣ* mouse; akin to OE *mūs* mouse] (14c) **1 a :** a substance with a penetrating persistent odor obtained from a sac beneath the abdominal skin of the male musk deer and used as a perfume fixative; *also* **:** a similar substance from another animal or a synthetic substitute **b :** the odor of musk; *also* **:** an odor resembling musk esp. in heaviness or persistence **2 :** any of various plants with musky odors; *esp* **:** MUSK PLANT

musk deer *n* (1681) **:** any of a genus (*Moschus*) of small heavy-limbed hornless deer of central Asian uplands with tusked musk-producing males

mus·keg \ˈməs-ˌkeg, -ˌkāg\ *n* [Cree *maske·k*] (1806) **1 :** BOG; *esp* **:** a sphagnum bog of northern No. America often with tussocks **2 :** a usu. thick deposit of partially decayed vegetable matter of wet boreal regions

mus·kel·lunge \ˈməs-kə-ˌlənj\ *n, pl* **muskellunge** [alter. of CanF *maskinongé,* fr. Ojibwa *ma·skino·še·*] (1777) **:** a large No. American pike (*Esox masquinongy*) that has dark markings, may weigh over 60 pounds (27 kilograms), and is a valuable sport fish

mus·ket \ˈməs-kət\ *n* [MF *mousquet,* fr. OIt *moschetto* small artillery piece, sparrow hawk, fr. dim. of *mosca* fly, fr. L *musca* — more at MIDGE] (ca. 1587) **:** a heavy large-caliber muzzle-loading usu. smoothbore shoulder firearm; *broadly* **:** a shoulder gun carried by infantry

mus·ke·teer \ˌməs-kə-ˈtir\ *n* [modif. of MF *mousquetaire,* fr. *mousquet*] (1590) **1 :** a soldier armed with a musket **2** [fr. the musketeers' friendship in the novel *Les Trois Mousquetaires* (1844) by Alexandre Dumas] **:** a good friend **:** BUDDY

mus·ket·ry \ˈməs-kə-trē\ *n* (1646) **1 :** MUSKETS **2 :** MUSKETEERS **3 a :** musket fire **b :** the art or science of using small arms esp. in battle

mus·kie *or* **mus·ky** \ˈməs-kē\ *n, pl* **muskies** (1894) **:** MUSKELLUNGE

musk·mel·on \ˈməsk-ˌme-lən\ *n* (1573) **:** a usu. sweet edible melon that is the fruit of an annual trailing or climbing Asian vine (*Cucumis melo*) of the gourd family: as **a :** any of various melons (*C. melo reticulatus*) with netted skin and musky odor that include most of the muskmelons cultivated in No. America; *esp* **:** CANTALOUPE 1 **b :** WINTER MELON 1

Mus·ko·ge·an *or* **Mus·kho·ge·an** \mə-ˈskō-gē-ən\ *n* (1891) **:** a language family of southeastern U.S. that includes Muskogee

Mus·ko·gee \mə-ˈskō-gē\ *n, pl* **Muskogee** *or* **Muskogees** [Creek *ma·skó·ki, maskó·ki,* a self-designation] (1775) **1 :** a member of an American Indian people of Georgia and eastern Alabama constituting the nucleus of the Creek confederacy **2 :** the language of the Muskogees and of some of the Seminoles

musk ox *n* (1744) **:** a heavyset shaggy-coated wild ox (*Ovibos moschatus*) of tundra regions of Greenland, Canada, and Alaska with the males producing a strong musky odor from glands beneath the eyes

musk plant *n* (1837) **:** a yellow-flowered perennial No. American herb (*Mimulus moschatus*) of the snapdragon family that has hairy foliage and sometimes a musky odor

musk·rat \ˈməsk-ˌrat\ *n, pl* **muskrat** *or* **muskrats** [prob. by folk etymology fr. a word of Algonquian origin; akin to Massachusett *musquash* muskrat] (1607) **:** an aquatic rodent (*Ondatra zibethica*) of the U.S. and Canada with a long scaly laterally compressed tail, webbed hind feet, and dark glossy brown fur; *also* **:** its fur or pelt

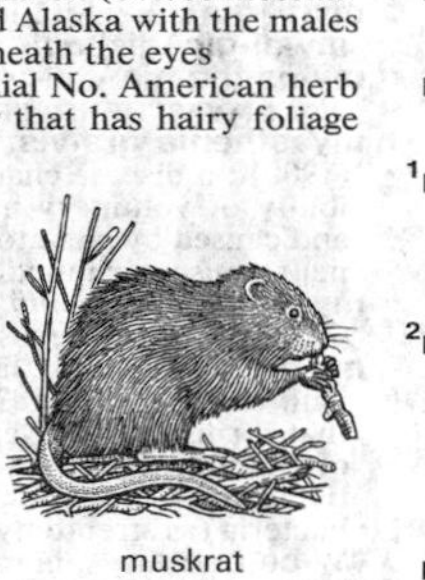

muskrat

musk rose *n* (1577) **:** a rose (*Rosa moschata*) of the Mediterranean region with white flowers having a musky odor

musk thistle *n* (ca. 1731) **:** a Eurasian thistle (*Carduus nutans*) that has nodding musky flower heads and is naturalized in eastern No. America

musk turtle *n* (1868) **:** any of various small American freshwater turtles (esp. genus *Sternotherus*) that have musk glands; *esp* **:** a small dark turtle (*S. odoratus*) capable of producing a foul odor

musky \ˈməs-kē\ *adj* **musk·i·er; -est** (1613) **:** having an odor of or resembling musk — **musk·i·ness** *n*

Mus·lim \ˈməz-ləm, ˈmus-, ˈmuz-\ *n* [Ar *muslim,* lit., one who submits (to God)] (ca. 1615) **1 :** an adherent of Islam **2 :** BLACK MUSLIM — **Muslim** *adj*

Muslim era *n* (1948) **:** ISLAMIC ERA

mus·lin \ˈməz-lən\ *n* [F *mousseline,* fr. It *mussolina,* fr. Ar *mawṣilī* of Mosul, fr. al-*Mawṣil* Mosul, Iraq] (1609) **:** a plain-woven sheer to coarse cotton fabric

mus·quash \ˈməs-ˌkwäsh, -ˌkwȯsh\ *n* [Massachusett] (1633) **:** MUSKRAT

[1]**muss** \ˈməs\ *n* [origin unknown] (1591) **1** *obs* **a :** a game in which players scramble for small objects thrown to the ground **b :** SCRAMBLE **2** *slang* **:** a confused conflict **:** ROW **3 :** a state of disorder **:** MESS

[2]**muss** *vt* (1835) **:** to make untidy **:** DISARRANGE

mus·sel \ˈmə-səl\ *n* [ME *muscle,* fr. OE *muscelle,* fr. VL **muscula,* fr. L *musculus* muscle, mussel] (bef. 12c) **1 :** a marine bivalve mollusk (esp. genus *Mytilus*) usu. having a dark elongated shell **2 :** a freshwater bivalve mollusk (as of *Unio, Anodonta,* or related genera) that is esp. abundant in rivers of the central U.S. and has a shell with a lustrous nacreous lining

Mus·sul·man *also* **Mus·sal·man** \ˈmə-səl-mən\ *n, pl* **Mus·sul·men** \-mən\ *or* **Mussulmans** [Turk *müslüman* & Pers *musulmān,* modif. of Ar *muslim*] (ca. 1583) **:** MUSLIM

mussy \ˈmə-sē\ *adj* **muss·i·er; -est** (ca. 1859) **:** characterized by clutter or muss **:** MESSY — **muss·i·ly** \ˈmə-sə-lē\ *adv* — **muss·i·ness** \ˈmə-sē-nəs\ *n*

[1]**must** \məs(t), ˈməst\ *vb, pres & past all persons* **must** [ME *moste,* fr. OE *mōste,* past indic. & subj. of *mōtan* to be allowed to, have to; akin to OHG *muozan* to be allowed to, have to] *verbal auxiliary* (bef. 12c) **1 a :** be commanded or requested to ⟨you ~ stop⟩ **b :** be urged to **:** ought by all means to ⟨you ~ read that book⟩ **2 :** be compelled by physical necessity to ⟨one ~ eat to live⟩ **:** be required by immediate or future need or purpose to ⟨we ~ hurry to catch the bus⟩ **3 a :** be obliged to **:** be compelled by social considerations to ⟨I ~ say you're looking well⟩ **b :** be required by law, custom, or moral conscience to ⟨we ~ obey the rules⟩ **c :** be determined to ⟨if you ~ go at least wait for me⟩ **d :** be unreasonably or perversely compelled to ⟨why ~ you argue⟩ **4 :** be logically inferred or supposed to ⟨it ~ be time⟩ **5 :** be compelled by fate or by natural law to ⟨what ~ be will be⟩ **6 :** was or were presumably certain to **:** was or were bound to ⟨if he did it she ~ have known⟩ **7** *dial* **:** MAY, SHALL — used chiefly in questions ~ *vi, archaic* **:** to be obliged to go ⟨I ~ to Coventry —Shak.⟩

[2]**must** \ˈməst\ *n* (1616) **1 :** an imperative need or duty **:** REQUIREMENT **2 :** an indispensable item **:** ESSENTIAL ⟨exercise is a ~⟩

[3]**must** *n* [ME, fr. OE, fr. L *mustum*] (bef. 12c) **:** the expressed juice of fruit and esp. grapes before and during fermentation; *also* **:** the pulp and skins of the crushed grapes

[4]**must** *n* [ME (Sc) *moist,* fr. MF *must,* alter. of *musc* musk] (15c) **1 :** MUSK **2 :** MOLD, MUSTINESS

mus·tache *also* **mous·tache** \ˈməs-ˌtash, (ˌ)mə-ˈstash\ *n* [MF *moustache,* fr. OIt *mustaccio,* fr. MGk *moustaki,* dim. of Gk *mystak-, mystax* upper lip, mustache] (1585) **1 :** the hair growing on the human upper lip; *esp* **:** such hair grown and often trimmed in a particular style **2 :** hair or bristles about the mouth of a mammal — **mus·tached** *also* **mous·tached** *adj*

mus·ta·chio *also* **mous·ta·chio** \(ˌ)mə-ˈsta-shē-ˌō, -ˈstä-, -shō\ *n, pl* **-chios** [Sp & It; Sp *mostacho,* fr. It *mustaccio,* fr. OIt] (1588) **:** MUSTACHE; *esp* **:** a large mustache — **mus·ta·chioed** *also* **mous·ta·chioed** \-shē-ˌōd, -shōd\ *adj*

mus·tang \ˈməs-ˌtaŋ\ *n* [MexSp *mestengo,* fr. Sp, stray, fr. *mesteño* strayed, fr. *mesta* annual roundup of cattle that disposed of strays, fr. ML (*animalia*) *mixta* mixed animals] (1808) **1 :** a small hardy naturalized horse of U.S. western plains directly descended from horses brought in by the Spaniards; *also* **:** BRONC **2** *slang* **:** a commissioned officer (as in the U.S. Navy) who has risen from the ranks

mus·tard \ˈməs-tərd\ *n* [ME, fr. AF *mustarde,* fr. *must* must, fr. L *mustum*] (13c) **1 a :** a pungent yellow powder of the seeds of any of several common mustards (*Brassica hirta, B. nigra,* or *B. juncea*) used as a condiment or in medicine as a stimulant and diuretic, an emetic, or a counterirritant **b** *slang* **:** ZEST **2 :** any of several herbs (genus *Brassica* of the family Cruciferae syn. Brassicaceae, the mustard family) with lobed leaves, yellow flowers, and linear beaked pods **3 :** a dark to moderate yellow — **mus·tardy** \-tər-dē\ *adj*

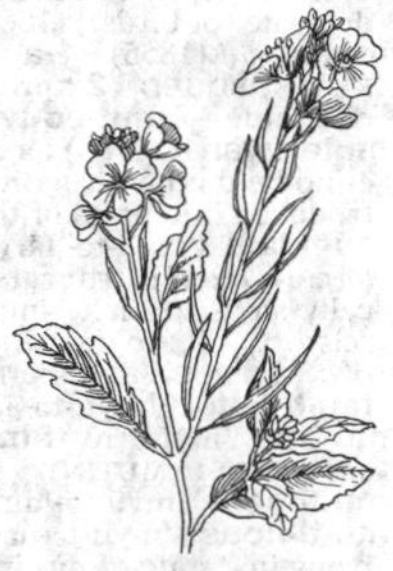

mustard 1a

mustard gas *n* (1917) **:** an irritant vesicant oily liquid $C_4H_8Cl_2S$ used esp. as a chemical weapon

mustard plaster *n* (1810) **:** a counterirritant and rubefacient plaster containing powdered mustard

[1]**mus·ter** \ˈməs-tər\ *n* [ME *mustre,* fr. AF *mostre, monstre,* fr. *mustrer*] (14c) **1 :** a representative specimen **:** SAMPLE **2 a :** an act of assembling; *specif* **:** formal military inspection **b :** critical examination **c :** an assembled group **:** COLLECTION **d :** INVENTORY

[2]**muster** *vb* **mus·tered; mus·ter·ing** \-t(ə-)riŋ\ [ME *mustren* to show, muster, fr. AF *mustrer, monstrer,* fr. L *monstrare* to show, fr. *monstrum* evil omen, monster — more at MONSTER] *vt* (15c) **1 a :** to cause to gather **:** CONVENE **b :** to enroll formally — usu. used with *in* or *into* ⟨was ~*ed* into the army⟩ **c :** to call the roll of **2 a :** to bring together **:** COLLECT **b :** to call forth **:** ROUSE **3 :** to amount to **:** COMPRISE ~ *vi* **:** to come together **:** CONGREGATE ***syn*** see SUMMON

muster out *vt* (1834) **:** to discharge from service

muster roll *n* (1605) **:** INVENTORY, ROSTER; *specif* **:** a register of the officers and men in a military unit or ship's company

musth *also* **must** \ˈməst\ *n* [Hindi & Urdu *mast* intoxicated, fr. Pers] (1878) **:** a periodic state of the bull elephant characterized esp. by aggressive behavior and usu. connected with the rutting season

must–have \ˈməst-ˌhav\ *n* (1980) **:** something that is essential to have or obtain — **must–have** *adj*

mustn't \ˈmə-sᵊnt\ (1741) **:** must not

must–see \ˈməst-ˈsē\ *n* (1946) **:** something (as a film) that must or should be seen — **must–see** *adj*

musty \ˈməs-tē\ *adj* **must·i·er; -est** [[4]*must*] (1530) **1 a :** impaired by damp or mildew **:** MOLDY **b :** tasting of mold **c :** smelling of damp and decay **:** FUSTY **2 a :** TRITE, STALE ⟨~ prose⟩ **b** (1) **:** ANTIQUATED ⟨~ customs⟩ (2) **:** SUPERANNUATED ***syn*** see MALODOROUS — **must·i·ly** \ˈməs-tə-lē\ *adv* — **must·i·ness** \-tē-nəs\ *n*

mu·ta·ble \ˈmyü-tə-bəl\ *adj* [ME, fr. L *mutabilis,* fr. *mutare* to change; akin to OE *mīthan* to conceal, Skt *mināti* he exchanges, deceives] (14c) **1 :** prone to change **:** INCONSTANT **2 a :** capable of change or of being changed **b :** capable of or liable to mutation — **mu·ta·bil·i·ty** \ˌmyü-tə-ˈbi-lə-tē\ *n* — **mu·ta·bly** \ˈmyü-tə-blē\ *adv*

mu·ta·gen \ˈmyü-tə-jən\ *n* [ISV *muta*tion + *-gen*] (1933) **:** an agent (as a chemical or various radiations) that tends to increase the frequency or extent of mutation — **mu·ta·gen·ic** \ˌmyü-tə-ˈje-nik\ *adj* — **mu·ta·gen·i·cal·ly** \-ni-k(ə-)lē\ *adv*

mu·ta·gen·e·sis \ˌmyü-tə-ˈje-nə-səs\ *n* [NL] (1948) **:** the occurrence or induction of mutation

mu·ta·ge·nic·i·ty \-jə-ˈni-sə-tē\ *n* (1956) **:** the capacity to induce mutations

mu·tant \ˈmyü-tᵊnt\ *adj* [L *mutant-, mutans,* prp. of *mutare*] (1903) **:** of, relating to, or produced by mutation — **mutant** *n*

mu·tase \ˈmyü-ˌtās, -ˌtāz\ *n* [ISV *mut-* (fr. L *mutare*) + *-ase*] (1938) **:** any of various enzymes that catalyze molecular rearrangements and esp. those involving the transfer of phosphate from one hydroxyl group to another in the same molecule

mu·tate \ˈmyü-ˌtāt, myü-ˈ\ *vb* **mu·tat·ed; mu·tat·ing** [L *mutatus,* pp. of *mutare*] *vi* (1818) **:** to undergo mutation ~ *vt* **:** to cause to undergo mutation — **mu·ta·tive** \ˈmyü-ˌtā-tiv, -tə-tiv\ *adj*

mu·ta·tion \myü-ˈtā-shən\ *n* (14c) **1 :** a significant and basic alteration **:** CHANGE **2 :** UMLAUT **3 a :** a relatively permanent change in hereditary material involving either a physical change in chromosome relations or a biochemical change in the codons that make up genes; *also* **:** the process of producing a mutation **b :** an individual, strain, or trait resulting from mutation — **mu·ta·tion·al** \-shnəl, -shə-nᵊl\ *adj* — **mu·ta·tion·al·ly** *adv*

mu·ta·tis mu·tan·dis \m(y)ü-ˈtä-təs-m(y)ü-ˈtän-dəs, -ˈtā-təs-, -ˈtan-\ *adv* [ME, fr. ML] (15c) **1 :** with the necessary changes having been made **2 :** with the respective differences having been considered

mutch·kin \ˈməch-kən\ *n* [ME (Sc) *muchekyn*] (15c) **:** a Scottish unit of liquid capacity equal to 0.90 pint (0.42 liter)

[1]**mute** \ˈmyüt\ *adj* **mut·er; mut·est** [ME *muet, mut,* fr. AF, fr. *mu, mute,* fr. L *mutus,* prob. fr. *mu,* representation of a muttered sound] (1513) **1 :** unable to speak **:** lacking the power of speech **2 :** characterized by absence of speech: as **a :** felt or experienced but not expressed ⟨touched her hand in ~ sympathy⟩ **b :** refusing to plead directly or stand trial ⟨the prisoner stands ~⟩ **3 :** remaining silent, undiscovered, or unrecognized **4 a :** contributing nothing to the pronunciation of a word ⟨the *b* in *plumb* is ~⟩ **b :** contributing to the pronunciation of a word but not representing the nucleus of a syllable ⟨the *e* in *mate* is ~⟩ — **mute·ly** *adv* — **mute·ness** *n*

[2]**mute** *n* (1530) **1 :** STOP 9 **2 :** a person who cannot or does not speak **3 :** a device attached to or inserted into a musical instrument to soften or alter its tone

[3]**mute** *vt* **mut·ed; mut·ing** (1883) **1 :** to muffle, reduce, or eliminate the sound of **2 :** to tone down **:** SOFTEN, SUBDUE ⟨~ a color⟩

[4]**mute** *vi* **mut·ed; mut·ing** [ME, fr. AF **meutir,* short for *ameutir,* alter. of OF *esmeltir,* of Gmc origin; akin to MD *smelten* to melt, make fluid, defecate (of birds)] (15c) *of a bird* **:** to evacuate the cloaca

muted *adj* (1855) **1 a :** being mute **:** SILENT **b :** toned down **:** LOW-KEY, SUBDUED **2 :** provided with or produced or modified by the use of a mute — **mut·ed·ly** *adv*

mute swan *n* (1785) **:** a common white swan (*Cygnus olor*) that produces no loud notes, is native to Europe and western Asia, and has been introduced into parts of the U.S.

mu·ti·late \ˈmyü-tə-ˌlāt\ *vt* **-lat·ed; -lat·ing** [L *mutilatus,* pp. of *mutilare,* fr. *mutilus* truncated, maimed] (1534) **1 :** to cut up or alter radically so as to make imperfect ⟨the child *mutilated* the book with his scissors⟩ **2 :** to cut off or permanently destroy a limb or essential part of **:** CRIPPLE ***syn*** see MAIM — **mu·ti·la·tion** \ˌmyü-tə-ˈlā-shən\ *n* — **mu·ti·la·tor** \ˈmyü-tə-ˌlā-tər\ *n*

mu·tine \ˈmyü-tᵊn\ *vi* **mu·tined; mu·tin·ing** [MF (*se*) *mutiner*] (1555) *obs* **:** REBEL, MUTINY

mu·ti·neer \ˌmyü-tə-ˈnir\ *n* (1604) **:** one that mutinies

mu·ti·nous \ˈmyü-tə-nəs, ˈmyüt-nəs\ *adj* (1578) **1 a :** disposed to or being in a state of mutiny **:** REBELLIOUS ⟨a ~ crew⟩ **b :** TURBULENT, UNRULY **2 :** of, relating to, or constituting mutiny ⟨~ threats⟩ — **mu·ti·nous·ly** *adv* — **mu·ti·nous·ness** *n*

mu·ti·ny \ˈmyü-tə-nē, ˈmyüt-nē\ *n, pl* **-nies** [*mutine* to rebel, fr. MF (*se*) *mutiner,* fr. *mutin* mutinous, fr. *meute* revolt, fr. VL **movita,* fr. fem. of *movitus,* alter. of L *motus,* pp. of *movēre* to move] (1540) **1** *obs* **:** TUMULT, STRIFE **2 :** forcible or passive resistance to lawful authority; *esp* **:** concerted revolt (as of a naval crew) against discipline or a superior officer ***syn*** see REBELLION — **mutiny** *vi*

mut·ism \ˈmyü-ˌti-zəm\ *n* [F *mutisme,* fr. L *mutus* mute] (1824) **:** the condition of being mute

mutt \ˈmət\ *n* [short for *muttonhead* dull-witted person] (1899) **1 :** a stupid or insignificant person **:** FOOL **2 :** a mongrel dog **:** CUR

mut·ter \ˈmə-tər\ *vb* [ME *muteren,* of imit. origin] *vi* (14c) **1 :** to utter sounds or words indistinctly or with a low voice and with the lips partly closed **2 :** to murmur complainingly or angrily **:** GRUMBLE ~ *vt* **:** to utter esp. in a low or imperfectly articulated manner — **mutter** *n* — **mut·ter·er** \-tər-ər\ *n*

mut·ton \ˈmə-tᵊn\ *n* [ME *motoun,* mutton, sheep, fr. AF *mutun* ram, sheep, mutton, of Celt origin; akin to OIr *molt* wether] (13c) **:** the flesh of a mature sheep used for food — **mut·tony** \ˈmə-tᵊn-ē, ˈmət-nē\ *adj*

mut·ton·chops \ˈmə-tᵊn-ˌchäps\ *n pl* (1865) **:** side-whiskers that are narrow at the temple and broad and round by the lower jaws — called also *muttonchop whiskers*

mut·ton·fish \-ˌfish\ *n* [fr. its flavor] (1735) **:** a common snapper (*Lutjanus analis*) of the warmer parts of the western Atlantic that is usu. olive green and sometimes nearly white or tinged with rosy red and that is an important food and sport fish — called also *mutton snapper*

mu·tu·al \ˈmyü-chə-wəl, -chəl, -chü-əl; ˈmyüch-wəl\ *adj* [MF *mutuel,* fr. L *mutuus* lent, borrowed, mutual, fr. *mutare* to change — more at MUTABLE] (15c) **1 a :** directed by each toward the other or the others ⟨~ affection⟩ **b :** having the same feelings one for the other ⟨they had long been ~ enemies⟩ **c :** shared in common ⟨enjoying their ~ hobby⟩ **d :** JOINT **2 :** characterized by intimacy **3 :** of or relating to a plan whereby the members of an organization share in the profits and expenses; *specif* **:** of, relating to, or taking the form of an insurance method in which the policyholders constitute the members of the insuring company — **mu·tu·al·ly** *adv*

mutual fund *n* (1934) **:** an open-end investment company that invests money of its shareholders in a usu. diversified group of securities of other corporations

mu·tu·al·ism \ˈmyü-chə-wə-ˌli-zəm, ˈmyü-chə-ˌli-, ˈmyüch-wə-ˌli-\ *n* (1849) **1 :** the doctrine or practice of mutual dependence as the condition of individual and social welfare **2 :** mutually beneficial association between different kinds of organisms — **mu·tu·al·ist** \-list\ *n* — **mu·tu·al·is·tic** \ˌmyü-chə-wə-ˈlis-tik, ˌmyü-chə-ˈlis-, ˌmyüch-wə-ˈlis-\ *adj*

mu·tu·al·i·ty \ˌmyü-chə-ˈwa-lə-tē\ *n* (ca. 1586) **1 :** the quality or state of being mutual **2 :** a sharing of sentiments **:** INTIMACY

mu·tu·al·ize \ˈmyü-chə-wə-ˌlīz, ˈmyü-chə-ˌlīz, ˈmyüch-wə-ˌlīz\ *vt* **-ized; -iz·ing** (1812) **:** to make mutual — **mu·tu·al·i·za·tion** \ˌmyü-chə-wə-lə-ˈzā-shən, ˌmyü-chə-lə-, ˌmyüch-wə-lə-\ *n*

mutually exclusive *adj* (1874) **:** being related such that each excludes or precludes the other ⟨*mutually exclusive* events⟩; *also* **:** INCOMPATIBLE ⟨their outlooks were not *mutually exclusive*⟩

mu·tu·el \ˈmyü-chə-wəl, -chəl, -chü-əl; ˈmyüch-wəl\ *n* (1908) **:** PARI-MUTUEL

muu·muu \ˈmü-ˌmü\ *n* [Hawaiian *mu'umu'u,* fr. *mu'umu'u* cut off] (1923) **:** a loose often long dress having bright colors and patterns and adapted from the dresses orig. distributed by missionaries to the native women of Hawaii

Mu·zak \ˈmyü-ˌzak\ *trademark* — used for recorded background music

mu·zhik *also* **mou·jik** *or* **mu·jik** \mü-ˈzhēk, -ˈzhik\ *n* [Russ] (1568) **:** a Russian peasant

[1]**muz·zle** \ˈmə-zəl\ *n* [ME *mosel,* fr. MF *musel,* fr. OF **mus* mouth of an animal, fr. ML *musus*] (15c) **1 :** the projecting jaws and nose of an animal **:** SNOUT **2 a :** a fastening or covering for the mouth of an animal used to prevent eating or biting **b :** something (as censorship) that restrains normal expression **3 :** the open end of an implement; *esp* **:** the discharging end of a weapon

[2]**muzzle** *vt* **muz·zled; muz·zling** \ˈməz-liŋ, ˈmə-zə-\ (15c) **1 :** to fit with a muzzle **2 a :** GAG ⟨*muzzled* the regime's critics⟩ **b :** RESTRAIN, RESTRICT ⟨the Pentagon's efforts to ~ press access —Joe Strupp⟩ ⟨the low prices *muzzled* competition⟩ — **muz·zler** \-lər\ *n*

muz·zy \ˈmə-zē\ *adj* **muz·zi·er; -est** [perh. blend of *muddled* and *fuzzy*] (ca. 1728) **1 a :** deficient in brightness **:** DULL, GLOOMY ⟨a ~ day⟩ **b :** lacking in clarity and precision ⟨his conclusions can be ~ and naive —*Times Lit. Supp.*⟩ **2 :** muddled or confused in mind — **muz·zi·ly** \ˈmə-zə-lē\ *adv* — **muz·zi·ness** \ˈmə-zē-nəs\ *n*

mv *or* **mV** *abbr* millivolt

MV *abbr* **1** main verb **2** mean variation **3** motor vessel

MVD *abbr* [Russ *Ministerstvo vnutrennikh del*] Ministry of Internal Affairs

MVP *abbr* most valuable player

mW *abbr* milliwatt

MW *abbr* megawatt

MWe *abbr* megawatts electric

MX \ˌem-ˈeks\ *n* [*m*issile, e*x*perimental] (1976) **:** a mobile ICBM having up to 10 independently targeted nuclear warheads

[1]**my** \ˈmī, mə\ *adj* [ME, fr. OE *mīn,* fr. *mīn,* suppletive gen. of *ic* I; akin to OE *mē* me] (12c) **1 :** of or relating to me or myself esp. as possessor, agent, object of an action, or familiar person ⟨~ car⟩ ⟨~ injuries⟩ ⟨~ man⟩ **2** — used interjectionally to express surprise and sometimes reduplicated ⟨~ oh ~⟩; used also interjectionally with names of various parts of the body to express doubt or disapproval ⟨~ foot⟩

[2]**my** *abbr* million years

my- *or* **myo-** *comb form* [NL, fr. Gk, fr. *mys* mouse, muscle — more at MOUSE] **:** muscle ⟨*myo*globin⟩ **:** muscle and ⟨*myo*neural⟩

mya *abbr* million years ago

my·al·gia \mī-ˈal-j(ē-)ə\ *n* [NL] (1860) **:** pain in one or more muscles — **my·al·gic** \-jik\ *adj*

my·as·the·nia \ˌmī-əs-ˈthē-nē-ə\ *n* [NL] (ca. 1856) **:** muscular debility; *also* **:** MYASTHENIA GRAVIS — **my·as·then·ic** \-ˈthe-nik\ *adj or n*

myasthenia gra·vis \-ˈgra-vəs, -ˈgrä-\ *n* [NL, lit., grave myasthenia] (1900) **:** a disease characterized by progressive weakness and exhaustibility of voluntary muscles without atrophy or sensory disturbance and caused by an autoimmune attack on acetylcholine receptors at the neuromuscular junction

myc- *or* **myco-** *comb form* [NL, fr. Gk *mykēt-, mykēs* fungus; akin to Gk *myxa* nasal mucus] **:** fungus ⟨*myco*logy⟩ ⟨*myc*osis⟩

my·ce·li·um \mī-ˈsē-lē-əm\ *n, pl* **-lia** \-lē-ə\ [NL, fr. *myc-* + Gk *hēlos* nail, wart, callus] (1836) **:** the mass of interwoven filamentous hyphae that forms esp. the vegetative portion of the thallus of a fungus and is often submerged in another body (as of soil or organic matter or the tissues of a host); *also* **:** a similar mass of filaments formed by some bacteria (as streptomyces) — **my·ce·li·al** \-əl\ *adj*

My·ce·nae·an \ˌmī-sə-ˈnē-ən\ *also* **My·ce·ni·an** \mī-ˈsē-nē-ən\ *adj* (1598) **1 :** of, relating to, or characteristic of Mycenae, its people, or the period (1400 to 1100 B.C.) of Mycenae's political ascendancy **2 :** characteristic of the Bronze Age Mycenaean culture of the eastern Mediterranean area — **Mycenaean** *n*

my·ce·to·ma \ˌmī-sə-ˈtō-mə\ *n, pl* **-mas** *also* **-ma·ta** \-mə-tə\ [NL, fr. Gk *mykēt-, mykēs*] (1863) **:** a condition marked by invasion of the deep subcutaneous tissues with fungi or actinomycetes; *also* **:** a tumorous mass occurring in mycetoma — **my·ce·to·ma·tous** \-mə-təs\ *adj*

my·ce·to·zo·an \mī-ˌsē-tə-ˈzō-ən\ *n* [NL *Mycetozoa,* order of protozoans, fr. Gk *mykēt-, mykēs* + NL *-zoa*] (1881) **:** SLIME MOLD — **mycetozoan** *adj*

-mycin *n comb form* [*streptomycin*] **:** substance obtained from a fungus-like bacterium ⟨erythro*mycin*⟩

my·co·bac·te·ri·um \ˌmī-kō-bak-ˈtir-ē-əm\ *n* [NL] (1909) **:** any of a genus (*Mycobacterium*) of nonmotile aerobic acid-fast bacteria that include numerous saprophytes and the pathogens causing tuberculosis and leprosy — **my·co·bac·te·ri·al** \-ē-əl\ *adj*

my·co·flo·ra \ˌmī-kə-ˈflōr-ə\ *n* [NL] (1945) **:** the fungi characteristic of a region or special environment

mycol *abbr* mycology

my·col·o·gy \mī-ˈkä-lə-jē\ *n* [NL *mycologia,* fr. *myc-* + L *-logia* -logy] (1836) **1 :** a branch of biology dealing with fungi **2 :** fungal life — **my·co·log·i·cal** \ˌmī-kə-ˈlä-ji-kəl\ *adj* — **my·co·log·i·cal·ly** \ˌmī-kə-ˈlä-ji-k(ə-)lē\ *adv* — **my·col·o·gist** \mī-ˈkä-lə-jist\ *n*

my·coph·a·gist \mī-ˈkä-fə-jist\ *n* [*mycophagy,* fr. *myc-* + *-phagy*] (1861) **:** one that eats fungi (as mushrooms) — **my·coph·a·gy** \-jē\ *n*

my·coph·a·gous \-gəs\ *adj* (ca. 1909) **:** feeding on fungi

my·co·phile \ˈmī-kō-ˌfī(-ə)l\ *n* (1885) **:** a devotee of mushrooms; *esp* **:** one whose hobby is hunting wild edible mushrooms

my·co·plas·ma \ˌmī-kō-ˈplaz-mə\ *n, pl* **-mas** *also* **-ma·ta** \-mə-tə\ [NL] (1955) **:** any of a genus (*Mycoplasma* of the family Mycoplasmataceae) of pleomorphic gram-negative chiefly nonmotile bacteria that lack a cell wall and are mostly parasitic usu. in mammals — called also *pleuropneumonia-like organism* — **my·co·plas·mal** \-məl\ *adj*

mycoplasma–like organism *n* (1967) **:** PHYTOPLASMA

my·cor·rhi·za \ˌmī-kə-ˈrī-zə\ *n, pl* **-zae** \-ˌzē\ *also* **-zas** [NL, fr. *myc-* + Gk *rhiza* root — more at ROOT] (1895) **:** the symbiotic association of the mycelium of a fungus with the roots of a seed plant — **my·cor·rhi·zal** \-zəl\ *adj*

my·co·sis \mī-ˈkō-səs\ *n, pl* **my·co·ses** \-ˌsēz\ [NL] (1876) **:** infection with or disease caused by a fungus — **my·cot·ic** \-ˈkä-tik\ *adj*

my·co·tox·in \ˌmī-kə-ˈtäk-sən\ *n* (1962) **:** a toxic substance produced by a fungus and esp. a mold

my·dri·a·sis \mə-ˈdrī-ə-səs\ *n* [L, fr. Gk] (ca. 1775) **:** excessive or prolonged dilatation of the pupil of the eye — **myd·ri·at·ic** \ˌmi-drē-ˈa-tik\ *adj or n*

myel- *or* **myelo-** *comb form* [NL, fr. Gk, fr. *myelos,* prob. fr. *myōn* cluster of muscles, fr. *mys* mouse, muscle — more at MOUSE] **:** bone marrow **:** spinal cord ⟨*myel*encephalon⟩

my·e·len·ceph·a·lon \ˌmī-ə-len-ˈse-fə-ˌlän, -lən\ *n* [NL] (1871) **:** the posterior part of the developing vertebrate hindbrain or the corresponding part of the adult brain composed of the medulla oblongata — **my·e·len·ce·phal·ic** \-ˌlen(t)-sə-ˈfa-lik\ *adj*

my·e·lin \ˈmī-ə-lən\ *n* [ISV] (1873) **:** a soft white somewhat fatty material that forms a thick layer around the axons of some neurons — **my·e·lin·ic** \ˌmī-ə-ˈli-nik\ *adj*

my·e·lin·at·ed \ˈmī-ə-lə-ˌnā-təd\ *adj* (1899) **:** having a myelin sheath ⟨∼ nerve fibers⟩

myelin sheath *n* (1891) **:** a layer of myelin surrounding the axons of some neurons — called also *medullary sheath*

my·e·li·tis \ˌmī-ə-ˈlī-təs\ *n, pl* **-lit·i·des** \-ˈli-tə-ˌdēz\ [NL] (1835) **:** inflammation of the spinal cord or of the bone marrow

my·e·lo·blast \ˈmī-ə-lə-ˌblast\ *n* [ISV] (ca. 1904) **:** a large mononuclear nongranular bone-marrow cell; *esp* **:** one that is a precursor of a myelocyte — **my·e·lo·blas·tic** \ˌmī-ə-lə-ˈblas-tik\ *adj*

my·e·lo·cyte \ˈmī-ə-lə-ˌsīt\ *n* [ISV] (1891) **:** a bone-marrow cell; *esp* **:** a motile cell with cytoplasmic granules that gives rise to the granulocytes of the blood and occurs abnormally in the circulating blood — **my·e·lo·cyt·ic** \ˌmī-ə-lə-ˈsi-tik\ *adj*

my·e·lo·fi·bro·sis \ˌmī-ə-lō-fī-ˈbrō-səs\ *n* [NL] (1937) **:** an anemic condition in which bone marrow becomes fibrotic and the liver and spleen usu. exhibit a development of blood-cell precursors — **my·e·lo·fi·brot·ic** \-ˈbrä-tik\ *adj*

my·e·log·e·nous \ˌmī-ə-ˈlä-jə-nəs\ *adj* [ISV] (1876) **:** of, relating to, originating in, or produced by the bone marrow ⟨∼ sarcoma⟩

myelogenous leukemia *n* (1904) **:** leukemia characterized by proliferation of myeloid tissue (as of the bone marrow and spleen) and an abnormal increase in the number of granulocytes, myelocytes, and myeloblasts in the circulating blood — called also *myelocytic leukemia, myeloid leukemia*

my·e·loid \ˈmī-ə-ˌlȯid\ *adj* [ISV] (1857) **:** of, relating to, or resembling bone marrow

my·e·lo·ma \ˌmī-ə-ˈlō-mə\ *n, pl* **-mas** *also* **-ma·ta** \-mə-tə\ [NL] (ca. 1857) **:** a primary tumor of the bone marrow — **my·e·lo·ma·tous** \-mə-təs\ *adj*

my·e·lop·a·thy \-ˈlä-pə-thē\ *n, pl* **-thies** [ISV] (ca. 1891) **:** a disease or disorder of the spinal cord or bone marrow — **my·e·lo·path·ic** \ˌmī-ə-lō-ˈpa-thik\ *adj*

my·e·lo·pro·lif·er·a·tive \ˈmī-ə-lō-prə-ˈli-f(ə-)rə-tiv, -fə-ˌrā-\ *adj* (1951) **:** of, relating to, or being a disorder (as leukemia) marked by excessive proliferation of bone marrow elements and esp. blood cell precursors

my·ia·sis \mī-ˈī-ə-səs, mē-\ *n, pl* **my·ia·ses** \-ˌsēz\ [NL, fr. Gk *myia* fly — more at MIDGE] (1837) **:** infestation with fly maggots

My·lar \ˈmī-ˌlär\ *trademark* — used for a polyester film

my·nah *or* **my·na** \ˈmī-nə\ *n* [Hindi & Urdu *mainā* hill mynah, fr. Skt *madana,* a kind of bird] (1769) **:** any of various Asian starlings (esp. genera *Acridotheres, Gracula,* and *Sturnus*); *esp* **:** a dark brown slightly crested bird (*A. tristis*) of southeastern Asia with a white tail tip and wing markings and bright yellow bill and feet — compare HILL MYNAH

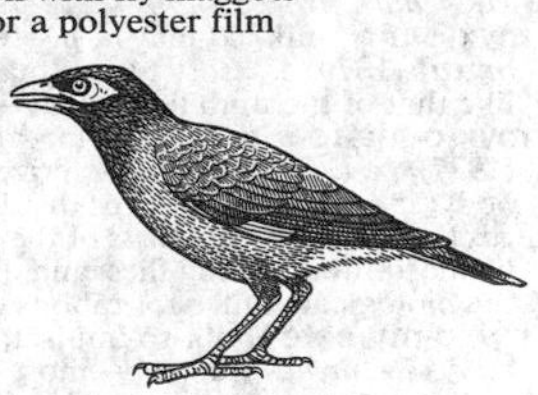

mynah

myn·heer \mə-ˈner\ *n* [D *mijnheer,* fr. *mijn* my + *heer* master, sir] (1652) **:** a male Netherlander — used as a title equivalent to *Mr.*

myo- — see MY-

myo·blast \ˈmī-ə-ˌblast\ *n* [ISV] (1884) **:** an undifferentiated cell capable of giving rise to muscle cells

myocardial infarction *n* (1927) **:** HEART ATTACK

myo·car·di·tis \ˌmī-ə-(ˌ)kär-ˈdī-təs\ *n* [NL] (1866) **:** inflammation of the myocardium

myo·car·di·um \ˌmī-ə-ˈkär-dē-əm\ *n* [NL, fr. *my-* + Gk *kardia* heart — more at HEART] (1879) **:** the middle muscular layer of the heart wall — **myo·car·di·al** \-dē-əl\ *adj*

my·oc·lo·nus \ˌmī-ˈä-klə-nəs\ *n* [NL] (1883) **:** irregular involuntary contraction of a muscle usu. resulting from functional disorder of controlling motor neurons; *also* **:** a condition characterized by myoclonus — **myo·clon·ic** \ˌmī-ə-ˈklä-nik\ *adj*

myo·elec·tric \ˌmī-ō-i-ˈlek-trik\ *also* **myo·elec·tri·cal** \-tri-kəl\ *adj* (ca. 1919) **:** of, relating to, or utilizing electricity generated by muscle

myo·fi·bril \ˌmī-ə-ˈfī-brəl, -ˈfi-\ *n* [NL *myofibrilla,* fr. *my-* + *fibrilla* fibril] (1898) **:** any of the longitudinal parallel contractile elements of a muscle cell that are composed of myosin and actin — **myo·fi·bril·lar** \-brə-lər\ *adj*

myo·fil·a·ment \-ˈfi-lə-mənt\ *n* (1949) **:** one of the individual filaments of actin or myosin that make up a myofibril

myo·gen·ic \-ˈje-nik\ *adj* [ISV] (1904) **:** taking place or functioning in ordered rhythmic fashion because of the inherent properties of cardiac muscle rather than specific neural stimuli ⟨a ∼ heartbeat⟩

myo·glo·bin \-ˈglō-bən, ˈmī-ə-ˌ\ *n* [ISV] (1925) **:** a red iron-containing protein pigment in muscles that is similar to hemoglobin

myo·ino·si·tol \ˌmī-ō-i-ˈnō-sə-ˌtȯl, -ˌtōl\ *n* (1951) **:** a biologically active inositol that is a component of many phospholipids and occurs widely in plants, animals, and microorganisms

my·ol·o·gy \mī-ˈä-lə-jē\ *n* [F or NL; F *myologie,* fr. NL *myologia,* fr. *my-* + L *-logia* -logy] (1649) **:** the scientific study of muscles

my·o·ma \mī-ˈō-mə\ *n, pl* **-mas** *also* **-ma·ta** \-mə-tə\ [NL] (1875) **:** a tumor consisting of muscle tissue — **my·o·ma·tous** \-mə-təs\ *adj*

myo·mec·to·my \ˌmī-ə-ˈmek-tə-mē\ *n, pl* **-mies** (1886) **:** surgical removal of a myoma or fibroid

myo·neu·ral \ˌmī-ə-ˈnu̇r-əl, -ˈnyu̇r-\ *adj* (1905) **:** of, relating to, or connecting muscles and nerves ⟨∼ junctions⟩

my·op·a·thy \mī-ˈä-pə-thē\ *n, pl* **-thies** [ISV] (ca. 1849) **:** a disorder of muscle tissue or muscles — **myo·path·ic** \ˌmī-ə-ˈpa-thik\ *adj*

my·ope \ˈmī-ˌōp\ *n* [F, fr. LL *myops* myopic, fr. Gk *myōps,* fr. *myein* to be closed + *ōps* eye, face — more at EYE] (1728) **:** a myopic person

my·o·pia \mī-ˈō-pē-ə\ *n* [NL, fr. Gk *myōpia,* fr. *myōp-, myōps*] (ca. 1752) **1 :** a condition in which the visual images come to a focus in front of the retina of the eye resulting esp. in defective vision of distant objects **2 :** a lack of foresight or discernment **:** a narrow view of something — **my·o·pic** \-ˈō-pik, -ˈä-\ *adj* — **my·o·pi·cal·ly** \-pi-k(ə-)lē\ *adv*

my·o·sin \ˈmī-ə-sən\ *n* [ISV *my-* + 2*-ose* + 1*-in*] (1942) **:** a fibrous globulin of muscle that can split ATP and that reacts with actin in muscle contraction to form actomyosin

myosis, myotic *var of* MIOSIS, MIOTIC

myo·si·tis \ˌmī-ə-ˈsī-təs\ *n* [NL, irreg. fr. Gk *mys* muscle, mouse] (ca. 1819) **:** soreness of voluntary muscle due to inflammation

myo·tome \ˈmī-ə-ˌtōm\ *n* [ISV] (1894) **:** the portion of an embryonic somite from which skeletal musculature is produced

myo·to·nia \ˌmī-ə-ˈtō-nē-ə\ *n* [NL] (1886) **:** tonic spasm of one or more muscles; *also* **:** a condition characterized by such spasms — **myo·ton·ic** \-ˈtä-nik\ *adj*

myotonic dystrophy *n* (1963) **:** a muscular disorder that is characterized by dystrophic muscle weakness and myotonia affecting multiple bodily systems and that is caused by an abnormally high number of repeats of a codon in the genetic material

Myr *abbr* million years

1**myr·i·ad** \ˈmir-ē-əd\ *n* [Gk *myriad-, myrias,* fr. *myrioi* countless, ten thousand] (1555) **1 :** ten thousand **2 :** a great number ⟨a ∼ of ideas⟩
usage Recent criticism of the use of *myriad* as a noun, both in the plural form *myriads* and in the phrase *a myriad of,* seems to reflect a mistaken belief that the word was originally and is still properly only an adjective. As the entries here show, however, the noun is in fact the older form, dating to the 16th century. The noun *myriad* has appeared in the works of such writers as Milton (plural *myriads*) and Thoreau (*a myriad of*), and it continues to occur frequently in reputable English. There is no reason to avoid it.

2**myriad** *adj* (1765) **1 :** INNUMERABLE ⟨those ∼ problems⟩; *also* **:** both numerous and diverse ⟨∼ topics⟩ **2 :** having innumerable aspects or elements ⟨the ∼ activity of the new land —Meridel Le Sueur⟩

myr·ia·pod *also* **myr·io·pod** \ˈmir-ē-ə-ˌpäd\ *n* [ultim. fr. Gk *myrioi* + *pod-, pous* foot — more at FOOT] (1826) **:** any of a group (Myriapoda) of arthropods having the body made up of numerous similar segments nearly all of which bear true jointed legs and including the millipedes and centipedes — **myriapod** *also* **myriopod** *adj*

my·ris·tic acid \mə-ˈris-tik-, mī-\ *n* [ISV, fr. NL *Myristica,* genus of trees] (1841) **:** a crystalline fatty acid $C_{14}H_{28}O_{2}$ occurring esp. in the form of glycerides in most fats

myrmeco- *comb form* [Gk *myrmēko-,* fr. *myrmēk-, myrmēx* — more at PISMIRE] **:** ant ⟨*myrmeco*philous⟩

myr·me·col·o·gy \ˌmər-mə-ˈkä-lə-jē\ *n* [ISV] (ca. 1902) **:** the scientific study of ants — **myr·me·co·log·i·cal** \-kə-ˈlä-ji-kəl\ *adj* — **myr·me·col·o·gist** \-ˈkä-lə-jist\ *n*

myr·me·co·phile \ˈmər-mi-kə-ˌfī(-ə)l\ *n* [ISV] (1898) **:** an organism that habitually shares an ant nest

myr·me·coph·i·lous \ˌmər-mə-ˈkä-fə-ləs\ *adj* (1866) **:** fond of, associated with, or benefited by ants

myr·mi·don \ˈmər-mə-ˌdän, -dən\ *n* [ME *Mirmydon,* L *Myrmidon-, Myrmido,* fr. Gk *Myrmidōn*] (15c) **1** *cap* **:** a member of a legendary Thessalian people who accompanied their king Achilles in the Trojan War **2 :** a loyal follower; *esp* **:** a subordinate who executes orders unquestioningly or unscrupulously

myrrh \ˈmər\ *n* [ME *myrre,* fr. OE, fr. L *myrrha,* fr. Gk, of Sem origin; akin to Ar *murr* myrrh] (bef. 12c) **:** a yellowish-brown to reddish-brown aromatic gum resin with a bitter slightly pungent taste obtained from a tree (esp. *Commiphora abyssinica* of the family Burseraceae) of eastern Africa and Arabia; *also* **:** a mixture of myrrh and labdanum

myr·tle \ˈmər-tᵊl\ *n, often attrib* [ME *mirtille,* fr. AF, fr. ML *myrtillus,* fr. L *myrtus,* fr. Gk *myrtos*] (1562) **1 a :** a common evergreen bushy shrub (*Myrtus communis* of the family Myrtaceae, the myrtle family) of southern Europe with oval to lance-shaped shiny leaves, fragrant white or rosy flowers, and black berries **b :** any of the chiefly tropical shrubs or trees comprising the myrtle family **2 a :** 1PERIWINKLE 1a **b :** CALIFORNIA LAUREL

my·self \mī-ˈself, mə-, *Southern also* -ˈsef\ *pron* (bef. 12c) **1 :** that identical one that is I — used reflexively ⟨I'm going to get ∼ a new suit⟩, for emphasis ⟨I ∼ will go⟩, or in absolute constructions ⟨∼ a tourist, I nevertheless avoided other tourists⟩ **2 :** my normal, healthy, or sane condition ⟨didn't feel ∼ yesterday⟩
usage *Myself* is often used where *I* or *me* might be expected: as subject ⟨to wonder what *myself* will say —Emily Dickinson⟩ ⟨others and *myself* continued to press for the legislation⟩, after *as, than,* or *like* ⟨an

\ə\ **abut** \ᵊ\ kitten, F table \ər\ **further** \a\ **ash** \ā\ **ace** \ä\ **mop, mar**
\au̇\ **out** \ch\ **chin** \e\ **bet** \ē\ **easy** \g\ **go** \i\ **hit** \ī\ **ice** \j\ **job**
\ŋ\ **sing** \ō\ **go** \ȯ\ **law** \ȯi\ **boy** \th\ **thin** \t͟h\ **the** \ü\ **loot** \u̇\ **foot**
\y\ **yet** \zh\ **vision, beige** \k̲, ⁿ, œ, ue, ʸ\ *see* Guide to Pronunciation

aversion to paying such people as *myself* to tutor⟩ ⟨was enough to make a better man than *myself* quail⟩ ⟨old-timers like *myself*⟩, and as object ⟨now here you see *myself* with the diver⟩ ⟨for my wife and *myself* it was a happy time⟩. Such uses almost always occur when the speaker or writer is referring to himself or herself as an object of discourse rather than as a participant in discourse. The other reflexive personal pronouns are similarly but less frequently used in the same circumstances. Critics have frowned on these uses since about the turn of the century, prob. unaware that they serve a definite purpose. Users themselves are as unaware as the critics—they simply follow their instincts. These uses are standard.

mys·ta·gogue \'mis-tə-ˌgäg\ *n* [L *mystagogus*, fr. Gk *mystagōgos*, fr. *mystēs* initiate (perh. akin to Gk *myein* to be closed) + *agein* to lead — more at AGENT] (ca. 1550)   **1** : one who initiates another into a mystery cult   **2** : one who understands or teaches mystical doctrines — **mys·ta·go·gy** \-ˌgä-jē, -ˌgō-\ *n*

mys·te·ri·ous \mis-'tir-ē-əs\ *adj* (1599)   **1 a** : of, relating to, or constituting mystery ⟨the ~ ways of God⟩   **b** : exciting wonder, curiosity, or surprise while baffling efforts to comprehend or identify : MYSTIFYING ⟨heard a ~ noise⟩ ⟨a ~ stranger⟩   **2** : stirred by or attracted to the inexplicable — **mys·te·ri·ous·ly** *adv* — **mys·te·ri·ous·ness** *n*

¹mys·tery \'mis-t(ə-)rē\ *n, pl* **-ter·ies** [ME *mysterie*, fr. L *mysterium*, fr. Gk *mystērion*, fr. *mystēs* initiate] (14c)   **1 a** : a religious truth that one can know only by revelation and cannot fully understand   **b** (1) : any of the 15 events (as the Nativity, the Crucifixion, or the Assumption) serving as a subject for meditation during the saying of the rosary   (2) *cap* : a Christian sacrament; *specif* : EUCHARIST   **c** (1) : a secret religious rite believed (as in Eleusinian and Mithraic cults) to impart enduring bliss to the initiate   (2) : a cult devoted to such rites   **2 a** : something not understood or beyond understanding : ENIGMA   **b** *obs* : a private secret   **c** : the secret or specialized practices or ritual peculiar to an occupation or a body of people ⟨the *mysteries* of the tailor's craft⟩   **d** : a piece of fiction dealing usu. with the solution of a mysterious crime   **3** : profound, inexplicable, or secretive quality or character ⟨the ~ of her smile⟩

syn MYSTERY, PROBLEM, ENIGMA, RIDDLE, PUZZLE mean something which baffles or perplexes. MYSTERY applies to what cannot be fully understood by reason or less strictly to whatever resists or defies explanation ⟨the *mystery* of the stone monoliths⟩. PROBLEM applies to a question or difficulty calling for a solution or causing concern ⟨*problems* created by high technology⟩. ENIGMA applies to utterance or behavior that is very difficult to interpret ⟨his suicide remains an *enigma*⟩. RIDDLE suggests an enigma or problem involving paradox or apparent contradiction ⟨the *riddle* of the reclusive pop star⟩. PUZZLE applies to an enigma or problem that challenges ingenuity for its solution ⟨the thief's motives were a *puzzle* for the police⟩.

²mystery *n, pl* **-ter·ies** [ME ministry, office, craft, fr. AF *mesterie*, fr. LL *misterium, mysterium*, alter. of *ministerium* service, occupation, fr. *minister* servant — more at MINISTER] (14c)   **1** *archaic* : TRADE, CRAFT   **2** *archaic* : a body of persons engaged in a particular trade, business, or profession : GUILD   **3** : MYSTERY PLAY

mystery play *n* [²*mystery*] (1852) : a medieval drama based on scriptural incidents (as the creation of the world, the Flood, or the life, death, and resurrection of Christ) — compare MIRACLE PLAY

¹mys·tic \'mis-tik\ *adj* [ME *mistik*, fr. L *mysticus* of mysteries, fr. Gk *mystikos*, fr. *mystēs* initiate] (14c)   **1** : MYSTICAL 1a   **2** : of or relating to mysteries or esoteric rites : OCCULT   **3** : of or relating to mysticism or mystics   **4 a** : MYSTERIOUS   **b** : OBSCURE, ENIGMATIC   **c** : inducing a feeling of awe or wonder   **d** : having magical properties

²mystic *n* (1679)   **1** : a follower of a mystical way of life   **2** : an advocate of a theory of mysticism

mys·ti·cal \'mis-ti-kəl\ *adj* (15c)   **1 a** : having a spiritual meaning or reality that is neither apparent to the senses nor obvious to the intelligence ⟨the ~ food of the sacrament⟩   **b** : involving or having the nature of an individual's direct subjective communion with God or ultimate reality ⟨the ~ experience of the Inner Light⟩   **2** : MYSTERIOUS, UNINTELLIGIBLE   **3 a** : MYSTIC 2   **b** : MYSTIC 3 — **mys·ti·cal·ly** \-k(ə-)lē\ *adv*

mys·ti·cism \'mis-tə-ˌsi-zəm\ *n* (1735)   **1** : the experience of mystical union or direct communion with ultimate reality reported by mystics   **2** : the belief that direct knowledge of God, spiritual truth, or ultimate reality can be attained through subjective experience (as intuition or insight)   **3 a** : vague speculation : a belief without sound basis   **b** : a theory postulating the possibility of direct and intuitive acquisition of ineffable knowledge or power

mys·ti·fi·ca·tion \ˌmis-tə-fə-'kā-shən\ *n* (1815)   **1 a** : an act or instance of mystifying   **b** : an obscuring esp. of capitalist or social dynamics (as by making them equivalent to natural laws) that is seen in Marxist thought as an impediment to critical consciousness ⟨the ~ of the sources of wealth —Henry Staten⟩   **2** : the quality or state of being mystified   **3** : something designed to mystify

mys·ti·fy \'mis-tə-ˌfī\ *vt* **-fied; -fy·ing** [F *mistifier*, fr. *mystère* mystery, fr. L *mysterium*] (1814)   **1** : to perplex the mind of : BEWILDER   **2** : to

make mysterious or obscure ⟨~ an interpretation of a prophecy⟩ — **mys·ti·fi·er** \-ˌfī(-ə)r\ *n* — **mys·ti·fy·ing·ly** \-ˌfī-iŋ-lē\ *adv*

mys·tique \mi-'stēk\ *n* [F, fr. *mystique*, adj., mystic, fr. L *mysticus*] (1891)   **1** : an air or attitude of mystery and reverence developing around something or someone   **2** : the special esoteric skill essential in a calling or activity

myth \'mith\ *n* [Gk *mythos*] (1830)   **1 a** : a usu. traditional story of ostensibly historical events that serves to unfold part of the world view of a people or explain a practice, belief, or natural phenomenon   **b** : PARABLE, ALLEGORY   **2 a** : a popular belief or tradition that has grown up around something or someone; *esp* : one embodying the ideals and institutions of a society or segment of society ⟨seduced by the American ~ of individualism —Orde Coombs⟩   **b** : an unfounded or false notion   **3** : a person or thing having only an imaginary or unverifiable existence   **4** : the whole body of myths

myth·i·cal \'mi-thi-kəl\ *or* **myth·ic** \-thik\ *adj* (1669)   **1** : based on or described in a myth esp. as contrasted with history   **2** *usu mythical* : existing only in the imagination : FICTITIOUS, IMAGINARY ⟨constructed a ~ all-star team⟩   **3** *usu mythic* : having qualities suitable to myth : LEGENDARY ⟨the twilight of a *mythic* professional career —Clayton Riley⟩   *syn* see FICTITIOUS — **myth·i·cal·ly** \-thi-k(ə-)lē\ *adv*

myth·i·cize \'mi-thə-ˌsīz\ *vt* **-cized; -ciz·ing** (1840)   **1** : to turn into or envelop in myth   **2** : to treat as myth — **myth·i·ciz·er** *n*

myth·mak·er \'mith-ˌmā-kər\ *n* (1871) : a creator of myths or of mythical situations or lore — **myth·mak·ing** \-kiŋ\ *n*

my·thog·ra·phy \mi-'thä-grə-fē\ *n* [Gk *mythographia*, fr. *mythos* + *-graphia* -graphy] (1851)   **1** : the representation of mythical subjects in art   **2** : a critical compilation of myths — **my·thog·ra·pher** \-fər\ *n*

myth·o·log·i·cal \ˌmi-thə-'lä-ji-kəl\ *also* **myth·o·log·ic** \-jik\ *adj* (1614)   **1** : of or relating to mythology or myths : dealt with in mythology   **2** : lacking factual basis or historical validity : MYTHICAL, FABULOUS — **myth·o·log·i·cal·ly** \-ji-k(ə-)lē\ *adv*

my·thol·o·gize \mi-'thä-lə-ˌjīz\ *vb* **-gized; -giz·ing** *vt* (1603)   **1** *obs* : to explain the mythological significance of   **2** : to build a myth around : MYTHICIZE ~ *vi*   **1** : to relate, classify, and explain myths   **2** : to create or perpetuate myths — **my·thol·o·giz·er** *n*

my·thol·o·gy \mi-'thä-lə-jē\ *n, pl* **-gies** [F or LL; F *mythologie*, fr. LL *mythologia* interpretation of myths, fr. Gk, legend, myth, fr. *mythologein* to relate myths, fr. *mythos* + *logos* speech — more at LEGEND] (1603)   **1** : an allegorical narrative   **2** : a body of myths: as   **a** : the myths dealing with the gods, demigods, and legendary heroes of a particular people   **b** : MYTHOS 2 ⟨cold war ~⟩   **3** : a branch of knowledge that deals with myth   **4** : a popular belief or assumption that has grown up around someone or something : MYTH 2a ⟨defective *mythologies* that ignore masculine depth of feeling —Robert Bly⟩ — **my·thol·o·ger** \-jər\ *n* — **my·thol·o·gist** \-jist\ *n*

mytho·ma·nia \ˌmi-thə-'mā-nē-ə, -nyə\ *n* [NL, fr. Gk *mythos* + LL *mania* mania] (ca. 1909) : an excessive or abnormal propensity for lying and exaggerating — **mytho·ma·ni·ac** \-nē-ˌak\ *n or adj*

mytho·poe·ia \ˌmi-thə-'pē-ə\ *n* [Gk *mythopoiia*, fr. *mythopoiein* to make a myth, fr. *mythos* + *poiein* to make — more at POET] (1846) : a creating of myth : a giving rise to myths — **mytho·poe·ic** \-'pē-ik\ *also* **mytho·po·et·ic** \-pō-'e-tik\ *or* **mytho·po·et·i·cal** \-ti-kəl\ *adj*

my·thos \'mi-ˌthäs, -ˌthäs\ *n, pl* **my·thoi** \-ˌthói\ [Gk] (1753)   **1 a** : MYTH 1a   **b** : MYTHOLOGY 2a   **2** : a pattern of beliefs expressing often symbolically the characteristic or prevalent attitudes in a group or culture ⟨the starving artist ~⟩   **3** : THEME, PLOT

mythy \'mi-thē\ *adj* (1931) : resembling, concerned with, or of a subject for myth ⟨a ~ theme⟩

my word *interj* (1841) — used to express surprise or astonishment

myx·ede·ma \ˌmik-sə-'dē-mə\ *n* [NL, fr. Gk *myxa* lamp wick, nasal mucus + NL *edema* edema — more at MUCUS] (1877) : severe hypothyroidism characterized by firm inelastic edema, dry skin and hair, and loss of mental and physical vigor — **myx·ede·ma·tous** \-'de-mə-təs, -'dē-\ *adj*

myx·o·ma \mik-'sō-mə\ *n, pl* **-mas** *also* **-ma·ta** \-mə-tə\ [NL, fr. Gk *myxa*] (1870) : a soft tumor made up of gelatinous connective tissue like that of the umbilical cord — **myx·o·ma·tous** \-mə-təs\ *adj*

myx·o·ma·to·sis \mik-ˌsō-mə-'tō-səs\ *n* [NL, fr. *myxomat-, myxoma*] (1927) : a condition characterized by the presence of myxomas in the body; *specif* : a severe virus disease of rabbits that is caused by a poxvirus (species *Myxoma virus* of the genus *Leporipoxvirus*) and transmitted by mosquitoes, biting flies, and direct contact and that has been used in the biological control of rabbits esp. in Australia

myxo·my·cete \ˌmik-sō-'mī-ˌsēt, ˌmik-sō-(ˌ)mī-'\ *n* [ultim. fr. Gk *myxa* + *mykēt-, mykēs* fungus — more at MYC-] (1875) : SLIME MOLD

myxo·vi·rus \'mik-sə-ˌvī-rəs\ *n* [NL, fr. Gk *myxa* + NL *virus* virus; fr. its affinity for certain mucins] (1955) : any of a former family (Myxoviridae) of single-stranded RNA viruses that included the orthomyxoviruses and the paramyxoviruses — **myxo·vi·ral** \ˌmik-sə-'vī-rəl\ *adj*

N

[1]n \ˈen\ *n, pl* **n's** *or* **ns** \ˈenz\ *often cap, often attrib* (bef. 12c) **1 a :** the 14th letter of the English alphabet **b :** a graphic representation of this letter **c :** a speech counterpart of orthographic *n* **2 :** a graphic device for reproducing the letter *n* **3 a :** one designated *n* esp. as the 14th in order or class **b :** an indefinite number; *esp* **:** a constant integer or a variable taking on integral values **4 :** something shaped like the letter N **5 :** the haploid or gametic number of chromosomes **6 :** EN 1
[2]n *abbr* **1** name **2** nano- **3** navy **4** net **5** neuter **6** *usu ital* neutron **7** noon **8** normal **9** north; northern **10** note **11** noun **12** number
[1]N *abbr* newton
[2]N *symbol* nitrogen
-n — see -EN
'n \ən, ᵊn\ *conj* [by shortening] **:** THAN
'n' *also* **'n** \ən, ᵊn\ *conj* **:** AND ⟨fish *'n'* chips⟩
Na *symbol* [NL *natrium*] sodium
NA *abbr* **1** national association **2** no account **3** North America **4** not applicable **5** not available
NAACP *abbr* National Association for the Advancement of Colored People
naan *also* **nan** \ˈnän, ˈnan\ *n* [Hindi & Urdu & Pers; Hindi & Urdu *nān* bread, fr. Pers] (1839) **:** a round flat leavened bread esp. of the Indian subcontinent
nab \ˈnab\ *vt* **nabbed; nab·bing** [perh. alter. of E dial. *nap*] (1686) **1 :** to catch or seize in arrest **:** APPREHEND **2 :** to seize suddenly
nabe \ˈnāb\ *n* [by shortening & alter. fr. *neighborhood*] (1935) **1 :** a neighborhood theater — usu. used in pl. with *the* **2 :** NEIGHBORHOOD 4
na·bob \ˈnā-ˌbäb\ *n* [Hindi *navāb* & Urdu *nawāb,* fr. Ar *nuwwāb,* pl. of *nā'ib* governor] (1612) **1 :** a provincial governor of the Mogul empire in India **2 :** a person of great wealth or prominence
na·celle \nə-ˈsel\ *n* [F, lit., small boat, fr. LL *navicella,* dim. of L *navis* ship — more at NAVE] (1904) **:** a streamlined enclosure (as for an engine) on an aircraft
na·cho \ˈnä-(ˌ)chō\ *n, pl* **nachos** [AmerSp, perh. fr. Sp *nacho* flat-nosed] (1949) **:** a tortilla chip topped with melted cheese and often additional savory toppings (as hot peppers or refried beans)
na·cre \ˈnā-kər\ *n* [F, fr. MF, fr. OIt *naccara* drum, nacre, fr. Ar *naqqāra* drum] (1718) **:** MOTHER-OF-PEARL
na·cre·ous \ˈnā-krē-əs, -k(ə-)rəs\ *adj* (ca. 1828) **:** possessing the qualities of, consisting of, or abounding in nacre; *also* **:** IRIDESCENT
NAD \ˌen-(ˌ)ā-ˈdē\ *n* [*n*icotinamide *a*denine *d*inucleotide] (ca. 1962) **:** a coenzyme $C_{21}H_{27}N_7O_{14}P_2$ of numerous dehydrogenases that occurs in most cells and plays an important role in all phases of intermediary metabolism as an oxidizing agent or when in the reduced form as a reducing agent for various metabolites — called also *nicotinamide adenine dinucleotide, diphosphopyridine nucleotide, DPN*
na·da \ˈnä-də\ *n* [Sp, fr. L *(res) nata* situation, circumstance, lit., a thing come into being] (1867) **:** NOTHING
Na–Dene \nä-ˈdā-(ˌ)nā, -ˈde-, -nē\ *n* [*na-* (fr. Haida *na* to dwell & Tlingit *na* people) + *Dene* Déné] (1915) **:** a hypothetically related group of American Indian languages that includes the Athabascan family, Tlingit, and Haida
NADH \en-(ˌ)ā-(ˌ)dē-ˈāch\ *n* [*NAD* + *H,* symbol for hydrogen] (1965) **:** the reduced form of NAD
na·dir \ˈnā-ˌdir, ˈnā-dər\ *n* [ME, fr. MF, fr. Ar *naḍhīr* opposite] (15c) **1 :** the point of the celestial sphere that is directly opposite the zenith and vertically downward from the observer **2 :** the lowest point

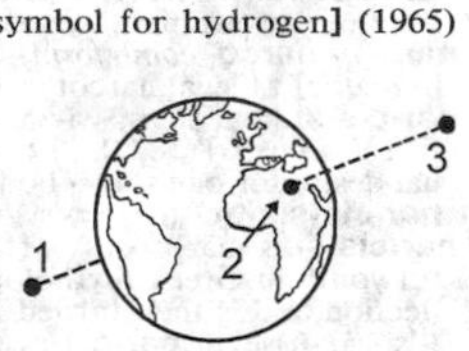

nadir 1: *1* nadir, *2* observer, *3* zenith

NADP \ˌen-(ˌ)ā-(ˌ)dē-ˈpē\ *n* [*n*icotinamide *a*denine *d*inucleotide *p*hosphate] (ca. 1961) **:** a coenzyme $C_{21}H_{28}N_7O_{17}P_3$ of numerous dehydrogenases (as that acting on glucose-6-phosphate) that occurs esp. in red blood cells and plays a role in intermediary metabolism similar to NAD but acting often on different metabolites — called also *nicotinamide adenine dinucleotide phosphate, TPN, triphosphopyridine nucleotide*
NADPH \ˌen-(ˌ)ā-(ˌ)dē-(ˌ)pē-ˈāch\ *n* [*NADP* + *H,* symbol for hydrogen] (1964) **:** the reduced form of NADP
NAFTA *abbr* North American Free Trade Agreement
[1]nag \ˈnag\ *n* [ME *nagge;* akin to D *negge* small horse] (15c) **:** HORSE; *esp* **:** one that is old or in poor condition
[2]nag *vb* **nagged; nag·ging** [prob. of Scand origin; akin to ON *nagga* to moan, complain] *vi* (ca. 1828) **1 :** to find fault incessantly **:** COMPLAIN **2 :** to be a persistent source of annoyance or distraction ~ *vt* **1 :** to irritate by constant scolding or urging **2 :** BADGER, WORRY — **nag·ger** *n* — **nagging** *adj* — **nag·ging·ly** \ˈna-giŋ-lē\ *adv*
[3]nag *n* (1925) **:** one who nags habitually
na·ga·na \nə-ˈgä-nə\ *n* [Zulu *unakane, ulunakane*] (1895) **:** trypanosomiasis (esp. when caused by *Trypanosoma brucei*) of domestic animals
nah \ˈna, ˈnä\ *adv* (1920) **:** not so **:** NO
Nah *abbr* Nahum
Na·huatl \ˈnä-ˌwä-tᵊl\ *n* [Sp *náhuatl,* fr. Nahuatl *Nāhuatl*] (1873) **:** a group of closely related Uto-Aztecan languages that includes the speech of several peoples (as the Aztecs) of central and southern Mexico and Central America — **Na·huat·lan** \nä-ˈwät-lən\ *adj or n*
Na·hum \ˈnā-əm, -həm\ *n* [Heb *Naḥūm*] **1 :** a Hebrew prophet of the seventh century B.C. **2 :** a prophetic book of canonical Jewish and Christian Scripture — see BIBLE table
NAIA *abbr* National Association of Intercollegiate Athletes
na·iad \ˈnā-əd, ˈnī-, -ˌad\ *n, pl* **na·iads** *or* **na·ia·des** \-ə-ˌdēz\ [ME, fr. MF or L; MF *naïade,* fr. L *naiad-, naias,* fr. Gk, fr. *nan* to flow — more at NOURISH] (14c) **1 :** any of the nymphs in classical mythology living in and giving life to lakes, rivers, springs, and fountains **2 :** an aquatic insect nymph (as of a mayfly, dragonfly, damselfly, or stone fly) **3 :** any of a genus (*Najas* of the family Najadaceae) of submerged aquatic plants
[1]na·ïf *or* **na·if** \nä-ˈēf\ *adj* [F] (1598) **:** NAIVE
[2]naïf *or* **naif** *n* (1893) **:** a naive person
[1]nail \ˈnāl\ *n* [ME, fr. OE *nægl;* akin to OHG *nagal* nail, fingernail, L *unguis* fingernail, toenail, claw, Gk *onyx*] (bef. 12c) **1 a :** a horny sheath protecting the upper end of each finger and toe of humans and most other primates **b :** a structure (as a claw) that terminates a digit and corresponds to a nail **2 :** a slender usu. pointed and headed fastener designed to be pounded in
[2]nail *vt* (bef. 12c) **1 :** to fasten with or as if with a nail **2 :** to fix in steady attention ⟨~*ed* his eye on the crack⟩ **3 a :** CATCH, TRAP **b :** to expose usu. so as to discredit **c :** to arrest or punish for an offense **4 a :** STRIKE, HIT **b :** to put out (a runner) in baseball **5 :** to perform or complete perfectly or impressively ⟨~*ed* a jump shot⟩ **6 :** to gain or win decisively — often used with *down* ⟨~ down their consent⟩ **7 :** to settle, establish, or represent clearly and unmistakably — often used with *down* **8** *usu vulgar* **:** to copulate with — **nail·er** *n*
nail bed *n* (1893) **:** the vascular epidermis upon which most of the fingernail or toenail rests that has a longitudinally ridged surface often visible through the nail
nail–bit·er \ˈnāl-ˌbī-tər\ *n* (1971) **:** something (as a close contest) that induces tension or anxiety — **nail–bit·ing** \-tiŋ\ *adj*
nail·brush \-ˌbrəsh\ *n* (1802) **:** a small firm-bristled brush for cleaning the hands and esp. the fingernails
nail file *n* (1862) **:** a small narrow instrument (as of metal or cardboard) with a rough or emery surface that is used for shaping fingernails
nain·sook \ˈnān-ˌsu̇k\ *n* [Hindi & Urdu *nainsukh,* lit., eye's delight] (1790) **:** a soft lightweight muslin
nai·ra \ˈnī-rə\ *n* [alter. of *Nigeria*] (1972) — see MONEY table
na·ive *or* **na·ïve** \nä-ˈēv, nī-\ *adj* **na·iv·er; -est** [F *naïve,* fem. of *naïf,* fr. OF, inborn, natural, fr. L *nativus* native] (1654) **1 :** marked by unaffected simplicity **:** ARTLESS, INGENUOUS **2 a :** deficient in worldly wisdom or informed judgment; *esp* **:** CREDULOUS **b :** not previously subjected to experimentation or a particular experimental situation ⟨made the test with ~ rats⟩; *also* **:** not having previously used a particular drug (as marijuana) **c :** not having been exposed previously to an antigen ⟨~ T cells⟩ **3 a :** SELF-TAUGHT, PRIMITIVE **b :** produced by or as if by a self-taught artist ⟨~ murals⟩ ***syn*** see NATURAL — **na·ive·ly** *or* **na·ïve·ly** *adv* — **na·ive·ness** *n*
na·ive·té *also* **na·ive·te** *or* **na·ïve·té** \nä-ˌē-və-ˈtā, -ˌē-və-; nä-ˈēv-ˌtā, -ˈē-və-; nī-\ *n* [F *naïveté,* fr. OF, inborn character, fr. *naif*] (1673) **1 :** a naive remark or action **2 :** the quality or state of being naive
na·ive·ty *also* **na·ïve·ty** \nä-ˈē-və-tē, -ˈēv-tē, nī-\ *n, pl* **-ties** (1708) *chiefly Brit* **:** NAÏVETÉ
na·ked \ˈnā-kəd, *esp Southern* ˈne-kəd\ *adj* [ME, fr. OE *nacod;* akin to OHG *nackot* naked, L *nudus,* Gk *gymnos*] (bef. 12c) **1 :** not covered by clothing **:** NUDE **2 :** devoid of customary or natural covering **:** BARE: as **a :** not enclosed in a scabbard **b :** not provided with a shade **c** *of a plant or one of its parts* **:** lacking pubescence or enveloping or subtending parts **d :** lacking foliage or vegetation **e** *of an animal or one of its parts* **:** lacking an external covering (as of hair, feathers, or shell) **3 a :** scantily supplied or furnished **b :** lacking embellishment **:** UNADORNED **4 :** UNARMED, DEFENSELESS **5 :** lacking confirmation or support **6 :** devoid of concealment or disguise **7 :** unaided by any optical device or instrument ⟨the ~ eye⟩ **8 :** not backed by the writer's ownership of the commodity contract or security ***syn*** see BARE — **na·ked·ly** *adv* — **na·ked·ness** *n*
naked mole rat *n* (1983) **:** a mole rat (*Heterocephalus glaber* of the family Bathyergidae) found in Ethiopia, Somalia, and Kenya that has nearly hairless wrinkled skin and is practically blind
nak·fa \ˈnäk-ˌfä\ *n, pl* **nakfa** [Tigrinya *naq'fa,* fr. *Nakfa,* town in Eritrea and site of a victory over Ethiopian forces in 1988] (1996) — see MONEY table
na·led \ˈnā-ˌled\ *n* [origin unknown] (ca. 1962) **:** a nonpersistent organophosphate insecticide $C_4H_7Br_2Cl_2O_4P$ used esp. to control crop pests and mosquitoes
na·li·dix·ic acid \ˌnā-lə-ˈdik-sik-\ *n* [perh. fr. *na*phthyr*idi*ne ($C_8H_6N_2$ — fr. *naphth-* + *pyridine*) + carbo*xylic acid*] (1962) **:** an antibacterial agent $C_{12}H_{12}N_2O_3$ that is used esp. in the treatment of genitourinary infections
na·lor·phine \na-ˈlȯr-ˌfēn\ *n* [*N-al*lyl + *morphine*] (ca. 1953) **:** a white crystalline compound $C_{19}H_{21}NO_3$ that is derived from morphine and is used in the form of its hydrochloride as a respiratory stimulant to counteract poisoning by morphine and similar narcotic drugs
nal·ox·one \na-ˈläk-ˌsōn\ *n* [*N-al*lyl + hydr*oxy-* + *-one*] (1964) **:** a synthetic potent antagonist $C_{19}H_{21}NO_4$ of narcotic drugs and esp. morphine that is administered esp. in the form of its hydrochloride
nal·trex·one \nal-ˈtrek-ˌsōn\ *n* [*N-al*lyl + *trex-* (as in *methotrexate*) + *-one*] (1973) **:** a synthetic opiate antagonist $C_{20}H_{23}NO_4$ administered in the form of its hydrochloride
nam·by–pam·by \ˌnam-bē-ˈpam-bē\ *adj* [*Namby Pamby,* nickname given to Ambrose Philips] (1741) **1 :** lacking in character or substance **:** INSIPID **2 :** WEAK, INDECISIVE — **namby–pamby** *n*
[1]name \ˈnām\ *n* [ME, fr. OE *nama;* akin to OHG *namo* name, L *nomen,* Gk *onoma, onyma*] (bef. 12c) **1 a :** a word or phrase that constitutes the distinctive designation of a person or thing **b :** a word or symbol used in logic to designate an entity **2 :** a descriptive often disparaging epithet ⟨called him ~*s*⟩ **3 a :** REPUTATION ⟨gave the town a bad ~⟩ **b :** an illustrious record **:** FAME ⟨made a ~ for himself in golf⟩ **c :** a person or thing with a reputation **4 :** FAMILY, CLAN **5 :** appearance as opposed to reality ⟨a friend in ~ only⟩ **6 :** one referred to by a name ⟨praise his holy ~⟩ — **in the name of 1 :** by authority of ⟨open *in the name of* the law⟩ **2 :** for the reason of **:** using the excuse of ⟨called for reforms *in the name of* progress⟩
[2]name *vt* **named; nam·ing** (bef. 12c) **1 :** to give a name to **:** CALL **2 a :** to mention or identify by name ⟨refused to ~ a suspect⟩ **b :** to accuse by name **3 :** to nominate for office **:** APPOINT **4 :** to decide on **:** CHOOSE ⟨~ the day for the wedding⟩ **5 :** to mention explicitly **:** SPECIFY ⟨unwilling to ~ a price⟩ — **nam·er** *n*

[3]name *adj* (1598) **1 :** of, relating to, or bearing a name ⟨~ tags⟩ **2 :** appearing in the name of a literary or theatrical production **3 a :** having an established reputation **b :** featuring celebrities
name·able *also* **nam·able** \ˈnā-mə-bəl\ *adj* (1780) **1 :** worthy of being named : MEMORABLE **2 :** capable of being named : IDENTIFIABLE
name–call·ing \ˈnām-ˌkȯ-liŋ\ *n* (1853) : the use of offensive names esp. to win an argument or to induce rejection or condemnation (as of a person or project) without objective consideration of the facts
name day *n* (1721) : the feast day of the saint after whom one is named
name–drop·ping \-ˌdrä-piŋ\ *n* (1950) : the studied but seemingly casual mention of prominent persons as associates done to impress others — **name–drop** \-ˌdräp\ *vi* — **name–drop·per** \ˌdrä-pər\ *n*
name·less \ˈnām-ləs\ *adj* (14c) **1 :** OBSCURE, UNDISTINGUISHED **2 :** not known by name : ANONYMOUS **3 :** having no legal right to a name : ILLEGITIMATE **4 :** not having been given a name : UNNAMED **5 :** not marked with a name ⟨a ~ grave⟩ **6 a :** incapable of precise description : INDEFINABLE **b :** too repulsive or distressing to describe — **name·less·ly** *adv* — **name·less·ness** *n*
name·ly \ˈnām-lē\ *adv* (14c) : that is to say : TO WIT
name of the game (1966) **1 :** the essential quality or matter ⟨patience is the *name of the game* in coastal duck hunting —Dick Beals⟩ **2 :** the fundamental goal of an activity
name·plate \-ˌplāt\ *n* (ca. 1859) : something (as a plate or plaque) bearing a name (as of a resident or manufacturer)
name·sake \-ˌsāk\ *n* [prob. fr. *name's sake*] (1646) : one that has the same name as another; *esp* : one who is named after another or for whom another is named
nan *var of* NAAN
nana \ˈna-nə\ *n* [prob. of baby-talk origin] (ca. 1844) : GRANDMOTHER
nance \ˈnan(t)s\ *n* [short for *nancy,* fr. the name *Nancy*] (1920) **1** *often disparaging* : an effeminate male **2** *often disparaging* : HOMOSEXUAL
NAND \ˈnand\ *n* [*not AND*] (1958) : a computer logic circuit that produces an output which is the inverse of that of an AND circuit
nan·di·na \nan-ˈdī-nə, -ˈdē-\ *n* [NL, fr. Jp *nanten*] (ca. 1890) : a widely cultivated Asian evergreen shrub (*Nandina domestica*) of the barberry family having red berries
nan·dro·lone \ˈnan-drə-ˌlōn\ *n* [perh. fr. *nor-* + *andr-* + [1]*-ol* + testoster*one*] (1963) : a semisynthetic anabolic steroid $C_{18}H_{26}O_2$ derived from testosterone and used chiefly in the form of various ester derivatives
nan·keen \ˌnan-ˈkēn\ *n* [*Nanking* (Nanjing), China] (1755) **1 :** a durable brownish yellow cotton fabric orig. loomed by hand in China **2** *pl* : trousers made of nankeen
Nan·kin \ˈnan-ˈkin, ˈnän-\ *or* **Nan·king** \-ˈkiŋ\ *n* [*Nanking* (Nanjing), China] (1761) : Chinese porcelain decorated in blue on a white ground
nan·no·plank·ton \ˌna-nō-ˈplaŋ(k)-tən, -ˌtän\ *n* [NL, fr. Gk *nanos, nannos* dwarf + NL *plankton* plankton] (1912) : the smallest plankton that consists of those organisms (as bacteria) passing through nets of very fine mesh silk cloth
nan·ny *also* **nan·nie** \ˈna-nē\ *n, pl* **nannies** [prob. of baby-talk origin] (1795) : a child's nurse or caregiver
nanny goat *n* [*Nanny,* nickname for *Anne*] (1788) : a female goat
nano- *comb form* [ISV, fr. Gk *nanos* dwarf] **1 :** one billionth (10^{-9}) part of ⟨*nano*second⟩ **2 :** nanotechnology ⟨*nano*machine⟩ **3 :** nanoscale ⟨*nano*particle⟩ ⟨*nano*tube⟩
nano·crys·tal \ˈna-nə-ˌkris-tᵊl\ *n* (1984) : a nanoscale crystal — **nano·crys·tal·line** \-ˈkris-tə-lən *also* -ˌlīn, -ˌlēn\ *adj*
nano·gram \ˈna-nə-ˌgram\ *n* [ISV] (1951) : one billionth of a gram
nano·ma·chine \-mə-ˌshēn\ *n* (1986) : a microscopic machine constructed by the use of nanotechnology
nano·me·ter \ˈna-nə-ˌmē-tər\ *n* [ISV] (1963) : one billionth of a meter
nano·par·ti·cle \-ˌpär-ti-kəl\ *n* (1983) : a microscopic particle whose size is measured in nanometers
nano·scale \-ˌskāl\ *adj* (1986) : having dimensions measured in nanometers
nano·sec·ond \-ˌse-kənd, -kənt\ *n* [ISV] (1959) **1 :** one billionth of a second **2 :** a very brief moment
nano·struc·ture \ˈna-nə-ˌstrək-chər\ *n* (1978) : a nanoscale structure; *esp* : an arrangement, structure, or part of something of molecular dimensions — **nano·struc·tured** \-chərd\ *adj*
nano·tech \ˈna-nō-ˌtek\ *n* (1991) : NANOTECHNOLOGY
nano·tech·nol·o·gy \ˌna-nō-tek-ˈnä-lə-jē\ *n* (1974) : the science of manipulating materials on an atomic or molecular scale esp. to build microscopic devices (as robots) — **nano·tech·no·log·i·cal** \-ˌtek-nə-ˈlä-ji-kəl\ *adj* — **nano·tech·nol·o·gist** \-tek-ˈnä-lə-jist\ *n*
nano·tes·la \ˈna-nō-ˌtes-lə\ *n* (1968) : a unit of magnetic flux density equal to 10^{-9} tesla
nano·tube \-ˌtüb\ *n* (1992) : a microscopic tube whose diameter is measured in nanometers; *esp* : one of pure carbon : BUCKYTUBE
Nan·tua sauce \nänⁿ(n)-ˈtwä-\ *n* [*Nantua,* France] (ca. 1961) : a cream sauce flavored with shellfish (as lobster)
Na·o·mi \nā-ˈō-mē\ *n* [Heb *Nāʿŏmī*] (1540) : the mother-in-law of the Old Testament heroine Ruth
[1]nap \ˈnap\ *vi* **napped; nap·ping** [ME *nappen,* fr. OE *hnappian;* akin to OHG *hnaffezen* to doze] (bef. 12c) **1 :** to sleep briefly esp. during the day : DOZE **2 :** to be off guard
[2]nap *n* (14c) : a short sleep esp. during the day : SNOOZE
[3]nap *n* [ME *noppe,* fr. MD, flock of wool, nap] (15c) : a hairy or downy surface (as on a fabric) — **nap·less** \-ləs\ *adj* — **napped** \ˈnapt\ *adj*
[4]nap *vt* **napped; nap·ping** (1620) : to raise a nap on (fabric or leather)
[5]nap *n* [fr. to go *nap* (to make all the points in the card game Napoleon)] (1895) *Brit* : a pick or recommendation as a good bet to win a contest (as a horse race); *also* : one named in a nap
[6]nap *vt* **napped; nap·ping** (1927) *Brit* : to pick or single out in a nap
napa cabbage \ˈna-pə-\ *n, often cap N* [perh. fr. Jp dial. *nappa* greens] (1980) : CHINESE CABBAGE b
napa leather *n* [*Napa,* California] (1897) : a glove leather made by tawing sheepskins with a soap-and-oil mixture; *also* : a similar soft leather
[1]na·palm \ˈnā-ˌpäm, -ˌpälm *also* ˈna- *also* nə-ˈpä(l)m\ *n* [*na*phthene + *palm*itate] (1942) **1 :** a thickener consisting of a mixture of aluminum soaps used in jelling gasoline (as for incendiary bombs) **2 :** fuel jelled with napalm
[2]napalm *vt* (1950) : to assault with napalm
nape \ˈnāp, ˈnap\ *n* [ME] (14c) : the back of the neck
na·pery \ˈnā-p(ə-)rē\ *n* [ME, fr. AF *naperie,* fr. *nape* tablecloth — more at NAPKIN] (14c) : household linen; *esp* : TABLE LINEN
Naph·ta·li \ˈnaf-tə-ˌlī\ *n* [Heb *Naphtālī*] (14c) : a son of Jacob and the traditional eponymous ancestor of one of the tribes of Israel
naph·tha \ˈnaf-thə, ÷ˈnap-\ *n* [L, fr. Gk, of Iranian origin; akin to Pers *neft* naphtha] (1543) **1 :** any of various volatile often flammable liquid hydrocarbon mixtures used chiefly as solvents and diluents **2 :** PETROLEUM
naph·tha·lene \-ˌlēn\ *n* [alter. of earlier *naphthaline,* irreg. fr. *naphtha*] (1821) : a crystalline aromatic hydrocarbon $C_{10}H_8$ usu. obtained by distillation of coal tar and used esp. in organic synthesis
naph·thene \ˈnaf-ˌthēn, ÷ˈnap-\ *n* (1884) : CYCLOPARAFFIN — **naph·then·ic** \ˌnaf-ˈthē-nik, ÷ˌnap-, -ˈthe-\ *adj*
naph·thol \ˈnaf-ˌthȯl, ÷ˈnap-, -ˌthōl\ *n* [ISV] (1849) **1 :** either of two isomeric derivatives $C_{10}H_8O$ of naphthalene used as antiseptics and in the manufacture of dyes **2 :** any of various hydroxy derivatives of naphthalene that resemble the simpler phenols
naph·thyl·amine \naf-ˈthi-lə-ˌmēn, ÷nap-\ *n* [ISV] (1857) : either of two isomeric crystalline bases $C_{10}H_9N$ used esp. as dye intermediates
na·pi·er grass \ˈnā-pē-ər-\ *n* [*Napier,* town in So. Africa] (1919) : a tall stout African perennial grass (*Pennisetum purpureum*) that resembles sugarcane and is widely grown for forage — called also *elephant grass*
Na·pier·ian logarithm \nə-ˈpir-ē-ən-, nā-\ *n* [John *Napier*] (1816) : NATURAL LOGARITHM
Na·pi·er's bones \ˈnā-pē-ərz-\ *n* (ca. 1658) : a set of graduated rods (as of wood or bone) invented by John Napier and used for multiplication and division based on the principles of logarithms
na·pi·form \ˈnā-pə-ˌfȯrm\ *adj* [L *napus* turnip (perh. fr. Gk *napy, sinapy* mustard) + ISV *-iform*] (ca. 1841) : globular at the top and tapering off abruptly ⟨a ~ root⟩
nap·kin \ˈnap-kən\ *n* [ME *nappekin,* fr. *nape* tablecloth, fr. AF, fr. L *mappa* napkin] (14c) **1 :** a piece of material (as cloth or paper) used at table to wipe the lips or fingers and protect the clothes **2 :** a small cloth or towel: as **a** *dial Brit* : HANDKERCHIEF **b** *chiefly Scot* : KERCHIEF **c** *chiefly Brit* : DIAPER 3 **3 :** SANITARY NAPKIN
na·po·leon \nə-ˈpōl-yən, -ˈpō-lē-ən\ *n* [F *napoléon,* fr. *Napoléon* Napoleon I] (1814) **1 :** a former French 20-franc gold coin **2 :** an oblong pastry with a filling of cream, custard, or jelly **3** *cap* : one like Napoleon I (as in ambition)
nappe \ˈnap\ *n* [F, tablecloth, sheet, nappe, fr. OF *nape* — more at NAPKIN] (1904) **1 :** SHEET 6 **2 :** a large mass of rock thrust over other rocks **3 :** one of the two sheets that lie on opposite sides of the vertex and together make up a cone
[1]nap·py \ˈna-pē\ *n* [obs. *nappy,* adj., foaming] (ca. 1550) *chiefly Scot* : LIQUOR; *specif* : ALE
[2]nappy *n, pl* **nappies** [E dial. *nap* bowl, fr. ME, fr. OE *hnæpp;* akin to OHG *hnapf* bowl] (ca. 1864) : a rimless shallow open serving dish
[3]nappy *n, pl* **nappies** [*nap*kin + [4]*-y*] (1927) *chiefly Brit* : DIAPER 3
[4]nappy *adj* **nap·pi·er; -est** [[3]*nap*] (1785) : KINKY 1
na·prap·a·thy \nə-ˈpra-pə-thē\ *n* [Czech *naprava* correction + E *-pathy*] (1909) : a system of treatment by manipulation of connective tissue and adjoining structures and by dietary measures that is held to facilitate the recuperative and regenerative processes of the body
na·prox·en \nə-ˈpräk-sən\ *n* [*na*phthyl (a derivative of naphthalene) + *pro*pionic acid + *ox*y + *-en* (as in *ibuprofen*)] (1971) : an analgesic and antipyretic NSAID $C_{14}H_{14}O_3$ often used in the form of its sodium salt
narc *also* **nark** \ˈnärk\ *n* [short for *narcotics agent*] (1967) *slang* : a person (as a government agent) who investigates narcotics violations
narc- *or* **narco-** *comb form* **1** [GK *narkē*] : deep sleep ⟨*narco*lepsy⟩ **2** [*narcotic*] : illegal narcotics ⟨*narco*-terrorism⟩
nar·cis·sism \ˈnär-sə-ˌsi-zəm\ *n* [G *Narzissismus,* fr. *Narziss* Narcissus, fr. L *Narcissus*] (1822) **1 :** EGOISM, EGOCENTRISM **2 :** love of or sexual desire for one's own body — **nar·cis·sist** \ˈnär-sə-sist\ *n or adj* — **nar·cis·sis·tic** \ˌnär-sə-ˈsis-tik\ *adj*
nar·cis·sus \när-ˈsi-səs\ *n* [L, fr. Gk *Narkissos*] (14c) **1** *cap* : a beautiful youth in Greek mythology who pines away for love of his own reflection and is then turned into the narcissus flower **2** *pl* **nar·cis·si** \-ˈsi-ˌsī, -(ˌ)sē\ *or* **nar·cis·sus·es** *or* **narcissus** [NL, genus name, fr. L, narcissus, fr. Gk *narkissos*] : DAFFODIL; *esp* : one whose flowers have a short corona and are usu. borne separately
nar·co \ˈnär-(ˌ)kō\ *n, pl* **narcos** (1955) *slang* : NARC
nar·co·lep·sy \ˈnär-kə-ˌlep-sē\ *n, pl* **-sies** [ISV] (1880) : a condition characterized by brief attacks of deep sleep often occurring with cataplexy and hypnagogic hallucinations — **nar·co·lep·tic** \ˌnär-kə-ˈlep-tik\ *adj*
nar·co·lep·tic \ˌnär-kə-ˈlep-tik\ *n* (1928) : a person who is subject to attacks of narcolepsy
nar·co·sis \när-ˈkō-səs\ *n, pl* **-co·ses** \-ˌsēz\ [NL, fr. Gk *narkōsis,* action of benumbing, fr. *narkoun*] (ca. 1693) : a state of stupor, unconsciousness, or arrested activity produced by the influence of narcotics or other chemical or physical agents — compare NITROGEN NARCOSIS
nar·co–ter·ror·ism \ˈnär-(ˌ)kō-ˈter-ər-ˌi-zəm\ *n* (1982) : terrorism financed by profits from illegal drug trafficking — **nar·co–ter·ror·ist** \-ist\ *n*
[1]nar·cot·ic \när-ˈkä-tik\ *n* [ME *narkotik,* fr. MF *narcotique,* fr. *narcotique,* adj., fr. ML *narcoticus,* fr. Gk *narkōtikos,* fr. *narkoun* to benumb, fr. *narkē* numbness — more at SNARE] (14c) **1 a :** a drug (as opium or morphine) that in moderate doses dulls the senses, relieves pain, and induces profound sleep but in excessive doses causes stupor, coma, or convulsions **b :** a drug (as marijuana or LSD) subject to restriction similar to that of addictive narcotics whether physiologically addictive and narcotic or not **2 :** something that soothes, relieves, or lulls
[2]narcotic *adj* (1526) **1 a :** having the properties of or yielding a narcotic **b :** inducing mental lethargy **2 :** of, induced by, or concerned with narcotics **3 :** of, involving, or intended for narcotic addicts — **nar·cot·i·cal·ly** \-ti-k(ə-)lē\ *adv*
nar·co·tize \ˈnär-kə-ˌtīz\ *vb* **-tized; -tiz·ing** [ISV] *vt* (1526) **1 a :** to treat with or subject to a narcotic **b :** to put into narcosis **2 :** to soothe to unconsciousness or unawareness ~ *vi* : to act as a narcotic
nard \ˈnärd\ *n* [ME *narde,* fr. OE, fr. L *nardus,* fr. Gk *nardos,* of Sem origin; akin to Heb *nērd* nard] (bef. 12c) : SPIKENARD 1b
na·res \ˈner-(ˌ)ēz\ *n pl* [ME, fr. L, pl. of *naris;* akin to L *nasus* nose — more at NOSE] (14c) : the pair of openings of the nose or nasal cavity
nar·ghi·le \ˈnär-gə-lē\ *or* **nar·gi·leh** \-ˌle\ *n* [Pers *nārgīla,* fr. *nārgīl* coconut, of Indo-Aryan origin; akin to Skt *nārikela* coconut; fr. the orig-

inal material used in making its bowl] (1758) : a water pipe for smoking that originated in the Near East

1**nark** \'närk\ *n* [perh. fr. Romany *nak* nose] (ca. 1860) *Brit* : STOOL PIGEON 1

2**nark** *var of* NARC

3**nark** *vt* [origin unknown] (1888) *Brit* : IRRITATE, ANNOY

Nar·ra·gan·sett *also* **Nar·ra·gan·set** \ˌna-rə-'gan(t)-sət\ *n, pl* **-sett** *or* **-setts** *also* **-set** *or* **-sets** [modif. of Narragansett *Nahicans, Nayohygunsic,* locale on Narragansett Bay] (1622) **1** : a member of an American Indian people of Rhode Island **2** : the Algonquian language of the Narragansett people

nar·rate \'ner-ˌāt, 'na-ˌrat, na-'rāt\ *vt* **nar·rat·ed; nar·rat·ing** [L *narratus,* pp. of *narrare,* fr. L *gnarus* knowing; akin to L *gnoscere, noscere* to know — more at KNOW] (1656) : to tell (as a story) in detail; *also* : to provide spoken commentary for (as a movie or television show) — **nar·ra·tor** \'ner-ˌā-tər, 'na-ˌrā-, na-'rā-, nə-; 'ner-ə-, 'na-rə-\ *n*

nar·ra·tion \na-'rā-shən, nə-\ *n* (15c) **1** : the act or process or an instance of narrating **2** : STORY, NARRATIVE — **nar·ra·tion·al** \-shnəl, -shə-nᵊl\ *adj*

nar·ra·tive \'ner-ə-tiv, 'na-rə-\ *n* (1567) **1** : something that is narrated : STORY, ACCOUNT **2** : the art or practice of narration **3** : the representation in art of an event or story; *also* : an example of such a representation — **narrative** *adj* — **nar·ra·tive·ly** *adv*

nar·ra·tol·o·gy \ˌner-ə-'tä-lə-jē, ˌna-rə-\ *n* (1976) : the study of structure in narratives — **nar·ra·to·log·i·cal** \-tə-'lä-ji-kəl\ *adj* — **nar·ra·tol·o·gist** \-'tä-lə-jist\ *n*

1**nar·row** \'ner-(ˌ)ō, 'na-(ˌ)rō\ *adj* [ME *narowe,* fr. OE *nearu;* akin to OHG *narwa* scar] (bef. 12c) **1 a** : of slender width ⟨a long and ~ room⟩ **b** : of less than standard or usual width ⟨a ~ sidewalk⟩ **c** *of a textile* : woven in widths usu. less than 18 inches (46 centimeters) **2** : limited in size or scope ⟨a ~ interpretation⟩ **3 a** : illiberal in views or disposition : PREJUDICED **b** *chiefly dial* : STINGY, NIGGARDLY **4 a** : barely sufficient : CLOSE ⟨won by a ~ margin⟩ **b** : barely successful ⟨a ~ escape⟩ **5** : minutely precise : METICULOUS ⟨a ~ inspection⟩ **6** *of an animal ration* : relatively rich in protein as compared with carbohydrate and fat **7** : TENSE 3 — **nar·row·ly** *adv* — **nar·row·ness** *n*

2**narrow** *vt* (bef. 12c) **1** : to decrease the breadth or extent of : CONTRACT — often used with *down* **2** : to decrease the scope or sphere of : LIMIT — often used with *down* ⟨~ down the choices⟩ ~ *vi* : to lessen in width or extent : CONTRACT — often used with *down*

3**narrow** *n* (13c) : a narrow part or passage; *specif* : a strait connecting two bodies of water — usu. used in pl. but sing. or pl. in constr.

nar·row·band \-ˌband\ *adj* (1950) : operating at, responsive to, or including a narrow range of frequencies

narrow boat *n* (1861) *Brit* : a barge with a beam of less than seven feet (2.1 meters)

nar·row·cast·ing \-ˌkas-tiŋ\ *n* (1928) : radio or television transmission aimed at a narrowly defined area or audience (as paying subscribers)

nar·row–mind·ed \-'mīn-dəd\ *adj* (1625) : lacking in tolerance or breadth of vision : PETTY — **nar·row–mind·ed·ly** *adv* — **nar·row–mind·ed·ness** *n*

nar·thex \'när-ˌtheks\ *n* [LGk *narthēx,* fr. Gk, giant fennel, cane, casket] (ca. 1673) **1** : the portico of an ancient church **2** : a vestibule leading to the nave of a church

nar·whal \'när-ˌwäl, -ˌhwäl, -wəl\ *also* **nar·whale** \-ˌwāl, -ˌhwāl\ *n* [Norw & Dan *narhval* & Sw *narval,* prob. modif. of Icel *náhvalur,* fr. ON *nāhvalr,* fr. *nār* corpse + *hvalr* whale; fr. its color] (1646) : an arctic cetacean (*Monodon monoceros*) about 20 feet (6 meters) long with the male having a long twisted ivory tusk

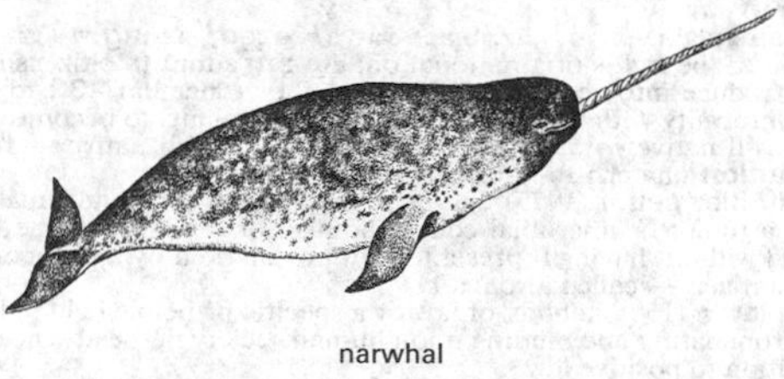

narwhal

nary \'ner-ē\ *adj* [alter. of *ne'er a*] (1848) *dial* : not any : not one ⟨I must have it back as I have ~ other copy —Flannery O'Connor⟩ — **nary a** *or* **nary an** : not a single ⟨survived the accident with *nary a* scratch⟩

NAS *abbr* **1** National Academy of Sciences **2** naval air station

NASA *abbr* National Aeronautics and Space Administration

1**na·sal** \'nā-zəl\ *n* [ME, fr. AF, fr. *nes* nose, fr. L *nasus* — more at NOSE] (14c) **1** : the nosepiece of a helmet **2** : a nasal part **3** : a nasal consonant

2**nasal** *adj* (1656) **1** : of or relating to the nose **2 a** : uttered with the soft palate lowered and with passage of air through the nose (as with \m\, \n\, \ŋ\, \ō^{n}\, or \a^{n}\) **b** : characterized by resonance produced through the nose **3** *of a musical tone* : SHARP, PENETRATING — **na·sal·i·ty** \nā-'za-lə-tē\ *n* — **na·sal·ly** \'nā-zə-lē, 'nāz-lē\ *adv*

na·sal·ize \'nā-zə-ˌlīz\ *vb* **-ized; -iz·ing** *vt* (1817) : to make nasal or pronounce as a nasal sound — **na·sal·i·za·tion** \ˌnā-zə-lə-'zā-shən\ *n*

NASCAR *abbr* National Association for Stock Car Auto Racing

na·scence \'na-sᵊn(t)s, 'nā-\ *n* (1570) : NASCENCY

na·scen·cy \-sᵊn(t)-sē\ *n, pl* **-cies** (1682) : BIRTH, ORIGIN

na·scent \'na-sᵊnt, 'nā-\ *adj* [L *nascent-, nascens,* prp. of *nasci* to be born — more at NATION] (ca. 1624) : coming or having recently come into existence ⟨a ~ middle class⟩ ⟨her ~ singing career⟩

NASD *abbr* National Association of Securities Dealers

naso- *comb form* [L *nasus* nose] **1** : nose and ⟨*naso*pharynx⟩ **2** : nasal ⟨*naso*gastric⟩

na·so·gas·tric \ˌnā-zō-'gas-trik\ *adj* (1942) : being or performed by intubation of the stomach through the nasal passages ⟨a ~ tube⟩

na·so·pha·ryn·geal \-fə-'rin-j(ē-)əl, -ˌfa-rən-'jē-əl\ *adj* (1872) : of, relating to, or affecting the nose and pharynx or the nasopharynx

na·so·phar·ynx \-'fa-riŋ(k)s\ *n* [NL] (1877) : the upper part of the pharynx continuous with the nasal passages

nas·tic \'nas-tik\ *adj* [Gk *nastos* close-pressed, fr. *nassein* to press] (1908) : of, relating to, or constituting a movement of a plant part caused by disproportionate growth or increase of turgor in one surface

nas·tur·tium \nə-'stər-shəm, na-\ *n* [L, a cress] (1704) : any of a genus (*Tropaeolum* of the family Tropaeolaceae, the nasturtium family) of herbs of Central and So. America with showy spurred flowers and pungent edible seeds and leaves; *esp* : either of two widely cultivated ornamentals (*T. majus* and *T. minus*)

nas·ty \'nas-tē\ *adj* **nas·ti·er; -est** [ME] (14c) **1 a** : disgustingly filthy **b** : physically repugnant **2** : INDECENT, OBSCENE **3** : MEAN, TAWDRY **4 a** : extremely hazardous or harmful ⟨a ~ undertow⟩ **b** : causing severe pain or suffering ⟨a ~ wound⟩ ⟨a ~ fall⟩ **c** : sharply unpleasant : DISAGREEABLE ⟨~ weather⟩ **5 a** : difficult to understand or deal with ⟨a ~ problem⟩ ⟨a ~ curveball⟩ **b** : psychologically unsettling : TRYING ⟨a ~ fear that she was lost⟩ **6** : lacking in courtesy or sportsmanship ⟨a ~ trick⟩ ***syn*** see DIRTY — **nas·ti·ly** \-tə-lē\ *adv* — **nas·ti·ness** \-tē-nəs\ *n* — **nasty** *n*

NASW *abbr* National Association of Social Workers

nat *abbr* **1** national **2** native **3** natural

na·tal \'nā-tᵊl\ *adj* [ME, fr. L *natalis,* fr. *natus,* pp. of *nasci* to be born — more at NATION] (15c) **1** : NATIVE **2** : of, relating to, or present at birth; *esp* : associated with one's birth ⟨a ~ star⟩

na·tal·i·ty \nā-'ta-lə-tē, nə-\ *n, pl* **-ties** (1888) : BIRTHRATE

na·tant \'nā-tᵊnt\ *adj* [ME *natand,* fr. L *natant-, natans,* prp. of *natare* to swim; akin to L *nare* to swim; akin to Gk *nein, nēchein* to swim, Skt *snāti* he bathes] (15c) : swimming or floating in water ⟨~ decapods⟩

na·ta·tion \nā-'tā-shən, na-\ *n* (1542) : the action or art of swimming

na·ta·to·ri·al \ˌnā-tə-'tōr-ē-əl, ˌna-\ *or* **na·ta·to·ry** \'nā-tə-ˌtōr-ē, 'na-\ *adj* (1816) **1** : of or relating to swimming **2** : adapted to or characterized by swimming ⟨a ~ leg of an aquatic insect⟩

na·ta·to·ri·um \ˌnā-tə-'tōr-ē-əm, ˌna-\ *n* [LL, fr. L *natare*] (ca. 1889) : an indoor swimming pool

natch \'nach\ *adv* [by shortening & alter. fr. *naturally*] (ca. 1945) *slang* : of course : NATURALLY

Natch·ez \'na-chəz\ *n, pl* **Natchez** [F, pl. of *Nacha, Natché,* a Natchez town] (1764) **1** : a member of an American Indian people of southwestern Mississippi **2** : the language of the Natchez people

na·tes \'nā-ˌtēz\ *n pl* [L, pl. of *natis* buttock] (ca. 1706) : BUTTOCKS

nathe·less \'nāth-ləs\ *or* **nath·less** \'nath-\ *adv* [ME, fr. OE *nā thē lǣs* not the less] (bef. 12c) *archaic* : NEVERTHELESS, NOTWITHSTANDING

na·tion \'nā-shən\ *n* [ME *nacioun,* fr. AF *naciun,* fr. L *nation-, natio* birth, race, nation, fr. *nasci* to be born; akin to L *gignere* to beget — more at KIN] (14c) **1 a** (1) : NATIONALITY 5a (2) : a politically organized nationality (3) : a non-Jewish nationality ⟨why do the ~*s* conspire —Ps 2:1 (RSV)⟩ **b** : a community of people composed of one or more nationalities and possessing a more or less defined territory and government **c** : a territorial division containing a body of people of one or more nationalities and usu. characterized by relatively large size and independent status **2** *archaic* : GROUP, AGGREGATION **3** : a tribe or federation of tribes (as of American Indians)

1**na·tion·al** \'nash-nəl, 'na-shə-nᵊl\ *adj* (1580) **1** : of or relating to a nation **2** : NATIONALIST **3** : comprising or characteristic of a nationality **4** : belonging to or maintained by the federal government **5** : of, relating to, or being a coalition government formed by most or all major political parties usu. in a crisis — **na·tion·al·ly** *adv*

2**national** *n* (1887) **1** : one that owes allegiance to or is under the protection of a nation without regard to the more formal status of citizen or subject **2** : a competition that is national in scope — usu. used in pl. ***syn*** see CITIZEN

national bank *n* (1736) **1** : CENTRAL BANK **2** : a bank operating under federal charter and supervision

national forest *n* (1897) : a usu. forested area of considerable extent that is preserved by government decree from private exploitation and is harvested only under supervision

national guard *n* (1792) **1** : a military establishment serving as a national constabulary and defense force **2** *cap* : a militia force recruited by each state of the U.S., equipped by the federal government, and jointly maintained subject to the call of either

national guardsman *n, often cap* (1961) : a member of a national guard

national income *n* (1878) : the aggregate of earnings from a nation's current production including compensation of employees, interest, rental income, and profits of business after taxes

na·tion·al·ise *chiefly Brit var of* NATIONALIZE

na·tion·al·ism \'nash-nə-ˌli-zəm, 'na-shə-nə-ˌli-zəm\ *n* (1844) **1** : loyalty and devotion to a nation; *esp* : a sense of national consciousness exalting one nation above all others and placing primary emphasis on promotion of its culture and interests as opposed to those of other nations or supranational groups **2** : a nationalist movement or government

1**na·tion·al·ist** \-list\ *n* (1715) **1** : an advocate of or believer in nationalism **2** : a member of a political party or group advocating national independence or strong national government

2**nationalist** *adj* (1884) **1** : of, relating to, or advocating nationalism **2** : of, relating to, or being a political group advocating or associated with nationalism

na·tion·al·is·tic \ˌnash-nə-'lis-tik, ˌna-shə-nə-'lis-tik\ *adj* (1866) **1** : of, favoring, or characterized by nationalism ⟨~ election speeches⟩ **2** : NATIONAL 1 — **na·tion·al·is·ti·cal·ly** \-ti-k(ə-)lē\ *adv*

na·tion·al·i·ty \ˌna-shə-'na-lə-tē, ˌnash-'na-\ *n, pl* **-ties** (1691) **1** : national character **2** : NATIONALISM 1 **3 a** : national status; *specif* : a legal relationship involving allegiance on the part of an individual and usu. protection on the part of the state **b** : membership in a particular nation **4** : political independence or existence as a separate nation **5 a** : a people having a common origin, tradition, and language and capable of forming or actually constituting a nation-state **b** : an ethnic group constituting one element of a larger unit (as a nation)

na·tion·al·ize \ˈnash-nə-ˌlīz, ˈna-shə-nə-ˌlīz\ *vt* **-ized; -iz·ing** (1800) **1** : to give a national character to **2** : to invest control or ownership of in the national government — **na·tion·al·i·za·tion** \ˌnash-nə-lə-ˈzā-shən, ˌna-shə-nə-lə-\ *n* — **na·tion·al·iz·er** \ˈnash-nə-ˌlī-zər, ˌna-shə-nə-ˌlī-zər\ *n*

national monument *n* (1879) : a place of historic, scenic, or scientific interest set aside for preservation usu. by presidential proclamation

national park *n* (1868) : an area of special scenic, historical, or scientific importance set aside and maintained by a national government and in the U.S. by an act of Congress

national seashore *n* (1962) : a recreational area adjacent to a seacoast and maintained by the federal government

national socialism *n, often cap N&S* (1931) : NAZISM — **national socialist** *adj, often cap N&S*

na·tion·hood \ˈnā-shən-ˌhu̇d\ *n* (1850) **1** : NATIONALITY 1 **2** : NATIONALITY 3a **3** : NATIONALITY 4

na·tion–state \ˈnā-shən-ˈstāt, -ˌstāt\ *n* (1918) : a form of political organization under which a relatively homogeneous people inhabits a sovereign state; *esp* : a state containing one as opposed to several nationalities

[1]**na·tion·wide** \ˌnā-shən-ˈwīd\ *adj* (1912) : extending throughout a nation

[2]**nationwide** *adv* (1926) : throughout the nation

[1]**na·tive** \ˈnā-tiv\ *adj* [ME *natif,* fr. MF, fr. L *nativus,* fr. *natus,* pp. of *nasci* to be born — more at NATION] (14c) **1** : INBORN, INNATE ⟨~ talents⟩ **2** : belonging to a particular place by birth **3** *archaic* : closely related **4** : belonging to or associated with one by birth **5** : NATURAL, NORMAL **6 a** : grown, produced, or originating in a particular place or in the vicinity : LOCAL **b** : living or growing naturally in a particular region : INDIGENOUS **7** : SIMPLE, UNAFFECTED **8 a** : constituting the original substance or source **b** : found in nature esp. in an unadulterated form ⟨mining ~ silver⟩ **9** *chiefly Austral* : having a usu. superficial resemblance to a specified English plant or animal **10** *cap* : of, relating to, or being a member of an aboriginal people of No. or So. America : NATIVE AMERICAN — **na·tive·ly** *adv* — **na·tive·ness** *n*

syn NATIVE, INDIGENOUS, ENDEMIC, ABORIGINAL mean belonging to a locality. NATIVE implies birth or origin in a place or region and may suggest compatibility with it ⟨*native* tribal customs⟩. INDIGENOUS applies to species or races and adds to NATIVE the implication of not having been introduced from elsewhere ⟨maize is *indigenous* to America⟩. ENDEMIC implies being peculiar to a region ⟨edelweiss is *endemic* in the Alps⟩. ABORIGINAL implies having no known race preceding in occupancy of the region ⟨the *aboriginal* peoples of Australia⟩.

[2]**native** *n* (1535) **1** : one born or reared in a particular place **2 a** : an original or indigenous inhabitant **b** : something indigenous to a particular locality **3** : a local resident; *esp* : a person who has always lived in a place as distinguished from a visitor or a temporary resident

Native American *n* (1737) : a member of any of the aboriginal peoples of the western hemisphere; *esp* : a Native American of No. America and esp. the U.S. — compare AMERICAN INDIAN — **Native American** *adj*

na·tiv·ism \ˈnā-ti-ˌvi-zəm\ *n* (1844) **1** : a policy of favoring native inhabitants as opposed to immigrants **2** : the revival or perpetuation of an indigenous culture esp. in opposition to acculturation — **na·tiv·ist** \-vist\ *n or adj* — **na·tiv·is·tic** \ˌnā-ti-ˈvis-tik\ *adj*

na·tiv·i·ty \nə-ˈti-və-tē, nā-\ *n, pl* **-ties** [ME *nativite,* fr. AF *nativité,* fr. ML *nativitat-, nativitas,* fr. LL, birth, fr. L *nativus*] (14c) **1** : the process or circumstances of being born : BIRTH; *esp, cap* : the birth of Jesus **2** : a horoscope at or of the time of one's birth **3** : the place of origin

natl *or* **nat'l** *abbr* national

NATO *abbr* North Atlantic Treaty Organization

na·tri·ure·sis \ˌnā-trē-yu̇-ˈrē-səs\ *n* [NL, fr. *natrium* sodium (fr. ISV *natron*) + *uresis* urination, fr. Gk *ourēsis,* fr. *ourein* to urinate — more at URINE] (1957) : excessive loss of sodium in the urine — **na·tri·uret·ic** \-ˈre-tik\ *adj or n*

na·tro·lite \ˈnā-trə-ˌlīt\ *n* [G *Natrolith,* fr. *Natron* (fr. F) + *-lith* -lite] (ca. 1805) : a hydrous silicate of sodium and aluminum that is related to zeolite

na·tron \ˈnā-ˌträn, -trən\ *n* [F, fr. Sp *natrón,* fr. Ar *naṭrūn,* fr. Gk *nitron* — more at NITER] (1684) : a hydrous native sodium carbonate used in ancient times in embalming, in ceramic pastes, and as a cleansing agent

[1]**nat·ter** \ˈna-tər\ *vi* [prob. imit.] (1942) : CHATTER 2

[2]**natter** *n* (1943) *chiefly Brit* : idle talk or conversation : CHAT

nat·ty \ˈna-tē\ *adj* **nat·ti·er; -est** [perh. alter. of earlier *netty,* fr. obs. *net* neat, clean] (1557) : trimly neat and tidy : SMART ⟨~ clothes⟩ ⟨a ~ dresser⟩ — **nat·ti·ly** \ˈna-tə-lē\ *adv* — **nat·ti·ness** \ˈna-tē-nəs\ *n*

[1]**nat·u·ral** \ˈna-chə-rəl, ˈnach-rəl\ *adj* [ME, fr. AF *naturel,* fr. L *naturalis* of nature, fr. *natura* nature] (14c) **1** : based on an inherent sense of right and wrong ⟨~ justice⟩ **2 a** : being in accordance with or determined by nature **b** : having or constituting a classification based on features existing in nature **3 a (1)** : begotten as distinguished from adopted; *also* : LEGITIMATE **(2)** : being a relation by actual consanguinity as distinguished from adoption ⟨~ parents⟩ **b** : ILLEGITIMATE ⟨a ~ child⟩ **4** : having an essential relation with someone or something : following from the nature of the one in question ⟨his guilt is a ~ deduction from the evidence⟩ **5** : implanted or being as if implanted by nature : seemingly inborn ⟨a ~ talent for art⟩ **6** : of or relating to nature as an object of study and research **7** : having a specified character by nature ⟨a ~ athlete⟩ **8 a** : occurring in conformity with the ordinary course of nature : not marvelous or supernatural ⟨~ causes⟩ **b** : formulated by human reason alone rather than revelation ⟨~ religion⟩ ⟨~ rights⟩ **c** : having a normal or usual character ⟨events followed their ~ course⟩ **9** : possessing or exhibiting the higher qualities (as kindliness and affection) of human nature ⟨a noble . . . brother . . . ever most kind and ~ —Shak.⟩ **10 a** : growing without human care; *also* : not cultivated ⟨~ prairie unbroken by the plow⟩ **b** : existing in or produced by nature : not artificial ⟨~ turf⟩ ⟨~ curiosities⟩ **c** : relating to or being natural food **11 a** : being in a state of nature without spiritual enlightenment : UNREGENERATE ⟨~ man⟩ **b** : living in or as if in a state of nature untouched by the influences of civilization and society **12 a** : having a physical or real existence as contrasted with one that is spiritual, intellectual, or fictitious ⟨a corporation is a legal but not a ~ person⟩ **b** : of, relating to, or operating in the physical as opposed to the spiritual world ⟨~ laws describe phenomena of the physical universe⟩ **13 a** : closely resembling an original : true to nature **b** : marked by easy simplicity and freedom from artificiality, affectation, or constraint **c** : having a form or appearance found in nature **14 a** : having neither flats nor sharps ⟨the ~ scale of C major⟩ **b** : being neither sharp nor flat **c** : having the pitch modified by the natural sign **15** : of an off-white or beige color — **nat·u·ral·ness** \-nəs\ *n*

syn NATURAL, INGENUOUS, NAIVE, UNSOPHISTICATED, ARTLESS mean free from pretension or calculation. NATURAL implies lacking artificiality and self-consciousness and having a spontaneousness suggesting the natural rather than the man-made world ⟨her unaffected, *natural* manner⟩. INGENUOUS implies inability to disguise or conceal one's feelings or intentions ⟨the *ingenuous* enthusiasm of children⟩. NAIVE suggests lack of worldly wisdom often connoting credulousness and unchecked innocence ⟨politically *naive*⟩. UNSOPHISTICATED implies a lack of experience and training necessary for social ease and adroitness ⟨*unsophisticated* adolescents⟩. ARTLESS suggests a naturalness resulting from unawareness of the effect one is producing on others ⟨*artless* charm⟩. ***syn*** see in addition REGULAR

[2]**natural** *n* (1533) **1** : one born without the usual powers of reason and understanding **2 a** : a sign ♮ placed on any degree of the musical staff to nullify the effect of a preceding sharp or flat **b** : a note or tone affected by the natural sign **3** : a result or combination that immediately wins the stake in a game; *specif* : a throw of 7 or 11 on the first cast in craps **4 a** : one having natural skills, talents, or abilities **b** : something that is likely to become an immediate success **c** : one that is obviously suitable for a specific purpose **5** : AFRO

natural childbirth *n* (1933) : a system of managing childbirth in which the mother receives preparatory education in order to remain conscious during and assist in delivery with minimal or no use of drugs or anesthetics

natural family planning *n* (1975) : a method of birth control that involves abstention from sexual intercourse during the period of ovulation which is determined through observation and measurement of bodily symptoms

natural food *n* (1917) : food that has undergone minimal processing and contains no preservatives or artificial additives

natural gas *n* (1825) **1** : gas issuing from the earth's crust through natural openings or bored wells; *esp* : a combustible mixture of methane and other hydrocarbons used chiefly as a fuel and raw material **2** : gas manufactured from organic matter (as coal)

natural history *n* (1567) **1** : a treatise on some aspect of nature **2** : the natural development of something (as an organism or disease) over a period of time **3** : the study of natural objects esp. in the field from an amateur or popular point of view

nat·u·ral·ise *Brit var of* NATURALIZE

nat·u·ral·ism \ˈna-chə-rə-ˌli-zəm, ˈnach-rə-\ *n* (ca. 1641) **1** : action, inclination, or thought based only on natural desires and instincts **2** : a theory denying that an event or object has a supernatural significance; *specif* : the doctrine that scientific laws are adequate to account for all phenomena **3** : realism in art or literature; *specif* : a theory or practice in literature emphasizing scientific observation of life without idealization and often including elements of determinism

nat·u·ral·ist \-list\ *n* (1587) **1** : one that advocates or practices naturalism **2** : a student of natural history; *esp* : a field biologist

nat·u·ral·is·tic \ˌna-chə-rə-ˈlis-tik, ˌnach-rə-\ *also* **nat·u·ral·ist** \ˈna-chə-rə-list, ˈnach-rə-\ *adj* (1838) : of, characterized by, or according with naturalism — **nat·u·ral·is·ti·cal·ly** \ˌna-chə-rə-ˈlis-ti-k(ə-)lē, ˌnach-rə-\ *adv*

nat·u·ral·ize \ˈna-chə-rə-ˌlīz, ˈnach-rə-\ *vb* **-ized; -iz·ing** *vt* (1559) **1** : to confer the rights of a national on; *esp* : to admit to citizenship **2** : to introduce into common use or into the vernacular **3** : to bring into conformity with nature **4** : to cause (as a plant) to become established as if native ~ *vi* : to become established as if native — **nat·u·ral·i·za·tion** \ˌna-chə-rə-lə-ˈzā-shən, ˌnach-rə-\ *n*

natural killer cell *n* (1975) : a large granular lymphocyte capable of killing a tumor or microbial cell without prior exposure to the target cell and without having it presented with or marked by a histocompatibility antigen — called also *NK cell*

natural law *n* (15c) : a body of law or a specific principle held to be derived from nature and binding upon human society in the absence of or in addition to positive law

natural logarithm *n* (1816) : a logarithm with *e* as a base

nat·u·ral·ly \ˈna-chər-ə-lē, ˈnach-rə-, ˈna-chər-\ *adv* (14c) **1** : by nature : by natural character or ability ⟨~ timid⟩ **2** : according to the usual course of things : as might be expected ⟨we ~ dislike being hurt⟩ **3 a** : without artificial aid ⟨hair that curls ~⟩ **b** : without affectation ⟨speak ~⟩ **4** : with truth to nature : REALISTICALLY

natural number *n* (1763) **1** : the number 1 or any number (as 3, 12, 432) obtained by adding 1 to it one or more times : a positive integer **2** : any of the positive integers together with 0 : a nonnegative integer

natural philosophy *n* (14c) : NATURAL SCIENCE; *esp* : PHYSICAL SCIENCE — **natural philosopher** *n*

natural resource *n* (1870) **1** *pl* : industrial materials and capacities (as mineral deposits and waterpower) supplied by nature **2** : RESOURCE 1b, c

natural science *n* (14c) : any of the sciences (as physics, chemistry, or biology) that deal with matter, energy, and their interrelations and transformations or with objectively measurable phenomena — **natural scientist** *n*

natural selection *n* (1857) : a natural process that results in the survival and reproductive success of individuals or groups best adjusted to their environment and that leads to the perpetuation of genetic qualities best suited to that particular environment

natural theology *n* (1675) : theology deriving its knowledge of God from the study of nature independent of special revelation

na·ture \ˈnā-chər\ *n* [ME, fr. MF, fr. L *natura,* fr. *natus,* pp. of *nasci* to be born — more at NATION] (14c) **1 a** : the inherent character or basic constitution of a person or thing : ESSENCE **b** : DISPOSITION, TEMPERAMENT **2 a** : a creative and controlling force in the universe **b** : an inner force or the sum of such forces in an individual **3** : a kind or class usu. distinguished by fundamental or essential characteristics ⟨documents of a confidential ~⟩ ⟨acts of a ceremonial ~⟩ **4** : the physical constitution or drives of an organism; *esp* : an excretory organ or function — used in phrases like *the call of nature* **5** : a spontaneous attitude (as of generosity) **6** : the external world in its entirety **7 a** : humankind's original or natural condition **b** : a simplified mode of life resembling this condition **8** : the genetically controlled qualities of an organism **9** : natural scenery ***syn*** see TYPE

na·tur·ism \ˈnā-chə-ˌri-zəm\ *n* (1847) **1 a** : NATURALISM 1 **b** : NATURALISM 2 **2** : the worship of the forces of nature **3** : NUDISM — **na·tur·ist** \-rist\ *n*

na·tu·rop·a·thy \ˌnā-chə-ˈrä-pə-thē\ *n* (1901) : a system of treatment of disease that avoids drugs and surgery and emphasizes the use of natural agents (as air, water, and herbs) and physical means (as tissue manipulation and electrotherapy) — **na·tu·ro·path** \ˈnā-chər-ə-ˌpath, ˈna-\ *n* — **na·tu·ro·path·ic** \ˌnā-chər-ə-ˈpa-thik, ˌna-; nə-ˌtyu̇r-ə-, -ˌtu̇r-\ *adj*

Nau·ga·hyde \ˈnȯ-gə-ˌhīd, ˈnä-\ *trademark* — used for vinyl-coated fabrics

[1]**naught** *also* **nought** \ˈnȯt, ˈnät\ *pron* [ME *nought,* fr. OE *nāwiht,* fr. *nā* no + *wiht* creature, thing — more at NO, WIGHT] (bef. 12c) : NOTHING ⟨efforts came to ∼⟩

[2]**naught** *also* **nought** *n* (bef. 12c) **1** : NOTHINGNESS, NONEXISTENCE **2** : the arithmetical symbol 0 : ZERO, CIPHER

naugh·ty \ˈnȯ-tē, ˈnä-\ *adj* **naugh·ti·er; -est** [ME *noughti,* fr. *nought*] (14c) **1 a** *archaic* : vicious in moral character : WICKED **b** : guilty of disobedience or misbehavior **2** : lacking in taste or propriety — **naugh·ti·ly** \ˈnȯ-tə-lē, ˈnä-\ *adv* — **naugh·ti·ness** \ˈnȯ-tē-nəs, ˈnä-\ *n*

nau·ma·chia \nȯ-ˈmā-kē-ə, -ˈma-\ *n, pl* **-chi·ae** \-kē-ˌē, -kē-ˌī\ *or* **-chi·as** [L, fr. Gk, naval battle, fr. *naus* ship + *machesthai* to fight — more at NAVE] (1596) **1** : an ancient Roman spectacle representing a naval battle **2** : a place for naumachiae

nau·pli·us \ˈnȯ-plē-əs\ *n, pl* **-plii** \-plē-ˌī, -ˌē\ [NL, fr. L, a shellfish, fr. Gk *nauplios*] (1836) : a crustacean larva in usu. the first stage after leaving the egg and with three pairs of appendages, a median eye, and little or no segmentation

nau·sea \ˈnȯ-zē-ə, -sē-ə; ˈnȯ-zhə, -shə\ *n* [L, seasickness, nausea, fr. Gk *nautia, nausia,* fr. *nautēs* sailor — more at NAUTICAL] (1569) **1** : a stomach distress with distaste for food and an urge to vomit **2** : extreme disgust — **nau·se·ant** \-zhē-ənt, -shē-, -zē-, -sē-\ *n or adj*

nau·se·ate \ˈnȯ-zhē-ˌāt, -shē-, -zē-, -sē-\ *vb* **-at·ed; -at·ing** *vi* (1625) **1** : to become affected with nausea **2** : to feel disgust ∼ *vt* : to affect with nausea or disgust

nauseating *adj* (1645) : causing nausea or esp. disgust ***usage*** see NAUSEOUS — **nau·se·at·ing·ly** *adv*

nau·seous \ˈnȯ-shəs, ˈnȯ-zē-əs\ *adj* (1612) **1** : causing nausea or disgust : NAUSEATING **2** : affected with nausea or disgust — **nau·seous·ly** *adv* — **nau·seous·ness** *n*

usage Those who insist that *nauseous* can properly be used only in sense 1 and that in sense 2 it is an error for *nauseated* are mistaken. Current evidence shows these facts: *nauseous* is most frequently used to mean physically affected with nausea, usu. after a linking verb such as *feel* or *become;* figurative use is quite a bit less frequent. Use of *nauseous* in sense 1 is much more often figurative than literal, and this use appears to be losing ground to *nauseating. Nauseated* is used more widely than *nauseous* in sense 2.

naut *abbr* nautical

nautch \ˈnȯch\ *n* [Hindi *nāc* & Urdu *nāch,* fr. Skt *nṛtya,* fr. *nṛtyati* he dances] (1809) : an entertainment in India consisting chiefly of dancing by professional dancing girls

nau·ti·cal \ˈnȯ-ti-kəl, ˈnä-\ *adj* [L *nauticus,* fr. Gk *nautikos,* fr. *nautēs* sailor, fr. *naus* ship — more at NAVE] (1552) : of, relating to, or associated with seamen, navigation, or ships — **nau·ti·cal·ly** \-k(ə-)lē\ *adv*

nautical mile *n* (1834) : any of various units of distance used for sea and air navigation based on the length of a minute of arc of a great circle of the earth and differing because the earth is not a perfect sphere: as **a** : a British unit equal to 6080 feet (1853.2 meters) **b** : an international unit equal to exactly 1852 meters (6076.115 feet or 1.15 statute miles) used officially in the U.S. since July 1, 1954

nau·ti·loid \ˈnȯ-tə-ˌlȯid, ˈnä-\ *n* (ca. 1728) : any of a subclass (Nautiloidea) of cephalopods bearing an external straight, curved, or spiral shell that were abundant chiefly in the Paleozoic but are represented in the recent fauna only by the nautiluses — **nautiloid** *adj*

nau·ti·lus \ˈnȯ-tə-ləs, ˈnä-\ *n, pl* **-lus·es** *or* **-li** \-tə-ˌlī, -ˌlē\ [NL, fr. L, paper nautilus, fr. Gk *nautilos,* lit., sailor, fr. *naus* ship] (1601) **1** : any of a genus (*Nautilus*) of cephalopod mollusks of the So. Pacific and Indian oceans with a spiral chambered shell that is pearly on the inside — called also *chambered nautilus* **2** : PAPER NAUTILUS

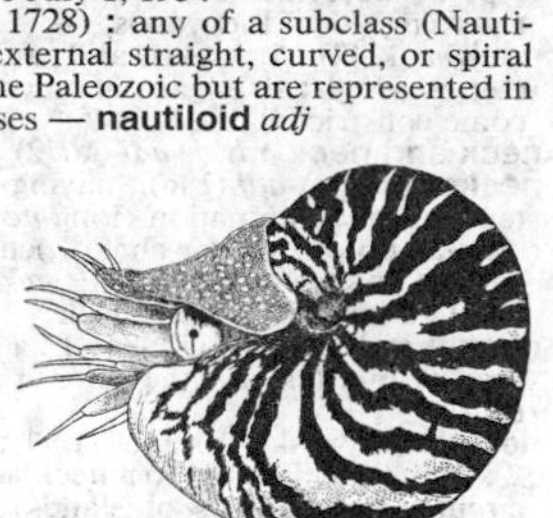

nautilus 1

nav *abbr* **1** naval **2** navigable; navigation

nav·aid \ˈna-ˌvād\ *n* [*navigation aid*] (1956) : a device or system (as a radar beacon) that provides a navigator with navigational data

Na·va·jo *also* **Na·va·ho** \ˈna-və-ˌhō, ˈnä-\ *n, pl* **-jo** *or* **-jos** *also* **-ho** *or* **-hos** [Sp (*Apache de*) *Navajó,* lit., Apache of Navajó, fr. *Navajó,* area occupied by Navajos, prob. fr. Tewa (Pueblo Indian language of northern New Mexico) *navahu·,* lit., arroyo with planted fields] (1780) **1** : a member of an American Indian people of northern New Mexico and Arizona **2** : the language of the Navajo people

na·val \ˈnā-vəl\ *adj* [ME, fr. L *navalis,* fr. *navis* ship] (15c) **1** *obs* : of or relating to ships or shipping **2 a** : of or relating to a navy **b** : consisting of or involving warships

naval architect *n* (ca. 1885) : one who designs ships

naval stores *n pl* [fr. their former use in the construction and maintenance of wooden sailing vessels] (1677) : products (as turpentine, pitch, and rosin) obtained from resinous conifers and esp. pines

[1]**nave** \ˈnāv\ *n* [ME, fr. OE *nafu;* akin to OE *nafela* navel] (bef. 12c) : the hub of a wheel

[2]**nave** *n* [ML *navis,* fr. L, ship; akin to OE *nōwend* sailor, Gk *naus* ship, Skt *nau*] (1673) : the main part of the interior of a church; *esp* : the long narrow central hall in a cruciform church that rises higher than the aisles flanking it to form a clerestory

na·vel \ˈnā-vəl\ *n* [ME, fr. OE *nafela;* akin to OHG *nabalo* navel, L *umbilicus,* Gk *omphalos*] (bef. 12c) **1** : a depression in the middle of the abdomen that marks the point of former attachment of the umbilical cord or yolk stalk **2** : the central point : MIDDLE

navel–gaz·ing \ˈnā-vəl-ˈgā-ziŋ\ *n* (1963) : useless or excessive self-contemplation

navel orange *n* (1888) : a seedless orange having a pit at the apex where the fruit encloses a small secondary fruit — called also *navel*

[1]**na·vic·u·lar** \nə-ˈvi-kyə-lər\ *adj* [ME *naviculare,* fr. L *navicula* boat, dim. of *navis*] (15c) **1** : shaped like a boat ⟨a ∼ bone⟩ **2** : of, relating to, or involving a navicular bone ⟨∼ disease⟩

[2]**navicular** *n* [NL (*os*) *naviculare* a navicular bone] (1816) : a navicular bone: **a** : one situated on the big-toe side of the tarsus in humans — called also *scaphoid* **b** : SCAPHOID 2 **c** : one situated in the hoof of a horse behind the coffin bone

nav·i·ga·ble \ˈna-vi-gə-bəl\ *adj* (15c) **1 a** : deep enough and wide enough to afford passage to ships ⟨∼ waterways⟩ **b** : capable of being navigated ⟨∼ terrain⟩ **2** : capable of being steered — **nav·i·ga·bil·i·ty** \ˌna-vi-gə-ˈbi-lə-tē\ *n* — **nav·i·ga·bly** \ˈna-vi-gə-blē\ *adv*

nav·i·gate \ˈna-və-ˌgāt\ *vb* **-gat·ed; -gat·ing** [L *navigatus,* pp. of *navigare,* fr. *navis* ship + *-igare* (fr. *agere* to drive) — more at AGENT] *vi* (1588) **1** : to travel by water : SAIL **2** : to steer a course through a medium; *specif* : to operate an airplane **3** : GET AROUND, MOVE ∼ *vt* **1 a** : to sail over, on, or through **b** : to make one's way over or through : TRAVERSE **2 a** : to steer or manage (a boat) in sailing **b** : to operate or control the course of (as an airplane)

nav·i·ga·tion \ˌna-və-ˈgā-shən\ *n* (1547) **1** : the act or practice of navigating **2** : the science of getting ships, aircraft, or spacecraft from place to place; *esp* : the method of determining position, course, and distance traveled **3** : ship traffic or commerce — **nav·i·ga·tion·al** \-shnəl, -shə-nᵊl\ *adj* — **nav·i·ga·tion·al·ly** *adv*

nav·i·ga·tor \ˈna-və-ˌgā-tər\ *n* (1590) : one that navigates or is qualified to navigate

nav·vy \ˈna-vē\ *n, pl* **navvies** [by shortening & alter. fr. *navigator* construction worker on a canal] (ca. 1834) *chiefly Brit* : an unskilled laborer

na·vy \ˈnā-vē\ *n, pl* **navies** [ME *navie,* fr. AF, fr. L *navigia* ships, fr. *navigare*] (14c) **1** : a group of ships : FLEET **2** : a nation's ships of war and of logistic support **3** *often cap* : the complete naval establishment of a nation including yards, stations, ships, and personnel **4** : a dark grayish purplish blue

navy bean *n* (1856) : a white-seeded kidney bean grown esp. for its nutritious seeds; *also* : its seed

Navy Cross *n* (1919) : a U.S. Navy decoration awarded for extraordinary heroism in operations against an armed enemy

navy yard *n* (1771) : a yard where naval vessels are built or repaired

na·wab \nə-ˈwäb\ *n* [Urdu *nawāb*] (1758) : NABOB

[1]**nay** \ˈnā\ *adv* [ME, fr. ON *nei,* fr. *ne* not + *ei* ever — more at NO, AYE] (13c) : NO

[2]**nay** *n* (14c) **1** : DENIAL, REFUSAL **2 a** : a negative reply or vote **b** : one who votes no

[3]**nay** *conj* (1560) : not merely this but also : not only so but ⟨the letter made him happy, ∼, ecstatic⟩

nay·say·er \ˈnā-ˌsā-ər, -ˌser\ *n* (1721) : one who denies, refuses, opposes, or is skeptical or cynical about something — **nay–say·ing** \-ˌsā-iŋ\ *n*

Naz·a·rene \ˌna-zə-ˈrēn\ *n* [ME *Nazaren,* fr. LL *Nazarenus,* fr. Gk *Nazarēnos,* fr. *Nazareth* Nazareth, Palestine] (13c) **1** : a native or resident of Nazareth **2 a** : CHRISTIAN 1a **b** : a member of the Church of the Nazarene that is a Protestant denomination deriving from the merging of three holiness groups, stressing sanctification, and following Methodist polity — **Nazarene** *adj*

Na·zi \ˈnät-sē, ˈnat-\ *n* [G, by shortening & alter. fr. *Nationalsozialist,* fr. *national* national + *Sozialist* socialist] (1930) **1** : a member of a German fascist party controlling Germany from 1933 to 1945 under Adolf Hitler **2** *often not cap* **a** : one who espouses the beliefs and policies of the German Nazis : FASCIST **b** : one who is likened to a German Nazi : a harshly domineering, dictatorial, or intolerant person — **nazi** *adj, often cap* — **na·zi·fi·ca·tion** \ˌnät-si-fə-ˈkā-shən, ˌnat-\ *n, often cap* — **na·zi·fy** \ˈnät-si-ˌfī, ˈnat-\ *vt, often cap*

Naz·i·rite *or* **Naz·a·rite** \ˈna-zə-ˌrīt\ *n* [LL *nazaraeus,* fr. Gk *naziraios, nazaraios,* fr. Heb *nāzīr,* lit., consecrated] (1560) : a Jew of biblical times consecrated to God by a vow to avoid drinking wine, cutting the hair, and being defiled by the presence of a corpse — **Naz·i·rit·ism** \-ˌrī-ˌti-zəm\ *n*

Na·zism \ˈnät-ˌsi-zəm, ˈnat-\ *also* **Na·zi·ism** \-sē-ˌi-zəm\ *n* [*Nazi* + *-ism*] (1934) : the body of political and economic doctrines held and put into effect by the Nazis in Germany from 1933 to 1945 including the totalitarian principle of government, predominance of esp. Germanic groups assumed to be racially superior, and supremacy of the führer

Nb *symbol* niobium

NB *abbr* **1** New Brunswick **2** northbound **3** nota bene — often not cap

NBA *abbr* **1** National Basketball Association **2** National Boxing Association

NBC *abbr* **1** National Broadcasting Company **2** nuclear, biological, and chemical

NBS *abbr* National Bureau of Standards

NC *abbr* **1** no charge **2** no credit **3** North Carolina **4** nurse corps

NCAA *abbr* National Collegiate Athletic Association

NCO \ˌen-(ˌ)sē-ˈō\ *n* (ca. 1810) : NONCOMMISSIONED OFFICER

NC–17 \ˈen-ˈsē-ˌse-vən-ˈtēn\ *certification mark* — used to certify that a motion picture is of such a nature that no one under the age of 17 can be admitted; compare G, PG, PG-13, R

nd *abbr* no date

\ə\ **abut** \ᵊ\ kitten, F table \ər\ **further** \a\ **ash** \ā\ **ace** \ä\ **mop, mar** \au̇\ **out** \ch\ **chin** \e\ **bet** \ē\ **easy** \g\ **go** \i\ **hit** \ī\ **ice** \j\ **job** \ŋ\ **sing** \ō\ **go** \ȯ\ **law** \ȯi\ **boy** \th\ **thin** \t͟h\ **the** \ü\ **loot** \u̇\ **foot** \y\ **yet** \zh\ **vision, beige** \k̲, ⁿ, œ, ue, ʸ\ *see* Guide to Pronunciation

Nd *symbol* neodymium
ND *abbr* **1** doctor of naturopathy **2** North Dakota
-nd *symbol* — used after the figure 2 to indicate the ordinal number *second* ⟨*2nd*⟩ ⟨*72nd*⟩
N Dak *abbr* North Dakota
NDE *abbr* near-death experience
NDP *abbr* New Democratic Party (Canad)
Ne *symbol* neon
NE *abbr* **1** Nebraska **2** New England **3** no effects **4** northeast
né \ˈnā\ *adj* [F, lit., born — more at NÉE] (1905) **1** — used to indicate the original, former, or legal name of a man ⟨Robert Roe, ~ John Doe⟩ **2 :** originally or formerly called
ne- *or* **neo-** *comb form* [Gk, fr. *neos* new — more at NEW] **1 a :** new : recent ⟨*Neo*gene⟩ **b :** new and different period or form of ⟨*Neo*platonism⟩ : in a new and different form or manner ⟨*Neo*platonic⟩ **c :** New World ⟨*Neo*tropical⟩ **d :** new and abnormal ⟨*neo*plasm⟩ **2 :** new chemical compound isomeric with or otherwise related to (such) a compound ⟨*neo*stigmine⟩
NEA *abbr* **1** National Education Association **2** National Endowment for the Arts
Ne·an·der·thal \nē-ˈan-dər-ˌtȯl, -ˌthȯl; nā-ˈän-dər-ˌtäl\ *n* [*Neanderthal,* valley in western Germany] (1874) **1** *or* **Ne·an·der·tal** \-ˌtȯl, -ˌtäl\ **:** a hominid (*Homo neanderthalensis* syn *H. sapiens neanderthalensis*) known from skeletal remains in Europe, northern Africa, and western Asia that lived from about 30,000 to 200,000 years ago — called also *Neanderthal man* **2 :** one who suggests a caveman in appearance, mentality, or behavior — **Neanderthal** *or* **Neandertal** *adj* — **Ne·an·der·thal·oid** \-ˌtȯ-ˌlȯid, -ˌthȯ-, -ˌtä-\ *adj or n*
[1]**neap** \ˈnēp\ *adj* [ME *neep,* fr. OE *nēp* being at the stage of neap tide] (bef. 12c) **:** of, relating to, or constituting a neap tide
[2]**neap** *n* (15c) **:** NEAP TIDE
Ne·a·pol·i·tan \ˌnē-ə-ˈpä-lə-tən\ *n* [ME, fr. L *neapolitanus* of Naples, fr. Gk *neapolitēs* citizen of Naples, fr. *Neapolis* Naples] (15c) **:** a native or inhabitant of Naples, Italy — **Neapolitan** *adj*
Neapolitan ice cream *n* (1895) **:** a brick of from two to four layers of ice cream of different flavors
neap tide *n* (1548) **:** a tide of minimum range occurring at the first and the third quarters of the moon
[1]**near** \ˈnir\ *adv* [ME *ner,* partly fr. *ner* nearer, fr. OE *nēar,* comparative of *nēah* nigh; partly fr. ON *nær* nearer, compar. of *nā-* nigh — more at NIGH] (13c) **1 :** at, within, or to a short distance or time ⟨sunset was drawing ~⟩ **2 :** ALMOST, NEARLY ⟨was ~ dead⟩ **3 :** in a close or intimate manner : CLOSELY ⟨~ related⟩ **4** *archaic* **:** in a frugal manner
[2]**near** *prep* (13c) **:** close to ⟨beaches ~ the city⟩ ⟨seemed to be ~ death⟩
[3]**near** *adj* (14c) **1 a :** not far distant in time, place, or degree ⟨in the ~ future⟩ **b :** almost happening : narrowly missed or avoided ⟨a ~ win in the primary⟩ ⟨a ~ midair collision⟩ **c :** nearly not happening ⟨a ~ escape⟩ **2 :** closely related or intimately associated ⟨her ~*est* and dearest friend⟩ **3 a :** being the closer of two ⟨the ~ side⟩ **b :** being the left-hand one of a pair ⟨the ~ wheel of a cart⟩ **4 :** DIRECT, SHORT ⟨the ~*est* road⟩ **5 :** STINGY, CLOSEFISTED **6 a :** closely resembling the standard or typical ⟨a ~ desert⟩ **b :** approximating the genuine ⟨~ silk⟩ — **near·ness** *n*
[4]**near** *vb* (ca. 1522) **:** APPROACH
near beer *n* (1909) **:** any of various malt liquors considered nonalcoholic because they contain less than a specified percentage of alcohol
near·by \nir-ˈbī, ˈnir-ˌ\ *adv or adj* (15c) **:** close at hand
Ne·arc·tic \ˌnē-ˈärk-tik, -ˈär-tik\ *adj* (1858) **:** of, relating to, or being the biogeographic subregion that includes Greenland and No. America north of tropical Mexico
near field communication *n* (1996) **:** a technology for digitally transmitting information over short distances (usu. between a smartphone and another device) using radio waves
near gale *n* (1958) **:** MODERATE GALE — see BEAUFORT SCALE table
near–in·fra·red \ˌnir-ˌin-frə-ˈred, -(ˌ)frä-\ *adj* (1950) **:** of or relating to the shorter wavelengths of radiation in the infrared spectrum and esp. to those between 0.7 and 2.5 micrometers
near·ly \ˈnir-lē\ *adv* (1561) **1 :** in a close manner or relationship ⟨~ related⟩ **2 a :** almost but not quite ⟨~ identical⟩ ⟨~ a year later⟩ **b :** to the least extent ⟨not ~ as good as we expected⟩
near miss *n* (1940) **1 a :** a miss (as with a bomb) close enough to cause damage **b :** something that falls just short of success **2 a :** a near collision (as between aircraft) **b :** CLOSE CALL
near money *n* (1936) **:** assets (as savings accounts or government bonds) quickly and easily converted to cash
near point *n* (1876) **:** the point nearest the eye at which an object is accurately focused on the retina at full accommodation
near·shore \ˈnir-ˈshȯr, ˈnir-ˌ\ *adj* (1896) **:** extending outward an indefinite but usu. short distance from shore ⟨~ sediments⟩
near·side \-ˌsīd\ *adj* (1723) *Brit* **:** LEFT-HAND 1 — **nearside** *n*
near·sight·ed \-ˌsī-təd\ *adj* (1686) **:** able to see near things more clearly than distant ones : MYOPIC — **near·sight·ed·ly** *adv*
near·sight·ed·ness \ˈnir-ˌsī-təd-nəs\ *n* (1811) **:** MYOPIA
near–ul·tra·vi·o·let \ˌnir-ˌəl-trə-ˈvī-(ə-)lət\ *adj* (1951) **:** of, relating to, or being the longest wavelengths of radiation in the ultraviolet spectrum esp. between 300 and 400 nanometers
[1]**neat** \ˈnēt\ *n, pl* **neat** *or* **neats** [ME *neet,* fr. OE *nēat;* akin to OHG *nōz* head of cattle, OE *nēotan* to make use of, Lith *nauda* use] (bef. 12c) **:** the common domestic bovine (*Bos taurus*)
[2]**neat** *adj* [MF *net,* fr. L *nitidus* bright, neat, fr. *nitēre* to shine; prob. akin to MIr *níam* luster] (15c) **1 :** free from dirt and disorder : habitually clean and orderly **2 a :** free from admixture or dilution : STRAIGHT ⟨~ brandy⟩ ⟨~ cement⟩ **b :** free from irregularity : SMOOTH ⟨~ silk⟩ **3 :** marked by tasteful simplicity ⟨a ~ outfit⟩ **4 a :** PRECISE, SYSTEMATIC **b :** marked by skill or ingenuity : ADROIT **5 :** NET ⟨~ profit⟩ **6 :** FINE, ADMIRABLE — **neat·ly** *adv* — **neat·ness** *n*
[3]**neat** *adv* (ca. 1578) **1 :** in a neat manner ⟨his hair combed back ~ —J. M. Cain⟩ **2 :** without admixture or dilution : STRAIGHT
neat·en \ˈnē-tᵊn\ *vt* **neat·ened; neat·en·ing** \ˈnēt-niŋ, ˈnē-tᵊn-iŋ\ (1828) **1 :** to set in order : make neat **2 :** to finish (as a piece of sewing) carefully
neath \ˈnēth\ *prep* (ca. 1582) *dial* **:** BENEATH
neat·herd \ˈnēt-ˌhərd\ *n* (14c) **:** HERDSMAN
neat·nik \ˈnēt-nik\ *n* (1959) **:** a person who is compulsively neat
neat's–foot oil \ˈnēts-ˌfu̇t-\ *n* (1639) **:** a pale yellow fatty oil made esp. from the bones of cattle and used chiefly as a leather dressing
neb \ˈneb\ *n* [ME, fr. OE; akin to ON *nef* beak] (bef. 12c) **1 a :** the beak of a bird or tortoise : BILL **b** *chiefly dial* **:** a person's mouth **c :** NOSE 1, SNOUT **2 :** NIB, TIP
Neb *or* **Nebr** *abbr* Nebraska
NEB *abbr* New English Bible
neb·bish \ˈne-bish\ *n* [Yiddish *nebekh* poor, unfortunate, fr. Czech *nebohý*] (1907) **:** a timid, meek, or ineffectual person — **neb·bishy** \-bi-shē\ *adj*
neb·u·la \ˈne-byə-lə\ *n, pl* **-lae** \-ˌlē, -ˌlī\ *also* **-las** [NL, fr. L, mist, cloud; akin to OHG *nebul* fog, Gk *nephelē, nephos* cloud] (1718) **1 :** any of numerous clouds of gas or dust in interstellar space **2 :** GALAXY 1b; *esp* **:** a galaxy other than the Milky Way galaxy — not used technically — **neb·u·lar** \-lər\ *adj*
nebular hypothesis *n* (1833) **:** a hypothesis in astronomy: the solar system has evolved from a hot gaseous nebula
neb·u·lize \ˈne-byə-ˌlīz\ *vt* **-lized; -liz·ing** [L *nebula*] (1867) **:** to reduce to a fine spray — **neb·u·li·za·tion** \ˌne-byə-lə-ˈzā-shən\ *n* — **neb·u·liz·er** \ˈne-byə-ˌlī-zər\ *n*
neb·u·los·i·ty \ˌne-byə-ˈlä-sə-tē\ *n, pl* **-ties** (1762) **1 :** the quality or state of being nebulous **2 :** nebulous matter; *also* **:** NEBULA 1
neb·u·lous \ˈne-byə-ləs\ *adj* [L *nebulosus* misty, fr. *nebula*] (1674) **1 :** of, relating to, or resembling a nebula : NEBULAR **2 :** INDISTINCT, VAGUE — **neb·u·lous·ly** *adv* — **neb·u·lous·ness** *n*
nec·es·sar·i·ly \ˌne-sə-ˈser-ə-lē\ *adv* (14c) **1 :** of necessity : UNAVOIDABLY **2 :** as a logical result or consequence
[1]**nec·es·sary** \ˈne-sə-ˌser-ē\ *adj* [ME *necessarie,* fr. L *necessarius,* fr. *necesse* necessary, prob. fr. *ne-* not + *cedere* to withdraw — more at NO] (14c) **1 :** absolutely needed : REQUIRED **2 a :** of an inevitable nature : INESCAPABLE **b** (1) **:** logically unavoidable (2) **:** that cannot be denied without contradiction **c :** determined or produced by the previous condition of things **d :** COMPULSORY
[2]**necessary** *n, pl* **-sar·ies** (14c) **:** an indispensable item : ESSENTIAL
necessary condition *n* (1651) **1 :** a state of affairs that must prevail if another is to occur : PREREQUISITE **2 :** a proposition whose falsity assures the falsity of another
ne·ces·si·tar·i·an·ism \ni-ˌse-sə-ˈter-ē-ə-ˌni-zəm\ *n* (1825) **:** the theory that results follow by invariable sequence from causes — **ne·ces·si·tar·i·an** \-ˈter-ē-ən\ *adj or n*
ne·ces·si·tate \ni-ˈse-sə-ˌtāt\ *vt* **-tat·ed; -tat·ing** (1625) **1 :** to make necessary : REQUIRE **2 :** FORCE, COMPEL — **ne·ces·si·ta·tion** \-ˌse-sə-ˈtā-shən\ *n*
ne·ces·si·tous \ni-ˈse-sə-təs\ *adj* (1611) **1 :** NEEDY, IMPOVERISHED **2 :** URGENT, PRESSING **3 :** NECESSARY — **ne·ces·si·tous·ly** *adv* — **ne·ces·si·tous·ness** *n*
ne·ces·si·ty \ni-ˈse-sə-tē, -ˈses-tē\ *n, pl* **-ties** [ME *necessite,* fr. AF *necessité,* fr. L *necessitat-, necessitas,* fr. *necesse*] (14c) **1 :** the quality or state of being necessary **2 a :** pressure of circumstance **b :** physical or moral compulsion **c :** impossibility of a contrary order or condition **3 :** the quality or state of being in need; *esp* **:** POVERTY **4 a :** something that is necessary : REQUIREMENT **b :** an urgent need or desire — **of necessity :** in such a way that it cannot be otherwise; *also* **:** as a necessary consequence ⟨further changes will occur *of necessity*⟩
[1]**neck** \ˈnek\ *n* [ME *nekke,* fr. OE *hnecca;* akin to OHG *hnac* nape] (bef. 12c) **1 a** (1) **:** the part of an animal that connects the head with the body (2) **:** the siphon of a bivalve mollusk (as a clam) **b :** the part of a garment that covers or is next to the neck **2 :** a relatively narrow part suggestive of a neck: as **a** (1) **:** the constricted end of a bottle (2) **:** the slender proximal end of a fruit **b :** CERVIX 2 **c :** the part of a stringed musical instrument extending from the body and supporting the fingerboard and strings **d :** a narrow stretch of land **e :** STRAIT 1b **f :** the part of a tooth between the crown and the root — see TOOTH illustration **g :** a column of solidified magma of a volcanic pipe or laccolith **3 :** a narrow margin ⟨won by a ~⟩ **4 :** REGION, PART ⟨my ~ of the woods⟩
[2]**neck** *vt* (1842) **1 :** to kiss and caress amorously **2 :** to reduce in diameter ~ *vi* **1 :** to engage in amorous kissing and caressing **2 :** to become constricted : NARROW
neck and neck *adv or adj* (1672) **:** very close (as in a race)
necked \ˈnekt\ *adj* (14c) **:** having a neck esp. of a specified kind — often used in combination ⟨long-*necked*⟩
neck·er·chief \ˈne-kər-chəf, -(ˌ)chif, -ˌchēf\ *n, pl* **-chiefs** *also* **-chieves** *see* HANDKERCHIEF *pl*\ [ME *nekkerchef,* fr. *nekke* + *kerchef* kerchief] (14c) **:** a kerchief for the neck
neck·ing \ˈne-kiŋ\ *n* (1798) **1 :** a narrow molding near the top of a column or pilaster **2 :** the act or practice of kissing and caressing amorously
neck·lace \ˈne-kləs\ *n* (1577) **1 :** an ornament worn around the neck **2 :** something likened to a necklace esp. in forming a linked series or a circular pattern ⟨a ~ of islands⟩
neck·line \ˈnek-ˌlīn\ *n* (1904) **:** the line of the neck opening of a garment
neck–rein \-ˌrān\ *vi* (1940) *of a saddle horse* **:** to respond to the pressure of a rein on one side of the neck by turning in the opposite direction ~ *vt* **:** to direct (a horse) by pressures of the rein on the neck
neck·tie \-ˌtī\ *n* (1838) **:** a narrow length of material worn about the neck and tied in front; *esp* **:** FOUR-IN-HAND
neck·wear \-ˌwer\ *n* (1870) **:** articles of clothing (as ties and scarves) worn about the neck
necr- *or* **necro-** *comb form* [LL, fr. Gk *nekr-, nekro-,* fr. *nekros* dead body — more at NOXIOUS] **1 :** those that are dead ⟨*necro*philia⟩ **2 :** one that is dead ⟨*necr*opsy⟩
ne·crol·o·gy \nə-ˈkrä-lə-jē, ne-\ *n, pl* **-gies** [NL *necrologium,* fr. *necr-* + *-logium* (as in ML *eulogium* eulogy)] (1799) **1 :** OBITUARY **2 :** a list of the recently dead — **nec·ro·log·i·cal** \ˌne-krə-ˈlä-ji-kəl\ *adj* — **ne·crol·o·gist** \nə-ˈkrä-lə-jist, ne-\ *n*
nec·ro·man·cy \ˈne-krə-ˌman(t)-sē\ *n* [alter. of ME *nigromancie,* fr. AF, fr. ML *nigromantia,* by folk etymology fr. LL *necromantia,* fr. LGk *nekromanteia,* fr. Gk *nekr-* + *-manteia* -mancy] (15c) **1 :** conjuration of the spirits of the dead for purposes of magically revealing the future or influencing the course of events **2 :** MAGIC, SORCERY — **nec·ro-**

man·cer \-sər\ *n* — **nec·ro·man·tic** \ˌne-krə-ˈman-tik\ *adj* — **nec·ro·man·ti·cal·ly** \-ti-k(ə-)lē\ *adv*

ne·croph·a·gous \nə-ˈkrä-fə-gəs, ne-\ *adj* (1835) **:** feeding on corpses or carrion ⟨~ insects⟩

nec·ro·phil·ia \ˌne-krə-ˈfi-lē-ə\ *n* [NL] (1892) **:** obsession with and usu. erotic interest in or stimulation by corpses — **nec·ro·phil·i·ac** \-ˈfi-lē-ˌak\ *adj or n* — **nec·ro·phil·ic** \-ˈfi-lik\ *adj*

ne·croph·i·lism \nə-ˈkrä-fə-ˌli-zəm, ne-\ *n* (1864) **:** NECROPHILIA

ne·crop·o·lis \nə-ˈkrä-pə-ləs, ne-\ *n, pl* **-lis·es** *or* **-les** \-ˌlēz\ *or* **-leis** \-ˌlās\ *or* **-li** \-ˌlī, -ˌlē\ [LL, city of the dead, fr. Gk *nekropolis,* fr. *nekr-* + *-polis* -polis] (1819) **:** CEMETERY; *esp* **:** a large elaborate cemetery of an ancient city

1**nec·rop·sy** \ˈne-ˌkräp-sē\ *n, pl* **-sies** (1856) **:** AUTOPSY 1; *esp* **:** an autopsy performed on an animal

2**necropsy** *vt* **-sied; -sy·ing** (1927) **:** to perform an autopsy on

ne·cro·sis \nə-ˈkrō-səs, ne-\ *n, pl* **ne·cro·ses** \-ˌsēz\ [LL, fr. Gk *nekrōsis,* fr. *nekroun* to make dead, fr. *nekros* dead body] (1665) **:** usu. localized death of living tissue — **ne·crot·ic** \-ˈkrä-tik\ *adj*

nec·ro·tiz·ing \ˈne-krə-ˌtī-ziŋ\ *adj* [Gk *nekrōtikos* necrotic, fr. *nekroun*] (1899) **:** causing or undergoing necrosis ⟨~ infections⟩ ⟨~ tissue⟩

necrotizing fasciitis *n* (1967) **:** a severe soft tissue infection by bacteria (as Group A streptococci) that is marked by edema and necrosis of subcutaneous tissues with involvement of adjacent fascia and by painful red swollen skin over affected areas

nec·tar \ˈnek-tər\ *n* [L, fr. Gk *nektar*] (1555) **1 a :** the drink of the Greek and Roman gods **b :** something delicious to drink **c :** a beverage of fruit juice and pulp ⟨apricot ~⟩ **2 :** a sweet liquid that is secreted by the nectaries of a plant and is the chief raw material of honey — **nec·tar·ous** \-t(ə-)rəs\ *adj*

nec·tar·ine \ˌnek-tə-ˈrēn\ *n* [obs. *nectarine,* adj., like nectar] (1611) **:** a peach with a smooth-skinned fruit that is a frequent somatic mutation of the normal peach; *also* **:** its fruit

nec·tary \ˈnek-t(ə-)rē\ *n, pl* **-tar·ies** [NL *nectarium,* irreg. fr. L *nectar* + *-arium* -ary] (1759) **:** a plant gland that secretes nectar

née *or* **nee** \ˈnā\ *adj* [F *née,* fem. of *né,* lit., born, pp. of *naître* to be born, fr. L *nasci* — more at NATION] (1758) **1 —** used to identify a woman by her maiden family name **2 :** originally or formerly called ⟨the Brewers ~ Pilots who also are in their third year —Fred Ciampa⟩

1**need** \ˈnēd\ *n* [ME *ned,* fr. OE *nīed, nēd;* akin to OHG *nōt* distress, need, OPruss *nautin* need] (bef. 12c) **1 :** necessary duty **:** OBLIGATION **2 a :** a lack of something requisite, desirable, or useful **b :** a physiological or psychological requirement for the well-being of an organism **3 :** a condition requiring supply or relief **4 :** lack of the means of subsistence **:** POVERTY

2**need** *vb* **need·ed; need·ing; needs** *or (auxiliary)* **need** *vi* (bef. 12c) **1 :** to be needful or necessary **2 :** to be in want **~** *vt* **:** to be in need of **:** REQUIRE **~** *verbal auxiliary* **:** be under necessity or obligation to ⟨you ~ not answer⟩ ⟨she ~ only wait⟩

1**need·ful** \ˈnēd-fəl\ *adj* (12c) **1 :** being in need **2 :** NECESSARY, REQUISITE — **need·ful·ly** \-fə-lē\ *adv* — **need·ful·ness** *n*

2**needful** *n* (1709) **1 :** something needed or requisite **2 :** MONEY

1**nee·dle** \ˈnē-dᵊl\ *n* [ME *nedle,* fr. OE *nǣdl;* akin to OHG *nādala* needle, *nājan* to sew, L *nēre* to spin, Gk *nēn*] (bef. 12c) **1 a :** a small slender usu. steel instrument that has an eye for thread or surgical sutures at one end and that is used for sewing **b :** any of various devices for carrying thread and making stitches (as in crocheting or knitting) **c** (1) **:** a slender hollow instrument for introducing material into or removing material from the body (as by insertion under the skin) (2) **:** any of various slender hollow devices used to introduce matter (as air) into or remove it from an object (as a ball) **2 a :** a slender bar of magnetized steel that when allowed to turn freely (as in a compass) indicates the direction of a magnetic field (as of the earth) **b :** a slender usu. sharp-pointed indicator on a dial **3 a :** a slender pointed object resembling a needle: as (1) **:** a pointed crystal (2) **:** a sharp rock (3) **:** OBELISK **b :** a needle-shaped leaf (as of a conifer) **c :** a slender rod (as of jewel or steel) with a rounded tip used in a phonograph to transmit vibrations from a record **:** STYLUS **d :** a slender pointed rod controlling a fine inlet or outlet (as in a valve) **4 :** a teasing or gibing remark — **nee·dle·like** \ˈnē-dᵊl-ˌ(l)īk\ *adj*

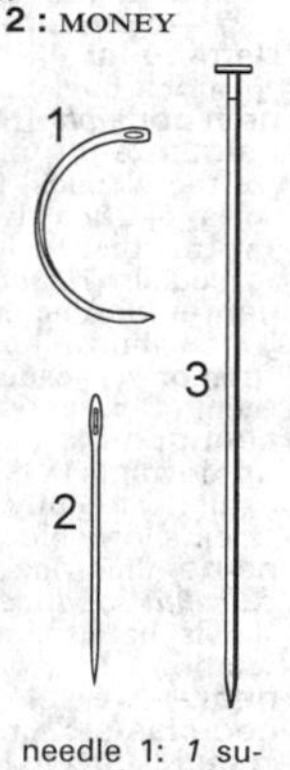

needle 1: *1* suture, *2* sewing, *3* knitting

2**needle** *vb* **nee·dled; nee·dling** \ˈnēd-liŋ, ˈnē-dᵊl-iŋ\ *vt* (ca. 1715) **1 :** to sew or pierce with or as if with a needle **2 a :** TEASE, TORMENT **b :** to incite to action by repeated gibes ⟨*needled* the boy into a fight⟩ **~** *vi* **:** SEW, EMBROIDER — **nee·dler** \ˈnēd-lər, ˈnē-dᵊl-ər\ *n*

nee·dle·fish \ˈnē-dᵊl-ˌfish\ *n* (1601) **1 :** any of a family (Belonidae) of elongate carnivorous chiefly marine bony fishes that are silvery with blue or green backs and have long slender jaws and sharp teeth **2 :** PIPEFISH

nee·dle–nose pliers \ˈnē-dᵊl-ˌnōz-\ *n pl but sing or pl in constr* (1971) **:** pliers with long slender jaws used for grasping small or thin objects

nee·dle·point \-ˌpȯint\ *n* (1865) **1 :** lace worked with a needle over a paper pattern **2 :** embroidery done on canvas usu. in simple even stitches across counted threads — **needlepoint** *adj*

need·less \ˈnēd-ləs\ *adj* (14c) **:** not needed **:** UNNECESSARY ⟨~ waste⟩ — **need·less·ly** *adv* — **need·less·ness** *n* — **needless to say :** as is self-evident or to be expected

nee·dle·stick \ˈnē-dᵊl-ˌstik\ *n* (1976) **:** an accidental puncture of the skin with an unsterilized instrument (as a syringe) — called also *needlestick injury*

nee·dle·wom·an \ˈnē-dᵊl-ˌwu̇-mən\ *n* (1535) **:** a woman who does needlework; *esp* **:** SEAMSTRESS

nee·dle·work \-ˌwərk\ *n* (14c) **1 :** work done with a needle; *esp* **:** work (as embroidery) other than plain sewing **2 :** the occupation of one who does needlework — **nee·dle·work·er** \-ˌwər-kər\ *n*

needn't \ˈnē-dᵊnt\ (1778) **:** need not

needs \ˈnēdz\ *adv* [ME *nedes,* fr. OE *nēdes,* fr. gen. of *nēd* need] (bef. 12c) **:** of necessity **:** NECESSARILY ⟨must ~ be recognized⟩

needy \ˈnē-dē\ *adj* **need·i·er; -est** (12c) **1 :** being in want **:** POVERTY-STRICKEN ⟨~ families⟩ **2 :** marked by want of affection, attention, or emotional support ⟨emotionally ~⟩ — **need·i·ness** *n*

neem \ˈnēm\ *n* [Hindi & Urdu *nīm,* fr. Skt *nimba*] (1813) **:** a large tropical Asian tree (*Azadirachta indica*) of the mahogany family having a bitter bark used as a tonic and leaves and seeds that have insecticidal and antiseptic properties and yield a medicinal aromatic oil

neep \ˈnēp\ *n* [ME *nepe,* fr. OE *nǣp,* fr. L *napus* — more at NAPIFORM] (bef. 12c) *chiefly Scot* **:** TURNIP

ne'er \ˈner\ *adv* (13c) **:** NEVER

ne'er–do–well \-du̇-ˌwel\ *n* (1736) **:** an idle worthless person — **ne'er–do–well** *adj*

ne·far·i·ous \ni-ˈfer-ē-əs\ *adj* [L *nefarius,* fr. *nefas* crime, fr. *ne-* not + *fas* right, divine law; perh. akin to Gk *themis* law, *tithenai* to place — more at DO] (ca. 1609) **:** flagrantly wicked or impious **:** EVIL ***syn*** see VICIOUS — **ne·far·i·ous·ly** *adv*

neg *abbr* **1** negative **2** negotiable

ne·gate \ni-ˈgāt\ *vt* **ne·gat·ed; ne·gat·ing** [L *negatus,* pp. of *negare* to say no, deny, fr. *neg-* no, not (akin to *ne-* not) — more at NO] (ca. 1623) **1 :** to deny the existence or truth of **2 :** to cause to be ineffective or invalid ***syn*** see NULLIFY — **negate** *n* — **ne·ga·tor** \-ˈgā-tər\ *n*

ne·ga·tion \ni-ˈgā-shən\ *n* (15c) **1 a :** the action or logical operation of negating or making negative **b :** a negative statement, judgment, or doctrine; *esp* **:** a logical proposition formed by asserting the falsity of a given proposition — see TRUTH TABLE table **2 a :** something that is the absence of something actual **:** NONENTITY **b :** something considered the opposite of something regarded as positive — **ne·ga·tion·al** \-shnəl, -shə-nᵊl\ *adj*

1**neg·a·tive** \ˈne-gə-tiv\ *adj* (15c) **1 a :** marked by denial, prohibition, or refusal ⟨received a ~ answer⟩; *also* **:** marked by absence, withholding, or removal of something positive ⟨the ~ motivation of shame —Garrett Hardin⟩ **b** (1) **:** denying a predicate of a subject or a part of a subject ⟨"no A is B" is a ~ proposition⟩ (2) **:** denoting the absence or the contradictory of something ⟨*nontoxic* is a ~ term⟩ (3) **:** expressing negation ⟨~ particles such as *no* and *not*⟩ **c :** ADVERSE, UNFAVORABLE ⟨the reviews were mostly ~⟩ **2 a :** lacking positive qualities; *esp* **:** DISAGREEABLE **b :** marked by features of hostility, withdrawal, or pessimism that hinder or oppose constructive treatment or development ⟨a ~ outlook⟩ ⟨~ criticism⟩ **c :** promoting a person or cause by criticizing or attacking the competition ⟨ran a ~ campaign⟩ ⟨~ advertising⟩ **3 a** (1) **:** less than zero and opposite in sign to a positive number that when added to the given number yields zero ⟨−2 is a ~ number⟩ (2) **:** having more outgo than income **:** constituting a loss ⟨~ cash flow⟩ ⟨~ worth⟩ **b :** extending or generated in a direction opposite to an arbitrarily chosen regular direction or position ⟨~ angle⟩ **4 a :** being, relating to, or charged with electricity of which the electron is the elementary unit **b :** having more electrons than protons ⟨a ~ ion⟩ **c** (1) **:** having lower electric potential and constituting the part toward which the current flows from the external circuit ⟨the ~ pole⟩ (2) **:** being the electron-emitting electrode of an electron tube **5 a :** not affirming the presence of a condition, substance, or organism suspected to be present; *also* **:** having a test result indicating the absence esp. of a condition, substance, or organism ⟨she is HIV ~⟩ **b :** directed or moving away from a source of stimulation ⟨~ tropism⟩ **c :** less than the pressure of the atmosphere ⟨~ pressure⟩ **6 :** having the light and dark parts in approximately inverse relation to those of the original photographic subject **7** *of a lens* **:** diverging light rays and forming a virtual inverted image — **neg·a·tive·ly** *adv* — **neg·a·tive·ness** *n* — **neg·a·tiv·i·ty** \ˌne-gə-ˈti-və-tē\ *n*

2**negative** *n* (1571) **1 a** (1) **:** a reply that indicates the withholding of assent **:** REFUSAL (2) *archaic* **:** a right of veto (3) *obs* **:** an adverse vote **:** VETO **b :** a proposition which denies or contradicts another; *esp* **:** the one of a pair of propositions in which negation is expressed **2 a :** something that is the opposite or negation of something else **b :** DRAWBACK, LIABILITY **3 a :** an expression (as the word *no*) of negation or denial **b :** a negative number **4 :** the side that upholds the contradictory proposition in a debate **5 :** a negative photographic image on transparent material used for printing positive pictures; *also* **:** the material that carries such an image **6 :** a reverse impression taken from a piece of sculpture or ceramics **7 :** a negative result (as of a test) ⟨a high rate of false ~*s*⟩; *also* **:** a test yielding such a result

3**negative** *vt* **-tived; -tiv·ing** (1706) **1 a :** to refuse assent to **b :** to reject by or as if by a vote **2 :** to demonstrate the falsity of **3 :** to deny the truth, reality, or validity of **4 :** NEUTRALIZE, COUNTERACT

negative feedback *n* (1934) **:** feedback that tends to dampen a process by applying the output against the initial conditions

negative income tax *n* (1966) **:** a system of federal subsidy payments to families with incomes below a stipulated level

negative transfer *n* (1921) **:** the impeding of learning or performance in a situation by learned responses carried over from another situation

neg·a·tiv·ism \ˈne-gə-ti-ˌvi-zəm\ *n* (1824) **1 :** an attitude of mind marked by skepticism esp. about nearly everything affirmed by others **2 :** a tendency to refuse to do, to do the opposite of, or to do something at variance with what is asked — **neg·a·tiv·ist** \-vist\ *n or adj* — **neg·a·tiv·is·tic** \ˌne-gə-ti-ˈvis-tik\ *adj*

1**ne·glect** \ni-ˈglekt\ *vt* [L *neglectus,* pp. of *neglegere, neclegere,* fr. *nec-* not (akin to *ne-* not) + *legere* to gather — more at NO, LEGEND] (1529) **1 :** to give little attention or respect to **:** DISREGARD **2 :** to leave undone or unattended to esp. through carelessness — **ne·glect·er** *n*

syn NEGLECT, DISREGARD, IGNORE, OVERLOOK, SLIGHT, FORGET mean to pass over without giving due attention. NEGLECT implies giving insufficient attention to something that merits one's attention ⟨habitually *neglected* his studies⟩. DISREGARD suggests voluntary inattention ⟨*disregarded* the wishes of his family⟩. IGNORE implies a failure to regard something obvious ⟨*ignored* the snide remark⟩. OVERLOOK suggests disregarding or ignoring through haste or lack of care ⟨in my rush I *overlooked* a key example⟩. SLIGHT implies contemptuous or disdainful disregarding or omitting ⟨*slighted* several major authors in her survey⟩. FORGET may suggest either a willful ignoring or a failure to impress something on one's mind ⟨*forget* what others say⟩.

[2]**neglect** *n* (1588) **1 :** an act or instance of neglecting something **2 :** the condition of being neglected

ne·glect·ful \ni-ˈglek(t)-fəl\ *adj* (1624) **:** given to neglecting **:** CARELESS, HEEDLESS ***syn*** see NEGLIGENT — **ne·glect·ful·ly** \-fə-lē\ *adv* — **ne·glect·ful·ness** *n*

neg·li·gee *also* **neg·li·gé** \ˌne-glə-ˈzhā, ˈne-glə-ˌ\ *n* [F *négligé*, fr. pp. of *négliger* to neglect, fr. L *neglegere*] (1756) **1 :** a woman's long flowing usu. sheer dressing gown **2 :** carelessly informal or incomplete attire

neg·li·gence \ˈne-gli-jən(t)s\ *n* (14c) **1 a :** the quality or state of being negligent **b :** failure to exercise the care that a reasonably prudent person would exercise in like circumstances **2 :** an act or instance of being negligent

neg·li·gent \-jənt\ *adj* [ME, fr. AF & L; AF, fr. L *neglegent-*, *neglegens*, prp. of *neglegere*] (14c) **1 a :** marked by or given to neglect esp. habitually or culpably **b :** failing to exercise the care expected of a reasonably prudent person in like circumstances **2 :** marked by a carelessly easy manner — **neg·li·gent·ly** *adv*

syn NEGLIGENT, NEGLECTFUL, LAX, SLACK, REMISS mean culpably careless or indicative of such carelessness. NEGLIGENT implies inattention to one's duty or business ⟨*negligent* about writing a note of thanks⟩. NEGLECTFUL adds a more disapproving implication of laziness or deliberate inattention ⟨a society callously *neglectful* of the poor⟩. LAX implies a blameworthy lack of strictness, severity, or precision ⟨a reporter *lax* about accurate quotation⟩. SLACK implies want of due or necessary diligence or care ⟨*slack* workmanship⟩. REMISS implies blameworthy carelessness shown in slackness, forgetfulness, or neglect ⟨had been *remiss* in their familial duties⟩.

neg·li·gi·ble \ˈne-gli-jə-bəl\ *adj* [L *neglegere, negligere*] (1829) **:** so small or unimportant or of so little consequence as to warrant little or no attention **:** TRIFLING ⟨a ~ error⟩ — **neg·li·gi·bil·i·ty** \ˌne-gli-jə-ˈbi-lə-tē\ *n* — **neg·li·gi·bly** \ˈne-gli-jə-blē\ *adv*

ne·go·tia·ble \ni-ˈgō-sh(ē-)ə-bəl\ *adj* (1758) **:** capable of being negotiated: as **a :** transferable from one person to another by being delivered with or without endorsement so that the title passes to the transferee ⟨~ securities⟩ **b :** capable of being traversed, dealt with, or accomplished ⟨a difficult but ~ road⟩ ⟨~ demands⟩ **c :** open to discussion or dispute — **ne·go·tia·bil·i·ty** \-ˌgō-sh(ē-)ə-ˈbi-lə-tē\ *n*

ne·go·ti·ant \-ˈgō-sh(ē-)ənt\ *n* (1611) **:** one that negotiates

ne·go·ti·ate \ni-ˈgō-shē-ˌāt, ÷-sē-\ *vb* **-at·ed; -at·ing** [L *negotiatus*, pp. of *negotiari* to carry on business, fr. *negotium* business, fr. *neg-* not + *otium* leisure — more at NEGATE] *vi* (1599) **:** to confer with another so as to arrive at the settlement of some matter ~ *vt* **1 a :** to deal with (some matter or affair that requires ability for its successful handling) **:** MANAGE **b :** to arrange for or bring about through conference, discussion, and compromise ⟨~ a treaty⟩ **2 a :** to transfer (as a bill of exchange) to another by delivery or endorsement **b :** to convert into cash or the equivalent value ⟨~ a check⟩ **3 a :** to successfully travel along or over ⟨~ a turn⟩ **b :** COMPLETE, ACCOMPLISH ⟨~ the trip in two hours⟩ — **ne·go·ti·a·tor** \-ˌā-tər\ *n* — **ne·go·ti·a·to·ry** \-sh(ē-)ə-ˌtȯr-ē, ÷-sē-\ *adj*

ne·go·ti·a·tion \ni-ˌgō-shē-ˈā-shən, ÷-sē-\ *n* (15c) **:** the action or process of negotiating or being negotiated — often used in pl.

Ne·gress \ˈnē-grəs\ *n* (1786) *sometimes offensive* **:** a black woman or girl

Ne·gril·lo \ni-ˈgri-(ˌ)lō, -ˈgrē-(ˌ)yō\ *n, pl* **-los** *or* **-loes** [Sp, dim. of *negro*] (1853) **:** a member of a people (as Pygmies) belonging to a group of dark-skinned peoples of small stature that live in Africa

Ne·gri·to \nə-ˈgrē-(ˌ)tō\ *n, pl* **-tos** *or* **-toes** [Sp, dim. of *negro*] (1812) **:** a member of a people (as the Andamanese) belonging to a group of dark-skinned peoples of small stature that live in Oceania and the southeastern part of Asia

ne·gri·tude \ˈne-grə-ˌtüd, ˈnē-, -ˌtyüd\ *n* [F *négritude*, fr. *nègre* Negro + *-i-* + *-tude*] (1950) **1 :** a consciousness of and pride in the cultural and physical aspects of the African heritage **2 :** the state or condition of being black

Ne·gro \ˈnē-(ˌ)grō\ *n, pl* **Negroes** [Sp or Pg, fr. *negro* black, fr. L *nigr-*, *niger*] (1555) *sometimes offensive* **:** a member of a race of humankind native to Africa and classified according to physical features (as dark skin pigmentation) — **Negro** *adj, sometimes offensive* — **ne·groid** \ˈnē-ˌgrȯid\ *adj or n, often cap, sometimes offensive* — **Ne·gro·ness** \-grō-nəs\ *n, sometimes offensive*

ne·gro·phobe \ˈnē-grə-ˌfōb\ *n, often cap* (1900) **:** one who strongly dislikes or fears black people — **ne·gro·pho·bia** \ˌnē-grə-ˈfō-bē-ə\ *n, often cap*

[1]**ne·gus** \ˈnē-gəs, ni-ˈgüs\ *n* [Amharic *nəgus*, fr. Geez *nĕgūša nagašt* king of kings] (1594) **:** KING — used as a title of the sovereign of Ethiopia

[2]**ne·gus** \ˈnē-gəs\ *n* [Francis *Negus* †1732 Eng. colonel] (1743) **:** a beverage of wine, hot water, sugar, lemon juice, and spices

Neh *abbr* Nehemiah

NEH *abbr* National Endowment for the Humanities

Ne·he·mi·ah \ˌnē-(h)ə-ˈmī-ə\ *n* [Heb *Nĕḥemyāh*] (14c) **1 :** a Jewish leader of the fifth century B.C. who supervised the rebuilding of the Jerusalem city walls and instituted religious reforms in the city **2 :** a narrative and historical book of canonical Jewish and Christian Scripture — see BIBLE table

Ne·he·mi·as \-ˈmī-əs\ *n* [LL, fr. Heb *Nĕḥemyāh*] (1535) **:** NEHEMIAH

NEI *abbr* not elsewhere included

neigh \ˈnā\ *vi* [ME *neyen*, fr. OE *hnǣgan*; akin to MHG *nēgen* to neigh] (bef. 12c) **:** to make the prolonged cry of a horse — **neigh** *n*

[1]**neigh·bor** \ˈnā-bər\ *n* [ME, fr. OE *nēahgebūr* (akin to OHG *nāhgibūr*); akin to OE *nēah* near and OE *gebūr* dweller — more at NIGH, BOOR] (bef. 12c) **1 :** one living or located near another **2 :** FELLOW MAN

[2]**neighbor** *adj* (1530) **:** being immediately adjoining or relatively near

[3]**neighbor** *vb* **neigh·bored; neigh·bor·ing** \-b(ə-)riŋ\ *vt* (ca. 1586) **:** to adjoin immediately or lie relatively near to ~ *vi* **1 :** to live or be located as a neighbor **2 :** to associate in a neighborly way

neigh·bor·hood \ˈnā-bər-ˌhu̇d\ *n* (15c) **1 :** neighborly relationship **2 :** the quality or state of being neighbors **:** PROXIMITY **3 a :** a place or region near **:** VICINITY **b :** an approximate amount, extent, or degree ⟨cost in the ~ of $100⟩ **4 a :** the people living near one another **b :** a section lived in by neighbors and usu. having distinguishing characteristics **5 :** the set of all points belonging to a given set whose distances from a given point are less than a given positive number; *broadly* **:** a set that contains a neighborhood

neigh·bor·ly \-lē\ *adj* (1558) **:** of, relating to, or characteristic of congenial neighbors; *esp* **:** FRIENDLY ⟨a ~ welcome⟩ ***syn*** see AMICABLE — **neigh·bor·li·ness** *n*

neigh·bour \-bər\ *chiefly Brit var of* NEIGHBOR

[1]**nei·ther** \ˈnē-thər *also* ˈnī-\ *conj* [ME, alter. (influenced by *either*) of *nauther, nother*, fr. OE *nāhwæther, nōther*, fr. *nā, nō* not + *hwæther* which of two, whether] (12c) **1 :** not either ⟨~ black nor white⟩ **2 :** also not ⟨~ did I⟩

usage Although use with *or* is neither archaic nor wrong, *neither* is usu. followed by *nor*. A few commentators think that *neither* must be limited in reference to two, but reference to more than two has been quite common since the 17th century ⟨rigid enforcement of antique decorum will help *neither* language, literature, nor literati —James Sledd⟩.

[2]**neither** *pron* (13c) **:** not the one or the other of two or more

usage Some commentators insist that *neither* must be used with a singular verb. It generally is, but esp. when a prepositional phrase intervenes between it and the verb, a plural verb is quite common ⟨*neither* of those ideal solutions are in sight —C. P. Snow⟩.

[3]**neither** *adj* (14c) **:** not either ⟨~ hand⟩

[4]**neither** *adv* (1551) **1** *chiefly dial* **:** EITHER **2 :** similarly not **:** also not ⟨just as the serf was not permitted to leave the land, so ~ was his offspring —G. G. Coulton⟩

nek·ton \ˈnek-tən, -ˌtän\ *n* [G *Nekton*, fr. Gk *nēkton*, neut. of *nēktos* swimming, fr. *nēchein* to swim — more at NATANT] (1893) **:** free-swimming aquatic animals essentially independent of wave and current action — **nek·ton·ic** \nek-ˈtä-nik\ *adj*

nel·son \ˈnel-sən\ *n* [prob. fr. the name *Nelson*] (1889) **:** a wrestling hold marked by the application of leverage against an opponent's arm, neck, and head — compare FULL NELSON, HALF NELSON

nemat- *or* **nemato-** *comb form* [NL, fr. Gk *nēmat-*, fr. *nēmat-*, *nēma*, fr. *nēn* to spin — more at NEEDLE] **1 :** thread ⟨*nemato*cyst⟩ **2 :** nematode ⟨*nemato*logy⟩

ne·mat·ic \ni-ˈma-tik\ *adj* [ISV *nemat-* + [1]*-ic*] (1923) **:** of, relating to, or being the phase of a liquid crystal characterized by arrangement of the long axes of the molecules in parallel lines but not layers — compare CHOLESTERIC, SMECTIC

nem·a·ti·cide *or* **nem·a·to·cide** \ˈne-mə-tə-ˌsīd, ni-ˈma-tə-\ *n* (1898) **:** a substance or preparation used to destroy nematodes — **nem·a·ti·ci·dal** *or* **nem·a·to·ci·dal** \ˌne-mə-tə-ˈsī-dᵊl, ni-ˌma-tə-\ *adj*

nem·a·to·cyst \-ˌsist\ *n* [ISV] (1875) **:** one of the stinging organelles of coelenterates used in catching prey

nem·a·tode \ˈne-mə-ˌtōd\ *n* [ultim. fr. Gk *nēmat-*, *nēma*] (1865) **:** any of a phylum (Nematoda or Nemata) of elongated cylindrical worms parasitic in animals or plants or free-living in soil or water — called also *roundworm*

nem·a·tol·o·gy \ˌne-mə-ˈtä-lə-jē\ *n* (ca. 1916) **:** a branch of zoology that deals with nematodes — **nem·a·to·log·i·cal** \ˌne-mə-tə-ˈlä-ji-kəl\ *adj* — **nem·a·tol·o·gist** \ˌne-mə-ˈtä-lə-jist\ *n*

Nem·bu·tal \ˈnem-byə-ˌtȯl\ *trademark* — used for the sodium salt of pentobarbital

nem con *abbr* [NL *nemine contradicente*] no one contradicting

ne·mer·te·an \ni-ˈmər-tē-ən\ *n* [ultim. fr. Gk *Nēmertēs* Nemertes, one of the Nereids] (1861) **:** any of a phylum (Nemertea syn. Rhynchocoela) of often vividly colored usu. long dorsoventrally flattened marine worms that typically burrow in the mud or sand along seacoasts — called also *ribbon worm* — **nem·er·tine** \ˈne-mər-ˌtīn\ *adj or n*

nem·e·sis \ˈne-mə-səs\ *n* [L, fr. Gk] (1561) **1** *cap* **:** the Greek goddess of retributive justice **2** *pl* **-e·ses** \-ˌsēz\ **a :** one that inflicts retribution or vengeance **b :** a formidable and usu. victorious rival or opponent **3** *pl* **-eses a :** an act or effect of retribution **b :** BANE 2

ne·moph·i·la \ni-ˈmä-fə-lə\ *n* [NL, fr. Gk *nemos* wooded pasture + *philos* loving] (1838) **:** any of a genus (*Nemophila*) of annual herbs of the waterleaf family chiefly of western No. America that are cultivated for their showy blue or white sometimes spotted flowers

ne·ne \ˈnā-(ˌ)nā\ *n* [Hawaiian *nēnē*] (1902) **:** an endangered goose (*Branta sandvicensis* syn. *Nesochen sandvicensis*) of the Hawaiian Islands that usu. inhabits waterless uplands and feeds on berries and vegetation

neo- — see NE-

neo·clas·sic \ˌnē-ō-ˈkla-sik\ *or* **neo·clas·si·cal** \-si-kəl\ *adj* (1877) **:** of, relating to, or constituting a revival or adaptation of the classical esp. in literature, music, art, or architecture — **neo·clas·si·cism** \-ˈkla-sə-ˌsi-zəm\ *n* — **neo·clas·si·cist** \-sist\ *n or adj*

neo·co·lo·nial·ism \ˌnē-ō-kə-ˈlō-nyə-ˌli-zəm, -ˈlō-nē-ə-ˌli-\ *n* (1961) **:** the economic and political policies by which a great power indirectly maintains or extends its influence over other areas or people — **neo·co·lo·nial** \-ˈlōn-yəl, -ˈlō-nē-əl\ *adj* — **neo·co·lo·nial·ist** \-yə-list, -ə-list\ *n or adj*

neo·con \ˈnē-ō-ˌkän\ *n* (1979) **:** NEOCONSERVATIVE

neo·con·ser·va·tive \ˌnē-ō-kən-ˈsər-və-tiv\ *n* (1952) **1 :** a former liberal espousing political conservatism **2 :** a conservative who advocates the assertive promotion of democracy and U.S. national interest in international affairs including through military means — **neo·con·ser·va·tism** \-və-ˌti-zəm\ *n* — **neoconservative** *adj*

neo·cor·tex \ˌnē-ō-ˈkȯr-ˌteks\ *n* [NL; fr. its being the cortex of the phylogenetically most recently developed part of the brain] (1909) **:** the large 6-layered dorsal region of the cerebral cortex that is unique to mammals; *broadly* **:** the mammalian cerebral cortex

neo·cor·ti·cal \-ˈkȯr-ti-kəl\ *adj* (1909) **:** of or relating to the neocortex

neo–Dar·win·ian \-där-ˈwi-nē-ən\ *adj* (1895) **:** of or relating to neo-Darwinism — **neo–Darwinian** *n*

neo–Dar·win·ism \-ˈdär-wə-ˌni-zəm\ *n* (ca. 1900) **:** a theory of evolution that is a synthesis of Darwin's theory in terms of natural selection and modern population genetics — **neo–Dar·win·ist** \-ˈdär-wə-nist\ *n*

neo·dym·i·um \ˌnē-ō-ˈdi-mē-əm\ *n* [NL, fr. *ne-* + *-dymium* (fr. *didymium*)] (1885) **:** a silver-white to yellow metallic element of the rare-earth group that is used esp. in magnets and lasers — see ELEMENT table

neo–Ex·pres·sion·ism \-ik-ˈspre-shə-ˌni-zəm\ *n, often cap N* (1961) **:** a revival of expressionism in art characterized by intense colors, dramatic usu. figural forms, and emotive subject matter — **neo–Ex·pres·sion·ist** \-nist\ *n or adj, often cap N*

neo–Freud·ian \-ˈfrȯi-dē-ən\ *adj, often cap N* (1932) **:** of or relating to a school of psychoanalysis that differs from Freudian orthodoxy in emphasizing the importance of social and cultural factors in the development of an individual's personality — **neo–Freudian** *n, often cap N*

Neo·gene \ˈnē-ə-ˌjēn\ *adj* [ISV *ne-* + *-gene* (fr. Gk *-genēs* born) — more at -GEN] (1859) **:** of, relating to, or being the later portion of the Tertiary including the Miocene and Pliocene or the corresponding system of rocks — **Neogene** *n*

neo–Goth·ic \ˌnē-ō-ˈgä-thik\ *adj* (1878) **:** of, relating to, or constituting a revival or adaptation of the Gothic esp. in literature or architecture

neo–im·pres·sion·ism \ˌnē-ō-im-ˈpre-shə-ˌni-zəm\ *n, often cap N&I* [F *néo-impressionnisme,* fr. *né-* ne- + *impressionnisme* impressionism] (1892) **:** a late 19th century French art theory and practice characterized by an attempt to make impressionism more precise in form and the use of a pointillistic painting technique — **neo–im·pres·sion·ist** \-ˈpre-sh(ə-)nist\ *adj or n, often cap N&I*

Neo–Lat·in \-ˈla-tᵊn\ *n* [ISV] (1850) **1 :** NEW LATIN **2 :** ROMANCE 5

neo·lib·er·al \-ˈli-b(ə-)rəl\ *n* (1921) **:** a liberal who de-emphasizes traditional liberal doctrines in order to seek progress by more pragmatic methods — **neoliberal** *adj* — **neo·lib·er·al·ism** \-b(ə-)rə-ˌli-zəm\ *n*

neo·lith \ˈnē-ə-ˌlith\ *n* [back-formation fr. *neolithic*] (1880) **:** a Neolithic stone implement

neo·lith·ic \ˌnē-ə-ˈli-thik\ *adj* (1865) **1** *cap* **:** of or relating to the latest period of the Stone Age characterized by polished stone implements **2 :** belonging to an earlier age and now outmoded

ne·ol·o·gism \nē-ˈä-lə-ˌji-zəm\ *n* [F *néologisme,* fr. *ne-* + *log-* + *-isme* -ism] (1872) **1 :** a new word, usage, or expression **2** *psychology* **:** a new word that is coined esp. by a person affected with schizophrenia and is meaningless except to the coiner — **ne·ol·o·gis·tic** \-ˌä-lə-ˈjis-tik\ *adj*

neo–Mal·thu·sian \ˌnē-ō-mal-ˈthü-zhən, -mȯl-, -ˈthyü-\ *adj* (1879) **:** advocating control of population growth (as by contraception) — **neo–Malthusian** *n* — **neo–Mal·thu·sian·ism** \-zhə-ˌni-zəm\ *n*

neo·my·cin \ˌnē-ə-ˈmī-sᵊn\ *n* (1949) **:** a broad-spectrum highly toxic antibiotic or mixture of antibiotics produced by a streptomyces (*Streptomyces fradiae*) and used medically esp. to treat local infections

[1]**ne·on** \ˈnē-ˌän\ *n* [Gk, neut. of *neos* new — more at NEW] (1898) **1 :** a colorless odorless mostly inert gaseous element that is found in minute amounts in air and is used in electric lamps — see ELEMENT table **2 a :** a discharge lamp in which the gas contains a large proportion of neon **b :** a sign composed of such lamps **c :** the illumination provided by such lamps or signs — **ne·oned** \-ˌänd\ *adj*

[2]**neon** *adj* (1904) **1 :** of, relating to, or using neon **2 :** extremely bright **:** FLUORESCENT ⟨~ yellow⟩

neo·na·tal \ˌnē-ō-ˈnā-tᵊl\ *adj* (1894) **:** of, relating to, or affecting the newborn and esp. the human infant during the first month after birth ⟨~ mortality⟩ — **neo·na·tal·ly** \-tᵊl-ē\ *adv*

ne·o·nate \ˈnē-ə-ˌnāt\ *n* [NL *neonatus,* fr. *ne-* + L *natus,* pp. of *nasci* to be born — more at NATION] (1925) **:** a newborn child; *esp* **:** a child less than a month old

neo·na·tol·o·gy \ˌnē-ə-nā-ˈtä-lə-jē\ *n* (1960) **:** a branch of medicine concerned with the care, development, and diseases of newborn infants — **neo·na·tol·o·gist** \-jist\ *n*

neo–Na·zi \ˌnē-ō-ˈnät-sē, -ˈnat-\ *n* (1938) **:** a member of a group espousing the programs and policies of Hitler's Nazis — **neo–Nazi** *adj* — **neo–Na·zism** \-ˈnät-ˌsi-zəm, -ˈnat-\ *n*

neo·or·tho·dox \ˌnē-ō-ˈȯr-thə-ˌdäks\ *adj* (1913) **:** of or relating to a 20th century movement in Protestant theology characterized by a reaction against liberalism and emphasis on various scripturally based Reformation doctrines — **neo·or·tho·doxy** \-ˌdäk-sē\ *n*

neo–pa·gan \-ˈpā-gən\ *n* (1868) **:** a person who practices a contemporary form of paganism (as Wicca) — **neo–pagan** *adj* — **neo–pa·gan·ism** \-ˈpā-gə-ˌni-zəm\ *n*

neo·phil·ia \ˌnē-ə-ˈfi-lē-ə\ *n* (1899) **:** love of or enthusiasm for what is new or novel — **neo·phil·i·ac** \-lē-ˌak\ *n*

neo·phyte \ˈnē-ə-ˌfīt\ *n* [ME, fr. LL *neophytus,* fr. Gk *neophytos,* fr. *neophytos* newly planted, newly converted, fr. *ne-* + *phyein* to bring forth — more at BE] (14c) **1 :** a new convert **:** PROSELYTE **2 :** NOVICE 1 **3 :** TYRO, BEGINNER

neo·pla·sia \ˌnē-ə-ˈplā-zh(ē-)ə\ *n* [NL] (1871) **1 :** the formation of tumors **2 :** a tumorous condition

neo·plasm \ˈnē-ə-ˌpla-zəm\ *n* [ISV] (1863) **:** TUMOR 2

neo·plas·tic \ˌnē-ə-ˈplas-tik\ *adj* [ISV] (1871) **1 :** of, relating to, or constituting a tumor or neoplasia **2 :** of or relating to de Stijl

neo·plas·ti·cism \-tə-ˌsi-zəm\ *n* [F *néo-plasticisme,* fr. *ne-* + *plastique* plastic + *-isme* -ism] (1933) **:** DE STIJL — **neo·plas·ti·cist** \-sist\ *n*

Neo·pla·to·nism \ˌnē-ō-ˈplā-tᵊn-ˌi-zəm\ *n* (1832) **1 :** Platonism modified in later antiquity to accord with Aristotelian, post-Aristotelian, and eastern conceptions that conceives of the world as an emanation from an ultimate indivisible being with whom the soul is capable of being reunited in trance or ecstasy **2 :** a doctrine similar to ancient Neoplatonism — **Neo·pla·ton·ic** \-plə-ˈtä-nik, -plā-\ *adj* — **Neo·pla·to·nist** \-ˈplā-tᵊn-ist\ *n*

neo·prene \ˈnē-ə-ˌprēn\ *n* [*ne-* + chloro*prene*] (1937) **:** a synthetic rubber made by the polymerization of chloroprene, characterized by superior resistance (as to oils), and used esp. for special-purpose clothing (as gloves and wet suits)

neo·re·al·ism \ˌnē-ō-ˈrē-ə-ˌli-zəm\ *n* (1950) **:** a movement esp. in Italian filmmaking characterized by the simple direct depiction of lower-class life — **neo·re·al·ist** \-list\ *adj or n* — **neo·re·al·is·tic** \-ˌrē-ə-ˈlis-tik\ *adj*

neo–scho·las·ti·cism \ˌnē-ō-skə-ˈlas-tə-ˌsi-zəm\ *n* (1881) **:** a movement among Catholic scholars aiming to restate medieval Scholasticism in a manner suited to present intellectual needs — **neo·scho·las·tic** \-ˈlas-tik\ *adj*

neo·stig·mine \ˌnē-ə-ˈstig-ˌmēn\ *n* [*ne-* + *-stigmine* (as in *physostigmine*)] (1941) **:** a cholinergic drug used in the form of its bromide $C_{12}H_{19}BrN_2O_2$ or a methyl sulfate derivative $C_{13}H_{22}N_2O_6S$ esp. in the diagnosis and treatment of myasthenia gravis and in the treatment of urinary bladder or bowel atony

ne·o·te·ny \nē-ˈä-tə-nē\ *n* [NL *neotenia,* fr. *ne-* + Gk *teinein* to stretch — more at THIN] (1901) **1 :** retention of some larval or immature characters in adulthood **2 :** attainment of sexual maturity during the larval stage — **ne·o·ten·ic** \ˌnē-ə-ˈte-nik\ *adj*

ne·o·ter·ic \ˌnē-ə-ˈter-ik\ *adj* [LL *neotericus,* fr. LGk *neōterikos,* fr. Gk youthful, fr. *neōterios,* compar. of *neos* new, young — more at NEW] (1577) **:** recent in origin **:** MODERN

neo·trop·i·cal \ˌnē-ō-ˈträ-pi-kəl\ *also* **neo·trop·ic** \-pik\ *adj, often cap* [ISV] (1858) **:** of, relating to, or constituting the tropical New World biogeographic region that extends south, east, and west from the central plateau of Mexico

neo·trop·ics \-ˈträ-piks\ *n pl, often cap* (1923) **:** the neotropical region

neo·type \ˈnē-ə-ˌtīp\ *n* (1905) **:** a type specimen that is selected subsequent to the description of a species to replace a preexisting type that has been lost or destroyed

NEP *abbr* New Economic Policy

Ne·pali \nə-ˈpȯ-lē, -ˈpä-, -ˈpa-\ *n, pl* **Nepali** *also* **Ne·pal·is** [Hindi *naipālī* of Nepal, fr. Skt *naipālīya,* fr. *Nepāla* Nepal] (1882) **1 :** a native or inhabitant of Nepal **2 :** an Indo-Aryan language spoken in Nepal — **Nepali** *adj*

ne·pen·the \nə-ˈpen(t)-thē\ *n* [L *nepenthes,* fr. Gk *nēpenthes,* neut. of *nēpenthēs* banishing pain and sorrow, fr. *nē-* not + *penthos* grief, sorrow; akin to Gk *pathos* suffering — more at NO, PATHOS] (1577) **1 :** a potion used by the ancients to induce forgetfulness of pain or sorrow **2 :** something capable of causing oblivion of grief or suffering — **ne·pen·the·an** \-thē-ən\ *adj*

nep·e·ta \ˈne-pə-tə\ *n* [NL, fr. L, an aromatic herb] (1633) **:** CATMINT

neph·e·line \ˈne-fə-ˌlēn\ *also* **neph·e·lite** \-ˌlīt\ *n* [F *néphéline,* fr. Gk *nephelē* cloud — more at NEBULA] (ca. 1814) **:** a hexagonal mineral that is a usu. glassy crystalline silicate of sodium, potassium, and aluminum common in igneous rocks — **neph·e·lin·ic** \ˌne-fə-ˈli-nik\ *adj*

neph·e·lin·ite \ˈne-fə-lə-ˌnīt\ *n* [ISV] (ca. 1863) **:** a silica-deficient igneous rock having nepheline as the predominant mineral — **neph·e·lin·it·ic** \ˌne-fə-lə-ˈni-tik\ *adj*

neph·e·lom·e·ter \ˌne-fə-ˈlä-mə-tər\ *n* [Gk *nephelē* cloud + ISV *-meter*] (1884) **1 :** an instrument for measuring the extent or degree of cloudiness **2 :** an instrument for determining the concentration or particle size of suspensions by means of transmitted or reflected light — **neph·e·lo·met·ric** \ˌne-fə-lō-ˈme-trik\ *adj* — **neph·e·lo·met·ri·cal·ly** \-tri-k(ə-)lē\ *adv* — **neph·e·lom·e·try** \-ˈlä-mə-trē\ *n*

neph·ew \ˈne-(ˌ)fyü, *chiefly Brit* -(ˌ)vyü\ *n* [ME *nevew,* fr. AF *nevou, neveu,* fr. L *nepot-, nepos* grandson, nephew; akin to OE *nefa* grandson, nephew, Skt *napāt* grandson] (14c) **1 a :** a son of one's brother or sister or of one's brother-in-law or sister-in-law **b :** an illegitimate son of an ecclesiastic **2** *obs* **:** a lineal descendant; *esp* **:** GRANDSON

nephr- *or* **nephro-** *comb form* [NL, fr. Gk, fr. *nephros* — more at NEPHRITIS] **:** kidney ⟨*nephr*ic⟩ ⟨*nephro*logy⟩

ne·phrec·to·my \ni-ˈfrek-tə-mē\ *n, pl* **-mies** [ISV] (1880) **:** the surgical removal of a kidney — **ne·phrec·to·mize** \-ˌmīz\ *vt*

neph·ric \ˈne-frik\ *adj* (1887) **:** RENAL

ne·phrid·i·um \ni-ˈfri-dē-əm\ *n, pl* **-ia** \-dē-ə\ [NL] (1877) **:** a tubular glandular excretory organ characteristic of various invertebrates — **ne·phrid·i·al** \-dē-əl\ *adj*

neph·rite \ˈne-ˌfrīt\ *n* [G *Nephrit,* fr. Gk *nephros;* fr. its formerly being worn as a remedy for kidney diseases] (1794) **:** a compact tremolite or actinolite that is the commoner and less valuable kind of jade and that varies in color from white to dark green or black

ne·phrit·ic \ni-ˈfri-tik\ *adj* (1580) **1 :** RENAL **2 :** of, relating to, or affected with nephritis

ne·phri·tis \ni-ˈfrī-təs\ *n, pl* **ne·phrit·i·des** \-ˈfri-tə-ˌdēz\ [LL, fr. Gk, fr. *nephros* kidney; prob. akin to ME *nere* kidney] (1566) **:** acute or chronic inflammation of the kidney caused by infection, degenerative process, or vascular disease

ne·phrol·o·gy \ni-ˈfrä-lə-jē\ *n* (ca. 1842) **:** a branch of medicine concerned with the kidneys — **ne·phrol·o·gist** \-jist\ *n*

neph·ron \ˈne-ˌfrän\ *n* [G, fr. Gk *nephros*] (1932) **:** a single excretory unit of the vertebrate kidney

ne·phrop·a·thy \ni-ˈfrä-pə-thē\ *n, pl* **-thies** [ISV] (ca. 1900) **:** an abnormal state of the kidney; *esp* **:** one associated with or secondary to some other pathological process — **neph·ro·path·ic** \ˌne-frə-ˈpa-thik\ *adj*

ne·phro·sis \ni-ˈfrō-səs\ *n* [NL] (1909) **:** a noninflammatory disease of the kidneys chiefly affecting function of the nephrons; *also* **:** NEPHROTIC SYNDROME — **ne·phrot·ic** \-ˈfrä-tik\ *adj or n*

neph·ro·stome \ˈne-frə-ˌstōm\ *n* [NL *nephrostoma,* fr. *nephr-* + *stoma* stoma] (1888) **:** the ciliated funnel-shaped coelomic opening of a typical nephridium

nephrotic syndrome *n* (1931) **:** an abnormal condition that is marked by deficiency of albumin in the blood and its excretion in the urine due to altered permeability of the glomerular basement membranes

neph·ro·tox·ic \ˌne-frə-ˈtäk-sik\ *adj* (1902) **:** poisonous to the kidney ⟨~ drugs⟩; *also* **:** resulting from or marked by poisoning of the kidney ⟨~ effects⟩ — **neph·ro·tox·ic·i·ty** \-täk-ˈsi-sə-tē\ *n*

ne plus ul·tra \ˌnā-ˌpləs-ˈəl-trə, ˌnē-\ *n* [NL, (go) no more beyond] (1637) **1 :** the highest point capable of being attained **:** ACME **2 :** the most profound degree of a quality or state

nep·o·tism \ˈne-pə-ˌti-zəm\ *n* [F *népotisme,* fr. It *nepotismo,* fr. *nepote* nephew, fr. L *nepot-, nepos* grandson, nephew — more at NEPHEW] (1670) **:** favoritism (as in appointment to a job) based on kinship — **nep·o·tis·tic** \ˌne-pə-ˈtis-tik\ *adj*

Nep·tune \ˈnep-ˌtün, -ˌtyün\ *n* [L *Neptunus*] (bef. 12c) **1 a :** the Roman god of the sea — compare POSEIDON **b :** OCEAN **2 :** the planet eighth in order from the sun — see PLANET table — **Nep·tu·ni·an** \nep-ˈtü-nē-ən, -ˈtyü-\ *adj*

nep·tu·ni·um \nep-ˈtü-nē-əm, -ˈtyü-\ *n* [NL, fr. ISV *Neptune*] (1941) **:** a radioactive metallic element that is chemically similar to uranium and is obtained in nuclear reactors esp. as a by-product in the production of plutonium — see ELEMENT table

nerd \ˈnərd\ *n* [perh. fr. *nerd,* a creature in the children's book *If I Ran the Zoo* (1950) by Dr. Seuss (Theodor Geisel)] (1951) **:** an unstylish, unattractive, or socially inept person; *esp* **:** one slavishly devoted to intel-

\ə\ **abut** \ᵊ\ **kitten, F table** \ər\ **further** \a\ **ash** \ā\ **ace** \ä\ **mop, mar** \au̇\ **out** \ch\ **chin** \e\ **bet** \ē\ **easy** \g\ **go** \i\ **hit** \ī\ **ice** \j\ **job** \ŋ\ **sing** \ō\ **go** \ȯ\ **law** \ȯi\ **boy** \th\ **thin** \t͟h\ **the** \ü\ **loot** \u̇\ **foot** \y\ **yet** \zh\ **vision, beige** \k̲, ⁿ, œ, ue, ʸ\ *see* Guide to Pronunciation

lectual or academic pursuits ⟨computer ~*s*⟩ — **nerd·i·ness** \ˈnər-dē-nəs\ *n* — **nerd·ish** \ˈnər-dish\ *adj* — **nerdy** \-dē\ *adj*

ne·re·id \ˈnir-ē-əd\ *n* [NL *Nereidae,* fr. *Nereis,* a genus, fr. L, Nereid] (1840) : any of a family (Nereidae) of chiefly marine polychaete worms; *esp* : any of a genus (*Nereis*) of usu. large often greenish worms — **nereid** *adj*

Ne·re·id \ˈnir-ē-əd\ *n* [L *Nereid-, Nereis,* fr. Gk *Nēreid-, Nēreis,* fr. *Nēreus* Nereus] (1606) : any of the sea nymphs fathered by Nereus

Ne·re·us \ˈnir-ē-əs\ *n* [L, fr. Gk *Nēreus*] (1513) : a sea-god in Greek mythology

ne·rit·ic \nə-ˈri-tik\ *adj* [ISV, perh. fr. NL *Nerita,* genus of marine snails] (1891) : of, relating to, inhabiting, or constituting the belt or region of shallow water adjoining the seacoast

ne·rol \ˈnir-ˌȯl, ˈner-\ *n* [ISV *ner-* (fr. *neroli oil*) + [1]*-ol*] (1869) : a liquid alcohol $C_{10}H_{18}O$ that has a rose scent and is used in perfumery

ner·o·li oil \ˈner-ə-lē-\ *n* [F *néroli,* fr. It *neroli,* fr. Anna Maria de La Trémoille, princess of *Nerola fl*1670] (1849) : a fragrant pale yellow essential oil obtained from flowers chiefly of the sour orange and used esp. in cologne and as a flavoring

nerts \ˈnərts\ *n pl* [alter. of *nuts*] (1929) *slang* : NONSENSE, NUTS — often used interjectionally

ner·va·tion \ˌnər-ˈvā-shən\ *n* (1849) : an arrangement or system of nerves; *also* : VENATION

[1]**nerve** \ˈnərv\ *n* [L *nervus* sinew, nerve; akin to Gk *neuron* sinew, nerve, *nēn* to spin — more at NEEDLE] (14c) **1** : SINEW, TENDON ⟨strain every ~⟩ **2** : any of the filamentous bands of nervous tissue that connect parts of the nervous system with the other organs, conduct nerve impulses, and are made up of axons and dendrites together with protective and supportive structures **3 a** : power of endurance or control : FORTITUDE, STRENGTH **b** : ASSURANCE, BOLDNESS; *also* : presumptuous audacity : GALL **4 a** : a sore or sensitive point ⟨her remark touched a ~⟩ **b** *pl* : nervous agitation or irritability : NERVOUSNESS ⟨a case of ~*s*⟩ **5** : VEIN 3 **6** : the sensitive pulp of a tooth ***syn*** see TEMERITY

[2]**nerve** *vt* **nerved; nerv·ing** (ca. 1749) : to give strength or courage to : supply with physical or moral force

nerve cell *n* (1858) : NEURON; *also* : CELL BODY

nerve center *n* (1868) **1** : CENTER 2c **2** : a source of leadership, organization, control, or energy ⟨the financial *nerve center* of the nation⟩

nerve cord *n* (1877) **1** : the pair of closely united ventral longitudinal nerves with their segmental ganglia that is characteristic of many elongate invertebrates (as earthworms) **2** : the dorsal tubular cord of nervous tissue above the notochord of a chordate that comprises or develops into the central nervous system

nerved \ˈnərvd\ *adj* (1800) **1 a** : VEINED ⟨a ~ wing⟩ **b** : having veins or nerves esp. of a specified kind or number — used in combination ⟨fan-*nerved* leaves⟩ **2** : showing courage or strength

nerve ending *n* (ca. 1890) : a structure forming the distal end of a nerve axon — see NEURON illustration

nerve fiber *n* (ca. 1847) : any of the processes (as axons or dendrites) of a neuron

nerve gas *n* (1940) : an organophosphate chemical weapon that interferes with normal nerve transmission and induces intense bronchial spasm with resulting inhibition of respiration

nerve growth factor *n* (1958) : a protein that promotes development of the sensory and sympathetic nervous systems and is required for maintenance of sympathetic neurons

nerve impulse *n* (1900) : the progressive physicochemical change in the membrane of a nerve fiber that follows stimulation and serves to transmit a record of sensation from a receptor or an instruction to act to an effector — called also *nervous impulse*

nerve·less \ˈnərv-ləs\ *adj* (1742) **1** : lacking strength or courage : FEEBLE **2** : exhibiting control or balance : POISED, COOL — **nerve·less·ly** *adv* — **nerve·less·ness** *n*

nerve net *n* (1904) : a network of neurons apparently continuous with one another and conducting impulses in all directions; *also* : a primitive nervous system (as in a jellyfish) consisting of such a network

nerve–rack·ing *or* **nerve–wrack·ing** \ˈnərv-ˌra-kiŋ\ *adj* (1812) : extremely trying on the nerves ⟨a ~ ordeal⟩

nerve trunk *n* (1851) : a bundle of nerve fibers enclosed in a connective tissue sheath

ner·vos·i·ty \ˌnər-ˈvä-sə-tē\ *n* (1787) : the quality or state of being nervous

ner·vous \ˈnər-vəs\ *adj* (14c) **1** *archaic* : SINEWY, STRONG **2** : marked by strength of thought, feeling, or style : SPIRITED ⟨a vibrant tight-packed ~ style of writing⟩ **3** : of, relating to, or composed of neurons **4 a** : of or relating to the nerves; *also* : originating in or affected by the nerves ⟨~ energy⟩ **b** : easily excited or irritated : JUMPY **c** : TIMID, APPREHENSIVE ⟨a ~ smile⟩ ⟨~ of strangers⟩ **5 a** : tending to produce nervousness or agitation : UNEASY ⟨a ~ situation⟩ **b** : appearing or acting unsteady, erratic, or irregular — used of inanimate things ***syn*** see VIGOROUS — **ner·vous·ly** *adv* — **ner·vous·ness** *n*

nervous breakdown *n* (1905) : an attack of mental or emotional disorder esp. when of sufficient severity to require hospitalization

nervous Nel·lie *or* **nervous Nel·ly** \-ˈne-lē\ *n, pl* **nervous Nellies** *often cap 1st N* [fr. the name *Nellie*] (1926) : a timid or worrisome person

nervous system *n* (1726) : the bodily system that in vertebrates is made up of the brain and spinal cord, nerves, ganglia, and parts of the receptor organs and that receives and interprets stimuli and transmits impulses to the effector organs — compare CENTRAL NERVOUS SYSTEM; AUTONOMIC NERVOUS SYSTEM, PERIPHERAL NERVOUS SYSTEM

ner·vure \ˈnər-vyər\ *n* [F, fr. *nerf* sinew, fr. L *nervus*] (1816) : VEIN 3

nervy \ˈnər-vē\ *adj* **nerv·i·er; -est** (1607) **1** *archaic* : SINEWY, STRONG **2 a** : showing or expressive of calm courage : BOLD **b** : marked by effrontery or presumption : BRASH **3** : EXCITABLE, NERVOUS — **nerv·i·ly** \-və-lē\ *adv* — **nerv·i·ness** \-vē-nəs\ *n*

NES *abbr* not elsewhere specified

ne·science \ˈne-sh(ē-)ən(t)s, ˈnē-, -sē-ən(t)s\ *n* [LL *nescientia,* fr. L *nescient-, nesciens,* prp. of *nescire* not to know, fr. *ne-* not + *scire* to know — more at NO, SCIENCE] (1612) : lack of knowledge or awareness : IGNORANCE — **ne·scient** \-sh(ē-)ənt, -sē-ənt\ *adj*

ness \ˈnes\ *n* [ME *nasse,* fr. OE *næss;* akin to OE *nasu* nose — more at NOSE] (bef. 12c) : CAPE, PROMONTORY

-ness *n suffix* [ME *-nes,* fr. OE; akin to OHG *-nissa* -ness] : state : condition : quality : degree ⟨good*ness*⟩

Nes·sel·rode \ˈne-səl-ˌrōd\ *n* [Count Karl R. *Nesselrode* †1862 Russ. statesman] (1840) : a mixture of candied fruits, nuts, and maraschino used in puddings, pies, and ice cream

Nes·sus \ˈne-səs\ *n* [L, fr. Gk *Nessos*] (14c) : a centaur slain by Hercules for trying to carry away Hercules' wife but avenged by means of a poisoned garment that causes Hercules to die in torment

[1]**nest** \ˈnest\ *n* [ME, fr. OE; akin to OHG *nest* nest, L *nidus*] (bef. 12c) **1 a** : a bed or receptacle prepared by an animal and esp. a bird for its eggs and young **b** : a place or specially modified structure serving as an abode of animals and esp. of their immature stages ⟨an ants' ~⟩ **c** : a receptacle resembling a bird's nest **2 a** : a place of rest, retreat, or lodging : HOME ⟨grown children who have left the ~⟩ **b** : DEN, HANGOUT **3** : the occupants or frequenters of a nest **4 a** : a group of similar things ⟨a ~ of giant mountains —Helen MacInnes⟩ **b** : HOTBED 2 ⟨a ~ of rebellion⟩ **5** : a group of objects made to fit close together or one within another **6** : an emplaced group of weapons

[2]**nest** *vi* (13c) **1** : to build or occupy a nest : settle in or as if in a nest **2** : to fit compactly together or within one another : EMBED ~ *vt* **1** : to form a nest for **2** : to pack compactly together **3** : to form a hierarchy, series, or sequence of with each member, element, or set contained in or containing the next ⟨~*ed* subroutines⟩

nest egg *n* (14c) **1** : a natural or artificial egg left in a nest esp. to induce a hen to continue to lay there **2** : a fund of money accumulated as a reserve

nest·er \ˈnes-tər\ *n* (1880) **1** *West* : a homesteader or squatter who takes up land on open range for a farm **2** : one that nests

nes·tle \ˈne-səl\ *vb* **nes·tled; nes·tling** \-s(ə-)liŋ\ [ME, fr. OE *nestlian,* fr. *nest*] *vi* (bef. 12c) **1** *archaic* : NEST 1 **2** : to settle snugly or comfortably **3** : to lie in an inconspicuous or sheltered manner ~ *vt* **1** : to settle, shelter, or house in or as if in a nest ⟨the children were *nestled* all snug in their beds —Clement Moore⟩ **2** : to press closely and affectionately ⟨~*s* a kitten in her arms⟩ — **nes·tler** \-s(ə-)lər\ *n*

nest·ling \ˈnest-liŋ\ *n* (14c) : a young bird that has not left the nest

Nes·tor \ˈnes-tər, -ˌtȯr\ *n* [L, fr. Gk *Nestōr*] (14c) **1** : a king of Pylos who serves in his old age as a counselor to the Greeks at Troy **2** *often not cap* : one who is a patriarch or leader in a field

Nes·to·ri·an \ne-ˈstȯr-ē-ən\ *adj* (1565) **1** : of or relating to the doctrine ascribed to Nestorius and ecclesiastically condemned in 431 that divine and human persons remained separate in the incarnate Christ **2** : of or relating to a church separating from Byzantine Christianity after 431, centering in Persia, and surviving chiefly in Asia Minor — **Nestorian** *n* — **Nes·to·ri·an·ism** \-ə-ˌni-zəm\ *n*

[1]**net** \ˈnet\ *n* [ME *nett,* fr. OE; akin to OHG *nezzi* net] (bef. 12c) **1 a** : an open-meshed fabric twisted, knotted, or woven together at regular intervals **b** : something made of net: as (1) : a device for catching fish, birds, or insects (2) : a fabric barricade which divides a court in half (as in tennis or volleyball) and over which a ball or shuttlecock must be hit to be in play (3) : the fabric that encloses the sides and back of the goal in various games (as soccer or hockey) **2** : an entrapping device or situation ⟨caught in the ~ of suspicious circumstances⟩ **3** : something resembling a net in reticulation (as of lines, fibers, or figures) **4 a** : a group of communications stations operating under unified control **b** : NETWORK 4 **5** *often cap* : INTERNET — **net·less** \-ləs\ *adj* — **net·like** \-ˌlīk\ *adj* — **net·ty** \ˈne-tē\ *adj*

[2]**net** *vt* **net·ted; net·ting** (1593) **1** : to cover or enclose with or as if with a net **2** : to catch in or as if in a net **3** : to cover with or as if with a network **4 a** : to hit (a ball) into the net for the loss of a point in a racket game **b** : to hit (a ball or puck) into the goal for a score (as in hockey or soccer); *also* : to score (a point or goal) by netting a ball or puck — **net·ter** *n*

[3]**net** *adj* [ME, clean, pure, fr. AF — more at NEAT] (15c) **1** : free from all charges or deductions: as **a** : remaining after the deduction of all charges, outlay, or loss ⟨~ earnings⟩ ⟨~ worth⟩ — compare GROSS **b** : excluding all tare ⟨~ weight⟩ **2** : excluding all nonessential considerations : BASIC, FINAL ⟨the ~ result⟩ ⟨~ effect⟩

[4]**net** *vt* **net·ted; net·ting** (1758) **1 a** : to receive by way of profit : CLEAR **b** : to produce by way of profit : YIELD **2** : to get possession of : GAIN

[5]**net** *n* (ca. 1904) **1** : a net amount, profit, weight, or price **2** : the score of a golfer in a handicap match after deducting his or her handicap from the gross score **3** : ESSENCE, GIST

net·book \ˈnet-ˌbu̇k\ *n* (2007) : a small portable computer designed primarily for wireless Internet access

Neth *abbr* Netherlands

neth·er \ˈne-t͟hər\ *adj* [ME, fr. OE *nithera,* fr. *nither* down; akin to OHG *nidar* down, Skt *ni*] (bef. 12c) **1** : situated down or below : LOWER **2** : situated or believed to be situated beneath the earth's surface

neth·er·most \-ˌmōst\ *adj* (14c) : farthest down : LOWEST

neth·er·world \-ˌwərld\ *n* (1632) **1** : the world of the dead **2** : UNDERWORLD 4 ⟨the ~ of deceit . . . and espionage —R. M. Nixon⟩ **3** : NO-MAN'S-LAND 2 ⟨lost in a bureaucratic ~⟩

net·i·quette \ˈne-ti-kət, -ˌket\ *n* [blend of *net* and *etiquette*] (1982) : etiquette governing communication on the Internet

net·i·zen \ˈne-tə-zən *also* -sən\ *n* [blend of *net* and *citizen*] (1984) : an active participant in the online community of the Internet

net·mind·er \ˈnet-ˌmīn-dər\ *n* (1937) : GOALKEEPER

net·roots \ˈnet-ˌrüts, -ˌru̇ts\ *n pl* (2003) : the grassroots political activists who communicate via the Internet esp. by blogs

net·su·ke \ˈnets-(ˌ)kā, -kē, -ke *also* ˈnet-sü-\ *n, pl* **netsuke** *or* **netsukes** [Jp] (1876) : a small and often intricately carved toggle (as of wood or ivory) used to fasten a small container to a kimono sash

nett *Brit var of* NET

netting *n* (1567) **1** : NETWORK 1 **2** : the act or process of making a net or network **3** : the act, process, or right of fishing with a net

[1]**net·tle** \ˈne-tᵊl\ *n* [ME, fr. OE *netel;* akin to OHG *nazza* nettle, Gk *adikē*] (bef. 12c) **1** : any of a genus (*Urtica* of the family Urticaceae, the nettle family) of chiefly coarse herbs armed with stinging

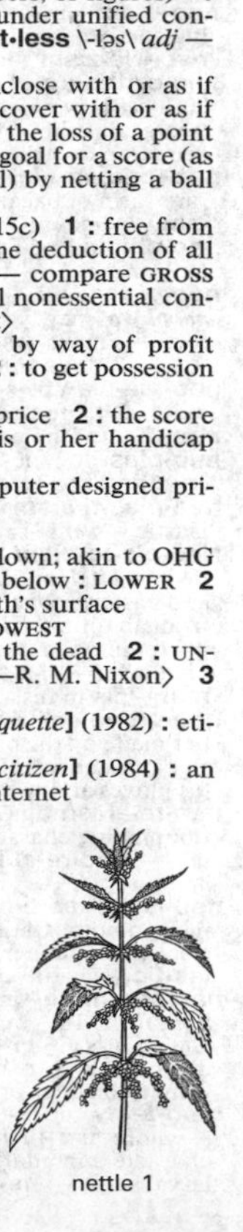

nettle 1

hairs **2 :** any of various prickly or stinging plants other than the true nettles (genus *Urtica*)

[2]**nettle** *vt* **net·tled; net·tling** \ˈnet-liŋ, ˈne-tᵊl-iŋ\ (15c) **1 :** to strike or sting with or as if with nettles **2 :** to arouse to sharp but transitory annoyance or anger ***syn*** see IRRITATE

nettle rash *n* (1740) **:** HIVES

net·tle·some \ˈne-tᵊl-səm\ *adj* (1766) **:** causing vexation **:** IRRITATING

net–veined \ˈnet-ˌvānd\ *adj* (1860) **:** having veins arranged in a fine network ‹a ∼ leaf› — see VENATION illustration; compare PARALLEL-VEINED — **net venation** *n*

net–winged \-ˌwiŋd\ *adj* (ca. 1890) **:** having wings with a fine network of veins

[1]**net·work** \ˈnet-ˌwərk\ *n* (1535) **1 :** a fabric or structure of cords or wires that cross at regular intervals and are knotted or secured at the crossings **2 :** a system of lines or channels resembling a network **3 a :** an interconnected or interrelated chain, group, or system ‹a ∼ of hotels› **b :** a system of computers, peripherals, terminals, and databases connected by communications lines **4 a :** a group of radio or television stations linked by wire or radio relay **b :** a radio or television company that produces programs for broadcast over such a network **5 :** a usu. informally interconnected group or association of persons (as friends or professional colleagues)

[2]**network** *vt* (1887) **1 :** to cover with or as if with a network ‹a continent . . . so ∼*ed* with navigable rivers and canals —*Lamp*› **2** *chiefly Brit* **:** to distribute for broadcast on a television network; *also* **:** BROADCAST 3 **3 :** to join (as computers) in a network ∼ *vi* **:** to engage in networking — **net·work·er** \-ˌwər-kər\ *n*

net·work·ing *n* (1967) **1 :** the exchange of information or services among individuals, groups, or institutions; *specif* **:** the cultivation of productive relationships for employment or business **2 :** the establishment or use of a computer network

Neuf·châ·tel \ˌnü-shä-ˈtel, ˌnyü-, ˌnə(r)-\ *n* [F, fr. *Neufchâtel,* France] (ca. 1865) **:** a soft unripened cheese similar to cream cheese but containing less fat and more moisture

neume \ˈnüm, ˈnyüm\ *n* [ME, fr. ML *pneuma, neuma,* fr. Gk *pneuma* breath — more at PNEUMATIC] (14c) **:** any of various symbols used in the notation of Gregorian chant — **neu·mat·ic** \nu̇-ˈma-tik, nyu̇-\ *adj*

neur- *or* **neuro-** *comb form* [NL, fr. Gk, nerve, sinew, fr. *neuron* — more at NERVE] **1 :** nerve ‹*neur*al› ‹*neuro*logy› **2 :** neural **:** neural and ‹*neuro*muscular›

neu·ral \ˈnu̇r-əl, ˈnyu̇r-\ *adj* (ca. 1847) **1 :** of, relating to, or affecting a nerve or the nervous system **2 :** situated in the region of or on the same side of the body as the brain and spinal cord **:** DORSAL — **neu·ral·ly** \-ə-lē\ *adv*

neural arch *n* (1854) **:** the cartilaginous or bony arch enclosing the spinal cord on the dorsal side of a vertebra

neural crest *n* (ca. 1885) **:** the ridge of one of the folds forming the neural tube that gives rise to the spinal ganglia and various structures of the autonomic nervous system

neu·ral·gia \nu̇-ˈral-jə, nyu̇-\ *n* [NL] (ca. 1834) **:** acute paroxysmal pain radiating along the course of one or more nerves usu. without demonstrable changes in the nerve structure — **neu·ral·gic** \-jik\ *adj*

neural network *n* (1951) **:** a computer architecture in which a number of processors are interconnected in a manner suggestive of the connections between neurons in a human brain and which is able to learn by a process of trial and error — called also *neural net*

neural plate *n* (1888) **:** a thickened plate of ectoderm along the dorsal midline of the early vertebrate embryo that gives rise to the neural tube and neural crests

neural tube *n* (1888) **:** the hollow longitudinal dorsal tube formed by infolding and subsequent fusion of the opposite ectodermal folds in the vertebrate embryo that gives rise to the brain and spinal cord

neur·amin·i·dase \ˌnu̇r-ə-ˈmi-nə-ˌdās, ˌnyu̇r-, -ˌdāz\ *n* [*neuramini*c acid, an amino acid + *-ide* + *-ase*] (1957) **:** a hydrolytic enzyme that occurs on the surface of the pneumococcus, influenza-causing viruses, and some paramyxoviruses as an antigen and that splits mucoproteins by breaking a glucoside link

neur·as·the·nia \ˌnu̇r-əs-ˈthē-nē-ə, ˌnyu̇r-\ *n* [NL] (ca. 1856) **:** a psychological disorder marked esp. by easy fatigability and often by lack of motivation, feelings of inadequacy, and psychosomatic symptoms — compare CHRONIC FATIGUE SYNDROME — **neur·as·then·ic** \-ˈthe-nik, -ˈthē-\ *adj or n* — **neur·as·then·i·cal·ly** \-ni-k(ə-)lē\ *adv*

neu·ri·lem·ma \ˌnu̇r-ə-ˈle-mə, ˌnyu̇r-\ *n* [NL, fr. *neur-* + Gk *eilēma* covering, coil, fr. *eilein* to wind; akin to Gk *eilyein* to wrap — more at VOLUBLE] (1852) **:** the plasma membrane surrounding a Schwann cell of a myelinated nerve fiber and separating layers of myelin — **neu·ri·lem·mal** \-ˈle-məl\ *adj*

neu·ri·tis \nu̇-ˈrī-təs, nyu̇-\ *n, pl* **-rit·i·des** \-ˈri-tə-ˌdēz\ *or* **-ri·tis·es** [NL] (1840) **:** an inflammatory or degenerative lesion of a nerve marked esp. by pain, sensory disturbances, and impaired or lost reflexes — **neu·rit·ic** \-ˈri-tik\ *adj or n*

neu·ro·ac·tive \ˌnu̇r-ō-ˈak-tiv, ˌnyu̇r-\ *adj* (1961) **:** stimulating neural tissue

neu·ro·anat·o·my \-ə-ˈna-tə-mē\ *n* (ca. 1899) **:** the anatomy of nervous tissue and the nervous system — **neu·ro·an·a·tom·i·cal** \-ˌa-nə-ˈtä-mi-kəl\ *also* **neu·ro·an·a·tom·ic** \-mik\ *adj* — **neu·ro·anat·o·mist** \-ə-ˈna-tə-mist\ *n*

neu·ro·bi·ol·o·gy \-bī-ˈä-lə-jē\ *n* (1906) **:** a branch of the life sciences that deals with the anatomy, physiology, and pathology of the nervous system — **neu·ro·bi·o·log·i·cal** \-ˌbī-ə-ˈlä-ji-kəl\ *adj* — **neu·ro·bi·ol·o·gist** \-bī-ˈä-lə-jist\ *n*

neu·ro·blas·to·ma \-blas-ˈtō-mə\ *n, pl* **-mas** *also* **-ma·ta** \-mə-tə\ [NL, fr. ISV *neuroblast* embryonic ganglion cell, fr. *neur-* + *-blast* -blast] (1910) **:** a malignant tumor formed of embryonic ganglion cells

neu·ro·chem·is·try \-ˈke-mə-strē\ *n* (1924) **1 :** the study of the chemical makeup and activities of nervous tissue **2 :** chemical processes and phenomena related to the nervous system — **neu·ro·chem·i·cal** \-ˈke-mi-kəl\ *adj or n* — **neu·ro·chem·ist** \-ˈke-mist\ *n*

neu·ro·de·gen·er·a·tive \-di-ˈje-nə-rə-tiv, -ˈjen-rə-; -ˈje-nə-ˌrā-; -dē-\ *adj* (1907) **:** relating to or marked by degeneration of nervous tissue

neu·ro·en·do·crine \-ˈen-də-krən, -ˌkrīn, -ˌkrēn\ *adj* (1922) **1 :** of, relating to, or being a hormonal substance that influences the activity of nerves **2 :** of, relating to, or functioning in neurosecretion

neu·ro·en·do·cri·nol·o·gy \-ˌen-də-kri-ˈnä-lə-jē, -(ˌ)krī-\ *n* (1922) **:** a branch of the life sciences dealing with neurosecretion and the physiological interaction between the central nervous system and the endocrine system — **neu·ro·en·do·cri·no·log·i·cal** \-ˌkri-nə-ˈlä-ji-kəl, -ˌkrī-, -ˌkrē-\ *adj* — **neu·ro·en·do·cri·nol·o·gist** \-kri-ˈnä-lə-jist, -(ˌ)krī-\ *n*

neu·ro·fi·bril \-ˈfī-brəl, -ˈfi-\ *n* [NL *neurofibrilla,* fr. *neur-* + *fibrilla* fibril] (1898) **:** a fine proteinaceous fibril that is found in cytoplasm (as of a neuron or a paramecium) and is capable of conducting excitation — **neu·ro·fi·bril·lary** \-brə-ˌler-ē\ *adj*

neurofibrillary tangle *n* (1973) **:** a pathological accumulation of paired helical filaments composed of abnormally formed tau protein that is found chiefly in the cytoplasm of neurons of the brain and esp. the cerebral cortex and hippocampus and that occurs typically in Alzheimer's disease

neu·ro·fi·bro·ma \-fī-ˈbrō-mə\ *n* (ca. 1892) **:** a fibroma composed of nervous and connective tissue and produced by proliferation of Schwann cells

neu·ro·fi·bro·ma·to·sis \-(ˌ)fī-ˌbrō-mə-ˈtō-səs\ *n* [NL, fr. *neurofibromat-, neurofibroma*] (1896) **:** a disorder inherited as an autosomal dominant and characterized esp. by brown spots on the skin, neurofibromas of peripheral nerves, and deformities of subcutaneous tissue and bone

neu·ro·gen·ic \ˌnu̇r-ə-ˈje-nik, ˌnyu̇r-\ *adj* (1901) **1 :** forming, originating in, or controlled by nervous tissue ‹∼ heartbeat› **2 :** induced or modified by nervous factors; *esp* **:** disordered because of abnormally altered neural relations — **neu·ro·gen·i·cal·ly** \-ni-k(ə-)lē\ *adv*

neu·ro·glia \nu̇-ˈrō-glē-ə, nyu̇-, -ˈrä-; ˌn(y)u̇r-ə-ˈglē-ə, -ˈglī-\ *n, pl* **neuroglia** [NL, fr. *neur-* + MGk *glia* glue — more at CLAY] (1873) **:** GLIA — **neu·ro·gli·al** \-əl\ *adj*

neu·ro·hor·mon·al \ˌnu̇r-ō-hȯr-ˈmō-nᵊl, ˌnyu̇r-\ *adj* (ca. 1935) **1 :** involving both neural and hormonal mechanisms **2 :** of, relating to, or being a neurohormone

neu·ro·hor·mone \-ˈhȯr-ˌmōn\ *n* [ISV] (1935) **:** a hormone (as acetylcholine or norepinephrine) produced by or acting on nervous tissue

neu·ro·hu·mor \-ˈhyü-mər, -ˈyü-\ *n* (1932) **:** NEUROHORMONE; *esp* **:** NEUROTRANSMITTER — **neu·ro·hu·mor·al** \-mə-rəl\ *adj*

neu·ro·hy·poph·y·sis \-hī-ˈpä-fə-səs\ *n* [NL] (1912) **:** the portion of the pituitary gland that is composed of the infundibulum and posterior lobe and is concerned with the secretion of various hormones — **neu·ro·hy·po·phy·se·al** *or* **neu·ro·hy·po·phy·si·al** \-(ˌ)hī-ˌpä-fə-ˈsē-əl, -ˌhī-pə-fə-, -ˈzē-, -ˌhī-pə-ˈfi-zē-\ *adj*

neu·ro·im·ag·ing \ˌn(y)u̇r-ō-ˈi-mə-jiŋ\ *n* (1983) **:** a clinical specialty concerned with producing images of the brain by noninvasive techniques (as computed tomography and magnetic resonance imaging); *also* **:** imaging of the brain by these techniques

neurol *abbr* neurological; neurology

neu·ro·lep·tic \ˌnu̇r-ə-ˈlep-tik, ˌnyu̇r-\ *n* [F *neuroleptique,* fr. *neur-* + *-leptique* affecting, fr. Gk *lēptikos* seizing, fr. *lambanein* to take, seize — more at LATCH] (1958) **:** ANTIPSYCHOTIC — **neuroleptic** *adj*

neu·rol·o·gist \nu̇-ˈrä-lə-jist, nyu̇-\ *n* (1832) **:** one specializing in neurology; *esp* **:** a physician skilled in the diagnosis and treatment of disease of the nervous system

neu·rol·o·gy \-jē\ *n* [NL *neurologia,* fr. *neur-* + *-logia* -logy] (ca. 1681) **:** the scientific study of the nervous system esp. in respect to its structure, functions, and abnormalities — **neu·ro·log·i·cal** \ˌnu̇r-ə-ˈlä-ji-kəl, ˌnyu̇r-\ *or* **neu·ro·log·ic** \-jik\ *adj* — **neu·ro·log·i·cal·ly** \-ji-k(ə-)lē\ *adv*

neu·ro·ma \nu̇-ˈrō-mə, nyu̇-\ *n, pl* **-mas** *also* **-ma·ta** \-mə-tə\ [NL] (ca. 1847) **:** a tumor or mass growing from a nerve and usu. consisting of nerve fibers

neu·ro·mus·cu·lar \ˌnu̇r-ō-ˈməs-kyə-lər, ˌnyu̇r-\ *adj* [ISV] (1864) **:** of or relating to nerves and muscles; *esp* **:** jointly involving or affecting nervous and muscular elements ‹a ∼ junction› ‹a ∼ disease›

neu·ron \ˈnü-ˌrän, ˈnyü-; ˈnu̇r-ˌän, ˈnyu̇r-\ *n* [NL *neuron,* fr. Gk, nerve, sinew — more at NERVE] (1891) **:** a grayish or reddish granular cell with specialized processes that is the fundamental functional unit of nervous tissue — **neu·ro·nal** \ˈnu̇r-ə-nᵊl, ˈnyu̇r-; nu̇-ˈrō-nᵊl, nyu̇-\ *also* **neu·ron·ic** \nu̇-ˈrä-nik, nyu̇-\ *adj*

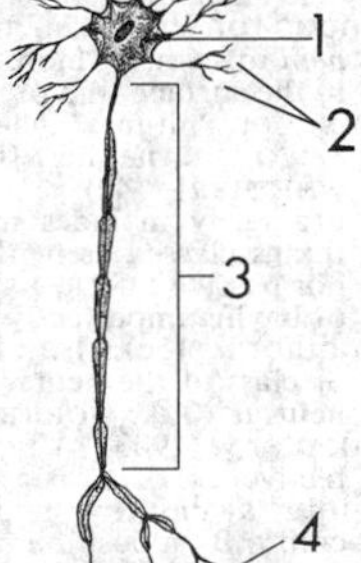

neuron: *1* cell body, *2* dendrite, *3* axon, *4* nerve ending

neu·rone \ˈn(y)u̇r-ˌōn, ˈn(y)ü-ˌrōn\ *chiefly Brit var of* NEURON

neu·ro·pa·thol·o·gy \ˌnu̇r-ō-pə-ˈthä-lə-jē, ˌnyu̇r-, -pa-\ *n* [ISV] (1853) **:** pathology of the nervous system — **neu·ro·path·o·log·ic** \-ˌpa-thə-ˈlä-jik\ *or* **neu·ro·path·o·log·i·cal** \-ji-kəl\ *adj* — **neu·ro·pa·thol·o·gist** \-pə-ˈthä-lə-jist, -pa-\ *n*

neu·rop·a·thy \nu̇-ˈrä-pə-thē, nyu̇-\ *n, pl* **-thies** [ISV] (ca. 1857) **:** an abnormal and usu. degenerative state of the nervous system or nerves; *also* **:** a systemic condition that stems from a neuropathy — **neu·ro·path·ic** \ˌnu̇r-ə-ˈpa-thik, ˌnyu̇r-\ *adj* — **neu·ro·path·i·cal·ly** \-thi-k(ə-)lē\ *adv*

neu·ro·pep·tide \ˌnu̇r-ə-ˈpep-ˌtīd, ˌnyu̇r-\ *n* (1975) **:** an endogenous peptide that influences neural activity or functioning

neu·ro·phar·ma·col·o·gy \ˌnu̇r-ō-ˌfär-mə-ˈkä-lə-jē, ˌnyu̇r-\ *n* (1950) **1 :** a branch of medical science dealing with the action of drugs on and in the nervous system **2 :** the properties and reactions of a drug on and in the nervous system — **neu·ro·phar·ma·co·log·i·cal** \-kə-ˈlä-ji-kəl\ *also* **neu·ro·phar·ma·co·log·ic** \-jik\ *adj* — **neu·ro·phar·ma·col·o·gist** \-ˈkä-lə-jist\ *n*

neu·ro·phys·i·ol·o·gy \-ˌfi-zē-ˈä-lə-jē\ *n* (1868) **:** physiology of the nervous system — **neu·ro·phys·i·o·log·i·cal** \-ə-ˈlä-ji-kəl\ *also* **neu·ro-**

phys·i·o·log·ic \-jik\ *adj* — **neu·ro·phys·i·o·log·i·cal·ly** \-ji-k(ə-)lē\ *adv* — **neu·ro·phys·i·ol·o·gist** \-ˈä-lə-jist\ *n*

neu·ro·plas·tic·i·ty \ˌnu̇r-ō-pla-ˈsti-sə-tē\ *n* (1985) : PLASTICITY 4

neu·ro·pro·tec·tive \ˌnu̇r-ō-prə-ˈtek-tiv, nyu̇r-\ *adj* (1987) : serving to protect neurons from injury or degeneration ⟨~ drugs⟩

neu·ro·psy·chi·a·try \-sə-ˈkī-ə-trē, -sī-\ *n* (1918) : a branch of medicine concerned with both neurology and psychiatry — **neu·ro·psy·chi·at·ric** \-ˌsī-kē-ˈa-trik\ *adj* — **neu·ro·psy·chi·at·ri·cal·ly** \-tri-k(ə-)lē\ *adv* — **neu·ro·psy·chi·a·trist** \-sə-ˈkī-ə-trist, -sī-\ *n*

neu·ro·psy·chol·o·gy \-sī-ˈkä-lə-jē\ *n* (ca. 1893) : a science concerned with the integration of psychological observations on behavior and the mind with neurological observations on the brain and nervous system — **neu·ro·psy·cho·log·i·cal** \-ˌsī-kə-ˈlä-ji-kəl\ *adj* — **neu·ro·psy·chol·o·gist** \-sī-ˈkä-lə-jist\ *n*

neu·rop·ter·an \nu̇-ˈräp-tə-rən, nyu̇-\ *n* [ultim. fr. Gk *neur-* + *pteron* wing — more at FEATHER] (ca. 1842) : any of an order (Neuroptera) of usu. net-winged insects that include the lacewings and ant lions — **neuropteran** *adj* — **neu·rop·ter·ous** \-rəs\ *adj*

neu·ro·ra·di·ol·o·gy \ˌnu̇r-ō-ˌrā-dē-ˈä-lə-jē, ˌnyu̇r-\ *n* (1938) : radiology of the nervous system — **neu·ro·ra·dio·log·i·cal** \-ə-ˈlä-ji-kəl\ *adj* — **neu·ro·ra·di·ol·o·gist** \-ˈä-lə-jist\ *n*

neu·ro·sci·ence \-ˈsī-ən(t)s\ *n* (1963) : a branch (as neurophysiology) of the life sciences that deals with the anatomy, physiology, biochemistry, or molecular biology of nerves and nervous tissue and esp. with their relation to behavior and learning — **neu·ro·sci·en·tif·ic** \-ˌsī-ən-ˈti-fik\ *adj* — **neu·ro·sci·en·tist** \-ˈsī-ən-tist\ *n*

neu·ro·se·cre·tion \-si-ˈkrē-shən\ *n* (1941) **1** : the process of producing a secretion by neurons **2** : a secretion produced by neurosecretion — **neu·ro·se·cre·to·ry** \-ˈkrē-tə-rē\ *adj*

neu·ro·sen·so·ry \-ˈsen(t)-sə-rē, -ˈsen(t)s-rē\ *adj* (1929) : of or relating to afferent nerves

neu·ro·sis \nu̇-ˈrō-səs, nyu̇-\ *n, pl* **-ro·ses** \-ˌsēz\ [NL] (ca. 1784) : a mental and emotional disorder that affects only part of the personality, is accompanied by a less distorted perception of reality than in a psychosis, does not result in disturbance of the use of language, and is accompanied by various physical, physiological, and mental disturbances (as visceral symptoms, anxieties, or phobias)

neu·ros·po·ra \nu̇-ˈräs-p(ə-)rə, nyu̇-\ *n* [NL, fr. *neur-* + *spora* spore] (1928) : any of a genus (*Neurospora* of the family Sordariaceae) of ascomycetous fungi which are used extensively in genetic research and have black perithecia and persistent asci and some of which have salmon-pink or orange spore masses and are severe pests in bakeries

neu·ro·sur·gery \-ˈsər-jə-rē, -ˈsərj-rē\ *n* (1904) : surgery of nervous structures (as nerves, the brain, or the spinal cord) — **neu·ro·sur·geon** \-ˈsər-jən\ *n* — **neu·ro·sur·gi·cal** \-ˈsər-ji-kəl\ *adj*

[1]**neu·rot·ic** \nu̇-ˈrä-tik\ *adj* (1866) : of, relating to, constituting, or affected with neurosis — **neu·rot·i·cal·ly** \-ti-k(ə-)lē\ *adv*

[2]**neurotic** *n* (1896) **1** : one affected with a neurosis **2** : an emotionally unstable individual

neu·rot·i·cism \nu̇-ˈrä-tə-ˌsi-zəm, nyu̇-\ *n* (1900) : a neurotic character, condition, or trait

neu·ro·tox·ic \ˌnu̇r-ō-ˈtäk-sik, ˌnyu̇r-\ *adj* (ca. 1903) : toxic to the nerves or nervous tissue — **neu·ro·tox·ic·i·ty** \-ˌtäk-ˈsi-sə-tē\ *n*

neu·ro·tox·in \-ˈtäk-sən\ *n* [ISV] (1902) : a poisonous complex esp. of protein that acts on the nervous system

neu·ro·trans·mis·sion \-tran(t)s-ˈmi-shən, -tranz-\ *n* (1961) : the transmission of nerve impulses across a synapse

neu·ro·trans·mit·ter \-tran(t)s-ˈmi-tər, -tranz-\ *n* (1961) : a substance (as norepinephrine or acetylcholine) that transmits nerve impulses across a synapse

neu·ro·trop·ic \-ˈträ-pik\ *adj* [ISV] (1903) : having an affinity for or localizing selectively in nerve tissue ⟨the ~ rabies virus⟩

neu·ru·la \ˈnu̇r-ə-lə, ˈnyu̇r-, -yə-lə\ *n, pl* **-lae** \-ˌlē\ *or* **-las** [NL, fr. *neur-* + L *-ula* -ule] (ca. 1890) : an early vertebrate embryo which follows the gastrula and in which nervous tissue begins to differentiate and the basic pattern of the vertebrate begins to emerge — **neu·ru·la·tion** \ˌnu̇r-ə-ˈlā-shən, ˌnyu̇r-, -yə-\ *n*

neus·ton \ˈnü-ˌstän, ˈnyü-\ *n* [G, fr. Gk, neut. of *neustos* swimming, fr. *nein* to swim — more at NATANT] (1928) : minute organisms that float in the surface film of water

[1]**neu·ter** \ˈnü-tər, ˈnyü-\ *adj* [ME *neutre,* fr. MF & L; MF *neutre,* fr. L *neuter,* lit., neither, fr. *ne-* not + *uter* which of two — more at NO, WHETHER] (14c) **1 a** : of, relating to, or constituting the gender that ordinarily includes most words or grammatical forms referring to things classed as neither masculine nor feminine **b** : neither active nor passive : INTRANSITIVE **2** : taking no side : NEUTRAL **3** : lacking or having imperfectly developed or nonfunctional generative organs

[2]**neuter** *n* (15c) **1 a** : a noun, pronoun, adjective, or inflectional form or class of the neuter gender **b** : the neuter gender **2** : one that is neutral **3 a** : WORKER 2 **b** : a spayed or castrated animal

[3]**neuter** *vt* (1903) **1** : CASTRATE, ALTER **2** : to remove the force or effectiveness of

[1]**neu·tral** \ˈnü-trəl, ˈnyü-\ *n* (15c) **1** : one that is neutral **2** : a neutral color **3** : a position of disengagement (as of gears)

[2]**neutral** *adj* [ME *neuterall* mutually neutralizing, fr. ML **neutralis,* back-formation fr. *neutralitas* middle ground, fr. L *neutralis* neuter, fr. *neutr-, neuter*] (1549) **1** : not engaged on either side; *specif* : not aligned with a political or ideological grouping ⟨a ~ nation⟩ **2** : of or relating to a neutral state or power ⟨~ territory⟩ **3 a** : not decided or pronounced as to characteristics : INDIFFERENT **b** (1) : ACHROMATIC (2) : nearly achromatic **c** (1) : NEUTER 3 (2) : lacking stamens or pistils **d** : neither acid nor basic **e** : not electrically charged **4** : produced with the tongue in the position it has when at rest ⟨the ~ vowels of \-ˈbəv\ *above*⟩ — **neu·tral·ly** \-trə-lē\ *adv* — **neu·tral·ness** *n*

neu·tral·ise *Brit var of* NEUTRALIZE

neu·tral·ism \ˈnü-trə-ˌli-zəm, ˈnyü-\ *n* (1579) **1** : NEUTRALITY **2** : a policy or the advocacy of neutrality esp. in international affairs — **neu·tral·ist** \-list\ *n* — **neu·tral·is·tic** \ˌnü-trə-ˈlis-tik, ˌnyü-\ *adj*

neu·tral·i·ty \nü-ˈtra-lə-tē, nyü-\ *n* (15c) : the quality or state of being neutral; *esp* : refusal to take part in a war between other powers

neu·tral·i·za·tion \ˌnü-trə-lə-ˈzā-shən, ˌnyü-\ *n* (1808) **1** : an act or process of neutralizing **2** : the quality or state of being neutralized

neu·tral·ize \ˈnü-trə-ˌlīz, ˈnyü-\ *vb* **-ized; -iz·ing** *vt* (1759) **1** : to make chemically neutral **2 a** : to counteract the activity or effect of : make ineffective ⟨propaganda that is difficult to ~⟩ **b** : KILL, DESTROY **3** : to make electrically inert by combining equal positive and negative quantities **4** : to invest (as a territory or a nation) with conventional or obligatory neutrality conferring inviolability during a war **5** : to make neutral by blending with the complementary color **6** : to give (as a pair of phonemes) a nondistinctive form or pronunciation ⟨\t\ and \d\ are *neutralized* when pronounced as flaps⟩ ~ *vi* : to undergo neutralization — **neu·tral·iz·er** *n*

neutral red *n* (1890) : a basic dye used chiefly as a biological stain and acid-base indicator

neutral spirits *n pl but sing or pl in constr* (1919) : ethanol of 190 or higher proof used esp. for blending other alcoholic liquors

neutral zone *n* (1948) : the portion of an ice hockey rink between the attacking and defensive zones

neu·tri·no \nü-ˈtrē-(ˌ)nō, nyü-\ *n, pl* **-nos** [It, fr. *neutro* neutral, neuter, fr. L *neutr-, neuter*] (1934) : an uncharged elementary particle that is believed to have a very small mass, that has any of three forms, and that interacts only rarely with other particles — **neu·tri·no·less** \-ləs\ *adj*

neu·tron \ˈnü-ˌträn, ˈnyü-\ *n* [prob. fr. *neutral*] (1932) : an uncharged elementary particle that has a mass nearly equal to that of the proton and is present in all known atomic nuclei except the hydrogen nucleus — **neu·tron·ic** \nü-ˈträ-nik, nyü-\ *adj*

neutron activation analysis *n* (1951) : an analytical method used to determine the chemical elements comprising a material by bombarding it with neutrons to produce radioactive atoms whose emissions are indicative of the elements present — called also *neutron activation*

neutron bomb *n* (1959) : a nuclear bomb designed to produce lethal neutrons but less blast and fire damage than other nuclear bombs

neutron star *n* (1934) : a dense celestial object that consists primarily of closely packed neutrons and that results from the collapse of a much larger stellar body

neu·tro·pe·nia \ˌn(y)ü-trə-ˈpē-nē-ə\ *n* [NL, fr. *neutro-* (fr. ISV *neutrophil*) + *-penia*] (ca. 1927) : leukopenia in which the decrease in white blood cells is chiefly in neutrophils — **neu·tro·pe·nic** \-ˈpē-nik\ *adj*

[1]**neu·tro·phil** \ˈnü-trə-ˌfil, ˈnyü-\ *or* **neu·tro·phil·ic** \ˌnü-trə-ˈfi-lik, ˌnyü-\ *adj* [ISV *neutro-* (fr. L *neutr-, neuter* neither) + *-phil*] (ca. 1890) : staining to the same degree with acid or basic dyes ⟨~ granulocytes⟩

[2]**neutrophil** *n* (1897) : a granulocyte that is the chief phagocytic white blood cell of the blood

Nev *abbr* Nevada

né·vé \nā-ˈvā\ *n* [F dial. (Swiss), fr. VL **nivatum,* fr. L *niv-, nix* snow — more at SNOW] (1843) : the partially compacted granular snow that forms the surface part of the upper end of a glacier; *broadly* : a field of granular snow

nev·er \ˈne-vər\ *adv* [ME, fr. OE *nǣfre,* fr. *ne* not + *ǣfre* ever — more at NO] (bef. 12c) **1** : not ever : at no time ⟨I ~ met her⟩ **2** : not in any degree : not under any condition ⟨~ the wiser for his experience⟩

never mind *conj* (1954) : MUCH LESS, LET ALONE — used esp. in negative contexts to add to one term another denoting something less likely ⟨with this knee I can hardly walk, *never mind* run⟩

nev·er·more \ˌne-vər-ˈmȯr\ *adv* (12c) : never again

nev·er–nev·er land \ˌne-vər-ˈne-vər-\ *n* (1900) : an ideal or imaginary place

nev·er·the·less \ˌne-vər-t͟hə-ˈles\ *adv* (14c) : in spite of that : HOWEVER ⟨her childish but ~ real delight —Richard Corbin⟩

ne·vi·ra·pine \nə-ˈvir-ə-ˌpēn, -ˈvī-rə-\ *n* [perh. fr. *ne-* (by reversal of *en*zyme) + *viral* + dipyridodi*azepin*one, class of drugs to which nevirapine belongs] (1991) : an antiretroviral drug $C_{15}H_{14}N_4O$ that inhibits reverse transcriptase and is administered orally in combination with at least one other antiretroviral in the treatment of infection by HIV-1 and AIDS

ne·vus \ˈnē-vəs\ *n, pl* **ne·vi** \-ˌvī\ [NL, fr. L *naevus*] (ca. 1836) : a congenital or acquired usu. highly pigmented area on the skin that is either flat or raised : MOLE

[1]**new** \ˈnü, *chiefly Brit* ˈnyü, *in place names usu* (ˌ)nü *or* nə *or* (ˌ)ni\ *adj* [ME, fr. OE *nīwe;* akin to OHG *niuwi* new, L *novus,* Gk *neos*] (bef. 12c) **1** : having recently come into existence : RECENT, MODERN **2 a** (1) : having been seen, used, or known for a short time : NOVEL ⟨rice was a ~ crop for the area⟩ (2) : UNFAMILIAR ⟨visit ~ places⟩ **b** : being other than the former or old ⟨a steady flow of ~ money⟩ **3** : having been in a relationship or condition but a short time ⟨~ to the job⟩ ⟨a ~ wife⟩ **4 a** : beginning as the resumption or repetition of a previous act or thing ⟨a ~ day⟩ ⟨the ~ edition⟩ **b** : made or become fresh ⟨awoke a ~ person⟩ **c** : relating to or being a new moon **5** : different from one of the same category that has existed previously ⟨~ realism⟩ **6** : of dissimilar origin and usu. of superior quality ⟨a ~ strain of hybrid corn⟩ **7** *cap* : MODERN 3; *esp* : having been in use after medieval times — **new·ish** \ˈnü-ish, ˈnyü-\ *adj* — **new·ness** *n*

syn NEW, NOVEL, ORIGINAL, FRESH mean having recently come into existence or use. NEW may apply to what is freshly made and unused ⟨*new* brick⟩ or has not been known before ⟨*new* designs⟩ or not experienced before ⟨starts the *new* job⟩. NOVEL applies to what is not only new but strange or unprecedented ⟨a *novel* approach to the problem⟩. ORIGINAL applies to what is the first of its kind to exist ⟨a man without one *original* idea⟩. FRESH applies to what has not lost its qualities of newness such as liveliness, energy, brightness ⟨a *fresh* start⟩.

[2]**new** *adv* (bef. 12c) : NEWLY, RECENTLY — usu. used in combination

[1]**new age** *adj, often cap N&A* (1949) **1** : of, relating to, or being New Age **2** : CONTEMPORARY, MODERN ⟨*new age* grocery stores⟩

[2]**new age** *n* (1971) **1** *cap* : an eclectic group of cultural attitudes arising in late 20th century Western society that are adapted from those of a variety of ancient and modern cultures, that emphasize beliefs (as reincarnation, holism, pantheism, and occultism) outside the mainstream, and that advance alternative approaches to spirituality, right living, and health **2** : a soft soothing form of instrumental music often used to promote relaxation — **New Ager** *n* — **New Agey** \-ˈā-jē\ *adj*

newb \ˈnüb\ *n* [by shortening] (1983) : NEWBIE

new·bie \ˈnü-bē, ˈnyü-\ *n, often attrib* [irreg. fr. *new*] (1970) : NEWCOMER; *esp* : a newcomer to cyberspace

new blood *n* (1851) : persons who are accepted into a group or organization and are expected to provide fresh ideas and vitality

[1]**new·born** \-ˌbȯrn\ *adj* (14c) **1** : recently born **2** : born anew

[2]**newborn** *n, pl* **newborn** *or* **newborns** (1879) : a newborn individual

New·burg *or* **New·burgh** \ˈnü-ˌbərg, ˈnyü-\ *adj* [origin unknown] (1890) : served with a sauce made of cream, butter, sherry, and egg yolks ⟨lobster ~⟩ ⟨shrimp ~⟩

New·cas·tle disease \ˈnü-ˌka-səl-, ˈnyü-; n(y)ü-ˈ\ *n* [*Newcastle* upon Tyne, England] (1927) : a contagious often fatal virus disease of birds and esp. the domestic chicken that is caused by a paramyxovirus (species *Newcastle disease virus* of the genus *Avulavirus*) and that is marked by respiratory and nervous symptoms

new·com·er \ˈnü-ˌkə-mər, ˈnyü-\ *n* (15c) **1** : one recently arrived **2** : BEGINNER, ROOKIE

New Criticism *n* (1941) : an analytic literary criticism that is marked by concentration on the language, imagery, and emotional or intellectual tensions in literary works — **New Critic** *n* — **New Critical** *adj*

New Deal *n* [fr. the supposed resemblance to the situation of freshness and equality of opportunity afforded by a fresh deal in a card game] (1932) : the legislative and administrative program of President F. D. Roosevelt designed to promote economic recovery and social reform during the 1930s; *also* : the period of this program — **New Dealer** *n* — **New Deal·ish** \-ˈdē-lish\ *adj* — **New Deal·ism** \-ˈdē(ə)-ˌli-zəm\ *n*

new drug *n* (ca. 1951) : a drug that has not been declared safe and effective by qualified experts under the conditions prescribed, recommended, or suggested in the label and that may be a new chemical formula or an established drug prescribed for use in a new way

new economics *n pl but usu sing in constr* (1928) : an economic concept that is a logical extension of Keynesianism and that holds that appropriate fiscal and monetary maneuvering can maintain healthy economic growth and prosperity indefinitely

new·el \ˈnü-əl, ˈnyü-\ *n* [ME *nowell,* fr. AF *nuel, noel* stone of a fruit, stone cut to form a newel, fr. LL *nucalis* like a nut, fr. L *nuc-, nux* nut — more at NUT] (14c) **1** : an upright post about which the steps of a circular staircase wind **2** : a post at the foot of a straight stairway or one at a landing

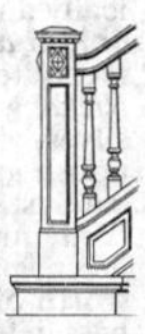

newel 2

New English Bible *n* (1957) : a translation of the Bible by a British interdenominational committee first published in its entirety in 1970

new·fan·gled \ˈnü-ˈfaŋ-gəld\ *adj* [ME, fr. *newefangel,* fr. *new* + OE *-*fangol,* fr. *fōn* (pp. *fangen*) to take, seize — more at PACT] (15c) **1** : attracted to novelty **2** : of the newest style or kind ⟨had many ~ gadgets in the kitchen⟩ — **new·fan·gled·ness** *n*

new–fash·ioned \-ˈfa-shənd\ *adj* (1575) **1** : made in a new fashion or form **2** : UP-TO-DATE

new·found \-ˈfau̇nd\ *adj* (15c) : newly found ⟨a ~ friend⟩

New·found·land \ˈnü-fən(d)-lənd, ˈnyü-, -ˌland; n(y)ü-ˈfau̇nd-lənd\ *n* [*Newfoundland,* Canada] (1773) : any of a breed of very large heavy highly intelligent black, black-and-white, brown, or gray dogs having a thick coat and prob. developed in Newfoundland

New·gate \ˈnü-ˌgāt, ˈnyü-, -gət\ *n* (14c) : a London prison razed in 1902

New Historicism *n* (1986) : a method of literary criticism that emphasizes the historicity of a text by relating it to the configurations of power, society, or ideology in a given time — **New Historicist** *adj or n*

new·ie \ˈnü-ē, ˈnyü-\ *n* (1834) : something new

new jack *adj, often cap N&J* [[1]*jack* (man, guy)] (1987) **1** : of, relating to, or consisting of new jack swing ⟨*new jack* grooves⟩ **2** : of, relating to, or being urban, hip, and usu. black ⟨the *new jack* generation⟩

new jack swing *n, often cap N&J&S* (1989) : pop music usu. performed by black musicians that combines elements of jazz, funk, rap, and rhythm and blues

New Jer·sey tea \nü-ˈjər-zē-, nyü-\ *n* [*New Jersey,* state of U.S.; fr. the use of its leaves as a substitute for tea during the American Revolution] (1759) : a low deciduous shrub (*Ceanothus americanus*) of the buckthorn family that is found in the eastern U.S. and has dull green leaves and small white flowers borne in large terminal panicles

New Je·ru·sa·lem \-jə-ˈrü-s(ə-)ləm, -zə-ləm; -ˈrüz-ləm\ *n* [fr. the phrase "the holy city, *New Jerusalem*" (Rev 21:2)] (1535) **1** : the final abode of souls redeemed by Christ **2** : an ideal earthly community

New Journalism *n* (1967) : journalism that features the author's subjective responses to people and events and that often includes fictional techniques meant to illuminate and dramatize those responses — **New Journalist** *n*

New Latin *n* (ca. 1889) : Latin as used since the end of the medieval period esp. in scientific description and classification

New Left *n* (1960) : a political movement originating esp. among students in the 1960s, favoring confrontational tactics, often breaking with older leftist ideologies, and concerned esp. with antiwar, antinuclear, feminist, and ecological issues — **new leftist** *n, often cap N&L*

new·ly \ˈnü-lē, ˈnyü-\ *adv* (bef. 12c) **1** : LATELY, RECENTLY ⟨a ~ married couple⟩ ⟨~ affluent⟩ **2** : ANEW, AFRESH ⟨~ painted⟩

new·ly·wed \-ˌwed\ *n* (1908) : a person recently married

new·mar·ket \ˈnü-ˌmär-kət, ˈnyü-\ *n* [*Newmarket,* England] (1837) : a long close-fitting coat worn in the 19th century

new math *n* (1964) : basic mathematics taught with emphasis on abstraction and the principles of set theory — called also *new mathematics*

new moon *n* (bef. 12c) **1** : the moon's phase when it is in conjunction with the sun so that its dark side is toward the earth; *also* : the thin crescent moon seen shortly after sunset for a few days after the actual occurrence of the new moon phase **2** : the first day of each Jewish month marked by a special liturgy

new potato *n* (1765) : a small moist tender thin-skinned potato harvested early in the growing season

New Right *n* (1966) : a political movement made up esp. of Protestants, opposed esp. to secular humanism, and concerned with issues esp. of church and state, patriotism, laissez-faire economics, pornography, and abortion

news \ˈnüz, ˈnyüz\ *n pl but sing in constr, often attrib* (15c) **1 a** : a report of recent events **b** : previously unknown information ⟨I've got ~ for you⟩ **c** : something having a specified influence or effect ⟨the rain was good ~ for lawns and gardens —Garrison Keillor⟩ ⟨the virus was bad ~⟩ **2 a** : material reported in a newspaper or news periodical or on a newscast **b** : matter that is newsworthy **3** : NEWSCAST — **news·less** \-ləs\ *adj*

news agency *n* (1873) : an organization that supplies news to subscribing newspapers, periodicals, and newscasters

news·agent \ˈnüz-ˌā-jənt, ˈnyüz-\ *n* (1851) *chiefly Brit* : NEWSDEALER

news·boy \-ˌbȯi\ *n* (1764) : one who delivers or sells newspapers

news·break \-ˌbrāk\ *n* (1944) : a newsworthy event

news·cast \-ˌkast\ *n* [*news* + broad*cast*] (ca. 1939) : a radio or television broadcast of news — **news·cast·er** \-ˌkas-tər\ *n*

news conference *n* (1946) : PRESS CONFERENCE

news·deal·er \-ˌdē-lər\ *n* (1861) : a dealer in newspapers, magazines, and often paperback books

news·group \-ˌgrüp\ *n* (1983) : an electronic bulletin board on the Internet that is devoted to a particular topic

news·hound \-ˌhau̇nd\ *n* (1918) : an aggressive journalist

new·sie \ˈnü-zē\ *n* (1971) : a person who works in the news industry; *esp* : REPORTER

news·let·ter \-ˌle-tər\ *n* (1903) : a small publication (as a leaflet or newspaper) containing news of interest chiefly to a special group

news·mag·a·zine \-ˌma-gə-ˌzēn, -ˈzēn\ *n* (1923) **1** : a usu. weekly magazine devoted chiefly to summarizing and analyzing news **2** : MAGAZINE 4c

news·man \-mən, -ˌman\ *n* (1596) : a person who gathers, reports, or comments on the news : REPORTER, CORRESPONDENT

news·mon·ger \-ˌməŋ-gər, -ˌmäŋ-\ *n* (1592) : a person who is active in gathering and repeating news; *esp* : GOSSIP

New South *n* (1887) : the southern U.S. in the years since the American Civil War

[1]**news·pa·per** \ˈnüz-ˌpā-pər, ˈnyüz-, ˈn(y)üs-\ *n* (1670) **1** : a paper that is printed and distributed usu. daily or weekly and that contains news, articles of opinion, features, and advertising **2** : an organization that publishes a newspaper **3** : the paper of a newspaper : NEWSPRINT

[2]**newspaper** *vi* (1943) : to do newspaper work

news·pa·per·man \-ˌman\ *n* (1806) : a person who owns or is employed by a newspaper

news·pa·per·wom·an \-ˌwu̇-mən\ *n* (1881) : a woman who owns or is employed by a newspaper

new·speak \ˈnü-ˌspēk, ˈnyü-\ *n, often cap* [*Newspeak,* a language "designed to diminish the range of thought," in the novel *1984* (1949) by George Orwell] (1950) : propagandistic language marked by euphemism, circumlocution, and the inversion of customary meanings

news·peo·ple \ˈnüz-ˌpē-pəl, ˈnyüz-\ *n pl* (1972) : REPORTERS

news·per·son \-ˌpər-sᵊn\ *n* (1973) : REPORTER

news·print \-ˌprint\ *n* (1909) : paper made chiefly from groundwood pulp and used mostly for newspapers

news·read·er \-ˌrē-dər\ *n* (1925) *chiefly Brit* : a news broadcaster

news·reel \-ˌrēl\ *n* (1916) : a short movie dealing with current events

news·room \-ˌrüm, -ˌru̇m\ *n* (1929) **1** : a place (as an office) where news is prepared for publication or broadcast **2** : NEWSSTAND

news·stand \-ˌstand\ *n* (1866) : a place (as an outdoor stall) where newspapers and periodicals are sold

New Style *adj* (1615) : using or according to the Gregorian calendar

news·week·ly \-ˌwē-klē\ *n* (1947) : a weekly newspaper or newsmagazine

news·wire \-ˌwī(-ə)r\ *n* (1972) : WIRE SERVICE

news·wom·an \-ˌwu̇-mən\ *n* (1928) : a woman who is a reporter

news·wor·thy \-ˌwər-t͟hē\ *adj* (1932) : interesting enough to the general public to warrant reporting — **news·wor·thi·ness** \-t͟hē-nəs\ *n*

news·writ·ing \-ˌrī-tiŋ\ *n* (1916) : JOURNALISM 1a

newsy \ˈnü-zē, ˈnyü-\ *adj* **news·i·er; -est** (1832) **1** : containing or filled with news ⟨~ letters⟩ **2** : NEWSWORTHY — **news·i·ness** *n*

newt \ˈnüt, ˈnyüt\ *n* [ME, alter. (resulting from misdivision of *an ewte*) of *ewte* — more at EFT] (15c) : any of various small salamanders (family Salamandridae) that are usu. semiaquatic as adults

New Testament *n* (14c) : the second part of the Christian Bible comprising the canonical Gospels and Epistles and also the book of Acts and book of Revelation — see BIBLE table

new·ton \ˈnü-tᵊn, ˈnyü-\ *n* [Sir Isaac *Newton*] (1904) : the unit of force in the meter-kilogram-second system equal to the force required to impart an acceleration of one meter per second per second to a mass of one kilogram

New·to·ni·an \nü-ˈtō-nē-ən, nyü-, -nyən\ *adj* (1713) **1** : of or relating to Sir Isaac Newton or his doctrines **2** : CLASSICAL 4b(2)

new town *n* (1918) : an urban development comprising a small to medium-sized city with a broad range of housing and planned industrial, commercial, and recreational facilities

new variant Creutzfeldt–Jakob disease *n* (1996) : VARIANT CREUTZFELDT-JAKOB DISEASE — abbr. *nvCJD*

new wave *n, often cap N&W* (1960) **1** : a cinematic movement that is characterized by improvisation, abstraction, and subjective symbolism and that often makes use of experimental photographic techniques **2** : a new movement in a particular field **3** : popular music less raw than punk rock and typically including unconventional melodies, exaggerated beats, and quirky lyrics **4** : DERNIER CRI; *esp* : fashion that is strikingly outrageous — **new–wave** \ˈnü-ˈwāv, ˈnyü-, -ˌwāv\ *adj* — **new wav·er** \-ˈwā-vər\ *n*

New World *n* (1555) : WESTERN HEMISPHERE; *esp* : the continental landmass of No. and So. America

New Year *n* (13c) **1** : the calendar year about to start or recently started **2 a** *usu* **New Year's** : NEW YEAR'S DAY **b** : the first days of a calendar year **3** : ROSH HASHANAH

New Year's Day *n* (13c) : the first day of the calendar year observed as a legal holiday in many countries

New York·ese \ˌn(y)ü-ˌyȯr-ˈkēz\ *n* (1894) : American English as spoken in New York City and surrounding areas

New York minute *n* (1980) : INSTANT, FLASH

[1]**next** \ˈnekst\ *adj* [ME, fr. OE *nīehst,* superl. of *nēah* nigh — more at NIGH] (bef. 12c) **1** : immediately adjacent (as in place, rank, or time) **2** : any other considered hypothetically ⟨knew it as well as the ~ man⟩

[2]**next** *prep* (bef. 12c) : nearest or adjacent to

\ə\ **abut** \ᵊ\ kitten, F table \ər\ **further** \a\ **ash** \ā\ **ace** \ä\ **mop, mar** \au̇\ **out** \ch\ **chin** \e\ **bet** \ē\ **easy** \g\ **go** \i\ **hit** \ī\ **ice** \j\ **job** \ŋ\ **sing** \ō\ **go** \ȯ\ **law** \ȯi\ **boy** \th\ **thin** \t͟h\ **the** \ü\ **loot** \u̇\ **foot** \y\ **yet** \zh\ **vision, beige** \k̟, ⁿ, œ, ue, ʸ\ *see* Guide to Pronunciation

[3]**next** *adv* (14c) **1 :** in the time, place, or order nearest or immediately succeeding ⟨~ we drove home⟩ ⟨the ~ closest school⟩ **2 :** on the first occasion to come ⟨when ~ we meet⟩

[4]**next** *n* (15c) : one that is next ⟨from one day to the ~⟩

next–door \ˈneks(t)-ˈdȯr\ *adj* (1744) : located or living in the next building, house, apartment, or room; *broadly* : NEARBY, ADJACENT

next door *adv* (1579) : in or to the next building, house, apartment, or room ⟨lives *next door*⟩; *broadly* : in or at an adjacent place — **next door to** : NEXT TO

next friend *n* (1579) : a person admitted to or appointed by a court to act for the benefit of a person (as an infant) lacking full legal capacity

next of kin (ca. 1548) : one or more persons in the nearest degree of relationship to another person

[1]**next to** *prep* (14c) **1 :** immediately following or adjacent to **2 :** in comparison to ⟨*next to* you I'm wealthy⟩

[2]**next to** *adv* (1667) : very nearly : ALMOST ⟨it was *next to* impossible to see in the fog⟩

nex·us \ˈnek-səs\ *n, pl* **nex·us·es** \-sə-səz\ *or* **nex·us** \-səs, -ˌsüs\ [L, fr. *nectere* to bind] (1663) **1 :** CONNECTION, LINK; *also* : a causal link **2 :** a connected group or series **3 :** CENTER, FOCUS

Nez Percé *or* **Nez Perce** \ˈnez-ˈpərs, ˈnes-ˈpers, ÷ˈnā-per-ˈsā\ *n, pl* **Nez Percé** *or* **Nez Per·cés** *same or* -ˈpər-səz, -ˈper-; ÷-per-ˈsā(z)\ *or* **Nez Perce** *or* **Nez Per·ces** *same or* -ˈpər-səz, -ˈper-\ [F, lit., pierced nose] (1812) **1 :** a member of an American Indian people of Idaho, Washington, and Oregon **2 :** the language of the Nez Percé people

NF *abbr* **1** Newfoundland **2** no funds

NFC *abbr* National Football Conference

NFL *abbr* National Football League

Nfld *abbr* Newfoundland

NFP *abbr* natural family planning

NFS *abbr* not for sale

ng *abbr* nanogram

NG *abbr* **1** national guard **2** no good

NGF *abbr* nerve growth factor

NGO *abbr* nongovernmental organization

NGU *abbr* nongonococcal urethritis

ngul·trum \eŋ-ˈgu̇l-trəm, en-\ *n* [Tibetan] (1973) — see MONEY table

ngwee \eŋ-ˈgwē, en-\ *n, pl* **ngwee** [Bemba, lit., bright] (1966) — see *kwacha* at MONEY table

NH *abbr* **1** never hinged **2** New Hampshire

NHL *abbr* National Hockey League

Ni *symbol* nickel

ni·a·cin \ˈnī-ə-sən\ *n* [*ni*cotinic *ac*id + [1]*-in*] (1942) : an acid $C_6H_5NO_2$ of the vitamin B complex found widely in animals and plants and used esp. against pellagra; *also* : NICOTINAMIDE — called also *nicotinic acid*

ni·a·cin·amide \ˌnī-ə-ˈsi-nə-ˌmīd\ *n* (1942) : a compound $C_6H_6N_2O$ of the vitamin B complex found esp. as a constituent of coenzymes and used similarly to niacin — called also *nicotinamide*

Ni·ag·a·ra \nī-ˈa-g(ə-)rə\ *n* [*Niagara* Falls] (1841) : an overwhelming flood : TORRENT ⟨a ~ of protests⟩

ni·al·amide \nī-ˈa-lə-ˌmīd\ *n* [*ni*cotinic acid + *amyl* + *amide*] (1959) : a synthetic antidepressant drug $C_{16}H_{18}N_4O_2$ that is an inhibitor of monoamine oxidase

nib \ˈnib\ *n* [prob. alter. of *neb*] (1585) **1 :** BILL, BEAK **2 a :** the sharpened point of a quill pen **b :** PEN POINT; *also* : each of the two divisions of a pen point **3 :** a small pointed or projecting part

[1]**nib·ble** \ˈni-bəl\ *vb* **nib·bled; nib·bling** \-b(ə-)liŋ\ [origin unknown] *vt* (ca. 1512) **1 a :** to bite gently **b :** to eat or chew in small bits **2 :** to take away bit by bit ⟨waves *nibbling* the shore⟩ ~ *vi* **1 :** to take gentle, small, or cautious bites; *also* : SNACK **2 :** to deal with something as if by nibbling — **nib·bler** \-b(ə-)lər\ *n*

[2]**nibble** *n* (1658) **1 :** an act of nibbling **2 :** a very small quantity or portion (as of food); *also* : SNACK **3 :** a tentative expression of interest

Ni·be·lung \ˈnē-bə-ˌlu̇ŋ\ *n, pl* **-lungs** *also* **-lung·en** \-ˌlu̇ŋ-ən\ [G] (1814) **1 :** a member of a race of dwarfs in Germanic legend **2 :** any of the followers of Siegfried **3 :** any of the Burgundian kings in the medieval German *Nibelungenlied*

nibs \ˈnibz\ *n pl but sing in constr* [origin unknown] (ca. 1821) : an important or self-important person — usu. used in the phrases *his nibs* or *her nibs* as if a title of honor

NIC *abbr* **1** network interface card **2** newly industrialized country; newly industrializing country

ni·cad \ˈnī-ˌkad\ *n, often cap N&C* [[1]*ni*ckel + *cad*mium] (1955) : a rechargeable storage battery that has a nickel cathode and a cadmium anode

nice \ˈnīs\ *adj* **nic·er; nic·est** [ME, foolish, wanton, fr. AF, silly, simple, fr. L *nescius* ignorant, fr. *nescire* not to know — more at NESCIENCE] (14c) **1** *obs* **a :** WANTON, DISSOLUTE **b :** COY, RETICENT **2 a :** showing fastidious or finicky tastes : PARTICULAR ⟨too ~ a palate to enjoy junk food⟩ **b :** exacting in requirements or standards : PUNCTILIOUS ⟨a ~ code of honor⟩ **3 :** possessing, marked by, or demanding great or excessive precision and delicacy ⟨~ measurements⟩ **4** *obs* : TRIVIAL **5 a :** PLEASING, AGREEABLE ⟨a ~ time⟩ ⟨a ~ person⟩ **b :** well-executed ⟨~ shot⟩ **c :** APPROPRIATE, FITTING ⟨not a ~ word for a formal occasion⟩ **6 a :** socially acceptable : WELL-BRED ⟨from a ~ family⟩ **b :** VIRTUOUS, RESPECTABLE ⟨was taught that ~ girls don't do that⟩ **7 :** POLITE, KIND ⟨that's ~ of you to say⟩ ***syn*** see CORRECT — **nice** *adv* — **nice·ly** *adv* — **nice·ness** *n*

Ni·cene \ˈnī-ˌsēn, nī-ˈ\ *adj* [ME, fr. LL *nicaenus,* fr. L *Nicaea* Nicaea, fr. Gk *Nikaia*] (14c) **1 :** of or relating to Nicaea or the Nicaeans **2 :** of or relating to the ecumenical church council held in Nicaea in A.D. 325 or to the Nicene Creed

Nicene Creed *n* (ca. 1569) : a Christian creed expanded from a creed issued by the first Nicene Council, beginning "I believe in one God," and used in liturgical worship

nice–nel·ly \ˈnīs-ˈne-lē\ *adj, often cap 2d N* [fr. the name *Nelly*] (1925) **1 :** marked by euphemism **2 :** PRUDISH — **nice nelly** *n, often cap 2d N* — **nice–nel·ly·ism** \-ˌi-zəm\ *n, often cap 2d N*

nice·ty \ˈnī-sə-tē, -stē\ *n, pl* **-ties** [ME *nicete,* fr. AF *niceté* foolishness, fr. *nice,* adj.] (14c) **1 :** the quality or state of being nice **2 :** an elegant, delicate, or civilized feature ⟨enjoy the *niceties* of life⟩ **3 :** a fine point or distinction : SUBTLETY ⟨the *niceties* of table manners⟩ **4 :** careful attention to details : delicate exactness : PRECISION **5 :** delicacy of taste or feeling : FASTIDIOUSNESS

[1]**niche** \ˈnich *also* ˈnēsh *or* ˈnish\ *n* [F, fr. MF, fr. *nicher* to nest, fr. VL **nidicare,* fr. L *nidus* nest — more at NEST] (1611) **1 a :** a recess in a wall esp. for a statue **b :** something that resembles a niche **2 a :** a place, employment, status, or activity for which a person or thing is best fitted ⟨finally found her ~⟩ **b :** a habitat supplying the factors necessary for the existence of an organism or species **c :** the ecological role of an organism in a community esp. in regard to food consumption **d :** a specialized market

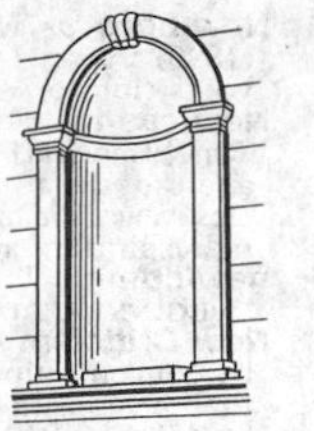
niche 1a

[2]**niche** *vt* **niched; nich·ing** (1752) : to place in or as if in a niche

Ni·chrome \ˈnī-ˌkrōm\ *trademark* — used for an alloy of nickel, chromium, and iron

[1]**nick** \ˈnik\ *n* [ME *nyke,* prob. alter. of *nocke* nock] (15c) **1 a :** a small notch, groove, or chip **b :** a small cut or wound **c :** a break in one strand of two-stranded DNA caused by a missing phosphodiester bond **2 :** a final critical moment ⟨in the ~ of time⟩ **3** *slang Brit* : PRISON; *also* : POLICE STATION **4** *Brit* : CONDITION ⟨in good ~⟩

[2]**nick** *vt* (1523) **1 :** to jot down : RECORD **2 a :** to make a nick in : NOTCH, CHIP **b :** to cut into or wound slightly ⟨~*ed* himself shaving⟩ **3 :** to cut short ⟨cold weather, which ~*ed* steel and automobile output —*Time*⟩ **4 :** to catch at the right point or time **5 :** CHEAT, OVERCHARGE **6 a** *slang Brit* : ARREST **b** *slang Brit* : STEAL ~ *vi* **1 :** to make petty attacks : SNIPE **2 :** to complement one another genetically and produce superior offspring

nick·el *also* **nick·le** \ˈni-kəl\ *n* [prob. fr. Sw *nickel,* fr. G *Kupfernickel* niccolite (mineral containing nickel arsenide) prob. fr. *Kupfer* copper + *Nickel* goblin; fr. the deceptive copper color of niccolite] (1755) **1 :** a silver-white hard malleable ductile metallic element capable of a high polish and resistant to corrosion that is used chiefly in alloys and as a catalyst — see ELEMENT table **2 a (1) :** the U.S. 5-cent piece regularly containing 25 percent nickel and 75 percent copper **(2) :** the Canadian 5-cent piece **b :** five cents **3** *slang* : a packet containing five dollars worth of an illicit drug (as marijuana) — called also *nickel bag* **4 :** a pass defense in football that employs five defensive backs

[1]**nick·el–and–dime** \ˌni-kəl-ən-ˈdīm\ *adj* (1941) **1 :** involving or offering only a small amount of money **2 :** SMALL-TIME

[2]**nickel–and–dime** *vt* **nick·eled–and–dimed** \ˌni-kəld-ən-ˈdīmd\ *or* **nick·el–and–dimed** \-ən-ˈdīmd\; **nick·el·ing–and–dim·ing** \-ˈdī-miŋ\ *or* **nickel–and–diming** (1961) **1 :** to impair, weaken, or defeat piecemeal (as through a series of small incursions or excessive attention to minor details) **2 :** to treat (as a person or situation) by paying excessive attention to small amounts of money often with a detrimental effect

nick·el·if·er·ous \ˌni-kə-ˈli-f(ə-)rəs\ *adj* (1821) : containing nickel

nick·el·ode·on \ˌni-kə-ˈlō-dē-ən\ *n* [prob. fr. *nickel* + *-odeon* (as in *melodeon* music hall)] (1907) **1 :** an early movie theater to which admission usu. cost five cents **2 :** JUKEBOX

nickel silver *n* (1860) : GERMAN SILVER

[1]**nick·er** \ˈni-kər\ *vi* **nick·ered; nick·er·ing** \-k(ə-)riŋ\ [perh. alter. of *neigh*] (1641) : NEIGH, WHINNY — **nicker** *n*

[2]**nicker** *n* [perh. fr. *nicker* one that nicks] (1910) *slang Brit* : [1]POUND 2a

nicknack *var of* KNICKKNACK

[1]**nick·name** \ˈnik-ˌnām\ *n* [ME *nekename* additional name, alter. (resulting from misdivision of *an ekename*) of *ekename,* fr. *eke* eke, also + *name* name] (15c) **1 :** a usu. descriptive name given instead of or in addition to the one belonging to a person, place, or thing **2 :** a familiar form of a proper name (as of a person or a city)

[2]**nickname** *vt* (1536) **1 :** MISNAME, MISCALL **2 :** to give a nickname to — **nick·nam·er** *n*

ni·co·ti·a·na \ni-ˌkō-shē-ˈa-nə, -ˈä-nə, -ˈā-nə\ *n* [NL, fr. *herba nicotiana,* lit., Nicot's herb, fr. Jean *Nicot* †1600 Fr. diplomat and scholar] (1600) : any of several tobaccos (as *Nicotiana alata*) grown for their showy flowers

nic·o·tin·amide \ˌni-kə-ˈtē-nə-ˌmīd, -ˈti-\ *n* [ISV] (1895) : NIACINAMIDE

nicotinamide adenine dinucleotide *n* (1961) : NAD

nicotinamide adenine dinucleotide phosphate *n* (1963) : NADP

nic·o·tine \ˈni-kə-ˌtēn\ *n* [F, fr. NL *nicotiana*] (1819) : a poisonous alkaloid $C_{10}H_{14}N_2$ that is the chief active principle of tobacco and is used as an insecticide

nic·o·tin·ic \ˌni-kə-ˈtē-nik, -ˈti-\ *adj* [ISV] (1873) : relating to, resembling, producing, or mediating the effects produced by nicotine on nerve fibers at autonomic ganglia and at the neuromuscular junctions of voluntary muscle which increases activity in small doses and inhibits it in larger doses ⟨~ receptors⟩ — compare MUSCARINIC

nicotinic acid *n* (1873) : NIACIN

nic·ti·tate \ˈnik-tə-ˌtāt\ *vi* **-tat·ed; -tat·ing** [alter. of *nictate* to wink, fr. L *nictatus,* pp. of *nictare* — more at CONNIVE] (1713) : WINK

nictitating membrane *n* (1713) : a thin membrane found in many vertebrates at the inner angle or beneath the lower lid of the eye and capable of extending across the eyeball

NICU *abbr* neonatal intensive care unit

NIDDM *abbr* non-insulin-dependent diabetes mellitus

ni·dic·o·lous \nī-ˈdi-kə-ləs\ *adj* [L *nidus* nest + E *-colous* — more at NEST] (ca. 1902) **1 :** reared for a time in a nest **2 :** living in a nest; *esp* : sharing the nest of another kind of animal

ni·di·fi·ca·tion \ˌni-də-fə-ˈkā-shən, ˌnī-\ *n* [ML *nidification-, nidificatio,* fr. L *nidificare* to build a nest, fr. *nidus* nest] (1658) : the act, process, or technique of building a nest

ni·dif·u·gous \nī-ˈdi-fyə-gəs\ *adj* [L *nidus* nest + *fugere* to flee — more at FUGITIVE] (1896) : leaving the nest soon after hatching

ni·dus \ˈnī-dəs\ *n, pl* **ni·di** \ˈnī-ˌdī\ *or* **ni·dus·es** [NL, fr. L] (1742) **1 :** a nest or breeding place; *esp* : a place or substance in an animal or plant where bacteria or other organisms lodge and multiply **2 :** a place where something originates, develops, or is located

niece \ˈnēs\ *n* [ME *nece* granddaughter, niece, fr. AF *nece, niece,* fr. LL *neptia,* fr. L *neptis;* akin to L *nepot-, nepos* grandson, nephew — more at NEPHEW] (14c) **1 :** a daughter of one's brother, sister, brother-in-law, or sister-in-law **2 :** an illegitimate daughter of an ecclesiastic

[1]**ni·el·lo** \nē-ˈe-(ˌ)lō\ *n, pl* **ni·el·li** \-(ˌ)lē\ *or* **niellos** [It, fr. ML *nigellum,* fr. neut. of L *nigellus* blackish, dim. of *niger* black] (1816) **1 :** any of

several black enamel-like alloys usu. of sulfur with silver, copper, and lead **2** : the art or process of decorating metal with incised designs filled with niello **3** : a piece of metal or an object decorated with niello

[2]**niello** *vt* (1866) : to inlay or ornament with niello

ni·fed·i·pine \nə-ˈfe-də-ˌpēn, -pən\ *n* [prob. *nitr-* + *-fe-* (fr. *phenyl*) + *-dipine* (by alter. & shortening fr. *pyridine*)] (1974) : a calcium channel blocker $C_{17}H_{18}N_2O_6$ that is a coronary vasodilator used esp. in the treatment of angina pectoris

Nifl·heim \ˈni-vəl-ˌhām\ *n* [ON *Niflheimr*] : the abode of the dead in Norse mythology

[1]**nif·ty** \ˈnif-tē\ *adj* **nif·ti·er; -est** [origin unknown] (1865) : very good : very attractive : FINE ⟨~ clothes⟩ — **nif·ti·ly** \ˈnif-tə-lē\ *adv*

[2]**nifty** *n, pl* **nifties** (1918) : something that is nifty; *esp* : a clever or neatly turned phrase or joke

ni·gel·la \nī-ˈje-lə\ *n* [NL, fr. LL, a black-seeded plant, fr. fem. of L *nigellus*] (14c) : any of a genus (*Nigella*) of erect annual herbs of the buttercup family having dissected threadlike leaves and usu. blue or white flowers; *esp* : LOVE-IN-A-MIST

Ni·ger–Con·go \ˌnī-jər-ˈkäŋ-(ˌ)gō\ *n* [*Niger* (river) + *Congo* (river)] (ca. 1950) : a language family that includes the Mande and Kwa branches and that is spoken by most of the indigenous peoples of west, central, and south Africa

[1]**nig·gard** \ˈni-gərd\ *n* [ME, of Scand origin; akin to ON *hnøggr* niggardly; akin to OE *hnēaw* niggardly] (14c) : a meanly covetous and stingy person : MISER — **niggard** *adj*

[2]**niggard** *vi* (ca. 1600) *obs* : to act niggardly ~ *vt, obs* : to treat in a niggardly manner

nig·gard·ly \-lē\ *adj* (1571) **1** : grudgingly mean about spending or granting : BEGRUDGING **2** : provided in meanly limited supply ***syn*** see STINGY — **nig·gard·li·ness** *n* — **niggardly** *adv*

nig·ger \ˈni-gər\ *n* [alter. of earlier *neger*, fr. MF *negre*, fr. Sp or Pg *negro*, fr. *negro* black, fr. L *niger*] (1574) **1** *usu offensive; see usage paragraph below* : a black person **2** *usu offensive; see usage paragraph below* : a member of any dark-skinned race **3** : a member of a socially disadvantaged class of persons ⟨it's time for somebody to lead all of America's ~*s* . . . all the people who feel left out of the political process —Ron Dellums⟩

usage *Nigger* in senses 1 and 2 can be found in the works of such writers of the past as Joseph Conrad, Mark Twain, and Charles Dickens, but it now ranks as perhaps the most offensive and inflammatory racial slur in English. Its use by and among blacks is not always intended or taken as offensive, but, except in sense 3, it is otherwise a word expressive of racial hatred and bigotry.

[1]**nig·gle** \ˈni-gəl\ *vb* **nig·gled; nig·gling** \-g(ə-)liŋ\ [origin unknown] *vi* (ca. 1616) **1 a** : TRIFLE **b** : to spend too much effort on minor details **2** : to find fault constantly in a petty way : CARP ⟨she haggles, she ~*s*, she wears out our patience —Virginia Woolf⟩ **3** : GNAW ~ *vt* : to give stingily or in tiny portions — **nig·gler** \-g(ə-)lər\ *n*

[2]**niggle** *n* (1886) *chiefly Brit* : a trifling doubt, objection, or complaint

nig·gling \ˈni-g(ə-)liŋ\ *adj* (1599) : PETTY; *also* : bothersome or persistent esp. in a petty or tiresome way ⟨~ injuries⟩ — **niggling** *n* — **nig·gling·ly** \-lē\ *adv*

[1]**nigh** \ˈnī\ *adv* [ME, fr. OE *nēah*; akin to OHG *nāh*, adv., nigh, prep., nigh, after, ON *nā-* nigh] (bef. 12c) **1** : near in place, time, or relationship — often used with *on*, *onto*, or *unto* **2** : NEARLY, ALMOST

[2]**nigh** *adj* (bef. 12c) **1** : CLOSE, NEAR **2** *chiefly dial* : DIRECT, SHORT **3** : being on the left side ⟨the ~ horse⟩

[3]**nigh** *prep* (bef. 12c) : NEAR

[4]**nigh** *vt* (13c) : to draw or come near to : APPROACH ~ *vi* : to draw near

[1]**night** \ˈnīt\ *n* [ME, fr. OE *niht*; akin to OHG *naht* night, L *noct-*, *nox*, Gk *nykt-*, *nyx*] (bef. 12c) **1** : the time from dusk to dawn when no sunlight is visible **2 a** : an evening or night taken as an occasion or point of time ⟨the opening ~⟩ **b** : an evening set aside for a particular purpose **3 a** : the quality or state of being dark **b** : a condition or period felt to resemble the darkness of night: as **(1)** : a period of dreary inactivity or affliction **(2)** : absence of moral values **c** : the beginning of darkness : NIGHTFALL — **night·less** \-ləs\ *adj*

[2]**night** *adj* (bef. 12c) **1** : of, relating to, or associated with the night ⟨~ air⟩ **2** : intended for use at night ⟨a ~ lamp⟩ **3 a** : existing, occurring, or functioning at night ⟨~ baseball⟩ ⟨a ~ nurse⟩ **b** : active or functioning best at night ⟨~ people⟩

night and day *adv* (bef. 12c) : all the time : CONTINUALLY

night blindness *n* (1754) : reduced visual capacity in faint light (as at night) — **night–blind** \ˈnīt-ˌblīnd\ *adj*

night–blooming cereus *n* (1832) : any of several night-blooming cacti; *esp* : a slender sprawling or climbing cactus (*Selenicereus grandiflorus*) often cultivated for its large showy fragrant white flowers

night·cap \ˈnīt-ˌkap\ *n* (14c) **1** : a cloth cap worn with nightclothes **2** : a usu. alcoholic drink taken at the end of the day **3** : the final race or contest of a day's sports; *esp* : the second game of a baseball doubleheader

night·clothes \-ˌklō(th)z\ *n pl* (1602) : garments for wear in bed

[1]**night·club** \-ˌkləb\ *n* (1894) : a place of entertainment open at night usu. serving food and liquor and providing music and space for dancing and often having a floor show

[2]**nightclub** *vi* (1936) : to patronize nightclubs — **night·club·ber** *n*

night court *n* (1934) : a criminal court in a large city that sits at night (as for rapid disposition of criminal charges and the granting of bail)

night crawler *n* (1924) : EARTHWORM; *esp* : a large earthworm found on the soil surface at night and used for fish bait

night·dress \ˈnīt-ˌdres\ *n* (ca. 1714) **1** : NIGHTGOWN **2** : NIGHTCLOTHES

night·fall \ˈnīt-ˌfȯl\ *n* (1700) : the close of the day : DUSK

night·glow \-ˌglō\ *n* (1951) : airglow seen during the night

night·gown \-ˌgau̇n\ *n* (14c) **1** *archaic* : DRESSING GOWN **2** : a loose garment for wear in bed

night·hawk \-ˌhȯk\ *n* (1611) **1 a** : any of a genus (*Chordeiles*) of American nightjars related to the whip-poor-will **b** : a common European nightjar (*Caprimulgus europaeus*) **2** : a person who habitually is active late at night

night heron *n* (1784) : any of various widely distributed nocturnal or crepuscular herons (esp. genus *Nycticorax*)

night·ie \ˈnī-tē\ *or* **nighty** *n, pl* **night·ies** [*nightgown* + *-ie*] (1871) : a nightgown for a woman or child

night·in·gale \ˈnī-tən-ˌgāl, -tiŋ-\ *n* [ME, alter. of OE *nihtegale*, fr. *niht* + *galan* to sing — more at YELL] (13c) : an Old World thrush (*Luscinia megarhynchos* syn. *Erithacus megarhynchos*) noted for the sweet usu. nocturnal song of the male; *also* : any of various other birds noted for their sweet song or for singing at night

night·jar \ˈnīt-ˌjär\ *n* [fr. its harsh sound] (1630) : any of a family (Caprimulgidae) of medium-sized long-winged crepuscular or nocturnal birds (as the whip-poor-wills and nighthawks) having a short bill, short legs, and soft mottled plumage and feeding on insects which they catch on the wing — called also *goatsucker*

night latch *n* (1854) : a door lock having a spring bolt operated from the outside by a key and from the inside by a knob

night letter *n* (1910) : a telegram sent at night at a reduced rate for delivery the following morning

night·life \ˈnīt-ˌlīf\ *n* (1852) : the activity of or entertainment provided for pleasure-seekers at night (as in nightclubs); *also* : establishments providing nightlife

night–light \-ˌlīt\ *n* (1839) : a light kept burning throughout the night

[1]**night·long** \-ˌlȯŋ\ *adj* (1612) : lasting the whole night ⟨~ festivities⟩

[2]**night·long** \-ˈlȯŋ\ *adv* (1870) : through the whole night

[1]**night·ly** \-lē\ *adj* (bef. 12c) **1** : happening, done, or used by night or every night **2** : of or relating to the night or every night

[2]**nightly** *adv* (15c) : every night; *also* : at or by night

night·mare \ˈnīt-ˌmer\ *n* [ME, fr. [1]*night* + [1]*mare*] (14c) **1** : an evil spirit formerly thought to oppress people during sleep **2** : a frightening dream that usu. awakens the sleeper **3** : something (as an experience, situation, or object) having the monstrous character of a nightmare or producing a feeling of anxiety or terror — **nightmare** *adj* — **night·mar·ish** \-ˌmer-ish\ *adj* — **night·mar·ish·ly** *adv*

night owl *n* (1845) : a person who keeps late hours at night

night rail \-ˌrāl\ *n* [*night* + *rail*, a woman's loose garment] (1554) *archaic* : NIGHTGOWN

night raven *n* (bef. 12c) : a bird that cries at night

night rider *n* (1877) : a member of a secret band who ride masked at night doing acts of violence for the purpose of punishing or terrorizing

nights \ˈnīts\ *adv* (bef. 12c) : in the nighttime repeatedly : on any night ⟨works ~⟩

night·scope \ˈnīt-ˌskōp\ *n* (1972) : an optical device usu. using infrared radiation that enables a person to see objects in the dark better

night·shade \-ˌshād\ *n* (bef. 12c) **1** : any of a genus (*Solanum* of the family Solanaceae, the nightshade family) of herbs, shrubs, and trees having alternate leaves, cymose flowers, and fruits that are berries and including some poisonous weeds, various ornamentals, and important crop plants (as the potato and eggplant) **2** : BELLADONNA 1

night·shirt \-ˌshərt\ *n* (1843) : a nightgown resembling a shirt

night·side \-ˌsīd\ *n* (1848) : the side of a celestial body (as the earth, the moon, or a planet) not in daylight

night soil *n* (ca. 1774) : human feces used esp. for fertilizing the soil

night·spot \ˈnīt-ˌspät\ *n* (1933) : NIGHTCLUB

night·stand \-ˌstand\ *n* (1892) : NIGHT TABLE

night·stick \-ˌstik\ *n* (1887) : a police officer's club

night sweats *n pl* (ca. 1754) : profuse sweating during sleep that is sometimes a symptom of febrile disease

night table *n* (1788) : a small bedside table or stand

night terror *n* (1896) : a sudden awakening in dazed terror that occurs in children during slow-wave sleep, is often preceded by a sudden shrill cry uttered in sleep, and is not remembered when the child awakes — usu. used in pl.

night·time \-ˌtīm\ *n, often attrib* (14c) : the time from dusk to dawn

night·walk·er \-ˌwȯ-kər\ *n* (15c) **1** : a person who roams about at night esp. with criminal intent **2** : PROSTITUTE, STREETWALKER

NIH *abbr* **1** National Institutes of Health **2** not invented here

ni·hil·ism \ˈnī-(h)ə-ˌli-zəm, ˈnē-\ *n* [G *Nihilismus*, fr. L *nihil* nothing — more at NIL] (ca. 1817) **1 a** : a viewpoint that traditional values and beliefs are unfounded and that existence is senseless and useless **b** : a doctrine that denies any objective ground of truth and esp. of moral truths **2 a** : a doctrine or belief that conditions in the social organization are so bad as to make destruction desirable for its own sake independent of any constructive program or possibility **b** *cap* : the program of a 19th century Russian party advocating revolutionary reform and using terrorism and assassination — **ni·hil·ist** \-list\ *n or adj* — **ni·hil·is·tic** \ˌnī-(h)ə-ˈlis-tik, ˌnē-\ *adj*

-nik *n suffix* [Yiddish, fr. Pol & Ukrainian] : one connected with or characterized by being ⟨beat*nik*⟩

Ni·ke \ˈnī-kē\ *n* [Gk *Nikē*] (1850) : the Greek goddess of victory

nil \ˈnil\ *n* [L, nothing, contr. of *nihil*, fr. OL *nihilum*, fr. *ne-* not + *hilum* trifle — more at NO] (1833) : NOTHING, ZERO — **nil** *adj*

nile green *n, often cap N* [*Nile* River, Africa] (1871) : a pale yellow green

Nile perch *n* (1926) : a large predaceous food fish (*Lates niloticus*) of the rivers and lakes of northern and central Africa that may exceed 200 pounds (91 kilograms) in weight

nil·gai \ˈnil-ˌgī\ *n* [Hindi & Urdu *nīlgāy*] (1882) : a large bluish-gray antelope (*Boselaphus tragocamelus*) of India and eastern Pakistan with the male having short horns, a black mane, and tuft of long hair on the throat

nill \ˈnil\ *vb* [ME *nilen*, fr. OE *nyllan*, fr. *ne* not + *wyllan* to wish — more at NO, WILL] *vi* (bef. 12c) *archaic* : to be unwilling : will not ⟨will you ~ you, I will marry you —Shak.⟩ ~ *vt, archaic* : REFUSE

Ni·lot·ic \nī-ˈlä-tik\ *adj* [L *Niloticus*, fr. Gk *Neilōtēs*, fr. *Neilos* Nile] (1653) **1** : of or relating to the Nile or the peoples of the Nile basin **2** : of, relating to, or being the languages of the Nilotic people

nil·po·tent \ˈnil-ˌpō-tənt\ *adj* [L *nil* nothing + *potent-*, *potens* having power — more at POTENT] (1870) : equal to zero when raised to some power ⟨~ matrices⟩

\ə\ **abut** \ə\ **kitten**, F **table** \ər\ **further** \a\ **ash** \ā\ **ace** \ä\ **mop, mar**
\au̇\ **out** \ch\ **chin** \e\ **bet** \ē\ **easy** \g\ **go** \i\ **hit** \ī\ **ice** \j\ **job**
\ŋ\ **sing** \ō\ **go** \ȯ\ **law** \ȯi\ **boy** \th\ **thin** \th\ **the** \ü\ **loot** \u̇\ **foot**
\y\ **yet** \zh\ **vision, beige** \k, n, œ, ue, y\ *see* Guide to Pronunciation

[1]**nim** \ˈnim\ *vb* **nimmed; nim·ming** [earlier *nim* to take, fr. ME *nimen,* fr. OE *niman*] *vt* (12c) *archaic* : STEAL, FILCH ~ *vi, archaic* : THIEVE

[2]**nim** *n* [prob. fr. [1]*nim*] (1901) : any of various games in which counters are laid out in one or more piles and each player in turn draws one or more counters with the object of taking the last counter, forcing the opponent to take it, or taking the most or fewest counters

nim·ble \ˈnim-bəl\ *adj* **nim·bler** \-b(ə-)lər\; **nim·blest** \-b(ə-)ləst\ [ME *nimel,* fr. OE *numol* holding much, fr. *niman* to take; akin to OHG *neman* to take, Gk *nemein* to distribute, manage, *nomos* pasture, *nomos* usage, custom, law] (14c) **1** : quick and light in motion : AGILE ⟨~ fingers⟩ **2 a** : marked by quick, alert, clever conception, comprehension, or resourcefulness ⟨a ~ mind⟩ **b** : RESPONSIVE, SENSITIVE ⟨a ~ listener⟩ — **nim·ble·ness** \-bəl-nəs\ *n* — **nim·bly** \-blē\ *adv*

nim·bo·stra·tus \ˌnim-bō-ˈstrā-təs, -ˈstra-\ *n* [NL, fr. L *nimbus* + NL *stratus* stratus] (ca. 1909) : a low dark layer of gray cloud usu. producing light continuous rain or snow — see CLOUD illustration

nim·bus \ˈnim-bəs\ *n, pl* **nim·bi** \-ˌbī, -ˌbē\ *or* **nim·bus·es** [L, rainstorm, cloud; prob. akin to L *nebula* cloud — more at NEBULA] (1616) **1 a** : a luminous vapor, cloud, or atmosphere about a god or goddess when on earth **b** : a cloud or atmosphere (as of romance) about a person or thing **2** : an indication (as a circle) of radiant light or glory about the head of a drawn or sculptured divinity, saint, or sovereign **3 a** : a rain cloud **b** : THUNDERHEAD; *also* : CUMULUS 2

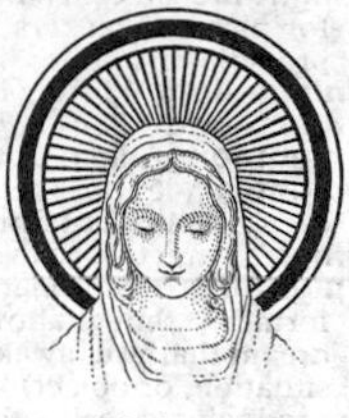

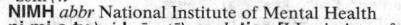

nimbus 2

NIMBY \ˈnim-bē\ *n* [*n*ot *i*n *m*y *b*ack*y*ard] (1980) : opposition to the locating of something considered undesirable (as a prison or incinerator) in one's neighborhood — **NIMBY·ism** \-ˌi-zəm\ *n*

NIMH *abbr* National Institute of Mental Health

ni·mi·e·ty \ni-ˈmī-ə-tē\ *n, pl* **-ties** [LL *nimietas,* fr. L *nimius* too much, adj., fr. *nimis,* adv.] (ca. 1564) : EXCESS, REDUNDANCY

nim·i·ny–pim·i·ny \ˌni-mə-nē-ˈpi-mə-nē\ *adj* [prob. alter. of *namby-pamby*] (1786) : affectedly refined : FINICKY

Nim·rod \ˈnim-ˌräd\ *n* [Heb *Nimrōdh*] (15c) **1** : a descendant of Ham represented in Genesis as a mighty hunter and a king of Shinar **2** *not cap* : HUNTER **3** *not cap, slang* : IDIOT, JERK

nin·com·poop \ˈnin-kəm-ˌpüp, ˈniŋ-\ *n* [origin unknown] (1676) : FOOL, SIMPLETON — **nin·com·poop·ery** \-ˌpü-pə-rē\ *n*

nine \ˈnīn\ *n* [ME, fr. *nyne,* adj., fr. OE *nigon;* akin to OHG *niun* nine, L *novem,* Gk *ennea*] (bef. 12c) **1** — see NUMBER table **2** : the ninth in a set or series ⟨wears a ~⟩ **3** : something having nine units or members: as **a** *cap* : the nine Muses **b** : a baseball team **c** : the first or last nine holes of an 18-hole golf course — **nine** *adj* — **nine** *pron, pl in constr* — **to the nines 1** : to perfection **2** : in a highly elaborate or showy manner ⟨dressed *to the nines*⟩

nine days' wonder *n* (1594) : something or someone that creates a short-lived sensation — called also *nine day wonder*

nine·fold \ˈnīn-ˌfōld, -ˈfōld\ *adj* (bef. 12c) **1** : being nine times as great or as many **2** : having nine units or members — **nine·fold** \-ˈfōld\ *adv*

nine·pin \-ˌpin\ *n* (ca. 1580) **1** *pl but sing in constr* : a bowling game resembling tenpins played without the headpin or having the nine pins in a diamond-shaped configuration with one pin in the center **2** : a pin used in ninepins

nine·teen \nīn-ˈtēn, ˈnīn-ˌ\ *n* [ME *nynetene,* adj., fr. OE *nigontēne,* fr. *nigon* + *-tīene* (akin to OE *tīen* ten) — more at TEN] (bef. 12c) — see NUMBER table — **nineteen** *adj* — **nineteen** *pron, pl in constr* — **nine·teenth** \-ˈtēn(t)th, -ˌtēn(t)th\ *adj or n*

nine–to–fiv·er \ˈnīn-tə-ˈfī-vər\ *n* (1959) : one who works at a job with regular daytime hours

nine·ty \ˈnīn-tē\ *n, pl* **nineties** [ME *ninety,* adj., fr. OE *nigontig,* short for *hundnigontig,* fr. *hundnigontig,* n., group of 90, fr. *hund-,* lit., hundred + *nigon* nine + *-tig* group of 10; akin to OE *tīen* ten] (bef. 12c) **1** — see NUMBER table **2** *pl* : the numbers 90 to 99; *specif* : the years 90 to 99 in a lifetime or century — **nine·ti·eth** \-tē-əth\ *adj or n* — **ninety** *adj* — **ninety** *pron, pl in constr*

nin·hy·drin \nin-ˈhī-drən\ *n* [fr. *Ninhydrin,* a trademark] (1913) : a poisonous crystalline oxidizing agent $C_9H_6O_4$ used esp. as an analytical reagent

nin·ja \ˈnin-jə, -(ˌ)jä\ *n, pl* **ninja** *also* **ninjas** [Jp, fr. *nin-* persevere, conceal, move stealthily + *-ja* person] (1964) : a person trained in ancient Japanese martial arts and employed esp. for espionage and assassinations

nin·ny \ˈni-nē\ *n, pl* **ninnies** [perh. by shortening & alter. fr. *an innocent*] (1593) : FOOL, SIMPLETON

nin·ny·ham·mer \ˈni-nē-ˌha-mər\ *n* (1592) : NINNY

ni·non \ˈnē-ˌnän\ *n* [prob. fr. F *Ninon,* nickname for *Anne*] (1911) : a smooth sheer fabric

ninth \ˈnīn(t)th\ *n, pl* **ninths** \ˈnīn(t)s, ˈnīn(t)ths\ (13c) **1** — see NUMBER table **2 a** : a musical interval embracing an octave and a second **b** : the tone at this interval **c** : a chord containing a ninth — **ninth** *adj or adv*

ninth cranial nerve *n* (ca. 1961) : GLOSSOPHARYNGEAL NERVE

ni·o·bate \ˈnī-ə-ˌbāt\ *n* [NL *niob*ium + E [1]*-ate*] (1845) : a salt containing an anionic grouping of niobium and oxygen

Ni·o·be \ˈnī-ə-bē\ *n* [L, fr. Gk *Niobē*] (14c) : a daughter of Tantalus and wife of Amphion who while weeping for her slain children is turned into a stone from which her tears continue to flow

ni·o·bi·um \nī-ˈō-bē-əm\ *n* [NL, fr. L *Niobe;* fr. its occurrence in tantalite] (1845) : a lustrous light gray ductile metallic element that resembles tantalum chemically and is used in alloys — see ELEMENT table

[1]**nip** \ˈnip\ *vb* **nipped; nip·ping** [ME *nippen;* akin to MD *nipen* to pinch, ON *hnippa* to prod] *vt* (14c) **1 a** : to catch hold of and squeeze tightly between two surfaces, edges, or points : PINCH, BITE ⟨the dog *nipped* his ankle⟩ **b** : to pinch in (as a garment) ⟨a dress *nipped* at the waist⟩ **2 a** : to sever by or as if by pinching sharply **b** : to destroy the growth, progress, or fulfillment of ⟨*nipped* in the bud⟩ **3** : to injure or make numb with cold : CHILL **4** : SNATCH, STEAL **5** : to defeat by a small margin ~ *vi* **1** : to move briskly, nimbly, or quickly **2** *chiefly Brit* : to make a quick trip

[2]**nip** *n* (1549) **1** : something that nips: as **a** *archaic* : a sharp biting comment **b** : a sharp stinging cold ⟨a ~ in the air⟩ **c** : a biting or pungent flavor : TANG **2** : the act of nipping : PINCH, BITE **3** : the region of a squeezing or crushing device (as a calender) where the rolls or jaws are closest together **4** : a small portion

[3]**nip** *n* [prob. fr. *nipperkin,* a liquor container] (ca. 1796) : a small quantity of liquor : SIP; *also* : a very small bottle of liquor

[4]**nip** *vi* **nipped; nip·ping** (1887) : to take liquor in nips : TIPPLE

ni·pa \ˈnē-pə\ *n* [prob. fr. It, fr. Malay *nipah* nipa palm] (1779) : thatch made of leaves of the nipa palm

nip and tuck \ˌnip-ən(d)-ˈtək\ *adj or adv* (1832) : being so close that the lead or advantage shifts rapidly from one opponent to another

nipa palm *n* (1779) : a southeast Asian palm (*Nipa fruticans*) growing chiefly along rivers and estuaries and having a short underground trunk and large erect pinnate leaves

nip·per \ˈni-pər\ *n* (1541) **1** : any of various devices (as pincers) for nipping — usu. used in pl. **2 a** *chiefly Brit* : a boy employed as a helper (as of a carter or hawker) **b** : CHILD; *esp* : a small boy

nipping *adj* (1547) : SHARP, CHILLING — **nip·ping·ly** \-lē\ *adv*

nip·ple \ˈni-pəl\ *n* [earlier *neble, nible,* prob. dim. of *neb, nib*] (ca. 1530) **1** : the protuberance of a mammary gland upon which in the female the lactiferous ducts open and from which milk is drawn **2 a** : an artificial teat through which a bottle-fed infant nurses **b** : a device with an orifice through which the discharge of a liquid can be regulated **3 a** : a protuberance resembling or suggesting the nipple of a breast **b** : a small projection through which oil or grease is injected into machinery **4** : a pipe coupling consisting of a short piece of threaded tubing — **nip·pled** \-pəld\ *adj*

Nip·pon·ese \ˌni-pə-ˈnēz, -ˈnēs\ *adj* [*Nippon,* Japan] (1859) : JAPANESE — **Nipponese** *n*

nip·py \ˈni-pē\ *adj* **nip·pi·er; -est** (1575) **1** : marked by a tendency to nip ⟨a ~ dog⟩ **2** : brisk, quick, or nimble in movement : SNAPPY **3** : PUNGENT, SHARP **4** : CHILLY, CHILLING ⟨a ~ day⟩ — **nip·pi·ly** \ˈni-pə-lē\ *adv* — **nip·pi·ness** \ˈni-pē-nəs\ *n*

nip–up \ˈnip-ˌəp\ *n* (1938) : a spring from a supine position to a standing position

ni·qab *also* **ni·qaab** \ni-ˈkäb\ *n* [Ar *niqāb*] (1936) : a veil for covering the hair and face except for the eyes that is worn by some Muslim women

nir·va·na \nir-ˈvä-nə, (ˌ)nər-\ *n, often cap* [Skt *nirvāṇa,* lit., act of extinguishing, fr. *nis-* out + *vāti* it blows — more at WIND] (1801) **1** : the final beatitude that transcends suffering, karma, and samsara and is sought esp. in Buddhism through the extinction of desire and individual consciousness **2 a** : a place or state of oblivion to care, pain, or external reality; *also* : BLISS, HEAVEN **b** : a goal hoped for but apparently unattainable : DREAM — **nir·van·ic** \-ˈvä-nik, -ˈva-\ *adj*

Ni·san \ˈni-sᵊn, nē-ˈsän\ *n* [Heb *Nīsān*] (14c) : the seventh month of the civil year or the first month of the ecclesiastical year in the Jewish calendar — see MONTH table

ni·sei \nē-ˈsā, ˈnē-ˌ\ *n, pl* **nisei** *often cap* [Jp, lit., second generation, fr. *ni* second + *sei* generation] (1929) : a son or daughter of Japanese immigrants who is born and educated in America and esp. in the U.S.

ni·si \ˈnī-ˌsī\ *adj* [L, unless, fr. *ne-* not + *si* if] (ca. 1836) : taking effect at a specified time unless previously modified or avoided by cause shown, further proceedings, or a condition fulfilled ⟨a decree ~⟩

Nis·sen hut \ˈni-sᵊn-\ *n* [Peter N. *Nissen* †1930 Brit. mining engineer] (1917) : a prefabricated shelter with a semicircular arching roof of corrugated iron sheeting and a concrete floor

NIST *abbr* National Institute of Standards and Technology

ni·sus \ˈnī-səs\ *n, pl* **ni·sus** \-səs, -ˌsüs\ [L, fr. *niti* to lean, rely, strive; akin to L *nictare* to wink — more at CONNIVE] (1699) : a mental or physical effort to attain an end : a perfective urge or endeavor

[1]**nit** \ˈnit\ *n* [ME *nite,* fr. OE *hnitu;* akin to OHG *hniz* nit, Gk *konid-, konis*] (bef. 12c) **1** : the egg of a louse or other parasitic insect; *also* : the insect itself when young **2** : a minor shortcoming

[2]**nit** *n* (ca. 1903) *chiefly Brit* : NITWIT

NIT *abbr* National Invitational Tournament

nite *var of* NIGHT

ni·ter \ˈnī-tər\ *n* [ME *nitre* natron, fr. MF, fr. L *nitrum,* fr. Gk *nitron,* fr. Egypt *ntry*] (1667) **1** : POTASSIUM NITRATE **2** *archaic* : CHILE SALTPETER

nit·ery *also* **nit·er·ie** \ˈnī-tə-rē\ *n, pl* **nit·er·ies** [*nite* + *-ery* (as in *eatery*); *niterie* fr. *nite* + F *-erie* -ery] (ca. 1934) : NIGHTCLUB

nit·id \ˈni-təd\ *adj* [L *nitidus* — more at NEAT] (1619) : BRIGHT, LUSTROUS

ni·ti·nol \ˈnī-tə-ˌnȯl, -ˌnōl\ *n* [*ni*ckel + *ti*tanium + *-nol* (fr. *N*aval *O*rdnance *L*aboratory, where it was created)] (1968) : a nonmagnetic alloy of titanium and nickel that after being deformed returns to its original shape upon being reheated

nit·pick \ˈnit-ˌpik\ *vb* [back-formation fr. *nit-picking*] *vi* (1966) : to engage in nit-picking ~ *vt* : to criticize by nit-picking — **nitpick** *n* — **nit·pick·er** *n* — **nit·picky** \-ˌpi-kē\ *adj*

nit–pick·ing \ˈnit-ˌpi-kiŋ\ *n* [[1]*nit*] (1956) : minute and usu. unjustified criticism

nitr- *or* **nitro-** *comb form* [*niter*] **1** : nitrogen ⟨*nitr*ide⟩ **2** *usu* **nitro-** : containing the monovalent group NO_2 ⟨*nitro*benzene⟩

ni·trate \ˈnī-ˌtrāt, -trət\ *n* [F, fr. *nitrique*] (1788) **1** : a salt or ester of nitric acid **2** : sodium nitrate or potassium nitrate used as a fertilizer

nitrate of soda (1841) : sodium nitrate used as a fertilizer

ni·tra·tion \nī-ˈtrā-shən\ *n* (1887) : the process of adding a nitro group to an organic compound — **ni·trate** \ˈnī-ˌtrāt\ *vt* — **ni·tra·tor** \-ˌtrā-tər\ *n*

ni·tre *chiefly Brit var of* NITER

ni·tric acid \ˈnī-trik-\ *n* [F *nitrique,* fr. *nitre* niter, fr. MF] (1788) : a corrosive liquid inorganic acid HNO_3 used esp. as an oxidizing agent, in nitrations, and in making organic compounds (as fertilizers, explosives, and dyes)

nitric oxide *n* (1807) : a colorless poisonous gas NO formed by oxidation of nitrogen or ammonia that is present in the atmosphere and also in mammals where it is synthesized from arginine and oxygen and acts as a vasodilator and as a mediator of cell-to-cell communication

[1]**ni·tride** \ˈnī-ˌtrīd\ *n* [ISV] (1850) : a binary compound of nitrogen with a more electropositive element

[2]**nitride** *vt* **ni·trid·ed; ni·trid·ing** (1928) : to case-harden (as steel) by causing the surface to absorb nitrogen

ni·tri·fi·ca·tion \ˌnī-trə-fə-ˈkā-shən\ *n* (1827) : the oxidation (as by bacteria) of ammonium salts to nitrites and the further oxidation of nitrites to nitrates
ni·tri·fi·er \ˈnī-trə-ˌfī(-ə)r\ *n* (1903) : any of the nitrifying bacteria
ni·tri·fy·ing \ˈnī-trə-ˌfī-iŋ\ *adj* [F *nitrifier* to convert into nitrite, fr. *nitr-*] (1827) : active in or relating to nitrification ⟨~ organisms⟩
nitrifying bacteria *n pl* (1925) : bacteria of a family (Nitrobacteraceae) comprising gram-negative bacteria commonly found in the soil and obtaining energy through the process of nitrification
ni·trile \ˈnī-trəl, -ˌtrī(-ə)l\ *n* [ISV *nitr-* + *-il, -ile* (fr. L *-ilis* [1]-ile)] (1848) : an organic cyanide containing the group CN which on hydrolysis yields an acid with elimination of ammonia
ni·trite \ˈnī-ˌtrīt\ *n* (1788) : a salt or ester of nitrous acid
[1]**ni·tro** \ˈnī-(ˌ)trō\ *adj* [*nitr-*] (1881) : containing or being the monovalent group NO_2 united through nitrogen
[2]**nitro** *n, pl* **nitros** (1903) : any of various nitrated products; *specif* : NITROGLYCERIN
ni·tro·ben·zene \ˌnī-trō-ˈben-ˌzēn, -ben-ˈ\ *n* [ISV] (1868) : a poisonous yellow oily liquid $C_6H_5NO_2$ with an almond odor that is used esp. in chemical synthesis (as of aniline)
ni·tro·cel·lu·lose \-ˈsel-yə-ˌlōs, -ˌlōz\ *n* [ISV] (1882) : any of several nitric-acid esters of cellulose used esp. for making explosives, plastics, and varnishes
ni·tro·fu·ran \ˌnī-trō-ˈfyu̇r-ˌan, -fyu̇-ˈran\ *n* (1930) : any of several nitro derivatives of furan used as bacteria-inhibiting agents
ni·tro·gen \ˈnī-trə-jən\ *n, often attrib* [F *nitrogène,* fr. *nitre* niter + *-gène* -gen] (1794) : a colorless tasteless odorless element that as a diatomic gas is relatively inert and constitutes 78 percent of the atmosphere and that is a constituent of organic compounds found in all living tissues — see ELEMENT table — **ni·trog·e·nous** \nī-ˈträ-jə-nəs\ *adj*
ni·tro·ge·nase \nī-ˈträ-jə-ˌnās, ˈnī-trə-jə-; -ˌnāz\ *n* (1934) : an enzyme of various nitrogen-fixing bacteria that catalyzes the reduction of molecular nitrogen to ammonia
nitrogen balance *n* (1944) : the difference between nitrogen intake and nitrogen loss in the body or the soil
nitrogen cycle *n* (1908) : a continuous series of natural processes by which nitrogen passes successively from air to soil to organisms and back to air or soil involving principally nitrogen fixation, nitrification, decay, and denitrification
nitrogen dioxide *n* (1869) : a toxic reddish brown gas NO_2 that is a strong oxidizing agent, is produced by combustion (as of fossil fuels), and is an atmospheric pollutant (as in smog)
nitrogen fixation *n* (1895) : the conversion of atmospheric nitrogen into a combined form (as ammonia) through chemical and esp. biological action (as that of soil rhizobia)
nitrogen–fixer *n* (1912) : any of various soil microorganisms that are involved in nitrogen fixation
nitrogen–fixing *adj* (1899) : capable of nitrogen fixation ⟨~ bacteria⟩
nitrogen mustard *n* (1943) : any of various toxic blistering compounds analogous to mustard gas but containing nitrogen instead of sulfur
nitrogen narcosis *n* (1937) : a state of euphoria and confusion similar to that of alcohol intoxication which occurs when nitrogen in normal air enters the bloodstream at increased pressure (as in deep-water diving) — called also *rapture of the deep*
nitrogen oxide *n* (1869) : any of several oxides of nitrogen most of which are produced in combustion and are considered to be atmospheric pollutants: as **a** : NITRIC OXIDE **b** : NITROGEN DIOXIDE **c** : NITROUS OXIDE
nitrogen tetroxide *n* (1869) : a colorless toxic gas N_2O_4 that is a dimer of nitrogen dioxide and that in liquid form is used as an oxidizer in rocket engines
ni·tro·glyc·er·in *or* **ni·tro·glyc·er·ine** \ˌnī-trə-ˈglis-rən, -ˈgli-sə-\ *n* [ISV] (1857) : an oily explosive poisonous liquid $C_3H_5N_3O_9$ used chiefly in making dynamite and in medicine as a vasodilator
ni·tro·meth·ane \ˌnī-trō-ˈme-ˌthān, *Brit usu* -ˈmē-\ *n* (1872) : a liquid nitroparaffin CH_3NO_2 that is used as an industrial solvent, in chemical synthesis, and as a fuel for rockets and high-performance engines
ni·tro·par·af·fin \-ˈpa-rə-fən\ *n* [ISV] (1892) : any of various nitro derivatives of alkanes
nitros- *or* **nitroso-** *comb form* [NL *nitrosus* nitrous] : containing the group NO ⟨*nitros*amine⟩
ni·tro·sa·mine \nī-ˈtrō-sə-ˌmēn\ *n* (1878) : any of various organic compounds which are characterized by the grouping NNO and some of which are powerful carcinogens
ni·trous \ˈnī-trəs\ *adj* [NL *nitrosus,* fr. L, full of natron, fr. *nitrum* natron — more at NITER] (1601) *archaic* : of, relating to, or containing niter
nitrous acid *n* (1788) : an unstable acid HNO_2 known only in solution or in the form of its salts or esters
nitrous oxide *n* (1798) : a colorless gas N_2O that when inhaled produces loss of sensibility to pain preceded by exhilaration and sometimes laughter, that is used esp. as an anesthetic in dentistry and as a fuel, and that is an atmospheric pollutant and greenhouse gas produced by combustion — called also *laughing gas*
nit·ty–grit·ty \ˈni-tē-ˌgri-tē, ˌni-tē-ˈ\ *n* [origin unknown] (1956) : what is essential and basic : specific practical details ⟨get down to the ~ of the problem⟩ — **nitty–gritty** *adj*
nit·wit \ˈnit-ˌwit\ *n* [prob. fr. G dial. *nit* not + E *wit*] (ca. 1922) : a scatterbrained or stupid person
NIU *abbr* network interface unit
[1]**nix** \ˈniks\ *n* [G *nichts* nothing] (1789) : NOTHING
[2]**nix** *vt* (ca. 1903) : VETO, REJECT ⟨the court ~*ed* the merger⟩
[3]**nix** *adv* (1902) : NO — used to express disagreement or the withholding of permission; often used with *on* ⟨they said ~ on our plan⟩
[4]**nix** *n* [G, fr. OHG *nihhus;* akin to OE *nicor* water monster and perh. to Gk *nizein* to wash] (1833) : a water sprite of Germanic folklore
nix·ie \ˈnik-sē\ *n* [G *Nixe* female nix, fr. OHG *nichessa,* fem. of *nihhus* nix] (1816) : [4]NIX
ni·zam \ni-ˈzäm, ˈnī-ˌzam, nī-ˈ\ *n* [Hindi & Urdu *nizām,* order, governor, ultim. fr. Ar *niḍhām*] (1768) : one of a line of sovereigns of Hyderabad, India, reigning from 1713 to 1950 — **ni·zam·ate** \ni-ˈzä-ˌmāt, nī-ˈza-\ *n*
NJ *abbr* New Jersey
NK cell \ˌen-ˈkā-\ *n* (1979) : NATURAL KILLER CELL
NKVD *abbr* [Russ *Narodnyĭ komissariat vnutrennikh del*] People's Commissariat of Internal Affairs
NL *abbr* **1** National League **2** Newfoundland and Labrador
NLCS *abbr* National League Championship Series
NLF *abbr* National Liberation Front
NLRB *abbr* National Labor Relations Board
nm *abbr* **1** nanometer **2** nautical mile
NM *abbr* New Mexico
NMDA \ˌen-(ˌ)em-(ˌ)dē-ˈā\ *n* [*N-m*ethyl-*D-a*spartate] (1986) : a synthetic amino acid $C_5H_9NO_4$ that binds selectively to a subset of glutamate receptors on neurons where the binding of glutamate results in the opening of calcium channels
N Mex *abbr* New Mexico
NMHA *abbr* National Mental Health Association
NMI *abbr* no middle initial
NMR *abbr* nuclear magnetic resonance
NNE *abbr* north-northeast
NNW *abbr* north-northwest
[1]**no** \ˈnō\ *adv* [ME, fr. OE *nā,* fr. *ne* not + *ā* always; akin to ON & OHG *ne* not, L *ne-,* Gk *nē-* — more at AYE] (bef. 12c) **1 a** *chiefly Scot* : NOT **b** — used as a function word to express the negative of an alternative choice or possibility ⟨shall we go out to dinner or ~⟩ **2** : in no respect or degree — used in comparisons ⟨you're ~ better than the rest of us⟩ **3** : not so — used to express negation, dissent, denial, or refusal ⟨~, I'm not going⟩ **4** — used with a following adjective to imply a meaning expressed by the opposite positive statement ⟨in ~ uncertain terms⟩ **5** — used as a function word to emphasize a following negative or to introduce a more emphatic, explicit, or comprehensive statement ⟨it's big, ~, it's gigantic⟩ **6** — used as an interjection to express surprise, doubt, or incredulity **7** — used in combination with a verb to form a compound adjective ⟨*no*-bake pie⟩ **8** : in negation ⟨shook his head ~⟩
[2]**no** *adj* (12c) **1 a** : not any ⟨~ parking⟩ ⟨~ disputing the decision⟩ **b** : hardly any : very little ⟨finished in ~ time⟩ **2** : not a : quite other than a ⟨he's ~ expert⟩ **3** — used in combination with a noun to form a compound adjective ⟨a *no*-nonsense realist⟩
[3]**no** \ˈnō\ *n, pl* **noes** *or* **nos** \ˈnōz\ (1588) **1** : an act or instance of refusing or denying by the use of the word *no* : DENIAL ⟨received a firm ~ in reply⟩ **2 a** : a negative vote or decision **b** *pl* : persons voting in the negative
[4]**no** *abbr* **1** north; northern **2** [L *numero,* abl. of *numerus*] number
[1]**No** *var of* NOH
[2]**No** *symbol* nobelium
NOAA *abbr* National Oceanic and Atmospheric Administration
no–account *adj* (1845) **1** : of no importance : TRIFLING **2** : not amounting to anything : SHIFTLESS ⟨her ~ son⟩ — **no–account** *n*
No·a·chi·an \nō-ˈā-kē-ən\ *adj* [Heb *Nōaḥ* Noah] (1678) **1** : of or relating to the patriarch Noah or his time **2** : ANCIENT, ANTIQUATED
No·ah \ˈnō-ə\ *n* [Heb *Nōaḥ*] (bef. 12c) : an Old Testament patriarch who built the ark in which he, his family, and living creatures of every kind survived the Flood
[1]**nob** \ˈnäb\ *n* [prob. alter. of *knob*] (ca. 1700) **1** : HEAD 1 **2** : a jack of the same suit as the starter in cribbage that scores one point for the holder — usu. used in the phrases *his nob* or *his nobs*
[2]**nob** *n* [perh. fr. [1]*nob*] (1703) *chiefly Brit* : one in a superior position in life
nob·ble \ˈnä-bəl\ *vt* **nob·bled; nob·bling** \-b(ə-)liŋ\ [perh. irreg. freq. of *nab*] (1847) **1** *Brit* : to incapacitate (a racehorse) esp. by drugging **2** *slang, Brit* **a** : to win over to one's side **b** : STEAL **c** : SWINDLE, CHEAT **d** : to get hold of : CATCH — **nob·bler** \-b(ə-)lər\ *n*
nob·by \ˈnä-bē\ *adj* **nob·bi·er; -est** (1788) : CHIC, SMART
No·bel·ist \nō-ˈbe-list\ *n* (1938) : a winner of a Nobel Prize
no·bel·i·um \nō-ˈbe-lē-əm\ *n* [NL, fr. Alfred B. *Nobel*] (1957) : a radioactive metallic element produced artificially — see ELEMENT table
No·bel Prize \nō-ˈbel-, ˈnō-ˌbel-\ *n* (1900) : any of various annual prizes (as in peace, literature, medicine) established by the will of Alfred Nobel for the encouragement of persons who work for the interests of humanity — called also *Nobel*
no·bil·i·ty \nō-ˈbi-lə-tē\ *n* [ME *nobilite,* fr. AF *nobilité,* fr. L *nobilitat-, nobilitas,* fr. *nobilis*] (14c) **1** : the quality or state of being noble in character, quality, or rank **2** : the body of persons forming the noble class in a country or state : ARISTOCRACY
[1]**no·ble** \ˈnō-bəl\ *adj* **no·bler** \-b(ə-)lər\; **no·blest** \-b(ə-)ləst\ [ME, fr. AF, fr. L *nobilis* well-known, noble, fr. *noscere* to come to know — more at KNOW] (13c) **1 a** : possessing outstanding qualities : ILLUSTRIOUS **b** : FAMOUS, NOTABLE ⟨~ deeds⟩ **2** : of high birth or exalted rank : ARISTOCRATIC **3 a** : possessing very high or excellent qualities or properties ⟨~ wine⟩ **b** : very good or excellent **4** : grand or impressive esp. in appearance ⟨~ edifice⟩ **5** : possessing, characterized by, or arising from superiority of mind or character or of ideals or morals : LOFTY ⟨a ~ ambition⟩ **6** : chemically inert or inactive esp. toward oxygen ⟨a ~ metal such as platinum⟩ — compare BASE 6a ***syn*** see MORAL — **no·ble·ness** \-bəl-nəs\ *n* — **no·bly** \-blē *also* -bə-lē\ *adv*
[2]**noble** *n* (14c) **1** : a person of noble rank or birth **2** : an old English gold coin equivalent to 6*s* 8*d*
noble gas *n* (1902) : any of a group of rare gases that include helium, neon, argon, krypton, xenon, and usu. radon and that exhibit great stability and extremely low reaction rates — called also *inert gas*
no·ble·man \ˈnō-bəl-mən\ *n* (14c) : a man of noble rank : PEER
noble rot *n* (1905) : a botrytis fungus (*Botrytis cinerea*) that infects various usu. overripe wine grapes causing shriveling which results in increased sugar and flavor content and is responsible for the characteristic flavor of sauternes and related wines
noble savage *n* (1670) : a mythic conception of people belonging to non-European cultures as having innate natural simplicity and virtue

\ə\ **abut** \ᵊ\ **kitten,** F **table** \ər\ **further** \a\ **ash** \ā\ **ace** \ä\ **mop, mar** \au̇\ **out** \ch\ **chin** \e\ **bet** \ē\ **easy** \g\ **go** \i\ **hit** \ī\ **ice** \j\ **job** \ŋ\ **sing** \ō\ **go** \ȯ\ **law** \ȯi\ **boy** \th\ **thin** \t͟h\ **the** \ü\ **loot** \u̇\ **foot** \y\ **yet** \zh\ **vision, beige** \k̲, ⁿ, œ, ue, ʸ\ *see* Guide to Pronunciation

uncorrupted by European civilization; *also* : a person exemplifying this conception
no·blesse \nō-ˈbles\ *n* [ME, fr. AF *noblesce,* fr. *noble*] (13c) **1 :** noble birth or condition **2 :** the members esp. of the French nobility
no·blesse oblige \nō-ˈbles-ə-ˈblēzh\ *n* [F, lit., nobility obligates] (1837) **:** the obligation of honorable, generous, and responsible behavior associated with high rank or birth
no·ble·wom·an \ˈnō-bəl-ˌwu̇-mən\ *n* (13c) **:** a woman of noble rank **:** PEERESS
[1]**no·body** \ˈnō-bə-dē, -ˌbä-dē\ *pron* (14c) **:** no person **:** not anybody
[2]**nobody** *n, pl* **no·bod·ies** (1581) **:** a person of no influence or consequence
no–brain·er \ˈnō-ˈbrā-nər\ *n* (1973) **:** something that requires a minimum of thought
no·ce·bo \ˌnō-ˈsē-(ˌ)bō\ *n, pl* **-bos** [L, I will be harmful; after *placebo*] (1961) **:** a harmless substance that when taken by a patient is associated with harmful effects due to negative expectations or the psychological condition of the patient
no·cent \ˈnō-sᵊnt\ *adj* [ME, fr. L *nocent-, nocens,* fr. prp. of *nocēre* to harm, hurt — more at NOXIOUS] (15c) **:** HARMFUL
no·ci·cep·tive \ˌnō-si-ˈsep-tiv\ *adj* [L *nocēre* + E *-i-* + *receptive*] (1904) **1** *of a stimulus* **:** PAINFUL, INJURIOUS **2 :** of, induced by, or responding to a nociceptive stimulus ⟨~ pain⟩ ⟨a ~ nerve pathway⟩
no·ci·cep·tor \ˌnō-si-ˈsep-tər\ *n* (1967) **:** a receptor (as in the skin) for nociceptive stimuli **:** a pain sense organ
[1]**nock** \ˈnäk\ *n* [ME *nocke* notched tip on the end of a bow; akin to MD *nocke* summit] (14c) **1 :** one of the notches cut in either of two tips of horn fastened on the ends of a bow or in the bow itself for holding the string **2 a :** the part of an arrow having a notch for the bowstring **b :** the notch itself
[2]**nock** *vt* (14c) **1 :** to make a nock in (a bow or arrow) **2 :** to fit (an arrow) against the bowstring
no contest *n* (1952) **:** NOLO CONTENDERE
noct·am·bu·list \näk-ˈtam-byə-list\ *n* [L *noct-, nox* night + *-ambulist* (as in *somnambulist*) — more at NIGHT] (ca. 1731) **:** a person who walks while asleep **:** SLEEPWALKER
noc·ti·lu·cent cloud \ˌnäk-tə-ˈlü-sᵊnt-\ *n* [*noctilucent* ultim. fr. L *noct-* + *lucent-, lucens* lucent] (1910) **:** a luminous thin usu. colored cloud seen esp. at twilight at a height of about 50 miles (80 kilometers)
noc·tu·id \ˈnäk-chə-wəd, ˈnäk-tə-\ *n* [NL *Noctuidae,* fr. *Noctua,* genus of moths, fr. L, the little owl (*Athene noctua*); akin to L *nox* night] (1894) **:** any of a large family (Noctuidae) of medium-sized often dull-colored moths with larvae (as cutworms and armyworms) that are often destructive agricultural pests — **noctuid** *adj*
noc·turn \ˈnäk-ˌtərn\ *n* [ME *nocturne,* fr. AF, fr. ML *nocturna,* fr. L, fem. of *nocturnus*] (14c) **:** a principal division of the office of matins
noc·tur·nal \näk-ˈtər-nᵊl\ *adj* [ME, fr. AF or LL; AF *nocturnel,* fr. LL *nocturnalis,* fr. L *nocturnus* of night, nocturnal, fr. *noct-, nox* night] (15c) **1 :** of, relating to, or occurring in the night ⟨a ~ journey⟩ **2 :** active at night ⟨a ~ predator⟩ — **noc·tur·nal·ly** \-nᵊl-ē\ *adv*
noc·turne \ˈnäk-ˌtərn\ *n* [F, adj., nocturnal, fr. L *nocturnus*] (1814) **:** a work of art dealing with evening or night; *esp* **:** a dreamy pensive composition for the piano — compare AUBADE 3
noc·u·ous \ˈnä-kyə-wəs\ *adj* [L *nocuus,* fr. *nocēre* to harm — more at NOXIOUS] (1635) **:** HARMFUL — **noc·u·ous·ly** *adv*
[1]**nod** \ˈnäd\ *vb* **nod·ded; nod·ding** [ME *nodden;* perh. akin to OHG *hnotōn* to shake] *vi* (14c) **1 :** to make a quick downward motion of the head whether deliberately (as in expressing assent or salutation) or involuntarily (as from drowsiness) **2 :** to incline or sway from the vertical as though ready to fall **3 :** to bend or sway the upper part gently downward or forward **:** bob gently **4 :** to make a slip or error in a moment of abstraction ~ *vt* **1 :** to incline (as the head) downward or forward **2 :** to bring, invite, or send by a nod ⟨*nodded* us in⟩ **3 :** to signify by a nod ⟨*nodded* their approval⟩ — **nod·der** *n*
[2]**nod** *n* (ca. 1541) **1 :** the act or an instance of nodding ⟨gave a ~ of greeting⟩ **2 :** an indication esp. of approval or recognition
nod·al \ˈnō-dᵊl\ *adj* (1830) **:** being, relating to, or located at or near a node — **no·dal·i·ty** \nō-ˈda-lə-tē\ *n* — **nod·al·ly** \ˈnō-dᵊl-ē\ *adv*
nodding *adj* (1565) **1 :** bending downward or forward **:** DROOPING ⟨~ flowers⟩ **2 :** SLIGHT, SUPERFICIAL ⟨a ~ acquaintance⟩
nod·dle \ˈnä-dᵊl\ *n* [ME *nodle* back of the head or neck] (1572) **:** HEAD, PATE
nod·dy \ˈnä-dē\ *n, pl* **noddies** [prob. short for obs. *noddypoll,* alter. of *hoddypoll* fumbling inept person] (ca. 1530) **1 :** a stupid person **2 :** any of several stout-bodied terns (esp. genus *Anous*) of warm seas
node \ˈnōd\ *n* [ME, fr. L *nodus* knot, node; akin to MIr *naidm* bond] (15c) **1 a :** a pathological swelling or enlargement (as of a rheumatic joint) **b :** a discrete mass of one kind of tissue enclosed in tissue of a different kind **2 :** an entangling complication (as in a drama) **:** PREDICAMENT **3 :** either of the two points where the orbit of a planet or comet intersects the ecliptic; *also* **:** either of the points at which the orbit of an earth satellite crosses the plane of the equator **4 a :** a point, line, or surface of a vibrating body or system that is free or relatively free from vibratory motion **b :** a point at which a wave has an amplitude of zero **5 a :** a point at which subsidiary parts originate or center **b :** a point on a stem at which a leaf or leaves are inserted **c :** a point at which a curve intersects itself in such a manner that the branches have different tangents **d :** VERTEX 1b
node of Ran·vier \-ˈräⁿ-vē-ˌā\ [Louis A. *Ranvier* †1922 Fr. histologist] (ca. 1885) **:** a small gap in the myelin sheath of a myelinated nerve fiber
nod off *vi* (1914) **:** to fall asleep
no·dose \ˈnō-ˌdōs\ *adj* [L *nodosus,* fr. *nodus*] (1687) **:** having numerous or conspicuous protuberances — **no·dos·i·ty** \nō-ˈdä-sə-tē\ *n*
nod·u·lar \ˈnä-jə-lər\ *adj* (1794) **:** of, relating to, characterized by, or occurring in the form of nodules ⟨~ lesions⟩
nod·u·la·tion \ˌnä-jə-ˈlā-shən\ *n* (1872) **1 :** the process of forming nodules and esp. root nodules containing symbiotic bacteria **2 :** NODULE
nod·ule \ˈnä-(ˌ)jül\ *n* [ME, fr. L *nodulus,* dim. of *nodus*] (15c) **:** a small mass of rounded or irregular shape: as **a :** a small rounded lump of a mineral or mineral aggregate **b :** a swelling on a leguminous root that contains symbiotic bacteria **c :** a small abnormal knobby bodily protuberance (as a tumorous growth or a calcification near an arthritic joint)
no·dus \ˈnō-dəs\ *n, pl* **no·di** \ˈnō-ˌdī, -ˌdē\ [L, knot, node] (ca. 1738) **:** COMPLICATION, DIFFICULTY
no·el \nō-ˈel\ *n* [F *noël* Christmas, carol, fr. OF *Nael (Deu), Noel* Christmas, fr. L *natalis* birthday, fr. *natalis* natal] (1811) **1 :** a Christmas carol **2** *cap* **:** CHRISTMAS
noes *pl of* NO
no·et·ic \nō-ˈe-tik\ *adj* [Gk *noētikos* intellectual, fr. *noein* to think, fr. *nous* mind] (1653) **:** of, relating to, or based on the intellect
no–fault *adj* (1967) **1 :** of, relating to, or being a motor vehicle insurance plan under which someone involved in an accident is compensated usu. up to a stipulated limit for actual losses (as for property damage, medical bills, and lost wages) by that person's own insurance company regardless of who is responsible for the accident **2 :** of, relating to, or being a divorce law under which neither party is held responsible for the breakup of the marriage **3 :** characterized by the absence of a prevailing sense of individual responsibility (as for behavior)
no–frills \ˈnō-ˈfrilz\ *adj* (1960) **:** offering or providing only the essentials **:** not fancy, elaborate, or luxurious ⟨a ~ airline⟩
nog \ˈnäg\ *n* [origin unknown] (1693) **1 :** a strong ale formerly brewed in Norfolk, England **2** [by shortening] **:** EGGNOG
nog·gin \ˈnä-gən\ *n* [origin unknown] (1630) **1 :** a small mug or cup **2 :** a small quantity (as a gill) of drink **3 :** a person's head
nog·ging \ˈnä-gən, -giŋ\ *n* [*nog* wooden block the size of a brick] (1825) **:** rough brick masonry used to fill in the open spaces of a wooden frame
no–go *adj* (1971) **:** being an area into which entry is forbidden or dangerous ⟨~ tourist areas⟩
[1]**no–good** \ˈnō-ˈgu̇d\ *adj* (1908) **:** having no worth, virtue, use, or chance of success ⟨a ~ scoundrel⟩
[2]**no–good** \ˈnō-ˌgu̇d\ *n* (1924) **:** a no-good person or thing
no–good·nik \ˌnō-ˈgu̇d-nik\ *n* (1936) **:** NO-GOOD, LOWLIFE
Noh *also* **No** \ˈnō\ *n, pl* **Noh** *also* **No** [Jp *nō,* lit., talent] (1871) **:** classic Japanese dance-drama having a heroic theme, a chorus, and highly stylized action, costuming, and scenery
[1]**no–hit** *adj* (1900) **:** of, relating to, or being a baseball game or a part of a game in which a pitcher allows the opposition no base hits
[2]**no–hit** *vt* (1967) **:** to give up no base hits to ⟨~ them for five innings⟩
no–hit·ter \ˌnō-ˈhi-tər\ *n* (1947) **:** a no-hit game in baseball
no–holds–barred \ˌnō-ˌhōl(d)z-ˈbärd\ *adj* (1961) **:** free of restrictions or hampering conventions ⟨a ~ contest⟩
no–hop·er \ˈnō-ˈhō-pər\ *n* (ca. 1943) *chiefly Brit* **:** one that has no chance of success
no·how \ˈnō-ˌhau̇\ *adv* (1775) **1 :** in no manner or way **:** not at all ⟨was ~ equal to the task⟩ **2** *dial* **:** ANYHOW
noil \ˈnȯi(-ə)l\ *n* [origin unknown] (ca. 1624) **:** short fiber removed during the combing of a textile fiber and often separately spun into yarn
noir \ˈnwär\ *n* [short for *film noir*] (1980) **1 :** crime fiction featuring hard-boiled cynical characters and bleak sleazy settings **2 :** FILM NOIR — **noir** *adj* — **noir·ish** \-ish\ *adj*
[1]**noise** \ˈnȯiz\ *n* [ME, fr. AF, disturbance, noise, fr. L *nausea* nausea] (13c) **1 :** loud, confused, or senseless shouting or outcry **2 a :** SOUND; *esp* **:** one that lacks agreeable musical quality or is noticeably unpleasant **b :** any sound that is undesired or interferes with one's hearing of something **c :** an unwanted signal or a disturbance (as static or a variation of voltage) in an electronic device or instrument (as radio or television); *broadly* **:** a disturbance interfering with the operation of a usu. mechanical device or system **d :** electromagnetic radiation (as light or radio waves) that is composed of several frequencies and that involves random changes in frequency or amplitude **e :** irrelevant or meaningless data or output occurring along with desired information **3 :** common talk **:** RUMOR; *esp* **:** SLANDER **4 :** something that attracts attention ⟨the play . . . will make little ~ in the world —Brendan Gill⟩ **5 :** something spoken or uttered **6 :** a style of rock music that is loud, often discordant, and usu. uses electronic noise (as feedback) — **noise·less** \-ləs\ *adj* — **noise·less·ly** *adv*
[2]**noise** *vb* **noised; nois·ing** *vi* (14c) **1 :** to talk much or loudly **2 :** to make a noise ~ *vt* **:** to spread by rumor or report — usu. used with *about* or *abroad* ⟨the scandal was quickly *noised* about⟩
noise·mak·er \ˈnȯiz-ˌmā-kər\ *n* (1574) **:** one that makes noise; *esp* **:** a device (as a horn or rattle) used to make noise at parties — **noise·mak·ing** \-kiŋ\ *n or adj*
noise pollution *n* (1966) **:** annoying or harmful noise (as of automobiles or jet airplanes) in an environment
noi·sette \nwə-ˈzet, nwä-\ *n* [F, dim. of *nois* choice cut of meat, lit., nut, fr. OF, fr. L *nux* — more at NUT] (1891) **:** a small piece of lean meat
noi·some \ˈnȯi-səm\ *adj* [ME *noysome,* fr. *noy* annoyance, alter. of *anoi,* fr. AF *anui,* fr. *anuier* to harass, annoy — more at ANNOY] (14c) **1 :** NOXIOUS, HARMFUL **2 a :** offensive to the senses and esp. to the sense of smell ⟨~ garbage⟩ **b :** highly obnoxious or objectionable ⟨~ habits⟩ ***syn*** see MALODOROUS — **noi·some·ly** *adv* — **noi·some·ness** *n*
noisy \ˈnȯi-zē\ *adj* **nois·i·er; -est** (1693) **1 :** making noise **2 :** full of or characterized by noise or clamor ⟨a ~ office⟩ **3 :** noticeably showy, gaudy, or bright **:** CONSPICUOUS — **nois·i·ly** \ˈnȯi-zə-lē\ *adv* — **nois·i·ness** \-zē-nəs\ *n*
no·li me tan·ge·re \ˌnō-lē-(ˌ)mē-ˈtan-jə-rē, -ˌlī-, -(ˌ)mā-, -ˈtäŋ-gə-ˌrā\ *n* [L, do not touch me; fr. Jesus' words to Mary Magdalene (Jn 20:17)] (1591) **:** a warning against touching or interference
nol·le pro·se·qui \ˌnä-lē-ˈprä-sə-ˌkwī\ *n* [L, to be unwilling to pursue] (1681) **:** an entry on the record of a legal action denoting that the prosecutor or plaintiff will proceed no further in an action or suit either as a whole or as to some count or as to one or more of several defendants
no·lo \ˈnō-(ˌ)lō\ *n* (1914) **:** NOLO CONTENDERE
no–load \ˈnō-ˈlōd\ *adj* (1963) **:** charging no sales commission ⟨a ~ mutual fund⟩ — **no–load** \ˈnō-ˌlōd\ *n*
no·lo con·ten·de·re \ˈnō-(ˌ)lō-kən-ˈten-də-rē\ *n* [L, I do not wish to contend] (1872) **:** a plea in a criminal prosecution that without admitting guilt subjects the defendant to conviction but does not preclude denying the truth of the charges in a collateral proceeding
nol–pros \ˈnäl-ˈpräs\ *vt* **nol–prossed; nol–pros·sing** [*nolle prosequi*] (ca. 1878) **:** to discontinue by entering a nolle prosequi
no·ma \ˈnō-mə\ *n* [NL, fr. Gk *nomē,* fr. *nemein* to spread (of an ulcer), lit., to graze, pasture — more at NIMBLE] (1834) **:** a spreading invasive gangrene chiefly of the lining of the cheek and lips that is usu. fatal and

occurs most often in persons severely debilitated by disease or profound nutritional deficiency

no·mad \ˈnō-ˌmad, *Brit also* ˈnä-\ *n* [L *nomad-, nomas* member of a wandering pastoral people, fr. Gk, fr. *nemein*] (1579) **1 :** a member of a people who have no fixed residence but move from place to place usu. seasonally and within a well-defined territory **2 :** an individual who roams about — **nomad** *adj* — **no·mad·ism** \ˈnō-ˌma-ˌdi-zəm\ *n*

no·mad·ic \nō-ˈma-dik\ *adj* (ca. 1818) **1 :** of, relating to, or characteristic of nomads ⟨a ~ tribe⟩ **2 :** roaming about from place to place aimlessly, frequently, or without a fixed pattern of movement

no–man's–land \ˈnō-ˌmanz-ˌland\ *n* (14c) **1 a :** an area of unowned, unclaimed, or uninhabited land **b :** an unoccupied area between opposing armies **c :** an area not suitable or used for occupation or habitation ⟨downtown was a retailing ~⟩ **2 :** an anomalous, ambiguous, or indefinite area esp. of operation, application, or jurisdiction ⟨the ~ between art and science⟩

nom·bril \ˈnäm-brəl\ *n* [MF, lit., navel, ultim. fr. L *umbilicus*] (1562) **:** the center point of the lower half of an armorial escutcheon

nom de guerre \ˌnäm-di-ˈger\ *n, pl* **noms de guerre** \ˌnäm(z)-di-\ [F, lit., war name] (1679) **:** PSEUDONYM

nom de plume \-ˈplüm\ *n, pl* **noms de plume** \ˌnäm(z)-di-\ [F, pen name; prob. coined in E] (1823) **:** PSEUDONYM, PEN NAME

nome \ˈnōm\ *n* [Gk *nomos* pasture, district — more at NIMBLE] (ca. 1727) **:** a province of ancient Egypt

no·men \ˈnō-mən\ *n, pl* **no·mi·na** \ˈnä-mə-nə, ˈnō-\ [L *nomin-, nomen* name — more at NAME] (ca. 1890) **:** the second of the three usual names of an ancient Roman male — compare COGNOMEN, PRAENOMEN

no·men·cla·tor \ˈnō-mən-ˌklā-tər\ *n* [L, slave whose duty was to announce the names of persons met during a political campaign, fr. *nomen* + *calare* to call — more at LOW] (1585) **1 :** a book containing collections or lists of words **2** *archaic* **:** one who announces the names of guests or of persons generally **3 :** one who gives names to or invents names for things

no·men·cla·to·ri·al \ˌnō-mən-klə-ˈtȯr-ē-əl\ *adj* (1885) **:** relating to or connected with nomenclature

no·men·cla·ture \ˈnō-mən-ˌklā-chər *also* nō-ˈmen-klə-ˌchu̇r, -ˈmeŋ-, -chər, -ˌtyu̇r, -ˌtu̇r\ *n* [L *nomenclatura* assigning of names, fr. *nomen* + *calatus,* pp. of *calare*] (1610) **1 :** NAME, DESIGNATION **2 :** the act or process or an instance of naming **3 a :** a system or set of terms or symbols esp. in a particular science, discipline, or art **b :** an international system of standardized New Latin names used in biology for kinds and groups of kinds of animals and plants — **no·men·cla·tur·al** \ˌnō-mən-ˈklāch-rəl, -ˈklā-chə-\ *adj*

no·men con·ser·van·dum \ˈnō-mən-ˌkän(t)-sər-ˈvan-dəm\ *n, pl* **no·mi·na con·ser·van·da** \ˈnä-mə-nə-ˌkän(t)-sər-ˈvan-də, ˈnō-\ [NL, name to be kept] (1916) **:** a biological taxonomic name that is preserved by special sanction in exception to the usual rules

nomen du·bi·um \-ˈdü-bē-əm, -ˈdyü-\ *n, pl* **nomina du·bia** \-bē-ə\ [NL, doubtful name] (1937) **:** a taxonomic name that cannot be assigned with certainty to any taxonomic group because the description is insufficient for identification and the original specimens no longer exist

nomen nu·dum \-ˈnü-dəm, -ˈnyü-\ *n, pl* **nomina nu·da** \-də\ [NL, bare name] (1900) **:** a proposed taxonomic name that is invalid because the group designated is not described or illustrated sufficiently for recognition, that has no nomenclatural status, and that consequently can be used as though never previously proposed

¹nom·i·nal \ˈnä-mə-nᵊl, ˈnäm-nəl\ *adj* [ME *nominalle,* fr. ML *nominalis,* fr. L, of a name, fr. *nomin-, nomen* name — more at NAME] (15c) **1 :** of, relating to, or being a noun or a word or expression taking a noun construction **2 a :** of, relating to, or constituting a name **b :** bearing the name of a person **3 a :** existing or being something in name or form only ⟨~ head of his party⟩ **b :** of, being, or relating to a designated or theoretical size that may vary from the actual **:** APPROXIMATE ⟨the pipe's ~ size⟩ **c :** TRIFLING, INSIGNIFICANT ⟨his involvement was ~⟩ ⟨charged only ~ rent⟩ **4** *of a rate of interest* **a :** equal to the annual rate of simple interest that would obtain if interest were not compounded when in fact it is compounded and paid for periods of less than a year **b :** equal to the percentage by which a repaid loan exceeds the principal borrowed with no adjustment made for inflation **5 :** being according to plan **:** SATISFACTORY ⟨everything was ~ during the launch⟩ — **nom·i·nal·ly** *adv*

²nominal *n* (1904) **:** a word or word group functioning as a noun

nom·i·nal·ism \ˈnä-mə-nə-ˌli-zəm, ˈnäm-nə-ˌli-zəm\ *n* (1844) **1 :** a theory that there are no universal essences in reality and that the mind can frame no single concept or image corresponding to any universal or general term **2 :** the theory that only individuals and no abstract entities (as essences, classes, or propositions) exist — compare ESSENTIALISM, REALISM — **nom·i·nal·ist** \-ist, -list\ *n* — **nominalist** *or* **nom·i·nal·is·tic** \ˌnä-mə-nə-ˈlis-tik, ˌnäm-nə-ˈlis-\ *adj*

nominal value *n* (1788) **:** PAR 1b

nominal wages *n pl* (1851) **:** wages measured in money as distinct from actual purchasing power

nom·i·nate \ˈnä-mə-ˌnāt\ *vt* **-nat·ed; -nat·ing** [L *nominatus,* pp. of *nominare,* fr. *nomin-, nomen* name — more at NAME] (1545) **1 :** DESIGNATE, NAME **2 a :** to appoint or propose for appointment to an office or place **b :** to propose as a candidate for election to office **c :** to propose for an honor ⟨~ her for player of the year⟩ **3 :** to enter (a horse) in a race — **nom·i·nat·able** \-ˌnā-tə-bəl\ *adj* — **nom·i·na·tor** \-ˌnā-tər\ *n* — **nom·i·nee** \ˌnä-mə-ˈnē\ *n*

nom·i·na·tion \ˌnä-mə-ˈnā-shən\ *n* (15c) **1 :** the act, process, or an instance of nominating **2 :** the state of being nominated

nom·i·na·tive \ˈnäm-nə-tiv, ˈnä-mə-; *2 & 3 are also* ˈnä-mə-ˌnā-\ *adj* [ME *nominatyf,* fr. AF or L; AF *nominatif,* fr. L *(casus) nominativus* nominative case, fr. *nominare;* fr. the traditional use of the nominative form in naming a noun] (14c) **1 a :** marking typically the subject of a verb esp. in languages that have relatively full inflection ⟨~ case⟩ **b :** of or relating to the nominative case ⟨a ~ ending⟩ **2 :** nominated or appointed by nomination **3 :** bearing a person's name — **nominative** *n*

no·mo·gram \ˈnä-mə-ˌgram, ˈnō-\ *n* [Gk *nomos* law + ISV *-gram* — more at NIMBLE] (1908) **:** a graphic representation that consists of several lines marked off to scale and arranged in such a way that by using a straightedge to connect known values on two lines an unknown value can be read at the point of intersection with another line

no·mo·graph \-ˌgraf\ *n* (ca. 1909) **:** NOMOGRAM — **no·mo·graph·ic** \ˌnä-mə-ˈgra-fik, ˌnō-\ *adj* — **no·mog·ra·phy** \nō-ˈmä-grə-fē\ *n*

no·mo·log·i·cal \ˌnä-mə-ˈlä-ji-kəl, ˌnō-\ *adj* [*nomology* science of physical and logical laws, fr. Gk *nomos* + E *-logy*] (1845) **:** relating to or expressing basic physical laws or rules of reasoning ⟨~ universals⟩

no·mo·thet·ic \-ˈthe-tik\ *adj* [Gk *nomothetikos* of legislation, fr. *nomothetēs* lawgiver, fr. *nomos* law + *-thetēs* one who establishes, fr. *tithenai* to put — more at DO] (1658) **:** relating to, involving, or dealing with abstract, general, or universal statements or laws

-nomy *n comb form* [Gk *-nomia,* fr. *nomos*] **:** system of laws governing or sum of knowledge regarding a (specified) field ⟨agro*nomy*⟩

non- \(ˈ)nän *also* ˌnən *or* ˈnən *before* ˈ*-stressed syllable,* ˌnän *also* ˌnən *before* ˌ*-stressed or unstressed syllable; the variant with* ə *is also to be understood at pronounced entries, though not shown*\ *prefix* [ME, fr. AF, fr. L *non* not, fr. OL *noenum,* fr. *ne-* not + *oinom,* neut. of *oinos* one — more at NO, ONE] **1 :** not **:** other than **:** reverse of **:** absence of ⟨*non*toxic⟩ ⟨*non*linear⟩ **2 :** of little or no consequence **:** unimportant **:** worthless ⟨*non*issues⟩ ⟨*non*system⟩ **3 :** lacking the usual esp. positive characteristics of the thing specified ⟨*non*celebration⟩ ⟨*non*art⟩

non·abra·sive
non·ab·sorb·able
non·ab·sor·bent
non·ab·sorp·tive
non·ab·stract
non·ac·a·dem·ic
non·ac·cep·tance
non·ac·count·able
non·ac·cred·it·ed
non·ac·cru·al
non·achieve·ment
non·ac·id
non·acid·ic
non·ac·quis·i·tive
non·act·ing
non·ac·tion
non·ac·ti·vat·ed
non·ac·tor
non·adap·tive
non·ad·dict
non·ad·dic·tive
non·ad·he·sive
non·adi·a·bat·ic
non·ad·ja·cent
non·ad·mir·er
non·ad·mis·sion
non·aero·sol
non·aes·thet·ic
non·af·fil·i·at·ed
non·af·flu·ent
non–Af·ri·can
non·ag·gres·sion
non·ag·gres·sive
non·ag·ri·cul·tur·al
non·al·co·hol·ic
non·al·ler·gen·ic
non·al·ler·gic
non·al·pha·bet·ic
non·alu·mi·num
non·am·big·u·ous
non–Amer·i·can
non·an·a·lyt·ic
non·an·a·tom·ic
non·an·i·mal
non·an·swer
non·an·tag·o·nis·tic
non·an·thro·po·log·i·cal
non·an·thro·pol·o·gist
non·an·ti·bi·ot·ic
non·an·ti·gen·ic
non·ap·pear·ance
non·aquat·ic
non·aque·ous
non·ar·a·ble
non·ar·bi·trar·i·ness
non·ar·bi·trary
non·ar·chi·tect
non·ar·chi·tec·ture
non·ar·gu·ment
non·aris·to·crat·ic
non·ar·o·mat·ic
non·art
non·art·ist
non·ar·tis·tic
non·as·cet·ic
non·as·pi·rin
non·as·ser·tive
non·as·so·ci·at·ed
non·as·tro·nom·i·cal
non·ath·lete
non·ath·let·ic
non·atom·ic
non·at·tached
non·at·tach·ment
non·at·ten·dance
non·at·tend·er
non·au·di·to·ry
non·au·thor
non·au·thor·i·tar·i·an
non·au·to·mat·ed
non·au·to·mat·ic
non·au·to·mo·tive
non·au·ton·o·mous
non·avail·abil·i·ty
non·bac·te·ri·al
non·bar·bi·tu·rate
non·bary·on·ic
non·ba·sic
non·bear·ing
non·be·hav·ior·al
non·be·ing
non·be·lief
non·be·liev·er
non·bel·lig·er·en·cy
non·bel·lig·er·ent
non·bet·ting
non·bib·li·cal
non·bib·lio·graph·ic
non·bi·na·ry
non·bind·ing
non·bio·de·grad·able
non·bio·graph·i·cal
non·bi·o·log·i·cal
non·bi·o·log·i·cal·ly
non·bi·ol·o·gist
non·bit·ing
non·black
non·body
non·bond·ed
non·bot·a·nist
non·brand
non·break·able
non·breath·ing
non·breed·er
non·breed·ing
non·broad·cast
non·build·ing
non·burn·able
non·buy·ing
non·cab·i·net
non·cak·ing
non·call·able
non·cam·pus
non·can·cel·able
non·can·cer·ous
non·can·ni·bal·is·tic
non·ca·non·i·cal
non·cap·i·tal
non·cap·i·tal·ist
non·car·cin·o·gen
non·car·ci·no·gen·ic
non·car·di·ac
non·ca·reer
non·car·ri·er
non·cash
non·ca·su·al
non–Cath·o·lic
non·caus·al
non·cel·e·bra·tion
non·ce·leb·ri·ty
non·cel·lu·lar
non·cel·lu·los·ic
non–Celt·ic
non·cen·tral
non·cer·tif·i·cat·ed
non·cer·ti·fied
non·char·ac·ter
non·char·is·mat·ic
non·chau·vin·ist
non·chem·i·cal
non–Chris·tian
non·chro·no·log·i·cal
non·church
non·church·go·er
non·cir·cu·lar
non·cir·cu·lat·ing
non·cit·i·zen
non·clan·des·tine
non·class
non·clas·si·cal
non·clas·si·fied
non·class·room
non·cler·i·cal
non·cling
non·clin·i·cal
non·clog·ging
non·co·er·cive
non·cog·ni·tive
non·co·her·ent
non·co·in·ci·dence
non·co·i·tal
non·cok·ing
non·co·la
non·col·lec·tor
non·col·lege
non·col·le·giate
non·col·lin·ear
non·col·or
non·col·ored
non·col·or·fast
non·com·bat
non·com·bat·ive
non·com·bus·ti·ble
non·com·mer·cial
non·com·mit·ment
non·com·mit·ted
non·com·mu·ni·cat·ing
non·com·mu·ni·ca·tion
non·com·mu·ni·ca·tive
non·com·mu·nist
non·com·mu·ni·ty
non·com·mu·ta·tive
non·com·mu·ta·tiv·i·ty
non·com·pa·ra·bil·i·ty
non·com·pa·ra·ble
non·com·pat·i·ble
non·com·pe·ti·tion
non·com·pet·i·tive
non·com·pet·i·tor
non·com·ple·men·ta·ry
non·com·plex
non·com·pli·ance
non·com·pli·ant
non·com·pli·cat·ed
non·com·ply·ing
non·com·pos·er
non·com·pound
non·com·pre·hen·sion
non·com·press·ible
non·com·put·er
non·com·put·er·ized
non·con·cep·tu·al
non·con·cern
non·con·clu·sion
non·con·cur·rent
non·con·dens·able
non·con·di·tioned
non·con·duct·ing
non·con·duc·tion
non·con·duc·tive
non·con·fer·ence
non·con·fi·dence
non·con·fi·den·tial
non·con·flict·ing

\ə\ **abut** \ᵊ\ kitten, F table \ər\ **further** \a\ **ash** \ā\ **ace** \ä\ **mop, mar** \au̇\ **out** \ch\ **chin** \e\ **bet** \ē\ **easy** \g\ **go** \i\ **hit** \ī\ **ice** \j\ **job** \ŋ\ **sing** \ō\ **go** \ȯ\ **law** \ȯi\ **boy** \th\ **thin** \t͟h\ **the** \ü\ **loot** \u̇\ **foot** \y\ **yet** \zh\ **vision, beige** \k, ⁿ, œ, ue, ʸ\ *see* Guide to Pronunciation

non·con·fron·ta·tion
non·con·fron·ta·tion·al
non·con·gru·ent
non·con·ju·gat·ed
non·con·nec·tion
non·con·scious
non·con·sec·u·tive
non·con·sen·su·al
non·con·ser·va·tion
non·con·ser·va·tive
non·con·sol·i·dat·ed
non·con·stant
non·con·sti·tu·tion·al
non·con·struc·tion
non·con·struc·tive
non·con·sum·er
non·con·sum·ing
non·con·sump·tion
non·con·sump·tive
non·con·tact
non·con·tem·po·rary
non·con·tig·u·ous
non·con·tin·gent
non·con·tin·u·ous
non·con·tract
non·con·trac·tu·al
non·con·tra·dic·tion
non·con·tra·dic·to·ry
non·con·trib·u·to·ry
non·con·trol·la·ble
non·con·trolled
non·con·trol·ling
non·con·tro·ver·sial
non·con·ven·tion·al
non·con·vert·ible
non·co·pla·nar
non·core
non·cor·po·rate
non·cor·re·la·tion
non·cor·rod·ible
non·cor·rod·ing
non·cor·ro·sive
non·coun·try
non·coun·ty
non·cov·er·age
non·cre·a·tive
non·cre·a·tiv·i·ty
non·cre·den·tialed
non·crime
non·crim·i·nal
non·cri·sis
non·crit·i·cal
non·crush·able
non·crys·tal·line
non·cul·i·nary
non·cul·ti·vat·ed
non·cul·ti·va·tion
non·cul·tur·al
non·cu·mu·la·tive
non·cur·rent
non·cus·tom·er
non·cy·clic
non·cy·cli·cal
non·dance
non·danc·er
non–Dar·win·i·an
non·de·cep·tive
non·de·ci·sion
non·de·creas·ing
non·de·duc·tive
non·de·fense
non·de·fer·ra·ble
non·de·form·ing
non·de·gen·er·ate
non·de·grad·able
non·de·gree
non·del·e·gate
non·de·lib·er·ate
non·de·lin·quent
non·de·liv·ery
non·de·mand·ing
non·dem·o·crat·ic
non·de·nom·i·na·tion·al
non·de·nom·i·na·tion·al·ism
non·de·part·men·tal
non·de·pen·dent
non·de·plet·able
non·de·plet·ing
non·de·po·si·tion
non·de·pressed
non·de·riv·a·tive
non·de·scrip·tive
non·de·sert
non·de·tach·able
non·de·ter·min·is·tic
non·de·vel·op·ment
non·de·vi·ant
non·di·a·bet·ic
non·di·a·lyz·able
non·di·dac·tic
non·dif·fus·ible

non·di·men·sion·al
non·dip·lo·mat·ic
non·di·rect·ed
non·di·rec·tion·al
non·dis·abled
non·dis·clo·sure
non·dis·count
non·dis·cre·tion·ary
non·dis·crim·i·na·tion
non·dis·crim·i·na·to·ry
non·dis·cur·sive
non·dis·per·sive
non·dis·rup·tive
non·di·ver·si·fied
non·doc·tor
non·doc·tri·naire
non·doc·u·men·ta·ry
non·dog·mat·ic
non·dol·lar
non·do·mes·tic
non·dom·i·nant
non·dra·mat·ic
non·driv·er
non·drug
non·du·ra·ble
non·earn·ing
non·ec·cle·si·as·ti·cal
non·econ·o·mist
non·ed·i·ble
non·ed·i·to·ri·al
non·ed·u·ca·tion
non·ed·u·ca·tion·al
non·ef·fec·tive
non·elas·tic
non·elect·ed
non·elec·tion
non·elec·tive
non·elec·tric
non·elec·tri·cal
non·elec·tron·ic
non·el·e·men·ta·ry
non·elite
non·emer·gen·cy
non·emo·tion·al
non·em·phat·ic
non·em·pir·i·cal
non·em·ploy·ee
non·em·ploy·ment
non·emp·ty
non·en·cap·su·lat·ed
non·end·ing
non·en·er·gy
non·en·force·abil·i·ty
non·en·force·ment
non·en·gage·ment
non·en·gi·neer·ing
non·en·ter·tain·ment
non·en·zy·mat·ic
non·en·zy·mic
non·equi·lib·ri·um
non·equiv·a·lence
non·equiv·a·lent
non·erot·ic
non·es·tab·lished
non·es·tab·lish·ment
non·es·ter·i·fied
non·eth·i·cal
non·eth·nic
non–Eu·ro·pe·an
non·eval·u·a·tive
non·ev·i·dence
non·ex·clu·sive
non·ex·ec·u·tive
non·ex·empt
non·ex·is·ten·tial
non·ex·ot·ic
non·ex·pend·able
non·ex·per·i·men·tal
non·ex·pert
non·ex·plan·a·to·ry
non·ex·ploi·ta·tion
non·ex·ploit·a·tive
non·ex·ploit·ive
non·ex·plo·sive
non·ex·posed
non·ex·tant
non·fact
non·fac·tor
non·fac·tu·al
non·fac·ul·ty
non·fad·ing
non·fa·mil·ial
non·fam·i·ly
non·fan
non·farm
non·farm·er
non·fa·tal
non·fat·ten·ing
non·fat·ty
non·fed·er·al
non·fed·er·at·ed
non·fem·i·nist
non·fil·a·men·tous
non·fil·ter·able

non·fi·nal
non·fi·nan·cial
non·fi·nite
non·fis·sion·able
non·flu·o·res·cent
non·fly·ing
non·food
non·for·feit·able
non·for·fei·ture
non·for·mal
non·fos·sil
non·frat·er·ni·za·tion
non·freez·ing
non·friv·o·lous
non·fro·zen
non·fuel
non·ful·fill·ment
non·func·tion·al
non·func·tion·ing
non·game
non·gas·eous
non·gay
non·ge·net·ic
non·gen·i·tal
non·geo·met·ri·cal
non·ghet·to
non·glam·or·ous
non·glare
non·golf·er
non·gov·ern·ment
non·gov·ern·men·tal
non·grad·ed
non·grad·u·ate
non·gram·mat·i·cal
non·gran·u·lar
non·grav·i·ta·tion·al
non·greasy
non·gre·gar·i·ous
non·grow·ing
non·growth
non·guest
non·ha·lo·ge·nat·ed
non·hand·i·capped
non·hap·pen·ing
non·har·dy
non·har·mon·ic
non·haz·ard·ous
non·heme
non·he·mo·lyt·ic
non·he·red·i·tary
non·het·ero·sex·u·al
non·hi·er·ar·chi·cal
non–His·pan·ic
non·his·tor·i·cal
non·home
non·ho·mo·ge·neous
non·ho·mol·o·gous
non·ho·mo·sex·u·al
non·hor·mon·al
non·hos·pi·tal
non·hos·pi·tal·ized
non·hos·tile
non·hous·ing
non·hu·man
non·hunt·er
non·hunt·ing
non·hy·gro·scop·ic
non·hys·ter·i·cal
non·ide·al
non·iden·ti·ty
non·ide·o·log·i·cal
non·im·age
non·im·i·ta·tive
non·im·mi·grant
non·im·mune
non·im·pact
non·im·pli·ca·tion
non·im·por·ta·tion
non·in·clu·sion
non·in·creas·ing
non·in·cum·bent
non·in·de·pen·dence
non–In·di·an
non·in·dig·e·nous
non·in·di·vid·u·al
non–In·do–Eu·ro·pe·an
non·in·dus·tri·al
non·in·dus·tri·al·ized
non·in·dus·try
non·in·fect·ed
non·in·fec·tious
non·in·fec·tive
non·in·fest·ed
non·in·flam·ma·ble
non·in·flam·ma·to·ry
non·in·fla·tion·ary
non·in·flec·tion·al
non·in·flu·ence
non·in·for·ma·tion
non·in·fringe·ment
non·ini·tial
non·in·i·ti·ate
non·in·ju·ry
non·in·sect

non·in·sec·ti·cid·al
non·in·stall·ment
non·in·sti·tu·tion·al
non·in·sti·tu·tion·al·ized
non·in·struc·tion·al
non·in·stru·men·tal
non·in·sur·ance
non·in·sured
non·in·te·gral
non·in·te·grat·ed
non·in·tel·lec·tu·al
non·in·ter·act·ing
non·in·ter·ac·tive
non·in·ter·change·able
non·in·ter·course
non·in·ter·est
non·in·ter·fer·ence
non·in·ter·sect·ing
non·in·tim·i·dat·ing
non·in·tox·i·cant
non·in·tox·i·cat·ing
non·in·tru·sive
non·in·tu·i·tive
non·ion·iz·ing
non·ir·ra·di·at·ed
non·ir·ri·gat·ed
non·ir·ri·tant
non·ir·ri·tat·ing
non–Jap·a·nese
non–Jew
non–Jew·ish
non·join·er
non·ju·di·cial
non·ju·ry
non·jus·ti·cia·ble
non·ko·sher
non·la·bor
non·land·own·er
non·lan·guage
non·law·yer
non·lead·ed
non·league
non·le·gal
non·le·gume
non·le·gu·mi·nous
non·le·thal
non·lex·i·cal
non·li·brar·i·an
non·li·brary
non·life
non·lin·e·al
non·lin·e·ar
non·lin·e·ar·i·ty
non·lin·guis·tic
non·liq·uid
non·lit·er·al
non·lit·er·ary
non·liv·ing
non·lo·cal
non·log·i·cal
non·lu·mi·nous
non·mag·net·ic
non·main·stream
non·ma·jor
non·ma·lig·nant
non·mal·lea·ble
non·mam·ma·li·an
non·man·age·ment
non·man·a·ge·ri·al
non·man·u·al
non·man·u·fac·tur·ing
non·mar·i·tal
non·mar·ket
non–Marx·ist
non·ma·te·ri·al
non·ma·te·ri·al·is·tic
non·math·e·mat·i·cal
non·math·e·ma·ti·cian
non·ma·tric·u·lat·ed
non·mean·ing·ful
non·mea·sur·able
non·meat
non·me·chan·i·cal
non·mech·a·nis·tic
non·med·i·cal
non·meet·ing
non·mem·ber
non·mem·ber·ship
non·men·tal
non·mer·cu·ri·al
non·meta·mer·ic
non·met·a·phor·i·cal
non·met·ric
non·met·ri·cal
non·met·ro
non·met·ro·pol·i·tan
non·mi·cro·bi·al
non·mi·grant
non·mi·gra·to·ry
non·mil·i·tant
non·mil·i·tary
non·mi·met·ic
non·mi·nor·i·ty

non·mo·bile
non·mo·lec·u·lar
non·mon·e·tar·ist
non·mon·e·tary
non·mon·ey
non·mo·nog·a·mous
non·mo·tile
non·mo·tor·ized
non·mov·ing
non·mu·nic·i·pal
non·mu·sic
non·mu·si·cal
non·mu·si·cian
non–Mus·lim
non·mu·tant
non·my·e·lin·at·ed
non·mys·ti·cal
non·nar·ra·tive
non·na·tion·al
non·na·tive
non·nat·u·ral
non·ne·ces·si·ty
non·neg·li·gent
non·ne·go·tia·ble
non·net·work
non·neu·ral
non·news
non·ni·trog·e·nous
non·nor·ma·tive
non·nov·el
non·nu·cle·at·ed
non·nu·mer·i·cal
non·nu·tri·tious
non·nu·tri·tive
non·ob·scene
non·ob·ser·vance
non·ob·ser·vant
non·ob·vi·ous
non·oc·cu·pa·tion·al
non·oc·cur·rence
non·of·fi·cial
non·ohm·ic
non·oily
non·op·er·at·ic
non·op·er·at·ing
non·op·er·a·tion·al
non·op·er·a·tive
non·op·ti·mal
non·or·gan·ic
non·or·tho·dox
non·over·lap·ping
non·own·er
non·ox·i·diz·ing
non·paid
non·par·al·lel
non·par·a·sit·ic
non·par·ent
non·par·tic·i·pant
non·par·tic·i·pat·ing
non·par·tic·i·pa·tion
non·par·tic·i·pa·to·ry
non·par·ty
non·pas·sive
non·past
non·pay·ing
non·pay·ment
non·per·for·mance
non·per·form·er
non·per·ish·able
non·per·mis·sive
non·per·son·al
non·pe·tro·le·um
non·phi·los·o·pher
non·phil·o·soph·i·cal
non·pho·ne·mic
non·pho·net·ic
non·phos·phate
non·pho·to·graph·ic
non·phys·i·cal
non·phy·si·cian
non·pla·nar
non·plas·tic
non·play
non·play·ing
non·po·et·ic
non·poi·son·ous
non·po·lar·iz·able
non·po·lice
non·po·lit·i·cal
non·po·lit·i·cal·ly
non·pol·i·ti·cian
non·pol·lut·ing
non·poor
non·po·rous
non·pos·ses·sion
non·prac·ti·cal
non·prac·tic·ing
non·preg·nant
non·print
non·prob·lem
non·pro·duc·ing
non·pro·fes·sion·al
non·pro·fes·sion·al·ly
non·pro·fes·so·ri·al

non·pro·gram
non·pro·gram·mer
non·pro·gres·sive
non·pro·pri·etary
non·psy·chi·at·ric
non·psy·chi·a·trist
non·psy·cho·log·i·cal
non·psy·chot·ic
non·pub·lic
non·pu·ni·tive
non·pur·po·sive
non·quan·ti·fi·able
non·quan·ti·ta·tive
non·ra·cial
non·ra·cial·ly
non·ra·dio·ac·tive
non·rail·road
non·ran·dom
non·ran·dom·ness
non·rat·ed
non·ra·tio·nal
non·re·ac·tive
non·re·ac·tor
non·re·al·is·tic
non·re·ap·point·ment
non·re·ceipt
non·re·cip·ro·cal
non·rec·og·ni·tion
non·re·cy·cla·ble
non·re·duc·ing
non·re·dun·dant
non·re·fill·able
non·re·flect·ing
non·reg·u·lat·ed
non·reg·u·la·tion
non·rel·a·tive
non·rel·e·vant
non·re·li·gious
non·re·new·able
non·re·new·al
non·re·pay·able
non·rep·re·sen·ta·tive
non·re·pro·duc·tive
non·res·i·den·tial
non·res·o·nant
non·re·spon·dent
non·re·spond·er
non·re·sponse
non·re·spon·sive
non·re·strict·ed
non·re·trac·tile
non·ret·ro·ac·tive
non·re·us·able
non·re·vers·ible
non·rev·o·lu·tion·ary
non·rig·id
non·ri·ot·er
non·ri·ot·ing
non·ro·tat·ing
non·rou·tine
non·roy·al
non·rub·ber
non·rul·ing
non·ru·mi·nant
non–Rus·sian
non·sal·able
non·sa·line
non·sa·pon·i·fi·able
non·schiz·o·phren·ic
non·school
non·sci·en·tif·ic
non·sci·en·tist
non·sea·son·al
non·sec·re·tory
non·se·cure
non·sed·i·ment·able
non·seg·re·gat·ed
non·seg·re·ga·tion
non·se·lect·ed
non·se·lec·tive
non–self–gov·ern·ing
non·sen·sa·tion·al
non·sen·si·tive
non·sen·su·ous
non·sen·tence
non·sep·tate
non·se·quen·tial
non·se·quen·tial·ly
non·se·ri·ous
non·sex·ist
non·sex·u·al
non·shrink
non·shrink·able
non·sign·er
non·si·mul·ta·neous
non·sink·able
non·skat·er
non·skel·e·tal
non·ski·er
non·smok·er
non·smok·ing
non·so·cial·ist
non·so·lar
non·so·lu·tion

non·spa·tial
non·speak·er
non·speak·ing
non·spe·cial·ist
non·spe·cif·ic
non·spe·cif·i·cal·ly
non·spec·tac·u·lar
non·spec·u·la·tive
non·speech
non·spher·i·cal
non·sta·tion·ary
non·sta·tis·ti·cal
non·steady
non·sto·ry
non·stra·te·gic
non·struc·tur·al
non·struc·tured
non·stu·dent
non·style
non·sub·ject
non·sub·jec·tive
non·sub·si·dized
non·suc·cess
non·sug·ar
non·su·per·im·pos·able
non·su·per·vi·so·ry
non·sur·gi·cal
non·swim·mer
non·sym·bol·ic
non·sym·met·ric
non·sym·met·ri·cal
non·syn·chro·nous
non·sys·tem·at·ic
non·sys·tem·ic
non·tar·iff
non·tax·able
non·teach·ing
non·tech·ni·cal
non·tem·po·ral
non·ten·ured
non·ter·mi·nal
non·the·at·ri·cal
non·the·ist
non·the·is·tic
non·theo·log·i·cal
non·the·o·ret·i·cal
non·ther·a·peu·tic
non·think·ing
non·tid·al
non·to·bac·co
non·ton·al
non·to·tal·i·tar·i·an
non·tox·ic
non·tra·di·tion·al
non·trans·fer·able
non·treat·ment
non·triv·i·al
non·trop·i·cal
non·tur·bu·lent
non·typ·i·cal
non·unan·i·mous
non·uni·form
non·uni·for·mi·ty
non·union·ized
non·unique
non·unique·ness
non·uni·ver·sal
non·uni·ver·si·ty
non·ur·ban
non·ur·gent
non·util·i·tar·i·an
non·util·i·ty
non·uto·pi·an
non·val·id
non·va·lid·i·ty
non·vas·cu·lar
non·veg·e·tar·i·an
non·ven·om·ous
non·vet·er·an
non·vi·a·ble
non·view·er
non·vi·ral
non·vir·gin
non·vis·cous
non·vi·su·al
non·vo·cal
non·vo·ca·tion·al
non·vol·ca·nic
non·vol·un·tary
non·vot·er
non·vot·ing
non·wage
non·war
non·win·ning
non·woody
non·work
non·work·er
non·work·ing
non·writ·er
non·yel·low·ing

non·ad·di·tive \ˈnän-ˈa-də-tiv\ *adj* (1926) **1 :** not having a numerical value equal to the sum of values for the component parts **2 :** of, relating to, or being a genic effect that is not additive — **non·ad·di·tiv·i·ty** \ˌnän-ˌa-də-ˈti-və-tē\ *n*

non·age \ˈnä-nij, ˈnō-\ *n* [ME, fr. AF, fr. *non-* + *age* age] (15c) **1 :** MINORITY 1 **2 a :** a period of youth **b :** lack of maturity

no·na·ge·nar·i·an \ˌnō-nə-jə-ˈner-ē-ən, ˌnä-\ *n* [L *nonagenarius* containing ninety, fr. *nonageni* ninety each, fr. *nonaginta* ninety, fr. *nona-* (akin to *novem* nine) + *-ginta* (akin to *viginti* twenty) — more at NINE, VIGESIMAL] (1804) **:** a person whose age is in the nineties — **nonagenarian** *adj*

no·na·gon \ˈnō-nə-ˌgän\ *n* [L *nonus* ninth + E *-gon* — more at NOON] (ca. 1639) **:** a polygon of nine angles and nine sides

non·aligned \ˌnän-ə-ˈlīnd\ *adj* (1960) **:** not allied with other nations and esp. with either the Communist or the non-Communist blocs — **non·align·ment** \-mənt\ *n*

non·al·le·lic \ˌnän-ə-ˈlē-lik, -ˈle-\ *adj* (1945) **:** not behaving as alleles toward one another ⟨~ genes⟩

no–name \ˈnō-ˌnām\ *adj* (1942) **:** having a name that is not readily recognized by the public ⟨a ~ product⟩ ⟨a ~ baseball team⟩ — **no–name** *n*

non–A, non–B hepatitis \ˈnän-ˈā-ˈnän-ˈbē-\ *n* (1976) **:** hepatitis clinically similar to hepatitis A and hepatitis B but caused by a different virus; *esp* **:** HEPATITIS C

non·bank \ˈnän-ˈbaŋk\ *n, often attrib* (1939) **:** a business that is not an officially established bank but offers many similar services — **non·bank·ing** \-ˈbaŋ-kiŋ\ *adj*

non·bond·ing \-ˈbän-diŋ\ *adj* (1952) **:** relating to, being, or occupying a molecular orbital that neither promotes nor inhibits bond formation between atoms ⟨a ~ electron⟩

¹**non·book** \-ˈbu̇k\ *adj* (1949) **:** being something other than a book; *esp* **:** being a library holding (as a microfilm) that is not a book

²**non·book** \-ˌbu̇k\ *n* (1960) **:** a book of little literary merit which is often a compilation (as of pictures, press clippings, or speeches)

non·busi·ness \-ˈbiz-nəs, -nəz\ *adj* (1927) **:** not related to business; *esp* **:** not related to one's primary business

non·ca·lo·ric \ˌnän-kə-ˈlȯr-ik\ *adj* (1950) **:** free from or very low in calories ⟨a ~ drink⟩

non·can·di·date \ˈnän-ˈkan-də-ˌdāt, -ˈka-nə-, -dət\ *n* (1944) **:** a person who is not a candidate; *esp* **:** one who has refused to be a candidate for a particular political office — **non·can·di·da·cy** \-də-sē\ *n*

¹**nonce** \ˈnän(t)s\ *n* [ME *nanes,* alter. (fr. misdivision of *then anes* in such phrases as *to then anes* for the one purpose) of *anes* one purpose, irreg. fr. *an, on* one — more at ONE] (13c) **1 :** the one, particular, or present occasion, purpose, or use ⟨for the ~⟩ **2 :** the time being

²**nonce** *adj* (1884) **:** occurring, used, or made only once or for a special occasion ⟨a ~ word⟩

non·cha·lance \ˌnän-shə-ˈlän(t)s; ˈnän-shə-ˌlän(t)s, -lən(t)s\ *n* (1678) **:** the quality or state of being nonchalant

non·cha·lant \-ˈlänt, -ˌlänt, -lənt\ *adj* [F, fr. OF, fr. prp. of *nonchaloir* to disregard, fr. *non-* + *chaloir* to concern, fr. L *calēre* to be warm — more at LEE] (ca. 1734) **:** having an air of easy unconcern or indifference ***syn*** see COOL — **non·cha·lant·ly** *adv*

non·chro·mo·som·al \ˌnän-ˌkrō-mə-ˈsō-məl\ *adj* (1960) **1 :** not situated on a chromosome **2 :** not involving chromosomes

non·cod·ing \(ˈ)nän-ˈkō-diŋ\ *adj* (1976) **:** not specifying the genetic code ⟨a ~ DNA sequence⟩

non·com \ˈnän-ˌkäm\ *n* (1883) **:** NONCOMMISSIONED OFFICER

non·com·bat·ant \ˌnän-kəm-ˈba-tᵊnt *also* ˈnän-ˈkäm-bə-tənt\ *n* (1811) **:** one that does not engage in combat: as **a :** a member (as a chaplain) of the armed forces whose duties do not include fighting **b :** CIVILIAN — **noncombatant** *adj*

non·com·e·do·gen·ic \(ˈ)nän-ˌkä-mə-dō-ˈje-nik\ *adj* [*non-* + *comedo* + *-genic*] (1983) **:** not tending to clog pores (as by the formation of blackheads) ⟨a ~ cosmetic⟩

non·com·mis·sioned officer \ˌnän-kə-ˈmi-shənd-\ *n* (1703) **:** a subordinate officer (as a sergeant) in the army, air force, or marine corps appointed from among enlisted personnel

non·com·mit·tal \-kə-ˈmi-tᵊl\ *adj* (1829) **1 :** giving no clear indication of attitude or feeling ⟨a ~ reply⟩ **2 :** having no clear or distinctive character — **non·com·mit·tal·ly** \-tᵊl-ē\ *adv*

non com·pos men·tis \ˌnän-ˌkäm-pəs-ˈmen-təs, ˌnōn-\ *adj* [L, lit., not having mastery of one's mind] (1607) **:** not of sound mind

non·con·cur \ˌnän-kən-ˈkər\ *vi* (1732) **:** to refuse or fail to concur — **non·con·cur·rence** \-ˈkər-ən(t)s, -ˈkə-rən(t)s\ *n*

non·con·duc·tor \-kən-ˈdək-tər\ *n* (1751) **:** a substance that conducts heat, electricity, or sound only in very small degree

non·con·form \-kən-ˈfȯrm\ *vi* [back-formation fr. *nonconformist*] (1681) **:** to fail to conform — **non·con·form·er** *n*

non·con·for·mance \-ˈfȯr-mən(t)s\ *n* (1786) **:** failure to conform

non·con·form·ism \-ˈfȯr-ˌmi-zəm\ *n* (1844) **:** NONCONFORMITY

non·con·form·ist \-ˈfȯr-mist\ *n* (1619) **1** *often cap* **:** a person who does not conform to an established church; *esp* **:** one who does not conform to the Church of England **2 :** a person who does not conform to a generally accepted pattern of thought or action — **nonconformist** *adj, often cap*

non·con·for·mi·ty \-ˈfȯr-mə-tē\ *n* (1618) **1 a :** failure or refusal to conform to an established church **b** *often cap* **:** the movement or principles of English Protestant dissent **c** *often cap* **:** the body of English Nonconformists **2 :** refusal to conform to an established or conventional creed, rule, or practice **3 :** absence of agreement or correspondence

non·co·op·er·a·tion \ˌnän-kō-ˌä-pə-ˈrā-shən\ *n* (1795) **:** failure or refusal to cooperate; *specif* **:** refusal through civil disobedience of a people to cooperate with the government of a country — **non·co·op·er·a·tion·ist** \-sh(ə-)nist\ *n* — **non·co·op·er·a·tor** \-ˈä-pə-ˌrā-tər\ *n*

non·co·op·er·a·tive \-ˈä-p(ə-)rə-tiv, -pə-ˌrā-\ *adj* (1922) **:** of, relating to, or characterized by noncooperation

non·cred·it \ˈnän-ˈkre-dət\ *adj* (1965) **:** not offering credit toward a degree ⟨~ courses⟩

non·cross·over \-ˈkrȯ-ˌsō-vər\ *adj* (1916) **:** having or being chromosomes that have not participated in genetic crossing-over

non·cus·to·di·al \-kə-ˈstō-dē-əl\ *adj* (1973) **:** of or being a parent who does not have sole custody of a child or who has custody a smaller portion of the time

non·dairy \-ˈder-ē, ˈnän-ˌ\ *adj* (1968) **:** containing no milk or milk products ⟨~ whipped topping⟩

non·de·duct·ible \ˌnän-di-ˈdək-tə-bəl\ *adj* (1943) **:** not deductible; *esp* **:** not deductible for income tax purposes ⟨a ~ contribution⟩ — **non·de·duct·ibil·i·ty** \-ˌdək-tə-ˈbi-lə-tē\ *n*

non·de·fense \ˌnän-di-ˈfen(t)s\ *adj* (1961) **:** not used or intended for or associated with the military ⟨~ spending⟩

non·de·script \ˌnän-di-ˈskript\ *adj* [*non-* + L *descriptus,* pp. of *describere* to describe] (1789) **1 :** belonging or appearing to belong to no particular class or kind **:** not easily described **2 :** lacking distinctive or interesting qualities **:** DULL, DRAB — **nondescript** *n*

non·de·struc·tive \-di-ˈstrək-tiv\ *adj* (1926) **:** not destructive; *specif* **:** not causing destruction of material being investigated or treated ⟨~ testing of metal⟩ — **non·de·struc·tive·ly** *adv* — **non·de·struc·tive·ness** *n*

non·dia·paus·ing \ˌnän-ˌdī-ə-ˈpȯ-ziŋ\ *adj* (1963) **1 :** not having a diapause **2 :** not being in a state of diapause

non·di·rec·tive \ˌnän-də-ˈrek-tiv, -(ˌ)dī-\ *adj* (1931) **:** of, relating to, or being psychotherapy, counseling, or interviewing in which the counselor refrains from interpretation or explanation but encourages the client (as by repeating phrases) to talk freely

non·dis·junc·tion \ˌnän-dis-ˈjəŋ(k)-shən\ *n* [ISV] (1913) **:** failure of homologous chromosomes or sister chromatids to separate subsequent to metaphase in meiosis or mitosis so that one daughter cell has both and the other neither of the chromosomes — **non·dis·junc·tion·al** \-shnəl, -shə-nᵊl\ *adj*

non·dis·tinc·tive \-di-ˈstiŋ(k)-tiv\ *adj* (1916) *of a speech sound* **:** having no signaling value

non·di·vid·ing \ˌnän-də-ˈvī-diŋ\ *adj* (1945) **:** not undergoing cell division

non·dor·mant \ˈnän-ˈdȯr-mənt\ *adj* (1940) **1 :** being in such a condition that germination is possible ⟨~ seeds⟩ **2 :** being in active vegetative growth ⟨~ plants⟩

non·drink·er \-ˈdriŋ-kər\ *n* (1899) **:** a person who abstains from alcoholic beverages — **non·drink·ing** \-kiŋ\ *adj*

non·dry·ing oil \-ˈdrī-iŋ-\ *n* (1877) **:** a highly saturated oil (as olive oil) that is unable to solidify when exposed in a thin film to air

¹**none** \ˈnən\ *pron, sing or pl in constr* [ME, fr. OE *nān,* fr. *ne* not + *ān* one — more at NO, ONE] (bef. 12c) **1 :** not any **2 :** not one **:** NOBODY **3 :** not any such thing or person **4 :** no part **:** NOTHING

²**none** *adj* (bef. 12c) *archaic* **:** not any **:** NO

³**none** *adv* (1651) **1 :** by no means **:** not at all ⟨~ too soon to begin⟩ **2 :** in no way **:** to no extent ⟨~ the worse for wear⟩

⁴**none** \ˈnōn\ *n, often cap* [LL *nona,* fr. L, 9th hour of the day from sunrise — more at NOON] (1845) **:** the fifth of the canonical hours

non·eco·nom·ic \ˌnän-ˌe-kə-ˈnä-mik, -ˌē-kə-\ *adj* (1920) **:** not economic; *esp* **:** having no economic importance or implication

non·elec·tro·lyte \ˌnän-ə-ˈlek-trə-ˌlīt\ *n* (1891) **:** a substance that does not readily ionize when dissolved or melted and is a poor conductor of electricity

non·en·ti·ty \-ˈen-tə-tē, -ˈe-nə-\ *n* (ca. 1600) **1 :** something that does not exist or exists only in the imagination **2 :** NONEXISTENCE **3 :** a person or thing of little consequence or significance

nones \ˈnōnz\ *n pl but sing or pl in constr* [ME *nonys,* fr. AF *nones,* fr. L *nonae,* fr. fem. pl. of *nonus* ninth] (14c) **1 :** the ninth day before the ides according to ancient Roman reckoning **2** *often cap* **:** ⁴NONE

non·es·sen·tial \ˌnän-i-ˈsen(t)-shəl\ *adj* (1751) **1 :** not essential **2 :** being a substance synthesized by the body in sufficient quantity to satisfy dietary needs ⟨~ amino acids⟩ — compare ESSENTIAL 2b — **nonessential** *n*

\ə\ **a**but \ᵊ\ kitten, F table \ər\ f**ur**ther \a\ **a**sh \ā\ **a**ce \ä\ m**o**p, m**a**r \au̇\ **ou**t \ch\ **ch**in \e\ b**e**t \ē\ **ea**sy \g\ **g**o \i\ h**i**t \ī\ **i**ce \j\ **j**ob \ŋ\ si**ng** \ō\ g**o** \ȯ\ l**aw** \ȯi\ b**oy** \th\ **th**in \t͟h\ **th**e \ü\ l**oo**t \u̇\ f**oo**t \y\ **y**et \zh\ vi**s**ion, bei**g**e \k̲, ⁿ, œ, ue, ʸ\ *see* Guide to Pronunciation

none·such \ˈnən-ˌsəch\ *n* (1590) : a person or thing without an equal — **nonesuch** *adj*

no·net \nō-ˈnet\ *n* [It *nonetto,* fr. *nono* ninth, fr. L *nonus* — more at NOON] (1865) : a combination of nine instruments or voices; *also* : a musical composition for such a combination

none·the·less \ˌnən-t͟hə-ˈles\ *adv* (1847) : NEVERTHELESS

non–eu·clid·e·an \ˌnän-yü-ˈkli-dē-ən\ *adj, often cap E* (1872) : not assuming or in accordance with all the postulates of Euclid's *Elements* ⟨~ geometry⟩

non·event \ˈnän-i-ˌvent, ˌnän-i-ˈ\ *n* (1962) **1 a :** an expected event that fails to take place or to satisfy expectations **b :** an often highly publicized event of little intrinsic interest or significance **2 :** an occurrence that is officially ignored

non·ex·is·tence \ˌnän-ig-ˈzis-tən(t)s\ *n* (1646) : absence of existence : the negation of being — **non·ex·is·tent** \-tənt\ *adj*

non·fat \ˈnän-ˈfat\ *adj* (1926) : lacking fat solids : having fat solids removed ⟨~ milk⟩

non·fea·sance \ˈnän-ˈfē-zᵊn(t)s\ *n* [*non-* + obs. E *feasance* doing, execution] (1596) : failure to act; *esp* : failure to do what ought to be done

non·fer·rous \-ˈfer-əs\ *adj* (1887) **1 :** not containing, including, or relating to iron **2 :** of or relating to metals other than iron

non·fic·tion \-ˈfik-shən\ *n* (1909) : literature or cinema that is not fictional — **non·fic·tion·al** \ˌnän-ˈfik-shnəl, -shə-nᵊl\ *adj*

non·fig·u·ra·tive \ˈnän-ˈfi-gyə-rə-tiv, -ˈfi-gə-\ *adj* (1934) : NONOBJECTIVE 2

non·flam·ma·ble \-ˈfla-mə-bəl\ *adj* (1915) : not flammable; *specif* : not easily ignited and not burning rapidly if ignited — **non·flam·ma·bil·i·ty** \ˌnän-ˌfla-mə-ˈbi-lə-tē\ *n*

non·flow·er·ing \ˈnän-ˈflau̇(-ə)r-iŋ\ *adj* (ca. 1934) : producing no flowers; *specif* : lacking a flowering stage in the life cycle

non·flu·en·cy \-ˈflü-ən(t)-sē\ *n, pl* **-cies** (ca. 1945) **1 :** lack of fluency **2 :** an instance of nonfluency

non·gon·o·coc·cal \ˌnän-ˌgä-nə-ˈkä-kəl\ *adj* (1961) : not caused by a gonococcus ⟨sexually transmitted ~ urethritis⟩

non gra·ta \ˌnän-ˈgra-tə, -ˈgrä-\ *adj* [*persona non grata*] (1925) : not approved : UNWELCOME

non·green \ˈnän-ˈgrēn\ *adj* (1897) : not green; *specif* : containing no chlorophyll ⟨~ saprophytes⟩

non·he·ro \ˈnän-ˈhē-(ˌ)rō, -ˈhir-(ˌ)ō\ *n* (1940) : ANTIHERO

non·his·tone \-ˈhis-ˌtōn\ *adj* (ca. 1966) : relating to or being any of the eukaryotic proteins (as DNA polymerase) that form complexes with DNA but are not classified as histones

non–Hodg·kin's lymphoma \ˈnän-ˈhäj-kənz-\ *n* (1972) : any of the numerous malignant lymphomas (as Burkitt's lymphoma) that are not classified as Hodgkin's disease

non·iden·ti·cal \ˌnän-(ˌ)ī-ˈden-ti-kəl, -ə-ˈden-\ *adj* (1890) **1 :** DIFFERENT **2 :** FRATERNAL 2 ⟨~ twins⟩

no·nil·lion \nō-ˈnil-yən\ *n, often attrib* [F, fr. L *nonus* ninth + F *-illion* (as in *million*) — more at NOON] (1690) — see NUMBER table

non·in·duc·tive \ˌnän-in-ˈdək-tiv\ *adj* (1893) : not inductive; *esp* : having negligible inductance

non–insulin–dependent diabetes *n* (1978) : TYPE 2 DIABETES

non–insulin–dependent diabetes mellitus *n* (1979) : TYPE 2 DIABETES — abbr. *NIDDM*

non·in·ter·laced \ˌnän-ˌin-tər-ˈlāst\ *adj* (1980) : not interlaced; *specif* : of, relating to, or using a method of video scanning (as for a television or computer screen) in which the horizontal lines of each frame are drawn consecutively in a single pass

non·in·ter·ven·tion \-ˌin-tər-ˈven(t)-shən\ *n* (1831) : the state or policy of not intervening ⟨~ in the affairs of other countries⟩ — **non·in·ter·ven·tion·ist** \-ˈven(t)-sh(ə-)nist\ *n or adj*

non·in·va·sive \-in-ˈvā-siv, -ziv\ *adj* (1968) **1 :** not tending to spread; *specif* : not tending to infiltrate and destroy healthy tissue ⟨~ cancer of the bladder⟩ **2 :** not being or involving an invasive medical procedure ⟨~ imaging techniques⟩ — **non·in·va·sive·ly** *adv*

non·in·volve·ment \-in-ˈvälv-mənt, -ˈvȯlv- *also* -ˈväv-, -ˈvȯv-\ *n* (1936) : absence of involvement or emotional attachment — **non·in·volved** \-ˈvä(l)vd, -ˈvȯ(l)vd\ *adj*

non·ion·ic \-(ˌ)ī-ˈä-nik\ *adj* (1929) : not ionic; *esp* : not dependent on a surface-active anion for effect ⟨~ surfactants⟩

non·is·sue \ˈnän-ˈi-(ˌ)shü\ *n* (1964) : an issue of little importance, validity, or concern

non·join·der \ˈnän-ˈjȯin-dər\ *n* (1833) : failure to include a necessary party to a suit at law

non·judg·men·tal \ˌnän-ˌjəj-ˈmen-tᵊl\ *adj* (1952) : avoiding judgments based on one's personal and esp. moral standards — **non·judg·men·tal·ly** *adv*

non·jur·ing \ˈnän-ˈju̇r-iŋ\ *adj* [*non-* + L *jur*are to swear — more at JURY] (1691) : not swearing allegiance — used esp. of a member of a party in Great Britain that would not swear allegiance to William and Mary or to their successors

non·ju·ror \-ˈju̇r-ər, -ˈju̇r-ˌȯr\ *n* (1691) : a person refusing to take an oath esp. of allegiance, supremacy, or abjuration; *specif* : one of the beneficed clergy in England and Scotland refusing to take an oath of allegiance to William and Mary or to their successors after the revolution of 1688

non·lit·er·ate \-ˈli-t(ə-)rət\ *adj* (1947) **1 :** not literate **2 :** having no written language — **nonliterate** *n*

non·met·al \-ˈme-tᵊl\ *n* (ca. 1864) : a chemical element (as boron, carbon, or nitrogen) that lacks the characteristics of a metal

non·me·tal·lic \ˌnän-mə-ˈta-lik\ *adj* (1815) **1 :** not metallic **2 :** of, relating to, or being a nonmetal

non·mor·al \ˈnän-ˈmȯr-əl, -ˈmär-\ *adj* (ca. 1866) : not falling into or existing in the sphere of morals or ethics

non·neg·a·tive \-ˈne-gə-tiv\ *adj* (1885) : not negative: as **a :** being either positive or zero **b :** taking on nonnegative values ⟨a ~ function⟩

non·nu·cle·ar \-ˈnü-klē-ər, -ˈnyü-, ÷-kyə-lər\ *adj* (1953) **1 :** not nuclear: as **a :** being a weapon whose destructive power is not derived from a nuclear reaction **b :** not operated by, using, or produced by nuclear energy **c :** not using or involving nuclear weapons **2 :** not having nuclear weapons ⟨a ~ country⟩

no–no \ˈnō-ˌnō\ *n, pl* **no–no's** *or* **no–nos** (ca. 1942) **1 :** something unacceptable or forbidden **2 :** NO-HITTER

non·ob·jec·tive \ˌnän-əb-ˈjek-tiv\ *adj* (1905) **1 :** not objective **2 :** representing or intended to represent no natural or actual object, figure, or scene ⟨~ art⟩ — **non·ob·jec·tiv·ism** \-ti-ˌvi-zəm\ *n* — **non·ob·jec·tiv·ist** \-vist\ *n* — **non·ob·jec·tiv·i·ty** \-ˌäb-ˌjek-ˈti-və-tē, -əb-\ *n*

non ob·stan·te \ˌnän-əb-ˈstan-tē, ˌnōn-\ *prep* [ME, fr. ML] (15c) : NOTWITHSTANDING

non–oil \ˈnän-ˈȯi(-ə)l\ *adj* (1970) **1 :** not relating to, containing, or derived from oil **2 :** being a net importer of petroleum or petroleum products ⟨~ nations⟩

no–nonsense *adj* (1855) : tolerating no nonsense : SERIOUS, BUSINESSLIKE ⟨a ~ manager⟩

non·or·gas·mic \ˌnän-ȯr-ˈgaz-mik\ *adj* (1973) : not capable of experiencing orgasm

no·nox·y·nol–9 \nä-ˈnäk-si-ˌnȯl-ˈnīn, nə-, -ˌnōl-\ *n* [*non*yl (the radical C_9H_{19}) + *oxy-* + phe*nol* + *9* (fr. the fact that the compounds it contains have an average of nine ethylene oxide groups per molecule)] (1980) : a spermicide used in contraceptive products

non·para·met·ric \-ˌpa-rə-ˈme-trik\ *adj* (1942) : not involving the estimation of parameters of a statistical function ⟨~ statistical tests⟩

1**non·pa·reil** \ˌnän-pə-ˈrel\ *adj* [ME *nounparalle,* fr. MF *nompareil,* fr. *non-* + *pareil* equal, fr. VL **pariculus,* fr. L *par* equal] (15c) : having no equal

2**nonpareil** *n* (1593) **1 :** an individual of unequaled excellence : PARAGON **2 a :** a small flat disk of chocolate covered with white sugar pellets **b :** sugar in small pellets of various colors

non·par·ti·san \ˈnän-ˈpär-tə-zən, -sən\ *adj* (1885) : not partisan; *esp* : free from party affiliation, bias, or designation ⟨~ ballot⟩ ⟨a ~ board⟩ — **non·par·ti·san·ship** \-ˌship\ *n*

non·pas·ser·ine \-ˈpa-sə-ˌrīn\ *adj* (ca. 1909) : not passerine; *esp* : of, relating to, or being any of various arboreal birds (as pigeons, woodpeckers, hummingbirds, and kingfishers) that are not passerines

non·patho·gen·ic \ˌnän-ˌpa-thə-ˈje-nik\ *adj* (1884) : not capable of inducing disease — compare AVIRULENT

non·peak \ˈnän-ˈpēk\ *adj* (ca. 1914) : OFF-PEAK

non·per·form·ing \ˌnän-pə(r)-ˈfȯr-miŋ\ *adj* (1979) : not producing the expected return ⟨~ loans⟩ ⟨~ assets⟩

non·per·sis·tent \-pər-ˈsis-tənt, -ˈzis-\ *adj* (1900) : not persistent: as **a :** decomposed rapidly by environmental action ⟨~ insecticides⟩ **b :** capable of being transmitted by a vector for only a relatively short time ⟨~ viruses⟩

non·per·son \ˈnän-ˈpər-sᵊn\ *n* (ca. 1909) : a person who is regarded as nonexistent: as **a :** UNPERSON **b :** one having no social or legal status

non pla·cet \ˈnän-ˈplā-sət, ˈnōn-\ *n* [L, it does not please] (1589) : a negative vote

1**non·plus** \ˌnän-ˈpləs\ *n* [L *non plus* no more] (1582) : a state of bafflement or perplexity : QUANDARY

2**nonplus** *vt* **-plussed** *also* **-plused** \-ˈpləst\; **-plus·sing** *also* **-plus·ing** \-ˈplə-siŋ\ (1591) : to cause to be at a loss as to what to say, think, or do : PERPLEX ***syn*** see PUZZLE

non·point \ˈnän-ˈpȯint\ *adj* (1977) : being a source of pollution (as runoff from farmland) that is not a point source; *also* : being pollution or a pollutant that does not arise from a single indentifiable source

non·po·lar \ˌnän-ˈpō-lər\ *adj* (1892) : not polar; *esp* : consisting of molecules not having a dipole ⟨a ~ solvent⟩

non pos·su·mus \ˈnän-ˈpä-sə-məs, ˈnōn-\ *n* [L, we cannot] (1883) : a statement expressing inability to do something

non·pre·scrip·tion \ˌnän-pri-ˈskrip-shən\ *adj* (1958) : capable of being bought without a doctor's prescription ⟨~ drugs⟩

non·pro·duc·tive \-prə-ˈdək-tiv\ *adj* (1868) : not productive: as **a :** failing to produce or yield : UNPRODUCTIVE ⟨a ~ oil well⟩ **b :** not directly concerned with production ⟨the ~ labor of clerks and inspectors⟩ **c** *of a cough* : DRY 3a — **non·pro·duc·tive·ness** *n*

non·prof·it \ˈnän-ˈprä-fət\ *adj* (1896) : not conducted or maintained for the purpose of making a profit ⟨a ~ organization⟩ — **nonprofit** *n*

non·pro·lif·er·a·tion \ˌnän-prə-ˌli-fə-ˈrā-shən\ *adj* (1964) : providing for the stoppage of proliferation (as of nuclear arms) ⟨~ treaty⟩ — **nonproliferation** *n*

non·pros \ˈnän-ˈpräs\ *vt* **non·prossed; non·pros·sing** [*non pros*equitur] (1755) : to enter a non prosequitur against

non pro·se·qui·tur \ˌnän-prə-ˈse-kwə-tər, ˌnōn-\ *n* [LL, he does not prosecute] (1768) : a judgment entered against a plaintiff for failure to appear to prosecute a suit

non·pro·tein \ˈnän-ˈprō-ˌtēn, -ˈprō-tē-ən\ *adj* (1926) : not being or derived from protein ⟨the ~ part of an enzyme⟩ ⟨~ nitrogen⟩

non·read·er \-ˈrē-dər\ *n* (1924) **1 :** one who does not or cannot read **2 :** a child who is slow in learning to read — **non·read·ing** \-diŋ\ *adj*

non·re·com·bi·nant \ˌnän-(ˌ)rē-ˈkäm-bə-nənt\ *adj* (1962) : not exhibiting the results of genetic recombination — **nonrecombinant** *n*

non·re·course \ˈnän-ˈrē-ˌkȯrs, -ri-ˈ\ *adj* (1926) : being or based on an agreement in which the lender has no right of recourse to the borrower's assets beyond stated limits ⟨a ~ note⟩ ⟨a ~ loan⟩

non·re·cur·rent \ˌnän-ri-ˈkər-ənt, -ˈkə-rənt\ *adj* (ca. 1864) : not recurring

non·re·cur·ring \-ri-ˈkər-iŋ, -ˈkə-riŋ\ *adj* (ca. 1864) : NONRECURRENT; *specif* : unlikely to happen again — used of financial transactions that affect a profit and loss statement abnormally

non·re·fund·able \-ri-ˈfən-də-bəl\ *adj* (1963) : not subject to refunding or being refunded ⟨a ~ bond⟩ ⟨a ~ fee⟩

non·rel·a·tiv·is·tic \-ˌre-lə-ti-ˈvis-tik\ *adj* (1930) **1 :** not based on or involving the theory of relativity ⟨~ equations⟩ ⟨~ kinematics⟩ **2 :** of, relating to, or being a body moving at less than a relativistic velocity — **non·rel·a·tiv·is·ti·cal·ly** \-ˈvis-ti-k(ə-)lē\ *adv*

non·rep·re·sen·ta·tion·al \-ˌre-pri-ˌzen-ˈtā-shnəl, -zən-, -shə-nᵊl\ *adj* (1923) : NONOBJECTIVE 2 ⟨a ~ sculpture⟩ — **non·rep·re·sen·ta·tion·al·ism** \-shnə-ˌli-zəm, -shə-nᵊl-ˌi-zəm\ *n*

non·res·i·dence \ˈnän-ˈre-zə-dən(t)s, -ˈrez-dən(t)s, -ˌden(t)s\ *n* (1585) : the state or fact of being nonresident

non·res·i·den·cy \-ˈre-zə-dən(t)-sē, -ˈrez-dən(t)-, -ˌden(t)-\ *n* (1584) : NONRESIDENCE

non·res·i·dent \-ˈre-zə-dənt, -ˈrez-dənt, -ˌdent\ *adj* (1540) : not residing in a particular place — **nonresident** *n*

non·re·sis·tance \ˌnän-ri-ˈzis-tən(t)s\ *n* (1643) : the principles or practice of passive submission to constituted authority even when unjust or oppressive; *also* : the principle or practice of not resisting violence by force

non·re·sis·tant \-tənt\ *adj* (1702) : not resistant; *specif* : susceptible to the effects of a deleterious agent (as an insecticide, a pathogen, or an extreme environmental condition) — **nonresistant** *n*

non·re·stric·tive \-ri-ˈstrik-tiv\ *adj* (1916) : not restrictive; *specif* : not limiting the reference of a modified word or phrase

nonrestrictive clause *n* (1916) : a descriptive clause that is not essential to the definiteness of the meaning of the word it modifies (as *who is retired* in "my father, who is retired, does volunteer work")

non·re·turn·able \-ri-ˈtər-nə-bəl\ *adj* (1903) : not returnable; *specif* : not returnable to a dealer in exchange for a deposit ⟨~ bottles⟩ — **nonreturnable** *n*

non·sched·uled \-ˈske-(ˌ)jüld, -jəld\ *adj* (1947) : licensed to transport by air without a regular schedule ⟨~ airlines⟩

[1]non·sci·ence \-ˈsī-ən(t)s\ *n* (1855) : something (as a discipline) that is not a science

[2]nonscience *adj* (1944) : of or relating to fields other than science

non·se·cre·tor \ˌnän-si-ˈkrē-tər\ *n* (1944) : an individual of blood group A, B, or AB who does not secrete the antigens characteristic of these blood groups in bodily fluids (as saliva)

non·sec·tar·i·an \-(ˌ)sek-ˈter-ē-ən\ *adj* (1831) : not having a sectarian character : not affiliated with or restricted to a particular religious group

non·self \ˈnän-ˈself, *Southern also* -ˈsef\ *n* (1874) : material that is foreign to the body of an organism

[1]non·sense \ˈnän-ˌsen(t)s, ˈnän(t)-sən(t)s\ *n* (1614) **1 a** : words or language having no meaning or conveying no intelligible ideas **b** (1) : language, conduct, or an idea that is absurd or contrary to good sense (2) : an instance of absurd action **2 a** : things of no importance or value : TRIFLES **b** : affected or impudent conduct ⟨took no ~ from subordinates⟩ **3** : genetic information consisting of one or more codons that do not code for any amino acid and usu. cause termination of the molecular chain in protein synthesis — **non·sen·si·cal** \ˌnän-ˈsen(t)-si-kəl\ *adj* — **non·sen·si·cal·ly** \-k(ə-)lē\ *adv* — **non·sen·si·cal·ness** \-kəl-nəs\ *n*

[2]nonsense *adj* (1799) **1** : consisting of an arbitrary grouping of speech sounds or symbols ⟨\ˈshrȯg-ˌthī-əmpth\ is a ~ word⟩ ⟨a ~ syllable⟩ **2** : consisting of one or more codons that are genetic nonsense — compare ANTISENSE, MISSENSE

nonsense verse *n* (1799) : humorous or whimsical verse that features absurd characters and actions and often contains evocative but meaningless nonce words

non se·qui·tur \ˈnän-ˈse-kwə-tər *also* -ˌtu̇r\ *n* [L, it does not follow] (1540) **1** : an inference that does not follow from the premises; *specif* : a fallacy resulting from a simple conversion of a universal affirmative proposition or from the transposition of a condition and its consequent **2** : a statement (as a response) that does not follow logically from or is not clearly related to anything previously said

non·sig·nif·i·cant \ˌnän-sig-ˈni-fi-kənt\ *adj* (1902) : not significant: as **a** : INSIGNIFICANT **b** : MEANINGLESS **c** : having or yielding a value lying within limits between which variation is attributed to chance ⟨a ~ statistical test⟩ — **non·sig·nif·i·cant·ly** *adv*

non·skid \-ˈskid\ *adj* (1904) : designed or equipped to prevent skidding

non·slip \-ˈslip\ *adj* (1903) : designed to reduce or prevent slipping

non·so·cial \-ˈsō-shəl\ *adj* (1902) : not socially oriented : lacking a social component

non·sport·ing \-ˈspȯr-tiŋ\ *adj* (1894) : lacking the qualities characteristic of a hunting dog

non·stan·dard \-ˈstan-dərd\ *adj* (1923) **1** : not standard **2** : not conforming in pronunciation, grammatical construction, idiom, or word choice to the usage generally characteristic of educated native speakers of a language — compare SUBSTANDARD

non·start·er \-ˈstär-tər\ *n* (1902) **1** : one that does not start **2** : someone or something that is not productive or effective ⟨his son has been, in politics a ~ —Anthony Lejeune⟩

non·ste·roi·dal \ˌnän-stə-ˈrȯi-dᵊl\ *also* **non·ste·roid** \ˈnän-ˈstir-ˌȯid, -ˈster-\ *adj* (1964) : of, relating to, or being a compound and esp. a drug that is not a steroid ⟨a ~ painkiller⟩ — **nonsteroid** *n*

non·stick \ˈnän-ˈstik\ *adj* [[3]*stick*] (1958) **1** : allowing easy removal of cooked food particles ⟨a ~ coating in a frying pan⟩ **2** : having a nonstick surface ⟨a ~ frying pan⟩

[1]non·stop \ˈnän-ˈstäp\ *adj* (1902) : done, made, or held without a stop : not easing or letting up — **nonstop** *adv*

[2]nonstop *n* (1975) : a nonstop airplane flight

non·suit \ˈnän-ˈsüt\ *n* [ME, fr. AF *nounsuyte,* fr. *noun-* non- + *siute* pursuit, legal suit — more at SUIT] (14c) : a judgment against a plaintiff for failure to prosecute a case or inability to establish a prima facie case — **nonsuit** *vt*

non·sup·port \ˌnän-sə-ˈpȯrt\ *n* (1909) : failure to support; *specif* : failure (as of a parent) to honor a statutory or contractual obligation to provide maintenance

non·sys·tem \ˈnän-ˈsis-təm\ *n* (1964) : a system that lacks effective organization

non·tar·get \-ˈtär-gət\ *adj* (1945) : not being the intended object of action by a particular agent ⟨effect of insecticides on ~ organisms⟩

non·ter·mi·nat·ing \-ˈtər-mə-ˌnā-tiŋ\ *adj* (ca. 1908) : not terminating or ending; *esp* : being a decimal for which there is no place to the right of the decimal point such that all places farther to the right contain the entry 0 ⟨1/3 gives the ~ decimal .33333 . . . ⟩

non·ther·mal \-ˈthər-məl\ *adj* (ca. 1964) : not produced by heat; *specif* : of, relating to, or being radiation having a spectrum that is not the spectrum of a blackbody

non·threat·en·ing \-ˈthret-niŋ, -ˈthre-tᵊn-iŋ\ *adj* (1963) **1** : not constituting a threat ⟨a ~ illness⟩ **2** : not likely to cause anxiety ⟨a ~ environment⟩; *also* : INNOCUOUS 2

non·ti·tle \-ˈtī-tᵊl\ *adj* (1968) : of, relating to, or being an athletic contest in which a title is not at stake

non trop·po \ˈnän-ˈtrō-(ˌ)pō, ˈnōn-\ *adv or adj* [It, lit., not too much] (ca. 1854) : without excess — used to qualify a direction in music

non–U \ˈnän-ˈyü\ *adj* (1954) : not characteristic of the upper classes

non·union \-ˈyün-yən\ *adj* (1863) **1** : not belonging to or connected with a trade union ⟨~ carpenters⟩ **2** : not recognizing or favoring trade unions or their members **3** : not produced or worked on by members of a trade union ⟨~ lettuce⟩

non·use \ˈnän-ˈyüs\ *n* (1542) **1** : failure to use ⟨~ of available material⟩ **2** : the fact or condition of not being used

non·us·er \-ˈyü-zər\ *n* (1646) : one who does not make use of something (as an available public facility or a harmful drug)

non·van·ish·ing \-ˈva-ni-shiŋ\ *adj* (1907) : not zero or becoming zero

non·vec·tor \-ˈvek-tər\ *n* (1956) : an organism (as an insect) that does not transmit a particular pathogen (as a virus)

non·ver·bal \-ˈvər-bəl\ *adj* (1924) : not verbal: as **a** : being other than verbal ⟨~ factors⟩ **b** : involving minimal use of language ⟨~ tests⟩ **c** : ranking low in verbal skill ⟨a ~ child⟩ — **non·ver·bal·ly** \-bə-lē\ *adv*

non·vin·tage \-ˈvin-tij\ *adj* (1924) : undated and usu. blended to approximate a standard ⟨a ~ wine⟩

non·vi·o·lence \-ˈvī-ə-lən(t)s\ *n* (1920) **1** : abstention from violence as a matter of principle; *also* : the principle of such abstention **2 a** : the quality or state of being nonviolent : avoidance of violence **b** : nonviolent demonstrations for the purpose of securing political ends

non·vi·o·lent \-lənt\ *adj* (1920) : abstaining or free from violence — **non·vi·o·lent·ly** *adv*

non·vol·a·tile \-ˈvä-lə-tᵊl\ *adj* (1866) : not volatile: as **a** : not vaporizing readily ⟨a ~ solvent⟩ **b** *of a computer memory* : retaining data when power is shut off

non–West·ern \-ˈwes-tərn\ *adj* (1902) **1** : not being part of the western tradition ⟨~ countries⟩ **2** : of or relating to non-Western societies ⟨~ values⟩

non·white \-ˈhwīt, -ˈwīt\ *n* (1927) : a person whose features and esp. whose skin color are distinctively different from those of peoples of northwestern Europe; *esp* : one who has black African ancestors — **nonwhite** *adj*

non·word \-ˈwərd\ *n* (1961) : a word that has no meaning, is not known to exist, or is disapproved

non·wo·ven \-ˈwō-vən\ *adj* (1945) **1** : made of fibers held together by interlocking or bonding (as by chemical or thermal means) : not woven, knitted, or felted ⟨~ fabric⟩ **2** : made of nonwoven fabric ⟨a ~ dress⟩ — **nonwoven** *n*

non·ze·ro \-ˈzir-(ˌ)ō\ *adj* (1905) **1** : being, having, or involving a value other than zero **2** : having phonetic content ⟨~ affixes⟩

[1]noo·dle \ˈnü-dᵊl\ *n* [perh. alter. of *noddle*] (1753) **1** : a stupid person : SIMPLETON **2** : HEAD, NOGGIN

[2]noodle *n* [G *Nudel*] (1779) : a food paste made usu. with egg and shaped typically in ribbon form

[3]noodle *vi* **noo·dled; noo·dling** \ˈnüd-liŋ, ˈnü-dᵊl-iŋ\ [imit.] (ca. 1937) : to improvise on an instrument in an informal or desultory manner

noog·ie \ˈnu̇-gē\ *n* [origin unknown] (1972) : the act of rubbing one's knuckles on a person's head so as to produce a mildly painful sensation

nook \ˈnu̇k\ *n* [ME *noke, nok*] (14c) **1** *chiefly Scot* : a right-angled corner **2 a** : an interior angle formed by two meeting walls **b** : a secluded or sheltered place or part ⟨searched every ~ and cranny⟩ **c** : a small often recessed section of a larger room ⟨a breakfast ~⟩

nooky *or* **nook·ie** \ˈnu̇-kē\ *n* [perh. fr. *nook* + [4]-*y*] (1928) **1** *often vulgar* : the female partner in sexual intercourse **2** *often vulgar* : SEXUAL INTERCOURSE

noon \ˈnün\ *n* [ME, fr. OE *nōn* ninth hour from sunrise, fr. L *nona,* fr. fem. of *nonus* ninth; akin to L *novem* nine — more at NINE] (13c) **1** : MIDDAY; *specif* : 12 o'clock at midday **2** *archaic* : MIDNIGHT — used chiefly in the phrase *noon of night* **3** : the highest point

noon·day \-ˌdā\ *n* (1535) : MIDDAY

no one *pron* (bef. 12c) : no person : NOBODY

noon·ing \ˈnü-niŋ, -nən\ *n* (ca. 1652) **1** *chiefly dial* : a meal eaten at noon **2** *chiefly dial* : a period at noon for eating or resting

noon·tide \ˈnün-ˌtīd\ *n* (12c) **1** : NOONTIME **2** : the culminating point

noon·time \-ˌtīm\ *n* (14c) : the time of noon : MIDDAY

[1]noose \ˈnüs, *Brit also* ˈnüz\ *n* [ME *nose*] (15c) **1** : a loop with a slipknot that binds closer the more it is drawn **2** : something that snares like a noose

[2]noose *vt* **noosed; noos·ing** (1600) **1** : to secure by a noose **2** : to make a noose in or of

noo·sphere \ˈnō-ə-ˌsfir\ *n* [ISV *noo-* mind (fr. Gk *noos, nous*) + *sphere* sphere] (1945) : the sphere of human consciousness and mental activity esp. in regard to its influence on the biosphere and in relation to evolution

Noot·ka \ˈnu̇t-kə\ *n, pl* **Nootka** *or* **Nootkas** [*Nootka* Sound, Vancouver Island] (1796) **1** : a member of a group of American Indian peoples inhabiting the west coast of Vancouver Island **2** : the Wakashan language of the Nootka people

no·ot·ro·pic \ˌnō-ə-ˈtrō-pik\ *n* [ISV *noo-* + *-tropic*] (1976) : a substance that enhances cognition and memory and facilitates learning — **nootropic** *adj*

no·pal \nō-ˈpäl, -ˈpal; ˈnō-pəl\ *n, pl* **nopals** *or* **no·pal·es** \nō-ˈpä-lās, -ˈpa-\ [Sp, fr. Nahuatl *nohpalli*] (1730) **1** : any of a genus (*Nopalea*) of cacti of Mexico and Central America that differ from the prickly pears in having erect petals and scarlet flowers with the stamens much longer than the petals; *broadly* : PRICKLY PEAR **2** : a fleshy young tender stem segment of the prickly pear cactus (esp. *Opuntia ficus-indica*) or the nopal cactus used as food

no·pa·li·to \nō-pä-ˈlē-tō\ *n* [MexSp, fr. dim. of *nopal*] (1902) : NOPAL 2

no–par *or* **no–par–value** *adj* (1922) : having no nominal value ⟨~ stocks⟩

nope \ˈnōp, *or with glottal stop instead of* p\ *adv* [by alter.] (1888) : NO

[1]nor \nər, ˈnȯr, *Southern also* ˈnär\ *conj* [ME, contr. of *nother* neither, nor, fr. *nother,* pron. & adj., neither — more at NEITHER] (14c) **1** — used as a function word to introduce the second or last member or the second and each following member of a series of items each of which is negated ⟨neither here ~ there⟩ ⟨not done by you ~ me ~ anyone⟩

\ə\ **abut** \ᵊ\ **kitten**, F table \ər\ **further** \a\ **ash** \ā\ **ace** \ä\ **mop, mar** \au̇\ **out** \ch\ **chin** \e\ **bet** \ē\ **easy** \g\ **go** \i\ **hit** \ī\ **ice** \j\ **job** \ŋ\ **sing** \ō\ **go** \ȯ\ **law** \ȯi\ **boy** \th\ **thin** \t͟h\ **the** \ü\ **loot** \u̇\ **foot** \y\ **yet** \zh\ **vision, beige** \k̲, ⁿ, œ, ue, ʸ\ *see* Guide to Pronunciation

2 — used as a function word to introduce and negate a following clause or phrase **3** *chiefly Brit* : NEITHER ***usage*** see [1]NEITHER

[2]**nor** *conj* [ME, perh. fr. [1]*nor*] (15c) *dial* : THAN

nor- *comb form* [*nor*mal] : homologue containing one less methyl group ⟨*nor*epinephrine⟩

NOR \ˈnȯr\ *n* [*not OR*] (1957) : a computer logic circuit that produces an output that is the inverse of that of an OR circuit

NORAD *abbr* North American Air Defense Command

nor·adren·a·line *also* **nor·adren·a·lin** \ˌnȯr-ə-ˈdre-nᵊl-ən\ *n* (1932) : NOREPINEPHRINE

nor·ad·ren·er·gic \ˌnȯr-ˌa-drə-ˈnər-jik\ *adj* [*noradren*aline + *-ergic*] (1963) : liberating, activated by, or involving norepinephrine in the transmission of nerve impulses ⟨~ nerve endings⟩ ⟨~ nerve fibers⟩

[1]**Nor·dic** \ˈnȯr-dik\ *adj* [F *nordique,* fr. *nord* north, fr. OF *north,* fr. OE] (1898) **1** : of or relating to the Germanic peoples of northern Europe and esp. of Scandinavia **2** : of or relating to a group or physical type of the Caucasian race characterized by tall stature, long head, light skin and hair, and blue eyes **3 a** : of or relating to competitive ski events involving cross-country racing, ski jumping, or biathlon — compare ALPINE **b** : of, relating to, or being cross-country skiing

[2]**Nordic** *n* (1901) **1** : a native of northern Europe **2** : a person of Nordic physical type **3** : a member of the peoples of Scandinavia

nor'easter *var of* NORTHEASTER 2

nor·epi·neph·rine \ˈnȯr-ˌe-pə-ˈne-frən\ *n* (1945) : a monoamine $C_8H_{11}NO_3$ that is a neurotransmitter in postganglionic neurons of the sympathetic nervous system and in some parts of the central nervous system, is a vasopressor hormone of the adrenal medulla, and is a precursor of epinephrine in its major biosynthetic pathway

nor·eth·in·drone \ˌnȯr-ˈe-thən-ˌdrōn\ *n* [*nor-* + *ethin*yl + hy*dr-* + *-one* (as in *progesterone*)] (1958) : a synthetic progestational hormone $C_{20}H_{26}O_2$ used in birth control pills often in the form of its acetate

Nor·folk Island pine \ˈnȯr-fək-, -ˌfȯk-\ *n* (1803) : an evergreen tree (*Araucaria heterophylla* syn. *A. excelsa*) of the araucaria family that is native to Australia and Norfolk Island and that is often grown as a houseplant — called also *Norfolk pine*

Norfolk jacket *n* [*Norfolk,* England] (1866) : a loose-fitting belted single-breasted jacket with box pleats

Norfolk terrier *n* (1964) : any of a breed of dogs developed in England and resembling the Norwich terrier but having folded-over ears

no·ri \ˈnō-rē, ˈnȯr-ē\ *n* [Jp] (1892) : dried laver seaweed pressed into thin sheets and used esp. as a seasoning or as a wrapper for sushi

nor·land \ˈnȯr-lənd\ *n* (ca. 1578) *chiefly dial* : NORTHLAND

norm \ˈnȯrm\ *n* [L *norma,* lit., carpenter's square] (1674) **1** : an authoritative standard : MODEL **2** : a principle of right action binding upon the members of a group and serving to guide, control, or regulate proper and acceptable behavior **3** : AVERAGE: as **a** : a set standard of development or achievement usu. derived from the average or median achievement of a large group **b** : a pattern or trait taken to be typical in the behavior of a social group **c** : a widespread or usual practice, procedure, or custom ⟨standing ovations became the ~⟩ **4 a** : a real-valued nonnegative function defined on a vector space with value analogous to length and satisfying the conditions that the function is zero if and only if the vector is zero, the function of the product of a scalar and a vector is equal to the product of the absolute value of the scalar and the function of the vector, and the function of the sum of two vectors is less than or equal to the sum of the functions of the two vectors; *specif* : the square root of the sum of the squares of the absolute values of the elements of a matrix or of the components of a vector **b** : the greatest distance between two successive points of a set of points that partition an interval into smaller intervals ***syn*** see AVERAGE

[1]**nor·mal** \ˈnȯr-məl\ *adj* [L *normalis,* fr. *norma*] (ca. 1696) **1** : PERPENDICULAR; *esp* : perpendicular to a tangent at a point of tangency **2 a** : according with, constituting, or not deviating from a norm, rule, or principle **b** : conforming to a type, standard, or regular pattern **3** : occurring naturally ⟨~ immunity⟩ **4 a** : of, relating to, or characterized by average intelligence or development **b** : free from mental disorder : SANE **5 a** *of a solution* : having a concentration of one gram equivalent of solute per liter **b** : containing neither basic hydroxyl nor acid hydrogen ⟨~ silver phosphate⟩ **c** : not associated ⟨~ molecules⟩ **d** : having a straight-chain structure ⟨~ butyl alcohol⟩ **6** *of a subgroup* : having the property that every coset produced by operating on the left by a given element is equal to the coset produced by operating on the right by the same element **7** : relating to, involving, or being a normal curve or normal distribution ⟨~ approximation to the binomial distribution⟩ **8** *of a matrix* : having the property of commutativity under multiplication by the transpose of the matrix each of whose elements is a conjugate complex number with respect to the corresponding element of the given matrix ***syn*** see REGULAR — **nor·mal·i·ty** \nȯr-ˈma-lə-tē\ *n* — **nor·mal·ly** \ˈnȯr-mə-lē\ *adv*

[2]**normal** *n* (ca. 1738) **1 a** : a normal line **b** : the portion of a normal line to a plane curve between the curve and the x-axis **2** : one that is normal **3** : a form or state regarded as the norm : STANDARD

normal curve *n* (1894) : the symmetrical bell-shaped curve of a normal distribution

nor·mal·cy \ˈnȯr-məl-sē\ *n* (1857) : the state or fact of being normal

normal distribution *n* (1897) : a probability density function that approximates the distribution of many random variables (as the proportion of outcomes of a particular sort in a large number of independent repetitions of an experiment in which the probabilities remain constant from trial to trial) and that has the form

$$f(x)=\frac{1}{\sigma\sqrt{2\pi}}\,e^{-\frac{1}{2}\left(\frac{x-\mu}{\sigma}\right)^2}$$

where μ is the mean and σ is the standard deviation — compare NORMAL CURVE

nor·mal·ise *Brit var of* NORMALIZE

nor·mal·ize \ˈnȯr-mə-ˌlīz\ *vt* **-ized; -iz·ing** (1865) **1** : to make conform to or reduce to a norm or standard **2** : to make normal (as by a transformation of variables) **3** : to bring or restore (as relations between countries) to a normal condition — **nor·mal·iz·able** \-ˌlī-zə-bəl\ *adj* — **nor·mal·i·za·tion** \ˌnȯr-mə-lə-ˈzā-shən\ *n*

nor·mal·iz·er \ˈnȯr-mə-ˌlī-zər\ *n* (1926) **1** : one that normalizes **2 a** : a subgroup consisting of those elements of a group for which the group operation with regard to a given element is commutative **b** : the set of elements of a group for which the group operation with regard to every element of a given subgroup is commutative

normal school *n* [trans. of F *école normale;* fr. the fact that the first French school so named was intended to serve as a model] (1838) : a usu. 2-year school for training chiefly elementary teachers

Nor·man \ˈnȯr-mən\ *n* [ME, fr. AF *Normant,* fr. ON *Northmann-, Northmathr* Norseman, fr. *northr* north + *mann-, mathr* man; akin to OE *north* north and to OE *man* man] (13c) **1** : a native or inhabitant of Normandy: **a** : one of the Scandinavian conquerors of Normandy in the 10th century **b** : one of the Norman-French conquerors of England in 1066 **2** : NORMAN-FRENCH — **Norman** *adj*

Norman architecture *n* (1797) : a Romanesque style first appearing in and near Normandy about A.D. 950; *also* : architecture resembling or imitating this style

nor·mande \nȯr-ˈmand\ *adj* [F, fr. fem. of *normand* Norman, fr. *Normandy,* France] (1868) : prepared with any of several foods traditionally associated with Normandy (as cream, apples, or cider)

Norman–French *n* (1605) **1** : the French language of the medieval Normans **2** : the modern dialect of Normandy

nor·ma·tive \ˈnȯr-mə-tiv\ *adj* [F *normatif,* fr. *norme* norm, fr. L *norma*] (1878) **1** : of, relating to, or determining norms or standards ⟨~ tests⟩ **2** : conforming to or based on norms ⟨~ behavior⟩ ⟨~ judgments⟩ **3** : prescribing norms ⟨~ rules of ethics⟩ ⟨~ grammar⟩ — **nor·ma·tive·ly** *adv* — **nor·ma·tive·ness** *n*

normed \ˈnȯrmd\ *adj* (1935) : being a mathematical entity upon which a norm is defined ⟨a ~ vector space⟩

nor·mo·ten·sive \ˌnȯr-mō-ˈten(t)-siv\ *adj* [*norm*al + *-o-* + *-tensive* (as in *hypotensive*)] (ca. 1941) : having normal blood pressure — **normotensive** *n*

nor·mo·ther·mia \-ˈthər-mē-ə\ *n* [NL, fr. *norm*alis normal + *-o-* + *-thermia* -thermy] (1898) : normal body temperature — **nor·mo·ther·mic** \-mik\ *adj*

Norn \ˈnȯrn\ *n* [ON] (1846) : any of the three Norse goddesses of fate

nor·o·virus \ˈnȯr-ə-ˌvī-rəs\ *n* [NL, fr. E *Nor*walk virus + NL *-o-* + *virus*] (2002) : any of a genus (*Norovirus* of the family *Caliciviridae*) of small round single-stranded RNA viruses; *specif* : NORWALK VIRUS

[1]**Norse** \ˈnȯrs\ *n, pl* **Norse** [prob. fr. obs. D *noorsch,* adj., Norwegian, Scandinavian, alter. of obs. D *noordsch* northern, fr. D *noord* north; akin to OE *north* north] (ca. 1688) **1 a** : NORWEGIAN 2 **b** : any of the western Scandinavian dialects or languages **c** : the Scandinavian group of Germanic languages **2** *pl* **a** : SCANDINAVIANS **b** : NORWEGIANS

[2]**Norse** *adj* (1768) **1** : of or relating to ancient Scandinavia or the language of its inhabitants **2** : NORWEGIAN

Norse·man \ˈnȯrs-mən\ *n* (1817) : any of the ancient Scandinavians

[1]**north** \ˈnȯrth\ *adv* [ME, fr. OE; akin to OHG *nord* north and perh. to Gk *nerteros* lower, infernal] (bef. 12c) : to, toward, or in the north

[2]**north** *adj* (bef. 12c) **1** : situated toward or at the north ⟨the ~ entrance⟩ **2** : coming from the north ⟨a ~ wind⟩

[3]**north** *n* (13c) **1 a** : the direction of the north terrestrial pole : the direction to the left of one facing east **b** : the compass point directly opposite to south **2** *cap* **a** : regions or countries lying to the north of a specified or implied point of orientation **b** : the industrially and economically developed nations of the world — compare SOUTH 5 **3** *often cap* **a** : the one of four positions at 90-degree intervals that lies to the north or at the top of a diagram **b** : a person occupying this position in the course of a specified activity (as the game of bridge)

Northants *abbr* Northamptonshire

north·bound \ˈnȯrth-ˌbau̇nd\ *adj* (1877) : traveling or headed north

north by east (1720) : a compass point that is one point east of due north : N11°15′E

north by west (1698) : a compass point that is one point west of due north : N11°15′W

[1]**north·east** \nȯrth-ˈēst, *naut* nȯr-ˈēst\ *adv* (bef. 12c) : to, toward, or in the northeast

[2]**northeast** *adj* (bef. 12c) **1** : coming from the northeast ⟨a ~ wind⟩ **2** : situated toward or at the northeast ⟨the ~ corner⟩

[3]**northeast** *n* (12c) **1 a** : the general direction between north and east **b** : the point midway between the north and east compass points **2** *cap* : regions or countries lying to the northeast of a specified or implied point of orientation

northeast by east (ca. 1771) : a compass point that is one point east of due northeast : N56°15′E

northeast by north (1725) : a compass point that is one point north of due northeast : N33°45′E

north·east·er \nȯrth-ˈē-stər, nȯr-ˈē-\ *n* (1774) **1** : a strong northeast wind **2** *or* **nor'·east·er** \nȯr-ˈē-\ : a storm with northeast winds

north·east·er·ly \nȯrth-ˈē-stər-lē\ *adv or adj* (1739) **1** : from the northeast **2** : toward the northeast

north·east·ern \-stərn\ *adj* (14c) **1** *often cap* : of, relating to, or characteristic of a region conventionally designated Northeast **2** : lying toward or coming from the northeast — **north·east·ern·most** \-stərn-ˌmōst\ *adj*

North·east·ern·er \-stə(r)-nər\ *n* (1860) : a native or inhabitant of a northeastern region (as of the U.S.)

[1]**north·east·ward** \nȯrth-ˈēs-twərd, nȯr-ˈēs-\ *adv or adj* (1553) : toward the northeast — **north·east·wards** \-twərdz\ *adv*

[2]**northeastward** *n* (1581) : NORTHEAST

north·er \ˈnȯr-t͟hər\ *n* (1820) **1** : a strong north wind **2** : a storm with north winds

[1]**north·er·ly** \-lē\ *adj or adv* [[3]*north* + *-erly* (as in *easterly*)] (1551) **1** : situated toward or belonging to the north ⟨the ~ border⟩ **2** : coming from the north ⟨a ~ wind⟩

[2]**northerly** *n, pl* **-lies** (1955) : a wind from the north

[1]**north·ern** \ˈnȯr-t͟hə(r)n\ *adj* [ME *northerne,* fr. OE; akin to OHG *nordrōni* northern, OE *north* north] (bef. 12c) **1** *cap* **a** : of, relating to, or characteristic of a region conventionally designated North **b** : of, relating to, or constituting the northern dialect **2 a** : lying toward the north **b** : coming from the north ⟨a ~ storm⟩ — **north·ern·most** \-ˌmōst\ *adj*

[2]**northern** *n* (1950) **1** *cap* : the dialect of English spoken in the part of the U.S. north of a line running northwest through central New Jersey, below the northern tier of counties in Pennsylvania, through northern

Ohio, Indiana, and Illinois, across central Iowa, and through the northwest corner of So. Dakota **2 :** 3PIKE 1a

northern corn rootworm *n* (1952) **:** a corn rootworm (*Diabrotica barberi* syn. *D. longicornis*) often destructive to Indian corn in the northern parts of the central and eastern U.S.

Northern Cross *n* (ca. 1909) **:** a cross formed by six stars in Cygnus

North•ern•er \ˈnȯr-t͟hə(r)-nər\ *n* (1599) **:** a native or inhabitant of the North; *esp* **:** a native or resident of the northern part of the U.S.

northern harrier *n* (1980) **:** a widely distributed brown or grayish hawk (*Circus cyaneus*) that inhabits open and marshy regions and has a conspicuous white patch on the rump — called also *marsh hawk*

northern hemisphere *n, often cap N&H* (ca. 1699) **:** the half of the earth that lies north of the equator

northern lights *n pl* (14c) **:** AURORA BOREALIS

northern oriole *n* (1957) **:** an American oriole (*Icterus galbula*) that includes the Baltimore oriole and the Bullock's oriole when they are considered subspecies rather than separate species

northern pike *n* (1856) **:** 3PIKE 1a

northern spotted owl *n* (1899) **:** a rare spotted owl (*Strix occidentalis caurina*) of old forests on the Pacific coast of No. America from northern California to southern British Columbia

northern white cedar *n* (1910) **:** an arborvitae (*Thuja occidentalis*) of eastern No. America that has branchlets in horizontal planes; *also* **:** its wood — called also *white cedar*

North Germanic *n* (ca. 1930) **:** a subdivision of the Germanic languages including Icelandic, Norwegian, Swedish, and Danish — see INDO-EUROPEAN LANGUAGES table

north•ing \ˈnȯr-thiŋ, -t͟hiŋ\ *n* (1669) **1 :** difference in latitude to the north from the last preceding point of reckoning **2 :** northerly progress

north•land \ˈnȯrth-ˌland, -lənd\ *n, often cap* (bef. 12c) **:** land in the north **:** the north of a country

North•man \ˈnȯrth-mən\ *n* (bef. 12c) **:** NORSEMAN

north–north•east \ˈnȯrth-ˌnȯrth-ˈēst, -ˌnȯr-ˈēst\ *n* (14c) **:** a compass point that is two points east of due north **:** N22°30′E

north–north•west \ˈnȯrth-ˌnȯr(th)-ˈwest\ *n* (14c) **:** a compass point that is two points west of due north **:** N22°30′W

north pole *n* (14c) **1 a** *often cap N&P* **:** the northernmost point of the earth; *broadly* **:** the corresponding point of a celestial body (as a planet) **b :** the zenith of the heavens as viewed from the north terrestrial pole **2** *of a magnet* **:** the pole that points toward the north when the magnet is freely suspended

north–seeking pole *n* (ca. 1920) **:** NORTH POLE 2

North Star *n* (14c) **:** the star of the northern hemisphere toward which the axis of the earth points — called also *polestar*

1**North•um•bri•an** \nȯr-ˈthəm-brē-ən\ *adj* (1602) **1 :** of, relating to, or characteristic of ancient Northumbria, its people, or its language **2 :** of, relating to, or characteristic of Northumberland, its people, or its language

2**Northumbrian** *n* (1611) **1 :** a native or inhabitant of ancient Northumbria **2 :** a native or inhabitant of Northumberland **3 a :** the Old English dialect of Northumbria **b :** the Modern English dialect of Northumberland

1**north•ward** \ˈnȯrth-wərd\ *adv or adj* (bef. 12c) **:** toward the north — **north•wards** \-wərdz\ *adv*

2**northward** *n* (14c) **:** northward direction or part ⟨sail to the ∼⟩

1**north•west** \nȯrth-ˈwest, *naut* nȯr-ˈwest\ *adv* (bef. 12c) **:** to, toward, or in the northwest

2**northwest** *adj* (bef. 12c) **1 :** coming from the northwest ⟨a ∼ wind⟩ **2 :** situated toward or at the northwest ⟨the ∼ corner⟩

3**northwest** *n* (12c) **1 a :** the general direction between north and west **b :** the point midway between the north and west compass points **2** *cap* **:** regions or countries lying to the northwest of a specified or implied point of orientation

northwest by north (ca. 1771) **:** a compass point that is one point north of due northwest **:** N33°45′W

northwest by west (1725) **:** a compass point that is one point west of due northwest **:** N56°15′W

north•west•er \nȯr(th)-ˈwes-tər\ *n* (1737) **:** a strong northwest wind

north•west•er•ly \-lē\ *adv or adj* (ca. 1611) **1 :** from the northwest **2 :** toward the northwest

north•west•ern \-ˈwes-tərn\ *adj* (1612) **1** *often cap* **:** of, relating to, or characteristic of a region conventionally designated Northwest **2 :** lying toward or coming from the northwest — **north•west•ern•most** \-ˌmōst\ *adj*

North•west•ern•er \-ˈwes-tə(r)-nər\ *n* (1855) **:** a native or inhabitant of the Northwest and esp. of the northwestern part of the U.S.

1**north•west•ward** \-ˈwes-twərd\ *adv or adj* (14c) **:** toward the northwest — **north•west•wards** \-twərdz\ *adv*

2**northwestward** *n* (1765) **:** NORTHWEST

nor•trip•ty•line \nȯr-ˈtrip-tə-ˌlēn\ *n* [*nor-* + *-tript-* (perh. fr. *tri*cyclic + he*pt*a-) + *-yl* + 2*-ine*] (1962) **:** a tricyclic antidepressant $C_{19}H_{21}N$ used in the form of its hydrochloride

Nor•walk virus \ˈnȯr-ˌwȯk-\ *n* [*Norwalk*, Ohio, site of an outbreak of the virus in 1968] (1983) **:** a highly infectious norovirus (species *Norwalk* virus) that causes acute gastroenteritis in humans

Nor•way lobster \ˈnȯr-ˌwā-\ *n* (ca. 1909) **:** LANGOUSTINE

Norway maple *n* (1797) **:** a Eurasian maple (*Acer platanoides*) with dark green or often reddish or red veined leaves that is much planted for shade in the U.S.

Norway rat *n* (1759) **:** BROWN RAT

Norway spruce *n* (1797) **:** a widely cultivated spruce (*Picea abies*) of northern Europe that has a pyramidal shape, spreading branches and pendulous branchlets, dark foliage, and long pendulous cones

Nor•we•gian \nȯr-ˈwē-jən\ *n* [ML *Norwegia* Norway] (1605) **1 a :** a native or inhabitant of Norway **b :** a person of Norwegian descent **2 :** the Germanic language of the Norwegian people — **Norwegian** *adj*

Norwegian elkhound *n* (1930) **:** any of a Norwegian breed of hardy short-bodied medium-sized dogs with erect ears and a very heavy coat of gray hairs with black tips

Nor•wich terrier \ˈnȯr-(ˌ)wich-, *Brit* ˈnär-ich- *or* ˈnär-ij-\ *n* [*Norwich*, England] (1931) **:** any of an English breed of small active low-set terriers that have a long straight wiry coat and erect ears

nos *abbr* numbers

NOS *abbr* not otherwise specified

1**nose** \ˈnōz\ *n* [ME, fr. OE *nosu;* akin to OHG *nasa* nose, L *nasus*] (bef. 12c) **1 a :** the part of the face that bears the nostrils and covers the anterior part of the nasal cavity; *broadly* **:** this part together with the nasal cavity **b :** the anterior part of the head at the top or end of the muzzle **:** SNOUT, PROBOSCIS **2 a :** the sense of smell **:** OLFACTION **b :** AROMA, BOUQUET **3 :** the vertebrate olfactory organ **4 a :** the forward end or projection of something **b :** the projecting or working end of a tool **5 :** the stem of a boat or its protective metal covering **6 a :** the nose as a symbol of prying or meddling curiosity or interference **b :** a knack for discovery or understanding ⟨a keen ∼ for absurdity⟩ — **on the nose 1 a :** at or to a target point ⟨the bombs landed right *on the nose*⟩ **b (1) :** on target **:** ACCURATE **(2) :** ACCURATELY **2 :** to win — used of horse or dog racing bets — **under one's nose :** extremely near to one ⟨the answer was right *under our noses*⟩; *also* **:** brazenly in or as if in one's presence ⟨embezzling funds right *under his nose*⟩

2**nose** *vb* **nosed; nos•ing** *vt* (ca. 1587) **1 :** to detect by or as if by smell **:** SCENT **2 a :** to push or move with the nose **b :** to move (as a vehicle) ahead slowly or cautiously ⟨*nosed* my car into the parking space⟩ **3 :** to touch or rub with the nose **:** NUZZLE ∼ *vi* **1 :** to use the nose in examining, smelling, or showing affection **2 a :** to search impertinently **:** PRY **b :** POKE 2a **3 :** to move ahead slowly or cautiously ⟨the boat *nosed* around the bend⟩ **4 :** to move the forward end in a specified direction ⟨the plane *nosed* up⟩ **5 :** to advance into a slight lead

nose•band \ˈnōz-ˌband\ *n* (ca. 1611) **:** the part of a headstall that passes over a horse's nose

1**nose•bleed** \-ˌblēd\ *n* (1848) **:** an attack of bleeding from the nose

2**nosebleed** *adj* (1978) **:** extremely or excessively high ⟨seats in the ∼ section⟩ ⟨∼ stock prices⟩

nose cone *n* (1949) **:** a protective cone constituting the forward end of an aerospace vehicle

nosed \ˈnōzd\ *adj* (1505) **:** having a nose esp. of a specified kind — usu. used in combination ⟨snub-*nosed*⟩

nose•dive \ˈnōz-ˌdīv\ *n* (1912) **1 :** a downward nose-first plunge of a flying object (as an airplane) **2 :** a sudden extreme drop ⟨stock prices took a ∼⟩ — **nose–dive** *vi*

no–see–um \nō-ˈsē-əm\ *n* [fr. the words (as supposedly spoken by American Indians) *no see um* you don't see them] (1842) **:** BITING MIDGE

nose•gay \ˈnōz-ˌgā\ *n* [ME, fr. *nose* nose + *gay* ornament, lit., something gay, fr. *gay*] (15c) **:** a small bunch of flowers **:** POSY

nose•guard \-ˌgärd\ *n* (1950) **:** a defensive lineman in football who plays opposite the offensive center

nose out *vt* (ca. 1630) **1 :** to discover often by prying **2 :** to defeat or surpass by a narrow margin

nose•piece \-ˌpēs\ *n* (ca. 1611) **1 :** a piece of armor for protecting the nose **2 :** the end piece of a microscope body to which an objective is attached **3 :** the bridge of a pair of eyeglasses

nose tackle *n* (1975) **:** NOSEGUARD

nose•wheel \-ˌhwēl, -ˌwēl\ *n* (1934) **:** a landing-gear wheel under the nose of an airplane

nos•ey par•ker \ˈnō-zē-ˈpär-kər\ *n, often cap N&P* [prob. fr. the name *Parker*] (1907) *chiefly Brit* **:** BUSYBODY

1**nosh** \ˈnäsh\ *vi* [Yiddish *nashn*, fr. MHG *nasehen* to eat on the sly] (1931) **:** to eat a snack **:** MUNCH ⟨∼*ing* on pizza⟩ — **nosh•er** *n*

2**nosh** *n* (1941) **:** a light meal **:** SNACK

1**no–show** \ˈnō-ˌshō, -ˈshō\ *n* (1941) **1 :** a person who reserves space (as on an airplane) but neither uses nor cancels the reservation **2 :** a person who buys a ticket but does not attend; *broadly* **:** a person who is expected but who does not show up **3 :** failure to show up

2**no–show** *adj* (1975) **:** of, relating to, or being a job for which the holder is paid but performs few duties or is rarely present for work

nosing *n* (ca. 1775) **:** the usu. rounded edge of a stair tread that projects over the riser; *also* **:** a similar rounded projection

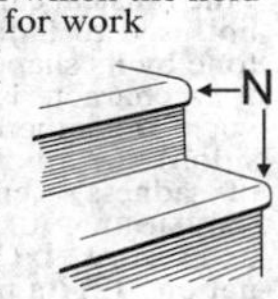

N nosing

nos•o•co•mi•al \ˌnä-sə-ˈkō-mē-əl\ *adj* [LL *nosocomium* hospital, fr. LGk *nosokomeion*, fr. Gk *nosokomos* one who tends the sick, fr. *nosos* disease + *-komos;* akin to Gk *kamnein* to suffer, toil, Skt *śāmyati* he tires] (ca. 1843) **:** acquired or occurring in a hospital ⟨∼ infection⟩

no•sol•o•gy \nō-ˈsä-lə-jē, -ˈzä-\ *n* [prob. fr. NL *nosologia*, fr. Gk *nosos* disease + NL *-logia* -logy] (ca. 1721) **1 :** a classification or list of diseases **2 :** a branch of medical science that deals with classification of diseases — **no•so•log•i•cal** \ˌnō-sə-ˈlä-ji-kəl\ *or* **no•so•log•ic** \-jik\ *adj* — **no•so•log•i•cal•ly** \-ji-k(ə-)lē\ *adv*

nos•tal•gia \nä-ˈstal-jə, nə- *also* nȯ-, nō-; nə-ˈstäl-\ *n* [NL, fr. Gk *nostos* return home + NL *-algia;* akin to Gk *neisthai* to return, OE *genesan* to survive, Skt *nasate* he approaches] (1729) **1 :** the state of being homesick **:** HOMESICKNESS **2 :** a wistful or excessively sentimental yearning for return to or of some past period or irrecoverable condition; *also* **:** something that evokes nostalgia — **nos•tal•gic** \-jik\ *adj or n* — **nos•tal•gi•cal•ly** \-ji-k(ə-)lē\ *adv* — **nos•tal•gist** \-jist\ *n*

nos•toc \ˈnäs-ˌtäk\ *n* [NL] (1650) **:** any of a genus (*Nostoc*) of usu. filamentous cyanobacteria that fix nitrogen

nos•tril \ˈnäs-trəl\ *n* [ME *nosethirl*, fr. OE *nosthyrl*, fr. *nosu* nose + *thyrel* hole; akin to OE *thurh* through] (bef. 12c) **1 :** either of the external nares; *broadly* **:** either of the nares with the adjoining passage on the same side of the septum **2 :** either fleshy lateral wall of the nose

nos•trum \ˈnäs-trəm\ *n* [L, neut. of *noster* our, ours, fr. *nos* we — more at US] (1602) **1 :** a medicine of secret composition recommended by its preparer but usu. without scientific proof of its effectiveness **2 :** a usu. questionable remedy or scheme **:** PANACEA ⟨an audience eager to believe he had found the ∼ for all of society's ills —Warren Sloat⟩

nosy *or* **nos•ey** \ˈnō-zē\ *adj* **nos•i•er; -est** [1*nose*] (1882) **:** of prying or inquisitive disposition or quality **:** INTRUSIVE — **nos•i•ly** \ˈnō-zə-lē\ *adv* — **nos•i•ness** \-zē-nəs\ *n*

\ə\ **a**but \ᵊ\ kitten, F table \ər\ **fur**ther \a\ **a**sh \ā\ **a**ce \ä\ m**o**p, m**a**r
\au̇\ **ou**t \ch\ **ch**in \e\ b**e**t \ē\ **ea**sy \g\ **g**o \i\ h**i**t \ī\ **i**ce \j\ **j**ob
\ŋ\ si**ng** \ō\ g**o** \ȯ\ l**aw** \ȯi\ b**oy** \th\ **th**in \t͟h\ **th**e \ü\ l**oo**t \u̇\ f**oo**t
\y\ **y**et \zh\ vi**si**on, beige \k̟, ⁿ, œ, ue, ʸ\ *see* Guide to Pronunciation

not \ˈnät\ *adv* [ME, alter. of *nought,* fr. *nought,* pron. — more at NAUGHT] (13c) **1** — used as a function word to make negative a group of words or a word **2** — used as a function word to stand for the negative of a preceding group of words ‹is sometimes hard to see and sometimes ∼›

NOT \ˈnät\ *n* [*not*] (1947) **:** a logical operator that produces a statement that is the inverse of an input statement

nota *pl of* NOTUM

no·ta be·ne \ˌnō-tə-ˈbē-nē, -ˈbe-\ [L, mark well] (ca. 1721) — used to call attention to something important

no·ta·bil·i·ty \ˌnō-tə-ˈbi-lə-tē\ *n, pl* **-ties** (1832) **:** a notable or prominent person

[1]**no·ta·ble** \ˈnō-tə-bəl, *for 2 also* ˈnä-\ *adj* (14c) **1 a :** worthy of note **:** REMARKABLE **b :** DISTINGUISHED, PROMINENT **2** *archaic* **:** efficient or capable in performance of housewifely duties — **no·ta·ble·ness** *n*

[2]**no·ta·ble** \ˈnō-tə-bəl\ *n* (1815) **1 :** a person of note **:** NOTABILITY **2** *pl, often cap* **:** a group of persons summoned esp. in monarchical France to act as a deliberative body

no·ta·bly \ˈnō-tə-blē\ *adv* (14c) **1 :** in a notable manner **:** to a high degree ‹was ∼ impressed› **2 :** ESPECIALLY, PARTICULARLY ‹other powers, ∼ Britain and the United States —C. A. Fisher›

no·tar·i·al \nō-ˈter-ē-əl\ *adj* (15c) **1 :** of, relating to, or characteristic of a notary public **2 :** done or executed by a notary public — **no·tar·i·al·ly** \-ə-lē\ *adv*

no·ta·ri·za·tion \ˌnō-tə-rə-ˈzā-shən\ *n* (1932) **1 :** the act, process, or an instance of notarizing **2 :** the notarial certificate appended to a document

no·ta·rize \ˈnō-tə-ˌrīz\ *vt* **-rized; -riz·ing** (1926) **:** to acknowledge or attest as a notary public

no·ta·ry public \ˈnō-tə-rē-\ *n, pl* **notaries public** *or* **notary publics** [ME *notary* clerk, notary public, fr. L *notarius* clerk, secretary, fr. *notarius* of shorthand, fr. *nota* note, shorthand character] (15c) **:** a public officer who attests or certifies writings (as a deed) to make them authentic and takes affidavits, depositions, and protests of negotiable paper — called also *notary*

no·tate \ˈnō-ˌtāt\ *vt* **no·tat·ed; no·tat·ing** [back-formation fr. *notation*] (1903) **:** to put into notation

no·ta·tion \nō-ˈtā-shən\ *n* [L *notation-, notatio,* fr. *notare* to note] (1584) **1 :** ANNOTATION, NOTE **2 a :** the act, process, method, or an instance of representing by a system or set of marks, signs, figures, or characters **b :** a system of characters, symbols, or abbreviated expressions used in an art or science or in mathematics or logic to express technical facts or quantities — **no·ta·tion·al** \-shnəl, -shə-nᵊl\ *adj*

[1]**notch** \ˈnäch\ *n* [perh. alter. (fr. misdivision of *an otch*) of **otch,* fr. MF *oche*] (1577) **1 a :** a V-shaped indentation **b :** a slit made to serve as a record **c :** a rounded indentation cut into the pages of a book on the edge opposite the spine **2 :** a deep close pass **:** GAP **3 :** DEGREE, STEP — **notched** \ˈnächt\ *adj*

[2]**notch** *vt* (1600) **1 :** to cut or make a notch in **2 a :** to mark or record by a notch **b :** SCORE, ACHIEVE — sometimes used with *up*

notch·back \ˈnäch-ˌbak\ *n* (1965) **:** an automobile with a trunk whose lid forms a distinct deck; *also* **:** the back of such an automobile

[1]**note** \ˈnōt\ *vt* **not·ed; not·ing** [ME, fr. AF *noter,* fr. L *notare* to mark, note, fr. *nota*] (13c) **1 a :** to notice or observe with care **b :** to record or preserve in writing **2 a :** to make special mention of or remark on **b :** INDICATE, SHOW — **not·er** *n*

[2]**note** *n* [ME, fr. AF, fr. L *nota* mark, character, written note] (13c) **1 a** (1) *obs* **:** MELODY, SONG (2) **:** TONE 2a (3) **:** CALL, SOUND; *esp* **:** the musical call of a bird **b :** a written symbol used to indicate duration and pitch of a tone by its shape and position on the staff **2 a :** a characteristic feature (as of odor or flavor) **b :** something (as an emotion or disposition) like a note in tone or resonance ‹a ∼ of sadness› ‹end on a high ∼› **3 a** (1) **:** MEMORANDUM (2) **:** a condensed or informal record **b** (1) **:** a brief comment or explanation (2) **:** a printed comment or reference set apart from the text **c** (1) **:** a written promise to pay a debt (2) **:** a piece of paper money (3) **:** a government or corporate bond usu. with a maturity of between two and ten years **d** (1) **:** a short informal letter (2) **:** a formal diplomatic communication **e :** a scholarly or technical essay shorter than an article and restricted in scope **f :** a sheet of notepaper **4 a :** DISTINCTION, REPUTATION ‹a figure of international ∼› **b :** OBSERVATION, NOTICE ‹took full ∼ of the proceedings› **c :** KNOWLEDGE, INFORMATION ***syn*** see SIGN

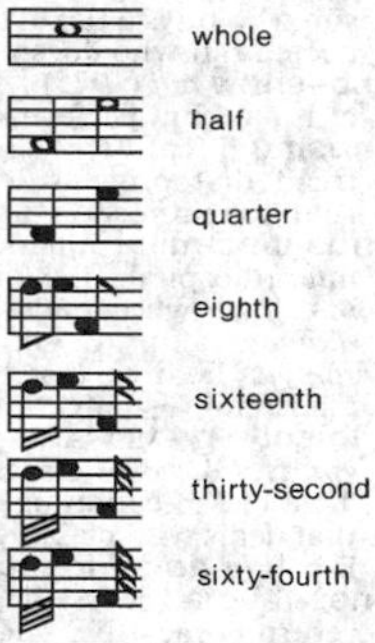
whole
half
quarter
eighth
sixteenth
thirty-second
sixty-fourth
[2]note 1b

note·book \ˈnōt-ˌbu̇k\ *n* (1579) **1 :** a book for notes or memoranda **2 :** a portable microcomputer that is similar to but usu. smaller than a laptop computer

note·case \-ˌkās\ *n* (1838) *Brit* **:** WALLET 2a

noted *adj* (14c) **:** well-known by reputation **:** EMINENT, CELEBRATED ***syn*** see FAMOUS — **not·ed·ly** *adv* — **not·ed·ness** *n*

note·less \ˈnōt-ləs\ *adj* (ca. 1616) **:** not noticed **:** UNDISTINGUISHED

note of hand (ca. 1738) **:** PROMISSORY NOTE

note·pad \ˈnōt-ˌpad\ *n* (1922) **:** [3]PAD 4

note·pa·per \-ˌpā-pər\ *n* (1849) **:** writing paper suitable for notes

note·wor·thy \-ˌwər-t͟hē\ *adj* (1552) **:** worthy of or attracting attention esp. because of some special excellence ‹a ∼ contribution› — **note·wor·thi·ly** \-t͟hə-lē\ *adv* — **note·wor·thi·ness** \-t͟hē-nəs\ *n*

not–for–profit *adj* (1935) **:** NONPROFIT

noth·er *or* **'noth·er** \ˈnə-t͟hər\ *adj* [alter. (fr. misdivision of *another*) of *other,* adj.] (ca. 1909) **:** OTHER — used esp. in the phrase *a whole nother;* used chiefly in speech or informal prose

[1]**noth·ing** \ˈnə-thiŋ\ *pron* [ME, fr. OE *nān thing, nāthing,* fr. *nān* no + *thing* thing — more at NONE] (bef. 12c) **1 :** not any thing **:** no thing ‹leaves ∼ to the imagination› **2 :** no part **3 :** one of no interest, value, or consequence ‹they mean ∼ to me› — **nothing doing :** by no means **:** definitely no — **nothing for it :** no alternative ‹*nothing for it* but to start over›

[2]**nothing** *adv* (12c) **:** not at all **:** in no degree — **nothing like :** not nearly ‹it's *nothing like* thorough enough›

[3]**nothing** *n* (1535) **1 a :** something that does not exist **b :** the absence of all magnitude or quantity; *also* **:** ZERO 1a **c :** NOTHINGNESS, NONEXISTENCE **2 :** someone or something of no or slight value or size **3 :** a light, playful, or frivolous remark — usu. used in pl. ‹whispered sweet ∼*s*› — **for nothing 1 :** without reason **2 :** at no charge

[4]**nothing** *adj* (1611) **:** of no account **:** WORTHLESS

noth·ing·ness \-nəs\ *n* (ca. 1631) **1 :** the quality or state of being nothing: as **a :** NONEXISTENCE **b :** utter insignificance **c :** DEATH **2 :** something insignificant or valueless **3 :** VOID, EMPTINESS

[1]**no·tice** \ˈnō-təs\ *n* [ME, fr. AF, knowledge, notification, fr. L *notitia* acquaintance, awareness, fr. *notus* known, fr. pp. of *noscere* to come to know — more at KNOW] (15c) **1 a** (1) **:** warning or intimation of something **:** ANNOUNCEMENT (2) **:** the announcement of a party's intention to quit an agreement or relation at a specified time (3) **:** the condition of being warned or notified — usu. used in the phrase *on notice* **b :** INFORMATION, INTELLIGENCE **2 a :** ATTENTION, HEED **b :** polite or favorable attention **:** CIVILITY **3 :** a written or printed announcement **4 :** a short critical account or review

[2]**notice** *vt* **no·ticed; no·tic·ing** (15c) **1 :** to give notice of **2 a :** to comment upon **:** REVIEW **3 a :** to treat with attention or civility **b :** to take notice of **:** MARK **4 :** to give a formal notice to — **no·tic·er** *n*

no·tice·able \ˈnō-tə-sə-bəl\ *adj* (1796) **1 :** worthy of notice **2 :** likely to be noticed — **no·tice·ably** \-blē\ *adv*

syn NOTICEABLE, REMARKABLE, PROMINENT, OUTSTANDING, CONSPICUOUS, SALIENT, STRIKING mean attracting notice or attention. NOTICEABLE applies to something unlikely to escape observation ‹a piano recital with no *noticeable* errors›. REMARKABLE applies to something so extraordinary or exceptional as to invite comment ‹a film of *remarkable* intelligence and wit›. PROMINENT applies to something commanding notice by standing out from its surroundings or background ‹a doctor who occupies a *prominent* position in the town›. OUTSTANDING applies to something that rises above and excels others of the same kind ‹honored for her *outstanding* contributions to science›. CONSPICUOUS applies to something that is obvious and unavoidable to the sight or mind ‹*conspicuous* bureaucratic waste›. SALIENT applies to something of significance that merits the attention given it ‹the *salient* points of the speech›. STRIKING applies to something that impresses itself powerfully and deeply upon the observer's mind or vision ‹the region's *striking* poverty›.

notice board *n* (1854) *chiefly Brit* **:** a board bearing a notice or on which notices may be posted; *esp* **:** BULLETIN BOARD

no·ti·fi·able \ˈnō-tə-ˌfī-ə-bəl, ˌnō-tə-ˈ\ *adj* (1889) **:** required by law to be reported to official health authorities ‹a ∼ disease›

no·ti·fi·ca·tion \ˌnō-tə-fə-ˈkā-shən\ *n* (14c) **1 :** the act or an instance of notifying **2 :** a written or printed matter that gives notice

no·ti·fy \ˈnō-tə-ˌfī\ *vt* **-fied; -fy·ing** [ME *notifien,* fr. AF *notifier* to make known, fr. LL *notificare,* fr. L *notus* known] (14c) **1** *obs* **:** to point out **2 :** to give notice of or report the occurrence of ‹he *notified* his intention to sue› **3 :** to give formal notice to ‹∼ a family of the death of a relation› ***syn*** see INFORM — **no·ti·fi·er** \-ˌfī(-ə)r\ *n*

no–till \ˈnō-ˈtil\ *n* (1968) **:** NO-TILLAGE

no–till·age \-ˈti-lij\ *n* (1968) **:** a system of farming that consists of planting a narrow slit trench without tillage and with the use of herbicides to suppress weeds

no·tion \ˈnō-shən\ *n* [L *notion-, notio,* fr. *noscere*] (1537) **1 a** (1) **:** an individual's conception or impression of something known, experienced, or imagined (2) **:** an inclusive general concept (3) **:** a theory or belief held by a person or group **b :** a personal inclination **:** WHIM **2** *obs* **:** MIND, INTELLECT **3** *pl* **:** small useful items **:** SUNDRIES ***syn*** see IDEA

no·tion·al \ˈnō-shnəl, -shə-nᵊl\ *adj* (1597) **1 :** THEORETICAL, SPECULATIVE **2 :** existing in the mind only **:** IMAGINARY **3 :** given to foolish or fanciful moods or ideas **4 a :** of, relating to, or being a notion or idea **:** CONCEPTUAL **b** (1) **:** presenting an idea of a thing, action, or quality ‹*has* is ∼ in *he has luck,* relational in *he has gone*› (2) **:** of or representing what exists or occurs in the world of things as distinguished from syntactic categories — **no·tion·al·i·ty** \ˌnō-shə-ˈna-lə-tē\ *n* — **no·tion·al·ly** \ˈnō-shnə-lē, -shə-nᵊl-ē\ *adv*

no·to·chord \ˈnō-tə-ˌkȯrd\ *n* [Gk *nōton, nōtos* back + L *chorda* cord — more at CORD] (1848) **:** a longitudinal flexible rod of cells that in the lowest chordates (as a lancelet or a lamprey) and in the embryos of the higher vertebrates forms the supporting axis of the body — **no·to·chord·al** \ˌnō-tə-ˈkȯr-dᵊl\ *adj*

no·to·ri·e·ty \ˌnō-tə-ˈrī-ə-tē\ *n, pl* **-ties** [MF or ML; MF *notorieté,* fr. ML *notorietat-, notorietas,* fr. *notorius*] (ca. 1650) **1 :** the quality or state of being notorious **2 :** a notorious person

no·to·ri·ous \nō-ˈtȯr-ē-əs, nə-\ *adj* [ML *notorius,* fr. LL *notorium* information, indictment, fr. L *noscere* to come to know — more at KNOW] (1534) **:** generally known and talked of; *esp* **:** widely and unfavorably known ***syn*** see FAMOUS

no·to·ri·ous·ly \-lē\ *adv* (1512) **1 :** in a notorious manner **2 :** as is notorious **:** as is very well known ‹∼, they never got along›

no–trump *adj* (1902) **:** being a bid, contract, or hand suitable to play without any suit being trumps — **no–trump** *n*

Notts *abbr* Nottinghamshire

no·tum \ˈnō-təm\ *n, pl* **no·ta** \ˈnō-tə\ [NL, fr. Gk *nōton* back] (1877) **:** the dorsal surface of a thoracic segment of an insect

[1]**not·with·stand·ing** \ˌnät-with-ˈstan-diŋ, -wit͟h-\ *prep* [ME *notwithstanding,* fr. *not* + *withstanding,* prp. of *withstonden* to withstand] (14c) **:** DESPITE ‹∼ their inexperience, they were an immediate success› — often used after its object ‹the motion passed, our objection ∼›

[2]**notwithstanding** *adv* (15c) **:** NEVERTHELESS, HOWEVER

[3]**notwithstanding** *conj* (15c) **:** ALTHOUGH

nou·gat \ˈnü-gət, *esp Brit* -ˌgä\ *n* [F, fr. Occitan, fr. Old Occitan *nogat,* fr. *noga* nut, fr. VL **nuca,* fr. L *nuc-, nux* — more at NUT] (1827) **:** a confection of nuts or fruit pieces in a sugar paste

nought *var of* NAUGHT

nou·me·non \ˈnü-mə-ˌnän\ *n, pl* **-na** \-nə, -ˌnä\ [G, fr. Gk *nooumenon* that which is apprehended by thought, fr. neut. of pres. pass. part. of *noein* to think, conceive, fr. *nous* mind] (1796) **:** a posited object or event as it appears in itself independent of perception by the senses — **nou·men·al** \-mə-nᵊl\ *adj*

noun \ˈnau̇n\ *n* [ME *nowne,* fr. AF *nom, noun* name, noun, fr. L *nomen* — more at NAME] (14c) **:** any member of a class of words that typically can be combined with determiners to serve as the subject of a verb, can be interpreted as singular or plural, can be replaced with a pronoun, and refer to an entity, quality, state, action, or concept

noun phrase *n, often cap N&P* (1923) **:** a phrase formed by a noun and all its modifiers and determiners; *broadly* **:** any syntactic element (as a clause, clitic, pronoun, or zero element) with a noun's function (as the subject of a verb or the object of a verb or preposition) — abbr. *NP*

nour·ish \ˈnər-ish, ˈnə-rish\ *vt* [ME *nurishen,* fr. AF *nuriss-,* stem of *nurrir, norrir,* fr. L *nutrire* to suckle, nourish; akin to Gk *nan* to flow, *noteros* damp, Skt *snauti* it drips] (14c) **1 :** NURTURE, REAR **2 :** to promote the growth of ⟨no occasions to exercise the feelings nor ~ passion —L. O. Coxe⟩ **3 a :** to furnish or sustain with nutriment **:** FEED **b :** MAINTAIN, SUPPORT ⟨their profits . . . ~ other criminal activities —Beverly Smith⟩ — **nour·ish·er** *n*

nour·ish·ing \ˈnər-i-shiŋ, ˈnə-ri-\ *adj* (14c) **:** giving nourishment **:** NUTRITIOUS

nour·ish·ment \ˈnər-ish-mənt, ˈnə-rish-\ *n* (15c) **1 a :** FOOD, NUTRIMENT **b :** SUSTENANCE 3 ⟨books for intellectual ~⟩ **2 :** the act of nourishing **:** the state of being nourished

nous *n* [Gk *noos, nous* mind] (1678) **1** \ˈnüs *also* ˈnau̇s\ **:** MIND, REASON: as **a :** an intelligent purposive principle of the world **b :** the divine reason regarded in Neoplatonism as the first emanation of God **2** \ˈnau̇s\ *chiefly Brit* **:** COMMON SENSE, ALERTNESS

nou·veau \nü-ˈvō\ *adj* [F, fr. MF *novel*] (1828) **:** newly arrived or developed

nou·veau riche \ˌnü-ˌvō-ˈrēsh\ *n, pl* **nou·veaux riches** *same*\ [F, lit., new rich] (1801) **:** a person newly rich **:** PARVENU

nou·velle \nü-ˈvel\ *adj* [*nouvelle* cuisine] (1976) **1 :** of or relating to nouvelle cuisine ⟨a ~ restaurant⟩ **2 :** TRENDY, NOVEL

nouvelle cuisine *n* [F, lit., new cuisine] (1975) **:** a form of French cuisine that uses little flour or fat and stresses light sauces and the use of fresh seasonal produce; *also* **:** a national or regional cuisine that stresses lightness and freshness in preparation ⟨American *nouvelle cuisine*⟩

nouvelle vague \-ˈväg\ *n* [F] (1959) **1 :** NEW WAVE 1 **2 :** NEW WAVE 2

Nov *abbr* November

[1]**no·va** \ˈnō-və\ *n, pl* **novas** *or* **no·vae** \-(ˌ)vē, -ˌvī\ [NL, fem. of L *novus* new] (1927) **:** a star that suddenly increases its light output tremendously and then fades away to its former obscurity in a few months or years — **no·va·like** \-və-ˌlīk\ *adj*

[2]**nova** *n, often cap* [short for *Nova Scotia salmon*] (1964) **:** cured and smoked salmon; *esp* **:** salmon that has been cured in a mixture of salt and sugar and smoked at a low temperature

no·vac·u·lite \nō-ˈva-kyə-ˌlīt\ *n* [L *novacula* razor] (1796) **:** a very hard fine-grained siliceous rock used for whetstones and possibly of sedimentary origin

no·va·tion \nō-ˈvā-shən\ *n* [LL *novation-, novatio* renewal, legal novation, fr. L *novare* to make new, fr. *novus*] (1682) **:** the substitution of a new legal obligation for an old one

[1]**nov·el** \ˈnä-vəl\ *adj* [ME, fr. AF, new, fr. L *novellus,* fr. dim. of *novus* new — more at NEW] (15c) **1 :** new and not resembling something formerly known or used **2 :** original or striking esp. in conception or style ⟨a ~ scheme to collect money⟩ ***syn*** see NEW

[2]**novel** *n* [It *novella*] (1639) **1 :** an invented prose narrative that is usu. long and complex and deals esp. with human experience through a usu. connected sequence of events **2 :** the literary genre consisting of novels — **nov·el·is·tic** \ˌnä-və-ˈlis-tik\ *adj* — **nov·el·is·ti·cal·ly** \-ti-k(ə-)lē\ *adv*

nov·el·ette \ˌnä-və-ˈlet\ *n* (1814) **:** NOVELLA 2

nov·el·ett·ish \-ˈle-tish\ *adj* (1904) **:** of, relating to, or characteristic of a novelette; *esp* **:** SENTIMENTAL

nov·el·ist \ˈnäv-list, ˈnä-və-\ *n* (1728) **:** a writer of novels

nov·el·ize \ˈnä-və-ˌlīz\ *vt* **-ized; -iz·ing** (1828) **:** to convert into the form of a novel ⟨~ a play⟩ — **nov·el·i·za·tion** \ˌnä-və-lə-ˈzā-shən\ *n*

no·vel·la \nō-ˈve-lə\ *n, pl* **novellas** *or* **no·vel·le** \-ˈve-lē\ [It, fr. fem. of *novello* new, fr. L *novellus*] (1898) **1** *pl novelle* **:** a story with a compact and pointed plot **2** *pl usu novellas* **:** a work of fiction intermediate in length and complexity between a short story and a novel

nov·el·ty \ˈnä-vəl-tē\ *n, pl* **-ties** [ME *novelte,* fr. AF *novelté,* fr. *novel*] (14c) **1 :** something new or unusual **2 :** the quality or state of being novel **:** NEWNESS **3 :** a small manufactured article intended mainly for personal or household adornment — usu. used in pl. **4 :** something (as a song or food item) that provides often fleeting amusement and is often based on a theme — often used attributively

[1]**No·vem·ber** \nō-ˈvem-bər, nə-\ *n* [ME *Novembre,* fr. AF, fr. L *November,* ninth month of the early Roman calendar, fr. *novem* nine — more at NINE] (13c) **:** the 11th month of the Gregorian calendar

[2]**November** (1956) — a communications code word for the letter *n*

no·vem·de·cil·lion \ˌnō-ˌvem-di-ˈsil-yən\ *n, often attrib* [L *novemdecim* nineteen (fr. *novem* + *decem* ten) + E *-illion* (as in *million*) — more at TEN] (ca. 1934) — see NUMBER table

no·ve·na \nō-ˈvē-nə\ *n* [ML, fr. L, fem. of *novenus* nine each, fr. *novem*] (1853) **:** a Roman Catholic period of prayer lasting nine consecutive days

nov·ice \ˈnä-vəs\ *n* [ME, fr. AF, fr. ML *novicius,* fr. L, newly imported, fr. *novus* — more at NEW] (14c) **1 :** a person admitted to probationary membership in a religious community **2 :** BEGINNER, TYRO

no·vi·tiate \nō-ˈvi-shət, nə-\ *n* [F *noviciat,* fr. ML *noviciatus,* fr. *novicius*] (1600) **1 :** the period or state of being a novice **2 :** a house where novices are trained **3 :** NOVICE

no·vo·bi·o·cin \ˌnō-və-ˈbī-ə-sən\ *n* [*novo-* (perh. modif. of L *niveus* snowy, specific epithet of the bacterium *Streptomyces niveus*) + *bi-* + *-mycin*] (1956) **:** a weak dibasic acid $C_{31}H_{36}N_2O_{11}$ that is highly toxic to humans and is sometimes used as an antimicrobial drug in some serious cases of staphylococcic and urinary tract infection

No·vo·cain \ˈnō-və-ˌkān\ *trademark* — used for a preparation containing the hydrochloride of procaine

no·vo·caine \-ˌkān\ *n* [ISV *novo-* (fr. L *novus* new) + *cocaine*] (1906) **:** procaine in the form of its hydrochloride; *broadly* **:** a local anesthetic

[1]**now** \ˈnau̇\ *adv* [ME, fr. OE *nū;* akin to OHG *nū* now, L *nunc,* Gk *nyn*] (bef. 12c) **1 a :** at the present time or moment **b :** in the time immediately before the present ⟨thought of them just ~⟩ **c :** in the time immediately to follow **:** FORTHWITH ⟨come in ~⟩ **2** — used with the sense of present time weakened or lost to express command, request, or admonition ⟨~ hear this⟩ ⟨~ you be sure to write⟩ **3** — used with the sense of present time weakened or lost to introduce an important point or indicate a transition (as of ideas) ⟨~, this may seem reasonable at first⟩ **4 :** SOMETIMES ⟨~ one and ~ another⟩ **5 :** under the present circumstances **6 :** at the time referred to ⟨~ the trouble began⟩ **7 :** by this time ⟨has been teaching ~ for twenty years⟩

[2]**now** *conj* (bef. 12c) **:** in view of the fact that **:** SINCE — often followed by *that* ⟨~ that we are here⟩

[3]**now** *n* (12c) **:** the present time or moment ⟨been ill up to ~⟩

[4]**now** *adj* (14c) **1 :** of or relating to the present time **:** EXISTING ⟨the ~ president⟩ **2 a :** excitingly new ⟨~ clothes⟩ **b :** constantly aware of what is new ⟨~ people⟩ ⟨the ~ generation⟩

NOW *abbr* National Organization for Women

now·a·days \ˈnau̇-(ə-)ˌdāz\ *adv* [ME *now a dayes,* fr. [1]*now* + *a dayes* during the day] (14c) **:** at the present time

now and then *adv* (15c) **:** from time to time **:** OCCASIONALLY ⟨*now and then* we go off to the country⟩

no·way *adv* (13c) **1** \ˈnō-ˌwā\ *or* **no·ways** \-ˌwāz\ **:** NOWISE **2** *usu* **no way** \-ˈwā\ **:** not so **:** NO — used emphatically

[1]**no·where** \ˈnō-ˌ(h)wer, -(h)wər\ *adv* (bef. 12c) **1 :** not in or at any place **2 :** to no place **3 :** not at all **:** not to the least extent — usu. used with *near* ⟨~ near as serious⟩ ⟨~ near enough⟩

[2]**nowhere** *n* (1831) **1 :** a nonexistent place **2 :** an unknown, distant, or obscure place or state ⟨rose to fame out of ~⟩ — **miles from nowhere :** in an extremely remote place

[3]**nowhere** *adj* (1970) **:** of or relating to a remote or relatively unknown location ⟨a ~ town⟩

no·wheres \ˈnō-ˌ(h)werz, -(h)wərz\ *adv* (ca. 1866) *chiefly dial* **:** NOWHERE

no·wheres·ville \ˈnō-ˌ(h)werz-ˌvil, -(h)wərz-\ *n* (1965) **:** NOWHERE: as **a :** a location lacking identifying or individualizing qualities **b :** a place or state denoting failure or relative obscurity ⟨a career heading towards ~⟩

no·whith·er \ˈnō-ˌhwi-t͟hər, -ˌwi-t͟hər; ˌnō-ˈ\ *adv* (bef. 12c) **:** to or toward no place

no–win \ˈnō-ˈwin, -ˌwin\ *adj* (1962) **:** not likely to give victory, success, or satisfaction **:** that cannot be won ⟨a ~ situation⟩ ⟨a ~ war⟩

no·wise \ˈnō-ˌwīz\ *adv* (14c) **:** not at all

now·ness \ˈnau̇-nəs\ *n* (1674) **:** the quality or state of existing or occurring in or belonging to the present time

nowt \ˈnau̇t *also* ˈnōt\ *dial Eng var of* NOUGHT

NO_x *abbr* nitrogen oxide

nox·ious \ˈnäk-shəs\ *adj* [ME *noxius,* fr. L, fr. *noxa* harm; akin to L *nocēre* to harm, *nec-, nex* violent death, Gk *nekros* dead body] (15c) **1 a :** physically harmful or destructive to living beings ⟨~ waste⟩ **b :** constituting a harmful influence on mind or behavior; *esp* **:** morally corrupting ⟨~ doctrines⟩ **2 :** DISAGREEABLE, OBNOXIOUS ***syn*** see PERNICIOUS — **nox·ious·ly** *adv* — **nox·ious·ness** *n*

noz·zle \ˈnä-zəl\ *n* [dim. of *nose*] (1683) **1 a :** a projecting vent of something **b :** a short tube with a taper or constriction used (as on a hose) to speed up or direct a flow of fluid **c :** a part in a rocket engine that accelerates the exhaust gases from the combustion chamber to a high velocity **2** *slang* **:** NOSE

np *abbr* **1** no pagination **2** no place (of publication)

Np *symbol* neptunium

NP *abbr* **1** neuropsychiatric; neuropsychiatry **2** no protest **3** notary public **4** noun phrase **5** nurse-practitioner

NPN *abbr* nonprotein nitrogen

NPR *abbr* National Public Radio

NPS *abbr* National Park Service

nr *abbr* near

NR *abbr* not rated

NRA *abbr* **1** National Recovery Administration **2** National Rifle Association

NRC *abbr* **1** National Research Council **2** Nuclear Regulatory Commission

ns *also* **nsec** *abbr* nanosecond

Ns *abbr* nimbostratus

NS *abbr* **1** new series **2** New Style **3** not specified **4** not sufficient **5** Nova Scotia

NSA *abbr* National Security Agency

NSAID \ˈen-ˌsed *also* -ˌsād\ *n* [*n*on*s*teroidal *a*nti-*i*nflammatory *d*rug] (1982) **:** a nonsteroidal anti-inflammatory drug (as aspirin and ibuprofen)

NSC *abbr* National Security Council

NSF *abbr* **1** National Science Foundation **2** not sufficient funds

NSW *abbr* New South Wales

NT *abbr* **1** New Territories **2** New Testament **3** Northern Territory **4** Northwest Territories

-n't *vb comb form* **:** not ⟨*isn't*⟩

nth \ˈen(t)th\ *adj* [*n* (indefinite number) + *-th*] (1827) **1 :** numbered with an unspecified or indefinitely large ordinal number ⟨for the ~ time⟩ **2 :** EXTREME, UTMOST ⟨to the ~ degree⟩

NTP *abbr* normal temperature and pressure

NTSB *abbr* National Transportation Safety Board

NTSC *abbr* **1** National Television Standards Committee **2** National Television Systems Committee

n–type \ˈen-ˌtīp\ *adj* [*negative* + *type*] (1946) **:** relating to or being a semiconductor in which charge is carried by electrons — compare P-TYPE

nu \ˈnü, ˈnyü\ *n* [Gk *ny,* of Sem origin; akin to Heb *nūn* nun] (1638) **:** the 13th letter of the Greek alphabet — see ALPHABET table

\ə\ **abut** \ᵊ\ kitten, F table \ər\ **further** \a\ ash \ā\ ace \ä\ mop, mar \au̇\ **out** \ch\ **chin** \e\ bet \ē\ **easy** \g\ go \i\ **hit** \ī\ ice \j\ **job** \ŋ\ sing \ō\ **go** \ȯ\ **law** \ȯi\ boy \th\ **thin** \t͟h\ **the** \ü\ **loot** \u̇\ **foot** \y\ yet \zh\ **vision,** beige \k̲, ⁿ, œ, ue, ʸ\ *see* Guide to Pronunciation

NU *abbr* **1** name unknown **2** Nunavut
nu·ance \'nü-ˌän(t)s, 'nyü-, -ˌäⁿs; nü-', nyü-'\ *n* [F, fr. MF, shade of color, fr. *nuer* to make shades of color, fr. *nue* cloud, fr. L *nubes;* perh. akin to W *nudd* mist] (1781) **1 :** a subtle distinction or variation **2 :** a subtle quality : NICETY **3 :** sensibility to, awareness of, or ability to express delicate shadings (as of meaning, feeling, or value) — **nu·anced** \-ˌän(t)st, -'än(t)st\ *adj*
nub \'nəb\ *n* [alter. of E dial. *knub,* prob. fr. LG *knubbe*] (1727) **1 :** KNOB, LUMP **2 :** NUBBIN **3 :** GIST, POINT ⟨the ~ of the problem⟩
nub·bin \'nə-bən\ *n* [perh. dim. of *nub*] (1692) **1 :** something (as an ear of Indian corn) that is small for its kind, stunted, undeveloped, or imperfect **2 :** a small usu. projecting part or bit **3 :** NUB 3
nub·ble \'nə-bəl\ *n* [dim. of *nub*] (1818) **:** a small knob or lump — **nub·bly** \-b(ə-)lē\ *adj*
nub·by \'nə-bē\ *adj* **nub·bi·er; -est** [*nub* + [1]*-y*] (ca. 1876) **1 :** having or being like nubbles **2 :** having nubs ⟨a ~ knit fabric⟩
Nu·bi·an \'nü-bē-ən, 'nyü-\ *n* (15c) **1 a :** a native or inhabitant of Nubia **b :** a member of one of the group of dark-skinned peoples that formed a powerful empire between Egypt and Ethiopia from the 6th to the 14th centuries **2 :** any of several languages spoken in central and northern Sudan — **Nubian** *adj*
nu·bile \'nü-ˌbī(-ə)l, 'nyü-, -bəl\ *adj* [F, fr. L *nubilis,* fr. *nubere* to marry — more at NUPTIAL] (ca. 1642) **1 :** of marriageable condition or age **2 :** sexually attractive — used of a young woman — **nu·bil·i·ty** \nü-'bi-lə-tē, nyü-\ *n*
nu·buck \'n(y)ü-ˌbək\ *n, often attrib* [perh. fr. *nu-* (alter. of [1]*new*) + [1]*buck*] (1926) **:** a soft sueded leather
nu·cel·lus \nü-'se-ləs, nyü-\ *n, pl* **nu·cel·li** \-'se-ˌlī\ [NL, fr. L *nucella* small nut, fr. *nuc-, nux* nut — more at NUT] (1882) **:** the central and chief part of a plant ovule that encloses the female gametophyte — **nu·cel·lar** \-'se-lər\ *adj*
nu·chal \'nü-kəl, 'nyü-\ *adj* [ML *nucha* nape, fr. Ar *nukhā'* spinal marrow] (1835) **:** of, relating to, or lying in the region of the nape
nucle- *or* **nucleo-** *comb form* [F *nuclé-, nucléo-,* fr. NL *nucleus*] **1 :** nucleus ⟨*nucleo*plasm⟩ **2 :** nucleic acid ⟨*nucleo*protein⟩
nu·cle·ar \'nü-klē-ər, 'nyü-, ÷-kyə-lər\ *adj* (1846) **1 :** of, relating to, or constituting a nucleus **2 a :** of or relating to the atomic nucleus ⟨~ reaction⟩ ⟨~ physics⟩ **b :** used in or produced by a nuclear reaction (as fission) ⟨~ fuel⟩ ⟨~ waste⟩ ⟨~ energy⟩ **c (1) :** being a weapon whose destructive power derives from an uncontrolled nuclear reaction **(2) :** of, produced by, or involving nuclear weapons ⟨the ~ age⟩ ⟨~ war⟩ **(3) :** armed with nuclear weapons ⟨~ powers⟩ **d :** of, relating to, or powered by nuclear energy ⟨a ~ submarine⟩ ⟨the ~ debate⟩ ⟨a ~ plant⟩ **3 :** CRAZY, BERSERK — usu. used in the phrase *go nuclear*

usage Though disapproved of by many, pronunciations ending in \-kyə-lər\ have been found in widespread use among educated speakers including scientists, lawyers, professors, congressmen, U.S. cabinet members, and at least two U.S. presidents and one vice president. While most common in the U.S., these pronunciations have also been heard from British and Canadian speakers.

nuclear family *n* (1947) **:** a family group that consists only of father, mother, and children
nuclear magnetic resonance *n* (1942) **:** the magnetic resonance of an atomic nucleus; *also* **:** chemical analysis that uses such resonance esp. to study molecular structure
nuclear medicine *n* (1952) **:** a branch of medicine dealing with the use of radioactive materials in the diagnosis and treatment of disease
nuclear membrane *n* (1888) **:** a double membrane enclosing a cell nucleus and having its outer part continuous with the endoplasmic reticulum — called also *nuclear envelope;* see CELL illustration
nuclear sap *n* (1877) **:** the clear homogeneous ground substance of a cell nucleus
nuclear winter *n* (1983) **:** the chilling of climate that is hypothesized to be a consequence of nuclear war and to result from the prolonged blockage of sunlight by high-altitude dust clouds produced by nuclear explosions
nu·cle·ase \'nü-klē-ˌās, 'nyü-, -ˌāz\ *n* (1902) **:** any of various enzymes that promote hydrolysis of nucleic acids
nu·cle·ate \'nü-klē-ˌāt, 'nyü-\ *vb* **-at·ed; -at·ing** [LL *nucleatus,* pp. of *nucleare* to become stony, fr. L *nucleus*] *vt* (ca. 1864) **1 :** to form into a nucleus **:** CLUSTER **2 :** to act as a nucleus for **3 :** to supply nuclei to ~ *vi* **1 :** to form a nucleus **2 :** to act as a nucleus **3 :** to begin to form — **nu·cle·ation** \ˌnü-klē-'ā-shən, ˌnyü-\ *n* — **nu·cle·a·tor** \'nü-klē-ˌā-tər, 'nyü-\ *n*
nu·cle·at·ed \'nü-klē-ˌā-təd, 'nyü-\ *or* **nu·cle·ate** \-klē-ət\ *adj* [L *nucleatus,* fr. *nucleus* kernel] (1845) **1 :** having a nucleus or nuclei ⟨~ cells⟩ **2** *usu nucleate* **:** originating or occurring at nuclei ⟨*nucleate* boiling⟩
nu·cle·ic acid \nu̇-'klē-ik-, -'klā-, nyü-\ *n* [fr. their occurrence in cell nuclei] (1892) **:** any of various complex organic acids (as DNA or RNA) that are composed of nucleotide chains
nu·cle·in \'nü-klē-ən, 'nyü-\ *n* (1878) **1 :** NUCLEOPROTEIN **2 :** NUCLEIC ACID
nu·cle·o·cap·sid \ˌnü-klē-ō-'kap-səd, ˌnyü-\ *n* (1963) **:** the nucleic acid and surrounding protein coat in a virus
nu·cle·oid \'nü-klē-ˌȯid, 'nyü-\ *n* (1938) **:** the DNA-containing area of a prokaryotic cell (as a bacterium)
nu·cle·o·lus \nü-'klē-ə-ləs, nyü-\ *n, pl* **-li** \-ˌlī\ [NL, fr. L, dim. of *nucleus*] (1845) **:** a spherical body of the nucleus of most eukaryotes that becomes enlarged during protein synthesis, is associated with a nucleolus organizer, and contains the DNA templates for ribosomal RNA — see CELL illustration — **nu·cle·o·lar** \-lər\ *adj*
nucleolus organizer *n* (1939) **:** the specific part of a chromosome with which a nucleolus is associated esp. during its reorganization after nuclear division — called also *nucleolar organizer*
nu·cle·on \'nü-klē-ˌän, 'nyü-\ *n* [ISV] (1923) **1 :** a proton or neutron esp. in the atomic nucleus **2 :** a hypothetical single entity with one-half unit of isospin that can manifest itself as either a proton or a neutron — **nu·cle·on·ic** \ˌnü-klē-'ä-nik, ˌnyü-\ *adj*
nu·cle·on·ics \ˌnü-klē-'ä-niks, ˌnyü-\ *n pl but sing or pl in constr* (1937) **:** a branch of physical science that deals with nucleons or with all phenomena of the atomic nucleus
nu·cle·o·phile \'nü-klē-ə-ˌfī(-ə)l, 'nyü-\ *n* (1943) **:** a nucleophilic substance (as an electron-donating reagent)
nu·cle·o·phil·ic \ˌnü-klē-ə-'fi-lik, ˌnyü-\ *adj* (1933) **1** *of an atom, ion, or molecule* **:** having an affinity for atomic nuclei **:** being an electron donor **2 :** involving a nucleophilic species ⟨a ~ reaction⟩ — compare ELECTROPHILIC — **nu·cle·o·phil·i·cal·ly** \-li-k(ə-)lē\ *adv* — **nu·cle·o·phi·lic·i·ty** \-klē-ō-fi-'li-sə-tē\ *n*
nu·cle·o·plasm \'nü-klē-ə-ˌpla-zəm, 'nyü-\ *n* [ISV] (1888) **:** the protoplasm of a nucleus — **nu·cle·o·plas·mic** \-klē-ə-'plaz-mik\ *adj*
nu·cle·o·pro·tein \ˌnü-klē-ō-'prō-ˌtēn, ˌnyü-, -'prō-tē-ən\ *n* [ISV] (1907) **:** a compound that consists of a protein (as a histone) conjugated with a nucleic acid (as a DNA) and that is the principal constituent of the hereditary material in chromosomes
nu·cle·o·side \'nü-klē-ə-ˌsīd, 'nyü-\ *n* [ISV *nucle-* + [2]*-ose* + *-ide*] (1911) **:** a compound (as guanosine or adenosine) that consists of a purine or pyrimidine base combined with deoxyribose or ribose and is found esp. in DNA or RNA
nu·cle·o·some \-ˌsōm\ *n* (1962) **:** any of the repeating globular subunits of chromatin that consist of a complex of DNA and histone — **nu·cle·o·so·mal** \ˌnü-klē-ə-'sō-məl, ˌnyü-\ *adj*
nu·cle·o·syn·the·sis \ˌnü-klē-ō-'sin(t)-thə-səs, ˌnyü-\ *n* [NL] (1960) **:** the production of a chemical element from simpler nuclei (as of hydrogen) esp. in a star — **nu·cle·o·syn·thet·ic** \-sin-'the-tik\ *adj*
nu·cle·o·tid·ase \ˌnü-klē-ə-'tī-ˌdās, ˌnyü-, -ˌdāz\ *n* (1911) **:** a phosphatase that promotes hydrolysis of a nucleotide (as into a nucleoside and phosphoric acid)
nu·cle·o·tide \'nü-klē-ə-ˌtīd, 'nyü-\ *n* [ISV, irreg. fr. *nucle-* + *-ide*] (1908) **:** any of several compounds that consist of a ribose or deoxyribose sugar joined to a purine or pyrimidine base and to a phosphate group and that are the basic structural units of nucleic acids (as RNA and DNA) — compare NUCLEOSIDE
nu·cle·us \'nü-klē-əs, 'nyü-\ *n, pl* **nu·clei** \-klē-ˌī\ *also* **nu·cle·us·es** [NL, fr. L, kernel, fr. *nuc-, nux* nut — more at NUT] (1704) **1 a :** the small bright body in the head of a comet **b :** the small brighter and denser portion of a galaxy **2 :** a central point, group, or mass about which gathering, concentration, or accretion takes place: as **a :** a cellular organelle of eukaryotes that is essential to cell functions (as reproduction and protein synthesis), is composed of nucleoplasm and a nucleoprotein-rich network from which chromosomes and nucleoli arise, and is enclosed in a definite membrane — see CELL illustration **b :** a mass of gray matter or group of cell bodies of neurons in the central nervous system **c :** a characteristic and stable complex of atoms or groups in a molecule; *esp* **:** RING ⟨the naphthalene ~⟩ **d :** the positively charged central portion of an atom that comprises nearly all of the atomic mass and that consists of protons and usu. neutrons **3 :** the peak of sonority in the utterance of a syllable **4 :** a basic or essential part **:** CORE ⟨players who are the ~ of the team⟩
nu·clide \'nü-ˌklīd, 'nyü-\ *n* [*nucl*eus + Gk *eidos* form, species — more at IDOL] (1947) **:** a species of atom characterized by the constitution of its nucleus and hence by the number of protons, the number of neutrons, and the energy content — **nu·clid·ic** \nü-'kli-dik, nyü-\ *adj*
[1]**nude** \'nüd, 'nyüd\ *adj* **nud·er; nud·est** [L *nudus* naked — more at NAKED] (1531) **1 :** lacking something essential esp. to legal validity ⟨a ~ contract⟩ **2 a :** devoid of a natural or conventional covering; *esp* **:** not covered by clothing or a drape **b (1) :** of the color of a white person's flesh **(2) :** giving the appearance of nudity ⟨a ~ dress⟩ **c :** featuring nudes ⟨a ~ movie⟩ **d :** frequented by naked people ⟨a ~ beach⟩ ***syn*** see BARE — **nude** *adv* — **nude·ly** *adv* — **nude·ness** *n* — **nu·di·ty** \'nü-də-tē, 'nyü-\ *n*
[2]**nude** *n* (1708) **1 a :** a representation of a nude human figure **b :** a nude person **2 :** the condition of being nude ⟨in the ~⟩
nudge \'nəj\ *vb* **nudged; nudg·ing** [origin unknown] *vt* (1675) **1 :** to touch or push gently; *esp* **:** to seek the attention of by a push of the elbow **2 :** to prod lightly **:** urge into action **3 :** APPROACH ⟨its circulation is *nudging* the four million mark —Bennett Cerf⟩ ~ *vi* **:** to give a nudge — **nudge** *n* — **nudg·er** *n*
nu·di·branch \'nü-də-ˌbraŋk, 'nyü-\ *n, pl* **-branchs** [NL *Nudibranchia,* fr. L *nudus* + Gk *branchia* gills] (1844) **:** any of an order (Nudibranchia) of marine opisthobranch mollusks without a shell in the adult state and without true gills — **nudibranch** *adj*

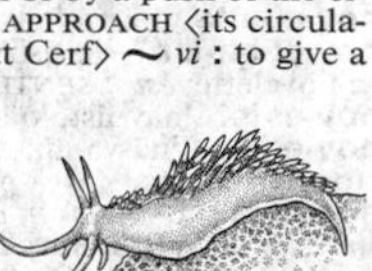
nudibranch

nud·ism \'nü-ˌdi-zəm, 'nyü-\ *n* (1929) **:** the practice of going nude esp. in sexually mixed groups and during periods of time spent at specially secluded places — **nud·ist** \'nü-dist, 'nyü-\ *adj or n*
nud·nik *also* **nud·nick** \'nu̇d-nik\ *n* [Yiddish *nudnik,* fr. *nudyen* to bore, fr. Pol *nudzić,* fr. *nuda* boredom] (1947) **:** a person who is a bore or nuisance
Nu·er \'nü-ər\ *n, pl* **Nuer** [prob. ultim. fr. Nuer *naað,* a self-designation] (1861) **1 :** a member of a Nilotic people of southern Sudan **2 :** the language of the Nuer people
nu·ga·to·ry \'nü-gə-ˌtȯr-ē, 'nyü-\ *adj* [L *nugatorius,* fr. *nugari* to trifle, fr. *nugae* trifles] (1603) **1 :** of little or no consequence **:** TRIFLING, INCONSEQUENTIAL **2 :** having no force **:** INOPERATIVE ***syn*** see VAIN
nug·get \'nə-gət\ *n* [origin unknown] (1852) **1 :** a solid lump; *esp* **:** a native lump of precious metal **2 :** TIDBIT 2 ⟨~*s* of wisdom⟩ **3 :** a small usu. rounded piece of food ⟨chicken ~*s*⟩
nui·sance \'nü-sᵊn(t)s, 'nyü-\ *n* [ME *nusaunce, noisaunce,* fr. AF, fr. *nuisir, nuire* to harm, fr. L *nocēre* — more at NOXIOUS] (15c) **1 :** HARM, INJURY **2 :** one that is annoying, unpleasant, or obnoxious **:** PEST
nuisance tax *n* (1924) **:** an excise tax collected in small amounts on a wide range of commodities directly from the consumer
[1]**nuke** \'nük, 'nyük\ *n* [by shortening & alter. fr. *nuclear*] (1959) **1 :** a nuclear weapon **2 :** a nuclear-powered electric generating station
[2]**nuke** *vt* **nuked; nuk·ing** (1967) **1 :** to attack or destroy with or as if with nuclear bombs **2 :** MICROWAVE
[1]**null** \'nəl\ *adj* [AF *nul,* lit., not any, fr. L *nullus,* fr. *ne-* not + *ullus* any; akin to L *unus* one — more at NO, ONE] (ca. 1567) **1 :** having no legal or binding force **:** INVALID **2 :** amounting to nothing **:** NIL **3 :** having no value **:** INSIGNIFICANT **4 a :** having no elements ⟨~ set⟩ **b :** having zero as a limit ⟨~ sequence⟩ **c** *of a matrix* **:** having all elements

equal to zero **5 a :** indicating usu. by a zero reading on a scale when a given quantity (as current or voltage) is zero or when two quantities are equal — used of an instrument **b :** being or relating to a method of measurement in which an unknown quantity (as of electric current) is compared with a known quantity of the same kind and found equal by a null detector **6 :** of, being, or relating to zero **7 :** ZERO 1c

[2]**null** *n* (1605) **1 :** ZERO 3a(1) **2 a :** a condition of a radio receiver when minimum or zero signal is received **b :** a minimum or zero value of an electric current or of a radio signal

[3]**null** *vt* (1643) **:** to make null

nul·lah \ˈnə-lə\ *n* [Hindi & Urdu *nālā*] (1776) **:** GULLY, RAVINE

null and void *adj* (1669) **:** having no force, binding power, or validity

null hypothesis *n* (1935) **:** a statistical hypothesis to be tested and accepted or rejected in favor of an alternative; *specif* **:** the hypothesis that an observed difference (as between the means of two samples) is due to chance alone and not due to a systematic cause

nul·li·fi·ca·tion \ˌnə-lə-fə-ˈkā-shən\ *n* (1798) **1 :** the act of nullifying **:** the state of being nullified **2 :** the action of a state impeding or attempting to prevent the operation and enforcement within its territory of a law of the U.S. **3 :** JURY NULLIFICATION — **nul·li·fi·ca·tion·ist** \-sh(ə-)nist\ *n*

nul·li·fi·er \ˈnə-lə-ˌfī(-ə)r\ *n* (1832) **:** one that nullifies; *specif* **:** one maintaining the right of nullification against the U.S. government

nul·li·fy \ˈnə-lə-ˌfī\ *vt* **-fied; -fy·ing** [LL *nullificare,* fr. L *nullus*] (1595) **1 :** to make null; *esp* **:** to make legally null and void **2 :** to make of no value or consequence

syn NULLIFY, NEGATE, ANNUL, ABROGATE, INVALIDATE mean to deprive of effective or continued existence. NULLIFY implies counteracting completely the force, effectiveness, or value of something ⟨a penalty *nullified* the touchdown⟩. NEGATE implies the destruction or canceling out of each of two things by the other ⟨the arguments *negate* each other⟩. ANNUL suggests making ineffective or nonexistent often by legal or official action ⟨the treaty *annuls* all previous agreements⟩. ABROGATE is like ANNUL but more definitely implies a legal or official act ⟨a law to *abrogate* trading privileges⟩. INVALIDATE implies making something powerless or unacceptable by declaration of its logical or moral or legal unsoundness ⟨the court *invalidated* the statute⟩.

nul·lip·a·rous \ˌnə-ˈli-pə-rəs\ *adj* [NL *nullipara* one who has never borne an offspring, fr. L *nullus* not any + *-para* -para] (1859) **:** of, relating to, or being a female that has not borne offspring

nul·li·ty \ˈnə-lə-tē\ *n, pl* **-ties** (1570) **1 a :** the quality or state of being null; *esp* **:** legal invalidity **b** (1) **:** NOTHINGNESS; *also* **:** INSIGNIFICANCE (2) **:** a mere nothing **:** NONENTITY **2 :** one that is null; *specif* **:** an act void of legal effect **3 :** the number of elements in a basis of a null-space

null–space \ˈnəl-ˌspās\ *n* (1884) **:** a subspace of a vector space consisting of vectors that under a given linear transformation are mapped onto zero

num *abbr* numeral

Num *or* **Numb** *abbr* Numbers

numb \ˈnəm\ *adj* [ME *nomen,* fr. pp. of *nimen* to take — more at NIM] (14c) **1 :** devoid of sensation esp. as a result of cold or anesthesia **2 :** devoid of emotion **:** INDIFFERENT — **numb** *vt* — **numb·ly** \ˈnəm-lē\ *adv* — **numb·ness** *n*

[1]**num·ber** \ˈnəm-bər\ *n* [ME *nombre,* fr. AF, fr. L *numerus*] (14c) **1 a** (1) **:** a sum of units **:** TOTAL (2) **:** COMPLEMENT 1b (3) **:** an indefinite usu. large total ⟨a ~ of members were absent⟩ ⟨the ~ of elderly is rising⟩ (4) *pl* **:** a numerous group **:** MANY (5) **:** a numerical preponderance **b** (1) **:** the characteristic of an individual by which it is treated as a unit or of a collection by which it is treated in terms of units (2) **:** an ascertainable total ⟨bugs beyond ~⟩ **c** (1) **:** a unit belonging to an abstract mathematical system and subject to specified laws of succession, addition, and multiplication; *esp* **:** NATURAL NUMBER (2) **:** an element (as *π*) of any of many mathematical systems obtained by extension of or analogy with the natural number system (3) *pl* **:** ARITHMETIC **2 :** a distinction of word form to denote reference to one or more than one; *also* **:** a form or group of forms so distinguished **3** *pl* **a** (1) **:** metrical structure **:** METER (2) **:** metrical lines **:** VERSES **b** *archaic* **:** musical sounds **:** NOTES **4 a :** a word, symbol, letter, or combination of symbols representing a number **b :** a numeral or combination of numerals or other symbols used to identify or designate ⟨dialed the wrong ~⟩ **c** (1) **:** a member of a sequence or collection designated by esp. consecutive numbers (as an issue of a periodical) (2) **:** a position in a numbered sequence **d :** a group of one kind ⟨not of their ~⟩ **5 :** one singled out from a group **:** INDIVIDUAL: as **a :** GIRL, WOMAN ⟨met an attractive ~ at the dance⟩ **b** (1) **:** a musical, theatrical, or literary selection or production (2) **:** ROUTINE, ACT **c :** STUNT, TRICK **d :** an act of transforming or impairing ⟨tripped and did a ~ on her knee⟩ **e :** an item of merchandise and esp. clothing **6 :** insight into a person's ability or character ⟨had my ~⟩ **7** *pl but sing or pl in constr* **a :** a form of lottery in which an individual wagers on the appearance of a certain combination of digits (as in regularly published numbers) — called also *numbers game* **b :** [2]POLICY 2a **8** *pl* **a :** figures representing amounts of money usu. in dollars spent, earned, or involved **b** (1) **:** STATISTICS 2; *esp* **:** individual statistics (as of an athlete) (2) **:** RATING 3c **9 :** a person represented by a number or considered without regard to individuality ⟨at the university I was just a ~⟩ **10 :** LIFETIME 1a — used with *up* ⟨the old feeling that comes to men in combat . . . that your ~ was up —Geoffrey Norman⟩ ***usage*** see AMOUNT — **by the numbers 1 :** in unison to a specific count or cadence **2 :** in a systematic, routine, or mechanical manner

☞ The Table of Numbers is on the following page.

[2]**number** *vb* **num·bered; num·ber·ing** \-b(ə-)riŋ\ *vt* (14c) **1 :** COUNT, ENUMERATE **2 :** to claim as part of a total **:** INCLUDE **3 :** to restrict to a definite number ⟨your days are ~*ed*⟩ **4 :** to assign a number to ⟨~ the pages⟩ **5 :** to amount to in number **:** TOTAL ⟨the crew ~*s* 100⟩ ~ *vi* **1 :** to reach a total number **2 :** to call off numbers in sequence — **num·ber·able** \-b(ə-)rə-bəl\ *adj* — **num·ber·er** \-bər-ər\ *n*

number cruncher *n* (1966) **1 :** a computer that performs fast numerical calculations esp. on large amounts of data **2 :** a person concerned with numerical data (as statistics) — **number crunching** *n*

num·ber·less \ˈnəm-bər-ləs\ *adj* (1573) **:** INNUMERABLE, COUNTLESS

number line *n* (1956) **:** a line of infinite extent whose points correspond to the real numbers according to their distance in a positive or negative direction from a point arbitrarily taken as zero

[1]**number one** *n* (ca. 1705) **1 :** one's own interests or welfare **:** ONESELF ⟨looking out for *number one*⟩ — often written *No. 1* **2 :** one that is first in rank, importance, or influence — often written *No. 1*

[2]**number one** *adj* (1839) **1 :** first in rank, importance, or influence **:** FOREMOST ⟨cancer is the country's *number one* killer⟩ — often written *No. 1* **2 :** of highest or of high quality

number plate *n* (1920) *chiefly Brit* **:** LICENSE PLATE

Num·bers \ˈnəm-bərz\ *n pl but sing in constr* (14c) **:** the mainly narrative fourth book of canonical Jewish and Christian Scripture — see BIBLE table

number theory *n* (1864) **:** the study of the properties of integers — **number theoretic** *adj* — **number theorist** *n*

numb·ing \ˈnə-miŋ\ *adj* (1581) **:** tending or serving to make numb or spiritless ⟨losing by a ~ margin⟩ ⟨a ~ lecture⟩ — **numb·ing·ly** *adv*

numbskull *var of* NUMSKULL

nu·men \ˈnü-mən, ˈnyü-\ *n, pl* **nu·mi·na** \-mə-nə\ [L, nod, divine will, numen; akin to L *nutare* to nod, Gk *neuein*] (1616) **:** a spiritual force or influence often identified with a natural object, phenomenon, or place

nu·mer·a·ble \ˈnüm-rə-bəl, ˈnü-mə-; ˈnyüm-, ˈnyü-mə-\ *adj* [L *numerabilis,* fr. *numerare* to count] (1570) **:** capable of being counted

nu·mer·acy \ˈn(y)üm-rə-sē, ˈn(y)ü-mə-\ *n* [L *numerus* number + E *-acy* (as in *literacy*)] (1959) **:** the capacity for quantitative thought and expression — **nu·mer·ate** \ˈnüm-rət, ˈnü-mə-; ˈnyüm-, ˈnyü-mə-\ *adj*

[1]**nu·mer·al** \ˈnüm-rəl, ˈnü-mə-; ˈnyüm-, ˈnyü-mə-\ *adj* [ME, fr. LL *numeralis,* fr. L *numerus*] (14c) **1 :** of, relating to, or expressing numbers **2 :** consisting of numbers or numerals — **nu·mer·al·ly** *adv*

[2]**numeral** *n* (1686) **1 :** a conventional symbol that represents a number **2** *pl* **:** numbers that designate by year a school or college class and that are awarded for distinction in an extracurricular activity

nu·mer·ate \ˈnü-mə-ˌrāt, ˈnyü-\ *vt* **-at·ed; -at·ing** [L *numeratus,* pp. of *numerare* to count, fr. *numerus*] (1657) **:** ENUMERATE

nu·mer·a·tion \ˌnü-mə-ˈrā-shən, ˌnyü-\ *n* (15c) **1 a :** the act or process or an instance of counting or numbering; *also* **:** a system of counting or numbering **b :** an act or instance of designating by a number **2 :** the art of reading in words numbers expressed by numerals

nu·mer·a·tor \ˈnü-mə-ˌrā-tər, ˈnyü-\ *n* (1542) **1 :** the part of a fraction that is above the line and signifies the number to be divided by the denominator **2 :** one that numbers

[1]**nu·mer·ic** \nu̇-ˈmer-ik, nyu̇-\ *adj* (ca. 1828) **:** NUMERICAL; *esp* **:** denoting a number or a system of numbers ⟨a ~ code⟩ ⟨a ~ sign⟩

[2]**nu·mer·ic** *n* (1879) **:** NUMBER, NUMERAL

nu·mer·i·cal \nu̇-ˈmer-i-kəl, nyu̇-\ *adj* [L *numerus*] (1628) **1 :** of or relating to numbers ⟨the ~ superiority of the enemy⟩ **2 :** expressed in or involving numbers or a number system ⟨~ standing in a class⟩ ⟨a ~ code⟩ — **nu·mer·i·cal·ly** \-k(ə-)lē\ *adv*

numerical analysis *n* (1853) **:** the study of quantitative approximations to the solutions of mathematical problems including consideration of and bounds to the errors involved

numerical taxonomy *n* (1962) **:** taxonomy in which many quantitatively measured characters are given equal weight in the determination of taxa and the construction of diagrams indicating systematic relationships — **numerical taxonomic** *adj* — **numerical taxonomist** *n*

nu·mer·ol·o·gy \ˌnü-mə-ˈrä-lə-jē, ˌnyü-\ *n* [L *numerus* + E *-o-* + *-logy*] (1911) **:** the study of the occult significance of numbers — **nu·mer·o·log·i·cal** \-mə-rə-ˈlä-ji-kəl\ *adj* — **nu·mer·ol·o·gist** \-mə-ˈrä-lə-jist\ *n*

nu·me·ro uno \ˈnü-mə-rō-ˈü-(ˌ)nō, ˈnyü-\ *n, pl* **numero unos** [It *numero uno* or Sp *número uno*] (1968) **:** NUMBER ONE — **numero uno** *adj*

nu·mer·ous \ˈnüm-rəs, ˈnü-mə-; ˈnyüm-, ˈnyü-mə-\ *adj* [ME, fr. L *numerosus,* fr. *numerus*] (15c) **:** consisting of great numbers of units or individuals ⟨born into a ~ family⟩; *also* **:** MANY ⟨received ~ complaints⟩ — **nu·mer·ous·ly** *adv* — **nu·mer·ous·ness** *n*

nu·mi·nous \ˈnü-mə-nəs, ˈnyü-\ *adj* [L *numin-, numen* numen] (1647) **1 :** SUPERNATURAL, MYSTERIOUS **2 :** filled with a sense of the presence of divinity **:** HOLY **3 :** appealing to the higher emotions or to the aesthetic sense **:** SPIRITUAL — **nu·mi·nous·ness** \-nəs\ *n*

nu·mis·mat·ic \ˌnü-məz-ˈma-tik, -məs-, ˌnyü-\ *adj* [F *numismatique,* fr. L *nomismat-, nomisma* coin, fr. Gk, current coin, fr. *nomizein* to use, fr. *nomos* custom, law — more at NIMBLE] (1792) **1 :** of or relating to numismatics **2 :** of or relating to currency **:** MONETARY — **nu·mis·mat·i·cal·ly** \-ti-k(ə-)lē\ *adv*

nu·mis·mat·ics \-tiks\ *n pl but sing in constr* (ca. 1828) **:** the study or collection of coins, tokens, and paper money and sometimes related objects (as medals) — **nu·mis·ma·tist** \nü-ˈmiz-mə-tist, nyü-\ *n*

num·mu·lar \ˈnəm-yə-lər\ *adj* [F *nummulaire,* fr. L *nummulus,* dim. of *nummus* coin, prob. fr. Gk *nomimos* customary, fr. *nomos*] (1846) **:** characterized by circular or oval lesions or drops ⟨~ dermatitis⟩

num·mu·lit·ic limestone \ˌnəm-yə-ˈli-tik-\ *n* [NL *Nummulites,* genus of foraminifers, fr. L *nummulus*] (1833) **:** the most widely distributed and distinctive formation of the Eocene in Europe, Asia, and northern Africa

num·skull *or* **numb·skull** \ˈnəm-ˌskəl\ *n* [*numb* + *skull*] (1717) **1 :** a thick or muddled head **2 :** a dull or stupid person **:** DUNCE

[1]**nun** \ˈnən\ *n* [ME, fr. OE *nunne,* fr. LL *nonna*] (bef. 12c) **:** a woman belonging to a religious order; *esp* **:** one under solemn vows of poverty, chastity, and obedience — **nun·like** \-ˌlīk\ *adj*

[2]**nun** \ˈnün\ *n* [Heb *nūn*] (ca. 1567) **:** the 14th letter of the Hebrew alphabet — see ALPHABET table

nun·a·tak \ˈnə-nə-ˌtak\ *n* [Inuit (Greenland) *nunataq*] (1877) **:** a hill or mountain completely surrounded by glacial ice

Nunc Di·mit·tis \ˌnəŋk-də-ˈmi-təs, ˌnu̇ŋk-\ *n* [L, now lettest thou depart; fr. the first words of the canticle] (1552) **:** the prayer of Simeon in Luke 2:29–32 used as a canticle

nun·cha·ku \ˈnən-ˌchək, ˌnən-ˈchä-kü\ *n, pl* **nun·cha·kus** *or* **nun-**

\ə\ **abut** \ᵊ\ kitten, F table \ər\ **further** \a\ ash \ā\ ace \ä\ mop, mar \au̇\ **out** \ch\ **chin** \e\ bet \ē\ **easy** \g\ go \i\ **hit** \ī\ ice \j\ job \ŋ\ sing \ō\ go \ȯ\ **law** \ȯi\ **boy** \th\ **thin** \t͟h\ **the** \ü\ **loot** \u̇\ **foot** \y\ yet \zh\ vision, beige \k̲, ⁿ, œ, ue, ʸ\ *see* Guide to Pronunciation

TABLE OF NUMBERS

CARDINAL NUMBERS[1]

NAME[2]	SYMBOL Arabic	Roman[3]
zero *or* naught *or* cipher	0	
one	1	I
two	2	II
three	3	III
four	4	IV
five	5	V
six	6	VI
seven	7	VII
eight	8	VIII
nine	9	IX
ten	10	X
eleven	11	XI
twelve	12	XII
thirteen	13	XIII
fourteen	14	XIV
fifteen	15	XV
sixteen	16	XVI
seventeen	17	XVII
eighteen	18	XVIII
nineteen	19	XIX
twenty	20	XX
twenty-one	21	XXI
twenty-two	22	XXII
twenty-three	23	XXIII
twenty-four	24	XXIV
twenty-five	25	XXV
twenty-six	26	XXVI
twenty-seven	27	XXVII
twenty-eight	28	XXVIII
twenty-nine	29	XXIX
thirty	30	XXX
thirty-one	31	XXXI
thirty-two *etc*	32	XXXII
forty	40	XL
forty-one *etc*	41	XLI
fifty	50	L
sixty	60	LX
seventy	70	LXX
eighty	80	LXXX
ninety	90	XC
one hundred	100	C
one hundred and one *or* one hundred one	101	CI
one hundred and two *etc*	102	CII
two hundred	200	CC
three hundred	300	CCC
four hundred	400	CD
five hundred	500	D
six hundred	600	DC
seven hundred	700	DCC
eight hundred	800	DCCC
nine hundred	900	CM
one thousand *or* ten hundred *etc*	1,000	M
two thousand *etc*	2,000	MM
five thousand	5,000	$\overline{\text{V}}$
ten thousand	10,000	$\overline{\text{X}}$
one hundred thousand	100,000	$\overline{\text{C}}$
one million	1,000,000	$\overline{\text{M}}$

ORDINAL NUMBERS[4]

NAME[5]	SYMBOL[6]
first	1st
second	2d *or* 2nd
third	3d *or* 3rd
fourth	4th
fifth	5th
sixth	6th
seventh	7th
eighth	8th
ninth	9th
tenth	10th
eleventh	11th
twelfth	12th
thirteenth	13th
fourteenth	14th
fifteenth	15th
sixteenth	16th
seventeenth	17th
eighteenth	18th
nineteenth	19th
twentieth	20th
twenty-first	21st
twenty-second	22d *or* 22nd
twenty-third	23d *or* 23rd
twenty-fourth	24th
twenty-fifth	25th
twenty-sixth	26th
twenty-seventh	27th
twenty-eighth	28th
twenty-ninth	29th
thirtieth	30th
thirty-first	31st
thirty-second *etc*	32d *or* 32nd
fortieth	40th
forty-first	41st
forty-second *etc*	42d *or* 42nd
fiftieth	50th
sixtieth	60th
seventieth	70th
eightieth	80th
ninetieth	90th
hundredth *or* one hundredth	100th
hundred and first *or* one hundred and first	101st
hundred and second *etc*	102d *or* 102nd
two hundredth	200th
three hundredth	300th
four hundredth	400th
five hundredth	500th
six hundredth	600th
seven hundredth	700th
eight hundredth	800th
nine hundredth	900th
thousandth *or* one thousandth	1,000th
two thousandth *etc*	2,000th
ten thousandth	10,000th
hundred thousandth *or* one hundred thousandth	100,000th
millionth *or* one millionth	1,000,000th

[1] The cardinal numbers are used in simple counting or in answer to "how many?" The words for these numbers may be used as nouns (he counted to *twelve*), as pronouns (*twelve* were found), or as adjectives (*twelve* girls).

[2] In formal contexts the numbers one to one hundred and in less formal contexts the numbers one to nine are commonly written out in words, while larger numbers are given in numerals. In nearly all contexts a number occurring at the beginning of a sentence is usually written out. Except in very formal contexts numerals are invariably used for dates. Arabic numbers from 1,000 to 9,999 are often written without commas or spaces (1000, 9999). Year numbers are always written without commas (1783).

[3] The Roman numerals are written either in capitals or in lowercase letters.

[4] The ordinal numbers are used to show the order of succession in which such items as names, objects, and periods of time are considered (the *twelfth* month; the *fourth* row of seats; the *18th* century).

[5] Each of the terms for the ordinal numbers excepting *first* and *second* is used in designating one of a number of parts into which a whole may be divided (a *fourth*; a *sixth*; a *tenth*) and as the denominator in fractions designating the number of such parts constituting a certain portion of a whole (*one fourth*; *three fifths*). When used as nouns the fractions are usually written as two words, although they are regularly hyphenated as adjectives (a *two-thirds* majority). When fractions are written in numerals, the cardinal symbols are used (¼, ⅗, ⅝).

[6] The Arabic symbols for the cardinal numbers may be read as ordinals in certain contexts (January 1 = January first; 2 Samuel = Second Samuel). The Roman numerals are sometimes read as ordinals (Henry IV = Henry the Fourth); sometimes they are written with the ordinal suffixes (XIXth Dynasty).

DENOMINATIONS ABOVE ONE MILLION

American system[1] NAME	VALUE IN POWERS OF TEN	NUMBER OF ZEROS[2]	NUMBER OF GROUPS OF THREE 0'S AFTER 1,000	*British system*[1] NAME	VALUE IN POWERS OF TEN	NUMBER OF ZEROS[2]	POWERS OF 1,000,000
billion	10^9	9	2	milliard	10^9	9	—
trillion	10^{12}	12	3	billion	10^{12}	12	2
quadrillion	10^{15}	15	4	trillion	10^{18}	18	3
quintillion	10^{18}	18	5	quadrillion	10^{24}	24	4
sextillion	10^{21}	21	6	quintillion	10^{30}	30	5
septillion	10^{24}	24	7	sextillion	10^{36}	36	6
octillion	10^{27}	27	8	septillion	10^{42}	42	7
nonillion	10^{30}	30	9	octillion	10^{48}	48	8
decillion	10^{33}	33	10	nonillion	10^{54}	54	9
undecillion	10^{36}	36	11	decillion	10^{60}	60	10
duodecillion	10^{39}	39	12	undecillion	10^{66}	66	11
tredecillion	10^{42}	42	13	duodecillion	10^{72}	72	12
quattuordecillion	10^{45}	45	14	tredecillion	10^{78}	78	13
quindecillion	10^{48}	48	15	quattuordecillion	10^{84}	84	14
sexdecillion	10^{51}	51	16	quindecillion	10^{90}	90	15
septendecillion	10^{54}	54	17	sexdecillion	10^{96}	96	16
octodecillion	10^{57}	57	18	septendecillion	10^{102}	102	17
novemdecillion	10^{60}	60	19	octodecillion	10^{108}	108	18
vigintillion	10^{63}	63	20	novemdecillion	10^{114}	114	19
centillion	10^{303}	303	100	vigintillion	10^{120}	120	20
				centillion	10^{600}	600	100

[1] The American system of numeration for denominations above one million was modeled on the French system but more recently the French system has been changed to correspond to the German and British systems. In the American system each of the denominations above 1,000 millions (the American *billion*) is 1,000 times the preceding one (one trillion = 1,000 billions; one quadrillion = 1,000 trillions). In the British system the first denomination above 1,000 millions (the British *milliard*) is 1,000 times the preceding one, but each of the denominations above 1,000 milliards (the British *billion*) is 1,000,000 times the preceding one (one trillion = 1,000,000 billions; one quadrillion = 1,000,000 trillions). In recent years, however, British usage reflects widespread and increasing use of the values of the American system in place of those of the British system.

[2] For convenience in reading large numerals, the thousands, millions, and larger denominations are usually separated by commas (21,530; 1,155,465) or especially in technical contexts by spaces (1 155 465). Serial numbers (as social security numbers) are often written with hyphens (042-24-4705).

chaku [Jp dial. (Okinawa)] (1970) : a weapon that consists of two hardwood sticks joined at their ends by a short length of rawhide, cord, or chain

nun·ci·a·ture \ˈnən(t)-sē-ə-ˌchu̇r, ˈnu̇n(t)-, -chər, -ˌtyu̇r, -ˌtu̇r\ *n* [It *nunciatura,* fr. *nuncio*] (1652) **1 :** a papal diplomatic mission headed by a nuncio **2 :** the office or period of office of a nuncio

nun·cio \ˈnən(t)-sē-ˌō, ˈnu̇n(t)-\ *n, pl* **-ci·os** [It, fr. L *nuntius* messenger, message] (1528) **:** a papal legate of the highest rank permanently accredited to a civil government

nun·cle \ˈnəŋ-kəl\ *n* [by alter. (fr. misdivision of *an uncle*)] (ca. 1589) *chiefly dial* **:** UNCLE

nun·cu·pa·tive \ˈnən-kyu̇-ˌpā-tiv, ˈnəŋ-; ˌnən-ˈkyü-pə-\ *adj* [ML *nuncupativus,* fr. LL, so-called, fr. L *nuncupatus,* pp. of *nuncupare* to name, prob. ultim. fr. *nomen* name + *capere* to take — more at NAME, HEAVE] (1546) **:** not written **:** ORAL ⟨a ~ will⟩

nun·nery \ˈnən-rē, ˈnə-nə-\ *n, pl* **-ner·ies** (14c) **:** a convent of nuns

nuoc mam \nü-ˈäk-ˈmäm\ *n* [Vietnamese *nước mắm,* lit., salted fish sauce] (1919) **:** a sauce made of fish (as anchovies) fermented in brine

Nu·pe \ˈnü-(ˌ)pā\ *n, pl* **Nupe** *or* **Nupes** (1883) **:** a member of a people of west central Nigeria; *also* **:** the language of the Nupe people

[1]**nup·tial** \ˈnəp-shəl, -chəl, ÷-shə-wəl, ÷-chə-wəl\ *adj* [L *nuptialis,* fr. *nuptiae,* pl., wedding, fr. *nubere* to marry; perh. akin to Gk *nymphē* bride, nymph] (15c) **1 :** of or relating to marriage or the marriage ceremony **2 :** characteristic of or occurring in the breeding season ⟨~ flight⟩

[2]**nuptial** *n* (ca. 1555) **:** MARRIAGE, WEDDING — usu. used in pl.

nup·tial·i·ty \ˌnəp-shē-ˈa-lə-tē, -chē-\ *n, pl* **-ties** (1899) **:** the marriage rate

Nur·i·stani \ˌnu̇r-ə-ˈstä-nē, ˌnyu̇r-\ *n* [*Nuristan,* Afghanistan] (1951) **1 :** a member of a group of peoples of the Hindu Kush in northeastern Afghanistan **2 :** the family of languages spoken by the Nuristanis that constitutes a distinct branch of Indo-Iranian

[1]**nurse** \ˈnərs\ *n* [ME *norice, norce, nurse,* fr. AF *nurice,* fr. LL *nutricia,* fr. L, fem. of *nutricius* nourishing — more at NUTRITIOUS] (13c) **1 a :** a woman who suckles an infant not her own **:** WET NURSE **b :** a woman who takes care of a young child **:** DRY NURSE **2 :** one that looks after, fosters, or advises **3 :** a person who cares for the sick or infirm; *specif* **:** a licensed health-care professional who practices independently or is supervised by a physician, surgeon, or dentist and who is skilled in promoting and maintaining health — compare LICENSED PRACTICAL NURSE, REGISTERED NURSE **4 a :** a worker form of a social insect (as an ant or a bee) that cares for the young **b :** a female mammal used to suckle the young of another

[2]**nurse** *vb* **nursed; nurs·ing** [ME *nurshen* to suckle, nourish, contr. of *nurishen*] *vt* (14c) **1 a :** to nourish at the breast **:** SUCKLE **b :** to take nourishment from the breast of **2 :** REAR, EDUCATE **3 a :** to promote the development or progress of **b :** to manage with care or economy ⟨*nursed* the business through hard times⟩ ⟨*nursed* a 1–0 lead⟩ **c :** to take charge of and watch over **4 a :** to care for and wait on (as a sick person) **b :** to attempt to cure by care and treatment **5 :** to hold in one's memory or consideration ⟨~ a grievance⟩ **6 a :** to use, handle, or operate carefully so as to conserve energy or avoid injury or pain ⟨~ a sprained ankle⟩ **b :** to use sparingly **c :** to consume slowly or over a long period ⟨~ a cup of coffee⟩ ~ *vi* **1 a :** to feed an offspring from the breast **b :** to feed at the breast **:** SUCK **2 :** to act or serve as a nurse — **nurs·er** *n*

nurse·maid \ˈnərs-ˌmād\ *n* (1657) **:** a girl or woman who is regularly employed to look after children

nurse–mid·wife \-ˈmid-ˌwīf\ *n* (1952) **:** a registered nurse with additional training as a midwife who delivers infants and provides prenatal and postpartum care, newborn care, and some routine care (as gynecological exams) of women — **nurse–mid·wife·ry** \-ˌmid-ˈwi-f(ə-)rē, -ˈwī-; -ˈmid-ˌwī-\ *n*

nurse–prac·ti·tion·er \-prak-ˈti-sh(ə-)nər\ *n* (1969) **:** a registered nurse who is qualified through advanced training to assume some of the duties and responsibilities formerly assumed only by a physician

nurs·ery \ˈnərs-rē, ˈnər-sə-\ *n, pl* **-er·ies** (14c) **1** *obs* **:** attentive care **:** FOSTERAGE **2 a :** a child's bedroom **b :** a place where children are temporarily cared for in their parents' absence **c :** DAY NURSERY **3 a :** something that fosters, develops, or promotes **b :** a place in which persons are trained or educated **4 :** an area where plants are grown for transplanting, for use as stocks for budding and grafting, or for sale **5 :** a place where young animals grow or are cared for

nurs·ery·man \-mən\ *n* (1672) **:** one whose occupation is the cultivation of plants (as trees and shrubs) esp. for sale

nursery rhyme *n* (1816) **:** a short rhyme for children that often tells a story

nursery school *n* (1835) **:** a school for children usu. under five years

nurse's aide *n* (1943) **:** a worker who assists trained nurses in a hospital by performing unspecialized services (as giving baths)

nurse shark *n* [alter. of *nusse*] (1851) **:** any of various sharks (as family Ginglymostomatidae); *esp* **:** a shark (*Ginglymostoma cirratum*) of warm waters

nursing *n* (1860) **1 :** the profession of a nurse ⟨schools of ~⟩ **2 :** the duties of a nurse ⟨proper ~ is difficult work⟩

nursing home *n* (1896) **:** a privately operated establishment providing maintenance and personal or nursing care for persons (as the aged or the chronically ill) who are unable to care for themselves properly

nurs·ling \ˈnərs-liŋ\ *n* (1557) **1 :** one that is solicitously cared for **2 :** a nursing child

nur·tur·ance \ˈnər-chə-rən(t)s\ *n* (ca. 1938) **:** affectionate care and attention — **nur·tur·ant** \-rənt\ *adj*

[1]**nur·ture** \ˈnər-chər\ *n* [ME *norture, nurture,* fr. AF *nureture,* fr. LL *nutritura* act of nursing, fr. L *nutritus,* pp. of *nutrire* to suckle, nourish — more at NOURISH] (14c) **1 :** TRAINING, UPBRINGING **2 :** something that nourishes **:** FOOD **3 :** the sum of the environmental factors influencing the behavior and traits expressed by an organism

[2]**nurture** *vt* **nur·tured; nur·tur·ing** \ˈnərch-riŋ, ˈnər-chə-\ (15c) **1 :** to supply with nourishment **2 :** EDUCATE **3 :** to further the development of **:** FOSTER — **nur·tur·er** \ˈnər-chər-ər\ *n*

[1]**nut** \ˈnət\ *n* [ME *nute, note,* fr. OE *hnutu;* akin to OHG *nuz* nut and perh. to L *nux* nut] (bef. 12c) **1 a** (1) **:** a hard-shelled dry fruit or seed with a separable rind or shell and interior kernel (2) **:** the kernel of a nut **b :** a dry indehiscent one-seeded fruit with a woody pericarp **2 a :** a hard problem or undertaking **b :** CORE, HEART **3 :** a perforated block usu. of metal that has an internal screw thread and is used on a bolt or screw for tightening or holding something **4 :** the ridge in a stringed instrument (as a violin) over which the strings pass on the upper end of the fingerboard **5 :** a small lump (as of butter) **6 a :** a foolish, eccentric, or crazy person **b :** ENTHUSIAST ⟨a movie ~⟩ **7** *pl* **:** NONSENSE — often used interjectionally **8** *slang* **:** a person's head **9** *usu vulgar* **:** TESTIS **10 :** the amount of money that must be earned in order to break even **11 :** EN 1 — **nut·like** \-ˌlīk\ *adj*

[2]**nut** *vi* **nut·ted; nut·ting** (1604) **:** to gather or seek nuts

nu·tate \ˈnü-ˌtāt, ˈnyü-\ *vi* **nu·tat·ed; nu·tat·ing** (1880) **:** to exhibit or undergo nutation

nu·ta·tion \nü-ˈtā-shən, nyü-\ *n* [L *nutation-, nutatio,* fr. *nutare* to nod, rock — more at NUMEN] (1612) **1** *archaic* **:** the act of nodding the head **2 :** oscillatory movement of the axis of a rotating body (as the earth) **:** WOBBLE **3 :** a spontaneous usu. spiral movement of a growing plant part — **nu·ta·tion·al** \-shnəl, -shə-nᵊl\ *adj*

nut–brown \ˈnət-ˈbrau̇n\ *adj* (14c) **:** of the color of a brown nut

nut·case \-ˌkās\ *n* (1959) **:** NUT 6a

nut·crack·er \-ˌkra-kər\ *n* (ca. 1548) **:** an implement for cracking nuts

nut·gall \-ˌgȯl\ *n* (15c) **:** a gall that resembles a nut; *esp* **:** such a gall produced on oaks

nut grass *n* (1775) **:** a perennial sedge (*Cyperus rotundus*) of wide distribution that has slender rootstocks bearing small edible tubers resembling nuts; *also* **:** a related sedge (*C. esculentus*)

nut·hatch \ˈnət-ˌhach\ *n* [ME *notehache,* fr. *note* nut + *-hache;* akin to OE *tohaccian* to hack — more at HACK] (14c) **:** any of various small tree-climbing chiefly insectivorous birds (family Sittidae and esp. genus *Sitta*) that have a compact body, a narrow bill, a short tail, and sometimes a black cap

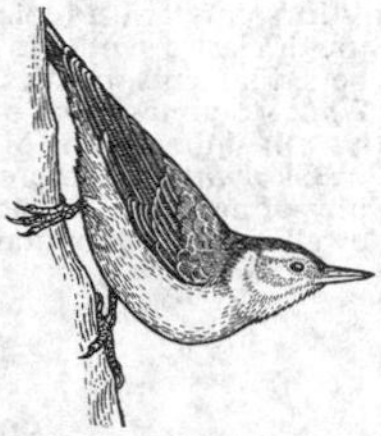

nuthatch

nut·house \ˈnət-ˌhau̇s\ *n* (1900) *slang* **:** a mental hospital

nut·let \ˈnət-lət\ *n* (1856) **1 a :** a small nut **b :** a small fruit similar to a nut **2 :** the stone of a drupelet

nut·meg \ˈnət-ˌmeg, -ˌmāg\ *n* [ME *notemigge, notemuge,* ultim. fr. Old Occitan *noz muscada,* fr. *noz* nut (fr. L *nuc-, nux*) + *muscada,* fem. of *muscat* musky — more at MUSCAT] (15c) **1 :** an aromatic seed produced by an evergreen tree (*Myristica fragrans* of the family Myristicaceae, the nutmeg family) native to the Moluccas; *also* **:** the ground seed used as a spice — compare MACE 2 **2 :** a tree yielding nutmeg

nut·pick \ˈnət-ˌpik\ *n* (1862) **:** a small sharp-pointed implement for extracting the kernels from nuts

nu·tra·ceu·ti·cal *also* **nu·tri·ceu·ti·cal** \ˌnü-trə-ˈsü-ti-kəl\ *n* [*nutri*tive + [2]*pharmaceutical*] (1990) **:** a foodstuff (as a fortified food or dietary supplement) that provides health benefits in addition to its basic nutritional value

nu·tria \ˈnü-trē-ə, ˈnyü-\ *n* [AmerSp, fr. Sp, otter, modif. of L *lutra;* prob. akin to OE *oter* otter] (1820) **1 :** the durable usu. light brown fur of a nutria **2 :** a large So. American semiaquatic rodent (*Myocastor coypus*) with webbed hind feet and a round nearly hairless tail that has been introduced into parts of Europe, Asia, and No. America

[1]**nu·tri·ent** \ˈnü-trē-ənt, ˈnyü-\ *adj* [L *nutrient-, nutriens,* prp. of *nutrire* to nourish — more at NOURISH] (1650) **:** furnishing nourishment

[2]**nutrient** *n* (ca. 1828) **:** a nutritive substance or ingredient

nu·tri·ment \ˈnü-trə-mənt, ˈnyü-\ *n* [ME, fr. L *nutrimentum,* fr. *nutrire*] (15c) **:** something that nourishes or promotes growth, provides energy, repairs body tissues, and maintains life

nu·tri·tion \nu̇-ˈtri-shən, nyu̇-\ *n* [ME *nutricioun,* fr. LL *nutrition-, nutritio,* fr. L *nutrire*] (15c) **1 :** the act or process of nourishing or being nourished; *specif* **:** the sum of the processes by which an animal or plant takes in and utilizes food substances **2 :** NOURISHMENT 1 — **nu·tri·tion·al** \-ˈtrish-nəl, -ˈtri-shə-nᵊl\ *adj* — **nu·tri·tion·al·ly** *adv*

nu·tri·tion·ist \-ˈtri-sh(ə-)nist\ *n* (1926) **:** a specialist in the study of nutrition

nu·tri·tious \nu̇-ˈtri-shəs, nyu̇-\ *adj* [L *nutricius,* fr. *nutric-, nutrix* nurse, fr. *nutrire* to nourish — more at NOURISH] (1665) **:** NOURISHING — **nu·tri·tious·ly** *adv* — **nu·tri·tious·ness** *n*

nu·tri·tive \ˈnü-trə-tiv, ˈnyü-\ *adj* (14c) **1 :** of or relating to nutrition **2 :** NOURISHING — **nu·tri·tive·ly** *adv*

nutritive ratio *n* (1897) **:** the ratio of digestible protein to other nutrients in a foodstuff or ration

nuts \ˈnəts\ *adj* (1785) **1 :** ENTHUSIASTIC, KEEN ⟨~ for animals and children —Rick Reilly⟩ **2 :** INSANE, CRAZY ⟨said that it was a novel and all the people who said otherwise were ~ —Flannery O'Connor⟩

nuts and bolts *n* (1967) **1 :** the working parts or elements **2 :** the practical workings of a machine or enterprise as opposed to theoretical considerations or speculative possibilities — **nuts–and–bolts** *adj*

nut·sedge \ˈnət-ˌsej\ *n* (ca. 1909) **:** NUT GRASS

nut·shell \ˈnət-ˌshel\ *n* (13c) **1 :** the hard external covering in which the kernel of a nut is enclosed **2 :** something of small size, amount, or scope — **in a nutshell :** in a very brief statement

nut·ter \ˈnə-tər\ *n* (1958) *slang Brit* **:** NUT 6a

nut·ty \ˈnə-tē\ *adj* **nut·ti·er; -est** (15c) **1 :** having or producing nuts **2 :** having a flavor like that of nuts **3 :** ECCENTRIC, SILLY; *also* **:** mentally unbalanced — **nut·ti·ly** \-tə-lē\ *adv* — **nut·ti·ness** *n*

Nuu–Chah–Nulth *also* **Nuu Chah Nulth** \ˌnü-ˈchä-nu̇l\ *n, pl* **Nuu–Chah–Nulth** *also* **Nuu Chah Nulth** [Nootka *nuča·ńuł,* lit., all along the mountains] (1979) **:** NOOTKA

nux vom·i·ca \ˈnəks-ˈvä-mi-kə\ *n, pl* **nux vomica** [NL, lit., emetic nut] (14c) **1 :** the poisonous disk-shaped seed of a tree (*Strychnos nux-vomica* of the family Loganiaceae) of southern Asia that contains several alkaloids and esp. strychnine and brucine; *also* **:** the tree yielding nux vomica **2 :** a drug containing nux vomica

\ə\ **abut** \ᵊ\ **kitten,** F table \ər\ **further** \a\ **ash** \ā\ **ace** \ä\ **mop, mar** \au̇\ **out** \ch\ **chin** \e\ **bet** \ē\ **easy** \g\ **go** \i\ **hit** \ī\ **ice** \j\ **job** \ŋ\ **sing** \ō\ **go** \ȯ\ **law** \ȯi\ **boy** \th\ **thin** \th\ **the** \ü\ **loot** \u̇\ **foot** \y\ **yet** \zh\ **vision, beige** \k, ⁿ, œ, ue, ʸ\ *see* Guide to Pronunciation

Nu·yo·ri·can \,nü-yòr-'rē-kən\ *n* [blend of AmerSp *nuyorquino* New Yorker and E *Puerto Rican*] (1974) : a person of Puerto Rican birth or descent who is a current or former resident of New York City — **Nuyorican** *adj*

nuz·zle \'nə-zəl\ *vb* **nuz·zled; nuz·zling** \'nəz-liŋ, 'nə-zə-lən\ [ME *noselen* to bring the nose toward the ground, fr. *nose*] *vi* (1530) **1** : to work with or as if with the nose; *esp* : to root, rub, or snuff something **2** : to lie close or snug ~ *vt* **1** : to root, rub, or touch with or as if with the nose **2** : to rub or push gently (as one's face) against something

NV *abbr* **1** Nevada **2** nonvoting

nvCJD *abbr* new variant Creutzfeldt-Jakob disease

NW *abbr* northwest

NWS *abbr* National Weather Service

NWT *abbr* Northwest Territories

NY *abbr* New York

ny·a·la \ä-lə\ *n, pl* **nyalas** *or* **nyala** [of Bantu origin; akin to Venda *dzi-nyálà* nyala buck] (1899) : an antelope (*Tragelaphus angasii*) of southeastern Africa with vertical white stripes on the sides of the body, a dorsal crest of hair from the neck to the base of the tail, and in the male shaggy black hair along the underside; *also* : a related antelope (*T. buxtoni*) of Ethiopia

NYC *abbr* New York City

nyc·ta·lo·pia \,nik-tə-'lō-pē-ə\ *n* [NL, fr. L *nyctalops* suffering from night blindness, fr. Gk *nyktalops*, fr. *nykt-, nyx* night + *alaos* blind + *ōp-, ōps* eye — more at NIGHT, EYE] (1684) : NIGHT BLINDNESS

ny·lon \'nī-,län\ *n* [coined word] (1938) **1** : any of numerous strong tough elastic synthetic polyamide materials that are fashioned into fibers, filaments, bristles, or sheets and used esp. in textiles and plastics **2** *pl* : stockings made of nylon

nymph \'nim(p)f\ *n* [ME *nimphe*, fr. MF, fr. L *nympha* bride, nymph, fr. Gk *nymphē* — more at NUPTIAL] (14c) **1** : any of the minor divinities of nature in classical mythology represented as beautiful maidens dwelling in the mountains, forests, trees, and waters **2** : GIRL **3** : any

of various immature insects; *esp* : a larva of an insect (as a grasshopper, true bug, or mayfly) with incomplete metamorphosis that differs from the imago esp. in size and in its incompletely developed wings and genitalia — **nymph·al** \'nim(p)-fəl\ *adj*

nym·pha·lid \nim-'fa-ləd, 'nim-fə-ləd\ *n* [NL *Nymphalidae*, ultim. fr. L *nympha* nymph] (1897) : any of a family (Nymphalidae) of butterflies (as a mourning cloak or fritillary) with the first pair of legs being hairy, reduced in size, and useless for walking — **nymphalid** *adj*

nym·phet *also* **nym·phette** \nim-'fet, 'nim(p)-fət\ *n* (1955) : a sexually precocious girl barely in her teens; *also* : a sexually attractive young woman

nym·pho \'nim(p)-(,)fō\ *n, pl* **nymphos** [short for *nymphomaniac*] (ca. 1910) : a person affected by nymphomania : NYMPHOMANIAC

nym·pho·lep·sy \'nim(p)-fə-,lep-sē\ *n* [*nympholept*, fr. Gk *nympholēptos* frenzied, lit., caught by nymphs, fr. *nymphē* + *lambanein* to seize — more at LATCH] (1775) **1** : a demonic enthusiasm held by the ancients to seize one bewitched by a nymph **2** : a frenzy of emotion — **nym·pho·lept** \-,lept\ *n* — **nym·pho·lep·tic** \,nim(p)-fə-'lep-tik\ *adj*

nym·pho·ma·nia \,nim(p)-fə-'mā-nē-ə, -nyə\ *n* [NL, fr. *nymphae* inner lips of the vulva (fr. L, pl. of *nympha*) + LL *mania* mania] (1702) : excessive sexual desire by a female — **nym·pho·ma·ni·ac** \-nē-,ak\ *n or adj* — **nym·pho·ma·ni·a·cal** \-mə-'nī-ə-kəl\ *adj*

Ny·norsk \nü-'nȯrsk, nyü-, nœ-\ *n* [Norw, lit., new Norwegian] (1931) : a literary form of Norwegian based on the spoken dialects of Norway — compare BOKMÅL

NYSE *abbr* New York Stock Exchange

nys·tag·mus \nis-'tag-məs\ *n* [NL, fr. Gk *nystagmos* drowsiness, fr. *nystazein* to doze; prob. akin to Lith *snusti* to doze] (1776) : a rapid involuntary oscillation of the eyeballs — **nys·tag·mic** \-mik\ *adj*

nys·ta·tin \'nis-tə-tən\ *n* [*New York State* (where it was developed) + [1]-*in*] (1952) : an antifungal antibiotic that is derived from a soil actinomycete (*Streptomyces noursei*) and is used esp. to treat candidiasis

NZ *abbr* New Zealand

[1]o \'ō\ *n, pl* **o's** *or* **os** \'ōz\ *often cap, often attrib* (bef. 12c) **1 a** : the 15th letter of the English alphabet **b** : a graphic representation of this letter **c** : a speech counterpart of orthographic *o* **2** : a graphic device for reproducing the letter *o* **3** : one designated *o* esp. as the 15th in order or class **4** : something shaped like the letter O; *esp* : ZERO

[2]o *abbr* **1** ocean **2** ohm **3** old **4** order **5** over

[1]O *var of* OH

[2]O *n* (1929) : the one of the four ABO blood groups characterized by the absence of antigens designated by the letters A and B and by the presence of antibodies against these antigens

[3]O *abbr* **1** offense **2** Ohio **3** [NL *octarius*] pint

[4]O *symbol* oxygen

[1]o- *or* **oo-** *comb form* [Gk *ōi-, ōio-*, fr. *ōion* — more at EGG] : egg ⟨*oology*⟩; *specif* : ovum ⟨*oogonium*⟩

[2]o- *abbr* orth- *or* ortho-

-o- [Gk, thematic vowel of many nouns and adjectives in combination] — used as a connective vowel orig. to join word elements of Greek origin and now also to join word elements of Latin or other origin ⟨*speedometer*⟩ ⟨*elastomer*⟩

[1]-o *n suffix* [perh. fr. [1]*oh*] : one that is, has the qualities of, or is associated with ⟨*bucko*⟩

[2]-o *interj suffix* [prob. fr. [1]*oh*] — in interjections formed from other parts of speech ⟨*cheerio*⟩ ⟨*righto*⟩

o' \ə\ *or* \ȯ, ō\ *prep* [ME *o, o-*, contr. of *on & of*] (13c) **1** *chiefly dial* : ON **2** : OF ⟨one o'clock⟩

o/a *abbr* on or about

oaf \'ōf\ *n, pl* **oafs** [alter. of *auf, alfe* goblin's child, prob. fr. ME *alven, elven* elf, fairy, fr. OE *ælfen* nymphs; akin to OE *ælf* elf — more at ELF] (1692) **1** : a stupid person : BOOB **2** : a big clumsy slow-witted person — **oaf·ish** \'ō-fish\ *adj* — **oaf·ish·ly** *adv* — **oaf·ish·ness** *n*

oak \'ōk\ *n, pl* **oaks** *or* **oak** *often attrib* [ME *ook*, fr. OE *āc*; akin to OHG *eih* oak and perh. to Gk *aigilōps*, a kind of oak] (bef. 12c) **1 a** : any of a genus (*Quercus*) of trees or shrubs of the beech family that produce acorns; *also* : any of various plants related to or resembling the oaks **b** : the tough hard durable wood of an oak tree **2** : the leaves of an oak used as decoration — **oak·en** \'ō-kən\ *adj*

oak apple *n* (15c) : a large round gall produced on oak leaves and twigs by a gall wasp (esp. *Amphibolips confluenta*)

oak–leaf cluster *n* (1918) : a bronze or silver cluster of oak leaves and acorns added to various military decorations to signify a second or subsequent award of the basic decoration

oak 1a: *1 acorn, 2 leaf*

oak·moss \'ōk-,mȯs\ *n* (1728) : any of several lichens (as *Evernia prunastri*) that grow on oak trees and yield a resin used in perfumery

oa·kum \'ō-kəm\ *n* [ME *okum*, fr. OE *ācumba* tow, fr. *ā-* (separative & perfective prefix) + -*cumba* (akin to OE *camb* comb) — more at ABIDE] (15c) : loosely twisted hemp or jute fiber impregnated with tar or a tar derivative and used in caulking seams and packing joints

oak wilt *n* (1942) : a destructive disease of oak trees that is caused by a fungus (*Ceratocystis fagacearum*) and is characterized by wilting, discoloration, and defoliation

[1]oar \'ȯr\ *n* [ME *oor*, fr. OE *ār*; akin to ON *ār* oar] (bef. 12c) **1** : a long pole with a broad blade at one end used for propelling or steering a boat **2** : OARSMAN — **oared** \'ȯrd\ *adj*

[2]oar *vi* (15c) : to progress by or as if by using oars ~ *vt* : to propel with or as if with oars : ROW

oar·fish \'ȯr-,fish\ *n* (1860) : a marine bony fish (*Regalecus glesne*) of subtropical waters with a narrow soft body from 20 to 30 feet (6 to 9 meters) long, a red dorsal fin running the entire length of the body, and red-tipped anterior rays rising above the head

oar·lock \-,läk\ *n* (bef. 12c) : a usu. U-shaped device for holding an oar in place

oars·man \'ȯrz-mən\ *n* (1701) : one who rows esp. in a racing crew — **oars·man·ship** \-,ship\ *n*

oars·wom·an \-,wu̇-mən\ *n* (1843) : a woman who is an oarsman

OAS *abbr* Organization of American States

OASDI *abbr* Old-Age, Survivors, and Disability Insurance

oa·sis \ō-'ā-səs\ *n, pl* **oa·ses** \-,sēz\ [LL, fr. Gk] (1613) **1** : a fertile or green area in an arid region (as a desert) **2** : something that provides refuge, relief, or pleasant contrast

oast \'ōst\ *n* [ME *ost*, fr. OE *āst;* akin to MD *eest* kiln, L *aestus* heat, *aestas* summer — more at EDIFY] (bef. 12c) : a usu. conical kiln used for drying hops, malt, or tobacco — called also *oast·house* \-,haus\

oat \'ōt\ *n, often attrib* [ME *ote*, fr. OE *āte*] (bef. 12c) **1 a** : any of several grasses (genus *Avena*); *esp* : a widely cultivated cereal grass (*A. sativa*) **b** : a crop or plot of the oat; *also* : the seed of an oat — usu. used in pl. but sing. or pl. in constr. **2** *archaic* : a reed instrument made of an oat straw — **feel one's oats** : to act in a newly self-confident and often self-important manner

oat·cake \'ōt-,kāk\ *n* (14c) : a thin flat oatmeal cake

oat cell *n* (1903) : any of the small round or oval cells with a high ratio of nuclear protoplasm to cytoplasm that resemble oat grains and are characteristic of a small-cell lung cancer

oat·en \'ō-t³n\ *adj* (14c) : of or relating to oats, oat straw, or oatmeal

oat·er \'ō-tər\ *n* (1946) : WESTERN 2

oat grass *n* (1578) : WILD OAT 1a; *broadly* : any of several grasses resembling the oat

oath \'ōth\ *n, pl* **oaths** \'ōthz, 'ōths\ [ME *ooth*, fr. OE *āth*; akin to OHG *eid* oath, MIr *oeth*] (bef. 12c) **1 a** (1) : a solemn usu. formal calling upon God or a god to witness to the truth of what one says or to witness that one sincerely intends to do what one says (2) : a solemn attestation of the truth or inviolability of one's words **b** : something (as a promise) corroborated by an oath **2** : an irreverent or careless use of a sacred name; *broadly* : SWEARWORD

oat·meal \'ōt-,mēl, ōt-'mēl\ *n* (14c) **1 a** : meal made from oats **b** : rolled oats **2** : porridge made from ground or rolled oats

OAU *abbr* Organization of African Unity
ob *abbr* **1** [L *obiit*] he died; she died **2** observation
Ob *or* **Obad** *abbr* Obadiah
OB *abbr* obstetric; obstetrician; obstetrics
ob- *prefix* [NL, fr. L, in the way, against, toward, fr. *ob* in the way of, on account of; akin to OCS *o, ob* on, around] **:** inversely ⟨obovate⟩
Oba·di·ah \ˌō-bə-ˈdī-ə\ *n* [Heb *ʿŌbhadhyāh*] (1587) **1 :** a Hebrew prophet **2 :** a prophetic book of canonical Jewish and Christian Scripture — see BIBLE table
[1]**ob·bli·ga·to** \ˌä-blə-ˈgä-(ˌ)tō\ *adj* [It, obligatory, fr. pp. of *obbligare* to oblige, fr. L *obligare* — more at OBLIGE] (1794) **:** not to be omitted **:** OBLIGATORY — used as a direction in music; compare AD LIBITUM
[2]**obbligato** *n, pl* **-tos** *also* **-ti** \-ˈgä-tē\ (1839) **1 :** an elaborate esp. melodic part accompanying a solo or principal melody and usu. played by a single instrument ⟨a song with violin ~⟩ **2 :** ACCOMPANIMENT 2b; *esp* **:** an attendant background sound
ob·cor·date \ˌäb-ˈkȯr-ˌdāt\ *adj* (ca. 1775) **:** heart-shaped with the notch apical ⟨~ leaf⟩
ob·du·ra·cy \ˈäb-də-rə-sē, -dyə-; äb-ˈdu̇r-ə-, əb-, -ˈdyu̇r-\ *n, pl* **-cies** (1597) **:** the quality or state of being obdurate
ob·du·rate \ˈäb-də-rət, -dyə-; äb-ˈdu̇r-ət, əb-, -ˈdyu̇r-\ *adj* [ME, fr. L *obduratus,* pp. of *obdurare* to harden, fr. *ob-* against + *durus* hard — more at DURING] (15c) **1 a :** stubbornly persistent in wrongdoing **b :** hardened in feelings **2 :** resistant to persuasion or softening influences ***syn*** see INFLEXIBLE — **ob·du·rate·ly** *adv* — **ob·du·rate·ness** *n*
OBE *abbr* **1** officer of the Order of the British Empire **2** out-of-body experience
obe·ah \ˈō-bē-ə\ *also* **obi** \ˈō-bē\ *n, often cap* [of African origin; akin to Ibo *díbìà* folk healer] (ca. 1711) **:** a system of belief among blacks chiefly of the British West Indies and the Guianas that is characterized by the use of magic ritual to ward off misfortune or to cause harm
obe·di·ence \ō-ˈbē-dē-ən(t)s, ə-\ *n* (13c) **1 a :** an act or instance of obeying **b :** the quality or state of being obedient **2 :** a sphere of jurisdiction; *esp* **:** an ecclesiastical or sometimes secular dominion
obe·di·ent \-ənt\ *adj* [ME, fr. AF, fr. L *oboedient-, oboediens,* fr. prp. of *oboedire* to obey] (13c) **:** submissive to the restraint or command of authority **:** willing to obey — **obe·di·ent·ly** *adv*
syn OBEDIENT, DOCILE, TRACTABLE, AMENABLE mean submissive to the will of another. OBEDIENT implies compliance with the demands or requests of one in authority ⟨*obedient* to the government⟩. DOCILE implies a predisposition to submit readily to control or guidance ⟨a *docile* child⟩. TRACTABLE suggests having a character that permits easy handling or managing ⟨*tractable* animals⟩. AMENABLE suggests a willingness to yield or cooperate because of a desire to be agreeable or because of a natural open-mindedness ⟨*amenable* to new ideas⟩.
obei·sance \ō-ˈbē-sᵊn(t)s, ə-, -ˈbā-\ *n* [ME *obeisaunce* obedience, obeisance, fr. AF *obeisance,* fr. *obeissant,* prp. of *obeir* to obey] (14c) **1 :** a movement of the body made in token of respect or submission **:** BOW **2 :** acknowledgment of another's superiority or importance **:** HOMAGE ⟨makes ~ to her mentors⟩ — **obei·sant** \-sᵊnt\ *adj* — **obei·sant·ly** *adv*
obe·lia \ō-ˈbēl-yə\ *n* [NL] (1868) **:** any of a genus (*Obelia*) of small colonial marine hydroids with colonies branched like trees
obe·lisk \ˈä-bə-ˌlisk *also* ˈō-\ *n* [MF *obelisque,* fr. L *obeliscus,* fr. Gk *obeliskos,* fr. dim. of *obelos*] (1569) **1 :** an upright 4-sided usu. monolithic pillar that gradually tapers as it rises and terminates in a pyramid **2 a :** OBELUS **b :** DAGGER 2b
obe·lize \-ˌlīz\ *vt* **-lized; -liz·ing** (ca. 1656) **:** to designate or annotate with an obelus
obe·lus \-ləs\ *n, pl* **ob·e·li** \-ˌlī, -ˌlē\ [ME, fr. LL, fr. Gk *obelos* spit, pointed pillar, obelus] (14c) **1 :** a symbol – or ÷ used in ancient manuscripts to mark a questionable passage **2 :** the symbol ÷
Ober·on \ˈō-bə-ˌrän, -rən\ *n* [MF, fr. OF *Auberon*] (ca. 1533) **:** the king of the fairies in medieval folklore
obese \ō-ˈbēs\ *adj* [L *obesus,* fr. *ob-* against + *esus,* pp. of *edere* to eat — more at OB-, EAT] (1651) **:** having excessive body fat
obe·si·ty \ō-ˈbē-sə-tē\ *n* (ca. 1611) **:** a condition characterized by the excessive accumulation and storage of fat in the body

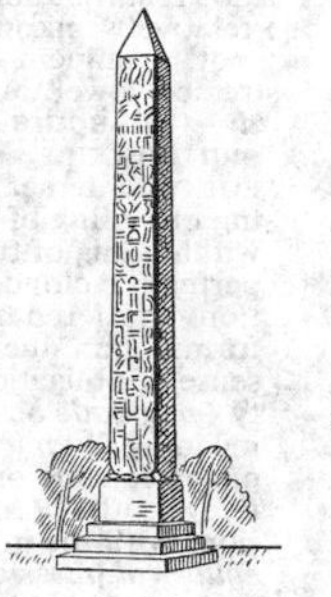

obelisk 1

obe·so·gen·ic \ə-ˌbē-sə-ˈje-nik\ *adj* [*obese* + *-o-* + *-genic*] (1986) **:** promoting excessive weight gain **:** producing obesity ⟨an ~ environment⟩
obey \ō-ˈbā, ə-\ *vb* **obeyed; obey·ing** [ME *obeien,* fr. AF *obeir,* fr. L *oboedire,* fr. *ob-* toward + *-oedire* (akin to *audire* to hear) — more at OB-, AUDIBLE] *vt* (14c) **1 :** to follow the commands or guidance of **2 :** to conform to or comply with ⟨~ an order⟩ ⟨falling objects ~ the laws of physics⟩ ~ *vi* **:** to behave obediently — **obey·er** *n*
ob·fus·cate \ˈäb-fə-ˌskāt; äb-ˈfəs-ˌkāt, əb-\ *vb* **-cat·ed; -cat·ing** [LL *obfuscatus,* pp. of *obfuscare,* fr. L *ob-* in the way + *fuscus* dark brown — more at OB-, DUSK] *vt* (1577) **1 a :** DARKEN **b :** to make obscure ⟨~ the issue⟩ **2 :** CONFUSE ⟨~ the reader⟩ ~ *vi* **:** to be evasive, unclear, or confusing — **ob·fus·ca·tion** \ˌäb-(ˌ)fəs-ˈkā-shən\ *n* — **ob·fus·ca·to·ry** \äb-ˈfəs-kə-ˌtȯr-ē, əb-\ *adj*
ob–gyn \ˌō-(ˌ)bē-ˈjin, -(ˌ)jē-(ˌ)wī-ˈen\ *n, pl* **ob–gyns** [*ob*stetrician *gyne*cologist] (ca. 1960) **:** a physician who specializes in obstetrics and gynecology
OB–GYN *abbr* obstetrics-gynecology
obi \ˈō-bē\ *n* [Jp] (1876) **:** a broad sash worn with a Japanese kimono
Obie \ˈō-bē\ *n* [*O.B.,* abbr. for *off Broadway*] (1956) **:** an award presented annually by a professional organization for notable achievement in plays performed off-Broadway
obit \ō-ˈbit, ˈō-bət, *esp Brit* ˈä-bit\ *n* [ME death, service marking the anniversary of a death, fr. AF, fr. L *obitus* death, fr. *obire* to go to meet, die, fr. *ob-* in the way + *ire* to go — more at ISSUE] (15c) **:** OBITUARY
obi·ter dic·tum \ˌō-bə-tər-ˈdik-təm, ˌä-\ *n, pl* **obiter dic·ta** \-tə\ [LL, lit., something said in passing] (1812) **1 :** an incidental and collateral opinion that is uttered by a judge but is not binding **2 :** an incidental remark or observation
obit·u·ary \ə-ˈbi-chə-ˌwer-ē, ō-, -ˈbi-chə-rē\ *n, pl* **-ar·ies** [ML *obituarium,* fr. L *obitus* death] (1703) **:** a notice of a person's death usu. with a short biographical account — **obit·u·ar·ist** \-ˈbi-chə-ˌwer-ist, -ˈbi-chə-rist\ *n* — **obituary** *adj*
obj *abbr* object; objective
[1]**ob·ject** \ˈäb-jikt, -(ˌ)jekt\ *n* [ME, fr. ML *objectum,* fr. L, neut. of *objectus,* pp. of *obicere* to throw in the way, present, hinder, fr. *ob-* in the way + *jacere* to throw — more at OB-, JET] (14c) **1 a :** something material that may be perceived by the senses ⟨I see an ~ in the distance⟩ **b :** something that when viewed stirs a particular emotion (as pity) ⟨look to the tragic loading of this bed . . . the ~ poisons sight; let it be hid —Shak.⟩ **2 a :** something mental or physical toward which thought, feeling, or action is directed ⟨an ~ for study⟩ ⟨the ~ of my affection⟩ ⟨delicately carved art ~*s*⟩ **b :** something physical that is perceived by an individual and becomes an agent for psychological identification ⟨the mother is the primary ~ of the child⟩ **3 a :** the goal or end of an effort or activity **:** PURPOSE, OBJECTIVE ⟨their ~ is to investigate the matter thoroughly⟩ **b :** a cause for attention or concern ⟨money is no ~⟩ **4 :** a thing that forms an element of or constitutes the subject matter of an investigation or science **5 a :** a noun or noun equivalent (as a pronoun, gerund, or clause) denoting the goal or result of the action of a verb **b :** a noun or noun equivalent in a prepositional phrase **6 a :** a data structure in object-oriented programming that can contain functions as well as data, variables, and other data structures **b :** a discrete entity (as a window or icon) in computer graphics that can be manipulated independently of other such entities ***syn*** see INTENTION — **ob·ject·less** \-ləs\ *adj* — **ob·ject·less·ness** *n*
[2]**ob·ject** \əb-ˈjekt\ *vb* [ME, fr. L *objectus,* pp. of *obicere* to throw in the way, object] *vt* (15c) **:** to put forth in opposition or as an objection ⟨~*ed* that the statement was misleading⟩ ~ *vi* **1 :** to oppose something firmly and usu. with words or arguments **2 :** to feel distaste for something — **ob·jec·tor** \-ˈjek-tər\ *n*
[3]**object** *same as* [1]\ *adj* (1959) **:** of, relating to, or being object code ⟨an ~ file⟩
ob·ject ball \ˈäb-jik(t)-, -(ˌ)jek(t)-\ *n* (1856) **:** the ball first struck by the cue ball in pool or billiards; *also* **:** a ball hit by the cue ball
object code *n* (1961) **:** a computer program after translation from source code usu. into machine language by a compiler
ob·jec·ti·fy \əb-ˈjek-tə-ˌfī\ *vt* **-fied; -fy·ing** (ca. 1837) **1 :** to treat as an object or cause to have objective reality **2 :** to give expression to (as an abstract notion, feeling, or ideal) in a form that can be experienced by others ⟨it is the essence of the fairy tale to ~ differing facets of the child's emotional experience —John Updike⟩ — **ob·jec·ti·fi·ca·tion** \-ˌjek-tə-fə-ˈkā-shən\ *n*
ob·jec·tion \əb-ˈjek-shən\ *n* (14c) **1 :** an act of objecting **2 a :** a reason or argument presented in opposition **b :** a feeling or expression of disapproval
ob·jec·tion·able \-sh(ə-)nə-bəl\ *adj* (1781) **:** UNDESIRABLE, OFFENSIVE — **ob·jec·tion·able·ness** *n* — **ob·jec·tion·ably** \-blē\ *adv*
[1]**ob·jec·tive** \əb-ˈjek-tiv, äb-\ *adj* (1647) **1 a :** relating to or existing as an object of thought without consideration of independent existence — used chiefly in medieval philosophy **b :** of, relating to, or being an object, phenomenon, or condition in the realm of sensible experience independent of individual thought and perceptible by all observers **:** having reality independent of the mind ⟨~ reality⟩ ⟨our reveries . . . are significantly and repeatedly shaped by our transactions with the ~ world —Marvin Reznikoff⟩ — compare SUBJECTIVE 3a **c** *of a symptom of disease* **:** perceptible to persons other than the affected individual — compare SUBJECTIVE 4c **d :** involving or deriving from sense perception or experience with actual objects, conditions, or phenomena ⟨~ awareness⟩ ⟨~ data⟩ **2 :** relating to, characteristic of, or constituting the case of words that follow prepositions or transitive verbs **3 a :** expressing or dealing with facts or conditions as perceived without distortion by personal feelings, prejudices, or interpretations ⟨~ art⟩ ⟨an ~ history of the war⟩ ⟨an ~ judgment⟩ **b** *of a test* **:** limited to choices of fixed alternatives and reducing subjective factors to a minimum ***syn*** see MATERIAL, FAIR — **ob·jec·tive·ly** *adv* — **ob·jec·tive·ness** *n* — **ob·jec·tiv·i·ty** \ˌäb-ˌjek-ˈti-və-tē, əb-\ *n*
[2]**objective** *n* (1835) **1 :** a lens or system of lenses that forms an image of an object **2 a :** something toward which effort is directed **:** an aim, goal, or end of action **b :** a strategic position to be attained or a purpose to be achieved by a military operation ***syn*** see INTENTION
objective complement *n* (1870) **:** a noun, adjective, or pronoun used in the predicate as complement to a verb and as qualifier of its direct object (as *chairman* in "we elected him chairman")
objective correlative *n* (1919) **:** something (as a situation or chain of events) that symbolizes or objectifies a particular emotion and that may be used in creative writing to evoke a desired emotional response in the reader
ob·jec·tiv·ism \əb-ˈjek-ti-ˌvi-zəm, äb-\ *n* (1854) **1 :** any of various theories asserting the validity of objective phenomena over subjective experience; *esp* **:** REALISM 2a **2 :** an ethical theory that moral good is objectively real or that moral precepts are objectively valid **3 :** a 20th century movement in poetry growing out of imagism and putting stress on form — **ob·jec·tiv·ist** \-vist\ *adj or n* — **ob·jec·tiv·is·tic** \-ˌjek-ti-ˈvis-tik\ *adj*
ob·ject language \ˈäb-jikt-, -(ˌ)jekt-\ *n* (1937) **:** TARGET LANGUAGE
ob·ject lesson \ˈäb-jikt-, -(ˌ)jekt-\ *n* (1831) **:** something that serves as a practical example of a principle or abstract idea
ob·ject–ori·ent·ed \-ˌȯr-ē-ˌen-təd\ *adj* (1981) **:** relating to, used in, or implemented by object-oriented programming ⟨an ~ language⟩
object–oriented programming *n* (1981) **:** computer programming in which programming objects are used to form additional objects and are arranged into hierarchies and in which a single object member (as a variable or function) may be used in several different but related ways
ob·jet d'art \ˌȯb-ˌzhā-ˈdär\ *n, pl* **ob·jets d'art** *same*\ [F, lit., art object] (1865) **1 :** an article of some artistic value **2 :** CURIO — called also *objet*

ob·jet trou·vé \ˈȯb-ˌzhä-trü-ˈvā\ *n, pl* **objets trouvés** *same*\ [F, lit., found object] (1937) **:** a natural or discarded object found by chance and held to have aesthetic value

ob·jur·ga·tion \ˌäb-jər-ˈgā-shən\ *n* [ME *objurgacyon,* fr. MF or L; MF *objurgation,* fr. L *objurgation-, objurgatio,* fr. *objurgare* to scold, blame, fr. *ob-* against + *jurgare* to quarrel, lit., to take to law, fr. *jur-, jus* law + *-igare* (fr. *agere* to lead) — more at OB-, JUST, AGENT] (15c) **:** a harsh rebuke — **ob·jur·gate** \ˈäb-jər-ˌgāt\ *vt* — **ob·jur·ga·to·ry** \əb-ˈjər-gə-ˌtȯr-ē\ *adj*

obl *abbr* **1** oblique **2** oblong

ob·lan·ceo·late \(ˌ)äb-ˈlan(t)-sē-ə-ˌlāt\ *adj* (1839) **:** inversely lanceolate ⟨an ~ leaf⟩ — see LEAF illustration

ob·last \ˈä-ˌblast, ˈȯ-, -bləst\ *n, pl* **oblasts** *also* **ob·las·ti** \-ˌblas-tē, -bləs-\ [Russ *oblast'*] (ca. 1886) **:** a political subdivision of Imperial Russia or a republic of the U.S.S.R. or of the Russian Federation

[1]**ob·late** \ä-ˈblāt, ˈä-ˌ\ *adj* [prob. fr. NL *oblatus,* fr. *ob-* + *-latus* (as in *prolatus* prolate)] (1705) **:** flattened or depressed at the poles ⟨an ~ spheroid⟩ — **ob·late·ness** *n*

[2]**ob·late** \ˈä-ˌblāt\ *n* [ML *oblatus,* lit., one offered up, fr. L, pp. of *offerre* — more at OFFER] (1864) **1 :** a layman living in a monastery under a modified rule and without vows **2 :** a member of one of several Roman Catholic communities of men or women

ob·la·tion \ə-ˈblā-shən, ō-\ *n* [ME *oblacioun,* fr. AF *oblation,* fr. LL *oblation-, oblatio,* fr. L *offerre*] (15c) **1 :** the act of making a religious offering; *specif, cap* **:** the act of offering the eucharistic elements to God **2 :** something offered in worship or devotion **:** a holy gift offered usu. at an altar or shrine

[1]**ob·li·gate** \ˈä-blə-ˌgāt\ *vt* **-gat·ed; -gat·ing** [L *obligatus,* pp. of *obligare*] (1533) **1 :** to bind legally or morally **:** CONSTRAIN **2 :** to commit (as funds) to meet an obligation

[2]**ob·li·gate** \ˈä-bli-gət, -blə-ˌgāt\ *adj* (1887) **1 :** restricted to one particularly characteristic mode of life ⟨an ~ parasite⟩ **2 :** biologically essential for survival ⟨~ mutualism⟩ — **ob·li·gate·ly** *adv*

ob·li·ga·tion \ˌä-blə-ˈgā-shən\ *n* (14c) **1 :** the action of obligating oneself to a course of action (as by a promise or vow) **2 a :** something (as a formal contract, a promise, or the demands of conscience or custom) that obligates one to a course of action **b :** a debt security (as a mortgage or corporate bond) **c :** a commitment (as by a government) to pay a particular sum of money; *also* **:** an amount owed under such an obligation ⟨unable to meet its ~*s,* the company went into bankruptcy⟩ **3 a :** a condition or feeling of being obligated **b :** a debt of gratitude **4 :** something one is bound to do **:** DUTY, RESPONSIBILITY

oblig·a·to·ry \ə-ˈbli-gə-ˌtȯr-ē, ä- *also* ˈä-bli-gə-\ *adj* (15c) **1 :** binding in law or conscience **2 :** relating to or enforcing an obligation ⟨a writ ~⟩ **3 :** MANDATORY, REQUIRED ⟨~ military service⟩; *also* **:** so commonplace as to be a convention, fashion, or cliché ⟨the ~ death scene in opera⟩ **4 :** OBLIGATE 1 — **oblig·a·to·ri·ly** \ə-ˌbli-gə-ˈtȯr-ə-lē, ä- *also* ˌä-bli-gə-\ *adv*

oblige \ə-ˈblīj\ *vb* **obliged; oblig·ing** [ME, fr. AF *obliger,* fr. L *obligare,* lit., to bind to, fr. *ob-* toward + *ligare* to bind — more at LIGATURE] *vt* (14c) **1 :** to constrain by physical, moral, or legal force or by the exigencies of circumstance ⟨*obliged* to find a job⟩ **2 a :** to put in one's debt by a favor or service ⟨we are much *obliged* for your help⟩ **b :** to do a favor for ⟨always ready to ~ a friend⟩ ~ *vi* **:** to do something as or as if as a favor ***syn*** see FORCE — **oblig·er** *n*

ob·li·gee \ˌä-blə-ˈjē\ *n* (1574) **:** one to whom another is obligated (as by a contract); *specif* **:** one who is protected by a surety bond

obliging *adj* (1632) **:** willing to do favors **:** HELPFUL ***syn*** see AMIABLE — **oblig·ing·ly** \-jiŋ-lē\ *adv* — **oblig·ing·ness** *n*

ob·li·gor \ˌä-blə-ˈgȯr, -ˈjȯr\ *n* (1541) **:** one who is bound by a legal obligation

[1]**oblique** \ō-ˈblēk, ə-, -ˈblīk; *military usu* ī\ *adj* [ME *oblike,* fr. L *obliquus*] (15c) **1 a :** neither perpendicular nor parallel **:** INCLINED **b :** having the axis not perpendicular to the base ⟨an ~ cone⟩ **c :** having no right angle ⟨an ~ triangle⟩ **2 a :** not straightforward **:** INDIRECT; *also* **:** OBSCURE **b :** DEVIOUS, UNDERHANDED **3 :** situated obliquely and having one end not inserted on bone ⟨~ muscles⟩ **4 :** taken from an airplane with the camera directed horizontally or diagonally downward ⟨an ~ photograph⟩ — **oblique·ly** *adv* — **oblique·ness** *n*

[2]**oblique** *n* (ca. 1608) **1 :** something (as a line) that is oblique **2 :** any of several oblique muscles; *esp* **:** any of the thin flat muscles forming the middle and outer layers of the lateral walls of the abdomen

[3]**oblique** *adv* (1687) **:** at a 45 degree angle ⟨to the right ~, march⟩

oblique angle *n* (1688) **:** an acute or obtuse angle

oblique case *n* (1530) **:** a grammatical case other than the nominative or vocative

obliq·ui·ty \ō-ˈbli-kwə-tē, ə-\ *n, pl* **-ties** (15c) **1 :** deviation from moral rectitude or sound thinking **2 a :** deviation from parallelism or perpendicularity; *also* **:** the amount of such deviation **b :** the angle between the planes of the earth's equator and orbit having a value of about 23°27′ ⟨~ of the ecliptic⟩ **3 a :** indirectness or deliberate obscurity of speech or conduct **b :** an obscure or confusing statement

oblit·er·ate \ə-ˈbli-tə-ˌrāt, ō-\ *vt* **-at·ed; -at·ing** [L *oblitteratus,* pp. of *oblitterare,* fr. *ob-* ob- + *littera* letter] (1600) **1 a :** to remove utterly from recognition or memory **b :** to remove from existence **:** destroy utterly all trace, indication, or significance of **c :** to cause to disappear (as a bodily part or a scar) or collapse (as a duct conveying body fluid) **:** REMOVE 4 ⟨a blood vessel *obliterated* by inflammation⟩ **2 :** to make undecipherable or imperceptible by obscuring or wearing away **3 :** CANCEL 4 — **oblit·er·a·tion** \-ˌbli-tə-ˈrā-shən\ *n* — **oblit·er·a·tor** \-ˈbli-tə-ˌrā-tər\ *n*

oblit·er·a·tive \ə-ˈbli-tə-ˌrā-tiv, ō-, -rə-tiv\ *adj* (ca. 1812) **:** inducing or characterized by obliteration: as **a :** causing or accompanied by closure or collapse of a lumen ⟨~ arterial disease⟩ **b :** tending to make inconspicuous ⟨~ behavior⟩

obliv·i·on \ə-ˈbli-vē-ən, ō-, ä-\ *n* [ME, fr. AF, fr. L *oblivion-, oblivio,* fr. *oblivisci* to forget, perh. fr. *ob-* in the way + *levis* smooth — more at OB-, LEVIGATE] (14c) **1 :** the fact or condition of forgetting or having forgotten; *esp* **:** the condition of being oblivious **2 :** the condition or state of being forgotten or unknown

obliv·i·ous \-vē-əs\ *adj* (15c) **1 :** lacking remembrance, memory, or mindful attention **2 :** lacking active conscious knowledge or awareness — usu. used with *of* or *to* — **obliv·i·ous·ly** *adv* — **obliv·i·ous·ness** *n*

ob·long \ˈä-ˌblȯŋ\ *adj* [ME, fr. AF *oblonge,* fr. L *oblongus,* fr. *ob-* toward + *longus* long — more at LONG] (15c) **:** deviating from a square, circular, or spherical form by elongation in one dimension ⟨an ~ piece of paper⟩ ⟨an ~ melon⟩ — **oblong** *n*

ob·lo·quy \ˈä-blə-kwē\ *n, pl* **-quies** [ME *obloquie,* fr. AF, fr. LL *obloquium,* fr. *obloqui* to speak against, fr. *ob-* against + *loqui* to speak] (15c) **1 :** a strongly condemnatory utterance **:** abusive language **2 :** the condition of one that is discredited **:** bad repute ***syn*** see ABUSE

ob·nox·ious \äb-ˈnäk-shəs, əb-\ *adj* [L *obnoxius,* fr. *ob* in the way of, exposed to + *noxa* harm — more at NOXIOUS] (1597) **1** *archaic* **:** exposed to something unpleasant or harmful — used with *to* **2** *archaic* **:** deserving of censure **3 :** odiously or disgustingly objectionable **:** highly offensive — **ob·nox·ious·ly** *adv* — **ob·nox·ious·ness** *n*

ob·nu·bi·late \äb-ˈnü-bə-ˌlāt, -ˈnyü-\ *vt* **-lat·ed; -lat·ing** [L *obnubilatus,* pp. of *obnubilare,* fr. *ob-* in the way + *nubilare* to be cloudy, fr. *nubilus* cloudy, fr. *nubes* cloud — more at OB-, NUANCE] (1583) **:** BECLOUD, OBSCURE — **ob·nu·bi·la·tion** \-ˌnü-bə-ˈlā-shən, -ˌnyü-\ *n*

OBO *abbr* or best offer

oboe \ˈō-(ˌ)bō\ *n* [It, fr. F *hautbois* — more at HAUTBOIS] (1794) **:** a double-reed woodwind instrument having a conical tube, a brilliant penetrating tone, and a usual range from B flat below middle C upward for over 2½ octaves — **obo·ist** \ˈō-(ˌ)bō-ist\ *n*

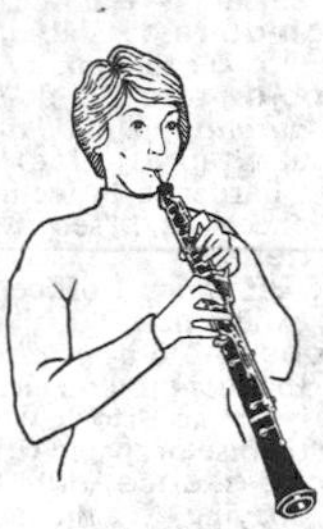
oboe

obol \ˈä-bəl, ˈō-\ *n* [L *obolus,* fr. Gk *obolos, obelos,* lit., spit] (ca. 1670) **:** an ancient Greek coin or weight equal to ⅙ drachma

ob·ovate \(ˌ)äb-ˈō-ˌvāt\ *adj* (1785) **:** ovate with the narrower end basal ⟨~ leaves⟩ — see LEAF illustration

ob·ovoid \-ˌvȯid\ *adj* (1819) **:** ovoid with the broad end toward the apex ⟨an ~ fruit⟩

ob·scene \äb-ˈsēn, əb-\ *adj* [MF, fr. L *obscenus, obscaenus*] (1593) **1 :** disgusting to the senses **:** REPULSIVE **2 a :** abhorrent to morality or virtue; *specif* **:** designed to incite to lust or depravity **b :** containing or being language regarded as taboo in polite usage ⟨~ lyrics⟩ **c :** repulsive by reason of crass disregard of moral or ethical principles ⟨an ~ misuse of power⟩ **d :** so excessive as to be offensive ⟨~ wealth⟩ ⟨~ waste⟩ ***syn*** see COARSE — **ob·scene·ly** *adv*

ob·scen·i·ty \-ˈse-nə-tē *also* -ˈsē-\ *n, pl* **-ties** (1589) **1 :** the quality or state of being obscene **2 :** something (as an utterance or act) that is obscene

ob·scur·ant \äb-ˈskyu̇r-ənt, əb-\ *or* **ob·scu·ran·tic** \ˌäb-skyə-ˈran-tik\ *adj* (1878) **:** tending to make obscure ⟨~ language⟩ — **obscurant** *n*

ob·scu·ran·tism \äb-ˈskyu̇r-ən-ˌti-zəm, əb-; ˌäb-skyu̇-ˈran-\ *n* (1834) **1 :** opposition to the spread of knowledge **:** a policy of withholding knowledge from the general public **2 a :** a style (as in literature or art) characterized by deliberate vagueness or abstruseness **b :** an act or instance of obscurantism — **ob·scu·ran·tist** \-ən-tist, -ˈran-tist\ *n or adj*

[1]**ob·scure** \äb-ˈskyu̇r, əb-\ *adj* [ME, fr. AF *oscur, obscur,* fr. L *obscurus*] (15c) **1 a :** DARK, DIM **b :** shrouded in or hidden by darkness **c :** not clearly seen or easily distinguished **:** FAINT ⟨~ markings⟩ **2 :** not readily understood or clearly expressed; *also* **:** MYSTERIOUS **3 :** relatively unknown: as **a :** REMOTE, SECLUDED ⟨an ~ village⟩ **b :** not prominent or famous ⟨an ~ poet⟩ **4 :** constituting the unstressed vowel \ə\ or having unstressed \ə\ as its value — **ob·scure·ly** *adv* — **ob·scure·ness** *n*

syn OBSCURE, DARK, VAGUE, ENIGMATIC, CRYPTIC, AMBIGUOUS, EQUIVOCAL mean not clearly understandable. OBSCURE implies a hiding or veiling of meaning through some inadequacy of expression or withholding of full knowledge ⟨*obscure* poems⟩. DARK implies an imperfect or clouded revelation often with ominous or sinister suggestion ⟨muttered *dark* hints of revenge⟩. VAGUE implies a lack of clear formulation due to inadequate conception or consideration ⟨a *vague* sense of obligation⟩. ENIGMATIC stresses a puzzling, mystifying quality ⟨*enigmatic* occult writings⟩. CRYPTIC implies a purposely concealed meaning ⟨*cryptic* hints of hidden treasure⟩. AMBIGUOUS applies to language capable of more than one interpretation ⟨an *ambiguous* directive⟩. EQUIVOCAL applies to language left open to differing interpretations with the intention of deceiving or evading ⟨moral precepts with *equivocal* phrasing⟩.

[2]**obscure** *vt* **ob·scured; ob·scur·ing** (15c) **1 :** to make dark, dim, or indistinct **2 :** to conceal or hide by or as if by covering **3 :** to reduce (a vowel) to the value \ə\ — **ob·scu·ra·tion** \ˌäb-skyu̇-ˈrā-shən\ *n*

[3]**obscure** *n* (1667) **:** OBSCURITY

ob·scu·ri·ty \äb-ˈskyu̇r-ə-tē, əb-\ *n, pl* **-ties** (14c) **1 :** one that is obscure **2 :** the quality or state of being obscure

ob·se·qui·ous \əb-ˈsē-kwē-əs, äb-\ *adj* [ME, compliant, fr. L *obsequiosus,* fr. *obsequium* compliance, fr. *obsequi* to comply, fr. *ob-* toward + *sequi* to follow — more at OB-, SUE] (15c) **:** marked by or exhibiting a fawning attentiveness ***syn*** see SUBSERVIENT — **ob·se·qui·ous·ly** *adv* — **ob·se·qui·ous·ness** *n*

ob·se·quy \ˈäb-sə-kwē\ *n, pl* **-quies** [ME *obsequie,* fr. AF, fr. ML *obsequiae* (pl.), alter. of L *exsequiae,* fr. *exsequi* to follow out, execute — more at EXECUTION] (15c) **:** a funeral or burial rite — usu. used in pl.

ob·serv·able \əb-ˈzər-və-bəl\ *adj* (1609) **1 :** NOTEWORTHY **2 :** capable of being observed **:** DISCERNIBLE — **ob·serv·abil·i·ty** \-ˌzər-və-ˈbi-lə-tē\ *n* — **observable** *n* — **ob·serv·ably** \-ˈzər-və-blē\ *adv*

ob·ser·vance \əb-ˈzər-vən(t)s\ *n* (13c) **1 a :** a customary practice, rite, or ceremony ⟨Sabbath ~*s*⟩ **b :** a rule governing members of a religious order **2 :** an act or instance of following a custom, rule, or law ⟨~ of the speed limits⟩ **3 :** an act or instance of watching

[1]**ob·ser·vant** \-vənt\ *adj* (1602) **1 a :** paying strict attention **:** WATCHFUL ⟨an ~ spectator⟩ **b :** KEEN, PERCEPTIVE **2 :** careful in observing (as rites, laws, or customs) **:** MINDFUL ⟨pious and religiously ~ families —Sidney Hook⟩ ⟨always ~ of the amenities⟩ — **ob·ser·vant·ly** *adv*

[2]**observant** *n* (1605) *obs* **:** an assiduous or obsequious servant or attendant

[1]**ob·ser·va·tion** \ˌäb-sər-ˈvā-shən, -zər-\ *n* [MF, fr. L *observation-, observatio,* fr. *observare*] (1535) **1 a :** an act or instance of observing a custom, rule, or law **b :** OBSERVANCE 3 **2 a :** an act of recognizing and

noting a fact or occurrence often involving measurement with instruments ⟨weather ~*s*⟩ **b :** a record or description so obtained **3 :** a judgment on or inference from what one has observed; *broadly* **:** REMARK, STATEMENT **4** *obs* **:** attentive care **:** HEED **5 :** the condition of one that is observed ⟨under ~ at the hospital⟩ — **ob·ser·va·tion·al** \-shnəl, -shə-nᵊl\ *adj* — **ob·ser·va·tion·al·ly** *adv*

²**observation** *adj* (1872) **:** designed for use in viewing something (as scenery) or in making observations ⟨an ~ tower⟩ ⟨the ~ platform⟩

ob·ser·va·to·ry \əb-ˈzər-və-ˌtȯr-ē\ *n, pl* **-ries** [prob. fr. NL *observatorium,* fr. L *observare*] (1676) **1 :** a building or place given over to or equipped for observation of natural phenomena (as in astronomy); *also* **:** an institution whose primary purpose is making such observations **2 :** a situation or structure commanding a wide view

ob·serve \əb-ˈzərv\ *vb* **ob·served; ob·serv·ing** [ME, fr. AF *observer,* fr. L *observare* to guard, watch, observe, fr. *ob-* in the way, toward + *servare* to keep — more at CONSERVE] *vt* (14c) **1 :** to conform one's action or practice to (as a law, rite, or condition) **:** comply with **2 :** to inspect or take note of as an augury, omen, or presage **3 :** to celebrate or solemnize (as a ceremony or festival) in a customary or accepted way **4 a :** to watch carefully esp. with attention to details or behavior for the purpose of arriving at a judgment **b :** to make a scientific observation on or of **5 :** to come to realize or know esp. through consideration of noted facts **6 :** to utter as a remark ~ *vi* **1 a :** to take notice **b :** to make observations **:** WATCH **2 :** REMARK, COMMENT ***syn*** see KEEP — **ob·serv·ing·ly** \-ˈzər-viŋ-lē\ *adv*

ob·serv·er \əb-ˈzər-vər\ *n* (ca. 1550) **:** one that observes: as **a :** a representative sent to observe but not participate officially in an activity (as a meeting or war) **b :** an expert analyst and commentator in a particular field ⟨political ~*s*⟩

ob·sess \əb-ˈses, äb-\ *vb* [L *obsessus,* pp. of *obsidēre* to frequent, besiege, fr. *ob-* against + *sedēre* to sit — more at OB-, SIT] *vt* (1531) **:** to haunt or excessively preoccupy the mind of ⟨was ~*ed* with the idea⟩ ~ *vi* **:** to engage in obsessive thinking **:** become obsessed with an idea

ob·ses·sion \äb-ˈse-shən, əb-\ *n* (1680) **1 :** a persistent disturbing preoccupation with an often unreasonable idea or feeling; *broadly* **:** compelling motivation ⟨an ~ with profits⟩ **2 :** something that causes an obsession — **ob·ses·sion·al** \-ˈsesh-nəl, -ˈse-shə-nᵊl\ *adj* — **ob·ses·sion·al·ly** *adv*

ob·ses·sive \äb-ˈse-siv, əb-\ *adj* (1901) **1 a :** tending to cause obsession **b :** excessive often to an unreasonable degree **2 :** of, relating to, or characterized by obsession **:** deriving from obsession — **obsessive** *n* — **ob·ses·sive·ly** *adv* — **ob·ses·sive·ness** *n*

obsessive–compulsive *adj* (1927) **:** relating to, characterized by, or affected with recurring obsessions and compulsions esp. as symptoms of a neurotic state ⟨~ disorder⟩ — **obsessive–compulsive** *n*

ob·sid·i·an \əb-ˈsi-dē-ən\ *n* [NL *obsidianus,* fr. L *obsidianus lapis,* false MS reading for *obsianus lapis,* lit., stone of Obsius, fr. *Obsius,* its supposed discoverer] (1796) **:** a dark natural glass formed by the cooling of molten lava

ob·so·lesce \ˌäb-sə-ˈles\ *vb* **-lesced; -lesc·ing** [L *obsolescere*] *vi* (1873) **:** to be or become obsolescent ~ *vt* **:** to make obsolescent

ob·so·les·cence \-ˈle-sᵊn(t)s\ *n* (ca. 1828) **:** the process of becoming obsolete or the condition of being nearly obsolete ⟨the gradual ~ of machinery⟩ ⟨reduced to ~⟩

ob·so·les·cent \-sᵊnt\ *adj* (1755) **:** going out of use **:** becoming obsolete — **ob·so·les·cent·ly** *adv*

¹**ob·so·lete** \ˌäb-sə-ˈlēt, ˈäb-sə-ˌ\ *adj* [L *obsoletus,* fr. pp. of *obsolescere* to grow old, become disused, perh. fr. *ob-* toward + *solēre* to be accustomed] (1579) **1 a :** no longer in use or no longer useful ⟨an ~ word⟩ **b :** of a kind or style no longer current **:** OLD-FASHIONED ⟨an ~ technology⟩ **2** *of a plant or animal part* **:** indistinct or imperfect as compared with a corresponding part in related organisms **:** VESTIGIAL ***syn*** see OLD — **ob·so·lete·ly** *adv* — **ob·so·lete·ness** *n*

²**obsolete** *vt* **-let·ed; -let·ing** (1640) **:** to make obsolete

ob·sta·cle \ˈäb-sti-kəl, -ˌsti-\ *n* [ME, fr. AF, fr. L *obstaculum,* fr. *obstare* to stand in front of, fr. *ob-* in the way + *stare* to stand — more at OB-, STAND] (14c) **:** something that impedes progress or achievement

obstacle course *n* (1943) **:** a military training course filled with obstacles (as hurdles, fences, walls, and ditches) that must be negotiated; *broadly* **:** a series of obstacles that must be overcome

ob·stet·ric \əb-ˈste-trik, äb-\ *or* **ob·stet·ri·cal** \-tri-kəl\ *adj* [modif. of L *obstetricius,* fr. *obstetric-, obstetrix* midwife, fr. *obstare*] (1742) **:** of, relating to, or associated with childbirth or obstetrics — **ob·stet·ri·cal·ly** \-tri-k(ə-)lē\ *adv*

ob·ste·tri·cian \ˌäb-stə-ˈtri-shən\ *n* (ca. 1828) **:** a physician specializing in obstetrics

ob·stet·rics \əb-ˈste-triks, äb-\ *n pl but sing or pl in constr* (ca. 1819) **:** a branch of medical science that deals with birth and with its antecedents and sequels

ob·sti·na·cy \ˈäb-stə-nə-sē\ *n, pl* **-cies** (14c) **1 a :** the quality or state of being obstinate **:** STUBBORNNESS **b :** the quality or state of being difficult to remedy, relieve, or subdue ⟨the ~ of tuberculosis⟩ **2 :** an instance of being obstinate

ob·sti·nate \ˈäb-stə-nət\ *adj* [ME, fr. AF *obstinat,* L *obstinatus,* pp. of *obstinare* to be resolved, fr. *ob-* in the way + *-stinare* (akin to *stare* to stand)] (14c) **1 :** perversely adhering to an opinion, purpose, or course in spite of reason, arguments, or persuasion ⟨~ resistance to change⟩ **2 :** not easily subdued, remedied, or removed ⟨~ fever⟩ — **ob·sti·nate·ly** *adv* — **ob·sti·nate·ness** *n*

syn OBSTINATE, DOGGED, STUBBORN, PERTINACIOUS, MULISH mean fixed and unyielding in course or purpose. OBSTINATE implies usu. an unreasonable persistence ⟨an *obstinate* proponent of conspiracy theories⟩. DOGGED suggests an admirable often tenacious and unwavering persistence ⟨pursued the story with *dogged* perseverance⟩. STUBBORN implies sturdiness in resisting change which may or may not be admirable ⟨a person too *stubborn* to admit error⟩. PERTINACIOUS suggests an annoying or irksome persistence ⟨a *pertinacious* salesclerk refusing to take no for an answer⟩. MULISH implies a thoroughly unreasonable obstinacy ⟨a *mulish* determination to have his own way⟩.

ob·strep·er·ous \əb-ˈstre-p(ə-)rəs, äb-\ *adj* [L *obstreperus,* fr. *obstrepere* to clamor against, fr. *ob-* against + *strepere* to make a noise] (ca. 1600) **1 :** marked by unruly or aggressive noisiness **:** CLAMOROUS ⟨~ merriment⟩ **2 :** stubbornly resistant to control **:** UNRULY ***syn*** see VOCIFEROUS — **ob·strep·er·ous·ly** *adv* — **ob·strep·er·ous·ness** *n*

ob·struct \əb-ˈstrəkt, äb-\ *vt* [L *obstructus,* pp. of *obstruere,* fr. *ob-* in the way + *struere* to build, heap up — more at OB-, STREW] (1590) **1 :** to block or close up by an obstacle **2 :** to hinder from passage, action, or operation **:** IMPEDE **3 :** to cut off from sight ⟨a wall ~*s* the view⟩ ***syn*** see HINDER — **ob·struc·tive** \-ˈstrək-tiv\ *adj or n* — **ob·struc·tive·ness** *n* — **ob·struc·tor** \-tər\ *n*

ob·struc·tion \əb-ˈstrək-shən, äb-\ *n* (1533) **1 a :** the state of being obstructed; *esp* **:** a condition of being clogged or blocked **b :** an act of obstructing **2 :** something that obstructs

ob·struc·tion·ism \-shə-ˌni-zəm\ *n* (1879) **:** deliberate interference with the progress or business esp. of a legislative body — **ob·struc·tion·ist** \-sh(ə-)nist\ *n or adj* — **ob·struc·tion·is·tic** \-ˌstrək-shə-ˈnis-tik\ *adj*

ob·tain \əb-ˈtān, äb-\ *vb* [ME *obteinen,* fr. AF & L; AF *obtenir,* fr. L *obtinēre* to hold on to, possess, obtain, fr. *ob-* in the way + *tenēre* to hold — more at THIN] *vt* (15c) **:** to gain or attain usu. by planned action or effort ~ *vi* **1** *archaic* **:** SUCCEED **2 :** to be generally recognized or established **:** PREVAIL — **ob·tain·abil·i·ty** \-ˌtā-nə-ˈbi-lə-tē\ *n* — **ob·tain·able** \-ˈtā-nə-bəl\ *adj* — **ob·tain·er** *n* — **ob·tain·ment** \-ˈtān-mənt\ *n*

ob·tect \əb-ˈtekt, äb-\ *also* **ob·tect·ed** \-ˈtek-təd\ *adj* [L *obtectus,* pp. of *obtegere* to cover over, fr. *ob-* in the way + *tegere* to cover — more at THATCH] (1816) *of a pupa* **:** enclosed in a firm case or covering with the appendages held tightly against the body

ob·trude \əb-ˈtrüd, äb-\ *vb* **ob·trud·ed; ob·trud·ing** [L *obtrudere* to thrust at, fr. *ob-* in the way + *trudere* to thrust — more at OB-, THREAT] *vt* (ca. 1609) **1 :** to thrust out **:** EXTRUDE **2 :** to force or impose (as oneself or one's ideas) without warrant or request ~ *vi* **:** to become unduly prominent or interfering **:** INTRUDE — **ob·trud·er** *n*

ob·tru·sion \-ˈtrü-zhən\ *n* [LL *obtrusion-, obtrusio,* fr. L *obtrudere*] (1579) **1 :** an act of obtruding **2 :** something that is obtruded

ob·tru·sive \-ˈtrü-siv, -ziv\ *adj* (1667) **1 a :** forward in manner or conduct ⟨~ behavior⟩ **b :** undesirably prominent **2 :** thrust out **:** PROTRUDING ⟨a sharp ~ edge⟩ ***syn*** see IMPERTINENT — **ob·tru·sive·ly** *adv* — **ob·tru·sive·ness** *n*

ob·tund \äb-ˈtənd\ *vt* [ME, fr. L *obtundere*] (14c) **:** to reduce the edge or violence of **:** DULL ⟨~*ed* reflexes⟩

ob·tu·ra·tion \ˌäb-tyə-ˈrā-shən, -tə-\ *n* [L *obturation-, obturatio,* fr. *obturare* to obstruct] (1610) **:** OBSTRUCTION, CLOSURE — **ob·tu·rate** \ˈäb-tyə-ˌrāt, -tə-\ *vt*

ob·tu·ra·tor \ˈäb-tyə-ˌrā-tər, -tə-\ *n* [NL, fr. L *obturare*] (ca. 1741) **:** one (as a prosthetic device) that closes or blocks up an opening (as a fissure in the palate)

ob·tuse \äb-ˈtüs, əb-, -ˈtyüs\ *adj* **ob·tus·er; -est** [ME, fr. L *obtusus* blunt, dull, fr. pp. of *obtundere* to beat against, blunt, fr. *ob-* against + *tundere* to beat — more at OB-, CONTUSION] (15c) **1 a :** not pointed or acute **:** BLUNT **b (1)** *of an angle* **:** exceeding 90 degrees but less than 180 degrees **(2) :** having an obtuse angle ⟨an ~ triangle⟩ — see TRIANGLE illustration **c** *of a leaf* **:** rounded at the free end **2 a :** lacking sharpness or quickness of sensibility or intellect **:** INSENSITIVE, STUPID **b :** difficult to comprehend **:** not clear or precise in thought or expression ***syn*** see DULL — **ob·tuse·ly** *adv* — **ob·tuse·ness** *n*

obv *abbr* obverse

¹**ob·verse** \äb-ˈvərs, əb-, ˈäb-ˌ\ *adj* [L *obversus,* fr. pp. of *obvertere* to turn toward, fr. *ob-* toward + *vertere* to turn — more at OB-, WORTH] (ca. 1656) **1 :** facing the observer or opponent **2 :** having the base narrower than the top ⟨an ~ leaf⟩ **3 :** constituting the obverse of something **:** OPPOSITE — **ob·verse·ly** *adv*

²**ob·verse** \ˈäb-ˌvərs, äb-ˈ, əb-ˈ\ *n* (1658) **1 :** the side of a coin or currency note bearing the chief device and lettering; *broadly* **:** a front or principal surface **2 :** a counterpart having the opposite orientation or force ⟨their rise was merely the ~ of the Empire's fall —A. J. Toynbee⟩; *also* **:** OPPOSITE 1 ⟨joy and its ~, sorrow⟩ **3 :** a proposition inferred immediately from another by denying the opposite of what the given proposition affirms ⟨the ~ of "all *A* is *B*" is "no *A* is not *B*"⟩

ob·vi·ate \ˈäb-vē-ˌāt\ *vt* **-at·ed; -at·ing** [LL *obviatus,* pp. of *obviare* to meet, withstand, fr. L *obviam*] (1598) **:** to anticipate and prevent (as a situation) or make unnecessary (as an action) — **ob·vi·a·tion** \ˌäb-vē-ˈā-shən\ *n*

ob·vi·ous \ˈäb-vē-əs\ *adj* [L *obvius,* fr. *obviam* in the way, fr. *ob* in the way of + *viam,* acc. of *via* way — more at OB-, VIA] (1603) **1** *archaic* **:** being in the way or in front **2 :** easily discovered, seen, or understood ***syn*** see EVIDENT — **ob·vi·ous·ness** *n*

ob·vi·ous·ly \-lē\ *adv* (1638) **1 :** in an obvious manner ⟨showed his anger ~⟩ **2 :** as is plainly evident ⟨~, something is wrong⟩

OC *abbr* **1** off center **2** officer candidate **3** on center **4** on course **5** over-the-counter

oca *also* **oka** \ˈō-kə\ *n* [Sp, fr. Quechua *oqa*] (1604) **:** either of two So. American wood sorrels (*Oxalis crenata* and *O. tuberosa*) cultivated for their edible tubers; *also* **:** the tuber of an oca

oc·a·ri·na \ˌä-kə-ˈrē-nə\ *n* [It, fr. It dial., dim. of *oca* goose, fr. LL *auca,* ultim. fr. L *avis* bird — more at AVIARY] (1877) **:** a simple wind instrument typically having an oval body with finger holes and a projecting mouthpiece

Oc·cam's razor *also* **Ock·ham's razor** \ˈä-kəmz-\ *n* [William of *Occam*] (ca. 1837) **:** a scientific and philosophic rule that entities should not be multiplied unnecessarily which is interpreted as requiring that the simplest of competing theories be preferred to the more complex or that explanations of unknown phenomena be sought first in terms of known quantities

¹**oc·ca·sion** \ə-ˈkā-zhən\ *n* [ME, fr. AF or L; AF, fr. L *occasion-, occasio,* fr. *occidere* to fall, fall down, fr. *ob-* toward + *cadere* to fall — more at OB-, CHANCE] (14c) **1 :** a favorable opportunity or circumstance ⟨did not have ~ to talk with them⟩ **2 a :** a state of affairs that provides a ground or reason ⟨the ~ of the discord was their mutual intolerance⟩ **b :** an occurrence or condition that brings something about; *esp* **:** the immediate inciting circumstance as distinguished from the fundamen-

\ə\ **abut** \ᵊ\ kitten, F table \ər\ **fur**ther \a\ **ash** \ā\ **ace** \ä\ m**o**p, m**a**r
\au̇\ **out** \ch\ **chin** \e\ **bet** \ē\ **easy** \g\ **go** \i\ **hit** \ī\ **ice** \j\ **job**
\ŋ\ **sing** \ō\ **go** \ȯ\ **law** \ȯi\ **boy** \th\ **thin** \t͟h\ **the** \ü\ **loot** \u̇\ **foot**
\y\ **yet** \zh\ vi**si**on, bei**ge** \k, ⁿ, œ, ue, ʸ\ *see* Guide to Pronunciation

tal cause ⟨his insulting remark was the ~ of a bitter quarrel⟩ **3 a** : HAPPENING, INCIDENT **b** : a time at which something happens : INSTANCE **4 a** : a need arising from a particular circumstance **b** *archaic* : a personal want or need — usu. used in pl. **5** *pl* : AFFAIRS, BUSINESS **6** : a special event or ceremony : CELEBRATION — **on occasion** : from time to time

[2]**occasion** *vt* **-sioned; -sion·ing** \-ˈkāzh-niŋ, -ˈkā-zhə-\ (15c) : BRING ABOUT, CAUSE

oc·ca·sion·al \-ˈkāzh-nəl, -ˈkā-zhə-nᵊl\ *adj* (ca. 1631) **1 a** : of or relating to a particular occasion ⟨a budget able to meet ~ demands as well as regular ones⟩ **b** : created for a particular occasion ⟨~ verse⟩ **2** : acting as the occasion or contributing cause of something **3** : encountered, occurring, appearing, or taken at irregular or infrequent intervals ⟨~ visitors⟩ ⟨an ~ vacation⟩ **4** : acting in a specified capacity from time to time ⟨an ~ lecturer⟩ **5** : designed or constructed to be used as the occasion demands ⟨~ furniture⟩

oc·ca·sion·al·ly \-ˈkāzh-nə-lē, -ˈkā-zhə-nᵊl-ē\ *adv* (1630) : on occasion : NOW AND THEN ⟨dines out ~⟩

Oc·ci·dent \ˈäk-sə-dənt, -ˌdent\ *n* [ME, fr. AF, fr. L *occident-, occidens,* fr. prp. of *occidere* to fall, set (of the sun)] (14c) : WEST 2a

oc·ci·den·tal \ˌäk-sə-ˈden-tᵊl\ *adj, often cap* (14c) **1** : of, relating to, or situated in the Occident : WESTERN **2** : of or relating to Occidentals — **oc·ci·den·tal·ly** *adv*

Occidental *n* (1857) : a member of one of the occidental peoples; *esp* : a person of European ancestry

Oc·ci·den·tal·ism \ˌäk-sə-ˈden-tə-ˌli-zəm\ *n* (1839) : the characteristic features of occidental peoples or culture

oc·ci·den·tal·ize \-tə-ˌlīz\ *vt* **-ized; -iz·ing** *often cap* (1870) : to make occidental (as in culture)

oc·cip·i·tal \äk-ˈsi-pə-tᵊl\ *adj* (1541) : of, relating to, or located within or near the occiput or the occipital bone — **occipital** *n* — **oc·cip·i·tal·ly** *adv*

occipital bone *n* (1679) : a compound bone that forms the posterior part of the skull and bears a condyle by which the skull articulates with the atlas

occipital condyle *n* (ca. 1860) : an articular surface on the occipital bone by which the skull articulates with the atlas

occipital lobe *n* (1882) : the posterior lobe of each cerebral hemisphere that bears the visual cortex and has the form of a 3-sided pyramid

oc·ci·put \ˈäk-sə-(ˌ)pət\ *n, pl* **occiputs** *or* **oc·cip·i·ta** \äk-ˈsi-pə-tə\ [ME, fr. L *occipit-, occiput,* fr. *ob-* against + *capit-, caput* head — more at OB-, HEAD] (14c) : the back part of the head or skull

Oc·ci·tan \ˈäk-sə-ˌtan\ *n* [F, fr. ML *occitanus,* fr. Old Occitan *oc* yes (contrasted with OF *oïl* yes) + ML *-itanus* (perh. as in *aquitanus* of Aquitaine)] (1958) : a Romance language spoken in southern France — **Occitan** *adj*

oc·clude \ə-ˈklüd, ä-\ *vb* **oc·clud·ed; oc·clud·ing** [L *occludere,* fr. *ob-* in the way + *claudere* to shut, close — more at CLOSE] *vt* (1597) **1** : to close up or block off : OBSTRUCT ⟨a thrombus *occluding* a coronary artery⟩; *also* : CONCEAL **2** : SORB ~ *vi* **1** : to come into contact with cusps of the opposing teeth fitting together ⟨his teeth do not ~ properly⟩ **2** : to become occluded

occluded front *n* (ca. 1938) : OCCLUSION 2

oc·clu·sal \ə-ˈklü-səl, ä-, -zəl\ *adj* (1897) : of or relating to the grinding or biting surface of a tooth or to occlusion of the teeth

oc·clu·sion \ə-ˈklü-zhən\ *n* [L *occludere*] (ca. 1645) **1** : the act of occluding : the state of being occluded: as **a** : the complete obstruction of the breath passage in the articulation of a speech sound **b** : the bringing of the opposing surfaces of the teeth of the two jaws into contact; *also* : the relation between the surfaces when in contact **c** : the inclusion or sorption of gas trapped during solidification of a material **2** : the front formed by a cold front overtaking a warm front and lifting the warm air above the earth's surface

oc·clu·sive \-siv, -ziv\ *adj* [L *occlusus,* pp. of *occludere*] (1888) **1** : serving to occlude **2** : characterized by occlusion

[1]**oc·cult** \ə-ˈkəlt, ä-\ *vt* [L *occultare,* freq. of *occulere*] (1500) : to shut off from view or exposure : COVER, ECLIPSE — **oc·cult·er** *n*

[2]**oc·cult** \ə-ˈkəlt, ä-; ˈä-ˌkəlt\ *adj* [L *occultus,* fr. pp. of *occulere* to cover up, fr. *ob-* in the way + *-culere* (akin to *celare* to conceal) — more at OB-, HELL] (1533) **1** : not revealed : SECRET **2** : not easily apprehended or understood : ABSTRUSE, MYSTERIOUS **3** : hidden from view : CONCEALED **4** : of or relating to the occult **5** : not manifest or detectable by clinical methods alone ⟨~ carcinoma⟩; *also* : not present in macroscopic amounts ⟨~ blood in a stool⟩ — **oc·cult·ly** *adv*

[3]**occult** *same as* [2]\ *n* (1923) : matters regarded as involving the action or influence of supernatural or supernormal powers or some secret knowledge of them — used with *the*

oc·cul·ta·tion \ˌä-(ˌ)kəl-ˈtā-shən\ *n* (15c) **1** : the state of being hidden from view or lost to notice **2** : the interruption of the light from a celestial body or of the signals from a spacecraft by the intervention of a celestial body; *esp* : an eclipse of a star or planet by the moon

oc·cult·ism \ə-ˈkəl-ˌti-zəm, ä-; ˈä-ˌkəl-\ *n* (1881) : occult theory or practice : belief in or study of the action or influence of supernatural or supernormal powers — **oc·cult·ist** \-tist\ *n*

oc·cu·pan·cy \ˈä-kyə-pən(t)-sē\ *n, pl* **-cies** (1596) **1** : the fact or condition of holding, possessing, or residing in or on something ⟨~ of the estate⟩ **2** : the act or fact of taking or having possession (as of unowned land) to acquire ownership **3** : the fact or condition of being occupied ⟨~ by more than 400 persons is unlawful⟩ **4** : the use to which a property is put ⟨industrial ~⟩ **5** : a building or part of a building intended to be occupied (as by a tenant)

oc·cu·pant \-pənt\ *n* (1596) **1** : one who acquires title by occupancy **2** : one who occupies a particular place; *esp* : RESIDENT

oc·cu·pa·tion \ˌä-kyə-ˈpā-shən\ *n* [ME *occupacioun,* fr. AF *occupaciun,* fr. L *occupation-, occupatio,* fr. *occupare*] (14c) **1 a** : an activity in which one engages ⟨pursuing pleasure has been his major ~⟩ **b** : the principal business of one's life : VOCATION **2 a** : the possession, use, or settlement of land : OCCUPANCY **b** : the holding of an office or position **3 a** : the act or process of taking possession of a place or area : SEIZURE **b** : the holding and control of an area by a foreign military force **c** : the military force occupying a country or the policies carried out by it *syn* see WORK — **oc·cu·pa·tion·al** \-shnəl, -shə-nᵊl\ *adj* — **oc·cu·pa·tion·al·ly** *adv*

occupational therapy *n* (1915) : therapy based on engagement in meaningful activities of daily life (as self-care skills, education, work, or social interaction) esp. to enable or encourage participation in such activities despite impairments or limitations in physical or mental functioning — **occupational therapist** *n*

oc·cu·py \ˈä-kyə-ˌpī\ *vt* **-pied; -py·ing** [ME *occupien* to take possession of, occupy, fr. AF *occupier, occuper,* fr. L *occupare,* fr. *ob-* toward + *-cupare* (akin to *capere* to seize) — more at OB-, HEAVE] (14c) **1** : to engage the attention or energies of **2 a** : to take up (a place or extent in space) ⟨this chair is *occupied*⟩ ⟨the fireplace will ~ this corner of the room⟩ **b** : to take or fill (an extent in time) ⟨the hobby *occupies* all of my free time⟩ **3 a** : to take or hold possession or control of ⟨enemy troops *occupied* the ridge⟩ **b** : to fill or perform the functions of (an office or position) **4** : to reside in as an owner or tenant — **oc·cu·pi·er** \-ˌpī(-ə)r\ *n*

oc·cur \ə-ˈkər\ *vi* **oc·curred; oc·cur·ring** \-ˈkər-iŋ, -ˈkə-riŋ\ [L *occurrere,* fr. *ob-* in the way + *currere* to run — more at OB-, CAR] (1534) **1** : to be found or met with : APPEAR **2** : to come into existence : HAPPEN **3** : to come to mind ⟨an idea that has *occurred* to me⟩

oc·cur·rence \ə-ˈkər-ən(t)s, -ˈkə-rən(t)s\ *n* (1539) **1** : something that occurs ⟨a startling ~⟩ **2** : the action or instance of occurring ⟨the repeated ~ of petty theft in the locker room⟩

syn OCCURRENCE, EVENT, INCIDENT, EPISODE, CIRCUMSTANCE mean something that happens or takes place. OCCURRENCE may apply to a happening without intent, volition, or plan ⟨an encounter that was a chance *occurrence*⟩. EVENT usu. implies an occurrence of some importance and frequently one having antecedent cause ⟨the *events* following the assassination⟩. INCIDENT suggests an occurrence of brief duration or secondary importance ⟨a minor wartime *incident*⟩. EPISODE stresses the distinctiveness or apartness of an incident ⟨a brief romantic *episode* in a life devoted to work⟩. CIRCUMSTANCE implies a specific detail attending an action or event as part of its setting or background ⟨couldn't recall the exact *circumstances*⟩.

[1]**oc·cur·rent** \ə-ˈkər-ənt, -ˈkə-rənt\ *adj* [ME, fr. MF, fr. L *occurrent-, occurrens,* prp. of *occurrere*] (15c) **1** : occurring at a particular time or place : CURRENT **2** : INCIDENTAL

[2]**occurrent** *n* (1535) : something that occurs as distinguished from something that continues to exist

OCD *abbr* obsessive-compulsive disorder

ocean \ˈō-shən\ *n, often attrib* [ME *occean,* fr. AF, fr. L *oceanus,* fr. Gk *Ōkeanos,* a river thought of as encircling the earth, ocean] (14c) **1 a** : the whole body of salt water that covers nearly three fourths of the surface of the earth **b** : any of the large bodies of water (as the Atlantic Ocean) into which the great ocean is divided **2** : a very large or unlimited space or quantity

ocean·ar·i·um \ˌō-shə-ˈner-ē-əm\ *n, pl* **-iums** *or* **-ia** \-ē-ə\ (1938) : a large marine aquarium

ocean·front \ˈō-shən-ˌfrənt\ *n* (1919) : a shore area on the ocean

ocean·go·ing \-ˌgō-iŋ\ *adj* (1885) : of, relating to, or designed for travel on the ocean

oce·an·ic \ˌō-shē-ˈa-nik\ *adj* (1656) **1 a** : of or relating to the ocean **b** : occurring in or frequenting the ocean and esp. the open sea as distinguished from littoral or neritic waters **2** : VAST, GREAT

Oce·anid \ō-ˈsē-ə-nəd\ *n* [Gk *ōkeanid-, ōkeanis,* fr. *Ōkeanos* Oceanus] (1842) : any of the ocean nymphs that are daughters of Oceanus and Tethys in Greek mythology

ocean·og·ra·phy \ˌō-shə-ˈnä-grə-fē\ *n* [ISV] (1859) : a science that deals with the oceans and includes the delimitation of their extent and depth, the physics and chemistry of their waters, marine biology, and the exploitation of their resources — **ocean·og·ra·pher** \-fər\ *n* — **ocean·o·graph·ic** \-nə-ˈgra-fik\ *also* **ocean·o·graph·i·cal** \-fi-kəl\ *adj* — **ocean·o·graph·i·cal·ly** \-fi-k(ə-)lē\ *adv*

ocean·ol·o·gy \ˌō-shə-ˈnä-lə-jē\ *n* (ca. 1864) : OCEANOGRAPHY; *specif* : the science of marine resources and technology — **ocean·ol·o·gist** \-ˈnä-lə-jist\ *n*

ocean perch *n* (1943) : any of several marine scorpaenid food fishes (genus *Sebastes*): **a** : REDFISH a; *also* : a related food fish (*S. fasciatus*) **b** : one (*S. alutus*) abundant in the northeastern Pacific from Japan to the Bering Sea to southern California

ocean sunfish *n* (1629) : a large bony fish (*Mola mola* of the family Molidae, order Tetraodontiformes) having high dorsal and anal fins and a body nearly oval in outline and attaining a length of 10 feet (3 meters) and a weight in excess of 2 tons (1.8 metric tons)

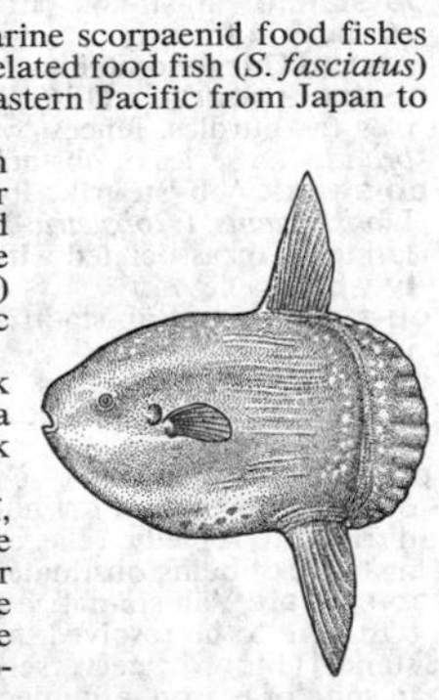
ocean sunfish

Oce·anus \ō-ˈsē-ə-nəs\ *n* [L, fr. Gk *Ōkeanos*] (1567) : a Titan who rules over a great river encircling the earth in Greek mythology

ocel·lus \ō-ˈse-ləs\ *n, pl* **ocel·li** \-ˈse-ˌlī, -(ˌ)lē\ [NL, fr. L, dim. of *oculus* eye — more at EYE] (1819) **1** : a minute simple eye or eyespot of an invertebrate **2** : an eyelike colored spot (as on a peacock feather or the wings of some butterflies) — **ocel·lar** \ō-ˈse-lər\ *adj*

oce·lot \ˈä-sə-ˌlät, ˈō-\ *n* [F, fr. Nahuatl *ōcēlōtl* jaguar] (1774) : a medium-sized American wildcat (*Felis pardalis*) that ranges from Texas to northern Argentina and has a tawny-yellow or grayish coat dotted and striped with black

ocher *or* **ochre** \ˈō-kər\ *n* [ME *oker,* fr. MF & L; MF *ocre,* fr. L *ochra,* fr. Gk *ōchra,* fr. fem. of *ōchros* yellow] (14c) **1** : an earthy usu. red or yellow and often impure iron ore used as a pigment **2** : the color of ocher; *esp* : the color of yellow ocher — **ocher·ous** \ˈō-k(ə-)rəs\ *or* **ochre·ous** \ˈō-k(ə-)rəs, -krē-əs\ *adj*

och·loc·ra·cy \ä-ˈklä-krə-sē\ *n* [Gk & MF; MF *ochlocratie,* fr. Gk *ochlokratia,* fr. *ochlos* mob + *-kratia* -cracy] (1584) : government by the mob : mob rule — **och·lo·crat** \ˈä-klə-ˌkrat\ *n* — **och·lo·crat·ic** \ˌä-klə-ˈkra-tik\ *or* **och·lo·crat·i·cal** \-ti-kəl\ *adj*

oci·cat \ˈä-sē-ˌkat\ *n* [blend of *ocelot* and *cat*] (1967) : any of a breed of domestic cats developed by crossing Siamese, American shorthair, and Abyssinian cats and having a short spotted coat

-ock *n suffix* [ME *-oc*, fr. OE] : small one ⟨hill*ock*⟩

Ockham's razor *var of* OCCAM'S RAZOR

o'·clock \ə-ˈkläk, ō-\ *adv* [contr. of *of the clock*] (1535) **1** : according to the clock ⟨the time is three ∼⟩ **2** — used for indicating position or direction as if on a clock dial that is oriented vertically or horizontally ⟨an airplane approaching at six ∼⟩

oco·ti·llo \ˌō-kə-ˈtē-(ˌ)yō\ *n, pl* **-llos** [MexSp, dim. of *ocote*, a resinous pine tree (*Pinus montezuma*), fr. Nahuatl *ocotl* pine, torch made of pine] (1856) : a thorny scarlet-flowered candlewood (*Fouquieria splendens* of the family Fouquieriaceae) of the southwestern U.S. and Mexico

OCR *abbr* optical character reader; optical character recognition

OCS *abbr* **1** officer candidate school **2** Old Church Slavic; Old Church Slavonic

Oct *abbr* October

octa- *or* **octo-** *also* **oct-** *comb form* [Gk *okta-, oktō-, okt-* (fr. *oktō*) & L *octo-, oct-*, fr. *octo* — more at EIGHT] : eight ⟨*octane*⟩ ⟨*octoroon*⟩

oc·ta·gon \ˈäk-tə-ˌgän\ *n* [L *octagonum*, fr. Gk *oktagōnon*, fr. octa- + *-gōnon* -gon] (1639) : a polygon of eight angles and eight sides — **oc·tag·o·nal** \äk-ˈta-gə-nᵊl\ *adj* — **oc·tag·o·nal·ly** \-nᵊl-ē\ *adv*

oc·ta·he·dral \ˌäk-tə-ˈhē-drəl\ *adj* (1758) **1** : having eight plane faces **2** : of, relating to, or formed in octahedrons — **oc·ta·he·dral·ly** \-drə-lē\ *adv*

oc·ta·he·dron \-drən\ *n, pl* **-drons** *or* **-dra** \-drə\ [Gk *oktaedron*, fr. octa- + *-edron* -hedron] (1570) : a solid bounded by eight plane faces

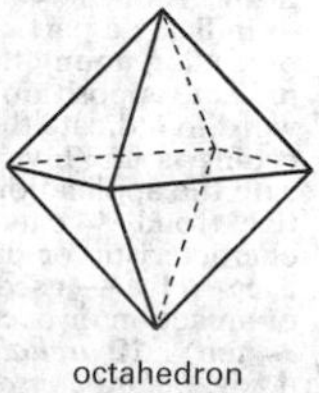

oc·tal \ˈäk-tᵊl\ *adj* (1948) : of, relating to, or being a number system with a base of eight

oc·tam·e·ter \äk-ˈta-mə-tər\ *n* [LL, having eight feet, fr. LGk *oktametros*, fr. okta- + *metron* measure — more at MEASURE] (1889) : a line of verse consisting of eight metrical feet

oc·tane \ˈäk-ˌtān\ *n* [ISV] (ca. 1872) **1** : any of several isomeric liquid alkanes C_8H_{18} **2** : OCTANE NUMBER

octane number *n* (1931) : a number that is used to measure the antiknock properties of a liquid motor fuel (as gasoline) with a higher number indicating a smaller likelihood of knocking — called also *octane rating*; compare CETANE NUMBER

oc·tant \ˈäk-tənt\ *n* [L *octant-, octans* eighth of a circle, fr. *octo*] (1731) **1** : an instrument for observing altitudes of a celestial body from a moving ship or aircraft **2** : any of the eight parts into which a space is divided by three coordinate planes

oc·ta·pep·tide \ˌäk-tə-ˈpep-ˌtīd\ *n* (1931) : a protein fragment or molecule (as oxytocin or vasopressin) that consists of eight amino acids linked in a polypeptide chain

oc·tave \ˈäk-tiv, -ˌtāv\ *n* [ME, fr. AF, fr. ML *octava*, fr. L, fem. of *octavus* eighth, fr. *octo* eight — more at EIGHT] (14c) **1** : an 8-day period of observances beginning with a festival day **2 a** : a stanza of eight lines : OTTAVA RIMA **b** : the first eight lines of an Italian sonnet **3 a** : a musical interval embracing eight diatonic degrees **b** : a tone or note at this interval **c** : the harmonic combination of two tones an octave apart **d** : the whole series of notes, tones, or digitals comprised within this interval and forming the unit of the modern scale **e** : an organ stop giving tones an octave above those corresponding to the keys **4** : the interval between two frequencies (as in an electromagnetic spectrum) having a ratio of 2 to 1 **5** : a group of eight

oc·ta·vo \äk-ˈtā-(ˌ)vō, -ˈtä-\ *n, pl* **-vos** [L, abl. of *octavus* eighth] (1582) : the size of a piece of paper cut eight from a sheet; *also* : a book, a page, or paper of this size

oc·tet \äk-ˈtet\ *n* (1864) **1** : a musical composition for eight instruments or voices **2** : a group or set of eight: as **a** : OCTAVE 2b **b** : the performers of an octet

oc·til·lion \äk-ˈtil-yən\ *n* [F, fr. MF, fr. oct- octa- + *-illion* (as in *million*)] (1690) — see NUMBER table

Oc·to·ber \äk-ˈtō-bər\ *n* [ME *Octobre*, fr. OE & AF; OE *October*, fr. L, 8th month of the early Roman calendar, fr. *octo*; AF, fr. L *October*] (bef. 12c) : the 10th month of the Gregorian calendar

oc·to·de·cil·lion \ˌäk-tō-di-ˈsil-yən\ *n* [L *octodecim* eighteen + E *-illion* (as in *million*)] (1939) — see NUMBER table

oc·to·ge·nar·i·an \ˌäk-tə-jə-ˈner-ē-ən\ *n* [L *octogenarius* containing eighty, fr. *octogeni* eighty each, fr. *octoginta* eighty, fr. *octo* eight + *-ginta* (akin to *viginti* twenty) — more at VIGESIMAL] (1815) : a person whose age is in the eighties — **octogenarian** *adj*

oc·to·ploid \ˈäk-tə-ˌploid\ *adj* [ISV] (1925) : having a chromosome number eight times the basic haploid chromosome number — **octoploid** *n*

oc·to·pod \ˈäk-tə-ˌpäd\ *n* [ultim. fr. Gk *oktōpod-, oktōpous* scorpion, fr. *oktō-* octa- + *pod-, pous* foot — more at FOOT] (ca. 1836) : any of an order (Octopoda) of cephalopod mollusks (as an octopus or argonaut) that have eight arms bearing sessile suckers — **octopod** *adj*

oc·to·pus \ˈäk-tə-pəs, -ˌpůs\ *n, pl* **-pus·es** *or* **-pi** \-ˌpī\ [NL *Octopod-, Octopus*, fr. Gk *oktōpous*] (1758) **1** : any of a genus (*Octopus*) of cephalopod mollusks that have eight muscular arms equipped with two rows of suckers; *broadly* : any octopod excepting the paper nautilus **2** : something that resembles an octopus esp. in having many centrally directed branches

oc·to·roon \ˌäk-tə-ˈrün\ *n* [*octa-* + *-roon* (as in *quadroon*)] (1861) : a person of one-eighth black ancestry

oc·to·syl·lab·ic \ˌäk-tə-sə-ˈla-bik\ *adj* [LL *octosyllabus*, fr. Gk *oktasyllabos*, fr. *okta-* octa- + *syllabē* syllable] (ca. 1771) **1** : consisting of eight syllables **2** : composed of verses of eight syllables — **octosyllabic** *n*

oc·to·syl·la·ble \ˈäk-tə-ˌsi-lə-bəl, ˌäk-tə-ˈ\ *n* (ca. 1846) : a word or line of eight syllables

oc·to·thorpe *or* **oc·to·thorp** \ˈäk-tə-ˌthorp, -tō-\ *n* [*octo-* + *thorp*, of unknown origin; fr. the eight points on its circumference] (1971) : the symbol #

¹**oc·u·lar** \ˈä-kyə-lər\ *adj* [LL *ocularis* of eyes, fr. L *oculus* eye] (ca. 1575) **1 a** : done or perceived by the eye ⟨∼ inspection⟩ **b** : based on what has been seen ⟨∼ testimony⟩ **2 a** : of or relating to the eye ⟨∼ muscles⟩ **b** : resembling an eye in form or function

²**ocular** *n* (1835) : EYEPIECE

oc·u·lar·ist \ˈä-kyə-lə-rist\ *n* (1866) : a person who makes and fits artificial eyes

oc·u·list \ˈä-kyə-list\ *n* [F *oculiste*, fr. L *oculus*] (1615) **1** : OPHTHALMOLOGIST **2** : OPTOMETRIST

oc·u·lo·mo·tor \ˌä-kyə-lə-ˈmō-tər\ *adj* [L *oculus* eye + E *-o-* + *motor*] (ca. 1890) **1** : moving or tending to move the eyeball **2** : of or relating to the oculomotor nerve

oculomotor nerve *n* (1881) : either of the pair of chiefly motor nerves that comprise the third pair of cranial nerves, arise from the midbrain, and supply four muscles of the eye

oc·u·lus \ˈä-kyə-ləs\ *n, pl* **oc·u·li** \-ˌlī, -ˌlē\ [L, lit., eye — more at EYE] (1848) **1** : a circular or oval window **2** : a circular opening at the top of a dome

od *or* **odd** \ˈäd\ *interj, often cap* [euphemism for *God*] (1695) *archaic* — used as a mild oath

¹**OD** \ˌō-ˈdē\ *n* [*overdose*] (ca. 1960) **1** : an overdose of a narcotic **2** : one who has taken an OD

²**OD** *vi* **OD'd** *or* **ODed; OD'ing; OD's** (1966) **1** : to become ill or die of an OD **2** : to have or experience too much of something — usu. used with *on* ⟨∼ on television⟩

³**OD** *abbr* **1** doctor of optometry **2** [L *oculus dexter*] right eye **3** officer of the day **4** olive drab **5** on demand **6** outside diameter; outside dimension **7** overdraft; overdrawn

oda·lisque \ˈō-də-ˌlisk\ *n* [F, fr. Turk *odalık*, fr. *oda* room] (ca. 1681) **1** : a female slave **2** : a concubine in a harem

odd \ˈäd\ *adj* [ME *odde*, fr. ON *odde* point of land, triangle, odd number; akin to OE *ord* point of a weapon] (14c) **1 a** : being without a corresponding mate ⟨an ∼ shoe⟩ **b** (1) : left over after others are paired or grouped (2) : separated from a set or series **2 a** : somewhat more than the indicated approximate quantity, extent, or degree — usu. used in combination ⟨300-*odd* pages⟩ **b** (1) : left over as a remainder ⟨had a few ∼ dollars left after paying his bills⟩ (2) : constituting a small amount ⟨had some ∼ change in her pocket⟩ **3 a** : being any of the integers (as –3, –1, +1, and +3) that are not divisible by two without leaving a remainder **b** : marked by an odd number of units **c** : being a function such that $f(-x) = -f(x)$ where the sign is reversed but the absolute value remains the same if the sign of the independent variable is reversed **4 a** : not regular, expected, or planned ⟨worked at ∼ jobs⟩ **b** : encountered or experienced from time to time : OCCASIONAL **5** : having an out-of-the-way location : REMOTE **6** : differing markedly from the usual or ordinary or accepted : PECULIAR *syn* see STRANGE — **odd·ness** *n*

odd·ball \ˈäd-ˌbȯl\ *n* (1948) : one that is eccentric — **oddball** *adj*

Odd Fellow *n* [Independent Order of *Odd Fellows*] (1795) : a member of a major benevolent and fraternal order

odd·i·ty \ˈä-də-tē\ *n, pl* **-ties** (1713) **1** : an odd person, thing, event, or trait **2** : the quality or state of being odd

odd lot *n* (1913) : a number or quantity other than the usual unit in transactions; *esp* : a quantity of less than 100 shares of stock

odd·ly \ˈäd-lē\ *adv* (1610) **1** : in an odd manner **2** : as is odd ⟨was quite happy, ∼ enough⟩

odd man out *n* (1873) : a person who differs from the other members of a group

odd·ment \ˈäd-mənt\ *n* (1796) **1 a** : something left over : REMNANT **b** *pl* : ODDS AND ENDS **2** : something odd : ODDITY

odd permutation *n* (1927) : a permutation that is produced by the successive application of an odd number of interchanges of pairs of elements

odd–pin·nate \ˈäd-ˈpi-ˌnāt\ *adj* (ca. 1890) : having leaflets on each side of the petiole and having a single leaflet at the tip of the petiole — see LEAF illustration — **odd-pin·nate·ly** *adv*

odds \ˈädz\ *n pl but sing or pl in constr* (ca. 1520) **1 a** *archaic* : INEQUALITIES **b** *obs* : degree of unlikeness **2 a** : an amount by which one thing exceeds or falls short of another ⟨won the election by considerable ∼⟩ **b** (1) : a difference favoring one of two opposed things ⟨overwhelming ∼⟩ (2) : a difference in terms of advantage or disadvantage ⟨what's the ∼, if thinking so makes them happy —Flora Thompson⟩ **c** (1) : the probability that one thing is so or will happen rather than another : CHANCES ⟨the ∼ are against it⟩ (2) : the ratio of the probability of one event to that of an alternative event **3** : DISAGREEMENT, VARIANCE — usu. used with *at* ⟨faculty and administration often are at ∼ on everything —W. E. Brock *b*1930⟩ **4 a** : special favor : PARTIALITY **b** : an allowance granted by one making a bet to one accepting the bet and designed to equalize the chances favoring one of the bettors **c** : the ratio between the amount to be paid off for a winning bet and the amount of the bet — **by all odds** : in every way : without question ⟨*by all odds* the best book of the year⟩

odds and ends *n pl* (ca. 1746) **1 a** : miscellaneous articles **b** : miscellaneous small matters (as of business) to be attended to **2** : miscellaneous remnants or leftovers ⟨*odds and ends* of food⟩

odds·mak·er \ˈädz-ˌmā-kər\ *n* (1931) : one who figures betting odds

odds–on \ˈädz-ˈȯn, -ˈän\ *adj* (1890) **1** : having or viewed as having a better than even chance to win ⟨the ∼ favorite⟩ **2** : not involving much risk : pretty sure ⟨an ∼ bet⟩

odd trick *n* (1837) : each trick in excess of six won by declarer's side at bridge — compare BOOK 9

ode \ˈōd\ *n* [MF *or* LL; MF, fr. LL, fr. Gk *ōidē*, lit., song, fr. *aeidein, aidein* to sing; akin to Gk *audē* voice] (1588) : a lyric poem usu. marked by exaltation of feeling and style, varying length of line, and complexity of stanza forms — **od·ist** \-ist\ *n*

-ode *n comb form* [Gk *-odos*, fr. *hodos*] **1** : way : path ⟨electr*ode*⟩ **2** : electrode ⟨di*ode*⟩

ode·um \ō-ˈdē-əm, ˈō-dē-\ *n, pl* **odea** \-ə\ [L & Gk; L, fr. Gk *ōideion*, fr. *ōidē* song] (1616) **1** : a small roofed theater of ancient Greece and Rome used chiefly for competitions in music and poetry **2** : a theater or concert hall

od·ic \ˈō-dik\ *adj* (1863) : of, relating to, or forming an ode

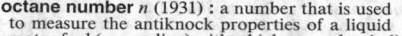

octahedron

\ə\ abut \ᵊ\ kitten, F table \ər\ further \a\ ash \ā\ ace \ä\ mop, mar
\aů\ out \ch\ chin \e\ bet \ē\ easy \g\ go \i\ hit \ī\ ice \j\ job
\ŋ\ sing \ō\ go \ȯ\ law \ȯi\ boy \th\ thin \th\ the \ü\ loot \ů\ foot
\y\ yet \zh\ vision, beige \k, ⁿ, œ, ᵫ, �\ *see* Guide to Pronunciation

odif·er·ous \ō-ˈdi-f(ə-)rəs\ *adj* [by contr.] (15c) : ODORIFEROUS
Odin \ˈō-dᵊn\ *n* [Dan, fr. ON *Ōthinn*] (1690) : the supreme god and creator in Norse mythology
odi·ous \ˈō-dē-əs\ *adj* [ME, fr. AF, fr. L *odiosus,* fr. *odium*] (14c) : arousing or deserving hatred or repugnance : HATEFUL ⟨an ~ crime⟩ ⟨a false and ~ comparison⟩ — **odi·ous·ly** *adv* — **odi·ous·ness** *n*
odi·um \ˈō-dē-əm\ *n* [L, hatred, fr. *odisse* to hate; akin to OE *atol* terrible, Gk *odyssasthai* to be angry] (1602) **1** : the state or fact of being subjected to hatred and contempt as a result of a despicable act or blameworthy circumstance **2** : hatred and condemnation accompanied by loathing or contempt : DETESTATION **3** : disrepute or infamy attached to something : OPPROBRIUM
odom·e·ter \ō-ˈdä-mə-tər\ *n* [F *odomètre,* fr. Gk *hodometron,* fr. *hodos* way, road + *metron* measure — more at MEASURE] (1791) : an instrument for measuring the distance traveled (as by a vehicle)
odo·nate \ˈō-də-ˌnāt, ō-ˈdä-(ˌ)nāt\ *n* [irreg. fr. Gk *odous, odōn* tooth] (1947) : any of an order (Odonata) of predaceous insects comprising the dragonflies and damselflies — **odonate** *adj*
odont- *or* **odonto-** *comb form* [F, fr. Gk, *odont-, odous* — more at TOOTH] : tooth ⟨*odonto*blast⟩
-odont *adj comb form* [Gk *odont-, odous* tooth] : having teeth of a (specified) nature ⟨acr*odont*⟩
-odontia *n comb form* [NL, fr. Gk *odont-, odous*] : form, condition, or mode of treatment of the teeth ⟨orth*odontia*⟩
odon·to·blast \ō-ˈdän-tə-ˌblast\ *n* [ISV] (1878) : any of the elongated radially arranged cells on the surface of the dental pulp that secrete dentin — **odon·to·blas·tic** \-ˌdän-tə-ˈblas-tik\ *adj*
odon·to·glos·sum \ō-ˌdän-tə-ˈglä-səm\ *n* [NL, fr. Gk *odont-* + *glōssa* tongue — more at GLOSS] (1880) : any of a genus (*Odontoglossum*) of widely cultivated tropical American orchids
odon·toid process \ō-ˈdän-ˌtȯid-\ *n* (ca. 1819) : a toothlike process projecting from the anterior end of the centrum of the axis vertebra on which the atlas vertebra rotates
odor \ˈō-dər\ *n* [ME *odour,* fr. AF *odur,* fr. L *odor;* akin to L *olēre* to smell, Gk *ozein* to smell, *osmē* smell, odor] (13c) **1 a** : a quality of something that stimulates the olfactory organ : SCENT **b** : a sensation resulting from adequate stimulation of the olfactory organ : SMELL **2 a** : a characteristic or predominant quality : FLAVOR ⟨the ~ of sanctity⟩ **b** : REPUTE, ESTIMATION ⟨in bad ~⟩ **3** *archaic* : something that emits a sweet or pleasing scent : PERFUME ***syn*** see SMELL — **odored** \ˈō-dərd\ *adj* — **odor·less** \-dər-ləs\ *adj*
odor·ant \ˈō-də-rənt\ *n* (1935) : an odorous substance; *esp* : one added to a dangerous odorless substance to warn of its presence
odor·if·er·ous \ˌō-də-ˈri-f(ə-)rəs\ *adj* (15c) **1** : yielding an odor : ODOROUS **2** : morally offensive ⟨~ legislation⟩ — **odor·if·er·ous·ly** *adv* — **odor·if·er·ous·ness** *n*
odor·ize \ˈō-də-ˌrīz\ *vt* **-ized; -iz·ing** (1884) : to make odorous : SCENT
odor·ous \ˈō-də-rəs\ *adj* (15c) : having an odor: as **a** : FRAGRANT **b** : MALODOROUS — **odor·ous·ly** *adv* — **odor·ous·ness** *n*
syn ODOROUS, FRAGRANT, REDOLENT, AROMATIC mean emitting and diffusing scent. ODOROUS applies to whatever has a strong distinctive smell whether pleasant or unpleasant ⟨*odorous* cheeses should be tightly wrapped⟩. FRAGRANT applies to things (as flowers or spices) with sweet or agreeable odors ⟨a *fragrant* rose⟩. REDOLENT applies usu. to a place or thing impregnated with odors ⟨the kitchen was *redolent* of garlic and tomatoes⟩. AROMATIC applies to things emitting pungent often fresh odors ⟨an *aromatic* blend of tobaccos⟩.
odour *chiefly Brit var of* ODOR
Odys·se·an \ō-ˈdi-sē-ən ("*Odysseus*"), ˌä-də-ˈsē-ən ("*journey*")\ *adj* (ca. 1711) : of, relating to, or characteristic of Odysseus or his journey
Odys·seus \ō-ˈdi-sē-əs, -ˈdis-yəs, -ˈdi-shəs, -ˈdi-ˌshüs\ *n* [Gk] (1616) : a king of Ithaca and Greek leader in the Trojan War who after the war wanders 10 years before reaching home
od·ys·sey \ˈä-də-sē\ *n, pl* **-seys** [the *Odyssey,* epic poem attributed to Homer recounting the long wanderings of Odysseus] (1889) **1** : a long wandering or voyage usu. marked by many changes of fortune **2** : an intellectual or spiritual wandering or quest
Oe *abbr* oersted
OECD *abbr* Organization for Economic Cooperation and Development
oe·cu·men·i·cal *esp Brit* ˌē-\ *chiefly Brit var of* ECUMENICAL
OED *abbr* Oxford English Dictionary
oe·de·ma *chiefly Brit var of* EDEMA
oe·di·pal \ˈe-də-pəl, ˈē-\ *adj, often cap* (1939) : of, relating to, or resulting from the Oedipus complex — **oe·di·pal·ly** \-pə-lē\ *adv, often cap*
[1]**Oe·di·pus** \-pəs\ *n* [L, fr. Gk *Oidipous*] (1557) : the son of Laius and Jocasta who in fulfillment of an oracle unknowingly kills his father and marries his mother
[2]**Oedipus** *adj* (1910) : OEDIPAL
Oedipus complex *n* (1910) : the positive libidinal feelings of a child toward the parent of the opposite sex and hostile or jealous feelings toward the parent of the same sex that in Freudian psychoanalytic theory may be a source of adult personality disorder when unresolved
oeil–de–boeuf \ˌə(r)-də-ˈbəf\ *n, pl* **oeils–de–boeuf** *same*\ [F *œil-de-bœuf,* lit., ox's eye] (1849) : OCULUS 1
oeil·lade \ˌə(r)-ˈyäd, œ-\ *n* [MF *œillade,* fr. *oeil* eye, fr. OF *oil,* fr. L *oculus* — more at EYE] (1592) : a glance of the eye; *esp* : OGLE
OEM \ˌō-(ˌ)ē-ˈem\ *n* [*o*riginal *e*quipment *m*anufacturer] (1968) : one that produces complex equipment (as a computer system) from components usu. bought from other manufacturers
oenology *var of* ENOLOGY
Oe·no·ne \ē-ˈnō-nē\ *n* [L, fr. Gk *Oinōnē*] (1566) : a nymph who is abandoned by her husband Paris for Helen of Troy
oe·no·phile \ˈē-nə-ˌfī(-ə)l\ *n* [F *œnophile,* fr. *œno-* (fr. Gk *oinos* wine) + *-phile* -phile — more at WINE] (1930) : a lover or connoisseur of wine
OEO *abbr* Office of Economic Opportunity
OER *abbr* officer efficiency report
[1]**o'er** \ˈȯr\ *adv* (1592) : OVER
[2]**o'er** *prep* (1593) : OVER
oer·sted \ˈər-stəd\ *n* [Hans Christian *Oersted*] (1930) : the unit of magnetic field strength in the centimeter-gram-second system
oe·soph·a·gus *chiefly Brit var of* ESOPHAGUS
oestr- *or* **oestro-** *chiefly Brit var of* ESTR-
oeu·vre \ˈə(r)-vrə, ˈœvrᵊ\ *n, pl* **oeuvres** *same*\ [F *œuvre,* lit., work, fr. OF *ovre,* L *opera* — more at OPERA] (1875) : a substantial body of work constituting the lifework of a writer, an artist, or a composer
[1]**of** \əv, *before consonants also* ə; ˈəv, ˈäv\ *prep* [ME, off, of, fr. OE, adv. & prep.; akin to OHG *aba* off, away, L *ab* from, away, Gk *apo*] (bef. 12c) **1** — used as a function word to indicate a point of reckoning ⟨north ~ the lake⟩ **2 a** — used as a function word to indicate origin or derivation ⟨a man ~ noble birth⟩ **b** — used as a function word to indicate the cause, motive, or reason ⟨died ~ flu⟩ **c** : BY ⟨plays ~ Shakespeare⟩ **d** : on the part of ⟨very kind ~ you⟩ **e** : occurring in ⟨a fish ~ the western Atlantic⟩ **3** — used as a function word to indicate the component material, parts, or elements or the contents ⟨throne ~ gold⟩ ⟨cup ~ water⟩ **4 a** — used as a function word to indicate the whole that includes the part denoted by the preceding word ⟨most ~ the army⟩ **b** — used as a function word to indicate a whole or quantity from which a part is removed or expended ⟨gave ~ his time⟩ **5 a** : relating to : ABOUT ⟨stories ~ her travels⟩ **b** : in respect to ⟨slow ~ speech⟩ **6 a** — used as a function word to indicate belonging or a possessive relationship ⟨king ~ England⟩ **b** — used as a function word to indicate relationship between a result determined by a function or operation and a basic entity (as an independent variable) ⟨a function ~ *x*⟩ ⟨the product ~ two numbers⟩ **7** — used as a function word to indicate something from which a person or thing is delivered ⟨eased ~ her pain⟩ or with respect to which someone or something is made destitute ⟨robbed ~ all their belongings⟩ **8 a** — used as a function word to indicate a particular example belonging to the class denoted by the preceding noun ⟨the city ~ Rome⟩ **b** — used as a function word to indicate apposition ⟨that fool ~ a husband⟩ **9 a** — used as a function word to indicate the object of an action denoted or implied by the preceding noun ⟨love ~ nature⟩ **b** — used as a function word to indicate the application of a verb ⟨cheats him ~ a dollar⟩ or of an adjective ⟨fond ~ candy⟩ **10** — used as a function word to indicate a characteristic or distinctive quality or possession ⟨a woman ~ courage⟩ **11 a** — used as a function word to indicate the position in time of an action or occurrence ⟨died ~ a Monday⟩ **b** : BEFORE ⟨quarter ~ ten⟩ **12** *archaic* : ON ⟨a plague ~ all cowards —Shak.⟩
[2]**of** \əv, *before consonants also* ə\ *verbal auxiliary* [by alter.] (ca. 1800) *nonstand* : HAVE — used in place of the contraction *'ve* often in representations of uneducated speech ⟨I could ~ beat them easy —Ring Lardner⟩
OF *abbr* outfield
ofay \ˈō-ˌfā, ō-ˈ\ *n* [origin unknown] (1925) *usu disparaging* : a white person
[1]**off** \ˈȯf\ *adv* [ME *of,* fr. OE — more at OF] (bef. 12c) **1 a** (1) : from a place or position ⟨march ~⟩; *specif* : away from land ⟨ship stood ~ to sea⟩ (2) : at a distance in space or time ⟨stood 10 paces ~⟩ ⟨a long way ~⟩ **b** : from a course : ASIDE ⟨turned ~ into a bypath⟩; *specif* : away from the wind **c** : into an unconscious state ⟨dozed ~⟩ **2 a** : so as to be separated from support ⟨rolled to the edge of the table and ~⟩ or close contact ⟨blew the lid ~⟩ ⟨the handle came ~⟩ **b** : so as to be divided ⟨surface marked ~ into squares⟩ **3 a** : to a state of discontinuance or suspension ⟨shut ~ an engine⟩ **b** — used as an intensifier ⟨drink ~ a glass⟩ ⟨finish it ~⟩ **4** : in absence from or suspension of regular work or service ⟨take time ~ for lunch⟩ **5** : OFFSTAGE
[2]**off** *prep* (bef. 12c) **1 a** — used as a function word to indicate physical separation or distance from a position of rest, attachment, or union ⟨take it ~ the table⟩ ⟨a path ~ the main walk⟩ ⟨a shop just ~ the main street⟩ **b** : to seaward of ⟨two miles ~ shore⟩ **2** : from the possession or charge of ⟨had his wallet stolen ~ him⟩ **3** — used as a function word to indicate the object of an action ⟨borrowed a dollar ~ him⟩ ⟨dined ~ oysters⟩ **4 a** — used as a function word to indicate the suspension of an occupation or activity ⟨~ duty⟩ ⟨~ liquor⟩ **b** : below the usual standard or level of ⟨~ his game⟩
[3]**off** *adj* (1666) **1 a** : SEAWARD **b** : RIGHT **c** : more removed or distant ⟨the ~ side of the building⟩ **2 a** : started on the way ⟨~ on a spree⟩ **b** : not taking place or staying in effect : CANCELED ⟨the deal was ~⟩ **c** : not operating **d** : not placed so as to permit operation **3 a** : not corresponding to fact : INCORRECT ⟨~ in his reckoning⟩ **b** : POOR, SUBNORMAL **c** : not entirely sane : ECCENTRIC **d** : REMOTE, SLIGHT ⟨an ~ chance⟩ **4 a** : spent off duty ⟨reading on his ~ days⟩ **b** : marked by a periodic decline in activity or business ⟨traveled in the ~ season for lower prices⟩ **5 a** : OFF-COLOR **b** : INFERIOR ⟨~ grade of oil⟩; *also* : affected with putrefaction **c** : DOWN ⟨stocks were ~⟩ **6** : CIRCUMSTANCED ⟨worse ~⟩
[4]**off** *vi* (1717) : to go away : DEPART — used chiefly as an imperative ⟨~, or I'll shoot⟩ ~ *vt, slang* : KILL, MURDER
[5]**off** *abbr* office; officer; official
-off \ˌȯf\ *n comb form* [run*off*] : competition : contest ⟨bake-*off*⟩
of·fal \ˈȯ-fəl, ˈä-\ *n* [ME, fr. *of* off + *fall*] (14c) **1** : the waste or by-product of a process: as **a** : trimmings of a hide **b** : the by-products of milling used esp. for stock feeds **c** : the viscera and trimmings of a butchered animal removed in dressing : VARIETY MEAT **2** : RUBBISH
off and on *adv* (1535) : with periodic cessation : INTERMITTENTLY ⟨rained *off and on* all day⟩
[1]**off·beat** \ˈȯf-ˌbēt\ *n* (ca. 1928) : an unaccented beat or portion of a beat in a musical measure
[2]**off·beat** \-ˈbēt\ *adj* (1938) : ECCENTRIC, UNCONVENTIONAL
off–brand \ˈȯf-ˌbrand\ *adj* (1892) : not identified with a major brand name ⟨~ sneakers⟩
off Broadway *n, often cap O* [fr. its usu. being produced in smaller theaters outside of the Broadway theatrical district] (1954) : a part of the New York professional theater stressing fundamental and artistic values and formerly engaging in experimentation — **off–Broadway** *adj or adv, often cap O*
off·cast \ˈȯf-ˌkast\ *adj* (1571) : cast off : DISCARDED — **offcast** *n*
off–col·or \ˈȯf-ˈkə-lər\ *or* **off–col·ored** \-lərd\ *adj* (1854) **1 a** : not having the right or standard color **b** : being out of sorts **2 a** : of doubtful propriety : DUBIOUS **b** : verging on the indecent ⟨~ remarks⟩
off·cut \ˈȯf-ˌkət\ *n* (ca. 1664) *chiefly Brit* : something that is cut off (as a waste piece of lumber)
of·fend \ə-ˈfend\ *vb* [ME, fr. AF *offendre,* fr. L *offendere* to strike against, offend, fr. *ob-* against + *-fendere* to strike — more at OB-, DEFEND] *vi* (14c) **1 a** : to transgress the moral or divine law : SIN ⟨if it be

a sin to covet honor, I am the most ~*ing* soul alive —Shak.⟩ **b :** to violate a law or rule : do wrong ⟨~ against the law⟩ **2 a :** to cause difficulty, discomfort, or injury ⟨took off his shoe and removed the ~*ing* pebble⟩ **b :** to cause dislike, anger, or vexation ⟨thoughtless words that ~ needlessly⟩ ~ *vt* **1 a :** VIOLATE, TRANSGRESS **b :** to cause pain to : HURT **2** *obs* **:** to cause to sin or fall **3 :** to cause to feel vexation or resentment usu. by violation of what is proper or fitting ⟨was ~*ed* by their language⟩ — **of·fend·er** *n*

syn OFFEND, OUTRAGE, AFFRONT, INSULT mean to cause hurt feelings or deep resentment. OFFEND need not imply an intentional hurting but it may indicate merely a violation of the victim's sense of what is proper or fitting ⟨hoped that my remarks had not *offended* her⟩. OUTRAGE implies offending beyond endurance and calling forth extreme feelings ⟨*outraged* by their accusations⟩. AFFRONT implies treating with deliberate rudeness or contemptuous indifference to courtesy ⟨deeply *affronted* by his callousness⟩. INSULT suggests deliberately causing humiliation, hurt pride, or shame ⟨*insulted* every guest at the party⟩.

of·fense *or* **of·fence** \ə-ˈfen(t)s, *esp for 3* ˈä-ˌfen(t)s, ˈȯ-\ *n* [ME, fr. AF, fr. L *offensa,* fr. fem. of *offensus,* pp. of *offendere*] (14c) **1 a** *obs* **:** an act of stumbling **b** *archaic* **:** a cause or occasion of sin : STUMBLING BLOCK **2 :** something that outrages the moral or physical senses **3 a :** the act of attacking : ASSAULT **b :** the means or method of attacking or of attempting to score **c :** the offensive team or members of a team playing offensive positions **d :** scoring ability **4 a :** the act of displeasing or affronting **b :** the state of being insulted or morally outraged ⟨takes ~ at the slightest criticism⟩ **5 a :** a breach of a moral or social code : SIN, MISDEED **b :** an infraction of law; *esp* **:** MISDEMEANOR — **of·fense·less** \-ləs\ *adj*

syn OFFENSE, RESENTMENT, UMBRAGE, PIQUE, DUDGEON, HUFF mean an emotional response to or an emotional state resulting from a slight or indignity. OFFENSE implies hurt displeasure ⟨takes deep *offense* at racial slurs⟩. RESENTMENT suggests lasting indignation or ill will ⟨harbored a lifelong *resentment* of his brother⟩. UMBRAGE may suggest hurt pride, resentment, or suspicion of another's motives ⟨took *umbrage* at the offer of advice⟩. PIQUE applies to a transient feeling of wounded vanity ⟨in a *pique* I foolishly declined the invitation⟩. DUDGEON suggests an angry fit of indignation ⟨stormed out of the meeting in high *dudgeon*⟩. HUFF implies a peevish short-lived spell of anger usu. at a petty cause ⟨in a *huff* he slammed the door⟩.

syn OFFENSE, SIN, VICE, CRIME, SCANDAL mean a transgression of law. OFFENSE applies to the infraction of any law, rule, or code ⟨at that school no *offense* went unpunished⟩. SIN implies an offense against moral or religious law ⟨the *sin* of blasphemy⟩. VICE applies to a habit or practice that degrades or corrupts ⟨regarded gambling as a *vice*⟩. CRIME implies a serious offense punishable by the law of the state ⟨the *crime* of murder⟩. SCANDAL applies to an offense that outrages the public conscience ⟨a career ruined by a sex *scandal*⟩.

1**of·fen·sive** \ə-ˈfen(t)-siv, *esp for 1* ˈä-ˌfen(t)-, ˈȯ-\ *adj* (ca. 1564) **1 a :** making attack : AGGRESSIVE **b :** of, relating to, or designed for attack ⟨~ weapons⟩ **c :** of or relating to an attempt to score in a game or contest; *also* **:** of or relating to a team in possession of the ball or puck **2 :** giving painful or unpleasant sensations : NAUSEOUS, OBNOXIOUS ⟨an ~ odor⟩ **3 :** causing displeasure or resentment ⟨~ remarks⟩ — **of·fen·sive·ly** *adv* — **of·fen·sive·ness** *n*

2**offensive** *n* (1687) **1 :** the act of an attacking party **2 :** ATTACK

1**of·fer** \ˈȯ-fər, ˈä-\ *vb* **of·fered; of·fer·ing** \-f(ə-)riŋ\ [ME *offren,* in sense 1, fr. OE *offrian,* fr. LL *offerre,* fr. L, to present, tender, fr. *ob-* toward + *ferre* to carry; in other senses, fr. AF *offrir,* fr. L *offerre* — more at BEAR] *vt* (bef. 12c) **1 a :** to present as an act of worship or devotion : SACRIFICE **b :** to utter (as a prayer) in devotion **2 a :** to present for acceptance or rejection : TENDER ⟨was ~*ed* a job⟩ **b :** to present in order to satisfy a requirement ⟨candidates for degrees may ~ French as one of their foreign languages⟩ **3 a :** PROPOSE, SUGGEST ⟨~ a solution to a problem⟩ **b :** to declare one's readiness or willingness ⟨~*ed* to help me⟩ **4 a :** to try or begin to exert : PUT UP ⟨~*ed* stubborn resistance⟩ **b :** THREATEN ⟨~*ed* to strike him with his cane⟩ **5 :** to make available : AFFORD; *esp* **:** to place (merchandise) on sale **6 :** to present in performance or exhibition **7 :** to propose as payment : BID ~ *vi* **1 :** to present something as an act of worship or devotion : SACRIFICE **2** *archaic* **:** to make an attempt **3 :** to present itself **4 :** to make a proposal (as of marriage)

2**offer** *n* (15c) **1 a :** a presenting of something for acceptance ⟨considering job ~*s* from several firms⟩ ⟨an ~ of marriage⟩ **b :** an undertaking to do an act or give something on condition that the party to whom the proposal is made do some specified act or make a return promise **2** *obs* **:** OFFERING **3 :** a price named by one proposing to buy : BID **4 a :** ATTEMPT, TRY **b :** an action or movement indicating a purpose or intention — **on offer** *chiefly Brit* **:** being offered esp. for sale

of·fer·ing \ˈȯ-f(ə-)riŋ, ˈä-\ *n* (bef. 12c) **1 a :** the act of one who offers **b :** something offered; *esp* **:** a sacrifice ceremonially offered as a part of worship **c :** a contribution to the support of a church **2 :** something offered for sale or patronage ⟨latest ~*s* of the leading novelists⟩ **3 :** a course of instruction or study

of·fer·to·ry \ˈȯ-fə(r)-ˌtȯr-ē, ˈä-\ *n, pl* **-ries** [ME *offertorie,* fr. ML *offertorium,* fr. LL *offerre*] (14c) **1** *often cap* **a :** the eucharistic offering of bread and wine to God before they are consecrated **b :** a verse from a Psalm said or sung at the beginning of the offertory **2 a :** the period of collection and presentation of the offerings of the congregation at public worship **b :** a musical composition played or sung during an offertory

off–gas·sing \ˈȯf-ˌga-siŋ\ *n* (1966) **:** the emission of esp. noxious gases (as from a building material)

1**off·hand** \ˈȯf-ˈhand, -ˌhand\ *adv* (1680) **:** without premeditation or preparation : EXTEMPORE ⟨couldn't give the figures ~⟩

2**offhand** *adj* (1692) **1 :** CASUAL, INFORMAL ⟨a relaxed, ~ manner⟩ **2 :** done or made offhand ⟨~ excuses⟩

off·hand·ed \-ˈhan-dəd, -ˌhan-\ *adj* (1812) **:** OFFHAND — **off·hand·ed·ly** *adv* — **off·hand·ed·ness** *n*

off–hour \ˈȯf-ˌau̇(-ə)r\ *n* (1898) **1 :** a period of time other than a rush hour **2 :** a period of time other than regular business hours

of·fice \ˈä-fəs, ˈȯ-\ *n* [ME, fr. AF, fr. L *officium* service, duty, office, fr. *opus* work + *facere* to make, do — more at OPERATE, DO] (13c) **1 a :** a special duty, charge, or position conferred by an exercise of governmental authority and for a public purpose : a position of authority to exercise a public function and to receive whatever emoluments may belong to it **b :** a position of responsibility or some degree of executive authority **2** [ME, fr. AF, fr. LL *officium,* fr. L] **:** a prescribed form or service of worship; *specif, cap* **:** DIVINE OFFICE **3 :** a religious or social ceremonial observance : RITE **4 a :** something that one ought to do or must do : an assigned or assumed duty, task, or role **b :** the proper or customary action of something : FUNCTION **c :** something done for another : SERVICE **5 :** a place where a particular kind of business is transacted or a service is supplied: as **a :** a place in which the functions of a public officer are performed **b :** the directing headquarters of an enterprise or organization **c :** the place in which a professional person conducts business **6** *pl, chiefly Brit* **:** the apartments, attached buildings, or outhouses in which the activities attached to the service of a house are carried on **7 a :** a major administrative unit in some governments ⟨British Foreign *Office*⟩ **b :** a subdivision of some government departments ⟨Patent *Office*⟩ ***syn*** see FUNCTION

office boy *n* (1842) **:** a boy or man employed for odd jobs in a business office

of·fice·hold·er \-ˌhōl-dər\ *n* (1787) **:** one holding a public office

1**of·fi·cer** \ˈä-fə-sər, ˈȯ-\ *n* [ME, fr. AF, fr. ML *officiarius,* fr. L *officium*] (14c) **1 a** *obs* **:** AGENT **b :** one charged with police duties **2 :** one who holds an office of trust, authority, or command ⟨the ~*s* of the bank⟩ ⟨chief executive ~⟩ **3 a :** one who holds a position of authority or command in the armed forces; *specif* **:** COMMISSIONED OFFICER **b :** the master or any of the mates of a merchant or passenger ship

2**officer** *vt* (1670) **1 :** to furnish with officers **2 :** to command or direct as an officer

officer of arms (ca. 1500) **:** any of the officers (as king of arms, herald, or pursuivant) of a monarch or government responsible for devising and granting armorial bearings

1**of·fi·cial** \ə-ˈfi-shəl *also* ō-\ *n* (14c) **1 :** one who holds or is invested with an office : OFFICER ⟨government ~*s*⟩ **2 :** one who administers the rules of a game or sport esp. as a referee or umpire

2**official** *adj* (ca. 1585) **1 :** of or relating to an office, position, or trust ⟨~ duties⟩ **2 :** holding an office **3 a :** AUTHORITATIVE, AUTHORIZED ⟨~ statement⟩ **b :** prescribed or recognized as authorized ⟨an ~ language⟩ **c :** described by the U.S. Pharmacopeia or the National Formulary **4 :** befitting or characteristic of a person in office ⟨extended an ~ greeting⟩ — **of·fi·cial·ly** \-ˈfi-sh(ə-)lē\ *adv*

of·fi·cial·dom \-ˈfi-shəl-dəm\ *n* (1863) **:** officials as a class

of·fi·cial·ese \-ˌfi-shə-ˈlēz, -ˈlēs\ *n* (1884) **:** the characteristic language of official statements : wordy, pompous, or obscure language

of·fi·cial·ism \-ˈfi-shə-ˌli-zəm\ *n* (1854) **:** lack of flexibility and initiative combined with excessive adherence to regulations in the behavior of usu. government officials

of·fi·ci·ant \ə-ˈfi-shē-ənt\ *n* (1844) **:** one (as a priest) that officiates at a religious rite

1**of·fi·ci·ary** \ə-ˈfi-shē-ˌer-ē, ō-, ä-\ *n, pl* **-ar·ies** [ML *officiarius*] (1611) **1 :** OFFICER, OFFICIAL **2 :** a body of officers or officials

2**officiary** *adj* (1612) **:** connected with, derived from, or having a title or rank by virtue of holding an office ⟨~ earl⟩

of·fi·ci·ate \ə-ˈfi-shē-ˌāt\ *vb* **-at·ed; -at·ing** *vi* (1623) **1 :** to perform a ceremony, function, or duty ⟨~ at a wedding⟩ **2 :** to act in an official capacity : act as an official (as at a sports contest) ~ *vt* **1 :** to carry out (an official duty or function) **2 :** to serve as a leader or celebrant of (a ceremony) **3 :** to administer the rules of (a game or sport) esp. as a referee or umpire — **of·fi·ci·a·tion** \-ˌfi-shē-ˈā-shən\ *n*

of·fi·ci·nal \ə-ˈfi-sə-nᵊl, ȯ-, ä-; ˌȯ-fə-ˈsī-nᵊl, ˌä-\ *adj* [ML *officinalis* of a storeroom, fr. *officina* storeroom, fr. L, workshop, fr. *opific-, opifex* workman, fr. *opus* work + *facere* to do] (ca. 1720) **:** MEDICINAL ⟨a monograph on ~ flora⟩

of·fi·cious \ə-ˈfi-shəs\ *adj* [L *officiosus,* fr. *officium* service, office] (1565) **1** *archaic* **a :** KIND, OBLIGING **b :** DUTIFUL **2 :** volunteering one's services where they are neither asked nor needed : MEDDLESOME **3 :** INFORMAL, UNOFFICIAL ***syn*** see IMPERTINENT — **of·fi·cious·ly** *adv* — **of·fi·cious·ness** *n*

off·ing \ˈȯ-fiŋ, ˈä-\ *n* [1*off*] (1608) **1 :** the part of the deep sea seen from the shore **2 :** the near or foreseeable future ⟨in the ~⟩

off·ish \ˈȯ-fish\ *adj* [1*off*] (1827) **:** STANDOFFISH — **off·ish·ness** *n*

off–key \ˈȯf-ˈkē\ *adj or adv* (1927) **1 :** varying in pitch from the proper tone of a melody **2 :** IRREGULAR, ANOMALOUS

off–kil·ter \-ˈkil-tər\ *adj* (ca. 1944) **1 :** not in perfect balance : a bit askew **2 :** ECCENTRIC, UNCONVENTIONAL ⟨~ characters⟩ ⟨an ~ approach⟩

off–la·bel \ˈȯf-ˌlā-bəl\ *adj* (1988) **:** of, relating to, or being a drug used to treat a condition for which it has not been officially approved

off–lim·its \ˈȯf-ˈli-məts\ *adj* (1945) **:** not to be entered or patronized by a designated class (as military personnel); *also* **:** not to be interfered with, considered, or spoken of ⟨the subject of sex was ~ in her family⟩

off–line \-ˈlīn\ *adj* (1950) **:** not connected to or served by a system and esp. a computer or telecommunications system; *also* **:** done independently of such a system ⟨~ activities⟩ — **off–line** *adv*

off–load \(ˌ)ȯf-ˈlōd, ˈȯf-ˌ\ *vb* (1850) **:** UNLOAD

off of *prep* (1567) **:** OFF

usage The *of* is often criticized as superfluous, a comment that is irrelevant because *off of* is an idiom. It is much more common in speech than in edited writing and is more common in American English than in British.

off–off–Broadway *n, often cap both Os* [fr. its relation to off Broadway being analogous to the relation of off Broadway to Broadway] (1965) **:** an avant-garde theatrical movement in New York — **off–off–Broadway** *adj or adv, often cap both Os*

off–peak \ˈȯf-ˈpēk\ *adj* (1920) **:** not being in the period of maximum use or business : not peak ⟨telephone rates during ~ hours⟩

off–price \ˈȯf-ˈprīs\ *adj* (1952) **:** of, relating to, selling, or being discounted merchandise ⟨an ~ store⟩ ⟨~ apparel⟩

\ə\ **abut** \ᵊ\ **kitten, F table** \ər\ **further** \a\ **ash** \ā\ **ace** \ä\ **mop, mar**
\au̇\ **out** \ch\ **chin** \e\ **bet** \ē\ **easy** \g\ **go** \i\ **hit** \ī\ **ice** \j\ **job**
\ŋ\ **sing** \ō\ **go** \ȯ\ **law** \ȯi\ **boy** \th\ **thin** \t͟h\ **the** \ü\ **loot** \u̇\ **foot**
\y\ **yet** \zh\ **vision, beige** \k̲, ⁿ, œ, ue, ʸ\ *see* Guide to Pronunciation

off·print \'ȯf-ˌprint\ *n* (1885) **:** a separately printed excerpt (as a magazine article) — **offprint** *vt*
off–put·ting \-ˌpu̇-tiŋ\ *adj* (1828) **:** that puts one off **:** REPELLENT, DISCONCERTING ⟨an ~ attitude⟩ — **off–put·ting·ly** \-lē\ *adv*
off–ramp \-ˌramp\ *n* (1954) **:** a ramp by which one leaves a limited-access highway
off–road \'ȯf-'rōd\ *adj* (1968) **:** of, relating to, done with, or being a vehicle designed esp. to operate away from public roads
off–road·er \-'rō-dər\ *n* (1971) **1 :** a driver of an off-road vehicle **2 :** an off-road vehicle
off·scour·ing \-ˌskau̇(-ə)r-iŋ\ *n* (1526) **1 :** someone rejected by society **:** OUTCAST **2 :** something that is scoured off **:** REFUSE
off·screen \'ȯf-'skrēn\ *adv or adj* (1935) **1 :** out of sight of the motion picture or television viewer **2 :** in private life
off–sea·son \'ȯf-ˌsē-zᵊn\ *n* (1848) **:** a time of suspended or reduced activity; *esp* **:** the time during which an athlete is not training or competing
1**off·set** \'ȯf-ˌset\ *n* (ca. 1555) **1 a** *archaic* **:** OUTSET, START **b :** CESSATION **2 a** (1) **:** a short prostrate lateral shoot arising from the base of a plant (2) **:** a small bulb arising from the base of another bulb **b :** a lateral or collateral branch (as of a family or race) **:** OFFSHOOT **c :** a spur from a range of hills **3 a :** a horizontal ledge on the face of a wall formed by a diminution of its thickness above **b :** DISPLACEMENT **c :** an abrupt change in the dimension or profile of an object or the part set off by such change **4 :** something that sets off to advantage or embellishes something else **:** FOIL **5 :** an abrupt bend in an object by which one part is turned aside out of line **6 :** something that serves to counterbalance or to compensate for something else; *esp* **:** either of two balancing ledger items **7 a :** unintentional transfer of ink (as from a freshly printed sheet) **b :** a printing process in which an inked impression from a plate is first made on a rubber-blanketed cylinder and then transferred to the paper being printed — **offset** *adj or adv*
2**off·set** \'ȯf-ˌset, *vt senses are also* ȯf-'\ *vb* **-set; -set·ting** *vt* (1792) **1 a :** to place over against something **:** BALANCE ⟨credits ~ debits⟩ **b :** to serve as a counterbalance for **:** COMPENSATE ⟨his speed ~ his opponent's greater weight⟩ **2 :** to form an offset in ⟨~ a wall⟩ ~ *vi* **:** to become marked by offset
off·shoot \'ȯf-ˌshüt\ *n* (1710) **1 a :** a collateral or derived branch, descendant, or member **:** OUTGROWTH **b :** a lateral branch (as of a mountain range) **2 :** a branch of a main stem esp. of a plant
1**off·shore** \'ȯf-'shȯr\ *adv* (1720) **1 :** from the shore **:** SEAWARD; *also* **:** at a distance from the shore **2 :** outside the country **:** ABROAD
2**off·shore** \'ȯf-ˌ\ *adj* (1845) **1 :** coming or moving away from the shore toward the water ⟨an ~ breeze⟩ **2 a :** situated off the shore but within waters under a country's control ⟨~ fisheries⟩ **b :** distant from the shore — compare INSHORE **3 :** situated or operating in a foreign country ⟨~ mutual funds⟩ ⟨~ banking⟩
3**off·shore** \'ȯf-ˌ\ *prep* (1965) **:** off the shore of
off·side \'ȯf-'sīd\ *adv or adj* (1867) **:** illegally in advance of the ball or puck
off–site \-'sīt\ *adj or adv* (1946) **:** not located or occurring at the site of a particular activity
off–speed \-'spēd\ *adj* (1965) **:** being slower than usual or expected ⟨throwing ~ pitches⟩
off·spring \'ȯf-ˌspriŋ\ *n, pl* **offspring** *also* **offsprings** [ME *ofspring,* fr. OE, fr. *of* off + *springan* to spring] (bef. 12c) **1 a :** the product of the reproductive processes of an animal or plant **:** YOUNG, PROGENY **b :** CHILD **2 a :** PRODUCT, RESULT ⟨scholarly manuscripts—the labored ~*s* of PhDs —Donna Martin⟩ **b :** OFFSHOOT 1a
off·stage \'ȯf-'stāj, -ˌstāj\ *adv or adj* (1921) **1 :** on a part of the stage not visible to the audience **2 :** in private life ⟨known ~ as a kindly person⟩ **3 :** behind the scenes **:** out of the public view ⟨much of the important work of the conference was done ~⟩
off–the–books *adj* (1980) **:** not reported or recorded ⟨~ transactions⟩ ⟨~ covert operations⟩ — **off the books** *adv*
off–the–cuff *adj* (1938) **:** not prepared in advance **:** SPONTANEOUS, INFORMAL ⟨~ remarks⟩ — **off–the–cuff** *adv*
off–the–peg *adj* (1922) *chiefly Brit* **:** READY-MADE 1
off–the–rack *adj* (1965) **:** READY-MADE 1 ⟨~ suits⟩
off–the–record *adj* (1933) **:** given or made in confidence and not for publication ⟨~ comments⟩
off–the–shelf *adj* (1950) **:** available as a stock item **:** not specially designed or custom-made ⟨~ software⟩
off–the–wall *adj* (1953) **:** highly unusual **:** BIZARRE ⟨an ~ sense of humor⟩
off·track \'ȯf-'trak\ *adv or adj* (1944) **:** away from a racetrack ⟨betting ~⟩ ⟨~ bookies⟩
off–white \'ȯf-'hwīt, -'wīt\ *n* (1927) **:** a yellowish or grayish white
off year *n* (1873) **1 :** a year in which no major election is held **2 :** a year of diminished activity or production ⟨an *off year* for auto sales⟩
oft \'ȯft\ *adv* [ME, fr. OE; akin to OHG *ofto* often] (bef. 12c) **:** OFTEN
of·ten \'ȯ-fən, ÷'ȯf-tən\ *adv* [ME, alter. of *oft*] (14c) **:** many times **:** FREQUENTLY
of·ten·times \-ˌtīmz\ *or* **oft·times** \'ȯf(t)-ˌtīmz\ *adv* (14c) **:** OFTEN, REPEATEDLY
ogee *also* **OG** \ō-ˌjē\ *n* [obs. E *ogee* ogive; fr. the use of such moldings in ogives] (1677) **1 :** a molding with an S-shaped profile **2 :** a pointed arch having on each side a reversed curve near the apex — see ARCH illustration
ogham *or* **ogam** \'ä-gəm, 'ō-; 'ō(-ə)m\ *n* [Ir *ogham,* fr. MIr *ogom, ogum*] (1729) **:** the alphabetic system of fifth and sixth century Irish in which an alphabet of 20 letters is represented by notches for vowels and lines for consonants and which is known principally from inscriptions cut on the edges of rough standing tombstones — **ogham·ic** \ä-'gä-mik, ō-; 'ō-(ə-)mik\ *adj* — **ogham·ist** \'ä-gə-mist, 'ō-; 'ō-(ə-)mist\ *n*
ogi·val \ō-'jī-vəl\ *adj* (1841) **:** of, relating to, or having the form of an ogive or an ogee
ogive \'ō-ˌjīv\ *n* [ME *oggif* stone comprising an arch, fr. MF *augive, ogive* diagonal arch] (1611) **1 a :** a diagonal arch or rib across a Gothic vault **b :** a pointed arch **2 :** a graph of a cumulative distribution function or a cumulative frequency distribution **3 :** OGEE 1
1**ogle** \'ō-gəl *also* 'ä-\ *vb* **ogled; ogling** \-g(ə-)liŋ\ [prob. fr. LG *oegeln,* fr. *oog* eye; akin to OHG *ouga* eye — more at EYE] *vi* (1682) **:** to glance with amorous invitation or challenge ~ *vt* **1 :** to eye amorously or provocatively **2 :** to look at esp. with greedy or interested attention — **ogler** \-g(ə-)lər\ *n*
2**ogle** *n* (1694) **:** an amorous or coquettish glance
ogre \'ō-gər\ *n* [F, prob. ultim. fr. L *Orcus,* god of the underworld] (1713) **1 :** a hideous giant of fairy tales and folklore that feeds on human beings **:** MONSTER **2 :** a dreaded person or object — **ogre·ish** \'ō-g(ə-)rish\ *adj*
ogress \'ō-g(ə-)rəs\ *n* (1713) **:** a female ogre
1**oh** *also* **O** \(')ō\ *interj* [ME *o*] (13c) **1** — used to express an emotion (as surprise or desire) or in response to physical stimuli **2** — used in direct address ⟨~, waiter! Will you come here, please?⟩ **3** — used to express acknowledgment or understanding of a statement **4** — used to introduce an example or approximation
2**oh** \'ō\ *n* [*o;* fr. the similarity of the symbol for zero (0) to the letter *O*] (1936) **:** ZERO
OH *abbr* Ohio
ohia \ō-'hē-ə\ *n* [Hawaiian *'ōhi'a*] (1824) **:** LEHUA
ohia lehua *n* [Hawaiian *'ōhi'a-lehua*] (1888) **:** LEHUA
ohm \'ōm\ *n* [Georg Simon *Ohm*] (1867) **:** the practical meter-kilogram-second unit of electric resistance equal to the resistance of a circuit in which a potential difference of one volt produces a current of one ampere — **ohm·ic** \'ō-mik\ *adj* — **ohm·i·cal·ly** \-mi-k(ə-)lē\ *adv*
ohm·me·ter \'ō(m)-ˌmē-tər\ *n* [ISV] (ca. 1890) **:** an instrument for indicating resistance in ohms directly
OHMS *abbr* on Her Majesty's service; on His Majesty's service
Ohm's law \'ōmz-\ *n* (1863) **:** a law in electricity: the strength of a direct current is directly proportional to the potential difference and inversely proportional to the resistance of the circuit
-oholic *var of* -AHOLIC
-oic *adj suffix* [F *-oïque* (as in *acide caproïque* caproic acid)] **:** containing carboxyl or a derivative ⟨benz*oic* acid⟩
1**-oid** *n suffix* **:** something resembling a (specified) object or having a (specified) quality ⟨glob*oid*⟩
2**-oid** *adj suffix* [L *-oïdes,* fr. Gk *-oeidēs,* fr. *-o-* + *eidos* appearance, form — more at WISE] **:** resembling **:** having the form or appearance of ⟨petal*oid*⟩
oid·i·um \ō-'i-dē-əm\ *n, pl* **-ia** \-dē-ə\ [NL, fr. *o-* + *-idium*] (1857) **1 a :** any of a genus (*Oidium* of the family Moniliaceae) of imperfect fungi many of which are now considered to be conidial stages of various powdery mildews **b :** one of the small conidia borne in chains by various fungi (as an oidium) — called also *arthrospore* **2 :** a powdery mildew esp. of grapes caused by an oidium
1**oil** \'ȯi(-ə)l\ *n, often attrib* [ME *oile,* fr. AF, fr. L *oleum* olive oil, fr. Gk *elaion,* fr. *elaia* olive] (13c) **1 a :** any of numerous unctuous combustible substances that are liquid or can be liquefied easily on warming, are soluble in ether but not in water, and leave a greasy stain on paper or cloth **b** (1) **:** PETROLEUM (2) **:** the petroleum industry **2 :** a substance (as a cosmetic preparation) of oily consistency ⟨bath ~⟩ **3 a :** an oil color used by an artist **b :** a painting done in oil colors **4 :** unctuous or flattering speech
2**oil** *vt* (15c) **:** to smear, rub over, furnish, or lubricate with oil ~ *vi* **:** to take on fuel oil — **oil the hand** *or* **oil the palm :** BRIBE, TIP
oil beetle *n* (1658) **:** any of various blister beetles (genus *Meloe* or a related genus) that emit a yellowish liquid from the leg joints when disturbed
oil·bird \'ȯi(-ə)l-ˌbərd\ *n* (ca. 1890) **:** a nocturnal bird (*Steatornis caripensis*) of northern So. America and Trinidad that is related to the nightjars, feeds chiefly on the fatty fruits of various palms, and has fatty young from which an oil used esp. in cooking is extracted — called also *guacharo*
oil cake *n* (1743) **:** the solid residue after extracting the oil from seeds (as of cotton)
oil·can \'ȯi(-ə)l-ˌkan\ *n* (1839) **:** a can for oil; *esp* **:** a spouted can designed to release oil drop by drop (as for lubricating machinery)
oil·cloth \-ˌklȯth\ *n* (1796) **:** cloth treated with oil or paint and used for table and shelf coverings
oil color *n* (1539) **1 :** a pigment used for oil paint **2 :** OIL PAINT
oiled \'ȯi(-ə)ld\ *adj* (1530) **1 :** lubricated, treated, or covered with or as if with oil ⟨~ paper⟩ **2** *slang* **:** DRUNK 1a
oil·er \'ȯi-lər\ *n* (ca. 1846) **1 :** a person who oils something **2 :** a receptacle or device for applying oil **3** *pl* **:** OILSKIN 3 **4 :** an auxiliary naval vessel used for refueling at sea
oil field *n* (1884) **:** a region rich in petroleum deposits; *esp* **:** one that has been brought into production
oil gland *n* (ca. 1836) **:** a gland (as of the skin) that produces an oily secretion: as **a :** a sebaceous gland **b :** UROPYGIAL GLAND
oil·man \'ȯi(-ə)l-mən, -ˌman\ *n* (1865) **1 :** an oil company executive **2 :** an oil field worker
oil of vitriol (1580) **:** concentrated sulfuric acid
oil of wintergreen (1857) **:** the methyl ester of salicylic acid that is used as a flavoring and as a counterirritant
oil paint *n* (1790) **:** paint in which a drying oil is the vehicle
oil painting *n* (1699) **1 a :** the act or art of painting in oil colors **b :** a picture painted in oils **2 :** painting that uses pigments orig. ground in oil
oil palm *n* (1858) **:** an African pinnate-leaved palm (*Elaeis guineensis*) cultivated for its clustered fruit whose flesh and seeds yield oil
oil pan *n* (1908) **:** the lower section of the crankcase used as a lubricating-oil reservoir on an internal combustion engine
oil patch *n* (ca. 1952) **1 :** OIL FIELD **2 :** the petroleum industry
oil·seed \'ȯi(-ə)l-ˌsēd\ *n* (1562) **:** a seed or crop (as flaxseed) grown mainly for oil
oil shale *n* (1873) **:** a rock (as shale) from which oil can be recovered by distillation
oil·skin \'ȯi(-ə)l-ˌskin\ *n* (1786) **1 :** an oiled waterproof cloth used for coverings and garments **2 :** an oilskin raincoat **3** *pl* **:** an oilskin suit of coat and trousers
oil slick *n* (1889) **:** a film of oil floating on water
oil·stone \'ȯi(-ə)l-ˌstōn\ *n* (1585) **:** a whetstone for use with oil
oil well *n* (1847) **:** a well from which petroleum is obtained
oily \'ȯi-lē\ *adj* **oil·i·er; -est** (14c) **1 :** of, relating to, or consisting of oil **2 a :** covered or impregnated with oil ⟨~ rags⟩ **b :** relatively high in naturally secreted oils ⟨~ skin⟩ ⟨~ hair⟩ **3 :** excessively

smooth or suave in manner — **oil·i·ly** \ˈȯi-lə-lē\ *adv* — **oil·i·ness** \-lē-nəs\ *n*

oink \ˈȯiŋk\ *n* [imit.] (1938) **:** the natural noise of a hog — **oink** *vi*

oint·ment \ˈȯint-mənt\ *n* [ME, alter. of *oynement,* fr. AF *uignement, oignement,* ultim. fr. L *unguentum,* fr. *unguere* to anoint; akin to OHG *ancho* butter, Skt *anakti* he salves] (14c) **:** a salve or unguent for application to the skin

oi·ti·ci·ca \ˌȯi-tə-ˈsē-kə\ *n* [Pg, fr. Tupi *witisíka,* fr. *wití,* the tree *Licania tomentosa* + *isíka* resin] (1901) **:** any of several So. American trees; *esp* **:** a Brazilian tree (*Licania rigida*) with seeds that yield a drying oil similar to tung oil

OJ *abbr* orange juice

Ojib·wa *or* **Ojib·way** *or* **Ojib·we** \ō-ˈjib-(ˌ)wā\ *n, pl* **Ojibwa** *or* **Ojibwas** *or* **Ojibway** *or* **Ojibways** *or* **Ojibwe** *or* **Ojibwes** [Ojibwa *očipweˑ,* an Ojibwa band] (1700) **1 :** a member of an American Indian people of the region around Lake Superior and westward **2 :** an Algonquian language of the Ojibwa people

OJT *abbr* on-the-job training

[1]**OK** *or* **okay** \ō-ˈkā, *in assenting or agreeing also* ˈō-ˌkā\ *adv or adj* [abbr. of *oll korrect,* facetious alter. of *all correct*] (1839) **:** ALL RIGHT

[2]**OK** *or* **okay** \ō-ˈkā\ *n* (1841) **:** APPROVAL, ENDORSEMENT

[3]**OK** *or* **okay** \ō-ˈkā\ *vt* **OK'd** *or* **okayed; OK'·ing** *or* **okay·ing** (1888) **:** APPROVE, AUTHORIZE

[4]**OK** *abbr* Oklahoma

oka *var of* OCA

oka·pi \ō-ˈkä-pē\ *n* [Mvuba (language spoken west of Lake Edward, Democratic Republic of the Congo)] (1900) **:** an African ungulate mammal (*Okapia johnstoni*) that is closely related to the giraffe but has a relatively short neck, a coat typically of solid reddish chestnut on the trunk, yellowish white on the cheeks, and purplish-black and cream rings on the upper parts of the legs

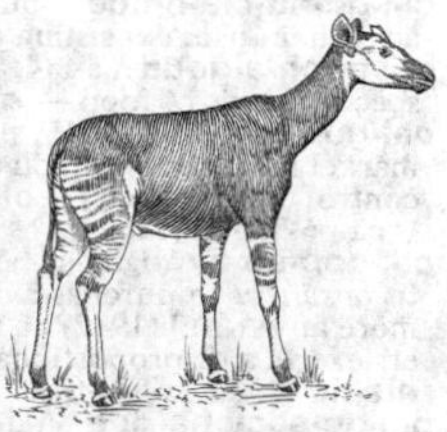

okapi

okey·doke \ˌō-kē-ˈdōk\ *or* **okey·do·key** \-ˈdō-kē\ *adv* [redupl. of *OK*] (ca. 1932) — used to express assent

Okie \ˈō-kē\ *n* [*Ok*lahoma + *-ie*] (1918) *sometimes disparaging* **:** a migrant agricultural worker; *esp* **:** one from Oklahoma in the 1930s

Okla *abbr* Oklahoma

okra \ˈō-krə, *Southern also* -krē\ *n* [of African origin; akin to Ibo *ókùrù* okra] (1679) **1 :** a tall annual herb (*Abelmoschus esculentus*) of the mallow family that is cultivated for its mucilaginous green pods used esp. in soups or stews; *also* **:** the pods of this plant **2 :** [1]GUMBO 1

[1]**-ol** *n suffix* [ISV, fr. *alcohol*] **:** chemical compound (as an alcohol or phenol) containing hydroxyl ⟨glycer*ol*⟩ ⟨cres*ol*⟩

[2]**-ol** — see -OLE

[3]**-ol** *n comb form* [ISV, fr. L *oleum* oil — more at OIL] **:** hydrocarbon chemically related to benzene ⟨xyl*ol*⟩

olal·lie·ber·ry \ˈō-lə-lē-ˌber-ē\ *n* [Chinook jargon *olallie* berry, prob. fr. Lower Chinook *úlali* camas patch, fr. *ú-lalχ* camas + *-iχ,* deictic suffix] (1968) **:** a blackish berry that is a hybrid of a loganberry and youngberry, resembles an elongated blackberry, and is grown chiefly along the western U.S. coast

[1]**old** \ˈōld; *for sense 9 usu* ˈōl\ *adj* [ME, fr. OE *eald;* akin to OHG *alt* old, L *alere* to nourish, *alescere* to grow, *altus* high, deep] (bef. 12c) **1 a :** dating from the remote past **:** ANCIENT ⟨~ traditions⟩ **b :** persisting from an earlier time ⟨an ~ ailment⟩ ⟨they brought up the same ~ argument⟩ **c :** of long standing ⟨an ~ friend⟩ **2 a :** distinguished from an object of the same kind by being of an earlier date ⟨many still used the ~ name⟩ **b** *cap* **:** belonging to an early period in the development of a language or literature ⟨*Old* Persian⟩ **3 :** having existed for a specified period of time ⟨a child three years ~⟩ **4 :** of, relating to, or originating in a past era ⟨~ chronicles record the event⟩ **5 a :** advanced in years or age ⟨an ~ person⟩ **b :** showing the characteristics of age ⟨looked ~ at 20⟩ **6 :** EXPERIENCED ⟨an ~ trooper speaking of the last war⟩ **7 :** FORMER ⟨his ~ students⟩ **8 a :** showing the effects of time or use **:** WORN, AGED ⟨~ shoes⟩ **b :** no longer in use **:** DISCARDED ⟨~ rags⟩ **c :** of a grayish or dusty color ⟨~ mauve⟩ **d :** TIRESOME ⟨gets ~ fast⟩ **9 a :** long familiar ⟨same ~ story⟩ ⟨good ~ Joe⟩ **b** — used as an intensive ⟨a high ~ time⟩ **c** — used to express an attitude of affection or amusement ⟨a big ~ dog⟩ ⟨flex the ~ biceps⟩ ⟨any ~ time⟩

syn OLD, ANCIENT, VENERABLE, ANTIQUE, ANTIQUATED, ARCHAIC, OBSOLETE mean having come into existence or use in the more or less distant past. OLD may apply to either actual or merely relative length of existence ⟨*old* houses⟩ ⟨an *old* sweater of mine⟩. ANCIENT applies to occurrence, existence, or use in or survival from the distant past ⟨*ancient* accounts of dragons⟩. VENERABLE stresses the impressiveness and dignity of great age ⟨the family's *venerable* patriarch⟩. ANTIQUE applies to what has come down from a former or ancient time ⟨collected *antique* Chippendale furniture⟩. ANTIQUATED implies being discredited or outmoded or otherwise inappropriate to the present time ⟨*antiquated* teaching methods⟩. ARCHAIC implies having the character or characteristics of a much earlier time ⟨the play used *archaic* language to convey a sense of period⟩. OBSOLETE may apply to something regarded as no longer acceptable or useful even though it is still in existence ⟨a computer that makes earlier models *obsolete*⟩.

[2]**old** *n* (13c) **1 :** one of a specified age — usu. used in combination ⟨a 3-year-*old*⟩ **2 :** old or earlier time — used in the phrase *of old* ⟨the cavalry of ~⟩

old boy *n* (1868) **1** *often cap O&B, Brit* **:** an alumnus esp. of a boys' school **2 :** a man who is a member of a long-standing and usu. influential clique esp. in a professional, business, or social sphere

Old Bulgarian *n* (1861) **:** OLD CHURCH SLAVIC

Old Catholic *n* (1871) **:** a member of one of various hierarchical and liturgical churches separating from the Roman Catholic Church at various times since the 18th century

Old Christmas *n* (1863) *chiefly Midland* **:** EPIPHANY 1

Old Church Slavic *n* (ca. 1929) **:** the Slavic language used in the liturgical and Biblical translations of Cyril and Methodius as attested in manuscripts of the 10th and 11th centuries — called also *Old Church Slavonic;* see INDO-EUROPEAN LANGUAGES table

old country *n, often cap O&C* (1782) **:** an emigrant's country of origin; *esp* **:** one in Europe — usu. used with *the*

old·en \ˈōl-dən\ *adj* (14c) **:** of or relating to a bygone era

Old English *n* (1579) **1 a :** the language of the English people from the time of the earliest documents in the seventh century to about 1100 — see INDO-EUROPEAN LANGUAGES table **b :** English of any period before Modern English **2 :** BLACK LETTER

Old English sheepdog *n* (1890) **:** any of a breed of tailless dogs developed in England and having a profuse blue-gray and white coat

old·fan·gled \ˈōl(d)-ˈfaŋ-gəld\ *adj* [*old* + *-fangled* (as in *newfangled*)] (1842) **:** OLD-FASHIONED

[1]**old–fash·ioned** \-ˈfa-shənd\ *adj* (1593) **1 a :** of, relating to, or characteristic of a past era ⟨wears an ~ black bow tie —Green Peyton⟩ **b :** adhering to customs of a past era **2 :** OUTMODED — **old–fash·ioned·ly** \-shən(d)-lē\ *adv* — **old–fash·ioned·ness** \-nəs\ *n*

[2]**old–fashioned** *n* (1901) **:** a cocktail usu. made with whiskey, bitters, sugar, a twist of lemon peel, and a small amount of water or soda

Old French *n* (1708) **:** the French language from the 9th to the 16th century; *esp* **:** French from the 9th to the 13th century — see INDO-EUROPEAN LANGUAGES table

Old Glory *n* (1862) **:** the flag of the U.S.

old gold *n* (1879) **:** a dark yellow

old–growth \ˈōl(d)-ˈgrōth\ *adj* (1868) **:** of, relating to, or being a forest characterized by the presence of large old trees, numerous snags and woody debris, and a multilayered canopy and that is usu. in a late stage of ecological succession — **old growth** *n*

old guard *n, often cap O&G* (1849) **1 :** the conservative and esp. older members of an organization (as a political party) **2 :** a group of established prestige and influence

old hand *n* (ca. 1785) **:** HAND 10e

old hat *adj* (1911) **1 :** OLD-FASHIONED **2 :** lacking in freshness **:** TRITE

Old High German *n* (1849) **:** High German exemplified in documents prior to ca. 1150 — see INDO-EUROPEAN LANGUAGES table

old·ie \ˈōl-dē\ *n* (1874) **:** one that is old; *esp* **:** a popular song of an earlier day

Old Ionic *n* (ca. 1889) **:** the Greek dialect of the Homeric epics

Old Iranian *n* (1888) **:** any Iranian language in use in the period B.C.

Old Irish *n* (1876) **:** the Irish in use from the seventh century to about 950 — see INDO-EUROPEAN LANGUAGES table

old·ish \ˈōl-dish\ *adj* (ca. 1669) **:** somewhat old or elderly

old lady *n* (1836) **1 :** WIFE **2 :** MOTHER **3 :** GIRLFRIEND; *esp* **:** one with whom a man cohabits

Old Latin *n* (ca. 1889) **:** Latin used in the early inscriptions and in literature prior to the classical period

old–line \ˈōl(d)-ˈlīn\ *adj* (1856) **1 a :** having a reputation or authority based on length or proven quality of service ⟨an ~ firm⟩ **b :** of established prestige and influence ⟨~ families⟩ **2 :** adhering to traditional policies or practices **:** CONSERVATIVE

old maid *n* (ca. 1530) **1 :** SPINSTER 3 **2 :** a prim fussy person ⟨he was a real *old maid* about burning rubbish —R. C. Ruark⟩ **3 :** a simple card game in which cards are matched in pairs and the player holding the unmatched card at the end loses — **old–maid·ish** \ˈōl(d)-ˈmā-dish\ *adj* — **old–maid·ish·ness** \-nəs\ *n*

old man *n* (1673) **1 a :** HUSBAND **b :** FATHER **2** *cap* **:** one in authority; *esp* **:** COMMANDING OFFICER **3 :** BOYFRIEND; *esp* **:** one with whom a woman cohabits

old–man's beard \ˈōl(d)-ˈmanz-\ *n* (1742) **1 :** any of several clematises (esp. *Clematis vitalba*) having plumose styles **2 :** a greenish-gray pendulous lichen (*Usnea barbata*) growing on trees

old master *n* (1697) **:** a work of art by an established master and esp. by any of the distinguished painters of the 16th, 17th, or early 18th century; *also* **:** such an artist

Old Nick \ˈōl(d)-ˈnik\ *n* (ca. 1643) — used as a name of the devil

Old Norse *n* (1844) **:** the North Germanic language of the Scandinavian peoples prior to about 1350 — see INDO-EUROPEAN LANGUAGES table

Old Occitan *n* (1985) **:** the Occitan language as attested in documents from about 1100 to 1500

Old Persian *n* (1867) **:** an ancient Iranian language known from cuneiform inscriptions from the sixth and fifth centuries B.C. — see INDO-EUROPEAN LANGUAGES table

Old Prussian *n* (1841) **:** a Baltic language used in East Prussia until the 17th century — see INDO-EUROPEAN LANGUAGES table

old rose *n* (1891) **:** a variable color averaging a grayish red

Old Saxon *n* (1841) **:** the language of the Saxons of northwest Germany until about the 12th century — see INDO-EUROPEAN LANGUAGES table

old–school *adj* (1803) **1 :** adhering to traditional policies or practices ⟨an ~ coach⟩ **2 :** characteristic or evocative of an earlier or original style, manner, or form ⟨~ music⟩

old school *n* (1749) **:** adherents of traditional policies and practices

old school tie *n* (1932) **1 a :** an attitude of conservatism, aplomb, and upper-class solidarity associated with English public school graduates **b :** a necktie displaying the colors of an English public school **2 :** clannishness among members of an established clique

old–shoe \ˈōl(d)-ˈshü\ *adj* (1944) **:** characterized by familiarity or freedom from restraint **:** COMFORTABLE, UNPRETENTIOUS

old sledge *n* (1830) **:** SEVEN-UP

old–squaw \ˈōl(d)-ˈskwȯ\ *n* (1838) **:** a common sea duck (*Clangula hyemalis*) of the more northern parts of the northern hemisphere — called also *long-tailed duck*

old·ster \ˈōl(d)-stər\ *n* (1848) **:** an old or elderly person

old style *n* (1617) **1** *cap O&S* **:** a style of reckoning time used before the adoption of the Gregorian calendar **2 :** a style of type distin-

\ə\ **a**but \ᵊ\ kitten, F table \ər\ **fur**ther \a\ **a**sh \ā\ **a**ce \ä\ m**o**p, m**ar**
\au̇\ **ou**t \ch\ **ch**in \e\ b**e**t \ē\ **ea**sy \g\ **g**o \i\ h**i**t \ī\ **i**ce \j\ **j**ob
\ŋ\ si**ng** \ō\ g**o** \ȯ\ l**aw** \ȯi\ b**oy** \th\ **th**in \t͟h\ **th**e \ü\ l**oo**t \u̇\ f**oo**t
\y\ **y**et \zh\ vi**s**ion, beige \k, ⁿ, œ, ue, ʸ\ *see* Guide to Pronunciation

guished by graceful irregularity among individual letters, bracketed serifs, and but slight contrast between light and heavy strokes
Old Style *adj* (1678) : using or according to the Julian calendar
Old Swedish *n* (ca. 1909) : the Swedish language as exemplified in documents prior to about 1350
Old Testament *n* (14c) : the first part of the Christian Bible containing the books of the Jewish canon of Scripture — see BIBLE table
old–time \ˈōl(d)-ˈtīm\ *adj* (1824) **1** : of, relating to, or characteristic of an earlier period ⟨~ songs⟩ **2** : of long standing ⟨~ residents⟩
old–tim·er \-ˈtī-mər, -ˌtī-mər\ *n* (1856) **1 a** : VETERAN **b** : OLDSTER **2** : something that is old-fashioned : ANTIQUE
old–timey \ˈōl(d)-ˈtī-mē\ *adj* (1850) : of a kind or style prevalent in or reminiscent of an earlier time ⟨~ music⟩
Old Welsh *n* (1882) : the Welsh language exemplified in documents prior to about 1150 — see INDO-EUROPEAN LANGUAGES table
old·wife \ˈōl(d)-ˌwīf\ *n* (1588) **1** : any of several marine fishes (as an alewife, menhaden, or triggerfish) **2** : OLD-SQUAW
old wives' tale *n* (ca. 1590) : an often traditional belief that is not based on fact : SUPERSTITION
old–world \ˈōl(d)-ˈwər(-ə)ld\ *adj* (1830) : of, relating to, or characteristic of the Old World; *esp* : having the charm or picturesque qualities of the Old World ⟨narrow ~ streets⟩
Old World *n* (ca. 1596) : the eastern hemisphere exclusive of Australia; *specif* : the continent of Europe
ole \ˈōl\ *adj* [by alter.] (ca. 1832) : OLD
ole- *or* **oleo-** *comb form* [F *olé-*, *oléo-*, fr. L *ole-*, fr. *oleum* — more at OIL] : oil ⟨*oleograph*⟩
-ole *also* **-ol** *n comb form* [ISV, fr. L *oleum*] **1** : chemical compound containing a 5-membered usu. heterocyclic ring ⟨pyrr*ole*⟩ **2** : chemical compound not containing hydroxyl ⟨eucalypt*ol*⟩ — esp. in names of ethers ⟨safr*ole*⟩
olé \ō-ˈlā\ *n* [Sp] (1922) : [2]BRAVO
ole·ag·i·nous \ˌō-lē-ˈa-jə-nəs\ *adj* [ME, fr. MF *oleagineux*, fr. L *oleagineus* of an olive tree, fr. *olea* olive tree, fr. Gk *elaia*] (1634) **1** : resembling or having the properties of oil : OILY; *also* : containing or producing oil **2** : marked by an offensively ingratiating manner or quality — **ole·ag·i·nous·ly** *adv* — **ole·ag·i·nous·ness** *n*
ole·an·der \ˈō-lē-ˌan-dər, ˌō-lē-ˈ\ *n* [ML, alter. of *arodandrum*, *lorandrum*, perh. alter. of L *rhododendron* — more at RHODODENDRON] (1545) : a poisonous evergreen shrub (*Nerium oleander*) of the dogbane family with clusters of fragrant white to red flowers
ole·an·do·my·cin \ˌō-lē-ˌan-də-ˈmī-sᵊn\ *n* [*oleandrose*, a sugar derived from oleandrin (a glycoside contained in oleander leaves) + *-o-* + *-mycin*] (1956) : an antibiotic $C_{35}H_{61}NO_{12}$ produced by a streptomyces (*Streptomyces antibioticus*)
ole·as·ter \ˈō-lē-ˌas-tər, ˌō-lē-ˈ\ *n* [ME, fr. L, fr. *olea*] (14c) : any of several plants (genus *Elaeagnus* of the family Elaeagnaceae, the oleaster family) having alternate leaves and small often fragrant flowers with four stamens; *esp* : RUSSIAN OLIVE
ole·ate \ˈō-lē-ˌāt\ *n* (ca. 1823) : a salt or ester of oleic acid
olec·ra·non \ō-ˈle-krə-ˌnän\ *n* [NL, fr. Gk *ōlekranon*, fr. *ōlenē* elbow + *kranion* skull — more at ELL, CRANIUM] (ca. 1741) : the process of the ulna projecting behind the elbow joint
ole·fin \ˈō-lə-fən\ *n* [ISV, fr. F *(gaz) oléfiant* ethylene, fr. L *oleum*] (1860) **1** : ALKENE **2** : a synthetic fiber (as polypropylene) derived from an alkene — **ole·fin·ic** \ˌō-lə-ˈfi-nik\ *adj*
oleic acid \ō-ˈlē-ik-, -ˈlā-\ *n* (1819) : a monounsaturated fatty acid $C_{18}H_{34}O_2$ obtained from natural fats and oils
ole·in \ˈō-lē-ən\ *n* [F *oléine*, fr. L *oleum*] (1838) **1** : an ester of glycerol and oleic acid **2** : the liquid portion of a fat
oleo \ˈō-lē-ˌō\ *n* [short for *oleomargarine*] (1884) : MARGARINE
oleo·graph \ˈō-lē-ə-ˌgraf\ *n* [ISV] (1873) : a chromolithograph printed on cloth to imitate an oil painting
oleo·mar·ga·rine \ˌō-lē-ō-ˈmär-jə-rən, -ˌrēn; -ˈmärj-rən\ *n* [F *oléomargarine*, fr. *olé-* + *margarine* margarine] (1873) : MARGARINE
oleo·res·in \ˌō-lē-ō-ˈre-zᵊn\ *n* [ISV] (ca. 1846) **1** : a natural plant product (as copaiba) containing chiefly essential oil and resin; *esp* : TURPENTINE 1b **2** : a preparation consisting essentially of oil holding resin in solution — **oleo·res·in·ous** \-ˈre-zᵊn-əs, -ˈrez-nəs\ *adj*
oles·tra \ō-ˈles-trə\ *n* [prob. by shortening & alter. fr. *(sucrose) polyester*] (1987) : a noncaloric fat substitute consisting of a series of compounds that are sucrose esters of six to eight fatty acids resistant to absorption by the digestive system because of their large size
ole·um \ˈō-lē-əm\ *n* [L, olive oil — more at OIL] (ca. 1823) **1** *pl* **olea** \-lē-ə\ : OIL **2** *pl* **oleums** : a heavy oily strongly corrosive solution of sulfur trioxide in anhydrous sulfuric acid
O level *n* (1949) **1** : the lowest of three levels of standardized British examinations in a secondary school subject; *also* : successful completion of an O-level examination in a particular subject — called also *Ordinary level*; compare A LEVEL, S LEVEL **2 a** : the level of education required to pass an O-level examination **b** : a course leading to an O-level examination
ol·fac·tion \äl-ˈfak-shən, ōl-\ *n* (ca. 1846) **1** : the sense of smell **2** : the act or process of smelling
ol·fac·tom·e·ter \ˌäl-ˌfak-ˈtä-mə-tər, ˌōl-\ *n* (1889) : an instrument for measuring the sensitivity of the sense of smell esp. in regard to intensity, concentration, or quality of an odor
ol·fac·to·ry \äl-ˈfak-t(ə-)rē, ōl-\ *adj* [L *olfactorius*, fr. *olfacere* to smell, fr. *olēre* to smell + *facere* to do — more at ODOR, DO] (ca. 1658) : of or relating to the sense of smell — **ol·fac·to·ri·ly** \-t(ə-)rə-lē\ *adv*
olfactory bulb *n* (ca. 1860) : a bulbous anterior projection of the olfactory lobe that is the place of termination of the olfactory nerves and is esp. well developed in lower vertebrates (as fishes)
olfactory lobe *n* (ca. 1860) : an anterior projection of each cerebral hemisphere that is continuous anteriorly with the olfactory nerve
olfactory nerve *n* (1670) : either of the pair of nerves that are the first cranial nerves and that arise in the olfactory neurosensory cells of the nasal mucous membrane and pass to the anterior part of the cerebrum
olig- *or* **oligo-** *comb form* [ML, fr. Gk, fr. *oligos*; perh. akin to Arm *ałkat* scant] : few ⟨*oligo*phagous⟩
ol·i·garch \ˈä-lə-ˌgärk, ˈō-\ *n* [Gk *oligarchēs*, fr. *olig-* + *-archēs* -arch] (ca. 1610) : a member or supporter of an oligarchy
ol·i·gar·chic \ˌä-lə-ˈgär-kik, ˌō-\ *or* **ol·i·gar·chi·cal** \-ki-kəl\ *adj* (1586) : of, relating to, or based on an oligarchy
ol·i·gar·chy \ˈä-lə-ˌgär-kē, ˈō-\ *n, pl* **-chies** (1542) **1** : government by the few **2** : a government in which a small group exercises control esp. for corrupt and selfish purposes; *also* : a group exercising such control **3** : an organization under oligarchic control
Ol·i·go·cene \ˈä-li-gō-ˌsēn, ˈō-; ə-ˈli-gə-\ *adj* [ISV] (ca. 1859) : of, relating to, or being an epoch of the Tertiary between the Eocene and Miocene or the corresponding series of rocks — see GEOLOGIC TIME table — **Oligocene** *n*
ol·i·go·chaete \-ˌkēt\ *n* [NL *Oligochaeta*, ultim. fr. Gk *olig-* + *chaitē* long hair] (1896) : any of a class or order (Oligochaeta) of hermaphroditic terrestrial or aquatic annelids (as an earthworm) that lack a specialized head — **oligochaete** *adj*
ol·i·go·clase \ˈä-li-gō-ˌklās, ˈō-, -ˌklāz; ə-ˈli-gə-\ *n* [G *Oligoklas*, fr. *olig-* olig- + Gk *klasis* breaking, fr. *klan* to break — more at CLAST] (1832) : a mineral of the plagioclase series
ol·i·go·den·dro·cyte \ˈä-li-gō-ˈden-drə-ˌsīt, ˈō-; ə-ˌli-gə-\ *n* [ISV, fr. *olig-* + *dendr-* + *-cyte*] (1932) : a glial cell resembling an astrocyte but smaller with few and slender processes having few branches
ol·i·go·den·drog·lia \-den-ˈdrä-glē-ə, -ˈdrō-\ *n* [NL, fr. ISV *oligodendrocyte* + NL *glia*] (1924) : glia made up of oligodendrocytes that forms the myelin sheath around axons in the central nervous system — **ol·i·go·den·drog·li·al** \-glē-əl\ *adj*
olig·o·mer \ə-ˈli-gə-mər\ *n* (1952) : a polymer or polymer intermediate containing relatively few structural units — **olig·o·mer·ic** \-ˌli-gə-ˈmer-ik\ *adj* — **olig·o·mer·i·za·tion** \-mə-rə-ˈzā-shən\ *n*
ol·i·go·nu·cle·o·tide \-ˈnü-klē-ə-ˌtīd, -ˈnyü-\ *n* (1942) : a short nucleic-acid chain usu. consisting of up to approximately 20 nucleotides
ol·i·goph·a·gous \ˌä-lə-ˈgä-fə-gəs, ˌō-\ *adj* (1920) : eating only a few specific kinds of food — **ol·i·goph·a·gy** \-ˈgä-fə-jē\ *n*
ol·i·gop·o·ly \-ˈgä-pə-lē\ *n* [*olig-* + *-poly* (as in *monopoly*)] (1895) : a market situation in which each of a few producers affects but does not control the market — **ol·i·gop·o·list** \-list\ *n* — **ol·i·gop·o·lis·tic** \-ˌgä-pə-ˈlis-tik\ *adj*
ol·i·gop·so·ny \-ˈgäp-sə-nē\ *n* [*olig-* + Gk *opsōnia* purchase of victuals, fr. *opsōnein* to purchase victuals, fr. *opson* food + *ōneisthai* to buy — more at VENAL] (1942) : a market situation in which each of a few buyers exerts a disproportionate influence on the market — **ol·i·gop·so·nis·tic** \-ˌgäp-sə-ˈnis-tik\ *adj*
ol·i·go·sac·cha·ride \ˌä-li-gō-ˈsa-kə-ˌrīd, ˌō-; ə-ˈli-gə-\ *n* [ISV] (1930) : a saccharide (as a disaccharide) that contains a known small number of monosaccharide units
ol·i·go·tro·phic \-ˈtrō-fik\ *adj* [ISV] (1928) : having a deficiency of plant nutrients that is usu. accompanied by an abundance of dissolved oxygen ⟨clear ~ lakes⟩
olio \ˈō-lē-ˌō\ *n, pl* **oli·os** [modif. of Sp *olla*] (ca. 1643) **1** : OLLA PODRIDA 1 **2 a** : a miscellaneous mixture : HODGEPODGE **b** : a miscellaneous collection (as of literary or musical selections)
ol·i·va·ceous \ˌä-lə-ˈvā-shəs\ *adj* (1776) : OLIVE 1
[1]**ol·ive** \ˈä-liv, -ləv\ *n* [ME, fr. AF, fr. L *oliva*, fr. Gk *elaia*] (13c) **1 a** : a Mediterranean evergreen tree (*Olea europaea* of the family Oleaceae, the olive family) cultivated for its drupaceous fruit that is an important food and source of oil; *also* : the fruit **b** : any of various shrubs and trees resembling the olive **2** : any of several colors resembling that of the unripe fruit of the olive tree that are yellowish green **3** : an oval eminence on each ventrolateral aspect of the medulla oblongata
[2]**olive** *adj* (1657) **1** : of the color olive or olive green **2** : approaching olive in color or complexion
olive branch *n* (14c) **1** : a branch of the olive tree esp. when used as a symbol of peace **2** : an offer or gesture of conciliation or goodwill
olive drab *n* (1878) **1** : a grayish olive **2 a** : a wool or cotton fabric of an olive drab color **b** : a uniform of this fabric
olive green *n* (1699) : a greenish olive
olive oil *n* (ca. 1741) : a pale yellow to yellowish-green nondrying oil obtained from olives and used chiefly as a salad oil and in cooking
Ol·i·ver \ˈä-lə-vər\ *n* [ME, fr. OF] (14c) : the close friend of Roland in the Charlemagne legends
olive ridley *n* (1980) : a relatively small sea turtle (*Lepidochelys olivacea*) that has a uniformly olive-colored carapace and is found along coasts and in the open sea of the tropical parts of the Pacific, Indian, and Atlantic oceans — called also *olive ridley turtle*
ol·iv·ine \ˈä-lə-ˌvēn\ *n* [G *Olivin*, fr. L *oliva*] (1794) : a usu. greenish mineral that is a complex silicate of magnesium and iron used esp. in refractories — compare PERIDOT — **ol·iv·in·ic** \ˌä-lə-ˈvi-nik\ *or* **ol·iv·in·it·ic** \-və-ˈni-tik\ *adj*
ol·la \ˈä-lə, ˈȯi-ə\ *n* [Sp, fr. L *olla*, *aulla* pot; akin to Skt *ukhā* pot and prob. to Goth *auhns* oven] (1622) : a large bulging widemouthed earthenware vessel sometimes with looped handles used (as by Pueblo Indians) for storage, cooking, or as a container for water

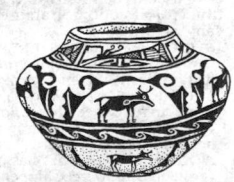

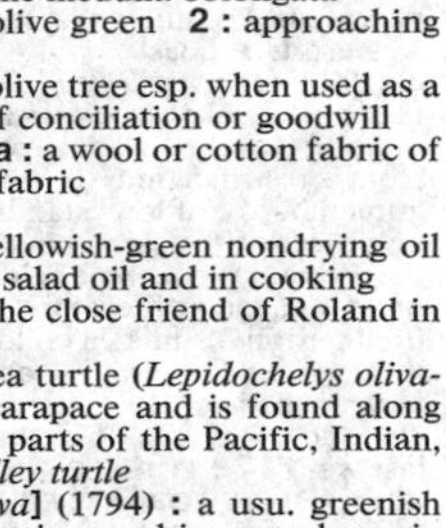
olla

ol·la po·dri·da \-pə-ˈdrē-də\ *n, pl* **olla podridas** \-ˈdrē-dəz\ *also* **ollas podridas** [Sp, lit., rotten pot] (1599) **1** : a rich highly seasoned stew of meat and vegetables usu. including sausage and chick-peas that is slowly simmered and is a traditional Spanish and Latin-American dish **2** : HODGEPODGE
ol·lie \ˈä-lē\ *n* [*Ollie*, nickname of Alan Gelfand *b*1963 U.S. skateboarder] (1979) **1** : a maneuver in skateboarding in which the skater kicks the tail of the board down while jumping in order to make the board pop into the air **2** : a maneuver in snowboarding in which the rider transfers weight from the front to the back foot to snap the board up off the ground — **ollie** *vb*
Ol·mec \ˈäl-ˌmek, ˈōl-\ *n* [Nahuatl *Ōlmēcah*, a coastal people in Aztec history, fr. *Ōlmān*, their homeland, prob. fr. *ōlli* rubber] (1880) : an ancient people of the southern east coast of Mexico who flourished about 1200 to 400 B.C.
olo·li·u·qui \ˌō-lō-lē-ˈü-kē\ *n* [Sp *ololiuque*, fr. Nahuatl *ololiuhqui*, lit., something rolled into a ball] (1915) : a woody-stemmed Mexican vine (*Rivea corymbosa* syn. *Turbina corymbosa*) of the morning glory family having small fleshy fruits with single seeds that are used esp. by the native Indians for medicinal, narcotic, and religious purposes
olo·ro·so \ˌō-lə-ˈrō-(ˌ)sō\ *n, pl* **-sos** [Sp, fr. *oloroso* fragrant, fr. *olor*

odor, fr. L, fr. *olēre* to smell — more at ODOR] (1876) : a dry full-bodied Spanish sherry

olym·pi·ad \ə-ˈlim-pē-ˌad, ō-\ *n, often cap* [ME *Olympias,* fr. L *Olympiad-, Olympias,* fr. Gk, fr. *Olympia,* site of ancient Olympic Games] (14c) **1 :** one of the 4-year intervals between Olympic Games by which time was reckoned in ancient Greece **2 :** a quadrennial celebration of the modern Olympic Games; *also* **:** a competition or series of competitions resembling an olympiad esp. in variety or challenge

[1]**Olym·pi·an** \-pē-ən\ *adj* (15c) **1 :** of or relating to Mount Olympus in Thessaly **2 :** befitting or characteristic of an Olympian; *esp* **:** LOFTY ⟨his . . . formula of glib simplicity and ~ arrogance —Richard Pollak⟩

[2]**Olympian** *adj* (1593) **1 :** of or relating to the ancient Greek region of Olympia **2 :** of, relating to, or constituting the Olympic Games

[3]**Olympian** *n* (1606) **:** a participant in Olympic Games

[4]**Olympian** *n* (1843) **1 :** one of the ancient Greek deities dwelling on Olympus **2 :** a being of lofty detachment or superior attainments

Olympian Games *n pl* (1593) **:** OLYMPIC GAMES 1

Olym·pia oyster \ə-ˈlim-pē-ə-, ō-\ *n* [*Olympia,* Washington] (1908) **:** a small flavorful native oyster (*Ostrea lurida*) of the Puget Sound area of the Pacific coast of No. America — called also *Olympia*

Olym·pic \ə-ˈlim-pik, ō-\ *adj* (1590) **1 :** [2]OLYMPIAN 1 **2 :** of or relating to the Olympic Games

Olympic Games *n pl* (ca. 1610) **1 :** an ancient Panhellenic festival held every fourth year and made up of contests of sports, music, and literature with the victor's prize a crown of wild olive **2 :** a modified revival of the ancient Olympic Games consisting of international athletic contests that are held at separate winter and summer gatherings at four year intervals — called also *Olympics*

Olym·pus \ə-ˈlim-pəs, ō-\ *n* [L, fr. Gk *Olympos*] (15c) **:** a mountain in Thessaly that in Greek mythology is the abode of the gods

om \ˈōm\ *n* [Skt] (1788) **:** a mantra consisting of the sound \ˈōm\ and used in contemplation of ultimate reality

OM *abbr* order of merit

-oma *n suffix, pl* **-omas** *also* **-omata** [L *omat-, -oma,* fr. Gk *-ōmat-, -ōma,* fr. *-ō-* (stem vowel of causative verbs in *-oun*) + *-mat-, -ma,* suffix denoting result — more at -MENT] **:** tumor ⟨aden*oma*⟩ ⟨fibr*oma*⟩

Oma·ha \ˈō-mə-ˌhȯ, -ˌhä\ *n, pl* **Omaha** *or* **Omahas** [Omaha *umą́hą,* a self-designation] (1814) **1 :** a member of an American Indian people of northeastern Nebraska **2 :** the Siouan language of the Omaha

oma·sum \ō-ˈmā-səm\ *n, pl* **oma·sa** \-sə\ [NL, fr. L, tripe of a bullock] (1556) **:** the third chamber of the ruminant stomach that is situated between the reticulum and the abomasum — compare RUMEN

OMB *abbr* Office of Management and Budget

om·bre \ˈäm-bər; ˈäm-brē, ˈəm-, -ˌbrā\ *n* [F or Sp; F *hombre,* fr. Sp, lit., man — more at HOMBRE] (ca. 1661) **:** an old three-handed card game popular in Europe esp. in the 17th and 18th centuries

om·bré \ˈäm-ˌbrā\ *adj* [F, pp. of *ombrer* to shade, fr. It *ombrare,* fr. *ombra* shade, fr. L *umbra* — more at UMBRAGE] (1893) **:** having colors or tones that shade into each other — used esp. of fabrics in which the color is graduated from light to dark — **ombré** *n*

om·buds·man \ˈäm-ˌbu̇dz-mən, ˈȯm-, -bədz-, -ˌman; äm-ˈbu̇dz-, ȯm-\ *n, pl* **-men** \-mən\ [Sw, lit., representative, fr. ON *umbothsmathr,* fr. *umboth* commission + *mathr* man] (1959) **1 :** a government official (as in Sweden or New Zealand) appointed to receive and investigate complaints made by individuals against abuses or capricious acts of public officials **2 :** one that investigates, reports on, and helps settle complaints — **om·buds·man·ship** \-ˌship\ *n*

om·buds·per·son \-ˌpər-sᵊn\ *n* (1974) **:** OMBUDSMAN 2

-ome *n suffix* [NL *-oma,* fr. L, -oma] **:** mass ⟨phyll*ome*⟩

ome·ga \ō-ˈmā-gə, -ˈmē-, -ˈme-\ *n* [ME, fr. Gk *ō mega,* lit., large o] (15c) **1 :** the 24th and last letter of the Greek alphabet — see ALPHABET table **2 :** the extreme or final part **:** END **3 a :** a negatively charged elementary particle that has a mass 3270 times the mass of an electron — called also *omega minus* **b :** a very short-lived unstable meson with mass 1532 times the mass of an electron — called also *omega meson*

ome·ga–3 \-ˈthrē\ *adj* (1967) **:** being or composed of polyunsaturated fatty acids that have the final double bond in the hydrocarbon chain between the third and fourth carbon atoms from the end of the molecule opposite that of the carboxyl group and that are found esp. in fish, fish oils, green leafy vegetables, and some nuts and vegetable oils

om·e·let *or* **om·e·lette** \ˈäm-lət, ˈä-mə-\ *n* [F *omelette,* alter. of MF *amelette, alemette,* alter. of *alemelle* thin plate, ultim. fr. L *lamella,* dim. of *lamina*] (ca. 1611) **:** beaten eggs cooked without stirring until set and served folded in half

omen \ˈō-mən\ *n* [L *omin-, omen*] (1582) **:** an occurrence or phenomenon believed to portend a future event **:** AUGURY

omen·tum \ō-ˈmen-təm\ *n, pl* **-ta** \-tə\ *or* **-tums** [L; perh. akin to L *induere* to put on, *exuere* to take off — more at EXUVIAE] (1682) **:** a fold of peritoneum connecting or supporting abdominal structures (as the stomach and liver); *also* **:** a fold of peritoneum free at one end — **omen·tal** \-ˈmen-tᵊl\ *adj*

omep·ra·zole \ō-ˈme-prə-ˌzōl, -ˈmē-, -ˌzȯl\ *n* [ISV *omepr-* (of unknown origin) + benzimid*azole*] (1984) **:** a benzimidazole derivative $C_{17}H_{19}N_3O_3S$ that inhibits gastric acid secretion

omer \ˈō-mər\ *n* [Heb *ʿōmer*] (ca. 1608) **1 :** an ancient Hebrew unit of dry capacity equal to ¹⁄₁₀ ephah **2 a** *often cap* **:** the sheaf of barley traditionally offered in Jewish Temple worship on the second day of the Passover **b** *cap* **:** a 7-week liturgical period of anticipation for Shavuot beginning with the second day of the Passover

OMG *or* **omg** *abbr* oh my God

om·i·cron \ˈä-mə-ˌkrän, ˈō-, *Brit* ō-ˈmī-(ˌ)krän\ *n* [ME, fr. Gk *o mikron,* lit., small o] (15c) **:** the 15th letter of the Greek alphabet — see ALPHABET table

om·i·nous \ˈä-mə-nəs\ *adj* (1580) **:** being or exhibiting an omen **:** PORTENTOUS; *esp* **:** foreboding or foreshadowing evil **:** INAUSPICIOUS — **om·i·nous·ly** *adv* — **om·i·nous·ness** *n*

syn OMINOUS, PORTENTOUS, FATEFUL mean having a menacing or threatening aspect. OMINOUS implies having a menacing, alarming character foreshadowing evil or disaster ⟨*ominous* rumblings from the volcano⟩. PORTENTOUS suggests being frighteningly big or impressive but now seldom definitely connotes forewarning of calamity ⟨an eerie and *portentous* stillness⟩. FATEFUL suggests being of momentous or decisive importance ⟨the *fateful* conference that led to war⟩.

omis·si·ble \ō-ˈmi-sə-bəl\ *adj* (1816) **:** that may be omitted

omis·sion \ō-ˈmi-shən, ə-\ *n* [ME *omissioun,* fr. AF *omission,* fr. LL *omission-, omissio,* fr. L *omittere*] (14c) **1 a :** something neglected or left undone **b :** apathy toward or neglect of duty **2 :** the act of omitting **:** the state of being omitted

omit \ō-ˈmit, ə-\ *vt* **omit·ted; omit·ting** [ME *omitten,* fr. L *omittere,* fr. *ob-* toward + *mittere* to let go, send — more at OB-] (15c) **1 :** to leave out or leave unmentioned ⟨~*s* one important detail⟩ **2 :** to leave undone **:** FAIL **3** *obs* **:** DISREGARD **4** *obs* **:** GIVE UP

om·ma·tid·i·um \ˌä-mə-ˈti-dē-əm\ *n, pl* **-tid·ia** \-dē-ə\ [NL, fr. Gk *ommat-, omma* eye; akin to Gk *ōps* eye — more at EYE] (1884) **:** one of the elements corresponding to a small simple eye that make up the compound eye of an arthropod — **om·ma·tid·i·al** \-dē-əl\ *adj*

omni- *comb form* [L, fr. *omnis*] **:** all **:** universally ⟨*omni*directional⟩

[1]**om·ni·bus** \ˈäm-ni-(ˌ)bəs\ *n* [F, fr. L, for all, dat. pl. of *omnis*] (1829) **1 :** a usu. automotive public vehicle designed to carry a large number of passengers **:** BUS **2 :** a book containing reprints of a number of works

[2]**omnibus** *adj* (1842) **1 :** of, relating to, or providing for many things at once **2 :** containing or including many items ⟨an ~ bill⟩

om·ni·com·pe·tent \ˌäm-ni-ˈkäm-pə-tənt\ *adj* (1827) **:** able to handle any situation; *esp* **:** having the authority or legal capacity to act in all matters — **om·ni·com·pe·tence** \-tən(t)s\ *n*

om·ni·di·rec·tion·al \ˌäm-ni-də-ˈrek-shnəl, -ˌnī-, -(ˌ)dī-, -shə-nᵊl\ *adj* (1927) **:** being in or involving all directions; *esp* **:** receiving or sending radio waves equally well in all directions ⟨~ antenna⟩

om·ni·far·i·ous \ˌäm-nə-ˈfer-ē-əs\ *adj* [LL *omnifarius,* fr. L *omni-* + *-farius* (as in *multifarius* diverse) — more at MULTIFARIOUS] (1653) **:** of all varieties, forms, or kinds ⟨~ interests⟩

om·nif·i·cent \äm-ˈni-fə-sənt\ *adj* [L *omni-* + E *-ficent* (as in *magnificent*)] (1677) **:** unlimited in creative power

om·nip·o·tence \äm-ˈni-pə-tən(t)s\ *n* (15c) **1 :** the quality or state of being omnipotent **2 :** an agency or force of unlimited power

[1]**om·nip·o·tent** \-tənt\ *adj* [ME, fr. AF, fr. L *omnipotent-, omnipotens,* fr. *omni-* + *potent-, potens* potent] (14c) **1** *often cap* **:** ALMIGHTY 1 **2 :** having virtually unlimited authority or influence ⟨an ~ ruler⟩ **3** *obs* **:** ARRANT — **om·nip·o·tent·ly** *adv*

[2]**omnipotent** *n* (1600) **1 :** one who is omnipotent **2** *cap* **:** GOD 1

om·ni·pres·ence \ˌäm-ni-ˈpre-zᵊn(t)s\ *n* (1601) **:** the quality or state of being omnipresent **:** UBIQUITY

om·ni·pres·ent \-zᵊnt\ *adj* (1609) **:** present in all places at all times

om·ni·range \ˈäm-ni-ˌrānj\ *n* (1946) **:** a system of radio navigation in which any bearing relative to a special radio transmitter on the ground may be chosen and flown by an airplane pilot — called also *omnidirectional range*

om·ni·science \äm-ˈni-shən(t)s\ *n* [ML *omniscientia,* fr. L *omni-* + *scientia* knowledge — more at SCIENCE] (ca. 1610) **:** the quality or state of being omniscient

om·ni·scient \-shənt\ *adj* [NL *omniscient-, omnisciens,* back-formation fr. ML *omniscientia*] (ca. 1604) **1 :** having infinite awareness, understanding, and insight **2 :** possessed of universal or complete knowledge — **om·ni·scient·ly** *adv*

om·ni·um–gath·er·um \ˌäm-nē-əm-ˈga-t͟hə-rəm\ *n, pl* **omnium–gatherums** [L *omnium* (gen. pl. of *omnis*) + E *gather* + L *-um,* noun ending] (1530) **:** a miscellaneous collection (as of things or persons)

om·ni·vore \ˈäm-ni-ˌvȯr\ *n* [NL *omnivora,* neut. pl. of *omnivorus,* fr. L] (1887) **:** one that is omnivorous

om·niv·o·rous \äm-ˈniv-rəs, -ˈni-və-\ *adj* [L *omnivorus,* fr. *omni-* + *-vorus* -vorous] (ca. 1656) **1 :** feeding on both animal and vegetable substances **2 :** avidly taking in everything as if devouring or consuming ⟨an ~ reader⟩ — **om·niv·o·rous·ly** *adv*

om·pha·los \ˈäm(p)-fə-ˌläs, -ləs\ *n* [Gk, navel — more at NAVEL] (1855) **:** a central point **:** HUB, FOCAL POINT

om·pha·lo·skep·sis \ˌäm(p)-fə-lō-ˈskep-səs\ *n* [NL, fr. Gk *omphalos* + *skepsis* examination — more at SPY] (1925) **:** contemplation of one's navel as an aid to meditation; *also* **:** NAVEL-GAZING

[1]**on** \ˈȯn, ˈän\ *prep* [ME *an, on,* prep. & adv., fr. OE; akin to OHG *ana* on, Gk *ana* up, on] (bef. 12c) **1 a** — used as a function word to indicate position in contact with and supported by the top surface of ⟨the book is lying ~ the table⟩ **b** — used as a function word to indicate position in or in contact with an outer surface ⟨the fly landed ~ the ceiling⟩ ⟨I have a cut ~ my finger⟩ ⟨paint ~ the wall⟩ **c** — used as a function word to indicate position in close proximity with ⟨a village ~ the sea⟩ ⟨stay ~ your opponent⟩ **d** — used as a function word to indicate the location of something ⟨~ the left⟩ ⟨~ the south side of the house⟩ ⟨~ the farm⟩ **2 a** — used as a function word to indicate a source of attachment or support ⟨~ a string⟩ ⟨stand ~ one foot⟩ ⟨hang it ~ a nail⟩ **b** — used as a function word to indicate a source of dependence ⟨you can rely ~ me⟩ ⟨feeds ~ insects⟩ ⟨lives ~ a pension⟩ **c** — used as a function word to indicate means of conveyance ⟨~ the bus⟩ **d** — used as a function word to indicate presence in the possession of ⟨had a knife ~ him⟩ **3** — used as a function word to indicate a time frame during which something takes place ⟨a parade ~ Sunday⟩ or an instant, action, or occurrence when something begins or is done ⟨~ cue⟩ ⟨~ arriving home, I found your letter⟩ ⟨news ~ the hour⟩ ⟨cash ~ delivery⟩ **4** *archaic* **:** OF **5 a** — used as a function word to indicate manner of doing something; often used with *the* ⟨~ the sly⟩ ⟨keep everything ~ the up-and-up⟩ **b** — used as a function word to indicate means or agency ⟨cut myself ~ a knife⟩ ⟨talk ~ the telephone⟩ **c** — used as a function word to indicate a medium of expression ⟨~ stage⟩ ⟨best show ~ television⟩ **6 a (1)** — used as a function word to indicate active involvement in a condition or status ⟨~ the increase⟩ ⟨~ the lookout⟩ **(2) :** regularly using or showing the effects of using ⟨~ drugs⟩ **b** — used as a function word to indicate involvement or participation ⟨~ tour⟩ ⟨~ the team⟩ ⟨~ duty⟩ **c** — used as a function word to indicate inclusion ⟨put it ~ the agenda⟩ **d** — used as a function word to indicate position or status in proper relationship with a standard or objective ⟨~ schedule⟩ **7 a** — used as a function word to indicate reason, ground, or basis (as for an action, opinion, or com-

putation) ⟨I have it ~ good authority⟩ ⟨~ one condition⟩ ⟨the interest will be 10 cents ~ the dollar⟩ **b** — used as a function word to indicate the cause or source ⟨profited ~ the sale of stock⟩ **c** — used as a function word to indicate the focus of obligation or responsibility ⟨drinks are ~ the house⟩ ⟨put the blame ~ me⟩ **8 a** — used as a function word to indicate the object of collision, opposition, or hostile action ⟨bumped my head ~ a limb⟩ ⟨an attack ~ religion⟩ ⟨pulled a gun ~ me⟩ **b** — used as a function word to indicate the object with respect to some disadvantage, handicap, or detriment ⟨has three inches in height ~ me⟩ ⟨a 3-game lead ~ the second-place team⟩ ⟨the joke's ~ me⟩ **9 a** — used as a function word to indicate destination or the focus of some action, movement, or directed effort ⟨crept up ~ him⟩ ⟨feast your eyes ~ this⟩ ⟨working ~ my skiing⟩ ⟨made a payment ~ the loan⟩ **b** — used as a function word to indicate the focus of feelings, determination, or will ⟨have pity ~ me⟩ ⟨keen ~ sports⟩ ⟨a curse ~ you⟩ **c** — used as a function word to indicate the object with respect to some misfortune or disadvantageous event ⟨the crops died ~ them⟩ **d** — used as a function word to indicate the subject of study, discussion, or consideration ⟨a book ~ insects⟩ ⟨reflect ~ that a moment⟩ ⟨agree ~ price⟩ **e :** with respect to ⟨go light ~ the salt⟩ ⟨short ~ cash⟩ **10** — used as a function word to indicate reduplication or succession in a series ⟨loss ~ loss⟩

[2]**on** *adv* (bef. 12c) **1 a :** in or into a position of contact with an upper surface esp. so as to be positioned for use or operation ⟨put the plates ~⟩ **b :** in or into a position of being attached to or covering a surface; *esp* : in or into the condition of being worn ⟨put his new shoes ~⟩ **2 a :** forward or at a more advanced point in space or time ⟨went ~ home⟩ ⟨later ~⟩ **b :** in continuance or succession ⟨rambled ~⟩ ⟨and so ~⟩ **3 :** into operation or a position permitting operation ⟨switched the light ~⟩

[3]**on** *adj* (ca. 1541) **1 :** engaged in an activity or function (as a dramatic role) **2 a (1) :** being in operation ⟨the radio is ~⟩ **(2) :** placed so as to permit operation ⟨the switch is ~⟩ **b :** taking place or being broadcast ⟨the game is ~⟩ **3 :** aware of something — usu. used with *to* ⟨my boss was ~ to me⟩ **4 :** INTENDED, PLANNED ⟨has nothing ~ for tonight⟩ **5** *Brit* : talking or harping incessantly — used with *about* **6** *chiefly Brit* : regarded as possible or feasible — usu. used in negative constructions **7 a :** engaged in or as if in a performance ⟨the comedian was always ~⟩ **b :** being at a high level of performance

ON *or* **Ont** *abbr* Ontario

[1]**-on** *n suffix* [ISV, alter. of *-one*] : chemical compound not a ketone or other oxo compound ⟨parathi*on*⟩

[2]**-on** *n suffix* [fr. *-on* (in *ion*)] **1 :** subatomic particle ⟨nucle*on*⟩ **2 a :** unit : quantum ⟨phot*on*⟩ ⟨magnet*on*⟩ **b :** basic hereditary component ⟨cistr*on*⟩ ⟨oper*on*⟩

[3]**-on** *n suffix* [NL, fr. *-on* (in *argon*)] : noble gas ⟨rad*on*⟩

on–again, off–again *adj* (1948) : existing briefly and in an intermittent unpredictable way ⟨*on-again, off-again* fads⟩

on•a•ger \ˈä-ni-jər\ *n* [ME, wild ass, fr. L, fr. Gk *onagros,* fr. *onos* ass + *agros* field — more at ACRE] (14c) **1 :** an Asian wild ass (*Equus hemionus onager* syn. *E. onager*) that usu. has a broad dorsal stripe and is related to the kiang **2** [LL, fr. L] : a heavy catapult used in ancient and medieval times

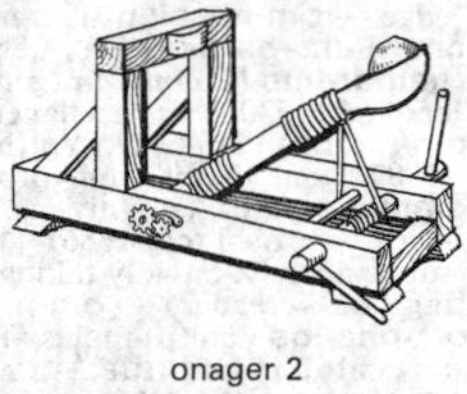

onager 2

on and off *adv* (1748) : OFF AND ON — **on–and–off** *adj*

onan•ism \ˈō-nə-ˌni-zəm\ *n* [prob. fr. NL *onanismus,* fr. *Onan,* son of Judah (Gen 38:9)] (ca. 1741) **1 :** MASTURBATION **2 :** COITUS INTERRUPTUS **3 :** SELF-GRATIFICATION — **onan•is•tic** \ˌō-nə-ˈnis-tik\ *adj*

on•board \ˈȯn-ˈbȯrd, ˈän-\ *adj* (1960) : carried within or occurring aboard a vehicle (as a satellite or an automobile) ⟨an ~ computer⟩

[1]**once** \ˈwən(t)s\ *adv* [ME *ones,* fr. gen. of *on* one] (12c) **1 :** one time and no more ⟨rode a horse only ~⟩ **2 :** at any one time : under any circumstances : EVER ⟨didn't ~ thank me⟩ **3 :** at some indefinite time in the past : FORMERLY ⟨was ~ a booming mining town⟩ **4 :** by one degree of relationship ⟨first cousin ~ removed⟩ — **once and for all 1 :** with finality : DEFINITIVELY **2 :** for the last time — **once in a while :** NOW AND THEN

[2]**once** *n* (13c) : one single time : one time at least ⟨please be on time this ~⟩ — **at once 1 :** at the same time : SIMULTANEOUSLY **2 :** IMMEDIATELY **3 :** [2]BOTH ⟨*at once* funny and sad⟩

[3]**once** *adj* (1691) : that once was : FORMER ⟨a ~ successful actor⟩

[4]**once** *conj* (1761) : at the moment when : AS SOON AS ⟨~ she spoke, I recognized her⟩

once–over \ˌwən(t)s-ˈō-vər, ˈwən(t)s-ˌ\ *n* (1913) : a swift examination or survey; *esp* : a swift comprehensive appraising glance ⟨gave me the ~⟩

once that *conj* (1874) : ONCE

on•cho•cer•ci•a•sis \ˌäŋ-kō-ˌsər-ˈkī-ə-səs\ *n, pl* **-a•ses** \-ˌsēz\ [NL, fr. *Onchocerca,* genus of worms] (1911) : infestation with or disease caused by filarial worms (genus *Onchocerca*); *esp* : a human disease marked by subcutaneous nodules, dermatitis, and visual impairment and caused by a worm (*O. volvulus*) found in Africa and tropical America which is transmitted by the bite of a female blackfly — called also *river blindness*

on•cid•i•um \än-ˈsi-dē-əm, äŋ-ˈki-\ *n* [NL, fr. Gk *onkos* barbed hook — more at ANGLE] (ca. 1868) : any of a genus (*Oncidium*) of showy tropical American chiefly epiphytic orchids

onco- *comb form* [NL, fr. Gk *onkos* bulk, mass; akin to Gk *enenkein* to carry — more at ENOUGH] : tumor ⟨*onco*logy⟩

on•co•gene \ˈäŋ-kō-ˌjēn\ *n* (1969) : a gene having the potential to cause a normal cell to become cancerous

on•co•gen•e•sis \ˌäŋ-kō-ˈje-nə-səs\ *n* [NL] (ca. 1932) : the induction or formation of tumors

on•co•gen•ic \-ˈje-nik\ *adj* (1936) **1 :** relating to tumor formation **2 :** tending to cause tumors — **on•co•ge•nic•i•ty** \-jə-ˈni-sə-tē\ *n*

on•col•o•gy \än-ˈkä-lə-jē, äŋ-\ *n* (ca. 1857) : the study of tumors — **on•co•log•i•cal** \ˌäŋ-kə-ˈlä-ji-kəl\ *also* **on•co•log•ic** \-jik\ *adj* — **on•col•o•gist** \än-ˈkä-lə-jist, äŋ-\ *n*

on•com•ing \ˈȯn-ˌkə-miŋ, ˈän-\ *adj* (1844) **1 a :** coming nearer in time or space ⟨the ~ year⟩ ⟨an ~ car⟩ **b :** FUTURE ⟨looked forward to his ~ visit⟩ **2 :** EMERGENT, RISING ⟨the ~ generation⟩

[1]**one** \ˈwən\ *adj* [ME *on, an,* fr. OE *ān;* akin to OHG *ein* one, L *unus* (OL *oinos*), Skt *eka*] (bef. 12c) **1 :** being a single unit or thing ⟨~ day at a time⟩ **2 a :** being one in particular ⟨early ~ morning⟩ **b :** being preeminently what is indicated ⟨~ fine person⟩ **3 a :** being the same in kind or quality ⟨both of ~ species⟩ **b (1) :** constituting a unified entity of two or more components ⟨the combined elements form ~ substance⟩ **(2) :** being in agreement or union ⟨am ~ with you on this⟩ **4 a :** SOME 1 ⟨will see you again ~ day⟩ **b :** being a certain individual specified by name ⟨~ John Doe made a speech⟩ **5 :** ONLY 2a ⟨the ~ person she wanted to marry⟩

[2]**one** *n* (bef. 12c) **1** — see NUMBER table **2 :** the number denoting unity **3 a :** the first in a set or series — often used with an attributive noun ⟨day ~⟩ **b :** an article of clothing of a size designated *one* ⟨wears a ~⟩ **4 :** a single person or thing ⟨has the ~ but needs the other⟩ **5 :** a one-dollar bill — **at one :** at harmony : in a state of agreement — **for one :** as one example ⟨I *for one* disagree⟩

[3]**one** *pron* (13c) **1 :** a certain indefinitely indicated person or thing ⟨saw ~ of his friends⟩ **2 a :** an individual of a vaguely indicated group : anyone at all ⟨~ never knows⟩ **b** — used as a third person substitute for a first person pronoun ⟨I'd like to read more but ~ doesn't have the time⟩ **3 :** a single instance of a specified action ⟨felt like belting him ~ —John Casey⟩

usage Sense 2a is usu. a sign of a formal style. A formal style excludes the participation of the reader or hearer; thus *one* is used where a less formal style might address the reader directly ⟨for the consequences of such choices, *one* has only oneself to thank —Walker Gibson⟩. This generic *one* has never been common in informal use in either British or American English, and people who start sentences with *one* often shift to another pronoun more natural to casual discourse ⟨when *one* is learning the river, he is not allowed to do or think about anything else —Mark Twain⟩. Use of *one* to replace a first-person pronoun—sense 2b—has occas. been criticized. It is more common in British English than in American ⟨I'm watching this pretty carefully and I hope that the issue will come up in the Lords and *one* may be able to speak about it —Donald Coggan⟩.

-one *n suffix* [ISV, alter. of *-ene*] : ketone or related or analogous compound or class of compounds ⟨lact*one*⟩ ⟨quin*one*⟩

one another *pron* (1526) : EACH OTHER ***usage*** see EACH OTHER

one–armed bandit \ˈwən-ˈärm(d)-\ *also* **one–arm bandit** *n* (1934) : SLOT MACHINE 2

one–bag•ger \-ˈba-gər\ *n* (1952) : SINGLE 2

one–dimensional *adj* (1883) **1 :** having one dimension **2 :** lacking depth : SUPERFICIAL ⟨~ characters⟩ — **one–dimensionality** *n*

one•fold \ˈwən-ˌfōld, -ˈfōld\ *adj* (bef. 12c) : constituting a single undivided whole

one–hand•ed \-ˈhan-dəd\ *adj* (15c) **1 :** having or using only one hand ⟨could beat him up ~⟩ **2 a :** designed for or requiring the use of only one hand **b :** effected by the use of only one hand

one–horse \-ˈhȯrs\ *adj* (1739) **1 :** drawn or operated by one horse **2 :** SMALL, SMALL-TIME ⟨a ~ town⟩

Onei•da \ō-ˈnī-də\ *n, pl* **Oneida** *or* **Oneidas** [Oneida *oneˑyóteʔ,* lit., standing rock] (1666) **1 :** a member of an American Indian people orig. of New York **2 :** the Iroquoian language of the Oneida people

onei•ric \ō-ˈnī-rik\ *adj* [Gk *oneiros* dream; akin to Arm *anurǰ* dream] (1859) : of or relating to dreams : DREAMY — **onei•ri•cal•ly** \-ri-k(ə-)lē\ *adv*

onei•ro•man•cy \ō-ˈnī-rə-ˌman(t)-sē\ *n* [Gk *oneiros* + E *-mancy*] (1652) : divination by means of dreams

one–lin•er \ˌwən-ˈlī-nər\ *n* (1967) **1 :** a very succinct joke or witticism **2 :** a succinct or meaningful and esp. accurate statement

one–man *adj* (1842) : of or relating to just one individual: as **a :** consisting of only one individual ⟨a ~ committee⟩ **b (1) :** done, presented, or produced by only one individual ⟨a ~ stage play⟩ **(2) :** featuring the work of a single artist (as a painter) ⟨a ~ show of oils⟩ **c :** designed for or limited to one individual

one–man band *n* (1925) **1 :** a musician who plays several instruments during a solo performance **2 :** a person who alone undertakes or is responsible for several tasks

one•ness \ˈwən-nəs\ *n* (ca. 1555) : the quality or state or fact of being one: as **a :** SINGLENESS **b :** INTEGRITY, WHOLENESS **c :** HARMONY **d :** SAMENESS, IDENTITY **e :** UNITY, UNION

one–night•er \ˌwən-ˈnī-tər\ *n* (ca. 1937) : ONE-NIGHT STAND

one–night stand *n* (1880) **1 :** a performance (as of a play or concert) given (as by a traveling group of actors or musicians) only once in each of a series of localities **2 a :** a locality used for one-night stands **b :** a stopover for a one-night stand **3 :** a sexual encounter limited to a single occasion; *also* : a partner in such an encounter

one–note \ˈwən-ˈnōt\ *adj* (1969) : unvarying in tone or emphasis : MONOTONOUS ⟨a ~ campaigner⟩

one–off \ˌwən-ˈȯf\ *adj* (1934) **1 :** limited to a single time, occasion, or instance : ONE-SHOT ⟨~ gigs⟩ **2 :** SINGULAR, UNIQUE ⟨a ~ design⟩ — **one–off** *n*

one–on–one \ˌwən-ȯn-ˈwən, ˌwən-än-\ *adj or adv* (1967) **1 :** playing directly against a single opposing player **2 :** involving a direct encounter between one person and another

one–piece *adj* (1880) : consisting of or made in a single undivided piece ⟨a ~ bathing suit⟩ — **one–piece** *n* — **one–piec•er** \ˈwən-ˈpē-sər\ *n*

oner•ous \ˈä-nə-rəs, ˈō-\ *adj* [ME, fr. MF *honereus,* fr. L *onerosus,* fr. *oner-, onus* burden; akin to Skt *anas* cart] (14c) **1 :** involving, imposing, or constituting a burden : TROUBLESOME ⟨an ~ task⟩ **2 :** having legal obligations that outweigh the advantages ⟨an ~ contract⟩ — **oner•ous•ly** *adv* — **oner•ous•ness** *n*

syn ONEROUS, BURDENSOME, OPPRESSIVE, EXACTING mean imposing hardship. ONEROUS stresses being laborious and heavy esp. because distasteful ⟨the *onerous* task of cleaning up the mess⟩. BURDENSOME suggests causing mental as well as physical strain ⟨*burdensome* responsibilities⟩. OPPRESSIVE implies extreme harshness or severity in what is imposed ⟨the *oppressive* tyranny of a police state⟩. EXACTING implies rigor or sternness rather than tyranny or injustice in the demands made or in the one demanding ⟨an *exacting* employer⟩.

one·self \(ˌ)wən-ˈself, *Southern also* -ˈsef\ *also* **one's self** \(ˌ)wən-, ˌwənz-\ *pron* (1548) **1 :** a person's self : one's own self — used reflexively as object of a preposition or verb or for emphasis in various constructions **2 :** one's normal, healthy, or sane condition or self — **be oneself :** to conduct oneself in a usual or fitting manner

one–shot \ˈwən-ˌshät\ *adj* (1927) **1 :** that is complete or effective through being done or used or applied only once ⟨there is no easy ~ answer to the problem⟩ **2 :** that is not followed by something else of the same kind ⟨a ~ tax cut⟩ — **one–shot** *n*

one–sid·ed \ˈwən-ˈsī-dəd\ *adj* (ca. 1802) **1 a** (1) **:** having one side prominent : LOPSIDED (2) **:** having or occurring on one side only **b :** limited to one side : PARTIAL ⟨a ~ interpretation⟩ **2 :** UNILATERAL ⟨a ~ decision⟩ — **one–sid·ed·ly** *adv* — **one–sid·ed·ness** *n*

ones place *n* (1976) **:** UNITS PLACE

one–step \ˈwən-ˌstep\ *n* (1911) **1 :** a ballroom dance in 2/4 time marked by quick walking steps backward and forward **2 :** music used for the one-step — **one–step** *vi*

one–stop \-ˈstäp\ *adj* (1933) **:** providing or offering a comprehensive range of goods or services at one location; *also* **:** provided or offered at such a location ⟨~ shopping⟩

one–tailed \ˈwən-ˈtāl(d)\ *also* **one–tail** \-ˈtāl\ *adj* (1947) **:** being a statistical test for which the critical region consists of all values of the test statistic greater than a given value or less than a given value but not both — compare TWO-TAILED

[1]**one·time** \ˈwən-ˈtīm\ *adj* (1850) **1 :** FORMER, SOMETIME ⟨a ~ actor⟩ **2 :** occurring only once : ONE-SHOT

[2]**onetime** *adv* (1886) **:** FORMERLY

one–to–one \ˌwən-tə-ˈwən, -də-\ *adj* (1873) **1 :** pairing each element of a set uniquely with an element of another set **2 :** ONE-ON-ONE 2

one–track *adj* (1926) **:** marked by often narrowly restricted attention to or absorption in just one thing ⟨a ~ mind⟩

one–trick pony *n* (1980) **:** one that is skilled in only one area; *also* **:** one that has success only once

one–two \ˈwən-ˈtü, -ˌtü\ *n* (1809) **1 :** a combination of two quick blows in rapid succession in boxing; *esp* **:** a left jab followed at once by a hard blow with the right hand **2** *or* **one–two punch :** two forces combining to produce a marked effect

one–up \ˌwən-ˈəp, ˈwən-\ *vt* [back-formation fr. *one-upmanship*] (1963) **:** to practice one-upmanship on

one up *adj* (1919) **:** being in a position of advantage — usu. used with *on*

one–up·man·ship \ˌwən-ˈəp-mən-ˌship\ *also* **one–ups·man·ship** \-ˈəps-mən-\ *n* (1952) **:** the art or practice of outdoing or keeping one jump ahead of a friend or competitor ⟨engaged in a round of verbal ~⟩

one–way *adj* (1824) **1 :** that moves in or allows movement in only one direction ⟨a ~ street⟩ **2 :** ONE-SIDED, UNILATERAL ⟨a ~ conversation⟩ **3 :** that functions in only one of two or more ways

on·go·ing \ˈȯn-ˌgō-iŋ, ˈän-, -ˌgō(-)iŋ\ *adj* (1877) **1 a :** being actually in process **b :** CONTINUING **2 :** continuously moving forward : GROWING — **on·go·ing·ness** \-nəs\ *n*

on·ion \ˈən-yən\ *n* [ME, fr. AF *oignon,* fr. L *union-, unio*] (14c) **1 :** a widely cultivated Asian herb (*Allium cepa*) of the lily family with pungent edible bulbs; *also* **:** its bulb **2 :** any of various plants of the same genus as the onion — **on·iony** \-yə-nē\ *adj*

onion dome *n* (1941) **:** a dome (as of a church) having the general shape of an onion — **onion–domed** *adj*

onion ring *n* (1946) **:** a ring of sliced onion coated with batter or crumbs and fried

on·ion·skin \-ˌskin\ *n* (1879) **:** a thin strong translucent paper of very light weight

oni·um \ˈō-nē-əm\ *adj* [*-onium*] (1905) **:** being or characterized by a usu. complex cation

-onium *n suffix* [NL, fr. *ammonium*] **:** an ion having a positive charge ⟨hydr*onium*⟩ — compare -IUM 1b

on·line \ˈȯn-ˈlīn, ˈän-ˈlīn\ *adj* (1950) **:** connected to, served by, or available through a system and esp. a computer or telecommunications system (as the Internet) ⟨an ~ database⟩; *also* **:** done while connected to such a system ⟨~ shopping⟩ — **online** *adv*

on·look·er \ˈȯn-ˌlu̇-kər, ˈän-\ *n* (1606) **:** one that looks on; *esp* **:** a passive spectator — **on·look·ing** \-kiŋ\ *adj*

[1]**on·ly** \ˈōn-lē\ *adj* [ME, fr. OE *ānlīc,* fr. *ān* one — more at ONE] (bef. 12c) **1 :** unquestionably the best : PEERLESS **2 a :** alone in a class or category : SOLE ⟨the ~ one left⟩ ⟨the ~ known species⟩ **b :** having no brother or sister ⟨an ~ child⟩ **3 :** FEW ⟨one of the ~ areas not yet explored⟩

[2]**only** *adv* (14c) **1 a :** as a single fact or instance and nothing more or different : MERELY ⟨has ~ lost one election —George Orwell⟩ **b :** SOLELY, EXCLUSIVELY ⟨known ~ to him⟩ **2 :** at the very least ⟨it was ~ too true⟩ **3 a :** in the final outcome ⟨will ~ make you sick⟩ **b :** with nevertheless the final result ⟨won the battles, ~ to lose the war⟩ **4 a :** as recently as : not before ⟨~ last week⟩ ⟨~ in the last year did she get recognition⟩ **b :** in the immediate past ⟨~ just talked to her⟩

usage The placement of *only* in a sentence has been a source of studious commentary since the 18th century, most of it intended to prove by force of argument that prevailing standard usage is wrong. After 200 years of preachment the following observations may be made: the position of *only* in standard spoken English is not fixed, since ambiguity is avoided through sentence stress; in casual prose that keeps close to the rhythms of speech *only* is often placed where it would be in speech; and in edited and more formal prose *only* tends to be placed immediately before the word or words it modifies.

[3]**only** *conj* (14c) **1 a :** with the restriction that : BUT ⟨you may go, ~ come back early⟩ **b :** and yet : HOWEVER ⟨they look very nice, ~ we can't use them⟩ **2 :** were it not that : EXCEPT ⟨I'd introduce you to her, ~ you'd win her —Jack London⟩

ono \ˈō-(ˌ)nō\ *n, pl* **ono** *or* **onos** [Hawaiian] **:** [3]WAHOO

on·o·mas·tic \ˌä-nə-ˈmas-tik\ *adj* [Gk *onomastikos,* fr. *onomazein* to name, fr. *onoma* name — more at NAME] (1716) **:** of, relating to, or consisting of a name or names — **on·o·mas·ti·cal·ly** \-ti-k(ə-)lē\ *adv*

on·o·mas·tics \-tiks\ *n pl but sing or pl in constr* (1930) **1 a :** the science or study of the origins and forms of words esp. as used in a specialized field **b :** the science or study of the origin and forms of proper names of persons or places **2 :** the system underlying the formation and use of words esp. for proper names or of words used in a specialized field — **on·o·mas·ti·cian** \ˌä-nə-mas-ˈti-shən\ *n*

on·o·ma·tol·o·gy \ˌä-nə-mə-ˈtä-lə-jē\ *n* [F *onomatologie,* fr. Gk *onomat-, onoma* name + F *-logie* -logy] (1845) **:** ONOMASTICS — **on·o·ma·tol·o·gist** \-jist\ *n*

on·o·mato·poe·ia \ˌä-nə-ˌmä-tə-ˈpē-ə, -ˌma-\ *n* [LL, fr. Gk *onomatopoiia,* fr. *onomat-, onoma* name + *poiein* to make — more at POET] (ca. 1577) **1 :** the naming of a thing or action by a vocal imitation of the sound associated with it (as *buzz, hiss*) **2 :** the use of words whose sound suggests the sense — **on·o·mato·poe·ic** \-ˈpē-ik\ *or* **on·o·mato·po·et·ic** \-pō-ˈe-tik\ *adj* — **on·o·mato·poe·i·cal·ly** \-ˈpē-ə-k(ə-)lē\ *or* **on·o·mato·po·et·i·cal·ly** \-pō-ˈe-ti-k(ə-)lē\ *adv*

On·on·da·ga \ˌä-nə(n)-ˈdȯ-gə, -ˈdā-, -ˈdä-\ *n, pl* **-ga** *or* **-gas** [Onondaga *onǫ́·tàˀke,* the chief Onondaga town] (1684) **1 :** a member of an American Indian people of New York and Canada **2 :** the Iroquoian language of the Onondaga people

on–ramp \ˈȯn-ˌramp, ˈän-\ *n* (1958) **:** a ramp by which one enters a limited-access highway

on·rush \-ˌrəsh\ *n* (1841) **1 :** a rushing forward or onward **2 :** ONSET — **on·rush·ing** \-ˌrə-shiŋ\ *adj*

on–screen \ˈȯn-ˈskrēn, ˈän-\ *adv or adj* (1955) **1 :** in a motion picture or a television program **2 :** on a computer or television screen

on·set \-ˌset\ *n* (1535) **1 :** ATTACK, ASSAULT ⟨withstand the ~ of the army⟩ **2 :** BEGINNING, COMMENCEMENT ⟨the ~ of winter⟩

on·shore \ˈȯn-ˌshȯr, ˈän-\ *adj* (1875) **1 :** coming or moving from the water toward or onto the shore ⟨an ~ wind⟩ **2 a :** situated on or near the shore as distinguished from being in deep or open water **b :** situated on land **3 :** DOMESTIC 2 ⟨~ markets⟩ — **on·shore** \ˈȯn-ˈ, ˈän-ˈ\ *adv*

on·side \-ˈsīd\ *adv or adj* (1871) **:** not offside : in a position legally to play or receive the ball or puck

onside kick *n* (1926) **:** a kickoff in football in which the ball travels just far enough to be legally recoverable by the kicking team

on–site \-ˈsīt\ *adv or adj* (1946) **:** at a particular place esp. of business ⟨printed ~⟩ ⟨~ day care⟩

on·slaught \ˈän-ˌslȯt, ˈȯn-\ *n* [modif. of D *aanslag* act of striking; akin to OE *an* on and to OE *slēan* to strike — more at SLAY] (ca. 1625) **:** an esp. fierce attack; *also* **:** something resembling such an attack ⟨an ~ of technological changes⟩

on·stage \ˈȯn-ˈstāj, ˈän-, -ˌstāj\ *adv or adj* (1925) **:** on or onto a stage : on a part of the stage visible to the audience

on·stream \ˈȯn-ˈstrēm, ˈän-\ *adv or adj* (1930) **:** in or into production ⟨plants scheduled to come ~⟩

ont- *or* **onto-** *comb form* [NL, fr. LGk, fr. Gk *ont-, ōn,* prp. of *einai* to be — more at IS] **1 :** being : existence ⟨*onto*logy⟩ **2 :** organism ⟨*onto*geny⟩

-ont *n comb form* [Gk *ont-, ōn,* prp.] **:** cell : organism ⟨dipl*ont*⟩

on–tar·get \ˈän-ˈtär-gət\ *adj* (1967) **:** exactly appropriate : ACCURATE ⟨~ advice⟩

on–the–job *adj* (1946) **:** of, relating to, or being something (as training or experience) learned, gained, or done while working at a job

on·tic \ˈän-tik\ *adj* (1942) **:** of, relating to, or having real being — **on·ti·cal·ly** \-ti-k(ə-)lē\ *adv*

[1]**on·to** \ˈȯn-(ˌ)tü, ˈän-\ *prep* (1581) **1 :** to a position on **2 :** in or into a state of awareness about ⟨put me ~ your methods⟩ **3 —** used as a function word to indicate a set each element of which is the image of at least one element of another set ⟨a function mapping the set *S* ~ the set *T*⟩

[2]**onto** *adj* (1942) **:** mapping elements in such a way that every element in one set is the image of at least one element in another set ⟨a function that is one-to-one and ~⟩

on·to·gen·e·sis \ˌän-tə-ˈje-nə-səs\ *n* [NL] (1875) **:** ONTOGENY

on·to·ge·net·ic \-jə-ˈne-tik\ *adj* [ISV] (1878) **1 :** of, relating to, or appearing in the course of ontogeny **2 :** based on visible morphological characters — **on·to·ge·net·i·cal·ly** \-ti-k(ə-)lē\ *adv*

on·tog·e·ny \än-ˈtä-jə-nē\ *n* [ISV] (1872) **:** the development or course of development esp. of an individual organism

on·to·log·i·cal \ˌän-tə-ˈlä-ji-kəl\ *adj* (1782) **1 :** of or relating to ontology **2 :** relating to or based upon being or existence — **on·to·log·i·cal·ly** \-k(ə-)lē\ *adv*

ontological argument *n* (1877) **:** an argument for the existence of God based upon the meaning of the term *God*

on·tol·o·gy \än-ˈtä-lə-jē\ *n* [NL *ontologia,* fr. *ont-* + *-logia* -logy] (ca. 1721) **1 :** a branch of metaphysics concerned with the nature and relations of being **2 :** a particular theory about the nature of being or the kinds of things that have existence — **on·tol·o·gist** \-jist\ *n*

onus \ˈō-nəs\ *n* (ca. 1640) **1** [L — more at ONEROUS] **a :** BURDEN **b :** a disagreeable necessity : OBLIGATION **c :** BLAME **d :** STIGMA **2** [NL *onus (probandi),* lit., burden of proving] **:** BURDEN OF PROOF

[1]**on·ward** \ˈȯn-wərd, ˈän-\ *also* **on·wards** \-wərdz\ *adv* (15c) **:** toward or at a point lying ahead in space or time : FORWARD

[2]**onward** *adj* (1674) **:** directed or moving onward : FORWARD

on·y·choph·o·ran \ˌä-ni-ˈkä-fə-rən\ *n* [NL *Onychophora,* group name, fr. Gk *onych-, onyx* claw + *-phoros* -phore] (ca. 1890) **:** PERIPATUS — **onychophoran** *adj*

-onym *n comb form* [Gk *-ōnymon,* fr. *onyma* — more at NAME] **:** name : word ⟨ant*onym*⟩

on·yx \ˈä-niks\ *n* [ME *oniche, onyx,* fr. AF & L; AF, fr. L *onych-, onyx,* fr. Gk, lit., claw, nail — more at NAIL] (14c) **:** a translucent chalcedony in parallel layers of different colors

oo- — see O-

oo·cyst \ˈō-ə-ˌsist\ *n* [ISV] (1875) **:** ZYGOTE; *specif* **:** a sporozoan zygote undergoing sporogenous development

oo·cyte \ˈō-ə-ˌsīt\ *n* [ISV] (1895) **:** an egg before maturation : a female gametocyte

OOD *abbr* officer of the deck

O'o·dham \ˈō-ə-ˌdäm\ *n, pl* **O'odhams** *or* **O'odham** [O'odham *ʔóʔdham* people] (1985) **1 a** : TOHONO O'ODHAM **b** : a member of either the Pima or Tohono O'odham peoples **2** : the Uto-Aztecan language spoken by the Pimas and Tohono O'odhams

oo·dles \ˈü-dᵊlz\ *n pl but sing or pl in constr* [origin unknown] (ca. 1867) : a great quantity : LOT

oog·a·mous \ō-ˈä-gə-məs\ *adj* (1888) : having or involving a small motile male gamete and a large immobile female gamete — **oog·a·my** \-mē\ *n*

oo·gen·e·sis \ˌō-ə-ˈje-nə-səs\ *n* [NL] (ca. 1879) : formation and maturation of the egg — **oo·ge·net·ic** \-jə-ˈne-tik\ *adj*

oo·go·ni·um \ˌō-ə-ˈgō-nē-əm\ *n, pl* **-nia** \-nē-ə\ [NL] (1867) **1** : a female sexual organ in various algae and fungi that corresponds to the archegonium of ferns and mosses **2** : a descendant of a primordial germ cell that gives rise to oocytes — **oo·go·ni·al** \-nē-əl\ *adj*

[1]**ooh** \ˈü\ *interj* (1604) — used to express amazement, joy, or surprise

[2]**ooh** *vi* (1951) : to exclaim in amazement, joy, or surprise ⟨∼*ing* and aahing over the new automobiles⟩ — **ooh** *n*

oo·lite \ˈō-ə-ˌlīt\ *n* [prob. fr. F *oolithe,* fr. *oo-* o- + *-lithe* -lite] (1785) : a rock consisting of small round grains usu. of calcium carbonate cemented together — **oo·lit·ic** \ˌō-ə-ˈli-tik\ *adj*

ool·o·gist \ō-ˈä-lə-jist\ *n* (1863) **1** : a person specializing in the study of birds' eggs **2** : a collector of birds' eggs — **ool·o·gy** \-jē\ *n*

oo·long \ˈü-ˌlȯŋ\ *n* [Chin (Xiamen) *oōlióng(dê),* lit., black dragon (tea)] (1845) : tea made from leaves that have been partially oxidized before firing

oom·pah \ˈüm-(ˌ)pä, ˈu̇m-\ *also* **oom·pah–pah** \ˌüm-(ˌ)pä-ˈpä, ˌu̇m-\ *n* [imit.] (1877) : a repeated rhythmic bass accompaniment esp. in a band; *also* : music featuring such accompaniment — **oompah** *vb*

oomph \ˈu̇m(p)f\ *n* [imit. of a sound made under exertion] (1936) **1** : personal charm or magnetism : GLAMOUR **2** : SEX APPEAL **3** : PUNCH, VITALITY

oo·pho·rec·to·my \ˌō-ə-fə-ˈrek-tə-mē\ *n, pl* **-mies** [NL *oophoron* ovary (fr. *o-* + Gk *-phoron,* neut. of *-phoros* -phore) + E *-ectomy*] (1872) : the surgical removal of an ovary — called also *ovariectomy*

oops *or* **whoops** *also* **woops** \ˈ(w)u̇(ə)ps\ *interj* (1933) — used typically to express mild apology, surprise, or dismay

Oort cloud \ˈȯrt-\ *n* [Jan *Oort* †1992 Dutch astronomer] (1974) : a spherical shell of cometary bodies believed to surround the sun far beyond the orbits of the outermost planets and from which some are dislodged when perturbed to fall toward the sun — compare KUIPER BELT

oo·spore \ˈō-ə-ˌspȯr\ *n* [ISV] (1865) : a spore (as of a fungus) produced by heterogamous fertilization

oo·the·ca \ˌō-ə-ˈthē-kə\ *n, pl* **oo·the·cae** \-ˈthē-(ˌ)kē, -(ˌ)sē\ [NL] (ca. 1856) : a firm-walled and distinctive egg case (as of a cockroach) — **oo·the·cal** \-ˈthē-kəl\ *adj*

oo·tid \ˈō-ə-ˌtid\ *n* [irreg. fr. *o-* + *-id*] (1904) : an egg cell that results from the second meiotic division of an oocyte and that develops into a mature egg

[1]**ooze** \ˈüz\ *n* [ME *wose,* fr. OE *wāse* mire; akin to ON *veisa* stagnant water] (bef. 12c) **1** : a soft deposit (as of mud, slime, or shells) on the bottom of a body of water **2** : a piece of soft wet plastic ground

[2]**ooze** *vb* **oozed; ooz·ing** [ME *wosen,* fr. *wose* sap] *vi* (14c) **1** : to pass or flow slowly through or as if through small openings or interstices **2** : to move slowly or imperceptibly ⟨the crowd began to ∼ forward —Bruce Marshall⟩ **3 a** : to exude moisture **b** : to exude something often in a faintly repellent manner ⟨∼ with sympathy⟩ ∼ *vt* **1** : to emit slowly **2** : EXUDE 2 ⟨∼ confidence⟩

[3]**ooze** *n* [ME *wose* sap, juice, fr. OE *wōs;* akin to OHG *waso* damp] (1587) **1** : a decoction of vegetable material used for tanning leather **2** : the act of oozing **3** : something that oozes

oozy \ˈü-zē\ *adj* **ooz·i·er; -est** (14c) **1** : containing or composed of ooze : resembling ooze **2** : exuding moisture : SLIMY

[1]**op** \ˈäp\ *n* (1964) : OPTICAL ART

[2]**op** *abbr* **1** operation; operative; operator **2** opportunity **3** opus

OP *abbr* **1** observation post **2** out of print

opac·i·ty \ō-ˈpa-sə-tē\ *n, pl* **-ties** [MF *opacité* shadiness, fr. L *opacitat-, opacitas,* fr. *opacus* shaded, dark] (1560) **1 a** : obscurity of sense : UNINTELLIGIBLENESS **b** : the quality or state of being mentally obtuse : DULLNESS **2** : the quality or state of a body that makes it impervious to the rays of light; *broadly* : the relative capacity of matter to obstruct the transmission of radiant energy **3** : an opaque spot in a normally transparent structure (as the lens of the eye)

opah \ˈō-pə, -ˌpä\ *n* [perh. fr. Ibo *úbà*] (1750) : a large elliptical laterally compressed marine bony fish (*Lampris guttatus* of the family Lampridae) with brilliant colors

opal \ˈō-pəl\ *n* [L *opalus,* fr. Gk *opallios,* ultim. fr. Skt *upala* stone, jewel] (ca. 1586) : a usu. amorphous mineral that is a hydrated silica softer and less dense than quartz and typically with definite and often marked iridescent play of colors and is used esp. as a gem

opal·es·cent \ˌō-pə-ˈle-sᵊnt\ *adj* (ca. 1813) : reflecting an iridescent light — **opal·es·cence** \-sᵊn(t)s\ *n* — **opal·es·cent·ly** \-sᵊnt-lē\ *adv*

opal·ine \ˈō-pə-ˌlīn, -ˌlēn\ *adj* (1784) : resembling opal

opaque \ō-ˈpāk\ *adj* [L *opacus*] (1641) **1** : exhibiting opacity : blocking the passage of radiant energy and esp. light **2 a** : hard to understand or explain ⟨∼ prose⟩ **b** : OBTUSE, THICKHEADED — **opaque** *n* — **opaque·ly** *adv* — **opaque·ness** *n*

opaque projector *n* (1951) : a projector using reflected light for projecting an image of an opaque object or matter on an opaque support

op art \ˈäp-\ *n* (1964) : OPTICAL ART — **op artist** *n*

op cit *abbr* [L *opere citato*] in the work cited

ope \ˈōp\ *vb* **oped; op·ing** (15c) *archaic* : OPEN

OPEC *abbr* Organization of Petroleum Exporting Countries

op–ed \ˈäp-ˈed\ *n, often cap O&E, often attrib* [short for *opposite editorial*] (1970) : a page of special features usu. opposite the editorial page of a newspaper; *also* : a feature on such a page

[1]**open** \ˈō-pən, -pᵊm\ *adj* **open·er** \ˈōp-nər, ˈō-pə-\; **open·est** \ˈōp-nəst, ˈō-pə-\ [ME, fr. OE; akin to OHG *offan* open, OE *ūp* up] (bef. 12c) **1** : having no enclosing or confining barrier : accessible on all or nearly all sides ⟨cattle grazing on an ∼ range⟩ **2 a (1)** : being in a position or adjustment to permit passage : not shut or locked ⟨an ∼ door⟩ **(2)** : having a barrier (as a door) so adjusted as to allow passage ⟨the house was ∼⟩ **b** : having the lips parted ⟨stood there with his mouth wide ∼⟩ **c** : not buttoned or zipped ⟨an ∼ shirt⟩ **3 a** : completely free from concealment : exposed to general view or knowledge ⟨their hostilities eventually erupted with ∼ war⟩ **b** : exposed or vulnerable to attack or question : SUBJECT ⟨∼ to doubt⟩ **c** : being an operation or surgical procedure in which an incision is made such that the tissues are fully exposed **4 a** : not covered with a top, roof, or lid ⟨an ∼ car⟩ ⟨her eyes were ∼⟩ **b** : having no protective covering ⟨∼ wiring⟩ ⟨an ∼ wound⟩ **5** : not restricted to a particular group or category of participants ⟨∼ to the public⟩ ⟨∼ housing⟩: as **a** : enterable by both amateur and professional contestants ⟨an ∼ tournament⟩ **b** : enterable by a registered voter regardless of political affiliation ⟨an ∼ primary⟩ **6** : fit to be traveled over : presenting no obstacle to passage or view ⟨the ∼ road⟩ ⟨∼ country⟩ **7** : having the parts or surfaces laid out in an expanded position : spread out : UNFOLDED ⟨an ∼ book⟩ **8 a (1)** : LOW 13 **(2)** : formed with the tongue in a lower position ⟨Italian has an ∼ and a close *e*⟩ **b (1)** : having clarity and resonance unimpaired by undue tension or constriction of the throat ⟨an ∼ vocal tone⟩ **(2)** *of a tone* : produced by an open string or on a wind instrument by the lip without the use of slides, valves, or keys **9 a** : available to follow or make use of ⟨the only course ∼ to us⟩ **b** : not taken up with duties or engagements ⟨keep an hour ∼ on Friday⟩ **c** : not finally decided : subject to further consideration ⟨the salary is ∼⟩ ⟨an ∼ question⟩ **d** : available for a qualified applicant : VACANT ⟨the job is still ∼⟩ **e** : remaining available for use or filling until canceled ⟨an ∼ order for more items⟩ **f** : available for future purchase ⟨these items are in ∼ stock⟩ **g** : available for breeding : not now pregnant ⟨an ∼ heifer⟩ **h** : not proprietary : available to third party developers ⟨∼ source code⟩ **10 a** : characterized by ready accessibility and usu. generous attitude: as **(1)** : generous in giving **(2)** : willing to hear and consider or to accept and deal with : RESPONSIVE **(3)** : free from reserve or pretense : FRANK **b** : accessible to the influx of new factors (as foreign goods) ⟨an ∼ market⟩ **11 a** : having openings, interruptions, or spaces ⟨∼ mesh⟩: as **(1)** : being porous and friable ⟨∼ soil⟩ **(2)** : sparsely distributed : SCATTERED ⟨∼ population⟩ **(3)** *of a compound* : having components separated by a space in writing or printing (as *opaque projector*) **b** : not made up of a continuous closed circuit of channels ⟨the insect circulatory system is ∼⟩ **12 a** *of an organ pipe* : not stopped at the top **b** *of a string on a musical instrument* : not stopped by the finger **13** : being in operation ⟨an ∼ microphone⟩; *esp* : ready for business, patronage, or use ⟨the store is ∼ from 9 to 5⟩ ⟨the new highway will be ∼ next week⟩ **14 a (1)** : characterized by lack of effective regulation of various commercial enterprises ⟨an ∼ town⟩ **(2)** : not repressed by legal controls ⟨∼ gambling⟩ **b** : free from checking or hampering restraints ⟨an ∼ economy⟩ **c** : relatively unguarded by opponents ⟨passed to an ∼ teammate⟩ **15** : having been opened by a first ante, bet, or bid ⟨the bidding is ∼⟩ **16** *of punctuation* : characterized by sparing use esp. of the comma **17 a** : containing none of its endpoints ⟨an ∼ interval⟩ **b** : being a set or composed of sets each point of which has a neighborhood all of whose points are contained in the set ⟨the interior of a sphere is an ∼ set⟩ **18 a** : being an incomplete electrical circuit **b** : not allowing the flow of electricity ⟨an ∼ switch⟩ **19** *of a universe* : having insufficient mass to halt expansion gravitationally ***syn*** see FRANK, LIABLE — **open** *adv* — **open·ly** \ˈō-pən-lē\ *adv* — **open·ness** \-pə(n)-nəs\ *n*

[2]**open** *vb* **opened** \ˈō-pənd, ˈō-pᵊmd\; **open·ing** \ˈōp-niŋ, ˈō-pə-\ *vt* (bef. 12c) **1 a** : to move (as a door) from a closed position **b** : to make available for entry or passage by turning back (as a barrier) or removing (as a cover or an obstruction) **2 a** : to make available for or active in a regular function ⟨∼ a new store⟩ **b** : to make accessible for a particular purpose ⟨∼*ed* new land for settlement⟩ **c** : to initiate access to (a computer file) prior to use **3 a** : to disclose or expose to view : REVEAL **b** : to make more discerning or responsive : ENLIGHTEN ⟨must ∼ our minds to the problems⟩ **c** : to bring into view or come in sight of by changing position **4 a** : to make an opening in ⟨∼*ed* the boil⟩ **b** : to loosen and make less compact ⟨∼ the soil⟩ **5** : to spread out : UNFOLD ⟨∼*ed* the book⟩ **6 a** : to enter upon : BEGIN ⟨∼*ed* the meeting⟩ **b** : to commence action in a card game by making (a first bid), putting a first bet in (the pot), or playing (a card or suit) as first lead **7** : to restore or recall (as an order) from a finally determined state to a state in which the parties are free to prosecute or oppose ∼ *vi* **1** : to become open ⟨the office ∼*ed* early⟩ **2 a** : to spread out : EXPAND ⟨the wound ∼*ed* under the strain⟩ **b** : to become disclosed ⟨a beautiful vista ∼*ed* before us⟩ **3** : to become enlightened or responsive **4** : to give access ⟨the rooms ∼ onto a hall⟩ **5** : SPEAK OUT 2 ⟨finally he ∼*ed* freely on the subject⟩ **6 a** : to begin a course or activity **b** : to make a bet, bid, or lead in commencing a round or hand of a card game **7** : to provide the opening performance of a show before the main event — **open·abil·i·ty** \ˌōp-nə-ˈbi-lə-tē, ˌō-pə-\ *n* — **open·able** \ˈōp-nə-bəl, ˈō-pə-\ *adj*

[3]**open** *n* (13c) **1** : OPENING **2** : open and unobstructed space: as **a** : OPEN AIR **b** : open water **3** : an open contest, competition, or tournament **4** : a public or unconcealed state or position

open admission *n* (1969) : OPEN ENROLLMENT 2

open adoption *n* (1973) : an adoption that involves contact between biological and adoptive parents and sometimes between biological parents and the adopted child

open–air *adj* (1830) : OUTDOOR

open air *n* (15c) : the space where air is unconfined; *esp* : OUTDOORS

open–and–shut *adj* (1841) **1** : perfectly simple : OBVIOUS **2** : easily settled ⟨an ∼ case of grand larceny⟩

open arms *n pl* (1735) : an eager or warm welcome ⟨greeted them with *open arms*⟩

open bar *n* (1960) : a bar (as at a wedding reception) at which drinks are served free — compare CASH BAR

open·cast \ˈō-pən-ˌkast\ *adj* (1713) *chiefly Brit* : worked from a surface open to the air ⟨an ∼ mine⟩ ⟨∼ mining⟩

open chain *n* (1880) : an arrangement of atoms represented in a structural formula by a chain whose ends are not joined so as to form a ring

open city *n* (1914) : a city that is not occupied or defended by military forces and that is not allowed to be bombed under international law

open dating *n* (1971) : the marking of perishable food products with a clearly readable date indicating when the food was packaged or the last date on which it should be sold or used

open door *n* (1526) **1** : a recognized right of admittance : freedom of access; *also* : a policy providing such freedom **2** : a policy giving opportunity for commercial relations with a country to all nations on equal terms — **open–door** *adj*

open–end *adj* (1917) **:** organized to allow for contingencies: as **a :** permitting additional debt to be incurred under the original indenture subject to specified conditions ⟨an ~ mortgage⟩ **b :** having a fluctuating capitalization of shares that are issued or redeemed at the current net asset value or at a figure in fixed ratio to this ⟨an ~ investment company⟩ — compare CLOSED-END

open–end·ed \ˌō-pən-ˈen-dəd\ *adj* (1825) **:** not rigorously fixed: as **a :** adaptable to the developing needs of a situation **b :** permitting or designed to permit spontaneous and unguided responses — **open–end·ed·ness** *n*

open enrollment *n* (1964) **1 :** the voluntary enrollment of a student in a public school other than the one assigned on the basis of residence **2 :** enrollment on demand as a student in an institution of higher learning irrespective of formal qualifications

open·er \ˈōp-nər, ˈō-pə-\ *n* (15c) **:** one that opens ⟨a bottle ~⟩: as **a** *pl* **:** cards of sufficient value for a player to open the betting in a poker game **b :** the first item, contest, or event of a series — **for openers :** to begin with

open–eyed \ˌō-pən-ˈīd\ *adj* (1601) **1 :** having the eyes open **2 :** carefully observant **:** DISCERNING

open–faced \-ˈfāst\ *also* **open–face** \-ˈfās\ *adj* (1918) **:** served without a covering layer (as of bread or pastry) ⟨an ~ sandwich⟩

open·hand·ed \-ˈhan-dəd\ *adj* (1593) **:** GENEROUS, MUNIFICENT — **open·hand·ed·ly** *adv* — **open·hand·ed·ness** *n*

open–heart *adj* (1960) **:** of, relating to, or performed on a heart temporarily stopped and relieved of circulatory function and surgically opened for repair of defects or damage ⟨~ surgery⟩

open·heart·ed \ˌō-pən-ˈhär-təd\ *adj* (1611) **1 :** candidly straightforward **:** FRANK **2 :** responsive to emotional appeal — **open·heart·ed·ly** *adv* — **open·heart·ed·ness** *n*

open–hearth *adj* (1881) **:** of, relating to, involving, or produced in the open-hearth process ⟨~ steel⟩

open–hearth process *n* (1882) **:** a process of making steel from pig iron in a reverberatory furnace equipped with a regenerator

open house *n* (15c) **1 :** ready and usu. informal hospitality or entertainment for all comers **2 :** a house or apartment open for inspection esp. by prospective buyers or tenants

open·ing \ˈōp-niŋ, ˈō-pə-\ *n* (13c) **1 a :** an act or instance of making or becoming open **b :** an act or instance of beginning **:** COMMENCEMENT; *esp* **:** a formal and usu. public event by which something new is put officially into operation **2 :** something that is open: as **a** (1) **:** BREACH, APERTURE (2) **:** an open width **:** SPAN **b :** an area without trees or with scattered usu. mature trees that occurs as a break in a forest **c :** two pages that face one another in a book **3 :** something that constitutes a beginning: as **a :** a usu. planned series of moves made at the beginning of a game of chess or checkers — compare ENDGAME, MIDDLE GAME **b :** a first performance **4 a :** OCCASION, CHANCE **b :** an opportunity for employment

open–label *adj* (1979) **:** being or relating to a clinical trial in which the treatment given to each subject is not concealed from either the experimenters or the subject ⟨an ~ multicenter study⟩ — compare DOUBLE-BLIND, SINGLE-BLIND

open letter *n* (1878) **:** a published letter of protest or appeal usu. addressed to an individual but intended for the general public

open loop *n* (1947) **:** a control system for an operation or process in which there is no self-correcting action as there is in a closed loop

open marriage *n* (1971) **:** a marriage in which the partners agree to let each other have sexual partners outside the marriage

open mike *n* (1978) **:** an event in which amateurs may perform (as at a coffeehouse) usu. without auditioning first

open–mind·ed \ˌō-pən-ˈmīn-dəd\ *adj* (1828) **:** receptive to arguments or ideas — **open–mind·ed·ly** *adv* — **open–mind·ed·ness** *n*

open·mouthed \ˌō-pən-ˈmau̇t͟hd, -ˈmau̇tht\ *adj* (15c) **1 :** CLAMOROUS, VOCIFEROUS **2 :** having the mouth wide open **3 :** struck with amazement or wonder — **open·mouth·ed·ly** \-ˈmau̇-t͟həd-lē, -thəd-\ *adv* — **open·mouth·ed·ness** \-ˈmau̇-t͟həd-nəs, -thəd-\ *n*

open–pol·li·nat·ed \ˌō-pən-ˈpä-lə-ˌnā-təd\ *adj* (1925) **:** pollinated by natural agencies (as wind or insects) without human intervention

open season *n* (ca. 1890) **1 :** a period when it is legal to kill or catch game or fish protected at other times by law **2 :** a time during which someone or something is the object of sustained attack or criticism

open secret *n* (1828) **:** a supposedly secret but generally known matter

open sentence *n* (1937) **:** a statement (as in mathematics) that contains at least one blank or unknown and that becomes true or false when the blank is filled or a quantity is substituted for the unknown

open ses·a·me \-ˈse-sə-mē\ *n* [fr. *open sesame,* the magical command used by Ali Baba to open the door of the robbers' den in *Ali Baba and the Forty Thieves*] (ca. 1837) **:** something that unfailingly brings about a desired end

open shop *n* (1903) **:** an establishment in which eligibility for employment and retention on the payroll are not determined by membership or nonmembership in a labor union though there may be an agreement by which a union is recognized as sole bargaining agent

open sight *n* (1591) **:** a firearm rear sight having an open notch

open stance *n* (1948) **:** a stance (as in golf) in which the forward foot is farther from the line of play than the back foot — compare CLOSED STANCE

open syllable *n* (1891) **:** a syllable ended by a vowel or diphthong

open up *vt* (1582) **1 :** to make available **2 :** to make plain or visible **:** DISCLOSE **3 :** to open by cutting into ~ *vi* **1 :** to spread out or come into view ⟨the road *opens up* ahead⟩ **2 :** to commence firing **3 :** to become communicative ⟨tried to get the patient to *open up*⟩

open·work \ˈō-pən-ˌwərk\ *n, often attrib* (1598) **:** work constructed so as to show openings through its substance **:** work that is perforated or pierced ⟨wrought-iron ~⟩ — **open–worked** \-ˌwərkt\ *adj*

[1]**opera** *pl of* OPUS

[2]**op·era** \ˈä-p(ə-)rə, *Southern also* ˈä-prē\ *n* [It, work, opera, fr. L, work, pains; akin to L *oper-, opus* — more at OPERATE] (1644) **1 :** a drama set to music and made up of vocal pieces with orchestral accompaniment and orchestral overtures and interludes; *specif* **:** GRAND OPERA **2 :** the score of a musical drama **3 :** the performance of an opera; *also* **:** a house where operas are performed

op·er·a·ble \ˈä-p(ə-)rə-bəl\ *adj* (1646) **1 :** fit, possible, or desirable to use **:** PRACTICABLE **2 :** likely to result in a favorable outcome upon surgical treatment ⟨an ~ cancer⟩ — **op·er·a·bil·i·ty** \ˌä-p(ə-)rə-ˈbi-lə-tē\ *n* — **op·er·a·bly** \ˈä-pə-rə-blē\ *adv*

op·éra bouffe \ˈō-pā-rä-ˈbüf, ˈä-p(ə-)rə-\ *n* [F, fr. It *opera buffa*] (1870) **:** satirical comic opera

opera buf·fa \-ˈbü-fə\ *n* [It, lit., comic opera] (1770) **:** an 18th century farcical comic opera with dialogue in recitative

opéra co·mique \-kä-ˈmēk, -kō-\ *n* [F, lit., comic opera] (1744) **:** an opera characterized by spoken dialogue interspersed between the arias and ensemble numbers — compare GRAND OPERA

opera glass *n* (1738) **:** a small low-power binocular without prisms for use at the opera or theater — often used in pl.

op·era·go·er \ˈä-p(ə-)rə-ˌgō-ər\ *n* (1850) **:** a person who frequently goes to operas — **op·era·go·ing** \-ˌgō-iŋ, -ˌgȯ(-)iŋ\ *n*

opera hat *n* (1810) **:** a man's collapsible top hat

opera house *n* (1720) **:** a theater devoted principally to the performance of operas; *broadly* **:** THEATER

op·er·and \ˌä-pə-ˈrand\ *n* [L *operandum,* neut. of gerundive of *operari*] (1853) **:** something (as a quantity or data) that is operated on (as in a mathematical operation); *also* **:** the address in a computer instruction of data to be operated on

[1]**op·er·ant** \ˈä-pə-rənt\ *adj* (15c) **1 :** functioning or tending to produce effects **:** EFFECTIVE ⟨an ~ conscience⟩ **2 :** of or relating to the observable or measurable **3 :** of, relating to, or being an operant or operant conditioning ⟨~ behavior⟩ — **op·er·ant·ly** *adv*

[2]**operant** *n* (1937) **:** behavior (as bar pressing by a rat to obtain food) that operates on the environment to produce rewarding and reinforcing effects

operant conditioning *n* (1941) **:** conditioning in which the desired behavior or increasingly closer approximations to it are followed by a rewarding or reinforcing stimulus — compare CLASSICAL CONDITIONING

opera se·ria \-ˈser-ē-ə, -ˈsir-\ *n* [It, lit., serious opera] (ca. 1854) **:** an 18th century opera with a heroic or legendary subject

op·er·ate \ˈä-pə-ˌrāt, ˈä-ˌprāt\ *vb* **-at·ed; -at·ing** [L *operatus,* pp. of *operari* to work, fr. *oper-, opus* work; akin to OE *efnan* to perform, Skt *apas* work] *vi* (1588) **1 :** to perform a function **:** exert power or influence ⟨factors *operating* against our success⟩ **2 :** to produce an appropriate effect ⟨the drug *operated* quickly⟩ **3 a :** to perform an operation or a series of operations **b :** to perform surgery **c :** to carry on a military or naval action or mission **4 :** to follow a course of conduct that is often irregular ⟨crooked gamblers *operating* in the club⟩ ~ *vt* **1 :** BRING ABOUT, EFFECT **2 a :** to cause to function **:** WORK **b :** to put or keep in operation **3 :** to perform an operation on; *esp* **:** to perform surgery on

op·er·at·ic \ˌä-pə-ˈra-tik\ *adj* (1749) **1 :** of or relating to opera **2 :** grand, dramatic, or romantic in style or effect — **op·er·at·i·cal·ly** \-ti-k(ə-)lē\ *adv*

operating *adj* (1808) **:** of, relating to, or used for or in operations ⟨~ expenses⟩ ⟨a hospital ~ room⟩

operating system *n* (1961) **:** software that controls the operation of a computer and directs the processing of programs (as by assigning storage space in memory and controlling input and output functions)

op·er·a·tion \ˌä-pə-ˈrā-shən\ *n* [ME *operacioun,* fr. MF *operation,* fr. L *operation-, operatio,* fr. *operari*] (14c) **1 :** performance of a practical work or of something involving the practical application of principles or processes **2 a :** an exertion of power or influence ⟨the ~ of a drug⟩ **b :** the quality or state of being functional or operative ⟨the plant is now in ~⟩ **c :** a method or manner of functioning ⟨a machine of very simple ~⟩ **3 :** EFFICACY, POTENCY — archaic except in legal usage **4 :** a procedure performed on a living body usu. with instruments esp. for the repair of damage or the restoration of health **5 :** any of various mathematical or logical processes (as addition) of deriving one entity from others according to a rule **6 a :** a usu. military action, mission, or maneuver including its planning and execution **b** *pl* **:** the office on the flight line of an airfield where pilots file clearance for flights and where flying from the field is controlled **c** *pl* **:** the agency of an organization charged with carrying on the principal planning and operating functions of a headquarters and its subordinate units **7 :** a business transaction esp. when speculative **8 :** a single step performed by a computer in the execution of a program **9 :** a usu. small business or establishment ⟨ran a struggling ~⟩

op·er·a·tion·al \-shnəl, -shə-nᵊl\ *adj* (ca. 1909) **1 :** of or relating to operation or to an operation ⟨the ~ gap between planning and production⟩ **2 :** of, relating to, or based on operations **3 a :** of, engaged in, or connected with execution of military or naval operations in campaign or battle **b :** ready for or in condition to undertake a destined function — **op·er·a·tion·al·ly** *adv*

op·er·a·tion·al·ism \-shnə-ˌli-zəm, -shə-nə-ˌli-zəm\ *n* (1931) **:** a view that the concepts or terms used in nonanalytic scientific statements must be definable in terms of identifiable and repeatable operations — **op·er·a·tion·al·ist** \-list, -ist\ *n* — **op·er·a·tion·al·is·tic** \-ˌrā-shnə-ˈlis-tik, -shə-nə-ˈlis-tik\ *adj*

op·er·a·tion·ism \ˌä-pə-ˈrā-shə-ˌni-zəm\ *n* (1935) **:** OPERATIONALISM — **op·er·a·tion·ist** \-sh(ə-)nist\ *n*

operations research *n* (1945) **:** the application of scientific and esp. mathematical methods to the study and analysis of problems involving complex systems — called also *operational research*

[1]**op·er·a·tive** \ˈä-p(ə-)rə-tiv, ˈä-pə-ˌrā-\ *adj* (15c) **1 a :** producing an appropriate effect **:** EFFICACIOUS **b :** most significant or essential ⟨the ~ word in a phrase⟩ **2 :** exerting force or influence **:** OPERATING **3 a :** having to do with physical operations (as of machines) **b :** WORKING ⟨an ~ craftsman⟩ **4 :** based on or consisting of an operation ⟨~ dentistry⟩ — **op·er·a·tive·ly** *adv* — **op·er·a·tive·ness** *n*

[2]**operative** *n* (ca. 1810) **:** OPERATOR: as **a :** ARTISAN, MECHANIC **b :** a secret agent **c :** PRIVATE DETECTIVE **d :** a person who works toward achieving the objectives of a larger interest ⟨political ~s⟩

\ə\ **abut** \ᵊ\ **kitten, F table** \ər\ **further** \a\ **ash** \ā\ **ace** \ä\ **mop, mar** \au̇\ **out** \ch\ **chin** \e\ **bet** \ē\ **easy** \g\ **go** \i\ **hit** \ī\ **ice** \j\ **job** \ŋ\ **sing** \ō\ **go** \ȯ\ **law** \ȯi\ **boy** \th\ **thin** \t͟h\ **the** \ü\ **loot** \u̇\ **foot** \y\ **yet** \zh\ **vision, beige** \ḵ, ⁿ, œ, ue, ʸ\ *see* Guide to Pronunciation

op·er·a·tor \'ä-pə-,rā-tər, 'ä-,prā-\ *n* (1611) **1 :** one that operates: as **a :** one that operates a machine or device **b :** one that operates a business **c :** one that performs surgical operations **d :** one that deals in stocks or commodities **2 a :** MOUNTEBANK, FRAUD **b :** a shrewd and skillful person who knows how to circumvent restrictions or difficulties **3 a :** something and esp. a symbol that denotes or performs a mathematical or logical operation **b :** a mathematical function **4 :** a binding site in a DNA chain at which a genetic repressor binds to inhibit the initiation of transcription of messenger RNA by one or more nearby structural genes — called also *operator gene*; compare OPERON — **op·er·a·tor·less** *adj*

[1]**oper·cu·lar** \ō-'pər-kyə-lər\ *adj* (1830) **:** of, relating to, or constituting an operculum

[2]**opercular** *n* (ca. 1890) **:** an opercular part (as a bone or scale)

oper·cu·late \ō-'pər-kyə-lət\ *also* **oper·cu·lat·ed** \-,lā-təd\ *adj* (ca. 1775) **:** having an operculum

oper·cu·lum \ō-'pər-kyə-ləm\ *n, pl* **-la** \-lə\ *also* **-lums** [NL, fr. L, cover, fr. *operire* to shut, cover] (1681) **1 :** a body process or part that suggests a lid: as **a :** a horny or shelly plate on the posterior dorsal surface of the foot in many gastropod mollusks that closes the shell when the animal is retracted **b :** the covering of the gills of a fish — see FISH illustration **2 :** a lid or covering flap (as of a moss capsule)

op·er·et·ta \,ä-pə-'re-tə\ *n* [It, dim. of *opera*] (1770) **:** a usu. romantic comic opera that includes songs and dancing — **op·er·et·tist** \-'re-tist\ *n*

op·er·on \'ä-pə-,rän\ *n* [F *opéron,* fr. *opérer* to bring about, effect (fr. L *operari*) + *-on* [2]-on] (1961) **:** a group of closely linked genes that produces a single messenger RNA molecule in transcription and that consists of structural genes and regulating elements (as an operator and promoter)

op·er·ose \'ä-pə-,rōs\ *adj* [L *operosus,* fr. *oper-, opus* work — more at OPERATE] (1662) **:** TEDIOUS, WEARISOME — **op·er·ose·ly** *adv* — **op·er·ose·ness** *n*

Ophe·lia \ō-'fēl-yə\ *n* (ca. 1601) **:** the daughter of Polonius in Shakespeare's *Hamlet*

ophid·i·an \ō-'fi-dē-ən\ *adj* [ultim. fr. Gk *ophis*] (1883) **:** of, relating to, or resembling snakes — **ophidian** *n*

Ophir \'ō-fər\ *n* [Heb *Ōphīr*] (14c) **:** a biblical land of uncertain location but reputedly rich in gold

ophit·ic \ä-'fi-tik, ō-\ *adj* [*ophite* serpentine (stone), fr. L *ophites,* fr. Gk *ophitēs* (*lithos*), fr. *ophitēs* snakelike, fr. *ophis* snake; akin to Skt *ahi* snake and prob. to L *anguis* snake, *anguilla* eel, Gk *enchelys* eel, *echidna* viper, *echinos* hedgehog, OE *igil*] (1875) **:** having or being a rock fabric in which lath-shaped plagioclase crystals are enclosed in later formed augite

ophi·u·roid \,ō-fē-'yu̇r-,ȯid, ,ä-\ *n* [NL *Ophiuroidea,* group name, fr. *Ophiura,* genus name, fr. Gk *ophis* + *oura* tail — more at ASS] (ca. 1879) **:** BRITTLE STAR — **ophiuroid** *adj*

ophthalm- *or* **ophthalmo-** *comb form* [Gk, fr. *ophthalmos*] **:** eye ⟨*ophthalmo*logy⟩

oph·thal·mia \äf-'thal-mē-ə, äp-\ *n* [ME *obtalmia,* fr. LL *ophthalmia,* fr. Gk, fr. *ophthalmos* eye; akin to Gk *ōps* eye — more at EYE] (14c) **:** inflammation of the conjunctiva or the eyeball

oph·thal·mic \-mik\ *adj* (ca. 1741) **1 :** of, relating to, or situated near the eye **2 :** supplying or draining the eye or structures in the region of the eye ⟨~ artery⟩

oph·thal·mol·o·gist \,äf-thə(l)-'mä-lə-jist, ,äp-, -,thal-\ *n* (1834) **:** a physician who specializes in ophthalmology — compare OPTICIAN, OPTOMETRIST

oph·thal·mol·o·gy \-'mä-lə-jē\ *n* (ca. 1842) **:** a branch of medical science dealing with the structure, functions, and diseases of the eye — **oph·thal·mo·log·ic** \-mə-'lä-jik\ *or* **oph·thal·mo·log·i·cal** \-ji-kəl\ *adj* — **oph·thal·mo·log·i·cal·ly** \-ji-k(ə-)lē\ *adv*

oph·thal·mo·scope \äf-'thal-mə-,skōp, äp-\ *n* [ISV] (ca. 1857) **:** an instrument for use in viewing the interior of the eye and esp. the retina — **oph·thal·mo·scop·ic** \(,)äf-,thal-mə-'skä-pik, (,)äp-\ *adj* — **oph·thal·mos·co·py** \,äf-thəl-'mäs-kə-pē, ,äp-, -,thal-\ *n*

-opia *n comb form* [NL, fr. Gk *-ōpia,* fr. *ōps*] **1 :** condition of having (such) vision ⟨diplo*pia*⟩ **2 :** condition of having (such) a visual defect ⟨hyper*opia*⟩

[1]**opi·ate** \'ō-pē-ət, -,āt\ *n* (15c) **1 a :** a drug (as morphine or codeine) containing or derived from opium and tending to induce sleep and alleviate pain; *broadly* **:** NARCOTIC 1a **b :** OPIOID 1 **2 :** something that induces rest or inaction or quiets uneasiness

[2]**opiate** *adj* (1543) **1 a :** containing or mixed with opium **b :** of, relating to, binding, or being an opiate ⟨~ receptors⟩ **2 a :** inducing sleep **:** NARCOTIC **b :** causing dullness or inaction

opine \ō-'pīn\ *vb* **opined; opin·ing** [ME, fr. MF & L; MF *opiner,* fr. L *opinari* to have an opinion] *vi* (15c) **:** to express opinions ~ *vt* **:** to state as an opinion

opin·ion \ə-'pin-yən\ *n* [ME, fr. AF, fr. L *opinion-, opinio,* fr. *opinari*] (14c) **1 a :** a view, judgment, or appraisal formed in the mind about a particular matter **b :** APPROVAL, ESTEEM **2 a :** belief stronger than impression and less strong than positive knowledge **b :** a generally held view **3 a :** a formal expression of judgment or advice by an expert **b :** the formal expression (as by a judge, court, or referee) of the legal reasons and principles upon which a legal decision is based — **opin·ioned** \-yənd\ *adj*

syn OPINION, VIEW, BELIEF, CONVICTION, PERSUASION, SENTIMENT mean a judgment one holds as true. OPINION implies a conclusion thought out yet open to dispute ⟨each expert seemed to have a different *opinion*⟩. VIEW suggests a subjective opinion ⟨very assertive in stating his *views*⟩. BELIEF implies often deliberate acceptance and intellectual assent ⟨a firm *belief* in her party's platform⟩. CONVICTION applies to a firmly and seriously held belief ⟨the *conviction* that animal life is as sacred as human⟩. PERSUASION suggests a belief grounded on assurance (as by evidence) of its truth ⟨was of the *persuasion* that everything changes⟩. SENTIMENT suggests a settled opinion reflective of one's feelings ⟨her feminist *sentiments* are well-known⟩.

opin·ion·at·ed \-yə-,nā-təd\ *adj* (1601) **:** unduly adhering to one's own opinion or to preconceived notions — **opin·ion·at·ed·ly** *adv* — **opin·ion·at·ed·ness** *n*

opin·ion·a·tive \-,nā-tiv\ *adj* (1536) **1 :** of, relating to, or consisting of opinion **:** DOCTRINAL **2 :** OPINIONATED — **opin·ion·a·tive·ly** *adv* — **opin·ion·a·tive·ness** *n*

[1]**opi·oid** \'ō-pē-,ȯid\ *adj* (1967) **1 :** possessing some properties characteristic of opiate narcotics but not derived from opium **2 :** of, involving, or induced by an opioid

[2]**opioid** *n* (1967) **1 :** any of a group of endogenous neural polypeptides (as an endorphin or enkephalin) that bind esp. to opiate receptors and mimic some of the pharmacological properties of opiates — called also *opioid peptide* **2 :** a synthetic drug possessing narcotic properties similar to opiates but not derived from opium; *broadly* **:** OPIATE 1a

opis·tho·branch \ə-'pis-thə-,braŋk\ *n, pl* **-branchs** [NL *Opisthobranchia,* fr. Gk *opisthen* behind (akin to Gk *epi* on) + *branchia* gills — more at EPI-] (ca. 1856) **:** any of a subclass (Opisthobranchia) of marine gastropod mollusks that have the gills when present posterior to the heart and often lack a shell — **opisthobranch** *adj*

opi·um \'ō-pē-əm\ *n* [ME, fr. L, fr. Gk *opion,* fr. dim. of *opos* sap] (14c) **1 :** a bitter brownish addictive narcotic drug that consists of the dried latex obtained from immature seed capsules of the opium poppy **2 :** something having an effect like that of opium

opium poppy *n* (1863) **:** an annual Eurasian poppy (*Papaver somniferum*) cultivated since antiquity as the source of opium, for its edible oily seeds, or for its showy flowers

opos·sum \(ə-)'pä-səm\ *n, pl* **opossums** *also* **opossum** [earlier *apossoun, opassom,* Virginia Algonquian, fr. Algonquian **wa·p-* white + **-a?θemw-* dog] (1610) **1 :** any of a family (Didelphidae) of American marsupials that usu. have a pointed snout and prehensile tail; *esp* **:** a common omnivorous largely nocturnal mammal (*Didelphis virginiana*) of No. America that has grayish to blackish fur with white on the cheeks and is an expert climber **2 :** any of several Australian phalangers

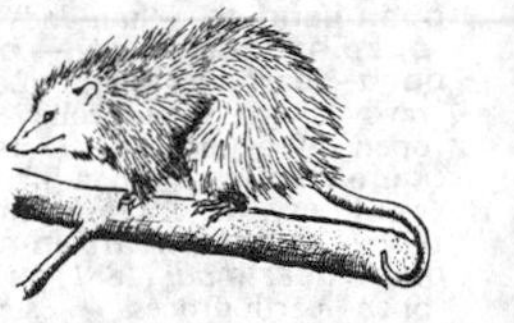
opossum 1

opp *abbr* opposite

[1]**op·po·nent** \ə-'pō-nənt\ *n* [L *opponent-, opponens,* prp. of *opponere*] (1560) **1 :** one that takes an opposite position (as in a debate, contest, or conflict) **2 :** a muscle that opposes or counteracts and limits the action of another

[2]**opponent** *adj* (1647) **1 :** ANTAGONISTIC, OPPOSING **2 :** situated in front

op·por·tune \,ä-pər-'tün, -'tyün\ *adj* [ME, fr. MF *opportun,* fr. L *opportunus,* fr. *ob-* toward + *portus* port, harbor — more at OB-, FORD] (15c) **1 :** suitable or convenient for a particular occurrence ⟨an ~ moment⟩ **2 :** occurring at an appropriate time ⟨an ~ offer of assistance⟩ — **op·por·tune·ly** *adv* — **op·por·tune·ness** \-'t(y)ün-nəs\ *n*

op·por·tun·ism \-'tü-,ni-zəm, -'tyü-\ *n* (1870) **:** the art, policy, or practice of taking advantage of opportunities or circumstances often with little regard for principles or consequences

op·por·tun·ist \-'tü-nist, -'tyü-\ *n* (1879) **:** one that is opportunistic or that practices opportunism — **opportunist** *adj*

op·por·tu·nis·tic \-tü-'nis-tik, -tyü-\ *adj* (1892) **:** taking advantage of opportunities as they arise: as **a :** exploiting opportunities with little regard to principle or consequences ⟨a politician considered ~⟩ **b :** feeding on whatever food is available ⟨~ feeders⟩ **c :** being or caused by a usu. harmless microorganism that can become pathogenic when the host's resistance is impaired ⟨~ infections⟩ — **op·por·tu·nis·ti·cal·ly** \-ti-k(ə-)lē\ *adv*

op·por·tu·ni·ty \,ä-pər-'tü-nə-tē, -'tyü-\ *n, pl* **-ties** (14c) **1 :** a favorable juncture of circumstances ⟨the halt provided an ~ for rest and refreshment⟩ **2 :** a good chance for advancement or progress

opportunity cost *n* (1911) **:** the added cost of using resources (as for production or speculative investment) that is the difference between the actual value resulting from such use and that of an alternative (as another use of the same resources or an investment of equal risk but greater return)

op·pos·able \ə-'pō-zə-bəl\ *adj* (ca. 1812) **1 :** capable of being opposed or resisted **2 :** capable of being placed against one or more of the remaining digits of a hand or foot ⟨the ~ human thumb⟩ — **op·pos·abil·i·ty** \-,pō-zə-'bi-lə-tē\ *n*

op·pose \ə-'pōz\ *vt* **op·posed; op·pos·ing** [F *opposer,* fr. L *opponere* (perf. indic. *opposui*), fr. *ob-* against + *ponere* to place — more at OB-, POSITION] (1579) **1 :** to place over against something so as to provide resistance, counterbalance, or contrast **2 :** to place opposite or against something **3 :** to offer resistance to — **op·pos·er** *n*

syn OPPOSE, COMBAT, RESIST, WITHSTAND mean to set oneself against someone or something. OPPOSE can apply to any conflict, from mere objection to bitter hostility or warfare ⟨*opposed* the plan⟩. COMBAT stresses the forceful or urgent countering of something ⟨*combat* disease⟩. RESIST implies an overt recognition of a hostile or threatening force and a positive effort to counteract or repel it ⟨*resisting* temptation⟩. WITHSTAND suggests a more passive resistance ⟨trying to *withstand* peer pressure⟩.

op·posed \-'pōzd\ *adj* (15c) **:** set or placed in opposition **:** CONTRARY ⟨with politicians, as ~ to soap, you cannot return what you have bought —Felix G. Rohatyn⟩

op·pose·less \ə-'pōz-ləs\ *adj* (1605) *archaic* **:** IRRESISTIBLE

[1]**op·po·site** \'ä-pə-zət, 'äp-sət\ *adj* [ME, fr. MF, fr. L *oppositus,* pp. of *opponere*] (14c) **1 a :** set over against something that is at the other end or side of an intervening line or space ⟨~ interior angles⟩ ⟨~ ends of a diameter⟩ **b :** situated in pairs on an axis with each member being separated from the other by half the circumference of the axis ⟨~ leaves⟩ — compare ALTERNATE **2 a :** occupying an opposing and often antagonistic position ⟨~ sides of the question⟩ **b :** diametrically different (as in nature or character) ⟨~ meanings⟩ **3 :** contrary to one another or to a thing specified **:** REVERSE ⟨gave them ~ directions⟩ **4 :** being the other of a pair that are corresponding or complementary in position, function, or nature ⟨members of the ~ sex⟩ **5 :** of, relating to, or being the side of a baseball field that is near the first base line for a right-handed batter and near the third base line for a left-handed batter — **op·po·site·ly** *adv* — **op·po·site·ness** *n*

syn OPPOSITE, CONTRADICTORY, CONTRARY, ANTITHETICAL mean being so far apart as to be or seem irreconcilable. OPPOSITE applies to things in sharp contrast or in conflict ⟨*opposite* views on foreign aid⟩. CONTRADICTORY applies to two things that completely negate each other so that if one is true or valid the other must be untrue or invalid ⟨made *contradictory* predictions about whether the market would rise or fall⟩. CONTRARY implies extreme divergence or diametrical opposition ⟨*contrary* assessments of the war situation⟩. ANTITHETICAL stresses clear and unequivocal diametrical opposition ⟨a law that is *antithetical* to the very idea of democracy⟩.

[2]**opposite** *n* (15c) **1 :** something that is opposed to some other often specified thing **2 :** ANTONYM **3 :** ADDITIVE INVERSE; *esp* **:** the additive inverse of a real number

[3]**opposite** *adv* (1667) **:** on or to an opposite side

[4]**opposite** *prep* (1758) **1 :** across from and usu. facing or on the same level with ⟨sat ∼ each other⟩ **2 :** in a role complementary to ⟨played ∼ the leading man in the comedy⟩

opposite number *n* (1906) **:** a member of a system or class who holds relatively the same position as a particular member in a corresponding system or class **:** COUNTERPART

op·po·si·tion \ˌä-pə-ˈzi-shən\ *n* (14c) **1 :** a configuration in which one celestial body is opposite another (as the sun) in the sky or in which the elongation is near or equal to 180 degrees **2 :** the relation between two propositions having the same subject and predicate but differing in quantity or quality or both **3 :** an act of setting opposite or over against **:** the condition of being so set **4 :** hostile or contrary action or condition **5 a :** something that opposes; *specif* **:** a body of persons opposing something **b** *often cap* **:** a political party opposing and prepared to replace the party in power — **op·po·si·tion·al** \-ˈzish-nəl, -ˈzi-shə-nᵊl\ *adj*

op·po·si·tion·ist \-ˈzi-sh(ə-)nist\ *n* (1773) **:** a member of an opposition — **oppositionist** *adj*

op·press \ə-ˈpres\ *vt* [ME, fr. AF *oppresser,* fr. L *oppressus,* pp. of *opprimere,* fr. *ob-* against + *premere* to press — more at OB-, PRESS] (14c) **1 a** *archaic* **:** SUPPRESS **b :** to crush or burden by abuse of power or authority **2 :** to burden spiritually or mentally **:** weigh heavily upon ***syn*** see WRONG — **op·pres·sor** \-ˈpre-sər\ *n*

op·pres·sion \ə-ˈpre-shən\ *n* (14c) **1 a :** unjust or cruel exercise of authority or power **b :** something that oppresses esp. in being an unjust or excessive exercise of power **2 :** a sense of being weighed down in body or mind **:** DEPRESSION

op·pres·sive \ə-ˈpre-siv\ *adj* (ca. 1677) **1 :** unreasonably burdensome or severe ⟨∼ legislation⟩ **2 :** TYRANNICAL **3 :** overwhelming or depressing to the spirit or senses ⟨an ∼ climate⟩ ***syn*** see ONEROUS — **op·pres·sive·ly** *adv* — **op·pres·sive·ness** *n*

op·pro·bri·ous \ə-ˈprō-brē-əs\ *adj* (14c) **1 :** expressive of opprobrium **:** SCURRILOUS ⟨∼ language⟩ **2 :** deserving of opprobrium **:** INFAMOUS — **op·pro·bri·ous·ly** *adv* — **op·pro·bri·ous·ness** *n*

op·pro·bri·um \-brē-əm\ *n* [L, fr. *opprobrare* to reproach, fr. *ob* in the way of + *probrum* reproach; akin to L *pro* forward and to L *ferre* to carry, bring — more at OB-, FOR, BEAR] (1656) **1 :** something that brings disgrace **2 a :** public disgrace or ill fame that follows from conduct considered grossly wrong or vicious **b :** CONTEMPT, REPROACH

op·pugn \ə-ˈpyün, ä-\ *vt* [ME, fr. L *oppugnare,* fr. *ob-* against + *pugnare* to fight — more at OB-, PUNGENT] (15c) **1 :** to fight against **2 :** to call in question — **op·pugn·er** *n*

Ops \ˈäps\ *n* [L] (14c) **:** the Roman goddess of abundance and the wife of Saturn

op·sin \ˈäp-sən\ *n* [prob. fr. *rhodopsin*] (1951) **:** any of various colorless proteins that in combination with retinal or a related prosthetic group form a visual pigment (as rhodopsin) in a reaction reversible by light

-opsis *n comb form, pl* **-opses** *or* **-opsides** [NL, fr. Gk, fr. *opsis* appearance, vision] **:** structure resembling a (specified) thing ⟨cary*opsis*⟩

op·son·ic \äp-ˈsä-nik\ *adj* (1903) **:** of, relating to, or involving opsonin

op·so·nin \ˈäp-sə-nən\ *n* [L *opsonare* to buy provisions, cater (fr. Gk *opsōnein*) + E [1]-*in* — more at OLIGOPSONY] (1903) **:** any of various proteins (as antibodies or complement) that bind to foreign particles and cells (as bacteria) making them more susceptible to the action of phagocytes

-opsy *n comb form* [Gk *-opsia,* fr. *opsis*] **:** examination ⟨necr*opsy*⟩

[1]**opt** \ˈäpt\ *vi* [F *opter,* fr. L *optare*] (1877) **:** to make a choice; *esp* **:** to decide in favor of something ⟨∼*ed* for a tax increase —Tom Wicker⟩

[2]**opt** *abbr* **1** optical; optician; optics **2** option; optional

op·ta·tive \ˈäp-tə-tiv\ *adj* (15c) **1 a :** of, relating to, or constituting a verbal mood that is expressive of wish or desire **b :** of, relating to, or constituting a sentence that is expressive of wish or hope **2 :** expressing desire or wish — **optative** *n* — **op·ta·tive·ly** *adv*

[1]**op·tic** \ˈäp-tik\ *adj* [ME, fr. ML *opticus,* fr. Gk *optikos,* fr. *opsesthai* to be going to see; akin to Gk *opsis* appearance, *ōps* eye — more at EYE] (14c) **:** of or relating to vision or the eye

[2]**optic** *n* (1600) **1 :** EYE **2 a :** any of the elements (as lenses, mirrors, or light guides) of an optical instrument or system — usu. used in pl. **b :** an optical instrument

op·ti·cal \ˈäp-ti-kəl\ *adj* (1570) **1 :** of or relating to the science of optics **2 a :** of or relating to vision **:** VISUAL **b :** VISIBLE 1 ⟨∼ wavelength⟩ **c :** of, relating to, or being objects that emit light in the visible range of frequencies ⟨an ∼ galaxy⟩ **d :** using the properties of light to aid vision ⟨an ∼ instrument⟩ **3 a :** of, relating to, or utilizing light esp. instead of other forms of energy ⟨∼ microscopy⟩ **b :** involving the use of light-sensitive devices to acquire information for a computer ⟨∼ character recognition⟩ **4 :** of or relating to optical art — **op·ti·cal·ly** \-k(ə-)lē\ *adv*

optical activity *n* (1877) **:** ability of a chemical substance to rotate the plane of vibration of polarized light to the right or left

optical art *n* (1964) **:** nonobjective art characterized by the use of straight or curved lines or geometric patterns often for an illusory effect (as of motion)

optical bench *n* (1883) **:** an apparatus that is fitted for the convenient location and adjustment of light sources and optical devices and that is used for the observation and measurement of optical phenomena

optical disk *n* (1977) **:** a disk with a plastic coating on which information (as music, visual images, or computer data) is recorded digitally (as in the form of tiny pits) and which is read by using a laser

optical fiber *n* (1962) **:** a single fiber-optic strand

optical glass *n* (1840) **:** flint or crown glass of well-defined characteristics used esp. for making lenses

optical illusion *n* (1794) **:** ILLUSION 2a(1)

optically active *adj* (1875) **:** capable of rotating the plane of vibration of polarized light to the right or left — used of compounds, molecules, or atoms

optical rotation *n* (1895) **:** the angle through which the plane of vibration of polarized light that traverses an optically active substance is rotated

optic axis *n* (1664) **:** a line in a doubly refracting medium that is parallel to the direction in which all components of plane-polarized light travel with the same speed

optic chiasma *n* (1872) **:** the X-shaped partial decussation on the undersurface of the hypothalamus through which the optic nerves are continuous with the brain — called also *optic chiasm*

optic cup *n* (ca. 1885) **:** the optic vesicle after invaginating to form a 2-layered cup from which the retina and pigmented layer of the eye will develop — called also *eyecup*

optic disk *n* (1871) **:** BLIND SPOT 1a

op·ti·cian \äp-ˈti-shən\ *n* (1737) **1 :** a maker of or dealer in optical items and instruments **2 :** a person who reads prescriptions for visual correction, orders lenses, and dispenses eyeglasses and contact lenses — compare OPHTHALMOLOGIST, OPTOMETRIST

optic lobe *n* (1844) **:** either of two prominences of the midbrain concerned with vision

optic nerve *n* (1615) **:** either of the second pair of cranial nerves that pass from the retina to the optic chiasma and conduct visual stimuli to the brain — see EYE illustration

op·tics \ˈäp-tiks\ *n pl but sing in constr* (1579) **:** a science that deals with the genesis and propagation of light, the changes that it undergoes and produces, and other phenomena closely associated with it

optic vesicle *n* (ca. 1885) **:** an evagination of each lateral wall of the embryonic vertebrate forebrain from which the nervous structures of the eye develop

op·ti·mal \ˈäp-tə-məl\ *adj* (1890) **:** most desirable or satisfactory **:** OPTIMUM — **op·ti·mal·i·ty** \ˌäp-tə-ˈma-lə-tē\ *n* — **op·ti·mal·ly** \-mə-lē\ *adv*

op·ti·mi·sa·tion, op·ti·mise *Brit var of* OPTIMIZATION, OPTIMIZE

op·ti·mism \ˈäp-tə-ˌmi-zəm\ *n* [F *optimisme,* fr. L *optimum,* n., best, fr. neut. of *optimus* best; akin to L *ops* power — more at OPULENT] (1759) **1 :** a doctrine that this world is the best possible world **2 :** an inclination to put the most favorable construction upon actions and events or to anticipate the best possible outcome — **op·ti·mist** \-mist\ *n* — **op·ti·mis·tic** \ˌäp-tə-ˈmis-tik\ *adj* — **op·ti·mis·ti·cal·ly** \-ti-k(ə-)lē\ *adv*

Op·ti·mist \ˈäp-tə-mist\ *n* [*Optimist (Club)*] (1911) **:** a member of a major international service club

op·ti·mi·za·tion \ˌäp-tə-mə-ˈzā-shən\ *n* (1857) **:** an act, process, or methodology of making something (as a design, system, or decision) as fully perfect, functional, or effective as possible; *specif* **:** the mathematical procedures (as finding the maximum of a function) involved in this

op·ti·mize \ˈäp-tə-ˌmīz\ *vt* **-mized; -miz·ing** (1857) **:** to make as perfect, effective, or functional as possible — **op·ti·miz·er** \-ˌmī-zər\ *n*

op·ti·mum \ˈäp-tə-məm\ *n, pl* **-ma** \-mə\ *also* **-mums** [L] (1879) **1 :** the amount or degree of something that is most favorable to some end; *esp* **:** the most favorable condition for the growth and reproduction of an organism **2 :** greatest degree attained or attainable under implied or specified conditions — **optimum** *adj*

[1]**op·tion** \ˈäp-shən\ *n* [F, fr. L *option-, optio* free choice; akin to L *optare* to choose] (1593) **1 :** an act of choosing **2 a :** the power or right to choose **:** freedom of choice **b :** a privilege of demanding fulfillment of a contract on any day within a specified time **c :** a contract conveying a right to buy or sell designated securities, commodities, or property interest at a specified price during a stipulated period; *also* **:** the right conveyed by an option **d :** a right of an insured person to choose the form in which payments due on a policy shall be made or applied **3 :** something that may be chosen: as **a :** an alternative course of action ⟨didn't have many ∼*s* open⟩ **b :** an item that is offered in addition to or in place of standard equipment **4 :** an offensive football play in which a back may choose whether to pass or run with the ball — called also *option play* ***syn*** see CHOICE

[2]**option** *vt* (1926) **1 :** to grant or take an option on **2 :** to acquire the exclusive right to use (an author's work) as the basis for a motion picture ⟨the studio ∼*ed* the novel for a film⟩

op·tion·al \ˈäp-shnəl, -shə-nᵊl\ *adj* (1765) **:** involving an option **:** not compulsory — **op·tion·al·i·ty** \ˌäp-shə-ˈna-lə-tē\ *n* — **op·tion·al·ly** *adv*

opto- *comb form* [Gk *optos,* verbal of *opsesthai* — more at OPTIC] **1 :** vision ⟨*opto*metry⟩ **2 :** optic and ⟨*opto*electronics⟩

op·to·elec·tron·ics \ˌäp-(ˌ)tō-i-lek-ˈträ-niks, -ē-lek-\ *n pl but sing in constr* (1959) **:** a branch of electronics that deals with electronic devices for emitting, modulating, transmitting, and sensing light — **op·to·elec·tron·ic** \-nik\ *adj*

op·to·ki·net·ic \ˌäp-tō-kə-ˈne-tik, -kī-\ *adj* (1925) **:** of, relating to, or involving movements of the eyes

op·tom·e·trist \äp-ˈtä-mə-trist\ *n* (1903) **:** a specialist licensed to practice optometry — compare OPHTHALMOLOGIST, OPTICIAN

op·tom·e·try \-trē\ *n* [ISV] (1886) **:** the health-care profession concerned esp. with examining the eye for defects and faults of refraction, with prescribing correctional lenses or eye exercises, with diagnosing diseases of the eye, and with treating such diseases or referring them for treatment — **op·to·met·ric** \ˌäp-tə-ˈme-trik\ *adj*

opt out *vi* (1951) **:** to choose not to participate in something — often used with *of* ⟨*opted out* of the project⟩

op·u·lence \ˈä-pyə-lən(t)s\ *n* (ca. 1510) **1 :** WEALTH, AFFLUENCE **2 :** ABUNDANCE, PROFUSION

op·u·lent \-lənt\ *adj* [L *opulentus,* fr. *ops* power, help; akin to L *opus* work] (1523) **:** exhibiting or characterized by opulence: as **a :** having

\ə\ **abut** \ᵊ\ **kitten**, F table \ər\ **further** \a\ **ash** \ā\ **ace** \ä\ **mop**, **mar**
\au̇\ **out** \ch\ **chin** \e\ **bet** \ē\ **easy** \g\ **go** \i\ **hit** \ī\ **ice** \j\ **job**
\ŋ\ **sing** \ō\ **go** \ȯ\ **law** \ȯi\ **boy** \th\ **thin** \t͟h\ **the** \ü\ **loot** \u̇\ **foot**
\y\ **yet** \zh\ **vision, beige** \k, ⁿ, œ, ue, ʸ\ *see* Guide to Pronunciation

a large estate or property : WEALTHY ⟨hoping to marry an ~ widow⟩ **b** : amply or plentifully provided or fashioned often to the point of ostentation ⟨living in ~ comfort⟩ ***syn*** see RICH — **op·u·lent·ly** *adv*

opun·tia \ō-ˈpən(t)-sh(ē-)ə\ *n* [L, a plant, fr. fem. of *opuntius* of Opus, fr. *Opunt-, Opus* Opus, ancient city in Greece] (1601) : any of a large genus (*Opuntia*) of American cacti with usu. yellow flowers and flat or terete joints usu. studded with tubercles bearing spines or prickly hairs — compare CHOLLA, PRICKLY PEAR

opus \ˈō-pəs\ *n, pl* **op·era** \ˈō-pə-rə, ˈä-\ *also* **opus·es** \ˈō-pə-səz\ [L *oper-, opus* — more at OPERATE] (1809) : WORK; *esp* : a musical composition or set of compositions usu. numbered in the order of its issue

opus·cule \ō-ˈpəs-(ˌ)kyül\ *n* [F, fr. L *opusculum,* dim. of *opus*] (ca. 1656) : a small or petty work : OPUSCULUM

opus·cu·lum \ō-ˈpəs-kyə-ləm\ *n, pl* **-la** \-lə\ [L] (1654) : a minor work (as of literature) — usu. used in pl.

[1]**or** \ər, ˈȯr, *Southern also* ˈär\ *conj* [ME, alter. of *other,* alter. of OE *oththe;* akin to OHG *eddo* or] (13c) **1** — used as a function word to indicate an alternative ⟨coffee ~ tea⟩ ⟨sink ~ swim⟩, the equivalent or substitutive character of two words or phrases ⟨lessen ~ abate⟩, or approximation or uncertainty ⟨in five ~ six days⟩ **2** *archaic* : EITHER **3** *archaic* : WHETHER **4** — used in logic as a sentential connective that forms a complex sentence which is true when at least one of its constituent sentences is true; compare DISJUNCTION

[2]**or** *prep* [ME, fr. *or,* adv., early, before, fr. ON *ār;* akin to OE *ǣr* early — more at ERE] (13c) *archaic* : BEFORE

[3]**or** *conj* (13c) *archaic* : BEFORE

[4]**or** \ˈȯr\ *n* [ME, fr. AF, gold, fr. L *aurum* — more at AUREUS] (15c) : the heraldic color gold or yellow

[1]**OR** \ˈȯr\ *n* [[1]*or*] (ca. 1956) : a logical operator that requires either of two inputs to be present or conditions to be met for an output to be made or a statement to be executed ⟨~ gate in a computer⟩

[2]**OR** *abbr* **1** operating room **2** operational research; operations research **3** Oregon **4** owner's risk **5** own recognizance

[1]**-or** *n suffix* [ME, fr. AF *-ur, -our, -eour* & L *-or;* AF *-ur, -our,* fr. L *-or;* AF *-eour,* fr. L *-ator,* fr. *-a-,* v. stem + *-tor,* agent suffix; akin to Gk *-tōr,* agent suffix, Skt *-tā*] : one that does a (specified) thing ⟨grant*or*⟩

[2]**-or** *n suffix* [ME, fr. AF, fr. L] : condition : activity ⟨demean*or*⟩

ora *pl of* OS

or·ache *or* **or·ach** \ˈȯr-ich, ˈär-\ *n* [ME *orage, arage,* fr. AF *orasche, arache,* fr. VL **atripic-, atrapex,* fr. Gk *atraphaxys*] (14c) : any of various herbs (genus *Atriplex*) of the goosefoot family that include some (as *A. hortensis*) with edible leaves

or·a·cle \ˈȯr-ə-kəl, ˈär-\ *n* [ME, fr. AF, fr. L *oraculum,* fr. *orare* to speak — more at ORATION] (15c) **1 a** : a person (as a priestess of ancient Greece) through whom a deity is believed to speak **b** : a shrine in which a deity reveals hidden knowledge or the divine purpose through such a person **c** : an answer or decision given by an oracle **2 a** : a person giving wise or authoritative decisions or opinions **b** : an authoritative or wise expression or answer

orac·u·lar \ȯ-ˈra-kyə-lər, ə-\ *adj* [L *oraculum*] (1631) **1** : resembling an oracle (as in solemnity of delivery) **2** : of, relating to, or being an oracle ***syn*** see DICTATORIAL — **orac·u·lar·i·ty** \-ˌra-kyə-ˈlar-ə-tē\ *n* — **orac·u·lar·ly** \-ˈra-kyə-lər-lē\ *adv*

ora·cy \ˈȯr-ə-sē, ˈär-\ *n* [*oral* + *-acy* (as in *literacy*)] (1965) : proficiency in oral expression and comprehension

[1]**oral** \ˈȯr-əl, ˈär-\ *adj* [L *or-, os* mouth; akin to ON *ōss* mouth of a river, Skt *ās* mouth] (1628) **1 a** : uttered by the mouth or in words : SPOKEN ⟨~ traditions⟩ **b** : using speech or the lips esp. in teaching the deaf **2 a** : of, given through, or involving the mouth ⟨~ health⟩ ⟨an ~ vaccine⟩ **b** : being on or relating to the same surface as the mouth **3 a** : of, relating to, or characterized by the first stage of psychosexual development in psychoanalytic theory during which libidinal gratification is derived from intake (as of food), by sucking, and later by biting **b** : of, relating to, or characterized by personality traits of passive dependency and aggressiveness — **oral·i·ty** \ȯ-ˈra-lə-tē, ō-\ *n* — **oral·ly** \ˈȯr-ə-lē, ˈär-\ *adv*

[2]**oral** *n* (1876) : an oral examination — usu. used in pl.

oral contraceptive *n* (1959) : BIRTH CONTROL PILL

oral history *n* (1955) **1** : tape-recorded historical information obtained in interviews concerning personal experiences and recollections; *also* : the study of such information **2** : a written work based on oral history — **oral historian** *n*

oral·ism \ˈȯr-ə-ˌli-zəm, ˈär-\ *n* (1883) : advocacy or use of the oral method of teaching the deaf — **oral·ist** \-list\ *n*

oral sex *n* (1973) : oral stimulation of the genitals : CUNNILINGUS, FELLATIO

orang \ə-ˈraŋ\ *n* (1778) : ORANGUTAN

[1]**or·ange** \ˈär-inj, ˈär(-ə)nj; *chiefly Northern & Midland* ˈȯr-inj, ˈȯr(-ə)nj\ *n* [ME, fr. AF *orrange, araunge,* fr. Old Occitan *auranja,* fr. Ar *nāranj,* fr. Pers *nārang,* fr. Skt *nāraṅga* orange tree] (14c) **1 a** : a globose berry with a yellowish to reddish-orange rind and a sweet edible pulp **b** : any of various small evergreen citrus trees (genus *Citrus*) with glossy ovate leaves, hard yellow wood, fragrant white flowers, and fruits that are oranges **2** : any of several trees or fruits resembling the orange **3** : any of a group of colors that are between red and yellow in hue

[2]**orange** *adj* (1542) **1** : of or relating to the orange **2** : of the color orange

Orange *adj* (1795) : of, relating to, or sympathizing with Orangemen — **Or·ange·ism** \ˈär-in-ˌji-zəm, ˈär(-ə)n-, ˈȯr-in-, ˈȯr(-ə)n-\ *n*

or·ange·ade \ˌär-in-ˈjād, ˌär(-ə)n-, ˌȯr-in-, ˌȯr(-ə)n-\ *n* [F, fr. *orange* + *-ade*] (1706) : a beverage of sweetened orange juice mixed with water

orange chromide *n* [*chromide,* ultim. fr. Gk *chromis,* a sea fish] (1933) : an Asian freshwater cichlid fish (*Etroplus maculatus*) that is orange or yellow with red spots and is often kept in tropical aquariums

orange hawkweed *n* (1855) : a European hawkweed (*Hieracium aurantiacum*) that has flower heads with bright orange-red rays and is a troublesome weed esp. in northeastern No. America

Or·ange·man \ˈär-inj-mən, ˈär(-ə)nj-, ˈȯr-inj-, ˈȯr(-ə)nj-\ *n* [William III of England, prince of *Orange*] (1796) **1** : a member of a secret society organized in the north of Ireland in 1795 to defend the British sovereign and to support the Protestant religion **2** : a Protestant Irishman esp. of Ulster

orange peel *n* (ca. 1909) : a rough surface (as on porcelain) like that of an orange

orange pekoe *n* (1840) : tea made from the smallest and youngest leaves of the shoot

orange roughy \-ˈrə-fē\ *n* [*roughy* the marine fish *Arripis georgianus,* short for *tommy rough,* fr. *Tommy,* given name + *rough,* prob. alter. of [1]*ruff*] (1979) : a reddish-orange fish (*Hoplostethus atlanticus*) of deep subtropical and tropical waters that has firm white flesh and is caught commercially chiefly in the waters of New Zealand

or·ange·ry *also* **or·ange·rie** \ˈär-inj-rē, ˈär(-ə)nj-, ˈȯr-inj-, ˈȯr(-ə)nj-\ *n, pl* **-ries** (1664) : a protected place and esp. a greenhouse for growing oranges in cool climates

or·ange·wood \ˈär-inj-ˌwu̇d, ˈär(-ə)nj-, ˈȯr-inj-, ˈȯr(-ə)nj-\ *n* (1884) : the wood of the orange tree used esp. in turnery and carving

or·ang·ey *or* **or·angy** \ˈär-in-jē, ˈär(-ə)n-, ˈȯr-in-, ˈȯr(-ə)n-\ *adj* (1778) : resembling or suggestive of an orange (as in flavor or color)

or·ang·ish \ˈär-in-jish, ˈär(-ə)n-, ˈȯr-in-, ˈȯr(-ə)n-\ *adj* (1888) : somewhat orange

orang·u·tan \ə-ˈraŋ-ə-ˌtaŋ, -ˈraŋ-gə-, -ˌtan\ *n* [Bazaar Malay (Malay-based pidgin), fr. Malay *orang* man + *hutan* forest] (1691) : a largely herbivorous arboreal anthropoid ape (*Pongo pygmaeus*) of Borneo and Sumatra that is about ⅔ as large as the gorilla and has brown skin, long sparse reddish-brown hair, and very long arms

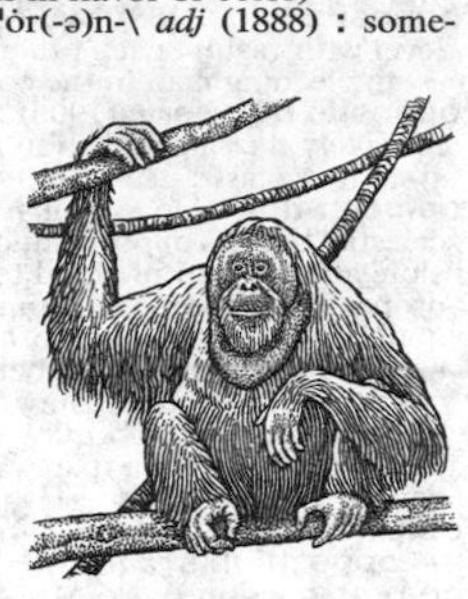
orangutan

orate \ȯ-ˈrāt, ˈȯr-ˌāt\ *vi* **orat·ed; orat·ing** [back-formation fr. *oration*] (1669) : to speak in an elevated and often pompous manner

ora·tion \ə-ˈrā-shən, ȯ-\ *n* [L *oration-, oratio* speech, oration, fr. *orare* to plead, speak, pray; akin to Hitt *ariya-* to consult an oracle and perh. to Gk *ara* prayer] (1502) : an elaborate discourse delivered in a formal and dignified manner

or·a·tor \ˈȯr-ə-tər, ˈär-\ *n* (15c) **1** : one who delivers an oration **2** : one distinguished for skill and power as a public speaker

Or·a·to·ri·an \ˌȯr-ə-ˈtȯr-ē-ən, ˌär-\ *n* (ca. 1656) : a member of the Congregation of the Oratory of St. Philip Neri founded in Rome in 1575 and comprising independent communities of secular priests under obedience but without vows — **Oratorian** *adj*

or·a·tor·i·cal \ˌȯr-ə-ˈtȯr-i-kəl, ˌär-ə-ˈtär-\ *adj* (1589) : of, relating to, or characteristic of an orator or oratory — **or·a·tor·i·cal·ly** \-k(ə-)lē\ *adv*

or·a·to·rio \ˌȯr-ə-ˈtȯr-ē-ˌō, ˌär-\ *n, pl* **-ri·os** [It, fr. the *Oratorio* di San Filippo Neri (Oratory of St. Philip Neri) in Rome] (1731) : a lengthy choral work usu. of a religious nature consisting chiefly of recitatives, arias, and choruses without action or scenery

[1]**or·a·to·ry** \ˈȯr-ə-ˌtȯr-ē, ˈär-\ *n, pl* **-ries** [ME *oratorie,* fr. AF, fr. LL *oratorium,* fr. L *orare*] (14c) **1** : a place of prayer; *esp* : a private or institutional chapel **2** *cap* : an Oratorian congregation, house, or church

[2]**oratory** *n* [L *oratoria,* fr. fem. of *oratorius* oratorical, fr. *orare*] (1594) **1** : the art of speaking in public eloquently or effectively **2 a** : public speaking that employs oratory **b** : public speaking that is characterized by the use of stock phrases and that appeals chiefly to the emotions

[1]**orb** \ˈȯrb\ *n* [ME, fr. MF *orbe,* fr. L *orbis* circle, disk, orb] (15c) **1** : any of the concentric spheres in old astronomy surrounding the earth and carrying the celestial bodies in their revolutions **2** *archaic* : something circular : CIRCLE, ORBIT **3** : a spherical body; *esp* : a spherical celestial object **4** : EYE **5** : a sphere surmounted by a cross symbolizing kingly power and justice

[2]**orb** *vt* (1600) **1** : to form into a disk or circle **2** *archaic* : ENCIRCLE, SURROUND, ENCLOSE ~ *vi, archaic* : to move in an orbit

or·bic·u·lar \ȯr-ˈbi-kyə-lər\ *adj* [ME *orbiculer,* fr. MF or LL; MF *orbiculaire,* fr. LL *orbicularis,* fr. L *orbiculus,* dim. of *orbis*] (15c) : SPHERICAL, CIRCULAR — **or·bic·u·lar·ly** \-ˈbi-kyə-lər-lē\ *adv*

or·bic·u·late \ȯr-ˈbi-kyə-lət\ *adj* (ca. 1760) : circular or nearly circular in outline ⟨an ~ leaf⟩ — see LEAF illustration

[1]**or·bit** \ˈȯr-bət\ *n* [ME, fr. ML *orbita,* fr. L, rut, track, prob. fr. *orbis*] (15c) : the bony socket of the eye — **or·bit·al** \ˈȯr-bə-tᵊl\ *adj*

[2]**orbit** *n* [L *orbita* path, rut, orbit] (1696) **1 a** : a path described by one body in its revolution about another (as by the earth about the sun or by an electron about an atomic nucleus); *also* : one complete revolution of a body describing such a path **b** : a circular path **2** : a range or sphere of activity or influence ⟨within the president's ~⟩ ***syn*** see RANGE — **orbital** *adj*

[3]**orbit** *vt* (1943) **1** : to revolve in an orbit around : CIRCLE **2** : to send up and make revolve in an orbit ⟨~ a satellite⟩ ~ *vi* : to travel in circles

orbital *n* [*orbital,* adj.] (1932) : a mathematically described region around a nucleus in an atom or molecule that may contain zero, one, or two electrons

or·bit·er \-bə-tər\ *n* (1951) : one that orbits: as **a** : a spacecraft designed to orbit a celestial body without landing on its surface **b** : SPACE SHUTTLE

orb weaver *n* (1889) : any of a family (Araneidae) of spiders that have eight similar eyes and typically spin a large elaborate wheel-shaped flat web

orb web *n* (1889) : a web made by an orb weaver

or·ca \ˈȯr-kə\ *n* [NL *Orca,* genus name, fr. L, a whale, prob. modif. of Gk *oryg-, oryx* — more at ORYX] (1866) : KILLER WHALE

Or·ca·di·an \ȯr-ˈkā-dē-ən\ *n* [L *Orcades* Orkney Islands] (1661) : a native or inhabitant of the Orkney Islands — **Orcadian** *adj*

or·chard \ˈȯr-chərd\ *n* [ME, fr. OE *ortgeard,* fr. *ort-* (fr. L *hortus* garden) + *geard* yard — more at YARD] (bef. 12c) : a planting of fruit trees, nut trees, or sugar maples; *also* : the trees of such a planting

orchard grass *n* (1765) : a widely grown tall stout hay and pasture grass (*Dactylis glomerata*) of Eurasia that grows in tufts and has loose open panicles — called also *cocksfoot*

or·chard·ist \ˈȯr-chər-dist\ *n* (1794) : an owner or supervisor of orchards

or·ches·tra \ˈȯr-kəs-trə, -ˌkes-\ *n* [L, fr. Gk *orchēstra,* fr. *orcheisthai* to dance; perh. akin to Skt *ṛghāyati* he trembles, he rages] (1606) **1 a** : the circular space used by the chorus in front of the proscenium in an

ancient Greek theater **b :** a corresponding semicircular space in a Roman theater used for seating important persons **2 a :** the space in front of the stage in a modern theater that is used by an orchestra **b :** the forward section of seats on the main floor of a theater **c :** the main floor of a theater **3 :** a group of musicians including esp. string players organized to perform ensemble music — compare BAND
or·ches·tral \ȯr-ˈkes-trəl\ *adj* (ca. 1811) **1 :** of, relating to, or composed for an orchestra **2 :** suggestive of an orchestra or its musical qualities — **or·ches·tral·ly** \-trə-lē\ *adv*
or·ches·trate \ˈȯr-kə-ˌstrāt\ *vt* **-trat·ed; -trat·ing** (1880) **1 a :** to compose or arrange (music) for an orchestra **b :** to provide with orchestration ⟨~ a ballet⟩ **2 :** to arrange or combine so as to achieve a desired or maximum effect ⟨*orchestrated* preparations for the banquet⟩ — **or·ches·tra·tor** *also* **or·ches·trat·er** \-ˌstrā-tər\ *n*
or·ches·tra·tion \ˌȯr-kə-ˈstrā-shən\ *n* (ca. 1859) **1 :** the arrangement of a musical composition for performance by an orchestra; *also* **:** orchestral treatment of a musical composition **2 :** harmonious organization ⟨develop a world community through ~ of cultural diversities —L. K. Frank⟩ — **or·ches·tra·tion·al** \-shnəl, -shə-nᵊl\ *adj*
or·chid \ˈȯr-kəd\ *n* [irreg. fr. NL *Orchis*] (1845) **1 :** any of a large family (Orchidaceae, the orchid family) of perennial epiphytic or terrestrial monocotyledonous plants that usu. have showy 3-petaled flowers with the middle petal enlarged into a lip and differing from the others in shape and color **2 :** a light purple — **or·chid·like** \-ˌlīk\ *adj*

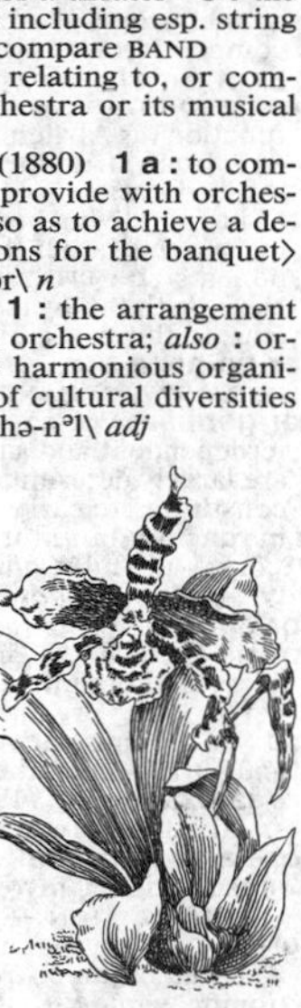
orchid 1

or·chi·da·ceous \ˌȯr-kə-ˈdā-shəs\ *adj* [NL *Orchidaceae,* family name, fr. *Orchis*] (1838) **1 :** of, relating to, or resembling the orchids **2 :** SHOWY, OSTENTATIOUS
or·chi·ec·to·my \ˌȯr-kē-ˈek-tə-mē\ *n, pl* **-mies** [Gk *orchis* + E *-ectomy*] (ca. 1894) **:** surgical removal of one or both testes
or·chis \ˈȯr-kəs\ *n* [NL, fr. L, orchid, fr. Gk, testicle, orchid; akin to MIr *uirgge* testicle] (1562) **:** ORCHID; *esp* **:** any of a genus (*Orchis*) of orchids with fleshy roots and a spurred lip
ord *abbr* **1** order **2** ordnance
or·dain \ȯr-ˈdān\ *vb* [ME *ordeinen,* fr. AF *ordener, ordeiner,* fr. LL *ordinare,* fr. L, to put in order, appoint, fr. *ordin-, ordo* order] *vt* (14c) **1 :** to invest officially (as by the laying on of hands) with ministerial or priestly authority **2 a :** to establish or order by appointment, decree, or law **:** ENACT ⟨we the people . . . do ~ and establish this Constitution —*U.S. Constitution*⟩ **b :** DESTINE, FOREORDAIN ~ *vi* **:** to issue an order — **or·dain·er** *n* — **or·dain·ment** \-ˈdān-mənt\ *n*
or·deal \ȯr-ˈdē(-ə)l, ˈȯr-ˌ\ *n* [ME *ordal,* fr. OE *ordāl;* akin to OHG *urteil* judgment, OE *dāl* division — more at DEAL] (bef. 12c) **1 :** a primitive means used to determine guilt or innocence by submitting the accused to dangerous or painful tests believed to be under supernatural control ⟨~ by fire⟩ **2 :** a severe trial or experience
[1]**or·der** \ˈȯr-dər\ *vb* **or·dered; or·der·ing** \ˈȯr-d(ə-)riŋ\ [ME, fr. *ordre,* n.] *vt* (13c) **1 :** to put in order **:** ARRANGE **2 a :** to give an order to **:** COMMAND **b :** DESTINE, ORDAIN ⟨so ~*ed* by the gods⟩ **c :** to command to go or come to a specified place ⟨~*ed* back to the base⟩ **d :** to give an order for ⟨~ a meal⟩ ~ *vi* **1 :** to bring about order **:** REGULATE **2 a :** to issue orders **:** COMMAND **b :** to give or place an order — **or·der·able** \-ə-bəl\ *adj* — **or·der·er** \-dər-ər\ *n*
syn ORDER, ARRANGE, MARSHAL, ORGANIZE, SYSTEMATIZE, METHODIZE mean to put persons or things into their proper places in relation to each other. ORDER suggests a straightening out so as to eliminate confusion ⟨*ordered* her business affairs⟩. ARRANGE implies a setting in sequence, relationship, or adjustment ⟨*arranged* the files numerically⟩. MARSHAL suggests gathering and arranging in preparation for a particular operation or effective use ⟨*marshaling* the facts for argument⟩. ORGANIZE implies arranging so that the whole aggregate works as a unit with each element having a proper function ⟨*organized* the volunteers into teams⟩. SYSTEMATIZE implies arranging according to a predetermined scheme ⟨*systematized* billing procedures⟩. METHODIZE suggests imposing an orderly procedure rather than a fixed scheme ⟨*methodizes* every aspect of daily living⟩. ***syn*** see in addition COMMAND
[2]**order** *n* [ME, fr. AF *ordre,* fr. ML & L; ML *ordin-, ordo* ecclesiastical order, fr. L, arrangement, group, class; akin to L *ordiri* to lay the warp, begin] (14c) **1 a :** a group of people united in a formal way: as **(1) :** a fraternal society ⟨the Masonic *Order*⟩ **(2) :** a community under a religious rule; *esp* **:** one requiring members to take solemn vows **b :** a badge or medal of such a society; *also* **:** a military decoration **2 a :** any of the several grades of the Christian ministry **b** *pl* **:** the office of a person in the Christian ministry **c** *pl* **:** ORDINATION **3 a :** a rank, class, or special group in a community or society **b :** a class of persons or things grouped according to quality, value, or natural characteristics: as **(1) :** a category of taxonomic classification ranking above the family and below the class **(2) :** the broadest category in soil classification **4 a (1) :** RANK, LEVEL ⟨a statesman of the first ~⟩ **(2) :** CATEGORY, CLASS ⟨in emergencies of this ~ —R. B. Westerfield⟩ **b (1) :** the arrangement or sequence of objects or of events in time ⟨listed the items in ~ of importance⟩ ⟨the batting ~⟩ **(2) :** a sequential arrangement of mathematical elements **c :** DEGREE 12a, b **d (1) :** the number of times differentiation is applied successively ⟨derivatives of higher ~⟩ **(2)** *of a differential equation* **:** the order of the derivative of highest order **e :** the number of columns or

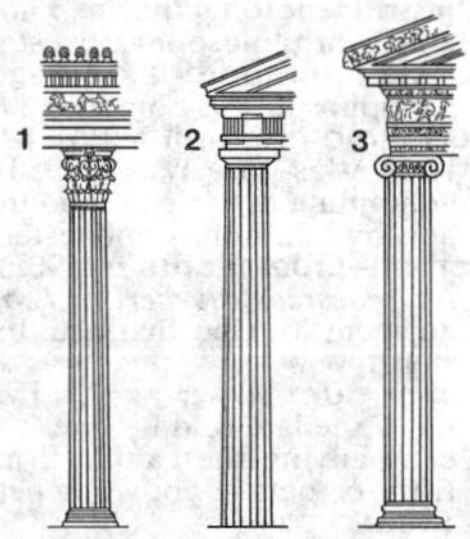

order 8b: *1* Corinthian, *2* Doric, *3* Ionic

rows or columns and rows in a magic square, determinant, or matrix ⟨the ~ of a matrix with 2 rows and 3 columns is 2 by 3⟩ **f :** the number of elements in a finite mathematical group **5 a (1) :** a sociopolitical system ⟨was opposed to changes in the established ~⟩ **(2) :** a particular sphere or aspect of a sociopolitical system ⟨the present economic ~⟩ **b :** a regular or harmonious arrangement ⟨the ~ of nature⟩ **6 a :** a prescribed form of a religious service **:** RITE **b :** the customary mode of procedure esp. in debate ⟨point of ~⟩ **7 a :** the state of peace, freedom from confused or unruly behavior, and respect for law or proper authority ⟨promised to restore law and ~⟩ **b :** a specific rule, regulation, or authoritative direction **:** COMMAND **8 a :** a style of building **b :** a type of column and entablature forming the unit of a style **9 a :** state or condition esp. with regard to functioning or repair ⟨things were in terrible ~⟩ **b :** a proper, orderly, or functioning condition ⟨their passports were in ~⟩ ⟨the phone is out of ~⟩ **10 a :** a written direction to pay money to someone **b :** a commission to purchase, sell, or supply goods or to perform work **c :** goods or items bought or sold **d :** an assigned or requested undertaking ⟨landing men on the moon was a tall ~⟩ **11 :** ORDER OF THE DAY ⟨flat roofs were the ~ in the small villages⟩ — **or·der·less** \-ləs\ *adj* — **in order :** APPROPRIATE, DESIRABLE ⟨an apology is *in order*⟩ — **in order to :** for the purpose of — **on order :** in the process of being ordered — **on the order of 1 :** after the fashion of **:** LIKE ⟨a genius *on the order of* Newton —D. B. Botkin⟩ **2 :** ABOUT, APPROXIMATELY ⟨spent *on the order of* two million dollars⟩ — **to order :** according to the specifications of an order ⟨shoes made *to order*⟩
order arms *n* [fr. the command *order arms!*] (1847) **1 :** a command to return the rifle to order arms from present arms or to drop the hand from a hand salute **2 :** a position in the manual of arms in which the rifle is held vertically beside the right leg with the butt resting on the ground
or·dered \ˈȯr-dərd\ *adj* (1579) **:** characterized by order: as **a :** marked by regularity or discipline ⟨led an ~ life⟩ **b :** marked by regular or harmonious arrangement or disposition ⟨an ~ landscape⟩ ⟨the ~ crystal structure⟩ **c :** having elements arranged or identified according to a rule: as **(1) :** having the property that every pair of different elements is related by a transitive relationship that is not symmetric **(2) :** having elements labeled by ordinal numbers ⟨an ~ triple has a first, second, and third element⟩
or·der·li·ness \ˈȯrd-ər-lē-nəs\ *n* (1571) **:** the quality or state of being orderly
[1]**or·der·ly** \-lē\ *adj* (1570) **1 a (1) :** arranged or disposed in some order or pattern **:** REGULAR ⟨~ rows of houses⟩ **(2) :** marked by order **:** TIDY ⟨keeps an ~ desk⟩ **b :** governed by law **:** REGULATED ⟨an ~ universe⟩ **c :** METHODICAL ⟨an ~ mind⟩ **2 :** well behaved **:** PEACEFUL ⟨an ~ crowd⟩ — **orderly** *adv*
[2]**orderly** *n, pl* **-lies** (1781) **1 :** a soldier assigned to perform various services (as carrying messages) for a superior officer **2 :** a hospital attendant who does routine or heavy work (as cleaning, carrying supplies, or moving patients)
order of battle (1702) **1 :** the disposition of troops or ships ready for combat **2 :** a tabular compilation of units, commanders, equipment, and their locations in a theater of operation
order of business [*order of business* (predetermined sequence of matters to be dealt with by an assembly)] (ca. 1890) **:** a matter which must be dealt with **:** TASK ⟨the budget was the first *order of business* at the committee meeting⟩
order of magnitude (1875) **:** a range of magnitude extending from some value to ten times that value
order of the day (1698) **1 :** the business or tasks appointed for an assembly for a given day **2 :** the characteristic or dominant feature or activity ⟨growth and change are the *order of the day* in every field —Ruth G. Strickland⟩
[1]**or·di·nal** \ˈȯrd-nəl, ˈȯrd-ə-nəl\ *n* (14c) **1** *cap* [ME, fr. ML *ordinale,* fr. LL, neut. of *ordinalis*] **:** a book of rites for the ordination of deacons, priests, and bishops **2** [LL *ordinalis,* fr. *ordinalis,* adj.] **:** ORDINAL NUMBER
[2]**ordinal** *adj* [LL *ordinalis,* fr. L *ordin-, ordo*] (1599) **1 :** of a specified order or rank in a series **2 :** of or relating to a taxonomic order
ordinal number *n* (1607) **1 :** a number designating the place (as first, second, or third) occupied by an item in an ordered sequence — see NUMBER table **2 :** a number assigned to an ordered set that designates both the order of its elements and its cardinal number
or·di·nance \ˈȯrd-nən(t)s, ˈȯr-də-nən(t)s\ *n* [ME, fr. AF & ML; AF *ordenance* order, disposition, fr. ML *ordinantia,* fr. L *ordinant-, ordinans,* prp. of *ordinare* to put in order — more at ORDAIN] (14c) **1 a :** an authoritative decree or direction **:** ORDER **b :** a law set forth by a governmental authority; *specif* **:** a municipal regulation **2 :** something ordained or decreed by fate or a deity **3 :** a prescribed usage, practice, or ceremony ***syn*** see LAW
or·di·nand \ˌȯr-də-ˈnand\ *n* [LL *ordinandus,* gerundive of *ordinare* to ordain] (ca. 1842) **:** a candidate for ordination
[1]**or·di·nary** \ˈȯr-də-ˌner-ē\ *n, pl* **-nar·ies** [ME *ordinarie,* fr. AF & ML; AF, fr. ML *ordinarius,* fr. L *ordinarius,* adj.] (14c) **1 a (1) :** a prelate exercising original jurisdiction over a specified territory or group **(2) :** a clergyman appointed formerly in England to attend condemned criminals **b :** a judge of probate in some states of the U.S. **2** *often cap* **:** the parts of the Mass that do not vary from day to day **3 :** the regular or customary condition or course of things — usu. used in the phrase *out of the ordinary* **4 a** *Brit* **:** a meal served to all comers at a fixed price **b** *chiefly Brit* **:** a tavern or eating house serving regular meals **5 :** a common heraldic charge (as the bend) of simple form
[2]**ordinary** *adj* [ME *ordinarie,* fr. L *ordinarius,* fr. *ordin-, ordo* order] (15c) **1 :** of a kind to be expected in the normal order of events **:** ROUTINE, USUAL ⟨an ~ day⟩ **2 :** having or constituting immediate or original jurisdiction; *also* **:** belonging to such jurisdiction **3 a :** of common quality, rank, or ability ⟨an ~ teenager⟩ **b :** deficient in

quality : POOR, INFERIOR ⟨~ wine⟩ *syn* see COMMON — **or·di·nar·i·ly** \ˌȯr-də-ˈner-ə-lē\ *adv* — **or·di·nar·i·ness** \ˈȯr-də-ˌner-ē-nəs\ *n*

ordinary–language philosophy *n* (1957) : a trend in philosophical analysis that seeks to resolve philosophical perplexity by revealing sources of puzzlement in the misunderstanding of ordinary language

Ordinary level *n* (1947) : O LEVEL

ordinary seaman *n* (1702) : a seaman of some experience but not as skilled as an able seaman

ordinary share *n* (1891) *Brit* : a share of common stock

or·di·nate \ˈȯr-dᵊn-ət, ˈȯr-də-nət, -ˌnāt\ *n* [NL *(linea) ordinate (applicata),* lit., line applied in an orderly manner] (1676) : the Cartesian coordinate obtained by measuring parallel to the y-axis — compare ABSCISSA

or·di·na·tion \ˌȯr-də-ˈnā-shən\ *n* (14c) : the act or an instance of ordaining : the state of being ordained

ord·nance \ˈȯrd-nən(t)s\ *n* [ME *ordinaunce,* fr. AF *ordenance* disposition, preparation, military provisions — more at ORDINANCE] (14c) **1 a** : military supplies including weapons, ammunition, combat vehicles, and maintenance tools and equipment **b** : a service of the army charged with the procuring, distributing, and safekeeping of ordnance **2** : CANNON, ARTILLERY

or·do \ˈȯr-(ˌ)dō\ *n, pl* **ordos** *or* **or·di·nes** \ˈȯr-də-ˌnēz\ [ML, fr. L, order] (1849) : a list of offices and feasts of the Roman Catholic Church for each day of the year

or·don·nance \ˌȯr-də-ˈnä^{n}s\ *n* [F, alter. of MF *ordenance* ordinance] (1644) : disposition of the parts (as of a literary composition) with regard to one another and the whole : ARRANGEMENT

Or·do·vi·cian \ˌȯr-də-ˈvi-shən\ *adj* [L *Ordovices,* ancient people in northern Wales] (1879) : of, relating to, or being the period between the Cambrian and the Silurian or the corresponding system of rocks — see GEOLOGIC TIME table — **Ordovician** *n*

or·dure \ˈȯr-jər\ *n* [ME, fr. AF, fr. *ord* dirty, foul, fr. L *horridus* horrid] (14c) **1** : EXCREMENT **2** : something that is morally degrading

[1]**ore** \ˈȯr\ *n, often attrib* [ME *or, oor,* partly fr. OE *ōra* ore; partly fr. OE *ār* brass; akin to OHG *ēr* bronze, L *aes* copper, bronze] (bef. 12c) **1** : a naturally occurring mineral containing a valuable constituent (as metal) for which it is mined and worked **2** : a source from which valuable matter is extracted

[2]**ore** \ˈər-ə\ *n, pl* **ore** [Sw *öre* & Dan & Norw *øre*] (1716) — see *krona, krone* at MONEY table

Ore *or* **Oreg** *abbr* Oregon

ore·ad \ˈȯr-ē-ˌad, -ē-əd\ *n* [ME *oreades,* pl., fr. L *oread-, oreas,* fr. Gk *oreiad-, oreias,* fr. *oreios* of a mountain, fr. *oros* mountain — more at ORIENT] (14c) : any of the nymphs of mountains and hills in Greek mythology

orec·chi·et·te \ō-ˌrä-kē-ˈe-tā\ *n* [It, pl. of *orecchietta,* dim. of *orecchia* ear, fr. L *auricula* — more at AURICLE] (1973) : small oval pasta

ore dressing *n* (1831) : mechanical preparation (as by crushing) and concentration (as by flotation) of ore

oreg·a·no \ə-ˈre-gə-ˌnō\ *n* [AmerSp *orégano,* fr. Sp, wild marjoram, fr. L *origanum* — more at ORIGANUM] (1771) **1** : a bushy perennial mint (*Origanum vulgare*) that is used as a seasoning and a source of aromatic oil — called also *origanum, wild marjoram* **2** : any of several plants (genera *Lippia* and *Coleus*) other than oregano of the vervain or mint families

Or·e·gon grape \ˈȯr-i-gən-, ˈär-, -ˌgän-\ *n* [*Oregon,* state of the U.S.] (ca. 1857) : an evergreen shrub (*Mahonia aquifolium*) of the barberry family that has yellow flowers, bears edible bluish-black berries, and is native to western No. America

Or·eo \ˈȯr-ē-(ˌ)ō, ˈär-\ *n* [fr. *Oreo,* trademark for a chocolate cookie with a white cream filling] (1969) *usu disparaging* : a black person who adopts the characteristic mentality and behavior of white middle-class society

Ores·tes \ə-ˈres-(ˌ)tēz, ȯ-\ *n* [L, fr. Gk *Orestēs*] (15c) : the son of Agamemnon and Clytemnestra who with his sister Electra avenges his father by killing his mother and her lover Aegisthus

org *abbr* **1** organic **2** organization; organized

or·gan \ˈȯr-gən\ *n* [ME, partly fr. OE *organa,* fr. L *organum,* fr. Gk *organon,* lit., tool, instrument; partly fr. AF *organe,* fr. L *organum;* akin to Gk *ergon* work — more at WORK] (bef. 12c) **1 a** *archaic* : any of various musical instruments; *esp* : WIND INSTRUMENT **b** (1) : a keyboard instrument in which sets of pipes are sounded by compressed air and produce a variety of timbres — called also *pipe organ* (2) : REED ORGAN (3) : an electronic keyboard instrument that approximates the sounds and resources of the pipe organ (4) : any of various similar cruder instruments **2 a** : a differentiated structure (as a heart, kidney, leaf, or stem) consisting of cells and tissues and performing some specific function in an organism **b** : bodily parts performing a function or cooperating in an activity ⟨the eyes and related structures that make up the visual ~*s*⟩ **3** : a subordinate group or organization that performs specialized functions ⟨the various ~*s* of government⟩ **4** : PERIODICAL

organ- *or* **organo-** *comb form* [Gk *organon*] **1** : organ ⟨*organo*genesis⟩ **2** : organic ⟨*organo*mercurial⟩

or·gan·dy *also* **or·gan·die** \ˈȯr-gən-dē\ *n, pl* **-dies** [F *organdi*] (1835) : a very fine transparent muslin with a stiff finish

or·gan·elle \ˌȯr-gə-ˈnel\ *n* [NL *organella,* fr. L *organum*] (1920) : a specialized cellular part (as a mitochondrion, lysosome, or ribosome) that is analogous to an organ

or·gan–grind·er \ˈȯr-gən-ˌgrīn-dər\ *n* (ca. 1807) : one that cranks a hand organ; *esp* : a street musician who operates a barrel organ

[1]**or·gan·ic** \ȯr-ˈga-nik\ *adj* (1517) **1** *archaic* : INSTRUMENTAL **2 a** : of, relating to, or arising in a bodily organ **b** : affecting the structure of the organism **3 a** (1) : of, relating to, or derived from living organisms ⟨~ evolution⟩ (2) : of, relating to, yielding, or involving the use of food produced with the use of feed or fertilizer of plant or animal origin without employment of chemically formulated fertilizers, growth stimulants, antibiotics, or pesticides ⟨~ farming⟩ ⟨~ produce⟩ **b** (1) : of, relating to, or containing carbon compounds (2) : relating to, being, or dealt with by a branch of chemistry concerned with the carbon compounds of living beings and most other carbon compounds **4 a** : forming an integral element of a whole : FUNDAMENTAL ⟨incidental music rather than ~ parts of the action —Francis Fergusson⟩ **b** : having systematic coordination of parts : ORGANIZED ⟨an ~ whole⟩ **c** : having the characteristics of an organism : developing in the manner of a living plant or animal ⟨society is ~⟩ **5** : of, relating to, or constituting the law by which a government or organization exists — **or·gan·i·cal·ly** \-ni-k(ə-)lē\ *adv* — **or·ga·nic·i·ty** \ˌȯr-gə-ˈni-sə-tē\ *n*

[2]**organic** *n* (1942) : an organic substance: as **a** : a fertilizer of plant or animal origin **b** : a pesticide whose active component is an organic compound or a mixture of organic compounds **c** : a food produced by organic farming

organic brain syndrome *n* (1966) : an acute or chronic mental dysfunction (as Alzheimer's disease) resulting chiefly from physical changes in brain structure and characterized esp. by impaired cognition

or·gan·i·cism \ȯr-ˈga-nə-ˌsi-zəm\ *n* [ISV] (1883) **1 a** : the explanation of life and living processes in terms of the levels of organization of living systems rather than in terms of the properties of their smallest components **b** : VITALISM **2** : any of various theories that attribute to society or the universe as a whole an existence or characteristics analogous to those of a biological organism — **or·gan·i·cist** \-sist\ *n or adj*

or·ga·ni·sa·tion, or·ga·nise, or·ga·nis·er *Brit var of* ORGANIZATION, ORGANIZE, ORGANIZER

or·gan·ism \ˈȯr-gə-ˌni-zəm\ *n* (ca. 1774) **1** : a complex structure of interdependent and subordinate elements whose relations and properties are largely determined by their function in the whole **2** : an individual constituted to carry on the activities of life by means of organs separate in function but mutually dependent : a living being — **or·gan·is·mic** \ˌȯr-gə-ˈniz-mik\ *also* **or·gan·is·mal** \-məl\ *adj* — **or·gan·is·mi·cal·ly** \-mi-k(ə-)lē\ *adv*

or·gan·ist \ˈȯr-gə-nist\ *n* (1591) : a person who plays the organ

[1]**or·ga·ni·za·tion** \ˌȯr-gə-nə-ˈzā-shən, ˌȯrg-nə-\ *n* (15c) **1 a** : the act or process of organizing or of being organized **b** : the condition or manner of being organized **2 a** : ASSOCIATION, SOCIETY ⟨charitable ~*s*⟩ **b** : an administrative and functional structure (as a business or a political party); *also* : the personnel of such a structure

[2]**organization** *adj* (1949) : characterized by complete conformity to the standards and requirements of an organization ⟨an ~ man⟩

or·ga·ni·za·tion·al \-shnəl, -shə-n^{ə}l\ *adj* (1881) **1** : of or relating to an organization : involving organization ⟨the ~ state of a crystal⟩ **2** : ORGANIZATION — **or·ga·ni·za·tion·al·ly** *adv*

or·ga·nize \ˈȯr-gə-ˌnīz\ *vb* **-nized; -niz·ing** *vt* (15c) **1** : to cause to develop an organic structure **2** : to form into a coherent unity or functioning whole : INTEGRATE ⟨trying to ~ her thoughts⟩ **3 a** : to set up an administrative structure for **b** : to persuade to associate in an organization; *esp* : UNIONIZE **4** : to arrange by systematic planning and united effort ~ *vi* **1** : to undergo physical or organic organization **2** : to arrange elements into a whole of interdependent parts **3** : to form an organization; *specif* : to form or persuade workers to join a union *syn* see ORDER — **or·gan·iz·able** \ˌȯr-gə-ˈnī-zə-bəl\ *adj*

organized *adj* (1817) **1** : having a formal organization to coordinate and carry out activities ⟨~ baseball⟩ ⟨~ crime⟩ **2** : affiliated by membership in an organization (as a union) ⟨~ steelworkers⟩

or·ga·niz·er \ˈȯr-gə-ˌnī-zər\ *n* (1849) **1** : one that organizes **2** : a region of a developing embryo or a substance produced by such a region that is capable of inducing a specific type of development in undifferentiated tissue — called also *inductor*

or·gan·o·chlo·rine \ˌȯr-gə-nō-ˈklȯr-ˌēn, ȯr-ˌga-nə-, -ən\ *adj* (1961) : of, relating to, or being a chlorinated hydrocarbon and esp. one used as a pesticide (as aldrin, DDT, or dieldrin) — **organochlorine** *n*

organ of Cor·ti \-ˈkȯr-tē\ [Alfonso *Corti* †1876 Ital. anatomist] (1867) : a complex epithelial structure in the cochlea that rests on the internal surface of the basilar membrane and in mammals is the chief part of the ear by which sound is directly perceived

or·gan·o·gen·e·sis \ˌȯr-gə-nō-ˈje-nə-səs, ȯr-ˌga-nə-\ *n* [NL] (ca. 1860) : the origin and development of bodily organs — compare MORPHOGENESIS — **or·gan·o·ge·net·ic** \-jə-ˈne-tik\ *adj*

or·gan·o·lep·tic \ˌȯr-gə-nō-ˈlep-tik, ȯr-ˌga-nə-\ *adj* [F *organoleptique,* fr. *organ-* + Gk *lēptikos* disposed to take, fr. *lambanein* to take — more at LATCH] (1852) **1** : being, affecting, or relating to qualities (as taste, color, odor, and feel) of a substance (as a food or drug) that stimulate the sense organs ⟨~ research⟩ **2** : involving use of the sense organs ⟨~ evaluation of foods⟩ — **or·gan·o·lep·ti·cal·ly** \-ti-k(ə-)lē\ *adv*

or·gan·o·mer·cu·ri·al \ˌȯr-gə-nō-(ˌ)mər-ˈkyu̇r-ē-əl, ȯr-ˌga-nə-\ *n* (1938) : an organic compound or a pharmaceutical preparation containing mercury

or·gan·o·me·tal·lic \-mə-ˈta-lik\ *adj* [ISV] (1852) : of, relating to, or being an organic compound that usu. contains a metal or metalloid bonded directly to carbon — **organometallic** *n*

or·ga·non \ˈȯr-gə-ˌnän\ *n* [Gk, lit., tool — more at ORGAN] (1610) : an instrument for acquiring knowledge; *specif* : a body of principles of scientific or philosophic investigation

or·gan·o·phos·phate \ˌȯr-gə-nō-ˈfäs-ˌfāt, ȯr-ˌga-nō-\ *n* (1949) : an organophosphorus compound (as a pesticide) — **organophosphate** *adj*

or·gan·o·phos·pho·rus \-ˈfäs-f(ə-)rəs\ *also* **or·gan·o·phos·pho·rous** \-fäs-ˈfȯr-əs\ *adj* (1950) : of, relating to, or being a phosphorus-containing organic compound and esp. a pesticide (as malathion) that acts by inhibiting cholinesterase — **organophosphorus** *n*

organ–pipe cactus *n* (1908) : any of several tall upright cacti (as *Lemaireocereus thurberi* or *L. marginatus*) of the southwestern U.S. and adjacent Mexico that usu. branch at the base to form several upright stems

or·ga·num \ˈȯr-gə-nəm\ *n* [ML, fr. L, organ] (1782) **1** : early polyphony of the late Middle Ages that consists of one or more voice parts accompanying the cantus firmus often in parallel motion at a fourth, fifth, or octave above or below; *also* : a composition in this style **2** : ORGANON

or·gan·za \ȯr-ˈgan-zə\ *n* [prob. alter. of *Lorganza,* a trademark] (1820) : a sheer dress fabric (as of silk or nylon) resembling organdy

or·gan·zine \ˈȯr-gən-ˌzēn\ *n* [F or It; F *organsin,* fr. It *organzino*] (1699) : a raw silk yarn used for warp threads in fine fabrics

[1]**or·gasm** \ˈȯr-ˌga-zəm\ *n* [NL *orgasmus,* fr. Gk *orgasmos,* fr. *organ* to grow ripe, be lustful; prob. akin to Skt *ūrjā* sap, strength] (ca. 1763) : intense or paroxysmal excitement; *esp* : an explosive discharge of neuromuscular tensions at the height of sexual arousal that is usu. accompanied by the ejaculation of semen in the male and by vaginal contractions in the female — **or·gas·mic** \ȯr-ˈgaz-mik\ *also* **or·gas·tic** \-ˈgas-tik\ *adj*

[2]**orgasm** *vi* (1972) : to experience orgasm

or·geat \'ȯr-ˌzhä(t)\ *n* [F, fr. MF, fr. *orge* barley, fr. L *hordeum;* akin to OHG *gersta* barley] (1754) **:** a sweet almond-flavored nonalcoholic syrup used as a cocktail ingredient or food flavoring

or·gi·as·tic \ˌȯr-jē-'as-tik\ *adj* [Gk *orgiastikos,* fr. *orgiazein* to celebrate orgies, fr. *orgia*] (1846) **1 :** of, relating to, or marked by orgies **2 :** characterized by unrestrained emotion **:** FRENZIED — **or·gi·as·ti·cal·ly** \-ti-k(ə-)lē\ *adv*

or·gone \'ȯr-ˌgōn\ *n, often attrib* [G *Orgon,* fr. *Org*asmus orgasm and *or*ganisch organic + *-on* ²-on] (1942) **:** a vital energy held to pervade nature and be a factor in health in the theories of Wilhelm Reich

or·gu·lous \'ȯr-gyə-ləs, -gə-\ *adj* [ME, fr. AF *orguillus,* fr. *orguil* pride, of Gmc origin; akin to OHG *urguol* distinguished] (13c) **:** PROUD

or·gy \'ȯr-jē\ *n, pl* **orgies** [MF *orgie,* fr. L *orgia,* pl., fr. Gk; akin to Gk *ergon* work — more at WORK] (ca. 1561) **1 :** secret ceremonial rites held in honor of an ancient Greek or Roman deity and usu. characterized by ecstatic singing and dancing **2 a :** drunken revelry **b :** a sexual encounter involving many people; *also* **:** an excessive sexual indulgence **3 :** excessive indulgence in something esp. to satisfy an inordinate appetite or craving ⟨an ~ of destruction⟩ ⟨a national ~ of thrill seeking and risk taking —K. T. Greenfeld⟩

-oria *pl of* -ORIUM

-orial *adj suffix* [ME, fr. L *-orius* -ory + ME *-al*] **:** of, belonging to, or connected with ⟨combinat*orial*⟩

orib·a·tid \ō-'ri-bə-təd, ˌȯr-ə-'ba-təd\ *n* [NL *Oribatidae* (coextensive with *Oribatoidea*), fr. *Oribata,* genus name, fr. Gk *oribatēs* walking the mountains, fr. *oros* mountain + *-batēs,* fr. *bainein* to go — more at ORIENT, COME] (1875) **:** any of a superfamily (Oribatoidea) of small oval eyeless nonparasitic mites having a heavily sclerotized integument with a leathery appearance — **oribatid** *adj*

ori·el window \'ȯr-ē-əl-\ *n* [ME, porch, oriel, fr. AF *oriol*] (14c) **:** a large bay window projecting from a wall and supported by a corbel or bracket — called also *oriel*

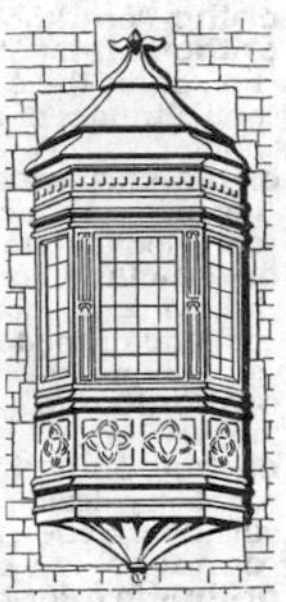

oriel window

¹**ori·ent** \'ȯr-ē-ənt, -ē-ˌent\ *n* [ME, fr. AF, fr. L *orient-, oriens,* fr. prp. of *oriri* to rise; akin to Skt *r̥ṇoti* he moves, arises, Gk *ornynai* to rouse, *oros* mountain] (14c) **1** *archaic* **:** EAST 1b **2** *cap* **:** EAST 2 **3 a :** a pearl of great luster **b :** the luster of a pearl

²**orient** *adj* (15c) **1** *archaic* **:** ORIENTAL 1 **2 a :** LUSTROUS, SPARKLING ⟨~ gems⟩ **b** *archaic* **:** RADIANT, GLOWING **3** *archaic* **:** rising in the sky

³**ori·ent** \'ȯr-ē-ˌent\ *vt* [F *orienter,* fr. MF, fr. *orient*] (ca. 1741) **1 a :** to cause to face or point toward the east; *specif* **:** to build (a church or temple) with the longitudinal axis pointing eastward and the chief altar at the eastern end **b :** to set or arrange in any determinate position esp. in relation to the points of the compass **c :** to ascertain the bearings of **2 a :** to set right by adjusting to facts or principles **b :** to acquaint with the existing situation or environment **3 :** to direct (as a book or film) toward the interests of a particular group **4 :** to cause the axes of the molecules of to assume the same direction

ori·en·tal \ˌȯr-ē-'en-tᵊl\ *adj* (14c) **1** *often cap* **:** of, relating to, or situated in Asia **2 a :** of superior grade, luster, or value **b :** being corundum or sapphire but simulating another gem in color **3** *often cap, sometimes offensive* **:** ASIAN **4** *cap* **:** of, relating to, or constituting the biogeographic region that includes Asia south and southeast of the Himalayas and the Malay Archipelago west of Wallace's line — **ori·en·tal·ly** \-tᵊl-ē\ *adv*

Oriental *n* (15c) **1** *sometimes offensive* **:** ASIAN; *esp* **:** one who is a native of east Asia or is of east Asian descent **2 :** ORIENTAL RUG **3 :** ORIENTAL SHORTHAIR

oriental fruit moth *n* (ca. 1921) **:** a small nearly cosmopolitan moth (*Grapholita molesta* syn. *Cydia molesta*) prob. of Japanese origin whose larva is injurious to the twigs and fruit of orchard trees and esp. the peach — called also *oriental peach moth*

Ori·en·ta·lia \ˌȯr-ē-ən-'tāl-yə, -ˌen-, -'tā-lē-ə\ *n pl* [NL] (1903) **:** materials concerning, characteristic of, or from Asia

ori·en·tal·ism \ˌȯr-ē-'en-tə-ˌli-zəm\ *n, often cap* (1769) **1 :** something (as a style or manner) associated with or characteristic of Asia or Asians **2 :** scholarship or learning in Asian subjects or languages — **ori·en·tal·ist** \-tə-list\ *n or adj, often cap*

ori·en·tal·ize \-tə-ˌlīz\ *vb* **-ized; -iz·ing** *vt* (1823) *often cap* **:** to make Asian **:** give Asian qualities to ~ *vi, often cap* **:** to adopt Asian characteristics — **ori·en·tal·i·za·tion** \-ˌen-tə-lə-'zā-shən, -ˌlī-'zā-\ *n, often cap*

Oriental poppy *n* (1731) **:** an Asian perennial poppy (*Papaver orientale*) that is commonly cultivated for its large showy flowers

Oriental rug *n* (1881) **:** a handwoven or hand-knotted one-piece rug or carpet made in a country of central or southern Asia — called also *Oriental carpet*

Oriental shorthair *n* (1974) **:** a slender short-haired domestic cat of a breed resembling the Siamese in conformation but having a solid-colored coat in a wide range of colors

ori·en·tate \'ȯr-ē-ən-ˌtāt, -ˌen-\ *vb* **-tat·ed; -tat·ing** *vi* (1848) **:** to face or turn to the east ~ *vt* **:** ORIENT

orientated *adj, chiefly Brit* (1950) **:** ORIENTED

ori·en·ta·tion \ˌȯr-ē-ən-'tā-shən, -ˌen-\ *n* (1839) **1 a :** the act or process of orienting or of being oriented **b :** the state of being oriented; *broadly* **:** ARRANGEMENT, ALIGNMENT **2 a :** a usu. general or lasting direction of thought, inclination, or interest **b :** a person's self-identification as heterosexual, homosexual, or bisexual ⟨sexual ~⟩ **3 :** change of position by organs, organelles, or organisms in response to external stimulus — **ori·en·ta·tion·al** \-shnəl, -shə-nᵊl\ *adj* — **ori·en·ta·tion·al·ly** *adv*

ori·ent·ed \'ȯr-ē-ˌen-təd\ *adj* (1937) **:** intellectually, emotionally, or functionally directed ⟨humanistically ~ scholars⟩ ⟨market-*oriented* production⟩

ori·en·teer \ˌȯr-ē-ən-'tir, -ˌen-\ *n* [back-formation fr. *orienteering*] (1965) **:** a person who engages in orienteering

ori·en·teer·ing \ˌȯr-ē-ən-'tir-iŋ, -ˌen-\ *n* [modif. of Sw *orientering,* fr. *orientera* to orient] (1948) **:** a cross-country race in which each participant uses a map and compass to navigate between checkpoints along an unfamiliar course

or·i·fice \'ȯr-ə-fəs, 'är-\ *n* [ME, fr. MF & LL; MF, fr. LL *orificium,* fr. L *or-, os* mouth + *facere* to make, do — more at ORAL, DO] (15c) **:** an opening (as a vent, mouth, or hole) through which something may pass — **or·i·fi·cial** \ˌȯr-ə-'fi-shəl, ˌär-\ *adj*

ori·flamme \'ȯr-ə-ˌflam, 'är-\ *n* [ME *oriflamble,* the banner of St. Denis, fr. MF, fr. OF *ori flambe,* small flag] (1600) **:** a banner, symbol, or ideal inspiring devotion or courage

ori·ga·mi \ˌȯr-ə-'gä-mē\ *n* [Jp, fr. *ori* fold + *kami* paper] (1956) **:** the Japanese art or process of folding squares of paper into representational shapes

orig·a·num \ə-'ri-gə-nəm\ *n* [ME, fr. L, wild marjoram, fr. Gk *origanon*] (14c) **:** any of several aromatic mints (esp. genus *Origanum*) used as seasonings; *esp* **:** OREGANO 1

or·i·gin \'ȯr-ə-jən, 'är-\ *n* [ME *origine,* fr. L *origin-, origo,* fr. *oriri* to rise — more at ORIENT] (15c) **1 :** ANCESTRY, PARENTAGE **2 a :** rise, beginning, or derivation from a source **b :** the point at which something begins or rises or from which it derives ⟨the ~ of the custom⟩; *also* **:** something that creates, causes, or gives rise to another ⟨a spring is the ~ of the brook⟩ **3 :** the more fixed, central, or larger attachment of a muscle **4 :** the intersection of coordinate axes

syn ORIGIN, SOURCE, INCEPTION, ROOT mean the point at which something begins its course or existence. ORIGIN applies to the things or persons from which something is ultimately derived and often to the causes operating before the thing itself comes into being ⟨an investigation into the *origin* of baseball⟩. SOURCE applies more often to the point where something springs into being ⟨the *source* of the Nile⟩ ⟨the *source* of recurrent trouble⟩. INCEPTION stresses the beginning of something without implying causes ⟨the business has been a success since its *inception*⟩. ROOT suggests a first, ultimate, or fundamental source often not easily discerned ⟨the real *root* of the violence⟩.

¹**orig·i·nal** \ə-'rij-ə-nᵊl, -'rij-nəl\ *n* (14c) **1** *archaic* **:** the source or cause from which something arises; *specif* **:** ORIGINATOR **2 a :** that from which a copy, reproduction, or translation is made **b :** a work composed firsthand **3 a :** a person of fresh initiative or inventive capacity **b :** a unique or eccentric person

²**original** *adj* (14c) **1 :** of, relating to, or constituting an origin or beginning **:** INITIAL ⟨the ~ part of the house⟩ **2 a :** not secondary, derivative, or imitative ⟨an ~ composition⟩ **b :** being the first instance or source from which a copy, reproduction, or translation is or can be made **3 :** independent and creative in thought or action **:** INVENTIVE ⟨an ~ artist⟩ ***syn*** see NEW

original equipment manufacturer *n* (1967) **:** OEM

orig·i·nal·i·ty \ə-ˌri-jə-'na-lə-tē\ *n* (1742) **1 :** the quality or state of being original **2 :** freshness of aspect, design, or style **3 :** the power of independent thought or constructive imagination

orig·i·nal·ly \ə-'ri-jə-nᵊl-ē; -'rij-nə-lē, -'ri-jən-\ *adv* (14c) **1** *archaic* **:** by origin or derivation **:** INHERENTLY **2 :** in the beginning **:** in the first place **:** INITIALLY **3 :** in a fresh or original manner

original sin *n* (14c) **1 :** the state of sin that according to Christian theology characterizes all human beings as a result of Adam's fall **2 :** a wrong of great magnitude ⟨the *original sin* of slavery⟩

orig·i·nate \ə-'ri-jə-ˌnāt\ *vb* **-nat·ed; -nat·ing** *vt* (1667) **:** to give rise to **:** INITIATE ~ *vi* **:** to take or have origin **:** BEGIN ***syn*** see SPRING — **orig·i·na·tion** \-ˌri-jə-'nā-shən\ *n* — **orig·i·na·tor** \-'ri-jə-ˌnā-tər\ *n*

orig·i·na·tive \ə-'ri-jə-ˌnā-tiv, -nə-\ *adj* (1811) **:** having ability to originate **:** CREATIVE — **orig·i·na·tive·ly** *adv*

O–ring \'ō-ˌriŋ\ *n* (1946) **:** a ring (as of synthetic rubber) used as a gasket

ori·ole \'ȯr-ē-ˌōl, -ē-əl\ *n* [NL *oriolus,* fr. ML, fr. OF *oriol,* fr. L *aureolus* golden-colored, dim. of *aureus* golden — more at AUREUS] (1768) **1 :** any of various usu. brightly colored Old World passerine birds (family Oriolidae and esp. genus *Oriolus*) **2 :** any of various New World passerine birds (family Icteridae and esp. genus *Icterus*) of which the males are usu. black and yellow or black and orange

Ori·on \ə-'rī-ən, ō-\ *n* [L, fr. Gk *Ōriōn*] (14c) **1** [L (gen. *Orionis*)] **:** a constellation on the equator east of Taurus represented on charts by the figure of a hunter with belt and sword **2 :** a giant hunter slain by Artemis in Greek mythology

ori·sha \'ȯr-ə-ˌshä\ *n, pl* **orishas** *also* **orisha** [Yoruba *òrìṣà*] (1860) **:** a Yoruba deity; *also* **:** one identified with a Roman Catholic saint in Santeria

or·is·mol·o·gy \ˌȯr-əz-'mä-lə-jē, ˌär-\ *n* [Gk *horismos* definition (fr. *horizein* to define) + E *-logy* — more at HORIZON] (1816) **:** the science of defining technical terms — **or·is·mo·log·i·cal** \ˌȯr-əz-mə-'lä-ji-kəl, ˌär-; ō-ˌriz-\ *adj*

or·i·son \'ȯr-ə-sən, 'är-, -zən\ *n* [ME, fr. AF *ureisun, oreison,* fr. LL *oration-, oratio,* fr. L, oration] (13c) **:** PRAYER

-orium *n suffix, pl* **-oriums** *or* **-oria** [L, fr. neut. of *-orius* -ory] **:** ¹-ORY ⟨haust*orium*⟩

Ori·ya \ō-'rē-ə\ *n* (1801) **:** the Indo-Aryan language of Orissa, India

Or·lean·ist \'ȯr-lē-ə-nist, ȯr-'lē-(ə-)nist\ *n* (1834) **:** a supporter of the Orleans family in its claim to the throne of France by descent from a younger brother of Louis XIV

Or·lon \'ȯr-ˌlän\ *trademark* — used for an acrylic fiber

or·lop deck \'ȯr-ˌläp-\ *n* [ME *overlop* deck of a single decker, fr. MLG *overlōp,* lit., something that overleaps] (1758) **:** the lowest deck in a ship having four or more decks

Or·mazd \'ȯr-(ˌ)məzd, -ˌmazd\ *n* [Pers *Urmazd,* fr. MPers, fr. Av *Ahuramazdāh-*] (1603) **:** AHURA MAZDA

or·mo·lu \'ȯr-mə-ˌlü\ *n, often attrib* [F *or moulu,* lit., ground gold] (1765) **:** golden or gilded brass or bronze used for decorative purposes (as in mounts for furniture)

¹**or·na·ment** \'ȯr-nə-mənt\ *n* [ME, fr. AF *urnement, ornement,* fr. L *ornamentum,* fr. *ornare*] (13c) **1** *archaic* **:** a useful accessory **2 a :** something that lends grace or beauty **b :** a manner or quality that

adorns **3 :** one whose virtues or graces add luster to a place or society **4 :** the act of adorning or being adorned **5 :** an embellishing note not belonging to the essential harmony or melody — called also *embellishment, fioritura*

²**or·na·ment** \-ˌment\ *vt* (1656) **:** to provide with ornament **:** EMBELLISH *syn* see ADORN

¹**or·na·men·tal** \ˌȯr-nə-ˈmen-tᵊl\ *adj* (1646) **:** of, relating to, or serving as ornament; *specif* **:** grown as an ornamental — **or·na·men·tal·ly** \-tᵊl-ē\ *adv*

²**ornamental** *n* (1650) **:** a decorative object; *esp* **:** a plant cultivated for its beauty rather than for use

or·na·men·ta·tion \ˌȯr-nə-mən-ˈtā-shən, -ˌmen-\ *n* (1706) **1 :** something that ornaments **:** EMBELLISHMENT **2 :** the act or process of ornamenting **:** the state of being ornamented

or·nate \ȯr-ˈnāt\ *adj* [ME *ornat,* fr. L *ornatus,* pp. of *ornare* to furnish, embellish; akin to L *ordo* order — more at ORDER] (15c) **1 :** marked by elaborate rhetoric or florid style **2 :** elaborately or excessively decorated ⟨an ~ mantle⟩ — **or·nate·ly** *adv* — **or·nate·ness** *n*

or·nery \ˈȯr-nə-rē, ˈär-; ˈȯrn-rē, ˈärn-\ *adj* **or·neri·er; -est** [alter. of *ordinary*] (1816) **:** having an irritable disposition **:** CANTANKEROUS — **or·neri·ness** *n*

ornith- *or* **ornitho-** *comb form* [L, fr. Gk, fr. *ornith-, ornis* — more at ERNE] **:** bird ⟨*ornitho*logy⟩

or·nith·ic \ȯr-ˈni-thik\ *adj* [Gk *ornithikos,* fr. *ornith-, ornis*] (1854) **:** of, relating to, or characteristic of birds

or·ni·thine \ˈȯr-nə-ˌthēn\ *n* [ISV *ornith*uric acid (a compound of which ornithine is a component, found in the urine of birds) + ²*-ine*] (1881) **:** a crystalline amino acid $C_5H_{12}N_2O_2$ that functions esp. in urea production as a carrier by undergoing conversion to citrulline and then arginine in reaction with ammonia and carbon dioxide followed by recovery along with urea by enzymatic hydrolysis of arginine

or·nith·is·chi·an \ˌȯr-nə-ˈthis-kē-ən\ *n* [NL *Ornithischia,* fr. *ornith-* + *ischium*] (1933) **:** any of an order (Ornithischia) of herbivorous dinosaurs (as a stegosaurus) that have the pubis of the pelvis rotated backward to a position parallel and close to the ischium — compare SAURISCHIAN — **ornithischian** *adj*

or·ni·thol·o·gy \ˌȯr-nə-ˈthä-lə-jē\ *n, pl* **-gies** [NL *ornithologia,* fr. *ornith-* + *-logia* -logy] (1676) **1 :** a treatise on ornithology **2 :** a branch of zoology dealing with birds — **or·ni·tho·log·i·cal** \-thə-ˈlä-ji-kəl\ *also* **or·ni·tho·log·ic** \-jik\ *adj* — **or·ni·tho·log·i·cal·ly** \-ji-k(ə-)lē\ *adv* — **or·ni·thol·o·gist** \-ˈthä-lə-jist\ *n*

or·nith·o·pod \ȯr-ˈni-thə-ˌpäd, ˈȯr-ni-thə-\ *n* [ultim. fr. Gk *ornith-* + *pod-, pous* foot — more at FOOT] (ca. 1889) **:** any of a suborder (Ornithopoda) of bipedal ornithischian dinosaurs (as a hadrosaur) with digitigrade walking limbs usu. having only three functional toes

or·ni·thop·ter \ˈȯr-nə-ˌthäp-tər\ *n* [ISV *ornith-* + *-pter* (as in *helicopter*)] (1908) **:** an aircraft designed to derive its chief support and propulsion from flapping wings

or·ni·tho·sis \ˌȯr-nə-ˈthō-səs\ *n, pl* **-tho·ses** \-ˌsēz\ [NL] (1939) **:** PSITTACOSIS

¹**oro-** *comb form* [Gk *oros* — more at ORIENT] **:** mountain ⟨*oro*graphy⟩

²**oro-** *comb form* [L *or-, os* — more at ORAL] **:** mouth ⟨*oro*pharynx⟩

oro·gen·e·sis \ˌȯr-ə-ˈje-nə-səs\ *n* [NL] (1886) **:** OROGENY — **oro·ge·net·ic** \-jə-ˈne-tik\ *adj*

orog·e·ny \ȯ-ˈrä-jə-nē\ *n* [ISV] (1890) **:** the process of mountain formation esp. by folding of the earth's crust — **oro·gen·ic** \ˌȯr-ə-ˈje-nik\ *adj*

oro·graph·ic \ˌȯr-ə-ˈgra-fik\ *also* **oro·graph·i·cal** \-fi-kəl\ *adj* (ca. 1803) **:** of or relating to mountains; *esp* **:** associated with or induced by the presence of mountains ⟨~ rainfall⟩

orog·ra·phy \ȯ-ˈrä-grə-fē\ *n* [ISV] (ca. 1846) **:** a branch of physical geography that deals with mountains

Oro·mo \ȯ-ˈrō-(ˌ)mō, ō-\ *n, pl* **Oromos** *or* **Oromo** [Oromo (western dial.) *oromoo,* a self-designation, prob. fr. obs. pl. of *orma* person, stranger] (1893) **1 :** a member of a Cushitic-speaking people of southern Ethiopia and adjacent parts of Kenya **2 :** the Cushitic language of the Oromo

oro·pha·ryn·geal \ˌȯr-ə-ˌfa-rən-ˈjē-əl, -fə-ˈrin-j(ē-)əl\ *adj* (1885) **1 :** of or relating to the oropharynx **2 :** of or relating to the mouth and pharynx

oro·phar·ynx \-ˈfa-riŋ(k)s\ *n* (1887) **:** the part of the pharynx that is below the soft palate and above the epiglottis and is continuous with the mouth

oro·tund \ˈȯr-ə-ˌtənd, ˈär-\ *adj* [modif. of L *ore rotundo,* lit., with round mouth] (ca. 1799) **1 :** marked by fullness, strength, and clarity of sound **:** SONOROUS ⟨an ~ voice⟩ **2 :** POMPOUS, BOMBASTIC ⟨an ~ speech⟩ — **oro·tun·di·ty** \ˌȯr-ə-ˈtən-də-tē, ˌär-\ *n*

¹**or·phan** \ˈȯr-fən\ *n* [ME, fr. LL *orphanus,* fr. Gk *orphanos;* akin to OHG *erbi* inheritance, L *orbus* orphaned] (15c) **1 :** a child deprived by death of one or usu. both parents **2 :** a young animal that has lost its mother **3 :** one deprived of some protection or advantage ⟨~*s* of the storm⟩ **4 :** a first line (as of a paragraph) separated from its related text and appearing at the bottom of a printed page or column — **orphan** *adj* — **or·phan·hood** \-ˌhu̇d\ *n*

²**orphan** *vt* **or·phaned; or·phan·ing** \ˈȯr-fə-niŋ, ˈȯrf-niŋ\ (1814) **:** to cause to become an orphan

or·phan·age \ˈȯr-fə-nij, ˈȯrf-nij\ *n* (ca. 1580) **1 :** the state of being an orphan **2 :** an institution for the care of orphans

orphan drug *n* (1981) **:** a drug that is not developed or marketed because its extremely limited use makes it unprofitable

orphan's court *n* (1713) **:** a probate court with jurisdiction in some states over the affairs of minors and the administration of estates

Or·pheus \ˈȯr-ˌfyüs, -fē-əs\ *n* [L, fr. Gk] (14c) **:** a poet and musician in Greek mythology who almost rescues his wife Eurydice from Hades by charming Pluto and Persephone with his lyre

or·phic \ˈȯr-fik\ *adj* (1655) **1** *cap* **:** of or relating to Orpheus or the rites or doctrines ascribed to him **2 :** MYSTIC, ORACULAR **3 :** FASCINATING, ENTRANCING — **or·phi·cal·ly** \-fi-k(ə-)lē\ *adv*

Or·phism \ˈȯr-ˌfi-zəm\ *n* [*Orpheus,* its reputed founder] (1880) **:** a mystic Greek religion offering initiates purification of the soul from innate evil and release from the cycle of reincarnation

or·phrey \ˈȯr-frē\ *n, pl* **orphreys** [ME *orfrey,* fr. AF *orfreis,* fr. ML *aurifrigium,* fr. L *aurum* gold + *Phrygius* Phrygian — more at AUREUS] (13c) **1 a :** elaborate embroidery **b :** a piece of such embroidery **2 :** an ornamental border or band esp. on an ecclesiastical vestment

or·pi·ment \ˈȯr-pə-mənt\ *n* [ME, fr. AF, fr. L *auripigmentum,* fr. *aurum* + *pigmentum* pigment] (14c) **:** a rare orange to lemon-yellow mineral consisting of a native trisulfide of arsenic

or·pine \ˈȯr-pən\ *n* [ME *orpin,* fr. AF, fr. *orpiment*] (14c) **:** an herb (*Sedum telephium* of the family Crassulaceae, the orpine family) that has fleshy leaves and pink or purple flowers and was formerly used in folk medicine; *broadly* **:** SEDUM

Or·ping·ton \ˈȯr-piŋ-tən\ *n* [*Orpington,* England] (1897) **:** any of an English breed of large deep-chested domestic chickens

or·rery \ˈȯr-ər-ē, ˈär-\ *n, pl* **or·rer·ies** [Charles Boyle †1731 4th Earl of *Orrery*] (1713) **:** an apparatus showing the relative positions and motions of bodies in the solar system by balls moved by a clockwork

or·ris \ˈȯr-əs, ˈär-\ *n* [prob. alter. of ME *ireos,* fr. ML, alter. of L *iris* iris] (1545) **:** ORRISROOT

or·ris·root \-ˌrüt, -ˌru̇t\ *n* (1598) **:** the fragrant rootstock of any of three European irises (*Iris florentina, I. germanica,* and *I. pallida*) used esp. in perfumery

ort \ˈȯrt\ *n* [ME, fr. MLG *orte*] (15c) **:** a morsel left at a meal **:** SCRAP

orth- *or* **ortho-** *comb form* [Gk, fr. *orthos* straight, right, true; akin to Skt *ūrdhva* high, upright] **1 :** straight **:** upright **:** vertical ⟨*ortho*grade⟩ **2 :** perpendicular ⟨*ortho*rhombic⟩ **3 :** correct **:** corrective ⟨*ortho*dontia⟩ **4 a :** hydrated or hydroxylated to the highest degree ⟨*ortho*phosphoric acid⟩ **b :** involving substitution at or characterized by or having the relationship of two neighboring positions in the benzene ring ⟨*ortho*-xylene⟩

or·thi·con \ˈȯr-thi-ˌkän\ *n* [ISV *orth-* + *icono*scope] (1939) **:** a camera tube similar to but more sensitive than an iconoscope in which the charges are scanned by a low-velocity beam

or·tho \ˈȯr-(ˌ)thō\ *adj* (1904) **:** ORTHOCHROMATIC

or·tho·cen·ter \ˈȯr-thə-ˌsen-tər\ *n* [ISV] (1869) **:** the common intersection of the three altitudes of a triangle or their extensions or of the several altitudes of a polyhedron provided these latter exist and meet in a point

or·tho·chro·mat·ic \ˌȯr-thə-krō-ˈma-tik\ *adj* [ISV] (1887) **1 :** of, relating to, or producing tone values of light and shade in a photograph that correspond to the tones in nature **2 :** sensitive to all colors except red

or·tho·clase \ˈȯr-thə-ˌklās, -ˌklāz\ *n* [G *Orthoklas,* fr. *orth-* + Gk *klasis* breaking, fr. *klan* to break — more at CLAST] (1849) **:** a monoclinic mineral of the feldspar group consisting of a silicate of potassium and aluminum

or·tho·don·tia \ˌȯr-thə-ˈdän(t)-sh(ē-)ə\ *n* [NL] (ca. 1849) **:** ORTHODONTICS

or·tho·don·tics \-ˈdän-tiks\ *n pl but sing in constr* (1909) **:** a branch of dentistry dealing with irregularities of the teeth (as malocclusion) and their correction (as by braces) — **or·tho·don·tic** \-tik\ *adj* — **or·tho·don·ti·cal·ly** \-ti-k(ə-)lē\ *adv* — **or·tho·don·tist** \-ˈdän-tist\ *n*

¹**or·tho·dox** \ˈȯr-thə-ˌdäks\ *adj* [ME *orthodoxe,* fr. MF or LL; MF *orthodoxe,* fr. LL *orthodoxus,* fr. LGk *orthodoxos,* fr. Gk *orth-* + *doxa* opinion — more at DOXOLOGY] (15c) **1 a :** conforming to established doctrine esp. in religion **b :** CONVENTIONAL **2** *cap* **:** of, relating to, or constituting any of various conservative religious or political groups: as **a :** EASTERN ORTHODOX **b :** of or relating to Orthodox Judaism — **or·tho·dox·ly** *adv*

²**orthodox** *n, pl* **orthodox** *also* **or·tho·dox·es** (1587) **1 :** one that is orthodox **2** *cap* **:** a member of an Eastern Orthodox church

Orthodox Judaism *n* (1904) **:** Judaism that adheres to the Torah and Talmud as interpreted in an authoritative rabbinic law code and applies their principles and regulations to modern living — compare CONSERVATIVE JUDAISM, REFORM JUDAISM

or·tho·doxy \ˈȯr-thə-ˌdäk-sē\ *n, pl* **-dox·ies** (1630) **1 :** the quality or state of being orthodox **2 :** an orthodox belief or practice **3** *cap* **a :** Eastern Orthodox Christianity **b :** ORTHODOX JUDAISM

or·tho·epy \ˈȯr-thə-ˌwe-pē, ȯr-ˈthō-ə-pē\ *n* [NL *orthoepia,* fr. Gk *orthoepeia,* fr. *orth-* + *epos* word — more at VOICE] (1668) **1 :** the customary pronunciation of a language **2 :** the study of the pronunciation of a language — **or·tho·ep·ic** \ˌȯr-thə-ˈwe-pik\ *adj* — **or·tho·ep·i·cal·ly** \-pi-k(ə-)lē\ *adv* — **or·tho·epist** \ˈȯr-thə-ˌwe-pist, ȯr-ˈthō-ə-pist\ *n*

or·tho·gen·e·sis \ˌȯr-thə-ˈje-nə-səs\ *n* [NL] (1895) **:** variation of organisms in successive generations that in some esp. former evolutionary theories takes place in some predestined direction resulting in progressive evolutionary trends independent of external factors — **or·tho·ge·net·ic** \-jə-ˈne-tik\ *adj* — **or·tho·ge·net·i·cal·ly** \-ti-k(ə-)lē\ *adv*

or·thog·o·nal \ȯr-ˈthä-gə-nᵊl\ *adj* [MF, fr. L *orthogonius,* fr. Gk *orthogōnios,* fr. *orth-* + *gōnia* angle — more at -GON] (1612) **1 a :** intersecting or lying at right angles **b :** having perpendicular slopes or tangents at the point of intersection ⟨~ curves⟩ **2 :** having a sum of products or an integral that is zero or sometimes one under specified conditions: as **a** *of real-valued functions* **:** having the integral of the product of each pair of functions over a specific interval equal to zero **b** *of vectors* **:** having the scalar product equal to zero **c** *of a square matrix* **:** having the sum of products of corresponding elements in any two rows or any two columns equal to one if the rows or columns are the same and equal to zero otherwise **:** having a transpose with which the product equals the identity matrix **3** *of a linear transformation* **:** having a matrix that is orthogonal **:** preserving length and distance **4 :** composed of mutually orthogonal elements ⟨an ~ basis of a vector space⟩ **5 :** statistically independent — **or·thog·o·nal·i·ty** \-ˌthä-gə-ˈna-lə-tē\ *n* — **or·thog·o·nal·ly** \-ˈthä-gə-nᵊl-ē\ *adv*

or·thog·o·nal·ize \ȯr-ˈthä-gə-nə-ˌlīz\ *vt* **-ized; -iz·ing** (1930) **:** to make orthogonal — **or·thog·o·nal·i·za·tion** \-ˌthä-gə-nə-lə-ˈzā-shən\ *n*

or·tho·grade \ˈȯr-thə-ˌgrād\ *adj* (1902) **:** walking with the body upright

or·tho·graph·ic \ˌȯr-thə-ˈgra-fik\ *also* **or·tho·graph·i·cal** \-fi-kəl\ *adj* (1706) **1 :** of, relating to, being, or prepared by orthographic projection ⟨an ~ map⟩ **2 a :** of or relating to orthography **b :** correct in spelling — **or·tho·graph·i·cal·ly** \-fi-k(ə-)lē\ *adv*

orthographic projection *n* (1668) **1 :** projection of a single view of an object (as a view of the front) onto a drawing surface in which the lines of projection are perpendicular to the drawing surface **2 :** the representation of related views of an object as if they were all in the same plane and projected by orthographic projection

or·thog·ra·phy \ȯr-ˈthä-grə-fē\ *n* [ME *ortografie,* fr. AF, fr. L *orthographia,* fr. Gk, fr. *orth-* + *graphein* to write — more at CARVE] (15c)

1 a : the art of writing words with the proper letters according to standard usage **b** : the representation of the sounds of a language by written or printed symbols **2** : a part of language study that deals with letters and spelling

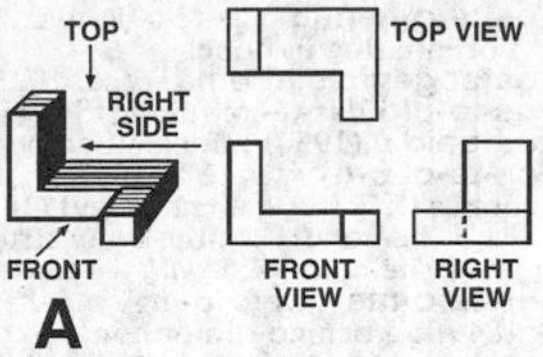

orthographic projection 2: object *A* with top view, front view, and right view

or·tho·mo·lec·u·lar \ˌȯr-thə-mə-ˈle-kyə-lər\ *adj* (1968) : relating to, based on, using, or being a theory according to which disease may be cured by providing the optimum amounts of substances (as vitamins) normally present in the body ⟨~ therapy⟩ ⟨~ psychiatry⟩

or·tho·myxo·vi·rus \ˌȯr-thō-ˈmik-sə-ˌvī-rəs\ *n* [NL, fr. *orth-* + *myxovirus*] (1973) : any of a family (*Orthomyxoviridae*) of single-stranded RNA viruses that have a spherical or filamentous virion with numerous surface projections of glycoprotein and include the causative agents of influenza

or·tho·nor·mal \ˌȯr-thə-ˈnȯr-məl\ *adj* (1932) **1** *of real-valued functions* : orthogonal with the integral of the square of each function over a specified interval equal to one **2** : being or composed of orthogonal elements of unit length ⟨~ basis of a vector space⟩

or·tho·pe·dic *also* **or·tho·pae·dic** \ˌȯr-thə-ˈpē-dik\ *adj* [F *orthopédique,* fr. *orthopédie* orthopedics, fr. *orth-* + Gk *paid-, pais* child — more at FEW] (1840) **1** : of, relating to, or employed in orthopedics **2** : marked by or affected with a skeletal deformity, disorder, or injury — **or·tho·pe·di·cal·ly** \-ˈpē-di-k(ə-)lē\ *adv*

or·tho·pe·dics *also* **or·tho·pae·dics** \-ˈpē-diks\ *n pl but sing or pl in constr* (ca. 1853) : a branch of medicine concerned with the correction or prevention of deformities, disorders, or injuries of the skeleton and associated structures (as tendons and ligaments) — **or·tho·pe·dist** \-ˈpē-dist\ *n*

or·tho·phos·phate \ˌȯr-thə-ˈfäs-ˌfāt\ *n* (1859) : a salt or ester of orthophosphoric acid

or·tho·phos·pho·ric acid \ˌȯr-thə-ˌfäs-ˈfȯr-ik-, -ˈfär-; -ˈfäs-f(ə-)rik-\ *n* [ISV] (1866) : PHOSPHORIC ACID 1

or·tho·psy·chi·a·try \-sə-ˈkī-ə-trē, -(ˌ)sī-\ *n* (ca. 1927) : psychiatry concerned esp. with the prevention and treatment of mental and behavioral disorders in youth — **or·tho·psy·chi·at·ric** \-ˌsī-kē-ˈa-trik\ *adj* — **or·tho·psy·chi·a·trist** \-sə-ˈkī-ə-trist, -(ˌ)sī-\ *n*

or·thop·tera \ȯr-ˈthäp-tə-rə\ *n pl* [NL, order name, fr. *orth-* + Gk *pteron* wing — more at FEATHER] (1828) : insects that are orthopterans

or·thop·ter·an \ȯr-ˈthäp-tə-rən\ *n* [NL *Orthoptera*] (ca. 1842) : any of an order (Orthoptera) of insects (as crickets and grasshoppers) characterized by biting mouthparts, two pairs of wings or none, enlarged hind femurs, and an incomplete metamorphosis — **orthopteran** *adj* — **or·thop·ter·ist** \-rist\ *n* — **or·thop·ter·oid** \-ˌrȯid\ *n or adj*

or·tho·rhom·bic \ˌȯr-thə-ˈräm-bik\ *adj* [ISV] (ca. 1859) : of, relating to, or constituting a system of crystallization characterized by three unequal axes at right angles to each other

or·tho·scop·ic \-ˈskä-pik\ *adj* [ISV *orth-* + *-scopic* (as in *microscopic*)] (1853) : giving an image in correct and normal proportions

or·tho·sis \ȯr-ˈthō-səs\ *n, pl* **or·tho·ses** \-ˌsēz\ [NL, fr. Gk *orthōsis* straightening, fr. *orthoun* to straighten, fr. *orthos*] (1958) : ORTHOTIC

or·tho·stat·ic \ˌȯr-thə-ˈsta-tik\ *adj* (1902) : of, relating to, or caused by an upright posture ⟨~ hypotension⟩

or·thot·ic \ȯr-ˈthä-tik\ *n* [NL *orthosis*] (1955) : a device (as a brace or splint) for supporting, immobilizing, or treating muscles, joints, or skeletal parts which are weak, ineffective, deformed, or injured

or·thot·ics \-tiks\ *n pl but sing in constr* (1957) : a branch of mechanical and medical science that deals with the design and fitting of orthotics — **or·thot·ic** \-tik\ *adj* — **or·tho·tist** \ȯr-ˈthä-tist, ˈȯr-thə-tist\ *n*

or·thot·ro·pous \ȯr-ˈthä-trə-pəs\ *adj* [ISV] (1830) : having the ovule straight and upright with the micropyle at the apex

or·to·lan \ˈȯr-tə-lən\ *n* [F or It; F, fr. It *ortolano,* lit., gardener, fr. L *hortulanus,* fr. *hortulus,* dim. of *hortus* garden — more at YARD] (1656) : an Old World bunting (*Emberiza hortulana*) having a greenish-gray head and breast, streaky brown back and wings, and a yellow throat

ORV *abbr* off-road vehicle

Or·vie·to \ȯr-ˈvyā-(ˌ)tō\ *n* [*Orvieto,* Italy] (1846) : a usu. dry Italian white wine

[1]**-ory** *n suffix* [L *-orium,* fr. neut. of *-orius,* adj. suffix] **1** : place of or for ⟨observat*ory*⟩ **2** : something that serves for ⟨cremat*ory*⟩

[2]**-ory** *adj suffix* [ME *-orie,* fr. AF & L; AF, fr. L *-orius*] **1** : of, relating to, or characterized by ⟨gustat*ory*⟩ **2** : serving for, producing, or maintaining ⟨justificat*ory*⟩

oryx \ˈȯr-iks, ˈär-\ *n, pl* **oryx** *or* **oryx·es** [NL, fr. L, a gazelle, fr. Gk, pickax, antelope, kind of whale, fr. *oryssein* to dig; akin to L *runcare* to grub up, weed, Skt *luñcati* he plucks] (1535) : any of a small genus (Oryx) of large heavily built African and Arabian antelopes that have a light-colored coat with dark conspicuous markings esp. on the face — compare GEMSBOK

or·zo \ˈȯrd-(ˌ)zō\ *n* [It, lit., barley, fr. L *hordeum* — more at ORGEAT] (ca. 1929) : rice-shaped pasta

[1]**os** \ˈäs\ *n, pl* **os·sa** \ˈä-sə\ [L *oss-, os* — more at OSSEOUS] (15c) : BONE

[2]**os** \ˈōs\ *n, pl* **ora** \ˈȯr-ə\ [L *or-, os* — more at ORAL] (1737) : ORIFICE

Os *symbol* osmium

OS *abbr* **1** [L *oculus sinister*] left eye **2** Old Style **3** operating system **4** out of stock

Osage \ō-ˈsāj, ˈō-ˌ\ *n, pl* **Osag·es** *or* **Osage** [F, prob. fr. an Algonquian language, fr. Osage *wažáže,* a self-designation] (1698) **1** : a member of an American Indian people orig. of Missouri **2** : the Siouan language of the Osage people

Osage orange *n* (1817) : an ornamental usu. thorny U.S. tree (*Maclura pomifera*) of the mulberry family with shiny ovate leaves and hard bright orange wood; *also* : its yellowish-green globose fruit

Os·can \ˈäs-kən\ *n* [L *Oscus*] (1753) **1** : a member of a people of ancient Italy occupying Campania **2** : the language of the Oscan people — see INDO-EUROPEAN LANGUAGES table

[1]**Os·car** \ˈäs-kər\ *trademark* — used esp. for any of a number of golden statuettes awarded annually by a professional organization for notable achievement in motion pictures

[2]**Oscar** (1952) — a communications code word for the letter *o*

os·cil·late \ˈä-sə-ˌlāt\ *vi* **-lat·ed; -lat·ing** [L *oscillatus,* pp. of *oscillare* to swing, fr. *oscillum* swing] (1726) **1 a** : to swing backward and forward like a pendulum **b** : to move or travel back and forth between two points **2** : to vary between opposing beliefs, feelings, or theories **3** : to vary above and below a mean value ***syn*** see SWING — **os·cil·la·to·ry** \ˈä-sə-lə-ˌtȯr-ē\ *adj*

os·cil·la·tion \ˌä-sə-ˈlā-shən\ *n* (1658) **1** : the action or state of oscillating **2** : VARIATION, FLUCTUATION **3** : a flow of electricity changing periodically from a maximum to a minimum; *esp* : a flow periodically changing direction **4** : a single swing (as of an oscillating body) from one extreme limit to the other — **os·cil·la·tion·al** \-shnəl, -shə-nᵊl\ *adj*

os·cil·la·tor \ˈä-sə-ˌlā-tər\ *n* (1835) **1** : one that oscillates **2** : a device for producing alternating current; *esp* : a radio-frequency or audio-frequency generator

oscillo- *comb form* [ISV, fr. L *oscillare*] : wave : oscillation ⟨*oscillo*scope⟩

os·cil·lo·gram \ä-ˈsi-lə-ˌgram, ə-\ *n* [ISV] (1903) : a record made by an oscillograph or oscilloscope

os·cil·lo·graph \-ˌgraf\ *n* [ISV] (1893) : an instrument for recording alternating current wave forms or other electrical oscillations — **os·cil·lo·graph·ic** \ä-ˌsi-lə-ˈgra-fik, ˌä-sə-lə-\ *adj* — **os·cil·lo·graph·i·cal·ly** \-fi-k(ə-)lē\ *adv* — **os·cil·log·ra·phy** \ˌä-sə-ˈlä-grə-fē\ *n*

os·cil·lo·scope \ä-ˈsi-lə-ˌskōp, ə-\ *n* [ISV] (1906) : an instrument in which the variations in a fluctuating electrical quantity appear temporarily as a visible wave form on the fluorescent screen of a cathode-ray tube — **os·cil·lo·scop·ic** \ä-ˌsi-lə-ˈskä-pik, ˌä-sə-lə-\ *adj*

os·cine \ˈä-ˌsīn\ *adj* [NL *Oscines,* suborder name, fr. L, pl. of *oscin-, oscen* songbird, bird giving omens by its cry, fr. *obs-, ob-* in front of, in the way + *canere* to sing — more at OB-, CHANT] (1883) : of or relating to a large suborder (Oscines) of passerine birds (as larks, shrikes, finches, orioles, and crows) characterized by a vocal apparatus highly specialized for singing — **oscine** *n*

Os·co–Um·bri·an \ˌäs-kō-ˈəm-brē-ən\ *n* [L *Oscus* + E *Umbrian*] (1894) : a subdivision of the Italic branch of the Indo-European language family containing Oscan and Umbrian

os·cu·late \ˈäs-kyə-ˌlāt\ *vt* **-lat·ed; -lat·ing** [L *osculatus,* pp. of *osculari,* fr. *osculum* kiss, fr. dim. of *os* mouth — more at ORAL] (ca. 1656) : KISS

os·cu·la·tion \ˌäs-kyə-ˈlā-shən\ *n* (ca. 1658) : the act of kissing; *also* : KISS — **os·cu·la·to·ry** \ˈäs-kyə-lə-ˌtȯr-ē\ *adj*

os·cu·lum \ˈäs-kyə-ləm\ *n* [NL, fr. L, dim. of *os* mouth] (1887) : an excurrent opening of a sponge

[1]**-ose** *adj suffix* [L *-osus*] : full of : having : possessing the qualities of ⟨cym*ose*⟩

[2]**-ose** *n suffix* [F, fr. *glucose*] **1** : carbohydrate ⟨amyl*ose*⟩; *esp* : sugar ⟨pent*ose*⟩ **2** : primary hydrolysis product ⟨prote*ose*⟩

Osee \ˈō-ˌzē, ō-ˈzā-ə\ *n* [LL, fr. Heb *Hōshēaʿ*] (1526) : HOSEA

oset·ra *also* **os·set·ra** \(ˌ)ō-ˈse-trə\ *n* [modif. of Russ *osëtr* sturgeon] (1955) : a golden or brownish caviar from a sturgeon (as *Acipenser gueldenstaedtii* of the Caspian Sea) with roe somewhat smaller than the beluga and having a usu. nutty flavor; *also* : the fish — compare SEVRUGA

OSHA *abbr* Occupational Safety and Health Administration

osier \ˈō-zhər\ *n* [ME, fr. AF, fr. ML *auseria* osier bed] (14c) **1** : any of various willows (esp. *Salix viminalis*) whose pliable twigs are used for furniture and basketry **2** : a willow rod used in basketry **3** : any of several American dogwoods; *esp* : RED OSIER

Osi·ris \ō-ˈsī-rəs\ *n* [L, fr. Gk, fr. Egypt *Wsỉr*] (1613) : the Egyptian god of the underworld and husband and brother of Isis

-osis *n suffix, pl* **-oses** *or* **-osises** [NL, fr. Gk *-ōsis,* fr. *-ō-* (stem of causative verbs in *-oun*) + *-sis*] **1 a** : action : process : condition ⟨hyp*nosis*⟩ **b** : abnormal or diseased condition ⟨leuk*osis*⟩ **2** : increase : formation ⟨leukocyt*osis*⟩

Os·man·li \äz-ˈman-lē\ *n* [Turk *osmanlı,* fr. *Osman,* founder of the Ottoman Empire] (1813) **1** : OTTOMAN 1 **2** : TURKISH

os·me·te·ri·um \ˌäz-mə-ˈtir-ē-əm\ *n, pl* **-ria** \-ē-ə\ [NL, irreg. fr. Gk *osmē* odor] (1816) : a protrusible glandular process of swallowtail larvae that emits a disagreeable odor for defensive purposes

osmic acid *n* (1842) : OSMIUM TETROXIDE

os·mi·um \ˈäz-mē-əm\ *n* [NL, fr. Gk *osmē* odor] (1804) : a blue-gray or blue-black hard brittle very heavy polyvalent metallic element with a high melting point that is used esp. as a catalyst and in hard alloys — see ELEMENT table

osmium tetroxide *n* (1869) : a crystalline compound OsO_4 that is an oxide of osmium, has a poisonous irritating vapor, and is used as a catalyst, oxidizing agent, and biological fixative and stain

os·mol *or* **os·mole** \ˈäz-ˌmōl, ˈäs-\ *n* [blend of *osmosis* and *mol* (5mole)] (1942) : a standard unit of osmotic pressure based on a one molal concentration of an ion in a solution

os·mo·lal·i·ty \ˌäz-mō-ˈla-lə-tē, ˌäs-\ *n, pl* **-ties** [*osmol* + 1*-al* + *-ity*] (ca. 1944) : the concentration of an osmotic solution esp. when measured in osmols or milliosmols per 1000 grams of solvent — **os·mo·lal** \äz-ˈmō-ləl, äs-\ *adj*

os·mo·lar·i·ty \ˌäz-mō-ˈla-rə-tē, ˌäs-\ *n, pl* **-ties** [*osmol* + *-ar* + *-ity*] (1948) : the concentration of an osmotic solution esp. when measured in osmols or milliosmols per liter of solution — **os·mo·lar** \äz-ˈmō-lər, äs-\ *adj*

os·mom·e·ter \äz-ˈmä-mə-tər, äs-\ *n* [*osmosis* + *-meter*] (1854) : an apparatus for measuring osmotic pressure — **os·mo·met·ric** \ˌäz-mə-ˈme-trik, ˌäs-\ *adj* — **os·mom·e·try** \äz-ˈmä-mə-trē\ *n*

os·mo·reg·u·la·tion \ˈäz-mō-ˌre-gyə-ˈlā-shən, ˈäs-\ *n* [*osmosis* + *regulation*] (1927) : regulation of osmotic pressure esp. in the body of a living organism — **os·mo·reg·u·la·to·ry** \-ˈre-gyə-lə-ˌtȯr-ē\ *adj*

os·mo·sis \äz-ˈmō-səs, äs-\ *n* [NL, short for *endosmosis*] (1867) **1** : movement of a solvent (as water) through a semipermeable membrane (as of a living cell) into a solution of higher solute concentration

\ə\ **abut** \ᵊ\ **kitten, F table** \ər\ **further** \a\ **ash** \ā\ **ace** \ä\ **mop, mar** \au̇\ **out** \ch\ **chin** \e\ **bet** \ē\ **easy** \g\ **go** \i\ **hit** \ī\ **ice** \j\ **job** \ŋ\ **sing** \ō\ **go** \ȯ\ **law** \ȯi\ **boy** \th\ **thin** \t͟h\ **the** \ü\ **loot** \u̇\ **foot** \y\ **yet** \zh\ **vision, beige** \k, ⁿ, œ, ue, ʸ\ *see* Guide to Pronunciation

that tends to equalize the concentrations of solute on the two sides of the membrane **2 :** a process of absorption or diffusion suggestive of the flow of osmotic action; *esp* : a usu. effortless often unconscious assimilation ⟨learned a number of languages by ~ —Roger Kimball⟩

os·mot·ic \-ˈmä-tik\ *adj* (1854) **:** of, relating to, caused by, or having the properties of osmosis — **os·mot·i·cal·ly** \-ti-k(ə-)lē\ *adv*

osmotic pressure *n* (1888) **:** the pressure produced by or associated with osmosis and dependent on molar concentration and absolute temperature: as **a :** the maximum pressure that develops in a solution separated from a solvent by a membrane permeable only to the solvent **b :** the pressure that must be applied to a solution to just prevent osmosis

osmotic shock *n* (1950) **:** a rapid change in the osmotic pressure (as by transfer to a medium of different concentration) affecting a living system

os·mun·da \äz-ˈmən-də\ *n* [NL, fr. ML, fr. OF *osmonde*] (1789) **:** any of a genus (*Osmunda*) of rather large ferns (as the cinnamon fern) with pinnate or bipinnate fronds and fibrous creeping rhizomes

os·prey \ˈäs-prē, -ˌprā\ *n, pl* **ospreys** [ME *ospray*, fr. AF **osfraie*, fr. L *ossifraga*, a bird of prey] (15c) **1 :** a large fish-eating hawk (*Pandion haliaetus*) with long wings that is dark brown above and mostly pure white below **2 :** a feather trimming used for millinery

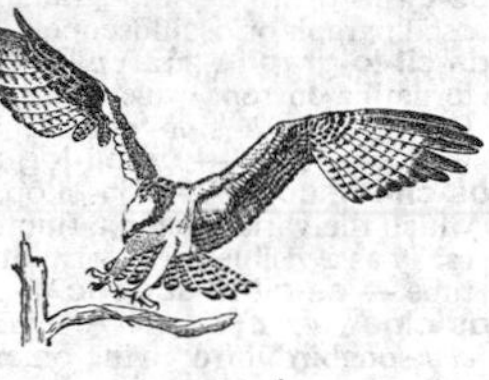
osprey 1

OSS *abbr* Office of Strategic Services

ossa *pl of* OS

os·se·in \ˈä-sē-ən\ *n* [ISV, fr. L *oss-, os*] (1857) **:** the collagen of bones

os·se·ous \ˈä-sē-əs\ *adj* [L *osseus*, fr. *oss-, os* bone; akin to Gk *osteon* bone, Skt *asthi*] (1682) **:** BONY 1

Os·sete \ä-ˌsēt\ *also* **Os·set** \ˈä-sət, -ˌset\ *n* [Russ *osetin*, fr. *Osetiya* Ossetia, fr. Georgian *Oseti*, fr. *osi* Ossete] (1814) **:** a member of a people of the central Caucasus — **Os·se·tian** \ä-ˈsē-shən\ *adj or n*

Os·set·ic \ä-ˈse-tik\ *n* (1841) **:** the Iranian language of the Ossetes

Os·si·an·ic \ˌä-sē-ˈa-nik, -shē-\ *adj* (1808) **:** of, relating to, or resembling the legendary Irish bard Ossian, the poems ascribed to him, or the rhythmic prose style used by James Macpherson in the poems he claimed to have translated from Ossian

os·si·cle \ˈä-si-kəl\ *n* [L *ossiculum*, dim. of *oss-, os*] (1578) **:** a small bone or bony structure (as the malleus, incus, or stapes) — **os·sic·u·lar** \ä-ˈsi-kyə-lər\ *adj*

os·si·fi·ca·tion \ˌä-sə-fə-ˈkā-shən\ *n* (1697) **1 a :** the natural process of bone formation **b :** the hardening (as of muscular tissue) into a bony substance **2 :** a mass or particle of ossified tissue **3 :** a tendency toward or state of being molded into a rigid, conventional, sterile, or unimaginative condition

os·si·frage \ˈä-sə-frij, -ˌfrāj\ *n* [L *ossifraga*, a bird of prey, fr. fem. of *ossifragus* bone-breaking, fr. *oss-, os* + *frangere* to break — more at BREAK] (1601) **:** LAMMERGEIER

os·si·fy \ˈä-sə-ˌfī\ *vb* **-fied; -fy·ing** [L *oss-, os* + E *-ify*] *vi* (1713) **1 :** to change into bone **2 :** to become hardened or conventional and opposed to change ~ *vt* **1 :** to change (as cartilage) into bone **2 :** to make rigidly conventional and opposed to change

os·so bu·co *also* **os·so buc·co** \ˌō-sō-ˈbü-(ˌ)kō, ˌȯ-sō-\ *n* [It *ossobuco* veal shank, lit., pierced bone] (1923) **:** a dish of veal shanks braised with vegetables, white wine, and seasoned stock

os·su·ary \ˈä-shə-ˌwer-ē, -syə-, -sə-\ *n, pl* **-ar·ies** [LL *ossuarium*, fr. L, neut. of *ossuarius* of bones, fr. OL *ossua*, pl. of *oss-, os*] (1658) **:** a depository for the bones of the dead

oste- *or* **osteo-** *comb form* [NL, fr. Gk, fr. *osteon* — more at OSSEOUS] **:** bone ⟨*oste*al⟩ ⟨*osteo*myelitis⟩

os·te·al \ˈäs-tē-əl\ *adj* [ISV] (1877) **:** of, relating to, or resembling bone; *also* **:** affecting or involving bone or the skeleton

os·te·i·tis \ˌäs-tē-ˈī-təs\ *n* [NL] (ca. 1847) **:** inflammation of bone

os·ten·si·ble \ä-ˈsten(t)-sə-bəl, ə-\ *adj* [F, fr. L *ostensus*, pp. of *ostendere* to show, fr. *obs-, ob-* in the way + *tendere* to stretch — more at OB-, THIN] (ca. 1771) **1 :** intended for display **:** open to view **2 :** being such in appearance **:** plausible rather than demonstrably true or real ⟨the ~ purpose for the trip⟩ ***syn*** see APPARENT

os·ten·si·bly \-blē\ *adv* (1765) **1 :** in an ostensible manner **2 :** to all outward appearances

os·ten·sive \ä-ˈsten(t)-siv\ *adj* (1782) **1 :** OSTENSIBLE 2 **2 :** of, relating to, or constituting definition by exemplifying the thing or quality being defined — **os·ten·sive·ly** *adv*

os·ten·so·ri·um \ˌäs-tən-ˈsȯr-ē-əm, -ˌten-\ *n, pl* **-ria** \-ē-ə\ [ML, fr. L *ostendere*] (ca. 1772) **:** MONSTRANCE

os·ten·ta·tion \ˌäs-tən-ˈtā-shən\ *n* [ME *ostentacion*, fr. MF, fr. L *ostentation-, ostentatio*, fr. *ostentare* to display, freq. of *ostendere*] (15c) **1 :** excessive display **:** PRETENTIOUSNESS **2** *archaic* **:** an act of displaying

os·ten·ta·tious \-shəs\ *adj* (1673) **:** marked by or fond of conspicuous or vainglorious and sometimes pretentious display ***syn*** see SHOWY — **os·ten·ta·tious·ly** *adv* — **os·ten·ta·tious·ness** *n*

os·te·o·ar·thri·tis \ˌäs-tē-ō-är-ˈthrī-təs\ *n* [NL] (1878) **:** arthritis marked by degeneration of the cartilage and bone of joints — **os·te·o·ar·thrit·ic** \-ˈthri-tik\ *adj*

os·te·o·blast \ˈäs-tē-ə-ˌblast\ *n* [ISV] (1875) **:** a bone-forming cell — **os·te·o·blas·tic** \ˌäs-tē-ə-ˈblas-tik\ *adj*

os·te·o·clast \ˈäs-tē-ə-ˌklast\ *n* [ISV *oste-* + Gk *klastos* broken — more at CLAST] (1872) **:** any of the large multinucleate cells closely associated with areas of bone resorption — **os·te·o·clas·tic** \ˌäs-tē-ə-ˈklas-tik\ *adj*

os·te·o·cyte \ˈäs-tē-ə-ˌsīt\ *n* (1942) **:** a cell that is characteristic of adult bone and is isolated in a lacuna of the bone substance

os·te·o·gen·e·sis \ˌäs-tē-ə-ˈje-nə-səs\ *n* [NL] (1830) **:** development and formation of bone

osteogenesis im·per·fec·ta \-ˌim-(ˌ)pər-ˈfek-tə\ *n* [NL, imperfect osteogenesis] (ca. 1901) **:** a hereditary disease marked esp. by extreme brittleness of bones and caused by defective or insufficient collagen

os·te·o·gen·ic \ˌäs-tē-ə-ˈje-nik\ *adj* (1867) **1 :** producing bone **2 :** originating in bone

osteogenic sarcoma *n* (ca. 1923) **:** OSTEOSARCOMA

1**os·te·oid** \ˈäs-tē-ˌȯid\ *adj* [ISV] (1840) **:** resembling bone

2**osteoid** *n* (1934) **:** uncalcified bone matrix

os·te·ol·o·gy \ˌäs-tē-ˈä-lə-jē\ *n* [NL *osteologia*, fr. Gk, description of bones, fr. *oste-* + *-logia* -logy] (1670) **1 :** a branch of anatomy dealing with the bones **2 :** the bony structure of an organism — **os·te·o·log·i·cal** \-tē-ə-ˈlä-ji-kəl\ *adj* — **os·te·ol·o·gist** \-tē-ˈä-lə-jist\ *n*

os·te·o·ma \ˌäs-tē-ˈō-mə\ *n, pl* **-mas** *also* **-ma·ta** \-mə-tə\ [NL] (ca. 1849) **:** a benign tumor composed of bone tissue

os·te·o·ma·la·cia \ˌäs-tē-ō-mə-ˈlā-sh(ē-)ə\ *n* [NL, fr. *oste-* + Gk *malakia* softness, fr. *malakos* soft — more at MOLLIFY] (ca. 1834) **:** a disease of adults that is characterized by softening of the bones and is analogous to rickets in the young

os·te·o·my·e·li·tis \-ˌmī-ə-ˈlī-təs\ *n* [NL] (1854) **:** an infectious usu. painful inflammatory disease of bone often of bacterial origin that may result in the death of bone tissue

os·te·o·path \ˈäs-tē-ə-ˌpath\ *n* (1897) **:** a practitioner of osteopathy

os·te·op·a·thy \ˌäs-tē-ˈä-pə-thē\ *n* [NL *osteopathia*, fr. *oste-* + L *-pathia* -pathy] (1899) **:** a system of medical practice based on a theory that diseases are due chiefly to loss of structural integrity which can be restored by manipulation of the parts supplemented by therapeutic measures (as use of drugs or surgery) — **os·te·o·path·ic** \ˌäs-tē-ə-ˈpa-thik\ *adj* — **os·te·o·path·i·cal·ly** \-thi-k(ə-)lē\ *adv*

os·teo·phyte \ˈäs-tē-ə-ˌfīt\ *n* (1846) **:** a pathological bony outgrowth

os·te·o·plas·ty \ˈäs-tē-ə-ˌplas-tē\ *n* (ca. 1860) **:** plastic surgery on bone; *esp* **:** replacement of lost bone tissue or reconstruction of defective bony parts — **os·te·o·plas·tic** \ˌäs-tē-ə-ˈplas-tik\ *adj*

os·te·o·po·ro·sis \ˌäs-tē-ō-pə-ˈrō-səs\ *n, pl* **-ro·ses** \-ˌsēz\ [NL, fr. *oste-* + *porosis* rarefaction, fr. *porus* pore + *-osis*] (1846) **:** a condition that affects esp. older women and is characterized by decrease in bone mass with decreased density and enlargement of bone spaces producing porosity and fragility — **os·te·o·po·rot·ic** \-ˈrä-tik\ *adj*

os·te·o·sar·co·ma \-sär-ˈkō-mə\ *n, pl* **-mas** *also* **-ma·ta** \-mə-tə\ [NL] (ca. 1826) **:** a sarcoma derived from bone or containing bone tissue

osti·na·to \ˌäs-tə-ˈnä-(ˌ)tō, ˌȯs-\ *n, pl* **-tos** *also* **-ti** \-tē\ [It, obstinate, fr. L *obstinatus*] (ca. 1876) **:** a musical figure repeated persistently at the same pitch throughout a composition — compare IMITATION, SEQUENCE

os·ti·ole \ˈäs-tē-ˌōl\ *n* [NL *ostiolum*, fr. L, dim. of *ostium*] (ca. 1857) **:** a small bodily aperture, orifice, or pore

os·ti·um \ˈäs-tē-əm\ *n, pl* **os·tia** \-tē-ə\ [NL, fr. L, door, mouth of a river; akin to L *os* mouth — more at ORAL] (1828) **:** a mouthlike opening in a bodily part (as a fallopian tube or a blood vessel)

ostler *var of* HOSTLER

os·to·my \ˈäs-tə-mē\ *n, pl* **-mies** [*colostomy*] (1957) **:** an operation (as a colostomy) to create an artificial passage for bodily elimination

-ostosis *n comb form, pl* **-ostoses** *or* **-ostosises** [NL, fr. Gk *-ostōsis*, fr. *osteon* bone — more at OSSEOUS] **:** ossification of a (specified) part or to a (specified) degree ⟨hyper*ostosis*⟩

os·tra·cise *Brit var of* OSTRACIZE

os·tra·cism \ˈäs-trə-ˌsi-zəm\ *n* (1588) **1 :** a method of temporary banishment by popular vote without trial or special accusation practiced in ancient Greece **2 :** exclusion by general consent from common privileges or social acceptance

os·tra·cize \-ˌsīz\ *vt* **-cized; -ciz·ing** [Gk *ostrakizein* to banish by voting with potsherds, fr. *ostrakon* shell, potsherd — more at OYSTER] (1649) **1 :** to exile by ostracism **2 :** to exclude from a group by common consent

os·tra·cod \ˈäs-trə-ˌkäd\ *also* **os·tra·code** \-ˌkōd\ *n* [ultim. fr. Gk *ostrakon*] (1865) **:** any of a subclass (Ostracoda) of very small aquatic crustaceans that have the body enclosed in a bivalve carapace, the body segmentation obscured, the abdomen rudimentary, and only seven pairs of appendages

os·tra·co·derm \ˈäs-trə-kō-ˌdərm, äs-ˈtra-kə-\ *n* [ultim. fr. Gk *ostrakon* + *derma* skin — more at DERM-] (1891) **:** any of the early fossil jawless fishes of the Lower Paleozoic usu. having a bony covering of plates or scales

os·tra·con \ˈäs-trə-ˌkän\ *n, pl* **-tra·ca** \-trə-kə\ [Gk *ostrakon* potsherd, shell — more at OYSTER] (1883) **:** a fragment (as of pottery) containing an inscription — usu. used in pl.

os·trich \ˈäs-trich, ˈȯs- *also* -trij\ *n* [ME, fr. AF *ostriz, ostrige*, fr. VL **avis struthio*, fr. L *avis* bird + LL *struthio* ostrich — more at STRUTHIOUS] (13c) **1 a :** a swift-footed 2-toed flightless ratite bird (*Struthio camelus*) of Africa that is the largest of existing birds and often weighs 300 pounds (140 kilograms) **b :** RHEA **c :** leather made from ostrich skin **2** [fr. the belief that the ostrich when pursued hides its head in the sand and believes itself to be unseen] **:** one who attempts to avoid danger or difficulty by refusing to face it — **os·trich·like** \-ˌlīk\ *adj*

ostrich fern *n* (1882) **:** any of a genus (*Matteuccia*) of temperate-zone ferns; *esp* **:** a tall fern (*M. struthiopteris*) with graceful arched fronds which are the source of edible fiddleheads

Os·tro·goth \ˈäs-trə-ˌgäth\ *n* [ME, fr. LL *Ostrogothi*, pl.] (14c) **:** a member of the eastern division of the Goths — **Os·tro·goth·ic** \ˌäs-trə-ˈgä-thik\ *adj*

Os·we·go tea \ä-ˈswē-gō-\ *n* [*Oswego* River, N. Y.] (1752) **:** a No. American mint (*Monarda didyma*) with showy scarlet irregular flowers

OT *abbr* **1** occupational therapist; occupational therapy **2** Old Testament **3** overtime

ot- *or* **oto-** *comb form* [Gk *ōt-, ōto-*, fr. *ōt-, ous* — more at EAR] **:** ear ⟨*ot*itis⟩ **:** ear and ⟨*oto*laryngology⟩

OTA *abbr* Office of Technology Assessment

OTB *abbr* offtrack betting

OTC *abbr* over-the-counter

Othel·lo \ə-ˈthe-(ˌ)lō, ō-\ *n* (1604) **:** a Moor in the military service of Venice, husband of Desdemona, and protagonist of Shakespeare's tragedy *Othello*

1**oth·er** \ˈə-t͟hər\ *adj* [ME, fr. OE *ōther;* akin to OHG *andar* other, Skt *antara*] (bef. 12c) **1 a :** being the one (as of two or more) remaining or not included ⟨held on with one hand and waved with the ~ one⟩ **b :** being the one or ones distinct from that or those first mentioned or implied ⟨taller than the ~ boys⟩ **c :** SECOND ⟨every ~ day⟩ **2 :** not the same : DIFFERENT ⟨any ~ color would have been better⟩ ⟨something ~ than it seems to be⟩ **3** : ADDITIONAL ⟨sold in the U.S. and 14 ~ countries⟩ **4 a** : recently past ⟨the ~ evening⟩ **b** : FORMER ⟨in ~ times⟩ **5** : disturbingly or threateningly different : ALIEN, EXOTIC

[2]**other** *n* (bef. 12c) **1 a** : one that remains of two or more **b** : a thing opposite to or excluded by something else ⟨went from one side to the ~⟩ ⟨nature as the ~ of culture⟩ **2** : a different or additional one ⟨the ~*s* came later⟩ **3 a** : one (as another person) that is psychologically differentiated from the self **b** *often cap* : one considered by members of a dominant group as alien, exotic, threatening, or inferior (as because of different racial, sexual, or cultural characteristics)

[3]**other** *pron, sometimes pl in constr* (bef. 12c) **1** *obs* **a** : one of two that remains **b** : each preceding one **2** : a different or additional one ⟨something or ~⟩

[4]**other** *adv* (13c) : OTHERWISE — used with *than* ⟨was unable to see them ~ than by going to their home⟩

oth·er–di·rect·ed \ˌə-t͟hər-də-ˈrek-təd, -dī-\ *adj* (1950) : directed in thought and action primarily by external norms rather than by one's own scale of values — **oth·er–di·rect·ed·ness** *n*

oth·er·guess \ˈə-t͟hər-ˌges\ *adj* [alter. of E dial. *othergates*] (1632) *archaic* : DIFFERENT

oth·er·ness \ˈə-t͟hər-nəs\ *n* (1587) **1** : the quality or state of being other or different **2** : something that is other or different

[1]**other than** *prep* (14c) : with the exception of : EXCEPT FOR, BESIDES ⟨*other than* that, nothing happened⟩

[2]**other than** *conj* (1605) : EXCEPT, BUT ⟨cannot be changed *other than* by judicial order⟩

oth·er·where \-ˌhwer, -ˌwer\ *adv* (14c) : ELSEWHERE

oth·er·while \-ˌhwī(-ə)l, -ˌwī(-ə)l\ *also* **oth·er·whiles** \-ˌhwī(-ə)lz, -ˌwī(-ə)lz\ *adv* (13c) *chiefly dial* : at another time

[1]**oth·er·wise** \-ˌwīz\ *pron* [ME, fr. OE (*on*) *ōthre wīsan* in another manner] (bef. 12c) : something or anything else : something to the contrary ⟨was ordered to testify and could not do ~⟩

[2]**otherwise** *adv* (13c) **1** : in a different way or manner ⟨glossed over or ~ handled —*Playboy*⟩ **2** : in different circumstances ⟨might ~ have left⟩ **3** : in other respects ⟨an ~ flimsy farce —*Current Biog.*⟩ **4** : if not ⟨do what I tell you, ~ you'll be sorry⟩ **5** : NOT — paired with an adjective, adverb, noun, or verb to indicate its contrary or to suggest an indefinite alternative ⟨people whose deeds, admirable or ~ —John Fischer⟩ ⟨almost thirty thousand women, Irish and ~ —J. M. Burns⟩ ⟨his opinion as to the success or ~ of it —*Austral. Dict. of Biog.*⟩

[3]**otherwise** *adj* (14c) : DIFFERENT ⟨if conditions were ~⟩

other woman *n* (1680) : a woman with whom a married man has an affair — usu. used with *the*

oth·er·world \ˈə-t͟hər-ˌwərld\ *n* (13c) : a world beyond death or beyond present reality

oth·er·world·ly \ˌə-t͟hər-ˈwərl(d)-lē\ *adj* (1879) **1 a** : of, relating to, or resembling that of a world other than the actual world **b** : devoted to preparing for a world to come **2** : devoted to intellectual or imaginative pursuits — **oth·er·world·li·ness** *n*

[1]**-otic** *adj suffix* [Gk *-ōtikos*, fr. *-ōtos*, ending of verbals, fr. *-o-* (stem of causative verbs in *-oun*) + *-tos*, suffix forming verbals — more at -ED] : of, relating to, or characterized by a (specified) action, process, or condition ⟨symbi*otic*⟩

[2]**-otic** *adj comb form* [Gk *ōtikos* of the ear, fr. *ōt-, ous* ear] : having (such) a relationship to the ear ⟨dich*otic*⟩

oti·ose \ˈō-shē-ˌōs, ˈō-tē-\ *adj* [L *otiosus*, fr. *otium* leisure] (1794) **1** : producing no useful result : FUTILE **2** : being at leisure : IDLE **3** : lacking use or effect : FUNCTIONLESS ***syn*** see VAIN — **oti·ose·ly** *adv* — **oti·ose·ness** *n* — **oti·os·i·ty** \ˌō-shē-ˈä-sə-tē, ˌō-tē-\ *n*

oti·tis \ō-ˈtī-təs\ *n* [NL] (ca. 1799) : inflammation of the ear

otitis me·dia \-ˈmē-dē-ə\ *n* [NL] (1874) : inflammation of the middle ear marked esp. by pain, fever, dizziness, and hearing loss

oto·cyst \ˈō-tə-ˌsist\ *n* [ISV; fr. its probable auditory function] (1877) : a fluid-containing organ of many invertebrates that contains an otolith : STATOCYST — **oto·cys·tic** \ˌō-tə-ˈsis-tik\ *adj*

oto·lar·yn·gol·o·gy \ˌō-tō-ˌla-rən-ˈgä-lə-jē\ *n* (1897) : a medical specialty concerned esp. with the ear, nose, and throat — **oto·lar·yn·go·log·i·cal** \-gə-ˈlä-ji-kəl\ *adj* — **oto·lar·yn·gol·o·gist** \-ˈgä-lə-jist\ *n*

oto·lith \ˈō-tə-ˌlith\ *n* [F *otolithe*, fr. *ot-* + *-lithe* -lith] (ca. 1836) : a calcareous concretion in the inner ear of a vertebrate or in the otocyst of an invertebrate — **oto·lith·ic** \ˌō-tə-ˈli-thik\ *adj*

otol·o·gy \ō-ˈtä-lə-jē\ *n* [*ot-* + *-logy*] (1842) : a science that deals with the ear and its diseases — **oto·log·ic** \ˌō-tə-ˈlä-jik\ *also* **oto·log·i·cal** \-ji-kəl\ *adj* — **otol·o·gist** \ō-ˈtä-lə-jist\ *n*

oto·rhi·no·lar·yn·gol·o·gy \ˌō-tō-ˌrī-nō-ˌla-rən-ˈgä-lə-jē\ *n* (ca. 1900) : OTOLARYNGOLOGY — **oto·rhi·no·lar·yn·go·log·i·cal** \-gə-ˈlä-ji-kəl\ *adj* — **oto·rhi·no·lar·yn·gol·o·gist** \-ˈgä-lə-jist\ *n*

oto·scle·ro·sis \ˌō-tō-sklə-ˈrō-səs\ *n* [NL] (1901) : growth of spongy bone in the inner ear that causes progressively increasing deafness

oto·scope \ˈō-tə-ˌskōp\ *n* (1853) : an instrument with lighting and magnifying systems used for visual examination of the tympanic membrane and the canal connecting it to the exterior of the body

oto·tox·ic \ˌō-tə-ˈtäk-sik\ *adj* (1951) : producing, involving, or being adverse effects on organs or nerves involved in hearing or balance ⟨an ~ drug⟩ — **oto·tox·ic·i·ty** \-täk-ˈsi-sə-tē\ *n*

OTR *abbr* occupational therapist, registered

OTS *abbr* officers' training school

ot·ta·va \ō-ˈtä-və\ *adv or adj* [It, octave, fr. ML *octava*] (1848) : at an octave higher or lower than written — used as a direction in music

ottava ri·ma \-ˈrē-mə\ *n, pl* **ottava rimas** [It, lit., eighth rhyme] (1820) : a stanza of eight lines of heroic verse with a rhyme scheme of *abababcc*

Ot·ta·wa \ˈä-tə-wə, -ˌwä, -ˌwȯ\ *n, pl* **-was** *or* **-wa** [F *Outaoua*, fr. Ojibwa (eastern dial.) *ota·wa·*] (1687) : a member of an American Indian people of Michigan and southern Ontario

ot·ter \ˈä-tər\ *n, pl* **otters** *also* **otter** [ME *oter*, fr. OE *otor*; akin to OHG *ottar* otter, Gk *hydōr* water — more at WATER] (bef. 12c) **1** : any of various largely aquatic carnivorous mammals (as genus *Lutra* or *Enhydra*) of the weasel family that usu. have webbed and clawed feet and dark brown fur **2** : the fur or pelt of an otter

ot·ter·hound \-ˌhau̇nd\ *n* [fr. its use in hunting otters] (1590) : any of a breed of large hounds that originated in Great Britain and have a rough outer and inner coat, webbed feet, and a keen sense of smell

otto *var of* ATTAR

ot·to·man \ˈä-tə-mən\ *n* (1605) **1** *cap* **a** : a member of a Turkish dynasty founded by Osman I that ruled the Ottoman Empire **b** : a citizen or functionary of the Ottoman Empire **2** [F *ottomane*, fr. fem. of *ottoman*, adj.] **a** : an upholstered often overstuffed seat or couch usu. without a back **b** : an overstuffed footstool **3** : a heavy clothing fabric characterized by pronounced crosswise ribs

Ot·to·man \ˈä-tə-mən\ *adj* [F, adj. & n., prob. fr. It *ottomano*, fr. Ar *ʿothmānī*, fr. *ʿOthmān* Osman I, founder of the Ottoman Empire] (1603) : of or relating to the Ottoman Empire or its citizens

oua·bain \wä-ˈbä-ən, ˈwä-ˌbän\ *n* [ISV, fr. F *ouabaïo*, an African tree, fr. Somali *waabayyo* arrow poison] (1893) : a poisonous glycoside $C_{29}H_{44}O_{12}$ obtained from several African shrubs or trees (genera *Strophanthus* and *Acokanthera*) of the dogbane family and used medically like digitalis and in Africa as an arrow poison

ou·bli·ette \ˌü-blē-ˈet\ *n* [F, fr. MF, fr. *oublier* to forget, fr. OF *oblier*, fr. VL **oblitare*, freq. of L *oblivisci* to forget — more at OBLIVION] (1819) : a dungeon with an opening only at the top

[1]**ouch** \ˈau̇ch\ *n* [ME, alter. (fr. misdivision of *a nouche*) of *nouche*, fr. AF *nusche, nouche*, of Gmc origin; akin to OHG *nusca* clasp] (14c) **1** *obs* : CLASP, BROOCH **2 a** : a setting for a precious stone **b** : JEWEL, ORNAMENT; *esp* : a buckle or brooch set with precious stones

[2]**ouch** *interj* [origin unknown] (1838) — used esp. to express sudden pain

oud \ˈüd\ *n* [Ar *ʿūd*, lit., wood] (1738) : a musical instrument of the lute family used in southwest Asia and northern Africa

[1]**ought** \ˈȯt\ *verbal auxiliary* [ME *oughte* (1st & 3d sing. pres. indic.), fr. *oughte*, 1st & 3d sing. past indic. & subj. of *owen* to own, owe — more at OWE] (12c) — used to express obligation ⟨~ to pay our debts⟩, advisability ⟨~ to take care of yourself⟩, natural expectation ⟨~ to be here by now⟩, or logical consequence ⟨the result ~ to be infinity⟩

[2]**ought** \ˈȯ(k)t\ *vt* [ME *oughte*, 1st & 3d sing. past indic. of *owen*] (13c) **1** *chiefly Scot* : POSSESS **2** *chiefly Scot* : OWE

[3]**ought** \ˈȯt\ *n* (1678) : moral obligation : DUTY

[4]**ought** \ˈȯt, ˈät\ *archaic var of* AUGHT

oughtn't \ˈȯ-t^{ə}nt\ (1884) : ought not

ou·gui·ya \ü-ˈgwē-ə, -ˈgē-ə\ *n, pl* **ouguiya** [Ar dial. *ūgīya*, fr. Ar *ūqīya*, lit., ounce] (1973) — see MONEY table

Oui·ja \ˈwē-jə, -jē\ *trademark* — used for a board with the alphabet and other signs on it that is used with a planchette to seek spiritualistic or telepathic messages

[1]**ounce** \ˈau̇n(t)s\ *n* [ME, fr. AF *unce*, fr. L *uncia* 12th part, ounce, fr. *unus* one — more at ONE] (14c) **1 a** : a unit of weight equal to $1/12$ troy pound — see WEIGHT table **b** : a unit of weight equal to $1/16$ avoirdupois pound **c** : a small amount ⟨an ~ of sense⟩ **2** : FLUID OUNCE

[2]**ounce** *n* [ME *unce* lynx, fr. MF, alter. (by misdivision, as if *l'once* the ounce) of *lonce*, prob. fr. OIt *lonza*, fr. MGk *lynk-, lynx*, fr. Gk] (1774) : SNOW LEOPARD

our \är, ˈau̇(-ə)r\ *adj* [ME *oure*, fr. OE *ūre*; akin to OHG *unsēr* our, OE *ūs* us] (bef. 12c) : of or relating to us or ourselves or ourself esp. as possessors or possessor, agents or agent, or objects or object of an action ⟨~ throne⟩ ⟨~ actions⟩ ⟨~ being chosen⟩

Our Father *n* [fr. the opening words] (1882) : LORD'S PRAYER

ours \ˈau̇(-ə)rz, ärz\ *pron, sing or pl in constr* (14c) : that which belongs to us — used without a following noun as a pronoun equivalent in meaning to the adjective *our*

our·self \är-ˈself, au̇(-ə)r-\ *pron* (14c) : MYSELF — used to refer to the single-person subject when *we* is used instead of *I* (as by a sovereign) ⟨will keep ~ till supper time alone —Shak.⟩

our·selves \-ˈselvz\ *pron pl* (15c) **1** : those identical ones that are we — used reflexively ⟨we're doing it solely for ~⟩, for emphasis ⟨we ~ will never go⟩, or in absolute constructions ⟨~ no longer young, we can sympathize with those who are old⟩; compare WE 1 **2** : our normal, healthy, or sane condition ⟨just not ~ today⟩

-ous *adj suffix* [ME, fr. AF *-us, -ous*, fr. L *-osus*] **1** : full of : abounding in : having : possessing the qualities of ⟨clamor*ous*⟩ ⟨poison*ous*⟩ **2** : having a valence lower than in compounds or ions named with an adjective ending in *-ic* ⟨mercur*ous*⟩

ousel *var of* OUZEL

Ou·shak *also* **Ushak** \ü-ˈshäk\ *n, often attrib* [fr. *Oushak, Ushak* (Uşak), town in Turkey] (1901) : a heavy wool Oriental rug characterized esp. by bright primary colors and an elaborate medallion pattern

oust \ˈau̇st\ *vt* [ME, fr. AF *oster, ouster* to take off, remove, oust, fr. LL *obstare* to ward off, fr. L, to stand in the way, fr. *ob-* in the way + *stare* to stand — more at OB-, STAND] (15c) **1 a** : to remove from or dispossess of property or position by legal action, by force, or by the compulsion of necessity **b** : to take away (as a right or authority) : BAR, REMOVE **2** : to take the place of : SUPPLANT ***syn*** see EJECT

oust·er \ˈau̇s-tər\ *n* [AF, fr. *oster, ouster* to oust] (1531) **1 a** : a wrongful dispossession **b** : a judgment removing an officer or depriving a corporation of a franchise **2** : EXPULSION

[1]**out** \ˈau̇t\ *adv* [ME, fr. OE *ūt*; akin to OHG *ūz* out, Gk *hysteros* later, Skt *ud* up, out] (bef. 12c) **1 a (1)** : in a direction away from the inside or center ⟨went ~ into the garden⟩ **(2)** : OUTSIDE ⟨it's raining ~⟩ **b** : from among others **c** : away from the shore **d** : away from home or work ⟨~ to lunch⟩ **e** : away from a particular place **2 a** : so as to be missing or displaced from the usual or proper place ⟨left a word ~⟩ ⟨threw his shoulder ~⟩ **b** : into the possession or control of another ⟨lend ~ money⟩ **c** : into a state of loss or defeat ⟨was voted ~⟩ **d** : into a state of vexation ⟨they do not mark me, and that brings me ~ —Shak.⟩ **e** : into groups or shares ⟨sorted ~ her notes⟩ ⟨parceled ~ the farm⟩ **3 a** : to the point of depletion, extinction, or exhaustion ⟨the food ran ~⟩ ⟨turn the light ~⟩ ⟨all tuckered ~⟩ **b** : to completion or satisfaction ⟨hear me ~⟩ ⟨work the problem ~⟩ **c** : to the full or a great extent or degree ⟨all decked ~⟩ ⟨stretched ~ on the floor⟩ **4 a** : in or into the open ⟨the sun came ~⟩ **b** : OUT LOUD ⟨cried ~⟩ **c** : in or into public circulation ⟨the evening paper isn't ~ yet⟩ ⟨hand ~ pamphlets⟩ ⟨the library book is still ~⟩ **5 a** : at an end

⟨before the day is ~⟩ **b :** in or into an insensible or unconscious state ⟨she was ~ cold⟩ **c :** in or into a useless state ⟨landed the plane with one engine ~⟩ **d :** so as to end the offensive turn of another player, a side, or oneself in baseball ⟨threw him ~⟩ ⟨fly ~⟩ **6** — used on a two-way radio circuit to indicate that a message is complete and no reply is expected

[2]**out** *vt* (bef. 12c) **1 :** EJECT, OUST **2 :** to identify publicly as being such secretly ⟨wanted to ~ pot smokers⟩; *esp* **:** to identify as being a closet homosexual ~ *vi* **:** to become publicly known ⟨the truth will ~⟩

[3]**out** *prep* (13c) — used as a function word to indicate an outward movement ⟨ran ~ the door⟩ ⟨looked ~ the window⟩

[4]**out** *adj* (13c) **1 a :** situated outside **:** EXTERNAL **b :** OUT-OF-BOUNDS **2 :** situated at a distance **:** OUTLYING ⟨the ~ islands⟩ **3 :** not being in power **4 :** ABSENT **5 :** removed by the defense from play as a batter or base runner in a baseball inning ⟨two men ~⟩ **6 :** directed outward or serving to direct something outward ⟨the ~ basket⟩ **7 :** not being in vogue or fashion **8 :** not to be considered **:** out of the question **9 :** DETERMINED 1 ⟨was ~ to get revenge⟩ **10 :** engaged in or attempting a particular activity ⟨won on his first time ~⟩ **11 :** publicly known or identified as a homosexual

[5]**out** *n* (1717) **1 :** OUTSIDE **2 :** one who is out of office or power or on the outside ⟨a matter of ~*s* versus ins⟩ **3 a :** an act or instance of putting a player out or of being put out in baseball **b :** a player that is put out **4 :** a way of escaping from an embarrassing or difficult situation — **on the outs :** on unfriendly terms **:** at variance

out- *prefix* [[1]*out*] **:** in a manner that exceeds or surpasses and sometimes overpowers or defeats ⟨*out*maneuver⟩

out·achieve
out·act
out·bar·gain
out·bid
out·bitch
out·bluff
out·box
out·brag
out·brawl
out·bulk
out·buy
out·catch
out·charge
out·climb
out·coach
out·com·pete
out·dance
out·daz·zle
out·de·bate
out·de·liv·er
out·de·sign
out·drag
out·dress
out·drink
out·drive
out·du·el
out·earn
out·eat
out·fight
out·fig·ure
out·fish
out·fly
out·fum·ble
out·gain
out·glit·ter
out·gross
out·hit
out·ho·mer
out·hunt
out·hus·tle
out·jump
out·kick
out·kill
out·last
out·leap
out·learn
out·man
out·ma·neu·ver
out·ma·nip·u·late
out·march
out·mus·cle
out·or·ga·nize
out·pass
out·per·form
out·pitch
out·play
out·plot
out·pol·i·tick
out·poll
out·pop·u·late
out·pow·er
out·pray
out·preach
out·price
out·pro·duce
out·prom·ise
out·punch
out·rate
out·re·bound
out·re·pro·duce
out·ri·val
out·roar
out·row
out·rush
out·sail
out·scheme
out·scoop
out·score
out·shout
out·sing
out·sit
out·skate
out·soar
out·spar·kle
out·speed
out·sprint
out·stride
out·swear
out·swim
out·talk
out·think
out·throw
out·trade
out·vie
out·vote
out·wait
out·walk
out·watch
out·wres·tle
out·write
out·yell
out·yield

out·age \ˈau̇-tij\ *n* (1899) **1 :** a quantity or bulk of something lost in transportation or storage **2 a :** a failure or interruption in use or functioning **b :** a period of interruption esp. of electric current

out–and–out \ˌau̇t-ᵊn(d)-ˈau̇t\ *adj* (1813) **:** being such completely at all times, in every way, or from every point of view ⟨an ~ fraud⟩

out–and–out·er \-ˈau̇-tər\ *n* (ca. 1812) **:** one who goes to extremes

out·back \ˈau̇t-ˈbak, -ˌbak\ *n* (1893) **:** isolated rural country esp. of Australia

out·bal·ance \ˌau̇t-ˈba-lən(t)s\ *vt* (1644) **:** OUTWEIGH

[1]**out·board** \ˈau̇t-ˌbȯrd\ *adj* (ca. 1823) **1 :** situated outboard **2 :** having, using, or limited to the use of an outboard motor

[2]**outboard** *adv* (ca. 1848) **1 :** outside a ship's bulwarks **:** in a lateral direction from the hull **2 :** in a position closer or closest to either of the wingtips of an airplane or to the sides of an automobile

[3]**outboard** *n* (1935) **1 :** OUTBOARD MOTOR **2 :** a boat with an outboard motor

outboard motor *n* (1909) **:** a small internal combustion engine with propeller integrally attached for mounting at the stern of a small boat

out·bound \ˈau̇t-ˌbau̇nd\ *adj* (1598) **:** outward bound ⟨~ traffic⟩

out–box \ˈau̇t-ˌbäks\ *n* (1970) **:** a box or tray (as on a desk) for holding outgoing interoffice mail

out·brave \ˌau̇t-ˈbrāv\ *vt* (1589) **1 :** to face or resist defiantly **2 :** to exceed in courage

out·break \ˈau̇t-ˌbrāk\ *n* (1602) **1 a :** a sudden or violent increase in activity or currency ⟨the ~ of war⟩ **b :** a sudden rise in the incidence of a disease ⟨an ~ of measles⟩ **c :** a sudden increase in numbers of a harmful organism and esp. an insect within a particular area ⟨an ~ of locusts⟩ **2 :** INSURRECTION, REVOLT

out·breed *vt* **-bred** \-ˌbred, -ˈbred\; **-breed·ing** (ca. 1909) **1** \ˈau̇t-ˌbrēd\ **:** to subject to outbreeding **2** \ˌau̇t-ˈ-\ **:** to breed faster than

out·breed·ing \ˈau̇t-ˌbrē-diŋ\ *n* (1901) **:** the interbreeding of individuals or stocks that are relatively unrelated

out·build·ing \ˈau̇t-ˌbil-diŋ\ *n* (1626) **:** a building (as a stable or a woodshed) separate from but accessory to a main house

out·burst \-ˌbərst\ *n* (1657) **1 :** a violent expression of feeling ⟨an ~ of anger⟩ **2 :** a surge of activity or growth ⟨new ~*s* of creative power —C. E. Montague⟩ **3 :** ERUPTION ⟨volcanic ~*s*⟩

out·bye *or* **out·by** \üt-ˈbī\ *adv* [ME (Sc) *out-by,* fr. *out* + *by*] (15c) *chiefly Scot* **:** a short distance away; *also* **:** OUTDOORS

out·cast \ˈau̇t-ˌkast\ *n* (14c) **1 :** one that is cast out or refused acceptance (as by society) **:** PARIAH **2** [Sc *cast out* to quarrel] *Scot* **:** QUARREL — **outcast** *adj*

out·caste \-ˌkast\ *n* (1876) **1 :** one who has been ejected from a Hindu caste for violation of its customs or rules **2 :** one who has no caste

out·class \ˌau̇t-ˈklas\ *vt* (1870) **:** to excel or surpass so decisively as to be or appear to be of a higher class

out·come \ˈau̇t-ˌkəm\ *n* (1788) **:** something that follows as a result or consequence ⟨a surprising ~⟩ ⟨patient ~*s* of bypass surgery⟩

[1]**out·crop** \ˈau̇t-ˌkräp\ *n* (1805) **1 :** a coming out of bedrock or of an unconsolidated deposit to the surface of the ground **2 :** the part of a rock formation that appears at the surface of the ground

[2]**out·crop** \ˈau̇t-ˌkräp, ˌau̇t-ˈ-\ *vi* (ca. 1847) **1 :** to project from the surrounding soil ⟨ledges *outcropping* from the eroded slope⟩ **2 :** to come to the surface **:** APPEAR

out·crop·ping \ˈau̇t-ˌkrä-piŋ\ *n* (1872) **:** OUTCROP

[1]**out·cross** \ˈau̇t-ˌkrȯs\ *n* (1890) **1 :** a cross between relatively unrelated individuals **2 :** the progeny of an outcross

[2]**outcross** *vt* (1918) **:** to cross with a relatively unrelated individual or strain

out·cry \ˈau̇t-ˌkrī\ *n* (14c) **1 a :** a loud cry **:** CLAMOR **b :** a vehement protest **2 :** AUCTION

out·dat·ed \ˌau̇t-ˈdā-təd\ *adj* (1616) **:** no longer current **:** OUTMODED — **out·dat·ed·ly** *adv* — **out·dat·ed·ness** *n*

out·dis·tance \ˌau̇t-ˈdis-tən(t)s\ *vt* (1857) **:** to go far ahead of (as in a race) **:** OUTSTRIP

out·do \-ˈdü\ *vt* **-did** \-ˈdid\; **-done** \-ˈdən\; **-do·ing** \-ˈdü-iŋ\; **-does** \-ˈdəz\ (1607) **1 :** to go beyond in action or performance **2 :** DEFEAT, OVERCOME ***syn*** see EXCEED

out·door \ˈau̇t-ˌdȯr; ˈau̇t-ˈ-\ *also* **out·doors** \-ˌdōrz, -ˌdȯrz; ˈau̇t-ˈ-\ *adj* [*out (of) door, out (of) doors*] (1748) **1 :** of or relating to the outdoors **2 a :** performed outdoors ⟨~ sports⟩ **b :** OUTDOORSY ⟨an ~ couple⟩ **3 :** not enclosed **:** having no roof ⟨an ~ restaurant⟩

[1]**out·doors** \ˌau̇t-ˈdȯrz; ˈau̇t-ˈ-\ *adv* (1755) **:** outside a building **:** in or into the open air

[2]**outdoors** *n pl but sing in constr* (1830) **1 :** a place or location away from the confines of a building **2 :** the world away from human habitations

out·doors·man \-mən\ *n* (1918) **:** one who spends much time in the outdoors or in outdoor activities — **out·doors·man·ship** \-ˌship\ *n*

out·doorsy \ˌau̇t-ˈdȯr-zē\ *adj* (1936) **1 :** relating to, characteristic of, or appropriate for the outdoors **2 :** fond of outdoor activities

out·draw \ˌau̇t-ˈdrȯ\ *vt* **-drew** \-ˈdrü\; **-drawn** \-ˈdrȯn\; **-draw·ing** (ca. 1909) **1 :** to attract a larger audience or following than **2 :** to draw a handgun more quickly than

out·er \ˈau̇-tər\ *adj* [ME, fr. [4]*out* + [1]*-er*] (13c) **1 :** existing independent of mind **:** OBJECTIVE **2 a :** situated farther out ⟨the ~ limits⟩ **b :** being away from a center **c :** situated or belonging on the outside

out·er·coat \ˈau̇-tər-ˌkōt\ *n* (1948) **:** COAT 1a

out·er·course \ˈau̇-tər-ˌkȯrs\ *n* [*outer* + *intercourse*] (1986) **:** sexual activity between individuals that does not involve vaginal or anal intercourse

outer ear *n* (1701) **:** the outer visible portion of the ear that collects and directs sound waves toward the tympanic membrane by way of a canal which extends inward through the temporal bone

out·er·most \ˈau̇-tər-ˌmōst\ *adj* (14c) **:** farthest out

outer planet *n* (1941) **:** any of the planets Jupiter, Saturn, Uranus, and Neptune whose orbits lie beyond the asteroid belt

outer space *n* (1879) **:** space immediately outside the earth's atmosphere; *broadly* **:** interplanetary or interstellar space

out·er·wear \ˈau̇-tər-ˌwer\ *n* (1883) **1 :** clothing for outdoor wear **2 :** outer clothing as opposed to underwear

out·face \ˌau̇t-ˈfās\ *vt* (ca. 1529) **1 :** to cause to waver or submit by or as if by staring **2 :** to confront unflinchingly **:** DEFY

out·fall \ˈau̇t-ˌfȯl\ *n* (1629) **:** the outlet of a body of water (as a river or lake); *esp* **:** the mouth of a drain or sewer

out·field \-ˌfēld\ *n* (1868) **1 :** the part of a baseball field beyond the infield and between the foul lines **2 :** the baseball defensive positions comprising right field, center field, and left field; *also* **:** the players who occupy these positions — **out·field·er** \-ˌfēl-dər\ *n*

[1]**out·fit** \ˈau̇t-ˌfit\ *n* (ca. 1769) **1 :** the act of fitting out or equipping (as for a voyage or expedition) **2 a :** a set of tools or equipment esp. for the practice of a trade **b :** a clothing ensemble often for a special occasion or activity **c :** physical, mental, or moral endowments or resources **3 :** a group that works as a team **:** ORGANIZATION; *esp* **:** a military unit

[2]**outfit** *vb* **out·fit·ted; out·fit·ting** *vt* (1847) **1 :** to furnish with an outfit **2 :** SUPPLY ⟨*outfitting* every family with shoes —*Amer. Guide Series: Vt.*⟩ ~ *vi* **:** to acquire an outfit ***syn*** see FURNISH

out·fit·ter \-ˌfi-tər\ *n* (1846) **:** one that outfits: as **a :** HABERDASHER **b :** a business providing equipment, supplies, and often trained guides (as for hunting trips); *also* **:** a guide working for such an outfitter

out·flank \ˌau̇t-ˈflaŋk\ *vt* (1765) **1 :** to get around the flank of (an opposing force) **2 :** GET AROUND, CIRCUMVENT

[1]**out·flow** \ˈau̇t-ˌflō, ˌau̇t-ˈ-\ *vi* (ca. 1580) **:** to flow out

[2]**out·flow** \ˈau̇t-ˌflō\ *n* (ca. 1800) **1 :** a flowing out ⟨the ~ of dollars⟩ **2 :** something that flows out ⟨~ of a sewage treatment plant⟩

out·foot \ˌau̇t-ˈfu̇t\ *vt* (1737) **:** to outdo in speed **:** OUTSTRIP

out·fox \-ˈfäks\ *vt* (1924) **:** OUTSMART

out–front \-ˈfrənt\ *adj* (1968) **:** FRANK, OPEN

out·gas \ˈau̇t-ˌgas, ˌau̇t-ˈ-\ *vt* (1921) **1 :** to remove occluded gases from usu. by heating; *broadly* **:** to remove gases from **2 :** to remove (gases) from a material or a space ~ *vi* **:** to lose gases

out·gen·er·al \ˌau̇t-ˈjen-rəl, -ˈje-nə-\ *vt* (1767) **:** to surpass in generalship **:** OUTMANEUVER

[1]**out·go** \ˌau̇t-ˈgō\ *vt* (1530) **:** to go beyond **:** OUTDO

[2]**out·go** \ˈau̇t-ˌgō\ *n, pl* **outgoes** (ca. 1640) **1 :** something that goes out; *specif* **:** EXPENDITURE **2 a :** the act of going out **b :** DEPARTURE **3 :** OUTLET 1a

out·go·ing \ˈau̇t-ˌgō-iŋ, -ˌgȯ(-)iŋ\ *adj* (1633) **1 a :** going away **:** DEPARTING ⟨an ~ ship⟩ **b :** retiring or withdrawing from a place or position ⟨the ~ president⟩ **c :** directed to an intended recipient ⟨~ mail⟩ **2 :** openly friendly and responsive **:** EXTROVERTED — **out·go·ing·ness** *n*

out·go·ings \-ˌgō-iŋz, -ˌgȯ(-)iŋz\ *n pl* (1765) *Brit* : costs incurred : EXPENSES

out–group \ˈau̇t-ˌgrüp\ *n* (ca. 1907) : a group that is distinct from one's own and so usu. an object of hostility or dislike — compare IN-GROUP 1

out·grow \ˌau̇t-ˈgrō\ *vt* **-grew** \-ˈgrü\; **-grown** \-ˈgrōn\; **-grow·ing** (1594) **1** : to grow or increase faster than ⟨mankind is ~*ing* food supplies —R. C. Murphy⟩ **2** : to grow too large or too mature for ⟨*outgrew* his best suit⟩ ⟨the need to ~ the habit of war —Norman Cousins⟩

out·growth \ˈau̇t-ˌgrōth\ *n* (1837) **1** : a process or product of growing out ⟨an ~ of hair⟩ **2** : CONSEQUENCE, BY-PRODUCT ⟨crime is often an ~ of poverty⟩

out·guess \ˌau̇t-ˈges\ *vt* (1911) : to anticipate the expectations, intentions, or actions of : OUTWIT

out·gun \-ˈgən\ *vt* (1691) : to surpass in firepower; *broadly* : OUTDO

out·haul \ˈau̇t-ˌhȯl\ *n* (1840) : a rope used to haul a sail taut along a spar

out–Her·od \ˌau̇t-ˈher-əd\ *vt* [*out-* + *Herod* the Great, depicted in medieval mystery plays as a blustering tyrant] (1602) : to exceed in violence or extravagance — usu. used in the phrase *out-Herod Herod*

out·house \ˈau̇t-ˌhau̇s\ *n* (14c) : OUTBUILDING; *esp* : PRIVY 1a

out·ing \ˈau̇-tiŋ\ *n* (1821) **1** : a brief usu. outdoor pleasure trip **2** : an athletic competition or race; *also* : an appearance therein **3** : a usu. public presentation or appearance (as in a particular role) ⟨her first ~ as a novelist⟩ **4** : the public disclosure of the covert homosexuality of a prominent person esp. by homosexual activists

out·land \ˈau̇t-ˌland, -lənd\ *n* (bef. 12c) **1** : a foreign land **2** *pl* : the outlying regions of a country : PROVINCES — **outland** *adj*

out·land·er \-ˌlan-dər, -lən-\ *n* (1598) : a person who belongs to another region, culture, or group : FOREIGNER, STRANGER

out·land·ish \ˌau̇t-ˈlan-dish\ *adj* (bef. 12c) **1** : of or relating to another country : FOREIGN **2 a** : strikingly out of the ordinary : BIZARRE ⟨an ~ costume⟩ **b** : exceeding proper or reasonable limits or standards **3** : remote from civilization ***syn*** see STRANGE — **out·land·ish·ly** *adv* — **out·land·ish·ness** *n*

[1]**out·law** \ˈau̇t-ˌlȯ\ *n* [ME *outlawe*, fr. OE *ūtlaga*, fr. ON *ūtlagi*, fr. *ūt* out (akin to OE *ūt* out) + *lag-*, *lǫg* law — more at OUT, LAW] (bef. 12c) **1** : a person excluded from the benefit or protection of the law **2 a** : a lawless person or a fugitive from the law **b** : a person or organization under a ban or restriction **c** : one that is unconventional or rebellious **3** : an animal (as a horse) that is wild and unmanageable — **outlaw** *adj*

[2]**outlaw** *vt* (bef. 12c) **1 a** : to deprive of the benefit and protection of law : declare to be an outlaw **b** : to make illegal ⟨~*ed* dueling⟩ **2** : to place under a ban or restriction **3** : to remove from legal jurisdiction or enforcement — **out·law·ry** \ˈau̇t-ˌlȯr-ē\ *n*

[1]**out·lay** \ˌau̇t-ˈlā, ˌau̇t-ˈ\ *vt* **-laid** \-ˈlād, -ˈlād\; **-lay·ing** (1802) : to lay out (money) : EXPEND

[2]**out·lay** \ˈau̇t-ˌlā\ *n* (1798) **1** : the act of expending **2** : EXPENDITURE, PAYMENT ⟨~*s* for national defense⟩

out·let \ˈau̇t-ˌlet, -lət\ *n* [ME *ut-lete*, fr. *ut* out + *-lete* watercourse, fr. OE *gelǣt*, fr. *lǣtan* to let] (13c) **1 a** : a place or opening through which something is let out : EXIT, VENT **b** : a means of release or satisfaction for an emotion or impulse ⟨sexual ~*s*⟩ **c** : a medium of expression or publication **d** : a publication or broadcast organization ⟨media ~*s*⟩ **2** : a stream flowing out of a lake or pond **3 a** : a market for a commodity **b** : an agency (as a store) through which a product is marketed ⟨retail ~*s*⟩ **4** : a receptacle for the plug of an electrical device

outlet pass *n* (ca. 1975) : a pass made in basketball by the player taking a defensive rebound to a teammate to start a fast break

out·li·er \-ˌlī(-ə)r\ *n* (1676) **1** : a person whose residence and place of business are at a distance **2** : something (as a geological feature) that is situated away from or classed differently from a main or related body **3** : a statistical observation that is markedly different in value from the others of the sample

[1]**out·line** \ˈau̇t-ˌlīn\ *n* (1662) **1 a** : a line that marks the outer limits of an object or figure : BOUNDARY **b** : SHAPE **2 a** : a style of drawing in which contours are marked without shading **b** : a sketch in outline **3 a** : a condensed treatment of a particular subject ⟨an ~ of world history⟩ **b** : a summary of a written work : SYNOPSIS **4** : a preliminary account of a project : PLAN **5** : a fishing line set out overnight

syn OUTLINE, CONTOUR, PROFILE, SILHOUETTE mean the line that bounds and gives form to something. OUTLINE applies to a line marking the outer limits or edges of a body or mass ⟨traced the *outline* of his hand⟩. CONTOUR stresses the quality of an outline or a bounding surface as being smooth, jagged, curving, or sharply angled ⟨a car with flowing *contours*⟩. PROFILE suggests a varied and sharply defined outline against a lighter background ⟨a portrait of her face in *profile*⟩. SILHOUETTE suggests a shape esp. of a head or figure with all detail blacked out in shadow leaving only the outline clearly defined ⟨photograph in *silhouette* against a bright sky⟩.

[2]**outline** *vt* (ca. 1790) **1** : to draw the outline of **2** : to indicate the principal features or different parts of ⟨*outlined* their responsibilities⟩

out·live \ˌau̇t-ˈliv\ *vt* (15c) **1** : to live beyond or longer than ⟨*outlived* most of his friends⟩ ⟨~ its usefulness⟩ **2** : to survive the effects of ⟨universities . . . ~ many political and social changes —J. B. Conant⟩

out·look \ˈau̇t-ˌlu̇k\ *n* (1667) **1 a** : a place offering a view **b** : a view from a particular place **2** : POINT OF VIEW ⟨a positive ~ on life⟩ **3** : the act of looking out **4** : the prospect for the future ⟨the ~ for steel demand in the U.S. —*Wall Street Jour.*⟩ ***syn*** see PROSPECT

out loud *adv* (1821) : loudly enough to be heard : ALOUD

out·ly·ing \ˈau̇t-ˌlī-iŋ\ *adj* (ca. 1690) : remote from a center or main body ⟨~ areas⟩

out·match \ˌau̇t-ˈmach\ *vt* (1603) : to prove superior to : OUTDO

out–mi·grant \ˈau̇t-ˌmī-grənt\ *n* (1945) : one that out-migrates

out–mi·grate \-ˌgrāt\ *vi* (1953) : to leave one region or community in order to settle in another esp. as part of a large-scale and continuing movement of population — compare IN-MIGRATE — **out–mi·gra·tion** \ˌau̇t-mī-ˈgrā-shən\ *n*

out·mode \ˌau̇t-ˈmōd\ *vt* **out·mod·ed; out·mod·ing** [*out (of) mode*] (1906) : to make unfashionable or obsolete

out·mod·ed \-ˈmō-dəd\ *adj* (1903) **1** : not being in style **2** : no longer acceptable, current, or usable ⟨~ customs⟩

out·most \ˈau̇t-ˌmōst\ *adj* (12c) : farthest out : OUTERMOST

out·num·ber \ˌau̇t-ˈnəm-bər\ *vt* (1670) : to exceed in number

out of *prep* (bef. 12c) **1 a** (1) — used as a function word to indicate direction or movement from within to the outside of ⟨walked *out of* the room⟩ (2) — used as a function word to indicate a change in quality, state, or form ⟨woke up *out of* a deep sleep⟩ **b** (1) — used as a function word to indicate a position or situation beyond the range, limits, or sphere of ⟨*out of* control⟩ (2) — used as a function word to indicate a position or state away from the usual or expected ⟨*out of* practice⟩ **2** — used as a function word to indicate origin, source, or cause ⟨a remarkable colt *out of* an ordinary mare⟩ ⟨built *out of* old lumber⟩ ⟨fled *out of* fear⟩ **3** — used as a function word to indicate exclusion from or deprivation of ⟨cheated him *out of* his savings⟩ ⟨*out of* breath⟩ **4** — used as a function word to indicate choice or selection from a group ⟨one *out of* four survived⟩ **5** — used as a function word to indicate the center of an enterprise or activity ⟨runs her business *out of* her home⟩ — **out of it** **1** : not part of a group, activity, or fashion **2** : in a dazed or confused state

out–of–body *adj* (1970) : relating to or involving a feeling of separation from one's body and of being able to view oneself and others from an external perspective ⟨an ~ experience⟩

out–of–bounds \ˌau̇t-ə(v)-ˈbau̇n(d)z\ *adv or adj* (1798) : outside the prescribed boundaries or limits

out–of–date \-ˈdāt\ *adj* (1592) : OUTMODED, OBSOLETE

out–of–door \-ˈdȯr\ *or* **out–of–doors** \-ˈdȯrz\ *adj* (1800) : OUTDOOR

out–of–doors *n pl but sing in constr* (1819) : OUTDOORS

out of doors *adv* (1603) : OUTDOORS

out–of–pock·et \-ˈpä-kət\ *adj* (1885) : requiring an outlay of cash ⟨~ expenses⟩

out–of–sight \ˌau̇-də-ˈsīt\ *adj* (1876) *slang* : WONDERFUL

out–of–the–way \ˌau̇t-ə(v)-thə-ˈwā\ *adj* (1704) **1** : UNUSUAL ⟨~ information⟩ **2** : being off the beaten track ⟨an ~ restaurant⟩

out·pace \ˌau̇t-ˈpās\ *vt* (1611) **1** : to surpass in speed **2** : OUTDO

out·pa·tient \ˈau̇t-ˌpā-shənt\ *n, often attrib* (1715) : a patient who is not hospitalized overnight but who visits a hospital, clinic, or associated facility for diagnosis or treatment — compare INPATIENT

out·place·ment \ˌau̇t-ˈplās-mənt, ˈau̇t-ˌ\ *n* (1970) : the process of easing unwanted or unneeded executives out of a company by providing company-paid assistance in finding them new jobs

out·point \ˌau̇t-ˈpȯint\ *vt* (1883) **1** : to sail closer to the wind than **2** : to win more points than (as in a boxing match)

out·port \ˈau̇t-ˌpȯrt\ *n* (1642) **1** *chiefly Brit* : a port other than the main port of a country **2** : a small fishing village esp. in Newfoundland

out·post \ˈau̇t-ˌpōst\ *n* (1757) **1 a** : a security detachment dispatched by a main body of troops to protect it from enemy surprise **b** : a military base established by treaty or agreement in another country **2 a** : an outlying or frontier settlement **b** : an outlying branch or position of a main organization or group

[1]**out·pour** \ˌau̇t-ˈpȯr, ˈau̇t-ˌ\ *vt* (1671) : to pour out

[2]**out·pour** \ˈau̇t-ˌpȯr\ *n* (1864) : OUTPOURING

out·pour·ing \ˈau̇t-ˌpȯr-iŋ\ *n* (15c) **1** : the act of pouring out ⟨an ~ of emotion⟩ **2** : something that pours out or is poured out : OUTFLOW

out·pull \ˌau̇t-ˈpu̇l\ *vt* (1926) : OUTDRAW 1

[1]**out·put** \ˈau̇t-ˌpu̇t\ *n* (ca. 1858) **1** : something produced: as **a** : mineral, agricultural, or industrial production ⟨steel ~⟩ **b** : mental or artistic production ⟨literary ~⟩ **c** : the amount produced by a person in a given time **d** : power or energy produced or delivered by a machine or system (as for storage or for conversion in kind or in characteristics) ⟨generator ~⟩ ⟨solar X-ray ~⟩ **e** : the information produced by a computer **2** : the act, process, or an instance of producing **3** : the terminal for the output on an electrical device

[2]**output** *vt* **out·put·ted** *or* **output; out·put·ting** (1858) : to produce as output

out·race \ˌau̇t-ˈrās\ *vt* (1657) : OUTPACE

[1]**out·rage** \ˈau̇t-ˌrāj\ *n* [ME, fr. AF *utrage, outrage* insult, excess, fr. *outre, utre* beyond, fr. L *ultra* — more at ULTRA-] (14c) **1** : an act of violence or brutality **2 a** : INJURY, INSULT ⟨do no ~*s* on silly women or poor passengers —Shak.⟩ **b** : an act that violates accepted standards of behavior or taste ⟨an ~ alike against decency and dignity —John Buchan⟩ **3** : the anger and resentment aroused by injury or insult

[2]**outrage** *vt* **out·raged; out·rag·ing** (1590) **1 a** : RAPE **b** : to violate the standards or principles of ⟨he has *outraged* respectability past endurance —John Braine⟩ **2** : to arouse anger or resentment in usu. by some grave offense ⟨was *outraged* by the accusation⟩ ***syn*** see OFFEND

out·ra·geous \(ˌ)au̇t-ˈrā-jəs\ *adj* (14c) **1 a** : exceeding the limits of what is usual **b** : not conventional or matter-of-fact : FANTASTIC **2** : VIOLENT, UNRESTRAINED **3 a** : going beyond all standards of what is right or decent ⟨an ~ disregard of human rights⟩ **b** : deficient in propriety or good taste ⟨~ language⟩ ⟨~ manners⟩ — **out·ra·geous·ly** *adv* — **out·ra·geous·ness** *n*

out·range \ˌau̇t-ˈrānj\ *vt* (1858) : to surpass in range

out·rank \-ˈraŋk\ *vt* (1842) **1** : to rank higher than **2** : to exceed in importance

ou·tré \ü-ˈtrā\ *adj* [F, fr. pp. of *outrer* to go beyond, carry to excess, fr. OF *ultrer, utrer*, fr. *ultre, outre* beyond] (1722) : violating convention or propriety : BIZARRE

[1]**out·reach** \ˌau̇t-ˈrēch\ *vt* (ca. 1568) **1 a** : to surpass in reach **b** : EXCEED ⟨the demand ~*es* the supply⟩ **2** : to get the better of by trickery ~ *vi* **1** : to go too far **2** : to reach out

[2]**out·reach** \ˈau̇t-ˌrēch\ *n* (1870) **1** : the act of reaching out **2** : the extent or limit of reach ⟨the ~ of the Ohio floods —Clifton Johnson⟩ **3** : the extending of services or assistance beyond current or usual limits ⟨an ~ program⟩; *also* : the extent of such services or assistance

[1]**out·ride** \ˌau̇t-ˈrīd\ *vt* **-rode** \-ˈrōd\; **-rid·den** \-ˈri-dᵊn\; **-rid·ing** \-ˈrī-diŋ\ (1530) **1** : to ride better, faster, or farther than : OUTSTRIP **2** : to ride out (a storm)

[2]**out·ride** \ˈau̇t-ˌrīd\ *n* (1880) : an unstressed syllable or group of syllables added to a foot in sprung rhythm but not counted in the scansion

out·rid·er \-ˌrī-dər\ *n* (ca. 1530) **1** : a mounted attendant **2** : one who escorts or clears the way for a vehicle or person **3** : FORERUNNER, HARBINGER ⟨~*s* of a new political movement⟩

out·rig·ger \ˈau̇t-ˌri-gər\ *n* (1742) **1 a** : a projection with a float or a shaped log at the end attached to a boat to prevent capsizing **b** : a spar or projecting beam run out from a ship's side to help secure the masts or from a mast to extend a rope or sail **2** : a boat equipped with an outrigger **3** : a projecting member run out from a main structure to provide additional stability or to support something; *esp* : a projecting frame to support the elevator or tailplanes of an airplane or the rotor of a helicopter

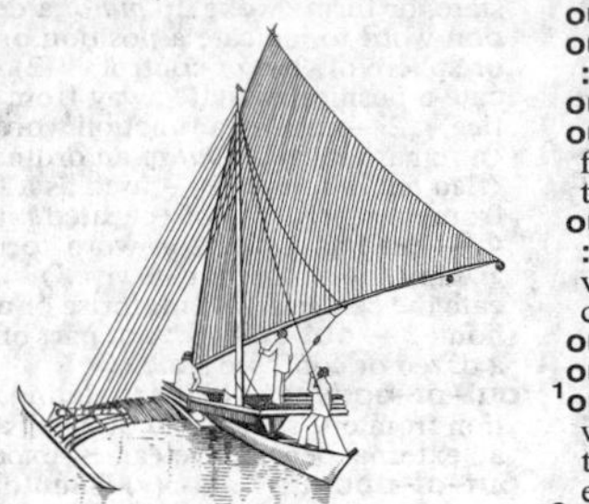

outrigger 2

[1]**out·right** \ˌau̇t-ˈrīt\ *adv* (14c) **1** *archaic* : straight ahead : DIRECTLY **2** : in entirety : COMPLETELY ⟨rejected the proposal ~⟩ **3** : without restraint or reservation ⟨laughed ~⟩ **4** : on the spot : INSTANTANEOUSLY ⟨was killed ~⟩ **5** : without lien or encumbrance ⟨purchased the property ~ for cash⟩

[2]**out·right** \ˈau̇t-ˌrīt\ *adj* (1532) **1 a** : being completely or exactly what is stated ⟨an ~ lie⟩ **b** : given without reservation ⟨~ grants for research⟩ **c** : made without encumbrance or lien ⟨an ~ sale⟩ **2** *archaic* : proceeding directly onward — **out·right·ly** *adv*

out·run \ˌau̇t-ˈrən\ *vt* **-ran** \-ˈran\; **-run; -run·ning** (1526) **1** : to run faster than **2** : EXCEED, SURPASS ⟨his ambitions ~ his abilities⟩

out·sell \-ˈsel\ *vt* **-sold** \-ˈsōld\; **-sell·ing** (1609) **1** *archaic* : to exceed in value **2** : to exceed in number of items sold **3** : to surpass in selling or salesmanship

out·set \ˈau̇t-ˌset\ *n* (1759) : BEGINNING, START

out·shine \ˌau̇t-ˈshīn\ *vb* **-shone** \-ˈshōn, *esp Brit* -ˈshän\ *or* **-shined; -shin·ing** *vt* (1596) **1 a** : to shine brighter than **b** : to excel in splendor or showiness **2** : OUTDO, SURPASS ⟨*outshone* most of the other films in quality —Kathleen Karr⟩ ~ *vi* : to shine out

out·shoot \ˌau̇t-ˈshüt\ *vt* **-shot** \-ˈshät\; **-shoot·ing** (1530) **1** : to surpass in shooting or making shots **2** : to shoot or go beyond

[1]**out·side** \ˌau̇t-ˈsīd, ˈau̇t-ˌ\ *n* (1502) **1 a** : a place or region beyond an enclosure or boundary: as (1) : the world beyond the confines of an institution (as a prison) (2) *often cap, in Alaska* : the world beyond the territory or state of Alaska; *esp* : the 48 contiguous states **b** : the area farthest from a specified point of reference: as (1) : the side of home plate farthest from the batter (2) : the part of a playing area toward the sidelines (3) : the part of a playing area away from the goal **2** : an outer side or surface **3** : an outer manifestation : APPEARANCE **4** : the extreme limit of a guess : MAXIMUM ⟨the crowd numbered 10,000 at the ~⟩

[2]**outside** *adj* (1634) **1 a** : of, relating to, or being on or toward the outer side or surface ⟨the ~ edge⟩ **b** : of, relating to, or being on or toward the outer side of a curve or turn **c** : of, relating to, or being on or near the outside ⟨an ~ pitch⟩ **2 a** : situated or performed outside a particular place **b** : connected with or giving access to the outside ⟨~ telephone line⟩ **3** : MAXIMUM **4 a** : not included or originating in a particular group or organization ⟨blamed the riot on ~ agitators⟩ **b** : not belonging to one's regular occupation or duties ⟨~ interests⟩ **5** : barely possible : REMOTE ⟨an ~ chance⟩ **6** : made or done from the outside ⟨borrowed a basketball and practiced his ~ shot⟩

[3]**outside** *adv* (1813) **1** : on or to the outside **2** : OUTDOORS

[4]**outside** *prep* (1826) **1** — used as a function word to indicate movement to or position on the outer side of **2** : beyond the limits of ⟨~ the scope of this report⟩ ⟨~ the law⟩ **3** : EXCEPT

outside of *prep* (ca. 1840) **1** : OUTSIDE **2** : ASIDE FROM

out·sid·er \ˌau̇t-ˈsī-dər, ˈau̇t-ˌ\ *n* (1800) **1** : a person who does not belong to a particular group **2** *chiefly Brit* : a contender not expected to win — **out·sid·er·ness** *n*

out·sight \ˈau̇t-ˌsīt\ *n* (1605) : the power or act of perceiving external things ⟨the clear-eyed insight and ~ of the born writer —*New Yorker*⟩

[1]**out·size** \ˈau̇t-ˌsīz\ *n* (1845) : an unusual size; *esp* : a size larger than the standard

[2]**outsize** *also* **out·sized** \-ˌsīzd\ *adj* (1880) **1** : unusually large or heavy **2** : exaggerated or extravagant in size or degree

out·skirt \ˈau̇t-ˌskərt\ *n* (1596) : a part remote from the center : BORDER — usu. used in pl. ⟨on the ~*s* of town⟩

out·slick \ˌau̇t-ˈslik\ *vt* (1926) : to get the better of esp. by trickery or cunning

out·smart \ˌau̇t-ˈsmärt\ *vt* (1924) : to get the better of; *esp* : OUTWIT

out·sole \ˈau̇t-ˌsōl\ *n* (1884) : the outside sole of a boot or shoe

out·source \ˈau̇t-ˌsȯrs\ *vt* (1979) : to procure (as some goods or services needed by a business or organization) under contract with an outside supplier ⟨decided to ~ some back-office operations⟩

out·speak \ˌau̇t-ˈspēk\ *vt* **-spoke** \-ˈspōk\; **-spo·ken** \-ˈspō-kən\; **-speak·ing** (1603) **1** : to excel in speaking **2** : to declare openly or boldly

out·spend \-ˈspend\ *vt* (1586) **1** : to exceed the limits of in spending ⟨~*s* his income⟩ **2** : to spend more than ⟨*outspent* the other candidates⟩

out·spent \-ˈspent\ *adj* (1652) : completely worn out : EXHAUSTED ⟨spurred him, like an ~ horse, to death —P. B. Shelley⟩

out·spo·ken \ˌau̇t-ˈspō-kən\ *adj* (ca. 1808) **1** : direct and open in speech or expression : FRANK ⟨~ in his criticism —*Current Biog.*⟩ **2** : spoken or expressed without reserve ⟨his ~ advocacy of gun control⟩ — **out·spo·ken·ly** *adv* — **out·spo·ken·ness** \-kən-nəs\ *n*

out·spread \ˌau̇t-ˈspred\ *vt* **-spread; -spread·ing** (14c) : to spread out

out·stand \ˌau̇t-ˈstand\ *vb* **-stood; -stand·ing** *vt* (1571) : to endure beyond ⟨I have *outstood* my time —Shak.⟩ ~ *vi* : STAND OUT

out·stand·ing \au̇t-ˈstan-diŋ, ˈau̇t-ˌ\ *adj* (1611) **1** : standing out : PROJECTING **2 a** : UNPAID ⟨left several bills ~⟩ **b** : continuing to exist : UNRESOLVED ⟨a long ~ problem in astronomy⟩ **c** *of securities* : publicly issued and sold **3 a** : standing out from a group : CONSPICUOUS **b** : marked by eminence and distinction ***syn*** see NOTICEABLE — **out·stand·ing·ly** \-diŋ-lē\ *adv*

out·stare \ˌau̇t-ˈster\ *vt* (1596) : OUTFACE 1

out·sta·tion \ˈau̇t-ˌstā-shən\ *n* (1844) : a remote or outlying station

out·stay \ˌau̇t-ˈstā\ *vt* (1600) **1** : OVERSTAY 1 ⟨~*ed* their welcome⟩ **2** : to surpass in staying power ⟨~*ed* his competitors⟩

out·stretch \ˌau̇t-ˈstrech\ *vt* (15c) : to stretch out : EXTEND

out·strip \ˌau̇t-ˈstrip\ *vt* [*out-* + obs. *strip* to move fast] (1580) **1** : to go faster or farther than **2** : to get ahead of ⟨has civilization *outstripped* the ability of its users to use it? —Margaret Mead⟩ ***syn*** see EXCEED

out·take \ˈau̇t-ˌtāk\ *n* (1902) **1** : a passage outward : FLUE, VENT **2** : something that is taken out: as **a** : a take that is not used in an edited version of a film or videotape **b** : a recorded musical selection not included in a record album

out–there \ˈau̇t-ˈt͟her\ *adj* (1991) : UNCONVENTIONAL ⟨~ styles⟩

out·turn \ˈau̇t-ˌtərn\ *n* (1800) : a quantity produced : OUTPUT

[1]**out·ward** \ˈau̇t-wərd\ *adj* (bef. 12c) **1** : moving, directed, or turned toward the outside or away from a center ⟨an ~ flow⟩ **2** : situated on the outside : EXTERIOR **3** : of or relating to the body or to appearances rather than to the mind or the inner life ⟨~ beauty⟩ **4** : EXTERNAL

[2]**outward** *or* **out·wards** \-wərdz\ *adv* (bef. 12c) **1** : toward the outside **2** *obs* : on the outside : EXTERNALLY

[3]**outward** *n* (1606) : external form, appearance, or reality

out·ward–bound \ˌau̇t-wərd-ˈbau̇nd\ *adj* (1602) : bound in an outward direction or to foreign parts ⟨an ~ ship⟩

out·ward·ly \ˈau̇t-wərd-lē\ *adv* (14c) **1 a** : on the outside : EXTERNALLY **b** : toward the outside **2** : in outward state, behavior, or appearance ⟨was ~ friendly⟩

out·ward·ness \-nəs\ *n* (1580) **1** : the quality or state of being external **2** : concern with or responsiveness to outward things

out·wash \ˈau̇t-ˌwȯsh, -ˌwäsh\ *n* (1894) : detritus consisting chiefly of gravel and sand carried by running water from the melting ice of a glacier and laid down in stratified deposits

out·wear \ˌau̇t-ˈwer\ *vt* **-wore** \-ˈwȯr\; **-worn** \-ˈwȯrn\; **-wear·ing** (ca. 1541) **1** : WEAR OUT, EXHAUST **2** : to last longer than ⟨a fabric that ~*s* others⟩

out·weigh \-ˈwā\ *vt* (1597) : to exceed in weight, value, or importance ⟨the advantages ~ the disadvantages⟩

out·wit \ˌau̇t-ˈwit\ *vt* **-wit·ted; -wit·ting** (1643) **1** : to get the better of by superior cleverness : OUTSMART **2** *archaic* : to surpass in wisdom

out·with \ˈau̇t-ˌwith\ *prep* (13c) *chiefly Scot* : OUTSIDE

[1]**out·work** \ˌau̇t-ˈwərk\ *vt* (13c) **1** : WORK OUT, COMPLETE **2** : to work harder, faster, or better than

[2]**out·work** \ˈau̇t-ˌwərk\ *n* (ca. 1615) : a minor defensive position constructed outside a fortified area

out·work·er \-ˌwər-kər\ *n* (1813) *chiefly Brit* : a person who works at home for a business firm

out·worn \ˌau̇t-ˈwȯrn\ *adj* (1565) : no longer useful or acceptable : OUTMODED ⟨an ~ social system⟩

out–year \ˈau̇t-ˌyir\ *n* (1981) : the year beyond a current fiscal year — usu. used in pl. except when attrib.

ou·zel *also* **ou·sel** \ˈü-zəl\ *n* [ME *ousel,* fr. OE *ōsle* — more at MERLE] (bef. 12c) **1 a** : BLACKBIRD 1a **b** : RING OUZEL **2** : DIPPER 2

ou·zo \ˈü-(ˌ)zō, -(ˌ)zȯ\ *n* [ModGk] (1897) : a colorless anise-flavored unsweetened Greek liqueur

ov- *or* **ovi-** *or* **ovo-** *comb form* [L *ov-, ovi-,* fr. *ovum* — more at EGG] : egg ⟨*ovicide*⟩ : ovum ⟨*oviduct*⟩

ova *pl of* OVUM

[1]**oval** \ˈō-vəl\ *n* (1570) **1** : an oval figure or object **2** : a racetrack in the shape of an oval or a rectangle having rounded corners

[2]**oval** *adj* [ML *ovalis,* fr. LL, of an egg, fr. L *ovum*] (1577) : having the shape of an egg; *also* : broadly elliptical — **oval·i·ty** \ō-ˈva-lə-tē\ *n* — **oval·ly** \-və-lē\ *adv* — **oval·ness** *n*

ov·al·bu·min \ˌä-val-ˈbyü-mən, ˌō-\ *n* (ca. 1836) **1** : the principal albumin of white of egg; *esp* : the crystalline part of egg albumins **2** : dried whites of eggs

Oval Office *n* [fr. the *Oval Office,* the U.S. president's office in the west wing of the White House] (1962) : the seat of the executive department of the U.S. government

oval window *n* (1683) : an oval opening between the middle ear and the vestibule having the base of the stapes or columella attached to its membrane

Ovam·bo \ō-ˈvam-(ˌ)bō, -ˈväm-\ *n, pl* **Ovambo** *or* **Ovambos** (1853) **1** : a member of a Bantu people of northern Namibia **2** : the Bantu language of the Ovambo people

ovar·i·an \ō-ˈver-ē-ən\ *also* **ovar·i·al** \-ē-əl\ *adj* (ca. 1834) : of, relating to, or involving an ovary ⟨~ cancer⟩

ovari·ec·to·my \ō-ˌver-ē-ˈek-tə-mē\ *n, pl* **-mies** (1889) : OOPHORECTOMY — **ovari·ec·to·mized** \-ˌmīzd\ *adj*

ovar·i·ole \ō-ˈver-ē-ˌōl\ *n* [NL **ovariolum,* dim. of *ovarium*] (1877) : one of the tubes of which the ovaries of most insects are composed

ovar·i·ot·o·my \ō-ˌver-ē-ˈä-tə-mē\ *n, pl* **-mies** (1844) **1** : surgical incision of an ovary **2** : OOPHORECTOMY

ova·ry \ˈō-və-rē, ˈōv-rē\ *n, pl* **-ries** [NL *ovarium,* fr. L *ovum* egg] (1658) **1** : one of the typically paired essential female reproductive organs that produce eggs and in vertebrates female sex hormones **2** : the enlarged rounded usu. basal portion of the pistil or gynoecium of an angiospermous plant that bears the ovules and consists of one or more carpels — see FLOWER illustration

ovate \ˈō-ˌvāt\ *adj* (1760) **1** : shaped like an egg **2** : having an outline like a longitudinal section of an egg with the basal end broader ⟨~ leaves⟩ — see LEAF illustration

ova·tion \ō-ˈvā-shən\ *n* [L *ovation-, ovatio,* fr. *ovare* to exult; akin to Gk *euoi,* interjection used in bacchic revels] (1533) **1** : a ceremony attending the entering of Rome by a general who had won a victory of less importance than that for which a triumph was granted **2** : an expression or demonstration of popular acclaim esp. by enthusiastic applause ⟨received a standing ~⟩

ov·en \ˈə-vən\ *n* [ME, fr. OE *ofen;* akin to OHG *ofan* oven and perh. to Gk *ipnos* oven] (bef. 12c) : a chamber used for baking, heating, or drying

ov·en·bird \-ˌbərd\ *n* [fr. the shape of its nest] (ca. 1825) **1** : any of various chiefly So. American small brown passerine birds (family Furnariidae, esp. genus *Furnarius*) **2** : an American warbler (*Seiurus aurocapillus*) that builds a dome-shaped nest on the ground

ov·en·proof \-ˌprüf\ *adj* (1939) : capable of withstanding the temperature range of a kitchen oven ⟨~ dishes⟩

¹**over** \ˈō-vər\ *adv* [ME, adv. & prep., fr. OE *ofer;* akin to OHG *ubar* (prep.) above, beyond, over, L *super,* Gk *hyper*] (bef. 12c) **1 a** : across a barrier or intervening space; *esp* : across the goal line in football **b** : forward beyond an edge or brink and often down ⟨wandered too near the cliff and fell ~⟩ **c** : across the brim ⟨soup boiled ~⟩ **d** : so as to bring the underside up ⟨turned his cards ~⟩ **e** : from a vertical to a prone or inclined position ⟨knocked the lamp ~⟩ **f** : from one person or side to another ⟨hand it ~⟩ **g** : ACROSS ⟨got his point ~⟩ **h** : to one's home ⟨invite some friends ~⟩ **i** : on the other side of an intervening space ⟨the next town ~⟩ **j** : to agreement or concord ⟨won them ~⟩ **2 a** (1) : beyond some quantity, limit, or norm often by a specified amount or to a specified degree ⟨show ran a minute ~⟩ (2) : in an excessive manner : INORDINATELY **b** : till a later time (as the next day) : OVERNIGHT ⟨stay ~⟩ ⟨sleep ~⟩ **3 a** : ABOVE **b** : so as to cover the whole surface ⟨windows boarded ~⟩ **4** — used on a two-way radio circuit to indicate that a message is complete and a reply is expected **5 a** : THROUGH ⟨read it ~⟩; *also* : in an intensive or comprehensive manner **b** : once more : AGAIN ⟨do it ~⟩

²**over** *prep* (bef. 12c) **1** — used as a function word to indicate motion or situation in a position higher than or above another ⟨towered ~ his mother⟩ ⟨flew ~ the lake⟩ ⟨rode ~ the old Roman road⟩ **2 a** — used as a function word to indicate the possession of authority, power, or jurisdiction in regard to some thing or person ⟨respected those ~ him⟩ **b** — used as a function word to indicate superiority, advantage, or preference ⟨a big lead ~ the others⟩ **c** — used as a function word to indicate one that is overcome, circumvented, or disregarded ⟨passed ~ the governor's veto⟩ **3 a** : more than ⟨cost ~ $5⟩ **b** : ABOVE 4 **4 a** — used as a function word to indicate position upon or movement down upon ⟨laid a blanket ~ the child⟩ ⟨hit him ~ the head⟩ **b** (1) : all through or throughout ⟨showed me ~ the house⟩ ⟨went ~ his notes⟩ (2) — used as a function word connecting one mathematical set and another whose elements are coefficients or values of parameters used to form elements of the first set ⟨polynomials ~ the field of real numbers⟩ **c** — used as a function word to indicate a particular medium or channel of communication ⟨~ the radio⟩ **5** — used as a function word to indicate position on or motion to the other side or beyond ⟨lives ~ the way⟩ ⟨fell ~ the edge⟩ **6 a** : THROUGHOUT, DURING ⟨~ the past 25 years⟩ **b** : until the end of ⟨stay ~ Sunday⟩ **7 a** — used as a function word to indicate an object of solicitude, interest, consideration, or reference ⟨the Lord watches ~ his own⟩ **b** — used as a function word to indicate the object of an expressed or implied occupation, activity, or concern ⟨trouble ~ money⟩ ⟨met with advisers ~ lunch⟩

³**over** *adj* (bef. 12c) **1 a** : UPPER, HIGHER **b** : OUTER, COVERING **c** : EXCESSIVE ⟨~ imagination⟩ **2 a** : not used up : REMAINING ⟨something ~ to provide for unusual requirements —J. A. Todd⟩ **b** : having or showing an excess or surplus **3** : being at an end ⟨the day is ~⟩ **4** : fried on both sides ⟨ordered two eggs ~⟩ — **over easy** : fried on one side then turned and fried lightly on the other side ⟨eggs *over easy*⟩

⁴**over** *vt* **overed; over·ing** \ˈō-və-riŋ, ˈōv-riŋ\ (1837) : to leap over

over- *prefix* **1** : so as to exceed or surpass ⟨*overachieve*⟩ **2** : EXCESSIVE ⟨*over*stimulation⟩ **3** : to an excessive degree ⟨*over*thin⟩

over·ab·stract
over·abun·dance
over·abun·dant
over·ac·cen·tu·ate
over·ad·just·ment
over·ad·ver·tise
over·ag·gres·sive
over·alert
over·am·bi·tious
over·am·bi·tious·ness
over·am·pli·fied
over·anal·y·sis
over·an·a·lyt·i·cal
over·an·a·lyze
over·anx·i·ety
over·anx·ious
over·ap·pli·ca·tion
over·arous·al
over·ar·range
over·ar·tic·u·late
over·as·sert
over·as·ser·tion
over·as·ser·tive
over·as·sess·ment
over·at·ten·tion
over·bake
over·beat
over·be·jew·eled
over·bill
over·bleach
over·boil
over·bold
over·bor·row
over·breath·ing
over·brief
over·bright
over·broad
over·browse
over·bru·tal
over·burn
over·busy
over·care·ful
over·cau·tion
over·cau·tious
over·cen·tral·i·za·tion
over·cen·tral·ize
over·chill

over·civ·i·lized
over·claim
over·clas·si·fi·ca·tion
over·clas·si·fy
over·clean
over·clear
over·coach
over·com·mer·cial·i·za·tion
over·com·mer·cial·ize
over·com·mu·ni·cate
over·com·mu·ni·ca·tion
over·com·plex
over·com·pli·ance
over·com·pli·cate
over·com·pli·cat·ed
over·com·press
over·con·cen·tra·tion
over·con·cern
over·con·cerned
over·con·fi·dence
over·con·fi·dent
over·con·fi·dent·ly
over·con·sci·en·tious
over·con·scious
over·con·ser·va·tive
over·con·struct
over·con·sume
over·con·sump·tion
over·con·trol
over·cook
over·cool
over·cor·rect
over·count
over·cred·u·lous
over·crit·i·cal
over·cul·ti·va·tion
over·cure
over·dec·o·rate
over·dec·o·ra·tion
over·de·mand·ing
over·de·pen·dence
over·de·pen·dent
over·dif·fer·en·ti·a·tion
over·di·rect
over·dis·count
over·di·ver·si·ty

over·doc·u·ment
over·dra·mat·ic
over·dra·ma·tize
over·drink
over·dry
over·ea·ger
over·ea·ger·ness
over·ear·nest
over·ed·it
over·ed·u·cate
over·ed·u·cat·ed
over·ed·u·ca·tion
over·elab·o·rate
over·elab·o·ra·tion
over·em·bel·lish
over·emote
over·emo·tion·al
over·em·pha·sis
over·em·pha·size
over·em·phat·ic
over·en·am·ored
over·en·cour·age
over·en·er·get·ic
over·en·gi·neer
over·en·rolled
over·en·ter·tained
over·en·thu·si·asm
over·en·thu·si·as·tic
over·equipped
over·es·ti·mate
over·es·ti·ma·tion
over·eval·u·a·tion
over·ex·ag·ger·ate
over·ex·ag·ger·a·tion
over·ex·cite
over·ex·cit·ed
over·ex·er·cise
over·ex·ert
over·ex·er·tion
over·ex·pand
over·ex·pan·sion
over·ex·pec·ta·tion
over·ex·plain
over·ex·plic·it
over·ex·ploit
over·ex·ploi·ta·tion
over·ex·trac·tion

over·ex·trap·o·la·tion
over·ex·trav·a·gant
over·ex·u·ber·ant
over·fac·ile
over·fa·mil·iar
over·fa·mil·iar·i·ty
over·fas·tid·i·ous
over·fat
over·fa·vor
over·fer·til·i·za·tion
over·fer·til·ize
over·fo·cus
over·fond
over·ful·fill
over·fund
over·fussy
over·gen·er·al·i·za·tion
over·gen·er·al·ize
over·gen·er·os·i·ty
over·gen·er·ous
over·gen·er·ous·ly
over·glam·or·ize
over·gov·ern
over·han·dle
over·har·vest
over·hasty
over·ho·mog·e·nize
over·hunt
over·hunt·ing
over·hype
over·ide·al·ize
over·iden·ti·fi·ca·tion
over·iden·ti·fy
over·imag·i·na·tive
over·im·press
over·in·debt·ed·ness
over·in·dulge
over·in·dul·gence
over·in·dul·gent
over·in·dus·tri·al·ize
over·in·flate
over·in·flat·ed
over·in·fla·tion
over·in·form
over·in·formed
over·in·ge·nious
over·in·ge·nu·ity
over·in·sis·tent
over·in·tel·lec·tu·al·i·za·tion
over·in·tel·lec·tu·al·ize
over·in·tense
over·in·ten·si·ty
over·in·ter·pre·ta·tion
over·in·vest·ment
over·la·bor
over·la·bored
over·lad·en
over·large
over·lav·ish
over·lend
over·length
over·length·en
over·light
over·lit·er·al
over·lit·er·ary

over·load
over·long
over·loud
over·lush
over·man·age
over·man·nered
over·ma·ture
over·ma·tu·ri·ty
over·med·i·cate
over·med·i·ca·tion
over·mighty
over·milk
over·mine
over·mix
over·mod·est
over·mod·est·ly
over·mus·cled
over·nice
over·nour·ish
over·nu·tri·tion
over·ob·vi·ous
over·op·er·ate
over·opin·ion·at·ed
over·op·ti·mism
over·op·ti·mist
over·op·ti·mis·tic
over·op·ti·mis·ti·cal·ly
over·or·ches·trate
over·or·ga·nize
over·or·ga·nized
over·or·na·ment
over·pack·age
over·par·tic·u·lar
over·pay
over·pay·ment
over·ped·al
over·peo·ple
over·plan
over·plant
over·plot
over·po·tent
over·praise
over·pre·cise
over·pre·scribe
over·pre·scrip·tion
over·priv·i·leged
over·prize
over·pro·cess
over·pro·duce
over·pro·duc·tion
over·pro·gram
over·prom·ise
over·pro·mote
over·pro·tect
over·pro·tec·tion
over·pro·tec·tive
over·pro·tec·tive·ness
over·pump
over·re·act
over·re·ac·tion
over·re·fined
over·re·fine·ment
over·reg·u·late
over·reg·u·la·tion
over·re·li·ance

over·re·port
over·re·spond
over·rich
over·rig·id
over·salt
over·san·guine
over·sat·u·rate
over·sat·u·ra·tion
over·sauce
over·scru·pu·lous
over·se·cre·tion
over·sen·si·tive
over·sen·si·tive·ness
over·sen·si·tiv·i·ty
over·se·ri·ous
over·se·ri·ous·ly
over·ser·vice
over·sim·plis·tic
over·smoke
over·so·lic·i·tous
over·so·phis·ti·cat·ed
over·spe·cial·i·za·tion
over·spe·cial·ize
over·spec·u·late
over·spec·u·la·tion
over·sta·bil·i·ty
over·staff
over·stim·u·late
over·stim·u·la·tion
over·stock
over·strain
over·stress
over·stretch
over·struc·tured
over·sub·tle
over·suds
over·sup·ply
over·sus·pi·cious
over·sweet
over·sweet·en
over·sweet·ness
over·swing
over·talk
over·talk·a·tive
over·tax
over·tax·a·tion
over·thin
over·think
over·tight·en
over·tip
over·tired
over·train
over·treat
over·treat·ment
over·use
over·uti·li·za·tion
over·uti·lize
over·vi·o·lent
over·viv·id
over·wa·ter
over·wea·ry
over·wind
over·with·hold
over·zeal·ous
over·zeal·ous·ness

over·achiev·er \ˌō-vər-ə-ˈchē-vər\ *n* (1952) : one who achieves success over and above the standard or expected level esp. at an early age — **over·achieve** \-ˈchēv\ *vi* — **over·achieve·ment** \-mənt\ *n*

over·act \ˌō-vər-ˈakt\ *vi* (1611) **1** : to act more than is necessary **2** : to overact a part ~ *vt* : to exaggerate in acting — **over·ac·tion** \-ˈak-shən\ *n*

over·ac·tive \-ˈak-tiv\ *adj* (1647) : excessively or abnormally active ⟨~ glands⟩ ⟨an ~ imagination⟩ — **over·ac·tiv·i·ty** \-ˌak-ˈti-və-tē\ *n*

over against *prep* (1517) : as opposed to : in contrast with

¹**over·age** \ˌō-vər-ˈāj\ *also* **over·aged** \-ˈājd\ *adj* [¹*over* + *age*] (15c) **1** : too old to be useful **2** : older than is normal for one's position, function, or grade

²**over·age** \ˈō-və-rij, ˈōv-rij\ *n* [³*over* + *-age*] (1909) : SURPLUS, EXCESS

¹**over·all** \ˌō-vər-ˈȯl\ *adv* (13c) **1** : ALL OVER 1 ⟨the pattern used ~⟩ **2** : from one end to the other ⟨600 feet long ~⟩ **3 a** : in view of all the circumstances or conditions ⟨~, the sale was a success⟩ **b** : as a whole : GENERALLY ⟨doesn't do as well ~⟩ **c** : with everyone or everything taken into account ⟨was third ~ in earnings⟩ ⟨got 31 miles to the gallon ~⟩

²**over·all** \ˈō-vər-ˌȯl\ *n* (1797) **1 a** *pl, archaic* : loose protective trousers worn over regular clothes **b** *usu pl* : trousers of strong material usu. with a bib and shoulder straps **2** *chiefly Brit* : a loose-fitting protective smock worn over regular clothing

³**over·all** \ˌō-vər-ˈȯl, ˈō-vər-ˌ\ *adj* (1894) **1** : including everything **2** : viewed as a whole : GENERAL

over·alled \ˈō-vər-ˌȯld\ *adj* (1908) : wearing overalls

over and above *prep* (15c) : in addition to : BESIDES

overall 1b

over and over *adv* (15c) : REPEATEDLY
over·arch·ing \ˌō-vər-ˈär-chiŋ\ *adj* (1720) **1** : forming an arch overhead **2** : dominating or embracing all else ⟨~ goals⟩
over·arm \ˈō-vər-ˌärm\ *adj* (1864) **1** : OVERHAND **2** *of a swimming stroke* : made with the arm lifted out of the water and stretched forward over the shoulder to begin the stroke
over·awe \ˌō-vər-ˈȯ\ *vt* (1579) : to restrain or subdue by awe
[1]**over·bal·ance** \ˌō-vər-ˈba-lən(t)s\ *vt* (1608) **1** : OUTWEIGH **2** : to cause to lose balance
[2]**over·bal·ance** \ˈō-vər-ˌ\ *n* (ca. 1659) : something more than an equivalent
over·bear \ˌō-vər-ˈber\ *vt* **-bore** \-ˈbȯr\; **-borne** \-ˈbȯrn\ *also* **-born** \-ˈbȯrn\; **-bear·ing** (1535) **1** : to bring down by superior weight or force : OVERWHELM **2 a** : to domineer over **b** : to surpass in importance or cogency : OUTWEIGH
overbearing *adj* (1614) **1 a** : tending to overwhelm : OVERPOWERING **b** : decisively important : DOMINANT **2** : harshly and haughtily arrogant ***syn*** see PROUD — **over·bear·ing·ly** \-iŋ-lē\ *adv*
over·bid \ˌō-vər-ˈbid\ *vb* **-bid; -bid·ding** *vi* (ca. 1616) **1** : to bid in excess of value **2 a** : to bid more than the scoring capacity of a hand at cards **b** *Brit* : to make a higher bid than the preceding one ~ *vt* : to bid beyond or in excess of; *esp* : to bid more than the value of (one's hand at cards) — **over·bid** \ˈō-vər-ˌbid\ *n*
over·bite \ˈō-vər-ˌbīt\ *n* (1887) : the projection of the upper front teeth over the lower in the normal occlusal position of the jaws
over·blouse \-ˌblau̇s, -ˌblau̇z\ *n* (1921) : a usu. fitted or belted blouse worn untucked
[1]**over·blown** \ˌō-vər-ˈblōn\ *adj* [[3]*blow*] (1616) : past the prime of bloom ⟨~ roses⟩
[2]**overblown** *adj* [[1]*blow*] (1864) **1** : excessively large in girth : PORTLY **2** : INFLATED ⟨~ claims⟩ ⟨~ rhetoric⟩; *also* : PRETENTIOUS
over·board \ˈō-vər-ˌbȯrd\ *adv* (bef. 12c) **1** : over the side of a ship or boat into the water **2** : to extremes of enthusiasm **3** : into discard : ASIDE
over·book \ˌō-vər-ˈbu̇k\ *vt* (1903) : to issue reservations for (as an airplane flight) in excess of the space available ~ *vi* : to issue reservations in excess of the space available
over·bought \-ˈbȯt\ *adj* (1929) : not likely to show an immediate rise in price because of prior heavy buying and accompanying price rises ⟨an ~ market⟩
over·breed \-ˈbrēd\ *vt* (ca. 1961) : to breed (a plant or animal) to excess esp. without regard to the quality of the breeding stock ⟨*overbred* dogs⟩
over·build \-ˈbild\ *vb* **-built** \-ˈbilt\; **-build·ing** *vt* (1601) : to build beyond the actual demand of ~ *vi* : to build houses or commercial developments in excess of demand
[1]**over·bur·den** \-ˈbər-dᵊn\ *vt* (1532) : to place an excessive burden on
[2]**over·bur·den** \ˈō-vər-ˌbər-dᵊn\ *n* (1855) : material overlying a deposit of useful geological materials or bedrock
over·buy \ˌō-vər-ˈbī\ *vb* **-bought** \-ˈbȯt\; **-buy·ing** *vt* (1745) : to buy in excess of needs or demand ~ *vi* : to make purchases beyond one's needs or in excess of one's ability to pay
over·call \-ˈkȯl\ *vt* (ca. 1903) : to make a higher bid than (the previous bid or bidder) in a card game ~ *vi* : to bid over an opponent's bid in bridge when one's partner has not bid or doubled — **over·call** \ˈō-vər-ˌkȯl\ *n*
over·ca·pac·i·ty \ˌō-vər-kə-ˈpa-sə-tē, -ˈpas-tē\ *n* (1928) : excessive capacity for production or services in relation to demand
over·cap·i·tal·ize \-ˈka-pə-tə-ˌlīz, -ˈkap-tə-\ *vt* (1890) **1** : to put a nominal value on the capital of (a corporation) higher than actual cost or fair market value **2** : to capitalize beyond what the business or the profit-making prospects warrant — **over·cap·i·tal·i·za·tion** \-ˌka-pə-tə-lə-ˈzā-shən, -ˌkap-tə-\ *n*
[1]**over·cast** *vt* **-cast; -cast·ing** (14c) **1** \ˌō-vər-ˈkast, ˈō-vər-ˌ\ : DARKEN, OVERSHADOW **2** \ˈō-vər-ˌ\ : to sew (raw edges of a seam) with long slanting widely spaced stitches to prevent raveling
[2]**over·cast** \ˈō-vər-ˌkast, ˌō-vər-ˈ\ *adj* (1536) : clouded over ⟨an ~ day⟩
[3]**over·cast** \ˈō-vər-ˌkast\ *n* (1637) : COVERING; *esp* : a covering of clouds over the sky
over·cast·ing \ˈō-vər-ˌkas-tiŋ\ *n* (1859) : the act of stitching raw edges of fabric to prevent raveling; *also* : the stitching so done
overcast stitch *n* (1852) : a small close embroidery stitch sometimes done over a foundation thread and used to form outlines
over·charge \ˌō-vər-ˈchärj\ *vt* (14c) **1** : to charge too much or too fully **2** : to fill too full **3** : EXAGGERATE, OVERDRAW ~ *vi* : to make an excessive charge — **over·charge** \ˈō-vər-ˌ\ *n*
over·class \ˈō-vər-ˌklas\ *n* (1982) : the highest social stratum : the segment of a society usu. having the most wealth, influence, education, and prestige — compare *underclass*
over·cloud \ˌō-vər-ˈklau̇d\ *vt* (1592) : to overspread with or as if with clouds
over·coat \ˈō-vər-ˌkōt\ *n* (1802) **1** : a warm coat worn over indoor clothing **2** : a protective coating (as of paint)
over·come \ˌō-vər-ˈkəm\ *vb* **-came** \-ˈkām\; **-come; -com·ing** [ME, fr. OE *ofercuman,* fr. *ofer* over + *cuman* to come] *vt* (bef. 12c) **1** : to get the better of : SURMOUNT ⟨~ difficulties⟩ **2** : OVERWHELM ~ *vi* : to gain the superiority : WIN ***syn*** see CONQUER — **over·com·er** *n*
over·com·mit \-kə-ˈmit\ *vt* (1951) : to commit excessively: as **a** : to obligate (as oneself) beyond the ability for fulfillment **b** : to allocate (resources) in excess of the capacity for replenishment — **over·com·mit·ment** \-mənt\ *n*
over·com·pen·sa·tion \-ˌkäm-pən-ˈsā-shən, -ˌpen-\ *n* (1912) : excessive compensation; *specif* : excessive reaction to a feeling of inferiority, guilt, or inadequacy leading to an exaggerated attempt to overcome the feeling — **over·com·pen·sate** \-ˈkäm-pən-ˌsāt\ *vb* — **over·com·pen·sa·to·ry** \-kəm-ˈpen(t)-sə-ˌtȯr-ē\ *adj*
over·crowd \ˌō-vər-ˈkrau̇d\ *vt* (1766) : to cause to be too crowded ~ *vi* : to crowd together too much
over·cut \-ˈkət\ *vt* (1906) : to cut excessively; *specif* : to cut timber from (a forest) in excess of annual growth or an allotted annual amount
over·de·sign \-di-ˈzīn\ *vt* (1951) : to design in a manner that is excessively complex or that exceeds usual standards (as of sturdiness or safety)
over·de·ter·mined \-di-ˈtər-mənd\ *adj* (1917) **1** : excessively determined **2** : having more than one determining psychological factor
over·de·vel·op \-di-ˈve-ləp\ *vt* (1869) : to develop excessively; *esp* : to subject (exposed photographic material) to a developing solution for excessive time or at excessive temperature, agitation, or concentration — **over·de·vel·op·ment** \-mənt\ *n*
over·di·ag·no·sis \-ˌdī-ig-ˈnō-səs, -əg-\ *n* (1978) : the diagnosis of a condition or disease more often than it is actually present — **over·di·ag·nose** \-ˈdī-ig-ˌnōs, -ˌnōz, -ˌdī-ig-ˈ, -əg-\ *vt*
over·do \ˌō-vər-ˈdü\ *vb* **-did** \-ˈdid\; **-done** \-ˈdən\; **-do·ing** \-ˈdü-iŋ\; **-does** \-ˈdəz\ *vt* (bef. 12c) **1 a** : to do in excess **b** : to use to excess **c** : EXAGGERATE **2** : to cook too long **3** : EXHAUST ~ *vi* : to go to extremes
over·dog \ˈō-vər-ˌdȯg\ *n* [[3]*over* + under*dog*] (1938) : one that is dominant or victorious
over·dom·i·nance \ˌō-vər-ˈdä-mə-nən(t)s, -ˈdäm-nən(t)s\ *n* (1947) : the condition wherein a heterozygote produces a phenotype more extreme or better adapted than that of the homozygote — **over·dom·i·nant** \-nənt\ *adj*
[1]**over·dose** \ˈō-vər-ˌdōs\ *n* (1700) **1** : too great a dose (as of a therapeutic agent); *also* : a lethal or toxic amount (as of a drug) **2** : an excessive quantity or amount ⟨an ~ of fun⟩ — **over·dos·age** \ˌō-vər-ˈdō-sij\ *n*
[2]**over·dose** \ˌō-vər-ˈdōs\ *vt* (1700) : to give an overdose or too many doses to ~ *vi* : to take or experience an overdose — usu. used with *on*
over·draft \ˈō-vər-ˌdraft\ *n* (1845) **1** : an act of overdrawing at a bank : the state of being overdrawn; *also* : the sum overdrawn **2** : LINE OF CREDIT
over·draw \ˌō-vər-ˈdrȯ\ *vb* **-drew** \-ˈdrü\; **-drawn** \-ˈdrȯn\; **-draw·ing** *vt* (1734) **1** : to draw checks on (a bank account) for more than the balance ⟨the account was *overdrawn*⟩ **2** : EXAGGERATE, OVERSTATE ~ *vi* : to make an overdraft
over·drawn *adj* (1817) : having an overdrawn account
[1]**over·dress** \ˌō-vər-ˈdres\ *vt* (1704) : to dress or adorn to excess ⟨felt ~*ed* for the occasion in his tuxedo⟩ ~ *vi* : to dress oneself to excess ⟨it's better to ~ for the party than be too casual⟩
[2]**over·dress** \ˈō-vər-ˌdres\ *n* (1812) : a dress worn over another
over·drive \ˈō-vər-ˌdrīv\ *n* (1926) **1** : an automotive transmission gear that transmits to the drive shaft a speed greater than engine speed **2** : a state of heightened activity ⟨going into rhetorical ~⟩
[1]**over·dub** \ˈō-vər-ˌdəb\ *n* (ca. 1965) **1** : the act or an instance of overdubbing **2** : recorded sound that is overdubbed ⟨vocal ~*s*⟩
[2]**over·dub** \ˌō-vər-ˈdəb\ *vt* (1967) : to transfer (recorded sound) onto a recording that bears sound recorded earlier in order to produce a combined effect
over·due \-ˈdü, -ˈdyü\ *adj* (1763) **1 a** : unpaid when due ⟨an ~ bill⟩ **b** : delayed beyond an appointed time ⟨an ~ train⟩ ⟨~ library books⟩ **2** : too great : EXCESSIVE ⟨an ~ share of the profits⟩ **3** : more than ready ⟨~ for a haircut⟩
over·eat \ˌō-vər-ˈēt\ *vi* **over·ate** \-ˈāt\; **over·eat·en** \-ˈē-tᵊn\; **over·eat·ing** (1599) : to eat to excess — **over·eat·er** \ˌō-vər-ˈē-tər, ˈō-vər-ˌ\ *n*
over·ex·pose \ˌō-vər-ik-ˈspōz\ *vt* (1869) : to expose excessively: as **a** : to expose (as film) to excessive radiation (as light) **b** : to expose (as a celebrity) to excessive publicity esp. to the extent that attraction is diminished — **over·ex·po·sure** \-ˈspō-zhər\ *n*
over·ex·tend \ˌō-vər-ik-ˈstend\ *vt* (1937) : to extend or expand beyond a safe or reasonable point; *esp* : to commit (oneself) financially beyond what can be paid — **over·ex·ten·sion** \-ˈsten(t)-shən\ *n*
over·fa·tigue \ˌō-vər-fə-ˈtēg\ *n* (1727) : excessive fatigue esp. when carried beyond the recuperative capacity of the individual — **over·fa·tigued** \-ˈtēgd\ *adj*
over·feed \ˌō-vər-ˈfēd\ *vb* **-fed** \-ˈfed\; **-feed·ing** *vt* (1608) : to feed to excess ~ *vi* : to eat to excess
over·fill \-ˈfil\ *vt* (13c) : to fill to overflowing ~ *vi* : to become full to overflowing
over·fish \-ˈfish\ *vt* (1867) : to fish to the detriment of (a fishing ground) or to the depletion of (a kind of organism)
over·flight \ˈō-vər-ˌflīt\ *n* (1950) : a passage over an area in an aircraft
[1]**over·flow** \ˌō-vər-ˈflō\ *vt* (bef. 12c) **1** : to cover with or as if with water : INUNDATE **2** : to flow over the brim of **3** : to cause to overflow ~ *vi* **1** : to flow over bounds **2** : to fill a space to capacity and spread beyond its limits ⟨the crowd ~*ed* into the street⟩
[2]**over·flow** \ˈō-vər-ˌflō\ *n* (1568) **1** : a flowing over : INUNDATION **2** : something that flows over : SURPLUS **3** : an outlet or receptacle for surplus liquid
over·fly \ˌō-vər-ˈflī\ *vt* **-flew** \-ˈflü\; **-flown** \-ˈflōn\; **-fly·ing** (14c) : to fly over; *esp* : to pass over in an aircraft or spacecraft
over·gar·ment \ˈō-vər-ˌgär-mənt\ *n* (15c) : an outer garment
over·glaze \-ˌglāz\ *adj* (1879) : applied or suitable for applying on top of a fired glaze ⟨~ enamels⟩ — **overglaze** *n*
over·graze \ˌō-vər-ˈgrāz\ *vt* (1919) : to allow animals to graze (as a pasture) to the point of damaging vegetational cover
over·grow \ˌō-vər-ˈgrō\ *vb* **-grew** \-ˈgrü\; **-grown** \-ˈgrōn\; **-grow·ing** *vt* (14c) **1** : to grow over so as to cover with herbage **2** : to grow beyond or rise above : OUTGROW ~ *vi* **1** : to grow excessively **2** : to become grown over — **over·growth** \ˈō-vər-ˌgrōth\ *n*
overgrown *adj* (1603) : grown abnormally or excessively large ⟨dismissed him as an ~ adolescent⟩
[1]**over·hand** \ˈō-vər-ˌhand\ *adj* (1656) : made with the hand brought forward and down from above shoulder level — **overhand** *adv* — **over·hand·ed** \ˌō-vər-ˈhan-dəd\ *adv or adj*
[2]**overhand** *vt* (1871) : to sew with short vertical stitches
[3]**overhand** *n* (ca. 1934) : an overhand stroke (as in handball)
overhand knot *n* (1840) : a small knot often used to prevent the end of a cord from fraying — see KNOT illustration
[1]**over·hang** \ˈō-vər-ˌhaŋ, ˌō-vər-ˈ\ *vb* **-hung** \-ˌhəŋ, -ˈhəŋ\; **-hang·ing** *vt* (1592) **1** : to project over **2** : to impend over : THREATEN ~ *vi* : to project so as to be over something
[2]**over·hang** \ˈō-vər-ˌhaŋ\ *n* (1864) **1** : something that overhangs; *also* : the extent of the overhanging **2** : the part of the bow or stern of a ship that projects over the water above the waterline **3** : a projection of the roof or upper story of a building beyond the wall of the lower part **4** : an excess amount of a commodity or security the selling of

which often drives down the value of that kind of commodity or security ⟨share ~⟩

over·haul \ˌō-vər-ˈhȯl\ *vt* (1705) **1 a :** to examine thoroughly **b** (1) : REPAIR (2) : to renovate, remake, revise, or renew thoroughly **2 :** to haul or drag over **3 :** OVERTAKE — **over·haul** \ˈō-vər-ˌhȯl\ *n*

1**over·head** \ˌō-vər-ˈhed\ *adv* (15c) : above one's head : ALOFT

2**over·head** \ˈō-vər-ˌhed\ *adj* (1874) **1 a :** operating, lying, or coming from above **b :** having the driving part above the part driven ⟨valves operated by an ~ camshaft⟩ **2 :** of or relating to overhead ⟨~ costs⟩

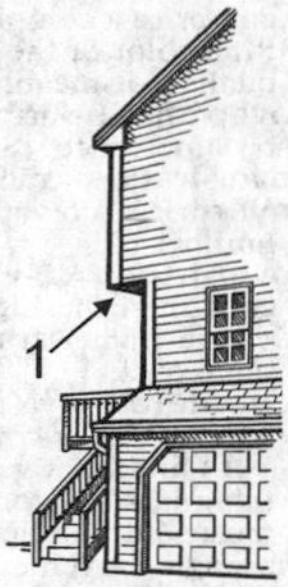

1 overhang 3

3**over·head** \ˈō-vər-ˌhed\ *n* (1914) **1 :** business expenses (as rent, insurance, or heating) not chargeable to a particular part of the work or product **2 :** CEILING; *esp* : the ceiling of a ship's compartment **3 :** a stroke in a racket game made above head height : SMASH

overhead projector *n* (1951) : a projector for projecting onto a vertical screen magnified images of graphic material on a horizontal transparency illuminated from below — called also *overhead*

over·hear \ˌō-vər-ˈhir\ *vb* **-heard** \-ˈhərd\; **-hear·ing** \-ˈhir-iŋ\ *vt* (1549) : to hear without the speaker's knowledge or intention ~ *vi* : to overhear something

over·heat \-ˈhēt\ *vt* (14c) **1 :** to heat to excess **2 :** to stimulate or agitate unduly ~ *vi* : to become heated beyond a safe or desirable point

over·heat·ed \-ˈhē-təd\ *adj* (1693) **1 :** PERFERVID **2 :** characterized by marked inflation from an increase in demand and a decrease in supply ⟨an ~ economy⟩

over·is·sue \ˌō-vər-ˈi-(ˌ)shü\ *n* (1803) : an issue exceeding the limit of capital, credit, or authority — **over·is·su·ance** \-ˈi-shə-wən(t)s\ *n* — **overissue** *vt*

over·joyed \-ˈjȯid\ *adj* (1594) : feeling great joy

1**over·kill** \ˌō-vər-ˈkil\ *vt* (1957) : to obliterate (a target) with more nuclear force than required

2**over·kill** \ˈō-vər-ˌkil\ *n* (1958) **1 :** a destructive capacity greatly exceeding that required for a given target **2 :** an excess of something (as a quantity or an action) beyond what is required or suitable for a particular purpose ⟨publicity ~⟩ ⟨an ~ in weaponry⟩ **3 :** killing in excess of what is intended or required

1**over·land** \ˈō-vər-ˌland, -lənd\ *adv* (12c) : by, on, or across land

2**overland** *adj* (1800) : going or accomplished over the land instead of by sea ⟨~ emigrants⟩ ⟨an ~ route⟩

over·lap \ˌō-vər-ˈlap\ *vt* (1704) **1 :** to extend over or past and cover a part of **2 :** to have something in common with ~ *vi* **1 :** to occupy the same area in part **2 :** to have something in common — **over·lap** \ˈō-vər-ˌlap\ *n*

1**over·lay** \ˌō-vər-ˈlā\ *vt* **-laid** \-ˈlād\; **-lay·ing** (14c) **1 a :** to lay or spread over or across : SUPERIMPOSE **b :** to prepare an overlay for **2 :** OVERLIE 2

2**over·lay** \ˈō-vər-ˌlā\ *n* (1794) : a covering either permanent or temporary: as **a :** an ornamental veneer **b :** a decorative and contrasting design or article placed on top of a plain one **c :** a transparent sheet containing graphic matter to be superimposed on another sheet

over·leaf \ˈō-vər-ˌlēf, -ˈlēf\ *adv* (1843) : on the other side of a leaf (as of a book) ⟨find the answers ~⟩

over·leap \ˌō-vər-ˈlēp\ *vt* **-leaped** *or* **-leapt** \-ˈlēpt *also* -ˈlept\; **-leap·ing** \-ˈlē-piŋ\ (bef. 12c) **1 :** to leap over or across **2 :** to defeat (oneself) by going too far

over·learn \-ˈlərn\ *vt* (1874) : to continue to study or practice after attaining proficiency

over·lie \-ˈlī\ *vt* **-lay** \-ˈlā\; **-lain** \-ˈlān\; **-ly·ing** \-ˈlī-iŋ\ (13c) **1 :** to lie over or upon **2 :** to cause the death of by lying upon

1**over·look** \-ˈlu̇k\ *vt* (14c) **1 :** to look over : INSPECT **2 a :** to look down upon from above **b :** to rise above or afford a view of **3 a :** to look past : MISS **b :** IGNORE 1 **c :** EXCUSE 2 **4 :** SUPERINTEND, OVERSEE **5 :** to look on with the evil eye : BEWITCH ***syn*** see NEGLECT

2**over·look** \ˈō-vər-ˌlu̇k\ *n* (1861) : a place from which one may look down on a scene below ⟨plenty of ~*s* and trails —Thelma H. Bell⟩

over·lord \ˈō-vər-ˌlȯrd\ *n* (13c) **1 :** a lord over other lords : a lord paramount **2 a :** an absolute or supreme ruler **b :** one having great power or authority ⟨a corporate ~⟩ — **over·lord·ship** \-ˌship, ˌō-vər-ˈ\ *n*

over·ly \ˈō-vər-lē\ *adv* (1806) : to an excessive degree : TOO

1**over·man** \-mən, -ˌman\ *n* (13c) **1 :** a man in authority over others; *specif* : FOREMAN **2** \-ˌman\ [trans. of G *Übermensch*] : SUPERMAN 1

2**over·man** \ˌō-vər-ˈman\ *vt* (ca. 1637) : to have or get too many personnel for the needs of ⟨~ a ship⟩

over·man·tel \ˈō-vər-ˌman-tᵊl\ *n* (1882) : an ornamental structure (as a painting) above a mantelpiece — **overmantel** *adj*

over·mas·ter \ˌō-vər-ˈmas-tər\ *vt* (14c) : OVERPOWER, SUBDUE

over·mas·ter·ing \-ˈmas-tə-riŋ\ *adj* (1645) : DOMINANT 1a, b ⟨~ behavior⟩ ⟨the ~ question⟩

over·match \-ˈmach\ *vt* (14c) **1 :** to be more than a match for : DEFEAT **2 :** to match with a superior opponent

1**over·much** \-ˈməch\ *adj* (13c) : too much

2**overmuch** *adv* (14c) : in too great a degree

3**over·much** \ˈō-vər-ˌməch, ˌō-vər-ˈ\ *n* (14c) : too great an amount

1**over·night** \ˌō-vər-ˈnīt\ *adv* (14c) **1 a :** on the evening before **b :** during the night ⟨stayed away ~⟩ **2 :** very quickly or suddenly ⟨became famous ~⟩

2**overnight** *adj* (1824) **1 :** of, lasting, or staying the night **2 :** SUDDEN, RAPID ⟨an ~ sensation⟩ **3 :** traveling during the night ⟨an ~ train⟩ **4 a :** accomplished by a mail service within one day's time ⟨~ delivery⟩ **b :** delivered within one day's time ⟨~ mail⟩

3**overnight** \ˈō-vər-ˌnīt, ˌō-vər-ˈ\ *vi* (1891) : to stay overnight ~ *vt* : to send (as a package or letter) by a mail service for delivery within one day's time

4**over·night** \ˈō-vər-ˌnīt\ *n* (1959) : an overnight stay

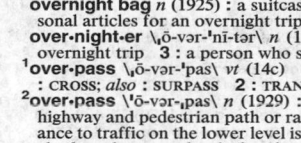

overnight bag *n* (1925) : a suitcase of a size to carry clothing and personal articles for an overnight trip — called also *overnight case*

over·night·er \ˌō-vər-ˈnī-tər\ *n* (1949) **1 :** OVERNIGHT BAG **2 :** an overnight trip **3 :** a person who stays overnight

1**over·pass** \ˌō-vər-ˈpas\ *vt* (14c) **1 :** to pass across, over, or beyond : CROSS; *also* : SURPASS **2 :** TRANSGRESS **3 :** DISREGARD, IGNORE

2**over·pass** \ˈō-vər-ˌpas\ *n* (1929) : a crossing of two highways or of a highway and pedestrian path or railroad at different levels where clearance to traffic on the lower level is obtained by elevating the higher level; *also* : the upper level of such a crossing

over·per·suade \ˌō-vər-pər-ˈswād\ *vt* (1624) : to persuade to act contrary to one's conviction or preference — **over·per·sua·sion** \-ˈswā-zhən\ *n*

over·plaid \ˈō-vər-ˌplad\ *n* (1923) : a textile design consisting of a plaid pattern superimposed on another plaid or on a textured ground; *also* : a fabric with such a design — **over·plaid·ed** *adj*

over·play \ˌō-vər-ˈplā\ *vt* (1767) **1 a :** to present (as a dramatic role) extravagantly : EXAGGERATE **b :** to place too much emphasis on **2 :** to rely too much on the strength of — usu. used in the phrase *overplay one's hand* **3 :** to strike a golf ball beyond (a putting green) ~ *vi* : to exaggerate a part or effect

over·plus \ˈō-vər-ˌpləs\ *n* [ME, part trans. of MF *surplus*] (14c) : SURPLUS

over·pop·u·late \ˌō-vər-ˈpäp-yə-ˌlāt\ *vt* (1828) : to populate too densely : furnish or provide with more than the environment or market will bear ~ *vi* : to become overly populous

over·pop·u·la·tion \ˌō-vər-ˌpä-pyə-ˈlā-shən\ *n* (1802) : the condition of having a population so dense as to cause environmental deterioration, an impaired quality of life, or a population crash

over·pow·er \ˌō-vər-ˈpau̇(-ə)r\ *vt* (1593) **1 :** to overcome by superior force : SUBDUE **2 :** to affect with overwhelming intensity ⟨the stench ~*ed* us⟩ **3 :** to provide with more power than is needed or desirable ⟨a dangerously ~*ed* car⟩ — **over·pow·er·ing·ly** \-ˈpau̇(-ə)r-iŋ-lē\ *adv*

over·pre·dict \ˌō-vər-pri-ˈdikt\ *vt* (1954) : to predict by an amount that exceeds the actual value ⟨~ inflation⟩ — **over·pre·dic·tion** \-ˈdik-shən\ *n*

over·pres·sure \ˈō-vər-ˌpre-shər\ *n* (1644) : pressure significantly above what is usual or normal

over·price \ˌō-vər-ˈprīs\ *vt* (1605) : to price too high

1**over·print** \ˌō-vər-ˈprint\ *vt* (1863) : to print over with something additional

2**over·print** \ˈō-vər-ˌ\ *n* (1876) : something added by or as if by overprinting; *esp* : a printed marking added to a postage or revenue stamp esp. to alter the original or to commemorate a special event

over·proof \ˌō-vər-ˈprüf\ *adj* (1807) : containing more alcohol than proof spirit

over·pro·por·tion \-prə-ˈpȯr-shən\ *vt* (1642) : to make disproportionately large

over·qual·i·fied \-ˈkwä-lə-ˌfīd\ *adj* (1954) : having more education, training, or experience than a job calls for

over·rate \ˈō-vər-ˌrāt\ *vt* (1610) : to rate, value, or estimate too highly ⟨~*s* his importance to the team⟩

over·reach \ˌō-və(r)-ˈrēch\ *vt* (14c) **1 :** to reach above or beyond : OVERTOP **2 :** to defeat (oneself) by seeking to do or gain too much **3 :** to get the better of esp. in dealing and bargaining and typically by unscrupulous or crafty methods ~ *vi* **1** *of a horse* : to strike the forefoot with the front part of the hind foot **2 a :** to go to excess **b :** EXAGGERATE **3 :** to overreach oneself — **over·reach** \ˈō-və(r)-ˌrēch, ˌō-və(r)-ˈ\ *n* — **over·reach·er** \-ˌrē-chər, -ˈrē-chər\ *n*

over·rep·re·sent·ed \ˈō-və(r)-ˌre-pri-ˈzen-təd\ *adj* (1900) : represented excessively; *esp* : having representatives in a proportion higher than the average — **over·rep·re·sen·ta·tion** \-ˌre-pri-ˌzen-ˈtā-shən, -zən-\ *n*

1**over·ride** \-ˈrīd\ *vt* **-rode** \-ˈrōd\; **-rid·den** \-ˈri-dᵊn\; **-rid·ing** \-ˈrī-diŋ\ (bef. 12c) **1 :** to ride over or across : TRAMPLE **2 :** to ride (as a horse) too much or too hard **3 a :** to prevail over : DOMINATE **b :** to set aside : ANNUL ⟨~ a veto⟩ **c :** to neutralize the action of (as an automatic control) **4 :** to extend or pass over; *esp* : OVERLAP

2**over·ride** \ˈō-və(r)-ˌrīd\ *n* (1931) **1 :** a commission paid to managerial personnel on sales made by subordinates **2 :** ROYALTY 5a **3 :** a device or system used to override a control **4 :** an act or an instance of overriding

overriding *adj* (1830) : CHIEF, PRINCIPAL ⟨an ~ concern⟩

over·ripe \ˌō-və(r)-ˈrīp\ *adj* (1671) **1 :** passed beyond maturity or ripeness toward decay ⟨an ~ pear⟩ **2 a :** DECADENT **b :** lacking originality or vigor ⟨~ prose⟩ — **over–ripe·ness** \-nəs\ *n*

over·rule \-ˈrül\ *vt* (1576) **1 :** to rule over : GOVERN **2 :** to prevail over : OVERCOME **3 a :** to rule against **b :** to set aside : REVERSE

1**over·run** \-ˈrən\ *vt* **-ran** \-ˈran\; **-run; -run·ning** (bef. 12c) **1 a** (1) : to defeat decisively and occupy the positions of (2) : to invade and occupy or ravage **b :** to spread or swarm over : INFEST **2 a :** to run or go beyond or past ⟨the plane *overran* the runway⟩ **b :** EXCEED ⟨~ a budget⟩ **c :** to readjust (set type) by shifting letters or words from one line into another **3 :** to flow over ⟨the river *overran* its banks⟩

2**over·run** \ˈō-və(r)-ˌrən\ *n* (1898) **1 :** an act or instance of overrunning; *esp* : an exceeding of the costs estimated in a contract for development and manufacture of new equipment **2 :** the amount by which something overruns **3 :** a run in excess of the quantity ordered by a customer

over·scale \ˈō-vər-ˌskāl\ *or* **over·scaled** \-ˌskāld\ *adj* (1953) : OVERSIZE ⟨an ~ coat⟩ ⟨an ~ sofa⟩

over·sea \ˌō-vər-ˈsē, ˈō-vər-ˌ\ *adj or adv* (12c) *chiefly Brit* : OVERSEAS

1**over·seas** \ˌō-vər-ˈsēz\ *adv* (1533) : beyond or across the sea ⟨lived ~ for a time⟩

2**over·seas** \ˈō-vər-ˌsēz\ *adj* (1892) **1 :** of or relating to movement, transport, or communication over the sea ⟨an ~ liner⟩ **2 :** situated, originating in, or relating to lands beyond the sea ⟨~ installations⟩ ⟨~ immigrants⟩

overseas cap *n* (1920) : GARRISON CAP
over·see \ˌō-vər-ˈsē\ *vt* **-saw** \-ˈsȯ\; **-seen** \-ˈsēn\; **-see·ing** (bef. 12c) **1** : SURVEY, WATCH **2 a** : INSPECT, EXAMINE **b** : SUPERVISE
over·seed \ˈō-vər-ˌsēd\ *vt* (1970) : to seed (an existing stand) with another type of plant ⟨~*ed* the Bermuda grass with ryegrass⟩
over·seer \ˈō-və(r)-ˌsir, -ˌsē-ər, ˌō-və(r)-ˈ\ *n* (1523) : SUPERVISOR, SUPERINTENDENT
over·sell \ˌō-vər-ˈsel\ *vt* **-sold** \-ˈsōld\; **-sell·ing** (ca. 1879) **1 a** : to sell too much or too many to **b** : to sell too much or too many of **2** : to make excessive claims for — **over·sell** \ˈō-vər-ˌsel\ *n*
over·set \-ˈset\ *vt* **-set; -set·ting** (1583) **1 a** : to disturb mentally or physically : UPSET **b** : to turn or tip over : OVERTURN **2** : to set too much type matter for — **over·set** \ˈō-vər-ˌset\ *n*
over·sexed \ˌō-vər-ˈsekst\ *adj* (1898) : exhibiting an excessive sexual drive or interest
over·shad·ow \-ˈsha-(ˌ)dō\ *vt* (bef. 12c) **1** : to cast a shadow over **2** : to exceed in importance : OUTWEIGH
over·shirt \ˈō-vər-ˌshərt\ *n* (1805) : a shirt usu. worn over another shirt without being tucked in
over·shoe \-ˌshü\ *n* (1823) : an outer shoe; *esp* : GALOSH
over·shoot \ˌō-vər-ˈshüt\ *vt* **-shot** \-ˈshät\; **-shoot·ing** (14c) **1** : to pass swiftly beyond **2** : to shoot or pass over or beyond so as to miss — **over·shoot** \ˈō-vər-ˌshüt\ *n*
[1]**over·shot** \ˈō-vər-ˌshät\ *adj* (ca. 1535) **1** : actuated by the weight of water passing over and flowing from above ⟨an ~ waterwheel⟩ **2 a** : having the upper jaw extending beyond the lower **b** : projecting beyond the lower jaw
[2]**overshot** *n* (1945) : a pattern or weave featuring filling threads which pass two or more warp yarns before reentering the fabric
over·sight \ˈō-vər-ˌsīt\ *n* (15c) **1 a** : watchful and responsible care **b** : regulatory supervision ⟨congressional ~⟩ **2** : an inadvertent omission or error
over·sim·ple \ˌō-vər-ˈsim-pəl\ *adj* (15c) : too simple : not thoroughgoing or exhaustive ⟨~ theories⟩ — **over·sim·ply** \-plē\ *adv*
over·sim·pli·fy \-ˈsim-plə-ˌfī\ *vt* (1923) : to simplify to such an extent as to bring about distortion, misunderstanding, or error ~ *vi* : to engage in undue or extreme simplification — **over·sim·pli·fi·ca·tion** \-ˌsim-plə-fə-ˈkā-shən\ *n*
over·size \ˌō-vər-ˈsīz\ *or* **over·sized** \-ˈsīzd\ *adj* (1853) : being of more than standard or ordinary size ⟨~ pillows⟩ ⟨an ~ shirt⟩
over·skirt \ˈō-vər-ˌskərt\ *n* (1869) : a skirt worn over another skirt
over·sleep \ˌō-vər-ˈslēp\ *vb* **-slept** \-ˈslept\; **-sleep·ing** *vi* (14c) : to sleep beyond the time for waking ~ *vt* : to allow (oneself) to oversleep
over·slip \ˌō-vər-ˈslip\ *vt* (15c) *obs* : ESCAPE
over·sold \ˌō-vər-ˈsōld\ *adj* (1926) : likely to show a rise in price because of prior heavy selling and accompanying decline in price ⟨an ~ stock⟩
over·soul \ˈō-vər-ˌsōl\ *n* (ca. 1844) : the absolute reality and basis of all existences conceived as a spiritual being in which the ideal nature imperfectly manifested in human beings is perfectly realized
over·spend \ˌō-vər-ˈspend\ *vb* **-spent** \-ˈspent\; **-spend·ing** *vt* (ca. 1618) **1** : to spend or use to excess : EXHAUST **2** : to exceed in expenditure ~ *vi* : to spend beyond one's means — **over·spend·er** *n*
over·spill \ˈō-vər-ˌspil\ *n* (1884) **1** : the act or an instance of spilling over **2** *chiefly Brit* : the movement of excess urban population into less crowded areas
over·spread \ˌō-vər-ˈspred\ *vt* **-spread; -spread·ing** (bef. 12c) : to spread over or above — **over·spread** \ˈō-vər-ˌspred\ *n*
over·state \-ˈstāt\ *vt* (1803) : to state in too strong terms : EXAGGERATE ⟨*overstated* his qualifications⟩ — **over·state·ment** \-mənt\ *n*
over·stay \-ˈstā\ *vt* (1646) : to stay beyond the time or the limits of
over·steer \ˈō-vər-ˌstir\ *n* (1936) : the tendency of an automobile to steer into a sharper turn than the driver intends sometimes with a thrusting of the rear to the outside; *also* : the action or an instance of oversteer
over·step \ˌō-vər-ˈstep\ *vt* (bef. 12c) : EXCEED, TRANSGRESS
over·stored \ˈō-vər-ˌstȯrd\ *adj* (1967) : having more stores than the market will support ⟨an ~ industry⟩
over·sto·ry \ˈō-vər-ˌstȯr-ē\ *n* (1925) **1** : the layer of foliage in a forest canopy **2** : the trees contributing to an overstory
over·strew \ˌō-vər-ˈstrü\ *vt* **-strewed; -strewed** *or* **-strewn** \-ˈstrün\; **-strew·ing** (ca. 1570) **1** : to strew or scatter about **2** : to cover here and there
over·stride \-ˈstrīd\ *vt* **-strode** \-ˈstrōd\; **-strid·den** \-ˈstri-dᵊn\; **-strid·ing** \-ˈstrī-diŋ\ (13c) **1 a** : to stride over, across, or beyond **b** : BESTRIDE **2** : to stride faster than or beyond
over·strung \-ˈstrəŋ\ *adj* (1810) : too highly strung : too sensitive
over·stuff \-ˈstəf\ *vt* (1715) **1** : to stuff too full **2** : to cover (as a chair or sofa) completely and deeply with upholstery
over·sub·scribe \-səb-ˈskrīb\ *vt* (1891) : to subscribe for more of than is available — **over·sub·scrip·tion** \-ˈskrip-shən\ *n*
overt \ō-ˈvərt, ˈō-(ˌ)vərt\ *adj* [ME, fr. AF, fr. pp. of *ovrir* to open, fr. VL **operire*, alter. of L *aperire*] (14c) : open to view : MANIFEST ⟨~ hostility⟩ — **overt·ly** *adv* — **overt·ness** *n*
over·take \ˌō-vər-ˈtāk\ *vt* **-took** \-ˈtu̇k\; **-tak·en** \-ˈtā-kən\; **-tak·ing** [ME, fr. [1]*over* + *taken* to take] (13c) **1 a** : to catch up with **b** : to catch up with and pass by **2** : to come upon suddenly
over–the–counter *adj* (1921) **1** : not traded or effected on an organized securities exchange ⟨~ transactions⟩ ⟨~ securities⟩ **2** : sold lawfully without prescription ⟨an ~ pain reliever⟩
over–the–hill *adj* (1946) **1** : past one's prime **2** : advanced in age
over–the–top *adj* (1984) : extremely or excessively flamboyant or outrageous ⟨an ~ performance⟩
over–the–transom *adj* (ca. 1952) : offered without prior arrangement esp. for publication : UNSOLICITED ⟨an ~ manuscript⟩
over·throw \ˌō-vər-ˈthrō\ *vt* **-threw** \-ˈthrü\; **-thrown** \-ˈthrōn\; **-throw·ing** (14c) **1** : OVERTURN, UPSET **2** : to cause the downfall of : BRING DOWN, DEFEAT **3** : to throw a ball over or past (as a base or a receiver) — **over·throw** \ˈō-vər-ˌthrō\ *n*
over·time \ˈō-vər-ˌtīm\ *n* (1536) **1** : time in excess of a set limit: as **a** : working time in excess of a standard day or week **b** : an extra period of play in a contest **2** : the wage paid for overtime — **overtime** *adv*
over·tone \-ˌtōn\ *n* (1867) **1 a** : one of the higher tones produced simultaneously with the fundamental and that with the fundamental comprise a complex musical tone : HARMONIC 1a **b** : HARMONIC 2 **2** : the color of the light reflected (as by a paint) **3** : a secondary effect, quality, or meaning : SUGGESTION, CONNOTATION
over·top \ˌō-vər-ˈtäp\ *vt* (ca. 1594) **1** : to rise above the top of **2** : to be superior to **3** : SURPASS
over·trade \-ˈtrād\ *vi* (1734) : to trade beyond one's capital
over·trick \ˈō-vər-ˌtrik\ *n* (1903) : a card trick won in excess of the number bid
over·trump \ˌō-vər-ˈtrəmp\ *vt* (1746) : to trump with a higher trump card than the highest previously played on the same trick ~ *vi* : to play a higher trump card than the highest previously played on the same trick
[1]**over·ture** \ˈō-və(r)-ˌchu̇r, -chər, -ˌtyu̇r, -ˌtu̇r\ *n* [ME, lit., opening, fr. AF, fr. VL **opertura*, alter. of L *apertura* — more at APERTURE] (15c) **1 a** : an initiative toward agreement or action : PROPOSAL **b** : something introductory : PRELUDE **2 a** : the orchestral introduction to a musical dramatic work **b** : an orchestral concert piece written esp. as a single movement in sonata form
[2]**overture** *vt* **-tured; -tur·ing** (ca. 1650) **1** : to put forward as an overture **2** : to make or present an overture to
[1]**over·turn** \ˌō-vər-ˈtərn\ *vt* (13c) **1** : to cause to turn over : UPSET ⟨~*ed* the vase⟩ **2 a** : INVALIDATE, DESTROY **b** : REVERSE 2a ⟨~ a court ruling⟩ ~ *vi* : UPSET, TURN OVER
[2]**over·turn** \ˈō-vər-ˌtərn\ *n* (ca. 1592) **1** : the act of overturning : the state of being overturned **2** : the sinking of surface water and rise of bottom water in a lake or sea that results from changes in temperature that commonly occur in spring and fall
over·val·ue \ˌō-vər-ˈval-(ˌ)yü\ *vt* (1597) : to assign an excessive or fictitious value to — **over·valu·a·tion** \-ˌval-yə-ˈwā-shən\ *n*
over·view \ˈō-vər-ˌvyü\ *n* (1588) : a general survey : SUMMARY
over·volt·age \ˌō-vər-ˈvōl-tij\ *n* (1907) **1** : the excess potential required for the discharge of an ion at an electrode over and above the equilibrium potential of the electrode **2** : voltage in excess of the normal operating voltage of a device or circuit
over·wear \-ˈwer\ *vt* **-wore** \-ˈwȯr\; **-worn** \-ˈwȯrn\; **-wear·ing** (1578) : WEAR OUT, EXHAUST
over·ween·ing \-ˈwē-niŋ\ *adj* [ME *overwening*, prp. of *overwenen* to be arrogant, fr. *over* + *wenen* to ween] (14c) **1** : ARROGANT, PRESUMPTUOUS **2** : IMMODERATE, EXAGGERATED — **over·ween·ing·ly** *adv*
over·weigh \-ˈwā\ *vt* (13c) **1** : to exceed in weight **2** : OPPRESS 2
[1]**over·weight** \ˈō-vər-ˌwāt, *2 is usu* ˌō-vər-ˈ\ *n* (1552) **1** : weight over and above what is required or allowed **2** : excessive or burdensome weight
[2]**over·weight** \ˌō-vər-ˈwāt\ *vt* (1603) **1** : to give too much weight or consideration to **2** : to weight excessively
[3]**over·weight** \ˌō-vər-ˈwāt\ *adj* (1638) : exceeding expected, normal, or proper weight; *esp* : exceeding the bodily weight normal for one's age, height, and build
over·whelm \ˌō-vər-ˈhwelm, -ˈwelm\ *vt* [ME, fr. [1]*over* + *whelmen* to turn over, cover up] (14c) **1** : UPSET, OVERTHROW **2 a** : to cover over completely : SUBMERGE **b** : to overcome by superior force or numbers **c** : to overpower in thought or feeling
over·whelm·ing \-ˈ(h)wel-miŋ\ *adj* (1702) : tending or serving to overwhelm ⟨~ force⟩; *also* : EXTREME, GREAT ⟨~ indifference⟩ ⟨an ~ majority⟩
over·whelm·ing·ly *adv* (1667) **1 a** : to an overwhelming extent ⟨an ~ powerful army⟩ **b** : EXTREMELY ⟨~ mediocre⟩ **2** : mostly by far ⟨the workers were ~ female⟩
[1]**over·win·ter** \ˌō-vər-ˈwin-tər\ *vi* (bef. 12c) : to last through or pass the winter
[2]**overwinter** *adj* (1900) : occurring during the period spanning the winter
over with *adj* (1899) : being at an end : FINISHED, COMPLETED
over·work \ˌō-vər-ˈwərk\ *vt* (1530) **1** : to cause to work too hard, too long, or to exhaustion ⟨~*ed* the horses⟩ **2 a** : to work too much on ⟨~ bread dough⟩ **b** : to make excessive use of ⟨~*ed* tunes⟩ ~ *vi* : to work too much or too long : OVERDO — **overwork** *n*
over·write \ˌō-və(r)-ˈrīt\ *vb* **-wrote** \-ˈrōt\; **-writ·ten** \-ˈri-tᵊn\; **-writ·ing** \-ˈrī-tiŋ\ *vt* (1658) **1** : to write over the surface of **2** : to write in inflated or overly elaborate style ~ *vi* : to write too much or in an overly elaborate style
over·wrought \-ˈrȯt\ *adj* [pp. of *overwork*] (1638) **1** : extremely excited : AGITATED **2** : elaborated to excess : OVERDONE
ovi- *or* **ovo-** — see OV-
ovi·cide \ˈō-və-ˌsīd\ *n* [ISV] (1913) : an agent that kills eggs; *esp* : an insecticide effective against the egg stage — **ovi·cid·al** \ˌō-və-ˈsī-dᵊl\ *adj*
ovi·duct \ˈō-və-ˌdəkt\ *n* [NL *oviductus*, fr. *ov-* + *ductus* duct] (1672) : a tube that allows for the passage of eggs from an ovary — **ovi·duc·tal** \ˌō-və-ˈdək-tᵊl\ *adj*
ovine \ˈō-ˌvīn\ *adj* [LL *ovinus*, fr. L *ovis* sheep — more at EWE] (1676) : of, relating to, or resembling sheep — **ovine** *n*
ovip·a·rous \ō-ˈvi-p(ə-)rəs\ *adj* [L *oviparus*, fr. *ov-* + *-parus* -parous] (1646) : producing eggs that develop and hatch outside the maternal body; *also* : involving the production of such eggs
ovi·pos·it \ˈō-və-ˌpä-zət, ˌō-və-ˈ\ *vi* [prob. back-formation fr. *ovipositor*] (1816) : to lay eggs — used esp. of insects — **ovi·po·si·tion** \ˌō-və-pə-ˈzi-shən\ *n* — **ovi·po·si·tion·al** \-ˈzish-nəl, -ˈzi-shə-nᵊl\ *adj*
ovi·pos·i·tor \ˈō-və-ˌpä-zə-tər, ˌō-və-ˈ\ *n* [NL, fr. L *ov-* + *positor* one that places, fr. *ponere* to place — more at POSITION] (1816) : a specialized organ (as of an insect) for depositing eggs — see INSECT illustration
ovi·rap·tor \ˈō-və-ˌrap-tər\ *n* [NL, fr. *ov-* + L *raptor* plunderer — more at RAPTOR] (1927) : any of a genus (*Oviraptor*) of bipedal theropod dinosaurs of the late Cretaceous having a toothless muscular jaw, clawed finger and toes, and a crested skull and that are thought to have exhibited brooding behavior
ovoid \ˈō-ˌvȯid\ *also* **ovoi·dal** \ō-ˈvȯi-dᵊl\ *adj* [F *ovoïde*, fr. L *ovum* egg — more at EGG] (ca. 1828) : resembling an egg in shape : OVATE ⟨an ~ fruit⟩ — **ovoid** *n*
ovo–lac·to vegetarian \ˈō-vō-ˈlak-tō-\ *n* (1977) : LACTO-OVO VEGETARIAN
ovo·lo \ˈō-və-ˌlō\ *n, pl* **-los** [It, dim. of *uovo, ovo* egg, fr. L *ovum*] (ca. 1639) : a rounded convex molding
ovo·tes·tis \ˌō-vō-ˈtes-təs\ *n* [NL] (1877) : a hermaphrodite gonad

ovo·vi·vip·a·rous \ˌō-vō-ˌvī-ˈvi-p(ə-)rəs\ *adj* (1801) **:** producing eggs that develop within the maternal body (as of various fishes or reptiles) and hatch within or immediately after release from the parent — **ovo·vi·vip·a·rous·ly** *adv* — **ovo·vi·vip·a·rous·ness** *n*

ovu·late \ˈäv-yə-ˌlāt, ˈōv-, -lət\ *adj* (1861) **:** bearing an ovule

ovu·la·tion \ˌäv-yə-ˈlā-shən, ˌōv-\ *n* (1848) **:** the discharge of a mature ovum from the ovary — **ovu·late** \ˈäv-yə-ˌlāt, ˈōv-\ *vb*

ovu·la·to·ry \ˈäv-yə-lə-ˌtōr-ē, ˈōv-\ *adj* (1931) **:** of, relating to, or involving ovulation ⟨the ∼ cycle⟩

ovule \ˈäv-(ˌ)yül, ˈōv-\ *n* [NL *ovulum*, dim. of L *ovum*] (1829) **1 :** an outgrowth of the ovary of a seed plant that is a megasporangium and encloses an embryo sac within a nucellus **2 :** a small egg; *esp* **:** one in an early stage of growth

ovum \ˈō-vəm\ *n, pl* **ova** \-və\ [NL, fr. L, egg — more at EGG] (ca. 1706) **:** a female gamete **:** MACROGAMETE — called also *egg cell*

ow \ˈau̇, ˈü\ *interj* [fr. *ow*, interj. expressing surprise, fr. ME] (1865) — used esp. to express sudden pain

OW *abbr* one-way

owe \ˈō\ *vb* **owed; ow·ing** [ME, to possess, own, owe, fr. OE *āgan*; akin to OHG *eigun* (1st & 3d pl. pres. indic.) possess, Skt *īśe* he possesses] *vt* (bef. 12c) **1 a** *archaic* **:** POSSESS, OWN **b :** to have or bear (an emotion or attitude) to someone or something ⟨∼*s* the boss a grudge⟩ **2 a** (1) **:** to be under obligation to pay or repay in return for something received **:** be indebted in the sum of ⟨∼*s* me $5⟩ (2) **:** to be under obligation to render (as duty or service) ⟨I ∼ you a favor⟩ **b :** to be indebted to ⟨∼*s* the grocer for supplies⟩ **3 :** to be indebted for ⟨*owed* his wealth to his father⟩ ⟨∼*s* much to good luck⟩ ∼ *vi* **1 :** to be in debt ⟨∼*s* for his house⟩ **2 :** to be attributable ⟨an idea that ∼*s* to Greek philosophy⟩ — **owe it :** to have a responsibility to do something to satisfy an obligation or duty ⟨*owes it* to voters to explain his reasons⟩

owing *adj* (15c) **:** due to be paid ⟨has bills ∼⟩

owing to *prep* (1667) **:** BECAUSE OF ⟨absent *owing to* illness⟩

owl \ˈau̇(-ə)l\ *n* [ME *owle*, fr. OE *ūle*; akin to OHG *uwila* owl] (bef. 12c) **:** any of an order (Strigiformes) of chiefly nocturnal birds of prey with a large head and eyes, short hooked bill, strong talons, and soft fluffy often brown-mottled plumage

owl·et \ˈau̇-lət\ *n* (1542) **:** a small or young owl

owl·ish \ˈau̇-lish\ *adj* (1611) **:** resembling or suggesting an owl — **owl·ish·ly** *adv* — **owl·ish·ness** *n*

owl monkey *n* (ca. 1890) **:** any of several small nocturnal monkeys (genus *Aotus*) of Central and So. American tropical forests that have round heads, large eyes, and densely furred bodies — called also *douroucouli*

[1]**own** \ˈōn\ *adj* [ME *owen*, fr. OE *āgen*; akin to OHG *eigan* own, ON *eiginn*, OE *āgan* to possess — more at OWE] (bef. 12c) **1 :** belonging to oneself or itself — usu. used following a possessive case or possessive adjective ⟨cooked my ∼ dinner⟩ **2** — used to express immediate or direct kinship ⟨an ∼ son⟩ ⟨an ∼ sister⟩

[2]**own** *vt* (bef. 12c) **1 a :** to have or hold as property **:** POSSESS **b :** to have power or mastery over ⟨wanted to ∼ his own life⟩ **2 :** to acknowledge to be true, valid, or as claimed **:** ADMIT ⟨∼ a debt⟩ ∼ *vi* **:** to acknowledge something to be true, valid, or as claimed — used with *to* or *up* ***syn*** see ACKNOWLEDGE — **own·er** \ˈō-nər\ *n*

[3]**own** *pron, sing or pl in constr* (bef. 12c) **:** one or ones belonging to oneself — used after a possessive and without a following noun ⟨gave out books so that each of us had our ∼⟩ ⟨a room of your ∼⟩ — **on one's own 1 :** for or by oneself **:** independently of assistance or control ⟨made the decision *on his own*⟩ **2 :** left to rely entirely on one's own resources ⟨if you mess up, you're *on your own*⟩

own·er·ship \ˈō-nər-ˌship\ *n* (1583) **1 :** the state, relation, or fact of being an owner **2 :** a group or organization of owners

ox \ˈäks\ *n, pl* **ox·en** \ˈäk-sən\ *also* **ox** [ME, fr. OE *oxa*; akin to OHG *ohso* ox, Skt *ukṣā* bull, and perh. to Skt *ukṣati* he moistens, Gk *hygros* wet — more at HUMOR] (bef. 12c) **1 :** a domestic bovine mammal (*Bos taurus*); *broadly* **:** a bovine mammal **2 :** an adult castrated male domestic ox

ox- *or* **oxo-** *comb form* [F, fr. *oxygène*] **:** oxygen ⟨*ox*acillin⟩

ox·a·cil·lin \ˌäk-sə-ˈsi-lən\ *n* [*ox-* + *azole* + *penicillin*] (1962) **:** a semisynthetic penicillin administered in the form of its hydrated sodium salt $C_{19}H_{18}N_3NaO_5S{\cdot}H_2O$ to treat infections caused by penicillin-resistant staphylococci

ox·a·late \ˈäk-sə-ˌlāt\ *n* (1788) **:** a salt or ester of oxalic acid

ox·al·ic acid \(ˌ)äk-ˈsa-lik-\ *n* [F (*acide*) *oxalique*, fr. L *oxalis*] (1790) **:** a poisonous strong acid $(COOH)_2$ or $H_2C_2O_4$ that occurs in various plants (as spinach) as oxalates and is used esp. as a bleaching or cleaning agent and as a chemical intermediate

ox·al·is \äk-ˈsa-ləs\ *n* [NL, genus name, fr. L, wood sorrel, fr. Gk, fr. *oxys* sharp — more at OXYGEN] (ca. 1706) **:** WOOD SORREL

ox·a·lo·ac·e·tate \ˌäk-sə-lō-ˈa-sə-ˌtāt\ *also* **ox·al·ac·e·tate** \ˌäk-sə-ˈla-\ *n* (1891) **:** a salt or ester of oxaloacetic acid

ox·a·lo·ace·tic acid \ˌäk-sə-lō-ə-ˈsē-tik-\ *also* **ox·al·ace·tic acid** \ˌäk-sə-lə-ˈsē-tik-\ *n* [*oxalic* + *acetic acid*] (1896) **:** a crystalline acid $C_4H_4O_5$ that is formed by reversible oxidation of malic acid (as in carbohydrate metabolism via the Krebs cycle) and in reversible transamination reactions (as from aspartic acid)

ox·a·lo·suc·cin·ic acid \ˈäk-sə-lō-sək-ˌsi-nik-, äk-ˈsa-lō-\ *n* [*oxalic* + *succinic acid*] (1925) **:** a tricarboxylic acid $C_6H_6O_7$ that is formed as an intermediate in the Krebs cycle

ox·az·e·pam \äk-ˈsa-zə-ˌpam\ *n* [hydr*oxy-* + di*azepam*] (1964) **:** a benzodiazepine tranquilizer $C_{15}H_{11}ClN_2O_2$

ox·blood \ˈäks-ˌbləd\ *n* (1705) **:** a moderate reddish brown

ox·bow \ˈäks-ˌbō\ *n* (14c) **1 :** a U-shaped frame forming a collar about an ox's neck and holding the yoke in place **2 :** something (as a bend in a river) resembling an oxbow — **oxbow** *adj*

Ox·bridge \ˈäks-ˌbrij\ *adj* [*Ox*ford + Cam*bridge*] (1955) **:** of, relating to, or characteristic of Oxford and Cambridge Universities — compare PLATEGLASS, REDBRICK 2

ox·cart \-ˌkärt\ *n* (1749) **:** a cart drawn by oxen

ox·eye \-ˌī\ *n* (15c) **:** any of several composite plants (as of the genera *Chrysanthemum* or *Heliopsis*) having heads with both disk and ray flowers; *esp* **:** DAISY 1b

oxeye daisy *n* (ca. 1763) **:** DAISY 1b

Oxfam *abbr* Oxford Committee for Famine Relief

ox·ford \ˈäks-fərd\ *n* [*Oxford*, England] (1886) **1 :** a low shoe laced or tied over the instep **2 :** a soft durable cotton or synthetic fabric made in plain or basket weaves — called also *oxford cloth*

Oxford down *n, often cap D* [*Oxfordshire*, England] (1859) **:** any of a Down breed of large hornless sheep developed by crossing Cotswolds and Hampshires — called also *Oxford*

Oxford movement *n* (1841) **:** a High Church movement within the Church of England begun at Oxford in 1833

ox·heart \ˈäks-ˌhärt\ *n* (1870) **:** any of various large sweet cherries

ox·i·dant \ˈäk-sə-dənt\ *n* (1884) **:** OXIDIZING AGENT — **oxidant** *adj*

ox·i·dase \ˈäk-sə-ˌdās, -ˌdāz\ *n* [ISV] (1896) **:** any of various enzymes that catalyze oxidations; *esp* **:** one able to react directly with molecular oxygen — **ox·i·da·sic** \ˌäk-sə-ˈdā-sik, -zik\ *adj*

ox·i·da·tion \ˌäk-sə-ˈdā-shən\ *n* [F, fr. *oxider, oxyder* to oxidize, fr. *oxide*] (1791) **1 :** the act or process of oxidizing **2 :** the state or result of being oxidized — **ox·i·da·tive** \ˈäk-sə-ˌdā-tiv\ *adj* — **ox·i·da·tive·ly** *adv*

oxidation–reduction *n* (1909) **:** a chemical reaction in which one or more electrons are transferred from one atom or molecule to another

oxidation state *n* (1942) **:** a positive or negative number that represents the effective charge of an atom or element and that indicates the extent or possibility of its oxidation ⟨the usual *oxidation state* of sodium is +1 and of oxygen −2⟩ — called also *oxidation number*

oxidative phosphorylation *n* (1945) **:** the synthesis of ATP by phosphorylation of ADP for which energy is obtained by electron transport and which takes place in the mitochondria during aerobic respiration

ox·ide \ˈäk-ˌsīd\ *n* [F *oxide, oxyde*, fr. *ox-* (fr. *oxygène* oxygen) + *-ide* (fr. *acide* acid)] (1790) **:** a binary compound of oxygen with a more electropositive element or group — **ox·id·ic** \äk-ˈsi-dik\ *adj*

ox·i·dise, ox·i·dis·er *chiefly Brit var of* OXIDIZE, OXIDIZER

ox·i·dize \ˈäk-sə-ˌdīz\ *vb* **-dized; -diz·ing** *vt* (1806) **1 :** to combine with oxygen **2 :** to dehydrogenate esp. by the action of oxygen **3 :** to change (a compound) by increasing the proportion of the electronegative part or change (an element or ion) from a lower to a higher positive valence **:** remove one or more electrons from (an atom, ion, or molecule) ∼ *vi* **:** to become oxidized — **ox·i·diz·able** \ˌäk-sə-ˈdī-zə-bəl\ *adj*

ox·i·diz·er \-ˌdī-zər\ *n* (1875) **:** OXIDIZING AGENT; *esp* **:** one used to support the combustion of a rocket propellant

oxidizing agent *n* (1830) **:** a substance that oxidizes something esp. chemically (as by accepting electrons)

ox·i·do·re·duc·tase \ˈäk-sə-dō-ri-ˈdək-ˌtās, -ˌtāz\ *n* [*oxid*ation + *-o-* + *reduct*ion + *-ase*] (1922) **:** an enzyme that catalyzes an oxidation-reduction reaction

ox·ime \ˈäk-ˌsēm\ *n* [ISV *ox-* + *-ime* (fr. *imide*)] (ca. 1890) **:** any of various compounds containing the divalent group C=NOH and obtained chiefly by the action of hydroxylamine on aldehydes and ketones

ox·im·e·ter \äk-ˈsi-mə-tər\ *n* [ISV *ox-* + *-i-* + *-meter*] (1929) **:** an instrument for measuring continuously the degree of oxygen saturation of the circulating blood — **ox·im·e·try** \äk-ˈsi-mə-trē\ *n*

ox·lip \ˈäk-ˌslip\ *n* [ME **oxeslippe*, fr. OE *oxanslyppe*, lit., ox dung, fr. *oxa* ox + *slypa, slyppe* paste — more at SLIP] (bef. 12c) **:** a Eurasian primula (*Primula elatior*) having usu. yellow flowers

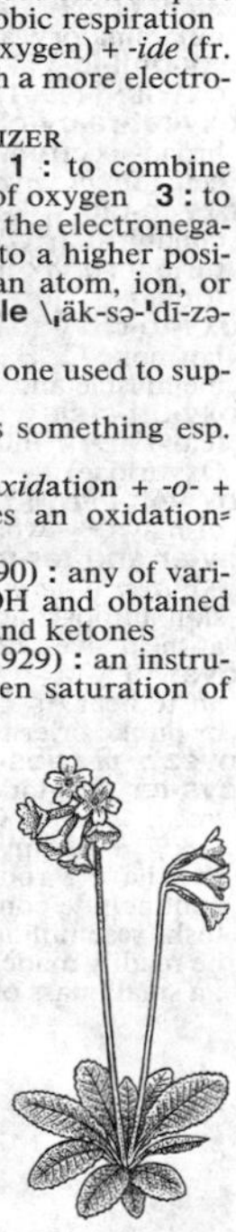
oxlip

oxo \ˈäk-(ˌ)sō\ *adj* [*ox-*] (ca. 1926) **:** containing oxygen

oxo- — see OX-

Oxon *abbr* **1** [ML *Oxonia*] Oxford **2** [ML *Oxoniensis*] of Oxford **3** Oxfordshire

Ox·o·ni·an \äk-ˈsō-nē-ən\ *n* [ML *Oxonia* Oxford] (ca. 1540) **:** a student or graduate of Oxford University — **Oxonian** *adj*

ox·peck·er \ˈäks-ˌpe-kər\ *n* (ca. 1848) **:** either of two small dull-colored African birds (*Buphagus erythrorhynchus* and *B. africanus*) of the starling family that feed on ticks which they pick from the backs of infested cattle and wild mammals

ox·tail \ˈäks-ˌtāl\ *n* (15c) **:** the tail of a beef animal; *esp* **:** the skinned tail used for food (as in soup)

ox·ter \ˈäk-stər\ *n* [ME (Sc), alter. of OE *ōxta*; akin to OE *eax* axis, axle — more at AXIS] (15c) **1** *chiefly Scot & Irish* **:** ARMPIT 1 **2** *chiefly Scot & Irish* **:** ARM

ox·tongue \ˈäks-ˌtəŋ\ *n* (14c) **:** a European hawkweed (*Picris echioides*) that has yellow flowers and is now naturalized in the eastern U.S.

oxy \ˈäk-sē\ *adj* [F, fr. *oxygène* oxygen] (1910) **:** containing oxygen or additional oxygen — often used in combination ⟨*oxy*hemoglobin⟩

oxy·acet·y·lene \ˌäk-sē-ə-ˈse-tə-lən, -ˌlēn\ *adj* [ISV] (1909) **:** of, relating to, or utilizing a mixture of oxygen and acetylene ⟨an ∼ torch⟩

oxy·co·done \ˌäk-sē-ˈkō-ˌdōn\ *n* [*oxy* + *codeine* + *-one*] (1966) **:** a narcotic analgesic $C_{18}H_{21}NO_4$ used esp. in the form of its hydrochloride

ox·y·gen \ˈäk-si-jən\ *n, often attrib* [F *oxygène*, fr. Gk *oxys*, adj., acidic, lit., sharp + F *-gène* -gen; akin to L *acer* sharp — more at EDGE] (1788) **1 :** a reactive element that is found in water, in most rocks and minerals, in numerous organic compounds, and as a colorless tasteless odorless diatomic gas constituting 21 percent of the atmosphere, that is capable of combining with all elements except the inert gases, that is active in physiological processes, and that is involved esp. in combustion — see ELEMENT table **2 :** something that sustains or fuels ⟨disagreement is the true ∼ of these magazines —Joseph Epstein⟩ — **ox·y·gen·less** \ˈäk-si-jən-ləs\ *adj*

[1]**ox·y·gen·ate** \ˈäk-si-jə-ˌnāt, äk-ˈsi-jə-\ *vt* **-at·ed; -at·ing** (1788) **:** to impregnate, combine, or supply (as blood) with oxygen — **ox·y·gen·a·tion** \ˌäk-si-jə-ˈnā-shən, äk-ˌsi-jə-\ *n*

[2]**oxygenate** *n* (1975) **:** an oxygen-containing substance (as ethanol) used esp. in gasoline to promote more complete combustion

ox·y·gen·a·tor \ˈäk-si-jə-ˌnā-tər, äk-ˈsi-jə-\ *n* (ca. 1864) **:** one that oxygenates; *specif* **:** an apparatus that oxygenates the blood extracorporeally (as during open-heart surgery)

\ə\ **abut** \ᵊ\ **kitten**, F **table** \ər\ **further** \a\ **ash** \ā\ **ace** \ä\ **mop, mar**
\au̇\ **out** \ch\ **chin** \e\ **bet** \ē\ **easy** \g\ **go** \i\ **hit** \ī\ **ice** \j\ **job**
\ŋ\ **sing** \ō\ **go** \ȯ\ **law** \ȯi\ **boy** \th\ **thin** \th̲\ **the** \ü\ **loot** \u̇\ **foot**
\y\ **yet** \zh\ **vision, beige** \k̲, ⁿ, œ, ue, ʸ\ *see* Guide to Pronunciation

oxygen cycle *n* (1935) : the cycle whereby atmospheric oxygen is converted to carbon dioxide in animal respiration and regenerated by green plants in photosynthesis

oxygen debt *n* (1923) : a cumulative deficit of oxygen available for oxidative metabolism that develops during periods of intense bodily activity and must be made good when the body returns to rest

oxygen demand *n* (1950) : BIOCHEMICAL OXYGEN DEMAND

ox·y·gen·ic \ˌäk-si-'je-nik\ *adj* (1850) **1** : of or relating to oxygen **2** : generating or producing oxygen ⟨∼ photosynthesis⟩

oxygen mask *n* (1920) : a device worn over the nose and mouth through which oxygen is supplied from a storage tank

oxygen tent *n* (1925) : a canopy which can be placed over a bedridden person and within which a flow of oxygen can be maintained

oxy·he·mo·glo·bin \ˌäk-si-'hē-mə-ˌglō-bən\ *n* [ISV] (1873) : hemoglobin loosely combined with oxygen that it releases to the tissues

oxy·hy·dro·gen \-'hī-drə-jən\ *adj* (1827) : of, relating to, or utilizing a mixture of oxygen and hydrogen ⟨an ∼ torch⟩

ox·y·mo·ron \ˌäk-sē-'mȯr-ˌän\ *n, pl* **-mo·rons** *also* **-mo·ra** \-'mȯr-ə\ [LGk *oxymōron*, fr. neut. of *oxymōros* pointedly foolish, fr. Gk *oxys* sharp, keen + *mōros* foolish] (1657) : a combination of contradictory or incongruous words (as *cruel kindness*); *broadly* : something (as a concept) that is made up of contradictory or incongruous elements — **ox·y·mo·ron·ic** \-mə-'rä-nik, -mō-\ *adj* — **ox·y·mo·ron·i·cal·ly** \-ni-k(ə-)lē\ *adv*

oxy·phen·bu·ta·zone \ˌäk-sē-ˌfen-'byü-tə-ˌzōn\ *n* [*oxy* + *phenylbutazone*] (1959) : a phenylbutazone derivative $C_{19}H_{20}N_2O_3$ having antiinflammatory, analgesic, and antipyretic effects

oxy·phil·ic \ˌäk-si-'fi-lik\ *adj* [Gk *oxys* acidic + E *-phil* — more at OXYGEN] (1901) : ACIDOPHILIC

oxy·tet·ra·cy·cline \-ˌte-trə-'sī-ˌklēn\ *n* (1953) : a yellow crystalline broad-spectrum antibiotic $C_{22}H_{24}N_2O_9$ produced by a soil actinomycete (*Streptomyces rimosus*)

oxy·to·cic \ˌäk-si-'tō-sik\ *adj* [ISV, fr. Gk *oxys* sharp, quick + *tokos* childbirth, fr. *tiktein* to bear — more at THANE] (1873) : hastening parturition; *also* : inducing contraction of uterine smooth muscle — **oxy·tocic** *n*

oxy·to·cin \-'tō-sᵊn\ *n* [ISV, fr. *oxytocic*] (1928) : a pituitary octapeptide hormone $C_{43}H_{66}N_{12}O_{12}S_2$ that stimulates esp. the contraction of uterine muscle and the secretion of milk

oxy·uri·a·sis \ˌäk-si-yü-'rī-ə-səs\ *n* [NL, fr. *Oxyuris*, genus of worms] (ca. 1909) : infestation with or disease caused by pinworms (family Oxyuridae)

oy \'ȯi\ *interj* [Yiddish] (1892) — used esp. to express exasperation or dismay ⟨∼, what a mess⟩

oy·er and ter·mi·ner \ˌȯi-ər-ən(d)-'tər-mə-nər\ *n* [ME, part trans. of AF *oyer et terminer*, lit., to hear and determine] (15c) **1** : a commission authorizing a British judge to hear and determine a criminal case at the assizes **2** : a high criminal court in some U.S. states

¹**oyez** \ō-'yez, -'yā, -'yes, 'ō-ˌ\ *vb imper* [ME, fr. AF, hear ye, imper. pl. of *oir* to hear, fr. L *audire* — more at AUDIBLE] (15c) — used by a court or public crier to gain attention before a proclamation

²**oyez** *n, pl* **oyes·ses** \-'ye-səz, -ˌye-səz\ (15c) : a cry of oyez

oys·ter \'ȯis-tər\ *n, often attrib* [ME *oistre*, fr. AF, fr. L *ostrea*, fr. Gk *ostreon*; akin to Gk *ostrakon* shell, *osteon* bone — more at OSSEOUS] (13c) **1 a** : any of various marine bivalve mollusks (family Ostreidae) that have a rough irregular shell closed by a single adductor muscle and include commercially important shellfish **b** : any of various mollusks resembling or related to the oysters **2** : something that is or can be readily made to serve one's personal ends ⟨the world was her ∼⟩ **3** : a small mass of muscle contained in a concavity of the pelvic bone on

each side of the back of a fowl **4** : an extremely taciturn person **5** : a grayish-white color

oyster bed *n* (1591) : a place where oysters grow or are cultivated

oys·ter·catch·er \-ˌka-chər, -ˌke-\ *n* (1731) : any of a family (Haematopodidae containing a single genus *Haematopus*) of wading birds that have stout legs, a heavy wedge-shaped bill, and often black-and-white plumage

oyster crab *n* (1756) : a tiny crab (*Pinnotheres ostreum*) that lives as a commensal in the gill cavity of the oyster

oyster cracker *n* (1857) : a small salted usu. round cracker

oyster drill *n* (1925) : DRILL 4a

oystercatcher

oys·ter·ing \'ȯis-t(ə-)riŋ\ *n* (1662) : the act or business of taking oysters for the market or for food

oys·ter·man \'ȯis-tər-mən\ *n* (1552) : one who gathers, opens, breeds, or sells oysters

oyster mushroom *n* (1875) : an edible mushroom (*Pleurotus ostreatus*) that grows esp. on deciduous trees and deadwood

oyster plant *n* (1821) : SALSIFY

oysters Rocke·fel·ler \-'rä-ki-ˌfe-lər\ *n pl* [prob. fr. John D. *Rockefeller* †1937] (1939) : a dish of oysters on the half shell cooked with various savory toppings typically including chopped spinach and a seasoned sauce

oz *abbr* [obs It *onza* (now *oncia*)] ounce; ounces

Oz \'äz\ *n* [fr. *Oz*, mythical land in a series of books by L. Frank Baum] (1931) : an ideal or fantastical place

ozo·ke·rite \ˌō-zō-'kir-ˌīt\ *n, also* **ozo·ce·rite** \-'sir-\ *n* [G *Ozokerit*, fr. Gk *ozein* to smell + *kēros* wax — more at CERUMEN] (ca. 1837) : a waxy mineral mixture of hydrocarbons that is colorless or white when pure and often of unpleasant odor and is used esp. in making candles and in electrotyping

ozon·a·tion \ˌō-(ˌ)zō-'nā-shən\ *n* (1854) : the treatment or combination of a substance or compound with ozone — **ozon·ate** \'ō-(ˌ)zō-ˌnāt, -zə-\ *vt*

ozone \'ō-ˌzōn\ *n* [G *Ozon*, fr. Gk *ozōn*, prp. of *ozein* to smell — more at ODOR] (ca. 1840) **1** : a triatomic very reactive form of oxygen that is a bluish irritating gas of pungent odor, that is a major air pollutant in the lower atmosphere but a beneficial component of the upper atmosphere, and that is used for oxidizing, bleaching, disinfecting, and deodorizing **2** : pure and refreshing air ⟨relished the ∼ of morning⟩ — **ozon·ic** \ō-'zō-nik, -'zä-\ *adj*

ozone hole *n* (1986) : an area of the ozone layer (as near the south pole) that is seasonally depleted of ozone

ozone layer *n* (1929) : an atmospheric layer at heights of about 20 to 30 miles (32 to 48 kilometers) that is normally characterized by high ozone content which blocks most solar ultraviolet radiation from entry into the lower atmosphere

ozon·ide \'ō-(ˌ)zō-ˌnīd\ *n* (1867) : a compound formed by the addition of ozone to a double or triple bond of an organic compound

ozon·ize \-ˌnīz\ *vt* **-ized; -iz·ing** (1850) : to treat, impregnate, or combine with ozone — **ozon·i·za·tion** \ˌō-(ˌ)zō-nə-'zā-shən\ *n* — **ozon·iz·er** \'ō-(ˌ)zō-ˌnī-zər\ *n*

ozo·no·sphere \ō-'zō-nə-ˌsfir\ *n* (1933) : OZONE LAYER

P

¹**p** \'pē\ *n, pl* **p's** *or* **ps** \'pēz\ *often cap, often attrib* (bef. 12c) **1 a** : the 16th letter of the English alphabet **b** : a graphic representation of this letter **c** : a speech counterpart of orthographic *p* **2** : a graphic device for reproducing the letter *p* **3** : one designated *p* esp. as the 16th in order or class **4** [abbr. for *pass*] **a** : a grade rating a student's work as passing **b** : one graded or rated with a P **5** : something shaped like the letter P

²**p** *abbr* **1** page; pages **2** parental generation **3** part **4** participle **5** past **6** pater **7** pawn **8** pence; penny **9** per **10** peseta **11** peso **12** petite **13** piano **14** pico- **15** pint **16** pipe **17** pitch **18** pole **19** port **20** power **21** pro **22** progressive **23** proton **24** purl

¹**P** *abbr* **1** pressure **2** [F *poids*] weight

²**P** *symbol* phosphorus

p- *abbr* para-

pa \'pä, 'pȯ\ *n* [short for *papa*] (ca. 1629) : FATHER

¹**Pa** *abbr* **1** pascal **2** Pennsylvania

²**Pa** *symbol* protactinium

¹**PA** \ˌ(ˌ)pē-'ā\ *n* (1970) : PHYSICIAN ASSISTANT

²**PA** *abbr* **1** Pennsylvania **2** *chiefly Brit* per annum **3** personal assistant **4** power amplifier **5** power of attorney **6** press agent **7** professional association **8** public address **9** purchasing agent

pa·'an·ga \pä-'äŋ-gə, -'äŋ-ə\ *n* [Tongan, lit., seed from a species of vine] (1966) — see MONEY table

PABA \'pa-bə, 'pä-; ˌpē-(ˌ)ā-ˌbē-(ˌ)ä\ *n* [*para-aminobenzoic acid*] (1943) : PARA-AMINOBENZOIC ACID

pab·lum \'pa-bləm\ *n* [fr. *Pablum*, a trademark for an infant cereal] (1932) : PABULUM 3

pab·u·lum \'pa-byə-ləm\ *n* [L, food, fodder; akin to L *pascere* to feed — more at FOOD] (1733) **1** : FOOD; *esp* : a suspension or solution of nutrients in a state suitable for absorption **2** : intellectual sustenance **3** : something (as writing or speech) that is insipid, simplistic, or bland

Pac *abbr* Pacific

PAC *abbr* political action committee

pa·ca \'pä-kə, 'pa-\ *n* [Pg, fr. Tupi *páka*] (1657) : either of two large nocturnal chiefly Central and So. American rodents (*Agouti paca* syn. *Cuniculus paca* and *A. taczanowskii* syn. *C. taczanowskii*) that typically have a white-spotted brownish coat

¹**pace** \'pās\ *n* [ME *pas*, fr. AF, stride, step, fr. L *passus*, fr. *pandere* to spread — more at FATHOM] (14c) **1 a** : rate of movement; *esp* : an established rate of locomotion **b** : rate of progress; *specif* : parallel rate of growth or development ⟨supplies kept ∼ with demand⟩ **c** : an example to be emulated; *specif* : first place in a competition ⟨three strokes off the ∼ —*Time*⟩ **d** (1) : rate of performance or delivery : TEMPO ⟨a steady ∼⟩ ⟨on ∼ to set a record⟩; *esp* : SPEED ⟨serves with great ∼⟩ ⟨a ∼ bowler in cricket⟩ (2) : rhythmic animation : FLUENCY ⟨writes with color, with zest, and with ∼ —Amy Loveman⟩ **2** : a manner of walking : TREAD **3 a** : STEP 2a(1) **b** : any of various units of distance based on the length of a human step **4 a** *pl* : an exhibition or test of skills or capacities ⟨the trainer put the tiger through its ∼s⟩ **b** : GAIT; *esp* : a fast 2-beat gait (as of the horse) in which the legs move in lateral pairs and support the animal alternately on the right and left legs

[2]**pace** *vb* **paced; pac·ing** *vi* (1513) **1 a :** to walk with often slow or measured tread **b :** to move along : PROCEED **2 :** to go at a pace — used esp. of a horse ~ *vt* **1 a :** to measure by pacing — often used with *off* ⟨*paced* off a 10-yard penalty⟩ **b :** to cover at a walk ⟨could hear him *pacing* the floor⟩ **2 :** to cover (a course) by pacing — used of a horse **3 a :** to set or regulate the pace of ⟨taught them how to ~ their solos for . . . impact —Richard Goldstein⟩; *also* **:** to establish a moderate or steady pace for (oneself) **b (1) :** to go before : PRECEDE **(2) :** to set an example for : LEAD **c :** to keep pace with

[3]**pa·ce** \ˈpä-(ˌ)sē; ˈpä-(ˌ)chā, -(ˌ)kā\ *prep* [L, abl. of *pac-, pax* peace, permission — more at PACT] (1863) **:** contrary to the opinion of — usu. used as an expression of deference to someone's contrary opinion; usu. ital. ⟨easiness is a virtue in grammar, ~ old-fashioned grammarians —Philip Howard⟩

pace car *n* (1965) **:** an automobile that leads the field of competitors through a pace lap but does not participate in the race

pace lap *n* (1971) **:** a lap of an auto racecourse by the entire field of competitors before the start of a race to allow the engines to warm up and to permit a flying start

pace·mak·er \ˈpās-ˌmā-kər\ *n* (1884) **1 a :** one that sets the pace for another **b :** one that takes the lead or sets an example **2 a :** a group of cells or a body part (as the sinus node of the heart) that serves to establish and maintain a rhythmic activity **b :** an electrical device for stimulating or steadying the heartbeat or reestablishing the rhythm of an arrested heart — **pace·mak·ing** \-kiŋ\ *n*

pac·er \ˈpā-sər\ *n* (ca. 1661) **1 :** one that paces; *specif* **:** a horse whose predominant gait is the pace **2 :** PACEMAKER

pace·set·ter \ˈpās-ˌse-tər\ *n* (1895) **:** PACEMAKER 1 — **pace·set·ting** \-tiŋ\ *adj*

pa·chi·si \pə-ˈchē-zē\ *n* [Hindi & Urdu *pacīsī*, fr. *pacīs* twenty-five] (1867) **:** an ancient board game played with dice and counters on a cruciform board in which players attempt to be the first to reach the home square

pa·chu·co \pə-ˈchü-(ˌ)kō\ *n, pl* **-cos** [AmerSp] (1943) **:** a young Mexican-American having a taste for flashy clothes and a special jargon and usu. belonging to a neighborhood gang

pachy·derm \ˈpa-ki-ˌdərm\ *n* [F *pachyderme,* fr. Gk *pachydermos* thick-skinned, fr. *pachys* thick + *derma* skin; akin to Skt *bahu* dense, much — more at DERM-] (1838) **:** any of various nonruminant mammals (as an elephant, a rhinoceros, or a hippopotamus) of a former group (Pachydermata) that have hooves or nails resembling hooves and usu. thick skin; *esp* **:** ELEPHANT

pachy·der·ma·tous \ˌpa-ki-ˈdər-mə-təs\ *adj* [ultim. fr. Gk *pachys* + *dermat-, derma* skin] (1823) **1 :** of or relating to the pachyderms **2 a :** THICK, THICKENED ⟨~ skin⟩ **b :** CALLOUS, INSENSITIVE

pach·y·san·dra \ˌpa-ki-ˈsan-drə\ *n* [NL, irreg. fr. Gk *pachys* + NL *-andrus* -androus] (1813) **:** any of a genus (*Pachysandra*) of perennial evergreen plants of the box family often used as a ground cover

pachy·tene \ˈpa-ki-ˌtēn\ *n* [ISV *pachy-* (fr. Gk *pachys*) + *-tene*] (1912) **:** the stage of meiotic prophase that immediately follows the zygotene and that is characterized by paired chromosomes thickened and visibly divided into chromatids and by the occurrence of crossing-over — **pachytene** *adj*

pa·cif·ic \pə-ˈsi-fik\ *adj* [ME *pacifique,* fr. L *pacificus,* fr. *pac-, pax* peace + *-i-* + *-ficus* -fic — more at PACT] (ca. 1548) **1 a :** tending to lessen conflict : CONCILIATORY **b :** rejecting the use of force as an instrument of policy **2 a :** having a soothing appearance or effect ⟨mild ~ breezes⟩ **b :** mild of temper : PEACEABLE **3** *cap* **:** of, relating to, bordering on, or situated near the Pacific Ocean — **pa·cif·i·cal·ly** \-fi-k(ə-)lē\ *adv*

pac·i·fi·ca·tion \ˌpa-sə-fə-ˈkā-shən\ *n* (15c) **1 a :** the act or process of pacifying : the state of being pacified **b :** the act of forcibly suppressing or eliminating a population considered to be hostile **2 :** a treaty of peace

pa·cif·i·ca·tor \pə-ˈsi-fə-ˌkā-tər\ *n* (1539) **:** PACIFIER 1

pa·cif·i·cism \pə-ˈsi-fə-ˌsi-zəm\ *n* (1910) **:** PACIFISM — **pa·cif·i·cist** \-sist\ *n*

Pacific salmon *n* (1888) **:** any of several anadromous salmonid fishes (genus *Oncorhynchus*) chiefly of the northern Pacific including the coho, sockeye salmon, chum salmon, chinook salmon, and pink salmon

Pacific time \pə-ˈsi-fik-\ *n* [*Pacific* Ocean] (1883) **:** the time of the eighth time zone west of Greenwich that includes the Pacific coastal region of the U.S. — see TIME ZONE illustration

Pacific yew *n* (ca. 1890) **:** a small or medium slow-growing irregularly branched yew (*Taxus brevifolia*) of the Pacific coast of the U.S. and Canada that yields a fine-grained hardwood and is the source of paclitaxel

pac·i·fi·er \ˈpa-sə-ˌfī(-ə)r\ *n* (1533) **1 :** one that pacifies **2 :** a usu. nipple-shaped device for babies to suck or bite on

pac·i·fism \ˈpa-sə-ˌfi-zəm\ *n* [F *pacifisme,* fr. *pacifique* pacific] (1902) **1 :** opposition to war or violence as a means of settling disputes; *specif* **:** refusal to bear arms on moral or religious grounds **2 :** an attitude or policy of nonresistance — **pac·i·fist** \-fist\ *n*

pac·i·fist \ˈpa-sə-fist\ *or* **pac·i·fis·tic** \ˌpa-sə-ˈfis-tik\ *adj* (1908) **1 :** of, relating to, or characteristic of pacifism or pacifists **2 :** strongly and actively opposed to conflict and esp. war — **pac·i·fis·ti·cal·ly** \ˌpa-sə-ˈfis-ti-k(ə-)lē\ *adv*

pac·i·fy \ˈpa-sə-ˌfī\ *vt* **-fied; -fy·ing** [ME *pacifien,* fr. AF *pacifier,* fr. L *pacificare,* fr. *pac-, pax* peace] (15c) **1 a :** to allay the anger or agitation of : SOOTHE ⟨~ a crying child⟩ **b :** APPEASE, PROPITIATE **2 a :** to restore to a tranquil state : SETTLE ⟨made an attempt to ~ the commotion⟩ **b :** to reduce to a submissive state : SUBDUE ⟨forces moved in to ~ the country⟩ — **pac·i·fi·able** \ˌpa-sə-ˈfī-ə-bəl\ *adj*

syn PACIFY, APPEASE, PLACATE, MOLLIFY, PROPITIATE, CONCILIATE mean to ease the anger or disturbance of. PACIFY suggests a soothing or calming ⟨*pacified* by a sincere apology⟩. APPEASE implies quieting insistent demands by making concessions ⟨*appease* their territorial ambitions⟩. PLACATE suggests changing resentment or bitterness to goodwill ⟨a move to *placate* local opposition⟩. MOLLIFY implies soothing hurt feelings or rising anger ⟨a speech that *mollified* the demonstrators⟩. PROPITIATE implies averting anger or malevolence esp. of a superior being ⟨*propitiated* his parents by dressing up⟩. CONCILIATE suggests ending an estrangement by persuasion, concession, or settling of differences ⟨*conciliating* the belligerent nations⟩.

Pa·cin·i·an corpuscle \pə-ˈsi-nē-ən-\ *n* [Filippo *Pacini* †1883 Ital. anatomist] (ca. 1860) **:** a pressure-sensitive mechanoreceptor that is an oval capsule terminating some sensory nerve fibers esp. in the skin

[1]**pack** \ˈpak\ *n, often attrib* [ME, of LG or D origin; akin to MLG & MD *pak* pack] (13c) **1 a :** a bundle arranged for convenience in carrying esp. on the back **b :** a group or pile of related objects **c (1) :** a number of individual components packaged as a unit ⟨a ~ of gum⟩ **(2) :** CONTAINER **(3) :** a compact unitized assembly to perform a specific function **(4) :** a stack of magnetic disks in a container for use as a storage device **2 a :** the contents of a bundle **b :** a large amount or number : HEAP ⟨a ~ of lies⟩ **c :** a full set of playing cards **3 a :** an act or instance of packing **b :** a method of packing **4 a :** a set of persons with a common interest : CLIQUE **b :** an organized unit (as of Cub Scouts) **5 a (1) :** a group of domesticated animals trained to hunt or run together **(2) :** a group of often predatory animals of the same kind ⟨a wolf ~⟩ **(3) :** a large group of individuals massed together (as in a race) **b :** WOLF PACK **6 :** a concentrated or compacted mass (as of snow or ice) **7 :** wet absorbent material for therapeutic application to the body **8 a :** a cosmetic paste for the face **b :** an application or treatment of oils or creams for conditioning the scalp and hair **9 :** material used in packing

[2]**pack** *vt* (14c) **1 a :** to make into a compact bundle **b :** to fill completely ⟨fans ~*ed* the stadium⟩ **c :** to fill with packing ⟨~ a joint in a pipe⟩ **d :** to load with a pack ⟨~ a mule⟩ **e :** to put in a protective container ⟨goods ~*ed* for shipment⟩ **2 a :** to crowd together **b :** to increase the density of : COMPRESS **3 a :** to cause or command to go without ceremony ⟨~*ed* him off to school⟩ **b :** to bring to an end : GIVE UP — used with *up* or *in* ⟨might ~ up the assignment⟩; used esp. in the phrase *pack it in* **4 :** to gather into tight formation : make a pack of (as hounds) **5 :** to cover or surround with a pack **6 a :** to transport on foot or on the back of an animal ⟨~ a canoe overland⟩ **b :** to wear or carry as equipment ⟨~ a gun⟩ **c :** to be supplied or equipped with : POSSESS ⟨a storm ~*ing* hurricane winds⟩ **d :** to make or be capable of making (an impact) ⟨a book that ~*s* a man-sized punch —C. J. Rolo⟩ ~ *vi* **1 a :** to go away without ceremony : DEPART ⟨simply ~*ed* up and left⟩ **b :** QUIT, STOP — used with *up* or *in* ⟨why don't you ~ in, before you kill yourself —Millard Lampell⟩ **2 a :** to stow goods and equipment for transportation **b :** to be suitable for packing ⟨a knit dress ~*s* well⟩ **3 a :** to assemble in a group : CONGREGATE **b :** to crowd together **4 :** to become built up or compacted in a layer or mass ⟨the ore ~*ed* into a stony mass⟩ **5 a :** to carry goods or equipment **b :** to travel with one's baggage (as by horse) — **pack·abil·i·ty** \ˌpa-kə-ˈbi-lə-tē\ *n* — **pack·able** \ˈpa-kə-bəl\ *adj*

[3]**pack** *vt* [obs. *pack* to make a secret agreement] (1587) **1 :** to influence the composition of so as to bring about a desired result ⟨~ a jury⟩ **2** *archaic* **:** to arrange (the cards in a pack) so as to cheat

[4]**pack** *adj* [perh. fr. obs. *pack* to make a secret agreement] (1701) *chiefly Scot* **:** INTIMATE

[1]**pack·age** \ˈpa-kij\ *n* (1611) **1** *archaic* **:** the act or process of packing **2 a :** a small or moderate-sized pack : PARCEL **b :** a commodity or a unit of a product uniformly wrapped or sealed **c :** a preassembled unit **3 :** a covering wrapper or container **4 :** something that suggests a package: as **a :** PACKAGE DEAL **b :** a radio or television series offered for sale at a lump sum **c :** contract benefits gained through collective bargaining **d :** a ready-made computer program or collection of related software **e :** a travel arrangement contract that offers for a fixed price transportation, accommodations, and often sightseeing and entertainment **f :** a collection of related items; *esp* **:** one to be considered or acted on together ⟨presented his tax ~ to the nation⟩

[2]**package** *vt* **pack·aged; pack·ag·ing** (1921) **1 a :** to make into a package; *esp* **:** to produce as an entertainment package **b :** to present (as a product) in such a way as to heighten its appeal to the public **2 :** to enclose in a package or covering — **pack·ag·er** *n*

package deal *n* (ca. 1948) **1 :** an offer or agreement involving a number of related items or one making acceptance of one item dependent on the acceptance of another **2 :** the items offered in a package deal

package store *n* (ca. 1918) **:** a store that sells bottled or canned alcoholic beverages for consumption off the premises

pack animal *n* (1836) **:** an animal used for carrying packs

pack·board \ˈpak-ˌbȯrd\ *n* (1939) **:** a usu. canvas-covered light wood or metal frame with shoulder straps used for carrying goods and equipment

packed \ˈpakt\ *adj* (1777) **1 a :** COMPRESSED ⟨~ snow⟩ **b :** that is crowded or stuffed — often used in combination ⟨an action-*packed* story⟩ **2 :** filled to capacity ⟨played to a ~ house⟩

pack·er \ˈpa-kər\ *n* (14c) **1 :** one that packs: as **a :** one engaged in processing food (as meat) and distributing it to retailers **b :** an automotive vehicle with a closed body and a compressing device (as for compacting rubbish) in the rear **2 :** PORTER 1 **3 :** one that conveys goods by means of a pack

pack·et \ˈpa-kət\ *n* [ME *pekette, pakat,* fr. AF *pacquet,* of Gmc origin; akin to MD *pak* pack] (15c) **1 a :** a small bundle or parcel **b :** a small thin package **c** *Brit* **(1) :** PAY ENVELOPE **(2) :** SALARY, PAYCHECK **d** *chiefly Brit* **:** a considerable amount ⟨that trip will cost a ~⟩ **2 a :** a number of letters dispatched at one time **b :** a small group, cluster, or mass **3 :** a passenger boat usu. carrying mail and cargo **4** *Brit* **:** a pack of cigarettes **5 :** a short fixed-length section of data that is transmitted as a unit in an electronic communications network

pack·horse \ˈpak-ˌhȯrs\ *n* (ca. 1500) **:** a horse used as a pack animal

pack ice *n* (1850) **:** sea ice formed into a mass by the crushing together of pans, floes, and brash

pack·ing \ˈpa-kiŋ\ *n* (14c) **1 a :** the action or process of packing something; *also* **:** a method of packing **b :** the processing of food and esp. meat for future sale **2 :** material (as a covering or stuffing) used to

protect packed goods (as for shipping); *also* : material used for making airtight or watertight ⟨~ for a faucet⟩
pack·ing·house \-ˌhau̇s\ *n* (1834) : an establishment for slaughtering livestock and processing and packing meat, meat products, and by-products; *also* : one for processing and packing other foodstuffs — called also *packing plant*
pack journalism *n* (1972) : journalism that is practiced by reporters in a group and that is marked by uniformity of news coverage and lack of original thought or initiative
pack·man \ˈpak-mən\ *n* (ca. 1625) : PEDDLER
pack rat *n* (1885) **1** : WOOD RAT; *esp* : a bushy-tailed rodent (*Neotoma cinerea*) of western No. America that has well-developed cheek pouches and that hoards food and miscellaneous objects **2** : a person who collects or hoards esp. unneeded items
pack·sack \ˈpak-ˌsak\ *n* (1851) : a case (as of canvas) held on the back by shoulder straps and used to carry gear esp. when traveling on foot
pack·sad·dle \-ˌsa-dᵊl\ *n* (14c) : a saddle designed to support loads on the backs of pack animals
pack·thread \-ˌthred\ *n* (14c) : strong thread or small twine used for sewing or tying packs or parcels
pac·li·tax·el \ˌpa-kli-ˈtak-sᵊl\ *n* [*Pac*ific yew + *-litax-* (perh. fr. *Taxus brevifolia*) + *-el* (alter. of [1]*-ol* or [3]*-ol*)] (1992) : an antineoplastic drug $C_{47}H_{51}NO_{14}$ orig. derived from the bark of the Pacific yew but now typically derived as a semisynthetic product of the English yew and used to treat ovarian cancer
pact \ˈpakt\ *n* [ME, fr. MF, fr. L *pactum*, fr. neut. of *pactus*, pp. of *pacisci* to agree, contract; akin to OE *fōn* to seize, L *pax* peace, *pangere* to fix, fasten, Gk *pēgnynai*] (15c) : [4]COMPACT; *esp* : an international treaty
[1]**pad** \ˈpad\ *vb* **pad·ded; pad·ding** [perh. fr. MD *paden* to follow a path, fr. *pad* path] *vt* (1553) : to traverse on foot ~ *vi* : to go on foot : WALK; *esp* : to walk with or as if with padded feet ⟨the dog *padded* along beside him⟩ ⟨*padding* around in bedroom slippers⟩
[2]**pad** *n* [MD *pad*] (1567) **1** *dial Brit* : PATH **2** : a horse that moves along at an easy pace **3** *archaic* : FOOTPAD
[3]**pad** *n* [origin unknown] (1570) **1 a** : a thin flat mat or cushion: as (1) : a piece of soft stuffed material used as or under a saddle (2) : padding used to shape an article of clothing (3) : a guard worn to shield body parts against impact (4) : a piece of usu. folded absorbent material (as gauze) used as a surgical dressing or protective covering (5) : a component of certain brake systems (as disc brakes) consisting of a plate covered with a frictional material **b** : a piece of material saturated with ink for inking the surface of a rubber stamp **2 a** : the foot of an animal **b** : the cushioned thickening of the underside of the toes of an animal **3** : a floating leaf of a water plant **4** : a collection of sheets of paper glued together at one end **5 a** (1) : a section of an airstrip used for warm-ups or turnarounds (2) : an area used for helicopter takeoffs and landings **b** : LAUNCHPAD **c** : a horizontal concrete surface (as for parking a mobile home) **6 a** : BED **b** : living quarters
[4]**pad** *vt* **pad·ded; pad·ding** (1827) **1 a** : to furnish with a pad or padding **b** : MUTE, MUFFLE **2** : to expand or increase esp. with needless, misleading, or fraudulent matter ⟨~ the sales figures⟩ — often used with *out* ⟨they ~ out their bibliographies —J. P. Kenyon⟩
[5]**pad** *n* [imit.] (1594) : a soft muffled or slapping sound
padding *n* (1828) : material with which something is padded
[1]**pad·dle** \ˈpa-dᵊl\ *vi* **pad·dled; pad·dling** \ˈpad-liŋ, ˈpa-dᵊl-iŋ\ [origin unknown] (1530) **1** : to move the hands or feet about in shallow water **2** *archaic* : to use the hands or fingers in toying or caressing **3** : TODDLE — **pad·dler** \ˈpad-lər, ˈpa-dᵊl-ər\ *n*
[2]**paddle** *n* [ME *padell* spade-shaped tool for cleaning a plow] (1624) **1 a** : a usu. wooden implement that has a long handle and a broad flattened blade and that is used to propel and steer a small craft (as a canoe) **b** : an implement often with a short handle and a broad flat blade that is used for stirring, mixing, or hitting; *esp* : one used to hit a ball in any of various games (as table tennis) **c** : a small usu. numbered sign that is raised by a bidder at an auction to signal a bid **d** : a flat electrode that is the part of a defibrillator placed on the chest of a patient and through which a shock of electricity is discharged **2 a** : any of the broad boards at the circumference of a paddle wheel or waterwheel **b** : any of the broad blades attached to a shaft (as in an ice cream machine) and used for stirring **3** : a computer input device with a dial used to control linear movement of a cursor on a computer display
[3]**paddle** *vb* **pad·dled; pad·dling** \ˈpad-liŋ, ˈpa-dᵊl-iŋ\ *vi* (1677) : to go on or through water by or as if by means of a paddle or paddle wheel ~ *vt* **1 a** : to propel by a paddle **b** : to transport in a paddled craft ⟨*paddled* us to shore in his canoe⟩ **2 a** : to beat or stir with or as if with a paddle (as in washing or dyeing) **b** : to punish by or as if by beating with a paddle — **pad·dler** \ˈpad-lər, ˈpa-dᵊl-ər\ *n*
pad·dle·ball \ˈpa-dᵊl-ˌbȯl\ *n* (1935) : a game like handball played by hitting the ball with a paddle; *also* : the ball used in this game
pad·dle·board \-ˌbȯrd\ *n* (1938) : a long narrow buoyant board used for riding the surf or in rescuing swimmers
pad·dle·boat \-ˌbōt\ *n* (1874) : a boat propelled by a paddle wheel
pad·dle·fish \-ˌfish\ *n* (1807) : any of a family (Polyodontidae) of ganoid fishes; *esp* : a large food fish (*Polyodon spathula*) of the Mississippi River valley with a long paddle-shaped snout and with roe used in caviar

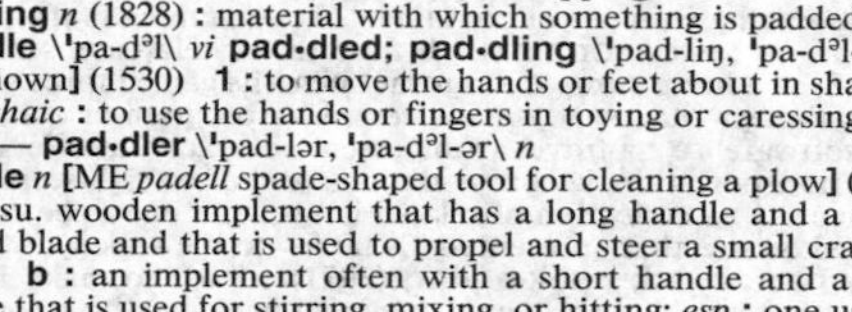

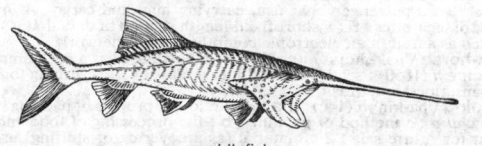

paddlefish

paddle tennis *n* (1925) : a game like tennis that is played with a paddle and rubber ball on a small court
paddle wheel *n* (1685) : a wheel with paddles around its circumference used to propel a boat
paddle wheeler *n* (1924) : a steamer propelled by a paddle wheel
pad·dock \ˈpa-dək, -dik\ *n* [alter. of ME *parrok*, fr. OE *pearroc*, fr. ML *parricus*] (1622) **1 a** : a usu. enclosed area used esp. for pasturing or exercising animals; *esp* : an enclosure where racehorses are saddled and paraded before a race **b** *Austral & NewZeal* : an often enclosed field **2** : an area at an automobile racecourse where racing cars are parked
pad·dy *also* **padi** \ˈpa-dē\ *n, pl* **paddies** *also* **pad·is** [Malay *padi*] (1623) **1** : RICE; *esp* : threshed unmilled rice **2** : wet land in which rice is grown
Pad·dy \ˈpa-dē\ *n, pl* **Paddies** [fr. *Paddy*, Hiberno-English nickname for *Patrick*] (1780) *often offensive* : IRISHMAN
pad·dy wagon \ˈpa-dē-\ *n* [prob. fr. *Paddy*] (1930) : an enclosed motortruck used by police to carry prisoners — called also *Black Maria*, *patrol wagon*
pad·lock \ˈpad-ˌläk\ *n* [ME *padlok*, fr. *pad-* (of unknown origin) + *lok* lock] (15c) : a removable lock with a shackle that can be passed through a staple or link and then secured — **padlock** *vt*
pa·dre \ˈpä-(ˌ)drā, -drē\ *n* [Sp or It or Pg, lit., father, fr. L *pater* — more at FATHER] (1584) **1** : a Christian clergyman; *esp* : PRIEST **2** : a military chaplain
pa·dro·ne \pə-ˈdrō-nē\ *n, pl* **-nes** *or* **-ni** \-nē\ [It, protector, owner, fr. L *patronus* patron] (1670) **1 a** : MASTER **b** : an Italian innkeeper **2** : a person who secures employment esp. for Italian immigrants
pad thai \ˈpäd-ˈtī, ˈpad-\ *n, often cap T* [Thai *phàd thaj*, lit., Thai stir-fried mixture] (1978) : a Thai dish consisting of rice noodles stir-fried usu. with any of various additional ingredients (as bean sprouts, peanuts, chicken, shrimp, and egg)
pad·u·a·soy \ˈpa-jə-wə-ˌsȯi, ˈpaj-wə-\ *n* [alter. of earlier *poudesoy*, fr. F *pou-de-soie*] (1663) : a corded silk fabric; *also* : a garment made of it
pae·an \ˈpē-ən\ *n* [L, hymn of thanksgiving esp. addressed to Apollo, fr. Gk *paian, paiōn*, fr. *Paian, Paiōn*, epithet of Apollo in the hymn] (1589) **1** : a joyous song or hymn of praise, tribute, thanksgiving, or triumph **2** : a work that praises or honors its subject : ENCOMIUM, TRIBUTE
paed- *or* **paedo-** — see PED-
pae·di·at·ric, pae·di·a·tri·cian, pae·di·at·rics *chiefly Brit var of* PEDIATRIC, PEDIATRICIAN, PEDIATRICS
pae·do·gen·e·sis *also* **pe·do·gen·e·sis** \ˌpē-dō-ˈje-nə-səs\ *n* [NL] (ca. 1871) : reproduction by young or larval animals : NEOTENY — **pae·do·ge·net·ic** \-jə-ˈne-tik\ *or* **pae·do·gen·ic** \-ˈje-nik\ *adj* — **pae·do·ge·net·i·cal·ly** \-jə-ˈne-ti-k(ə-)lē\ *adv*
pae·do·mor·phic \ˌpē-də-ˈmȯr-fik\ *adj* (1891) : of, relating to, involving, or exhibiting paedomorphosis or paedomorphism
pae·do·mor·phism \-ˈmȯr-ˌfi-zəm\ *n* (ca. 1891) : retention in the adult of infantile or juvenile characters
pae·do·mor·pho·sis \-ˈmȯr-fə-səs\ *n* [NL, fr. *paed-* + Gk *morphōsis* formation, fr. *morphoun* to form, fr. *morphē* form] (1922) : phylogenetic change that involves retention of juvenile characters by the adult
pa·el·la \pä-ˈe-lə, -ˈä-; -ˈāl-yə, -ˈā-yə\ *n* [Catal, lit., pot, pan, fr. MF *paelle*, fr. L *patella* small pan — more at PATELLA] (ca. 1892) : a saffron-flavored dish containing rice, meat, seafood, and vegetables
pae·on \ˈpē-ən, -ˌän\ *n* [L, fr. Gk *paiōn*, fr. *paian, paiōn* paean] (1603) : a metrical foot of four syllables with one long and three short syllables (as in classical prosody) or with one stressed and three unstressed syllables (as in English prosody)
pa·gan \ˈpā-gən\ *n* [ME, fr. LL *paganus*, fr. L, civilian, country dweller, fr. *pagus* country district; akin to L *pangere* to fix — more at PACT] (14c) **1** : HEATHEN 1; *esp* : a follower of a polytheistic religion (as in ancient Rome) **2** : one who has little or no religion and who delights in sensual pleasures and material goods : an irreligious or hedonistic person **3** : NEO-PAGAN — **pagan** *adj* — **pa·gan·ish** \-gə-nish\ *adj*
pa·gan·ism \ˈpā-gə-ˌni-zəm\ *n* (15c) **1 a** : pagan beliefs or practices **b** : a pagan religion **2** : the quality or state of being a pagan
pa·gan·ize \-ˌnīz\ *vb* **-ized; -iz·ing** *vt* (1615) : to make pagan ~ *vi* : to become pagan — **pa·gan·iz·er** *n*
[1]**page** \ˈpāj\ *n* [ME, fr. AF] (14c) **1 a** (1) : a youth being trained for the medieval rank of knight and in the personal service of a knight (2) : a youth attendant on a person of rank esp. in the medieval period **b** : a boy serving as an honorary attendant at a formal function (as a wedding) **2** : one employed to deliver messages, assist patrons, serve as a guide, or attend to similar duties **3** : an act or instance of paging ⟨a ~ came over the loudspeaker⟩ ⟨got a ~ from the client⟩
[2]**page** *vt* **paged; pag·ing** (15c) **1** : to wait on or serve in the capacity of a page **2** : to summon by repeatedly calling out the name of **3** : to send a message to via a pager
[3]**page** *n* [MF, fr. L *pagina*; akin to L *pangere* to fix, fasten — more at PACT] (1589) **1 a** : one of the leaves of a publication or manuscript; *also* : a single side of one of these leaves **b** : the material printed or written on a page **2 a** : a written record **b** : a noteworthy event or period **3 a** : a sizable subdivision of computer memory; *also* : a block of information that fills a page and can be transferred as a unit between the internal and external storage of a computer **b** : the block of information found at a single World Wide Web address
[4]**page** *vb* **paged; pag·ing** *vt* (1628) : to number or mark the pages of ~ *vi* : to turn the pages (as of a book or magazine) esp. in a steady or haphazard manner — usu. used with *through*
pag·eant \ˈpa-jənt\ *n* [ME *pagyn, padgeant*, lit., scene of a play, fr. AF *pagine, pagent*, fr. ML *pagina*, perh. fr. L, page] (14c) **1 a** : a mere show : PRETENSE **b** : an ostentatious display **2** : SHOW, EXHIBITION; *esp* : an elaborate colorful exhibition or spectacle often with music that consists of a series of tableaux, of a loosely unified drama, or of a procession usu. with floats **3** : PAGEANTRY 1
pag·eant·ry \ˈpa-jən-trē\ *n* (1608) **1** : pageants and the presentation of pageants **2** : colorful, rich, or splendid display : SPECTACLE **3** : mere show : empty display
page boy *n* (1874) **1** : a boy serving as a page **2** *usu* **pageboy** : an often shoulder-length hairdo with the ends of the hair rolled under
[1]**pag·er** \ˈpā-jər\ *n* (1901) : one that pages; *esp* : a small radio receiver that beeps, vibrates, or flashes to alert the user to an incoming message which is usu. displayed on a small screen
[2]**pager** *n* (1966) : one having or covering a specified number or kind of pages — used in combination ⟨her essay was a 15-*pager*⟩
Pag·et's disease \ˈpa-jəts-\ *n* [Sir James *Paget* †1899 Eng. surgeon] (1880) **1** : a rare form of breast cancer initially manifested as a scaly

red rash on the nipple and areola **2 :** a chronic disease in which the bones become enlarged, weak, and deformed

page–turn·er \ˈpāj-ˌtər-nər\ *n* (1972) **:** an engrossing book or story

pag·i·nate \ˈpa-jə-ˌnāt\ *vt* **-nat·ed; -nat·ing** [L *pagina* page] (1884) **:** [4]PAGE

pag·i·na·tion \ˌpa-jə-ˈnā-shən\ *n* (1841) **1 :** the action of paging **:** the condition of being paged **2 a :** the numbers or marks used to indicate the sequence of pages (as of a book) **b :** the number and arrangement of pages or an indication of these

pa·go·da \pə-ˈgō-də\ *n* [Pg *pagode* statue of a deity, Hindu or Buddhist temple] (1588) **:** a tower in eastern Asia usu. with roofs curving upward at the division of each of several stories and erected as a temple or memorial

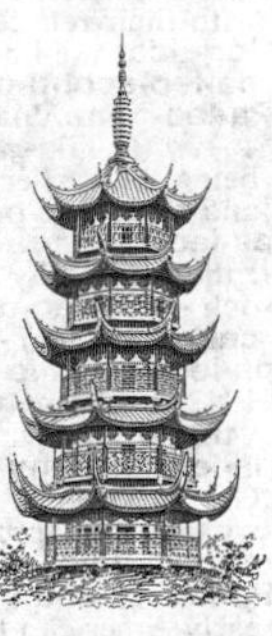

pagoda

PAH *abbr* polycyclic aromatic hydrocarbon

Pah·la·vi \ˈpa-lə-(ˌ)vē, ˈpä-\ *n* [Pers *pahlavī,* fr. *Pahlav* Parthia, fr. OPers *Parthava-*] (1773) **1 :** the Iranian language of Sassanian Persia — see INDO-EUROPEAN LANGUAGES table **2 :** a script used for writing Pahlavi

[1]**paid** \ˈpād\ *past and past part of* PAY

[2]**paid** *adj* (1817) **1 :** marked by the receipt of pay ⟨~ vacation time⟩ **2 :** being or having been paid or paid for ⟨a ~ official⟩ ⟨a ~ political announcement⟩

pail \ˈpāl\ *n* [ME *payle, paille*] (14c) **1 :** a usu. cylindrical container with a handle **:** BUCKET **2 :** the quantity that a pail contains — **pail·ful** \-ˌfu̇l\ *n*

pail·lard \pī-ˈyär, pā-ˈyär\ *n* [F *paillarde,* fr. *Paillard,* late 19th cent. Fr. restaurateur] (1972) **:** a piece of beef or veal usu. pounded thin and grilled

pail·lette \pī-ˈyet, pā-ˈyet, pə-ˈlet\ *n* [F, fr. *paille* straw — more at PALLET] (1876) **1 :** a small shiny object (as a spangle) applied in clusters as a decorative trimming (as on women's clothing) **2 :** a trimming made of paillettes

[1]**pain** \ˈpān\ *n* [ME, fr. AF *peine,* fr. L *poena,* fr. Gk *poinē* payment, penalty; akin to Gk *tinein* to pay, *tinesthai* to punish, Av *kaēnā* revenge, Skt *cayate* he revenges] (14c) **1 :** PUNISHMENT **2 a :** usu. localized physical suffering associated with bodily disorder (as a disease or an injury); *also* **:** a basic bodily sensation induced by a noxious stimulus, received by naked nerve endings, characterized by physical discomfort (as pricking, throbbing, or aching), and typically leading to evasive action **b :** acute mental or emotional distress or suffering **:** GRIEF **3** *pl* **:** the throes of childbirth **4** *pl* **:** trouble, care, or effort taken to accomplish something ⟨was at ~*s* to reassure us⟩ **5 :** one that irks or annoys or is otherwise troublesome — often used in such phrases as *pain in the neck* — **pain·less** \-ləs\ *adj* — **pain·less·ly** *adv* — **pain·less·ness** *n* — **on pain of** *or* **under pain of :** subject to penalty or punishment of ⟨made to leave the country *on pain of* death⟩

[2]**pain** *vt* (14c) **1 :** to make suffer or cause distress to **:** HURT **2** *archaic* **:** to put (oneself) to trouble or exertion ~ *vi* **1** *archaic* **:** SUFFER **2 :** to give or have a sensation of pain

pained \ˈpānd\ *adj* (14c) **1 :** feeling pain **:** HURT **2 :** expressing or involving pain ⟨a ~ expression⟩ ⟨with ~ surprise⟩

pain·ful \ˈpān-fəl\ *adj* **pain·ful·ler** \-fə-lər\; **pain·ful·lest** (14c) **1 a :** feeling or giving pain ⟨a ~ injury⟩ **b :** IRKSOME, ANNOYING **2 :** requiring effort or exertion ⟨a long ~ trip⟩ **3** *archaic* **:** CAREFUL, DILIGENT — **pain·ful·ly** \-f(ə-)lē\ *adv* — **pain·ful·ness** \-fəl-nəs\ *n*

pain·kill·er \-ˌki-lər\ *n* (1853) **:** something (as a drug) that relieves pain — **pain·kill·ing** \-liŋ\ *adj*

[1]**pains·tak·ing** \ˈpān-ˌstā-kiŋ\ *n* (1538) **:** the action of taking pains **:** diligent care and effort

[2]**painstaking** *adj* (1696) **:** taking pains **:** expending, showing, or involving diligent care and effort — **pains·tak·ing·ly** \-kiŋ-lē\ *adv*

[1]**paint** \ˈpānt\ *vb* [ME, fr. AF *paint, peint,* pp. of *peindre,* fr. L *pingere* to tattoo, embroider, paint; akin to OE *fāh* variegated, Gk *poikilos* variegated, *pikros* sharp, bitter] *vt* (13c) **1 a (1) :** to apply color, pigment, or paint to **(2) :** to color with a cosmetic **b (1) :** to apply with a movement resembling that used in painting **(2) :** to treat with a liquid by brushing or swabbing ⟨~ the wound with iodine⟩ **2 a (1) :** to produce in lines and colors on a surface by applying pigments **(2) :** to depict by such lines and colors **b :** to decorate, adorn, or variegate by applying lines and colors **c :** to produce or evoke as if by painting ⟨~*s* glowing pictures of the farm⟩ **3 :** to touch up or cover over by or as if by painting **4 :** to depict as having specified or implied characteristics ⟨~*s* them whiter than the evidence justifies —Oliver La Farge⟩ ~ *vi* **1 :** to practice the art of painting **2 :** to use cosmetics

[2]**paint** *n* (1602) **1 :** the action of painting **:** something produced by painting **2 :** MAKEUP; *esp* **:** a cosmetic to add color **3 a (1) :** a mixture of a pigment and a suitable liquid to form a closely adherent coating when spread on a surface in a thin coat **(2) :** the pigment used in this mixture esp. when in the form of a cake ⟨a box of ~*s*⟩ **b :** an applied coating of paint **4 :** a powerful muscular pinto having quarter horse or Thoroughbred ancestry; *broadly* **:** PINTO — called also *paint horse* **5 :** FREE THROW LANE **6 :** computer-generated color design ⟨a ~ program⟩

paint·ball \ˈpānt-ˌbȯl\ *n* (1987) **:** a game in which two teams try to capture each other's flag while defending their own using compressed-air guns that shoot paint-filled pellets

paint·brush \ˈpānt-ˌbrəsh\ *n* (1815) **1 :** a brush for applying paint **2 a :** INDIAN PAINTBRUSH 1 **b :** ORANGE HAWKWEED

painted bunting *n* (ca. 1811) **:** a brightly colored bunting (*Passerina ciris*) that is found from the southern U.S. to Panama

painted cup *n* (1787) **:** INDIAN PAINTBRUSH 1

painted lady *n* (1753) **1 :** a migratory nymphalid butterfly (*Vanessa cardui*) with wings mottled in brown, orange, black, and white **2 :** PROSTITUTE 1a

painted trillium *n* (1855) **:** a trillium (*Trillium undulatum*) of northeastern No. America that has a solitary flower with white petals streaked with purple

painted turtle *n* (1876) **:** a No. American freshwater turtle (*Chrysemys picta*) having a greenish to black carapace with yellow, red, or olive bordered scutes and a yellow plastron

[1]**paint·er** \ˈpān-tər\ *n* (14c) **:** one that paints: as **a :** an artist who paints **b :** one who applies paint esp. as an occupation

[2]**pain·ter** \ˈpān-tər\ *n* [ME *paynter,* prob. fr. MF dial. (Normandy) *pentoir, penteur* clothesline, fr. *pendre* to hang — more at PENDANT] (14c) **:** a line used for securing or towing a boat

[3]**pain·ter** *n* [alter. of *panther*] (ca. 1764) **:** COUGAR 1

paint·er·ly \ˈpān-tər-lē\ *adj* (ca. 1586) **1 :** of, relating to, or typical of a painter **:** ARTISTIC ⟨~ attention to detail⟩ **2 :** suggestive or characteristic of a painting or of the art of painting ⟨~ photography⟩; *esp* **:** marked by an openness of form which is not linear and in which sharp outlines are lacking ⟨~ brushwork⟩ — **paint·er·li·ness** *n*

painter's colic *n* (ca. 1834) **:** intestinal colic associated with obstinate constipation due to chronic lead poisoning

paint·ing \ˈpān-tiŋ\ *n* (13c) **1 :** a product of painting; *esp* **:** a work produced through the art of painting **2 :** the art or occupation of painting

paint·work \ˈpānt-ˌwərk\ *n* (1764) **1** *chiefly Brit* **:** PAINT 3b **2** *chiefly Brit* **:** work with paint

[1]**pair** \ˈper\ *n, pl* **pairs** *or* **pair** [ME *paire,* fr. AF, fr. L *paria* equal things, fr. neut. pl. of *par* equal] (14c) **1 a (1) :** two corresponding things designed for use together ⟨a ~ of shoes⟩ **(2) :** two corresponding bodily parts or members ⟨a ~ of hands⟩ **b :** something made up of two corresponding pieces ⟨a ~ of trousers⟩ **2 a :** two similar or associated things: as **(1) :** two mated animals **(2) :** a couple in love, engaged, or married ⟨were a devoted ~⟩ **(3) :** two playing cards of the same value or denomination and esp. of the same rank **(4) :** two horses harnessed side by side **(5) :** two members of a deliberative body that agree not to vote on a specific issue during a time agreed on; *also* **:** an agreement not to vote made by the two members **b :** a partnership esp. of two players in a contest against another partnership **3** *chiefly dial* **:** a set or series of small objects (as beads)

[2]**pair** *vt* (1606) **1 a :** to make a pair of — often used with *off* or *up* ⟨~*ed* off the animals⟩ **b :** to cause to be a member of a pair **c :** to arrange a voting pair between **2 :** to arrange in pairs ~ *vi* **1 :** to constitute a member of a pair ⟨a sock that didn't ~⟩ **2 a :** to become associated with another — often used with *off* or *up* ⟨~*ed* up with an old friend⟩ **b :** to become grouped or separated into pairs — often used with *off* ⟨~*ed* off for the next dance⟩

pair–bond \-ˌbänd\ *n* (1940) **:** a monogamous relationship — **pair–bond·ing** *n*

paired–associate learning *n* (1966) **:** the learning of syllables, digits, or words in pairs (as in the study of a foreign language) so that one member of the pair evokes recall of the other

pair of compasses (1563) **:** COMPASS 3c

pair of virginals (1542) **:** VIRGINAL

pair production *n* (1934) **:** the transformation of a quantum of radiant energy simultaneously into an electron and a positron when the quantum interacts with the intense electric field near a nucleus

pai·sa \pī-ˈsä\ *n* [ultim. fr. Hindi & Urdu *paisā,* a quarter-anna coin, fr. Old Indo-Aryan **padāṁśa* quarter part; akin to Skt *pada* footstep and *aṁśa* part] (1884) **1** *pl* **paisa** — see *rupee, taka* at MONEY table **2** *pl* **pai·se** \-ˈsā\ — see *rupee* at MONEY table

pais·ley \ˈpāz-lē\ *adj, often cap* [*Paisley,* Scotland] (1790) **1 :** made typically of soft wool and woven or printed with colorful curved abstract figures **2 :** marked by designs, patterns, or figures typically used in paisley fabrics ⟨a ~ print⟩ — **paisley** *n*

Pai·ute *also* **Pi·ute** \ˈpī-ˌyüt\ *n* [alter. of *Pie-Utaw,* alter. of *Paiuches,* pl., fr. AmerSp *Payuchis* Southern Paiutes] (1827) **1 :** a member of an American Indian people orig. of Utah, Arizona, Nevada, and California **2 :** either of the two Uto-Aztecan languages of the Paiute people

pa·ja·ma \pə-ˈjä-mə, -ˈja-\ *n* [Hindi & Urdu *pājāma,* fr. Pers *pā* leg + *jāma* garment] (1883) **:** PAJAMAS — **pa·ja·maed** \-məd\ *adj*

pa·ja·mas \-məz\ *n pl* [pl. of *pajama*] (1800) **1 :** loose lightweight trousers formerly much worn in the Near East **2 :** a loose usu. two-piece lightweight suit designed esp. for sleeping or lounging — called also *pj's*

pak choi *var of* BOK CHOY

pa·ke·ha \ˈpä-kə-ˌhä, ˈpa-kē-ə\ *n, pl* **pakeha** *or* **pakehas** *often cap* [Maori] (1832) *chiefly NewZeal* **:** a person who is not of Maori descent; *esp* **:** a white person

Paki \ˈpa-kē, ˈpä-\ *n* [short for *Pakistani*] (1964) *chiefly Brit, usu offensive* **:** an immigrant from Pakistan or a neighboring south Asian country

[1]**pal** \ˈpal\ *n* [Romany *phral, phal* brother, friend, fr. Skt *bhrātṛ* brother; akin to OE *brōthor* brother] (ca. 1682) **:** a close friend — **pal·ship** \-ˌship\ *n*

[2]**pal** *vi* **palled; pal·ling** (1879) **:** to be or become pals **:** associate as pals ⟨they've *palled* around for years⟩

[1]**pal·ace** \ˈpa-ləs\ *n* [ME *palais,* fr. AF, fr. L *palatium,* fr. *Palatium,* the Palatine Hill in Rome where the emperors' residences were built] (13c) **1 a :** the official residence of a chief of state (as a monarch or a president) **b** *chiefly Brit* **:** the official residence of an archbishop or bishop **2 a :** a large stately house **b :** a large public building **c :** a highly decorated place for public amusement or refreshment ⟨a movie ~⟩

[2]**palace** *adj* (14c) **1 :** of or relating to a palace **2 :** of, relating to, or involving the intimates of a chief executive ⟨a ~ revolution⟩ ⟨~ politics⟩ **3 :** LUXURIOUS, DELUXE

pal·a·din \ˈpa-lə-dən\ *n* [MF, fr. It *paladino,* fr. OF *palatin,* fr. ML *palatinus* courtier, fr. LL, imperial official — more at PALATINE] (1592) **1 :** a trusted military leader (as for a medieval prince) **2 :** a leading champion of a cause

palae- *or* **palaeo-** *chiefly Brit var of* PALE-

pa·laes·tra \pə-ˈles-trə\ *n, pl* **-trae** \-(ˌ)trē\ [ME *palestre* arena, fr. L *palaestra* place for wrestling, fr. Gk *palaistra,* fr. *palaiein* to wrestle] (1580) **1 :** a school in ancient Greece or Rome for sports (as wrestling) **2 :** GYMNASIUM

pa·lan·quin \ˌpa-lən-ˈkēn, -ˈkwin, -ˈkin, ˈpa-lən-ˌ; pə-ˈlaŋ-kwən\ *n* [Pg *palanquim,* fr. Malay or Jav *pelangki,* of Indo-Aryan origin; akin to

\ə\ **abut** \ᵊ\ **kitten,** F table \ər\ **further** \a\ **ash** \ā\ **ace** \ä\ **mop, mar** \au̇\ **out** \ch\ **chin** \e\ **bet** \ē\ **easy** \g\ **go** \i\ **hit** \ī\ **ice** \j\ **job** \ŋ\ **sing** \ō\ **go** \ȯ\ **law** \ȯi\ **boy** \th\ **thin** \t͟h\ **the** \ü\ **loot** \u̇\ **foot** \y\ **yet** \zh\ **vision, beige** \k, ⁿ, œ, ue, ʸ\ *see* Guide to Pronunciation

Bengali *pālaṅka* bed] (1588) **:** a conveyance formerly used esp. in eastern Asia usu. for one person that consists of an enclosed litter borne on the shoulders of men by means of poles

pal·at·able \ˈpa-lə-tə-bəl\ *adj* (1664) **1 :** agreeable to the palate or taste **2 :** agreeable or acceptable to the mind — **pal·at·abil·i·ty** \ˌpa-lə-tə-ˈbi-lə-tē\ *n* — **pal·at·able·ness** *n* — **pal·at·ably** \ˈpa-lə-tə-blē\ *adv*

syn PALATABLE, APPETIZING, SAVORY, TASTY, TOOTHSOME mean agreeable or pleasant esp. to the sense of taste. PALATABLE often applies to something that is found to be merely agreeable ⟨butterflies that birds find *palatable*⟩. APPETIZING suggests a whetting of the appetite and applies to aroma and appearance as well as taste ⟨*appetizing* hors d'oeuvres⟩. SAVORY applies to both taste and aroma and suggests piquancy and often spiciness ⟨dumplings with *savory* fillings⟩. TASTY implies a pronounced taste ⟨a tart and *tasty* pie⟩. TOOTHSOME stresses the notion of agreeableness and sometimes implies tenderness or daintiness ⟨an enticing array of *toothsome* desserts⟩.

pal·a·tal \ˈpa-lə-tᵊl\ *adj* (1668) **1 a :** formed with some part of the tongue near or touching the hard palate posterior to the teethridge ⟨the \sh\ and \y\ in English and the \k\ of *ich* \ik\ in German are examples of ~ consonants⟩ **b** *of a vowel* **:** FRONT 2 **2 :** of, relating to, forming, or affecting the palate — **palatal** *n* — **pal·a·tal·ly** \-tᵊl-ē\ *adv*

pal·a·tal·i·za·tion \ˌpa-lə-tə-lə-ˈzā-shən\ *n* (1863) **1 :** the quality or state of being palatalized **2 :** an act or instance of palatalizing an utterance ⟨in rapid speech the \t\ in *got* undergoes ~ before *you* to yield \ˈgächə\⟩

pal·a·tal·ize \ˈpa-lə-tə-ˌlīz\ *vt* **-ized; -iz·ing** (1867) **:** to pronounce as or change into a palatal sound

pal·ate \ˈpa-lət\ *n* [ME, fr. L *palatum*] (14c) **1 :** the roof of the mouth separating the mouth from the nasal cavity **2 a :** a usu. intellectual taste or liking ⟨too ornate for my ~⟩ **b :** the sense of taste

pa·la·tial \pə-ˈlā-shəl\ *adj* [L *palatium* palace] (1733) **1 :** of, relating to, or being a palace **2 :** suitable to a palace **:** MAGNIFICENT — **pa·la·tial·ly** \-shə-lē\ *adv* — **pa·la·tial·ness** *n*

pa·lat·i·nate \pə-ˈla-tə-nət\ *n* (ca. 1580) **:** the territory of a palatine

[1]**pal·a·tine** \ˈpa-lə-ˌtīn\ *adj* [ME, fr. L *palatinus* imperial, fr. *palatium*] (15c) **1 a :** possessing royal privileges **b :** of or relating to a palatine or a palatinate **2 a :** of or relating to a palace esp. of a Roman or Holy Roman emperor **b :** PALATIAL

[2]**palatine** \-ˌtīn, *3 is also* -ˌtēn\ *n* [LL *palatinus* imperial official, fr. L *palatinus*, adj.] (1591) **1 a :** a feudal lord having sovereign power within his domains **b :** a high officer of an imperial palace **2** *cap* **:** a native or inhabitant of the Palatinate **3** [F, fr. Elisabeth Charlotte of Bavaria †1722 Princess *Palatine*] **:** a fur cape or stole covering the neck and shoulders

[3]**palatine** \-ˌtīn\ *adj* [F *palatin*, fr. L *palatum* palate] (ca. 1656) **:** of, relating to, or lying near the palate

[4]**palatine** \-ˌtīn\ *n* (1854) **:** either of a pair of bones that are situated behind and between the maxillae and in humans are of extremely irregular form

[1]**pa·lav·er** \pə-ˈla-vər, -ˈlä-\ *n* [Pg *palavra* word, speech, fr. LL *parabola* parable, speech] (1735) **1 a :** a long parley usu. between persons of different cultures or levels of sophistication **b :** CONFERENCE, DISCUSSION **2 a :** idle talk **b :** misleading or beguiling speech

[2]**palaver** *vb* **pa·lav·ered; pa·lav·er·ing** \pə-ˈla-və-riŋ, -ˈlä-; -ˈlav-riŋ, -ˈläv-\ *vi* (1773) **1 :** to talk profusely or idly **2 :** PARLEY ~ *vt* **:** to use palaver to **:** CAJOLE

pa·laz·zo \pə-ˈlät-(ˌ)sō\ *n, pl* **pa·laz·zi** \-(ˌ)sē\ [It, fr. L *palatium* palace] (ca. 1666) **:** a large imposing building (as a museum or a place of residence) esp. in Italy

[1]**pale** \ˈpāl\ *n* [ME, fr. AF *pel, pal* stake, fr. L *palus* — more at POLE] (12c) **1** *archaic* **:** PALISADE, PALING **2 a :** one of the stakes of a palisade **b :** PICKET **3 a :** a space or field having bounds **:** ENCLOSURE **b :** a territory or district within certain bounds or under a particular jurisdiction **4 :** an area or the limits within which one is privileged or protected (as from censure) ⟨conduct that was beyond the ~⟩ **5 :** a perpendicular stripe on a heraldic shield

[2]**pale** *vt* **paled; pal·ing** (14c) **:** to enclose with pales **:** FENCE

[3]**pale** *adj* **pal·er; pal·est** [ME, fr. AF, fr. L *pallidus*, fr. *pallēre* to be pale — more at FALLOW] (14c) **1 :** deficient in color or intensity of color **:** PALLID ⟨a ~ complexion⟩ **2 :** not bright or brilliant **:** DIM ⟨a ~ sun shining through the fog⟩ **3 :** FEEBLE, FAINT ⟨a ~ imitation⟩ **4 :** deficient in chroma ⟨a ~ pink⟩ — **pale·ly** \ˈpāl-lē\ *adv* — **pale·ness** \-nəs\ *n* — **pal·ish** \ˈpā-lish\ *adj*

[4]**pale** *vb* **paled; pal·ing** *vi* (14c) **:** to become pale ~ *vt* **:** to make pale

pale- *or* **paleo-** *comb form* [Gk *palai-, palaio-* ancient, fr. *palaios*, fr. *palai* long ago; prob. akin to Gk *tēle* far off, Skt *carama* last] **1 :** involving or dealing with ancient forms or conditions ⟨*paleo*botany⟩ **2 :** early **:** primitive **:** archaic ⟨*Paleo*lithic⟩

pa·lea \ˈpā-lē-ə\ *n, pl* **pa·le·ae** \-lē-ˌē\ [NL, fr. L, chaff — more at PALLET] (1753) **1 :** one of the chaffy scales on the receptacle of many composite plants **2 :** the upper bract that with the lemma encloses the flower in grasses — **pa·le·al** \-lē-əl\ *adj*

pale ale *n* (1708) **:** a usu. medium-colored very dry heavily hopped ale

Pa·le·arc·tic \ˌpā-lē-ˈärk-tik, -ˈär-tik\ *adj* (1858) **:** of, relating to, or being a biogeographic region or subregion that includes Europe, Asia north of the Himalayas, and Africa north of the Sahara

pale·face \ˈpāl-ˌfās\ *n* (1822) **:** a white person

pa·leo·an·thro·pol·o·gy \ˌpā-lē-ō-ˌan(t)-thrə-ˈpä-lə-jē, *esp Brit* ˌpa-\ *n* (1916) **:** a branch of anthropology dealing with fossil hominids — **pa·leo·an·thro·po·log·i·cal** \-pə-ˈlä-ji-kəl\ *adj* — **pa·leo·an·thro·pol·o·gist** \-ˈpä-lə-jist\ *n*

pa·leo·bi·ol·o·gy \-bī-ˈä-lə-jē\ *n* (1893) **:** a branch of paleontology concerned with the biology of fossil organisms — **pa·leo·bi·o·log·i·cal** \-bī-ə-ˈlä-ji-kəl\ *also* **pa·leo·bi·o·log·ic** \-ˈlä-jik\ *adj* — **pa·leo·bi·ol·o·gist** \-bī-ˈä-lə-jist\ *n*

pa·leo·bot·a·ny \-ˈbä-tə-nē, -ˈbät-nē\ *n* [ISV] (1872) **:** a branch of botany dealing with fossil plants — **pa·leo·bo·tan·i·cal** \-bə-ˈta-ni-kəl\ *also* **pa·leo·bo·tan·ic** \-ˈta-nik\ *adj* — **pa·leo·bo·tan·i·cal·ly** \-nik(ə-)lē\ *adv* — **pa·leo·bot·a·nist** \-ˈbä-tə-nist, -ˈbät-nist\ *n*

Pa·leo·cene \ˈpā-lē-ə-ˌsēn, *esp Brit* ˈpa-\ *adj* [ISV] (1877) **:** of, relating to, or being the earliest epoch of the Tertiary or the corresponding series of rocks — see GEOLOGIC TIME table — **Paleocene** *n*

pa·leo·cli·mat·ic \-klī-ˈma-tik, -klə-\ *adj* (1893) **:** of, relating to, or being a climate distinctive to a past geological age

pa·leo·cli·ma·tol·o·gy \ˌpā-lē-ō-ˌklī-mə-ˈtä-lə-jē, *esp Brit* ˌpa-\ *n* [ISV] (ca. 1909) **:** a science dealing with the climate of past ages — **pa·leo·cli·ma·tol·o·gist** \-jist\ *n*

pa·leo·con·ser·va·tive \-kən-ˈsər-və-tiv\ *n* (1981) **:** a conservative espousing traditional principles and policies — **paleoconservative** *adj*

pa·leo·ecol·o·gy \-i-ˈkä-lə-jē, -e-ˈkä-\ *n* (1898) **:** a branch of ecology that is concerned with the characteristics of ancient environments and with their relationships to ancient plants and animals — **pa·leo·eco·log·i·cal** \-ˌē-kə-ˈlä-ji-kəl, -ˌe-kə-\ *also* **pa·leo·eco·log·ic** \-jik\ *adj* — **pa·leo·ecol·o·gist** \-i-ˈkä-lə-jist, -e-ˈkä-\ *n*

Pa·leo·gene \ˈpā-lē-ə-ˌjēn, *esp Brit* ˈpa-\ *adj* [G *Paläogen*, fr. *palä-* pale- + *-gen* (fr. Gk *-genēs* born) — more at -GEN] (1882) **:** of, relating to, or being the earlier part of the Tertiary including the Paleocene, Eocene, and Oligocene or the corresponding series of rocks — **Paleogene** *n*

pa·leo·ge·og·ra·phy \ˌpā-lē-ō-jē-ˈä-grə-fē, *esp Brit* ˌpa-\ *n* [ISV] (1881) **:** the geography of ancient times or of a particular past geological epoch — **pa·leo·geo·graph·ic** \-ˌjē-ə-ˈgra-fik\ *or* **pa·leo·geo·graph·i·cal** \-fi-kəl\ *adj* — **pa·leo·geo·graph·i·cal·ly** \-fi-k(ə-)lē\ *adv*

pa·leo·graph·ic \-ə-ˈgra-fik\ *or* **pa·leo·graph·i·cal** \-fi-kəl\ *adj* (ca. 1842) **:** relating to writings of former times — **pa·leo·graph·i·cal·ly** \-fi-k(ə-)lē\ *adv*

pa·le·og·ra·phy \ˌpā-lē-ˈä-grə-fē, *esp Brit* ˌpa-\ *n* [NL *palaeographia*, fr. Gk *palai-* pale- + *-graphia* -graphy] (1806) **1 :** the study of ancient writings and inscriptions **2 a :** an ancient manner of writing **b :** ancient writings — **pa·le·og·ra·pher** \-fər\ *n*

Pa·leo–In·di·an \ˌpā-lē-ō-ˈin-dē-ən, *esp Brit* ˌpa-\ *n* (1940) **:** one of the early American hunting people of Asian origin extant in the late Pleistocene — **Paleo–Indian** *adj*

Pa·leo·lith·ic \ˌpā-lē-ə-ˈli-thik, *esp Brit* ˌpa-\ *adj* [ISV] (1865) **:** of or relating to the earliest period of the Stone Age characterized by rough or chipped stone implements

pa·leo·mag·ne·tism \ˌpā-lē-ō-ˈmag-nə-ˌti-zəm, *esp Brit* ˌpa-\ *n* (1854) **1 :** the intensity and direction of residual magnetization in ancient rocks **2 :** a science that deals with paleomagnetism — **pa·leo·mag·net·ic** \-mag-ˈne-tik\ *adj* — **pa·leo·mag·net·i·cal·ly** \-ti-k(ə-)lē\ *adv* — **pa·leo·mag·ne·tist** \-ˈmag-nə-tist\ *n*

pa·le·on·tol·o·gy \ˌpā-lē-ˌän-ˈtä-lə-jē, -ən-, *esp Brit* ˌpa-\ *n* [F *paléontologie*, fr. *palé-* pale- + Gk *onta* existing things (fr. neut. pl. of *ont-, ōn*, prp. of *einai* to be) + F *-logie* -logy — more at IS] (1837) **:** a science dealing with the life of past geological periods as known from fossil remains — **pa·le·on·to·log·i·cal** \-ˌän-tə-ˈlä-ji-kəl\ *also* **pa·le·on·to·log·ic** \-jik\ *adj* — **pa·le·on·tol·o·gist** \-ˌän-ˈtä-lə-jist, -ən-\ *n*

pa·leo·pa·thol·o·gy \ˌpā-lē-ō-pə-ˈthä-lə-jē, -pa-ˈthä-, *esp Brit* ˌpa-lē-\ *n* (1893) **:** a branch of pathology concerned with ancient diseases as evidenced esp. in fossil or other remains — **pa·leo·path·o·log·i·cal** \-ˌpa-thə-ˈlä-ji-kəl\ *adj* — **pa·leo·pa·thol·o·gist** \-pə-ˈthä-lə-jist, -pa-\ *n*

Pa·leo·zo·ic \ˌpā-lē-ə-ˈzō-ik, *esp Brit* ˌpa-\ *adj* (1838) **:** of, relating to, originating in, or being an era of geological history that extends from the beginning of the Cambrian to the close of the Permian and is marked by the culmination of nearly all classes of invertebrates except the insects and in the later epochs by the appearance of terrestrial plants, amphibians, and reptiles; *also* **:** relating to the corresponding system of rocks — see GEOLOGIC TIME table — **Paleozoic** *n*

pa·leo·zo·ol·o·gy \-zō-ˈä-lə-jē, -zə-ˈwä-\ *n* [ISV] (1857) **:** a branch of paleontology dealing with ancient and fossil animals — **pa·leo·zoo·log·i·cal** \-ˌzō-ə-ˈlä-ji-kəl\ *adj* — **pa·leo·zo·ol·o·gist** \-jist\ *n*

pal·ette \ˈpa-lət\ *n* [F, fr. MF, dim. of *pale* spade, fr. L *pala*; prob. akin to L *pangere* to fix — more at PACT] (1622) **1 :** a thin oval or rectangular board or tablet that a painter holds and mixes pigments on **2 a :** the set of colors put on the palette **b (1) :** a particular range, quality, or use of color **(2) :** a comparable range, quality, or use of available elements ⟨a rich ~ of tones and timbres⟩ ⟨a ~ of flavors⟩

palette knife *n* (1759) **:** a knife with usu. a flexible steel blade and no cutting edge used to mix colors or to apply colors (as to a painting)

pal·frey \ˈpȯl-frē\ *n, pl* **palfreys** [ME, fr. AF *palefrei*, fr. ML *palafredus*, fr. LL *paraveredus* post-horse for secondary roads, fr. Gk *para-* beside, subsidiary + LL *veredus* post-horse, fr. a Gaulish word akin to W *gorwydd* horse; akin to OIr *réidid* he rides — more at PARA-, RIDE] (13c) *archaic* **:** a saddle horse other than a warhorse; *esp* **:** a lady's light easy-gaited horse

Pa·li \ˈpä-lē\ *n* [Skt *pāli* row, series of Buddhist sacred texts] (1800) **:** an Indo-Aryan language used as the liturgical and scholarly language of Theravada Buddhism — see INDO-EUROPEAN LANGUAGES table

pal·i·mo·ny \ˈpa-lə-ˌmō-nē\ *n* [blend of *pal* and *alimony*] (1979) **:** a court-ordered allowance paid by one member of a couple formerly living together out of wedlock to the other

pa·limp·sest \ˈpa-ləm(p)-ˌsest, pə-ˈlim(p)-\ *n* [L *palimpsestus*, fr. Gk *palimpsēstos* scraped again, fr. *palin* + *psēn* to rub, scrape; akin to Skt *psāti, babhasti* he chews] (1825) **1 :** writing material (as a parchment or tablet) used one or more times after earlier writing has been erased **2 :** something having usu. diverse layers or aspects apparent beneath the surface ⟨Canada . . . is a ~, an overlay of classes and generations —Margaret Atwood⟩

pal·in·drome \ˈpa-lən-ˌdrōm\ *n* [Gk *palindromos* running back again, fr. *palin* back, again + *dramein* to run; akin to Gk *polos* axis, pole — more at POLE, DROMEDARY] (ca. 1629) **:** a word, verse, or sentence (as "Able was I ere I saw Elba") or a number (as 1881) that reads the same backward or forward — **pal·in·drom·ic** \ˌpa-lən-ˈdrō-mik, -ˈdrä-\ *adj* — **pal·in·drom·ist** \ˈpa-lən-ˌdrō-mist\ *n*

paling *n* (15c) **1 :** a fence of pales or pickets **2 :** wood for making pales **3 :** a pale or picket for a fence

pal·in·gen·e·sis \ˌpa-lən-ˈje-nə-səs\ *n* [NL, fr. Gk *palin* again + L *genesis* genesis] (1668) **:** METEMPSYCHOSIS — **pal·in·ge·net·ic** \-jə-ˈne-tik\ *adj*

pal·in·ode \ˈpa-lə-ˌnōd\ *n* [Gk *palinōidia*, fr. *palin* + *aeidein* to sing — more at ODE] (1579) **1 :** an ode or song recanting or retracting something in an earlier poem **2 :** a formal retraction

[1]**pal·i·sade** \ˌpa-lə-ˈsād\ *n* [F *palissade*, ultim. fr. L *palus* stake — more at POLE] (1600) **1 a :** a fence of stakes esp. for defense **b :** a long strong stake pointed at the top and set close with others as a defense **2 :** a line of bold cliffs

[2]**palisade** *vt* **-sad·ed; -sad·ing** (1632) **:** to fortify with palisades
palisade cell *n* (1875) **:** a cell of the palisade layer
palisade layer *n* (1914) **:** a layer of columnar cells rich in chloroplasts found beneath the upper epidermis of foliage leaves — called also *palisade mesophyll, palisade parenchyma, palisade tissue*; compare SPONGY PARENCHYMA
[1]**pall** \ˈpȯl\ *vb* [ME, short for *appallen* to become pale — more at APPALL] *vi* (14c) **1 :** to lose strength or effectiveness **2 :** to lose in interest or attraction ⟨his humor began to ~ on us⟩ **3 :** DWINDLE ⟨our enthusiasm soon *~ed*⟩ ~ *vt* **1 :** to cause to become insipid **2 :** to deprive of pleasure in something by satiating ***syn*** see SATIATE
[2]**pall** *n* [ME, cloak, mantle, fr. OE *pæll,* fr. L *pallium*] (14c) **1 :** PALLIUM 1a **2 a :** a square of linen usu. stiffened with cardboard that is used to cover the chalice **b** (1) **:** a heavy cloth draped over a coffin (2) **:** a coffin esp. when holding a body **3 a :** something that covers or conceals; *esp* **:** an overspreading element that produces an effect of gloom ⟨a ~ of thick black smoke⟩ ⟨a ~ of suspicion⟩ **b :** a feeling of gloom ⟨his absence cast a ~ over the celebration⟩
[3]**pall** *vt* (15c) **:** to cover with a pall **:** DRAPE
Pal·la·di·an \pə-ˈlā-dē-ən, -ˈlä-\ *adj* (1731) **:** of or relating to a revived classical style in architecture based on the works of Andrea Palladio — **Pal·la·di·an·ism** \-ə-ˌni-zəm\ *n*
[1]**pal·la·di·um** \pə-ˈlā-dē-əm\ *n* [ME, fr. L, fr. Gk *palladion,* fr. *Pallad-, Pallas*] (14c) **1** *cap* **:** a statue of Pallas whose preservation was believed to ensure the safety of Troy **2** *pl* **pal·la·dia** \-dē-ə\ **:** SAFEGUARD 2a
[2]**palladium** *n* [NL, fr. *Pallad-, Pallas,* an asteroid] (1803) **:** a silver-white ductile malleable metallic element that is used esp. in electrical contacts, as a catalyst, and in alloys — see ELEMENT table — **pal·la·dous** \pə-ˈlā-dəs\ *adj*
Pal·las \ˈpa-ləs\ *n* [L *Pallad-, Pallas,* fr. Gk] (14c) **:** ATHENA
pall·bear·er \ˈpȯl-ˌber-ər\ *n* [[2]*pall*] (1707) **:** a person who helps to carry the coffin at a funeral; *also* **:** a member of the escort or honor guard of the coffin who does not actually help to carry it
[1]**pal·let** \ˈpa-lət\ *n* [ME *paillet,* fr. AF *paillete* bundle of straw, fr. *paille* straw, fr. L *palea* chaff, straw; akin to Skt *palāva* chaff] (14c) **1 :** a straw-filled tick or mattress **2 :** a small, hard, or temporary bed
[2]**pallet** *n* [MF *palette,* lit., small shovel — more at PALETTE] (1558) **1 :** a wooden flat-bladed instrument **2 :** a lever or surface in a timepiece that receives an impulse from the escapement wheel and imparts motion to a balance or pendulum **3 :** a portable platform for handling, storing, or moving materials and packages (as in warehouses, factories, or vehicles)
pal·let·ise *Brit var of* PALLETIZE
pal·let·ize \ˈpa-lə-ˌtīz\ *vt* **-ized; -iz·ing** (1944) **:** to place on, transport, or store by means of pallets — **pal·let·i·za·tion** \ˌpa-lə-tə-ˈzā-shən\ *n* — **pal·let·iz·er** \ˈpa-lə-ˌtī-zər\ *n*
pal·lette \pa-ˈlet\ *n* [alter. of *palette*] (1834) **:** one of the plates at the armpits of a suit of armor — see ARMOR illustration
pal·li·al \ˈpa-lē-əl\ *adj* [NL *pallium*] (1836) **1 :** of, relating to, or produced by the mantle of a mollusk or brachiopod **2 :** of or relating to the cerebral cortex
pal·liasse \pal-ˈyas\ *n* [modif. of F *paillasse,* fr. *paille* straw] (1763) **:** a thin straw mattress used as a pallet
pal·li·ate \ˈpa-lē-ˌāt\ *vt* **-at·ed; -at·ing** [ME, fr. LL *palliatus,* pp. of *palliare* to cloak, conceal, fr. L *pallium* cloak] (15c) **1 :** to reduce the violence of (a disease); *also* **:** to ease (symptoms) without curing the underlying disease **2 :** to cover by excuses and apologies **3 :** to moderate the intensity of ⟨trying to ~ the boredom⟩ — **pal·li·a·tion** \ˌpa-lē-ˈā-shən\ *n* — **pal·li·a·tor** \ˈpa-lē-ˌā-tər\ *n*
[1]**pal·li·a·tive** \ˈpa-lē-ˌā-tiv, ˈpal-yə-\ *adj* (15c) **:** serving to palliate ⟨~ surgery⟩ ⟨~ care⟩ — **pal·lia·tive·ly** *adv*
[2]**palliative** *n* (1724) **:** something that palliates
pal·lid \ˈpa-ləd\ *adj* [L *pallidus* — more at PALE] (1590) **1 :** deficient in color **:** WAN ⟨a ~ countenance⟩ **2 :** lacking sparkle or liveliness **:** DULL ⟨a ~ entertainment⟩ — **pal·lid·ly** *adv* — **pal·lid·ness** *n*
pal·li·dot·o·my \ˌpa-li-ˈdä-tə-mē\ *n, pl* **-mies** [NL *(globus) pallidus* structure within the corpus striatum, lit., pale globe + ISV *-tomy*] (1951) **:** the surgical inactivation of a part of the basal ganglia in the treatment of involuntary movements (as in Parkinson's disease)
pal·li·um \ˈpa-lē-əm\ *n, pl* **-lia** \-lē-ə\ *or* **-li·ums** [ME, fr. L] (12c) **1 a :** a white woolen band with pendants in front and back worn over the chasuble by a pope or archbishop as a symbol of full episcopal authority **b :** a draped rectangular cloth worn as a cloak by men of ancient Greece and Rome **2** [NL, fr. L, cloak] **a :** CEREBRAL CORTEX **b** (1) **:** the mantle of a mollusk or brachiopod (2) **:** the mantle of a bird
pall–mall \ˌpel-ˈmel, ˌpal-ˈmal, *US often* ˌpȯl-ˈmȯl\ *n* [MF *pallemaille,* fr. It *pallamaglio,* fr. *palla* ball (of Gmc origin; akin to OHG *balla* ball) + *maglio* mallet, fr. L *malleus* — more at BALL, MAUL] (1598) **:** a 17th century game in which each player attempts to drive a wooden ball with a mallet down an alley and through a raised ring in as few strokes as possible; *also* **:** the alley in which it is played
pal·lor \ˈpa-lər\ *n* [ME, fr. L, fr. *pallēre* to be pale — more at FALLOW] (15c) **:** deficiency of color esp. of the face **:** PALENESS
pal·ly \ˈpa-lē\ *adj* (1895) **:** sharing the relationship of pals **:** INTIMATE
[1]**palm** \ˈpäm, ˈpälm, ˈpȯm, ˈpȯlm\ *n* [ME, OE, fr. L *palma* palm of the hand, palm tree; fr. the resemblance of the tree's leaves to the outstretched hand; akin to Gk *palamē* palm of the hand, OE *folm,* OIr *lám* hand] (bef. 12c) **1 :** any of a family (Palmae syn. Arecaceae) of mostly tropical or subtropical monocotyledonous trees, shrubs, or vines with usu. a simple stem and a terminal crown of large pinnate or fan-shaped leaves **2 :** a leaf of the palm as a symbol of victory or rejoicing; *also* **:** a branch (as of laurel) similarly used **3 :** a symbol of triumph or superiority; *also* **:** VICTORY, TRIUMPH **4 :** an addition to a military decoration in the form of a palm frond esp. to indicate a second award of the basic decoration — **palm·like** \-ˌlīk\ *adj*

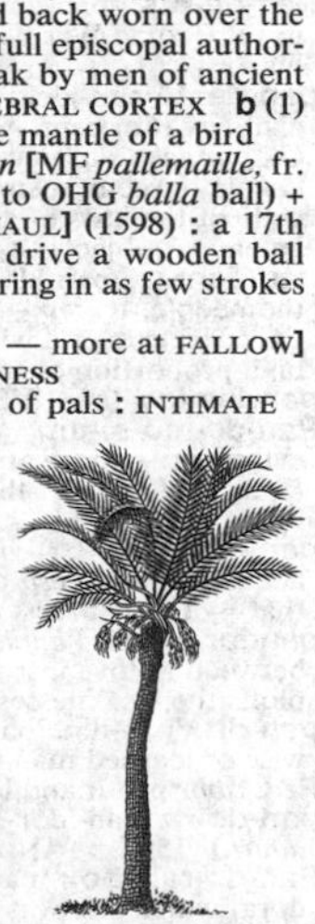

[1]palm 1

[2]**palm** *n* [ME *paume, palme,* fr. AF, fr. L *palma*] (14c) **1 :** the somewhat concave part of the human hand between the bases of the fingers and the wrist or the corresponding part of the forefoot of a lower mammal **2 :** a flat expanded part esp. at the end of a base or stalk (as of an anchor) **3** [L *palmus,* fr. *palma*] **:** a unit of length based on the breadth or length of the hand **4 :** something (as a part of a glove) that covers the palm of the hand **5 :** an act of palming (as of cards)
[3]**palm** *vt* (1673) **1 a :** to conceal in or with the hand ⟨~ a card⟩ **b :** to take or pick up stealthily **c :** to hand stealthily ⟨*~ed* him a dollar bill⟩ **2 :** to impose by fraud ⟨a second imposter to be *~ed* upon you —Sir Walter Scott⟩ **3 :** to touch with the palm: as **a :** to stroke with the palm or hand **b :** to allow (a basketball) to come to rest momentarily in the hand while dribbling thus committing a violation
pal·mar \ˈpal-mər, ˈpä-, ˈpäl-, ˈpȯ-, ˈpȯl-\ *adj* (1656) **:** of, relating to, or involving the palm of the hand
pal·ma·ry \ˈpal-mə-rē, ˈpä-, ˈpäl-, ˈpȯ-, ˈpȯl-\ *adj* [L *palmarius* deserving the palm, fr. *palma*] (1657) **:** OUTSTANDING, BEST
pal·mate \ˈpal-ˌmāt, ˈpä-, ˈpäl-, ˈpȯ-, ˈpȯl-\ *also* **pal·mat·ed** \-ˌmā-təd\ *adj* (1661) **:** resembling a hand with the fingers spread: as **a :** having lobes radiating from a common point ⟨a ~ leaf⟩ — see LEAF illustration **b :** having the distal portion broad, flat, and lobed ⟨a ~ antler⟩ — **pal·mate·ly** *adv* — **pal·ma·tion** \pal-ˈmā-shən, pä-, ˈpäl-, ˈpȯ-, ˈpȯl-\ *n*
palmed \ˈpämd, ˈpälmd, ˈpȯmd, ˈpȯlmd\ *adj* (15c) **:** having a palm of a specified kind — used in combination ⟨leather-*palmed* gloves⟩
palm·er \ˈpä-mər, ˈpäl-, ˈpȯ-, ˈpȯl-\ *n* (13c) **:** a person wearing two crossed palm leaves as a sign of a pilgrimage made to the Holy Land
palm·er·worm \-ˌwərm\ *n* (1560) **:** a caterpillar that suddenly appears in great numbers devouring herbage
pal·mette \ˌpal-ˈmet\ *n* [F, fr. *palme* palm, fr. L *palma*] (1850) **:** a decorative motif suggestive of a palm
pal·met·to \pal-ˈme-(ˌ)tō *also* pä-, päl-, pȯ-, pȯl-\ *n, pl* **-tos** *or* **-toes** [modif. of Sp *palmito,* fr. *palma* palm, fr. L] (1615) **1 :** any of several usu. low-growing fan-leaved palms; *esp* **:** CABBAGE PALMETTO **2 :** strips of the leaf blade of a palmetto used in weaving
palmetto bug *n* (1973) *chiefly Southern* **:** COCKROACH
palm·ist \ˈpä-mist, ˈpäl-, ˈpȯ-, ˈpȯl-\ *n* [prob. back-formation fr. *palmistry*] (1877) **:** one who practices palmistry
palm·ist·ry \ˈpä-mə-strē, ˈpäl-, ˈpȯ-, ˈpȯl-\ *n* [ME *pawmestry,* prob. fr. *paume* palm + *maistrie* mastery] (15c) **:** the art or practice of reading a person's character or future from the lines on the palms
pal·mi·tate \ˈpal-mə-ˌtāt, ˈpä-, ˈpäl-, ˈpȯ-, ˈpȯl-\ *n* (1852) **:** a salt or ester of palmitic acid
pal·mit·ic acid \(ˌ)pal-ˈmi-tik-, (ˌ)pä-, (ˌ)päl-, (ˌ)pȯ-, (ˌ)pȯl-\ *n* [ISV, fr. *palmitin*] (1857) **:** a waxy crystalline saturated fatty acid $C_{16}H_{32}O_2$ occurring free or in the form of esters (as glycerides) in most fats and fatty oils and in several essential oils and waxes
pal·mi·tin \ˈpal-mə-tən, ˈpä-, ˈpäl-, ˈpȯ-, ˈpȯl-\ *n* [F *palmitine,* prob. fr. *palmite* pith of the palm tree, fr. Sp *palmito*] (1855) **:** an ester of glycerol and palmitic acid; *esp* **:** a solid ester found in animal fats
palm off *vt* (1822) **1 :** to dispose of usu. by trickery or guile **2 :** PASS OFF 2 ⟨*palming* himself *off* as a minister —Toni Morrison⟩
palm oil *n* (1625) **:** an edible fat obtained from the flesh of the fruit of several palms and used esp. in soap and lubricating greases
Palm Sunday *n* [fr. the palm branches strewn in Christ's way] (bef. 12c) **:** the Sunday before Easter celebrated in commemoration of Christ's triumphal entry into Jerusalem
palm·top \ˈpä(l)m-ˌtäp, ˈpȯ(l)m-\ *n* [[2]*palm* + lap*top*] (1987) **:** a small portable computer easily held in the palm of the hand
palmy \ˈpä-mē, ˈpäl-, ˈpȯ-, ˈpȯl-\ *adj* **palm·i·er; -est** (1602) **1 :** marked by prosperity **:** FLOURISHING ⟨the ~ days of the British drama —Oscar Wilde⟩ **2 :** abounding in or bearing palms
pal·my·ra \pal-ˈmī-rə\ *n* [Pg *palmeira,* fr. *palma* palm, fr. L] (1698) **:** a tall fan-leaved palm (*Borassus flabellifer*) of India cultivated for its hard resistant wood, fiber, and sugar-rich sap — called also *palmyra palm*
pal·o·mi·no \ˌpa-lə-ˈmē-(ˌ)nō\ *n, pl* **-nos** [AmerSp, fr. Sp, like a dove, fr. L *palumbinus,* fr. *palumbes* ringdove; akin to Gk *peleia* dove, L *pallēre* to be pale — more at FALLOW] (1914) **:** a horse that is pale cream to gold in color and has a flaxen or white mane and tail
pa·loo·ka \pə-ˈlü-kə\ *n* [origin unknown] (1924) **1 :** an inexperienced or incompetent boxer **2 :** OAF, LOUT
pal·o·ver·de \ˌpa-lō-ˈver-(ˌ)dā, ˌpä-, -ˈvər-\ *n* [MexSp, lit., green tree] (1854) **1 :** any of several small spiny trees or shrubs (genus *Cercidium*) of the legume family that have greenish branches and are found chiefly in dry regions of the southwestern U.S. and Mexico **2 :** JERUSALEM THORN
[1]**palp** \ˈpalp\ *vt* [MF *palper,* fr. L *palpare*] (1534) **:** TOUCH, FEEL
[2]**palp** *n* [NL *palpus*] (1842) **:** PALPUS
pal·pa·ble \ˈpal-pə-bəl\ *adj* [ME, fr. LL *palpabilis,* fr. L *palpare* to stroke, caress — more at FEEL] (14c) **1 :** capable of being touched or felt **:** TANGIBLE **2 :** easily perceptible **:** NOTICEABLE ⟨a ~ difference⟩ **3 :** easily perceptible by the mind **:** MANIFEST ***syn*** see PERCEPTIBLE — **pal·pa·bil·i·ty** \ˌpal-pə-ˈbi-lə-tē\ *n* — **pal·pa·bly** \ˈpal-pə-blē\ *adv*
pal·pate \ˈpal-ˌpāt\ *vt* **pal·pat·ed; pal·pat·ing** [prob. back-formation fr. *palpation,* fr. L *palpation-, palpatio,* fr. *palpare*] (ca. 1852) **:** to examine by touch esp. medically — **pal·pa·tion** \pal-ˈpā-shən\ *n*
pal·pe·bral \pal-ˈpē-brəl\ *adj* [LL *palpebralis,* fr. L *palpebra* eyelid; akin to L *palpare*] (1840) **:** of, relating to, or located on or near the eyelids
pal·pi·tant \ˈpal-pə-tənt\ *adj* (1837) **:** marked by trembling or throbbing
pal·pi·tate \ˈpal-pə-ˌtāt\ *vi* **-tat·ed; -tat·ing** [L *palpitatus,* pp. of *palpitare,* freq. of *palpare* to stroke] (ca. 1623) **:** to beat rapidly and strongly **:** THROB — **pal·pi·ta·tion** \ˌpal-pə-ˈtā-shən\ *n*
pal·pus \ˈpal-pəs\ *n, pl* **pal·pi** \-ˌpī, -(ˌ)pē\ [NL, fr. L, caress, soft palm of the hand, fr. *palpare*] (1813) **:** a segmented usu. tactile or gustatory process on an arthropod mouthpart — see INSECT illustration
pals·grave \ˈpȯlz-ˌgrāv\ *n* [D *paltsgrave*] (1539) **:** COUNT PALATINE 1a
pal·sied \ˈpȯl-zēd\ *adj* (1550) **:** affected with or as if with palsy

1pal·sy \ˈpȯl-zē\ *n, pl* **palsies** [ME *palesie,* alter. of *parlesey,* fr. AF *paralisie,* fr. L *paralysis*] (14c) **1 :** PARALYSIS **2 :** a condition marked by uncontrollable tremor of the body or a part
2palsy *vt* **pal·sied; pal·sy·ing** (1615) **:** to affect with or as if with palsy
3palsy \ˈpal-zē\ *adj* (1951) **:** PALSY-WALSY
palsy–walsy \ˌpal-zē-ˈwal-zē\ *adj* [redupl. of *palsy*] (1943) *slang* **:** being or appearing to be very intimate
pal·ter \ˈpȯl-tər\ *vi* **pal·tered; pal·ter·ing** \-t(ə-)riŋ\ [origin unknown] (1600) **1 :** to act insincerely or deceitfully **:** EQUIVOCATE **2 :** HAGGLE, CHAFFER ***syn*** see LIE — **pal·ter·er** \-tər-ər\ *n*
pal·try \ˈpȯl-trē\ *adj* **pal·tri·er; -est** [obs. *paltry* trash, fr. dial. *palt, pelt* piece of coarse cloth, trash; akin to MLG *palte* rag] (1570) **1 :** INFERIOR, TRASHY **2 :** MEAN, DESPICABLE ⟨a ~ trick⟩ **3 :** TRIVIAL ⟨a ~ excuse⟩ **4 :** MEAGER, MEASLY ⟨made a ~ donation⟩ — **pal·tri·ness** *n*
pa·lu·dal \pə-ˈlü-dᵊl, ˈpal-yə-dᵊl\ *adj* [L *palud-, palus* marsh; akin to Skt *palvala* pond] (ca. 1820) **:** of or relating to marshes or fens **:** MARSHY
paly \ˈpā-lē\ *adj* (1513) *archaic* **:** somewhat pale **:** PALLID
pal·y·nol·o·gy \ˌpa-lə-ˈnä-lə-jē\ *n* [Gk *palynein* to sprinkle, fr. *palē* fine meal] (1944) **:** a branch of science dealing with pollen and spores — **pal·y·no·log·i·cal** \-nə-ˈlä-ji-kəl\ *also* **pal·y·no·log·ic** \-jik\ *adj* — **pal·y·no·log·i·cal·ly** \-ji-k(ə-)lē\ *adv* — **pal·y·nol·o·gist** \-ˈnä-lə-jist\ *n*
pam·pa \ˈpam-pə, ˈpäm-\ *n, pl* **pam·pas** \-pəz, -pəs\ [AmerSp, fr. Quechua] (1704) **:** an extensive generally grass-covered plain of temperate So. America east of the Andes **:** PRAIRIE
pam·pas grass \-pəz-, -pəs-\ *n* (ca. 1851) **:** a So. American grass (*Cortaderia selloana*) often grown for ornament that has showy white panicles borne on tall stems
pam·pe·an \ˈpam-pē-ən, ˈpäm-, pam-ˈ, päm-ˈ\ *adj* (1839) **:** of or relating to the pampas of So. America or their Indian inhabitants
pam·per \ˈpam-pər\ *vt* **pam·pered; pam·per·ing** \-p(ə-)riŋ\ [ME, prob. of D origin; akin to D dial. *pamperen* to pamper] (14c) **1** *archaic* **:** to cram with rich food **:** GLUT **2 a :** to treat with extreme or excessive care and attention ⟨~*ed* their guests⟩ **b :** GRATIFY, HUMOR ⟨enabled him to ~ his wanderlust —*New Yorker*⟩ ***syn*** see INDULGE — **pam·per·er** \-pər-ər\ *n*
pam·pe·ro \pam-ˈper-(ˌ)ō, päm-\ *n, pl* **-ros** [AmerSp, fr. *pampa*] (1818) **:** a strong cold wind from the west or southwest that sweeps over the pampas
pam·phlet \ˈpam(p)-flət\ *n* [ME *pamflet* unbound booklet, fr. *Pamphilus seu De Amore* Pamphilus or On Love, popular Latin love poem of the 12th cent.] (14c) **:** an unbound printed publication with no cover or with a paper cover
1pam·phle·teer \ˌpam(p)-flə-ˈtir\ *n* (1642) **:** a writer of pamphlets attacking something or urging a cause
2pamphleteer *vi* (1698) **1 :** to write and publish pamphlets **2 :** to engage in partisan arguments indirectly in writings
1pan \ˈpan\ *n* [ME *panne,* fr. OE (akin to OHG *phanna* pan), fr. L *patina,* fr. Gk *patanē*] (bef. 12c) **1 a :** a usu. broad, shallow, and open container for domestic use (as for cooking) **b :** any of various similar usu. metal receptacles: as **(1) :** the hollow part of the lock in a firelock or flintlock gun that receives the priming **(2) :** either of the receptacles in a pair of scales **(3) :** a round shallow usu. metal container for separating metal (as gold) from waste by washing **c** *Brit* **:** TOILET 3b; *also* **:** BOWL 3b **d :** STEEL DRUM **2 a (1) :** a natural basin or depression in land **(2) :** a similar artificial basin (as for evaporating brine) **b :** a drifting fragment of the flat thin ice that forms in bays or along the shore **3 :** HARDPAN 1 **4** *slang* **:** FACE **5 :** a harsh criticism
2pan *vb* **panned; pan·ning** *vt* (1839) **1 a :** to wash in a pan for the purpose of separating heavy particles **b :** to separate (as gold) by panning **c :** to place in a pan **2 :** to criticize severely ⟨the show was *panned*⟩ ~ *vi* **1 :** to wash material (as earth or gravel) in a pan in search of metal (as gold) **2 :** to yield precious metal in the process of panning — usu. used with *out*
3pan \ˈpän\ *n* [Hindi & Urdu *pān,* fr. Skt *parṇa* wing, leaf — more at FERN] (1616) **1 :** a betel leaf **2 :** a masticatory of betel nut, mineral lime, and pan
4pan \ˈpan\ *n* [short for *panorama*] (ca. 1922) **1 :** the process of panning a motion-picture or video camera **2 :** a shot in which the camera is panned
5pan \ˈpan\ *vb* **panned; pan·ning** *vt* (1930) **:** to rotate (as a motion-picture camera) so as to keep an object in the picture or secure a panoramic effect ~ *vi* **1 :** to pan a motion-picture or video camera **2** *of a camera* **:** to undergo panning
1Pan \ˈpan\ *n* [L, fr. Gk] (14c) **:** a Greek god of pastures, flocks, and shepherds usu. represented as having the legs, horns, and ears of a goat
2Pan *abbr* Panama
PAN *abbr* peroxyacetyl nitrate
pan- *comb form* [Gk, fr. *pan,* neut. of *pant-, pas* all, every; akin to Toch B *pont-* all] **1 :** all **:** completely ⟨*pan*chromatic⟩ **2 a :** involving all of a (specified) group or region ⟨*Pan*-American⟩ **b :** advocating or involving the union of a (specified) group ⟨*Pan*-Slavism⟩ **3 :** whole **:** general ⟨*pan*leukopenia⟩
pan·a·cea \ˌpa-nə-ˈsē-ə\ *n* [L, fr. Gk *panakeia,* fr. *panakēs* all-healing, fr. *pan-* + *akos* remedy] (1548) **:** a remedy for all ills or difficulties **:** CURE-ALL — **pan·a·ce·an** \-ˈsē-ən\ *adj*
pa·nache \pə-ˈnash, -ˈnäsh\ *n* [MF *pennache,* fr. OIt *pennacchio,* fr. LL *pinnaculum* small wing — more at PINNACLE] (1553) **1 :** an ornamental tuft (as of feathers) esp. on a helmet **2 :** dash or flamboyance in style and action **:** VERVE

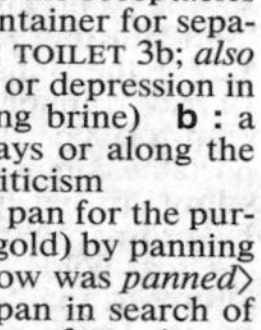
panache 1

pa·na·da \pə-ˈnä-də\ *n* [Sp, fr. *pan* bread, fr. L *panis* — more at FOOD] (ca. 1598) **:** a paste of flour or bread crumbs and water or stock used as a base for sauce or a binder for forcemeat or stuffing
Pan–Af·ri·can·ism \ˌpan-ˈa-fri-kə-ˌni-zəm\ *n* (1952) **:** a movement for the political union of all the African nations — **Pan–Af·ri·can** \-kən\ *adj* — **Pan–Af·ri·can·ist** \-kə-nist\ *n or adj*
pan·a·ma \ˈpa-nə-ˌmä, -ˌmȯ\ *n, often cap* [AmerSp *panamá,* fr. *Panama,* Central America] (1848) **:** a lightweight hat of natural-colored straw hand-plaited of narrow strips from the young leaves of the jipijapa; *also* **:** a machine-made imitation of this
Panama Red *n* (1967) **:** marijuana of a reddish tint that is of Panamanian origin and is held to be very potent
Pan–Amer·i·can \ˌpa-nə-ˈmer-ə-kən\ *adj* (1889) **:** of, relating to, or involving the independent republics of No. and So. America
Pan–Amer·i·can·ism \-kə-ˌni-zəm\ *n* (1901) **:** a movement for greater cooperation among the Pan-American nations
Pan–Ar·ab·ism \ˌpan-ˈa-rə-ˌbi-zəm, -ˈer-ə-\ *n* (1920) **:** a movement for the political union of all Arab nations — **pan–Arab** \-ˈa-rəb, -ˈer-əb\ *adj* — **pan–Ar·ab·ist** \-ˈa-rə-bist, -ˈer-ə-\ *adj or n*
pan·a·tela *or* **pan·e·tela** \ˌpa-nə-ˈte-lə\ *n* [Sp, fr. AmerSp, a long thin biscuit, ultim. fr. L *panis* bread] (1847) **:** a long slender straight-sided cigar
1pan·cake \ˈpan-ˌkāk\ *n* (14c) **:** a flat cake made of thin batter and cooked (as on a griddle) on both sides
2pancake *vb* **pan·caked; pan·cak·ing** *vi* (1911) **:** to make a pancake landing ~ *vt* **1 :** to cause to pancake **2 :** to knock flat
Pan–Cake \ˈpan-ˌkāk\ *trademark* — used for a cosmetic in semimoist cake form
pancake landing *n* (1928) **:** a landing in which the airplane is stalled usu. unintentionally above the landing surface causing it to drop abruptly in an approximately horizontal position with little forward motion
pan·cet·ta \(ˌ)pan-ˈche-tə\ *n* [It, fr. dim. of *pancia* belly, paunch, fr. L *pantic-, pantex*] (1954) **:** unsmoked bacon used esp. in Italian cuisine
pan·chax \ˈpan-ˌkaks\ *n* [NL] (1961) **:** any of various small brilliantly colored Old World killifishes (genus *Aplocheilus*) often kept in tropical aquariums
Pan·chen Lama \ˈpän-chən-\ *n* [*Panchen* fr. Chin (Beijing) *bānchán*] (1794) **:** the lama who is the chief spiritual adviser of the Dalai Lama
pan·chro·mat·ic \ˌpan-krō-ˈma-tik\ *adj* [ISV] (1903) **:** sensitive to light of all colors in the visible spectrum ⟨~ film⟩
pan·cra·ti·um \pan-ˈkrā-shē-əm\ *n* [L, fr. Gk *pankration,* fr. *pan-* + *kratos* strength — more at HARD] (1603) **:** an ancient Greek athletic contest involving both boxing and wrestling
pan·cre·as \ˈpaŋ-krē-əs, ˈpan-\ *n* [NL, fr. Gk *pankreas* sweetbread, fr. *pan-* + *kreas* flesh, meat — more at RAW] (1578) **:** a large lobulated gland of vertebrates that secretes digestive enzymes and the hormones insulin and glucagon — **pan·cre·at·ic** \ˌpaŋ-krē-ˈa-tik, ˌpan-\ *adj*
pancreat- *comb form* [NL, fr. Gk *pankreat-, pancreas*] **:** pancreas ⟨*pancreat*ic⟩
pan·cre·a·tec·to·my \ˌpaŋ-krē-ə-ˈtek-tə-mē, ˌpan-\ *n, pl* **-mies** (ca. 1900) **:** surgical removal of all or part of the pancreas — **pan·cre·a·tec·to·mized** \-ˌmīzd\ *adj*
pancreatic duct *n* (1784) **:** a duct leading from the pancreas and opening into the duodenum
pancreatic juice *n* (ca. 1666) **:** a clear alkaline secretion of pancreatic enzymes (as trypsin and lipase) that flows into the duodenum and acts on food already acted on by the gastric juice and saliva
pan·cre·a·tin \pan-ˈkrē-ə-tən; ˈpaŋ-krē-, ˈpan-\ *n* (ca. 1860) **:** a mixture of enzymes from the pancreatic juice; *also* **:** a preparation containing such a mixture
pan·cre·a·ti·tis \ˌpaŋ-krē-ə-ˈtī-təs, ˌpan-\ *n, pl* **-tit·i·des** \-ˈti-tə-ˌdēz\ [NL] (ca. 1842) **:** inflammation of the pancreas
pan·cre·o·zy·min \-krē-ō-ˈzī-mən\ *n* [*pancreas* + *-o-* + *zym-* + *1-in*] (1943) **:** CHOLECYSTOKININ
pan·cy·to·pe·nia \ˌpan-ˌsī-tə-ˈpē-nē-ə\ *n* [NL, fr. *pan-* + *cyt-* + *-penia*] (ca. 1941) **:** an abnormal reduction in the number of erythrocytes, white blood cells, and blood platelets in the blood; *also* **:** a disorder (as aplastic anemia) characterized by such a reduction
pan·da \ˈpan-də\ *n* [F, perh. fr. a language of the southeast Himalayas] (1835) **1 :** RED PANDA **2 :** a large black-and-white mammal (*Ailuropoda melanoleuca*) of chiefly central China that feeds primarily on bamboo shoots and is now usu. classified with the bears (family Ursidae) — called also *giant panda*
panda car *n* [fr. its black-and-white coloration] (1967) *Brit* **:** a police patrol car
pan·da·nus \pan-ˈdā-nəs, -ˈda-\ *n, pl* **-ni** \-nī\ [NL, genus name, fr. Malay *pandan* screw pine] (1830) **:** SCREW PINE; *also* **:** a fiber made from screw-pine leaves and used for woven products (as mats)
Pan·da·rus \ˈpan-də-rəs\ *n* [L, fr. Gk *Pandaros*] (14c) **:** a Lycian archer in the Trojan War who in medieval legend procures Cressida for Troilus
pan·dect \ˈpan-ˌdekt\ *n* [LL *Pandectae,* the Pandects, digest of Roman civil law (6th cent. A.D.), fr. L, pl. of *pandectes* encyclopedic work, fr. Gk *pandektēs* all-receiving, fr. *pan-* + *dechesthai* to receive; akin to Gk *dokein* to seem, seem good — more at DECENT] (1553) **1 :** a complete code of the laws of a country or system of law **2 :** a treatise covering an entire subject
1pan·dem·ic \pan-ˈde-mik\ *adj* [LL *pandemus,* fr. Gk *pandēmos* of all the people, fr. *pan-* + *dēmos* people — more at DEMAGOGUE] (1666) **:** occurring over a wide geographic area and affecting an exceptionally high proportion of the population ⟨~ malaria⟩
2pandemic *n* (ca. 1853) **:** a pandemic outbreak of a disease
Pan·de·mo·ni·um \ˌpan-də-ˈmō-nē-əm\ *n* [NL, fr. Gk *pan-* + *daimōn* evil spirit — more at DEMON] (1667) **1 :** the capital of Hell in Milton's *Paradise Lost* **2 :** the infernal regions **:** HELL **3** *not cap* **:** a wild uproar **:** TUMULT
1pan·der \ˈpan-dər\ *vi* **pan·dered; pan·der·ing** \-d(ə-)riŋ\ (1523) **:** to act as a pander; *esp* **:** to provide gratification for others' desires ⟨films that ~ to the basest emotions⟩ — **pan·der·er** \-dər-ər\ *n*
2pander *n* [ME *Pandare* Pandarus, fr. L *Pandarus*] (1530) **1 a :** a go-between in love intrigues **b :** PIMP **2 :** someone who caters to or exploits the weaknesses of others
pan·dit \ˈpan-dət, ˈpən-\ *n* [Hindi *paṇḍit,* fr. Skt *paṇḍita*] (ca. 1828) **:** a wise or learned man in India — often used as an honorary title
P&L *abbr* profit and loss
pan·do·ra \pan-ˈdȯr-ə\ *n* [It, fr. LL *pandura* 3-stringed lute, fr. Gk *pandoura*] (1597) **:** BANDORE
Pan·do·ra's box \pan-ˈdȯr-əz-\ *n* [fr. the box, sent by the gods to Pandora, which she was forbidden to open and which loosed a swarm of evils upon humankind when she opened it out of curiosity] (1579) **:** a prolific source of troubles

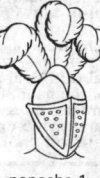

pan·dow·dy \pan-ˈdau̇-dē\ *n, pl* **-dies** [origin unknown] (1805) **:** a deep-dish spiced apple dessert sweetened with sugar, molasses, or maple syrup and covered with a rich crust
pan·dy \ˈpan-dē\ *vt* **pan·died; pan·dy·ing** [prob. fr. L *pande,* imper. sing. of *pandere* to spread out (the hand), command of the schoolmaster to the boy — more at FATHOM] (1863) *Brit* **:** to punish (a schoolboy) with a blow on the palm of the hand esp. with a ferule
pane \ˈpān\ *n* [ME *pan, pane* strip of cloth, pane, fr. AF *pan, panne,* fr. L *pannus* cloth, rag — more at VANE] (14c) **:** a piece, section, or side of something: as **a :** a framed sheet of glass in a window or door **b :** one of the sections into which a sheet of postage stamps is cut for distribution — **paned** \ˈpānd\ *adj* — **pane·less** \-ləs\ *adj*
pan·e·gy·ric \ˌpa-nə-ˈjir-ik, -ˈjī-rik\ *n* [L *panegyricus,* fr. Gk *panēgyrikos,* fr. *panēgyrikos* of or for a festival assembly, fr. *panēgyris* festival assembly, fr. *pan-* + *agyris* assembly; akin to Gk *ageirein* to gather] (1603) **:** a eulogistic oration or writing; *also* **:** formal or elaborate praise ***syn*** see ENCOMIUM — **pan·e·gy·ri·cal** \-ˈjir-i-kəl, -ˈjī-ri-\ *adj* — **pan·e·gy·ri·cal·ly** \-k(ə-)lē\ *adv*
pan·e·gy·rist \ˌpa-nə-ˈjir-ist, -ˈjī-rist\ *n* (1605) **:** EULOGIST
1pan·el \ˈpa-nᵊl\ *n* [ME, piece of cloth, jury list on a piece of parchment, fr. AF, fr. VL **pannellus,* dim. of L *pannus*] (14c) **1 a** (1) **:** a schedule containing names of persons summoned as jurors (2) **:** the group of persons so summoned (3) **:** JURY 1 **b** (1) **:** a group of persons selected for some service (as investigation or arbitration) ⟨a ~ of experts⟩ (2) **:** a group of persons who discuss before an audience a topic of public interest; *also* **:** PANEL DISCUSSION (3) **:** a group of entertainers or guests engaged as players in a quiz or guessing game on a radio or television program **2 :** a separate or distinct part of a surface: as **a :** a fence section **:** HURDLE **b** (1) **:** a thin usu. rectangular board set in a frame (as in a door) (2) **:** a usu. sunken or raised section of a surface set off by a margin (3) **:** a flat usu. rectangular piece of construction material (as plywood or precast masonry) made to form part of a surface **c :** a vertical section of fabric (as a gore) **d :** COMIC STRIP; *also* **:** a frame of a comic strip **3 :** a thin flat piece of wood on which a picture is painted; *also* **:** a painting on such a surface **4 a :** a section of a switchboard **b :** a usu. vertical mount for controls or dials (as of instruments of measurement)
2panel *vt* **-eled** *or* **-elled; -el·ing** *or* **-el·ling** (15c) **:** to furnish or decorate with panels ⟨*paneled* the living room⟩
panel discussion *n* (1936) **:** a formal discussion by a panel
paneling *also* **panelling** *n* (1824) **:** panels joined in a continuous surface; *esp* **:** decorative wood panels so joined
pan·el·ist \ˈpa-nᵊl-ist\ *n* (1951) **:** a member of a discussion or advisory panel or of a radio or television panel
panel truck *n* (1910) **:** a small motortruck with a fully enclosed body
panetela *var of* PANATELA
pan·et·to·ne \ˌpä-nə-ˈtō-nē, ˌpa-\ *n* [It, fr. *panetto* small loaf, dim. of *pane* bread, fr. L *panis* — more at FOOD] (1922) **:** a usu. yeast-leavened bread containing raisins and candied fruit
pan·fish \ˈpan-ˌfish\ *n* (1796) **:** a small food fish (as a sunfish) usu. taken with hook and line and not available on the market
pan·fry \ˈpan-ˌfrī, pan-ˈfrī\ *vt* (ca. 1929) **:** to cook in a frying pan with a small amount of fat
pan·ful \ˈpan-ˌfu̇l\ *n* (ca. 1740) **:** as much or as many as a pan will hold
1pang \ˈpaŋ\ *n* [origin unknown] (15c) **1 :** a brief piercing spasm of pain **2 :** a sharp attack of mental anguish ⟨~*s* of remorse⟩
2pang *vt* (1502) **:** to cause to have pangs **:** TORMENT
pan·ga \ˈpäŋ-gə\ *n* [Swahili] (1925) **:** MACHETE
pan·gen·e·sis \ˌpan-ˈje-nə-səs\ *n* [NL] (1868) **:** a disproven hypothetical mechanism of heredity in which the cells throw off particles that collect in the reproductive products or in buds so that the egg or bud contains particles from all parts of the parent — **pan·ge·net·ic** \-jə-ˈne-tik\ *adj*
Pan·gloss·ian \pan-ˈglä-sē-ən, paŋ-, -ˈglȯ-\ *adj* [*Pangloss,* optimistic tutor in Voltaire's *Candide* (1759)] (1831) **:** marked by the view that all is for the best in this best of possible worlds **:** excessively optimistic
pan·go·la grass \pan-ˈgō-lə-, paŋ-\ *n* [alter. of *Pongola grass,* fr. the *Pongola* River, So. Africa] (1948) **:** a rapid-growing perennial grass (*Digitaria decumbens*) of southern Africa that has been introduced into the southern U.S. as a pasture grass
pan·go·lin \ˈpaŋ-gə-lən, ˈpan-\ *n* [Malay dial. *pĕngguling*] (1774) **:** any of a family (Manidae of the order Pholidota) of Asian and African toothless mammals having the body covered dorsally with large imbricated horny scales — called also *scaly anteater*
1pan·han·dle \ˈpan-ˌhan-dᵊl\ *n* (1856) **:** a narrow projection of a larger territory (as a state) ⟨the Oklahoma *Panhandle*⟩
2panhandle *vb* **pan·han·dled; pan·han·dling** \-ˌhan(d)-liŋ, -ˌhan-dᵊl-iŋ\ [back-formation fr. *panhandler,* prob. fr. *panhandle,* n.; fr. the extended forearm] *vi* (1894) **:** to stop people on the street and ask for food or money **:** BEG ~ *vt* **1 :** to accost on the street and beg from **2 :** to get by panhandling — **pan·han·dler** \-ˌhan(d)-lər, -ˌhan-dᵊl-ər\ *n*
Pan·hel·len·ic \ˌpan-hə-ˈle-nik\ *adj* (1847) **1 :** of or relating to all Greece or all the Greeks **2 :** of or relating to the Greek-letter sororities or fraternities in American colleges and universities or to an association representing them
pan·hu·man \ˌpan-ˈhyü-mən, -ˈyü-\ *adj* (1900) **:** of or relating to all humanity ⟨the ~ problem of evil —R. K. Merton⟩
1pan·ic \ˈpa-nik\ *adj* [F *panique,* fr. Gk *panikos,* lit., of Pan, fr. *Pan*] (1603) **1 :** of, relating to, or resembling the mental or emotional state believed induced by the god Pan ⟨~ fear⟩ **2 :** of, relating to, or arising from a panic ⟨~ buying⟩ **3 :** of or relating to the god Pan
2panic *n* (1708) **1 a :** a sudden overpowering fright; *also* **:** acute extreme anxiety **b :** a sudden unreasoning terror often accompanied by mass flight ⟨widespread ~ in the streets⟩ **c :** a sudden widespread fright concerning financial affairs that results in a depression of values caused by extreme measures for protection of property (as securities) **2** *slang* **:** one that is very funny ***syn*** see FEAR — **pan·icky** \ˈpa-ni-kē\ *adj*
3panic *vb* **pan·icked** \-nikt\; **pan·ick·ing** *vt* (1827) **1 :** to affect with panic **2 :** to cause to laugh uproariously ⟨~ an audience with a gag⟩ ~ *vi* **:** to be affected with panic
panic attack *n* (1966) **:** an episode of intense fear or apprehension that is of sudden onset
panic button *n* (ca. 1950) **:** something setting off a precipitous emergency response ⟨there was no pushing of *panic buttons* at the White House, no rushing of troops —J. C. Harsch⟩
panic disorder *n* (1979) **:** an anxiety disorder characterized by recurrent unexpected panic attacks
pan·ic grass \ˈpa-nik-\ *n* [ME *panik,* fr. L *panicum* foxtail millet, fr. *panus* stalk of a panicle] (1597) **:** any of various grasses (*Panicum* and related genera) including some important forage and cereal grasses
pan·i·cle \ˈpa-ni-kəl\ *n* [L *panicula,* dim. of *panus*] (1597) **1 :** a compound racemose inflorescence — see INFLORESCENCE illustration **2 :** a pyramidal loosely branched flower cluster — **pan·i·cled** \-kəld\ *adj* — **pa·nic·u·late** \pa-ˈni-kyə-lət, pə-\ *adj*
pan·ic–strick·en \ˈpa-nik-ˌstri-kən\ *adj* (1804) **:** overcome with panic
pan·i·cum \ˈpa-ni-kəm\ *n* [NL, fr. L, foxtail millet] (1844) **:** any of a large and widely distributed genus (*Panicum*) of annual and perennial grasses that have 1- to 2-flowered spikelets arranged in a panicle
pa·ni·no \pə-ˈnē-nō\ *n, pl* **pa·ni·ni** \pə-ˈnē-nē\ [It, dim. of *pane* bread, fr. L *panis* — more at FOOD] (1955) **:** a usu. grilled sandwich made with Italian bread
Pan·ja·bi \ˌpən-ˈjä-bē, -ˈja-\ *n* [Hindi & Urdu *pañjābī,* fr. *pañjābī* of Punjab] (1854) **:** PUNJABI 1
pan·jan·drum \pan-ˈjan-drəm\ *n, pl* **-drums** *also* **-dra** \-drə\ [Grand *Panjandrum,* burlesque title of an imaginary personage in some nonsense lines by Samuel Foote] (1856) **:** a powerful personage or pretentious official
pan·leu·ko·pe·nia \ˌpan-ˌlü-kə-ˈpē-nē-ə\ *n* [NL] (1940) **:** an acute usu. fatal epizootic disease esp. of cats that is caused by a parvovirus (species *Feline panleukopenia virus* of the genus *Parvovirus*) and is marked by fever, diarrhea and dehydration, and destruction of white blood cells
pan·mic·tic \ˌpan-ˈmik-tik\ *adj* [*pan-* + Gk *miktos,* verbal of *mignynai* to mix] (1943) **:** of, relating to, or exhibiting panmixia
pan·mix·ia \-ˈmik-sē-ə\ *n* [NL, fr. *pan-* + Gk *mixis* act of mingling, mating, fr. *mignynai* to mix — more at MIX] (1889) **:** random mating within a breeding population
panne \ˈpan\ *n* [F, fr. OF *penne, panne* fur used for lining, fr. L *pinna* feather, wing — more at PEN] (ca. 1794) **1 :** a silk or rayon velvet with lustrous pile flattened in one direction — called also *panne velvet* **2 :** a heavy silk or rayon satin with high luster and waxy smoothness
pan·nier *also* **pan·ier** \ˈpan-yər, ˈpa-nē-ər\ *n* [ME *panier,* fr. AF *paner, panier,* fr. L *panarium,* fr. *panis* bread — more at FOOD] (13c) **1 :** a large container: as **a :** a basket often carried on the back of an animal or the shoulders of a person **b :** one of a pair of packs or baskets hung over the rear wheel of a vehicle (as a bicycle) **2 a :** one of a pair of hoops formerly used to expand women's skirts at the sides **b :** an overskirt draped at the sides of a skirt for an effect of fullness

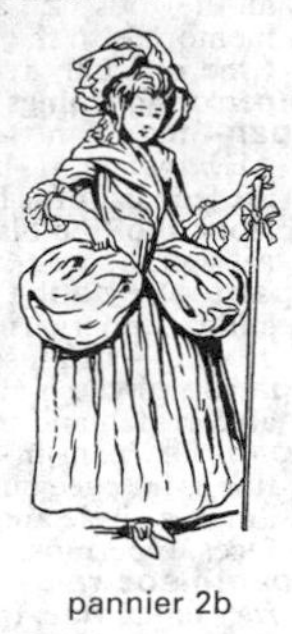
pannier 2b

pan·ni·kin \ˈpa-ni-kən\ *n* [¹*pan* + *-nikin* (as in *cannikin*)] (1823) *Brit* **:** a small pan or cup
panocha *var of* PENUCHE
pan·o·plied \ˈpa-nə-plēd\ *adj* (1832) **:** dressed in or having a panoply
pan·o·ply \ˈpa-nə-plē\ *n, pl* **-plies** [Gk *panoplia,* fr. *pan-* + *hopla* arms, armor, pl. of *hoplon* tool, weapon — more at HOPLITE] (1632) **1 a :** a full suit of armor **b :** ceremonial attire **2 :** something forming a protective covering **3 a :** a magnificent or impressive array ⟨the full ~ of a military funeral⟩ **b :** a display of all appropriate appurtenances ⟨no need for the ~ of power⟩
pan·op·tic \pa-ˈnäp-tik\ *adj* [Gk *panoptēs* all-seeing, fr. *pan-* + *opsesthai* to be going to see — more at OPTIC] (1826) **:** being or presenting a comprehensive or panoramic view ⟨a ~ view of the city⟩
pan·o·rama \ˌpa-nə-ˈra-mə, -ˈrä-\ *n* [*pan-* + Gk *horama* sight, fr. *horan* to see — more at WARY] (1796) **1 a :** CYCLORAMA 1 **b :** a picture exhibited a part at a time by being unrolled before the spectator **2 a :** an unobstructed or complete view of an area in every direction **b :** a comprehensive presentation of a subject ⟨a ~ of American history⟩ **c :** RANGE **3 :** a mental picture of a series of images or events — **pan·o·ram·ic** \-ˈra-mik\ *adj* — **pan·o·ram·i·cal·ly** \-mi-k(ə-)lē\ *adv*
pan out *vi* [²*pan*] (1868) **:** TURN OUT; *esp* **:** SUCCEED ⟨the signs revealed that the experiment wasn't *panning out* —Ronald Reagan⟩
pan·pipe \ˈpan-ˌpīp\ *n* [*Pan,* its traditional inventor] (1820) **:** a primitive wind instrument consisting of a series of short vertical pipes of graduated length bound together with the mouthpieces in an even row — often used in pl.
pan·sex·u·al \ˌpan-ˈsek-sh(ə-)wəl, -shəl\ *adj* (1926) **:** exhibiting or implying many forms of sexual expression — **pan·sex·u·al·i·ty** \ˌpan-ˌsek-shə-ˈwa-lə-tē\ *n*
Pan–Slav·ism \ˌpan-ˈslä-ˌvi-zəm, -ˈsla-\ *n* (1850) **:** a political and cultural movement orig. emphasizing the cultural ties between the Slavic peoples but later associated with Russian expansionism — **Pan–Slavic** \-ˈslä-vik, -ˈsla-\ *adj* — **Pan–Slav·ist** \-ˈslä-vist, -ˈsla-\ *n*
1pan·sy \ˈpan-zē\ *n, pl* **pansies** [ME *pancy, pensee,* fr. MF *pensée,* fr. *pensée* thought, fr. fem. of *pensé,* pp. of *penser* to think, fr. L *pensare* to ponder — more at PENSIVE] (15c) **1 :** a garden plant (*Viola wittrockiana*) derived chiefly from the hybridization of the European Johnny-jump-up (*Viola tricolor*) with other wild violets; *also* **:** its flower **2 a** *usu disparaging* **:** a weak or effeminate man or boy **b** *usu disparaging* **:** a male homosexual
2pansy *adj* (1929) *usu disparaging* **:** EFFEMINATE 1; *also* **:** HOMOSEXUAL
1pant \ˈpant\ *vb* [ME, modif. of AF *panteiser,* fr. VL **phantasiare* to have hallucinations, fr. Gk *phantasioun,* fr. *phantasia* appearance, imagination — more at FANCY] *vi* (14c) **1 a :** to breathe quickly, spasmodically, or in a labored manner **b :** to run panting **c :** to move with or make a throbbing or puffing sound **2 :** to long eagerly **:** YEARN **3 :** THROB, PULSATE ~ *vt* **:** to utter with panting **:** GASP

[2]**pant** *n* (1513) **1 a :** a panting breath **b :** the visible movement of the chest accompanying such a breath **2 :** a throbbing or puffing sound

[3]**pant** *n* [short for *pantaloons*] (1840) **1 :** an outer garment covering each leg separately and usu. extending from the waist to the ankle — usu. used in pl. **2** *pl, chiefly Brit* **:** men's underpants **3** *pl* **:** PANTIE — **with one's pants down :** in an embarrassing position (as of being unprepared to act)

[4]**pant** *adj* (1892) **:** of or relating to pants ⟨a ~ leg⟩

pant- *or* **panto-** *comb form* [Gk, fr. *pant-, pas* — more at PAN-] **:** all ⟨*pant*isocracy⟩

Pan·ta·gru·el \ˌpan-tə-ˈgrü-əl; pan-ˈta-grə-wəl, -ˌwel\ *n* [F] (1598) **:** the huge son of Gargantua in Rabelais's *Pantagruel* — **Pan·ta·gru·el·ian** \ˌpan-tə-grü-ˈe-lē-ən, (ˌ)pan-ˌta-grə-ˈwe-\ *adj*

pan·ta·lets *or* **pan·ta·lettes** \ˌpan-tə-ˈlets\ *n pl* [*pantaloons*] (1834) **:** long drawers with a ruffle at the bottom of each leg worn esp. by women and children in the first half of the 19th century

pan·ta·loon \ˌpan-tə-ˈlün\ *n* [MF & OIt; MF *Pantalon,* fr. OIt *Pantaleone, Pantalone*] (ca. 1590) **1 a** *or* **pan·ta·lo·ne** \-tə-ˈlō-nē\ *cap* **:** a character in the commedia dell'arte that is usu. a skinny old dotard who wears spectacles, slippers, and a tight-fitting combination of trousers and stockings **b :** a buffoon in pantomimes **2** *pl* **a :** wide breeches worn esp. in England during the reign of Charles II **b :** close-fitting trousers usu. having straps passing under the instep and worn esp. in the 19th century **3 :** loose-fitting usu. shorter than ankle-length trousers

pan·tech·ni·con \pan-ˈtek-ni-kən\ *n* [short for *pantechnicon van,* fr. *pantechnicon* storage warehouse] (1891) *Brit* **:** [3]VAN 1

pan·the·ism \ˈpan(t)-thē-ˌi-zəm\ *n* [F *panthéisme,* fr. *panthéiste* pantheist, fr. E *pantheist,* fr. *pan-* + Gk *theos* god] (1732) **1 :** a doctrine that equates God with the forces and laws of the universe **2 :** the worship of all gods of different creeds, cults, or peoples indifferently; *also* **:** toleration of worship of all gods (as at certain periods of the Roman empire) — **pan·the·ist** \-thē-ist\ *n* — **pan·the·is·tic** \ˌpan(t)-thē-ˈis-tik\ *also* **pan·the·is·ti·cal** \-ti-kəl\ *adj* — **pan·the·is·ti·cal·ly** \-ti-k(ə-)lē\ *adv*

pan·the·on \ˈpan(t)-thē-ˌän, -ən\ *n* [ME *Panteon,* a temple at Rome, fr. L *Pantheon,* fr. Gk *pantheion* temple of all the gods, fr. neut. of *pantheios* of all gods, fr. *pan-* + *theos* god] (14c) **1 :** a temple dedicated to all the gods **2 :** a building serving as the burial place of or containing memorials to the famous dead of a nation **3 :** the gods of a people; *esp* **:** the officially recognized gods **4 :** a group of illustrious or notable persons or things

pan·ther \ˈpan(t)-thər\ *n, pl* **panthers** *also* **panther** [ME *pantere,* fr. AF *panthere,* fr. L *panthera,* fr. Gk *panthēr*] (13c) **1 :** LEOPARD: as **a :** a leopard of a hypothetical exceptionally large fierce variety **b :** a leopard of the black color phase **2 :** COUGAR 1 — compare FLORIDA PANTHER **3 :** JAGUAR

pant·ie *or* **panty** \ˈpan-tē\ *n, pl* **pant·ies** [[3]*pant*] (1908) **:** a woman's or child's undergarment covering the lower trunk and made with closed crotch — usu. used in pl.

pantie girdle *n* (1941) **:** a woman's girdle having a sewed-in or detachable crotch and made with or without garters and bones

pan·tile \ˈpan-ˌtī(-ə)l\ *n* [[1]*pan*] (1640) **1 :** a roofing tile whose cross section is an ogee curve **2 :** a roofing tile of which the cross section is an arc of a circle and which is laid with alternate convex and concave surfaces uppermost — **pan·tiled** \-ˌtī(-ə)ld\ *adj*

pant·i·soc·ra·cy \ˌpan-tə-ˈsä-krə-sē, ˌpan-ˌtī-\ *n, pl* **-cies** [*pant-* + *isocracy* equal rule, fr. Gk *isokratia,* fr. *is-* + *-kratia* -cracy] (1794) **:** a utopian community in which all rule equally — **pant·i·so·crat·ic** \ˌpan-ˌtī-sə-ˈkra-tik\ *or* **pant·i·so·crat·i·cal** \-ˈkra-ti-kəl\ *adj* — **pant·i·soc·ra·tist** \ˌpan-tə-ˈsä-krə-tist, ˌpan-ˌtī-\ *n*

pan·to \ˈpan-(ˌ)tō\ *n, pl* **pantos** (1852) *Brit* **:** PANTOMIME 2c

pan·to·fle \pan-ˈtō-fəl, -ˈtä-, -ˈtü-; ˈpan-tə-fəl\ *n* [ME (Sc) *pantuifil,* fr. MF *pantoufle*] (15c) **:** SLIPPER

pan·to·graph \ˈpan-tə-ˌgraf\ *n* [F *pantographe,* fr. *pant-* + *-graphe* -graph] (1723) **1 :** an instrument for copying something (as a map) on a predetermined scale consisting of four light rigid bars jointed in parallelogram form; *also* **:** any of various extensible devices of similar construction (as for use as brackets or gates) **2 :** an electrical trolley carried by a collapsible and adjustable frame — **pan·to·graph·ic** \ˌpan-tə-ˈgra-fik\ *adj*

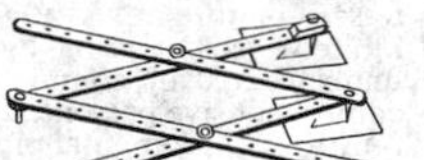

pantograph 1

[1]**pan·to·mime** \ˈpan-tə-ˌmīm\ *n* [L *pantomimus,* fr. *pant-* + *mimus* mime] (1589) **1 :** PANTOMIMIST **2 a :** an ancient Roman dramatic performance featuring a solo dancer and a narrative chorus **b :** any of various dramatic or dancing performances in which a story is told by expressive bodily or facial movements of the performers **c :** a British theatrical entertainment of the Christmas season based on a nursery tale and featuring topical songs, tableaux, and dances **3 a :** conveyance of a story by bodily or facial movements esp. in drama or dance **b :** the art or genre of conveying a story by bodily movements only — **pan·to·mim·ic** \ˌpan-tə-ˈmi-mik\ *adj*

[2]**pantomime** *vb* **-mimed; -mim·ing** *vi* (1768) **:** to engage in pantomime ~ *vt* **:** to represent by pantomime

pan·to·mim·ist \ˈpan-tə-ˌmī-mist, -ˌmi-\ *n* (ca. 1823) **1 :** an actor or dancer in pantomimes **2 :** a composer of pantomimes

pan·to·the·nate \ˌpan-tə-ˈthe-ˌnāt, pan-ˈtä-thə-ˌnāt\ *n* (ca. 1934) **:** a salt or ester of pantothenic acid

pan·to·then·ic acid \ˌpan-tə-ˈthe-nik-, -ˈthē-\ *n* [Gk *pantothen* from all sides, fr. *pant-, pas* all — more at PAN-] (1933) **:** a viscous oily acid $C_9H_{17}NO_5$ of the vitamin B complex found in all living tissues

pan·trop·i·cal \ˌpan-ˈträ-pi-kəl\ *also* **pan·trop·ic** \-pik\ *adj* (1923) **:** occurring or distributed throughout the tropical regions of the earth

pan·try \ˈpan-trē\ *n, pl* **pantries** [ME *panetrie,* fr. AF *paneterie,* fr. *paneter* servant in charge of the pantry, fr. *pain* bread, fr. L *panis* — more at FOOD] (14c) **1 :** a room or closet used for storage (as of provisions) or from which food is brought to the table **2 :** a room (as in a hotel or hospital) for preparation of foods on order

pan·try·man \-mən\ *n* (ca. 1567) **:** a person in charge of or working in a pantry (as in a hotel or hospital)

pants suit *n* (1964) **:** PANTSUIT

pant·suit \ˈpant-ˌsüt\ *n* (1964) **:** a woman's ensemble consisting usu. of a long jacket and pants of the same material — **pant·suit·ed** *adj*

panty hose *n* (1963) **:** a one-piece undergarment for women that consists of hosiery made with a panty-style top — usu. pl. in constr.

panty raid *n* (ca. 1952) **:** a raid on a women's dormitory by college men usu. to obtain panties as trophies

panty·waist \ˈpan-tē-ˌwāst\ *n* (ca. 1936) **1 :** a child's garment consisting of short pants buttoned to a waist **2 :** SISSY — **pantywaist** *adj*

pan·zer \ˈpan-zər, ˈpän(t)-sər\ *n* [G *Panzer* tank, armor, coat of mail, fr. MHG *panzier,* fr. OF *panciere,* fr. *pance, panche* belly — more at PAUNCH] (ca. 1939) **:** TANK 3; *specif* **:** a German tank of World War II

panzer division *n* (ca. 1939) **:** a German armored division

[1]**pap** \ˈpap\ *n* [ME *pappe;* of imit. origin] (13c) **1** *chiefly dial* **:** NIPPLE, TEAT **2 :** something shaped like a nipple

[2]**pap** *n* [ME] (15c) **1 :** a soft food for infants or invalids **2 :** political patronage **3 :** something lacking solid value or substance

pa·pa \ˈpä-pə, *chiefly Brit* pə-ˈpä\ *also* **pop·pa** \ˈpä-pə\ *n* [F (baby talk)] (1677) **:** FATHER

Pa·pa \pə-ˈpä, ˈpä-pə\ (1952) — a communications code word for the letter *p*

pa·pa·cy \ˈpā-pə-sē\ *n, pl* **-cies** [ME *papacie,* fr. ML *papatia,* fr. LL *papa* pope — more at POPE] (14c) **1 :** the office of pope **2 :** a succession or line of popes **3 :** the term of a pope's reign **4** *cap* **:** the system of government of the Roman Catholic Church of which the pope is the supreme head

Pa·pa·go \ˈpä-pə-ˌgō, ˈpa-\ *n, pl* **Papago** *or* **Papagos** [Sp *pápago,* earlier *papabos,* short for *papabi-ootam,* fr. O'odham *bá·bawĭ-ʔóʔodham,* lit., tepary bean people] (1839) **:** TOHONO O'ODHAM

pa·pa·in \pə-ˈpā-ən, -ˈpī-ən\ *n* [ISV, fr. *papaya*] (ca. 1889) **:** a protease in the juice of unripe papaya that is used esp. as a tenderizer for meat and in medicine (as in the topical debridement of necrotic tissue)

pa·pal \ˈpā-pəl\ *adj* [ME, fr. AF, fr. ML *papalis,* fr. LL *papa*] (14c) **:** of or relating to a pope or to the Roman Catholic Church; *also* **:** resembling a pope or that of a pope — **pa·pal·ly** \-pə-lē\ *adv*

papal cross *n* (ca. 1889) **:** a figure of a cross having a long upright shaft and three crossbars with the longest at or somewhat above its middle and the two other successively shorter crossbars above the longest one — see CROSS illustration

papal infallibility *n* (1831) **:** the Roman Catholic doctrine that the pope cannot err when speaking ex cathedra in defining a doctrine of Christian faith or morals

Pa·pa·ni·co·laou smear \ˌpä-pə-ˈnē-kə-ˌlaù-, ˌpa-pə-ˈni-\ *n* [George N. *Papanicolaou* †1962 Am. medical scientist] (1950) **:** PAP SMEAR

Papanicolaou test *n* (1946) **:** PAP SMEAR

pa·pa·raz·zo \ˌpä-pə-ˈrät-(ˌ)sō\ *n, pl* **-raz·zi** \-(ˌ)sē\ [It, fr. *Paparazzo,* surname of such a photographer in the film *La dolce vita* (1959) by Federico Fellini] (1961) **:** a freelance photographer who aggressively pursues celebrities for the purpose of taking candid photographs

pa·pav·er·ine \pə-ˈpa-və-ˌrēn; -ˈpav-rən, -ˈpa-və-\ *n* [ISV, fr. L *papaver* poppy] (1857) **:** a crystalline alkaloid $C_{20}H_{21}NO_4$ found in opium or made synthetically that is used usu. in the form of its hydrochloride chiefly as an antispasmodic for its ability to relax smooth muscle

papaw *var of* PAWPAW

pa·pa·ya \pə-ˈpī-ə\ *n* [Sp, of AmerInd origin; akin to Arawak *papáia* papaya] (1598) **:** a tropical American tree (*Carica papaya* of the family Caricaceae, the papaya family) having an oblong to globose yellow edible fruit with numerous black seeds in a central cavity; *also* **:** its fruit

[1]**pa·per** \ˈpā-pər\ *n* [ME *papir,* fr. AF, fr. L *papyrus* papyrus, paper, fr. Gk *papyros* papyrus] (14c) **1 a** (1) **:** a felted sheet of usu. vegetable fibers laid down on a fine screen from a water suspension (2) **:** a similar sheet of other material (as plastic) **b :** a piece of paper **2 a :** a piece of paper containing a written or printed statement **:** DOCUMENT ⟨pedigree ~*s*⟩ **b :** a piece of paper containing writing or print **c :** a formal written composition often designed for publication and often intended to be read aloud ⟨presented a scholarly ~ at the meeting⟩ **d :** a piece of written schoolwork **3 :** a paper container or wrapper **4 :** NEWSPAPER **5 :** the negotiable notes or instruments of commerce **6 :** WALLPAPER **7 :** TICKETS; *esp* **:** free passes **8 :** PAPERBACK — **on paper 1 :** in writing ⟨wants these promises *on paper*⟩ **2 :** in theory ⟨the plan looks good *on paper*⟩ **3 :** figured at face value ⟨*on paper* the stock was worth nearly a million dollars⟩

[2]**paper** *vb* **pa·pered; pa·per·ing** \ˈpā-p(ə-)riŋ\ *vt* (1594) **1** *archaic* **:** to put down or describe in writing **2 :** to fold or enclose in paper **3 :** to cover or line with paper; *esp* **:** to apply wallpaper to **4 :** to fill by giving out free passes ⟨~ the theater for opening night⟩ **5 :** to cover (an area) with advertising bills, circulars, or posters ~ *vi* **:** to hang wallpaper — **pa·per·er** \-pər-ər\ *n*

[3]**paper** *adj* (1594) **1 a :** made of paper, cardboard, or papier-mâché ⟨a ~ bag⟩ **b :** PAPERY **2 :** of or relating to clerical work or written communication **3 :** existing only in theory **:** NOMINAL ⟨a ~ blockade⟩ **4 :** admitted by free passes ⟨a ~ audience⟩ **5 :** finished with a crisp smooth surface similar to that of paper ⟨~ taffeta⟩

pa·per·back \ˈpā-pər-ˌbak\ *n* (1899) **:** a book with a flexible paper binding — **paperback** *also* **pa·per·backed** \-ˌbakt\ *adj*

pa·per·bark \ˈpā-pər-ˌbärk\ *n* (1842) **:** any of several chiefly Australian trees (genus *Melaleuca*) of the myrtle family having papery bark; *esp* **:** CAJEPUT

paper birch *n* (1810) **:** a No. American birch (*Betula papyrifera*) with peeling white bark and toothed ovate leaves

pa·per·board \ˈpā-pər-ˌbȯrd\ *n* (1549) **:** CARDBOARD

pa·per·bound \-ˌbaùnd\ *n* (1950) **:** PAPERBACK — **paperbound** *adj*

pa·per·boy \-ˌbȯi\ *n* (1876) **:** a boy who delivers newspapers **:** NEWSBOY

paper chromatography *n* (1948) **:** chromatography that uses paper strips or sheets as the adsorbent stationary phase through which a solution flows

paper clip *n* (1875) **:** a length of wire bent into flat loops that is used to hold papers together

paper cutter *n* (ca. 1828) **1 :** PAPER KNIFE **2 :** a machine or device for cutting or trimming sheets of paper to required dimensions

pa·per·hang·er \ˈpā-pər-ˌhaŋ-ər\ *n* (1796) **1 :** one that applies wallpaper **2** *slang* **:** one who passes worthless checks

pa·per·hang·ing \-ˌhaŋ-iŋ\ *n* (1873) **:** the act of applying wallpaper

paper knife *n* (ca. 1807) **1 :** a knife for slitting envelopes or uncut pages **2 :** the knife of a paper cutter

pa·per·less \ˈpā-pər-ləs\ *adj* (1969) **:** recording or relaying information by electronic media rather than on paper ⟨~ offices⟩

pa·per·mak·er \ˈpā-pər-ˌmā-kər\ *n* (ca. 1580) **:** one that makes paper — **pa·per·mak·ing** \-kiŋ\ *n*

paper money *n* (1691) **1 :** money consisting of government notes and banknotes **2 :** BANK MONEY

paper mulberry *n* (1777) **:** an Asian tree (*Broussonetia papyrifera*) of the mulberry family that is widely grown as a shade tree

paper nautilus *n* (1835) **:** a pelagic cephalopod (genus *Argonauta*) of which the female has a delicate papery shell

paper over *vt* (1910) **1 :** to gloss over, explain away, or patch up (as major differences or disparities) esp. in order to maintain a semblance of unity or agreement **2 :** HIDE, CONCEAL

paper profit *n* (1893) **:** a profit that can be realized only by selling something (as a security) that has appreciated in market value

pa·per–thin \ˈpā-pər-ˌthin\ *adj* (1928) **:** extremely thin ⟨~ partitions⟩

paper tiger *n* (1850) **:** one that is outwardly powerful or dangerous but inwardly weak or ineffectual

paper trail *n* (1955) **:** documents (as financial records) from which a person's actions may be traced or opinions learned

pa·per–train \ˈpā-pər-ˌtrān\ *vt* (1971) **:** to train (as a dog) to defecate and urinate on paper indoors

paper wasp *n* (1893) **:** a vespid wasp (esp. genus *Polistes*) that builds a nest of papery material

pa·per·weight \-ˌwāt\ *n* (1822) **:** a usu. small heavy object used to hold down loose papers (as on a desk)

pa·per·white \-ˌ(h)wīt\ *n* (1806) **:** a polyanthus narcissus bearing clusters of small very fragrant pure white flowers

pa·per·work \-ˌwərk\ *n* (1917) **:** routine clerical or record-keeping work often incidental to a more important task

pa·pery \ˈpā-p(ə-)rē\ *adj* (1627) **:** resembling paper in thinness or consistency ⟨~ leaves⟩ ⟨~ silk⟩ — **pa·per·i·ness** *n*

pa·pe·terie \ˈpa-pə-trē, ˌpa-pə-ˈ\ *n* [F] (ca. 1847) **:** packaged fancy stationery

[1]**Pa·phi·an** \ˈpā-fē-ən\ *n* [L *paphius,* fr. Gk *paphios,* fr. *Paphos,* ancient city of Cyprus that was the center of worship of Aphrodite] (1598) **1** *often not cap* **:** PROSTITUTE **2 :** a native or inhabitant of Paphos

[2]**Paphian** *adj* (1605) **1 :** of or relating to illicit love **:** WANTON **2 :** of or relating to Paphos or its people

Pa·pia·men·to \ˌpä-pyə-ˈmen-(ˌ)tō\ *also* **Pa·pia·men·tu** \-(ˌ)tü\ *n* [Sp, fr. Papiamento *papya* talk + *-mentu* -ment] (1923) **:** a Spanish-based creole language of Netherlands Antilles

pa·pier col·lé \ˌpā-ˌpyā-(ˌ)kō-ˈlā, ˌpa-\ *n, pl* **papiers collés** \-ˌpyā-(ˌ)kō-ˈlā(z)\ [F, glued paper] (1935) **:** COLLAGE

[1]**pa·pier–mâ·ché** \ˌpā-pər-mə-ˈshā, ˌpa-ˌpyā-mə-, -(ˌ)ma-\ *n* [F, lit., chewed paper] (1753) **:** a light strong molding material of wastepaper pulped with glue and other additives

[2]**papier–mâché** *adj* (1753) **1 :** formed of papier-mâché **2 :** UNREAL, ARTIFICIAL

pa·pil·i·o·na·ceous \pə-ˌpi-lē-ə-ˈnā-shəs\ *adj* [L *papilion-, papilio* butterfly — more at PAVILION] (1668) **:** having a corolla (as in the bean or pea) with usu. five petals that include a large upper petal enclosing two lateral wings and a lower carina of two united petals

pa·pil·la \pə-ˈpi-lə\ *n, pl* **pa·pil·lae** \-ˈpi-(ˌ)lē, -ˌlī\ [L, nipple, fr. dim. of *papula* pimple; akin to Lith *papas* nipple] (1713) **:** a small projecting body part similar to a nipple in form: **a :** a vascular process of connective tissue extending into and nourishing the root of a hair, feather, or developing tooth — see HAIR illustration **b :** any of the vascular protuberances of the dermal layer of the skin extending into the epidermal layer and often containing tactile corpuscles **c :** any of the small protuberances on the upper surface of the tongue often containing taste buds — **pap·il·lary** \ˈpa-pə-ˌler-ē, *esp Brit* pə-ˈpi-lə-rē\ *adj* — **pa·pil·late** \ˈpa-pə-ˌlāt, pə-ˈpi-lət\ *adj* — **pa·pil·lose** \ˈpa-pə-ˌlōs, pə-ˈpi-ˌlōs\ *adj*

pap·il·lo·ma \ˌpa-pə-ˈlō-mə\ *n, pl* **-mas** *also* **-ma·ta** \-mə-tə\ [NL] (1866) **:** a benign tumor (as a wart) due to overgrowth of epithelial tissue on papillae of vascular connective tissue (as of the skin) — **pap·il·lo·ma·tous** \-ˈlō-mə-təs\ *adj*

pap·il·lo·ma·vi·rus \-ˌvī-rəs\ *n* [NL] (1960) **:** any of a family (*Papillomaviridae*) of viruses that contain a single molecule of circular double-stranded DNA and cause papillomas in mammals — compare HUMAN PAPILLOMAVIRUS

pa·pil·lon \ˌpä-pē-ˈyōⁿ, ˌpa-\ *n* [F, lit., butterfly, fr. L *papilion-, papilio*] (1907) **:** any of a European breed of small slender toy spaniels having large erect heavily fringed ears

pa·pil·lote \ˌpä-pē-ˈyōt, ˌpa-\ *n* [F, fr. *papillon* butterfly] (1818) **:** a greased usu. paper wrapper in which food (as meat or fish) is cooked

pa·pist \ˈpā-pist\ *n, often cap* [MF or NL; MF *papiste,* fr. *pape* pope; NL *papista,* fr. LL *papa* pope] (1534) *usu disparaging* **:** ROMAN CATHOLIC — **papist** *adj, usu disparaging*

pa·pist·ry \ˈpā-pə-strē\ *n* (1535) *usu disparaging* **:** the Roman Catholic religion

pa·poose \pa-ˈpüs, pə-\ *n* [Narragansett *papoòs*] (1634) **:** a young child of American Indian parents

pa·po·va·vi·rus \pə-ˈpō-və-ˌvī-rəs\ *n* [*pa*pilloma + *po*lyoma + *va*cuolating + *virus*] (1935) **:** any of a former family (Papovaviridae) of double-stranded DNA viruses that included the papillomaviruses and polyomaviruses

pap·par·del·le \ˌpä-pär-ˈde-lā\ *n* [It] (1899) **:** pasta in the form of wide ribbons

pap·pose \ˈpa-ˌpōs\ *adj* (1691) **:** having or being a pappus

pap·pus \ˈpa-pəs\ *n, pl* **pap·pi** \ˈpa-ˌpī, -ˌpē\ [L, fr. Gk *pappos*] (ca. 1704) **:** an appendage or tuft of appendages that crowns the ovary or fruit in various seed plants and functions in dispersal of the fruit

pap·py \ˈpa-pē\ *n* (1763) *chiefly Southern & Midland* **:** PAPA

pa·pri·ka \pə-ˈprē-kə, pa-\ *n* [Hung, fr. Serbian & Croatian, fr. *papar* ground pepper, ultim. fr. L *piper* — more at PEPPER] (1843) **:** a usu. mild red condiment consisting of the dried finely ground pods of various sweet peppers; *also* **:** a sweet pepper used for making paprika

Pap smear \ˈpap-\ *n* [George N. *Papanicolaou* †1962 Am. medical scientist] (1952) **:** a method for the early detection of cancer esp. of the uterine cervix that involves the staining of exfoliated cells using a special technique which differentiates diseased tissue — called also *Papanicolaou smear, Papanicolaou test, Pap test*

Pap·u·an \ˈpa-pyə-wən, -pə-\ *n* (1814) **1 :** a native or inhabitant of Papua **2 :** a member of any of the native peoples of New Guinea and adjacent areas of Melanesia **3 :** any of a heterogeneous group of languages spoken in New Guinea, New Britain, and the Solomon islands — **Papuan** *adj*

pap·u·lar \ˈpa-pyə-lər\ *adj* (ca. 1820) **:** consisting of or characterized by papules

pap·ule \ˈpa-(ˌ)pyül\ *n* [L *papula*] (1864) **:** a small solid usu. conical elevation of the skin

pap·y·rol·o·gy \ˌpa-pə-ˈrä-lə-jē\ *n* [ISV] (1898) **:** the study of papyrus manuscripts — **pap·y·rol·o·gist** \-jist\ *n*

pa·py·rus \pə-ˈpī-rəs\ *n, pl* **pa·py·ri** \-ˈpī-(ˌ)rē, -rī\ *or* **pa·py·rus·es** [ME, fr. L — more at PAPER] (14c) **1 :** a tall perennial sedge (*Cyperus papyrus*) of the Nile valley **2 :** the pith of the papyrus plant esp. when made into strips and pressed into a material to write on **3 a :** a writing on papyrus **b :** a written scroll made of papyrus

[1]**par** \ˈpär\ *n* [L, one that is equal, fr. *par* equal] (1622) **1 a :** the established value of the monetary unit of one country expressed in terms of the monetary unit of another country using the same metal as the standard of value **b :** the face amount of an instrument of value (as a check or note): as (1) **:** the monetary value assigned to each share of stock in the charter of a corporation (2) **:** the principal of a bond **2 :** common level **:** EQUALITY — usu. used with *on* ⟨judged the recording to be on a ~ with previous ones⟩ **3 a :** an amount taken as an average or norm **b :** an accepted standard; *specif* **:** a usual standard of physical condition or health **4 :** the score standard for each hole of a golf course; *also* **:** a score equal to par — **par** *adj* — **par for the course :** not unusual **:** NORMAL

[2]**par** *vt* **parred; par·ring** (1950) **:** to score par on (a hole)

[1]**pa·ra** \ˈpär-ə\ *n, pl* **paras** *or* **para** [Turk, fr. Pers *pāra,* lit., piece, scrap] (1687) **1 a :** any of several monetary units of the Turkish Empire **b :** a coin representing one para **2** [Serbian & Croatian, fr. Turk] — see *dinar* at MONEY table

[2]**para** *abbr* paragraph

[1]**para-** *or* **par-** *prefix* [Gk, fr. *para;* akin to Gk *pro* before — more at FOR] **1 :** beside **:** alongside of **:** beyond **:** aside from ⟨*para*thyroid⟩ ⟨*par*enteral⟩ **2 a :** closely related to ⟨*par*aldehyde⟩ **b :** involving substitution at or characterized by two opposite positions in the benzene ring that are separated by two carbon atoms ⟨*para*dichlorobenzene⟩ **3 a :** faulty **:** abnormal ⟨*par*esthesia⟩ **b :** associated in a subsidiary or accessory capacity ⟨*para*medical⟩ **c :** closely resembling **:** almost ⟨*para*typhoid⟩

[2]**para-** *comb form* [*parachute*] **:** parachute ⟨*para*trooper⟩

-para *n comb form, pl* **-paras** *or* **-parae** [L, fr. *parere* to give birth to — more at PARE] **:** woman delivered of (so many) children ⟨primi*para*⟩

para–ami·no·ben·zo·ic acid \ˌpa-rə-ə-ˌmē-ˌnō-ˌben-ˈzō-ik-, ˌpa-rə-ˌa-mə-(ˌ)nō-\ *n* [ISV] (1906) **:** a colorless para-substituted aminobenzoic acid that is a growth factor of the vitamin B complex and is used as a sunscreen — called also *PABA*

para–ami·no·sal·i·cyl·ic acid \-ˌsa-lə-ˈsi-lik-\ *n* (1946) **:** the white crystalline para-substituted isomer of aminosalicylic acid that is made synthetically and is used in the treatment of tuberculosis

para·bi·o·sis \ˌpa-rə-(ˌ)bī-ˈō-səs, -bē-\ *n* [NL] (1903) **1 :** reversible suspension of obvious vital activities **2 :** anatomical and physiological union of two organisms — **para·bi·ot·ic** \-ˈä-tik\ *adj* — **para·bi·ot·i·cal·ly** \-ti-k(ə-)lē\ *adv*

par·a·ble \ˈpa-rə-bəl\ *n* [ME, fr. AF, fr. LL *parabola,* fr. Gk *parabolē* comparison, fr. *paraballein* to compare, fr. *para-* + *ballein* to throw — more at DEVIL] (14c) **:** EXAMPLE; *specif* **:** a usu. short fictitious story that illustrates a moral attitude or a religious principle

pa·rab·o·la \pə-ˈra-bə-lə\ *n* [NL, fr. Gk *parabolē,* lit., comparison] (1579) **1 :** a plane curve generated by a point moving so that its distance from a fixed point is equal to its distance from a fixed line **:** the intersection of a right circular cone with a plane parallel to an element of the cone **2 :** something bowl-shaped (as an antenna or microphone reflector)

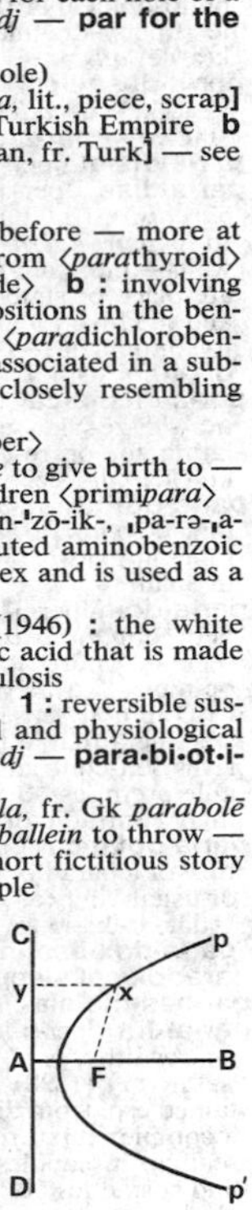

parabola 1: *F* fixed point; *CD* fixed line; *x* moving point; *AB* axis; *xy* distance from *x* to *CD; pp'* parabola

par·a·bol·ic \ˌpa-rə-ˈbä-lik\ *adj* [in sense 1, fr. LL *parabola* parable; in sense 2, fr. NL *parabola*] (1669) **1 :** expressed by or being a parable **:** ALLEGORICAL **2 :** of, having the form of, or relating to a parabola ⟨motion in a ~ curve⟩ — **par·a·bol·i·cal·ly** \-li-k(ə-)lē\ *adv*

pa·rab·o·loid \pə-ˈra-bə-ˌlȯid\ *n* (ca. 1702) **:** a surface all of whose intersections by planes are either parabolas and ellipses or parabolas and hyperbolas — **pa·rab·o·loi·dal** \-ˌra-bə-ˈlȯi-dᵊl\ *adj*

para·cet·a·mol \ˌpa-rə-ˈsē-tə-ˌmȯl\ *n* [ˈ*para-* + *acet*yl + *am*ino + phen*ol*] (1957) *Brit* **:** ACETAMINOPHEN

[1]**para·chute** \ˈper-ə-ˌshüt, ˈpa-rə-\ *n* [F, fr. *para-* (as in *parasol*) + *chute* fall — more at CHUTE] (1785) **1 :** a device for slowing the descent of a person or object through the air that consists of a fabric canopy beneath which the person or object is suspended **2 :** PATAGIUM **3 :** a device or structure suggestive of a parachute in form, use, or operation — **para·chut·ic** \ˌper-ə-ˈshü-tik, ˌpa-rə-\ *adj*

[2]**parachute** *vb* **-chut·ed; -chut·ing** *vt* (1809) **:** to convey by means of a parachute ~ *vi* **:** to descend by means of a parachute

parachute pants *n pl* (1977) **:** baggy casual pants of lightweight fabric often with an elastic or drawstring at the waist and the cuffs

para·chut·ist \ˈper-ə-ˌshü-tist, ˈpa-rə-\ *n* (1888) **:** one that parachutes: as **a :** PARATROOPER **b :** a person who parachutes as a sport

Par·a·clete \ˈpa-rə-ˌklēt\ *n* [ME *Paraclyte,* fr. LL *Paracletus, Paraclitus,* fr. Gk *Paraklētos,* lit., advocate, intercessor, fr. *parakalein* to invoke, fr. *para-* + *kalein* to call — more at LOW] (15c) **:** HOLY SPIRIT

\ə\ **abut** \ᵊ\ **kitten,** F **table** \ər\ **further** \a\ **ash** \ā\ **ace** \ä\ **mop, mar** \au̇\ **out** \ch\ **chin** \e\ **bet** \ē\ **easy** \g\ **go** \i\ **hit** \ī\ **ice** \j\ **job** \ŋ\ **sing** \ō\ **go** \ȯ\ **law** \ȯi\ **boy** \th\ **thin** \t͟h\ **the** \ü\ **loot** \u̇\ **foot** \y\ **yet** \zh\ **vision, beige** \k, ⁿ, œ, ue, ʸ\ *see* Guide to Pronunciation

para·crine \ˈpa-rə-krən, -ˌkrīn\ *adj* [¹*para-* + *-crine* (as in *endocrine*)] (1972) : of, relating to, promoted by, or being a substance secreted by a cell and acting on adjacent cells — compare AUTOCRINE

¹**pa·rade** \pə-ˈrād\ *n* [F, fr. MF, fr. *parer* to prepare — more at PARE] (ca. 1656) **1** : a pompous show : EXHIBITION **2 a** : the ceremonial formation of a body of troops before a superior officer **b** : a place where troops assemble regularly for parade **3 a** : an informal procession **b** : a public procession **c** : a usu. lengthy array or succession ⟨a ~ of visitors⟩ **4 a** : a place for strolling **b** : those who promenade

²**parade** *vb* **pa·rad·ed; pa·rad·ing** *vt* (1686) **1** : to cause to maneuver or march : MARSHAL **2** : PROMENADE **3** : to exhibit ostentatiously ~ *vi* **1** : to march in or as if in a procession **2** : PROMENADE **3 a** : SHOW OFF **b** : MASQUERADE ⟨myths which ~ as modern science —M. R. Cohen⟩ ***syn*** see SHOW — **pa·rad·er** *n*

para·di·chlo·ro·ben·zene \ˌpa-rə-ˌdī-ˌklȯr-ə-ˈben-ˌzēn, -ˌben-ˈ\ *n* [ISV] (1876) : a white crystalline compound $C_6H_4Cl_2$ made by chlorinating benzene and used esp. as a moth repellent and deodorizer

par·a·did·dle \ˈpa-rə-ˌdi-dᵊl\ *n* [origin unknown] (1927) : a quick succession of drumbeats slower than a roll and alternating left- and right-hand strokes in a typical L-R-L-L, R-L-R-R pattern

par·a·digm \ˈper-ə-ˌdīm, ˈpa-rə- *also* -ˌdim\ *n* [LL *paradigma*, fr. Gk *paradeigma*, fr. *paradeiknynai* to show side by side, fr. *para-* + *deiknynai* to show — more at DICTION] (15c) **1** : EXAMPLE, PATTERN; *esp* : an outstandingly clear or typical example or archetype **2** : an example of a conjugation or declension showing a word in all its inflectional forms **3** : a philosophical and theoretical framework of a scientific school or discipline within which theories, laws, and generalizations and the experiments performed in support of them are formulated; *broadly* : a philosophical or theoretical framework of any kind — **par·a·dig·mat·ic** \ˌper-ə-dig-ˈma-tik, ˌpa-rə-\ *adj* — **par·a·dig·mat·i·cal·ly** \-ti-k(ə-)lē\ *adv*

par·a·di·sa·i·cal \ˌper-ə-ˌdī-ˈsā-ə-kəl, -ˈzā-, ˌpa-rə-\ *or* **par·a·di·sa·ic** \-ˈsā-ik, -ˈzā-\ *adj* [*paradise* + *-aic* (as in *Hebraic*) + *-al*] (1754) : PARADISIACAL — **par·a·di·sa·i·cal·ly** \-ə-k(ə-)lē\ *adv*

par·a·dis·al \ˌper-ə-ˈdī-səl, -zəl, ˈpa-rə-\ *adj* (1560) : PARADISIACAL

par·a·dise \ˈper-ə-ˌdīs, -ˌdīz, ˈpa-rə-\ *n* [ME *paradis*, fr. AF, fr. LL *paradisus*, fr. Gk *paradeisos*, lit., enclosed park, of Iranian origin; akin to Av *pairi-daēza-* enclosure; akin to Gk *peri* around and to Gk *teichos* wall — more at PERI-, DOUGH] (12c) **1 a** : EDEN 2 **b** : an intermediate place or state where the souls of the righteous await resurrection and the final judgment **c** : HEAVEN **2** : a place or state of bliss, felicity, or delight — **par·a·dis·ial** \ˌper-ə-ˈdi-sē-əl, -zē-, ˌpa-rə-\ *also* **par·a·dis·i·cal** \-si-kəl, -zi-\ *adj*

par·a·di·si·a·cal \ˌper-ə-də-ˈsī-ə-kəl, -ˌdī-, -ˈzī-, ˌpa-rə-\ *or* **par·a·dis·i·ac** \-ˈdi-zē-ˌak, -sē-\ *adj* [LL *paradisiacus*, fr. *paradisus*] (1649) : of, relating to, or resembling paradise — **par·a·di·si·a·cal·ly** \-də-ˈsī-ə-k(ə-)lē, -ˌdī-, -ˈzī-\ *adv*

pa·ra·dor \ˌpä-rä-ˈt͟hȯr\ *n, pl* **pa·ra·dor·es** \-ˈt͟hȯr-ās\ *or* **paradors** [Sp, inn, fr. *parar* to stop, lodge for the night, fr. L *parare* to prepare — more at PARE] (1845) : a usu. government-operated hostelry found esp. in Spain

par·a·dox \ˈper-ə-ˌdäks, ˈpa-rə-\ *n* [L *paradoxum*, fr. Gk *paradoxon*, fr. neut. of *paradoxos* contrary to expectation, fr. *para-* + *dokein* to think, seem — more at DECENT] (1540) **1** : a tenet contrary to received opinion **2 a** : a statement that is seemingly contradictory or opposed to common sense and yet is perhaps true **b** : a self-contradictory statement that at first seems true **c** : an argument that apparently derives self-contradictory conclusions by valid deduction from acceptable premises **3** : one (as a person, situation, or action) having seemingly contradictory qualities or phases

par·a·dox·i·cal \ˌper-ə-ˈdäk-si-kəl, ˌpa-rə-\ *adj* (1598) **1 a** : of the nature of a paradox **b** : inclined to paradoxes **2** : not being the normal or usual kind ⟨a ~ pulse⟩ ⟨~ drug reactions⟩ — **par·a·dox·i·cal·i·ty** \-ˌdäk-si-ˈka-lə-tē\ *n* — **par·a·dox·i·cal·ly** \-ˈdäk-si-k(ə-)lē\ *adv* — **par·a·dox·i·cal·ness** \-kəl-nəs\ *n*

paradoxical sleep *n* (1964) : REM SLEEP

par·aes·the·sia *chiefly Brit var of* PARESTHESIA

par·af·fin \ˈper-ə-fən, ˈpa-rə-\ *n* [G, fr. L *parum* too little (akin to Gk *pauros* little, *paid-*, *pais* child) + *affinis* bordering on — more at FEW, AFFINITY] (1838) **1 a** : a waxy crystalline flammable substance obtained esp. from distillates of wood, coal, petroleum, or shale oil that is a complex mixture of hydrocarbons and is used chiefly in coating and sealing, in candles, in rubber compounding, and in pharmaceuticals and cosmetics **b** : any of various mixtures of similar hydrocarbons including mixtures that are semisolid or oily **2** : ALKANE **3** *chiefly Brit* : KEROSENE — **par·af·fin·ic** \ˌper-ə-ˈfi-nik, pa-rə-\ *adj*

para·for·mal·de·hyde \ˌpa-rə-fȯr-ˈmal-də-ˌhīd, -fər-\ *n* (1894) : a white powder $(CH_2O)_x$ that consists of a polymer of formaldehyde and is used esp. as a disinfectant

para·gen·e·sis \ˌpa-rə-ˈje-nə-səs\ *n* [NL] (1853) : the formation of minerals in contact in such a manner as to affect one another's development — **para·ge·net·ic** \-jə-ˈne-tik\ *adj* — **para·ge·net·i·cal·ly** \-ti-k(ə-)lē\ *adv*

para·glid·er \ˈpa-rə-ˌglī-dər\ *n* (1944) **1** : a modified parachute used for paragliding **2** : a person who paraglides

para·glid·ing \ˈpa-rə-ˌglī-diŋ\ *n* (1978) : the recreational sport of soaring from a slope or a cliff using a modified parachute — **para·glide** \-ˌglīd\ *vi*

¹**par·a·gon** \ˈper-ə-ˌgän, -gən, ˈpa-rə-\ *n* [MF, fr. OIt *paragone*, lit., touchstone, fr. *paragonare* to test on a touchstone, fr. Gk *parakonan* to sharpen, fr. *para-* + *akonē* whetstone, fr. *akē* point; akin to Gk *akmē* point — more at EDGE] (ca. 1548) : a model of excellence or perfection

²**paragon** *vt* (ca. 1586) **1** : to compare with : PARALLEL **2** : to put in rivalry : MATCH **3** *obs* : SURPASS

¹**par·a·graph** \ˈper-ə-ˌgraf, ˈpa-rə-\ *n* [ME *paragraf* marginal sign marking a paragraph, fr. AF *parogref*, fr. ML *paragraphus*, fr. Gk *paragraphos* line used to mark change of persons in a dialogue, fr. *paragraphein* to write alongside, fr. *para-* + *graphein* to write — more at CARVE] (1525) **1 a** : a subdivision of a written composition that consists of one or more sentences, deals with one point or gives the words of one speaker, and begins on a new usu. indented line **b** : a short composition or note that is complete in one paragraph **2** : a character (as ¶) used to indicate the beginning of a paragraph and as a reference mark — **par·a·graph·ic** \ˌper-ə-ˈgra-fik, ˌpa-rə-\ *adj*

²**paragraph** *vt* (1764) **1** : to write paragraphs about **2** : to divide into paragraphs ~ *vi* : to write paragraphs

par·a·graph·er \ˈper-ə-ˌgra-fər, ˈpa-rə-\ *n* (1822) : a writer of paragraphs esp. for the editorial page of a newspaper

para·in·flu·en·za \ˌpa-rə-ˌin-flü-ˈen-zə\ *n* (1959) : PARAINFLUENZA VIRUS; *also* : a respiratory illness caused by a parainfluenza virus

parainfluenza virus *n* (1959) : any of several paramyxoviruses (genera *Respirovirus* and *Rubulavirus*) that are a frequent cause of infections (as croup) of the lower respiratory tract esp. in infants and children

para·jour·nal·ism \ˌpar-ə-ˈjər-nᵊl-ˌi-zəm\ *n* (1965) : journalism that is heavily colored by the opinions of the reporter

par·a·keet \ˈper-ə-ˌkēt, ˈpa-rə-\ *n* [Sp & MF; Sp *periquito*, fr. MF *perroquet* parrot] (1581) : any of numerous usu. small slender parrots with a long graduated tail

para·lan·guage \ˈpa-rə-ˌlaŋ-gwij\ *n* (1958) : optional vocal effects (as tone of voice) that accompany or modify the phonemes of an utterance and that may communicate meaning

par·al·de·hyde \pa-ˈral-də-ˌhīd, pə-\ *n* (1857) : a colorless liquid polymer $C_6H_{12}O_3$ derived from acetaldehyde and used esp. as an anticonvulsant, sedative, and hypnotic

para·le·gal \ˌpa-rə-ˈlē-gəl\ *adj* (1966) : of, relating to, or being a paraprofessional who assists a lawyer — **para·le·gal** \ˈpar-ə-ˌlē-gəl\ *n*

para·lin·guis·tics \ˌpa-rə-liŋ-ˈgwis-tiks\ *n* (1958) : the study of paralanguage — **para·lin·guis·tic** \-tik\ *adj*

Par·a·li·pom·e·non \ˌpa-rə-lə-ˈpä-mə-ˌnän, -lī-\ *n* [ME, fr. LL, fr. Gk *Paraleipomenōn*, gen. of *Paraleipomena*, lit., things left out, fr. neut. pl. of passive prp. of *paraleipein* to leave out, fr. *para-* + *leipein* to leave; fr. its forming a supplement to Samuel and Kings — more at LOAN] (14c) : CHRONICLES

par·al·lac·tic \ˌpa-rə-ˈlak-tik\ *adj* [NL *parallacticus*, fr. Gk *parallaktikos*, fr. *parallaxis*] (1630) : of, relating to, or due to parallax

par·al·lax \ˈpa-rə-ˌlaks\ *n* [MF *parallaxe*, fr. Gk *parallaxis*, fr. *parallassein* to change, fr. *para-* + *allassein* to change, fr. *allos* other] (1580) : the apparent displacement or the difference in apparent direction of an object as seen from two different points not on a straight line with the object; *esp* : the angular difference in direction of a celestial body as measured from two points on the earth's orbit

¹**par·al·lel** \ˈper-ə-ˌlel, ˈpa-rə-, -ləl\ *adj* [L *parallelus*, fr. Gk *parallēlos*, fr. *para* beside + *allēlōn* of one another, fr. *allos* . . . *allos* one . . . another, fr. *allos* other — more at ELSE] (1549) **1 a** : extending in the same direction, everywhere equidistant, and not meeting ⟨~ rows of trees⟩ **b** : everywhere equally distant ⟨concentric spheres are ~⟩ **2 a** : having parallel sides ⟨a ~ reamer⟩ **b** : being or relating to an electrical circuit having a number of conductors in parallel **c** : arranged in parallel ⟨a ~ processor⟩ **d** : relating to or being a connection in a computer system in which the bits of a byte are transmitted over separate channels at the same time ⟨a ~ port⟩ — compare SERIAL **3 a (1)** : similar, analogous, or interdependent in tendency or development **(2)** : exhibiting parallelism in form, function, or development ⟨~ evolution⟩ **b** : readily compared : COMPANION **c** : having identical syntactical elements in corresponding positions; *also* : being such an element **d (1)** : having the same tonic — used of major and minor keys and scales **(2)** : keeping the same distance apart in musical pitch **4** : performed while keeping one's skis parallel ⟨~ turns⟩ ***syn*** see SIMILAR

²**parallel** *n* (1551) **1 a** : a parallel line, curve, or surface **b** : one of the imaginary circles on the surface of the earth paralleling the equator and marking the latitude; *also* : the corresponding line on a globe or map — see LATITUDE illustration **c** : a character ‖ used in printing esp. as a reference mark **2 a** : something equal or similar in all essential particulars : COUNTERPART **b** : SIMILARITY, ANALOGUE **3** : a comparison to show resemblance **4 a** : the state of being physically parallel **b** : an arrangement of electrical devices in a circuit in which the same potential difference is applied to two or more resistances with each resistance being on a different branch of the circuit — compare SERIES **c** : an arrangement or state that permits several operations or tasks to be performed simultaneously rather than consecutively — **in parallel** : in a parallel arrangement

³**parallel** *vt* (1598) **1** : to indicate analogy of : COMPARE **2 a** : to show something equal to : MATCH **b** : to correspond to **3** : to place so as to be parallel in direction with something **4** : to extend, run, or move in a direction parallel to

⁴**parallel** *adv* (ca. 1747) : in a parallel manner

parallel bars *n pl* (1868) **1** : a pair of usu. wooden bars supported horizontally above the floor at the same height or at different heights usu. by a common base and used in gymnastics **2** : an event in gymnastics competition in which even or uneven parallel bars are used

par·al·lel·e·pi·ped \ˌpa-rə-ˌle-lə-ˈpī-pəd *also* -ˌle-ˈle-pə-ˌped\ *n* [Gk *parallēlepipedon*, fr. *parallēlos* + *epipedon* plane surface, fr. neut. of *epipedos* flat, fr. *epi-* epi- + *pedon* ground; akin to L *ped-*, *pes* foot — more at FOOT] (1570) : a 6-faced polyhedron all of whose faces are parallelograms lying in pairs of parallel planes

par·al·lel·ism \ˈpa-rə-ˌle-ˌli-zəm, -lə-ˌli-\ *n* (1610) **1** : the quality or state of being parallel **2** : RESEMBLANCE, CORRESPONDENCE **3** : repeated syntactical similarities introduced for rhetorical effect **4** : a theory that mind and matter accompany one another but are not causally related **5** : the independent development of a similar trait in related species or lineages following divergence from a common ancestor

par·al·lel·o·gram \ˌpa-rə-ˈle-lə-ˌgram\ *n* [LL or Gk; LL *parallelogrammum*, fr. Gk *parallēlogrammon*, fr. neut. of *parallēlogrammos* bounded by parallel lines, fr. *parallēlos* + *grammē* line, fr. *graphein* to write — more at CARVE] (1570) : a quadrilateral with opposite sides parallel and equal

par·al·lel–veined \ˌpa-rə-ˌlel-ˈvānd, -ləl-\ *adj* (1861) *of a leaf* : having veins arranged nearly parallel to one another — see VENATION illustration; compare NET-VEINED

pa·ral·o·gism \pə-ˈra-lə-ˌji-zəm\ *n* [MF *paralogisme*, fr. LL *paralogismus*, fr. Gk *paralogismos*, fr. *paralogos* unreasonable, fr. *para-* + *logos* speech, reason — more at LEGEND] (1565) : a fallacious argument

Para·lym·pics \ˌpa-rə-ˈlim-piks\ *n pl* [*para*plegic + O*lympics*] (1953) : a series of international contests for athletes with disabilities that are associated with and held following the summer and winter Olympic Games — called also *Paralympic Games* — **Para·lym·pi·an** \-pē-ən\ *n* — **Para·lym·pic** \-pik\ *adj*

par·a·lyse *Brit var of* PARALYZE

pa·ral·y·sis \pə-ˈra-lə-səs\ *n, pl* **-y·ses** \-ˌsēz\ [L, fr. Gk, fr. *paralyein* to loosen, disable, fr. *para-* + *lyein* to loosen — more at LOSE] (1525) **1** : complete or partial loss of function esp. when involving the motion or sensation in a part of the body **2** : loss of the ability to move **3** : a state of powerlessness or incapacity to act

paralysis agi·tans \-ˈa-jə-ˌtanz\ *n* [NL, lit., shaking palsy] (1817) : PARKINSON'S DISEASE

[1]**par·a·lyt·ic** \ˌpa-rə-ˈli-tik\ *adj* [ME *paralytyk,* fr. AF *paralitik,* fr. L *paralyticus,* fr. Gk *paralytikos,* fr. *paralyein*] (14c) **1** : affected with, characterized by, or causing paralysis **2** : of, relating to, or resembling paralysis — **par·a·lyt·i·cal·ly** \-ti-k(ə-)lē\ *adv*

[2]**paralytic** *n* (14c) : one affected with paralysis

par·a·lyze \ˈper-ə-ˌlīz, ˈpa-rə-\ *vt* **-lyzed; -lyz·ing** [F *paralyser,* back-formation fr. *paralysie* paralysis, fr. L *paralysis*] (1804) **1** : to affect with paralysis **2** : to make powerless or ineffective **3** : UNNERVE **4** : STUN, STUPEFY **5** : to bring to an end : PREVENT, DESTROY — **par·a·ly·za·tion** \ˌper-ə-lə-ˈzā-shən, ˌpa-rə-\ *n* — **par·a·lyz·er** \ˈper-ə-ˌlī-zər, ˈpa-rə-\ *n* — **par·a·lyz·ing·ly** \-ˌlī-ziŋ-lē\ *adv*

para·mag·net \ˈpa-rə-ˌmag-nət\ *n* [back-formation fr. *paramagnetic*] (ca. 1900) : a paramagnetic substance

para·mag·net·ic \ˌpa-rə-mag-ˈne-tik\ *adj* [ISV] (ca. 1850) : being or relating to a magnetizable substance (as aluminum) that has small but positive susceptibility which varies little with magnetizing force — **para·mag·net·i·cal·ly** \-ti-k(ə-)lē\ *adv* — **para·mag·ne·tism** \-ˈmag-nə-ˌti-zəm\ *n*

par·a·me·cium \ˌpa-rə-ˈmē-sh(ē-)əm, -sē-əm\ *n, pl* **-cia** \-sh(ē-)ə, -sē-ə\ *also* **-ciums** [NL, fr. Gk *paramēkēs* oblong, fr. *para-* + *mēkos* length; akin to Gk *makros* long — more at MEAGER] (1752) : any of a genus (*Paramecium*) of ciliate chiefly freshwater protozoans that have an elongate body rounded at the anterior end and an oblique funnel-shaped buccal groove bearing the mouth at the extremity

para·med·ic \ˌpa-rə-ˈme-dik\ *also* **para·med·i·cal** \-di-kəl\ *n* (1967) **1** : a person who works in a health field in an auxiliary capacity to a physician (as by giving injections and taking X-rays) **2** : a specially trained medical technician licensed to provide a wide range of emergency services (as defibrillation and the intravenous administration of drugs) before or during transportation to a hospital — compare EMT

para·med·i·cal \ˌpa-rə-ˈme-di-kəl\ *also* **para·med·ic** \-dik\ *adj* (1921) : concerned with supplementing the work of highly trained medical professionals ⟨~ aides and technicians⟩

par·a·ment \ˈpa-rə-mənt\ *n* [ME, fr. ML *paramentum,* fr. *parare* to adorn, fr. L, to prepare — more at PARE] (15c) : an ornamental ecclesiastical hanging or vestment

pa·ram·e·ter \pə-ˈram-ə-tər\ *n* [NL, fr. *para-* + Gk *metron* measure — more at MEASURE] (1852) **1 a** : an arbitrary constant whose value characterizes a member of a system (as a family of curves); *also* : a quantity (as a mean or variance) that describes a statistical population **b** : an independent variable used to express the coordinates of a variable point and functions of them — compare PARAMETRIC EQUATION **2** : any of a set of physical properties whose values determine the characteristics or behavior of something ⟨~*s* of the atmosphere such as temperature, pressure, and density⟩ **3** : something represented by a parameter : a characteristic element; *broadly* : CHARACTERISTIC, ELEMENT, FACTOR ⟨political dissent as a ~ of modern life⟩ **4** : LIMIT, BOUNDARY — usu. used in pl. ⟨the ~*s* of science fiction⟩ — **para·met·ric** \ˌpa-rə-ˈme-trik\ *adj* — **para·met·ri·cal·ly** \-tri-k(ə-)lē\ *adv*

pa·ram·e·ter·ize \pə-ˈra-mə-tə-ˌrīz, -mə-ˌtrīz\ *or* **pa·ram·e·trize** \-ˈra-mə-ˌtrīz\ *vt* **-ter·ized** *or* **-trized; -ter·iz·ing** *or* **-triz·ing** (1940) : to express in terms of parameters — **pa·ram·e·ter·i·za·tion** \-ˌra-mə-tə-rə-ˈzā-shən, -mə-trə-\ *or* **pa·ram·e·tri·za·tion** \-mə-trə-\ *n*

parametric equation *n* (1909) : any of a set of equations that express the coordinates of the points of a curve as functions of one parameter or that express the coordinates of the points of a surface as functions of two parameters

para·mil·i·tary \ˌpa-rə-ˈmi-lə-ˌter-ē\ *adj* (1935) : of, relating to, being, or characteristic of a force formed on a military pattern esp. as a potential auxiliary military force ⟨a ~ border patrol⟩ ⟨~ training⟩ — **paramilitary** *n*

par·am·ne·sia \ˌpa-ˌram-ˈnē-zhə, -əm-\ *n* [NL, fr. *para-* + *-mnesia* (as in *amnesia*)] (1888) : a disorder of memory; *esp* : DÉJÀ VU 1

[1]**par·a·mount** \ˈper-ə-ˌmau̇nt, ˈpa-rə-\ *adj* [AF *paramont,* fr. *par* by (fr. L *per*) + *amunt* above, fr. *a* to (fr. L *ad*) + *munt* mountain — more at FOR, AT, MOUNT] (1531) : superior to all others : SUPREME ⟨a matter of ~ importance⟩ ***syn*** see DOMINANT — **par·a·mount·cy** \-ˌmau̇n(t)-sē\ *n* — **par·a·mount·ly** \-ˌmau̇nt-lē\ *adv*

[2]**paramount** *n* (1616) : a supreme ruler

par·amour \ˈpa-rə-ˌmu̇r\ *n* [ME, fr. *par amour* for the sake of love, willingly, fr. AF *par amur*] (14c) : an illicit lover

par·am·y·lum \ˌpa-ˈra-mə-ləm\ *n* [NL, fr. *para-* + L *amylum* starch — more at AMYL-] (1897) : a reserve carbohydrate that is found in various protozoans and algae and resembles starch

para·myxo·vi·rus \ˌpa-rə-ˈmik-sə-ˌvī-rəs\ *n* [NL] (1962) : any of a family (*Paramyxoviridae*) of single-stranded RNA viruses that include the parainfluenza viruses, the respiratory syncytial virus, and the causative agents of canine distemper, measles, mumps, Newcastle disease, and rinderpest

pa·rang \ˈpär-ˌaŋ\ *n* [Malay] (1839) : a short sword, cleaver, or machete common in Malaysia and Indonesia

para·noia \ˌper-ə-ˈnȯi-ə, ˌpa-rə-\ *n* [NL, fr. Gk, madness, fr. *paranous* demented, fr. *para-* + *nous* mind] (ca. 1811) **1** : a psychosis characterized by systematized delusions of persecution or grandeur usu. without hallucinations **2** : a tendency on the part of an individual or group toward excessive or irrational suspiciousness and distrustfulness of others — **para·noi·ac** \-ˈnȯi-ˌak, -ˈnȯi-ik\ *also* **para·noic** \-ˈnȯi(-i)k, -ˈnō-ik\ *adj or n* — **para·noi·cal·ly** \-ˈnȯi(-i)-k(ə-)lē, -ˈnō-i-k(ə-)lē\ *adv*

para·noid \ˈper-ə-ˌnȯid, ˌpa-rə-\ *also* **para·noi·dal** \ˌper-ə-ˈnȯi-dᵊl, ˌpa-rə-\ *adj* (1904) **1** : characterized by or resembling paranoia **2** : characterized by suspiciousness, persecutory trends, or megalomania **3** : extremely fearful — **paranoid** *n*

paranoid schizophrenia *n* (1940) : schizophrenia characterized esp. by persecutory or grandiose delusions or hallucinations or by delusional jealousy

para·nor·mal \ˌpa-rə-ˈnȯr-məl, ˈpa-rə-ˌ\ *adj* (ca. 1920) : not scientifically explainable : SUPERNATURAL — **paranormal** *n* — **para·nor·mal·i·ty** \ˌpa-rə-ˌnȯr-ˈma-lə-tē\ *n* — **para·nor·mal·ly** \-ˈnȯr-mə-lē\ *adv*

para·nymph \ˈpa-rə-ˌnim(p)f\ *n* [LL *paranymphus,* fr. Gk *paranymphos,* fr. *para-* + *nymphē* bride — more at NUPTIAL] (1600) **1** : a friend going with a bridegroom to fetch home the bride in ancient Greece; *also* : the bridesmaid conducting the bride to the bridegroom **2 a** : BEST MAN **b** : BRIDESMAID

par·a·pet \ˈpa-rə-pət, -ˌpet\ *n* [It *parapetto,* fr. *parare* to shield (fr. L, to prepare) + *petto* chest, fr. L *pectus* — more at PARE, PECTORAL] (1590) **1** : a wall, rampart, or elevation of earth or stone to protect soldiers **2** : a low wall or railing to protect the edge of a platform, roof, or bridge — called also *parapet wall* — **par·a·pet·ed** \-ˌpe-təd\ *adj*

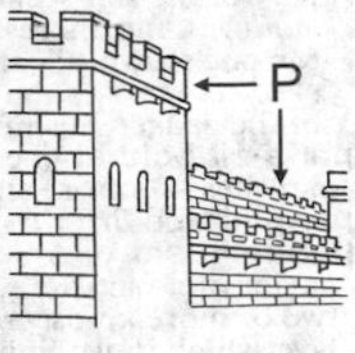

P parapet 1

pa·raph \ˈpa-rəf, pə-ˈraf\ *n* [MF, modif. of L *paragraphus* paragraph] (1584) : a flourish at the end of a signature

par·a·pher·na·lia \ˌper-ə-fə(r)-ˈnāl-yə, ˌpa-rə-\ *n pl but sing or pl in constr* [ML, ultim. fr. Gk *parapherna* bride's property beyond her dowry, fr. *para-* + *phernē* dowry, fr. *pherein* to bear — more at BEAR] (1651) **1** : the separate real or personal property of a married woman that she can dispose of by will and sometimes according to common law during her life **2** : personal belongings **3 a** : articles of equipment : FURNISHINGS **b** : accessory items : APPURTENANCES

para·phil·ia \ˌpa-rə-ˈfi-lē-ə\ *n* [NL] (1925) : a pattern of recurring sexually arousing mental imagery or behavior that involves unusual and esp. socially unacceptable sexual practices (as sadism or pedophilia) — **para·phil·iac** \-ˈfi-lē-ˌak\ *or* **para·phil·ic** \-ˈfi-lik\ *adj or n*

[1]**para·phrase** \ˈper-ə-ˌfrāz, ˈpa-rə-\ *n* [MF, fr. L *paraphrasis,* fr. Gk, fr. *paraphrazein* to paraphrase, fr. *para-* + *phrazein* to point out] (1548) **1** : a restatement of a text, passage, or work giving the meaning in another form **2** : the use or process of paraphrasing in studying or teaching composition

[2]**paraphrase** *vb* **-phrased; -phras·ing** *vi* (1596) : to make a paraphrase ~ *vt* : to make a paraphrase of — **para·phras·able** \ˌper-ə-ˈfrā-zə-bəl, ˌpa-rə-\ *adj* — **para·phras·er** *n*

para·phras·tic \ˌper-ə-ˈfras-tik, ˌpa-rə-\ *adj* [F *paraphrastique,* fr. Gk *paraphrastikos,* fr. *paraphrazein*] (ca. 1623) : having the nature of or being a paraphrase — **para·phras·ti·cal·ly** \-ti-k(ə-)lē\ *adv*

pa·raph·y·sis \pə-ˈra-fə-səs\ *n, pl* **-y·ses** \-ˌsēz\ [NL, fr. Gk, sucker, offshoot, fr. *paraphyein* to produce at the side, fr. *para-* + *phyein* to bring forth — more at BE] (1857) : one of the slender sterile filaments borne among the sporogenous or gametogenous organs in certain ferns, mosses, algae, and fungi

para·ple·gia \ˌpa-rə-ˈplē-j(ē-)ə\ *n* [NL, fr. Gk *paraplēgiē* hemiplegia, fr. *para-* + *-plēgia* -plegia] (ca. 1657) : paralysis of the lower half of the body with involvement of both legs — **para·ple·gic** \-jik\ *adj or n*

para·po·di·um \-ˈpō-dē-əm\ *n, pl* **-dia** \-dē-ə\ [NL] (1877) **1** : either of a pair of fleshy lateral processes borne by most segments of a polychaete worm **2** : a lateral expansion on each side of the foot usu. forming a broad swimming organ in some gastropods — **para·po·di·al** \-dē-əl\ *adj*

para·pro·fes·sion·al \-prə-ˈfesh-nəl, -ˈfe-shə-nᵊl\ *n* (1965) : a trained aide who assists a professional person (as a teacher or doctor) — **paraprofessional** *adj*

para·psy·chol·o·gy \ˌpa-rə-(ˌ)sī-ˈkä-lə-jē\ *n* [ISV] (1925) : a field of study concerned with the investigation of evidence for paranormal psychological phenomena (as telepathy, clairvoyance, and psychokinesis) — **para·psy·cho·log·i·cal** \-ˌsī-kə-ˈlä-ji-kəl\ *adj* — **para·psy·chol·o·gist** \-(ˌ)sī-ˈkä-lə-jist\ *n*

para·quat \ˈpa-rə-ˌkwät\ *n* [*para-* + *qua*ternary] (ca. 1961) : a highly toxic contact herbicide containing a salt of a cation $[C_{12}H_{14}N_2]^{2+}$

para·res·cue \ˈpa-rə-ˌres-(ˌ)kyü\ *n, often attrib* (1948) : a search and rescue mission by specially trained personnel who can parachute to the site ⟨a ~ team⟩ — **para·res·cue·man** \-ˌman, -mən\ *n* — **para·res·cu·er** \-ər\ *n*

para·ros·an·i·line \ˌpa-rə-ˌrō-ˈza-nᵊl-ən\ *n* [ISV [1]*para-* + *rosaniline* the compound $C_{20}H_{21}N_3O$, fr. L *rosa* rose + ISV *aniline*] (ca. 1879) : a white crystalline base $C_{19}H_{19}N_3O$ that is the parent compound of many dyes; *also* : its red chloride used esp. as a biological stain

Pa·ra rubber \ˈpa-rə-, pə-ˈrä-\ *n* [*Pará,* Brazil] (1857) : native rubber from So. American rubber trees (genus *Hevea* and esp. *H. brasiliensis*)

Para rubber tree *n* (1930) : a So. American rubber tree (*Hevea brasiliensis*)

para·sail·ing \ˈpa-rə-ˌsā-liŋ\ *n* (1967) : the recreational sport of soaring in a parachute while being towed usu. by a motorboat

par·a·sang \ˈpa-rə-ˌsaŋ\ *n* [L *parasanga,* fr. Gk *parasangēs,* of Iranian origin; akin to Pers *farsung* parasang] (1594) : any of various Persian units of distance; *esp* : an ancient unit of about four miles (six kilometers)

para·sex·u·al \ˌpa-rə-ˈsek-sh(ə-)wəl, -shəl\ *adj* (1954) : relating to or being reproduction that results in recombination of genes from different individuals but does not involve meiosis and formation of a zygote by fertilization as in sexual reproduction ⟨the ~ cycle in some fungi⟩ — **para·sex·u·al·i·ty** \-ˌsek-shə-ˈwa-lə-tē\ *n*

pa·ra·shah \ˈpär-ə-ˌshä\ *n* [Heb *pārāshāh,* lit., explanation] (ca. 1624) : a passage in Jewish Scripture dealing with a single topic; *specif* : a section of the Torah assigned for weekly reading in synagogue worship

par·a·site \ˈper-ə-ˌsīt, ˈpa-rə-\ *n* [MF, fr. L *parasitus,* fr. Gk *parasitos,* fr. *para-* + *sitos* grain, food] (1539) **1** : a person who exploits the hospitality of the rich and earns welcome by flattery **2** : an organism living in, with, or on another organism in parasitism **3** : something that resembles a biological parasite in dependence on something else for existence or support without making a useful or adequate return — **par·a·sit·ic** \ˌper-ə-ˈsi-tik, ˌpa-rə-\ *also* **par·a·sit·i·cal** \-ti-kəl\ *adj* — **par·a·sit·i·cal·ly** \-ti-k(ə-)lē\ *adv*

\ə\ **a**but \ᵊ\ kitten, F table \ər\ **fur**ther \a\ **a**sh \ā\ **a**ce \ä\ m**o**p, m**ar** \au̇\ **ou**t \ch\ **ch**in \e\ b**e**t \ē\ **ea**sy \g\ **g**o \i\ h**i**t \ī\ **i**ce \j\ **j**ob \ŋ\ si**ng** \ō\ g**o** \ȯ\ l**aw** \ȯi\ b**oy** \th\ **th**in \t͟h\ **th**e \ü\ l**oo**t \u̇\ f**oo**t \y\ **y**et \zh\ vi**si**on, bei**ge** \k̟, ⁿ, œ, ue, ʸ\ *see* Guide to Pronunciation *syn* PARASITE, SYCOPHANT, TOADY, LEECH, SPONGE mean a usu. obsequious flatterer or self-seeker. PARASITE applies to one who clings to a person of wealth, power, or influence or is useless to society ‹a jet-setter with an entourage of *parasites*›. SYCOPHANT adds to this a strong suggestion of fawning, flattery, or adulation ‹a powerful prince surrounded by *sycophants*›. TOADY emphasizes the servility and snobbery of the self-seeker ‹cultivated leaders of society and became their *toady*›. LEECH stresses persistence in clinging to or bleeding another for one's own advantage ‹a *leech* living off his family and friends›. SPONGE stresses the parasitic laziness, dependence, and opportunism of the cadger ‹a shiftless *sponge,* always looking for a handout›.

par·a·sit·i·cid·al \ˌper-ə-ˌsi-tə-ˈsī-dᵊl, ˌpa-rə-\ *adj* (1892) : destructive to parasites — **par·a·sit·i·cide** \-ˈsi-tə-ˌsīd\ *n*

par·a·sit·ise *Brit var of* PARASITIZE

par·a·sit·ism \ˈper-ə-sə-ˌti-zəm, -ˌsī-, ˌpa-rə-\ *n* (ca. 1611) **1 :** the behavior of a parasite **2 :** an intimate association between organisms of two or more kinds; *esp* : one in which a parasite obtains benefits from a host which it usu. injures **3 :** PARASITOSIS

par·a·sit·ize \-sə-ˌtīz, -ˌsī-\ *vt* **-ized; -iz·ing** (ca. 1890) : to infest or live on or with as a parasite — **par·a·sit·i·za·tion** \ˌper-ə-sə-tə-ˈzā-shən, -ˌsī-, ˌpa-rə-\ *n*

par·a·sit·oid \ˈper-ə-sə-ˌtȯid, -ˌsī-, ˌpa-rə-\ *n* (1922) : an insect and esp. a wasp that completes its larval development within the body of another insect eventually killing it and is free-living as an adult — **parasitoid** *adj*

par·a·si·tol·o·gy \ˌper-ə-sə-ˈtä-lə-jē, -ˌsī-, ˌpa-rə-\ *n* [L *parasitus* + ISV *-logy*] (1882) : a branch of biology dealing with parasites and parasitism esp. among animals — **par·a·si·to·log·i·cal** \-ˌsi-tə-ˈlä-ji-kəl, -ˌsī-\ *also* **par·a·si·to·log·ic** \-jik\ *adj* — **par·a·si·to·log·i·cal·ly** \-ji-k(ə-)lē\ *adv* — **par·a·si·tol·o·gist** \-sə-ˈtä-lə-jist, -ˌsī-\ *n*

par·a·sit·o·sis \-sə-ˈtō-səs, -ˌsī-\ *n, pl* **-o·ses** \-ˌsēz\ [NL] (ca. 1899) : infestation with or disease caused by parasites

par·a·sol \ˈper-ə-ˌsȯl, -ˌsäl, ˈpa-rə-\ *n* [F, fr. OIt *parasole,* fr. *parare* to shield + *sole* sun, fr. L *sol* — more at PARAPET, SOLAR] (1660) : a lightweight umbrella used as a sunshade

[1]**para·sym·pa·thet·ic** \ˌpa-rə-ˌsim-pə-ˈthe-tik\ *adj* [ISV] (1905) : of, relating to, being, or acting on the parasympathetic nervous system

[2]**parasympathetic** *n* (1925) **1 :** a parasympathetic nerve **2 :** PARASYMPATHETIC NERVOUS SYSTEM

parasympathetic nervous system *n* (ca. 1934) : the part of the autonomic nervous system that contains chiefly cholinergic fibers, that tends to induce secretion, to increase the tone and contractility of smooth muscle, and to slow heart rate, and that consists of a cranial and a sacral part — compare SYMPATHETIC NERVOUS SYSTEM

para·sym·pa·tho·mi·met·ic \ˌpar-ə-ˈsim-pə-(ˌ)thō-mī-ˈme-tik, -mə-\ *adj* [ISV] (1942) : simulating parasympathetic nervous action in physiological effect

para·syn·the·sis \ˌpa-rə-ˈsin(t)-thə-səs\ *n* [NL] (1862) : the formation of words by adding a derivative ending and prefixing a particle (as in *denationalize*) — **para·syn·thet·ic** \-sin-ˈthe-tik\ *adj*

para·tac·tic \ˌpa-rə-ˈtak-tik\ *also* **para·tac·ti·cal** \-ti-kəl\ *adj* (1871) : of or relating to parataxis — **para·tac·ti·cal·ly** \-ti-k(ə-)lē\ *adv*

para·tax·is \ˌpa-rə-ˈtak-səs\ *n* [NL, fr. Gk, act of placing side by side, fr. *paratassein* to place side by side, fr. *para-* + *tassein* to arrange] (ca. 1842) : the placing of clauses or phrases one after another without coordinating or subordinating connectives

para·thi·on \ˌpa-rə-ˈthī-ən, -ˌän\ *n* [*para-* + *thio*phosphate + [1]*-on*] (1947) : an extremely toxic insecticide $C_{10}H_{14}NO_5PS$

par·a·thor·mone \ˌpa-rə-ˈthȯr-ˌmōn\ *n* [fr. *Parathormone,* a trademark] (1925) : PARATHYROID HORMONE

[1]**para·thy·roid** \-ˈthī-ˌrȯid\ *n* (1895) : PARATHYROID GLAND

[2]**parathyroid** *adj* [ISV] (1895) : of, relating to, or produced by the parathyroid glands

para·thy·roid·ec·to·my \-ˌrȯi-ˈdek-tə-mē\ *n, pl* **-mies** (1903) : partial or complete excision of the parathyroid glands — **para·thy·roid·ec·to·mized** \-ˌmīzd\ *adj*

parathyroid gland *n* [ISV] (1895) : any of usu. four small endocrine glands that are adjacent to or embedded in the thyroid gland and produce parathyroid hormone

parathyroid hormone *n* (1953) : a hormone of the parathyroid gland that regulates the metabolism of calcium and phosphorus in the body

para·tran·sit \ˌpa-rə-ˈtran(t)-sət, -ˈtran-zət\ *n* (1973) : transportation service that supplements larger public transit systems by providing individualized rides without fixed routes or timetables

para·troop·er \ˈpa-rə-ˌtrü-pər\ *n* (1927) : a member of the paratroops

para·troops \-ˌtrüps\ *n pl* [[2]*para-*] (1940) : troops trained and equipped to parachute from an airplane — **para·troop** \-ˌtrüp\ *adj*

[1]**para·ty·phoid** \ˌpa-rə-ˈtī-ˌfȯid, -(ˌ)tī-ˈ\ *adj* [ISV] (1902) **1 :** resembling typhoid fever **2 :** of or relating to paratyphoid or its causative organisms ‹∼ infection›

[2]**paratyphoid** *n* (1902) : a salmonellosis that resembles typhoid fever and is commonly contracted by eating contaminated food — called also *paratyphoid fever*

para·vane \ˈpa-rə-ˌvān\ *n* [prob. fr. F *para-* warding off (as in *parachute*) + E *vane*] (1919) : a torpedo-shaped protective device with serrate teeth in its forward end used underwater by a ship in mined areas to sever the moorings of mines

par·boil \ˈpär-ˌbȯi(-ə)l\ *vt* [ME, fr. *parboilen* to boil thoroughly, fr. AF *parboiler, parbuillir,* fr. LL *perbullire,* fr. L *per-* thoroughly (fr. *per* through) + *bullire* to boil, fr. *bulla* bubble — more at FOR] (14c) : to boil briefly as a preliminary or incomplete cooking procedure

par·buck·le \ˈpär-ˌbə-kəl\ *n* [origin unknown] (1626) : a purchase for hoisting or lowering a cylindrical object by making fast the middle of a long rope aloft and looping both ends around the object which rests in the loops and rolls in them as the ends are hauled up or paid out; *also* : a single line made fast at one end and passed around an object that is used similarly — **parbuckle** *vt*

Par·cae \ˈpär-ˌkī, -ˌsē\ *n pl* [L] (1575) : FATE 4

[1]**par·cel** \ˈpär-səl\ *n* [ME, fr. AF *parcele,* fr. VL **particella,* fr. L *particula* small part — more at PARTICLE] (14c) **1 a :** FRAGMENT, PORTION **b :** a volume of a fluid (as air) considered as a single entity within a greater volume of the same fluid **2 :** a tract or plot of land **3 :** a company, collection, or group of persons, animals, or things : LOT ‹the whole story was a ∼ of lies› **4 a :** a wrapped bundle : PACKAGE **b :** a unit of salable merchandise

[2]**parcel** *adv* (15c) *archaic* : PARTLY

[3]**parcel** *adj* (15c) : PART-TIME, PARTIAL

[4]**parcel** *vt* **-celed** *or* **-celled; -cel·ing** *or* **-cel·ling** \ˈpär-s(ə-)liŋ\ (15c) **1 :** to divide into parts : DISTRIBUTE — often used with *out* **2 :** to make up into a parcel : WRAP **3 :** to cover (as a rope) with strips of canvas or tape

parcel post *n* (1837) **1 :** a mail service handling parcels **2 :** packages handled by parcel post

par·ce·nary \ˈpär-sə-ˌner-ē\ *n* [AF *parcenerie,* fr. *parcener*] (1544) : COPARCENARY 1

par·ce·ner \ˈpärs-nər, ˈpär-sə-nər\ *n* [AF, partner, joint heir, fr. OF *parcion* division, share, fr. L *partition-, partitio* — more at PARTITION] (1574) : COPARCENER

parch \ˈpärch\ *vb* [ME] *vt* (14c) **1 :** to toast under dry heat **2 :** to shrivel with heat **3 :** to dry or shrivel with cold ∼ *vi* : to become dry or scorched

parched \ˈpärcht\ *adj* (ca. 1552) : deprived of natural moisture; *also* : THIRSTY

Par·chee·si \pär-ˈchē-zē, pər-, *esp Brit* -sē\ *trademark* — used for a board game adapted from pachisi

parch·ment \ˈpärch-mənt\ *n* [ME *parchemin,* fr. AF, modif. of L *pergamena,* fr. Gk *pergamēnē,* fr. fem. of *Pergamēnos* of Pergamum, fr. *Pergamon* Pergamum] (14c) **1 :** the skin of a sheep or goat prepared for writing on **2 :** strong, tough, and often somewhat translucent paper made to resemble parchment **3 :** a parchment manuscript; *also* : an academic diploma

[1]**pard** \ˈpärd\ *n* [ME *parde,* fr. AF *pard,* fr. L *pardus,* fr. Gk *pardos*] (14c) : LEOPARD

[2]**pard** *n* [short for *pardner*] (1850) *chiefly dial* : PARTNER, CHUM

par·die *or* **par·di** *or* **par·dy** \pər-ˈdē, pär-\ *or* **per·die** \pər-, per-\ *interj* [ME *pardee,* fr. AF *par Dé* by God] (14c) *archaic* — used as a mild oath

pard·ner \ˈpärd-nər\ *n* [alter. of *partner*] (1795) *chiefly dial* : PARTNER, CHUM

[1]**par·don** \ˈpär-dᵊn\ *n* [ME, fr. AF *pardun, pardoun,* fr. *parduner*] (14c) **1 :** INDULGENCE 1 **2 :** the excusing of an offense without exacting a penalty **3 a :** a release from the legal penalties of an offense **b :** an official warrant of remission of penalty **4 :** excuse or forgiveness for a fault, offense, or discourtesy ‹I beg your ∼›

[2]**pardon** *vt* **par·doned; par·don·ing** \ˈpärd-niŋ, ˈpär-dᵊn-iŋ\ [ME, fr. AF *parduner,* fr. LL *perdonare* to grant freely, fr. L *per-* thoroughly + *donare* to give — more at PARBOIL, DONATION] (15c) **1 a :** to absolve from the consequences of a fault or crime **b :** to allow (an offense) to pass without punishment : FORGIVE **c :** to relieve of a penalty improperly assessed **2 :** TOLERATE *syn* see EXCUSE

par·don·able \ˈpärd-nə-bəl, ˈpär-dᵊn-ə-bəl\ *adj* (15c) : admitting of being pardoned : EXCUSABLE ‹∼ offenses› — **par·don·able·ness** *n* — **par·don·ably** \-blē\ *adv*

par·don·er \ˈpärd-nər, ˈpär-dᵊn-ər\ *n* (14c) **1 :** a medieval preacher delegated to raise money for religious works by soliciting offerings and granting indulgences **2 :** one that pardons

pare \ˈper\ *vt* **pared; par·ing** [ME, fr. AF *parer* to make, prepare, pare, fr. L *parare* to prepare, acquire; akin to L *parere* to give birth to, produce, Gk *porein* to give, present, Skt *pṛṇāti* he gives] (14c) **1 :** to trim off an outside, excess, or irregular part of ‹∼ apples› ‹*paring* his nails› **2 :** to diminish or reduce by or as if by paring ‹∼ expenses› ‹the novel was *pared* down to 200 pages› — **par·er** *n*

par·e·gor·ic \ˌpa-rə-ˈgȯr-ik, -ˈgär-\ *n* [F *parégorique* mitigating pain, fr. LL *paregoricus,* fr. Gk *parēgorikos,* fr. *parēgorein* to talk over, soothe, fr. *para-* + *agora* assembly, fr. *ageirein* to gather] (ca. 1827) : camphorated tincture of opium used esp. to relieve pain

pa·ren·chy·ma \pə-ˈreŋ-kə-mə\ *n* [NL, fr. Gk, visceral flesh, fr. *parenchein* to pour in beside, fr. *para-* + *en-* en- + *chein* to pour — more at FOUND] (1615) **1 :** the essential and distinctive tissue of an organ or an abnormal growth as distinguished from its supportive framework **2 :** a tissue of higher plants that consists of thin-walled living photosynthetic or storage cells capable of division even when mature and that makes up much of the substance of leaves and roots, the pulp of fruits, and parts of stems and supporting structures — **pa·ren·chy·mal** \pə-ˈreŋ-kə-məl, ˌpa-rən-ˈkī\ *adj* — **par·en·chy·ma·tous** \ˌpa-rən-ˈkī-mə-təs, -ˈki-\ *adj*

[1]**par·ent** \ˈper-ənt\ *n* [ME, fr. AF, fr. L *parent-, parens;* akin to L *parere* to give birth to] (15c) **1 a :** one that begets or brings forth offspring **b :** a person who brings up and cares for another **2 a :** an animal or plant that is regarded in relation to its offspring **b :** the material or source from which something is derived **c :** a group from which another arises and to which it usu. remains subsidiary ‹a ∼ company› — **parent** *adj* — **pa·ren·tal** \pə-ˈren-tᵊl\ *adj* — **pa·ren·tal·ly** \-tᵊl-ē\ *adv* — **par·ent·less** \ˈper-ənt-ləs\ *adj*

[2]**parent** *vt* (1663) : to be or act as the parent of : ORIGINATE, PRODUCE ∼ *vi* : to be or act as a parent

par·ent·age \ˈper-ən-tij\ *n* [ME, fr. AF, fr. *parent*] (15c) **1 a :** descent from parents or ancestors : LINEAGE ‹a person of noble ∼› **b :** DERIVATION, ORIGIN ‹a tradition of uncertain ∼› **2 :** PARENTHOOD

par·en·ter·al \pa-ˈren-tə-rəl\ *adj* [ISV *para-* + *enteral*] (ca. 1910) : situated or occurring outside the intestine; *esp* : introduced otherwise than by way of the intestines — **par·en·ter·al·ly** \-rə-lē\ *adv*

pa·ren·the·sis \pə-ˈren(t)-thə-səs\ *n, pl* **-the·ses** \-ˌsēz\ [LL, fr. Gk, lit., act of inserting, fr. *parentithenai* to insert, fr. *para-* + *en-* en- + *tithenai* to place — more at DO] (ca. 1550) **1 a :** an amplifying or explanatory word, phrase, or sentence inserted in a passage from which it is usu. set off by punctuation **b :** a remark or passage that departs from the theme of a discourse : DIGRESSION **2 :** INTERLUDE, INTERVAL **3 :** one or both of the curved marks ( ) used in writing and printing to enclose a parenthetical expression or to group a symbolic unit in a logical or mathematical expression — **par·en·thet·i·cal** \ˌper-ən-ˈthe-ti-kəl, pa-rən-\ *also* **par·en·thet·ic** \-tik\ *adj* — **par·en·thet·i·cal·ly** \-ti-k(ə-)lē\ *adv*

pa·ren·the·size \pə-ˈren(t)-thə-ˌsīz\ *vt* **-sized; -siz·ing** (1837) : to make a parenthesis of : enclose within parentheses

par·ent·hood \ˈper-ənt-ˌhu̇d\ *n* (1856) : the state of being a parent; *specif* : the position, function, or standing of a parent

par·ent·ing \ˈper-ən-tiŋ\ *n* (1958) **1** : the raising of a child by its parents **2** : the act or process of becoming a parent **3** : the taking care of someone in the manner of a parent
parent–teacher association *n, often cap P&T&A* (1915) : an organization of local groups of teachers and the parents of their pupils that works for the improvement of the schools and the benefit of the pupils
pa·re·sis \pə-ˈrē-səs, ˈpa-rə-\ *n, pl* **pa·re·ses** \-ˌsēz\ [NL, fr. Gk, fr. *parienai* to let fall, fr. *para-* + *hienai* to let go, send — more at JET] (1693) **1** : slight or partial paralysis **2** : GENERAL PARESIS — **pa·ret·ic** \pə-ˈre-tik\ *adj or n*
par·es·the·sia \ˌpar-əs-ˈthē-zhə\ *n* [NL, fr. *para-* + *-esthesia* (as in *anesthesia*)] (ca. 1860) : a sensation of pricking, tingling, or creeping on the skin that has no objective cause — **par·es·thet·ic** \-ˈthe-tik\ *adj*
pa·reu *or* **pa·reo** \ˈpär-ā-(ˌ)ü\ *n* [Tahitian] (1860) : a wraparound skirt usu. made from a rectangular piece of printed cloth and worn by men and women throughout Polynesia
pa·re·ve \ˈpär-(ə-)və\ *or* **par·ve** \ˈpär-və\ *adj* [Yiddish *parev*] (1939) : made without milk, meat, or their derivatives ⟨~ margarine⟩ — compare FLEISHIG, MILCHIG
par ex·cel·lence \ˌpär-ˌek-sə-ˈläⁿs\ *adj* [F, lit., by excellence] (1695) : being the best of a kind : PREEMINENT ⟨a chef *par excellence*⟩
par·fait \pär-ˈfā\ *n* [F, lit., something perfect, fr. *parfait* perfect, fr. L *perfectus*] (1894) **1** : a flavored custard containing whipped cream and syrup frozen without stirring **2** : a cold dessert made of layers of fruit, syrup, ice cream, and whipped cream
parfait glass *n* (ca. 1951) : a tall narrow glass with a short stem
par·fleche \ˈpär-ˌflesh\ *n* [CanF *parflèche*, fr. F *parer* to ward off + *flèche* arrow] (1827) **1** : a raw hide soaked in lye to remove the hair and dried **2** : an article (as a bag or case) made of parfleche
par·fo·cal \ˌpär-ˈfō-kəl\ *adj* [L *par* equal + E *focal*] (ca. 1886) : being or having lenses or lens sets (as eyepieces) with the corresponding focal points all in the same plane — **par·fo·cal·i·ty** \ˌpär-fō-ˈka-lə-tē\ *n* — **par·fo·cal·ize** \ˌpär-ˈfō-kə-ˌlīz\ *vt*
parge \ˈpärj\ *vt* **parged; parg·ing** (1701) : PARGET
[1]**par·get** \ˈpär-jət\ *vt* **-get·ed** *or* **-get·ted; -get·ing** *or* **-get·ting** [ME *pargetten*, fr. MF *parjeter*, lit., to throw out, fr. *par-* thoroughly (fr. L *per-*) + *jeter* to throw — more at JET] (14c) : to coat with plaster; *esp* : to apply ornamental or waterproofing plaster to
[2]**parget** *n* (14c) **1** : plaster, whitewash, or roughcast for coating a wall **2** : plasterwork esp. in raised ornamental figures on walls
par·gy·line \ˈpär-jə-ˌlēn\ *n* [pro*pargyl*, an alcohol + [2]*-ine*] (1961) : a monoamine oxidase inhibitor $C_{11}H_{13}N$ that is used in the form of its hydrochloride esp. as an antihypertensive agent
parhelic circle *n* (1890) : a luminous circle or halo parallel to the horizon at the altitude of the sun — called also *parhelic ring*
par·he·lion \pär-ˈhēl-yən\ *n, pl* **-lia** \-yə\ [L *parelion*, fr. Gk *parēlion*, fr. *para-* + *hēlios* sun — more at SOLAR] (1647) : any of several bright spots often tinged with color that often appear on the parhelic circle — called also *sun dog* — **par·he·lic** \-ˈhē-lik\ *adj*
pa·ri·ah \pə-ˈrī-ə\ *n* [Tamil *paṟaiyaṉ*, lit., drummer] (1613) **1** : a member of a low caste of southern India **2** : one that is despised or rejected : OUTCAST
par·i·an \ˈper-ē-ən\ *n* [*Parian*, adj.; fr. its suitability for making statuettes] (1847) : a porcelain composed essentially of kaolin and feldspar and usu. used unglazed in ornamental articles
Par·i·an \ˈper-ē-ən\ *adj* (1578) : of or relating to the island of Paros noted for its marble used extensively for sculpture in ancient times
Parian ware *n* (1860) **1** : PARIAN **2** : articles made of parian
[1]**pa·ri·e·tal** \pə-ˈrī-ə-tᵊl\ *adj* [ME, fr. ML *parietalis*, fr. *pariet-, paries* wall of a cavity or hollow organ, fr. L, wall] (15c) **1 a** : of or relating to the walls of a part or cavity **b** : of, relating to, or forming the upper posterior wall of the head **2** : attached to the main wall rather than the axis or a cross wall of a plant ovary — used of an ovule or a placenta **3** : of or relating to college living or its regulation; *esp* : of or relating to parietals
[2]**parietal** *n* (15c) **1** : a parietal part (as a bone, scale, or plate) **2** *pl* : the regulations governing the visiting privileges of members of the opposite sex in campus dormitories
parietal bone *n* (15c) : either of a pair of bones of the roof of the skull between the frontal bones and the occipital bones
parietal cell *n* (1875) : any of the large oval cells of the gastric mucous membrane that secrete hydrochloric acid
parietal lobe *n* (ca. 1889) : the middle division of each cerebral hemisphere that contains an area concerned with bodily sensations
pari–mu·tu·el \ˌper-i-ˈmyü-chə-wəl, -chəl, ˌpa-ri-; -ˈmyüch-wəl\ *n* [F *pari mutuel*, lit., mutual stake] (1881) **1** : a betting pool in which those who bet on competitors finishing in the first three places share the total amount bet minus a percentage for the management **2** : a machine for registering the bets and computing the payoffs in pari-mutuel betting
paring *n* (14c) **1** : the act of cutting away an edge or surface **2** : something pared off ⟨apple ~*s*⟩
paring knife *n* (ca. 1580) : a small short-bladed knife (as for paring fruit)
pa·ri pas·su \ˈpa-ri-ˈpa-(ˌ)sü\ *adv or adj* [L, with equal step] (1567) : at an equal rate or pace
Par·is \ˈpa-rəs\ *n* [L, fr. Gk] (14c) : a son of Priam whose abduction of Helen leads to the Trojan War
Par·is green \ˈpa-rəs-\ *n* [*Paris*, France] (1868) **1** : a very poisonous green copper and arsenic compound $C_4H_6As_6Cu_4O_{16}$ used esp. formerly as an insecticide and pigment **2** : a brilliant yellowish green
par·ish \ˈper-ish, ˈpa-rish\ *n* [ME *parisshe*, fr. AF *paroche, parosse*, fr. LL *parochia*, fr. LGk *paroikia*, fr. *paroikos* Christian, fr. Gk, stranger, fr. *para-* + *oikos* house — more at VICINITY] (14c) **1 a (1)** : the ecclesiastical unit of area committed to one pastor **(2)** : the residents of such an area **b** *Brit* : a subdivision of a county often coinciding with an original ecclesiastical parish and constituting the unit of local government **2** : a local church community composed of the members or constituents of a Protestant church **3** : a civil division of the state of Louisiana corresponding to a county in other states
pa·rish·ion·er \pə-ˈri-sh(ə-)nər\ *n* [ME *parisshoner*, prob. modif. of AF *parochien*, fr. *paroche*] (15c) : a member or inhabitant of a parish
[1]**par·i·ty** \ˈper-ə-tē, ˈpa-rə-\ *n, pl* **-ties** [L *paritas*, fr. *par* equal] (1608) **1** : the quality or state of being equal or equivalent **2 a** : equivalence of a commodity price expressed in one currency to its price expressed in another **b** : equality of purchasing power established by law between different kinds of money at a given ratio **3** : an equivalence between farmers' current purchasing power and their purchasing power at a selected base period maintained by government support of agricultural commodity prices **4 a** : the property of an integer with respect to being odd or even ⟨3 and 7 have the same ~⟩ **b (1)** : the state of being odd or even used as the basis of a method of detecting errors in binary-coded data **(2)** : PARITY BIT **5** : the property of oddness or evenness of a quantum mechanical function **6** : the symmetry of behavior in an interaction of a physical entity (as a subatomic particle) with that of its mirror image
[2]**parity** *n* [*-parous*] (1878) : the state or fact of having borne offspring; *also* : the number of children previously borne
parity bit *n* (1957) : a bit added to an array of bits (as on magnetic tape) to provide parity
[1]**park** \ˈpärk\ *n* [ME, fr. AF, fr. ML *parricus*, fr. pre-L **parra* pole, trellis] (13c) **1 a** : an enclosed piece of ground stocked with game and held by royal prescription or grant **b** : a tract of land that often includes lawns, woodland, and pasture attached to a country house and is used as a game preserve and for recreation **2 a** : a piece of ground in or near a city or town kept for ornament and recreation **b** : an area maintained in its natural state as a public property **3 a** : a space occupied by military vehicles, materials, or animals **b** : PARKING LOT **4** : an enclosed arena or stadium used esp. for ball games **5** : an area designed for a specified type of use (as industrial, commercial, or residential use) ⟨amusement ~*s*⟩ — **park·like** \ˈpärk-ˌlīk\ *adj*
[2]**park** *vt* (1526) **1** : to enclose in a park **2 a (1)** : to bring (a vehicle) to a stop and keep standing at the edge of a public way **(2)** : to leave temporarily on a public way or in a parking lot or garage **b** : to land and leave (as an airplane) **c** : to establish (as a satellite) in orbit **3 a** : to set and leave temporarily ⟨~*ed* his book on the chair⟩ **b** : to place, settle, or establish esp. for a considerable time ⟨kids ~*ed* in front of the TV⟩ ~ *vi* : to park a vehicle — **park·er** *n*
par·ka \ˈpär-kə\ *n* [Aleut, fr. Russ dial., ultim. fr. Nenets (Samoyedic language of northern Russia)] (1780) **1** : a hooded fur pullover garment for arctic wear **2** : a usu. lined fabric outerwear pullover or jacket
park·ing brake \ˈpär-kiŋ-\ *n* (1924) : EMERGENCY BRAKE
parking lot *n* (1924) : an area used for the parking of motor vehicles
parking meter *n* (1935) : a coin-operated device which registers the purchase of parking time for a motor vehicle
par·kin·so·nian \ˌpär-kən-ˈsō-nē-ən, -nyən\ *adj* (1906) **1** : of or similar to that of parkinsonism **2** : affected with parkinsonism and esp. Parkinson's disease
par·kin·son·ism \ˈpär-kən-sə-ˌni-zəm\ *n* (ca. 1923) **1** : PARKINSON'S DISEASE **2** : a neurological disorder resembling Parkinson's disease
Par·kin·son's disease \ˈpär-kən-sənz-\ *n* [James *Parkinson* †1824 Eng. physician] (1877) : a chronic progressive neurological disease chiefly of later life that is linked to decreased dopamine production in the substantia nigra and is marked esp. by tremor of resting muscles, rigidity, slowness of movement, impaired balance, and a shuffling gait — called also *paralysis agitans, Parkinson's, Parkinson's syndrome*
Parkinson's Law *n* [C. Northcote *Parkinson* †1993 Eng. historian] (1955) **1** : an observation in office organization: the number of subordinates increases at a fixed rate regardless of the amount of work produced **2** : an observation in office organization: work expands so as to fill the time available for its completion
park·land \ˈpärk-ˌland\ *n* (1862) : land with clumps of trees and shrubs in cultivated condition used as or suitable for use as a park
par·kour \pär-ˈku̇r, ˈpär-ˌku̇r\ *n* [F, alter. of *parcours* course, route, fr. ML *percursus*, fr. L *percurrere* to run through, fr. *per-* + *currere* to run] (2002) : the sport of traversing environmental obstacles by running, climbing, or leaping rapidly and efficiently
park·way \ˈpärk-ˌwā\ *n* (1887) : a broad landscaped thoroughfare
par·lance \ˈpär-lən(t)s\ *n* [MF, fr. OF, fr. *parler*] (1577) **1** : SPEECH; *esp* : formal debate or parley **2** : manner or mode of speech : IDIOM
par·lan·do \pär-ˈlän-(ˌ)dō\ *or* **par·lan·te** \-(ˌ)tā\ *adj* [*parlando* fr. It, verbal of *parlare* to speak, fr. ML *parabolare*; *parlante* fr. It, prp. of *parlare*] (ca. 1854) : delivered or performed in a style suggestive of speech — used as a direction in music
[1]**par·lay** \ˈpär-ˌlā, -lē\ *vt* [F *paroli*, n., parlay, fr. It dial., pl. of *parolo*, perh. fr. *paro* equal, fr. L *par*] (1828) **1** : to bet in a parlay **2 a** : to exploit successfully **b** : to increase or otherwise transform into something of much greater value
[2]**parlay** *n* (1904) : a series of two or more bets so set up in advance that the original stake plus its winnings are risked on the successive wagers; *broadly* : the fresh risking of an original stake together with its winnings
parle \ˈpär(-ə)l\ *vi* **parled; parl·ing** [ME, to parley, fr. AF *parler*] (14c) *archaic* : PARLEY — **parle** *n, archaic*
[1]**par·ley** \ˈpär-lē\ *vi* **par·leyed; par·ley·ing** (1570) : to speak with another : CONFER; *specif* : to discuss terms with an enemy
[2]**parley** *n, pl* **parleys** [ME *parlai* speech, prob. fr. MF *parlee*, fr. fem. of *parlé*, pp. of *parler* to speak, fr. ML *parabolare*, fr. LL *parabola* speech, parable — more at PARABLE] (1580) **1 a** : a conference for discussion of points in dispute **b** : a conference with an enemy **2** : DISCUSSION
par·lia·ment \ˈpär-lə-mənt *also* ˈpärl-yə-\ *n* [ME, fr. AF *parlement*, fr. *parler*] (13c) **1** : a formal conference for the discussion of public affairs; *specif* : a council of state in early medieval England **2 a** : an assemblage of the nobility, clergy, and commons called together by the British sovereign as the supreme legislative body in the United Kingdom **b** : a similar assemblage in another nation or state **3 a** : the supreme legislative body of a usu. major political unit that is a continuing institution comprising a series of individual assemblages **b** : the British House of Commons **4** : one of several principal courts of justice existing in France before the Revolution of 1789
par·lia·men·tar·i·an \ˌpär-lə-ˌmen-ˈter-ē-ən, -mən- *also* ˌpärl-yə-\ *n*

(1644) **1** *often cap* **:** an adherent of the parliament in opposition to the king during the English Civil War **2 :** an expert in the rules and usages of a deliberative assembly (as a parliament) **3 :** a member of a parliament

par·lia·men·ta·ry \-ˈmen-t(ə-)rē\ *adj* (1604) **1 a :** of or relating to a parliament **b :** enacted, done, or ratified by a parliament **2 :** of or adhering to the parliament as opposed to the king during the English Civil War **3 :** of, based on, or having the characteristics of parliamentary government **4 :** of or relating to members of a parliament **5 :** of or according to parliamentary law ‹∼ procedure›

parliamentary government *n* (1844) **:** a system of government having the real executive power vested in a cabinet composed of members of the legislature who are individually and collectively responsible to the legislature

parliamentary law *n* (1869) **:** the rules and precedents governing the proceedings of deliberative assemblies and other organizations

[1]**par·lor** \ˈpär-lər\ *n* [ME *parlour,* fr. AF, fr. *parler*] (13c) **1 :** a room used primarily for conversation or the reception of guests: as **a :** a room in a private dwelling for the entertainment of guests **b :** a conference chamber or private reception room **c :** a room in an inn, hotel, or club for conversation or semiprivate uses **2 :** any of various business places ‹a funeral ∼› ‹a beauty ∼›

[2]**parlor** *adj* (1552) **1 :** used in or suitable for a parlor ‹∼ furniture› **2 a :** fostered or advocated in comfortable seclusion without consequent action or application to affairs ‹∼ bolshevism› **b :** given to or characterized by fostering or advocating something (as a doctrine) in such a manner ‹∼ socialist›

parlor car *n* (1868) **:** an extra-fare railroad passenger car for day travel equipped with individual chairs

parlor game *n* (1872) **:** a game suitable for playing indoors

parlor grand *n* (1856) **:** a grand piano intermediate in length between a concert grand and a baby grand

par·lour \ˈpär-lər\ *chiefly Brit var of* PARLOR

par·lous \ˈpär-ləs\ *adj* [ME, alter. of *perilous*] (14c) **1** *obs* **:** dangerously shrewd or cunning **2 :** full of danger or risk — **par·lous·ly** *adv*

Par·me·san \ˈpär-mə-ˌzän, -ˌzhän, -zən, -ˌzan\ *n* [*Parmesan* of Parma, fr. MF *parmesan,* fr. north It dial. *parmežan*] (1538) **:** a very hard dry sharply flavored cheese that is sold grated or in wedges

par·mi·gia·na \ˌpär-mi-ˈjä-nə, -ˈzhän; ˈpär-mi-ˌzhän, -ˌzän\ *or* **par·mi·gia·no** \-ˈjä-(ˌ)nō\ *adj* [It *parmigiana,* fem. of *parmigiano* of Parma, fr. *Parma*] (ca. 1684) **:** made or covered with Parmesan cheese ‹veal ∼›

Par·nas·si·an \pär-ˈna-sē-ən\ *adj* (1629) **1** [L *parnassius* of Parnassus, fr. Gk *parnasios,* fr. *Parnasos* Parnassus, mountain in Greece sacred to Apollo and the Muses] **:** of or relating to poetry **2** [F *parnassien,* fr. *Parnasse* Parnassus; fr. *Le Parnasse contemporain* (1866), an anthology of poetry] **:** of or relating to a school of French poets of the second half of the 19th century emphasizing metrical form rather than emotion — **Parnassian** *n*

pa·ro·chi·al \pə-ˈrō-kē-əl\ *adj* [ME *parochiall,* fr. AF *parochial,* fr. LL *parochialis,* fr. *parochia* parish — more at PARISH] (14c) **1 :** of or relating to a church parish **2 :** of or relating to a parish as a unit of local government **3 :** confined or restricted as if within the borders of a parish **:** limited in range or scope (as to a narrow area or region) **:** PROVINCIAL, NARROW — **pa·ro·chi·al·ly** \-kē-ə-lē\ *adv*

pa·ro·chi·al·ism \-kē-ə-ˌli-zəm\ *n* (1847) **:** the quality or state of being parochial; *esp* **:** selfish pettiness or narrowness (as of interests, opinions, or views)

parochial school *n* (1755) **:** a private school maintained by a religious body usu. for elementary and secondary instruction

par·o·dist \ˈper-ə-dist, ˈpa-rə-\ *n* (1742) **:** a writer of parodies

[1]**par·o·dy** \ˈper-ə-dē, ˈpa-rə-\ *n, pl* **-dies** [L *parodia,* fr. Gk *parōidia,* fr. *para-* + *aidein* to sing — more at ODE] (1598) **1 :** a literary or musical work in which the style of an author or work is closely imitated for comic effect or in ridicule **2 :** a feeble or ridiculous imitation ***syn*** see CARICATURE — **pa·rod·ic** \pə-ˈrä-dik, pa-\ *adj* — **par·o·dis·tic** \ˌper-ə-ˈdis-tik, ˌpa-rə-\ *adj*

[2]**parody** *vt* **-died; -dy·ing** (ca. 1745) **1 :** to compose a parody on ‹∼ a poem› **2 :** to imitate in the manner of a parody

par·ol \ˈper-əl, ˈpa-rəl\ *n* [MF *parole*] (1590) **:** WORD OF MOUTH — **parol** *adj*

[1]**pa·role** \pə-ˈrōl\ *n* [F, speech, parole, fr. MF, fr. LL *parabola* speech — more at PARABLE] (1531) **1 :** a promise made with or confirmed by a pledge of one's honor; *esp* **:** the promise of a prisoner of war to fulfill stated conditions in consideration of his release **2 :** a watchword given only to officers of the guard and of the day **3 :** a conditional release of a prisoner serving an indeterminate or unexpired sentence **4 a :** language viewed as a specific individual usage **:** PERFORMANCE **b :** a linguistic act — compare LANGUE — **parole** *adj*

[2]**parole** *vt* **pa·roled; pa·rol·ing** (1781) **:** to release (a prisoner) on parole

pa·rol·ee \pə-ˌrō-ˈlē, -ˈrō-(ˌ); ˌper-ə-ˈlē, ˌpa-rə-\ *n* (1903) **:** one released on parole

par·o·no·ma·sia \ˌpa-rə-nō-ˈmā-zh(ē-)ə, ˌpa-ˌrä-nə-ˈmā-\ *n* [L, fr. Gk, fr. *paronomazein* to call with a slight change of name, fr. *para-* + *onoma* name — more at NAME] (1577) **:** a play on words **:** PUN — **par·o·no·mas·tic** \-ˈmas-tik\ *adj*

par·o·nym \ˈpa-rə-ˌnim\ *n* [LL *paronymon,* fr. Gk *parōnymon,* neut. of *parōnymos*] (ca. 1846) **:** a paronymous word

par·on·y·mous \pə-ˈrä-nə-məs, pa-\ *adj* [Gk *parōnymos,* fr. *para-* + *-ōnymos* (as in *homōnymos* homonymous)] (1656) **1 :** CONJUGATE 4 **2 a :** formed from a word in another language **b :** having a form similar to that of a cognate foreign word

pa·rot·id \pə-ˈrä-təd\ *adj* [NL *parotid-, parotis* parotid gland, fr. L, tumor near the ear, fr. Gk *parōtid-, parōtis,* fr. *para-* + *ōt-, ous* ear — more at EAR] (1687) **:** of or relating to the parotid gland

parotid gland *n* (ca. 1771) **:** a serous salivary gland situated on each side of the face below and in front of the ear

par·o·ti·tis \ˌpa-rō-ˈtī-təs\ *n* (1822) **:** inflammation of the parotid glands; *also* **:** MUMPS

par·ous \ˈper-əs\ *adj* [*-parous*] (ca. 1889) **:** having produced offspring

-parous *adj comb form* [L *-parus,* fr. *parere* to give birth to, produce — more at PARE] **:** giving birth to **:** producing ‹multi*parous*›

Par·ou·sia \ˌpär-ü-ˈsē-ə, pə-ˈrü-zē-ə\ *n* [Gk, lit., presence, fr. *paront-, parōn,* prp. of *pareinai* to be present, fr. *para-* + *einai* to be — more at IS] (1844) **:** SECOND COMING

par·ox·e·tine \pa-ˈräk-sə-ˌtēn\ *n* [perh. fr. ISV *par-* (alter. of pi*per*idine) + *ox-* + meth*yl* + [2]*-ine*] (1977) **:** a drug $C_{19}H_{20}FNO_3$ that enhances serotonin activity and is usu. administered in the form of its hydrochloride to treat depression

par·ox·ysm \ˈpa-rək-ˌsi-zəm *also* pə-ˈräk-\ *n* [ME *paroxism,* fr. ML *paroxysmus,* fr. Gk *paroxysmos,* fr. *paroxynein* to stimulate, fr. *para-* + *oxynein* to provoke, fr. *oxys* sharp — more at OXYGEN] (15c) **1 :** a fit, attack, or sudden increase or recurrence of symptoms (as of a disease) **:** CONVULSION ‹a ∼ of coughing› **2 :** a sudden violent emotion or action **:** OUTBURST ‹a ∼ of rage› — **par·ox·ys·mal** \ˌpa-rək-ˈsiz-məl *also* pə-ˌräk-\ *adj*

[1]**par·quet** \pär-ˈkā\ *vt* **par·queted** \-ˈkād\; **par·quet·ing** \-ˈkā-iŋ\ (1678) **1 :** to furnish with a floor of parquet **2 :** to make of parquetry

[2]**par·quet** \ˈpär-ˌkā, pär-ˈ\ *n* [F, fr. MF, small enclosure, fr. *parc* park] (1816) **1 a :** a patterned wood surface (as flooring or paneling); *esp* **:** one made of parquetry **b :** PARQUETRY **2 :** the main floor of a theater; *specif* **:** the part from the front of the stage to the parquet circle

parquet circle *n* (1854) **:** the part of the main floor of a theater that is beneath the galleries

par·que·try \ˈpär-kə-trē\ *n, pl* **-tries** (ca. 1842) **:** work in the form of usu. geometrically patterned wood laid or inlaid esp. for floors

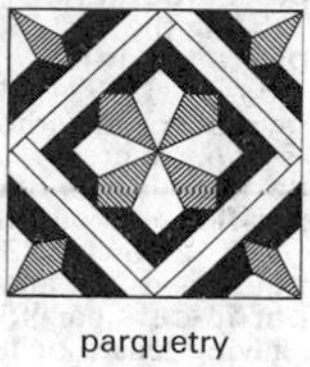
parquetry

parr \ˈpär\ *n, pl* **parr** *also* **parrs** [origin unknown] (ca. 1722) **:** a young salmon actively feeding in freshwater

par·rel *or* **par·ral** \ˈpa-rəl\ *n* [ME *perel, parelle,* short for *apparail* apparel (rigging)] (15c) **:** a rope loop or sliding collar by which a yard or spar is held to a mast in such a way that it may be hoisted or lowered

par·ri·cid·al \ˌpa-rə-ˈsī-dᵊl\ *adj* (1627) **:** of, relating to, or guilty of parricide

par·ri·cide \ˈpa-rə-ˌsīd\ *n* (1554) **1** [L *parricida* killer of a close relative, fr. *parri-* (perh. akin to Gk *pēos* kinsman by marriage) + *-cida* -cide] **:** one that murders his or her father, mother, or a close relative **2** [L *parricidium* murder of a close relative, fr. *parri-* + *-cidium* -cide] **:** the act of a parricide

[1]**par·rot** \ˈper-ət, ˈpa-rət\ *n* [prob. modif. of MF *perroquet*] (ca. 1525) **1 :** any of numerous widely distributed tropical birds (order Psittaciformes and esp. family Psittacidae) that are often crested and brightly colored, have a distinctive stout hooked bill and zygodactyl feet, and include some excellent mimics **2 :** a person who sedulously echoes another's words — **parrot** *adj*

[2]**parrot** *vt* (1596) **:** to repeat by rote

parrot fever *n* (1930) **:** PSITTACOSIS

parrot fish *n* (1712) **:** any of a family (Scaridae) of usu. brightly colored chiefly tropical marine fishes that have the teeth in each jaw fused into a cutting plate resembling a beak

par·ry \ˈper-ē, ˈpa-rē\ *vb* **par·ried; par·ry·ing** [prob. fr. F *parez,* imper. of *parer* to parry, fr. Old Occitan *parar,* fr. L *parare* to prepare — more at PARE] *vi* (1672) **1 :** to ward off a weapon or blow **2 :** to evade or turn aside something ∼ *vt* **1 :** to ward off (as a blow) **2 :** to evade esp. by an adroit answer ‹*parried* the question› — **parry** *n*

[1]**parse** \ˈpärs, *chiefly Brit* ˈpärz\ *vb* **parsed; pars·ing** [L *pars orationis* part of speech] *vt* (ca. 1553) **1 a :** to resolve (as a sentence) into component parts of speech and describe them grammatically **b :** to describe grammatically by stating the part of speech and explaining the inflection and syntactical relationships **2 :** to examine in a minute way **:** analyze critically ‹having trouble *parsing* . . . explanations for dwindling market shares —R. S. Anson› ∼ *vi* **1 :** to give a grammatical description of a word or a group of words **2 :** to admit of being parsed

[2]**parse** *n* (1963) **:** a product or an instance of parsing

par·sec \ˈpär-ˌsek\ *n* [*par*allax + *sec*ond] (1913) **:** a unit of measure for interstellar space that is equal to 3.26 light-years and is the distance to an object having a parallax of one second as seen from points separated by one astronomical unit

pars·er \ˈpär-sər\ *n* (ca. 1864) **:** one that parses; *specif* **:** a computer program that breaks down text into recognized strings of characters for further analysis

Par·si *also* **Par·see** \ˈpär-(ˌ)sē\ *n* [Pers *pārsī,* fr. *Pārs* Persia] (1583) **1 :** a Zoroastrian descended from Persian refugees settled principally at Mumbai (Bombay) **2 :** the Iranian dialect of the Parsi religious literature — **Par·si·ism** \-ˌi-zəm\ *n*

par·si·mo·ni·ous \ˌpär-sə-ˈmō-nē-əs\ *adj* (1598) **1 :** exhibiting or marked by parsimony; *esp* **:** frugal to the point of stinginess **2 :** SPARING, RESTRAINED ***syn*** see STINGY — **par·si·mo·ni·ous·ly** *adv*

par·si·mo·ny \ˈpär-sə-ˌmō-nē\ *n* [ME *parcimony,* fr. L *parsimonia,* fr. *parsus,* pp. of *parcere* to spare] (15c) **1 a :** the quality of being careful with money or resources **:** THRIFT **b :** the quality or state of being stingy **2 :** economy in the use of means to an end; *esp* **:** economy of explanation in conformity with Occam's razor

pars·ley \ˈpär-slē\ *n* [ME *persely,* fr. OE *petersilie,* fr. VL **petrosilium,* alter. of L *petroselinum,* fr. Gk *petroselinon,* fr. *petros* stone + *selinon* celery] (bef. 12c) **:** a European biennial herb (*Petroselinum crispum*) of the carrot family widely grown for its finely dissected curly or flat leaves which are used as an herb or garnish; *also* **:** the leaves

pars·leyed *also* **pars·lied** \-slēd\ *adj* (1916) **:** garnished or flavored with parsley ‹∼ potatoes›

pars·nip \ˈpär-snəp\ *n* [ME *passenep,* modif. of OF *pasnaie,* fr. L *pastinaca,* fr. *pastinum* 2-pronged dibble] (14c) **:** a Eurasian biennial herb (*Pastinaca sativa*) of the carrot family with large pinnate leaves and yellow flowers that is cultivated for its long tapered edible root which is cooked as a vegetable; *also* **:** the root

par·son \ˈpär-sᵊn\ *n* [ME *persone,* fr. AF, fr. ML *persona,* lit., person, fr. L] (13c) **1 :** RECTOR **2 :** CLERGYMAN; *esp* **:** a Protestant pastor

par·son·age \ˈpär-s(ə-)nij, ˈpär-sə-nij\ *n* (15c) **:** the house provided by a church for its pastor

Par·sons ta·ble \ˈpär-sᵊnz-\ *n* [*Parsons* School of Design, New York City] (1967) **:** a usu. rectangular table having straight legs that are flush with the edge of the top

[1]**part** \ˈpärt\ *n* [ME, fr. AF & OE, both fr. L *part-, pars;* perh. akin to L *parare* to prepare — more at PARE] (bef. 12c) **1 a (1) :** one of the often indefinite or unequal subdivisions into which something is or is re-

garded as divided and which together constitute the whole (2) : an essential portion or integral element **b** : one of several or many equal units of which something is composed or into which it is divisible : an amount equal to another amount ⟨mix one ~ of the powder with three ~*s* of water⟩ **c** (1) : an exact divisor of a quantity : ALIQUOT (2) : PARTIAL FRACTION **d** : one of the constituent elements of a plant or animal body: as (1) : ORGAN, MEMBER (2) *pl* : PRIVATE PARTS **e** : a division of a literary work **f** (1) : a vocal or instrumental line or melody in concerted music or in harmony (2) : a particular voice or instrument in concerted music; *also* : the score for it **g** : a constituent member of a machine or other apparatus; *also* : a spare part **2** : something falling to one in a division or apportionment : SHARE ⟨wanted no ~ of the proposal⟩ **3** : one's share or allotted task (as in an action) : DUTY ⟨one must do one's ~⟩ **4** : one of the opposing sides in a conflict or dispute **5** : a general area of indefinite boundaries — usu. used in pl. ⟨you're not from around these ~*s*⟩ ⟨took off for ~*s* unknown⟩ **6** : a function or course of action performed **7 a** : an actor's lines in a play **b** : the role of a character in a play **8** : a constituent of character or capacity : TALENT ⟨a man of many ~*s*⟩ **9** : the line where the hair is parted — **for one's part** : as far as one's share or interest is concerned ⟨*for my part*, I do not see that the difference is important —Mary McCarthy⟩ — **for the most part** : in general : on the whole ⟨*for the most part* the crowd was orderly⟩ — **in part** : in some degree : PARTIALLY — **on one's part** *or* **on the part of one** : with regard to the one specified

syn PART, PORTION, PIECE, MEMBER, DIVISION, SECTION, SEGMENT, FRAGMENT mean something less than the whole. PART is a general term appropriate when indefiniteness is required ⟨they ran only *part* of the way⟩. PORTION implies an assigned or allotted part ⟨cut the pie into six *portions*⟩. PIECE applies to a separate or detached part of a whole ⟨a puzzle with 500 *pieces*⟩. MEMBER suggests one of the functional units composing a body ⟨a structural *member*⟩. DIVISION applies to a large or diversified part ⟨the manufacturing *division* of the company⟩. SECTION applies to a relatively small or uniform part ⟨the entertainment *section* of the newspaper⟩. SEGMENT applies to a part separated or marked out by or as if by natural lines of cleavage ⟨the retired *segment* of the population⟩. FRAGMENT applies to a part produced by or as if by breaking off ⟨only a *fragment* of the play still exists⟩.

[2]**part** *vb* [ME, fr. AF *partir,* fr. L *partire* to divide, fr. *part-, pars*] *vi* (13c) **1 a** : to separate from or take leave of someone **b** : to take leave of one another **2** : to become separated into parts **3 a** : to go away : DEPART **b** : DIE **4** : to become separated, detached, or broken **5** : to relinquish possession or control ⟨hated to ~ with that money⟩ ~ *vt* **1 a** : to divide into parts **b** : to separate by combing on each side of a line **c** : to break or suffer the breaking of (as a rope or anchor chain) **2** : to divide into shares and distribute : APPORTION **3 a** : to remove from contact or association ⟨if aught but death ~ thee and me —Ruth 1:17(AV)⟩ **b** : to keep separate ⟨the narrow channel that ~*s* England from France⟩ **c** : to hold (as brawlers) apart **d** : to separate by a process of extraction, elimination, or secretion **4 a** *archaic* : LEAVE, QUIT **b** *dial Brit* : RELINQUISH, GIVE UP — **part company 1** : to end a relationship or association **2** : to diverge from another (as in opinion) — often used with *with* ***syn*** see SEPARATE

[3]**part** *adv* (1513) : PARTLY

[4]**part** *adj* (1818) : PARTIAL 1

[5]**part** *abbr* **1** participial; participle **2** particular

par·take \pär-ˈtāk, pər-\ *vb* **-took** \-ˈtu̇k\; **-tak·en** \-ˈtā-kən\; **-tak·ing** [back-formation fr. *partaker,* alter. of *part taker*] *vi* (1561) **1** : to take part in or experience something along with others ⟨~ in the revelry⟩ ⟨~ of the good life⟩ **2** : to have a portion (as of food or drink) **3** : to possess or share a certain nature or attribute ⟨the experience ~*s* of a mystical quality⟩ ~ *vt* : to take part in ***syn*** see SHARE — **par·tak·er** *n*

part and parcel *n* (15c) : an essential or integral component ⟨stress was *part and parcel* of the job⟩

part·ed \ˈpär-təd\ *adj* (1534) **1 a** : divided into parts **b** : cleft so that the divisions reach nearly but not quite to the base — usu. used in combination ⟨a 3-*parted* corolla⟩ **2** *archaic* : DEAD

par·terre \pär-ˈter\ *n* [F, fr. MF, fr. *par terre* on the ground] (ca. 1639) **1** : an ornamental garden with paths between the beds **2** : the part of the main floor of a theater that is behind the orchestra; *esp* : PARQUET CIRCLE

par·the·no·car·py \ˈpär-thə-nō-ˌkär-pē\ *n* [ISV, fr. Gk *parthenos* virgin + *karpos* fruit — more at HARVEST] (1911) : the production of fruits without fertilization ⟨bananas set fruit by ~ and without pollination⟩ — **par·the·no·car·pic** \ˌpär-thə-nō-ˈkär-pik\ *adj*

par·the·no·gen·e·sis \ˌpär-thə-nō-ˈje-nə-səs\ *n* [NL, fr. Gk *parthenos* + L *genesis* genesis] (1849) : reproduction by development of an unfertilized usu. female gamete that occurs esp. among lower plants and invertebrate animals — **par·the·no·ge·net·ic** \-jə-ˈne-tik\ *also* **par·the·no·gen·ic** \-ˈje-nik\ *adj* — **par·the·no·ge·net·i·cal·ly** \-ti-k(ə-)lē\ *adv*

Par·the·non \ˈpär-thə-ˌnän\ *n* [L, fr. Gk *Parthenōn*] (1776) : a Doric temple of Athena built on the acropolis at Athens in the fifth century B.C.

Par·thi·an \ˈpär-thē-ən\ *adj* (1565) **1** : of, relating to, or characteristic of ancient Parthia or its people **2** : relating to, being, or having the effect of a shot fired while in real or feigned retreat — **Parthian** *n*

[1]**par·tial** \ˈpär-shəl\ *adj* [ME *parcial,* fr. LL *partialis,* fr. L *part-, pars* part] (14c) **1** : of or relating to a part rather than the whole : not general or total ⟨a ~ solution⟩ **2** : inclined to favor one party more than the other : BIASED **3** : markedly fond of someone or something — used with *to* ⟨~ to pizza⟩

[2]**partial** *n* (1880) : OVERTONE 1a

partial denture *n* (1860) : a usu. removable artificial replacement of one or more teeth

partial derivative *n* (1889) : the derivative of a function of several variables with respect to one of them and with the remaining variables treated as constants

partial differential equation *n* (1845) : a differential equation containing at least one partial derivative

partial differentiation *n* (ca. 1890) : the process of finding a partial derivative

partial fraction *n* (1816) : one of the simpler fractions into the sum of which the quotient of two polynomials may be decomposed

par·tial·i·ty \pär-shē-ˈa-lə-tē, pär-ˈsha-lə-tē\ *n, pl* **-ties** (15c) **1** : the quality or state of being partial : BIAS **2** : a special taste or liking

par·tial·ly \ˈpär-sh(ə-)lē\ *adv* (15c) **1** *archaic* : in a biased manner : with partiality **2** : to some extent : in some degree

partially ordered *adj* (1941) : having some or all elements connected by a relation that is reflexive, transitive, and antisymmetric

partial pressure *n* (1857) : the pressure exerted by a (specified) component in a mixture of gases

partial product *n* (ca. 1823) : a product obtained by multiplying a multiplicand by one digit of a multiplier having more than one digit

par·ti·ble \ˈpär-tə-bəl\ *adj* (14c) : capable of being parted : DIVISIBLE ⟨a ~ inheritance⟩ — **par·ti·bil·i·ty** \ˌpär-tə-ˈbi-lə-tē\ *n*

par·tic·i·pant \pär-ˈti-sə-pənt, pər-\ *n* (1562) : one that participates — **participant** *adj*

par·tic·i·pate \pär-ˈti-sə-ˌpāt, pər-\ *vb* **-pat·ed; -pat·ing** [L *participatus,* pp. of *participare,* fr. *particip-, particeps* participant, fr. *part-, pars* part + *capere* to take — more at HEAVE] *vt* (1531) *archaic* : PARTAKE ~ *vi* **1** : to possess some of the attributes of a person, thing, or quality **2 a** : to take part ⟨always ~*s* in class discussions⟩ **b** : to have a part or share in something ***syn*** see SHARE — **par·tic·i·pa·tor** \-ˌpā-tər\ *n*

par·tic·i·pa·tion \(ˌ)pär-ˌti-sə-ˈpā-shən, pər-\ *n* (14c) **1** : the act of participating **2** : the state of being related to a larger whole

par·tic·i·pa·tion·al \-ˈpā-shnəl, -ˈpā-shə-nᵊl\ *adj* (1959) : PARTICIPATORY

par·tic·i·pa·tive \pär-ˈti-sə-pə-tiv, pər-, -ˌpā-tiv\ *adj* (1951) : relating to or involving participation; *esp* : of, relating to, or being a style of management in which subordinates participate in decision making

par·tic·i·pa·to·ry \pär-ˈti-sə-pə-ˌtȯr-ē, pər-\ *adj* (1881) : characterized by or involving participation; *esp* : providing the opportunity for individual participation ⟨~ democracy⟩ ⟨~ management⟩

par·ti·cip·i·al \ˌpär-tə-ˈsi-pē-əl\ *adj* [L *participialis,* fr. *participium*] (1591) : of, relating to, or formed with or from a participle — **par·ti·cip·i·al·ly** \-pē-ə-lē\ *adv*

par·ti·ci·ple \ˈpär-tə-ˌsi-pəl\ *n* [ME, fr. AF, modif. of L *participium,* fr. *particip-, particeps*] (14c) : a word having the characteristics of both verb and adjective; *esp* : an English verbal form that has the function of an adjective and at the same time shows such verbal features as tense and voice and capacity to take an object

par·ti·cle \ˈpär-ti-kəl\ *n* [ME, fr. L *particula,* fr. dim. of *part-, pars*] (14c) **1 a** : a minute quantity or fragment **b** : a relatively small or the smallest discrete portion or amount of something **2** *archaic* : a clause or article of a composition or document **3** : any of the basic units of matter and energy (as a molecule, atom, proton, electron, or photon) **4** : a unit of speech expressing some general aspect of meaning or some connective or limiting relation and including the articles, most prepositions and conjunctions, and some interjections and adverbs ⟨the ~ *up* has a perfective meaning in phrases such as *beat up* and *cut up*⟩ **5** : a small eucharistic wafer distributed to a Roman Catholic layman at Communion

particle accelerator *n* (1945) : ACCELERATOR d

par·ti·cle·board \-ˌbȯrd\ *n* (ca. 1957) : a composition board made of very small pieces of wood bonded together

particle physics *n* (1946) : a branch of physics dealing with the constitution, properties, and interactions of elementary particles esp. as revealed in experiments using particle accelerators — called also *high-energy physics* — **particle physicist** *n*

par·ti–col·or \ˈpär-tē-ˌkə-lər\ *or* **par·ti–col·ored** \-lərd\ *adj* [obs. E *party* parti-color, fr. ME *parti,* fr. AF, of two colors, fr. pp. of *partir* to divide] (1530) : showing different colors or tints; *esp* : having a predominant color broken by patches of one or more other colors ⟨a ~ cocker spaniel⟩ — **parti–color** *n*

[1]**par·tic·u·lar** \pə(r)-ˈti-kyə-lər, -k(ə-)lər\ *adj* [ME *particuler,* fr. AF, fr. LL *particularis,* fr. L *particula* small part] (14c) **1** : of, relating to, or being a single person or thing ⟨the ~ person I had in mind⟩ **2** *obs* : PARTIAL **3** : of, relating to, or concerned with details ⟨gave us a very ~ account of the trip⟩ **4 a** : distinctive among other examples or cases of the same general category : notably unusual ⟨suffered from measles of ~ severity⟩ **b** : being one unit or element among others ⟨~ incidents in a story⟩ **5 a** : denoting an individual member or subclass in logic **b** : affirming or denying a predicate to a part of the subject — used of a proposition in logic ⟨"some men are wise" is a ~ affirmative⟩ **6 a** : concerned over or attentive to details : METICULOUS ⟨a very ~ gardener⟩ **b** : nice in taste : FASTIDIOUS **c** : hard to please : EXACTING ***syn*** see CIRCUMSTANTIAL, SPECIAL

[2]**particular** *n* (15c) **1** *archaic* : a separate part of a whole **2 a** : an individual fact, point, circumstance, or detail ⟨a hero in every ~ —Ron Fimrite⟩ **b** : a specific item or detail of information — usu. used in pl. ⟨wanted to know all the ~*s* of the incident⟩ ⟨bill of ~*s*⟩ **3 a** : an individual or a specific subclass (as in logic) falling under some general concept or term **b** : a particular proposition in logic ***syn*** see ITEM — **in particular** : in distinction from others : SPECIFICALLY

par·tic·u·lar·ise *Brit var of* PARTICULARIZE

par·tic·u·lar·ism \pə(r)-ˈti-k(yə-)lə-ˌri-zəm *also* pär-\ *n* (1824) **1** : exclusive or special devotion to a particular interest **2** : a political theory that each political group has a right to promote its own interests and esp. independence without regard to the interests of larger groups **3** : a tendency to explain complex social phenomena in terms of a single causative factor — **par·tic·u·lar·ist** \-rist\ *n or adj* — **par·tic·u·lar·is·tic** \-ˌti-k(yə-)lə-ˈris-tik\ *adj*

par·tic·u·lar·i·ty \pə(r)-ˌti-kyə-ˈla-rə-tē *also* (ˌ)pär-\ *n, pl* **-ties** (1528) **1 a** : a minute detail : PARTICULAR **b** : an individual characteristic : PECULIARITY; *also* : SINGULARITY **2** : the quality or state of being particular as distinguished from universal **3 a** : attentiveness to detail : EXACTNESS **b** : the quality or state of being fastidious in behavior or expression

\ə\ **a**but \ᵊ\ kitten, F table \ər\ **fur**ther \a\ **a**sh \ā\ **a**ce \ä\ m**o**p, m**ar** \au̇\ **ou**t \ch\ **ch**in \e\ b**e**t \ē\ **ea**sy \g\ **g**o \i\ h**i**t \ī\ **i**ce \j\ **j**ob \ŋ\ si**ng** \ō\ g**o** \ȯ\ l**aw** \ȯi\ b**oy** \th\ **th**in \t͟h\ **th**e \ü\ l**oo**t \u̇\ f**oo**t \y\ **y**et \zh\ vi**si**on, beige \k, ⁿ, œ, ue, ʸ\ *see* Guide to Pronunciation

par·tic·u·lar·i·za·tion \-ˌti-k(yə-)lə-rə-ˈzā-shən\ *n* (1641) **:** the act of particularizing **:** the condition of being particularized
par·tic·u·lar·ize \pə(r)-ˈti-k(yə-)lə-ˌrīz *also* pär-\ *vb* **-ized; -iz·ing** *vt* (1593) **:** to state in detail **:** SPECIFY ~ *vi* **:** to go into details
par·tic·u·lar·ly \pə(r)-ˈti-kyə-(lər-)lē, -kyə-lə-lē; pə(r)-ˈti-k(ə-)lē; *also* pär-\ *adv* (14c) **1 :** in a particular manner **:** in detail **2 :** to an unusual degree ⟨a ~ dry summer⟩ **3 :** in particular **:** SPECIFICALLY
[1]**par·tic·u·late** \pär-ˈti-kyə-lət *also* -ˌlāt\ *adj* [L *particula*] (1871) **:** of or relating to minute separate particles
[2]**particulate** *n* (1942) **:** a particulate substance
particulate inheritance *n* (1889) **:** MENDELIAN INHERITANCE
[1]**part·ing** \ˈpär-tiŋ\ *n* (15c) **:** a place or point where a division or separation occurs — **parting of the ways 1 :** a point of separation or divergence **2 :** a place or time at which a choice must be made
[2]**parting** *adj* (1562) **:** given, taken, or done at parting ⟨a ~ kiss⟩
par·ti pris \ˈpär-ˌtē-ˈprē\ *n, pl* **partis pris** \-ˌtē-ˈprē(z)\ [F, lit., side taken] (1857) **:** a preconceived opinion **:** PREJUDICE — **parti pris** *adj*
[1]**par·ti·san** *also* **par·ti·zan** \ˈpär-tə-zən, -sən, -ˌzan, *chiefly Brit* ˌpär-tə-ˈzan\ *n* [MF *partisan,* fr. north It dial. *partižan,* fr. *part* part, party, fr. L *part-, pars* part] (1555) **1 :** a firm adherent to a party, faction, cause, or person; *esp* **:** one exhibiting blind, prejudiced, and unreasoning allegiance **2 a :** a member of a body of detached light troops making forays and harassing an enemy **b :** a member of a guerrilla band operating within enemy lines ***syn*** see FOLLOWER — **partisan** *adj* — **par·ti·san·ly** \-lē\ *adv* — **par·ti·san·ship** \-ˌship\ *n*
[2]**par·ti·san** *or* **par·ti·zan** \ˈpär-tə-zən, -sən\ *n* [MF *partisane,* fr. north It dial. *partižana,* fem. of *partižan*] (1556) **:** a weapon of the 16th and 17th centuries with long shaft and broad blade
par·ti·ta \pär-ˈtē-tə\ *n* [It, fr. *partire* to divide, fr. L — more at PART] (1880) **1 :** VARIATION 4 **2 :** SUITE 2b(1)
par·tite \ˈpär-ˌtīt\ *adj* [L *partitus,* fr. pp. of *partire*] (ca. 1570) **1 :** divided into a usu. specified number of parts **2 :** PARTED 1b ⟨a ~ leaf⟩
[1]**par·ti·tion** \pär-ˈti-shən, pər-\ *n* (15c) **1 :** the action of parting **:** the state of being parted **:** DIVISION **2 :** something that divides; *esp* **:** an interior dividing wall **3 :** one of the parts or sections of a whole
[2]**partition** *vt* (1653) **1 a :** to divide into parts or shares **b :** to divide (as a country) into two or more territorial units having separate political status **2 :** to separate or divide by a partition (as a wall) — often used with *off* — **par·ti·tion·er** \-ˈti-sh(ə-)nər\ *n*
par·ti·tion·ist \-ˈti-sh(ə-)nist\ *n* (ca. 1900) **:** an advocate of political partition
par·ti·tive \ˈpär-tə-tiv\ *adj* (14c) **1 :** serving to part or divide into parts **2 a :** of, relating to, or denoting a part ⟨a ~ construction⟩ **b :** serving to indicate the whole of which a part is specified ⟨~ genitive⟩ — **par·ti·tive·ly** *adv*
part·let \ˈpärt-lət\ *n* [ME (Sc) *patelet,* fr. MF *patelette,* fr. dim. of *patte* paw] (1519) **:** a 16th century chemisette with a band or collar
part·ly \ˈpärt-lē\ *adv* (1523) **:** in some measure or degree **:** PARTIALLY
[1]**part·ner** \ˈpärt-nər *also* ˈpärd-\ *n* [ME *partener,* alter. of *parcener,* fr. AF, coparcener — more at PARCENER] (14c) **1** *archaic* **:** one that shares **:** PARTAKER **2 a :** one associated with another esp. in an action **:** ASSOCIATE, COLLEAGUE **b :** either of two persons who dance together **c :** one of two or more persons who play together in a game against an opposing side **d :** a person with whom one shares an intimate relationship **:** one member of a couple **3 :** a member of a partnership esp. in a business; *also* **:** such membership **4 :** one of the heavy timbers that strengthen a ship's deck to support a mast — usu. used in pl. — **part·ner·less** \-ləs\ *adj*
[2]**partner** *vt* (1611) **1 :** to join or associate with another as partner **2 :** to provide with a partner ~ *vi* **:** to join as a partner
partners desk *n* (1950) **:** a large desk with an open kneehole which allows use of the desk by two people seated opposite each other
part·ner·ship \-ˌship\ *n* (1576) **1 :** the state of being a partner **:** PARTICIPATION **2 a :** a legal relation existing between two or more persons contractually associated as joint principals in a business **b :** the persons joined together in a partnership **3 :** a relationship resembling a legal partnership and usu. involving close cooperation between parties having specified and joint rights and responsibilities
part of speech (1509) **:** a traditional class of words distinguished according to the kind of idea denoted and the function performed in a sentence
par·ton \ˈpär-ˌtän\ *n* [*particle* + [2]*-on*] (1969) **:** a particle (as a quark or gluon) that is held to be a constituent of hadrons
par·tridge \ˈpär-trij, *dial* ˈpa-trij\ *n, pl* **partridge** *or* **par·tridg·es** [ME *partrich,* modif. of AF *perdriz,* alter. of OF *perdix,* fr. L *perdic-, perdix,* fr. Gk *perdik-, perdix*] (14c) **1 :** any of various typically medium-sized stout-bodied Old World gallinaceous birds (*Perdix, Alectoris,* and related genera) with variegated plumage that are often hunted as game **2 :** any of various related birds (as the American ruffed grouse or bobwhite) resembling the Old World partridges in size, habits, or value as game
par·tridge·ber·ry \-ˌber-ē\ *n* (1714) **:** a trailing evergreen plant (*Mitchella repens*) of the madder family native to the eastern U.S. and Canada with edible slightly acidic scarlet berries; *also* **:** its berry

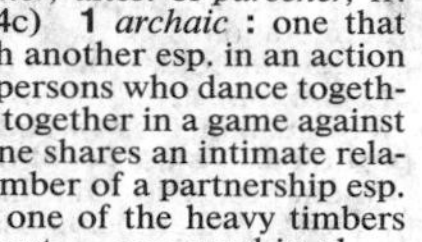

partridgeberry

part–song \ˈpärt-ˌsȯŋ\ *n* (1731) **:** a usu. unaccompanied song consisting of two or more voice parts with one part carrying the melody
part–time \ˈpärt-ˈtīm\ *adj* (1891) **:** involving or working less than customary or standard hours ⟨a ~ job⟩ ⟨~ students⟩ — **part–time** *adv* — **part–tim·er** \-ˌtī-mər, -ˈtī-\ *n*
[1]**par·tu·ri·ent** \pär-ˈtu̇r-ē-ənt, -ˈtyu̇r-\ *adj* [L *parturient-, parturiens,* prp. of *parturire* to be in labor, fr. *parere* to give birth to — more at PARE] (1592) **1 :** bringing forth or about to bring forth young **2 :** of or relating to parturition
[2]**parturient** *n* (1947) **:** a parturient individual
par·tu·ri·tion \ˌpär-chə-ˈri-shən, ˌpär-tyu̇-, ˌpär-tə-\ *n* [LL *parturition-, parturitio,* fr. L *parturire*] (1646) **:** the action or process of giving birth to offspring
part·way \ˈpärt-ˈwā\ *adv* (1822) **1 :** to some extent **:** PARTIALLY, PARTLY **2 :** at a point in the way or distance ⟨~ through the trip they met some friends⟩
[1]**par·ty** \ˈpär-tē\ *n, pl* **parties** [ME *partie* part, party, fr. AF, fr. *partir* to divide — more at PART] (14c) **1 :** a person or group taking one side of a question, dispute, or contest **2 :** a group of persons organized for the purpose of directing the policies of a government **3 :** a person or group participating in an action or affair ⟨a mountain-climbing ~⟩ ⟨a ~ to the transaction⟩ **4 :** a particular individual **:** PERSON ⟨an old ~ approaching 80⟩ **5 :** a detail of soldiers **6 :** a social gathering; *also* **:** the entertainment provided for it — **party** *adj*
[2]**party** *vi* **par·tied; par·ty·ing** (1919) **:** to attend or give parties; *broadly* **:** REVEL 1 — **par·ty·er** *also* **par·ti·er** \-tē-ər\ *n*
party animal *n* (1982) **:** a person known for frequent often wild partying
par·ty·go·er \ˈpär-tē-ˌgō-ər\ *n* (1831) **:** a person who attends a party or who attends parties frequently
party line *n* (1834) **1 :** the policy or practice of a political party **2 :** a single telephone circuit connecting two or more subscribers with the exchange — called also *party wire* **3 :** the principles or policies of an individual or organization; *also* **:** the explanation or interpretation usu. put forth ⟨the *party line* that her mother was a saint —Leslie Bennetts⟩ — **par·ty–lin·er** \ˌpär-tē-ˈlī-nər\ *n*
party poop·er \-ˈpü-pər\ *n* [[3]*poop* + *-er*] (1954) **:** a person who refuses to join in the fun of a party; *broadly* **:** one who refuses to go along with everyone else
party wall *n* (1667) **:** a wall which divides two adjoining properties and in which each of the owners shares the rights
pa·rure \pə-ˈru̇r\ *n* [F, lit., adornment, fr. OF *pareure,* fr. *parer* to prepare, adorn — more at PARE] (1818) **:** a matched set of ornaments (as jewelry)
par value *n* (1797) **:** PAR 1b(1)
parve *var of* PAREVE
par·ve·nu \ˈpär-və-ˌnü, -ˌnyü\ *n, pl* **-nus** \-ˌn(y)üz\ [F, fr. pp. of *parvenir* to arrive, fr. L *pervenire,* fr. *per* through + *venire* to come — more at FOR, COME] (1787) **:** one that has recently or suddenly risen to an unaccustomed position of wealth or power and has not yet gained the prestige, dignity, or manner associated with it — **parvenu** *adj*
par·ve·nue \-ˌnü, -ˌnyü\ *n* [F, *parvenue,* fem. of *parvenum,* pp.] (1826) **:** a woman who is a parvenu — **parvenue** *adj*
par·vis *also* **par·vise** \ˈpär-vəs\ *n* [ME *parvis,* fr. AF, modif. of LL *paradisus* enclosed park — more at PARADISE] (14c) **1 :** a court or enclosed space before a building (as a church) **2 :** a single portico or colonnade before a church
par·vo \ˈpär-(ˌ)vō\ *n* (1980) **:** PARVOVIRUS 2
par·vo·vi·rus \ˈpär-vō-ˌvī-rəs\ *n* [NL, fr. L *parvus* small (akin to Gk *pauros* small, *paid-, pais* child) + NL *-o-* + *virus* — more at FEW] (1965) **1 :** any of a family (*Parvoviridae*) of single-stranded DNA viruses that include the causative agents of fifth disease in humans, panleukopenia in cats, and parvovirus in dogs **2 :** a highly contagious febrile virus disease of dogs that is spread esp. by contact with infected feces, that is caused by a strain (Canine parvovirus) of the parvovirus causing panleukopenia in cats, and that is marked by loss of appetite, lethargy, often bloody diarrhea and vomiting, and sometimes death
pas \ˈpä\ *n, pl* **pas** \ˈpä(z)\ [F, fr. L *passus* step — more at PACE] (1707) **1 :** the right of precedence **2 :** a dance step or combination of steps
PAS *abbr* para-aminosalicylic acid
pas·cal \pas-ˈkal, päs-ˈkäl\ *n* [Blaise *Pascal*] (1956) **1 :** a unit of pressure in the meter-kilogram-second system equivalent to one newton per square meter **2** *cap P or all cap* **:** a structured computer programming language developed from Algol and designed to process both numerical and textual data
Pas·cal's triangle \pas-ˈkalz-, päs-ˈkälz-\ *n* (1886) **:** a system of numbers arranged in rows resembling a triangle with each row consisting of the coefficients in the expansion of $(a + b)^n$ for $n = 0, 1, 2, 3, \ldots$
Pasch \ˈpask\ *also* **Pas·cha** \ˈpäs-kə\ *n* [ME *pasche* Passover, Easter, fr. AF, fr. LL *pascha,* fr. LGk, fr. Gk, Passover, fr. Heb *pesaḥ*] (12c) **1 :** EASTER **2 :** PASSOVER — **pas·chal** \ˈpas-kəl\ *adj*
paschal full moon *n* (1892) **:** the 14th day of a lunar month occurring on or next after March 21 according to a fixed set of ecclesiastical calendar rules and without regard to the real moon
Paschal Lamb *n* (15c) **1 :** a lamb slain and eaten during the Passover celebration in ancient Judaism **2 :** AGNUS DEI 2
pas de bour·rée \ˌpä-də-bu̇-ˈrā\ *n, pl* **pas de bourrée** *same*\ *or* **pas de bour·rées** \-ˈrā(z)\ [F, lit., bourrée step] (1830) **:** a walking or running ballet step usu. executed on the points of the toes
pas de chat \-ˈshä\ *n, pl* **pas de chat** *same*\ [F, lit., cat's step] (1914) **:** a ballet leap from one foot to the other in which the feet are drawn up and the knees are bent so that the legs form a diamond
pas de deux \-ˈdə(r), -ˈdü\ *n, pl* **pas de deux** \-ˈdər(z), -ˈdə(z), -ˈdü(z)\ [F, lit., step for two] (ca. 1762) **1 :** a dance or figure for two performers **2 :** an intricate relationship or activity involving two parties or things
pas de qua·tre \-ˈkat, -ˈka-trə, -ˈkätrᵊ\ *n, pl* **pas de quatre** *same*\ [F, lit., step for four] (1846) **:** a dance or figure for four performers
pas de trois \-ˈtrwä, -ˈtwä\ *n, pl* **pas de trois** \-ˈtrwä(z), -ˈtwä(z)\ [F, lit., step for three] (ca. 1762) **:** a dance or figure for three performers
pa·se \ˈpä-(ˌ)sā\ *n* [Sp, lit., feint, fr. *pase* let him pass, fr. *pasar* to pass, fr. VL **passare*] (1937) **:** a movement of a cape by a matador in drawing a bull and taking his charge
pa·seo \pə-ˈsā-(ˌ)ō, pä-\ *n, pl* **pa·se·os** [Sp, fr. *pasear* to take a stroll, fr. *paso* passage, step, fr. L *passus*] (1832) **1 a :** a leisurely usu. evening stroll **:** PROMENADE **b :** a public walk or boulevard **2 :** a formal entrance march of bullfighters into an arena
[1]**pash** \ˈpash\ *vt* [ME *passhen*] (14c) *dial Eng* **:** SMASH
[2]**pash** *n* [origin unknown] (1611) *dial Eng* **:** HEAD
pa·sha \ˈpä-shə, ˈpa-; pə-ˈshä, -ˈshȯ\ *also* **ba·shaw** \bə-ˈshȯ\ *n* [Turk *paşa*] (1646) **:** a man of high rank or office (as in Turkey or northern Africa)
pash·mi·na \ˌpəsh-ˈmē-nə\ *n* [Pers, fr. *pashmin* woolen, fr. *pashm* wool] (1885) **:** a fine wool similar to cashmere made from the undercoat of domestic Himalayan goats; *also* **:** a shawl made from this wool
Pash·to \ˈpəsh-(ˌ)tō\ *also* **Push·tu** \-(ˌ)tü\ *n* [Pashto *pašto*] (1784) **:** the Iranian language of the Pashtuns

Pash·tun *also* **Push·tun** \ˌpəsh-ˈtün\ *n, pl* **Pashtuns** *also* **Pushtuns** *or* **Pashtun** *also* **Pushtun** [Pashto *paštun, paxtun*] (1815) : a member of a people of eastern and southern Afghanistan and adjacent parts of Pakistan

Pa·siph·aë \pə-ˈsi-fə-ˌē\ *n* [L, fr. Gk *Pasiphaē*] (14c) : the wife of Minos and mother of the Minotaur by a white bull

pasque·flow·er \ˈpask-ˌflau̇(-ə)r\ *n* [modif. of MF *passefleur,* fr. *passer* to pass + *fleur* flower] (1597) : any of several anemones with palmately compound leaves and large usu. white or purple early spring flowers

pas·qui·nade \ˌpas-kwə-ˈnād\ *n* [MF, fr. It *pasquinata,* fr. *Pasquino,* name given to a statue in Rome on which lampoons were posted] (1658) **1** : a lampoon posted in a public place **2** : satirical writing : SATIRE — **pasquinade** *vt*

[1]**pass** \ˈpas\ *vb* [ME, fr. AF *passer,* fr. VL **passare,* fr. L *passus* step — more at PACE] *vi* (13c) **1** : MOVE, PROCEED, GO **2 a** : to go away : DEPART **b** : DIE — often used with *on* **3 a** : to move in a path so as to approach and continue beyond something : move past; *esp* : to move past another vehicle going in the same direction **b** : to run the normal course — used of time or a period of time ⟨the hours ~ quickly⟩ **4 a** : to go or make one's way through ⟨allow no one to ~⟩ **b** : to go uncensured, unchallenged, or seemingly unnoticed ⟨let the remark ~⟩ **5** : to go from one quality, state, or form to another ⟨~*es* from a liquid to a gaseous state⟩ **6 a** : to sit in inquest or judgment **b** (1) : to render a decision, verdict, or opinion ⟨the court ~*ed* on the legality of wiretapping⟩ (2) : to become legally rendered ⟨judgment ~*ed* for the plaintiff⟩ **7** : to go from the control, ownership, or possession of one person or group to that of another ⟨the throne ~*ed* to the king's son⟩ ⟨title ~*es* to the buyer upon payment in full⟩ **8 a** : HAPPEN, OCCUR **b** : to take place or be exchanged as or in a social, personal, or business interaction ⟨words ~*ed*⟩ **9 a** : to become approved by a legislature or body empowered to sanction or reject ⟨the proposal ~*ed*⟩ **b** : to undergo an inspection, test, or course of study successfully **10 a** : to serve as a medium of exchange **b** : to be accepted or regarded ⟨drivel that ~*es* for literature⟩ **c** : to identify oneself or be identified as something one is not ⟨tried to ~ as an adult⟩ ⟨Mom could ~ as my sister⟩ **11 a** *obs* : to make a pass in fencing **b** : to throw or hit a ball or puck to a teammate — often used with *off* **12 a** (1) : to decline to bid, double, or redouble in a card game (2) : to withdraw from the current poker pot **b** : to let something go by without accepting or taking advantage of it — often used with *on* ⟨~*ed* on the cheesecake⟩ ⟨thanks for the offer, but I'll ~⟩ ~ *vt* **1** : to go beyond: as **a** : SURPASS, EXCEED ⟨~*es* all expectations⟩ **b** : to advance or develop beyond **c** : to go past (one moving in the same direction) **2 a** : to go by : proceed or extend beyond ⟨~ the school on their way to work⟩ **b** (1) : *obs* : NEGLECT, OMIT (2) : to omit a regularly scheduled declaration and payment of (a dividend) **3 a** : to go across, over, or through : CROSS **b** : to live through (as an experience or peril) : UNDERGO **c** : to go through (as a test) successfully **4 a** : to secure the approval of ⟨the bill ~*ed* the Senate⟩ **b** : to cause or permit to win approval or legal or official sanction ⟨~ a law⟩ **c** : to give approval or a passing grade to ⟨~ the students⟩ **5 a** : to let (as time or a period of time) go by esp. while involved in a leisure activity ⟨I'll read to ~ the time⟩ **b** : to let go unnoticed : OVERLOOK, DISREGARD **6 a** : PLEDGE **b** : to transfer the right to or property in ⟨~ title to a house⟩ **7 a** : to put in circulation ⟨~ bad checks⟩ **b** (1) : to transfer or transmit from one to another ⟨~ the salt⟩ ⟨~*ing* the savings on to customers⟩ (2) : to relay or communicate (as information) to another **c** : to cause or enable to go : TRANSPORT **d** : to throw or hit (a ball or puck) esp. to a teammate **8 a** : to pronounce (as a sentence or opinion) esp. judicially **b** : UTTER ⟨~*ed* a cutting remark⟩ **9 a** : to cause or permit to go past or through a barrier **b** : to move or cause to move in a particular manner or direction ⟨~*ed* my hand over my face⟩ ⟨~ the rope through the loop⟩ **c** : to cause to march or go by in order ⟨~ the troops in review⟩ **10** : to emit or discharge from a bodily part and esp. the bowels **11 a** : to give a base on balls to **b** : to hit a ball past (an opponent) in a game (as tennis) — **pass·er** *n* — **pass muster** : to gain approval or acceptance — **pass the buck** : to shift a responsibility to someone else — **pass the hat** : to take up a collection for money — **pass the time of day** : to exchange greetings or engage in pleasant conversation

[2]**pass** *n* [ME, fr. AF *pas,* fr. L *passus*] (14c) **1** : a means (as an opening, road, or channel) by which a barrier may be passed or access to a place may be gained; *esp* : a low place in a mountain range **2** : a position to be held usu. against odds

[3]**pass** *n* [[1]*pass*] (1523) **1** : REALIZATION ⟨brought his dream to ~⟩ **2** : the act or an instance of passing : PASSAGE **3** : a usu. distressing or bad state of affairs ⟨what has brought you to such a ~?⟩ **4 a** : a written permission to move about freely in a place or to leave or enter it **b** : a written leave of absence from a military post or station for a brief period **c** : a permit or ticket allowing free transportation or free admission **5** *archaic* : a thrust or lunge in fencing **6 a** : a transference of objects by sleight of hand or other deceptive means **b** : a moving of the hands over or along something **7** *archaic* : an ingenious sally (as of wit) **8** : the passing of an examination or course of study; *also* : the mark or certification of such passing **9** : a single complete mechanical operation; *also* : a single complete cycle of operations (as for processing, manufacturing, or printing) **10 a** (1) : a transfer of a ball or a puck from one player to another on the same team (2) : a ball or puck so transferred **b** : PASSING SHOT **11** : BASE ON BALLS **12** : an election not to bid, bet, or draw an additional card in a card game **13** : a throw of dice in the game of craps that wins the bet for the shooter — compare [3]CRAP 2, MISSOUT **14** : a single passage or movement (as of an airplane) over a place or toward a target **15 a** : EFFORT, TRY **b** : a sexually inviting gesture or approach **16** : PASE

[4]**pass** *abbr* passenger

pass·able \ˈpa-sə-bəl\ *adj* (15c) **1 a** : capable of being passed, crossed, or traveled on ⟨~ roads⟩ **b** : capable of being freely circulated **2** : good enough : ADEQUATE — **pass·ably** \-blē\ *adv*

pas·sa·ca·glia \ˌpä-sə-ˈkäl-yə, ˌpa-sə-ˈkal-yə\ *n* [modif. of Sp *pasacalle,* fr. *pasar* to pass + *calle* street, fr. L *callis* path — more at PASE] (1659) **1 a** : an old Italian or Spanish dance tune **b** : an instrumental musical composition consisting of variations usu. on a ground bass in moderately slow triple time **2** : an old dance performed to a passacaglia

pas·sa·do \pə-ˈsä-(ˌ)dō\ *n, pl* **-dos** *or* **-does** [modif. of MF *passade* (fr. OIt *passata*) or OIt *passata,* fr. *passare* to pass, fr. VL] (1588) *archaic* : a thrust in fencing with one foot advanced

[1]**pas·sage** \ˈpa-sij\ *n* (13c) **1 a** : a way of exit or entrance : a road, path, channel, or course by which something passes **b** : a corridor or lobby giving access to the different rooms or parts of a building or apartment **2 a** : the action or process of passing from one place, condition, or stage to another **b** : DEATH 1a **c** : a continuous movement or flow ⟨the ~ of time⟩ **3 a** (1) : a specific act of traveling or passing esp. by sea or air (2) : a privilege of conveyance as a passenger : ACCOMMODATIONS **b** : the passing of a legislative measure or law : ENACTMENT **4** : a right, liberty, or permission to pass **5 a** : something that happens or is done : INCIDENT **b** : something that takes place between two persons mutually **6 a** : a usu. brief portion of a written work or speech that is relevant to a point under discussion or noteworthy for content or style **b** : a phrase or short section of a musical composition **c** : a detail of a work of art (as a painting) **7** : the act or action of passing something or undergoing a passing **8** : incubation of a pathogen (as a virus) in culture, a living organism, or a developing egg

[2]**passage** *vb* **pas·saged; pas·sag·ing** *vi* (1824) : to go past or across : CROSS ~ *vt* : to subject to passage ⟨*passaged* a virus⟩

pas·sage·way \-ˌwā\ *n* (ca. 1606) : a way that allows passage

pas·sage·work \-ˌwərk\ *n* (1865) : a section of a musical composition characteristically unimportant thematically and consisting esp. of ornamental figures

pas·sant \ˈpa-sᵊnt\ *adj* [ME *passaunt,* fr. AF *passant,* fr. prp. of *passer* to pass] (15c) : walking with the farther forepaw raised — used of a heraldic animal

pass away *vi* (13c) **1** : to go out of existence **2** : DIE 1

pass·band \ˈpas-ˌband\ *n* (1922) : a band of frequencies (as in a radio circuit or a light filter) that is transmitted with maximum efficiency

pass·book \-ˌbu̇k\ *n* (1828) : BANKBOOK

pass degree *n* (1868) : a bachelor's degree without honors that is taken at a British university

pas·sé \pa-ˈsā\ *adj* [F, fr. pp. of *passer*] (1775) **1** : past one's prime **2 a** : OUTMODED **b** : behind the times

passed ball *n* (1861) : a baseball pitch not hit by the batter that passes the catcher when it should have been caught and allows a base runner to advance — compare WILD PITCH

passed pawn *n* (1797) : a chess pawn that has no enemy pawn in front of it on its own or an adjacent file

pas·sel \ˈpa-səl\ *n* [alter. of *parcel*] (1835) : a large number or amount

passe·men·terie \pas-ˈmen-t(ə-)rē\ *n* [F, fr. *passement* ornamental braid, fr. *passer*] (1794) : an ornamental edging or trimming (as tassels) made of braid, cord, gimp, beading, or metallic thread

pas·sen·ger \ˈpa-sᵊn-jər\ *n, often attrib* [ME *passager,* fr. AF, fr. *passage* path, way, passage, fr. *passer*] (14c) **1** : WAYFARER **2** : a traveler in a public or private conveyance

passenger pigeon *n* (1802) : an extinct but formerly abundant No. American migratory pigeon (*Ectopistes migratorius*)

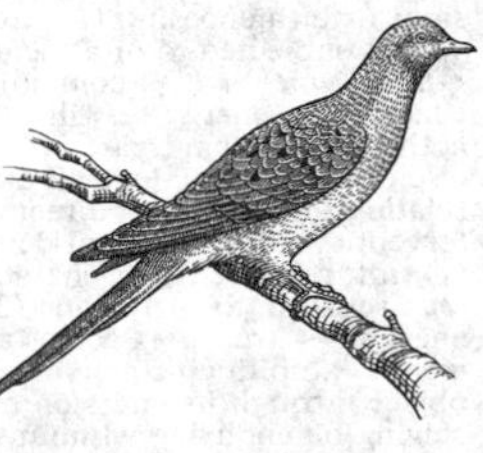
passenger pigeon

passe–par·tout \ˌpas-pər-ˈtü, -ˌpär-\ *n* [F, fr. *passe partout* pass everywhere] (1675) **1** : MASTER KEY **2 a** : [5]MAT **b** : a method of framing in which a picture, a mat, a glass, and a back (as of cardboard) are held together by strips of paper or cloth pasted over the edges **3** : a strong paper gummed on one side and used esp. for mounting pictures

pass·er–by \ˌpa-sər-ˈbī, ˈpa-sər-ˌ\ *n, pl* **pass·ers–by** \-sərz-\ (1567) : one who passes by

pas·ser·ine \ˈpa-sə-ˌrīn\ *adj* [L *passerinus* of sparrows, fr. *passer* sparrow] (1776) : of or relating to the largest order (Passeriformes) of birds which includes over half of all living birds and consists chiefly of altricial songbirds of perching habits — compare OSCINE — **passerine** *n*

pas seul \ˌpä-ˈsəl, -ˈsər(-ə)l\ *n* [F, lit., solo step] (1809) : a solo dance or dance figure

pass–fail \ˈpas-ˈfāl\ *adj* (1959) : being a system of grading whereby the grades "pass" and "fail" replace the traditional letter grades — **pass–fail** *n*

pas·si·ble \ˈpa-sə-bəl\ *adj* [ME, fr. MF & LL; MF *passible,* fr. LL *passibilis,* fr. L *passus,* pp. of *pati* to suffer — more at PATIENT] (14c) : capable of feeling or suffering

pas·sim \ˈpa-səm; ˈpa-ˌsim, ˈpä-\ *adv* [L, fr. *passus* scattered, fr. pp. of *pandere* to spread — more at FATHOM] (1634) : HERE AND THERE

[1]**pass·ing** \ˈpa-siŋ\ *n* (14c) : the act of one that passes or causes to pass; *esp* : DEATH 1a — **in passing** : by the way : INCIDENTALLY

[2]**passing** *adj* (14c) **1** : going by or past ⟨a ~ pedestrian⟩ **2** : having a brief duration ⟨a ~ whim⟩ **3** *obs* : SURPASSING **4** : SUPERFICIAL ⟨a ~ acquaintance⟩ ⟨a ~ resemblance⟩ **5 a** : of, relating to, or used in or for the act or process of passing ⟨~ lanes⟩ **b** : given on satisfactory completion of an examination or course of study ⟨a ~ grade⟩

[3]**passing** *adv* (14c) : to a surpassing degree : EXCEEDINGLY ⟨~ strange⟩

passing note *n* (1730) : a nonharmonic tone interposed between essential harmonic tones of adjacent chords — called also *passing tone*

passing shot *n* (1928) : a stroke (as in tennis) that drives the ball to one side and beyond the reach of an opponent

pas·sion \ˈpa-shən\ *n* [ME, fr. AF, fr. LL *passion-, passio* suffering, being acted upon, fr. L *pati* to suffer — more at PATIENT] (13c) **1** *often cap* **a** : the sufferings of Christ between the night of the Last Supper and his death **b** : an oratorio based on a gospel narrative of the Pas-

\ə\ **abut** \ᵊ\ kitten, F table \ər\ **further** \a\ **ash** \ā\ **ace** \ä\ **mop, mar** \au̇\ **out** \ch\ **chin** \e\ **bet** \ē\ **easy** \g\ **go** \i\ **hit** \ī\ **ice** \j\ **job** \ŋ\ **sing** \ō\ **go** \ȯ\ **law** \ȯi\ **boy** \th\ **thin** \t͟h\ **the** \ü\ **loot** \u̇\ **foot** \y\ **yet** \zh\ **vision, beige** \k, ⁿ, œ, ue, ʸ\ *see* Guide to Pronunciation

sion **2** *obs* : SUFFERING **3** : the state or capacity of being acted on by external agents or forces **4 a** (1) : EMOTION ⟨his ruling ~ is greed⟩ (2) *pl* : the emotions as distinguished from reason **b** : intense, driving, or overmastering feeling or conviction **c** : an outbreak of anger **5 a** : ardent affection : LOVE **b** : a strong liking or desire for or devotion to some activity, object, or concept **c** : sexual desire **d** : an object of desire or deep interest — **pas·sion·less** \-ləs\ *adj*

syn PASSION, FERVOR, ARDOR, ENTHUSIASM, ZEAL mean intense emotion compelling action. PASSION applies to an emotion that is deeply stirring or ungovernable ⟨was a slave to his *passions*⟩. FERVOR implies a warm and steady emotion ⟨read the poem aloud with great *fervor*⟩. ARDOR suggests warm and excited feeling likely to be fitful or short-lived ⟨the *ardor* of their honeymoon soon faded⟩. ENTHUSIASM applies to lively or eager interest in or admiration for a proposal, cause, or activity ⟨never showed much *enthusiasm* for sports⟩. ZEAL implies energetic and unflagging pursuit of an aim or devotion to a cause ⟨preaches with fanatical *zeal*⟩. ***syn*** see in addition FEELING

pas·sion·al \ˈpa-shə-nᵊl, ˈpash-nəl\ *adj* (15c) : of, relating to, or marked by passion

pas·sion·ate \ˈpa-sh(ə-)nət\ *adj* (15c) **1 a** : easily aroused to anger **b** : filled with anger : ANGRY **2 a** : capable of, affected by, or expressing intense feeling **b** : ENTHUSIASTIC, ARDENT **3** : swayed by or affected with sexual desire ***syn*** see IMPASSIONED — **pas·sion·ate·ly** *adv* — **pas·sion·ate·ness** *n*

pas·sion·flow·er \ˈpa-shən-ˌflau̇(-ə)r\ *n* [fr. the fancied resemblance of parts of the flower to the instruments of Christ's crucifixion] (1633) : any of a genus (*Passiflora* of the family Passifloraceae, the passionflower family) of chiefly tropical woody tendriled climbing vines or erect herbs with usu. showy flowers and pulpy often edible berries

passion fruit *n* (1752) : the edible fruit of a passionflower; *esp* : the small roundish purple or yellow fruit of a Brazilian passionflower (*Passiflora edulis*) grown commercially in warmer parts of the U.S. — compare GRANADILLA

Pas·sion·ist \ˈpa-sh(ə-)nist\ *n* [It *passionista,* fr. *passione* passion, fr. LL *passion-, passio*] (1832) : a member of a Roman Catholic mendicant order founded by St. Paul of the Cross in Italy in 1720 and devoted chiefly to missionary work and retreats

passion play *n, often cap 1st P* (1870) : a dramatic representation of the scenes connected with the passion and crucifixion of Jesus

Passion Sunday *n* (14c) : the fifth Sunday in Lent

Pas·sion·tide \ˈpa-shən-ˌtīd\ *n* (1847) : the last two weeks of Lent

Passion Week *n* (15c) **1** : HOLY WEEK **2** : the week between Passion Sunday and Palm Sunday

pas·siv·ate \ˈpa-si-ˌvāt\ *vt* **-at·ed; -at·ing** (1913) **1** : to make inactive or less reactive ⟨~ the surface of steel by chemical treatment⟩ **2** : to protect (as a solid-state device) against contamination by coating or surface treatment — **pas·siv·ation** \ˌpa-si-ˈvā-shən\ *n*

[1]**pas·sive** \ˈpa-siv\ *adj* [ME, fr. L *passivus,* fr. *passus,* pp.] (14c) **1 a** (1) : acted upon by an external agency (2) : receptive to outside impressions or influences **b** (1) : asserting that the grammatical subject of a verb is subjected to or affected by the action represented by that verb ⟨the ~ voice⟩ (2) : containing or yielding a passive verb form **c** (1) : lacking in energy or will : LETHARGIC (2) : tending not to take an active or dominant part **d** : induced by an outside agency ⟨~ exercise of a paralyzed leg⟩ **2 a** : not active or operating : INERT **b** : of, relating to, or making direct use of the sun's heat usu. without the intervention of mechanical devices ⟨a ~ solar house⟩ **c** : LATENT **d** (1) : of, relating to, or characterized by a state of chemical inactivity; *esp* : resistant to corrosion (2) : not involving expenditure of chemical energy ⟨~ transport across a cell membrane⟩ **e** *of an electronic element* : exhibiting no gain or control **f** : relating to the detection of an object through its emission of energy or sound ⟨~ sonar⟩ **3 a** : receiving or enduring without resistance : SUBMISSIVE **b** : existing or occurring without being active, open, or direct ⟨~ support⟩ **4** : of, relating to, or being business activity in which the investor does not actively participate in the generation of income ***syn*** see INACTIVE — **pas·sive·ly** *adv* — **pas·sive·ness** *n* — **pas·siv·i·ty** \pa-ˈsi-və-tē\ *n*

[2]**passive** *n* (1530) **1** : a passive verb form **2** : the passive voice of a language

passive–aggressive *adj* (1946) : being, marked by, or displaying behavior characterized by the expression of negative feelings, resentment, and aggression in an unassertive passive way (as through procrastination and stubbornness) — **passive–aggressive** *n*

passive immunity *n* (1895) : immunity acquired by transfer of antibodies (as by injection of serum from an individual with active immunity) — **passive immunization** *n*

pas·sive–ma·trix \ˈpa-siv-ˈmā-triks\ *adj* (1986) : of, relating to, or being an LCD in which the pixels are controlled in groups

passive resistance *n* (1819) : resistance esp. to a government or an occupying power characterized mainly by noncooperation

passive restraint *n* (1970) : a restraint (as a self-locking seat belt) that acts automatically to protect an automobile rider during a crash

passive smoking *n* (1971) : the involuntary inhalation of tobacco smoke (as from another's cigarette) esp. by a nonsmoker

passive transfer *n* (1935) : a local transfer of skin sensitivity from an allergic to a normal person by injection of serum from the former that is used esp. for identifying specific allergens when a high degree of allergic sensitivity is suspected

pas·siv·ism \ˈpa-si-ˌvi-zəm\ *n* (1872) : a passive attitude, behavior, or way of life — **pas·siv·ist** \-vist\ *n*

pass·key \ˈpas-ˌkē\ *n* (ca. 1817) **1** : MASTER KEY **2** : SKELETON KEY

pass off *vt* (1681) **1** : to make public or offer for sale with intent to deceive **2** : to give a false identity or character to

pass out *vi* (1899) **1** : DIE 1 **2** : to lose consciousness ~ *vt* : to reject (a deal in bridge) as unplayable because everyone has passed on the first round of bidding

Pass·over \ˈpas-ˌō-vər\ *n* [fr. the exemption of the Israelites from the slaughter of the firstborn in Egypt (Exod 12:23–27)] (1530) : a Jewish holiday beginning on the 14th of Nisan and commemorating the Hebrews' liberation from slavery in Egypt

pass over *vt* (14c) **1** : to ignore in passing **2** : to pay no attention to the claims of : DISREGARD

pass·port \ˈpas-ˌpȯrt\ *n* [ME (Sc) *pasport,* fr. MF *passeport,* fr. *passer* to pass + *port* port, fr. L *portus* — more at FORD] (15c) **1 a** : a formal document issued by an authorized official of a country to one of its citizens that is usu. necessary for exit from and reentry into the country, that allows the citizen to travel in a foreign country in accordance with visa requirements, and that requests protection for the citizen while abroad **b** : a license issued by a country permitting a foreign citizen to pass or take goods through its territory : SAFE-CONDUCT **c** : a document of identification required by law to be carried by persons residing or traveling within a country **2 a** : a permission or authorization to go somewhere **b** : something that secures admission, acceptance, or attainment ⟨education as a ~ to success⟩

pass–through *n* (1951) **1** : the act, action, or process of offsetting increased costs by raising prices **2** : an opening in a wall between two rooms through which something (as dishes) may be passed

pass up *vt* (1896) : to let go by without accepting or taking advantage of ⟨*pass up* a chance for promotion⟩; *also* : DECLINE, REJECT

pass·word \ˈpas-ˌwərd\ *n* (1799) **1** : something that enables one to pass or gain admission: as **a** : a spoken word or phrase required to pass by a guard **b** : a sequence of characters required for access to a computer system **2** : WATCHWORD

[1]**past** \ˈpast\ *adj* [ME, fr. pp. of *passen* to pass] (14c) **1 a** : AGO ⟨12 years ~⟩ **b** : just gone or elapsed ⟨for the ~ few months⟩ **2** : having existed or taken place in a period before the present : BYGONE **3** : of, relating to, or constituting a verb tense that is expressive of elapsed time and that in English is usu. formed by internal vowel change (as in *sang*) or by the addition of a suffix (as in *laughed*) **4** : having served as a specified officer in an organization ⟨~ president⟩

[2]**past** *prep* (14c) **1 a** : beyond the age for or of ⟨~ playing with dolls⟩ **b** : AFTER ⟨half ~ two⟩ **2 a** : at the farther side of : BEYOND **b** : in a course or direction going close to and then beyond ⟨drove ~ the house⟩ **3** *obs* : more than **4** : beyond the capacity, range, or sphere of ⟨~ belief⟩

[3]**past** *n* (1520) **1 a** : time gone by **b** : something that happened or was done in the past ⟨regret the ~⟩ **2 a** : the past tense of a language **b** : a verb form in the past tense **3** : a past life, history, or course of action; *esp* : one that is kept secret — **past·less** \ˈpas(t)-ləs\ *adj*

[4]**past** *adv* (1546) : so as to reach and go beyond a point near at hand ⟨drove ~⟩

pas·ta \ˈpäs-tə *also* ˈpas-\ *n* [It, fr. LL] (1847) **1** : paste in processed form (as macaroni) or in the form of fresh dough (as ravioli) **2** : a dish of cooked pasta

[1]**paste** \ˈpāst\ *n* [ME, fr. AF, fr. LL *pasta* dough, paste] (14c) **1 a** : a dough that contains a considerable proportion of fat and is used for pastry crust or fancy rolls **b** : a confection made by evaporating fruit with sugar or by flavoring a gelatin, starch, or gum arabic preparation **c** : a smooth food product made by evaporation or grinding ⟨tomato ~⟩ ⟨almond ~⟩ **d** : a shaped dough (as spaghetti or ravioli) prepared from semolina, farina, or wheat flour **2** : a soft plastic mixture or composition: as **a** : a preparation usu. of flour or starch and water used as an adhesive or a vehicle for mordant or color **b** : clay or a clay mixture used in making pottery or porcelain **3** : a brilliant glass of high lead content used for the manufacture of artificial gems

[2]**paste** *vt* **past·ed; past·ing** (ca. 1562) **1** : to cause to adhere by or as if by paste : STICK **2** : to cover with something pasted on

[3]**paste** *vt* **past·ed; past·ing** [alter. of *baste*] (1846) **1** : to strike hard at **2** : to beat or defeat soundly ⟨*pasted* their opponents 42–0⟩

[1]**paste·board** \ˈpās(t)-ˌbȯrd\ *n* (1562) **1** : a solid cardboard with a paper facing; *broadly* : CARDBOARD **2** : TICKET 2a

[2]**pasteboard** *adj* (1599) **1** : made of pasteboard **2** : SHAM, UNSUBSTANTIAL ⟨prefabricated plots and ~ heroes —Peter Andrews⟩

paste·down \-ˌdau̇n\ *n* (ca. 1888) : the outer leaf of an endpaper that is pasted down to the inside of the front or back cover of a book

[1]**pas·tel** \pas-ˈtel\ *n* [F, fr. It *pastello,* fr. LL *pastellus* woad, fr. dim. of *pasta*] (1662) **1** : a paste made of powdered pigment ranging from pale to deep colors and used for making crayons; *also* : a crayon made of such paste **2 a** : a drawing in pastel **b** : the process or art of drawing with pastels **3** : a light literary sketch **4** : any of various pale or light colors

[2]**pastel** *adj* (1884) **1 a** : of or relating to a pastel **b** : made with pastels **2** : pale and light in color **3** : lacking in body or vigor

pas·tel·ist *or* **pas·tel·list** \-ˈte-list\ *n* (1881) : an artist who works with pastels

pas·tern \ˈpas-tərn\ *n* [MF *pasturon,* fr. *pasture* pastern, fr. OF *empasturer* to hobble (a horse), fr. *pasture* tether, modif. of LL (*chorda*) *pastoria,* fr. L, fem. of *pastorius* of a herdsman, fr. *pastor* herdsman — more at PASTOR] (ca. 1530) **1** : a part of the foot of an equine extending from the fetlock to the top of the hoof — see HORSE illustration **2** : a part of the leg of an animal other than an equine that corresponds to the pastern

paste·up \ˈpāst-ˌəp\ *n* (ca. 1930) : MECHANICAL; *also* : the process of making mechanicals

pas·teur·ise *Brit var of* PASTEURIZE

pas·teur·i·za·tion \ˌpas-chə-rə-ˈzā-shən, ˌpas-tyə-, -tə-\ *n* (1886) **1** : partial sterilization of a substance and esp. a liquid (as milk) at a temperature and for a period of exposure that destroys objectionable organisms without major chemical alteration of the substance **2** : irradiation of food products

pas·teur·ize \ˈpas-chə-ˌrīz, ˈpas-tyə-, -tə-\ *vt* **-ized; -iz·ing** [Louis *Pasteur*] (1881) : to subject to pasteurization — **pas·teur·iz·er** *n*

pas·tic·cio \pas-ˈtē-ch(ē-ˌ)ō, pä-\ *n, pl* **-ci** \-(ˌ)chē\ *or* **-cios** [It, lit., baked meat dish, pie, fr. VL **pasticium,* fr. LL *pasta*] (1752) : PASTICHE

pas·tiche \pas-ˈtēsh, päs-\ *n* [F, fr. It *pasticcio*] (1878) **1** : a literary, artistic, musical, or architectural work that imitates the style of previous work; *also* : such stylistic imitation **2 a** : a musical, literary, or artistic composition made up of selections from different works : POTPOURRI **b** : HODGEPODGE — **pas·ti·cheur** \ˌpas-tē-ˈshər, ˌpäs-\ *n*

past·ies \ˈpās-tēz\ *n pl* [[2]*paste*] (ca. 1954) : small round coverings for a woman's nipples worn esp. by a stripteaser

pas·tille \pas-ˈtēl\ *also* **pas·til** \ˈpas-tᵊl\ *n* [F *pastille,* fr. L *pastillus* small loaf, lozenge; akin to L *panis* bread — more at FOOD] (1658) **1** : a small mass of aromatic paste for fumigating or scenting the air of a room **2** : LOZENGE 3

pas·time \ˈpas-ˌtīm\ *n* (15c) : something that amuses and serves to make time pass agreeably : DIVERSION

pas·ti·na \ˈpäs-tē-nə\ *n* [It, dim. of *pasta* pasta] (ca. 1948) : very small bits of pasta used in soup or broth

pas·tis \päs-ˈtēs\ *n* [F, fr. F dial. (Marseilles), lit., jumble, kind of pastry, fr. Occitan, fr. Old Occitan *pastitz* cake, fr. VL **pasticium*] (1926) : a French liqueur flavored with aniseed

pas·ti·tsio \päs-ˈtēt-sē-(ˌ)ō\ *also* **pastitso** \-ˈtēt-(ˌ)sō\ *n* [ModGk, fr. It *pasticcio*] (ca. 1950) : a Greek baked dish made of ground meat layered with pasta and usu. topped with white sauce and cheese

past master *n* (1762) **1 :** one who has held the office of worshipful master in a lodge of Freemasons or of master in a guild, club, or society **2** [alter. of *passed master*] : one who is expert : ADEPT

past·ness \ˈpas(t)-nəs\ *n* (1829) **1 :** the quality or state of being past **2 :** the subjective quality of something being remembered rather than immediately experienced ⟨almost any popular record . . . is apt to be tinged with ~ —Roy McMullen⟩

[1]**pas·tor** \ˈpas-tər\ *n* [ME *pastour,* fr. AF, fr. L *pastor* herdsman, fr. *pascere* to feed — more at FOOD] (14c) : a spiritual overseer; *esp* : a clergyman serving a local church or parish — **pas·tor·ship** \-ˌship\ *n*

[2]**pastor** *vt* **pas·tored; pas·tor·ing** \-t(ə-)riŋ\ (1623) : to serve as pastor of (as a church)

[3]**pas·tor** \päs-ˈtȯr\ *n* [Sp, fr. L] (14c) *chiefly Southwest* : HERDSMAN

[1]**pas·to·ral** \ˈpas-t(ə-)rəl\ *adj* [ME, fr. L *pastoralis,* fr. *pastor* herdsman] (15c) **1 a** (1) : of, relating to, or composed of shepherds or herdsmen (2) : devoted to or based on livestock raising **b :** of or relating to the countryside : not urban ⟨a ~ setting⟩ **c :** portraying or expressive of the life of shepherds or country people esp. in an idealized and conventionalized manner ⟨~ poetry⟩ **d :** pleasingly peaceful and innocent : IDYLLIC **2 a :** of or relating to spiritual care or guidance esp. of a congregation **b :** of or relating to the pastor of a church — **pas·to·ral·ly** \-t(ə-)rə-lē\ *adv* — **pas·to·ral·ness** *n*

[2]**pastoral** \ˈpas-t(ə-)rəl; *1d is often* ˌpas-tə-ˈräl, -ˈral\ *n* (1584) **1 a :** a literary work (as a poem or play) dealing with shepherds or rural life in a usu. artificial manner and typically drawing a contrast between the innocence and serenity of the simple life and the misery and corruption of city and esp. court life **b :** pastoral poetry or drama **c :** a rural picture or scene **d :** PASTORALE 1a **2 :** CROSIER 1 **3 :** a letter of a pastor to his charge: as **a :** a letter addressed by a bishop to his diocese **b :** a letter of the house of bishops of the Protestant Episcopal Church to be read in each parish

pas·to·rale \ˌpas-tə-ˈräl, -ˈral *also* -ˈrä-lē\ *n* [It, fr. *pastorale* of herdsmen, fr. L *pastoralis*] (1724) **1 a :** an instrumental or vocal composition having a pastoral theme **b :** an opera of the 16th or 17th centuries having a pastoral plot **2 :** PASTORAL 1a

Pastoral Epistle *n* (1836) : one of three New Testament letters including two addressed to Timothy and one to Titus that give advice on matters of church government and discipline

pas·to·ral·ism \ˈpas-t(ə-)rə-ˌli-zəm\ *n* (1854) **1 :** the quality or style characteristic of pastoral writing **2 a :** livestock raising **b :** social organization based on livestock raising as the primary economic activity — **pas·to·ral·ist** \-list\ *n or adj*

pas·tor·ate \ˈpas-t(ə-)rət\ *n* (1795) **1 :** the office, state, jurisdiction, or tenure of office of a pastor **2 :** a body of pastors

past participle *n* (1798) : a participle that typically expresses completed action, that is traditionally one of the principal parts of the verb, and that is traditionally used in English in the formation of perfect tenses in the active voice and of all tenses in the passive voice

past perfect *adj* (1889) : of, relating to, or constituting a verb tense that is traditionally formed in English with *had* and denotes an action or state as completed at or before a past time spoken of — **past perfect** *n*

pas·tra·mi *also* **pas·tromi** \pə-ˈsträ-mē\ *n* [Yiddish *pastrame,* fr. Rom *pastramă* pressed and cured meat] (1925) : a highly seasoned smoked beef prepared esp. from shoulder cuts

pas·try \ˈpās-trē\ *n, pl* **pastries** [[1]*paste*] (ca. 1538) **1 a :** PASTE 1a **b :** sweet baked goods made of dough having a high fat content **2 :** a piece of pastry

past tense *n* (1813) : a verb tense expressing action or state in or as if in the past: **a :** a verb tense expressive of elapsed time (as *wrote* in "on arriving I wrote a letter") **b :** a verb tense expressing action or state in progress or continuance or habitually done or customarily occurring at a past time (as *was writing* in "I was writing while he dictated" or *loved* in "their sons loved fishing")

pas·tur·age \ˈpas-chə-rij\ *n* (ca. 1533) : PASTURE

[1]**pas·ture** \ˈpas-chər\ *n* [ME, fr. AF, fr. LL *pastura,* fr. L *pastus,* pp. of *pascere* to feed — more at FOOD] (14c) **1 :** plants (as grass) grown for the feeding esp. of grazing animals **2 :** land or a plot of land used for grazing **3 :** the feeding of livestock : GRAZING

[2]**pasture** *vb* **pas·tured; pas·tur·ing** *vi* (14c) : GRAZE, BROWSE ~ *vt* **1 :** to feed (as cattle) on pasture **2 :** to use as pasture

pas·ture·land \ˈpas-chər-ˌland\ *n* (1591) : PASTURE 2

[1]**pas·ty** \ˈpas-tē\ *n, pl* **pasties** [ME *pastee,* fr. AF *pasté,* fr. *paste* dough, paste] (13c) **1 :** a meat pie **2 :** TURNOVER 5

[2]**pasty** \ˈpās-tē\ *adj* **past·i·er; -est** (1659) : resembling paste; *esp* : pallid and unhealthy in appearance — **past·i·ness** \-nəs\ *n*

PA system \ˌpē-ˈā-\ *n* (ca. 1936) : PUBLIC-ADDRESS SYSTEM

[1]**pat** \ˈpat\ *n* [ME *patte,* prob. of imit. origin] (15c) **1 :** a light blow esp. with the hand or a flat instrument **2 :** a light tapping often rhythmical sound **3 :** something (as butter) shaped into a small flat usu. square individual portion — **pat on the back :** an expression of approval

[2]**pat** *adv* (1578) : in a pat manner : APTLY, PERFECTLY ⟨has her part down ~⟩

[3]**pat** *vb* **pat·ted; pat·ting** *vt* (1591) **1 :** to strike lightly with a flat instrument **2 :** to flatten, smooth, or put into place or shape with light blows **3 :** to tap or stroke gently with the hand to soothe, caress, or show approval ~ *vi* : to strike or beat gently

[4]**pat** *adj* (1646) **1 a :** exactly suited to the purpose or occasion : APT **b :** suspiciously appropriate : CONTRIVED ⟨a ~ ending⟩ **2 :** learned, mastered, or memorized exactly **3 :** FIRM, UNYIELDING **4 :** reduced to a simple or mechanical form : STANDARD, TRITE ⟨~ answers⟩

[5]**pat** *abbr* patent

PAT *abbr* point after touchdown

pa·ta·ca \pə-ˈtä-kə\ *n* [Pg] (1928) — see MONEY table

pat–a–cake *var of* PATTY-CAKE

pa·ta·gi·um \pə-ˈtā-jē-əm\ *n, pl* **-gia** \-jē-ə\ [NL, fr. L, gold edging on a tunic] (1826) **1 :** the fold of skin connecting the forelimbs and hind limbs of some tetrapods (as flying squirrels) **2 :** the fold of skin in front of the main segments of a bird's wing

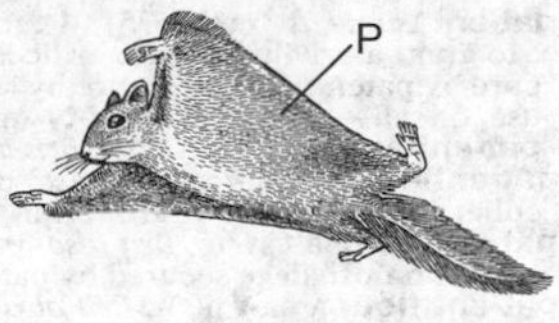

P patagium 1

[1]**patch** \ˈpach\ *n* [ME *pacche*] (14c) **1 :** a piece of material used to mend or cover a hole or a weak spot **2 :** a tiny piece of black silk or court plaster worn on the face or neck esp. by women to hide a blemish or to heighten beauty **3 a :** a piece of material (as adhesive plaster) used medically usu. to cover a wound **b :** a usu. disk-shaped piece of material that is worn on the skin and contains a substance (as a drug) that is absorbed at a constant rate through the skin into the bloodstream ⟨a nicotine ~⟩ **c :** a shield worn over the socket of an injured or missing eye **4 a :** a small piece : SCRAP **b :** a part or area distinct from that about it ⟨cabbage ~⟩ **c :** a period of time : SPELL ⟨was going through a rough ~⟩ **5 :** someone or something equal or comparable — usu. used in negative constructions ⟨the new chairman isn't a ~ on his predecessor⟩ **6 :** a piece of cloth sewed on a garment as an ornament or insignia; *esp* : SHOULDER PATCH **7 :** a temporary connection in a communication system (as a telephone hookup) **8 :** a minor correction or modification in a computer program

[2]**patch** *vt* (15c) **1 :** to mend, cover, or fill up a hole or weak spot in **2 :** to provide with a patch **3 a :** to make of patches or fragments **b :** to mend or put together esp. in hasty or shabby fashion — usu. used with *up* **c :** to apply a patch to (a computer program) **4 a :** to connect (as circuits) by a patch cord **b :** to connect (as a person or message) to a communication system esp. temporarily ⟨they ~*ed* him into the conference call⟩ ***syn*** see MEND

[3]**patch** *n* [perh. by folk etymology fr. It dial. *paccio*] (1549) : FOOL, DOLT

patch·board \ˈpach-ˌbȯrd\ *n* (1934) : a switchboard in which circuits are interconnected by patch cords

patch cord *n* (1926) : a wire with a plug at each end that is used to connect electrical devices

patch·ou·li *also* **patch·ou·ly** \ˈpa-chə-lē, pə-ˈchü-lē\ *n* [Tamil *paccuḷi*] (1845) : a heavy perfume made from the fragrant essential oil of a southeast Asian mint (*Pogostemon cablin*); *also* : the plant itself

patch pocket *n* (1895) : a flat pocket applied to the outside of a garment

patch test *n* (1933) : a test for determining allergic sensitivity that is made by applying to the unbroken skin small pads soaked with the allergen to be tested

patch·work \ˈpach-ˌwərk\ *n, often attrib* (1692) **1 :** something composed of miscellaneous or incongruous parts : HODGEPODGE **2 :** pieces of cloth of various colors and shapes sewn together to form a covering; *also* : something resembling such a covering ⟨a ~ of fields⟩

patchwork quilt *n* (1840) **1 :** a quilt made of patchwork **2 :** PATCHWORK 1

patchy \ˈpa-chē\ *adj* **patch·i·er; -est** (1798) **1 :** marked by, consisting of, or diversified with patches **2 :** irregular in appearance, makeup, or quality — **patch·i·ly** \ˈpa-chə-lē\ *adv* — **patch·i·ness** \ˈpa-chē-nəs\ *n*

pat down *vt* (ca. 1957) : FRISK

pate \ˈpāt\ *n* [ME] (14c) **1 :** HEAD **2 :** the crown of the head **3** *chiefly disparaging* : BRAIN — **pat·ed** \ˈpā-təd\ *adj*

pâte \ˈpät\ *n* [F, lit., paste, fr. OF *paste*] (1863) : PASTE 2b

pâ·té *also* **pate** \pä-ˈtā, pa-\ *n* [F, fr. MF *pasté* — more at PASTY] (1706) **1 :** a meat or fish pie or patty **2 :** a spread of finely chopped or pureed seasoned meat ⟨chicken liver ~⟩

pâ·té de foie gras \(ˌ)pä-ˌtā-də-ˌfwä-ˈgrä, (ˌ)pa-ˌtā-\ *n, pl* **pâ·tés de foie gras** \-ˌtā(z)-\ [F, lit., pâté of fat liver] (1827) : a pâté of fat goose liver and usu. truffles sometimes with added fat pork

pa·tel·la \pə-ˈte-lə\ *n, pl* **-lae** \-ˈte-(ˌ)lē, -ˌlī\ *or* **-las** [L, fr. dim. of *patina* shallow dish] (1693) : a thick flat triangular movable bone that forms the anterior point of the knee and protects the front of the joint — called also *kneecap* — **pa·tel·lar** \-ˈte-lər\ *adj*

pat·en \ˈpa-tᵊn\ *n* [ME, fr. AF *patene,* fr. ML & L; ML *patina,* fr. L, shallow dish, fr. Gk *patanē*] (14c) **1 :** a plate usu. made of precious metal and used to carry the bread at the Eucharist **2 a :** PLATE **b :** something (as a metal disk) resembling a plate

pa·ten·cy \ˈpa-tᵊn(t)-sē, ˈpā-\ *n* (1656) : the quality or state of being patent

[1]**pat·ent** *1–3 are* ˈpa-tᵊnt, *chiefly Brit* ˈpā-; *4* ˈpā-; *5* ˈpā-, ˈpa-; *6–7* ˈpa-, ˈpā-, *Brit usu* ˈpā-\ *adj* [ME, fr. AF, fr. L *patent-, patens,* fr. prp. of *patēre* to be open — more at FATHOM] (14c) **1 a :** open to public inspection — used chiefly in the phrase *letters patent* **b** (1) : secured by letters patent or by a patent to the exclusive control and possession of a particular individual or party (2) : protected by a patent : made under a patent ⟨~ locks⟩ **c :** protected by a trademark or a brand name so as to establish proprietary rights analogous to those conveyed by letters patent or a patent : PROPRIETARY ⟨~ drugs⟩ **2 :** of, relating to, or concerned with the granting of patents esp. for inventions ⟨a ~ lawyer⟩ **3 :** making exclusive or proprietary claims or pretensions **4 :** affording free passage : UNOBSTRUCTED ⟨a ~ opening⟩ **5 :** PATULOUS, SPREADING ⟨a ~ calyx⟩ **6** *archaic* : ACCESSIBLE, EXPOSED **7 :** readily visible or intelligible : OBVIOUS ***syn*** see EVIDENT — **pat·ent·ly** *adv*

[2]**pat·ent** \ˈpa-tᵊnt, *Brit also* ˈpā-\ *n* (14c) **1 :** an official document conferring a right or privilege : LETTERS PATENT **2 a :** a writing securing for a term of years the exclusive right to make, use, or sell an invention **b :** the monopoly or right so granted **c :** a patented invention **3 :** PRIVILEGE, LICENSE **4 :** an instrument making a conveyance of public lands; *also* : the land so conveyed **5 :** PATENT LEATHER

[3]**pat·ent** \same as [2]\ *vt* (1675) **1 :** to obtain or grant a patent right to **2 :** to grant a privilege, right, or license to by patent **3 :** to obtain or secure by patent; *esp* : to secure by letters patent exclusive right to make, use, or sell — **pat·ent·abil·i·ty** \ˌpa-tᵊn-tə-ˈbi-lə-tē, *Brit also* ˌpā-\ *n* — **pat·ent·able** \ˈpa-tᵊn-tə-bəl, *Brit also* ˈpā-\ *adj*

pat·ent·ed \ˈpa-tᵊn-təd, *Brit also* ˈpā-\ *adj* (1951) **:** originated by or peculiar to one person or group : INDIVIDUALIZED

pat·en·tee \ˌpa-tᵊn-ˈtē, *Brit also* ˌpā-\ *n* (15c) **:** one to whom a grant is made or a privilege secured by patent

pat·ent flour \ˈpa-tᵊn(t)-, *Brit also* ˈpā-\ *n* (1886) **:** a high-grade wheat flour that consists solely of endosperm

pat·ent leather \ˈpa-tᵊn(t)-, *Brit usu* ˈpā-\ *n* (1829) **:** a leather with a hard smooth glossy surface

patent medicine *n* (1770) **:** a packaged nonprescription drug which is protected by a trademark and whose contents are incompletely disclosed; *also* : any drug that is a proprietary

patent office *n* (1696) **:** a government office for examining claims to patents and granting patents

pat·en·tor \ˈpa-tᵊn-tər, ˌpa-tᵊn-ˈtȯr, *Brit also* ˈpā-, ˌpā-\ *n* (ca. 1890) **:** one that grants a patent

patent right *n* (1805) **:** a right granted by letters patent; *esp* : the exclusive right to an invention

pa·ter *n* (14c) **1** \ˈpä-ˌter\ *often cap* : PATERNOSTER **2** \ˈpā-tər\ [L] *chiefly Brit* : FATHER

pa·ter·fa·mil·i·as \ˌpa-tər-fə-ˈmi-lē-əs, ˌpä-, ˌpā-\ *n, pl* **pa·tres·fa·mil·i·as** \ˌpā-ˌtrēz-, ˌpä-ˌtrās-\ [ME, fr. L, fr. *pater* father + *familias,* archaic gen. of *familia* household — more at FATHER, FAMILY] (15c) **1 :** the male head of a household **2 :** the father of a family **3 :** a man who originates or is a leading figure in something (as a movement, discipline, or enterprise)

pa·ter·nal \pə-ˈtər-nᵊl\ *adj* [ME, fr. LL *paternalis,* fr. L *paternus* paternal, fr. *pater*] (15c) **1 a :** of or relating to a father **b :** like that of a father ⟨~ benevolence⟩ **2 :** received or inherited from one's male parent **3 :** related through one's father ⟨~ grandfather⟩ — **pa·ter·nal·ly** \-nᵊl-ē\ *adv*

pa·ter·nal·ism \pə-ˈtər-nə-ˌli-zəm\ *n* (1881) **1 :** a system under which an authority undertakes to supply needs or regulate conduct of those under its control in matters affecting them as individuals as well as in their relations to authority and to each other **2 :** a policy or practice based on or characteristic of paternalism — **pa·ter·nal·ist** \-nə-list\ *n or adj* — **pa·ter·nal·is·tic** \-ˌtər-nə-ˈlis-tik\ *adj* — **pa·ter·nal·is·ti·cal·ly** \-ti-k(ə-)lē\ *adv*

[1]**pa·ter·ni·ty** \pə-ˈtər-nə-tē\ *n* (1582) **1 :** the quality or state of being a father **2 :** origin or descent from a father

[2]**paternity** *adj* (1926) **1 :** granted to a father ⟨~ leave⟩ ⟨~ rights⟩ **2 :** of or relating to the determination of paternity ⟨a ~ suit⟩

paternity test *n* (1926) **:** a test esp. of DNA or genetic traits to determine whether a given man could be the biological father of a given child

pa·ter·nos·ter \ˌpä-tər-ˈnäs-tər, ˈpa-tər-ˌ, ˈpä-ˌter-ˈ, -ˈnäs-ˌter\ *n* [ME, fr. OE, fr. ML, fr. L *pater noster* our father, fr. the opening words] (bef. 12c) **1** *often cap* : LORD'S PRAYER **2 :** a word formula repeated as a prayer or magical charm

[1]**path** \ˈpath, ˈpäth\ *n, pl* **paths** \ˈpathz, ˈpaths, ˈpäthz, ˈpäths\ [ME, fr. OE *pæth;* akin to OHG *pfad* path] (bef. 12c) **1 :** a trodden way **2 :** a track specially constructed for a particular use **3 a :** COURSE, ROUTE **b :** a way of life, conduct, or thought **4 a :** the continuous series of positions or configurations that can be assumed in any motion or process of change by a moving or varying system **b :** a sequence of arcs in a network that can be traced continuously without retracing any arc **5 :** PATHWAY 2

[2]**path** *or* **pathol** *abbr* pathological; pathology

path- *or* **patho-** *comb form* [NL, fr. Gk, fr. *pathos,* lit., suffering — more at PATHOS] **:** pathological state : disease ⟨*patho*gen⟩

-path *n comb form* [G, back-formation fr. *-pathie* -pathy] **1 :** practitioner of a (specified) system of medicine that emphasizes one aspect of disease or its treatment ⟨naturo*path*⟩ **2** [ISV, fr. Gk *-pathēs,* adj., suffering, fr. *pathos*] **a :** one suffering from a disorder (of such a part or system) ⟨psycho*path*⟩ **b :** one perceiving ⟨tele*path*⟩

Pa·than \pə-ˈtän, ˌpä-\ *n* [Hindi & Urdu *Paṭhān,* fr. Pashto (eastern dial.) *Paxtana,* pl. of *Paxtun*] (1638) **:** PASHTUN

path·break·ing \ˈpath-ˌbrā-kiŋ\ *adj* (1914) **:** TRAILBLAZING

pa·thet·ic \pə-ˈthe-tik\ *adj* [MF or LL; MF *pathetique,* fr. LL *patheticus,* fr. Gk *pathētikos* capable of feeling, pathetic, fr. *paschein* (aor. *pathein*) to experience, suffer — more at PATHOS] (1598) **1 :** having a capacity to move one to either compassionate or contemptuous pity **2 :** marked by sorrow or melancholy : SAD **3 :** pitifully inferior or inadequate ⟨the restaurant's ~ service⟩ **4 :** ABSURD, LAUGHABLE ⟨a ~ costume⟩ ***syn*** see MOVING — **pa·thet·i·cal** \-ti-kəl\ *adj* — **pa·thet·i·cal·ly** \-ti-k(ə-)lē\ *adv*

pathetic fallacy *n* (1856) **:** the ascription of human traits or feelings to inanimate nature (as in *cruel sea*)

path·find·er \ˈpath-ˌfīn-dər, ˈpäth-\ *n* (1840) **:** one that discovers a way; *esp* : one that explores untraversed regions to mark out a new route — **path·find·ing** \-diŋ\ *n or adj*

path·less \-ləs\ *adj* (1591) **:** UNTRODDEN, TRACKLESS — **path·less·ness** *n*

patho·bi·ol·o·gy \ˌpa-thō-bī-ˈä-lə-jē\ *n* (ca. 1909) **:** PATHOLOGY

path·o·gen \ˈpa-thə-jən\ *n* [ISV] (1880) **:** a specific causative agent (as a bacterium or virus) of disease

path·o·gen·e·sis \ˌpa-thə-ˈje-nə-səs\ *n* [NL] (1876) **:** the origination and development of a disease

path·o·ge·net·ic \-jə-ˈne-tik\ *adj* [ISV] (1838) **1 :** of or relating to pathogenesis **2 :** PATHOGENIC 2

path·o·gen·ic \-ˈje-nik\ *adj* [ISV] (1852) **1 :** PATHOGENETIC 1 **2 :** causing or capable of causing disease — **path·o·ge·nic·i·ty** \-jə-ˈni-sə-tē\ *n*

pa·tho·gno·mon·ic \ˌpa-thə(g)-nō-ˈmä-nik\ *adj* [Gk *pathognōmonikos,* fr. *path-* + *gnōmonikos* fit to judge, fr. *gnōmōn* interpreter; akin to Gk *gignōskein* to know — more at KNOW] (1625) **:** distinctively characteristic of a particular disease

pa·thog·ra·phy \pə-ˈthä-grə-fē\ *n* (1917) **:** biography that focuses on a person's illnesses, misfortunes, or failures; *also* : sensational or morbid biography

path·o·log·i·cal \ˌpa-thə-ˈlä-ji-kəl\ *also* **path·o·log·ic** \-jik\ *adj* (1688) **1 :** of or relating to pathology **2 :** altered or caused by disease; *also* : indicative of disease **3 :** being such to a degree that is extreme, excessive, or markedly abnormal ⟨a ~ liar⟩ ⟨~ fear⟩ — **path·o·log·i·cal·ly** \-ji-k(ə-)lē\ *adv*

pa·thol·o·gist \pə-ˈthä-lə-jist, pa-\ *n* (1650) **:** a specialist in pathology; *specif* : one who interprets and diagnoses the changes caused by disease in tissues and body fluids

pa·thol·o·gize \pə-ˈthä-lə-ˌjīz\ *vt* **-gized; -giz·ing** (1649) **:** to view or characterize as medically or psychologically abnormal ⟨natural hormonal shifts have been *pathologized* —Joyce C. Mills⟩

pa·thol·o·gy \-jē\ *n, pl* **-gies** [NL *pathologia* & MF *pathologie,* fr. Gk *pathologia* study of the emotions, fr. *path-* + *-logia* -logy] (1611) **1 :** the study of the essential nature of diseases and esp. of the structural and functional changes produced by them **2 :** something abnormal: **a :** the structural and functional deviations from the normal that constitute disease or characterize a particular disease **b :** deviation from propriety or from an assumed normal state of something nonliving or nonmaterial **c :** deviation giving rise to social ills ⟨connections between these *pathologies* . . . and crime —Wendy Kaminer⟩

path·o·phys·i·ol·o·gy \ˌpa-thō-ˌfi-zē-ˈä-lə-jē\ *n* (1947) **:** the physiology of abnormal states; *specif* : the functional changes that accompany a particular syndrome or disease — **path·o·phys·i·o·log·i·cal** \-zē-ə-ˈlä-ji-kəl\ *or* **path·o·phys·i·o·log·ic** \-jik\ *adj*

pa·thos \ˈpā-ˌthäs, -ˌthȯs, -ˌthōs *also* ˈpa-\ *n* [Gk, suffering, experience, emotion, fr. *paschein* (aor. *pathein*) to experience, suffer; perh. akin to Lith *kęsti* to suffer] (1591) **1 :** an element in experience or in artistic representation evoking pity or compassion **2 :** an emotion of sympathetic pity

path·way \ˈpath-ˌwā, ˈpäth-\ *n* (15c) **1 :** PATH, COURSE **2 :** a line of communication over interconnecting neurons extending from one organ or center to another; *also* : a network of interconnecting neurons along which a nerve impulse travels **3 :** the sequence of usu. enzyme-catalyzed reactions by which one substance is converted into another ⟨metabolic ~*s*⟩

-pathy *n comb form* [L *-pathia,* fr. Gk *-patheia,* fr. *-pathēs* suffering, fr. *pathos*] **1 :** feeling : suffering ⟨em*pathy*⟩ : perception ⟨tele*pathy*⟩ **2 :** disorder of (such) a part or kind ⟨neuro*pathy*⟩ **3 :** system of medicine based on (such) a factor ⟨osteo*pathy*⟩

pa·tience \ˈpā-shən(t)s\ *n* (13c) **1 :** the capacity, habit, or fact of being patient **2** *chiefly Brit* : SOLITAIRE 2

[1]**pa·tient** \ˈpā-shənt\ *adj* [ME *pacient,* fr. AF, fr. L *patient-, patiens,* fr. prp. of *pati* to suffer; perh. akin to Gk *pēma* suffering] (14c) **1 :** bearing pains or trials calmly or without complaint **2 :** manifesting forbearance under provocation or strain **3 :** not hasty or impetuous **4 :** steadfast despite opposition, difficulty, or adversity **5 a :** able or willing to bear — used with *of* **b :** SUSCEPTIBLE, ADMITTING ⟨~ of one interpretation⟩ — **pa·tient·ly** *adv*

[2]**patient** *n* (14c) **1 a :** an individual awaiting or under medical care and treatment **b :** the recipient of any of various personal services **2 :** one that is acted upon

patient dumping *n* (1973) **:** DUMPING 2

pa·ti·na \pə-ˈtē-nə, ˈpa-tə-nə\ *n, pl* **pa·ti·nas** \-nəz\ *or* **pa·ti·nae** \-ˌnē, -ˌnī\ [It, fr. L, shallow dish — more at PATEN] (1748) **1 a :** a usu. green film formed naturally on copper and bronze by long exposure or artificially (as by acids) and often valued aesthetically for its color **b :** a surface appearance of something grown beautiful esp. with age or use **2 :** an appearance or aura that is derived from association, habit, or established character **3 :** a superficial covering or exterior

pat·i·nate \ˈpa-tə-ˌnāt\ *vb* **-nat·ed; -nat·ing** *vt* (1880) **:** to give a patina to ~ *vi* : to take on a patina — usu. used in the past participle ⟨*patinated* bronze⟩ — **pat·i·na·tion** \ˌpa-tə-ˈnā-shən\ *n*

[1]**pa·tine** \pa-ˈtēn\ *n* [F, fr. It *patina*] (1883) **:** PATINA

[2]**patine** *vt* **pa·tined; pa·tin·ing** (1896) **:** to cover with a patina

pa·tio \ˈpa-tē-ˌō *also* ˈpä-\ *n, pl* **pa·ti·os** [Sp] (1828) **1 :** COURTYARD; *esp* : an inner court open to the sky **2 :** a recreation area that adjoins a dwelling, is often paved, and is adapted esp. to outdoor dining

pa·tis·se·rie *or* **pâ·tis·se·rie** \pə-ˈti-sə-rē, pä-\ *n* [F *pâtisserie,* fr. MF *pastiserie,* fr. *pasticier* to make pastry, fr. OF **pastitz* cake, fr. VL **pasticium,* fr. LL *pasta* dough] (1784) **1 :** PASTRY 1b **2 :** a pastry shop

pâ·tis·sier *or* **pa·tis·sier** \pä-tis-ˈyā\ *n* [F *pâtissier,* fr. OF *pasticier,* fr. OF **pastitz* cake] (ca. 1905) **:** a pastry chef

pa·tois \ˈpa-ˌtwä, ˈpä-\ *n, pl* **pa·tois** \-ˌtwäz\ [F] (1643) **1 a :** a dialect other than the standard or literary dialect **b :** uneducated or provincial speech **2 :** the characteristic special language of an occupational or social group : JARGON

patr- *or* **patri-** *or* **patro-** *comb form* [*patr-, patri-* fr. L, fr. *patr-, pater; patr-, patro-* fr. Gk, fr. *patr-, patēr* — more at FATHER] **:** father ⟨*patr*istic⟩

pa·tri·arch \ˈpā-trē-ˌärk\ *n* [ME *patriarche,* fr. AF, fr. LL *patriarcha,* fr. Gk *patriarchēs,* fr. *patria* lineage (fr. *patr-, patēr* father) + *-archēs* -arch — more at FATHER] (13c) **1 a :** one of the scriptural fathers of the human race or of the Hebrew people **b :** a man who is father or founder **c** (1) **:** the oldest member or representative of a group (2) **:** a venerable old man **d :** a man who is head of a patriarchy **2 a :** any of the bishops of the ancient or Eastern Orthodox sees of Constantinople, Alexandria, Antioch, and Jerusalem or the ancient and Western see of Rome with authority over other bishops **b :** the head of any of various Eastern churches **c :** a Roman Catholic bishop next in rank to the pope with purely titular or with metropolitan jurisdiction **3 :** a Mormon of the Melchizedek priesthood empowered to perform the ordinances of the church and pronounce blessings within a stake or prescribed jurisdiction

pa·tri·ar·chal \ˌpā-trē-ˈär-kəl\ *adj* (15c) **:** of, relating to, or being a patriarch or patriarchy

patriarchal cross *n* (ca. 1727) **:** a chiefly heraldic cross denoting a cardinal's or archbishop's rank and having two crossbars of which the lower is the longer and intersects the upright above or at its center — called also *cross of Lorraine;* see CROSS illustration

pa·tri·arch·ate \ˈpā-trē-ˌär-kət, -ˌkāt\ *n* (1617) **1 a :** the office, jurisdiction, or time in office of a patriarch **b :** the residence or headquarters of a patriarch **2 :** PATRIARCHY

pa·tri·ar·chy \-ˌär-kē\ *n, pl* **-chies** (1632) **1 :** social organization marked by the supremacy of the father in the clan or family, the legal dependence of wives and children, and the reckoning of descent and inheritance in the male line; *broadly* : control by men of a disproportionately large share of power **2** : a society or institution organized according to the principles or practices of patriarchy

pa·tri·cian \pə-ˈtri-shən\ *n* [ME *patricion*, fr. AF *patrician*, fr. L *patricius*, fr. *patres* senators, fr. pl. of *pater* father — more at FATHER] (15c) **1** : a member of one of the original citizen families of ancient Rome **2 a** : a person of high birth : ARISTOCRAT **b** : a person of breeding and cultivation — **patrician** *adj*

pa·tri·ci·ate \-ˈtri-shē-ət, -ˌāt\ *n* (ca. 1656) **1** : the position or dignity of a patrician **2** : a patrician class

pat·ri·cide \ˈpa-trə-ˌsīd\ *n* (1593) **1** [L *patricida*, fr. *patr-* + *-cida* -cide] : one who murders his or her own father **2** [LL *patricidium*, fr. L *patr-* + *-cidium* -cide] : the murder of one's own father — **pat·ri·cid·al** \ˌpa-trə-ˈsī-dᵊl\ *adj*

pat·ri·lin·eal \ˌpa-trə-ˈli-nē-əl\ *adj* (1904) : relating to, based on, or tracing descent through the paternal line ⟨a ~ society⟩

pat·ri·mo·ny \ˈpa-trə-ˌmō-nē\ *n* [ME *patrimoine, patrimonie*, fr. AF *patremoine*, fr. L *patrimonium*, fr. *patr-, pater* father] (14c) **1 a** : an estate inherited from one's father or ancestor **b** : anything derived from one's father or ancestors : HERITAGE **2** : an estate or endowment belonging by ancient right to a church — **pat·ri·mo·ni·al** \ˌpa-trə-ˈmō-nē-əl\ *adj*

pa·tri·ot \ˈpā-trē-ət, -ˌät, *chiefly Brit* ˈpa-trē-ət\ *n* [MF *patriote* compatriot, fr. LL *patriota*, fr. Gk *patriōtēs*, fr. *patria* lineage, fr. *patr-, patēr* father] (1605) : one who loves his or her country and supports its authority and interests

pa·tri·ot·ic \ˌpā-trē-ˈä-tik, *chiefly Brit* ˌpa-\ *adj* (1757) **1** : inspired by patriotism **2** : befitting or characteristic of a patriot — **pa·tri·ot·i·cal·ly** \-ti-k(ə-)lē\ *adv*

pa·tri·ot·ism \ˈpā-trē-ə-ˌti-zəm, *chiefly Brit* ˈpa-\ *n* (ca. 1726) : love for or devotion to one's country

Patriots' Day *n* (1897) : the third Monday in April observed as a legal holiday in Maine and Massachusetts in commemoration of the battles of Lexington and Concord in 1775

pa·tris·tic \pə-ˈtris-tik\ *also* **pa·tris·ti·cal** \-ti-kəl\ *adj* (ca. 1828) : of or relating to the church fathers or their writings

pa·tris·tics \-tiks\ *n pl but sing in constr* (1847) : the study of the writings and background of the church fathers

Pa·tro·clus \pə-ˈtrō-kləs, -ˈträ-\ *n* [L, fr. Gk *Patroklos*] (15c) : a Greek hero and friend of Achilles slain by Hector at Troy

[1]**pa·trol** \pə-ˈtrōl\ *n* (1664) **1 a** : the action of traversing a district or beat or of going the rounds along a chain of guards for observation or the maintenance of security **b** : the person performing such an action **c** : a unit of persons or vehicles employed for reconnaissance, security, or combat **2** : a subdivision of a Boy Scout troop or Girl Scout troop

[2]**patrol** *vb* **pa·trolled; pa·trol·ling** [F *patrouiller*, fr. MF, to tramp around in the mud, fr. *patte* paw — more at PATTEN] *vi* (1691) : to carry out a patrol ~ *vt* : to carry out a patrol of — **pa·trol·ler** *n*

pa·trol·man \pə-ˈtrōl-mən\ *n* (1867) : one who patrols; *esp* : a police officer assigned to a beat

patrol wagon *n* (1887) : PADDY WAGON

pa·tron \ˈpā-trən, *for 6 also* pa-ˈtrōⁿ\ *n* [ME, fr. AF, fr. ML & L; ML *patronus* patron saint, patron of a benefice, pattern, fr. L, defender, fr. *patr-, pater*] (14c) **1 a** : a person chosen, named, or honored as a special guardian, protector, or supporter **b** : a wealthy or influential supporter of an artist or writer **c** : a social or financial sponsor of a social function (as a ball or concert) **2** : one that uses wealth or influence to help an individual, an institution, or a cause **3** : one who buys the goods or uses the services offered esp. by an establishment **4** : the holder of the right of presentation to an English ecclesiastical benefice **5** : a master in ancient times who freed his slave but retained some rights over him **6** [F, fr. MF] : the proprietor of an establishment (as an inn) esp. in France **7** : the chief male officer in some fraternal lodges having both men and women members — **pa·tron·al** \ˈpā-trə-nᵊl; *Brit* pə-ˈtrō-nᵊl, pa-\ *adj*

pa·tron·age \ˈpa-trə-nij, ˈpā-\ *n* (14c) **1** : ADVOWSON **2** : the support or influence of a patron **3** : kindness done with an air of superiority **4** : business or activity provided by patrons ⟨the new branch library is expected to have a heavy ~⟩ **5 a** : the power to make appointments to government jobs esp. for political advantage **b** : the distribution of jobs on the basis of patronage **c** : jobs distributed by patronage

pa·tron·ess \ˈpā-trə-nəs\ *n* (15c) : a woman who is a patron

pa·tron·ise *Brit var of* PATRONIZE

pa·tron·ize \ˈpā-trə-ˌnīz, ˈpa-\ *vt* **-ized; -iz·ing** (1589) **1** : to act as patron of : provide aid or support for **2** : to adopt an air of condescension toward : treat haughtily or coolly **3** : to be a frequent or regular customer or client of — **pa·tron·i·za·tion** \ˌpā-trə-nə-ˈzā-shən, pa-\ *n* — **pa·tron·iz·ing·ly** \ˈpā-trə-ˌnī-ziŋ-lē, ˈpa-\ *adv*

patron saint *n* (1717) **1** : a saint to whose protection and intercession a person, a society, a church, or a place is dedicated **2** : an original leader or prime exemplar

pat·ro·nym·ic \ˌpa-trə-ˈni-mik\ *n* [ultim. fr. Gk *patrōnymia* patronymic, fr. *patr-* + *onyma* name — more at NAME] (1612) : a name derived from that of the father or a paternal ancestor usu. by the addition of an affix — **patronymic** *adj*

pa·troon \pə-ˈtrün\ *n* [F *patron* & Sp *patrón*, fr. ML *patronus*, fr. L, patron] (1743) **1** *archaic* : the captain or officer commanding a ship **2** [D, fr. F *patron*] : the proprietor of a manorial estate esp. in New York orig. granted under Dutch rule but in some cases existing until the mid-19th century

pat·sy \ˈpat-sē\ *n, pl* **pat·sies** [perh. fr. It *pazzo* fool] (1903) : a person who is easily manipulated or victimized : PUSHOVER

pat·ten \ˈpa-tᵊn\ *n* [ME *patin*, fr. AF, fr. *pate* paw, hoof, fr. VL **patta*, of imit. origin] (14c) : a clog, sandal, or overshoe often with a wooden sole or metal device to elevate the foot and increase the wearer's height or aid in walking in mud

[1]**pat·ter** \ˈpa-tər\ *vb* [ME *patren*, fr. *paternoster*] *vt* (14c) : to say or speak in a rapid or mechanical manner ~ *vi* **1** : to recite prayers (as paternosters) rapidly or mechanically **2** : to talk glibly and volubly **3** : to speak or sing rapid-fire words in a theatrical performance — **pat·ter·er** \-tər-ər\ *n*

[2]**patter** *n* (1758) **1** : a specialized lingo : CANT; *esp* : the jargon of criminals (as thieves) **2** : the spiel of a street hawker or of a circus barker **3** : empty chattering talk **4 a** (1) : the rapid-fire talk of a comedian (2) : the talk with which an entertainer accompanies a routine **b** : the words of a comic song or of a rapidly spoken usu. humorous monologue introduced into such a song

[3]**patter** *vb* [freq. of [3]*pat*] *vi* (1611) **1** : to strike or pat rapidly and repeatedly **2** : to run with quick light-sounding steps ~ *vt* : to cause to patter

[4]**patter** *n* (1844) : a quick succession of light sounds or pats

[1]**pat·tern** \ˈpa-tərn\ *n* [ME *patron*, fr. AF, fr. ML *patronus*] (14c) **1** : a form or model proposed for imitation : EXEMPLAR **2** : something designed or used as a model for making things ⟨a dressmaker's ~⟩ **3** : an artistic, musical, literary, or mechanical design or form **4** : a natural or chance configuration ⟨frost ~*s*⟩ ⟨the ~ of events⟩ **5** : a length of fabric sufficient for an article (as of clothing) **6 a** : the distribution of shrapnel, bombs on a target, or shot from a shotgun **b** : the grouping made on a target by bullets **7** : a reliable sample of traits, acts, tendencies, or other observable characteristics of a person, group, or institution ⟨a behavior ~⟩ ⟨spending ~*s*⟩ **8 a** : the flight path prescribed for an airplane that is coming in for a landing **b** : a prescribed route to be followed by a pass receiver in football **9** : TEST PATTERN **10** : a discernible coherent system based on the intended interrelationship of component parts ⟨foreign policy ~*s*⟩ **11** : frequent or widespread incidence ⟨a ~ of dissent⟩ ⟨a ~ of violence⟩ ***syn*** see MODEL — **pat·terned** \-tərnd\ *adj* — **pat·tern·less** *adj*

[2]**pattern** *vt* (ca. 1586) **1** *dial chiefly Eng* **a** : MATCH **b** : IMITATE **2** : to make, adapt, or fashion according to a pattern **3** : to furnish, adorn, or mark with a design ~ *vi* : to form a pattern

pat·tern·ing \ˈpa-tər-niŋ\ *n* (1862) **1** : decoration, composition, or configuration according to a pattern **2** : physical therapy esp. for neurological impairment based on a theory holding that repeated manipulation of body parts to simulate normal motor developmental activity (as crawling or walking) promotes neurological development or repair

pat·ty *also* **pat·tie** \ˈpa-tē\ *n, pl* **patties** [F *pâté* pâté] (1710) **1** : a little pie **2 a** : a small flat cake of chopped food ⟨a hamburger ~⟩ **b** : a small flat candy ⟨a peppermint ~⟩ **3** : PATTY SHELL

pat·ty–cake \ˈpa-tē-ˌkāk\ *or* **pat–a–cake** \ˈpa-də-ˌkāk, ˈpat-ə-\ *n* [fr. the opening words of the rhyme] (1889) : a game in which two participants (as mother and child) clap their hands together to the rhythm of an accompanying nursery rhyme

pat·ty·pan \ˈpa-tē-ˌpan\ *n* [*pattypan* pan for baking patties] (1900) : a roundish summer squash having a scalloped edge — called also *cymling*

patty shell *n* (1909) : a shell of puff pastry made to hold a creamed meat, fish, or vegetable filling

pat·u·lous \ˈpa-chə-ləs\ *adj* [L *patulus*, fr. *patēre* to be open — more at FATHOM] (1616) : spreading widely from a center ⟨a tree with ~ branches⟩

pat·zer \ˈpät-sər, ˈpat-\ *also* **pot·zer** \ˈpät-\ *n* [prob. fr. G *Patzer* bungler, fr. *patzen* to blunder] (1959) : an inept chess player

pau·ci·ty \ˈpȯ-sə-tē\ *n* [ME *paucite*, fr. L *paucitat-, paucitas*, fr. *paucus* little — more at FEW] (15c) **1** : smallness of number : FEWNESS **2** : smallness of quantity : DEARTH

Paul \ˈpȯl\ *n* [L *Paulus*, fr. Gk *Paulos*] (bef. 12c) : an early Christian apostle and missionary and author of several New Testament epistles

Paul Bun·yan \-ˈbən-yən\ *n* (1925) : a giant lumberjack of American folklore

Pau·li exclusion principle \ˈpau̇-lē-\ *n* [Wolfgang *Pauli*] (1926) : EXCLUSION PRINCIPLE — called also *Pauli principle*

Pau·line \ˈpȯ-ˌlīn\ *adj* (1817) : of or relating to the apostle Paul, his epistles, or the doctrine or theology implicit in his epistles

Paul·ist \ˈpȯ-list\ *n* (ca. 1883) : a member of the Roman Catholic Congregation of the Missionary Priests of St. Paul the Apostle founded by I. T. Hecker in the U.S. in 1858

pau·low·nia \pȯ-ˈlō-nē-ə\ *n* [NL, fr. Anna *Pavlovna* †1865 Russ. princess] (1843) : any of a genus (*Paulownia*) of Chinese trees of the snapdragon family; *esp* : one (*P. tomentosa*) widely cultivated for its panicles of fragrant violet flowers

paunch \ˈpȯnch, ˈpänch\ *n* [ME, fr. AF **panche, pance*, fr. L *pantic-, pantex*] (14c) **1 a** : the belly and its contents **b** : POTBELLY **2** : RUMEN

paunchy \ˈpȯn-chē, ˈpän-\ *adj* **paunch·i·er; -est** (1598) : having a potbelly — **paunch·i·ness** *n*

pau·per \ˈpȯ-pər\ *n* [L, poor — more at POOR] (1516) **1** : a person destitute of means except such as are derived from charity; *specif* : one who receives aid from funds designated for the poor **2** : a very poor person — **pau·per·ism** \-pə-ˌri-zəm\ *n*

pau·per·ize \ˈpȯ-pə-ˌrīz\ *vt* **-ized; -iz·ing** (1834) : to reduce to poverty — **pau·per·i·za·tion** \ˌpȯ-pə-rə-ˈzā-shən\ *n*

pau·piette \pō-ˈpyet\ *n* [F *paupiette*, fr. It *polpetta* meat croquette, dim. of *polpa* pulp, flesh, fr. L *pulpa*] (1889) : a thin slice of meat or fish wrapped around a forcemeat filling

[1]**pause** \ˈpȯz\ *n* [ME, fr. L *pausa*, fr. Gk *pausis*, fr. *pauein* to stop] (15c) **1** : a temporary stop **2 a** : a break in a verse **b** : a brief suspension of the voice to indicate the limits and relations of sentences and their parts **3** : temporary inaction esp. as caused by uncertainty : HESITATION **4 a** : the sign denoting a fermata **b** : a mark (as a period or comma) used in writing or printing to indicate or correspond to a pause of voice **5** : a reason or cause for pausing (as to reconsider) ⟨a thought that should give one ~⟩ **6** : a function of an electronic device that pauses a recording

[2]**pause** *vb* **paused; paus·ing** *vi* (15c) **1** : to stop temporarily **2** : to linger for a time ~ *vt* : to cause to pause : STOP

pa·vane \pə-ˈvän, -ˈvan\ *also* **pa·van** *same or* ˈpa-vən\ *n* [MF *pavane*, fr. It dial. *pavana*, fr. fem. of *pavano* of Padua, fr. *Pava* (Tuscan *Padova*) Padua] (1535) **1** : a stately court dance by couples that was introduced from southern Europe into England in the 16th century **2** : mu-

910 pave • PCI

sic for the pavane; *also* : music having the slow duple rhythm of a pavane

pave \ˈpāv\ *vt* **paved; pav·ing** [ME, fr. AF *paver,* fr. L *pavire* to strike, pound; perh. akin to Gk *paiein* to strike] (14c) **1** : to lay or cover with material (as asphalt or concrete) that forms a firm level surface for travel **2** : to cover firmly and solidly as if with paving material **3** : to serve as a covering or pavement of — **pave the way** : to prepare a smooth easy way : facilitate development

pa·vé \pa-ˈvā\ *also* **pa·véed** *or* **pa·véd** \pa-ˈvād\ *or* **pa·ve** \pa-ˈvā\ *adj* [*pavé* fr. F, fr. pp. of *paver* to pave] (1903) *of jewels* : set as close together as possible to conceal a metal base

pave·ment \ˈpāv-mənt\ *n* [ME, fr. AF, fr. L *pavimentum,* fr. *pavire*] (13c) **1** : a paved surface: as **a** : the artificially covered surface of a public thoroughfare **b** *chiefly Brit* : SIDEWALK **2** : the material with which something is paved **3** : something that suggests a pavement (as in flatness, hardness, and extent of surface)

pav·er \ˈpā-vər\ *n* (15c) **1** : one that paves **2** : PAVEMENT 2

[1]**pa·vil·ion** \pə-ˈvil-yən\ *n* [ME *pavilloun, pavillioun,* fr. AF, fr. L *papilion-, papilio* butterfly; perh. akin to OHG *fifaltra* butterfly] (13c) **1 a** : a large often sumptuous tent **b** : something resembling a canopy or tent ⟨tree ferns spread their delicate ~*s* —Blanche E. Baughan⟩ **2 a** : a part of a building projecting from the rest **b** : one of several detached or semidetached units into which a building is sometimes divided **3 a** : a usu. open sometimes ornamental structure in a garden, park, or place of recreation that is used for entertainment or shelter **b** : a temporary structure erected at an exposition by an individual exhibitor **4** : the lower faceted part of a brilliant below the girdle — see BRILLIANT illustration

[2]**pavilion** *vt* (14c) : to furnish or cover with or put in a pavilion

paving *n* (15c) : PAVEMENT

pav·ior *or* **pav·iour** \ˈpāv-yər\ *n* [ME *pavier,* fr. *paven* to pave] (15c) *Brit* : PAVER

pav·lo·va \pav-lə-və, pav-ˈlō-\ *n, often cap* [Anna *Pavlova*] (1926) : a dessert of Australian and New Zealand origin consisting of a meringue shell topped with whipped cream and usu. fruit

Pav·lov·i·an \pav-ˈlō-vē-ən, -ˈlō-; -ˈlō-fē-\ *adj* (1926) **1** : of or relating to Ivan Pavlov or to his work and theories ⟨~ conditioning⟩ **2** : being or expressing a conditioned or predictable reaction : AUTOMATIC ⟨the candidates gave ~ answers⟩

[1]**paw** \ˈpȯ\ *n* [ME, fr. AF *powe, poe*] (14c) **1** : the foot of a quadruped (as a lion or dog) that has claws; *broadly* : the foot of an animal **2** : a human hand esp. when large or clumsy

[2]**paw** *vt* (15c) **1** : to touch or strike at with a paw **2** : to feel or touch clumsily, rudely, or sexually **3** : to scrape or beat with or as if with a hoof **4** : to flail at or grab for wildly ~ *vi* **1** : to beat or scrape something with or as if with a hoof **2** : to touch or strike with a paw **3** : to feel or touch someone or something clumsily, rudely, or sexually **4** : to flail or grab wildly **5** : to search esp. carelessly or roughly ⟨~*ed* through the box of discount items⟩

paw·ky \ˈpȯ-kē\ *adj* [obs. E dial. *pawk* trick] (ca. 1640) *chiefly Brit* : artfully shrewd : CANNY

pawl \ˈpȯl\ *n* [perh. modif. of D *pal* pawl] (1730) : a pivoted tongue or sliding bolt on one part of a machine that is adapted to fall into notches or interdental spaces on another part so as to permit motion in only one direction

[1]**pawn** \ˈpȯn, ˈpän\ *n* [ME *pown,* fr. AF *peoun, paun,* fr. ML *pedon-, pedo* foot soldier, fr. L *ped-, pes* foot — more at FOOT] (14c) **1** : one of the chessmen of least value having the power to move only forward ordinarily one square at a time, to capture only diagonally forward, and to be promoted to any piece except a king upon reaching the eighth rank **2** : one that can be used to further the purposes of another

[2]**pawn** *n* [ME *paun,* fr. MF dial. (Walloon, Flanders) *pan*] (15c) **1 a** : something delivered to or deposited with another as security for a loan **b** : HOSTAGE **2** : the state of being pledged **3** : something used as a pledge : GUARANTY **4** : the act of pawning

[3]**pawn** *vt* (ca. 1566) : to deposit in pledge or as security esp. in exchange for money — **pawn·er** \ˈpȯ-nər, ˈpä-\ *also* **paw·nor** *same or* pȯ-ˈnȯr, pä-\ *n*

pawn·bro·ker \ˈpȯn-ˌbrō-kər, ˈpän-\ *n* (1658) : one who lends money in exchange for personal property that can be sold if the loan is not repaid by a certain time — **pawn·bro·king** \-kiŋ\ *n*

Paw·nee \pȯ-ˈnē, pä-\ *n, pl* **Pawnee** *or* **Pawnees** [of Siouan origin; akin to Osage *ppáį* Pawnee, Omaha *ppáði*] (1698) : a member of an American Indian people orig. of Kansas and Nebraska

pawn off *vt* (1832) : to get rid of or pass off usu. by deception : PALM OFF

pawn·shop \ˈpȯn-ˌshäp, ˈpän-\ *n* (1749) : a pawnbroker's shop

paw·paw *also* **pa·paw** *n* [prob. modif. of Sp *papaya*] (1624) **1** \pə-ˈpȯ\ : PAPAYA **2** \ˈpä-(ˌ)pȯ, ˈpȯ-\ : a No. American tree (*Asimina triloba*) of the custard-apple family with purple flowers and an edible green-skinned fruit; *also* : its fruit

pax \ˈpaks, ˈpäks\ *n* [ME, fr. ML, fr. L, peace — more at PEACE] (14c) **1** : a tablet decorated with a sacred figure (as of Christ) and sometimes ceremonially kissed by participants at mass **2** : the kiss of peace in the Mass **3** : PEACE; *esp, cap* : a period of general stability in international affairs under the influence of dominant military power — usu. used in combination with a latinized name ⟨*Pax* Americana⟩

[1]**pay** \ˈpā\ *vb* **paid** \ˈpād\ *also in sense 7* **payed; pay·ing** [ME, fr. AF *paier,* fr. L *pacare* to pacify, fr. *pac-, pax* peace] *vt* (13c) **1 a** : to make due return to for services rendered or property delivered **b** : to engage for money : HIRE ⟨you couldn't ~ me to do that⟩ **2 a** : to give in return for goods or service ⟨~ wages⟩ **b** : to discharge indebtedness for : SETTLE ⟨~ a bill⟩ **c** : to make a disposal or transfer of (money) **3** : to give or forfeit in expiation or retribution ⟨~ the penalty⟩ **4 a** : to make compensation for **b** : to requite according to what is deserved ⟨~ them back⟩ **5** : to give, offer, or make freely or as fitting ⟨~ attention⟩ ⟨~ your respects⟩ **6 a** : to return value or profit to ⟨it ~*s* you to stay open⟩ **b** : to bring in as a return ⟨an investment ~*ing* five percent⟩ **7** : to slacken (as a rope) and allow to run out — used with *out* ~ *vi* **1** : to discharge a debt or obligation **2** : to be worth the expense or effort ⟨crime doesn't ~⟩ **3** : to suffer the consequences of an act — **pay one's dues** **1** : to earn a right or position through experience, suffering, or hard work **2** *also* **pay dues** : PAY *vi* 3 — **pay one's way** *or* **pay one's own way** : to pay one's share of expenses — **pay the piper** : to bear the cost of something — **pay through the nose** : to pay exorbitantly or dearly

syn PAY, COMPENSATE, REMUNERATE, SATISFY, REIMBURSE, INDEMNIFY, REPAY, RECOMPENSE mean to give money or its equivalent in return for something. PAY implies the discharge of an obligation incurred ⟨*paid* their bills⟩. COMPENSATE implies a making up for services rendered ⟨an attorney well *compensated* for her services⟩. REMUNERATE clearly suggests paying for services rendered and may extend to payment that is generous or not contracted for ⟨promised to *remunerate* the searchers handsomely⟩. SATISFY implies paying a person what is required by law ⟨all creditors will be *satisfied* in full⟩. REIMBURSE implies a return of money that has been spent for another's benefit ⟨*reimbursed* employees for expenses⟩. INDEMNIFY implies making good a loss suffered through accident, disaster, or warfare ⟨*indemnified* the families of the dead miners⟩. REPAY stresses paying back an equivalent in kind or amount ⟨*repay* a favor with a favor⟩. RECOMPENSE suggests due return in amends, friendly repayment, or reward ⟨passengers were *recompensed* for the delay⟩.

[2]**pay** *n* (14c) **1** : something paid for a purpose and esp. as a salary or wage : REMUNERATION **2 a** : the act or fact of paying or being paid **b** : the status of being paid by an employer : EMPLOY **3** : a person viewed with respect to reliability or promptness in paying debts or bills **4 a** : ore or a natural deposit that yields metal and esp. gold in profitable amounts **b** : an oil-yielding stratum or zone

[3]**pay** *adj* (1856) **1** : containing or leading to something precious or valuable **2** : equipped with a coin slot for receiving a fee for use ⟨a ~ telephone⟩ **3** : requiring payment

[4]**pay** *vt* **payed** *also* **paid; pay·ing** [obs. F *peier,* fr. L *picare,* fr. *pic-, pix* pitch — more at PITCH] (1610) : to coat with a waterproof composition

pay·able \ˈpā-ə-bəl\ *adj* (14c) **1** : that may, can, or must be paid **2** : PROFITABLE

pay–as–you–go *adj* (1840) : of or relating to a system or policy of paying bills when due or of paying for goods and services when purchased

pay·back \ˈpā-ˌbak\ *n* (1718) **1** : REQUITAL **2** : a return on an investment equal to the original capital outlay; *also* : the period of time elapsed before an investment is recouped

pay–cable *n* (1971) : pay-TV utilizing a cable television system

pay·check \ˈpā-ˌchek\ *n* (1899) **1** : a check in payment of wages or salary **2** : WAGES, SALARY

pay·day \-ˌdā\ *n* (1529) : a regular day on which wages are paid

pay dirt *n* (1853) **1** : earth or ore that yields a profit to a miner **2** : a useful or remunerative discovery or object

pay down *vt* (1975) : to reduce (a debt) by repaying in part

PAYE *abbr, Brit* pay as you earn

pay·ee \(ˌ)pā-ˈē\ *n* (1758) : one to whom money is or is to be paid

pay envelope *n* (1901) : an envelope containing one's wages

pay·er \ˈpā-ər\ *also* **pay·or** \ˈpā-ər, (ˌ)pā-ˈȯr\ *n* (14c) : one that pays; *esp* : the person by whom a bill or note has been or should be paid

pay·load \ˈpā-ˌlōd\ *n* (1914) **1** : the load carried by a vehicle exclusive of what is necessary for its operation; *esp* : the load carried by an aircraft or spacecraft consisting of things (as passengers or instruments) necessary to the purpose of the flight **2** : the weight of a payload

pay·mas·ter \-ˌmas-tər\ *n* (1537) : an officer or agent whose duty it is to pay salaries or wages

pay·ment \ˈpā-mənt\ *n* (14c) **1** : the act of paying **2** : something that is paid : PAY **3** : REQUITAL

pay·nim \ˈpā-nəm\ *n* [ME *painim,* fr. AF *paenisme* heathendom, fr. LL *paganismus,* fr. *paganus* pagan] (13c) *archaic* : PAGAN; *esp* : MUSLIM

[1]**pay·off** \ˈpā-ˌȯf\ *n* (1905) **1 a** : PROFIT, REWARD **b** : RETRIBUTION **2** : the act or occasion of receiving money or material gain esp. as compensation or as a bribe **3** : the climax of an incident or enterprise; *specif* : the denouement of a narrative **4** : a decisive fact or factor resolving a situation or bringing about a definitive conclusion

[2]**payoff** *adj* (1932) : yielding results in the final test : DECISIVE

pay off *vt* (1607) **1 a** : to pay (a debt or a creditor) in full **b** : to give all due wages to; *esp* : to pay in full and discharge (an employee) **c** : BRIBE **2** : to inflict retribution on **3** : to allow (a thread or rope) to run off a spool or drum ~ *vi* : to yield returns

pay·o·la \pā-ˈō-lə\ *n* [[1]*pay* + *-ola* (as in *Pianola,* trademark for a player piano)] (1938) : undercover or indirect payment (as to a disc jockey) for a commercial favor (as for promoting a particular recording)

pay·out \ˈpā-ˌau̇t\ *n* (1943) : the act of paying out : PAYOFF

pay–per–view *n* (1978) : a cable television service by which customers can order access to a particular broadcast for a fee

pay phone *n* (1936) : a usu. coin-operated public telephone

pay·roll \ˈpā-ˌrōl\ *n* (1740) **1** : a paymaster's or employer's list of those entitled to pay and of the amounts due to each **2** : the sum necessary for distribution to those on a payroll; *also* : the money to be distributed

payt *abbr* payment

pay–TV *n* (1954) : a service providing noncommercial television programming (as recent movies and entertainment specials) by means of a scrambled signal to subscribers who are provided with a decoder — called also *pay television;* compare PAY-CABLE, SUBSCRIPTION TV

pay up *vi* (15c) : to pay what is due ~ *vt* : to pay in full

pay·wall \ˈpā-ˌwȯl\ *n* [[1]*pay* + *firewall*] (2004) : a system that prevents Internet users from accessing certain Web content without a paid subscription

pb *abbr* paperback

Pb *symbol* [L *plumbum*] lead

PB *abbr* **1** personal best **2** power brakes

PB&J *abbr* peanut butter and jelly

PBB \ˌpē-(ˌ)bē-ˈbē\ *n* (ca. 1975) : POLYBROMINATED BIPHENYL

PBS *abbr* Public Broadcasting Service

PBX \ˌpē-(ˌ)bē-ˈeks\ *n* [*p*rivate *b*ranch e*x*change] (1944) : a private telephone switchboard

pc *abbr* **1** parsec **2 a** [L *post cibum*] after a meal **b** [*post cibos*] after meals

[1]**PC** \ˌpē-ˈsē\ *n, pl* **PCs** *or* **PC's** (1977) : PERSONAL COMPUTER

[2]**PC** *abbr* **1** peace corps **2** percent; percentage **3** political correctness; politically correct **4** postcard **5** printed circuit **6** professional corporation

PCB \ˌpē-(ˌ)sē-ˈbē\ *n* (1966) : POLYCHLORINATED BIPHENYL

PCI *abbr* peripheral component interconnect

1**PCP** \ˌpē-(ˌ)sē-ˈpē\ *n* [*p*henyl + *c*ycl- + *p*iperidine] (ca. 1970) : PHENCYCLIDINE
2**PCP** *abbr* **1** Pneumocystis carinii pneumonia **2** primary care physician; primary care provider
PCR *abbr* polymerase chain reaction
pct *abbr* percent; percentage
pd *abbr* paid
Pd *symbol* palladium
PD *abbr* **1** per diem **2** police department **3** postal district **4** potential difference **5** program director **6** public defender **7** public domain
1**PDA** \ˌpē-(ˌ)dē-ˈā\ *n* [*p*ersonal *d*igital *a*ssistant] (1992) : a small handheld device equipped with a microprocessor that is used esp. for storing and organizing personal information (as addresses and schedules)
2**PDA** *abbr* public display of affection
pdf *or* **PDF** \ˌpē-(ˌ)dē-ˈef\ *n* [*p*ortable *d*ocument *f*ormat] (1992) : a computer file format for the transmission of a multimedia document that is not intended to be edited further and appears unaltered in most computer environments; *also* : a document that uses this format
PDQ \ˌpē-(ˌ)dē-ˈkyü\ *adv, often not cap* [abbr. of *pretty damned quick*] (1875) : IMMEDIATELY
PDT *abbr* Pacific daylight time
pe \ˈpā\ *n* [Heb *pē*] (1823) : the 17th letter of the Hebrew alphabet — see ALPHABET table
PE *abbr* **1** physical education **2** Prince Edward Island **3** printer's error **4** probable error **5** professional engineer
P/E *abbr* price/earnings
pea \ˈpē\ *n, pl* **peas** *also* **pease** \ˈpēz\ *often attrib* [back-formation fr. ME *pease* (taken as a pl.), fr. OE *pise,* fr. L *pisa,* pl. of *pisum,* fr. Gk *pison*] (1611) **1 a** : a variable annual Eurasian vine (*Pisum sativum*) of the legume family that is cultivated esp. for its rounded smooth or wrinkled edible protein-rich seeds **b** : the seed of the pea **c** *pl* : the immature pods of the pea with their included seeds **2** : any of various leguminous plants related to or resembling the pea — usu. used in combination or with a qualifying term ⟨chick*pea*⟩ ⟨black-eyed ~⟩; *also* : the seed of such a plant **3** : something resembling a pea (as in size or shape)

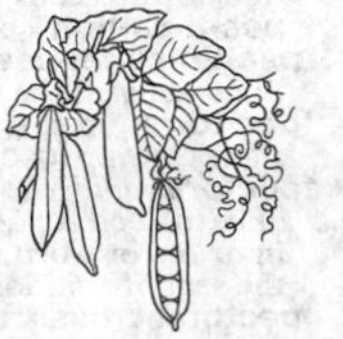

pea 1a

pea aphid *n* (1925) : a widely distributed aphid (*Acyrthosiphon pisum*) that is a serious pest on legumes (as alfalfa, pea, and clover)
pea bean *n* (1778) **1** : a small white dried kidney bean; *esp* : NAVY BEAN **2** : a plant that is a source of pea beans
1**peace** \ˈpēs\ *n* [ME *pees,* fr. AF *pes, pees,* fr. L *pac-, pax;* akin to L *pacisci* to agree — more at PACT] (12c) **1** : a state of tranquillity or quiet: as **a** : freedom from civil disturbance **b** : a state of security or order within a community provided for by law or custom ⟨a breach of the ~⟩ **2** : freedom from disquieting or oppressive thoughts or emotions **3** : harmony in personal relations **4 a** : a state or period of mutual concord between governments **b** : a pact or agreement to end hostilities between those who have been at war or in a state of enmity **5** — used interjectionally to ask for silence or calm or as a greeting or farewell — **at peace** : in a state of concord or tranquillity
2**peace** *vi* (14c) *obs* : to be, become, or keep silent or quiet
peace•able \ˈpē-sə-bəl\ *adj* (14c) **1 a** : disposed to peace : not contentious or quarrelsome **b** : quietly behaved **2** : free from strife or disorder — **peace•able•ness** *n* — **peace•ably** \-blē\ *adv*
peace corps *n* (1960) : a body of trained personnel sent as volunteers esp. to assist underdeveloped nations
peace dividend *n* (1968) : a portion of funds made available for nondefense spending by a reduction in the defense budget (as after a war)
peace•ful \ˈpēs-fəl\ *adj* (14c) **1** : PEACEABLE 1 **2** : untroubled by conflict, agitation, or commotion : QUIET, TRANQUIL **3** : of or relating to a state or time of peace **4** : devoid of violence or force ***syn*** see CALM — **peace•ful•ly** \-fə-lē\ *adv* — **peace•ful•ness** *n*
peace•keep•ing \ˈpēs-ˌkē-piŋ\ *n* (1910) : the preserving of peace; *esp* : international enforcement and supervision of a truce between hostile states or communities — **peace•keep•er** \-pər\ *n*
peace•mak•er \-ˌmā-kər\ *n* (15c) : one who makes peace esp. by reconciling parties at variance — **peace•mak•ing** \-kiŋ\ *n or adj*
peace•nik \-ˌnik\ *n* (1962) : an opponent of war; *specif* : one who participates in antiwar demonstrations
peace offering *n* (ca. 1530) : a gift or service for the purpose of procuring peace or reconciliation
peace officer *n* (1714) : a civil officer (as a police officer) whose duty it is to preserve the public peace
peace pipe *n* (1760) : CALUMET
peace sign *n* (1968) **1** : a sign made by holding the palm outward and forming a V with the index and middle fingers and used to indicate the desire for peace **2** : PEACE SYMBOL
peace symbol *n* (1970) : the symbol ☮ used to signify peace
peace•time \ˈpēs-ˌtīm\ *n* (1551) : a time when a nation is not at war
1**peach** \ˈpēch\ *n* [ME *peche,* fr. AF *pesche, peche* (the fruit), fr. LL *persica,* fr. L (*malum*) *persicum,* lit., Persian fruit] (14c) **1 a** : a low spreading freely branching Chinese tree (*Prunus persica*) of the rose family that has lanceolate leaves and sessile usu. pink flowers and is widely cultivated in temperate areas for its edible fruit which is a single-seeded drupe with a hard central stone, a pulpy white or yellow flesh, and a thin fuzzy skin **b** : the edible fruit of the peach **2** : a moderate yellowish pink **3** : one resembling a peach (as in sweetness, beauty, or excellence)
2**peach** *vb* [ME *pechen,* short for *apechen* to accuse, fr. AF *apecher, empecher* to ensnare — more at IMPEACH] *vt* (1560) : to inform against : BETRAY ~ *vi* : to turn informer : BLAB
peach leaf curl *n* (1888) : leaf curl of the peach that is caused by a fungus (*Taphrina deformans*)
peach tree borer *n* (1850) : a blue-black clearwing moth (*Synanthedon exitiosa* syn. *Sanninoidea exitiosa*) with the female having an orange band on the abdomen and whose white brown-headed larva bores in the wood of stone fruit trees (as the peach)
peachy \ˈpē-chē\ *adj* **peach•i•er; -est** (1599) **1** : resembling a peach **2** : unusually fine : DANDY
peachy keen *adj* (1948) : PEACHY 2
pea•coat \ˈpē-ˌkōt\ *n* [*pea-* (as in *pea jacket*) + *coat*] (1790) : a heavy woolen double-breasted jacket orig. worn by sailors
1**pea•cock** \ˈpē-ˌkäk\ *n* [ME *pecok,* fr. *pe-* (fr. OE *pēa* peafowl, fr. L *pavon-, pavo* peacock) + *cok* cock] (14c) **1** : a male peafowl distinguished by a crest of upright feathers and by greatly elongated loosely webbed upper tail coverts which are mostly tipped with iridescent spots and are erected and spread in a shimmering fan usu. as a courtship display; *broadly* : PEAFOWL **2** : one making a proud display of oneself : SHOW-OFF — **pea•cock•ish** \-ˌkä-kish\ *adj* — **pea•cocky** \-kē\ *adj*
2**peacock** *vi* (1818) : SHOW OFF
peacock blue *n* (1881) : a moderate greenish blue
peacock flower *n* (1884) : ROYAL POINCIANA
pea•fowl \ˈpē-ˌfau̇(-ə)l\ *n* [*pea-* (as in *peacock*) + *fowl*] (1804) : either of two very large terrestrial pheasants (*Pavo cristatus* and *P. muticus*) of southeastern Asia and India that are often reared as ornamental fowls
pea green *n* (1752) : a moderate yellow green
pea•hen \ˈpē-ˌhen\ *n* [ME *pehenne,* fr. *pe-* + *henne* hen] (15c) : a female peafowl
pea jacket \ˈpē-\ *n* [by folk etymology fr. D *pijjekker,* fr. *pij,* a kind of cloth + *jekker* jacket] (1721) : PEACOAT
1**peak** \ˈpēk\ *n* [perh. alter. of *pike*] (1530) **1** : a pointed or projecting part of a garment; *esp* : the visor of a cap or hat **2** : PROMONTORY **3** : a sharp or pointed end **4 a** (1) : the top of a hill or mountain ending in a point (2) : a prominent mountain usu. having a well-defined summit **b** : something resembling a mountain peak **5 a** : the upper aftermost corner of a fore-and-aft sail **b** : the narrow part of a ship's bow or stern or the part of the hold in it **6 a** : the highest level or greatest degree **b** : a high point in a course of development esp. as represented on a graph **7** : WIDOW'S PEAK ***syn*** see SUMMIT
2**peak** *vi* (1577) : to reach a maximum (as of capacity, value, or activity) — often used with *out* ~ *vt* : to cause to come to a peak, point, or maximum
3**peak** *adj* (1903) : being at or reaching the maximum ⟨~ levels⟩ ⟨~ output⟩; *also* : of, relating to, or being a period of maximum intensity or activity ⟨~ business hours⟩
4**peak** *vi* [origin unknown] (1605) **1** : to grow thin or sickly **2** : to dwindle away
5**peak** *vt* [fr. *apeak* held vertically] (1626) **1** : to set (as a gaff) nearer the perpendicular **2** : to hold (oars) with blades well raised
1**peaked** \ˈpēkt *also* ˈpē-kəd\ *adj* (15c) : having a peak : POINTED ⟨~ lapels⟩ ⟨a ~ hill⟩ — **peaked•ness** \ˈpēk(t)-nəs, ˈpē-kəd-nəs\ *n*
2**peak•ed** \ˈpē-kəd *also* ˈpi-kəd\ *adj* [4*peak*] (1800) : being pale and wan or emaciated : SICKLY
peak flow meter *n* (1962) : a device that measures the maximum rate of air flow out of the lungs during forced expiration and that is used esp. for monitoring lung capacity of asthmatics
peaky \ˈpē-kē\ *adj* (1821) : 2PEAKED
1**peal** \ˈpēl\ *n* [ME, appeal, summons to church, short for *appel* appeal, fr. *appelen* to appeal] (14c) **1 a** : the loud ringing of bells **b** : a complete set of changes on a given number of bells **c** : a set of bells tuned to the tones of the major scale for change ringing **2** : a loud sound or succession of sounds ⟨~*s* of laughter⟩
2**peal** *vi* (1631) : to give out peals ~ *vt* : to utter or give forth loudly
pea•like \ˈpē-ˌlīk\ *adj* (1711) **1** : resembling a pea esp. in size, firmness, and shape **2** *of a flower* : being showy and papilionaceous
1**pea•nut** \ˈpē-(ˌ)nət\ *n* (1802) **1** : a low-branching widely cultivated annual herb (*Arachis hypogaea*) of the legume family with showy yellow flowers having a peduncle which elongates and bends into the soil where the ovary ripens into a pod containing one to three oily edible seeds; *also* : its seed or seed-containing pod **2** : an insignificant or tiny person **3** *pl* : a trifling amount **4** : a pellet usu. made of polystyrene foam that is used esp. as packing material
2**peanut** *adj* (1836) : INSIGNIFICANT, PETTY ⟨~ politics⟩
peanut oil *n* (1862) : a colorless to yellow fatty nondrying oil that is obtained from peanuts and is used chiefly as a salad oil, in margarine, in soap, and as a vehicle in pharmaceutical preparations and cosmetics
pear \ˈper\ *n* [ME *pere,* fr. OE *peru,* fr. VL **pira,* fr. L, pl. of *pirum*] (bef. 12c) **1** : a pome fruit of a tree (genus *Pyrus,* esp. *P. communis*) of the rose family that typically has a pale green or brownish skin, a firm juicy flesh, and an oblong shape in which a broad base end tapers upward to a narrow stem end **2** : a tree bearing pears
1**pearl** \ˈpər(-ə)l\ *n* [ME *perle,* fr. AF, prob. fr. VL **pernula,* dim. of L *perna* upper leg, kind of sea mussel; akin to OE *fiersn* heel, Gk *pternē*] (14c) **1 a** : a dense variously colored and usu. lustrous concretion formed of concentric layers of nacre as an abnormal growth within the shell of some mollusks and used as a gem **b** : MOTHER-OF-PEARL **2** : one that is very choice or precious **3** : something resembling a pearl intrinsically or physically **4** : a nearly neutral slightly bluish medium gray
2**pearl** *vt* (14c) **1** : to set or adorn with pearls **2** : to sprinkle or bead with pearly drops **3** : to form into small round grains **4** : to give a pearly color or luster to ~ *vi* **1** : to form drops or beads like pearls **2** : to fish or search for pearls — **pearl•er** \ˈpər-lər\ *n*
3**pearl** *adj* (1610) **1 a** : of, relating to, or resembling pearl **b** : made of or adorned with pearls **2** : having medium-sized grains ⟨~ barley⟩
4**pearl** *n or vt* [alter. of *purl*] (1824) *Brit* : PICOT
pearl•es•cent \ˌpər-ˈle-sᵊnt\ *adj* (1936) : having a pearly luster ⟨a ~ lacquer⟩ — **pearl•es•cence** \-sᵊn(t)s\ *n*
pearl essence *n* (1854) : a translucent substance that occurs in the silvery scales of various fish (as herring) and is used in making artificial pearls, lacquers, and plastics
pearl gray *n* (1796) **1** : a yellowish to light gray **2** : a pale blue
Pearl Harbor *n* [*Pearl Harbor,* Oahu, Hawaii, Am. naval station attacked without warning by the Japanese on December 7, 1941] (1942) : a surprise attack often with devastating effect

\ə\ **abut** \ᵊ\ kitten, F table \ər\ **fur**ther \a\ **a**sh \ā\ **a**ce \ä\ m**o**p, m**a**r
\au̇\ **ou**t \ch\ **ch**in \e\ b**e**t \ē\ **ea**sy \g\ **g**o \i\ h**i**t \ī\ **i**ce \j\ **j**ob
\ŋ\ si**ng** \ō\ g**o** \ȯ\ l**aw** \ȯi\ b**oy** \th\ **th**in \t͟h\ **th**e \ü\ l**oo**t \u̇\ f**oo**t
\y\ **y**et \zh\ vi**s**ion, beige \k̲, ⁿ, œ, ue, ʸ\ *see* Guide to Pronunciation

pearl·ite \ˈpər(-ə)-ˌlīt\ *n* [F *perlite,* fr. *perle* pearl] (1888) **:** the lamellar mixture of ferrite and cementite in slowly cooled iron-carbon alloys occurring normally as a principal constituent of both steel and cast iron — **pearl·it·ic** \ˌpər-ˈli-tik\ *adj*
pearl·ized \ˈpər(-ə)-ˌlīzd\ *adj* (1937) **:** given a pearlescent surface or finish
pearl millet *n* (ca. 1890) **:** a tall cereal grass (*Pennisetum glaucum* syn. *P. americanum*) that has large leaves and dense round spikes and is widely grown for its seeds and for forage
pearl onion *n* (1880) **:** a very small usu. pickled onion used esp. in appetizers and as a garnish
pearly \ˈpər-lē\ *adj* **pearl·i·er; -est** (15c) **1 :** resembling, containing, or adorned with pearls or mother-of-pearl **2 :** highly precious
pearly everlasting *n* (1857) **:** an everlasting (*Anaphalis margaritacea*) that has herbage covered with white woolly hairs and corymbose heads with white scarious involucres
pearly nautilus *n* (ca. 1800) **:** NAUTILUS 1
pear psylla *n* (1904) **:** a yellowish or greenish jumping plant louse (*Psylla pyricola*) that is often destructive to the pear
pear–shaped \ˈper-ˌshāpt\ *adj* (1758) **1 :** having an oval shape markedly tapering at one end **2** *of a vocal tone* **:** free from harshness, thinness, or nasality
peart \ˈpirt\ *adj* [alter. of *pert*] (ca. 1520) *chiefly Southern & Midland* **:** being in good spirits **:** LIVELY — **peart·ly** *adv*
peas·ant \ˈpe-zᵊnt\ *n* [ME *paissaunt,* fr. AF *paisant, pesaunt,* fr. *pais, paiis* country, fr. LL *pagensis* inhabitant of a district, fr. L *pagus* district; akin to L *pangere* to fix — more at PACT] (15c) **1 :** a member of a European class of persons tilling the soil as small landowners or as laborers; *also* **:** a member of a similar class elsewhere **2 :** a usu. uneducated person of low social status
peas·ant·ry \-zᵊn-trē\ *n* (ca. 1553) **1 :** PEASANTS **2 :** the position, rank, or behavior of a peasant
pease·cod *or* **peas·cod** \ˈpēz-ˌkäd\ *n* [ME *pesecod,* fr. *pese* + *cod* bag, husk — more at CODPIECE] (14c) **:** a pea pod
pea·shoot·er \ˈpē-ˌshü-tər\ *n* (1803) **:** a toy blowgun that uses peas for projectiles
pea soup *n* (1711) **1 :** a thick purée made of dried peas **2 :** a thick fog
[1]**peat** \ˈpēt\ *n, often attrib* [ME *pete* piece of peat, fr. ML *peta,* prob. of Celt origin; akin to Cornish *peyth* bit, W *peth* thing] (14c) **1 :** TURF 2b **2 :** partially carbonized vegetable tissue formed by partial decomposition in water of various plants (as mosses of the genus *Sphagnum*) — **peaty** \ˈpē-tē\ *adj*
[2]**peat** *n* [origin unknown] (1599) **:** a bold lively woman
peat moss *n* (1880) **:** SPHAGNUM
pea·vey *or* **pea·vy** \ˈpē-vē\ *n, pl* **peaveys** *or* **peavies** [Joseph *Peavey* †1873 Am. blacksmith] (1870) **:** a lumberman's lever that has a pivoting hooked arm and metal spike at one end — called also *cant dog;* compare CANT HOOK
[1]**peb·ble** \ˈpe-bəl\ *n* [ME *pobble,* fr. OE *papolstān,* fr. *papol-* (of unknown origin) + *stān* stone] (14c) **1 :** a small usu. rounded stone esp. when worn by the action of water **2 :** transparent and colorless quartz **:** ROCK CRYSTAL **3 :** an irregular, crinkled, or grainy surface — **peb·bly** \-b(ə-)lē\ *adj*
[2]**pebble** *vt* **peb·bled; peb·bling** \-b(ə-)liŋ\ (1605) **1 :** to pelt with pebbles **2 :** to pave or cover with pebbles or something resembling pebbles **3 :** to grain (as leather) so as to produce a rough and irregularly indented surface
pec \ˈpek\ *n* (1944) **:** PECTORAL MUSCLE — usu. used in pl.
pe·can \pi-ˈkän, -ˈkan; ˈpē-ˌkan\ *n* [AmerF *pacane,* fr. Illinois *pakani*] (1772) **1 :** a large hickory (*Carya illinoinensis* syn. *C. illinoensis*) that has roughish bark and hard but brittle wood and is widely grown in the warmer parts of the U.S. and in Mexico for its edible nut **2 :** the wood of the pecan tree **3 :** the smooth oblong thin-shelled nut of the pecan tree
pec·ca·dil·lo \ˌpe-kə-ˈdi-(ˌ)lō\ *n, pl* **-loes** *or* **-los** [Sp *pecadillo,* dim. of *pecado* sin, fr. L *peccatum,* fr. neut. of *peccatus,* pp. of *peccare*] (1600) **:** a slight offense
pec·cant \ˈpe-kənt\ *adj* [L *peccant-, peccans,* prp. of *peccare* to stumble, sin] (ca. 1604) **1 :** guilty of a moral offense **:** SINNING **2 :** violating a principle or rule **:** FAULTY — **pec·cant·ly** *adv*
pec·ca·ry \ˈpe-kə-rē\ *n, pl* **-ries** [of Cariban origin; akin to Suriname Carib *paki:ra* peccary] (1697) **:** any of several largely nocturnal gregarious American mammals resembling the related pigs: as **a :** a grizzled animal (*Tayassu tajacu*) with an indistinct white collar **b :** a blackish animal (*Tayassu pecari*) with a whitish mouth region

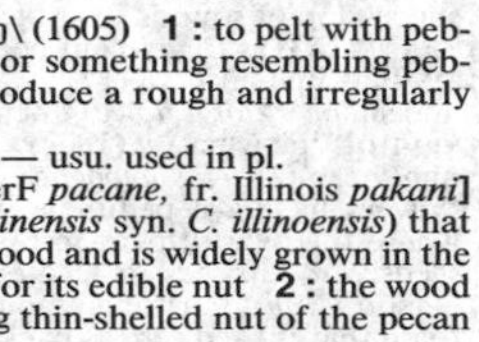
peccary

pec·ca·vi \pe-ˈkä-(ˌ)wē, -(ˌ)vē; -ˈkā-ˌvī\ *n* [L, I have sinned, fr. *peccare*] (1553) **:** an acknowledgment of sin
[1]**peck** \ˈpek\ *n* [ME *pek,* fr. AF] (13c) **1 —** see WEIGHT table **2 :** a large quantity or number
[2]**peck** *vb* [ME, perh. fr. MLG *pekken*] *vt* (14c) **1 a :** to strike or pierce esp. repeatedly with the bill or a pointed tool **b :** to make by pecking ⟨∼ a hole⟩ **2 :** to pick up with the bill ∼ *vi* **1 a :** to strike, pierce, or pick up something with or as if with the bill **b :** CARP, NAG **2 :** to eat reluctantly and in small bites ⟨∼ at food⟩
[3]**peck** *n* (ca. 1591) **1 :** an impression or hole made by pecking **2 :** a quick sharp stroke **3 :** a quick light kiss ⟨a ∼ on the cheek⟩
peck·er \ˈpe-kər\ *n* (1587) **1 :** one that pecks **2** *chiefly Brit* **:** COURAGE **3** *often vulgar* **:** PENIS
peck·er·wood \ˈpe-kər-ˌwu̇d\ *n* [prob. inversion of *woodpecker*] (1904) *often disparaging* **:** a rural white Southerner
pecking order *also* **peck order** *n* (1928) **1 :** the basic pattern of social organization within a flock of poultry in which each bird pecks another lower in the scale without fear of retaliation and submits to pecking by one of higher rank; *broadly* **:** a dominance hierarchy in a group of social animals **2 :** a social hierarchy
peck·ish \ˈpe-kish\ *adj* [[2]*peck*] (1785) **1** *chiefly Brit* **:** HUNGRY **2 :** CROTCHETY
Peck·sniff·ian \pek-ˈsni-fē-ən\ *adj* [Seth *Pecksniff,* character in *Martin Chuzzlewit* (1843–44) by Charles Dickens] (1849) **:** unctuously hypocritical **:** PHARISAICAL
pecky \ˈpe-kē\ *adj* [[3]*peck*] (1848) **1 :** marked by lenticular or finger-shaped pockets of decay caused by fungi ⟨∼ cypress⟩ **2 :** containing discolored or shriveled grains ⟨∼ rice⟩
pec·o·ri·no \ˌpe-kə-ˈrē-(ˌ)nō\ *n, often cap* [It, fr. *pecorino* of sheep, fr. *pecora* sheep, ewe, fr. L, domestic animals, fr. pl. of *pecus* cattle — more at FEE] (1908) **:** any of various cheeses of Italian origin made from sheep's milk
pec·ten \ˈpek-tən\ *n, pl* **pectens** [NL *pectin-, pecten,* fr. L, comb, scallop] (1682) **1 :** SCALLOP 1a **2** *pl usu* **pec·ti·nes** \-tə-ˌnēz\ **:** a body part that resembles a comb; *esp* **:** a folded vascular pigmented membrane projecting into the vitreous humor in the eye of a bird or reptile
pec·tic \ˈpek-tik\ *adj* [F *pectique,* fr. Gk *pēktikos* coagulating, fr. *pēgnynai* to fix, coagulate — more at PACT] (1830) **:** of, relating to, or derived from pectin
pectic acid *n* (1830) **:** any of various water-insoluble substances formed by hydrolyzing the methyl ester groups of pectins
pec·tin \ˈpek-tən\ *n* [F *pectine,* fr. *pectique*] (1838) **:** any of various water-soluble substances that bind adjacent cell walls in plant tissues and yield a gel which is the basis of fruit jellies; *also* **:** a commercial product rich in pectins
pec·ti·na·ceous \ˌpek-tə-ˈnā-shəs\ *adj* (ca. 1844) **:** of, relating to, or containing pectin
pec·ti·nate \ˈpek-tə-ˌnāt\ *adj* [L *pectinatus,* fr. *pectin-, pecten* comb; akin to Gk *kten-, kteis* comb] (1793) **:** having narrow parallel projections or divisions suggestive of the teeth of a comb ⟨∼ antennae⟩ — **pec·ti·na·tion** \ˌpek-tə-ˈnā-shən\ *n*
pec·tin·es·ter·ase \ˌpek-tə-ˈnes-tə-ˌrās, -ˌrāz\ *n* (1945) **:** an enzyme that catalyzes the hydrolysis of pectins into pectic acids and methanol
[1]**pec·to·ral** \ˈpek-t(ə-)rəl\ *n* (15c) **1 :** something worn on the breast **2 :** PECTORAL MUSCLE
[2]**pectoral** *adj* [MF or L; MF, fr. L *pectoralis,* fr. *pector-, pectus* breast; akin to Toch A *päśśäm* breasts, OIr *ucht* breast] (1578) **1 :** of, situated in or on, or worn on the chest **2 :** coming from the breast or heart as the seat of emotion
pectoral cross *n* (ca. 1735) **:** a cross worn on the breast esp. by a prelate
pectoral fin *n* (1769) **:** either of the fins of a fish that correspond to the forelimbs of a quadruped
pectoral girdle *n* (ca. 1890) **:** SHOULDER GIRDLE
pectoral muscle *n* (1615) **:** any of the muscles which connect the ventral walls of the chest with the bones of the upper arm and shoulder and of which there are two on each side of the human body
pec·u·late \ˈpe-kyə-ˌlāt\ *vt* **-lat·ed; -lat·ing** [L *peculatus,* pp. of *peculari,* fr. *peculium*] (1802) **:** EMBEZZLE — **pec·u·la·tion** \ˌpe-kyə-ˈlā-shən\ *n* — **pec·u·la·tor** \ˈpe-kyə-ˌlā-tər\ *n*
[1]**pe·cu·liar** \pi-ˈkyül-yər\ *adj* [ME *peculier,* fr. L *peculiaris* of private property, special, fr. *peculium* private property, fr. *pecu* cattle; akin to L *pecus* cattle — more at FEE] (15c) **1 :** characteristic of only one person, group, or thing **:** DISTINCTIVE **2 :** different from the usual or normal: **a :** SPECIAL, PARTICULAR **b :** ODD, CURIOUS **c :** ECCENTRIC, QUEER ***syn*** see CHARACTERISTIC, STRANGE — **pe·cu·liar·ly** *adv*
[2]**peculiar** *n* (1562) **:** something exempt from ordinary jurisdiction; *esp* **:** a church or parish exempt from the jurisdiction of the ordinary in whose territory it lies
pe·cu·liar·i·ty \pi-ˌkyül-ˈya-rə-tē, -ˌkyü-lē-ˈa-\ *n, pl* **-ties** (1646) **1 :** the quality or state of being peculiar **2 :** a distinguishing characteristic **3 :** ODDITY, QUIRK
pe·cu·ni·ary \pi-ˈkyü-nē-ˌer-ē\ *adj* [L *pecuniarius,* fr. *pecunia* money — more at FEE] (1502) **1 :** consisting of or measured in money **2 :** of or relating to money — **pe·cu·ni·ar·i·ly** \-ˌkyü-nē-ˈer-ə-lē\ *adv*
ped \ˈped\ *n* [Gk *pedon* ground; akin to L *ped-, pes* foot — more at FOOT] (1951) **:** a natural soil aggregate
ped- *or* **pedo-** *or* **paed-** *or* **paedo-** *comb form* [Gk *paid-, paido-,* fr. *paid-, pais* child, boy — more at FEW] **:** child ⟨*ped*iatric⟩ **:** childhood ⟨*paedo*genesis⟩
-ped *or* **-pede** *n comb form* [L *ped-, pes*] **:** foot ⟨maxilli*ped*⟩
ped·a·gog·i·cal \ˌpe-də-ˈgä-ji-kəl, -ˈgō-\ *also* **ped·a·gog·ic** \-jik\ *adj* (1619) **:** of, relating to, or befitting a teacher or education — **ped·a·gog·i·cal·ly** \-ji-k(ə-)lē\ *adv*
ped·a·gog·ics \-jiks\ *n pl but sing in constr* (ca. 1859) **:** PEDAGOGY
ped·a·gogue *also* **ped·a·gog** \ˈpe-də-ˌgäg\ *n* [ME *pedagoge,* fr. L *paedagogus,* fr. Gk *paidagōgos,* slave who escorted children to school, fr. *paid-* ped- + *agōgos* leader, fr. *agein* to lead — more at AGENT] (14c) **:** TEACHER, SCHOOLMASTER; *esp* **:** a dull, formal, or pedantic teacher
ped·a·go·gy \ˈpe-də-ˌgō-jē *also* -ˌgä-, *esp Brit* -ˌgä-gē\ *n* (ca. 1623) **:** the art, science, or profession of teaching; *esp* **:** EDUCATION 2
[1]**ped·al** \ˈpe-dᵊl\ *n* [MF *pedale,* fr. It, fr. L *pedalis,* adj.] (1618) **1 :** a lever pressed by the foot in the playing of a musical instrument (as an organ or piano) **2 :** a foot lever or treadle by which a part is activated in a mechanism
[2]**ped·al** *adj* [L *pedalis,* fr. *ped-, pes*] (1618) **1** \ˈpe-dᵊl *also* ˈpē-\ **:** of or relating to the foot **2** \ˈpe-\ **:** of, relating to, or involving a pedal
[3]**ped·al** \ˈpe-dᵊl\ *vb* **ped·aled** *also* **ped·alled; ped·al·ing** *also* **ped·al·ling** \ˈpe-dᵊl-iŋ, ˈped-liŋ\ *vi* (1883) **1 :** to ride a bicycle **2 :** to use or work a pedal ∼ *vt* **:** to work the pedals of
pedal bone *n* (1881) **:** COFFIN BONE
pe·dal·fer \pə-ˈdal-fər, -ˌfer\ *n* [Gk *ped*on ground + E *al*umen + L *ferrum* iron] (1928) **:** a soil that lacks a hardened layer of accumulated carbonates
ped·al–note \ˈpe-dᵊl-ˌnōt\ *n* [fr. the playing of the lowest notes on the organ by means of pedals] (ca. 1828) **1 :** PEDAL POINT **2 :** one of the lowest tones that can be sounded on a brass instrument being an octave below the normal usable range and representing the fundamental of the harmonic series
ped·a·lo \ˈpe-də-(ˌ)lō\ *n, pl* **-los** [F *pédalo,* fr. *pédale* pedal + *-o* (perh. as in *meccano* children's construction set)] (1945) *chiefly Brit* **:** a small recreational paddleboat powered by pedals
pedal point *n* (1852) **:** a single tone usu. the tonic or dominant that is normally sustained in the bass and sounds against changing harmonies in the other parts
pedal pushers *n pl* (1944) **:** women's and girls' calf-length trousers

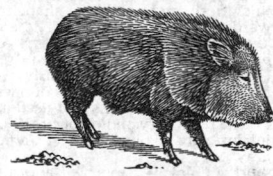

pedal steel *n* (1965) **:** a box-shaped musical instrument with legs that has usu. 10 strings which can be altered in pitch by the use of pedals and which are plucked while being pressed with a movable steel bar — called also *pedal steel guitar*

ped·ant \ˈpe-dᵊnt\ *n* [MF, fr. It *pedante*] (1588) **1** *obs* **:** a male schoolteacher **2 a :** one who makes a show of knowledge **b :** one who is unimaginative or who unduly emphasizes minutiae in the presentation or use of knowledge **c :** a formalist or precisionist in teaching

pe·dan·tic \pi-ˈdan-tik\ *adj* (1628) **1 :** of, relating to, or being a pedant **2 :** narrowly, stodgily, and often ostentatiously learned **3 :** UNIMAGINATIVE, DULL — **pe·dan·ti·cal·ly** \-ˈdan-ti-k(ə-)lē\ *adv*

ped·ant·ry \ˈpe-dᵊn-trē\ *n, pl* **-ries** (1612) **1 :** pedantic presentation or application of knowledge or learning **2 :** an instance of pedantry

ped·dle \ˈpe-dᵊl\ *vb* **ped·dled; ped·dling** \ˈped-liŋ, ˈpe-dᵊl-iŋ\ [back-formation fr. *peddler,* fr. ME *pedlere,* alter. of *pedder* peddler] *vi* (1532) **1 :** to travel about with wares for sale; *broadly* **:** SELL **2 :** to be busy with trifles **:** PIDDLE ~ *vt* **1 :** to sell or offer for sale from place to place **:** HAWK; *broadly* **:** SELL **2 :** to deal out or seek to disseminate **3 :** to offer or promote as valuable

ped·dler *also* **ped·lar** \ˈped-lər\ *n* (14c) **:** one who peddles: as **a :** one who offers merchandise (as fresh produce) for sale along the street or from door to door **b :** one who deals in or promotes something intangible (as a personal asset or an idea) ⟨influence ~*s*⟩

ped·er·ast \ˈpe-də-ˌrast\ *n* [Gk *paiderastēs,* lit., lover of boys, fr. *paid-* ped- + *erastēs* lover, fr. *erasthai* to love — more at EROS] (1638) **:** a man who desires or engages in sexual activity with a boy — **ped·er·as·tic** \ˌpe-də-ˈras-tik\ *adj* — **ped·er·as·ty** \ˈpe-də-ˌras-tē\ *n*

[1]**ped·es·tal** \ˈpe-dəs-tᵊl\ *n* [MF *piedestal,* fr. OIt *piedestallo,* fr. *pie di stallo* foot of a stall] (1563) **1 a :** the support or foot of a late classic or neoclassic column — see COLUMN illustration **b :** the base of an upright structure **2 :** BASE, FOUNDATION **3 :** a position of esteem

[2]**pedestal** *vt* **-taled** *or* **-talled; -tal·ing** *or* **-tal·ling** (1648) **:** to place on or furnish with a pedestal

[1]**pe·des·tri·an** \pə-ˈdes-trē-ən\ *adj* [L *pedestr-, pedester,* lit., going on foot, fr. *ped-, pes* foot — more at FOOT] (1716) **1 :** COMMONPLACE, UNIMAGINATIVE **2 a :** going or performed on foot **b :** of, relating to, or designed for walking ⟨a ~ mall⟩

[2]**pedestrian** *n* (1770) **:** a person going on foot **:** WALKER

pe·des·tri·an·ism \-ə-ˌni-zəm\ *n* (1808) **1 a :** the practice of walking **b :** fondness for walking for exercise or recreation **2 :** the quality or state of being unimaginative or commonplace

pe·di·at·ric \ˌpē-dē-ˈa-trik\ *adj* (1850) **:** of or relating to pediatrics

pe·di·a·tri·cian \ˌpē-dē-ə-ˈtri-shən\ *also* **pe·di·a·trist** \ˌpē-dē-ˈa-trist, pē-ˈdī-ə-\ *n* (1903) **:** a specialist in pediatrics

pe·di·at·rics \ˌpē-dē-ˈa-triks\ *n pl but sing or pl in constr* (ca. 1857) **:** a branch of medicine dealing with the development, care, and diseases of children

pedi·cab \ˈpe-di-ˌkab\ *n* [L *ped-, pes* + E *cab*] (1922) **:** a tricycle with a 2-seat passenger compartment covered by a usu. folding top and a separate seat for a driver who pedals

ped·i·cel \ˈpe-də-ˌsel\ *n* [NL *pedicellus,* dim. of L *pediculus*] (1682) **:** a slender basal part of an organism or one of its parts: as **a :** a plant stalk that supports a fruiting or spore-bearing organ **b :** a narrow basal attachment (as of the abdomen of an ant) of an animal organ or part — **ped·i·cel·late** \ˌpe-də-ˈse-lət\ *adj*

ped·i·cle \ˈpe-di-kəl\ *n* [L *pediculus,* fr. dim. of *ped-, pes*] (1626) **1 :** PEDICEL b **2 :** the part of a skin or tissue graft left attached to the original site during the preliminary stages of union — **ped·i·cled** \-kəld\ *adj*

pe·dic·u·late \pi-ˈdi-kyə-lət\ *adj* [ultim. fr. L *pediculus* little foot, pedicel] (1882) **:** of or relating to an order (Lophiiformes syn. Pediculati) of marine bony fishes (as a batfish or goosefish) with pectoral fins at the end of an armlike process and part of the dorsal fin modified into a lure — **pediculate** *n*

pe·dic·u·lo·sis \pi-ˌdi-kyə-ˈlō-səs\ *n, pl* **-lo·ses** \-ˌsēz\ [NL, fr. L *pediculus* louse, dim. of *pedis* louse] (1876) **:** infestation with lice

pe·dic·u·lous \pi-ˈdi-kyə-ləs\ *adj* [L *pediculosus,* fr. *pediculus*] (ca. 1540) **:** infested with lice **:** LOUSY

pedi·cure \ˈpe-di-ˌkyu̇r\ *n* [F *pédicure,* fr. L *ped-, pes* foot + *curare* to take care, fr. *cura* care] (1784) **1 :** a person who provides care for the feet, toes, and nails **2 a :** care of the feet, toes, and nails **b :** a single treatment of these parts — **pedi·cur·ist** \-ˌkyu̇r-ist\ *n*

ped·i·gree \ˈpe-də-ˌgrē\ *n* [ME *pedegru,* fr. AF *pé de grue,* lit., crane's foot; fr. the shape made by the lines of a genealogical chart] (15c) **1 :** a register recording a line of ancestors **2 a :** an ancestral line **:** LINEAGE **b :** the origin and the history of something; *broadly* **:** BACKGROUND, HISTORY **3 a :** a distinguished ancestry **b :** the recorded purity of breed of an individual or strain — **ped·i·greed** \-ˌgrēd\ *or* **pedigree** *adj*

ped·i·ment \ˈpe-də-mənt\ *n* [alter. of obs. E *periment,* prob. alter. of E *pyramid*] (1664) **1 :** a triangular space that forms the gable of a low-pitched roof and that is usu. filled with relief sculpture in classical architecture; *also* **:** a similar form used as a decoration **2 :** a broad gently sloping bedrock surface with low relief that is situated at the base of a steeper slope and is usu. thinly covered with alluvial gravel and sand — **ped·i·men·tal** \ˌpe-də-ˈmen-tᵊl\ *adj* — **ped·i·ment·ed** \ˈpe-də-ˌmen-təd\ *adj*

pedi·palp \ˈpe-də-ˌpalp\ *n* [NL *pedipalpus,* fr. *ped-, pes* foot + *palpus* palpus] (1826) **:** either of the second pair of appendages of an arachnid (as a spider) that are borne near the mouth and are often modified for a special (as sensory) function

pedo- — see PED-

ped·o·cal \ˈpe-də-ˌkal\ *n* [Gk *pedon* earth + L *calc-, calx* lime — more at PED, CHALK] (1928) **:** a soil that includes a definite hardened layer of accumulated carbonates — **ped·o·cal·ic** \ˌpe-də-ˈka-lik\ *adj*

[1]**pedogenesis** *var of* PAEDOGENESIS

[2]**ped·o·gen·e·sis** \ˌpe-də-ˈje-nə-səs\ *n* [NL, fr. Gk *pedon* + L *genesis*] (1935) **:** the formation and development of soil — **ped·o·gen·ic** \-ˈje-nik\ *also* **ped·o·ge·net·ic** \-jə-ˈne-tik\ *adj*

pe·dol·o·gy \pi-ˈdä-lə-jē, pe-\ *n* [Gk *pedon* + ISV *-logy*] (1900) **:** SOIL SCIENCE — **pe·do·log·i·cal** \ˌpe-də-ˈlä-ji-kəl\ *also* **ped·o·log·ic** \-jik\ *adj* — **pe·dol·o·gist** \pi-ˈdä-lə-jist, pe-\ *n*

pe·dom·e·ter \pi-ˈdä-mə-tər\ *n* [F *pédomètre,* fr. L *ped-, pes* foot + F *-mètre* -meter — more at FOOT] (1723) **:** an instrument usu. in watch form that records the distance a person covers on foot by responding to the body motion at each step

pe·do·phile \ˈpe-də-ˌfī(-ə)l, ˈpē-\ *n* (1941) **:** one affected with pedophilia

pe·do·phil·ia \ˌpe-də-ˈfi-lē-ə, ˌpē-\ *n* [NL] (1906) **:** sexual perversion in which children are the preferred sexual object — **pe·do·phil·i·ac** \-ˈfi-lē-ˌak\ *or* **pe·do·phil·ic** \-ˈfi-lik\ *adj*

ped·or·thics \pə-ˈdȯr-thiks\ *n pl but sing or pl in constr* [L *ped-, pes* + E *orth-* + *-ics*] (1974) **:** the art and practice of designing, making, and fitting therapeutic shoes for relieving painful or disabling conditions of the feet — **ped·or·thic** \-thik\ *adj* — **ped·or·thist** \-thist\ *n*

pe·dun·cle \ˈpē-ˌdəŋ-kəl, pi-ˈ\ *n* [NL *pedunculus,* dim. of L *ped-, pes*] (1702) **1 :** a stalk bearing a flower or flower cluster or a fructification **2 :** a narrow part by which some larger part or the whole body of an organism is attached **:** STALK, PEDICEL **3 :** a narrow stalk by which a tumor or polyp is attached — **pe·dun·cled** \-kəld\ *adj* — **pe·dun·cu·lar** \pi-ˈdəŋ-kyə-lər\ *adj*

pe·dun·cu·lat·ed \pi-ˈdəŋ-kyə-ˌlā-təd\ *also* **pe·dun·cu·late** \-lət\ *adj* [NL *pedunculus*] (1752) **:** having, growing on, or being attached by a peduncle ⟨a ~ tumor⟩

[1]**pee** \ˈpē\ *n* (1602) **1 :** the letter *p* **2** *pl* **pee** *Brit* **:** PENNY

[2]**pee** *vi* **peed; pee·ing** [euphemism fr. the initial letter of *piss*] (ca. 1825) *sometimes vulgar* **:** URINATE

[3]**pee** *n* (1880) **1** *sometimes vulgar* **:** URINE **2** *sometimes vulgar* **:** an act of urination

[1]**peek** \ˈpēk\ *vi* [ME *piken*] (14c) **1 a :** to look furtively **b :** to peer through a crack or hole or from a place of concealment — often used with *in* or *out* **2 :** to take a brief look **:** GLANCE

[2]**peek** *n* (1636) **1 :** a furtive look **2 :** a brief look **:** GLANCE

[1]**peek·a·boo** \ˈpē-kə-ˌbü\ *n* [[1]*peek* + [1]*boo*] (1600) **:** a game for amusing a baby by repeatedly hiding one's face or body and popping back into view exclaiming "Peekaboo!"

[2]**peekaboo** *adj* (1895) **1 :** trimmed with eyelet embroidery ⟨a ~ blouse⟩ **2 :** made of a sheer or transparent fabric; *also* **:** revealing usu. small areas of skin **3 :** offering only limited display or disclosure esp. of a teasing sort ⟨~ publicity⟩

[1]**peel** \ˈpēl\ *vb* [ME *pelen,* fr. AF *peler,* fr. L *pilare* to remove the hair from, fr. *pilus* hair] *vt* (13c) **1 :** to strip off an outer layer of **2 :** to remove by stripping ⟨~ the label off the can⟩ ~ *vi* **1 a :** to come off in sheets or scales **b :** to lose an outer layer (as of skin) ⟨his face is ~*ing*⟩ **2 :** to take off one's clothes **3 :** to break away from a group or formation — often used with *off* — **peel·able** \ˈpē-lə-bəl\ *adj*

[2]**peel** *n* (14c) **1 :** the skin or rind of a fruit **2 :** a thin layer of organic material that is embedded in a film of collodion and stripped from the surface of an object (as a plant fossil) for microscopic study **3 :** CHEMICAL PEEL

[3]**peel** *n* [ME *pele,* fr. AF, fr. L *pala*] (14c) **:** a usu. long-handled spade-shaped instrument that is used chiefly by bakers for getting something (as bread or pies) into or out of the oven

[4]**peel** *n* [ME (Sc) *pel,* fr. ME, stockade, stake, fr. AF, stake, fr. L *palus* — more at POLE] (1726) **:** a medieval small massive fortified tower along the Scottish-English border — called also *peel tower*

[1]**peel·er** \ˈpē-lər\ *n* (1597) **1 :** one that peels **2 :** a crab that is about to shed its shell **3 :** a log of wood (as Douglas fir) suitable for cutting into veneer — called also *peeler log*

[2]**peeler** *n* [Sir Robert *Peel*] (1816) *Brit* **:** POLICE OFFICER

peel·ing \ˈpē-liŋ\ *n* (1598) **:** a peeled-off piece or strip

peel off *vi* (1941) **1 :** to veer away from an airplane formation esp. for diving or landing **2 :** DEPART, LEAVE

[1]**peen** \ˈpēn\ *vt* (ca. 1522) **:** to draw, bend, or flatten by or as if by hammering with a peen

[2]**peen** *n* [prob. of Scand origin; akin to Norw *penn* peen] (1683) **:** a usu. hemispherical or wedge-shaped end of the head of a hammer that is opposite the face and is used esp. for bending, shaping, or cutting the material struck

[1]**peep** \ˈpēp\ *vi* [ME *pepen,* of imit. origin] (15c) **1 :** to utter a feeble shrill sound as of a bird newly hatched **:** CHEEP **2 :** to utter the slightest sound

[2]**peep** *n* (15c) **1 :** a feeble shrill sound **:** CHEEP **2 :** a slight utterance esp. of complaint or protest **3 :** any of several small sandpipers

[3]**peep** *vb* [ME *pepen,* perh. alter. of *piken* to peek] *vi* (15c) **1 a :** to peer through or as if through a crevice **b :** to look cautiously or slyly **2 :** to begin to emerge from or as if from concealment **:** show slightly ~ *vt* **1 :** to put forth or cause to protrude slightly **2** *slang* **:** to have a look at **:** SEE, WATCH

[4]**peep** *n* (1530) **1 :** a first glimpse or faint appearance ⟨at the ~ of dawn⟩ **2 a :** a brief look **:** GLANCE **b :** a furtive look

[1]**peep·er** \ˈpē-pər\ *n* (1607) **1 :** one that peeps; *specif* **:** VOYEUR **2 :** EYE

[2]**peeper** *n* (ca. 1586) **1 :** one that makes a peeping sound **2 :** any of various tree frogs that peep shrilly; *esp* **:** SPRING PEEPER

peep·hole \ˈpēp-ˌhōl\ *n* (ca. 1570) **:** a hole or crevice to peep through

Peeping Tom \-ˈtäm\ *n* [*Peeping Tom,* legendary citizen of Coventry who watched Lady Godiva riding naked] (1769) **:** a pruriently prying person **:** VOYEUR — **Peeping Tom·ism** \-ˈtä-ˌmi-zəm\ *n*

peeps \ˈpēps\ *n pl* [by shortening & alter.] *slang* (1847) **:** PEOPLE1

peep show *n* (1801) **:** an entertainment (as a film) or object (as a small picture) that is viewed through a small opening or a magnifying glass and is usu. sexually explicit

peep sight *n* (1866) **:** a rear sight for a gun having an adjustable metal piece pierced with a small hole to peep through in aiming

pee·pul *or* **pi·pal** \ˈpē-(ˌ)pəl\ *n* [Hindi & Urdu *pīpal,* fr. Skt *pippala*] (1783) **:** a large long-lived fig (*Ficus religiosa*) found from India to southeastern Asia

[1]**peer** \ˈpir\ *n* [ME, fr. AF *per,* fr. *per,* adj., equal, fr. L *par*] (13c) **1 :** one that is of equal standing with another **:** EQUAL; *esp* **:** one belonging to the same societal group esp. based on age, grade, or status **2** *archaic* **:** COMPANION **3 a :** a member of one of the five ranks (as duke, mar-

quess, earl, viscount, or baron) of the British peerage **b :** NOBLE 1 — **peer** *adj*

[2]**peer** *vt* (14c) *archaic* **:** RIVAL, MATCH

[3]**peer** *vi* [perh. by shortening & alter. fr. *appear*] (1580) **1 :** to look narrowly or curiously; *esp* **:** to look searchingly at something difficult to discern **2 :** to come slightly into view **:** emerge partly

peer·age \ˈpir-ij\ *n* (15c) **1 :** the body of peers **2 :** the rank or dignity of a peer **3 :** a book containing a list of peers with their genealogy, history, and titles

peer·ess \ˈpir-əs\ *n* (1688) **1 :** the wife or widow of a peer **2 :** a woman who holds in her own right the rank of a peer

peer·less \ˈpir-ləs\ *adj* (14c) **:** MATCHLESS, INCOMPARABLE

peer review *n* (1969) **:** a process by which something proposed (as for research or publication) is evaluated by a group of experts in the appropriate field — **peer–review** *vt*

[1]**peeve** \ˈpēv\ *vt* **peeved; peev·ing** [back-formation fr. *peevish*] (1901) **:** to make peevish or resentful **:** ANNOY ***syn*** see IRRITATE

[2]**peeve** *n* (1909) **1 :** a feeling or mood of resentment **2 :** a particular grievance or source of aggravation

pee·vish \ˈpē-vish\ *adj* [ME *pevish* spiteful] (15c) **1 :** querulous in temperament or mood **:** FRETFUL **2 :** perversely obstinate ⟨a ~ child⟩ **3 :** marked by ill temper — **pee·vish·ly** *adv* — **pee·vish·ness** *n*

pee·wee \ˈpē-(ˌ)wē\ *n* [imit.] (1793) **1 :** PEWEE **2 :** one that is diminutive or small; *esp* **:** a small child **3 :** an age-specific level of youth sports; *also* **:** a member of a team in a peewee league — **peewee** *adj*

pee·wit *also* **pe·wit** \ˈpē-ˌwit, ˈpyü-ət\ *n* [imit.] (ca. 1529) **:** any of several birds; *esp* **:** LAPWING

[1]**peg** \ˈpeg\ *n* [ME *pegge,* prob. fr. MD] (15c) **1 a :** a small usu. cylindrical pointed or tapered piece (as of wood) used to pin down or fasten things or to fit into or close holes **:** PIN, PLUG **b** *Brit* **:** CLOTHESPIN **c :** a predetermined level at which something (as a price) is fixed **2 a :** a projecting piece used as a support or boundary marker **b :** something (as a fact or issue) used as a support, pretext, or reason ⟨a news ~ for the story⟩ **3 a :** one of the movable wooden pegs set in the head of a stringed instrument (as a violin) that are turned to regulate the pitch of the strings — see VIOLIN illustration **b :** a step or degree esp. in estimation **4 :** a pointed prong or claw for catching or tearing **5** *Brit* **:** DRINK ⟨poured himself out a stiff ~ —Dorothy Sayers⟩ **6 :** something (as a leg) resembling a peg **7 :** THROW; *esp* **:** a hard throw in baseball made in an attempt to put out a base runner

[2]**peg** *vb* **pegged; peg·ging** *vt* (1543) **1 a :** to put a peg into **b** *Brit* **:** to pin (laundry) on a clothesline **2 :** to attach or fix as if with a peg: as **a :** to pin down **:** RESTRICT **b :** to fix or hold (as prices or wage increases) at a predetermined level or rate **c :** to place in a definite category **:** IDENTIFY ⟨was *pegged* as an intellectual⟩ **3 :** to mark by pegs **4 :** THROW ~ *vi* **1 :** to work steadily and diligently — often used with *away* **2 :** to move along vigorously or hastily **:** HUSTLE

[3]**peg** *or* **pegged** *adj* (1681) **:** wide at the top and narrow at the bottom ⟨~ pants⟩

PEG *abbr* polyethylene glycol

Peg·a·sus \ˈpe-gə-səs\ *n* [L (gen. *Pegasi*), fr. Gk *Pēgasos*] (14c) **1 :** a winged horse that causes the stream Hippocrene to spring from Mount Helicon with a blow of his hoof **2** *archaic* **:** poetic inspiration **3 :** a northern constellation near the vernal equinoctial point

peg·board \ˈpeg-ˌbȯrd\ *n* (1952) **:** material (as fiberboard) with regularly spaced perforations into which hooks may be inserted for the storage or display of articles

peg leg *n* [[1]peg] (1769) **:** an artificial leg; *esp* **:** one fitted at the knee

peg·ma·tite \ˈpeg-mə-ˌtīt\ *n* [F, fr. Gk *pēgmat-, pēgma* something fastened together, fr. *pēgnynai* to fasten together — more at PACT] (ca. 1828) **:** a coarse variety of granite occurring in dikes or veins — **peg·ma·tit·ic** \ˌpeg-mə-ˈti-tik\ *adj*

peg out *vi* (1854) *chiefly Brit* **:** DIE

peg–top \ˈpeg-ˈtäp\ *or* **peg–topped** \-ˈtäpt\ *adj* (1858) **:** PEG

peg top *n* (1747) **1** \ˈpeg-ˈtäp\ **:** a pear-shaped top that is made to spin on the sharp metal peg in its base by the unwinding of a string wound round its center **2** *pl* \-ˌtäps\ **:** peg trousers

PEI *abbr* Prince Edward Island

pei·gnoir \pān-ˈwär, pen-\ *n* [F, lit., garment worn while combing the hair, fr. MF, fr. *peigner* to comb the hair, fr. L *pectinare,* fr. *pectin-, pecten* comb — more at PECTINATE] (1835) **:** a woman's loose negligee or dressing gown

[1]**pe·jo·ra·tive** \pi-ˈjȯr-ə-tiv, -ˈjär- *also* ˈpe-jə-rə-tiv *or* ˈpē- *or* -ˌrā- *or* ˈpej-rə- *or* ˈpēj-\ *n* (1882) **:** a pejorative word or phrase

[2]**pejorative** *adj* [LL *pejoratus,* pp. of *pejorare* to make or become worse, fr. L *pejor* worse; akin to Skt *padyate* he falls, L *ped-, pes* foot — more at FOOT] (ca. 1888) **:** having negative connotations; *esp* **:** tending to disparage or belittle **:** DEPRECIATORY — **pe·jo·ra·tive·ly** *adv*

peke \ˈpēk\ *n, often cap* (1910) **:** PEKINGESE 2

Pe·kin \pi-ˈkin, ˈpē-ˌ\ *n* [*Pekin, Peking* (Beijing), China] (1885) **:** any of a breed of large white ducks of Chinese origin used for meat production

Pe·king duck \ˈpē-ˌkiŋ-, ˈpā-\ *n* (1955) **:** a Chinese dish consisting of roasted duck meat and strips of crispy duck skin topped with scallions and sauce and wrapped in thin pancakes

Pe·king·ese *or* **Pe·kin·ese** \ˌpē-kə-ˈnēz, -ˈnēs; -kiŋ-ˈēz, -ˈēs\ *n, pl* **Pekingese** *or* **Pekinese** (1849) **1 a :** the Chinese dialect of Beijing **b :** a native or resident of Beijing **2 :** any of a Chinese breed of small short-legged dogs with a broad flat face and a profuse long soft coat

Peking man *n* (1926) **:** an extinct Pleistocene hominid known from skeletal and cultural remains in cave deposits at Zhoukoudianzhen, China and classified with the direct ancestor (*Homo erectus*) of modern humans

pe·koe \ˈpē-(ˌ)kō *also* ˈpe-\ *n* [Chin (Xiamen) *pek-ho*] (1713) **:** a tea made from young leaves slightly larger than those of orange pekoe

pel·age \ˈpe-lij\ *n* [F, fr. MF, fr. *poil* hair, fr. OF *peil,* fr. L *pilus*] (1734) **:** the hairy covering of a mammal

[1]**Pe·la·gian** \pə-ˈlā-j(ē-)ən\ *n* (15c) **:** one agreeing with Pelagius in denying original sin and consequently in holding that individuals have perfect freedom to do either right or wrong

[2]**Pelagian** *adj* (15c) **:** of or relating to Pelagians or Pelagianism

Pe·la·gian·ism \-j(ē-)ə-ˌni-zəm\ *n* (1581) **:** the teaching of Pelagius or Pelagians

pe·lag·ic \pə-ˈla-jik\ *adj* [L *pelagicus,* fr. Gk *pelagikos,* fr. *pelagos* sea — more at PLAGAL] (ca. 1656) **:** of, relating to, or living or occurring in the open sea **:** OCEANIC ⟨~ sediment⟩ ⟨~ birds⟩ — **pelagic** *n*

pel·ar·go·ni·um \ˌpe-lär-ˈgō-nē-əm, -lər-\ *n* [NL, fr. Gk *pelargos* stork (akin to Gk *pelios* livid, *polios* gray) + NL *-nium* (as in *Geranium*) — more at FALLOW] (1813) **:** any of a genus (*Pelargonium*) of southern African herbs of the geranium family with showy flowers of usu. red, pink, or white distinguished by a spurred calyx and irregular corolla — called also *geranium, storksbill*; compare ROSE GERANIUM

Pe·las·gian \pə-ˈlaz-j(ē-)ən, -ˈlaz-gē-ən\ *n* [Gk *pelasgios,* adj., Pelasgian, fr. *Pelasgoi* Pelasgians] (15c) **:** a member of an ancient people mentioned by classical writers as early inhabitants of Greece and the eastern islands of the Mediterranean — **Pelasgian** *adj*

pe·lec·y·pod \pə-ˈle-sə-ˌpäd\ *n* [NL *Pelecypoda,* group name, fr. Gk *pelekys* ax (akin to Skt *paraśu* ax) + *pod-, pous* foot — more at FOOT] (1875) **:** LAMELLIBRANCH

pel·er·ine \ˌpe-lə-ˈrēn, ˈpe-lə-rən\ *n* [prob. fr. F *pèlerine*] (1744) **:** a woman's narrow cape made of fabric or fur and usu. with long ends hanging down in front

Pe·leus \ˈpēl-ˌyüs, ˈpē-lē-əs\ *n* [L, fr. Gk *Pēleus*] (15c) **:** a son of Aeacus who becomes by the goddess Thetis the father of Achilles

pelf \ˈpelf\ *n* [ME, fr. AF *pelfre* booty] (14c) **:** MONEY, RICHES

pel·i·can \ˈpe-li-kən\ *n* [ME, fr. OE *pellican,* fr. LL *pelecanus,* fr. Gk *pelekan*] (bef. 12c) **:** any of a genus (*Pelecanus*) of large web-footed fish-eating birds with a very large bill and distensible gular pouch

pe·lisse \pə-ˈlēs, pe-\ *n* [F, fr. OF *pelice,* fr. LL *pellicia,* fr. fem. of *pellicius* made of skin, fr. L *pellis* skin — more at FELL] (1713) **1 :** a long cloak or coat made of fur or lined or trimmed with fur **2 :** a woman's loose lightweight cloak with wide collar and fur trimming

pel·la·gra \pə-ˈla-grə, -ˈlā-, -ˈlä-\ *n* [It, fr. *pelle* skin (fr. L *pellis*) + *-agra* (as in *podagra,* fr. L)] (ca. 1811) **:** a disease marked by dermatitis, gastrointestinal disorders, and mental disturbances and associated with a diet deficient in niacin — **pel·la·grous** \-grəs\ *adj*

[1]**pel·let** \ˈpe-lət\ *n* [ME *pelote,* fr. AF, fr. VL **pilota,* dim. of L *pila* ball] (14c) **1 a :** a usu. small rounded, spherical, or cylindrical body (as of food or medicine) **b :** a wad of indigestible material (as of bones and fur) regurgitated by a bird of prey **2 :** any of various projectiles fired from a weapon (as an air rifle) — **pel·let·al** \-lə-tᵊl\ *adj*

[2]**pellet** *vt* (1607) **1 :** PELLETIZE **2 :** to strike with pellets

pellet gun *n* (1952) **:** AIR GUN 1

pel·let·ise *Brit var of* PELLETIZE

pel·let·ize \ˈpe-lə-ˌtīz\ *vt* **-ized; -iz·ing** (1942) **1 :** to form or compact into pellets ⟨~ ore⟩ **2 :** to coat (seeds) with a soluble material (as to facilitate ease of handling) — **pel·let·i·za·tion** \ˌpe-lə-tə-ˈzā-shən\ *n* — **pel·let·iz·er** \ˈpe-lə-ˌtī-zər\ *n*

pel·li·cle \ˈpe-li-kəl\ *n* [MF *pellicule,* fr. ML *pellicula,* fr. L, dim. of *pellis*] (15c) **:** a thin skin or film: as **a :** an outer membrane of some protozoans (as euglenoids or paramecia) **b :** a film that reflects a part of the light falling upon it and transmits the rest and that is used for dividing a beam of light (as in a photographic device)

pel·li·to·ry \ˈpe-lə-ˌtȯr-ē\ *n, pl* **-ries** [ME *peletre, pelytory,* fr. AF *peletre, peretre,* fr. ML *peletrum, piretrum,* alter. of L *pyrethrum* — more at PYRETHRUM] (15c) **1 :** a southern European composite plant (*Anacyclus pyrethrum*) resembling yarrow — called also *pellitory-of-Spain* **2 :** any of a genus (*Parietaria*) of herbs of the nettle family with alternate leaves and inconspicuous flowers — called also *pellitory-of-the-wall*

pell–mell \ˌpel-ˈmel\ *adv* [MF *pelemele*] (1590) **1 :** in mingled confusion or disorder ⟨papers strewn ~ on the desk⟩ **2 :** in confused haste ⟨ran ~ for the door⟩ — **pell–mell** *adj or n*

pel·lu·cid \pə-ˈlü-səd\ *adj* [L *pellucidus,* fr. *per* through + *lucidus* lucid — more at FOR] (1563) **1 :** admitting maximum passage of light without diffusion or distortion ⟨a ~ stream⟩ **2 :** reflecting light evenly from all surfaces **3 :** easy to understand — **pel·lu·cid·ly** \pə-ˈlü-səd-lē\ *adv*

pel·met \ˈpel-mət\ *n* [prob. modif. of F *palmette* palmette] (1812) **:** a short valance or small cornice for concealing curtain fixtures

Pe·lops \ˈpē-ˌläps, ˈpe-\ *n* [L, fr. Gk] (15c) **:** a son of Tantalus served by his father to the gods for food but later restored to life by them

pe·lo·rus \pə-ˈlȯr-əs\ *n* [origin unknown] (1854) **:** a navigational instrument resembling a mariner's compass without magnetic needles and having two sight vanes by which bearings are taken

pe·lo·ta \pə-ˈlō-tə\ *n* [Sp, fr. OF *pelote* little ball — more at PELLET] (1807) **1 :** a court game related to jai alai **2 :** the ball used in jai alai

pel·o·ton \ˌpe-lə-ˈtän, ˈpe-lə-ˌtän\ *n* [F, lit., ball — more at PLATOON] (1951) **:** the main body of riders in a bicycle race

[1]**pelt** \ˈpelt\ *n* [ME, prob. fr. *pelett* animal skin, fr. AF *pelette* — more at PELTRY] (15c) **1 :** a usu. undressed skin with its hair, wool, or fur **2 :** a skin stripped of hair or wool for tanning

[2]**pelt** *vt* (1568) **:** to strip off the skin or pelt of (an animal)

[3]**pelt** *vb* [ME] *vt* (15c) **1 a :** to strike with a succession of blows or missiles ⟨~*ed* him with stones⟩ **b :** to assail vigorously or persistently ⟨~*ed* her with accusations⟩ **2 :** HURL, THROW ⟨~*ed* snowballs at them⟩ **3 :** to beat or dash repeatedly against ⟨hailstones ~*ing* the roof⟩ ~ *vi* **1 :** to deliver a succession of blows or missiles **2 :** to beat incessantly **3 :** to move rapidly and vigorously **:** HURRY — **pelt·er** *n*

[4]**pelt** *n* (ca. 1540) **:** BLOW, WHACK

pel·tate \ˈpel-ˌtāt\ *adj* [L *pelta* small shield, fr. Gk *peltē*] (ca. 1760) **:** shaped like a shield; *specif* **:** having the stem or support attached to the lower surface instead of at the base or margin ⟨~ leaves⟩ — see LEAF illustration

pelt·ing \ˈpel-tiŋ\ *adj* [prob. fr. E dial. *pelt* piece of trash] (1540) *archaic* **:** PALTRY, INSIGNIFICANT

pelt·ry \ˈpel-trē\ *n, pl* **peltries** [ME, fr. AF *pelterie,* fr. *peleter* furrier, fr. *pelette* small skin, fr. *pel* skin, fr. L *pellis* — more at FELL] (15c) **:** PELTS, FURS; *esp* **:** raw undressed skins — often used in pl.

pel·vic \ˈpel-vik\ *adj* (1799) **:** of, relating to, or located in or near the pelvis — **pelvic** *n*

pelvic fin *n* (1882) **:** one of the paired fins of a fish that are homologous with the hind limbs of a quadruped

pelvic girdle *n* (1862) **:** a bony or cartilaginous arch that supports the hind limbs of a vertebrate

pelvic inflammatory disease *n* (1921) **:** inflammation of the female reproductive tract (as the fallopian tubes and ovaries) that occurs esp.

as a result of a sexually transmitted disease and is a leading cause of infertility in women

pel•vis \ˈpel-vəs\ *n, pl* **pel•vis•es** \-və-səz\ *or* **pel•ves** \-ˌvēz\ [NL, fr. L, basin; perh. akin to OE & ON *full* cup] (1615) **1 :** a basin-shaped structure in the skeleton of many vertebrates that is formed by the pelvic girdle and adjoining bones of the spine **2 :** the cavity of the pelvis **3 :** the funnel-shaped cavity of the kidney into which urine is discharged

pel•y•co•saur \ˈpe-li-kə-ˌsȯr\ *n* [ultim. fr. Gk *pelyc-, pelyx* bowl + *sauros* lizard] (1904) **:** any of an order (Pelycosauria) of primitive chiefly Permian quadruped synapsid reptiles often having extreme development of the dorsal vertebral processes

Pem•broke table \ˈpem-ˌbrōk-, -ˌbru̇k-\ *n* [*Pembroke,* Wales] (1778) **:** a small 4-legged table originating in the Georgian period and having two drop leaves and a drawer

Pembroke Welsh corgi *n* (1938) **:** any of a breed of Welsh corgis with pointed ears, straight forelegs, and a short tail — called also *Pembroke*

pem•mi•can *also* **pem•i•can** \ˈpe-mi-kən\ *n* [Cree *pimihkaːn*] (1791) **:** a concentrated food used by No. American Indians and consisting of lean meat dried, pounded fine, and mixed with melted fat; *also* **:** a similar preparation (as of dried beef, flour, molasses, suet) used for emergency rations

pem•o•line \ˈpe-mə-ˌlēn\ *n* [origin unknown] (1961) **:** a synthetic drug $C_9H_8N_2O_2$ that is a mild stimulant of the central nervous system

pem•phi•gus \ˈpem(p)-fi-gəs, pem-ˈfī-\ *n* [NL, fr. Gk *pemphig-, pemphix* pustule] (ca. 1779) **:** an autoimmune disease marked by blisters on skin and mucous membranes and often by itching or burning

[1]**pen** \ˈpen\ *vt* **penned; pen•ning** [ME *pennen,* fr. OE *-pennian*] (13c) **:** to shut in or as if in a pen

[2]**pen** *n* [ME, perh. fr. *pennen*] (14c) **1 a :** a small enclosure for animals **b :** the animals in a pen ⟨a ~ of sheep⟩ **2 :** a small place of confinement or storage **3 :** a protected dock or slip for a submarine **4 :** BULL PEN 2

[3]**pen** *n* [ME *penne,* fr. AF, feather, pen, fr. L *penna, pinna* feather; akin to Gk *pteron* wing — more at FEATHER] (14c) **1 :** an implement for writing or drawing with ink or a similar fluid: as **a :** QUILL **b :** PEN POINT **c :** a penholder containing a pen point **d :** FOUNTAIN PEN **e :** BALLPOINT **2 a :** a writing instrument regarded as a means of expression ⟨enlisted the ~*s* of the best writers —F. H. Chase⟩ **b :** WRITER **3 :** the internal horny feather-shaped shell of a squid **4 :** STYLUS d

[4]**pen** *vt* **penned; pen•ning** (15c) **:** WRITE, INDITE ⟨~ a letter⟩

[5]**pen** *n* [origin unknown] (ca. 1550) **:** a female swan

[6]**pen** *n* (1884) **:** PENITENTIARY

[7]**pen** *abbr* peninsula

PEN *abbr* International Association of Poets, Playwrights, Editors, Essayists and Novelists

pe•nal \ˈpē-nᵊl\ *adj* [ME, fr. AF, fr. L *poenalis,* fr. *poena* punishment — more at PAIN] (15c) **1 :** of, relating to, or involving punishment, penalties, or punitive institutions **2 :** liable to punishment ⟨a ~ offense⟩ **3 :** used as a place of confinement and punishment ⟨a ~ colony⟩ — **pe•nal•ly** \-nᵊl-ē\ *adv*

penal code *n* (1828) **:** a code of laws concerning crimes and offenses and their punishment

pe•nal•ise *Brit var of* PENALIZE

pe•nal•ize \ˈpē-nə-ˌlīz, ˈpe-\ *vt* **-ized; -iz•ing** (1868) **1 :** to inflict a penalty on **2 :** to put at a serious disadvantage — **pe•nal•i•za•tion** \-nə-lə-ˈzā-shən\ *n*

pen•al•ty \ˈpe-nᵊl-tē\ *n, pl* **-ties** [ME *penalte,* fr. MF *penalité,* fr. ML *poenalitas,* fr. L *poenalis*] (15c) **1 :** the suffering in person, rights, or property that is annexed by law or judicial decision to the commission of a crime or public offense **2 :** the suffering or the sum to be forfeited to which a person agrees to be subjected in case of nonfulfillment of stipulations **3 a :** disadvantage, loss, or hardship due to some action **b :** a disadvantage (as loss of yardage, time, or possession of the ball or an addition to or subtraction from the score) imposed on a team or competitor for violation of the rules of a sport **4 :** points scored in bridge by the side that defeats the opposing contract — usu. used in pl. — **penalty** *adj*

penalty box *n* (1931) **:** an area alongside an ice hockey rink to which penalized players are confined for the duration of their penalty

penalty kick *n* (1889) **1 :** a free kick in rugby **2 :** a free kick at the goal in soccer made from a point 12 yards in front of the goal and allowed for certain violations within a designated area around the goal

penalty shot *n* (ca. 1948) **:** an unhindered shot at the goal in ice hockey awarded to an individual for certain violations by an opponent

[1]**pen•ance** \ˈpe-nən(t)s\ *n* [ME, fr. AF, fr. ML *poenitentia* penitence] (14c) **1 :** an act of self-abasement, mortification, or devotion performed to show sorrow or repentance for sin **2 :** a sacramental rite that is practiced in Roman, Eastern, and some Anglican churches and that consists of private confession, absolution, and a penance directed by the confessor **3 :** something (as a hardship or penalty) resembling an act of penance (as in compensating for an offense)

[2]**penance** *vt* **pen•anced; pen•anc•ing** (ca. 1600) **:** to impose penance on

Pe•na•tes \pə-ˈnā-tēz, -ˈnä-\ *n pl* [L, fr. *penus* food, provisions] (1513) **:** the Roman gods of the household worshipped in close connection with Vesta and with the Lares

pence \ˈpen(t)s\ *pl of* PENNY

pen•cel *or* **pen•cil** \ˈpen(t)-səl\ *n* [ME *pencel,* fr. AF *pencel, penuncel*] (13c) **:** PENNONCEL

pen•chant \ˈpen-chənt, *esp Brit* ˈpä^{n}-ˌshä^{n}\ *n* [F, fr. prp. of *pencher* to incline, fr. VL **pendicare,* fr. L *pendere* to weigh] (1672) **:** a strong and continued inclination; *broadly* **:** LIKING ***syn*** see LEANING

[1]**pen•cil** \ˈpen(t)-səl\ *n* [ME *pensel,* fr. AF *pincel,* fr. VL **penicellus,* alter. of L *penicillus,* dim. of *peniculus* brush, fr. dim. of *penis* tail, penis] (14c) **1 :** an artist's brush **2 :** an artist's individual skill or style **3 a :** an implement for writing, drawing, or marking consisting of or containing a slender cylinder or strip of a solid marking substance **b :** a small medicated or cosmetic roll or stick for local applications **4 :** a set of geometric objects each pair of which has a common property ⟨the lines in a plane through a point comprise a ~ of lines⟩ **5 :** something (as a beam of radiation) long and thin like a pencil

[2]**pencil** *vt* **-ciled** *or* **-cilled; -cil•ing** *or* **-cil•ling** \-s(ə-)liŋ\ (ca. 1532) **1 :** to paint, draw, write, or mark with a pencil **2 :** to plan or designate tentatively — used with *in* ⟨~*ed* him in as the nominee⟩

pen•cil•ing *or* **pen•cil•ling** *n* (1706) **:** the work of the pencil or brush; *also* **:** a product of this

pencil pusher *n* (1881) **:** a person who does predominantly paperwork

pen•dant *also* **pen•dent** \ˈpen-dənt; *3 & 4 are also* ˈpe-nənt, *5 is also* pä^{n}-ˈdä^{n}\ *n* [ME *pendaunt,* fr. AF *pendant,* fr. prp. of *pendre* to hang, fr. VL **pendere,* fr. L *pendēre;* akin to L *pendere* to weigh, estimate, pay, *pondus* weight] (14c) **1 :** something suspended: as **a :** an ornament (as on a necklace) allowed to hang free **b :** an electrical fixture suspended from the ceiling **2 :** a hanging ornament of roofs or ceilings much used in the later styles of Gothic architecture **3 :** a length of line usu. used as a connector on a boat or ship; *esp* **:** a short rope hanging from a spar and having at its free end a block or spliced thimble **4** *chiefly Brit* **:** PENNANT 1a **5 a :** COMPANION PIECE **b :** something secondary or supplementary

pen•den•cy \ˈpen-dən(t)-sē\ *n* (1637) **:** the state of being pending ⟨the ~ of the litigation⟩

pen•dent *or* **pen•dant** \ˈpen-dənt\ *adj* [ME *pendaunt*] (14c) **1 :** jutting or leaning over **:** OVERHANGING ⟨a ~ cliff⟩ **2 :** supported from above **:** SUSPENDED ⟨icicles ~ from the eaves⟩ **3 :** remaining undetermined **:** PENDING

pen•den•tive \pen-ˈden-tiv\ *n* [F *pendentif,* fr. L *pendent-, pendens,* prp. of *pendēre*] (ca. 1741) **:** one of the concave triangular members that support a dome over a square space

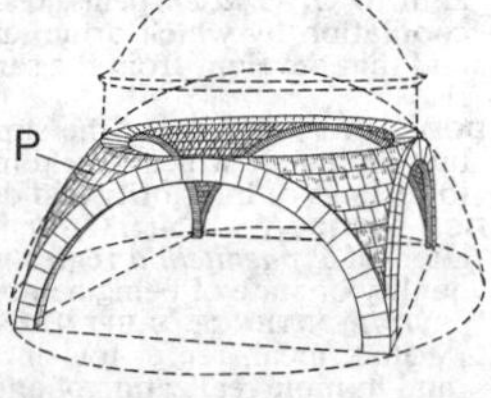

P pendentive

[1]**pend•ing** \ˈpen-diŋ\ *prep* [F *pendant,* fr. prp. of *pendre*] (1642) **1 :** DURING **2 :** while awaiting ⟨~ approval⟩

[2]**pending** *adj* (1797) **1 :** not yet decided **:** being in continuance ⟨the case is still ~⟩ **2 :** IMMINENT, IMPENDING

pen•du•lar \ˈpen-jə-lər, ˈpen-dyə-, -də-\ *adj* (1875) **:** being or resembling the movement of a pendulum

pen•du•lous \-ləs\ *adj* [L *pendulus,* fr. *pendēre* to hang] (ca. 1605) **1** *archaic* **:** poised without visible support **2 a :** suspended so as to swing freely ⟨branches hung with ~ vines⟩ **b :** inclined or hanging downward ⟨~ jowls⟩ **3 :** marked by vacillation, indecision, or uncertainty — **pen•du•lous•ness** *n*

pen•du•lum \-ləm\ *n* [NL, fr. L, neut. of *pendulus*] (1660) **1 :** a body suspended from a fixed point so as to swing freely to and fro under the action of gravity and commonly used to regulate movements (as of clockwork) **2 :** something (as a state of affairs) that alternates between opposites

Pe•nel•o•pe \pə-ˈne-lə-pē\ *n* [L, fr. Gk *Pēnelopē*] (14c) **:** the wife of Odysseus who waits faithfully for him during his 20 years' absence

pe•ne•plain *also* **pe•ne•plane** \ˈpē-ni-ˌplān, ˈpe-\ *n* [L *paene, pene* almost + E *plain* or *plane*] (1889) **:** a land surface of considerable area and slight relief shaped by erosion

pen•e•tra•ble \ˈpe-nə-trə-bəl\ *adj* (1538) **:** capable of being penetrated — **pen•e•tra•bil•i•ty** \ˌpe-nə-trə-ˈbi-lə-tē\ *n*

pen•e•tra•lia \ˌpe-nə-ˈtrā-lē-ə\ *n pl* [L, neut. pl. of *penetralis* inner, fr. *penetrare* to penetrate] (1668) **:** the innermost or most private parts

pen•e•trance \ˈpe-nə-trən(t)s\ *n* [ISV, fr. L *penetrare*] (1934) **:** the proportion of individuals of a particular genotype that express its phenotypic effect in a given environment

[1]**pen•e•trant** \-trənt\ *adj* (1543) **:** PENETRATING

[2]**penetrant** *n* (ca. 1734) **:** one that penetrates or is capable of penetrating

pen•e•trate \ˈpe-nə-ˌtrāt\ *vb* **-trat•ed; -trat•ing** [L *penetratus,* pp. of *penetrare,* fr. *penitus* deep within, far; akin to L *penus* provisions] *vt* (ca. 1530) **1 a :** to pass into or through **b :** to enter by overcoming resistance **:** PIERCE **c :** to gain entrance to **2 a :** to see into or through **b :** to discover the inner contents or meaning of **3 :** to affect profoundly with feeling **4 :** to diffuse through or into ~ *vi* **1 a :** to pass, extend, pierce, or diffuse into or through something **b :** to pierce something with the eye or mind **2 :** to affect deeply the senses or feelings ***syn*** see ENTER

penetrating *adj* (1593) **1 :** having the power of entering, piercing, or pervading ⟨a ~ shriek⟩ **2 :** ACUTE, DISCERNING ⟨~ insights into life⟩ — **pen•e•trat•ing•ly** \-ˌtrā-tiŋ-lē\ *adv*

pen•e•tra•tion \ˌpe-nə-ˈtrā-shən\ *n* (1605) **1 a :** the power to penetrate; *esp* **:** the ability to discern deeply and acutely **b :** the depth to which something penetrates **c :** the extent to which a commercial product or agency is familiar or sells in a market **2 :** the act or process of penetrating: as **a :** the act of entering a country so that actual establishment of influence is accomplished **b :** an attack that penetrates the enemy's front or territory ***syn*** see DISCERNMENT

pen•e•tra•tive \ˈpe-nə-ˌtrā-tiv\ *adj* (15c) **1 :** tending to penetrate **:** PIERCING **2 :** ACUTE ⟨~ observations⟩ **3 :** IMPRESSIVE ⟨a ~ speaker⟩

pen•e•trom•e•ter \ˌpe-nə-ˈträ-mə-tər\ *n* [L *penetrare* + ISV *-meter*] (1905) **:** an instrument for measuring firmness or consistency (as of soil)

pen•gö \ˈpeŋ-ˌgə(r), -ˌgœ\ *n, pl* **pengö** *or* **pengös** [Hung *pengő,* lit., jingling] (1925) **:** the basic monetary unit of Hungary from 1925 to 1946

pen•guin \ˈpen-gwən, ˈpeŋ-\ *n* [obs. E *penguin* great auk, perh. fr. W *pen gwyn* white head (applied to the bird in winter plumage)] (1588) **:** any of various erect short-legged flightless aquatic birds (family Spheniscidae) of the southern hemisphere

pen•hold•er \ˈpen-ˌhōl-dər\ *n* (1815) **:** a holder or handle for a pen point

-penia *n comb form* [NL, fr. Gk *penia*] **:** deficiency ⟨leuko*penia*⟩

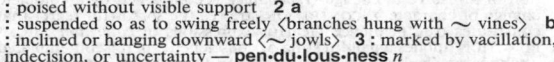

\ə\ **abut** \ᵊ\ **kitten,** F table \ər\ **further** \a\ **ash** \ā\ **ace** \ä\ **mop, mar** \au̇\ **out** \ch\ **chin** \e\ **bet** \ē\ **easy** \g\ **go** \i\ **hit** \ī\ **ice** \j\ **job** \ŋ\ **sing** \ō\ **go** \ȯ\ **law** \ȯi\ **boy** \th\ **thin** \t͟h\ **the** \ü\ **loot** \u̇\ **foot** \y\ **yet** \zh\ **vision, beige** \k̟, ^{n}, œ, ue, ^{y}\ *see* Guide to Pronunciation

pen·i·cil·la·mine \ˌpe-nə-ˈsi-lə-ˌmēn\ *n* [*penicill*in + *amine*] (1943) **:** an amino acid $C_5H_{11}NO_2S$ that is obtained from penicillins and is used esp. in the treatment of cystinuria, rheumatoid arthritis, and poisoning by metals (as copper or lead)
pen·i·cil·late \ˌpe-nə-ˈsi-lət, -ˌlāt\ *adj* [L *penicillus* brush — more at PENCIL] (1819) **:** furnished with a tuft of fine filaments ⟨a ~ stigma⟩
pen·i·cil·lin \ˌpe-nə-ˈsi-lən\ *n* [NL *Penicillium*] (1929) **1 :** any of several relatively nontoxic antibiotic acids of the general formula $C_9H_{11}N_2O_4SR$ that are produced by molds (genus *Penicillium* and esp. *P. notatum* or *P. chrysogenum*) or synthetically and are used esp. against gram-positive cocci; *also* **:** a mixture of such acids **2 :** a salt or ester of a penicillin or a mixture of such salts or esters
pen·i·cil·lin·ase \-ˈsi-lə-ˌnās, -ˌnāz\ *n* (1940) **:** BETA-LACTAMASE
pen·i·cil·li·um \-ˈsi-lē-əm\ *n, pl* **-lia** \-lē-ə\ [NL, fr. L *penicillus*] (1867) **:** any of a genus (*Penicillium*) of fungi (as a blue mold) that are found chiefly on moist nonliving organic matter (as decaying fruit) and have been grouped with the imperfect fungi but are now often placed with the ascomycetes
pe·nile \ˈpē-ˌnī(-ə)l\ *adj* (ca. 1861) **:** of, relating to, or affecting the penis
pen·in·su·la \pə-ˈnin(t)-s(ə-)lə, -shə-lə\ *n* [L *paeninsula*, fr. *paene* almost + *insula* island] (1538) **:** a portion of land nearly surrounded by water and connected with a larger body by an isthmus; *also* **:** a piece of land jutting out into the water whether with or without a well-defined isthmus — **pen·in·su·lar** \-s(ə-)lər, -shə-lər\ *adj*
pe·nis \ˈpē-nəs\ *n, pl* **pe·nis·es** *also* **pe·nes** \ˈpē-(ˌ)nēz\ [L, penis, tail; akin to OHG *faselt* penis, Gk *peos*] (1668) **:** a male erectile organ of copulation by which urine and semen are discharged from the body and that develops from the same embryonic mass of tissue as the clitoris
penis envy *n* (1924) **:** the supposed coveting of the penis by a young human female which is held in Freudian psychoanalytic theory to lead to feelings of inferiority and defensive or compensatory behavior
pen·i·tence \ˈpe-nə-tən(t)s\ *n* [ME, fr. AF *penitance*, fr. ML *poenitentia*, alter. of L *paenitentia* regret, fr. *paenitent-, paenitens*, prp.] (13c) **:** the quality or state of being penitent **:** sorrow for sins or faults
syn PENITENCE, REPENTANCE, CONTRITION, COMPUNCTION, REMORSE mean regret for sin or wrongdoing. PENITENCE implies sad and humble realization of and regret for one's misdeeds ⟨absolution is dependent upon sincere *penitence*⟩. REPENTANCE adds the implication of a resolve to change ⟨*repentance* accompanied by a complete change of character⟩. CONTRITION stresses the sorrowful regret that constitutes true penitence ⟨tearful expressions of *contrition*⟩. COMPUNCTION implies a painful sting of conscience esp. for contemplated wrongdoing ⟨had no *compunctions* about taking back what is mine⟩. REMORSE suggests prolonged and insistent self-reproach and mental anguish for past wrongs and esp. for those whose consequences cannot be remedied ⟨thieves untroubled by feelings of *remorse*⟩.
[1]**pen·i·tent** \-tənt\ *adj* [ME, fr. MF & L; MF *penitent*, fr. L *paenitent-, paenitens*, fr. prp. of *paenitēre* to cause regret, feel regret, perh. fr. *paene* almost] (14c) **:** feeling or expressing humble or regretful pain or sorrow for sins or offenses **:** REPENTANT — **pen·i·tent·ly** *adv*
[2]**penitent** *n* (14c) **1 :** a person who repents of sin **2 :** a person under church censure but admitted to penance or reconciliation esp. under the direction of a confessor
pen·i·ten·tial \ˌpe-nə-ˈten(t)-shəl\ *adj* (1508) **:** of or relating to penitence or penance — **pen·i·ten·tial·ly** \-ˈten(t)-sh(ə-)lē\ *adv*
[1]**pen·i·ten·tia·ry** \ˌpe-nə-ˈten(t)-sh(ə-)rē\ *n, pl* **-ries** [ME *penitenciary*, fr. ML *poenitentiarius*, fr. *poenitentia*] (15c) **1 a :** an officer in some Roman Catholic dioceses vested with power from the bishop to deal with cases of a nature normally handled only by the bishop **b** *cap* **:** a cardinal presiding over a tribunal of the Roman curia concerned with dispensations and indulgences **2 :** a public institution in which offenders against the law are confined for detention or punishment; *specif* **:** a state or federal prison in the U.S.
[2]**pen·i·ten·tia·ry** \ˌpe-nə-ˈten(t)-sh(ə-)rē, *1 also* -ˈten(t)-shē-ˌer-ē\ *adj* (1577) **1 :** PENITENTIAL **2 :** of, relating to, or incurring confinement in a penitentiary
pen·knife \ˈpen-ˌnīf\ *n* [ME; fr. its original use for mending quill pens] (15c) **:** a small pocketknife usu. with only one blade
pen·light *also* **pen·lite** \-ˌlīt\ *n* (1945) **:** a small flashlight resembling a fountain pen in size or shape
pen·man \-mən\ *n* (1539) **1 a :** CALLIGRAPHER **b :** COPYIST, SCRIBE **c :** a person with a specified quality or kind of handwriting ⟨a poor ~⟩ **2 :** AUTHOR
pen·man·ship \-ˌship\ *n* (1695) **1 :** the art or practice of writing with the pen **2 :** quality or style of handwriting
Penn *or* **Penna** *abbr* Pennsylvania
pen name *n* (ca. 1864) **:** an author's pseudonym
pen·nant \ˈpe-nənt\ *n* [alter. of *pendant*] (1698) **1 a :** any of various nautical flags tapering usu. to a point or swallowtail and used for identification or signaling **b :** a flag or banner longer in the fly than in the hoist; *esp* **:** one that tapers to a point **2 :** a flag emblematic of championship (as in a baseball league); *also* **:** the championship itself
pen·nate \ˈpe-ˌnāt\ *adj* [irreg. fr. NL *Pennales*] (1938) **:** of, relating to, or being usu. elongate bilaterally symmetrical diatoms of an order (Pennales) having a raphe or a similar structure
pen·ne \ˈpe(n)-(ˌ)nā\ *n, pl* **penne** [It, pl. of *penna*, lit., quill, feather, pen, fr. L *pinna* feather & *penna* wing — more at PEN] (1919) **:** short thick diagonally cut tubular pasta
pen·ni \ˈpe-nē\ *n, pl* **pen·nia** \-nē-ə\ *also* **penni** *or* **pen·nis** \-nēz\ [Finn] (ca. 1893) **:** a former monetary unit equal to 1/100 Finnish markka
pen·ni·less \ˈpe-ni-ləs\ *adj* (14c) **:** destitute of money
pen·non \ˈpe-nən\ *n* [ME, fr. AF *penun*, dim. of *penne* quill, wing feather — more at PEN] (14c) **1 a :** a long usu. triangular or swallow-tailed streamer typically attached to the head of a lance as an ensign **b :** PENNANT 1a **2 :** WING, PINION
pen·non·cel *or* **pen·on·cel** \ˈpe-nən-ˌsel\ *n* [ME *penoncell*, fr. AF *penuncel*, dim. of *penun*] (14c) **:** a small pennon used in late medieval or Renaissance times
Penn·syl·va·nia Dutch \ˌpen(t)-səl-ˈvā-nyə-, -nē-ə-\ *n* (ca. 1824) **1 :** a people orig. of eastern Pennsylvania whose characteristic cultural traditions go back to the German migrations of the 18th century **2 :** a dialect of German spoken mainly in Amish communities esp. in Pennsylvania, Ohio, and Indiana — **Pennsylvania Dutchman** *n*
Pennsylvania German *n* (1869) **:** PENNSYLVANIA DUTCH
Penn·syl·va·nian \-ˈvā-nyən, -nē-ən\ *adj* (1698) **1 :** of or relating to Pennsylvania or its people **2 :** of, relating to, or being the period of the Paleozoic era in No. America between the Mississippian and Permian or the corresponding system of rocks — see GEOLOGIC TIME table — **Pennsylvanian** *n*
pen·ny \ˈpe-nē\ *n, pl* **pennies** \-nēz\ *or* **pence** \ˈpen(t)s\ *often attrib* [ME, fr. OE *penning, penig*; akin to OHG *pfenning*, a coin] (bef. 12c) **1 a :** a monetary unit of the United Kingdom formerly equal to 1/240 pound but now equal to 1/100 pound **b :** a similar monetary unit of any of various other countries in or formerly in the Commonwealth of Nations — see *pound* at MONEY table **c :** a coin representing one penny **2 :** DENARIUS **3** *pl pennies* **:** CENT **4 :** a former monetary unit equal to 1/100 Irish pound **5 :** a trivial amount **6 :** a piece or sum of money ⟨that will cost a pretty ~⟩
-penny *adj comb form* [*penny*; perh. fr. the original price per hundred] **:** being a (designated) nail size ⟨an eight*penny* nail⟩
pen·ny–an·te \ˈpe-nē-ˈan-tē\ *adj* (1865) **:** SMALL-TIME, TWO-BIT
penny ante *n* (1855) **:** poker played for very low stakes
penny arcade *n* (1908) **:** an amusement center having coin-operated devices for entertainment
penny candy *n* (ca. 1940) **:** inexpensive candy orig. costing a penny apiece
pen·ny·cress \ˈpe-nē-ˌkres\ *n* (1713) **:** a Eurasian cruciferous herb (*Thlaspi arvense*) with round flat pods that is widely naturalized in the New World
penny dreadful *n* (ca. 1873) **:** a novel of violent adventure or crime — **penny–dreadful** *adj*
penny loafer *n* (1968) **:** a loafer with a strap across the upper orig. used for holding a penny
pen·ny–pinch·ing \-ˌpin-chiŋ\ *n* (1935) **:** FRUGALITY, PARSIMONY — **pen·ny–pinch·er** \-chər\ *n* — **penny–pinching** *adj*
pen·ny·roy·al \ˌpen-ē-ˈrȯi(-ə)l, ˈpe-ni-ˌrī(-ə)l\ *n* [prob. alter. of AF *puliol real*, fr. *puliol* pennyroyal (ultim. fr. L *puleium*) + *real* royal] (1530) **1 :** a European perennial mint (*Mentha pulegium*) with small aromatic leaves **2 :** an aromatic No. American mint (*Hedeoma pulegioides*) that has blue or violet flowers borne in axillary tufts and yields an oil used in folk medicine or to drive away mosquitoes
penny stock *n* (ca. 1920) **:** a usu. unlisted highly speculative stock usu. selling for a dollar or less
pen·ny·weight \ˈpe-nē-ˌwāt\ *n* (14c) — see WEIGHT table
pen·ny·whistle \-ˌhwi-səl, -ˌwi-\ *n* (1789) **1 :** a small fipple flute **2 :** a toy whistle
pen·ny–wise \-ˌwīz\ *adj* [fr. the phrase *penny-wise and pound-foolish*] (1607) **:** wise or prudent only in dealing with small sums or matters
pen·ny·wort \-ˌwərt, -ˌwȯrt\ *n* (14c) **:** any of several usu. round-leaved plants (as of the genus *Hydrocotyle* of the carrot family)
pen·ny·worth \ˈpe-nē-ˌwərth, *Brit often* ˈpe-nərth\ *n, pl* **pennyworth** *or* **pennyworths** (bef. 12c) **1 :** a penny's worth **2 :** value for the money spent **:** BARGAIN **3 :** a small quantity **:** MODICUM
Pe·nob·scot \pə-ˈnäb-ˌskät, -skət\ *n, pl* **-scot** *or* **-scots** [earlier *Panawamske*, fr. Eastern Abenaki *pαnáwαhpskek*, a village name, lit., where the rocks widen] (1624) **:** a member of an American Indian people of the Penobscot River valley and Penobscot Bay region of Maine
pe·nol·o·gy \pi-ˈnä-lə-jē\ *n* [Gk *poinē* penalty + E *-logy* — more at PAIN] (1838) **:** a branch of criminology dealing with prison management and the treatment of offenders — **pe·no·log·i·cal** \ˌpē-nə-ˈlä-ji-kəl\ *adj* — **pe·nol·o·gist** \pi-ˈnä-lə-jist\ *n*
pen pal *n* (1938) **:** a friend made and kept through correspondence
pen point *n* (ca. 1864) **:** a small thin convex metal device that tapers to a split point, fits into a holder, and is used for writing or drawing
pen pusher *n* (1911) **:** PENCIL PUSHER
[1]**pen·sion** \ˈpen(t)-shən\ *n* [ME, fr. AF, fr. L *pension-, pensio*, fr. *pendere* to pay — more at PENDANT] (14c) **1** \ˈpen(t)-shən\ **:** a fixed sum paid regularly to a person: **a** *archaic* **:** WAGE **b :** a gratuity granted (as by a government) as a favor or reward **c :** one paid under given conditions to a person following retirement from service or to surviving dependents **2** \pänˢ-ˈyōⁿ\ [F, fr. MF] **a :** accommodations esp. at a continental European hotel or boardinghouse **:** ROOM AND BOARD **b** *also* **pen·sio·ne** \pen(t)-ˈsyō-(ˌ)nā\ [*pensione*, fr. It] **:** a hotel or boardinghouse esp. in continental Europe — **pen·sion·less** \ˈpen(t)-shən-ləs\ *adj*
[2]**pension** *vt* **pen·sioned; pen·sion·ing** \ˈpen(t)-sh(ə-)niŋ\ (1702) **1 :** to grant or pay a pension to **2 :** to dismiss or retire from service with a pension ⟨~*ed* off his faithful old servant⟩
pen·sion·able \ˈpen(t)-sh(ə-)nə-bəl\ *adj* (1882) *chiefly Brit* **:** of, relating to, qualified for, or qualifying for a pension ⟨~ employees⟩ ⟨a ~ post⟩
pen·sion·ary \ˈpen(t)-shə-ˌner-ē\ *n, pl* **-ar·ies** (1536) **:** PENSIONER; *esp* **:** HIRELING — **pensionary** *adj*
pen·sion·er \ˈpen(t)-sh(ə-)nər\ *n* (15c) **1 :** a person who receives or lives on a pension **2** *obs* **a :** GENTLEMAN-AT-ARMS **b :** RETAINER **c :** MERCENARY, HIRELING
pen·sive \ˈpen(t)-siv\ *adj* [ME *pensif*, fr. AF, fr. *penser* to think, fr. L *pensare* to ponder, freq. of *pendere* to weigh — more at PENDANT] (14c) **1 :** musingly or dreamily thoughtful **2 :** suggestive of sad thoughtfulness — **pen·sive·ly** *adv* — **pen·sive·ness** *n*
pen·ste·mon *also* **pent·ste·mon** \pen(t)-ˈstē-mən, ˈpen(t)-stə-\ *n* [NL, fr. *penta-* + Gk *stēmōn* warp, thread — more at STAMEN] (1760) **:** any of a genus (*Penstemon*) of chiefly American herbs of the snapdragon family with showy tubular flowers
pen·stock \ˈpen-ˌstäk\ *n* (ca. 1607) **1 :** a sluice or gate for regulating a flow (as of water) **2 :** a conduit or pipe for conducting water
pent \ˈpent\ *adj* [prob. fr. pp. of obs. E *pend* to confine] (1550) **:** shut up **:** CONFINED, REPRESSED ⟨a ~ crowd⟩ ⟨*pent-up* feelings⟩
penta- *or* **pent-** *comb form* [Gk, fr. *pente* — more at FIVE] **1 :** five ⟨*penta*hedron⟩ **2 :** containing five atoms or groups ⟨*pent*ane⟩
pen·ta·chlo·ro·phe·nol \ˌpen-tə-ˌklȯr-ə-ˈfē-ˌnōl, -fi-ˈ\ *n* (1879) **:** a crystalline compound C_6Cl_5OH used esp. as a wood preservative and fungicide and a disinfectant
pen·ta·cle \ˈpen-ti-kəl\ *n* [ML **pentaculum*, prob. fr. Gk *pente*] (1594) **:** PENTAGRAM
pen·tad \ˈpen-ˌtad\ *n* [Gk *pentad-, pentas*, fr. *pente*] (1653) **:** a group of five

pen·ta·gon \ˈpen-tə-ˌgän\ *n* [Gk *pentagōnon,* fr. neut. of *pentagōnos* pentagonal, fr. *penta-* + *gōnia* angle — more at -GON] (1570) **:** a polygon of five angles and five sides

Pentagon *n* [the *Pentagon* building, headquarters of the Department of Defense] (1945) **:** the U.S. military leadership

pen·tag·o·nal \pen-ˈta-gə-nᵊl\ *adj* (1571) **1 :** having five sides and five angles **2 :** having a pentagon as a cross section or as a base ⟨a ~ pyramid⟩ — **pen·tag·o·nal·ly** \-nᵊl-ē\ *adv*

Pen·ta·gon·ese \ˌpen-tə-ˌgä-ˈnēz, -ˈnēs\ *n* (1950) **:** military jargon

pen·ta·gram \ˈpen-tə-ˌgram\ *n* [Gk *pentagrammon,* fr. *penta-* + *-grammon* (akin to *gramma* letter) — more at GRAM] (1825) **:** a figure of a 5-pointed star usu. made with alternate points connected by a continuous line and used as a magic or occult symbol; *also* **:** a similar 6-pointed star (as a Solomon's seal)

pen·ta·he·dron \ˌpen-tə-ˈhē-drən\ *n* [NL] (1590) **:** a solid bounded by five faces — **pen·ta·he·dral** \-drəl\ *adj*

pen·tam·er·ous \pen-ˈta-mə-rəs\ *adj* [NL *pentamerus,* fr. *penta-* (fr. Gk) + *-merus* -merous] (1821) **:** divided into or consisting of five parts; *specif* **:** having each floral whorl consisting of five or a multiple of five members

pen·tam·e·ter \pen-ˈta-mə-tər\ *n* [L, fr. Gk *pentametros* having five metrical feet, fr. *penta-* + *metron* measure — more at MEASURE] (1580) **:** a line of verse consisting of five metrical feet

pent·am·i·dine \pen-ˈta-mə-ˌdēn, -dən\ *n* (1941) **:** a drug used chiefly in the form of its salt $C_{23}H_{36}N_4O_{10}S_2$ esp. to treat protozoal infections (as leishmaniasis) and to prevent AIDS-related pneumonia

pen·tane \ˈpen-ˌtān\ *n* [ISV] (1872) **:** any of three isomeric alkanes C_5H_{12} that occur esp. in petroleum

pen·tan·gle \ˈpent-ˌaŋ-gəl, ˈpen-ˌtaŋ-\ *n* (14c) **:** PENTAGRAM

pen·ta·pep·tide \ˌpen-tə-ˈpep-ˌtīd\ *n* (1905) **:** a polypeptide that contains five amino acid residues

pen·ta·ploid \ˈpen-tə-ˌplȯid\ *adj* (1921) **:** having or being a chromosome number that is five times the basic number — **pentaploid** *n* — **pen·ta·ploi·dy** \-ˌplȯi-dē\ *n*

pen·tar·chy \ˈpen-ˌtär-kē\ *n* [Gk *pentarchia,* fr. *penta-* + *-archia* -archy] (ca. 1586) **:** a group of five countries or districts each under its own ruler or government

Pen·ta·teuch \ˈpen-tə-ˌtük, -ˌtyük\ *n* [ME *Penteteuke,* fr. LL *Pentateuchus,* fr. Gk *Pentateuchos,* fr. *penta-* + *teuchos* tool, vessel, book, fr. *teuchein* to make — more at DOUGHTY] (15c) **:** the first five books of Jewish and Christian Scriptures

pen·tath·lete \pen-ˈtath-ˌlēt, ÷-ˈta-thə-\ *n* (1828) **:** an athlete participating in a pentathlon

pen·tath·lon \pen-ˈtath-lən, -ˌlän, ÷-ˈta-thə-\ *n* [Gk, fr. *penta-* + *athlon* contest] (1603) **:** an athletic contest involving participation by each contestant in five different events; *esp* **:** MODERN PENTATHLON

pen·ta·ton·ic \ˌpen-tə-ˈtä-nik\ *adj* (1864) **:** consisting of five tones; *specif* **:** being or relating to a scale in which the tones are arranged like a major scale with the fourth and seventh tones omitted

pen·ta·va·lent \ˌpen-tə-ˈvā-lənt\ *adj* (1866) **:** having a valence of five

pen·taz·o·cine \pen-ˈta-zə-ˌsēn\ *n* [prob. fr. *penta-* + *az-* + *octa-* + *²-ine*] (1963) **:** a synthetic analgesic drug $C_{19}H_{27}NO$ that is less addictive than morphine

Pen·te·cost \ˈpen-ti-ˌkȯst, -ˌkäst\ *n* [ME, fr. OE *pentecosten,* fr. LL *pentecoste,* fr. Gk *pentēkostē,* lit., fiftieth day, fr. *pentēkostos* fiftieth, fr. *pentēkonta* fifty, fr. *penta-* + *-konta* (akin to L *viginti* twenty) — more at VIGESIMAL] (bef. 12c) **1 :** SHAVUOT **2 :** a Christian feast on the seventh Sunday after Easter commemorating the descent of the Holy Spirit on the apostles — called also *Whitsunday*

[1]**Pen·te·cos·tal** \ˌpen-ti-ˈkäs-tᵊl, -ˈkȯs-\ *adj* (ca. 1663) **1 :** of, relating to, or suggesting Pentecost **2 :** of, relating to, or constituting any of various Christian religious bodies that emphasize individual experiences of grace, spiritual gifts (as glossolalia and faith healing), expressive worship, and evangelism — **Pen·te·cos·tal·ism** \-tə-ˌli-zəm\ *n* — **Pen·te·cos·tal·ist** \-tə-list\ *n or adj*

[2]**Pentecostal** *n* (1904) **:** a member of a Pentecostal religious body

pent·house \ˈpent-ˌhau̇s\ *n* [alter. of ME *pentis,* fr. AF *apentiz,* fr. *apent,* pp. of *apendre, appendre* to attach, hang against — more at APPEND] (14c) **1 a :** a shed or roof attached to and sloping from a wall or building **b :** a smaller structure joined to a building **:** ANNEX **2 :** a structure or dwelling on the roof or top floor of a building

pen·ti·men·to \ˌpen-tə-ˈmen-(ˌ)tō\ *n, pl* **-ti** \-(ˌ)tē\ [It, lit., repentance, correction, fr. *pentire* to repent, fr. L *paenitēre* — more at PENITENT] (1823) **:** a reappearance in a painting of an original drawn or painted element which was eventually painted over by the artist

pent·land·ite \ˈpent-lən-ˌdīt\ *n* [F, fr. Joseph *Pentland* †1873 Irish scientist] (ca. 1858) **:** a bronzy yellow mineral that is an isometric nickel iron sulfide and the principal ore of nickel

pen·to·bar·bi·tal \ˌpen-tə-ˈbär-bə-ˌtȯl\ *n* [*penta-* + *-o-* + *barbital*] (1931) **:** a granular barbiturate $C_{11}H_{18}N_2O_3$ used esp. in the form of its sodium or calcium salt as a sedative, hypnotic, and antispasmodic

pen·to·bar·bi·tone \-ˌtōn\ *n* [*penta-* + *-o-* + *barbitone*] (1938) *Brit* **:** PENTOBARBITAL

pen·to·san \ˈpen-tə-ˌsan\ *n* [ISV] (1892) **:** any of various polysaccharides that yield only pentoses on hydrolysis and occur widely in plants

pen·tose \ˈpen-ˌtōs, -ˌtōz\ *n* [ISV] (1890) **:** a monosaccharide $C_5H_{10}O_5$ (as ribose) that contains five carbon atoms in the molecule

Pen·to·thal \ˈpen-tə-ˌthȯl\ *trademark* — used for thiopental

pent·ox·ide \pent-ˈäk-ˌsīd\ *n* [ISV] (1851) **:** an oxide containing five atoms of oxygen in the molecule

pentstemon *var of* PENSTEMON

pen·tyl·ene·tet·ra·zol \ˌpen-tə-ˌlēn-ˈte-trə-ˌzȯl, -ˌzōl\ *n* [*penta-* + *methylene* + *tetrazole* (CH_2N_4)] (1949) **:** an analeptic drug $C_6H_{10}N_4$

pe·nu·che \pə-ˈnü-chē\ *also* **pa·no·cha** \pə-ˈnō-chə\ *n* [MexSp *panocha* raw sugar, fr. Sp, ear of maize, ultim. fr. L *panicula* panicle — more at PANICLE] (1871) **:** fudge made usu. of brown sugar, butter, cream or milk, and nuts

pe·nult \ˈpē-ˌnəlt, pi-ˈ\ *n* [L *paenultima* penult, fr. fem. of *paenultimus* almost last, fr. *paene* almost + *ultimus* last — more at ULTIMATE] (1537) **:** the next to the last member of a series; *esp* **:** the next to the last syllable of a word

pen·ul·ti·ma \pi-ˈnəl-tə-mə\ *n* [L] (1589) **:** PENULT

pen·ul·ti·mate \pi-ˈnəl-tə-mət\ *adj* (1677) **1 :** next to the last ⟨the ~ chapter of a book⟩ **2 :** of or relating to a penult ⟨a ~ accent⟩ — **pen·ul·ti·mate·ly** *adv*

pen·um·bra \pə-ˈnəm-brə\ *n, pl* **-brae** \-(ˌ)brē, -ˌbrī\ *or* **-bras** [NL, fr. L *paene* almost + *umbra* shadow — more at UMBRAGE] (1665) **1 a :** a space of partial illumination (as in an eclipse) between the perfect shadow on all sides and the full light **b :** a shaded region surrounding the dark central portion of a sunspot **2 :** a surrounding or adjoining region in which something exists in a lesser degree **:** FRINGE **3 :** a body of rights held to be guaranteed by implication in a civil constitution **4 :** something that covers, surrounds, or obscures **:** SHROUD ⟨a ~ of secrecy⟩ ⟨a ~ of somber dignity has descended over his reputation —James Atlas⟩ — **pen·um·bral** \-brəl\ *adj*

pe·nu·ri·ous \pə-ˈnu̇r-ē-əs, -ˈnyu̇r-\ *adj* (1590) **1 :** marked by or suffering from penury **2 :** given to or marked by extreme stinting frugality ***syn*** see STINGY — **pe·nu·ri·ous·ly** *adv* — **pe·nu·ri·ous·ness** *n*

pen·u·ry \ˈpen-yə-rē\ *n* [ME, fr. L *penuria, paenuria* want; perh. akin to L *paene* almost] (14c) **1 :** a cramping and oppressive lack of resources (as money); *esp* **:** severe poverty **2 :** extreme and often niggardly frugality ***syn*** see POVERTY

pe·on \ˈpē-ˌän, -ən *also* pā-ˈōn *for 2, Brit also* ˈpyün *for 1*\ *n, pl* **peons** *or* **pe·o·nes** \pā-ˈō-nēz\ [Pg *peão* & F *pion,* fr. ML *pedon-, pedo* foot soldier — more at PAWN] (1609) **1 :** any of various workers in India, Sri Lanka, or Malaysia: as **a :** INFANTRYMAN **b :** ORDERLY **2** [Sp *peón,* fr. L *pedon-, pedo*] **:** a member of the landless laboring class in Spanish America **3** *pl peons* **a :** a person held in compulsory servitude to a master for the working out of an indebtedness **b :** DRUDGE, MENIAL

pe·on·age \ˈpē-ə-nij\ *n* (1844) **1 a :** the use of laborers bound in servitude because of debt **b :** a system of convict labor by which convicts are leased to contractors **2 :** the condition of a peon

pe·o·ny \ˈpē-ə-nē\ *n, pl* **-nies** [ME *piony,* fr. AF *peonie, pioiné,* fr. L *paeonia,* fr. Gk *paiōnia,* fr. *Paiōn* Paeon, physician of the gods] (14c) **1 :** any of a genus (*Paeonia* of the family Paeoniaceae) of chiefly Eurasian plants with large often double flowers **2 :** the flower of a peony

[1]**peo·ple** \ˈpē-pəl\ *n, pl* **people** [ME *peple,* fr. AF *pople, peple, peuple,* fr. L *populus*] (13c) **1** *pl* **:** humans making up a group or assembly or linked by a common interest **2** *pl* **:** HUMAN BEINGS, PERSONS — often used in compounds instead of *persons* ⟨sales*people*⟩; often used attributively ⟨~ skills⟩ **3** *pl* **:** the members of a family or kinship **4** *pl* **:** the mass of a community as distinguished from a special class ⟨disputes between the ~ and the nobles⟩ — often used by Communists to distinguish Communists from other people **5** *pl* **peoples :** a body of persons that are united by a common culture, tradition, or sense of kinship, that typically have common language, institutions, and beliefs, and that often constitute a politically organized group **6 :** lower animals usu. of a specified kind or situation **7 :** the body of enfranchised citizens of a state — **peo·ple·less** \-pə(l)-ləs\ *adj*

[2]**people** *vt* **peo·pled; peo·pling** \-p(ə-)liŋ\ [ME, fr. AF *popler, poeplier,* fr. *pople*] (15c) **1 :** to supply or fill with people **2 :** to dwell in **:** INHABIT

peo·ple·hood \ˈpē-pəl-ˌhu̇d\ *n* (ca. 1899) **1 :** the quality or state of constituting a people **2 :** the awareness of the underlying unity that makes the individual a part of a people

people mover *n* (1968) **:** any of various rapid-transit systems (as of moving sidewalks or automated driverless cars) for shuttling people

[1]**pep** \ˈpep\ *n* [short for *pepper*] (1908) **:** brisk energy or initiative and high spirits

[2]**pep** *vt* **pepped; pep·ping** (1912) **:** to inject pep into ⟨~ him up⟩

pep·er·o·mia \ˌpe-pə-ˈrō-mē-ə\ *n* [NL, fr. Gk *peperi* pepper + *homoios* like, similar — more at HOMEO-] (1882) **:** any of a genus (*Peperomia*) of fleshy tropical herbs of the pepper family often cultivated for their showy variegated leaves

pe·pi·no \pə-ˈpē-(ˌ)nō\ *n, pl* **-nos** [AmerSp, fr. Sp, cucumber, fr. OSp *pepón* melon, fr. L *pepon-, pepo*] (1890) **:** a bushy perennial plant (*Solanum muricatum*) of the nightshade family that is native to temperate uplands of So. America and has an edible usu. purple-marked yellow fruit; *also* **:** the fruit

pe·pi·ta \pe-ˈpē-tä\ *n* [Sp] (1942) **:** the edible seed of a pumpkin or squash often dried or toasted

pep·los \ˈpe-pləs, -ˌpläs\ *also* **pep·lus** \-pləs\ *n* [L *peplus,* fr. Gk *peplos*] (1738) **:** a garment worn like a shawl by women of ancient Greece

pep·lum \ˈpe-pləm\ *n* [L, fr. Gk *peplon* peplos] (1866) **:** a short section attached to the waistline of a blouse, jacket, or dress — **pep·lumed** \-pləmd\ *adj*

pe·po \ˈpē-(ˌ)pō\ *n, pl* **pepos** [L, a melon — more at PUMPKIN] (ca. 1849) **:** an indehiscent fleshy one-celled many-seeded berry (as a pumpkin, squash, melon, or cucumber) that has a hard rind and is the characteristic fruit of the gourd family

[1]**pep·per** \ˈpe-pər\ *n* [ME *peper,* fr. OE *pipor,* fr. L *piper,* fr. Gk *peperi*] (bef. 12c) **1 a :** either of two pungent products from the fruit of an Indian plant (*Piper nigrum*) that are used chiefly as condiments: (1) **:** BLACK PEPPER (2) **:** WHITE PEPPER **b :** any of several products similar to pepper that are obtained from plants of the same genus ⟨cubeb ~⟩ **c :** any of various pungent condiments of plants unrelated to the pepper ⟨Szechuan ~⟩ **2 :** any of a genus (*Piper* of the family Piperaceae, the pepper family) of tropical mostly jointed climbing shrubs with aromatic leaves; *esp* **:** a woody vine (*P. nigrum*) with spicate flowers that is widely cultivated in the tropics for its red berries from which black pepper and white pepper are prepared **3 a :** CAPSICUM 1; *esp* **:** one (*Capsicum annuum*) whose fruits are hot peppers or sweet peppers **b :** the hollow fruit of a pepper that is usu. green when unripe and red or yellow when ripe — **pepper** *adj*

[2]**pepper** *vt* **pep·pered; pep·per·ing** \ˈpe-p(ə-)riŋ\ (bef. 12c) **1 a :** to sprinkle or season with pepper **b :** to shower with or as if with shot or other missiles **2 :** to hit with or as if with rapid repeated blows **3 :** to sprinkle or cover as if with pepper ⟨~*ed* the report with statistics⟩ ⟨a face ~*ed* with freckles⟩ — **pep·per·er** \-pər-ər\ *n*

[3]**pepper** *n* [prob. fr. [2]*pep* + [2]*-er*] (1943) : a baseball practice or warm-up game in which usu. several fielders toss the ball a short distance to a single batter who hits it back

pep·per–and–salt \ˌpe-pər(-ə)n(d)-ˈsȯlt\ *adj* (1751) : SALT-AND-PEPPER

pep·per·box \ˈpe-pər-ˌbäks\ *n* (1546) **1** : a small usu. cylindrical box or bottle with a perforated top used for sprinkling pepper on food **2** : a pistol of the late 18th century with five or six revolving barrels

pep·per·corn \-ˌkȯrn\ *n* (bef. 12c) : a dried berry of the black pepper

peppered moth *n* (ca. 1832) : a European geometrid moth (*Biston betularia*) that typically has white wings with small black specks but also occurs as a solid black form esp. in areas where the air is heavily polluted by industry

pep·per·grass \ˈpe-pər-ˌgras\ *n* (15c) : any of a genus (*Lepidium*) of cresses; *esp* : GARDEN CRESS

pepper mill *n* (1739) : a hand mill for grinding peppercorns

pep·per·mint \-ˌmint, -mənt, *in rapid speech* ˈpep-mənt *or* -ᵊm-ənt\ *n* (1696) **1 a** : a pungent and aromatic mint (*Mentha piperita*) with dark green lanceolate leaves and whorls of small pink flowers in spikes **b** : any of several mints (as *M. arvensis*) that are related to the peppermint **2** : candy flavored with peppermint — **pep·per·minty** \ˈpe-pər-ˌmin-tē\ *adj*

peppermint 1a

pep·per·o·ni \ˌpe-pə-ˈrō-nē\ *n* [It *peperoni* cayenne peppers, pl. of *peperone,* aug. of *pepe* pepper, fr. L *piper* — more at PEPPER] (1921) : a highly seasoned beef and pork sausage

pepper pot *n* (1679) **1** *Brit* : PEPPERBOX 1 **2 a** : a highly seasoned West Indian stew of vegetables and meat or fish **b** : a thick soup of tripe, meat, dumplings, and vegetables highly seasoned esp. with crushed peppercorns — called also *Philadelphia pepper pot*

pepper shaker *n* (1895) : a container with a perforated top for sprinkling pepper

pepper spray *n* (1989) : a temporarily disabling aerosol that is composed partly of capsicum oleoresin and causes irritation and blinding of the eyes and inflammation of the nose, throat, and skin

pep·per·tree \ˈpe-pər-ˌtrē\ *n* (ca. 1692) : a So. American evergreen tree (*Schinus molle*) of the cashew family grown as a shade tree in mild climates

pep·pery \ˈpe-p(ə-)rē\ *adj* (1699) **1** : of, relating to, or having the qualities of pepper : HOT, PUNGENT ⟨a ~ taste⟩ **2** : having a hot temper : TOUCHY ⟨a ~ boss⟩ **3** : FIERY, STINGING ⟨a ~ satire⟩ — **pep·per·i·ness** \-nəs\ *n*

pep pill *n* (1937) : any of various stimulant drugs in pill or tablet form

pep·py \ˈpe-pē\ *adj* **pep·pi·er; -est** (1918) : full of pep — **pep·pi·ness** *n*

pep·sin \ˈpep-sən\ *n* [G, fr. Gk *pepsis* digestion, fr. *pessein*] (ca. 1844) **1** : a protease of the stomach that breaks down most proteins to polypeptides **2** : a preparation containing pepsin that is obtained from the stomach esp. of the hog and is used esp. as a digestive aid

pep·sin·o·gen \pep-ˈsi-nə-jən\ *n* [ISV] (1878) : a granular zymogen of the gastric glands that is readily converted into pepsin in a slightly acid medium

pep talk *n* (1925) : a usu. brief, intense, and emotional talk designed to influence or encourage an audience

pep·tic \ˈpep-tik\ *adj* [L *pepticus,* fr. Gk *peptikos,* fr. *peptos* cooked, fr. *peptein, pessein* to cook, digest — more at COOK] (1651) **1** : relating to or promoting digestion : DIGESTIVE **2** : of, relating to, producing, or caused by pepsin ⟨~ digestion⟩ **3** : connected with or resulting from the action of digestive juices ⟨a ~ ulcer⟩

pep·ti·dase \ˈpep-tə-ˌdās, -ˌdāz\ *n* (1918) : an enzyme that hydrolyzes simple peptides or their derivatives

pep·tide \ˈpep-ˌtīd\ *n* [ISV, fr. *peptone*] (1906) : any of various amides that are derived from two or more amino acids by combination of the amino group of one acid with the carboxyl group of another and are usu. obtained by partial hydrolysis of proteins — **pep·tid·ic** \pep-ˈti-dik\ *adj*

peptide bond *n* (1935) : the chemical bond between carbon and nitrogen in a peptide linkage

peptide linkage *n* (1925) : the divalent group CONH that unites the amino acid residues in a peptide

pep·ti·do·gly·can \ˌpep-tə-dō-ˈglī-ˌkan\ *n* (1966) : a polymer that is composed of polysaccharide and peptide chains and is found esp. in bacterial cell walls — called also *mucopeptide, murein*

pep·tone \ˈpep-ˌtōn\ *n* [G *Pepton,* fr. Gk, neut. of *peptos* cooked] (1860) : any of various water-soluble products of partial hydrolysis of proteins

Pe·quot \ˈpē-ˌkwät\ *n* [Narragansett *Pequttôog*] (1631) : a member of an American Indian people of what is now eastern Connecticut

[1]**per** \ˈpər\ *prep* [L, through, by means of, by — more at FOR] (14c) **1** : by the means or agency of : THROUGH ⟨~ bearer⟩ **2** : with respect to every member of a specified group : for each **3** : according to — often used with *as* ⟨~ instructions⟩ ⟨as ~ usual⟩

usage *Per* occurs most frequently in business contexts; its use outside such contexts is often criticized but is quite widespread, esp. in sense 2. Its most common and natural nonbusiness uses always involve figures, usu. in relation to price ⟨$150 *per* performance⟩, automobiles ⟨32 miles *per* gallon⟩ ⟨55 miles *per* hour⟩, or sports ⟨averages 15 points and 9 rebounds *per* game⟩.

[2]**per** *adv* (1899) : for each : APIECE ⟨a bargain at $3.50 ~⟩

[3]**per** *abbr* **1** period **2** person

per- *prefix* [L, through, throughout, thoroughly, detrimental to, fr. *per*] **1** : throughout : thoroughly ⟨*per*use⟩ **2 a** : containing the largest possible or a relatively large proportion of a (specified) chemical element ⟨*per*chloroethylene⟩ **b** : containing an element in its highest or a high oxidation state ⟨*per*chloric acid⟩

[1]**per·ad·ven·ture** \ˈpər-əd-ˌven-chər, ˈper-; ˌpər-əd-ˈ, ˌper-\ *adv* [ME *par aventure,* fr. AF, by chance] (14c) *archaic* : PERHAPS, POSSIBLY

[2]**peradventure** *n* (1627) **1** : DOUBT ⟨a fact established beyond ~⟩ **2** : CHANCE 4a ⟨beyond ~ of doubt⟩

per·am·bu·late \pə-ˈram-byə-ˌlāt\ *vb* **-lat·ed; -lat·ing** [L *perambulatus,* pp. of *perambulare,* fr. *per-* through + *ambulare* to walk] *vt* (1568) **1** : to travel over or through esp. on foot : TRAVERSE **2** : to make an official inspection of (a boundary) on foot ~ *vi* : STROLL — **per·am·bu·la·tion** \-ˌram-byə-ˈlā-shən\ *n* — **per·am·bu·la·to·ry** \-ˈram-byə-lə-ˌtȯr-ē\ *adj*

per·am·bu·la·tor \pə-ˈram-byə-ˌlā-tər, *for 2 also* ˈpram-\ *n* (1611) **1** : one that perambulates **2** *chiefly Brit* : a baby carriage

per an·num \(ˌ)pər-ˈa-nəm\ *adv* [ML] (1531) : in or for each year

per·bo·rate \(ˌ)pər-ˈbȯr-ˌāt\ *n* [ISV] (1881) : a salt that is a compound of a borate with hydrogen peroxide

perc *abbr* **1** perchloroethylene **2** percolation

per·cale \(ˌ)pər-ˈkāl, ˈpər-ˌ; (ˌ)pər-ˈkal\ *n* [ultim. fr. Pers *pargāla*] (1840) : a fine closely woven cotton cloth variously finished for clothing, sheeting, and industrial uses

per·ca·line \ˌpər-kə-ˈlēn\ *n* [F, fr. *percale*] (ca. 1858) : a lightweight cotton fabric; *esp* : a glossy fabric used for bookbindings

per cap·i·ta \(ˌ)pər-ˈka-pə-tə\ *adv or adj* [ML, by heads] (1682) **1** : equally to each individual **2** : per unit of population : by or for each person ⟨the highest income *per capita* of any state in the union⟩

per·ceive \pər-ˈsēv\ *vt* **per·ceived; per·ceiv·ing** [ME, fr. AF *perceivre,* fr. L *percipere,* fr. *per-* thoroughly + *capere* to take — more at HEAVE] (14c) **1 a** : to attain awareness or understanding of **b** : to regard as being such ⟨*perceived* threats⟩ ⟨was *perceived* as a loser⟩ **2** : to become aware of through the senses; *esp* : SEE, OBSERVE — **per·ceiv·able** \-ˈsē-və-bəl\ *adj* — **per·ceiv·ably** \-blē\ *adv* — **per·ceiv·er** *n*

[1]**per·cent** \pər-ˈsent\ *adv* [earlier *per cent,* fr. *per* + L *centum* hundred — more at HUNDRED] (1568) : in the hundred : of each hundred

[2]**percent** *n, pl* **percent** *or* **percents** (1667) **1** *pl percent* **a** : one part in a hundred **b** : PERCENTAGE ⟨a large ~ of their income⟩ **2** *percents pl, Brit* : securities bearing a specified rate of interest

[3]**percent** *adj* (1888) **1** : reckoned on the basis of a whole divided into 100 parts **2** : paying interest at a specified percent

per·cent·age \pər-ˈsen-tij\ *n* (ca. 1789) **1 a** : a part of a whole expressed in hundredths ⟨a high ~ of students attended⟩ **b** : the result obtained by multiplying a number by a percent ⟨the ~ equals the rate times the base⟩ **2 a** : a share of winnings or profits **b** : ADVANTAGE, PROFIT ⟨no ~ in going around looking like an old sack of laundry —Wallace Stegner⟩ **3** : an indeterminate part : PROPORTION **4 a** : PROBABILITY **b** : favorable odds

percentage point *n* (1958) : one hundredth of a whole : PERCENT ⟨interest rates rose one *percentage point* from 6.5 percent to 7.5 percent⟩

per·cen·tile \pər-ˈsen-ˌtī(-ə)l\ *n* (1885) : a value on a scale of 100 that indicates the percent of a distribution that is equal to or below it ⟨a score in the 95th ~⟩

per cen·tum \pər-ˈsen-təm\ *n* [*per* + L *centum*] (ca. 1565) : PERCENT

per·cept \ˈpər-ˌsept\ *n* [back-formation fr. *perception*] (ca. 1837) : an impression of an object obtained by use of the senses : SENSE-DATUM

per·cep·ti·ble \pər-ˈsep-tə-bəl\ *adj* (1567) : capable of being perceived esp. by the senses ⟨a ~ change in her tone⟩ ⟨a barely ~ light⟩ — **per·cep·ti·bil·i·ty** \-ˌsep-tə-ˈbi-lə-tē\ *n* — **per·cep·ti·bly** \-blē\ *adv*

syn PERCEPTIBLE, SENSIBLE, PALPABLE, TANGIBLE, APPRECIABLE, PONDERABLE mean apprehensible as real or existent. PERCEPTIBLE applies to what can be discerned by the senses often to a minimal extent ⟨a *perceptible* difference in sound to a careful listener⟩. SENSIBLE applies to whatever is clearly apprehended through the senses or impresses itself strongly on the mind ⟨an abrupt, *sensible* drop in temperature⟩. PALPABLE applies either to what has physical substance or to what is obvious and unmistakable ⟨the tension in the air was almost *palpable*⟩. TANGIBLE suggests what is capable of being handled or grasped both physically and mentally ⟨no *tangible* evidence of UFOs⟩. APPRECIABLE applies to what is distinctly discernible by the senses or definitely measurable ⟨an *appreciable* increase in income⟩. PONDERABLE suggests having definitely measurable weight or importance ⟨exerted a *ponderable* influence on world events⟩.

per·cep·tion \pər-ˈsep-shən\ *n* [L *perception-, perceptio* act of perceiving, fr. *percipere*] (14c) **1 a** : a result of perceiving : OBSERVATION **b** : a mental image : CONCEPT **2** *obs* : CONSCIOUSNESS **3 a** : awareness of the elements of environment through physical sensation ⟨color ~⟩ **b** : physical sensation interpreted in the light of experience **4 a** : quick, acute, and intuitive cognition : APPRECIATION **b** : a capacity for comprehension ***syn*** see DISCERNMENT — **per·cep·tion·al** \-shnəl, -shə-nᵊl\ *adj*

per·cep·tive \pər-ˈsep-tiv\ *adj* (1656) **1** : responsive to sensory stimuli : DISCERNING ⟨a ~ eye⟩ **2 a** : capable of or exhibiting keen perception : OBSERVANT ⟨a ~ scholar⟩ **b** : characterized by sympathetic understanding or insight — **per·cep·tive·ly** *adv* — **per·cep·tive·ness** *n* — **per·cep·tiv·i·ty** \(ˌ)pər-ˌsep-ˈti-və-tē\ *n*

per·cep·tu·al \(ˌ)pər-ˈsep-chə-wəl, -chəl, -shwəl\ *adj* [*percept* + *-ual* (as in *conceptual*)] (1878) : of, relating to, or involving perception esp. in relation to immediate sensory experience — **per·cep·tu·al·ly** *adv*

Per·ce·val \ˈpər-sə-vəl\ *n* [OF] (14c) : a knight of King Arthur who wins a sight of the Holy Grail

[1]**perch** \ˈpərch\ *n* [ME *perche,* fr. AF, fr. L *pertica* pole] (14c) **1** : a bar or peg on which something is hung **2 a** : a roost for a bird **b** : a resting place or vantage point : SEAT **c** : a prominent position ⟨his new ~ as president⟩ **3** *chiefly Brit* : ROD 2

[2]**perch** *vi* (14c) : to alight, settle, or rest on a perch, a height, or a precarious spot ~ *vt* : to place on a perch, a height, or a precarious spot

[3]**perch** *n, pl* **perch** *or* **perch·es** [ME *perche,* fr. AF, fr. L *perca,* fr. Gk *perkē;* akin to OHG *faro* colored, L *porcus,* a spiny fish] (14c) **1 a** : a small European freshwater bony fish (*Perca fluviatilis* of the family Percidae, the perch family) **b** : YELLOW PERCH **2** : any of numerous bony fishes (as of the families Percidae, Centrarchidae, and Serranidae)

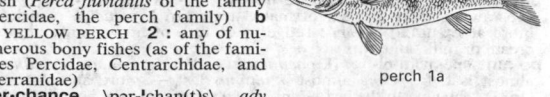

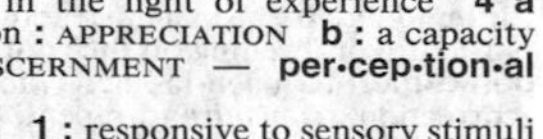
perch 1a

per·chance \pər-ˈchan(t)s\ *adv* [ME *parchaunce,* fr. AF *par chance,* by chance] (14c) : PERHAPS, POSSIBLY

Per·che·ron \ˈpər-chə-ˌrän, -shə-\ *n* [F] (1875) : any of a breed of powerful rugged draft horses that originated in the Perche region of France

per·chlo·rate \(ˌ)pər-ˈklȯr-ˌāt, -ət\ *n* [ISV] (1826) : a salt or ester of perchloric acid

per·chlo·ric acid \(ˌ)pər-ˈklȯr-ik-\ *n* (1818) : a fuming corrosive strong acid $HClO_4$ that is the most highly oxidized acid of chlorine and a powerful oxidizing agent when heated

per·chlo·ro·eth·y·lene \(ˌ)pər-ˌklȯr-ō-ˈe-thə-ˌlēn\ *n* (1873) : a colorless nonflammable toxic liquid C_2Cl_4 used often as a solvent in dry cleaning and for removal of grease from metals

per·cip·i·ence \pər-ˈsi-pē-ən(t)s\ *n* (ca. 1774) : PERCEPTION 4

[1]**per·cip·i·ent** \-ənt\ *n* [L *percipient-, percipiens,* prp. of *percipere* to perceive] (1662) **1 :** one that perceives **2 :** a person on whose mind a telepathic impulse or message is held to fall

[2]**percipient** *adj* (1692) : capable of or characterized by perception : DISCERNING ⟨a ~ critic⟩ — **per·cip·i·ent·ly** *adv*

per·co·late \ˈpər-kə-ˌlāt, ÷-kyə-\ *vb* **-lat·ed; -lat·ing** [L *percolatus,* pp. of *percolare,* fr. *per-* through + *colare* to sieve — more at PER-, COLANDER] *vt* (1626) **1 a :** to cause (a solvent) to pass through a permeable substance (as a powdered drug) esp. for extracting a soluble constituent **b :** to prepare (coffee) in a percolator **2 :** to be diffused through : PENETRATE ~ *vi* **1 :** to ooze or trickle through a permeable substance : SEEP **2 a :** to become percolated **b :** to become lively or effervescent **3 :** to spread gradually ⟨allow the sunlight to ~ into our rooms —Norman Douglas⟩ **4 :** SIMMER 2a ⟨the feud had been *percolating* for a long time⟩ — **per·co·la·tion** \ˌpər-kə-ˈlā-shən\ *n*

per·co·la·tor \ˈpər-kə-ˌlā-tər, ÷-kyə-\ *n* (ca. 1842) : one that percolates; *specif* : a coffeepot in which boiling water rising through a tube is repeatedly deflected downward through a perforated basket containing ground coffee beans to extract their essence

per con·tra \(ˌ)pər-ˈkän-trə\ *adv* [It, by the opposite side (of the ledger)] (1554) **1 a :** on the contrary **b :** by way of contrast **2 :** as an offset

per cu·ri·am \(ˌ)pər-ˈkyu̇r-ē-ˌäm, -ˈku̇r-\ *adv or adj* [ML *per curiam,* lit., by the court] (1685) : by the court as a whole rather than by a single justice and usu. without extended discussion ⟨a *per curiam* decision⟩

per·cuss \pər-ˈkəs\ *vt* [L *percussus,* pp. of *percutere*] (1560) : to tap sharply; *esp* : to practice percussion on

per·cus·sion \pər-ˈkə-shən\ *n* [ME, fr. AF *percussioun,* fr. L *percussion-, percussio,* fr. *percutere* to beat, fr. *per-* thoroughly + *quatere* to shake] (15c) **1 :** the act of percussing: as **a :** the striking of a percussion cap so as to set off the charge in a firearm **b :** the beating or striking of a musical instrument **c :** the act or technique of tapping the surface of a body part to learn the condition of the parts beneath by the resultant sound **2 :** the striking of sound on the ear **3 :** percussion instruments that form a section of a band or orchestra — **percussion** *adj*

percussion cap *n* (1823) : CAP 5

percussion instrument *n* (1872) : a musical instrument (as a drum, xylophone, or maraca) sounded by striking, shaking, or scraping

per·cus·sion·ist \pər-ˈkə-sh(ə-)nist\ *n* (1939) : one skilled in the playing of percussion instruments

per·cus·sive \pər-ˈkə-siv\ *adj* (1793) **1 :** of or relating to percussion; *esp* : operative or operated by striking **2 :** having powerful impact — **per·cus·sive·ly** *adv* — **per·cus·sive·ness** *n*

per·cu·ta·ne·ous \ˌpər-kyü-ˈtā-nē-əs\ *adj* (1887) : effected, occurring, or performed through the skin — **per·cu·ta·ne·ous·ly** *adv*

perdie *var of* PARDIE

[1]**per di·em** \(ˌ)pər-ˈdē-əm, -ˈdī-\ *adv* [ML] (1520) : by the day : for each day

[2]**per diem** *adj* (1809) **1 :** based on use or service by the day : DAILY **2 :** paid by the day

[3]**per diem** *n, pl* **per diems** (1812) **1 :** a daily allowance **2 :** a daily fee

per·di·tion \pər-ˈdi-shən\ *n* [ME *perdicion,* fr. AF *perdiciun,* LL *perdition-, perditio,* fr. L *perdere* to destroy, fr. *per-* through + *dare* to give — more at PER-, DATE] (14c) **1 a** *archaic* : utter destruction **b** *obs* : LOSS **2 a :** eternal damnation **b :** HELL

[1]**per·du** *or* **per·due** \ˈpər-(ˌ)dü, -(ˌ)dyü; (ˌ)pər-ˈ\ *n* [F *sentinelle perdue,* lit., lost sentinel] (1605) *obs* : a soldier assigned to extremely hazardous duty

[2]**per·du** *or* **per·due** \per-ˈdœ\ *adj* [F *perdu,* masc., & *perdue,* fem., fr. pp. of *perdre* to lose, fr. L *perdere*] (1612) : remaining out of sight

per·du·ra·ble \(ˌ)pər-ˈdu̇r-ə-bəl, -ˈdyu̇r-; ˈpər-jə-rə-\ *adj* [ME, long-lasting, eternal, fr. AF *pardurable,* fr. LL *perdurabilis,* fr. L *perdurare* to endure, fr. *per-* throughout + *durare* to last — more at DURING] (14c) : very durable — **per·du·ra·bil·i·ty** \(ˌ)pər-ˌdu̇r-ə-ˈbil-ət-ē, -ˌdyu̇r-; ˌpər-jə-rə-\ *n* — **per·du·ra·bly** \(ˌ)pər-ˈdu̇r-ə-blē, -ˈdyu̇r-; ˈpər-jə-rə-\ *adv*

per·dure \(ˌ)pər-ˈdu̇r, -ˈdyu̇r\ *vi* **per·dured; per·dur·ing** [ME, fr. AF *pardurer,* L *perdurare*] (15c) : to continue to exist : LAST

père \ˈper\ *n* [F *père,* fr. OF *paire, perre,* fr. L *pater* — more at FATHER] (1802) : FATHER — used after a name to distinguish a father from a son; compare FILS

per·e·gri·nate \ˈper-ə-grə-ˌnāt\ *vb* **-nat·ed; -nat·ing** *vi* (1593) : to travel esp. on foot : WALK ~ *vt* : to walk or travel over : TRAVERSE — **per·e·gri·na·tion** \ˌper-ə-grə-ˈnā-shən\ *n*

per·e·grine \ˈper-ə-grən, -ˌgrēn\ *adj* [MF *peregrin,* fr. ML *peregrinus,* fr. L, foreign — more at PILGRIM] (1599) : having a tendency to wander

peregrine falcon *n* [ME *faukon peregryn,* fr. ML *falco peregrinus,* lit., pilgrim falcon; fr. the young being captured wandering from their nests, which were too inaccessible to reach easily] (14c) : a swift nearly cosmopolitan falcon (*Falco peregrinus*) often used in falconry — called also *peregrine*

pe·remp·to·ry \pə-ˈrem(p)-t(ə-)rē\ *adj* [ME *peremptorie,* fr. AF, fr. LL & L; LL *peremptorius,* fr. L, destructive, fr. *perimere* to take entirely, destroy, fr. *per-* thoroughly + *emere* to take — more at REDEEM] (15c) **1 a :** putting an end to or precluding a right of action, debate, or delay; *specif* : not providing an opportunity to show cause why one should not comply ⟨a ~ mandamus⟩ **b :** admitting of no contradiction **2 :** expressive of urgency or command ⟨a ~ call⟩ **3 a :** characterized by often imperious or arrogant self-assurance ⟨how insolent of late he is become, how proud, how ~ —Shak.⟩ **b :** indicative of a peremptory attitude or nature : HAUGHTY ⟨a ~ tone⟩ ⟨~ disregard of an objection⟩ ***syn*** see MASTERFUL — **pe·remp·to·ri·ly** \-ˈrem(p)-t(ə-)rə-lē; -ˌrem(p)-ˈtȯr-ə-lē\ *adv* — **pe·remp·to·ri·ness** \-ˈrem(p)-t(ə-)rē-nəs\ *n*

peremptory challenge *n* (ca. 1531) : a challenge (as of a juror) made as of right without assigning any cause

pe·ren·nate \ˈper-ə-ˌnāt, pə-ˈre-ˌnāt\ *vi* **-nat·ed; -nat·ing** [L *perennatus,* pp. of *perennare,* fr. *perennis*] (ca. 1623) : to live over from one growing season to another ⟨a *perennating* rhizome⟩ — **per·en·na·tion** \ˌper-ə-ˈnā-shən\ *n*

pe·ren·ni·al \pə-ˈre-nē-əl\ *adj* [L *perennis,* fr. *per-* throughout + *annus* year — more at PER-, ANNUAL] (1644) **1 :** present at all seasons of the year **2 :** persisting for several years usu. with new herbaceous growth from a perennating part ⟨~ asters⟩ **3 a :** PERSISTENT, ENDURING ⟨~ favorites⟩ **b :** continuing without interruption : CONSTANT, PERPETUAL ⟨the ~ quest for certainty⟩ ⟨a ~ student⟩ **c :** regularly repeated or renewed : RECURRENT ⟨death is a ~ literary theme⟩ ***syn*** see CONTINUAL — **perennial** *n* — **pe·ren·ni·al·ly** \-nē-ə-lē\ *adv*

pe·re·on \pə-ˈrē-ˌän\ *or* **pe·rei·on** \-ˈrī-\ *n* [NL, fr. Gk *peraiōn,* prp. of *peraioun* to transport, fr. *peraios* situated beyond, fr. *pera* beyond; akin to Gk *poros* passage — more at FARE] (1855) : the thorax or the seven metameres comprising the thorax of some crustaceans (as a decapod)

pe·reo·pod \pə-ˈrē-ə-ˌpäd\ *or* **pe·reio·pod** \-ˈrī-\ *n* [NL *perion* + E *-pod*] (1893) : an appendage of the pereon

per·e·stroi·ka \ˌper-ə-ˈstrȯi-kə\ *n* [Russ *perestroĭka,* lit., restructuring] (1986) : the policy of economic and governmental reform instituted by Mikhail Gorbachev in the Soviet Union during the mid-1980s

perf *abbr* **1** perforated **2** performance

[1]**per·fect** \ˈpər-fikt\ *adj* [ME *parfit,* fr. AF, fr. L *perfectus,* fr. pp. of *perficere* to carry out, perfect, fr. *per-* thoroughly + *facere* to make, do — more at DO] (14c) **1 a :** being entirely without fault or defect : FLAWLESS ⟨a ~ diamond⟩ **b :** satisfying all requirements : ACCURATE **c :** corresponding to an ideal standard or abstract concept ⟨a ~ gentleman⟩ **d :** faithfully reproducing the original; *specif* : LETTER-PERFECT **e :** legally valid **2 :** EXPERT, PROFICIENT ⟨practice makes ~⟩ **3 a :** PURE, TOTAL **b :** lacking in no essential detail : COMPLETE **c** *obs* : SANE **d :** ABSOLUTE, UNEQUIVOCAL ⟨enjoys ~ happiness⟩ **e :** of an extreme kind : UNMITIGATED ⟨a ~ brat⟩ ⟨an act of ~ foolishness⟩ **4** *obs* : MATURE **5 :** of, relating to, or constituting a verb form or verbal that expresses an action or state completed at the time of speaking or at a time spoken of **6** *obs* **a :** CERTAIN, SURE **b :** CONTENTED, SATISFIED **7** *of a musical interval* : belonging to the consonances unison, fourth, fifth, and octave which retain their character when inverted and when raised or lowered by a half step become augmented or diminished **8 a :** sexually mature and fully differentiated ⟨a ~ insect⟩ **b :** having both stamens and pistils in the same flower ⟨a ~ flower⟩ — **per·fect·ness** \-fik(t)-nəs\ *n*

syn PERFECT, WHOLE, ENTIRE, INTACT mean not lacking or faulty in any particular. PERFECT implies the soundness and the excellence of every part, element, or quality of a thing frequently as an unattainable or theoretical state ⟨a *perfect* set of teeth⟩. WHOLE suggests a completeness or perfection that can be sought, gained, or regained ⟨felt like a *whole* person again after vacation⟩. ENTIRE implies perfection deriving from integrity, soundness, or completeness of a thing ⟨the *entire* Beethoven corpus⟩. INTACT implies retention of perfection of a thing in its natural or original state ⟨the boat survived the storm *intact*⟩.

[2]**per·fect** \pər-ˈfekt *also* ˈpər-fikt\ *vt* (14c) **1 :** to bring to final form **2 :** to make perfect : IMPROVE, REFINE — **per·fect·er** *n*

[3]**per·fect** \ˈpər-fikt\ *n* (1841) : the perfect tense of a language; *also* : a verb form in the perfect tense

per·fec·ta \pər-ˈfek-tə\ *n* [AmerSp *quiniela perfecta* perfect quiniela] (1967) : a bet in which the bettor picks the first and second place finishers in order — compare QUINIELA, TRIFECTA

perfect binding *n* (1926) : a book binding in which a layer of adhesive holds the pages and cover together — **per·fect–bound** \ˈpər-fik(t)-ˈbau̇nd\ *adj*

perfect game *n* (ca. 1949) : a baseball game in which a pitcher allows no hits, no runs, and no opposing batter to reach first base

per·fect·ible \pər-ˈfek-tə-bəl *also* ˈpər-fik-\ *adj* (1635) : capable of improvement or perfection (as in moral state) — **per·fect·ibil·i·ty** \pər-ˌfek-tə-ˈbi-lə-tē *also* ˌpər-fik-\ *n*

per·fec·tion \pər-ˈfek-shən\ *n* [ME *perfeccioun,* fr. AF *perfection,* fr. L *perfection-, perfectio,* fr. *perficere*] (13c) **1 :** the quality or state of being perfect: as **a :** freedom from fault or defect : FLAWLESSNESS **b :** MATURITY **c :** the quality or state of being saintly **2 a :** an exemplification of supreme excellence **b :** an unsurpassable degree of accuracy or excellence **3 :** the act or process of perfecting

per·fec·tion·ism \-shə-ˌni-zəm\ *n* (ca. 1846) **1 a :** the doctrine that the perfection of moral character constitutes a person's highest good **b :** the theological doctrine that a state of freedom from sin is attainable on earth **2 :** a disposition to regard anything short of perfection as unacceptable — **per·fec·tion·ist** \-sh(ə-)nist\ *n or adj* — **per·fec·tion·is·tic** \-ˌfek-shə-ˈnis-tik\ *adj*

per·fec·tive \pər-ˈfek-tiv *also* ˈpər-fik-\ *adj* (1596) **1** *archaic* **a :** tending to make perfect **b :** becoming better **2 :** expressing action as complete or as implying the notion of completion, conclusion, or result ⟨~ verb⟩ — **perfective** *n* — **per·fec·tive·ly** *adv* — **per·fec·tive·ness** *n* — **per·fec·tiv·i·ty** \pər-ˌfek-ˈti-və-tē *also* ˌpər-fik-\ *n*

per·fect·ly \ˈpər-fik(t)-lē\ *adv* (14c) **1 :** in a perfect manner **2 :** to a complete or adequate extent : QUITE ⟨was ~ happy until now⟩

perfect number *n* (14c) : an integer (as 6 or 28) the sum of whose integral factors including 1 but excluding itself is equal to itself

per·fec·to \pər-ˈfek-(ˌ)tō\ *n, pl* **-tos** [Sp, perfect, fr. L *perfectus*] (1894) : a cigar that is thick in the middle and tapers at each end

perfect participle *n* (1862) : PAST PARTICIPLE

perfect pitch *n* (1949) : ABSOLUTE PITCH 2

perfect square *n* (1856) : an integer (as 9 or 36) whose square root is an integer

\ə\ **abut** \ᵊ\ **kitten, F table** \ər\ **further** \a\ **ash** \ā\ **ace** \ä\ **mop, mar** \au̇\ **out** \ch\ **chin** \e\ **bet** \ē\ **easy** \g\ **go** \i\ **hit** \ī\ **ice** \j\ **job** \ŋ\ **sing** \ō\ **go** \ȯ\ **law** \ȯi\ **boy** \th\ **thin** \t͟h\ **the** \ü\ **loot** \u̇\ **foot** \y\ **yet** \zh\ **vision, beige** \k̟, ⁿ, œ, ue, ʸ\ *see* Guide to Pronunciation

perfect storm *n* (1936) : a critical or disastrous situation created by a powerful concurrence of factors

per·fer·vid \(ˌ)pər-ˈfər-vəd, ˈpər-\ *adj* [NL *perfervidus,* fr. L *per-* thoroughly + *fervidus* fervid] (1856) : marked by overwrought or exaggerated emotion : excessively fervent ***syn*** see IMPASSIONED

per·fid·i·ous \(ˌ)pər-ˈfi-dē-əs\ *adj* (1572) : of, relating to, or characterized by perfidy ***syn*** see FAITHLESS — **per·fid·i·ous·ly** *adv* — **per·fid·i·ous·ness** *n*

per·fi·dy \ˈpər-fə-dē\ *n, pl* **-dies** [L *perfidia,* fr. *perfidus* faithless, fr. *per-* detrimental to + *fides* faith — more at PER-, FAITH] (1592) **1** : the quality or state of being faithless or disloyal : TREACHERY **2** : an act or an instance of disloyalty

per·fluo·ro·car·bon \pər-ˌflȯr-ō-ˈkär-bən, -ˌflu̇r-\ *n* (1947) : any of various hydrocarbon derivatives in which all hydrogen atoms have been replaced with fluorine and that include blood substitutes used in emulsified form

per·fo·li·ate \ˌpər-ˈfō-lē-ət, ˈpər-\ *adj* [NL *perfoliata,* an herb having leaves pierced by the stem, fr. L *per* through + *foliata,* fem. of *foliatus* foliate] (1687) : having the basal part naturally united around the stem ⟨a ~ leaf of a honeysuckle⟩

per·fo·rate \ˈpər-fə-ˌrāt\ *vb* **-rat·ed; -rat·ing** [L *perforatus,* pp. of *perforare* to bore through, fr. *per-* through + *forare* to bore — more at BORE] *vt* (1538) **1** : to make a hole through; *esp* : to make a line of holes in to facilitate separation **2** : to pass through or into by or as if by making a hole ~ *vi* : to penetrate a surface — **per·fo·rate** \ˈpər-f(ə-)rət, -fə-ˌrāt\ *adj* — **per·fo·ra·tor** \-fə-ˌrā-tər\ *n*

perforated *adj* (1578) **1** : having a hole or perforations; *esp* : having a specified number of perforations in 20 millimeters ⟨the stamps are ~ 10⟩ **2** : characterized by perforation ⟨a ~ ulcer⟩

per·fo·ra·tion \ˌpər-fə-ˈrā-shən\ *n* (15c) **1** : the act or process of perforating **2 a** : a hole or pattern made by or as if by piercing or boring **b** : one of the series of holes (as between rows of postage stamps) in a sheet that serve as an aid in separation

per·force \pər-ˈfȯrs\ *adv* [ME *par force,* fr. AF, by force] (14c) **1** *obs* : by physical coercion **2** : by force of circumstances

per·form \pə(r)-ˈfȯrm\ *vb* [ME, fr. AF *parfurmer,* alter. of *perforner, parfurnir,* fr. *par-, per-* thoroughly (fr. L *per-*) + *furnir* to complete — more at FURNISH] *vt* (14c) **1** : to adhere to the terms of : FULFILL ⟨~ a contract⟩ **2** : CARRY OUT, DO **3 a** : to do in a formal manner or according to prescribed ritual **b** : to give a rendition of : PRESENT ~ *vi* **1** : to carry out an action or pattern of behavior : ACT, FUNCTION **2** : to give a performance : PLAY — **per·form·abil·i·ty** \-ˌfȯr-mə-ˈbi-lə-tē\ *n* — **per·form·able** \-ˈfȯr-mə-bəl\ *adj* — **per·form·er** \-ˈfȯr-mər\ *n*

syn PERFORM, EXECUTE, DISCHARGE, ACCOMPLISH, ACHIEVE, EFFECT, FULFILL mean to carry out or into effect. PERFORM implies action that follows established patterns or procedures or fulfills agreed-upon requirements and often connotes special skill ⟨*performed* gymnastics⟩. EXECUTE stresses the carrying out of what exists in plan or in intent ⟨*executed* the hit-and-run⟩. DISCHARGE implies execution and completion of appointed duties or tasks ⟨*discharged* his duties⟩. ACCOMPLISH stresses the successful completion of a process rather than the means of carrying it out ⟨*accomplished* everything they set out to do⟩. ACHIEVE adds to ACCOMPLISH the implication of conquered difficulties ⟨*achieve* greatness⟩. EFFECT adds to ACHIEVE an emphasis on the inherent force in the agent capable of surmounting obstacles ⟨*effected* sweeping reforms⟩. FULFILL implies a complete realization of ends or possibilities ⟨*fulfilled* their ambitions⟩.

per·for·mance \pə(r)-ˈfȯr-mən(t)s\ *n* (15c) **1 a** : the execution of an action **b** : something accomplished : DEED, FEAT **2** : the fulfillment of a claim, promise, or request : IMPLEMENTATION **3 a** : the action of representing a character in a play **b** : a public presentation or exhibition ⟨a benefit ~⟩ **4 a** : the ability to perform : EFFICIENCY **b** : the manner in which a mechanism performs ⟨engine ~⟩ **5** : the manner of reacting to stimuli : BEHAVIOR **6** : the linguistic behavior of an individual : PAROLE; *also* : the ability to speak a certain language — compare COMPETENCE 3

performance art *n* (1971) : a nontraditional art form often with political or topical themes that typically features a live presentation to an audience or onlookers (as on a street) and draws on such arts as acting, poetry, music, dance, or painting — **performance artist** *n*

per·for·ma·tive \-ˈfȯr-mə-tiv\ *adj* (1955) : being or relating to an expression that serves to effect a transaction or that constitutes the performance of the specified act by virtue of its utterance ⟨a ~ verb such as *promise*⟩ — compare CONSTATIVE — **performative** *n*

per·for·ma·to·ry \-mə-ˌtȯr-ē\ *adj* (1949) : PERFORMATIVE; *also* : of or relating to performance

performing *adj* (1889) : of, relating to, or constituting an art (as drama) that involves public performance ⟨the ~ arts⟩

1**per·fume** \ˈpər-ˌfyüm, (ˌ)pər-ˈ\ *n* [MF *perfum,* prob. fr. Old Occitan, fr. *perfumar* to perfume, fr. *per-* thoroughly (fr. L) + *fumar* to smoke, fr. L *fumare,* fr. *fumus* smoke — more at FUME] (1533) **1** : the scent of something sweet-smelling **2** : a substance that emits a pleasant odor; *esp* : a fluid preparation of natural essences (as from plants or animals) or synthetics and a fixative used for scenting ***syn*** see FRAGRANCE

2**per·fume** \(ˌ)pər-ˈfyüm, ˈpər-ˌ\ *vt* **per·fumed; per·fum·ing** (1531) : to fill or imbue with an odor

per·fum·er \pə(r)-ˈfyü-mər, ˈpər-ˌ\ *n* (ca. 1580) : one that makes or sells perfumes

per·fum·ery \pə(r)-ˈfyü-mə-rē, -ˈfyüm-rē\ *n, pl* **-er·ies** (1800) **1 a** : the art or process of making perfume **b** : the products made by a perfumer **2** : an establishment where perfumes are made

per·func·to·ry \pər-ˈfəŋ(k)-t(ə-)rē\ *adj* [LL *perfunctorius,* fr. L *perfungi* to accomplish, get through with, fr. *per-* through + *fungi* to perform — more at PER-, FUNCTION] (1593) **1** : characterized by routine or superficiality : MECHANICAL ⟨a ~ smile⟩ **2** : lacking in interest or enthusiasm — **per·func·to·ri·ly** \-t(ə-)rə-lē\ *adv* — **per·func·to·ri·ness** \-t(ə-)rē-nəs\ *n*

per·fus·ate \(ˌ)pər-ˈfyü-ˌzāt, -zət\ *n* (1915) : a fluid (as a solution pumped through the heart) that is perfused

per·fuse \(ˌ)pər-ˈfyüz\ *vt* **per·fused; per·fus·ing** [ME, fr. L *perfusus,* pp. of *perfundere* to pour over, fr. *per-* through + *fundere* to pour — more at FOUND] (15c) **1** : SUFFUSE **2 a** : to cause to flow or spread : DIFFUSE **b** : to force a fluid through (an organ or tissue) esp. by way of the blood vessels — **per·fu·sion** \-ˈfyü-zhən\ *n*

per·fu·sion·ist \(ˌ)pər-ˈfyü-zhə-nist\ *n* (1964) : a certified medical technician responsible for extracorporeal oxygenation of the blood during open-heart surgery and for the operation and maintenance of equipment (as a heart-lung machine) controlling it

per·go·la \ˈpər-gə-lə, pər-ˈgō-\ *n* [It, fr. L *pergula*] (1675) **1** : ARBOR, TRELLIS **2** : a structure usu. consisting of parallel colonnades supporting an open roof of girders and cross rafters

1**per·haps** \pər-ˈhaps, ˈpraps\ *adv* [*per* + *hap*] (1528) : possibly but not certainly : MAYBE

2**perhaps** *n* (1534) : something open to doubt or conjecture

pe·ri \ˈpir-ē\ *n* [Pers *perī* fairy, genius, fr. MPers *parīk;* akin to Av *pairikā* sorceress] (ca. 1780) **1** : a supernatural being in Persian folklore descended from fallen angels and excluded from paradise until penance is accomplished **2** : a beautiful and graceful girl

peri- *prefix* [L, fr. Gk, around, in excess, fr. *peri;* akin to Gk *peran* to pass through — more at FARE] **1** : all around : about ⟨*peri*scope⟩ **2** : near ⟨*peri*helion⟩ **3** : enclosing : surrounding ⟨*peri*neurium⟩

peri·anth \ˈper-ē-ˌan(t)th\ *n* [NL *perianthium,* fr. *peri-* + Gk *anthos* flower — more at ANTHOLOGY] (ca. 1806) : the floral structure comprised of the calyx and corolla esp. when the two whorls are fused — see FLOWER illustration

peri·apt \ˈper-ē-ˌapt\ *n* [MF or Gk; MF *periapte,* fr. Gk *periapton,* fr. *periaptein* to fasten around (oneself), fr. *peri-* + *haptein* to fasten] (1584) : AMULET

peri·car·di·al \ˌper-ə-ˈkär-dē-əl\ *adj* (1654) : of, relating to, or affecting the pericardium; *also* : situated around the heart

peri·car·di·tis \-ˌkär-ˈdī-təs\ *n* [NL] (ca. 1783) : inflammation of the pericardium

peri·car·di·um \-ˈkär-dē-əm\ *n, pl* **-dia** \-dē-ə\ [ME, fr. ML, fr. Gk *perikardion,* neut. of *perikardios* around the heart, fr. *peri-* + *kardia* heart — more at HEART] (15c) **1** : the conical sac of serous membrane that encloses the heart and the roots of the great blood vessels of vertebrates **2** : a cavity or space that contains the heart of an invertebrate and in arthropods is a part of the hemocoel

peri·carp \ˈper-ə-ˌkärp\ *n* [NL *pericarpium,* fr. Gk *perikarpion* pod, fr. *peri-* + *-karpion* -carp] (1759) : the ripened and variously modified walls of a plant ovary — see ENDOCARP illustration

peri·chon·dri·um \ˌper-ə-ˈkän-drē-əm\ *n, pl* **-dria** \-drē-ə\ [NL, fr. *peri-* + Gk *chondros* grain, cartilage] (1741) : the membrane of fibrous connective tissue that invests cartilage except at joints — **peri·chon·dral** \-drəl\ *adj*

pe·ric·o·pe \pə-ˈri-kə-pē\ *n* [LL, fr. Gk *perikopē* section, fr. *peri-* + *kopē* act of cutting, fr. *koptein* to cut — more at CAPON] (1658) : a selection from a book; *specif* : LECTION 1

peri·cra·ni·um \ˌper-ə-ˈkrā-nē-əm\ *n, pl* **-nia** \-nē-ə\ [ME *pericraneum,* fr. ML, fr. Gk *perikranion,* neut. of *perikranios* around the skull, fr. *peri-* + *kranion* skull — more at CRANIUM] (15c) : the external periosteum of the skull — **peri·cra·ni·al** \-nē-əl\ *adj*

peri·cy·cle \ˈper-ə-ˌsī-kəl\ *n* [F *péricycle,* fr. Gk *perikyklos* spherical, fr. *peri-* + *kyklos* circle — more at WHEEL] (ca. 1892) : a thin layer of parenchymatous or sclerenchymatous cells that surrounds the stele in most vascular plants — **peri·cy·clic** \ˌper-ə-ˈsī-klik, -ˈsi-\ *adj*

peri·derm \ˈper-ə-ˌdərm\ *n* [NL *peridermis,* fr. *peri-* + *-dermis*] (1849) : an outer layer of tissue; *esp* : a cortical protective layer of many roots and stems that typically consists of phellem, phellogen, and phelloderm

pe·rid·i·um \pə-ˈri-dē-əm\ *n, pl* **pe·rid·ia** \-dē-ə\ [NL, fr. Gk *pēridion,* dim. of *pēra* leather bag] (ca. 1823) : the outer envelope of the sporophore of many fungi

per·i·dot \ˈper-ə-ˌdät, -ˌdō(t)\ *n* [F *péridot,* fr. OF *peritot*] (ca. 1706) : a deep yellowish-green transparent variety of olivine used as a gem — **per·i·do·tic** \ˌper-ə-ˈdä-tik, -ˈdō-\ *adj*

pe·ri·do·tite \pə-ˈri-də-ˌtīt\ *n* [F *péridotite,* fr. *péridot*] (1878) : any of a group of granular igneous rocks composed of ferromagnesian minerals and esp. olivine — **pe·ri·do·tit·ic** \pə-ˌri-də-ˈti-tik\ *adj*

peri·gee \ˈper-ə-(ˌ)jē\ *n* [MF, fr. NL *perigeum,* fr. Gk *perigeion,* fr. neut. of *perigeios* near the earth, fr. *peri-* + *gē* earth] (1594) : the point in the orbit of an object (as a satellite) orbiting the earth that is nearest to the center of the earth; *also* : the point nearest a planet or a satellite (as the moon) reached by an object orbiting it — compare APOGEE — **peri·ge·an** \ˌper-ə-ˈjē-ən\ *adj*

pe·rig·y·nous \pə-ˈri-jə-nəs\ *adj* [NL *perigynus,* fr. *peri-* + *-gynus* -gynous] (1807) : borne on a ring or cup of the receptacle surrounding a pistil ⟨~ petals⟩; *also* : having perigynous stamens and petals ⟨~ flowers⟩ — **pe·rig·y·ny** \-nē\ *n*

peri·he·lion \ˌper-ə-ˈhēl-yən\ *n, pl* **-he·lia** \-ˈhēl-yə\ [NL, fr. *peri-* + Gk *hēlios* sun — more at SOLAR] (1666) : the point in the path of a celestial body (as a planet) that is nearest to the sun — compare APHELION — **peri·he·lial** \-ˈhēl-yəl\ *adj*

peri·kar·y·on \-ˈka-rē-ˌän, -ən\ *n, pl* **-kar·ya** \-ē-ə\ [NL, fr. *peri-* + Gk *karyon* nut, kernel — more at CAREEN] (1897) : CELL BODY — **peri·kar·y·al** \-ē-əl\ *adj*

1**per·il** \ˈper-əl, ˈpe-rəl\ *n* [ME, fr. AF, fr. L *periculum* — more at FEAR] (13c) **1** : exposure to the risk of being injured, destroyed, or lost : DANGER ⟨fire put the city in ~⟩ **2** : something that imperils : RISK ⟨lessen the ~s of the streets⟩

2**peril** *vt* **-iled** *also* **-illed; -il·ing** *also* **-il·ling** (1567) : to expose to danger

pe·ril·la \pə-ˈri-lə\ *n* [NL] (1900) : any of a genus (*Perilla*) of Asian mints that have a bilabiate fruiting calyx and rugose nutlets

per·il·ous \ˈper-ə-ləs, ˈpe-rə-\ *adj* (14c) : full of or involving peril ⟨a ~ journey⟩ ***syn*** see DANGEROUS — **per·il·ous·ly** *adv* — **per·il·ous·ness** *n*

peri·lune \ˈper-ə-ˌlün\ *n* [*peri-* + L *luna* moon — more at LUNAR] (1960) : the point in the path of a body orbiting the moon that is nearest to the center of the moon — compare APOLUNE

peri·lymph \-ˌlim(p)f\ *n* [ISV] (ca. 1839) : the fluid between the membranous and bony labyrinths of the ear

peri·men·o·pause \ˌper-ē-ˈme-nə-ˌpȯz, -ˈmē-\ *n* (1962) : the period around the onset of menopause that is often marked by various physical signs (as hot flashes and menstrual irregularity) — **peri·men·o·paus·al** \-ˌme-nə-ˈpȯ-zəl, -ˌmē-\ *adj*

pe·rim·e·ter \pə-ˈri-mə-tər\ *n* [ME *perimetre,* fr. L *perimetros,* fr. Gk, fr. *peri-* + *metron* measure — more at MEASURE] (15c) **1 a** : the boundary of a closed plane figure **b** : the length of a perimeter **2** : a line or strip bounding or protecting an area **3 :** outer limits — often used in pl. **4 :** the part of a basketball court outside the three-point line

peri·my·si·um \ˌper-ə-ˈmi-zhē-əm, -zē-\ *n, pl* **-sia** \-zhē-ə, -zē-\ [NL, irreg. fr. *peri-* + Gk *mys* mouse, muscle — more at MOUSE] (ca. 1842) **:** the connective-tissue sheath that surrounds a muscle and forms sheaths for the bundles of muscle fibers

peri·na·tal \-ˈnā-tᵊl\ *adj* (1952) **:** occurring in, concerned with, or being in the period around the time of birth ⟨∼ mortality⟩ ⟨∼ care⟩ — **peri·na·tal·ly** \-tᵊl-(l)ē\ *adv*

peri·na·tol·o·gy \ˌper-ə-ˌnā-ˈtä-lə-jē\ *n* (1969) **:** a branch of medicine concerned with perinatal care — **peri·na·tol·o·gist** \-jist\ *n*

per·i·ne·um \ˌper-ə-ˈnē-əm\ *n, pl* **-nea** \-ˈnē-ə\ [ME, fr. LL *perinaion*, fr. Gk, fr. *peri-* + *inan* to empty out; perh. akin to Skt *iṣṇāti* he sets in motion] (15c) **:** an area of tissue that marks externally the approximate boundary of the outlet of the pelvis and gives passage to the urinogenital ducts and rectum; *also* **:** the area between the anus and the posterior or part of the external genitalia — **per·i·ne·al** \-ˈnē-əl\ *adj*

peri·neu·ri·um \ˌper-ə-ˈnùr-ē-əm, -ˈnyùr-\ *n, pl* **-ria** \-ē-ə\ [NL, fr. *peri-* + Gk *neuron* nerve — more at NERVE] (ca. 1842) **:** the connective-tissue sheath that surrounds a bundle of nerve fibers

¹**pe·ri·od** \ˈpir-ē-əd\ *n* [ME *periode*, fr. MF, fr. ML, L, & Gk; ML *periodus* period of time, punctuation mark, fr. L & Gk; L, rhetorical period, fr. Gk *periodos* circuit, period of time, rhetorical period, fr. *peri-* + *hodos* way] (ca. 1530) **1 :** the completion of a cycle, a series of events, or a single action **2 a** (1) **:** an utterance from one full stop to another **:** SENTENCE (2) **:** a well-proportioned sentence of several clauses (3) **:** PERIODIC SENTENCE **b :** a musical structure or melodic section usu. composed of two or more contrasting or complementary phrases and ending with a cadence **3 a :** the full pause with which the utterance of a sentence closes **b :** END, STOP **4** *obs* **:** GOAL, PURPOSE **5 a** (1) **:** a point . used to mark the end (as of a declarative sentence or an abbreviation) (2) — used interjectionally to emphasize the finality of the preceding statement ⟨I don't remember — ∼⟩ **b :** a rhythmical unit in Greek verse composed of a series of two or more cola **6 a :** a portion of time determined by some recurring phenomenon **b** (1) **:** the interval of time required for a cyclic motion or phenomenon to complete a cycle and begin to repeat itself (2) **:** a number *k* that does not change the value of a periodic function *f* when added to the independent variable; *esp* **:** the smallest such number **c :** a single cyclic occurrence of menstruation **7 a :** a chronological division **:** STAGE **b :** a division of geologic time longer than an epoch and included in an era **c :** a stage of culture having a definable place in time and space **8 a :** one of the divisions of the academic day **b :** one of the divisions of the playing time of a game

syn PERIOD, EPOCH, ERA, AGE mean a division of time. PERIOD may designate an extent of time of any length ⟨*periods* of economic prosperity⟩. EPOCH applies to a period begun or set off by some significant or striking quality, change, or series of events ⟨the steam engine marked a new *epoch* in industry⟩. ERA suggests a period of history marked by a new or distinct order of things ⟨the *era* of global communications⟩. AGE is used frequently of a fairly definite period dominated by a prominent figure or feature ⟨the *age* of Samuel Johnson⟩.

²**period** *adj* (1905) **:** of, relating to, or representing a particular historical period ⟨∼ furniture⟩ ⟨∼ costumes⟩

pe·ri·od·ic \ˌpir-ē-ˈä-dik\ *adj* (1642) **1 a :** occurring or recurring at regular intervals **b :** occurring repeatedly from time to time **2 a**

: consisting of or containing a series of repeated stages, processes, or digits **:** CYCLIC ⟨∼ decimals⟩ ⟨a ∼ vibration⟩ **b :** being a function any value of which recurs at regular intervals **3 :** expressed in or characterized by periodic sentences

per·iod·ic acid \ˌpər-(ˌ)ī-ˈä-dik-\ *n* [ISV *per-* + *iodic*] (1836) **:** any of the strongly oxidizing acids (as H_5IO_6 or HIO_4) that are the most highly oxidized acids of iodine

¹**pe·ri·od·i·cal** \ˌpir-ē-ˈä-di-kəl\ *adj* (1601) **1 :** PERIODIC 1 **2 a :** published with a fixed interval between the issues or numbers **b :** published in, characteristic of, or connected with a periodical

²**periodical** *n* (1798) **:** a periodical publication

periodical cicada *n* (1890) **:** SEVENTEEN-YEAR LOCUST

pe·ri·od·i·cal·ly \ˌpir-ē-ˈä-di-k(ə-)lē\ *adv* (1646) **1 :** at regular intervals of time **2 :** from time to time **:** FREQUENTLY

pe·ri·od·ic·i·ty \ˌpir-ē-ə-ˈdi-sə-tē\ *n* (1833) **:** the quality, state, or fact of being regularly recurrent or having periods

periodic law *n* (1872) **:** a law in chemistry: the elements when arranged in the order of their atomic numbers show a periodic variation of atomic structure and of most of their properties

periodic sentence *n* (ca. 1928) **:** a usu. complex sentence that has no subordinate or trailing elements following its principal clause (as in "yesterday while I was walking down the street, I saw him")

periodic table *n* (1895) **:** an arrangement of chemical elements based on the periodic law

pe·ri·od·i·za·tion \ˌpir-ē-ə-də-ˈzā-shən\ *n* (1938) **:** division (as of history) into periods

peri·odon·tal \ˌper-ē-ō-ˈdän-tᵊl\ *adj* (1854) **1 :** investing or surrounding a tooth **2 :** of or affecting periodontal tissues or regions ⟨∼ diseases⟩ — **peri·odon·tal·ly** \-tᵊl-ē\ *adv*

periodontal membrane *n* (1899) **:** the fibrous connective-tissue layer covering the cementum of a tooth and holding it in place in the jawbone

peri·odon·tics \-ˈdän-tiks\ *n pl but sing in constr* [NL *periodontium* periodontal tissue, fr. *peri-* + Gk *odont-, odous, odōn* tooth — more at TOOTH] (ca. 1944) **:** a branch of dentistry that deals with diseases of the supporting and investing structures of the teeth including the gums, cementum, periodontal membranes, and alveolar bone — **peri·odon·tist** \-ˈdän-tist\ *n*

peri·odon·ti·tis \ˌper-ē-(ˌ)dän-ˈtī-təs\ *n* [NL] (1872) **:** inflammation of the supporting structures of the teeth and esp. the periodontal membrane

peri·odon·tol·o·gy \-ˌdän-ˈtä-lə-jē\ *n* (1914) **:** PERIODONTICS

period piece *n* (1940) **:** a work (as of literature, art, furniture, cinema, or music) whose special value lies in its evocation of a historical period

peri·onych·i·um \ˌper-ē-ō-ˈni-kē-əm\ *n, pl* **-ia** \-kē-ə\ [NL, fr. *peri-* + Gk *onych-, onyx* nail — more at NAIL] (ca. 1879) **:** the tissue bordering the root and sides of a fingernail or toenail

peri·op·er·a·tive \ˌper-ē-ˈä-p(ə-)rə-tiv, -pə-ˌrā-\ *adj* (1966) **:** relating to, occurring in, or being the period around the time of a surgical operation ⟨∼ morbidity⟩ ⟨∼ nursing⟩

peri·os·te·al \ˌper-ē-ˈäs-tē-əl\ *adj* (1830) **1 :** situated around or produced external to bone **2 :** of, relating to, or involving the periosteum

peri·os·te·um \-tē-əm\ *n, pl* **-tea** \-tē-ə\ [NL, fr. LL *periosteon*, fr. Gk, neut. of *periosteos* around the bone, fr. *peri-* + *osteon* bone — more at OSSEOUS] (1597) **:** the membrane of connective tissue that closely invests all bones except at the articular surfaces

---

PERIODIC TABLE

This is a common long form of the table. Roman numerals and letters heading the vertical columns indicate the groups. (There are differences of opinion regarding the letter designations, but those given here are probably the most generally used. Also, international standards favor numbering the groups 1–18 from left to right using Arabic numerals, but the designations shown below remain quite common.) The horizontal rows represent the periods, with two series removed from the two very long periods and represented below the main table. Atomic numbers are given above the symbols for the elements. Compare ELEMENT table.

IA[1]												IIIA	IVA	VA	VIA	VIIA[3]	VIIIA[4]
1 H	IIA[2]															1 H	2 He
3 Li	4 Be											5 B	6 C	7 N	8 O	9 F	10 Ne
11 Na	12 Mg	IIIB	IVB	VB	VIB	VIIB		VIII			IB	IIB	13 Al	14 Si	15 P	16 S	17 Cl	18 Ar
19 K	20 Ca	21 Sc	22 Ti	23 V	24 Cr	25 Mn	26 Fe	27 Co	28 Ni	29 Cu	30 Zn	31 Ga	32 Ge	33 As	34 Se	35 Br	36 Kr
37 Rb	38 Sr	39 Y	40 Zr	41 Nb	42 Mo	43 Tc	44 Ru	45 Rh	46 Pd	47 Ag	48 Cd	49 In	50 Sn	51 Sb	52 Te	53 I	54 Xe
55 Cs	56 Ba	57 *La	72 Hf	73 Ta	74 W	75 Re	76 Os	77 Ir	78 Pt	79 Au	80 Hg	81 Tl	82 Pb	83 Bi	84 Po	85 At	86 Rn
87 Fr	88 Ra	89 #Ac	104 Rf	105 Db	106 Sg	107 Bh	108 Hs	109 Mt	110 Ds	111 Rg	112 Cn						

*LANTHANIDE SERIES	58 Ce	59 Pr	60 Nd	61 Pm	62 Sm	63 Eu	64 Gd	65 Tb	66 Dy	67 Ho	68 Er	69 Tm	70 Yb	71 Lu
#ACTINIDE SERIES	90 Th	91 Pa	92 U	93 Np	94 Pu	95 Am	96 Cm	97 Bk	98 Cf	99 Es	100 Fm	101 Md	102 No	103 Lr

[1] Group IA (excluding hydrogen) comprises the alkali metals.
[2] Group IIA comprises the alkaline earth metals.
[3] Group VIIA (excluding hydrogen) comprises the halogens.
[4] Group VIIIA (also called group Zero) comprises the noble gases.

peri·os·ti·tis \-ˌäs-ˈtī-təs\ *n* [NL] (1843) : inflammation of the periosteum

[1]**peri·pa·tet·ic** \ˌper-ə-pə-ˈte-tik\ *n* (15c) **1** *cap* : a follower of Aristotle or adherent of Aristotelianism **2** : PEDESTRIAN, ITINERANT **3** *pl* : movement or journeys hither and thither

[2]**peripatetic** *adj* [MF & L; MF *peripatetique,* fr. L *peripateticus,* fr. Gk *peripatētikos,* fr. *peripatein* to walk up and down, discourse while pacing (as did Aristotle), fr. *peri-* + *patein* to tread; akin to Skt *patha* path — more at FIND] (1566) **1** *cap* : ARISTOTELIAN **2 a** : of, relating to, or given to walking **b** : moving or traveling from place to place : ITINERANT — **peri·pa·tet·i·cal·ly** \-ti-k(ə-)lē\ *adv* — **Peri·pa·tet·i·cism** \-ˈte-tə-ˌsi-zəm\ *n*

pe·rip·a·tus \pə-ˈri-pə-təs\ *n* [NL, genus name, fr. Gk *peripatos* act of walking about, fr. *peri-* + *patein* to tread] (ca. 1931) : any of a class or phylum (Onychophora) of primitive tropical wormlike invertebrates that appear intermediate between annelid worms and arthropods

peri·pe·teia \ˌper-ə-pə-ˈtē-ə, -ˈtī-\ *n* [Gk, fr. *peripiptein* to fall around, change suddenly, fr. *peri-* + *piptein* to fall — more at FEATHER] (1591) : a sudden or unexpected reversal of circumstances or situation esp. in a literary work

pe·rip·e·ty \pə-ˈri-pə-tē\ *n, pl* **-ties** (1753) : PERIPETEIA

[1]**pe·riph·er·al** \pə-ˈri-f(ə-)rəl\ *adj* (1808) **1** : of, relating to, involving, or forming a periphery or surface part **2 a** : of, relating to, affecting, or being part of the peripheral nervous system ⟨~ nerves⟩ ⟨~ neuritis⟩ **b** : of, relating to, or being blood in the systemic circulation ⟨~ lymphocytes⟩ **3** : of, relating to, or being the outer part of the field of vision ⟨good ~ vision⟩ **4** : AUXILIARY, SUPPLEMENTARY ⟨~ equipment⟩; *also* : of or relating to computer peripherals — **pe·riph·er·al·ly** *adv*

[2]**peripheral** *n* (1966) : a device connected to a computer to provide communication (as input and output) or auxiliary functions (as additional storage)

peripheral nervous system *n* (1896) : the part of the nervous system that is outside the central nervous system and comprises the cranial nerves excepting the optic nerve, the spinal nerves, and the autonomic nervous system

peripheral neuropathy *n* (1938) : a disease or degenerative state of the peripheral nerves in which motor, sensory, or vasomotor nerve fibers may be affected and which is marked by muscle weakness and atrophy, pain, and numbness

pe·riph·ery \pə-ˈri-f(ə-)rē\ *n, pl* **-er·ies** [MF *peripherie,* fr. LL *peripheria,* fr. Gk *periphereia,* fr. *peripherein* to carry around, fr. *peri-* + *pherein* to carry — more at BEAR] (1571) **1** : the perimeter of a circle or other closed curve; *also* : the perimeter of a polygon **2** : the external boundary or surface of a body **3 a** : the outward bounds of something as distinguished from its internal regions or center : CONFINES **b** : an area lying beyond the strict limits of a thing

pe·riph·ra·sis \pə-ˈri-frə-səs\ *n, pl* **-ra·ses** \-ˌsēz\ [L, fr. Gk, fr. *periphrazein* to express periphrastically, fr. *peri-* + *phrazein* to point out] (1533) **1** : use of a longer phrasing in place of a possible shorter form of expression **2** : an instance of periphrasis

peri·phras·tic \ˌper-ə-ˈfras-tik\ *adj* (1805) **1** : of, relating to, or characterized by periphrasis **2** : formed by the use of function words or auxiliaries instead of by inflection ⟨*more fair* is a ~ comparative⟩ — **peri·phras·ti·cal·ly** \-ti-k(ə-)lē\ *adv*

pe·riph·y·ton \pə-ˈri-fə-ˌtän\ *n* [NL, fr. Gk *periphytos* (verbal of *periphyein* to grow around, fr. *peri-* + *phyein* to bring forth, grow) + *-on* (as in *plankton*) — more at BE] (1945) : organisms (as some algae) that live attached to underwater surfaces — **peri·phyt·ic** \ˌper-ə-ˈfi-tik\ *adj*

peri·plasm \ˈper-ə-ˌpla-zəm\ *n* (1961) : the region in a gram-negative bacterium between the plasma membrane and an outer surrounding membrane that contains esp. enzymes and a thin layer of peptidoglycan — **peri·plas·mic** \ˌper-ə-ˈplaz-mik\ *adj*

peri·plast \ˈper-ə-ˌplast\ *n* (1853) : PLASMA MEMBRANE; *also* : a proteinaceous subcellular layer below the plasma membrane esp. of a euglena

pe·rique \pə-ˈrēk\ *n* [LaF *périque*] (1882) : an aromatic fermented Louisiana tobacco used in smoking mixtures

peri·scope \ˈper-ə-ˌskōp\ *n* [ISV] (1879) : a tubular optical instrument containing lenses and mirrors by which an observer obtains an otherwise obstructed field of view

peri·scop·ic \ˌper-ə-ˈskä-pik\ *adj* (1804) **1** : providing a view all around or on all sides ⟨~ lens⟩ **2** : of or relating to a periscope

per·ish \ˈper-ish, ˈpe-rish\ *vb* [ME *perisshen,* fr. AF *periss-,* stem of *perir,* fr. L *perire,* fr. *per-* detrimentally + *ire* to go — more at PER-, ISSUE] *vi* (13c) **1** : to become destroyed or ruined : cease to exist ⟨recollection of a past already long since ~*ed* —Philip Sherrard⟩ ⟨guard against your mistakes or your attempts (~ the thought) to cheat —C. B. Davis⟩ **2** *chiefly Brit* : DETERIORATE, SPOIL ~ *vt* **1** *chiefly Brit* : to cause to die : DESTROY **2** : WEAKEN, BENUMB

per·ish·able \ˈper-i-shə-bəl, ˈpe-ri-\ *adj* (1611) : liable to perish : liable to spoil or decay ⟨such ~ products as fruit, vegetables, butter, and eggs⟩ — **per·ish·abil·i·ty** \ˌper-i-shə-ˈbi-lə-tē, ˌpe-ri-\ *n* — **perishable** *n*

periscope

pe·ris·so·dac·tyl \pə-ˈri-sə-ˌdak-tᵊl\ *n* [NL *Perissodactyla,* fr. Gk *perissos* excessive, odd in number + *daktylos* finger, toe] (ca. 1852) : any of an order (Perissodactyla) of nonruminant ungulate mammals (as a horse, a tapir, or a rhinoceros) that usu. have an odd number of toes, molar teeth with transverse ridges on the grinding surface, and the posterior premolars resembling true molars — **perissodactyl** *adj*

peri·stal·sis \ˌper-ə-ˈstȯl-səs, -ˈstäl-, -ˈstal-\ *n, pl* **-stal·ses** \-ˌsēz\ [NL, fr. Gk *peristaltikos* peristaltic] (1859) : successive waves of involuntary contraction passing along the walls of a hollow muscular structure (as the esophagus or intestine) and forcing the contents onward

peri·stal·tic \-tik\ *adj* [Gk *peristaltikos,* fr. *peristellein* to wrap around, fr. *peri-* + *stellein* to place] (1655) **1** : of, relating to, resulting from, or being peristalsis **2** : having an action suggestive of peristalsis

peristaltic pump *n* (1962) : a pump in which fluid is forced along by waves of contraction produced mechanically on flexible tubing

peri·stome \ˈper-ə-ˌstōm\ *n* [NL *peristoma,* fr. *peri-* + Gk *stoma* mouth — more at STOMACH] (ca. 1796) **1** : the fringe of teeth surrounding the orifice of a moss capsule **2** : the region around the mouth in various invertebrates — **peri·sto·mi·al** \ˌper-ə-ˈstō-mē-əl\ *adj*

peri·style \ˈper-ə-ˌstī(-ə)l\ *n* [F *péristyle,* fr. L *peristylum,* fr. Gk *peristylon,* fr. neut. of *peristylos* surrounded by a colonnade, fr. *peri-* + *stylos* pillar — more at STEER] (1612) **1** : a colonnade surrounding a building or court **2** : an open space enclosed by a colonnade

peri·the·ci·um \ˌper-ə-ˈthē-shē-əm, -sē-\ *n, pl* **-cia** \-shē-ə, -sē-\ [NL, fr. *peri-* + Gk *thēkion,* dim. of *thēkē* case — more at TICK] (ca. 1832) : a spherical, cylindrical, or flask-shaped hollow fruiting body in various ascomycetous fungi that contains the asci and usu. opens by a terminal pore — **peri·the·cial** \-ˈthē-sh(ē-)əl, -sē-əl\ *adj*

peri·to·ne·um \ˌper-ə-tə-ˈnē-əm\ *n, pl* **-ne·ums** \-ˈnē-əmz\ *or* **-nea** \-ˈnē-ə\ [ME, fr. LL, fr. Gk *peritonaion,* neut. of *peritonaios* stretched around, fr. *peri-* + *teinein* to stretch — more at THIN] (15c) : the smooth transparent serous membrane that lines the cavity of the abdomen of a mammal and is folded inward over the abdominal and pelvic viscera — **peri·to·ne·al** \-ˈnē-əl\ *adj* — **peri·to·ne·al·ly** \-ə-lē\ *adv*

peri·to·ni·tis \ˌper-ə-tə-ˈnī-təs\ *n* [NL] (1776) : inflammation of the peritoneum

pe·rit·ri·chous \pə-ˈri-tri-kəs\ *adj* [*peri-* + Gk *trich-, thrix* hair] (1877) **1** : having flagella uniformly distributed over the body ⟨~ bacteria⟩ **2** : having a spiral line of modified cilia around the oral disk ⟨~ protozoa⟩ — **pe·rit·ri·chous·ly** *adv*

peri·wig \ˈper-i-ˌwig\ *n* [modif. of MF *perruque* — more at PERUKE] (1529) : PERUKE — **peri·wigged** \-ˌwigd\ *adj*

[1]**per·i·win·kle** \ˈper-i-ˌwiŋ-kəl\ *n* [ME *perwinke,* fr. OE *perwince,* fr. VL **pervinca,* short for L *vincapervinca*] (bef. 12c) **1** : any of several trailing or woody evergreen herbs of the dogbane family: as **a (1)** : a European creeper (*Vinca minor*) widely cultivated as a ground cover and for its blue or white flowers — called also *myrtle* **(2)** : a trailing plant (*Vinca major*) with large blue flowers that is used as a ground cover and in window boxes **b** : ROSY PERIWINKLE **2** : a light purplish blue — called also *periwinkle blue*

[2]**periwinkle** *n* [ME **periwinkle,* alter. of OE *pīnewincle,* fr. L *pina,* a kind of mussel (fr. Gk) + OE *-wincle* (akin to Dan *vincle* snail shell)] (ca. 1530) : any of various gastropod mollusks: as **a** : any of a genus (*Littorina*) of edible littoral marine snails; *also* : any of various similar or related marine snails **b** : any of several No. American freshwater snails

per·jure \ˈpər-jər\ *vt* **per·jured; per·jur·ing** \ˈpər-jə-riŋ, ˈpərj-riŋ\ [AF *parjurer, perjurer,* fr. L *perjurare,* fr. *per-* detrimentally, for the worse + *jurare* to swear — more at PER-, JURY] (1535) **1** : to make a perjurer of (oneself) **2** *obs* : to cause to commit perjury

per·jur·er \ˈpər-jər-ər\ *n* (15c) : a person guilty of perjury

per·ju·ri·ous \(ˌ)pər-ˈju̇r-ē-əs\ *adj* (1602) : marked by perjury ⟨~ testimony⟩ — **per·ju·ri·ous·ly** *adv*

per·ju·ry \ˈpər-jə-rē, ˈpərj-rē\ *n* (14c) : the voluntary violation of an oath or vow either by swearing to what is untrue or by omission to do what has been promised under oath : false swearing

[1]**perk** \ˈpərk\ *vb* [ME] *vi* (14c) **1 a** : to thrust up the head, stretch out the neck, or carry the body in a bold or insolent manner **b** : to stick up or out jauntily **2** : to gain in vigor or cheerfulness esp. after a period of weakness or depression — usu. used with *up* ⟨he's ~*ed* up noticeably⟩ ~ *vt* **1** : to make smart or spruce in appearance : FRESHEN, IMPROVE — often used with *up* **2** : to thrust up quickly or impudently

[2]**perk** *vi* (1656) : PERCOLATE

[3]**perk** *n* (1824) : PERQUISITE — usu. used in pl.

perky \ˈpər-kē\ *adj* **perk·i·er; -est** (1855) **1** : briskly self-assured : COCKY **2** : JAUNTY ⟨a ~ . . . waltz —*New Yorker*⟩ — **perk·i·ly** \-kə-lē\ *adv* — **perk·i·ness** \-kē-nəs\ *n*

per·lite \ˈpər-ˌlīt\ *n* [F, fr. *perle* pearl] (1833) : volcanic glass that has a concentric structure, appears as if composed of concretions, is usu. grayish and sometimes spherulitic, and when heated expands to form a lightweight aggregate used esp. in concrete and plaster and as a medium for potting plants — **per·lit·ic** \ˌpər-ˈli-tik\ *adj*

[1]**perm** \ˈpərm\ *n* (1927) : PERMANENT

[2]**perm** *vt* (1928) : to give (hair) a permanent wave

per·ma·cul·ture \ˈpər-mə-ˌkəl-chər\ *n* [ˈ*perma*nent + agri*culture*] (1978) : an agricultural system or method that seeks to integrate human activity with natural surroundings so as to create highly efficient self-sustaining ecosystems

per·ma·frost \ˈpər-mə-ˌfrȯst\ *n* [*perma*nent + *frost*] (1943) : a permanently frozen layer at variable depth below the surface in frigid regions of a planet (as earth)

per·ma·nence \ˈpər-mə-nən(t)s, ˈpərm-nən(t)s\ *n* (15c) : the quality or state of being permanent : DURABILITY

per·ma·nen·cy \-nən(t)-sē\ *n, pl* **-cies** (1555) **1** : PERMANENCE **2** : something permanent

[1]**per·ma·nent** \-nənt\ *adj* [ME, fr. AF *parmanant,* fr. L *permanent-, permanens,* prp. of *permanēre* to endure, fr. *per-* throughout + *manēre* to remain — more at PER-, MANSION] (15c) : continuing or enduring without fundamental or marked change : STABLE ***syn*** see LASTING — **per·ma·nent·ly** *adv* — **per·ma·nent·ness** *n*

[2]**permanent** *n* (1925) : a long-lasting hair wave or straightening produced by mechanical and chemical means — called also *permanent wave*

permanent magnet *n* (1828) : a magnet that retains its magnetism after removal of the magnetizing force

permanent press *n* (1964) **1** : the process of treating a fabric with a chemical (as a resin) and heat for setting the shape and for aiding wrinkle resistance **2** : material treated by permanent press **3** : the condition of material treated by permanent press — **permanent–press** *adj*

permanent tissue *n* (1875) : plant tissue that has completed its growth and differentiation and is usu. incapable of meristematic activity

permanent tooth *n* (1836) : any of the second set of teeth of a mammal that follow the milk teeth, typically persist into old age, and in humans are 32 in number

per·man·ga·nate \(ˌ)pər-ˈmaŋ-gə-ˌnāt\ *n* (1841) **1** : a salt containing the anion MnO_4^-; *esp* : POTASSIUM PERMANGANATE **2** : the anion MnO_4^- of a permanganate

per·me·abil·i·ty \ˌpər-mē-ə-ˈbi-lə-tē\ *n* (1759) **1 :** the quality or state of being permeable **2 :** the property of a magnetizable substance that determines the degree in which it modifies the magnetic flux in the region occupied by it in a magnetic field

per·me·able \ˈpər-mē-ə-bəl\ *adj* (15c) **:** capable of being permeated **:** PENETRABLE; *esp* **:** having pores or openings that permit liquids or gases to pass through ⟨a ∼ membrane⟩ ⟨∼ limestone⟩

per·me·ase \ˈpər-mē-ˌās, -ˌāz\ *n* [ISV *perme-* (fr. *permeate*) + *-ase*] (1957) **:** a substance that catalyzes the transport of another substance across a cell membrane

per·me·ate \ˈpər-mē-ˌāt\ *vb* **-at·ed; -at·ing** [L *permeatus,* pp. of *permeare,* fr. *per-* through + *meare* to go, pass; akin to MW *mynet* to go, Czech *mijet* to pass] *vi* (1656) **:** to diffuse through or penetrate something ∼ *vt* **1 :** to spread or diffuse through ⟨a room *permeated* with tobacco smoke⟩ **2 :** to pass through the pores or interstices of — **per·me·ative** \-ˌā-tiv\ *adj*

per·me·ation \ˌpər-mē-ˈā-shən\ *n* (ca. 1623) **1 :** the quality or state of being permeated **2 :** the action or process of permeating

per men·sem \(ˌ)pər-ˈmen(t)-səm\ *adv* [ML] (1647) **:** by the month

per·meth·rin \(ˌ)pər-ˈme-thrən\ *n* [*per-* + *methyl* + pyreth*rin*] (1976) **:** a synthetic pyrethroid $C_{21}H_{20}Cl_2O_3$ used esp. as an insecticide

Perm·ian \ˈpər-mē-ən, ˈper-\ *adj* [*Perm,* former province in eastern Russia] (1841) **:** of, relating to, or being the last period of the Paleozoic era or the corresponding system of rocks — see GEOLOGIC TIME table — **Permian** *n*

per mill \(ˌ)pər-ˈmil\ *adv* [*per* + L *mille* thousand] (1721) **:** per thousand — **per·mil·lage** \(ˌ)pər-ˈmi-lij\ *n*

per·mis·si·ble \pər-ˈmi-sə-bəl\ *adj* [ME, fr. ML *permissibilis,* fr. L *permissus,* pp. of *permittere*] (15c) **:** that may be permitted **:** ALLOWABLE — **per·mis·si·bil·i·ty** \-ˌmi-sə-ˈbi-lə-tē\ *n* — **per·mis·si·ble·ness** \-ˈmi-sə-bəl-nəs\ *n* — **per·mis·si·bly** \-blē\ *adv*

per·mis·sion \pər-ˈmi-shən\ *n* [ME, fr. AF, fr. L *permission-, permissio,* fr. *permittere*] (15c) **1 :** the act of permitting **2 :** formal consent **:** AUTHORIZATION

per·mis·sive \pər-ˈmi-siv\ *adj* [ME *permyssyf,* fr. MF *permissif,* fr. L *permissus*] (15c) **1** *archaic* **:** granted on sufferance **:** TOLERATED **2 a :** granting or tending to grant permission **:** TOLERANT **b :** deficient in firmness or control **:** INDULGENT, LAX **3 :** allowing discretion **:** OPTIONAL ⟨reduced the ∼ retirement age from 65 to 62⟩ — **per·mis·sive·ly** *adv* — **per·mis·sive·ness** *n*

[1]**per·mit** \pər-ˈmit\ *vb* **per·mit·ted; per·mit·ting** [ME *permitten,* fr. L *permittere* to let through, permit, fr. *per-* through + *mittere* to let go, send] *vt* (15c) **1 :** to consent to expressly or formally ⟨∼ access to records⟩ **2 :** to give leave **:** AUTHORIZE **3 :** to make possible ⟨the design ∼*s* easy access⟩ ∼ *vi* **:** to give an opportunity **:** ALLOW ⟨if time ∼*s*⟩ — **per·mit·tee** \pər-ˌmi(t)-ˈtē, ˌpər-mi(t)-\ *n* — **per·mit·ter** *n*

[2]**per·mit** \ˈpər-ˌmit, pər-ˈ\ *n* (1682) **1 :** a written warrant or license granted by one having authority ⟨a gun ∼⟩ **2 :** PERMISSION

[3]**per·mit** \ˈpər-ˌmit, pər-ˈ\ *n* [perh. by folk etymology fr. Sp *palometa,* a kind of pompano, fr. dim. of *paloma* dove, fr. L *palumba, palumbes* — more at PALOMINO] (ca. 1945) **:** either of two pompanos (*Trachinotus falcatus* and *T. goodei*) that are important game fishes of temperate to tropical waters of the western Atlantic

per·mit·tiv·i·ty \ˌpər-ˌmi-ˈti-və-tē, -mə-\ *n* [[1]*permit* + *-ivity* (as in *selectivity*)] (1887) **:** the ability of a material to store electrical potential energy under the influence of an electric field measured by the ratio of the capacitance of a capacitor with the material as dielectric to its capacitance with vacuum as dielectric — called also *dielectric constant*

per·mu·ta·tion \ˌpər-myü-ˈtā-shən\ *n* [ME *permutacioun* exchange, transformation, fr. AF, fr. L *permutation-, permutatio,* fr. *permutare*] (14c) **1 :** often major or fundamental change (as in character or condition) based primarily on rearrangement of existent elements ⟨the system has gone through several ∼*s*⟩; *also* **:** a form or variety resulting from such change ⟨technology available in various ∼*s*⟩ **2 a :** the act or process of changing the lineal order of an ordered set of objects **b :** an ordered arrangement of a set of objects — **per·mu·ta·tion·al** \-shnəl, -shə-nᵊl\ *adj*

permutation group *n* (1904) **:** a group whose elements are permutations and in which the product of two permutations is a permutation whose effect is the same as the successive application of the first two

per·mute \pər-ˈmyüt\ *vt* **per·mut·ed; per·mut·ing** [ME, to exchange, fr. AF or L; AF *permuter,* fr. L *permutare,* fr. *per-* + *mutare* to change — more at MUTABLE] (1878) **:** to change the order or arrangement of; *esp* **:** to arrange in all possible ways — **per·mut·able** \-ˈmyü-tə-bəl\ *adj*

per·ni·cious \pər-ˈni-shəs\ *adj* [ME, fr. AF, fr. L *perniciosus,* fr. *pernicies* destruction, fr. *per-* + *nec-, nex* violent death — more at NOXIOUS] (15c) **1 :** highly injurious or destructive **:** DEADLY **2** *archaic* **:** WICKED — **per·ni·cious·ly** *adv* — **per·ni·cious·ness** *n*

syn PERNICIOUS, BANEFUL, NOXIOUS, DELETERIOUS, DETRIMENTAL mean exceedingly harmful. PERNICIOUS implies irreparable harm done through evil or insidious corrupting or undermining ⟨the claim that pornography has a *pernicious* effect on society⟩. BANEFUL implies injury through poisoning or destroying ⟨the *baneful* notion that discipline destroys creativity⟩. NOXIOUS applies to what is both offensive and injurious to the health of a body or mind ⟨*noxious* chemical fumes⟩. DELETERIOUS applies to what has an often unsuspected harmful effect ⟨a diet found to have *deleterious* effects⟩. DETRIMENTAL implies obvious harmfulness to something specified ⟨the *detrimental* effects of excessive drinking⟩.

pernicious anemia *n* (1874) **:** a severe megaloblastic anemia that is marked by a progressive decrease in the number of red blood cells and by pallor, weakness, and gastrointestinal and nervous disturbances and is caused by malabsorption of vitamin B_{12} due to the absence of intrinsic factor

per·nick·e·ty \pər-ˈni-kə-tē\ *adj* [origin unknown] (ca. 1818) *chiefly Brit* **:** PERSNICKETY

Per·nod \per-ˈnō, ˌpər-\ *trademark* — used for a French liqueur

pe·ro·ne·al \ˌper-ō-ˈnē-əl, pə-ˈrō-nē-\ *adj* [NL *peroneus,* fr. *perone* fibula, fr. Gk *peronē,* lit., pin, fr. *peirein* to pierce — more at DIAPIR] (1831) **:** of, relating to, or located near the fibula

per·oral \(ˌ)pər-ˈȯr-əl, per-, -ˈär-\ *adj* [ISV] (1908) **:** occurring through or by way of the mouth — **per·oral·ly** \-ə-lē\ *adv*

per·o·rate \ˈper-ə-ˌrāt *also* ˈpər-\ *vi* **-rat·ed; -rat·ing** [L *peroratus,* pp. of *perorare* to declaim at length, wind up an oration, fr. *per-* through + *orare* to speak — more at PER-, ORATION] (1603) **1 :** to deliver a long or grandiloquent oration **2 :** to make a peroration

per·o·ra·tion \ˌper-ə-ˈrā-shən *also* ˌpər-\ *n* [ME *peroracyon,* fr. L *peroration-, peroratio,* fr. *perorare*] (15c) **1 :** the concluding part of a discourse and esp. an oration **2 :** a highly rhetorical speech — **per·o·ra·tion·al** \ˌper-ə-ˈrā-shnəl, ˌpər-, -shə-nᵊl\ *adj*

pe·rov·skite \pə-ˈräv-ˌskīt, -ˈräf-\ *n* [G *Perowskit,* fr. Count L. A. *Perovskiĭ* †1856 Russ. statesman] (1840) **:** a yellow, brown, or grayish-black mineral consisting of an oxide of calcium and titanium and sometimes containing rare earth elements

per·ox·i·dase \pə-ˈräk-sə-ˌdās, -ˌdāz\ *n* (1900) **:** an enzyme that catalyzes the oxidation of various substances by peroxides

per·ox·i·da·tion \pə-ˌräk-sə-ˈdā-shən\ *n* (1839) **:** oxidation to the greatest possible extent resulting esp. in formation of a peroxide

[1]**per·ox·ide** \pə-ˈräk-ˌsīd\ *n* (1804) **:** a compound (as hydrogen peroxide) in which oxygen is visualized as joined to oxygen — **per·ox·id·ic** \-ˌräk-ˈsi-dik\ *adj*

[2]**peroxide** *vt* **-id·ed; -id·ing** (1906) **:** to treat with a peroxide; *esp* **:** to bleach (hair) with hydrogen peroxide

[3]**peroxide** *adj* (1920) **:** having or being bleached hair ⟨a ∼ blonde⟩

per·ox·i·some \pə-ˈräk-sə-ˌsōm\ *n* [*peroxide* + [3]*-some*] (1965) **:** a cytoplasmic cell organelle containing enzymes (as catalase) which act in oxidative reactions and esp. in the production and decomposition of hydrogen peroxide — **per·ox·i·som·al** \-ˌräk-sə-ˈsō-məl\ *adj*

peroxy- *comb form* [ISV *per-* + *oxy*] **:** containing the divalent group O–O ⟨*peroxy*acetyl nitrate⟩

per·oxy·ace·tyl nitrate \pə-ˌräk-sē-ə-ˈsē-tᵊl-; -ˈa-sə-tᵊl-, -ˌtēl-\ *n* (1963) **:** a toxic compound $C_2H_3O_5N$ found esp. in smog

[1]**perp** \ˈpərp\ *n* (1981) **:** a perpetrator esp. of a crime

[2]**perp** *abbr* perpendicular

per·pend \(ˌ)pər-ˈpend\ *vb* [ME, fr. L *perpendere,* fr. *per-* thoroughly + *pendere* to weigh — more at PER-, PENDANT] *vt* (15c) **:** to reflect on carefully **:** PONDER ∼ *vi* **:** to be attentive **:** REFLECT

[1]**per·pen·dic·u·lar** \ˌpər-pən-ˈdi-kyə-lər\ *adj* [ME *perpendiculer,* fr. MF, fr. L *perpendicularis,* fr. *perpendiculum* plumb line, fr. *per-* + *pendēre* to hang — more at PENDANT] (14c) **1 a :** standing at right angles to the plane of the horizon **:** exactly upright **b :** being at right angles to a given line or plane **2 :** extremely steep **:** PRECIPITOUS **3** *often cap* **:** of or relating to a medieval English Gothic style of architecture in which vertical lines predominate **4 :** relating to, uniting, or consisting of individuals of dissimilar type or on different levels ***syn*** see VERTICAL — **per·pen·dic·u·lar·i·ty** \-ˌdi-kyə-ˈla-rə-tē\ *n* — **per·pen·dic·u·lar·ly** \-ˈdi-kyə-lər-lē\ *adv*

[2]**perpendicular** *n* (1571) **:** a line at right angles to a line or plane (as of the horizon)

per·pe·trate \ˈpər-pə-ˌtrāt\ *vt* **-trat·ed; -trat·ing** [L *perpetratus,* pp. of *perpetrare,* fr. *per-* through + *patrare* to accomplish, fr. *pater* father — more at FATHER] (1537) **1 :** to bring about or carry out (as a crime or deception) **:** COMMIT **2 :** to produce, perform, or execute (something likened to a crime) ⟨∼ a pun⟩ — **per·pe·tra·tion** \ˌpər-pə-ˈtrā-shən\ *n* — **per·pe·tra·tor** \ˈpər-pə-ˌtrā-tər\ *n*

per·pet·u·al \pər-ˈpe-chə-wəl, -chəl; -ˈpech-wəl\ *adj* [ME *perpetuel,* fr. AF, fr. L *perpetuus* uninterrupted, fr. *per-* through + *petere* to go to — more at FEATHER] (14c) **1 a :** continuing forever **:** EVERLASTING ⟨∼ motion⟩ **b (1) :** valid for all time ⟨a ∼ right⟩ **(2) :** holding (as an office) for life or for an unlimited time **2 :** occurring continually **:** indefinitely long-continued ⟨∼ problems⟩ **3 :** blooming continuously throughout the season ***syn*** see CONTINUAL — **per·pet·u·al·ly** *adv*

perpetual calendar *n* (1895) **:** a table for finding the day of the week for any one of a wide range of dates

perpetual check *n* (ca. 1909) **:** an endless succession of checks to which an opponent's king may be subjected to force a draw in chess

per·pet·u·ate \pər-ˈpe-chə-ˌwāt\ *vt* **-at·ed; -at·ing** [L *perpetuatus,* pp. of *perpetuare,* fr. *perpetuus*] (1530) **:** to make perpetual or cause to last indefinitely ⟨∼ the species⟩ — **per·pet·u·a·tion** \-ˌpe-chə-ˈwā-shən\ *n* — **per·pet·u·a·tor** \-ˈpe-chə-ˌwā-tər\ *n*

per·pe·tu·i·ty \ˌpər-pə-ˈtü-ə-tē, -ˈtyü-\ *n, pl* **-ties** [ME *perpetuite,* fr. AF *perpetuité,* fr. L *perpetuitat-, perpetuitas,* fr. *perpetuus*] (15c) **1 :** ETERNITY 2 **2 :** the quality or state of being perpetual ⟨bequeathed to them in ∼⟩ **3 a :** the condition of an estate limited so that it will not take effect or vest within the period fixed by law **b :** an estate so limited **4 :** an annuity payable forever

per·phe·na·zine \(ˌ)pər-ˈfē-nə-ˌzēn, -ˈfe-\ *n* [blend of *piperazine* and *phen-*] (1957) **:** a phenothiazine tranquilizer $C_{21}H_{26}ClN_3OS$ that is used esp. to control psychotic symptoms (as anxiety and agitation)

per·plex \pər-ˈpleks\ *vt* [obs. *perplex,* adj., involved, perplexed, fr. L *perplexus,* fr. *per-* thoroughly + *plexus* involved, fr. pp. of *plectere* to braid, twine — more at PER-, PLY] (1593) **1 :** to make unable to grasp something clearly or to think logically and decisively about something ⟨her attitude ∼*es* me⟩ ⟨a ∼*ing* problem⟩ **2 :** to make intricate or involved **:** COMPLICATE ***syn*** see PUZZLE

per·plexed \-ˈplekst\ *adj* (15c) **1 :** filled with uncertainty **:** PUZZLED **2 :** full of difficulty — **per·plexed·ly** \-ˈplek-səd-lē, -ˈplekst-lē\ *adv*

per·plex·i·ty \pər-ˈplek-sə-tē\ *n, pl* **-ties** [ME *perplexite,* fr. MF *perplexité,* fr. LL *perplexitat-, perplexitas,* fr. L *perplexus*] (14c) **1 :** the state of being perplexed **:** BEWILDERMENT **2 :** something that perplexes **3 :** ENTANGLEMENT

per·qui·site \ˈpər-kwə-zət\ *n* [ME, property acquired by means other than inheritance, fr. AF *perquisit,* ML *perquisitum,* fr. neut. of *perquisitus,* pp. of *perquirere* to purchase, acquire, fr. L, to search for thoroughly, fr. *per-* thoroughly + *quaerere* to seek] (15c) **1 :** a privilege, gain, or profit incidental to regular salary or wages; *esp* **:** one expected or promised **2 :** GRATUITY, TIP **3 :** something held or claimed as an exclusive right or possession

per·ron \ˈper-ən, pe-rōⁿ\ *n* [F, fr. OF, fr. *perre, pierre* rock, stone, fr. L *petra,* fr. Gk] (1723) **:** an outdoor stairway leading up to a building entrance; *also* **:** a platform at its top

per·ry \ˈper-ē\ *n* [ME *peirrie,* fr. AF *peré,* fr. VL **piratum,* fr. L *pirum* pear] (14c) : fermented pear juice often made sparkling

pers *abbr* **1** person; personal **2** personnel

perse \ˈpərs\ *adj* [ME *pers,* fr. AF, fr. ML *persus*] (15c) : of a dark grayish blue resembling indigo

[1]**per se** \(ˌ)pər-ˈsā *also* per-ˈsā *or* (ˌ)pər-ˈsē\ *adv* [L] (1572) : by, of, or in itself or oneself or themselves : as such : INTRINSICALLY

[2]**per se** *adj* (ca. 1655) : being such inherently, clearly, or as a matter of law ⟨a *per se* conflict of interest⟩

per second per second *adv* (1922) : per second every second — used of acceleration

per·se·cute \ˈpər-si-ˌkyüt\ *vt* **-cut·ed; -cut·ing** [ME, fr. MF *persecuter,* back-formation fr. *persecuteur* persecutor, fr. LL *persecutor,* fr. *persequi* to persecute, fr. L, to pursue, fr. *per-* through + *sequi* to follow — more at SUE] (15c) **1 :** to harass or punish in a manner designed to injure, grieve, or afflict; *specif* : to cause to suffer because of belief **2 :** to annoy with persistent or urgent approaches (as attacks, pleas, or importunities) : PESTER ***syn*** see WRONG — **per·se·cu·tee** \ˌpər-si-ˌkyü-ˈtē\ *n* — **per·se·cu·tive** \ˈpər-si-ˌkyü-tiv\ *adj* — **per·se·cu·tor** \-ˌkyü-tər\ *n* — **per·se·cu·to·ry** \-kyü-ˌtȯr-ē, -ˌkyü-tə-rē\ *adj*

per·se·cu·tion \ˌpər-si-ˈkyü-shən\ *n* (14c) **1 :** the act or practice of persecuting esp. those who differ in origin, religion, or social outlook **2 :** the condition of being persecuted, harassed, or annoyed

Per·se·id \ˈpər-sē-əd\ *n* [L *Perseus;* fr. their appearing to radiate from a point in Perseus] (1876) : any of a group of meteors that appear annually about August 11

Per·seph·o·ne \pər-ˈse-fə-nē\ *n* [L, fr. Gk *Persephonē*] (1567) : a daughter of Zeus and Demeter abducted by Pluto to reign with him over the underworld

Per·seus \ˈpər-ˌsüs, -sē-əs\ *n* [L, fr. Gk] (14c) **1 :** a son of Zeus and Danaë and slayer of Medusa **2** [L (gen. *Persei*), fr. Gk] **:** a northern constellation between Taurus and Cassiopeia

per·se·ver·ance \ˌpər-sə-ˈvir-ən(t)s\ *n* (14c) : the action or condition or an instance of persevering : STEADFASTNESS

per·sev·er·a·tion \pər-ˌse-və-ˈrā-shən\ *n* [L *perseveration-, perseveratio,* fr. *perseverare*] (1910) : continuation of something (as repetition of a word) usu. to an exceptional degree or beyond a desired point — **per·sev·er·ate** \-ˈse-və-ˌrāt\ *vi* — **per·sev·er·a·tive** \-ˌrā-tiv\ *adj*

per·se·vere \ˌpər-sə-ˈvir\ *vi* **-vered; -ver·ing** [ME, fr. AF *parseverer,* fr. L *perseverare,* fr. *per-* through + *severus* severe] (14c) : to persist in a state, enterprise, or undertaking in spite of counterinfluences, opposition, or discouragement — **per·se·ver·ing·ly** *adv*

Per·sian \ˈpər-zhən, *esp Brit* -shən\ *n* (14c) **1 :** one of the people of Persia: as **a :** one of the ancient Iranians who under Cyrus and his successors founded an empire in southwest Asia **b :** a member of one of the peoples forming the modern Iranian nationality **2 a :** any of several Iranian languages dominant in Persia at different periods **b :** the modern language of Iran and western Afghanistan — see INDO-EUROPEAN LANGUAGES table **3 :** a thin soft silk formerly used esp. for linings **4 :** PERSIAN CAT — **Persian** *adj*

Persian cat *n* (1821) : any of a breed of stocky round-headed domestic cats that have a long silky coat and thick ruff

Persian cat

Persian lamb *n* (1889) **1 :** a pelt that is obtained from a newborn karakul lamb slightly older than those yielding broadtail and that is characterized by very silky tightly curled glossy fur **2 :** the young of the karakul sheep that furnishes skins used in furriery

per·si·flage \ˈpər-si-ˌfläzh, ˈper-\ *n* [F, fr. *persifler* to banter, fr. *per-* thoroughly + *siffler* to whistle, hiss, boo, ultim. fr. L *sibilare*] (1757) : frivolous bantering talk : light raillery

per·sim·mon \pər-ˈsi-mən\ *n* [Virginia Algonquian *pessemmin*] (1612) **1 :** any of a genus (*Diospyros*) of trees of the ebony family with hard fine wood, oblong leaves, and small bell-shaped flowers; *esp* : an eastern U.S. tree (*D. virginiana*) or a Japanese tree (*D. kaki*) **2 :** the usu. orange several-seeded globular berry of a persimmon that is edible when fully ripe but usu. extremely astringent when unripe

per·sist \pər-ˈsist, -ˈzist\ *vi* [MF *persister,* fr. L *persistere,* fr. *per-* + *sistere* to take a stand, stand firm; akin to L *stare* to stand — more at STAND] (1538) **1 :** to go on resolutely or stubbornly in spite of opposition, importunity, or warning **2** *obs* : to remain unchanged or fixed in a specified character, condition, or position **3 :** to be insistent in the repetition or pressing of an utterance (as a question or an opinion) **4 :** to continue to exist esp. past a usual, expected, or normal time ***syn*** see CONTINUE — **per·sist·er** *n*

per·sis·tence \pər-ˈsis-tən(t)s, -ˈzis-\ *n* (1546) **1 :** the action or fact of persisting **2 :** the quality or state of being persistent; *esp* : PERSEVERANCE

per·sis·ten·cy \-tən(t)-sē\ *n* (1597) : PERSISTENCE 2

per·sis·tent \-tənt\ *adj* [L *persistent-, persistens,* prp. of *persistere*] (1826) **1 :** existing for a long or longer than usual time or continuously: as **a :** retained beyond the usual period ⟨a ~ leaf⟩ **b :** continuing without change in function or structure ⟨~ gills⟩ **c :** effective in the open for an appreciable time usu. through slow volatilizing ⟨mustard gas is ~⟩ **d :** degraded only slowly by the environment ⟨~ pesticides⟩ **e :** remaining infective for a relatively long time in a vector after an initial period of incubation ⟨~ viruses⟩ **2 a :** continuing or inclined to persist in a course **b :** continuing to exist despite interference or treatment ⟨a ~ cough⟩ ⟨has been in a ~ vegetative state for two years⟩ — **per·sis·tent·ly** *adv*

per·snick·e·ty \pər-ˈsni-kə-tē\ *adj* [alter. of *pernickety*] (1915) **1 a :** fussy about small details : FASTIDIOUS ⟨a ~ teacher⟩ **b :** having the characteristics of a snob **2 :** requiring great precision ⟨a ~ job⟩ — **per·snick·e·ti·ness** \-nəs\ *n*

per·son \ˈpər-sᵊn\ *n* [ME, fr. AF *persone,* fr. L *persona* actor's mask, character in a play, person, prob. fr. Etruscan *phersu* mask, fr. Gk *prosōpa,* pl. of *prosōpon* face, mask — more at PROSOPOPOEIA] (13c) **1 :** HUMAN, INDIVIDUAL — sometimes used in combination esp. by those who prefer to avoid *man* in compounds applicable to both sexes ⟨chair*person*⟩ ⟨spokes*person*⟩ **2 :** a character or part in or as if in a play : GUISE **3 a :** one of the three modes of being in the Trinitarian Godhead as understood by Christians **b :** the unitary personality of Christ that unites the divine and human natures **4 a** *archaic* : bodily appearance **b :** the body of a human being; *also* : the body and clothing ⟨unlawful search of the ~⟩ **5 :** the personality of a human being : SELF **6 :** one (as a human being, a partnership, or a corporation) that is recognized by law as the subject of rights and duties **7 :** reference of a segment of discourse to the speaker, to one spoken to, or to one spoken of as indicated by means of certain pronouns or in many languages by verb inflection — **per·son·hood** \-ˌhu̇d\ *n* — **in person :** in one's bodily presence ⟨the movie star appeared *in person*⟩

per·so·na \pər-ˈsō-nə, -ˌnä\ *n, pl* **per·so·nae** \-(ˌ)nē, -ˌnī\ *or* **personas** [L] (1909) **1 :** a character assumed by an author in a written work **2 a** *pl personas* [NL, fr. L] : an individual's social facade or front that esp. in the analytic psychology of C. G. Jung reflects the role in life the individual is playing — compare ANIMA **b :** the personality that a person (as an actor or politician) projects in public : IMAGE **3** *pl personae* : a character in a fictional presentation (as a novel or play) — usu. used in pl. ⟨comic *personae*⟩

per·son·able \ˈpərs-nə-bəl, ˈpər-sə-nə-bəl\ *adj* (15c) : pleasant or amiable in person : ATTRACTIVE — **per·son·able·ness** *n*

per·son·age \ˈpərs-nij, ˈpər-sə-nij\ *n* (15c) **1 :** a person of rank, note, or distinction; *esp* : one distinguished for presence and personal power **2 :** a human individual : PERSON **3 :** a dramatic, fictional, or historical character; *also* : IMPERSONATION

per·so·na gra·ta \pər-ˈsō-nə-ˈgra-tə, -ˈgrä-\ *adj* [NL, acceptable person] (1882) : personally acceptable or welcome

[1]**per·son·al** \ˈpərs-nəl, ˈpər-sə-nəl\ *adj* [ME, fr. AF *personel,* fr. LL *personalis,* fr. L *persona*] (14c) **1 :** of, relating to, or affecting a particular person : PRIVATE, INDIVIDUAL ⟨~ ambition⟩ ⟨~ financial gain⟩ **2 a :** done in person without the intervention of another; *also* : proceeding from a single person **b :** carried on between individuals directly ⟨a ~ interview⟩ **3 :** relating to the person or body **4 :** relating to an individual or an individual's character, conduct, motives, or private affairs often in an offensive manner ⟨a ~ insult⟩ **5 a :** being rational and self-conscious ⟨~, responsive government is still possible —John Fischer⟩ **b :** having the qualities of a person rather than a thing or abstraction ⟨a ~ devil⟩ **6 :** of, relating to, or constituting personal property ⟨a ~ estate⟩ **7 :** denoting grammatical person **8 :** intended for private use or use by one person ⟨a ~ stereo⟩

[2]**personal** *n* (1861) **1 :** a short newspaper paragraph relating to the activities of a person or a group or to personal matters **2 :** a short personal communication in a special column of the classified ads section of a newspaper or periodical **3 :** PERSONAL FOUL

personal computer *n* (1976) : a general-purpose computer equipped with a microprocessor and designed to run esp. commercial software (as a word processor or Internet browser) for an individual user

personal digital assistant *n* (1992) : PDA

personal effects *n pl* (1818) : privately owned items (as clothing and jewelry) normally worn or carried on the person

personal equation *n* (1845) : variation (as in observation) occasioned by the personal peculiarities of an individual; *also* : a correction or allowance made for such variation

personal foul *n* (ca. 1829) : a foul in a game (as basketball) involving usu. physical contact with or deliberate roughing of an opponent — compare TECHNICAL FOUL

per·son·al·ise *Brit var of* PERSONALIZE

per·son·al·ism \ˈpərs-nə-ˌli-zəm, ˈpər-sə-nə-\ *n* (ca. 1846) : a doctrine emphasizing the significance, uniqueness, and inviolability of personality — **per·son·al·ist** \-list\ *n or adj* — **per·son·al·is·tic** \ˌpərs-nə-ˈlis-tik, ˌpər-sə-nə-\ *adj*

per·son·al·i·ty \ˌpər-sə-ˈna-lə-tē, ˌpər-ˈsna-\ *n, pl* **-ties** [ME *personalite,* fr. AF *personalité,* fr. LL *personalitat-, personalitas,* fr. *personalis*] (15c) **1 a :** the quality or state of being a person **b :** personal existence **2 a :** the condition or fact of relating to a particular person; *specif* : the condition of referring directly to or being aimed disparagingly or hostilely at an individual **b :** an offensively personal remark ⟨angrily resorted to *personalities*⟩ **3 a :** the complex of characteristics that distinguishes an individual or a nation or group; *esp* : the totality of an individual's behavioral and emotional characteristics **b :** a set of distinctive traits and characteristics ⟨the energetic ~ of the city⟩ **4 a :** distinction or excellence of personal and social traits; *also* : a person having such quality **b :** a person of importance, prominence, renown, or notoriety ⟨a TV ~⟩ ***syn*** see DISPOSITION

personality inventory *n* (1932) : any of several tests that attempt to characterize the personality of an individual by objective scoring of replies to a large number of questions concerning his or her own behavior — compare MINNESOTA MULTIPHASIC PERSONALITY INVENTORY

personality test *n* (1914) : any of several tests that consist of standardized tasks designed to determine various aspects of the personality or the emotional status of the individual examined

per·son·al·ize \ˈpərs-nə-ˌlīz, ˈpər-sə-nə-\ *vt* **-ized; -iz·ing** (ca. 1741) **1 :** PERSONIFY **2 :** to make personal or individual; *specif* : to mark as the property of a particular person ⟨*personalized* stationery⟩ — **per·son·al·i·za·tion** \ˌpərs-nə-lə-ˈzā-shən, ˌpər-sə-nə-\ *n*

per·son·al·ly \ˈpərs-nə-lē, ˈpər-sə-nə-\ *adv* (14c) **1 :** in person ⟨attend to the matter ~⟩ **2 :** as a person : in personality ⟨~ attractive but not very trustworthy⟩ **3 :** for oneself : as far as oneself is concerned ⟨~, I don't want to go⟩ **4 :** in a personal manner ⟨don't take this ~⟩

personal pronoun *n* (1668) : a pronoun (as *I, you,* or *they*) that expresses a distinction of person

personal property *n* (1833) : property other than real property consisting of things temporary or movable : CHATTELS

personal tax *n* (ca. 1935) : DIRECT TAX

per·son·al·ty \ˈpərs-nəl-tē, ˈpər-sə-nəl-\ *n, pl* **-ties** [ME, fr. AF *personalté,* fr. LL *personalitat-, personalitas* personality] (15c) : PERSONAL PROPERTY

per·so·na non gra·ta \pər-ˈsō-nə-ˌnän-ˈgra-tə, -ˈgrä-\ *adj* [NL, unacceptable person] (1904) : personally unacceptable or unwelcome

per·son·ate \ˈpər-sə-ˌnāt\ *vt* **-at·ed; -at·ing** (1591) **1 a :** IMPERSONATE, REPRESENT **b :** to assume without authority and with fraudulent intent (some character or capacity) **2 :** to invest with personality or personal characteristics ⟨*personating* their gods ridiculous, and themselves past shame —John Milton⟩ — **per·son·a·tion** \ˌpər-sə-ˈnā-shən\ *n* — **per·son·a·tive** \ˈpər-sə-ˌnā-tiv\ *adj* — **per·son·a·tor** \-ˌnā-tər\ *n*

per·son–hour \ˈpər-sᵊn-ˌau̇(-ə)r\ *n* (1975) **:** a unit of one hour's work by one person

per·son·i·fi·ca·tion \pər-ˌsä-nə-fə-ˈkā-shən\ *n* (ca. 1755) **1 :** attribution of personal qualities; *esp* **:** representation of a thing or abstraction as a person or by the human form **2 :** a divinity or imaginary being representing a thing or abstraction **3 :** EMBODIMENT, INCARNATION

per·son·i·fy \pər-ˈsä-nə-ˌfī\ *vt* **-fied; -fy·ing** (ca. 1741) **1 :** to conceive of or represent as a person or as having human qualities or powers **2 :** to be the embodiment or personification of **:** INCARNATE ⟨a teacher who *personified* patience⟩ — **per·son·i·fi·er** \-ˌfī(-ə)r\ *n*

per·son·nel \ˌpər-sə-ˈnel\ *n* [F, fr. G *Personale, Personal,* fr. ML *personale,* fr. LL, neut. of *personalis* personal] (1837) **1 a :** a body of persons usu. employed (as in a factory or organization) **b personnel** *pl* **:** PERSONS **2 :** a division of an organization concerned with personnel

person of interest (1937) **:** a person who is believed to be possibly involved in a crime but has not been charged or arrested

[1]**per·spec·tive** \pər-ˈspek-tiv\ *n* [ME *perspectyf,* fr. ML *perspectivum,* fr. neut. of *perspectivus* of sight, optical, fr. L *perspectus,* pp. of *perspicere* to look through, see clearly, fr. *per-* through + *specere* to look — more at PER-, SPY] (14c) *archaic* **:** an optical glass (as a telescope)

[2]**perspective** *n* [MF, prob. modif. of OIt *prospettiva,* fr. *prospetto* view, prospect, fr. L *prospectus* — more at PROSPECT] (1563) **1 a :** the technique or process of representing on a plane or curved surface the spatial relation of objects as they might appear to the eye; *specif* **:** representation in a drawing or painting of parallel lines as converging in order to give the illusion of depth and distance **b :** a picture in perspective **2 a :** the interrelation in which a subject or its parts are mentally viewed ⟨places the issues in proper ~⟩; *also* **:** POINT OF VIEW **b :** the capacity to view things in their true relations or relative importance ⟨trying to maintain my ~⟩ **3 a :** a visible scene; *esp* **:** one giving a distinctive impression of distance **:** VISTA **b :** a mental view or prospect ⟨gain a broader ~ on the situation⟩ **4 :** the appearance to the eye of objects in respect to their relative distance and positions — **per·spec·tiv·al** \pər-ˈspek-ti-vəl, ˌpər-(ˌ)spek-ˈtī-vəl\ *adj*

[3]**perspective** *adj* [ME, optical, fr. ML *perspectivus*] (1570) **1** *obs* **:** aiding the vision ⟨his eyes should be like unto the wrong end of a ~ glass —Alexander Pope⟩ **2 :** of, relating to, employing, or seen in perspective ⟨~ drawing⟩ — **per·spec·tive·ly** *adv*

Per·spex \ˈpər-ˌspeks\ *trademark* — used for an acrylic plastic

per·spi·ca·cious \ˌpər-spə-ˈkā-shəs\ *adj* [L *perspicac-, perspicax,* fr. *perspicere*] (1640) **:** of acute mental vision or discernment **:** KEEN ***syn*** see SHREWD — **per·spi·ca·cious·ly** *adv* — **per·spi·ca·cious·ness** *n* — **per·spi·cac·i·ty** \-ˈka-sə-tē\ *n*

per·spic·u·ous \pər-ˈspi-kyə-wəs\ *adj* [L *perspicuus* transparent, perspicuous, fr. *perspicere*] (1586) **:** plain to the understanding esp. because of clarity and precision of presentation ⟨a ~ argument⟩ ***syn*** see CLEAR — **per·spi·cu·i·ty** \ˌpər-spə-ˈkyü-ə-tē\ *n* — **per·spic·u·ous·ly** \pər-ˈspi-kyə-wəs-lē\ *adv* — **per·spic·u·ous·ness** *n*

per·spi·ra·tion \ˌpər-spə-ˈrā-shən\ *n* (1626) **1 :** the action or process of perspiring **2 :** a saline fluid secreted by the sweat glands **:** SWEAT

per·spi·ra·to·ry \pər-ˈspī-rə-ˌtȯr-ē, ˈpər-sp(ə-)rə-\ *adj* (1725) **:** of, relating to, secreting, or inducing perspiration

per·spire \pər-ˈspī(-ə)r\ *vi* **per·spired; per·spir·ing** [F *perspirer,* fr. MF, fr. L *per-* through + *spirare* to blow, breathe — more at PER-] (ca. 1682) **:** to emit matter through the skin; *specif* **:** to secrete and emit perspiration

per stir·pes \pər-ˈstər-pēz, per-ˈstir-pās\ *adv or adj* [L, by familial stocks] (1682) **:** in equal shares to each member of a specified class with the share of a deceased member divided proportionately among his or her beneficiaries (as children) ⟨the estate was divided *per stirpes*⟩

per·suad·able \pər-ˈswā-də-bəl\ *adj* (ca. 1598) **:** capable of being persuaded

per·suade \pər-ˈswād\ *vt* **per·suad·ed; per·suad·ing** [L *persuadēre,* fr. *per-* thoroughly + *suadēre* to advise, urge — more at SWEET] (15c) **1 :** to move by argument, entreaty, or expostulation to a belief, position, or course of action **2 :** to plead with **:** URGE — **per·suad·er** *n*

per·sua·si·ble \-ˈswā-zə-bəl, -ˈswā-sə-\ *adj* [ME, *plausible,* fr. MF, fr. L *persuasibilis* persuasive, fr. *persuasus,* pp. of *persuadēre*] (1502) **:** PERSUADABLE

per·sua·sion \pər-ˈswā-zhən\ *n* [ME *persuasioun,* fr. MF or L; MF *persuasion,* fr. L *persuasion-, persuasio,* fr. *persuadēre*] (14c) **1 a :** the act or process or an instance of persuading **b :** a persuading argument **c :** the ability to persuade **:** PERSUASIVENESS **2 :** the condition of being persuaded **3 a :** an opinion held with complete assurance **b :** a system of religious beliefs; *also* **:** a group adhering to a particular system of beliefs **4 :** KIND, SORT ***syn*** see OPINION

per·sua·sive \-ˈswā-siv, -ziv\ *adj* (15c) **:** tending to persuade — **per·sua·sive·ly** *adv* — **per·sua·sive·ness** *n*

pert \ˈpərt\ *adj* [ME, evident, attractive, saucy, short for *apert* evident, fr. AF, fr. L *apertus* open, fr. pp. of *aperire* to open] (14c) **1 a :** saucily free and forward **:** flippantly cocky and assured **b :** being trim and chic **:** JAUNTY ⟨a ~ little hat⟩ **c :** piquantly stimulating ⟨is a ~ notion⟩ **2 :** LIVELY, VIVACIOUS — **pert·ly** *adv* — **pert·ness** *n*

per·tain \pər-ˈtān\ *vi* [ME *perteinen,* fr. AF *partenir, purteiner,* fr. L *pertinēre* to reach to, belong, fr. *per-* through + *tenēre* to hold — more at THIN] (14c) **1 a (1) :** to belong as a part, member, accessory, or product **(2) :** to belong as an attribute, feature, or function ⟨the destruction ~*ing* to war⟩ **(3) :** to belong as a duty or right ⟨rights that ~ to fatherhood⟩ **b :** to be appropriate to something ⟨which rule ~*s*?⟩ **2 :** to have reference ⟨books ~*ing* to birds⟩

per·ti·na·cious \ˌpər-tə-ˈnā-shəs\ *adj* [L *pertinac-, pertinax,* fr. *per-* thoroughly + *tenac-, tenax* tenacious, fr. *tenēre*] (1626) **1 a :** adhering resolutely to an opinion, purpose, or design **b :** perversely persistent **2 :** stubbornly tenacious ***syn*** see OBSTINATE — **per·ti·na·cious·ly** *adv* — **per·ti·na·cious·ness** *n* — **per·ti·nac·i·ty** \-ˈna-sə-tē\ *n*

per·ti·nence \ˈpər-tə-nən(t)s, ˈpərt-nən(t)s\ *n* (1659) **:** the quality or state of being pertinent **:** RELEVANCE

per·ti·nen·cy \-tə-nən(t)-sē, -nən(t)-sē\ *n* (1598) **:** PERTINENCE

per·ti·nent \ˈpər-tə-nənt, ˈpərt-nənt\ *adj* [ME, fr. AF, fr. L *pertinent-, pertinens,* prp. of *pertinēre*] (14c) **:** having a clear decisive relevance to the matter in hand ***syn*** see RELEVANT — **per·ti·nent·ly** *adv*

per·turb \pər-ˈtərb\ *vt* [ME, fr. MF *perturber,* fr. L *perturbare* to throw into confusion, fr. *per-* + *turbare* to disturb — more at TURBID] (14c) **1 :** to cause to be worried or upset **:** DISQUIET **2 :** to throw into confusion **:** DISORDER **3 :** to cause to experience a perturbation ***syn*** see DISCOMPOSE — **per·turb·able** \-ˈtər-bə-bəl\ *adj*

per·tur·ba·tion \ˌpər-tər-ˈbā-shən, ˌpər-ˌtər-\ *n* (14c) **1 :** the action of perturbing **:** the state of being perturbed **2 :** a disturbance of motion, course, arrangement, or state of equilibrium; *esp* **:** a disturbance of the regular and usu. elliptical course of motion of a celestial body that is produced by some force additional to that which causes its regular motion — **per·tur·ba·tion·al** \-shnəl, -shə-nᵊl\ *adj*

per·tus·sis \pər-ˈtə-səs\ *n* [NL, fr. L *per-* thoroughly + *tussis* cough] (ca. 1799) **:** WHOOPING COUGH

pe·ruke \pə-ˈrük\ *n* [MF *perruque,* fr. OIt *parrucca, perrucca* hair, wig] (ca. 1573) **:** WIG; *specif* **:** one of a type popular from the 17th to the early 19th century — **pe·ruked** \-ˈrükt\ *adj*

peruke

pe·ruse \pə-ˈrüz\ *vt* **pe·rused; pe·rus·ing** [ME, to use up, deal with in sequence, fr. L *per-* thoroughly + ME *usen* to use] (1532) **1 a :** to examine or consider with attention and in detail **:** STUDY **b :** to look over or through in a casual or cursory manner **2 :** READ; *esp* **:** to read over in an attentive or leisurely manner — **pe·rus·al** \-ˈrü-zəl\ *n* — **pe·rus·er** *n*

perv \ˈpərv\ *n* (1944) **:** PERVERT

per·vade \pər-ˈvād\ *vt* **per·vad·ed; per·vad·ing** [L *pervadere* to go through, pervade, fr. *per-* through + *vadere* to go — more at PER-, WADE] (1659) **:** to become diffused throughout every part of

per·va·sion \pər-ˈvā-zhən\ *n* (1661) **:** the action of pervading or condition of being pervaded

per·va·sive \pər-ˈvā-siv, -ziv\ *adj* (ca. 1750) **:** pervading or tending to pervade ⟨a ~ odor⟩ — **per·va·sive·ly** *adv* — **per·va·sive·ness** *n*

pervasive developmental disorder *n* (ca. 1981) **:** AUTISM SPECTRUM DISORDER

per·verse \(ˌ)pər-ˈvərs, ˈpər-ˌ\ *adj* [ME, fr. AF *purvers, pervers,* fr. L *perversus,* fr. pp. of *pervertere*] (14c) **1 a :** turned away from what is right or good **:** CORRUPT **b :** IMPROPER, INCORRECT **c :** contrary to the evidence or the direction of the judge on a point of law ⟨~ verdict⟩ **2 a :** obstinate in opposing what is right, reasonable, or accepted **:** WRONGHEADED **b :** arising from or indicative of stubbornness or obstinacy **3 :** marked by peevishness or petulance **:** CRANKY **4 :** marked by perversion ***syn*** see CONTRARY — **per·verse·ly** *adv* — **per·verse·ness** *n* — **per·ver·si·ty** \pər-ˈvər-sə-tē, -stē\ *n*

per·ver·sion \pər-ˈvər-zhən, -shən\ *n* (14c) **1 :** the action of perverting **:** the condition of being perverted **2 :** a perverted form; *esp* **:** an aberrant sexual practice or interest esp. when habitual

per·ver·sive \-ˈvər-siv, -ziv\ *adj* (1817) **1 :** perverting or tending to pervert **2 :** arising from or indicative of perversion

[1]**per·vert** \pər-ˈvərt\ *vt* [ME, fr. AF *purvertir, pervertir,* fr. L *pervertere* to overturn, corrupt, pervert, fr. *per-* thoroughly + *vertere* to turn — more at PER-, WORTH] (14c) **1 a :** to cause to turn aside or away from what is good or true or morally right **:** CORRUPT **b :** to cause to turn aside or away from what is generally done or accepted **:** MISDIRECT **2 a :** to divert to a wrong end or purpose **:** MISUSE **b :** to twist the meaning or sense of **:** MISINTERPRET ***syn*** see DEBASE — **per·vert·er** *n*

[2]**per·vert** \ˈpər-ˌvərt\ *n* (ca. 1661) **:** one that has been perverted; *specif* **:** one given to some form of sexual perversion

per·vert·ed \pər-ˈvər-təd\ *adj* (14c) **1 :** CORRUPT **2 :** marked by perversion — **per·vert·ed·ly** *adv* — **per·vert·ed·ness** *n*

per·vi·ous \ˈpər-vē-əs\ *adj* [L *pervius,* fr. *per-* through + *via* way — more at PER-, WAY] (ca. 1614) **1 :** ACCESSIBLE ⟨~ to reason⟩ **2 :** PERMEABLE ⟨~ soil⟩ — **per·vi·ous·ness** *n*

Pe·sach \ˈpā-ˌsäk\ *n* [Heb *pesaḥ*] (1613) **:** PASSOVER

pes·ca·tar·i·an *or* **pes·ce·tar·i·an** \ˌpe-skə-ˈter-ē-ən\ *n* [prob. fr. It *pesce* fish (fr. L *piscis*) + E *vegetarian*] (1993) **:** one whose diet includes fish but no other meat

pe·se·ta \pə-ˈsā-tə\ *n* [Sp, fr. dim. of *peso*] (1801) **:** the basic monetary unit of Spain until 2002

pe·se·wa \pə-ˈsā-wə\ *n, pl* **pesewas** *or* **pesewa** [Twi *pésewa,* lit., penny, penny's worth of gold dust] (1965) — see *cedi* at MONEY table

pesky \ˈpes-kē\ *adj* **pesk·i·er; -est** [prob. irreg. fr. *pest* + [1]*-y*] (1775) **:** TROUBLESOME, VEXATIOUS ⟨~ issues⟩

pe·so \ˈpā-(ˌ)sō, ˈpe-\ *n, pl* **pesos** [Sp, lit., weight, fr. L *pensum* — more at POISE] (1555) **1 :** an old silver coin of Spain and Spanish America equal to eight reals **2** — see MONEY table

pes·sa·ry \ˈpe-sə-rē\ *n, pl* **-ries** [ME *pessarie,* fr. AF, fr. LL *pessarium,* fr. *pessus, pessum* pessary, fr. Gk *pessos* oval stone for playing checkers, pessary] (14c) **1 :** a vaginal suppository **2 :** a device worn in the vagina to support the uterus, remedy a malposition, or prevent conception

pes·si·mism \ˈpe-sə-ˌmi-zəm *also* ˈpe-zə-\ *n* [F *pessimisme,* fr. L *pessimus* worst — more at PEJORATIVE] (1815) **1 :** an inclination to emphasize adverse aspects, conditions, and possibilities or to expect the worst possible outcome **2 a :** the doctrine that reality is essentially evil **b :** the doctrine that evil overbalances happiness in life — **pes·si·mist** \-mist\ *n*

pes·si·mis·tic \ˌpe-sə-ˈmis-tik *also* ˌpe-zə-\ *adj* (1868) **:** of, relating to, or characterized by pessimism **:** GLOOMY ***syn*** see CYNICAL — **pes·si·mis·ti·cal·ly** \-ti-k(ə-)lē\ *adv*

pest \ˈpest\ *n* [MF *peste,* fr. L *pestis*] (1513) **1 :** an epidemic disease associated with high mortality; *specif* **:** PLAGUE **2 :** something resembling a pest in destructiveness; *esp* **:** a plant or animal detrimental to humans or human concerns (as agriculture or livestock production) **3 :** one that pesters or annoys **:** NUISANCE — **pesty** \ˈpes-tē\ *adj*

\ə\ **a**but \ᵊ\ kitten, F table \ər\ **fur**ther \a\ **a**sh \ā\ **a**ce \ä\ m**o**p, m**a**r \au̇\ **ou**t \ch\ **ch**in \e\ b**e**t \ē\ **ea**sy \g\ **g**o \i\ h**i**t \ī\ **i**ce \j\ **j**ob \ŋ\ si**ng** \ō\ g**o** \ȯ\ l**aw** \ȯi\ b**oy** \th\ **th**in \t͟h\ **th**e \ü\ l**oo**t \u̇\ f**oo**t \y\ **y**et \zh\ vi**s**ion, beige \k, ⁿ, œ, ue, ʸ\ *see* Guide to Pronunciation

pes·ter \ˈpes-tər\ *vt* **pes·tered; pes·ter·ing** \-t(ə-)riŋ\ [modif. of MF *empestrer* to hobble, embarrass, fr. VL **impastoriare,* fr. L *in-* + LL *pastoria* tether — more at PASTERN] (1533) **1** *obs* : OVERCROWD **2** : to harass with petty irritations : ANNOY ***syn*** see WORRY

pest·hole \ˈpest-ˌhōl\ *n* (1862) : a place liable to epidemic disease

pest·house \-ˌhau̇s\ *n* (1614) : a shelter or hospital for those infected with a pestilential or contagious disease

pes·ti·cide \ˈpes-tə-ˌsīd\ *n* (ca. 1925) : an agent used to destroy pests — **pes·ti·ci·dal** \ˌpes-tə-ˈsī-dᵊl\ *adj*

pes·tif·er·ous \pes-ˈti-f(ə-)rəs\ *adj* [ME, fr. L *pestifer* pestilential, noxious, fr. *pestis* + *-fer* -ferous] (15c) **1** : dangerous to society : PERNICIOUS **2 a** : carrying or propagating infection : PESTILENTIAL **b** : infected with a pestilential disease **3** : TROUBLESOME, ANNOYING — **pes·tif·er·ous·ly** *adv* — **pes·tif·er·ous·ness** *n*

pes·ti·lence \ˈpes-tə-lən(t)s\ *n* (14c) **1** : a contagious or infectious epidemic disease that is virulent and devastating; *esp* : BUBONIC PLAGUE **2** : something that is destructive or pernicious ⟨I'll pour this ~ into his ear —Shak.⟩

pes·ti·lent \-lənt\ *adj* [ME, fr. L *pestilent-, pestilens* pestilential, fr. *pestis*] (14c) **1** : destructive of life : DEADLY **2** : injuring or endangering society : PERNICIOUS **3** : causing displeasure or annoyance **4** : INFECTIOUS, CONTAGIOUS ⟨a ~ disease⟩ — **pes·ti·lent·ly** *adv*

pes·ti·len·tial \ˌpes-tə-ˈlen(t)-shəl\ *adj* (14c) **1 a** : causing or tending to cause pestilence : DEADLY **b** : of or relating to pestilence **2** : morally harmful : PERNICIOUS **3** : giving rise to vexation or annoyance : IRRITATING — **pes·ti·len·tial·ly** \-ˈlen(t)-sh(ə-)lē\ *adv*

[1]**pes·tle** \ˈpe-səl, ˈpes-tᵊl\ *n* [ME *pestel,* fr. AF, fr. L *pistillum,* fr. *pinsere* to pound, crush; akin to Gk *ptissein* to crush, Skt *pinaṣṭi* he pounds] (14c) **1** : a usu. club-shaped implement for pounding or grinding substances in a mortar — see MORTAR illustration **2** : any of various devices for pounding, stamping, or pressing

[2]**pestle** *vb* **pes·tled; pes·tling** \ˈpe-s(ə-)liŋ, ˈpes-tᵊl-iŋ\ *vt* (15c) *archaic* : to beat, pound, or pulverize with or as if with a pestle ~ *vi* : to work with a pestle : use a pestle

pes·to \ˈpes-(ˌ)tō\ *n* [It, fr. *pesto,* adj., pounded, fr. *pestare* to pound, fr. LL *pistare,* freq. of L *pinsere*] (1937) : a sauce made esp. of fresh basil, garlic, oil, pine nuts, and grated cheese

[1]**pet** \ˈpet\ *n* [perh. back-formation fr. ME *pety* small — more at PETTY] (1508) **1 a** : a pampered and usu. spoiled child **b** : a person who is treated with unusual kindness or consideration : DARLING **2** : a domesticated animal kept for pleasure rather than utility

[2]**pet** *adj* (1584) **1** : kept or treated as a pet **2** : expressing fondness or endearment ⟨a ~ name⟩ **3** : FAVORITE ⟨a ~ project⟩

[3]**pet** *vb* **pet·ted; pet·ting** *vt* (1629) **1 a** : to treat as a pet **b** : to stroke in a gentle or loving manner **2** : to treat with unusual kindness and consideration : PAMPER ~ *vi* : to engage in amorous embracing, caressing, and kissing : NECK — **pet·ter** *n*

[4]**pet** *n* [origin unknown] (1581) : a fit of peevishness, sulkiness, or anger

[5]**pet** *vi* **pet·ted; pet·ting** (1629) : to take offense : SULK

[6]**pet** *abbr* petroleum

Pet *abbr* Peter

PET *abbr* positron-emission tomography

peta- *comb form* [ISV, modif. of Gk *penta-* penta-] : quadrillion (10^{15}) ⟨*peta*-electron volts⟩

pet·al \ˈpe-tᵊl\ *n* [NL *petalum,* fr. Gk *petalon;* akin to Gk *petannynai* to spread out — more at FATHOM] (ca. 1726) : one of the modified often brightly colored leaves of the corolla of a flower — see FLOWER illustration — **pet·aled** *or* **pet·alled** \-tᵊld\ *adj* — **pet·al·like** \-tᵊl-ˌ(l)īk\ *adj*

pet·al·oid \ˈpe-tə-ˌlȯid\ *adj* (1730) **1** : resembling a flower petal **2** : consisting of petaloid elements

pet·al·ous \ˈpe-tə-ləs\ *adj* (1686) **1** : having petals **2** : having (such or so many) petals — used in combination ⟨poly*petalous*⟩

pe·tard \pə-ˈtär(d)\ *n* [MF, fr. *peter* to break wind, fr. *pet* expulsion of intestinal gas, fr. L *peditum,* fr. neut. of *peditus,* pp. of *pedere* to break wind; akin to Gk *bdein* to break wind] (1598) **1** : a case containing an explosive to break down a door or gate or breach a wall **2** : a firework that explodes with a loud report

pet·a·sos *or* **pet·a·sus** \ˈpe-tə-səs\ *n* [L & Gk; L *petasus,* fr. Gk *petasos;* akin to Gk *petannynai* to spread out] (1577) : a broad-brimmed low-crowned hat worn by ancient Greeks and Romans; *esp* : the winged hat of Hermes

pet·cock \ˈpet-ˌkäk\ *n* [*pet-* (perh. fr. *petty*) + *cock*] (ca. 1864) : a small cock, faucet, or valve for releasing a gas (as air) or draining

pe·te·chia \pə-ˈtē-kē-ə\ *n, pl* **-chi·ae** \-kē-ˌī\ [NL, fr. It *petecchia,* ultim. fr. L *impetigo*] (ca. 1784) : a minute reddish or purplish spot containing blood that appears in skin or mucous membrane as a result of localized hemorrhage — **pe·te·chi·al** \-kē-əl\ *adj*

[1]**pe·ter** \ˈpē-tər\ *vi* [origin unknown] (1846) **1** : to diminish gradually and come to an end : GIVE OUT — usu. used with *out* ⟨novelists whose creative impetus seems largely to have ~*ed* out —*Times Lit. Supp.*⟩ **2** : to become exhausted — usu. used with *out*

[2]**peter** *n* [fr. the name *Peter*] (ca. 1902) *often vulgar* : PENIS

Pe·ter \ˈpē-tər\ *n* [LL *Petrus,* fr. Gk *Petros,* fr. *petra* rock] **1** : a fisherman of Galilee and one of the twelve apostles **2** : either of two hortatory letters written to early Christians and included as books of the New Testament — see BIBLE table

Peter Pan \-ˈpan\ *n* (1904) **1** : a boy in Sir James Barrie's play *Peter Pan* who lives without growing older in a never-never land **2** : an adult who does not want to grow up : one who hangs on to adolescent interests and attitudes

Peter Pan collar *n* (1908) : a usu. small flat close-fitting collar with rounded ends that meet at the top in front

Peter Principle *n* [Laurence J. *Peter* †1990 Am. (Canad.-born) educator] (1968) : an observation: in a hierarchy employees tend to rise to the level of their incompetence

Peter's pence *n pl but sing in constr* [ME; fr. the tradition that St. Peter founded the papal see] (14c) **1** : an annual tribute of a penny formerly paid by each householder in England to the papal see **2** : a voluntary annual contribution made by Roman Catholics to the pope

pet·i·o·lar \ˌpe-tē-ˈō-lər\ *adj* (1760) : of, relating to, or proceeding from a petiole

pet·i·o·late \ˈpe-tē-ə-ˌlāt, ˌpe-tē-ˈō-lət\ *adj* (ca. 1753) : having a stalk or petiole

pet·i·ole \ˈpe-tē-ˌōl\ *n* [NL *petiolus,* fr. L *petiolus, peciolus* small foot, fruit stalk, prob. alter. of L **pediciolus,* dim. of *pediculus,* dim. of *ped-, pes* foot — more at FOOT] (1753) **1** : a slender stem that supports the blade of a foliage leaf **2** : PEDUNCLE; *specif* : a slender abdominal segment joining the rest of the abdomen to the thorax in some insects — **pet·i·oled** \-ˌōld\ *adj*

pet·i·o·lule \ˈpe-tē-ō-ˌlül, ˌpe-tē-ˈōl-(ˌ)yül\ *n* [NL *petiolulus,* dim. of *petiolus*] (1832) : a stalk of a leaflet of a compound leaf

pet·it \ˈpe-tē\ *adj* [ME, small, minor, fr. AF, small] (14c) : PETTY 1 — used chiefly in legal compounds

pe·tit bourgeois \pə-ˈtē-, ˌpe-tē-\ *n* [F, lit., small bourgeois] (1828) **1** : a member of the petite bourgeoisie **2** : PETITE BOURGEOISIE — **petit bourgeois** *adj*

[1]**pe·tite** \pə-ˈtēt\ *adj* [F, fem. of *petit*] (1784) : having a small trim figure — usu. used of a woman — **pe·tite·ness** *n*

[2]**petite** *n* (ca. 1929) : a clothing size for short women

petite bourgeoisie *n* [F, lit., small bourgeoisie] (1916) : the lower middle class including esp. small shopkeepers and artisans

petite si·rah *also* **petite sy·rah** \-sə-ˈrä\ *n, often cap P & S* [F *petite syrah,* lit., little syrah (a grape variety)] (1948) : a dry red wine of spicy fruitiness made from a grape grown chiefly in California; *also* : the grape

pe·tit four \ˌpe-tē-ˈfȯr, pə-ˌtē-, -ˈfu̇r\ *n, pl* **petits fours** *or* **petit fours** \-ˈfȯrz, -ˈfu̇r(z)\ [F, lit., small oven] (1884) : a small cake cut from pound or sponge cake and frosted

[1]**pe·ti·tion** \pə-ˈti-shən\ *n* [ME, fr. AF, fr. L *petition-, petitio,* fr. *petere* to seek, request — more at FEATHER] (14c) **1** : an earnest request : ENTREATY **2 a** : a formal written request made to an official person or organized body (as a court) **b** : a document embodying such a formal written request **3** : something asked or requested — **pe·ti·tion·ary** \-ˈti-shə-ˌner-ē\ *adj*

[2]**petition** *vb* **pe·ti·tioned; pe·ti·tion·ing** \-ˈti-sh(ə-)niŋ\ *vt* (1607) : to make a request to : SOLICIT ~ *vi* : to make a request; *esp* : to make a formal written request — **pe·ti·tion·er** \-sh(ə-)nər\ *n*

pe·ti·tio prin·ci·pii \pə-ˈtē-tē-ˌō-(ˌ)priŋ-ˈki-pē-ˌē\ *n* [ML, lit., postulation of the beginning, begging the question] (ca. 1531) : a logical fallacy in which a premise is assumed to be true without warrant or in which what is to be proved is implicitly taken for granted

pet·it jury \ˈpe-tē-\ *n* (15c) : a jury of 12 persons impaneled to try and to decide finally upon the facts at issue in causes for trial in a court

petit larceny *n* (ca. 1580) : larceny involving property of a value below a legally established minimum

pe·tit–maî·tre \pə-ˌtē-ˈmātrᵊ\ *n, pl* **petits–maîtres** *same*\ [F, lit., small master] (1711) : DANDY, FOP

pe·tit mal \ˈpe-tē-ˌmal, -ˌmäl\ *n* [F, lit., small illness] (1874) : epilepsy characterized by mild seizures marked by diminished awareness usu. with a blank stare but not by loss of consciousness; *also* : one of these seizures — compare GRAND MAL

pet·it point \ˈpe-tē-ˌpȯint\ *n* [F, lit., small point] (ca. 1882) : TENT STITCH; *also* : embroidery made with this stitch

pet peeve *n* (ca. 1919) : a frequent subject of complaint

petr- *or* **petri-** *or* **petro-** *comb form* [NL, fr. Gk *petr-, petro-,* fr. *petros* stone & *petra* rock] **1** : stone : rock ⟨*petro*logy⟩ **2** : petroleum ⟨*petro*dollar⟩

pe·tra·le sole \pə-ˈträ-lē-\ *n* [*petrale* prob. fr. It dial., a flatfish] (1953) : a flounder (*Eopsetta jordani*) chiefly of the Pacific waters of No. America that is an important food fish — called also *petrale*

Pe·trar·chan sonnet \pi-ˈträr-kən-, ˌpē-, (ˌ)pe-\ *n* [*Petrarch* (Francesco Petrarca)] (ca. 1909) : ITALIAN SONNET

pe·trel \ˈpe-trəl, ˈpē-\ *n* [alter. of earlier *pitteral*] (1676) : any of numerous seabirds (esp. families Procellariidae and Hydrobatidae); *esp* : one of the smaller long-winged birds that fly far from land — compare STORM PETREL

pe·tri dish \ˈpē-trē-\ *n* [Julius R. *Petri* †1921 Ger. bacteriologist] (ca. 1892) **1** : a small shallow dish of thin glass or plastic with a loose cover used esp. for cultures in bacteriology **2** : something (as a place or situation) that fosters development or innovation ⟨the college was a *petri dish* for radical views⟩

pet·ri·fac·tion \ˌpe-trə-ˈfak-shən\ *n* (15c) **1** : the process of petrifying **2** : something petrified **3** : the quality or state of being petrified

pet·ri·fi·ca·tion \ˌpe-trə-fə-ˈkā-shən\ *n* (ca. 1611) : PETRIFACTION

pet·ri·fy \ˈpe-trə-ˌfī\ *vb* **-fied; -fy·ing** [MF *petrifier,* fr. *petr-* + *-ifier* -ify] *vt* (1594) **1** : to convert (organic matter) into stone or a substance of stony hardness by the infiltration of water and the deposition of dissolved mineral matter **2** : to make rigid or inert like stone: **a** : to make lifeless or inactive : DEADEN ⟨slogans are apt to ~ a man's thinking —*Saturday Rev.*⟩ **b** : to confound with fear, amazement, or awe ⟨a novel about an airline pilot that will ~ you —Martin Levin⟩ ~ *vi* : to become stone or of stony hardness or rigidity

Pe·trine \ˈpē-ˌtrīn\ *adj* [LL *Petrus* Peter] (1841) **1** : of, relating to, or characteristic of the apostle Peter or the doctrines associated with his name **2** : of, relating to, or characteristic of Peter the Great or his reign

pet·ro·chem·i·cal \ˌpe-trō-ˈke-mi-kəl\ *n* (1942) : a chemical isolated or derived from petroleum or natural gas — **pet·ro·chem·is·try** \-ˈke-mə-strē\ *n*

pet·ro·dol·lar \ˈpe-trō-ˌdä-lər\ *n* (1974) : a dollar's worth of foreign exchange obtained by a petroleum-exporting country through sales abroad — usu. used in pl.

pet·ro·gen·e·sis \ˌpe-trō-ˈje-nə-səs\ *n* [NL] (1901) : the origin or formation of rocks — **pet·ro·ge·net·ic** \-jə-ˈne-tik\ *adj*

pet·ro·glyph \ˈpe-trə-ˌglif\ *n* [F *pétroglyphe,* fr. *pétr-* petr- + *-glyphe* (as in *hiéroglyphe* hieroglyph)] (1870) : a carving or inscription on a rock

pe·trog·ra·phy \pə-ˈträ-grə-fē, pe-\ *n* [NL *petrographia,* fr. *petr-* + L *-graphia* -graphy] (1651) : the description and systematic classification of rocks — **pe·trog·ra·pher** \-fər\ *n* — **pet·ro·graph·ic** \ˌpe-trə-ˈgra-fik\ *or* **pet·ro·graph·i·cal** \-fi-kəl\ *adj* — **pet·ro·graph·i·cal·ly** \-fi-k(ə-)lē\ *adv*

pet·rol \ˈpe-trəl, -ˌträl\ *n* [F *essence de pétrole,* lit., essence of petroleum] (1895) *chiefly Brit* : GASOLINE

pet·ro·la·tum \ˌpe-trə-ˈlā-təm, -ˈlä-\ *n* [NL, fr. ML *petroleum*] (1887) : PETROLEUM JELLY

pe·tro·leum \pə-ˈtrō-lē-əm, -ˈtrōl-yəm\ *n* [ME, fr. ML, fr. L *petr-* + *oleum* oil — more at OIL] (15c) : an oily flammable bituminous liquid that may vary from almost colorless to black, occurs in many places in the upper strata of the earth, is a complex mixture of hydrocarbons with small amounts of other substances, and is prepared for use as gasoline, naphtha, or other products by various refining processes

petroleum jelly *n* (1883) **:** a neutral unctuous odorless tasteless substance obtained from petroleum and used esp. in ointments and dressings

pe·trol·o·gy \pə-ˈträ-lə-jē, pe-\ *n* [ISV] (1811) **:** a science that deals with the origin, history, occurrence, structure, chemical composition, and classification of rocks — **pet·ro·log·ic** \ˌpe-trə-ˈlä-jik\ *or* **pet·ro·log·i·cal** \-ji-kəl\ *adj* — **pet·ro·log·i·cal·ly** \-ji-k(ə-)lē\ *adv* — **pe·trol·o·gist** \pə-ˈträ-lə-jist, pe-\ *n*

pet·ro·nel \ˌpe-trə-ˈnel\ *n* [perh. modif. of MF *poitrinal, petrinal,* fr. *poitrinal* of the chest, fr. *poitrine* chest, ultim. fr. L *pector-, pectus* — more at PECTORAL] (ca. 1577) **:** a portable firearm resembling a carbine of large caliber

pe·tro·sal \pə-ˈtrō-səl\ *adj* [NL *petrosa* petrous portion of the temporal bone, fr. L, fem. of *petrosus*] (1713) **:** of, relating to, or situated in the region of the petrous portion of the temporal bone or capsule of the inner ear

pe·trous \ˈpe-trəs, ˈpē-\ *adj* [ME, fr. AF **petros,* fr. L *petrosus,* fr. *petra* rock, fr. Gk] (14c) **:** of, relating to, or constituting the exceptionally hard and dense portion of the human temporal bone that contains the internal auditory organs

PET scan \ˈpet-\ *n* (1980) **:** a sectional view of the body constructed by positron-emission tomography — **PET scanner** *n* — **PET scanning** *n*

[1]**pet·ti·coat** \ˈpe-tē-ˌkōt\ *n* [ME *petycote* short tunic, petticoat, fr. *pety* small + *cote* coat] (15c) **1 :** a skirt worn by women, girls, or young children: as **a :** an outer skirt formerly worn by women and small children **b :** a fancy skirt made to show below a draped-up overskirt **c :** an underskirt usu. a little shorter than outer clothing and often made with a ruffled, pleated, or lace edge **d** *archaic* **:** the skirt of a woman's riding habit **2 a :** a garment characteristic or typical of women **b :** WOMAN **3 :** something (as a valance) resembling a petticoat — **pet·ti·coat·ed** \-ˌkō-təd\ *adj*

[2]**petticoat** *adj* (1620) **:** of, relating to, or exercised by women **:** FEMALE

pet·ti·fog·ger \ˈpe-tē-ˌfó-gər, -ˌfä-\ *n* [prob. fr. *petty* + obs. E *fogger* pettifogger] (1564) **1 :** a lawyer whose methods are petty, underhanded, or disreputable **:** SHYSTER **2 :** one given to quibbling over trifles — **pet·ti·fog·ging** \-giŋ\ *adj or n* — **pet·ti·fog·gery** \-g(ə-)rē\ *n*

petting zoo *n* (1965) **:** a collection of farm animals or gentle exotic animals for children to pet and feed

pet·tish \ˈpe-tish\ *adj* [prob. fr. [4]*pet*] (ca. 1552) **:** FRETFUL, PEEVISH — **pet·tish·ly** *adv* — **pet·tish·ness** *n*

pet·ti·toes \ˈpe-tē-ˌtōz\ *n pl* [pl. of obs. *pettytoe* offal] (ca. 1555) **1 :** the feet of a pig used as food **2 :** TOES, FEET

pet·ty \ˈpe-tē\ *adj* **pet·ti·er; -est** [ME *pety* small, minor, alter. of *petit*] (14c) **1 :** having secondary rank or importance **:** MINOR, SUBORDINATE **2 :** having little or no importance or significance **3 :** marked by or reflective of narrow interests and sympathies **:** SMALL-MINDED — **pet·ti·ly** \ˈpe-tə-lē\ *adv* — **pet·ti·ness** \ˈpe-tē-nəs\ *n*

petty cash *n* (1715) **:** cash kept on hand for payment of minor items

petty larceny *n* (ca. 1580) **:** PETIT LARCENY

petty officer *n* (1744) **:** a subordinate officer in the navy or coast guard appointed from among the enlisted men — compare NONCOMMISSIONED OFFICER

petty officer first class *n* (1917) **:** an enlisted man in the navy or coast guard ranking above a petty officer second class and below a chief petty officer

petty officer second class *n* (1917) **:** an enlisted man in the navy or coast guard ranking above a petty officer third class and below a petty officer first class

petty officer third class *n* (1917) **:** an enlisted man in the navy or coast guard ranking above a seaman and below a petty officer second class

pet·u·lance \ˈpe-chə-lən(t)s\ *n* (1535) **:** the quality or state of being petulant **:** PEEVISHNESS

pet·u·lan·cy \-lən(t)-sē\ *n* (1537) *archaic* **:** PETULANCE

pet·u·lant \-lənt\ *adj* [L or MF; MF, fr. L *petulant-, petulans;* akin to L *petere* to go to, attack, seek — more at FEATHER] (1598) **1 :** insolent or rude in speech or behavior **2 :** characterized by temporary or capricious ill humor **:** PEEVISH — **pet·u·lant·ly** *adv*

pe·tu·nia \pi-ˈtün-yə, -ˈtyün-\ *n* [NL, fr. obs. F *petun* tobacco, fr. Tupi *petíma*] (1825) **:** any of a genus (*Petunia*) of tropical So. American herbs of the nightshade family with flowers having funnel-shaped corollas

pew \ˈpyü\ *n* [ME *pewe,* fr. MF dial. (Picardy) *puie* balustrade, fr. L *podia,* pl. of *podium* parapet, podium, fr. Gk *podion* base, dim. of *pod-, pous* foot — more at FOOT] (14c) **1 :** a compartment in the auditorium of a church providing seats for several persons **2 :** one of the benches with backs and sometimes doors fixed in rows in a church

pe·wee \ˈpē-(ˌ)wē\ *n* [imit.] (1796) **:** any of various small largely gray or olive-colored American flycatchers (genus *Contopus*)

pew·hold·er \ˈpyü-ˌhōl-dər\ *n* (1822) **:** a renter or owner of a pew

pewit *var of* PEEWIT

pew·ter \ˈpyü-tər\ *n* [ME, fr. AF *peutre,* fr. VL **piltrum*] (14c) **1 :** any of various alloys having tin as chief component; *esp* **:** a dull alloy with lead formerly used for domestic utensils **2 :** utensils of pewter **3 :** a bluish gray — **pewter** *adj*

pew·ter·er \ˈpyü-tər-ər\ *n* (14c) **:** one that makes pewter utensils

pey·o·te \pā-ˈō-tē\ *also* **pey·otl** \-ˈō-tᵊl\ *n* [MexSp *peyote,* fr. Nahuatl *peyotl* peyote cactus] (1849) **1 :** a hallucinogenic drug containing mescaline that is derived from peyote buttons and used esp. in the religious ceremonies of some American Indian peoples **2 :** a small low spineless cactus (*Lophophora williamsii*) of the southwestern U.S. and Mexico having rounded stems covered with jointed tubercles — called also *mescal*

peyote button *n* (1921) **:** one of the dried discoid tops of the peyote cactus

pf *abbr* **1** personal foul **2** pfenning **3** picofarad **4** [It *più forte*] louder **5** preferred

PFC *or* **Pfc** *abbr* private first class

PFD *abbr* personal flotation device

pfen·nig \ˈfe-nig, -nik, *G* ˈ(p)fe-nik\ *n, pl* **pfennig** *also* **pfen·nigs** \ˈfe-nigz, -niks\ *or* **pfen·ni·ge** \ˈ(p)fe-ni-gə, -ni-yə\ [G, fr. OHG *pfenning* — more at PENNY] (1549) **:** a former monetary unit equal to 1/100 deutsche mark

p53 \ˌpē-ˌfif-tē-ˈthrē\ *n* [fr. *p53,* the protein made by the gene, fr. *protein* + *53,* the gene's molecular weight] (1990) **:** a tumor suppressor gene that in an inactivated form tends to be associated with a high risk of certain cancers

PFLAG *abbr* Parents, Families, and Friends of Lesbians and Gays

pg *abbr* **1** page **2** picogram

[1]**PG** *abbr* **1** postgraduate **2** prostaglandin

[2]**PG** \ˈpē-ˈjē\ *certification mark* — used to certify that a motion picture is of such a nature that all ages may be allowed admission but parental guidance is suggested; compare G, NC-17, PG-13, R

PGA *abbr* Professional Golfers' Association

PG–13 \-ˌthər(t)-ˈtēn\ *certification mark* — used to certify that a motion picture is of such a nature that persons of all ages may be admitted but parental guidance is suggested esp. for children under 13; compare G, NC-17, PG, R

pH \ˈpē-ˈāch\ *n* [G, fr. *P*otenz power + *H* (symbol for hydrogen)] (1909) **:** a measure of acidity and alkalinity of a solution that is a number on a scale on which a value of 7 represents neutrality and lower numbers indicate increasing acidity and higher numbers increasing alkalinity and on which each unit of change represents a tenfold change in acidity or alkalinity and that is the negative logarithm of the effective hydrogen-ion concentration or hydrogen-ion activity in gram equivalents per liter of the solution; *also* **:** the condition represented by a pH number

PH *abbr* **1** pinch hit **2** public health **3** Purple Heart

Phae·dra \ˈfē-drə\ *n* [L, fr. Gk *Phaidra*] (14c) **:** a daughter of Minos who marries Theseus and falls in love with her stepson Hippolytus

Pha·ë·thon \ˈfā-ə-tən, -ˌthän\ *n* [L, fr. Gk *Phaethōn*] (14c) **:** a son of Helios who drives his father's sun-chariot through the sky but loses control and is struck down by a thunderbolt of Zeus

pha·eton \ˈfā-ə-tən\ *n* [*Phaëthon*] (1742) **1 :** any of various light four-wheeled horse-drawn vehicles **2 :** TOURING CAR

phage \ˈfāj *also* ˈfäzh\ *n* [by shortening] (1925) **:** BACTERIOPHAGE

-phage *n comb form* [Gk *-phagos* one that eats, fr. *-phagos* -phagous] **:** virus or cell that destroys cells ⟨bacterio*phage*⟩ ⟨macro*phage*⟩

-phagia *n comb form* [NL, fr. Gk] **:** -PHAGY ⟨dys*phagia*⟩

phago·cyte \ˈfa-gə-ˌsīt\ *n* [ISV, fr. Gk *phagein* + NL *-cyta* -cyte] (ca. 1884) **:** a cell (as a white blood cell) that engulfs and consumes foreign material (as microorganisms) and debris — **phago·cyt·ic** \ˌfa-gə-ˈsi-tik\ *adj*

phago·cy·tize \ˈfa-gə-sə-ˌtīz, -ˌsī-\ *vt* **-tized; -tiz·ing** (1913) **:** PHAGOCYTOSE

phago·cy·tose \-sə-ˌtōs, -sī-, -ˌtōz\ *vt* **-tosed; -tos·ing** [back-formation fr. *phagocytosis*] (1905) **:** to consume by phagocytosis

phago·cy·to·sis \ˌfa-gə-sə-ˈtō-səs, -sī-\ *n, pl* **-to·ses** \-ˌsēz\ [NL] (1889) **:** the engulfing and usu. the destruction of particulate matter by phagocytes — **phago·cy·tot·ic** \-ˈtä-tik\ *adj*

-phagous *adj comb form* [Gk *-phagos,* fr. *phagein* to eat — more at BAKSHEESH] **:** eating ⟨sapro*phagous*⟩

-phagy *n comb form, pl* **-phagies** [Gk *-phagia,* fr. *phagein*] **:** eating of a (specified) type or substance ⟨geo*phagy*⟩

phal·ae·nop·sis \ˌfa-lə-ˈnäp-səs\ *n, pl* **-nopsis** *also* **-nop·ses** \-ˌsēz\ [NL, fr. Gk *phalaina* moth + *-opsis*] (1846) **:** any of a genus (*Phalaenopsis*) of ornamental epiphytic orchids of southeastern Asia and Australia having fleshy leaves and large showy flowers with broad lateral petals

pha·lange \ˈfā-ˌlanj, fə-ˈ, fā-ˈ\ *n* [F, fr. Gk *phalang-, phalanx*] (1688) **:** PHALANX 2

pha·lan·ge·al \ˌfā-lən-ˈjē-əl, ˌfa-; fə-ˈlan-jē-, fā-\ *adj* (1828) **:** of or relating to a phalanx or the phalanges

pha·lan·ger \fə-ˈlan-jər, ˈfā-ˌ\ *n* [NL, fr. Gk *phalang-, phalanx*] (ca. 1774) **:** any of various small to medium-sized marsupial mammals (family Phalangeridae) of the Australian region that are chiefly arboreal and nocturnal and usu. densely furred

phal·an·stery \ˈfa-lən-ˌster-ē\ *n, pl* **-ster·ies** [F *phalanstère* dwelling of a Fourierist community, fr. L *phalang-, phalanx* + F *-stère* (as in *monastère* monastery)] (1839) **1 a :** a Fourierist cooperative community **b :** a self-contained structure housing such a community **2 :** something resembling a Fourierist phalanstery

pha·lanx \ˈfā-ˌlaŋ(k)s, *Brit usu* ˈfa-\ *n, pl* **pha·lanx·es** *or* **pha·lan·ges** \fə-ˈlan-(ˌ)jēz, fā-, ˈfā-, *Brit usu* fa-\ [L *phalang-, phalanx,* fr. Gk, battle line, digital bone, lit., log — more at BALK] (1553) **1 :** a body of heavily armed infantry in ancient Greece formed in close deep ranks and files; *broadly* **:** a body of troops in close array **2** *pl phalanges* **:** one of the digital bones of the hand or foot of a vertebrate **3** *pl usu phalanxes* **a :** a massed arrangement of persons, animals, or things ⟨a ~ of armed guards⟩ **b :** an organized body of persons ⟨a ~ of lawyers⟩

phal·a·rope \ˈfa-lə-ˌrōp\ *n, pl* **-ropes** *also* **-rope** [F, fr. NL *phalaropod-, phalaropus,* fr. Gk *phalaris* coot + *pod-, pous* foot; akin to Gk *phalios* having a white spot — more at BALD, FOOT] (1771) **:** any of a genus (*Phalaropus*) of small shorebirds related to sandpipers but distinguished by their lobed toes and preference for swimming

phal·lic \ˈfa-lik\ *adj* (1704) **1 :** of or relating to phallicism ⟨a ~ cult⟩ **2 :** of, relating to, or resembling a phallus **3 :** relating to or being the stage of psychosexual development in psychoanalytic theory that follows the anal stage and during which a child becomes interested in his or her own sexual organs — **phal·li·cal·ly** \-li-k(ə-)lē\ *adv*

phal·li·cism \ˈfa-lə-ˌsi-zəm\ *n* (1883) **:** the worship of the generative principle as symbolized by the phallus

phal·lo·cen·tric \ˌfa-lə-ˈsen-trik\ *adj* (1927) **:** centered on or emphasizing the masculine viewpoint — **phal·lo·cen·trism** \-ˈsen-ˌtri-zəm\ *n*

phal·lo·crat·ic \ˌfa-lə-ˈkra-tik, -(ˌ)lō-\ *adj* (1975) **:** relating to, resulting from, or advocating masculine power and dominance

phal·lus \ˈfa-ləs\ *n, pl* **phal·li** \ˈfa-ˌlī, -ˌlē\ *or* **phal·lus·es** [L, fr. Gk *phallos* penis, representation of the penis; prob. akin to L *flare* to blow

\ə\ **abut** \ᵊ\ **kitten**, F table \ər\ **further** \a\ **ash** \ā\ **ace** \ä\ **mop, mar**
\au̇\ **out** \ch\ **chin** \e\ **bet** \ē\ **easy** \g\ **go** \i\ **hit** \ī\ **ice** \j\ **job**
\ŋ\ **sing** \ō\ **go** \ȯ\ **law** \ȯi\ **boy** \th\ **thin** \t͟h\ **the** \ü\ **loot** \u̇\ **foot**
\y\ **yet** \zh\ **vision, beige** \k̲, ⁿ, œ, ue, ʸ\ *see* Guide to Pronunciation

— more at BLOW] (ca. 1613) **1 :** a symbol or representation of the penis **2 :** PENIS

-phane *n comb form* [Gk *phanēs* appearing, fr. *phainein* to show — more at FANCY] **:** substance having a (specified) form, quality, or appearance ⟨hydro*phane*⟩

phan·er·o·gam \ˈfa-nə-rə-ˌgam, fə-ˈner-ə-\ *n* [F *phanérogame,* ultim. fr. Gk *phaneros* visible (fr. *phainein*) + *gamos* marriage] (1861) **:** a seed plant or flowering plant **:** SPERMATOPHYTE

phan·er·o·phyte \ˈfa-nə-rə-ˌfīt, fə-ˈner-ə-\ *n* [Gk *phaneros* + ISV *-phyte*] (1913) **:** a perennial plant that bears its perennating buds well above the surface of the ground

Phan·er·o·zo·ic \ˌfa-nə-rə-ˈzō-ik\ *adj* [Gk *phaneros* + E 2*-zoic*] (1930) **:** of, relating to, or being an eon of geologic history that comprises the Paleozoic, Mesozoic, and Cenozoic or the corresponding systems of rocks — see GEOLOGIC TIME table — **Phanerozoic** *n*

phan·tasm *also* **fan·tasm** \ˈfan-ˌta-zəm\ *n* [ME *fantasme,* fr. AF *fantosme, fantasme,* fr. L *phantasma,* fr. Gk, fr. *phantazein* to present to the mind — more at FANCY] (13c) **1 :** a product of fantasy: as **a :** delusive appearance **:** ILLUSION **b :** GHOST, SPECTER **c :** a figment of the imagination **2 :** a mental representation of a real object — **phan·tas·mal** \fan-ˈtaz-məl\ *adj* — **phan·tas·mic** \-mik\ *adj*

phan·tas·ma \fan-ˈtaz-mə\ *n, pl* **-ma·ta** \-mə-tə\ [L] (1598) **:** PHANTASM 1

phan·tas·ma·go·ria \(ˌ)fan-ˌtaz-mə-ˈgȯr-ē-ə\ *n* [F *phantasmagorie,* fr. *phantasme* phantasm (fr. OF *fantasme*) + *-agorie* (perh. fr. Gk *agora* assembly) — more at AGORA] (ca. 1802) **1 :** an exhibition of optical effects and illusions **2 a :** a constantly shifting complex succession of things seen or imagined **b :** a scene that constantly changes **3 :** a bizarre or fantastic combination, collection, or assemblage — **phan·tas·ma·gor·ic** \-ˈgȯr-ik, -ˈgär-\ *or* **phan·tas·ma·gor·i·cal** \-i-kəl\ *adj*

phantasy *var of* FANTASY

1phan·tom \ˈfan-təm\ *n* [ME *fantosme, fantome,* fr. AF *fantosme* phantasm] (14c) **1 a :** something apparent to sense but with no substantial existence **:** APPARITION **b :** something elusive or visionary **c :** an object of continual dread or abhorrence ⟨the ~ of disease and want⟩ **2 :** something existing in appearance only **3 :** a representation of something abstract, ideal, or incorporeal ⟨she was a ~ of delight —William Wordsworth⟩ — **phan·tom·like** \-ˌlīk\ *adv or adj*

2phantom *adj* (15c) **1 :** of the nature of, suggesting, or being a phantom **:** ILLUSORY **2 :** FICTITIOUS, DUMMY ⟨~ voters⟩

phantom limb *n* (1871) **:** an often painful sensation of the presence of a limb that has been amputated — called also *phantom pain*

phar *abbr* **1** pharmacopoeia **2** pharmacy

pha·raoh \ˈfer-(ˌ)ō, ˈfā-(ˌ)rō\ *n, often cap* [ME *pharao,* fr. OE, fr. LL *pharaon-, pharao,* fr. Gk *pharaō,* fr. Heb *parʿōh,* fr. Egypt *pr-ʿ3*] (bef. 12c) **1 :** a ruler of ancient Egypt **2 :** TYRANT

pharaoh ant *n* (ca. 1947) **:** a small red ant (*Monomorium pharaonis*) that is a common household pest

phar·a·on·ic \ˌfer-ā-ˈä-nik\ *adj, often cap* [F *pharaonique,* fr. *pharaon* pharaoh, fr. LL *Pharaon-, Pharao*] (ca. 1828) **1 :** of, relating to, or characteristic of a pharaoh or the pharaohs **2 :** enormous in size or magnitude ⟨~ construction projects⟩

phar·i·sa·ic \ˌfa-rə-ˈsā-ik\ *adj* [LL *pharisaicus,* fr. LGk *pharisaikos,* fr. Gk *pharisaios* Pharisee] (ca. 1618) **1 :** PHARISAICAL **2** *cap* **:** of or relating to the Pharisees

phar·i·sa·ical \-ˈsā-ə-kəl\ *adj* (1531) **:** marked by hypocritical censorious self-righteousness — **phar·i·sa·ical·ly** \-k(ə-)lē\ *adv* — **phar·i·sa·ical·ness** \-kəl-nəs\ *n*

phar·i·sa·ism \ˈfa-rə-(ˌ)sā-ˌi-zəm\ *n* [NL *pharisaismus,* fr. Gk *pharisaios*] (1583) **1** *cap* **:** the doctrines or practices of the Pharisees **2** *often cap* **:** pharisaical character, spirit, or attitude **:** HYPOCRISY

phar·i·see \ˈfa-rə-(ˌ)sē\ *n* [ME *pharise,* fr. OE *farise,* fr. LL *pharisaeus,* fr. Gk *pharisaios,* fr. Aram *pĕrīshayyā,* pl. of *pĕrīshā,* lit., separated] (bef. 12c) **1** *cap* **:** a member of a Jewish sect of the intertestamental period noted for strict observance of rites and ceremonies of the written law and for insistence on the validity of their own oral traditions concerning the law **2 :** a pharisaical person

pharm *abbr* pharmaceutical; pharmacist; pharmacy

phar·ma \ˈfär-mə\ *n* [short for *pharmaceutical*] (1992) **:** a pharmaceutical company; *also* **:** large pharmaceutical companies as a group

1phar·ma·ceu·ti·cal \ˌfär-mə-ˈsü-ti-kəl\ *adj* [LL *pharmaceuticus,* fr. Gk *pharmakeutikos,* fr. *pharmakeuein* to administer drugs — more at PHARMACY] (1640) **:** of, relating to, or engaged in pharmacy or the manufacture and sale of pharmaceuticals ⟨a ~ company⟩ — **phar·ma·ceu·ti·cal·ly** \-ti-k(ə-)lē\ *adv*

2pharmaceutical *n* (1881) **:** a medicinal drug

phar·ma·cist \ˈfär-mə-sist\ *n* (1834) **:** a person licensed to engage in pharmacy

pharmaco- *comb form* [Gk *pharmako-,* fr. *pharmakon*] **:** medicine **:** drug ⟨*pharmaco*logy⟩

phar·ma·co·dy·nam·ics \ˌfär-mə-kō-dī-ˈna-miks, -də-\ *n pl but sing in constr* (ca. 1842) **:** a branch of pharmacology dealing with the reactions between drugs and living systems — **phar·ma·co·dy·nam·ic** \-mik\ *adj* — **phar·ma·co·dy·nam·i·cal·ly** \-mi-k(ə-)lē\ *adv*

phar·ma·co·ge·net·ics \ˌfär-mə-kō-je-ˈne-tiks\ *n pl but sing in constr* (1960) **:** the study of how genetic differences among individuals cause varied responses to a drug

phar·ma·co·ge·no·mics \ˌfär-mə-kō-jē-ˈnō-miks\ *n pl but sing in constr* (1997) **:** the science concerned with ways to compensate for genetic differences in patients which cause varied responses to a single drug — **phar·ma·co·ge·no·mic** \-mik\ *adj*

phar·ma·cog·no·sy \ˌfär-mə-ˈkäg-nə-sē\ *n* [ISV, fr. Gk *pharmakon* + *-gnōsia* knowledge, fr. *gnōsis* — more at GNOSIS] (ca. 1885) **:** a branch of pharmacology dealing with medicinal substances of biological origin and esp. medicinal substances obtained from plants — **phar·ma·cog·nos·tic** \-ˌkäg-ˈnäs-tik\ *or* **phar·ma·cog·nos·ti·cal** \-ti-kəl\ *adj*

phar·ma·co·ki·net·ics \-kō-kə-ˈne-tiks, -kō-kī-\ *n pl but sing in constr* (1960) **1 :** the study of the bodily absorption, distribution, metabolism, and excretion of drugs **2 :** the characteristic interactions of a drug and the body in terms of its absorption, distribution, metabolism, and excretion — **phar·ma·co·ki·net·ic** \-tik\ *adj*

phar·ma·col·o·gy \ˌfär-mə-ˈkä-lə-jē\ *n* (1704) **1 :** the science of drugs including their origin, composition, pharmacokinetics, therapeutic use, and toxicology **2 :** the properties and reactions of drugs esp. with relation to their therapeutic value — **phar·ma·co·log·i·cal** \-kə-ˈlä-ji-kəl\ *also* **phar·ma·co·log·ic** \-jik\ *adj* — **phar·ma·co·log·i·cal·ly** \-ji-k(ə-)lē\ *adv* — **phar·ma·col·o·gist** \-ˈkä-lə-jist\ *n*

phar·ma·co·poe·ia *also* **phar·ma·co·pe·ia** \-kə-ˈpē-ə\ *n* [NL, fr. LGk *pharmakopoiia* preparation of drugs, fr. Gk *pharmako-* + *poiein* to make — more at POET] (1621) **1 :** a book describing drugs, chemicals, and medicinal preparations; *esp* **:** one issued by an officially recognized authority and serving as a standard **2 :** a collection or stock of drugs — **phar·ma·co·poe·ial** *also* **phar·ma·co·pe·ial** \-əl\ *adj*

phar·ma·co·ther·a·py \ˌfär-mə-kō-ˈther-ə-pē\ *n* (ca. 1903) **:** the treatment of disease and esp. mental illness with drugs

phar·ma·cy \ˈfär-mə-sē\ *n, pl* **-cies** [LL *pharmacia* administration of drugs, fr. Gk *pharmakeia,* fr. *pharmakeuein* to administer drugs, fr. *pharmakon* magic charm, poison, drug] (1651) **1 :** the art, practice, or profession of preparing, preserving, compounding, and dispensing medical drugs **2 a :** a place where medicines are compounded or dispensed **b :** DRUGSTORE **3 :** PHARMACOPOEIA 2

PharmD *abbr* doctor of pharmacy

pha·ryn·geal \ˌfa-rən-ˈjē-əl, fə-ˈrin-j(ē-)əl\ *adj* [NL *pharyngeus,* fr. *pharyng-, pharynx*] (ca. 1823) **:** relating to or located or produced in the region of the pharynx

phar·yn·gi·tis \ˌfa-rən-ˈjī-təs\ *n, pl* **-git·i·des** \-ˈji-tə-ˌdēz\ (ca. 1844) **:** inflammation of the pharynx

phar·ynx \ˈfa-riŋ(k)s\ *n, pl* **pha·ryn·ges** \fə-ˈrin-(ˌ)jēz\ *also* **phar·ynx·es** [NL *pharyng-, pharynx,* fr. Gk, throat, pharynx; akin to ON *barki* throat and prob. to L *ferire* to strike — more at BORE] (1677) **1 :** the muscular tubular passage of the vertebrate digestive and respiratory tracts extending from the back of the nasal cavity and mouth to the esophagus — compare NASOPHARYNX, OROPHARYNX **2 :** a differentiated part of the alimentary canal in some invertebrates that may be thickened and muscular, eversible and toothed, or adapted as a suctorial organ

1phase \ˈfāz\ *n* [NL *phasis,* fr. Gk, appearance of a star, phase of the moon, fr. *phainein* to show (middle voice, to appear) — more at FANCY] (ca. 1750) **1 :** a particular appearance or state in a regularly recurring cycle of changes ⟨~s of the moon⟩ **2 a :** a distinguishable part in a course, development, or cycle ⟨the early ~s of her career⟩ **b :** an aspect or part (as of a problem) under consideration **3 :** the point or stage in a period of uniform circular motion, harmonic motion, or the periodic changes of any magnitude varying according to a simple harmonic law to which the rotation, oscillation, or variation has advanced from its standard position or assumed instant of starting **4 :** a homogeneous, physically distinct, and mechanically separable portion of matter present in a nonhomogeneous physicochemical system **5 :** an individual or subgroup distinguishably different in appearance or behavior from the norm of the group to which it belongs; *also* **:** the distinguishing peculiarity — **pha·sic** \ˈfā-zik\ *adj* — **in phase :** in a synchronized or correlated manner — **out of phase :** in an unsynchronized manner **:** not in correlation

2phase *vt* **phased; phas·ing** (1904) **1 :** to adjust so as to be in a synchronized condition **2 :** to conduct or carry out by planned phases **3 :** to introduce in stages — usu. used with *in* ⟨~ in new models⟩

phase–contrast *adj* (1934) **:** of or employing the phase-contrast microscope

phase–contrast microscope *n* (1947) **:** a microscope that translates differences in phase of the light transmitted through or reflected by the object into differences of intensity in the image — called also *phase microscope*

phase·down \ˈfāz-ˌdau̇n\ *n* (1964) **:** a gradual reduction (as in operations or size) **:** a slowing down by phases

phase down *vt* (1970) **:** to reduce the size or amount of by phases ⟨*phase down* the program⟩ ~ *vi* **:** to undergo reduction by phases

phase modulation *n* (1930) **:** modulation of the phase of a radio carrier wave by voice or other signal

phase·out \ˈfāz-ˌau̇t\ *n* (1958) **:** a gradual stopping (as in operations or production) **:** a closing down by phases

phase out *vt* (1940) **:** to discontinue the practice, production, or use of by phases ~ *vi* **:** to stop production or operation by phases

-phasia *n comb form* [NL, fr. Gk, speech, fr. *phasis* utterance, fr. *phanai* to speak, say — more at BAN] **:** speech disorder of a (specified) type ⟨dys*phasia*⟩

phas·mid \ˈfaz-məd\ *n* [NL *Phasmida,* group name, fr. *Phasma,* type genus, fr. Gk, apparition, fr. *phainein* to show — more at FANCY] (1872) **:** any of an order (Phasmatodea syn. Phasmida) of large cylindrical or sometimes flattened chiefly tropical insects (as a walking stick) that have long legs, strictly phytophagous habits, and incomplete metamorphosis and that include forms resembling leaves or twigs — **phasmid** *adj*

phat \ˈfat\ *adj* **phat·ter; phat·test** [prob. alter. of 1*fat*] (1963) *slang* **:** highly attractive or gratifying **:** EXCELLENT ⟨a ~ beat moving through my body —Tara Roberts⟩

phat·ic \ˈfa-tik\ *adj* [Gk *phatos,* verbal of *phanai* to speak] (1922) **:** of, relating to, or being speech used for social or emotive purposes rather than for communicating information — **phat·i·cal·ly** \-ti-k(ə-)lē\ *adv*

PhB *abbr* [NL *philosophiae baccalaureus*] bachelor of philosophy

PhD *abbr* [NL *philosophiae doctor*] doctor of philosophy

pheas·ant \ˈfe-zᵊnt\ *n, pl* **pheasant** *or* **pheasants** [ME *fesaunt,* fr. AF *fesant, faisan,* fr. L *phasianus,* fr. Gk (*ornis*) *phasianos,* fr. *phasianos* of the Phasis River, fr. *Phasis,* river in Colchis] (13c) **1 :** any of numerous large often long-tailed and brightly colored Old World gallinaceous birds (*Phasianus* and related genera of the family Phasianidae) including many raised as ornamental or game birds — compare RING-NECKED PHEASANT **2 :** any of various birds resembling a pheasant

phel·lem \ˈfe-ˌlem\ *n* [Gk *phellos* cork + E *-em* (as in *phloem*)] (ca. 1887) **:** a layer of usu. suberized cells produced outwardly by a phellogen

phel·lo·derm \ˈfe-lə-ˌdərm\ *n* [Gk *phellos* + ISV *-derm*] (1875) **:** a layer of parenchyma produced inwardly by a phellogen

phel·lo·gen \ˈfe-lə-jən\ *n* [Gk *phellos* + ISV *-gen*] (1875) **:** a secondary meristem that initiates phellem and phelloderm in the periderm of a stem or root — called also *cork cambium*

phen- *or* **pheno-** *comb form* [obs. *phene* benzene, fr. F *phène,* fr. Gk *phainein* to show; fr. its occurrence in illuminating gas — more at FANCY] **1 :** related to or derived from benzene ⟨*phen*ol⟩ **2 :** containing phenyl ⟨*pheno*barbital⟩

phe·na·caine \ˈfē-nə-ˌkān, ˈfe-\ *n* [prob. fr. *phen*etidine + *acet-* + *-caine*] (1907) : a crystalline base $C_{18}H_{22}N_2O_2$ or its hydrochloride used as a local anesthetic

phen·ac·e·tin \fi-ˈna-sə-tən\ *n* [ISV] (ca. 1887) : a white crystalline compound $C_{10}H_{13}NO_2$ formerly used to ease pain or fever but withdrawn because of its serious side effects — called also *acetophenetidin*

phen·a·kite \ˈfe-nə-ˌkīt, ˈfē-\ *or* **phen·a·cite** \-ˌsīt\ *n* [G *Phenakit,* fr. Gk *phenak-, phenax* deceiver; fr. its being easily mistaken for quartz] (ca. 1834) : a hard glassy mineral that consists of a silicate of beryllium and occurs esp. in rhombohedral crystals

phen·an·threne \fə-ˈnan-ˌthrēn\ *n* [ISV *phen-* + *anthracene*] (1882) : a crystalline tricyclic aromatic hydrocarbon $C_{14}H_{10}$ of coal tar isomeric with anthracene

phen·a·zine \ˈfe-nə-ˌzēn\ *n* [ISV] (1893) : a yellowish crystalline base $C_{12}H_8N_2$ used esp. in organic synthesis

phen·cy·cli·dine \(ˌ)fen-ˈsi-klə-ˌdēn, -ˈsī-, -dən\ *n* [*phen-* + *cycl-* + *-idine*] (1959) : a piperidine derivative $C_{17}H_{25}N$ used chiefly in the form of its hydrochloride esp. as a veterinary anesthetic and sometimes illicitly as a psychedelic drug — called also *angel dust, PCP*

phe·net·ic \fi-ˈne-tik\ *adj* [*phen*otype + *-etic* (as in *genetic*)] (1960) : of or relating to taxonomic analysis that emphasizes the overall similarities of characteristics among biological taxa without regard to phylogenetic relationships

phe·net·ics \-tiks\ *n pl but sing in constr* (ca. 1960) : a system of biological classification based on phenetic methods — **phe·net·i·cist** \-ˈne-tə-sist\ *n*

phen–fen \ˈfen-ˌfen\ *n* (1984) : FEN-PHEN

phen·met·ra·zine \(ˌ)fen-ˈme-trə-ˌzēn\ *n* [*phen*yl + *met*hyl + *tetra-* + *azine*] (1956) : a sympathomimetic stimulant $C_{11}H_{15}NO$ used in the form of its hydrochloride as an appetite suppressant

phe·no·bar·bi·tal \ˌfē-nō-ˈbär-bə-ˌtȯl\ *n* (1919) : a crystalline barbiturate $C_{12}H_{12}N_2O_3$ used as a hypnotic, sedative, and anticonvulsant

phe·no·bar·bi·tone \-bə-ˌtōn\ *n* (ca. 1932) *chiefly Brit* : PHENOBARBITAL

phe·no·copy \ˈfē-nə-ˌkä-pē\ *n* [ISV *pheno*type + *copy*] (1937) : a phenotypic variation that is caused by unusual environmental conditions and resembles the normal expression of a genotype other than its own

phe·no·cryst \-ˌkrist\ *n* [F *phénocryste,* fr. Gk *phainein* to show + *krystallos* crystal — more at FANCY] (1893) : one of the prominent embedded crystals of a porphyry — **phe·no·crys·tic** \ˌfē-nə-ˈkris-tik\ *adj*

phe·nol \ˈfē-ˌnōl, -ˌnȯl, fi-ˈ\ *n* [ISV *phen-* + ³*-ol*] (ca. 1852) **1** : a corrosive poisonous crystalline acidic compound C_6H_5OH present in the tars of coal and wood that in dilute solution is used as a disinfectant **2** : any of various acidic compounds analogous to phenol and regarded as hydroxyl derivatives of aromatic hydrocarbons

phe·no·late \ˈfē-nə-ˌlāt\ *n* (1885) : PHENOXIDE

phe·no·lat·ed \ˈfē-nə-ˌlā-təd\ *adj* (1923) : treated, mixed, or impregnated with phenol

¹**phe·no·lic** \fi-ˈnō-lik, -ˈnä-\ *adj* (ca. 1872) **1 a** : of, relating to, or having the characteristics of a phenol **b** : containing or derived from a phenol **2** : of, relating to, or being a phenolic

²**phenolic** *n* (1926) **1** : a usu. thermosetting resin or plastic made by condensation of a phenol with an aldehyde and used esp. for molding and insulating and in coatings and adhesives — called also *phenolic resin* **2** : PHENOL 2

phe·nol·o·gy \fi-ˈnä-lə-jē\ *n* [*pheno*mena + *-logy*] (ca. 1884) **1** : a branch of science dealing with the relations between climate and periodic biological phenomena (as bird migration or plant flowering) **2** : periodic biological phenomena that are correlated with climatic conditions — **phe·no·log·i·cal** \ˌfē-nə-ˈlä-ji-kəl\ *adj* — **phe·no·log·i·cal·ly** \-k(ə-)lē\ *adv*

phe·nol·phtha·lein \ˌfē-nᵊl-ˈtha-lē-ən, -ˈtha-ˌlēn, -ˈthā-\ *n* [ISV *phenol* + *phthalein* any of various xanthene dyes, fr. *phthalic acid*] (1875) : a white or yellowish-white crystalline compound $C_{20}H_{14}O_4$ used in analysis as an indicator because its solution is brilliant red in alkalies and is decolorized by acids and in medicine as a laxative

phenol red *n* (1916) : a red crystalline compound $C_{19}H_{14}O_5S$ used esp. as an acid-base indicator

phe·nom \ˈfē-ˌnäm, fi-ˈnäm\ *n* (ca. 1890) : PHENOMENON; *esp* : a person of phenomenal ability or promise

phe·nom·e·na \fi-ˈnä-mə-nə, -ˌnä\ *n, pl* **-nas** (1576) *nonstand* : PHENOMENON

usage *Phenomena* has been in occasional use as a singular for more than 400 years and its plural *phenomenas* for more than 350. Our evidence shows that it is primarily a speech form used by poets, critics, and professors, among others, but one that sometimes turns up in edited prose ⟨the Borgia were, in modern terms, a media *phenomena* —*Economist*⟩. It is etymologically no more irregular than *stamina, agenda,* and *candelabra,* but it has nowhere near the frequency of use that they have, and while they are standard, *phenomena* is still rather borderline.

phe·nom·e·nal \fi-ˈnä-mə-nᵊl\ *adj* (1825) : relating to or being a phenomenon: as **a** : known through the senses rather than through thought or intuition **b** : concerned with phenomena rather than with hypotheses **c** : EXTRAORDINARY, REMARKABLE ***syn*** see MATERIAL — **phe·nom·e·nal·ly** \-nᵊl-ē\ *adv*

phe·nom·e·nal·ism \-nə-ˌli-zəm\ *n* (ca. 1865) **1** : a theory that limits knowledge to phenomena only **2** : a theory that all knowledge is of phenomena and that what is construed to be perception of material objects is simply perception of sense-data — **phe·nom·e·nal·ist** \-list\ *n or adj* — **phe·nom·e·nal·is·tic** \-ˌnä-mə-nə-ˈlis-tik\ *adj* — **phe·nom·e·nal·is·ti·cal·ly** \-ti-k(ə-)lē\ *adv*

phe·nom·e·no·log·i·cal \fi-ˌnä-mə-nə-ˈlä-ji-kəl\ *adj* (ca. 1858) **1** : of or relating to phenomenology **2** : PHENOMENAL **3** : of or relating to phenomenalism — **phe·nom·e·no·log·i·cal·ly** \-k(ə-)lē\ *adv*

phe·nom·e·nol·o·gy \fi-ˌnä-mə-ˈnä-lə-jē\ *n, pl* **-gies** [G *Phänomenologie,* fr. *Phänomenon* phenomenon + *-logie* -logy] (ca. 1797) **1** : the study of the development of human consciousness and self-awareness as a preface to or a part of philosophy **2 a (1)** : a philosophical movement that describes the formal structure of the objects of awareness and of awareness itself in abstraction from any claims concerning existence **(2)** : the typological classification of a class of phenomena ⟨the ~ of religion⟩ **b** : an analysis produced by phenomenological investigation — **phe·nom·e·nol·o·gist** \-jist\ *n*

phe·nom·e·non \fi-ˈnä-mə-ˌnän, -nən\ *n, pl* **-na** \-nə, -ˌnä\ *or* **-nons** [LL *phaenomenon,* fr. Gk *phainomenon,* fr. neut. of *phainomenos,* prp. of *phainesthai* to appear, middle voice of *phainein* to show — more at FANCY] (1605) **1** *pl phenomena* : an observable fact or event **2** *pl phenomena* **a** : an object or aspect known through the senses rather than by thought or intuition **b** : a temporal or spatiotemporal object of sensory experience as distinguished from a noumenon **c** : a fact or event of scientific interest susceptible to scientific description and explanation **3 a** : a rare or significant fact or event **b** *pl phenomenons* : an exceptional, unusual, or abnormal person, thing, or occurrence ***usage*** see PHENOMENA

phe·no·thi·a·zine \ˌfē-nō-ˈthī-ə-ˌzēn\ *n* [ISV] (1894) **1** : a greenish-yellow crystalline compound $C_{12}H_9NS$ used as an anthelmintic and insecticide esp. in veterinary practice **2** : any of various phenothiazine derivatives (as chlorpromazine) that are used as tranquilizing agents esp. in the treatment of schizophrenia

phe·no·type \ˈfē-nə-ˌtīp\ *n* [G *Phänotypus,* fr. Gk *phainein* to show + *typos* type] (ca. 1911) : the observable properties of an organism that are produced by the interaction of the genotype and the environment — **phe·no·typ·ic** \ˌfē-nə-ˈti-pik\ *also* **phe·no·typ·i·cal** \-pi-kəl\ *adj* — **phe·no·typ·i·cal·ly** \-pi-k(ə-)lē\ *adv*

phen·ox·ide \fi-ˈnäk-ˌsīd\ *n* (1888) : a salt of a phenol esp. in its capacity as a weak acid

phen·ter·mine \ˈfen-tər-ˌmēn\ *n* [prob. fr. *phen*yl + *ter*t- (fr. *tertiary*) + *amine*] (1962) : an anorectic drug $C_{10}H_{15}N$ used in the form of its hydrochloride to treat obesity

phen·tol·amine \fen-ˈtä-lə-ˌmēn, -mən\ *n* [*phen-* + *tol*uidine + *amine*] (1952) : an adrenergic blocking agent $C_{17}H_{19}N_3O$ used esp. in the diagnosis and treatment of hypertension due to pheochromocytoma

phe·nyl \ˈfe-nᵊl, ˈfē-\ *n* [ISV] (ca. 1850) : a monovalent aryl radical C_6H_5– derived from benzene by removal of one hydrogen atom — often used in combination — **phe·nyl·ic** \fi-ˈni-lik\ *adj*

phe·nyl·al·a·nine \ˌfe-nᵊl-ˈa-lə-ˌnēn, ˌfē-\ *n* [ISV] (ca. 1883) : an essential amino acid $C_9H_{11}NO_2$ that is converted in the normal body to tyrosine

phen·yl·bu·ta·zone \ˌfe-nᵊl-ˈbyü-tə-ˌzōn\ *n* [*phenyl* + *but*yric acid + py*razalone* ($C_3H_4N_2O$)] (1952) : a drug $C_{19}H_{20}N_2O_2$ that is used for its analgesic and anti-inflammatory properties esp. in the treatment of arthritis, gout, and bursitis

phen·yl·eph·rine \-ˈe-ˌfrēn, -frən\ *n* [*phenyl* + epi*nephrine*] (ca. 1947) : a sympathomimetic agent $C_9H_{13}NO_2$ that is used in the form of its hydrochloride as a vasoconstrictor, a mydriatic, a nasal decongestant, and by injection to raise the blood pressure

phen·yl·eth·yl·amine \ˌfe-nᵊl-ˌe-thəl-ˈa-ˌmēn, ˌfē-\ *n* (1910) : a neurotransmitter $C_8H_{11}N$ that is an amine resembling amphetamine in structure and pharmacological properties; *also* : any of its derivatives

phe·nyl·ke·ton·uria \ˌfe-nᵊl-ˌkē-tᵊn-ˈu̇r-ē-ə, ˌfē-, -ˈyu̇r-\ *n* [NL, fr. ISV *phenyl* + *ketone* + NL *-uria*] (1935) : an inherited metabolic disorder caused by an enzyme deficiency resulting in accumulation of phenylalanine and its metabolites in the blood causing usu. severe mental retardation and seizures unless phenylalanine is restricted from the diet beginning at birth — abbr. *PKU* — **phe·nyl·ke·ton·uric** \-ˈu̇r-ik, -ˈyu̇r-\ *n or adj*

phen·yl·pro·pa·nol·amine \ˌfe-nᵊl-ˌprō-pə-ˈnō-lə-ˌmēn, ˌfē-, -ˈnō-; -nō-ˈla-ˌmēn\ *n* [*phenyl* + *propane* + ¹*-ol* + *amine*] (1947) : a sympathomimetic drug $C_9H_{13}NO$ used in the form of its hydrochloride esp. as a nasal and bronchial decongestant and as an appetite suppressant

phen·yl·thio·car·ba·mide \ˌfe-nᵊl-ˌthī-ō-ˈkär-bə-ˌmīd, ˌfē-\ *n* (1879) : a crystalline compound $C_7H_8N_2S$ that is extremely bitter or tasteless depending on the presence or absence of a single dominant gene in the taster — called also *phenylthiourea, PTC*

phen·yl·thio·urea \-ˌthī-ō-yu̇-ˈrē-ə\ *n* (1896) : PHENYLTHIOCARBAMIDE

phe·nyt·o·in \fə-ˈni-tə-wən\ *n* [di*phenyl*hydan*toin*] (1941) : a crystalline anticonvulsant compound $C_{15}H_{12}N_2O_2$ used in the form of its sodium salt in the treatment of epilepsy — called also *diphenylhydantoin*

pheo·chro·mo·cy·to·ma \ˌfē-ə-ˌkrō-mə-sə-ˈtō-mə, -sī-\ *n, pl* **-mas** *also* **-ma·ta** \-mə-tə\ [NL, fr. ISV *pheochromocyte* chromaffin cell (fr. *pheochrome* chromaffin — fr. Gk *phaios* dusky, gray + ISV *-chrome* — + *-cyte*) + NL *-oma*] (1929) : a tumor that is derived from chromaffin cells and is usu. associated with paroxysmal or sustained hypertension

phe·re·sis \fə-ˈrē-səs\ *n, pl* **phe·re·ses** \-ˌsēz\ [prob. back-formation fr. *plasmapheresis*] (1975) : APHERESIS

pher·o·mone \ˈfer-ə-ˌmōn\ *n* [ISV *phero-* (fr. Gk *pherein* to carry) + *-mone* (as in *hormone*) — more at BEAR] (1959) : a chemical substance that is usu. produced by an animal and serves esp. as a stimulus to other individuals of the same species for one or more behavioral responses — **pher·o·mon·al** \ˌfer-ə-ˈmō-nᵊl\ *adj*

phew *a voiceless bilabial fricative usu followed by a voiceless* (y)ü *or* ᵫ *sound; often read as* ˈf(y)ü\ *interj* (1604) **1** — used to express relief or fatigue **2** — used to express disgust at or as if at an unpleasant odor

phi \ˈfī\ *n* [MGk, fr. Gk *phei*] (1638) : the 21st letter of the Greek alphabet — see ALPHABET table

phi·al \ˈfī(-ə)l\ *n* [ME, fr. L *phiala,* fr. Gk *phialē*] (14c) : VIAL

Phi Be·ta Kap·pa \ˌfī-ˌbā-tə-ˈka-pə\ *n* [*Phi Beta Kappa* (*Society*), fr. *phi* + *beta* + *kappa,* initials of the society's Gk motto *philosophia biou kybernētēs* philosophy the guide of life] (1912) : a person winning high scholastic distinction in an American college or university and being elected to membership in a national honor society founded in 1776

Phil *abbr* Philippians

phil- *or* **philo-** *comb form* [Gk, fr. *philos* dear, friendly] : loving : having an affinity for ⟨*philo*progenitive⟩

¹**-phil** *or* **-phile** *n comb form* [F *-phile,* fr. Gk *-philos* -philous] : lover : one having an affinity for or a strong attraction to ⟨acido*phil*⟩ ⟨Slavo*phile*⟩

²**-phil** *or* **-phile** *adj comb form* [NL *-philus,* fr. L, fr. Gk *-philos*] : loving : having a fondness or affinity for ⟨Franco*phile*⟩

\ə\ abut \ᵊ\ kitten, F table \ər\ further \a\ ash \ā\ ace \ä\ mop, mar \au̇\ out \ch\ chin \e\ bet \ē\ easy \g\ go \i\ hit \ī\ ice \j\ job \ŋ\ sing \ō\ go \ȯ\ law \ȯi\ boy \th\ thin \t͟h\ the \ü\ loot \u̇\ foot \y\ yet \zh\ vision, beige \k̲, ⁿ, œ, ᵫ, ʸ\ see Guide to Pronunciation

Phil·a·del·phia lawyer \ˌfi-lə-ˈdel-fyə-, -fē-ə-\ *n* [*Philadelphia,* Pa.] (1788) : a lawyer knowledgeable in the most minute aspects of the law

Philadelphia pepper pot *n* (1929) : PEPPER POT 2b

phil·a·del·phus \ˌfi-lə-ˈdel-fəs\ *n* [NL, fr. Gk *philadelphos* brotherly, fr. *phil-* + *adelphos* brother — more at -ADELPHOUS] (1783) : MOCK ORANGE 1

phi·lan·der \fə-ˈlan-dər\ *vi* **-dered; -der·ing** \-d(ə-)riŋ\ [fr. obs. *philander* lover, philanderer, prob. fr. the name *Philander*] (1737) *of a man* : to have casual or illicit sex with a woman or with many women; *esp* : to be sexually unfaithful to one's wife — **phi·lan·der·er** \-dər-ər\ *n*

phil·an·throp·ic \ˌfi-lən-ˈthrä-pik\ *also* **phil·an·throp·i·cal** \-pi-kəl\ *adj* (1789) **1** : of, relating to, or characterized by philanthropy : HUMANITARIAN **2** : dispensing or receiving aid from funds set aside for humanitarian purposes — **phil·an·throp·i·cal·ly** \-pi-k(ə-)lē\ *adv*

phi·lan·thro·pist \fə-ˈlan(t)-thrə-pist\ *n* (ca. 1736) : one who practices philanthropy

phi·lan·thro·poid \-ˌpȯid\ *n* [blend of *philanthropist* and *anthropoid*] (1945) : a person who works for a philanthropic organization

phi·lan·thro·py \-pē\ *n, pl* **-pies** [LL *philanthropia,* fr. Gk *philanthrōpia,* fr. *philanthrōpos* loving people, fr. *phil-* + *anthrōpos* human being] (ca. 1623) **1** : goodwill to fellowmen; *esp* : active effort to promote human welfare **2 a** : a philanthropic act or gift **b** : an organization distributing or supported by philanthropic funds

phi·lat·e·list \fə-ˈla-tə-list\ *n* (ca. 1865) : a specialist in philately : one who collects or studies stamps

phi·lat·e·ly \fə-ˈla-tə-lē\ *n* [F *philatélie,* fr. *phil-* + Gk *ateleia* tax exemption, fr. *atelēs* free from tax, fr. *a-* + *telos* tax; perh. akin to Gk *tlēnai* to bear; fr. the fact that a stamped letter frees the recipient from paying the mailing charges — more at TOLERATE] (ca. 1865) : the collection and study of postage and imprinted stamps : stamp collecting — **phil·a·tel·ic** \ˌfi-lə-ˈte-lik\ *adj* — **phil·a·tel·i·cal·ly** \-li-k(ə-)lē\ *adv*

Phi·le·mon \fə-ˈlē-mən, fī-\ *n* [Gk *Philēmōn*] (14c) **1** : a friend and probable convert of the apostle Paul **2** : a letter written by St. Paul to a Christian living in the area of Colossae and included as a book in the New Testament — see BIBLE table **3** : a poor aged Phrygian in Greek mythology who with his wife Baucis treats a disguised Zeus hospitably and is rewarded by him with a splendid temple

phil·har·mon·ic \ˌfi-lər-ˈmä-nik, -(ˌ)lär-; ˌfil-(ˌ)här-\ *n* [F *philharmonique,* lit., loving harmony, fr. It *filarmonico,* fr. *fil-* phil- + *armonia* harmony, fr. L *harmonia*] (1843) : SYMPHONY ORCHESTRA

phil·hel·lene \(ˌ)fil-ˈhe-ˌlēn\ *or* **phil·hel·len·ic** \ˌfil-hə-ˈle-nik\ *adj* [Gk *philellēn,* fr. *phil-* + *Hellēn* Hellene] (ca. 1825) : admiring Greece or the Greeks — **philhellene** *n* — **phil·hel·le·nism** \(ˌ)fil-ˈhe-lə-ˌni-zəm\ *n* — **phil·hel·le·nist** \-nist\ *n*

-philia *n comb form* [NL, fr. Gk *philia* friendship, fr. *philos* dear] **1** : friendly feeling toward ⟨Franco*philia*⟩ **2** : tendency toward ⟨hemo*philia*⟩ **3** : abnormal appetite or liking for ⟨necro*philia*⟩

¹-philiac *n comb form* [NL *-philia* + Gk *-akos,* adj. suffix] **1** : one having a tendency toward ⟨hemo*philiac*⟩ **2** : one having an abnormal appetite or liking for ⟨copro*philiac*⟩

²-philiac *adj comb form* **1** : having an abnormal appetite or liking for ⟨pedo*philiac*⟩ **2** : having admiration or partiality for ⟨Anglo*philiac*⟩

-philic *adj comb form* [Gk *-philos* -philous] : having an affinity for : loving ⟨acido*philic*⟩

Phi·lip·pi·ans \fə-ˈli-pē-ənz\ *n pl but sing in constr* [short for *Epistle to the Philippians*] (1549) : a hortatory letter written by St. Paul to the Christians of Philippi and included as a book in the New Testament — see BIBLE table

phi·lip·pic \fə-ˈli-pik\ *n* [MF *philippique,* fr. L & Gk; L *philippica, orationes philippicae,* speeches of Cicero against Mark Antony, trans. of Gk *philippikoi logoi,* speeches of Demosthenes against Philip II of Macedon, lit., speeches relating to Philip] (1592) : a discourse or declamation full of bitter condemnation : TIRADE

Phil·ip·pine mahogany \ˈfi-lə-ˌpēn-\ *n* [*Philippine* Islands] (ca. 1924) : any of several Philippine dipterocarp timber trees (genera *Shorea, Parashorea,* and *Pentacme*) with wood resembling that of the true mahoganies; *also* : its wood

phi·lis·tia \fə-ˈlis-tē-ə\ *n, often cap* [*Philistia,* ancient country of southwest Palestine] (1857) : the class or world of cultural philistines

Phi·lis·tine \ˈfi-lə-ˌstēn; fə-ˈlis-tən, -ˌtēn; ˈfi-lə-stən\ *n* (14c) **1** : a native or inhabitant of ancient Philistia **2** *often not cap* **a** : a person who is guided by materialism and is usu. disdainful of intellectual or artistic values **b** : one uninformed in a special area of knowledge — **philistine** *adj, often cap* — **phi·lis·tin·ism** \-lə-ˌstē-ˌni-zəm; -ˈlis-tə-, -ˌtē-, -lə-stə-\ *n, often cap*

Phil·lips \ˈfi-ləps\ *adj* [fr. *Phillips,* a trademark, fr. Henry M. *Phillips* †1958 Am. engineer] (1935) : of, relating to, or being a screw having a head with a cross slot or the corresponding screwdriver

phil·lu·men·ist \fi-ˈlü-mə-nist\ *n* [*phil-* + L *lumen* light — more at LUMINARY] (1943) : one who collects matchbooks or matchbox labels

Phi·loc·te·tes \fi-ˈläk-tə-ˌtēz, ˌfi-läk-ˈtē-tēz\ *n* [Gk *Philoktētēs*] (14c) : a Greek archer who uses the bow of Hercules to slay Paris at Troy

phil·o·den·dron \ˌfi-lə-ˈden-drən\ *n, pl* **-drons** *also* **-dra** \-drə\ [NL, fr. Gk, neut. of *philodendros* loving trees, fr. *phil-* + *dendron* tree — more at DENDR-] (1877) : any of various aroid plants (as of the genus *Philodendron*) that are cultivated for their showy foliage

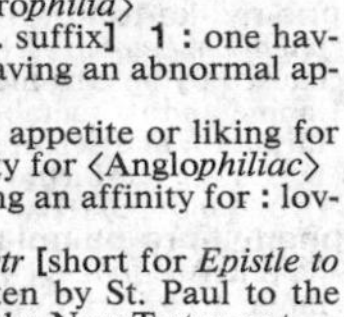

philodendron

phi·lol·o·gy \fə-ˈlä-lə-jē *also* fī-\ *n* [F *philologie,* fr. L *philologia* love of learning and literature, fr. Gk, fr. *philologos* fond of learning and literature, fr. *phil-* + *logos* word, speech — more at LEGEND] (1612) **1** : the study of literature and of disciplines relevant to literature or to language as used in literature **2 a** : LINGUISTICS; *esp* : historical and comparative linguistics **b** : the study of human speech esp. as the vehicle of literature and as a field of study that sheds light on cultural history — **phil·o·log·i·cal** \ˌfi-lə-ˈlä-ji-kəl\ *adj* — **phil·o·log·i·cal·ly** \-k(ə-)lē\ *adv* — **phi·lol·o·gist** \fə-ˈlä-lə-jist *also* fī-\ *n*

Phil·o·mel \ˈfi-lə-ˌmel\ *n* [L *Philomela* Philomela, nightingale] (1579) : NIGHTINGALE

Phil·o·me·la \ˌfi-lə-ˈmē-lə\ *n* [L, fr. Gk *Philomēlē*] (14c) : an Athenian princess in Greek mythology raped and deprived of her tongue by her brother-in-law Tereus, avenged by the killing of his son, and changed into a nightingale while fleeing from him

phil·o·pro·gen·i·tive \ˌfi-lə-prō-ˈje-nə-tiv\ *adj* [*phil-* + L *progenitus,* pp. of *progignere* to beget — more at PROGENITOR] (1865) **1** : tending to produce offspring : PROLIFIC **2** : of, relating to, or characterized by love of offspring — **phil·o·pro·gen·i·tive·ness** *n*

philos *abbr* philosophy

phi·lo·sophe \ˌfē-lə-ˈzȯf\ *n* [F, lit., philosopher] (1779) : one of the deistic or materialistic writers and thinkers of the 18th century French Enlightenment

phi·los·o·pher \fə-ˈlä-s(ə-)fər\ *n* [ME *philosophe, philosophre,* fr. AF, fr. L *philosophus,* fr. Gk *philosophos,* fr. *phil-* + *sophia* wisdom, fr. *sophos* wise] (14c) **1 a** : a person who seeks wisdom or enlightenment : SCHOLAR, THINKER **b** : a student of philosophy **2 a** : a person whose philosophical perspective makes meeting trouble with equanimity easier **b** : an expounder of a theory in a particular area of experience **c** : one who philosophizes

philosopher's stone *n* (14c) : an imaginary stone, substance, or chemical preparation believed to have the power of transmuting baser metals into gold and sought by alchemists; *broadly* : an elusive or imaginary key to success — called also *philosophers' stone*

phil·o·soph·i·cal \ˌfi-lə-ˈsä-fi-kəl *also* -ˈzä-\ *also* **phil·o·soph·ic** \-fik\ *adj* (14c) **1 a** : of or relating to philosophers or philosophy **b** : based on philosophy **2** : characterized by the attitude of a philosopher; *specif* : calm or unflinching in the face of trouble, defeat, or loss — **phil·o·soph·i·cal·ly** \-fi-k(ə-)lē\ *adv*

philosophical analysis *n* (1936) : ANALYTIC PHILOSOPHY

phi·los·o·phise *Brit var of* PHILOSOPHIZE

phi·los·o·phize \fə-ˈlä-sə-ˌfīz\ *vb* **-phized; -phiz·ing** *vi* (1594) **1** : to reason in the manner of a philosopher **2** : to expound a moralizing and often superficial philosophy ~ *vt* : to consider from or bring into conformity with a philosophical point of view — **phi·los·o·phiz·er** *n*

phi·los·o·phy \fə-ˈlä-s(ə-)fē\ *n, pl* **-phies** [ME *philosophie,* fr. AF, fr. L *philosophia,* fr. Gk, fr. *philosophos* philosopher] (14c) **1 a** (1) : all learning exclusive of technical precepts and practical arts (2) : the sciences and liberal arts exclusive of medicine, law, and theology ⟨a doctor of ~⟩ (3) : the 4-year college course of a major seminary **b** (1) *archaic* : PHYSICAL SCIENCE (2) : ETHICS **c** : a discipline comprising as its core logic, aesthetics, ethics, metaphysics, and epistemology **2 a** : pursuit of wisdom **b** : a search for a general understanding of values and reality by chiefly speculative rather than observational means **c** : an analysis of the grounds of and concepts expressing fundamental beliefs **3 a** : a system of philosophical concepts **b** : a theory underlying or regarding a sphere of activity or thought ⟨the ~ of war⟩ **4 a** : the most basic beliefs, concepts, and attitudes of an individual or group **b** : calmness of temper and judgment befitting a philosopher

philosophy of life (1760) **1** : an overall vision of or attitude toward life and the purpose of life **2** [trans. of G *Lebensphilosophie*] : any of various philosophies that emphasize human life or life in general

-philous *adj comb form* [Gk *-philos,* fr. *philos* dear, friendly] : loving : having an affinity for ⟨hygro*philous*⟩

phil·ter \ˈfil-tər\ *n* [MF *philtre,* fr. L *philtrum,* fr. Gk *philtron;* akin to Gk *philos* dear] (ca. 1587) **1** : a potion credited with magical power **2** : a potion, drug, or charm held to have the power to arouse sexual passion

phil·tre *chiefly Brit var of* PHILTER

phi phenomenon *n* (ca. 1928) : apparent motion resulting from an orderly sequence of stimuli (as lights flashed in rapid succession a short distance apart on a sign) without any actual motion being presented to the eye

phish·ing \ˈfi-shiŋ\ *n* [alter. (influenced by *phreaking*) of *fishing*] (1997) : a scam by which an e-mail user is duped into revealing personal or confidential information which the scammer can use illicitly — **phisher** \-shər\ *n*

phiz \ˈfiz\ *n* [by shortening & alter. fr. *physiognomy*] (1685) : FACE

phleb- *or* **phlebo-** *comb form* [Gk *phleb-, phlebo-,* fr. *phleb-, phleps;* perh. akin to Gk *phlyein, phlyzein* to boil over — more at FLUID] : vein ⟨*phleb*itis⟩

phle·bi·tis \fli-ˈbī-təs\ *n* [NL] (ca. 1834) : inflammation of a vein

phle·bol·o·gy \fli-ˈbä-lə-jē\ *n* [ISV] (1893) : a branch of medicine concerned with the veins

phle·bo·to·mus fever \fli-ˈbä-tə-məs-\ *n* [NL *Phlebotomus,* genus of sand flies] (ca. 1923) : SANDFLY FEVER

phle·bot·o·my \fli-ˈbä-tə-mē\ *n, pl* **-mies** [ME *fleobotomie,* fr. MF *flebothomie,* fr. LL *phlebotomia,* fr. Gk, fr. *phleb-* + *-tomia* -tomy] (14c) : the letting of blood for transfusion, diagnosis, or experiment, and esp. formerly in the treatment of disease — called also *venesection* — **phle·bot·o·mist** \-mist\ *n*

Phleg·e·thon \ˈfle-gə-ˌthän\ *n* [L, fr. Gk *Phlegethōn*] (14c) : a river of fire in Hades

phlegm \ˈflem\ *n* [ME *fleume,* fr. AF, fr. LL *phlegmat-, phlegma,* fr. Gk, flame, inflammation, phlegm, fr. *phlegein* to burn — more at BLACK] (13c) **1** : the one of the four humors in early physiology that was considered to be cold and moist and to cause sluggishness **2** : viscid mucus secreted in abnormal quantity in the respiratory passages **3 a** : dull or apathetic coldness or indifference **b** : intrepid coolness or calm fortitude — **phlegmy** \ˈfle-mē\ *adj*

phleg·mat·ic \fleg-ˈma-tik\ *adj* (14c) **1** : resembling, consisting of, or producing the humor phlegm **2** : having or showing a slow and stolid temperament ***syn*** see IMPASSIVE — **phleg·mat·i·cal·ly** \-ti-k(ə-)lē\ *adv*

phlo·em \ˈflō-ˌem\ *n* [G, fr. Gk *phloios, phloos* bark; perh. akin to Gk *phlein* to teem, abound, *phlyein, phlyzein* to boil over — more at FLUID] (1875) : a complex tissue in the vascular system of higher plants that consists mainly of sieve tubes and elongated parenchyma cells usu. with fibers and that functions in translocation and in support and storage — compare XYLEM

phloem necrosis *n* (1923) : a pathological state in a plant characterized by brown discoloration and disintegration of the phloem; *esp* : a fatal disease of the American elm caused by a phytoplasma transmitted by a leafhopper (*Scaphoideus luteolus*)

phloem ray *n* (1875) : a vascular ray or part of a vascular ray that is located in phloem — compare XYLEM RAY

phlo·gis·tic \flō-ˈjis-tik\ *adj* (1732) **1** [Gk *phlogistos*] **:** of or relating to inflammations and fevers **2** [NL *phlogiston*] **:** of or relating to phlogiston

phlo·gis·ton \-tən\ *n* [NL, fr. Gk, neut. of *phlogistos* inflammable, fr. *phlogizein* to set on fire, fr. *phlog-, phlox* flame, fr. *phlegein*] (1733) **:** the hypothetical principle of fire regarded formerly as a material substance

phlog·o·pite \ˈflä-gə-ˌpīt\ *n* [G *Phlogopit,* fr. Gk *phlogōpos* fiery-looking, fr. *phlog-, phlox* + *ōps* face — more at EYE] (1850) **:** a usu. brown to red form of mica

phlox \ˈfläks\ *n, pl* **phlox** *or* **phlox·es** [NL, fr. L, a flower, fr. Gk, flame, wallflower] (ca. 1706) **:** any of a genus (*Phlox* of the family Polemoniaceae, the phlox family) of American annual or perennial herbs that have usu. pink, purplish, white, or variegated flowers, a salverform corolla with the stamens on its tube, and a 3-valved capsular fruit

pH meter *n* **:** an apparatus for measuring the strength or the amount of acid present in a mixture or solution — called also *acidimeter*

pho \ˈfə, ˈfō\ *n* [Vietnamese *phở*] (1935) **:** a soup made of beef or chicken broth and rice noodles

-phobe *n comb form* [Gk *-phobos* fearing] **:** one fearing or averse to (something specified) ⟨Franco*phobe*⟩

pho·bia \ˈfō-bē-ə\ *n* [*-phobia*] (1786) **:** an exaggerated usu. inexplicable and illogical fear of a particular object, class of objects, or situation

-phobia *n comb form* [NL, fr. LL, fr. Gk, fr. *-phobos* fearing, fr. *phobos* fear, flight, fr. *phebesthai* to flee; akin to Lith *bėgti* to flee, OCS *běžati*] **1 :** exaggerated fear of ⟨acro*phobia*⟩ **2 :** intolerance or aversion for ⟨photo*phobia*⟩

pho·bic \ˈfō-bik\ *adj* (1897) **:** of, relating to, affected with, or constituting phobia — **phobic** *n*

-phobic *adj comb form* [F *-phobique,* fr. LL *-phobicus,* fr. Gk *-phobikos,* fr. *-phobia*] **1 a :** having an intolerance or aversion for ⟨photo*phobic*⟩ ⟨Anglo*phobic*⟩ **b :** exhibiting a phobia for ⟨claustro*phobic*⟩ **2 :** lacking affinity for ⟨hydro*phobic*⟩

phoe·be \ˈfē-bē\ *n* [imit.] (1700) **:** any of a genus (*Sayornis*) of the tyrant flycatcher family; *esp* **:** a flycatcher (*S. phoebe*) of the eastern U.S. that has a slight crest and is plain grayish brown above and yellowish white below

Phoe·be \ˈfē-bē\ *n* [L, fr. Gk *Phoibē,* fr. *phoibē,* fem. of *phoibos*] (1567) **:** ARTEMIS

Phoe·bus \ˈfē-bəs\ *n* [L, fr. Gk *Phoibos,* fr. *phoibos* radiant] (14c) **1 :** APOLLO **2** *not cap* **:** SUN

Phoe·ni·cian \fi-ˈnē-shən, -ˈni-\ *n* (14c) **1 :** a native or inhabitant of ancient Phoenicia **2 :** the Semitic language of ancient Phoenicia — **Phoenician** *adj*

phoe·nix \ˈfē-niks\ *n* [ME *fenix,* fr. OE, fr. L *phoenix,* fr. Gk *phoinix*] (bef. 12c) **:** a legendary bird which according to one account lived 500 years, burned itself to ashes on a pyre, and rose alive from the ashes to live another period; *also* **:** a person or thing likened to the phoenix — **phoe·nix·like** \-ˌlīk\ *adj*

phon- *or* **phono-** *comb form* [L, fr. Gk *phōn-, phōno-,* fr. *phōnē* — more at BAN] **:** sound **:** voice **:** speech ⟨*phon*ate⟩ ⟨*phono*graph⟩

pho·nate \ˈfō-ˌnāt\ *vi* **pho·nat·ed; pho·nat·ing** (1876) **:** to produce vocal sounds and esp. speech — **pho·na·tion** \fō-ˈnā-shən\ *n*

[1]**phone** \ˈfōn\ *n* [Gk *phōnē*] (ca. 1866) **:** a speech sound considered as a physical event without regard to its place in the sound system of a language

[2]**phone** *n* [by shortening] (1880) **1 :** TELEPHONE **2 :** EARPHONE

[3]**phone** *vb* **phoned; phon·ing** (1885) **:** TELEPHONE

[1]**-phone** *n comb form* [Gk *-phōnos* sounding, fr. *phōnē*] **1 :** sound ⟨homo*phone*⟩ — often in names of musical instruments and sound-transmitting devices ⟨radio*phone*⟩ ⟨xylo*phone*⟩ **2 :** speaker of (a specified language) ⟨Franco*phone*⟩

[2]**-phone** *adj comb form* [F, fr. Gk *-phōnos*] **:** of or relating to a population that speaks (a specified language) ⟨Franco*phone*⟩

phone card *n* (1982) **:** a prepaid card used for making telephone calls

phone–in \ˈfōn-ˌin\ *n* (1963) **:** a call-in show (as on radio)

pho·ne·mat·ic \ˌfō-nē-ˈma-tik\ *adj* (1935) **:** PHONEMIC

pho·neme \ˈfō-ˌnēm\ *n* [F *phonème,* fr. Gk *phōnēmat-, phōnēma* speech sound, utterance, fr. *phōnein* to sound] (1894) **:** any of the abstract units of the phonetic system of a language that correspond to a set of similar speech sounds (as the velar \k\ of *cool* and the palatal \k\ of *keel*) which are perceived to be a single distinctive sound in the language

pho·ne·mic \fə-ˈnē-mik, fō-\ *adj* (1921) **1 :** of, relating to, or having the characteristics of a phoneme **2 a :** constituting members of different phonemes (as \n\ and \m\ in English) **b :** DISTINCTIVE 2 — **pho·ne·mi·cal·ly** \-mi-k(ə-)lē\ *adv*

pho·ne·mics \-miks\ *n pl but sing in constr* (1934) **1 :** a branch of linguistic analysis involving the study of phonemes **2 :** the structure of a language in terms of phonemes — **pho·ne·mi·cist** \-mə-sist\ *n*

phone sex *n* (1982) **1 :** prerecorded sex-oriented telephone messages available to those who call a commercial service **2 :** sex-oriented telephone conversations (as with an operator employed by a commercial service or with a lover)

phone tag *n* (1984) **:** TELEPHONE TAG

pho·net·ic \fə-ˈne-tik\ *adj* [NL *phoneticus,* fr. Gk *phōnētikos,* fr. *phōnein* to sound with the voice, fr. *phōnē* voice] (1803) **1 :** representing the sounds and other phenomena of speech: as **a :** constituting an alteration of ordinary spelling that better represents the spoken language, that employs only characters of the regular alphabet, and that is used in a context of conventional spelling **b :** representing speech sounds by means of symbols that have one value only **c :** employing for speech sounds more than the minimum number of symbols necessary to represent the significant differences in a speaker's speech **2 a :** of or relating to spoken language or speech sounds **b :** of or relating to the science of phonetics — **pho·net·i·cal·ly** \-ti-k(ə-)lē\ *adv*

phonetic alphabet *n* (1848) **1 :** a set of symbols (as the IPA) used for phonetic transcription **2 :** any of various systems of identifying letters of the alphabet by means of code words in voice communication

pho·ne·ti·cian \ˌfō-nə-ˈti-shən *also* ˌfä-\ *n* (1877) **:** a specialist in phonetics

pho·net·ics \fə-ˈne-tiks\ *n pl but sing in constr* (1836) **1 :** the system of speech sounds of a language or group of languages **2 a :** the study and systematic classification of the sounds made in spoken utterance **b :** the practical application of this science to language study

pho·nic \ˈfä-nik *also* ˈfō-\ *adj* (1823) **1 :** of, relating to, or producing sound **:** ACOUSTIC **2 a :** of or relating to the sounds of speech **b :** of or relating to phonics — **pho·ni·cal·ly** \-ni-k(ə-)lē\ *adv*

pho·nics \ˈfä-niks, *1 is also* ˈfō-\ *n pl but sing in constr* (ca. 1684) **1 :** the science of sound **:** ACOUSTICS **2 :** a method of teaching beginners to read and pronounce words by learning the phonetic value of letters, letter groups, and esp. syllables

pho·no \ˈfō-(ˌ)nō\ *n, pl* **phonos** (1903) **:** PHONOGRAPH

pho·no·car·dio·gram \ˌfō-nə-ˈkär-dē-ə-ˌgram\ *n* [ISV] (1911) **:** a graphic representation of heart sounds made by means of a microphone, amplifier, and recording equipment

pho·no·car·di·og·ra·phy \-ˌkär-dē-ˈä-grə-fē\ *n* (1916) **:** the process of producing a phonocardiogram — **pho·no·car·dio·graph** \-ˈkär-dē-ə-ˌgraf\ *n* — **pho·no·car·dio·graph·ic** \-ˌkär-dē-ə-ˈgra-fik\ *adj*

pho·no·gram \ˈfō-nə-ˌgram\ *n* [ISV] (1864) **1 :** a character or symbol used to represent a word, syllable, or phoneme **2 :** a succession of orthographic letters that occurs with the same phonetic value in several words (as the *ight* of *bright, fight,* and *flight*)

pho·no·graph \ˈfō-nə-ˌgraf\ *n* (1877) **:** an instrument for reproducing sounds by means of the vibration of a stylus or needle following a spiral groove on a revolving disc or cylinder

pho·nog·ra·pher \fə-ˈnä-grə-fər, fō-\ *n* (1845) **:** a specialist in phonography

pho·no·graph·ic \ˌfō-nə-ˈgra-fik, *1 is also* ˌfä-\ *adj* (1828) **1 :** of or relating to phonography **2 :** of or relating to a phonograph — **pho·no·graph·i·cal·ly** \-fi-k(ə-)lē\ *adv*

pho·nog·ra·phy \fə-ˈnä-grə-fē, fō-\ *n* (1701) **1 :** spelling based on pronunciation **2 :** a system of shorthand writing based on sound

pho·no·lite \ˈfō-nə-ˌlīt\ *n* [F, fr. G *Phonolith,* fr. *phon-* + *-lith;* fr. its ringing sound when struck] (1831) **:** a gray or green volcanic rock consisting essentially of orthoclase and nepheline

pho·nol·o·gy \fə-ˈnä-lə-jē, fō-\ *n* (1798) **1 :** the science of speech sounds including esp. the history and theory of sound changes in a language or in two or more related languages **2 :** the phonetics and phonemics of a language at a particular time — **pho·no·log·i·cal** \ˌfō-nə-ˈlä-ji-kəl *also* ˌfä-\ *also* **pho·no·log·ic** \-jik\ *adj* — **pho·no·log·i·cal·ly** \-ji-k(ə-)lē\ *adv* — **pho·nol·o·gist** \fə-ˈnä-lə-jist, fō-\ *n*

pho·non \ˈfō-ˌnän\ *n* [*phon-* + [2]*-on*] (1932) **:** a quantum of vibrational energy (as in a crystal)

pho·no·tac·tics \ˌfō-nə-ˈtak-tiks\ *n pl but sing in constr* (1956) **:** the area of phonology concerned with the analysis and description of the permitted sound sequences of a language — **pho·no·tac·tic** \-tik\ *adj*

[1]**pho·ny** *also* **pho·ney** \ˈfō-nē\ *adj* **pho·ni·er; -est** [perh. alter. of *fawney* gilded brass ring used in the fawney rig, a confidence game, fr. Ir *fáinne* ring, fr. OIr *ánne* — more at ANUS] (1893) **:** not genuine or real: as **a** (1) **:** intended to deceive or mislead (2) **:** intended to defraud **:** COUNTERFEIT **b :** arousing suspicion **:** probably dishonest ⟨something ~ about the story⟩ **c :** having no basis in fact **:** FICTITIOUS ⟨~ publicity stories⟩ **d :** FALSE, SHAM ⟨a ~ name⟩ **e :** making a false show: as (1) **:** HYPOCRITICAL (2) **:** SPECIOUS ⟨has a ~ poetic elegance —*New Republic*⟩ — **pho·ni·ly** \ˈfō-ni-lē\ *adv* — **pho·ni·ness** \ˈfō-nē-nəs\ *n*

[2]**phony** *also* **phoney** *n, pl* **pho·nies** *also* **phoneys** (1902) **:** one that is phony

[3]**phony** *vt* **pho·nied; pho·ny·ing** (1940) **:** COUNTERFEIT, FAKE — often used with *up* ⟨a paper *phonied* up on the spur of the moment —William Faulkner⟩

-phony *also* **-phonia** *n comb form* [L *-phonia,* fr. Gk *-phōnia,* fr. *-phōnos* sounding — more at -PHONE] **1 :** sound ⟨tele*phony*⟩ **2** *usu* *-phonia* **:** speech disorder of a (specified) type ⟨dys*phonia*⟩

pho·ny–ba·lo·ney *or* **pho·ney–baloney** \-bə-ˈlō-nē\ *adj* (1936) **:** PHONY e

phoo·ey \ˈfü-ē\ *interj* (1919) — used to express repudiation or disgust

pho·rate \ˈfȯr-ˌāt\ *n* [*phos*phorus + thio*ate* salt of a thio acid] (1959) **:** a very toxic organophosphate systemic insecticide $C_7H_{17}O_2PS_3$

-phore *n comb form* [NL *-phorus,* fr. Gk *-phoros,* fr. *-phoros* (adj. comb. form) carrying, fr. *pherein* to carry — more at BEAR] **:** carrier ⟨gameto*phore*⟩

-phoresis *n comb form, pl* **-phoreses** [NL, fr. Gk *phorēsis* act of carrying, fr. *phorein* to carry, wear, freq. of *pherein*] **:** transmission ⟨electro*phoresis*⟩

phos·gene \ˈfäz-ˌjēn\ *n* [Gk *phōs* light + *-genēs* born, produced — more at FANCY, -GEN; fr. its originally having been obtained by the action of sunlight] (1812) **:** a colorless gas $COCl_2$ of unpleasant odor that is a severe respiratory irritant that has been used in chemical warfare

phosph- *or* **phospho-** *comb form* [*phosphorus*] **1 :** phosphorus ⟨*phos*phide⟩ **2 :** phosphate ⟨*phospho*fructokinase⟩

phos·pha·tase \ˈfäs-fə-ˌtās, -ˌtāz\ *n* (1912) **:** an enzyme that accelerates the hydrolysis and synthesis of organic esters of phosphoric acid and the transfer of phosphate groups to other compounds: **a :** ALKALINE PHOSPHATASE **b :** ACID PHOSPHATASE

phos·phate \ˈfäs-ˌfāt\ *n* [F, fr. *acide phosphorique* phosphoric acid] (1788) **1 a** (1) **:** a salt or ester of a phosphoric acid (2) **:** the trivalent anion PO_4^{3-} derived from phosphoric acid H_3PO_4 **b :** an organic compound of phosphoric acid in which the acid group is bound to nitrogen or a carboxyl group in a way that permits useful energy to be released (as in metabolism) **2 :** an effervescent drink of carbonated water with a small amount of phosphoric acid flavored with fruit syrup **3 :** a phosphatic material used for fertilizers

phosphate rock *n* (1869) **:** a rock that consists largely of calcium phosphate usu. together with other minerals (as calcium carbonate), is used in making fertilizers, and is a source of phosphorus compounds

phos·phat·ic \fäs-ˈfa-tik, -ˈfā-\ *adj* (1818) **:** of, relating to, or containing phosphoric acid or phosphates ⟨~ fertilizers⟩

phos·pha·tide \ˈfäs-fə-ˌtīd\ *n* [ISV] (1884) **:** PHOSPHOLIPID — **phos·pha·tid·ic** \ˌfäs-fə-ˈti-dik\ *adj*

\ə\ **abut** \ᵊ\ kitten, F table \ər\ **fur**ther \a\ **ash** \ā\ **ace** \ä\ **mop, mar** \au̇\ **out** \ch\ **chin** \e\ **bet** \ē\ **easy** \g\ **go** \i\ **hit** \ī\ **ice** \j\ **job** \ŋ\ **sing** \ō\ **go** \ȯ\ **law** \ȯi\ **boy** \th\ **thin** \t͟h\ **the** \ü\ **loot** \u̇\ **foot** \y\ **yet** \zh\ **vision, beige** \k̲, ⁿ, œ, ue, ʸ\ *see* Guide to Pronunciation

phos·pha·ti·dyl \ˌfäs-fə-ˈtī-dᵊl, fäs-ˈfa-tə-dᵊl\ *n* (1941) **:** any of several monovalent groups $(RCOO)_2C_3H_5OPO(OH)$ that are derived from phosphatidic acids

phos·pha·ti·dyl·cho·line \ˌfäs-fə-ˌtī-dᵊl-ˈkō-ˌlēn, (ˌ)fäs-ˌfa-tə-dᵊl-\ *n* (1954) **:** LECITHIN

phos·pha·ti·dyl·eth·a·nol·amine \-ˌe-thə-ˈnä-lə-ˌmēn, -ˈnō-\ *n* (1942) **:** any of a group of phospholipids that occur esp. in blood plasma and the white matter of the central nervous system — called also *cephalin*

phos·pha·tize \ˈfäs-fə-ˌtīz\ *vt* **-tized; -tiz·ing** (1866) **1 :** to treat with phosphoric acid or a phosphate **2 :** to change to a phosphate or phosphates — **phos·pha·ti·za·tion** \ˌfäs-fə-tə-ˈzā-shən, -ˌfä-\ *n*

phos·pha·tu·ria \ˌfäs-fə-ˈtu̇r-ē-ə, -ˈtyu̇r-\ *n* [NL, fr. ISV *phosphate* + NL *-uria*] (1876) **:** the excessive discharge of phosphates in the urine

phos·phene \ˈfäs-ˌfēn\ *n* [ISV *phos-* + Gk *phainein* to show — more at FANCY] (ca. 1860) **:** a luminous impression due to excitation of the retina

phos·phide \-ˌfīd\ *n* [ISV] (1849) **:** a binary compound of phosphorus with a more electropositive element or group

phos·phine \-ˌfēn\ *n* [ISV] (1869) **1 :** any of various derivatives of phosphine analogous to amines but weaker as bases **2 :** a colorless poisonous flammable gas PH_3 that is a weaker base than ammonia and that is used esp. to fumigate stored grain

phos·phite \-ˌfīt\ *n* (1788) **:** a salt or ester of phosphorous acid

phos·pho·cre·a·tine \ˌfäs-(ˌ)fō-ˈkrē-ə-ˌtēn\ *n* [ISV] (1927) **:** a compound $C_4H_{10}N_3O_5P$ of creatine and phosphoric acid that is found esp. in vertebrate muscle where it is an energy source for muscle contraction

phos·pho·di·es·ter·ase \-dī-ˈes-tə-ˌrās, -ˌrāz\ *n* (1932) **:** a phosphatase (as from snake venom) that acts on diesters (as some nucleotides) to hydrolyze only one of the two ester groups

phos·pho·enol·pyr·uvate \ˌfäs-ˌfō-ə-ˌnȯl-pī-ˈrü-ˌvāt, -ˌnōl-, -ˌpī(-ə)r-ˈyü-\ *n* (1956) **:** a salt or ester of phosphoenolpyruvic acid

phos·pho·enol·pyr·uvic acid \-pī-ˈrü-vik-, -pī(-ə)r-ˈyü-vik-\ *n* (1959) **:** the phosphate $H_2C{=}C(OPO_3H_2)COOH$ of the enol form of pyruvic acid that is formed as an intermediate in carbohydrate metabolism

phos·pho·fruc·to·ki·nase \ˌfäs-(ˌ)fō-ˌfrək-tō-ˈkī-ˌnās, -ˌfrük-, -ˌfru̇k-, -ˌnāz\ *n* [*phosph-* + *fructose* + *kinase*] (1947) **:** an enzyme that functions in carbohydrate metabolism and esp. in glycolysis by catalyzing the transfer of a second phosphate (as from ATP) to fructose

phos·pho·glu·co·mu·tase \-ˌglü-kō-ˈmyü-ˌtās, -ˌtāz\ *n* (1938) **:** an enzyme found in all plant and animal cells that catalyzes the reversible isomerization of glucose-1-phosphate to glucose-6-phosphate

phos·pho·glyc·er·al·de·hyde \-ˌgli-sə-ˈral-də-ˌhīd\ *n* (1941) **:** a phosphate of glyceraldehyde $C_3H_5O_3(H_2PO_3)$ that is formed esp. in anaerobic metabolism of carbohydrates by the splitting of a diphosphate of fructose

phos·pho·glyc·er·ate \ˌfäs-fō-ˈgli-sə-ˌrāt\ *n* (1901) **:** a salt or ester of phosphoglyceric acid

phos·pho·gly·cer·ic acid \-gli-ˈser-ik-\ *n* (1857) **:** either of two isomeric acid phosphates $C_3H_5O_3(OPO_3H_2)$ of glyceric acid that are formed as intermediates in photosynthesis and in carbohydrate metabolism

phos·pho·ki·nase \ˌfäs-fō-ˈkī-ˌnās, -ˌnāz\ *n* (1946) **:** KINASE

phos·pho·li·pase \-ˈlī-ˌpās, -ˌpāz\ *n* (1945) **:** any of several enzymes that hydrolyze lecithins or phosphatidylethanolamines — called also *lecithinase*

phos·pho·lip·id \-ˈli-pəd\ *n* (1928) **:** any of numerous lipids (as lecithins and phosphatidylethanolamines) in which phosphoric acid as well as a fatty acid is esterified to glycerol and which are found in all living cells and in the bilayers of cell membranes

phos·pho·mono·es·ter·ase \-ˌmä-nō-ˈes-tə-ˌrās, -ˌrāz\ *n* (1932) **:** a phosphatase that acts on monoesters

phos·pho·ni·um \fäs-ˈfō-nē-əm\ *n* [NL] (1871) **:** a monovalent cation PH_4^+ analogous to ammonium and derived from phosphine; *also* **:** an organic derivative of phosphonium (as $(C_2H_5)_4P^+$)

phos·pho·pro·tein \ˌfäs-fō-ˈprō-ˌtēn, -ˈprō-tē-ən\ *n* (ca. 1908) **:** any of various proteins (as casein) that contain combined phosphoric acid

phos·phor \ˈfäs-fər, -ˌfȯr\ *also* **phos·phore** \-ˌfȯr, -fər\ *n* [L *phosphorus,* fr. Gk *phōsphoros,* lit., light bringer, fr. *phōsphoros* light-bearing, fr. *phōs* light + *pherein* to carry, bring — more at FANCY, BEAR] (1705) **1 :** a phosphorescent substance **2 :** a luminescent substance that emits light when excited by radiation (as electrons) and is used esp. in fluorescent lamps and cathode-ray tubes

phosphor bronze *n* (1875) **:** a bronze of great hardness, elasticity, and toughness that contains a small amount of phosphorus

phos·pho·resce \ˌfäs-fə-ˈres\ *vi* **-resced; -resc·ing** [prob. back-formation fr. *phosphorescent*] (1794) **:** to exhibit phosphorescence

phos·pho·res·cence \-ˈre-sᵊn(t)s\ *n* (1796) **1 :** luminescence that is caused by the absorption of radiations (as light or electrons) and continues for a noticeable time after these radiations have stopped — compare FLUORESCENCE **2 :** an enduring luminescence without sensible heat

phos·pho·res·cent \-sᵊnt\ *adj* (1766) **:** exhibiting phosphorescence — **phos·pho·res·cent·ly** *adv*

phos·pho·ric \fäs-ˈfȯr-ik, -ˈfär-; ˈfäs-f(ə-)rik\ *adj* (1784) **:** of, relating to, or containing phosphorus esp. with a valence higher than in phosphorous compounds

phosphoric acid *n* (1784) **1 :** a syrupy or deliquescent tribasic acid H_3PO_4 used esp. in preparing phosphates (as for fertilizers), in rust-proofing metals, and esp. formerly as a flavoring in soft drinks — called also *orthophosphoric acid* **2 :** a compound (as pyrophosphoric acid or metaphosphoric acid) consisting of phosphate groups linked directly to each other by oxygen

phos·pho·rite \ˈfäs-fə-ˌrīt\ *n* (1796) **1 :** a fibrous concretionary apatite **2 :** PHOSPHATE ROCK — **phos·pho·rit·ic** \ˌfäs-fə-ˈri-tik\ *adj*

phos·pho·rol·y·sis \ˌfäs-fə-ˈrä-lə-səs\ *n* [NL] (1937) **:** a reversible reaction analogous to hydrolysis in which phosphoric acid functions in a manner similar to that of water with the formation of a phosphate (as glucose-1-phosphate in the breakdown of liver glycogen) — **phos·pho·ro·lyt·ic** \-rō-ˈli-tik\ *adj*

phos·pho·rous \ˈfäs-f(ə-)rəs; fäs-ˈfȯr-əs\ *adj* (1788) **:** of, relating to, or containing phosphorus esp. with a valence lower than in phosphoric compounds

phosphorous acid *n* (1788) **:** a deliquescent crystalline acid H_3PO_3 used esp. as a reducing agent and in making phosphites

phos·pho·rus \ˈfäs-f(ə-)rəs\ *n, often attrib* [NL, fr. Gk *phōsphoros* light-bearing — more at PHOSPHOR] (1645) **1 :** a phosphorescent substance or body; *esp* **:** one that shines or glows in the dark **2** *also* **phos·pho·rous** *same*\ **:** a nonmetallic element of the nitrogen family that occurs widely esp. as phosphates — see ELEMENT table

phos·pho·ryl \ˈfäs-fə-ˌril\ *n* [ISV] (1869) **:** a usu. trivalent group PO

phos·phor·y·lase \fäs-ˈfȯr-ə-ˌlās, -ˌlāz\ *n* (1939) **:** any of the enzymes that catalyze phosphorolysis with the formation of organic phosphates

phos·phor·y·late \-ˌlāt\ *vt* **-lat·ed; -lat·ing** (1937) **:** to cause (an organic compound) to take up or combine with phosphoric acid or a phosphorus-containing group — **phos·phor·y·la·tive** \-ˌlā-tiv\ *adj*

phos·phor·y·la·tion \ˌfäs-ˌfȯr-ə-ˈlā-shən\ *n* (1925) **:** the process of phosphorylating a chemical compound either by reaction with inorganic phosphate or by transfer of phosphate from another organic phosphate; *esp* **:** the enzymatic conversion of carbohydrates into their phosphoric esters in metabolic processes

phot- *or* **photo-** *comb form* [Gk *phōt-, phōto-,* fr. *phōt-, phōs* — more at FANCY] **1 :** light **:** radiant energy ⟨*photon*⟩ ⟨*photography*⟩ **2 :** photograph **:** photographic ⟨*photoengraving*⟩ **3 :** photoelectric ⟨*photocell*⟩

pho·tic \ˈfō-tik\ *adj* (1843) **1 :** of, relating to, or involving light esp. in relation to organisms **2 :** penetrated by light esp. of the sun ⟨the ~ zone of the ocean⟩ — **pho·ti·cal·ly** \ˈfō-ti-k(ə-)lē\ *adv*

1**pho·to** \ˈfō-(ˌ)tō\ *n, pl* **photos** (1860) **:** PHOTOGRAPH

2**photo** *vb* (1868) **:** PHOTOGRAPH

3**photo** *adj* (1888) **:** PHOTOGRAPHIC 1

pho·to·ag·ing \ˌfō-tō-ˈā-jiŋ\ *n* (1986) **:** the cumulative detrimental effects (as wrinkles or dark spots) on skin that result from long-term exposure to sunlight and esp. ultraviolet light

pho·to·au·to·tro·phic \ˌfō-tō-ˌȯ-tə-ˈtrō-fik\ *adj* (1943) **:** autotrophic and utilizing energy from light ⟨green plants are ~⟩ — **pho·to·au·to·troph** \-ˈȯ-tə-ˌtrōf\ *n* — **pho·to·au·to·tro·phi·cal·ly** \-ˌȯ-tə-ˈtrō-fi-k(ə-)lē\ *adv*

pho·to·bi·ol·o·gy \ˌfō-tō-(ˌ)bī-ˈä-lə-jē\ *n* [ISV] (1935) **:** a branch of biology that deals with the effects on living organisms of radiant energy (as light) — **pho·to·bi·o·log·i·cal** \-ˌbī-ə-ˈlä-ji-kəl\ *also* **pho·to·bi·o·log·ic** \-ˈlä-jik\ *adj* — **pho·to·bi·ol·o·gist** \-(ˌ)bī-ˈä-lə-jist\ *n*

pho·to·cath·ode \-ˈka-ˌthōd\ *n* [ISV] (1930) **:** a cathode that emits electrons when exposed to radiant energy and esp. light

pho·to·cell \ˈfō-tə-ˌsel\ *n* [ISV] (1891) **:** PHOTOELECTRIC CELL

pho·to·chem·i·cal \ˌfō-tō-ˈke-mi-kəl\ *adj* (1857) **1 :** of, relating to, or resulting from the chemical action of radiant energy and esp. light ⟨~ smog⟩ **2 :** of or relating to photochemistry ⟨~ studies⟩ — **pho·to·chem·i·cal·ly** \-k(ə-)lē\ *adv*

pho·to·chem·is·try \-ˈke-mə-strē\ *n* (1867) **1 :** a branch of chemistry that deals with the effect of radiant energy in producing chemical changes **2 a :** photochemical properties ⟨the ~ of gases⟩ **b :** photochemical processes ⟨~ of vision⟩ — **pho·to·chem·ist** \-ˈke-mist\ *n*

pho·to·chro·mic \ˌfō-tə-ˈkrō-mik\ *adj* [*phot-* + *chrom-* + *1-ic*] (1953) **1 :** capable of changing color on exposure to radiant energy (as light) ⟨~ glass⟩ **2 :** of, relating to, or utilizing the change of color shown by a photochromic substance ⟨a ~ process⟩ — **pho·to·chro·mism** \-ˌmi-zəm\ *n*

pho·to·co·ag·u·la·tion \-kō-ˌa-gyə-ˈlā-shən\ *n* (1961) **:** a surgical process of coagulating tissue by means of a precisely oriented high-energy light source (as a laser)

pho·to·com·pose \ˌfō-tō-kəm-ˈpōz\ *vt* (1929) **:** to set (as reading matter) by photocomposition — **pho·to·com·pos·er** *n*

pho·to·com·po·si·tion \-ˌkäm-pə-ˈzi-shən\ *n* (1929) **:** composition of text directly on film or photosensitive paper for reproduction

pho·to·con·duc·tive \-kən-ˈdək-tiv\ *adj* (1929) **:** having, involving, or operating by photoconductivity

pho·to·con·duc·tiv·i·ty \-ˌkän-ˌdək-ˈti-və-tē, -kən-\ *n* (1929) **:** electrical conductivity that is affected by exposure to electromagnetic radiation (as light)

1**pho·to·copy** \ˈfō-tə-ˌkä-pē\ *n* [ISV] (ca. 1909) **:** a copy of usu. printed material made with a process in which an image is formed by the action of light usu. on an electrically charged surface

2**photocopy** *vt* (1944) **:** to make a photocopy of ~ *vi* **:** to make a photocopy — **pho·to·copi·er** *n*

pho·to·cur·rent \ˈfō-tō-ˌkər-ənt, -ˌkə-rənt\ *n* (1913) **:** a stream of electrons produced by photoelectric or photovoltaic effects

pho·to·de·com·po·si·tion \-ˌdē-ˌkäm-pə-ˈzi-shən\ *n* (1888) **:** PHOTOLYSIS

pho·to·de·grad·able \-di-ˈgrā-də-bəl\ *adj* (1971) **:** chemically degradable by the action of light ⟨~ plastics⟩

pho·to·de·tec·tor \-di-ˈtek-tər\ *n* (1947) **:** any of various devices for detecting and measuring the intensity of radiant energy through photoelectric action

pho·to·di·ode \-ˈdī-ˌōd\ *n* (1945) **:** a photoelectric semiconductor device for detecting and often measuring radiant energy (as light)

pho·to·dis·in·te·gra·tion \-dis-ˌin-tə-ˈgrā-shən\ *n* (1935) **:** disintegration of the nucleus of an atom caused by absorption of radiant energy (as light) — **pho·to·dis·in·te·grate** \-ˈin-tə-ˌgrāt\ *vt*

pho·to·dis·so·ci·a·tion \-di-ˌsō-sē-ˈā-shən, -shē-\ *n* (1925) **:** dissociation of the molecules of a substance (as water) caused by absorption of radiant energy — **pho·to·dis·so·ci·ate** \-ˈsō-sē-ˌāt, -shē-\ *vb*

pho·to·du·pli·ca·tion \-ˌdü-plə-ˈkā-shən, -ˌdyü-\ *n* (1941) **:** the process of making photocopies — **pho·to·du·pli·cate** \-ˈdü-plə-ˌkāt, -ˈdyü-\ *vb* — **pho·to·du·pli·cate** \-pli-kət\ *n*

pho·to·dy·nam·ic \-(ˌ)dī-ˈna-mik\ *adj* [ISV] (1909) **:** of, relating to, or having the property of intensifying or inducing a toxic reaction to light (as in the destruction of cancer cells stained with a light-sensitive dye) in a living system — **pho·to·dy·nam·i·cal·ly** \-mi-k(ə-)lē\ *adv*

pho·to·elec·tric \ˌfō-tō-i-ˈlek-trik\ *adj* [ISV] (ca. 1879) **:** involving, relating to, or utilizing any of various electrical effects due to the interaction of radiation (as light) with matter — **pho·to·elec·tri·cal·ly** \-tri-k(ə-)lē\ *adv*

photoelectric cell *n* (1891) **:** an electronic device whose electrical properties are modified by the action of light

photoelectric effect *n* (1892) **:** the emission of free electrons from a metal surface when light strikes it

pho·to·elec·tron \ˌfō-tō-i-ˈlek-ˌträn\ *n* [ISV] (1912) **:** an electron released in photoemission — **pho·to·elec·tron·ic** \-ˌlek-ˈträ-nik\ *adj*
pho·to·emis·sion \-i-ˈmi-shən\ *n* (1916) **:** the release of electrons from a usu. solid material (as a metal) by means of energy supplied by incidence of radiation and esp. light — **pho·to·emis·sive** \-ˈmi-siv\ *adj*
pho·to·en·grave \-in-ˈgrāv\ *vt* [back-formation fr. *photoengraving*] (1892) **:** to make a photoengraving of — **pho·to·en·grav·er** *n*
pho·to·en·grav·ing *n* (1872) **1 :** a photomechanical process for making linecuts and halftone cuts by photographing an image on a metal plate and then etching **2 a :** a plate made by photoengraving **b :** a print made from such a plate
pho·to–es·say \ˈfō-tō-ˌe-ˌsā\ *n* (1944) **:** a group of photographs (as in a book or magazine) arranged to explore a theme or tell a story
pho·to·ex·ci·ta·tion \ˌfō-tō-ˌek-ˌsī-ˈtā-shən, -ˌek-sə-\ *n* (1918) **:** the process of exciting the atoms or molecules of a substance by the absorption of radiant energy — **pho·to·ex·cit·ed** \-ik-ˈsī-təd, -ek-\ *adj*
photo finish *n* (1936) **1 :** a race or finish in which contestants are so close that a photograph of them as they cross the finish line has to be examined to determine the winner **2 :** a close contest
pho·to·fin·ish·er \ˌfō-tō-ˈfi-ni-shər\ *n* (ca. 1934) **:** one that develops and prints photographic film — **pho·to·fin·ish·ing** \-shiŋ\ *n*
pho·to·flash \ˈfō-tō-ˌflash\ *n* (1930) **:** FLASH 6f(2)
pho·to·flood \-ˌfləd\ *n* (1933) **:** an electric lamp that provides intense sustained illumination for taking photographs
pho·tog \fə-ˈtäg\ *n* [short for *photographer*] (ca. 1906) **:** one who takes photographs **:** PHOTOGRAPHER
pho·to·ge·nic \ˌfō-tə-ˈje-nik, -ˈjē-\ *adj* (1839) **1 :** produced or precipitated by light ⟨~ dermatitis⟩ **2 :** producing or generating light **:** PHOSPHORESCENT ⟨~ bacteria⟩ **3 :** suitable for being photographed esp. because of visual appeal ⟨a ~ smile⟩ — **pho·to·ge·ni·cal·ly** \-ni-k(ə-)lē\ *adv*
pho·to·ge·ol·o·gy \ˌfō-tō-jē-ˈä-lə-jē\ *n* (1941) **:** a branch of geology concerned with the identification and study of geological features through the study of aerial or orbital photographs — **pho·to·geo·log·ic** \-ˌjē-ə-ˈlä-jik\ *also* **pho·to·geo·log·i·cal** \-ji-kəl\ *adj* — **pho·to·ge·ol·o·gist** \-ˈä-lə-jist\ *n*
pho·to·gram \ˈfō-tə-ˌgram\ *n* [ISV] (1859) **:** a photographic image made by placing objects between light-sensitive paper and a light source
pho·to·gram·me·try \ˌfō-tə-ˈgra-mə-trē\ *n* [ISV *photogram* photograph (fr. *phot-* + *-gram*) + *-metry*] (1875) **:** the science of making reliable measurements by the use of photographs and esp. aerial photographs (as in surveying) — **pho·to·gram·met·ric** \-grə-ˈme-trik\ *adj* — **pho·to·gram·me·trist** \-ˈgra-mə-trist\ *n*
¹**pho·to·graph** \ˈfō-tə-ˌgraf\ *n* (1839) **:** a picture or likeness obtained by photography
²**photograph** *vt* (1839) **:** to take a photograph of ~ *vi* **1 :** to take a photograph **2 :** to appear as an image in a photograph ⟨an actress who ~*s* well⟩
pho·tog·ra·pher \fə-ˈtä-grə-fər\ *n* (1843) **:** one who practices photography; *esp* **:** one who makes a business of taking photographs
pho·to·graph·ic \ˌfō-tə-ˈgra-fik\ *adj* (1839) **1 :** relating to, obtained by, or used in photography **2 :** representing nature and human beings with the exactness of a photograph **3 :** capable of retaining vivid impressions ⟨a ~ memory⟩ — **pho·to·graph·i·cal·ly** \-fi-k(ə-)lē\ *adv*
pho·tog·ra·phy \fə-ˈtä-grə-fē\ *n* (1839) **:** the art or process of producing images by the action of radiant energy and esp. light on a sensitive surface (as film or an optical sensor)
pho·to·gra·vure \ˌfō-tə-grə-ˈvyu̇r\ *n* [F, fr. *phot-* + *gravure*] (1879) **:** a process for printing from an intaglio plate prepared by photographic methods
pho·to·in·duced \ˌfō-tō-in-ˈdüst, -ˈdyüst\ *adj* (1947) **:** induced by the action of light — **pho·to·in·duc·tion** \-ˈdək-shən\ *n* — **pho·to·in·duc·tive** \-ˈdək-tiv\ *adj*
pho·to·in·ter·pre·ta·tion \-in-ˌtər-prə-ˈtā-shən, -pə-\ *n* (1923) **:** the science of identifying and describing objects in photographs — **pho·to·in·ter·pret·er** \-ˈtər-prə-tər, -pə-\ *n*
pho·to·ion·i·za·tion \-ˌī-ə-nə-ˈzā-shən\ *n* (1914) **:** ionization (as in the ionosphere) of a molecule or atom caused by absorption of radiant energy — **pho·to·ion·ize** \-ˈī-ə-ˌnīz\ *vt*
pho·to·jour·nal·ism \ˌfō-tō-ˈjər-nə-ˌli-zəm\ *n* (1938) **:** journalism in which written copy is subordinate to pictorial usu. photographic presentation of news stories or in which a high proportion of pictorial presentation is used; *broadly* **:** news photography — **pho·to·jour·nal·ist** \-nə-list\ *n* — **pho·to·jour·nal·is·tic** \-ˌjər-nə-ˈlis-tik\ *adj*
pho·to·ki·ne·sis \-kə-ˈnē-səs, -kī-\ *n* [NL] (1905) **:** motion or activity induced by light — **pho·to·ki·net·ic** \-ˈne-tik\ *adj*
pho·to·li·thog·ra·phy \-li-ˈthä-grə-fē\ *n* [ISV] (1856) **1 :** lithography in which photographically prepared plates are used **2 :** a process involving the photographic transfer of a pattern to a surface for etching (as in producing an integrated circuit) — **pho·to·lith·o·graph** \-ˈli-thə-ˌgraf\ *n or vt* — **pho·to·lith·o·graph·ic** \-ˌli-thə-ˈgra-fik\ *adj* — **pho·to·lith·o·graph·i·cal·ly** \-fi-k(ə-)lē\ *adv*
pho·tol·y·sis \fō-ˈtä-lə-səs\ *n* [NL] (1911) **:** chemical decomposition by the action of radiant energy (as light) — **pho·to·lyt·ic** \ˌfō-tə-ˈli-tik\ *adj* — **pho·to·lyt·i·cal·ly** \-ti-k(ə-)lē\ *adv*
pho·to·lyze \ˈfō-tə-ˌlīz\ *vt* **-lyzed; -lyz·ing** (1936) **:** to cause to undergo photolysis — **pho·to·lyz·able** \-ˌlī-zə-bəl\ *adj*
pho·to·map \ˈfō-tō-ˌmap\ *n* (1939) **:** a photograph which is taken vertically from above (as from an airplane) and upon which a grid and data pertinent to maps have been added — **photomap** *vb*
pho·to·mask \-ˌmask\ *n* (1965) **:** MASK 2d
pho·to·me·chan·i·cal \ˌfō-tō-mi-ˈka-ni-kəl\ *adj* [ISV] (1884) **:** relating to or involving any of various processes for producing printed matter from a photographically prepared surface — **pho·to·me·chan·i·cal·ly** \-ni-k(ə-)lē\ *adv*
pho·tom·e·ter \fō-ˈtä-mə-tər\ *n* [NL *photometrum,* fr. *phot-* + *-metrum* -meter] (1778) **:** an instrument for measuring luminous intensity, luminous flux, illumination, or brightness
pho·to·met·ric \ˌfō-tə-ˈme-trik\ *adj* (ca. 1828) **:** of or relating to photometry or the photometer — **pho·to·met·ri·cal·ly** \-tri-k(ə-)lē\ *adv*
pho·tom·e·try \fō-ˈtä-mə-trē\ *n* [NL *photometria,* fr. *phot-* + *-metria* -metry] (1824) **:** a branch of science that deals with measurement of the intensity of light; *also* **:** the practice of using a photometer
pho·to·mi·cro·graph \ˌfō-tə-ˈmī-krə-ˌgraf\ *n* (1858) **:** a photograph of a microscope image — **pho·to·mi·cro·graph·ic** \-ˌmī-krə-ˈgra-fik\ *adj* — **pho·to·mi·crog·ra·phy** \-mī-ˈkrä-grə-fē\ *n*
pho·to·mon·tage \-män-ˈtäzh, -mōⁿ(n)-\ *n* [ISV] (1931) **:** montage using photographic images; *also* **:** a picture made by photomontage
pho·to·mor·pho·gen·e·sis \ˌfō-tə-ˌmȯr-fə-ˈje-nə-səs\ *n* [NL] (1959) **:** plant morphogenesis controlled by radiant energy (as light) — **pho·to·mor·pho·gen·ic** \-ˈje-nik\ *adj*
pho·to·mo·sa·ic \-mō-ˈzā-ik\ *n* (1942) **:** an image composed of many smaller photographs; *esp* **:** MOSAIC 6
pho·to·mul·ti·pli·er tube \ˌfō-tō-ˈməl-tə-ˌplī(-ə)r-\ *n* (1941) **:** a vacuum tube that detects light esp. from dim sources through the use of photoemission and successive instances of secondary emission to produce enough electrons to generate a useful current — called also *photomultiplier*
pho·to·mu·ral \-ˈmyu̇r-əl\ *n* (1927) **:** an enlarged photograph usu. several yards long used on walls esp. as decoration
pho·ton \ˈfō-ˌtän\ *n* [*phot-* + ²*-on*] (1916) **1 :** a unit of intensity of light at the retina equal to the illumination received per square millimeter of a pupillary area from a surface having a brightness of one candle per square meter **2 :** a quantum of electromagnetic radiation — **pho·ton·ic** \fō-ˈtä-nik\ *adj*
pho·to·neg·a·tive \ˌfō-tō-ˈne-gə-tiv\ *adj* (1914) **:** exhibiting negative phototropism or phototaxis
pho·ton·ics \fō-ˈtä-niks\ *n pl but sing in constr* (1952) **:** a branch of physics that deals with the properties and applications of photons esp. as a medium for transmitting information
pho·to·nu·cle·ar \ˌfō-tō-ˈnü-klē-ər, -ˈnyü-, ÷-kyə-lər\ *adj* (1941) **:** relating to or caused by the incidence of radiant energy (as gamma rays) on atomic nuclei
pho·to–off·set \-ˈȯf-ˌset\ *n* (1926) **:** offset printing from photolithographic plates
photo op \-ˈäp\ *n* (1981) **:** PHOTO OPPORTUNITY
photo opportunity *n* (1972) **:** a situation or event that lends itself to and is often arranged expressly for the taking of pictures that give favorable publicity to the individuals photographed
pho·to·ox·i·da·tion \-ˌäk-sə-ˈdā-shən\ *n* (1888) **:** oxidation under the influence of radiant energy (as light) — **pho·to·ox·i·da·tive** \-ˈäk-sə-ˌdā-tiv\ *adj* — **pho·to·ox·i·dize** \-ˈäk-sə-ˌdīz\ *vb*
pho·to·pe·ri·od \-ˈpir-ē-əd\ *n* (1920) **:** a recurring cycle of light and dark periods of constant length; *also* **:** PHOTOPHASE 2 — **pho·to·pe·ri·od·ic** \-ˌpir-ē-ˈä-dik\ *adj* — **pho·to·pe·ri·od·i·cal·ly** \-di-k(ə-)lē\ *adv*
pho·to·pe·ri·od·ism \-ˈpir-ē-ə-ˌdi-zəm\ *n* (ca. 1911) **:** a plant's or animal's response or capacity to respond to photoperiod
pho·to·phase \ˈfō-tə-ˌfāz\ *n* (1944) **1 :** LIGHT REACTION **2 :** the light period of a photoperiodic cycle of light and dark
pho·to·pho·bia \ˌfō-tə-ˈfō-bē-ə\ *n* [NL] (ca. 1799) **:** intolerance to light; *esp* **:** painful sensitiveness to strong light
pho·to·pho·bic \-ˈfō-bik\ *adj* (1858) **1 a :** shunning or avoiding light **b :** growing best under reduced illumination **2 :** of or relating to photophobia
pho·to·phore \ˈfō-tə-ˌfȯr\ *n* [ISV] (1898) **:** a light-emitting organ; *esp* **:** one of the luminous spots on various marine mostly deep-sea fishes
pho·to·phos·phor·y·la·tion \ˈfō-tō-ˌfäs-ˌfȯr-ə-ˈlā-shən\ *n* (1956) **:** the synthesis of ATP from ADP and phosphate that occurs in a plant using radiant energy absorbed during photosynthesis
phot·opic \fōt-ˈō-pik, -ˈä-pik\ *adj* [NL *photopia,* fr. *phot-* + *-opia*] (1915) **:** relating to or being vision in bright light with light-adapted eyes that is mediated by the cones of the retina
pho·to·play \ˈfō-tō-ˌplā\ *n* (1910) **:** MOTION PICTURE 2
pho·to·po·la·rim·e·ter \ˌfō-tō-ˌpō-lə-ˈri-mə-tər\ *n* (ca. 1889) **:** an instrument used to measure the intensity and polarization of reflected light (as from clouds enveloping a planet)
pho·to·poly·mer \ˌfō-tō-ˈpä-lə-mər\ *n* (1932) **:** a photosensitive plastic used esp. in the manufacture of printing plates
pho·to·pos·i·tive \-ˈpä-zə-tiv, -ˈpäz-tiv\ *adj* (1914) **:** exhibiting positive phototropism or phototaxis
pho·to·prod·uct \-ˈprä-(ˌ)dəkt\ *n* (1926) **:** a product of a photochemical reaction
pho·to·re·ac·tion \-rē-ˈak-shən\ *n* (1909) **:** a photochemical reaction
pho·to·re·ac·ti·va·tion \-rē-ˌak-tə-ˈvā-shən\ *n* (1949) **:** repair of DNA (as of a bacterium) esp. by a light-dependent enzymatic reaction after damage by ultraviolet irradiation — **pho·to·re·ac·ti·vat·ing** \-ˈak-tə-ˌvā-tiŋ\ *adj*
pho·to–re·al·ism \ˌfō-tō-ˈrē-ə-ˌli-zəm\ *n* (1961) **:** realism in painting characterized by extremely meticulous depiction of detail — **pho·to–re·al·ist** \-list\ *n or adj* — **pho·to–re·al·is·tic** \ˌfō-tō-ˌrē-ə-ˈlis-tik\ *adj*
pho·to·re·cep·tion \-ri-ˈsep-shən\ *n* (1902) **:** perception of waves in the range of visible light; *specif* **:** VISION — **pho·to·re·cep·tive** \-ˈsep-tiv\ *adj*
pho·to·re·cep·tor \-ˈsep-tər\ *n* (1906) **:** a receptor for light stimuli
pho·to·re·con·nais·sance \-ri-ˈkä-nə-zən(t)s *also* -sən(t)s\ *n* (1940) **:** reconnaissance in which aerial photographs are taken
pho·to·re·duc·tion \-ri-ˈdək-shən\ *n* (1888) **:** chemical reduction under the influence of radiant energy (as light) **:** photochemical reduction — **pho·to·re·duce** \-ri-ˈdüs, -ˈdyüs\ *vt*
pho·to·re·frac·tive ker·a·tec·to·my \ˌfō-tō-ri-ˌfrak-tiv-ˌker-ə-ˈtek-tə-mē\ *n* (1986) **:** surgical removal of part of the corneal surface using an excimer laser in order to correct for myopia — compare RADIAL KERATOTOMY
pho·to·re·pro·duc·tion \-ˌrē-prə-ˈdək-shən\ *n* (1939) **:** reproduction by photographic means; *also* **:** PHOTOCOPY
pho·to·re·sist \ˈfō-tō-ri-ˌzist, ˌfō-tō-ri-ˈ\ *n* (1953) **:** a photosensitive resin that loses its resistance to chemical etching when exposed to radiation and is used esp. in the transference of a circuit pattern to a semiconductor chip during the production of an integrated circuit

\ə\ **abut** \ᵊ\ **kitten, F table** \ər\ **further** \a\ **ash** \ā\ **ace** \ä\ **mop, mar**
\au̇\ **out** \ch\ **chin** \e\ **bet** \ē\ **easy** \g\ **go** \i\ **hit** \ī\ **ice** \j\ **job**
\ŋ\ **sing** \ō\ **go** \ȯ\ **law** \ȯi\ **boy** \th\ **thin** \t͟h\ **the** \ü\ **loot** \u̇\ **foot**
\y\ **yet** \zh\ **vision, beige** \k̲, ⁿ, œ, ue, ʸ\ *see* Guide to Pronunciation

pho·to·res·pi·ra·tion \ˌfō-tō-ˌres-pə-ˈrā-shən\ *n* (1945) : a light-dependent process in some plants resulting in the oxidation of glycolic acid and release of carbon dioxide that under some environmental conditions (as high temperature) tends to inhibit photosynthesis
pho·to·sen·si·tive \-ˈsen(t)-s(ə-)tiv\ *adj* (1886) **1** : sensitive to the action of radiant energy **2** : being or caused by an abnormal reaction to sunlight — **pho·to·sen·si·tiv·i·ty** \-ˌsen(t)-sə-ˈti-və-tē\ *n*
pho·to·sen·si·ti·za·tion \-ˌsen(t)-s(ə-)tə-ˈzā-shən\ *n* (ca. 1923) **1** : the process of photosensitizing **2** : the condition of being photosensitized; *esp* : the development of an abnormal capacity to react to sunlight typically by edematous swelling and dermatitis
pho·to·sen·si·tize \-ˈsen(t)-sə-ˌtīz\ *vt* (ca. 1923) : to sensitize to the influence of radiant energy and esp. light — **pho·to·sen·si·tiz·er** *n*
pho·to·set \ˈfō-tō-ˌset\ *vt* **-set; -set·ting** (1957) : PHOTOCOMPOSE — **pho·to·set·ter** *n*
pho·to·shop \ˈfō-(ˌ)tō-ˌshäp\ *vt, often cap* [*Photoshop*, trademark for an image-manipulation software product] (1992) : to alter (a digital image) with Photoshop software or other image-editing software esp. in a way that distorts reality (as for deliberately deceptive purposes)
pho·to·sphere \ˈfō-tə-ˌsfir\ *n* (1664) **1** : a sphere of light or radiance **2** : the luminous surface layer of the sun or a star — **pho·to·spher·ic** \ˌfō-tə-ˈsfir-ik, -ˈsfer-\ *adj*
[1]**pho·to·stat** \ˈfō-tə-ˌstat\ *n* [fr. *Photostat*, a trademark] (1911) : a device for making a photographic copy of graphic matter; *also* : a copy made by this device
[2]**photostat** *vt* **-stated** *also* **-statted; -stating** *also* **-statting** (1914) : to copy by a photostat
pho·to·stat·ic \ˌfō-tə-ˈsta-tik\ *adj* (1919) : of, made by, or using a photostat ⟨a ~ copy⟩ ⟨a ~ process⟩
pho·to·syn·thate \ˌfō-tō-ˈsin-ˌthāt\ *n* [*photosynthesis* + [1]*-ate*] (1913) : a product of photosynthesis
pho·to·syn·the·sis \-ˈsin(t)-thə-səs\ *n* [NL] (1898) : synthesis of chemical compounds with the aid of radiant energy and esp. light; *esp* : formation of carbohydrates from carbon dioxide and a source of hydrogen (as water) in the chlorophyll-containing cells (as of green plants) exposed to light — **pho·to·syn·the·size** \-ˌsīz\ *vi* — **pho·to·syn·thet·ic** \-sin-ˈthe-tik\ *adj* — **pho·to·syn·thet·i·cal·ly** \-ti-k(ə-)lē\ *adv*
pho·to·sys·tem \ˈfō-tō-ˌsis-təm\ *n* (1964) : either of two photochemical reaction centers consisting chiefly of photosynthetic pigments complexed with protein and occurring in chloroplasts: **a** : one that absorbs light with a wavelength of about 700 nanometers — called also *photosystem I* **b** : one that absorbs light with a wavelength of about 680 nanometers — called also *photosystem II*
pho·to·tac·tic \ˌfō-tō-ˈtak-tik\ *adj* [ISV] (1882) : of, relating to, or exhibiting phototaxis — **pho·to·tac·ti·cal·ly** \-ti-kə-lē\ *adv*
pho·to·tax·is \-ˈtak-səs\ *n* [NL] (ca. 1889) : a taxis in which light is the directive factor
pho·to·te·leg·ra·phy \-tə-ˈle-grə-fē\ *n* [ISV] (1886) : FACSIMILE 2
pho·to·ther·a·py \ˌfō-tō-ˈther-ə-pē\ *n* (1899) : LIGHT THERAPY
pho·to·tox·ic \-ˈtäk-sik\ *adj* (1942) **1** : rendering the skin susceptible to damage (as sunburn or blisters) upon exposure to light and esp. ultraviolet light ⟨~ antibiotics⟩ **2** : induced by a phototoxic substance — **pho·to·tox·ic·i·ty** \-täk-ˈsi-sə-tē\ *n*
pho·to·tran·sis·tor \-tran-ˈzis-tər, -tran(t)-ˈsis-\ *n* (1950) : a photoconductive semiconductor device used esp. as a photodetector
pho·to·tro·pic \ˌfō-tə-ˈtrō-pik, -ˈträ-\ *adj* (ca. 1890) : of, relating to, or capable of phototropism — **pho·to·tro·pi·cal·ly** \-pi-k(ə-)lē\ *adv*
pho·tot·ro·pism \fō-ˈtä-trə-ˌpi-zəm\ *n* [ISV] (1899) : a tropism in which light is the orienting stimulus
pho·to·tube \ˈfō-tō-ˌtüb, -ˌtyüb\ *n* (1930) : an electron tube having a photoemissive cathode whose released electrons are drawn to the anode by reason of its positive potential
pho·to·type·set·ting \ˌfō-tō-ˈtīp-ˌse-tiŋ\ *n* (1931) : PHOTOCOMPOSITION; *esp* : photocomposition done on a keyboard or tape-operated composing machine — **pho·to·type·set·ter** *n*
pho·to·vol·ta·ic \-väl-ˈtā-ik, -vōl-\ *adj* [ISV] (ca. 1889) : of, relating to, or utilizing the generation of a voltage when radiant energy falls on the boundary between dissimilar substances (as two different semiconductors) — **photovoltaic** *n*
phr *abbr* phrase
phrag·mi·tes \frag-ˈmī-ˌtēz\ *n* [NL, fr. Gk *phragmitēs* growing in hedges, fr. *phragma* fence, hedge, fr. *phrassein* to enclose] (1877) : any of a genus (*Phragmites*) of widely distributed reeds with tall stems and large showy panicles resembling plumes
phrag·mo·plast \ˈfrag-mō-ˌplast\ *n* [ISV *phragmo-* (fr. Gk *phragmos* fence, fr. *phrassein* to enclose) + *-plast*] (1912) : the enlarged barrel-shaped spindle that is characteristic of the later stages of plant mitosis and within which the cell plate forms
phras·al \ˈfrā-zəl\ *adj* (1871) : of, relating to, or consisting of a phrase ⟨~ prepositions⟩ — **phras·al·ly** \-zə-lē\ *adv*
phrasal verb *n* (1925) : a phrase (as *take off* or *look down on*) that combines a verb with a preposition or adverb or both and that functions as a verb whose meaning is different from the combined meanings of the individual words
[1]**phrase** \ˈfrāz\ *n* [L *phrasis*, fr. Gk, fr. *phrazein* to point out, explain, tell] (1530) **1** : a characteristic manner or style of expression : DICTION **2 a** : a brief expression; *esp* : CATCHPHRASE **b** : WORD **3** : a short musical thought typically two to four measures long closing with a cadence **4** : a word or group of words forming a syntactic constituent with a single grammatical function ⟨an adverbial ~⟩ **5** : a series of dance movements comprising a section of a pattern
[2]**phrase** *vt* **phrased; phras·ing** (1570) **1 a** : to express in words or in appropriate or telling terms **b** : to designate by a descriptive word or phrase **2** : to divide into melodic phrases
phrase book *n* (1594) : a book containing idiomatic expressions of a foreign language and their translation
phrase·mak·er \ˈfrāz-ˌmā-kər\ *n* (1822) **1** : one who coins impressive phrases **2** : one given to making fine-sounding but often hollow and meaningless phrases — **phrase·mak·ing** \-kiŋ\ *n*
phrase·mon·ger \-ˌməŋ-gər, -ˌmäŋ-\ *n* (1611) : PHRASEMAKER 2 — **phrase·mon·ger·ing** \-g(ə-)riŋ\ *n*
phra·se·o·log·i·cal \ˌfrā-zē-ə-ˈlä-ji-kəl\ *adj* (1664) **1 a** : expressed in formal often sententious phrases **b** : marked by frequently insincere use of such phrases **2** : of or relating to phraseology
phra·se·ol·o·gist \ˌfrā-zē-ˈä-lə-jist, frā-ˈzä-\ *n* (1713) : one who uses sententious or insincere phrases
phra·se·ol·o·gy \-jē\ *n, pl* **-gies** [NL *phraseologia*, irreg. fr. Gk *phrasis* + *-logia* -logy] (1664) **1** : a manner of organizing words and phrases into longer elements : STYLE **2** : choice of words
phrasing *n* (1611) **1** : style of expression : PHRASEOLOGY **2** : the act, method, or result of grouping notes into musical phrases
phra·try \ˈfrā-trē\ *n, pl* **phratries** [Gk *phratria*, fr. *phratēr* member of the same clan, member of a phratry — more at BROTHER] (1833) **1** : a kinship group forming a subdivision of a Greek phyle **2** : a tribal subdivision; *specif* : an exogamous group typically comprising several totemic clans
phreak \ˈfrēk\ *n* [alter. of [1]*freak*] (1972) : PHREAKER
phreak·er \ˈfrē-kər\ *n* (1984) : one who gains illegal access to the telephone system — **phreak·ing** \-kiŋ\ *n*
phre·at·ic \frē-ˈa-tik\ *adj* [Gk *phreat-*, *phrear* well; akin to Arm *ałbiwr* spring, OHG *brunno* — more at BURN] (ca. 1890) **1** : of, relating to, or being groundwater **2** : of, relating to, or being an explosion caused by steam derived from groundwater
phre·at·o·phyte \frē-ˈa-tə-ˌfīt\ *n* [Gk *phreat-*, *phrear* well + E *-o-* + *-phyte*] (1920) : a deep-rooted plant that obtains its water from the water table or the layer of soil just above it — **phre·at·o·phyt·ic** \-ˌa-tə-ˈfi-tik\ *adj*
phre·net·ic *archaic var of* FRENETIC
-phrenia *n comb form* [NL, fr. Gk *phren-*, *phrēn* diaphragm, mind] : disordered condition of mental functions ⟨hebe*phrenia*⟩
phren·ic \ˈfre-nik\ *adj* [NL *phrenicus*, fr. Gk *phren-*, *phrēn*] (1697) **1** : of or relating to the diaphragm **2** : of or relating to the mind
phre·nol·o·gy \fri-ˈnä-lə-jē\ *n* [Gk *phren-*, *phrēn*] (1805) : the study of the conformation of the skull based on the belief that it is indicative of mental faculties and character — **phre·no·log·i·cal** \ˌfre-nə-ˈlä-ji-kəl, ˌfrē-\ *adj* — **phre·nol·o·gist** \fri-ˈnä-lə-jist\ *n*
phren·sy *archaic var of* FRENZY
Phry·gian \ˈfri-j(ē-)ən\ *n* (15c) **1** : a native or inhabitant of ancient Phrygia **2** : the extinct Indo-European language of the Phrygians — see INDO-EUROPEAN LANGUAGES table — **Phrygian** *adj*
phthal·ate \ˈtha-ˌlāt\ *n* (ca. 1866) : any of various salts or esters of phthalic acid used esp. as plasticizers and in solvents
phthal·ic acid \ˈtha-lik-\ *n* [ISV, short for obs. *naphthalic acid*, fr. *naphthalene*] (1857) : any of three isomeric acids $C_8H_6O_4$ obtained by oxidation of various benzene derivatives
phthalic anhydride *n* (1855) : a crystalline cyclic acid anhydride $C_8H_4O_3$ used esp. in making alkyd resins
phtha·lo·cy·a·nine \ˌtha-lō-ˈsī-ə-ˌnēn, ˌthā-\ *n* [ISV *phthal*ic acid + *-o-* + *cyanine*] (1933) : a bright greenish-blue crystalline compound $C_{32}H_{18}N_8$; *also* : any of several metal derivatives that are brilliant fast blue to green dyes or pigments
phthis·ic \ˈti-zik\ *n* [ME *tisike*, fr. AF, fr. L *phthisicus* suffering from tuberculosis, fr. Gk *phthisikos*, fr. *phthisis*] (14c) : PHTHISIS — **phthisic** *or* **phthis·i·cal** \-zi-kəl\ *adj*
phthi·sis \ˈthī-səs, ˈtī-, ˈthi-, ˈti-\ *n, pl* **phthi·ses** \-ˌsēz\ [L, fr. Gk, fr. *phthinein* to waste away; akin to Skt *kṣiṇoti* he destroys] (1526) : a progressively wasting or consumptive condition; *esp* : pulmonary tuberculosis
phyco- *comb form* [Gk *phykos* seaweed] : algae ⟨*phyco*logy⟩
phy·co·cy·a·nin \ˌfī-kō-ˈsī-ə-nən\ *n* [ISV *phyco-* + *cyan-* + [1]*-in*] (1875) : any of various bluish-green protein pigments found in cyanobacteria
phy·co·er·y·thrin \-ˈer-i-thrən\ *n* [ISV *phyco-* + *erythr-* + [1]*-in*] (ca. 1868) : any of the red protein pigments in the cells of red algae
phy·col·o·gy \fī-ˈkä-lə-jē\ *n* (ca. 1847) : the study or science of algae — called also *algology* — **phy·co·log·i·cal** \ˌfī-kə-ˈlä-ji-kəl\ *adj* — **phy·col·o·gist** \fī-ˈkä-lə-jist\ *n*
phy·co·my·cete \ˌfī-kō-ˈmī-ˌsēt, -ˌmī-ˈsēt\ *n* [ultim. fr. Gk *phykos* + *mykēt-*, *mykēs* fungus — more at MYC-] (ca. 1900) : any of a large class (Phycomycetes) of lower fungi that are in many respects similar to algae and are now often assigned to subdivisions (as Mastigomycotina and Zygomycota) — **phy·co·my·ce·tous** \-ˌmī-ˈsē-təs\ *adj*
phyl- *or* **phylo-** *comb form* [L, fr. Gk, fr. *phylē*, *phylon*; akin to Gk *phyein* to bring forth — more at BE] : tribe : race : phylum ⟨*phylo*geny⟩
phy·lac·tery \fə-ˈlak-t(ə-)rē\ *n, pl* **-ter·ies** [ME *philaterie*, fr. ML *philaterium*, alter. of LL *phylacterium*, fr. Gk *phylaktērion* amulet, phylactery, fr. *phylassein* to guard, fr. *phylak-*, *phylax* guard] (14c) **1** : either of two small square leather boxes containing slips inscribed with scriptural passages and traditionally worn on the left arm and on the head by observant Jewish men and esp. adherents of Orthodox Judaism during morning weekday prayers **2** : AMULET

phylactery 1

phy·le \ˈfī-(ˌ)lē\ *n, pl* **phy·lae** \-ˌlē\ [Gk *phylē* tribe, phyle] (1863) : the largest political subdivision among the ancient Athenians
phy·let·ic \fī-ˈle-tik\ *adj* [ISV *phyl-* + *-etic* (as in *genetic*)] (1881) : of or relating to evolutionary change in a single line of descent without branching — **phy·let·i·cal·ly** \-ti-k(ə-)lē\ *adv*
phyll- *or* **phyllo-** *comb form* [NL, fr. Gk, fr. *phyllon* — more at BLADE] : leaf ⟨*phyll*ome⟩
-phyll *n comb form* [NL *-phyllum*, fr. Gk *phyllon* leaf] : leaf ⟨sporo*phyll*⟩
phyl·la·ry \ˈfi-lə-rē\ *n, pl* **-ries** [NL *phyllarium*, fr. Gk *phyllarion*, dim. of *phyllon* leaf] (1857) : one of the involucral bracts subtending the flower head of a composite plant
phyl·lo *also* **filo** *or* **fil·lo** \ˈfē-(ˌ)lō, ˈfī-\ *n* [ModGk, sheet of pastry dough, lit., leaf, fr. Gk *phyllon*] (1950) : extremely thin dough that is layered to produce a flaky pastry
phyl·lo·clade \ˈfi-lə-ˌklād\ *n* [NL *phyllocladium*, fr. *phyll-* + Gk *klados* branch — more at HOLT] (1884) : a flattened stem or branch (as a joint of a cactus) that functions as a leaf

phyl·lode \ˈfi-ˌlōd\ *n* [NL *phyllodium,* fr. Gk *phyllōdēs* like a leaf, fr. *phyllon* leaf] (1848) **:** a flat expanded petiole that replaces the blade of a foliage leaf, fulfills the same functions, and is analogous to a cladophyll

phyl·lome \ˈfi-ˌlōm\ *n* [ISV] (1875) **:** a plant part that is a leaf or is phylogenetically derived from a leaf

phyl·lo·tac·tic \ˌfi-lə-ˈtak-tik\ *adj* (1857) **:** of or relating to phyllotaxis

phyl·lo·tax·is \ˌfi-lə-ˈtak-səs\ *also* **phyl·lo·taxy** \ˈfi-lə-ˌtak-sē\ *n* [NL *phyllotaxis,* fr. *phyll-* + *-taxis*] (1857) **1 :** the arrangement of leaves on a stem and in relation to one another **2 :** the study of phyllotaxis and of the laws that govern it

-phyllous *adj comb form* [NL *-phyllus,* fr. Gk *-phyllos,* fr. *phyllon* leaf — more at BLADE] **:** having (such or so many) leaves, leaflets, or leaflike parts ⟨hetero*phyllous*⟩

phyl·lox·e·ra \ˌfi-ˌläk-ˈsir-ə, fə-ˈläk-sə-rə\ *n* [NL, fr. *phyll-* + Gk *xēros* dry] (1880) **:** any of several plant lice (family Phylloxeridae); *esp* **:** one (*Daktulosphaira vitifoliae* syn. *Viteus vitifoliae*) orig. of No. America but introduced into Europe and elsewhere that produces galls on the leaves and roots of grape vines and is a serious pest esp. of vinifera grapes in wine-producing regions

phy·lo·ge·net·ic \ˌfī-lō-jə-ˈne-tik\ *adj* [ISV, fr. NL *phylogenesis* phylogeny, fr. *phyl-* + *genesis*] (1877) **1 :** of or relating to phylogeny **2 :** based on natural evolutionary relationships **3 :** acquired in the course of phylogenetic development **:** RACIAL — **phy·lo·ge·net·i·cal·ly** \-ti-k(ə-)lē\ *adv*

phy·log·e·ny \fī-ˈlä-jə-nē\ *n, pl* **-nies** [ISV] (ca. 1872) **1 :** the evolutionary history of a kind of organism **2 :** the evolution of a genetically related group of organisms as distinguished from the development of the individual organism **3 :** the history or course of the development of something (as a word or custom)

phy·lum \ˈfī-ləm\ *n, pl* **phy·la** \-lə\ [NL, fr. Gk *phylon* tribe, race — more at PHYL-] (1876) **1 a :** a direct line of descent within a group **b :** a group that constitutes or has the unity of a phylum; *specif* **:** a primary category in biological taxonomy esp. of animals that ranks above the class and below the kingdom — compare DIVISION 10 **2 :** a group of languages related more remotely than those of a family or stock

phys *abbr* **1** physical **2** physics

phys ed \ˈfiz-ˈed\ *n* (1955) **:** PHYSICAL EDUCATION

physi- *or* **physio-** *comb form* [L, fr. Gk, fr. *physis* — more at PHYSICS] **1 :** nature ⟨*physio*graphy⟩ **2 :** physical ⟨*physio*therapy⟩

phys·iat·rist \ˌfi-zē-ˈa-trist\ *n* [*physiatrics* physical medicine, fr. Gk *physis* + ISV *-iatrics*] (ca. 1947) **:** a physician who specializes in physiatry

phys·iat·ry \ˌfi-zē-ˈa-trē, fə-ˈzī-ə-trē\ *n* [alter. of *physiatrics*] (1947) **:** PHYSICAL MEDICINE AND REHABILITATION

[1]**phys·ic** \ˈfi-zik\ *n* [ME *physik* natural science, art of medicine, fr. AF *phisique, fisik,* fr. L *physica,* sing., natural science, fr. Gk *physikē,* fr. fem. of *physikos* — more at PHYSICS] (14c) **1 a :** the art or practice of healing disease **b :** the practice or profession of medicine **2 :** a medicinal agent or preparation; *esp* **:** PURGATIVE **3** *archaic* **:** NATURAL SCIENCE

[2]**physic** *vt* **phys·icked; phys·ick·ing** (14c) **1 :** to treat with or administer medicine to; *esp* **:** PURGE **2 :** HEAL, CURE

[1]**phys·i·cal** \ˈfi-zi-kəl\ *adj* [ME *phisicale* medical, fr. ML *physicalis,* fr. L *physica*] (1580) **1 a :** of or relating to natural science **b** (1) **:** of or relating to physics (2) **:** characterized or produced by the forces and operations of physics **2 a :** having material existence **:** perceptible esp. through the senses and subject to the laws of nature ⟨everything ~ is measurable by weight, motion, and resistance —Thomas De Quincey⟩ **b :** of or relating to material things **3 a :** of or relating to the body ⟨~ abuse⟩ **b** (1) **:** concerned or preoccupied with the body and its needs **:** CARNAL ⟨~ appetites⟩ (2) **:** SEXUAL ⟨a ~ love affair⟩ ⟨~ attraction⟩ **c :** characterized by esp. rugged and forceful physical activity **:** ROUGH ⟨a ~ hockey game⟩ ⟨a ~ player⟩ ***syn*** see MATERIAL — **phys·i·cal·ly** \-k(ə-)lē\ *adv* — **phys·i·cal·ness** \-kəl-nəs\ *n*

[2]**physical** *n* (1934) **:** PHYSICAL EXAMINATION

physical anthropology *n* (1873) **:** anthropology concerned with the comparative study of human evolution, variation, and classification esp. through measurement and observation — compare CULTURAL ANTHROPOLOGY — **physical anthropologist** *n*

physical education *n* (1830) **:** instruction in the development and care of the body ranging from simple calisthenic exercises to a course of study providing training in hygiene, gymnastics, and the performance and management of athletic games

physical examination *n* (ca. 1884) **:** an examination of the bodily functions and condition of an individual

physical geography *n* (1774) **:** geography that deals with the exterior physical features and changes of the earth

phys·i·cal·ism \ˈfi-zi-kə-ˌli-zəm\ *n* (1931) **:** a thesis that the descriptive terms of scientific language are reducible to terms which refer to spatiotemporal things or events or to their properties — **phys·i·cal·ist** \-list\ *n or adj* — **phys·i·cal·is·tic** \ˌfi-zi-kə-ˈlis-tik\ *adj*

phys·i·cal·i·ty \ˌfi-zə-ˈka-lə-tē\ *n, pl* **-ties** (1660) **1 :** intensely physical orientation **:** predominance of the physical usu. at the expense of the mental, spiritual, or social **2 :** a physical aspect or quality

phys·i·cal·ize \ˈfi-zi-kə-ˌlīz\ *vt* **-ized; -iz·ing** (1947) **:** to give physical form or expression to ⟨her gestures *physicalized* her major points⟩

physical medicine and rehabilitation *n* (1939) **:** a medical specialty concerned with treating disabling disorders and injuries by physical means (as by the use of electrotherapy, therapeutic exercise, or pharmaceutical pain control) — called also *physiatry, physical medicine*

physical science *n* (1802) **:** any of the natural sciences (as physics, chemistry, and astronomy) that deal primarily with nonliving materials — **physical scientist** *n*

physical therapy *n* (1922) **:** the treatment of disease, injury, or disability by physical and mechanical means (as massage, regulated exercise, water, light, heat, and electricity) — **physical therapist** *n*

phy·si·cian \fə-ˈzi-shən\ *n* [ME *phisicien, fisicien,* fr. AF, fr. *phisique* medicine] (13c) **1 :** a person skilled in the art of healing; *specif* **:** one educated, clinically experienced, and licensed to practice medicine as usu. distinguished from surgery **2 :** one exerting a remedial or salutary influence

physician assistant *n* (1970) **:** a person certified to provide basic medical services usu. under the supervision of a licensed physician — called also *PA, physician's assistant*

physician–assisted suicide *n* (1987) **:** suicide by a patient facilitated by means (as a drug prescription) or by information (as an indication of a lethal dosage) provided by a physician aware of the patient's intent

phys·i·cist \ˈfi-zə-sist, ˈfiz-sist\ *n* (ca. 1840) **1 :** a specialist in physics **2** *archaic* **:** a person skilled in natural science

phys·i·co·chem·i·cal \ˌfi-zi-kō-ˈke-mi-kəl\ *adj* (1664) **1 :** being physical and chemical **2 :** of or relating to chemistry that deals with the physicochemical properties of substances — **phys·i·co·chem·i·cal·ly** \-k(ə-)lē\ *adv*

phys·ics \ˈfi-ziks\ *n pl but sing or pl in constr* [L *physica,* pl., natural science, fr. Gk *physika,* fr. neut. pl. of *physikos* of nature, fr. *physis* growth, nature, fr. *phyein* to bring forth — more at BE] (1715) **1 :** a science that deals with matter and energy and their interactions **2 a :** the physical processes and phenomena of a particular system **b :** the physical properties and composition of something

phys·io·crat \ˈfi-zē-ə-ˌkrat\ *n, often cap* [F *physiocrate,* fr. *physi-* physi- + *-crate* -crat] (1798) **:** a member of a school of political economists founded in 18th century France and characterized chiefly by a belief that government policy should not interfere with the operation of natural economic laws and that land is the source of all wealth — **phys·io·crat·ic** \ˌfi-zē-ə-ˈkra-tik\ *adj, often cap*

phys·i·og·nom·ic \ˌfi-zē-ə(g)-ˈnä-mik\ *also* **phys·i·og·nom·i·cal** \-mi-kəl\ *adj* (1588) **:** of, relating to, or characteristic of physiognomy or the physiognomy — **phys·i·og·nom·i·cal·ly** \-mi-k(ə-)lē\ *adv*

phys·i·og·no·my \ˌfi-zē-ˈä(g)-nə-mē\ *n, pl* **-mies** [ME *phisonomie,* fr. AF *phisenomie,* fr. LL *physiognomia, physiognomia,* fr. Gk *physiognōmonia,* fr. *physiognōmōn* judging character by the features, fr. *physis* nature, physique, appearance + *gnōmōn* interpreter — more at GNOMON] (14c) **1 :** the art of discovering temperament and character from outward appearance **2 :** the facial features held to show qualities of mind or character by their configuration or expression **3 :** external aspect; *also* **:** inner character or quality revealed outwardly

phys·i·og·ra·phy \ˌfi-zē-ˈä-grə-fē\ *n* [prob. fr. F *physiographie,* fr. *physi-* + *-graphie* -graphy] (ca. 1828) **:** PHYSICAL GEOGRAPHY — **phys·i·og·ra·pher** \-fər\ *n* — **phys·io·graph·ic** \ˌfi-zē-ō-ˈgra-fik\ *also* **phys·io·graph·i·cal** \-fi-kəl\ *adj*

physiol *abbr* physiologist; physiology

phys·i·o·log·i·cal \ˌfi-zē-ə-ˈlä-ji-kəl\ *or* **phys·i·o·log·ic** \-jik\ *adj* (1814) **1 :** of or relating to physiology **2 :** characteristic of or appropriate to an organism's healthy or normal functioning ⟨the sodium level was ~⟩ **3 :** differing in, involving, or affecting physiological factors ⟨a ~ strain of bacteria⟩ — **phys·i·o·log·i·cal·ly** \-ji-k(ə-)lē\ *adv*

physiological psychology *n* (1888) **:** a branch of psychology that deals with the effects of normal and pathological physiological processes on mental life — called also *psychophysiology*

physiological saline *n* (1896) **:** a solution of a salt or salts that is essentially isotonic with tissue fluids or blood

phys·i·ol·o·gy \ˌfi-zē-ˈä-lə-jē\ *n* [L *physiologia* natural science, fr. Gk, fr. *physi-* + *-logia* -logy] (1615) **1 :** a branch of biology that deals with the functions and activities of life or of living matter (as organs, tissues, or cells) and of the physical and chemical phenomena involved — compare ANATOMY **2 :** the organic processes and phenomena of an organism or any of its parts or of a particular bodily process — **phys·i·ol·o·gist** \-jist\ *n*

phys·io·pa·thol·o·gy \ˈfi-zē-ō-pə-ˈthä-lə-jē, -pa-\ *n* (ca. 1889) **:** a branch of biology or medicine that combines physiology and pathology esp. in the study of altered bodily function in disease — **phys·io·path·o·log·ic** \-ˌpa-thə-ˈlä-jik\ *or* **phys·io·path·o·log·i·cal** \-ji-kəl\ *adj*

phys·io·ther·a·py \ˌfi-zē-ō-ˈther-ə-pē\ *n* [NL *physiotherapia,* fr. *physi-* + *therapia* therapy] (ca. 1903) **:** PHYSICAL THERAPY — **phys·io·ther·a·pist** \-pist\ *n*

phy·sique \fə-ˈzēk\ *n* [F, fr. *physique* physical, bodily, fr. L *physicus* of nature, fr. Gk *physikos*] (1804) **:** the form or structure of a person's body **:** bodily makeup

phy·so·stig·mine \ˌfī-sə-ˈstig-ˌmēn\ *n* [ISV, fr. NL *Physostigma,* genus of vines that bear the Calabar bean] (1864) **:** a crystalline tasteless alkaloid $C_{15}H_{21}N_3O_2$ from the Calabar bean that is used in medicine esp. in the form of its salicylate for its anticholinesterase activity

phyt- *or* **phyto-** *comb form* [NL, fr. Gk, fr. *phyton,* fr. *phyein* to bring forth — more at BE] **:** plant ⟨*phyto*phagous⟩

phy·tane \ˈfī-ˌtān\ *n* (ca. 1907) **:** an isoprenoid hydrocarbon $C_{20}H_{42}$ that is found esp. associated with fossilized plant remains from the Precambrian and later eras

-phyte *n comb form* [ISV, fr. Gk *phyton* plant] **1 :** plant having a (specified) characteristic or habitat ⟨xero*phyte*⟩ **2 :** pathological outgrowth ⟨osteo*phyte*⟩

-phytic *adj comb form* [ISV, fr. Gk *phyton* plant] **:** like a plant ⟨holo*phytic*⟩

phy·to·alex·in \ˌfī-tō-ə-ˈlek-sən\ *n* [ISV *phyt-* + *alexin* substance combating infection, fr. Gk *alexein* to ward off, protect; akin to Skt *rakṣati* he protects] (1949) **:** any of various antimicrobial chemical substances produced by plants to combat infection by a pathogen (as a fungus)

[1]**phy·to·chem·i·cal** \-ˈke-mi-kəl\ *adj* (ca. 1858) **:** of, relating to, or being phytochemistry — **phy·to·chem·i·cal·ly** \-mi-k(ə-)lē\ *adv*

[2]**phytochemical** *n* (1985) **:** a chemical compound (as beta-carotene) occurring naturally in plants

phy·to·chem·is·try \-ˈke-mə-strē\ *n* (1837) **:** the chemistry of plants, plant processes, and plant products — **phy·to·chem·ist** \-ˈke-mist\ *n*

phy·to·chrome \ˈfī-tə-ˌkrōm\ *n* (1960) **:** any of a group of proteins bound to light-absorbing pigments in many plants that play a role in initiating floral and developmental processes when activated by red or near-infrared radiation

phy·to·es·tro·gen \ˌfī-tō-ˈes-trə-jən\ *n* (1964) **:** a chemical compound (as genistein) that occurs naturally in plants and has estrogenic properties

phy·to·fla·gel·late \ˌfī-tō-ˈfla-jə-lət, -ˌlāt; -flə-ˈje-\ *n* (1935) **:** any of various organisms (as dinoflagellates) that are considered a subclass (Phytomastigophora syn. Phytomastigina) usu. of algae by botanists and of protozoans by zoologists and that have many characteristics in common with typical algae

phy·to·ge·og·ra·phy \ˌfī-tō-jē-ˈä-grə-fē\ *n* [ISV] (ca. 1847) **:** the biogeography of plants — **phy·to·ge·og·ra·pher** \-fər\ *n* — **phy·to·geo·graph·i·cal** \-ˌjē-ə-ˈgra-fi-kəl\ *or* **phy·to·geo·graph·ic** \-fik\ *adj* — **phy·to·geo·graph·i·cal·ly** \-fi-k(ə-)lē\ *adv*

phy·to·he·mag·glu·ti·nin \-ˌhē-mə-ˈglü-tə-nən\ *n* (1949) **:** a proteinaceous hemagglutinin of plant origin used esp. to induce mitosis (as in lymphocytes)

phy·to·hor·mone \-ˈhȯr-ˌmōn\ *n* [ISV] (1933) **:** PLANT HORMONE

phy·to·lith \ˈfī-tə-ˌlith\ *n* (1958) **:** a microscopic siliceous particle that is formed by a plant and that is highly resistant to decomposition ⟨ancient vegetation revealed by ∼*s*⟩

phy·ton \ˈfī-ˌtän\ *n* [NL, fr. Gk, plant] (1846) **1 :** a structural unit of a plant consisting of a leaf and its associated portion of stem **2 :** the smallest part of a stem, root, or leaf that when severed may grow into a new plant — **phy·ton·ic** \fī-ˈtä-nik\ *adj*

phy·to·nu·tri·ent \ˌfī-tō-ˈnü-trē-ənt, -ˈnyü-\ *n* (1994) **:** a bioactive plant-derived compound (as resveratrol) associated with positive health effects

phy·to·path·o·gen \ˌfī-tō-ˈpa-thə-jən\ *n* (ca. 1930) **:** an organism parasitic on a plant host — **phy·to·path·o·gen·ic** \-ˌpa-thə-ˈje-nik\ *adj*

phy·to·pa·thol·o·gy \-pə-ˈthä-lə-jē, -pa-\ *n* [ISV] (ca. 1859) **:** plant pathology — **phy·to·path·o·log·i·cal** \-ˌpa-thə-ˈlä-ji-kəl\ *adj*

phy·toph·a·gous \fī-ˈtä-fə-gəs\ *adj* (1826) **:** feeding on plants

phy·to·plank·ter \ˌfī-tō-ˈplaŋ(k)-tər\ *n* (1944) **:** a planktonic plant

phy·to·plank·ton \-ˈplaŋ(k)-tən, -ˌtän\ *n* [ISV] (1897) **:** planktonic plant life — **phy·to·plank·ton·ic** \-plaŋ(k)-ˈtä-nik\ *adj*

phy·to·plas·ma \ˌfī-tə-ˈplaz-mə\ *n* [NL] (1994) **:** any of a group of bacteria that are related to mycoplasmas, cause plant diseases (as aster yellows) by infecting phloem tissue, are transmitted esp. by homopteran insect vectors, and have proved extremely difficult to grow in artificial media — called also *mycoplasma-like organism*

phy·to·so·ci·ol·o·gy \-ˌsō-sē-ˈä-lə-jē, -shē-\ *n* (1928) **:** a branch of ecology concerned esp. with the structure, composition, and interrelationships of plant communities — **phy·to·so·cio·log·i·cal** \-sē-ə-ˈlä-ji-kəl\ *adj*

phy·tos·ter·ol \fī-ˈtäs-tə-ˌrȯl, -ˌrōl\ *n* [ISV] (1898) **:** any of various sterols derived from plants

phy·to·tox·ic \ˌfī-tə-ˈtäk-sik\ *adj* (1926) **:** poisonous to plants — **phy·to·tox·ic·i·ty** \-ˌtäk-ˈsi-sə-tē\ *n*

[1]**pi** \ˈpī\ *n, pl* **pis** \ˈpīz\ [MGk, fr. Gk *pei,* of Sem origin; akin to Heb *pē* pe] (1638) **1 :** the 16th letter of the Greek alphabet — see ALPHABET table **2 a :** the symbol π denoting the ratio of the circumference of a circle to its diameter **b :** the ratio itself **:** a transcendental number having a value rounded to eight decimal places of 3.14159265

[2]**pi** *also* **pie** \ˈpī\ *n, pl* **pies** [origin unknown] (ca. 1659) **1 :** type that is spilled or mixed **2 :** a pi character or matrix

[3]**pi** *also* **pie** *vb* **pied; pi·ing** *or* **pie·ing** *vt* (1889) **:** to spill or throw (type or type matter) into disorder ∼ *vi* **:** to become pied

[4]**pi** *also* **pie** *adj* (ca. 1940) **1 :** not intended to appear in final printing ⟨∼ lines⟩ **2 :** capable of being inserted only by hand ⟨∼ characters⟩

PI *abbr* **1** Philippine Islands **2** private investigator **3** programmed instruction

pi·al \ˈpī-əl, ˈpē-\ *adj* (1889) **:** of or relating to the pia mater

pia ma·ter \ˈpī-ə-ˌmā-tər, ˈpē-ə-ˌmä-\ *n* [ME, fr. ML, fr. L, tender mother] (14c) **:** the thin vascular membrane that invests the brain and spinal cord internal to the arachnoid and dura mater

pi·a·nism \ˈpē-ə-ˌni-zəm\ *n* (1844) **1 :** the art or technique of piano playing **2 :** the composition or adaptation of music for the piano

[1]**pi·a·nis·si·mo** \ˌpē-ə-ˈni-sə-ˌmō\ *adv or adj* [It, fr. *piano* softly] (1724) **:** very softly — used as a direction in music

[2]**pianissimo** *n, pl* **-mi** \-(ˌ)mē\ *or* **-mos** (1830) **:** a passage played, sung, or spoken very softly

pi·a·nist \pē-ˈa-nist, ˈpē-ə-\ *n* (ca. 1828) **:** a person who plays the piano; *esp* **:** a skilled or professional performer on the piano

pi·a·nis·tic \ˌpē-ə-ˈnis-tik\ *adj* (1881) **1 :** of, relating to, or characteristic of the piano **2 :** skilled in or well adapted to piano playing — **pi·a·nis·ti·cal·ly** \-ti-k(ə-)lē\ *adv*

[1]**pi·a·no** \pē-ˈä-(ˌ)nō\ *adv or adj* [It, fr. LL *planus* smooth, fr. L, level — more at FLOOR] (1683) **:** at a soft volume **:** SOFT — used as a direction in music

[2]**pi·ano** \pē-ˈa-(ˌ)nō *also* -ˈä-\ *n, pl* **pianos** [It, short for *pianoforte,* fr. *gravicembalo col piano e forte,* lit., harpsichord with soft and loud; fr. the fact that its tones could be varied in loudness] (1803) **:** a musical instrument having steel wire strings that sound when struck by felt-covered hammers operated from a keyboard

piano accordion *n* (1860) **:** an accordion with a keyboard for the right hand resembling and corresponding to the middle register of a piano keyboard

pi·ano·forte \pē-ˈa-nə-ˌfȯrt, -ˈä-, -ˌfȯr-tē; -ˌa-nə-ˈfȯr-tē, -ˌä-\ *n* [It] (1767) **1 :** FORTEPIANO **2 :** PIANO

piano hinge *n* (1926) **:** a hinge that has a thin pin joint and extends along the full length of the part to be moved

pi·as·sa·va \ˌpē-ə-ˈsä-və\ *n* [Pg *piassaba,* fr. Tupi *piasáβa*] (1835) **1 :** any of several stiff coarse fibers obtained from palms and used esp. in cordage or brushes **2 :** a palm yielding piassava; *esp* **:** either of two Brazilian palms (*Attalea funifera* and *Leopoldinia piassaba*)

pi·as·tre *also* **pi·as·ter** \pē-ˈas-tər, -ˈäs-\ *n* [F *piastre,* fr. It *piastra* thin metal plate, coin, fr. L *emplastra, emplastrum* plaster] (1592) **1 :** PIECE OF EIGHT **2** — see *pound* at MONEY table

pi·az·za \pē-ˈa-zə, -ˈä-, *1 is usu* -ˈat-sə, -ˈät-\ *n, pl* **piazzas** *or* **pi·az·ze** \-ˈat-(ˌ)sā, -ˈät-\ [It, fr. L *platea* broad street — more at PLACE] (1563) **1** *pl piazze* **:** an open square esp. in an Italian town **2 a :** an arcaded and roofed gallery **b** *dial* **:** VERANDA, PORCH

pi·broch \ˈpē-ˌbräk, -ˌbräk\ *n* [ScGael *pìobaireachd* pipe music] (1719) **:** a set of martial or mournful variations for the Scottish Highland bagpipe

[1]**pic** \ˈpik\ *n, pl* **pics** *or* **pix** \ˈpiks\ [short for *picture*] (1884) **1 :** PHOTOGRAPH **2 :** MOTION PICTURE

[2]**pic** \ˈpik, ˈpēk\ *n* [Sp *pica,* fr. *picar* to prick] (1926) **:** the picador's lance

[1]**pi·ca** \ˈpī-kə\ *n* [NL, fr. L, magpie — more at PIE] (1563) **:** an abnormal desire to eat substances (as chalk or ashes) not normally eaten

[2]**pica** *n* [prob. fr. ML, collection of church rules] (1588) **1 :** 12-point type **2 :** a unit of about 1/6 inch used in measuring typographic material **3 :** a typewriter type providing 10 characters to the linear inch and six lines to the vertical inch

pic·a·dor \ˈpi-kə-ˌdȯr, ˌpi-kə-ˈ\ *n, pl* **picadors** \-ˌdȯrz, -ˈdȯrz\ *or* **pic·a·do·res** \ˌpi-kə-ˈdȯr-ēz\ [Sp, fr. *picar* to prick, fr. VL **piccare* — more at PIKE] (1797) **:** a horseman in a bullfight who jabs the bull with a lance to weaken its neck and shoulder muscles

[1]**pi·ca·resque** \ˌpi-kə-ˈresk, ˌpē-\ *adj* [Sp *picaresco,* fr. *pícaro*] (1810) **:** of or relating to rogues or rascals; *also* **:** of, relating to, suggesting, or being a type of fiction dealing with the episodic adventures of a usu. roguish protagonist ⟨a ∼ novel⟩

[2]**picaresque** *n* (1895) **:** one that is picaresque

pi·ca·ro \ˈpē-kä-ˌrō\ *n, pl* **-ros** [Sp *pícaro*] (1623) **:** ROGUE, BOHEMIAN

[1]**pic·a·roon** *or* **pick·a·roon** \ˌpi-kə-ˈrün\ *n* [Sp *picarón,* aug. of *pícaro*] (1624) **1 :** PIRATE **2 :** PICARO

[2]**picaroon** *vi* (1625) **:** to act as a pirate

[1]**pic·a·yune** \ˌpi-kē-ˈyün\ *n* [Occitan *picaioun,* a small coin, fr. *picaio* money, fr. *pica* to jingle, of imit. origin] (1804) **1 a :** a Spanish half real piece formerly current in the South **b :** HALF DIME **2 :** something trivial

[2]**picayune** *adj* (1836) **:** of little value **:** PALTRY; *also* **:** PETTY, SMALL-MINDED — **pic·a·yun·ish** \-ˈyü-nish\ *adj*

pic·ca·lil·li \ˌpi-kə-ˈli-lē\ *n* [prob. alter. of *pickle*] (1845) **:** a relish of chopped vegetables and spices

[1]**pic·co·lo** \ˈpi-kə-ˌlō\ *adj* [It, small] (ca. 1854) **:** smaller than ordinary size ⟨a ∼ banjo⟩

[2]**piccolo** *n, pl* **-los** [It, short for *piccolo flauto* small flute] (1856) **:** a small shrill flute whose range is an octave higher than that of an ordinary flute — **pic·co·lo·ist** \-ˌlō-ist\ *n*

pice \ˈpīs\ *n, pl* **pice** [Hindi *paisā*] (1615) **:** PAISA

pi·ce·ous \ˈpī-sē-əs\ *adj* [L *piceus,* fr. *pic-, pix* pitch — more at PITCH] (1826) **:** of, relating to, or resembling pitch; *esp* **:** glossy brownish black in color ⟨an insect with a ∼ abdomen⟩

pi·cho·line \ˌpē-shō-ˈlēn\ *n* [F, fr. Occitan *pichoulino*] (ca. 1959) **:** a medium-sized brine-cured green olive of French origin

[1]**pick** \ˈpik\ *vb* [ME *piken,* partly fr. OE **pīcian* (akin to MD *picken* to prick); partly fr. MF *piquer* to prick — more at PIKE] *vt* (14c) **1 :** to pierce, penetrate, or break up with a pointed instrument ⟨∼*ed* the hard clay⟩ **2 a :** to remove bit by bit ⟨∼ meat from bones⟩ **b :** to remove covering or adhering matter from ⟨∼ the bones⟩ **3 a :** to gather by plucking ⟨∼ apples⟩ **b :** CHOOSE, SELECT ⟨tried to ∼ the shortest route⟩ **c :** to make (one's way) slowly and carefully ⟨∼*ed* his way through the rubble⟩ **4 a :** PILFER, ROB ⟨∼ pockets⟩ **b :** to obtain useful information from by questioning — used in such phrases as *pick the brains of* **5 :** PROVOKE ⟨∼ a quarrel⟩ **6 a :** to dig into **:** PROBE ⟨∼*ing* his teeth⟩ **b :** to pluck (as a guitar) with a pick or with the fingers **c :** to loosen or pull apart with a sharp point ⟨∼ wool⟩ **7 :** to unlock with a device (as a wire) other than the key ⟨∼ a lock⟩ ∼ *vi* **1 :** to use or work with a pick **2 :** to gather or harvest something by plucking **3 :** PILFER — used in the phrase *picking and stealing* **4 :** to eat sparingly or mincingly ⟨∼*ing* listlessly at his dinner⟩ — **pick and choose :** to select with care and deliberation — **pick at :** to criticize repeatedly esp. for minor faults **:** NAG — **pick on :** to single out for criticism, teasing, or bullying ⟨*picked on* smaller boys⟩; *also* **:** to single out for a particular purpose or for special attention

[2]**pick** *n* (15c) **1 :** a blow or stroke with a pointed instrument **2 a :** the act or privilege of choosing or selecting **:** CHOICE ⟨take your ∼⟩ **b :** the best or choicest one ⟨the ∼ of the herd⟩ **c :** one that is picked ⟨his ∼ for vice president⟩ **3 :** the portion of a crop gathered at one time ⟨the first ∼ of peaches⟩ **4 :** a screen in basketball

[3]**pick** *n* [ME *pik*] (14c) **1 :** a heavy wooden-handled iron or steel tool pointed at one or both ends — compare MATTOCK **2 a :** TOOTHPICK **b :** PICKLOCK **c :** a small thin piece (as of plastic or metal) used to pluck the strings of a stringed instrument **3 :** one of the points on the forepart of the blade of a skate used in figure skating **4 :** a comb with long widely spaced teeth used to give height to a hairstyle

[4]**pick** *vt* [ME *pykken* to pitch (a tent); akin to ME *picchen* to pitch] (1523) **1** *chiefly dial* **:** to throw or thrust with effort **:** HURL **2 :** to throw (a shuttle) across the loom

[5]**pick** *n* (1627) **1** *dial Eng* **a :** the act of pitching or throwing **b :** something thrown **2 a :** a throw of the shuttle **b :** a filling thread

pickaback *var of* PIGGYBACK

pick–and–roll \ˈpik-ən(d)-ˈrōl\ *n* (ca. 1961) **:** a basketball play in which a player sets a screen and then cuts toward the basket for a pass

pick–and–shovel *adj* (1895) **:** done with or as if with a pick and shovel **:** LABORIOUS

pick·a·nin·ny *or* **pic·a·nin·ny** \ˈpi-kə-ˌni-nē, ˌpi-kə-ˈ\ *n, pl* **-nies** [prob. ultim. fr. Pg *pequenino,* dim. of *pequeno* small] (1653) *often offensive* **:** a black child

pick·ax \ˈpik-ˌaks\ *n* [ME *pecaxe,* alter. of *pikois,* fr. AF *picois,* fr. *pic* pick, fr. L *picus* woodpecker — more at PIE] (15c) **:** [3]PICK 1

[1]**pick·ed** \ˈpi-kəd\ *adj* [ME, fr. [3]*pick*] (14c) *chiefly dial* **:** POINTED, PEAKED

[2]**picked** \ˈpikt\ *adj* [[1]*pick*] (ca. 1548) **:** CHOICE, PRIME

pick·eer \pi-ˈkir\ *vi* [prob. modif. of F *picorer* to maraud, perh. fr. MF *pecore* sheep, fr. OIt *pecora* — more at PECORINO] (ca. 1645) *archaic* **:** to skirmish in advance of an army; *also* **:** SCOUT, RECONNOITER

pick·er \ˈpi-kər\ *n* (14c) **:** one that picks: as **a :** a worker who picks something (as crops) **b :** a tool, implement, or machine used in picking something **c :** a musician who picks a stringed instrument (as a banjo)

pick·er·el \ˈpi-k(ə-)rəl\ *n, pl* **-el** *or* **-els** [ME *pikerel,* dim. of *pike*] (13c) **1 a** *dial chiefly Brit* **:** a young or small pike **b :** either of two fishes resembling but smaller than the related northern pike: (1) **:** CHAIN PICKEREL (2) **:** one (*Esox americanus*) of eastern No. America having green or red fins and a black bar below and slanting away from the eye **2 :** WALLEYE 3

pick·er·el·weed \-ˌwēd\ *n* (1836) **:** a shallow-water monocotyledonous perennial plant (*Pontederia cordata*) chiefly of the eastern U.S. and Canada with large leaves and a spike of purplish-blue flowers

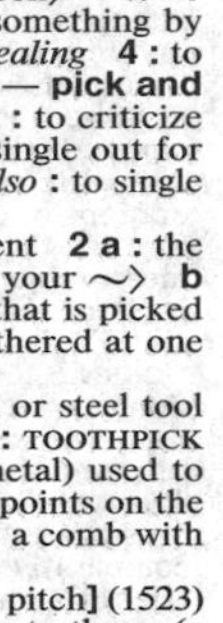

pickerelweed

[1]**pick·et** \ˈpi-kət\ *n* [F *piquet,* fr. MF, fr. *piquer* to prick — more at PIKE] (ca. 1702) **1 :** a pointed or sharpened stake, post, or pale **2 a :** a detached body of soldiers serving to guard an army from surprise **b :** a detachment kept ready in camp for such duty **c :** SENTRY **3 :** a person posted by a labor organization at a place of work affected by a strike; *also* **:** a person posted for a demonstration or protest

[2]**picket** *vt* (1745) **1 :** to enclose, fence, or fortify with pickets **2 a :** to guard with a picket **b :** to post as a picket **3 :** TETHER **4 a :** to post pickets at **b :** to walk or stand in front of as a picket ~ *vi* **:** to serve as a picket — **pick·et·er** *n*

pick·et·boat \ˈpi-kət-ˌbōt\ *n* (1866) **:** a craft used (as by the coast guard) for harbor patrol

picket line *n* (1856) **1 :** a position held by a line of military pickets **2 :** a line of people picketing a business, organization, or institution

pick·ings \ˈpi-kiŋz, -kənz\ *n pl* (1642) **:** something that is picked or picked up: as **a :** gleanable or eatable fragments **:** SCRAPS **b :** yield or return for effort expended ⟨easy ~⟩ ⟨slim ~⟩

[1]**pick·le** \ˈpi-kəl\ *n* [ME *pykyl, pekill* sauce, gravy, fr. or akin to MD *peeckel* brine] (15c) **1 :** a solution or bath for preserving or cleaning: as **a :** a brine or vinegar solution in which foods are preserved **b :** any of various baths used in industrial cleaning or processing **2 :** a difficult situation **:** PLIGHT ⟨could see no way out of the ~ I was in —R. L. Stevenson⟩ **3 :** an article of food that has been preserved in brine or in vinegar; *specif* **:** a cucumber that has been so preserved

[2]**pickle** *vt* **pick·led; pick·ling** \-k(ə-)liŋ\ (1570) **1 :** to treat, preserve, or clean in or with a pickle **2 :** to give a light finish to (as furniture) by bleaching or painting and wiping

[3]**pickle** *n* [perh. fr. Sc *pickle* to trifle, pilfer] (1552) **1** *Scot* **:** GRAIN, KERNEL **2** *Scot* **:** a small quantity

pickled *adj* (ca. 1552) **1 :** preserved in or cured with pickle ⟨~ herring⟩ **2 :** DRUNK 1a ⟨gets thoroughly ~ before dinner —*New Yorker*⟩

pick·le·weed \ˈpi-kəl-ˌwēd\ *n* (ca. 1925) **:** any of several succulent plants having leaves often reduced to scales or sheaths: as **a :** GLASSWORT **b :** a shrub (*Allenrolfea occidentalis*) of the goosefoot family growing in moist saline soils of the southwestern U.S. **c :** SALTWORT 2

pick·lock \ˈpik-ˌläk\ *n* (1553) **1 :** BURGLAR **2 :** a tool for picking locks

pick–me–up \ˈpik-mē-ˌəp\ *n* (1867) **:** something that stimulates or restores **:** TONIC, BRACER ⟨my usual morning ~⟩

pick·off \ˈpik-ˌȯf\ *n* (1939) **:** a baseball play in which a base runner is picked off

pick off *vt* (1810) **1 :** to shoot or bring down esp. one by one **2 :** to put out (a base runner who is off base) with a quick throw (as from the pitcher or catcher) **3 :** INTERCEPT ⟨*picked off* a pass⟩

pick out *vt* (1540) **1 :** DISCERN, MAKE OUT **2 :** to play the notes of by ear or one by one ⟨*picking out* tunes on the piano⟩

pick over *vt* (1839) **:** to examine in order to select the best or remove the unwanted

pick·pock·et \ˈpik-ˌpä-kət\ *n* (1591) **:** a thief who picks pockets

pick·proof \-ˌprüf\ *adj* (1933) **:** designed to prevent picking ⟨a ~ lock⟩

pick·thank \-ˌthaŋk\ *n* [fr. *pick a thank* to seek someone's favor] (15c) *archaic* **:** SYCOPHANT

[1]**pick·up** \ˈpik-ˌəp\ *n* (1848) **1 :** one that is picked up: as **a :** a hitchhiker who is given a ride **b :** a temporary chance acquaintance **c :** a player acquired from another team **2 :** the act or process of picking up: as **a :** a revival of business activity **b :** ACCELERATION **c :** the act or technique of making the acquaintance of a previously unknown person esp. for amorous purposes **3 :** the conversion of mechanical movements into electrical impulses in the reproduction of sound; *also* **:** a device (as on a phonograph) for making such conversion **4 a :** the reception of sound or an image into a radio or television transmitting apparatus for conversion into electrical signals **b :** a device (as a microphone or a television camera) for converting sound or the image of a scene into electrical signals **5 :** a light truck having an enclosed cab and an open body with low sides and tailgate — called also *pickup truck* **6 :** a pickup game ⟨playing ~⟩

[2]**pickup** *adj* (1909) **:** utilizing or comprising local or available personnel esp. without formal organization ⟨a ~ basketball game⟩ ⟨a ~ band⟩

pick up *vt* (14c) **1 a :** to take hold of and lift up **b :** to gather together **:** COLLECT ⟨*picked up* all the pieces⟩ **c :** to clean up **:** TIDY **2 :** to take (passengers or freight) into a vehicle **3 a :** to acquire casually or by chance ⟨*picked up* a valuable antique at an auction⟩ **b :** to acquire by study or experience **:** LEARN ⟨*picking up* a great deal of knowledge in the process —Robert Schleicher⟩ **c :** to obtain esp. by payment **:** BUY ⟨*picked up* some groceries⟩ **d :** to acquire (a player) esp. from another team through a trade or by financial recompense **e :** to accept for the purpose of paying ⟨offered to *pick up* the tab⟩ **f :** to come down with **:** CATCH ⟨*picked up* a cold⟩ **g :** GAIN, EARN ⟨*picked up* a few yards on the last play⟩ ⟨*picked up* her first victory⟩ **4 a :** to enter informally into conversation or companionship with (a previously unknown person) ⟨had a brief affair with a girl he *picked up* in a bar⟩ **b :** to take into custody ⟨the police *picked up* the fugitive⟩ **5 a :** to catch sight of **:** PERCEIVE ⟨*picked up* the harbor lights⟩ **b :** to come to and follow ⟨*picked up* the outlaw's trail⟩ **c :** to bring within range of sight or hearing ⟨*pick up* distant radio signals⟩ **d :** UNDERSTAND, CATCH ⟨didn't *pick up* the hint⟩ **6 a :** REVIVE **b :** INCREASE **7 :** to resume after a break **:** CONTINUE ⟨*pick up* the discussion tomorrow⟩ **8 :** to assume responsibility for guarding (an opponent) in an athletic contest ~ *vi* **1 :** to recover or increase speed, vigor, or activity **:** IMPROVE ⟨after the strike, business *picked up*⟩ ⟨the wind began to *pick up*⟩ **2 :** to put things in order ⟨was always *picking up* after her⟩ **3 :** to pack up one's belongings ⟨couldn't just *pick up* and leave⟩ — **pick up on 1 a :** UNDERSTAND, APPRECIATE **b :** to become aware of **:** NOTICE **2 :** to adopt as one's own **:** TAKE UP

Pick·wick·ian \(ˌ)pik-ˈwi-kē-ən\ *adj* [Samuel *Pickwick,* character in the novel *Pickwick Papers* (1836–37) by Charles Dickens] (1836) **1 :** marked by simplicity and generosity **2 :** intended or taken in a sense other than the obvious or literal one

picky \ˈpi-kē\ *adj* **pick·i·er; -est** (1900) **:** FUSSY, CHOOSY ⟨a ~ eater⟩

pi·clo·ram \ˈpi-klə-ˌram, ˈpī-\ *n* [*pic*olinic acid (acid obtained by oxidation of picoline) + *chlor-* + *am*ine] (1965) **:** a systemic herbicide $C_6H_3Cl_3N_2O_2$ that is persistent in the soil

[1]**pic·nic** \ˈpik-(ˌ)nik\ *n, often attrib* [G or F; G *Picknick,* fr. F *pique-nique*] (1826) **1 :** an excursion or outing with food usu. provided by members of the group and eaten in the open; *also* **:** the food provided for a picnic **2 a :** a pleasant or amusingly carefree experience ⟨I don't expect being married to be a ~ —Josephine Pinckney⟩ **b :** an easy task or feat **3 :** a shoulder of pork with much of the butt removed — **pic·nic·ky** \-(ˌ)ni-kē\ *adj*

[2]**picnic** *vi* **pic·nicked; pic·nick·ing** (1842) **:** to go on a picnic **:** eat in picnic fashion — **pic·nick·er** *n*

pico- *comb form* [ISV, prob. fr. Sp *pico* small amount, lit., peak, beak] **1 :** one trillionth (10^{-12}) part of ⟨*pico*gram⟩ **2 :** very small ⟨*pico*rnavirus⟩

pi·co·gram \ˈpē-kō-ˌgram, -kə-\ *n* [ISV] (1951) **:** one trillionth of a gram

pic·o·line \ˈpi-kə-ˌlēn, ˈpī-\ *n* [L *pic-, pix* pitch + ISV [1]*-ol* + [2]*-ine* — more at PITCH] (1853) **:** any of the three liquid isomeric pyridine derivatives C_6H_7N used chiefly as solvents and in organic synthesis

pi·co·mole \ˈpē-kō-ˌmōl, -kə-\ *n* (1968) **:** one trillionth of a mole

pi·cor·na·vi·rus \(ˌ)pē-ˌkȯr-nə-ˈvī-rəs\ *n* [*pico-* + *RNA* + *virus*] (1962) **:** any of a family (*Picornaviridae*) of small single-stranded RNA viruses that include the causative agents of encephalomyocarditis, hepatitis A, poliomyelitis, foot-and-mouth disease, and hand, foot and mouth disease — compare COXSACKIE VIRUS, ECHOVIRUS, ENTEROVIRUS, RHINOVIRUS

pi·co·sec·ond \ˌpē-kō-ˈse-kənd, -kənt\ *n* [ISV] (ca. 1962) **:** one trillionth of a second

pi·cot \ˈpē-(ˌ)kō, pē-ˈ\ *n* [F, lit., small point, fr. MF, fr. *pic* prick, fr. *piquer* to prick — more at PIKE] (ca. 1882) **:** one of a series of small ornamental loops forming an edging on ribbon or lace

pic·o·tee \ˌpi-kə-ˈtē\ *n* [F *picoté* pointed, fr. *picoter* to mark with points, fr. *picot*] (1727) **:** a flower (as some carnations or tulips) having one basic color with a margin of another color

picr- *or* **picro-** *comb form* [F, fr. Gk *pikr-, pikro-,* fr. *pikros* — more at PAINT] **:** bitter ⟨*picr*ic acid⟩

pic·ric acid \ˈpi-krik-\ *n* [ISV] (1852) **:** a toxic yellow crystalline phenol derivative $C_6H_3N_3O_7$ structurally similar to TNT and used esp. as a high explosive and as a dye or mordant

pic·ro·tox·in \ˌpi-krō-ˈtäk-sən\ *n* [ISV] (1815) **:** a poisonous bitter crystalline stimulant and convulsive substance $C_{30}H_{34}O_{13}$ obtained from the berry of a southeast Asian vine (*Anamirta cocculus*) and used intravenously as an antidote for barbiturate poisoning

Pict \ˈpikt\ *n* [ME *Pictes,* pl., Picts, fr. OE *Pihtas,* fr. LL *Picti*] (bef. 12c) **:** a member of a people of the north of Scotland who are first noted in historical records in the late third century and who became amalgamated with the Scots in the mid-eighth century — **Pict·ish** \ˈpik-tish\ *adj or n*

pic·to·gram \ˈpik-tə-ˌgram\ *n* [ISV *picto-* (fr. L *pictus*) + *-gram*] (1910) **:** PICTOGRAPH

pic·to·graph \-ˌgraf\ *n* [L *pictus* + E *-o-* + *-graph*] (1851) **1 :** an ancient or prehistoric drawing or painting on a rock wall **2 :** one of the symbols belonging to a pictorial graphic system **3 :** a diagram representing statistical data by pictorial forms — **pic·to·graph·ic** \ˌpik-tə-ˈgra-fik\ *adj*

pic·tog·ra·phy \pik-ˈtä-grə-fē\ *n* (1851) **:** use of pictographs **:** PICTURE WRITING 1

[1]**pic·to·ri·al** \pik-ˈtȯr-ē-əl\ *adj* [LL *pictorius,* fr. L *pictor* painter — more at PICTURESQUE] (1646) **1 :** of or relating to a painter, a painting, or the painting or drawing of pictures ⟨~ perspective⟩ **2 a :** of, relating to, or consisting of pictures ⟨~ records⟩ **b :** illustrated by pictures ⟨~ weekly⟩ **c :** consisting of or displaying the characteristics of pictographs **d :** suggesting or conveying visual images ⟨~ poetry⟩ — **pic·to·ri·al·ly** \-ē-ə-lē\ *adv* — **pic·to·ri·al·ness** *n*

[2]**pictorial** *n* (1844) **:** a periodical having much pictorial matter

pic·to·ri·al·ism \-ē-ə-ˌli-zəm\ *n* (1869) **1 :** the use or creation of pictures or visual images **2 :** a movement or technique in photography emphasizing artificial often romanticized pictorial qualities — **pic·to·ri·al·ist** \-list\ *adj or n*

pic·to·ri·al·ize \pik-ˈtȯr-ē-ə-ˌlīz\ *vt* **-ized; -iz·ing** (1870) **:** to represent by a picture or illustrate with pictures — **pic·to·ri·al·i·za·tion** \-ˌtȯr-ē-ə-lə-ˈzā-shən\ *n*

[1]**pic·ture** \ˈpik-chər\ *n* [ME, fr. L *pictura,* fr. *pictus,* pp. of *pingere* to paint — more at PAINT] (15c) **1 :** a design or representation made by various means (as painting, drawing, or photography) **2 a :** a description so vivid or graphic as to suggest a mental image or give an accurate idea of something ⟨the book gives a detailed ~ of what is happening⟩ **b :** a mental image **3 :** IMAGE, COPY ⟨he was the ~ of his father⟩ ⟨she was the very ~ of health⟩ **4 a :** a transitory visible image or reproduction **b :** MOTION PICTURE **c** *pl* **:** MOVIES **5 :** TABLEAU 2 **6 :** SITUATION ⟨took a hard look at his financial ~⟩

[2]**picture** *vt* **pic·tured; pic·tur·ing** \ˈpik-chə-riŋ, ˈpik-shriŋ\ (15c) **1 :** to paint or draw a representation, image, or visual conception of **:** DEPICT; *also* **:** ILLUSTRATE **2 :** to describe graphically in words **3 :** to form a mental image of **:** IMAGINE

picture–book *adj* (1922) **:** suitable for or suggestive of a picture book: as **a :** PICTURESQUE **b :** PICTURE-PERFECT

picture book *n* (1847) **:** a book that consists wholly or chiefly of pictures

picture hat *n* (1887) **:** a woman's dressy hat with a broad brim

picture–perfect *adj* (1981) **:** completely flawless **:** PERFECT ⟨made a ~ landing⟩

pic·ture·phone \ˈpik-chər-ˌfōn\ *n* (1956) **:** VIDEOPHONE

picture–postcard *adj* (1907) **:** PICTURESQUE 1 ⟨a ~ village⟩

picture puzzle *n* (1898) **:** JIGSAW PUZZLE

pic·tur·esque \ˌpik-chə-ˈresk\ *adj* [F & It; F *pittoresque,* fr. It *pittoresco,* fr. *pittore* painter, fr. L *pictor,* fr. *pingere*] (1703) **1 a :** resembling a picture **:** suggesting a painted scene **b :** charming or quaint in appearance **2 :** evoking mental images **:** VIVID ***syn*** see GRAPHIC — **pic·tur·esque·ly** *adv* — **pic·tur·esque·ness** *n*

picture tube *n* (1937) **:** a cathode-ray tube on which the picture appears in a television

\ə\ **abut** \ᵊ\ kitten, F table \ər\ **further** \a\ **ash** \ā\ **ace** \ä\ mop, mar \au̇\ **out** \ch\ **chin** \e\ **bet** \ē\ **easy** \g\ **go** \i\ **hit** \ī\ **ice** \j\ **job** \ŋ\ **sing** \ō\ **go** \ȯ\ **law** \ȯi\ **boy** \th\ **thin** \t͟h\ **the** \ü\ **loot** \u̇\ **foot** \y\ **yet** \zh\ **vision,** beige \k, ⁿ, œ, ue, ʸ\ *see* Guide to Pronunciation

picture window *n* (1938) **:** an outsize usu. single-paned window designed to frame an exterior view

picture writing *n* (1741) **1 :** the recording of events or expression of messages by pictures representing actions or facts **2 :** the record or message represented by picture writing

pic·tur·ize \ˈpik-chə-ˌrīz\ *vt* **-ized; -iz·ing** (ca. 1846) **:** to make a picture of **:** present in pictures; *esp* **:** to make into a motion picture ‹~ a novel› — **pic·tur·i·za·tion** \ˌpik-chə-rə-ˈzā-shən\ *n*

PID *abbr* pelvic inflammatory disease

pid·dle \ˈpi-dᵊl\ *vi* **pid·dled; pid·dling** \ˈpid-liŋ, ˈpi-dᵊl-iŋ\ [origin unknown] (1545) **1 :** DAWDLE, PUTTER **2 :** URINATE

pid·dling \ˈpid-lən, -liŋ; ˈpi-dᵊl-ən, -iŋ\ *adj* (1559) **:** TRIVIAL, PALTRY

pid·dly \ˈpid-lē\ *adj* (1946) **:** TRIVIAL, PIDDLING

pid·dock \ˈpi-dək, -dik\ *n* [origin unknown] (1851) **:** a bivalve mollusk (family Pholadidae, esp. genera *Pholas* and *Barnea*) that bores holes in wood, clay, and rocks

pid·gin \ˈpi-jən\ *n* [*pidgin English*] (1876) **:** a simplified speech used for communication between people with different languages — **pid·gin·i·za·tion** \ˌpi-jə-nə-ˈzā-shən\ *n* — **pid·gin·ize** \ˈpi-jə-ˌnīz\ *vt*

pidgin English *n, often cap P* [Chinese Pidgin English *pidgin* business] (1859) **:** an English-based pidgin; *esp* **:** one orig. used in parts of east Asia

[1]**pie** \ˈpī\ *n* [ME, fr. AF, fr. L *pica;* akin to L *picus* woodpecker, OHG *speh*] (13c) **:** MAGPIE

[2]**pie** *n* [ME] (14c) **1 :** a meat dish baked with biscuit or pastry crust — compare POTPIE **2 :** a dessert consisting of a filling (as of fruit or custard) in a pastry shell or topped with pastry or both **3 a :** AFFAIR, BUSINESS ‹she wanted her finger . . . in every possible social ~ —Mary Deasy› **b :** a whole regarded as divisible into shares ‹giving the less fortunate . . . a larger share of the economic ~ —R. M. Hutchins›

[3]**pie** *var of* PI

[1]**pie·bald** \ˈpī-ˌbȯld\ *adj* (1589) **1 :** composed of incongruous parts **2 :** of different colors; *esp* **:** spotted or blotched with black and white

[2]**piebald** *n* (1765) **:** a piebald animal (as a horse)

[1]**piece** \ˈpēs\ *n* [ME, fr. AF, fr. VL **pettia,* of Gaulish origin; akin to W *peth* thing] (13c) **1 :** a part of a whole: as **a :** FRAGMENT ‹~*s* of broken glass› **b :** any of the individual members comprising a unit — often used in combination ‹a five-*piece* band› ‹a three-*piece* suit› **c :** PORTION, ALLOCATION ‹a ~ of the jackpot› **2 :** an object or individual regarded as a unit of a kind or class ‹a ~ of fruit› **3 :** a usu. unspecified distance ‹down the road a ~› **4 :** a standard quantity (as of length, weight, or size) in which something is made or sold **5 :** a literary, journalistic, artistic, dramatic, or musical composition **6 :** FIREARM **7 :** COIN; *also* **:** TOKEN **8 :** a movable object used in playing a board game; *specif* **:** a chessman other than a pawn **9 :** OPINION, VIEW ‹spoke his ~› **10 a** *usu vulgar* **:** an act of copulation **b** *usu vulgar* **:** the female partner in sexual intercourse **11 :** INSTANCE, EXAMPLE ‹silly ~ of nonsense› ‹a nice ~ of acting› ***syn*** see PART — **of a piece :** ALIKE, CONSISTENT — **piece of one's mind :** a severe scolding **:** TONGUE-LASHING — **piece of the action :** a share in activity or profit — **to pieces 1 :** without reserve or restraint **:** COMPLETELY **2 :** into fragments; *also* **:** into component parts **3 :** out of control ‹went *to pieces* from shock›

[2]**piece** *vt* **pieced; piec·ing** (15c) **1 :** to repair, renew, or complete by adding pieces **:** PATCH **2 :** to join into a whole — often used with *together* ‹his new book . . . has been *pieced* together from talks —Merle Miller› — **piec·er** *n*

piece by piece *adv* (1560) **:** by degrees **:** PIECEMEAL

pièce de ré·sis·tance \pē-ˌes-də-rə-ˌzē-ˈstän(t)s, -rā-, -ˈstäⁿs\ *n, pl* **pièces de ré·sis·tance** *same*\ [F, lit., piece of resistance] (1839) **1 :** the chief dish of a meal **2 :** an outstanding item or event **:** SHOWPIECE

piece–dye \ˈpēs-ˌdī\ *vt* (1920) **:** to dye after weaving or knitting

piece goods *n pl* (1665) **:** cloth fabrics sold from the bolt at retail in lengths specified by the customer — called also *yard goods*

[1]**piece·meal** \ˈpēs-ˌmēl, -ˈmēl\ *adv* (14c) **1 :** one piece at a time **:** GRADUALLY **2 :** in pieces or fragments **:** APART

[2]**piecemeal** *adj* (1600) **:** done, made, or accomplished piece by piece or in a fragmentary way ‹~ reforms in the system›

piece of cake (1935) **:** something easily done **:** CINCH, BREEZE

piece of eight (1610) **:** an old Spanish peso of eight reals

piece of work (1928) **:** a complicated, difficult, or eccentric person

piece·wise \ˈpēs-ˌwīz\ *adv* (1674) **:** with respect to a number of discrete intervals, sets, or pieces ‹~ continuous functions›

piece·work \-ˌwərk\ *n* (1549) **:** work done by the piece and paid for at a set rate per unit — **piece·work·er** \-ˌwər-kər\ *n*

pie chart *n* (1922) **:** a circular chart cut by radii into segments illustrating relative magnitudes or frequencies — called also *circle graph*

pie·crust \ˈpī-ˌkrəst\ *n* (1582) **:** the pastry shell of a pie

[1]**pied** \ˈpīd\ *adj* (14c) **:** of two or more colors in blotches; *also* **:** wearing or having a parti-colored coat ‹a ~ horse›

[2]**pied** *past and past part of* PI *or of* PIE

pied–à–terre \pē-ˌā-də-ˈter, -ˌā-dä-; ˌpyā-dä-\ *n, pl* **pieds–à–terre** *same*\ [F, lit., foot to the ground] (1829) **:** a temporary or second lodging

pied·mont \ˈpēd-ˌmänt\ *adj* [*Piedmont,* region of Italy] (1855) **:** lying or formed at the base of mountains — **piedmont** *n*

pied piper *n, often cap both Ps* [the *Pied Piper,* hero of a German folktale who charmed the rats of Hameln, Germany, into a river] (1925) **1 :** one that offers strong but delusive enticement **2 :** a leader who makes irresponsible promises **3 :** a charismatic person who attracts followers

pie–eyed \ˈpī-ˌīd\ *adj* (1904) **:** INTOXICATED

pie–faced \-ˌfāst\ *adj* (ca. 1912) **:** having a round, smooth, or blank face

pie·hole \ˈpī-ˌhōl\ *n* (1993) *slang* **:** MOUTH 1a

pieing *pres part of* PI *or of* PIE

pie in the sky (1911) **:** an unrealistic enterprise or prospect of prosperity — **pie–in–the–sky** *adj*

pie·plant \ˈpī-ˌplant\ *n* (1838) **:** garden rhubarb

pier \ˈpir\ *n* [ME *per,* fr. OE, fr. ML *pera*] (12c) **1 :** an intermediate support for the adjacent ends of two bridge spans **2 :** a structure (as a breakwater) extending into navigable water for use as a landing place or promenade or to protect or form a harbor **3 :** a vertical structural support: as **a :** the wall between two openings **b :** PILLAR, PILASTER **c :** a vertical member that supports the end of an arch or lintel **d :** an auxiliary mass of masonry used to stiffen a wall **4 :** a structural mount (as for a telescope) usu. of stonework, concrete, or steel

pierce \ˈpirs\ *vb* **pierced; pierc·ing** [ME *percen,* fr. AF *percer,* fr. VL **pertusiare,* fr. L *pertusus,* pp. of *pertundere* to perforate, fr. *per-* through + *tundere* to beat — more at PER-, CONTUSION] *vt* (14c) **1 a :** to run into or through as a pointed weapon does **:** STAB **b :** to enter or thrust into sharply or painfully **2 :** to make a hole through **:** PERFORATE **3 :** to force or make a way into or through **4 :** to penetrate with the eye or mind **:** DISCERN **5 :** to penetrate so as to move or touch the emotions of ~ *vi* **:** to force a way into or through something ***syn*** see ENTER — **pierc·er** *n*

pierced *adj* (14c) **1 :** having holes; *esp* **:** decorated with perforations **2 :** having the flesh punctured for the attachment of a piece of jewelry ‹~ ears› ‹a ~ tongue› **3 :** designed for pierced ears ‹~ earrings›

[1]**piercing** *adj* (14c) **:** PENETRATING: as **a :** LOUD, SHRILL ‹~ cries› **b :** PERCEPTIVE ‹~ eyes› **c :** penetratingly cold **:** BITING ‹a ~ wind› **d :** CUTTING, INCISIVE ‹~ sarcasm› — **pierc·ing·ly** \ˈpir-siŋ-lē\ *adv*

[2]**piercing** *n* (1977) **:** a piece of jewelry (as a ring or stud) that is attached to pierced flesh

pier glass *n* (1703) **:** a large high mirror; *esp* **:** one designed to occupy the wall space between windows — called also *pier mirror*

Pi·eri·an \pī-ˈir-ē-ən, -ˈer-\ *adj* (1591) **1 :** of or relating to the region of Pieria in ancient Macedonia or to the Muses who were once worshipped there **2 :** of or relating to learning or poetry

pie·ro·gi *also* **pi·ro·gi** \pə-ˈrō-gē, pi-\ *n, pl* **-gi** *also* **-gies** [Pol, pl. of *pieróg* dumpling, pierogi] (1811) **:** a case of dough filled with a savory filling (as of meat, cheese, or vegetables) and cooked by boiling and then panfrying

Pier·rot \ˈpē-ə-ˌrō\ *n* [F, dim. of *Pierre* Peter] (ca. 1770) **:** a stock comic character of old French pantomime usu. having a whitened face and wearing loose white clothes

pier table *n* (1765) **:** a table to be placed under a pier glass

pies *pl of* PI *or of* PIE

pie safe *n* (1951) **:** a cupboard whose doors have decoratively pierced tin panels for ventilation

pie·tà \ˌpē-(ˌ)ā-ˈtä, pyā-\ *n, often cap* [It, lit., pity, fr. L *pietat-, pietas*] (1644) **:** a representation of the Virgin Mary mourning over the dead body of Christ

pi·e·tism \ˈpī-ə-ˌti-zəm\ *n* (1697) **1** *cap* **:** a 17th century religious movement originating in Germany in reaction to formalism and intellectualism and stressing Bible study and personal religious experience **2 a :** emphasis on devotional experience and practices **b :** affectation of devotion — **pi·e·tist** \ˈpī-ə-tist\ *adj or n, often cap*

pi·e·tis·tic \ˌpī-ə-ˈtis-tik\ *adj* (1830) **1 :** of or relating to Pietism **2 a :** of or relating to religious devotion or devout persons **b :** marked by overly sentimental or emotional devotion to religion **:** RELIGIOSE — **pi·e·tis·ti·cal·ly** \-ti-k(ə-)lē\ *adv*

pi·e·ty \ˈpī-ə-tē\ *n, pl* **pi·e·ties** [F *pieté* piety, pity, fr. OF, fr. L *pietat-, pietas,* fr. *pius* dutiful, pious] (1579) **1 :** the quality or state of being pious: as **a :** fidelity to natural obligations (as to parents) **b :** dutifulness in religion **:** DEVOUTNESS **2 :** an act inspired by piety **3 :** a conventional belief or standard **:** ORTHODOXY ***syn*** see FIDELITY

piezo- *comb form* [Gk *piezein* to press; perh. akin to Skt *pīḍayati* he squeezes] **:** pressure ‹*piezo*meter›

pi·e·zo·elec·tric \pē-ˌā-(ˌ)zō-ə-ˈlek-trik, pē-ˌāt-(ˌ)sō-\ *adj* [ISV] (1883) **:** of, relating to, marked by, or functioning by means of piezoelectricity — **pi·e·zo·elec·tri·cal·ly** \-tri-k(ə-)lē\ *adv*

pi·e·zo·elec·tric·i·ty \-ˌlek-ˈtri-s(ə-)tē\ *n* [ISV] (1883) **:** electricity or electric polarity due to pressure esp. in a crystalline substance (as quartz)

pi·e·zom·e·ter \ˌpē-ə-ˈzä-mə-tər, pē-ˌāt-ˈsä-\ *n* (1820) **:** an instrument for measuring pressure or compressibility; *esp* **:** one for measuring the change of pressure of a material subjected to hydrostatic pressure — **pi·e·zo·met·ric** \pē-ˌā-zə-ˈme-trik, pē-ˌāt-sə-\ *adj*

[1]**pif·fle** \ˈpi-fəl\ *vi* **pif·fled; pif·fling** \-f(ə-)liŋ\ [perh. blend of *piddle* and *trifle*] (ca. 1878) **:** to talk or act in a trivial, inept, or ineffective way

[2]**piffle** *n* (1890) **:** trivial nonsense ‹pseudo-scientific ~›

pif·fling \ˈpi-flən, -f(ə-)liŋ\ *adj* (1864) **:** of little worth or importance **:** TRIVIAL

[1]**pig** \ˈpig\ *n, often attrib* [ME *pigge*] (13c) **1 a :** a young domesticated swine not yet sexually mature; *broadly* **:** a wild or domestic swine **b :** an animal related to or resembling the pig **2 a :** PORK **b :** the dressed carcass of a young swine weighing less than 130 pounds (60 kilograms) **c :** PIGSKIN **3 :** a dirty, gluttonous, or repulsive person **4 :** a crude casting of metal (as iron) **5** *slang* **:** an immoral woman **6** *slang, usu disparaging* **:** POLICE OFFICER — **pig·like** \-ˌlīk\ *adj*

[2]**pig** *vb* **pigged; pig·ging** *vi* (15c) **1 :** FARROW **2 :** to live like a pig ‹~ it› ~ *vt* **:** FARROW

pig·boat \ˈpig-ˌbōt\ *n* (1921) **:** SUBMARINE

[1]**pi·geon** \ˈpi-jən\ *n* [ME, fr. AF *pygoun, pijun,* fr. LL *pipion-, pipio* young bird, fr. L *pipire* to chirp] (14c) **1 :** any of a widely distributed family (Columbidae, order Columbiformes) of birds with a stout body, rather short legs, and smooth and compact plumage; *esp* **:** a member of any of numerous varieties of the rock dove that exist in domestication and in the feral state in cities and towns throughout most of the world **2 :** a young woman **3 :** an easy mark **:** DUPE **4 :** CLAY PIGEON

[2]**pigeon** *n* [alter. of *pidgin*] (1826) **:** an object of special concern **:** accepted business or interest ‹tennis was not his ~›

pigeon breast *n* (1842) **:** a deformity of the chest marked by sharp projection of the sternum

pigeon hawk *n* (ca. 1728) **:** MERLIN — used for one of No. America

[1]**pi·geon·hole** \ˈpi-jən-ˌhōl\ *n* (1577) **1 :** a hole or small recess for pigeons to nest **2 :** a small open compartment (as in a desk or cabinet) for keeping letters or documents **3 :** a neat category which usu. fails to reflect actual complexities

[2]**pigeonhole** *vt* (1840) **1 a :** to place in or as if in the pigeonhole of a desk **b :** to lay aside **:** SHELVE ‹his reports continued to be *pigeonholed* and his advice not taken —Walter Mills› **2 :** to assign to an often restrictive category **:** CLASSIFY — **pi·geon·hol·er** \-ˌhō-lər\ *n*

pi·geon·ite \ˈpi-jə-ˌnīt\ *n* [*Pigeon* Point, northeast Minn. + [1]*-ite*] (1900) **:** a monoclinic mineral of the pyroxene group

pi·geon–liv·ered \ˈpi-jən-ˌli-vərd\ *adj* (1602) **:** GENTLE, MILD

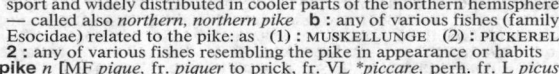

pigeon pea *n* (1725) **:** a leguminous shrubby herb (*Cajanus cajan*) with trifoliate leaves, yellow flowers, and flattened pods that is much cultivated esp. in the tropics; *also* **:** its small highly nutritious seed

pi·geon–toed \ˈpi-jən-ˌtōd\ *adj* (1786) **:** having the toes and forefoot turned inward

pi·geon·wing \-ˌwiŋ\ *n* (ca. 1808) **:** a fancy dance step executed by jumping and striking the legs together

pig·fish \ˈpig-ˌfish\ *n* (1860) **:** a saltwater grunt (*Orthopristis chrysoptera*) that is a food fish found from Long Island, N.Y., southward

pig·gery \ˈpi-gə-rē\ *n, pl* **-ger·ies** (1781) **1 :** a place where swine are kept **2 :** swinish behavior

pig·gin \ˈpi-gən\ *n* [ME *pygyn*] (14c) **:** a small wooden pail with one stave extended upward as a handle

piggin

pig·gish \ˈpi-gish\ *adj* (1820) **1 :** of, relating to, or suggestive of a pig ⟨a ~ snort⟩ **2 :** having qualities associated with a pig — **pig·gish·ly** *adv* — **pig·gish·ness** *n*

pig·gy \ˈpi-gē\ *adj* **pig·gi·er; -est** (ca. 1845) **:** PIGGISH

1**pig·gy·back** \ˈpi-gē-ˌbak\ *also* **pick·a·back** \ˈpi-gē-, ˈpi-kə-\ *adv* [alter. of earlier *a pick pack,* of unknown origin] (1565) **1 :** up on the back and shoulders **2 :** on or as if on the back of another; *esp* **:** on a railroad flatcar

2**piggyback** *also* **pickaback** *n* (ca. 1590) **1 :** the act of carrying piggyback **2 :** the movement of loaded truck trailers on railroad flatcars

3**piggyback** *also* **pickaback** *adj* (1823) **1 :** marked by being up on the shoulders and back ⟨a child needs hugging, tussling, and ~ rides —Benjamin Spock⟩ **2 :** carried or transported piggyback: as **a :** of or relating to the hauling of truck trailers on railroad flatcars **b :** being or relating to something carried into space as an extra load by a vehicle (as a spacecraft)

4**piggyback** *also* **pickaback** *vt* (1952) **1 :** to carry up on the shoulders and back **2 :** to haul (as a truck trailer) by railroad car **3 :** to set up or cause to function in conjunction with something larger, more important, or already in existence or operation ~ *vi* **:** to function or be carried on or as if on the back of another

piggy bank *n* (1941) **:** a coin bank often in the shape of a pig

pig·head·ed \ˈpig-ˌhe-dəd\ *adj* (1620) **:** willfully or perversely unyielding **:** OBSTINATE — **pig·head·ed·ly** *adv* — **pig·head·ed·ness** *n*

pig in a blanket *n, pl* **pigs in a blanket** *or* **pigs in blankets** (1926) **:** a frankfurter served in a wrapper of baked dough

pig in a poke (1562) **:** something offered in such a way as to obscure its real nature or worth ⟨unwilling to buy a *pig in a poke*⟩

pig iron *n* (1665) **:** crude iron that is the direct product of the blast furnace and is refined to produce steel, wrought iron, or ingot iron

pig latin *n, often cap L* (1938) **:** a jargon that is made by systematic alteration of English (as *ipskay the ointjay* for *skip the joint*)

pig·let \ˈpi-glət\ *n* (1861) **:** a small usu. young swine

1**pig·ment** \ˈpig-mənt\ *n* [ME, spice, dye, fr. L *pigmentum* coloring substance, fr. *pingere* to paint — more at PAINT] (14c) **1 :** a substance that imparts black or white or a color to other materials; *esp* **:** a powdered substance that is mixed with a liquid in which it is relatively insoluble and used esp. to impart color to coating materials (as paints) or to inks, plastics, and rubber **2 :** a coloring matter in animals and plants esp. in a cell or tissue; *also* **:** any of various related colorless substances — **pig·men·tary** \-mən-ˌter-ē\ *adj*

2**pig·ment** \-ˌment, -mənt\ *vt* (1900) **:** to color with or as if with pigment

pig·men·ta·tion \ˌpig-mən-ˈtā-shən, -ˌmen-\ *n* (1866) **:** coloration with or deposition of pigment; *esp* **:** an excessive deposition of bodily pigment

pigmy *var of* PYGMY

pi·gno·li \pēn-ˈyō-lē\ *or* **pi·gno·lia** \-lē-ə\ *n, pl* **-li** *or* **-lis** *or* **-lia** *or* **-lias** [*pignoli* fr. It, pl. of *pignolo, pinolo,* fr. *pigna, pina* pine cone, fr. L *pinea; pignolia* perh. modif. of *pignoli* — more at PINEAL] (1893) **:** PINE NUT

pig·nut \ˈpig-ˌnət\ *n* (1666) **1 :** any of several bitter-flavored hickory nuts **2 :** a hickory (as *Carya glabra* and *C. cordiformis*) bearing pignuts

pig out *vi* (1977) **:** to eat greedily **:** GORGE — **pig–out** \ˈpig-ˌau̇t\ *n*

pig·pen \-ˌpen\ *n* (1803) **1 :** a pen for pigs **2 :** a dirty slovenly place

pig·skin \-ˌskin\ *n* (1852) **1 :** the skin of a swine or leather made of it **2 a :** a jockey's saddle **b :** FOOTBALL 2a

pig·stick \-ˌstik\ *vi* (1891) **:** to hunt the wild boar on horseback with a spear — **pig·stick·er** *n*

pig·sty \ˈpig-ˌstī\ *n* (1580) **:** PIGPEN

pig·tail \-ˌtāl\ *n* (1688) **1 :** tobacco in small twisted strands or rolls **2 :** a tight braid of hair

pig·tailed \-ˌtāld\ *adj* (1754) **:** wearing a pigtail ⟨~ little girls⟩

pig·weed \-ˌwēd\ *n* (ca. 1801) **:** any of various vigorous weedy plants esp. of the goosefoot or amaranth families

piing *pres part of* PI *or of* PIE

PIK *abbr* payment in kind

pi·ka \ˈpē-kə, ˈpī-\ *n* [perh. fr. Evenki (Tungusic language of Siberia)] (1827) **:** any of various short-eared small lagomorph mammals (family Ochotonidae) of rocky uplands of Asia and western No. America with relatively short hind legs — called also *coney, rock rabbit*

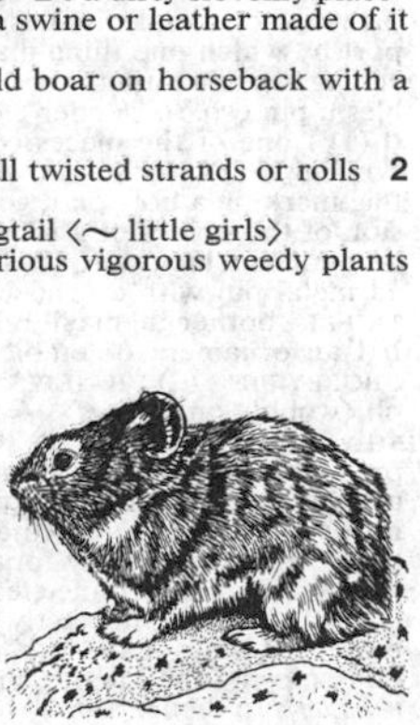
pika

pi·ka·ke \ˈpē-kä-ˌkā\ *n* [Hawaiian *pīkake,* lit., peacock, fr. E] (1933) **:** an evergreen climbing jasmine (*Jasminum sambac*) of Asia long cultivated for its profuse fragrant white flowers

1**pike** \ˈpīk\ *n* [ME, fr. OE *pīc* pickax] (13c) **1 :** PIKESTAFF 1 **2 :** a sharp point or spike; *also* **:** the tip of a spear — **piked** \ˈpīkt\ *adj*

2**pike** *n* [ME, perh. of Scand origin; akin to Norw dial. *pīk* pointed mountain] (13c) *dial Eng* **:** a mountain or hill having a peaked summit — used esp. in place names

3**pike** *n, pl* **pike** *or* **pikes** [ME, fr. 1*pike*] (14c) **1 a :** a large elongate long-snouted freshwater bony fish (*Esox lucius*) valued for food and sport and widely distributed in cooler parts of the northern hemisphere — called also *northern, northern pike* **b :** any of various fishes (family Esocidae) related to the pike: as (1) **:** MUSKELLUNGE (2) **:** PICKEREL **2 :** any of various fishes resembling the pike in appearance or habits

4**pike** *n* [MF *pique,* fr. *piquer* to prick, fr. VL **piccare,* perh. fr. L *picus* woodpecker — more at PIE] (ca. 1511) **:** a heavy spear with a very long shaft used by infantry esp. in Europe from the Middle Ages to the 18th century

5**pike** *vt* **piked; pik·ing** (1798) **:** to pierce, kill, or wound with a pike

6**pike** *vi* **piked; pik·ing** [ME *pyken* (refl.)] (1526) **1 :** to leave abruptly ⟨get lonely and sore, and ~ out —Sinclair Lewis⟩ **2 :** to make one's way ⟨~ along⟩

7**pike** *n* (1812) **1 :** TURNPIKE **2 :** a railroad or railroad line or system — **down the pike 1 :** in the course of events ⟨the greatest boxer to come *down the pike* in years⟩ **2 :** in the future ⟨today's advances only hint at what's *down the pike*⟩

8**pike** *n* [perh. fr. 3*pike*] (1928) **:** a body position (as in diving) in which the hips are bent, the knees are straight, and the hands touch the toes or clasp the legs behind or just above the knees

pike·man \ˈpīk-mən\ *n* (ca. 1550) **:** a soldier armed with a pike

pike·min·now \ˈpīk-ˌmi-(ˌ)nō\ *n* (1998) **:** SQUAWFISH

pike perch *n* (1842) **:** a fish (as the walleye) of the perch family that resembles the pike

pik·er \ˈpī-kər\ *n* [*pike* to play cautiously, of unknown origin] (ca. 1889) **1 :** one who gambles or speculates with small amounts of money **2 :** one who does things in a small way; *also* **:** TIGHTWAD, CHEAPSKATE

pike·staff \ˈpīk-ˌstaf\ *n* (14c) **1 :** a spiked staff for use on slippery ground **2 :** the staff of a foot soldier's pike

pi·ki \ˈpē-kē\ *n* [Hopi *píki*] (ca. 1889) **:** bread made esp. from blue cornmeal and baked in thin sheets by the Indians of the southwestern U.S.

pi·laf *also* **pi·laff** \pi-ˈläf, -ˈlȯf; ˈpē-ˌ\ *or* **pi·lau** *or* **pi·law** \pi-ˈlō, -ˈlȯ, ˈpē-(ˌ); *Southern often* ˈpər-(ˌ)lü, -(ˌ)lō\ *n* [Turk & Pers; Turk *pilav,* fr. Pers *pilāv*] (ca. 1612) **:** a dish made of seasoned rice and often meat

pi·las·ter \pi-ˈlas-tər, ˈpī-ˌlas-\ *n* [MF *pilastre,* fr. It *pilastro*] (1575) **:** an upright architectural member that is rectangular in plan and is structurally a pier but architecturally treated as a column and that usu. projects a third of its width or less from the wall

1 pilaster

Pi·la·tes \pə-ˈlä-tēz\ *n* [Joseph H. *Pilates* †1967 U.S. (Ger.-born) fitness instructor] (1934) **:** an exercise regimen typically performed with the use of specialized apparatus

pil·chard \ˈpil-chərd\ *n* [origin unknown] (ca. 1530) **1 :** a fish (*Sardina pilchardus*) of the herring family that occurs in great schools along the coasts of Europe — compare SARDINE 1 **2 :** any of several sardines related to the European pilchard

1**pile** \ˈpī(-ə)l\ *n* [ME, dart, quill, pole driven into the ground, fr. OE *pīl,* fr. L *pilum* javelin] (12c) **1 :** a long slender column usu. of timber, steel, or reinforced concrete driven into the ground to carry a vertical load **2 :** a wedge-shaped heraldic charge usu. placed vertically with the broad end up **3 a :** a target-shooting arrowhead without cutting edges **b** [L *pilum*] **:** an ancient Roman foot soldier's heavy javelin

2**pile** *vt* **piled; pil·ing** (15c) **:** to drive piles into

3**pile** *vb* **piled; pil·ing** [ME, fr. 4*pile*] *vt* (14c) **1 :** to lay or place in a pile **:** STACK **2 a :** to heap in abundance **:** LOAD ⟨*piled* potatoes on his plate⟩ **b :** to collect little by little into a mass — usu. used with *up* ~ *vi* **1 :** to form a pile or accumulation — usu. used with *up* **2 :** to move or press forward in or as if in a mass **:** CROWD ⟨*piled* into a car⟩

4**pile** *n* [ME pier of a bridge, stack, heap, fr. MF *pille* pier of a bridge, fr. L *pila* pillar] (15c) **1 a** (1) **:** a quantity of things heaped together (2) **:** a heap of wood for burning a corpse or a sacrifice **b :** any great number or quantity **:** LOT **2 :** a large building or group of buildings **3 :** a great amount of money **:** FORTUNE **4 :** REACTOR 3b

5**pile** *n* [ME, fr. AF *peil, pil* hair, coat with thick nap, fr. L *pilus* hair] (15c) **1 :** a coat or surface of usu. short close fine furry hairs **2 :** a velvety surface produced by an extra set of filling yarns that form raised loops which are cut and sheared — **pile·less** \ˈpī(-ə)l-ləs\ *adj*

6**pile** *n* [ME *pilez,* pl., fr. ML *pili,* perh. fr. L *pila* ball] (15c) **1 :** a single hemorrhoid **2** *pl* **:** HEMORRHOIDS

pi·le·at·ed \ˈpī-lē-ˌā-təd, ˈpi-\ *adj* (ca. 1728) **:** having a crest covering the pileum

pileated woodpecker *n* (1782) **:** a large red-crested No. American woodpecker (*Dryocopus pileatus*) that is black with white on the face, neck, and undersides of the wings

piled *adj* (15c) **:** having a pile ⟨a deep-*piled* rug⟩

pile driver *n* (1772) **:** a machine for driving down piles with a drop hammer or a steam or air hammer

pi·le·um \ˈpī-lē-əm\ *n, pl* **pi·lea** \-lē-ə\ [NL, fr. L *pileus, pileum* felt cap; akin to Gk *pilos* felt] (1874) **:** the top of the head of a bird from the bill to the nape

pile·up \ˈpī(-ə)l-ˌəp\ *n* (ca. 1929) **1 :** a collision involving usu. several motor vehicles **2 a :** a jammed tangled mass or pile (as of motor vehicles or people) resulting from collision or accumulation **b :** ACCUMULATION

pi·le·us \ˈpī-lē-əs\ *n, pl* **pi·lei** \-lē-ˌī\ [NL, fr. L] (1715) **1** [L] **:** a pointed or close-fitting cap worn by ancient Romans **2 :** the convex, concave, or flattened spore-bearing structure of some basidiomycetes that is attached superiorly to the stem and typically is expanded with gills or pores on the underside — called also *cap*

pile·wort \ˈpī(-ə)l-ˌwərt, -ˌwȯrt\ *n* [ME *pyle wort;* fr. its use in treating piles] (15c) **:** LESSER CELANDINE

\ə\ **abut** \ᵊ\ kitten, F table \ər\ **further** \a\ **ash** \ā\ **ace** \ä\ mop, mar \au̇\ **out** \ch\ **chin** \e\ bet \ē\ **easy** \g\ **go** \i\ **hit** \ī\ **ice** \j\ **job** \ŋ\ **sing** \ō\ **go** \ȯ\ **law** \ȯi\ **boy** \th\ **thin** \t͟h\ **the** \ü\ **loot** \u̇\ **foot** \y\ yet \zh\ **vision**, beige \k, ⁿ, œ, ue, ʸ\ *see* Guide to Pronunciation

pil·fer \ˈpil-fər\ *vb* **pil·fered; pil·fer·ing** \-f(ə-)riŋ\ [MF *pelfrer,* fr. *pelfre* booty] *vi* (ca. 1548) **:** STEAL; *esp* **:** to steal stealthily in small amounts and often again and again ~ *vt* **:** STEAL; *esp* **:** to steal in small quantities ***syn*** see STEAL — **pil·fer·able** \-f(ə-)rə-bəl\ *adj* — **pil·fer·age** \-f(ə-)rij\ *n* — **pil·fer·er** \-fər-ər\ *n* — **pil·fer·proof** \-ˌprüf\ *adj*
pil·gar·lic \pil-ˈgär-lik\ *n* [*pilled garlic*] (ca. 1529) **1 a :** a bald head **b :** a bald-headed man **2 :** a man looked upon with humorous contempt or mock pity
pil·grim \ˈpil-grəm\ *n* [ME, fr. AF *pelerin, pilegrin,* fr. LL *pelegrinus,* alter. of L *peregrinus* foreigner, fr. *peregrinus,* adj., foreign, fr. *peregri* abroad, fr. *per* through + *agr-, ager* land — more at FOR, ACRE] (13c) **1 :** one who journeys in foreign lands **:** WAYFARER **2 :** one who travels to a shrine or holy place as a devotee **3** *cap* **:** one of the English colonists settling at Plymouth in 1620
[1]**pil·grim·age** \ˈpil-grə-mij\ *n* (14c) **1 :** a journey of a pilgrim; *esp* **:** one to a shrine or a sacred place **2 :** the course of life on earth
[2]**pilgrimage** *vi* **-aged; -ag·ing** (14c) **:** to go on a pilgrimage
pilgrim bottle *n* (1874) **:** COSTREL
piling *n* (15c) **:** a structure of piles; *also* **:** PILE
Pi·li·pi·no \ˌpi-lə-ˈpē-(ˌ)nō, ˌpē-\ *n* [Tag, lit., Philippine, fr. Sp *Filipino*] (1936) **:** FILIPINO 3
[1]**pill** \ˈpil\ *vb* [ME *pilen, pillen,* partly fr. OE *pilian* to peel, partly fr. AF *piler* to rob] *vi* (12c) *dial chiefly Eng* **:** to come off in flakes or scales **:** PEEL ~ *vt* **1** *archaic* **:** to subject to depredation or extortion **2** *dial* **:** to peel or strip off
[2]**pill** *n* [ME *pylle,* fr. AF *pile* & MD *pille,* both ultim. fr. L *pilula,* fr. dim. of *pila* ball] (14c) **1 a :** a usu. medicinal or dietary preparation in a small rounded mass to be swallowed whole **b** *often cap* **:** BIRTH CONTROL PILL — usu. used with *the* **2 :** something repugnant or unpleasant that must be accepted or endured **3 :** something resembling a pill in size or shape **4 :** a disagreeable or tiresome person
[3]**pill** *vt* (1736) **1 :** to dose with pills **2 :** BLACKBALL ~ *vi* **:** to become rough with or mat into little balls ⟨brushed woolens often ~⟩
[1]**pil·lage** \ˈpi-lij\ *n* [ME *pilage,* fr. AF, fr. *piler* to rob, plunder] (14c) **1 :** the act of looting or plundering esp. in war **2 :** something taken as booty
[2]**pillage** *vb* **pil·laged; pil·lag·ing** *vt* (ca. 1593) **:** to plunder ruthlessly **:** LOOT ~ *vi* **:** to take booty ***syn*** see RAVAGE — **pil·lag·er** *n*
[1]**pil·lar** \ˈpi-lər\ *n* [ME *piler,* fr. AF, fr. ML *pilare,* fr. L *pila*] (13c) **1 a :** a firm upright support for a superstructure **:** POST **b :** a usu. ornamental column or shaft; *esp* **:** one standing alone for a monument **2 a :** a supporting, integral, or upstanding member or part ⟨a ~ of society⟩ **b :** a fundamental precept ⟨the five ~s of Islam⟩ **3 :** a solid mass of coal, rock, or ore left standing to support a mine roof **4 :** a body part that resembles a column — **pil·lar·less** *adj* — **from pillar to post :** from one place or one predicament to another
[2]**pillar** *vt* (1787) **:** to provide or strengthen with or as if with pillars
pil·lar–box \ˈpi-lər-ˌbäks\ *n* (1855) *Brit* **:** a pillar-shaped mailbox
pill·box \ˈpil-ˌbäks\ *n* (1702) **1 :** a box for pills; *esp* **:** a shallow round box of pasteboard **2 :** a small low concrete emplacement for machine guns and antitank weapons **3 :** a small round hat without a brim; *specif* **:** a woman's shallow hat with a flat crown and straight sides
pill bug *n* [[2]*pill;* fr. its rolling into a ball when disturbed] (1843) **:** WOOD LOUSE; *esp* **:** a wood louse capable of curling itself into a ball
[1]**pil·lion** \ˈpil-yən\ *n* [ScGael or Ir; ScGael *pillean,* dim. of *peall* covering, couch; Ir *pillín,* dim. of *peall* covering, couch] (1503) **1 a :** a light saddle for women consisting chiefly of a cushion **b :** a pad or cushion put on behind a man's saddle chiefly for a woman to ride on **2** *chiefly Brit* **:** a motorcycle or bicycle saddle for a passenger
[2]**pillion** *adv* (1852) *chiefly Brit* **:** on or as if on a pillion ⟨ride ~⟩
[1]**pil·lo·ry** \ˈpi-lə-rē, ˈpil-rē\ *n, pl* **-ries** [ME, fr. AF *pilori*] (13c) **1 :** a device formerly used for publicly punishing offenders consisting of a wooden frame with holes in which the head and hands can be locked **2 :** a means for exposing one to public scorn or ridicule
[2]**pillory** *vt* **-ried; -ry·ing** (ca. 1600) **1 :** to set in a pillory as punishment **2 :** to expose to public contempt, ridicule, or scorn
[1]**pil·low** \ˈpi-(ˌ)lō\ *n* [ME *pilwe,* fr. OE *pyle* (akin to OHG *pfuliwi*), fr. L *pulvinus*] (bef. 12c) **1 a :** a support for the head of a reclining person; *esp* **:** one consisting of a cloth bag filled with feathers, down, sponge rubber, or plastic fiber **b :** something resembling a pillow esp. in form **2 :** a cushion or pad tightly stuffed and used as a support for the design and tools in making lace with a bobbin — **pil·lowy** \ˈpi-lə-wē\ *adj*
[2]**pillow** *vt* (1629) **1 :** to rest or lay on or as if on a pillow **2 :** to serve as a pillow for ~ *vi* **:** to lay or rest one's head on or as if on a pillow
pillow block *n* (1814) **:** a block or standard to support a journal (as of a shaft) **:** BEARING
pil·low·case \ˈpi-lə-ˌkās, -lō-\ *n* (1633) **:** a removable covering for a pillow
pillow lace *n* [fr. its being worked over a pillow on which the pattern is marked] (1815) **:** lace made with a bobbin
pillow slip *n* (1793) **:** PILLOWCASE
pillow talk *n* (1914) **:** intimate conversation between lovers in bed
pi·lo·car·pine \ˌpī-lə-ˈkär-ˌpēn\ *n* [ISV, fr. NL *Pilocarpus jaborandi,* species of tropical shrubs] (1875) **:** a miotic alkaloid $C_{11}H_{16}N_2O_2$ obtained from jaborandi that is used chiefly in the form of its hydrochloride or nitrate esp. in the treatment of glaucoma
pi·lo·ni·dal \ˌpī-lə-ˈnī-dᵊl\ *adj* [L *pilus* hair + *nidus* nest] (1880) **:** of, relating to, or being a hair-containing cyst of the skin in the lower-back region near the upper crease of the buttocks
pi·lose \ˈpī-ˌlōs\ *adj* [L *pilosus,* fr. *pilus* hair] (1712) **:** covered with usu. soft hair — **pi·los·i·ty** \pī-ˈlä-sə-tē\ *n*
[1]**pi·lot** \ˈpī-lət\ *n* [MF *pilote,* fr. It *pilota,* alter. of *pedota,* fr. MGk **pēdōtēs,* fr. Gk *pēda* steering oars, pl. of *pēdon* oar; prob. akin to Gk *pod-, pous* foot — more at FOOT] (15c) **1 a :** one employed to steer a ship **:** HELMSMAN **b :** a person who is qualified and usu. licensed to conduct a ship into and out of a port or in specified waters **c :** a person who flies or is qualified to fly an aircraft or spacecraft **2 :** GUIDE, LEADER **3 :** COWCATCHER **4 :** a piece that guides a tool or machine part **5 :** a television show produced and filmed or taped as a sample of a proposed series **6 :** PILOT LIGHT 1 — **pi·lot·less** \-ləs\ *adj*
[2]**pilot** *vt* (1613) **1 :** to act as a guide to **:** lead or conduct over a usu. difficult course **2 a :** to set and conn the course of ⟨~ a ship⟩ **b :** to act as pilot of ⟨~ a plane⟩ ***syn*** see GUIDE
[3]**pilot** *adj* (1915) **:** serving as a guiding or tracing device, an activating or auxiliary unit, or a trial apparatus or operation ⟨a ~ study⟩
pi·lot·age \ˈpī-lə-tij\ *n* (ca. 1618) **1 :** the action or business of piloting **2 :** the compensation paid to a licensed ship's pilot
pilot biscuit *n* (1836) **:** HARDTACK — called also *pilot bread*
pilot engine *n* (1838) **:** a locomotive going in advance of a train to make sure that the way is clear
pilot fish *n* (1592) **:** a pelagic carangid fish (*Naucrates ductor*) that has dark vertical stripes and often swims in company with a shark
pi·lot·house \ˈpī-lət-ˌhau̇s\ *n* (1842) **:** a deckhouse for a ship's helmsman containing the steering wheel, compass, and navigating equipment
pilot light *n* (1881) **1 :** a small permanent flame used to ignite gas at a burner **2 :** an indicator light showing where a switch or circuit breaker is located or whether a motor is in operation or power is on — called also *pilot lamp*
pilot officer *n* (1919) **:** a commissioned officer in the British air force who ranks with a second lieutenant in the army
pilot whale *n* (1867) **:** either of two chiefly dark gray to black medium-sized toothed whales (*Globicephala melaena* and *G. macrorhynchus*) of temperate to tropical waters — called also *blackfish*
pil·sner *or* **pil·sen·er** \ˈpils-nər, ˈpilz-, ˈpil-zə-\ *n* [G, lit., of Pilsen (Plzeň), city in the Czech Republic] (1875) **1 :** a light beer with a strong flavor of hops **2 :** a tall slender footed glass for beer
Pilt·down man \ˈpilt-ˌdau̇n-\ *n* [*Piltdown,* East Sussex, England] (1913) **:** a supposedly very early hominid erroneously reconstructed in the early 1900s from what was later determined to be human skull fragments and an orangutan lower jaw planted by a hoaxer
pil·ule \ˈpil-(ˌ)yül\ *n* [MF, fr. L *pilula* pill — more at PILL] (1543) **:** a little pill
pi·lus \ˈpī-ləs\ *n, pl* **pi·li** \-ˌlī\ [L] (1760) **:** a hair or a structure (as on the surface of a bacterial cell) resembling a hair
Pi·ma \ˈpē-mə\ *n, pl* **Pimas** *or* **Pima** [AmerSp, short for earlier *Pimahitos, Pima Aytos,* fr. O'odham (18th cent.) *pimahaitu* nothing] (1829) **1 :** a member of an American Indian people of southern Arizona and northern Mexico **2 :** O'ODHAM 2 — **Pi·man** \-mən\ *adj*
pi·ma cotton \ˈpē-mə-, ˈpi-\ *n* [*Pima* County, Arizona] (1925) **:** a cotton that produces fiber of exceptional strength and firmness and that was developed in the southwestern U.S. by selection and breeding of Egyptian cottons
pi·men·to \pə-ˈmen-(ˌ)tō\ *n, pl* **-tos** *or* **-to** [Sp *pimienta* allspice, pepper, fr. LL *pigmenta,* pl. of *pigmentum* plant juice, fr. L, pigment] (1660) **1 :** ALLSPICE **2 :** PIMIENTO 1
pimento cheese *n* (1910) **:** a Neufchâtel, process, cream, or occas. cheddar cheese to which ground pimientos have been added
pi–me·son \ˈpī-ˈme-ˌzän, -ˈmā-, -ˈmē-, -ˌsän\ *n* [[1]*pi*] (1947) **:** PION
pi·mien·to \pə-ˈmen-(ˌ)tō, pəm-ˈyen-\ *n, pl* **-tos** [Sp, fr. *pimienta*] (1843) **1 :** any of various bluntly conical thick-fleshed sweet peppers of European origin that have a distinctive mild sweet flavor and are used esp. as a garnish, as a stuffing for olives, and as a source of paprika **2 :** a plant that bears pimientos
[1]**pimp** \ˈpimp\ *n* [prob. akin to Brit. dial. *pimp* small bundle of sticks, ME *pymple* papule, G *Pimpf* young boy, kid, lit., little fart, *Pumpf, Pumps* fart] (1701) **:** a criminal who is associated with, usu. exerts control over, and lives off the earnings of one or more prostitutes
[2]**pimp** *vt* (1745) **:** to make use of often dishonorably for one's own gain or benefit ~ *vi* **:** to work as a pimp
pim·per·nel \ˈpim-pər-ˌnel, -pər-nəl\ *n* [ME *pimpernele,* fr. AF, fr. LL *pimpinella,* a medicinal herb] (15c) **:** any of a genus (*Anagallis*) of herbs of the primrose family; *esp* **:** SCARLET PIMPERNEL
pimp·ing \ˈpim-pən, -piŋ\ *adj* [prob. akin to ME *pymple* papule — more at PIMP] (1640) **1 :** PETTY, INSIGNIFICANT **2** *chiefly dial* **:** PUNY, SICKLY
pim·ple \ˈpim-pəl\ *n* [ME *pymple;* akin to OE *piplian* to break out in pimples, and prob. to E *pimp* — more at PIMP] (14c) **1 :** a small inflamed elevation of the skin **:** PAPULE; *esp* **:** PUSTULE **2 :** a swelling or protuberance like a pimple — **pim·pled** \-pəld\ *adj* — **pim·ply** \-p(ə-)lē\ *adj*
pimp·mo·bile \ˈpimp-mō-ˌbēl, -mə-\ *n* (1971) **:** an ostentatious luxury car of a kind characteristically used by a pimp
[1]**pin** \ˈpin\ *n* [ME, fr. OE *pinn* (akin to OHG *pfinn* peg), perh. fr. L *pinna* quill, feather — more at PEN] (bef. 12c) **1 a :** a piece of solid material (as wood or metal) used esp. for fastening things together or as a support by which one thing may be suspended from another **b** *obs* **:** the center peg of a target; *also* **:** the center itself **c :** something that resembles a pin esp. in slender elongated form ⟨an electrical connector ~⟩ **d** (1) **:** one of the pieces constituting the target in various games (as bowling) (2) **:** the peg at which a quoit is pitched (3) **:** the staff of the flag marking a hole on a golf course **e :** a peg for regulating the tension of the strings of a musical instrument **f :** the part of a key stem that enters a lock **g :** a belaying pin **2 a** (1) **:** a very thin small pointed metal pin with a head used esp. for fastening cloth (2) **:** LITTLE, TRIFLE ⟨bother them all! I don't care a ~ about them —Bram Stoker⟩ **b :** an ornament or emblem fastened to clothing with a pin **c** (1) **:** BOBBY PIN (2) **:** HAIRPIN (3) **:** SAFETY PIN **3 :** LEG — usu. used in pl. ⟨wobbly on his ~*s*⟩ **4 :** a fall in wrestling
[2]**pin** *vt* **pinned; pin·ning** (14c) **1 a :** to fasten, join, or secure with a pin **b :** to hold fast or immobile **c :** to present (a young woman) with a fraternity pin as a pledge of affection **2 a :** FASTEN ⟨*pinned* his hopes on a miracle⟩ ⟨~ the blame on someone else⟩ **b :** to assign the blame or responsibility for ⟨~ the robbery on a night watchman⟩ **c :** to define or determine clearly or precisely — usu. used with *down* ⟨it is hard to ~ down exactly when things changed —Katharine Whittemore⟩ **3 a :** to make (a chess opponent's piece) unable to move without exposing the king to check or a valuable piece to capture **b** *of a wrestler* **:** to secure a fall over (an opponent)
[3]**pin** *adj* (ca. 1523) **1 :** of or relating to a pin **2** *of leather* **:** having a grain suggesting the heads of pins
PIN *abbr* personal identification number
pi·ña cloth \ˈpēn-yə-\ *n* [Sp *piña* pineapple, pinecone, fr. L *pinea* pinecone — more at PINEAL] (1856) **:** a lustrous transparent cloth of Philippine origin that is woven of silky pineapple fibers
pi·ña co·la·da \ˈpēn-yə-kō-ˈlä-də, ˈpē-nə-\ *n* [Sp, lit., strained pineapple] (1920) **:** a tall drink made of rum, cream of coconut, and pineapple juice mixed with ice

pin·a·fore \ˈpi-nə-ˌfȯr\ *n* [²*pin* + *afore*] (1782) **:** a sleeveless usu. low-necked garment fastened in the back and worn as an apron or dress — **pin·a·fored** \-ˌfȯrd\ *adj*

pi·ña·ta *or* **pi·na·ta** \pēn-ˈyä-tə\ *n* [Sp *piñata,* lit., pot, fr. It *pignatta,* prob. fr. *pigna* pinecone — more at PIGNOLI] (1883) **:** a decorated vessel (as of papier-mâché) filled with candies, fruits, and gifts and hung up to be broken with sticks by blindfolded persons as part of esp. Latin-American festivities (as at Christmas or for a birthday party)

pin·ball \ˈpin-ˌbȯl\ *vi* (1974) **:** to move abruptly from one place to another

pinball machine *n* (1936) **:** an amusement device in which a ball propelled by a plunger scores points as it rolls down a slanting surface among pins and targets — called also *pinball game*

pin·bone \ˈpin-ˌbōn\ *n* (1640) **:** the hipbone esp. of a quadruped — see COW illustration

pince–nez \paⁿs-ˈnā, pan(t)s-\ *n, pl* **pince–nez** \-ˈnā(z)\ [F, fr. *pincer* to pinch + *nez* nose, fr. L *nasus* — more at NOSE] (1876) **:** eyeglasses clipped to the nose by a spring

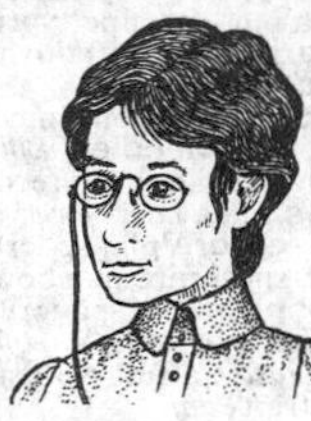
pince-nez

pin·cer \ˈpin(t)-sər, *esp for 1 US often* ˈpin-chər\ *n* [ME *pinceour,* fr. AF **pinceour, pinchure,* fr. AF **pincher, pincer* to pinch, fr. VL **pinctiare, *punctiare,* fr. L *punctum* puncture — more at POINT] (14c) **1** *pl* **a :** an instrument having two short handles and two grasping jaws working on a pivot and used for gripping things **b :** a claw (as of a lobster) resembling a pair of pincers **:** CHELA **2 :** PINCER MOVEMENT — **pin·cer·like** \-ˌlīk\ *adj*

pincer movement *n* (1938) **1 :** a military attack by two coordinated forces that close in on an enemy position from different directions **2 :** a combination of two forces acting against an opposing force

[1]**pinch** \ˈpinch\ *vb* [ME, fr. AF **pincher, pincer*] *vt* (14c) **1 a :** to squeeze between the finger and thumb or between the jaws of an instrument **b :** to prune the tip of (a plant or shoot) usu. to induce branching **c :** to squeeze or compress painfully **d :** to cause physical or mental pain to **e** (1) **:** to cause to appear thin, haggard, or shrunken (2) **:** to cause to shrivel or wither **2 a :** to subject to strict economy or want **:** STRAITEN **b :** to restrain or limit narrowly **:** CONSTRICT **3 a :** STEAL **b :** ARREST **4 :** to sail too close to the wind ~ *vi* **1 :** COMPRESS, SQUEEZE **2 :** to be miserly or closefisted **3 :** to press painfully **4 :** NARROW, TAPER ⟨the road ~*ed* down to a trail —Cecelia Holland⟩ — **pinch pennies :** to practice strict economy

[2]**pinch** *n* (15c) **1 a :** a critical juncture **:** EMERGENCY **b** (1) **:** PRESSURE, STRESS (2) **:** HARDSHIP, PRIVATION **c :** DEFICIT **2 a :** an act of pinching **:** SQUEEZE **b :** as much as may be taken between the finger and thumb ⟨a ~ of snuff⟩ **c :** a very small amount **3 :** a marked thinning of a vein or bed **4 a :** THEFT **b :** a police raid; *also* **:** ARREST *syn* see JUNCTURE

[3]**pinch** *adj* (1912) **1 :** SUBSTITUTE ⟨~ runner⟩ **2 :** hit by a pinch hitter ⟨a ~ homer⟩

pinch bar *n* (1837) **:** a bar similar in form and use to a crowbar and sometimes having an end adapted for pulling spikes or inserting under a heavy wheel that is to be rolled

pinch·beck \ˈpinch-ˌbek\ *n* [Christopher *Pinchbeck* †1732 Eng. watchmaker] (1734) **1 :** an alloy of copper and zinc used esp. to imitate gold in jewelry **2 :** something counterfeit or spurious — **pinchbeck** *adj*

pinch·er \ˈpin-chər\ *n* (15c) **1 :** one that pinches **2** *pl* **:** PINCERS

pinch–hit \ˈpinch-ˈhit, ˌpinch-\ *vi* [back-formation fr. *pinch hitter*] (1915) **1 :** to act or serve in place of another **2 :** to bat in the place of another player esp. when a hit is particularly needed

pinch hit *n* (1927) **:** a hit made by a pinch hitter

pinch hitter *n* (1912) **:** one that pinch-hits

pinch·pen·ny \ˈpinch-ˌpe-nē\ *adj* (1582) **:** STINGY, NIGGARDLY

pin curl *n* (1896) **:** a curl made usu. by dampening a strand of hair with water or lotion, coiling it, and securing it by a hairpin or clip

pin·cush·ion \ˈpin-ˌku̇-shən\ *n* (1632) **:** a small cushion in which pins may be stuck ready for use

pincushion flower *n* (1856) **:** any of several scabiouses (esp. *Scabiosa atropurpurea, S. caucasica,* or *S. columbaria*)

[1]**Pin·dar·ic** \pin-ˈda-rik\ *adj* (1640) **1 :** of or relating to the poet Pindar **2 :** written in the manner or style characteristic of Pindar

[2]**Pindaric** *n* (1671) **1 :** a Pindaric ode **2** *pl* **:** loose irregular verses similar to those used in Pindaric odes

[1]**pine** \ˈpīn\ *n, often attrib* [ME, fr. OE *pīn,* fr. L *pinus;* prob. akin to Gk *pitys* pine] (bef. 12c) **1 :** any of a genus (*Pinus* of the family Pinaceae, the pine family) of coniferous evergreen trees that have slender elongated needles and include some valuable timber trees and ornamentals **2 :** the straight-grained white or yellow usu. durable and resinous wood of a pine varying from extreme softness in the white pine to hardness in the longleaf pine **3 :** any of various Australian coniferous trees (as of the genera *Callitris* or *Araucaria*) **4 :** PINEAPPLE **5 :** BENCH 1c — **pin·ey** *also* **piny** \ˈpī-nē\ *adj*

[2]**pine** *vi* **pined; pin·ing** [ME, fr. OE *pīnian* to suffer, fr. **pīn* punishment, fr. L *poena* — more at PAIN] (14c) **1 :** to lose vigor, health, or flesh (as through grief) **:** LANGUISH **2 :** to yearn intensely and persistently esp. for something unattainable ⟨they still *pined* for their lost wealth⟩ *syn* see LONG

pi·ne·al \ˈpī-nē-əl, pī-ˈ\ *adj* [F *pinéal,* fr. MF, fr. L *pinea* pinecone, fr. fem. of *pineus* of pine, fr. *pinus*] (1681) **:** of, relating to, or secreted by the pineal gland ⟨a ~ tumor⟩ ⟨the ~ hormone melatonin⟩

pi·ne·al·ec·to·my \ˌpī-nē-ə-ˈlek-tə-mē, pī-ˌnē-\ *n* (1915) **:** surgical removal of the pineal gland — **pi·ne·al·ec·to·mize** \-tə-ˌmīz\ *vt*

pineal gland *n* (1712) **:** a small usu. conical appendage of the brain of all craniate vertebrates that functions primarily as an endocrine gland secreting melatonin and that in a few reptiles has the essential structure of an eye — called also *pineal, pineal body, pineal organ*

pine·ap·ple \ˈpī-ˌna-pəl\ *n* (1588) **1 a :** a tropical monocotyledonous plant (*Ananas comosus* of the family Bromeliaceae, the pineapple family) that has rigid spiny-margined recurved leaves and a short stalk with a dense oblong head of small abortive flowers **b :** the large edible multiple fruit of the pineapple that consists of the sweet succulent fleshy inflorescence **2 :** a hand grenade

pineapple guava *n* (ca. 1924) **:** FEIJOA

pineapple sage *n* (1950) **:** a Mexican salvia (*Salvia elegans* syn. *S. rutilans*) having a scent of pineapple that is cultivated as an annual

pine·cone \ˈpīn-ˌkōn\ *n* (1695) **:** a cone of a pine tree

pine·drops \ˈpīn-ˌdräps\ *n pl but sing or pl in constr* (1857) **1 :** a purplish-brown leafless saprophytic plant (*Pterospora andromedea*) of the wintergreen family with racemose drooping white flowers **2 :** BEECHDROPS

pine·land \ˈpīn-ˌland, -lənd\ *n* (ca. 1658) **:** land naturally dominated by pine forests

pine marten *n* (1768) **:** an American marten (*Martes americana*) found mainly in coniferous forests; *also* **:** a Eurasian marten (*Martes martes*)

pi·nene \ˈpī-ˌnēn\ *n* [ISV, fr. L *pinus*] (1885) **:** either of two liquid isomeric unsaturated bicyclic terpene hydrocarbons $C_{10}H_{16}$ of which one is a major constituent of wood turpentine

pine nut *n* (bef. 12c) **:** the edible seed of any of several pines — compare PIÑON

pin·ery \ˈpī-nə-rē, ˈpīn-rē\ *n, pl* **-er·ies** (1758) **1 :** a hothouse or area where pineapples are grown **2 :** a grove or forest of pine

pine·sap \ˈpīn-ˌsap\ *n* (1840) **:** any of several yellowish or reddish parasitic or saprophytic herbs (genus *Monotropa*) of the wintergreen family resembling the Indian pipe

pine siskin *n* (1887) **:** a No. American finch (*Carduelis pinus* of the family Fringillidae) with streaked plumage

pine snake *n* (1791) **:** a large constricting colubrid snake (*Pituophis melanoleucus*) that is typically white and black and occurs esp. in coastal regions of eastern No. America from New Jersey southward into Mexico — compare BULL SNAKE

pine tar *n* (1855) **:** tar obtained by destructive distillation of pinewood and used esp. in roofing and soaps and in the treatment of skin diseases

pi·ne·tum \pī-ˈnē-təm\ *n, pl* **pi·ne·ta** \-ˈnē-tə\ [L, fr. *pinus*] (1842) **:** a plantation of pine trees; *esp* **:** a scientific collection of living coniferous trees

pine·wood \ˈpīn-ˌwu̇d\ *n* (1601) **1 :** the wood of the pine tree **2 :** a wood of pines — often used in pl. but sing. or pl. in constr.

piney woods *n pl* (1800) **:** woodland of the southern U.S. in which pines are the dominant tree

pin·feath·er \ˈpin-ˌfe-t͟hər\ *n* (ca. 1775) **:** a feather not fully developed; *esp* **:** a feather just emerging through the skin

pin·fish \-ˌfish\ *n* (1878) **:** a small compressed dark green grunt (*Lagodon rhomboides*) that has sharp dorsal spines and occurs along the Atlantic coast

pin·fold \-ˌfōld\ *n* [ME, fr. OE *pundfald,* fr. *pund-* enclosure + *fald* fold] (13c) **1 :** [2]POUND 1a **2 :** a place of restraint

[1]**ping** \ˈpiŋ\ *n* [imit.] (1835) **1 :** a sharp sound like that of a striking bullet **2 :** KNOCK 2b

[2]**ping** *vi* (1855) **1 :** to make a ping **2 :** to ricochet with a ping ⟨gravel ~*ing* off . . . the car —Margaret Atwood⟩ ~ *vt* **:** to cause to ping ⟨~ a bell⟩

ping·er \ˈpiŋ-ər\ *n* (1957) **:** a device for producing pulses of sound (as for marking an underwater site or detecting an underwater object)

pin·go \ˈpiŋ-(ˌ)gō\ *n, pl* **pingos** [Inuit *pinguq*] (1938) **:** a low hill or mound forced up by hydrostatic pressure in an area underlain by permafrost

[1]**ping–pong** \ˈpiŋ-ˌpäŋ, -ˌpȯŋ\ *vb* (1952) **:** SHIFT, BOUNCE

[2]**ping–pong** *n* (1934) **:** something resembling a game of table tennis; *esp* **:** a series of usu. verbal exchanges between two parties ⟨a ~ of absurdist dialogue —Lawrence O'Toole⟩

Ping–Pong \ˈpiŋ-ˌpäŋ, -ˌpȯŋ\ *trademark* — used for table tennis

pin·head \ˈpin-ˌhed\ *n* (1593) **1 :** the head of a pin **2 :** something very small or insignificant **3 :** a very dull or stupid person **:** FOOL

pin·head·ed \-ˌhe-dəd\ *adj* (1901) **:** DULL, STUPID — **pin·head·ed·ness** *n*

pin·hole \-ˌhōl\ *n* (1612) **:** a small hole made by, for, or as if by a pin

[1]**pin·ion** \ˈpin-yən\ *n* [ME, prob. modif. of AF **empignon, enpenoun* flight feathers, ultim. fr. VL **pinnion-, pinnio,* fr. L *pinna* feather — more at PEN] (15c) **1 :** the terminal section of a bird's wing including the carpus, metacarpus, and phalanges; *broadly* **:** WING **2 :** FEATHER, QUILL; *also* **:** FLIGHT FEATHERS — **pin·ioned** \-yənd\ *adj*

[2]**pinion** *vt* (1558) **1 a :** to disable or restrain by binding the arms **b :** to bind fast **:** SHACKLE **2 :** to restrain (a bird) from flight esp. by cutting off the pinion of one wing

[3]**pinion** *n* [F *pignon,* fr. MF *peignon,* fr. *peigne* comb, fr. L *pecten* — more at PECTINATE] (1659) **1 :** a gear with a small number of teeth designed to mesh with a larger wheel or rack **2 :** the smaller of a pair or the smallest of a train of gear wheels

[1]**pink** \ˈpiŋk\ *n* [ME, fr. MD *pinke*] (15c) **:** a ship with a narrow overhanging stern — called also *pinkie*

[2]**pink** *n* [origin unknown] (1573) **1 :** any of a genus (*Dianthus* of the family Caryophyllaceae, the pink family) of chiefly Eurasian herbs having usu. pink, red, or white flowers **2 a :** the very embodiment **:** PARAGON **b** (1) **:** one dressed in the height of fashion (2) **:** ELITE **c :** highest degree possible **:** HEIGHT ⟨keep their house in the ~ of repair —Rebecca West⟩ — **in the pink :** in the best of health or condition

[3]**pink** *n* (1678) **1 :** any of a group of colors bluish red to red in hue, of medium to high lightness, and of low to moderate saturation **2 a :** the scarlet color of a fox hunter's coat; *also* **:** a fox hunter's coat of this color **b :** pink-colored clothing **c** *pl* **:** light-colored trousers formerly worn by army officers **3 :** PINKO

[4]**pink** *adj* (1720) **1 :** of the color pink **2 :** holding moderately radical and usu. socialistic political or economic views **3 :** emotionally moved **:** EXCITED — often used as an intensive ⟨tickled ~⟩ — **pink·ness** *n*

[5]**pink** *vt* [ME, to thrust] (1503) **1 a :** to perforate in an ornamental pattern **b :** to cut a saw-toothed edge on **2 a :** PIERCE, STAB **b :** to wound by irony, criticism, or ridicule

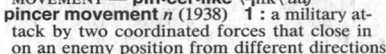

\ə\ **abut** \ᵊ\ kitten, F table \ər\ **further** \a\ **ash** \ā\ **ace** \ä\ **mop, mar** \au̇\ **out** \ch\ **chin** \e\ **bet** \ē\ **easy** \g\ **go** \i\ **hit** \ī\ **ice** \j\ **job** \ŋ\ **sing** \ō\ **go** \ȯ\ **law** \ȯi\ **boy** \th\ **thin** \t͟h\ **the** \ü\ **loot** \u̇\ **foot** \y\ **yet** \zh\ **vision, beige** \k̲, ⁿ, œ, ue, ʸ\ *see* Guide to Pronunciation

pink bollworm *n* (1906) : a small dark brown moth (*Pectinophora gossypiella*) whose pinkish larva bores into the flowers and bolls of cotton and is a destructive pest in most cotton-growing regions

pink–collar *adj* (1975) : of, relating to, or constituting a class of employees in occupations (as nursing and clerical jobs) traditionally held by women

pink elephants *n pl* (1940) : hallucinations arising esp. from heavy drinking or use of narcotics ⟨began to see *pink elephants*⟩

pink·eye \ˈpiŋk-ˌī\ *n* (1855) : an acute highly contagious conjunctivitis of humans and certain domestic animals

1**pin·kie** \ˈpiŋ-kē\ *n* [prob. fr. D *pinkje* small pink, dim. of *pink,* fr. MD *pinke*] (1840) : 1PINK

2**pinkie** *or* **pin·ky** \ˈpiŋ-kē\ *n, pl* **pinkies** [prob. fr. D *pinkje,* dim. of *pink* little finger] (ca. 1808) : LITTLE FINGER

pinking shears *n pl* (ca. 1939) : shears with a saw-toothed inner edge on the blades for making a zigzag cut

pink·ish \ˈpiŋ-kish\ *adj* (1784) : somewhat pink; *esp* : tending to be pink in politics — **pink·ish·ness** *n*

pink lady *n* (1931) : a cocktail consisting of gin, brandy, lemon juice, grenadine, and white of egg shaken with ice and strained

pink·ly \ˈpiŋ-klē\ *adv* (1836) : in a pink manner : with a pink hue

pink noise *n* (1961) : a mixture of sound waves with an intensity that diminishes proportionally with frequency to yield approximately equal energy per octave — compare WHITE NOISE

pinko \ˈpiŋ-(ˌ)kō\ *n, pl* **pink·os** *also* **pink·oes** (1936) : a person who holds advanced liberal or moderately radical political or economic views

pink·root \ˈpiŋk-ˌrüt, -ˌru̇t\ *n* (1763) : any of several American plants (genus *Spigelia*) related to the nux vomica and used as anthelmintics; *esp* : a U.S. woodland herb (*S. marilandica*) sometimes cultivated for its showy red and yellow flowers

pink salmon *n* (1905) : a small spotted Pacific salmon (*Oncorhynchus gorbuscha*) native to the northern Pacific Ocean and adjacent rivers

pink sheet *n* (1963) **1** : a daily listing of over-the-counter stocks and their prices **2** : any of a group of lightly traded over-the-counter stocks

pink slip *n* (1915) : a notice from an employer that a recipient's employment is being terminated — **pink–slip** *vt*

pin money *n* (1697) **1 a** : money given by a man to his wife for her own use **b** : money set aside for the purchase of incidentals **2** : a trivial amount of money ⟨worked for *pin money*⟩

pin·na \ˈpi-nə\ *n, pl* **pin·nae** \ˈpi-ˌnē, -ˌnī\ *or* **pinnas** [NL, fr. L, feather, wing — more at PEN] (1719) **1 a** : a projecting body part (as a feather, wing, or fin) **b** : the largely cartilaginous projecting portion of the external ear — see EAR illustration **2** : a leaflet or primary division of a pinnate leaf or frond

pin·nace \ˈpi-nəs\ *n* [MF *pinace,* prob. fr. OSp *pinaza,* fr. *pino* pine, fr. L *pinus*] (1538) **1** : a light sailing ship; *esp* : one used as a tender **2** : any of various ship's boats

1**pin·na·cle** \ˈpi-ni-kəl\ *n* [ME *pinacle,* fr. AF, fr. LL *pinnaculum* small wing, gable, fr. L *pinna* wing, battlement] (14c) **1** : an upright architectural member generally ending in a small spire and used esp. in Gothic construction to give weight esp. to a buttress **2** : a structure or formation suggesting a pinnacle; *specif* : a lofty peak **3** : the highest point of development or achievement : ACME ***syn*** see SUMMIT

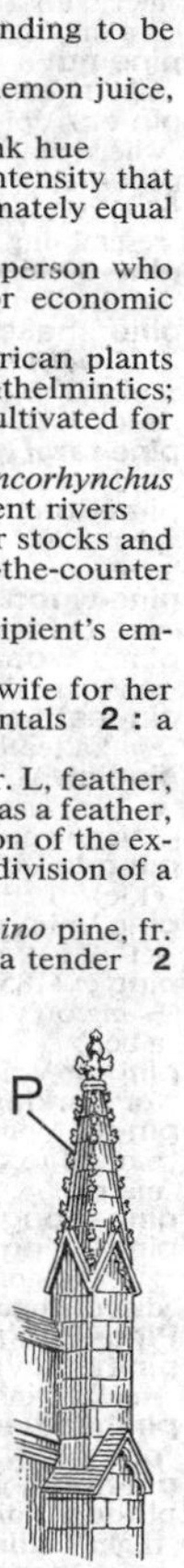

P pinnacle 1

2**pinnacle** *vt* **-cled; -cling** \-k(ə-)liŋ\ (14c) **1** : to surmount with a pinnacle **2** : to raise or rear on a pinnacle

pin·nate \ˈpi-ˌnāt\ *adj* [NL *pinnatus,* fr. L, feathered, fr. *pinna* feather, wing, fin] (ca. 1727) : resembling a feather esp. in having similar parts arranged on opposite sides of an axis like the barbs on the rachis of a feather ⟨a ~ leaf⟩ — see LEAF illustration — **pin·nate·ly** *adv*

pin·nat·i·fid \pə-ˈna-tə-fəd, -ˌfid\ *adj* [NL *pinnatifidus,* fr. *pinnatus* + L *-fidus* -fid] (ca. 1753) : cleft in a pinnate manner ⟨a ~ leaf⟩

pin·ner \ˈpi-nər\ *n* (1652) **1** : a woman's cap with long lappets worn in the 17th and 18th centuries **2** : one that pins

pin·ni·ped \ˈpi-nə-ˌped\ *n* [ultim. fr. L *pinna* + *ped-, pes* foot — more at FOOT] (1866) : any of an order or suborder (Pinnipedia) of aquatic carnivorous mammals (as a seal or walrus) with all four limbs modified into flippers — **pinniped** *adj*

pin·nule \ˈpin-(ˌ)yül\ *n* [NL *pinnula,* fr. L, dim. of *pinna*] (1748) **1** : any of the secondary branches of a plumose organ esp. of a crinoid **2** : one of the ultimate divisions of a twice pinnate leaf

pin·ny \ˈpi-nē\ *n, pl* **pinnies** [by shortening & alter.] (1851) *chiefly Brit* : PINAFORE

pin oak *n* (1813) : a pyramidally crowned deciduous oak (*Quercus palustris*) esp. of wet regions of the eastern U.S. that has deeply cleft toothed leaves and rather small nearly hemispherical acorns

pi·noch·le \ˈpē-ˌnə-kəl\ *n* [modif. of G dial. *Binokel,* a game resembling bezique, fr. F dial. *binocle*] (1864) : a card game played with a 48-card pack containing two each of A, K, Q, J, 10, 9 in each suit with the object to score points by melding certain combinations of cards or by winning tricks that contain scoring cards; *also* : the meld of queen of spades and jack of diamonds scoring 40 points in this game

pi·no·cy·to·sis \ˌpi-nə-sə-ˈtō-səs, ˌpī-, -ˌsī-\ *n, pl* **-to·ses** \-ˌsēz\ [NL, fr. Gk *pinein* to drink + NL *cyt-* + *-osis* — more at POTABLE] (1895) : the uptake of fluid and dissolved substances by a cell by invagination and pinching off of the cell membrane — **pi·no·cy·tot·ic** \-ˈtä-tik\ *or* **pi·no·cyt·ic** \ˌpi-nə-ˈsī-tik, ˌpī-\ *adj* — **pi·no·cy·tot·i·cal·ly** \-ti-k(ə-)lē\ *adv*

pi·no·le \pi-ˈnō-lē\ *n* [AmerSp, fr. Nahuatl *pinolli*] (1842) **1** : a finely ground flour made from parched corn **2** : any of various flours resembling pinole and ground from the seeds of other plants

pi·ñon *or* **pin·yon** \ˈpin-ˌyōn, -ˌyän, -yən; pin-ˈyōn\ *n, pl* **pi·ñons** *or* **pin·yons** *or* **pi·ño·nes** \pin-ˈyō-nēz\ [AmerSp *piñón,* fr. Sp, pine nut, fr. *piña* pinecone, fr. L *pinea* — more at PINEAL] (1831) : any of various small pines (as *Pinus quadrifolia, P. cembroides, P. edulis,* and *P. monophylla*) of western No. America with edible seeds; *also* : the edible seed of a piñon

pi·not blanc \ˈpē-(ˌ)nō-ˈblä^n, pē-ˈnō-\ *n, often cap P&B* [F, lit., white Pinot (a grape variety)] (ca. 1948) : a dry white wine similar to chardonnay

pinot gri·gio \-ˈgrē-j(ē-)ō, -zh(ē-)ō\ *n, often cap P&G* [It, lit., gray Pinot] (1976) : a dry white wine that is produced in Italy

pinot noir \-ˈnwär\ *n, often cap P&N* [F, lit., black Pinot] (1941) : a dry red wine produced from the same grape as French burgundy

1**pin·point** \ˈpin-ˌpȯint\ *n* (1849) **1** : something that is extremely small or insignificant **2** : the point of a pin **3** : an extremely small or sharp point

2**pinpoint** *adj* (1897) **1** : extremely fine or precise **2** : located, fixed, or directed with extreme precision ⟨~ targets⟩ **3** : small as a pinpoint

3**pinpoint** *vt* (1917) **1** : to locate or aim with great precision or accuracy ⟨~ a source⟩ **2 a** : to fix, determine, or identify with precision ⟨~ the cause⟩ **b** : to cause to stand out conspicuously : HIGHLIGHT

1**pin·prick** \ˈpin-ˌprik\ *n* (ca. 1860) **1** : a small puncture made by or as if by a pin **2** : a petty irritation or annoyance

2**pinprick** *vt* (1899) : to administer pinpricks to ~ *vi* : to administer pinpricks

PINS *abbr* persons in need of supervision

pins and needles *n pl* (1813) : a pricking tingling sensation in a limb growing numb or recovering from numbness — **on pins and needles** : in a nervous or jumpy state of anticipation

pin·set·ter \ˈpin-ˌse-tər\ *n* (1916) : an employee or a mechanical device that spots pins in a bowling alley

pin·spot·ter \-ˌspä-tər\ *n* (1946) : PINSETTER

pin·stripe \-ˌstrīp\ *n, often attrib* (1897) : a very thin stripe esp. on a fabric; *also* : a suit with such stripes — often used in pl. — **pin–striped** \-ˌstrīpt\ *adj*

pint \ˈpīnt\ *n* [ME *pinte,* fr. MF, prob. fr. VL **pincta,* fem. of *pinctus,* pp. of L *pingere* to paint; fr. the use of a painted mark on a container to show its capacity — more at PAINT] (14c) **1** — see WEIGHT table **2** : a pint pot or vessel

1**pin·ta** \ˈpin-tə, -ˌtä\ *n* [AmerSp, fr. Sp, spot, mark, fr. VL **pincta*] (1825) : a chronic skin disease that is endemic in tropical America, that occurs successively as an initial papule, a generalized eruption, and a patchy loss of pigment, and that is caused by a treponemal spirochete (*Treponema careteum*) morphologically indistinguishable from the causative agent of syphilis

2**pinta** \ˈpīn-tə\ *n* [*pint* + *-a* (as in *cuppa*)] (1959) *Brit* : a pint of milk

pin–ta·ble \ˈpin-ˌtā-bəl\ *n* (1936) *Brit* : PINBALL MACHINE

pin·tail \ˈpin-ˌtāl\ *n, pl* **pintail** *or* **pintails** (1768) : a bird having elongated central tail feathers; *esp* : a slender duck (*Anas acuta*) of the northern hemisphere with the male having a brown head, a white breast with a white line continuing up the side of the neck, and chiefly gray upperparts

pin·tle \ˈpin-tᵊl\ *n* [ME *pintel,* lit., penis, fr. OE; akin to MLG *pint* penis, OE *pinn* pin] (15c) : a usu. upright pivot pin on which another part turns

1**pin·to** \ˈpin-(ˌ)tō\ *n, pl* **pintos** *also* **pintoes** [AmerSp, fr. *pinto* spotted, fr. obs. Sp, fr. VL **pinctus*] (1860) : a horse or pony of various breeding that is marked with patches of white and another color — compare PAINT, PIEBALD, SKEWBALD

2**pinto** *adj* (1865) : PIED, MOTTLED

pinto bean *n* (1913) : a mottled kidney bean that is grown for food and for stock feed

pint–size \ˈpīnt-ˌsīz\ *or* **pint–sized** \-ˌsīzd\ *adj* (1936) : SMALL

1**pin·up** \ˈpin-ˌəp\ *n* (1943) : something fastened to a wall: as **a** : a photograph or poster of a person considered to have glamorous qualities **b** : something (as a lamp) designed for wall attachment

2**pinup** *adj* (1941) **1** : of or relating to pinups ⟨male ~ calendars⟩ **2** : designed for hanging on a wall ⟨a ~ lamp⟩

pinup girl *n* (1941) : a girl or woman whose glamorous qualities make her a suitable subject for a pinup

pin·wale \ˈpin-ˌwāl\ *adj* (1949) *of a fabric* : made with narrow wales

pin·weed \-ˌwēd\ *n* (1814) : any of a genus (*Lechea*) of herbs of the rockrose family with slender stems, many small leaves, and tiny flowers

1**pin·wheel** \-ˌhwēl, -ˌwēl\ *n* (1869) **1** : a fireworks device in the form of a revolving wheel of colored fire **2** : a toy consisting of lightweight vanes that revolve at the end of a stick **3** : something (as a galaxy) shaped like a pinwheel

2**pinwheel** *vi* (ca. 1934) : to move like a pinwheel

pin·worm \-ˌwərm\ *n* (ca. 1864) **1** : any of numerous small nematode worms (family Oxyuridae) that infest the intestines and esp. the cecum of various vertebrates; *esp* : a worm (*Enterobius vermicularis*) parasitic in humans **2** : any of several rather slender insect larvae that burrow in plant tissue

pinx *abbr* [L *pinxit*] he painted it; she painted it

pinx·ter flower \ˈpiŋ(k)-stər-\ *n* [D *pinkster* Whitsuntide] (1857) : a deciduous pink-flowered azalea (*Rhododendron periclymenoides* syn. *R. nudiflorum*) native to rich moist woodlands of eastern No. America

pin·yin \ˈpin-ˈyin\ *n, often cap* [Chin (Beijing) *pīnyīn* to spell phonetically, fr. *pīn* to arrange + *yīn* sound, pronunciation] (1963) : a system for romanizing Chinese ideograms in which tones are indicated by diacritics and unaspirated consonants are transcribed as voiced — compare WADE-GILES

pinyon *var of* PIÑON

pi·on \ˈpī-ˌän\ *n* [contr. of *pi-meson*] (1950) : a meson that is a combination of up and down quarks and antiquarks, that may be positive, negative, or neutral, and that has a mass about 270 times that of the electron — **pi·on·ic** \pī-ˈä-nik\ *adj*

1**pi·o·neer** \ˌpī-ə-ˈnir\ *n* [MF *pionier,* fr. OF *peonier* foot soldier, fr. *peon* foot soldier, fr. ML *pedon-, pedo* — more at PAWN] (1523) **1** : a member of a military unit usu. of construction engineers **2 a** : a person or group that originates or helps open up a new line of thought or activity or a new method or technical development **b** : one of the first to settle in a territory **3** : a plant or animal capable of establishing itself in a bare, barren, or open area and initiating an ecological cycle

2**pioneer** *vi* (1780) : to act as a pioneer ⟨~*ed* in the development of airplanes⟩ ~ *vt* **1** : to open or prepare for others to follow; *also* : SETTLE **2** : to originate or take part in the development of

3**pioneer** *adj* (1836) **1** : ORIGINAL, EARLIEST **2** : relating to or being a pioneer; *esp* : of, relating to, or characteristic of early settlers or their time

pi·ous \ˈpī-əs\ *adj* [ME, fr. L *pius*] (15c) **1 a :** marked by or showing reverence for deity and devotion to divine worship **b :** marked by conspicuous religiosity ⟨a hypocrite—a thing all ~ words and uncharitable deeds —Charles Reade⟩ **2 :** sacred or devotional as distinct from the profane or secular : RELIGIOUS ⟨a ~ opinion⟩ **3 :** showing loyal reverence for a person or thing : DUTIFUL **4 a :** marked by sham or hypocrisy **b :** marked by self-conscious virtue : VIRTUOUS **5 :** deserving commendation : WORTHY ⟨a ~ effort⟩ — **pi·ous·ly** *adv* — **pi·ous·ness** *n*

¹pip \ˈpip\ *n* [ME *pippe,* fr. MD (akin to OHG *pfiffiz*), fr. VL **pipita,* alter. of L *pituita* phlegm, pip; perh. akin to Gk *pitys* pine — more at PINE] (15c) **1 a :** a disorder of a bird marked by formation of a scale or crust on the tongue **b :** the scale or crust of this disorder **2 a :** any of various human ailments; *esp* **:** a slight nonspecific disorder **b** *chiefly Brit* **:** a feeling of irritation or annoyance

²pip *vb* **pipped; pip·ping** [imit.] *vi* (1598) **1 :** ¹PEEP 1 **2 :** to break through the shell of the egg ⟨the chick *pipped*⟩ ~ *vt* **:** to break open (the shell of an egg) in hatching

³pip *n* [origin unknown] (1604) **1 a :** one of the dots used on dice and dominoes to indicate numerical value **b :** SPOT 2c **2 a :** SPOT, SPECK **b :** ¹SPIKE 6a; *also* **:** BLIP **3 :** an individual rootstock of the lily of the valley **4 :** a diamond-shaped insignia of rank worn by a second lieutenant, lieutenant, or captain in the British army

⁴pip *n* [short for *pippin*] (1797) **1 :** a small fruit seed; *esp* **:** one of a several-seeded fleshy fruit **2 :** one extraordinary of its kind

⁵pip *vt* **pipped; pip·ping** [prob. fr. *pip* to blackball, fr. ³*pip* or ⁴*pip*] (1880) *Brit* **:** to beat by a narrow margin

⁶pip *n* [imit.] (1907) *chiefly Brit* **:** a short high-pitched tone

pip·age *or* **pipe·age** \ˈpī-pij\ *n* (1612) **1 a :** transportation by means of pipes **b :** the charge for such transportation **2 :** material for pipelines : PIPING

pipal *var of* PEEPUL

¹pipe \ˈpīp\ *n* [ME, fr. OE *pīpa* (akin to OHG *pfīfa* pipe), fr. VL **pipa* pipe, fr. L *pipare* to peep, of imit. origin] (bef. 12c) **1 a :** a tubular wind instrument; *specif* **:** a small fipple flute held in and played by the left hand **b :** one of the tubes of a pipe organ: (1) : FLUE PIPE (2) : REED PIPE **c :** BAGPIPE — usu. used in pl. **d** (1) : VOICE, VOCAL CORD — usu. used in pl. (2) : PIPING 1 **2 a :** a long tube or hollow body for conducting a liquid, gas, or finely divided solid or for structural purposes **b :** a means of transmission (as of television signals or computer data) ⟨a broadband fiber-optic ~⟩ **3 a :** a tubular or cylindrical object, part, or passage **b :** a roughly cylindrical and vertical geological formation **c :** the eruptive channel opening into the crater of a volcano **4 a :** a large cask of varying capacity used esp. for wine and oil **b :** any of various units of liquid capacity based on the size of a pipe; *esp* **:** a unit equal to two hogsheads **5 :** a device for smoking usu. consisting of a tube having a bowl at one end and a mouthpiece at the other **6 :** SNAP 2c, CINCH — **pipe·ful** \-ˌfu̇l\ *n* — **pipe·less** \ˈpīp-ləs\ *adj* — **pipe·like** \ˈpīp-ˌlīk\ *adj*

²pipe *vb* **piped; pip·ing** *vi* (bef. 12c) **1 a :** to play on a pipe **b :** to convey orders by signals on a boatswain's pipe **2 a :** to speak in a high or shrill voice **b :** to emit a shrill sound ~ *vt* **1 a :** to play (a tune) on a pipe **b :** to utter in the shrill tone of a pipe **2 a :** to lead or cause to go with pipe music **b** (1) : to call or direct by the boatswain's pipe (2) : to receive aboard or attend the departure of by sounding a boatswain's pipe **3 :** to trim with piping **4 :** to furnish or equip with pipes **5 :** to convey by or as if by pipes; *esp* **:** to transmit by wire or coaxial cable **6 :** NOTICE

pipe clay *n* (1732) **:** highly plastic grayish-white clay used esp. in making tobacco pipes and for whitening leather

pipe cleaner *n* (1861) **:** something used to clean the inside of a pipe; *specif* **:** a piece of flexible wire in which tufted fabric is twisted and which is used to clean the stem of a tobacco pipe

pipe down *vi* [²*pipe*] (1876) **:** to stop talking or making noise

pipe dream *n* [fr. the fantasies brought about by the smoking of opium] (1890) **:** an illusory or fantastic plan, hope, or story

pipe·fish \ˈpīp-ˌfish\ *n* (1769) **:** any of various fishes (family Syngnathidae) that are related to the sea horses and have a tube-shaped snout and a long slender body covered with bony plates

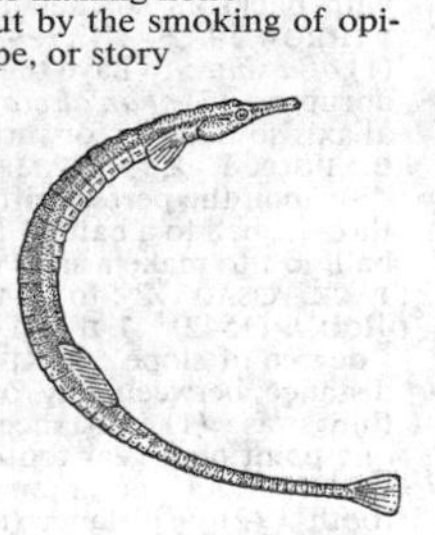
pipefish

pipe fitter *n* (1860) **:** a worker who installs and repairs piping

pipe fitting *n* (1858) **1 :** the work of a pipe fitter **2 :** a piece (as a coupling or elbow) used to connect pipes or as accessory to a pipe

pipe·line \ˈpīp-ˌlīn\ *n* (1856) **1 a :** a line of pipe with pumps, valves, and control devices for conveying liquids, gases, or finely divided solids **b :** PIPE 2b **2 :** a direct channel for information **3 :** a process or channel of supply ⟨an arms ~⟩ **4 :** a state of development, preparation, or production ⟨several projects in the ~⟩; *also* **:** the system for such processes ⟨a strong product ~⟩ **5 :** a course of individual advancement or development esp. to fill organizational needs

pipe organ *n* (1862) **:** ORGAN 1b(1)

pip·er \ˈpī-pər\ *n* (bef. 12c) **:** one that plays on a pipe

pi·per·a·zine \pi-ˈper-ə-ˌzēn, pī-\ *n* [ISV *piper*idine + *azine*] (1889) **:** a crystalline heterocyclic base $C_4H_{10}N_2$ used esp. as an anthelmintic

pi·per·i·dine \pi-ˈper-ə-ˌdēn, pī-\ *n* [ISV *piperine* + *-idine*] (1854) **:** a toxic liquid heterocyclic base $C_5H_{11}N$ that has a peppery ammoniacal odor and is obtained usu. by hydrolysis of piperine

pip·er·ine \ˈpi-pə-ˌrēn\ *n* [prob. fr. F *pipérine,* fr. L *piper* pepper] (1820) **:** a white crystalline alkaloid $C_{17}H_{19}NO_3$ that is the chief active constituent of pepper

pi·per·o·nal \pī-ˈper-ə-ˌnal\ *n* [ISV *piperine* + *-one* + ³*-al*] (1869) **:** a crystalline aldehyde $C_8H_6O_3$ with an odor of heliotrope

pi·per·o·nyl bu·tox·ide \pī-ˈper-ə-ˌnil-byü-ˈtäk-ˌsīd, -nᵊl-\ *n* [*piperon*al + *-yl* + *butyl* + *oxide*] (1945) **:** an insecticide $C_{19}H_{30}O_5$; *esp* **:** an oily liquid containing this compound that is used chiefly as a synergist (as for pyrethrin insecticides)

pipe·stone \ˈpīp-ˌstōn\ *n* (1804) **:** a pink or mottled pink-and-white argillaceous stone used esp. by American Indians to make carved objects (as tobacco pipes)

pipe stop *n* (ca. 1906) **:** an organ stop composed of flue pipes

pi·pette *also* **pi·pet** \pī-ˈpet\ *n* [F *pipette,* dim. of *pipe* pipe, cask, fr. VL **pipa, *pippa* pipe] (1839) **:** a small piece of apparatus which typically consists of a narrow tube into which fluid is drawn by suction (as for dispensing or measurement) and retained by closing the upper end — **pipette** *also* **pipet** *vb*

pipe up *vi* (1853) **:** SPEAK UP

pipe wrench *n* (ca. 1875) **:** a wrench for gripping and turning a cylindrical object (as a pipe) usu. by use of two serrated jaws so designed as to grip the pipe when turning in one direction only

¹piping *n* (13c) **1 a :** a sound, note, or call like that of a pipe **b :** the music of a pipe **2 :** a quantity or system of pipes **3 :** trimming stitched in seams or along edges (as of clothing, slipcovers, or curtains)

²piping *adj* (15c) **1 :** SHRILL ⟨a ~ voice⟩ **2 :** TRANQUIL ⟨~ times of peace —Shak.⟩

piping hot *adj* (14c) **:** very hot

piping plover *n* (1828) **:** a small pale plover (*Charadrius melodus*) chiefly of eastern No. America

pip·is·trelle \ˌpi-pə-ˈstrel\ *n* [F, fr. It *pipistrello* bat, alter. of *vipistrello,* ultim. fr. L *vespertilion-, vespertilio* — more at VESPERTILIAN] (1771) **:** any of a genus (*Pipistrellus* of the family Vespertilionidae) of bats typically appearing in early evening and exhibiting erratic flight; *esp* **:** one (*P. pipistrellus*) of Eurasia and northern Africa

pip·it \ˈpi-pət\ *n* [imit.] (1745) **:** any of various small songbirds (family Motacillidae and esp. genus *Anthus*) resembling the lark

pip·kin \ˈpip-kən\ *n* [perh. fr. *pipe*] (1554) **:** a small earthenware or metal pot usu. with a horizontal handle

pip·pin \ˈpi-pən\ *n* [ME *pepin,* fr. AF] (15c) **1 :** a crisp tart apple having usu. yellow or greenish-yellow skin strongly flushed with red and used esp. for cooking **2 :** a highly admired or very admirable person or thing

pip–pip \ˌpi(p)-ˈpip\ *interj* [prob. fr. *pip-pip,* imitating the sound of a horn] (1907) *Brit* — used to express farewell

pip·sis·se·wa \pip-ˈsi-sə-ˌwȯ\ *n* [perh. fr. Eastern Abenaki *kpi-pskʷáhsawe,* lit., flower of the woods] (1789) **:** any of a genus (*Chimaphila,* esp. *C. umbellata*) of evergreen herbs of the wintergreen family with astringent leaves used as a tonic and diuretic

pip–squeak \ˈpip-ˌskwēk\ *n* (1910) **:** one that is small or insignificant

pi·quan·cy \ˈpē-kən(t)-sē, ˈpi-kwən(t)-\ *n* (1664) **:** the quality or state of being piquant

pi·quant \ˈpē-kənt, -ˌkänt; ˈpi-kwənt\ *adj* [MF, fr. prp. of *piquer*] (1616) **1 :** engagingly provocative; *also* **:** having a lively arch charm **2 :** agreeably stimulating to the palate; *esp* **:** SPICY ***syn*** see PUNGENT — **pi·quant·ly** *adv* — **pi·quant·ness** *n*

¹pique \ˈpēk\ *n* (1551) **:** a transient feeling of wounded vanity : RESENTMENT ⟨a fit of ~⟩ ***syn*** see OFFENSE

²pique *vt* **piqued; piqu·ing** [F *piquer,* lit., to prick — more at PIKE] (1669) **1 :** to arouse anger or resentment in : IRRITATE ⟨what ~s linguistic conservatives —T. H. Middleton⟩ **2 a :** to excite or arouse esp. by a provocation, challenge, or rebuff ⟨sly remarks to ~ their curiosity⟩ **b :** PRIDE ⟨he ~s himself on his skill as a cook⟩ ***syn*** see PROVOKE

pi·qué *or* **pi·que** \pi-ˈkā, ˈpē-ˌ\ *n* [F *piqué,* fr. pp. of *piquer* to prick, quilt] (1852) **1 :** a durable ribbed clothing fabric of cotton, rayon, or silk **2 :** decoration of a tortoiseshell or ivory object with inlaid fragments of gold or silver

pi·quet \pi-ˈkā, -ˈket\ *n* [F] (1646) **:** a two-handed card game played with 32 cards

pir·ac·e·tam \ˌpī(-ə)r-ˈa-sə-ˌtam\ *n* [ISV *pir-* (alter. of *pyrrolidine,* a pyrrole derivative) + *acetam*ide] (1972) **:** an amine $C_6H_{10}N_2O_2$ that has been used as a nootropic

pi·ra·cy \ˈpī-rə-sē\ *n, pl* **-cies** [ML *piratia,* fr. LGk *peirateia,* fr. Gk *peiratēs* pirate] (1537) **1 :** an act of robbery on the high seas; *also* **:** an act resembling such robbery **2 :** robbery on the high seas **3 a :** the unauthorized use of another's production, invention, or conception esp. in infringement of a copyright **b :** the illicit accessing of broadcast signals

pi·ra·gua \pə-ˈrä-gwə, -ˈra-\ *n* [Sp] (ca. 1599) **1 :** DUGOUT 1 **2 :** a 2-masted flat-bottomed boat

pi·ra·nha \pə-ˈrä-nə; -ˈrän-yə, -ˈran-\ *n, pl* **pi·ra·nhas** *or* **piranha** [Pg, fr. Tupi *pirája, pirãʸa,* fr. *pirá* fish + *ája, ãʸa* tooth] (1861) **:** any of various usu. small So. American characin fishes (genera *Serrasalmus* and *Pygocentrus*) that have very sharp teeth, often appear in schools, and include some that may attack and inflict dangerous wounds upon humans and large animals — called also *caribe*

pi·ra·ru·cu \pi-ˌrär-ə-ˈkü\ *n* [Pg, fr. Tupi *pirawrukú,* fr. *pirá* fish + *urukú* annatto] (1840) **:** a very large edible bony fish (*Arapaima gigas* of the family Osteoglossidae) of the rivers of northern So. America

¹pi·rate \ˈpī-rət\ *n* [ME, fr. MF or L; MF, fr. L *pirata,* fr. Gk *peiratēs,* fr. *peiran* to attempt — more at FEAR] (14c) **:** one who commits or practices piracy — **pi·rat·i·cal** \pə-ˈra-ti-kəl, pī-\ *adj* — **pi·rat·i·cal·ly** \-k(ə-)lē\ *adv*

²pirate *vb* **pi·rat·ed; pi·rat·ing** *vt* (1577) **1 :** to commit piracy on **2 :** to take or appropriate by piracy: as **a :** to reproduce without authorization esp. in infringement of copyright **b :** to lure away from another employer by offers of betterment ~ *vi* **:** to commit or practice piracy

PIRG *abbr* Public Interest Research Group

piriform *var of* PYRIFORM

pirn \ˈpərn, *2 is also* ˈpirn\ *n* [ME] (15c) **1 :** QUILL 1a(1) **2** *chiefly Scot* **:** a device resembling a reel

pirogi *var of* PIEROGI

pi·rogue \ˈpē-ˌrōg\ *n* [F, fr. Sp *piragua,* fr. Carib *piraua*] (1666) **1 :** DUGOUT 1 **2 :** a boat like a canoe

\ə\ **abut** \ᵊ\ kitten, F table \ər\ **further** \a\ **ash** \ā\ **ace** \ä\ mop, mar \au̇\ **out** \ch\ **chin** \e\ bet \ē\ **easy** \g\ **go** \i\ **hit** \ī\ **ice** \j\ **job** \ŋ\ **sing** \ō\ **go** \ȯ\ **law** \ȯi\ **boy** \th\ **thin** \t͟h\ **the** \ü\ **loot** \u̇\ **foot** \y\ yet \zh\ **vision,** beige \k, ⁿ, œ, ue, ʸ\ *see* Guide to Pronunciation

piro·plasm \ˈpir-ə-ˌpla-zəm\ *or* **piro·plas·ma** \ˌpir-ə-ˈplaz-mə\ *n, pl* **piroplasms** *or* **piro·plas·ma·ta** \ˌpir-ə-ˈplaz-mə-tə\ [NL *Piroplasma,* genus of piroplasms] (1901) : BABESIA

pi·rosh·ki *or* **pi·rozh·ki** \pi-ˈrōsh-kē, ˌpir-əsh-ˈkē\ *n pl* [Russ *pirozhki,* pl. of *pirozhok,* dim. of *pirog* pastry] (1912) : small pastries with meat, cheese, or vegetable filling

pir·ou·ette \ˌpir-ə-ˈwet\ *n* [F, lit., teetotum] (1706) : a rapid whirling about of the body; *esp* : a full turn on the toe or ball of one foot in ballet — **pirouette** *vi*

pis *pl of* PI

pis al·ler \ˌpē-za-ˈlā\ *n, pl* **pis al·lers** \-ˈlā(z)\ [F, lit., to go worst] (1676) : a last resource or device

pis·ca·to·ri·al \ˌpis-kə-ˈtȯr-ē-əl\ *adj* (1828) : PISCATORY

pis·ca·to·ry \ˈpis-kə-ˌtȯr-ē\ *adj* [L *piscatorius,* fr. *piscari* to fish, fr. *piscis*] (1633) : of, relating to, or dependent on fish or fishing

Pi·sce·an \ˈpī-sē-ən, ˈpi-sē-, ˈpis-kē-\ *n* (1925) : PISCES 2b

Pi·sces \ˈpī-(ˌ)sēz *also* ˈpi-ˌsēz *or* ˈpis-ˌkās\ *n pl but sing in constr* [ME, fr. L (gen. *Piscium*), fr. pl. of *piscis* fish — more at FISH] **1** : a zodiacal constellation directly south of Andromeda **2 a** : the 12th sign of the zodiac in astrology — see ZODIAC table **b** : one born under this sign

pi·sci·cul·ture \ˈpī-sə-ˌkəl-chər, ˈpi-sə-, ˈpis-kə-\ *n* [prob. fr. F, fr. L *piscis* + F *culture* culture] (1856) : the cultivation of fish

pi·sci·na \pə-ˈsē-nə, -ˈsī-\ *n* [ML, fr. L, fishpond, fr. *piscis*] (1774) : a basin with a drain near the altar of a church for disposing of water from liturgical ablutions

pi·scine \ˈpī-ˌsēn, ˈpi-ˌsīn, ˈpis-ˌkīn\ *adj* [L *piscinus,* fr. *piscis*] (1799) : of, relating to, or characteristic of fish

pi·sci·vore \ˈpī-sə-ˌvȯr, ˈpi-\ *n* [back-formation fr. *piscivorous*] (1973) : a fish-eating animal

pi·sciv·o·rous \pə-ˈsi-və-rəs, pī-\ *adj* [L *piscis* + E *-vorous*] (1668) : feeding on fishes

pish \ˈpish\ *interj* (1592) — used to express disdain or contempt

[1]**pi·si·form** \ˈpī-sə-ˌfȯrm\ *adj* [L *pisum* pea + E *-iform* — more at PEA] (1767) : resembling a pea in size or shape

[2]**pisiform** *n* (ca. 1771) : a bone on the ulnar side of the carpus in most mammals

pis·mire \ˈpis-ˌmī(-ə)r, ˈpiz-\ *n* [ME *pissemire,* fr. *pisse* urine + *mire* ant, of Scand origin; akin to ON *maurr* ant; akin to L *formica* ant, Gk *myrmēx*] (14c) : ANT

pis·mo clam \ˈpiz-(ˌ)mō-\ *n, often cap P* [*Pismo* Beach, Calif.] (1913) : a thick-shelled clam (*Tivela stultorum*) of the southwest coast of No. America used extensively for food

pi·so \ˈpē-(ˌ)sō\ *n, pl* **pisos** [prob. fr. Tag, fr. Sp *peso*] (ca. 1975) : the peso of the Philippines

pi·so·lite \ˈpī-sə-ˌlīt\ *n* [NL *pisolithus,* fr. Gk *pisos* pea + *-lithos* -lith] (1708) : a limestone composed of pisiform concretions — **pi·so·lit·ic** \ˌpī-sə-ˈli-tik\ *adj*

[1]**piss** \ˈpis\ *vb* [ME, fr. AF *pisser,* fr. VL **pissiare,* of imit. origin] *vi* (14c) *sometimes vulgar* : URINATE ~ *vt, sometimes vulgar* : to urinate in or on

[2]**piss** *n* (14c) **1** *sometimes vulgar* : URINE **2** *sometimes vulgar* : an act of urinating — often used with *take*

piss and vinegar *n* (ca. 1942) *sometimes vulgar* : VIM, SPUNK

piss·ant \ˈpis-ˌant\ *n, often attrib* [*pissant* ant, fr. *[1]piss* + *ant*] (1945) *sometimes vulgar* : one that is insignificant — used as a generalized term of abuse

piss away *vt* (1949) *sometimes vulgar* : to fritter away : SQUANDER

pissed \ˈpist\ *adj* (1929) **1** *chiefly Brit, sometimes vulgar* : DRUNK 1a **2** *sometimes vulgar* : ANGRY, IRRITATED — often used with *off*

pissing contest *n* (1982) *sometimes vulgar* : a competition between rivals to determine superiority, predominance, or leadership — called also *pissing match*

piss off *vt* (ca. 1946) *sometimes vulgar* : ANGER, IRRITATE ~ *vi, Brit, sometimes vulgar* : to leave immediately : SCRAM — usu. used as a command

pis·soir \pi-ˈswär\ *n* [F, fr. MF, fr. *pisser* to urinate, fr. OF *pisser, pissier*] (1919) : a public urinal usu. located on the street in some European countries

piss–poor \ˈpis-ˌpu̇r, -ˌpȯr\ *adj* (1946) *sometimes vulgar* : very bad : extremely poor

pis·ta·chio \pə-ˈsta-sh(ē-ˌ)ō, -ˈstä-\ *n, pl* **-chios** [It *pistacchio,* fr. L *pistacium* pistachio nut, fr. Gk *pistakion,* fr. *pistakē* pistachio tree, of Iranian origin; akin to Pers *pistah* pistachio tree] (1598) : a small Asian tree (*Pistacia vera*) of the cashew family whose drupaceous fruit contains a greenish edible seed; *also* : its seed

pis·ta·reen \ˌpis-tə-ˈrēn\ *n* [prob. modif. of Sp *peseta* peseta] (1744) : an old Spanish silver piece circulating at a debased rate

piste \ˈpēst\ *n* [F, fr. MF, fr. OIt *pista,* fr. *pistare* to trample down, pound — more at PISTON] (ca. 1741) : TRAIL; *esp* : a downhill ski trail

pis·til \ˈpis-tᵊl\ *n* [NL *pistillum,* fr. L, pestle — more at PESTLE] (ca. 1741) : a single carpel or group of fused carpels usu. differentiated into an ovary, style, and stigma — see FLOWER illustration

pis·til·late \ˈpis-tə-ˌlāt\ *adj* (ca. 1828) : having pistils; *specif* : having pistils but no stamens

pis·tol \ˈpis-tᵊl\ *n* [MF *pistole,* fr. G, fr. MHG *pischulle,* fr. Czech *píšťala,* lit., pipe, fife; akin to Czech *pištět* to squeak] (ca. 1570) **1** : a handgun whose chamber is integral with the barrel; *broadly* : HANDGUN **2** : a notably sharp, spirited, or energetic person — **pistol** *vt*

pis·tole \pis-ˈtōl\ *n* [MF] (1592) : an old gold 2-escudo piece of Spain; *also* : any of several old gold coins of Europe of approximately the same value

pis·tol·eer \ˌpis-tə-ˈlir\ *n* (1832) : one who is armed with a pistol

pis·to·le·ro \ˌpis-tə-ˈler-ō\ *n, pl* **-ros** [Sp, fr. *pistola* pistol] (1936) : GUNMAN

pistol grip *n* (1874) **1** : a grip of a shotgun or rifle shaped like a pistol stock **2** : a handle shaped like a pistol stock

pistol–whip *vt* (ca. 1942) : to beat with a pistol

pis·ton \ˈpis-tən\ *n* [F, fr. It *pistone,* fr. *pistare* to pound, fr. OIt, fr. ML, fr. L *pistus,* pp. of *pinsere* to crush — more at PESTLE] (1704) **1** : a sliding piece moved by or moving against fluid pressure which usu. consists of a short cylindrical body fitting within a cylindrical chamber or vessel along which it moves back and forth **2** : a sliding valve moving in a cylinder in a brass instrument which when depressed by a finger knob serves to lower the instrument's pitch

piston pin *n* (1897) : WRIST PIN

piston ring *n* (1867) : a springy split metal ring for sealing the gap between a piston and the cylinder wall

piston rod *n* (1786) : CONNECTING ROD

[1]**pit** \ˈpit\ *n* [ME, fr. OE *pytt* (akin to OHG *pfuzzi* well), fr. L *puteus* well, pit] (bef. 12c) **1 a (1)** : a hole, shaft, or cavity in the ground **(2)** : MINE **(3)** : a scooped-out place used for burning something (as charcoal) **b** : an area often sunken or depressed below the adjacent floor area: as **(1)** : an enclosure in which animals are made to fight each other **(2)** : a space at the front of a theater for the orchestra **(3)** : an area in a securities or commodities exchange in which members trade (as stocks) **2 a** : HELL 1a — used with *the* **b** : a place or situation of futility, misery, or degradation **c** *pl* : WORST ⟨it's the ~*s*⟩ **3** : a hollow or indentation esp. in the surface of an organism: as **a** : a natural hollow in the surface of the body **b** : one of the indented scars left in the skin by a pustular disease : POCKMARK **c** : a minute depression in the secondary wall of a plant cell functioning in the intercellular movement of water and dissolved material **4** : any of the areas alongside an auto racecourse used for refueling and repairing the cars during a race — often used in pl. with *the*

[2]**pit** *vb* **pit·ted; pit·ting** *vt* (15c) **1 a** : to place, cast, bury, or store in a pit **b** : to make pits in; *esp* : to scar or mark with pits **2 a** : to set (as gamecocks) into or as if into a pit to fight **b** : to set into opposition or rivalry — usu. used with *against* ~ *vi* **1** : to become marked with pits; *esp* : to preserve for a time an indentation made by pressure **2** : to make a pit stop

[3]**pit** *n* [D, fr. MD — more at PITH] (1841) : the stone of a drupaceous fruit

[4]**pit** *vt* **pit·ted; pit·ting** (1906) : to remove the pit from (a fruit)

[1]**pi·ta** \ˈpē-tə\ *n* [Sp & Pg] (1698) **1** : any of several fiber-yielding plants (as an agave) **2** : the fiber of a pita; *also* : any of several fibers from other sources

[2]**pita** *n* [ModGk] (1945) : a thin flat bread that can be separated easily into two layers to form a pocket — called also *pita bread*

pit–a–pat \ˌpit-i-ˈpat\ *n* [imit.] (1582) : PITTER-PATTER — **pit–a–pat** *adv or adj* — **pit–a–pat** *vi*

pit boss *n* (1939) : a person who supervises the gaming tables in a casino

pit bull *n* (1930) **1** : a dog (as an American Staffordshire terrier) of any of several breeds or a real or apparent hybrid with one or more of these breeds that was developed and is now often trained for fighting and is noted for strength and stamina **2** : an aggressive and tenacious person

pit bull terrier *n* (1945) **1** : PIT BULL 1 **2** : AMERICAN PIT BULL TERRIER

[1]**pitch** \ˈpich\ *n* [ME *pich,* fr. OE *pic,* fr. L *pic-, pix;* akin to Gk *pissa* pitch, OCS *pĭcĭlŭ*] (bef. 12c) **1** : a black or dark viscous substance obtained as a residue in the distillation of organic materials and esp. tars **2** : any of various bituminous substances **3** : resin obtained from various conifers and often used medicinally **4** : any of various artificial mixtures resembling resinous or bituminous pitches

[2]**pitch** *vt* (bef. 12c) : to cover, smear, or treat with or as if with pitch

[3]**pitch** *vb* [ME *pichen* to thrust, drive, fix firmly, prob. fr. OE **piccan,* fr. VL **piccare* — more at PIKE] *vt* (13c) **1** : to erect and fix firmly in place ⟨~ a tent⟩ **2** : to throw usu. with a particular objective or toward a particular point ⟨~ hay onto a wagon⟩: as **a** : to throw (a baseball) to a batter **b** : to toss (as coins) so as to fall at or near a mark ⟨~ pennies⟩ **c** : to put aside or discard by or as if by throwing ⟨~*ed* the trash into the bin⟩ **3 a** : to present or advertise esp. in a high-pressure way : PLUG, PROMOTE **b** : to attempt to persuade esp. with a sales pitch **c** : to present (a movie or program idea) for consideration (as by a TV producer) **4 a (1)** : to cause to be at a particular level or of a particular quality ⟨a test ~*ed* at a 5th-grade reading level⟩ **(2)** : to set in a particular musical key **b** : to cause to be set at a particular angle : SLOPE **5** : to utter glibly and insincerely **6 a** : to use as a starting pitcher **b** : to play as pitcher **7** : to hit (a golf ball) in a high arc with backspin so that it rolls very little after striking the green **8** : THROW 14 ⟨~ a fit⟩ ~ *vi* **1 a** : to fall precipitately or headlong **b (1)** *of a ship* : to have the bow alternately plunge precipitately and rise abruptly **(2)** *of an aircraft, missile, or spacecraft* : to turn about a lateral axis so that the forward end rises or falls in relation to the after end **c** : BUCK 1 **2** : ENCAMP **3** : to hit upon or happen upon something ⟨~ upon the perfect gift⟩ **4** : to incline downward : SLOPE **5 a** : to throw a ball to a batter **b** : to play ball as a pitcher **c** : to pitch a golf ball **6** : to make a sales pitch ***syn*** see THROW — **pitch into 1** : ATTACK, ASSAIL **2** : to set to work on energetically

[4]**pitch** *n* (1542) **1 a** : SLOPE; *also* : degree of slope : RAKE **b** : the distance between any of various things: as **(1)** : distance between one point on a gear tooth and the corresponding point on the next tooth **(2)** : distance from any point on the thread of a screw to the corresponding point on an adjacent thread measured parallel to the axis **c** : the theoretical distance a propeller would advance longitudinally in one revolution **d** : the number of teeth or of threads per inch **e** : a unit of width of type based on the number of times a letter can be set in a linear inch **2** : the action or a manner of pitching; *esp* : an up-and-down movement — compare YAW **3** *archaic* : TOP, ZENITH **4 a** : the relative level, intensity, or extent of some quality or state ⟨tensions rose to a feverish ~⟩ **b (1)** : the property of a sound and esp. a musical tone that is determined by the frequency of the waves producing it : highness or lowness of sound **(2)** : a standard frequency for tuning instruments **c (1)** : the

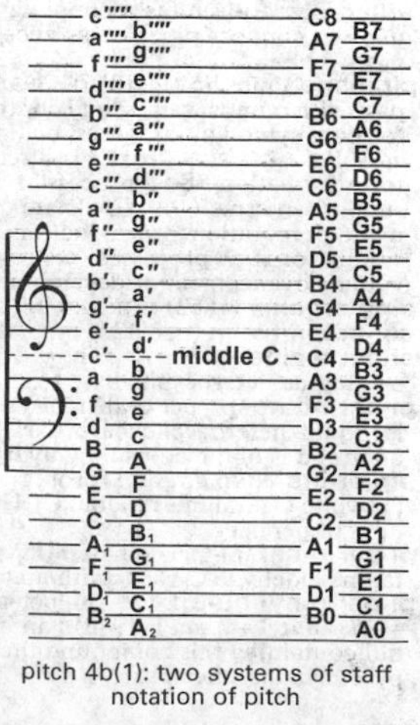
c'''''
a'''' b''''
f'''' g''''
d'''' e''''
b''' c''''
g''' a'''
e''' f'''
c''' d'''
a'' b''
f'' g''
d'' e''
b' c''
g' a'
e' f'
c' d' middle C
a b
f g
d e
B c
G A
E F
C D
A_1 B_1
F_1 G_1
D_1 E_1
B_2 C_1
A_2
C8 B7
A7 G7
F7 E7
D7 C7
B6 A6
G6 F6
E6 D6
C6 B5
A5 G5
F5 E5
D5 C5
B4 A4
G4 F4
E4 D4
C4 B3
A3 G3
F3 E3
D3 C3
B2 A2
G2 F2
E2 D2
C2 B1
A1 G1
F1 E1
D1 C1
B0 A0
pitch 4b(1): two systems of staff notation of pitch

difference in the relative vibration frequency of the human voice that contributes to the total meaning of speech (2) : a definite relative pitch that is a significant phenomenon in speech **5 a** : a steep place : DECLIVITY **b** : the portion of a route (as in mountain climbing or caving) between belay points **6** *chiefly Brit* **a** : an outdoor site (as for camping or doing business) **b** : PLAYING FIELD 1 **7** : an all-fours game in which the first card led is a trump **8 a** : an often high-pressure sales presentation **b** : ADVERTISEMENT **c** : RECOMMENDATION, PLUG ⟨made a ~ for tax cuts⟩ **9 a** : the delivery of a baseball by a pitcher to a batter **b** : a baseball so thrown **c** : PITCHOUT 2 — **pitched** \ˈpicht\ *adj*

pitch–black \ˈpich-ˈblak\ *adj* (1599) : extremely dark or black

pitch·blende \ˈpich-ˌblend\ *n* [part trans. of G *Pechblende,* fr. *Pech* pitch + *Blende* blende] (1770) : a brown to black mineral that consists of massive uraninite, has a distinctive luster, contains radium, and is the chief ore-mineral source of uranium

pitch–dark \ˈpich-ˈdärk\ *adj* (1827) : extremely dark : PITCH-BLACK

pitched battle *n* (1596) : an intensely fought battle in which the opposing forces are locked in close combat

[1]**pitch·er** \ˈpi-chər\ *n* [ME *picher,* fr. AF, fr. ML *bicarius* drinking cup] (13c) **1** : a container for holding and pouring liquids that usu. has a lip or spout and a handle **2** : a modified leaf of a pitcher plant in which the hollowed petiole and base of the blade form an elongated receptacle — **pitch·er·ful** \-ˌfu̇l\ *n*

[2]**pitcher** *n* (ca. 1722) : one that pitches; *specif* : the player who pitches in a game of baseball

pitcher plant *n* (1819) : a plant (esp. family Sarraceniaceae, the pitcher-plant family) with pitcher-shaped leaves in which insects are trapped and digested by means of a fluid secreted by the leaves

pitch·fork \ˈpich-ˌfȯrk\ *n* (13c) : a long-handled fork that has two or three long somewhat curved prongs and is used esp. in pitching hay — **pitchfork** *vt*

pitch in *vi* (1843) **1** : to begin to work **2** : to contribute to a common endeavor

pitch·man \ˈpich-mən\ *n* (1918) : a man who makes a sales pitch: as **a** : one who sells merchandise on the streets or from a concession **b** : one who does radio or TV commercials

pitch·out \ˈpich-ˌau̇t\ *n* (1903) **1** : a pitch in baseball deliberately out of reach of the batter to enable the catcher to put out a base runner esp. with a throw **2** : a lateral pass in football between two backs behind the line of scrimmage — **pitch out** *vi*

pitch–per·fect \ˈpich-ˈpər-fikt\ *adj* (1970) : sensitive to or having exactly the right tone or style ⟨a ~ translation⟩

pitch pine *n* (1676) **1** : any of several pines that yield pitch; *esp* : a 3-leaved pine (*Pinus rigida*) of eastern No. America **2** : the wood of a pitch pine

pitch pipe *n* (1711) : a small reed pipe or flue pipe producing one or more tones to establish the pitch in singing or in tuning an instrument

pitch·pole \ˈpich-ˌpōl\ *vb* [*pitchpole* somersault, fr. [3]*pitch* + *pole, poll* head] *vi* (1851) : to turn end over end ⟨the catamaran *pitchpoled*⟩ ~ *vt* : to cause to turn end over end

pitch·wom·an \-ˌwu̇-mən\ *n* (1957) : a woman who makes a sales pitch

pitchy \ˈpi-chē\ *adj* (15c) **1 a** : full of pitch : TARRY **b** : of, relating to, or having the qualities of pitch **2** : PITCH-BLACK

pit·e·ous \ˈpi-tē-əs\ *adj* (14c) : of a kind to move to pity or compassion — **pit·e·ous·ly** *adv* — **pit·e·ous·ness** *n*

pit·fall \ˈpit-ˌfȯl\ *n* (14c) **1** : TRAP, SNARE; *specif* : a pit flimsily covered or camouflaged and used to capture and hold animals or men **2** : a hidden or not easily recognized danger or difficulty

[1]**pith** \ˈpith\ *n* [ME, fr. OE *pitha;* akin to MD & MLG *pit* pith, pit] (bef. 12c) **1 a** : a usu. continuous central strand of spongy tissue in the stems of most vascular plants that prob. functions chiefly in storage **b** : any of various loose spongy plant tissues that resemble true pith **c** : the soft or spongy interior of a part of the body **2 a** : the essential part : CORE **b** : substantial quality (as of meaning) **3** : IMPORTANCE

[2]**pith** *vt* (1805) **1 a** : to kill (as cattle) by piercing or severing the spinal cord **b** : to destroy the spinal cord or central nervous system of (as a frog) usu. by passing a wire or needle up and down the vertebral canal **2** : to remove the pith from (a plant stem)

pit·head \ˈpit-ˌhed\ *n* (1839) *chiefly Brit* : the top of a mining pit or coal shaft; *also* : the immediately adjacent ground and buildings

pith helmet *n* (1889) : TOPEE

pith ray *n* (1902) : MEDULLARY RAY

pithy \ˈpi-thē\ *adj* **pith·i·er; -est** (1562) **1** : consisting of or abounding in pith **2** : having substance and point : tersely cogent ***syn*** see CONCISE — **pith·i·ly** \ˈpi-thə-lē\ *adv* — **pith·i·ness** \ˈpi-thē-nəs\ *n*

piti·able \ˈpi-tē-ə-bəl\ *adj* (15c) **1** : deserving or exciting pity : LAMENTABLE ⟨~ victims⟩ **2** : of a kind to evoke mingled pity and contempt esp. because of inadequacy ⟨a ~ excuse⟩ ***syn*** see CONTEMPTIBLE — **piti·able·ness** *n* — **piti·ably** \-blē\ *adv*

piti·er \ˈpi-tē-ər\ *n* (1601) : one that pities

piti·ful \ˈpi-ti-fəl\ *adj* (14c) **1** *archaic* : full of pity : COMPASSIONATE **2 a** : deserving or arousing pity or commiseration **b** : exciting pitying contempt (as by meanness or inadequacy) ⟨~ wages⟩ — **piti·ful·ly** \-f(ə-)lē\ *adv* — **piti·ful·ness** \-fəl-nəs\ *n*

piti·less \ˈpi-ti-ləs\ *adj* (15c) : devoid of pity : HARSH, CRUEL — **piti·less·ly** *adv* — **piti·less·ness** *n*

pit·man \ˈpit-mən\ *n* (1703) **1** *pl* **pit·men** \-mən\ : a man who works in or near a pit: as **a** *Brit* : MINER **b** : a sawyer who stands below the timber **2** *pl* **pitmans** : CONNECTING ROD

pi·ton \ˈpē-ˌtän\ *n* [F] (1893) : a spike, wedge, or peg that is driven into a rock or ice surface as a support (as for a mountain climber)

pi·tot–stat·ic tube \ˌpē-ˌtō-ˈsta-tik-\ *n, often cap P* (1926) : a device that consists of a pitot tube and a static tube and that measures pressures in such a way that the relative speed of a fluid can be determined

pi·tot tube \ˈpē-ˌtō-\ *n, often cap P* [F (*tube de*) *Pitot,* fr. Henri *Pitot* †1771 Fr. physicist] (ca. 1859) **1** : a device that consists of a tube having a short right-angled bend which is placed vertically in a moving body of fluid (as air) with the mouth of the bent part directed upstream and that is used with a manometer to measure the velocity of fluid flow **2** : PITOT-STATIC TUBE

pit saw *n* (1679) : a handsaw worked by two persons one of whom stands on or above the log being sawed into planks and the other below it usu. in a pit

pit stop *n* (1932) **1** : a stop at the pits during an automobile race **2 a** (1) : a stop (as during a trip) for fuel, food, or rest or for use of a restroom (2) : a temporary deviation from a direct or usual course ⟨a career *pit stop* . . . where he worked temporarily in between TV jobs —Mark Lorando⟩ **b** (1) : a place where a pit stop is or can be made (2) : an establishment providing food or drink

pit·tance \ˈpi-tᵊn(t)s\ *n* [ME *pitance,* fr. AF, piety, pity, dole, portion, fr. ML *pietantia,* fr. *pietant-, pietans,* prp. of *pietari* to be charitable, fr. L *pietas* piety — more at PITY] (14c) : a small portion, amount, or allowance; *also* : a meager wage or remuneration

pitted *adj* (bef. 12c) : marked with pits

pit·ter–pat·ter \ˈpi-tər-ˌpa-tər, ˈpi-tē-ˌ\ *n* [redupl. of [4]*patter*] (15c) : a rapid succession of light sounds or beats : PATTER — **pitter–patter** \ˌpi-tər-ˈ, ˌpi-tē-ˈ\ *adv or adj* — **pitter–patter** *same as adv*\ *vi*

pitting *n* (1665) **1** : an arrangement of pits **2** : the action or process of forming pits **3** : the bringing of gamecocks together to fight

pit·tos·po·rum \pə-ˈtäs-pə-rəm\ *n* [NL, fr. Gk *pitta, pissa* pitch + *spora* seed — more at PITCH, SPORE] (1789) : any of various Old World shrubs or trees (genus *Pittosporum* of the family Pittosporaceae) planted esp. as ornamentals in warm regions

[1]**pi·tu·i·tary** \pə-ˈtü-ə-ˌter-ē, -ˈtyü-\ *adj* [L *pituita* phlegm; fr. the former belief that the pituitary gland secreted phlegm — more at PIP] (1615) **1** : of or relating to the pituitary gland **2** : caused or characterized by secretory disturbances of the pituitary gland ⟨~ dwarfism⟩

[2]**pituitary** *n, pl* **-tar·ies** (1845) : PITUITARY GLAND

pituitary gland *n* (1825) : a small oval endocrine organ that is attached to the infundibulum of the brain, consists of an epithelial anterior lobe joined by an intermediate part to a posterior lobe of nervous origin, and produces various internal secretions directly or indirectly impinging on most basic body functions — called also *hypophysis, pituitary body*; see BRAIN illustration

pit viper *n* (ca. 1885) : any of various mostly New World vipers (subfamily Crotalinae of the family Viperidae) with a sensory pit on each side of the head and hollow perforated retractable fangs

[1]**pity** \ˈpi-tē\ *n, pl* **pit·ies** [ME *pite,* fr. AF *pité,* fr. L *pietat-, pietas* piety, pity, fr. *pius* pious] (13c) **1 a** : sympathetic sorrow for one suffering, distressed, or unhappy **b** : capacity to feel pity **2** : something to be regretted ⟨it's a ~ you can't go⟩

syn PITY, COMPASSION, COMMISERATION, CONDOLENCE, SYMPATHY mean the act or capacity for sharing the painful feelings of another. PITY implies tender or sometimes slightly contemptuous sorrow for one in misery or distress ⟨felt *pity* for the captives⟩. COMPASSION implies pity coupled with an urgent desire to aid or to spare ⟨treats the homeless with great *compassion*⟩. COMMISERATION suggests pity expressed outwardly in exclamations, tears, or words of comfort ⟨murmurs of *commiseration* filled the loser's headquarters⟩. CONDOLENCE applies chiefly to formal expression of grief to one who has suffered loss ⟨expressed their *condolences* to the widow⟩. SYMPATHY often suggests a tender concern but can also imply a power to enter into another's emotional experience of any sort ⟨went to my best friend for *sympathy*⟩ ⟨in *sympathy* with her desire to locate her natural parents⟩.

[2]**pity** *vb* **pit·ied; pity·ing** *vt* (15c) : to feel pity for ~ *vi* : to feel pity

pitying *adj* (1589) : expressing or feeling pity — **pity·ing·ly** \-iŋ-lē\ *adv*

pit·y·ri·a·sis \ˌpi-ti-ˈrī-ə-səs\ *n* [NL, fr. Gk, fr. *pityron* scurf] (ca. 1693) : any of various skin conditions of humans or domestic animals marked by dry scaling patches of skin

più \ˈpyü, pē-ˈü\ *adv* [It, fr. L *plus*] (1724) : MORE — used to qualify an adverb or adjective used as a direction in music

Piute *var of* PAIUTE

[1]**piv·ot** \ˈpi-vət\ *n* [F] (1611) **1** : a shaft or pin on which something turns **2 a** : a person, thing, or factor having a major or central role, function, or effect **b** : a key player or position; *specif* : an offensive position of a basketball player standing usu. with back to the basket to relay passes, shoot, or provide a screen for teammates **3** : the action of pivoting; *esp* : the action in basketball of stepping with one foot while keeping the other foot at its point of contact with the floor

[2]**pivot** *adj* (1796) **1** : turning on or as if on a pivot **2** : PIVOTAL

[3]**pivot** *vi* (1841) : to turn on or as if on a pivot ~ *vt* **1** : to provide with, mount on, or attach by a pivot **2** : to cause to pivot — **pivot·able** \-və-tə-bəl\ *adj*

piv·ot·al \ˈpi-və-tᵊl\ *adj* (1844) **1** : of, relating to, or constituting a pivot **2** : vitally important : CRITICAL — **piv·ot·al·ly** \-tᵊl-ē\ *adv*

piv·ot·man \ˈpi-vət-ˌman\ *n* (ca. 1814) : one who plays the pivot; *specif* : a center on a basketball team

pivot tooth *n* (1842) : an artificial crown attached to the root of a tooth by a usu. metallic pin — called also *pivot crown*

pix *pl of* PIC

pix·el \ˈpik-səl, -ˌsel\ *n* [*pix* + *element*] (1969) **1** : any of the small discrete elements that together constitute an image (as on a television or computer screen) **2** : any of the detecting elements of a charge-coupled device used as an optical sensor

pix·e·lat·ed \ˈpik-sə-ˌlā-təd\ *adj* [*pixel* + *-ated* (after *pixilated*)] (1982) *of an image* : displayed in such a manner that individual pixels are discernible

[1]**pix·ie** *also* **pixy** \ˈpik-sē\ *n, pl* **pix·ies** [origin unknown] (ca. 1630) **1** : FAIRY; *specif* : a cheerful mischievous sprite **2** : a usu. petite vivacious woman or girl — **pix·ie·ish** \-sē-ish\ *adj*

[2]**pixie** *also* **pixy** *adj* (1943) : playfully mischievous — **pixi·ness** *n*

pix·i·lat·ed *also* **pix·il·lat·ed** \ˈpik-sə-ˌlā-təd\ *adj* [irreg. fr. *pixie*] (1848) **1** : somewhat unbalanced mentally; *also* : BEMUSED **2** : WHIMSICAL ⟨~ pleasures⟩ — **pix·i·la·tion** \ˌpik-sə-ˈlā-shən\ *n*

pizz *abbr* pizzicato

piz·za \ˈpēt-sə\ *n* [It, perh. of Gmc origin; akin to OHG *bizzo, pizzo* bite, bit, *bīzan* to bite — more at BITE] (1845) : a dish made typically of flattened bread dough spread with a savory mixture usu. including tomatoes and cheese and often other toppings and baked — called also *pizza pie* — **pizza·like** \-ˌlīk\ *adj*

\ə\ **abut** \ᵊ\ **kitten,** F **table** \ər\ **further** \a\ **ash** \ā\ **ace** \ä\ **mop, mar**
\au̇\ **out** \ch\ **chin** \e\ **bet** \ē\ **easy** \g\ **go** \i\ **hit** \ī\ **ice** \j\ **job**
\ŋ\ **sing** \ō\ **go** \ȯ\ **law** \ȯi\ **boy** \th\ **thin** \t͟h\ **the** \ü\ **loot** \u̇\ **foot**
\y\ **yet** \zh\ **vision, beige** \k̲, ⁿ, œ, ue, ʸ\ *see* Guide to Pronunciation

piz·zazz *or* **pi·zazz** \pə-ˈzaz\ *n* [origin unknown] (1937) : the quality of being exciting or attractive: as **a** : GLAMOUR **b** : VITALITY — **piz·zazzy** *or* **pi·zazzy** \-ˈza-zē\ *adj*
piz·ze·ria \ˌpēt-sə-ˈrē-ə\ *n* [It, fr. *pizza*] (ca. 1912) : an establishment where pizzas are made or sold
¹piz·zi·ca·to \ˌpit-si-ˈkä-(ˌ)tō\ *n, pl* **-ca·ti** \-ˈkä-(ˌ)tē\ (1845) : a note or passage played by plucking strings
²pizzicato *adv or adj* [It, pp. of *pizzicare* to pluck] (ca. 1854) : by means of plucking instead of bowing — used as a direction in music; compare ARCO
piz·zle \ˈpi-zəl\ *n* [prob. fr. D dial. *pezel;* akin to LG *pesel* pizzle] (1523) **1** : the penis of an animal **2** : a whip made of a bull's pizzle
pj's \ˈpē-ˌjāz\ *n pl* [*pajamas*] (1951) : PAJAMAS
pk *abbr* **1** park **2** peak **3** peck **4** pike
¹PK \ˌpē-ˈkā\ *n* (1943) : PSYCHOKINESIS
²PK *abbr* preacher's kid
pkg *abbr* package
pkt *abbr* packet
PKU *abbr* phenylketonuria
pkwy *abbr* parkway
pl *abbr* **1** place **2** plate
PL *abbr* **1** private line **2** public law **3** public library
pla·ca·ble \ˈpla-kə-bəl, ˈplā-\ *adj* (1586) : easily placated : TOLERANT, TRACTABLE — **pla·ca·bil·i·ty** \ˌpla-kə-ˈbi-lə-tē, ˌplā-\ *n* — **pla·ca·bly** \ˈpla-kə-blē, ˈplā-\ *adv*
¹plac·ard \ˈpla-kərd, -ˌkärd\ *n* [ME *placquart* formal document, fr. MF *placard,* fr. *plaquer* to make adhere, plate — more at PLAQUE] (1560) **1** : a notice posted in a public place : POSTER **2** : a small card or metal plaque
²plac·ard \-ˌkärd, -kərd\ *vt* (1813) **1 a** : to cover with or as if with posters **b** : to post in a public place **2** : to announce by or as if by posting
pla·cate \ˈplā-ˌkāt, ˈpla-\ *vt* **pla·cat·ed; pla·cat·ing** [L *placatus,* pp. of *placare* — more at PLEASE] (1678) : to soothe or mollify esp. by concessions : APPEASE ***syn*** see PACIFY — **pla·cat·er** *n* — **pla·cat·ing·ly** \-ˌkā-tiŋ-lē\ *adv* — **pla·ca·tion** \plā-ˈkā-shən, pla-\ *n* — **pla·ca·tive** \ˈplā-ˌkā-tiv, ˈpla-\ *adj* — **pla·ca·to·ry** \ˈplā-kə-ˌtȯr-ē, ˈpla-\ *adj*
¹place \ˈplās\ *n* [ME, fr. AF, open space, fr. L *platea* broad street, fr. Gk *plateia (hodos),* fr. fem. of *platys* broad, flat; akin to Skt *pṛthu* broad, L *planta* sole of the foot] (13c) **1 a** : physical environment : SPACE **b** : a way for admission or transit **c** : physical surroundings : ATMOSPHERE **2 a** : an indefinite region or expanse ⟨all over the ~⟩ **b** : a building or locality used for a special purpose ⟨a ~ of learning⟩ ⟨a fine eating ~⟩ **c** *archaic* : the three-dimensional compass of a material object **3 a** : a particular region, center of population, or location ⟨a nice ~ to visit⟩ **b** : a building, part of a building, or area occupied as a home ⟨our summer ~⟩ **4** : a particular part of a surface or body : SPOT **5** : relative position in a scale or series: as **a** : position in a social scale ⟨kept them in their ~⟩ **b** : a step in a sequence ⟨in the first ~, it's none of your business⟩ **c** : a position at the conclusion of a competition ⟨finished in last ~⟩ **6 a** : a proper or designated niche or setting ⟨the ~ of education in society⟩ **b** : an appropriate moment or point ⟨this is not the ~ to discuss compensation —Robert Moses⟩ **c** : a distinct condition, position, or state of mind ⟨the postfeminist generation is in a different ~ —Betty Friedan⟩ **7 a** : an available seat or accommodation ⟨needs a ~ to stay⟩ **b** : an empty or vacated position ⟨new ones will take their ~⟩ **8** : the position of a figure in relation to others of a row or series; *esp* : the position of a digit within a numeral **9 a** : remunerative employment : JOB **b** : prestige accorded to one of high rank : STATUS ⟨an endless quest for preferment and ~ —*Time*⟩ **10** : a public square : PLAZA **11** : a small street or court **12** : second place at the finish (as of a horse race) — **in place 1** *also* **into place a** : in an original or proper position **b** : established, instituted, or operational ⟨systems *in place*⟩ **2** : in the same spot without forward or backward movement ⟨run *in place*⟩ — **in place of** : as a substitute or replacement for : INSTEAD OF — **out of place 1** : not in the proper or usual location **2** : IMPROPER, INAPPROPRIATE
²place *vb* **placed; plac·ing** *vt* (15c) **1 a** : to put in or as if in a particular place or position : SET **b** : to present for consideration ⟨a question *placed* before the group⟩ **c** : to put in a particular state ⟨~ a performer under contract⟩ **d** : to direct to a desired spot **e** : to cause (the voice) to produce free and well resonated singing or speaking tones **2 a** : to assign to a position in a series or category : RANK **b** : ESTIMATE ⟨*placed* the value of the estate too high⟩ **c** : to identify by connecting with an associated context ⟨couldn't quite ~ her face⟩ ⟨police *placed* them at the crime scene⟩ **3** : to distribute in an orderly manner : ARRANGE **4** : to appoint to a position **5** : to find a place (as a home or employment) for **6 a** : to give (an order) to a supplier **b** : to give an order for ⟨~ a bet⟩ **c** : to try to establish a connection for ⟨~ a telephone call⟩ ~ *vi* : to earn a given spot in a competition; *specif* : to come in second (as in a horse race) — **place·able** \ˈplā-sə-bəl\ *adj*
pla·ce·bo \plə-ˈsē-(ˌ)bō\ *n, pl* **-bos** [L, I shall please] (1785) **1 a** : a usu. pharmacologically inert preparation prescribed more for the mental relief of the patient than for its actual effect on a disorder **b** : an inert or innocuous substance used esp. in controlled experiments testing the efficacy of another substance (as a drug) **2** : something tending to soothe
placebo effect *n* (1950) : improvement in the condition of a patient that occurs in response to treatment but cannot be considered due to the specific treatment used
place·hold·er \ˈplās-ˌhōl-dər\ *n* (1958) : a symbol in a mathematical or logical expression that may be replaced by the name of any element of a set
¹place·kick \ˈplās-ˌkik\ *n* (1856) : the kicking of a ball (as a football) placed or held in a stationary position on the ground
²placekick *vt* (1856) **1** : to kick (a ball) from a stationary position **2** : to score by means of a placekick — **place·kick·er** *n*
place·less \-ləs\ *adj* (14c) **1** : lacking a fixed location **2** : indistinguishable from other such places in appearance or character ⟨a ~ parking complex —T. J. Jablonsky⟩ — **place·less·ly** *adv* — **place·less·ness** *n*
place·man \-mən\ *n* (1741) : a political appointee to a public office esp. in 18th century Britain
place mat *n* (1928) : a small often rectangular table mat on which a place setting is laid
place·ment \ˈplās-mənt\ *n* (1844) **1** : an act or instance of placing: as **a** : an accurately hit ball (as in tennis) that an opponent cannot return **b** : the assignment of a person to a suitable place (as a job or a class in school) **2** : PLACEKICK
placement test *n* (1928) : a test usu. given to a student entering an educational institution to determine specific knowledge or proficiency in various subjects for the purpose of assignment to appropriate courses or classes
place–name \ˈplās-ˌnām\ *n* (1868) : the name of a geographic locality
pla·cen·ta \plə-ˈsen-tə\ *n, pl* **-centas** *or* **-cen·tae** \-ˈsen-(ˌ)tē\ [NL, fr. L, flat cake, fr. Gk *plakoenta,* acc. of *plakoeis,* fr. *plak-, plax* flat surface — more at FLUKE] (1691) **1** : the vascular organ in mammals except monotremes and marsupials that unites the fetus to the maternal uterus and mediates its metabolic exchanges through a more or less intimate association of uterine mucosal with chorionic and usu. allantoic tissues; *also* : an analogous organ in another animal **2** : a sporangium-bearing surface; *esp* : the part of the carpel bearing ovules
¹pla·cen·tal \plə-ˈsen-tᵊl\ *adj* (1791) **1** : of, relating to, having, or occurring by means of a placenta **2** : EUTHERIAN
²placental *n* (1839) : a placental mammal : EUTHERIAN
pla·cen·ta·tion \ˌpla-sᵊn-ˈtā-shən, plə-ˌsen-\ *n* (1760) **1** : the arrangement of placentas and ovules in a plant ovary **2 a** : the development of the placenta and attachment of the fetus to the uterus during pregnancy **b** : the morphological type of a placenta
¹plac·er \ˈplā-sər\ *n* (1579) : one that places: as **a** : one that deposits or arranges **b** : one of the winners in a competition
²plac·er \ˈpla-sər\ *n, often attrib* [Sp, fr. Catal, submarine plain, fr. *plaza* place, fr. L *platea* broad street — more at PLACE] (1848) : an alluvial, marine, or glacial deposit containing particles of valuable mineral and esp. of gold ⟨~ gold⟩
place setting *n* (1944) : a set of dishes and flatware constituting a table service for one person
place value *n* (1911) : the value of the place of a digit in a numeral
plac·id \ˈpla-səd\ *adj* [L *placidus,* fr. *placēre* to please — more at PLEASE] (1626) : serenely free of interruption or disturbance ⟨~ skies⟩ ⟨a ~ disposition⟩; *also* : COMPLACENT 1 ***syn*** see CALM — **pla·cid·i·ty** \pla-ˈsi-də-tē, plə-\ *n* — **plac·id·ly** \ˈpla-səd-lē\ *adv* — **plac·id·ness** *n*
plack·et \ˈpla-kət\ *n* [origin unknown] (1605) **1 a** : a slit in a garment (as a skirt) often forming the closure **b** *archaic* : a pocket esp. in a woman's skirt **2** *archaic* **a** : PETTICOAT **b** : WOMAN
plac·o·derm \ˈpla-kə-ˌdərm\ *n* [NL *Placodermi,* ultim. fr. GK *plak-, plax* + *derma* skin — more at DERM-] (ca. 1865) : any of a class (Placodermi) of extinct chiefly Devonian fishes with an armor of bony plates and primitive jaw structures
plac·oid \ˈpla-ˌkȯid\ *adj* [Gk *plak-, plax* flat surface] (1842) : of, relating to, or being a scale of dermal origin with an enamel-tipped spine characteristic of the elasmobranchs
pla·gal \ˈplā-gəl\ *adj* [ML *plagalis,* ultim. fr. Gk *plagios* oblique, sideways, fr. *plagos* side; akin to L *plaga* net, region, Gk *pelagos* sea] (1597) **1** *of a church mode* : having the keynote on the fourth scale step — compare AUTHENTIC 4a **2** *of a cadence* : progressing from the subdominant chord to the tonic — compare AUTHENTIC 4b
plage \ˈpläzh\ *n* [F, beach, luminous surface, fr. It *piaggia* beach, fr. LL *plagia,* fr. Gk *plagios* oblique] (1888) **1** : the beach of a seaside resort **2** : a bright region on the sun caused by the light emitted by clouds of calcium or hydrogen and often associated with a sunspot
pla·gia·rise *Brit var of* PLAGIARIZE
pla·gia·rism \ˈplā-jə-ˌri-zəm *also* -jē-ə-\ *n* (1621) **1** : an act or instance of plagiarizing **2** : something plagiarized — **pla·gia·rist** \-rist\ *n* — **pla·gia·ris·tic** \ˌplā-jə-ˈris-tik *also* -jē-ə-\ *adj*
pla·gia·rize \ˈplā-jə-ˌrīz *also* -jē-ə-\ *vb* **-rized; -riz·ing** [*plagiary*] *vt* (1716) : to steal and pass off (the ideas or words of another) as one's own : use (another's production) without crediting the source ~ *vi* : to commit literary theft : present as new and original an idea or product derived from an existing source — **pla·gia·riz·er** *n*
pla·gia·ry \ˈplā-jē-ˌer-ē, -jə-rē\ *n, pl* **-ries** [Latin *plagiarius,* lit., kidnapper, fr. *plagium* netting of game, kidnapping, fr. *plaga* net, trap] (1601) **1** *archaic* : one that plagiarizes **2** : PLAGIARISM
pla·gio·clase \ˈplā-j(ē-)ə-ˌklās, ˈpla-, -ˌklāz\ *n* [Gk *plagios* oblique + *klasis* breaking, fr. *klan* to break — more at CLAST] (ca. 1868) : a triclinic feldspar; *esp* : one having calcium or sodium in its composition
pla·gio·tro·pic \ˌplā-j(ē-)ə-ˈtrō-pik, ˌpla-, -ˈträ-\ *adj* [Gk *plagios* + ISV *-tropic*] (1898) : having the longer axis inclined away from the vertical
¹plague \ˈplāg\ *n* [ME *plage,* fr. LL *plaga,* fr. L, blow; akin to L *plangere* to strike — more at PLAINT] (14c) **1 a** : a disastrous evil or affliction : CALAMITY **b** : a destructively numerous influx ⟨a ~ of locusts⟩ **2 a** : an epidemic disease causing a high rate of mortality : PESTILENCE **b** : a virulent contagious febrile disease that is caused by a bacterium (*Yersinia pestis*) and that occurs in bubonic, pneumonic, and septicemic forms — called also *black death* **3 a** : a cause of irritation : NUISANCE **b** : a sudden unwelcome outbreak ⟨a ~ of burglaries⟩
²plague *vt* **plagued; plagu·ing** (15c) **1** : to smite, infest, or afflict with or as if with disease, calamity, or natural evil **2 a** : to cause worry or distress to : HAMPER, BURDEN **b** : to disturb or annoy persistently ***syn*** see WORRY — **plagu·er** *n*
plagu·ey *also* **plaguy** \ˈplā-gē, ˈple-\ *adj* (1615) : causing irritation or annoyance : TROUBLESOME — **plaguey** *adv* — **plagu·i·ly** \-gə-lē\ *adv*
plaice \ˈplās\ *n, pl* **plaice** [ME, fr. AF *plais,* fr. LL *platessa*] (14c) : any of various flatfishes; *esp* : a large European flounder (*Pleuronectes platessa*) having red spots and used for food
plaid \ˈplad\ *n* [ScGael *plaide*] (1512) **1** : a rectangular length of tartan worn over the left shoulder as part of the Scottish national costume **2 a** : a twilled woolen fabric with a tartan pattern **b** : a fabric with a pattern of tartan or an imitation of tartan **3 a** : TARTAN 1 **b** : a pattern of unevenly spaced repeated stripes crossing at right angles — **plaid** *adj* — **plaid·ed** \ˈpla-dəd\ *adj*
¹plain \ˈplān\ *vi* [ME, fr. AF *pleindre, plaindre,* fr. L *plangere* to lament — more at PLAINT] (14c) *archaic* : COMPLAIN
²plain *n* [ME, fr. AF, fr. L *planum,* fr. neut. of *planus* flat, plain — more at FLOOR] (14c) **1 a** : an extensive area of level or rolling treeless

country **b :** a broad unbroken expanse **2 :** something free from artifice, ornament, or extraneous matter

[3]**plain** *adj* (14c) **1** *archaic* **:** EVEN, LEVEL **2 :** lacking ornament **:** UNDECORATED **3 :** free of extraneous matter **:** PURE **4 :** free of impediments to view **:** UNOBSTRUCTED **5 a** (1) **:** evident to the mind or senses **:** OBVIOUS ⟨it's perfectly ~ that they will resist⟩ (2) **:** CLEAR ⟨let me make my meaning ~⟩ **b :** marked by outspoken candor **:** free from duplicity or subtlety **:** BLUNT ⟨~ talk⟩ **6 a :** belonging to the masses **:** COMMON **b :** lacking special distinction or affectation **:** ORDINARY **7 :** characterized by simplicity **:** not complicated ⟨~ home-cooked meals⟩ **8 :** lacking beauty or ugliness ***syn*** see COMMON, EVIDENT, FRANK — **plain·ly** *adv* — **plain·ness** \'plān-nəs\ *n*

[4]**plain** *adv* (14c) **:** in a plain manner **:** without obscurity or ambiguity ⟨saw them clearly and told you ~ —*Amer. Documentation*⟩

[5]**plain** *adv* [partly fr. ME *plein* entire, complete, fr. AF, full, fr. L *plenus;* partly fr. [3]*plain* — more at FULL] (1535) **:** ABSOLUTELY 1 ⟨~ wrong⟩

plain·chant \'plān-ˌchant\ *n* [F *plain-chant,* lit., plain song] (ca. 1741) **:** PLAINSONG

plain·clothes \'plān-'klō(th)z\ *adj* (1866) **:** dressed in civilian clothes while on duty — used esp. of a police officer

plain·clothes·man \'plān-'klō(th)z-mən, -ˌman\ *n* (1899) **:** a plainclothes police officer

plain–Jane \'plān-'jān\ *adj* [fr. the name *Jane*] (1936) **:** not fancy or glamorous **:** ORDINARY

plain Jane \-'jān\ *n* (1912) **:** one that is plain

plain–laid \'plān-'lād\ *adj* (1881) *of a rope* **:** consisting of three strands laid right-handed — compare CABLE–LAID

Plain People *n* (1904) **:** members of any of various Protestant groups (as Mennonites) esp. in the U.S. who wear distinctively plain clothes and adhere to a simple and traditional style of life excluding many conveniences of modern technology

Plains \'plānz\ *adj* (1844) **:** of or relating to No. American Indians of the Great Plains or to their culture

plain sailing *n* (1756) **:** easy progress over an unobstructed course

plains·man \'plānz-mən\ *n* [Great *Plains* + *man*] (1870) **:** an inhabitant of the plains

plain·song \'plān-ˌsȯŋ\ *n* (1513) **:** a monophonic rhythmically free liturgical chant of any of various Christian rites; *esp* **:** GREGORIAN CHANT

plain·spo·ken \-'spō-kən\ *adj* (1678) **:** CANDID, FRANK — **plain·spo·ken·ness** \-kən-nəs\ *n*

plaint \'plānt\ *n* [ME, fr. AF, fr. L *planctus,* fr. *plangere* to strike, beat one's breast, lament; akin to OHG *fluokhōn* to curse, Gk *plēssein* to strike] (13c) **1 :** LAMENTATION, WAIL **2 :** PROTEST, COMPLAINT

plain·text \'plān-ˌtekst\ *n* (1918) **:** the intelligible form of an encrypted text or of its elements — compare CIPHERTEXT

plain·tiff \'plān-təf\ *n* [ME *plaintif,* fr. AF, fr. *pleintif,* adj.] (14c) **:** a person who brings a legal action — compare DEFENDANT

plain·tive \'plān-tiv\ *adj* [ME *plaintif* grieving, fr. AF *pleintif, plaintif,* fr. *plaint*] (1579) **:** expressive of suffering or woe **:** MELANCHOLY ⟨a ~ sigh⟩ — **plain·tive·ly** *adv* — **plain·tive·ness** *n*

plain–vanilla *adj* (1959) **:** lacking special features or qualities **:** BASIC

plain weave *n* (1888) **:** a weave in which the threads interlace alternately

plain–woven *adj* (1879) **:** made in plain weave

[1]**plait** \'plāt, 'plat\ *n* [ME *pleit,* fr. AF *pleit, plei, pli,* fr. VL **plicitum,* fr. neut. of L *plicitus,* pp. of *plicare* to fold — more at PLY] (14c) **1 :** PLEAT **2 :** a braid of material (as hair or straw); *specif* **:** PIGTAIL

[2]**plait** *vt* (14c) **1 :** PLEAT 1 **2 a :** to interweave the strands or locks of **:** BRAID **b :** to make by plaiting ⟨~ a basket⟩ — **plait·er** *n*

plait·ing \'plā-tiŋ\ *n* (15c) **:** the interlacing of strands **:** BRAIDING

[1]**plan** \'plan\ *n* [F, plane, foundation, ground plan; partly fr. L *planum* level ground, fr. neut. of *planus* level; partly fr. F *planter* to plant, fix in place, fr. LL *plantare* — more at FLOOR, PLANT] (1706) **1 :** a drawing or diagram drawn on a plane: as **a :** a top or horizontal view of an object **b :** a large-scale map of a small area **2 a :** a method for achieving an end **b :** an often customary method of doing something **:** PROCEDURE **c :** a detailed formulation of a program of action **d :** GOAL, AIM **3 :** an orderly arrangement of parts of an overall design or objective **4 :** a detailed program (as for payment or the provision of some service) ⟨pension ~⟩ — **plan·less** \-ləs\ *adj* — **plan·less·ly** *adv* — **plan·less·ness** *n*

syn PLAN, DESIGN, PLOT, SCHEME, PROJECT mean a method devised for making or doing something or achieving an end. PLAN always implies mental formulation and sometimes graphic representation ⟨*plans* for a house⟩. DESIGN often suggests a particular pattern and some degree of achieved order or harmony ⟨a *design* for a new dress⟩. PLOT implies a laying out in clearly distinguished sections with attention to their relations and proportions ⟨the *plot* of the play⟩. SCHEME stresses calculation of the end in view and may apply to a plan motivated by craftiness and self-interest ⟨a *scheme* to defraud the government⟩. PROJECT often stresses imaginative scope and vision ⟨a *project* to develop the waterfront⟩.

[2]**plan** *vb* **planned; plan·ning** *vt* (1728) **1 :** to arrange the parts of **:** DESIGN ⟨~ a new layout⟩ **2 :** to devise or project the realization or achievement of ⟨*planned* their escape⟩ **3 :** to have in mind **:** INTEND ⟨~*s* to leave soon⟩ ~ *vi* **1 :** to make plans ⟨~ ahead⟩ **2 :** to have a specified intention — used with *on* ⟨~*s* on going⟩ — **plan·ner** *n*

plan- *or* **plano-** *comb form* [L *planus*] **1 :** flat ⟨*plano*graphy⟩ **2 :** flat and ⟨*plano*-concave⟩

pla·nar \'plā-nər, -ˌnär\ *adj* (1850) **1 :** of, relating to, or lying in a plane **2 :** two-dimensional in quality — **pla·nar·i·ty** \plā-'na-rə-tē\ *n*

pla·nar·ia \plə-'ner-ē-ə\ *n, pl* **-ia** *also* **-ias** [NL, fr. fem. of LL *planarius* lying on a plane, fr. L *planum* plane] (1855) **:** any of a genus (*Planaria*) of 2-eyed planarian worms; *broadly* **:** PLANARIAN

pla·nar·i·an \-ē-ən\ *n* [NL *Planaria*] (ca. 1858) **:** TRICLAD; *esp* **:** any of various dark-colored freshwater triclad flatworms (family Planariidae) with two eyespots and a triangular head

pla·na·tion \plā-'nā-shən\ *n* (1877) **:** the condition or process of becoming flattened

plan B *n* (1977) **:** an alternative plan of action for use if the original plan should fail

plan·chet \'plan-chət\ *n* [dim. of *planch* flat plate, fr. MF *planche*] (1611) **1 :** a metal disk to be stamped as a coin **2 :** a small metal or plastic disk

plan·chette \plan-'shet\ *n* [F, fr. OF, dim. of *planche* plank, fr. L *planca*] (1860) **:** a small triangular or heart-shaped board supported on casters at two points and a vertical pencil at a third and believed to produce automatic writing when lightly touched by the fingers; *also* **:** a similar board without a pencil

Planck's constant \'plän(k)s-, 'plaŋ(k)s-\ *n* [Max K. E. L. *Planck*] (1910) **:** a constant that gives the unvarying ratio of the energy of a quantum of radiation to its frequency and that has an approximate value of 6.626×10^{-34} J·s — symbol *h*

[1]**plane** \'plān\ *vb* **planed; plan·ing** [ME, fr. AF *planer,* fr. LL *planare,* fr. L *planus* level — more at FLOOR] *vt* (14c) **1 a :** to make smooth or even **:** LEVEL **b :** to make smooth or even by use of a plane **2 :** to remove by or as if by planing — often used with *away* or *off* ~ *vi* **1 :** to work with a plane **2 :** to do the work of a plane — **plan·er** *n*

[2]**plane** *n* [ME, fr. AF, fr. L *platanus,* fr. Gk *platanos;* prob. akin to Gk *platys* broad — more at PLACE] (14c) **:** any of a genus (*Platanus* of the family Platanaceae, the plane-tree family) of chiefly deciduous trees with large palmately lobed leaves, flowers in globose heads, and usu. scaling bark — called also *buttonwood, plane tree, sycamore*

[3]**plane** *n* [ME, fr. AF, fr. LL *plana,* fr. *planare*] (14c) **:** a tool for smoothing or shaping a wood surface

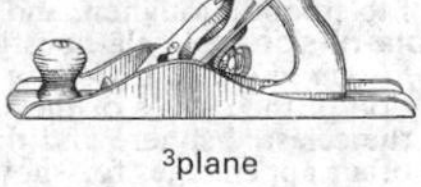

[3]plane

[4]**plane** *n* [L *planum,* fr. neut. of *planus* level] (1571) **1 a :** a surface in which if any two points are chosen a straight line joining them lies wholly in that surface **b :** a flat or level surface **2 :** a level of existence, consciousness, or development ⟨on the intellectual ~⟩ **3 a :** one of the main supporting surfaces of an airplane **b** [by shortening] **:** AIRPLANE

[5]**plane** *adj* [L *planus*] (14c) **1 :** having no elevations or depressions **:** FLAT **2 a :** of, relating to, or dealing with geometric planes **b :** lying in a plane ⟨a ~ curve⟩ ***syn*** see LEVEL

[6]**plane** *vi* **planed; plan·ing** [ME, fr. MF *planer,* fr. *plain* level, plain] (15c) **1 a :** to fly while keeping the wings motionless **b :** to skim across the surface of the water **2 :** to travel by airplane

plane angle *n* (1570) **:** an angle that for a given dihedral angle is formed by two intersecting lines each of which lies on a face of the dihedral angle and is perpendicular to the edge of the face

plane geometry *n* (1747) **:** a branch of elementary geometry that deals with plane figures

plane·load \'plān-ˌlōd\ *n* (1941) **:** a load that fills an airplane

plane of polarization (1831) **:** the plane in which the magnetic-vibration component of plane-polarized electromagnetic radiation lies

plane–polarized *adj* (ca. 1853) **:** vibrating in a single plane ⟨*plane-polarized* light waves⟩

pla·ner tree \'plā-nər-\ *n* [J. J. *Planer* †1789 Ger. botanist] (ca. 1810) **:** a deciduous tree (*Planera aquatica*) of the elm family growing chiefly in wet southeastern U.S. soils and having an oval ribbed nutlike drupe

plan·et \'pla-nət\ *n* [ME *planete,* fr. AF, fr. LL *planeta,* modif. of Gk *planēt-, planēs,* lit., wanderer, fr. *planasthai* to wander — more at FLOOR] (13c) **1 a :** any of the seven celestial bodies sun, moon, Venus, Jupiter, Mars, Mercury, and Saturn that in ancient belief have motions of their own among the fixed stars **b** (1) **:** any of the large bodies that revolve around the sun in the solar system (2) **:** a similar body associated with another star **c :** EARTH — usu. used with *the* **2 :** a celestial body held to influence the fate of human beings **3 :** a person or thing of great importance **:** LUMINARY — **plan·et·like** \-ˌlīk\ *adj*

plane table *n* (1607) **:** an instrument consisting essentially of a drawing board on a tripod with a ruler pointed at the object observed and used for plotting the lines of a survey directly from observation

plan·e·tar·i·um \ˌpla-nə-'ter-ē-əm\ *n, pl* **-i·ums** *or* **-ia** \-ē-ə\ (1734) **1 :** a model or representation of the solar system **2 a :** an optical device for projecting various celestial images and effects **b :** a building or room housing such a projector

plan·e·tary \'pla-nə-ˌter-ē\ *adj* (1607) **1 a :** of, relating to, being, or resembling a planet **b :** ERRATIC, WANDERING **c :** having a motion like that of a planet ⟨~ electrons⟩ **d :** IMMENSE ⟨the scope of this project has reached ~ proportions⟩ **2 a :** of, relating to, or belonging to the

PLANETS

NAME	SYMBOL	MEAN DISTANCE FROM THE SUN astronomical units	million miles	million kilometers	SIDEREAL PERIOD OF REVOLUTION days or years	SIDEREAL PERIOD OF ROTATION hours or days	EQUATORIAL DIAMETER miles	kilometers	MASS relative to Earth
Mercury	☿	0.39	35.99	57.91	87.97 d.	58.65 d.	3,033	4,879	0.06
Venus	♀	0.72	67.25	108.21	224.70 d.	243.02 d.	7,522	12,104	0.82
Earth	⊕	1.00	92.98	149.60	365.26 d.	23.93 h.	7,928	12,756	1.00
Mars	♂	1.52	141.67	227.94	686.99 d.	24.62 h.	4,222	6,794	0.11
Jupiter	♃	5.20	483.78	778.41	11.86 y.	9.92 h.	88,865	142,984	317.82
Saturn	♄	9.54	886.72	1,426.73	29.47 y.	10.66 h.	74,914	120,536	95.16
Uranus	⛢	19.19	1,784.32	2,870.97	84.02 y.	17.24 h.	31,770	51,118	14.54
Neptune	♆	30.07	2,795.68	4,498.25	164.79 y.	16.11 h.	30,782	49,528	17.15

earth : TERRESTRIAL **b :** GLOBAL, WORLDWIDE ⟨~ politics⟩ **3 :** having or consisting of an epicyclic train of gear wheels

planetary nebula *n* (1785) : a usu. compact luminous ring-shaped nebula that is composed of matter which has been ejected from a hot star at its center

planetary science *n* (1969) : PLANETOLOGY — **planetary scientist** *n*

plan·e·tes·i·mal \ˌpla-nə-ˈte-sə-məl, -zə-məl\ *n* [*planet* + *-esimal* (as in *infinitesimal*)] (1903) : any of numerous small celestial bodies that may have existed at an early stage of the development of the solar system

planetesimal hypothesis *n* (1904) : a hypothesis in astronomy: the planets have evolved by aggregation from planetesimals

plan·et·oid \ˈpla-nə-ˌtȯid\ *n* (1803) : a small body resembling a planet; *esp* : ASTEROID — **plan·et·oi·dal** \ˌpla-nə-ˈtȯi-dᵊl\ *adj*

plan·et·ol·o·gy \ˌpla-nə-ˈtä-lə-jē\ *n, pl* **-gies** (1865) : a branch of astronomy that deals with the condensed matter of the solar system and esp. with the planets and their moons — **plan·et·o·log·i·cal** \ˌpla-nə-tə-ˈlä-ji-kəl\ *adj* — **plan·et·ol·o·gist** \ˌpla-nə-ˈtä-lə-jist\ *n*

planet wheel *n* (1799) : a gear wheel that revolves around the wheel with which it meshes in an epicyclic train

plan·et·wide \ˈpla-nət-ˈwīd\ *adj* (1969) : extending throughout or involving an entire planet

plan·form \ˈplan-ˌfȯrm\ *n* (1908) : the contour of an object (as an airplane) or mass as viewed from above

plan·gen·cy \ˈplan-jən(t)-sē\ *n* (1858) : the quality or state of being plangent

plan·gent \-jənt\ *adj* [L *plangent-, plangens,* prp. of *plangere* to strike, lament — more at PLAINT] (1666) **1 :** having a loud reverberating sound ⟨a ~ roar⟩ **2 :** having an expressive and esp. plaintive quality ⟨~ lyrics⟩ — **plan·gent·ly** *adv*

pla·nim·e·ter \plā-ˈni-mə-tər, plə-\ *n* [F *planimètre,* fr. L *planum* plane + F *-mètre* -meter] (ca. 1858) : an instrument for measuring the area of a plane figure by tracing its boundary line

pla·ni·met·ric \ˌplā-nə-ˈme-trik\ *adj* (ca. 1828) **1 :** of, relating to, or made by means of a planimeter ⟨~ measurements⟩ **2** *of a map* **:** having no indications of relief — **pla·ni·met·ri·cal·ly** \-tri-k(ə-)lē\ *adv*

planing *adj* (1919) : having or being a hull designed to lift partially from the water's surface at high speeds ⟨~ boats⟩

plan·ish \ˈpla-nish\ *vt* [ME *planysshen,* fr. AF *planiss-,* stem of *planir* to make smooth, fr. *plain, plan* level, fr. L *planus* — more at FLOOR] (14c) : to smooth, toughen, and finish (metal) by hammering lightly

pla·ni·sphere \ˈplā-nə-ˌsfir\ *n* [alter. of ME *planisperie,* fr. ML *planisphaerium,* fr. L *planum* plane + *sphaera* sphere] (14c) : a representation of the circles of the sphere on a plane; *esp* : a polar projection of the celestial sphere and the stars on a plane with adjustable circles or other appendages for showing celestial phenomena for any given time — **pla·ni·spher·ic** \ˌplā-nə-ˈsfir-ik, -ˈsfer-\ *adj*

[1]**plank** \ˈplaŋk\ *n* [ME, fr. AF *plaunke, planche,* fr. L *planca*] (13c) **1 a :** a heavy thick board; *esp* : one 2 to 4 inches (5 to 10 centimeters) thick and at least 8 inches (20 centimeters) wide **b :** an object made of a plank or planking **c :** PLANKING **2 a :** an article in the platform of a political party **b :** a principal item of a policy or program

[2]**plank** *vt* (15c) **1 :** to cover, build, or floor with planks **2 :** to set down forcefully — usu. used with *down* **3 :** to cook and serve on a board

plank·ing \ˈplaŋ-kiŋ\ *n* (15c) **1 :** the act or process of covering or fitting with planks **2 :** a quantity of planks

plank·ter \ˈplaŋ(k)-tər\ *n* [Gk *planktēr* wanderer, fr. *plazesthai*] (1935) : a planktonic organism

plank·ton \ˈplaŋ(k)-tən, -ˌtän\ *n* [G, fr. Gk, neut. of *planktos* drifting, fr. *plazesthai* to wander, drift, middle voice of *plazein* to drive astray; akin to L *plangere* to strike — more at PLAINT] (1889) : the passively floating or weakly swimming usu. minute animal and plant life of a body of water — **plank·ton·ic** \plaŋ(k)-ˈtä-nik\ *adj*

planning *n* (1730) : the act or process of making or carrying out plans; *specif* : the establishment of goals, policies, and procedures for a social or economic unit ⟨city ~⟩ ⟨business ~⟩

plano- — see PLAN-

pla·no–con·cave \ˌplā-nō-(ˌ)kän-ˈkāv, -ˈkän-ˌ\ *adj* (1693) : flat on one side and concave on the other

pla·no–con·vex \-(ˌ)kän-ˈveks, -ˈkän-ˌ, -kən-ˈ\ *adj* (1665) : flat on one side and convex on the other

plan·o·gram \ˈpla-nə-ˌgram\ *n* [*plan-* (taken as combining form of [1]*plan*) + *-gram*] (1986) : a schematic drawing or plan for displaying merchandise in a store so as to maximize sales

pla·nog·ra·phy \plā-ˈnä-grə-fē, plə-\ *n* (ca. 1909) : a process (as lithography) for printing from a plane surface — **pla·no·graph·ic** \ˌplā-nə-ˈgra-fik\ *adj*

plan position indicator *n* (1932) : a radarscope having a sweep synchronized with a usu. rotating antenna so that the radar return can be used to find range and bearing

[1]**plant** \ˈplant\ *vb* [ME, fr. OE *plantian,* fr. LL *plantare* to plant, fix in place, fr. L, to plant, fr. *planta* plant] *vt* (bef. 12c) **1 a :** to put or set in the ground for growth ⟨~ seeds⟩ **b :** to set or sow with seeds or plants **c :** IMPLANT **2 a :** ESTABLISH, INSTITUTE **b :** COLONIZE, SETTLE **c :** to place (animals) in a new locality **d :** to stock with animals **3 a :** to place in or on the ground **b :** to place firmly or forcibly ⟨~*ed* a hard blow on his chin⟩ **4 a :** CONCEAL **b :** to covertly place for discovery, publication, or dissemination ~ *vi* : to plant something — **plant·able** \ˈplan-tə-bəl\ *adj*

[2]**plant** *n* [ME *plante,* fr. OE, fr. L *planta*] (bef. 12c) **1 a :** a young tree, vine, shrub, or herb planted or suitable for planting **b :** any of a kingdom (Plantae) of multicellular eukaryotic mostly photosynthetic organisms typically lacking locomotive movement or obvious nervous or sensory organs and possessing cellulose cell walls **2 a :** the land, buildings, machinery, apparatus, and fixtures employed in carrying on a trade or an industrial business **b :** a factory or workshop for the manufacture of a particular product; *also* : POWER PLANT **c :** the total facilities available for production or service **d :** the buildings and other physical equipment of an institution **3 :** an act of planting **4 :** something or someone planted — **plant·like** \-ˌlīk\ *adj*

Plan·tag·e·net \plan-ˈta-jə-nət, -ˈtaj-nət\ *adj* [*Plantagenet,* nickname of the family adopted as surname] (ca. 1562) : of or relating to a royal house ruling England from 1154 to 1485 ⟨the ~ kings⟩ — **Plantagenet** *n*

[1]**plan·tain** \ˈplan-tᵊn\ *n* [ME, fr. AF, fr. L *plantagin-, plantago,* fr. *planta* sole of the foot; fr. its broad leaves — more at PLACE] (13c) : any of a genus (*Plantago* of the family Plantaginaceae, the plantain family) of herbs with basal rosettes of usu. lanceolate or elliptical leaves and spikes of minute greenish flowers

[2]**plantain** *n* [Sp *plántano, plátano* plane tree, banana tree, fr. ML *plantanus* plane tree, alter. of L *platanus* — more at PLANE] (1582) **1 :** the angular greenish starchy fruit of the plantain that is a staple food in the tropics when cooked **2 :** a banana plant (*Musa paradisiaca*)

plantain lily *n* (1882) : HOSTA

plan·tar \ˈplan-tər, -ˌtär\ *adj* [L *plantaris,* fr. *planta* sole — more at PLACE] (ca. 1706) : of or relating to the sole of the foot ⟨~ wart⟩

plantar fasciitis *n* (1940) : inflammation of the dense fibrous band of tissue of the sole of the foot that is marked esp. by heel or arch pain

plan·ta·tion \plan-ˈtā-shən\ *n* (15c) **1 :** a usu. large group of plants and esp. trees under cultivation **2 :** a settlement in a new country or region ⟨Plymouth *Plantation*⟩ **3 a :** a place that is planted or under cultivation **b :** an agricultural estate usu. worked by resident labor

plant·er \ˈplan-tər\ *n* (14c) **1 :** one that cultivates plants: as **a** (1) **:** FARMER (2) **:** one who owns or operates a plantation **b :** a planting machine or implement **2 :** one who settles or founds a place and esp. a new colony **3 :** a container in which ornamental plants are grown

planter's punch *n* (1878) : a punch of rum, lime or lemon juice, sugar, water, and sometimes bitters

plant food *n* (1853) **1 :** FOOD 1b **2 :** FERTILIZER

plant hormone *n* (1932) : an organic substance other than a nutrient that in minute amounts modifies a plant physiological process; *esp* : one produced by a plant and active elsewhere than at the site of production

plan·ti·grade \ˈplan-tə-ˌgrād\ *adj* [F, fr. L *planta* sole + F *-grade*] (1827) : walking on the sole with the heel touching the ground ⟨humans are ~⟩ — **plantigrade** *n*

plant·ing \ˈplan-tiŋ\ *n* (1535) : an area where plants are grown for commercial or decorative purposes; *also* : the plants grown in such an area

plant kingdom *n* (1858) : a basic group of natural objects that includes all living and extinct plants — compare ANIMAL KINGDOM, MINERAL KINGDOM

plant·let \ˈplant-lət\ *n* (ca. 1711) : a small or young plant

plant louse *n* (1763) : APHID; *also* : any of various small insects (as a jumping plant louse) of similar habits

plan·to·cra·cy \plan-ˈtä-krə-sē\ *n* [*plant*er + *-o-* + *-cracy*] (1840) **1 :** a ruling class made up of planters **2 :** government by planters

plan·u·la \ˈplan-yə-lə\ *n, pl* **-lae** \-ˌlē, -ˌlī\ [NL, fr. L *planus* level, flat — more at FLOOR] (1835) : the very young usu. flattened oval or oblong free-swimming ciliated larva of a coelenterate

plaque \ˈplak\ *n* [F, fr. MF, metal sheet, fr. *plaquer* to plate, fr. MD *placken* to piece, patch; akin to MD *placke* piece, MHG *placke* patch] (1845) **1 a :** an ornamental brooch; *esp* : the badge of an honorary order **b :** a flat thin piece (as of metal) used for decoration **c :** a commemorative or identifying inscribed tablet **2 a :** a localized abnormal patch on a body part or surface **b :** a sticky usu. colorless film on teeth that is formed by and harbors bacteria **c :** an atherosclerotic lesion **d :** a histopathologic lesion of brain tissue that is characteristic of Alzheimer's disease and consists of a dense proteinaceous core composed primarily of beta-amyloid that is often surrounded and infiltrated by a cluster of degenerating axons and dendrites **3 :** a clear area in a bacterial culture produced by viral destruction of cells

[1]**plash** \ˈplash\ *n* [prob. imit.] (ca. 1522) : SPLASH

[2]**plash** *vi* (1542) : to cause a splashing or spattering effect ~ *vt* : to break the surface of (water) : SPLASH

-plasia *or* **-plasy** *n comb form* [NL *-plasia,* fr. Gk *plasis* molding, fr. *plassein*] : development : formation ⟨hyper*plasia*⟩ ⟨homo*plasy*⟩

plasm \ˈpla-zəm\ *n* [LL *plasma* something molded] (1747) : PLASMA — compare GERMPLASM

plasm- *or* **plasmo-** *comb form* [F, fr. NL *plasma*] : plasma ⟨*plasm*odium⟩ ⟨*plasmo*lysis⟩

-plasm *n comb form* [G *-plasma,* fr. NL *plasma*] : formative or formed material (as of a cell or tissue) ⟨endo*plasm*⟩

plas·ma \ˈplaz-mə\ *n* [G, fr. LL, something molded, fr. Gk, fr. *plassein* to mold — more at PLASTER] (1517) **1 :** a green faintly translucent quartz **2** [NL, fr. LL] **a :** the fluid part of blood, lymph, or milk as distinguished from suspended material; *esp* : BLOOD PLASMA **b :** the juice that can be expressed from muscle **3 :** PROTOPLASM **4 :** a collection of charged particles (as in the atmospheres of stars or in a metal) containing about equal numbers of positive ions and electrons and exhibiting some properties of a gas but differing from a gas in being a good conductor of electricity and in being affected by a magnetic field **5 :** a display (as a television screen) consisting of discrete cells of plasma sandwiched between two layers of glass and electrodes such that each cell emits light when it receives an electric current — **plas·mat·ic** \plaz-ˈma-tik\ *adj*

plasma cell *n* (1895) : a lymphocyte that is a mature antibody-secreting B cell

plas·ma·gel \ˈplaz-mə-ˌjel\ *n* (ca. 1923) : gelated cytoplasm; *esp* : the outer firm zone of a pseudopodium

plas·ma·gene \-ˌjēn\ *n* [ISV] (1939) : a self-replicating extranuclear determiner of hereditary characteristics

plasma jet *n* (1957) : a stream of very hot ionized plasma; *also* : a device for producing such a stream

plas·ma·lem·ma \ˌplaz-mə-ˈle-mə\ *n* [NL, fr. *plasma* + Gk *lemma* husk — more at LEMMA] (ca. 1923) : PLASMA MEMBRANE

plasma membrane *n* (1893) : a semipermeable limiting layer of cell protoplasm — called also *cell membrane*; see CELL illustration

plas·ma·phe·re·sis \ˌplaz-mə-fə-ˈrē-səs, -ˈfer-ə-səs\ *n* [NL, fr. *plasm-* + Gk *aphairesis* taking off — more at APHAERESIS] (1914) : a process for removing blood plasma without depleting the donor or patient of other blood constituents (as red blood cells) by separating out the plasma from the whole blood and returning the rest to the donor's or patient's circulatory system

plas·ma·sol \ˈplaz-mə-ˌsäl, -ˌsȯl, -ˌsōl\ *n* (ca. 1923) : cytoplasm in the form of a sol esp. in a pseudopodium or amoeboid cell

plasma torch *n* (1959) : a device that heats a gas by electrical means to form a plasma for high-temperature operations (as melting metal)

plas·mid \ˈplaz-məd\ *n* [*plasma* + ^{2}*-id*] (1952) **:** an extrachromosomal ring of DNA esp. of bacteria that replicates autonomously

plas·min \-mən\ *n* (ca. 1866) **:** a proteolytic enzyme that dissolves the fibrin of blood clots

plas·min·o·gen \plaz-ˈmi-nə-jən\ *n* (1945) **:** the precursor of plasmin that is found in blood plasma and serum

plas·mo·des·ma \ˌplaz-mə-ˈdez-mə\ *also* **plas·mo·desm** \ˈplaz-mə-ˌde-zəm\ *n, pl* **-des·ma·ta** \-ˈdez-mə-tə\ *or* **-des·mas** \-ˈdez-məz\ [NL *plasmodesma,* fr. *plasma* + Gk *desmat-, desma* bond, fr. *dein* to bind — more at DIADEM] (1905) **:** one of the cytoplasmic strands passing through openings in some plant cell walls and forming connections with adjacent cells

plas·mo·di·um \plaz-ˈmō-dē-əm\ *n, pl* **-dia** \-dē-ə\ [NL, fr. *plasm-* + *-odium* thing resembling, fr. Gk *-ōdēs* like] (1875) **1 a :** a motile multinucleate mass of protoplasm resulting from fusion of uninucleate amoeboid cells; *also* **:** an organism (as a stage of a slime mold) that consists of such a structure **b :** SYNCYTIUM 1 **2 :** a sporozoan parasite (genus *Plasmodium*) that is the causative agent of malaria

plas·mog·a·my \plaz-ˈmä-gə-mē\ *n* [ISV] (1912) **:** fusion of the cytoplasm of two or more cells as distinguished from fusion of nuclei

plas·mol·y·sis \plaz-ˈmä-lə-səs\ *n* [NL] (1883) **:** shrinking of the cytoplasm away from the wall of a living cell due to outward osmotic flow of water — **plas·mo·lyt·ic** \ˌplaz-mə-ˈli-tik\ *adj*

plas·mo·lyze \ˈplaz-mə-ˌlīz\ *vb* **-lyzed; -lyz·ing** *vt* (1888) **:** to subject to plasmolysis ~ *vi* **:** to undergo plasmolysis

-plast *n comb form* [F *-plaste* thing molded, fr. LL *-plastus,* fr. Gk *-plastos,* fr. *plastos* molded, fr. *plassein*] **:** organized particle or granule **:** cell ⟨chromo*plast*⟩

^{1}**plas·ter** \ˈplas-tər\ *n* [ME, fr. OE, fr. L *emplastrum,* fr. Gk *emplastron,* fr. *emplassein* to plaster on, fr. *en-* + *plassein* to mold, plaster; perh. akin to L *planus* level, flat — more at FLOOR] (bef. 12c) **1 :** a medicated or protective dressing that consists of a film (as of cloth or plastic) spread with a usu. medicated substance ⟨adhesive ~⟩; *broadly* **:** something applied to heal and soothe **2 :** a pasty composition (as of lime, water, and sand) that hardens on drying and is used for coating walls, ceilings, and partitions — **plas·tery** \-t(ə-)rē\ *adj*

^{2}**plaster** *vb* **plas·tered; plas·ter·ing** \-t(ə-)riŋ\ *vt* (14c) **1 :** to overlay or cover with plaster **:** COAT **2 :** to apply a plaster to **3 a :** to cover over or conceal as if with a coat of plaster **b :** to apply as a coating or incrustation **c :** to smooth down with a sticky or shiny substance ⟨~*ed* his hair down⟩ **4 :** to fasten or apply tightly to another surface **5 :** to treat with plaster of paris **6 :** to affix to or place on esp. conspicuously or in quantity **7 :** to inflict heavy damage or loss on esp. by a concentrated or unremitting attack ~ *vi* **:** to apply plaster — **plas·ter·er** \-tər-ər\ *n*

plas·ter·board \ˈplas-tər-ˌbȯrd\ *n* (1897) **:** DRYWALL

plaster cast *n* (1825) **1 :** a sculptor's model in plaster of paris **2 :** a rigid dressing of gauze impregnated with plaster of paris

plastered *adj* (1902) **:** DRUNK, INTOXICATED

plastering *n* (15c) **1 :** a coating of or as if of plaster **2 :** a decisive defeat

plaster of par·is \-ˈpa-rəs\ *often cap 2d P* [*Paris,* France] (15c) **:** a white powdery slightly hydrated calcium sulfate $CaSO_4 \cdot \frac{1}{2}H_2O$ or $2CaSO_4 \cdot H_2O$ made by calcining gypsum and used chiefly for casts and molds in the form of a quick-setting paste with water

plaster saint *n* (1890) **:** a person without human failings

plas·ter·work \ˈplas-tər-ˌwərk\ *n* (1600) **:** plastering often ornate in design used to finish architectural constructions

^{1}**plas·tic** \ˈplas-tik\ *adj* [L *plasticus* of molding, fr. Gk *plastikos,* fr. *plassein* to mold, form] (1632) **1 :** FORMATIVE, CREATIVE ⟨~ forces in nature⟩ **2 a :** capable of being molded or modeled ⟨~ clay⟩ **b :** capable of adapting to varying conditions **:** PLIABLE ⟨ecologically ~ animals⟩ **3 :** SCULPTURAL **4 :** made or consisting of a plastic **5 :** capable of being deformed continuously and permanently in any direction without rupture **6 :** of, relating to, or involving plastic surgery **7 :** having a quality suggestive of mass-produced plastic goods; *esp* **:** ARTIFICIAL 4 ⟨~ smiles⟩ **8 :** relating to, characterized by, or exhibiting neural plasticity

syn PLASTIC, PLIABLE, PLIANT, DUCTILE, MALLEABLE, ADAPTABLE mean susceptible of being modified in form or nature. PLASTIC applies to substances soft enough to be molded yet capable of hardening into the desired fixed form ⟨*plastic* materials allow the sculptor greater freedom⟩. PLIABLE suggests something easily bent, folded, twisted, or manipulated ⟨*pliable* rubber tubing⟩. PLIANT may stress flexibility and sometimes connote springiness ⟨an athletic shoe with a *pliant* sole⟩. DUCTILE applies to what can be drawn out or extended with ease ⟨*ductile* metals such as copper⟩. MALLEABLE applies to what may be pressed or beaten into shape ⟨the *malleable* properties of gold⟩. ADAPTABLE implies the capability of being easily modified to suit other conditions, needs, or uses ⟨computer hardware that is *adaptable*⟩.

^{2}**plastic** *n* (1905) **1 :** a plastic substance; *specif* **:** any of numerous organic synthetic or processed materials that are mostly thermoplastic or thermosetting polymers of high molecular weight and that can be made into objects, films, or filaments **2 :** credit cards used for payment — called also *plastic money* — **plas·ticky** \ˈplas-ti-kē\ *adj*

-plastic *adj comb form* [Gk *-plastikos,* fr. *plassein*] **1 :** developing **:** forming ⟨thrombo*plastic*⟩ **2 :** of or relating to (something designated by a term ending in *-plasm, -plast, -plasty,* or *-plasy*) ⟨homo*plastic*⟩ ⟨neo*plastic*⟩

plas·ti·cal·ly \ˈplas-ti-k(ə-)lē\ *adv* (1835) **1 :** in a plastic manner **2 :** with respect to plastic qualities

plastic art *n* (1804) **1 :** art (as sculpture or bas-relief) characterized by modeling **:** three-dimensional art **2 :** visual art (as painting, sculpture, or film) esp. as distinguished from art that is written (as poetry or music) — often used in pl.

plastic foam *n* (1943) **:** EXPANDED PLASTIC

Plas·ti·cine \ˈplas-tə-ˌsēn\ *trademark* — used for a plastic modeling paste

plas·tic·i·ty \pla-ˈsti-sə-tē\ *n* (ca. 1783) **1 :** the quality or state of being plastic; *esp* **:** capacity for being molded or altered **2 :** the ability to retain a shape attained by pressure deformation **3 :** the capacity of organisms with the same genotype to vary in developmental pattern, in phenotype, or in behavior according to varying environmental conditions **4 :** the capacity for continuous alteration of the neural pathways and synapses of the living brain and nervous system in response to experience or injury

plas·ti·cize \ˈplas-tə-ˌsīz\ *vt* **-cized; -ciz·ing** (1919) **1 :** to make plastic **2 :** to treat with a plastic ⟨a *plasticized* mattress cover⟩ — **plas·ti·ci·za·tion** \ˌplas-tə-sə-ˈzā-shən\ *n*

plas·ti·ciz·er \ˈplas-tə-ˌsī-zər\ *n* (1925) **:** one that plasticizes; *specif* **:** a chemical added esp. to rubbers and resins to impart flexibility, workability, or stretchability

plastic money *n* (1974) **:** PLASTIC 2

plastic surgeon *n* (1946) **:** a specialist in plastic surgery

plastic surgery *n* (1842) **:** surgery done to repair, restore, or improve lost, injured, defective, or misshapen body parts

plas·tic·ware \ˈplas-tik-ˌwer\ *n* (1964) **:** articles made of plastic

plas·tid \ˈplas-təd\ *n* [G, fr. Gk *plastos* molded] (1885) **:** any of various cytoplasmic organelles (as an amyloplast or chloroplast) of photosynthetic cells that serve in many cases as centers of special metabolic activities — **plas·tid·i·al** \pla-ˈsti-dē-əl\ *adj*

plas·ti·na·tion \ˌplas-tə-ˈnā-shən\ *n* [ISV *plasti*c + *-ination* (as in *calcination*)] (1981) **:** a technique for the preservation of biological tissue that involves replacing water and fat in tissue with a polymer (as silicone or polyester) to produce a dry durable specimen for anatomical study

plas·ti·sol \ˈplas-tə-ˌsäl, -ˌsȯl\ *n* [*plastic* + ^{4}*sol*] (1946) **:** a substance consisting of a mixture of a resin and a plasticizer that can be molded, cast, or made into a continuous film by application of heat

plas·to·cy·a·nin \ˌplas-tō-ˈsī-ə-nən\ *n* [Gk *plastos* + E *cyan-* + ^{1}*-in*] (1961) **:** a copper-containing protein that acts as an intermediary in photosynthetic electron transport

plas·to·qui·none \ˌplas-(ˌ)tō-kwi-ˈnōn, -ˈkwi-ˌ\ *n* [Gk *plastos* + E *quinone*] (1958) **:** a plant substance that is related to vitamin K and plays a role in photosynthetic phosphorylation

plas·tral \ˈplas-trəl\ *adj* (1888) **:** of or relating to a plastron

plas·tron \ˈplas-trən\ *n* [MF, fr. OIt *piastrone,* aug. of *piastra* thin metal plate — more at PIASTRE] (ca. 1507) **1 a :** a metal breastplate formerly worn under the hauberk **b :** a quilted pad worn in fencing to protect the chest, waist, and the side on which the weapon is held **2 :** the ventral part of the shell of a tortoise or turtle consisting typically of nine symmetrically placed bones overlaid by horny plates **3 a :** a trimming like a bib for a woman's dress **b :** DICKEY 1a **4 :** a thin film of air held by water-repellent hairs of some aquatic insects

-plasty *n comb form* [F *-plastie,* fr. LGk *-plastia* molding, fr. Gk *-plastēs* molder, fr. *plassein*] **:** plastic surgery ⟨osteo*plasty*⟩

-plasy — see -PLASIA

^{1}**plat** \ˈplat\ *vt* **plat·ted; plat·ting** [ME, alter. of *plaiten*] (14c) **:** PLAIT

^{2}**plat** *n* (14c) **:** PLAIT

^{3}**plat** *n* [ME, prob. alter. of *plot*] (15c) **1 :** a small piece of ground (as a lot or quadrat) **:** PLOT **2 :** a plan, map, or chart of a piece of land with actual or proposed features (as lots); *also* **:** the land represented

^{4}**plat** *vt* **plat·ted; plat·ting** (1751) **:** to make a plat of

^{5}**plat** *abbr* **1** plateau **2** platoon

plat·an \ˈpla-tᵊn\ *n* [ME, fr. L *platanus* — more at PLANE] (14c) **:** ^{2}PLANE

plat du jour \ˌplä-də-ˈzhu̇r, ˌpla-\ *n, pl* **plats du jour** *same*\ [F, lit., plate of the day] (1906) **:** a dish that is featured by a restaurant on a particular day

^{1}**plate** \ˈplāt\ *n* [ME, fr. AF, fr. *plate,* fem. of *plat* flat, fr. VL **plattus,* prob. fr. Gk *platys* broad, flat — more at PLACE] (14c) **1 a :** a smooth flat thin piece of material **b** (1) **:** forged, rolled, or cast metal in sheets usu. thicker than ¼ inch (6 millimeters) (2) **:** a very thin layer of metal deposited on a surface of base metal by plating **c :** one of the broad metal pieces used in armor; *also* **:** armor of such plates **d** (1) **:** a thin relatively flat anatomical part (as a lamina of bone) of an animal body; *esp* **:** SCUTE (2) **:** the thin under portion of the forequarter of beef; *esp* **:** the fatty back part — see BEEF illustration **e :** HOME PLATE **f :** any of the large movable segments into which the earth's lithosphere is divided according to the theory of plate tectonics **2** [ME; partly fr. AF *plate* plate, bullion; partly fr. OSp *plata* silver, fr. VL **platta* metal plate, fr. fem. of *plattus* flat] **a** *obs* **:** a silver coin **b :** precious metal; *esp* **:** silver bullion **3** [ME, fr. AF *plat, plate* dish, plate, fr. *plat* flat] **a :** domestic hollowware made of or plated with gold, silver, or base metals **b :** a shallow usu. circular vessel from which food is eaten or served **c** (1) **:** a quantity to fill a plate **:** PLATEFUL (2) **:** a main course served on a plate (3) **:** food and service supplied to one person ⟨a dinner at $10 a ~⟩ **d** (1) **:** a prize given to the winner in a contest (2) *Brit* **:** a horse race in which the contestants compete for a prize of fixed value rather than stakes **e :** a dish or pouch passed during collections **f :** a flat glass or plastic dish used chiefly for culturing microorganisms **4 a :** a prepared surface from which printing is done **b :** a sheet of material (as glass or plastic) coated with a light-sensitive photographic emulsion **c :** a metallic grid with its interstices filled with active material that forms one of the structural units of a battery **d :** LICENSE PLATE **5 :** a horizontal structural member that provides bearing and anchorage esp. for the trusses of a roof or the rafters **6 :** the part of a denture that fits to the mouth; *broadly* **:** DENTURE **7 :** a full-page illustration often on different paper from the text pages **8 :** a schedule of matters to deal with ⟨have a lot on my ~ now⟩ — **plate·like** \-ˌlīk\ *adj* — **on a plate :** without having been earned **:** as a gift ⟨goals were handed to them *on a plate*⟩

^{2}**plate** *vt* **plat·ed; plat·ing** (14c) **1 :** to cover or equip with plate: as **a :** to provide with armor plate **b :** to cover with an adherent layer mechanically, chemically, or electrically; *also* **:** to deposit (as a layer) on a surface **2 :** to make a printing surface from or for **3 :** to fix or secure with a plate **4 :** to cause (as a runner) to score in baseball **5 :** to arrange (food) on a plate

^{1}**pla·teau** \pla-ˈtō, ˈpla-ˌ\ *n, pl* **plateaus** *or* **pla·teaux** \-ˈtōz, -ˌtōz\ [F, fr. MF, platter, fr. *plat* flat] (1796) **1 a :** a usu. extensive land area having a relatively level surface raised sharply above adjacent land on at least one side : TABLELAND **b** : a similar undersea feature **2 a** : a region of little or no change in a graphic representation **b** : a relatively stable level, period, or condition **3** : a level of attainment or achievement ⟨the 500-point ~⟩

[2]**plateau** *vi* (1939) : to reach a level, period, or condition of stability or maximum attainment

plate·ful \ˈplāt-ˌfu̇l\ *n* (1766) **1** : a quantity to fill a plate; *also* : a generous helping **2** : a large number or amount ⟨a ~ of problems⟩

plate·glass \ˈplāt-ˈglas, -ˌglas\ *adj, often cap* (1968) : of, relating to, or being the British universities founded in the latter half of the 20th century — compare OXBRIDGE, REDBRICK 2

plate glass *n* (ca. 1741) : rolled, ground, and polished sheet glass

plate·let \ˈplāt-lət\ *n* (1895) : a minute flattened body (as of ice or a mineral); *esp* : a minute colorless disklike body of mammalian blood that assists in blood clotting by adhering to other platelets and to damaged epithelium — called also *blood platelet, thrombocyte*

plate·mak·er \ˈplāt-ˌmā-kər\ *n* (1904) : a machine for making printing plates and esp. offset printing plates — **plate·mak·ing** \-kiŋ\ *n*

plat·en \ˈpla-tᵊn\ *n* [ME *plateine* thin metal plate, fr. AF, fr. *plate*] (1541) **1** : a flat plate; *esp* : one that exerts or receives pressure (as in a printing press) **2** : the roller of a typewriter or printer

plat·er \ˈplā-tər\ *n* (1777) **1** : one that plates **2 a** : a horse that runs chiefly in plate races **b** : a racehorse that competes in the lowest grade of races

plate rail *n* (1850) : a rail or narrow shelf along the upper part of a wall for holding plates or ornaments

plat·er·esque \ˌpla-tə-ˈresk\ *adj, often cap* [Sp *plateresco,* fr. *platero* silversmith, fr. *plata* silver] (ca. 1864) : of, relating to, or being a 16th century Spanish architectural style characterized by elaborate ornamentation suggestive of silver plate

plate tectonics *n pl but sing in constr* (1969) **1** : a theory in geology: the lithosphere of the earth is divided into a small number of plates which float on and travel independently over the mantle and much of the earth's seismic activity occurs at the boundaries of these plates **2** : the process and dynamics of tectonic plate movement; *also* : a similar process on a body other than earth — compare CONTINENTAL DRIFT — **plate–tectonic** *adj*

plat·form \ˈplat-ˌfȯrm\ *n, often attrib* [MF *plate-forme* diagram, map, lit., flat form] (1535) **1** : PLAN, DESIGN **2** : a declaration of the principles on which a group of persons stands; *esp* : a declaration of principles and policies adopted by a political party or a candidate **3 a (1)** : a usu. raised horizontal flat surface; *esp* : a raised flooring **(2)** : a device or structure incorporating or providing a platform; *esp* : such a structure on legs used for offshore drilling (as for oil) **b** : a place or opportunity for public discussion **4 a** : a usu. thick layer (as of cork) between the inner sole and outer sole of a shoe **b** : a shoe having such a sole **5 a** : a vehicle (as a satellite or aircraft) used for a particular purpose or to carry a usu. specified kind of equipment **b** : OPERATING SYSTEM; *also* : the computer architecture and equipment using a particular operating system

platform balance *n* (1811) : a balance having a platform on which objects are weighed — called also *platform scale*

platform rocker *n* (1944) : a chair that rocks on a stable platform

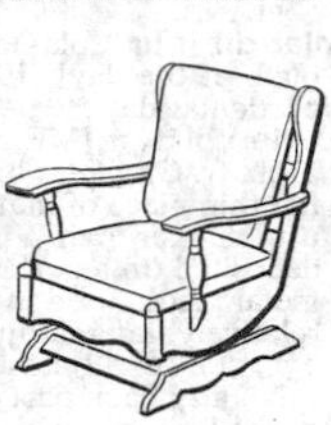

platform rocker

platform tennis *n* (1955) : a variation of paddle tennis that is played on a platform enclosed by a wire fence

pla·ti·na \plə-ˈtē-nə\ *n* [Sp] (1750) : PLATINUM

plating *n* (1765) **1** : the act or process of plating **2 a** : a coating of metal plates **b** : a thin coating of metal

plat·i·nize \ˈpla-tə-ˌnīz\ *vt* **-nized; -niz·ing** (1825) : to cover, treat, or combine with platinum or a compound of platinum

plat·i·no·cy·a·nide \ˌpla-tə-nō-ˈsī-ə-ˌnīd\ *n* (1845) : a fluorescent complex salt formed by the union of a compound of platinum and cyanide with another cyanide

[1]**plat·i·num** \ˈplat-nəm, ˈpla-tə-nəm\ *n, often attrib* [NL, fr. Sp *platina,* fr. dim. of *plata* silver — more at PLATE] (1808) **1** : a precious grayish-white noncorroding ductile malleable heavy metallic element that fuses with difficulty and is used esp. in chemical ware and apparatus, as a catalyst, and in dental and jewelry alloys — see ELEMENT table **2** : a moderate gray

[2]**platinum** *adj* (1971) : qualifying for a platinum record — **go platinum** : to have enough sales to qualify for a platinum record

platinum blonde *n* (1931) **1** : a person whose hair is of a pale silvery-blonde color **2** : the color of the hair of a platinum blonde

platinum record *n* (1978) : a platinum phonograph record awarded to a singer or group whose album has sold at least one million copies — compare GOLD RECORD

plat·i·tude \ˈpla-tə-ˌtüd, -ˌtyüd\ *n* [F, fr. *plat* flat, dull] (1812) **1** : the quality or state of being dull or insipid **2** : a banal, trite, or stale remark

plat·i·tu·di·nal \ˌpla-tə-ˈtüd-nəl, -ˈtyüd-; -ˈtü-də-nəl, -ˈtyü-\ *adj* (1870) : PLATITUDINOUS

plat·i·tu·di·nar·i·an \-ˌtü-də-ˈner-ē-ən, -ˌtyü-\ *n* (1855) : one given to the use of platitudes

plat·i·tu·di·nize \-ˈtü-də-ˌnīz, -ˈtyü-\ *vi* **-nized; -niz·ing** [*platitudinous*] (1868) : to utter platitudes

plat·i·tu·di·nous \-ˈtüd-nəs, -ˈtyüd-; -ˈtü-də-nəs, -ˈtyü-\ *adj* [*platitude* + *-inous* (as in *multitudinous*)] (1853) : having the characteristics of a platitude : full of platitudes ⟨~ remarks⟩ — **plat·i·tu·di·nous·ly** *adv*

pla·ton·ic \plə-ˈtä-nik, plā-\ *adj* [L *platonicus,* fr. Gk *platōnikos,* fr. *Platōn* Plato] (1533) **1** *cap* : of, relating to, or characteristic of Plato or Platonism **2 a** : relating to or based on platonic love; *also* : experiencing or professing platonic love **b** : of, relating to, or being a relationship marked by the absence of romance or sex **3** : NOMINAL, THEORETICAL — **pla·ton·i·cal·ly** \-ni-k(ə-)lē\ *adv*

platonic love *n, often cap P* (1631) **1** : love conceived by Plato as ascending from passion for the individual to contemplation of the universal and ideal **2** : a close relationship between two persons in which sexual desire is nonexistent or has been suppressed or sublimated

Pla·to·nism \ˈplā-tə-ˌni-zəm\ *n* (ca. 1570) **1 a** : the philosophy of Plato stressing esp. that actual things are copies of transcendent ideas and that these ideas are the objects of true knowledge apprehended by reminiscence **b** : NEOPLATONISM **2** : PLATONIC LOVE — **Pla·to·nist** \-tə-nist\ *n* — **Pla·to·nis·tic** \ˌplā-tə-ˈnis-tik\ *adj*

Pla·to·nize \ˈplā-tə-ˌnīz\ *vb* **-nized; -niz·ing** *vi* (1608) : to adopt, imitate, or conform to Platonic opinions ~ *vt* : to explain in accordance with or adapt to Platonic doctrines; *esp* : IDEALIZE

[1]**pla·toon** \plə-ˈtün, pla-\ *n* [F *peloton* small detachment, lit., ball, fr. MF *pelote* little ball — more at PELLET] (1637) **1** : a subdivision of a company-sized military unit normally consisting of two or more squads or sections **2** : a group of persons sharing a common characteristic or activity ⟨a ~ of waiters⟩; *esp* : a group of football players who are trained for either offense or defense and are sent into or withdrawn from the game as a body

[2]**platoon** *vt* (1963) : to play (one player) alternately with another player in the same position (as on a baseball team) ~ *vi* **1** : to alternate with another player at the same position **2** : to use alternate players at the same position

platoon sergeant *n* (1915) : a noncommissioned officer in the army ranking above a staff sergeant and below a first sergeant

Platt·deutsch \ˈplat-ˌdȯich, ˈplät-\ *n* [G, fr. D *Platduitsch,* lit., Low German, fr. *plat* flat, low + *duitsch* German] (1677) : the Low German speech of northern Germany comprising several dialects

plat·ter \ˈpla-tər\ *n* [ME *plater,* fr. AF, fr. *plat* plate] (13c) **1 a** : a large plate used esp. for serving meat **b** : PLATE 3c(2) **2** : a phonograph record — **plat·ter·ful** \-ˌfu̇l\ *n* — **on a platter** : without effort : very easily ⟨can have the presidency *on a platter* —Jonathan Daniels⟩

[1]**platy** \ˈplā-tē\ *adj* (1533) : resembling a plate; *also* : consisting of plates or flaky layers — used chiefly of soil or mineral formations

[2]**platy** \ˈpla-tē\ *n, pl* **platy** *or* **plat·ys** *or* **plat·ies** [NL *Platypoecilus,* former genus name of the fish] (1931) : either of two tropical American freshwater live-bearers (*Xiphophorus maculatus* and *X. variatus*) that have a highly variable often brilliant color and are popular aquarium fishes — called also *platy·fish* \-ˌfish\

platy·hel·minth \ˌpla-ti-ˈhel-ˌmin(t)th\ *n* [ultim. fr. Gk *platys* broad, flat + *helminth-, helmis* helminth] (ca. 1890) : FLATWORM — **platy·hel·min·thic** \-hel-ˈmin(t)-thik, -ˈmin-tik\ *adj*

platy·pus \ˈpla-ti-pəs, -ˌpu̇s\ *n, pl* **platy·pus·es** *also* **platy·pi** \-ˌpī, -ˌpē\ [NL, fr. Gk *platypous* flat-footed, fr. *platys* broad, flat + *pous* foot — more at PLACE, FOOT] (1799) : a small carnivorous aquatic monotreme mammal (*Ornithorhynchus anatinus*) of eastern Australia and Tasmania that has a fleshy bill resembling that of a duck, dense fur, webbed feet, and a broad flattened tail — called also *duck-billed platypus*

plat·yr·rhine \ˈpla-ti-ˌrīn\ *adj* (1857) **1** [NL *Platyrrhina,* fr. Gk *platyrrhin-, platyrrhis* broad-nosed, fr. *platys* + *rhin-, rhis* nose] : of, relating to, or being any of a division (Platyrrhina) of arboreal New World monkeys characterized by a broad nasal septum, usu. 36 teeth, and often a prehensile tail — compare CATARRHINE **2** [Gk *platyrrhin-, platyrrhis*] : having a short broad nose — **platyrrhine** *n*

plau·dit \ˈplȯ-dət\ *n* [L *plaudite* applaud, pl. imper. of *plaudere* to applaud] (1606) **1** : an act or round of applause **2** : enthusiastic approval — usu. used in pl. ⟨received the ~*s* of the critics⟩

plau·si·bil·i·ty \ˌplȯ-zə-ˈbi-lə-tē\ *n, pl* **-ties** (1649) **1** : the quality or state of being plausible **2** : something plausible

plau·si·ble \ˈplȯ-zə-bəl\ *adj* [L *plausibilis* worthy of applause, fr. *plausus,* pp. of *plaudere*] (1565) **1** : superficially fair, reasonable, or valuable but often specious ⟨a ~ pretext⟩ **2** : superficially pleasing or persuasive ⟨a swindler . . . , then a quack, then a smooth, ~ gentleman —R. W. Emerson⟩ **3** : appearing worthy of belief ⟨the argument was both powerful and ~⟩ — **plau·si·ble·ness** *n* — **plau·si·bly** \-blē\ *adv*

plau·sive \ˈplȯ-ziv, -siv\ *adj* [L *plausus,* pp.] (1600) **1** : manifesting praise or approval **2** *obs* : PLEASING **3** *archaic* : SPECIOUS

[1]**play** \ˈplā\ *n* [ME, fr. OE *plega;* akin to OE *plegan* to play, MD *pleyen*] (bef. 12c) **1 a** : SWORDPLAY **b** *archaic* : GAME, SPORT **c** : the conduct, course, or action of a game **d** : a particular act or maneuver in a game: as **(1)** : the action during an attempt to advance the ball in football **(2)** : the action in which a player is put out in baseball **e** : the action in which cards are played after bidding in a card game **f** : the moving of a piece in a board game (as chess) **g** : one's turn in a game ⟨it's your ~⟩ **2 a** *obs* : SEXUAL INTERCOURSE **b** : amorous flirtation : DALLIANCE **3 a** : recreational activity; *esp* : the spontaneous activity of children **b** : absence of serious or harmful intent : JEST ⟨said it in ~⟩ **c** : the act or an instance of playing on words or speech sounds **d** : GAMING, GAMBLING **4 a (1)** : an act, way, or manner of proceeding : MANEUVER ⟨that was a ~ to get your fingerprints —Erle Stanley Gardner⟩ **(2)** : DEAL, VENTURE **b (1)** : the state of being active, operative, or relevant ⟨other motives surely come into ~ —M. R. Cohen⟩ ⟨several issues are at ~⟩ **(2)** : brisk, fitful, or light movement ⟨the gem presented a dazzling ~ of colors⟩ **(3)** : free or unimpeded motion (as of a part of a machine); *also* : the length or measure of such motion **(4)** : scope or opportunity for action **(5)** : a function of an electronic device that causes a recording to play **5** : emphasis or publicity esp. in the news media ⟨wished the country received a better ~ in the American press —Hugh MacLennan⟩ **6** : a move or series of moves calculated to arouse friendly feelings — usu. used with *make* ⟨made a big ~ for the girl —Will Herman⟩ **7 a** : the stage representation of an action or story **b** : a dramatic composition : DRAMA ***syn*** see FUN — **in play** : in condition or position to be legitimately played — **out of play** : not in play

[2]**play** *vi* (bef. 12c) **1 a** : to engage in sport or recreation : FROLIC **b** : to have sexual relations; *esp* : to have promiscuous or illicit sexual relations — usu. used in the phrase *play around* **c (1)** : to move aimlessly about : TRIFLE **(2)** : to toy or fiddle around with something ⟨~*ed* with her food⟩ **(3)** : to deal or behave frivolously or mockingly : JEST **(4)** : to deal in a light, speculative, or sportive manner **(5)** : to make use of double meaning or of the similarity of sound of two words for stylistic or humorous effect **2 a** : to take advantage ⟨~*ing* on fears⟩ **b (1)** : FLUTTER, FRISK **(2)** : to move or operate in a lively, irregular, or intermittent manner **c** : to move or function freely within prescribed limits **d** : to produce a stream ⟨hoses ~*ing* on a fire⟩ **3 a (1)** : to perform music ⟨~ on a violin⟩ **(2)** : to sound in performance

⟨the organ is ~*ing*⟩ (3) **:** to emit sounds ⟨the radio is ~*ing*⟩ (4) **:** to reproduce recorded sounds ⟨a record is ~*ing*⟩ **b** (1) **:** to act in a dramatic production (2) **:** SHOW, RUN ⟨what's ~*ing* at the theater⟩ **c :** to be suitable for dramatic performance **d :** to act with special consideration so as to gain favor, approval, or sympathy ⟨might ~ to popular prejudices to serve his political ends —V. L. Parrington⟩ — often used in the phrase *play up to* **e :** to produce a specified impression in performance ⟨a movie that ~*s* like a sitcom⟩ **4 a :** to engage or take part in a game **b :** to perform in a position in a specified manner ⟨the outfielders were ~*ing* deep⟩ **c :** to perform an action during one's turn in a game **d :** GAMBLE **e** (1) **:** to behave or conduct oneself in a specified way ⟨~ safe⟩ (2) **:** to feign a specified state or quality ⟨~ dead⟩ (3) **:** to take part in or assent to some activity **:** COOPERATE ⟨~ along with his scheme⟩ (4) **:** to act so as to prove advantageous to another — usu. used in the phrase *play into the hands of* **5 :** to gain approval **:** GO OVER ⟨her idea did not ~ well⟩ ~ *vt* **1 a** (1) **:** to engage in or occupy oneself with ⟨~ baseball⟩ (2) **:** to engage in (an activity) as a game (3) **:** to deal with, handle, or manage (4) **:** EXPLOIT, MANIPULATE **b :** to pretend to engage in the activities of ⟨~ war⟩ ⟨children ~*ing* house⟩ **c** (1) **:** to amount to by one's efforts ⟨~*ed* an important role in their success⟩ (2) **:** to perform or execute for amusement or to deceive or mock ⟨~ a trick⟩ (3) **:** WREAK ⟨~ havoc⟩ (4) **:** to use or introduce as a political or rhetorical strategy ⟨~ the national security card⟩ **2 a** (1) **:** to put on a performance of (a play) (2) **:** to act in the character or part of (3) **:** to act or perform in ⟨~*ed* leading theaters⟩ **b :** to perform or act the part of ⟨~ the fool⟩ **3 a** (1) **:** to contend against in or as if in a game (2) **:** to use as a contestant in a game ⟨the coach did not ~ him⟩ (3) **:** to perform the duties associated with (a certain position) ⟨~*ed* quarterback⟩ (4) **:** to guard or move into position to defend against (an opponent) in a specified manner **b** (1) **:** to wager in a game **:** STAKE (2) **:** to make wagers on ⟨~ the races⟩ (3) **:** to speculate on or in ⟨~ the stock market⟩ (4) **:** to operate on the basis of ⟨~ a hunch⟩ **c :** to put into action in a game; *esp* **:** to remove (a playing card) from one's hand and place usu. faceup on a table in one's turn either as part of a scoring combination or as one's contribution to a trick **d :** to catch or pick up (a batted ball) **:** FIELD ⟨~*ed* the ball bare-handed⟩ **e :** to direct the course of (as a ball) **:** HIT ⟨~*ed* a wedge shot to the green⟩; *also* **:** to cause (a ball or puck) to rebound ⟨~*ed* the ball off the backboard⟩ **4 a :** to perform (music) on an instrument ⟨~ a waltz⟩ **b :** to perform music on ⟨~ the violin⟩ **c :** to perform music of (a certain composer) **d** (1) **:** to cause (as a radio or phonograph) to emit sounds (2) **:** to cause the recorded sound or image of (as a record or a magnetic tape) to be reproduced **5 a :** WIELD, PLY **b :** to discharge, fire, or set off with continuous effect ⟨~*ed* the hose on the burning building⟩ **c :** to cause to move or operate lightly and irregularly or intermittently **d :** to keep (a hooked fish) in action — **play·abil·i·ty** \ˌplā-ə-ˈbi-lə-tē\ *n* — **play·able** \ˈplā-ə-bəl\ *adj* — **play ball :** COOPERATE — **play both ends against the middle :** to set opposing interests against each other to one's own ultimate profit — **play by ear :** to deal with something without previous planning or instructions — **play games :** to try to hide the truth from someone by deceptive means — **play one's cards :** to act with the means available to one — **play possum :** to pretend to be asleep or dead — **play second fiddle :** to take a subordinate position — **play the field :** to date or have romantic connections with more than one person — **play the game :** to act according to a code or set of standards — **play with a full deck :** to be rational or sane — **play with fire :** to do something risky or dangerous — **play with oneself :** MASTURBATE

pla·ya \ˈplī-ə\ *n* [Sp, lit., beach, fr. LL *plagia* — more at PLAGE] (1854) **:** the flat-floored bottom of an undrained desert basin that becomes at times a shallow lake

play·act \ˈplā-ˌakt\ *vb* [back-formation fr. *playacting*] *vt* (1901) **:** ACT OUT 1a ~ *vi* **1 a :** to take part in theatrical performances esp. as a professional **b :** to make believe **2 :** to engage in theatrical or insincere behavior — **play·act·ing** *n*

play–action pass *n* (1964) **:** a pass play in football in which the quarterback fakes a handoff before passing the ball — called also *play-action*

play·back \ˈplā-ˌbak\ *n* (1929) **:** an act or instance of reproducing recorded sound or pictures often immediately after recording

play back *vt* (1949) **:** to perform a playback of (a usu. recently recorded disc or tape)

play·bill \ˈplā-ˌbil\ *n* (1616) **:** a bill advertising a play and usu. announcing the cast

Playbill *trademark* — used for a theater program

play·book \-ˌbu̇k\ *n* (1535) **1 :** one or more plays in book form **2 :** a notebook containing diagrammed football plays **3 :** a stock of usual tactics or methods ⟨straight from his opponent's political ~⟩

play·boy \-ˌbȯi\ *n* (1907) **:** a man who lives a life devoted chiefly to the pursuit of pleasure

play–by–play \ˈplā-ˌbī-ˌplā, ˌplā-ˌbī-ˈ\ *adj* (1931) **1 :** being or giving a running commentary on a sports event ⟨a radio ~ announcer⟩ **2 :** relating each event as it occurs — **play–by–play** *n*

play·date \ˈplā-ˌdāt\ *n* (1984) **:** a play session for small children arranged in advance by their parents

play down *vt* (1930) **:** to attach little importance to **:** MINIMIZE

played out *adj* (1856) **1 :** worn out or used up **2 :** tired out **:** SPENT

play·er \ˈplā-ər\ *n* (14c) **:** one that plays: as **a :** a person who plays a game **b :** MUSICIAN **c :** ACTOR **d :** a device that reproduces recorded material (as video images or music) from a usu. specified medium ⟨a CD ~⟩ **e :** one actively involved esp. in a competitive field or process **:** PARTICIPANT ⟨a key ~ in politics⟩

player piano *n* (1907) **:** a piano containing a mechanism by which it plays automatically

play·fel·low \ˈplā-ˌfe-(ˌ)lō\ *n* (1513) **:** PLAYMATE

play·field \-ˌfēld\ *n* (1883) **:** a playground for outdoor athletics

play·ful \ˈplā-fəl\ *adj* (13c) **1 :** full of play **:** FROLICSOME, SPORTIVE ⟨a ~ kitten⟩ **2 :** HUMOROUS, JOCULAR — **play·ful·ly** \-fə-lē\ *adv* — **play·ful·ness** *n*

play·girl \-ˌgər(-ə)l\ *n* (1912) **:** a woman who lives a life devoted chiefly to the pursuit of pleasure

play·go·er \-ˌgō-ər\ *n* (1822) **:** a person who frequently attends plays

play·ground \-ˌgrau̇nd\ *n* (1794) **1 :** a piece of land used for and usu. equipped with facilities for recreation esp. by children **2 :** an area known or suited for activity of a specified sort ⟨a vacation ~⟩

play·group \ˈplā-ˌgrüp\ *n* (1909) **:** an informal gathering of preschool children organized for the purpose of play and companionship

play·house \-ˌhau̇s\ *n* (bef. 12c) **1 :** THEATER **2 :** a small house for children to play in

play·ing card \ˈplā-iŋ-\ *n* (15c) **:** one of a set of 24 to 78 thin rectangular pieces of cardboard or plastic marked on one side to show its rank and suit and used in playing any of numerous games

playing field *n* (ca. 1584) **1 :** a field for various games; *esp* **:** the part of a field officially marked off for play **2 :** a set of conditions for competition — usu. used in such phrases as *a level playing field*

play·land \ˈplā-ˌland\ *n* (1918) **:** PLAYGROUND

play·let \-lət\ *n* (1884) **:** a short play

play·list \-ˌlist\ *n* (1972) **:** a list of recordings to be played on the air by a radio station; *also* **:** a similar list used for organizing a personal digital music collection

play·mak·er \-ˌmā-kər\ *n* (ca. 1942) **:** a player who leads the offense for a team (as in basketball or hockey) — **play·mak·ing** \-kiŋ\ *n or adj*

play·mate \-ˌmāt\ *n* (1591) **:** a companion in play

play–off \ˈplā-ˌȯf\ *n* (1895) **1 :** a final contest or series of contests to determine the winner between contestants or teams that have tied **2 :** a series of contests played after the end of the regular season to determine a championship — often used in pl.

play off *vt* (1606) **1 a :** to set in opposition for one's own gain **b :** to set in contrast **2 :** to complete the playing of (an interrupted contest) **3 :** to break (a tie) by a play-off

play out *vt* (1580) **1 a :** to perform to the end ⟨*play out* a role⟩ **b :** USE UP, FINISH **2 :** UNREEL, UNFOLD ⟨*played out* a length of line —Gordon Webber⟩ ~ *vi* **1 :** to become spent or exhausted **2 :** DEVELOP, UNFOLD ⟨see how things *play out*⟩

play·pen \ˈplā-ˌpen\ *n* (1931) **:** a portable usu. collapsible enclosure in which a baby or young child may play — called also *play yard*

play·room \-ˌrüm, -ˌru̇m\ *n* (1819) **:** a room equipped for children to play in

play·suit \-ˌsüt\ *n* (1908) **:** a sports and play outfit for women or children that consists usu. of a blouse and shorts

play therapy *n* (1939) **:** psychotherapy in which a child is encouraged to reveal feelings and conflicts in play rather than by verbalization

play·thing \ˈplā-ˌthiŋ\ *n* (1675) **1 :** TOY 3 **2 :** TOY 5

play·time \-ˌtīm\ *n* (1661) **:** a time for play or diversion

play up *vt* (1909) **:** EMPHASIZE; *also* **:** EXAGGERATE, OVEREMPHASIZE

play·wear \ˈplā-ˌwer\ *n* (1964) **:** informal clothing worn for leisure activities

play·wright \ˈplā-ˌrīt\ *n* [¹*play* + obs. *wright* maker — more at WRIGHT] (1616) **:** a person who writes plays

play·writ·ing *also* **play·wright·ing** \-ˌrī-tiŋ\ *n* (1709) **:** the writing of plays

pla·za \ˈpla-zə, ˈplä-\ *n* [Sp, fr. L *platea* broad street — more at PLACE] (1683) **1 a :** a public square in a city or town **b :** an open area usu. located near urban buildings and often featuring walkways, trees and shrubs, places to sit, and sometimes shops **2 :** a place on a thoroughfare (as a turnpike) at which all traffic must temporarily stop (as to pay tolls) **3 :** an area adjacent to an expressway which has service facilities (as a restaurant, gas station, and restrooms) **4 :** SHOPPING CENTER

PLC *abbr, Brit* public limited company

plea \ˈplē\ *n* [ME *ple, plede,* fr. AF *plai, pleit* fr. ML *placitum,* fr. L, decision, decree, fr. neut. of *placitus,* pp. of *placēre* to please, be decided — more at PLEASE] (13c) **1 :** a legal suit or action **2 :** an allegation made by a party in support of a cause: as **a :** an allegation of fact — compare DEMURRER **b** (1) **:** a defendant's answer to a plaintiff's declaration in common-law practice (2) **:** an accused person's answer to a charge or indictment in criminal practice **c :** a plea of guilty to an indictment **3 :** something offered by way of excuse or justification ⟨left early with the ~ of a headache⟩ **4 :** an earnest entreaty **:** APPEAL ⟨their ~ for understanding must be answered⟩ ***syn*** see APOLOGY

plea bar·gain·ing \-ˌbär-gə-niŋ\ *n* (1932) **:** the negotiation of an agreement between a prosecutor and a defendant whereby the defendant is permitted to plead guilty to a reduced charge — **plea–bargain** *vi* — **plea bargain** *n*

pleach \ˈplēch, ˈplāch\ *vt* [ME *plechen,* fr. AF **plecher, plesser,* fr. VL **plactiare,* alter. of L *plectere* to braid — more at PLY] (14c) **:** INTERLACE, PLAIT

plead \ˈplēd\ *vb* **plead·ed** \ˈplē-dəd\ *or* **pled** *also* **plead** \ˈpled\; **plead·ing** [ME *pleden, plaiden,* fr. AF *plaider, pleder,* fr. *plai* plea] *vi* (13c) **1 :** to argue a case or cause in a court of law **2 a :** to make an allegation in an action or other legal proceeding; *esp* **:** to answer the previous pleading of the other party by denying facts therein stated or by alleging new facts **b :** to conduct pleadings **3 :** to make a plea of a specified nature ⟨~ not guilty⟩ **4 a :** to argue for or against a claim **b :** to entreat or appeal earnestly ~ *vt* **1 :** to maintain (as a case or cause) in a court of law or other tribunal **2 :** to allege in or by way of a legal plea **3 :** to offer as a plea usu. in defense, apology, or excuse — **plead·able** \ˈplē-də-bəl\ *adj* — **plead·er** *n* — **plead·ing·ly** \ˈplē-diŋ-lē\ *adv*

pleading *n* (14c) **1 :** advocacy of a cause in a court of law **2 a :** one of the formal usu. written allegations and counter allegations made alternately by the parties in a legal action or proceeding **b :** the action or process performed by the parties in presenting such formal allegations until a single point at issue is produced **c :** the introduction of one of these allegations and esp. the first one **d :** the body of rules according to which these allegations are framed **3 :** the act or an instance of making a plea **4 :** a sincere entreaty

pleas·ance \ˈple-zᵊn(t)s\ *n* (14c) **1 :** a feeling of pleasure **:** DELIGHT **2 :** a pleasant rest or recreation place usu. attached to a mansion

\ə\ **abut** \ᵊ\ **kitten**, F table \ər\ **further** \a\ **ash** \ā\ **ace** \ä\ **mop, mar**
\au̇\ **out** \ch\ **chin** \e\ **bet** \ē\ **easy** \g\ **go** \i\ **hit** \ī\ **ice** \j\ **job**
\ŋ\ **sing** \ō\ **go** \ȯ\ **law** \ȯi\ **boy** \th\ **thin** \t͟h\ **the** \ü\ **loot** \u̇\ **foot**
\y\ **yet** \zh\ **vision, beige** \k̟, ⁿ, œ, ue, ʸ\ *see* Guide to Pronunciation

pleas·ant \ˈple-zᵊnt\ *adj* [ME *plesaunt,* fr. AF *plaisant,* fr. prp. of *plaisir*] (14c) **1 :** having qualities that tend to give pleasure : AGREEABLE ⟨a ~ day⟩ **2 :** having or characterized by pleasing manners, behavior, or appearance — **pleas·ant·ly** *adv* — **pleas·ant·ness** *n*

pleas·ant·ry \-zᵊn-trē\ *n, pl* **-ries** (1597) **1 :** a humorous act or remark : JEST **2 :** an agreeable playfulness in conversation : BANTER **3 :** a polite social remark ⟨exchanged *pleasantries*⟩

[1]**please** \ˈplēz\ *vb* **pleased; pleas·ing** [ME *plesen,* fr. AF *plaisir, pleisir, pleire,* fr. L *placēre;* akin to L *placare* to placate and perh. to Gk *plak-, plax* flat surface — more at FLUKE] *vi* (14c) **1 :** to afford or give pleasure or satisfaction **2 :** LIKE, WISH ⟨do as you ~⟩ **3** *archaic* **:** to have the kindness ⟨will you ~ to enter the carriage —Charles Dickens⟩ ~ *vt* **1 :** to give pleasure to : GRATIFY **2 :** to be the will or pleasure of ⟨may it ~ Your Majesty⟩ — **pleas·er** \ˈplē-zər\ *n*

[2]**please** *adv* (1667) **1 —** used as a function word to express politeness or emphasis in a request ⟨~ come in⟩ **2 —** used as a function word to express polite affirmation ⟨like some tea? *Please*⟩ **3 —** used as a function word to express scornful disagreement, disapproval, or disbelief ⟨you believe that? Oh, ~⟩

pleasing *adj* (14c) **:** giving pleasure : AGREEABLE ⟨the sun's ~ warmth⟩ — **pleas·ing·ly** \-lē\ *adv* — **pleas·ing·ness** *n*

plea·sur·able \ˈplezh-rə-bəl, ˈplāzh-; ˈple-zhə-, ˈplā-\ *adj* (1557) **:** PLEASANT, GRATIFYING — **plea·sur·abil·i·ty** \ˌplezh-rə-ˈbi-lə-tē, ˌplāzh-; ˌple-zhə-, ˌplā-\ *n* — **plea·sur·able·ness** \ˈplezh-rə-bəl-nəs, ˈplāzh-; ˈple-zhə-, ˈplā-\ *n* — **plea·sur·ably** \-blē\ *adv*

[1]**plea·sure** \ˈple-zhər, ˈplā-\ *n* [ME *plesure,* alter. of *plesir,* fr. AF *plaisir,* fr. *plaisir* to please] (14c) **1 :** DESIRE, INCLINATION ⟨wait upon his ~ —Shak.⟩ **2 :** a state of gratification **3 a :** sensual gratification **b :** frivolous amusement **4 :** a source of delight or joy

[2]**pleasure** *vb* **plea·sured; plea·sur·ing** \ˈplezh-riŋ, ˈplāzh-; ˈple-zhə-, ˈplā-\ *vt* (1537) **1 :** to give pleasure to : GRATIFY **2 :** to give sexual pleasure to ~ *vi* **1 :** to take pleasure : DELIGHT **2 :** to seek pleasure

pleasure dome *n* (1797) **:** a place of pleasurable entertainment or recreation : RESORT

plea·sure·less \ˈple-zhər-ləs, ˈplā-\ *adj* (1719) **:** giving no pleasure

pleasure principle *n* (1912) **:** a tendency for individual behavior to be directed toward immediate satisfaction of instinctual drives and immediate relief from pain or discomfort

[1]**pleat** \ˈplēt\ *vt* [ME *pleten,* fr. *pleit, plete* plait] (14c) **1 :** FOLD; *esp* **:** to arrange in pleats ⟨~ a skirt⟩ **2 :** PLAIT 2 — **pleat·er** *n*

[2]**pleat** *n* [ME *plete*] (15c) **:** a fold in cloth made by doubling material over on itself; *also* **:** something resembling such a fold — **pleat·less** \-ləs\ *adj*

pleath·er \ˈple-t͟hər\ *n* [blend of *plastic* and *leather*] (1982) **:** a plastic fabric made to look like leather

pleb \ˈpleb\ *n* (1795) **:** PLEBEIAN

plebe \ˈplēb\ *n* [obs. *plebe* common people, fr. F *plèbe,* fr. L *plebs*] (1833) **:** a freshman at a military or naval academy

[1]**ple·be·ian** \pli-ˈbē-ən\ *n* [L *plebeius* of the common people, fr. *plebs* common people] (1533) **1 :** a member of the Roman plebs **2 :** one of the common people — **ple·be·ian·ism** \-ə-ˌni-zəm\ *n*

[2]**plebeian** *adj* (1566) **1 :** of or relating to plebeians **2 :** crude or coarse in manner or style : COMMON — **ple·be·ian·ly** *adv*

pleb·i·scite \ˈple-bə-ˌsīt, -sət *also* -ˌsēt\ *n* [L *plebis scitum* law voted by the comitia, lit., decree of the common people] (1860) **:** a vote by which the people of an entire country or district express an opinion for or against a proposal esp. on a choice of government or ruler — **ple·bi·sci·ta·ry** \ple-ˈbi-sə-ˌter-ē, pli-; ˌple-bə-ˈsī-tə-rē\ *adj*

plebs \ˈplebz, ˈpleps\ *n, pl* **ple·bes** \ˈplē-(ˌ)bēz, ˈplā-ˌbās\ [L] (1647) **1 :** the general populace **2 :** the common people of ancient Rome

ple·cop·ter·an \pli-ˈkäp-tə-rən\ *n* [NL *Plecoptera,* group name, fr. Gk *plekein* to braid + *pteron* wing — more at PLY, FEATHER] (ca. 1890) **:** STONE FLY — **plecopteran** *adj*

plec·trum \ˈplek-trəm\ *n, pl* **plec·tra** \-trə\ *or* **plectrums** [L, fr. Gk *plēktron,* fr. *plēssein* to strike — more at PLAINT] (ca. 1552) **:** [3]PICK 2c

[1]**pledge** \ˈplej\ *n* [ME *plegge* security, fr. AF *plege,* fr. LL *plebium,* fr. **plebere* to pledge, prob. of Gmc origin; akin to OHG *pflegan* to take care of — more at PLIGHT] (14c) **1 a :** a bailment of a chattel as security for a debt or other obligation without involving transfer of title **b :** the chattel so delivered **c :** the contract incidental to such a bailment **2 a :** the state of being held as a security or guaranty **b :** something given as security for the performance of an act **3 :** a token, sign, or earnest of something else **4 :** a gage of battle **5 :** TOAST 3 **6 a :** a binding promise or agreement to do or forbear **b** (1) **:** a promise to join a fraternity, sorority, or secret society (2) **:** a person who has so promised

[2]**pledge** *vt* **pledged; pledg·ing** (15c) **1 :** to make a pledge of; *esp* **:** PAWN **2 :** to drink to the health of **3 :** to bind by a pledge **4 :** to promise the performance of by a pledge — **pledg·er** \ˈple-jər\ *or* **pled·gor** \ˈple-jər, ple-ˈjȯr\ *n*

pledg·ee \ple-ˈjē\ *n* (1766) **:** one to whom a pledge is given

pled·get \ˈple-jət\ *n* [origin unknown] (ca. 1540) **:** a compress or pad used to apply medication to or absorb discharges (as from a wound)

-plegia *n comb form* [NL, fr. Gk *-plēgia,* fr. *plēssein* to strike — more at PLAINT] **:** paralysis ⟨di*plegia*⟩

ple·iad \ˈplē-əd, ˈplā-, -ˌad, *chiefly Brit* ˈplī-\ *n* [F *Pléiade,* group of seven 16th cent. Fr. poets, fr. MF, group of seven tragic poets of ancient Alexandria, fr. Gk *Pleiad-, Pleias,* fr. sing. of *Pleiades*] (ca. 1839) **:** a group of usu. seven illustrious or brilliant persons or things

Pleiad *n* (14c) **:** any of the Pleiades

Ple·ia·des \ˈplē-ə-ˌdēz, ˈplā-, *chiefly Brit* ˈplī-\ *n pl* [L, fr. Gk] (14c) **1 :** the seven daughters of Atlas turned into a group of stars in Greek mythology **2 :** a conspicuous cluster of stars in the constellation Taurus that includes six stars in the form of a very small dipper

plein air \ˌplān-ˈer; ple-ˈner\ *adj* [F, open air] (1894) **1 :** of or relating to painting in outdoor daylight **2 :** of or relating to a branch of impressionism that attempts to represent outdoor light and air — **plein-air·ism** \plā-ˈner-ˌi-zəm, ple-\ *n* — **plein-air·ist** \-ist\ *n*

pleio- *or* **pleo-** *or* **plio-** *comb form* [Gk *pleiōn, pleōn* — more at PLUS] **:** more ⟨*pleio*tropic⟩ ⟨*pleo*morphic⟩ ⟨*Plio*cene⟩

pleio·tro·pic \ˌplī-ə-ˈtrō-pik, -ˈträ-\ *adj* (1938) **:** producing more than one effect; *esp* **:** having multiple phenotypic expressions ⟨a ~ gene⟩ — **plei·ot·ro·py** \plī-ˈä-trə-pē\ *n*

Pleis·to·cene \ˈplīs-tə-ˌsēn\ *adj* [Gk *pleistos* most + ISV *-cene;* akin to Gk *pleiōn* more] (1839) **:** of, relating to, or being the earlier epoch of the Quaternary or the corresponding series of rocks — see GEOLOGIC TIME table — **Pleistocene** *n*

ple·na·ry \ˈplē-nə-rē, ˈple-\ *adj* [ME, fr. LL *plenarius,* fr. L *plenus* full — more at FULL] (15c) **1 :** complete in every respect : ABSOLUTE, UNQUALIFIED ⟨~ power⟩ **2 :** fully attended or constituted by all entitled to be present ⟨a ~ session⟩ ***syn*** see FULL

plenary indulgence *n* (1648) **:** a remission of the entire temporal punishment for sin

ple·nip·o·tent \pli-ˈni-pə-tənt\ *adj* [LL *plenipotent-, plenipotens,* fr. L *plenus* + *potent-, potens* powerful — more at POTENT] (1658) **:** PLENIPOTENTIARY

[1]**plen·i·po·ten·tia·ry** \ˌple-nə-pə-ˈten(t)-sh(ə-)rē, -shē-ˌer-ē\ *adj* [ML *plenipotentiarius,* adj. & n., fr. LL *plenipotent-, plenipotens*] (ca. 1645) **1 :** invested with full power **2 :** of or relating to a plenipotentiary

[2]**plenipotentiary** *n, pl* **-ries** (ca. 1656) **:** a person and esp. a diplomatic agent invested with full power to transact business

plen·ish \ˈple-nish\ *vt* [ME (Sc) *plenyssen* to fill up, fr. AF *pleniss-,* stem of *plenir,* fr. *plein* full, fr. L *plenus*] (1513) *chiefly Brit* **:** EQUIP

plen·i·tude \ˈple-nə-ˌtüd, -ˌtyüd\ *n* [ME *plenitude,* fr. AF or L; AF, fr. L *plenitudo,* fr. *plenus*] (15c) **1 :** the quality or state of being full : COMPLETENESS **2 :** a great sufficiency : ABUNDANCE

plen·i·tu·di·nous \ˌple-nə-ˈtüd-nəs, -ˈtyüd-; -ˈtü-də-nəs, -ˈtyü-\ *adj* [L *plenitudin-, plenitudo*] (1895) **:** characterized by plenitude

plen·te·ous \ˈplen-tē-əs\ *adj* [ME *plentevous, plenteous,* fr. AF *plentivus,* fr. *plentif* abundant, fr. *plenté* plenty] (14c) **1 :** FRUITFUL, PRODUCTIVE ⟨a ~ harvest —J. G. Frazer⟩ — usu. used with *in* or *of* ⟨the seasons had been ~ in corn —George Eliot⟩ **2 :** constituting or existing in plenty ⟨~ grace with thee is found —Charles Wesley⟩ — **plen·te·ous·ly** *adv* — **plen·te·ous·ness** *n*

plen·ti·ful \ˈplen-ti-fəl\ *adj* (15c) **1 :** containing or yielding plenty ⟨a ~ land⟩ **2 :** characterized by, constituting, or existing in plenty — **plen·ti·ful·ly** \-f(ə-)lē\ *adv* — **plen·ti·ful·ness** *n*

syn PLENTIFUL, AMPLE, ABUNDANT, COPIOUS mean more than sufficient without being excessive. PLENTIFUL implies a great or rich supply ⟨peaches are *plentiful* this summer⟩. AMPLE implies a generous sufficiency to satisfy a particular requirement ⟨*ample* food to last the winter⟩. ABUNDANT suggests an even greater or richer supply than does PLENTIFUL ⟨streams *abundant* with fish⟩. COPIOUS stresses largeness of supply rather than fullness or richness ⟨*copious* examples of bureaucratic waste⟩.

plen·ti·tude \ˈplen-tə-ˌtüd, -ˌtyüd\ *n* [by alter. (influenced by *plenty*)] (1615) **:** PLENITUDE

[1]**plen·ty** \ˈplen-tē\ *n* [ME *plente,* fr. AF *plenté,* fr. LL *plenitat-, plenitas,* fr. L, fullness, fr. *plenus* full — more at FULL] (13c) **1 a :** a full or more than adequate amount or supply ⟨had ~ of time to finish the job⟩ **b :** a large number or amount ⟨in ~ of trouble⟩ **2 :** the quality or state of being copious : PLENTIFULNESS

[2]**plenty** *adj* (14c) **1 :** plentiful in amount, number, or supply ⟨if reasons were as ~ as blackberries —Shak.⟩ **2 :** AMPLE ⟨~ work to be done —*Time*⟩

usage Many commentators object to use of sense 2 in writing; it appears to be limited chiefly to spoken English. Sense 1 is literary but is no longer in common use.

[3]**plenty** *adv* (1842) **:** more than sufficiently : to a considerable degree ⟨the nights were ~ cold —F. B. Gipson⟩

usage Many handbooks advise avoiding the adverb *plenty* in writing; "use *very, quite,* or a more precise word," they advise. Actually *plenty* is often a more precise word than its recommended replacements; *very, fully,* or *quite* will not work as well in these typical quotations ⟨it's already *plenty* hot for us in the kitchen without some dolt opening the oven —C. H. Bridges⟩ ⟨may not be rising quite as rapidly as other health costs, but it is going up *plenty* fast —*Changing Times*⟩. It is not used in more formal writing.

ple·num \ˈple-nəm, ˈplē-\ *n* [NL, fr. L, neut. of *plenus*] (1678) **1 a :** a space or all space every part of which is full of matter **b :** an air-filled space in a structure; *esp* **:** one that receives air from a blower for distribution (as in a ventilation system) **2 :** a general assembly of all members esp. of a legislative body **3 :** the quality or state of being full

ple·och·ro·ism \plē-ˈä-krə-ˌwi-zəm\ *n* [ISV *pleochroic,* fr. *pleio-* + Gk *chrōs* skin, color] (1857) **:** the property of a crystal of showing different colors when viewed by light polarized in different directions — **pleo·chro·ic** \ˌplē-ə-ˈkrō-ik\ *adj*

pleo·mor·phic \ˌplē-ə-ˈmȯr-fik\ *adj* (1886) **:** able to assume different forms : POLYMORPHIC ⟨~ bacteria⟩ ⟨a ~ sarcoma⟩ — **pleo·mor·phism** \-ˌfi-zəm\ *n*

ple·o·nasm \ˈplē-ə-ˌna-zəm\ *n* [LL *pleonasmus,* fr. Gk *pleonasmos,* fr. *pleonazein* to be excessive, fr. *pleiōn, pleōn* more — more at PLUS] (1610) **1 :** the use of more words than those necessary to denote mere sense (as in *the man he said*) : REDUNDANCY **2 :** an instance or example of pleonasm — **ple·o·nas·tic** \ˌplē-ə-ˈnas-tik\ *adj* — **ple·o·nas·ti·cal·ly** \-ti-k(ə-)lē\ *adv*

ple·o·pod \ˈplē-ə-ˌpäd\ *n* [Gk *plein* to sail + E *-o-* + *-pod;* fr. its use in swimming — more at FLOW] (1888) **:** an abdominal limb of a crustacean

ple·ro·cer·coid \ˌplir-ō-ˈsər-ˌkȯid\ *n* [Gk *plērēs* full + *kerkos* tail — more at FULL] (1906) **:** the solid elongate infective larva of some tapeworms usu. occurring in the muscles of fishes

ple·si·o·saur \ˈplē-sē-ə-ˌsȯr, -zē-\ *n* [ultim. fr. Gk *plēsios* close (akin to Gk *pelas* near) + *sauros* lizard] (1839) **:** any of an order or suborder (Plesiosauria) of large carnivorous marine reptiles of the Mesozoic with dorsoventrally flattened bodies and limbs modified into flippers

pleth·o·ra \ˈple-thə-rə\ *n* [ML, fr. Gk *plēthōra,* lit., fullness, fr. *plēthein* to be full — more at FULL] (1541) **1 :** a bodily condition characterized by an excess of blood and marked by turgescence and a florid complexion **2 :** EXCESS, SUPERFLUITY; *also* **:** PROFUSION, ABUNDANCE — **ple·tho·ric** \plə-ˈthȯr-ik, ple-, -ˈthär-; ˈple-thə-rik\ *adj*

ple·thys·mo·gram \ple-ˈthiz-mə-ˌgram, plə-\ *n* (1894) **:** a tracing made by a plethysmograph

ple·thys·mo·graph \-ˌgraf\ *n* [ISV, fr. Gk *plēthysmos* increase, fr. *plēthynein* to increase, fr. *plēthys* mass, quantity, fr. *plēthein*] (1872) **:** an instrument for determining and registering variations in the size of an organ, limb, or part resulting from changes in the amount of blood present or passing through it — **ple·thys·mo·graph·ic** \-ˌthiz-mə-

ˈgra-fik\ *adj* — **ple·thys·mo·graph·i·cal·ly** \-fi-k(ə-)lē\ *adv* — **pleth·ys·mog·ra·phy** \ˌple-thiz-ˈmä-grə-fē\ *n*
pleu·ra \ˈplu̇r-ə\ *n, pl* **pleu·rae** \ˈplu̇r-ˌē, -ˌī\ *or* **pleuras** [ME, fr. ML, fr. Gk, rib, side] (15c) **:** the delicate serous membrane that lines each half of the thorax of mammals and is folded back over the surface of the lung of the same side — **pleu·ral** \ˈplu̇r-əl\ *adj*
pleu·ri·sy \ˈplu̇r-ə-sē\ *n* [ME *pleuresi,* fr. AF *pleuresie,* fr. LL *pleurisis,* alter. of L *pleuritis,* fr. Gk, fr. *pleura* side] (14c) **:** inflammation of the pleura that is typically characterized by sudden onset, painful and difficult respiration, and exudation of fluid or fibrinous material into the pleural cavity — **pleu·rit·ic** \plu̇-ˈri-tik\ *adj*
pleu·ro·pneu·mo·nia \ˌplu̇r-ō-nu̇-ˈmō-nyə, -ō-nyu̇-\ *n* [NL] (ca. 1725) **1 :** combined inflammation of the pleura and lungs **2 :** an acute febrile and often fatal respiratory disorder of cattle, goats, sheep, and related animals caused by a mycoplasma (*Mycoplasma mycoides*)
pleuropneumonia–like organism *n* (1935) **:** MYCOPLASMA
pleus·ton \ˈplü-stən, -ˌstän\ *n* [ISV *pleus-* (irreg. fr. Gk *plein* to sail, float) + *-on* (as in *plankton*)] (1943) **:** organisms living in the thin surface layer existing at the air-water interface of a body of water — **pleus·ton·ic** \plü-ˈstä-nik\ *adj*
plex *or* ˈ**plex** \ˈpleks\ *n* (1985) **:** MULTIPLEX
-plex *n comb form* [partly fr. L *-plex* (as in *duplex*); partly fr. *complex*] **1 :** a figure of a given power ⟨googol*plex*⟩ **2 :** a building divided into an often specified number of spaces (as apartments or movie theaters) ⟨four*plex*⟩ ⟨multi*plex*⟩
plex·i·form \ˈplek-sə-ˌfȯrm\ *adj* [NL *plexus* + E *-iform*] (ca. 1828) **:** of, relating to, or having the form or characteristics of a plexus
Plex·i·glas \ˈplek-si-ˌglas\ *trademark* — used for acrylic plastic sheets
plex·i·glass \ˈplek-si-ˌglas\ *n* [alter. of *Plexiglas*] (1935) **:** a transparent acrylic plastic often used in place of glass
plex·us \ˈplek-səs\ *n, pl* **plex·us·es** \-sə-səz\ [NL, fr. L *plectere* to braid — more at PLY] (1682) **1 :** a network of anastomosing or interlacing blood vessels or nerves **2 :** an interwoven combination of parts or elements in a structure or system
plf *abbr* plaintiff
pli·able \ˈplī-ə-bəl\ *adj* [ME, fr. AF, fr. *plier* to bend, fold — more at PLY] (14c) **1 a :** supple enough to bend freely or repeatedly without breaking **b :** yielding readily to others **:** COMPLAISANT **2 :** adjustable to varying conditions *syn* see PLASTIC — **pli·abil·i·ty** \ˌplī-ə-ˈbi-lə-tē\ *n* — **pli·able·ness** \ˈplī-ə-bəl-nəs\ *n* — **pli·ably** \-blē\ *adv*
pli·an·cy \ˈplī-ən(t)-sē\ *n* (1632) **:** the quality or state of being pliant
pli·ant \ˈplī-ənt\ *adj* (14c) **1 :** PLIABLE 1a **2 :** easily influenced **:** YIELDING **3 :** suitable for varied uses *syn* see PLASTIC — **pli·ant·ly** *adv* — **pli·ant·ness** *n*
pli·ca \ˈplī-kə\ *n, pl* **pli·cae** \-ˌkē, -ˌsē\ [ML, fr. L *plicare* to fold — more at PLY] (ca. 1660) **:** a fold or folded part; *esp* **:** a groove or fold of skin
pli·cate \ˈplī-ˌkāt\ *adj* [L *plicatus,* pp. of *plicare*] (ca. 1760) **1 :** folded lengthwise like a fan ⟨a ~ leaf⟩ **2 :** having the surface thrown up into or marked with parallel ridges ⟨~ wing cases⟩
pli·ca·tion \plī-ˈkā-shən\ *n* (14c) **1 :** the act or process of folding **:** the state of being folded **2 :** FOLD
plié \plē-ˈā\ *n* [F, fr. pp. of *plier* to bend] (1892) **:** a bending of the knees outward by a ballet dancer with the back held straight
pli·ers \ˈplī(-ə)rz\ *n pl but sing or pl in constr* [[2]*ply*] (ca. 1569) **:** a small pincers for holding small objects or for bending and cutting wire
[1]**plight** \ˈplīt\ *vt* [ME, fr. OE *plihtan* to endanger, fr. *pliht* danger; akin to OE *plēon* to expose to danger, OHG *pflegan* to take care of] (13c) **:** to put or give in pledge **:** ENGAGE ⟨~ his troth⟩ — **plight·er** *n*
[2]**plight** *n* (13c) **:** a solemnly given pledge **:** ENGAGEMENT
[3]**plight** *n* [ME *plight, plit* danger, condition, in part fr. OE *pliht;* in part fr. AF *plit, pleit, pli* condition, plight, lit., bending, fold — more at PLAIT] (13c) **:** an unfortunate, difficult, or precarious situation
plim·soll \ˈplim(p)-səl, ˈplim-ˌsȯl\ *n* [prob. fr. the supposed resemblance of the upper edge of the shoe's mudguard to the Plimsoll mark on a ship] (1907) *Brit* **:** SNEAKER 2
Plimsoll mark *n* [Samuel *Plimsoll* †1898 Eng. shipping reformer] (1884) **:** a load line or a set of load-line markings on an oceangoing cargo ship — called also *Plimsoll line*

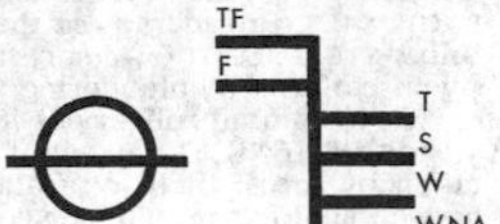

Plimsoll mark: *TF* tropical freshwater mark; *F* freshwater mark; *T* tropical load line; *S* summer load line; *W* winter load line; *WNA* winter load line, North Atlantic

[1]**plink** \ˈpliŋk\ *vb* [imit.] *vi* (1941) **1 :** to make a tinkling sound **2 :** to shoot at random targets in an informal and noncompetitive manner ~ *vt* **1 :** to cause to make a tinkling sound **2 :** to shoot at esp. in a casual manner — **plink·er** *n*
[2]**plink** *n* (1954) **:** a tinkling metallic sound
plinth \ˈplin(t)th\ *n* [L *plinthus,* fr. Gk *plinthos*] (1601) **1 a :** the lowest member of a base **:** SUBBASE **b :** a block upon which the moldings of an architrave or trim are stopped at the bottom **2 :** a usu. square block serving as a base; *broadly* **:** any of various bases or lower parts **3 :** a course of stones forming a continuous foundation or base course
plio- — see PLEIO-
Pli·o·cene \ˈplī-ə-ˌsēn\ *adj* (1831) **:** of, relating to, or being the latest epoch of the Tertiary or the corresponding series of rocks — see GEOLOGIC TIME table — **Pliocene** *n*
plique–à–jour \ˌplēk-(ˌ)ä-ˈzhu̇r\ *n* [F, lit., braid letting in daylight] (1878) **:** a style of enameling in which usu. transparent enamels are fused into the openings of a metal filigree to produce an effect suggestive of stained glass
plis·kie *or* **plis·ky** \ˈplis-kē\ *n, pl* **pliskies** [origin unknown] (1706) *chiefly Scot* **:** PRACTICAL JOKE, TRICK
plis·sé *or* **plis·se** \pli-ˈsā\ *n* [F *plissé,* fr. pp. of *plisser* to pleat, fr. MF, fr. *pli* fold, fr. *plier* to fold — more at PLY] (1859) **1 :** a fabric with a plissé finish **2 :** a textile finish of permanently puckered designs formed by treating with a sodium hydroxide solution
PLO *abbr* Palestine Liberation Organization
plod \ˈpläd\ *vb* **plod·ded; plod·ding** [origin unknown] *vi* (1562) **1 :** to work laboriously and monotonously **:** DRUDGE **2 a :** to walk heavily or slowly **:** TRUDGE **b :** to proceed slowly or tediously ⟨the movie's plot just ~*s* along⟩ ~ *vt* **:** to tread slowly or heavily along or over — **plod** *n* — **plod·der** *n* — **plod·ding·ly** \ˈplä-diŋ-lē\ *adv*
-ploid *adj comb form* [ISV, fr. *diploid* and *haploid*] **:** having or being a chromosome number that bears (such) a relationship to or is (so many) times the basic chromosome number of a given group ⟨poly*ploid*⟩
ploi·dy \ˈplȯi-dē\ *n* [fr. such words as *diploidy, hexaploidy*] (1939) **:** degree of repetition of the basic number of chromosomes
[1]**plonk** *var of* PLUNK
[2]**plonk** *n* [short for earlier *plink-plonk,* perh. modif. of F *vin blanc* white wine] (1930) *chiefly Brit* **:** cheap or inferior wine
plop \ˈpläp\ *vb* **plopped; plop·ping** [imit.] *vi* (1821) **1 :** to fall, drop, or move suddenly with a sound like that of something dropping into water **2 :** to allow the body to drop heavily — usu. used with *down* ⟨*plopped* down on the couch⟩ ~ *vt* **1 :** to set, drop, or throw heavily **2 :** to place or set carelessly or hastily ⟨*plopped* the money into stocks⟩ — **plop** *n*
plo·sion \ˈplō-zhən\ *n* (1899) **:** EXPLOSION 3
plo·sive \ˈplō-siv\ *n* [short for *explosive*] (1899) **:** STOP 9 — **plosive** *adj*
[1]**plot** \ˈplät\ *n* [ME, fr. OE] (bef. 12c) **1 a :** a small area of planted ground ⟨a vegetable ~⟩ **b :** a small piece of land in a cemetery **c :** a measured piece of land **:** LOT **2 :** GROUND PLAN, PLAT **3 :** the plan or main story (as of a movie or literary work) **4** [perh. back-formation fr. *complot*] **:** a secret plan for accomplishing a usu. evil or unlawful end **:** INTRIGUE **5 :** a graphic representation (as a chart) — **plot·less** \-ləs\ *adj* — **plot·less·ness** *n*
syn PLOT, INTRIGUE, MACHINATION, CONSPIRACY, CABAL mean a plan secretly devised to accomplish an evil or treacherous end. PLOT implies careful foresight in planning a complex scheme ⟨an assassination *plot*⟩. INTRIGUE suggests secret underhanded maneuvering in an atmosphere of duplicity ⟨backstairs *intrigue*⟩. MACHINATION implies a contriving of annoyances, injuries, or evils by indirect means ⟨the *machinations* of a party boss⟩. CONSPIRACY implies a secret agreement among several people usu. involving treason or great treachery ⟨a *conspiracy* to fix prices⟩. CABAL typically applies to political intrigue involving persons of some eminence ⟨a *cabal* among powerful senators⟩. *syn* see in addition PLAN
[2]**plot** *vb* **plot·ted; plot·ting** *vt* (1588) **1 a :** to make a plot, map, or plan of **b :** to mark or note on or as if on a map or chart **2 :** to lay out in plots **3 a :** to locate (a point) by means of coordinates **b :** to locate (a curve) by plotted points **c :** to represent (an equation) by means of a curve so constructed **4 :** to plan or contrive esp. secretly **5 :** to invent or devise the plot of (as a movie or a literary work) ~ *vi* **1 :** to form a plot **:** SCHEME **2 :** to be located by means of coordinates ⟨the data ~ at a single point⟩
plot·line \ˈplät-ˌlīn\ *n* (1952) **:** PLOT 3
plot·tage \ˈplä-tij\ *n* (1936) **:** the area included in a plot of land
plot·ter \ˈplä-tər\ *n* (1588) **:** one that plots: as **a :** a person who schemes or conspires **b :** a contriver of a literary plot **c :** a device for plotting; *specif* **:** an instrument that graphs computer output
plot·ty \ˈplä-tē\ *adj* **plot·ti·er; -est** (1897) **:** marked by intricacy of plot or intrigue ⟨a ~ novel⟩ — **plot·ti·ness** *n*
plough *chiefly Brit var of* PLOW
plough·man's lunch \ˈplau̇-mənz-\ *n* (1944) **:** a cold lunch served esp. in an English pub typically including bread, cheese, and pickled onions
plo·ver \ˈplə-vər, ˈplō-\ *n, pl* **plover** *or* **plovers** [ME, fr. AF *plover, pluvier,* fr. VL **pluviarius,* fr. L *pluvia* rain — more at PLUVIAL] (14c) **1 :** any of a family (Charadriidae) of shorebirds that differ from the sandpipers in having a short hard-tipped bill and usu. a stouter more compact build **2 :** any of various birds (as a turnstone or sandpiper) related to the plovers
[1]**plow** \ˈplau̇\ *n* [ME, fr. OE *plōh* hide of land; akin to OHG *pfluog* plow] (12c) **1 :** an implement used to cut, lift, and turn over soil esp. in preparing a seedbed **2 :** any of various devices (as a snowplow) operating like a plow
[2]**plow** *vt* (15c) **1 a :** to turn, break up, or work with a plow **b :** to make (as a furrow) with a plow **2 :** to cut into, open, or make furrows or ridges in with or as if with a plow **3 :** to cleave the surface of or move through (water) ⟨whales ~*ing* the ocean⟩ **4 :** to clear away snow from with a snowplow ⟨~ the street⟩ **5 :** to spend or invest (money) in substantial amounts — used with *into* ⟨~ money into stocks⟩ ~ *vi* **1 a :** to use a plow **b :** to undergo plowing **2 a :** to move forcefully into or through something ⟨the car ~*ed* into a fence⟩ **b :** to proceed steadily and laboriously ⟨had to ~ through a stack of letters⟩ — **plow·able** \-ə-bəl\ *adj* — **plow·er** \ˈplau̇(-ə)r\ *n*
plow back *vt* (1930) **:** to reinvest (profits) in a business — **plow·back** \ˈplau̇-ˌbak\ *n*
plow·boy \ˈplau̇-ˌbȯi\ *n* (1569) **1 :** a boy who leads the team drawing a plow **2 :** a country youth
plow·man \-mən, -ˌman\ *n* (13c) **1 :** a man who guides a plow **2 :** a farm laborer
plow·share \ˈplau̇-ˌsher\ *n* [ME *ploughshare,* fr. *plough* plow + *schare* plowshare — more at SHARE] (14c) **:** a part of a plow that cuts the furrow
plow under *vt* (1900) **:** to cause to disappear **:** BURY, OVERWHELM
ploy \ˈplȯi\ *n* [prob. fr. *employ*] (1697) **1 :** ESCAPADE, FROLIC **2 a :** a tactic intended to embarrass or frustrate an opponent **b :** a devised or contrived move **:** STRATAGEM ⟨a ~ to get her to open the door —Robert B. Parker⟩
pls *abbr* please
PLSS *abbr* portable life-support system
PLU *abbr* price lookup
[1]**pluck** \ˈplək\ *vb* [ME, fr. OE *pluccian;* akin to MHG *pflücken* to pluck] *vt* (bef. 12c) **1 :** to pull or pick off or out **2 a :** to remove something (as hairs) from by or as if by plucking ⟨~ one's eyebrows⟩ **b :** ROB, FLEECE **3 :** to move, remove, or separate forcibly or abruptly ⟨~*ed* the child from the middle of the street⟩ **4 a :** to pick, pull, or grasp at **b :** to play by sounding the strings with the fingers or a pick ~ *vi* **:** to make a sharp pull or twitch — **pluck·er** *n*

\ə\ **abut** \ᵊ\ **kitten**, F **table** \ər\ **further** \a\ **ash** \ā\ **ace** \ä\ **mop, mar**
\au̇\ **out** \ch\ **chin** \e\ **bet** \ē\ **easy** \g\ **go** \i\ **hit** \ī\ **ice** \j\ **job**
\ŋ\ **sing** \ō\ **go** \ȯ\ **law** \ȯi\ **boy** \th\ **thin** \t͟h\ **the** \ü\ **loot** \u̇\ **foot**
\y\ **yet** \zh\ **vision, beige** \k, ⁿ, œ, ue, ʸ\ *see* Guide to Pronunciation

[2]**pluck** *n* (15c) **1 :** an act or instance of plucking or pulling **2 :** the heart, liver, lungs, and trachea of a slaughtered animal esp. as an item of food **3 :** courageous readiness to fight or continue against odds **:** dogged resolution

plucky \ˈplə-kē\ *adj* **pluck·i·er; -est** (1840) **:** SPIRITED, BRAVE — **pluck·i·ly** \ˈplə-kə-lē\ *adv* — **pluck·i·ness** \ˈplə-kē-nəs\ *n*

[1]**plug** \ˈpləg\ *n* [D, fr. MD *plugge;* akin to MHG *pfloc* plug] (1606) **1 a :** a piece used to fill a hole **:** STOPPER **b :** an obtruding or obstructing mass of material resembling a stopper **2 :** a flat compressed cake of tobacco **3 :** a small core or segment removed from a larger object **4 :** something inferior; *esp* **:** an inferior often aged or unsound horse **5 a :** HYDRANT, FIREPLUG **b :** SPARK PLUG **6 :** an artificial fishing lure used primarily for casting and made with one or more sets of gang hooks **7 :** any of various devices resembling or functioning like a plug: as **a :** a male fitting for making an electrical connection to a live circuit by insertion in a receptacle (as an outlet) **b :** a device for connecting electric wires to a jack **8 :** a piece of favorable publicity or a favorable mention usu. incorporated in general matter

[2]**plug** *vb* **plugged; plug·ging** *vt* (1630) **1 a :** to stop, make tight, or secure by inserting a plug **b :** to remedy (a deficiency) as if by inserting a plug ⟨trying to ~ the gaps in their understanding⟩ **2 :** to hit with a bullet **:** SHOOT **3 :** to advertise or publicize insistently ~ *vi* **1 :** to become plugged — usu. used with *up* **2 :** to work doggedly and persistently ⟨*plugged* away at her homework⟩ **3 :** to fire shots — **plug·ger** *n* — **plug into 1 :** to connect or become connected to by or as if by means of a plug ⟨the city was *plugged into* the new highway system⟩ **2 :** to load into as if by means of a plug ⟨*plugged* the data *into* a computer⟩

plug and play *n* (1993) **:** a feature of a computer system by which peripherals are automatically detected and configured by the operating system — **plug–and–play** *adj*

plugged *adj* (1694) **1** *of a coin* **:** altered by the insertion of a plug of base metal **2 :** closed by or as if by a plug **:** OBSTRUCTED

plugged–in \ˈpləgd-ˈin\ *adj* (1968) **:** technologically or socially informed and connected ⟨~ teenagers⟩

plug hat *n* (1863) **:** a man's stiff hat (as a bowler or top hat)

[1]**plug–in** \ˈpləg-ˌin\ *adj* (1922) **:** designed to be connected to an electric circuit by plugging in ⟨a ~ toy⟩ ⟨a ~ circuit board⟩

[2]**plug–in** *n* (1946) **1 :** something that plugs in **2 :** a small piece of software that supplements a larger program (as a browser)

plug in *vi* (1893) **:** to establish an electric circuit by inserting a plug ~ *vt* **:** to attach or connect to an electric receptacle (as an outlet)

plug·o·la \(ˌ)plə-ˈgō-lə\ *n* [*plug* + *-ola* (as in *payola*)] (1959) **:** incidental advertising on radio or television that is not purchased like regular advertising

plug–ug·ly \ˈpləg-ˌəg-lē\ *n* (1856) **:** THUG, TOUGH; *esp* **:** one hired to intimidate

plum \ˈpləm\ *n, often attrib* [ME, fr. OE *plūme,* modif. of L *prunum* plum, fr. Gk *proumnon*] (bef. 12c) **1 :** any of various trees and shrubs (genus *Prunus*) of the rose family with globular to oval smooth-skinned edible fruits that are drupes with oblong seeds; *also* **:** the fruit **2 :** any of various trees with edible fruits resembling plums; *also* **:** the fruit **3 a :** a raisin when used in desserts **b :** SUGARPLUM **4 :** something superior or very desirable; *esp* **:** something desirable given in return for a favor **5 :** a dark reddish purple — **plum·like** \-ˌlīk\ *adj*

plum·age \ˈplü-mij\ *n* [ME, fr. MF, fr. OF, fr. *plume* feather — more at PLUME] (14c) **:** the feathers of a bird — **plum·aged** \-mijd\ *adj*

[1]**plumb** \ˈpləm\ *n* [ME, fr. AF *plum, plomb,* fr. L *plumbum* lead] (14c) **:** a lead weight attached to a line and used to indicate a vertical direction — **out of plumb** *or* **off plumb :** out of vertical or true

[2]**plumb** *adv* (15c) **1 :** straight down or up **:** VERTICALLY **2** *chiefly dial* **:** to a complete degree **:** ABSOLUTELY ⟨'you're ~ crazy', she remarked, with easy candor —*Harper's Weekly*⟩ **3 :** in a direct manner **:** EXACTLY; *also* **:** without interval of time **:** IMMEDIATELY

[3]**plumb** *vt* (15c) **1 :** to weight with lead **2 a :** to measure the depth of with a plumb **b :** to examine minutely and critically ⟨~*ing* the book's complexities⟩ **3 :** to adjust or test by a plumb line **4 :** to seal with lead **5** [back-formation fr. *plumber*] **:** to supply with or install as plumbing ~ *vi* **:** to work as a plumber

[4]**plumb** *adj* (15c) **1 :** exactly vertical or true **2 :** THOROUGH, COMPLETE ***syn*** see VERTICAL

plum·ba·go \ˌpləm-ˈbā-(ˌ)gō\ *n, pl* **-gos** [L *plumbagin-, plumbago* galena, fr. *plumbum*] (1747) **1** [NL, fr. L] **:** any of a genus (*Plumbago* of the family Plumbaginaceae, the plumbago family) of chiefly tropical herbs and shrubs with alternate leaves and spikes of showy flowers **2 :** GRAPHITE 1

plumb bob *n* (ca. 1840) **:** the metal bob of a plumb line

plumb·er \ˈplə-mər\ *n* [ME, fr. AF *plummer, plomner,* fr. L *plumbarius,* fr. *plumbum*] (15c) **1 :** a dealer or worker in lead **2 :** one who installs, repairs, and maintains piping, fittings, and fixtures involved in the distribution and use of water in a building **3 :** a person whose job is to prevent or put an end to leaks of sensitive information

plumber's helper *n* (1952) **:** PLUNGER d — called also *plumber's friend*

plumber's snake *n* (1938) **:** a long flexible rod or cable usu. of steel that is used to free clogged pipes

plumb·ing \ˈplə-miŋ\ *n* (1666) **1 :** the act of using a plumb **2 :** a plumber's occupation or trade **3 a :** the apparatus (as pipes and fixtures) concerned in the distribution and use of water in a building **b :** an internal system that resembles plumbing; *esp* **:** one consisting of conduits or channels for conveying fluids

plum·bism \ˈpləm-ˌbi-zəm\ *n* [L *plumbum* lead] (1876) **:** lead poisoning esp. when chronic

plumb line *n* (15c) **1 :** a line (as of cord) that has at one end a weight (as a plumb bob) and is used esp. to determine verticality **2 :** a line directed to the center of gravity of the earth **:** a vertical line

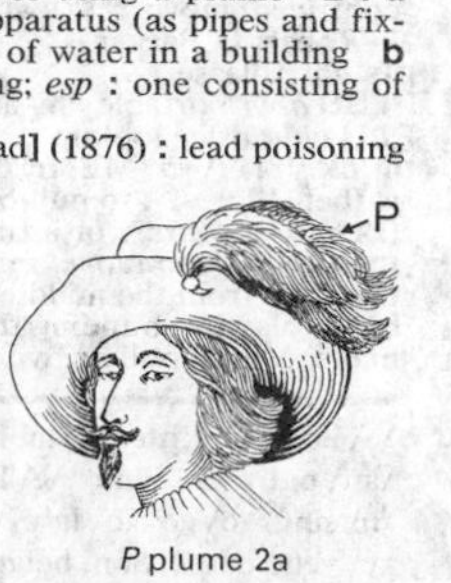

P plume 2a

[1]**plume** \ˈplüm\ *n* [ME, fr. AF, fr. L *pluma* small soft feather — more at FLEECE] (14c) **1 :** a feather of a bird: as **a :** a large conspicuous or showy feather **b :** CONTOUR FEATHER **c :** PLUMAGE **d :** a cluster of distinctive feathers **2 a :** material (as a feather, cluster of feathers, or a tuft of hair) worn as an ornament **b :** a token of honor or prowess **:** PRIZE **3 :** something resembling a feather (as in shape, appearance, or lightness): as **a :** a plumose appendage of a plant **b :** an elongated and usu. open and mobile column or band (as of smoke, exhaust gases, or blowing snow) **c :** an animal structure having a main shaft bearing many hairs or filamentous parts; *esp* **:** a full bushy tail **d :** any of several columns of molten rock rising from the earth's lower mantle that are theorized to drive tectonic plate movement and to underlie hot spots

[2]**plume** *vt* **plumed; plum·ing** (15c) **1 a :** to provide or deck with feathers **b :** to array showily **2 :** to indulge (oneself) in pride with an obvious or vain display of self-satisfaction **3** *of a bird* **a :** to preen and arrange the feathers of (itself) **b :** to preen and arrange (feathers)

plumed *adj* (15c) **:** provided with or adorned with or as if with a plume — often used in combination ⟨a white-*plumed* egret⟩

plume·let \ˈplüm-lət\ *n* (ca. 1847) **:** a small tuft or plume

plu·me·ria \plü-ˈmir-ē-ə\ *n* [NL, genus name, fr. Charles *Plumier* †1704 Fr. botanist] (1753) **:** FRANGIPANI

[1]**plum·met** \ˈplə-mət\ *n* [ME *plomet,* fr. AF *plumet, plomet,* fr. *plum* lead, lead weight — more at PLUMB] (14c) **:** PLUMB; *also* **:** PLUMB LINE

[2]**plummet** *vi* (1937) **1 :** to fall perpendicularly ⟨birds ~*ed* down⟩ **2 :** to drop sharply and abruptly ⟨prices ~*ed*⟩

plum·my \ˈplə-mē\ *adj* **plum·mi·er; -est** (1759) **1 a :** full of plums ⟨a rich ~ cake⟩ **b :** CHOICE, DESIRABLE ⟨got a ~ role in the movie⟩ **2 a :** having a plum color **b :** rich and mellow often to the point of affectation ⟨a ~ singing voice⟩

plu·mose \ˈplü-ˌmōs\ *adj* (ca. 1727) **1 :** having feathers or plumes **:** FEATHERED **2 :** FEATHERY ⟨~ setae⟩

[1]**plump** \ˈpləmp\ *vb* [ME] *vi* (14c) **1 :** to drop, sink, or come in contact suddenly or heavily ⟨~*ed* down in the chair⟩ **2 :** to favor or decide in favor of someone or something strongly or emphatically — used with *for* ~ *vt* **1 :** to drop, cast, or place suddenly or heavily **2 :** to give support and favorable publicity to

[2]**plump** *n* (15c) **:** a sudden plunge, fall, or blow; *also* **:** the sound made by a plump

[3]**plump** *adv* (1594) **1 :** with a sudden or heavy drop **2 a :** straight down **b :** straight ahead **3 :** without qualification **:** DIRECTLY ⟨~ out of luck⟩

[4]**plump** *n* [ME *plumpe*] (15c) *chiefly dial* **:** GROUP, FLOCK ⟨a ~ of ducks rose at the same time —H. D. Thoreau⟩

[5]**plump** *vb* [[6]*plump*] *vt* (1533) **:** to make plump ~ *vi* **:** to become plump

[6]**plump** *adj* [ME, dull, blunt, fr. MD *plomp*] (1569) **1 :** having a full rounded usu. pleasing form ⟨a ~ woman⟩ **2 :** AMPLE, ABUNDANT — **plump·ish** \ˈpləm-pish\ *adj*

plump·en \ˈpləm-pən\ *vb* (1687) **:** [5]PLUMP

[1]**plump·er** \ˈpləm-pər\ *n* [[5]*plump*] (1690) **:** an object carried in the mouth to fill out the cheeks

[2]**plumper** *n* [[1]*plump*] (ca. 1785) *chiefly Brit* **:** a vote for only one candidate when two or more are to be elected to the same office

[1]**plump·ly** \ˈpləm-plē\ *adv* (1611) **:** in a plump way ⟨a ~ pretty girl⟩

[2]**plumply** *adv* [[3]*plump*] (1786) **:** in a wholehearted manner and without hesitation or circumlocution **:** FORTHRIGHTLY

[1]**plump·ness** \ˈpləmp-nəs\ *n* (1545) **:** the quality or state of being plump

[2]**plumpness** *n* (1780) **:** freedom from hesitation or circumlocution

plum pudding *n* (1711) **:** a rich boiled or steamed pudding containing fruits and spices

plum tomato *n* (ca. 1900) **:** a small oblong tomato

plu·mule \ˈplü-(ˌ)myül\ *n* [NL *plumula,* fr. L, dim. of *pluma* small soft feather — more at FLEECE] (ca. 1741) **1 :** the primary bud of a plant embryo usu. situated at the apex of the hypocotyl and consisting of leaves and an epicotyl **2 :** a down feather

plumy \ˈplü-mē\ *adj* **plum·i·er; -est** (1582) **1 :** DOWNY **2 :** having or resembling plumes

[1]**plun·der** \ˈplən-dər\ *vb* **plun·dered; plun·der·ing** \-d(ə-)riŋ\ [G *plündern*] *vt* (1632) **1 a :** to take the goods of by force (as in war) **:** PILLAGE, SACK ⟨invaders ~*ed* the town⟩ **b :** to take by force or wrongfully **:** STEAL, LOOT ⟨~*ed* artifacts from the tomb⟩ **2 :** to make extensive use of as if by plundering **:** use or use up wrongfully ⟨~ the land⟩ ~ *vi* **:** to commit robbery or looting — **plun·der·er** \-dər-ər\ *n*

[2]**plunder** *n* (1643) **1 :** an act of plundering **:** PILLAGING **2 :** something taken by force, theft, or fraud **:** LOOT **3** *chiefly dial* **:** personal or household effects ***syn*** see SPOIL

plun·der·ous \-d(ə-)rəs\ *adj* (1845) **:** given to plundering

[1]**plunge** \ˈplənj\ *vb* **plunged; plung·ing** [ME, fr. AF *plunger,* fr. VL **plumbicare,* fr. L *plumbum* lead] *vt* (14c) **1 :** to cause to penetrate or enter quickly and forcibly into something ⟨*plunged* the dagger⟩ **2 :** to cause to enter a state or course of action usu. suddenly, unexpectedly, or violently ⟨*plunged* the nation into economic depression⟩ ~ *vi* **1 :** to thrust or cast oneself into or as if into water **2 a :** to become pitched or thrown headlong or violently forward and downward; *also* **:** to move oneself in such a manner ⟨*plunged* off the embankment⟩ **b :** to act with reckless haste **:** enter suddenly or unexpectedly ⟨*plunges* into project after project⟩ **c :** to bet or gamble heavily and recklessly **3 :** to descend or dip suddenly ⟨the stock's value *plunged*⟩

[2]**plunge** *n* (15c) **:** an act or instance of plunging **:** DIVE; *also* **:** SWIM

plung·er \ˈplən-jər\ *n* (1611) **:** one that plunges: as **a :** DIVER **b :** a reckless gambler or speculator **c** (1) **:** a sliding reciprocating piece driven by or against fluid pressure; *esp* **:** PISTON (2) **:** a piece with a motion like that of a ram or piston **d :** a rubber suction cup on a handle used to free plumbing traps and waste outlets of obstructions

plunk \ˈpləŋk\ *or* **plonk** \ˈpläŋk, ˈplȯŋk\ *vb* [imit.] *vt* (1805) **1 :** to pluck or hit so as to produce a quick, hollow, metallic, or harsh sound **2 :** to set down suddenly **:** PLUMP ~ *vi* **1 :** to make a plunking sound **2 :** to drop abruptly **:** DIVE **3 :** to come out in favor of someone or something **:** PLUMP — used with *for* — **plunk** *n* — **plunk·er** *n*

plunk down *vi* (1891) **:** to drop abruptly **:** settle into position ~ *vt* **1 a :** to put down usu. firmly or abruptly ⟨*plunked* the items *down* on the counter⟩ **b :** to settle (oneself) into position ⟨*plunked* himself *down* on the bench⟩ **2 :** to pay out ⟨reluctant to *plunk down* the money for a new car⟩

plu·per·fect \ˌplü-ˈpər-fikt\ *adj* [ME *pluperfyth,* modif. of LL *plusquamperfectus,* lit., more than perfect] (15c) **1 :** PAST PERFECT **2 :** utterly perfect or complete — **pluperfect** *n*

plu•ral \ˈplu̇r-əl\ *adj* [ME, fr. AF & L; AF *plurel,* fr. L *pluralis,* fr. *plur-, plus* more — more at PLUS] (14c) **1 :** of, relating to, or constituting a class of grammatical forms usu. used to denote more than one or in some languages more than two **2 :** relating to, consisting of, or containing more than one or more than one kind or class ⟨a ~ society⟩ — **plural** *n* — **plu•ral•ly** \-ə-lē\ *adv*

plu•ral•ism \ˈplu̇r-ə-ˌli-zəm\ *n* (1772) **1 :** the holding of two or more offices or positions (as benefices) at the same time **2 :** the quality or state of being plural **3 a :** a theory that there are more than one or more than two kinds of ultimate reality **b :** a theory that reality is composed of a plurality of entities **4 a :** a state of society in which members of diverse ethnic, racial, religious, or social groups maintain and develop their traditional culture or special interest within the confines of a common civilization **b :** a concept, doctrine, or policy advocating this state — **plu•ral•ist** \-list\ *adj or n* — **plu•ral•is•tic** \ˌplu̇r-ə-ˈlis-tik\ *adj* — **plu•ral•is•ti•cal•ly** \-ti-k(ə-)lē\ *adv*

plu•ral•i•ty \plu̇-ˈra-lə-tē\ *n, pl* **-ties** (14c) **1 a :** the state of being plural **b :** the state of being numerous **c :** a large number or quantity **2 :** PLURALISM 1; *also* **:** a benefice held by pluralism **3 a :** a number greater than another **b :** an excess of votes over those cast for an opposing candidate **c :** a number of votes cast for a candidate in a contest of more than two candidates that is greater than the number cast for any other candidate but not more than half the total votes cast

plu•ral•ize \ˈplu̇r-ə-ˌlīz\ *vt* **-ized; -iz•ing** (1803) **:** to make plural or express in the plural form — **plu•ral•i•za•tion** \ˌplu̇r-ə-lə-ˈzā-shən\ *n*

plu•rip•o•tent \plu̇-ˈri-pə-tənt\ *adj* [L *plur-, plus* more + E *potent*] (1916) **:** not fixed as to developmental potentialities; *esp* **:** capable of differentiating into one of many cell types ⟨~ stem cells⟩

[1]plus \ˈpləs\ *adj* [L, adv., more, fr. neut. of *plur-, plus,* adj.; akin to Gk *pleion* more, L *plenus* full — more at FULL] (1579) **1 :** algebraically positive **2 :** having, receiving, or being in addition to what is anticipated **3 a :** falling high in a specified range ⟨a grade of C ~⟩ **b :** greater than that specified **c :** possessing a specified quality to a high degree **4 :** electrically positive **5 :** relating to or being a particular one of the two mating types that are required for successful fertilization in sexual reproduction in some lower plantlike organisms (as a fungus)

[2]plus *n, pl* **plus•es** \ˈplə-səz\ *also* **plus•ses** (1654) **1 :** PLUS SIGN **2 :** an added quantity **3 :** a positive factor or quality **4 :** SURPLUS

[3]plus *prep* (1668) **1 :** increased by **:** with the addition of ⟨four ~ five⟩ ⟨principal ~ interest⟩ **2 :** BESIDES — used chiefly in speech and casual writing ⟨~ all this, as a sedative it has no equal —Groucho Marx⟩

[4]plus *conj* (ca. 1950) **1 :** AND ⟨eats alone, a hot beef sandwich ~ a BLT ~ apple pie —Garrison Keillor⟩ **2 :** in addition to which ⟨it's also pretty on my open shelves, ~ it smells good —Nikki Giovanni⟩
usage The preposition *plus* has long been used with a meaning equivalent to *and* (as in "two *plus* two"); people have come to use *plus* as a conjunction much like *and.* Sense 2 is considered to be an adverb by some. It is used chiefly in speech and in informal writing.

plus fours *n pl* (1920) **:** loose sports knickers made four inches longer than ordinary knickers

[1]plush \ˈpləsh\ *n* [MF *peluche*] (1594) **:** a fabric with an even pile longer and less dense than velvet pile

[2]plush *adj* (ca. 1645) **1 :** relating to, resembling, or made of plush **2 a :** notably luxurious **b :** RICH, FULL ⟨the ~ sound of his saxophone playing⟩ ⟨a ~, ripe wine⟩ — **plush•ly** *adv* — **plush•ness** *n*

plushy \ˈplə-shē\ *adj* **plush•i•er; -est** (1611) **1 :** having the texture of or covered with plush **2 :** LUXURIOUS, SHOWY — **plush•i•ness** *n*

plus/minus sign *n* (1971) **:** the sign ± used to indicate a quantity (as 2 in "the square root of 4 is ±2") taking on both an algebraically positive value and its negative and to indicate a plus or minus quantity (as 4 in "the population age was 30 ± 4 years") — called also *plus/minus symbol*

[1]plus or minus *adj* (1926) **:** indicating a quantity whose algebraically positive and negative values serve to bracket a range of values either alone or when added to and subtracted from a given number ⟨measured with an accuracy of *plus or minus* 3 feet⟩

[2]plus or minus *adv* (1849) **:** MORE OR LESS, APPROXIMATELY ⟨a dance for singles *plus or minus* age 30⟩

plus•sage \ˈplə-sij\ *n* (1924) **:** an additional amount

plus sign *n* (1841) **:** a sign + denoting addition or a positive quantity

plus–size \ˈpləs-ˈsīz\ *also* **plus–sized** \-ˈsīzd\ *adj* (1942) *of clothing* **:** extra large ⟨~ apparel⟩ — sometimes used of a person ⟨a ~ woman⟩

Plu•to \ˈplü-(ˌ)tō\ *n* [L *Pluton-, Pluto,* fr. Gk *Ploutōn*] (14c) **1 :** the Greek god of the underworld — compare DIS **2** [NL] **:** a dwarf planet occupying an orbit that crosses the orbit of Neptune
usage In 2006 the International Astronomical Union defined *planet* in such a way as to exclude Pluto, reclassifying it instead as a *dwarf planet.* Although discussion of the matter continues, the change has been widely accepted.

plu•toc•ra•cy \plü-ˈtä-krə-sē\ *n, pl* **-cies** [Gk *ploutokratia,* fr. *ploutos* wealth; akin to Gk *plein* to sail, float — more at FLOW] (1652) **1 :** government by the wealthy **2 :** a controlling class of the wealthy — **plu•to•crat** \ˈplü-tə-ˌkrat\ *n* — **plu•to•crat•ic** \ˌplü-tə-ˈkra-tik\ *adj* — **plu•to•crat•i•cal•ly** \-ti-k(ə-)lē\ *adv*

plu•ton \ˈplü-ˌtän\ *n* [prob. back-formation fr. *plutonic*] (1936) **:** a typically large body of intrusive igneous rock

plu•to•ni•an \plü-ˈtō-nē-ən\ *adj, often cap* (1667) **:** of, relating to, or characteristic of Pluto or the lower world **:** INFERNAL

plu•ton•ic \plü-ˈtä-nik\ *adj* [L *Pluton-, Pluto*] (1833) **1 :** formed by solidification of magma deep within the earth and crystalline throughout ⟨~ rock⟩ **2** *often cap* **:** PLUTONIAN

plu•to•ni•um \plü-ˈtō-nē-əm\ *n* [NL, fr. *Pluton-, Pluto,* the planet Pluto] (1942) **:** a radioactive metallic element similar chemically to uranium that is formed as the isotope 239 by decay of neptunium and found in minute quantities in pitchblende, that undergoes slow disintegration with the emission of an alpha particle to form uranium 235, and that is fissionable with slow neutrons to yield atomic energy — see ELEMENT table

[1]plu•vi•al \ˈplü-vē-əl\ *adj* [L *pluvialis,* fr. *pluvia* rain, fr. fem. of *pluvius* rainy, fr. *pluere* to rain — more at FLOW] (ca. 1656) **1 a :** of or relating to rain **b :** characterized by abundant rain **2** *of a geologic change* **:** resulting from the action of rain

[2]pluvial *n* (1929) **:** a prolonged period of wet climate

[1]ply \ˈplī\ *vb* **plied; ply•ing** [ME *plien,* short for *applien* to apply] *vt* (14c) **1 a :** to use or wield diligently ⟨busily ~*ing* his pen⟩ **b :** to practice or perform diligently ⟨~ a trade⟩ **2 :** to keep furnishing or supplying something to ⟨*plied* us with liquor⟩ **3 a :** to make a practice of rowing or sailing over or on ⟨the boat *plies* the river⟩ **b :** to go or travel regularly over, on, or through ⟨jets ~*ing* the skies⟩ ~ *vi* **1 :** to apply oneself steadily **2 :** to go or travel regularly

[2]ply *n, pl* **plies** [[3]*ply*] (1532) **1 a :** one of several layers (as of cloth) usu. sewn or laminated together **b :** one of the strands in a yarn **c :** one of the veneer sheets forming plywood **d :** a layer of a paper or cardboard **2 :** INCLINATION, BIAS

[3]ply *vt* **plied; ply•ing** [ME *plien* to fold, fr. AF *plier, pleier,* fr. L *plicare;* akin to OHG *flehtan* to braid, L *plectere,* Gk *plekein*] (ca. 1909) **:** to twist together ⟨~ two single yarns⟩

Plym•outh Rock \ˈpli-məth-\ *n* [*Plymouth Rock,* traditional site of Pilgrim landing in 1620] (1849) **:** any of a U.S. breed of medium-sized single-combed domestic chickens raised for eggs and meat

plyo•met•rics \ˌplī-ə-ˈme-triks\ *n pl but sing or pl in constr* [prob. irreg. fr. *plio-* + *-metrics* (as in *isometrics*)] (1981) **:** exercise involving repeated rapid stretching and contracting of muscles (as by jumping and rebounding) to increase muscle power — **plyo•met•ric** \-trik\ *adj*

ply•wood \ˈplī-ˌwu̇d\ *n* (1907) **:** a structural material consisting of sheets of wood glued or cemented together with the grains of adjacent layers arranged at right angles or at a wide angle

pm *abbr* **1** phase modulation **2** premium

Pm *symbol* promethium

PM *abbr* **1** paymaster **2** permanent magnet **3** postmaster **4** post meridiem — often not cap and often punctuated **5** postmortem **6** prime minister **7** provost marshal

PMB *abbr* private mailbox

PMDD *abbr* premenstrual dysphoric disorder

pmk *abbr* postmark

PMS \ˌpē-(ˌ)em-ˈes\ *n* (1976) **:** PREMENSTRUAL SYNDROME

pmt *abbr* payment

PN *abbr* promissory note

-pnea *or* **-pnoea** *n comb form* [NL, fr. Gk *-pnoia,* fr. *pnoia,* fr. *pnein* to breathe] **:** breath **:** breathing ⟨hyper*pnea*⟩ ⟨a*pnoea*⟩

pneum- *or* **pneumo-** *comb form* [NL, partly fr. Gk *pneum-* (fr. *pneuma*); partly fr. Gk *pneumōn* lung] **1 :** air **:** gas ⟨*pneumo*thorax⟩ **2 :** lung ⟨*pneumo*coniosis⟩ **3 :** respiration ⟨*pneumo*graph⟩ **4 :** pneumonia ⟨*pneumo*coccus⟩

pneu•ma \ˈnü-mə, ˈnyü-\ *n* [Gk] (1884) **:** SOUL, SPIRIT

pneumat- *or* **pneumato-** *comb form* [Gk, fr. *pneumat-, pneuma*] **1 :** air **:** vapor **:** gas ⟨*pneumato*lytic⟩ **2 :** respiration ⟨*pneumato*phore⟩

pneu•mat•ic \nu̇-ˈma-tik, nyu̇-\ *adj* [L *pneumaticus,* fr. Gk *pneumatikos,* fr. *pneumat-, pneuma* air, breath, spirit, fr. *pnein* to breathe — more at SNEEZE] (1659) **1 :** of, relating to, or using gas (as air or wind): **a :** moved or worked by air pressure **b (1) :** adapted for holding or inflated with compressed air **(2) :** having air-filled cavities **2 :** of or relating to the pneuma **:** SPIRITUAL **3 :** having a well-proportioned feminine figure; *esp* **:** having a full bust — **pneu•mat•i•cal•ly** \-ti-k(ə-)lē\ *adv* — **pneu•ma•tic•i•ty** \ˌnü-mə-ˈti-sə-tē, ˌnyü-\ *n*

pneu•ma•tol•o•gy \ˌnü-mə-ˈtä-lə-jē, ˌnyü-\ *n* [NL *pneumatologia,* fr. Gk *pneumat-, pneuma* + NL *-logia* -logy] (1678) **:** the study of spiritual beings or phenomena

pneu•ma•to•lyt•ic \ˌnü-mə-tə-ˈli-tik, ˌnyü-; (ˌ)n(y)ü-ˌma-\ *adj* [ISV] (1896) **:** formed or forming by hot vapors or superheated liquids under pressure — used esp. of minerals and ores

pneu•mat•o•phore \nu̇-ˈma-tə-ˌfȯr, nyu̇-\ *n* [ISV] (1859) **1 :** a muscular gas-containing sac that serves as a float on a siphonophore colony **2 :** a usu. partially exposed root of a wetland plant (as a mangrove) that functions esp. in the intake of oxygen from the atmosphere

pneu•mo•coc•cus \ˌnü-mə-ˈkä-kəs, ˌnyü-\ *n, pl* **-coc•ci** \-ˈkäk-ˌsī, -ˌsē; -ˈkä-ˌkī, -ˌkē\ [NL] (1890) **:** a bacterium (*Streptococcus pneumoniae*) that causes an acute pneumonia involving one or more lobes of the lung — **pneu•mo•coc•cal** \-ˈkä-kəl\ *adj*

pneu•mo•co•ni•o•sis \ˌnü-mō-ˌkō-nē-ˈō-səs, ˌnyü-\ *n, pl* **-o•ses** \-ˌsēz\ [NL, fr. *pneum-* + Gk *konis* dust — more at INCINERATE] (1881) **:** a disease of the lungs caused by the habitual inhalation of irritants (as mineral or metallic particles) — compare BLACK LUNG, SILICOSIS

Pneu•mo•cys•tis ca•ri•nii pneumonia \ˌnü-mə-ˈsis-təs-kə-ˈrī-nē-ˌē-, ˌnyü-\ *n* [NL *Pneumocystis carinii,* species name] (1964) **:** a pneumonia chiefly affecting immunocompromised individuals that is caused by a microorganism (*Pneumocystis carinii* syn. *P. jiroveci*), attacks esp. the interstitial and alveolar tissues of the lungs, and is characterized esp. by a nonproductive cough, shortness of breath, and fever — abbr. *PCP*

pneu•mo•graph \ˈnü-mə-ˌgraf, ˈnyü-\ *n* [ISV] (1878) **:** an instrument for recording thoracic movements or volume change during respiration

pneu•mo•nec•to•my \ˌnü-mə-ˈnek-tə-mē, ˌnyü-\ *n, pl* **-mies** [Gk *pneumōn* + ISV *-ectomy*] (1890) **:** excision of an entire lung or of one or more lobes of a lung

pneu•mo•nia \nu̇-ˈmō-nyə, nyu̇-\ *n* [NL, fr. Gk, fr. *pneumōn* lung, alter. of *pleumōn* — more at PULMONARY] (1603) **:** a disease of the lungs characterized esp. by inflammation and consolidation of lung tissue followed by resolution and by fever, chills, cough, and difficulty in breathing and that is caused esp. by infection

pneu•mon•ic \nu̇-ˈmä-nik, nyu̇-\ *adj* [NL *pneumonicus,* fr. Gk *pneumonikos,* fr. *pneumōn*] (1675) **1 :** of, relating to, or affecting the lungs ⟨~ plague⟩**:** PULMONIC, PULMONARY **2 :** of, relating to, or affected with pneumonia

pneu•mo•ni•tis \ˌnü-mə-ˈnī-təs, ˌnyü-\ *n* [NL, fr. Gk *pneumōn*] (ca. 1834) **:** inflammation of the lungs

pneu•mo•tho•rax \ˌnü-mə-ˈthȯr-ˌaks, ˌnyü-\ *n* [NL] (1821) **:** a condition in which air or other gas is present in the pleural cavity and which occurs spontaneously as a result of disease or injury of lung tissue, rupture of air-filled pulmonary cysts, or puncture of the chest wall or is induced as a therapeutic measure to collapse the lung

\ə\ **abut** \ᵊ\ **kitten, F table** \ər\ **further** \a\ **ash** \ā\ **ace** \ä\ **mop, mar** \au̇\ **out** \ch\ **chin** \e\ **bet** \ē\ **easy** \g\ **go** \i\ **hit** \ī\ **ice** \j\ **job** \ŋ\ **sing** \ō\ **go** \ȯ\ **law** \ȯi\ **boy** \th\ **thin** \t͟h\ **the** \ü\ **loot** \u̇\ **foot** \y\ **yet** \zh\ **vision, beige** \k̲, ⁿ, œ, ue, ʸ\ *see* Guide to Pronunciation

PnP *abbr* plug and play
pnxt *abbr* [L *pinxit*] he painted it; she painted it
po *abbr* [L *per os*] by mouth; orally
Po *symbol* polonium
PO *abbr* **1** petty officer **2** postal order **3** post office **4** purchase order
[1]**poach** \ˈpōch\ *vt* [ME *pocchen,* fr. MF *pocher,* fr. OF *poché* poached, lit., bagged, fr. *poche* bag, pocket — more at POUCH] (15c) : to cook in simmering liquid
[2]**poach** *vb* [MF *pocher,* of Gmc origin; akin to ME *poken* to poke] *vi* (1611) **1** : to encroach upon esp. for the purpose of taking something **2** : to trespass for the purpose of stealing game; *also* : to take game or fish illegally ~ *vt* **1** : to trespass on **2 a** : to take (game or fish) by illegal methods **b** : to appropriate (something) as one's own **c** : to attract (as an employee or customer) away from a competitor
[1]**poach·er** \ˈpō-chər\ *n* [[2]*poach*] (1614) **1** : one that trespasses or steals **2** : one who kills or takes wild animals (as game or fish) illegally
[2]**poacher** *n* [[1]*poach*] (1861) **1** : a covered pan containing a plate with depressions or shallow cups in each of which an egg can be cooked over steam rising from boiling water in the bottom of the pan **2** : a baking dish in which food (as fish) can be poached
POB *abbr* post office box
po·bla·no \pō-ˈblä-nō\ *n, pl* **-nos** [MexSp *(chile) poblano,* lit., chili pepper of Puebla (Mexico)] (1950) : a large usu. mild heart-shaped chili pepper esp. when fresh and dark green — compare ANCHO
po'·boy \ˈpō-ˌbȯi\ *also* **poor boy** *n* (1932) : SUBMARINE 2
po·chard \ˈpō-chərd\ *n* [origin unknown] (1552) : any of various rather heavy-bodied diving ducks (esp. genus *Aythya*) with a large head and with feet and legs placed far back under the body
[1]**pock** \ˈpäk\ *n* [ME *pokke,* fr. OE *pocc;* akin to MLG & MD *pocke* pock] (bef. 12c) : a pustule in an eruptive disease (as smallpox); *also* : a spot suggesting such a pustule
[2]**pock** *vt* (1841) : to mark with or as if with pocks : PIT
[1]**pock·et** \ˈpä-kət\ *n* [ME *poket,* fr. AF *poket, pochete,* dim. of *poke, pouche* bag — more at POUCH] (15c) **1 a** : a small bag carried by a person : PURSE **b** : a small bag that is sewed or inserted in a garment so that it is open at the top or side ⟨coat ~⟩ **2** : supply of money : MEANS **3** : RECEPTACLE, CONTAINER: as **a** : an opening at the corner or side of a billiard table **b** : a superficial pouch in some animals **4** : a small often isolated area or group ⟨~*s* of unemployment⟩: **a** : a cavity containing a deposit (as of gold, water, or gas) **b** : AIR POCKET **5** : a place for a batten made by sewing a strip on a sail **6 a** : BLIND ALLEY **b** : the position of a contestant in a race hemmed in by others **c** : an area formed by blockers from which a football quarterback attempts to pass **7** : the concave area at the base of the finger sections of a baseball glove or mitt in which the ball is normally caught — **pock·et·ful** \-ˌfu̇l\ *n* — **in one's pocket** : in one's control or possession — **in pocket** **1** : provided with funds **2** : in the position of having made a profit — **out of pocket** **1** : low on money or funds **2** : having suffered a loss **3** : from cash on hand
[2]**pocket** *vt* (1589) **1 a** : to put or enclose in or as if in one's pocket ⟨~*ed* the change⟩ **b** : to appropriate to one's own use : STEAL **c** : to refuse assent to (a bill) by a pocket veto **2** : to put up with : ACCEPT **3** : to set aside : SUPPRESS ⟨~*ed* his pride⟩ **4 a** : to hem in **b** : to drive (a ball) into a pocket of a pool table **5** : to cover or supply with pockets — **pock·et·able** \ˈpä-kə-tə-bəl\ *adj*
[3]**pocket** *adj* (1612) **1 a** : small enough to be carried in the pocket **b** : SMALL, MINIATURE ⟨a ~ park⟩ **2 a** : of or relating to money **b** : carried in or paid from one's own pocket
pocket battleship *n* (1930) : a small German battleship built so as to come within treaty limitations of tonnage and armament
pocket billiards *n pl but usu sing in constr* (1913) : POOL 2b
[1]**pock·et·book** \ˈpä-kət-ˌbu̇k\ *n* (1617) **1** *often* **pocket book** : a small esp. paperback book that can be carried in the pocket **2** : a flat typically leather folding case for money or personal papers that can be carried in a pocket or handbag **3 a** : PURSE **b** : HANDBAG 2 **4 a** : financial resources : INCOME **b** : economic interests
[2]**pocketbook** *adj* (1894) : relating to or involving economic interests
pocket borough *n* (1856) : an English constituency controlled before parliamentary reform by a single person or family
pocket edition *n* (1715) **1** : POCKETBOOK 1 **2** : a miniature form of something
pocket gopher *n* (1873) : GOPHER 2a
pock·et·knife \ˈpä-kət-ˌnīf\ *n* (1727) : a knife that has one or more blades that fold into the handle and that can be carried in the pocket
pocket money *n* (1632) : money for small personal expenses
pocket mouse *n* (1884) : any of various nocturnal burrowing rodents (family Heteromyidae) that resemble mice, live in arid parts of western No. America, and have long hind legs and tail and fur-lined cheek pouches
pock·et–size \ˈpä-kət-ˌsīz\ *also* **pock·et–sized** \-ˌsīzd\ *adj* (1907) **1** : of a size convenient for carrying in the pocket **2** : SMALL
pocket veto *n* (1842) : an indirect veto of a legislative bill by an executive through retention of the bill unsigned until after adjournment of the legislature — **pocket veto** *vt*
[1]**pock·mark** \ˈpäk-ˌmärk\ *n* (ca. 1673) : a mark, pit, or depressed scar caused by smallpox or acne; *also* : an imperfection or depression like a pockmark
[2]**pockmark** *vt* (1756) : to cover with or as if with pockmarks : PIT
pocky \ˈpä-kē\ *adj* (14c) : covered with pocks
po·co \ˈpō-(ˌ)kō, ˈpȯ-\ *adv* [It, little, fr. L *paucus* — more at FEW] (1724) : to a slight degree : SOMEWHAT — used to qualify a direction in music ⟨~ allegro⟩
po·co a po·co \ˈpō-kō-(ˌ)ä-ˈpō-(ˌ)kō, ˈpȯ-kō-(ˌ)ä-ˈpȯ-\ *adv* [It] (ca. 1854) : little by little : GRADUALLY — used as a direction in music
po·co·cu·ran·te \ˌpō-kō-kyu̇-ˈran-tē, -ku̇-\ *adj* [It *poco curante* caring little] (1815) : INDIFFERENT, NONCHALANT — **po·co·cu·ran·tism** \-ˈran-ˌti-zəm\ *n*
po·co·sin \pə-ˈkō-sᵊn\ *n* [prob. fr. Virginia or North Carolina Algonquian] (1634) : an upland swamp of the coastal plain of the southeastern U.S.
[1]**pod** \ˈpäd\ *n* [origin unknown] (1573) **1** : a bit socket in a brace **2** : a straight groove or channel in the barrel of an auger
[2]**pod** *n* [prob. alter. of *cod* bag — more at CODPIECE] (1688) **1** : a dry dehiscent pericarp or fruit that is composed of one or more carpels; *esp* : LEGUME **2 a** : an anatomical pouch **b** : a grasshopper egg case **3** : a tapered and roughly cylindrical body of ore or mineral **4** : a usu. protective container or housing: as **a** : a streamlined compartment (as for fuel) under the wings or fuselage of an aircraft **b** : a compartment (as for personnel, a power unit, or an instrument) on a ship or craft
[3]**pod** *vi* **pod·ded; pod·ding** (1734) : to produce pods
[4]**pod** *n* [origin unknown] (1832) : a number of animals (as whales) clustered together
POD *abbr* **1** payable on death **2** pay on delivery
-pod *n comb form* [Gk *-podos,* fr. *pod-, pous* foot — more at FOOT] : foot : part resembling a foot ⟨pleo*pod*⟩
po·dag·ra \pə-ˈda-grə\ *n* [ME, fr. L, fr. Gk, lit., foot trap, fr. *pod-, pous* + *agra* hunt, catch; prob. akin to Gk *agein* to drive, lead — more at AGENT] (14c) : a painful condition of the big toe caused by gout
pod·cast \ˈpäd-ˌkast\ *n* [*iPod,* trademark for a portable media player + broad*cast*] (2004) : a program (as of music or talk) made available in digital format for automatic download over the Internet — **podcast** *vb* — **pod·cast·er** *n*
pod corn *n* (1893) : corn of a variety (*Zea mays tunicata*) that has each individual kernel enclosed in a husk
po·de·sta \ˌpō-də-ˈstä\ *n* [It *podestà,* lit., power, fr. L *potestat-, potestas,* irreg. fr. *potis* able — more at POTENT] (1548) : a chief magistrate in a medieval Italian municipality
podgy \ˈpä-jē\ *adj* **podg·i·er; -est** [*podge* something pudgy] (1846) *chiefly Brit* : PUDGY
po·di·a·try \pə-ˈdī-ə-trē, pō-\ *n* [Gk *pod-, pous* + E *-iatry*] (1914) : the medical care and treatment of the human foot — called also *chiropody* — **po·di·at·ric** \ˌpō-dē-ˈa-trik\ *adj* — **po·di·a·trist** \pə-ˈdī-ə-trist, pō-\ *n*
po·di·um \ˈpō-dē-əm\ *n, pl* **podiums** *or* **po·dia** \-dē-ə\ [L — more at PEW] (1743) **1** : a low wall serving as a foundation or terrace wall: as **a** : one around the arena of an ancient amphitheater serving as a base for the tiers of seats **b** : the masonry under the stylobate of a temple **2 a** : a dais esp. for an orchestral conductor **b** : LECTERN
-podium *n comb form, pl* **-podia** [NL, fr. Gk *podion,* dim. of *pod-, pous* foot — more at FOOT] : foot : part resembling a foot ⟨pseudo*podium*⟩
podo·phyl·lin \ˌpä-də-ˈfi-lən\ *n* [ISV, fr. NL *Podophyllum*] (1851) : a resin obtained from podophyllum and used in medicine as a caustic
podo·phyl·lum \-ˈfi-ləm\ *n* [NL, fr. *Podophyllum,* genus of herbs including the mayapple] (1842) : the dried rhizome and rootlet of the mayapple that is used as a caustic or as a source of the more effective podophyllin
Po·dunk \ˈpō-ˌdəŋk\ *n* [*Podunk,* village in Mass. or locality in Conn.] (1846) : a small, unimportant, and isolated town
pod·zol *also* **pod·sol** \ˈpäd-ˌzȯl\ *n* [Russ] (1908) : any of a group of zonal soils that develop in a moist climate esp. under coniferous or mixed forest and have an organic mat and a thin organic-mineral layer above a light gray leached layer resting on a dark horizon that is marked by illuviation and enriched with amorphous clay — **pod·zol·ic** \päd-ˈzä-lik, -ˈzȯ-\ *adj*
pod·zol·i·za·tion *also* **pod·sol·i·za·tion** \ˌpäd-ˌzȯ-lə-ˈzā-shən\ *n* (1912) : a process of soil formation esp. in humid regions involving principally leaching of the upper layers with accumulation of material in lower layers and development of characteristic horizons; *specif* : the development of a podzol — **pod·zol·ize** \ˈpäd-ˌzȯ-ˌlīz\ *vb*
POE *abbr* **1** port of embarkation **2** port of entry
po·em \ˈpō-əm, -im, ˈpōm *also* ˈpȯ(-)im, ˈpō-ˌem\ *n* [MF *poeme,* fr. L *poema,* fr. Gk *poiēma,* fr. *poiein*] (15c) **1** : a composition in verse **2** : something suggesting a poem (as in expressiveness, lyricism, or formal grace) ⟨the house we stayed in . . . was itself a ~ —H. J. Laski⟩
po·e·sy \ˈpō-ə-zē, -sē\ *n, pl* **po·e·sies** [ME *poesie,* fr. MF, fr. L *poesis,* fr. Gk *poiēsis,* lit., creation, fr. *poiein*] (14c) **1 a** : a poem or body of poems **b** : POETRY **c** : artificial or sentimentalized poetic writing **2** : poetic inspiration
po·et \ˈpō-ət, -it *also* ˈpȯ(-)it\ *n* [ME, fr. AF *poete,* fr. L *poeta,* fr. Gk *poiētēs* maker, poet, fr. *poiein* to make; akin to Skt *cinoti* he gathers, heaps up] (14c) **1** : one who writes poetry : a maker of verses **2** : one (as a creative artist) of great imaginative and expressive capabilities and special sensitivity to the medium
po·et·as·ter \ˈpō-ə-ˌtas-tər\ *n* [NL, fr. L *poeta* + *-aster* -aster] (1599) : an inferior poet
po·et·ess \ˈpō-ə-təs, ˈpō-i- *also* ˈpȯ(-)i-\ *n* (1530) : a girl or woman who is a poet
po·et·ic \pō-ˈe-tik\ *adj* (1530) **1 a** : of, relating to, or characteristic of poets or poetry **b** : given to writing poetry **2** : written in verse **3** : having or expressing the qualities of poetry (as though aesthetic or emotional impact) ⟨her ~ beauty⟩
po·et·i·cal \-ti-kəl\ *adj* (14c) **1** : POETIC **2** : being beyond or above the truth of history or nature : IDEALIZED ⟨had ~ ideas about love⟩ — **po·et·i·cal·ly** \-k(ə-)lē\ *adv* — **po·et·i·cal·ness** \-ti-kəl-nəs\ *n*
po·et·i·cism \pō-ˈe-tə-ˌsi-zəm\ *n* (1926) : an archaic, trite, or strained expression in poetry
po·et·i·cize \-ˌsīz\ *vt* **-cized; -ciz·ing** (1804) : to give a poetic quality to
poetic justice *n* (ca. 1890) : an outcome in which vice is punished and virtue rewarded usu. in a manner peculiarly or ironically appropriate
poetic license *n* (1819) : LICENSE 4
po·et·ics \pō-ˈe-tiks\ *n pl but sing or pl in constr* (ca. 1741) **1 a** : a treatise on poetry or aesthetics **b** *also* **po·et·ic** \-tik\ : poetic theory or practice; *also* : a particular theory of poetry or sometimes other literary forms ⟨a feminist ~⟩ **2** : poetic feelings or utterances
po·et·ize \ˈpō-ə-ˌtīz\ *vb* **-ized; -iz·ing** *vi* (1581) : to compose poetry ~ *vt* : POETICIZE — **po·et·iz·er** *n*
poet laureate *n, pl* **poets laureate** *or* **poet laureates** (15c) **1** : a poet honored for achievement **2 a** : a poet appointed for life by an English sovereign as a member of the royal household and formerly expected to compose poems for court and national occasions **b** : a poet appointed annually by the U.S. Library of Congress as a consultant and typically involved in the promotion of poetry **3** : one regarded by a country or region as its most eminent or representative poet
po·et·ry \ˈpō-ə-trē, -i-trē *also* ˈpȯ(-)i-trē\ *n* (14c) **1 a** : metrical writing : VERSE **b** : the productions of a poet : POEMS **2** : writing that formulates a concentrated imaginative awareness of experience in language chosen and arranged to create a specific emotional response

through meaning, sound, and rhythm **3 a :** something likened to poetry esp. in beauty of expression **b :** poetic quality or aspect ⟨the ~ of dance⟩

po–faced \ˈpō-ˌfāst\ *adj* [perh. fr. *po* chamber pot, toilet, fr. F *pot* pot] (1934) *Brit* **:** having an assumed solemn, serious, or earnest expression or manner **:** piously or hypocritically solemn

pog·o·nip \ˈpä-gə-ˌnip\ *n* [Shoshone *payinappih* cloud] (1865) **:** a dense winter fog containing frozen particles that is formed in deep mountain valleys of the western U.S.

po·go·noph·o·ran \ˌpō-gə-ˈnä-fə-rən\ *n* [NL *Pogonophora,* fr. Gk *pōgōnophora,* neut. pl. of *pōgōnophoros* wearing a beard, fr. *pōgōn* beard + *-phoros* -phore] (1963) **:** any of a phylum (Pogonophora) of marine wormlike animals of uncertain systematic relationships that live in chitinous tubes on the floor of deep seas, have obscure segmentation, and lack a mouth and digestive tract — **pogonophoran** *adj*

po·go stick \ˈpō-(ˌ)gō-\ *n* [fr. *Pogo,* a trademark] (1921) **:** a pole with a strong spring at the bottom and two footrests on which a person stands and moves along with a series of jumps

[1]**po·grom** \ˈpō-grəm, ˈpä-; pō-ˈgräm, pə-\ *n* [Yiddish, fr. Russ, lit., devastation] (1903) **:** an organized massacre of helpless people; *specif* **:** such a massacre of Jews

[2]**pogrom** *vt* (1915) **:** to massacre or destroy in a pogrom

po·grom·ist \ˈpō-grə-mist, ˈpä-; pō-ˈgrä-, pə-\ *n* (1907) **:** one who organizes or takes part in a pogrom

po·gy \ˈpō-gē\ *n, pl* **pogies** [by shortening & alter. fr. *poghaden,* perh. fr. Eastern Abenaki] (ca. 1847) **:** MENHADEN

poi \ˈpȯi\ *n, pl* **poi** *or* **pois** [Hawaiian & Samoan] (1782) **:** a Hawaiian food of taro root cooked, pounded, and kneaded to a paste and often allowed to ferment

-poiesis *n comb form, pl* **-poieses** [NL, fr. Gk *poiēsis* creation — more at POESY] **:** production **:** formation ⟨hemato*poiesis*⟩

-poietic *adj comb form* [Gk *poiētikos* creative, fr. *poiētēs* maker — more at POET] **:** productive **:** formative ⟨hemato*poietic*⟩

poi·gnance \ˈpȯi-nyən(t)s *sometimes* ˈpȯi(g)-nən(t)s\ *n* (1769) **:** POIGNANCY

poi·gnan·cy \ˈpȯi-nyən(t)-sē *sometimes* ˈpȯi(g)-nən(t)-sē\ *n, pl* **-cies** (1730) **1 :** the quality or state of being poignant **2 :** an instance of poignancy

poi·gnant \ˈpȯi-nyənt *sometimes* ˈpȯi(g)-nənt\ *adj* [ME *poynaunt,* fr. AF *poinant, poignant,* prp. of *poindre* to prick, sting, fr. L *pungere* — more at PUNGENT] (14c) **1 :** pungently pervasive ⟨a ~ perfume⟩ **2 a** (1) **:** painfully affecting the feelings **:** PIERCING (2) **:** deeply affecting **:** TOUCHING **b :** designed to make an impression **:** CUTTING ⟨~ satire⟩ **3 a :** pleasurably stimulating **b :** being to the point **:** APT ***syn*** see PUNGENT, MOVING — **poi·gnant·ly** *adv*

poi·ki·lo·therm \pȯi-ˈkē-lə-ˌthərm, -ˈki-\ *n* [Gk *poikilos* variegated + ISV *-therm* — more at PAINT] (1920) **:** an organism (as a frog) with a variable body temperature that tends to fluctuate with and is similar to or slightly higher than the temperature of its environment **:** a cold-blooded organism — **poi·ki·lo·ther·mic** \ˌpȯi-kə-lō-ˈthər-mik\ *adj*

poi·lu \pwäl-ˈyü, pwä-ˈlü; ˈpwäl-ˌyü, ˈpwä-ˌlü; pwä-ˈlᵫ\ *n* [F, fr. *poilu* hairy, fr. MF, fr. *poil* hair, fr. OF *peil,* L *pilus*] (1914) **:** a French soldier; *esp* **:** a front-line soldier in World War I

poin·ci·ana \ˌpȯin(t)-sē-ˈa-nə, ˌp(w)än(t)-\ *n* [NL, fr. De *Poinci,* 17th cent. governor of part of the French West Indies] (1731) **:** any of several ornamental tropical trees or shrubs (genera *Caesalpinia* and *Delonix*) of the legume family formerly placed in their own genus (*Poinciana*) — compare ROYAL POINCIANA

poin·set·tia \pȯin-ˈse-tē-ə, ÷pȯint-, ÷-ˈse-tə\ *n* [NL, fr. Joel R. *Poinsett* †1851 Am. diplomat] (1836) **:** any of several spurges (genus *Euphorbia*) with flower clusters subtended by showy involucral bracts; *esp* **:** a showy Mexican and Central American plant (*E. pulcherrima*) with tapering usu. scarlet bracts that suggest petals and surround small yellow flowers

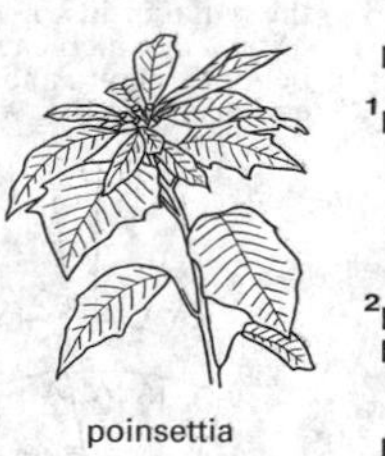

poinsettia

[1]**point** \ˈpȯint\ *n* [ME, partly fr. AF, prick, dot, moment, fr. L *punctum,* fr. neut. of *punctus,* pp. of *pungere* to prick; partly fr. AF *pointe* sharp end, fr. VL **puncta,* fr. L, fem. of *punctus,* pp. — more at PUNGENT] (13c) **1 a** (1) **:** an individual detail **:** ITEM (2) **:** a distinguishing detail ⟨tact is one of her strong ~*s*⟩ **b :** the most important essential in a discussion or matter ⟨missed the whole ~ of the joke⟩ **c :** COGENCY **2** *obs* **:** physical condition **3 :** an end or object to be achieved **:** PURPOSE ⟨did not see what ~ there was in continuing the discussion⟩ **4 a :** a geometric element that has zero dimensions and a location determinable by an ordered set of coordinates **b** (1) **:** a narrowly localized place having a precisely indicated position ⟨walked to a ~ 50 yards north of the building⟩ (2) **:** a particular place **:** LOCALITY ⟨have come from distant ~*s*⟩ **c** (1) **:** an exact moment ⟨at this ~ I was interrupted⟩ (2) **:** a time interval immediately before something indicated **:** VERGE ⟨at the ~ of death⟩ **d** (1) **:** a particular step, stage, or degree in development ⟨had reached the ~ where nothing seemed to matter anymore⟩ (2) **:** a definite position in a scale **5 a :** the terminal usu. sharp or narrowly rounded part of something **:** TIP **b :** a weapon or tool having such a part and used for stabbing or piercing: as (1) **:** ARROWHEAD (2) **:** SPEARHEAD **c** (1) **:** the contact or discharge extremity of an electric device (as a spark plug or distributor) (2) *chiefly Brit* **:** an electric outlet **6 a :** a projecting usu. tapering piece of land or a sharp prominence **b** (1) **:** the tip of a projecting body part (2) **:** TINE 2 (3) *pl* **:** the extremities or markings of the extremities of an animal esp. when of a color differing from the rest of the body **c :** a railroad switch **d :** the head of the bow of a stringed instrument **7 :** a short musical phrase; *esp* **:** a phrase in contrapuntal music **8 a :** a very small mark **b** (1) **:** PUNCTUATION MARK; *esp* **:** PERIOD 5a (1) (2) **:** DECIMAL POINT **9 :** a lace for tying parts of a garment together used esp. in the 16th and 17th centuries **10 :** one of usu. 11 divisions of a heraldic shield that determines the position of a charge **11 a :** one of the 32 equidistant spots of a compass card for indicating direction **b :** the difference of 11¼ degrees between two such successive points **c :** a direction indicated by a compass point ⟨from all ~*s* of the compass⟩ **12 :** a small detachment ahead of an advance guard or behind a rear guard **13 a :** NEEDLEPOINT 1 **b :** lace made with a bobbin **14 :** one of 12 spaces marked off on each side of a backgammon board **15 :** a unit of measurement: as **a** (1) **:** a unit of counting in the scoring of a game or contest (2) **:** a unit used in evaluating the strength of a bridge hand **b :** a unit of academic credit **c** (1) **:** a unit used in quoting prices (as of stocks, bonds, and commodities) (2) *pl* **:** a percentage of the face value of a loan often added as a placement fee or service charge (3) **:** a percentage of the profits of a business venture (as a motion-picture production) **d :** a unit of about ¹⁄₇₂ inch used esp. to measure the size of type **16 :** the action of pointing: as **a :** the rigidly intent attitude of a hunting dog marking game for a gunner **b :** the action in dancing of extending one leg and arching the foot so that only the tips of the toes touch the floor **17 :** a position of a player in various games (as lacrosse); *also* **:** the player of such a position **18 :** a number thrown on the first roll of the dice in craps which the player attempts to repeat before throwing a seven — compare MISSOUT, PASS 13 **19 :** credit accruing from creating a good impression ⟨scored ~*s* for hard work⟩ — **beside the point :** IRRELEVANT — **in point of :** with regard to **:** in the matter of ⟨*in point of* law⟩ ⟨*in point of* fact⟩ — **to the point :** RELEVANT, PERTINENT ⟨a suggestion that was *to the point*⟩

[2]**point** *vt* (14c) **1 a :** to furnish with a point **:** SHARPEN ⟨~*ing* a pencil with a knife⟩ **b :** to give added force, emphasis, or piquancy to ⟨~ up a remark⟩ **2 :** to scratch out the old mortar from the joints of (as a brick wall) and fill in with new material **3 a** (1) **:** to mark the pauses or grammatical divisions in **:** PUNCTUATE (2) **:** to separate (a decimal fraction) from an integer by a decimal point — usu. used with *off* **b :** to mark (as Hebrew words) with diacritics (as vowel points) **4 a** (1) **:** to indicate the position or direction of esp. by extending a finger ⟨~ the way home⟩ (2) **:** to direct someone's attention to ⟨~ the way to new knowledge —Elizabeth Hall⟩ — usu. used with *out* or *up* ⟨~ out a mistake⟩ ⟨~*s* up the difference⟩ **b** *of a hunting dog* **:** to indicate the presence and place of (game) by a point **5 a :** to cause to be turned in a particular direction ⟨~ a gun⟩ ⟨~*ed* the boat upstream⟩ **b :** to extend (a leg) and arch (the foot) in executing a point in dancing ~ *vi* **1 a :** to indicate the fact or probability of something specified ⟨everything ~*s* to a bright future⟩ **b :** to indicate the position or direction of something esp. by extending a finger ⟨~ at the map⟩ **c :** to direct attention ⟨can ~ with pride to their own traditions⟩ **d :** to point game ⟨a dog that ~*s* well⟩ **2 a :** to lie extended, aimed, or turned in a particular direction ⟨a directional arrow that ~*ed* to the north⟩ **b :** to execute a point in dancing **3** *of a ship* **:** to sail close to the wind **4 :** to train for a particular contest

point–and–click *adj* (1983) **:** of, relating to, or being a computer interface that allows the activation of a file or function by selection with a pointing device (as a mouse)

point–and–shoot *adj* (1975) **:** having or using preset or automatically adjusted controls (as for focus or shutter speed) ⟨a ~ camera⟩

point–blank \ˈpȯint-ˈblaŋk\ *adj* (1591) **1 a :** marked by no appreciable drop below initial horizontal line of flight **b :** so close to a target that a missile fired will travel in a straight line to the mark **2 :** DIRECT, BLUNT ⟨a ~ refusal⟩ — **point–blank** *adv*

point count *n* (1950) **:** a method of evaluating the strength of a hand in bridge by counting points for each high card and usu. for long or short suits; *also* **:** the value of a hand so evaluated

point d'ap·pui \ˌpwa^{n}(n)-da-ˈpwē\ *n, pl* **points d'appui** *same*\ [F, lit., point of support] (1819) **:** FOUNDATION, BASE

point–de·vice \ˌpȯint-di-ˈvīs\ *adj* [ME *at point devis* at a fixed point] (1526) *archaic* **:** marked by punctilious attention to detail **:** METICULOUS — **point–device** *adv, archaic*

pointe \ˈpwa^{n}(n)t\ *n* [F *pointe* (*du pied*), lit., tiptoe] (1846) **:** a ballet position in which the body is balanced on the extreme tip of the toe

[1]**point·ed** \ˈpȯin-təd\ *adj* (14c) **1 a :** having a point **b :** being an arch with a pointed crown; *also* **:** marked by the use of a pointed arch ⟨~ architecture⟩ **2 a :** being to the point **:** PERTINENT **b :** aimed at a particular person or group **3 :** CONSPICUOUS, MARKED ⟨~ indifference⟩ **4 :** having points that contrast in color with the basic coat color ⟨a ~ cat⟩ — **point·ed·ly** *adv* — **point·ed·ness** *n*

[2]**pointed** *adj* [short for *appointed*] (1523) *obs* **:** SET, FIXED

poin·telle \ˌpȯin-ˈtel\ *n* [perh. fr. [1]*point* + *-elle* (as in *dentelle* lace)] (1953) **:** an openwork design (as in knitted fabric) typically in the shape of chevrons; *also* **:** a fabric with this design

point·er \ˈpȯin-tər\ *n* (1574) **1 a** *pl, cap* **:** the two stars in the Big Dipper a line through which points to the North Star **b :** one that points out; *esp* **:** a rod used to direct attention **c :** a computer memory address that contains another address (as of desired data) **2 :** a large strong slender smooth-haired gundog that hunts by scent and indicates the presence of game by pointing **3 :** one that furnishes with points **4 :** a useful suggestion or hint **:** TIP

point estimate *n* (1966) **:** the single value assigned to a parameter in point estimation

point estimation *n* (1962) **:** estimation in which a single value is assigned to a parameter

point guard *n* (1970) **:** a guard in basketball who is chiefly responsible for running the offense

poin·til·lism \ˈpwa^{n}(n)-tē-ˌyi-zəm, ˈpȯin-tə-ˌli-zəm\ *n, often cap* [F *pointillisme,* fr. *pointiller* to stipple, fr. *point* spot, fr. OF — more at POINT] (1901) **:** the theory or practice in art of applying small strokes or dots of color to a surface so that from a distance they blend together — **poin·til·list** \ˌpwa^{n}(n)-tē-ˈyēst, ˈpȯin-tə-list\ *n*

poin·til·lis·tic \ˌpwa^{n}(n)-tē-ˈyis-tik, ˌpȯin-tə-ˈlis-\ *also* **poin·til·list** \ˌpwa^{n}(n)-tē-ˈyēst, ˈpȯin-tə-list\ *adj* (1922) **1 :** composed of many discrete details or parts **2 :** of, relating to, or characteristic of pointillism or pointillists

point lace *n* (1672) **:** NEEDLEPOINT 1

point·less \ˈpȯint-ləs\ *adj* (1582) **1 :** devoid of meaning **:** SENSELESS ⟨a ~ remark⟩ **2 :** devoid of effectiveness **:** FLAT ⟨~ attempts to be funny⟩ — **point·less·ly** *adv* — **point·less·ness** *n*

point man *n* (1944) **1 :** a soldier who goes ahead of a patrol **2 :** one who is in the forefront; *esp* **:** a principal spokesman or advocate ⟨the *point man* for the President's economic policy⟩
point mutation *n* (1925) **:** a gene mutation involving the substitution, addition, or deletion of a single nucleotide base
point of accumulation (1927) **:** LIMIT POINT
point of departure (1857) **:** a starting point esp. in a discussion
point of honor (1592) **:** a matter seriously affecting one's honor
point of inflection (1743) **:** INFLECTION POINT
point of no return (1941) **1 :** the point in the flight of an aircraft beyond which the remaining fuel will be insufficient for a return to the starting point with the result that the craft must proceed **2 :** a critical point at which turning back or reversal is not possible
point–of–purchase *adj* (1939) **:** of or relating to the place (as a supermarket aisle) where a decision to purchase is made ⟨~ displays⟩
point–of–service *adj* (1987) **:** of, relating to, or being a health-care insurance plan that allows enrollees to seek care from a physician affiliated with the service provider at a fixed co-payment or to choose a nonaffiliated physician and pay more — abbr. *POS*
point of view (1720) **:** a position or perspective from which something is considered or evaluated **:** STANDPOINT
point person *n* (1977) **:** POINT MAN 2
point set topology *n* (1957) **:** a branch of topology concerned with the properties and theory of topological spaces and metric spaces developed with emphasis on set theory
point–shav·ing \ˈpȯint-ˌshā-viŋ\ *n, often attrib* (1975) **:** an attempt (as by a member of the team favored to win) to influence the final score of a game so that the predicted winner wins by less than the point spread
point source *n* (1903) **1 :** a source of radiation (as light) that is concentrated at a point and considered as having no spatial extension **2 :** an identifiable confined source (as a smokestack or wastewater treatment plant) from which a pollutant is discharged or emitted
point spread *n* (ca. 1949) **:** the number of points by which an oddsmaker expects a favorite to defeat an underdog
point–to–point *n* (1898) **:** a cross-country steeplechase
pointy \ˈpȯin-tē\ *adj* **point·i·er; -est** (1644) **1 :** coming to a rather sharp point **2 :** having parts that stick out sharply here and there
pointy–head \ˈpȯin-tē-ˌhed\ *n* (1968) *usu disparaging* **:** INTELLECTUAL — **pointy–head·ed** \-ˌhe-dəd\ *adj*
[1]**poise** \ˈpȯiz\ *vb* **poised; pois·ing** [ME, to weigh, ponder, fr. AF *peiser, poiser,* fr. L *pensare* — more at PENSIVE] *vt* (1598) **1 a :** BALANCE; *esp* **:** to hold or carry in equilibrium ⟨carried a water jar *poised* on her head⟩ **b :** to hold supported or suspended without motion in a steady position ⟨*poised* her fork and gave her guest a knowing look —Louis Bromfield⟩ **2 :** to hold or carry (the head) in a particular way **3 :** to put into readiness **:** BRACE ~ *vi* **1 :** to become drawn up into readiness **2 :** HOVER
[2]**poise** *n* [ME *poyse* weight, heaviness, fr. AF *peis, pois,* fr. L *pensum,* fr. neut. of *pensus,* pp. of *pendere* to weigh — more at PENDANT] (1649) **1 :** a stably balanced state **:** EQUILIBRIUM ⟨a ~ between widely divergent impulses —F. R. Leavis⟩ **2 a :** easy self-possessed assurance of manner **:** gracious tact in coping or handling; *also* **:** the pleasantly tranquil interaction between persons of poise ⟨no angry outbursts marred the ~ of the meeting⟩ **b :** a particular way of carrying oneself **:** BEARING, CARRIAGE ***syn*** see TACT
[3]**poise** \ˈpwäz\ *n* [F, fr. Jean Louis Marie *Poiseuille* †1869 Fr. physician and anatomist] (1913) **:** a centimeter-gram-second unit of viscosity equal to the viscosity of a fluid that would require a shearing force of one dyne to impart to a one-square-centimeter area of an arbitrary layer of the fluid a velocity of one centimeter per second relative to another layer separated from the first by a distance of one centimeter
poised *adj* (1616) **:** having poise: **a :** marked by balance or equilibrium **b :** marked by easy composure of manner or bearing
poi·sha \ˈpȯi-shə\ *n, pl* **poisha** [Bengali *poisa,* prob. fr. Hindi *paisā*] (ca. 1976) **:** the paisa of Bangladesh
[1]**poi·son** \ˈpȯi-z^{ə}n\ *n* [ME, fr. AF *poisun* drink, potion, poison, fr. L *potion-, potio* drink — more at POTION] (13c) **1 a :** a substance that through its chemical action usu. kills, injures, or impairs an organism **b** (1) **:** something destructive or harmful (2) **:** an object of aversion or abhorrence **2 :** a substance that inhibits the activity of another substance or the course of a reaction or process ⟨a catalyst ~⟩
[2]**poison** *vt* **poi·soned; poi·son·ing** \ˈpȯiz-niŋ, ˈpȯi-z^{ə}n-iŋ\ (14c) **1 a :** to injure or kill with poison **b :** to treat, taint, or impregnate with or as if with poison **2 :** to exert a baneful influence on **:** CORRUPT ⟨~*ed* their minds⟩ **3 :** to inhibit the activity, course, or occurrence of ⟨on the night when he ~*ed* my rest —Charles Dickens⟩ — **poi·son·er** \ˈpȯiz-nər, ˈpȯi-z^{ə}n-ər\ *n*
[3]**poison** *adj* (ca. 1520) **1 :** POISONOUS, VENOMOUS ⟨a ~ plant⟩ ⟨a ~ tongue⟩ **2 :** impregnated with poison **:** POISONED ⟨a ~ arrow⟩
poison dart frog *n* (1968) **:** any of several small brightly colored frogs (family Dendrobatidae) of tropical Central and So. America that produce poisonous secretions sometimes used by native peoples to poison dart or arrow tips — called also *poison arrow frog*
poison gas *n* (1915) **:** a poisonous gas or a liquid or a solid giving off poisonous vapors designed (as in chemical warfare) to kill, injure, or disable by inhalation or contact
poison hemlock *n* (ca. 1818) **:** a large European biennial poisonous herb (*Conium maculatum*) of the carrot family that is naturalized in the U.S. and has finely divided leaves and small white flowers — compare WATER HEMLOCK
poison ivy *n* (1784) **1 a :** a climbing plant (*Toxicodendron radicans* syn. *Rhus radicans*) of the cashew family that is esp. common in the eastern and central U.S., that has ternate leaves, greenish flowers, and white berries, and that produces an acutely irritating oil causing a usu. intensely itching skin rash **b :** any of several plants closely related to poison ivy **2 :** a skin rash caused by poison ivy
poison oak *n* (1743) **1 :** any of several plants related to poison ivy and producing an oil with similar irritating properties: as **a :** a bushy plant (*Toxicodendron diversilobum* syn. *Rhus diversiloba*) of the Pacific coast **b :** a bushy plant (*Toxicodendron toxicarium* syn. *Rhus toxicodendron*) chiefly of the southeastern U.S. **2 :** POISON IVY 1a
poi·son·ous \ˈpȯiz-nəs, ˈpȯi-z^{ə}n-əs\ *adj* (1565) **1 :** DESTRUCTIVE, HARMFUL **2 :** having the properties or effects of poison **:** VENOMOUS **3 :** SPITEFUL, MALICIOUS — **poi·son·ous·ly** *adv*
poison–pen *adj* (1914) **:** written with malice and spite and usu. anonymously ⟨a ~ letter⟩
poison pill *n* (1983) **:** a financial tactic or provision used by a company to make an unwanted takeover prohibitively expensive or less desirable
poison sumac *n* (1817) **:** a swamp shrub (*Toxicodendron vernix* syn. *Rhus vernix*) chiefly of the eastern U.S. and Canada that has pinnate leaves, greenish flowers, and greenish white berries and produces an irritating oil — called also *poison dogwood*
poi·son·wood \ˈpȯi-z^{ə}n-ˌwu̇d\ *n* (1721) **:** a tree (*Metopium toxiferum*) of the cashew family that is native to Florida and the West Indies and has compound leaves, greenish paniculate flowers, and orange-yellow fruits and produces a severely irritating sap
Pois·son distribution \pwä-ˈsō^{n}-\ *n* [Siméon D. *Poisson* †1840 Fr. mathematician] (1922) **:** a probability density function that is often used as a mathematical model of the number of outcomes obtained in a suitable interval of time and space, that has its mean equal to its variance, that is used as an approximation to the binomial distribution, and that has the form

$$f(x) = \frac{e^{-\mu}\mu^{x}}{x!} \text{ where } \mu$$

is the mean and x takes on nonnegative integral values
Poisson's ratio *n* [S. *Poisson*] (1886) **:** the ratio of transverse to longitudinal strain in a material under tension
[1]**poke** \ˈpōk\ *n* [ME, fr. AF — more at POCKET] (13c) **1** *chiefly Southern & Midland* **:** BAG, SACK **2 a :** WALLET **b :** PURSE
[2]**poke** *vb* **poked; pok·ing** [ME; akin to MD *poken* to poke] *vt* (14c) **1 a** (1) **:** PROD, JAB ⟨*poked* him in the ribs⟩ (2) **:** to urge or stir by prodding or jabbing ⟨*poked* and scolded by the old folks —Upton Sinclair⟩ (3) **:** to cause to prod **:** THRUST ⟨*poked* a stick at the snake⟩ **b** (1) **:** PIERCE, STAB (2) **:** to produce by or as if by piercing, stabbing, or jabbing ⟨~ a hole⟩ ⟨*poked* holes in his heavily footnoted argument —David Stoll⟩ **c** (1) **:** HIT, PUNCH ⟨*poked* him in the nose⟩ (2) **:** to deliver (a blow) with the fist (3) **:** to hit (a blooper) in baseball **2 a :** to cause to project ⟨*poked* her head out of the window⟩ **b :** to make (one's way) by poking ⟨*poked* his way through the ruins⟩ **c :** to interpose or interject in a meddlesome manner ⟨asked him not to ~ his nose into other people's business⟩ ~ *vi* **1 a :** to make a prodding, jabbing, or thrusting movement esp. repeatedly **b :** to strike out at something **2 a :** to look about or through something without system **:** RUMMAGE ⟨*poking* around in the attic⟩ **b :** MEDDLE **3 :** to move or act slowly or aimlessly ⟨just *poked* around and didn't accomplish much⟩ **4 :** to become stuck out or forward **:** PROTRUDE — **poke fun at :** RIDICULE, MOCK
[3]**poke** *n* (ca. 1796) **1 a :** a quick thrust **:** JAB **b :** a blow with the fist **:** PUNCH **2 :** a projecting brim on the front of a woman's bonnet **3 :** a cutting remark **:** DIG
[4]**poke** *n* [perh. modif. of Virginia Algonquian *pocone, poughkone* puccoon] (1708) **:** POKEWEED
poke·ber·ry \ˈpōk-ˌber-ē\ *n* (1774) **:** the berry of the pokeweed; *also* **:** POKEWEED
[1]**pok·er** \ˈpō-kər\ *n* (1534) **:** one that pokes; *esp* **:** a metal rod for stirring a fire
[2]**po·ker** \ˈpō-kər\ *n* [prob. modif. of F *poque,* a card game similar to poker] (1836) **:** any of several card games in which a player bets that the value of his or her hand is greater than that of the hands held by others, in which each subsequent player must either equal or raise the bet or drop out, and in which the player holding the highest hand at the end of the betting wins the pot

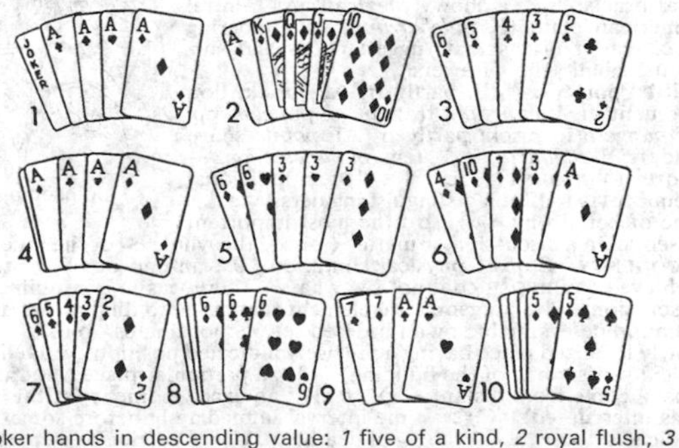

poker hands in descending value: *1* five of a kind, *2* royal flush, *3* straight flush, *4* four of a kind, *5* full house, *6* flush, *7* straight, *8* three of a kind, *9* two pair, *10* one pair

poker face *n* [[2]*poker;* fr. the poker player's need to conceal emotions during play] (1885) **:** an inscrutable face that reveals no hint of a person's thoughts or feelings — **po·ker–faced** \ˈpō-kər-ˌfāst\ *adj*
poke·weed \ˈpōk-ˌwēd\ *n* (1751) **:** a coarse American perennial herb (*Phytolacca americana* of the family Phytolaccaceae, the pokeweed family) with racemose white flowers, dark purple juicy berries, a poisonous root, and young shoots sometimes used as potherbs
po·key \ˈpō-kē\ *n, pl* **pokeys** [origin unknown] (ca. 1919) *slang* **:** JAIL
poky *or* **pok·ey** \ˈpō-kē\ *adj* **pok·i·er; -est** [[2]*poke*] (1844) **1 :** small and cramped **2 :** SHABBY, DULL **3 :** annoyingly slow — **pok·i·ly** \-kə-lē\ *adv* — **pok·i·ness** \-kē-nəs\ *n*
pol \ˈpäl\ *n* (ca. 1942) **:** POLITICIAN
Pol *abbr* Poland
Po·la·bi·an \pō-ˈlä-bē-ən, -ˈlā-\ *n* [*Polab,* ultim. fr. Polabian *po* on + *Lȧbi,* the Elbe River] (1866) **1** *or* **Po·lab** \pō-ˈläb\ **:** a member of a Slavic people formerly dwelling in the basin of the Elbe and on the Baltic coast of Germany **2 :** the extinct West Slavic language of the Polabians

Po·lack \ˈpō-ˌläk, -ˌlak\ *n* [Pol *polak*] (1574) **1** *obs* : a native or inhabitant of Poland **2** *usu disparaging* : a person of Polish birth or descent
Po·land Chi·na \ˈpō-lən(d)-ˈchī-nə\ *n* [*Poland,* Europe + *China,* Asia] (1879) : any of a U.S. breed of large white-marked black swine
[1]**po·lar** \ˈpō-lər\ *adj* [NL *polaris,* fr. L *polus* pole] (1551) **1 a** : of or relating to a geographic pole or the region around it **b** : coming from or having the characteristics of such a region **c** (1) : passing over a celestial body's north and south poles ⟨a satellite in a ~ orbit⟩ (2) : traveling in a polar orbit ⟨a ~ satellite⟩ **2** : of or relating to one or more poles (as of a magnet) **3** : serving as a guide ⟨a ~ principle⟩ ⟨a ~ theory⟩ **4** : diametrically opposite ⟨~ positions on the issue⟩ **5** : exhibiting polarity; *esp* : having a dipole or characterized by molecules having dipoles ⟨a ~ solvent⟩ **6** : resembling a pole or axis around which all else revolves : PIVOTAL ⟨~ events⟩ **7** : of, relating to, or expressed in polar coordinates ⟨~ equations⟩; *also* : of or relating to a polar coordinate system
[2]**polar** *n* (1848) : a straight line related to a point; *specif* : the straight line joining the points of contact of the tangents from a point exterior to a conic section
polar bear *n* (1781) : a large creamy-white carnivorous bear (*Ursus maritimus* syn. *Thalarctos maritimus*) that inhabits arctic regions
polar body *n* (1888) : a cell that separates from an oocyte during meiosis and that contains a nucleus produced in the first or second meiotic division and very little cytoplasm
polar circle *n* (1551) : either of the two parallels of latitude each at a distance from a pole of the earth equal to about 23 degrees 27 minutes
polar coordinate *n* (1816) : either of two numbers that locate a point in a plane by its distance from a fixed point on a line and the angle this line makes with a fixed line
polar front *n* (1920) : the boundary between the cold air of a polar region and the warmer air of lower latitudes
po·lar·im·e·ter \ˌpō-lə-ˈri-mə-tər\ *n* [ISV, fr. *polarization*] (1855) **1** : an instrument for determining the amount of polarization of light or the proportion of polarized light in a partially polarized ray **2** : a polariscope for measuring the amount of rotation of the plane of polarization esp. by liquids — **po·lar·i·met·ric** \pō-ˌla-rə-ˈme-trik\ *adj* — **po·lar·im·e·try** \ˌpō-lə-ˈri-mə-trē\ *n*
Po·lar·is \pə-ˈler-əs, -ˈlär-, -ˈla-rəs\ *n* [NL, fr. *polaris* polar] (1844) : NORTH STAR
po·lar·i·scope \pō-ˈla-rə-ˌskōp\ *n* [ISV, fr. *polarization*] (1829) **1** : an instrument for studying the properties of or examining substances in polarized light **2** : POLARIMETER 2 — **po·lar·i·scop·ic** \-ˌla-rə-ˈskä-pik\ *adj*
po·lar·ise *Brit var of* POLARIZE
po·lar·i·ty \pō-ˈler-ə-tē, pə-, -ˈla-rə-\ *n, pl* **-ties** (1646) **1** : the quality or condition inherent in a body that exhibits opposite properties or powers in opposite parts or directions or that exhibits contrasted properties or powers in contrasted parts or directions : the condition of having poles **2** : attraction toward a particular object or in a specific direction **3** : the particular state either positive or negative with reference to the two poles or to electrification **4 a** : diametrical opposition **b** : an instance of such opposition
polarity therapy *n* (1964) : a holistic discipline that seeks to achieve physical and emotional health through a system of touch, diet, exercise, and self-awareness designed to balance energy flows in the body
po·lar·i·za·tion \ˌpō-lə-rə-ˈzā-shən\ *n* (1812) **1** : the action of polarizing or state of being or becoming polarized: as **a** (1) : the action or process of affecting radiation and esp. light so that the vibrations of the wave assume a definite form (2) : the state of radiation affected by this process **b** : an increase in the resistance of an electrolytic cell often caused by the deposition of gas on one or both electrodes **c** : MAGNETIZATION **2 a** : division into two opposites **b** : concentration about opposing extremes of groups or interests formerly ranged on a continuum
po·lar·ize \ˈpō-lə-ˌrīz\ *vb* **-ized; -iz·ing** [F *polariser,* fr. NL *polaris* polar] *vt* (1811) **1** : to cause (as light waves) to vibrate in a definite pattern **2** : to give physical polarity to **3** : to break up into opposing factions or groupings ⟨a campaign that *polarized* the electorate⟩ **4** : CONCENTRATE 1 ⟨recreate a cohesive rock community by *polarizing* . . . an amorphous, fragmented audience —Ellen Willis⟩ ~ *vi* : to become polarized — **po·lar·iz·abil·i·ty** \ˌpō-lə-ˌrī-zə-ˈbi-lə-tē\ *n* — **po·lar·iz·able** \ˌpō-lə-ˈrī-zə-bəl\ *adj*
polar nucleus *n* (1882) : either of the two nuclei of a seed plant embryo sac that are destined to form endosperm
po·lar·og·ra·phy \ˌpō-lə-ˈrä-grə-fē\ *n* [ISV, fr. *polarization*] (1936) : a method of qualitative or quantitative analysis based on current-voltage curves obtained during electrolysis of a solution with a steadily increasing electromotive force — **po·lar·o·graph·ic** \pō-ˌla-rə-ˈgra-fik\ *adj* — **po·lar·o·graph·i·cal·ly** \-fi-k(ə-)lē\ *adv*
Po·lar·oid \ˈpō-lə-ˌrȯid\ *trademark* — used esp. for a light-polarizing material used esp. in eyeglasses and lamps to prevent glare or for a camera that produces developed pictures
po·lar·on \ˈpō-lə-ˌrän\ *n* [ISV *polar* + [2]*-on*] (1946) : a conducting electron in an ionic crystal together with the induced polarization of the surrounding lattice
pol·der \ˈpōl-dər\ *n* [D] (1604) : a tract of low land (as in the Netherlands) reclaimed from a body of water (as the sea)
[1]**pole** \ˈpōl\ *n* [ME, fr. OE *pāl* stake, pole, fr. L *palus* stake; akin to L *pangere* to fix — more at PACT] (bef. 12c) **1 a** : a long slender usu. cylindrical object (as a length of wood) **b** : a shaft which extends from the front axle of a wagon between wheelhorses and by which the wagon is drawn : TONGUE **c** : a long staff of wood, metal, or fiberglass used in the pole vault **2** : a varying unit of length; *esp* : one equal to a rod (16½ feet or about 5 meters) **3** : a tree with a breast-high diameter of from 4 to 12 inches (10 to 30 centimeters) **4** : the inside front row position on the starting line for a race
[2]**pole** *vb* **poled; pol·ing** *vt* (1573) **1** : to act upon with a pole **2** : to impel or push with a pole ~ *vi* **1** : to propel a boat with a pole **2** : to use ski poles to gain speed
[3]**pole** *n* [ME, fr. L *polus,* fr. Gk *polos* pivot, pole; akin to Gk *pelesthai* to become, Skt *carati* he moves, wanders — more at WHEEL] (14c) **1** : either extremity of an axis of a sphere and esp. of the earth's axis **2 a** : either of two related opposites **b** : a point of guidance or attraction **3 a** : either of the two terminals of an electric cell, battery, generator, or motor **b** : one of two or more regions in a magnetized body at which the magnetic flux density is concentrated **4** : either of two morphologically or physiologically differentiated areas at opposite ends of an axis in an organism or cell — see BLASTULA illustration **5 a** : the fixed point in a system of polar coordinates that serves as the origin **b** : the point of origin of two tangents to a conic section that determine a polar — **poles apart** : diametrically opposed
Pole \ˈpōl\ *n* [G, of Slavic origin; akin to Pol *Polak* Pole, *Polska* Poland, *pole* field] (1535) **1** : a native or inhabitant of Poland **2** : a person of Polish descent
[1]**pole·ax** \ˈpōl-ˌaks\ *n* [ME *polax, pollax,* fr. *pol, polle* poll + *ax*] (14c) **1** : a battle-ax with a short handle and often a hook or spike opposite the blade; *also* : one with a long handle used as an ornamental weapon **2** : an ax used in slaughtering cattle
[2]**poleax** *vt* (1882) : to attack, strike, or fell with or as if with a poleax
pole bean *n* (ca. 1770) : a cultivated bean that is usu. trained to grow upright on supports
pole·cat \ˈpōl-ˌkat\ *n, pl* **polecats** *or* **polecat** [ME *polcat,* prob. fr. MF *poul, pol* cock + ME *cat;* prob. fr. its preying on poultry — more at PULLET] (14c) **1** : any of several carnivorous mammals (as of the genera *Mustela* or *Vormela*) of the weasel family; *esp* : a brown to black European mammal (*M. putorius*) from which the domesticated ferret is derived **2** : SKUNK
pole dancing *n* (1994) : usu. solo dancing performed while using a fixed vertical pole as a prop — **pole dance** *n or vi* — **pole dancer** *n*
poleis *pl of* POLIS
pole·less \ˈpōl-ləs\ *adj* (1647) : having no pole
po·lem·ic \pə-ˈle-mik\ *n* [F *polémique,* fr. MF, fr. *polemique* controversial, fr. Gk *polemikos* warlike, hostile, fr. *polemos* war; perh. akin to Gk *pelemizein* to shake, OE eal*felo* baleful] (1638) **1 a** : an aggressive attack on or refutation of the opinions or principles of another **b** : the art or practice of disputation or controversy — usu. used in pl. but sing. or pl. in constr. **2** : an aggressive controversialist : DISPUTANT — **po·lem·i·cist** \-ˈle-mə-sist\ *n*
po·lem·i·cal \-mi-kəl\ *also* **po·lem·ic** \-mik\ *adj* (1640) **1** : of, relating to, or being a polemic : CONTROVERSIAL **2** : engaged in or addicted to polemics : DISPUTATIOUS — **po·lem·i·cal·ly** \-mi-k(ə-)lē\ *adv*
po·lem·i·cize \-ˈle-mə-ˌsīz\ *vi* **-cized; -ciz·ing** (1950) : to engage in controversy : deliver a polemic
po·le·mist \pə-ˈle-mist, ˈpä-lə-mist\ *n* (1825) : one skilled in or given to polemics
pol·e·mize \ˈpä-lə-ˌmīz\ *vi* **-mized; -miz·ing** (1828) : POLEMICIZE
pol·e·mo·ni·um \ˌpä-lə-ˈmō-nē-əm\ *n* [NL, fr. Gk *polemōnion,* a plant] (1733) : JACOB'S LADDER 1
po·len·ta \pō-ˈlen-tə, pə-, -ˌtä\ *n* [It, fr. L, crushed and hulled barley; akin to L *pollen* fine flour] (1764) : mush made of chestnut meal, cornmeal, semolina, or farina
pol·er \ˈpō-lər\ *n* (1848) : one that poles; *esp* : one that poles a boat
pole·star \ˈpōl-ˌstär\ *n* (1555) **1** : NORTH STAR **2 a** : a directing principle : GUIDE **b** : a center of attraction
pole vault *n* (1877) : a vault with the aid of a pole; *specif* : a field event consisting of a vault for height over a crossbar — **pole–vault** *vi* — **pole–vaulter** *n*
pole·ward \ˈpōl-wərd\ *adv or adj* (1835) : toward or in the direction of a pole of the earth ⟨as the sun moves ~⟩ ⟨~ variation in temperature⟩
[1]**po·lice** \pə-ˈlēs\ *vt* **po·liced; po·lic·ing** [in sense 1, fr. MF *policier,* fr. *police* conduct of public affairs; in other senses, fr. [2]*police*] (1589) **1** *archaic* : GOVERN **2** : to control, regulate, or keep in order by use of police **3** : to make clean and put in order **4 a** : to supervise the operation, execution, or administration of to prevent or detect and prosecute violations of rules and regulations **b** : to exercise such supervision over the policies and activities of **5** : to perform the functions of a police force in or over
[2]**police** *n, pl* **police** *often attrib* [F, fr. OF, fr. LL *politia* government, administration, fr. Gk *politeia,* fr. *politēs* citizen, fr. *polis* city, state; akin to Skt *pur* rampart, Lith *pilis* castle] (1716) **1 a** : the internal organization or regulation of a political unit through exercise of governmental powers esp. with respect to general comfort, health, morals, safety, or prosperity **b** : control and regulation of affairs affecting the general order and welfare of any unit or area **c** : the system of laws for effecting such control **2 a** : the department of government concerned primarily with maintenance of public order, safety, and health and enforcement of laws and possessing executive, judicial, and legislative powers **b** : the department of government charged with prevention, detection, and prosecution of public nuisances and crimes **3 a** : POLICE FORCE **b** *pl* : POLICE OFFICERS **4 a** : a private organization resembling a police force ⟨campus ~⟩ **b** *pl* : the members of a private police organization **5 a** : the action or process of cleaning and putting in order **b** : military personnel detailed to perform this function **6** : one attempting to regulate or censor a specified field or activity ⟨the fashion ~⟩
police action *n* (1933) : a localized military action undertaken without formal declaration of war by regular armed forces against persons held to be violators of international peace and order
police court *n* (1823) : a court of record that has jurisdiction over various minor offenses (as breach of the peace) and the power to bind over for trial in a superior court or for a grand jury persons accused of more serious offenses
police dog *n* (1908) **1** : a dog trained to assist police (as in drug detection) **2** : GERMAN SHEPHERD
police force *n* (1838) : a body of trained officers entrusted by a government with maintenance of public peace and order, enforcement of laws, and prevention and detection of crime
po·lice·man \pə-ˈlēs-mən\ *n* (1801) **1** : a member of a police force **2** : one held to resemble a policeman ⟨making the United States the ~ for the whole world —R. B. Long⟩
police officer *n* (1797) : a member of a police force

police power *n* (1827) : the inherent power of a government to exercise reasonable control over persons and property within its jurisdiction in the interest of the general security, health, safety, morals, and welfare except where legally prohibited
police procedural *n, pl* **police procedurals** (1967) : a mystery story written from the point of view of the police investigating the crime
police reporter *n* (1834) : a reporter regularly assigned to cover police news (as crimes and arrests)
police state *n* (1851) : a political unit characterized by repressive governmental control of political, economic, and social life usu. by an arbitrary exercise of power by police and esp. secret police in place of regular operation of administrative and judicial organs of the government according to publicly known legal procedures
police station *n* (1846) : the headquarters of the police for a locality
po·lice·wom·an \pə-ˈlēs-ˌwu̇-mən\ *n* (1853) : a woman who is a member of a police force
[1]**pol·i·cy** \ˈpä-lə-sē\ *n, pl* **-cies** *often attrib* [ME *policie* government, policy, fr. MF *police, policie* — more at POLICE] (15c) **1 a :** prudence or wisdom in the management of affairs **b :** management or procedure based primarily on material interest **2 a :** a definite course or method of action selected from among alternatives and in light of given conditions to guide and determine present and future decisions **b :** a high-level overall plan embracing the general goals and acceptable procedures esp. of a governmental body
[2]**policy** *n, pl* **-cies** [alter. of earlier *police,* fr. MF, certificate, fr. OIt *polizza,* modif. of ML *apodixa* receipt, fr. MGk *apodeixis,* fr. Gk, proof, fr. *apodeiknynai* to demonstrate — more at APODICTIC] (1565) **1 :** a writing whereby a contract of insurance is made **2 a :** a daily lottery in which participants bet that certain numbers will be drawn from a lottery wheel **b :** NUMBER 7a
pol·i·cy·hold·er \ˈpä-lə-sē-ˌhōl-dər\ *n* (1846) : the owner of an insurance policy
policy science *n* (1950) : a social science dealing with the making of high-level policy (as in a government or business)
po·lio \ˈpō-lē-ˌō\ *n* (1931) : POLIOMYELITIS
po·lio·my·eli·tis \ˌpō-lē-(ˌ)ō-ˌmī-ə-ˈlī-təs\ *n* [NL, fr. Gk *polios* gray + *myelos* marrow — more at FALLOW, MYEL-] (1878) : an acute infectious disease caused by the poliovirus and characterized by fever, motor paralysis, and atrophy of skeletal muscles often with permanent disability and deformity and marked by inflammation of nerve cells in the anterior gray matter in each lateral half of the spinal cord — called also *infantile paralysis*
po·lio·vi·rus \ˈpō-lē-(ˌ)ō-ˌvī-rəs\ *n* [NL, fr. *polio*myelitis + *virus*] (1953) : an enterovirus (species *Poliovirus*) occurring in three distinct serotypes that cause poliomyelitis — compare SALK VACCINE
po·lis \ˈpä-ləs\ *n, pl* **po·leis** \ˈpä-ˌlās\ [Gk — more at POLICE] (1884) : a Greek city-state; *broadly* : a state or society esp. when characterized by a sense of community
-polis *n comb form* [LL, fr. Gk, fr. *polis*] : city ⟨megalo*polis*⟩
po·li–sci \ˈpä-lē-ˈsī\ *n* (ca. 1914) : POLITICAL SCIENCE
[1]**pol·ish** \ˈpä-lish\ *vb* [ME *polisshen,* fr. AF *poliss-,* stem of *polir,* fr. L *polire*] *vt* (14c) **1 :** to make smooth and glossy usu. by friction : BURNISH **2 :** to smooth, soften, or refine in manners or condition **3 :** to bring to a highly developed, finished, or refined state : PERFECT ~ *vi* : to become smooth or glossy by or as if by friction — **pol·ish·er** *n*
[2]**polish** *n* (1679) **1 a :** a smooth glossy surface : LUSTER **b :** freedom from rudeness or coarseness : CULTURE **c :** a state of high development or refinement **2 :** the action or process of polishing **3 :** a preparation that is used to produce a gloss and often a color for the protection and decoration of a surface ⟨furniture ~⟩ ⟨nail ~⟩
[1]**Pol·ish** \ˈpō-lish\ *adj* [*Pole*] (1592) : of, relating to, or characteristic of Poland, the Poles, or Polish
[2]**Polish** *n* (1671) : the Slavic language of the Poles
polish off *vt* (1829) : to finish off or dispose of rapidly or completely
polit *abbr* political
po·lit·bu·ro \ˈpä-lət-ˌbyu̇r-(ˌ)ō, ˈpō-lət-, pə-ˈlit-\ *n* [Russ *politbyuro,* fr. *politicheskoe byuro* political bureau] (1925) : the principal policy-making and executive committee of a Communist party
po·lite \pə-ˈlīt\ *adj* **po·lit·er; -est** [ME (Sc) *polit,* L *politus,* fr. pp. of *polire*] (15c) **1 a :** of, relating to, or having the characteristics of advanced culture **b :** marked by refined cultural interests and pursuits esp. in arts and belles lettres **2 a :** showing or characterized by correct social usage **b :** marked by an appearance of consideration, tact, deference, or courtesy **c :** marked by a lack of roughness or crudities ⟨~ literature⟩ ***syn*** see CIVIL — **po·lite·ly** *adv* — **po·lite·ness** *n*
po·li·tesse \ˌpä-li-ˈtes, ˌpȯ-\ *n* [F, fr. MF, cleanness, fr. OIt *pulitezza,* fr. *pulito,* pp. of *pulire* to polish, clean, fr. L *polire*] (1713) : formal politeness : DECOROUSNESS
pol·i·tic \ˈpä-lə-ˌtik\ *adj* [ME *politik,* fr. MF *politique,* fr. L *politicus,* fr. Gk *politikos,* fr. *politēs* citizen — more at POLICE] (15c) **1 :** POLITICAL **2 :** characterized by shrewdness in managing, contriving, or dealing **3 :** sagacious in promoting a policy **4 :** shrewdly tactful ***syn*** see EXPEDIENT, SUAVE
po·lit·i·cal \pə-ˈli-ti-kəl\ *adj* [L *politicus*] (1551) **1 a :** of or relating to government, a government, or the conduct of government **b :** of, relating to, or concerned with the making as distinguished from the administration of governmental policy **2 :** of, relating to, involving, or involved in politics and esp. party politics **3 :** organized in governmental terms ⟨~ units⟩ **4 :** involving or charged or concerned with acts against a government or a political system ⟨~ prisoners⟩ — **po·lit·i·cal·ly** \-k(ə-)lē\ *adv*
political action committee *n* (1944) : a group formed (as by an industry or an issue-oriented organization) to raise and contribute money to the campaigns of candidates likely to advance the group's interests
political economy *n* (ca. 1687) **1 :** ECONOMICS **2 :** the theory or study of the role of public policy in influencing the economic and social welfare of a political unit — **political economist** *n*
po·lit·i·cal·ize \pə-ˈli-ti-kə-ˌlīz\ *vt* **-ized; -izing** (1869) : POLITICIZE — **po·lit·i·cal·i·za·tion** \-ˌli-ti-kə-lə-ˈzā-shən\ *n*
politically correct *adj* (1936) : conforming to a belief that language and practices which could offend political sensibilities (as in matters of sex or race) should be eliminated — **political correctness** *n*
political science *n* (1606) : a social science concerned chiefly with the description and analysis of political and esp. governmental institutions and processes — **political scientist** *n*
pol·i·ti·cian \ˌpä-lə-ˈti-shən\ *n* (1589) **1 :** a person experienced in the art or science of government; *esp* : one actively engaged in conducting the business of a government **2 a :** a person engaged in party politics as a profession **b :** a person primarily interested in political office for selfish or other narrow usu. short-sighted reasons
po·lit·i·cise *Brit var of* POLITICIZE
po·lit·i·cize \pə-ˈli-tə-ˌsīz\ *vt* **-cized; -ciz·ing** (1846) : to give a political tone or character to ⟨an attempt to ~ the civil service⟩ — **po·lit·i·ci·za·tion** \-ˌli-tə-sə-ˈzā-shən\ *n*
pol·i·tick \ˈpä-lə-ˌtik\ *vi* [back-formation fr. *politicking,* n., fr. *politics* + [3]*-ing*] (ca. 1934) : to engage in often partisan political discussion or activity — **pol·i·tick·er** *n*
po·lit·i·co \pə-ˈli-ti-ˌkō\ *n, pl* **-cos** *also* **-coes** [It *politico* or Sp *político,* ultim. fr. L *politicus* political] (1630) : POLITICIAN
pol·i·tics \ˈpä-lə-ˌtiks\ *n pl but sing or pl in constr* [Gk *politika,* fr. neut. pl. of *politikos* political] (ca. 1529) **1 a :** the art or science of government **b :** the art or science concerned with guiding or influencing governmental policy **c :** the art or science concerned with winning and holding control over a government **2 :** political actions, practices, or policies **3 a :** political affairs or business; *esp* : competition between competing interest groups or individuals for power and leadership (as in a government) **b :** political life esp. as a principal activity or profession **c :** political activities characterized by artful and often dishonest practices **4 :** the political opinions or sympathies of a person **5 a :** the total complex of relations between people living in society **b :** relations or conduct in a particular area of experience esp. as seen or dealt with from a political point of view ⟨office ~⟩ ⟨ethnic ~⟩
pol·i·ty \ˈpä-lə-tē\ *n, pl* **-ties** [LL *politia* — more at POLICE] (1538) **1 :** political organization **2 :** a specific form of political organization **3 :** a politically organized unit **4 a :** the form or constitution of a politically organized unit **b :** the form of government of a religious denomination
pol·ka \ˈpōl-kə, ˈpō-kə\ *n* [Czech, fr. *Polka* Polish woman, fem. of *Polák* Pole] (1843) **1 :** a lively couple dance of Bohemian origin in duple time with a basic pattern of hop-step-close-step **2 :** a lively originally Bohemian dance tune in 2/4 time — **polka** *vi*
pol·ka dot \ˈpō-kə-ˌdät\ *n* (1857) : a dot in a pattern of regularly distributed dots in textile design — **polka–dot** *or* **pol·ka–dot·ted** \-ˌdä-təd\ *adj*
[1]**poll** \ˈpōl\ *n* [ME *pol, polle,* fr. MLG] (14c) **1 :** HEAD **2 a :** the top or back of the head **b :** NAPE **3 :** the broad or flat end of a striking tool (as a hammer) **4 a** (1) **:** the casting or recording of the votes of a body of persons (2) **:** a counting of votes cast **b :** the place where votes are cast or recorded — usu. used in pl. ⟨at the ~*s*⟩ **c :** the period of time during which votes may be cast at an election **d :** the total number of votes recorded ⟨a heavy ~⟩ **5 a :** a questioning or canvassing of persons selected at random or by quota to obtain information or opinions to be analyzed **b :** a record of the information so obtained
[2]**poll** *vt* (14c) **1 a :** to cut off or cut short the hair or wool of : CROP, SHEAR **b :** to cut off or cut short (as wool) **2 a :** to cut off or back the top of (as a tree); *specif* : POLLARD **b :** to cut off or cut short the horns of (cattle) **3 a :** to receive and record the votes of **b :** to request each member of to declare a vote individually ⟨~ the assembly⟩ **4 :** to receive (as votes) in an election **5 :** to question or canvass in a poll **6 :** to test (as several computer terminals sharing a single line) in sequence for messages to be transmitted ~ *vi* : to cast one's vote at a poll — **poll·ee** \pō-ˈlē\ *n* — **poll·er** \ˈpō-lər\ *n*
pol·lack *or* **pol·lock** \ˈpä-lək\ *n, pl* **pollack** *or* **pollock** [ME *poullok,* perh. fr. ScotGael *pollag* or Ir *pollóg*] (15c) **1 :** a commercially important No. Atlantic food fish (*Pollachius virens*) related to and resembling the cods but darker **2 :** a commercially important northern Pacific food fish (*Theragra chalcogramma*) of the cod family that closely resembles the pollack — called also *walleye pollack*
[1]**pol·lard** \ˈpä-lərd\ *n* [[2]*poll*] (1611) : a tree cut back to the trunk to promote the growth of a dense head of foliage
[2]**pollard** *vt* (1670) : to make a pollard of (a tree)
polled \ˈpōld\ *adj* (1584) : having no horns
pol·len \ˈpä-lən\ *n* [NL *pollin-, pollen,* fr. L, fine flour] (ca. 1760) **1 :** a mass of microspores in a seed plant appearing usu. as a fine dust **2 :** a dusty bloom on the body of an insect
pollen basket *n* (1860) : a smooth area on each hind tibia of a bee that is edged by a fringe of stiff hairs and serves to collect and transport pollen — called also *corbicula*
pollen grain *n* (1835) : one of the granular microspores that occur in pollen and give rise to the male gametophyte of a seed plant
pol·len·iz·er *also* **pol·lin·iz·er** \ˈpä-lə-ˌnī-zər\ *n* [*pollenize* to pollinate] (1897) **1 :** a plant that is a source of pollen **2 :** POLLINATOR a
pollen mother cell *n* (1884) : a cell that is derived from the hypodermis of the pollen sac and that gives rise by meiosis to four cells each of which develops into a pollen grain
pollen sac *n* (1875) : one of the pouches of a seed plant anther in which pollen is formed
pollen tube *n* (1835) : a tube that is formed by a pollen grain and conveys the sperm nuclei to the embryo sac of an angiosperm or the archegonium of a gymnosperm
pol·lex \ˈpä-ˌleks\ *n, pl* **pol·li·ces** \ˈpä-lə-ˌsēz\ [NL *pollic-, pollex,* fr. L, thumb, big toe] (ca. 1836) : the first digit of the forelimb : THUMB
pollin- *comb form* [NL *pollin-, pollen*] : pollen ⟨*pollin*ate⟩
pol·li·nate \ˈpä-lə-ˌnāt\ *vt* **-nat·ed; -nat·ing** (1875) **1 :** to carry out the pollination of **2 :** to mark or smudge with pollen
pol·li·na·tion \ˌpä-lə-ˈnā-shən\ *n* (1875) : the transfer of pollen from an anther to the stigma in angiosperms or from the microsporangium to the micropyle in gymnosperms
pol·li·na·tor \ˈpä-lə-ˌnā-tər\ *n* (1903) : one that pollinates: as **a :** an agent (as an insect) that pollinates flowers **b :** POLLENIZER 1
pol·lin·i·um \pä-ˈli-nē-əm\ *n, pl* **-ia** \-nē-ə\ [NL, fr. *pollin-*] (1862) : a coherent mass of pollen grains often with a stalk bearing an adhesive disk that clings to insects
pol·li·no·sis *or* **pol·len·osis** \ˌpä-lə-ˈnō-səs\ *n* [NL *pollinosis,* fr. *pollin-*] (1925) : HAY FEVER

poll·ster \ˈpōl-stər\ *n* (1939) **:** one that conducts a poll or compiles data obtained by a poll
poll tax *n* (1692) **:** a tax of a fixed amount per person levied on adults and often linked to the right to vote
pol·lut·ant \pə-ˈlü-tᵊnt\ *n* (1892) **:** something that pollutes
pol·lute \pə-ˈlüt\ *vt* **pol·lut·ed; pol·lut·ing** [ME, fr. L *pollutus,* pp. of *polluere,* fr. *por-* (akin to L *per* through) + *-luere* (akin to L *lutum* mud, Gk *lyma* dirt, defilement) — more at FOR] (14c) **1 a :** to make ceremonially or morally impure **:** DEFILE **b :** DEBASE 1 ⟨using language to deceive or mislead ~*s* language —Linda C. Lederman⟩ **2 a :** to make physically impure or unclean **:** BEFOUL, DIRTY **b :** to contaminate (an environment) esp. with man-made waste ***syn*** see CONTAMINATE — **pol·lut·er** *n* — **pol·lut·ive** \-ˈlü-tiv\ *adj*
pol·lu·tion \pə-ˈlü-shən\ *n* (14c) **1 :** the action of polluting esp. by environmental contamination with man-made waste; *also* **:** the condition of being polluted **2 :** POLLUTANT
Pol·lux \ˈpä-ləks\ *n* [L, modif. of Gk *Polydeukēs*] (1526) **1 :** one of the Dioscuri **2 :** a first-magnitude star in the constellation Gemini
Pol·ly·an·na \ˌpä-lē-ˈa-nə\ *n* [*Pollyanna,* heroine of the novel *Pollyanna* (1913) by Eleanor Porter †1920 Am. fiction writer] (1921) **:** a person characterized by irrepressible optimism and a tendency to find good in everything — **Pollyanna** *adj* — **Pol·ly·an·na·ish** \-ˈa-nə-ish\ *also* **Pol·ly·an·nish** \-ˈa-nish\ *adj*
pol·ly·wog *or* **pol·li·wog** \ˈpä-lē-ˌwäg, -ˌwȯg\ *n* [alter. of ME *polwygle,* prob. fr. *pol* poll + *wiglen* to wiggle] (1838) **:** TADPOLE
po·lo \ˈpō-(ˌ)lō\ *n* [Balti, ball] (1872) **1 :** a game played by teams of players on horseback using mallets with long flexible handles to drive a wooden ball through goalposts **2 :** WATER POLO **3 :** POLO SHIRT — **po·lo·ist** \ˈpō-(ˌ)lō-ist\ *n*
polo coat *n* (1910) **:** a tailored overcoat that is made esp. of tan camel's hair and often has stitched edges and a half-belt on the back
po·lo·naise \ˌpä-lə-ˈnāz, ˌpō-\ *n* [F, fr. fem. of *polonais* Polish, fr. *Pologne* Poland, fr. ML *Polonia*] (1773) **1 :** an elaborate short-sleeved overdress with a fitted waist and a draped cutaway overskirt **2 a :** a stately Polish processional dance popular in 19th century Europe **b :** music for this dance in moderate ¾ time

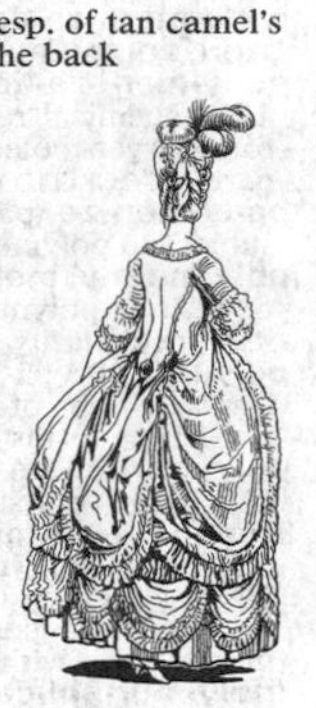
polonaise 1

po·lo–neck \ˈpō-(ˌ)lō-ˌnek\ *n* (1944) *chiefly Brit* **:** TURTLENECK
Po·lo·nia \pə-ˈlō-nē-ə, -nyə\ *n* [NL, Poland, fr. ML] (1944) **:** people of Polish descent living outside Poland
po·lo·ni·um \pə-ˈlō-nē-əm\ *n* [NL, fr. ML *Polonia*] (1898) **:** a radioactive metallic element that is similar chemically to tellurium and bismuth, occurs esp. in pitchblende and radium-lead residues, and emits an alpha particle to form an isotope of lead — see ELEMENT table
Po·lo·ni·us \pə-ˈlō-nē-əs\ *n* (ca. 1601) **:** a garrulous courtier and father of Ophelia and Laertes in Shakespeare's *Hamlet*
polo shirt *n* (1920) **:** a close-fitting pullover often knit shirt with short or long sleeves and turnover collar or banded neck
pol·ter·geist \ˈpōl-tər-ˌgīst\ *n* [G, fr. *poltern* to knock + *Geist* spirit] (1848) **:** a noisy usu. mischievous ghost held to be responsible for unexplained noises (as rappings)
[1]**pol·troon** \päl-ˈtrün\ *n* [MF *poultron,* fr. OIt *poltrone,* prob. akin to *poltro* colt, ultim. fr. L *pullus* young of an animal — more at FOAL] (ca. 1529) **:** a spiritless coward **:** CRAVEN
[2]**poltroon** *adj* (1645) **:** characterized by complete cowardice
pol·troon·ery \-ˈtrü-nə-rē, -ˈtrün-rē\ *n* (1590) **:** mean pusillanimity **:** COWARDICE
poly \ˈpä-lē\ *n, pl* **pol·ys** \-lēz\ *often attrib* [short for *polymer*] (1942) **:** a polymerized plastic or something made of this; *esp* **:** a polyester fiber, fabric, or garment
poly- *comb form* [Gk, fr. *polys;* akin to OHG *filu* many, Skt *puru,* L *plenus* full — more at FULL] **1 :** many **:** several **:** much **:** MULTI- ⟨*poly*chotomous⟩ ⟨*poly*gyny⟩ **2 a :** containing an indefinite number more than one of a (specified) substance ⟨*poly*sulfide⟩ **b :** polymeric **:** polymer of a (specified) monomer ⟨*poly*ethylene⟩ ⟨*poly*adenylic acid⟩
poly(A) \ˌpä-lē-ˈā\ *n* [*poly-* + *a*denylic acid] (1957) **:** RNA or a segment of RNA that is composed of a polynucleotide chain consisting entirely of adenylic acid residues and that codes for polylysine when functioning as messenger RNA in protein synthesis
poly·acryl·amide \ˌpä-lē-ə-ˈkri-lə-ˌmīd\ *n* (1944) **:** a polyamide of acrylic acid
poly·ac·ry·lo·ni·trile \ˌpä-lē-ˌa-krə-lō-ˈnī-trəl, -ˌtrēl\ *n* (1935) **:** a polymer of acrylonitrile used often as fibers
poly·ad·e·nyl·ic acid \ˌpä-lē-ˌa-də-ˈni-lik-\ *n* (1956) **:** POLY(A)
poly·al·co·hol \ˌpä-lē-ˈal-kə-ˌhȯl\ *n* (1900) **:** an alcohol (as a diol) that contains more than one hydroxyl group
poly·am·ide \ˌpä-lē-ˈa-ˌmīd, -məd\ *n* [ISV] (1929) **:** a compound characterized by more than one amide group; *esp* **:** a polymeric amide (as nylon)
poly·amine \ˈpä-lē-ə-ˌmēn, ˌpä-lē-ˈa-ˌmēn\ *n* (1861) **:** a compound characterized by more than one amino group
poly·am·o·ry \ˌpä-lē-ˈa-mə-rē\ *n, pl* **-ories** [*polyamor*ous (fr. *poly-* + *amorous*) + [2]*-y*] (1994) **:** the state or practice of having more than one open romantic relationship at a time — **poly·am·or·ist** \-rist\ *n* — **poly·am·o·rous** \-ˈa-mə-rəs, -ˈam-rəs\ *adj*
poly·an·dry \ˈpä-lē-ˌan-drē\ *n* [Gk *polyandros,* adj., having many husbands, fr. *poly-* + *andr-, anēr* man, husband — more at ANDR-] (1780) **:** the state or practice of having more than one husband or male mate at one time — compare POLYGAMY, POLYGYNY — **poly·an·drous** \ˌpä-lē-ˈan-drəs\ *adj*
poly·an·tha \ˌpä-lē-ˈan(t)-thə\ *n* [NL, fr. Gk *polyanthos* blooming] (1889) **:** any of numerous dwarf hybrid roses characterized by many large clusters of small flowers
poly·an·thus \-ˈan(t)-thəs\ *n, pl* **-an·thus·es** *also* **-an·thi** \-ˈan-ˌthī, -ˌthē\ [NL, fr. Gk *polyanthos* blooming, fr. *poly-* + *anthos* flower — more at ANTHOLOGY] (ca. 1727) **1 :** any of various hybrid primroses **2 :** a narcissus (*Narcissus tazetta*) having small white or yellow flowers arranged in umbels and having a spreading perianth
poly·atom·ic \-ə-ˈtä-mik\ *adj* [ISV] (1857) **:** containing more than one and esp. more than two atoms ⟨~ molecules⟩
poly·bro·mi·nat·ed biphenyl \ˌpä-lē-ˈbrō-mə-ˌnā-təd-\ *n* (1975) **:** any of several compounds that are similar to polychlorinated biphenyls in environmental toxicity and in structure but that have various hydrogen atoms replaced by bromine rather than chlorine — called also *PBB*
poly·bu·ta·di·ene \-ˌbyü-tə-ˈdī-ˌēn, -ˌdī-ˈ\ *n* (1939) **:** a synthetic rubber that has a high resistance to wear and is used esp. in the manufacture of tires
poly·car·bon·ate \-ˈkär-bə-ˌnāt, -nət\ *n* (1930) **:** any of various tough transparent thermoplastics characterized by high impact strength and high softening temperature
poly·cen·tric \-ˈsen-trik\ *adj* (1887) **:** having more than one center (as of development or control): as **a :** having several centromeres ⟨~ chromosomes⟩ **b :** characterized by polycentrism
poly·cen·trism \-ˈsen-ˌtri-zəm\ *n* (1956) **:** the existence of many centers of Communist ideological thought; *esp* **:** the existence of a number of autonomous national Communist movements
poly·chaete \ˈpä-lē-ˌkēt\ *n* [ultim. fr. Gk *polychaitēs* having much hair, fr. *poly-* + *chaitē* long hair] (1896) **:** any of a class (Polychaeta) of chiefly marine annelid worms (as clam worms) usu. with paired segmental appendages, separate sexes, and a free-swimming trochophore larva — **polychaete** *adj*
poly·chlo·ri·nat·ed biphenyl \ˌpä-lē-ˈklōr-ə-ˌnā-təd-\ *n* (1962) **:** any of several compounds that are produced by replacing hydrogen atoms in biphenyl with chlorine, have various industrial applications, and are toxic environmental pollutants which tend to accumulate in animal tissues — called also *PCB*
poly·chot·o·mous \-ˈkä-tə-məs\ *adj* [*poly-* + *-chotomous* (as in *dichotomous*)] (ca. 1858) **:** dividing or marked by division into many parts, branches, or classes — **poly·chot·o·my** \-mē\ *n*
poly·chro·mat·ic \-krō-ˈma-tik\ *adj* [Gk *polychrōmatos,* fr. *poly-* + *chrōmat-, chrōma* color — more at CHROMATIC] (ca. 1841) **1 :** showing a variety or a change of colors **:** MULTICOLORED **2 :** being or relating to radiation that is composed of more than one wavelength
poly·chro·mato·phil·ic \-krō-ˌma-tə-ˈfi-lik\ *adj* (1897) **:** stainable with more than one type of stain and esp. with both acid and basic dyes ⟨~ erythroblasts⟩ — **poly·chro·mato·phil·ia** \-ˈfi-lē-ə\ *n*
poly·chrome \ˈpä-lē-ˌkrōm\ *adj* [Gk *polychrōmos,* fr. *poly-* + *chrōma*] (1837) **:** relating to, made with, or decorated in several colors ⟨~ pottery⟩ — **polychrome** *vt* — **poly·chro·my** \-ˌkrō-mē\ *n*
poly·cis·tron·ic \ˌpä-lē-sis-ˈträ-nik\ *adj* (1963) **:** containing the genetic information of a number of cistrons ⟨~ messenger RNA⟩
poly·clin·ic \-ˈkli-nik\ *n* [ISV] (ca. 1889) **:** a clinic or hospital treating diseases of many sorts
poly·clon·al \-ˈklō-nəl\ *adj* (1914) **:** produced by, involving, or being cells derived from two or more cells of different ancestry or genetic constitution ⟨~ antibody synthesis⟩ ⟨~ activation of T cells⟩
poly·con·den·sa·tion \-ˌkän-ˌden-ˈsā-shən, -dən-\ *n* [ISV] (1936) **:** a chemical condensation leading to the formation of a compound of high molecular weight
poly·con·ic projection \ˌpä-lē-ˈkä-nik-\ *n* (ca. 1864) **:** a map projection consisting of a composite series of concentric cones each of which before being unrolled has been placed over a sphere so as to be tangent to a different parallel of latitude
poly·crys·tal·line \-ˈkris-tə-lən\ *adj* (1918) **1 :** consisting of crystals variously oriented **2 :** composed of more than one crystal — **poly·crys·tal** \ˈpä-lē-ˌkris-tᵊl\ *n*
poly·cy·clic \ˌpä-lē-ˈsī-klik, -ˈsi-\ *adj* [ISV] (1869) **:** having more than one cyclic component; *esp* **:** having two or more rings in the molecule
polycyclic aromatic hydrocarbon *n* (1951) **:** any of a class of hydrocarbon molecules that have multiple carbon rings, and that include carcinogenic substances and environmental pollutants — abbr. *PAH*
poly·cys·tic \-ˈsis-tik\ *adj* (1869) **:** having or involving more than one cyst ⟨~ kidneys⟩ ⟨a ~ disease⟩
polycystic kidney disease *n* (1948) **:** either of two hereditary diseases characterized by gradually enlarging bilateral cysts of the kidney which lead to reduced renal functioning or renal failure
polycystic ovary syndrome *n* (1967) **:** a variable disease that is marked by amenorrhea, hirsutism, obesity, infertility, and ovarian enlargement and is usu. initiated by an elevated level of luteinizing hormone, androgen, or estrogen which results in an abnormal cycle of gonadotropin release by the pituitary gland — called also *polycystic ovarian syndrome*
poly·cy·thae·mia *chiefly Brit var of* POLYCYTHEMIA
poly·cy·the·mia \-(ˌ)sī-ˈthē-mē-ə\ *n* [NL, fr. *poly-* + *cyt-* + *-hemia*] (ca. 1857) **:** a condition marked by an abnormal increase in the number of circulating red blood cells; *specif* **:** POLYCYTHEMIA VERA — **poly·cy·the·mic** \-mik\ *adj*
polycythemia ve·ra \-ˈvir-ə\ *n* [NL, true polycythemia] (ca. 1925) **:** polycythemia of unknown cause that is marked by increase in total blood volume and accompanied by nosebleed, distension of the circulatory vessels, and enlargement of the spleen — called also *erythremia*
poly·dac·tyl \-ˈdak-tᵊl\ *adj* [Gk *polydaktylos,* fr. *poly-* + *daktylos* digit] (1876) **:** having or causing polydactyly
poly·dac·ty·ly \-ˈdak-tə-lē\ *n* (1886) **:** the condition of having more than the normal number of fingers or toes
poly·dip·sia \-ˈdip-sē-ə\ *n* [NL, fr. *poly-* + Gk *dipsa* thirst] (1660) **:** excessive or abnormal thirst — **poly·dip·sic** \-sik\ *adj*
poly·dis·perse \-dis-ˈpərs\ *adj* [*poly-* + L *dispersus* dispersed, fr. pp. of *dispergere* to disperse] (1915) **:** of, relating to, or characterized by or as particles of varied sizes in the dispersed phase of a disperse system — **poly·dis·per·si·ty** \-ˈpər-sə-tē\ *n*
poly·elec·tro·lyte \ˌpä-lē-ə-ˈlek-trə-ˌlīt\ *n* (1947) **:** a substance of high molecular weight (as a protein) that is an electrolyte
poly·em·bry·o·ny \-ˈem-brē-ə-nē, -(ˌ)em-ˈbrī-\ *n* [ISV *poly-* + *embryon-* + [2]*-y*] (1849) **1 :** the condition of having several embryos **2 :** the pro-

duction of two or more embryos from one ovule or egg — **poly·em·bry·on·ic** \ˌem-brē-ˈä-nik\ *adj*

poly·ene \ˈpä-lē-ˌēn\ *n* [ISV] (1928) : an organic compound containing many double bonds; *esp* : one having the double bonds in a long aliphatic hydrocarbon chain — **poly·enic** \ˌpä-lē-ˈē-nik\ *adj*

[1]**poly·es·ter** \ˈpä-lē-ˌes-tər, ˌpä-lē-ˈ\ *n* [ISV] (1929) : any of a group of polymers that consist basically of repeated units of an ester and are used esp. in making fibers or plastics; *also* : a product (as a fiber or fabric) composed of polyester — **poly·es·ter·i·fi·ca·tion** \-e-ˌster-ə-fə-ˈkā-shən\ *n*

[2]**polyester** *adj* (1975) : characterized by inelegant or unsophisticated middle-class taste ⟨∼ suburbs⟩ ⟨∼ folks⟩

poly·es·trous \ˌpä-lē-ˈes-trəs\ *adj* (1900) : having more than one period of estrus in a year

poly·eth·yl·ene \-ˈe-thə-ˌlēn\ *n* (1862) : a polymer of ethylene; *esp* : any of various partially crystalline lightweight thermoplastics $(CH_2CH_2)_x$ that are resistant to chemicals and moisture, have good insulating properties, and are used esp. in packaging and insulation

polyethylene glycol *n* (1886) : any of a series of polymers $H(OCH_2CH_2)_nOH$ where *n* is greater than three that vary from viscous liquids to waxy solids and are used esp. as lubricants and in medical and biotechnological applications — abbr. *PEG*

po·lyg·a·la \pə-ˈli-gə-lə\ *n* [NL, genus name, fr. L, milkwort, fr. Gk *polygalon,* fr. *poly-* + *gala* milk — more at GALAXY] (1578) : MILKWORT

poly·gam·ic \ˌpä-lē-ˈga-mik\ *adj* (1819) : POLYGAMOUS

po·lyg·a·mous \pə-ˈli-gə-məs\ *adj* [Gk *polygamos,* fr. *poly-* + *-gamos* -gamous] (1613) **1 a** : relating to or practicing polygamy **b** : having more than one mate at one time ⟨baboons are ∼⟩ **2** : bearing both hermaphrodite and unisexual flowers on the same plant

po·lyg·a·my \-mē\ *n* (ca. 1591) **1** : marriage in which a spouse of either sex may have more than one mate at the same time — compare POLYANDRY, POLYGYNY **2** : the state of being polygamous — **po·lyg·a·mist** \-mist\ *n* — **po·lyg·a·mize** \-ˌmīz\ *vi*

poly·gene \ˈpä-lē-ˌjēn\ *n* [ISV] (1941) : any of a group of nonallelic genes that collectively control the inheritance of a quantitative character or modify the expression of a qualitative character — **poly·gen·ic** \ˌpä-lē-ˈjē-nik\ *adj*

poly·gen·e·sis \ˌpä-lē-ˈje-nə-səs\ *n* [NL] (ca. 1882) : development from more than one source

poly·ge·net·ic \-jə-ˈne-tik\ *adj* (1861) **1** : POLYPHYLETIC **2** : having many distinct sources

[1]**poly·glot** \ˈpä-lē-ˌglät\ *n* [[2]*polyglot*] (ca. 1645) **1** : one who is polyglot **2** *cap* : a book containing versions of the same text in several languages; *esp* : the Scriptures in several languages **3** : a mixture or confusion of languages or nomenclatures

[2]**polyglot** *adj* [Gk *polyglōttos,* fr. *poly-* + *glōtta* language — more at GLOSS] (ca. 1656) **1 a** : speaking or writing several languages : MULTILINGUAL **b** : composed of numerous linguistic groups ⟨a ∼ population⟩ **2** : containing matter in several languages ⟨a ∼ sign⟩ **3** : composed of elements from different languages **4** : widely diverse (as in ethnic or cultural origins) ⟨a ∼ cuisine⟩

poly·glot·ism *or* **poly·glot·tism** \-ˌglä-ˌti-zəm\ *n* (1882) : the use of many languages : the ability to speak many languages

poly·gon \ˈpä-lē-ˌgän\ *n* [LL *polygonum,* fr. Gk *polygōnon,* fr. neut. of *polygōnos* polygonal, fr. *poly-* + *gōnia* angle — more at -GON] (1571) **1** : a closed plane figure bounded by straight lines **2** : a closed figure on a sphere bounded by arcs of great circles — **po·lyg·o·nal** \pə-ˈli-gə-nᵊl\ *adj* — **po·lyg·o·nal·ly** \-nᵊl-ē\ *adv*

po·lyg·o·num \pə-ˈli-gə-nəm\ *n* [NL, fr. Gk *polygonon* knotgrass, fr. *poly-* + *gony* knee — more at KNEE] (ca. 1706) : any of a genus (*Polygonum*) of herbs of the buckwheat family with a prominent tubular sheath around the base of each petiole, thickened nodes, and flowers that are solitary and axillary or in spiked racemes — called also *knotweed*

poly·graph \ˈpä-lē-ˌgraf\ *n* (1871) : an instrument for recording variations of several different pulsations (as of physiological variables) simultaneously — compare LIE DETECTOR — **poly·graph·ic** \ˌpä-lē-ˈgra-fik\ *adj*

po·lyg·ra·pher \ˈpä-lē-ˌgra-fər, pə-ˈli-grə-fər\ *n* (ca. 1934) : one who operates a polygraph

po·lyg·ra·phist \ˈpä-lē-ˌgra-fist, pə-ˈli-grə-fist\ *n* (1954) : POLYGRAPHER

po·lyg·y·nous \pə-ˈli-jə-nəs\ *adj* (1874) : relating to or practicing polygyny ⟨∼ species of birds⟩

po·lyg·y·ny \-nē\ *n* (1780) : the state or practice of having more than one wife or female mate at a time — compare POLYANDRY, POLYGAMY

polyhedral angle *n* (ca. 1864) : a portion of space partly enclosed by three or more planes whose intersections meet in a vertex

poly·he·dron \ˌpä-lē-ˈhē-drən\ *n, pl* **-drons** *or* **-dra** \-drə\ [NL] (1570) : a solid formed by plane faces — **poly·he·dral** \-drəl\ *adj*

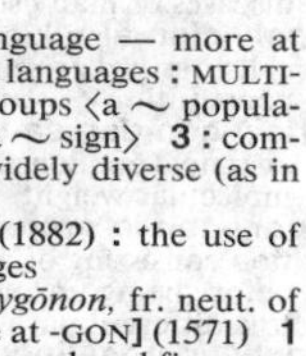

polyhedron

poly·he·dro·sis \ˌpä-lē-hē-ˈdrō-səs\ *n, pl* **-dro·ses** \-ˌsēz\ [NL, fr. *polyhedron*] (1947) : any of numerous diseases that affect specific insect larvae or decapod crustaceans, that are caused by double-stranded DNA viruses of a family (*Baculoviridae*) or by reoviruses of a genus (*Cypovirus*), and that are characterized by dissolution of tissues and accumulation of virus-containing granules in the resultant fluid

poly·his·tor \ˌpä-lē-ˈhis-tər\ *n* [Gk *polyistōr* very learned, fr. *poly-* + *istōr, histōr* learned — more at HISTORY] (1588) : POLYMATH — **poly·his·tor·ic** \-his-ˈtȯr-ik, -ˈtär-\ *adj*

poly·hy·droxy \-hī-ˈdräk-sē\ *adj* (ca. 1929) : containing more than one hydroxyl group in the molecule

Poly·hym·nia \ˌpä-lē-ˈhim-nē-ə\ *n* [L, fr. Gk *Polyymnia*] (1573) : the Greek Muse of sacred song

poly I:C \ˌpä-lē-ˈī-ˈsē\ *also* **poly I·poly C** \ˌpä-lē-ˈī-ˌpä-lē-ˈsē\ *n* [*poly-* + *i*nosinic acid + *c*ytidylic acid] (1969) : a synthetic 2-stranded RNA that induces interferon formation and is composed of one strand consisting entirely of cytosine-containing nucleotides and one strand consisting entirely of inosine-containing nucleotides

poly·iso·prene \ˌpä-lē-ˈī-sə-ˌprēn\ *n* (1935) : a polymer of isoprene occurring naturally in rubber and gutta-percha and also produced synthetically

poly·ke·tide \ˌpä-lē-ˈkē-ˌtīd\ *n* [ISV *poly-* + *ket-* + *-ide*] (1927) : any of a large class of diverse compounds that are characterized by more than two carbonyl groups connected by single intervening carbon atoms, that are produced esp. by certain bacteria and fungi, and that include various substances (as erythromycin and lovastatin) having antibiotic, anticancer, cholesterol-lowering, or immunosuppressive effects

poly·ly·sine \ˌpä-lē-ˈlī-ˌsēn\ *n* (1947) : a protein whose polypeptide chain consists entirely of lysine residues

poly·math \ˈpä-lē-ˌmath\ *n* [Gk *polymathēs* very learned, fr. *poly-* + *manthanein* to learn — more at MATHEMATICAL] (1621) : a person of encyclopedic learning — **polymath** *or* **poly·math·ic** \ˌpä-lē-ˈma-thik\ *adj* — **po·ly·ma·thy** \pə-ˈli-mə-thē, ˈpä-lə-ˌma-thē\ *n*

poly·mer \ˈpä-lə-mər\ *n* [ISV, back-formation fr. *polymeric,* fr. Gk *polymerēs* having many parts, fr. *poly-* + *meros* part — more at MERIT] (1866) : a chemical compound or mixture of compounds formed by polymerization and consisting essentially of repeating structural units — **poly·mer·ic** \ˌpä-lə-ˈmer-ik\ *adj* — **poly·mer·ism** \pə-ˈli-mə-ˌri-zəm, ˈpä-lə-mə-\ *n*

po·ly·mer·ase \pə-ˈlim-ə-rās; ˈpä-lə-mə-ˌrās, -ˌrāz\ *n* (1958) : any of several enzymes that catalyze the formation of DNA or RNA from precursor substances in the presence of preexisting DNA or RNA acting as a template — compare DNA POLYMERASE, RNA POLYMERASE

polymerase chain reaction *n* (1987) : an in vitro technique for rapidly synthesizing large quantities of a given DNA segment that involves separating the DNA into its two complementary strands, using DNA polymerase to synthesize two-stranded DNA from each single strand, and repeating the process — abbr. *PCR*

po·ly·mer·i·sa·tion, po·ly·mer·ise *chiefly Brit var of* POLYMERIZATION, POLYMERIZE

po·ly·mer·i·za·tion \pə-ˌli-mə-rə-ˈzā-shən, ˌpä-lə-mə-rə-\ *n* [ISV] (1872) **1** : a chemical reaction in which two or more molecules combine to form larger molecules that contain repeating structural units — compare ASSOCIATION 5 **2** : reduplication of parts in an organism

po·ly·mer·ize \pə-ˈli-mə-ˌrīz, ˈpä-lə-mə-\ *vb* **-ized; -iz·ing** *vt* (1865) : to subject to polymerization ∼ *vi* : to undergo polymerization

poly·meth·yl methacrylate \ˈpä-lē-ˌme-thəl-\ *n* (1936) : a thermoplastic resin of polymerized methyl methacrylate which is characterized by its optical clarity

poly·morph \ˈpä-lē-ˌmȯrf\ *n* [ISV] (ca. 1828) **1** : a polymorphic organism; *also* : one of the several forms of such an organism **2** : any of the crystalline forms of a polymorphic substance

poly·mor·phism \ˌpä-lē-ˈmȯr-ˌfi-zəm\ *n* (1839) : the quality or state of existing in or assuming different forms: as **a** (1) : existence of a species in several forms independent of the variations of sex (2) : existence of a gene in several allelic forms; *also* : a variation in a specific DNA sequence (3) : existence of a molecule (as an enzyme) in several forms in a single species **b** : the property of crystallizing in two or more forms with distinct structure — **poly·mor·phic** \-fik\ *adj* — **poly·mor·phi·cal·ly** \-fi-k(ə-)lē\ *adv*

poly·mor·pho·nu·cle·ar \-ˌmȯr-fə-ˈnü-klē-ər, -ˈnyü-\ *adj* (1897) *of a white blood cell* : having the nucleus complexly lobed — **polymorphonuclear** *n*

poly·mor·phous \-ˈmȯr-fəs\ *adj* [Gk *polymorphos,* fr. *poly-* + *-morphos* -morphous] (1785) : having, assuming, or occurring in various forms, characters, or styles : POLYMORPHIC ⟨a ∼ rash⟩ ⟨∼ sexuality⟩ — **poly·mor·phous·ly** *adv*

polymorphous perverse *adj* (1909) : relating to or exhibiting infantile sexual tendencies in which the genitals are not yet identified as the sole or principal sexual organs nor coitus as the goal of erotic activity

poly·myo·si·tis \ˌpä-lē-ˌmī-ə-ˈsī-təs\ *n* (1878) : inflammation of several muscles at once; *specif* : an inflammatory muscle disease of unknown cause that affects skeletal muscles chiefly closest to the trunk and is characterized esp. by muscle weakness and muscle and joint pain

poly·myx·in \ˌpä-lē-ˈmik-sən\ *n* [ISV, fr. NL *polymyxa,* fr. *poly-* + Gk *myxa* mucus — more at MUCUS] (1947) : any of several toxic antibiotics obtained from a soil bacterium (*Bacillus polymyxa*) and active against gram-negative bacteria

Poly·ne·sian \ˌpä-lə-ˈnē-zhən, -shən\ *n* (1807) **1** : a member of any of the indigenous peoples of Polynesia **2** : a group of Austronesian languages spoken in Polynesia — **Polynesian** *adj*

poly·neu·ri·tis \ˌpä-lē-nu̇-ˈrī-təs, -nyu̇-\ *n* [NL] (1886) : neuritis of several peripheral nerves at the same time

Poly·ni·ces \ˌpä-lə-ˈnī-sēz\ *n* [L, fr. Gk *Polyneikēs*] (15c) : a son of Oedipus for whom the Seven against Thebes mount their expedition

[1]**poly·no·mi·al** \ˌpä-lə-ˈnō-mē-əl\ *n* [*poly-* + *-nomial* (as in *binomial*)] (1674) : a mathematical expression of one or more algebraic terms each of which consists of a constant multiplied by one or more variables raised to a nonnegative integral power (as $a + bx + cx^2$)

[2]**polynomial** *adj* (ca. 1704) : relating to, composed of, or expressed as one or more polynomials ⟨∼ functions⟩ ⟨∼ equations⟩

poly·nu·cle·ar \ˌpä-lē-ˈnü-klē-ər, -ˈnyü-, ÷-kyə-lər\ *adj* [ISV] (1908) : chemically polycyclic esp. with respect to the benzene ring — used chiefly of aromatic hydrocarbons that are important as pollutants and possibly as carcinogens

polynuclear aromatic hydrocarbon *n* (1962) : POLYCYCLIC AROMATIC HYDROCARBON

poly·nu·cle·o·tide \-ˈnü-klē-ə-ˌtīd, -ˈnyü-\ *n* [ISV] (1911) : a polymeric chain of nucleotides

po·lyn·ya \ˌpä-lən-ˈyä\ *n, pl* **polynyas** *also* **po·lyn·yi** \-ˈyē\ [Russ *polyn'ya*] (1853) : an area of open water in sea ice

poly·ole·fin \ˌpä-lē-ˈō-lə-fən\ *n* (1930) : a polymer of an alkene (as polyethylene)

poly·oma·vi·rus \ˌpä-lē-ˈō-mə-ˌvī-rəs\ *n* [NL *polyoma,* fr. *poly-* + *-oma*] (1958) : any virus of a family (*Polyomaviridae* and esp. genus *Polyomavirus*) of double-stranded DNA viruses that induce tumors in specific mammals

poly·on·y·mous \ˌpä-lē-ˈä-nə-məs\ *adj* [Gk *polyōnymos,* fr. *poly-* + *onoma, onyma* name — more at NAME] (1678) : having or known by various names

pol·yp \ˈpä-ləp\ *n* [F *polype* octopus, nasal polyp, fr. OF *polipe,* fr. L *polypus,* fr. Gk *polypous,* fr. *poly-* + *pous* foot — more at FOOT] (1742) **1** : a coelenterate (as a coral) that has typically a hollow cylindrical

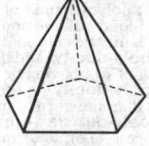

body closed and attached at one end and opening at the other by a central mouth surrounded by tentacles armed with nematocysts **2 :** a growth projecting from a mucous membrane (as of the colon or vocal cords) — **pol·yp·oid** \-lə-ˌpȯid\ *adj*
poly·pep·tide \ˌpä-lē-ˈpep-ˌtīd\ *n* [ISV] (1903) **:** a molecular chain of amino acids — **poly·pep·tid·ic** \-(ˌ)pep-ˈti-dik\ *adj*
poly·pet·al·ous \-ˈpe-tə-ləs\ *adj* [NL *polypetalus,* fr. *poly-* + *petalum* petal] (ca. 1704) **:** having or consisting of separate petals
poly·pha·gia \-ˈfā-j(ē-)ə\ *n* [Gk *polyphagia,* fr. *polyphagos*] (ca. 1693) **:** excessive appetite or eating
po·lyph·a·gous \pə-ˈli-fə-gəs\ *adj* [Gk *polyphagos* eating too much, fr. *poly-* + *-phagos* -phagous] (1815) **:** feeding on or utilizing many kinds of food — **po·lyph·a·gy** \-jē\ *n*
poly·phar·ma·cy \ˌpä-li-ˈfär-mə-sē\ *n* (1762) **:** the practice of administering or using multiple medications esp. concurrently (as in the treatment of a single disease or of several coexisting conditions)
poly·phase \ˈpä-lē-ˌfāz\ *adj* [ISV] (1891) **:** having or producing two or more phases ⟨a ~ machine⟩ ⟨a ~ current⟩
poly·pha·sic \ˌpä-lē-ˈfā-zik\ *adj* (1922) **:** consisting of two or more phases
Poly·phe·mus \ˌpä-lə-ˈfē-məs\ *n* [L, fr. Gk *Polyphēmos*] (14c) **:** a Cyclops whom Odysseus blinds in order to escape from his cave
poly·phe·nol \ˌpä-lē-ˈfē-ˌnōl, -fi-ˈ\ *n* [ISV] (1894) **:** a polyhydroxy phenol; *esp* **:** an antioxidant phytochemical — **poly·phe·no·lic** \-fi-ˈnō-lik, -ˈnä-\ *adj*
poly·phil·o·pro·gen·i·tive \-ˌfi-lə-prō-ˈje-nə-tiv\ *adj* (1919) **:** extremely prolific **:** PHILOPROGENITIVE
poly·phone \ˈpä-lē-ˌfōn\ *n* (1872) **:** a symbol or sequence of symbols having more than one phonemic value (as *a* in English)
poly·phon·ic \ˌpä-lē-ˈfä-nik\ *or* **po·lyph·o·nous** \pə-ˈli-fə-nəs\ *adj* (1782) **1 :** of, relating to, or marked by polyphony **2 :** being a polyphone — **poly·phon·i·cal·ly** \ˌpä-lē-ˈfä-ni-k(ə-)lē\ *or* **po·lyph·o·nous·ly** *adv*
polyphonic prose *n* (1916) **:** a freely rhythmical prose employing characteristic devices of verse (as alliteration and assonance)
po·lyph·o·ny \pə-ˈli-fə-nē\ *n* [Gk *polyphōnia* variety of tones, fr. *polyphōnos* having many tones or voices, fr. *poly-* + *phōnē* voice — more at BAN] (ca. 1864) **:** a style of musical composition employing two or more simultaneous but relatively independent melodic lines **:** COUNTERPOINT
poly·phy·let·ic \ˌpä-lē-(ˌ)fī-ˈle-tik\ *adj* [ISV, fr. Gk *polyphylos* of many tribes, fr. *poly-* + *phylē* tribe — more at PHYL-] (1875) **:** of, relating to, or derived from different ancestral stocks; *specif* **:** relating to or being a taxonomic group that includes members (as genera or species) from different ancestral lineages — **poly·phy·let·i·cal·ly** \-ti-k(ə-)lē\ *adv*
pol·yp·ide \ˈpä-lə-ˌpīd\ *n* [*polyp* + Gk *-idēs,* patronymic suffix] (1850) **:** one of the individual zooids of a bryozoan colony
poly·ploid \ˈpä-lē-ˌplȯid\ *adj* [ISV] (1920) **:** having or being a chromosome number that is a multiple greater than two of the monoploid number — **polyploid** *n* — **poly·ploi·dy** \-ˌplȯi-dē\ *n*
po·lyp·nea \pä-ˈlip-nē-ə, pə-\ *n* [NL] (ca. 1889) **:** rapid or panting respiration
poly·po·dy \ˈpä-lə-ˌpō-dē\ *n, pl* **-dies** [ME *polypodie,* fr. L *polypodium,* fr. Gk *polypodion,* fr. *poly-* + *pod-, pous* foot — more at FOOT] (14c) **:** any of a genus (*Polypodium*) of chiefly epiphytic ferns with creeping rhizomes; *esp* **:** either of two ferns (*P. vulgare* of Eurasia and *P. virginianum* of No. America) with relatively narrow entire segments
poly·pro·pyl·ene \ˌpä-lē-ˈprō-pə-ˌlēn\ *n* (1935) **:** any of various thermoplastic plastics or fibers that are polymers of propylene
po·lyp·tych \pä-ˈlip-ˌtik, pə-ˈlip-tik\ *n* [Gk *polyptychos* having many folds, fr. *poly-* + *ptychē* fold, fr. *ptyssein* to fold] (1859) **:** an arrangement of four or more panels (as of a painting) usu. hinged and folding together
poly·rhythm \ˈpä-lē-ˌri-t͟həm\ *n* (1929) **:** the simultaneous combination of contrasting rhythms in music — **poly·rhyth·mic** \ˌpä-lē-ˈrit͟h-mik\ *adj* — **poly·rhyth·mi·cal·ly** \-mi-k(ə-)lē\ *adv*
poly·ri·bo·nu·cle·o·tide \ˌpä-lē-ˌrī-bō-ˈnü-klē-ə-ˌtīd, -ˈnyü-\ *n* (1956) **:** a polynucleotide in which the mononucleotides are ribonucleotides
poly·ri·bo·some \-ˈrī-bə-ˌsōm\ *n* (1962) **:** a cluster of ribosomes linked together by a molecule of messenger RNA and forming the site of protein synthesis — **poly·ri·bo·som·al** \-ˌrī-bə-ˈsō-məl\ *adj*
poly·sac·cha·ride \-ˈsa-kə-ˌrīd\ *n* [ISV] (1892) **:** a carbohydrate that can be decomposed by hydrolysis into two or more molecules of monosaccharides; *esp* **:** one (as cellulose, starch, or glycogen) containing many monosaccharide units and marked by complexity
po·ly·se·mous \ˌpä-lē-ˈsē-məs, pə-ˈli-sə-məs\ *or* **po·ly·se·mic** \ˌpä-lē-ˈsē-mik\ *adj* [LL *polysemus,* fr. Gk *polysēmos,* fr. *poly-* + *sēma* sign] (1884) **:** having multiple meanings — **po·ly·se·my** \pə-ˈli-sə-mē, ˈpä-lē-ˌsē-mē\ *n*
poly·some \ˈpä-lē-ˌsōm\ *n* (1962) **:** POLYRIBOSOME
poly·sor·bate \ˌpä-lē-ˈsȯr-ˌbāt\ *n* (1950) **:** any of several emulsifiers used in the preparation of some pharmaceuticals or foods
po·lys·ti·chous \pə-ˈlis-ti-kəs\ *adj* [Gk *polystichos,* fr. *poly-* + *stichos* row — more at DISTICH] (ca. 1889) **:** arranged in several rows
poly·sty·rene \ˌpä-lē-ˈstī-ˌrēn\ *n* (1927) **:** a polymer of styrene; *esp* **:** a rigid transparent thermoplastic that has good physical and electrical insulating properties and is used esp. in molded products, foams, and sheet materials
poly·sul·fide \-ˈsəl-ˌfīd\ *n* [ISV] (1849) **:** a sulfide containing two or more atoms of sulfur in the molecule
poly·syl·lab·ic \-sə-ˈla-bik\ *adj* [ML *polysyllabus,* fr. Gk *polysyllabos,* fr. *poly-* + *syllabē* syllable] (1782) **1 :** having more than one and usu. more than three syllables **2 :** characterized by words of many syllables — **poly·syl·lab·i·cal·ly** \-bi-k(ə-)lē\ *adv*
poly·syl·la·ble \ˈpä-lē-ˌsi-lə-bəl, ˌpä-lē-ˈ\ *n* [modif. of ML *polysyllaba,* fr. fem. of *polysyllabus*] (1570) **:** a polysyllabic word
poly·syn·ap·tic \ˌpä-lē-sə-ˈnap-tik\ *adj* (1964) **:** involving two or more synapses in the central nervous system ⟨~ reflexes⟩ — **poly·syn·ap·ti·cal·ly** \-ti-k(ə-)lē\ *adv*
poly·syn·de·ton \-ˈsin-də-ˌtän\ *n* [NL, fr. LGk, neut. of *polysyndetos* using many conjunctions, fr. Gk *poly-* + *syndetos* bound together, conjunctive — more at ASYNDETON] (ca. 1577) **:** repetition of conjunctions in close succession (as in *we have ships and men and money*)
[1]**poly·tech·nic** \-ˈtek-nik\ *adj* [F *polytechnique,* fr. Gk *polytechnos* skilled in many arts, fr. *poly-* + *technē* art — more at TECHNICAL] (1801) **:** relating to or devoted to instruction in many technical arts or applied sciences
[2]**polytechnic** *n* (1836) **:** a polytechnic school
poly·tene \ˈpä-lē-ˌtēn\ *adj* [ISV] (1935) **:** relating to, being, or having chromosomes each of which consists of many strands with the corresponding chromomeres in contact — **poly·te·ny** \-ˌtē-nē\ *n*
poly·the·ism \ˈpä-lē-(ˌ)thē-ˌi-zəm\ *n* [F *polythéisme,* fr. LGk *polytheos* polytheistic, fr. Gk, of many gods, fr. *poly-* + *theos* god] (1613) **:** belief in or worship of more than one god — **poly·the·ist** \-ˌthē-ist\ *adj or n* — **poly·the·is·tic** \ˌpä-lē-thē-ˈis-tik\ *also* **poly·the·is·ti·cal** \-ˈis-ti-kəl\ *adj*
poly·thene \ˈpä-lə-ˌthēn\ *n* [by contr.] (1939) *chiefly Brit* **:** POLYETHYLENE
poly·to·nal·i·ty \ˌpä-lē-tō-ˈna-lə-tē\ *n* (1923) **:** the simultaneous use of two or more musical keys — **poly·ton·al** \-ˈtō-nᵊl\ *adj* — **poly·ton·al·ly** \-nᵊl-ē\ *adv*
poly·typ·ic \ˌpä-lē-ˈti-pik\ *adj* (1888) **:** represented by several or many types or subdivisions ⟨a ~ species of organism⟩
poly·un·sat·u·rat·ed \ˌpä-lē-ˌən-ˈsa-chə-ˌrā-təd\ *adj* (1932) *of an oil or fatty acid* **:** having many double or triple bonds in a molecule — compare MONOUNSATURATED
poly·ure·thane \ˌpä-lē-ˈyu̇r-ə-ˌthān\ *n* [ISV] (1944) **:** any of various polymers that contain NHCOO linkages and are used esp. in flexible and rigid foams, elastomers, and resins (as for coatings)
poly·uria \-ˈyu̇r-ē-ə\ *n* [NL] (ca. 1842) **:** excessive secretion of urine
poly·va·lent \-ˈvā-lənt *also* pə-ˈli-və-lənt\ *adj* [ISV] (1881) **1 :** having a chemical valence greater usu. than two **2 :** effective against, sensitive toward, or counteracting more than one toxin, microorganism, or antigen ⟨~ vaccines⟩ — **poly·va·lence** \-lən(t)s\ *n*
poly·vi·nyl \ˌpä-lē-ˈvī-nᵊl\ *adj* [ISV] (1927) **:** of, relating to, or being a polymerized vinyl compound, resin, or plastic — often used in combination
polyvinyl chloride *n* (1933) **:** a polymer of vinyl chloride used esp. for electrical insulation, films, and pipes — abbr. *PVC*
poly·wa·ter \ˈpä-lē-ˌwȯ-tər, -ˌwä-\ *n* [*poly*meric *water*] (1969) **:** water condensed into a glass capillary tube and formerly held to be a stable form with special properties
Pom \ˈpäm\ *n* (1912) *Austral & NewZeal, usu disparaging* **:** POMMY
pom·ace \ˈpə-məs, ˈpä-\ *n* [ME *pomys,* prob. fr. ML *pomacium* cider, fr. LL *pomum* apple, fr. L, fruit] (15c) **1 :** the dry or pulpy residue of material (as fruit, seeds, or fish) from which a liquid (as juice or oil) has been pressed or extracted **2 :** something crushed to a pulpy mass
po·ma·ceous \pō-ˈmā-shəs\ *adj* [NL *pomaceus,* fr. LL *pomum*] (1706) **1 :** of or relating to apples **2** [*pome*] **:** resembling a pome
po·made \pō-ˈmād, -ˈmäd\ *n* [MF *pommade* ointment formerly made from apples, fr. It *pomata,* fr. *pomo* apple, fr. LL *pomum*] (1562) **:** a perfumed ointment; *esp* **:** a fragrant hair dressing — **pomade** *vt*
po·man·der \ˈpō-ˌman-dər, pō-ˈ\ *n* [ME, modif. of AF *pomme de ambre,* lit., apple or ball of amber] (15c) **1 :** a mixture of aromatic substances enclosed in a perforated bag or box and used to scent clothes and linens or formerly carried as a guard against infection; *also* **:** a clove-studded orange or apple used for the same purposes **2 :** a box or hollow fruit-shaped ball for holding pomander
po·ma·tum \pō-ˈmā-təm, -ˈmä-\ *n* [NL, fr. LL *pomum* apple] (1562) **:** POMADE
pome \ˈpōm\ *n* [ME, fruit, fr. AF *pume, pomme* apple, fruit, ultim. fr. LL *pomum*] (15c) **:** a fleshy fruit (as an apple or pear) consisting of an outer thickened fleshy layer and a central core with usu. five seeds enclosed in a capsule
pome·gran·ate \ˈpä-mə-ˌgra-nət; ˈpäm-ˌgra-nət, ˈpəm-\ *n* [ME *poumgrenet,* fr. AF *pome garnette,* lit., seedy fruit] (14c) **1 :** a several-celled reddish berry that is about the size of an orange with a thick leathery skin and many seeds with pulpy crimson arils of tart flavor **2 :** a widely cultivated tropical Asian tree (*Punica granatum* of the family Punicaceae) bearing pomegranates
pom·e·lo \ˈpä-mə-ˌlō\ *n, pl* **-los** [prob. alter. of earlier *pompelmous,* fr. D *pompelmoes*] (1858) **1 :** GRAPEFRUIT **2** *or* **pum·me·lo** \ˈpə-\ **a :** a very large thick-rinded usu. pear-shaped citrus fruit differing from the closely related grapefruit esp. in its loose rind and often coarse dry pulp **b :** a large widely cultivated tropical tree (*Citrus maxima* syn. *C. grandis*) of southeast Asia that bears pomelos
Pom·er·a·nian \ˌpä-mə-ˈrā-nē-ən, -nyən\ *n* (1760) **1 :** any of a breed of long-haired compact toy dogs with a soft dense undercoat **2 :** a native or inhabitant of Pomerania — **Pomeranian** *adj*
pom·fret \ˈpäm-frət, ˈpəm-\ *n* [alter. of earlier *pamflet,* prob. fr. F *pample,* fr. Pg *pampo*] (1813) **1 :** any of a family (Bramidae) of usu. deep-bodied spiny-finned oceanic fishes some of which are used for food **2 :** a silvery deep-bodied marine food fish (*Pampus argenteus* of the family Stromateidae) of Asia
pom·mée \pä-ˈmā, ˌpə-\ *adj* [F, fr. MF *pomme* apple, ball] (1725) *of a heraldic cross* **:** having the end of each arm terminating in a ball or disk — see CROSS illustration
[1]**pom·mel** \ˈpə-məl, ˈpä-\ *n* [ME *pomel,* fr. AF, fr. VL **pomellum* ball, knob, fr. dim. of L *pomum* fruit] (14c) **1 :** the knob on the hilt of a sword or saber **2 :** the protuberance at the front and top of a saddle **3 :** either of a pair of removable rounded or U-shaped handles used on the top of a pommel horse
[2]**pom·mel** \ˈpə-məl\ *vt* **-meled** *or* **-melled; -mel·ing** *or* **-mel·ling** \ˈpə-mə-liŋ, ˈpəm-liŋ\ [ˈ*pommel*] (1530) **:** PUMMEL
pommel horse *n* (1908) **1 :** a gymnastics apparatus for swinging and balancing feats that consists of a padded rectangular or cylindrical form

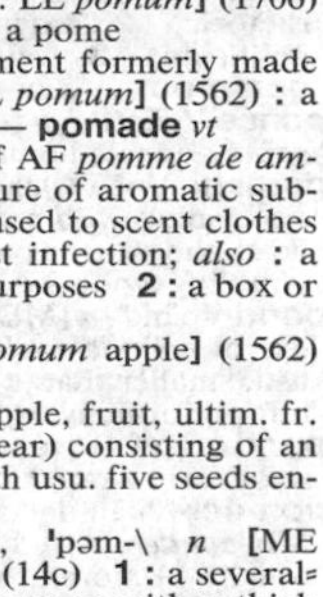

pommel horse 1

\ə\ **abut** \ᵊ\ **kitten,** F **table** \ər\ **further** \a\ **ash** \ā\ **ace** \ä\ **mop, mar** \au̇\ **out** \ch\ **chin** \e\ **bet** \ē\ **easy** \g\ **go** \i\ **hit** \ī\ **ice** \j\ **job** \ŋ\ **sing** \ō\ **go** \ȯ\ **law** \ȯi\ **boy** \th\ **thin** \t͟h\ **the** \ü\ **loot** \u̇\ **foot** \y\ **yet** \zh\ **vision, beige** \k̲, ⁿ, œ, ue, ʸ\ *see* Guide to Pronunciation

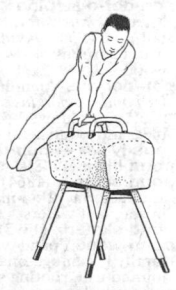

with two pommels on the top and that is supported in a horizontal position above the floor **2 :** an event in which the pommel horse is used

Pom·my *or* **Pom·mie** \ˈpä-mē\ *n, pl* **Pommies** [by shortening & alter. fr. *pomegranate,* alter. of *Jimmy Grant,* rhyming slang for *immigrant*] (1912) *Austral & NewZeal, usu disparaging* **:** BRITON; *esp* **:** an English immigrant

Po·mo \ˈpō-(ˌ)mō\ *n, pl* **Pomo** *or* **Pomos** [in part fr. Northern Pomo *pʰoʔmo·,* a village name, lit., at red earth hole; in part fr. Northern Pomo *pʰoʔmaʔ* one residing at (the place denoted by the preceding element)] (1852) **1 :** a member of a group of American Indian peoples of northern California **2 :** any of the family of languages spoken by the Pomo

po·mol·o·gy \pō-ˈmä-lə-jē\ *n* [NL *pomologia,* fr. L *pomum* fruit + *-logia* -logy] (1818) **:** the science and practice of growing fruit — **po·mo·log·i·cal** \ˌpō-mə-ˈlä-ji-kəl\ *adj* — **po·mol·o·gist** \pō-ˈmä-lə-jist\ *n*

pomp \ˈpämp\ *n* [ME, fr. AF *pompe,* fr. L *pompa* procession, pomp, fr. Gk *pompē* act of sending, escort, procession, pomp, fr. *pempein* to send] (14c) **1 :** a show of magnificence **:** SPLENDOR ⟨every day begins . . . in a ~ of flaming colours —F. D. Ommanney⟩ **2 :** a ceremonial or festival display (as a train of followers or a pageant) **3 a :** ostentatious display **:** VAINGLORY **b :** an ostentatious gesture or act

pom·pa·dour \ˈpäm-pə-ˌdȯr\ *n* [Marquise de *Pompadour*] (1756) **1 a :** a man's style of hairdressing in which the hair is combed into a high mound in front **b :** a woman's style of hairdressing in which the hair is brushed into a loose full roll around the face **2 :** hair dressed in a pompadour — **pom·pa·doured** \-ˌdȯrd\ *adj*

pom·pa·no \ˈpäm-pə-ˌnō, ˈpəm-\ *n, pl* **-no** *or* **-nos** [AmerSp *pámpano,* fr. Sp, a percoid fish (*Sparus auratus*), lit., vine leaf, fr. L *pampinus*] (1778) **1 :** a carangid food fish (*Trachinotus carolinus*) of the western Atlantic and Gulf of Mexico; *broadly* **:** any of several related fishes **2 :** a small bluish or greenish butterfish (*Peprilus simillimus*) of the Pacific coast of No. America

¹pom–pom \ˈpäm-ˌpäm\ *n* [alter. of *pompon*] (1873) **1 :** an ornamental ball or tuft used esp. on clothing, caps, or costumes **2 :** a handheld usu. brightly colored fluffy ball flourished by cheerleaders

²pom–pom *n* [imit.; fr. the sound of its discharge] (1899) **:** an automatic antiaircraft gun of 20 to 40 millimeters mounted esp. on ships

pom·pon \ˈpäm-ˌpän\ *n* [F, fr. MF *pompe* tuft of ribbons] (1751) **1 :** ¹POM-POM 1 **2 :** a chrysanthemum or dahlia with small rounded flower heads

pom·pos·i·ty \päm-ˈpä-sə-tē\ *n, pl* **-ties** (1620) **1 :** pompous demeanor, speech, or behavior **2 :** a pompous gesture, habit, or act

pomp·ous \ˈpäm-pəs\ *adj* (15c) **1 :** excessively elevated or ornate ⟨~ rhetoric⟩ **2 :** having or exhibiting self-importance **:** ARROGANT ⟨a ~ politician⟩ **3 :** relating to or suggestive of pomp **:** MAGNIFICENT — **pomp·ous·ly** *adv* — **pomp·ous·ness** *n*

ponce \ˈpän(t)s\ *n* [origin unknown] (1872) *Brit* **:** PIMP; *also, usu disparaging* **:** a male homosexual

pon·cho \ˈpän-(ˌ)chō\ *n, pl* **ponchos** [AmerSp, fr. Mapuche] (1717) **1 :** a blanket with a slit in the middle so that it can be slipped over the head and worn as a sleeveless garment **2 :** a waterproof garment resembling a poncho and having an integral hood

¹pond \ˈpänd\ *n* [ME *ponde* artificially confined body of water, prob. alter. of *pounde* enclosure — more at POUND] (14c) **:** a body of water usu. smaller than a lake ⟨a fishing ~⟩ — sometimes used with *the* to refer informally or facetiously to the Atlantic Ocean

²pond *vt* (1694) **:** to block (as a stream) to create a pond ~ *vi* **:** to collect in or form a pond

pon·der \ˈpän-dər\ *vb* **pon·dered; pon·der·ing** \-d(ə-)riŋ\ [ME, fr. MF *ponderer,* fr. L *ponderare* to weigh, ponder, fr. *ponder-, pondus* weight — more at PENDANT] *vt* (14c) **1 :** to weigh in the mind **:** APPRAISE ⟨~*ed* their chances of success⟩ **2 :** to think about **:** reflect on ⟨~*ed* the events of the day⟩ ~ *vi* **:** to think or consider esp. quietly, soberly, and deeply — **pon·der·er** \-dər-ər\ *n*

syn PONDER, MEDITATE, MUSE, RUMINATE mean to consider or examine attentively or deliberately. PONDER implies a careful weighing of a problem or, often, prolonged inconclusive thinking about a matter ⟨*pondered* the course of action⟩. MEDITATE implies a definite focusing of one's thoughts on something so as to understand it deeply ⟨*meditated* on the meaning of life⟩. MUSE suggests a more or less focused daydreaming as in remembrance ⟨*mused* upon childhood joys⟩. RUMINATE implies going over the same matter in one's thoughts again and again but suggests little of either purposive thinking or rapt absorption ⟨*ruminated* on past disappointments⟩.

pon·der·a·ble \ˈpän-d(ə-)rə-bəl\ *adj* [LL *ponderabilis,* fr. *ponderare*] (1813) **:** significant enough to be worth considering **:** APPRECIABLE ***syn*** see PERCEPTIBLE

pon·der·o·sa pine \ˌpän-də-ˈrō-sə-, -zə-\ *n* [NL *ponderosa,* specific epithet of *Pinus ponderosa,* fr. L, fem. of *ponderosus* ponderous] (1878) **:** a tall pine (*Pinus ponderosa*) of western No. America with long needles usu. in groups of two or three; *also* **:** its strong reddish straight-grained wood

pon·der·ous \ˈpän-d(ə-)rəs\ *adj* [ME, fr. AF *ponderus,* fr. L *ponderosus,* fr. *ponder-, pondus* weight] (15c) **1 :** of very great weight **2 :** unwieldy or clumsy because of weight and size **3 :** oppressively or unpleasantly dull **:** LIFELESS ⟨~ prose⟩ ***syn*** see HEAVY — **pon·der·ous·ly** *adv* — **pon·der·ous·ness** *n*

pond lily *n* (1748) **:** WATER LILY

pond scum *n* (1864) **1 :** any of various algae (esp. spirogyra) or cyanobacteria **2 :** a mass of tangled filaments of algae or cyanobacteria in stagnant waters

pond skater *n* (1895) **:** WATER STRIDER

pond·weed \ˈpänd-ˌwēd\ *n* (1578) **:** any of a genus (*Potamogeton* of the family Potamogetonaceae, the pondweed family) of aquatic plants with jointed usu. rooting stems, floating or submerged leaves, and spikes of greenish flowers

pone \ˈpōn\ *n* [modif. of Virginia Algonquian *appone*] (1634) *Southern & Midland* **:** CORN PONE

pon·gee \ˌpän-ˈjē, ˈpän-ˌ\ *n, often attrib* [Chin (Beijing) *běnjī,* fr. *běn* own + *jī* loom] (1711) **:** a thin soft fabric of Chinese origin woven from raw silk; *also* **:** an imitation of this fabric in cotton or a synthetic fiber (as of polyester or rayon)

pon·gid \ˈpän-jəd, ˈpäŋ-gəd\ *n* [ultim. fr. Kongo *mpongi* ape] (1950) **:** any of a family (Pongidae) of apes that includes the chimpanzee, gorilla, and orangutan — **pongid** *adj*

¹pon·iard \ˈpän-yərd\ *n* [MF *poignard,* fr. *poing* fist, fr. OF *puing,* fr. L *pugnus* fist — more at PUNGENT] (1588) **:** a dagger with a usu. slender blade of triangular or square cross section

²poniard *vt* (1601) **:** to pierce or kill with a poniard

pons \ˈpänz\ *n, pl* **pon·tes** \ˈpän-ˌtēz\ [NL, short for *pons Varolii*] (1831) **:** a broad mass of chiefly transverse nerve fibers in the mammalian brain stem lying ventral to the cerebellum at the anterior end of the medulla oblongata — see BRAIN illustration

pons asi·no·rum \ˈpänz-ˌa-sə-ˈnȯr-əm\ *n* [NL, lit., asses' bridge, name applied to the proposition that the base angles of an isosceles triangle are equal] (1751) **:** a critical test of ability or understanding; *also* **:** STUMBLING BLOCK

pons Va·ro·lii \-və-ˈrō-lē-ˌī, -lē-ˌē\ *n* [NL, lit., bridge of Varoli, fr. Costanzo *Varoli* †1575 Ital. surgeon and anatomist] (ca. 1693) **:** PONS

pon·ti·fex \ˈpän-tə-ˌfeks\ *n, pl* **pon·tif·i·ces** \pän-ˈti-fə-ˌsēz\ [L *pontific-, pontifex,* fr. *pont-, pons* bridge + *facere* to make — more at FIND, DO] (ca. 1580) **:** a member of the council of priests in ancient Rome

pon·tiff \ˈpän-təf\ *n* [F *pontif,* fr. L *pontific-, pontifex*] (1626) **1 :** PONTIFEX **2 :** BISHOP; *specif, often cap* **:** POPE 1

¹pon·tif·i·cal \pän-ˈti-fi-kəl\ *n* [ME, fr. AF, fr. ML *pontificale,* fr. neut. of *pontificalis*] (14c) **1 :** episcopal attire; *specif* **:** the insignia of the episcopal order worn by a prelate when celebrating a pontifical mass — usu. used in pl. **2 :** a book containing the forms for sacraments and rites performed by a bishop

²pontifical *adj* [ME, fr. AF, fr. L *pontificalis,* fr. *pontific-, pontifex*] (15c) **1 a :** of or relating to a pontiff or pontifex **b :** celebrated by a prelate of episcopal rank with distinctive ceremonies ⟨~ mass⟩ **2 :** POMPOUS **3 :** pretentiously dogmatic — **pon·tif·i·cal·ly** \-k(ə-)lē\ *adv*

¹pon·tif·i·cate \pän-ˈti-fi-kət, -ˌkāt\ *n* [ME, fr. L *pontificatus,* fr. *pontific-, pontifex*] (15c) **:** the state, office, or term of office of a pontiff

²pon·tif·i·cate \pän-ˈti-fə-ˌkāt\ *vi* **-cat·ed; -cat·ing** [ML *pontificatus,* pp. of *pontificare,* fr. L *pontific-, pontifex*] (1818) **1 a :** to officiate as a pontiff **b :** to celebrate pontifical mass **2 :** to speak or express opinions in a pompous or dogmatic way — **pon·tif·i·ca·tion** \(ˌ)pän-ˌti-fə-ˈkā-shən\ *n* — **pon·tif·i·ca·tor** \-ˌkā-tər\ *n*

pon·til \ˈpän-tᵊl\ *n* [F, perh. fr. It *puntello,* dim. of *punto* point, fr. L *punctus* — more at POINT] (1832) **:** PUNTY — called also *pontil rod*

pon·tine \ˈpän-ˌtīn\ *adj* [NL *pont-, pons* pons] (1889) **:** of or relating to the pons

Pont l'É·vêque \ˌpōⁿ-lā-ˈvek\ *n* [*Pont l'Évêque,* town in France] (ca. 1889) **:** a soft surface-ripened cheese firmer, yellower, and having less surface mold than Camembert

¹pon·toon \pän-ˈtün\ *n* [F *ponton,* fr. OF, fr. L *ponton-, ponto*] (1690) **1 :** a flat-bottomed boat (as a lighter); *esp* **:** a flat-bottomed boat or portable float used in building a floating temporary bridge **2 :** a float esp. of a seaplane

²pontoon *n* [perh. alter. of *vingt-et-un*] (ca. 1917) *Brit* **:** BLACKJACK 5

po·ny \ˈpō-nē\ *n, pl* **ponies** [prob. fr. obs. F *poulenet,* dim. of F *poulain* colt, fr. OF *pulain,* perh. fr. ML *pullamen* young animal, fr. L *pullus* — more at FOAL] (1659) **1 a :** a small horse; *esp* **:** one of any of several breeds of very small stocky animals noted for their gentleness and endurance **b :** a bronco, mustang, or similar horse of the western U.S. **c :** RACEHORSE — usu. used in pl. **2 :** something smaller than standard: as **a :** a small beer glass **b :** a small liqueur glass typically holding one ounce **3 :** a literal translation of a foreign language text; *esp* **:** one used surreptitiously by students in preparing or reciting lessons

pony express *n, often cap P&E* (1847) **:** a rapid postal and express system that operated across the western U.S. in 1860–61 by relays of horses and riders

po·ny·tail \ˈpō-nē-ˌtāl\ *n* (1951) **:** a hairstyle in which the hair is pulled together and banded usu. at the back of the head so as to resemble a pony's tail — **po·ny·tailed** \-ˌtāld\ *adj*

pony up *vb* **po·nied up; po·ny·ing up** [origin unknown] *vt* (1824) **:** to pay (money) esp. in settlement of an account ~ *vi* **:** PAY

Pon·zi scheme \ˈpän-zē-\ *n* [Charles *Ponzi* †1949 Am. (Ital.-born) swindler] (1973) **:** an investment swindle in which some early investors are paid off with money put up by later ones in order to encourage more and bigger risks

pon·zu \ˈpän-(ˌ)zü\ *n* [Jp *ponsu, ponzu* juice squeezed from sour oranges, fr. D *pons,* lit., punch, fr. E ⁴*punch*] (1972) **:** a tangy sauce made with citrus juice, rice wine vinegar, and soy sauce and used esp. on seafood

-poo \ˌpü, ˈpü\ *suffix* [origin unknown] — used as a derogatory diminutive ⟨cutesy-*poo*⟩

¹pooch \ˈpüch\ *vb* [alter. of ¹*pouch*] (ca. 1923) *chiefly dial* **:** BULGE

²pooch *n* [origin unknown] (1924) **:** DOG

pood \ˈpüd, ˈpüt\ *n* [Russ *pud,* fr. ORuss, fr. ON *pund* pound — more at POUND] (1554) **:** a Russian unit of weight equal to about 36.11 pounds (16.38 kilograms)

poo·dle \ˈpü-dᵊl\ *n* [G *Pudel,* short for *Pudelhund,* fr. *pudeln* to splash + *Hund* dog] (1810) **1 :** any of a breed of intelligent dogs that have a curly dense solid-colored coat and that are grouped into standard, miniature, and toy sizes which are often considered separate breeds — compare TOY POODLE **2 :** a fabric with a nubby or coarsely looped surface that resembles a poodle's coat — called also *poodle cloth*

¹poof \ˈpüf, ˈpu̇f\ *interj* (1824) — used to express disdain or dismissal or to suggest instantaneous occurrence

²poof *also* **poove** \ˈpüv, ˈpu̇v\ *n, pl* **poofs** *also* **pooves** [perh. alter. of ²*puff*] (ca. 1860) *Brit, usu disparaging* **:** a male homosexual

poof·ter \ˈpüf-tər, ˈpu̇f-\ *also* **poof·tah** \-tə\ *n* [by alter.] (1903) *Brit, usu disparaging* **:** POOF

pooh \ˈpü, ˈpu̇\ *interj* (1602) — used to express contempt or disapproval

pooh–bah *also* **poo–bah** \ˈpü-ˌbä, -ˌbȯ\ *n, often cap P&B* [*Pooh-Bah,* character in Gilbert and Sullivan's opera *The Mikado* (1885) bearing the title Lord-High-Everything-Else] (1888) **1 :** a person holding many offices or positions **2 :** a person in high position or of great influence

pooh–pooh \ˈpü-(ˌ)pü, pü-ˈ\ *also* **pooh** \ˈpü\ *vb* [*pooh*] *vi* (1827) **:** to express contempt or impatience ~ *vt* **:** to express contempt for or make light of **:** PLAY DOWN, DISMISS

¹pool \ˈpül\ *n* [ME, fr. OE *pōl;* akin to OHG *pfuol* pool] (bef. 12c) **1 a** (1) **:** a small and rather deep body of usu. fresh water (2) **:** a quiet place in a stream (3) **:** a body of water forming above a dam **b**

: something resembling a pool ⟨a ~ of light⟩ **2 :** a small body of standing liquid **3 :** a continuous area of porous sedimentary rock that yields petroleum or gas **4 :** SWIMMING POOL

2**pool** *vi* (1626) **1 :** to form a pool **2** *of blood* **:** to accumulate or become static (as in the veins of a bodily part)

3**pool** *n* [F *poule,* lit., hen, fr. OF, fem. of *poul* cock — more at PULLET] (1708) **1 a :** an aggregate stake to which each player of a game has contributed **b :** all the money bet by a number of persons on a particular event **2 a :** a game played on an English billiard table in which each of the players stakes a sum and the winner takes all **b :** any of various games of billiards played on an oblong table having 6 pockets with usu. 15 object balls **3 :** an aggregation of the interests or property of different persons made to further a joint undertaking by subjecting them to the same control and a common liability **4 :** a readily available supply: as **a :** the whole quantity of a particular material present in the body and available for function or the satisfying of metabolic demands **b :** a body product (as blood) collected from many donors and stored for later use **c :** a group of people available for some purpose ⟨a shrinking ~ of applicants⟩ ⟨typing ~⟩ **5 :** GENE POOL **6 :** a group of journalists from usu. several news organizations using pooled resources (as television equipment) to produce shared coverage esp. of events to which access is restricted

4**pool** *vt* (1879) **:** to combine (as resources) in a common pool or effort

pool·room \ˈpül-ˌrüm, -ˌru̇m\ *n* (1861) **1 :** a room in which bookmaking is carried on **2 :** a room for the playing of pool

1**pool·side** \-ˌsīd\ *n* (1921) **:** the area surrounding a swimming pool

2**poolside** *adv or adj* (1973) **:** at or near the side of a pool

1**poop** \ˈpüp\ *n* [ME, fr. AF *pope,* fr. L *puppis*] (15c) **1** *obs* **:** STERN **2 :** an enclosed superstructure at the stern of a ship above the main deck

2**poop** *vt* (1748) **1 :** to break over the stern of **2 :** to ship (a sea or wave) over the stern

3**poop** *vi* [earlier, to break wind, fr. ME *poupen* to make a gulping sound, of imit. origin] (ca. 1903) **:** DEFECATE

4**poop** *n* (1965) **:** FECES

5**poop** *vb* [origin unknown] *vt* (ca. 1932) *slang* **:** to put out of breath; *also* **:** to tire out ~ *vi, slang* **:** to become exhausted ⟨~ out⟩

6**poop** *n* [perh. fr. 4*poop*] (ca. 1941) *slang* **:** INFORMATION, SCOOP

poop deck *n* (1815) **:** a partial deck above a ship's main afterdeck

poop·er–scoop·er \ˈpü-pər-ˌskü-pər\ *n* [5*poop*] (1976) **:** a device used for picking up the excrement of a pet (as a dog) for disposal

poor \ˈpu̇r, ˈpȯr\ *adj* [ME *poure,* fr. AF *povre, pore,* fr. L *pauper;* akin to L *paucus* little and to L *parere* to give birth to, produce — more at FEW, PARE] (13c) **1 a :** lacking material possessions **b :** of, relating to, or characterized by poverty **2 a :** less than adequate **:** MEAGER **b :** small in worth **3 :** exciting pity ⟨you ~ thing⟩ **4 a :** inferior in quality or value **b :** HUMBLE, UNPRETENTIOUS **c :** MEAN, PETTY **5 :** LEAN, EMACIATED **6 :** BARREN, UNPRODUCTIVE — used of land **7 :** INDIFFERENT, UNFAVORABLE **8 :** lacking a normal or adequate supply of something specified — often used in combination ⟨oil-*poor* countries⟩ — **poor·ish** \-ish\ *adj* — **poor·ness** *n*

poor box *n* (1621) **:** a box (as in a church) for alms for the poor

poor boy *var of* PO'BOY

Poor Clare \-ˈkler\ *n* (1608) **:** a member of an austere order of nuns founded by St. Clare under the direction of St. Francis in Assisi, Italy, in 1212

poor farm *n* (1726) **:** a farm maintained at public expense for the support and employment of needy persons

poor·house \-ˌhau̇s\ *n* (1792) **:** a place maintained at public expense to house needy or dependent persons

poor law *n* (1752) **:** a law providing for or regulating the public relief or support of the poor

1**poor·ly** \ˈpu̇r-lē, ˈpȯr-\ *adv* (13c) **:** in a poor condition or manner; *esp* **:** in an inferior or imperfect way **:** BADLY ⟨sang ~⟩

2**poor·ly** *adj* (1749) **:** somewhat ill **:** INDISPOSED

poor–mouth \ˈpu̇r-ˌmau̇th, ˈpȯr-, -ˌmau̇th\ *vi* (1964) **:** to plead poverty as a defense or excuse ~ *vt* **:** to speak disparagingly of

poor mouth *n* (1764) **:** an exaggerated claim of poverty

poor–spir·it·ed \-ˈspir-ə-təd\ *adj* (1656) **:** lacking zest, confidence, or courage — **poor–spir·it·ed·ly** *adv* — **poor–spir·it·ed·ness** *n*

poor white *n* (1819) *often offensive* **:** WHITE TRASH

1**pop** \ˈpäp\ *vb* **popped; pop·ping** [ME *poppen,* of imit. origin] *vt* (15c) **1 :** to strike or knock sharply **:** HIT **2 :** to push, put, or thrust suddenly and often deftly ⟨~*s* a grape into her mouth⟩ ⟨*popped* in a CD⟩ **3 :** to cause to explode or burst open ⟨*popped* some popcorn⟩ ⟨~ the trunk⟩ **4 :** to fire at **:** SHOOT **5 :** to take (pills) esp. frequently or habitually **6 :** to open with a pop ⟨~ a cold beer⟩ ~ *vi* **1 a :** to go, come, or appear suddenly — often used with *up* ⟨images *popping* up on the screen⟩ ⟨~ in for a visit⟩ **b :** to escape or break away from something (as a point of attachment) usu. suddenly or unexpectedly **2 :** to make or burst with a sharp sound ⟨a balloon *popped*⟩ **3 :** to protrude from the sockets ⟨eyes *popping* with amazement⟩ **4 :** to shoot with a firearm **5 :** to hit a pop fly — often used with *up* or *out* — **pop the question :** to propose marriage

2**pop** *n* (1591) **1 :** a sharp explosive sound **2 :** a shot from a gun **3 :** SODA POP **4 :** POP FLY **5 :** power to hit a baseball hard ⟨a hitter with some ~ in his bat⟩ **6 :** a drink or shot of alcohol — **a pop 1 :** for each one **:** APIECE ⟨tickets at $10 *a pop*⟩ **2 :** for each attempt ⟨rushed for an average of five yards *a pop*⟩

3**pop** *adv* (1621) **:** like or with a pop **:** SUDDENLY — often used interjectionally

4**pop** *n* [short for *poppa*] (1838) **:** FATHER

5**pop** *adj* [by shortening] (1880) **1 :** POPULAR ⟨~ music⟩: as **a :** of or relating to popular music ⟨~ singer⟩ **b :** of or relating to the popular culture disseminated through the mass media ⟨~ psychology⟩ ⟨~ grammarians⟩ ⟨~ society⟩ **2 a :** of or relating to pop art ⟨~ painter⟩ **b :** having, using, or imitating themes or techniques characteristic of pop art ⟨~ movie⟩

6**pop** *n* (1935) **1 :** popular music **2 :** POP ART **3 :** pop culture

7**pop** *abbr* population

POP *abbr* point of purchase

pop art *n, often cap P&A* (1957) **:** art in which commonplace objects (as road signs, hamburgers, comic strips, or soup cans) are used as subject matter and are often physically incorporated in the work — **pop artist** *n, often cap P*

1**pop·corn** \ˈpäp-ˌkȯrn\ *n* (1823) **:** an Indian corn (*Zea mays praecox*) whose kernels on exposure to heat burst open to form a white starchy mass; *also* **:** the kernels esp. after popping

2**popcorn** *adj* (1950) **:** having widespread appeal but usu. offering little artistic merit or intellectual stimulation ⟨~ movies⟩

pope \ˈpōp\ *n* [ME, fr. OE *pāpa,* fr. LL *papa,* fr. Gk *pappas, papas,* title of bishops, lit., papa] (bef. 12c) **1** *often cap* **:** a prelate who as bishop of Rome is the head of the Roman Catholic Church **2 :** one that resembles a pope (as in authority) **3 a :** the Eastern Orthodox or Coptic patriarch of Alexandria **b :** a priest of an Eastern church

pop·ery \ˈpō-p(ə-)rē\ *n* (ca. 1534) *usu disparaging* **:** ROMAN CATHOLICISM

pop eye \ˈpäp-ˌī\ *n* [back-formation fr. *pop-eyed*] (1828) **:** an eye staring and bulging (as from excitement) — **pop–eyed** \-ˌīd\ *adj*

pop fly *n* (1887) **:** a high fly ball in baseball

pop·gun \ˈpäp-ˌgən\ *n* (1622) **:** a toy gun that usu. shoots a cork and produces a popping sound

pop·in·jay \ˈpä-pən-ˌjā\ *n* [ME *papejay* parrot, fr. MF *papegai, papejai,* fr. Ar *babghā'*] (1596) **:** a strutting supercilious person

pop·ish \ˈpō-pish\ *adj* [*pope*] (1528) *often disparaging* **:** ROMAN CATHOLIC

pop·lar \ˈpä-plər\ *n* [ME *popler,* fr. AF, fr. OF **pople* poplar, fr. L *populus*] (14c) **1 a :** any of a genus (*Populus*) of slender catkin-bearing quick-growing deciduous trees (as an aspen or cottonwood) of the willow family **b :** the wood of a poplar **2 :** TULIP TREE 1

pop·lin \ˈpä-plən\ *n* [F *papeline*] (1710) **:** a strong fabric in plain weave with crosswise ribs

pop·li·te·al \ˌpä-plə-ˈtē-əl *also* pä-ˈpli-tē-əl\ *adj* [NL *popliteus,* fr. L *poplit-, poples* knee joint, back of the knee] (1786) **:** of or relating to the back part of the leg behind the knee joint

pop off *vi* (1764) **1 a :** to die unexpectedly **b :** to leave suddenly **2 :** to talk thoughtlessly and often loudly or angrily

popover \ˈpäp-ˌō-vər\ *n* (1875) **:** a hollow quick bread shaped like a muffin and made from a thin batter of eggs, milk, and flour

poppa *var of* PAPA

pop·per \ˈpä-pər\ *n* (1750) **1 :** one that pops; *esp* **:** a utensil for popping corn **2** *slang* **:** a vial of amyl nitrite or butyl nitrite used illicitly as an inhalational aphrodisiac

pop·pet \ˈpä-pət\ *n* [ME *popet* — more at PUPPET] (15c) **1 a** *Midland* **:** DOLL **b** *obs* **:** MARIONETTE **2** *chiefly Brit* **:** DEAR **3 a :** an upright support or guide of a machine that is fastened at the bottom only **b :** a valve that rises perpendicularly to or from its seat

pop·pied \ˈpä-pēd\ *adj* (1818) **1** *archaic* **:** growing or overgrown with poppies **2 :** DROWSY

1**pop·ple** \ˈpä-pəl\ *n* [ME *popul,* fr. OE, fr. L *populus*] (14c) *chiefly dial* **:** POPLAR 1

2**popple** *n* [*popple,* vb., fr. ME *poplen* to bubble, ripple, prob. of imit. origin] (1875) **:** a choppy sea

pop·py \ˈpä-pē\ *n, pl* **poppies** [ME *popi,* fr. OE *popæg, popig,* modif. of L *papaver*] (bef. 12c) **1 a :** any of a genus (*Papaver* of the family Papaveraceae, the poppy family) of chiefly annual or perennial herbs with milky juice, showy regular flowers, and capsular fruits including the opium poppy and several forms cultivated as ornamentals **b :** an extract or decoction of poppy used medicinally **2 :** a strong reddish orange

pop·py·cock \ˈpä-pē-ˌkäk\ *n* [D dial. *pappekak,* lit., soft dung, fr. D *pap* pap + *kak* dung] (1865) **:** empty talk or writing **:** NONSENSE

pop·py·head \-ˌhed\ *n* (1839) **:** a raised ornament often in the form of a finial generally used on the tops of the upright ends of seats in Gothic churches

poppy seed *n* (14c) **:** the seed of a poppy used chiefly as a topping or flavoring for baked goods

pop quiz *n* (ca. 1960) **:** an unscheduled or unannounced quiz

Pop·si·cle \ˈpäp-ˌsi-kəl, -sə-\ *trademark* — used for flavored and colored water frozen on a stick

pop–top \ˈpäp-ˌtäp\ *n* (1965) **:** a closure that can be pulled by hand to open a can

pop·u·lace \ˈpä-pyə-ləs\ *n* [MF, fr. It *popolaccio* rabble, aug. of *popolo* the people, fr. L *populus*] (1572) **1 :** the common people **:** MASSES **2 :** POPULATION

pop·u·lar \ˈpä-pyə-lər\ *adj* [L *popularis,* fr. *populus* the people, a people] (1548) **1 :** of or relating to the general public **2 :** suitable to the majority: as **a :** adapted to or indicative of the understanding and taste of the majority ⟨a ~ history of the war⟩ **b :** suited to the means of the majority **:** INEXPENSIVE ⟨sold at ~ prices⟩ **3 :** frequently encountered or widely accepted ⟨a ~ theory⟩ **4 :** commonly liked or approved ⟨a very ~ girl⟩ ***syn*** see COMMON — **pop·u·lar·ly** *adv*

popular front *n, often cap P&F* (1936) **:** a coalition esp. of leftist political parties against a common opponent; *specif* **:** one sponsored and dominated by Communists as a device for gaining power

pop·u·lar·ise *Brit var of* POPULARIZE

pop·u·lar·i·ty \ˌpä-pyə-ˈla-rə-tē\ *n* (1601) **:** the quality or state of being popular

pop·u·lar·ize \ˈpä-pyə-lə-ˌrīz\ *vb* **-ized; -iz·ing** *vi* (1593) **:** to cater to popular taste ~ *vt* **:** to make popular: as **a :** to cause to be liked or esteemed **b :** to present in generally understandable or interesting form — **pop·u·lar·i·za·tion** \ˌpä-pyə-lə-rə-ˈzā-shən\ *n* — **pop·u·lar·iz·er** \ˈpä-pyə-lə-ˌrī-zər\ *n*

popular sovereignty *n* (1848) **1 :** a doctrine in political theory that government is created by and subject to the will of the people **2 :** a pre-Civil War doctrine asserting the right of the people living in a newly organized territory to decide by vote of their territorial legislature whether or not slavery would be permitted there

pop·u·late \ˈpä-pyə-ˌlāt\ *vt* **-lat·ed; -lat·ing** [ML *populatus,* pp. of *populare* to people, fr. L *populus* people] (1578) **1 :** to have a place in **:** OCCUPY, INHABIT **2 a :** to furnish or provide with inhabitants **:** PEOPLE **b :** to provide with members

\ə\ **abut** \ᵊ\ kitten, F table \ər\ **further** \a\ **ash** \ā\ **ace** \ä\ **mop, mar** \au̇\ **out** \ch\ **chin** \e\ **bet** \ē\ **easy** \g\ **go** \i\ **hit** \ī\ **ice** \j\ **job** \ŋ\ **sing** \ō\ **go** \ȯ\ **law** \ȯi\ **boy** \th\ **thin** \th\ **the** \ü\ **loot** \u̇\ **foot** \y\ **yet** \zh\ **vision, beige** \k, ⁿ, œ, ue, ʸ\ *see* Guide to Pronunciation

pop·u·la·tion \ˌpä-pyə-ˈlā-shən\ *n* [LL *population-, populatio,* fr. L *populus*] (1612) **1 a** : the whole number of people or inhabitants in a country or region **b** : the total of individuals occupying an area or making up a whole **c** : the total of particles at a particular energy level — used esp. of atoms in a laser **2** : the act or process of populating **3 a** : a body of persons or individuals having a quality or characteristic in common **b** (1) : the organisms inhabiting a particular locality (2) : a group of interbreeding organisms that represents the level of organization at which speciation begins **4** : a group of individual persons, objects, or items from which samples are taken for statistical measurement — **pop·u·la·tion·al** \-shnəl, -shə-nᵊl\ *adj*

population explosion *n* (1953) : a pyramiding of numbers of a biological population; *esp* : the recent great increase in human numbers resulting from increased survival and exponential population growth

[1]**pop·u·list** \ˈpä-pyə-list\ *n* [L *populus* the people] (1892) **1** : a member of a political party claiming to represent the common people; *esp, often cap* : a member of a U.S. political party formed in 1891 primarily to represent agrarian interests and to advocate the free coinage of silver and government control of monopolies **2** : a believer in the rights, wisdom, or virtues of the common people — **pop·u·lism** \-ˌli-zəm\ *n* — **pop·u·lis·tic** \ˌpä-pyə-ˈlis-tik\ *adj*

[2]**populist** *adj* (1893) **1** *often cap* : of, relating to, or characterized by populism **2 a** : POPULAR 1 **b** : POPULAR 2

pop·u·lous \ˈpä-pyə-ləs\ *adj* [ME, fr. L *populosus,* fr. *populus* people] (15c) **1 a** : densely populated **b** : having a large population **2 a** : NUMEROUS **b** : filled to capacity — **pop·u·lous·ly** *adv* — **pop·u·lous·ness** *n*

[1]**pop–up** \ˈpäp-ˌəp\ *n* (1906) **1** : POP FLY **2** : a component or device that pops up **3** : a pop-up book **4** : a pop-up window on a computer screen

[2]**pop–up** *adj* (1934) **1** : of, relating to, or having a component or device that pops up ⟨a ~ book⟩ **2** : appearing suddenly on a computer screen ⟨a ~ window⟩

por *abbr* portrait

por·bea·gle \ˈpȯr-ˌbē-gəl\ *n* [Corn *porgh-bugel*] (1758) : a viviparous mackerel shark (*Lamna nasus*) chiefly of the No. Atlantic and southwestern Pacific oceans with a pointed snout and crescent-shaped tail

por·ce·lain \ˈpȯr-s(ə-)lən\ *n* [MF *porcelaine* cowrie shell, porcelain, fr. It *porcellana,* fr. *porcello* vulva, lit., little pig, fr. L *porcellus,* dim. of *porcus* pig, vulva; fr. the shape of the shell — more at FARROW] (ca. 1530) **1** : a hard, fine-grained, sonorous, nonporous, and usu. translucent and white ceramic ware that consists essentially of kaolin, quartz, and a feldspathic rock and is fired at a high temperature — called also *hard-paste porcelain, true porcelain* **2** : SOFT-PASTE PORCELAIN — **por·ce·lain·like** \-ˌlīk\ *adj* — **por·ce·la·ne·ous** *or* **por·cel·la·ne·ous** \ˌpȯr-sə-ˈlā-nē-əs\ *adj*

porcelain enamel *n* (1883) : a fired-on opaque glassy coating on metal

por·ce·lain·ize \ˈpȯr-s(ə-)lə-ˌnīz\ *vt* **-ized; -iz·ing** (1951) : to fire a glassy coating on (as steel)

porch \ˈpȯrch\ *n* [ME *porche,* fr. AF, fr. L *porticus* portico, fr. *porta* gate; akin to L *portus* port — more at FORD] (14c) **1** : a covered area adjoining an entrance to a building and usu. having a separate roof **2** *obs* : PORTICO

por·cine \ˈpȯr-ˌsīn\ *adj* [L *porcinus,* fr. *porcus* pig — more at FARROW] (ca. 1656) : of, relating to, or suggesting swine : PIGGISH

por·ci·ni \pȯr-ˈchē-(ˌ)nē\ *n, pl* **porcini** *also* **porcinis** [It, pl. of *porcino,* short for *fungo porcino,* lit., porcine mushroom] (1976) : a large wild edible brownish boletus mushroom (*Boletus edulis*) — called also *cèpe*

por·ci·no \pȯr-ˈchē-(ˌ)nō\ *n, pl* **-ni** [It] (1976) : PORCINI

por·cu·pine \ˈpȯr-kyə-ˌpīn\ *n, pl* **porcupines** *also* **porcupine** [ME *porke despyne,* fr. MF *porc espin,* fr. OIt *porcospino,* fr. L *porcus* pig + *spina* spine, prickle] (15c) : any of various relatively large slow-moving chiefly herbivorous rodents having sharp erectile spines mingled with the hair and constituting an Old World terrestrial family (Hystricidae) and a New World chiefly arboreal family (Erethizontidae)

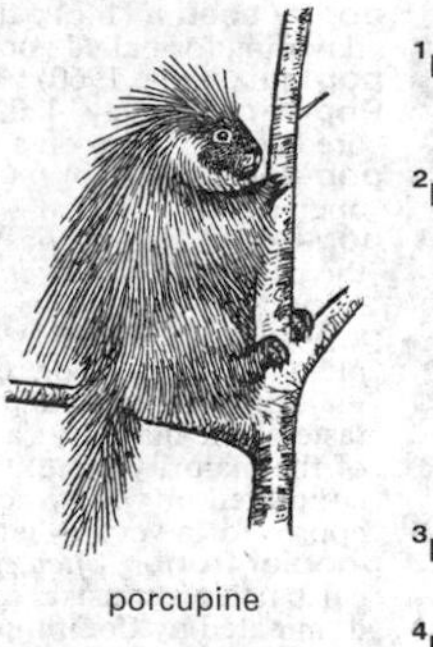
porcupine

porcupine fish *n* (1681) : any of several bony fishes (family Diodontidae) that have sharp spines covering the body and inflate themselves into a sphere when threatened; *esp* : a spotted chiefly tropical fish (*Diodon hystrix*) that is olive to brown above with white below

[1]**pore** \ˈpȯr\ *vi* **pored; por·ing** [ME *pouren*] (13c) **1** : to gaze intently **2** : to read or study attentively — usu. used with *over* **3** : to reflect or meditate steadily

[2]**pore** *n* [ME, fr. MF, fr. L *porus,* fr. Gk *poros* passage, pore — more at FARE] (14c) **1** : a minute opening esp. in an animal or plant; *esp* : one by which matter passes through a membrane **2** : a small interstice (as in soil) admitting absorption or passage of liquid — **pored** *adj*

pore fungus *n* (1922) : a fungus (family Boletaceae or Polyporaceae) having the spore-bearing surface within tubes or pores

por·gy \ˈpȯr-gē\ *n, pl* **porgies** *also* **porgy** [alter. of *pargo,* fr. Sp & Pg, fr. L *phager,* fr. Gk *phagros*] (1671) **1** : a blue-spotted silvery-red food fish (*Pagrus pagrus* of the family Sparidae) of the eastern and western Atlantic; *also* : any of various fishes (as a scup) of the same family **2** [alter. of *pogy*] : any of various bony fishes (as a menhaden) of families other than that of the porgy

pork \ˈpȯrk\ *n* [ME, fr. AF *porc* pig, fr. L *porcus* — more at FARROW] (14c) **1** : the fresh or salted flesh of swine when dressed for food **2** : government funds, jobs, or favors distributed by politicians to gain political advantage

pork barrel *n* (1909) : government projects or appropriations yielding rich patronage benefits; *also* : PORK 2

pork belly *n* (ca. 1950) : an uncured side of pork

pork·er \ˈpȯr-kər\ *n* (1657) **1** : HOG; *esp* : a young pig fattened for table use as fresh pork **2** : one resembling a fattened pig : FATTY

pork·pie hat \ˈpȯrk-ˌpī-\ *n* [fr. its shape] (1860) : a hat with a low telescoped crown, flat top, and flexible brim

[1]**porky** \ˈpȯr-kē\ *adj* **pork·i·er; -est** (1852) : resembling a pig : FAT

[2]**por·ky** \ˈpȯr-kē\ *n, pl* **porkies** (1900) : PORCUPINE

porn \ˈpȯrn\ *also* **por·no** \ˈpȯr-(ˌ)nō\ *n, often attrib* (1962) : PORNOGRAPHY

por·nog·ra·pher \pȯr-ˈnä-grə-fər\ *n* (1850) : one who produces pornography

por·nog·ra·phy \-fē\ *n* [Gk *pornographos,* adj., writing about prostitutes, fr. *pornē* prostitute + *graphein* to write; akin to Gk *pernanai* to sell, *poros* journey — more at FARE, CARVE] (1858) **1** : the depiction of erotic behavior (as in pictures or writing) intended to cause sexual excitement **2** : material (as books or a photograph) that depicts erotic behavior and is intended to cause sexual excitement **3** : the depiction of acts in a sensational manner so as to arouse a quick intense emotional reaction ⟨the ~ of violence⟩ — **por·no·graph·ic** \ˌpȯr-nə-ˈgra-fik\ *adj* — **por·no·graph·i·cal·ly** \-fi-k(ə-)lē\ *adv*

porny \ˈpȯr-ne\ *adj* **porn·i·er; -est** (1961) : of, relating to, involved in, or being pornography

po·ros·i·ty \pə-ˈrä-sə-tē, pȯ-\ *n, pl* **-ties** (14c) **1 a** : the quality or state of being porous **b** : the ratio of the volume of interstices of a material to the volume of its mass **2** : PORE

po·rous \ˈpȯr-əs\ *adj* (14c) **1 a** : possessing or full of pores **b** : containing vessels ⟨hardwood is ~⟩ **2 a** : permeable to fluids **b** : permeable to outside influences **3** : capable of being penetrated ⟨~ national boundaries⟩ — **po·rous·ly** *adv* — **po·rous·ness** *n*

por·phyr·ia \pȯr-ˈfir-ē-ə\ *n* [NL, fr. ISV *porphyrin*] (1923) : any of several usu. hereditary abnormalities of porphyrin metabolism characterized by excretion of excess porphyrins in the urine

por·phy·rin \ˈpȯr-fə-rən\ *n* [ISV, fr. Gk *porphyra* purple] (1910) : any of various compounds with a macrocyclic structure that consists essentially of four pyrrole rings joined by four =CH– groups; *esp* : one (as chlorophyll or hemoglobin) containing a central metal atom and usu. exhibiting biological activity

por·phy·rit·ic \ˌpȯr-fə-ˈri-tik\ *adj* [ME *porphiritike,* fr. ML *porphyriticus,* fr. Gk *porphyritikos,* fr. *porphyritēs* (*lithos*) porphyry] (15c) **1** : of or relating to porphyry **2** : having distinct crystals (as of feldspar) in a relatively fine-grained base

por·phy·rop·sin \ˌpȯr-fə-ˈräp-sən\ *n* [Gk *porphyra* purple + E *-opsin* (as in *rhodopsin*)] (1930) : a purple pigment in the retinal rods of freshwater fishes that resembles rhodopsin

por·phy·ry \ˈpȯr-f(ə-)rē\ *n, pl* **-ries** [ME *porphiri,* fr. ML *porphyrium,* alter. of L *porphyrites,* fr. Gk *porphyritēs* (*lithos*), lit., stone like Tyrian purple, fr. *porphyra* purple] (15c) **1** : a rock consisting of feldspar crystals embedded in a compact dark red or purple groundmass **2** : an igneous rock of porphyritic texture

[1]**por·poise** \ˈpȯr-pəs\ *n* [ME *porpoys,* fr. AF *porpeis,* fr. ML *porcopiscis,* fr. L *porcus* pig + *piscis* fish — more at FARROW, FISH] (14c) **1** : any of a family (Phocoenidae) of small gregarious toothed whales; *esp* : a blunt-snouted usu. largely black whale (*Phocoena phocoena*) of the No. Atlantic and No. Pacific that is five to eight feet (1.5 to 2.4 meters) long **2** : DOLPHIN 1a(1)

[2]**porpoise** *vi* (1909) **1** : to leap or plunge like a porpoise ⟨penguins . . . ~ out of the water —David Lewis⟩ **2** : to rise and fall repeatedly

por·rect \pə-ˈrekt, pä-\ *adj* [L *porrectus,* pp. of *porrigere* to stretch out, fr. *por-* forward + *regere* to direct — more at PORTEND, RIGHT] (15c) : extended forward ⟨~ antennae⟩

por·ridge \ˈpȯr-ij, ˈpär-\ *n* [alter. of *pottage*] (ca. 1643) : a soft food made by boiling meal of grains or legumes in milk or water until thick — **por·ridgy** \-i-jē\ *adj*

por·rin·ger \-ən-jər\ *n* [alter. of ME *potager, potynger,* fr. AF *potageer,* fr. *potage* pottage] (1522) : a low usu. metal bowl with a single and usu. flat and pierced handle

[1]**port** \ˈpȯrt\ *n* [ME, fr. OE & AF, fr. L *portus* — more at FORD] (bef. 12c) **1** : a place where ships may ride secure from storms : HAVEN **2 a** : a harbor town or city where ships may take on or discharge cargo **b** : AIRPORT **3** : PORT OF ENTRY

[2]**port** *n* [ME *porte,* fr. AF, gate, door, fr. L *porta* passage, gate; akin to L *portus* port] (bef. 12c) **1** *chiefly Scot* : GATE **2 a** : an opening (as in a valve seat or valve face) for intake or exhaust of a fluid **b** : the area of opening in a cylinder face of a passageway for the working fluid in an engine; *also* : such a passageway **c** : a small opening in a container or vessel esp. for viewing or for the controlled passage of material ⟨access ~⟩ **3 a** : an opening in a vessel's side (as for admitting light or loading cargo) **b** *archaic* : the cover for a porthole **4** : a hole in an armored vehicle or fortification through which guns may be fired **5** : a hardware interface by which a computer is connected to another device (as a printer, a mouse, or another computer); *broadly* : JACK 8

[3]**port** *n* [ME, fr. AF, fr. *porter* to carry, fr. L *portare*] (14c) **1** : the manner of bearing oneself **2** *archaic* : STATE 3 **3** : the position in which a military weapon is carried at the command *port arms*

[4]**port** *vt* [[5]*port*] (1580) : to turn or put (a helm) to the left — used chiefly as a command

[5]**port** *n* [prob. fr. [1]*port* or [2]*port*] (ca. 1644) : the left side of a ship or aircraft looking forward — called also *larboard;* compare STARBOARD — **port** *adj*

[6]**port** *n* [*Oporto,* Portugal] (1691) : a sweet fortified wine of rich taste and aroma made in Portugal; *also* : a similar wine made elsewhere

[7]**port** *vt* [perh. fr. [2]*port* (hardware interface)] (1984) : to translate (software) into a version for another computer or operating system

[8]**port** *abbr* **1** portable **2** portrait

Port *abbr* Portugal

portabella *or* **portabello** *var of* PORTOBELLO

por·ta·bil·i·ty \ˌpȯr-tə-ˈbi-lə-tē\ *n, pl* **-ties** (1667) **1** : the quality or state of being portable **2** : the transferability of a worker's benefits from one pension fund to another when the worker changes jobs

[1]**por·ta·ble** \ˈpȯr-tə-bəl\ *adj* [ME, fr. AF, fr. LL *portabilis,* fr. L *portare* to carry — more at FARE] (15c) **1 a** : capable of being carried or moved about ⟨a ~ TV⟩ **b** : characterized by portability ⟨a ~ pension⟩ **c** : usable on many computers with little or no modification ⟨~ software⟩ **2** *archaic* : BEARABLE — **por·ta·bly** \ˈpȯr-tə-blē\ *adv*

[2]**portable** *n* (1883) : something that is portable

[1]**por·tage** \ˈpȯr-tij, *3 is also* pȯr-ˈtäzh\ *n* [ME, fr. AF, fr. *porter* to carry] (15c) **1** : the labor of carrying or transporting **2** *archaic* : the cost of carrying : PORTERAGE **3 a** : the carrying of boats or goods overland

from one body of water to another or around an obstacle (as a rapids) **b** : the route followed in making such a transfer

²**por·tage** \ˈpȯr-tij, pȯr-ˈtäzh\ *vb* **por·taged; por·tag·ing** *vt* (1836) : to carry over a portage ~ *vi* : to move gear over a portage

¹**por·tal** \ˈpȯr-tᵊl\ *n* [ME, fr. AF, fr. ML *portale* city gate, porch, fr. neut. of *portalis* of a gate, fr. L *porta* gate — more at PORT] (14c) **1** : DOOR, ENTRANCE; *esp* : a grand or imposing one **2** : the whole architectural composition surrounding and including the doorways and porches of a church **3** : the approach or entrance to a bridge or tunnel **4** : a communicating part or area of an organism; *specif* : the point at which something (as a pathogen) enters the body **5** : a site serving as a guide or point of entry to the World Wide Web and usu. including a search engine or a collection of links to other sites arranged esp. by topic

²**portal** *adj* [NL *porta* transverse fissure of the liver, fr. L, gate] (1845) **1** : of or relating to the transverse fissure on the underside of the liver where most of the vessels enter **2** : of, relating to, or being a portal vein or a portal system ⟨~ circulation⟩

portal system *n* [*portal vein*] (1851) : a system of veins that begins and ends in capillaries

portal–to–portal *adj* (1943) : of or relating to the time spent by a worker in traveling between the entrance to an employer's property and the worker's actual job site (as in a mine) ⟨~ pay⟩

portal vein *n* [²*portal*] (1845) : a vein that collects blood from one part of the body and distributes it in another through capillaries; *esp* : a vein carrying blood from the digestive organs and spleen to the liver

por·ta·men·to \ˌpȯr-tə-ˈmen-(ˌ)tō\ *n, pl* **-men·ti** \-(ˌ)tē\ [It, lit., act of carrying, fr. *portare* to carry, fr. L] (1771) : a continuous gliding movement from one tone to another (as by the voice)

port arms *n* [fr. the command *port arms!*] (ca. 1890) : a position in the manual of arms in which the rifle is held diagonally in front of the body with the muzzle pointing upward to the left; *also* : a command to assume this position

por·ta·tive \ˈpȯr-tə-tiv\ *adj* [ME *portatif,* fr. MF, fr. L *portatus,* pp. of *portare*] (14c) : PORTABLE

port·cul·lis \pȯrt-ˈkə-ləs\ *n* [ME *port colice,* fr. AF *porte coliz,* lit., sliding door] (14c) : a grating of iron hung over the gateway of a fortified place and lowered between grooves to prevent passage

port de bras \ˌpȯr-də-ˈbrä\ *n* [F, lit., carriage of the arm] (1912) : the technique and practice of arm movement in ballet

Port du Sa·lut \ˌpȯr-də-sə-ˈlü, -sa-; -səl-ˈyü, -sal-\ *n* [F *port-du-salut, port-salut,* fr. *Port du Salut,* Trappist abbey in northwest France] (1881) : a semisoft pressed ripened cheese of usu. mild flavor originated by Trappist monks in France

Porte \ˈpȯrt\ *n* [F, short for *Sublime Porte,* lit., sublime gate; fr. the gate of the sultan's palace where justice was administered] (15c) : the government of the Ottoman empire

porte co·chere \ˌpȯrt-kō-ˈsher\ *n* [F *porte cochère,* lit., coach door] (1698) **1** : a passageway through a building or screen wall designed to let vehicles pass from the street to an interior courtyard **2** : a roofed structure extending from the entrance of a building over an adjacent driveway and sheltering those getting in or out of vehicles

por·tend \pȯr-ˈtend\ *vt* [ME, fr. L *portendere,* fr. *por-* forward (akin to *per* through) + *tendere* to stretch — more at FOR, THIN] (15c) **1** : to give an omen or anticipatory sign of **2** : INDICATE, SIGNIFY

por·tent \ˈpȯr-ˌtent\ *n* [L *portentum,* fr. neut. of *portentus,* pp. of *portendere*] (ca. 1587) **1** : something that foreshadows a coming event : OMEN, SIGN **2** : prophetic indication or significance **3** : MARVEL, PRODIGY

por·ten·tous \pȯr-ˈten-təs\ *adj* (15c) **1** : of, relating to, or constituting a portent ⟨suspense, ~ foreshadowing, hints of sinister and violent mysteries —Francine Prose⟩ **2** : eliciting amazement or wonder : PRODIGIOUS **3 a** : being a grave or serious matter ⟨~ decisions⟩ **b** : self-consciously solemn or important : POMPOUS ⟨~ declamation unsalted by the least trace of humor —W. H. Pritchard⟩ **c** : ponderously excessive ⟨that discipline's overwrought, ~ phrases —R. M. Coles⟩ ***syn*** see OMINOUS — **por·ten·tous·ly** *adv* — **por·ten·tous·ness** *n*

¹**por·ter** \ˈpȯr-tər\ *n* [ME, fr. AF, fr. LL *portarius,* fr. L *porta* gate — more at PORT] (13c) *chiefly Brit* : a person stationed at a door or gate to admit or assist those entering

²**porter** *n* [ME *portour,* fr. AF *porteour,* fr. LL *portator,* fr. L *portare* to carry — more at FARE] (14c) **1** : a person who carries burdens; *esp* : one employed to carry baggage for patrons at a hotel or transportation terminal **2** : a parlor-car or sleeping-car attendant who waits on passengers and makes up berths **3** [short for *porter's beer*] : a heavy dark brown beer brewed from browned or charred malt **4** : a person who does routine cleaning (as in a hospital or office)

³**porter** *vt* (1609) : to transport or carry as or as if by a porter ~ *vi* : to act as a porter

por·ter·age \-tə-rij\ *n* (15c) : a porter's work; *also* : the charge for it

por·ter·house \ˈpȯr-tər-ˌhau̇s\ *n* (ca. 1758) **1** : a house where malt liquor (as porter) is sold **2** : a large steak cut from the thick end of the short loin to contain a T-shaped bone and a large piece of tenderloin — see BEEF illustration

port·fo·lio \pȯrt-ˈfō-lē-ˌō\ *n, pl* **-li·os** [It *portafoglio,* fr. *portare* to carry (fr. L) + *foglio* leaf, sheet, fr. L *folium* — more at BLADE] (1722) **1** : a hinged cover or flexible case for carrying loose papers, pictures, or pamphlets **2** [fr. the use of such a case to carry documents of state] : the office and functions of a minister of state or member of a cabinet **3** : the securities held by an investor : the commercial paper held by a financial house (as a bank) **4** : a set of pictures (as drawings or photographs) usu. bound in book form or loose in a folder **5** : a selection of a student's work (as papers and tests) compiled over a period of time and used for assessing performance or progress

port·hole \ˈpȯrt-ˌhōl\ *n* [²*port*] (ca. 1591) **1** : an opening (as a window) with a cover or closure esp. in the side of a ship or aircraft **2** : a port through which to shoot **3** : ²PORT 2

Por·tia \ˈpȯr-shə\ *n* (1596) : the heroine in Shakespeare's *The Merchant of Venice*

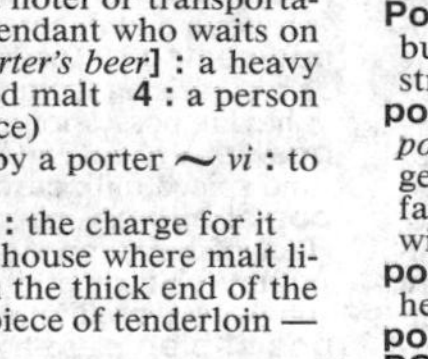

portico

por·ti·co \ˈpȯr-ti-ˌkō\ *n, pl* **-coes** *or* **-cos** [It, fr. L *porticus* — more at PORCH] (1605) : a colonnade or covered ambulatory esp. in classical architecture and often at the entrance of a building

por·tiere \pȯr-ˈtyer, -ˈtir; ˈpȯr-tē-ər\ *n* [F *portière,* fr. OF, fem. of *portier, porter* porter, doorkeeper] (1843) : a curtain hanging across a doorway

¹**por·tion** \ˈpȯr-shən\ *n* [ME *porcioun,* fr. AF, fr. L *portion-, portio;* akin to L *part-, pars* part] (14c) **1** : an individual's part or share of something: as **a** : a share received by gift or inheritance **b** : DOWRY **c** : enough food esp. of one kind to serve one person at one meal **2** : an individual's lot, fate, or fortune : one's share of good and evil **3** : an often limited part of a whole ***syn*** see PART, FATE

²**portion** *vt* **por·tioned; por·tion·ing** \-sh(ə-)niŋ\ (14c) **1** : to divide into portions : DISTRIBUTE ⟨~*ed* out the food equally⟩ **2** : to allot a dowry to : DOWER

por·tion·less \-shən-ləs\ *adj* (1782) : having no portion; *esp* : having no dowry or inheritance

port·land cement \ˈpȯrt-lən(d)-\ *n* [Isle of *Portland,* England; fr. its resemblance to a limestone found there] (1824) : a hydraulic cement made by finely pulverizing the clinker produced by calcining to incipient fusion a mixture of clay and limestone or similar materials

port·ly \ˈpȯrt-lē\ *adj* **port·li·er; -est** [³*port*] (15c) **1** : DIGNIFIED, STATELY **2** : heavy or rotund of body : STOUT — **port·li·ness** *n*

¹**port·man·teau** \pȯrt-ˈman-(ˌ)tō\ *n, pl* **-teaus** *or* **-teaux** \-(ˌ)tōz\ [MF *portemanteau,* fr. *porter* to carry + *manteau* mantle, fr. L *mantellum* — more at PORT] (1579) **1** : a large suitcase **2** : a word or morpheme whose form and meaning are derived from a blending of two or more distinct forms (as *smog* from *smoke* and *fog*)

²**portmanteau** *adj* (1909) **1** : combining more than one use or quality **2** : being a portmanteau ⟨a ~ word⟩

por·to·bel·lo \ˌpȯr-tə-ˈbe-(ˌ)lō\ *also* **por·ta·bel·la** \-lə\ *or* **por·ta·bel·lo** \ˌpȯr-tə-ˈbe-(ˌ)lō\ *n, pl* **-los** *also* **-las** [perh. alter. of It *prataiolo, prataiuolo* or dial. It *pratarolo* meadow mushroom, fr. *prato* meadow, fr. L *pratum*] (1986) : a large dark mature cultivated mushroom noted for its meaty texture that is of the same variety of button mushroom as the cremini

port of call (1858) **1** : an intermediate port where ships customarily stop for supplies, repairs, or transshipment of cargo **2** : a stop included on an itinerary

port of entry (1769) **1** : a place where foreign goods may be cleared through a customhouse **2** : a place where an alien may be permitted to enter a country

¹**por·trait** \ˈpȯr-trət, -ˌtrāt\ *n* [MF, fr. pp. of *portraire*] (1570) **1** : PICTURE; *esp* : a pictorial representation of a person usu. showing the face **2** : a sculptured figure : BUST **3** : a graphic portrayal in words

²**portrait** *adj* (1932) : of, relating to, or being a document having the vertical dimension longer than the horizontal dimension

por·trait·ist \-trə-tist, -ˌtrā-\ *n* (1859) : a maker of portraits

por·trai·ture \ˈpȯr-trə-ˌchu̇r, -chər, -ˌtyu̇r, -ˌtu̇r\ *n* (14c) **1** : the making of portraits : PORTRAYAL **2** : PORTRAIT

por·tray \pȯr-ˈtrā, pər-\ *vt* [ME *portraien,* fr. AF *purtraire,* fr. L *protrahere* to draw forth, reveal, expose — more at PROTRACT] (14c) **1** : to make a picture of : DEPICT **2 a** : to describe in words **b** : to play the role of : ENACT — **por·tray·er** *n*

por·tray·al \-ˈtrā(-ə)l\ *n* (1843) **1** : the act or process or an instance of portraying : REPRESENTATION **2** : PORTRAIT

por·tress \ˈpȯr-trəs\ *n* (15c) : a woman who is a porter: as **a** : a doorkeeper in a convent or apartment building **b** : CHARWOMAN

Port Roy·al·ist \pȯrt-ˈrȯi-ə-list\ *n* [F *port-royaliste,* fr. *Port-Royal,* a convent near Versailles, France] (ca. 1741) : a member or adherent of a 17th century French Jansenist lay community noted for its logicians and educators

Port Sa·lut \ˌpȯr-sə-ˈlü, -sa-; -səl-ˈyü, -sal-\ *n* (1881) : PORT DU SALUT

Por·tu·guese \ˈpȯr-chə-ˌgēz, -ˌgēs; ˌpȯr-chə-ˈ\ *n, pl* **Portuguese** [Pg *português,* adj. & n., fr. *Portugal*] (1534) **1 a** : a native or inhabitant of Portugal **b** : one who is of Portuguese descent **2** : the Romance language of Portugal and Brazil — **Portuguese** *adj*

Portuguese man–of–war *n, pl* **Portuguese man–of–wars** *also* **Portuguese men–of–war** (1707) : any of a genus (*Physalia* of the family Physaliidae) of large tropical and subtropical pelagic siphonophores having a crested bladderlike float which bears the colony comprised of three types of zooids on the lower surface with one of the three having nematocyst-equipped tentacles

Portuguese water dog *n* (1948) : any of a breed of medium-sized robust dogs that have a large broad head and curly or wavy coat and are strong swimmers

por·tu·laca \ˌpȯr-chə-ˈla-kə\ *n* [NL, fr. L, purslane, fr. *portula,* dim. of *porta* gate; fr. the lid of its capsule — more at PORT] (1548) : any of a genus (*Portulaca*) of chiefly tropical succulent herbs of the purslane family; *esp* : a widely cultivated So. American plant (*P. grandiflora*) with showy flowers and small conical leaves

port–wine stain \ˈpȯrt-ˈwīn-\ *n* (ca. 1909) : a reddish-purple superficial hemangioma of the skin commonly occurring as a birthmark

pos *abbr* **1** position **2** positive

POS *abbr* point-of-service

po·sa·da \pə-ˈsä-də\ *n* [Sp, fr. *posar* to lodge, fr. LL *pausare*] (1671) : an inn in Spanish-speaking countries

¹**pose** \ˈpōz\ *vb* **posed; pos·ing** [ME, fr. AF *poser,* fr. VL **pausare,* fr. LL, to stop, rest, pause, fr. L *pausa* pause] *vt* (14c) **1 a** : to set forth or offer for attention or consideration ⟨let me ~ a question⟩ **b** : to come to attention as : PRESENT ⟨smoking ~*s* a health risk⟩ **2 a** : to put or set in place **b** : to place (as a model) in a studied attitude ~ *vi* **1** : to assume a posture or attitude usu. for artistic purposes **2** : to affect an attitude or character usu. to deceive or impress ⟨*posed* as a doctor to gain access to the ward⟩

²**pose** *n* (1818) **1** : a sustained posture; *esp* : one assumed for artistic effect **2** : an attitude, role, or characteristic assumed for effect

syn POSE, AIR, AIRS, AFFECTATION, MANNERISM mean an adopted way of speaking or behaving. POSE implies an attitude deliberately as-

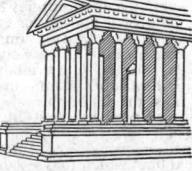

sumed in order to impress others ‹her shyness was just a *pose*›. AIR may suggest natural acquirement through environment or way of life ‹a traveler's sophisticated *air*›. AIRS always implies artificiality and pretentiousness ‹snobbish *airs*›. AFFECTATION applies to a trick of speech or behavior that strikes the observer as insincere ‹the posh accent is an *affectation*›. MANNERISM applies to an acquired eccentricity that has become a habit ‹gesturing with a cigarette was her most noticeable *mannerism*›.

[3]**pose** *vt* **posed; pos·ing** [short for earlier *appose,* fr. ME *apposen,* alter. of *opposen* to oppose] (1593) **:** PUZZLE, BAFFLE

Po·sei·don \pə-ˈsī-dᵊn\ *n* [L, fr. Gk *Poseidōn*] (1811) **:** the Greek god of the sea — compare NEPTUNE

[1]**pos·er** \ˈpō-zər\ *n* [[3]*pose*] (1793) **:** a puzzling or baffling question

[2]**poser** *n* [[1]*pose*] (1888) **:** a person who poses

po·seur \pō-ˈzər, ˈpō-zər\ *n* [F, lit., poser, fr. *poser*] (1869) **:** a person who pretends to be what he or she is not **:** an affected or insincere person

posh \ˈpäsh\ *adj* [origin unknown] (1918) **1 :** ELEGANT, FASHIONABLE ‹a ~ restaurant› **2** *Brit* **:** typical of or intended for the upper classes **:** HIGHFALUTIN ‹~ accents› — **posh·ly** *adv* — **posh·ness** *n*

pos·it \ˈpä-zət\ *vt* **pos·it·ed** \ˈpä-zə-təd, ˈpäz-təd\; **pos·it·ing** \ˈpä-zə-tiŋ, ˈpäz-tiŋ\ [L *positus,* pp. of *ponere*] (1647) **1 :** to dispose or set firmly **:** FIX **2 :** to assume or affirm the existence of **:** POSTULATE **3 :** to propose as an explanation **:** SUGGEST

[1]**po·si·tion** \pə-ˈzi-shən\ *n* [ME *posycion,* fr. AF *posicioun,* fr. L *position-, positio,* fr. *ponere* to lay down, put, place, fr. OL **posinere,* fr. *po-* away (akin to OCS *po-,* perfective prefix, Gk *apo* away) + L *sinere* to leave — more at OF] (14c) **1 :** an act of placing or arranging: as **a :** the laying down of a proposition or thesis **b :** an arranging in order **2 :** a point of view adopted and held to ‹made my ~ on the issue clear› **3 a :** the point or area occupied by a physical object **:** LOCATION ‹took her ~ at the head of the line› **b :** a certain arrangement of bodily parts ‹rose to a standing ~› **4 :** a market commitment in securities or commodities; *also* **:** the inventory of a market trader **5 a :** relative place, situation, or standing ‹is now in a ~ to make decisions on his own› **b :** social or official rank or status **c :** an employment for which one has been hired **:** JOB ‹a ~ with a brokerage firm› **d :** a situation that confers advantage or preference

[2]**position** *vt* **po·si·tioned; po·si·tion·ing** \pə-ˈzi-sh(ə-)niŋ\ (1817) **:** to put in a certain position ‹~*ed* the chairs around the room› ‹~*ed* the company in the global market›

po·si·tion·al \pə-ˈzi-sh(ə-)nəl\ *adj* (1571) **1 :** of, relating to, or fixed by position ‹~ astronomy› **2 :** involving little movement ‹~ warfare› **3 :** dependent on position or environment or context ‹the front-articulated \k\ in \kē\ *key* and the back-articulated \k\ in \kül\ *cool* are ~ variants› — **po·si·tion·al·ly** *adv*

positional notation *n* (1941) **:** a system of expressing numbers in which the digits are arranged in succession, the position of each digit has a place value, and the number is equal to the sum of the products of each digit by its place value

position effect *n* (1930) **:** a genetic effect in which the expression of a gene is influenced by its interaction with usu. adjacent genes and which is modified when the spatial relationships of the genes change (as by translocation)

position paper *n* (1949) **:** a detailed report that recommends a course of action on a particular issue

[1]**pos·i·tive** \ˈpä-zə-tiv, ˈpäz-tiv\ *adj* [ME, fr. AF, fr. L *positivus,* fr. *positus,* pp. of *ponere*] (14c) **1 a :** formally laid down or imposed **:** PRESCRIBED ‹~ laws› **b :** expressed clearly or peremptorily ‹her answer was a ~ *no*› **c :** fully assured **:** CONFIDENT ‹~ it was her book› **2 a :** of, relating to, or constituting the degree of comparison that is expressed in English by the unmodified and uninflected form of an adjective or adverb and denotes no increase or diminution **b (1) :** independent of changing circumstances **:** UNCONDITIONED ‹an insurance policy with ~ coverage› **(2) :** relating to or constituting a motion or device that is definite, unyielding, constant, or certain in its action ‹a ~ system of levers› **c (1) :** INCONTESTABLE ‹~ proof› **(2) :** UNQUALIFIED ‹a ~ disgrace› **3 a :** not fictitious **:** REAL ‹~ social tensions› **b :** active and effective in social or economic function rather than merely maintaining peace and order ‹a ~ government› **4 a :** indicating, relating to, or characterized by affirmation, addition, inclusion, or presence rather than negation, withholding, or absence ‹took the ~ approach and struck a new deal rather than canceling the contract› **b :** having rendition of light and shade similar in tone to the tones of the original subject ‹a ~ photographic image› **c :** contributing toward or characterized by increase or progression ‹take some ~ action› ‹~ cash flow› **d :** directed or moving toward a source of stimulation ‹a ~ taxis› **e :** real and numerically greater than zero ‹+2 is a ~ integer› **5 a (1) :** being, relating to, or charged with electricity of which the proton is the elementary unit and which predominates in a glass body after being rubbed with silk **(2) :** having more protons than electrons ‹a ~ ion› **b (1) :** having higher electric potential and constituting the part from which the current flows to the external circuit ‹the ~ terminal of a discharging storage battery› **(2) :** being an electron-collecting electrode of an electron tube **6 a :** marked by or indicating acceptance, approval, or affirmation ‹received a ~ response› **b :** affirming the presence esp. of a condition, substance, or organism suspected to be present ‹a ~ test for blood›; *also* **:** having a test result indicating the presence esp. of a condition, substance, or organism ‹HIV ~› **7** *of a lens* **:** converging light rays and forming a real inverted image **8 a :** having a good effect **:** FAVORABLE ‹a ~ role model› **b :** marked by optimism ‹the ~ point of view› ***syn*** see SURE — **pos·i·tive·ly** \-lē, *for emphasis often* ˌpä-zə-ˈtiv-\ *adv* — **pos·i·tive·ness** \ˈpä-zə-tiv-nəs, ˈpäz-tiv-\ *n*

[2]**positive** *n* (1530) **:** something positive: as **a (1) :** the positive degree of comparison in a language **(2) :** a positive form of an adjective or adverb **b :** something of which an affirmation can be made **:** REALITY **c :** a positive photograph or a print from a negative **d :** a positive result (as of a test); *also* **:** a test yielding such a result

positive definite *adj* (1907) **1 :** having a positive value for all values of the constituent variables ‹*positive definite* quadratic forms› **2** *of a matrix* **:** having the characteristic roots real and positive

positive feedback *n* (1934) **:** feedback that tends to magnify a process or increase its output

positive law *n* (14c) **:** law established or recognized by governmental authority — compare NATURAL LAW

pos·i·tiv·ism \ˈpä-zə-ti-ˌvi-zəm, ˈpäz-ti-\ *n* [F *positivisme,* fr. *positif* positive + *-isme* -ism] (1847) **1 a :** a theory that theology and metaphysics are earlier imperfect modes of knowledge and that positive knowledge is based on natural phenomena and their properties and relations as verified by the empirical sciences **b :** LOGICAL POSITIVISM **2 :** the quality or state of being positive — **pos·i·tiv·ist** \-vist\ *adj or n* — **pos·i·tiv·is·tic** \ˌpä-zə-ti-ˈvis-tik, ˌpäz-ti-\ *adj* — **pos·i·tiv·is·ti·cal·ly** \-ti-k(ə-)lē\ *adv*

pos·i·tiv·i·ty \ˌpä-zə-ˈti-və-tē\ *n, pl* **-ties** (1659) **1 :** the quality or state of being positive **2 :** something that is positive

pos·i·tron \ˈpä-zə-ˌträn\ *n* [*posi*tive + *-tron* (as in *electron*)] (1933) **:** a positively charged particle having the same mass and magnitude of charge as the electron and constituting the antiparticle of the electron — called also *antielectron*

positron–emission tomography *n* (1976) **:** tomography in which a cross-sectional image of regional metabolism is obtained by a usu. color-coded representation of the distribution of gamma radiation given off in the collision of electrons in cells with positrons emitted by radionuclides incorporated into metabolic substances that have been administered (as by injection)

pos·i·tro·ni·um \ˌpä-zə-ˈtrō-nē-əm\ *n* (1945) **:** a short-lived system that consists of a positron and an electron bound together and is suggestive of a hydrogen atom

po·so·le *or* **po·zo·le** \pō-ˈsō-(ˌ)lā\ *n* [MexSp, fr. Nahuatl *pozolli,* fr. the base of *pozōn-* boil, be covered with foam] (1931) **:** a thick soup chiefly of Mexico and the U.S. Southwest made with pork, hominy, garlic, and chili

poss *abbr* **1** possessive **2** possible

pos·se \ˈpä-sē\ *n* [ML *posse comitatus,* lit., power or authority of the county] (1645) **1 :** a large group often with a common interest **2 :** a body of persons summoned by a sheriff to assist in preserving the public peace usu. in an emergency **3 :** a group of people temporarily organized to make a search (as for a lost child) **4 :** ENTOURAGE 1

pos·sess \pə-ˈzes *also* -ˈses\ *vt* [ME, fr. MF *possesser* to have possession of, take possession of, fr. L *possessus,* pp. of *possidēre,* fr. *potis* able, having the power + *sedēre* to sit — more at POTENT, SIT] (14c) **1 a :** to have and hold as property **:** OWN **b :** to have as an attribute, knowledge, or skill **2 a :** to take into one's possession **b :** to enter into and control firmly **:** DOMINATE ‹was ~*ed* by demons› **c :** to bring or cause to fall under the influence, possession, or control of some emotional or intellectual response or reaction ‹melancholy ~*es* her› **3 a** *obs* **:** to instate as owner **b :** to make the owner or holder — used in passive construction to indicate simple possession ‹~*ed* of riches› ‹~*ed* of knowledge and experience› — **pos·ses·sor** *n*

pos·sessed *adj* (1534) **1 a (1) :** influenced or controlled by something (as an evil spirit, a passion, or an idea) **(2) :** MAD, CRAZED **b :** urgently desirous to do or have something **2** *obs* **:** held as a possession **3 :** SELF-POSSESSED, CALM — **pos·sessed·ly** \-ˈze-səd-lē, -ˈzest-lē *also* -ˈse-səd- *or* -ˈsest-\ *adv* — **pos·sessed·ness** \-ˈze-səd-nəs, -ˈzest-nəs *also* -ˈse-səd- *or* -ˈsest-\ *n*

pos·ses·sion \-ˈze-shən *also* -ˈse-\ *n* (14c) **1 a :** the act of having or taking into control **b :** control or occupancy of property without regard to ownership **c :** OWNERSHIP **d :** control of the ball or puck; *also* **:** an instance of having such control (as in football) ‹scored on their first two ~*s*› **2 :** something owned, occupied, or controlled **:** PROPERTY **3 a :** domination by something (as an evil spirit, a passion, or an idea) **b :** a psychological state in which an individual's normal personality is replaced by another **c :** SELF-POSSESSION — **pos·ses·sion·al** \-ˈzesh-nəl, -ˈze-shə-nᵊl *also* -ˈsesh-nəl *or* -ˈse-shə-nᵊl\ *adj* — **pos·ses·sion·less** \-ˈze-shən-ləs, -ˈse-\ *adj*

[1]**pos·ses·sive** \pə-ˈze-siv *also* -ˈse-\ *adj* (15c) **1 :** of, relating to, or constituting a word, a word group, or a grammatical case that denotes ownership or a relation analogous to ownership **2 :** manifesting possession or the desire to own or dominate — **pos·ses·sive·ly** *adv* — **pos·ses·sive·ness** *n*

[2]**possessive** *n* (15c) **1 :** a possessive word or word group **2 a :** the possessive case **b :** a word in the possessive case

possessive adjective *n* (1870) **:** a pronominal adjective expressing possession

possessive pronoun *n* (15c) **:** a pronoun that derives from a personal pronoun and denotes possession and analogous relationships

pos·ses·so·ry \pə-ˈze-sə-rē, -ˈzes-rē *also* -ˈse-sə-rē *or* -ˈses-rē\ *adj* (15c) **1 :** of, arising from, or having the nature of possession ‹~ rights› **2 :** having possession **3 :** characteristic of a possessor **:** POSSESSIVE

pos·set \ˈpä-sət\ *n* [ME *poshet, possot*] (15c) **:** a hot drink of sweetened and spiced milk curdled with ale or wine

pos·si·bil·i·ty \ˌpä-sə-ˈbi-lə-tē\ *n, pl* **-ties** (14c) **1 :** the condition or fact of being possible **2** *archaic* **:** one's utmost power, capacity, or ability **3 :** something that is possible **4 :** potential or prospective value — usu. used in pl. ‹the house had great *possibilities*›

pos·si·ble \ˈpä-sə-bəl\ *adj* [ME, fr. AF, fr. L *possibilis,* fr. *posse* to be able, fr. *potis, pote* able + *esse* to be — more at POTENT, IS] (14c) **1 a :** being within the limits of ability, capacity, or realization ‹a ~ but difficult task› **b :** being what may be conceived, be done, or occur according to nature, custom, or manners ‹the best ~ care› ‹the worst ~ circumstance› **2 a :** being something that may or may not occur ‹a ~ surprise visit› **b :** being something that may or may not be true or actual ‹~ explanation› **3 :** having an indicated potential ‹a ~ housing site›

syn POSSIBLE, PRACTICABLE, FEASIBLE mean capable of being realized. POSSIBLE implies that a thing may certainly exist or occur given the proper conditions ‹a *possible* route up the west face of the mountain›. PRACTICABLE implies that something may be effected by available means or under current conditions ‹a solution that is not *practicable* in the time available›. FEASIBLE applies to what is likely to work or be useful in attaining the end desired ‹commercially *feasible* for mass production›.

pos·si·bly \-blē\ *adv* (14c) **1 :** in a possible manner **:** by any possibility ‹that's all she could ~ do› **2 :** by merest chance **:** PERHAPS ‹~ he will recover› **3 :** it is possible or imaginable **:** CONCEIVABLY ‹a political libel which may ~ damage me —G. B. Shaw›

posslq *abbr* persons of the opposite sex sharing living quarters

pos·sum \ˈpä-səm\ *n* (1613) : OPOSSUM

[1]**post** \ˈpōst\ *n* [ME, fr. OE, fr. L *postis;* prob. akin to L *por-* forward and to L *stare* to stand — more at PORTEND, STAND] (bef. 12c) **1 :** a piece (as of timber or metal) fixed firmly in an upright position esp. as a stay or support : PILLAR, COLUMN **2 :** a pole or stake set up to mark or indicate something; *esp* : a pole that marks the starting or finishing point of a horse race **3 :** a metallic fitting attached to an electrical device (as a storage battery) for convenience in making connections **4 a :** GOALPOST **b :** a football passing play in which the receiver runs downfield before turning towards the middle of the field **5 :** the metal stem of a pierced earring

[2]**post** *vt* (1633) **1 a :** to publish, announce, or advertise by or as if by use of a placard **b :** to denounce by public notice **c :** to enter on a public listing **d :** to forbid (property) to trespassers under penalty of legal prosecution by notices placed along the boundaries **e :** SCORE ⟨~*ed* a 70 in the final round⟩ **2 :** to affix to a usual place (as a wall) for public notices : PLACARD **3 :** to publish (as a message) in an online forum (as an electronic bulletin board)

[3]**post** *n* [MF *poste* relay station, courier, fr. OIt *posta* relay station, fr. fem. of *posto,* pp. of *porre* to place, fr. L *ponere* — more at POSITION] (1507) **1** *obs* : COURIER **2** *archaic* **a :** one of a series of stations for keeping horses for relays **b :** the distance between any two such consecutive stations : STAGE **3** *chiefly Brit* **a :** a nation's organization for handling mail; *also* : the mail handled **b** (1) **:** a single dispatch of mail (2) **:** LETTER 2a **c :** POST OFFICE **d :** POSTBOX **4 :** something (as a message) that is published online

[4]**post** *vi* (1533) **1 :** to travel with post-horses **2 :** to ride or travel with haste : HURRY **3 :** to rise from the saddle and return to it in rhythm with a horse's trot ~ *vt* **1** *archaic* : to dispatch in haste **2 :** MAIL ⟨~ a letter⟩ **3 a :** to transfer or carry from a book of original entry to a ledger **b :** to make transfer entries in **4 :** to make familiar with a subject : INFORM ⟨kept her ~*ed* on the latest gossip⟩

[5]**post** *adv* (1549) : with post-horses : EXPRESS

[6]**post** *n* [MF *poste,* fr. OIt *posto,* fr. pp. of *porre* to place] (1598) **1 a :** the place at which a soldier is stationed; *esp* : a sentry's beat or station **b :** a station or task to which one is assigned **c :** the place at which a body of troops is stationed : CAMP **d :** a local subdivision of a veterans' organization **e :** one of two bugle calls sounded (as in the British army) at tattoo **2 a :** an office or position to which a person is appointed **b :** an area on a basketball court that is located just outside the free throw lane usu. near the basket; *also* : the offensive position of a player occupying the post **3 a :** TRADING POST, SETTLEMENT **b :** a trading station on the floor of a stock exchange

[7]**post** *vt* (1683) **1 a :** to station in a given place ⟨guards were ~*ed* at the doors⟩ **b :** to carry ceremoniously to a position ⟨~*ing* the colors⟩ **2** *chiefly Brit* : to assign to a unit, position, or location (as in the military or civil service) **3 :** to put up (as bond)

post- *prefix* [ME, fr. L, fr. *post;* akin to Lith *pas* at, Gk *apo* away from — more at OF] **1 a :** after : subsequent : later ⟨*post*date⟩ **b :** behind : posterior : following after ⟨*post*lude⟩ ⟨*post*consonantal⟩ **2 a :** subsequent to : later than ⟨*post*operative⟩ **b :** posterior to ⟨*post*orbital⟩

post·abor·tion
post·ac·ci·dent
post·ad·o·les·cent
post·am·pu·ta·tion
post·apart·heid
post·apoc·a·lyp·tic
post·ar·rest
post·atom·ic
post·at·tack
post·bac·ca·lau·re·ate
post·bib·li·cal
post·bour·geois
post·burn
post·cap·i·tal·ist
post–Chris·tian
post·co·i·tal
post·col·lege
post·col·le·giate
post·co·lo·nial
post·com·mu·nist
post·con·cep·tion
post·con·cert
post·con·quest
post·con·so·nan·tal
post·con·ven·tion
post·cop·u·la·to·ry
post·cor·o·nary
post·coup
post·crash
post·cri·sis
post–Dar·win·i·an
post·dead·line
post·de·bate
post·de·liv·ery
post·de·po·si·tion·al
post·de·pres·sion
post·de·val·u·a·tion
post·dive
post·di·ves·ti·ture
post·di·vorce
post·drug
post·ed·it·ing
post–Ein·stein·ian
post·elec·tion
post·en·ceph·a·lit·ic
post·ep·i·lep·tic
post·erup·tive
post·ex·er·cise
post·ex·pe·ri·ence
post·ex·po·sure
post·fire
post·flight
post·frac·ture
post·freeze
post–Freud·ian
post·game
post·gla·cial
post·grad·u·a·tion
post·har·vest
post·hem·or·rhag·ic
post·hol·i·day
post·ho·lo·caust
post·hos·pi·tal
post·im·pact
post·im·pe·ri·al
post·im·plan·ta·tion
post·in·au·gu·ral
post·in·de·pen·dence
post·in·dus·tri·al
post·in·fec·tion
post·in·jec·tion
post·in·oc·u·la·tion
post·ir·ra·di·a·tion
post·land·ing
post·launch
post·lib·er·a·tion
post·mar·i·tal
post·mas·tec·to·my
post·mat·ing
post·me·di·e·val
post·mid·night
post·neo·na·tal
post·or·gas·mic
post·pres·i·den·tial
post·pri·ma·ry
post·pris·on
post·psy·cho·an·a·lyt·ic
post·pu·ber·ty
post·pu·bes·cent
post·race
post·re·ces·sion
post–Ref·or·ma·tion
post·res·ur·rec·tion
post·re·tire·ment
post·rev·o·lu·tion·ary
post·ri·ot
post·ro·man·tic
post·sea·son
post·sec·ond·ary
post·show
post·stim·u·la·tion
post·stim·u·lus
post·strike
post·tax
post·teen
post·trau·mat·ic
post·treat·ment
post·trial
post·vac·ci·nal
post·vac·ci·na·tion
post·va·sec·to·my
post–Vic·to·ri·an
post·wean·ing
post·work·shop

post·age \ˈpō-stij\ *n* (1654) **1 :** the fee for postal service **2 :** adhesive stamps or printed indicia representing postal fees

postage–due stamp *n* (1893) : a special adhesive stamp that is applied by a post office to mail bearing insufficient postage

postage meter *n* (1927) : a machine that prints postal indicia on pieces of mail, records the amount of postage, and subtracts it from a total paid amount for which the machine has been set

postage–stamp *adj* (1938) : suggesting a postage stamp in size : very small ⟨~ yards⟩

postage stamp *n* (1840) : a government adhesive stamp or imprinted stamp for use on mail as evidence of prepayment of postage

post·al \ˈpōs-tᵊl\ *adj* (1843) **1 :** of or relating to the mails or the post office **2 :** conducted by mail ⟨~ chess⟩ **3 :** insanely or murderously violent — usu. used in the phrase *go postal*

postal card *n* (1872) **1 :** a card officially stamped and issued by the government for use in the mail **2 :** POSTCARD

postal order *n* (1883) *Brit* : MONEY ORDER

postal service *n* (1885) : POST OFFICE 1

postal union *n* (1875) : an association of governments that sets up uniform regulations and practices for international mail

post·ax·i·al \ˌpōst-ˈak-sē-əl\ *adj* (1872) : of or relating to the ulnar side of the vertebrate forelimb or the fibular side of the hind limb; *also* : of or relating to the side of an animal or side of one of its limbs that is posterior to the axis of its body or limbs

post·bag \ˈpōs(t)-ˌbag\ *n* (1813) **1** *Brit* : MAILBAG **2** *Brit* : a single batch of mail : LETTERS

post·bel·lum \ˌpōs(t)-ˈbe-ləm\ *adj* [L *post bellum* after the war] (1874) : of, relating to, or characteristic of the period following a war and esp. following the American Civil War

post·box \ˈpōs(t)-ˌbäks\ *n* (1754) : MAILBOX; *esp* : a public mailbox

post·boy \-ˌbȯi\ *n* (1707) : POSTILION

[1]**post·card** \ˈpōs(t)-ˌkärd\ *n* (1870) **1 :** POSTAL CARD 1 **2 :** a card on which a message may be written for mailing without an envelope and to which the sender must affix a stamp — **post·card·like** \-ˌlīk\ *adj*

[2]**postcard** *adj* (1924) : PICTURESQUE, PICTURE-POSTCARD ⟨a ~ village⟩

post·ca·va \ˌpōs(t)-ˈkā-və\ *n* [NL] (1882) : the inferior vena cava of vertebrates higher than fishes — **post·ca·val** \-vəl\ *adj*

post chaise *n* (1712) : a carriage usu. having a closed body on four wheels and seating two to four persons

post·clas·si·cal \ˌpōs(t)-ˈkla-si-kəl\ *or* **post·clas·sic** \-sik\ *adj* (1867) : of or relating to a period (as in art, literature, or civilization) following a classical one

post·code \ˈpōs(t)-ˌkōd\ *n* (1967) : a code (as of numbers and letters) used similarly to the zip code esp. in the United Kingdom and Australia

post–com·mu·nion \ˌpōs(t)-kə-ˈmyü-nyən\ *n, often cap P&C* [ML *postcommunion-, postcommunio,* fr. L *post-* + LL *communio* communion] (15c) : a liturgically variable prayer following the communion at Eucharist

post·con·sum·er \-kən-ˈsü-mər\ *adj* (1984) **1 :** discarded by an end consumer ⟨~ waste⟩ **2 :** having been used and recycled for reuse in another consumer product ⟨~ plastics⟩

post·cra·ni·al \-ˈkrā-nē-əl\ *adj* (1913) : of or relating to the part of the body caudal to the head ⟨~ skeleton⟩ — **post·cra·ni·al·ly** *adv*

post·date \ˌpōs(t)-ˈdāt, ˈpōs(t)-ˌ\ *vt* (1624) **1 a :** to date with a date later than that of execution ⟨~ a check⟩ **b :** to assign (an event) to a date subsequent to that of actual occurrence **2 :** to follow in time

post·di·lu·vi·an \ˌpōs(t)-də-ˈlü-vē-ən, -dī-\ *adj* [*post-* + L *diluvium* flood — more at DELUGE] (1680) : of or relating to the period after the flood described in the Bible — **postdiluvian** *n*

[1]**post·doc** \ˈpōs(t)-ˌdäk\ *n* (1968) : one engaged in postdoctoral study or research

[2]**postdoc** *adj* (1970) : POSTDOCTORAL

post·doc·tor·al \ˌpōs(t)-ˈdäk-t(ə-)rəl, ˈpōst-ˌ\ *also* **post·doc·tor·ate** \-t(ə-)rət\ *adj* (1936) : being beyond the doctoral level: **a :** of or relating to advanced academic or professional work beyond a doctor's degree ⟨a ~ fellowship⟩ **b :** engaged in such work ⟨~ scholars⟩

post·emer·gence \ˌpōst-i-ˈmər-jən(t)s\ *adj* (1940) : used or occurring in the stage between the emergence of a seedling and the maturity of a crop plant ⟨~ herbicides⟩ ⟨~ development⟩

[1]**post·er** \ˈpōs-tər\ *n* [[4]*post*] (1605) *archaic* : a swift traveler

[2]**poster** *n* [[2]*post*] (1838) : a bill or placard for posting often in a public place; *esp* : one that is decorative or pictorial

poster boy *n* (1978) : a male poster child

poster child *n* (1969) **1 :** a child who has a disease and is pictured in posters to solicit funds for combating the disease **2 :** a person having a public image that is identified with something (as a cause)

poster color *n* (1925) : an opaque watercolor paint with a gum- or glue-size binder sold usu. in jars — called also *poster paint*

poste res·tante \ˌpōst-ˌres-ˈtänt\ *n* [F, lit., waiting mail] (1768) *chiefly Brit* : GENERAL DELIVERY

poster girl *n* (1969) : a female poster child

[1]**pos·te·ri·or** \pō-ˈstir-ē-ər, pä-\ *adj* [L, compar. of *posterus* coming after, fr. *post* after — more at POST-] (1534) **1 :** later in time : SUBSEQUENT **2 :** situated behind: as **a :** CAUDAL **b** *of the human body or its parts* : DORSAL **3** *of a plant part* : ADAXIAL, SUPERIOR — **pos·te·ri·or·ly** *adv*

[2]**pos·te·ri·or** \pä-ˈstir-ē-ər, pō-\ *n* (ca. 1616) : the hinder parts of the body; *specif* : BUTTOCKS

posterior cruciate ligament *n* (1981) : a cruciate ligament of each knee that attaches the back of the tibia with the front of the femur and functions esp. to limit the backward motion of the tibia

pos·te·ri·or·i·ty \(ˌ)pō-ˌstir-ē-ˈȯr-ə-tē, (ˌ)pä-, -ˈär-\ *n* (14c) : the quality or state of being later or subsequent

pos·ter·i·ty \pä-ˈster-ə-tē\ *n* [ME *posterite,* fr. AF *pusterité,* fr. L *posteritat-, posteritas,* fr. *posterus* coming after] (14c) **1 :** the offspring of one progenitor to the furthest generation **2 :** all future generations

pos·tern \ˈpōs-tərn, ˈpäs-\ *n* [ME *posterne,* fr. AF, alter. of OF *posterle,* fr. LL *posterula,* dim. of *postera* back door, fr. L, fem. of *posterus*] (14c) **1 :** a back door or gate **2 :** a private or side entrance or way — **postern** *adj*

pos·tero·lat·er·al \ˌpäs-tə-rō-ˈla-t(ə-)rəl\ *adj* [*posterior* + *-o-* + *lateral*] (1852) : posterior and lateral in position or direction

poster session *n* (1974) : a presentation of information on a series of posters that may include drawings, photographs, charts, graphs, and textual data relating to a specific subject

post exchange *n* (1892) : a store at a military installation that sells merchandise and services to military personnel and authorized civilians

\ə\ **abut** \ᵊ\ kitten, F table \ər\ **further** \a\ **ash** \ā\ **ace** \ä\ **mop, mar** \au̇\ **out** \ch\ **chin** \e\ **bet** \ē\ **easy** \g\ **go** \i\ **hit** \ī\ **ice** \j\ **job** \ŋ\ **sing** \ō\ **go** \ȯ\ **law** \ȯi\ **boy** \th\ **thin** \t͟h\ **the** \ü\ **loot** \u̇\ **foot** \y\ **yet** \zh\ **vision, beige** \k̲, ⁿ, œ, ue, ʸ\ *see* Guide to Pronunciation

post·ex·il·ic \ˌpōst-(ˌ)eg-ˈzi-lik\ *adj* (1871) **:** of or relating to the period of Jewish history between the end of the exile in Babylon in 538 B.C. and A.D. 1

post·face \ˈpōs(t)-fəs, -ˌfās; pȯs-ˈfäs\ *n* [F, fr. *post-* + *-face* (as in *préface* preface)] (1782) **:** a brief article or note (as of explanation) placed at the end of a publication

post·fem·i·nist \ˌpōst-ˈfe-mə-nist\ *adj* (1983) **:** of, relating to, occurring in, or being the period following widespread advocacy and acceptance of feminism

post·fix \ˈpōs(t)-ˌfiks\ *adj* [*post-* + *-fix* (as in *prefix*)] (1973) **:** characterized by placement of an operator after its operand or after its two operands if it is a binary operator — compare INFIX, PREFIX

postfix notation *n* (1973) **:** REVERSE POLISH NOTATION

post–free \ˈpōs(t)-ˈfrē\ *adj* (1723) *chiefly Brit* **:** POSTPAID

post·gan·gli·on·ic \ˌpōs(t)-ˌgaŋ-glē-ˈä-nik\ *adj* (1897) **:** distal to a ganglion; *specif* **:** of, relating to, or being an axon arising from a cell body within an autonomic ganglion — compare PREGANGLIONIC

post·grad \ˈpōs(t)-ˌgrad\ *adj* (1926) **:** POSTGRADUATE — **postgrad** *n*

1**post·grad·u·ate** \ˌpōs(t)-ˈgra-jə-wət, -ˌwāt, -ˈgraj-wət\ *adj* (1858) **:** of, relating to, or engaged in formal studies after graduation **:** GRADUATE

2**postgraduate** *n* (ca. 1890) **:** a student continuing formal education after graduation from high school or college

1**post·haste** \ˈpōst-ˈhāst\ *n* [3*post*] (1545) *archaic* **:** great haste

2**posthaste** *adv* (1569) **:** with all possible speed

3**posthaste** *adj* (1604) *obs* **:** SPEEDY, IMMEDIATE ⟨requires your . . . ~ appearance —Shak.⟩

post hoc \ˈpōst-ˈhäk\ *adj* [NL *post hoc, ergo propter hoc* after this, therefore because of this] (1704) **1 :** relating to or being the fallacy of arguing from temporal sequence to a causal relation **2 :** formulated after the fact ⟨a *post hoc* rationalization⟩

post·hole \ˈpōst-ˌhōl\ *n* (1703) **:** a hole dug for a post

post horn *n* (1659) **:** a simple straight or coiled brass or copper small wind instrument with cupped mouthpiece used esp. by guards of mail coaches of the 18th and 19th centuries

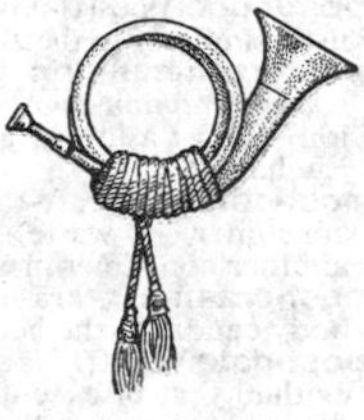

post horn

post–horse \ˈpōst-ˌhȯrs\ *n* [3*post*] (1527) **:** a horse for use esp. by couriers or mail carriers

post·hu·mous \ˈpäs-chə-məs *also* -tə-, -tyə-, -thə-; päst-ˈhyü-məs, ˈpōst-, -ˈyü-\ *adj* [L *posthumus,* alter. of *postumus* late-born, posthumous, fr. superl. of *posterus* coming after — more at POSTERIOR] (1619) **1 :** born after the death of the father **2 :** published after the death of the author **3 :** following or occurring after death ⟨~ fame⟩ — **post·hu·mous·ly** *adv* — **post·hu·mous·ness** *n*

post·hyp·not·ic \ˌpōst-hip-ˈnä-tik, -ip-\ *adj* [ISV] (1890) **:** of, relating to, or characteristic of the period following a hypnotic trance

pos·tiche \pȯs-ˈtēsh\ *n* [F, fr. Sp. *postizo*] (1876) **:** WIG; *esp* **:** TOUPEE 2

pos·tie \ˈpōs-tē\ *n* [by shortening & alter. fr. *postman*] (1871) *Brit* **:** LETTER CARRIER

pos·til·ion *or* **pos·til·lion** \pō-ˈstil-yən, pə-\ *n* [MF *postillon* mail carrier using post-horses, fr. It *postiglione,* fr. *posta* post — more at POST] (ca. 1611) **:** one who rides as a guide on the near horse of one of the pairs attached to a coach or post chaise esp. without a coachman

Post·im·pres·sion·ism \ˌpōst-im-ˈpre-shə-ˌni-zəm\ *n* [F *postimpressionisme,* fr. *post-* + *impressionisme* impressionism] (1910) **:** a theory or practice of art originating in France in the last quarter of the 19th century that in revolt against impressionism stresses variously volume, picture structure, or expressionism — **Post·im·pres·sion·ist** \-ˈpre-sh(ə-)nist\ *adj or n* — **Post·im·pres·sion·is·tic** \-ˌpre-shə-ˈnis-tik\ *adj*

1**post·ing** \ˈpōs-tiŋ\ *n* [4*post*] (1682) **1 :** the act of transferring an entry or item from a book of original entry to the proper account in a ledger **2 :** the record in a ledger account resulting from the transfer of an entry or item from a book of original entry

2**posting** *n* [7*post*] (1880) **:** appointment to a post or a command

3**posting** *n* [2*post*] (1991) **:** 3POST 4

post–Kant·ian \ˌpōs(t)-ˈkan-tē-ən, -ˈkän-\ *adj* (1843) **:** of or relating to the idealist philosophers (as Fichte, Schelling, and Hegel) following Kant and developing some of his ideas

post·lap·sar·i·an \-ˌlap-ˈser-ē-ən\ *adj* [*post-* + L *lapsus* slip, fall — more at LAPSE] (1733) **:** of, relating to, or characteristic of the time or state after the fall of humankind described in the Bible

post·lit·er·ate \-ˈli-tə-rət *also* -ˈli-trət\ *adj* (1960) **:** relating to or occurring after the introduction of the electronic media

post·lude \ˈpōst-ˌlüd\ *n* [*post-* + *-lude* (as in *prelude*)] (1851) **1 :** a closing piece of music; *esp* **:** an organ voluntary at the end of a church service **2 :** a closing phase (as of an epoch or a literary work)

post·man \ˈpōs(t)-mən, -ˌman\ *n* (1529) **:** MAILMAN

1**post·mark** \-ˌmärk\ *n* (1678) **:** an official postal marking on a piece of mail; *specif* **:** a mark showing the post office and date of mailing

2**postmark** *vt* (1716) **:** to put a postmark on

post·mas·ter \-ˌmas-tər\ *n* (1513) **1 :** one who has charge of a post office **2 :** one who has charge of a station for the accommodation of travelers or who supplies post-horses — **post·mas·ter·ship** \-ˌship\ *n*

postmaster general *n, pl* **postmasters general** (1626) **:** an official in charge of a national post office department or agency

post·men·o·paus·al \ˌpōs(t)-ˌme-nə-ˈpȯ-zəl, -ˌmē-\ *adj* (1928) **1 :** having undergone menopause **2 :** occurring or administered after menopause — **post·men·o·paus·al·ly** \-zə-lē\ *adv* — **post·men·o·pause** \-ˈme-nə-ˌpȯz, -ˈmē-\ *n*

post me·ri·di·em \-mə-ˈri-dē-əm, -ˌem\ *adj* [L] (1647) **:** being after noon — abbr. *PM*

post·mil·le·nar·i·an·ism \-ˌmi-lə-ˈner-ē-ə-ˌni-zəm\ *n* (ca. 1890) **:** POSTMILLENNIALISM — **postmillenarian** *adj or n*

post·mil·len·ni·al \-mə-ˈle-nē-əl\ *adj* (1851) **1 :** coming after or relating to the period after the millennium **2 :** holding or relating to postmillennialism

post·mil·len·ni·al·ism \-ə-ˌli-zəm\ *n* (1879) **:** the theological doctrine that the second coming of Christ will occur after the millennium — **post·mil·len·ni·al·ist** \-ə-list\ *n*

post·mis·tress \ˈpōs(t)-ˌmis-trəs\ *n* (1697) **:** a woman who is a postmaster

post·mod·ern \ˌpōs(t)-ˈmä-dərn, ÷-ˈmä-d(ə-)rən\ *adj* (1925) **1 :** of, relating to, or being an era after a modern one ⟨~ times⟩ ⟨a ~ metropolis⟩ **2 a :** of, relating to, or being any of various movements in reaction to modernism that are typically characterized by a return to traditional materials and forms (as in architecture) or by ironic self-reference and absurdity (as in literature) **b :** of, relating to, or being a theory that involves a radical reappraisal of modern assumptions about culture, identity, history, or language ⟨~ feminism⟩ — **post·mod·ern·ism** \-dər-ˌni-zəm\ *n* — **post·mod·ern·ist** \-nist\ *adj or n* — **post·mo·der·ni·ty** \-mə-ˈdər-ne-tē, -mä- *also* -ˈder-\ *n*

1**post·mor·tem** \ˌpōs(t)-ˈmȯr-təm\ *adj* [L *post mortem* after death] (1832) **1 :** done, occurring, or collected after death ⟨~ tissue specimens⟩ **2 :** following the event

2**postmortem** *n* (1846) **1 :** AUTOPSY 1 **2 :** an analysis or discussion of an event after it is over

postmortem examination *n* (1832) **:** AUTOPSY 1

post·na·sal drip \ˈpōst-ˌnā-zəl-\ *n* (ca. 1949) **:** flow of mucous secretion from the posterior part of the nasal cavity onto the wall of the pharynx occurring usu. as a chronic accompaniment of an allergic state

post·na·tal \ˌpōs(t)-ˈnā-tᵊl\ *adj* [ISV] (ca. 1859) **:** occurring or being after birth; *specif* **:** of or relating to an infant immediately after birth ⟨~ care⟩ — **post·na·tal·ly** *adv*

post·nup·tial \-ˈnəp-shəl, -chəl, ÷-chə-wəl\ *adj* (1807) **:** made or occurring after marriage or mating

post oak *n* [1*post*] (1775) **:** a white oak (*Quercus stellata*) of the eastern and central U.S. having hard durable wood

post office *n* (1652) **1 :** a government department or agency handling the transmission of mail **2 :** a local branch of a national post office handling the mail for a particular place or area **3 :** a game in which a player acting as postmaster or postmistress may exact a kiss from one of the opposite sex as payment for the pretended delivery of a letter

post–op \ˈpōst-ˈäp\ *adj* **:** POSTOPERATIVE — **post–op** *adv*

post·op·er·a·tive \ˌpōst-ˈä-p(ə-)rə-tiv, -pə-ˌrā-\ *adj* [ISV] (ca. 1890) **1 :** following a surgical operation ⟨~ care⟩ **2 :** having recently undergone a surgical operation ⟨a ~ patient⟩ — **post·op·er·a·tive·ly** *adv*

post·or·bit·al \-ˈȯr-bə-tᵊl\ *adj* (ca. 1836) **:** situated behind the eye socket

post·paid \ˈpōs(t)-ˈpād\ *adj* (1653) **:** having the postage paid by the sender and not chargeable to the receiver

post·par·tum \ˌpōs(t)-ˈpär-təm\ *adj* [NL *post partum* after birth] (1846) **1 :** occurring in or being the period following parturition ⟨~ depression⟩ **2 :** being in or used in the postpartum period ⟨~ mothers⟩ — **postpartum** *adv*

post–polio syndrome *n* (1985) **:** a condition that affects former poliomyelitis patients long after recovery from the disease and that is characterized by muscle weakness, joint and muscle pain, and fatigue

post·pone \(ˌ)pōs(t)-ˈpōn\ *vt* **post·poned; post·pon·ing** [L *postponere* to place after, postpone, fr. *post-* + *ponere* to place — more at POSITION] (ca. 1520) **1 :** to put off to a later time **:** DEFER **2 a :** to place later (as in a sentence) than the normal position in English ⟨~ an adjective⟩ **b :** to place later in order of precedence, preference, or importance ***syn*** see DEFER — **post·pon·able** \-ˈpō-nə-bəl\ *adj* — **post·pone·ment** \-ˈpōn-mənt\ *n* — **post·pon·er** *n*

post·po·si·tion \ˌpōs(t)-pə-ˈzi-shən, ˈpōs(t)-pə-ˌ\ *n* [F, fr. *postposer* to place after, fr. L *postponere* (perf. indic. *postposui*)] (ca. 1638) **:** the placing of a grammatical element after a word to which it is primarily related in a sentence; *also* **:** such a word or particle esp. when functioning as a preposition — **post·po·si·tion·al** \ˌpōs(t)-pə-ˈzish-nəl, -ˈzi-shə-nᵊl\ *adj* — **post·po·si·tion·al·ly** *adv*

post·pos·i·tive \-ˈpä-zə-tiv, -ˈpäz-tiv\ *adj* (1786) **:** placed after or at the end of another word — **post·pos·i·tive·ly** *adv*

post·pran·di·al \ˌpōs(t)-ˈpran-dē-əl\ *adj* (1820) **:** occurring after a meal — **post·pran·di·al·ly** \-ə-lē\ *adv*

post·pro·duc·tion \ˌpōs(t)-prə-ˈdək-shən, ˈpōs(t)-prə-ˌ, -prō-\ *n* (1953) **:** the period following filming or taping in which a motion picture or television show is readied for public presentation

post road *n* (1657) **:** a route over which mail is carried

post·script \ˈpōs(t)-ˌskript\ *n* [NL *postscriptum,* fr. L, neut. of *postscriptus,* pp. of *postscribere* to write after, fr. *post-* + *scribere* to write — more at SCRIBE] (1551) **:** a note or series of notes appended to a completed letter, article, or book

post–struc·tur·al·ism \ˌpōs(t)-ˈstrək-chə-rə-ˌli-zəm, -ˈstrək-shrə-\ *n* (1977) **:** a movement or theory (as deconstruction) that views the descriptive premise of structuralism as contradicted by reliance on borrowed concepts or differential terms and categories and sees inquiry as inevitably shaped by discursive and interpretive practices — **post–struc·tur·al·ist** *adj or n*

post·sur·gi·cal \ˌpōs(t)-ˈsər-ji-kəl\ *adj* (1962) **:** POSTOPERATIVE — **post·sur·gi·cal·ly** \-k(ə-)lē\ *adv*

post·syn·ap·tic \ˌpōs(t)-sə-ˈnap-tik\ *adj* (1909) **1 :** occurring after synapsis ⟨a ~ chromosome⟩ **2 :** of, occurring in, or being a nerve cell by which a wave of excitation is conveyed away from a synapse ⟨a ~ membrane⟩ — **post·syn·ap·ti·cal·ly** \-ti-k(ə-)lē\ *adv*

post·ten·sion \-ˈten(t)-shən\ *vt* (1950) **:** to apply tension to (reinforcing steel) after concrete has set

post·test \ˈpōs(t)-ˌtest\ *n* (ca. 1951) **:** a test given to students after completion of an instructional program or segment and often used in conjunction with a pretest to measure their achievement and the effectiveness of the program

post time *n* [1*post*] (1941) **:** the designated starting time of a horse race

post·tran·scrip·tion·al \ˌpōs(t)-tran(t)-ˈskrip-shnəl, -shə-nᵊl\ *adj* (1969) **:** occurring, acting, or existing after genetic transcription

post·trans·fu·sion \-tran(t)s-ˈfyü-zhən\ *adj* (1944) **1 :** caused by transfused blood **2 :** occurring after blood transfusion ⟨~ shock⟩

post·trans·la·tion·al \-tran(t)s-ˈlā-shnəl, -shə-nᵊl\ *adj* (1975) **:** occurring or existing after genetic translation

post–traumatic stress disorder *n* (1980) **:** a psychological reaction occurring after experiencing a highly stressing event (as wartime combat, physical violence, or a natural disaster) that is usu. characterized by depression, anxiety, flashbacks, recurrent nightmares, and avoidance of reminders of the event — abbr. *PTSD;* called also *post-traumatic stress syndrome*

pos·tu·lan·cy \'päs-chə-lən(t)-sē\ *n, pl* **-cies** (ca. 1883) **1 :** the quality or state of being a postulant **2 :** the period during which a person remains a postulant
pos·tu·lant \'päs-chə-lənt\ *n* [F, petitioner, candidate, postulant, fr. MF, fr. prp. of *postuler* to demand, solicit, fr. L *postulare*] (1759) **1 :** a person admitted to a religious order as a probationary candidate for membership **2 :** a person on probation before being admitted as a candidate for holy orders in the Episcopal Church
[1]**pos·tu·late** \'päs-chə-ˌlāt\ *vt* **-lat·ed; -lat·ing** [L *postulatus,* pp. of *postulare;* akin to L *poscere* to ask, OHG *forscōn* to search, Skt *pṛcchati* he asks — more at PRAY] (1593) **1 :** DEMAND, CLAIM **2 a :** to assume or claim as true, existent, or necessary **:** depend upon or start from the postulate of **b :** to assume as a postulate or axiom (as in logic or mathematics) — **pos·tu·la·tion** \ˌpäs-chə-'lā-shən\ *n* — **pos·tu·la·tion·al** \-shnəl, -shə-nᵊl\ *adj*
[2]**pos·tu·late** \'päs-chə-lət, -ˌlāt\ *n* [ML *postulatum,* fr. neut. of *postulatus,* pp. of *postulare* to assume, fr. L, to demand] (1646) **1 :** a hypothesis advanced as an essential presupposition, condition, or premise of a train of reasoning **2 :** AXIOM 3
pos·tu·la·tor \-ˌlā-tər\ *n* (1863) **:** an official who presents a plea for beatification or canonization in the Roman Catholic Church — compare DEVIL'S ADVOCATE
post up *vi* (1974) **:** to take up a position against a defender in the post in basketball while standing with one's back to the basket ~ *vt* **:** to post up against (a defender) in basketball
pos·tur·al \'päs-chə-rəl\ *adj* (1857) **:** of, relating to, or involving posture; *also* **:** ORTHOSTATIC
[1]**pos·ture** \'päs-chər\ *n* [MF, fr. It *postura,* fr. L *positura,* fr. *positus,* pp. of *ponere* to place — more at POSITION] (ca. 1586) **1 a :** the position or bearing of the body whether characteristic or assumed for a special purpose ⟨erect ~⟩ **b :** the pose of a model or artistic figure **2 :** state or condition at a given time esp. with respect to capability in particular circumstances ⟨maintain a competitive ~ in the market⟩ **3 :** a conscious mental or outward behavioral attitude
[2]**posture** *vb* **pos·tured; pos·tur·ing** *vt* (ca. 1645) **:** to cause to assume a given posture **:** POSE ~ *vi* **1 :** to assume a posture; *esp* **:** to strike a pose for effect **2 :** to assume an artificial or pretended attitude **:** ATTITUDINIZE — **pos·tur·er** \-chər-ər\ *n*
post·vo·cal·ic \ˌpōs(t)-vō-'ka-lik, -və-\ *adj* [ISV] (1892) **:** immediately following a vowel
post·war \'pōs(t)-ˌwär\ *adj* (1908) **:** occurring or existing after a war; *esp* **:** occurring or existing after World War II
po·sy \'pō-zē\ *n, pl* **posies** [alter. of *poesy*] (1533) **1 :** a brief sentiment, motto, or legend **2 a :** BOUQUET, NOSEGAY **b :** FLOWER
[1]**pot** \'pät\ *n* [ME, fr. OE *pott;* akin to MLG *pot* pot] (bef. 12c) **1 a :** a usu. rounded metal or earthen container used chiefly for domestic purposes (as in cooking or for holding liquids or growing plants); *also* **:** any of various technical or industrial vessels or enclosures resembling or likened to a household pot ⟨the ~ of a still⟩ **b :** POTFUL ⟨a ~ of coffee⟩ **2 :** an enclosed framework of wire, wood, or wicker for catching fish or lobsters **3 a :** a large amount (as of money) **b (1) :** the total of the bets at stake at one time **(2) :** one round in a poker game **c :** the common fund of a group **4 :** POTSHOT **5 :** POTBELLY **6 :** RUIN ⟨gone to ~⟩ **7** *Brit* **:** a shot in snooker in which a ball is pocketed **8 :** a vessel for urination and defecation: as **a :** TOILET 3b **b :** POTTY
[2]**pot** *vb* **pot·ted; pot·ting** *vt* (1616) **1 a :** to place in a pot **b :** to pack or preserve (as cooked and chopped meat) in a sealed pot, jar, or can often with aspic **2 :** to shoot with a potshot **3 :** to make or shape (earthenware) as a potter **4 :** to embed (as electronic components) in a container with an insulating or protective material (as plastic) ~ *vi* **:** to take a potshot
[3]**pot** *n* [perh. modif. of MexSp *potiguaya*] (1938) **:** MARIJUANA
[4]**pot** *abbr* **1** potential **2** potentiometer
[1]**po·ta·ble** \'pō-tə-bəl\ *adj* [ME, fr. LL *potabilis,* fr. L *potare* to drink; akin to L *bibere* to drink, Gk *pinein*] (15c) **:** suitable for drinking — **po·ta·bil·i·ty** \ˌpō-tə-'bi-lə-tē\ *n* — **po·ta·ble·ness** \'pō-tə-bəl-nəs\ *n*
[2]**potable** *n* (1623) **:** a liquid that is suitable for drinking; *esp* **:** an alcoholic beverage
po·tage \pȯ-'täzh\ *n* [MF, fr. OF, pottage] (1505) **:** a thick soup
pot ale *n* (1812) **:** the residue of fermented wort left in a still after the distillation of whiskey or alcohol and used for animal feed
pot·ash \'pät-ˌash\ *n* [sing. of *pot ashes*] (1748) **1 :** potassium carbonate esp. from wood ashes **2 :** potassium or a potassium compound esp. as used in agriculture or industry
po·tas·sic \pə-'ta-sik\ *adj* (1850) **:** of, relating to, or containing potassium
po·tas·si·um \pə-'ta-sē-əm\ *n, often attrib* [NL, fr. *potassa* potash, fr. E *potash*] (ca. 1807) **:** a silver-white soft light low-melting monovalent metallic element of the alkali metal group that occurs abundantly in nature esp. combined in minerals — see ELEMENT table
potassium–argon *adj* (1953) **:** being or relating to a method of dating paleontological or geological materials based on the radioactive decay of potassium to argon that has taken place in a specimen
potassium bromide *n* (1869) **:** a crystalline salt KBr with a saline taste that is used esp. as a sedative and in photography
potassium carbonate *n* (1866) **:** a white salt K_2CO_3 that forms a strongly alkaline solution and is used in making glass and soap
potassium chlorate *n* (1869) **:** a crystalline salt $KClO_3$ that is used as an oxidizing agent in matches, fireworks, and explosives
potassium chloride *n* (1869) **:** a crystalline salt KCl occurring as a mineral and in natural waters and used esp. as a fertilizer
potassium cyanide *n* (1869) **:** a very poisonous crystalline salt KCN used esp. in gold and silver extraction from ore
potassium dichromate *n* (1871) **:** a soluble salt $K_2Cr_2O_7$ forming large orange-red crystals used esp. in dyeing, in photography, and as an oxidizing agent
potassium hydroxide *n* (1869) **:** a white deliquescent solid KOH that dissolves in water with much heat to form a strongly alkaline and caustic liquid and is used chiefly in making soap and as a reagent
potassium nitrate *n* (1869) **:** a crystalline salt KNO_3 that occurs as a product of nitrification in arable soils, is a strong oxidizer, and is used esp. in making gunpowder, as a fertilizer, and in medicine
potassium permanganate *n* (1869) **:** a dark purple salt $KMnO_4$ used as an oxidizer and disinfectant
potassium sorbate *n* (1960) **:** a potassium salt $C_6H_7KO_2$ of sorbic acid used esp. as a food preservative
potassium sulfate *n* (1869) **:** a white crystalline compound K_2SO_4 used esp. as a fertilizer
po·ta·tion \pō-'tā-shən\ *n* [ME *potacioun,* fr. AF *potation,* fr. L *potation-, potatio* act of drinking, fr. *potare* to drink — more at POTABLE] (15c) **1 :** a usu. alcoholic drink or brew **2 :** the act or an instance of drinking or inhaling; *also* **:** the portion taken in one such act
po·ta·to \pə-'tā-(ˌ)tō, -tə, *dial* pə-'dā-, bə-\ *n, pl* **-toes** *often attrib* [Sp *batata,* fr. Taino] (1565) **1 :** SWEET POTATO **2 a :** an erect So. American herb (*Solanum tuberosum*) of the nightshade family widely cultivated for its edible starchy tuber **b :** the tuber of a potato — called also *Irish potato, spud, white potato*
potato beetle *n* (1866) **:** COLORADO POTATO BEETLE
potato blight *n* (1847) **:** any of several destructive fungus diseases of the potato
potato bug *n* (1799) **:** COLORADO POTATO BEETLE
potato chip *n* (1854) **:** a thin slice of white potato that has been cooked until crisp and then usu. salted
potato leafhopper *n* (1921) **:** a small green white-spotted leafhopper (*Empoasca fabae*) esp. of the eastern and southern U.S. that is a serious pest on many cultivated plants and esp. on the potato
potato pancake *n* (1865) **:** a fried flat cake of grated potato mixed with raw egg and usu. grated onion and spices
potato tu·ber·worm \-'tü-bər-ˌwərm, -'tyü-\ *n* (1920) **:** a grayish-brown moth (*Phthorimaea operculella*) whose larva mines the leaves and bores in the stems and tubers of the potato plant and often attacks other solanaceous plants (as tobacco and tomato)
pot–au–feu \ˌpät-ō-'fə(r), pȯ-tō-'fœ\ *n, pl* **pot–au–feu** [F, lit., pot on the fire] (1791) **:** a French boiled dinner of meat and vegetables
pot·bel·lied \'pät-ˌbe-lēd\ *adj* (1657) **:** having a potbelly
potbellied pig *n* (1985) **:** any of a breed of small pigs originating in southeastern Asia and having a straight tail, potbelly, swayback, and black, white, or black and white coat
potbellied stove *n* (1933) **:** a stove with a rounded or bulging body — called also *potbelly stove*
pot·bel·ly \'pät-ˌbe-lē\ *n* (1696) **1 :** an enlarged, swollen, or protruding abdomen **2 :** POTBELLIED STOVE
pot·boil \-ˌbȯi(-ə)l\ *vi* (1867) **:** to produce potboilers
pot·boil·er \-ˌbȯi-lər\ *n* (1862) **:** a usu. inferior work (as of art or literature) produced chiefly for profit
pot–bound \'pät-ˌbau̇nd\ *adj* (1850) *of a potted plant* **:** having roots so densely matted as to allow little or no space for further growth
pot·boy \-ˌbȯi\ *n* (1662) **:** a boy who serves drinks in a tavern
pot cheese *n* (1812) **:** COTTAGE CHEESE
po·teen *also* **po·theen** \pə-'tēn, -'chēn, -'tyēn, -'thēn\ *n* [Ir *poitín,* lit., small pot, dim. of *pota* pot] (1812) **:** whiskey illicitly distilled in Ireland
Po·tem·kin village \pə-'tem(p)-kən-\ *n* [Grigori *Potëmkin,* who supposedly built impressive fake villages along a route Catherine the Great was to travel] (1937) **:** an impressive facade or show designed to hide an undesirable fact or condition
po·tence \'pō-tᵊn(t)s\ *n* (15c) **:** POTENCY
po·ten·cy \'pō-tᵊn(t)-sē\ *n, pl* **-cies** (15c) **1 a :** FORCE, POWER **b :** the quality or state of being potent **c :** the ability or capacity to achieve or bring about a particular result **2 :** POTENTIALITY 1
[1]**po·tent** \'pō-tᵊnt\ *adj* [ME, fr. L *potent-, potens* (prp. of *posse* to be able), fr. L *potis, pote* able; akin to Goth brūth*faths* bridegroom, Gk *posis* husband, Skt *pati* master] (15c) **1 :** having or wielding force, authority, or influence **:** POWERFUL **2 :** achieving or bringing about a particular result **:** EFFECTIVE **3 a :** chemically or medicinally effective ⟨a ~ vaccine⟩ **b :** rich in a characteristic constituent ⟨a ~ drink⟩ **4 :** able to copulate — usu. used of the male — **po·tent·ly** *adv*
[2]**potent** *adj* [obs. E *potent* crutch] (1610) *of a heraldic cross* **:** having flat bars across the ends of the arms — see CROSS illustration
po·ten·tate \'pō-tᵊn-ˌtāt\ *n* (15c) **:** RULER, SOVEREIGN; *broadly* **:** one who wields great power or sway
[1]**po·ten·tial** \pə-'ten(t)-shəl\ *adj* [ME *potencial,* fr. LL *potentialis,* fr. *potentia* potentiality, fr. L, power, fr. *potent-, potens*] (14c) **1 :** existing in possibility **:** capable of development into actuality ⟨~ benefits⟩ **2 :** expressing possibility; *specif* **:** of, relating to, or constituting a verb phrase expressing possibility, liberty, or power by the use of an auxiliary with the infinitive of the verb (as in "it may rain") ***syn*** see LATENT — **po·ten·tial·ly** \-'ten(t)-sh(ə-)lē\ *adv*
[2]**potential** *n* (1817) **1 a :** something that can develop or become actual ⟨a ~ for violence⟩ **b :** PROMISE 2 **2 a :** any of various functions from which the intensity or the velocity at any point in a field may be readily calculated **b :** the work required to move a unit positive charge from a reference point (as at infinity) to a point in question **c :** POTENTIAL DIFFERENCE
potential difference *n* (1892) **:** the difference in potential between two points that represents the work involved or the energy released in the transfer of a unit quantity of electricity from one point to the other
potential energy *n* (1853) **:** the energy that a piece of matter has because of its position or nature or because of the arrangement of parts
po·ten·ti·al·i·ty \pə-ˌten(t)-shē-'a-lə-tē\ *n, pl* **-ties** (1625) **1 :** the ability to develop or come into existence **2 :** POTENTIAL 1
po·ten·ti·ate \pə-'ten(t)-shē-ˌāt\ *vt* **-at·ed; -at·ing** (1817) **:** to augment the effective or active or more effective or more active; *also* **:** to augment the activity of (as a drug) synergistically — **po·ten·ti·a·tion** \-ˌten(t)-shē-'ā-shən\ *n* — **po·ten·ti·a·tor** \-'ten(t)-shē-ˌā-tər\ *n*
po·ten·til·la \ˌpō-tᵊn-'ti-lə\ *n* [NL, fr. ML, garden heliotrope, fr. L *potent-, potens*] (1548) **:** CINQUEFOIL 1
po·ten·ti·om·e·ter \pə-ˌten(t)-shē-'ä-mə-tər\ *n* [ISV *potential* + *-o-* + *-meter*] (1881) **1 :** an instrument for measuring electromotive forces **2 :** VOLTAGE DIVIDER — **po·ten·ti·o·met·ric** \-sh(ē-)ə-'me-trik\ *adj*

\ə\ **a**but \ᵊ\ kitten, F table \ər\ **fur**ther \a\ **a**sh \ā\ **a**ce \ä\ m**o**p, m**a**r \au̇\ **ou**t \ch\ **ch**in \e\ b**e**t \ē\ **ea**sy \g\ **g**o \i\ h**i**t \ī\ **i**ce \j\ **j**ob \ŋ\ si**ng** \ō\ g**o** \ȯ\ l**aw** \ȯi\ b**oy** \th\ **th**in \t͟h\ **th**e \ü\ l**oo**t \u̇\ f**oo**t \y\ **y**et \zh\ vi**si**on, beige \k̟, ⁿ, œ, ue, ʸ\ *see* Guide to Pronunciation

pot·ful \'pät-ˌfu̇l\ n (14c) 1 : as much or as many as a pot will hold 2 : a large amount ⟨makes a ~ of money —John Corry⟩

pot hat n (1580) : a hat with a stiff crown; esp : DERBY

pot·head \'pät-ˌhed\ n (1957) : a person who frequently smokes marijuana

¹**poth·er** \'pä-thər\ n [origin unknown] (1591) 1 a : a confused or fidgety flurry of activity : COMMOTION b : agitated talk or controversy usu. over a trivial matter 2 : a choking cloud of dust or smoke 3 : mental turmoil

²**pother** vb **poth·ered; poth·er·ing** \'pä-thə-riŋ, 'päth-riŋ\ vt (1692) : to put into a pother ~ vi : to be in a pother

pot·herb \'pät-ˌərb, -ˌhərb\ n (1538) : a usu. leafy herb that is cooked for use as greens; also : one (as mint) used to season food

pot holder n (1888) : a small cloth pad used for handling hot cooking utensils or containers

pot·hole \'pät-ˌhōl\ n (1826) 1 a : a circular hole formed in the rocky bed of a river by the grinding action of stones or gravel whirled round by the water b : a sizable rounded often water-filled depression in land 2 : a pot-shaped hole in a road surface 3 : a usu. minor difficulty or setback ⟨hit a ~ in her comeback attempt⟩ — **pot·holed** \-ˌhōld\ adj

pot·hook \-ˌhu̇k\ n (15c) 1 : an S-shaped hook for hanging pots and kettles over an open fire 2 : a written character resembling a pothook

po·thos \'pō-ˌthäs\ n, pl pothos [NL, fr. Sinhalese pótā] (1822) : a southeast Asian climbing plant (Epipremnum aureum syn. Scindapsus aureus) of the arum family widely grown esp. as a houseplant for its leathery or waxy heart-shaped green leaves that are spotted or streaked with golden yellow or white

pot·house \-ˌhau̇s\ n (1598) : TAVERN 1

pot·hunt·er \-ˌhən-tər\ n (1750) 1 : one who hunts game for food 2 : an amateur archaeologist — **pot·hunt·ing** \-tiŋ\ n

po·tion \'pō-shən\ n [ME pocioun, fr. AF poisun, pocioun drink, potion, fr. L potion-, potio, fr. potare to drink — more at POTABLE] (14c) : a mixture of liquids (as liquor or medicine)

¹**pot·latch** \'pät-ˌlach\ n [Chinook Jargon patlač, fr. Nootka paƛpač] (ca. 1858) 1 : a ceremonial feast of the American Indians of the northwest coast marked by the host's lavish distribution of gifts or sometimes destruction of property to demonstrate wealth and generosity with the expectation of eventual reciprocation 2 Northwest : a social event or celebration

²**potlatch** vt (1898) 1 : to give (as a gift) esp. with the expectation of a gift in return 2 : to hold or give a potlatch for (as a tribe or group) ~ vi : to hold or give a potlatch

pot lik·ker \-ˌli-kər\ Southern & Midland var of POT LIQUOR

pot·line \'pät-ˌlīn\ n (1944) : a row of electrolytic cells used in the production of aluminum

pot liquor n (1742) : the liquid left in a pot after cooking something

pot·luck \'pät-ˌlək, 1b also -ˌlək\ n (1592) 1 a : the regular meal available to a guest for whom no special preparations have been made b : a communal meal to which people bring food to share — usu. used attributively ⟨a ~ supper⟩ 2 : whatever is offered or available in given circumstances or at a given time

pot marigold n (1760) : a calendula (Calendula officinalis) grown esp. for ornament

po·tom·e·ter \pō-ˈtä-mə-tər\ n [Gk poton drink (akin to Gk pinein to drink) + E -meter — more at POTABLE] (1884) : an apparatus for measuring the rate of transpiration in a plant by determining the amount of water absorbed

pot·pie \'pät-ˈpī, -ˌpī\ n (1702) : pastry-covered meat and vegetables cooked in a deep dish

pot·pour·ri \ˌpō-pu̇-ˈrē\ n [F pot pourri, lit., rotten pot] (1749) 1 : a mixture of flowers, herbs, and spices that is usu. kept in a jar and used for scent 2 : a miscellaneous collection : MEDLEY ⟨a ~ of the best songs and sketches —Current Biog.⟩

pot roast n (1881) : a piece of beef cooked by braising usu. on top of the stove

POTS abbr plain old telephone system; plain old telephone service

pot·sherd \'pät-ˌshərd\ n [ME pot-sherd, fr. pot + sherd shard] (14c) : a pottery fragment usu. unearthed as an archaeological relic

¹**pot·shot** \-ˌshät\ n [fr. the notion that such a shot is unsportsmanlike and worthy only of one whose object is to fill the cooking pot] (1843) 1 : a shot taken from ambush or at a random or easy target 2 : a critical remark made in a random or sporadic manner

²**potshot** vb potshot; pot·shot·ting vi (1913) : to take a potshot ~ vt : to attack or shoot with a potshot

pot sticker n (1968) : a crescent-shaped dumpling filled usu. with pork, steamed, and then fried

pot still n (1799) : a still used esp. in the distillation of Irish grain whiskey and Scotch malt whiskey in which the heat of the fire is applied directly to the pot containing the mash

pot·stone \'pät-ˌstōn\ n (1741) : a more or less impure steatite used esp. in prehistoric times to make cooking vessels

pot·tage \'pä-tij\ n [ME potage, fr. AF, fr. pot pot, of Gmc origin; akin to OE pott pot] (13c) : a thick soup of vegetables and often meat

pot·ted adj (ca. 1684) 1 : preserved in a pot, jar, or can ⟨~ meat⟩ 2 : planted or grown in a pot 3 : briefly and superficially summarized ⟨a dull, pedestrian ~ history —Times Lit. Supp.⟩ 4 slang : DRUNK 1a

¹**pot·ter** \'pä-tər\ n (bef. 12c) : one that makes pottery

²**potter** vi [prob. freq. of E dial. pote to poke] (1829) : PUTTER — **pot·ter·er** \'pä-tər-ər\ n — **pot·ter·ing·ly** \'pä-tə-riŋ-lē\ adv

potter's clay n (15c) : a plastic clay suitable for making pottery — called also potter's earth

potter's field n [fr. the mention in Mt 27:7 of the purchase of a potter's field for use as a graveyard] (1777) : a public burial place for paupers, unknown persons, and criminals

potter's wheel n (1567) : a usu. horizontal disk revolving on a vertical spindle and carrying the clay being shaped by a potter

potter's wheel

pot·tery \'pä-tə-rē\ n, pl -ter·ies (15c) 1 : a place where clayware is made and fired 2 a : the art or craft of the potter b : the manufacture of clayware from porcelain and stoneware and from brick and tile 3 : CLAYWARE; esp : earthenware as distinguished from porcelain and stoneware and from brick and tile

pot·tle \'pä-tᵊl\ n [ME potel, fr. AF, fr. pot] (14c) : a container holding a half gallon (1.9 liters)

pot·to \'pä-(ˌ)tō\ n, pl pottos [perh. fr. Wolof pata, a tailless monkey] (1763) : any of several African primates (genera Arctocebus and Perodicticus); esp : a nocturnal slow-moving arboreal primate (P. potto) with woolly brownish fur and a vestigial index finger

Pott's disease \'päts-\ n [Percivall Pott †1788 Eng. surgeon] (1835) : tuberculosis of the spine with destruction of bone resulting in curvature of the spine

¹**pot·ty** \'pä-tē\ adj pot·ti·er; -est [prob. fr. ¹pot] (ca. 1860) 1 Brit : TRIVIAL, INSIGNIFICANT 2 chiefly Brit : slightly crazy 3 : SNOBBISH

²**potty** n, pl potties (ca. 1942) 1 : a small child's pot for urination or defecation; also : POTTY-CHAIR 2 : TOILET, BATHROOM

pot·ty–chair \-ˌcher\ n (1941) : a child's chair having an open seat under which a receptacle is placed for toilet training

pot·ty–mouthed \-ˌmau̇thd, -ˌmau̇tht\ adj (1987) : given to the use of vulgar language — **potty mouth** n

potty training n (1946) : TOILET TRAINING — **potty train** vt

POTUS abbr president of the United States

potzer var of PATZER

¹**pouch** \'pau̇ch\ n [ME pouche, fr. AF, of Gmc origin; akin to OE pocca bag] (14c) 1 : a small drawstring bag carried on the person 2 a : a bag of small or moderate size for storing or transporting goods; specif : a lockable bag for first-class mail or diplomatic dispatches b chiefly Scot : POCKET c : PACKET 3 : an anatomical structure resembling a pouch — **pouched** \'pau̇cht\ adj

²**pouch** vt (ca. 1566) 1 : to put or form into or as if into a pouch 2 : to transmit by pouch ~ vi 1 : to bulge in a manner suggesting a pouch ⟨~ing cheeks⟩ 2 : to transmit mail or dispatches by pouch

pouchy \'pau̇-chē\ adj pouch·i·er; -est (1786) : having, tending to have, or resembling a pouch ⟨~ insomniac eyes —Graham Greene⟩

pouf also pouffe \'pu̇f\ n [F pouf, something inflated, of imit. origin] (1817) 1 : PUFF 3b(3) 2 : a bouffant or fluffy part of a garment or accessory 3 : OTTOMAN — **poufed or pouffed** \'pu̇ft\ adj

Pouil·ly–Fuis·sé \ˌpü-ˌyē-fwē-ˈsā\ n [Solutré-Pouilly and Fuissé, villages in France] (1927) : a dry white burgundy from an area west of Mâcon, France

Pouil·ly–Fu·mé \ˌpü-ˌyē-fü-ˈmā, -fwē-\ n [F, fr. Pouilly-sur-Loire, village in France + fumé, pp. of fumer to smoke, fr. L fumare, fr. fumus smoke — more at FUME] (1935) : a dry white wine from the Loire valley of France

pou·larde also pou·lard \pù-ˈlärd\ n [F poularde] (1733) : a fattened pullet used esp. for roasting

poult \'pōlt\ n [ME polet, pulte young fowl — more at PULLET] (15c) : a young fowl; esp : a young turkey

poul·ter·er \'pōl-tər-ər\ n [alter. of ME pulter, fr. AF pulleter] (1534) : one that deals in poultry

poul·ter's measure \'pōl-tərz-\ n [obs. poulter poulterer, fr. ME pulter; fr. the former practice of occas. giving one or two extra when counting eggs by dozens] (1575) : a meter in which lines of 12 and 14 syllables alternate

¹**poul·tice** \'pōl-təs\ n [ME pultes, fr. ML, lit., pap, fr. L, pl. of pult-, puls porridge] (15c) : a soft usu. heated and sometimes medicated mass spread on cloth and applied to sores or other lesions

²**poultice** vt -ticed; -tic·ing (1644) : to apply a poultice to

poul·try \'pōl-trē\ n [ME pultrie, fr. AF pulletrie, fr. pulleter poulterer, fr. pullet chicken — more at PULLET] (14c) : domesticated birds kept for eggs or meat

poul·try·man \-mən\ n (1538) 1 : one who raises domestic fowls esp. on a commercial scale for the production of eggs and meat 2 : one who deals in poultry or poultry products

¹**pounce** \'pau̇n(t)s\ n [ME, punching tool, dagger, talon — more at PUNCH] (15c) : the claw of a bird of prey

²**pounce** vi pounced; pounc·ing (1648) 1 a : to swoop upon and seize something with or as if with talons b : to seize upon and make capital of something (as another's blunder or an opportunity) 2 : to make a sudden assault or approach

³**pounce** n (1841) : the act of pouncing

⁴**pounce** vt pounced; pounc·ing [MF poncer, fr. ponce] (1535) : to dust, rub, finish, or stencil with pounce

⁵**pounce** n [F ponce pumice, fr. MF, fr. LL pomic-, pomex, alter. of L pumic-, pumex — more at FOAM] (1705) 1 : a fine powder formerly used to prevent ink from spreading 2 : a fine powder for making stenciled patterns

poun·cet–box \'pau̇n(t)-sət-\ n [prob. fr. MF *poncette small pounce bag] (1598) archaic : a box for carrying pomander

¹**pound** \'pau̇nd\ n, pl pounds also pound [ME, fr. OE pund, fr. L pondo pound, fr. abl. of pondus weight — more at PENDANT] (bef. 12c) 1 : any of various units of mass and weight; specif : a unit now in general use among English-speaking peoples equal to 16 avoirdupois ounces or 7000 grains or 0.4536 kilogram — see WEIGHT table 2 a : the basic monetary unit of the United Kingdom — called also pound sterling b : any of numerous basic monetary units of other countries — see MONEY table c : the basic monetary unit of Ireland from 1921 to 2001 d : ²LIRA e : the basic monetary unit of Cyprus from 1960 to 2008

²**pound** n [ME, enclosure, fr. OE pund-] (14c) 1 a : an enclosure for animals; esp : a public enclosure for stray or unlicensed animals ⟨a dog ~⟩ b : a depot for holding impounded personal property until redeemed by the owner ⟨a car ~⟩ 2 : a place or condition of confinement 3 : an enclosure within which fish are kept or caught; esp : the inner compartment of a fish trap or pound net

³**pound** vb [alter. of ME pounen, fr. OE pūnian] vt (bef. 12c) 1 : to reduce to powder or pulp by beating 2 a : to strike heavily or repeatedly b : to produce with or as if with repeated vigorous strokes — usu. used with out ⟨~ out a story on the typewriter⟩ c : to inculcate by insistent repetition : DRIVE ⟨day after day the facts were ~ed home to them —Ivy B. Priest⟩ d : to move, throw, or carry forcefully and aggressively ⟨~ the ball down the field⟩ 3 : to move along heavily or persistently ⟨~ed the pavement looking for work⟩ 4 : to drink or consume rapidly : SLUG ⟨~ down some beers⟩ ~ vi 1 : to strike

heavy repeated blows **2 :** PULSATE, THROB ⟨my heart was ~*ing*⟩ **3 a :** to move with or make a heavy repetitive sound **b :** to work hard and continuously — usu. used with *away*
[4]**pound** *n* (1863) : an act or sound of pounding
[1]**pound·age** \ˈpau̇n-dij\ *n* (1554) : IMPOUNDMENT 1
[2]**poundage** *n* (1599) **1 :** a charge per pound of weight **2 :** weight in pounds
pound·al \ˈpau̇n-dᵊl\ *n* [ˈ*pound* + *-al* (as in *quintal*)] (1879) : a unit of force equal to the force that would give a free mass of one pound an acceleration of one foot per second per second
pound cake *n* [fr. the original recipe prescribing a pound of each of the principal ingredients] (1743) : a rich butter cake made with a large proportion of eggs and shortening
[1]**pound·er** \ˈpau̇n-dər\ *n* (bef. 12c) **1 :** a tool used for pounding **2 :** one that pounds
[2]**pounder** *n* (1665) **1 :** a gun throwing a projectile of a specified weight — used in combination ⟨the ship was armed with six-*pounders*⟩ **2 :** one having a usu. specified weight or value in pounds — used in combination ⟨caught a ten-*pounder*⟩
pound–fool·ish \ˈpau̇n(d)-ˈfü-lish\ *adj* [fr. the phrase *penny-wise and pound-foolish*] (1598) : imprudent in dealing with large sums or large matters
pound mile *n* (1939) : the transport of one pound of mail or express for one mile
pound net *n* (1856) : a fish trap consisting of a netting arranged into a directing wing and an enclosure with a narrow entrance
pound of flesh (1827) : a payment or penalty exacted to fulfill a deal or punishment ⟨loan sharks taking their *pound of flesh*⟩
pound sign *n* (1895) **1 :** the symbol £ **2 :** the symbol #
[1]**pour** \ˈpȯr\ *vb* [ME] *vt* (14c) **1 a :** to cause to flow in a stream **b :** to dispense from a container ⟨~*ed* drinks for everyone⟩ **2 :** to supply or produce freely or copiously ⟨~*ed* money into the project⟩ **3 :** to give full expression to : VENT ⟨~*ed* out his feelings⟩ ~ *vi* **1 :** to move with a continuous flow **2 :** to rain hard **3 :** to move or come continuously : STREAM ⟨complaints ~*ed in*⟩ **4 :** to score easily or freely (as in basketball) — used with *in* ⟨~*ed* in 30 points⟩ — **pour·able** \ˈpȯr-ə-bəl\ *adj* — **pour·er** \-ər\ *n* — **pour·ing·ly** \-iŋ-lē\ *adv*
[2]**pour** *n* (1790) **1 :** the action of pouring : STREAM **2 a :** an instance of pouring or an amount poured **b :** a heavy fall of rain : DOWNPOUR
pour·boire \pu̇r-ˈbwär\ *n* [F, fr. *pour boire* for drinking] (1788) : TIP, GRATUITY
pour·par·ler \ˌpu̇r-pär-ˈlā\ *n* [F, fr. MF, fr. *pourparler* to discuss, fr. OF, fr. *pour* for, before + *parler* to speak — more at PURCHASE, PARLEY] (1709) : a discussion preliminary to negotiations
pour·point \ˈpu̇r-ˌpȯint, -ˌpwant\ *n* [ME *purpoint*, fr. AF, fr. OF *porpoint*, adj., quilted, fr. VL **perpunctus*, pp. of **perpungere* to perforate, fr. L *per* through + *pungere* to prick, pierce — more at PUNGENT] (14c) : a padded and quilted doublet
pour point *n* (1922) : the lowest temperature at which a substance flows under specified conditions
pousse–ca·fé \ˌpüs-(ˌ)ka-ˈfā\ *n* [F, lit., coffee chaser] (1862) : an after-dinner drink consisting of several liqueurs of different colors and specific gravities poured so as to remain in separate layers
pous·sette \pü-ˈset\ *vi* **pous·sett·ed; pous·sett·ing** [F, game in which contestants cross pins with each attempting to get his pin on top, fr. *pousser* to push] (1798) : to swing in a semicircle with hands joined with one's partner in a country-dance
[1]**pout** \ˈpau̇t\ *vb* [ME] *vi* (14c) **1 a :** to show displeasure by thrusting out the lips or wearing a sullen expression **b :** SULK **2 :** PROTRUDE ~ *vt* : to cause to protrude ⟨~*ed* her lips⟩
[2]**pout** *n* (1591) **1 :** a protrusion of the lips expressive of displeasure **2** *pl* : a fit of pique
[3]**pout** *n, pl* **pout** or **pouts** [prob. fr. ME **poute*, a fish with a large head, fr. OE *-pūte;* akin to ME *pouten* to pout] (1591) : any of several large-headed fishes (as a bullhead or eelpout)
pout·er \ˈpau̇-tər\ *n* (1793) **1 :** any of several breeds of domestic pigeons characterized by erect carriage and an inflatable crop **2 :** one that pouts
pou·tine \pü-ˈtēn\ *n* [CanF] (1982) *chiefly Canad* : a dish of French fries covered with brown gravy and cheese curds
pouty \ˈpau̇-tē\ *adj* **pout·i·er; -est** (1799) **1 :** SULKY 1 **2 :** expressive of displeasure
POV *abbr* point of view
pov·er·ty \ˈpä-vər-tē\ *n, often attrib* [ME *poverte*, fr. AF *poverté*, fr. L *paupertat-, paupertas*, fr. *pauper* poor — more at POOR] (12c) **1 a :** the state of one who lacks a usual or socially acceptable amount of money or material possessions **b :** renunciation as a member of a religious order of the right as an individual to own property **2 :** SCARCITY, DEARTH **3 a :** debility due to malnutrition **b :** lack of fertility
syn POVERTY, INDIGENCE, PENURY, WANT, DESTITUTION mean the state of one with insufficient resources. POVERTY may cover a range from extreme want of necessities to an absence of material comforts ⟨the extreme *poverty* of the slum dwellers⟩. INDIGENCE implies seriously straitened circumstances ⟨the *indigence* of her years as a graduate student⟩. PENURY suggests a cramping or oppressive lack of money ⟨a catastrophic illness that condemned them to years of *penury*⟩. WANT and DESTITUTION imply extreme poverty that threatens life itself through starvation or exposure ⟨lived in a perpetual state of *want*⟩ ⟨the widespread *destitution* in countries beset by famine⟩.
poverty line *n* (1901) : a level of personal or family income below which one is classified as poor according to governmental standards — called also *poverty level*
pov·er·ty–strick·en \-ˌstri-kən\ *adj* (1786) : very poor : DESTITUTE
[1]**pow** \ˈpō, ˈpau̇\ *n* [alter. of *poll*] (ca. 1500) : HEAD, POLL
[2]**pow** \ˈpau̇\ *n* [imit.] (ca. 1580) : a sound of a blow or explosion
POW \ˌpē-(ˌ)ō-ˈdə-bəl-(ˌ)yü, -bə-(ˌ)yü; -ˈdəb-(ˌ)yü\ *n* (ca. 1919) : PRISONER OF WAR
[1]**pow·der** \ˈpau̇-dər\ *vb* **pow·dered; pow·der·ing** \ˈpau̇-d(ə-)riŋ\ *vt* (13c) **1 :** to sprinkle or cover with or as if with powder **2 :** to reduce or convert to powder **3 :** to hit very hard ~ *vi* **1 :** to become powder **2 :** to apply cosmetic powder — **pow·der·er** \-dər-ər\ *n*
[2]**powder** *n, often attrib* [ME *poudre*, fr. AF *pudre, podre*, fr. L *pulver-, pulvis* dust; prob. akin to Skt *palāva* chaff] (14c) **1 :** matter in a finely divided state : particulate matter **2 a :** a preparation in the form of fine particles esp. for medicinal or cosmetic use **b :** fine dry light snow **3 :** any of various solid explosives used chiefly in gunnery and blasting — **pow·der·less** \-ləs\ *adj* — **pow·der·like** \-ˌlīk\ *adj*
powder blue *n* (1896) : a pale blue
powder horn *n* (1508) : a flask for carrying gunpowder; *esp* : one made of the horn of an ox or cow
powder keg *n* (1791) **1 :** a small usu. metal cask for holding gunpowder or blasting powder **2 :** something liable to explode
powder metallurgy *n* (1933) : a branch of science or an art concerned with the production of powdered metals or of metallic objects by compressing a powdered metal or alloy with or without other materials and heating without thoroughly melting to solidify and strengthen
powder monkey *n* (1697) : a person who carries or has charge of explosives (as in blasting operations)
powder–puff *adj* (1939) : of, relating to, or being a traditionally male activity or event done or played by women ⟨a ~ football game⟩
powder puff *n* (1697) : a small fluffy device (as a pad) for applying cosmetic powder
powder room *n* (1927) **1 :** a restroom for women **2 :** a lavatory in the main living area of a house
pow·dery \ˈpau̇-də-rē\ *adj* (15c) **1 a :** resembling or consisting of powder ⟨~ snow⟩ **b :** easily reduced to powder : CRUMBLING **2 :** covered with or as if with powder
powdery mildew *n* (1889) **1 :** an ascomycetous fungus (family Erysiphaceae) producing abundant powdery conidia on the host **2 :** a plant disease caused by a powdery mildew
[1]**pow·er** \ˈpau̇(-ə)r\ *n, often attrib* [ME, fr. AF *poer, pouer*, fr. *poer* to be able, fr. VL **potēre*, alter. of L *posse* — more at POTENT] (13c) **1 a** (1) : ability to act or produce an effect (2) : ability to get extra-base hits (3) : capacity for being acted upon or undergoing an effect **b :** legal or official authority, capacity, or right **2 a :** possession of control, authority, or influence over others **b :** one having such power; *specif* : a sovereign state **c :** a controlling group : ESTABLISHMENT — often used in the phrase *the powers that be* **d** *archaic* : a force of armed men **e** *chiefly dial* : a large number or quantity **3 a :** physical might **b :** mental or moral efficacy **c :** political control or influence **4** *pl* : an order of angels — see CELESTIAL HIERARCHY **5 a :** the number of times as indicated by an exponent that a number occurs as a factor in a product ⟨5 to the third ~ is 125⟩; *also* : the product itself ⟨8 is a ~ of 2⟩ **b :** CARDINAL NUMBER 2 **6 a :** a source or means of supplying energy; *esp* : ELECTRICITY **b :** MOTIVE POWER **c :** the time rate at which work is done or energy emitted or transferred **7 :** MAGNIFICATION 2b **8 :** [1]SCOPE 3 **9 :** the probability of rejecting the null hypothesis in a statistical test when a particular alternative hypothesis happens to be true
syn POWER, AUTHORITY, JURISDICTION, CONTROL, COMMAND, SWAY, DOMINION mean the right to govern or rule or determine. POWER implies possession of ability to wield force, authority, or influence ⟨the *power* to mold public opinion⟩. AUTHORITY implies power for a specific purpose within specified limits ⟨granted the *authority* to manage her estate⟩. JURISDICTION applies to official power exercised within prescribed limits ⟨the bureau having *jurisdiction* over parks⟩. CONTROL stresses the power to direct and restrain ⟨you are responsible for the students under your *control*⟩. COMMAND implies the power to make arbitrary decisions and compel obedience ⟨the army officer in *command*⟩. SWAY suggests the extent of exercised power or influence ⟨the empire extended its *sway* over the region⟩. DOMINION stresses sovereign power or supreme authority ⟨given *dominion* over all the animals⟩.
syn POWER, FORCE, ENERGY, STRENGTH, MIGHT mean the ability to exert effort. POWER may imply latent or exerted physical, mental, or spiritual ability to act or be acted upon ⟨the awesome *power* of flowing water⟩. FORCE implies the actual effective exercise of power ⟨used enough *force* to push the door open⟩. ENERGY applies to power expended or capable of being transformed into work ⟨a worker with boundless *energy*⟩. STRENGTH applies to the quality or property of a person or thing that makes possible the exertion of force or the withstanding of strain, pressure, or attack ⟨use weight training to build your *strength*⟩. MIGHT implies great or overwhelming power or strength ⟨the belief that *might* makes right⟩.
[2]**power** *vt* (1540) **1 :** to supply with power and esp. motive power **2 :** to give impetus to ~ *vi* **1 :** to move about by means of motive power **2 :** to move with great speed or force
[3]**power** *adj* (1822) **1 :** operated mechanically or electrically rather than manually ⟨a car with ~ locks⟩ ⟨~ tools⟩ **2 :** of, relating to, or utilizing strength ⟨plays a ~ game⟩; *also* : POWERFUL 1 ⟨a ~ critic⟩ **3 :** of, relating to, or being a meal at which influential people discuss business or politics ⟨a ~ lunch⟩
power base *n* (1959) : a base of political support
pow·er·boat \ˈpau̇(-ə)r-ˌbōt\ *n* (1830) : MOTORBOAT — **pow·er·boat·er** \-ˌbō-tər\ *n* — **pow·er·boat·ing** \-ˌbō-tiŋ\ *adj*
power broker *n* (1961) : a person (as in politics) able to exert strong influence through control of votes or individuals
power chord *n* (1977) : a combination of two tones consisting of a root and its fifth that is often used in rock music
pow·er–dive \-ˌdīv\ *vi* (1937) : to make a power dive ~ *vt* : to cause to power-dive
power dive *n* (1930) : a dive of an airplane accelerated by the power of the engine
power forward *n* (1969) : a basketball forward whose size and strength are used primarily in controlling play near the basket
pow·er·ful \ˈpau̇(-ə)r-fəl\ *adj* (15c) **1 :** having great power, prestige, or influence ⟨a ~ leader⟩ **2 :** leading to many or important deductions ⟨a ~ set of postulates⟩ — **pow·er·ful·ly** \-f(ə-)lē\ *adv*
power function *n* (1957) **1 :** a function of a parameter under statistical test whose value for a particular value of the parameter is the probability of rejecting the null hypothesis if that value of the parameter

\ə\ **abut** \ᵊ\ kitten, F table \ər\ **further** \a\ **ash** \ā\ **ace** \ä\ **mop, mar**
\au̇\ **out** \ch\ **chin** \e\ **bet** \ē\ **easy** \g\ **go** \i\ **hit** \ī\ **ice** \j\ **job**
\ŋ\ **sing** \ō\ **go** \ȯ\ **law** \ȯi\ **boy** \th\ **thin** \t͟h\ **the** \ü\ **loot** \u̇\ **foot**
\y\ **yet** \zh\ **vision, beige** \k̲, ⁿ, œ, ue, ʸ\ *see* Guide to Pronunciation

happens to be true **2 :** a function (as $f(x) = ax^k$) that equals the product of a constant and a power of the independent variable

pow·er·house \ˈpau̇(-ə)r-ˌhau̇s\ *n* (ca. 1889) **1 a :** POWER PLANT 1 **b :** a source of influence or inspiration **2 :** one having great power: as **a :** one having great drive, energy, or ability ⟨a ~ rock band⟩ **b :** an athletic team characterized by strong aggressive play

pow·er·less \-ləs\ *adj* (15c) **1 :** devoid of strength or resources ⟨~ victims⟩ **2 :** lacking the authority or capacity to act ⟨was ~ to help⟩ — **pow·er·less·ly** *adv* — **pow·er·less·ness** *n*

power mower *n* (1940) **:** a motor-driven lawn mower

power of attorney (1747) **:** a legal instrument authorizing one to act as the attorney or agent of the grantor

power pack *n* (1936) **:** a unit for converting a power supply (as from a battery or household electrical circuit) to a voltage suitable for an electronic device

power plant *n* (1890) **1 :** an electric utility generating station **2 :** an engine and related parts supplying the motive power of a self-propelled object (as a rocket or automobile)

power play *n* (1947) **1 :** a military, diplomatic, political, or administrative maneuver in which power is brought to bear **2 a :** a concentrated attack in football in which the ballcarrier is preceded by a mass of blockers **b :** a situation in ice hockey in which one team temporarily has more players on the ice than the other team because of a penalty

power politics *n pl but sing or pl in constr* (1926) **:** politics based primarily on the use of power (as military and economic strength) as a coercive force rather than on ethical precepts

power series *n* (1893) **:** an infinite series whose terms are successive integral powers of a variable multiplied by constants

power shovel *n* (1909) **:** a power-operated excavating machine consisting of a boom or crane that supports a lever arm with a large bucket at the end of it

power station *n* (1901) **:** POWER PLANT 1

power steering *n* (1932) **:** an automotive steering system with engine power used to amplify the torque applied at the steering wheel by the driver

power strip *n* (1980) **:** an electrical device consisting of a cord with a plug on one end and several sockets on the other

power structure *n* (1942) **1 :** a group of persons having control of an organization **:** ESTABLISHMENT **2 :** the hierarchical interrelationships existing within a controlling group

power sweep *n* (1964) **:** SWEEP 3e

power take–off *n* (1929) **:** a supplementary mechanism (as on a tractor) enabling the engine power to be used to operate nonautomotive apparatus (as a pump or saw)

power train *n* (1943) **:** the intervening mechanism by which power is transmitted from an engine to a propeller or axle that it drives; *also* **:** this mechanism plus the engine ⟨*power train* warranty⟩

power up *vt* (1970) **:** to cause to operate ⟨*power up* the computer⟩ — **pow·er–up** \ˈpau̇(-ə)r-ˌəp\ *n*

power walk *vi* (1984) **:** to walk quickly for exercise esp. while carrying or wearing weights

[1]**pow·wow** \ˈpau̇-ˌwau̇\ *n* [Narragansett *powwaw* or Massachusett *pauwau*] (1624) **1 :** an American Indian medicine man **2 a :** an American Indian ceremony (as for victory in war) **b :** an American Indian social gathering or fair usu. including competitive dancing **3 a :** a social get-together **b :** a meeting for discussion

[2]**powwow** *vi* (1642) **:** to hold a powwow

[1]**pox** \ˈpäks\ *n, pl* **pox** *or* **pox·es** [alter. of *pocks,* pl. of *pock*] (ca. 1530) **1 a :** a virus disease (as chicken pox) characterized by pustules or eruptions **b** *archaic* **:** SMALLPOX **c :** SYPHILIS **2 :** a disastrous evil **:** PLAGUE, CURSE ⟨a ~ on him⟩ — **poxy** \ˈpäk-sē\ *adj*

[2]**pox** *vt* (1601) *archaic* **:** to infect with a pox and esp. with syphilis

pox·vi·rus \ˈpäks-ˌvī-rəs\ *n* [NL] (1941) **:** any of a family (*Poxviridae*) of brick-shaped or ovoid double-stranded DNA viruses that have a surface lipoprotein membrane covered with tubular or globular structures and that include the vaccinia virus and the causative agents of cowpox, myxomatosis of rabbits, and smallpox

pozole *var of* POSOLE

poz·zo·la·na \ˌpät-sə-ˈlä-nə\ *or* **poz·zo·lan** \ˈpät-sə-lən\ *n* [It *pozzolana*] (ca. 1706) **:** finely divided siliceous or siliceous and aluminous material that reacts chemically with slaked lime at ordinary temperature and in the presence of moisture to form a strong slow-hardening cement — **poz·zo·la·nic** \ˌpät-sə-ˈla-nik, -ˈlä-\ *adj*

pp *abbr* **1** pages **2** per person **3** [L *per procurationem*] by proxy **4** pianissimo

PP *abbr* **1** parcel post **2** postpaid **3** prepaid

ppb *abbr* parts per billion

ppd *abbr* **1** postpaid **2** prepaid

PPI *abbr* plan position indicator

ppm *abbr* **1** pages per minute **2** parts per million

PPO \ˌpē-(ˌ)pē-ˈō\ *n, pl* **PPOs** [*p*referred *p*rovider *o*rganization] (1982) **:** an organization providing health care that gives economic incentives to the individual purchaser of a health-care contract to patronize certain physicians, laboratories, and hospitals that agree to supervision and reduced fees — compare HMO

PPS *abbr* [NL *post postscriptum*] an additional postscript

ppt *abbr* **1** parts per thousand **2** parts per trillion **3** precipitate

PPV *abbr* pay-per-view

PQ *abbr* Province of Quebec

pr *abbr* **1** pair **2** price **3** printed

[1]**Pr** *abbr* propyl

[2]**Pr** *symbol* praseodymium

[1]**PR** *or* **p.r.** \ˈpē-ˈär\ *n, often attrib* (1942) **:** PUBLIC RELATIONS ⟨had a job in ~⟩ ⟨the company's ~ rep⟩

[2]**PR** *abbr* **1** payroll **2** personal record **3** proportional representation **4** Puerto Rico

prac·ti·ca·ble \ˈprak-ti-kə-bəl\ *adj* (1648) **1 :** capable of being put into practice or of being done or accomplished **:** FEASIBLE ⟨a ~ plan⟩ **2 :** capable of being used **:** USABLE ⟨a ~ weapon⟩ ***syn*** see POSSIBLE — **prac·ti·ca·bil·i·ty** \ˌprak-ti-kə-ˈbi-lə-tē\ *n* — **prac·ti·ca·ble·ness** \ˈprak-ti-kə-bəl-nəs\ *n* — **prac·ti·ca·bly** \-blē\ *adv*

[1]**prac·ti·cal** \ˈprak-ti-kəl\ *adj* [ME, fr. LL *practicus,* fr. Gk *praktikos,* fr. *prassein* to pass over, fare, do; akin to Gk *peran* to pass through — more at FARE] (15c) **1 a :** of, relating to, or manifested in practice or action **:** not theoretical or ideal ⟨a ~ question⟩ ⟨for all ~ purposes⟩ **b :** being such in practice or effect **:** VIRTUAL ⟨a ~ failure⟩ **2 :** actively engaged in some course of action or occupation ⟨a ~ farmer⟩ **3 :** capable of being put to use or account **:** USEFUL ⟨he had a ~ knowledge of French⟩ **4 a :** disposed to action as opposed to speculation or abstraction **b (1) :** qualified by practice or practical training ⟨a good ~ mechanic⟩ **(2) :** designed to supplement theoretical training by experience **5 :** concerned with voluntary action and ethical decisions ⟨~ reason⟩ — **prac·ti·cal·i·ty** \ˌprak-ti-ˈka-lə-tē\ *n* — **prac·ti·cal·ness** \ˈprak-ti-kəl-nəs\ *n*

[2]**practical** *n* (1925) **:** an examination requiring demonstration of some practical skill ⟨a zoology ~⟩

practical art *n* (1830) **:** an art (as woodworking) that serves ordinary or material needs — usu. used in pl.

practical joke *n* (1776) **:** a prank intended to trick or embarrass someone or cause physical discomfort — **practical joker** *n*

prac·ti·cal·ly \ˈprak-ti-k(ə-)lē\ *adv* (1571) **1 :** in a practical manner ⟨look ~ at the problem⟩ **2 :** ALMOST, NEARLY ⟨~ everyone⟩

practical nurse *n* (1921) **:** a nurse who cares for the sick professionally without having the training or experience required of a registered nurse; *esp* **:** LICENSED PRACTICAL NURSE

practical theology *n* (1828) **:** the study of the institutional activities of religion (as preaching, church administration, pastoral care, and liturgics)

[1]**prac·tice** *also* **prac·tise** \ˈprak-təs\ *vb* **prac·ticed** *also* **prac·tised; prac·tic·ing** *also* **prac·tis·ing** [ME *practisen,* fr. MF *practiser,* fr. ML *practizare,* alter. of *practicare,* fr. *practica* practice, n., fr. LL *practice,* fr. Gk *praktikē,* fr. fem. of *praktikos*] *vt* (14c) **1 a :** CARRY OUT, APPLY ⟨~ what you preach⟩ **b :** to do or perform often, customarily, or habitually ⟨~ politeness⟩ **c :** to be professionally engaged in ⟨~ medicine⟩ **2 a :** to perform or work at repeatedly so as to become proficient ⟨~ the act⟩ **b :** to train by repeated exercises ⟨~ pupils in penmanship⟩ **3** *obs* **:** PLOT ~ *vi* **1 :** to do repeated exercises for proficiency **2 :** to pursue a profession actively **3** *archaic* **:** INTRIGUE **4 :** to do something customarily **5 :** to take advantage of someone ⟨he *practised* on their credulity with huge success —*Times Lit. Supp.*⟩ — **prac·tic·er** *n*

[2]**practice** *also* **practise** *n* (15c) **1 a :** actual performance or application ⟨ready to carry out in ~ what they advocated in principle⟩ **b :** a repeated or customary action ⟨had this irritating ~⟩ **c :** the usual way of doing something ⟨local ~*s*⟩ **d :** the form, manner, and order of conducting legal suits and prosecutions **2 a :** systematic exercise for proficiency ⟨~ makes perfect⟩ **b :** the condition of being proficient through systematic exercise ⟨get in ~⟩ **3 a :** the continuous exercise of a profession **b :** a professional business; *esp* **:** one constituting an incorporeal property ***syn*** see HABIT

practiced *also* **practised** *adj* (1568) **1 :** EXPERIENCED, SKILLED ⟨a ~ chef⟩ **2 :** learned by practice ⟨a ~ skill⟩

prac·tice–teach \ˈprak-təs-ˈtēch\ *vi* **-taught** \-ˈtȯt\; **-teach·ing** [back-formation fr. *practice teaching*] (1952) **:** to engage in practice teaching — **practice teacher** *n*

practice teaching *n* (ca. 1913) **:** teaching by a student under the supervision of an experienced teacher

practicing *also* **practising** *adj* (1625) **:** actively engaged in a specified career or way of life ⟨a ~ physician⟩

prac·ti·cum \ˈprak-ti-kəm\ *n* [G *Praktikum,* fr. LL *practicum,* neut. of *practicus* practical] (1904) **:** a course of study designed esp. for the preparation of teachers and clinicians that involves the supervised practical application of previously studied theory

prac·ti·tion·er \prak-ˈti-sh(ə-)nər\ *n* [alter. of earlier *practician,* fr. ME (Sc) *pratician,* fr. MF *practicien,* fr. *pratique* practice] (1535) **1 :** one who practices; *esp* **:** one who practices a profession **2** *Christian Science* **:** an authorized healer

Pra·der–Wil·li syndrome \ˈprä-dər-ˈvi-lē-\ *n* [Andrea *Prader b*1919 and Heinrich *Willi* †1971 Swiss pediatricians] (1964) **:** a genetic disorder characterized esp. by short stature, mental retardation, hypotonia, functionally deficient gonads, and uncontrolled appetite leading to extreme obesity

prae·ci·pe *also* **pre·ci·pe** \ˈpre-sə-ˌpē, ˈprē-\ *n* [ME *presepe,* fr. ML *praecipe,* fr. L, imper. of *praecipere* to instruct — more at PRECEPT] (15c) **1 :** any of various legal writs commanding a person to do something or to appear and show cause why he or she should not **2 :** a written order requesting a clerk or prothonotary of a court to issue a writ and specifying the contents of the writ

prae·mu·ni·re \ˌprē-myu̇-ˈnī(-ə)r-ē\ *n* [ME *praemunire facias,* fr. ML, that you cause to warn; fr. prominent words in the writ] (1529) **:** an offense against the English Crown punishable chiefly by forfeiture and orig. committed by asserting papal legal supremacy in England

prae·no·men \prē-ˈnō-mən\ *n, pl* **-nomens** *or* **-no·mi·na** \-ˈnä-mə-nə, -ˈnō-\ [L, fr. *prae-* pre- + *nomen* name — more at NAME] (1706) **:** the first of the usual three names of an ancient Roman male — compare COGNOMEN, NOMEN

praesidium *var of* PRESIDIUM

prae·tor *also* **pre·tor** \ˈprē-tər\ *n* [ME *pretor,* fr. L *praetor*] (15c) **:** an ancient Roman magistrate ranking below a consul and having chiefly judicial functions — **prae·to·ri·al** \prē-ˈtȯr-ē-əl\ *adj* — **prae·tor·ship** \ˈprē-tər-ˌship\ *n*

prae·to·ri·an *also* **pre·to·ri·an** \prē-ˈtȯr-ē-ən\ *adj* (15c) **1** *often cap* **:** of, forming, or resembling the Roman imperial bodyguard **2 :** of or relating to a praetor — **praetorian** *n, often cap*

prag·mat·ic \prag-ˈma-tik\ *also* **prag·mat·i·cal** \-ti-kəl\ *adj* [L *pragmaticus* skilled in law or business, fr. Gk *pragmatikos,* fr. *pragmat-, pragma* deed, fr. *prassein* to do — more at PRACTICAL] (1616) **1** *archaic* **a (1) :** BUSY **(2) :** OFFICIOUS **b :** OPINIONATED **2 :** relating to matters of fact or practical affairs often to the exclusion of intellectual or artistic matters **:** practical as opposed to idealistic ⟨~ men of power have had no time or inclination to deal with . . . social morality —K. B. Clark⟩ **3 :** relating to or being in accordance with philosophical pragmatism — **pragmatic** *n* — **prag·mat·i·cal·ly** \-ti-k(ə-)lē\ *adv*

prag·mat·i·cism \prag-ˈma-tə-ˌsi-zəm\ *n* (1905) **:** the philosophic doctrine of C. S. Peirce — **prag·mat·i·cist** \-sist\ *n*

prag·mat·ics \prag-ˈma-tiks\ *n pl but sing or pl in constr* (1937) **1 :** a branch of semiotics that deals with the relation between signs or linguistic expressions and their users **2 :** a branch of linguistics that is concerned with the relationship of sentences to the environment in which they occur

pragmatic sanction *n* (1643) **:** a solemn decree of a sovereign on a matter of primary importance and with the force of fundamental law

prag·ma·tism \'prag-mə-ˌti-zəm\ *n* (ca. 1864) **1 :** a practical approach to problems and affairs ⟨tried to strike a balance between principles and ~⟩ **2 :** an American movement in philosophy founded by C. S. Peirce and William James and marked by the doctrines that the meaning of conceptions is to be sought in their practical bearings, that the function of thought is to guide action, and that truth is preeminently to be tested by the practical consequences of belief — **prag·ma·tist** \-mə-tist\ *adj or n* — **prag·ma·tis·tic** \ˌprag-mə-'tis-tik\ *adj*

prai·rie \'prer-ē\ *n, often attrib* [F, fr. OF *praierie,* fr. VL **prataria,* fr. L *pratum* meadow] (ca. 1682) **1 :** land in or predominantly in grass **2 :** a tract of grassland: as **a :** a large area of level or rolling land in the Mississippi River valley that in its natural uncultivated state usu. has deep fertile soil, a cover of tall coarse grasses, and few trees **b :** one of the dry treeless plateaus east of the Rocky Mountains that merge on their east side with the prairies proper and are characterized by shorter grasses and drier less fertile soil

prairie chicken *n* (1691) **:** a grouse (*Tympanuchus cupido*) chiefly of the tallgrass prairies of the central U.S. with the male having yellowish-orange neck sacs which are inflated during courtship displays; *also* **:** a closely related smaller grouse (*T. pallidicinctus*) having reddish neck sacs

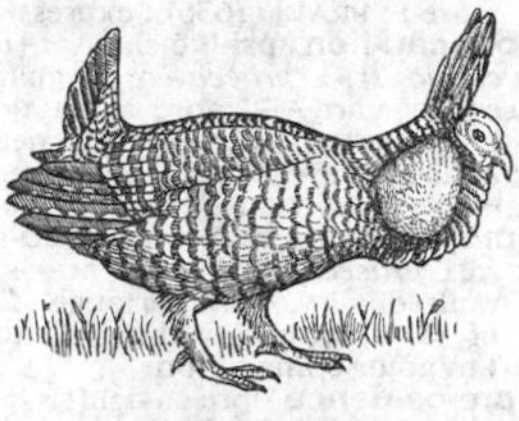

prairie chicken

prairie dog *n* (1774) **:** any of a genus (*Cynomys*) of gregarious burrowing rodents of the squirrel family chiefly of central and western U.S. plains; *esp* **:** a black-tailed rodent (*C. ludovicianus*) that usu. lives in extensive colonial burrows

prairie schooner *n* (1841) **:** a covered wagon used by pioneers in cross-country travel — called also *prairie wagon*

prairie soil *n* (1817) **:** any of a zonal group of soils developed in a temperate relatively humid climate under tall grass

prairie wolf *n* (1804) **:** COYOTE

^{1}**praise** \'prāz\ *vb* **praised; prais·ing** [ME *preisen,* fr. AF *preiser, priser* to appraise, esteem — more at PRIZE] *vt* (13c) **1 :** to express a favorable judgment of **:** COMMEND **2 :** to glorify (a god or saint) esp. by the attribution of perfections ~ *vi* **:** to express praise — **prais·er** *n*

^{2}**praise** *n* (14c) **1 a :** an expression of approval **:** COMMENDATION **b :** WORSHIP **2 a :** VALUE, MERIT **b** *archaic* **:** one that is praised

praise·wor·thy \'prāz-ˌwər-thē\ *adj* (15c) **:** LAUDABLE ⟨a ~ effort⟩ — **praise·wor·thi·ly** \-thə-lē\ *adv* — **praise·wor·thi·ness** \-thē-nəs\ *n*

Pra·krit \'prä-ˌkrit, -krət\ *n* [Skt *prākṛta,* fr. *prākṛta* natural, vulgar] (1766) **:** any or all of the ancient Indo-Aryan languages or dialects other than Sanskrit — see INDO-EUROPEAN LANGUAGES table

pra·line \'prä-ˌlēn, 'prā-, 'prō-\ *n* [F, fr. Count Plessis-*Praslin* †1675 Fr. soldier] (1723) **:** a confection of nuts and sugar: as **a :** almonds cooked in boiling sugar until brown and crisp **b :** a patty of creamy brown sugar and pecan meats

prall·tril·ler \'präl-ˌtri-lər\ *n* [G, fr. *prallen* to rebound + *Triller* trill] (ca. 1841) **:** a musical ornament made by a quick alternation of a principal tone with the tone above

^{1}**pram** \'präm, 'pram\ *n* [MD *praem* & MLG *prām*] (1548) **:** a small lightweight nearly flat-bottomed boat with a broad transom and usu. squared-off bow

^{2}**pram** \'pram\ *n* [by shortening & alter. fr. *perambulator*] (1884) *chiefly Brit* **:** BABY CARRIAGE

^{1}**prance** \'pran(t)s\ *vb* **pranced; pranc·ing** [ME *prauncen*] *vi* (14c) **1 :** to spring from the hind legs or move by so doing **2 :** to ride on a prancing horse **3 :** to walk or move in a spirited manner **:** STRUT; *also* **:** to dance about ~ *vt* **:** to cause (a horse) to prance — **pranc·er** \'pran(t)-sər\ *n*

^{2}**prance** *n* (1751) **:** an act or instance of prancing; *specif* **:** a prancing movement

pran·di·al \'pran-dē-əl\ *adj* [L *prandium* late breakfast, luncheon] (1820) **:** of or relating to a meal

prang \'praŋ\ *vt* [origin unknown] (1941) *chiefly Brit* **:** to have an accident with **:** cause to crash — **prang** *n, chiefly Brit*

^{1}**prank** \'praŋk\ *n* [obs. *prank* to play tricks] (ca. 1529) **:** TRICK: **a** *obs* **:** a malicious act **b :** a mildly mischievous act **c :** a ludicrous act

^{2}**prank** *vb* [prob. fr. D *pronken* to strut; akin to MHG *gebrunkel* glitter of metal] *vi* (15c) **:** to show oneself off ~ *vt* **:** to dress or adorn gaily or showily

prank·ish \'praŋ-kish\ *adj* (1827) **1 :** full of pranks ⟨a ~ child⟩ **2 :** having the nature of a prank ⟨~ acts⟩ — **prank·ish·ly** *adv* — **prank·ish·ness** *n*

prank·ster \'praŋ(k)-stər\ *n* (1927) **:** a person who plays pranks

prase \'prāz, 'prās\ *n* [F, fr. MF *prasse,* L *prasius,* fr. Gk *prasios,* fr. *prasios,* adj., of the color of a leek, fr. *prason* leek; akin to L *porrum* leek] (1788) **:** a chalcedony that is translucent and yellowish green

pra·seo·dym·i·um \ˌprā-zē-ō-'di-mē-əm, ˌprā-sē-\ *n* [NL, alter. of *praseodidymium,* irreg. fr. Gk *prasios,* adj. + NL *didymium* didymium] (1885) **:** a yellowish-white metallic element of the rare-earth group used esp. in alloys and in the form of its salts in coloring glass greenish yellow — see ELEMENT table

prat \'prat\ *n* [prob. fr. argot *prat* buttocks] (ca. 1961) *Brit* **:** a stupid or foolish person

prate \'prāt\ *vi* **prat·ed; prat·ing** [ME, fr. MD; akin to MLG *pratten* to pout] (15c) **:** to talk long and idly **:** CHATTER — **prate** *n* — **prat·er** *n* — **prat·ing·ly** \'prā-tiŋ-lē\ *adv*

prat·fall \'prat-ˌfȯl\ *n* [argot *prat* buttocks + *fall*] (1930) **1 :** a fall on the buttocks **2 :** a humiliating mishap or blunder

pra·tin·cole \'pra-tᵊn-ˌkōl, 'prā-, -tiŋ-\ *n* [ultim. fr. L *pratum* meadow + *incola* inhabitant, fr. *in-* + *colere* to cultivate — more at WHEEL] (1773) **:** any of several Old World shore-inhabiting birds (genera *Glareola* and *Stiltia* of the family Glareolidae) with a short bill and a forked tail

pra·tique \pra-'tēk\ *n* [F, lit., practice, fr. OF, fr. ML *practica* — more at PRACTICE] (1609) **:** clearance given an incoming ship by the health authority of a port

^{1}**prat·tle** \'pra-tᵊl\ *vb* **prat·tled; prat·tling** \'prat-liŋ, 'pra-tᵊl-iŋ\ [LG *pratelen;* akin to MD *praten* to prate] *vi* (1532) **1 :** PRATE **2 :** to utter or make meaningless sounds suggestive of the chatter of children **:** BABBLE ~ *vt* **:** to say in an unaffected or childish manner — **prattler** \'prat-lər, 'pra-tᵊl-ər\ *n* — **prat·tling·ly** \-liŋ-lē, -tᵊl-iŋ-\ *adv*

^{2}**prattle** *n* (1555) **1 :** trifling or empty talk **2 :** a sound that is meaningless, repetitive, and suggestive of the chatter of children

prau \'prau̇, 'prä-ˌü\ *or* **proa** \'prō-ə\ *n* [Malay *pĕrahu*] (1582) **:** any of various Indonesian boats usu. without a deck that are propelled esp. by sails or paddles

prav·a·stat·in \'pra-və-ˌsta-tᵊn\ *n* [ISV *pra-* (of unknown origin) + *-vastatin* (as in *lovastatin*)] (1987) **:** a drug $C_{23}H_{35}NaO_7$ that inhibits the production of cholesterol in the body and is used to treat hypercholesterolemia

^{1}**prawn** \'prȯn, 'prän\ *n* [ME *prane*] (15c) **:** any of various widely distributed edible decapod crustaceans: as **a :** one (as of the genera *Pandalus* and *Penaeus*) that resembles shrimps and has a large compressed abdomen **b :** SHRIMP; *esp* **:** a large shrimp **c :** LANGOUSTINE

^{2}**prawn** *vi* (1886) **:** to fish for or with prawns — **prawn·er** *n*

prax·e·ol·o·gy \ˌprak-sē-'ä-lə-jē\ *n* [alter. of earlier *praxiology,* fr. *praxis* + *-o-* + *-logy*] (1904) **:** the study of human action and conduct — **prax·e·o·log·i·cal** \-sē-ə-'lä-ji-kəl\ *adj*

prax·is \'prak-səs\ *n, pl* **prax·es** \-ˌsēz\ [ML, fr. Gk, doing, action, fr. *prassein* to do, practice — more at PRACTICAL] (1581) **1 :** ACTION, PRACTICE: as **a :** exercise or practice of an art, science, or skill **b :** customary practice or conduct **2 :** practical application of a theory

pray \'prā\ *vb* [ME, fr. AF *prier, praer, preier,* fr. L *precari,* fr. *prec-, prex* request, prayer; akin to OHG *frāga* question, *frāgēn* to ask, Skt *pṛcchati* he asks] *vt* (13c) **1 :** ENTREAT, IMPLORE — often used as a function word in introducing a question, request, or plea ⟨~ be careful⟩ **2 :** to get or bring by praying ~ *vi* **1 :** to make a request in a humble manner **2 :** to address God or a god with adoration, confession, supplication, or thanksgiving

^{1}**prayer** \'prer\ *n, often attrib* [ME, fr. AF *priere, praiere, preiere,* fr. ML *precaria,* fr. L, fem. of *precarius* obtained by entreaty, fr. *prec-, prex*] (14c) **1 a** (1) **:** an address (as a petition) to God or a god in word or thought ⟨said a ~ for the success of the voyage⟩ (2) **:** a set order of words used in praying **b :** an earnest request or wish **2 :** the act or practice of praying to God or a god ⟨kneeling in ~⟩ **3 :** a religious service consisting chiefly of prayers — often used in pl. **4 :** something prayed for **5 :** a slight chance ⟨haven't got a ~⟩

^{2}**pray·er** \'prā-ər, 'prer\ *n* [ME *prayere,* fr. *prayen* to pray + ^{2}*-er*] (14c) **:** one that prays **:** SUPPLICANT

prayer beads \'prer-\ *n pl* (1630) **:** a string of beads by which prayers are counted; *specif* **:** ROSARY

prayer book *n* (ca. 1597) **:** a book containing prayers and often other forms and directions for worship

prayer·ful \'prar-fəl, 'prer-\ *adj* (1626) **1 :** DEVOUT **2 :** EARNEST, SINCERE — **prayer·ful·ly** \-fə-lē\ *adv* — **prayer·ful·ness** *n*

prayer meeting *n* (1780) **:** a usu. informal gathering for worship and prayer; *esp* **:** a Protestant worship service usu. held on a week night — called also *prayer service*

prayer rug *n* (ca. 1890) **:** a small Oriental rug used by Muslims to kneel on when praying

prayer shawl *n* (1905) **:** TALLITH

prayer wheel *n* (1814) **:** a cylinder of wood or metal that revolves on an axis and contains written prayers and that is used in praying by Tibetan Buddhists

praying mantis *n* (ca. 1890) **:** MANTIS; *esp* **:** a European mantis (*Mantis religiosa*) that has been introduced into the U.S. — called also *praying mantid*

PRC *abbr* People's Republic of China

pre- *prefix* [L *prae-,* fr. *prae* in front of, before — more at FOR] **1 a** (1) **:** earlier than **:** prior to **:** before ⟨*Pre*cambrian⟩ ⟨*pre*historic⟩ (2) **:** preparatory or prerequisite to ⟨*pre*medical⟩ **b :** in advance **:** beforehand ⟨*pre*cancel⟩ ⟨*pre*pay⟩ **2 :** in front of **:** anterior to ⟨*pre*axial⟩ ⟨*pre*molar⟩

pre·ad·mis·sion	**pre·com·mit·ment**	**pre·dive**
pre·adult	**pre·com·pute**	**pre·draft**
pre·ag·ri·cul·tur·al	**pre·com·put·er**	**pre·drill**
pre·an·es·thet·ic	**pre·con·cert**	**pre·dy·nas·tic**
pre·an·nounce	**pre·con·cil·i·ar**	**pre·elec·tion**
pre·ap·prove	**pre·con·quest**	**pre·elec·tric**
pre·ar·range	**pre·con·so·nan·tal**	**pre·elec·tron·ic**
pre·ar·range·ment	**pre·con·struct·ed**	**pre·em·bar·go**
pre·as·sem·bled	**pre·con·ven·tion**	**pre·em·ploy·ment**
pre·as·sign	**pre·con·vic·tion**	**pre·en·roll·ment**
pre·bake	**pre·cool**	**pre·erect**
pre·bat·tle	**pre·cop·u·la·to·ry**	**pre·es·tab·lish**
pre·bib·li·cal	**pre·crash**	**pre·eth·i·cal**
pre·book	**pre·crease**	**pre·ex·per·i·ment**
pre·break·fast	**pre·cri·sis**	**pre·fade**
pre·cap·i·tal·ist	**pre·cut**	**pre·fas·cist**
pre·chill	**pre·dawn**	**pre·fem·i·nist**
pre–Christ·mas	**pre·de·fine**	**pre·feu·dal**
pre·clear	**pre·de·liv·ery**	**pre·fight**
pre·clear·ance	**pre·de·par·ture**	**pre·file**
pre·code	**pre·des·ig·nate**	**pre·filled**
pre·co·i·tal	**pre·de·val·u·a·tion**	**pre·fi·nance**
pre·col·lege	**pre·de·vel·op·ment**	**pre·fire**
pre·col·le·giate	**pre·din·ner**	**pre·flame**
pre·co·lo·nial	**pre·dis·charge**	**pre·for·mat**
pre·com·bus·tion	**pre·dis·cov·ery**	**pre·for·mu·late**

pre·fresh·man
pre·fro·zen
pre·game
pre·gen·i·tal
pre·har·vest
pre·head·ache
pre·hir·ing
pre·hol·i·day
pre·in·au·gu·ral
pre·in·cor·po·ra·tion
pre·in·duc·tion
pre·in·dus·tri·al
pre·in·ter·view
pre·in·va·sion
pre·kin·der·gar·ten
pre·launch
pre·life
pre·lit·er·ary
pre·log·i·cal
pre·lunch
pre·lun·cheon
pre·made
pre·man·u·fac·ture
pre·mar·i·tal
pre·mar·i·tal·ly
pre·mar·ket·ing
pre·mar·riage
pre·meal
pre·mea·sure
pre·me·di·e·val
pre·meet
pre·mei·ot·ic
pre·men·o·paus·al
pre·merg·er
pre·mi·gra·tion
pre·mod·ern
pre·mod·i·fi·ca·tion
pre·mod·i·fy
pre·moist·en
pre·mold
pre·molt
pre·mor·al
pre·my·cot·ic
pre·noon
pre·no·ti·fi·ca·tion
pre·no·ti·fy
pre·num·ber
pre·open·ing
pre·op·er·a·tion·al
pre·or·der
pre·paste
pre·per·for·mance
pre·pill
pre·plan
pre·por·tion
pre·pre·pared
pre·pres·i·den·tial
pre·press
pre·price
pre·pri·ma·ry
pre·pro·duc·tion
pre·pro·gram
pre·psy·che·del·ic
pre·pub·li·ca·tion
pre·punch
pre·pu·pal
pre·pur·chase
pre·qual·i·fi·ca·tion
pre·qual·i·fy
pre·race
pre·re·ces·sion
pre·re·cord·ed
pre·re·hears·al
pre·re·lease
pre·re·quire
pre·re·tire·ment
pre·re·turn
pre·re·view
pre·re·vi·sion·ist
pre·rev·o·lu·tion
pre·rev·o·lu·tion·ary
pre·rinse
pre·ri·ot
pre·rock
pre·ro·man·tic
pre·sale
pre·sched·ule
pre·screen
pre·sea·son
pre·sen·tence
pre·sen·tenc·ing
pre·ser·vice
pre·set·tle·ment
pre·show
pre·slaugh·ter
pre·sleep
pre·slice
pre·song
pre·spec·i·fy
pre·split
pre·stamp
pre·ster·il·ize
pre·stor·age
pre·strike
pre·struc·ture
pre·sum·mit
pre·sur·gery
pre·sweet·en
pre·symp·tom·at·ic
pre·tape
pre·tax
pre·tech·no·log·i·cal
pre·tele·vi·sion
pre·ter·mi·na·tion
pre·the·a·ter
pre·tour·na·ment
pre·train
pre·trav·el
pre·treat
pre·treat·ment
pre·trial
pre·trimmed
pre·type
pre·uni·fi·ca·tion
pre·uni·ver·si·ty
pre·vi·a·ble
pre·war
pre·warn
pre·wash
pre·wean·ing
pre·work
pre·wrap

preach \ˈprēch\ *vb* [ME *prechen,* fr. AF *precher,* fr. LL *praedicare,* fr. L, to proclaim, make known, fr. *prae-* pre- + *dicare* to proclaim — more at DICTION] *vi* (13c) **1 :** to deliver a sermon **2 :** to urge acceptance or abandonment of an idea or course of action; *specif* **:** to exhort in an officious or tiresome manner ~ *vt* **1 :** to set forth in a sermon ⟨~ the gospel⟩ **2 :** to advocate earnestly ⟨~*ed* revolution⟩ **3 :** to deliver (as a sermon) publicly **4 :** to bring, put, or affect by preaching ⟨~*ed* the . . . church out of debt —*Amer. Guide Series: Va.*⟩ — **preach·er** *n* — **preach·ing·ly** \ˈprē-chiŋ-lē\ *adv*

preach·ify \ˈprē-chə-ˌfī\ *vi* **-ified; -ify·ing** (1775) **:** to preach ineptly or tediously

preach·ment \ˈprēch-mənt\ *n* (14c) **1 :** the act or practice of preaching **2 :** SERMON, EXHORTATION; *specif* **:** a tedious or unwelcome one

preachy \ˈprē-chē\ *adj* **preach·i·er; -est** (1819) **:** marked by obvious moralizing **:** DIDACTIC ⟨put off by the speaker's ~ tone⟩ — **preach·i·ly** \-chə-lē\ *adv* — **preach·i·ness** \-chē-nəs\ *n*

pre·ad·ap·ta·tion \ˌprē-ˌa-ˌdap-ˈtā-shən\ *n* (1886) **:** a character of an organism or taxonomic group that takes on a function when none previously existed or that differs from its existing function which has been derived by evolution; *also* **:** the possession of one or more such characters

pre·adapt·ed \ˌprē-ə-ˈdap-təd\ *adj* (1758) **:** characterized by preadaptation

pre·adap·tive \-ˈdap-tiv\ *adj* (1915) **:** of, relating to, or characterized by preadaptation

pre·ad·o·les·cence \ˌprē-ˌa-də-ˈle-sᵊn(t)s\ *n* (1930) **:** the period of human development just preceding adolescence; *specif* **:** the period between the approximate ages of 9 and 12 — **pre·ad·o·les·cent** \-sᵊnt\ *adj or n*

pre·am·ble \ˈprē-ˌam-bəl, prē-ˈ\ *n* [ME, fr. MF *preambule,* fr. ML *preambulum,* fr. LL, neut. of *praeambulus* walking in front of, fr. L *prae-* + *ambulare* to walk] (14c) **1 :** an introductory statement; *esp* **:** the introductory part of a constitution or statute that usu. states the reasons for and intent of the law **2 :** an introductory fact or circumstance; *esp* **:** one indicating what is to follow

pre·amp \ˈprē-ˌamp\ *n* (1949) **:** PREAMPLIFIER

pre·am·pli·fi·er \(ˌ)prē-ˈam-plə-ˌfī(-ə)r\ *n* (1935) **:** an amplifier designed to amplify extremely weak electrical signals before they are fed to additional amplifier circuits

pre·atom·ic \ˌprē-ə-ˈtä-mik\ *adj* (1914) **:** of or relating to a time before the use of the atomic bomb and atomic energy

pre·ax·i·al \(ˌ)prē-ˈak-sē-əl\ *adj* (1872) **:** situated in front of an axis of the body

preb·end \ˈpre-bənd\ *n* [ME *prebende,* fr. AF, fr. ML *praebenda,* fr. LL, subsistence allowance granted by the state, fr. L, fem. of *praebendus,* gerundive of *praebēre* to offer, fr. *prae-* + *habēre* to hold — more at GIVE] (15c) **1 :** a stipend furnished by a cathedral or collegiate church to a clergyman (as a canon) in its chapter **2 :** PREBENDARY — **pre·ben·dal** \pri-ˈben-dᵊl, ˈpre-bən-\ *adj*

preb·en·dary \ˈpre-bən-ˌder-ē\ *n, pl* **-dar·ies** (15c) **1 :** a clergyman receiving a prebend for officiating and serving in the church **2 :** an honorary canon in a cathedral chapter

pre·bi·o·log·i·cal \ˌprē-ˌbī-ə-ˈlä-ji-kəl\ *also* **pre·bi·o·log·ic** \-jik\ *adj* (1953) **:** PREBIOTIC

pre·bi·ot·ic \ˌprē-bī-ˈä-tik\ *adj* (1958) **:** of, relating to, or being chemical or environmental precursors of the origin of life ⟨~ molecules⟩; *also* **:** existing or occurring before the origin of life

pre·cal·cu·lus \(ˌ)prē-ˈkal-kyə-ləs\ *adj* (1964) **:** relating to or being mathematical prerequisites for the study of calculus — **precalculus** *n*

Pre·cam·bri·an \(ˌ)prē-ˈkam-brē-ən, -ˈkām-\ *adj* (1864) **:** of, relating to, or being the earliest era of geological history or the corresponding system of rocks that is characterized esp. by the appearance of single-celled organisms and is equivalent to the Archean and Proterozoic eons — see GEOLOGIC TIME table — **Precambrian** *n*

[1]**pre·can·cel** \(ˌ)prē-ˈkan(t)-səl\ *vt* (1921) **:** to cancel (a postage stamp) in advance of use — **pre·can·cel·la·tion** \ˌprē-ˌkan(t)-sə-ˈlā-shən\ *n*

[2]**precancel** *n* (1929) **:** a precanceled postage stamp

pre·can·cer·ous \(ˌ)prē-ˈkan(t)s-rəs, -ˈkan(t)-sə-\ *adj* [ISV] (1882) **:** tending to become cancerous ⟨a ~ lesion⟩

pre·car·i·ous \pri-ˈker-ē-əs\ *adj* [L *precarius* obtained by entreaty, uncertain — more at PRAYER] (1646) **1 :** depending on the will or pleasure of another **2 :** dependent on uncertain premises **:** DUBIOUS ⟨~ generalizations⟩ **3 a :** dependent on chance circumstances, unknown conditions, or uncertain developments **b :** characterized by a lack of security or stability that threatens with danger ***syn*** see DANGEROUS — **pre·car·i·ous·ly** *adv* — **pre·car·i·ous·ness** *n*

pre·cast \ˌprē-ˈkast, ˈprē-ˌ\ *adj* (1914) **:** being concrete that is cast in the form of a structural element (as a panel or beam) before being placed in final position

prec·a·to·ry \ˈpre-kə-ˌtȯr-ē\ *adj* [LL *precatorius,* fr. L *precari* to pray — more at PRAY] (1636) **:** expressing a wish

pre·cau·tion \pri-ˈkȯ-shən\ *n* [F *précaution,* fr. LL *praecaution-, praecautio,* fr. L *praecavēre* to guard against, fr. *prae-* + *cavēre* to be on one's guard — more at HEAR] (1603) **1 :** care taken in advance **:** FORESIGHT ⟨warned of the need for ~⟩ **2 :** a measure taken beforehand to prevent harm or secure good **:** SAFEGUARD ⟨take the necessary ~*s*⟩ — **pre·cau·tion·ary** \-shə-ˌner-ē\ *adj*

pre·cede \pri-ˈsēd\ *vb* **pre·ced·ed; pre·ced·ing** [ME, fr. MF *preceder,* fr. L *praecedere,* fr. *prae-* pre- + *cedere* to go] *vt* (15c) **1 :** to surpass in rank, dignity, or importance **2 :** to be, go, or come ahead or in front of **3 :** to be earlier than **4 :** to cause to be preceded **:** PREFACE ~ *vi* **:** to go or come before

pre·ce·dence \ˈpre-sə-dən(t)s, pri-ˈsē-dᵊn(t)s\ *n* (1588) **1 a** *obs* **:** ANTECEDENT **b :** the fact of preceding in time **2 a :** the right to superior honor on a ceremonial or formal occasion **b :** the order of ceremonial or formal preference **c :** priority of importance ⟨your safety takes ~⟩

pre·ce·den·cy \-dən(t)-sē, -dᵊn(t)-sē\ *n* (1612) **:** PRECEDENCE

[1]**pre·ce·dent** \pri-ˈsē-dᵊnt, ˈpre-sə-dənt\ *adj* [ME, fr. AF, fr. L *praecedent-, praecedens,* prp. of *praecedere*] (15c) **:** prior in time, order, arrangement, or significance

[2]**prec·e·dent** \ˈpre-sə-dənt\ *n* (15c) **1 :** an earlier occurrence of something similar **2 a :** something done or said that may serve as an example or rule to authorize or justify a subsequent act of the same or an analogous kind ⟨a verdict that had no ~⟩ **b :** the convention established by such a precedent or by long practice **3 :** a person or thing that serves as a model

pre·ced·ing \pri-ˈsē-diŋ\ *adj* (15c) **:** that immediately precedes in time or place ⟨the ~ day⟩ ⟨~ paragraphs⟩

syn PRECEDING, ANTECEDENT, FOREGOING, PREVIOUS, PRIOR, FORMER, ANTERIOR mean being before. PRECEDING usu. implies being immediately before in time or in place ⟨the *preceding* sentence⟩. ANTECEDENT applies to order in time and may suggest a causal relation ⟨conditions *antecedent* to the revolution⟩. FOREGOING applies chiefly to statements ⟨the *foregoing* remarks⟩. PREVIOUS and PRIOR imply existing or occurring earlier, but PRIOR often adds an implication of greater importance ⟨a child from a *previous* marriage⟩ ⟨a *prior* obligation⟩. FORMER implies always a definite comparison or contrast with something that is latter ⟨the *former* name of the company⟩. ANTERIOR applies to position before or ahead of usu. in space, sometimes in time or order ⟨the *anterior* lobe of the brain⟩.

pre·cen·sor \(ˌ)prē-ˈsen(t)-sər\ *vt* (1942) **:** to censor (a publication or film) before its release to the public

pre·cen·tor \pri-ˈsen-tər\ *n* [L *praecentor,* fr. *praecinere* to lead in singing, fr. *prae-* + *canere* to sing — more at CHANT] (1613) **:** a leader of the singing of a choir or congregation — **pre·cen·to·ri·al** \ˌprē-ˌsen-ˈtȯr-ē-əl\ *adj* — **pre·cen·tor·ship** \pri-ˈsen-tər-ˌship\ *n*

pre·cept \ˈprē-ˌsept\ *n* [ME, fr. AF, fr. L *praeceptum,* fr. neut. of *praeceptus,* pp. of *praecipere* to take beforehand, instruct, fr. *prae-* + *capere* to take — more at HEAVE] (14c) **1 :** a command or principle intended esp. as a general rule of action **2 :** an order issued by legally constituted authority to a subordinate official ***syn*** see LAW

pre·cep·tive \pri-ˈsep-tiv\ *adj* (15c) **:** giving precepts **:** DIDACTIC

pre·cep·tor \pri-ˈsep-tər, ˈprē-ˌ\ *n* (15c) **1 a :** TEACHER, TUTOR **b :** the headmaster or principal of a school **2 :** the head of a preceptory of Knights Templars — **pre·cep·tor·ship** \-ˌship\ *n*

[1]**pre·cep·to·ri·al** \pri-ˌsep-ˈtȯr-ē-əl, ˌprē-\ *adj* (ca. 1741) **:** of, relating to, or making use of preceptors

[2]**preceptorial** *n* (ca. 1952) **:** a college course that emphasizes independent reading, discussion in small groups, and individual conferences with the teacher

pre·cep·to·ry \pri-ˈsep-t(ə-)rē, ˈprē-ˌ\ *n, pl* **-ries** (1540) **1 :** a subordinate house or community of the Knights Templars; *broadly* **:** COMMANDERY 1 **2 :** COMMANDERY 2

pre·cess \prē-ˈses, ˈprē-ˌ\ *vb* [back-formation fr. *precession*] *vi* (1892) **:** to progress with a movement of precession ~ *vt* **:** to cause to precess

pre·ces·sion \prē-ˈse-shən\ *n* [NL *praecession-, praecessio,* fr. ML, act of preceding, fr. L *praecedere* to precede] (1879) **:** a comparatively slow gyration of the rotation axis of a spinning body about another line intersecting it so as to describe a cone — **pre·ces·sion·al** \-ˈsesh-nəl, -ˈse-shə-nᵊl\ *adj*

precession of the equinoxes (1621) **:** a slow westward motion of the equinoxes along the ecliptic caused by the gravitational action of sun and moon upon the protuberant matter about the earth's equator

pre–Chris·tian \(ˌ)prē-ˈkris-chən, -ˈkrish-\ *adj* (1828) **:** of, relating to, or being a time before the beginning of the Christian era

pré·cieux \prā-ˈsyœ\ *or* **pré·cieuse** \-ˈsyœz\ *adj* [F *précieux,* masc., & *précieuse,* fem., lit., precious, fr. MF *precios*] (1727) **:** PRECIOUS 3

pre·cinct \ˈprē-ˌsiŋ(k)t\ *n* [ME, fr. ML *praecinctum,* fr. L, neut. of *praecinctus,* pp. of *praecingere* to gird, encircle, fr. *prae-* pre- + *cingere* to gird — more at CINCTURE] (15c) **1 :** a part of a territory with definite bounds or functions often established for administrative purposes **:** DISTRICT: as **a :** a subdivision of a county, town, city, or ward for election purposes **b :** a division of a city for police control **2 a :** an enclosure bounded by the walls of a building — often used in pl. **b :** a sphere of thought, action, or influence — often used in pl. **3 a** *pl* **:** the region immediately surrounding a place : ENVIRONS **b :** PLACE, LOCALE **4 :** BOUNDARY — often used in pl. ‹a ruined tower within the ~*s* of the squire's grounds —T. L. Peacock›

pre·ci·os·i·ty \ˌpre-shē-ˈä-sə-tē, -sē-\ *n, pl* **-ties** (1866) **1 :** fastidious refinement **2 :** an instance of preciosity

[1]**pre·cious** \ˈpre-shəs\ *adj* [ME, fr. AF *precios,* fr. L *pretiosus,* fr. *pretium* price — more at PRICE] (13c) **1 :** of great value or high price ‹~ jewels› **2 :** highly esteemed or cherished ‹a ~ friend› **3 :** excessively refined : AFFECTED ‹~ manners› **4 :** GREAT, THOROUGHGOING ‹a ~ scoundrel› — **pre·cious·ness** *n*

[2]**precious** *adv* (1595) **:** VERY, EXTREMELY ‹has ~ little to say›

pre·cious·ly *adv* (14c) **1 :** in a precious manner **2 :** PRECIOUS

precipe *var of* PRAECIPE

prec·i·pice \ˈpre-s(ə-)pəs\ *n* [F, fr. MF, fr. L *praecipitium,* fr. *praecipit-, praeceps* headlong, fr. *prae-* + *caput* head — more at HEAD] (1613) **1 :** a very steep or overhanging place **2 :** a hazardous situation; *broadly* **:** BRINK

pre·cip·i·ta·ble \pri-ˈsi-pə-tə-bəl\ *adj* (1670) **:** capable of being precipitated

pre·cip·i·tance \pri-ˈsi-pə-tən(t)s\ *n* (1667) **:** PRECIPITANCY

pre·cip·i·tan·cy \-tən(t)-sē\ *n* (1540) **:** undue hastiness or suddenness

[1]**pre·cip·i·tant** \-tənt\ *adj* (1671) **:** PRECIPITATE — **pre·cip·i·tant·ly** *adv* — **pre·cip·i·tant·ness** *n*

[2]**precipitant** *n* (ca. 1685) **:** a precipitating agent; *esp* **:** one that causes the formation of a precipitate

[1]**pre·cip·i·tate** \pri-ˈsi-pə-ˌtāt\ *vb* **-tat·ed; -tat·ing** [L *praecipitatus,* pp. of *praecipitare,* fr. *praecipit-, praeceps*] *vt* (1528) **1 a :** to throw violently **:** HURL ‹the quandaries into which the release of nuclear energy has *precipitated* mankind —A. B. Arons› **b :** to throw down **2 :** to bring about esp. abruptly ‹~ a scandal that would end with his expulsion —John Cheever› **3 a :** to cause to separate from solution or suspension **b :** to cause (vapor) to condense and fall or deposit ~ *vi* **1 a :** to fall headlong **b :** to fall or come suddenly into some condition **2 :** to move or act precipitately **3 a :** to separate from solution or suspension **b :** to condense from a vapor and fall as rain or snow — **pre·cip·i·ta·tive** \-ˌtā-tiv\ *adj* — **pre·cip·i·ta·tor** \-ˌtā-tər\ *n*

[2]**pre·cip·i·tate** \pri-ˈsi-pə-tət, -ˌtāt\ *n* [NL *praecipitatum,* fr. L, neut. of *praecipitatus*] (1594) **1 :** a substance separated from a solution or suspension by chemical or physical change usu. as an insoluble amorphous or crystalline solid **2 :** a product, result, or outcome of some process or action

[3]**pre·cip·i·tate** \pri-ˈsi-pə-tət\ *adj* (1615) **1 a :** falling, flowing, or rushing with steep descent **b :** PRECIPITOUS, STEEP **2 :** exhibiting violent or unwise speed — **pre·cip·i·tate·ly** *adv* — **pre·cip·i·tate·ness** *n*

syn PRECIPITATE, HEADLONG, ABRUPT, IMPETUOUS, SUDDEN mean showing undue haste or unexpectedness. PRECIPITATE stresses lack of due deliberation and implies prematureness of action ‹the army's *precipitate* withdrawal›. HEADLONG stresses rashness and lack of forethought ‹a *headlong* flight from arrest›. ABRUPT stresses curtness and a lack of warning or ceremony ‹an *abrupt* refusal›. IMPETUOUS stresses extreme impatience or impulsiveness ‹an *impetuous* lover proposing marriage›. SUDDEN stresses unexpectedness and sharpness or violence of action ‹flew into a *sudden* rage›.

pre·cip·i·ta·tion \pri-ˌsi-pə-ˈtā-shən\ *n* (1502) **1 :** the quality or state of being precipitate **:** HASTINESS **2 :** an act, process, or instance of precipitating; *esp* **:** the process of forming a precipitate **3 :** something precipitated: as **a :** a deposit on the earth of hail, mist, rain, sleet, or snow; *also* **:** the quantity of water deposited **b :** PRECIPITATE 1

pre·cip·i·tin \pri-ˈsi-pə-tən\ *n* [ISV, fr. *precipitate*] (1900) **:** an antibody that forms a precipitate when it unites with its antigen

pre·cip·i·tin·o·gen \pri-ˌsi-pə-ˈti-nə-jən\ *n* (1904) **:** an antigen that stimulates the production of a specific precipitin

pre·cip·i·tous \pri-ˈsi-pə-təs\ *adj* [F *précipiteux,* fr. MF, fr. L *precipitium* precipice] (1646) **1 :** PRECIPITATE 2 **2 a :** very steep, perpendicular, or overhanging in rise or fall ‹a ~ slope› **b :** having precipitous sides ‹a ~ gorge› **c :** having a very steep ascent ‹a ~ street› ***syn*** see STEEP — **pre·cip·i·tous·ly** *adv* — **pre·cip·i·tous·ness** *n*

pré·cis \prā-ˈsē, ˈprā-(ˌ)sē\ *n, pl* **pré·cis** \-ˈsēz, -(ˌ)sēz\ [F, fr. *précis* precise] (1760) **:** a concise summary of essential points, statements, or facts

pre·cise \pri-ˈsīs\ *adj* [ME, fr. MF *precis,* fr. L *praecisus,* pp. of *praecidere* to cut off, fr. *prae-* + *caedere* to cut] (15c) **1 :** exactly or sharply defined or stated **2 :** minutely exact **3 :** strictly conforming to a pattern, standard, or convention **4 :** distinguished from every other ‹at just that ~ moment› ***syn*** see CORRECT — **pre·cise·ness** *n*

pre·cise·ly *adv* (14c) **:** EXACTLY ‹~ two o'clock› — sometimes used as an intensive ‹was popular ~ because he was so kind›

pre·ci·sian \pri-ˈsi-zhən\ *n* (1571) **1 :** a person who stresses or practices scrupulous adherence to a strict standard esp. of religious observance or morality **2 :** PURITAN 1

[1]**pre·ci·sion** \pri-ˈsi-zhən\ *n* (1740) **1 :** the quality or state of being precise **:** EXACTNESS **2 a :** the degree of refinement with which an operation is performed or a measurement stated — compare ACCURACY 2b **b :** the accuracy (as in binary or decimal places) with which a number can be represented usu. expressed in terms of the number of computer words available for representation ‹double ~ arithmetic permits the representation of an expression by two computer words› **3 :** RELEVANCE 2 — **pre·ci·sion·ist** \-ˈsi-zhə-nist, -ˈsizh-nist\ *n*

[2]**precision** *adj* (1875) **1 :** adapted for extremely accurate measurement or operation **2 :** held to low tolerance in manufacture **3 :** marked by precision of execution

pre·clin·i·cal \(ˌ)prē-ˈkli-ni-kəl\ *adj* (1926) **1 :** of, relating to, or concerned with the period preceding clinical manifestations **2 :** of, relating to, or being the period in medical or dental education preceding the clinical study of medicine or dentistry **3 :** occurring prior to clinical testing ‹a ~ animal study of a new therapy›

pre·clude \pri-ˈklüd\ *vt* **pre·clud·ed; pre·clud·ing** [L *praecludere,* fr. *prae-* + *claudere* to close — more at CLOSE] (1629) **1** *archaic* **:** CLOSE **2 :** to make impossible by necessary consequence **:** rule out in advance — **pre·clu·sion** \-ˈklü-zhən\ *n* — **pre·clu·sive** \-ˈklü-siv, -ziv\ *adj* — **pre·clu·sive·ly** *adv*

pre·co·cial \pri-ˈkō-shəl\ *adj* [NL *praecoces* precocial birds, fr. L, pl. of *praecoc-, precox*] (ca. 1872) **:** capable of a high degree of independent activity from birth ‹ducklings are ~› — compare ALTRICIAL

pre·co·cious \pri-ˈkō-shəs\ *adj* [L *praecoc-, praecox* early ripening, precocious, fr. *prae-* + *coquere* to cook — more at COOK] (1650) **1 :** exceptionally early in development or occurrence ‹~ puberty› **2 :** exhibiting mature qualities at an unusually early age ‹a ~ child› — **pre·co·cious·ly** *adv* — **pre·co·cious·ness** *n* — **pre·coc·i·ty** \pri-ˈkä-sə-tē\ *n*

pre·cog·ni·tion \ˌprē-(ˌ)käg-ˈni-shən\ *n* [LL *praecognition-, praecognitio,* fr. L *praecognoscere* to know beforehand, fr. *prae-* + *cognoscere* to know — more at COGNITION] (ca. 1611) **:** clairvoyance relating to an event or state not yet experienced — **pre·cog·ni·tive** \(ˌ)prē-ˈkäg-nə-tiv\ *adj*

pre–Co·lum·bi·an \ˌprē-kə-ˈləm-bē-ən\ *adj* (1888) **:** preceding or belonging to the time before the arrival of Columbus in America

pre·con·ceive \ˌprē-kən-ˈsēv\ *vt* (1558) **:** to form (as an opinion) prior to actual knowledge or experience ‹*preconceived* notions›

pre·con·cep·tion \-kən-ˈsep-shən\ *n* (1625) **1 :** a preconceived idea **2 :** PREJUDICE

[1]**pre·con·di·tion** \-kən-ˈdi-shən\ *n* (1825) **:** PREREQUISITE

[2]**precondition** *vt* (1922) **:** to put in a proper or desired condition or frame of mind esp. in preparation

[1]**pre·con·scious** \(ˌ)prē-ˈkän(t)-shəs\ *adj* (1860) **:** not present in consciousness but capable of being recalled without encountering any inner resistance or repression — **pre·con·scious·ly** *adv*

[2]**preconscious** *n* (ca. 1922) **:** the preconscious part of the psyche esp. in psychoanalysis

pre·con·tact \ˌprē-ˈkän-ˌtakt\ *adj* (ca. 1909) **:** of or relating to the period before contact of an indigenous people with an outside culture

pre·cook \(ˌ)prē-ˈku̇k\ *vt* (1926) **:** to cook partially or entirely before final cooking or reheating

pre·cooked \(ˌ)prē-ˈku̇kt\ *adj* (1964) **:** CANNED 1 ‹a ~ speech›

pre·crit·i·cal \-ˈkri-ti-kəl\ *adj* (1881) **:** prior to the development of critical capacity

pre·cur·sor \pri-ˈkər-sər, ˈprē-ˌ\ *n* [ME *precursoure,* fr. L *praecursor,* fr. *praecurrere* to run before, fr. *prae-* pre- + *currere* to run — more at CURRENT] (15c) **1 a :** one that precedes and indicates the approach of another **b :** PREDECESSOR **2 :** a substance, cell, or cellular component from which another substance, cell, or cellular component is formed ***syn*** see FORERUNNER — **pre·cur·so·ry** \-ˈkərs-rē, -ˈkər-sə-\ *adj*

pred *abbr* predicate

pre·da·ceous *or* **pre·da·cious** \pri-ˈdā-shəs\ *adj* [L *praedari* to prey upon (fr. *praeda* prey) + E *-aceous* or *-acious* (as in *rapacious*) — more at PREY] (1713) **1 :** living by preying on other animals **:** PREDATORY **2** *usu predacious* **:** tending to devour or despoil **:** RAPACIOUS — **pre·da·ceous·ness** *n* — **pre·dac·i·ty** \-ˈda-sə-tē\ *n*

pre·date \(ˌ)prē-ˈdāt\ *vt* (ca. 1864) **:** ANTEDATE

pre·da·tion \pri-ˈdā-shən\ *n* [ME *predacion,* fr. L *praedation-, praedatio,* fr. *praedari*] (15c) **1 :** the act of preying or plundering **:** DEPREDATION **2 :** a mode of life in which food is primarily obtained by the killing and consuming of animals

predation pressure *n* (1942) **:** the effects of predation on a natural community esp. with respect to the survival of species preyed upon

pred·a·tor \ˈpre-də-tər, -ˌtȯr\ *n* (1912) **1 :** one that preys, destroys, or devours **2 :** an animal that lives by predation

pred·a·to·ry \ˈpre-də-ˌtȯr-ē\ *adj* (1589) **1 a :** of, relating to, or practicing plunder, pillage, or rapine **b :** inclined or intended to injure or exploit others for personal gain or profit ‹~ pricing practices› **2 :** living by predation **:** PREDACEOUS; *also* **:** adapted to predation

pre·de·cease \ˌprē-di-ˈsēs\ *vb* **-ceased; -ceas·ing** *vt* (1593) **:** to die before (another person) ~ *vi* **:** to die first — **predecease** *n*

pre·de·ces·sor \ˈpre-də-ˌse-sər, ˈprē-; ˌpre-də-ˈ, ˌprē-\ *n* [ME *predecessour,* fr. AF *predecessur,* fr. LL *praedecessor,* fr. L *prae-* pre- + *decessor* retiring governor, fr. *decedere* to depart, retire from office — more at DECEASE] (14c) **1 :** one that precedes; *esp* **:** a person who has previously occupied a position or office to which another has succeeded **2** *archaic* **:** ANCESTOR

pre·del·la \pri-ˈde-lə\ *n* [It, footrest, altar step, predella, fr. Langobardic (Gmc language of the Lombards) **predel-,* **pretel-,* lath, board; akin to OHG *bret* board, *bort* plank, ship's side — more at BOARD] (1853) **:** the base of an altarpiece; *esp* **:** one containing decorated panels depicting scenes related to the main panel or panels

pre·des·ti·nar·i·an \(ˌ)prē-ˌdes-tə-ˈner-ē-ən, ˌprē-des-\ *n* [*predestin*ation + *-arian*] (1667) **:** one who believes in predestination — **predestinarian** *adj* — **pre·des·ti·nar·i·an·ism** \-ē-ə-ˌni-zəm\ *n*

[1]**pre·des·ti·nate** \prē-ˈdes-tə-nət, -ˌnāt\ *adj* [ME, fr. L *praedestinatus,* pp. of *praedestinare*] (14c) **:** destined, fated, or determined beforehand

[2]**pre·des·ti·nate** \-ˌnāt\ *vt* **-nat·ed; -nat·ing** [ME, fr. L *praedestinatus,* pp.] (15c) **1 :** to foreordain to an earthly or eternal lot or destiny by divine decree **2** *archaic* **:** PREDETERMINE

pre·des·ti·na·tion \(ˌ)prē-ˌdes-tə-ˈnā-shən, ˌprē-des-\ *n* (14c) **1 :** the act of predestinating **:** the state of being predestinated **2 :** the doctrine that God in consequence of his foreknowledge of all events infallibly guides those who are destined for salvation

pre·des·ti·na·tor \prē-ˈdes-tə-ˌnā-tər\ *n* (1579) **1** *archaic* **:** PREDESTINARIAN **2 :** one that predestinates

pre·des·tine \(ˌ)prē-ˈdes-tən\ *vt* [ME, fr. AF or L; AF *predestiner,* fr. L *praedestinare,* fr. *prae-* + *destinare* to determine — more at DESTINE] (14c) **:** to destine, decree, determine, appoint, or settle beforehand; *esp* **:** PREDESTINATE 1

pre·de·ter·mi·na·tion \ˌprē-di-ˌtər-mə-ˈnā-shən\ *n* (1647) **1 :** the act of predetermining **:** the state of being predetermined: as **a :** the ordaining of events beforehand **b :** a fixing or settling in advance **2 :** a purpose formed beforehand

---

\ə\ **a**but \ᵊ\ **k**itten, F ta**ble** \ər\ **fur**ther \a\ **a**sh \ā\ **a**ce \ä\ m**o**p, m**a**r
\au̇\ **ou**t \ch\ **ch**in \e\ b**e**t \ē\ **ea**sy \g\ **g**o \i\ h**i**t \ī\ **i**ce \j\ **j**ob
\ŋ\ si**ng** \ō\ g**o** \ȯ\ l**aw** \ȯi\ b**oy** \th\ **th**in \t͟h\ **th**e \ü\ l**oo**t \u̇\ f**oo**t
\y\ **y**et \zh\ vi**si**on, bei**ge** \ḵ, ⁿ, œ, ue, ʸ\ *see* Guide to Pronunciation

pre·de·ter·mine \-di-ˈtər-mən\ *vt* [LL *praedeterminare,* fr. L *prae-* + *determinare* to determine] (1622) **1 a :** FOREORDAIN, PREDESTINE **b :** to determine beforehand **2 :** to impose a direction or tendency on beforehand

pre·de·ter·min·er \-di-ˈtər-mə-nər\ *n* (1959) **:** a limiting noun modifier (as *both* or *all*) characterized by occurrence before the determiner in a noun phrase

pre·di·a·be·tes \ˌprē-ˌdī-ə-ˈbē-tēz, -təs\ *n* (1935) **:** an asymptomatic abnormal state that precedes the development of clinically evident diabetes — **pre·di·a·bet·ic** \-ˈbe-tik\ *adj or n*

pre·di·al \ˈprē-dē-əl\ *adj* [ME *prediall,* fr. ML *praedialis,* fr. L *praedium* landed property, fr. *praed-, praes* bondsman, fr. *prae-* + *vad-, vas* surety — more at WED] (15c) **:** of or relating to land or its products

[1]**pred·i·ca·ble** \ˈpre-di-kə-bəl\ *n* [ML *praedicabile,* fr. neut. of *praedicabilis*] (1551) **:** something that may be predicated; *esp* **:** one of the five most general kinds of attribution in traditional logic that include genus, species, difference, property, and accident

[2]**predicable** *adj* [ML *praedicabilis,* fr. LL *praedicare* to predicate] (ca. 1598) **:** capable of being asserted

pre·dic·a·ment \pri-ˈdi-kə-mənt, *1 is usu* ˈpre-di-kə-\ *n* [ME, fr. LL *praedicamentum,* fr. *praedicare*] (14c) **1 :** the character, status, or classification assigned by a predication; *specif* **:** CATEGORY 1 **2 :** CONDITION, STATE; *esp* **:** a difficult, perplexing, or trying situation

[1]**pred·i·cate** \ˈpre-di-kət\ *n* [ME, fr. LL *praedicatum,* fr. neut. of *praedicatus*] (15c) **1 a :** something that is affirmed or denied of the subject in a proposition in logic **b :** a term designating a property or relation **2 :** the part of a sentence or clause that expresses what is said of the subject and that usu. consists of a verb with or without objects, complements, or adverbial modifiers — **pred·i·ca·tive** \-kə-tiv, -ˌkā-\ *adj* — **pred·i·ca·tive·ly** *adv*

[2]**pred·i·cate** \ˈpre-də-ˌkāt\ *vt* **-cat·ed; -cat·ing** [LL *praedicatus,* pp. of *praedicare* to assert, predicate logically, preach, fr. L, to proclaim, assert — more at PREACH] (ca. 1552) **1 a :** AFFIRM, DECLARE **b** *archaic* **:** PREACH **2 a :** to assert to be a quality, attribute, or property — used with following *of* ⟨∼*s* intelligence of humans⟩ **b :** to make (a term) the predicate in a proposition **3 :** FOUND, BASE — usu. used with *on* ⟨the theory is *predicated* on recent findings⟩ **4 :** IMPLY

[3]**pred·i·cate** \ˈpre-di-kət\ *adj* (1887) **:** completing the meaning of a copula ⟨∼ adjective⟩ ⟨∼ noun⟩

predicate calculus *n* (1950) **:** the branch of symbolic logic that uses symbols for quantifiers and for arguments and predicates of propositions as well as for unanalyzed propositions and logical connectives — called also *functional calculus;* compare PROPOSITIONAL CALCULUS

predicate nominative *n* (1887) **:** a noun or pronoun in the nominative or common case completing the meaning of a copula

pred·i·ca·tion \ˌpre-də-ˈkā-shən\ *n* [ME *predicacion,* fr. AF *predicaciun,* fr. L *praedication-, praedicatio,* fr. *praedicare*] (14c) **1** *archaic* **a :** an act of proclaiming or preaching **b :** SERMON **2 :** an act or instance of predicating: as **a :** the expression of action, state, or quality by a grammatical predicate **b :** the logical affirmation of something about another; *esp* **:** assignment of something to a class

pred·i·ca·to·ry \ˈpre-di-kə-ˌtȯr-ē\ *adj* [LL *praedicatorius,* fr. *praedicare* to preach] (1611) **:** of or relating to preaching

pre·dict \pri-ˈdikt\ *vb* [L *praedictus,* pp. of *praedicere,* fr. *prae-* pre- + *dicere* to say — more at DICTION] *vt* (1609) **:** to declare or indicate in advance; *esp* **:** foretell on the basis of observation, experience, or scientific reason ∼ *vi* **:** to make a prediction **syn** see FORETELL — **pre·dict·abil·i·ty** \-ˌdik-tə-ˈbi-lə-tē\ *n* — **pre·dict·able** \-ˈdik-tə-bəl\ *adj* — **pre·dic·tive** \-ˈdik-tiv\ *adj* — **pre·dic·tive·ly** \-lē\ *adv* — **pre·dic·tor** \-ˈdik-tər\ *n*

pre·dict·ably \-ˈdik-tə-blē\ *adv* (1914) **1 :** in a manner that can be predicted ⟨works quickly and ∼⟩ **2 :** as one could predict **:** as one would expect ⟨∼, the politicians howled⟩

pre·dic·tion \pri-ˈdik-shən\ *n* (1561) **1 :** an act of predicting **2 :** something that is predicted **:** FORECAST

pre·di·gest \ˌprē-dī-ˈjest, -də-\ *vt* (1663) **1 :** to subject to predigestion **2 :** to simplify for easy use ⟨∼*ed* classics for children⟩

pre·di·ges·tion \-ˈjes-chən, -ˈjesh-\ *n* (ca. 1612) **:** artificial or natural partial digestion of food ⟨enzymatic ∼⟩ ⟨microbial ∼⟩

pre·di·lec·tion \ˌpre-də-ˈlek-shən, ˌprē-\ *n* [F *prédilection,* fr. ML *praediligere* to love more, prefer, fr. L *prae-* + *diligere* to love — more at DILIGENT] (1742) **:** an established preference for something

syn PREDILECTION, PREPOSSESSION, PREJUDICE, BIAS mean an attitude of mind that predisposes one to favor something. PREDILECTION implies a strong liking deriving from one's temperament or experience ⟨a *predilection* for travel⟩. PREPOSSESSION suggests a fixed conception likely to preclude objective judgment of anything counter to it ⟨a *prepossession* against technology⟩. PREJUDICE usu. implies an unfavorable prepossession and connotes a feeling rooted in suspicion, fear, or intolerance ⟨a mindless *prejudice* against the unfamiliar⟩. BIAS implies an unreasoned and unfair distortion of judgment in favor of or against a person or thing ⟨a strong *bias* toward the plaintiff⟩.

pre·dis·pose \ˌprē-di-ˈspōz\ *vt* (1646) **1 :** to dispose in advance ⟨a good teacher ∼*s* children to learn⟩ **2 :** to make susceptible ⟨malnutrition ∼*s* one to disease⟩ ∼ *vi* **:** to bring about susceptibility **syn** see INCLINE — **pre·dis·po·si·tion** \ˌprē-ˌdis-pə-ˈzi-shən\ *n*

pred·nis·o·lone \pred-ˈni-sə-ˌlōn\ *n* [blend of *prednisone* and [1]*-ol*] (1955) **:** a glucocorticoid $C_{21}H_{28}O_5$ that is a dehydrogenated analog of cortisol and is used esp. as an anti-inflammatory drug

pred·ni·sone \ˈpred-nə-ˌsōn *also* -ˌzōn\ *n* [prob. fr. *pregnane* ($C_{21}H_{36}$) + *diene* (compound containing two double bonds) + cort*isone*] (1955) **:** a glucocorticoid $C_{21}H_{26}O_5$ that is a dehydrogenated analog of cortisone and is used as an anti-inflammatory agent, as an antineoplastic agent, and as an immunosuppressant

pre·doc·tor·al \(ˌ)prē-ˈdäk-t(ə-)rəl\ *adj* (1937) **:** of, relating to, or engaged in academic study leading to the doctoral degree

pre·dom·i·nance \pri-ˈdä-mə-nən(t)s, -ˈdäm-nən(t)s\ *n* (1592) **:** the quality or state of being predominant

pre·dom·i·nan·cy \-nən(t)-sē\ *n* (ca. 1598) **:** PREDOMINANCE

pre·dom·i·nant \-nənt\ *adj* [MF, fr. ML *praedominant-, praedominans,* prp. of *praedominari* to predominate, fr. L *prae-* + *dominari* to rule, govern — more at DOMINATE] (1576) **1 :** having superior strength, influence, or authority **:** PREVAILING **2 :** being most frequent or common **syn** see DOMINANT

pre·dom·i·nant·ly \-nənt-lē\ *adv* (1681) **:** for the most part **:** MAINLY

[1]**pre·dom·i·nate** \-nət\ *adj* [alter. of *predominant*] (1591) **:** PREDOMINANT

[2]**pre·dom·i·nate** \pri-ˈdä-mə-ˌnāt\ *vb* [ML *praedominatus,* pp. of *praedominari*] *vi* (1594) **1 :** to hold advantage in numbers or quantity **2 :** to exert controlling power or influence **:** PREVAIL ∼ *vt* **:** to exert control over **:** DOMINATE — **pre·dom·i·na·tion** \-ˌdä-mə-ˈnā-shən\ *n*

pre·dom·i·nate·ly \pri-ˈdä-mə-nət-lē\ *adv* (1594) **:** PREDOMINANTLY

pre·eclamp·sia \ˌprē-i-ˈklam(p)-sē-ə\ *n* [NL] (1923) **:** a serious condition developing in late pregnancy that is characterized by a sudden rise in blood pressure, excessive weight gain, generalized edema, proteinuria, severe headache, and visual disturbances and that may result in eclampsia if untreated — **pre·eclamp·tic** \-ˈklam(p)-tik\ *adj*

pre·emer·gence \ˌprē-ə-ˈmər-jən(t)s\ *adj* (1935) **:** used or occurring before emergence of seedlings above the ground ⟨∼ herbicides⟩

pre·emer·gent \-jənt\ *adj* (1959) **:** PREEMERGENCE

pree·mie *also* **pre·mie** \ˈprē-mē\ *n* [*pre*mature + *-ie*] (1927) **:** a premature baby

pre·em·i·nence \prē-ˈe-mə-nən(t)s\ *n* (13c) **:** the quality or state of being preeminent **:** SUPERIORITY

pre·em·i·nent \-nənt\ *adj* [ME, fr. LL *praeeminent-, praeeminens,* fr. L, prp. of *praeeminēre* to be outstanding, fr. *prae-* + *eminēre* to stand out — more at EMINENT] (15c) **:** having paramount rank, dignity, or importance **:** OUTSTANDING, SUPREME — **pre·em·i·nent·ly** *adv*

pre·empt \prē-ˈem(p)t\ *vb* [back-formation fr. *preemption*] *vt* (1850) **1 :** to acquire (as land) by preemption **2 :** to seize upon to the exclusion of others ⟨the movement was then ∼*ed* by a lunatic fringe⟩ **3 :** to replace with something considered to be of greater value or priority ⟨the program did not appear, having been ∼*ed* by a baseball game —Robert MacNeil⟩ **4 :** to gain a commanding or preeminent place in **5 :** to prevent from happening or taking place **:** FORESTALL ∼ *vi* **:** to make a preemptive bid in bridge — **pre·emp·tor** \-ˈem(p)-tər\ *n*

pre·emp·tion \-ˈem(p)-shən\ *n* [ML *praeemption-, praeemptio* previous purchase, fr. *praeemere* to buy before, fr. L *prae-* pre- + *emere* to buy — more at REDEEM] (1602) **1 a :** the right of purchasing before others; *esp* **:** one given by the government to the actual settler upon a tract of public land **b :** the purchase of something under this right **2 :** a prior seizure or appropriation **:** a taking possession before others **3 :** a doctrine in law according to which federal law supersedes state law when federal law is in conflict with a state law **4 :** a policy of launching a preemptive attack in order to prevent a suspected imminent attack

pre·emp·tive \-ˈem(p)-tiv\ *adj* (1855) **1 a :** of or relating to preemption **b :** having power to preempt **2** *of a bid in bridge* **:** higher than necessary and intended to shut out bids by the opponents **3 :** giving a stockholder first option to purchase new stock in an amount proportionate to his existing holdings **4 :** marked by the seizing of the initiative **:** initiated by oneself ⟨a ∼ attack⟩ — **pre·emp·tive·ly** *adv*

[1]**preen** \ˈprēn\ *n* [ME *prene,* fr. OE *prēon;* akin to MHG *pfrieme* awl] (bef. 12c) **1** *dial chiefly Brit* **:** PIN **2** *dial chiefly Brit* **:** BROOCH

[2]**preen** *vt* (1572) *chiefly Scot* **:** PIN

[3]**preen** *vb* [ME *prenen,* alter. of *proynen, prunen,* fr. AF *puroindre, proindre,* fr. *pur-* thoroughly + *uindre, oindre* to anoint, rub, fr. L *unguere* — more at PURCHASE, OINTMENT] *vt* (14c) **1** *of a bird* **:** to groom with the bill esp. by rearranging the barbs and barbules of the feathers and by distributing oil from the uropygial gland **2 :** to dress or smooth (oneself) up **:** PRIMP **3 :** to pride or congratulate (oneself) on an achievement ∼ *vi* **1 :** to make oneself sleek **2 :** to behave or speak with obvious pride or self-satisfaction — **preen·er** *n*

pre–en·gi·neered \ˌprē-ˌen-jə-ˈnird\ *adj* (1951) **:** constructed of or employing prefabricated modules ⟨a ∼ metal building⟩

pre·ex·il·ic \ˌprē-eg-ˈzi-lik\ *adj* (1880) **:** previous to the exile of the Jews to Babylon in about 600 B.C.

pre·ex·ist \ˌprē-ig-ˈzist\ *vi* (1599) **:** to exist earlier or before ∼ *vt* **:** ANTEDATE

pre·ex·is·tence \-ig-ˈzis-tən(t)s\ *n* (ca. 1652) **:** existence in a former state or previous to something else; *specif* **:** existence of the soul before its union with the body — **pre·ex·is·tent** \-tənt\ *adj*

pre·ex·ist·ing \ˌprē-ig-ˈzi-stiŋ\ *adj* (1585) **:** existing at an earlier time ⟨a ∼ medical condition⟩

pref *abbr* **1** preface **2** preference; preferred **3** prefix

[1]**pre·fab** \(ˌ)prē-ˈfab, ˈprē-ˌ\ *adj* (1937) **:** produced by prefabrication **:** PREFABRICATED ⟨a ∼ house⟩

[2]**prefab** *n* (1942) **:** a prefabricated structure

pre·fab·ri·cate \(ˌ)prē-ˈfa-bri-ˌkāt\ *vt* (1932) **1 :** to fabricate the parts of at a factory so that construction consists mainly of assembling and uniting standardized parts **2 :** to produce artificially — **pre·fab·ri·ca·tion** \ˌprē-ˌfa-bri-ˈkā-shən\ *n*

[1]**pref·ace** \ˈpre-fəs\ *n* [ME, fr. AF, fr. ML *prephatia,* alter. of L *praefation-, praefatio* foreword, fr. *praefari* to say beforehand, fr. *prae-* pre- + *fari* to say — more at BAN] (14c) **1** *often cap* **:** a variable doxology beginning with the Sursum Corda and ending with the Sanctus in traditional eucharistic liturgies **2 :** the introductory remarks of a speaker or author **3 :** APPROACH, PRELIMINARY

[2]**preface** *vb* **pref·aced; pref·ac·ing** *vi* (1619) **:** to make introductory remarks ∼ *vt* **1 :** to say or write as preface ⟨a note *prefaced* to the manuscript⟩ **2 :** PRECEDE, HERALD **3 :** to introduce by or begin with a preface **4 :** to stand in front of ⟨a porch ∼*s* the entrance⟩ **5 :** to be a preliminary to — **pref·ac·er** *n*

pref·a·to·ry \ˈpre-fə-ˌtȯr-ē\ *adj* [L *praefari*] (1675) **1 :** of, relating to, or constituting a preface ⟨∼ remarks⟩ **2 :** located in front

pre·fect \ˈprē-ˌfekt\ *n* [ME, fr. AF, fr. L *praefectus,* fr. pp. of *praeficere* to place at the head of, fr. *prae-* + *facere* to make — more at DO] (14c) **1 :** any of various high officials or magistrates of differing functions and ranks in ancient Rome **2 :** a chief officer or chief magistrate **3 :** a student monitor in a usu. private school

prefect apostolic *n* (ca. 1888) **:** a Roman Catholic clergyman and usu. a priest with quasi-episcopal jurisdiction over a district of a missionary territory

pre·fec·ture \ˈprē-ˌfek-chər\ *n* (15c) **1 :** the office or term of office of a prefect **2 :** the official residence of a prefect **3 :** the district governed by a prefect — **pre·fec·tur·al** \prē-ˈfek-chə-rəl, pri-\ *adj*

prefecture apostolic *n* (1911) **:** the district under a prefect apostolic

pre·fer \pri-ˈfər\ *vt* **pre·ferred; pre·fer·ring** [ME *preferren,* fr. AF *pre-*

ferrer, fr. L *praeferre* to put before, prefer, fr. *prae-* + *ferre* to carry — more at BEAR] (14c) **1 :** to promote or advance to a rank or position **2 :** to like better or best ⟨~*s* sports to reading⟩ ⟨~*s* to watch TV⟩ **3 :** to give (a creditor) priority **4** *archaic* **:** to put or set forward or before someone **:** RECOMMEND **5 :** to bring or lay against someone ⟨won't ~ charges⟩ **6 :** to bring forward or lay before one for consideration — **pre·fer·rer** *n*

pref·er·a·ble \ˈpre-f(ə-)rə-bəl, ˈpre-fər-bəl *also* pri-ˈfər-ə-bəl\ *adj* (1666) **:** having greater value or desirability **:** being preferred — **pref·er·a·bil·i·ty** \ˌpre-f(ə-)rə-ˈbi-lə-tē\ *n* — **pref·er·a·bly** \-blē\ *adv*

pref·er·ence \ˈpre-fərn(t)s, ˈpre-f(ə-)rən(t)s\ *n* [ME *preferraunce,* fr. MF *preferance,* fr. ML *praeferentia,* fr. L *praeferent-, praeferens,* prp. of *praeferre*] (15c) **1 a :** the act of preferring **:** the state of being preferred **b :** the power or opportunity of choosing **2 :** one that is preferred **3 :** the act, fact, or principle of giving advantages to some over others **4 :** priority in the right to demand and receive satisfaction of an obligation **5 :** ORIENTATION 2b ⟨sexual ~⟩ ***syn*** see CHOICE

pref·er·en·tial \ˌpre-fə-ˈren(t)-shəl\ *adj* (1849) **1 :** showing preference **2 :** employing or creating a preference in trade relations **3 :** designed to permit expression of preference among candidates ⟨a ~ primary⟩ **4 :** giving preference esp. in hiring to union members ⟨a ~ shop⟩ — **pref·er·en·tial·ly** \-ˈren(t)-sh(ə-)lē\ *adv*

pre·fer·ment \pri-ˈfər-mənt\ *n* (15c) **1 a :** advancement or promotion in dignity, office, or station **b :** a position or office of honor or profit **2 :** priority or seniority in right esp. to receive payment or to purchase property on equal terms with others **3 :** the act of bringing forward (as charges)

preferred provider *n* (1982) **1 :** PPO — usu. used attributively **2 :** a health-care provider (as a doctor or hospital) that is part of a PPO

preferred provider organization *n* (1982) **:** PPO

preferred stock *n* (ca. 1859) **:** stock guaranteed priority by a corporation's charter over common stock in the payment of dividends and usu. in the distribution of assets

pre·fig·u·ra·tion \(ˌ)prē-ˌfi-gyə-ˈrā-shən, -gə-\ *n* (14c) **1 :** the act of prefiguring **:** the state of being prefigured **2 :** something that prefigures — **pre·fig·u·ra·tive** \ˌprē-ˈfi-gyə-rə-tiv, -gə-\ *adj*

pre·fig·ure \ˌprē-ˈfi-gyər, *esp Brit* -ˈfi-gər\ *vt* [ME, fr. LL *praefigurare,* fr. L *prae-* pre- + *figurare* to shape, picture, fr. *figura* figure] (15c) **1 :** to show, suggest, or announce by an antecedent type, image, or likeness **2 :** to picture or imagine beforehand — **pre·fig·ure·ment** \-mənt\ *n*

[1]**pre·fix** *vt* [ME, fr. MF *prefixer,* fr. L *praefixus*] (15c) **1** \(ˌ)prē-ˈfiks\ **:** to fix or appoint beforehand **2** \ˈprē-ˌ, prē-ˈ\ [partly fr. [2]*prefix*] **:** to place in front; *esp* **:** to add as a prefix ⟨~ a syllable to a word⟩

[2]**pre·fix** \ˈprē-ˌfiks\ *n* [NL *praefixum,* fr. L, neut. of *praefixus,* pp. of *praefigere* to fasten before, fr. *prae-* + *figere* to fasten — more at FIX] (1646) **1 :** an affix attached to the beginning of a word, base, or phrase and serving to produce a derivative word or an inflectional form — compare SUFFIX **2 :** a title used before a person's name — **pre·fix·al** \ˈprē-ˌfik-səl, prē-ˈ\ *adj*

[3]**pre·fix** *same as* [2]\ *adj* (1971) **:** characterized by placement of an operator before its operand or before its two operands if it is a binary operator — compare INFIX, POSTFIX

[1]**pre·flight** \ˈprē-ˌflīt\ *adj* (1942) **:** preparing for or preliminary to flight (as of an aircraft) ⟨a ~ inspection⟩

[2]**preflight** *vt* (1945) **:** to inspect (as an aircraft) before a flight

[3]**preflight** *n* (1950) **:** a preflight inspection of an aircraft

pre·fo·cus \(ˌ)prē-ˈfō-kəs\ *vt* (1948) **:** to focus beforehand (as automotive headlights before installation)

pre·form \ˈprē-ˌfȯrm, (ˌ)prē-ˈ\ *vt* [L *praeformare,* fr. *prae-* + *formare* to form, fr. *forma* form] (1601) **1 :** to form or shape beforehand **2 :** to bring to approximate preliminary shape and size — **pre·form** \ˈprē-ˌfȯrm\ *n*

pre·for·ma·tion \ˌprē-fȯr-ˈmā-shən\ *n* (1732) **1 :** previous formation **2 :** the now discredited theory that every germ cell contains the organism of its kind fully formed and that development involves merely an increase in size — compare EPIGENESIS 1, HOMUNCULUS 2 — **pre·for·ma·tion·ist** \-sh(ə-)nist\ *n or adj*

[1]**pre·fron·tal** \(ˌ)prē-ˈfrən-tᵊl\ *adj* (1854) **:** anterior to or involving the anterior part of a frontal structure ⟨a ~ bone⟩

[2]**prefrontal** *n* (1854) **:** a prefrontal part (as a bone)

prefrontal cortex *n* (1964) **:** the gray matter of the anterior part of the frontal lobe that is highly developed in humans and plays a role in the regulation of complex cognitive, emotional, and behavioral functioning

pre·gan·gli·on·ic \ˌprē-ˌgaŋ-glē-ˈä-nik\ *adj* (1895) **:** proximal to a ganglion; *specif* **:** of, relating to, or being a usu. medullated axon arising from a cell body in the central nervous system and terminating in an autonomic ganglion — compare POSTGANGLIONIC

preg·gers \ˈpre-gərz\ *adj* [by alter.] (1942) **:** PREGNANT

preg·na·ble \ˈpreg-nə-bəl\ *adj* [alter. of ME *prenable,* fr. AF — more at IMPREGNABLE] (14c) **:** vulnerable to capture ⟨a ~ fort⟩ — **preg·na·bil·i·ty** \ˌpreg-nə-ˈbi-lə-tē\ *n*

preg·nan·cy \ˈpreg-nən(t)-sē\ *n, pl* **-cies** (15c) **1 :** the quality of being pregnant (as in meaning) **2 :** the condition of being pregnant **:** GESTATION **3 :** an instance of being pregnant

preg·nant \ˈpreg-nənt\ *adj* [ME, fr. L *praegnant-, praegnans* carrying a fetus, alter. of *praegnas,* fr. *prae-* pre- + *-gnas* (akin to *gignere* to give birth to) — more at KIN] (14c) **1** *archaic* **:** COGENT **2 :** abounding in fancy, wit, or resourcefulness **:** INVENTIVE ⟨all this has been said . . . by great and ~ artists —*Times Lit. Supp.*⟩ **3 :** rich in significance or implication ⟨the ~ phrases of the Bible —Edmund Wilson⟩ ⟨a ~ pause⟩ **4 :** containing a developing embryo, fetus, or unborn offspring within the body **:** GRAVID **5 :** having possibilities of development or consequence **:** involving important issues **:** MOMENTOUS ⟨draw inspiration from the heroic achievements of that ~ age —Kemp Malone⟩ **6** *obs* **:** INCLINED, DISPOSED ⟨your own most ~ and vouchsafed ear —Shak.⟩ **7 :** FULL, TEEMING — **preg·nant·ly** *adv*

preg·nen·o·lone \preg-ˈne-nə-ˌlōn\ *n* [ISV *pregnene* ($C_{21}H_{34}$) + [1]*-ol* + *-one*] (1936) **:** an unsaturated hydroxy steroid ketone $C_{21}H_{32}O_2$ that is formed by the oxidation of steroids (as cholesterol) and yields progesterone on dehydrogenation

pre·heat \(ˌ)prē-ˈhēt\ *vt* (1898) **:** to heat beforehand; *esp* **:** to heat (an oven) to a designated temperature before using for cooking — **pre·heat·er** *n*

pre·hen·sile \prē-ˈhen(t)-səl, -ˈhen-ˌsī(-ə)l\ *adj* [F *préhensile,* fr. L *prehensus,* pp. of *prehendere* to seize — more at GET] (ca. 1785) **1 :** adapted for seizing or grasping esp. by wrapping around ⟨~ tail⟩ **2 :** gifted with mental grasp or moral or aesthetic perception — **pre·hen·sil·i·ty** \(ˌ)prē-ˌhen-ˈsi-lə-tē\ *n*

pre·hen·sion \prē-ˈhen(t)-shən\ *n* (ca. 1828) **1 :** the act of taking hold, seizing, or grasping **2 a :** mental understanding **:** COMPREHENSION **b :** apprehension by the senses

pre–His·pan·ic \ˌprē-(h)i-ˈspa-nik\ *adj* (1919) **:** of, relating to, or being the time prior to Spanish conquests in the western hemisphere

pre·his·to·ri·an \ˌprē-(h)is-ˈtȯr-ē-ən\ *n* (1893) **:** an archaeologist who specializes in prehistory

pre·his·tor·ic \ˌprē-(h)is-ˈtȯr-ik, -ˈtär-\ *also* **pre·his·tor·i·cal** \-i-kəl\ *adj* (1832) **1 :** of, relating to, or existing in times antedating written history **2 :** of or relating to a language in a period of its development from which contemporary records of its sounds and forms have not been preserved **3 :** regarded as being outdated or outmoded ⟨~ attitudes⟩ — **pre·his·tor·i·cal·ly** \-i-k(ə-)lē\ *adv*

pre·his·to·ry \ˌprē-ˈhis-t(ə-)rē\ *n* (1871) **1 :** the study of prehistoric humankind **2 :** a history of the antecedents of an event, situation, or thing **3 :** the prehistoric period of human evolution

pre·hom·i·nid \-ˈhä-mə-nəd\ *n* [ultim. fr. L *pre-* + *homin-, homo* human being — more at HOMAGE] (1939) **:** any of various extinct primates resembling or ancestral to hominids — **prehominid** *adj*

pre·hu·man \(ˈ)prē-ˈhyü-mən, -ˈyü-\ *adj* (1844) **1 :** antedating the appearance of human beings **2 :** of, relating to, or being an extinct primate and esp. an extinct hominid that resembles or is ancestral to humans — **prehuman** *n*

pre·ig·ni·tion \ˌprē-ig-ˈni-shən\ *n* (1898) **:** ignition in an internal combustion engine while the inlet valve is open or before compression is completed

pre·im·plan·ta·tion \ˌprē-ˌim-ˌplan-ˈtā-shən\ *adj* (1945) **:** of, involving, or being an embryo before uterine implantation

pre·in·stall \(ˌ)prē-in-ˈstȯl\ *vt* (1983) **:** to install (as software) on a computer prior to sale — **pre·in·stal·la·tion** \-ˌin(t)-stə-ˈlā-shən\ *n*

pre·judge \(ˌ)prē-ˈjəj\ *vt* [MF *prejuger,* fr. L *praejudicare,* fr. *prae-* + *judicare* to judge — more at JUDGE] (1579) **:** to judge before hearing or before full and sufficient examination — **pre·judg·er** *n* — **pre·judg·ment** \-ˈjəj-mənt\ *n*

[1]**prej·u·dice** \ˈpre-jə-dəs\ *n* [ME, fr. AF, fr. L *praejudicium* previous judgment, damage, fr. *prae-* + *judicium* judgment — more at JUDICIAL] (13c) **1 :** injury or damage resulting from some judgment or action of another in disregard of one's rights; *esp* **:** detriment to one's legal rights or claims **2 a** (1) **:** preconceived judgment or opinion (2) **:** an adverse opinion or leaning formed without just grounds or before sufficient knowledge **b :** an instance of such judgment or opinion **c :** an irrational attitude of hostility directed against an individual, a group, a race, or their supposed characteristics ***syn*** see PREDILECTION

[2]**prejudice** *vt* **-diced; -dic·ing** (15c) **1 :** to injure or damage by some judgment or action (as in a case of law) **2 :** to cause to have prejudice

prejudiced *adj* (1579) **:** resulting from or having a prejudice or bias for or esp. against

prej·u·di·cial \ˌpre-jə-ˈdi-shəl\ *adj* (15c) **1 :** tending to injure or impair **:** DETRIMENTAL ⟨a transfer ~ to other creditors⟩ **2 :** leading to premature judgment or unwarranted opinion ⟨~ evidence⟩ — **prej·u·di·cial·ly** \-ˈdi-sh(ə-)lē\ *adv* — **prej·u·di·cial·ness** \-shəl-nəs\ *n*

pre–K \ˈprē-ˈkā\ *n* (1977) **:** PREKINDERGARTEN

pre·kin·der·gar·ten \(ˈ)prē-ˈkin-də(r)-ˌgär-tᵊn, -dᵊn\ *n, often attrib* (1925) **1 :** NURSERY SCHOOL **2 :** a class or program preceding kindergarten for children usu. from three to four years old

prel·a·cy \ˈpre-lə-sē\ *n, pl* **-cies** (14c) **1 :** the office or dignity of a prelate **2 :** episcopal church government

pre·lap·sar·i·an \ˌprē-ˌlap-ˈser-ē-ən\ *adj* [*pre-* + L *lapsus* slip, fall — more at LAPSE] (1879) **:** characteristic of or belonging to the time or state before the fall of humankind

prel·ate \ˈpre-lət *also* ˈprē-ˌlāt\ *n* [ME *prelat,* fr. AF, fr. ML *praelatus,* lit., one receiving preferment, fr. L (pp. of *praeferre* to prefer), fr. *prae-* + *latus,* pp. of *ferre* to carry — more at TOLERATE, BEAR] (13c) **:** an ecclesiastic (as a bishop or abbot) of superior rank

prel·a·ture \ˈpre-lə-ˌchu̇r, -chər, -ˌtyu̇r, -ˌtu̇r\ *n* (1607) **1 :** PRELACY 1 **2 :** a body of prelates

pre·lect \pri-ˈlekt\ *vi* [L *praelectus,* pp. of *praelegere,* fr. *prae-* + *legere* to read — more at LEGEND] (1785) **:** to discourse publicly **:** LECTURE — **pre·lec·tion** \-ˈlek-shən\ *n*

pre·lim \ˈprē-ˌlim, pri-ˈ\ *n or adj* (1891) **:** PRELIMINARY

[1]**pre·lim·i·nary** \pri-ˈli-mə-ˌner-ē\ *n, pl* **-nar·ies** [F *préliminaires,* pl., fr. ML *praeliminaris,* adj., preliminary, fr. L *prae-* pre- + *limin-, limen* threshold] (1656) **:** something that precedes or is introductory or preparatory: as **a :** a preliminary scholastic examination **b** *pl, Brit* **:** FRONT MATTER **c :** a preliminary heat or trial (as of a race) **d :** a minor match preceding the main event (as of a boxing card)

[2]**preliminary** *adj* (ca. 1667) **:** coming before and usu. forming a necessary prelude to something else ⟨~ studies⟩ ⟨~ results⟩ — **pre·lim·i·nar·i·ly** \-ˌli-mə-ˈner-ə-lē\ *adv*

pre·lit·er·ate \ˌprē-ˈli-t(ə-)rət\ *adj* (1925) **1 a :** not yet employing writing as a cultural medium **b :** lacking the use of writing **2 :** antedating the use of writing — **preliterate** *n*

pre·load \ˈprē-ˌlōd\ *vt* (1945) **:** to load in advance and esp. at a time removed from that of use ⟨~*ed* software⟩

[1]**pre·lude** \ˈprel-ˌyüd, ˈprāl-; ˈpre-ˌlüd, ˈprā-; *sense 1 also* ˈprē-ˌlüd\ *n* [MF, fr. ML *praeludium,* fr. L *praeludere* to play beforehand, fr. *prae-* + *ludere* to play — more at LUDICROUS] (1561) **1 :** an introductory performance, action, or event preceding and preparing for the principal or a more important matter **2 a :** a musical section or movement introducing the theme or chief subject (as of a fugue or suite) or serving as an introduction to an opera or oratorio **b :** an opening voluntary **c**

\ə\ **abut** \ᵊ\ **kitten,** F table \ər\ **further** \a\ **ash** \ā\ **ace** \ä\ **mop, mar**
\au̇\ **out** \ch\ **chin** \e\ **bet** \ē\ **easy** \g\ **go** \i\ **hit** \ī\ **ice** \j\ **job**
\ŋ\ **sing** \ō\ **go** \ȯ\ **law** \ȯi\ **boy** \th\ **thin** \t͟h\ **the** \ü\ **loot** \u̇\ **foot**
\y\ **yet** \zh\ **vision, beige** \k̲, ⁿ, œ, ue, ʸ\ *see* Guide to Pronunciation

: a separate concert piece usu. for piano or orchestra and based entirely on a short motif

[2]**prelude** *vb* **pre·lud·ed; pre·lud·ing** *vt* (1655) **1** : to serve as a prelude to **2** : to play as a prelude ~ *vi* : to give or serve as a prelude; *esp* : to play a musical introduction — **pre·lud·er** *n*

pre·lu·sion \pri-ˈlü-zhən\ *n* [L *praelusion-, praelusio,* fr. *praeludere*] (1597) : PRELUDE, INTRODUCTION

pre·lu·sive \-ˈlü-siv, -ziv\ *adj* (1605) : constituting or having the form of a prelude : INTRODUCTORY — **pre·lu·sive·ly** *adv*

pre·ma·lig·nant \ˌprē-mə-ˈlig-nənt\ *adj* (ca. 1897) : PRECANCEROUS

pre·man \(ˌ)prē-ˈman, ˈprē-ˌman\ *n* (1921) : any of several extinct primates ancestral to humans and esp. recent humans

pre·ma·ture \ˌprē-mə-ˈtyu̇r, -ˈtu̇r, -ˈchu̇r *also* ˌpre-\ *adj* [L *praematurus* too early, fr. *prae-* + *maturus* ripe, mature] (ca. 1529) : happening, arriving, existing, or performed before the proper, usual, or intended time; *esp* : born after a gestation period of less than 37 weeks ⟨~ babies⟩ — **premature** *n* — **pre·ma·ture·ly** *adv* — **pre·ma·ture·ness** *n* — **pre·ma·tu·ri·ty** \-ˈtyu̇r-ə-tē, -ˈtu̇r-, -ˈchu̇r-\ *n*

pre·max·il·la \ˌprē-mak-ˈsi-lə\ *n* [NL] (1866) : either of a pair of bones of the upper jaw of vertebrates between and in front of the maxillae — **pre·max·il·lary** \(ˌ)prē-ˈmak-sə-ˌler-ē, *chiefly Brit* ˌprē-mak-ˈsi-lə-rē\ *adj or n*

[1]**pre·med** \(ˌ)prē-ˈmed, ˈprē-ˌmed\ *n* (ca. 1928) : a premedical student or course of study

[2]**premed** *adj* (1950) : PREMEDICAL

pre·med·i·cal \(ˌ)prē-ˈme-di-kəl\ *adj* (1904) : preceding and preparing for the professional study of medicine

pre·med·i·tate \(ˌ)prē-ˈme-də-ˌtāt\ *vb* [L *praemeditatus,* pp. of *praemeditari,* fr. *prae-* + *meditari* to meditate] *vt* (ca. 1548) : to think about and revolve in the mind beforehand ~ *vi* : to think, consider, or deliberate beforehand — **pre·med·i·ta·tor** \-ˌtā-tər\ *n*

pre·med·i·tat·ed \-ˌtā-təd\ *adj* (1590) : characterized by fully conscious willful intent and a measure of forethought and planning ⟨~ murder⟩ — **pre·med·i·tat·ed·ly** *adv*

pre·med·i·ta·tion \(ˌ)prē-ˌme-də-ˈtā-shən\ *n* (15c) : an act or instance of premeditating; *specif* : consideration or planning of an act beforehand that shows intent to commit that act

pre·med·i·ta·tive \(ˌ)prē-ˈme-də-ˌtā-tiv\ *adj* (1858) : given to or characterized by premeditation

pre·men·stru·al \(ˌ)prē-ˈmen(t)-strə-wəl, -strəl\ *adj* (1885) : of, relating to, occurring in, or being the period just preceding menstruation ⟨~ tension⟩ ⟨~ symptoms⟩ — **pre·men·stru·al·ly** *adv*

premenstrual dysphoric disorder *n* (1985) : severe premenstrual syndrome characterized by symptoms (as depression and anxiety) that markedly interfere with normal daily functioning

premenstrual syndrome *n* (1944) : a varying group of symptoms manifested by some women prior to menstruation that may include emotional instability, irritability, insomnia, fatigue, anxiety, depression, headache, edema, and abdominal pain — called also *PMS*

premie *var of* PREEMIE

[1]**pre·mier** \pri-ˈmir, -ˈmyir, -ˈmē-ər; ˈprē-ˌ, ˈpre-ˌ\ *adj* [ME *primer, primier,* fr. AF, first, chief, fr. L *primarius* of the first rank — more at PRIMARY] (15c) **1** : first in position, rank, or importance **2** : first in time : EARLIEST

[2]**premier** *n* [F, fr. *premier,* adj., fr. OF] (1711) : PRIME MINISTER — **premier·ship** \-ˌship\ *n*

pre·mier dan·seur \prə-myā-dän-ˈsœr\ *n* [F] (1828) : the principal male dancer in a ballet company

[1]**pre·miere** \pri-ˈmyer, -ˈmir, -ˈmē-ər; ˌpri-mē-ˈer\ *adj* [alter. of [1]*premier*] (1768) : PREMIER

[2]**premiere** *also* **pre·mière** *same as* [1]PREMIERE\ *n* [F *première,* fr. fem. of *premier* first] (1889) **1** : a first performance or exhibition ⟨the ~ of a play⟩ **2** : the chief actress of a theatrical cast

[3]**premiere** *also* **pre·mière** *or* **pre·mier** *same as* [1]PREMIERE\ *vb* **premiered** *also* **pre·mièred; pre·mier·ing** *also* **pre·mièr·ing** *vt* (1933) : to give a first public performance of ~ *vi* **1** : to have a first public performance **2** : to appear for the first time as a star performer

pre·mière dan·seuse \prə-myer-dän-ˈsœz\ *n* [F] (1828) : PRIMA BALLERINA

pre·mil·le·nar·i·an·ism \ˌprē-ˌmi-lə-ˈner-ē-ə-ˌni-zəm\ *n* (1844) : PREMILLENNIALISM — **pre·mil·le·nar·i·an** \-ē-ən\ *adj or n*

pre·mil·len·ni·al \ˌprē-mə-ˈle-nē-əl\ *adj* (1846) **1** : coming before a millennium **2** : holding or relating to premillennialism — **pre·millen·ni·al·ly** \-nē-ə-lē\ *adv*

pre·mil·len·ni·al·ism \-nē-ə-ˌli-zəm\ *n* (1848) : the view that Christ's return will usher in a future millennium of Messianic rule mentioned in Revelation — **pre·mil·len·ni·al·ist** \-nē-ə-list\ *n*

[1]**prem·ise** *also* **prem·iss** \ˈpre-məs\ *n* [in sense 1, fr. ME *premisse,* fr. AF, fr. ML *praemissa,* fr. L, fem. of *praemissus,* pp. of *praemittere* to place ahead, fr. *prae-* pre- + *mittere* to send; in other senses, fr. ME *premisses,* fr. ML *praemissa,* fr. L, neut. pl. of *praemissus*] (14c) **1 a** : a proposition antecedently supposed or proved as a basis of argument or inference; *specif* : either of the first two propositions of a syllogism from which the conclusion is drawn **b** : something assumed or taken for granted : PRESUPPOSITION **2** *pl* : matters previously stated; *specif* : the preliminary and explanatory part of a deed or of a bill in equity **3** *pl* [fr. its being identified in the premises of the deed] **a** : a tract of land with the buildings thereon **b** : a building or part of a building usu. with its appurtenances (as grounds)

[2]**pre·mise** \ˈpre-məs *also* pri-ˈmīz\ *vt* **pre·mised; pre·mis·ing** (1526) **1 a** : to set forth beforehand as an introduction or a postulate **b** : to offer as a premise in an argument **2** : POSTULATE **3** : to base on certain assumptions

[1]**pre·mi·um** \ˈprē-mē-əm\ *n* [L *praemium* booty, profit, reward, fr. *prae-* + *emere* to take, buy — more at REDEEM] (1601) **1 a** : a reward or recompense for a particular act **b** : a sum over and above a regular price paid chiefly as an inducement or incentive **c** : a sum in advance of or in addition to the nominal value of something ⟨bonds callable at a ~ of six percent⟩ **d** : something given free or at a reduced price with the purchase of a product or service **2** : the consideration paid for a contract of insurance **3** : a high value or a value in excess of that normally or usu. expected ⟨put a ~ on accuracy⟩

[2]**premium** *adj* (1844) : of exceptional quality or amount; *also* : higher-priced

[1]**pre·mix** \(ˌ)prē-ˈmiks, ˈprē-ˌ\ *vt* (1927) : to mix before use

[2]**pre·mix** \ˈprē-ˌmiks\ *n* (1937) : a mixture of ingredients designed to be mixed with other ingredients before use

pre·mo·lar \(ˌ)prē-ˈmō-lər\ *adj* (ca. 1859) : situated in front of or preceding the molar teeth; *esp* : being or relating to those teeth of a mammal in front of the true molars and behind the canines when the latter are present — **premolar** *n*

pre·mon·ish \-ˈmä-nish\ *vt* (1526) *archaic* : FOREWARN ~ *vi, archaic* : to give warning in advance

pre·mo·ni·tion \ˌprē-mə-ˈni-shən, ˌpre-\ *n* [ME *premunition,* fr. AF, fr. ML *premunition-, premunitio,* alter. of LL *praemonitio,* fr. L *praemonēre* to warn in advance, fr. *prae-* + *monēre* to warn — more at MIND] (15c) **1** : previous notice or warning : FOREWARNING **2** : anticipation of an event without conscious reason : PRESENTIMENT

pre·mon·i·to·ry \pri-ˈmä-nə-ˌtȯr-ē\ *adj* (1647) : giving warning ⟨a ~ symptom⟩ — **pre·mon·i·to·ri·ly** \-ˌmä-nə-ˈtȯr-ə-lē\ *adv*

Pre·mon·stra·ten·sian \ˌprē-ˌmän(t)-strə-ˈten(t)-shən\ *n* [ML *praemonstratensis,* fr. *praemonstratensis* of Prémontré, fr. *Praemonstratus* Prémontré] (1695) : a member of an order of canons regular founded by St. Norbert at Prémontré near Laon, France, in 1120

pre·mune \(ˌ)prē-ˈmyün\ *adj* [back-formation fr. *premunition*] (1948) : exhibiting premunition

pre·mu·ni·tion \ˌprē-myu̇-ˈni-shən\ *n* [L *praemunition-, praemunitio* strengthening of an argument to forestall objections, fr. *praemunire* to fortify in advance, fr. *prae-* + *munire* to fortify — more at MUNITION] (1607) **1** *archaic* : an advance provision of protection **2 a** : resistance to a disease due to the existence of its causative agent in a state of physiological equilibrium in the host **b** : immunity to a particular infection due to previous presence of the causative agent

pre·name \ˈprē-ˌnām\ *n* (1894) : FORENAME

pre·na·tal \(ˌ)prē-ˈnā-tᵊl\ *adj* (1826) **1** : occurring, existing, or performed before birth ⟨~ care⟩ **2** : providing or receiving prenatal medical care ⟨a ~ clinic⟩ ⟨~ patients⟩ — **pre·na·tal·ly** \-tᵊl-ē\ *adv*

[1]**pre·nom·i·nate** \(ˌ)prē-ˈnä-mə-nət\ *adj* [LL *praenominatus,* pp. of *praenominare* to name before, fr. L *prae-* + *nominare* to name — more at NOMINATE] (1513) *obs* : previously mentioned

[2]**pre·nom·i·nate** \-ˌnāt\ *vt* (1547) *obs* : to mention previously

pre·no·tion \(ˌ)prē-ˈnō-shən, ˈprē-ˌ\ *n* [L *praenotion-, praenotio* preconception, fr. *prae-* + *notio* idea, conception — more at NOTION] (1588) **1** : PRESENTIMENT, PREMONITION **2** : PRECONCEPTION

[1]**pren·tice** \ˈpren-təs\ *n* [ME *prentis,* short for *apprentis*] (14c) : APPRENTICE 1, LEARNER — **prentice** *adj*

[2]**prentice** *vt* **pren·ticed; pren·tic·ing** (1598) : APPRENTICE

pre·nup·tial \(ˌ)prē-ˈnəp-shəl, -chəl, ÷-chə-wəl\ *adj* (1869) : made or occurring before marriage ⟨a ~ party⟩

prenuptial agreement *n* (1978) : an agreement made between a man and a woman before marrying in which they give up future rights to each other's property in the event of divorce or death — called also *pre·nup* \ˈprē-ˌnəp\, *prenuptial*

pre·oc·cu·pan·cy \(ˌ)prē-ˈä-kyə-pən(t)-sē\ *n* (ca. 1755) **1** : an act or the right of taking possession before another **2** : the condition of being completely busied or preoccupied

pre·oc·cu·pa·tion \(ˌ)prē-ˌä-kyə-ˈpā-shən\ *n* (1603) **1** : an act of preoccupying : the state of being preoccupied **2 a** : extreme or excessive concern with something **b** : something that preoccupies one

pre·oc·cu·pied \(ˌ)prē-ˈä-kyə-ˌpīd\ *adj* (1842) **1** : previously applied to another group and unavailable for use in a new sense — used of a biological generic or specific name **2 a** : lost in thought; *also* : absorbed in some preoccupation **b** : already occupied **syn** see ABSTRACTED

pre·oc·cu·py \-ˌpī\ *vt* [L *praeoccupare,* lit., to seize in advance, fr. *prae-* + *occupare* to seize, occupy] (1567) **1** : to engage or engross the interest or attention of beforehand or preferentially **2** : to take possession of or fill beforehand or before another

pre–op \ˈprē-ˈäp\ *adj* (1934) : PREOPERATIVE

pre·op·er·a·tive \(ˌ)prē-ˈä-p(ə-)rə-tiv, -pə-ˌrā-\ *adj* (1904) **1** : occurring before a surgical operation ⟨~ care⟩ **2** : having not yet undergone a surgical operation — **pre·op·er·a·tive·ly** *adv*

pre·or·dain \ˌprē-ȯr-ˈdān\ *vt* (1533) : to decree or ordain in advance : FOREORDAIN — **pre·or·dain·ment** \-mənt\ *n* — **pre·or·di·na·tion** \(ˌ)prē-ˌȯr-də-ˈnā-shən\ *n*

pre·ovu·la·to·ry \(ˌ)prē-ˈäv-yə-lə-ˌtȯr-ē, -ˈōv-\ *adj* (1935) : occurring or existing in or typical of the period immediately preceding ovulation

pre–owned \(ˌ)prē-ˈōnd, ˈprē-ˌ\ *adj* (1956) : SECONDHAND, USED

[1]**prep** \ˈprep\ *n* (1862) **1** : PREPARATION **2** : PREPARATORY SCHOOL **3** : a preliminary trial for a racehorse

[2]**prep** *vb* **prepped; prep·ping** *vi* (1915) **1** : to attend preparatory school **2** [short for *prepare*] : to get ready ~ *vt* : PREPARE; *esp* : to prepare for an operation or examination ⟨nurses *prepped* the patient⟩

pre·pack·age \(ˌ)prē-ˈpa-kij\ *vt* (1945) : to package (as food or a manufactured article) before offering for sale to the consumer

prep·a·ra·tion \ˌpre-pə-ˈrā-shən\ *n* [ME *preparacion,* fr. MF *preparation,* fr. L *praeparation-, praeparatio,* fr. *praeparare* to prepare] (14c) **1** : the action or process of making something ready for use or service or of getting ready for some occasion, test, or duty **2** : a state of being prepared **3** : a preparatory act or measure **4** : something that is prepared; *specif* : a medicinal substance made ready for use

[1]**pre·par·a·tive** \pri-ˈpa-rə-tiv\ *n* (14c) : something that prepares the way for or serves as a preliminary to something else : PREPARATION

[2]**preparative** *adj* (ca. 1530) : PREPARATORY — **pre·par·a·tive·ly** *adv*

pre·par·a·tor \pri-ˈpa-rə-tər\ *n* (1762) : one that prepares; *specif* : a person who prepares scientific specimens or museum displays

pre·pa·ra·to·ry \pri-ˈpa-rə-ˌtȯr-ē *also* ˈpre-p(ə-)rə-\ *adj* (15c) : preparing or serving to prepare for something : INTRODUCTORY — **pre·pa·ra·to·ri·ly** \pri-ˌpa-rə-ˈtȯr-ə-lē *also* ˌpre-p(ə-)rə-\ *adv*

preparatory school *n* (1822) **1** : a usu. private school preparing students primarily for college **2** *Brit* : a private elementary school preparing students primarily for British public schools

preparatory to *prep* (1649) : in preparation for

pre·pare \pri-ˈper\ *vb* **pre·pared; pre·par·ing** [ME, fr. MF *preparer,* fr. L *praeparare,* fr. *prae-* pre- + *parare* to procure, prepare — more at PARE] *vt* (15c) **1 a** : to make ready beforehand for some purpose, use, or activity ⟨~ food for dinner⟩ **b** : to put in a proper state of mind ⟨is *prepared* to listen⟩ **2** : to work out the details of : plan in advance ⟨*preparing* a campaign strategy⟩ **3 a** : to put together : COMPOUND

⟨~ a prescription⟩ **b :** to put into written form ⟨~ a report⟩ ~ *vi* **:** to get ready ⟨*preparing* for a career⟩ — **pre·par·er** *n*

prepared *adj* (1663) **:** subjected to a special process or treatment — **pre·pared·ly** \-ˈperd-lē, -ˈper-əd-\ *adv*

pre·pared·ness \pri-ˈper-əd-nəs *also* -ˈperd-nəs\ *n* (1590) **:** the quality or state of being prepared; *esp* **:** a state of adequate preparation in case of war

pre·pay \(ˌ)prē-ˈpā\ *vt* **-paid** \-ˈpād\; **-pay·ing** (1839) **:** to pay or pay the charge on in advance — **pre·pay·ment** \-ˈpā-mənt\ *n*

prepd *abbr* prepared

pre·pense \pri-ˈpen(t)s\ *adj* [by shortening & alter. fr. earlier *purpensed,* fr. ME, pp. of *purpensen* to deliberate, premeditate, fr. AF *purpenser,* fr. *pur-* thoroughly + *penser* to think — more at PURCHASE, PENSIVE] (1702) **:** planned beforehand **:** PREMEDITATED — usu. used postpositively ⟨malice ~⟩ — **pre·pense·ly** *adv*

pre·plant \ˌprē-ˈplant, ˈprē-ˌ\ *also* **pre·plant·ing** \-ˈplan-tiŋ\ *adj* (1961) **:** occurring or used before planting a crop ⟨~ soil fertilization⟩

pre·pon·der·ance \pri-ˈpän-d(ə-)rən(t)s\ *n* (1681) **1 :** a superiority in weight, power, importance, or strength **2 a :** a superiority or excess in number or quantity **b :** MAJORITY

pre·pon·der·an·cy \-d(ə-)rən(t)-sē\ *n* (1646) **:** PREPONDERANCE

pre·pon·der·ant \pri-ˈpän-d(ə-)rənt\ *adj* (15c) **1 :** having superior weight, force, or influence **2 :** having greater prevalence ***syn*** see DOMINANT — **pre·pon·der·ant·ly** *adv*

[1]**pre·pon·der·ate** \pri-ˈpän-də-ˌrāt\ *vb* **-at·ed; -at·ing** [L *praeponderatus,* pp. of *praeponderare,* fr. *prae-* + *ponder-, pondus* weight — more at PENDANT] *vi* (1623) **1 :** to exceed in weight **2 :** to exceed in influence, power, or importance **3 :** to exceed in numbers ~ *vt* **1** *archaic* **:** OUTWEIGH **2** *archaic* **:** to weigh down — **pre·pon·der·a·tion** \-ˌpän-də-ˈrā-shən, ˌprē-\ *n*

[2]**pre·pon·der·ate** \-ˈpän-də-rət\ *adj* (1802) **:** PREPONDERANT — **pre·pon·der·ate·ly** *adv*

prep·o·si·tion \ˌpre-pə-ˈzi-shən\ *n* [ME *preposicioun,* fr. AF *preposicion,* fr. L *praeposition-, praepositio,* fr. *praeponere* to put in front, fr. *prae-* pre- + *ponere* to put — more at POSITION] (14c) **:** a function word that typically combines with a noun phrase to form a phrase which usu. expresses a modification or predication — **prep·o·si·tion·al** \-ˈzish-nəl, -ˈzi-shə-nᵊl\ *adj* — **prep·o·si·tion·al·ly** *adv*

pre·pos·i·tive \pri-ˈpä-zə-tiv, -ˈpäz-tiv\ *adj* [LL *praepositivus,* fr. L *praepositus,* pp. of *praeponere*] (1583) **:** put before **:** PREFIXED — **pre·pos·i·tive·ly** *adv*

pre·pos·sess \ˌprē-pə-ˈzes *also* -ˈses\ *vt* (1614) **1** *obs* **:** to take previous possession of **2 :** to cause to be preoccupied **3 :** to influence beforehand esp. favorably

pre·pos·sess·ing \-ˈze-siŋ, -ˈse-\ *adj* (1642) **1** *archaic* **:** creating prejudice **2 :** tending to create a favorable impression **:** ATTRACTIVE

pre·pos·ses·sion \ˌprē-pə-ˈze-shən *also* -ˈse-\ *n* (1648) **1** *archaic* **:** prior possession **2 :** an attitude, belief, or impression formed beforehand **:** PREJUDICE **3 :** an exclusive concern with one idea or object **:** PREOCCUPATION ***syn*** see PREDILECTION

pre·pos·ter·ous \pri-ˈpäs-t(ə-)rəs\ *adj* [L *praeposterus,* lit., in the wrong order, fr. *prae-* + *posterus* hinder, following — more at POSTERIOR] (1542) **:** contrary to nature, reason, or common sense **:** ABSURD — **pre·pos·ter·ous·ly** *adv* — **pre·pos·ter·ous·ness** *n*

pre·po·ten·cy \(ˌ)prē-ˈpō-tᵊn(t)-sē\ *n* (1646) **1 :** the quality or state of being prepotent **:** PREDOMINANCE **2 :** unusual ability of an individual or strain to transmit its characters to offspring because of homozygosity for numerous dominant genes

pre·po·tent \-tᵊnt\ *adj* [ME, fr. L *praepotent-, praepotens,* fr. *prae-* + *potens* powerful — more at POTENT] (15c) **1 a :** having exceptional power, authority, or influence **b :** exceeding others in power **2 :** exhibiting genetic prepotency — **pre·po·tent·ly** *adv*

[1]**prep·py** *or* **prep·pie** \ˈpre-pē\ *n, pl* **prep·pies** [[1]*prep*] (1967) **1 :** a student at or a graduate of a preparatory school **2 :** a person deemed to dress or behave like a preppy

[2]**preppy** *or* **preppie** *adj* (1967) **1 :** relating to, characteristic of, or being a preppy **2 :** relating to or being a style of dress characterized esp. by classic clothing and neat appearance — **prep·pi·ly** \ˈpre-pə-lē\ *adv* — **prep·pi·ness** \ˈpre-pē-nəs\ *n*

pre·pran·di·al \(ˌ)prē-ˈpran-dē-əl\ *adj* (1822) **:** of, relating to, or suitable for the time just before dinner ⟨a ~ drink⟩

pre·preg \ˌprē-ˈpreg, ˈprē-ˌ\ *n* [*pre-* + im*preg*nated] (1954) **:** a reinforcing or molding material (as paper or glass cloth) already impregnated with a synthetic resin

[1]**pre·print** \ˈprē-ˌprint, ˌprē-ˈprint\ *n* (1889) **1 :** an issue of a technical paper often in preliminary form before its publication in a journal **2 :** something (as an advertisement) printed before the rest of the publication in which it is to appear

[2]**pre·print** \(ˌ)prē-ˈprint\ *vt* (1926) **:** to print in advance for later use

pre·pro·cess \(ˌ)prē-ˈprä-ˌses, -ˈprō-, -səs\ *vt* (1942) **:** to do preliminary processing of (as data) — **pre·pro·ces·sor** \-ˌse-sər; -sə-sər, -ˌsȯr\ *n*

pre·pro·fes·sion·al \ˌprē-prə-ˈfesh-nəl, -ˈfe-shə-nᵊl\ *adj* (1926) **:** of or relating to the period preceding specific study for or practice of a profession

prep school *n* (1895) **:** PREPARATORY SCHOOL

prepub *abbr* prepublication

pre·pu·ber·al \(ˌ)prē-ˈpyü-b(ə-)rəl\ *adj* (ca. 1935) **:** PREPUBERTAL

pre·pu·ber·tal \-bər-tᵊl\ *adj* (1859) **:** of, relating to, being in, or occurring in prepuberty ⟨~ children⟩ ⟨~ growth⟩

pre·pu·ber·ty \-bər-tē\ *n* (1922) **:** the period of development immediately preceding puberty

pre·pu·bes·cence \ˌprē-pyü-ˈbe-sᵊn(t)s\ *n* (1916) **:** PREPUBERTY

pre·pu·bes·cent \-sᵊnt\ *adj* (1904) **:** PREPUBERTAL — **prepubescent** *n*

pre·puce \ˈprē-ˌpyüs\ *n* [ME, fr. AF, fr. L *praeputium*] (15c) **:** FORESKIN; *also* **:** a similar fold of skin investing the clitoris — **pre·pu·tial** \prē-ˈpyü-shəl\ *adj*

pre·quel \ˈprē-kwəl\ *n* [*pre-* + *-quel* (as in *sequel*)] (1972) **:** a work (as a novel or a play) whose story precedes that of an earlier work

Pre–Ra·pha·el·ite \(ˌ)prē-ˈra-fē-ə-ˌlīt, -ˈrā-, -ˈrä-\ *n* (1850) **1 a :** a member of a brotherhood of artists formed in England in 1848 to restore the artistic principles and practices regarded as characteristic of Italian art before Raphael **b :** an artist or writer influenced by this brotherhood **2 :** a modern artist dedicated to restoring early Renaissance ideals or methods — **Pre–Raphaelite** *adj* — **Pre–Ra·pha·el·it·ism** \-ˌlī-ˌti-zəm\ *n*

pre·reg·is·tra·tion \ˌprē-ˌre-jə-ˈstrā-shən\ *n* (1967) **:** a special registration (as for returning students) prior to an official registration period — **pre·reg·is·ter** \(ˌ)prē-ˈre-jə-stər\ *vi*

pre·req·ui·site \(ˌ)prē-ˈre-kwə-zət\ *n* (1633) **:** something that is necessary to an end or to the carrying out of a function — **prerequisite** *adj*

pre·rog·a·tive \pri-ˈrä-gə-tiv\ *n* [ME, fr. AF & L; AF, fr. L *praerogativa,* Roman century voting first in the comitia, privilege, fr. fem. of *praerogativus* voting first, fr. *praerogatus,* pp. of *praerogare* to ask for an opinion before another, fr. *prae-* + *rogare* to ask — more at RIGHT] (15c) **1 a :** an exclusive or special right, power, or privilege: as **(1) :** one belonging to an office or an official body **(2) :** one belonging to a person, group, or class of individuals **(3) :** one possessed by a nation as an attribute of sovereignty **b :** the discretionary power inhering in the British Crown **2 :** a distinctive excellence — **pre·rog·a·tived** \-tivd\ *adj*

pres *abbr* **1** present **2** president

[1]**pres·age** \ˈpre-sij, *also* pri-ˈsāj\ *n* [ME, fr. L *praesagium,* fr. *praesagus* having a foreboding, fr. *prae-* + *sagus* prophetic — more at SEEK] (14c) **1 :** something that foreshadows or portends a future event **:** OMEN **2 :** an intuition or feeling of what is going to happen in the future **3** *archaic* **:** PROGNOSTICATION **4 :** warning or indication of the future — **pre·sage·ful** \pri-ˈsāj-fəl\ *adj*

[2]**pre·sage** \ˈpre-sij, pri-ˈsāj\ *vb* **pre·saged; pre·sag·ing** *vt* (1562) **1 :** to give an omen or warning of **:** FORESHADOW **2 :** FORETELL, PREDICT ~ *vi* **:** to make or utter a prediction — **pre·sag·er** *n, obs*

pre·sanc·ti·fied \(ˌ)prē-ˈsaŋ(k)-ti-ˌfīd\ *adj* (1758) **:** consecrated at a previous service — used of eucharistic elements

Presb *abbr* Presbyterian

pres·by·ope \ˈprez-bē-ˌōp; ˈpres-bē-, -pē-\ *n* [prob. fr. F, fr. NL *presbyopia*] (ca. 1857) **:** one affected with presbyopia

pres·by·o·pia \ˌprez-bē-ˈō-pē-ə, ˌpres-\ *n* [NL, fr. GK *presbys* old man + NL *-opia*] (1793) **:** a visual condition which becomes apparent esp. in middle age and in which loss of elasticity of the lens of the eye causes defective accommodation and inability to focus sharply for near vision — **pres·by·o·pic** \-ˈō-pik, -ˈä-\ *adj or n*

pres·by·ter \ˈprez-bə-tər, ˈpres-\ *n* [LL, elder, priest, fr. Gk *presbyteros,* compar. of *presbys* old man, elder; akin to Gk *pro* before and Gk *bainein* to go — more at FOR, COME] (1597) **1 :** a member of the governing body of an early Christian church **2 :** a member of the order of priests in churches having episcopal hierarchies that include bishops, priests, and deacons **3 :** ELDER 4b — **pres·byt·er·ate** \prez-ˈbi-tə-rət, pres-, -ˌrāt\ *n*

[1]**pres·by·te·ri·al** \ˌprez-bə-ˈtir-ē-əl, ˌpres-\ *adj* (ca. 1600) **:** of or relating to presbyters or a presbytery — **pres·by·te·ri·al·ly** \-ē-ə-lē\ *adv*

[2]**presbyterial** *n, often cap* (1928) **:** an organization of Presbyterian women associated with a presbytery

[1]**Pres·by·te·ri·an** \-ē-ən\ *n* (1640) **:** a member of a Presbyterian church

[2]**Presbyterian** *adj* (1641) **1** *often not cap* **:** characterized by a graded system of representative ecclesiastical bodies (as presbyteries) exercising legislative and judicial powers **2 :** of, relating to, or constituting a Protestant Christian church that is presbyterian in government and traditionally Calvinistic in doctrine — **Pres·by·te·ri·an·ism** \-ē-ə-ˌni-zəm\ *n*

pres·by·tery \ˈprez-bə-ˌter-ē, ˈpres-, -bə-trē\ *n, pl* **-ter·ies** [ME & LL; ME *presbytory* part of church reserved for clergy, fr. LL *presbyterium* group of presbyters, part of church reserved for clergy, fr. Gk *presbyterion* group of presbyters, fr. *presbyteros* elder, priest] (15c) **1 :** the part of a church reserved for the officiating clergy **2 :** a ruling body in presbyterian churches consisting of the ministers and representative elders from congregations within a district **3 :** the jurisdiction of a presbytery **4 :** the house of a Roman Catholic parish priest

[1]**pre·school** \ˈprē-ˌskül, (ˌ)prē-ˈ\ *adj* (1914) **:** of, relating to, or constituting the period in a child's life that ordinarily precedes attendance at elementary school

[2]**pre·school** \ˈprē-ˌskül\ *n* (ca. 1925) **:** a school for children usu. younger than those attending elementary school or kindergarten **:** NURSERY SCHOOL

pre·school·er \-ˌskü-lər\ *n* (1946) **1 :** a child not yet old enough for school **2 :** a child attending a preschool

pre·science \ˈpre-sh(ē-)ən(t)s, ˈprē-, -s(ē-)ən(t)s\ *n* [ME, fr. LL *praescientia,* fr. L *praescient-, praesciens,* prp. of *praescire* to know beforehand, fr. *prae-* + *scire* to know — more at SCIENCE] (14c) **:** foreknowledge of events: **a :** divine omniscience **b :** human anticipation of the course of events **:** FORESIGHT — **pre·scient** \-sh(ē-)ənt, -s(ē-)ənt\ *adj* — **pre·scient·ly** *adv*

pre·sci·en·tif·ic \ˌprē-ˌsī-ən-ˈti-fik\ *adj* (1858) **:** of, relating to, or having the characteristics of a period before the rise of modern science or a state prior to the application of the scientific method

pre·scind \pri-ˈsind\ *vb* [L *praescindere* to cut off in front, fr. *prae-* + *scindere* to cut — more at SHED] *vi* (1650) **:** to withdraw one's attention ~ *vt* **:** to detach for purposes of thought

pre·score \(ˌ)prē-ˈskȯr\ *vt* (1937) **:** to record (as sound) in advance for use when the corresponding scenes are photographed in making movies

pre·scribe \pri-ˈskrīb\ *vb* **pre·scribed; pre·scrib·ing** [ME, fr. L *praescribere* to write at the beginning, dictate, order, fr. *prae-* + *scribere* to write — more at SCRIBE] *vi* (15c) **1 :** to lay down a rule **:** DICTATE **2** [ME, fr. ML *praescribere,* fr. L, to write at the beginning] **:** to claim a title to something by right of prescription **3 :** to write or give medical prescriptions **4 :** to become by prescription invalid or unenforceable ~ *vt* **1 a :** to lay down as a guide, direction, or rule of action **:** ORDAIN **b :** to specify with authority **2 :** to designate or order the use of as a remedy ⟨*prescribed* a painkiller⟩ ⟨a *prescribed* burn to restore natural forest conditions⟩ — **pre·scrib·er** *n*

pre·script \ˈprē-ˌskript, pri-ˈ\ *adj* [ME, fr. L *praescriptus,* pp. of *praescribere*] (ca. 1540) : prescribed as a rule — **pre·script** \ˈprē-ˌskript\ *n*

pre·scrip·tion \pri-ˈskrip-shən\ *n* [partly fr. ME *prescripcion* establishment of a claim, fr. AF, fr. LL *praescription-, praescriptio,* fr. L, act of writing at the beginning, order, limitation of subject matter, fr. *praescribere;* partly fr. L *praescription-, praescriptio* order] (14c) **1 a** : the establishment of a claim of title to something under common law usu. by use and enjoyment for a period fixed by statute **b** : the right or title acquired under common law by such possession **2** : the process of making claim to something by long use and enjoyment **3** : the action of laying down authoritative rules or directions **4 a** : a written direction for a therapeutic or corrective agent; *specif* : one for the preparation and use of a medicine **b** : a prescribed medicine **c** : something (as a recommendation) resembling a doctor's prescription ⟨∼*s* for economic recovery⟩ **5 a** : ancient or long continued custom **b** : a claim founded upon ancient custom or long continued use **6** : something prescribed as a rule

prescription drug *n* (1951) : a drug that can be obtained only by means of a physician's prescription

pre·scrip·tive \pri-ˈskrip-tiv\ *adj* (1748) **1** : serving to prescribe ⟨∼ rules of usage⟩ **2** : acquired by, founded on, or determined by prescription or by long-standing custom — **pre·scrip·tive·ly** *adv*

pre·se·lect \ˌprē-sə-ˈlekt\ *vt* (ca. 1859) : to choose in advance usu. on the basis of a particular criterion — **pre·se·lec·tion** \-ˈlek-shən\ *n*

pre·sell \(ˌ)prē-ˈsel\ *vt* **-sold** \-ˈsōld\; **-sell·ing** (1947) **1** : to precondition (as a customer) for subsequent purchase or create advance demand for (as a product) esp. through marketing strategies **2** : to sell in advance ⟨raised money to publish the book by *preselling* film rights⟩

pres·ence \ˈpre-zᵊn(t)s\ *n* (14c) **1** : the fact or condition of being present **2 a** : the part of space within one's immediate vicinity **b** : the neighborhood of one of superior esp. royal rank **3** *archaic* : COMPANY 2a **4** : one that is present: as **a** : the actual person or thing that is present **b** : something present of a visible or concrete nature **5 a** : the bearing, carriage, or air of a person; *esp* : stately or distinguished bearing **b** : a noteworthy quality of poise and effectiveness ⟨the actor's commanding ∼⟩ **6** : something (as a spirit) felt or believed to be present

presence of mind (1665) : self-control so maintained in an emergency or in an embarrassing situation that one can say or do the right thing

1pres·ent \ˈpre-zᵊnt\ *n* [ME, fr. AF, fr. *presenter*] (13c) : something presented : GIFT

2pre·sent \pri-ˈzent\ *vb* [ME, fr. AF *presenter,* fr. L *praesentare,* fr. *praesent-, praesens,* adj.] *vt* (14c) **1 a** (1) : to bring or introduce into the presence of someone esp. of superior rank or status (2) : to introduce socially **b** : to bring (as a play) before the public **2** : to make a gift to **3** : to give or bestow formally **4 a** : to lay (as a charge) before a court as an object of inquiry **b** : to bring a formal public charge, indictment, or presentment against **5** : to nominate to a benefice **6 a** : to offer to view : SHOW **b** : to bring to one's attention ⟨this ∼*s* a problem⟩ **7** : to act the part of : PERFORM **8** : to aim, point, or direct (as a weapon) so as to face something or in a particular direction ∼ *vi* **1** : to present a weapon **2** : to become manifest **3** : to come forward as a patient **4** : to make a presentation ***syn*** see GIVE — **pre·sent·er** *n*

3pres·ent \ˈpre-zᵊnt\ *adj* [ME, fr. AF, fr. L *praesent-, praesens,* fr. prp. of *praeesse* to be before one, fr. *prae-* pre- + *esse* to be — more at IS] (14c) **1** : now existing or in progress **2 a** : being in view or at hand **b** : existing in something mentioned or under consideration **3** : constituting the one actually involved, at hand, or being considered **4** : of, relating to, or constituting a verb tense that is expressive of present time or the time of speaking **5** *obs* : ATTENTIVE **6** *archaic* : INSTANT, IMMEDIATE — **pres·ent·ness** *n*

4pres·ent \ˈpre-zᵊnt\ *n* (14c) **1 a** *obs* : present occasion or affair **b** *pl* : the present words or statements; *specif* : the legal instrument or other writing in which these words are used **2 a** : the present tense of a language **b** : a verb form in the present tense **3** : the present time — **at present** : at or during this time : NOW

pre·sent·able \pri-ˈzen-tə-bəl\ *adj* (ca. 1626) **1** : capable of being presented **2** : being in condition to be seen or inspected esp. by the critical — **pre·sent·abil·i·ty** \-ˌzen-tə-ˈbi-lə-tē\ *n* — **pre·sent·able·ness** \-ˈzen-tə-bəl-nəs\ *n* — **pre·sent·ably** \-blē\ *adv*

pre·sent arms \pri-ˈzent-\ *n* [fr. the command *present arms!*] (ca. 1884) **1** : a position in the manual of arms in which the rifle is held vertically in front of the body **2** : a command to assume the position of present arms or to give a hand salute

pre·sen·ta·tion \ˌprē-ˌzen-ˈtā-shən, ˌpre-zᵊn-, ˌprē-zᵊn-\ *n* (15c) **1 a** : the act of presenting **b** : the act, power, or privilege esp. of a patron of applying to the bishop or ordinary for instituting someone into a benefice **2** : something presented: as **a** : a symbol or image that represents something **b** : something offered or given : GIFT **c** : something set forth for the attention of the mind **d** : a descriptive or persuasive account (as by a salesman of a product) **e** : a presenting symptom or group of symptoms ⟨clinical ∼ of appendicitis⟩ **3** : the position in which the fetus lies in the uterus in labor with respect to the opening of the uterus **4** : an immediate object of perception, cognition, or memory **5** *often cap* : a church feast on November 21 celebrating the presentation of the Virgin Mary in the temple **6** : the method by which radio, navigation, or radar information is given to the operator (as the pilot of an airplane) — **pre·sen·ta·tion·al** \-shnəl, -shə-nᵊl\ *adj*

pre·sen·ta·tive \pri-ˈzen-tə-tiv, ˈpre-zᵊn-ˌtā-\ *adj* (ca. 1842) : known, knowing, or capable of being known directly rather than through cogitation

pres·ent–day \ˈpre-zᵊnt-ˈdā\ *adj* (1887) : now existing or occurring

pre·sen·tee \ˌpre-zᵊn-ˈtē, pri-ˌzen-\ *n* (15c) : one who is presented or to whom something is presented

pre·sen·tient \pri-ˈsen(t)-sh(ē-)ənt, ˈprē-; pri-ˈzen(t)-\ *adj* [L *praesentient-, praesentiens,* prp. of *praesentire*] (1814) : having a presentiment

pre·sen·ti·ment \pri-ˈzen-tə-mənt\ *n* [F *pressentiment,* fr. MF, fr. *pressentir* to have a presentiment, fr. L *praesentire* to feel beforehand, fr. *prae-* + *sentire* to feel — more at SENSE] (1714) : a feeling that something will or is about to happen : PREMONITION — **pre·sen·ti·men·tal** \-ˌzen-tə-ˈmen-tᵊl\ *adj*

pres·ent·ism \ˈpre-zᵊn-ˌti-zəm\ *n* [3*present*] (1923) : an attitude toward the past dominated by present-day attitudes and experiences — **pres·ent·ist** \-zᵊn-tist\ *adj*

pres·ent·ly \ˈpre-zᵊnt-lē\ *adv* (14c) **1 a** *archaic* : at once **b** : without undue delay : BEFORE LONG **2** : at the present time : NOW

usage Both senses 1b and 2 are flourishing in current English, but many commentators have objected to sense 2. Since this sense has been in continuous use since the 15th century, it is not clear why it is objectionable. Perhaps a note in the *Oxford English Dictionary* (1909) that the sense has been obsolete since the 17th century in literary English is to blame, but the note goes on to observe that the sense is in regular use in most English dialects. The last citation in that dictionary is from a 1901 Leeds newspaper, written in Standard English. Sense 2 is most common in contexts relating to business and politics ⟨the fastest-rising welfare cost is Medicaid, *presently* paid by the states and cities —William Safire⟩

pre·sent·ment \pri-ˈzent-mənt\ *n* (14c) **1** : the act of presenting to an authority a formal statement of a matter to be dealt with; *specif* : the notice taken or statement made by a grand jury of an offense from their own knowledge without a bill of indictment laid before them **2** : the act of offering at the proper time and place a document (as a bill of exchange) that calls for acceptance or payment by another **3 a** : the act of presenting to view or consciousness **b** : something set forth, presented, or exhibited **c** : the aspect in which something is presented

present participle *n* (1864) : a participle that typically expresses present action in relation to the time expressed by the finite verb in its clause and that in English is formed with the suffix *-ing* and is used in the formation of the progressive tenses

present perfect *adj* (1887) : of, relating to, or constituting a verb tense that is formed in English with *have* and that expresses action or state completed at the time of speaking — **present perfect** *n*

present tense *n* (14c) : the tense of a verb that expresses action or state in the present time and is used of what occurs or is true at the time of speaking and of what is habitual or characteristic or is always or necessarily true, that is sometimes used to refer to action in the past, and that is sometimes used for future events

present value *n* (1831) : the sum of money which if invested now at a given rate of compound interest will accumulate exactly to a specified amount at a specified future date

pres·er·va·tion·ist \ˌpre-zər-ˈvā-sh(ə-)nist\ *n* (1927) : one who advocates preservation (as of a biological species or a historical landmark)

1pre·ser·va·tive \pri-ˈzər-və-tiv\ *adj* (14c) : having the power of preserving

2preservative *n* (15c) : something that preserves or has the power of preserving; *specif* : an additive used to protect against decay, discoloration, or spoilage

1pre·serve \pri-ˈzərv\ *vb* **pre·served; pre·serv·ing** [ME, fr. ML *praeservare,* fr. LL, to observe beforehand, fr. L *prae-* + *servare* to keep, guard, observe — more at CONSERVE] *vt* (14c) **1** : to keep safe from injury, harm, or destruction : PROTECT **2 a** : to keep alive, intact, or free from decay **b** : MAINTAIN **3 a** : to keep or save from decomposition **b** : to can, pickle, or similarly prepare for future use **4** : to keep up and reserve for personal or special use ∼ *vi* **1** : to make preserves **2** : to raise and protect game for purposes of sport **3** : to be able to be preserved (as by canning) — **pre·serv·abil·i·ty** \-ˌzər-və-ˈbi-lə-tē\ *n* — **pre·serv·able** \-ˈzər-və-bəl\ *adj* — **pres·er·va·tion** \ˌpre-zər-ˈvā-shən\ *n* — **pre·serv·er** \pri-ˈzər-vər\ *n*

2preserve *n* (1600) **1** : fruit canned or made into jams or jellies or cooked whole or in large pieces in a syrup so as to keep its shape — often used in pl. **2** : an area restricted for the protection and preservation of natural resources (as animals or plants) ⟨a game ∼ for regulated hunting or fishing⟩ ⟨nature ∼*s*⟩ **3** : something regarded as reserved for certain persons

1pre·set \ˈprē-ˌset\ *vt* **-set; -set·ting** (1929) : to set in advance

2preset *n* (1953) : something (as a radio station) preprogrammed into a device

pre·shrink \(ˌ)prē-ˈshriŋk, *esp Southern* -ˈsriŋk\ *vt* **-shrank** \-ˈshraŋk, -ˈsraŋk\; **-shrunk** \-ˈshrəŋk, -ˈsrəŋk\ (1926) : to shrink (as a fabric) before making into a garment so that it will not shrink much when washed

pre·side \pri-ˈzīd\ *vi* **pre·sid·ed; pre·sid·ing** [L *praesidēre* to guard, preside over, fr. *prae-* + *sedēre* to sit — more at SIT] (1608) **1** : to exercise guidance, direction, or control **2 a** : to occupy the place of authority : act as president, chairman, or moderator **b** : to occupy a position similar to that of a president or chairman **3** : to occupy a position of featured instrumental performer — usu. used with *at* ⟨*presided* at the organ⟩ — **pre·sid·er** *n*

pres·i·den·cy \ˈpre-zə-dən(t)-sē, ˈprez-dən(t)- *also* ˈpre-zə-ˌden(t)-sē\ *n, pl* **-cies** (1591) **1 a** : the office of president **b** (1) : the office of president of the U.S. (2) : the American governmental institution comprising the office of president and various associated administrative and policy-making agencies **2** : the term during which a president holds office **3** : the action or function of one that presides : SUPERINTENDENCE **4** : a Mormon executive council of the church or a stake consisting of a president and two counselors

pres·i·dent \ˈpre-zə-dənt, ˈprez-dənt, ˈpre-zə-ˌdent *in rapid speech* ˈprezᵊnt\ *n* [ME, fr. AF, fr. L *praesident-, praesidens,* fr. prp. of *praesidēre*] (14c) **1** : an official chosen to preside over a meeting or assembly **2** : an appointed governor of a subordinate political unit **3** : the chief officer of an organization (as a corporation or institution) usu. entrusted with the direction and administration of its policies **4** : the presiding officer of a governmental body **5 a** : an elected official serving as both chief of state and chief political executive in a republic having a presidential government **b** : an elected official having the position of chief of state but usu. only minimal political powers in a republic having a parliamentary government — **pres·i·den·tial** \ˌpre-zə-ˈden(t)-shəl, ˌprez-ˈden(t)-\ *adj* — **pres·i·den·tial·ly** \-sh(ə-)lē\ *adv* — **pres·i·dent·ship** \ˈpre-zə-dənt-ˌship, ˈprez-dənt-, ˈpre-zə-ˌdent-\ *n*

presidential government *n* (1857) : a system of government in which the president is constitutionally independent of the legislature

Presidents' Day *n* (1952) : WASHINGTON'S BIRTHDAY 2

pre·sid·i·al \pri-ˈsi-dē-əl, -ˈzi-\ *adj* [LL *praesidialis,* fr. L *praesidium* garrison, fr. *praesid-, praeses* guard, governor, fr. *praesidēre*] (1611) **1** [F *présidial,* fr. MF, alter. of *presidal,* fr. LL *praesidalis* of a provincial governor, fr. L *praesid-, praeses*] : PROVINCIAL 1 **2 :** of, having, or constituting a garrison **3 :** of or relating to a president

pre·sid·i·ary \-dē-ˌer-ē\ *adj* (1599) : PRESIDIAL 2

pre·si·dio \pri-ˈsē-dē-ˌō, -ˈsi-, -ˈzē-, -ˈzi-\ *n, pl* **-di·os** [Sp, fr. L *praesidium*] (1763) : a garrisoned place; *esp* : a military post or fortified settlement in areas currently or orig. under Spanish control

pre·sid·i·um \pri-ˈsi-dē-əm, prē-, -ˈzi-\ *also* **prae·sid·i·um** \pri-, prē-, prī-\ *n, pl* **-ia** \-dē-ə\ *or* **-iums** [Russ *prezidium,* fr. L *praesidium* garrison] (1920) **1 :** a permanent executive committee selected esp. in Communist countries to act for a larger body **2 :** a nongovernmental executive committee

pre·sig·ni·fy \(ˌ)prē-ˈsig-nə-ˌfī\ *vt* [L *praesignificare,* fr. *prae-* + *significare* to signify] (1586) : to intimate or signify beforehand : PRESAGE

[1]**pre·soak** \(ˌ)prē-ˈsōk\ *vt* (1919) : to soak beforehand

[2]**pre·soak** \ˈprē-ˌsōk\ *n* (1919) **1 :** an instance of presoaking **2 :** a preparation used in presoaking clothes

pre–So·crat·ic \ˌprē-sə-ˈkra-tik, -sō-\ *adj* (1871) : of or relating to Greek philosophers before Socrates — **pre–Socratic** *n*

pre·sort \(ˌ)prē-ˈsȯrt\ *vt* (1951) : to sort (outgoing mail) by zip code usu. before delivery to a post office

[1]**press** \ˈpres\ *n* [ME *presse,* fr. AF, fr. *presser* to press] (13c) **1 a :** a crowd or crowded condition : THRONG **b :** a thronging or crowding forward or together **2 a :** an apparatus or machine by which a substance is cut or shaped, an impression of a body is taken, a material is compressed, pressure is applied to a body, liquid is expressed, or a cutting tool is fed into the work by pressure **b :** a building containing presses or a business using presses **3 :** CLOSET, CUPBOARD **4 a :** an action of pressing or pushing : PRESSURE **b :** an aggressive pressuring defense employed in basketball often over the entire court area **5 :** the properly smoothed and creased condition of a freshly pressed garment ⟨out of ~⟩ **6 a :** PRINTING PRESS **b :** the act or the process of printing **c :** a printing or publishing establishment **7 a :** the gathering and publishing or broadcasting of news : JOURNALISM **b :** newspapers, periodicals, and often radio and television news broadcasting **c :** news reporters, publishers, and broadcasters **d :** comment or notice in newspapers and periodicals ⟨is getting a good ~⟩ **8 :** any of various pressure devices (as one for keeping sporting gear from warping when not in use) **9 :** a lift in weight lifting in which the weight is raised to shoulder height and then smoothly extended overhead without assist from the legs — compare CLEAN AND JERK, SNATCH

[2]**press** *vb* [ME, fr. AF *presser,* fr. L *pressare,* freq. of *premere* to press; prob. akin to Russ na*peret'* to press] *vt* (14c) **1 :** to act upon through steady pushing or thrusting force exerted in contact : SQUEEZE **2 a :** ASSAIL, HARASS **b :** AFFLICT, OPPRESS **3 a :** to squeeze out the juice or contents of **b :** to squeeze with apparatus or instruments to a desired density, smoothness, or shape **4 a :** to exert influence on : CONSTRAIN **b :** to try hard to persuade : BESEECH, ENTREAT **5 :** to move by means of pressure **6 a :** to lay stress or emphasis on **b :** to insist on or request urgently **7 :** to follow through (a course of action) **8 :** to clasp in affection or courtesy **9 :** to make (a phonograph record) from a matrix ~ *vi* **1 :** to crowd closely : MASS **2 :** to force or push one's way **3 :** to seek urgently : CONTEND **4 :** to require haste or speed in action **5 :** to exert pressure **6 :** to take or hold a press **7 :** to employ a press in basketball — **press the flesh :** to greet and shake hands with people esp. while campaigning for political office

[3]**press** *vb* [alter. of obs. *prest* to enlist by giving pay in advance] *vt* (1578) **1 :** to force into service esp. in an army or navy : IMPRESS **2 a :** to take by authority esp. for public use : COMMANDEER **b :** to take and force into any usu. emergency service ~ *vi* : to impress men as soldiers or sailors

[4]**press** *n* (1599) **1 :** impressment into service esp. in a navy **2** *obs* **:** a warrant for impressing recruits

press agent *n* [[1]*press*] (1883) : an agent employed to establish and maintain good public relations through publicity — **press–agent** *vb* — **press–agent·ry** \-ˈā-jən-trē\ *n*

press·board \ˈpres-ˌbȯrd\ *n* (1847) **1 :** IRONING BOARD; *esp* : a small one for sleeves **2 :** a strong highly glazed composition board resembling vulcanized fiber

press box *n* (1889) : a space reserved for reporters (as at a stadium)

press cloth *n* (1899) : a cloth used between an iron and a garment

press conference *n* (1937) : an interview or announcement given by a public figure to the press by appointment

press·er \ˈpre-sər\ *n* (1503) **1 :** one that presses **2 :** PRESS CONFERENCE

press–gang \ˈpres-ˌgaŋ\ *n* [[4]*press*] (1693) : a detachment of men under command of an officer empowered to force men into military or naval service — **press–gang** *vt*

press·ing \ˈpre-siŋ\ *adj* (1591) **1 :** urgently important : CRITICAL ⟨a ~ issue⟩ **2 :** EARNEST, WARM — **press·ing·ly** \ˈpre-siŋ-lē\ *adv*

press kit *n* (1968) : a collection of promotional materials for distribution to the press

press·man \ˈpres-mən, -ˌman\ *n* (1598) **1 :** an operator of a press; *esp* : the operator of a printing press **2** *Brit* : NEWSPAPERMAN

press·mark \-ˌmärk\ *n* [[1]*press* (closet)] (1802) *chiefly Brit* : a mark or number assigned to a book to indicate its location in a library

press of sail (1794) : the fullest amount of sail that a ship can crowd on — called also *press of canvas*

pres·sor \ˈpre-ˌsȯr, -sər\ *adj* [LL, one that presses, fr. L *premere* to press — more at PRESS] (ca. 1890) : raising or tending to raise blood pressure; *also* : involving vasoconstriction

press·room \ˈpres-ˌrüm, -ˌru̇m\ *n* (1683) **1 :** a room in a printing plant containing the printing presses **2 :** a room (as at the White House) for the use of members of the press

press·run \-ˌrən\ *n* (1945) : a continuous operation of a printing press producing a specified number of copies; *also* : the number of copies printed

press secretary *n* (1945) : a person officially in charge of press relations for a usu. prominent public figure

press–up \ˈpres-(ˌ)əp\ *n* (1936) *Brit* : PUSH-UP

[1]**pres·sure** \ˈpre-shər\ *n* [ME, fr. AF, fr. LL *pressura,* fr. L, action of pressing, pressure, fr. *pressus,* pp. of *premere*] (14c) **1 a :** the burden of physical or mental distress **b :** the constraint of circumstance : the weight of social or economic imposition **2 :** the application of force to something by something else in direct contact with it : COMPRESSION **3** *archaic* : IMPRESSION, STAMP **4 a :** the action of a force against an opposing force **b :** the force or thrust exerted over a surface divided by its area **c :** ELECTROMOTIVE FORCE **5 :** the stress or urgency of matters demanding attention : EXIGENCY ⟨people who work well under ~⟩ **6 :** the force of selection that results from one or more agents and tends to reduce a population of organisms ⟨population ~⟩ ⟨predation ~⟩ **7 :** the pressure exerted in every direction by the weight of the atmosphere **8 :** a sensation aroused by moderate compression of a body part or surface — **pres·sure·less** *adj*

[2]**pressure** *vt* **pres·sured; pres·sur·ing** \ˈpre-sh(ə-)riŋ\ (1938) **1 :** to apply pressure to **2 :** PRESSURIZE **3 :** to cook in a pressure cooker

pressure cabin *n* (1935) : a pressurized cabin

pressure cooker *n* (1915) **1 :** an airtight utensil for quick cooking or preserving of foods by means of high-temperature steam under pressure **2 :** a situation or environment that is fraught with emotional or social pressures — **pressure–cook** *vb*

pressure gauge *n* (1862) : a gauge for indicating fluid pressure

pressure group *n* (1928) : an interest group organized to influence public and esp. government policy but not to elect candidates to office

pressure point *n* (1882) **1 :** a discrete point on the body to which pressure is applied (as in acupressure or reflexology) for therapeutic purposes **2 :** a point where a blood vessel can be compressed against underlying bone to slow blood flow and control bleeding

pressure suit *n* (1936) : an inflatable suit for high-altitude or space flight to protect the body from low pressure

pressure wave *n* (1942) : a wave (as a sound wave) in which the propagated disturbance is a variation of pressure in a material medium — called also *P-wave*

pres·sur·ise *Brit var of* PRESSURIZE

pres·sur·ize \ˈpre-shə-ˌrīz\ *vt* **-ized; -iz·ing** (1938) **1 :** to confine the contents of under a pressure greater than that of the outside atmosphere; *esp* : to maintain near-normal atmospheric pressure in during high-altitude or spaceflight (as by means of a supercharger) **2 :** to apply pressure to **3 :** to design to withstand pressure — **pres·sur·i·za·tion** \ˌpre-sh(ə-)rə-ˈzā-shən\ *n* — **pres·sur·iz·er** *n*

press·work \ˈpres-ˌwərk\ *n* (1771) : the operation, management, or product of a printing press; *esp* : the branch of printing concerned with the actual transfer of ink from form or plates to paper

prest \ˈprest\ *adj* [ME, fr. AF, fr. L *praestus* — more at PRESTO] (14c) *obs* : READY

pres·ti·dig·i·ta·tion \ˌpres-tə-ˌdi-jə-ˈtā-shən\ *n* [F, fr. *prestidigitateur* prestidigitator, fr. *preste* nimble, quick (fr. It *presto*) + L *digitus* finger — more at DIGIT] (1859) : SLEIGHT OF HAND, LEGERDEMAIN — **pres·ti·dig·i·ta·tor** \-ˈdi-jə-ˌtā-tər\ *n*

pres·tige \pre-ˈstēzh, -ˈstēj\ *n, often attrib* [F, fr. MF, conjuror's trick, illusion, fr. L *praestigiae,* pl., conjuror's tricks, fr. *praestringere* to graze, blunt, constrict, fr. *prae-* + *stringere* to bind tight — more at STRAIN] (1829) **1 :** standing or estimation in the eyes of people : weight or credit in general opinion **2 :** commanding position in people's minds ***syn*** see INFLUENCE — **pres·tige·ful** \-fəl\ *adj*

pres·ti·gious \pre-ˈsti-jəs, -ˈstē- *also* prə-\ *adj* [L *praestigiosus,* fr. *praestigiae*] (1546) **1** *archaic* : of, relating to, or marked by illusion, conjuring, or trickery **2 :** having prestige : HONORED — **pres·ti·gious·ly** *adv* — **pres·ti·gious·ness** *n*

pres·tis·si·mo \pre-ˈsti-sə-ˌmō\ *adv or adj* [It, fr. *presto* + *-issimo,* suffix denoting a high degree] (ca. 1724) : faster than presto — used as a direction in music

[1]**pres·to** \ˈpres-(ˌ)tō\ *interj* [It, quick, quickly, fr. L *praestus* ready, fr. *praesto* adv., on hand; akin to L *prae* before — more at FOR] (ca. 1599) — used to indicate the sudden appearance or occurrence of something often as if by magic

[2]**presto** *adv or adj* (1644) **1 :** suddenly as if by magic : IMMEDIATELY **2 :** at a rapid tempo — used as a direction in music

[3]**presto** *n, pl* **prestos** (1801) : a presto musical passage or movement

[1]**pre·stress** \(ˌ)prē-ˈstres\ *vt* (1934) : to introduce internal stresses into (as a structural beam) to counteract the stresses that will result from applied load (as in incorporating cables under tension in concrete)

[2]**pre·stress** \ˈprē-ˌstres, ˌprē-ˈ\ *n* (1934) **1 :** the stresses introduced in prestressing **2 :** the process of prestressing **3 :** the condition of being prestressed

pre·sum·able \pri-ˈzü-mə-bəl\ *adj* (1692) : capable of being presumed : acceptable as an assumption

pre·sum·ably \-blē\ *adv* (1846) : by reasonable assumption

pre·sume \pri-ˈzüm\ *vb* **pre·sumed; pre·sum·ing** [ME, fr. LL & AF; AF *presumer,* fr. LL *praesumere* to dare, fr. L, to anticipate, assume, fr. *prae-* + *sumere* to take — more at CONSUME] *vt* (14c) **1 :** to undertake without leave or clear justification : DARE **2 :** to expect or assume esp. with confidence **3 :** to suppose to be true without proof ⟨*presumed* innocent until proved guilty⟩ **4 :** to take for granted : IMPLY ~ *vi* **1 :** to act or proceed presumptuously or on a presumption **2 :** to go beyond what is right or proper — **pre·sumed·ly** \-ˈzü-məd-lē, -ˈzümd-lē\ *adv* — **pre·sum·er** *n*

presuming *adj* (15c) : PRESUMPTUOUS — **pre·sum·ing·ly** \-ˈzü-miŋ-lē\ *adv*

pre·sump·tion \pri-ˈzəm(p)-shən\ *n* [ME *presumpcioun,* fr. AF *presumption,* fr. LL & L; LL *praesumption-, praesumptio* presumptuous attitude, fr. L, assumption, fr. *praesumere*] (13c) **1 :** presumptuous attitude or conduct : AUDACITY **2 a :** an attitude or belief dictated by probability : ASSUMPTION **b :** the ground, reason, or evidence lending probability to a belief **3 :** a legal inference as to the existence or truth of a fact not certainly known that is drawn from the known or proved existence of some other fact

pre·sump·tive \-ˈzəm(p)-tiv\ *adj* (15c) **1 :** based on probability or presumption ⟨the ~ nominee⟩ **2 :** giving grounds for reasonable opinion or belief **3 :** being an embryonic precursor with the potential for

\ə\ **abut** \ᵊ\ **kitten**, F table \ər\ **further** \a\ **ash** \ā\ **ace** \ä\ **mop, mar**
\au̇\ **out** \ch\ **chin** \e\ **bet** \ē\ **easy** \g\ **go** \i\ **hit** \ī\ **ice** \j\ **job**
\ŋ\ **sing** \ō\ **go** \ȯ\ **law** \ȯi\ **boy** \th\ **thin** \th̲\ **the** \ü\ **loot** \u̇\ **foot**
\y\ **yet** \zh\ **vision, beige** \k̲, ⁿ, œ, ue, ʸ\ *see* Guide to Pronunciation

forming a particular structure or tissue in the normal course of development ⟨~ retina⟩ — **pre·sump·tive·ly** *adv*

pre·sump·tu·ous \pri-ˈzəm(p)-chə-wəs, -chəs, -shəs\ *adj* [ME, fr. AF *presumptious,* fr. LL *praesumptuosus,* irreg. fr. *praesumptio*] (14c) : overstepping due bounds (as of propriety or courtesy) : taking liberties — **pre·sump·tu·ous·ly** *adv* — **pre·sump·tu·ous·ness** *n*

pre·sup·pose \ˌprē-sə-ˈpōz\ *vt* [ME, fr. MF *presupposer,* fr. ML *praesupponere* (perf. indic. *praesupposui*), fr. L *prae-* + ML *supponere* to suppose — more at SUPPOSE] (15c) **1** : to suppose beforehand **2** : to require as an antecedent in logic or fact — **pre·sup·po·si·tion** \(ˌ)prē-ˌsə-pə-ˈzi-shən\ *n* — **pre·sup·po·si·tion·al** \-ˈzish-nəl, -ˈzi-shə-nᵊl\ *adj*

pre·syn·ap·tic \ˌprē-sə-ˈnap-tik\ *adj* (1937) : of, occurring in, or being a neuron by which a nerve impulse is conveyed to a synapse ⟨a ~ membrane⟩ ⟨a ~ neuron⟩ — **pre·syn·ap·ti·cal·ly** \-ti-k(ə-)lē\ *adv*

prêt–à–por·ter *or* **pret–a–por·ter** \ˌpret-ä-pȯr-ˈtā\ *n* [F, ready to wear] (1959) : ready-to-wear clothes

[1]**pre·teen** \ˈprē-ˈtēn, -ˌtēn\ *n* (1952) : a boy or girl not yet 13 years old

[2]**preteen** *adj* (1954) **1** : relating to or produced for children esp. in the 9 to 12 year-old age group ⟨~ fashions⟩ **2** : being younger than 13

pre·teen–ag·er \(ˌ)prē-ˈtē-nā-jər\ *n* (1965) : PRETEEN

[1]**pre·tend** \pri-ˈtend\ *vb* [ME, fr. AF *pretendre,* fr. L *praetendere* to allege as an excuse, lit., to stretch out, fr. *prae-* pre- + *tendere* to stretch — more at THIN] *vt* (15c) **1** : to give a false appearance of being, possessing, or performing ⟨does not ~ to be a psychiatrist⟩ **2 a** : to make believe : FEIGN ⟨he ~*ed* deafness⟩ **b** : to claim, represent, or assert falsely ⟨~*ing* an emotion he could not really feel⟩ **3** *archaic* : VENTURE, UNDERTAKE ~ *vi* **1** : to feign an action, part, or role esp. in play **2** : to put in a claim ⟨cannot ~ to any particular expertise —Clive Barnes⟩ ***syn*** see ASSUME

[2]**pretend** *adj* (1911) **1** : IMAGINARY, MAKE-BELIEVE ⟨had a ~ pal with whom he talked⟩ **2** : not genuine : MOCK ⟨~ pearls⟩ **3** : being a nonfunctional imitation ⟨a ~ train for the children to play in⟩

pre·tend·ed \pri-ˈten-dəd\ *adj* (15c) : professed or avowed but not genuine ⟨~ affection⟩ — **pre·tend·ed·ly** *adv*

pre·tend·er \pri-ˈten-dər\ *n* (1609) : one that pretends: as **a** : one who lays claim to something; *specif* : a claimant to a throne who is held to have no just title **b** : one who makes a false or hypocritical show

pre·tense *or* **pre·tence** \ˈprē-ˌten(t)s, pri-ˈ\ *n* [ME, prob. modif. of ML *pretensio,* irreg. fr. L *praetendere*] (15c) **1** : a claim made or implied; *esp* : one not supported by fact **2 a** : mere ostentation : PRETENTIOUSNESS ⟨confuse dignity with pomposity and ~ —Bennett Cerf⟩ **b** : a pretentious act or assertion **3** : an inadequate or insincere attempt to attain a certain condition or quality **4** : professed rather than real intention or purpose : PRETEXT ⟨was there under false ~*s*⟩ **5** : MAKE-BELIEVE, FICTION **6** : false show : SIMULATION ⟨saw through his ~ of indifference⟩

[1]**pre·ten·sion** \pri-ˈten(t)-shən\ *n* (15c) **1** : an allegation of doubtful value : PRETEXT **2** : a claim or an effort to establish a claim **3** : a claim or right to attention or honor because of merit **4** : an aspiration or intention that may or may not reach fulfillment ⟨has serious literary ~*s*⟩ **5** : VANITY, PRETENTIOUSNESS ***syn*** see AMBITION — **pre·ten·sion·less** \-ləs\ *adj*

[2]**pre·ten·sion** \ˌprē-ˈten(t)-shən\ *vt* [*pre-* + [2]*tension*] (1937) : PRESTRESS

pre·ten·tious \pri-ˈten(t)-shəs\ *adj* [F *prétentieux,* fr. *prétention* pretension, fr. ML *pretention-, pretentio,* fr. L *praetendere*] (1832) **1** : characterized by pretension: as **a** : making usu. unjustified or excessive claims (as of value or standing) ⟨the ~ fraud who assumes a love of culture that is alien to him —Richard Watts⟩ **b** : expressive of affected, unwarranted, or exaggerated importance, worth, or stature ⟨~ language⟩ ⟨~ houses⟩ **2** : making demands on one's skill, ability, or means : AMBITIOUS ⟨the ~ daring of the Green Mountain Boys in crossing the lake —*Amer. Guide Series: Vt.*⟩ ***syn*** see SHOWY — **pre·ten·tious·ly** *adv* — **pre·ten·tious·ness** *n*

[1]**pret·er·it** *or* **pret·er·ite** \ˈpre-tə-rət\ *adj* [ME *preterit,* fr. AF, fr. L *praeteritus,* fr. pp. of *praeterire* to go by, pass, fr. *praeter* beyond, past, by (fr. compar. of *prae* before) + *ire* to go — more at FOR, ISSUE] (14c) *archaic* : BYGONE, FORMER

[2]**preterit** *or* **preterite** *n* (14c) : PAST TENSE

pre·term \(ˌ)prē-ˈtərm, ˈprē-ˌ\ *adj* (1928) : of, relating to, being, or brought forth by premature birth ⟨a ~ infant⟩ ⟨~ labor⟩

pre·ter·mi·nal \(ˌ)prē-ˈtərm-nəl, -ˈtər-mə-\ *adj* (1947) : occurring or being in the period prior to death ⟨~ cancer⟩ ⟨a ~ patient⟩

pre·ter·mis·sion \ˌprē-tər-ˈmi-shən\ *n* [L *praetermission-, praetermissio,* fr. *praetermittere*] (1583) : the act or an instance of pretermitting : OMISSION

pre·ter·mit \-ˈmit\ *vt* **-mit·ted; -mit·ting** [L *praetermittere,* fr. *praeter* by, past + *mittere* to let go, send] (1513) **1** : to leave undone : NEGLECT **2** : to let pass without mention or notice : OMIT **3** : to suspend indefinitely ⟨the grand jury voted to ~ the case⟩

pre·ter·nat·u·ral \ˌprē-tər-ˈna-chə-rəl, -ˈnach-rəl\ *adj* [ML *praeternaturalis,* fr. L *praeter naturam* beyond nature] (1580) **1** : existing outside of nature **2** : exceeding what is natural or regular : EXTRAORDINARY ⟨wits trained to ~ acuteness by the debates —G. L. Dickinson⟩ **3** : inexplicable by ordinary means; *esp* : PSYCHIC ⟨~ phenomena⟩ — **pre·ter·nat·u·ral·ly** \-ˈna-chə-rə-lē, ˈnach-rə-, ˈna-chər-\ *adv* — **pre·ter·nat·u·ral·ness** \-ˈna-chə-rəl-nəs, -ˈnach-rəl-\ *n*

pre·test \ˈprē-ˌtest\ *n* (1926) : a preliminary test: as **a** : a test of the effectiveness or safety of a product prior to its sale **b** : a test to evaluate the preparedness of students for further studies — **pre·test** \(ˌ)prē-ˈtest\ *vt*

pre·text \ˈprē-ˌtekst\ *n* [L *praetextus,* fr. *praetexere* to assign as a pretext, screen, extend in front, fr. *prae-* + *texere* to weave — more at TECHNICAL] (1513) : a purpose or motive alleged or an appearance assumed in order to cloak the real intention or state of affairs ***syn*** see APOLOGY

pre·text·ing \ˈprē-ˌtek-stiŋ\ *n* (1992) : the practice of presenting oneself as someone else in order to obtain private information

pretor, pretorian *var of* PRAETOR, PRAETORIAN

pret·ti·fy \ˈpri-tə-ˌfī, ˈpər-, ˈpru̇-\ *vt* **-fied; -fy·ing** (1850) : to make pretty — **pret·ti·fi·ca·tion** \ˌpri-tə-fə-ˈkā-shən, ˌpər-, ˌpru̇-\ *n* — **pret·ti·fi·er** \ˈpri-tə-ˌfī(-ə)r, ˈpər-, ˈpru̇-\ *n*

pret·ti·ness \ˈpri-tē-nəs, ˈpər-, ˈpru̇-\ *n* (1617) **1** : the quality or state of being pretty **2** : something pretty

[1]**pret·ty** \ˈpri-tē, ˈpər- *also* ˈpru̇-\ *adj* **pret·ti·er; -est** [ME *praty, prety,* fr. OE *prættig* tricky, fr. *prætt* trick; akin to ON *prettr* trick] (bef. 12c) **1 a** : ARTFUL, CLEVER **b** : PAT, APT **2 a** : pleasing by delicacy or grace **b** : having conventionally accepted elements of beauty **c** : appearing or sounding pleasant or nice but lacking strength, force, manliness, purpose, or intensity ⟨~ words that make no sense —Elizabeth B. Browning⟩ **3 a** : MISERABLE, TERRIBLE ⟨a ~ mess you've gotten us into⟩ **b** *chiefly Scot* : STOUT **4** : moderately large : CONSIDERABLE ⟨a very ~ profit⟩ ⟨cost a ~ penny⟩ **5** : easy to enjoy : PLEASANT — usu. used in negative constructions ⟨reality is not so ~ —Caleb Solomon⟩ ***syn*** see BEAUTIFUL — **pret·ti·ly** \-tə-lē\ *adv* — **pret·ty·ish** \-tē-ish\ *adj*

[2]**pret·ty** \ˈpri-tē, ˈpər- *also* ˈpru̇-; *before "near(ly)" often* ˈpərt *or* ˈprit *or* ˈpru̇t\ *adv* (1565) **1 a** : in some degree : MODERATELY ⟨~ cold weather⟩ **b** : QUITE, MAINLY ⟨the wound was . . . ~ bad —Walt Whitman⟩ **2** : in a pretty manner : PRETTILY ⟨pop vocalists who can sing ~ —Gerald Levitch⟩ — **pretty much** : MAINLY, LARGELY

usage Some handbooks say that *pretty* is overworked and recommend using a more specific word or restricting *pretty* to informal or colloquial contexts. *Pretty* is used to tone down a statement and is in wide use in all forms of English. It is common in informal speech and writing but is neither rare nor wrong in serious discourse ⟨he may, if he be *pretty* well off or clever, qualify himself as a doctor —G. B. Shaw⟩ ⟨a return to those traditions of American foreign policy which worked *pretty* well for over a century —H. S. Commager⟩ ⟨the arguments for buying expensive books have to be *pretty* cogent —*Times Lit. Supp.*⟩.

[3]**pret·ty** \ˈpri-tē, ˈpər- *also* ˈpru̇-\ *n, pl* **pretties** (1736) **1** *pl* : dainty clothes; *esp* : LINGERIE **2** : a pretty person or thing

[4]**pret·ty** *same as* [3]\ *vt* **pret·tied; pret·ty·ing** (1909) : to make pretty — usu. used with *up* ⟨curtains to ~ up the room⟩

pretty boy *n* (1885) : a man who is notably good-looking; *also* : DANDY 1

pret·zel \ˈpret-səl\ *n* [G *Brezel,* ultim. fr. L *brachiatus* having branches like arms, fr. *brachium* arm — more at BRACE] (ca. 1838) : a brittle or chewy glazed usu. salted slender bread often shaped like a loose knot

prev *abbr* previous; previously

pre·vail \pri-ˈvāl\ *vi* [ME, fr. L *praevalēre,* fr. *prae-* pre- + *valēre* to be strong — more at WIELD] (15c) **1** : to gain ascendancy through strength or superiority : TRIUMPH **2** : to be or become effective or effectual **3** : to use persuasion successfully ⟨~*ed* on him to sing⟩ **4** : to be frequent : PREDOMINATE ⟨the west winds that ~ in the mountains⟩ **5** : to be or continue in use or fashion : PERSIST ⟨a custom that still ~*s*⟩

prev·a·lence \ˈpre-və-lən(t)s, ˈprev-lən(t)s\ *n* (1713) **1** : the quality or state of being prevalent **2** : the degree to which something is prevalent; *esp* : the percentage of a population that is affected with a particular disease at a given time

prev·a·lent \-lənt\ *adj* [L *praevalent-, praevalens* very powerful, fr. prp. of *praevalēre*] (1576) **1** *archaic* : POWERFUL **2** : being in ascendancy : DOMINANT **3** : generally or widely accepted, practiced, or favored : WIDESPREAD — **prevalent** *n* — **prev·a·lent·ly** *adv*

pre·var·i·cate \pri-ˈver-ə-ˌkāt, -ˈva-rə-\ *vi* **-cat·ed; -cat·ing** [L *praevaricatus,* pp. of *praevaricari* to act in collusion, lit., to straddle, fr. *prae-* + *varicare* to straddle, fr. *varus* bowlegged] (ca. 1631) : to deviate from the truth : EQUIVOCATE ***syn*** see LIE — **pre·var·i·ca·tion** \-ˌver-ə-ˈkā-shən, -ˈva-rə-\ *n* — **pre·var·i·ca·tor** \-ˈver-ə-ˌkā-tər, -ˈva-rə-\ *n*

pre·ve·nient \pri-ˈvēn-yənt\ *adj* [L *praevenient-, praeveniens,* prp. of *praevenire*] (ca. 1656) : ANTECEDENT, ANTICIPATORY — **pre·ve·nient·ly** *adv*

pre·vent \pri-ˈvent\ *vb* [ME, to anticipate, fr. L *praeventus,* pp. of *praevenire* to come before, anticipate, forestall, fr. *prae-* + *venire* to come — more at COME] *vt* (15c) **1** *archaic* **a** : to be in readiness for (as an occasion) **b** : to meet or satisfy in advance **c** : to act ahead of **d** : to go or arrive before **2** : to deprive of power or hope of acting or succeeding **3** : to keep from happening or existing ⟨steps to ~ war⟩ **4** : to hold or keep back : HINDER, STOP — often used with *from* ~ *vi* : to interpose an obstacle — **pre·vent·abil·i·ty** \-ˌven-tə-ˈbi-lə-tē\ *n* — **pre·vent·able** *also* **pre·vent·ible** \-ˈven-tə-bəl\ *adj* — **pre·vent·er** *n*

syn PREVENT, ANTICIPATE, FORESTALL mean to deal with beforehand. PREVENT implies taking advance measures against something possible or probable ⟨measures taken to *prevent* leaks⟩. ANTICIPATE may imply merely getting ahead of another by being a precursor or forerunner or it may imply checking another's intention by acting first ⟨*anticipated* the question by making a statement⟩. FORESTALL implies a getting ahead so as to stop or interrupt something in its course ⟨hoped to *forestall* the sale⟩.

pre·ven·ta·tive \-ˈven-tə-tiv\ *adj or n* (ca. 1666) : PREVENTIVE

pre·ven·tion \pri-ˈven(t)-shən\ *n* (1582) : the act of preventing or hindering

[1]**pre·ven·tive** \-ˈven-tiv\ *n* (ca. 1639) : something that prevents; *esp* : something used to prevent disease

[2]**preventive** *adj* (ca. 1626) : devoted to or concerned with prevention : PRECAUTIONARY ⟨~ steps against soil erosion⟩: as **a** : designed or serving to prevent the occurrence of disease ⟨~ medical care⟩ **b** : undertaken to forestall anticipated hostile action ⟨a ~ coup⟩ — **pre·ven·tive·ly** *adv* — **pre·ven·tive·ness** *n*

pre·ver·bal \(ˌ)prē-ˈvər-bəl\ *adj* (1921) **1** : occurring before the verb **2** : having not yet acquired the faculty of speech ⟨a ~ child⟩

[1]**pre·view** \ˈprē-ˌvyü\ *vt* (1607) **1** : to see beforehand; *specif* : to view or to show in advance of public presentation **2** : to give a preliminary survey of — **pre·view·er** \-ˌvyü-ər\ *n*

[2]**preview** *n* (1882) **1** : an advance statement, sample, or survey **2** : an advance showing or performance (as of a motion picture or play) **3** *also* **pre·vue** \-ˌvyü\ : a showing of clips from a motion picture advertised for appearance in the near future — called also *trailer*

pre·vi·ous \ˈprē-vē-əs\ *adj* [L *praevius* leading the way, fr. *prae-* pre- + *via* way — more at WAY] (1625) **1** : going before in time or order : PRIOR **2** : acting too soon : PREMATURE ⟨somewhat ~ in his conclusion⟩ ***syn*** see PRECEDING — **pre·vi·ous·ly** *adv* — **pre·vi·ous·ness** *n*

previous question *n* (ca. 1715) : a parliamentary motion to put the pending question to an immediate vote without further debate or amendment that if defeated has the effect of permitting resumption of debate

previous to *prep* (1698) : PRIOR TO, BEFORE

[1]**pre·vi·sion** \prē-ˈvi-zhən\ *n* [ME *previsioun,* fr. MF *prevision,* fr. LL *praevision-, praevisio,* fr. L *praevidēre* to foresee, fr. *prae-* + *vidēre* to see — more at WIT] (15c) **1 :** FORESIGHT, PRESCIENCE **2 :** FORECAST, PROGNOSTICATION — **pre·vi·sion·al** \-ˈvizh-nəl, -ˈvi-zhə-nᵊl\ *adj* — **pre·vi·sion·ary** \-ˈvi-zhə-ˌner-ē\ *adj*

[2]**prevision** *vt* **pre·vi·sioned; pre·vi·sion·ing** \-ˈvi-zhə-niŋ, -ˈvizh-niŋ\ (1891) **:** FORESEE

pre·vo·cal·ic \ˌprē-vō-ˈka-lik, -və-\ *adj* [ISV] (1899) **:** immediately preceding a vowel

pre·vo·ca·tion·al \ˌprē-vō-ˈkā-shnəl, -shə-nᵊl\ *adj* (1914) **:** given or required before admission to a vocational school

pre·writ·ing \ˈprē-ˌrī-tiŋ\ *n* (1968) **:** the formulation and organization of ideas preparatory to writing

prexy \ˈprek-sē\ *also* **prex** \ˈpreks\ *n, pl* **prex·ies** *also* **prex·es** [*prexy* fr. *prex,* by shortening & alter. fr. *president*] (1828) *slang* **:** PRESIDENT — used chiefly of a college president

[1]**prey** \ˈprā\ *n, pl* **prey** *also* **preys** [ME *preie,* fr. AF, fr. L *praeda;* akin to L *prehendere* to grasp, seize — more at GET] (13c) **1** *archaic* **:** SPOIL, BOOTY **2 a :** an animal taken by a predator as food **b :** one that is helpless or unable to resist attack **:** VICTIM ⟨was ~ to his own appetites⟩ **3 :** the act or habit of preying

[2]**prey** *vi* **preyed; prey·ing** [ME, fr. AF *preier,* fr. L *praedari,* fr. *praeda*] (14c) **1 :** to make raids for the sake of booty **2 a :** to seize and devour prey **b :** to commit violence or robbery or fraud **3 :** to have an injurious, destructive, or wasting effect ⟨worry ~*ed* upon his mind⟩ — **prey·er** *n*

prez \ˈprez\ *n, pl* **prez·es** \ˈpre-zəz\ [by shortening & alter.] (1936) *slang* **:** PRESIDENT

prf *abbr* proof

Pri·am \ˈprī-əm, -ˌam\ *n* [L *Priamus,* fr. Gk *Priamos*] (14c) **:** the father of Hector, Paris, and Cassandra and king of Troy during the Trojan War

pri·a·pic \prī-ˈā-pik, -ˈa-\ *adj* [L *priapus* lecher, fr. *Priapus*] (1786) **1 :** PHALLIC **2 :** relating to or preoccupied with virility or male sexual excitement

pri·a·pism \ˈprī-ə-ˌpi-zəm\ *n* [F *priapisme,* fr. MF, ultim. fr. Gk *Priapos* (traditionally portrayed in Greco-Roman art with an erect penis)] (1601) **:** an abnormal often painful persistent erection of the penis

Pri·a·pus \prī-ˈā-pəs\ *n* [L, fr. Gk *Priapos*] (14c) **:** a Greek and Roman god of gardens and male generative power

[1]**price** \ˈprīs\ *n* [ME *pris,* fr. AF, fr. L *pretium* price, money; prob. akin to Skt *prati-* against, in return — more at PROS-] (13c) **1** *archaic* **:** VALUE, WORTH **2 a :** the quantity of one thing that is exchanged or demanded in barter or sale for another **b :** the amount of money given or set as consideration for the sale of a specified thing **3 :** the terms for the sake of which something is done or undertaken: as **a :** an amount sufficient to bribe one ⟨believed every man had his ~⟩ **b :** a reward for the apprehension or death of a person ⟨an outlaw with a ~ on his head⟩ **4 :** the cost at which something is obtained ⟨the ~ of freedom is restraint —J. Irwin Miller⟩

[2]**price** *vt* **priced; pric·ing** (15c) **1 :** to set a price on **2 :** to find out the price of **3 :** to drive by raising prices excessively ⟨*priced* themselves out of the market⟩ — **pric·er** *n*

price–cut·ter \ˈprīs-ˌkə-tər\ *n* (1901) **:** one that reduces prices esp. to a level designed to cripple competition — **price–cut·ting** \-tiŋ\ *n*

priced *adj* (1733) **:** having a specified price — used in combination ⟨low-*priced* merchandise⟩

price–earnings ratio *n* (1961) **:** a measure of the value of a common stock determined as the ratio of its market price to its annual earnings per share and usu. expressed as a simple numeral

price–fix·ing \ˈprīs-ˌfik-siŋ\ *n* (1920) **:** the setting of prices artificially (as by producers or government) contrary to free market operations

price index *n* (1886) **:** an index number expressing the level of a group of commodity prices relative to the level of the prices of the same commodities during an arbitrarily chosen base period and used to indicate changes in the level of prices from one period to another

price·less \ˈprīs-ləs\ *adj* (1594) **1 a :** having a value beyond any price **:** INVALUABLE **b :** costly because of rarity or quality **:** PRECIOUS **2 :** having worth in terms of other than market value **3 :** delightfully amusing, odd, or absurd — **price·less·ly** *adv*

price point *n* (1900) **:** the standard price set by the manufacturer for a product

price support *n* (1945) **:** artificial maintenance of prices (as of a raw material) at some predetermined level usu. through government action

price tag *n* (1881) **1 :** a tag on merchandise showing the price at which it is offered for sale **2 :** PRICE, COST

price war *n* (1925) **:** commercial competition characterized by the repeated cutting of prices below those of competitors

pric·ey *also* **pricy** \ˈprī-sē\ *adj* **pric·i·er; -est** (1932) **:** EXPENSIVE

[1]**prick** \ˈprik\ *n* [ME *prikke,* fr. OE *prica;* akin to MD *pric* prick] (bef. 12c) **1 :** a mark or shallow hole made by a pointed instrument **2 a :** a pointed instrument or weapon **b :** a sharp projecting organ or part **3 :** an instance of pricking or the sensation of being pricked: as **a :** a nagging or sharp feeling of remorse, regret, or sorrow **b :** a slight sharply localized discomfort ⟨the ~ of a needle⟩ **4** *usu vulgar* **:** PENIS **5** *usu vulgar* **:** a spiteful or contemptible man often having some authority

[2]**prick** *vt* (bef. 12c) **1 :** to pierce slightly with a sharp point **2 :** to affect with anguish, grief, or remorse ⟨doubt began to ~ him —Philip Hale⟩ **3 :** to ride, guide, or urge on with or as if with spurs **:** GOAD **4 :** to mark, distinguish, or note by means of a small mark **5 :** to trace or outline with punctures **6 :** to remove (a young seedling) from the seedbed to another suitable for further growth — usu. used with *out* **7 :** to cause to be or stand erect ⟨a dog ~*ing* its ears⟩ ~ *vi* **1 a :** to prick something or cause a pricking sensation **b :** to feel discomfort as if from being pricked **2 a :** to urge a horse with the spur **b :** to ride fast **3 :** THRUST **4 :** to become directed upward **:** POINT — **prick up one's ears :** to listen intently

prick·er \ˈpri-kər\ *n* (14c) **1 :** one that pricks **2 a :** THORN, PRICKLE **b :** BRIAR

prick·et \ˈpri-kət\ *n* [ME *priket,* fr. *prikke*] (15c) **1 a :** a spike on which a candle is stuck **b :** a candlestick with such a point **2 :** a buck in the second year of life

[1]**prick·le** \ˈpri-kəl\ *n* [ME *prikle,* fr. OE *pricle;* akin to OE *prica* prick] (15c) **1 :** a fine sharp process or projection; *esp* **:** a sharp pointed emergence arising from the epidermis or bark of a plant **2 :** a prickling or tingling sensation

[2]**prickle** *vb* **prick·led; prick·ling** \-k(ə-)liŋ\ *vt* (1513) **1 :** to prick slightly **2 :** to produce prickles in ~ *vi* **:** to cause or feel a prickling, tingling, or stinging sensation

prick·ly \ˈpri-k(ə-)lē\ *adj* **prick·li·er; -est** (1578) **1 :** full of or covered with prickles; *esp* **:** distinguished from related kinds by the presence of prickles **2 :** marked by prickling **:** STINGING ⟨a ~ sensation⟩ **3 a :** TROUBLESOME, VEXATIOUS ⟨~ issues⟩ **b :** easily irritated ⟨had a ~ disposition⟩ — **prick·li·ness** *n*

prickly ash *n* (1709) **:** a prickly aromatic No. American shrub or small tree (*Zanthoxylum americanum*) of the rue family with yellowish flowers

prickly heat *n* (1736) **:** a noncontagious cutaneous eruption of red pimples with intense itching and tingling caused by inflammation around the sweat ducts

prickly pear *n* (1612) **1 :** OPUNTIA; *esp* **:** any of those with flat spiny joints — called also *prickly pear cactus;* compare CHOLLA **2 :** the pulpy pear-shaped edible fruit of various prickly pears (as *Opuntia ficus-indica*)

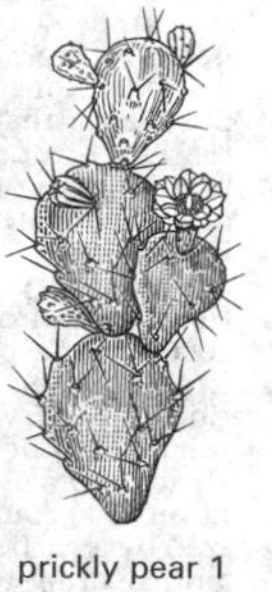
prickly pear 1

prickly poppy *n* (1724) **:** any of a genus (*Argemone*) of plants of the poppy family with white or yellow flowers and prickly leaves and fruits

[1]**pride** \ˈprīd\ *n* [ME, fr. OE *prȳde,* fr. *prūd* proud — more at PROUD] (bef. 12c) **1 :** the quality or state of being proud: as **a :** inordinate self-esteem **:** CONCEIT **b :** a reasonable or justifiable self-respect **c :** delight or elation arising from some act, possession, or relationship ⟨parental ~⟩ **2 :** proud or disdainful behavior or treatment **:** DISDAIN **3 a :** ostentatious display **b :** highest pitch **:** PRIME **4 :** a source of pride **:** the best in a group or class **5 :** a company of lions **6 :** a showy or impressive group ⟨a ~ of dancers⟩

[2]**pride** *vt* **prid·ed; prid·ing** (13c) **:** to indulge (as oneself) in pride

pride·ful \ˈprīd-fəl\ *adj* (15c) **:** full of pride: as **a :** DISDAINFUL, HAUGHTY **b :** EXULTANT, ELATED — **pride·ful·ly** \-fə-lē\ *adv* — **pride·ful·ness** *n*

pride of place (1605) **:** the highest or first position

prie–dieu \(ˌ)prē-ˈdyə(r), prē-ˈdyœ\ *n, pl* **prie–dieux** \-ˈdyə(r)(z), -ˈdyœ(z)\ [F, lit., pray God] (1760) **1 :** a kneeling bench designed for use by a person at prayer and fitted with a raised shelf on which the elbows or a book may be rested **2 :** a low armless upholstered chair with a high straight back

pri·er *also* **pry·er** \ˈprī(-ə)r\ *n* (1552) **:** one that pries; *esp* **:** an inquisitive person

priest \ˈprēst\ *n* [ME *preist,* fr. OE *prēost,* ultim. fr. LL *presbyter* — more at PRESBYTER] (bef. 12c) **:** one authorized to perform the sacred rites of a religion esp. as a mediatory agent between humans and God; *specif* **:** an Anglican, Eastern Orthodox, or Roman Catholic clergyman ranking below a bishop and above a deacon

priest·ess \ˈprēs-təs\ *n* (1654) **1 :** a woman authorized to perform the sacred rites of a religion **2 :** a woman regarded as a leader (as of a movement)

priest·hood \ˈprēst-ˌhu̇d, ˈprē-ˌstu̇d\ *n* (bef. 12c) **1 :** the office, dignity, or character of a priest **2 :** the whole body of priests **3 :** ELITE 1 ⟨the ~ of the art world⟩

priest·ly \ˈprēst-lē\ *adj* (bef. 12c) **1 :** of or relating to a priest or the priesthood **:** SACERDOTAL **2 :** characteristic of or befitting a priest — **priest·li·ness** *n*

priest–rid·den \ˈprēst-ˌri-dᵊn\ *adj* (1653) **:** controlled or oppressed by priests

[1]**prig** \ˈprig\ *n* [*prig* to steal] (1610) **:** THIEF

[2]**prig** *n* [prob. fr. [1]*prig*] (1676) **1** *archaic* **:** FOP **2** *archaic* **:** FELLOW, PERSON **3 :** one who offends or irritates by observance of proprieties (as of speech or manners) in a pointed manner or to an obnoxious degree — **prig·gery** \-gə-rē\ *n* — **prig·gish** \ˈpri-gish\ *adj* — **prig·gish·ly** *adv* — **prig·gish·ness** *n*

prig·gism \ˈpri-ˌgi-zəm\ *n* (ca. 1805) **:** stilted adherence to convention

[1]**prill** \ˈpril\ *vt* [origin unknown] (1944) **:** to convert (as a molten solid) into spherical pellets usu. by forming into drops in a spray and allowing the drops to solidify

[2]**prill** *n* (1952) **:** a pellet made by prilling

[1]**prim** \ˈprim\ *vt* **primmed; prim·ming** [origin unknown] (1706) **1 :** to give a prim or demure expression to ⟨*primming* her thin lips after every mouthful —John Buchan⟩ **2 :** to dress primly

[2]**prim** *adj* **prim·mer; prim·mest** (1709) **1 a :** stiffly formal and proper **:** DECOROUS **b :** PRUDISH **2 :** NEAT, TRIM ⟨~ hedges⟩ — **prim·ly** *adv* — **prim·ness** *n*

[3]**prim** *abbr* **1** primary **2** primitive

pri·ma ballerina \ˈprē-mə-\ *n* [It, leading ballerina] (1870) **:** the principal female dancer in a ballet company

pri·ma·cy \ˈprī-mə-sē\ *n* (14c) **1 :** the state of being first (as in importance, order, or rank) **:** PREEMINENCE ⟨the ~ of intellectual and esthetic over materialistic values —T. R. McConnell⟩ **2 :** the office, rank, or preeminence of an ecclesiastical primate

pri·ma don·na \ˌpri-mə-ˈdä-nə, ˌprē-\ *n, pl* **prima donnas** [It, lit., first lady] (1782) **1 :** a principal female singer in an opera or concert organization **2 :** a vain or undisciplined person who finds it difficult to work under direction or as part of a team

[1]**pri·ma fa·cie** \ˌprī-mə-ˈfā-shə, -shē, -sē *also* -shē-ˌē, -sē-ˌē\ *adv* [ME, fr. L] (15c) **:** at first view **:** on the first appearance

[2]**prima facie** *adj* (1800) **1 :** true, valid, or sufficient at first impression **:** APPARENT ⟨the theory . . . gives a *prima facie* solution —R. J. Butler⟩

\ə\ **abut** \ᵊ\ **kitten,** F **table** \ər\ **further** \a\ **ash** \ā\ **ace** \ä\ **mop, mar**
\au̇\ **out** \ch\ **chin** \e\ **bet** \ē\ **easy** \g\ **go** \i\ **hit** \ī\ **ice** \j\ **job**
\ŋ\ **sing** \ō\ **go** \ȯ\ **law** \ȯi\ **boy** \th\ **thin** \t͟h\ **the** \ü\ **loot** \u̇\ **foot**
\y\ **yet** \zh\ **vision, beige** \k̲, ⁿ, œ, ue, ʸ\ *see* Guide to Pronunciation

2 : SELF-EVIDENT **3** : legally sufficient to establish a fact or a case unless disproved ⟨*prima facie* evidence⟩

pri·mal \ˈprī-məl\ *adj* [ML *primalis,* fr. L *primus* first — more at PRIME] (1602) **1** : ORIGINAL, PRIMITIVE ⟨village life continued in its ~ innocence —Van Wyck Brooks⟩ **2** : first in importance : PRIMARY

pri·mal·i·ty \prī-ˈma-lə-tē\ *n* (1919) : the property of being a prime number

primal scream therapy *n* (1971) : psychotherapy in which the patient recalls and reenacts a particularly disturbing past experience usu. occurring early in life and expresses normally repressed anger or frustration esp. through spontaneous and unrestrained screams, hysteria, or violence — called also *primal therapy*

pri·mar·i·ly \prī-ˈmer-ə-lē *also* prə-, *chiefly Brit* ˈprī-mər-ə-lē\ *adv* (1601) **1** : for the most part : CHIEFLY ⟨has now become ~ a residential town —S. P. B. Mais⟩ **2** : in the first place : ORIGINALLY

[1]**pri·ma·ry** \ˈprī-ˌmer-ē, ˈprī-mə-rē, ˈprīm-rē\ *adj* [ME, fr. LL *primarius* basic, primary, fr. L, principal, fr. *primus*] (15c) **1** : first in order of time or development : PRIMITIVE ⟨the ~ stage of civilization⟩ ⟨the ~ lesion of a disease⟩ **2 a** : of first rank, importance, or value : PRINCIPAL ⟨the ~ purpose⟩ **b** : BASIC, FUNDAMENTAL ⟨security is a ~ need⟩ **c** : of, relating to, or constituting the principal quills of a bird's wing **d** : of or relating to agriculture, forestry, and the extractive industries or their products **e** : expressive of present or future time ⟨~ tense⟩ **f** : of, relating to, or constituting the strongest of the three or four degrees of stress recognized by most linguists ⟨the first syllable of *basketball* carries ~ stress⟩ **3 a** : DIRECT, FIRSTHAND ⟨~ sources of information⟩ **b** : not derivable from other colors, odors, or tastes **c** : preparatory to something else in a continuing process ⟨~ instruction⟩ **d** : of or relating to a primary school ⟨~ education⟩ **e** : of or relating to a primary election ⟨a ~ candidate⟩ **f** : belonging to the first group or order in successive divisions, combinations, or ramifications ⟨~ nerves⟩ **g** : directly derived from ores ⟨~ metals⟩ **h** : of, relating to, or being the amino acid sequence in proteins ⟨~ protein structure⟩ **4** : resulting from the substitution of one of two or more atoms or groups in a molecule ⟨a ~ amine⟩; *esp* : being or characterized by a carbon atom having a bond to only one other carbon atom **5** : of, relating to, involving, or derived from primary meristem ⟨~ tissue⟩ ⟨~ growth⟩ **6** : of, relating to, or involved in the production of organic substances by green plants ⟨~ productivity⟩ **7** : providing primary care ⟨a ~ physician⟩

[2]**primary** *n, pl* **-ries** (1656) **1** : something that stands first in rank, importance, or value : FUNDAMENTAL — usu. used in pl. **2** : the celestial body around which one or more other celestial bodies revolve; *esp* : the more massive usu. brighter component of a binary star system **3** : one of the usu. 9 or 10 strong quills on the distal joint of a bird's wing — see WING illustration **4 a** : PRIMARY COLOR **b** : the sensation of seeing primary colors **5 a** : CAUCUS **b** : an election in which qualified voters nominate or express a preference for a particular candidate or group of candidates for political office, choose party officials, or select delegates for a party convention **6** : the coil that is connected to the source of electricity in an induction coil or transformer — called also *primary coil*

primary atypical pneumonia *n* (ca. 1944) : any of a group of pneumonias (as Q fever and psittacosis) caused esp. by viruses, mycoplasmas, rickettsias, and chlamydias

primary care *n* (1970) : health care provided by a medical professional (as a general practitioner, pediatrician, or nurse) with whom a patient has initial contact and by whom the patient may be referred to a specialist — often used attributively ⟨a *primary care* physician⟩; called also *primary health care;* compare SECONDARY CARE, TERTIARY CARE

primary cell *n* (1902) : a cell that converts chemical energy into electrical energy by irreversible chemical reactions

primary color *n* (1817) : any of a set of colors from which all other colors may be derived

primary meristem *n* (1875) : meristem (as procambium) derived from the apical meristem

primary root *n* (1877) : the root of a plant that develops first and originates from the radicle

primary school *n* (1802) **1** : a school usu. including the first three grades of elementary school but sometimes also including kindergarten **2** : ELEMENTARY SCHOOL

primary syphilis *n* (ca. 1890) : the first stage of syphilis that is marked by the development of a chancre and the spread of the causative spirochete in the tissues of the body

primary tooth *n* (ca. 1898) : MILK TOOTH

primary wall *n* (1925) : the first-formed wall of a plant cell that is produced around the protoplast and usu. has plasmodesmata

pri·mate \ˈprī-ˌmāt *or esp for 1* -mət\ *n* [ME *primat,* fr. AF, fr. ML *primat-, primas* archbishop, fr. L, leader, fr. *primus*] (13c) **1** *often cap* : a bishop who has precedence in a province, a group of provinces, or a nation **2** *archaic* : one first in authority or rank : LEADER **3** [NL *Primates,* fr. L, pl. of *primat-, primas*] : any of an order (Primates) of mammals that are characterized esp. by advanced development of binocular vision, specialization of the appendages for grasping, and enlargement of the cerebral hemispheres and that include humans, apes, monkeys, and related forms (as lemurs and tarsiers) — **pri·mate·ship** \-ˌship\ *n* — **pri·ma·tial** \prī-ˈmā-shəl\ *adj*

pri·ma·tol·o·gy \ˌprī-mə-ˈtä-lə-jē\ *n* (1926) : the study of primates esp. other than recent humans (*Homo sapiens*) — **pri·ma·to·log·i·cal** \-mə-tə-ˈlä-ji-kəl\ *adj* — **pri·ma·tol·o·gist** \-mə-ˈtä-lə-jist\ *n*

pri·ma·vera \ˌprē-mə-ˈver-ə\ *adj* [It *(alla) primavera* in the style of springtime] (1976) : served with a mixture of fresh vegetables (as zucchini, snow peas, and broccoli) — usu. used postpositively ⟨pasta ~⟩

[1]**prime** \ˈprīm\ *n* [ME, fr. OE *prīm,* fr. L *prima hora* first hour] (bef. 12c) **1 a** *often cap* : the second of the canonical hours **b** : the first hour of the day usu. considered either as 6 a.m. or the hour of sunrise **2 a** : the earliest stage **b** : SPRING **c** : YOUTH **3** : the most active, thriving, or satisfying stage or period ⟨in the ~ of his life⟩ **4** : the chief or best individual or part : PICK ⟨~ of the flock, and choicest of the stall —Alexander Pope⟩ **5** : PRIME NUMBER **6 a** : the first note or tone of a musical scale : TONIC **b** : the interval between two notes on the same staff degree **7** : the symbol ′ used to distinguish arbitrary characters (as *a* and *a*′), to indicate a specific unit (as feet or minutes of time or angular measure), or to indicate the derivative of a function (as *p*′ or *f*′(*x*)) — compare DOUBLE PRIME **8** : PRIME RATE

[2]**prime** *adj* [ME, fr. AF, fem. of *prim* first, fr. L *primus;* akin to L *prior*] (14c) **1** : first in time : ORIGINAL **2 a** : of, relating to, or being a prime number — compare RELATIVELY PRIME **b** : having no polynomial factors other than itself and no monomial factors other than 1 ⟨a ~ polynomial⟩ **c** : expressed as a product of prime factors (as prime numbers and prime polynomials) ⟨a ~ factorization⟩ **3 a** : first in rank, authority, or significance : PRINCIPAL ⟨a ~ example⟩ **b** : having the highest quality or value ⟨~ farmland⟩ **c** : of the highest grade regularly marketed — used of meat and esp. beef **4** : not deriving from something else : PRIMARY — **prime·ly** *adv* — **prime·ness** *n*

[3]**prime** *vb* **primed; prim·ing** [prob. fr. [1]*prime*] *vt* (1513) **1** : FILL, LOAD **2 a** : to prepare for firing by supplying with priming **b** : to insert a primer into (a cartridge case) **3** : to apply the first color, coating, or preparation to ⟨~ a wall⟩ **4 a** : to put into working order by filling or charging with something ⟨~ a pump with water⟩ **b** : to supply with an essential prerequisite (as a hormone, nucleic acid, or antigen) for chemical or biological activity ⟨*primed* female mice with estrogen⟩ **5** : to instruct beforehand : COACH ⟨*primed* the witness⟩ **6** : STIMULATE ~ *vi* : to become prime — **prime the pump** : to take steps to encourage the growth or functioning of something

prime cost *n* (1698) : the combined total of raw material and direct labor costs incurred in production; *broadly* : cost less vendor's or agent's commission for charges

prime meridian *n* (ca. 1859) : the meridian of 0 degrees longitude which runs through the original site of the Royal Observatory at Greenwich, England, and from which other longitudes are reckoned

prime minister *n* (1655) **1** : the chief minister of a ruler or state **2** : the official head of a cabinet or ministry; *esp* : the chief executive of a parliamentary government — **prime ministerial** *adj* — **prime ministership** *n* — **prime ministry** *n*

prime mover *n* [trans. of ML *primus motor*] (1809) **1 a** : an initial source of motive power (as a windmill, waterwheel, turbine, or internal combustion engine) designed to receive and modify force and motion as supplied by some natural source and apply them to drive machinery **b** : a powerful tractor or truck usu. with all-wheel drive **2** : the self-moved being that is the source of all motion **3** : the original or most effective force in an undertaking or work ⟨education is . . . a *prime mover* of cultural and societal change —R. C. Buck⟩

prime number *n* (1570) : any integer other than 0 or ± 1 that is not divisible without remainder by any other integers except ± 1 and ± the integer itself

[1]**prim·er** \ˈpri-mər, *chiefly Brit* ˈprī-mər\ *n* [ME, layperson's prayer book, fr. AF, fr. ML *primarium,* fr. LL, neut. of *primarius* primary] (14c) **1** : a small book for teaching children to read **2** : a small introductory book on a subject **3** : a short informative piece of writing

[2]**prim·er** \ˈprī-mər\ *n* (1819) **1** : a device for priming; *esp* : a cap, tube, or wafer containing percussion powder or compound used to ignite an explosive charge **2** : material used in priming a surface — called also *prime coat* **3** : a molecule (as a short strand of RNA or DNA) whose presence is required for formation of another molecule (as a longer chain of DNA)

prime rate *n* (1958) : an interest rate formally announced by a bank to be the lowest available at a particular time to its most credit-worthy customers — called also *prime interest rate*

pri·me·ro \pri-ˈmer-(ˌ)ō, -ˈmir-\ *n* [modif. of Sp *primera,* fr. fem. of *primer* first, fr. L *primarius*] (1533) : a card game popular in the 16th and 17th centuries

prime time *n* (1958) **1** : the time period when the television or radio audience is the largest; *also* : television shows shown in prime time **2** : the choicest or busiest time **3** : BIG TIME 2 ⟨a pitcher not yet ready for *prime time*⟩ — **prime–time** *adj*

pri·me·val \prī-ˈmē-vəl\ *adj* [L *primaevus,* fr. *primus* first + *aevum* age — more at AYE] (1662) **1** : of or relating to the earliest ages (as of the world or human history) : ANCIENT, PRIMITIVE ⟨100 acres of ~ forest which has never felt an ax —Mary R. Zimmer⟩ **2** : PRIMORDIAL 1b — **pri·me·val·ly** \-və-lē\ *adv*

priming *n* (1598) **1** : the act of one that primes **2** : the explosive used in priming a charge **3** : [2]PRIMER 2

pri·mip·a·ra \prī-ˈmi-pə-rə\ *n, pl* **-ras** *or* **-rae** \-ˌrē, -ˌrī\ [L, fr. *primus* first + *-para* -para] (ca. 1842) **1** : an individual bearing a first offspring **2** : an individual that has borne only one offspring — **pri·mip·a·rous** \prī-ˈmi-pə-rəs\ *adj*

[1]**prim·i·tive** \ˈpri-mə-tiv\ *adj* [ME *primitif,* fr. L *primitivus* first formed, fr. *primitiae* first fruits, fr. *primus* first — more at PRIME] (14c) **1 a** : not derived : ORIGINAL, PRIMARY **b** : assumed as a basis; *esp* : AXIOMATIC ⟨~ concepts⟩ **2 a** : of or relating to the earliest age or period : PRIMEVAL ⟨the ~ church⟩ **b** : closely approximating an early ancestral type : little evolved ⟨~ mammals⟩ **c** : belonging to or characteristic of an early stage of development : CRUDE, RUDIMENTARY ⟨~ technology⟩ **d** : of, relating to, or constituting the assumed parent speech of related languages ⟨~ Germanic⟩ **3 a** : ELEMENTAL, NATURAL ⟨our ~ feelings of vengeance —John Mackwood⟩ **b** : of, relating to, or produced by a people or culture that is nonindustrial and often nonliterate and tribal ⟨~ art⟩ **c** : NAIVE **d** (1) : SELF-TAUGHT, UNTUTORED ⟨~ craftsmen⟩ (2) : produced by a self-taught artist ⟨a ~ painting⟩ — **prim·i·tive·ly** *adv* — **prim·i·tive·ness** *n* — **prim·i·tiv·i·ty** \ˌpri-mə-ˈti-və-tē\ *n*

[2]**primitive** *n* (15c) **1 a** : something primitive; *specif* : a primitive idea, term, or proposition **b** : a root word **2 a** (1) : an artist of an early period of a culture or artistic movement (2) : a later imitator or follower of such an artist **b** (1) : a self-taught artist (2) : an artist whose work is marked by directness and naïveté **c** : a work of art produced by a primitive artist **d** : a typically rough or simple usu. handmade and antique home accessory or furnishing **3 a** : a member of a primitive people **b** : an unsophisticated person

primitive streak *n* (1854) : an elongated band of cells that forms along the axis of a developing fertilized egg early in gastrulation and that is considered a forerunner of the neural tube and nervous system

prim·i·tiv·ism \ˈpri-mə-ti-ˌvi-zəm\ *n* (1861) **1** : primitive practices or procedures; *also* : a primitive quality or state **2 a** : belief in the superiority of a simple way of life close to nature **b** : belief in the superiority of nonindustrial society to that of the present **3** : the style of art of primitive peoples or primitive artists — **prim·i·tiv·ist** \-vist\ *n or adj* — **prim·i·tiv·is·tic** \ˌpri-mə-ti-ˈvis-tik\ *adj*

[1]**pri·mo** \ˈprē-(ˌ)mō\ *n, pl* **primos** [It, fr. *primo* first, fr. L *primus*] (1792) : the first or leading part (as in a duet or trio)

[2]**pri·mo** \ˈprē-(ˌ)mō, ˈprī-\ *adv* [L, fr. *primus*] (ca. 1901) : in the first place

[3]**pri·mo** \ˈprē-(ˌ)mō\ *adj* [prob. fr. It, chief, first] (1972) *slang* : of the finest quality : EXCELLENT

pri·mo·gen·i·tor \ˌprī-mō-ˈje-nə-tər\ *n* [LL, fr. L *primus* + *genitor* begetter, fr. *gignere* to beget — more at KIN] (1654) : ANCESTOR, FOREFATHER

pri·mo·gen·i·ture \-ˌchu̇r, -chər, -ˌtyu̇r, -ˌtu̇r\ *n* [LL *primogenitura,* fr. L *primus* + *genitura* birth, fr. *genitus,* pp. of *gignere*] (1602) **1 :** the state of being the firstborn of the children of the same parents **2 :** an exclusive right of inheritance belonging to the eldest son

pri·mor·di·al \prī-ˈmȯr-dē-əl\ *adj* [ME, fr. LL *primordialis,* fr. L *primordium* origin, fr. *primus* first + *ordiri* to begin — more at PRIME, ORDER] (14c) **1 a :** first created or developed : PRIMEVAL 1 **b :** existing in or persisting from the beginning (as of a solar system or universe) ⟨a ~ gas cloud⟩ **c :** earliest formed in the growth of an individual or organ : PRIMITIVE ⟨~ cells⟩ **2 :** FUNDAMENTAL, PRIMARY ⟨~ human joys —Sir Winston Churchill⟩ — **pri·mor·di·al·ly** \-dē-ə-lē\ *adv*

primordial soup *n* (1969) : a mixture of organic molecules in evolutionary theory from which life on earth originated

pri·mor·di·um \-dē-əm\ *n, pl* **-dia** \-dē-ə\ [NL, fr. L] (1855) : the rudiment or commencement of a part or organ

primp \ˈprimp\ *vb* [perh. alter. of [1]*prim*] *vt* (1801) : to dress, adorn, or arrange in a careful or finicky manner ~ *vi* : to dress or groom oneself carefully ⟨~*s* for hours before a date⟩

prim·rose \ˈprim-ˌrōz\ *n* [ME *primerose,* fr. AF, fr. *prime* first + *rose* rose — more at PRIME, ROSE] (14c) : any of a genus (*Primula* of the family Primulaceae, the primrose family) of perennial herbs with large tufted basal leaves and showy variously colored flowers — compare EVENING PRIMROSE

primrose path *n* (1601) **1 :** a path of ease or pleasure and esp. sensual pleasure ⟨himself the *primrose path* of dalliance treads —Shak.⟩ **2 :** a path of least resistance

primrose yellow *n* (1882) **1 :** a light to moderate greenish yellow **2 :** a light to moderate yellow

prim·u·la \ˈprim-yə-lə\ *n* [NL, fr. ML, fr. *primula veris,* lit., first fruit of spring] (1753) : PRIMROSE

pri·mum mo·bi·le \ˈprī-məm-ˈmō-bə-lē, ˈprē-\ *n, pl* **primum mobiles** [ME, fr. ML, lit., first moving thing] (15c) : the outermost concentric sphere conceived in medieval astronomy as carrying the spheres of the fixed stars and the planets in its daily revolution

pri·mus \ˈprī-məs\ *n, often cap* [ML, one who is first, magnate, fr. L, first — more at PRIME] (1724) : the presiding bishop of the Scottish Episcopal Church

pri·mus in·ter pa·res \ˈprī-məs-ˌin-tər-ˈpa-rēz, ˈprē-məs-\ *n* [L] (1813) : first among equals

prin *abbr* **1** principal **2** principle

prince \ˈprin(t)s\ *n* [ME, fr. AF, fr. L *princip-, princeps* leader, initiator, fr. *primus* first + *capere* to take — more at HEAVE] (13c) **1 a :** MONARCH, KING **b :** the ruler of a principality or state **2 :** a male member of a royal family; *esp* : a son of the sovereign **3 :** a nobleman of varying rank and status **4 :** one likened to a prince; *esp* : a man of high rank or of high standing in his class or profession — **prince·ship** \ˈprin(t)s-ˌship\ *n*

Prince Al·bert \-ˈal-bərt\ *n* [*Prince Albert* Edward (later Edward VII king of England)] (1884) : a double-breasted frock coat with the upper part fitted to the body

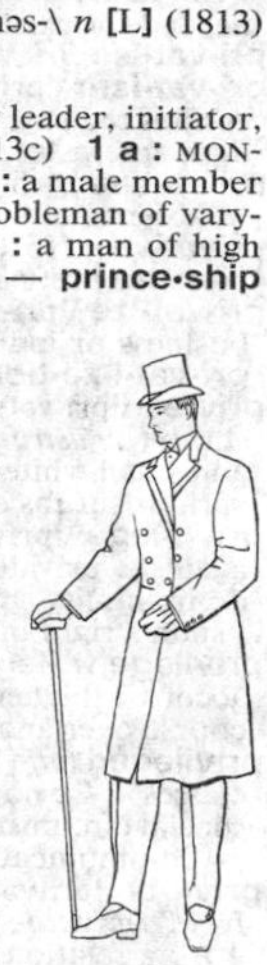

Prince Albert

Prince Charming *n* [*Prince Charming,* hero of the fairy tale *Cinderella* by Charles Perrault] (1856) : a suitor who fulfills the dreams of his beloved; *also* : a man of often specious charm toward women

prince consort *n, pl* **princes consort** (1858) : the husband of a reigning queen

prince·dom \ˈprin(t)s-dəm, -təm\ *n* (1560) **1 :** the jurisdiction, sovereignty, rank, or estate of a prince **2 :** PRINCIPALITY 3 — usu. used in pl.

prince·let \ˈprin(t)s-lət\ *n* (1682) : PRINCELING

prince·li·ness \-lē-nəs\ *n* (1571) **1 :** princely conduct or character **2 :** LUXURY, MAGNIFICENCE

prince·ling \ˈprin(t)s-liŋ\ *n* (1794) : a petty or insignificant prince

prince·ly \ˈprin(t)s-lē\ *adj* **prince·li·er; -est** (15c) **1 :** of or relating to a prince : ROYAL **2 :** befitting a prince : NOBLE, MAGNIFICENT ⟨~ manners⟩ ⟨a ~ sum⟩ — **princely** *adv*

Prince of Wales \-ˈwālz\ (15c) : the male heir apparent to the British throne — used as a title only after it has been specif. conferred by the sovereign

prince's feather *n* (1629) : a showy widely cultivated annual plant (*Amaranthus hypochondriacus* or *A. cruentus*) of the amaranth family having dense usu. red spikes of flowers

[1]**prin·cess** \ˈprin(t)-səs, ˈprin-ˌses, (*usual Brit*) prin-ˈses\ *n* (14c) **1** *archaic* : a woman having sovereign power **2 :** a female member of a royal family; *esp* : a daughter or granddaughter of a sovereign **3 :** the consort of a prince **4 :** one likened to a princess; *esp* : a woman of high rank or of high standing in her class or profession ⟨a pop music ~⟩

[2]**princess** *same as* [1]\ *or* **prin·cesse** \prin-ˈses\ *adj* [F *princesse* princess, fr. *prince*] (1867) : close-fitting and usu. with gores from neck to flaring hemline ⟨a ~ gown⟩

Princess Royal *n, pl* **Princesses Royal** (ca. 1649) : the eldest daughter of a British sovereign — a title granted for life and used only after it has been specif. conferred by the sovereign

[1]**prin·ci·pal** \ˈprin(t)-s(ə-)pəl, -sə-bəl\ *adj* [ME, fr. AF, fr. L *principalis,* fr. *princip-, princeps*] (14c) **1 :** most important, consequential, or influential : CHIEF ⟨the ~ ingredient⟩ ⟨the region's ~ city⟩ **2 :** of, relating to, or constituting principal or a principal ***usage*** see PRINCIPLE — **prin·ci·pal·ly** \-sə-p(ə-)lē, -sə-bə-lē, -splē\ *adv*

[2]**principal** *n* (14c) **1 :** a person who has controlling authority or is in a leading position: as **a :** a chief or head man or woman **b :** the chief executive officer of an educational institution **c :** one who engages another to act as an agent subject to general control and instruction; *specif* : the person from whom an agent's authority derives **d :** the chief or an actual participant in a crime **e :** the person primarily or ultimately liable on a legal obligation **f :** a leading performer : STAR **2 :** a matter or thing of primary importance: as **a** (1) **:** a capital sum earning interest, due as a debt, or used as a fund (2) **:** the corpus of an estate, portion, devise, or bequest **b :** the construction that gives shape and strength to a roof and is usu. one of several trusses; *broadly* : the most important member of a piece of framing ***usage*** see PRINCIPLE — **prin·ci·pal·ship** \ˈprin(t)-s(ə-)pəl-ˌship, -sə-bəl-\ *n*

principal diagonal *n* (1964) : the diagonal in a square matrix that runs from upper left to lower right

prin·ci·pal·i·ty \ˌprin(t)-sə-ˈpa-lə-tē\ *n, pl* **-ties** (14c) **1 a :** the state, office, or authority of a prince **b :** the position or responsibilities of a principal (as of a school) **2 :** the territory or jurisdiction of a prince : the country that gives title to a prince **3** *pl* : an order of angels — see CELESTIAL HIERARCHY

principal parts *n pl* (1870) : a series of verb forms from which all the other forms of a verb can be derived including in English the infinitive, the past tense, and the present and past participles

prin·cip·i·um \prin-ˈsi-pē-əm, prin-ˈki-\ *n, pl* **-ia** \-pē-ə\ [L, beginning, basis] (1600) : a fundamental principle

prin·ci·ple \ˈprin(t)-s(ə-)pəl, -sə-bəl\ *n* [ME, fr. MF *principe, principle,* fr. OF, fr. L *principium* beginning, fr. *princip-, princeps* initiator — more at PRINCE] (14c) **1 a :** a comprehensive and fundamental law, doctrine, or assumption **b** (1) **:** a rule or code of conduct (2) **:** habitual devotion to right principles ⟨a man of ~⟩ **c :** the laws or facts of nature underlying the working of an artificial device **2 :** a primary source : ORIGIN **3 a :** an underlying faculty or endowment ⟨such ~*s* of human nature as greed and curiosity⟩ **b :** an ingredient (as a chemical) that exhibits or imparts a characteristic quality **4** *cap, Christian Science* : a divine principle : GOD — **in principle :** with respect to fundamentals ⟨prepared to accept the proposition *in principle*⟩

usage Although nearly every handbook and many dictionaries warn against confusing *principle* and *principal,* many people still do. *Principle* is only a noun; *principal* is both adjective and noun. If you are unsure which noun you want, read the definitions in this dictionary.

prin·ci·pled \-s(ə-)pəld, -sə-bəld\ *adj* (1642) : exhibiting, based on, or characterized by principle — often used in combination

prin·cox \ˈprin-ˌkäks, ˈpriŋ-\ *n* [origin unknown] (1540) *archaic* : a pert youth : COXCOMB

prink \ˈpriŋk\ *vb* [prob. alter. of [2]*prank*] (1576) : PRIMP — **prink·er** *n*

[1]**print** \ˈprint\ *n* [ME *prente,* fr. AF, fr. *preint, prient,* pp. of *priendre* to press, fr. L *premere* — more at PRESS] (14c) **1 a :** a mark made by pressure : IMPRESSION **b :** something impressed with a print or formed in a mold **c :** FINGERPRINT **2 a :** printed state or form **b :** the printing industry **3 a :** PRINTED MATTER **b** *pl* : printed publications **4 :** printed letters : TYPE **5 a** (1) **:** a copy made by printing (2) **:** a reproduction of an original work of art (as a painting) made by a photomechanical process (3) **:** an original work of art (as a woodcut, etching, or lithograph) intended for graphic reproduction and produced by or under the supervision of the artist who designed it **b :** cloth with a pattern or figured design applied by printing; *also* : an article of such cloth **c :** a photographic or motion-picture copy; *esp* : one made from a negative — **in print :** procurable from the publisher — **out of print :** not procurable from the publisher

[2]**print** *vt* (14c) **1 a :** to impress something in or on **b :** to stamp (as a mark) in or on something **2 a :** to make a copy of by impressing paper against an inked printing surface **b** (1) **:** to impress (as wallpaper) with a design or pattern (2) **:** to impress (a pattern or design) on something **c :** to publish in print **d :** PRINT OUT; *also* : to display on a surface (as a computer screen) for viewing **3 :** to write in letters shaped like those of ordinary roman text type **4 :** to make (a positive picture) on a sensitized photographic surface from a negative or a positive ~ *vi* **1 a :** to work as a printer **b :** to produce printed matter **2 :** to produce something in printed form **3 :** to write or hand-letter in imitation of unjoined printed characters

[3]**print** *adj* (1953) : of, relating to, or writing for printed publications ⟨~ journalists⟩

print·able \ˈprin-tə-bəl\ *adj* (1837) **1 :** capable of being printed or of being printed from **2 :** considered fit to publish — **print·abil·i·ty** \ˌprin-tə-ˈbi-lə-tē\ *n*

printed circuit *n* (1946) : a circuit for electronic apparatus made by depositing conductive material in continuous paths from terminal to terminal on an insulating surface

printed matter *n* (1857) : matter printed by any of various mechanical processes that is eligible for mailing at a special rate

print·er \ˈprin-tər\ *n* (1504) : one that prints: as **a :** a person engaged in printing **b :** a device used for printing; *esp* : a machine for printing from photographic negatives **c :** a device (as an ink-jet printer) that produces printout

printer's devil *n* (1757) : an apprentice in a printing office

print·ery \ˈprin-tə-rē\ *n, pl* **-er·ies** (1638) : PRINTING OFFICE

print·head \ˈprint-ˌhed\ *n* (1968) : a usu. movable part of a computer printer that contains the printing elements

print·ing \ˈprin-tiŋ\ *n* (14c) **1 :** the act or product of one that prints **2 :** reproduction in printed form **3 :** the art, practice, or business of a printer **4 :** IMPRESSION 4c **5** *pl* : paper to be printed on

printing office *n* (1733) : an establishment where printing is done

printing press *n* (1578) : a machine that produces printed copies

print·less \ˈprint-ləs\ *adj* (1610) : making, bearing, or taking no imprint

print·mak·ing \-ˌmā-kiŋ\ *n* (1928) : the design and production of prints by an artist — **print·mak·er** \-kər\ *n*

print·out \ˈprint-ˌau̇t\ *n* (1953) : a printed record produced automatically (as by a computer)

print out *vt* (1953) : to make a printout of

[1]pri·on \ˈprī-ˌän\ *n* [NL, fr. Gk *priōn* saw, fr. *priein* to saw; fr. its sawlike bill] (1848) **:** any of several small petrels (genus *Pachyptila* of the family Procellariidae) of the southern hemisphere that are bluish gray above and white below

[2]pri·on \ˈprē-ˌän\ *n* [*pro*teinaceous + *in*fectious + *[2]-on*] (1982) **:** any of several protein particles that are abnormal forms of normal cellular proteins, that lack nucleic acid, and that in mammals have been implicated as the cause of prion diseases when accumulated in the mammalian brain

prion disease *n* (1986) **:** any of a group of spongiform encephalopathies that are caused by prions and that include bovine spongiform encephalopathy, Creutzfeldt-Jakob disease, kuru, scrapie, and variant Creutzfeldt-Jakob disease — called also *transmissible spongiform encephalopathy*

[1]pri·or \ˈprī(-ə)r\ *n* [ME, fr. OE & AF; both fr. ML, fr. LL, administrator, fr. L, former, superior] (bef. 12c) **1 :** the superior ranking next to the abbot of a monastery **2 :** the superior of a house or group of houses of any of various religious communities — **pri·or·ate** \ˈprī-ə-rət\ *n* — **pri·or·ship** \ˈprī(-ə)r-ˌship\ *n*

[2]prior *adj* [L, former, superior; akin to L *priscus* ancient, *prae* before — more at FOR] (1709) **1 :** earlier in time or order **2 :** taking precedence (as in importance) ***syn*** see PRECEDING — **pri·or·ly** *adv*

pri·or·ess \ˈprī-ə-rəs\ *n* (14c) **:** a nun corresponding in rank to a prior

pri·or·i·tize \prī-ˈȯr-ə-ˌtīz, -ˈär-; ˈprī-ə-rə-\ *vt* **-tized; -tiz·ing** (1961) **:** to list or rate (as projects or goals) in order of priority ***usage*** see -IZE — **pri·or·i·ti·za·tion** \prī-ˌȯr-ə-tə-ˈzā-shən, -är-; ˌprī-ə-rə-\ *n*

pri·or·i·ty \prī-ˈȯr-ə-tē, -ˈär-\ *n, pl* **-ties** (14c) **1 a (1) :** the quality or state of being prior **(2) :** precedence in date or position of publication — used of taxa **b (1) :** superiority in rank, position, or privilege **(2) :** legal precedence in exercise of rights over the same subject matter **2 :** a preferential rating; *esp* **:** one that allocates rights to goods and services usu. in limited supply ⟨that project has top ~⟩ **3 :** something given or meriting attention before competing alternatives

prior restraint *n* (1951) **:** governmental prohibition imposed on expression before the expression actually takes place

prior to *prep* (1706) **:** in advance of **:** BEFORE

usage Sometimes termed pompous or affected, *prior to* is a synonym of *before* that most often appears in rather formal contexts, such as the annual reports of corporations. It may occas. emphasize the notion of anticipation ⟨page makeup decisions are verified and approved *prior to* typesetting —*Publishers Weekly*⟩.

pri·o·ry \ˈprī-(ə-)rē\ *n, pl* **-ries** [ME *priorie,* fr. AF, fr. ML *prioria,* fr. *prior*] (13c) **:** a religious house under a prior or prioress

prise \ˈprīz\ *chiefly Brit var of* [5]PRIZE

prism \ˈpri-zəm\ *n* [LL *prismat-, prisma,* fr. Gk, lit., anything sawn, fr. *priein* to saw] (1570) **1 :** a polyhedron with two polygonal faces lying in parallel planes and with the other faces parallelograms **2 a :** a transparent body that is bounded in part by two nonparallel plane faces and is used to refract or disperse a beam of light **b :** a prism-shaped decorative glass luster **3 :** a crystal form whose faces are parallel to one axis; *esp* **:** one whose faces are parallel to the vertical axis **4 :** a medium that distorts, slants, or colors whatever is viewed through it

pris·mat·ic \priz-ˈma-tik\ *adj* (1709) **1 :** relating to, resembling, or constituting a prism **2 a :** formed by a prism **b :** resembling the colors formed by refraction of light through a prism ⟨~ effects⟩ **3 :** highly colored **:** BRILLIANT ⟨~ lyrics⟩ **4 :** having such symmetry that a general form with faces cutting all axes at unspecified intercepts is a prism ⟨~ crystals⟩ — **pris·mat·i·cal·ly** \-ti-k(ə-)lē\ *adv*

pris·ma·toid \ˈpriz-mə-ˌtȯid\ *n* [LL *prismat-, prisma* prism] (ca. 1890) **:** a polyhedron that has all of its vertices in two parallel planes

pris·moid \ˈpriz-ˌmȯid\ *n* (ca. 1704) **:** a prismatoid whose parallel bases have the same number of sides — **pris·moi·dal** \priz-ˈmȯi-dᵊl\ *adj*

[1]pris·on \ˈpri-zᵊn\ *n* [ME, fr. AF, fr. L *prehension-, prehensio* act of seizing, fr. *prehendere* to seize — more at GET] (12c) **1 :** a state of confinement or captivity **2 :** a place of confinement esp. for lawbreakers; *specif* **:** an institution (as one under state jurisdiction) for confinement of persons convicted of serious crimes — compare JAIL

[2]prison *vt* (14c) **:** IMPRISON, CONFINE

prison camp *n* (1864) **1 :** a camp for the confinement of reasonably trustworthy prisoners usu. employed on government projects **2 :** a camp for prisoners of war or political prisoners

pris·on·er \ˈpriz-nər, ˈpri-zᵊn-ər\ *n* (14c) **1 :** a person deprived of liberty and kept under involuntary restraint, confinement, or custody; *esp* **:** one on trial or in prison **2 :** someone restrained as if in prison ⟨a ~ of her own conscience⟩

prisoner of war (1660) **:** a person captured in war; *esp* **:** a member of the armed forces of a nation who is taken by the enemy during combat

prisoner's base *n* (ca. 1773) **:** a game in which players on each of two teams seek to tag and imprison players of the other team who have ventured out of their home territory

pris·sy \ˈpri-sē\ *adj* **pris·si·er; -est** [prob. blend of *prim* and *sissy*] (1895) **:** overly prim and precise **:** FINICKY — **pris·si·ly** \ˈpri-sə-lē\ *adv* — **pris·si·ness** \ˈpri-sē-nəs\ *n*

pris·tane \ˈpris-ˌtān\ *n* [L *pristis* shark, sawfish; fr. its occurrence in the liver oils of sharks] (1923) **:** an isoprenoid hydrocarbon $C_{19}H_{40}$ that usu. accompanies phytane

pris·tine \ˈpris-ˌtēn, pri-ˈstēn, *esp Brit* ˈpris-ˌtīn\ *adj* [L *pristinus;* akin to L *prior*] (1534) **1 :** belonging to the earliest period or state **:** ORIGINAL ⟨the hypothetical ~ lunar atmosphere⟩ **2 a :** not spoiled, corrupted, or polluted (as by civilization) **:** PURE ⟨a ~ forest⟩ **b :** fresh and clean as or as if new ⟨used books in ~ condition⟩ — **pris·tine·ly** *adv*

prith·ee \ˈpri-t͟hē, -thē\ *interj* [alter. of *(I) pray thee*] (ca. 1590) *archaic* — used to express a wish or request

priv *abbr* private; privately

pri·va·cy \ˈprī-və-sē, *esp Brit* ˈpri-\ *n, pl* **-cies** (15c) **1 a :** the quality or state of being apart from company or observation **:** SECLUSION **b :** freedom from unauthorized intrusion ⟨one's right to ~⟩ **2** *archaic* **:** a place of seclusion **3 a :** SECRECY **b :** a private matter **:** SECRET

pri·vat·do·zent *also* **pri·vat·do·cent** \prē-ˈvät-(ˌ)dō(t)-ˌsent\ *n, often cap* [G *Privatdozent,* fr. *privat* private + *Dozent* teacher, fr. L *docent-, docens,* prp. of *docēre* to teach — more at DOCILE] (1854) **:** an unsalaried university lecturer or teacher in German-speaking countries remunerated directly by students' fees

[1]pri·vate \ˈprī-vət\ *adj* [ME *privat,* fr. AF, fr. L *privatus,* fr. pp. of *privare* to deprive, release, fr. *privus* private, individual; prob. akin to L *pro* for, in front of — more at FOR] (14c) **1 a :** intended for or restricted to the use of a particular person, group, or class ⟨a ~ park⟩ **b :** belonging to or concerning an individual person, company, or interest ⟨a ~ house⟩ **c (1) :** restricted to the individual or arising independently of others ⟨~ opinion⟩ **(2) :** carried on by the individual independently of the usual institutions ⟨a doctor in ~ practice⟩; *also* **:** being educated by independent study or a tutor or in a private school ⟨~ students⟩ **d :** not general in effect ⟨a ~ statute⟩ **e :** of, relating to, or receiving hospital service in which the patient has more privileges than a semiprivate or ward patient **2 a (1) :** not holding public office or employment ⟨a ~ citizen⟩ **(2) :** not related to one's official position **:** PERSONAL ⟨~ correspondence⟩ **b :** being a private **3 a :** withdrawn from company or observation ⟨a ~ retreat⟩ **b :** not known or intended to be known publicly **:** SECRET **c :** preferring to keep personal affairs to oneself **:** valuing privacy highly **d :** unsuitable for public use or display **4 :** not having shares that can be freely traded on the open market ⟨a ~ company⟩ — **pri·vate·ly** *adv* — **pri·vate·ness** *n*

[2]private *n* (15c) **1** *archaic* **:** one not in public office **2** *obs* **:** PRIVACY **3** *pl* **:** PRIVATE PARTS **4 a :** a person of low rank in various organizations (as a police or fire department) **b :** an enlisted man of the lowest rank in the marine corps or of one of the two lowest ranks in the army — **in private :** not openly or in public

private detective *n* (1861) **:** PRIVATE INVESTIGATOR

private enterprise *n* (1844) **:** FREE ENTERPRISE

pri·va·teer \ˌprī-və-ˈtir\ *n* (1664) **:** an armed private ship licensed to attack enemy shipping; *also* **:** a sailor on such a ship — **privateer** *vi*

private eye *n* (1938) **:** PRIVATE INVESTIGATOR

private first class *n* (1918) **:** an enlisted man ranking in the army above a private and below a corporal and in the marine corps above a private and below a lance corporal

private investigator *n* (1940) **:** a person not a member of a police force who is licensed to do detective work (as investigation of suspected wrongdoing or searching for missing persons)

private label *n* (1950) **:** a label associated with a specific chain store; *also* **:** a brand or product having a private label — usu. hyphenated when used attributively ⟨*private-label* clothes⟩

private law *n* (1773) **:** a branch of law concerned with private persons, property, and relationships — compare PUBLIC LAW

private parts *n pl* (1737) **:** the external genital and excretory organs

private school *n* (1665) **:** a school that is established, conducted, and primarily supported by a nongovernmental agency

private treaty *n* (1858) **:** a sale of property on terms determined by conference of the seller and buyer — compare AUCTION

pri·va·tion \prī-ˈvā-shən\ *n* [ME *privacion,* fr. AF, fr. L *privation-, privatio,* fr. *privare* to deprive] (14c) **1 :** an act or instance of depriving **:** DEPRIVATION **2 :** the state of being deprived; *esp* **:** lack of what is needed for existence

pri·vat·ise *Brit var of* PRIVATIZE

pri·vat·ism \ˈprī-və-ˌti-zəm\ *n* [*private*] (1950) **:** the attitude of being uncommitted to or avoiding involvement in anything beyond one's immediate interests

[1]priv·a·tive \ˈpri-və-tiv\ *adj* (14c) **:** constituting or predicating privation or absence of a quality ⟨*non-* is a ~ prefix⟩ — **priv·a·tive·ly** *adv*

[2]privative *n* (1588) **:** a privative term, expression, or proposition; *also* **:** a privative prefix or suffix

pri·vat·ize \ˈprī-və-ˌtīz\ *vt* (1948) **:** to make private; *esp* **:** to change (as a business or industry) from public to private control or ownership — **pri·vat·i·za·tion** \ˌprī-və-tə-ˈzā-shən\ *n*

priv·et \ˈpri-vət\ *n* [origin unknown] (1542) **:** a Eurasian deciduous shrub (*Ligustrum vulgare*) of the olive family with semievergreen leaves and small white flowers that is widely used for hedges; *broadly* **:** any of various shrubs of the same genus

[1]priv·i·lege \ˈpriv-lij, ˈpri-və-\ *n* [ME, fr. AF, fr. L *privilegium* law for or against a private person, fr. *privus* private + *leg-, lex* law] (12c) **:** a right or immunity granted as a peculiar benefit, advantage, or favor; *esp* **:** such a right or immunity attached specif. to a position or an office

[2]privilege *vt* **-leged; -leg·ing** (14c) **1 :** to grant a privilege to **2 :** to accord a higher value or superior position to ⟨~ one mode of discourse over another⟩

privileged *adj* (14c) **1 :** having or enjoying one or more privileges ⟨~ classes⟩ **2 :** not subject to the usual rules or penalties because of some special circumstance; *esp* **:** not subject to disclosure in a court of law ⟨a ~ communication⟩

priv·i·ty \ˈpri-və-tē\ *n, pl* **-ties** [ME *privite* privacy, secret, fr. AF *privetė,* fr. ML *privitat-, privatas,* fr. L *privus* private — more at PRIVATE] (1523) **1 a :** a relationship between persons who successively have a legal interest in the same right or property **b :** an interest in a transaction, contract, or legal action to which one is not a party arising out of a relationship to one of the parties **2 :** private or joint knowledge of a private matter; *esp* **:** cognizance implying concurrence

[1]privy \ˈpri-vē\ *adj* [ME *prive,* fr. AF *privé,* fr. L *privatus* private] (14c) **1 a :** PRIVATE, WITHDRAWN **b :** SECRET **2 :** belonging or relating to a person in one's individual rather than official capacity **3 :** admitted as one sharing in a secret ⟨~ to the conspiracy⟩ — **priv·i·ly** \-və-lē\ *adv*

[2]privy *n, pl* **priv·ies** (14c) **1 a :** a small building having a bench with holes through which the user may defecate or urinate **b :** TOILET 3b **2 :** a person having a legal interest of privity

privy council *n* (14c) **1** *archaic* **:** a secret or private council **2** *cap P&C* **:** a body of officials and dignitaries chosen by the British monarch as an advisory council to the Crown usu. functioning through its committees **3 :** a usu. appointive advisory council to an executive — **privy councillor** *n*

privy purse *n* (1667) **:** an allowance for the private expenses of the British sovereign

prix fixe \ˈprē-ˈfēks, -ˈfiks\ *n* [F, fixed price] (1881) **:** a complete meal offered at a fixed price; *also* **:** the price charged

[1]prize \ˈprīz\ *n* [ME *pris* prize, price — more at PRICE] (14c) **1 :** something offered or striven for in competition or in contests of chance; *also* **:** PREMIUM 1d **2 :** something exceptionally desirable **3** *archaic* **:** a contest for a reward **:** COMPETITION

[2]prize *adj* (1803) **1 a :** awarded or worthy of a prize **b :** awarded as a prize **c :** entered for the sake of a prize ⟨a ~ drawing⟩ **2 :** outstanding of a kind ⟨raised ~ hogs⟩

[3]prize *vt* **prized; priz·ing** [ME *prisen,* fr. AF *priser, preiser* to appraise, esteem, fr. LL *pretiare,* fr. L *pretium* price, value — more at PRICE] (14c) **1 :** to estimate the value of **:** RATE **2 :** to value highly **:** ESTEEM ⟨a *prized* possession⟩ ***syn*** see APPRECIATE

[4]prize *n* [ME *prise,* fr. AF, taking, seizure, fr. *prendre* to take, fr. L *prehendere* — more at GET] (14c) **1 :** something taken by force, stratagem, or threat; *esp* **:** property lawfully captured at sea in time of war **2 :** an act of capturing or taking; *esp* **:** the wartime capture of a ship and its cargo at sea ***syn*** see SPOIL

[5]prize *vt* **prized; priz·ing** [*prize* lever] (1686) **:** to press, force, or move with a lever **:** PRY

prize·fight \ˈprīz-ˌfīt\ *n* (1749) **:** a professional boxing match — **prize·fight·er** \-ˌfī-tər\ *n*

prize·fight·ing \-ˌfī-tiŋ\ *n* (1706) **:** professional boxing

prize money *n* (1726) **1 :** a part of the proceeds of a captured ship formerly divided among the officers and men making the capture **2 :** money offered in prizes

priz·er \ˈprī-zər\ *n* (1599) *archaic* **:** one that contends for a prize

prize·win·ner \ˈprīz-ˌwi-nər\ *n* (1893) **:** a winner of a prize

prize·win·ning \-ˌwi-niŋ\ *adj* (1919) **:** having won or of a quality to win a prize ⟨a ~ design⟩

PRK *abbr* photorefractive keratectomy

prn *abbr* [L *pro re nata*] as needed; as the circumstances require

[1]pro \ˈprō\ *n, pl* **pros** [ME, fr. L, prep., for — more at FOR] (15c) **1 :** an argument or evidence in affirmation ⟨an appraisal of the ~*s* and cons⟩ **2 :** the affirmative side or one holding it

[2]pro *adv* [*pro-*] (15c) **:** on the affirmative side **:** in affirmation ⟨much has been written ~ and con⟩

[3]pro *prep* [L] (1817) **:** in favor of **:** FOR

[4]pro *n or adj* (1866) **:** PROFESSIONAL

PRO *abbr* public relations officer

[1]pro- *prefix* [NL, fr. L, fr. Gk, before, forward, forth, for, fr. *pro* — more at FOR] **1 a :** earlier than **:** prior to **:** before ⟨*pro*thalamion⟩ **b :** rudimentary **:** PROT- ⟨*pro*nucleus⟩ **c :** precursory ⟨*pro*insulin⟩ **2 a :** located in front of or at the front of **:** anterior to ⟨*pro*cephalic⟩ **b :** front **:** anterior ⟨*pro*thorax⟩ **3 :** projecting ⟨*pro*gnathous⟩

[2]pro- *prefix* [L *pro* in front of, before, for, forward — more at FOR] **1 :** taking the place of **:** substituting for ⟨*pro*cathedral⟩ ⟨*pro*caine⟩ **2 :** favoring **:** supporting **:** championing ⟨*pro*-American⟩

proa *var of* PRAU

pro·abor·tion \ˌprō-ə-ˈbȯr-shən\ *adj* (1972) **:** favoring the legalization of abortion — **pro–abor·tion·ist** \-sh(ə-)nist\ *n*

pro·ac·tive \(ˌ)prō-ˈak-tiv\ *adj* (1933) **1** [[1]*pro-*] **:** relating to, caused by, or being interference between previous learning and the recall or performance of later learning ⟨~ inhibition of memory⟩ **2** [[2]*pro-* + *reactive*] **:** acting in anticipation of future problems, needs, or changes — **pro·ac·tive·ly** *adv*

[1]pro–am \ˈprō-ˈam\ *adj* (1949) **:** of, relating to, or involving professionals teaming with or competing against amateurs

[2]pro–am *n* (1963) **:** a pro-am event or tournament

prob *abbr* **1** probable; probably **2** probate **3** problem

prob·a·bi·lism \ˈprä-bə-bə-ˌli-zəm\ *n* [F *probabilisme,* fr. L *probabilis* probable] (ca. 1843) **1 :** a theory that in disputed moral questions any solidly probable course may be followed even though an opposed course is or appears more probable **2 :** a theory that certainty is impossible esp. in the sciences and that probability suffices to govern belief and action — **prob·a·bi·list** \-list\ *adj or n*

prob·a·bi·lis·tic \ˌprä-bə-bə-ˈlis-tik\ *adj* (1864) **1 :** of or relating to probabilism **2 :** of, relating to, or based on probability — **prob·a·bi·lis·ti·cal·ly** *adv*

prob·a·bil·i·ty \ˌprä-bə-ˈbi-lə-tē\ *n, pl* **-ties** (15c) **1 :** the quality or state of being probable **2 :** something (as an event or circumstance) that is probable **3 a (1) :** the ratio of the number of outcomes in an exhaustive set of equally likely outcomes that produce a given event to the total number of possible outcomes **(2) :** the chance that a given event will occur **b :** a branch of mathematics concerned with the study of probabilities **4 :** a logical relation between statements such that evidence confirming one confirms the other to some degree

probability density *n* (1939) **:** PROBABILITY DENSITY FUNCTION; *also* **:** a particular value of a probability density function

probability density function *n* (1957) **1 :** PROBABILITY FUNCTION **2 :** a function of a continuous random variable whose integral over an interval gives the probability that its value will fall within the interval

probability distribution *n* (1920) **:** PROBABILITY FUNCTION; *also* **:** PROBABILITY DENSITY FUNCTION 2

probability function *n* (1906) **:** a function of a discrete random variable that gives the probability that the outcome associated with that variable will occur

[1]prob·a·ble \ˈprä-bə-bəl, ˈprä(b)-bəl\ *adj* [ME, fr. L *probabilis* commendable, probable, fr. *probare* to test, approve, prove — more at PROVE] (1606) **1 :** supported by evidence strong enough to establish presumption but not proof ⟨a ~ hypothesis⟩ **2 :** establishing a probability ⟨~ evidence⟩ **3 :** likely to be or become true or real ⟨~ outcome⟩

[2]probable *n* (1647) **:** one that is probable

probable cause *n* (ca. 1676) **:** a reasonable ground for supposing that a charge is well-founded

prob·a·bly \ˈprä-bə-blē, ˈprä(b)-blē\ *adv* (1613) **:** insofar as seems reasonably true, factual, or to be expected **:** without much doubt ⟨is ~ happy⟩ ⟨it will ~ rain⟩

pro·band \ˈprō-ˌband, prō-ˈ\ *n* [L *probandus,* gerundive of *probare*] (ca. 1929) **:** an individual affected with a disorder who is the first subject in a study (as of a genetic character in a family lineage)

[1]pro·bate \ˈprō-ˌbāt, *Brit also* -bit\ *n* [ME *probat,* fr. L *probatum,* neut. of *probatus,* pp. of *probare*] (15c) **1 a :** the action or process of proving before a competent judicial authority that a document offered for official recognition and registration as the last will and testament of a deceased person is genuine **b :** the judicial determination of the validity of a will **2 :** the officially authenticated copy of a probated will

[2]pro·bate \-ˌbāt\ *vt* **pro·bat·ed; pro·bat·ing** (1570) **1 :** to establish (a will) by probate as genuine and valid **2 :** to put (a convicted offender) on probation

probate court *n* (1786) **:** a court that has jurisdiction chiefly over the probate of wills and administration of deceased persons' estates

pro·ba·tion \prō-ˈbā-shən\ *n* [ME *probacioun,* fr. MF & L; MF *probation,* fr. L *probation-, probatio,* fr. *probare*] (15c) **1 :** critical examination and evaluation or subjection to such examination and evaluation **2 a :** subjection of an individual to a period of testing and trial to ascertain fitness (as for a job or school) **b :** the action of suspending the sentence of a convicted offender and giving the offender freedom during good behavior under the supervision of a probation officer **c :** the state or a period of being subject to probation — **pro·ba·tion·al** \-shnəl, -shə-nᵊl\ *adj* — **pro·ba·tion·al·ly** *adv* — **pro·ba·tion·ary** \-shə-ˌner-ē\ *adj*

pro·ba·tion·er \-sh(ə-)nər\ *n* (1603) **1 :** a person (as a newly admitted student nurse) whose fitness is being tested during a trial period **2 :** a convicted offender on probation

probation officer *n* (1880) **:** an officer appointed to investigate, report on, and supervise the conduct of convicted offenders on probation

pro·ba·tive \ˈprō-bə-tiv\ *adj* (15c) **1 :** serving to test or try **:** EXPLORATORY **2 :** serving to prove **:** SUBSTANTIATING

pro·ba·to·ry \ˈprō-bə-ˌtȯr-ē\ *adj* (1625) **:** PROBATIVE

[1]probe \ˈprōb\ *n* [ML *proba* examination, fr. L *probare*] (1580) **1 :** a slender medical instrument used esp. for exploration (as of a wound or body cavity) **2 a :** any of various testing devices or substances: as **(1) :** a pointed metal tip for making electrical contact with a circuit element being checked **(2) :** a usu. small object that is inserted into something so as to test conditions at a given point **(3) :** a device used to penetrate or send back information esp. from outer space or a celestial body **(4) :** a device (as an ultrasound generator) or a substance (as radioactively labeled DNA) used to obtain specific information for diagnostic or experimental purposes **b :** a pipe on the receiving airplane thrust into the drogue of the delivering airplane in air refueling **3 a :** the action of probing **b :** a penetrating or critical investigation **c :** a tentative exploratory advance or survey

[2]probe *vb* **probed; prob·ing** *vt* (1649) **1 :** to search into and explore very thoroughly **:** subject to a penetrating investigation **2 :** to examine with a probe ⟨unmanned vehicles *probed* space⟩ ~ *vi* **:** to make a searching exploratory investigation ***syn*** see ENTER — **prob·er** *n*

pro·ben·e·cid \prō-ˈbe-nə-səd\ *n* [irreg. fr. *propyl* + *benzoic acid*] (1950) **:** a drug $C_{13}H_{19}NO_4S$ that acts on renal tubular function and is used to increase the concentration of some drugs (as penicillin) in the blood by inhibiting their excretion and to increase the excretion of urates in gout

pro·bi·ot·ic \prō-bī-ˈä-tik, -bē-ˈä-\ *n* [[2]*pro-* + *-biotic* (as in *antibiotic*)] (1951) **:** a preparation (as a dietary supplement) containing live bacteria (as lactobacilli) that is taken orally to restore beneficial bacteria to the body; *also* **:** a bacterium of such a preparation — **probiotic** *adj*

prob·it \ˈprä-bət\ *n* [*prob*ability un*it*] (1934) **:** a unit of measurement of statistical probability based on deviations from the mean of a normal distribution

pro·bi·ty \ˈprō-bə-tē\ *n* [ME *probite,* fr. L *probitat-, probitas,* fr. *probus* honest — more at PROVE] (15c) **:** adherence to the highest principles and ideals **:** UPRIGHTNESS ***syn*** see HONESTY

[1]prob·lem \ˈprä-bləm, -bᵊm, -ˌblem\ *n* [ME *probleme,* fr. L *problema,* fr. Gk *problēma,* lit., obstacle, fr. *proballein* to throw forward, fr. *pro-* forward + *ballein* to throw — more at PRO-, DEVIL] (14c) **1 a :** a question raised for inquiry, consideration, or solution **b :** a proposition in mathematics or physics stating something to be done **2 a :** an intricate unsettled question **b :** a source of perplexity, distress, or vexation **c :** difficulty in understanding or accepting ⟨I have a ~ with your saying that⟩ ***syn*** see MYSTERY

[2]problem *adj* (1894) **1 :** dealing with a problem of conduct or social relationship ⟨a ~ play⟩ **2 :** difficult to deal with ⟨a ~ child⟩

[1]prob·lem·at·ic \ˌprä-blə-ˈma-tik\ *also* **prob·lem·at·i·cal** \-ti-kəl\ *adj* (1609) **1 a :** posing a problem **:** difficult to solve or decide **b :** not definite or settled **:** UNCERTAIN ⟨their future remains ~⟩ **c :** open to question or debate **:** QUESTIONABLE **2 :** expressing or supporting a possibility ***syn*** see DOUBTFUL — **prob·lem·at·i·cal·ly** \-ti-k(ə-)lē\ *adv*

[2]problematic *n* (1957) **:** something that is problematic **:** a problematic aspect or concern

prob·lem·a·tize \ˈprä-blə-mə-ˌtīz\ *vt* **-tized; -tiz·ing** (1910) **:** to consider or treat as a problem — **prob·lem·a·ti·za·tion** \ˌprä-blə-mə-tə-ˈzā-shən\ *n*

pro bono \ˌprō-ˈbō-(ˌ)nō\ *adj* [L *pro bono publico* for the public good] (1970) **:** being, involving, or doing professional and esp. legal work donated esp. for the public good ⟨*pro bono* work⟩ — **pro bono** *adv*

pro·bos·ci·de·an \prə-ˌbä-sə-ˈdē-ən\ *also* **pro·bos·cid·i·an** \prə-ˌbä-ˈsi-dē-ən, (ˌ)prō-\ *n* [ultim. fr. L *proboscid-, proboscis*] (1835) **:** any of an order (Proboscidea) of large mammals comprising the elephants and extinct related forms (as mastodons) — **proboscidean** *adj*

pro·bos·cis \prə-ˈbä-səs, -ˈbäs-kəs\ *n, pl* **-bos·cis·es** *also* **-bos·ci·des** \-ˈbä-sə-ˌdēz\ [L, fr. Gk *proboskis,* fr. *pro-* + *boskein* to feed] (1609) **1 a :** the trunk of an elephant; *also* **:** any long flexible snout **b :** the human nose esp. when prominent **2 :** any of various elongated or extensible tubular processes (as the sucking organ of a butterfly) of the oral region of an invertebrate

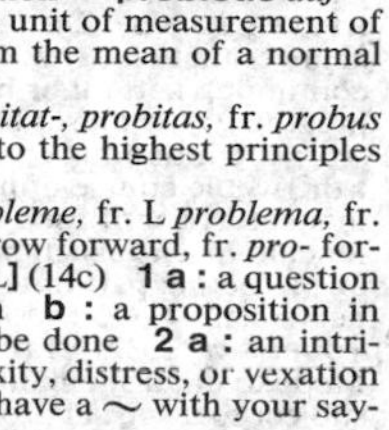

P proboscis 2

proboscis monkey *n* (1793) **:** a large long-tailed monkey (*Nasalis larvatus*) of Bornean forests that has a large nose which is long and pendulous in adult males

proc *abbr* proceedings

pro·caine \ˈprō-ˌkān\ *n* [ISV [2]*pro-* + *-caine*] (1918) **:** a basic ester $C_{13}H_{20}N_2O_2$ of para-aminobenzoic acid; *also* **:** its crystalline hydrochloride used as a local anesthetic

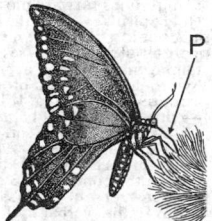

pro·cam·bi·um \(ˌ)prō-ˈkam-bē-əm\ *n* [NL] (1875) : the part of the primary meristem of a plant that forms cambium and primary vascular tissues — **pro·cam·bi·al** \-bē-əl\ *adj*

pro·car·ba·zine \prō-ˈkär-bə-ˌzēn, -zən\ *n* [*pro*pyl + *carb*amic acid + *azine*] (1965) : an antineoplastic drug $C_{12}H_{19}N_3O$ that is a monoamine oxidase inhibitor used in the form of its hydrochloride esp. in the palliative treatment of Hodgkin's disease

procaryote *var of* PROKARYOTE

pro·ca·the·dral \ˌprō-kə-ˈthē-drəl\ *n* (1868) : a parish church used as a cathedral

[1]**pro·ce·dur·al** \prə-ˈsē-jə-rəl, -ˈsēj-rəl\ *adj* (1889) : of or relating to procedure; *esp* : of or relating to the procedure used by courts or other bodies administering substantive law — **pro·ce·dur·al·ly** *adv*

[2]**procedural** *n* (1972) : a realist crime novel with a specific focus ⟨a courtroom ~⟩; *esp* : POLICE PROCEDURAL

procedural due process *n* (1938) : DUE PROCESS 1

pro·ce·dure \prə-ˈsē-jər\ *n* [F *procédure*, fr. MF, fr. *proceder*] (ca. 1611) **1 a** : a particular way of accomplishing something or of acting **b** : a step in a procedure **2 a** : a series of steps followed in a regular definite order ⟨legal ~⟩ ⟨a surgical ~⟩ **b** : a set of instructions for a computer that has a name by which it can be called into action **3 a** : a traditional or established way of doing things **b** : PROTOCOL 3a

pro·ceed \prō-ˈsēd, prə-\ *vi* [ME *proceden*, fr. AF *proceder*, fr. L *procedere*, fr. *pro-* forward + *cedere* to go — more at PRO-] (14c) **1** : to come forth from a source : ISSUE ⟨strange sounds *~ed* from the room⟩ **2 a** : to continue after a pause or interruption **b** : to go on in an orderly regulated way **3 a** : to begin and carry on an action, process, or movement **b** : to be in the process of being accomplished ⟨the work is *~ing* well⟩ **4** : to move along a course : ADVANCE ***syn*** see SPRING

pro·ceed·ing \-ˈsē-diŋ\ *n* (15c) **1** : legal action ⟨a divorce ~⟩ **2** : PROCEDURE **3** *pl* : EVENTS, HAPPENINGS **4** : TRANSACTION **5** *pl* : an official record of things said or done

pro·ceeds \ˈprō-ˌsēdz\ *n pl* (1665) **1** : the total amount brought in ⟨the ~ of a sale⟩ **2** : the net amount received (as for a check or from an insurance settlement) after deduction of any discount or charges

pro·ce·phal·ic \ˌprō-sə-ˈfa-lik\ *adj* (1874) : relating to, forming, or situated on or near the front of the head

pro·cer·coid \(ˌ)prō-ˈsər-ˌkȯid\ *n* [*pro-* + Gk *kerkos* tail] (1918) : the solid first parasitic larva of some tapeworms that develops usu. in the body cavity of a copepod

[1]**pro·cess** \ˈprä-ˌses, ˈprō-, -səs\ *n, pl* **pro·cess·es** \-ˌse-səz, -sə-, -ˌsēz\ [ME *proces*, fr. AF *procés*, fr. L *processus*, fr. *procedere*] (14c) **1 a** : PROGRESS, ADVANCE ⟨in the ~ of time⟩ **b** : something going on : PROCEEDING **2 a** (1) : a natural phenomenon marked by gradual changes that lead toward a particular result ⟨the ~ of growth⟩ (2) : a continuing natural or biological activity or function ⟨such life *~es* as breathing⟩ **b** : a series of actions or operations conducing to an end; *esp* : a continuous operation or treatment esp. in manufacture **3 a** : the whole course of proceedings in a legal action **b** : the summons, mandate, or writ used by a court to compel the appearance of the defendant in a legal action or compliance with its orders **4** : a prominent or projecting part of an organism or organic structure ⟨a bone ~⟩ ⟨a nerve cell ~⟩ **5** : [6]CONK

[2]**process** *vt* (1532) **1 a** : to proceed against by law : PROSECUTE **b** (1) : to take out a summons against (2) : to serve a summons on **2 a** : to subject to a special process or treatment (as in the course of manufacture or film development) **b** (1) : to subject to or handle through an established usu. routine set of procedures ⟨~ insurance claims⟩ (2) : to integrate sensory information received so that an action or response is generated ⟨the brain *~es* visual images relayed from the retina⟩ (3) : to subject to examination or analysis ⟨computers ~ data⟩ **c** : to work (hair) into a conk

[3]**process** *adj* (1888) **1** : treated or made by a special process esp. when involving synthesis or artificial modification **2** : made by or used in a mechanical or photomechanical duplicating process **3** : of or involving illusory effects usu. introduced during processing of the film

[4]**pro·cess** \prə-ˈses\ *vi* [back-formation fr. [1]*procession*] (1814) *chiefly Brit* : to move in a procession

pro·cess·able *also* **pro·cess·ible** \ˈprä-ˌse-sə-bəl, ˈprō-\ *adj* (1954) : suitable for processing : capable of being processed — **pro·cess·abil·i·ty** *also* **pro·cess·ibil·i·ty** \ˌprä-ˌse-sə-ˈbi-lə-tē, ˌprō-\ *n*

process cheese *n* (1926) : a cheese made by blending several lots of cheese — called also *processed cheese*

[1]**pro·ces·sion** \prə-ˈse-shən\ *n* [ME *processioun*, fr. AF *processiun*, fr. LL & L; LL *procession-, processio* religious procession, fr. L, act of proceeding, fr. *procedere*] (12c) **1 a** : a group of individuals moving along in an orderly often ceremonial way **b** : SUCCESSION, SEQUENCE **2 a** : continuous forward movement : PROGRESSION **b** : EMANATION ⟨the Holy Spirit's ~ from the Father⟩

[2]**procession** *vi* (1691) *archaic* : to go in procession

[1]**pro·ces·sion·al** \prə-ˈsesh-nəl, -ˈse-shə-nᵊl\ *n* (15c) **1** : a book containing material for a procession **2** : a musical composition (as a hymn) designed for a procession **3** : a ceremonial procession

[2]**processional** *adj* (ca. 1611) : of, relating to, or moving in a procession — **pro·ces·sion·al·ly** *adv*

pro·ces·sor \ˈprä-ˌse-sər, ˈprō-\ *n* (1909) **1** : one that processes ⟨scrap ~⟩ ⟨agricultural ~⟩ **2 a** (1) : COMPUTER (2) : CPU **b** : a computer program (as a compiler) that puts another program into a form acceptable to the computer **3** : FOOD PROCESSOR

pro·cès–ver·bal \prō-ˌsā-vər-ˈbäl, -(ˌ)ver-\ *n, pl* **pro·cès–ver·baux** \-ˈbō\ [F, lit., verbal trial] (1635) : an official written record

pro–choice \(ˌ)prō-ˈchȯis\ *adj* (1975) : favoring the legalization of abortion — **pro–choic·er** \-ˈchȯi-sər\ *n*

pro·claim \prō-ˈklām, prə-\ *vt* [ME *proclamen*, fr. AF or L; AF *proclamer*, fr. L *proclamare*, fr. *pro-* before + *clamare* to cry out — more at PRO-, CLAIM] (14c) **1 a** : to declare publicly, typically insistently, proudly, or defiantly and in either speech or writing : ANNOUNCE **b** : to give outward indication of : SHOW ⟨his manner *~ed* his genteel upbringing⟩ **2** : to declare or declare to be solemnly, officially, or formally ⟨~ an amnesty⟩ ⟨~ the country a republic⟩ **3** : to praise or glorify openly or publicly : EXTOL ⟨*~ed* the rescue workers' efforts⟩ ***syn*** see DECLARE — **pro·claim·er** *n*

proc·la·ma·tion \ˌprä-klə-ˈmā-shən\ *n* [ME *proclamacion*, fr. AF, fr. L *proclamation-, proclamatio*, fr. *proclamare*] (14c) **1** : the action of proclaiming : the state of being proclaimed **2** : something proclaimed; *specif* : an official formal public announcement

pro·clit·ic \(ˌ)prō-ˈkli-tik\ *n* [NL *procliticus*, fr. Gk *pro-* + LL *-cliticus* (as in *encliticus* enclitic)] (ca. 1864) : a clitic that is associated with a following word — **proclitic** *adj*

pro·cliv·i·ty \prō-ˈkli-və-tē\ *n, pl* **-ties** [L *proclivitas*, fr. *proclivis* sloping, prone, fr. *pro-* forward + *clivus* slope — more at PRO-, DECLIVITY] (ca. 1591) : an inclination or predisposition toward something; *esp* : a strong inherent inclination toward something objectionable ***syn*** see LEANING

Proc·ne \ˈpräk-nē\ *n* [L, fr. Gk *Proknē*] (ca. 1527) : the wife of Tereus who is changed into a swallow while fleeing from him

pro·con·sul \(ˌ)prō-ˈkän(t)-səl\ *n* [ME, fr. L, fr. *pro consule* for a consul] (14c) **1** : a governor or military commander of an ancient Roman province **2** : an administrator in a modern colony, dependency, or occupied area usu. with wide powers — **pro·con·su·lar** \-s(ə-)lər\ *adj* — **pro·con·su·late** \-s(ə-)lət\ *n* — **pro·con·sul·ship** \-səl-ˌship\ *n*

pro·cras·ti·nate \prə-ˈkras-tə-ˌnāt, prō-\ *vb* **-nat·ed; -nat·ing** [L *procrastinatus*, pp. of *procrastinare*, fr. *pro-* forward + *crastinus* of tomorrow, fr. *cras* tomorrow] *vt* (1588) : to put off intentionally and habitually ~ *vi* : to put off intentionally the doing of something that should be done ***syn*** see DELAY — **pro·cras·ti·na·tion** \-ˌkras-tə-ˈnā-shən\ *n* — **pro·cras·ti·na·tor** \-ˈkras-tə-ˌnā-tər\ *n*

pro·cre·ant \ˈprō-krē-ənt\ *adj* (1588) **1** : producing offspring **2** *archaic* : of or relating to procreation

pro·cre·ate \-ˌāt\ *vb* **-at·ed; -at·ing** [L *procreatus*, pp. of *procreare*, fr. *pro-* forth + *creare* to create — more at PRO-, CREATE] *vt* (1536) : to beget or bring forth (offspring) : PROPAGATE ~ *vi* : to beget or bring forth offspring : REPRODUCE — **pro·cre·ation** \ˌprō-krē-ˈā-shən\ *n* — **pro·cre·ative** \ˈprō-krē-ˌā-tiv\ *adj* — **pro·cre·ator** \-ˌā-tər\ *n*

pro·crus·te·an \prə-ˈkrəs-tē-ən, prō-\ *adj, often cap* (1832) **1** : of, relating to, or typical of Procrustes **2** : marked by arbitrary often ruthless disregard of individual differences or special circumstances

procrustean bed *n, often cap P* (1832) : a scheme or pattern into which someone or something is arbitrarily forced

Pro·crus·tes \prə-ˈkrəs-(ˌ)tēz, prō-\ *n* [L, fr. Gk *Prokroustēs*] (1567) : a villainous son of Poseidon in Greek mythology who forces travelers to fit into his bed by stretching their bodies or cutting off their legs

pro·cryp·tic \(ˌ)prō-ˈkrip-tik\ *adj* [*pro-* (as in *protect*) + *cryptic*] (1890) : of, relating to, or being a concealing pattern or shade of coloring esp. in insects

proc·to·dae·um \ˌpräk-tə-ˈdē-əm\ *n, pl* **-daea** \-ˈdē-ə\ *or* **-dae·ums** [NL, fr. Gk *prōktos* anus + *hodos* way] (1876) : the embryonic posterior ectodermal part of the alimentary canal

proc·tol·o·gy \präk-ˈtä-lə-jē\ *n* [Gk *prōktos* + E *-logy*] (1899) : a branch of medicine dealing with the structure and diseases of the anus, rectum, and sigmoid colon — **proc·to·log·ic** \ˌpräk-tə-ˈlä-jik\ *or* **proc·to·log·i·cal** \-ji-kəl\ *adj* — **proc·tol·o·gist** \präk-ˈtä-lə-jist\ *n*

proc·tor \ˈpräk-tər\ *n* [ME *procutour* procurator, proctor, alter. of *procuratour*] (14c) : SUPERVISOR, MONITOR; *specif* : one appointed to supervise students (as at an examination) — **proctor** *vb* — **proc·to·ri·al** \präk-ˈtȯr-ē-əl\ *adj* — **proc·tor·ship** \ˈpräk-tər-ˌship\ *n*

pro·cum·bent \prō-ˈkəm-bənt\ *adj* [L *procumbent-, procumbens*, prp. of *procumbere* to fall or lean forward, fr. *pro-* forward + *-cumbere* to lie down] (1668) **1** : being or having stems that trail along the ground without rooting **2** : lying face down

proc·u·ra·tion \ˌprä-kyə-ˈrā-shən\ *n* [ME *procuratioun*, fr. AF *procuration*, fr. L *procuration-, procuratio*, fr. *procurare*] (15c) **1 a** : the act of appointing another as one's agent or attorney **b** : the authority vested in one so appointed **2** : the action of obtaining something (as supplies) : PROCUREMENT

proc·u·ra·tor \ˈprä-kyə-ˌrā-tər\ *n* (14c) **1** : one that manages another's affairs : AGENT **2** : an officer of the Roman empire entrusted with management of the financial affairs of a province and often having administrative powers as agent of the emperor — **proc·u·ra·to·ri·al** \ˌprä-kyə-rə-ˈtȯr-ē-əl\ *adj*

pro·cure \prə-ˈkyu̇r, prō-\ *vb* **pro·cured; pro·cur·ing** [ME, fr. AF *procurer*, fr. LL *procurare*, fr. L, to take care of, fr. *pro-* for + *cura* care] *vt* (14c) **1 a** : to get possession of : obtain by particular care and effort **b** : to get and make available for promiscuous sexual intercourse **2** : BRING ABOUT, ACHIEVE ⟨*procured* the prisoner's release⟩ ~ *vi* : to procure women — **pro·cur·able** \-ˈkyu̇r-ə-bəl\ *adj*

pro·cure·ment \-ˈkyu̇r-mənt\ *n* (14c) : the act or process of procuring; *esp* : the obtaining of military supplies by a government

pro·cur·er \-ˈkyu̇r-ər\ *n* (1538) : one that procures; *esp* : PANDER

Pro·cy·on \ˈprō-sē-ˌän, ˈprä-, -ən\ *n* [L, fr. Gk *Prokyōn*, lit., fore-dog; fr. its rising before Sirius] (1658) : the brightest star in the constellation Canis Minor

[1]**prod** \ˈpräd\ *vb* **prod·ded; prod·ding** [origin unknown] *vt* (1535) **1 a** : to thrust a pointed instrument into : PRICK **b** : to incite to action : STIR **2** : to poke or stir as if with a prod ~ *vi* : to urge someone on — **prod·der** *n*

[2]**prod** *n* (ca. 1787) **1** : a pointed instrument used to prod **2** : an incitement to act ⟨needed a few *~s* to remember her lines⟩

[3]**prod** *abbr* product; production

Prod \ˈpräd\ *n* [by shortening & alter.] (1942) *chiefly Irish, often disparaging* : PROTESTANT 1b

[1]**prod·i·gal** \ˈprä-di-gəl\ *adj* [L *prodigus*, fr. *prodigere* to drive away, squander, fr. *pro-, prod-* forth + *agere* to drive — more at PRO-, AGENT] (15c) **1** : characterized by profuse or wasteful expenditure : LAVISH ⟨a ~ feast⟩ ⟨~ outlays for her clothes⟩ **2** : recklessly spendthrift ⟨the ~ prince⟩ **3** : yielding abundantly : LUXURIANT — often used with *of* ⟨nature has been so ~ of her bounty —H. T. Buckle⟩ ***syn*** see PROFUSE — **prod·i·gal·i·ty** \ˌprä-də-ˈga-lə-tē\ *n* — **prod·i·gal·ly** \ˈprä-di-g(ə-)lē\ *adv*

[2]**prodigal** *n* (1561) **1** : one who spends or gives lavishly and foolishly **2** : one who has returned after an absence

pro·di·gious \prə-ˈdi-jəs\ *adj* (15c) **1 a** *obs* : being an omen : PORTENTOUS **b** : resembling or befitting a prodigy : STRANGE, UNUSUAL **2** : exciting amazement or wonder **3** : extraordinary in bulk, quantity, or degree : ENORMOUS ***syn*** see MONSTROUS — **pro·di·gious·ly** *adv* — **pro·di·gious·ness** *n*

prod·i·gy \ˈprä-də-jē\ *n, pl* **-gies** [ME, fr. L *prodigium* omen, monster, fr. *pro-, prod-* + *-igium* (akin to *aio* I say) — more at ADAGE] (15c) **1 a :** a portentous event : OMEN **b :** something extraordinary or inexplicable **2 a :** an extraordinary, marvelous, or unusual accomplishment, deed, or event **b :** a highly talented child or youth

prodn *abbr* production

pro·dro·mal \(ˌ)prō-ˈdrō-məl\ *adj* (1716) : PRECURSORY; *esp* : marked by prodromes

pro·drome \ˈprō-ˌdrōm\ *n* [F, lit., precursor, fr. Gk *prodromos,* fr. *pro-* before + *dromos* act of running, racecourse — more at PRO-, DROMEDARY] (ca. 1834) : a premonitory symptom of disease

[1]**pro·duce** \prə-ˈdüs, prō-, -ˈdyüs\ *vb* **pro·duced; pro·duc·ing** [ME (Sc), fr. L *producere,* fr. *pro-* forward + *ducere* to lead — more at TOW] *vt* (15c) **1 :** to offer to view or notice **2 :** to give birth or rise to : YIELD **3 :** to extend in length, area, or volume ⟨~ a side of a triangle⟩ **4 :** to make available for public exhibition or dissemination: as **a :** to provide funding for ⟨search for backers to ~ the film⟩ **b :** to oversee the making of ⟨will ~ their new album⟩ **5 a :** to cause to have existence or to happen : BRING ABOUT **b :** to give being, form, or shape to : MAKE; *esp* : MANUFACTURE **6 :** to compose, create, or bring out by intellectual or physical effort **7 :** to cause to accrue ~ *vi* : to bear, make, or yield something — **pro·duc·ible** \-ˈdü-sə-bəl, -ˈdyü-\ *adj*

[2]**pro·duce** \ˈprä-(ˌ)düs, ˈprō- *also* -(ˌ)dyüs\ *n* (1695) **1 a :** something produced **b :** the amount produced : YIELD **2 :** agricultural products and esp. fresh fruits and vegetables as distinguished from grain and other staple crops **3 :** the progeny usu. of a female animal

pro·duc·er \prə-ˈdü-sər, prō-, -ˈdyü-\ *n* (1513) **1 :** one that produces; *esp* : one that grows agricultural products or manufactures crude materials into articles of use **2 :** a person who supervises or finances a work (as a staged or recorded performance) for exhibition or dissemination to the public **3 :** an autotrophic organism (as a green plant) viewed as a source of biomass that can be consumed by other organisms — compare CONSUMER

producer gas *n* (1895) : a fuel gas made by circulating air or a mixture of air and steam through a layer of incandescent fuel and consisting chiefly of carbon monoxide, hydrogen, and nitrogen

producer goods *n pl* (1948) : goods (as tools and raw materials) used to produce other goods and satisfy human wants only indirectly

prod·uct \ˈprä-(ˌ)dəkt\ *n* [in sense 1, fr. ME, fr. ML *productum,* fr. L, something produced, fr. neut. of *productus,* pp. of *producere;* in other senses, fr. L *productum*] (15c) **1 :** the number or expression resulting from the multiplication together of two or more numbers or expressions **2 a (1) :** something produced; *esp* : COMMODITY 1 **(2) :** something (as a service) that is marketed or sold as a commodity **b :** something resulting from or necessarily following from a set of conditions ⟨a ~ of his environment⟩ **3 :** the amount, quantity, or total produced **4 :** CONJUNCTION 5

pro·duc·tion \prə-ˈdək-shən, prō-\ *n* (15c) **1 a :** something produced : PRODUCT **b (1) :** a literary or artistic work **(2) :** a work presented to the public (as on the stage or screen or over the air) **c :** something exaggerated out of proportion to its importance **2 a :** the act or process of producing **b :** the creation of utility; *esp* : the making of goods available for use **3 :** total output esp. of a commodity or an industry **4** *often attrib* : something not specially designed or customized and usu. mass-produced ⟨a ~ car⟩ ⟨~ housing⟩ — **pro·duc·tion·al** \-shnəl, -shə-nᵊl\ *adj*

production control *n* (1929) : systematic planning, coordinating, and directing of all manufacturing activities and influences to insure having goods made on time, of adequate quality, and at reasonable cost

production line *n* (1935) : LINE 6j

pro·duc·tive \prə-ˈdək-tiv, prō-\ *adj* (1612) **1 :** having the quality or power of producing esp. in abundance ⟨~ fishing waters⟩ **2 :** effective in bringing about ⟨investigating committees have been ~ of much good —R. K. Carr⟩ **3 a :** yielding results, benefits, or profits **b :** yielding or devoted to the satisfaction of wants or the creation of utilities **4 :** continuing to be used in the formation of new words or constructions ⟨*un-* is a ~ prefix⟩ **5 :** raising mucus or sputum (as from the bronchi) ⟨a ~ cough⟩ — **pro·duc·tive·ly** *adv* — **pro·duc·tive·ness** *n*

pro·duc·tiv·i·ty \ˌprō-dək-ˈti-və-tē, ˌprä-, prə-ˌdək-\ *n* (ca. 1810) **1 :** the quality or state of being productive **2 :** the rate per unit area or per unit volume at which biomass consumable as food by other organisms is made by producers

product placement *n* (1982) : the inclusion of a product in a television program or film as a form of paid advertisement

pro·em \ˈprō-ˌem, -əm\ *n* [ME *proheme,* fr. AF *proeme,* fr. L *prooemium,* fr. Gk *prooimion,* fr. *pro-* + *oimē* song; prob. akin to Hitt *išamai-* song, Skt *syati* he binds — more at SINEW] (14c) **1 :** preliminary comment : PREFACE **2 :** PRELUDE — **pro·emi·al** \prō-ˈē-mē-əl, -ˈe-\ *adj*

pro·en·zyme \(ˌ)prō-ˈen-ˌzīm\ *n* [ISV] (ca. 1900) : ZYMOGEN

pro·es·trus \(ˌ)prō-ˈes-trəs\ *n* [NL] (1923) : a period immediately preceding estrus characterized by preparatory physiological changes

[1]**prof** \ˈpräf\ *n* (1838) : PROFESSOR

[2]**prof** *abbr* professional

pro–fam·i·ly \ˌprō-ˈfam-lē, -ˈfa-mə-\ *adj* (1926) **1 :** favoring or encouraging traditional family structures and values **2 :** opposing abortion and often birth control

prof·a·na·tion \ˌprä-fə-ˈnā-shən, ˌprō-\ *n* (1552) : the act or an instance of profaning

pro·fa·na·to·ry \prō-ˈfa-nə-ˌtȯr-ē, prə-, -ˈfā-\ *adj* (1853) : tending to profane : DESECRATING

[1]**pro·fane** \prō-ˈfān, prə-\ *vt* **pro·faned; pro·fan·ing** [ME *prophanen,* fr. AF *prophaner,* fr. L *profanare,* fr. *profanus*] (14c) **1 :** to treat (something sacred) with abuse, irreverence, or contempt : DESECRATE **2 :** to debase by a wrong, unworthy, or vulgar use — **pro·fan·er** *n*

[2]**profane** *adj* [ME *prophane,* fr. MF, fr. L *profanus,* fr. *pro-* before + *fanum* temple — more at PRO-, FEAST] (15c) **1 :** not concerned with religion or religious purposes : SECULAR **2 :** not holy because unconsecrated, impure, or defiled : UNSANCTIFIED **3 a :** serving to debase or defile what is holy : IRREVERENT **b :** OBSCENE, VULGAR **4 a :** not being among the initiated **b :** not possessing esoteric or expert knowledge — **pro·fane·ly** *adv* — **pro·fane·ness** \-ˈfān-nəs\ *n*

pro·fan·i·ty \prō-ˈfa-nə-tē, prə-\ *n, pl* **-ties** (1607) **1 a :** the quality or state of being profane **b :** the use of profane language **2 a :** profane language **b :** an utterance of profane language

pro·fess \prə-ˈfes, prō-\ *vb* [in sense 1, fr. ME, fr. *profes,* adj., having professed one's vows, fr. AF, fr. LL *professus,* fr. L, pp. of *profitēri* to profess, confess, fr. *pro-* before + *fatēri* to acknowledge; in other senses, fr. L *professus,* pp. — more at CONFESS] *vt* (14c) **1 :** to receive formally into a religious community following a novitiate by acceptance of the required vows **2 a :** to declare or admit openly or freely : AFFIRM **b :** to declare in words or appearances only : PRETEND, CLAIM **3 :** to confess one's faith in or allegiance to **4 a :** to practice or claim to be versed in (a calling or profession) **b :** to teach as a professor ~ *vi* **1 :** to make a profession or avowal **2** *obs* : to profess friendship

pro·fessed \-ˈfest\ *adj* (ca. 1524) **1 :** openly and freely declared or acknowledged : AFFIRMED **2 :** professing to be qualified; *also* : EXPERT

pro·fessed·ly \prə-ˈfe-səd-lē, -ˈfest-lē\ *adv* (1570) **1 :** by profession or declaration : AVOWEDLY **2 :** with pretense : ALLEGEDLY

pro·fes·sion \prə-ˈfe-shən\ *n* [ME *professioun,* fr. AF *profession,* fr. LL & L; LL *profession-, professio,* fr. L, public declaration, fr. *profitēri*] (13c) **1 :** the act of taking the vows of a religious community **2 :** an act of openly declaring or publicly claiming a belief, faith, or opinion : PROTESTATION **3 :** an avowed religious faith **4 a :** a calling requiring specialized knowledge and often long and intensive academic preparation **b :** a principal calling, vocation, or employment **c :** the whole body of persons engaged in a calling

[1]**pro·fes·sion·al** \prə-ˈfesh-nəl, -ˈfe-shə-nᵊl\ *adj* (1606) **1 a :** of, relating to, or characteristic of a profession **b :** engaged in one of the learned professions **c (1) :** characterized by or conforming to the technical or ethical standards of a profession **(2) :** exhibiting a courteous, conscientious, and generally businesslike manner in the workplace **2 a :** participating for gain or livelihood in an activity or field of endeavor often engaged in by amateurs ⟨a ~ golfer⟩ **b :** having a particular profession as a permanent career ⟨a ~ soldier⟩ **c :** engaged in by persons receiving financial return ⟨~ football⟩ **3 :** following a line of conduct as though it were a profession ⟨a ~ patriot⟩ — **pro·fes·sion·al·ly** *adv*

[2]**professional** *n* (1811) : one that is professional; *esp* : one that engages in a pursuit or activity professionally

professional corporation *n* (1970) : a corporation organized by one or more licensed individuals (as a doctor or lawyer) esp. for the purpose of providing professional services and obtaining tax advantages

pro·fes·sion·al·ism \-ˈfesh-nə-ˌli-zəm, -ˈfe-shə-nə-ˌli-\ *n* (1856) **1 :** the conduct, aims, or qualities that characterize or mark a profession or a professional person **2 :** the following of a profession (as athletics) for gain or livelihood

pro·fes·sion·al·ize \-ˌlīz\ *vt* **-ized; -iz·ing** (1856) : to give a professional character to — **pro·fes·sion·al·i·za·tion** \-ˌfesh-nə-lə-ˈzā-shən, -ˌfe-shə-nə-lə-\ *n*

pro·fes·sor \prə-ˈfe-sər\ *n* (14c) **1 :** one that professes, avows, or declares **2 a :** a faculty member of the highest academic rank at an institution of higher education **b :** a teacher at a university, college, or sometimes secondary school **c :** one that teaches or professes special knowledge of an art, sport, or occupation requiring skill — **pro·fes·so·ri·al** \ˌprō-fə-ˈsȯr-ē-əl, ˌprä-\ *adj* — **pro·fes·so·ri·al·ly** \-ē-ə-lē\ *adv* — **pro·fes·sor·ship** \prə-ˈfe-sər-ˌship\ *n*

pro·fes·sor·ate \prə-ˈfe-sə-rət\ *n* (1860) : the office, term of office, or position of a professor

pro·fes·so·ri·at \ˌprō-fə-ˈsȯr-ē-ət, ˌprä-, -ē-ˌat\ *or* **pro·fes·so·ri·ate** \-ət, -ˌāt\ *n* [modif. of F *professorat,* fr. *professeur* professor, fr. L *professor,* fr. *profitēri*] (1858) **1 :** the body of college and university teachers at an institution or in society **2 :** the office, duties, or position of a professor

[1]**prof·fer** \ˈprä-fər\ *vt* **prof·fered; prof·fer·ing** \-f(ə-)riŋ\ [ME *profren,* fr. AF *profrer, proffrir, porofrir,* fr. *por-* forth (fr. L *pro-*) + *offrir* to offer — more at PRO-] (14c) : to present for acceptance : TENDER, OFFER

[2]**proffer** *n* (14c) : OFFER, SUGGESTION

pro·fi·cien·cy \prə-ˈfi-shən(t)-sē\ *n* (1544) **1 :** advancement in knowledge or skill : PROGRESS **2 :** the quality or state of being proficient

pro·fi·cient \-shənt\ *adj* [L *proficient-, proficiens,* prp. of *proficere* to go forward, accomplish, fr. *pro-* forward + *facere* to make — more at PRO-, DO] (ca. 1590) : well advanced in an art, occupation, or branch of knowledge — **proficient** *n* — **pro·fi·cient·ly** *adv*

syn PROFICIENT, ADEPT, SKILLED, SKILLFUL, EXPERT mean having great knowledge and experience in a trade or profession. PROFICIENT implies a thorough competence derived from training and practice ⟨*proficient* in translating foreign languages⟩. ADEPT implies special aptitude as well as proficiency ⟨*adept* at doing long division⟩. SKILLED stresses mastery of technique ⟨a *skilled* surgeon⟩. SKILLFUL implies individual dexterity in execution or performance ⟨*skillful* drivers⟩. EXPERT implies extraordinary proficiency and often connotes knowledge as well as technical skill ⟨*expert* in the evaluation of wines⟩.

[1]**pro·file** \ˈprō-ˌfī(-ə)l\ *n* [It *profilo,* fr. *profilare* to draw in outline, fr. *pro-* forward (fr. L) + *filare* to spin, fr. LL — more at FILE] (1645) **1 :** a representation of something in outline; *esp* : a human head or face represented or seen in a side view **2 :** an outline seen or represented in sharp relief : CONTOUR **3 :** a side or sectional elevation: as **a :** a drawing showing a vertical section of the ground **b :** a vertical section of a soil from the ground surface to the underlying unweathered material **4 :** a set of data often in graphic form portraying the significant features of something ⟨a corporation's earnings ~⟩; *esp* : a graph representing the extent to which an individual exhibits traits or abilities as determined by tests or ratings **5 :** a concise biographical sketch **6 :** degree or level of public exposure ⟨trying to keep a low ~⟩ ⟨a job with a high ~⟩ ***syn*** see OUTLINE

[2]**profile** *vt* **pro·filed; pro·fil·ing** (1715) **1 :** to represent in profile or by a profile : produce (as by drawing, writing, or graphing) a profile of **2**

\ə\ **abut** \ᵊ\ kitten, F table \ər\ **further** \a\ **ash** \ā\ **ace** \ä\ **mop,** mar \au̇\ **out** \ch\ **chin** \e\ bet \ē\ **easy** \g\ **go** \i\ hit \ī\ **ice** \j\ **job** \ŋ\ **sing** \ō\ **go** \ȯ\ **law** \ȯi\ **boy** \th\ **thin** \t͟h\ **the** \ü\ **loot** \u̇\ **foot** \y\ yet \zh\ vision, beige \k, ⁿ, œ, ue, ʸ\ *see* Guide to Pronunciation

: to shape the outline of by passing a cutter around **3** : to subject to profiling — **pro·fil·er** *n*

profiling *n* (1980) : the act or process of extrapolating information about a person based on known traits or tendencies ⟨consumer ~⟩; *specif* : the act of suspecting or targeting a person on the basis of observed characteristics or behavior ⟨racial ~⟩

[1]**prof·it** \ˈprä-fət\ *n, often attrib* [ME, fr. AF, fr. L *profectus* advance, profit, fr. *proficere*] (14c) **1** : a valuable return : GAIN **2** : the excess of returns over expenditure in a transaction or series of transactions; *esp* : the excess of the selling price of goods over their cost **3** : net income usu. for a given period of time **4** : the ratio of profit for a given year to the amount of capital invested or to the value of sales **5** : the compensation accruing to entrepreneurs for the assumption of risk in business enterprise as distinguished from wages or rent — **prof·it·less** \-ləs\ *adj* — **prof·it·wise** \-ˌwīz\ *adv*

[2]**profit** *vi* (14c) **1** : to be of service or advantage : AVAIL **2** : to derive benefit : GAIN **3** : to make a profit ~ *vt* : to be of service to : BENEFIT

prof·it·able \ˈprä-fə-tə-bəl, ˈpräf-tə-bəl\ *adj* (14c) : affording profits : yielding advantageous returns or results — **prof·it·abil·i·ty** \ˌprä-fə-tə-ˈbi-lə-tē\ *n* — **prof·it·able·ness** \ˈprä-fə-tə-bəl-nəs\ *n* — **prof·it·ably** \-blē\ *adv*

profit and loss *n* (1588) : a summary account used at the end of an accounting period to collect the balances of the nominal accounts so that the net profit or loss may be shown

profit center *n* (1968) : a part of a corporation or its product line that is an important source of profits

prof·i·teer \ˌprä-fə-ˈtir\ *n* (1912) : one who makes what is considered an unreasonable profit esp. on the sale of essential goods during times of emergency — **profiteer** *vi*

pro·fit·er·ole \prə-ˈfi-tə-ˌrōl\ *n* [F, perh. fr. *profit* profit] (1884) : a miniature cream puff with a sweet or savory filling

profit sharing *n* (1881) : a system or process under which employees receive a part of the profits of an industrial or commercial enterprise

profit system *n* (1945) : FREE ENTERPRISE

prof·li·ga·cy \ˈprä-fli-gə-sē\ *n* (1738) : the quality or state of being profligate

[1]**prof·li·gate** \ˈprä-fli-gət, -ˌgāt\ *adj* [L *profligatus,* fr. pp. of *profligare* to strike down, fr. *pro-* forward, down + *-fligare* (akin to *fligere* to strike); akin to Gk *phlibein* to squeeze] (1617) **1** : wildly extravagant ⟨~ spending⟩ **2** : completely given up to dissipation and licentiousness ⟨leading a ~ life⟩ — **prof·li·gate·ly** *adv*

[2]**profligate** *n* (1709) : a person given to wildly extravagant and usu. grossly self-indulgent expenditure

pro·flu·ent \ˈprä-ˌflü-ənt, ˈprō-; prō-ˈflü-\ *adj* [ME, fr. L *profluent-, profluens,* prp. of *profluere* to flow forth, fr. *pro-* forth + *fluere* to flow — more at PRO-, FLUID] (15c) : flowing copiously or smoothly

pro for·ma \(ˌ)prō-ˈfȯr-mə\ *adj* [L, for form] (ca. 1580) **1** : made or carried out in a perfunctory manner or as a formality **2** : based on financial assumptions or projections: as **a** : reflecting a transaction (as a merger) or other development as if it had been or will be in effect for a past or future period ⟨a *pro forma* balance sheet⟩ **b** : excluding usu. extraordinary charges or expenses (as from acquisitions, restructuring, or the write-down of goodwill) often in order to present a more attractive financial report ⟨*pro forma* income⟩

pro forma invoice *n* (1857) : a document provided prior to or with a shipment of goods (as for export) that describes the items and terms of sale but does not have the function of a real invoice

[1]**pro·found** \prə-ˈfau̇nd, prō-\ *adj* [ME, fr. AF *parfunt, profond* deep, fr. L *profundus,* fr. *pro-* before + *fundus* bottom — more at PRO-, BOTTOM] (14c) **1 a** : having intellectual depth and insight **b** : difficult to fathom or understand **2 a** : extending far below the surface **b** : coming from, reaching to, or situated at a depth : DEEP-SEATED ⟨a ~ sigh⟩ **3 a** : characterized by intensity of feeling or quality **b** : all encompassing : COMPLETE ⟨~ sleep⟩ ⟨~ deafness⟩ — **pro·found·ly** \-ˈfau̇n(d)-lē\ *adv* — **pro·found·ness** \-ˈfau̇n(d)-nəs\ *n*

[2]**profound** *n* (1621) *archaic* : something that is very deep; *specif* : the depths of the sea

pro·fun·di·ty \prə-ˈfən-də-tē\ *n, pl* **-ties** [ME *profundite,* fr. L *profunditat-, profunditas* depth, fr. *profundus*] (15c) **1 a** : intellectual depth **b** : something profound or abstruse **2** : the quality or state of being profound or deep

pro·fuse \prə-ˈfyüs, prō-\ *adj* [ME, fr. L *profusus,* pp. of *profundere* to pour forth, fr. *pro-* forth + *fundere* to pour — more at FOUND] (15c) **1** : pouring forth liberally : EXTRAVAGANT ⟨~ in their thanks⟩ **2** : exhibiting great abundance : BOUNTIFUL ⟨a ~ harvest⟩ — **pro·fuse·ly** *adv* — **pro·fuse·ness** *n*

syn PROFUSE, LAVISH, PRODIGAL, LUXURIANT, LUSH, EXUBERANT mean giving or given out in great abundance. PROFUSE implies pouring forth without restraint ⟨*profuse* apologies⟩. LAVISH suggests an unstinted or unmeasured profusion ⟨a *lavish* party⟩. PRODIGAL implies reckless or wasteful lavishness threatening to lead to early exhaustion of resources ⟨*prodigal* spending⟩. LUXURIANT suggests a rich and splendid abundance ⟨a *luxuriant* beard⟩. LUSH suggests rich, soft luxuriance ⟨a *lush* green lawn⟩. EXUBERANT implies marked vitality or vigor in what produces abundantly ⟨an *exuberant* imagination⟩.

pro·fu·sion \-ˈfyü-zhən\ *n* (1545) **1** : lavish expenditure : EXTRAVAGANCE **2** : the quality or state of being profuse **3** : great quantity : lavish display or supply ⟨snow falling in ~⟩

[1]**prog** \ˈpräg\ *vi* **progged; prog·ging** [origin unknown] (1624) *chiefly dial* : to search about; *esp* : FORAGE

[2]**prog** *n* (1655) *chiefly dial* : FOOD, VICTUALS

[3]**prog** *abbr* **1** program **2** progressive

pro·gen·i·tor \prō-ˈje-nə-tər, prə-\ *n* [ME, fr. AF *progenitour,* fr. L *progenitor,* fr. *progignere* to beget, fr. *pro-* forth + *gignere* to beget — more at KIN] (14c) **1 a** : an ancestor in the direct line : FOREFATHER **b** : a biologically ancestral form **2** : PRECURSOR, ORIGINATOR ⟨~*s* of socialist ideas —*Times Lit. Supp.*⟩ ⟨~ cells⟩

prog·e·ny \ˈprä-jə-nē\ *n, pl* **-nies** [ME *progenie,* fr. AF, fr. L *progenies,* fr. *progignere*] (14c) **1 a** : DESCENDANTS, CHILDREN **b** : offspring of animals or plants **2** : OUTCOME, PRODUCT **3** : a body of followers, disciples, or successors

pro·ge·ria \prō-ˈjir-ē-ə\ *n* (1904) : a rare genetic disorder of childhood marked by slowed physical growth and characteristic signs (as baldness, wrinkled skin, and atherosclerosis) of rapid aging with death usu. occurring around puberty

pro·ges·ta·tion·al \ˌprō-ˌjes-ˈtā-shnəl, -shə-nᵊl\ *adj* (1923) : preceding pregnancy or gestation; *esp* : of, relating to, inducing, or constituting the modifications of the female mammalian system associated esp. with ovulation and corpus luteum formation ⟨~ hormones⟩

pro·ges·ter·one \prō-ˈjes-tə-ˌrōn\ *n* [*progestin* + *-sterone*] (1935) : a female steroid sex hormone $C_{21}H_{30}O_2$ that is secreted by the corpus luteum to prepare the endometrium for implantation and later by the placenta during pregnancy to prevent rejection of the developing embryo or fetus; *also* : a synthetic steroid resembling progesterone in action

pro·ges·tin \-ˈjes-tən\ *n* [*pro-* + *gest*ation + [1]*-in*] (1930) : PROGESTOGEN; *esp* : a synthetic progesterone (as levonorgestrel)

pro·ges·to·gen \-ˈjes-tə-jən\ *n* [*progest*ational + *-ogen* (as in *estrogen*)] (ca. 1941) : a naturally occurring or synthetic progestational steroid — **pro·ges·to·gen·ic** \-ˌjes-tə-ˈje-nik\ *adj*

pro·glot·tid \(ˌ)prō-ˈglä-təd\ *n* [NL *proglottis*] (1864) : a segment of a tapeworm containing both male and female reproductive organs

pro·glot·tis \(ˌ)prō-ˈglä-təs\ *n, pl* **-glot·ti·des** \-ˈglä-tə-ˌdēz\ [NL *proglottid-, proglottis,* fr. Gk *proglōttis* tip of the tongue, fr. *pro-* + *glōtta* tongue — more at GLOSS] (1855) : PROGLOTTID

prog·na·thism \ˈpräg-nə-ˌthi-zəm, präg-ˈnā-\ *n* (ca. 1864) : the condition marked by a prognathous jaw — **prog·na·thic** \präg-ˈna-thik, -ˈnā-\ *adj*

prog·na·thous \ˈpräg-nə-thəs\ *adj* (1836) : being or having an upper or lower jaw that projects abnormally forward

prog·no·sis \präg-ˈnō-səs\ *n, pl* **-no·ses** \-ˌsēz\ [LL, fr. Gk *prognōsis,* lit., foreknowledge, fr. *progignōskein* to know before, fr. *pro-* + *gignōskein* to know — more at KNOW] (1655) **1** : the prospect of recovery as anticipated from the usual course of disease or peculiarities of the case **2** : FORECAST, PROGNOSTICATION

[1]**prog·nos·tic** \präg-ˈnäs-tik\ *n* [ME *pronostique,* fr. MF, fr. L *prognosticum,* fr. Gk *prognōstikon,* fr. neut. of *prognōstikos* foretelling, fr. *progignōskein*] (15c) **1** : something that foretells : PORTENT **2** : PROGNOSTICATION, PROPHECY

[2]**prognostic** *adj* (1603) : of, relating to, or serving as ground for prognostication or a prognosis ⟨~ weather charts⟩ ⟨favorable ~ signs⟩

prog·nos·ti·cate \präg-ˈnäs-tə-ˌkāt\ *vt* **-cat·ed; -cat·ing** (15c) **1** : to foretell from signs or symptoms : PREDICT **2** : PRESAGE ***syn*** see FORETELL — **prog·nos·ti·ca·tive** \-ˌkā-tiv\ *adj* — **prog·nos·ti·ca·tor** \-ˌkā-tər\ *n*

prog·nos·ti·ca·tion \(ˌ)präg-ˌnäs-tə-ˈkā-shən\ *n* (15c) **1** : an indication in advance : FORETOKEN **2 a** : an act, the fact, or the power of prognosticating : FORECAST **b** : FOREBODING

pro·grade \ˈprō-ˌgrād\ *adj* [L *pro-* forward + E *-grade* (as in *retrograde*)] (1967) : having or being a direction of rotation or revolution that is counterclockwise as viewed from the north pole of the sky or a planet

[1]**pro·gram** \ˈprō-ˌgram, -grəm\ *n* [F *programme* agenda, public notice, fr. Gk *programma,* fr. *prographein* to write before, fr. *pro-* before + *graphein* to write — more at CARVE] (1633) **1** [LL *programma,* fr. Gk] : a public notice **2 a** : a brief usu. printed outline of the order to be followed, of the features to be presented, and the persons participating (as in a public performance) **b** : the performance of a program; *esp* : a performance broadcast on radio or television **3** : a plan or system under which action may be taken toward a goal **4** : CURRICULUM **5** : PROSPECTUS, SYLLABUS **6 a** : a plan for the programming of a mechanism (as a computer) **b** : a sequence of coded instructions that can be inserted into a mechanism (as a computer) **c** : a sequence of coded instructions (as genes or behavioral responses) that is part of an organism

[2]**program** *also* **programme** *vt* **-grammed** *or* **-gramed; -gram·ming** *or* **-gram·ing** (1896) **1 a** : to arrange or furnish a program of or for : BILL **b** : to enter in a program **2** : to work out a sequence of operations to be performed by (a mechanism) : provide with a program **3 a** : to insert a program for (a particular action) into or as if into a mechanism **b** : to control by or as if by a program **c** (1) : to code in an organism's program (2) : to provide with a biological program ⟨cells *programmed* to synthesize hemoglobin⟩ **4** : to predetermine the thinking, behavior, or operations of as if by computer programming ⟨children are *programmed* into violence —Lisa A. Richette⟩ — **pro·gram·ma·bil·i·ty** \(ˌ)prō-ˌgra-mə-ˈbi-lə-tē\ *n* — **pro·gram·ma·ble** \ˈprō-ˌgra-mə-bəl\ *adj or n*

program director *n* (1948) : one in charge of planning and scheduling program material for a radio or television station or network

pro·gram·mat·ic \ˌprō-grə-ˈma-tik\ *adj* (1896) **1** : relating to program music **2** : of, relating to, resembling, or having a program — **pro·gram·mat·i·cal·ly** \-ti-k(ə-)lē\ *adv*

programme *chiefly Brit var of* PROGRAM

programmed cell death *n* (1982) : APOPTOSIS

programmed instruction *n* (1961) : instruction through information given in small steps with each requiring a correct response by the learner before going on to the next step

pro·gram·mer *also* **pro·gram·er** \ˈprō-ˌgra-mər, -grə-\ *n* (ca. 1889) : one that programs: as **a** : a person who prepares and tests programs for devices (as computers) **b** : one that programs a mechanism **c** : one that prepares an instructional program **d** : a person who plans or prepares entertainment programs ⟨a television ~⟩

pro·gram·ming *also* **pro·gram·ing** \-miŋ\ *n* (1940) **1** : the planning, scheduling, or performing of a program **2 a** : the process of instructing or learning by means of an instructional program **b** : the process of preparing an instructional program

program music *n* (1879) : music intended to suggest a sequence of images or incidents

program trading *n* (1984) : computerized trading of large blocks of stocks in one market and stock index futures in another so as to take advantage of price differentials between the markets

[1]**prog·ress** \ˈprä-grəs, -ˌgres, *US also & Brit usu* ˈprō-ˌgres\ *n* [ME, fr. AF *progrés,* fr. L *progressus* advance, fr. *progredi* to go forth, fr. *pro-* forward + *gradi* to go — more at PRO-, GRADE] (15c) **1 a** (1) : a royal journey marked by pomp and pageant (2) : a state procession **b** : a tour or circuit made by an official (as a judge) **c** : an expedition, journey, or march through a region **2** : a forward or onward movement (as to an objective or to a goal) : ADVANCE **3** : gradual betterment; *esp*

: the progressive development of humankind — **in progress** : going on : OCCURRING

[2]**pro·gress** \prə-ˈgres\ *vi* (1539) **1** : to move forward : PROCEED **2** : to develop to a higher, better, or more advanced stage

pro·gres·sion \prə-ˈgre-shən\ *n* (15c) **1** : a sequence of numbers in which each term is related to its predecessor by a uniform law **2 a** : the action or process of progressing : ADVANCE **b** : a continuous and connected series : SEQUENCE **3 a** : succession of musical tones or chords **b** : the movement of musical parts in harmony **c** : SEQUENCE 2c — **pro·gres·sion·al** \-ˈgresh-nəl, -ˈgre-shə-nᵊl\ *adj*

[1]**pro·gres·sive** \prə-ˈgre-siv\ *adj* (ca. 1612) **1 a** : of, relating to, or characterized by progress **b** : making use of or interested in new ideas, findings, or opportunities **c** : of, relating to, or constituting an educational theory marked by emphasis on the individual child, informality of classroom procedure, and encouragement of self-expression **2** : of, relating to, or characterized by progression **3** : moving forward or onward : ADVANCING **4 a** : increasing in extent or severity ⟨a ~ disease⟩ **b** : increasing in rate as the base increases ⟨a ~ tax⟩ **5** *often cap* : of or relating to political Progressives **6** : of, relating to, or constituting a verb form that expresses action or state in progress at the time of speaking or a time spoken of **7** : of, relating to, or being a multifocal lens with a gradual transition between focal lengths ⟨~ bifocals⟩ **8** : or, relating to, or using a method of video scanning (as for television or a computer monitor) in which the horizontal lines of each frame are drawn successively from top to bottom — compare INTERLACED — **pro·gres·sive·ly** *adv* — **pro·gres·sive·ness** *n*

[2]**progressive** *n* (1846) **1 a** : one that is progressive **b** : one believing in moderate political change and esp. social improvement by governmental action **2** *cap* : a member of any of various U.S. political parties: as **a** : a member of a predominantly agrarian minor party that around 1912 split off from the Republicans; *specif* : BULL MOOSE **b** : a follower of Robert M. La Follette in the presidential campaign of 1924 **c** : a follower of Henry A. Wallace in the presidential campaign of 1948

Progressive Conservative *adj* (1944) : of or relating to a major political party in Canada traditionally advocating economic nationalism and close ties with the United Kingdom and the Commonwealth of Nations — **Progressive Conservative** *n*

pro·gres·siv·ism \prə-ˈgre-si-ˌvi-zəm\ *n* (1892) **1** : the principles, beliefs, or practices of progressives **2** *cap* : the political and economic doctrines advocated by the Progressives **3** : the theories of progressive education — **pro·gres·siv·ist** \-vist\ *n or adj* — **pro·gres·siv·is·tic** \-ˌgre-si-ˈvis-tik\ *adj*

pro·gres·siv·i·ty \ˌprō-(ˌ)gre-ˈsi-və-tē\ *n* (1883) : the quality or state of being a progressive tax

pro·hib·it \prō-ˈhi-bət, prə-\ *vt* [ME, fr. L *prohibitus,* pp. of *prohibēre* to keep off, fr. *pro-* forward + *habēre* to hold — more at PRO-, GIVE] (15c) **1** : to forbid by authority : ENJOIN **2 a** : to prevent from doing something **b** : PRECLUDE ***syn*** see FORBID

pro·hi·bi·tion \ˌprō-ə-ˈbi-shən *also* ˌprō-hə-\ *n* (14c) **1** : the act of prohibiting by authority **2** : an order to restrain or stop **3** *often cap* : the forbidding by law of the manufacture, transportation, and sale of alcoholic liquors except for medicinal and sacramental purposes

pro·hi·bi·tion·ist \-sh(ə-)nist\ *n* (1830) : one who favors prohibition; *esp, cap* : a member of a U.S. political party advocating prohibition

pro·hib·i·tive \prō-ˈhi-bə-tiv, prə-\ *adj* (15c) **1** : tending to prohibit or restrain **2** : tending to preclude use or purchase ⟨~ costs⟩ **3** : almost certain to perform as predicted ⟨a ~ favorite⟩ — **pro·hib·i·tive·ly** *adv* — **pro·hib·i·tive·ness** *n*

pro·hib·i·to·ry \-ˈhi-bə-ˌtȯr-ē\ *adj* (ca. 1591) : PROHIBITIVE

pro·in·su·lin \(ˌ)prō-ˈin(t)-s(ə-)lən\ *n* (1916) : a single-chain pancreatic polypeptide precursor of insulin that gives rise to the double chain of insulin by cleavage and loss of the middle part of the molecule

proj *abbr* **1** project **2** projector

[1]**proj·ect** \ˈprä-ˌjekt, -jikt *also* ˈprō-\ *n* [ME *projecte,* fr. ML *projectum,* fr. L, neut. of *projectus,* pp. of *proicere* to throw forward, fr. *pro-* + *jacere* to throw — more at JET] (15c) **1** : a specific plan or design : SCHEME **2** *obs* : IDEA **3** : a planned undertaking: as **a** : a definitely formulated piece of research **b** : a large usu. government-supported undertaking **c** : a task or problem engaged in usu. by a group of students to supplement and apply classroom studies **4** : a usu. public housing development consisting of houses or apartments built and arranged according to a single plan ***syn*** see PLAN

[2]**pro·ject** \prə-ˈjekt\ *vb* [AF *projecter,* fr. L *projectus,* pp.] *vt* (15c) **1 a** : to devise in the mind : DESIGN **b** : to plan, figure, or estimate for the future **2** : to throw or cast forward : THRUST **3** : to put or set forth : present for consideration **4** : to cause to jut out **5** : to cause (light or shadow) to fall into space or (an image) to fall on a surface **6** : to reproduce (as a point, line, or area) on a surface by motion in a prescribed direction **7** : to display outwardly esp. to an audience **8** : to attribute (one's own ideas, feelings, or characteristics) to other people or to objects ~ *vi* **1** : to jut out : PROTRUDE **2 a** : to come across vividly : give an impression **b** : to make oneself heard clearly — **project·able** \-ˈjek-tə-bəl\ *adj*

[1]**pro·jec·tile** \prə-ˈjek-tᵊl, -ˌtī(-ə)l, *chiefly Brit* ˈprä-jik-ˌtī(-ə)l\ *n* (1665) **1** : a body projected by external force and continuing in motion by its own inertia; *esp* : a missile for a weapon (as a firearm) **2** : a self-propelling weapon (as a rocket)

[2]**projectile** *adj* (1715) **1** : projecting or impelling forward ⟨a ~ force⟩ **2** : capable of being thrust forward

projectile vom·it·ing \-ˈvä-mə-tiŋ\ *n* (1862) : vomiting that is sudden and so vigorous that the vomitus is forcefully projected to a distance

pro·jec·tion \prə-ˈjek-shən\ *n* (1557) **1 a** : a systematic presentation of intersecting coordinate lines on a flat surface upon which features from a curved surface (as of the earth or the celestial sphere) may be mapped ⟨an equal-area map ~⟩ **b** : the process or technique of reproducing a spatial object upon a plane or curved surface or a line by projecting its points; *also* : a graph or figure so formed **2** : a transforming change **3** : the act of throwing or thrusting forward **4** : the forming of a plan : SCHEMING **5 a** (1) : a jutting out (2) : a part that juts out **b** : a view of a building or architectural element **6 a** : the act of perceiving a mental object as spatially and sensibly objective; *also* : something so perceived **b** : the attribution of one's own ideas, feelings, or attitudes to other people or to objects; *esp* : the externalization of blame, guilt, or responsibility as a defense against anxiety **7** : the display of motion pictures by projecting an image from them upon a screen **8 a** : the act of projecting esp. to an audience **b** : control of the volume, clarity, and distinctness of a voice to gain greater audibility **9** : an estimate of future possibilities based on a current trend — **pro·jec·tion·al** \-shnəl, -shə-nᵊl\ *adj*

syn PROJECTION, PROTRUSION, PROTUBERANCE, BULGE mean an extension beyond the normal line or surface. PROJECTION implies a jutting out esp. at a sharp angle ⟨those *projections* along the wall are safety hazards⟩. PROTRUSION suggests a thrusting out so that the extension seems a deformity ⟨the bizarre *protrusions* of a coral reef⟩. PROTUBERANCE implies a growing or swelling out in rounded form ⟨a skin disease marked by warty *protuberances*⟩. BULGE suggests an expansion caused by internal pressure ⟨*bulges* in the tile floor⟩.

projection booth *n* (ca. 1928) : a booth in a theater or hall for housing and operating a projector and esp. a motion-picture projector

pro·jec·tion·ist \prə-ˈjek-sh(ə-)nist\ *n* (1922) : one that makes projections: as **a** : CARTOGRAPHER **b** : a person who operates a motion-picture projector or television equipment

pro·jec·tive \prə-ˈjek-tiv\ *adj* (1682) **1** : relating to, produced by, or involving geometric projection **2** : of or relating to something that indicates the psychodynamic constitution of an individual ⟨~ tests⟩ — **pro·jec·tive·ly** *adv*

projective geometry *n* (1885) : a branch of geometry that deals with the properties of configurations that are unaltered by projection

pro·jec·tor \prə-ˈjek-tər\ *n* (1596) **1** : one that plans a project; *specif* : PROMOTER **2** : one that projects: as **a** : a device for projecting a beam of light **b** : an optical instrument for projecting an image upon a surface **c** : a machine for projecting motion pictures on a screen **3** : an imagined line from an object to a surface along which projection takes place

pro·jet \prō-ˈzhā, ˈprō-ˌ\ *n, pl* **projets** \-ˈzhā(z), -ˌzhā(z)\ [F, fr. MF *pourget,* fr. *pourjeter, projeter,* lit., to throw forward, fr. *por-* (fr. L *porro* forward; akin to Gk *pro-* forward) + *jeter* to throw — more at FOR, JET] (1808) **1** : PLAN; *esp* : a draft of a proposed measure or treaty **2** : a projected or proposed design

pro·kary·ote *also* **pro·cary·ote** \(ˌ)prō-ˈka-rē-ˌōt\ *n* [NL *Prokaryotes,* proposed subdivision of protists, fr. [1]*pro-* + *kary-* + *-otes,* pl. n. suffix, fr. Gk *-ōtos* — more at -OTIC] (1963) : any of the typically unicellular microorganisms that lack a distinct nucleus and membrane-bound organelles and that are classified as a kingdom (Prokaryotae syn. Monera) or into two domains (Bacteria and Archaea) — compare ARCHAEA, BACTERIUM, EUKARYOTE — **pro·kary·ot·ic** \-ˌka-rē-ˈä-tik\ *adj*

pro·lac·tin \prō-ˈlak-tən\ *n* [[2]*pro-* + *lact-* + [1]*-in*] (1932) : a protein hormone of the anterior lobe of the pituitary that induces lactation

pro·la·min *or* **pro·la·mine** \ˈprō-lə-mən, -ˌmēn\ *n* [ISV *proline* + *ammonia* + [1]*-in,* [2]*-ine*] (1908) : any of various simple proteins (as zein) that are found esp. in grass seeds and are soluble in alcohol

[1]**pro·lapse** \prō-ˈlaps, ˈprō-ˌ\ *n* [NL *prolapsus,* fr. LL, fall, fr. L *prolabi* to fall or slide forward, fr. *pro-* forward + *labi* to slide — more at PRO-, SLEEP] (ca. 1834) : the falling down or slipping of a body part from its usual position or relations

[2]**pro·lapse** \prō-ˈlaps\ *vi* **pro·lapsed; pro·laps·ing** (1876) : to undergo prolapse

pro·late \ˈprō-ˌlāt\ *adj* [L *prolatus* (pp. of *proferre* to bring forward, extend) fr. *pro-* forward + *-latus,* pp. of *ferre* to carry — more at BEAR, TOLERATE] (1694) : EXTENDED; *esp* : elongated in the direction of a line joining the poles ⟨a ~ spheroid⟩

prole \ˈprōl\ *n or adj* (1887) : PROLETARIAN

pro·leg \ˈprō-ˌleg, -ˌlāg\ *n* (1816) : a fleshy leg that occurs on an abdominal segment of some insect larvae but not in the adult

pro·le·gom·e·non \ˌprō-li-ˈgä-mə-ˌnän, -nən\ *n, pl* **-e·na** \-nə\ [Gk, neut. pres. pass. part. of *prolegein* to say beforehand, fr. *pro-* before + *legein* to say — more at LEGEND] (ca. 1652) : prefatory remarks; *specif* : a formal essay or critical discussion serving to introduce and interpret an extended work — **pro·le·gom·e·nous** \-nəs\ *adj*

pro·lep·sis \prō-ˈlep-səs\ *n, pl* **-lep·ses** \-ˌsēz\ [Gk *prolēpsis,* fr. *prolambanein* to take beforehand, fr. *pro-* before + *lambanein* to take — more at LATCH] (1578) : ANTICIPATION: as **a** : the representation or assumption of a future act or development as if presently existing or accomplished **b** : the application of an adjective to a noun in anticipation of the result of the action of the verb (as in "while yon slow oxen turn the *furrowed* plain") — **pro·lep·tic** \-ˈlep-tik\ *adj* — **pro·lep·ti·cal·ly** \-ti-k(ə-)lē\ *adv*

pro·le·tar·i·an \ˌprō-lə-ˈter-ē-ən\ *n* [L *proletarius,* fr. *proles* progeny, fr. *pro-* forth + *-oles* (akin to *alere* to nourish) — more at OLD] (1658) : a member of the proletariat — **proletarian** *adj*

pro·le·tar·i·an·ise *Brit var of* PROLETARIANIZE

pro·le·tar·i·an·ize \-ˈter-ē-ə-ˌnīz\ *vt* **-ized; -iz·ing** (1887) : to reduce to a proletarian status or level — **pro·le·tar·i·an·i·za·tion** \-ˌter-ē-ə-nə-ˈzā-shən\ *n*

pro·le·tar·i·at \ˌprō-lə-ˈter-ē-ət, -ē-ˌat\ *n* [F *prolétariat,* fr. L *proletarius*] (1847) **1** : the laboring class; *esp* : the class of industrial workers who lack their own means of production and hence sell their labor to live **2** : the lowest social or economic class of a community

pro–life \(ˌ)prō-ˈlīf\ *adj* (1971) : opposed to abortion — **pro–lif·er** \-ˈlī-fər\ *n*

pro·lif·er·ate \prə-ˈli-fə-ˌrāt\ *vb* **-at·ed; -at·ing** [back-formation fr. *proliferation,* fr. F *prolifération,* fr. *proliférer* to proliferate, fr. *prolifère* reproducing freely, fr. L *proles* + *-fer* -ferous] *vi* (1873) **1** : to grow by rapid production of new parts, cells, buds, or offspring **2** : to increase in number as if by proliferating : MULTIPLY ~ *vt* **1** : to cause to grow by proliferating **2** : to cause to increase in number or extent as if by proliferating — **pro·lif·er·a·tion** \-ˌli-fə-ˈrā-shən\ *n* — **pro·lif·er·a·tive** \-ˈli-fə-ˌrā-tiv, -f(ə-)rə-tiv\ *adj*

pro·lif·ic \prə-ˈli-fik\ *adj* [F *prolifique,* fr. MF, fr. L *proles* + MF *-fique* -fic] (1650) **1** : producing young or fruit esp. freely : FRUITFUL **2** *archaic* : causing abundant growth, generation, or reproduction **3**

: marked by abundant inventiveness or productivity ‹a ~ composer› ***syn*** see FERTILE — **pro·lif·i·ca·cy** \-ˈli-fi-kə-sē\ *n* — **pro·lif·i·cal·ly** \-fi-k(ə-)lē\ *adv* — **pro·lif·ic·ness** \-fik-nəs\ *n*

pro·li·fic·i·ty \ˌprō-lə-ˈfi-sə-tē\ *n* (1725) : prolific power or character

pro·line \ˈprō-ˌlēn\ *n* [G *Prolin,* contr. of *Pyrrolidin* pyrrolidine (C_4H_9N), fr. ISV *pyrrole* + *-idine*] (1904) : an amino acid $C_5H_9NO_2$ that can be synthesized by animals from glutamate

pro·lix \prō-ˈliks, ˈprō-(ˌ)\ *adj* [ME, fr. AF & L; AF *prolix,* fr. L *prolixus* extended, fr. *pro-* forward + *liquēre* to be fluid — more at LIQUID] (15c) **1** : unduly prolonged or drawn out : too long **2** : marked by or using an excess of words ***syn*** see WORDY — **pro·lix·i·ty** \prō-ˈlik-sə-tē\ *n* — **pro·lix·ly** *adv*

pro·loc·u·tor \prō-ˈlä-kyə-tər\ *n* [ME, fr. L, fr. *pro-* for + *locutor* speaker, fr. *loqui* to speak] (15c) **1** : one who speaks for another : SPOKESMAN **2** : presiding officer : CHAIRMAN

pro·log·ize \ˈprō-ˌlȯ-ˌgīz, -ˌlä-; -lə-ˌjīz\ *or* **pro·logu·ize** \-ˌlȯ-ˌgīz, -ˌlä-\ *vi* **-log·ized** *or* **-logu·ized; -log·iz·ing** *or* **-logu·iz·ing** (1608) : to write or speak a prologue

pro·logue *also* **pro·log** \ˈprō-ˌlȯg, -ˌläg\ *n* [ME *prolog,* fr. AF *prologue,* fr. L *prologus* preface to a play, fr. Gk *prologos* part of a Greek play preceding the entry of the chorus, fr. *pro-* before + *legein* to speak — more at PRO-, LEGEND] (14c) **1** : the preface or introduction to a literary work **2 a** : a speech often in verse addressed to the audience by an actor at the beginning of a play **b** : the actor speaking such a prologue **3** : an introductory or preceding event or development

pro·long \prə-ˈlȯŋ\ *vt* [ME, fr. MF *prolonguer,* fr. LL *prolongare,* fr. L *pro-* forward + *longus* long] (15c) **1** : to lengthen in time : CONTINUE **2** : to lengthen in extent, scope, or range ***syn*** see EXTEND — **pro·lon·ga·tion** \(ˌ)prō-ˌlȯŋ-ˈgā-shən, prə-\ *n* — **pro·long·er** \prə-ˈlȯŋ-ər\ *n*

pro·lu·sion \prō-ˈlü-zhən\ *n* [L *prolusion-, prolusio,* fr. *proludere* to play beforehand, fr. *pro-* before + *ludere* to play — more at LUDICROUS] (1601) **1** : a preliminary trial or exercise : PRELUDE **2** : an introductory and often tentative discourse — **pro·lu·so·ry** \-ˈlü-sə-rē, -zə-; -ˈlüz-rē, -ˈlüz-\ *adj*

[1]**prom** \ˈpräm\ *n* [short for *promenade*] (1894) **1** : a formal dance given by a high school or college class **2** *Brit* : PROMENADE 2

[2]**prom** *abbr* promontory

[1]**prom·e·nade** \ˌprä-mə-ˈnād, -ˈnäd\ *vb* **-nad·ed; -nad·ing** [[2]*promenade*] *vi* (1588) **1** : to take or go on a promenade **2** : to perform a promenade in a dance ~ *vt* : to walk about in or on — **prom·e·nad·er** *n*

[2]**promenade** *n* [F, fr. *promener* to take for a walk, fr. MF, alter. of OF *pourmener,* fr. *pour-* completely (fr. L *pro-*) + *mener* to lead — more at PRO-, AMENABLE] (1648) **1** : a place for strolling **2** : a leisurely walk or ride esp. in a public place for pleasure or display **3 a** : a ceremonious opening of a formal ball consisting of a grand march of all the guests **b** : a figure in a square dance in which couples move counterclockwise in a circle

promenade deck *n* (1829) : an upper deck or an area on a deck of a passenger ship where passengers stroll

Pro·me·the·an \prə-ˈmē-thē-ən\ *adj* (1594) : of, relating to, or resembling Prometheus, his experiences, or his art; *esp* : daringly original or creative

Pro·me·theus \-thē-əs, -ˌthyüs\ *n* [L, fr. Gk *Promētheus*] (14c) : a Titan who is chained and tortured by Zeus for stealing fire from heaven and giving it to humankind

pro·me·thi·um \-thē-əm\ *n* [NL, fr. L *Prometheus*] (1948) : a radioactive metallic element of the rare-earth group obtained as a fission product of uranium or from neutron-irradiated neodymium — see ELEMENT table

prom·i·nence \ˈprä-mə-nən(t)s, ˈpräm-nən(t)s\ *n* (1598) **1** : something prominent : PROJECTION ‹a rocky ~› **2** : the quality, state, or fact of being prominent or conspicuous **3** : a mass of gas resembling a cloud that arises from the chromosphere of the sun

prom·i·nent \-nənt\ *adj* [ME *promynent,* fr. L *prominent-, prominens,* fr. prp. of *prominēre* to jut forward, fr. *pro-* forward + *-minēre* (akin to *mont-, mons* mountain) — more at MOUNT] (15c) **1** : standing out or projecting beyond a surface or line : PROTUBERANT **2 a** : readily noticeable : CONSPICUOUS **b** : widely and popularly known : LEADING ***syn*** see NOTICEABLE — **prom·i·nent·ly** *adv*

pro·mis·cu·i·ty \ˌprä-mə-ˈskyü-ə-tē, ˌprō-\ *n, pl* **-ties** (ca. 1849) **1** : miscellaneous mingling or selection of persons or things : INDISCRIMINATENESS **2** : promiscuous sexual behavior

pro·mis·cu·ous \prə-ˈmis-kyə-wəs\ *adj* [L *promiscuus,* fr. *pro-* forth + *miscēre* to mix — more at PRO-, MIX] (1601) **1** : composed of all sorts of persons or things **2** : not restricted to one class, sort, or person : INDISCRIMINATE ‹education . . . cheapened through the ~ distribution of diplomas —Norman Cousins› **3** : not restricted to one sexual partner **4** : CASUAL, IRREGULAR ‹~ eating habits› — **pro·mis·cu·ous·ly** *adv* — **pro·mis·cu·ous·ness** *n*

[1]**prom·ise** \ˈprä-məs\ *n* [ME *promis,* fr. L *promissum,* fr. neut. of *promissus,* pp. of *promittere* to send forth, promise, fr. *pro-* forth + *mittere* to send] (15c) **1 a** : a declaration that one will do or refrain from doing something specified **b** : a legally binding declaration that gives the person to whom it is made a right to expect or to claim the performance or forbearance of a specified act **2** : reason to expect something ‹little ~ of relief›; *esp* : ground for expectation of success, improvement, or excellence ‹shows considerable ~› **3** : something that is promised

[2]**promise** *vb* **prom·ised; prom·is·ing** *vt* (15c) **1** : to pledge to do, bring about, or provide ‹~ aid› **2** *archaic* : WARRANT, ASSURE **3** *chiefly dial* : BETROTH **4** : to suggest beforehand : give promise of ‹dark clouds ~ rain› ~ *vi* **1** : to make a promise **2** : to give ground for expectation : be imminent — **prom·is·ee** \ˌprä-mə-ˈsē\ *n* — **prom·i·sor** \-ˈsȯr\ *also* **prom·is·er** \ˈprä-mə-sər\ *n*

promised land *n* (1604) : something and esp. a place or condition believed to promise final satisfaction or realization of hopes

promising *adj* (1597) : full of promise : likely to succeed or to yield good results ‹a ~ new medicine› — **prom·is·ing·ly** \-siŋ-lē\ *adv*

prom·is·so·ry \ˈprä-mə-ˌsȯr-ē\ *adj* [ME *promissorye,* fr. ML *promissorius,* fr. L *promittere*] (15c) : containing or conveying a promise or assurance

promissory note *n* (1710) : a written promise to pay at a fixed or determinable future time a sum of money to a specified individual or to bearer

pro·mo \ˈprō-(ˌ)mō\ *n, pl* **promos** *often attrib* [short for *promotional*] (1946) : a promotional announcement, blurb, or appearance

prom·on·to·ry \ˈprä-mən-ˌtȯr-ē\ *n, pl* **-ries** [L *promunturium, promonturium;* prob. akin to *prominēre* to jut forth — more at PROMINENT] (1548) **1 a** : a high point of land or rock projecting into a body of water **b** : a prominent mass of land overlooking or projecting into a lowland **2** : a bodily prominence

pro·mote \prə-ˈmōt\ *vt* **pro·mot·ed; pro·mot·ing** [ME, fr. L *promotus,* pp. of *promovēre,* lit., to move forward, fr. *pro-* forward + *movēre* to move] (14c) **1 a** : to advance in station, rank, or honor : RAISE **b** : to change (a pawn) into a piece in chess by moving to the eighth rank **c** : to advance (a student) from one grade to the next higher grade **2 a** : to contribute to the growth or prosperity of : FURTHER ‹~ international understanding› **b** : to help bring (as an enterprise) into being : LAUNCH **c** : to present (merchandise) for buyer acceptance through advertising, publicity, or discounting **3** *slang* : to get possession of by doubtful means or by ingenuity ***syn*** see ADVANCE — **pro·mot·abil·i·ty** \-ˌmō-tə-ˈbi-lə-tē\ *n* — **pro·mot·able** \-ˈmō-tə-bəl\ *adj*

pro·mot·er \-ˈmō-tər\ *n* (14c) **1** : one that promotes; *esp* : one who assumes the financial responsibilities of a sporting event (as a boxing match) including contracting with the principals, renting the site, and collecting gate receipts **2** *obs* : PROSECUTOR **3** : a substance that in very small amounts is able to increase the activity of a catalyst **4** : a binding site in a DNA chain at which RNA polymerase binds to initiate transcription of messenger RNA by one or more nearby structural genes

pro·mo·tion \prə-ˈmō-shən\ *n* (15c) **1** : the act or fact of being raised in position or rank : PREFERMENT **2** : the act of furthering the growth or development of something; *esp* : the furtherance of the acceptance and sale of merchandise through advertising, publicity, or discounting — **pro·mo·tion·al** \-shnəl, -shə-nᵊl\ *adj*

pro·mo·tive \-ˈmō-tiv\ *adj* (1644) : tending or serving to promote ‹measures ~ of good health› — **pro·mo·tive·ness** *n*

[1]**prompt** \ˈpräm(p)t\ *vt* [ME, fr. ML *promptare,* fr. L *promptus* prompt] (14c) **1** : to move to action : INCITE **2** : to assist (one acting or reciting) by suggesting or saying the next words of something forgotten or imperfectly learned : CUE **3** : to serve as the inciting cause of ‹evidence ~*ing* an investigation› — **prompt·er** *n*

[2]**prompt** *adj* (1784) : of or relating to prompting actors

[3]**prompt** *adj* [ME, fr. L *promptus* ready, prompt, fr. pp. of *promere* to bring forth, fr. *pro-* forth + *emere* to take — more at REDEEM] (15c) **1** : being ready and quick to act as occasion demands **2** : performed readily or immediately ‹~ assistance› ***syn*** see QUICK — **prompt·ly** \ˈpräm(p)t-lē, ˈpräm-plē\ *adv* — **prompt·ness** \ˈpräm(p)t-nəs, ˈprämp-nəs\ *n*

[4]**prompt** *n, pl* **prompts** \ˈpräm(p)ts, ˈprämps\ (ca. 1531) **1** [[1]*prompt*] : something that prompts : REMINDER **2** [[3]*prompt*] : a limit of time given for payment of an account for goods purchased; *also* : the contract by which this time is fixed

prompt·book \ˈpräm(p)t-ˌbu̇k, ˈprämp-ˌbu̇k\ *n* (1809) : a copy of a play with directions for performance used by a theater prompter

promp·ti·tude \ˈpräm(p)-tə-ˌtüd, -ˌtyüd\ *n* [ME, fr. LL *promptitudo,* fr. L *promptus*] (15c) : the quality or habit of being prompt : PROMPTNESS

prompt side *n* (1824) **1** : the side of the stage adjacent to the prompter's corner **2** : the side of the stage to the right of an actor facing the audience

pro·mul·gate \ˈprä-məl-ˌgāt; prō-ˈməl-, prə-ˈ, ˈprō-(ˌ)\ *vt* **-gat·ed; -gat·ing** [L *promulgatus,* pp. of *promulgare,* fr. *pro-* forward + *-mulgare* (prob. akin to *mulgēre* to milk, extract) — more at EMULSION] (1530) **1** : to make (as a doctrine) known by open declaration : PROCLAIM **2 a** : to make known or public the terms of (a proposed law) **b** : to put (a law) into action or force ***syn*** see DECLARE — **pro·mul·ga·tion** \ˌprä-məl-ˈgā-shən; ˌprō-(ˌ)məl-, (ˌ)prō-ˌ\ *n* — **pro·mul·ga·tor** \ˈprä-məl-ˌgā-tər; prō-ˈməl-, prə-ˈ, ˈprō-(ˌ)\ *n*

pro·na·tion \prō-ˈnā-shən\ *n* [*pronate,* fr. LL *pronatus,* pp. of *pronare* to bend forward, fr. L *pronus*] (1666) **1** : rotation of the hand and forearm so that the palm faces backwards or downwards **2** : rotation of the medial bones in the midtarsal region of the foot inward and downward so that in walking the foot tends to come down on its inner margin — **pro·nate** \ˈprō-ˌnāt\ *vb*

pro·na·tor \ˈprō-ˌnā-tər\ *n* (ca. 1741) : a muscle that produces pronation

prone \ˈprōn\ *adj* [ME, fr. L *pronus* bent forward, tending; akin to L *pro* forward — more at FOR] (14c) **1** : having a tendency or inclination : being likely ‹~ to forget names› ‹accident-*prone*› **2 a** : having the front or ventral surface downward **b** : lying flat or prostrate — **prone** *adv* — **prone·ly** *adv* — **prone·ness** \ˈprōn-nəs\ *n*

syn PRONE, SUPINE, PROSTRATE, RECUMBENT mean lying down. PRONE implies a position with the front of the body turned toward the supporting surface ‹push-ups require a *prone* position›. SUPINE implies lying on one's back and suggests inertness or abjectness ‹lying *supine* on the couch›. PROSTRATE implies lying full-length as in submission, defeat, or physical collapse ‹a runner fell *prostrate* at the finish line›. RECUMBENT implies the posture of one sleeping or resting ‹a patient comfortably *recumbent* in a hospital bed›. ***syn*** see in addition LIABLE

pro·neph·ros \(ˌ)prō-ˈne-frəs, -ˌfräs\ *n* [NL, fr. Gk *pro-* + *nephros* kidney — more at NEPHRITIS] (1881) : either member of the first and most anterior pair of the three successive paired vertebrate renal organs that functions in the adults of amphioxus and some lampreys, functions temporarily in larval fishes and amphibians, and is present but nonfunctional in embryos of reptiles, birds, and mammals — compare MESONEPHROS, METANEPHROS — **pro·neph·ric** \-frik\ *adj*

[1]**prong** \ˈprȯŋ, ˈpräŋ\ *n* [ME *pronge*] (15c) **1** : FORK **2** : a tine of a fork **3** : a slender pointed or projecting part: as **a** : a fang of a tooth **b** : a point of an antler **4** : something resembling a prong

[2]**prong** *vt* (1816) : to stab, pierce, or break up with a pronged device

pronged \ˈprȯŋd, ˈpräŋd\ *adj* (1767) **1** : having a usu. specified number of prongs — usu. used in combination ‹a 3-*pronged* fork› **2** : having a usu. specified number of parts or approaches ‹a 2-*pronged* strategy›

prong·horn \\'pròn̄-ˌhòrn, 'prän-\\ *n, pl* **pronghorn** *or* **pronghorns** (1823) : a swift horned ruminant mammal (*Antilocapra americana*) chiefly of grasslands and deserts of western No. America that resembles an antelope — called also *pronghorn antelope*

pro·nom·i·nal \\prō-'nä-mə-nᵊl, -'näm-nəl\\ *adj* [LL *pronominalis*, fr. L *pronomin-, pronomen*] (1680) **1** : of, relating to, or constituting a pronoun **2** : resembling a pronoun in identifying or specifying without describing ⟨the ∼ adjective *this* in *this* dog⟩ — **pro·nom·i·nal·ly** *adv*

pro·noun \\'prō-ˌnau̇n\\ *n* [ME, fr. AF, fr. L *pronomin-, pronomen*, fr. *pro-* for + *nomin-, nomen* name — more at PRO-, NAME] (1530) : any of a small set of

pronghorn

words in a language that are used as substitutes for nouns or noun phrases and whose referents are named or understood in the context

pro·nounce \\prə-'nau̇n(t)s\\ *vb* **pro·nounced; pro·nounc·ing** [ME, fr. AF *pronuncier*, fr. L *pronuntiare*, fr. *pro-* forth + *nuntiare* to report, fr. *nuntius* messenger — more at PRO-] *vt* (14c) **1 a** : to declare officially or ceremoniously ⟨the minister *pronounced* them husband and wife⟩ **2** : to declare authoritatively or as an opinion ⟨doctors *pronounced* him fit to resume duties⟩ **3 a** : to employ the organs of speech to produce ⟨∼ these words⟩; *esp* : to say correctly ⟨I can't ∼ his name⟩ **b** : to represent in printed characters the spoken counterpart of ⟨an orthographic representation⟩ ⟨both dictionaries ∼ *clique* the same⟩ **4** : RECITE ⟨speak the speech, I pray you, as I *pronounced* it to you —Shak.⟩ ∼ *vi* **1** : to pass judgment **2** : to produce the components of spoken language — **pro·nounce·abil·i·ty** \\-ˌnau̇n(t)-sə-'bi-lə-tē\\ *n* — **pro·nounce·able** \\-'nau̇n(t)-sə-bəl\\ *adj* — **pro·nounc·er** *n*

pro·nounced \\-'nau̇n(t)st\\ *adj* (ca. 1741) : strongly marked : DECIDED ⟨a ∼ dislike⟩ — **pro·nounc·ed·ly** \\-'nau̇n(t)-səd-lē, -'nau̇n(t)st-lē\\ *adv*

pro·nounce·ment \\prə-'nau̇n(t)s-mənt\\ *n* (1593) **1** : a usu. formal declaration of opinion **2** : an authoritative announcement

pronouncing *adj* (1764) : relating to or indicating pronunciation ⟨a ∼ dictionary⟩

pron·to \\'prän-ˌtō\\ *adv* [Sp, fr. L *promptus* prompt] (1911) : without delay

¹**pro·nu·clear** \\(ˌ)prō-'nü-klē-ər, -'nyü-, -÷-kyə-lər\\ *adj* [*pronucleus*] (ca. 1889) : of, relating to, or resembling a pronucleus

²**pronuclear** *adj* [²*pro-* + *nuclear*] (1971) : advocating the use of nuclear-powered generating stations

pro·nu·cle·us \\(ˌ)prō-'nü-klē-əs, -'nyü-\\ *n* [NL] (1880) : the haploid nucleus of a male or female gamete (as an egg or sperm) up to the time of fusion with that of another gamete in fertilization

pro·nun·ci·a·men·to \\prō-ˌnən(t)-sē-ə-'men-(ˌ)tō\\ *n, pl* **-tos** *or* **-toes** [modif. of Sp *pronunciamiento*, fr. *pronunciar* to pronounce, fr. L *pronuntiare*] (1835) : PROCLAMATION, PRONOUNCEMENT

pro·nun·ci·a·tion \\prə-ˌnən(t)-sē-'ā-shən *also* ÷-ˌnau̇n-sī-\\ *n* [ME *pronunciacion*, fr. AF *pronunciation*, fr. L *pronuntiation-, pronuntiatio*, fr. *pronuntiare*] (15c) : the act or manner of pronouncing something — **pro·nun·ci·a·tion·al** \\-shnᵊl, -shə-nᵊl\\ *adj*

¹**proof** \\'prüf\\ *n* [ME *prof, prove*, alter. of *preve*, fr. AF *preove*, fr. LL *proba*, fr. L *probare* to prove — more at PROVE] (13c) **1 a** : the cogency of evidence that compels acceptance by the mind of a truth or a fact **b** : the process or an instance of establishing the validity of a statement esp. by derivation from other statements in accordance with principles of reasoning **2** *obs* : EXPERIENCE **3** : something that induces certainty or establishes validity **4** *archaic* : the quality or state of having been tested or tried; *esp* : unyielding hardness **5** : evidence operating to determine the finding or judgment of a tribunal **6 a** *pl* **proofs** *or* **proof** : a copy (as of typeset text) made for examination or correction **b** : a test impression of an engraving, etching, or lithograph **c** : a coin that is struck from a highly polished die on a polished planchet, is not intended for circulation, and sometimes differs in metallic content from coins of identical design struck for circulation **d** : a test photographic print made from a negative **7** : a test applied to articles or substances to determine whether they are of standard or satisfactory quality **8 a** : the minimum alcoholic strength of proof spirit **b** : strength with reference to the standard for proof spirit; *specif* : alcoholic strength indicated by a number that is twice the percent by volume of alcohol present ⟨whiskey of 90 ∼ is 45 percent alcohol⟩

²**proof** *adj* (1592) **1** : able to resist or repel ⟨boots that were . . . ∼ against cold and wet —Robertson Davies⟩ — often used in combination ⟨wind*proof*⟩ **2** : used in proving or testing or as a standard of comparison **3** : of standard strength or quality or alcoholic content

³**proof** *vt* (1745) **1 a** : to make or take a proof or test of **b** : PROOFREAD **2** : to give a resistant quality to **3** : to activate (yeast) by mixing with water and sometimes sugar or milk — **proof·er** *n*

proof·read \\'prüf-ˌrēd\\ *vt* **-read** \\-ˌred\\; **-read·ing** [back-formation fr. *proofreader*] (1920) : to read and mark corrections in (as a proof)

proof·read·er \\-ˌrē-dər\\ *n* (1832) : a person who proofreads

proof spirit *n* (1712) : an alcoholic liquor or mixture of ethanol and water that contains 50 percent ethanol by volume at 60°F (16°C)

¹**prop** \\'präp\\ *n* [ME *proppe*, fr. MD, stopper; akin to MLG *proppe* stopper] (15c) : something that props or sustains : SUPPORT

²**prop** *vt* **propped; prop·ping** (1538) **1 a** : to support by placing something under or against — often used with *up* **b** : to support by placing against something **2** : SUSTAIN, STRENGTHEN — often used with *up* ⟨a government *propped* up by the military⟩

³**prop** *n* (1841) **1** : PROPERTY 3 ⟨stage ∼*s*⟩ **2** : something used in creating or enhancing a desired effect ⟨buy books . . . as cultural ∼*s* because they want to appear literate —John Powers⟩

⁴**prop** *n* (1914) : PROPELLER

⁵**prop** *abbr* **1** property **2** proposition **3** proprietor

prop- *comb form* [ISV, fr. *propionic* (*acid*)] : related to propionic acid ⟨*prop*ane⟩ ⟨*prop*yl⟩

pro·pae·deu·tic \\ˌprō-pi-'dü-tik, -'dyü-\\ *n* [Gk *propaideuein* to teach beforehand, fr. *pro-* before + *paideuein* to teach, fr. *paid-, pais* child—

more at PRO-, FEW] (1798) : preparatory study or instruction — **pro·paedeutic** *adj*

pro·pa·gan·da \ˌprä-pə-ˈgan-də, ˌprō-\ *n* [NL, fr. *Congregatio de propaganda fide* Congregation for propagating the faith, organization established by Pope Gregory XV †1623] (1718) **1** *cap* : a congregation of the Roman curia having jurisdiction over missionary territories and related institutions **2** : the spreading of ideas, information, or rumor for the purpose of helping or injuring an institution, a cause, or a person **3** : ideas, facts, or allegations spread deliberately to further one's cause or to damage an opposing cause; *also* : a public action having such an effect — **pro·pa·gan·dist** \-dist\ *n or adj* — **pro·pa·gan·dis·tic** \-ˌgan-ˈdis-tik\ *adj* — **pro·pa·gan·dis·ti·cal·ly** \-ti-k(ə-)lē\ *adv*

pro·pa·gan·dize \-ˈgan-ˌdīz\ *vb* **-dized; -diz·ing** *vt* (1844) : to subject to propaganda; *also* : to carry on propaganda for ~ *vi* : to carry on propaganda — **pro·pa·gan·diz·er** \-ˌdī-zər\ *n*

prop·a·gate \ˈprä-pə-ˌgāt\ *vb* **-gat·ed; -gat·ing** [L *propagatus,* pp. of *propagare* to set slips, propagate, fr. *propages* slip, offspring, fr. *pro-* before + *pangere* to fasten — more at PRO-, PACT] *vt* (ca. 1570) **1** : to cause to continue or increase by sexual or asexual reproduction **2** : to pass along to offspring **3 a** : to cause to spread out and affect a greater number or greater area : EXTEND **b** : to foster growing knowledge of, familiarity with, or acceptance of (as an idea or belief) : PUBLICIZE **c** : to transmit (as sound or light) through a medium ~ *vi* **1** : to multiply sexually or asexually **2** : INCREASE, EXTEND **3** : to travel through space or a material — used of wave energy (as light, sound, or radio waves) — **prop·a·ga·tive** \-ˌgā-tiv\ *adj* — **prop·a·ga·tor** \-ˌgā-tər\ *n*

prop·a·ga·tion \ˌprä-pə-ˈgā-shən\ *n* (15c) : the act or action of propagating: as **a** : increase (as of a kind of organism) in numbers **b** : the spreading of something (as a belief) abroad or into new regions **c** : enlargement or extension (as of a crack) in a solid body

prop·a·gule \ˈprä-pə-ˌgyül\ *n* [NL *propagulum,* fr. L *propages* slip] (1858) : a structure (as a cutting, a seed, or a spore) that propagates a plant

pro·pane \ˈprō-ˌpān\ *n* [ISV *prop-* + *-ane*] (1866) : a heavy flammable gaseous alkane C_3H_8 found in crude petroleum and natural gas and used esp. as fuel and in chemical synthesis

pro·pel \prə-ˈpel\ *vt* **pro·pelled; pro·pel·ling** [ME *propellen,* fr. L *propellere,* fr. *pro-* before + *pellere* to drive — more at FELT] (15c) : to drive forward or onward by or as if by means of a force that imparts motion

[1]**pro·pel·lant** *also* **pro·pel·lent** \-ˈpe-lənt\ *adj* (1644) : capable of propelling

[2]**propellant** *also* **propellent** *n* (1814) : something that propels: as **a** : an explosive for propelling projectiles **b** : fuel plus oxidizer used by a rocket engine **c** : a gas kept under pressure in a bottle or can for expelling the contents when the pressure is released

pro·pel·ler *also* **pro·pel·lor** \prə-ˈpe-lər\ *n* (1780) : one that propels; *esp* : a device that consists of a central hub with radiating blades placed and twisted so that each forms part of a helical surface and that is used to propel a vehicle (as a ship or airplane)

pro·pel·ler–head \prə-ˈpe-lər-ˌhed\ *n* [fr. cartoon images of science fiction fans wearing caps with a propeller protruding from the top] (1982) *often disparaging* : an enthusiast of technology and esp. of computers : TECHNOPHILE

pro·pend \prō-ˈpend\ *vi* [L *propendēre,* fr. *pro-* before + *pendēre* to hang — more at PENDANT] (1545) *obs* : INCLINE

pro·pense \prō-ˈpen(t)s\ *adj* [L *propensus,* pp. of *propendēre*] (1528) *archaic* : leaning or inclining toward : DISPOSED

pro·pen·si·ty \prə-ˈpen(t)-sə-tē\ *n, pl* **-ties** (1570) : an often intense natural inclination or preference ***syn*** see LEANING

[1]**prop·er** \ˈprä-pər\ *adj* [ME *propre* proper, own, fr. AF, fr. L *proprius* own] (14c) **1 a** : referring to one individual only **b** : belonging to one : OWN **c** : appointed for the liturgy of a particular day **d** : represented heraldically in natural color **2** : belonging characteristically to a species or individual : PECULIAR **3** *chiefly dial* : GOOD-LOOKING, HANDSOME **4** : very good : EXCELLENT **5** *chiefly Brit* : UTTER, ABSOLUTE **6** : strictly limited to a specified thing, place, or idea ⟨the city ~⟩ **7 a** : strictly accurate : CORRECT **b** *archaic* : VIRTUOUS, RESPECTABLE **c** : strictly decorous : GENTEEL **8** : marked by suitability, rightness, or appropriateness : FIT **9** : being a mathematical subset (as a subgroup) that does not contain all the elements of the inclusive set from which it is derived ***syn*** see FIT — **prop·er·ly** *adv* — **prop·er·ness** *n*

[2]**proper** *n* (15c) **1** : the parts of the Mass that vary according to the liturgical calendar **2** : the part of a missal or breviary containing the proper of the Mass and the offices proper to the holy days of the liturgical year

[3]**proper** *adv* (15c) *chiefly dial* : in a thorough manner : COMPLETELY

proper adjective *n* (1905) : an adjective that is formed from a proper noun and that is usu. capitalized in English

pro·per·din \prō-ˈpər-dᵊn\ *n* [prob. fr. [1]*pro-* + L *perdere* to destroy + E [1]*-in* — more at PERDITION] (1954) : a blood serum protein that participates in the activation of complement in a pathway which does not involve the presence of antibodies

proper fraction *n* (1674) : a fraction in which the numerator is less or of lower degree than the denominator

proper noun *n* (ca. 1890) : a noun that designates a particular being or thing, does not take a limiting modifier, and is usu. capitalized in English — called also *proper name*

prop·er·tied \ˈprä-pər-tēd\ *adj* (ca. 1772) : possessing property

prop·er·ty \ˈprä-pər-tē\ *n, pl* **-ties** [ME *proprete,* fr. AF *proprete,* fr. L *proprietat-, proprietas,* fr. *proprius* own] (14c) **1 a** : a quality or trait belonging and esp. peculiar to an individual or thing **b** : an effect that an object has on another object or on the senses **c** : VIRTUE 3 **d** : an attribute common to all members of a class **2 a** : something owned or possessed; *specif* : a piece of real estate **b** : the exclusive right to possess, enjoy, and dispose of a thing : OWNERSHIP **c** : something to which a person or business has a legal title **d** : one (as a performer) who is under contract and whose work is esp. valuable **e** : a book or script purchased for publication or production **3** : an article or object used in a play or motion picture except painted scenery and costumes ***syn*** see QUALITY — **prop·er·ty·less** \-ləs\ *adj* — **prop·er·ty·less·ness** \-nəs\ *n*

property damage insurance *n* (ca. 1946) : insurance protecting against all or part of an individual's legal liability for damage done (as by his or her automobile) to the property of another

property right *n* (1848) : a legal right or interest in or against specific property

property tax *n* (1808) : a tax levied on real or personal property

pro·phage \ˈprō-ˌfāj, -ˌfäzh\ *n* (1951) : an intracellular form of a bacteriophage in which it is harmless to the host, is usu. integrated into the hereditary material of the host, and reproduces when the host does

pro·phase \-ˌfāz\ *n* [ISV] (1884) **1** : the initial stage of mitosis and of the mitotic division of meiosis characterized by the condensation of chromosomes consisting of two chromatids, disappearance of the nucleolus and nuclear membrane, and formation of mitotic spindle **2** : the initial stage of the first division of meiosis in which the chromosomes become visible, homologous pairs of chromosomes undergo synapsis and crossing over, chiasmata appear, chromosomes condense with homologues visible as tetrads, and the nuclear membrane and nucleolus disappear — compare DIAKINESIS, DIPLOTENE, LEPTOTENE, PACHYTENE, ZYGOTENE — **pro·pha·sic** \(ˌ)prō-ˈfā-zik\ *adj*

proph·e·cy *also* **proph·e·sy** \ˈprä-fə-sē\ *n, pl* **-cies** *also* **-sies** [ME *prophecie,* fr. AF, fr. LL *prophetia,* fr. Gk *prophēteia,* fr. *prophētēs* prophet] (13c) **1** : an inspired utterance of a prophet **2** : the function or vocation of a prophet; *specif* : the inspired declaration of divine will and purpose **3** : a prediction of something to come

proph·e·size \ˈprä-fə-ˌsīz\ *vb* **-sized; -siz·ing** (1848) : PROPHESY

proph·e·sy \ˈprä-fə-ˌsī\ *vb* **-sied; -sy·ing** [ME *prophesien,* fr. AF **prophecier,* fr. OF, fr. *prophecie*] *vt* (14c) **1** : to utter by or as if by divine inspiration **2** : to predict with assurance or on the basis of mystic knowledge **3** : PREFIGURE ~ *vi* **1** : to speak as if divinely inspired **2** : to give instruction in religious matters : PREACH **3** : to make a prediction ***syn*** see FORETELL — **proph·e·si·er** \-ˌsī(-ə)r\ *n*

proph·et \ˈprä-fət\ *n* [ME *prophete,* fr. AF, fr. L *propheta,* fr. Gk *prophētēs,* fr. *pro* for + *phanai* to speak — more at FOR, BAN] (12c) **1** : one who utters divinely inspired revelations: as **a** *often cap* : the writer of one of the prophetic books of the Bible **b** *cap* : one regarded by a group of followers as the final authoritative revealer of God's will ⟨Muhammad, the *Prophet* of Allah⟩ **2** : one gifted with more than ordinary spiritual and moral insight; *esp* : an inspired poet **3** : one who foretells future events : PREDICTOR **4** : an effective or leading spokesman for a cause, doctrine, or group **5** *Christian Science* **a** : a spiritual seer **b** : disappearance of material sense before the conscious facts of spiritual Truth — **proph·et·hood** \-ˌhu̇d\ *n*

proph·et·ess \ˈprä-fə-təs\ *n* (14c) : a woman who is a prophet

pro·phet·ic \prə-ˈfe-tik\ *also* **pro·phet·i·cal** \-ˈfe-ti-kəl\ *adj* (15c) **1** : of, relating to, or characteristic of a prophet or prophecy **2** : foretelling events : PREDICTIVE — **pro·phet·i·cal·ly** \-ti-k(ə-)lē\ *adv*

Proph·ets \ˈprä-fəts\ *n pl* : the second part of the Hebrew Bible — see BIBLE table

[1]**pro·phy·lac·tic** \ˌprō-fə-ˈlak-tik *also* ˌprä-\ *adj* [Gk *prophylaktikos,* fr. *prophylassein* to be on guard, fr. *pro-* before + *phylassein* to guard, fr. *phylak-, phylax* guard] (1574) **1** : guarding from or preventing the spread or occurrence of disease or infection **2** : tending to prevent or ward off : PREVENTIVE — **pro·phy·lac·ti·cal·ly** \-ti-k(ə-)lē\ *adv*

[2]**prophylactic** *n* (1642) : something prophylactic; *esp* : a device and esp. a condom for preventing venereal infection or conception

pro·phy·lax·is \-ˈlak-səs\ *n, pl* **-lax·es** \-ˈlak-ˌsēz\ [NL, fr. Gk *prophylaktikos*] (ca. 1842) : measures designed to preserve health (as of an individual or of society) and prevent the spread of disease

[1]**pro·pine** \prə-ˈpēn, -ˈpīn\ *vt* **pro·pined; pro·pin·ing** [ME, fr. MF *propiner,* fr. L *propinare* to present, drink to someone's health, fr. Gk *propinein* lit., to drink first, fr. *pro-* + *pinein* to drink — more at POTABLE] (15c) *chiefly Scot* : to present or give esp. as a token of friendship

[2]**propine** *n* (15c) *Scot* : a gift in return for a favor

pro·pin·qui·ty \prə-ˈpiŋ-kwə-tē\ *n* [ME *propinquite,* fr. L *propinquitat-, propinquitas* kinship, proximity, fr. *propinquus* near, akin, fr. *prope* near — more at APPROACH] (14c) **1** : nearness of blood : KINSHIP **2** : nearness in place or time : PROXIMITY

pro·pi·o·nate \ˈprō-pē-ə-ˌnāt\ *n* [ISV] (1862) : a salt or ester of propionic acid

pro·pi·on·ic acid \ˌprō-pē-ˈä-nik-\ *n* [ISV [1]*pro-* + Gk *piōn* fat; akin to Skt *pīvan* swelling, fat] (1850) : a liquid sharp-odored fatty acid $C_3H_6O_2$ found in milk and distillates of wood, coal, and petroleum and used esp. as a mold inhibitor and flavoring agent

pro·pi·ti·ate \prō-ˈpi-shē-ˌāt\ *vt* **-at·ed; -at·ing** [L *propitiatus,* pp. of *propitiare,* fr. *propitius* propitious] (1583) : to gain or regain the favor or goodwill of : APPEASE ***syn*** see PACIFY — **pro·pi·ti·a·tor** \-ˌā-tər\ *n*

pro·pi·ti·a·tion \prō-ˌpi-shē-ˈā-shən\ *n* (14c) **1** : the act of propitiating **2** : something that propitiates; *specif* : an atoning sacrifice

pro·pi·ti·a·to·ry \prō-ˈpi-sh(ē-)ə-ˌtȯr-ē\ *adj* (1551) **1** : intended to propitiate : EXPIATORY **2** : of or relating to propitiation

pro·pi·tious \prə-ˈpi-shəs\ *adj* [ME *propycyous,* fr. AF *propicius,* fr. L *propitius,* prob. fr. *pro-* for + *petere* to seek — more at PRO-, FEATHER] (15c) **1** : favorably disposed : BENEVOLENT **2** : being a good omen : AUSPICIOUS ⟨~ sign⟩ **3** : tending to favor : ADVANTAGEOUS ***syn*** see FAVORABLE — **pro·pi·tious·ly** *adv* — **pro·pi·tious·ness** *n*

pro·plas·tid \(ˌ)prō-ˈplas-təd\ *n* [ISV] (1922) : a minute cytoplasmic body from which a plastid is formed

prop·man \ˈpräp-ˌman\ *n* (ca. 1937) : a man in charge of stage properties

prop·o·lis \ˈprä-pə-ləs\ *n* [ME *propoleos,* fr. ML, alter. of L *propolis,* fr. Gk, fr. *pro-* for + *polis* city — more at PRO-, POLICE] (15c) : a brownish resinous material of waxy consistency collected by bees from the buds of trees and used as a cement in repairing and maintaining the hive

pro·pone \prə-ˈpōn\ *vt* **pro·poned; pro·pon·ing** [ME (Sc), fr. L *proponere* — more at PROPOUND] (14c) **1** *Scot* : PROPOSE, PROPOUND **2** *Scot* : to put forward (a defense)

pro·po·nent \prə-ˈpō-nənt, ˈprō-ˌ\ *n* [L *proponent-, proponens,* prp. of *proponere*] (1588) : one who argues in favor of something : ADVOCATE

[1]**pro·por·tion** \prə-ˈpȯr-shən\ *n* [ME *proporcion,* fr. AF, fr. L *proportion-, proportio,* fr. *pro* for + *portion-, portio* portion — more at FOR] (14c) **1** : harmonious relation of parts to each other or to the whole : BALANCE, SYMMETRY **2 a** : proper or equal share ⟨each did her ~ of the work⟩ **b** : QUOTA, PERCENTAGE **3** : the relation of one

part to another or to the whole with respect to magnitude, quantity, or degree : RATIO **4** : SIZE, DIMENSION **5** : a statement of equality between two ratios in which the first of the four terms divided by the second equals the third divided by the fourth (as in 4/2=10/5) — compare EXTREME 1b, MEAN 1c — **in proportion** : PROPORTIONAL 1

2**proportion** *vt* **pro·por·tioned; pro·por·tion·ing** \-sh(ə-)niŋ\ (14c) **1** : to adjust (a part or thing) in size relative to other parts or things **2** : to make the parts of harmonious or symmetrical **3** : APPORTION, ALLOT

pro·por·tion·able \-sh(ə-)nə-bəl\ *adj* (14c) : PROPORTIONAL, PROPORTIONATE — **pro·por·tion·ably** \-blē\ *adv, archaic*

1**pro·por·tion·al** \prə-ˈpȯr-shnəl, -shə-nᵊl\ *n* (14c) : a number or quantity in a proportion

2**proportional** *adj* (15c) **1 a** : corresponding in size, degree, or intensity **b** : having the same or a constant ratio ⟨corresponding sides of similar triangles are ~⟩ **2** : regulated or determined in size or degree with reference to proportions ⟨a ~ system of immigration quotas⟩ — **pro·por·tion·al·i·ty** \-ˌpȯr-shə-ˈna-lə-tē\ *n* — **pro·por·tion·al·ly** \-ˈpȯr-shnə-lē, -shə-nᵊl-ē\ *adv*

proportional parts *n pl* (1728) : fractional parts of the difference between successive entries in a table for use in linear interpolation

proportional representation *n* (1870) : an electoral system designed to represent in a legislative body each political group or party in proportion to its actual voting strength in the electorate

proportional tax *n* (ca. 1943) : a tax in which the tax rate remains constant regardless of the amount of the tax base

1**pro·por·tion·ate** \prə-ˈpȯr-sh(ə-)nət\ *adj* (14c) : PROPORTIONAL 1 — **pro·por·tion·ate·ly** *adv*

2**pro·por·tion·ate** \-shə-ˌnāt\ *vt* **-at·ed; -at·ing** (1570) : to make proportionate : PROPORTION

pro·pos·al \prə-ˈpō-zəl\ *n* (ca. 1640) **1** : an act of putting forward or stating something for consideration **2 a** : something proposed : SUGGESTION **b** : OFFER; *specif* : an offer of marriage

pro·pose \prə-ˈpōz\ *vb* **pro·posed; pro·pos·ing** [ME, fr. AF *purposer, proposer,* fr. L *proponere* (perf. indic. *proposui*) — more at PROPOUND] *vi* (14c) **1** : to form or put forward a plan or intention ⟨man ~*s,* but God disposes⟩ **2** *obs* : to engage in talk or discussion **3** : to make an offer of marriage ~ *vt* **1 a** : to set before the mind (as for discussion, imitation, or action) ⟨~ a plan for settling the dispute⟩ **b** : to set before someone and esp. oneself as an aim or intent ⟨*proposed* to spend the summer in Italy⟩ **2 a** : to set forth for acceptance or rejection ⟨~ terms for peace⟩ ⟨~ a topic for debate⟩ **b** : to recommend to fill a place or vacancy : NOMINATE ⟨~ them for membership⟩ **c** : to offer as a toast ⟨~ the happiness of the couple⟩ — **pro·pos·er** *n*

1**prop·o·si·tion** \ˌprä-pə-ˈzi-shən\ *n* (14c) **1 a** (1) : something offered for consideration or acceptance : PROPOSAL (2) : a request for sexual intercourse **b** : the point to be discussed or maintained in argument usu. stated in sentence form near the outset **c** : a theorem or problem to be demonstrated or performed **2 a** : an expression in language or signs of something that can be believed, doubted, or denied or is either true or false **b** : the objective meaning of a proposition **3** : something of an indicated kind to be dealt with ⟨the farm was never a paying ~⟩ — **prop·o·si·tion·al** \-ˈzish-nəl, -ˈzi-shə-nᵊl\ *adj*

2**proposition** *vt* **-si·tioned; -si·tion·ing** \-ˈzi-sh(ə-)niŋ\ (1924) : to make a proposal to; *esp* : to suggest sexual intercourse to

propositional calculus *n* (1903) : the branch of symbolic logic that uses symbols for unanalyzed propositions and logical connectives only — called also *sentential calculus*; compare PREDICATE CALCULUS

propositional function *n* (1903) **1** : SENTENTIAL FUNCTION **2** : something that is designated or expressed by a sentential function

pro·pos·i·tus \prō-ˈpä-zə-təs\ *n, pl* **-i·ti** \-ˌtī\ [NL, fr. L, pp. of *proponere*] (1899) : the person immediately concerned : SUBJECT

pro·pound \prə-ˈpau̇nd\ *vt* [alter. of earlier *propone,* fr. ME (Sc) *proponen,* fr. L *proponere* to display, propound, fr. *pro-* before + *ponere* to put, place — more at PRO-, POSITION] (1537) : to offer for discussion or consideration — **pro·pound·er** *n*

pro·poxy·phene \prō-ˈpäk-sə-ˌfēn\ *n* [*prop-* + *oxy* + *-phene* (alter. of *phenyl*)] (1955) : a narcotic analgesic $C_{22}H_{29}NO_2$ structurally related to methadone but less addicting that is administered esp. in the form of its salts (as the hydrochloride)

pro·prae·tor *or* **pro·pre·tor** \(ˌ)prō-ˈprē-tər\ *n* [L *propraetor,* fr. *pro-* (as in *proconsul*) + *praetor*] (ca. 1580) : a praetor of ancient Rome sent out to govern a province

pro·pran·o·lol \prō-ˈpra-nə-ˌlȯl, -ˌlōl\ *n* [*pro*pyl + *propanol* + 1*-ol*] (1964) : a beta-blocker $C_{16}H_{21}NO_2$ used in the form of its hydrochloride in the treatment of abnormal heart rhythms and angina pectoris

1**pro·pri·e·tary** \prə-ˈprī-ə-ˌter-ē\ *n, pl* **-tar·ies** [ME *propietarie,* fr. AF, fr. ML *propietarius,* fr. LL, adj.] (15c) **1** : one that possesses, owns, or holds exclusive right to something; *specif* : PROPRIETOR 1 **2** : something that is used, produced, or marketed under exclusive legal right of the inventor or maker; *specif* : a drug (as a patent medicine) that is protected by secrecy, patent, or copyright against free competition as to name, product, composition, or process of manufacture **3** : a business secretly owned by and run as a cover for an intelligence organization

2**proprietary** *adj* [LL *proprietarius,* fr. L *proprietas* property — more at PROPERTY] (1589) **1** : of, relating to, or characteristic of a proprietor ⟨~ rights⟩ **2** : used, made, or marketed by one having the exclusive legal right ⟨a ~ process⟩ ⟨~ software⟩ **3** : privately owned and managed and run as a profit-making organization ⟨a ~ clinic⟩

pro·pri·e·tor \prə-ˈprī-ə-tər\ *n* [alter. of 1*proprietary*] (1637) **1** : one granted ownership of a colony (as one of the original American colonies) and full prerogatives of establishing a government and distributing land **2 a** : a person who has the legal right or exclusive title to something : OWNER **b** : one having an interest (as control or present use) less than absolute and exclusive right — **pro·pri·e·tor·ship** \-ˌship\ *n*

pro·pri·e·to·ri·al \prə-ˌprī-ə-ˈtȯr-ē-əl, prō-\ *adj* (1851) : PROPRIETARY 1

pro·pri·e·tress \-ˈprī-ə-trəs\ *n* (1692) : a woman who is a proprietor

pro·pri·e·ty \prə-ˈprī-ə-tē\ *n, pl* **-ties** [ME *propriete,* fr. AF *proprieté, proprété* property, quality of a person or thing — more at PROPERTY] (14c) **1** *obs* : true nature **2** *obs* : a special characteristic : PECULIARITY **3** : the quality or state of being proper : APPROPRIATENESS **4 a** : conformity to what is socially acceptable in conduct or speech **b** : fear of offending against conventional rules of behavior esp. between the sexes **c** *pl* : the customs and manners of polite society

pro·pri·o·cep·tion \ˌprō-prē-ō-ˈsep-shən\ *n* [*proprioceptive* + *-ion*] (1906) : the reception of stimuli produced within the organism

pro·pri·o·cep·tive \-ˈsep-tiv\ *adj* [L *proprius* own + E *-ceptive* (as in *receptive*)] (1906) : of, relating to, or being stimuli arising within the organism ⟨a ~ sensation⟩ ⟨~ feedback⟩

pro·pri·o·cep·tor \-tər\ *n* [NL, fr. L *proprius* + NL *-ceptor* (as in *receptor*)] (1906) : a sensory receptor (as a muscle spindle) excited by proprioceptive stimuli (as changes in limb position)

prop root *n* (1905) : a root that serves as a prop or support to the plant

props \präps\ *n pl but usu sing in constr* [short for *proper dues*] (1992) **1** *slang* : DUE a ⟨takes pains to give the man his ~ —Dan Epstein⟩ **2** *slang* : RESPECT ⟨teachers have to earn their ~ just like everybody else —Greg Donaldson⟩ **3** *slang* : CREDIT 6b ⟨at least deserves ~ for writing a song about something that rings true —Jim Abbott⟩

prop·to·sis \präp-ˈtō-səs, prō-ˈtō-\ *n* [NL, fr. LL, falling forward, fr. Gk *proptōsis,* fr. *propiptein* to fall forward, fr. *pro-* forward + *piptein* to fall — more at PRO-, FEATHER] (1676) : forward projection or displacement esp. of the eyeball

pro·pul·sion \prə-ˈpəl-shən\ *n* [L *propellere* to propel] (1626) **1** : the action or process of propelling **2** : something that propels

pro·pul·sive \-ˈpəl-siv\ *adj* [L *propulsus,* pp. of *propellere*] (1758) : tending or having power to propel ⟨~ force⟩

pro·pyl \ˈprō-pəl\ *n, often attrib* [ISV *prop-* + *-yl*] (1850) : either of two isomeric alkyl radicals C_3H_7 derived from propane — often used in combination

pro·py·lae·um \ˌprä-pə-ˈlē-əm, ˌprō-\ *n, pl* **-laea** \-ˈlē-ə\ [L, fr. Gk *propylaion,* fr. *pro-* before + *pylē* gate — more at PRO-] (ca. 1706) : a vestibule or entrance of architectural importance before a building or enclosure — often used in pl.

pro·pyl·ene \ˈprō-pə-ˌlēn\ *n* (1850) : a flammable gaseous hydrocarbon C_3H_6 obtained by cracking petroleum hydrocarbons and used chiefly in organic synthesis

propylene glycol *n* (1885) : a sweet hygroscopic viscous liquid $C_3H_8O_2$ made esp. from propylene and used esp. as an antifreeze and solvent, in brake fluids, and as a food preservative

pro ra·ta \(ˌ)prō-ˈrā-tə, -ˈrä-, -ˈra-\ *adv* [L] (1575) : proportionately according to an exactly calculable factor (as share or liability) — **pro rata** *adj*

pro·rate \(ˌ)prō-ˈrāt, ˈprō-ˌ\ *vb* **pro·rat·ed; pro·rat·ing** [*pro rata*] *vt* (1860) : to divide, distribute, or assess proportionately ~ *vi* : to make a pro rata distribution — **pro·ra·tion** \prō-ˈrā-shən\ *n*

pro·ro·gate \ˈprō-rə-ˌgāt\ *vt* **-gat·ed; -gat·ing** (1534) : PROROGUE — **pro·ro·ga·tion** \ˌprō-rə-ˈgā-shən\ *n*

pro·rogue \prə-ˈrōg\ *vb* **pro·rogued; pro·rogu·ing** [ME *prorogen,* fr. AF *proroger,* fr. L *prorogare,* fr. *pro-* before + *rogare* to ask — more at PRO-, RIGHT] *vt* (15c) **1** : DEFER, POSTPONE **2** : to terminate a session of (as a British parliament) by royal prerogative ~ *vi* : to suspend or end a legislative session

pros *pl of* PRO

pros- *prefix* [LL, fr. Gk, fr. *proti, pros* face to face with, toward, in addition to, near; akin to Skt *prati-* near, toward, against, in return, Gk *pro* before — more at FOR] : in front ⟨*pros*encephalon⟩

pro·sa·ic \prō-ˈzā-ik\ *adj* [LL *prosaicus,* fr. L *prosa* prose] (ca. 1656) **1 a** : characteristic of prose as distinguished from poetry : FACTUAL **b** : DULL, UNIMAGINATIVE ⟨~ advice⟩ **2** : EVERYDAY, ORDINARY ⟨heroic characters wasted in ~ lives —*Kirkus Reviews*⟩ — **pro·sa·i·cal·ly** \-ˈzā-ə-k(ə-)lē\ *adv*

pro·sa·ism \ˈprō-(ˌ)zā-ˌi-zəm\ *n* (1787) **1** : a prosaic manner, style, or quality **2** : a prosaic expression

pro·sa·ist *n* [L *prosa* prose] (1803) **1** \ˈprō-(ˌ)zā-ist, -zā-ˌist\ : a prose writer **2** \prō-ˈzā-ist\ : a prosaic person

pro·sa·teur \ˌprō-zə-ˈtər\ *n* [F, fr. It *prosatore,* fr. ML *prosator,* fr. L *prosa*] (1880) : a writer of prose

pro·sau·ro·pod \prō-ˈsȯr-ə-ˌpäd\ *n* [NL *Prosauropoda,* fr. 1*pro-* + *Sauropoda* — more at SAUROPOD] (1941) : any of a group (Prosauropoda) of chiefly herbivorous Triassic dinosaurs that are prob. ancestral to sauropods

pro·sce·ni·um \prō-ˈsē-nē-əm\ *n* [L, fr. Gk *proskēnion* front of the building forming the background for a dramatic performance, stage, fr. *pro-* + *skēnē* building forming the background for a dramatic performance — more at SCENE] (1606) **1 a** : the stage of an ancient Greek or Roman theater **b** : the part of a modern stage in front of the curtain **c** : the wall that separates the stage from the auditorium and provides the arch that frames it **2 a** : FOREGROUND 1 **b** : FOREGROUND 2

pro·sciut·to \prō-ˈshü-(ˌ)tō\ *n, pl* **-ti** \-(ˌ)tē\ *or* **-tos** [It, alter. of *presciutto,* fr. *pre-* (fr. L *prae-* pre-) + *asciutto* dried out, fr. L *exsuctus,* fr. pp. of *exsugere* to suck out, fr. *ex-* + *sugere* to suck — more at SUCK] (ca. 1929) : dry-cured spiced Italian ham usu. sliced thin

pro·scribe \prō-ˈskrīb\ *vt* **pro·scribed; pro·scrib·ing** [L *proscribere* to publish, proscribe, fr. *pro-* before + *scribere* to write — more at SCRIBE] (1560) **1** : to publish the name of as condemned to death with the property of the condemned forfeited to the state **2** : to condemn or forbid as harmful or unlawful : PROHIBIT — **pro·scrib·er** *n*

pro·scrip·tion \prō-ˈskrip-shən\ *n* [ME *proscripcion,* fr. L *proscription-, proscriptio,* fr. *proscribere*] (14c) **1** : the act of proscribing : the state of being proscribed **2** : an imposed restraint or restriction : PROHIBITION — **pro·scrip·tive** \-ˈskrip-tiv\ *adj* — **pro·scrip·tive·ly** *adv*

1**prose** \ˈprōz\ *n* [ME, fr. AF, fr. L *prosa,* fr. fem. of *prorsus, prosus,* straightforward, being in prose, contr. of *proversus,* pp. of *provertere* to turn forward, fr. *pro-* forward + *vertere* to turn — more at PRO-, WORTH] (14c) **1 a** : the ordinary language people use in speaking or writing **b** : a literary medium distinguished from poetry esp. by its greater irregularity and variety of rhythm and its closer correspon-

\ə\ **abut** \ᵊ\ **kitten,** F **table** \ər\ **further** \a\ **ash** \ā\ **ace** \ä\ **mop, mar**
\au̇\ **out** \ch\ **chin** \e\ **bet** \ē\ **easy** \g\ **go** \i\ **hit** \ī\ **ice** \j\ **job**
\ŋ\ **sing** \ō\ **go** \ȯ\ **law** \ȯi\ **boy** \th\ **thin** \t͟h\ **the** \ü\ **loot** \u̇\ **foot**
\y\ **yet** \zh\ **vision, beige** \k, ⁿ, œ, ue, ʸ\ *see* Guide to Pronunciation

dence to the patterns of everyday speech **2 :** a prosaic style, quality, or condition

[2]**prose** *adj* (14c) **1 :** of, relating to, or written in prose **2 :** PROSAIC

[3]**prose** *vi* **prosed; pros·ing** (1642) **1 :** to write prose **2 :** to write or speak in a prosaic manner

pro se \ˈprō-ˈsā, -ˈsē\ *adj or adv* [L] (1861) **:** on one's own behalf **:** without an attorney ⟨a *pro se* action⟩ ⟨a defendant's right to proceed *pro se*⟩

pro·sec·co \prō-ˈse-kō\ *n, pl* **-cos** [It, a grape variety, prob. fr. *Prosecco (Prosek),* town near Trieste] (1881) **:** a dry Italian sparkling wine

pro·sec·tor \prō-ˈsek-tər\ *n* [prob. fr. F *prosecteur,* fr. LL *prosector* anatomist, fr. L *prosecare* to cut away, fr. *pro-* forth + *secare* to cut — more at PRO-, SAW] (ca. 1857) **:** a person who makes dissections for anatomic demonstrations

pros·e·cute \ˈprä-si-ˌkyüt\ *vb* **-cut·ed; -cut·ing** [ME, fr. L *prosecutus,* pp. of *prosequi* to pursue — more at PURSUE] *vt* (15c) **1 :** to follow to the end **:** pursue until finished ⟨~ a war⟩ **2 :** to engage in **:** PERFORM **3 a :** to bring legal action against for redress or punishment of a crime or violation of law **b :** to institute legal proceedings with reference to ⟨~ a claim⟩ ~ *vi* **:** to institute and carry on a legal suit or prosecution — **pros·e·cut·able** \ˌprä-sə-ˈkyü-tə-bəl\ *adj*

prosecuting attorney *n* (1832) **:** an attorney who conducts proceedings in a court on behalf of the government **:** DISTRICT ATTORNEY

pros·e·cu·tion \ˌprä-si-ˈkyü-shən\ *n* (1567) **1 :** the act or process of prosecuting; *specif* **:** the institution and continuance of a criminal suit involving the process of pursuing formal charges against an offender to final judgment **2 :** the party by whom criminal proceedings are instituted or conducted **3** *obs* **:** PURSUIT

pros·e·cu·tor \ˈprä-si-ˌkyü-tər\ *n* (ca. 1670) **1 :** a person who institutes a prosecution before a court **2 :** PROSECUTING ATTORNEY

pros·e·cu·to·ri·al \ˌprä-si-kyü-ˈtȯr-ē-əl\ *adj* (1968) **:** of, relating to, or being a prosecutor or prosecution

[1]**pros·e·lyte** \ˈprä-sə-ˌlīt\ *n* [ME *proselite,* fr. AF *prosilite,* fr. LL *proselytus* proselyte, alien resident, fr. Gk *prosēlytos,* fr. *pros* near + *-ēlytos* (akin to *ēlythe* he went) — more at PROS-, ELASTIC] (14c) **:** a new convert (as to a faith or cause)

[2]**proselyte** *vb* **-lyt·ed; -lyt·ing** (1624) **:** PROSELYTIZE

pros·e·ly·tise *Brit var of* PROSELYTIZE

pros·e·ly·tism \ˈprä-sə-ˌlī-ˌti-zəm, ˈprä-s(ə-)lə-\ *n* (ca. 1660) **1 :** the act of becoming or condition of being a proselyte **:** CONVERSION **2 :** the act or process of proselytizing

pros·e·ly·tize \ˈprä-s(ə-)lə-ˌtīz\ *vb* **-tized; -tiz·ing** *vi* (1679) **1 :** to induce someone to convert to one's faith **2 :** to recruit someone to join one's party, institution, or cause ~ *vt* **:** to recruit or convert esp. to a new faith, institution, or cause — **pros·e·ly·ti·za·tion** \ˌprä-s(ə-)lə-tə-ˈzā-shən, ˌprä-sə-ˌlī-tə-\ *n* — **pros·e·ly·tiz·er** \ˈprä-s(ə-)lə-ˌtī-zər\ *n*

pro·sem·i·nar \(ˌ)prō-ˈse-mə-ˌnär\ *n* (ca. 1922) **:** a course of study like a graduate seminar but often open to advanced undergraduates

pros·en·ceph·a·lon \ˌpräs-ˌen-ˈse-fə-ˌlän, -lən\ *n* [NL] (1846) **:** FOREBRAIN — **pros·en·ce·phal·ic** \-sə-ˈfa-lik\ *adj*

prose poem *n* (1842) **:** a composition in prose that has some of the qualities of a poem — **prose poet** *n*

pros·er \ˈprō-zər\ *n* (1627) **1 :** a writer of prose **2 :** one who talks or writes tediously

Pro·ser·pi·na \prō-ˈsər-pə-nə\ *or* **Pros·er·pine** \ˈprä-sər-ˌpīn\ *n* [L] (14c) **:** PERSEPHONE

pro shop *n* (1932) **:** a shop at which equipment for a particular sport (as golf) is sold typically by a professional in that sport

pro·sim·i·an \prō-ˈsi-mē-ən\ *n* [NL *Prosimii,* fr. [1]*pro-* + L *simia* ape — more at SIMIAN] (ca. 1890) **:** any of a suborder (Prosimii) of lower primates (as lemurs and tarsiers) — **prosimian** *adj*

pro·sit \ˈprō-zət, -sət\ *or* **prost** \ˈprōst\ *interj* [G, fr. L *prosit* may it be beneficial, fr. *prodesse* to be useful — more at PROUD] (1846) — used to wish good health esp. before drinking

pro·so \ˈprō-(ˌ)sō\ *n* [Russ] (1917) **:** MILLET 1a

pros·o·branch \ˈprä-sə-ˌbraŋk\ *n, pl* **-branchs** [NL *Prosobranchia,* fr. *proso-* in front (fr. Gk *prosō* forward) + *branchia* gills (fr. Gk)] (1851) **:** any of a subclass (Prosobranchia) of gastropod mollusks that have the loop of visceral nerves twisted into a figure eight, the sexes usu. separate, and usu. an operculum — **prosobranch** *adj*

pro·sod·ic \prə-ˈsä-dik *also* -ˈzä-\ *or* **pro·sod·i·cal** \-di-kəl\ *adj* (1774) **:** of or relating to prosody — **pro·sod·i·cal·ly** \-di-k(ə-)lē\ *adv*

pros·o·dy \ˈprä-sə-dē, -zə-\ *n, pl* **-dies** [ME, fr. L *prosodia* accent of a syllable, fr. Gk *prosōidia* song sung to instrumental music, accent, fr. *pros* in addition to + *ōidē* song — more at PROS-, ODE] (15c) **1 :** the study of versification; *esp* **:** the systematic study of metrical structure **2 :** a particular system, theory, or style of versification **3 :** the rhythmic and intonational aspect of language — **pros·o·dist** \-dist\ *n*

pro·so·ma \(ˌ)prō-ˈsō-mə\ *n* [NL, fr. Gk *pro-* + *sōma* body] (1872) **:** the anterior region of the body of an invertebrate (as an arachnid) esp. when the segmentation is suppressed or obscured; *esp* **:** CEPHALOTHORAX

pros·o·pog·ra·phy \ˌprä-sə-ˈpä-grə-fē\ *n* [NL *prosopographia,* fr. Gk *prosōpon* person + *-graphia* -graphy] (1929) **:** a study that identifies and relates a group of persons or characters within a particular historical or literary context — **pros·o·po·graph·i·cal** \-pə-ˈgra-fi-kəl\ *adj*

pro·so·po·poe·ia \prə-ˌsō-pə-ˈpē-ə, ˌprä-sə-pə-\ *n* [L, fr. Gk *prosōpopoiia,* fr. *prosōpon* mask, person (fr. *pros-* + *ōps* face) + *poiein* to make — more at EYE, POET] (ca. 1555) **1 :** a figure of speech in which an imaginary or absent person is represented as speaking or acting **2 :** PERSONIFICATION

[1]**pros·pect** \ˈprä-ˌspekt\ *n* [ME, fr. L *prospectus* view, prospect, fr. *prospicere* to look forward, exercise foresight, fr. *pro-* forward + *specere* to look — more at PRO-, SPY] (15c) **1 :** EXPOSURE 3b **2 a (1) :** an extensive view **(2) :** a mental consideration **:** SURVEY **b :** a place that commands an extensive view **:** LOOKOUT **c :** something extended to the view **:** SCENE **d** *archaic* **:** a sketch or picture of a scene **3** *obs* **:** ASPECT **4 a :** the act of looking forward **:** ANTICIPATION **b :** a mental picture of something to come **:** VISION **c :** something that is awaited or expected **:** POSSIBILITY **d** *pl* **(1) :** financial expectations **(2) :** CHANCES **5 :** a place showing signs of containing a mineral deposit **6 a :** a potential buyer or customer **b :** a likely candidate for a job or position — **in prospect :** possible or likely for the future

syn PROSPECT, OUTLOOK, ANTICIPATION, FORETASTE mean an advance realization of something to come. PROSPECT implies expectation of a particular event, condition, or development of definite interest or concern ⟨the *prospect* of a quiet weekend⟩. OUTLOOK suggests a forecasting of the future ⟨a favorable *outlook* for the economy⟩. ANTICIPATION implies a prospect or outlook that involves advance suffering or enjoyment of what is foreseen ⟨the *anticipation* of her arrival⟩. FORETASTE implies an actual though brief or partial experience of something forthcoming ⟨the frost was a *foretaste* of winter⟩.

[2]**pros·pect** \ˈprä-ˌspekt, *chiefly Brit* prə-ˈ\ *vi* (1841) **:** to explore an area esp. for mineral deposits ~ *vt* **:** to inspect (a region) for mineral deposits; *broadly* **:** EXPLORE — **pros·pec·tor** \-ˌspek-tər, -ˈspek-\ *n*

pro·spec·tive \prə-ˈspek-tiv *also* ˈprä-ˌ, prō-ˈ, prä-ˈ\ *adj* (ca. 1699) **1 :** relating to or effective in the future **2 a :** likely to come about **:** EXPECTED ⟨the ~ benefits of this law⟩ **b :** likely to be or become ⟨a ~ mother⟩ — **pro·spec·tive·ly** *adv*

pro·spec·tus \prə-ˈspek-təs, prä-\ *n, pl* **-tus·es** [L, prospect] (1765) **1 :** a preliminary printed statement that describes an enterprise (as a business or publication) and that is distributed to prospective buyers, investors, or participants **2 :** something (as a statement or situation) that forecasts the course or nature of something

pros·per \ˈpräs-pər\ *vb* **pros·pered; pros·per·ing** \-p(ə-)riŋ\ [ME, fr. AF *prosperer,* fr. L *prosperare* to cause to succeed, fr. *prosperus* favorable] *vi* (14c) **1 :** to succeed in an enterprise or activity; *esp* **:** to achieve economic success **2 :** to become strong and flourishing ~ *vt* **:** to cause to succeed or thrive

pros·per·i·ty \prä-ˈsper-ə-tē\ *n* (13c) **:** the condition of being successful or thriving; *esp* **:** economic well-being

Pros·pero \ˈpräs-pə-ˌrō\ *n* (1610) **:** the rightful duke of Milan in Shakespeare's *The Tempest*

pros·per·ous \ˈpräs-p(ə-)rəs\ *adj* [ME, fr. ML *prosperosus,* fr. L *prosperus*] (15c) **1 :** AUSPICIOUS, FAVORABLE **2 a :** marked by success or economic well-being **b :** enjoying vigorous and healthy growth **:** FLOURISHING — **pros·per·ous·ly** *adv* — **pros·per·ous·ness** *n*

pross \ˈpräs\ *or* **pros·sie** \ˈprä-sē\ *or* **pros·tie** \ˈpräs-tē\ *n* (1902) *slang* **:** PROSTITUTE 1a

pros·ta·cy·clin \ˌpräs-tə-ˈsī-klən\ *n* [*prosta-* (as in *prostaglandin*) + *cycl-* + [1]*-in*] (1976) **:** a prostaglandin that is a metabolite of arachidonic acid, inhibits platelet aggregation, and dilates blood vessels

pros·ta·glan·din \ˌpräs-tə-ˈglan-dən\ *n* [*prosta*te *gland* + [1]*-in;* fr. its occurrence in the seminal fluid of animals] (1936) **:** any of various oxygenated unsaturated cyclic fatty acids of animals that are formed chiefly by the action of cyclooxygenase on arachidonic acid and perform a variety of hormonelike actions (as in controlling blood pressure or smooth muscle contraction)

pros·tate \ˈpräs-ˌtāt\ *n* [NL *prostata* prostate gland, fr. Gk *prostatēs,* fr. *proïstanai* to put in front, fr. *pro-* before + *histanai* to cause to stand — more at PRO-, STAND] (1646) **:** PROSTATE GLAND — **pros·tat·ic** \prä-ˈsta-tik\ *adj*

pros·ta·tec·to·my \ˌpräs-tə-ˈtek-tə-mē\ *n, pl* **-mies** (ca. 1890) **:** surgical removal or resection of the prostate gland

prostate gland *n* (ca. 1764) **:** a firm partly muscular partly glandular body that is situated about the base of the mammalian male urethra and that secretes an alkaline viscid fluid which is a major constituent of the semen

prostate–specific antigen *n* (1981) **:** a protease secreted by epithelial cells of the prostate gland that is used in the diagnosis of prostate cancer since its concentration in blood serum tends to be proportional to the clinical stage of the disease — abbr. *PSA*

pros·ta·tism \ˈpräs-tə-ˌti-zəm\ *n* (ca. 1900) **:** disease of the prostate; *esp* **:** a disorder resulting from obstruction of the bladder neck by an enlarged prostate gland

pros·ta·ti·tis \ˌpräs-tə-ˈtī-təs\ *n* [NL] (ca. 1844) **:** inflammation of the prostate gland

pros·the·sis \präs-ˈthē-səs, ˈpräs-thə-\ *n, pl* **-the·ses** \-ˌsēz\ [NL, fr. Gk, addition, fr. *prostithenai* to add to, fr. *pros-* in addition to + *tithenai* to put — more at PROS-, DO] (ca. 1900) **:** an artificial device to replace or augment a missing or impaired part of the body

pros·thet·ic \präs-ˈthe-tik\ *adj* (ca. 1890) **1 :** of or relating to a prosthesis or prosthetics **2 :** of, relating to, or constituting a nonprotein group of a conjugated protein — **pros·thet·i·cal·ly** \-ti-k(ə-)lē\ *adv*

pros·thet·ics \-tiks\ *n pl but sing or pl in constr* (ca. 1894) **:** the surgical or dental specialty concerned with the design, construction, and fitting of prostheses

pros·thet·ist \ˈpräs-thə-tist\ *n* (1902) **:** a specialist in prosthetics

pros·tho·don·tics \ˌpräs-thə-ˈdän-tiks\ *n pl but sing or pl in constr* [NL *prosthodontia,* fr. *prosthesis* + *-odontia*] (1947) **:** prosthetic dentistry — **pros·tho·don·tist** \-ˈdän-tist\ *n* (1917) **:** a specialist in prosthodontics

[1]**pros·ti·tute** \ˈpräs-tə-ˌtüt, -ˌtyüt\ *vt* **-tut·ed; -tut·ing** [L *prostitutus,* pp. of *prostituere,* fr. *pro-* before + *statuere* to station — more at PRO-, STATUTE] (1530) **1 :** to offer indiscriminately for sexual intercourse esp. for money **2 :** to devote to corrupt or unworthy purposes **:** DEBASE ⟨~ one's talents⟩ — **pros·ti·tu·tor** \-ˌtü-tər, -ˌtyü-\ *n*

[2]**prostitute** *adj* (1563) **:** devoted to corrupt purposes **:** PROSTITUTED

[3]**prostitute** *n* (1613) **1 a :** a woman who engages in promiscuous sexual intercourse esp. for money **:** WHORE **b :** a male who engages in sexual and esp. homosexual practices for money **2 :** a person (as a writer or painter) who deliberately debases his or her talents (as for money)

pros·ti·tu·tion \ˌpräs-tə-ˈtü-shən, -ˈtyü-\ *n* (1553) **1 :** the act or practice of engaging in promiscuous sexual relations esp. for money **2 :** the state of being prostituted **:** DEBASEMENT

pro·sto·mi·um \prō-ˈstō-mē-əm\ *n, pl* **-mia** \-mē-ə\ [NL, fr. Gk *pro-* + *stoma* mouth — more at STOMACH] (1870) **:** the portion of the head of an annelid worm (as an earthworm) that is situated in front of the mouth — **pro·sto·mi·al** \-mē-əl\ *adj*

[1]**pros·trate** \ˈprä-ˌstrāt\ *adj* [ME *prostrat,* fr. AF, fr. L *prostratus,* pp. of *prosternere,* fr. *pro-* before + *sternere* to spread out, throw down — more at STREW] (14c) **1 :** stretched out with face on the ground in adoration or submission; *also* **:** lying flat **2 :** completely overcome and lacking vitality, will, or power to rise ⟨was ~ from the heat⟩ **3 :** trailing on the ground **:** PROCUMBENT ⟨~ shrubs⟩ ***syn*** see PRONE

[2]**pros·trate** \ˈprä-ˌstrāt, *esp Brit* prä-ˈ\ *vt* **pros·trat·ed; pros·trat·ing** (15c) **1 :** to throw or put into a prostrate position **2 :** to put (oneself) in a humble and submissive posture or state ⟨the whole town had to ~ itself in official apology —Claudia Cassidy⟩ **3 :** to reduce to submission, helplessness, or exhaustion ⟨was *prostrated* with grief⟩

pros·tra·tion \prä-ˈstrā-shən\ *n* (14c) **1 a :** the act of assuming a prostrate position **b :** the state of being in a prostrate position : ABASEMENT **2 a :** complete physical or mental exhaustion : COLLAPSE **b :** the process of being made powerless or the condition of powerlessness ⟨the country suffered economic ~ after the war⟩

prosy \ˈprō-zē\ *adj* **pros·i·er; -est** [¹*prose*] (1814) : lacking in qualities that seize the attention or strike the imagination : COMMONPLACE; *esp* : tediously dull in speech or manner — **pros·i·ly** \-zə-lē\ *adv* — **pros·i·ness** \-zē-nəs\ *n*

Prot *abbr* Protestant

prot- *or* **proto-** *comb form* [Gk *prōt-, prōto-,* fr. *prōtos;* akin to Gk *pro* before — more at FOR] **1 a :** first in time ⟨*proto*history⟩ **b :** beginning : giving rise to ⟨*proto*planet⟩ **2 :** parent substance of a (specified) substance ⟨*prot*actinium⟩ **3 :** first formed : primary ⟨*proto*xylem⟩ **4** *cap* : relating to or constituting the recorded or assumed language that is ancestral to a language or to a group of related languages or dialects ⟨*Proto*-Indo-European⟩

prot·ac·tin·i·um \ˌprō-ˌtak-ˈti-nē-əm\ *n* [NL] (1918) : a shiny radioactive metallic element of relatively short life — see ELEMENT table

pro·tag·o·nist \prō-ˈta-gə-nist\ *n* [Gk *prōtagōnistēs,* fr. *prōt-* prot- + *agōnistēs* competitor at games, actor, fr. *agōnizesthai* to compete, fr. *agōn* contest, competition at games — more at AGONY] (1671) **1 a :** the principal character in a literary work (as a drama or story) **b :** a leading actor, character, or participant in a literary work or real event **2 :** a leader, proponent, or supporter of a cause : CHAMPION

prot·amine \ˈprō-tə-ˌmēn\ *n* [ISV *prot-* + *amine*] (1874) : any of various strongly basic proteins of relatively low molecular weight that are rich in arginine and are found associated esp. with DNA in place of histone in the sperm cells of various animals (as fish)

prot·a·sis \ˈprä-tə-səs\ *n, pl* **-a·ses** \-ˌsēz\ [LL, fr. Gk, premise of a syllogism, conditional clause, fr. *proteinein* to stretch out before, put forward, fr. *pro-* + *teinein* to stretch — more at THIN] (ca. 1568) **1 :** the introductory part of a play or narrative poem **2 :** the subordinate clause of a conditional sentence — compare APODOSIS — **pro·tat·ic** \prä-ˈta-tik, prō-\ *adj*

prote- *or* **proteo-** *comb form* [ISV, fr. F *protéine*] : protein ⟨*prote*ase⟩ ⟨*proteo*lysis⟩

pro·tea \ˈprō-tē-ə\ *n* [NL, fr. L *Proteus* Proteus] (1770) : any of a genus (*Protea* of the family Proteaceae, the protea family) of African evergreen shrubs often grown as ornamentals for their showy bracts and dense flower heads

pro·te·an \ˈprō-tē-ən, prō-ˈtē-\ *adj* (1598) **1 :** of or resembling Proteus in having a varied nature or ability to assume different forms **2 :** displaying great diversity or variety : VERSATILE

pro·te·ase \ˈprō-tē-ˌās, -ˌāz\ *n* [ISV] (1903) : any of numerous enzymes that hydrolyze proteins and are classified according to the most prominent functional group (as serine or cysteine) at the active site — called also *proteinase*

protease inhibitor *n* (1976) : a substance that inhibits the action of a protease; *specif* : any of various drugs (as indinavir) that inhibit the action of the protease of HIV so that the cleavage of viral proteins into mature functional infectious particles is prevented and that are used esp. in combination with other agents in the treatment of HIV infection

pro·tect \prə-ˈtekt\ *vb* [ME, fr. L *protectus,* pp. of *protegere,* fr. *pro-* in front + *tegere* to cover — more at PRO-, THATCH] *vt* (15c) **1 a :** to cover or shield from exposure, injury, damage, or destruction : GUARD **b :** DEFEND 1c ⟨~ the goal⟩ **2 :** to maintain the status or integrity of esp. through financial or legal guarantees: as **a :** to save from contingent financial loss **b :** to foster or shield from infringement or restriction ⟨salesmen with ~*ed* territories⟩ ⟨~ one's rights⟩; *specif* : to restrict competition for (as domestic industries) by means of tariffs or trade controls **3 :** DEFEND 5 ⟨~ a lead⟩ ~ *vi* : to provide a guard or shield ⟨~*s* against tooth decay⟩ ***syn*** see DEFEND — **pro·tect·able** \-ˈtek-tə-bəl\ *adj* — **pro·tec·tive** \-ˈtek-tiv\ *adj* — **pro·tec·tive·ly** *adv* — **pro·tec·tive·ness** *n*

pro·tec·tant \prə-ˈtek-tənt\ *n* (1935) : a protecting agent

pro·tec·tion \prə-ˈtek-shən\ *n* (14c) **1 :** the act of protecting : the state of being protected **2 a :** one that protects **b :** supervision or support of one that is smaller and weaker **c :** a contraceptive device (as a condom) **3 :** the freeing of the producers of a country from foreign competition in their home market by restrictions (as high duties) on foreign competitive goods **4 a :** immunity from prosecution purchased by criminals through bribery **b :** money extorted by racketeers posing as a protective association **5 :** COVERAGE 1a **6 :** anchoring equipment placed in cracks for safety while rock climbing

pro·tec·tion·ist \-sh(ə-)nist\ *n* (1844) : an advocate of government economic protection for domestic producers through restrictions on foreign competitors — **pro·tec·tion·ism** \-shə-ˌni-zəm\ *n* — **protectionist** *adj*

protective tariff *n* (1838) : a tariff intended primarily to protect domestic producers rather than to yield revenue

pro·tec·tor \prə-ˈtek-tər\ *n* (14c) **1 a :** one that protects : GUARDIAN **b :** a device used to prevent injury : GUARD **2 a :** one having the care of a kingdom during the king's minority : REGENT **b :** the executive head of the Commonwealth of England, Scotland, and Ireland from 1653 to 1659 — called also *Lord Protector of the Commonwealth* — **pro·tec·tor·ship** \-ˌship\ *n*

pro·tec·tor·al \-ˈtek-t(ə-)rəl\ *adj* (1657) : of or relating to a protector or protectorate

pro·tec·tor·ate \-ˈtek-t(ə-)rət\ *n* (1692) **1 a :** government by a protector **b** *cap* : the government of England (1653–59) under the Cromwells **c :** the rank, office, or period of rule of a protector **2 a :** the relationship of superior authority assumed by one power or state over a dependent one **b :** the dependent political unit or territory in such a relationship

pro·tec·to·ry \-ˈtek-t(ə-)rē\ *n, pl* **-ries** (1885) : an institution for the protection and care of usu. homeless or delinquent children

pro·tec·tress \-ˈtek-trəs\ *n* (1570) : a woman who is a protector

pro·té·gé \ˈprō-tə-ˌzhā, ˌprō-tə-ˈ\ *n* [F, fr. pp. of *protéger* to protect, fr. MF, fr. L *protegere*] (1787) : one who is protected or trained or whose career is furthered by a person of experience, prominence, or influence

pro·té·gée \ˈprō-tə-ˌzhā, ˌprō-tə-ˈ\ *n* [F, fem. of *protégé*] (1778) : a girl or woman who is a protégé

pro·tein \ˈprō-ˌtēn *also* ˈprō-tē-ən\ *n, often attrib* [F *protéine,* fr. LGk *prōteios* primary, fr. Gk *prōtos* first — more at PROT-] (ca. 1844) **1 :** any of various naturally occurring extremely complex substances that consist of amino-acid residues joined by peptide bonds, contain the elements carbon, hydrogen, nitrogen, oxygen, usu. sulfur, and occas. other elements (as phosphorus or iron), and include many essential biological compounds (as enzymes, hormones, or antibodies) **2 :** the total nitrogenous material in plant or animal substances

pro·tein·a·ceous \ˌprō-tə-ˈnā-shəs; ˌprō-ˌtē-(ə-)ˈnā-shəs\ *adj* (ca. 1844) : of, relating to, containing, resembling, or being protein

pro·tein·ase \ˈprō-tə-ˌnās, -ˌnāz; ˈprō-ˌtē-(ə-)ˌnās, -ˌnāz\ *n* [ISV] (1929) : PROTEASE

protein kinase *n* (1966) : any of a class of enzymes that catalyze the transfer of a phosphate group from ATP to one or more amino acids in the side chain of a protein resulting in a conformational change affecting protein function

protein kinase C *n* (1981) : a protein kinase that catalyzes the phosphorylation of specific serine or threonine amino acid residues

pro·tein·uria \ˌprō-tə-ˈnu̇r-ē-ə, -ˈnyu̇r-; ˌprō-tē(-ə)-ˈnu̇r-ē-ə, -ˈnyu̇r-\ *n* [NL, fr. ISV *protein* + NL *-uria*] (1911) : the presence of excess protein in the urine

pro tem \(ˌ)prō-ˈtem\ *adv* (1828) : PRO TEMPORE

pro tem·po·re \prō-ˈtem-pə-rē\ *adv* [ME, fr. L] (15c) : for the time being

pro·tend \prō-ˈtend\ *vb* [ME, fr. L *protendere,* fr. *pro-* + *tendere* to stretch — more at THIN] *vt* (15c) **1** *archaic* : to stretch forth **2** *archaic* : EXTEND ~ *vi, archaic* : STICK OUT, PROTRUDE

pro·ten·sive \-ˈten(t)-siv\ *adj* [L *protensus,* pp. of *protendere*] (1671) **1** *archaic* : having continuance in time **2** *archaic* : having lengthwise extent or extensiveness — **pro·ten·sive·ly** *adv*

pro·teo·gly·can \ˌprō-tē-ə-ˈglī-ˌkan\ *n* [ISV] (1968) : any of a class of glycoproteins of high molecular weight that are found esp. in the extracellular matrix of connective tissue

pro·te·ol·y·sis \ˌprō-tē-ˈä-lə-səs\ *n* [NL] (1880) : the hydrolysis of proteins or peptides with formation of simpler and soluble products

pro·teo·lyt·ic \ˌprō-tē-ə-ˈli-tik\ *adj* (1877) : of, relating to, or producing proteolysis — **pro·teo·lyt·i·cal·ly** \-ti-k(ə-)lē\ *adv*

pro·te·ome \ˈprō-tē-ˌōm\ *n* [*prote-* + *-ome* (as in *genome*)] (1995) : the complement of proteins expressed in a cell, tissue, or organism by a genome

pro·te·o·mics \ˌprō-tē-ˈō-miks\ *n pl but sing in constr* (1997) : a branch of biotechnology concerned with applying the techniques of molecular biology, biochemistry, and genetics to analyzing the structure, function, and interactions of the proteins produced by the genes of a particular cell, tissue, or organism, with organizing the information in databases, and with applications of the data — compare GENOMICS — **pro·te·o·mic** \-mik\ *adj*

pro·te·ose \ˈprō-tē-ˌōs, -ˌōz\ *n* [ISV] (ca. 1890) : any of various water-soluble protein derivatives formed by partial hydrolysis of proteins

Pro·te·ro·zo·ic \ˌprä-tə-rə-ˈzō-ik, ˌprō-\ *adj* [Gk *proteros* former, earlier (fr. *pro* before) + ISV *-zoic* — more at FOR] (1899) : of, relating to, or being the eon of geologic time or the corresponding segment of rocks that includes the interval between the Archean and Phanerozoic eons, exceeds in length all of subsequent geologic time, and is marked by rocks that contain fossils indicating the first appearance of eukaryotic organisms (as algae) — see GEOLOGIC TIME table — **Proterozoic** *n*

¹**pro·test** \ˈprō-ˌtest\ *n* [ME, fr. *protester*] (15c) **1 :** a solemn declaration of opinion and usu. of dissent: as **a :** a sworn declaration that payment of a note or bill has been refused and that all responsible signers or debtors are liable for resulting loss or damage **b :** a declaration made esp. before or while paying that a tax is illegal and that payment is not voluntary **2 :** the act of objecting or a gesture of disapproval ⟨resigned in ~⟩; *esp* : a usu. organized public demonstration of disapproval **3 :** a complaint, objection, or display of unwillingness usu. to an idea or a course of action ⟨went under ~⟩ **4 :** an objection made to an official or a governing body of a sport

²**pro·test** \prə-ˈtest, ˈprō-ˌ, prō-ˈ\ *vb* [ME, fr. AF *protester,* fr. L *protestari,* fr. *pro-* forth + *testari* to call to witness — more at PRO-, TESTAMENT] *vt* (15c) **1 :** to make solemn declaration or affirmation of ⟨~ my innocence⟩ **2 :** to execute or have executed a formal protest against (as a bill or note) **3 :** to make a statement or gesture in objection to ⟨~*ed* the abuses of human rights⟩ ~ *vi* **1 :** to make a protestation **2 :** to make or enter a protest ***syn*** see ASSERT — **pro·test·er** *or* **pro·tes·tor** \-ˈtes-tər, -ˌtes-\ *n*

¹**prot·es·tant** \ˈprä-təs-tənt, *2 is also* prə-ˈtes-\ *n* [MF, fr. L *protestant-, protestans,* prp. of *protestari*] (1539) **1** *cap* **a :** any of a group of German princes and cities presenting a defense of freedom of conscience against an edict of the Diet of Spires in 1529 intended to suppress the Lutheran movement **b :** a member of any of several church denominations denying the universal authority of the Pope and affirming the Reformation principles of justification by faith alone, the priesthood of all believers, and the primacy of the Bible as the only source of revealed truth; *broadly* : a Christian not of a Catholic or Eastern church **2 :** one who makes or enters a protest — **Prot·es·tant·ism** \ˈprä-təs-tən-ˌti-zəm\ *n*

²**protestant** *adj* (1539) **1** *cap* : of or relating to Protestants, their churches, or their religion **2 :** making or sounding a protest ⟨the two ~ ladies up and marched out —*Time*⟩

Protestant ethic *n* (1926) : an ethic that stresses the virtue of hard work, thrift, and self-discipline

pro·tes·ta·tion \ˌprä-təs-ˈtā-shən, ˌprō-, -ˌtes-\ *n* (14c) : the act of protesting : a solemn declaration or avowal

pro·te·us \ˈprō-tē-əs\ *n, pl* **-tei** \-tē-ˌī\ [NL, fr. L, Proteus] (1896) : any of a genus (*Proteus*) of aerobic usu. motile enterobacteria that include saprophytes in decaying organic matter and a common causative agent (*P. mirabilis*) of urinary tract infections

\ə\ **a**but \ᵊ\ kitten, F table \ər\ **fur**ther \a\ **a**sh \ā\ **a**ce \ä\ m**o**p, m**a**r
\au̇\ **ou**t \ch\ **ch**in \e\ b**e**t \ē\ **ea**sy \g\ **g**o \i\ h**i**t \ī\ **i**ce \j\ **j**ob
\ŋ\ si**ng** \ō\ g**o** \ȯ\ l**aw** \ȯi\ b**oy** \th\ **th**in \t͟h\ **th**e \ü\ l**oo**t \u̇\ f**oo**t
\y\ **y**et \zh\ vi**s**ion, bei**g**e \k̲, ⁿ, œ, ue, ʸ\ *see* Guide to Pronunciation

Pro·teus \'prō-ˌtyüs, -tē-əs, -ˌtüs\ *n* [L, fr. Gk *Prōteus*] (15c) : a Greek sea god capable of assuming different forms
pro·tha·la·mi·on \ˌprō-thə-'lā-mē-ən, -ˌän\ *or* **pro·tha·la·mi·um** \-mē-əm\ *n, pl* **-mia** \-mē-ə\ [NL, fr. Gk *pro-* + *-thalamion* (as in *epithalamion*)] (1597) : a song in celebration of a marriage
pro·thal·li·um \prō-'tha-lē-əm\ *n, pl* **-thal·lia** \-lē-ə\ [NL, fr. *pro-* + *thallus*] (1858) : PROTHALLUS
pro·thal·lus \(ˌ)prō-'tha-ləs\ *n* [NL] (1854) **1** : the gametophyte of a pteridophyte (as a fern) that is typically a small flat green thallus attached to the soil by rhizoids **2** : a greatly reduced structure of a seed plant corresponding to the pteridophyte prothallus

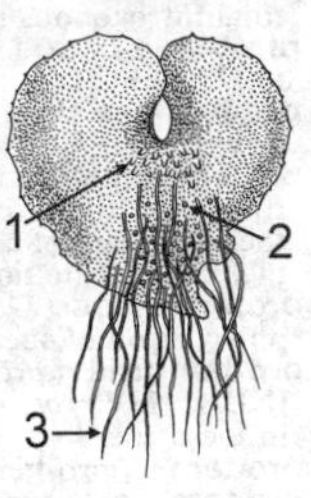

prothallus 1: *1* antheridium, *2* archegonium, *3* rhizoid

proth·e·sis \'prä-thə-səs\ *n, pl* **-e·ses** \-ˌsēz\ [LL, alter. of *prosthesis,* fr. Gk, lit., addition — more at PROSTHESIS] (ca. 1550) : the addition of a sound to the beginning of a word (as in Old French *estat*—whence English *estate*—from Latin *status*) — **pro·thet·ic** \prä-'the-tik\ *adj*
pro·tho·no·ta·ry \ˌprō-'thä-nə-ˌter-ē, ˌprō-thə-'nō-tə-rē\ *or* **pro·to·no·ta·ry** \prō-'tä-nə-ˌter-ē, ˌprō-tə-'nō-tə-rē\ *n, pl* **-ries** [ME *prothonotarie,* fr. LL *protonotarius,* fr. *prot-* + L *notarius* stenographer — more at NOTARY PUBLIC] (15c) : a chief clerk of any of various courts of law — **pro·tho·no·tar·i·al** \prō-ˌthä-nə-'ter-ē-əl, ˌpro-thə-nō-'ter-ē-əl\ *adj*
prothonotary warbler *n* (1783) : a large eastern No. American warbler (*Protonotaria citrea* of the family Parulidae) of wooded swamps that has a golden-yellow head and breast and bluish-gray wings
pro·tho·rac·ic \ˌprō-thə-'ra-sik\ *adj* (1826) : of or relating to the prothorax
prothoracic gland *n* (1887) : one of a pair of thoracic endocrine organs in some insects that control molting
pro·tho·rax \(ˌ)prō-'thȯr-ˌaks\ *n* [NL *prothorac-, prothorax,* fr. [1]*pro-* + *thorax*] (1826) : the anterior segment of the thorax of an insect — see INSECT illustration
pro·throm·bin \(ˌ)prō-'thräm-bən\ *n* [ISV] (1898) : a plasma protein produced in the liver in the presence of vitamin K and converted into thrombin in the clotting of blood
pro·tist \'prō-(ˌ)tist\ *n* [NL *Protista,* fr. Gk, neut. pl. of *prōtistos* very first, primal, fr. superl. of *prōtos* first — more at PROT-] (1889) : any of a diverse taxonomic group and esp. a kingdom (Protista syn. Protoctista) of eukaryotic organisms that are unicellular and sometimes colonial or less often multicellular and that typically include the protozoans, most algae, and often some fungi (as slime molds) — **pro·tis·tan** \prō-'tis-tən\ *adj or n*
pro·ti·um \'prō-tē-əm, 'prō-shē-\ *n* [NL, fr. Gk *prōtos* first] (1933) : the ordinary light hydrogen isotope of atomic mass 1
proto- — see PROT-
pro·to·cer·a·tops \ˌprō-(ˌ)tō-'ser-ə-ˌtäps\ *n* [NL, fr. *prot-* + *Ceratops,* a genus — more at CERATOPSIAN] (1979) : any of a genus (*Protoceratops*) of small herbivorous ceratopsian dinosaurs of the late Cretaceous that lacked horns
pro·to·col \'prō-tə-ˌkȯl, -ˌkōl, -ˌkäl, -kəl\ *n* [MF *prothocole,* fr. ML *protocollum,* fr. LGk *prōtokollon* first sheet of a papyrus roll bearing date of manufacture, fr. Gk *prōt-* prot- + *kollan* to glue together, fr. *kolla* glue; perh. akin to MD *helen* to glue] (1541) **1** : an original draft, minute, or record of a document or transaction **2 a** : a preliminary memorandum often formulated and signed by diplomatic negotiators as a basis for a final convention or treaty **b** : the records or minutes of a diplomatic conference or congress that show officially the agreements arrived at by the negotiators **3 a** : a code prescribing strict adherence to correct etiquette and precedence (as in diplomatic exchange and in the military services) ⟨a breach of ∼⟩ **b** : a set of conventions governing the treatment and esp. the formatting of data in an electronic communications system ⟨network ∼*s*⟩ **c** : CONVENTION 3a,b **4** : a detailed plan of a scientific or medical experiment, treatment, or procedure
pro·to·derm \'prō-tə-ˌdərm\ *n* [ISV] (ca. 1932) : the outer primary meristem of a plant or plant part
pro·to·gal·axy \ˌprō-tō-'ga-lək-sē\ *n* (1950) : a cloud of gas believed to be the precursor to a galaxy
pro·to·his·to·ry \-'his-t(ə-)rē\ *n* [ISV] (1903) : the study of human beings in the times that immediately antedate recorded history — **pro·to·his·to·ri·an** \-(h)is-'tȯr-ē-ən\ *n* — **pro·to·his·tor·ic** \-'tȯr-ik, -'tär-\ *adj*
pro·to·hu·man \-'hyü-mən, -'yü-\ *adj* (ca. 1909) : of, relating to, or resembling an early hominid (as an australopithecine) — **protohuman** *n*
pro·to·lan·guage \'prō-tō-ˌlaŋ-gwij\ *n* (1948) : an assumed or recorded ancestral language
pro·to·mar·tyr \'prō-tō-ˌmär-tər\ *n* [ME *prothomartir,* fr. MF, fr. LL *protomartyr,* fr. LGk *prōtomartyr-, prōtomartys,* fr. Gk *prōt-* + *martyr-, martys* martyr] (15c) : the first martyr in a cause or region
pro·ton \'prō-ˌtän\ *n* [Gk *prōton,* neut. of *prōtos* first — more at PROT-] (1920) : an elementary particle that is identical with the nucleus of the hydrogen atom, that along with the neutron is a constituent of all other atomic nuclei, that carries a positive charge numerically equal to the charge of an electron, and that has a mass of 1.673×10^{-27} kilogram — **pro·ton·ic** \prō-'tä-nik\ *adj*
pro·ton·ate \'prō-tə-ˌnāt\ *vb* **-at·ed; -at·ing** *vt* (1946) : to add a proton to ∼ *vi* : to acquire an additional proton — **pro·ton·ation** \ˌprō-tə-'nā-shən\ *n*
pro·to·ne·ma \ˌprō-tə-'nē-mə\ *n, pl* **-ne·ma·ta** \-'nē-mə-tə, -'ne-\ [NL *protonemat-, protonema,* fr. *prot-* + Gk *nēma* thread — more at NEMAT-] (1857) : the primary usu. filamentous thalloid stage of the gametophyte in mosses and in some liverworts comparable to the prothallus in ferns — **pro·to·ne·mal** \-'nē-məl\ *adj* — **pro·to·ne·ma·tal** \-'nē-mə-tᵊl, -'ne-\ *adj*
pro·ton·o·tary apostolic \prə-'tä-nə-ˌter-ē-, prō-tə-'nä-tə-rē-\ *or* **pro·thon·o·tary apostolic** \prə-'thä-nə-ˌter-ē-, ˌprō-thə-'nä-tə-rē-\ *n, pl* **protonotar·ies apostolic** *or* **prothonotar·ies apostolic** (1682) : a priest of the chief college of the papal curia who keeps records of consistories and canonizations and signs papal bulls; *also* : an honorary member of this college
proton pump inhibitor *n* (1983) : any of a group of drugs that inhibit the activity of pumps transporting hydrogen ions across cell membranes and are used to inhibit gastric acid secretion
proton synchrotron *n* (1947) : a synchrotron in which protons are accelerated by means of frequency modulation of the radio-frequency accelerating voltage so that they have energies of billions of electron volts
pro·to·path·ic \ˌprō-tə-'pa-thik\ *adj* [ISV, fr. MGk *prōtopathēs* affected first, fr. Gk *prōt-* prot- + *pathos* experience, suffering — more at PATHOS] (1905) : of, relating to, or being cutaneous sensory reception responsive only to strong rather crude stimuli
pro·to·phlo·em \-'flō-ˌem\ *n* (1884) : the first-formed phloem that develops from procambium, consists of narrow thin-walled cells, and is usu. associated with a region of rapid growth
pro·to·plan·et \'prō-tō-ˌpla-nət\ *n* (1949) : a hypothetical whirling gaseous mass within a giant cloud of gas and dust that rotates around a sun and is believed to give rise to a planet — **pro·to·plan·e·tary** \ˌprō-tō-'pla-nə-ˌter-ē\ *adj*
pro·to·plasm \'prō-tə-ˌpla-zəm\ *n* [G *Protoplasma,* fr. *prot-* + NL *plasma*] (1848) **1** : the organized colloidal complex of organic and inorganic substances (as proteins and water) that constitutes the living nucleus, cytoplasm, plastids, and mitochondria of the cell **2** : CYTOPLASM — **pro·to·plas·mic** \ˌprō-tə-'plaz-mik\ *adj*
pro·to·plast \'prō-tə-ˌplast\ *n* [MF *protoplaste,* fr. LL *protoplastus* first human, fr. Gk *prōtoplastos* first formed, fr. *prōt-* prot- + *plastos* formed, fr. *plassein* to mold — more at PLASTER] (1532) **1** : one that is formed first : PROTOTYPE **2** : a plant cell that has had its cell wall removed; *also* : the nucleus, cytoplasm, and plasma membrane of a cell as distinguished from inert walls and inclusions
pro·to·por·phy·rin \ˌprō-tō-'pȯr-f(ə-)rən\ *n* [ISV] (1925) : a purple porphyrin acid $C_{34}H_{34}N_4O_4$ obtained from hemin or heme by removal of bound iron
pro·to·star \'prō-tō-ˌstär\ *n* (1947) : a cloud of gas and dust in space believed to develop into a star
pro·to·stele \'prō-tə-ˌstēl, ˌprō-tə-'stē-lē\ *n* (1901) : a stele forming a solid rod with the phloem surrounding the xylem — **pro·to·ste·lic** \ˌprō-tə-'stē-lik\ *adj*
pro·to·stome \'prō-tə-ˌstōm\ *n* [NL *Protostomia,* fr. *prot-* + Gk *stoma* mouth — more at STOMACH] (1959) : any of a major group (Protostomia) of bilateral metazoan animals (as mollusks, annelids, and arthropods) characterized in typical forms by determinate and spiral cleavage, formation of a mouth and anus directly from the blastopore, and formation of the coelom by splitting of the embryonic mesoderm — compare DEUTEROSTOME
pro·to·troph \'prō-tə-ˌtrōf, -ˌträf\ *n* [back-formation fr. *prototrophic*] (1946) : a prototrophic individual
pro·to·tro·phic \ˌprō-tə-'trō-fik\ *adj* [ISV] (1900) : having the nutritional requirements of the normal or wild type — **pro·to·tro·phy** \prō-'tä-trə-fē\ *n*
pro·to·typ·al \ˌprō-tə-'tī-pəl\ *adj* (ca. 1693) : PROTOTYPICAL
pro·to·type \'prō-tə-ˌtīp\ *n* [F, fr. Gk *prōtotypon,* fr. neut. of *prōtotypos* archetypal, fr. *prōt-* + *typos* type] (1552) **1** : an original model on which something is patterned : ARCHETYPE **2** : an individual that exhibits the essential features of a later type **3** : a standard or typical example **4** : a first full-scale and usu. functional form of a new type or design of a construction (as an airplane)
pro·to·typ·i·cal \ˌprō-tə-'ti-pi-kəl\ *also* **pro·to·typ·ic** \-pik\ *adj* (1650) : of, relating to, or being a prototype — **pro·to·typ·i·cal·ly** \-pi-k(ə-)lē\ *adv*
pro·to·xy·lem \ˌprō-tə-'zī-ləm, -ˌlem\ *n* (1887) : the first-formed xylem developing from procambium and consisting of narrow cells with annular, spiral, or scalariform wall thickenings
pro·to·zo·al \ˌprō-tə-'zō-əl\ *adj* (1890) : of or relating to protozoans
pro·to·zo·an \-'zō-ən\ *n* [NL *Protozoa,* fr. *prot-* + *-zoa*] (ca. 1864) : any of a phylum or subkingdom (Protozoa) of chiefly motile and heterotrophic unicellular protists (as amoebas, trypanosomes, sporozoans, and paramecia) that are represented in almost every kind of habitat and include some pathogenic parasites of humans and domestic animals — **protozoan** *adj*
pro·to·zo·ol·o·gy \-zō-'ä-lə-jē, -zə-'wä-\ *n* [NL *Protozoa* + ISV *-logy*] (1904) : a branch of zoology dealing with protozoans — **pro·to·zo·ol·o·gist** \-zō-'ä-lə-jist, -zə-'wä-\ *n*
pro·to·zo·on \-'zō-ˌän\ *n, pl* **-zoa** \-'zō-ə\ [NL, fr. sing. of *Protozoa*] (ca. 1853) : PROTOZOAN
pro·tract \prō-'trakt, prə-\ *vt* [L *protractus,* pp. of *protrahere,* lit., to draw forward, fr. *pro-* forward + *trahere* to draw — more at PRO-] (1540) **1** *archaic* : DELAY, DEFER **2** : to prolong in time or space : CONTINUE **3** : to extend forward or outward — compare RETRACT 1 ***syn*** see EXTEND — **pro·trac·tive** \-'trak-tiv\ *adj*
protracted meeting *n* (1832) : a protracted revival meeting
pro·trac·tile \-'trak-tᵊl, -ˌtī(-ə)l\ *adj* [L *protractus*] (1828) : capable of being thrust out ⟨∼ jaws⟩
pro·trac·tion \-'trak-shən\ *n* [LL *protraction-, protractio* act of drawing out, fr. *protrahere*] (1535) **1** : the act of protracting : the state of being protracted **2** : the drawing to scale of an area of land
pro·trac·tor \-'trak-tər\ *n* (ca. 1611) **1 a** : one that protracts **b** : a muscle that extends a part **2** : an instrument for laying down and measuring angles in drawing and plotting
pro·trep·tic \prō-'trep-tik\ *n* [LL *protrepticus* hortatory, encouraging, fr. Gk *protreptikos,* fr. *protrepein* to turn forward, urge on, fr. *pro-* + *trepein* to turn] (1678) : an utterance (as a speech) designed to instruct and persuade — **protreptic** *adj*
pro·trude \prō-'trüd\ *vb* **pro·trud·ed; pro·trud·ing** [L *protrudere,* fr. *pro-* + *trudere* to thrust — more at THREAT] *vt* (1620) **1** *archaic* : to thrust forward **2** : to cause to project ∼ *vi* : to jut out from the surrounding surface or context ⟨a handkerchief *protruding* from his breast pocket⟩ — **pro·tru·si·ble** \-'trü-sə-bəl, -zə-\ *adj*
pro·tru·sion \prō-'trü-zhən\ *n* [L *protrudere*] (1646) **1** : the act of protruding : the state of being protruded **2** : something (as an anatomical part or excrescence) that protrudes ***syn*** see PROJECTION

pro·tru·sive \-ˈtrü-siv, -ziv\ *adj* (1676) **1** *archaic* : thrusting forward **2** : PROMINENT, PROTUBERANT ⟨a ~ jaw⟩ **3** : OBTRUSIVE, PUSHING ⟨a coarse ~ manner⟩ — **pro·tru·sive·ly** *adv* — **pro·tru·sive·ness** *n*
pro·tu·ber·ance \prō-ˈtü-b(ə-)rən(t)s, -ˈtyü-\ *n* (1646) **1** : something that is protuberant **2** : the quality or state of being protuberant ***syn*** see PROJECTION
pro·tu·ber·ant \-b(ə-)rənt\ *adj* [LL *protuberant-, protuberans,* prp. of *protuberare* to bulge out, fr. L *pro-* forward + *tuber* excrescence, swelling; perh. akin to L *tumēre* to swell — more at THUMB] (1646) : thrusting out from a surrounding or adjacent surface often as a rounded mass : PROMINENT ⟨~ eyes⟩ — **pro·tu·ber·ant·ly** *adv*
proud \ˈprau̇d\ *adj* [ME, fr. OE *prūd,* prob. fr. OF *prod, prud, prou* advantageous, just, wise, bold, fr. LL *prode* advantage, advantageous, back-formation fr. L *prodesse* to be advantageous, fr. *pro-, prod-* for, in favor + *esse* to be — more at PRO-, IS] (bef. 12c) **1** : feeling or showing pride: as **a** : having or displaying excessive self-esteem **b** : much pleased : EXULTANT **c** : having proper self-respect **2 a** : marked by stateliness : MAGNIFICENT **b** : giving reason for pride : GLORIOUS ⟨the ~*est* moment in her life⟩ **3** : VIGOROUS, SPIRITED ⟨a ~ steed⟩ **4** *chiefly Brit* : raised above a surrounding area ⟨a ~ design on a stamp⟩ — **proud·ly** *adv*
syn PROUD, ARROGANT, HAUGHTY, LORDLY, INSOLENT, OVERBEARING, SUPERCILIOUS, DISDAINFUL mean showing scorn for inferiors. PROUD may suggest an assumed superiority or loftiness ⟨too *proud* to take charity⟩. ARROGANT implies a claiming for oneself of more consideration or importance than is warranted ⟨a conceited and *arrogant* executive⟩. HAUGHTY suggests a consciousness of superior birth or position ⟨a *haughty* aristocrat⟩. LORDLY implies pomposity or an arrogant display of power ⟨a *lordly* condescension⟩. INSOLENT implies contemptuous haughtiness ⟨ignored by an *insolent* waiter⟩. OVERBEARING suggests a tyrannical manner or an intolerable insolence ⟨an *overbearing* supervisor⟩. SUPERCILIOUS implies a cool, patronizing haughtiness ⟨an aloof and *supercilious* manner⟩. DISDAINFUL suggests a more active and openly scornful superciliousness ⟨*disdainful* of their social inferiors⟩.
proud flesh *n* (14c) : an excessive growth of granulation tissue
proud·ful \ˈprau̇d-fəl\ *adj* (14c) *chiefly dial* : marked by or full of pride
proud·heart·ed \-ˈhär-təd\ *adj* (14c) : proud in spirit : HAUGHTY
proust·ite \ˈprü-ˌstīt\ *n* [F, fr. Joseph L. *Proust* †1826 Fr. chemist] (1835) : a mineral that consists of a red sulfide of silver and arsenic and occurs in crystals or massively
prov *abbr* **1** province; provincial **2** provisional
Prov *abbr* Proverbs
pro·vas·cu·lar \(ˌ)prō-ˈvas-kyə-lər\ *adj* (ca. 1948) : of, relating to, or being procambium
prove \ˈprüv\ *vb* **proved; proved** *or* **prov·en** \ˈprü-vən, *Brit also* ˈprō-\; **prov·ing** \ˈprü-viŋ\ [ME, fr. AF *prover, pruver,* fr. L *probare* to test, prove, fr. *probus* good, honest, fr. *pro-* for, in favor + *-bus* (akin to OE *bēon* to be) — more at PRO-, BE] *vt* (13c) **1** *archaic* : to learn or find out by experience **2 a** : to test the truth, validity, or genuineness of ⟨the exception ~*s* the rule⟩ ⟨~ a will at probate⟩ **b** : to test the worth or quality of; *specif* : to compare against a standard — sometimes used with *up* or *out* **c** : to check the correctness of (as an arithmetic result) **3 a** : to establish the existence, truth, or validity of (as by evidence or logic) ⟨~ a theorem⟩ ⟨the charges were never *proved* in court⟩ **b** : to demonstrate as having a particular quality or worth ⟨the vaccine has been *proven* effective after years of tests⟩ ⟨*proved* herself a great actress⟩ **4** : to show (oneself) to be worthy or capable ⟨eager to ~ myself in the new job⟩ ~ *vi* : to turn out esp. after trial or test ⟨the new drug *proved* effective⟩ — **prov·able** \ˈprü-və-bəl\ *adj* — **prov·able·ness** *n* — **prov·ably** \-blē\ *adv* — **prov·er** \ˈprü-vər\ *n*
usage The past participle *proven,* orig. the past participle of *preve,* a Middle English variant of *prove* that survived in Scotland, has gradually worked its way into standard English over the past three and a half centuries. It seems to have first become established in legal use and to have come only slowly into literary use. Tennyson was one of its earliest frequent users, prob. for metrical reasons. It was disapproved by 19th century grammarians, one of whom included it in a list of "words that are not words." Surveys made some 50 or 60 years ago indicated that *proved* was about four times as frequent as *proven.* But our evidence from the last 30 or 35 years shows this no longer to be the case. As a past participle *proven* is now about as frequent as *proved* in all contexts. As an attributive adjective ⟨*proved* or *proven* gas reserves⟩ *proven* is much more common than *proved.*
prov·e·nance \ˈpräv-nən(t)s, ˈprä-və-ˌnän(t)s\ *n* [F, fr. *provenir* to come forth, originate, fr. L *provenire,* fr. *pro-* forth + *venire* to come — more at PRO-, COME] (1785) **1** : ORIGIN, SOURCE **2** : the history of ownership of a valued object or work of art or literature
[1]**Pro·ven·çal** \ˌprō-ˌvän-ˈsäl, ˌprä-vən-, *sense 1 also* prə-ˈven(t)-səl\ *adj* [MF, fr. *Provence* Provence] (1589) **1** : of, relating to, or characteristic of Provence or the people of Provence **2** *or* **Pro·ven·çale** : cooked with garlic, onion, mushrooms, tomato, olive oil, and herbs ⟨scallops ~⟩
[2]**Pro·ven·çal** \ˌprō-ˌvän-ˈsäl, ˌprä-vən-\ *n* (1600) **1** : a native or inhabitant of Provence **2** : OCCITAN; *esp* : the dialect of Occitan spoken in Provence
prov·en·der \ˈprä-vən-dər\ *n* [ME, fr. AF *provende, provendre,* fr. ML *provenda,* alter. of *praebenda* prebend] (14c) **1** : dry food for domestic animals : FEED **2** : FOOD, VICTUALS
pro·ve·nience \prə-ˈvē-nyən(t)s, -nē-ən(t)s\ *n* [alter. of *provenance*] (1882) : ORIGIN, SOURCE
prov·en·ly \ˈprü-vən-lē, *Brit also* ˈprō-\ *adv* (1887) : demonstrably as stated : without doubt or uncertainty
pro·ven·tric·u·lus \ˌprō-ven-ˈtri-kyə-ləs\ *n, pl* **-li** \-ˌlī, -ˌlē\ [NL] (ca. 1836) **1** : the glandular or true stomach of a bird that is situated between the crop and gizzard **2** : a muscular dilatation of the foregut in most mandibulate insects that is armed internally with chitinous teeth or plates for grinding food **3** : the thin-walled sac in front of the gizzard of an earthworm
prove out *vi* (1941) : to turn out to be satisfactory or as expected
[1]**prov·erb** \ˈprä-ˌvərb\ *n* [ME *proverbe,* fr. AF, fr. L *proverbium,* fr. *pro-* + *verbum* word — more at WORD] (14c) **1** : a brief popular epigram or maxim : ADAGE **2** : BYWORD 4
[2]**proverb** *vt* (14c) **1** : to speak of proverbially **2** *obs* : to provide with a proverb
pro–verb \ˈprō-ˌvərb, -ˈvərb\ *n* (1907) : a form of the verb *do* used to avoid repetition of a verb (as *do* in "act as I do")
pro·ver·bi·al \prə-ˈvər-bē-əl\ *adj* (1548) **1** : of, relating to, or resembling a proverb **2** : that has become a proverb or byword : commonly spoken of ⟨the ~ smoking gun⟩ — **pro·ver·bi·al·ly** \-ə-lē\ *adv*
Prov·erbs \ˈprä-ˌvərbz\ *n pl but sing in constr* : a collection of moral sayings and counsels forming a book of canonical Jewish and Christian Scripture — see BIBLE table
pro·vide \prə-ˈvīd\ *vb* **pro·vid·ed; pro·vid·ing** [ME, fr. L *providēre,* lit., to see ahead, fr. *pro-* forward + *vidēre* to see — more at PRO-, WIT] *vi* (15c) **1** : to take precautionary measures ⟨~ for the common defense —*U.S. Constitution*⟩ **2** : to make a proviso or stipulation ⟨the Constitution . . . ~*s* for an elected two-chamber legislature —*Current Biog.*⟩ **3** : to make preparation to meet a need ⟨~ for entertainment⟩; *esp* : to supply something for sustenance or support ⟨~*s* for the poor⟩ ~ *vt* **1** *archaic* : to prepare in advance **2 a** : to supply or make available (something wanted or needed) ⟨*provided* new uniforms for the band⟩; *also* : AFFORD ⟨curtains ~ privacy⟩ **b** : to make something available to ⟨~ the children with free balloons⟩ **3** : to have as a condition : STIPULATE ⟨the contract ~*s* that certain deadlines will be met⟩
provided *conj* [ME, pp. of *providen* to provide] (15c) : on condition that : with the understanding : IF ***usage*** see PROVIDING
prov·i·dence \ˈprä-və-dən(t)s, -ˌden(t)s\ *n* [ME, fr. AF, fr. L *providentia,* fr. *provident-, providens*] (14c) **1 a** *often cap* : divine guidance or care **b** *cap* : God conceived as the power sustaining and guiding human destiny **2** : the quality or state of being provident
prov·i·dent \-dənt, -ˌdent\ *adj* [ME, fr. L *provident-, providens,* fr. prp. of *providēre*] (15c) **1** : making provision for the future : PRUDENT **2** : FRUGAL, SAVING — **prov·i·dent·ly** *adv*
prov·i·den·tial \ˌprä-və-ˈden(t)-shəl\ *adj* (1648) **1** : of, relating to, or determined by Providence **2** *archaic* : marked by foresight : PRUDENT **3** : occurring by or as if by an intervention of Providence ⟨a ~ escape⟩ ***syn*** see LUCKY — **prov·i·den·tial·ly** \-ˈden(t)-sh(ə-)lē\ *adv*
pro·vid·er \prə-ˈvī-dər\ *n* (1523) : one that provides ⟨health-care ~*s*⟩ ⟨an Internet ~⟩; *esp* : BREADWINNER
providing *conj* [ME, prp. of *providen*] (15c) : on condition that : in case
usage Although occas. still disapproved, *providing* is as well established as a conjunction as *provided* is. *Provided* is more common.
prov·ince \ˈprä-vən(t)s\ *n* [ME, fr. AF, fr. L *provincia*] (14c) **1 a** : a country or region brought under the control of the ancient Roman government **b** : an administrative district or division of a country **c** *pl* : all of a country except the metropolises **2 a** : a division of a country forming the jurisdiction of an archbishop or metropolitan **b** : a territorial unit of a religious order **3 a** : a biogeographic division of less rank than a region **b** : an area that exhibits essential continuity of geological history; *also* : one characterized by particular structural or petrological features **4 a** : proper or appropriate function or scope : SPHERE ⟨that question is outside my ~⟩ **b** : a department of knowledge or activity ***syn*** see FUNCTION
[1]**pro·vin·cial** \prə-ˈvin(t)-shəl\ *n* [in sense 1, fr. ME, fr. AF or ML; AF, fr. ML *provincialis,* fr. *provincia* ecclesiastical province; in other senses, fr. L *provincialis,* fr. *provincia* province] (14c) **1** : the superior of a province of a Roman Catholic religious order **2** : one living in or coming from a province **3 a** : a person of local or restricted interests or outlook **b** : a person lacking urban polish or refinement
[2]**provincial** *adj* (14c) **1** : of, relating to, or coming from a province **2 a** : limited in outlook : NARROW **b** : lacking the polish of urban society : UNSOPHISTICATED **3** : of or relating to a decorative style (as in furniture) marked by simplicity, informality, and relative plainness; *esp* : FRENCH PROVINCIAL — **pro·vin·cial·ly** \-ˈvin(t)-sh(ə-)lē\ *adv*
pro·vin·cial·ism \-shə-ˌli-zəm\ *n* (1770) **1** : a dialectal or local word, phrase, or idiom **2** : the quality or state of being provincial
pro·vin·cial·ist \-ˈvin(t)-sh(ə-)list\ *n* (1656) : a native or inhabitant of a province
pro·vin·ci·al·i·ty \prə-ˌvin(t)-shē-ˈa-lə-tē\ *n, pl* **-ties** (1782) **1** : PROVINCIALISM 2 **2** : an act or instance of provincialism
pro·vin·cial·ize \-ˈvin(t)-shə-ˌlīz\ *vt* **-ized; -iz·ing** (1829) : to make provincial — **pro·vin·cial·i·za·tion** \-ˌvin(t)-sh(ə-)lə-ˈzā-shən\ *n*
proving ground *n* (ca. 1890) **1** : a place for scientific experimentation or testing (as of vehicles or weapons) **2** : a place where something is developed or tried out
pro·vi·rus \(ˌ)prō-ˈvī-rəs\ *n* [NL] (1949) : a form of a virus that is integrated into the genetic material of a host cell and by replicating with it can be transmitted from one cell generation to the next without causing lysis — **pro·vi·ral** \-rəl\ *adj*
[1]**pro·vi·sion** \prə-ˈvi-zhən\ *n* [ME, fr. AF, fr. LL & L; LL *provision-, provisio* act of providing, fr. L, foresight, fr. *providēre* to see ahead — more at PROVIDE] (14c) **1 a** : the act or process of providing **b** : the fact or state of being prepared beforehand **c** : a measure taken beforehand to deal with a need or contingency : PREPARATION ⟨made ~ for replacements⟩ **2** : a stock of needed materials or supplies; *esp* : a stock of food — usu. used in pl. **3** : PROVISO, STIPULATION
[2]**provision** *vt* **pro·vi·sioned; pro·vi·sion·ing** \-ˈvi-zhə-niŋ, -ˈvizh-niŋ\ (1809) : to supply with provisions
[1]**pro·vi·sion·al** \prə-ˈvizh-nəl, -ˈvi-zhə-nᵊl\ *adj* (1601) : serving for the time being : TEMPORARY ⟨a ~ government⟩ — **pro·vi·sion·al·ly** *adv*
[2]**provisional** *n* (1886) : a postage stamp for use until a regular issue appears — compare DEFINITIVE
pro·vi·sion·ary \prə-ˈvi-zhə-ˌner-ē\ *adj* (1617) : PROVISIONAL
pro·vi·sion·er \-ˈvi-zhə-nər, -ˈvizh-nər\ *n* (1866) : a furnisher of provisions
pro·vi·so \prə-ˈvī-(ˌ)zō\ *n, pl* **-sos** *also* **-soes** [ME, fr. ML *proviso quod* provided that] (15c) **1** : an article or clause (as in a contract) that introduces a condition **2** : a conditional stipulation

\ə\ **abut** \ᵊ\ **kitten, F table** \ər\ **further** \a\ **ash** \ā\ **ace** \ä\ **mop, mar**
\au̇\ **out** \ch\ **chin** \e\ **bet** \ē\ **easy** \g\ **go** \i\ **hit** \ī\ **ice** \j\ **job**
\ŋ\ **sing** \ō\ **go** \ȯ\ **law** \ȯi\ **boy** \th\ **thin** \t͟h\ **the** \ü\ **loot** \u̇\ **foot**
\y\ **yet** \zh\ **vision, beige** \k̲, ⁿ, œ, ue, ʸ\ *see* Guide to Pronunciation

pro·vi·so·ry \-ˈvī-zə-rē, -ˈvīz-rē\ *adj* (ca. 1611) **1 :** containing or subject to a proviso : CONDITIONAL **2 :** PROVISIONAL

pro·vi·ta·min \(ˌ)prō-ˈvī-tə-mən\ *n* (1927) : a precursor of a vitamin convertible into the vitamin in an organism

Pro·vo \ˈprō-(ˌ)vō\ *n, pl* **Provos** [*Pro*visional I.R.A., name of the faction + [1]*-o*] (1971) : a member of the extremist faction of the Irish Republican Army

pro·vo·ca·teur \prō-ˌvä-kə-ˈtər\ *n* (1919) **1 :** AGENT PROVOCATEUR **2 :** one who provokes ⟨a political ~⟩

prov·o·ca·tion \ˌprä-və-ˈkā-shən\ *n* [ME *provocacioun,* fr. AF *provocacion,* fr. L *provocation-, provocatio,* fr. *provocare*] (14c) **1 :** the act of provoking : INCITEMENT **2 :** something that provokes, arouses, or stimulates

pro·voc·a·tive \prə-ˈvä-kə-tiv\ *adj* (15c) : serving or tending to provoke, excite, or stimulate ⟨a ~ question⟩ — **provocative** *n* — **pro·voc·a·tive·ly** *adv* — **pro·voc·a·tive·ness** *n*

pro·voke \prə-ˈvōk\ *vt* **pro·voked; pro·vok·ing** [ME, fr. AF **provoker, provocher,* fr. L *provocare,* fr. *pro-* forth + *vocare* to call, fr. *voc-, vox* voice — more at PRO-, VOICE] (14c) **1 a** *archaic* : to arouse to a feeling or action **b :** to incite to anger **2 a :** to call forth (as a feeling or action) : EVOKE ⟨~ laughter⟩ **b :** to stir up purposely ⟨~ a fight⟩ **c :** to provide the needed stimulus for ⟨will ~ a lot of discussion⟩ — **pro·vok·er** *n*

syn PROVOKE, EXCITE, STIMULATE, PIQUE, QUICKEN mean to arouse as if by pricking. PROVOKE directs attention to the response called forth ⟨my stories usually *provoke* laughter⟩. EXCITE implies a stirring up or moving profoundly ⟨news that *excited* anger and frustration⟩. STIMULATE suggests a rousing out of lethargy, quiescence, or indifference ⟨*stimulating* conversation⟩. PIQUE suggests stimulating by mild irritation or challenge ⟨that remark *piqued* my interest⟩. QUICKEN implies beneficially stimulating and making active or lively ⟨the high salary *quickened* her desire to have the job⟩. ***syn*** see in addition IRRITATE

provoking *adj* (1642) : causing mild anger : ANNOYING — **pro·vok·ing·ly** \-kiŋ-lē\ *adv*

pro·vo·lo·ne \ˌprō-və-ˈlō-nē, ˈprō-və-ˌlōn\ *n* [It, aug. of *provola,* a kind of cheese] (1912) : a usu. firm pliant often smoked cheese of Italian origin

pro·vost \ˈprō-ˌvōst, ˈprä-vəst, ˈprō-vəst, *esp attrib* ˌprō-(ˌ)vō\ *n* [ME, fr. OE *profost* & AF *provost,* fr. ML *propositus,* alter. of *praepositus,* fr. L, one in charge, director, fr. pp. of *praeponere* to place at the head — more at PREPOSITION] (bef. 12c) **1 :** the chief dignitary of a collegiate or cathedral chapter **2 :** the chief magistrate of a Scottish burgh **3 :** the keeper of a prison **4 :** a high-ranking university administrative officer

provost court *n* (1864) : a military court usu. for the trial of minor offenses within an occupied hostile territory

provost guard *n* (1862) : a police detail of soldiers under the authority of the provost marshal

provost marshal *n* (1535) : an officer who supervises the military police of a command

[1]**prow** \ˈprau̇\ *adj* [ME, fr. AF *pru, prou* — more at PROUD] (14c) *archaic* : VALIANT, GALLANT

[2]**prow** \ˈprau̇, *archaic* ˈprō\ *n* [MF *proue,* prob. fr. OIt dial. *prua,* fr. L *prora,* fr. Gk *prōira*] (1555) **1 :** the bow of a ship : STEM **2 :** a pointed projecting front part

prow·ess \ˈprau̇-əs *also* ˈprō-\ *n* [ME *prouesse,* fr. AF *pruesse, prowesse,* fr. *prou*] (13c) **1 :** distinguished bravery; *esp* : military valor and skill **2 :** extraordinary ability ⟨his ~ on the football field⟩

[1]**prowl** \ˈprau̇(-ə)l\ *vb* [ME *prollen*] *vi* (14c) : to move about or wander stealthily in or as if in search of prey ~ *vt* : to roam over in a predatory manner — **prowl·er** \ˈprau̇-lər\ *n*

[2]**prowl** *n* (1803) : an act or instance of prowling — **on the prowl :** in the act of prowling; *also* : in search of something ⟨his fourth wife had just left him, and he was *on the prowl* again —Mary McCarthy⟩

prowl car *n* (1937) : SQUAD CAR

prox *abbr* proximo

prox·e·mics \präk-ˈsē-miks\ *n pl but sing or pl in constr* [*prox*imity + *-emics* (as in *phonemics*)] (1963) : the study of the nature, degree, and effect of the spatial separation individuals naturally maintain (as in various social and interpersonal situations) and of how this separation relates to environmental and cultural factors — **prox·e·mic** \-mik\ *adj*

prox·i·mal \ˈpräk-sə-məl\ *adj* [L *proximus*] (1727) **1 :** situated close to : PROXIMATE **2 :** next to or nearest the point of attachment or origin, a central point, or the point of view; *esp* : located toward the center of the body — compare DISTAL **3 :** of, relating to, or being the mesial and distal surfaces of a tooth — **prox·i·mal·ly** \-mə-lē\ *adv*

proximal convoluted tubule *n* (ca. 1899) : the convoluted portion of the vertebrate nephron that lies between Bowman's capsule and the loop of Henle and functions esp. in the resorption of sugar, sodium and chloride ions, and water from the glomerular filtrate — called also *proximal tubule*

prox·i·mate \ˈpräk-sə-mət\ *adj* [L *proximatus,* pp. of *proximare* to approach, fr. *proximus* nearest, next, superl. of *prope* near — more at APPROACH] (1661) **1 :** immediately preceding or following (as in a chain of events, causes, or effects) ⟨~, rather than ultimate, goals —Reinhold Niebuhr⟩ **2 a :** very near : CLOSE **b :** soon forthcoming : IMMINENT — **prox·i·mate·ly** *adv* — **prox·i·mate·ness** *n*

prox·im·i·ty \präk-ˈsi-mə-tē\ *n* [MF *proximité,* fr. L *proximitat-, proximitas,* fr. *proximus*] (15c) : the quality or state of being proximate : CLOSENESS

proximity fuse *n* (1945) : a fuse for a projectile that uses the principle of radar to detect the presence of a target within the projectile's effective range

prox·i·mo \ˈpräk-sə-ˌmō\ *adj* [L *proximo mense* in the next month] (1855) : of or occurring in the next month after the present

proxy \ˈpräk-sē\ *n, pl* **prox·ies** [ME *proxi, procucie,* contr. of *procuracie,* fr. AF, fr. ML *procuratia,* alter. of L *procuratio* procuration] (15c) **1 :** the agency, function, or office of a deputy who acts as a substitute for another **2 a :** authority or power to act for another **b :** a document giving such authority; *specif* : a power of attorney authorizing a specified person to vote corporate stock **3 :** a person authorized to act for another : PROCURATOR — **proxy** *adj*

proxy marriage *n* (1900) : a marriage celebrated in the absence of one of the contracting parties who is represented at the ceremony by a proxy

Pro·zac \ˈprō-ˌzak\ *trademark* — used for a preparation of fluoxetine

PrP *abbr* prion protein

prude \ˈprüd\ *n* [F, good woman, prudish woman, short for *prudefemme* good woman, fr. OF *prode femme*] (1704) : a person who is excessively or priggishly attentive to propriety or decorum; *esp* : a woman who shows or affects extreme modesty

pru·dence \ˈprü-dᵊn(t)s\ *n* [ME, fr. AF, fr. L *prudentia,* alter. of *providentia* — more at PROVIDENCE] (14c) **1 :** the ability to govern and discipline oneself by the use of reason **2 :** sagacity or shrewdness in the management of affairs **3 :** skill and good judgment in the use of resources **4 :** caution or circumspection as to danger or risk

pru·dent \-dᵊnt\ *adj* [ME, fr. MF, fr. L *prudent-, prudens,* contr. of *provident-, providens* — more at PROVIDENT] (14c) : characterized by, arising from, or showing prudence: as **a :** marked by wisdom or judiciousness ⟨~ advice⟩ **b :** shrewd in the management of practical affairs ⟨~ investors⟩ **c :** marked by circumspection : DISCREET **d :** PROVIDENT, FRUGAL ***syn*** see WISE — **pru·dent·ly** *adv*

pru·den·tial \prü-ˈden(t)-shəl\ *adj* (15c) **1 :** of, relating to, or proceeding from prudence **2 :** exercising prudence esp. in business matters — **pru·den·tial·ly** \-ˈden(t)-sh(ə-)lē\ *adv*

prud·ery \ˈprü-d(ə-)rē\ *n, pl* **-er·ies** (1709) **1 :** the characteristic quality or state of a prude **2 :** a prudish act or remark

prud·ish \ˈprü-dish\ *adj* (1717) : marked by prudery : PRIGGISH — **prud·ish·ly** *adv* — **prud·ish·ness** *n*

pru·i·nose \ˈprü-ə-ˌnōs\ *adj* [L *pruinosus* covered with hoarfrost, fr. *pruina* hoarfrost — more at FREEZE] (ca. 1826) : covered with whitish dust or bloom ⟨~ stems⟩

[1]**prune** \ˈprün\ *n* [ME, fr. AF, plum, fr. L *prunum* — more at PLUM] (14c) : a plum dried or capable of drying without fermentation

[2]**prune** *vb* **pruned; prun·ing** [ME *prouynen,* prob. ultim. fr. OF *prooignier,* alter. of **porrooignier,* fr. *por-* completely (fr. L *pro-*) + *rooignier* to cut, prune, fr. VL **rotundiare* to cut around, fr. L *rotundus* round — more at PRO-, ROTUND] *vt* (15c) **1 a :** to reduce esp. by eliminating superfluous matter ⟨*pruned* the text⟩ ⟨~ the budget⟩ **b :** to remove as superfluous ⟨~ away all ornamentation⟩ **2 :** to cut off or cut back parts of for better shape or more fruitful growth ⟨~ the branches⟩ ~ *vi* : to cut away what is unwanted or superfluous — **prun·er** *n*

pru·nel·la \prü-ˈne-lə\ *also* **pru·nelle** \-ˈnel\ *n* [F *prunelle,* lit., sloe, fr. dim. of *prune* plum] (1670) **1 :** a twilled woolen dress fabric **2 :** a heavy woolen fabric used for the uppers of shoes

pruning hook *n* (1611) : a pole bearing a curved blade for pruning plants

pru·nus \ˈprü-nəs\ *n* [NL, fr. L, plum tree, fr. Gk *proumnē*] (1839) : any of a genus (*Prunus*) of drupaceous trees or shrubs of the rose family that have showy clusters of usu. white or pink flowers first appearing in the spring often before the leaves and including many grown for ornament or for their fruit (as the plum, cherry, or apricot)

pru·ri·ence \ˈpru̇r-ē-ən(t)s\ *n* (1781) : the quality or state of being prurient

pru·ri·en·cy \-ən(t)-sē\ *n* (1795) : PRURIENCE

pru·ri·ent \-ənt\ *adj* [L *prurient-, pruriens,* prp. of *prurire* to itch, crave; akin to L *pruna* glowing coal, Skt *ploṣati* he singes, and prob. to L *pruina* hoarfrost — more at FREEZE] (1592) : marked by or arousing an immoderate or unwholesome interest or desire; *esp* : marked by, arousing, or appealing to sexual desire — **pru·ri·ent·ly** *adv*

pru·ri·go \prü-ˈrī-(ˌ)gō, -ˈrē-\ *n* [NL, fr. L, itch, fr. *prurire*] (ca. 1646) : a chronic inflammatory skin disease marked by itching papules

pru·rit·ic \-ˈri-tik\ *adj* (1899) : of, relating to, or marked by itching

pru·ri·tus \-ˈrī-təs, -ˈrē-\ *n* [L, fr. *prurire*] (1653) : ITCH 1a

Prus·sian blue \ˈprə-shən-\ *n* [*Prussia,* Germany] (1724) **1 :** any of numerous blue iron pigments formerly regarded as ferric ferrocyanide **2 :** a dark blue crystalline hydrated ferric ferrocyanide $Fe_4[Fe(CN)_6]_3 \cdot xH_2O$ used as a test for ferric iron **3 :** a greenish blue

prus·sian·ise *Brit var of* PRUSSIANIZE

Prus·sian·ism \ˈprə-shə-ˌni-zəm\ *n* (1856) : the practices or policies (as the advocacy of militarism) held to be typically Prussian

prus·sian·ize \-ˌnīz\ *vt* **-ized; -iz·ing** *often cap* (1861) : to make Prussian in character or principle (as in authoritarian control or rigid discipline) — **prus·sian·i·za·tion** \ˌprə-shə-nə-ˈzā-shən\ *n*

prus·sic acid \ˈprə-sik-\ *n* [F *prussique,* fr. (*bleu de*) *Prusse* Prussian blue] (1790) : HYDROCYANIC ACID

pru·tah *or* **pru·ta** \prü-ˈtä\ *n, pl* **pru·toth** \-ˈtōt, -ˈtōth, -ˈtōs\ *or* **pru·tot** \-ˈtōt, -ˈtōs\ [ModHeb *pĕrūṭāh,* fr. LHeb, a small coin] (1949) **1 :** a former monetary unit of Israel equivalent to 1/1000 pound **2 :** a coin representing one prutah

[1]**pry** \ˈprī\ *vi* **pried; pry·ing** [ME *prien*] (14c) : to look closely or inquisitively; *also* : to make a nosy or presumptuous inquiry

[2]**pry** *vt* **pried; pry·ing** [prob. back-formation fr. [5]*prize*] (ca. 1806) **1 :** to raise, move, or pull apart with a lever : PRIZE **2 :** to extract, detach, or open with difficulty ⟨*pried* the secret out of my sister⟩

[3]**pry** *n* (1823) **1 :** a tool for prying **2 :** LEVERAGE

pryer *var of* PRIER

prying *adj* (1552) : inquisitive in an annoying, officious, or meddlesome way ***syn*** see CURIOUS — **pry·ing·ly** \-iŋ-lē\ *adv*

Prze·wal·ski's horse \pshə-ˈväl-skēz-, shə-, ˌpər-zhə-ˈväl-\ *n* [Nikolaĭ M. *Przheval'skiĭ* †1888 Russ. soldier & explorer] (1881) : a small stocky bay- or dun-colored wild horse (*Equus caballus przewalskii* syn. *E. przewalskii*) of central Asia having a large head and short erect mane and now existing chiefly in captivity — called also *Prze·wal·ski horse* \-skē-\

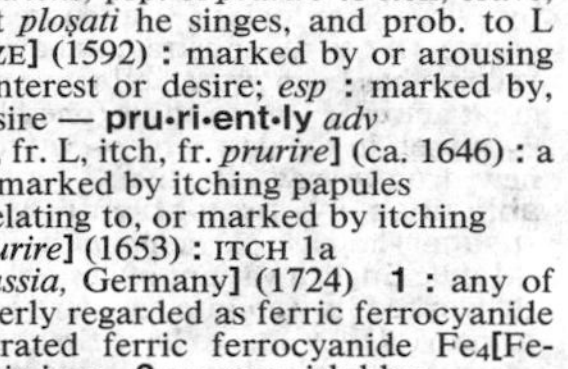

Przewalski's horse

ps *abbr* picosecond

Ps *or* **Psa** *abbr* Psalms

PS *abbr* **1** [NL *postscriptum*] postscript **2** power steering **3** public school

PSA *abbr* **1** prostate-specific antigen **2** public service announcement

psalm \ˈsäm, ˈsälm, ˈsȯm, ˈsȯlm\ *n, often cap* [ME, fr. OE *psealm,* fr. LL *psalmus,* fr. Gk *psalmos,* lit., twanging of a harp, fr. *psallein* to pluck, play a stringed instrument] (bef. 12c) **:** a sacred song or poem used in worship; *esp* **:** one of the biblical hymns collected in the Book of Psalms

psalm·book \-ˌbu̇k\ *n* (12c) *archaic* **:** PSALTER

psalm·ist \ˈsä-mist, ˈsäl-, ˈsȯ-, ˈsȯl\ *n* (15c) **:** a writer or composer of esp. biblical psalms

psalm·o·dy \ˈsä-mə-dē, ˈsäl-, ˈsȯ-, ˈsȯl\ *n* [ME *psalmodie,* fr. AF, fr. LL *psalmodia,* fr. LGk *psalmōidia,* lit., singing to the harp, fr. Gk *psalmos* + *aidein* to sing — more at ODE] (14c) **1 :** the act, practice, or art of singing psalms in worship **2 :** a collection of psalms

Psalms \ˈsämz, ˈsälmz, ˈsȯmz\ *n pl but sing in constr* **:** a collection of sacred poems forming a book of canonical Jewish and Christian Scripture — see BIBLE table

Psal·ter \ˈsäl-tər, ˈsȯl-\ *n* [ME, fr. OE *psalter* & AF *psaltier,* fr. LL *psalterium,* fr. LGk *psaltērion,* fr. Gk, psaltery] (bef. 12c) **:** the Book of Psalms; *also* **:** a collection of Psalms for liturgical or devotional use

psal·te·ri·um \säl-ˈtir-ē-əm, sȯl-\ *n, pl* **-ria** \-ē-ə\ [NL, fr. LL, psalter; fr. the resemblance of the folds to the pages of a book] (ca. 1846) **:** OMASUM

psal·tery *also* **psal·try** \ˈsäl-t(ə-)rē, ˈsȯl-\ *n, pl* **-ter·ies** *also* **-tries** [ME *psalterie,* fr. AF, fr. L *psalterium,* fr. Gk *psaltērion,* fr. *psallein* to play on a stringed instrument] (14c) **:** an ancient musical instrument resembling the zither

p's and q's \ˌpēz-ᵊn-ˈkyüz\ *n pl* [fr. the phrase *mind one's p's and q's,* alluding to the difficulty a child learning to write has in distinguishing between *p* and *q*] (1779) **1 :** something (as one's manners) that one should be mindful of ⟨better watch his *p's and q's* when I get a six-gun of my own —Jean Stafford⟩ **2 :** best behavior ⟨being on her *p's and q's* for two solid days was too much —Guy McCrone⟩

psec *abbr* picosecond

pse·phol·o·gy \sē-ˈfä-lə-jē\ *n* [Gk *psēphos* pebble, ballot, vote; fr. the use of pebbles by the ancient Greeks in voting] (1952) **:** the scientific study of elections — **pse·pho·log·i·cal** \ˌsē-fə-ˈlä-ji-kəl\ *adj* — **pse·phol·o·gist** \sē-ˈfä-lə-jist\ *n*

[1]**pseud** \ˈsüd\ *n* [short for *pseudo-intellectual*] (1964) *Brit* **:** a person who pretends to be an intellectual

[2]**pseud** *abbr* pseudonym; pseudonymous

pseud- *or* **pseudo-** *comb form* [Gk, fr. *pseudēs,* fr. *pseudesthai* to lie; akin to Arm *sut* lie and prob. to Gk *psychein* to breathe — more at PSYCH-] **1 :** false **:** spurious ⟨*pseudo*classic⟩ **2 :** temporary or substitute formation similar to (a specified thing) ⟨*pseudo*podium⟩ **3 :** resembling, isomeric with, or related to (a specified chemical compound) ⟨*pseudo*ephedrine⟩

pseud·ep·i·graph \sü-ˈde-pə-ˌgraf\ *n* (1884) **:** PSEUDEPIGRAPHON 2

pseud·epig·ra·phon \ˌsü-di-ˈpi-grə-ˌfän\ *n, pl* **-pha** \-fə\ [NL, sing. of *pseudepigrapha,* fr. Gk, neut. pl. of *pseudepigraphos* falsely inscribed, fr. *pseud-* + *epigraphein* to inscribe — more at EPIGRAM] (1692) **1** *pl* **:** APOCRYPHA **2 :** any of various pseudonymous or anonymous Jewish religious writings of the period 200 B.C. to A.D. 200; *esp* **:** one of such writings (as the Psalms of Solomon) not included in any canon of biblical Scripture — usu. used in pl.

pseud·epig·ra·phy \-fē\ *n* [Gk *pseudepigraphos*] (ca. 1842) **:** the ascription of false names of authors to works

pseu·do \ˈsü-(ˌ)dō\ *adj* [ME, fr. LL *pseudo-*] (15c) **:** being apparently rather than actually as stated **:** SHAM, SPURIOUS ⟨distinction between true and ~ humanism —K. F. Reinhardt⟩

pseu·do·cho·lin·es·ter·ase \ˈsü-dō-ˌkō-lə-ˈnes-tə-ˌrās, -ˌrāz\ *n* (1943) **:** CHOLINESTERASE 2

pseu·do·clas·sic \ˌsü-dō-ˈkla-sik\ *adj* (1899) **:** pretending to be or erroneously regarded as classic — **pseudoclassic** *n*

pseu·do·clas·si·cism \-ˈkla-sə-ˌsi-zəm\ *n* (1871) **:** imitative representation of classicism in literature and art

pseu·do·coel \ˈsü-də-ˌsēl\ *n* (1887) **:** a body cavity that is not a product of gastrulation and is not lined with a well-defined mesodermal membrane

pseu·do·coe·lom·ate \ˌsü-dō-ˈsē-lə-ˌmāt\ *n* (1940) **:** an invertebrate (as a nematode or rotifer) having a body cavity that is a pseudocoel — **pseudocoelomate** *adj*

pseu·do·cy·e·sis \-ˌsī-ˈē-səs\ *n* [NL, fr. *pseud-* + *cyesis* pregnancy, fr. Gk *kyēsis,* fr. *kyein* to be pregnant — more at CYME] (ca. 1817) **:** a psychosomatic state that occurs without conception and is marked by some of the physical symptoms and changes in hormonal balance of pregnancy

pseu·do·ephed·rine \ˌsü-dō-i-ˈfed-rən, *Brit also* -ˈe-fə-drən\ *n* (1974) **:** an isomer of ephedrine used in the form of its hydrochloride or sulfate esp. to relieve nasal congestion

pseu·do·mo·nad \ˌsü-də-ˈmō-ˌnad, -nəd\ *n* [NL *Pseudomonad-, Pseudomonas*] (1921) **:** any of a genus (*Pseudomonas*) of gram-negative rod-shaped motile bacteria including some that produce a greenish fluorescent water-soluble pigment and some that are saprophytes or plant or animal pathogens

pseu·do·mo·nas \-nəs\ *n, pl* **-mo·na·des** \-ˈmō-nə-ˌdēz, -ˈmä-\ [NL, fr. *pseud-* + *monad-, monas* monad] (1903) **:** PSEUDOMONAD

pseu·do·morph \ˈsü-də-ˌmȯrf\ *n* [prob. fr. F *pseudomorphe,* fr. *pseud-* + *-morphe* -morph] (1849) **1 :** a mineral having the characteristic outward form of another species **2 :** a deceptive or irregular form — **pseu·do·mor·phic** \ˌsü-də-ˈmȯr-fik\ *adj* — **pseu·do·mor·phism** \-ˌfi-zəm\ *n* — **pseu·do·mor·phous** \-fəs\ *adj*

pseu·do·nym \ˈsü-də-ˌnim\ *n* [F *pseudonyme,* fr. Gk *pseudōnymos* bearing a false name, fr. *pseud-* + *onyma* name — more at NAME] (1833) **:** a fictitious name; *esp* **:** PEN NAME

pseu·do·nym·i·ty \ˌsü-də-ˈni-mə-tē\ *n* (1877) **:** the use of a pseudonym; *also* **:** the fact or state of being signed with a pseudonym

pseu·don·y·mous \sü-ˈdä-nə-məs\ *adj* [Gk *pseudōnymos*] (ca. 1706) **:** bearing or using a fictitious name ⟨a ~ report⟩; *also* **:** being a pseudonym — **pseu·don·y·mous·ly** *adv* — **pseu·don·y·mous·ness** *n*

pseu·do·pa·ren·chy·ma \ˌsü-dō-pə-ˈreŋ-kə-mə\ *n* [NL] (1875) **:** compactly interwoven short-celled filaments esp. in fungi that resemble parenchyma of higher plants — **pseu·do·par·en·chy·ma·tous** \-ˌpa-rən-ˈki-mə-təs, -ˈkī-\ *adj*

pseu·do·pod \ˈsü-də-ˌpäd\ *n* [NL *pseudopodium*] (1874) **:** PSEUDOPODIUM — **pseu·dop·o·dal** \sü-ˈdä-pə-dᵊl\ *or* **pseu·do·po·di·al** \ˌsü-də-ˈpō-dē-əl\ *adj*

pseu·do·po·di·um \ˌsü-də-ˈpō-dē-əm\ *n, pl* **-po·dia** \-dē-ə\ [NL] (1854) **1 :** a temporary protrusion or retractile process of the cytoplasm of a cell that functions (as in an amoeba) esp. in a locomotor or food gathering capacity — see AMOEBA illustration **2 :** a slender leafless branch of the gametophyte in various mosses that often bears gemmae

pseu·do·preg·nan·cy \ˌsü-dō-ˈpreg-nən(t)-sē\ *n* (1860) **1 :** PSEUDOCYESIS **2 :** an anestrous state resembling pregnancy that occurs in various mammals usu. after an infertile copulation — **pseu·do·preg·nant** \-nənt\ *adj*

pseu·do·ran·dom \-ˈran-dəm\ *adj* (1949) **:** being or involving entities (as numbers) that are selected by a definite computational process but that satisfy one or more standard tests for statistical randomness

pseu·do·sci·ence \ˌsü-dō-ˈsī-ən(t)s\ *n* (1844) **:** a system of theories, assumptions, and methods erroneously regarded as scientific — **pseu·do·sci·en·tif·ic** \-ˌsī-ən-ˈti-fik\ *adj* — **pseu·do·sci·en·tist** \-ˈsī-ən-tist\ *n*

pseu·do·scor·pi·on \-ˈskȯr-pē-ən\ *n* [NL *Pseudoscorpiones,* fr. *pseud-* + L *scorpion-, scorpio* scorpion] (1835) **:** any of a widely distributed order (Pseudoscorpionida syn. Pseudoscorpiones) of tiny arachnids that have no caudal stinger and feed on tiny invertebrates (as insects and mites)

pseu·do·so·phis·ti·ca·tion \ˈsü-dō-sə-ˌfis-tə-ˈkā-shən\ *n* (1965) **:** false or feigned sophistication — **pseu·do·so·phis·ti·cat·ed** \-sə-ˈfis-ti-ˌkā-təd\ *adj*

pseu·do·tu·ber·cu·lo·sis \-tu̇-ˌbər-kyə-ˈlō-səs, -tyu̇-\ *n* [NL] (1900) **:** any of several diseases that are marked by the formation of granulomas resembling tubercular nodules and are caused by a bacterium (as *Yersinia pseudotuberculosis*) other than the tubercle bacillus

psf *abbr* pounds per square foot

PSG *abbr* platoon sergeant

pshaw \ˈshȯ\ *interj* (1656) — used to express irritation, disapproval, contempt, or disbelief

[1]**psi** \ˈsī, ˈpsī\ *n* [ME, fr. ML, fr. LGk, fr. Gk *psei*] (15c) **:** the 23d letter of the Greek alphabet — see ALPHABET table

[2]**psi** \ˈsī\ *n* [prob. by shortening & alter. fr. *psychic*] (1942) **:** parapsychological psychic phenomena or powers

[3]**psi** *abbr* pounds per square inch

psi·lo·cy·bin \ˌsī-lə-ˈsī-bən\ *n* [NL *Psilocybe,* fungus genus + [1]*-in*] (1958) **:** a hallucinogenic indole $C_{12}H_{17}N_2O_4P$ obtained from a fungus (as *Psilocybe mexicana* or *P. cubensis* syn. *Stropharia cubensis*)

psi·lo·phyte \ˈsī-lə-ˌfīt\ *n* [NL *Psilophyton,* genus of plants, fr. Gk *psilos* bare, mere (prob. akin to Gk *psēn* to rub) + *phyton* plant — more at PHYT-] (ca. 1911) **:** any of a division (Psilophyta) of simple dichotomously branched plants that first appeared during the Late Silurian, are now limited to two extant genera, lack true leaves and roots, and include the oldest known land plants with vascular tissue — **psi·lo·phyt·ic** \ˌsī-lə-ˈfi-tik\ *adj*

psi particle \ˈsī-, ˈpsī-\ *n* (1974) **:** J/PSI PARTICLE

psit·ta·cine \ˈsi-tə-ˌsīn\ *adj* [L *psittacinus,* fr. *psittacus* parrot, fr. Gk *psittakos*] (1874) **:** of or relating to the parrots — **psittacine** *n*

psit·ta·co·sis \ˌsi-tə-ˈkō-səs\ *n* [NL, fr. L *psittacus*] (1897) **:** an infectious disease of birds caused by a bacterium (*Chlamydia psittaci*), marked by diarrhea and wasting, and transmissible to humans in whom it occurs as a flu-like illness often accompanied by pneumonia — called also *ornithosis, parrot fever* — **psit·ta·co·tic** \-ˈkä-tik, -ˈkō-\ *adj*

pso·cid \ˈsō-səd\ *n* [ultim. fr. NL *Psocus,* genus of lice] (1891) **:** any of an order (Psocoptera syn. Corrodentia) of minute usu. winged primitive insects (as a book louse) having simple mouthparts

pso·ra·len \ˈsȯr-ə-lən\ *n* [NL *Psoralea,* genus of plants from which it is isolated + E *-en,* alter. of *-ene*] (1933) **:** a substance $C_{11}H_6O_3$ found in some plants that photosensitizes mammalian skin and is used in conjunction with ultraviolet light to treat psoriasis; *also* **:** any of various derivatives of psoralen having similar properties

pso·ri·a·sis \sə-ˈrī-ə-səs\ *n* [NL, fr. Gk *psōriasis,* fr. *psōrian* to have the itch, fr. *psōra* itch; akin to Gk *psēn* to rub] (ca. 1684) **:** a chronic skin disease characterized by circumscribed red patches covered with white scales — **pso·ri·at·ic** \ˌsȯr-ē-ˈa-tik\ *adj or n*

PST *abbr* Pacific standard time

[1]**psych** *or* **psyche** \ˈsīk\ *vt* **psyched; psych·ing** [by shortening] (1917) **1 :** PSYCHOANALYZE **2 a :** to anticipate correctly the intentions or actions of **:** OUTGUESS **b :** to analyze or figure out (as a problem or course of action) ⟨I ~*ed* it all out by myself and decided —David Hulburd⟩ **3 a :** to make psychologically uneasy **:** INTIMIDATE, SCARE ⟨pressure doesn't ~ me —Jerry Quarry⟩ — often used with *out* ⟨has a way of ~*ing* out the competition⟩ **b :** to make (as oneself) psychologically ready esp. for performance — often used with *up* ⟨~*ed* herself up for the race⟩

[2]**psych** *abbr* psychology

psych- *or* **psycho-** *comb form* [Gk, fr. *psychē* breath, principle of life, life, soul, fr. *psychein* to breathe; akin to Skt *babhasti* he blows] **1 :** mind **:** mental processes and activities ⟨*psycho*dynamic⟩ ⟨*psycho*logy⟩ **2 :** psychological methods ⟨*psycho*analysis⟩ ⟨*psycho*therapy⟩ **3 :** brain ⟨*psycho*surgery⟩ **4 :** mental and ⟨*psycho*somatic⟩

psych·as·the·nia \ˌsī-kəs-ˈthē-nē-ə\ *n* [NL] (1900) **:** a neurotic state characterized esp. by phobias, obsessions, or compulsions that one knows are irrational — **psych·as·then·ic** \-ˈthe-nik\ *adj or n*

psy·che \ˈsī-kē\ *n* [L, fr. Gk *psychē* soul] (1590) **1** *cap* **:** a princess loved by Cupid **2** [Gk *psychē*] **a :** SOUL, PERSONALITY ⟨the nation's consumer ~ —D. J. Kevles⟩ **b :** MIND 2

psy·che·de·lia \ˌsī-kə-ˈdēl-yə\ *n* [NL, fr. E *psychedelic*] (1967) **1 :** the world of people, phenomena, or items associated with psychedelic drugs **2 :** psychedelic music

\ə\ **abut** \ᵊ\ **kitten**, F **table** \ər\ **further** \a\ **ash** \ā\ **ace** \ä\ **mop, mar** \au̇\ **out** \ch\ **chin** \e\ **bet** \ē\ **easy** \g\ **go** \i\ **hit** \ī\ **ice** \j\ **job** \ŋ\ **sing** \ō\ **go** \ȯ\ **law** \ȯi\ **boy** \th\ **thin** \t͟h\ **the** \ü\ **loot** \u̇\ **foot** \y\ **yet** \zh\ **vision, beige** \k, ⁿ, œ,ue, ʸ\ *see* Guide to Pronunciation

[1]**psy·che·del·ic** \ˌsī-kə-ˈde-lik\ *n* [irreg. fr. *psych-* + Gk *dēloun* to show, fr. *dēlos* evident; akin to Skt *dīdeti* it shines, L *dies* day — more at DEITY] (1956) : a psychedelic drug (as LSD)
[2]**psychedelic** *adj* (1957) **1 a :** of, relating to, or being drugs (as LSD) capable of producing abnormal psychic effects (as hallucinations) and sometimes psychotic states **b :** produced by or associated with the use of psychedelic drugs ⟨a ~ experience⟩ **2 :** imitating, suggestive of, or reproducing effects (as distorted or bizarre images or sounds) resembling those produced by psychedelic drugs ⟨~ color schemes⟩ — **psy·che·del·i·cal·ly** \-ˈde-li-k(ə-)lē\ *adv*
psy·chi·a·try \sə-ˈkī-ə-trē, sī-\ *n* [prob. fr. F *psychiatrie,* fr. *psychiatre* psychiatrist, fr. *psych-* psych- + Gk *iatros* physician — more at -IATRY] (1828) : a branch of medicine that deals with mental, emotional, or behavioral disorders — **psy·chi·at·ric** \ˌsī-kē-ˈa-trik\ *adj* — **psy·chi·at·ri·cal·ly** \-tri-k(ə-)lē\ *adv* — **psy·chi·a·trist** \sə-ˈkī-ə-trist, sī-\ *n*
[1]**psy·chic** \ˈsī-kik\ *also* **psy·chi·cal** \-ki-kəl\ *adj* [Gk *psychikos* of the soul, fr. *psychē* soul] (1642) **1 :** of or relating to the psyche : PSYCHOGENIC **2 :** lying outside the sphere of physical science or knowledge : immaterial, moral, or spiritual in origin or force **3 :** sensitive to nonphysical or supernatural forces and influences : marked by extraordinary or mysterious sensitivity, perception, or understanding — **psy·chi·cal·ly** \-ki-k(ə-)lē\ *adv*
[2]**psychic** *n* (1871) **1 a :** a person apparently sensitive to nonphysical forces **b :** MEDIUM 2d **2 :** psychic phenomena
psy·cho \ˈsī-(ˌ)kō\ *n, pl* **psychos** [short for *psychopath*] (1942) : a deranged or psychopathic person — not used technically — **psycho** *adj*
psy·cho·acous·tics \ˌsī-kō-ə-ˈküs-tiks\ *n pl but sing in constr* (1948) : a branch of science dealing with the perception of sound, the sensations produced by sounds, and the problems of communication — **psy·cho·acous·tic** \-tik\ *adj*
psy·cho·ac·tive \ˌsī-kō-ˈak-tiv\ *adj* (1961) : affecting the mind or behavior ⟨~ drugs⟩
psy·cho·anal·y·sis \ˌsī-kō-ə-ˈna-lə-səs\ *n* [NL] (1906) : a method of analyzing psychic phenomena and treating emotional disorders that involves treatment sessions during which the patient is encouraged to talk freely about personal experiences and esp. about early childhood and dreams — **psy·cho·an·a·lyst** \-ˈa-nə-list\ *n*
psy·cho·an·a·lyt·ic \-ˌa-nə-ˈli-tik\ *also* **psy·cho·an·a·lyt·i·cal** \-ti-kəl\ *adj* (1906) : of, relating to, or employing psychoanalysis or its principles and techniques — **psy·cho·an·a·lyt·i·cal·ly** \-ti-k(ə-)lē\ *adv*
psy·cho·an·a·lyze \-ˈa-nə-ˌlīz\ *vt* (1911) : to treat by means of psychoanalysis
psy·cho·bab·ble \ˈsī-kō-ˌba-bəl\ *n* (1975) **1 :** a predominantly metaphorical language for expressing one's feelings **2 a :** psychological jargon **b :** trite or simplistic language derived from psychotherapy ⟨repeating the usual ~ about self-discovery —Mark Coleman⟩ — **psychobabble** *vi* — **psy·cho·bab·bler** \-ˌba-blər\ *n*
psy·cho·bi·og·ra·phy \ˌsī-kō-bī-ˈä-grə-fē, -bē-\ *n* (1931) : a biography written from a psychodynamic or psychoanalytic point of view; *also* : the application of such a point of view to the writing of a biography — **psy·cho·bi·og·ra·pher** \-fər\ *n* — **psy·cho·bio·graph·i·cal** \-ˌbī-ə-ˈgra-fi-kəl\ *adj*
psy·cho·bi·ol·o·gy \-bī-ˈä-lə-jē\ *n* [ISV] (1902) : the study of mental functioning and behavior in relation to other biological processes — **psy·cho·bi·o·log·i·cal** \-ˌbī-ə-ˈlä-ji-kəl\ *also* **psy·cho·bi·o·log·ic** \-jik\ *adj* — **psy·cho·bi·ol·o·gist** \-bī-ˈä-lə-jist\ *n*
psy·cho·chem·i·cal \-ˈke-mi-kəl\ *n* (1956) : a psychoactive chemical — **psychochemical** *adj*
psy·cho·dra·ma \-ˈdrä-mə, -ˈdra-\ *n* (1937) **1 :** an extemporized dramatization designed to afford catharsis and social relearning for one or more of the participants from whose life history the plot is abstracted **2 :** a dramatic narrative or work characterized by psychological overtones **3 :** an often ongoing psychological struggle; *also* : an expression of psychological turmoil — **psy·cho·dra·mat·ic** \-drə-ˈma-tik\ *adj*
psy·cho·dy·nam·ics \-dī-ˈna-miks, -də-\ *n pl but sing or pl in constr* (1874) **1 :** the psychology of mental or emotional forces or processes developing esp. in early childhood and their effects on behavior and mental states **2 :** explanation or interpretation (as of behavior or mental states) in terms of mental or emotional forces or processes **3 :** motivational forces acting esp. at the unconscious level — **psy·cho·dy·nam·ic** \-mik\ *adj* — **psy·cho·dy·nam·i·cal·ly** \-mi-k(ə-)lē\ *adv*
psy·cho·gen·e·sis \-ˈje-nə-səs\ *n* [NL] (1838) **1 :** the origin and development of mental functions, traits, or states **2 :** development from mental as distinguished from physical origins — **psy·cho·ge·net·ic** \-jə-ˈne-tik\ *adj*
psy·cho·gen·ic \-ˈje-nik\ *adj* (1902) : originating in the mind or in mental or emotional conflict — **psy·cho·gen·i·cal·ly** \-ni-k(ə-)lē\ *adv*
psy·cho·graph \ˈsī-kə-ˌgraf\ *n* (1916) : PSYCHOBIOGRAPHY
psy·cho·graph·ics \ˌsī-kə-ˈgra-fiks\ *n pl but sing or pl in constr* [*psych-* + *-graphics* (as in *demographics*)] (1968) : market research or statistics classifying population groups according to psychological variables (as attitudes, values, or fears); *also* : variables or trends identified through such research — **psy·cho·graph·ic** \-fik\ *adj* — **psy·cho·graph·i·cal·ly** \-fi-k(ə-)lē\ *adv*
psy·cho·his·to·ry \ˈsī-kō-ˌhis-t(ə-)rē\ *n* (1934) : historical analysis or interpretation using psychological and psychoanalytic methods; *also* : a work of history using such methods — **psy·cho·his·to·ri·an** \ˌsī-kō-(h)is-ˈtȯr-ē-ən, -ˈtär-\ *n* — **psy·cho·his·to·ri·cal** \-ˈtȯr-i-kəl, -ˈtär-\ *adj*
psy·cho·ki·ne·sis \ˌsī-kō-kə-ˈnē-səs, -kī-\ *n* [NL] (1914) : movement of physical objects by the mind without use of physical means — compare PRECOGNITION, TELEKINESIS — **psy·cho·ki·net·ic** \-ˈne-tik\ *adj*
psychol *abbr* psychological
psy·cho·lin·guis·tics \ˌsī-kō-liŋ-ˈgwis-tiks\ *n pl but sing in constr* (1936) : the study of the mental faculties involved in the perception, production, and acquisition of language — **psy·cho·lin·guist** \-ˈliŋ-gwist\ *n* — **psy·cho·lin·guis·tic** \-tik\ *adj*
psy·cho·log·i·cal \ˌsī-kə-ˈlä-ji-kəl\ *also* **psy·cho·log·ic** \-jik\ *adj* (ca. 1688) **1 a :** of or relating to psychology **b :** MENTAL **2 :** directed toward the will or toward the mind specif. in its conative function ⟨~ warfare⟩ — **psy·cho·log·i·cal·ly** \-ji-k(ə-)lē\ *adv*
psychological moment *n* (1871) : the occasion when the mental atmosphere is most certain to be favorable to the full effect of an action or event
psy·chol·o·gise *Brit var of* PSYCHOLOGIZE
psy·chol·o·gism \sī-ˈkä-lə-ˌji-zəm\ *n* (1858) : a theory that applies psychological conceptions to the interpretation of historical events or logical thought
psy·chol·o·gize \-ˌjīz\ *vb* **-gized; -giz·ing** *vi* (1810) : to speculate in psychological terms or on psychological motivations ~ *vt* : to explain or interpret in psychological terms
psy·chol·o·gy \-jē\ *n, pl* **-gies** [NL *psychologia,* fr. *psych-* + *-logia* -logy] (1653) **1 :** the science of mind and behavior **2 a :** the mental or behavioral characteristics of an individual or group **b :** the study of mind and behavior in relation to a particular field of knowledge or activity **3 :** a theory or system of psychology ⟨Freudian ~⟩ ⟨the ~ of Jung⟩ — **psy·chol·o·gist** \-jist\ *n*
psy·cho·met·ric \ˌsī-kə-ˈme-trik\ *adj* (1854) : of or relating to psychometrics or psychometry — **psy·cho·met·ri·cal·ly** \-tri-k(ə-)lē\ *adv*
psy·cho·me·tri·cian \-mə-ˈtri-shən\ *n* (ca. 1939) **1 :** a person (as a clinical psychologist) who is skilled in the administration and interpretation of objective psychological tests **2 :** a psychologist who devises, constructs, and standardizes psychometric tests
psy·cho·met·rics \-ˈme-triks\ *n pl but sing in constr* (ca. 1924) : the psychological theory or technique of mental measurement
psy·chom·e·try \sī-ˈkä-mə-trē\ *n* (ca. 1842) **1 :** divination of facts concerning an object or its owner through contact with or proximity to the object **2 :** PSYCHOMETRICS
psy·cho·mo·tor \ˌsī-kə-ˈmō-tər\ *adj* [ISV] (1878) : of or relating to motor action directly proceeding from mental activity
psy·cho·neu·ro·im·mu·nol·o·gy \ˌsī-kō-ˌn(y)u̇r-ō-ˌim-yə-ˈnä-lə-jē\ *n* (1982) : a branch of medicine that deals with the influence of emotional states (as stress) and nervous system activities on immune function esp. in relation to the onset and progression of disease
psy·cho·neu·ro·sis \ˌsī-kō-nu̇-ˈrō-səs, -nyu̇-\ *n* [NL] (1883) : NEUROSIS; *esp* : a neurosis based on emotional conflict in which an impulse that has been blocked seeks expression in a disguised response or symptom — **psy·cho·neu·rot·ic** \-ˈrä-tik\ *adj or n*
psy·cho·path \ˈsī-kə-ˌpath\ *n* [ISV] (1885) : a mentally ill or unstable person; *esp* : a person affected with antisocial personality disorder
[1]**psy·cho·path·ic** \ˌsī-kə-ˈpa-thik\ *adj* (1847) : of, relating to, or characterized by psychopathy or antisocial personality disorder — **psy·cho·path·i·cal·ly** \-thi-k(ə-)lē\ *adv*
[2]**psychopathic** *n* (ca. 1890) : PSYCHOPATH
psychopathic personality disorder *n* (ca. 1923) : ANTISOCIAL PERSONALITY DISORDER
psy·cho·pa·thol·o·gy \ˌsī-kō-pə-ˈthä-lə-jē, -pa-\ *n* [ISV] (1847) : the study of psychological and behavioral dysfunction occurring in mental disorder or in social disorganization; *also* : such dysfunction — **psy·cho·path·o·log·i·cal** \-ˌpa-thə-ˈlä-ji-kəl\ *also* **psy·cho·path·o·log·ic** \-jik\ *adj* — **psy·cho·path·o·log·i·cal·ly** \-ji-k(ə-)lē\ *adv* — **psy·cho·pa·thol·o·gist** \-pə-ˈthä-lə-jist, -pa-\ *n*
psy·chop·a·thy \sī-ˈkä-pə-thē\ *n, pl* **-thies** [ISV] (1847) : mental disorder esp. when marked by egocentric and antisocial activity
psy·cho·phar·ma·col·o·gy \ˌsī-kō-ˌfär-mə-ˈkä-lə-jē\ *n* (1920) : the study of the effect of drugs on the mind and behavior — **psy·cho·phar·ma·co·log·i·cal** \-mə-kə-ˈlä-ji-kəl\ *also* **psy·cho·phar·ma·co·log·ic** \-jik\ *adj* — **psy·cho·phar·ma·col·o·gist** \-ˈkä-lə-jist\ *n*
psy·cho·phys·i·cal \ˌsī-kō-ˈfi-zi-kəl\ *adj* (1847) : of or relating to psychophysics; *also* : sharing mental and physical qualities ⟨~ color perception⟩ — **psy·cho·phys·i·cal·ly** \-k(ə-)lē\ *adv*
psychophysical parallelism *n* (1894) : PARALLELISM 4
psy·cho·phys·ics \ˌsī-kō-ˈfi-ziks\ *n pl but sing in constr* [ISV] (1878) : a branch of psychology concerned with the effect of physical processes (as intensity of stimulation) on the mental processes of an organism — **psy·cho·phys·i·cist** \-ˈfi-zə-sist, -ˈfiz-sist\ *n*
psy·cho·phys·i·o·log·i·cal \ˌsī-kō-ˌfi-zē-ə-ˈlä-ji-kəl\ *also* **psy·cho·phys·i·o·log·ic** \-jik\ *adj* (1839) **1 :** of or relating to physiological psychology **2 :** combining or involving mental and bodily processes — **psy·cho·phys·i·o·log·i·cal·ly** \-ji-k(ə-)lē\ *adv*
psy·cho·phys·i·ol·o·gy \-ˌfi-zē-ˈä-lə-jē\ *n* [ISV] (1839) : PHYSIOLOGICAL PSYCHOLOGY — **psy·cho·phys·i·ol·o·gist** \-jist\ *n*
psy·cho·sex·u·al \-ˈsek-shə-wəl, -shwəl, -shəl\ *adj* (1897) **1 :** of or relating to the mental, emotional, and behavioral aspects of sexual development **2 :** of or relating to mental or emotional attitudes concerning sexual activity **3 :** of or relating to the physiological psychology of sex — **psy·cho·sex·u·al·ly** *adv*
psy·cho·sex·u·al·i·ty \-ˌsek-shə-ˈwa-lə-tē\ *n* (1910) : the psychic factors of sex
psy·cho·sis \sī-ˈkō-səs\ *n, pl* **-cho·ses** \-ˌsēz\ [NL] (1847) : fundamental derangement of the mind (as in schizophrenia) characterized by defective or lost contact with reality esp. as evidenced by delusions, hallucinations, and disorganized speech and behavior
psy·cho·so·cial \ˌsī-kō-ˈsō-shəl\ *adj* (1899) **1 :** involving both psychological and social aspects ⟨~ adjustment in marriage⟩ **2 :** relating social conditions to mental health ⟨~ medicine⟩ — **psy·cho·so·cial·ly** \-ˈsō-sh(ə-)lē\ *adv*
psy·cho·so·mat·ic \-sə-ˈma-tik\ *adj* [ISV] (1863) **1 :** of, relating to, concerned with, or involving both mind and body ⟨the ~ nature of man —Herbert Ratner⟩ **2 :** of, relating to, involving, or concerned with bodily symptoms caused by mental or emotional disturbance ⟨~ symptoms⟩ ⟨~ medicine⟩ — **psy·cho·so·mat·i·cal·ly** \-ti-k(ə-)lē\ *adv*
psy·cho·sur·gery \-ˈsər-jə-rē, -ˈsərj-rē\ *n* (1936) : cerebral surgery employed in treating psychic symptoms — **psy·cho·sur·geon** \-ˈsər-jən\ *n* — **psy·cho·sur·gi·cal** \-ˈsər-ji-kəl\ *adj*
psy·cho·syn·the·sis \-ˈsin(t)-thə-səs\ *n* (1919) : a form of psychotherapy combining psychoanalytic techniques with meditation and exercise
psy·cho·ther·a·peu·tic \-ˌther-ə-ˈpyü-tik\ *adj* [ISV] (ca. 1888) : of, relating to, or used in psychotherapy — **psy·cho·ther·a·peu·ti·cal·ly** \-ti-k(ə-)lē\ *adv*
psy·cho·ther·a·py \-ˈther-ə-pē\ *n* [ISV] (ca. 1890) : treatment of mental or emotional disorder or of related bodily ills by psychological means — **psy·cho·ther·a·pist** \-pist\ *n*
psy·chot·ic \sī-ˈkä-tik\ *adj* (ca. 1890) : of, relating to, marked by, or affected with psychosis ⟨a ~ patient⟩ ⟨~ behavior⟩ — **psychotic** *n* — **psy·chot·i·cal·ly** \-ti-k(ə-)lē\ *adv*

psy·choto·mi·met·ic \sī-ˌkä-tō-mə-ˈme-tik, -mī-\ *adj* [*psychotic* + *-o-* + *mimetic*] (1956) : of, relating to, involving, or inducing psychotic alteration of behavior and personality ⟨~ drugs⟩ — **psychotomimetic** *n* — **psy·choto·mi·met·i·cal·ly** \-ti-k(ə-)lē\ *adv*

psy·cho·tro·pic \ˌsī-kə-ˈtrō-pik\ *adj* (1948) : acting on the mind ⟨~ drugs⟩ — **psychotropic** *n*

psych–out \ˈsīk-ˌau̇t\ *n* (1971) : an act or an instance of psyching someone out

psychro- *comb form* [Gk, fr. *psychros,* fr. *psychein* to cool] : cold ⟨*psychro*meter⟩

psy·chrom·e·ter \sī-ˈkrä-mə-tər\ *n* [ISV] (ca. 1741) : a hygrometer consisting essentially of two similar thermometers with the bulb of one being kept wet so that the cooling that results from evaporation makes it register a lower temperature than the dry one and with the difference between the readings constituting a measure of the dryness of the atmosphere — **psy·chro·met·ric** \ˌsī-krə-ˈme-trik\ *adj* — **psy·chrom·e·try** \sī-ˈkrä-mə-trē\ *n*

psy·chro·phil·ic \ˌsī-krō-ˈfi-lik\ *adj* (1897) : thriving at a relatively low temperature ⟨~ bacteria⟩

psyl·la \ˈsi-lə\ *n* [NL, genus name, fr. Gk, flea; akin to L *pulex* flea, Skt *pluṣi*] (1852) : any of various plant lice (family Psyllidae) including economically important plant pests — compare PEAR PSYLLA

psyl·lid \ˈsi-ləd\ *n* [ultim. fr. NL *Psylla*] (1899) : PSYLLA — **psyllid** *adj*

psyl·li·um \ˈsi-lē-əm\ *n* [NL *psyllium,* fr. Gk *psyllion* fleawort, fr. *psylla*] (1598) : the seed of a fleawort (esp. *Plantago psyllium*) that has the property of swelling and becoming gelatinous when moist and is used as a mild laxative — called also *psyllium seed*

psy·ops \ˈsī-ˌäps\ *n pl, often attrib* [*ps*ychological *op*eration*s*] (1966) : military operations usu. aimed at influencing the enemy's state of mind through noncombative means (as distribution of leaflets)

psy·war \ˈsī-ˌwȯr\ *n* (1951) : psychological warfare

pt *abbr* **1** part **2** patient **3** payment **4** pint **5** point **6** port

Pt *symbol* platinum

PT *abbr* **1** Pacific time **2** part-time **3** physical therapist; physical therapy **4** physical training

pta *abbr* peseta

PTA *abbr* Parent-Teacher Association

ptar·mi·gan \ˈtär-mi-gən\ *n, pl* **-gan** *or* **-gans** [modif. of ScGael *tarmachan*] (1599) : any of various grouses (genus *Lagopus*) of northern regions with completely feathered feet

PT boat \ˌpē-ˈtē-, ˈpē-ˌ\ *n* [*p*atrol *t*orpedo] (1941) : a small fast patrol craft usu. armed with torpedoes, machine guns, and depth charges — called also *PT*

PTC \ˌpē-(ˌ)tē-ˈsē\ *n* (1932) : PHENYLTHIOCARBAMIDE

pte *abbr, Brit* private

pter·an·o·don \tə-ˈra-nə-ˌdän, -ˈrä-\ *n* [NL, fr. Gk *pteron* wing + *anodōn* toothless fr. *an-* + *odōn, odous* tooth — more at FEATHER, TOOTH] (1881) : any of a genus (*Pteranodon*) of Cretaceous pterosaurs having a backwardly directed bony crest on the skull and a wingspan of about 25 feet (7.7 meters)

pterid- *or* **pterido-** *comb form* [Gk *pterid-, pteris;* akin to Gk *pteron* wing, feather] : fern ⟨*pterido*logy⟩

pter·i·dine \ˈter-ə-ˌdēn\ *n* [ISV *pterin* + *-idine*] (1943) : a yellow crystalline bicyclic base $C_6H_4N_4$; *broadly* : any of a class of compounds (as the pterins) that have the bicyclic ring system of pteridine and include esp. various animal pigments

pter·i·dol·o·gy \ˌter-ə-ˈdä-lə-jē\ *n* (1855) : the study of ferns — **pter·i·do·log·i·cal** \ˌter-ə-də-ˈlä-ji-kəl\ *adj* — **pter·i·dol·o·gist** \-ˈdä-lə-jist\ *n*

pte·ri·do·phyte \tə-ˈri-də-ˌfīt, ˈter-ə-dō-\ *n* [NL *Pteridophyta,* fr. Gk *pterid-* + *phyton* plant — more at PHYT-] (1880) : any of a division (Pteridophyta) of vascular plants (as a fern) that have roots, stems, and leaves but lack flowers or seeds

pte·ri·do·sperm \tə-ˈri-də-ˌspərm, ˈter-ə-dō-\ *n* [ISV] (1904) : SEED FERN

pter·in \ˈter-ən\ *n* [ISV *pter-* (fr. Gk *pteron* wing) + [1]*-in;* fr. its being a factor in the pigments of butterfly wings] (1934) : any of various compounds that contain the bicyclic ring system characteristic of pteridine

ptero·dac·tyl \ˌter-ə-ˈdak-tᵊl\ *n* [NL *Pterodactylus,* genus of reptiles, fr. Gk *pteron* wing + *daktylos* finger — more at FEATHER] (1830) : any of various pterosaurs (suborder Pterodactyloidea) of the Late Jurassic and Cretaceous having a rudimentary tail and a beak with reduced dentition; *broadly* : PTEROSAUR

ptero·pod \ˈter-ə-ˌpäd\ *n* [NL *Pteropoda,* group name, fr. Gk *pteron* wing + NL *-poda*] (1835) : any of the opisthobranch mollusks comprising two orders (Thecosomata and Gymnosomata) and having the anterior lobes of the foot expanded into broad thin winglike swimming organs

ptero·saur \ˈter-ə-ˌsȯr\ *n* [NL *Pterosauria,* fr. Gk *pteron* wing + *sauros* lizard] (1862) : any of an order (Pterosauria) of extinct flying reptiles existing from the Late Triassic throughout the Jurassic and most of the Cretaceous and having a featherless wing membrane extending from the side of the body along the arm to the end of the greatly elongated fourth digit

pter·o·yl·glu·tam·ic acid \ˌter-ə-ˌwil-glü-ˈta-mik-\ *n* [ISV *pteroyl,* the radical $(C_{13}H_{11}N_6O)CO$ + *glutamic acid*] (1943) : FOLIC ACID

pte·ryg·i·um \te-ˈri-jē-əm\ *n, pl* **pte·ryg·ia** \-jē-ə\ *also* **-iums** [NL, fr. Gk *pterygion* little wing, fr. *pteryx*] (1657) : a fleshy mass of thickened conjunctiva that grows over part of the cornea usu. from the inner side of the eyeball and causes a disturbance of vision

[1]**pter·y·goid** \ˈter-ə-ˌgȯid\ *adj* [NL *pterygoides,* fr. Gk *pterygoeidēs,* lit., shaped like a wing, fr. *pteryg-, pteryx* wing; akin to Gk *pteron* wing — more at FEATHER] (1722) : of, relating to, or lying in the region of the inferior part of the sphenoid bone of the vertebrate skull

[2]**pterygoid** *n* (1831) : a pterygoid part (as a bone, muscle, or nerve)

pterygoid process *n* (1741) : a process extending downward from each side of the sphenoid bone in humans and other mammals

pter·y·la \ˈter-ə-lə\ *n, pl* **-lae** \-ˌlē, -ˌlī\ [NL, fr. Gk *pteron* + *hylē* wood, forest] (1867) : one of the definite areas of the skin of a bird on which feathers grow

ptg *abbr* printing

PTO *abbr* **1** Parent-Teacher Organization **2** please turn over **3** power takeoff

Ptol·e·ma·ic \ˌtä-lə-ˈmā-ik\ *adj* [Gk *Ptolemaikos,* fr. *Ptolemaios* Ptolemy] (1674) **1** : of or relating to the second century geographer and astronomer Ptolemy of Alexandria and esp. to his belief that the earth is at the center of the universe with the sun, moon, and planets revolving around it ⟨the ~ system⟩ **2** : of or relating to the Greco-Egyptian Ptolemies ruling Egypt from 323 to 30 B.C.

pto·maine \ˈtō-ˌmān, tō-ˈ\ *n* [It *ptomaina,* fr. Gk *ptōma* fall, fallen body, corpse, fr. *piptein* to fall — more at FEATHER] (1880) : any of various organic bases which are formed by the action of putrefactive bacteria on nitrogenous matter and some of which are poisonous

ptomaine poisoning *n* (1893) : food poisoning caused by bacteria or bacterial products

pto·sis \ˈtō-səs\ *n, pl* **pto·ses** \-ˌsēz\ [NL, fr. Gk *ptōsis* act of falling, fr. *piptein*] (1743) : a sagging or prolapse of an organ or part; *esp* : a drooping of the upper eyelid

PTSD *abbr* post-traumatic stress disorder

PTV *abbr* public television

Pty *abbr, Brit* proprietary

pty·a·lin \ˈtī-ə-lən\ *n* [Gk *ptyalon* saliva, fr. *ptyein* to spit — more at SPEW] (1845) : an amylase found in the saliva of many animals that converts starch into sugar

pty·a·lism \-ˌli-zəm\ *n* [NL *ptyalismus,* fr. Gk *ptyalismos,* fr. *ptyalizein* to salivate, fr. *ptyalon*] (1676) : an excessive flow of saliva

p–type \ˈpē-ˌtīp\ *adj* [*p*ositive *type*] (1946) : relating to or being a semiconductor in which charge is carried by holes — compare N-TYPE

Pu *symbol* plutonium

PU *abbr* pickup

[1]**pub** \ˈpəb\ *n* (ca. 1859) **1** *chiefly Brit* : PUBLIC HOUSE 2 **2** : an establishment where alcoholic beverages are sold and consumed

[2]**pub** *abbr* **1** public **2** publication **3** publicity **4** published; publisher; publishing

pub crawl *n* (1915) : a round of visits to a number of bars in succession — **pub–crawl** *vi* — **pub crawler** *n*

pu·ber·tal \ˈpyü-bər-tᵊl\ *or* **pu·ber·al** \ˈpyü-bə-rəl\ *adj* [*pubertal* fr. *puberty; puberal* fr. ML *puberalis,* fr. L *puber*] (ca. 1837) : of or relating to puberty

pu·ber·ty \ˈpyü-bər-tē\ *n* [ME *puberte,* fr. L *pubertas,* fr. *puber* pubescent] (14c) **1** : the condition of being or the period of becoming first capable of reproducing sexually marked by maturing of the genital organs, development of secondary sex characteristics, and in the human and in higher primates by the first occurrence of menstruation in the female **2** : the age at which puberty occurs often construed legally as 14 in boys and 12 in girls

pu·ber·u·lent \pyü-ˈber-ə-lənt, -yə-lənt\ *adj* [L *puber* pubescent + E *-ulent* (as in *pulverulent*)] (1847) : covered with fine pubescence

pu·bes \ˈpyü-(ˌ)bēz\ *n, pl* **pubes** [NL, fr. L, manhood, body hair, pubic region; akin to L *puber* pubescent] (ca. 1570) **1** : the hair that appears on the lower part of the hypogastric region at puberty **2** : the pubic region

pu·bes·cence \pyü-ˈbe-sᵊn(t)s\ *n* (15c) **1** : the quality or state of being pubescent **2** : a pubescent covering or surface

pu·bes·cent \-sᵊnt\ *adj* [L *pubescent-, pubescens,* prp. of *pubescere* to reach puberty, become covered as with hair, fr. *pubes*] (1646) **1 a** : arriving at or having reached puberty **b** : of or relating to puberty **2** : covered with fine soft short hairs — compare VILLOUS

pu·bic \ˈpyü-bik\ *adj* (1831) : of, relating to, or situated in or near the region of the pubes or the pubis

pu·bis \ˈpyü-bəs\ *n, pl* **pu·bes** \-(ˌ)bēz\ [NL *os pubis,* lit., bone of the pubic region] (1597) : the ventral and anterior of the three principal bones composing either half of the pelvis — called also *pubic bone*

publ *abbr* **1** publication **2** published; publisher; publishing

[1]**pub·lic** \ˈpə-blik\ *adj* [ME *publique,* fr. AF, fr. L *publicus;* akin to L *populus* people] (14c) **1 a** : exposed to general view : OPEN **b** : WELL-KNOWN, PROMINENT **c** : PERCEPTIBLE, MATERIAL **2 a** : of, relating to, or affecting all the people or the whole area of a nation or state ⟨~ law⟩ **b** : of or relating to a government **c** : of, relating to, or being in the service of the community or nation **3 a** : of or relating to people in general : UNIVERSAL **b** : GENERAL, POPULAR **4** : of or relating to business or community interests as opposed to private affairs : SOCIAL **5** : devoted to the general or national welfare : HUMANITARIAN **6 a** : accessible to or shared by all members of the community **b** : capitalized in shares that can be freely traded on the open market — often used with *go* **7** : supported by public funds and private contributions rather than by income from commercials ⟨~ radio⟩ ⟨~ television⟩ — **pub·lic·ness** *n*

[2]**public** *n* (15c) **1** : a place accessible or visible to the public — usu. used in the phrase *in public* **2** : the people as a whole : POPULACE **3** : a group of people having common interests or characteristics; *specif* : the group at which a particular activity or enterprise aims

public–address system *n* (1923) : an apparatus including a microphone and loudspeakers used for broadcasting (as to an audience in an auditorium)

pub·li·can \ˈpə-bli-kən\ *n* [ME, fr. AF, fr. L *publicanus* tax farmer, fr. *publicum* public revenue, fr. neut. of *publicus*] (13c) **1 a** : a Jewish tax collector for the ancient Romans **b** : a collector of taxes or tribute **2** *chiefly Brit* : the licensee of a public house

public assistance *n* (1884) : government aid to needy, aged, or disabled persons and to dependent children

pub·li·ca·tion \ˌpə-blə-ˈkā-shən\ *n* [ME *publicacioun,* fr. MF *publication,* fr. L *publication-, publicatio,* fr. *publicare,* fr. *publicus* public] (14c) **1** : the act or process of publishing **2** : a published work

public defender *n* (1918) : a lawyer usu. holding public office whose duty is to defend accused persons unable to pay for legal assistance

public domain *n* (1832) **1** : land owned directly by the government **2** : the realm embracing property rights that belong to the community at large, are unprotected by copyright or patent, and are subject to appropriation by anyone

\ə\ **abut** \ᵊ\ kitten, F table \ər\ **further** \a\ **ash** \ā\ **ace** \ä\ mop, mar
\au̇\ **out** \ch\ **chin** \e\ bet \ē\ **easy** \g\ **go** \i\ **hit** \ī\ **ice** \j\ **job**
\ŋ\ **sing** \ō\ **go** \ȯ\ **law** \ȯi\ **boy** \th\ **thin** \th̲\ **the** \ü\ **loot** \u̇\ **foot**
\y\ yet \zh\ **vision, beige** \k̲, ⁿ, œ, ue, ʸ\ *see* Guide to Pronunciation

public health *n* (1617) : the art and science dealing with the protection and improvement of community health by organized community effort and including preventive medicine and sanitary and social science
public house *n* (1658) **1** : INN, HOSTELRY **2** *chiefly Brit* : a licensed saloon or bar
pub·li·cise *Brit var of* PUBLICIZE
pub·li·cist \ˈpə-blə-sist\ *n* (1792) **1 a** : an expert in international law **b** : an expert or commentator on public affairs **2** : one that publicizes; *specif* : PRESS AGENT
pub·lic·i·ty \(ˌ)pə-ˈbli-sə-tē, -ˈblis-tē\ *n* (1788) **1** : the quality or state of being public **2 a** : an act or device designed to attract public interest; *specif* : information with news value issued as a means of gaining public attention or support **b** : the dissemination of information or promotional material **c** : paid advertising **d** : public attention or acclaim
pub·li·cize \ˈpə-blə-ˌsīz\ *vt* **-cized; -ciz·ing** (1844) : to bring to the attention of the public : ADVERTISE
pub·lic–key \ˈpə-blik-ˈkē\ *n, often attrib* (1977) : a cryptographic element that is the publicly shared half of an encryption code and that can be used only to encode messages
public land *n* (1789) : land owned by a government; *specif* : that part of the U.S. public domain subject to sale or disposal under the homestead laws
public law *n* (1761) **1** : a legislative enactment affecting the public at large **2** : a branch of law concerned with regulating the relations of individuals with the government and the organization and conduct of the government itself — compare PRIVATE LAW
pub·lic·ly \ˈpə-bli-klē\ *also* **pub·li·cal·ly** \-li-k(ə-)lē\ *adv* (1563) **1** : in a manner observable by or in a place accessible to the public : OPENLY **2 a** : by the people generally **b** : by a government
public officer *n* (1606) : a person who has been legally elected or appointed to office and who exercises governmental functions
public relations *n pl but usu sing in constr, often attrib* (1807) : the business of inducing the public to have understanding for and goodwill toward a person, firm, or institution; *also* : the degree of understanding and goodwill achieved
public sale *n* (1641) : AUCTION 1
public school *n* (1580) **1** : an endowed secondary boarding school in Great Britain offering a classical curriculum and preparation for the universities or public service **2** : a free tax-supported school controlled by a local governmental authority
public servant *n* (1671) : a government official or employee
public service *n* (ca. 1576) **1** : the business of supplying a commodity (as electricity or gas) or service (as transportation) to any or all members of a community **2** : a service rendered in the public interest **3** : governmental employment; *esp* : CIVIL SERVICE
public–service corporation *n* (1904) : a quasi-public corporation
public speaking *n* (1762) **1** : the act or process of making speeches in public **2** : the art of effective oral communication with an audience
public–spirited *adj* (1677) : motivated by devotion to the general welfare — **pub·lic–spir·it·ed·ness** *n*
public utility *n* (1903) : a business organization (as an electric company) performing a public service and subject to special governmental regulation
public works *n pl* (1606) : works (as schools, highways, docks) constructed for public use or enjoyment esp. when financed and owned by the government
pub·lish \ˈpə-blish\ *vb* [ME, modif. of AF *publier*, fr. L *publicare*, fr. *publicus* public] *vt* (14c) **1 a** : to make generally known **b** : to make public announcement of **2 a** : to disseminate to the public **b** : to produce or release for distribution; *specif* : PRINT 2c **c** : to issue the work of (an author) ~ *vi* **1** : to put out an edition **2** : to have one's work accepted for publication — **pub·lish·able** \-bli-shə-bəl\ *adj*
pub·lish·er \ˈpə-bli-shər\ *n* (15c) : one that publishes something; *esp* : a person or corporation whose business is publishing
pub·lish·ing \-shiŋ\ *n* (1580) : the business or profession of the commercial production and issuance of literature, information, musical scores or sometimes recordings, or art ⟨newspaper ~⟩ ⟨software ~⟩
puc·coon \(ˌ)pə-ˈkün\ *n* [Virginia Algonquian *poughkone*] (1612) **1** : any of several American plants (as bloodroot) yielding a red or yellow pigment **2** : a pigment from a puccoon
puce \ˈpyüs\ *n* [F, lit., flea, fr. OF *pulce*, fr. L *pulic-, pulex* — more at PSYLLA] (1833) : a dark red
[1]**puck** \ˈpək\ *n* [ME *puke*, fr. OE *pūca*; akin to ON *pūki* devil] (bef. 12c) **1** *archaic* : an evil spirit : DEMON **2** : a mischievous sprite : HOBGOBLIN; *specif, cap* : ROBIN GOODFELLOW
[2]**puck** *n* [E dial. *puck* to poke, hit, prob. fr. Ir *poc* butt, stroke in hurling, lit., buck (male deer)] (1891) : a vulcanized rubber disk used in ice hockey
pucka *var of* PUKKA
[1]**puck·er** \ˈpə-kər\ *vb* **puck·ered; puck·er·ing** \-k(ə-)riŋ\ [prob. irreg. fr. [1]*poke*] *vi* (1598) : to become wrinkled or constricted ~ *vt* : to contract into folds or wrinkles
[2]**pucker** *n* (ca. 1750) : a fold or wrinkle in a normally even surface
puck·ery \ˈpə-k(ə-)rē\ *adj* (1830) : that puckers or causes puckering
puck·ish \ˈpə-kish\ *adj* [[1]*puck*] (1874) : IMPISH, WHIMSICAL — **puck·ish·ly** *adv* — **puck·ish·ness** *n*
pud \ˈpu̇d\ *n* (1706) *Brit* : PUDDING
PUD *abbr* pickup and delivery
pud·ding \ˈpu̇-diŋ\ *n* [ME] (13c) **1** : BLOOD SAUSAGE **2 a** (1) : a boiled or baked soft food usu. with a cereal base ⟨corn ~⟩ ⟨bread ~⟩ (2) : a dessert of a soft, spongy, or thick creamy consistency ⟨chocolate ~⟩ (3) *Brit* : DESSERT 1 **b** : a dish often containing suet or having a suet crust and orig. boiled in a bag ⟨steak and kidney ~⟩
pudding stone *n* (1753) : CONGLOMERATE 1
[1]**pud·dle** \ˈpə-dᵊl\ *n* [ME *podel*; akin to LG *pudel* puddle, OE *pudd* ditch] (14c) **1** : a very small pool of usu. dirty or muddy water **2 a** : an earthy mixture (as of clay, sand, and gravel) worked while wet into a compact mass that becomes impervious to water when dry **b** : a thin mixture of soil and water for puddling plants
[2]**puddle** *vb* **pud·dled; pud·dling** \ˈpəd-liŋ, ˈpə-dᵊl-iŋ\ *vi* (15c) : to dabble or wade around in a puddle ~ *vt* **1** : to make muddy or turbid : MUDDLE **2 a** : to work (a wet mixture of earth or concrete) into a dense impervious mass **b** : to subject (iron) to the process of puddling **3 a** : to strew with puddles **b** : to compact (soil) esp. by working when too wet **c** : to dip the roots of (a plant) in a thin mud before transplanting — **pud·dler** \ˈpəd-lər, ˈpə-dᵊl-ər\ *n*
puddle duck *n* (1877) : DABBLER b
puddle jumper *n* (1942) *slang* : LIGHTPLANE
puddling *n* (1839) : the process of converting pig iron into wrought iron or rarely steel by subjecting it to heat and frequent stirring in a furnace in the presence of oxidizing substances
pu·den·cy \ˈpyü-dᵊn(t)-sē\ *n* [L *pudentia*, fr. *pudent-, pudens*, prp. of *pudēre* to be ashamed, make ashamed] (1611) : MODESTY
pu·den·dum \pyu̇-ˈden-dəm\ *n, pl* **-da** \-də\ [NL, sing. of L *pudenda*, fr. neut. pl. of *pudendus*, gerundive of *pudēre* to be ashamed] (1634) : the external genital organs of a human being and esp. of a woman — usu. used in pl. — **pu·den·dal** \-dᵊl\ *adj*
pudgy \ˈpə-jē\ *adj* **pudg·i·er; -est** [origin unknown] (1836) : being short and plump : CHUBBY — **pudg·i·ness** *n*
pu·di·bund \ˈpyü-də-ˌbənd\ *adj* [L *pudibundus*, fr. *pudēre* to be ashamed + *-bundus* (as in *moribundus* moribund)] (ca. 1656) : PRUDISH
pueb·lo \ˈpwe-(ˌ)blō; pü-ˈe-, pyü-\ *n, pl* **-los** [Sp, village, lit., people, fr. L *populus*] (1808) **1 a** : the communal dwelling of an American Indian village of Arizona, New Mexico, and adjacent areas consisting of contiguous flat-roofed stone or adobe houses in groups sometimes several stories high **b** : an American Indian village of the southwestern U.S. **2** *cap* : a member of a group of American Indian peoples of the southwestern U.S.
pu·er·ile \ˈpyu̇(-ə)r-əl, -ˌī(-ə)l\ *adj* [F or L; F *puéril*, fr. L *puerilis*, fr. *puer* boy, child; akin to Skt *putra* son, child and perh. to Gk *pais* boy, child — more at FEW] (1652) **1** : JUVENILE **2** : CHILDISH, SILLY ⟨~ remarks⟩ — **pu·er·ile·ly** \-ə(l)-lē, -ˌī(-ə)l-lē\ *adv* — **pu·er·il·i·ty** \ˌpyu̇(-ə)r-ˈi-lə-tē\ *n*
pu·er·il·ism \ˈpyu̇(-ə)r-ə-ˌli-zəm, ˈpyu̇(-ə)r-ˌī-\ *n* (1924) : childish behavior esp. as a symptom of mental disorder
pu·er·per·al \pyü-ˈər-p(ə-)rəl\ *adj* [L *puerpera* woman in childbirth, fr. *puer* child + *parere* to give birth to — more at PARE] (1768) : of, relating to, or occurring during childbirth or the period immediately following ⟨~ infection⟩ ⟨~ depression⟩
puerperal fever *n* (1768) : an abnormal condition that results from infection of the placental site following delivery or abortion and is characterized in mild form by fever but in serious cases the infection may spread through the uterine wall or pass into the bloodstream — called also *childbed fever, puerperal sepsis*
pu·er·pe·ri·um \ˌpyü-ər-ˈpir-ē-əm\ *n, pl* **-ria** \-ē-ə\ [L, fr. *puerpera*] (ca. 1890) : the period between childbirth and the return of the uterus to its normal size
[1]**puff** \ˈpəf\ *vb* [ME, fr. OE *pyffan*, of imit. origin] *vi* (bef. 12c) **1 a** (1) : to blow in short gusts (2) : to exhale forcibly **b** : to breathe hard : PANT **c** : to emit small whiffs or clouds (as of smoke) often as an accompaniment to vigorous action ⟨~ at a pipe⟩ **2** : to speak or act in a scornful, conceited, or exaggerated manner **3 a** : to become distended : SWELL — usu. used with *up* **b** : to open or appear in or as if in a puff **4** : to form a chromosomal puff ~ *vt* **1 a** : to emit, propel, blow, or expel by or as if by puffs : WAFT **b** : to draw on (as a cigar, cigarette, or pipe) with intermittent exhalations of smoke **2 a** : to distend with or as if with air or gas : INFLATE **b** : to make proud or conceited : ELATE **c** (1) : to praise extravagantly and usu. with exaggeration ⟨authors ~*ing* their own work⟩ (2) : ADVERTISE
[2]**puff** *n* (13c) **1 a** : an act or instance of puffing : WHIFF **b** : a slight explosive sound accompanying a puff **c** : a perceptible cloud or aura emitted in a puff **d** : DRAW 1a **2** : a light round hollow pastry **3 a** : a slight swelling : PROTUBERANCE **b** : a fluffy mass: as (1) : POUF 2 (2) : a small fluffy pad for applying cosmetic powder (3) : a soft loose roll of hair (4) : a quilted bed covering **4** : a commendatory or promotional notice or review **5** : an enlarged region of a chromosome that is associated with intensely active genes involved in RNA synthesis — **puff·i·ness** \ˈpə-fē-nəs\ *n* — **puffy** \ˈpə-fē\ *adj*
[3]**puff** *adj* (1943) : of, relating to, or designed for promotion or flattery ⟨a ~ piece in the paper⟩
puff adder *n* (1789) **1** : a large thick-bodied extremely venomous African viper (*Bitis arietans*) **2** : HOGNOSE SNAKE
puff·ball \ˈpəf-ˌbȯl\ *n* (1649) : any of various globose and often edible fungi (esp. family Lycoperdaceae) that discharge mature spores in a smokelike cloud when pressed or struck
puff·er \ˈpə-fər\ *n* (1629) **1** : one that puffs **2** : PUFFER FISH
puffer fish *n* (1927) **1** : any of a family (Tetraodontidae) of chiefly tropical scaleless marine bony fishes which can distend themselves to a globular form and most of which are highly poisonous — called also *blowfish, globefish, swellfish*; compare FUGU **2** : any of various fish of the same order (Tetraodontiformes) as the puffer fish
puff·ery \ˈpə-f(ə-)rē\ *n* (1782) : exaggerated commendation esp. for promotional purposes : HYPE
puf·fin \ˈpə-fən\ *n* [ME *pophyn*] (14c) : any of several seabirds (genera *Fratercula* and *Lunda*) of the northern hemisphere having a short neck and a deep grooved parti-colored laterally compressed bill
puff pastry *n* (1788) : a pastry dough containing many alternating layers of butter and dough or the light flaky pastry made from it — called also *puff paste*
[1]**pug** \ˈpəg\ *n* [obs. *pug* hobgoblin, monkey] (1751) **1** : any of a breed of small sturdy compact dogs of Asian origin with a smooth, short coat, tightly curled tail, short muzzle, and broad wrinkled face **2 a** : PUG NOSE **b** : a close knot or coil of hair : BUN
[2]**pug** *vt* **pugged; pug·ging** [origin unknown] (1843) : to work and mix (as clay) when wet esp. to make more homogeneous and easier to handle (as in throwing or molding wares)
[3]**pug** *n* [by shortening & alter. fr. *pugilist*] (1858) : [1]BOXER 1
[4]**pug** *n* [Hindi & Urdu *pag* foot, step] (1865) : FOOTPRINT; *esp* : a print of a wild mammal
pug·ga·ree *also* **pug·a·ree** *or* **pug·gree** \ˈpə-g(ə-)rē\ *n* [Hindi & Urdu *pagṛī* turban] (1665) : a light scarf wrapped around a sun helmet or used as a hatband
pu·gi·lism \ˈpyü-jə-ˌli-zəm\ *n* [L *pugil* boxer; akin to L *pugnus* fist — more at PUNGENT] (1791) : [1]BOXING — **pu·gi·lis·tic** \ˌpyü-jə-ˈlis-tik\ *adj*
pu·gi·list \ˈpyü-jə-list\ *n* (1790) : FIGHTER; *esp* : a professional boxer
pug·mark \ˈpəg-ˌmärk\ *n* (1922) : [4]PUG

pug mill *n* [[2]*pug*] (1824) **:** a machine in which materials (as clay and water) are mixed, blended, or kneaded into a desired consistency
pug·na·cious \ˌpəg-ˈnā-shəs\ *adj* [L *pugnac-, pugnax,* fr. *pugnare* to fight — more at PUNGENT] (1642) **:** having a quarrelsome or combative nature **:** TRUCULENT ***syn*** see BELLIGERENT — **pug·na·cious·ly** *adv* — **pug·na·cious·ness** *n* — **pug·nac·i·ty** \-ˈna-sə-tē\ *n*
pug nose *n* [[1]*pug*] (1777) **:** a nose having a slightly concave bridge and flattened nostrils — **pug–nosed** \ˈpəg-ˌnōzd\ *adj*
pui·sne \ˈpyü-nē\ *adj* [AF *puisné* younger — more at PUNY] (1688) *chiefly Brit* **:** inferior in rank ⟨~ judge⟩ — **puisne** *n*
puis·sance \ˈpwi-sᵊn(t)s, ˈpyü-ə-sən(t)s, pyü-ˈi-sᵊn(t)s\ *n* [ME, fr. AF *pussance, puissance,* fr. *pussant* able, powerful, fr. *poer* to be able, be powerful — more at POWER] (15c) **:** STRENGTH, POWER
puis·sant \-sᵊnt, -sənt\ *adj* (15c) **:** having puissance **:** POWERFUL
puke \ˈpyük\ *vb* **puked; puk·ing** [origin unknown] (ca. 1600) **:** VOMIT — **puke** *n*
puk·ka *also* **puc·ka** \ˈpə-kə\ *adj* [Hindi & Urdu *pakkā* cooked, ripe, solid, fr. Skt *pakva;* akin to Gk *pessein* to cook — more at COOK] (1776) **:** GENUINE, AUTHENTIC; *also* **:** FIRST-CLASS
pul \ˈpül\ *n, pl* **puls** \ˈpülz\ *or* **pul** [Pers *pūl*] (1927) — see *afghani* at MONEY table
pu·la \ˈpü-lə, ˈpyü-\ *n, pl* **pula** [Tswana, lit., rain (used as a greeting)] (1976) — see MONEY table
Pu·las·ki \pə-ˈlas-kē, pyü-\ *n* [Edward C. *Pulaski,* †1931 Am. forest ranger] (1924) **:** a single-bit ax with an adze-shaped hoe extending from the back
pul·chri·tude \ˈpəl-krə-ˌtüd, -ˌtyüd\ *n* [ME, fr. L *pulchritudin-, pulchritudo,* fr. *pulchr-, pulcher* beautiful] (15c) **:** physical comeliness — **pul·chri·tu·di·nous** \ˌpəl-krə-ˈtüd-nəs, -ˈtyüd-; -ˈtü-dᵊn-əs, -ˈtyü-\ *adj*
pule \ˈpyül\ *vi* **puled; pul·ing** [prob. imit.] (1534) **:** WHINE, WHIMPER
pu·li \ˈpu̇-lē, ˈpyü-\ *n, pl* **pu·lik** \-lik\ *or* **pulis** \-lēz\ [Hung] (1936) **:** any of a breed of medium-sized agile Hungarian sheepdogs with a thick woolly coat hanging in long thin cords
Pu·lit·zer Prize \ˈpu̇-lət-sər-, ˈpyü-\ *n* (1918) **:** any of various annual prizes (as for outstanding literary or journalistic achievement) established by the will of Joseph Pulitzer — called also *Pulitzer*
[1]**pull** \ˈpu̇l *also* ˈpəl\ *vb* [ME, fr. OE *pullian;* akin to MLG *pulen* to shell, cull] *vt* (bef. 12c) **1 a :** to exert force upon so as to cause or tend to cause motion toward the force **b :** to stretch (cooling candy) repeatedly ⟨~ taffy⟩ **c :** to strain abnormally ⟨~ a tendon⟩ **d :** to hold back (a racehorse) from winning **e :** to work (an oar) by drawing back strongly **2 a :** to draw out from the skin ⟨~ feathers from a rooster's tail⟩ **b :** to pluck from a plant or by the roots ⟨~ flowers⟩ ⟨~ turnips⟩ **c :** EXTRACT ⟨~ a tooth⟩ **3 :** to hit (a ball) toward the left from a right-handed swing or toward the right from a left-handed swing — compare PUSH **4 :** to draw apart **:** REND, TEAR **5 :** to print (as a proof) by impression **6 :** to remove from a place or situation ⟨~ the engine⟩ ⟨~*ed* the pitcher in the third inning⟩ ⟨~*ed* the show⟩ **7 :** to bring (a weapon) into the open ⟨~*ed* a knife⟩ **8 a :** PERFORM, CARRY OUT ⟨~ an all-nighter⟩ ⟨~ guard duty⟩ **b :** COMMIT, PERPETRATE ⟨~ a robbery⟩ ⟨~ a prank⟩ **9 a :** PUT ON, ASSUME ⟨~ a grin⟩ **b :** to act or behave in the manner of ⟨~*ed* a Horace Greely and went west —Steve Rushin⟩ **10 a :** to draw the support or attention of **:** ATTRACT ⟨~ votes⟩ — often used with *in* **b :** OBTAIN, SECURE ⟨~*ed* a B in the course⟩ **11 :** to demand or obtain an advantage over someone by the assertion of ⟨~ rank⟩ ~ *vi* **1 a :** to use force in drawing, dragging, or tugging **b :** to move esp. through the exercise of mechanical energy ⟨the car ~*ed* clear of the rut⟩ **c** (1) **:** to take a drink (2) **:** to draw hard in smoking ⟨~*ed* at a pipe⟩ **d :** to strain against the bit **2 :** to draw a gun **3 :** to admit of being pulled **4 :** to feel or express strong sympathy **:** ROOT ⟨~*ing* for my team to win⟩ **5** *of an offensive lineman in football* **:** to move back from the line of scrimmage and toward one flank to provide blocking for a ballcarrier — **pull·er** *n* — **pull a face :** to make a face **:** GRIMACE — **pull a fast one :** to perpetrate a trick or fraud — **pull punches** *also* **pull a punch :** to refrain from using all the force at one's disposal — **pull oneself together :** to regain one's composure — **pull one's leg :** to deceive someone playfully **:** HOAX — **pull one's weight :** to do one's full share of the work — **pull stakes** *or* **pull up stakes :** to move out **:** LEAVE — **pull strings** *also* **pull wires :** to exert hidden influence or control — **pull the plug 1 :** to disconnect a medical life-support system **2 :** to withdraw essential and esp. financial support — **pull the rug from under :** to weaken or unsettle esp. by removing support or assistance from — **pull the string :** to throw a changeup — **pull the trigger :** to make a decisive move or action — **pull the wool over one's eyes :** to blind to the true situation **:** HOODWINK — **pull together :** to work in harmony **:** COOPERATE
[2]**pull** *n, often attrib* (14c) **1 a :** the act or an instance of pulling **b** (1) **:** a draft of liquid (2) **:** an inhalation of smoke **c :** the effort expended in moving ⟨a long ~ uphill⟩ **d :** force required to overcome resistance to pulling ⟨a trigger with a four pound ~⟩ **2 a :** ADVANTAGE **b :** special influence **3 :** PROOF 6a **4 :** a device for pulling something or for operating by pulling ⟨a drawer ~⟩ **5 :** a force that attracts, compels, or influences **:** ATTRACTION **6 :** an injury resulting from abnormal straining or stretching ⟨a muscle ~⟩ ⟨a groin ~⟩
pull away *vi* (ca. 1934) **1 :** to draw oneself back or away **:** WITHDRAW **2 :** to move off or ahead
pull·back \ˈpu̇l-ˌbak\ *n* (1668) **:** a pulling back; *esp* **:** an orderly withdrawal of troops from a position or area
pull–down *adj* (1984) **:** being or appearing below a selected item (as an icon) in a window overlaying the original view on a computer display ⟨a ~ menu⟩
pull down *vt* (15c) **1 a :** DEMOLISH, DESTROY **b :** to hunt down **:** OVERCOME **2 a :** to bring to a lower level **:** REDUCE **b :** to depress in health, strength, or spirits **3 :** to draw or earn (as wages or salary)
pul·let \ˈpu̇-lət\ *n* [ME *polet,* fr. AF *pullet* young bird, chicken, dim. of *pulle, poule* young animal, fr. LL *pullus,* fr. L, young animal, chicken, sprout — more at FOAL] (14c) **:** a young hen; *specif* **:** a hen of the domestic chicken less than a year old
pul·ley \ˈpu̇-lē\ *n, pl* **pulleys** [ME *poley, pully,* fr. AF *pulie,* prob. ultim. fr. Gk *polos* axis, pole — more at POLE] (14c) **1 :** a sheave or small wheel with a grooved rim and with or without the block in which it runs used singly with a rope or chain to change the direction and point of application of a pulling force and in various combinations to increase the applied force esp. for lifting weights **2 :** a pulley or pulleys with ropes to form a tackle that constitutes one of the simple machines **3 :** a wheel used to transmit power by means of a band, belt, cord, rope, or chain passing over its rim

pulley 2

pull in *vt* (1605) **1 :** CHECK, RESTRAIN **2 :** ARREST ~ *vi* **:** to arrive at a destination or come to a stop
Pull·man \ˈpu̇l-mən\ *n* [George M. *Pullman*] (1867) **1 :** a railroad passenger car with specially comfortable furnishings for day or esp. for night travel **2 :** a large suitcase
pull off *vt* (1883) **:** to carry out despite difficulties **:** accomplish successfully against odds ⟨the team *pulled off* an upset⟩
pul·lo·rum disease \pə-ˈlȯr-əm-\ *n* [NL *pullorum* (specific epithet of *Salmonella pullorum*), fr. L, of chickens (gen. pl. of *pullus*)] (1929) **:** a destructive typically diarrheal salmonellosis esp. of young domestic chickens that is caused by a bacterium (*Salmonella pullorum*)
pull·out \ˈpu̇l-ˌau̇t\ *n* (1825) **1 :** the act or an instance of pulling out: as **a :** the action in which an airplane goes from a dive to horizontal flight **b :** PULLBACK **2 :** something that can be pulled out
pull out *vi* (1855) **1 :** LEAVE, DEPART **2 :** WITHDRAW
[1]**pull·over** \ˈpu̇l-ˌō-vər\ *n* (1899) **:** a pullover garment (as a sweater)
[2]**pullover** *adj* (1907) **:** put on by being pulled over the head
pull over *vi* (1930) **:** to steer one's vehicle to the side of the road ~ *vt* **:** to cause to pull over ⟨*pulled* him *over* for speeding⟩
pull quote *n* (1978) **:** a significant passage in an article, story, book, or speech that is quoted and used for drawing attention to its source
pull round *vi* (1891) *chiefly Brit* **:** to regain one's health ~ *vt, chiefly Brit* **:** to restore to good health
pull tab *n* (1963) **:** a metal tab (as on a can) pulled to open the container
pull through *vi* (1852) **:** to survive a dangerous or difficult situation ~ *vt* **:** to help survive a dangerous or difficult situation
pul·lu·late \ˈpəl-yə-ˌlāt\ *vi* **-lat·ed; -lat·ing** [L *pullulatus,* pp. of *pullulare,* fr. *pullulus,* dim. of *pullus* chicken, sprout — more at FOAL] (1619) **1 a :** GERMINATE, SPROUT **b :** to breed or produce freely ⟨the country's *pullulating* population⟩ **2 :** SWARM, TEEM ⟨the island *pullulated* with tourists⟩ — **pul·lu·la·tion** \ˌpəl-yə-ˈlā-shən\ *n*
pull–up \ˈpu̇l-ˌəp\ *n* (1938) **:** CHIN-UP
pull up *vt* (1623) **1 :** to bring to a stop **:** HALT **2 :** CHECK, REBUKE ~ *vi* **1 a :** to check oneself **b :** to come to an often abrupt halt **:** STOP **2 :** to draw even with others in a race
pul·mo·nary \ˈpu̇l-mə-ˌner-ē, ˈpəl-\ *adj* [L *pulmonarius,* fr. *pulmon-, pulmo* lung; akin to Gk *pleumōn* lung, Skt *kloman* right lung] (1704) **1 a :** of, relating to, affecting, or occurring in the lungs ⟨~ tissue⟩ ⟨~ edema⟩ **b :** carried on by the lungs ⟨~ respiration⟩ **2 :** PULMONATE **3 :** occurring in the pulmonary artery ⟨a ~ embolism⟩
pulmonary artery *n* (1704) **:** an artery that conveys venous blood from the heart to the lungs — see HEART illustration
pulmonary circulation *n* (ca. 1890) **:** the passage of blood from the right side of the heart through arteries to the lungs where it picks up oxygen and is returned to the left side of the heart by veins
pulmonary vein *n* (1704) **:** a valveless vein that returns oxygenated blood from the lungs to the heart
[1]**pul·mo·nate** \ˈpu̇l-mə-ˌnāt, ˈpəl-\ *adj* [L *pulmon-, pulmo* lung] (ca. 1859) **1 :** having lungs or organs resembling lungs **2 :** of or relating to a subclass (Pulmonata) of gastropod mollusks having a respiratory sac and comprising most land snails and slugs and many freshwater snails
[2]**pulmonate** *n* (1883) **:** a pulmonate gastropod
pul·mon·ic \pu̇l-ˈmä-nik, ˌpəl-\ *adj* [L *pulmon-, pulmo*] (1661) **:** PULMONARY
pul·mo·nol·o·gist \ˌpu̇l-mə-ˈnä-lə-jəst, ˌpəl-\ *n* [L *pulmon-, pulmo* + E *-ologist* (as in *cardiologist*)] (1979) **:** a specialist in the anatomy, physiology, and pathology of the lungs
pul·mo·tor \ˈpu̇l-ˌmō-tər, ˈpəl-\ *n* [fr. *Pulmotor,* a trademark] (1911) **:** a respiratory apparatus for pumping oxygen or air into and out of the lungs (as of an asphyxiated person)
[1]**pulp** \ˈpəlp\ *n* [ME *pulpe,* fr. L *pulpa* flesh, pulp] (14c) **1 a** (1) **:** the soft, succulent part of a fruit usu. composed of mesocarp (2) **:** stem pith when soft and spongy **b :** a soft mass of vegetable matter (as of apples) from which most of the water has been extracted by pressure **c :** the soft sensitive tissue that fills the central cavity of a tooth — see TOOTH illustration **d :** a material prepared by chemical or mechanical means from various materials (as wood or rags) for use in making paper and cellulose products **2 :** pulverized ore mixed with water **3 a :** pulpy condition or character **b :** something in such a condition or having such a character **4 :** a magazine or book printed on cheap paper (as newsprint) and often dealing with sensational material; *also* **:** sensational or tabloid writing — often used attributively ⟨~ fiction⟩ — **pulp·i·ness** \ˈpəl-pē-nəs\ *n* — **pulpy** \ˈpəl-pē\ *adj*
[2]**pulp** *vt* (1683) **1 :** to reduce to pulp ⟨~*ed* unsold copies of the book⟩ **2 :** to cause to appear pulpy **3 :** to deprive of the pulp ~ *vi* **:** to become pulp or pulpy — **pulp·er** *n*
pulp·al \ˈpəl-pəl\ *adj* (1903) **:** of or relating to pulp esp. of a tooth ⟨a ~ abscess⟩ — **pulp·al·ly** \ˈpəl-pə-lē\ *adv*
pul·pit \ˈpu̇l-ˌpit, ˈpəl-, -pət\ *n* [ME, fr. AF, fr. LL *pulpitum,* fr. L, staging, platform] (14c) **1 :** an elevated platform or high reading desk used in preaching or conducting a worship service **2 a :** the preaching profession **b :** a preaching position
pulp·wood \ˈpəlp-ˌwu̇d\ *n* (1885) **:** a wood (as of aspen, hemlock, pine, or spruce) used in making pulp for paper

\ə\ **abut** \ᵊ\ kitten, F table \ər\ **further** \a\ **ash** \ā\ **ace** \ä\ mop, mar \au̇\ **out** \ch\ **chin** \e\ bet \ē\ **easy** \g\ **go** \i\ **hit** \ī\ **ice** \j\ **job** \ŋ\ **sing** \ō\ **go** \ȯ\ **law** \ȯi\ **boy** \th\ **thin** \t͟h\ **the** \ü\ **loot** \u̇\ **foot** \y\ yet \zh\ **vision, beige** \k̟, ⁿ, œ, ue, ʸ\ *see* Guide to Pronunciation

pul·que \ˈpül-ˌkā; ˈpül-kē, ˈpu̇l-\ *n* [MexSp] (1693) **:** a Mexican alcoholic beverage made from the fermented sap of various agaves (as *Agave atrovirens*)

pul·sant \ˈpəl-sənt\ *adj* (1709) **:** pulsating with activity

pul·sar \ˈpəl-ˌsär\ *n* [*pulse* + *-ar* (as in *quasar*)] (1968) **:** a celestial source of pulsating electromagnetic radiation (as radio waves) characterized by a short relatively constant interval (as .033 second) between pulses that is held to be a rotating neutron star

pul·sate \ˈpəl-ˌsāt *also* ˌpəl-ˈ\ *vi* **pul·sat·ed; pul·sat·ing** [L *pulsatus*, pp. of *pulsare*, freq. of *pellere*] (1744) **1 :** to throb or move rhythmically **:** VIBRATE **2 :** to exhibit a pulse or pulsation **:** BEAT

pul·sa·tile \ˈpəl-sə-tᵊl, -ˌtī(-ə)l\ *adj* (1541) **:** of or marked by pulsation

pul·sa·tion \ˌpəl-ˈsā-shən\ *n* (15c) **1 :** rhythmical throbbing or vibrating (as of an artery); *also* **:** a single beat or throb **2 :** a periodically recurring alternate increase and decrease of a quantity (as pressure, volume, or voltage)

pul·sa·tor \ˈpəl-ˌsā-tər, ˌpəl-ˈ\ *n* (1890) **:** something that beats or throbs in working

[1]**pulse** \ˈpəls\ *n* [ME *puls*, prob. fr. AF *puuiz* gruel, fr. L *pult-, puls*, prob. fr. Gk *poltos*] (13c) **:** the edible seeds of various crops (as peas, beans, or lentils) of the legume family; *also* **:** a plant yielding pulse

[2]**pulse** *n* [ME *puls*, fr. AF, fr. L *pulsus*, lit., beating, fr. *pellere* to drive, push, beat — more at FELT] (14c) **1 a :** the regular expansion of an artery caused by the ejection of blood into the arterial system by the contractions of the heart **b :** the palpable beat resulting from such pulse as detected in a superficial artery; *also* **:** the number of individual beats in a specified time period (as one minute) ⟨a resting ~ of 70⟩ **2 a :** underlying sentiment or opinion or an indication of it **b :** VITALITY **3 a :** rhythmical beating, vibrating, or sounding **b :** BEAT, THROB **4 a :** a transient variation of a quantity (as electric current or voltage) whose value is normally constant **b (1) :** an electromagnetic wave or modulation thereof of brief duration **(2) :** a brief disturbance of pressure in a medium; *esp* **:** a sound wave or short train of sound waves **5 :** a dose of a substance esp. when applied over a short period of time ⟨~*s* of intravenous methylprednisolone⟩

[3]**pulse** *vb* **pulsed; puls·ing** *vi* (15c) **:** to exhibit a pulse or pulsation **:** THROB ~ *vt* **1 :** to drive by or as if by a pulsation **2 :** to cause to pulsate **3 a :** to produce or modulate (as electromagnetic waves) in the form of pulses ⟨*pulsed* waves⟩ **b :** to cause (an apparatus) to produce pulses — **puls·er** *n*

pulse–jet engine \ˈpəls-ˈjet-\ *n* (1946) **:** a jet engine designed to produce a pulsating thrust by the intermittent flow of hot gases

pulse oximeter *n* (1986) **:** a device that measures the oxygen saturation of arterial blood in a subject by utilizing a sensor attached typically to a finger, toe, or ear to determine the percentage of oxyhemoglobin in blood pulsating through a network of capillaries

pulv *abbr* [L *pulvis*] powder

pul·ver·a·ble \ˈpəl-və-rə-bəl, ˈpəlv-rə-\ *adj* (ca. 1617) **:** capable of being pulverized

pul·ver·ise *Brit var of* PULVERIZE

pul·ver·ize \ˈpəl-və-ˌrīz\ *vb* **-ized; -iz·ing** [ME, fr. LL *pulverizare*, fr. L *pulver-, pulvis* dust, powder — more at POWDER] *vt* (15c) **1 :** to reduce (as by crushing, beating, or grinding) to very small particles **:** ATOMIZE ⟨~ rock⟩ **2 :** ANNIHILATE, DEMOLISH ~ *vi* **:** to become pulverized — **pul·ver·iz·able** \ˌpəl-və-ˈrī-zə-bəl\ *adj* — **pul·ver·i·za·tion** \ˌpəl-və-rə-ˈzā-shən, ˌpəlv-rə-\ *n* — **pul·ver·iz·er** \ˈpəl-və-ˌrī-zər\ *n*

pul·ver·u·lent \ˌpəl-ˈver-yə-lənt, -ˈver-ə-\ *adj* [L *pulverulentus* dusty, fr. *pulver-, pulvis*] (ca. 1656) **1 :** consisting of or reducible to fine powder **2 :** being or looking dusty **:** CRUMBLY

pul·vi·nus \ˌpəl-ˈvī-nəs, -ˈvē-\ *n, pl* **-vi·ni** \-ˈvī-ˌnī, -ˈvē-(ˌ)nē\ [NL, fr. L, cushion] (ca. 1857) **:** a swelling at the base of a petiole or petiolule

pu·ma \ˈpü-mə, ˈpyü-\ *n, pl* **pumas** *also* **puma** [Sp, fr. Quechua] (1774) **:** COUGAR 1; *also* **:** the fur or pelt of a cougar

pum·ice \ˈpə-məs\ *n* [ME *pomis*, fr. AF *pomice*, fr. L *pumic-, pumex* — more at FOAM] (15c) **:** a volcanic glass full of cavities and very low in density that is used esp. in powder form for smoothing and polishing — **pu·mi·ceous** \pyü-ˈmi-shəs, ˌpə-\ *adj*

pum·ic·ite \ˈpə-mə-ˌsīt\ *n* (1916) **:** PUMICE

pum·mel \ˈpə-məl\ *vb* **-meled** *also* **-melled; -mel·ing** *also* **-mel·ling** \ˈpə-mə-liŋ, ˈpəm-liŋ\ [alter. of *pommel*] (1548) **:** POUND, BEAT

pummelo *var of* POMELO 2

[1]**pump** \ˈpəmp\ *n* [ME *pumpe, pompe;* akin to MLG *pumpe* pump, MD *pompe*] (15c) **1 :** a device that raises, transfers, delivers, or compresses fluids or that attenuates gases esp. by suction or pressure or both **2 :** HEART **3 :** an act or the process of pumping **4 :** an energy source (as light) for pumping atoms or molecules **5 :** a biological mechanism by which atoms, ions, or molecules are transported across cell membranes — compare SODIUM PUMP

[2]**pump** *vi* (1508) **1 :** to work a pump **:** raise or move a fluid with a pump **2 :** to exert oneself to pump or as if to pump something **3 :** to move in a manner that resembles the action of a pump handle ~ *vt* **1 a :** to raise (as water) with a pump **b :** to draw fluid from with a pump **2 :** to pour forth, deliver, or draw with or as if with a pump ⟨~*ed* money into the economy⟩ ⟨~ new life into the classroom⟩ **3 a :** to question persistently ⟨~*ed* him for the information⟩ **b :** to elicit by persistent questioning **4 a :** to operate by manipulating a lever **b :** to manipulate as if operating a pump handle ⟨~*ed* my hand warmly⟩ **c :** to cause to move with an action resembling that of a pump handle ⟨a runner ~*ing* her arms⟩ **5 :** to transport (as ions) against a concentration gradient by the expenditure of energy **6 a :** to excite (as atoms or molecules) esp. so as to cause emission of coherent monochromatic electromagnetic radiation (as in a laser) **b :** to energize (as a laser) by pumping — **pump iron :** to lift weights

[3]**pump** *n* [origin unknown] (1555) **:** a shoe that grips the foot chiefly at the toe and heel; *esp* **:** a close-fitting woman's dress shoe with a moderate to high heel

pumped \ˈpəm(p)t\ *adj* (1984) **:** filled with energetic excitement and enthusiasm ⟨~ for the football game⟩

pumped storage *n* (1927) **:** a hydroelectric system in which electricity is generated during periods of high demand by the use of water that has been pumped into a reservoir at a higher altitude during periods of low demand

pump·er \ˈpəm-pər\ *n* (1657) **:** one that pumps; *esp* **:** a fire truck equipped with a pump

pum·per·nick·el \ˈpəm-pər-ˌni-kəl\ *n* [G, fr. *pumpern* to break wind + *Nickel* goblin; fr. its reputed indigestibility] (1756) **:** a dark coarse sourdough bread made of unbolted rye flour

pump fake *n* (1977) **:** a fake in which a player simulates throwing a pass (as in football) or taking a shot (as in basketball) — **pump–fake** *vb*

pump·kin \ˈpəm(p)-kən, ÷ˈpəŋ-kən\ *n, often attrib* [alter. of earlier *pumpion*, modif. of F *popon, pompon* melon, pumpkin, fr. L *pepon-, pepo*, fr. Gk *pepōn*, fr. *pepōn* ripened; akin to Gk *pessein* to cook, ripen — more at COOK] (1654) **1 a :** a fruit of any of various cultivars of herbaceous plants (*Cucurbita pepo, C. maxima, C. moschata,* and *C. mixta* syn. *C. argyrosperma*) of the gourd family that is typically round and orange but may be another color or shape, that has a hard usu. smooth skin with shallow longitudinal grooves, and that is grown for ornamental use or for its fibrous pale flesh used esp. in baking or as feed for livestock **b :** any of several annual chiefly trailing American plants that bear pumpkins **2 :** a strong orange color

pump·kin·seed \-ˌsēd\ *n* (1814) **:** a brightly colored freshwater sunfish (*Lepomis gibbosus*) with a reddish spot on the operculum

pump priming *n* (1936) **:** government investment expenditures designed to induce a self-sustaining expansion of economic activity

pump up *vt* (1791) **1 a :** to fill with enthusiasm or excitement **b :** to fill with or as if with air **:** INFLATE **2 :** INCREASE 1

[1]**pun** \ˈpən\ *n* [perh. fr. It *puntiglio* fine point, quibble — more at PUNCTILIO] (1662) **:** the usu. humorous use of a word in such a way as to suggest two or more of its meanings or the meaning of another word similar in sound

[2]**pun** *vi* **punned; pun·ning** (1670) **:** to make puns

pu·na \ˈpü-nə\ *n* [AmerSp, fr. Quechua] (1613) **:** a treeless windswept tableland or basin in the higher Andes

[1]**punch** \ˈpənch\ *n* [ME *pounce, punche*, prob. alter. of *ponson, ponchon* puncheon] (14c) **1 a :** a tool usu. in the form of a short rod of steel that is variously shaped at one end for different operations (as forming, perforating, embossing, or cutting) **b :** a short tapering steel rod for driving the heads of nails below a surface **c :** a steel die faced with a letter in relief that is forced into a softer metal to form an intaglio matrix from which foundry type is cast **d :** a device or machine for cutting holes or notches (as in paper or cardboard) **2 :** a hole or notch from a perforating operation

[2]**punch** *vb* [ME *pouncen, punchen* to emboss, pierce, prob. fr. *pounce*, n.] *vt* (14c) **1 a :** PROD, POKE **b :** DRIVE, HERD ⟨~*ing* cattle⟩ **2 a :** to strike with a forward thrust esp. of the fist **b :** to drive or push forcibly by or as if by a punch **c :** to hit (a ball) with less than a full swing **3 :** to emboss, cut, perforate, or make with or as if with a punch **4 a :** to push down so as to produce a desired result ⟨~ buttons on a jukebox⟩ **b :** to hit or press down the operating mechanism of ⟨~ a typewriter⟩ **c :** to insert a time card into (a time clock) **d :** to produce by or as if by punching keys ⟨~ out a tune on the piano⟩ **e :** to enter (as data) by punching keys **5 :** to give emphasis to ~ *vi* **1 :** to perform the action of punching something **2 :** to move or push forward esp. by a sudden forceful effort ⟨~*ed* into enemy territory⟩ — **punch·er** *n*

[3]**punch** *n* (14c) **1 :** the action of punching **2 :** a quick blow with or as if with the fist **3 :** effective energy or forcefulness ⟨a story that packs a ~⟩ ⟨political ~⟩ — **punch·less** \ˈpənch-ləs\ *adj* — **to the punch :** to the first blow or to decisive action — usu. used with *beat*

[4]**punch** *n* [perh. fr. Hindi & Urdu *pãc* five, fr. Skt *pañca;* akin to Gk *pente* five; fr. its orig. having five ingredients — more at FIVE] (1632) **:** a hot or cold drink that is usu. a combination of hard liquor, wine, or beer and nonalcoholic beverages; *also* **:** a drink that is a mixture of nonalcoholic beverages

Punch–and–Judy show \ˌpənch-ən-ˈjü-dē-\ *n* (1870) **:** a traditional puppet show in which the little hook-nosed puppet Punch fights comically with his wife Judy

punch·ball \ˈpənch-ˌbȯl\ *n* (1932) **:** baseball adapted for small areas in which a rubber ball is hit with a fist instead of a bat

punch·board \-ˌbȯrd\ *n* (1912) **:** a small board that has many holes each filled with a rolled-up printed slip to be punched out on payment of a nominal sum in an effort to obtain a slip that entitles the player to a designated prize

punch bowl *n* (1680) **:** a large bowl from which a beverage (as punch) is served

punch card *n* (1919) **:** a card in which holes are punched in designated positions to represent data — called also *Hollerith card, punched card*

punch–drunk \ˈpənch-ˌdrəŋk\ *adj* [[2]*punch*] (1918) **1 :** suffering cerebral injury typically marked by mental confusion, incoordination, and slurred speech and usu. resulting from minute brain hemorrhages caused by repeated head blows in boxing **2 :** behaving as if punch-drunk **:** DAZED, CONFUSED

[1]**pun·cheon** \ˈpən-chən\ *n* [ME *ponson, punchon*, fr. AF *ponchon* pointed tool, support, ultim. fr. VL **punctiare* to prick, pierce, fr. L *punctum*, supine of *pungere* — more at PUNGENT] (14c) **1 :** a pointed tool for piercing or for working on stone **2 a :** a short upright framing timber **b :** a split log or heavy slab with the face smoothed

[2]**puncheon** *n* [ME *punchon*, fr. AF *ponchon*, prob. fr. MF *poinçon* mark on goods certifying their origin] (15c) **:** a large cask of varying capacity

punch in *vi* (1926) **:** to record the time of one's arrival or beginning work by punching a time clock

pun·chi·nel·lo \ˌpən-chə-ˈne-(ˌ)lō\ *n* [modif. of It dial. *polecenella*] (1666) **1** *cap* **:** a fat short humpbacked clown or buffoon in Italian puppet shows **2** *pl* **-los :** a squat grotesque person

punch·ing bag \ˈpən-chiŋ-\ *n* (1886) **1 :** a stuffed or inflated bag usu. suspended for free movement and punched for exercise or for training in boxing **2 :** one who is routinely abused or defeated by another

punch line *n* (1921) **:** the sentence, statement, or phrase (as in a joke) that makes the point

punch list *n* (1955) **:** a list of usu. minor tasks to be completed at the end of a project

punch–out \ˈpənch-ˌau̇t\ *n* (1973) **1 :** FISTFIGHT **2 :** STRIKEOUT

punch out *vi* (1928) **1 :** to record the time of one's stopping work or departure by punching a time clock **2 :** to bail out of an aircraft using an ejection seat ~ *vt* **1 :** to beat up **2 :** STRIKE OUT

punch press (1911) **:** a press equipped with cutting, shaping, or combination dies for working on material (as metal)

punch–up \ˈpənch-ˌəp\ *n* (1958) *chiefly Brit* **:** FISTFIGHT

punch up *vt* (ca. 1959) : to give energy or forcefulness to ⟨jokes added to *punch up* a speech⟩

punchy \ˈpən-chē\ *adj* **punch·i·er; -est** (1917) **1 a :** having punch : FORCEFUL, SPIRITED **b :** VIVID, VIBRANT ⟨~ video graphics⟩ **2 :** PUNCH-DRUNK 2

punc·tate \ˈpəŋk-ˌtāt\ *adj* [NL *punctatus,* fr. L *punctum* point — more at POINT] (ca. 1760) **1 :** marked with minute spots or depressions ⟨a ~ leaf⟩ **2 :** characterized by dots or points ⟨~ skin lesions⟩ — **punc·ta·tion** \ˌpəŋk-ˈtā-shən\ *n*

punc·til·io \ˌpəŋk-ˈti-lē-ˌō\ *n, pl* **-i·os** [It & Sp; It *puntiglio* point of honor, scruple, fr. Sp *puntillo,* fr. dim. of *punto* point, fr. L *punctum*] (1596) **1 :** a minute detail of conduct in a ceremony or in observance of a code **2 :** careful observance of forms (as in social conduct)

punc·til·i·ous \-lē-əs\ *adj* (1634) : marked by or concerned about precise accordance with the details of codes or conventions *syn* see CAREFUL — **punc·til·i·ous·ly** *adv* — **punc·til·i·ous·ness** *n*

punc·tu·al \ˈpəŋk-chə-wəl, -chəl\ *adj* [ME, having a sharp point, fr. ML *punctualis* of a point, fr. L *punctus* pricking, point, fr. *pungere* to prick — more at PUNGENT] (1675) : being on time : PROMPT — **punc·tu·al·i·ty** \ˌpəŋk-chə-ˈwa-lə-tē\ *n* — **punc·tu·al·ly** \ˈpəŋk-chə-wə-lē, -chə-lē\ *adv*

punc·tu·ate \ˈpəŋk-chə-ˌwāt\ *vb* **-at·ed; -at·ing** [ML *punctuatus,* pp. of *punctuare* to point, provide with punctuation marks, fr. L *punctus* point] *vt* (ca. 1766) **1 :** to mark or divide (written matter) with punctuation marks **2 :** to break into or interrupt at intervals ⟨the steady click of her needles *punctuated* the silence —Edith Wharton⟩ **3 :** ACCENTUATE, EMPHASIZE ~ *vi* : to use punctuation marks — **punc·tu·a·tor** \-ˌwā-tər\ *n*

punctuated equilibrium *n* (1978) : evolution that is characterized by long periods of stability in the characteristics of an organism and short periods of rapid change during which new forms appear esp. from small subpopulations of the ancestral form in restricted parts of its geographic range; *also* : a theory or model of evolution emphasizing this — compare GRADUALISM 2

punc·tu·a·tion \ˌpəŋk-chə-ˈwā-shən\ *n* (ca. 1539) **1 :** the act of punctuating : the state of being punctuated **2 :** the act or practice of inserting standardized marks or signs in written matter to clarify the meaning and separate structural units; *also* : a system of punctuation **3 :** something that contrasts or accentuates

punctuation mark *n* (1860) : any of various standardized marks or signs used in punctuation

PUNCTUATION MARKS

.	period (*or chiefly Brit* full stop)
,	comma
;	semicolon
:	colon
'	apostrophe
' '	quotation marks, single (*or chiefly Brit* inverted commas)
" "	quotation marks, double (*or chiefly Brit* inverted commas)
« »	guillemets
?	question mark
¿ ?	question marks, Spanish
!	exclamation point
¡ !	exclamation points, Spanish
‽	interrobang
@	at sign
/	slash (*or diagonal or slant or solidus or virgule*)
\	backslash
. . .	ellipsis
-	hyphen
⸗	double hyphen
–	dash (*or en dash*)
—	dash (*or em dash*)
~	swung dash
( )	parentheses
[ ]	brackets, square (*or brackets*)
⟨ ⟩	brackets, angle
{ }	braces (*or curly brackets*)

¹punc·ture \ˈpəŋk-chər\ *n* [ME, fr. L *punctura,* fr. *punctus,* pp. of *pungere*] (14c) **1 :** an act of puncturing **2 :** a hole, wound, or perforation made by puncturing **3 :** a minute depression

²puncture *vb* **punc·tured; punc·tur·ing** \ˈpəŋk-chə-riŋ, ˈpəŋk-shriŋ\ *vt* (1699) **1 :** to pierce with or as if with a pointed instrument or object **2 :** to make useless or ineffective as if by a puncture : DEFLATE ~ *vi* : to become punctured

puncture vine *n* (1911) : an Old World annual prostrate herb (*Tribulus terrestris*) of the caltrop family that has hard spiny pods and is a troublesome weed esp. in the western U.S. — called also *caltrop*

pun·dit \ˈpən-dət\ *n* [Hindi *paṇḍit,* fr. Skt *paṇḍita,* fr. *paṇḍita* learned] (1672) **1 :** PANDIT **2 :** a learned man : TEACHER **3 :** a person who gives opinions in an authoritative manner usu. through the mass media : CRITIC — **pun·dit·ry** \-də-trē\ *n*

pun·dit·oc·ra·cy \ˌpən-dət-ˈä-krə-sē\ *n, pl* **-cies** [*pundit* + *-cracy*] (1987) : a group of powerful and influential political commentators

pung \ˈpəŋ\ *n* [short for earlier *tow-pong,* fr. Algonquian origin; akin to Micmac *tobăgun* drag made with skin] (1825) *NewEng* : a sleigh with a box-shaped body

pun·gen·cy \ˈpən-jən(t)-sē\ *n* (1649) : the quality or state of being pungent

pun·gent \-jənt\ *adj* [L *pungent-, pungens,* prp. of *pungere* to prick, sting; akin to L *pugnus* fist, *pugnare* to fight, Gk *pygmē* fist] (1597) **1 :** sharply painful **2 :** having a stiff and sharp point ⟨~ leaves⟩ **3 a :** marked by a sharp incisive quality : CAUSTIC ⟨a ~ critic⟩ ⟨~ language⟩ **b :** being sharp and to the point **4 a :** causing a sharp or irri-

tating sensation; *esp* : ACRID **b :** having an intense flavor or odor ⟨a ~ chili⟩ — **pun·gent·ly** *adv*

syn PUNGENT, PIQUANT, POIGNANT, RACY mean sharp and stimulating to the mind or the senses. PUNGENT implies a sharp, stinging, or biting quality esp. of odors ⟨a cheese with a *pungent* odor⟩. PIQUANT suggests a power to whet the appetite or interest through tartness or mild pungency ⟨a *piquant* sauce⟩. POIGNANT suggests something sharply or piercingly effective in stirring one's emotions ⟨felt a *poignant* sense of loss⟩. RACY implies having a strongly characteristic natural quality fresh and unimpaired ⟨spontaneous, *racy* prose⟩.

pun·gle \ˈpəŋ-gəl\ *vb* **pun·gled; pun·gling** \ˈpəŋ-g(ə-)liŋ\ [Sp *póngale* put it down] *vt* (1851) : to make a payment or contribution of (money) — usu. used with *up* ~ *vi* : PAY, CONTRIBUTE — usu. used with *up*

¹Pu·nic \ˈpyü-nik\ *adj* [L *punicus,* fr. *Poenus* inhabitant of Carthage; akin to Gk *Phoinix* Phoenician] (1533) **1 :** of or relating to Carthage or the Carthaginians **2 :** FAITHLESS, TREACHEROUS

²Punic *n* (1673) : the Phoenician dialect of ancient Carthage

pun·ish \ˈpə-nish\ *vb* [ME *punisshen,* fr. AF *puniss-,* stem of *punir,* fr. L *punire,* fr. *poena* penalty — more at PAIN] *vt* (14c) **1 a :** to impose a penalty on for a fault, offense, or violation **b :** to inflict a penalty for the commission of (an offense) in retribution or retaliation **2 a :** to deal with roughly or harshly **b :** to inflict injury on : HURT ~ *vi* : to inflict punishment — **pun·ish·abil·i·ty** \ˌpə-nish-ə-ˈbi-lə-tē\ *n* — **pun·ish·able** \ˈpə-nish-ə-bəl\ *adj* — **pun·ish·er** *n*

syn PUNISH, CHASTISE, CASTIGATE, CHASTEN, DISCIPLINE, CORRECT mean to inflict a penalty on in requital for wrongdoing. PUNISH implies subjecting to a penalty for wrongdoing ⟨*punished* for stealing⟩. CHASTISE may apply to either the infliction of corporal punishment or to verbal censure or denunciation ⟨*chastised* his son for neglecting his studies⟩. CASTIGATE usu. implies a severe, typically public censure ⟨an editorial *castigating* the entire city council⟩. CHASTEN suggests any affliction or trial that leaves one humbled or subdued ⟨*chastened* by a landslide election defeat⟩. DISCIPLINE implies a punishing or chastening in order to bring under control ⟨parents must *discipline* their children⟩. CORRECT implies punishing aimed at reforming an offender ⟨the function of prison is to *correct* the wrongdoer⟩.

pun·ish·ment \ˈpə-nish-mənt\ *n* (15c) **1 :** the act of punishing **2 a :** suffering, pain, or loss that serves as retribution **b :** a penalty inflicted on an offender through judicial procedure **3 :** severe, rough, or disastrous treatment

pu·ni·tion \pyü-ˈni-shən\ *n* [ME *punicion,* fr. AF, fr. L *punition-, punitio,* fr. *punire*] (15c) : PUNISHMENT

pu·ni·tive \ˈpyü-nə-tiv\ *adj* [F *punitif,* fr. ML *punitivus,* fr. L *punitus,* pp. of *punire*] (1624) : inflicting, involving, or aiming at punishment ⟨severe ~ measures⟩ — **pu·ni·tive·ly** *adv* — **pu·ni·tive·ness** *n*

punitive damages *n pl* (1865) : damages awarded in excess of compensation to the plaintiff to punish a defendant for a serious wrong

Pun·jabi \ˌpən-ˈjä-bē, -ˈja-\ *n* [Hindi & Urdu *pañjābī,* fr. *pañjābī* of Punjab, fr. Pers *panjābī,* fr. *Panjāb* Punjab] (1846) **1 :** an Indo-Aryan language of the Punjab **2 :** a native or inhabitant of the Punjab region of the northwestern Indian subcontinent — **Punjabi** *adj*

¹punk \ˈpəŋk\ *n* [origin unknown] (1596) **1** *archaic* : PROSTITUTE **2** [prob. partly fr. ³*punk*] : NONSENSE, FOOLISHNESS **3 a :** a young inexperienced person : BEGINNER, NOVICE; *esp* : a young man **b :** a usu. petty gangster, hoodlum, or ruffian **c** *slang* : a young man used as a homosexual partner esp. in a prison **4 a :** PUNK ROCK **b :** a punk rock musician **c :** one who affects punk styles

²punk *adj* (1896) **1 :** very poor : INFERIOR ⟨played a ~ game⟩ **2 :** being in poor health ⟨said that she was feeling ~⟩ **3 a :** of or relating to punk rock **b :** relating to or being a style (as of dress or hair) inspired by punk rock — **punk·ish** \ˈpəŋ-kish\ *adj*

³punk *n* [perh. alter. of *spunk*] (1687) **1 :** wood so decayed as to be dry, crumbly, and useful for tinder **2 :** a preparation (as of a stick of coated wood) that burns slowly and is used to ignite fuses esp. of fireworks

pun·kah \ˈpəŋ-kə\ *n* [Hindi & Urdu *pākhā*] (1787) : a fan used esp. in India that consists of a canvas-covered frame suspended from the ceiling and that is operated by a cord

punk·er \ˈpəŋ-kər\ *n* (1977) : ¹PUNK 4b, c

pun·kie *also* **pun·ky** \ˈpəŋ-kē\ *n, pl* **punkies** [New York D *punki,* modif. of Delaware (Munsee) *pónkwas*] (1769) : BITING MIDGE

punk rock *n* (1971) : rock music marked by extreme and often deliberately offensive expressions of alienation and social discontent — **punk rocker** *n*

¹punky \ˈpəŋ-kē\ *adj* **punk·i·er; -est** [²*punk*] (1872) : resembling punk in being soft or rotted — **punk·i·ness** *n*

²punky *adj* [¹*punk*] (1972) : resembling or typical of a punk

pun·net \ˈpə-nət\ *n* [origin unknown] (ca. 1822) *Brit* : a small basket for fruits or vegetables

Pun·nett square \ˈpə-nət-\ *n* [Reginald C. *Punnett* †1967 Eng. geneticist] (1942) : an *n* × *n* square used in genetics to calculate the frequencies of the different genotypes and phenotypes among the offspring of a cross

pun·ny \ˈpə-nē\ *adj* **pun·ni·er; -est** (1947) : constituting or involving a pun

pun·ster \ˈpən(t)-stər\ *n* (1700) : one who is given to punning

¹punt \ˈpənt\ *n* [ME **punt,* fr. OE, fr. L *ponton-, ponto*] (bef. 12c) : a long narrow flat-bottomed boat with square ends usu. propelled with a pole

²punt *vt* (1816) : to propel (as a punt) with a pole

³punt *vi* [F *ponter,* fr. *ponte* point in some games, play against the banker, fr. Sp *punto* point, fr. L *punctum* — more at POINT] (1712) **1 :** to play at a gambling game against the banker **2** *Brit* : GAMBLE

⁴punt *vb* [origin unknown] *vt* (1845) : to kick (as a football or soccer ball) with the top of the foot before the ball which is dropped from the hands hits the ground ~ *vi* : to punt a ball

⁵punt *n* (1845) : the act or an instance of punting a ball

⁶punt \ˈpu̇nt\ *n* [Ir, pound, fr. E *pound*] (1975) : the monetary pound of Ireland

\ə\ abut \ᵊ\ kitten, F table \ər\ further \a\ ash \ā\ ace \ä\ mop, mar \au̇\ out \ch\ chin \e\ bet \ē\ easy \g\ go \i\ hit \ī\ ice \j\ job \ŋ\ sing \ō\ go \ȯ\ law \ȯi\ boy \th\ thin \t̲h̲\ the \ü\ loot \u̇\ foot \y\ yet \zh\ vision, beige \k̲, ⁿ, œ, ᴜᴇ, ᵜ\ *see* Guide to Pronunciation

punt·er \ˈpən-tər\ *n* (ca. 1706) **1 :** one that punts: as **a** *chiefly Brit* **:** a person who gambles; *esp* **:** one who bets against a bookmaker **b :** a person who uses a punt in boating **c :** a person who punts a ball **2** *chiefly Brit* **:** CUSTOMER, PATRON

punt formation *n* (1949) **:** an offensive football formation in which a back making a punt stands approximately 10 yards behind the line and the other backs are in blocking position close to the line

pun·ty \ˈpən-tē\ *n, pl* **punties** [F *pontil*] (1662) **:** a metal rod used for fashioning hot glass

pu·ny \ˈpyü-nē\ *adj* **pu·ni·er; -est** [AF *puisné* younger, weakly, lit., born afterward, fr. *puis* afterward + *né* born] (1593) **:** slight or inferior in power, size, or importance **:** WEAK — **pu·ni·ly** \ˈpyü-nə-lē\ *adv* — **pu·ni·ness** \ˈpyü-nē-nəs\ *n*

[1]**pup** \ˈpəp\ *n* [short for *puppy*] (1773) **1 :** a young dog; *also* **:** one of the young of various animals (as a seal or rat) **2 :** OFFSET 2a

[2]**pup** *vi* **pupped; pup·ping** (1787) **:** to give birth to pups

pu·pa \ˈpyü-pə\ *n, pl* **pu·pae** \-(ˌ)pē *also* -ˌpī\ *or* **pupas** [NL, fr. L *pupa* doll] (1815) **:** an intermediate usu. quiescent stage of a metamorphic insect (as a bee, moth, or beetle) that occurs between the larva and the imago, is usu. enclosed in a cocoon or protective covering, and undergoes internal changes by which larval structures are replaced by those typical of the imago — **pu·pal** \ˈpyü-pəl\ *adj*

pu·par·i·um \pyü-ˈper-ē-əm\ *n, pl* **pu·par·ia** \-ē-ə\ [NL, fr. *pupa*] (1815) **:** a rigid outer shell formed from the larval skin that covers some pupae (as of a dipteran fly)

pu·pate \ˈpyü-ˌpāt\ *vi* **pu·pat·ed; pu·pat·ing** (ca. 1879) **:** to become a pupa **:** pass through a pupal stage — **pu·pa·tion** \pyü-ˈpā-shən\ *n*

pup·fish \ˈpəp-ˌfish\ *n* (1949) **:** any of several killifishes (genus *Cyprinodon* of the family Cyprinodontidae) esp. of warm streams and springs of the western U.S.

[1]**pu·pil** \ˈpyü-pəl\ *n* [ME *pupille* minor ward, fr. AF, fr. L *pupillus* male ward (fr. dim. of *pupus* boy) & *pupilla* female ward, fr. dim. of *pupa* girl, doll] (1536) **1 :** a child or young person in school or in the charge of a tutor or instructor **:** STUDENT **2 :** one who has been taught or influenced by a famous or distinguished person

[2]**pupil** *n* [MF *pupille*, fr. L *pupilla*, fr. dim. of *pupa* doll; fr. the tiny image of oneself seen reflected in another's eye] (1567) **:** the contractile aperture in the iris of the eye — **pu·pil·lary** \ˈpyü-pə-ˌler-ē\ *adj*

pu·pil·age *or* **pu·pil·lage** \ˈpyü-pə-lij\ *n* (ca. 1599) **:** the state or period of being a pupil

pup·pet \ˈpə-pət\ *n, often attrib* [ME *popet* youth, doll, fr. MF *poupette*, dim. of **poupe* doll, fr. VL **puppa*, alter. of L *pupa*] (1538) **1 a :** a small-scale figure (as of a person or animal) usu. with a cloth body and hollow head that fits over and is moved by the hand **b :** MARIONETTE **2 :** DOLL 1 **3 :** one whose acts are controlled by an outside force or influence ⟨a ~ ruler⟩ — **pup·pet·like** \-ˌlīk\ *adj*

pup·pe·teer \ˌpə-pə-ˈtir\ *n* (ca. 1923) **:** one who manipulates puppets

pup·pet·ry \ˈpə-pə-trē\ *n, pl* **-ries** (1528) **1 :** the production or creation of puppets or puppet shows **2 :** the art of manipulating puppets

pup·py \ˈpə-pē\ *n, pl* **puppies** [ME *popi*, fr. MF *poupée* doll, toy, fr. **poupe*] (1567) **1 :** a young domestic dog; *specif* **:** one less than a year old **2 :** BABY 4 ⟨a computer that is one fast ~⟩ — **pup·py·hood** \-ˌhu̇d\ *n* — **pup·py·ish** \-ish\ *adj* — **pup·py·like** \-ˌlīk\ *adj*

puppy dog *n* (1595) **:** a domestic dog; *esp* **:** one having the lovable attributes of a puppy

puppy love *n* (1823) **:** transitory love or affection felt by a child or adolescent

puppy mill *n* (1973) **:** a commercial farming operation in which purebred dogs are raised in large numbers

pup tent *n* (1863) **:** a small usu. wedge-shaped tent for two persons

pu·pu \ˈpü-ˌpü\ *n* [Hawaiian *pūpū* appetizer] (1956) **:** an Asian dish served as an appetizer or main course and consisting of a variety of foods (as egg rolls, spareribs, and fried shrimp) ⟨~ platter⟩

Pu·ra·na \pu̇-ˈrä-nə\ *n, often cap* [Skt *purāṇa*, fr. *purāṇa* ancient, fr. *purā* formerly; akin to Skt *pura* before, Gk *para* beside, *pro* before — more at FOR] (1696) **:** one of a class of Hindu sacred writings chiefly from A.D. 300 to A.D. 750 comprising popular myths and legends and other traditional lore — **Pu·ra·nic** \-nik\ *adj*

pur·blind \ˈpər-ˌblīnd\ *adj* [ME *pur blind*, fr. *pur* purely, wholly, fr. *pur* pure] (14c) **1 a** *obs* **:** wholly blind **b :** partly blind **2 :** lacking in vision, insight, or understanding **:** OBTUSE — **pur·blind·ly** \-ˌblīn(d)-lē\ *adv* — **pur·blind·ness** \-ˌblīn(d)-nəs\ *n*

[1]**pur·chase** \ˈpər-chəs\ *vb* **pur·chased; pur·chas·ing** [ME *purchacen*, fr. AF *purchacer* to strive for, obtain, fr. *por-, pur-* thoroughly, to a conclusion (fr. L *pro-* forward, for) + *chacer* to pursue, chase — more at PRO-] *vt* (14c) **1 a** *archaic* **:** GAIN, ACQUIRE **b :** to acquire (real estate) by means other than descent **c :** to obtain by paying money or its equivalent **:** BUY **d :** to obtain by labor, danger, or sacrifice **2 :** to constitute the means for buying ⟨our dollars ~ less each year⟩ ~ *vi* **:** to purchase something — **pur·chas·able** \-chə-sə-bəl\ *adj* — **pur·chas·er** *n*

[2]**purchase** *n* (14c) **1 :** an act or instance of purchasing **2 :** something obtained esp. for a price in money or its equivalent **3 a (1) :** a mechanical hold or advantage applied to the raising or moving of heavy bodies **(2) :** an apparatus or device by which advantage is gained **b (1) :** an advantage (as a firm hold or position) used in applying one's power ⟨clutching the steering wheel for more ~ —Barry Crump⟩ **(2) :** a means of exerting power

pur·dah \ˈpər-də\ *n* [Hindi & Urdu *parda*, lit., screen, veil] (1865) **1 :** seclusion of women from public observation among Muslims and some Hindus esp. in India **2 :** a state of seclusion or concealment

pure \ˈpyu̇r\ *adj* **pur·er; pur·est** [ME *pur*, fr. AF, fr. L *purus*; akin to OHG *fowen* to sift, Skt *punāti* he cleanses, MIr *úr* fresh, new] (14c) **1 a (1) :** unmixed with any other matter ⟨~ gold⟩ **(2) :** free from dust, dirt, or taint ⟨~ springwater⟩ **(3) :** SPOTLESS, STAINLESS **b :** free from harshness or roughness and being in tune — used of a musical tone **c** *of a vowel* **:** characterized by no appreciable alteration of articulation during utterance **2 a :** being thus and no other **:** SHEER, UNMITIGATED ⟨~ folly⟩ **b (1) :** ABSTRACT, THEORETICAL ⟨~ research⟩ **(2) :** A PRIORI ⟨~ mechanics⟩ **c :** not directed toward exposition of reality or solution of practical problems ⟨~ literature⟩ **d :** being nonobjective and to be appraised on formal and technical qualities only ⟨~ form⟩ **3 a (1) :** free from what vitiates, weakens, or pollutes **(2) :** containing nothing that does not properly belong **b :** free from moral fault or guilt **c :** marked by chastity **:** CONTINENT **d (1) :** of pure blood and unmixed ancestry **(2) :** homozygous in and breeding true for one or more characters **e :** ritually clean **4 :** having exactly the talents or skills needed for a particular role ⟨a ~ shooter in basketball⟩ *syn* see CHASTE — **pure·ness** *n*

pure–blood·ed \ˈpyu̇r-ˌblə-dəd\ *or* **pure–blood** \-ˌbləd\ *adj* (1821) **:** FULL-BLOODED 1 — **pure·blood** \-ˌbləd\ *n*

pure·bred \-ˈbred, -ˌbred\ *adj* (1852) **:** bred from members of a recognized breed, strain, or kind without admixture of other blood over many generations — **pure·bred** \-ˌbred\ *n*

pure democracy *n* (1656) **:** democracy in which the power is exercised directly by the people rather than through representatives

[1]**pu·ree** *or* **pu·rée** \pyu̇-ˈrā, -ˈrē\ *n* [F *purée*, fr. MF, fr. fem. of *puré*, pp. of *purer* to purify, strain, fr. L *purare* to purify, fr. *purus*] (1707) **1 :** a paste or thick liquid suspension usu. made from cooked food ground finely **2 :** a thick soup made of pureed vegetables

[2]**puree** *or* **purée** *vt* **pu·reed** *or* **pu·réed; pu·ree·ing** *or* **pu·rée·ing** (1928) **:** to make a puree of

pure imaginary *n* (1947) **:** a complex number that is solely the product of a real number other than zero and the imaginary unit — **pure imaginary** *adj*

pure·ly \ˈpyu̇r-lē\ *adv* (14c) **1 a :** to a full extent **:** TOTALLY ⟨~ by accident⟩ **b :** WHOLLY, EXCLUSIVELY ⟨a selection based ~ on merit⟩ **2 :** without admixture of anything injurious or foreign **3 :** SIMPLY, MERELY ⟨read ~ for relaxation⟩ **4 :** in a chaste or innocent manner

pur·fle \ˈpər-fəl\ *vt* **pur·fled; pur·fling** \-f(ə-)liŋ\ [ME *purfilen*, fr. *purfil* embroidered border, fr. AF, fr. *pur* for, in place of (fr. L *pro-*) + *fil* thread, yarn — more at PRO-, FILE] (14c) **:** to ornament the border or edges of — **purfle** *n*

pur·ga·tion \ˌpər-ˈgā-shən\ *n* (14c) **:** the act or result of purging

[1]**pur·ga·tive** \ˈpər-gə-tiv\ *adj* [ME *purgatif*, fr. LL *purgativus*, fr. L *purgatus*, pp.] (15c) **:** purging or tending to purge

[2]**purgative** *n* (1576) **:** a purging medicine **:** CATHARTIC

pur·ga·to·ri·al \ˌpər-gə-ˈtȯr-ē-əl\ *adj* (15c) **1 :** of, relating to, or suggestive of purgatory **2 :** cleansing of sin **:** EXPIATORY

pur·ga·to·ry \ˈpər-gə-ˌtȯr-ē\ *n, pl* **-ries** [ME, fr. AF or ML; AF *purgatorie*, fr. ML *purgatorium*, fr. LL, neut. of *purgatorius* purging, fr. L *purgare*] (13c) **1 :** an intermediate state after death for expiatory purification; *specif* **:** a place or state of punishment wherein according to Roman Catholic doctrine the souls of those who die in God's grace may make satisfaction for past sins and so become fit for heaven **2 :** a place or state of temporary suffering or misery

[1]**purge** \ˈpərj\ *vb* **purged; purg·ing** [ME, fr. AF *purger*, fr. L *purigare*, *purgare* to purify, purge, fr. *purus* pure + *-igare* (akin to *agere* to drive, do) — more at ACT] *vt* (14c) **1 a :** to clear of guilt **b :** to free from moral or ceremonial defilement **2 a :** to cause evacuation from (as the bowels) **b (1) :** to make free of something unwanted ⟨~ a manhole of gas⟩ ⟨~ yourself of fear⟩ **(2) :** to free (as a boiler) of sediment or relieve (as a steam pipe) of trapped air by bleeding **c (1) :** to rid (as a nation or party) by a purge **(2) :** to get rid of ⟨the leaders had been *purged*⟩ ~ *vi* **1 :** to become purged **2 :** to have or produce frequent evacuations **3 :** to cause purgation — **purg·er** *n*

[2]**purge** *n* (1563) **1 :** something that purges; *esp* **:** PURGATIVE **2 a :** an act or instance of purging **b :** the removal of elements or members regarded as undesirable and esp. as treacherous or disloyal

pu·ri \ˈpu̇r-ē\ *n, pl* **puri** *or* **puris** [Hindi & Urdu *pūrī*, fr. Skt *pūra*] (1839) **:** a puffy fried wheat cake of India

pu·ri·fi·ca·tion \ˌpyu̇r-ə-fə-ˈkā-shən\ *n* (14c) **:** the act or an instance of purifying or of being purified

pu·ri·fi·ca·tor \ˈpyu̇r-ə-fə-ˌkā-tər\ *n* (1853) **1 :** a linen cloth used to wipe the chalice after celebration of the Eucharist **2 :** one that purifies

pu·ri·fi·ca·to·ry \pyu̇r-ˈi-fi-kə-ˌtȯr-ē, ˈpyu̇r-(ə-)fə-kə-\ *adj* (1610) **:** serving, tending, or intended to purify ⟨~ rituals⟩

pu·ri·fy \ˈpyu̇r-ə-ˌfī\ *vb* **-fied; -fy·ing** [ME *purifien*, fr. AF *purifier*, fr. L *purificare*, fr. L *purus* + *-ificare* -ify] *vt* (14c) **:** to make pure: as **a :** to clear from material defilement or imperfection **b :** to free from guilt or moral or ceremonial blemish **c :** to free from undesirable elements ~ *vi* **:** to grow or become pure or clean — **pu·ri·fi·er** \-ˌfī(-ə)r\ *n*

Pu·rim \ˈpu̇r-im, ˈpyu̇r-, -ˌēm; pu̇-ˈrim, pyu̇-, -ˈrēm\ *n* [Heb *pūrīm*, lit., lots; fr. the casting of lots by Haman (Esth 9:24–26)] (1535) **:** a Jewish holiday celebrated on the 14th of Adar in commemoration of the deliverance of the Jews from the massacre plotted by Haman

pu·rine \ˈpyu̇r-ˌēn\ *n* [G *Purin*, fr. L *purus* pure + NL *uricus* uric (fr. E *uric*) + G *-in* [2]-ine] (1898) **1 :** a crystalline base $C_5H_4N_4$ that is the parent of compounds of the uric-acid group **2 :** a derivative of purine; *esp* **:** a base (as adenine or guanine) that is a constituent of DNA or RNA

pur·ism \ˈpyu̇r-ˌi-zəm\ *n* (1803) **1 :** an example of rigid adherence to or insistence on purity or nicety esp. in use of words; *esp* **:** a word, phrase, or sense used chiefly by purists **2 :** the quality or practice of adherence to purity esp. in language

pur·ist \ˈpyu̇r-ist\ *n* (ca. 1706) **:** a person who adheres strictly and often excessively to a tradition; *esp* **:** one preoccupied with the purity of a language and its protection from the use of foreign or altered forms — **pu·ris·tic** \pyu̇-ˈris-tik\ *adj* — **pu·ris·ti·cal·ly** \-ti-k(ə-)lē\ *adv*

[1]**pu·ri·tan** \ˈpyu̇r-ə-tən\ *n* [prob. fr. LL *puritas* purity] (ca. 1567) **1** *cap* **:** a member of a 16th and 17th century Protestant group in England and New England opposing as unscriptural the ceremonial worship and the prelacy of the Church of England **2 :** one who practices or preaches a more rigorous or professedly purer moral code than that which prevails

[2]**puritan** *adj, often cap* (1581) **:** of or relating to puritans, the Puritans, or puritanism

pu·ri·tan·i·cal \ˌpyu̇r-ə-ˈta-ni-kəl\ *adj* (1604) **1 :** of, relating to, or characterized by a rigid morality **2 :** PURITAN — **pu·ri·tan·i·cal·ly** \-k(ə-)lē\ *adv*

pu·ri·tan·ism \ˈpyu̇r-ə-tᵊn-ˌi-zəm\ *n* (1573) **1** *cap* **:** the beliefs and practices characteristic of the Puritans **2 :** strictness and austerity esp. in matters of religion or conduct

pu·ri·ty \ˈpyu̇r-ə-tē\ *n* [ME *purete*, fr. AF *purité*, fr. LL *puritat-, puritas*, fr. L *purus* pure] (13c) **1 :** the quality or state of being pure **2 :** SATURATION 4a

Pur·kin·je cell \(ˌ)pər-ˈkin-jē-\ *n* [Jan *Purkinje*] (ca. 1890) : any of numerous nerve cells that occupy the middle layer of the cerebellar cortex and are characterized by a large globose body with massive dendrites directed outward and a single slender axon directed inward

Purkinje fiber *n* (ca. 1890) : any of the modified cardiac muscle fibers with few nuclei, granulated central cytoplasm, and sparse peripheral striations that make up a network of myocardial conducting tissue

¹**purl** \ˈpər(-ə)l\ *n* [ME] (14c) **1** : gold or silver thread or wire for embroidering or edging **2** : the intertwisting of thread that knots a stitch usu. along an edge **3** : PURL STITCH

²**purl** *vt* (1526) **1 a** : to embroider with gold or silver thread **b** : to edge or border with gold or silver embroidery **2** : to knit in purl stitch ~ *vi* : to do knitting in purl stitch

³**purl** *n* [perh. of Scand origin; akin to Norw *purla* to ripple] (ca. 1522) **1** : a purling or swirling stream or rill **2** : a gentle murmur or movement (as of purling water)

⁴**purl** *vi* (1591) **1** : EDDY, SWIRL **2** : to make a soft murmuring sound like that of a purling stream

pur·lieu \ˈpərl-(ˌ)yü, ˈpər-(ˌ)lü\ *n* [ME *purlewe* land severed from an English royal forest by perambulation, fr. AF *puralé* perambulation, fr. *puraler* to travel through, measure, fr. *pur-* thoroughly + *aler* to go — more at PURCHASE] (15c) **1 a** : an outlying or adjacent district **b** *pl* : ENVIRONS, NEIGHBORHOOD **2 a** : a frequently visited place : HAUNT **b** *pl* : CONFINES, BOUNDS

pur·lin \ˈpər-lən\ *n* [origin unknown] (15c) : a horizontal member in a roof

pur·loin \(ˌ)pər-ˈloin, ˈpər-\ *vt* [ME, to put away, misappropriate, fr. AF *purluigner* to prolong, postpone, set aside, fr. *pur-* forward + *luin, loing* at a distance, fr. L *longe*, fr. *longus* long — more at PURCHASE, LONG] (15c) : to appropriate wrongfully and often by a breach of trust *syn* see STEAL — **pur·loin·er** *n*

purl stitch *n* [¹*purl*] (1852) : a knitting stitch usu. made with the yarn at the front of the work by inserting the right needle into the front of a loop on the left needle from the right, catching the yarn with the right needle, and bringing it through to form a new loop — compare KNIT STITCH

pu·ro·my·cin \ˌpyur-ə-ˈmī-sᵊn\ *n* [*purine* + *-o-* + *-mycin*] (1953) : an antibiotic $C_{22}H_{29}N_7O_5$ that is obtained from an actinomycete (*Streptomyces albonіger*) and is a potent inhibitor of protein synthesis

¹**pur·ple** \ˈpər-pəl\ *adj* **pur·pler** \-p(ə-)lər\; **pur·plest** \-p(ə-)ləst\ [ME *purpel*, alter. of *purper*, fr. OE *purpuran* of purple, gen. of *purpure* purple color, fr. L *purpura*, fr. Gk *porphyra*] (bef. 12c) **1** : REGAL, IMPERIAL **2** : of the color purple **3 a** : highly rhetorical : ORNATE **b** : marked by profanity

²**purple** *n* (15c) **1 a** (1) : cloth dyed purple (2) : a garment of such color; *esp* : a purple robe worn as an emblem of rank or authority **b** (1) : TYRIAN PURPLE (2) : any of various colors that fall about midway between red and blue in hue **c** (1) : a mollusk (as of the genus *Purpura*) yielding a purple dye and esp. the Tyrian purple of ancient times (2) : a pigment or dye that colors purple **2 a** : imperial or regal rank or power **b** : high rank or station

³**purple** *vb* **pur·pled**; **pur·pling** \-p(ə-)liŋ\ *vt* (15c) : to make purple ~ *vi* : to become purple

purple coneflower *n* (ca. 1909) : any of a No. American genus (*Echinacea*, esp. *E. purpurea*) of coarse perennial composite herbs with thick rough leaves and long-stalked flower heads having purplish-brown cone-shaped disks and usu. pink to purplish rays

purple finch *n* (1754) : a finch (*Carpodacus purpureus*) of the U.S. and Canada living in the male a rosy-red head, breast, and rump

pur·ple·heart \ˈpər-pəl-ˌhärt\ *n* (1796) : a strong durable purplish wood that is obtained from various leguminous trees (genus *Peltogyne*) of Central and So. America; *also* : a tree producing such wood

Purple Heart *n* (1932) : a U.S. military decoration awarded to any member of the armed forces wounded or killed in action

purple loosestrife *n* (1548) : a perennial Eurasian marsh herb (*Lythrum salicaria*) of the loosestrife family that is naturalized in eastern No. America and has long spikes of purple flowers

purple martin *n* (1743) : a large swallow (*Progne subis*) of No. America the males of which have glossy purplish-blue plumage

purple passage *n* [trans. of L *pannus purpureus* purple patch; fr. the traditional splendor of purple cloth as contrasted with plainer materials] (1895) **1** : a passage conspicuous for brilliance or effectiveness in a work that is dull, commonplace, or uninspired **2** *chiefly Brit* : a piece of obtrusively ornate writing — called also *purple patch*

purple scale *n* (ca. 1909) : a brownish or purplish armored scale (*Lepidosaphes beckii*) that is destructive to citrus fruit

pur·plish \ˈpər-p(ə-)lish\ *adj* (1562) : somewhat purple

pur·ply \ˈpər-p(ə-)lē\ *adj* (1725) : PURPLISH

¹**pur·port** \ˈpər-ˌpȯrt\ *n* [ME, fr. AF, content, tenor, fr. *purporter* to carry, mean, purport, fr. *pur-* thoroughly + *porter* to carry — more at PURCHASE, PORT] (15c) : meaning conveyed, professed, or implied : IMPORT; *also* : SUBSTANCE, GIST

²**pur·port** \(ˌ)pər-ˈpȯrt\ *vt* (15c) **1** : to have the often specious appearance of being, intending, or claiming (something implied or inferred) ⟨a book that ~s to be an objective analysis⟩; *also* : CLAIM ⟨foreign novels which he ~s to have translated —Mary McCarthy⟩ **2** : INTEND, PURPOSE

pur·port·ed \-ˈpȯr-təd\ *adj* (1836) : REPUTED, ALLEGED ⟨took gullible tourists to ~ ancient sites⟩

pur·port·ed·ly \-lē\ *adv* (1942) : it is purported to : OSTENSIBLY, ALLEGEDLY

¹**pur·pose** \ˈpər-pəs\ *n* [ME *purpos*, fr. AF, fr. *purposer* to intend, propose, fr. L *proponere* (perf. indic. *proposui*) to propose — more at PROPOUND] (14c) **1 a** : something set up as an object or end to be attained : INTENTION **b** : RESOLUTION, DETERMINATION **2** : a subject under discussion or an action in course of execution *syn* see INTENTION — **on purpose** : by intent : INTENTIONALLY

²**purpose** *vt* **pur·posed**; **pur·pos·ing** (14c) : to propose as an aim to oneself

pur·pose–built \ˌpər-pəs-ˈbilt\ *adj* (1954) *chiefly Brit* : built for a particular purpose

pur·pose·ful \ˈpər-pəs-fəl\ *adj* (1853) **1** : having a purpose: as **a** : MEANINGFUL ⟨~ activities⟩ **b** : INTENTIONAL ⟨~ ambiguity⟩ **2** : full of determination ⟨was soft-spoken but ~⟩ — **pur·pose·ful·ly** \-fə-lē\ *adv* — **pur·pose·ful·ness** *n*

pur·pose·less \-ləs\ *adj* (ca. 1552) : having no purpose : AIMLESS, MEANINGLESS — **pur·pose·less·ly** *adv* — **pur·pose·less·ness** *n*

pur·pose·ly \-lē\ *adv* (15c) : with a deliberate or express purpose

pur·po·sive \ˈpər-pə-siv, (ˌ)pər-ˈpō-\ *adj* (1849) **1** : serving or effecting a useful function though not as a result of planning or design : having or tending to fulfill a conscious purpose or design : PURPOSEFUL — **pur·po·sive·ly** *adv* — **pur·po·sive·ness** *n*

pur·pu·ra \ˈpər-pyə-rə, -pə-rə\ *n* [NL, fr. L, purple color] (1753) : any of several hemorrhagic states characterized by patches of purplish discoloration resulting from extravasation of blood into the skin and mucous membranes — **pur·pu·ric** \ˌpər-ˈpyùr-ik\ *adj*

pur·pure \ˈpər-pyər\ *n* [ME, fr. OE, purple] (1535) : the heraldic color purple

¹**purr** \ˈpər\ *n* [imit.] (1601) : a low vibratory murmur typical of an apparently contented or pleased cat

²**purr** *vi* (1620) **1** : to make a purr or a sound like a purr ⟨cars ~ing along the highway⟩ **2 a** : to speak in a manner that resembles a purr **b** : to speak in a malicious catty manner — **purr·ing·ly** \-iŋ-lē\ *adv*

¹**purse** \ˈpərs\ *n* [ME *purs*, fr. OE, modif. of ML *bursa*, fr. LL, ox hide, fr. Gk *byrsa*] (bef. 12c) **1 a** (1) : a small bag for money (2) : a receptacle (as a pocketbook) for carrying money and often other small objects **b** : a receptacle (as a pouch) shaped like a purse **2 a** : RESOURCES, FUNDS **b** : a sum of money offered as a prize or present; *also* : the total amount of money offered in prizes for a given event — **purse·like** \-ˌlīk\ *adj*

²**purse** *vt* **pursed**; **purs·ing** (14c) **1** : to put into a purse **2** : PUCKER, KNIT ⟨*pursed* his brow⟩

purse–proud \ˈpərs-ˌpraùd\ *adj* (1681) : proud because of one's wealth esp. in the absence of other distinctions

purs·er \ˈpər-sər\ *n* [ME, fr. *purs* purse] (15c) **1** : an official on a ship responsible for papers and accounts and on a passenger ship also for the comfort and welfare of passengers **2** : a steward on an airliner

purse seine *n* (1862) : a large seine designed to be set by two boats around a school of fish and so arranged that after the ends have been brought together the bottom can be closed — **purse seiner** *n* — **purse seining** *n*

purse strings *n pl* (15c) : financial resources; *also* : control over these resources

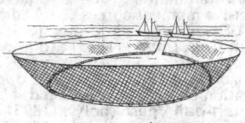

purse seine

purs·lane \ˈpər-slən, -ˌslān\ *n* [ME, fr. AF *porsulaigne*, fr. LL *porcillagin-, porcillago*, alter. of L *porcillaca*, alter. of *portulaca*] (14c) : any of a family (Portulacaceae, the purslane family) of cosmopolitan usu. succulent herbs; *esp* : a fleshy-leaved trailing plant (*Portulaca oleracea*) with tiny yellow flowers that is a common troublesome weed but is sometimes eaten as a potherb or in salads

pur·su·ance \pər-ˈsü-ən(t)s\ *n* (1605) : the act of pursuing; *esp* : a carrying out or into effect : PROSECUTION ⟨in ~ of his duties⟩

pur·su·ant to \-ˌant-\ *prep* (1628) : in carrying out : in conformity with : ACCORDING TO

pur·sue \pər-ˈsü, -ˈsyü\ *vb* **pur·sued**; **pur·su·ing** [ME, fr. AF *pursure, pursiure*, fr. L *prosequi*, fr. *pro-* forward + *sequi* to follow — more at PRO-, SUE] *vt* (14c) **1** : to follow in order to overtake, capture, kill, or defeat **2** : to find or employ measures to obtain or accomplish : SEEK ⟨~ a goal⟩ **3** : to proceed along ⟨~s a northern course⟩ **4 a** : to engage in ⟨~ a hobby⟩ **b** : to follow up or proceed with ⟨~ an argument⟩ **5** : to continue to afflict : HAUNT ⟨was *pursued* by horrible memories⟩ **6** : ²CHASE 1c ⟨*pursued* by dozens of fans⟩ ~ *vi* : to go in pursuit *syn* see CHASE — **pur·su·er** *n*

pur·suit \pər-ˈsüt, -ˈsyüt\ *n* [ME, fr. AF *pursute*, fr. *pursure*] (14c) **1** : the act of pursuing **2** : an activity that one engages in as a vocation, profession, or avocation : OCCUPATION *syn* see WORK

pursuit plane *n* (ca. 1918) : a fighter plane esp. of the period before World War II

pur·sui·vant \ˈpər-si-vənt, -swi-\ *n* [ME *pursevant* attendant of a herald, fr. AF *pursevaunt, pursuant*, lit., follower, fr. prp. of *pursure* to pursue] (14c) **1** : an officer of arms ranking below a herald but having similar duties **2** : FOLLOWER, ATTENDANT

¹**pur·sy** \ˈpə-sē, ˈpər-sē\ *adj* **pur·si·er; -est** [ME *pursi, pursif*, fr. AF *porsif*, alter. of **polsif*, fr. OF *pousser* to exert pressure, breathe heavily — more at PUSH] (15c) **1** : short-winded esp. because of corpulence **2** : FAT — **pur·si·ness** *n*

²**pursy** \ˈpər-sē\ *adj* **purs·i·er; -est** [¹*purse*] (1552) **1** : having a puckered appearance **2** : PURSE-PROUD

pur·te·nance \ˈpərt-nən(t)s, ˈpər-tᵊn-ən(t)s\ *n* [ME *portenaunce*, lit., appurtenance, fr. AF *partenance*, fr. *partenir* to belong — more at PERTAIN] (15c) : ENTRAILS, PLUCK

pu·ru·lence \ˈpyùr-ə-lən(t)s, ˈpyùr-yə-\ *n* (1597) : the quality or state of being purulent; *also* : PUS

pu·ru·lent \-lənt\ *adj* [L *purulentus*, fr. *pur-, pus* pus] (1597) **1** : containing, consisting of, or being pus ⟨a ~ discharge⟩ **2** : accompanied by suppuration

pur·vey \(ˌ)pər-ˈvā, ˈpər-ˌ\ *vt* **pur·veyed; pur·vey·ing** [ME *purveien*, fr. AF *purveier, purveer* to look at, foresee, provide, fr. L *providēre* to provide] (14c) **1** : to supply (as provisions) usu. as a matter of business **2** : PEDDLE 2

pur·vey·ance \-ˈən(t)s\ *n* (14c) : the act or process of purveying or procuring

pur·vey·or \-ər\ *n* (14c) **1** : one that purveys **2** : VICTUALLER, CATERER

pur·view \ˈpər-ˌvyü\ *n* [ME *purveu*, fr. AF *purveu est* it is provided (opening phrase of a statute)] (15c) **1 a** : the body or enacting part of a statute **b** : the limit, purpose, or scope of a statute **2** : the range or

---

\ə\ abut \ᵊ\ kitten, F table \ər\ further \a\ ash \ā\ ace \ä\ mop, mar
\aù\ out \ch\ chin \e\ bet \ē\ easy \g\ go \i\ hit \ī\ ice \j\ job
\ŋ\ sing \ō\ go \ȯ\ law \ȯi\ boy \th\ thin \ᵗh\ the \ü\ loot \ù\ foot
\y\ yet \zh\ vision, beige \k̲, ⁿ, œ, ᵫ, �\ see Guide to Pronunciation

limit of authority, competence, responsibility, concern, or intention **3** : range of vision, understanding, or cognizance

pus \ˈpəs\ *n* [L *pur-, pus* — more at FOUL] (15c) : thick opaque usu. yellowish-white fluid matter formed by suppuration and composed of exudate containing white blood cells, tissue debris, and microorganisms

Pu•sey•ism \ˈpyü-zē-ˌi-zəm, -sē-\ *n* [Edward Bouverie *Pusey*] (1838) : TRACTARIANISM — **Pu•sey•ite** \-ˌīt\ *n*

[1]**push** \ˈpu̇sh\ *vb* [ME *possen, pusshen,* prob. fr. OF *pousser* to exert pressure, fr. L *pulsare,* freq. of *pellere* to drive, strike — more at FELT] *vt* (13c) **1 a** : to press against with force in order to drive or impel **b** : to move or endeavor to move away or ahead by steady pressure without striking **2 a** : to thrust forward, downward, or outward **b** : to cause to increase : RAISE ⟨~ prices to record levels⟩ **c** : to try to move beyond or expand ⟨~ one's limits⟩ **d** : to hit (a ball) toward the right from a right-handed swing or toward the left from a left-handed swing — compare PULL **3 a** : to press or urge forward to completion **b** : to urge or press the advancement, adoption, or practice of ⟨~*ed* a bill in the legislature⟩; *esp* : to make aggressive efforts to sell ⟨we're ~*ing* ham this week⟩ **c** : to engage in the illicit sale of (narcotics) **4** : to bear hard upon so as to involve in difficulty ⟨poverty ~*ed* them to the breaking point⟩ **5** : to approach in age or number ⟨grandmother must be ~*ing* 75⟩ ~ *vi* **1** : to press against something with steady force in or as if in order to impel **2** : to press forward energetically against opposition **3** : to exert oneself continuously, vigorously, or obtrusively to gain an end ⟨~*ing* for higher wages⟩ — **push one's luck** : to take an increasing risk

[2]**push** *n* (ca. 1560) **1** : a vigorous effort to attain an end : DRIVE: **a** : a military assault or offensive **b** : an advance that overcomes obstacles **c** : a campaign to promote a product **2** : a time for action : EMERGENCY **3 a** : an act of pushing : SHOVE **b (1)** : a physical force steadily applied in a direction away from the body exerting it **(2)** : a nonphysical pressure : INFLUENCE, URGE **c** : vigorous enterprise or energy **4 a** : an exertion of influence to promote another's interests **b** : stimulation to activity : IMPETUS — **push comes to shove** : a decisive moment comes ⟨backed down when *push came to shove*⟩

PUSH *abbr* People United to Serve Humanity

push around *vt* (1923) : to impose on contemptuously : BULLY

push•back \ˈpu̇sh-ˌbak\ *n* (1942) **1** : the action of forcing an object backward **2** : resistance or opposition in response to a policy or regulation esp. by those affected

push•ball \ˈpu̇sh-ˌbȯl\ *n* (1895) : a game in which each of two sides endeavors to push an inflated orig. leather-covered ball six feet (1.8 meters) in diameter across its opponents' goal; *also* : the ball used

push–bike \-ˌbīk\ *n* (1910) *Brit* : BICYCLE — called also *push bicycle*

push broom *n* (1892) : a long-handled wide brush that is designed to be pushed and is used for sweeping

push–button *adj* (1916) **1** : operated or done by means of push buttons ⟨a ~ phone⟩ **2** : using or dependent on complex and more or less self-operating mechanisms that are put in operation by a simple act comparable to pushing a button ⟨~ warfare⟩

push button *n* (ca. 1874) : a small button or knob that when pushed operates something esp. by closing an electric circuit

push•cart \ˈpu̇sh-ˌkärt\ *n* (1853) : a cart or barrow pushed by hand

push•chair \-ˌcher\ *n* (1919) *chiefly Brit* : STROLLER

push•down \-ˌdau̇n\ *n* (1961) : a store of data (as in a computer) from which the most recently stored item must be the first retrieved — called also *pushdown list, pushdown stack*

push•er \ˈpu̇-shər\ *n* (1591) : one that pushes; *esp* : one that pushes illegal drugs

push•ing \ˈpu̇-shiŋ\ *adj* (1677) **1** : marked by ambition, energy, enterprise, and initiative **2** : marked by tactless forwardness or officious intrusiveness

push off *vi* (1740) : SET OUT ⟨we *pushed off* for home⟩

push on *vi* (1602) : to continue on one's way : PROCEED

push•over \ˈpu̇sh-ˌō-vər\ *n* (1906) **1** : something accomplished without difficulty : SNAP **2** : an opponent who is easy to defeat or a victim who is capable of no effective resistance **3** : someone unable to resist an attraction or appeal : SUCKER

push•pin \-ˌpin\ *n* (1907) : a pin that has a roughly cylindrical head and that is easily inserted and withdrawn (as from a bulletin board)

push–pull \-ˈpu̇l\ *adj* (1920) : relating to or being an arrangement of two electronic circuit elements (as transistors) such that an alternating input causes them to send current through a load alternately ⟨a ~ circuit⟩ — **push–pull** *n*

push•rod \ˈpu̇sh-ˌräd\ *n* (1908) : a rod actuated by a cam to open or close a valve of an internal combustion engine

Pushtu *var of* PASHTO

Pushtun *var of* PASHTUN

push–up \ˈpu̇sh-ˌəp\ *n* (1897) : a conditioning exercise performed in a prone position by raising and lowering the body with the straightening and bending of the arms while keeping the back straight and supporting the body on the hands and toes

pushy \ˈpu̇-shē\ *adj* **push•i•er; -est** (1874) : aggressive often to an objectionable degree : FORWARD — **push•i•ly** \ˈpu̇-shə-lē\ *adv* — **push•i•ness** \ˈpu̇-shē-nəs\ *n*

pu•sil•la•nim•i•ty \ˌpyü-sə-lə-ˈni-mə-tē *also* ˌpyü-zə-\ *n* (14c) : the quality or state of being pusillanimous : COWARDLINESS

pu•sil•lan•i•mous \-ˈla-nə-məs\ *adj* [LL *pusillanimis,* fr. L *pusillus* very small (dim. of *pusus* boy) + *animus* spirit; perh. akin to L *puer* child — more at PUERILE, ANIMATE] (15c) : lacking courage and resolution : marked by contemptible timidity ***syn*** see COWARDLY — **pu•sil•lan•i•mous•ly** *adv*

[1]**puss** \ˈpu̇s\ *n* [origin unknown] (1598) **1** : CAT **2** : GIRL

[2]**puss** *n* [Ir *pus* mouth] (1844) *slang* : FACE

puss•ley \ˈpəs-lē\ *n* [by alter.] (1775) : PURSLANE

[1]**pussy** \ˈpu̇-sē\ *n, pl* **puss•ies** [[1]*puss*] (1699) **1** : CAT **2** : a catkin of the pussy willow

[2]**pus•sy** \ˈpu̇-sē\ *n, pl* **pus•sies** [perh. of LG or Scand origin; akin to ON *pūss* pocket, pouch, LG *pūse* vulva, OE *pusa* bag] (1699) **1** *usu vulgar* : VULVA **2 a** *usu vulgar* : SEXUAL INTERCOURSE **b** *usu vulgar* : the female partner in sexual intercourse

[3]**pus•sy** \ˈpə-sē\ *adj* **pus•si•er; -est** (1888) : full of or resembling pus ⟨a ~ wound⟩

[4]**pus•sy** \ˈpu̇-sē\ *n, pl* **pus•sies** [short for *pussycat*] (ca. 1942) *slang* : a weak or cowardly man or boy : WIMP, SISSY

pussy•cat \ˈpu̇-sē-ˌkat\ *n* (1698) **1** : CAT **2** : one that is weak, compliant, or amiable : SOFTY

pussy•foot \ˈpu̇-sē-ˌfu̇t\ *vi* (1903) **1** : to tread or move warily or stealthily **2** : to refrain from committing oneself — **pussy•foot•er** *n*

pussy•toes \ˈpu̇-sē-ˌtōz\ *or* **puss•y's–toes** \-sēz-\ *n pl but sing or pl in constr* (1892) : any of a genus (*Antennaria*) of woolly or hoary chiefly temperate perennial composite herbs that have small usu. whitish discoid flower heads and a pappus formed of club-shaped bristles

pussy willow \ˈpu̇-sē-\ *n* (1851) : a willow (as the No. American *Salix discolor*) having large cylindrical silky catkins

pussy willow

[1]**pus•tu•lant** \ˈpəs-chə-lənt; ˈpəs-tyə-, -tə-\ *n* (1861) : an agent (as a chemical) that induces pustule formation

[2]**pustulant** *adj* (ca. 1890) : producing pustules

pus•tu•lar \-lər\ *adj* (1716) **1** : of, relating to, or resembling pustules **2** : covered with pustular prominences : PUSTULATED

pus•tu•lat•ed \-ˌlā-təd\ *adj* (1666) : covered with pustules

pus•tu•la•tion \ˌpəs-chə-ˈlā-shən, ˌpəs-tyə-, -tə-\ *n* (15c) **1** : the act of producing pustules : the state of having pustules **2** : PUSTULE

pus•tule \ˈpəs-(ˌ)chül, -(ˌ)tyül, -(ˌ)tül\ *n* [ME, fr. L *pustula;* akin to Lith *pusti* to blow, Gk *physa* breath] (14c) **1** : a small circumscribed elevation of the skin containing pus and having an inflamed base **2** : a small often distinctively colored elevation or spot resembling a blister or pimple

[1]**put** \ˈpu̇t\ *vb* **put; put•ting** [ME *putten;* akin to OE *putung* instigation, MD *poten* to plant] *vt* (12c) **1 a** : to place in a specified position or relationship : LAY ⟨~ the book on the table⟩ **b** : to move in a specified direction **c (1)** : to send (as a weapon or missile) into or through something : THRUST **(2)** : to throw with an overhand pushing motion ⟨~ the shot⟩ **d** : to bring into a specified state or condition ⟨a reapportionment . . . that was ~ into effect at the September primaries —*Current Biog.*⟩ **e** : to prescribe a specified regimen for — usu. used with *on* ⟨~ her on medication⟩ ⟨~ him on a diet⟩ **2 a** : to cause to endure or suffer something : SUBJECT ⟨~ traitors to death⟩ **b** : IMPOSE, INFLICT ⟨~ a special tax on luxuries⟩ **3 a** : to set before one for judgment or decision ⟨~ the question⟩ **b** : to call for a formal vote on ⟨~ the motion⟩ **4 a (1)** : to convey into another form ⟨want to ~ my feelings into words⟩ **(2)** : to translate into another language or style ⟨~ the poem into English⟩ **(3)** : ADAPT ⟨lyrics ~ to music⟩ **b** : EXPRESS, STATE ⟨*putting* it mildly⟩ **5 a** : to devote (oneself) to an activity or end ⟨~ himself to winning back their confidence⟩ **b** : APPLY ⟨~ her mind to the problem⟩ **c** : ASSIGN ⟨~ them to work⟩ **d** : to cause to perform an action : URGE ⟨~ the horse over the fence⟩ **e** : IMPEL, INCITE ⟨~ them into a frenzy⟩ **6 a** : REPOSE, REST ⟨~*s* his faith in reason⟩ **b** : INVEST 1 ⟨~ her money in the company⟩ **7 a** : to give as an estimate ⟨~ the time as about eleven⟩ **b** : ATTACH, ATTRIBUTE ⟨~*s* a high value on their friendship⟩ **c** : IMPUTE ⟨~ the blame on the partners⟩ **8** : BET, WAGER ⟨~ $2 on the favorite⟩ ~ *vi* **1** : to start in motion : GO; *esp* : to leave in a hurry **2** *of a ship* : to take a specified course ⟨~ down the river⟩ — **put forth 1 a** : ASSERT, PROPOSE **b** : to make public : ISSUE **2** : to bring into action : EXERT **3** : to produce or send out by growth ⟨*put forth* leaves⟩ **4** : to start out — **put forward** : PROPOSE ⟨*put forward* a theory⟩ — **put in mind** : REMIND — **put one's finger on** : IDENTIFY ⟨*put his finger on* the cause of the trouble⟩ — **put one's foot down** : to take a firm stand — **put one's foot in one's mouth** : to make a tactless or embarrassing blunder — **put paid to** *chiefly Brit* : to finish off : bring an end to — **put the arm on** *or* **put the bite on** : to ask for money — **put the finger on** : to inform on ⟨*put the finger on* . . . heroin pushers —Barrie Zwicker⟩ — **put the make on** : to make sexual advances toward — **put to bed** : to make the final preparations for printing (as a newspaper) — **put together 1** : to create as a unified whole : CONSTRUCT **2** : ADD, COMBINE

[2]**put** *n* (14c) **1** : a throw made with an overhand pushing motion; *specif* : the act or an instance of putting the shot **2** : an option to sell a specified amount of a security (as a stock) or commodity (as wheat) at a fixed price at or within a specified time — compare CALL 3d

[3]**put** *adj* (1841) : being in place : FIXED, SET ⟨stay ~ until I call⟩

put about *vt* (1607) *of a ship* : to cause to change course or direction ~ *vi* : to change course or direction : go on another tack

put across *vt* (1906) **1** : PUT OVER 3 **2** : to convey effectively or forcefully ⟨*put* her viewpoint *across* subtly⟩

pu•ta•men \pyü-ˈtā-mən\ *n* [NL, fr. L, hard outer covering, shell, fr. *putare* to clean, prune] (1877) : the large dark lateral part of the basal ganglion which comprises the external portion of the corpus striatum and which has connections to the caudate nucleus

put–and–take \ˌpu̇t-ᵊn-ˈtāk\ *n* (1921) : any of various games of chance played with a teetotum or with dice in which players contribute to a pool and take from it according to the instructions on the top or dice

pu•ta•tive \ˈpyü-tə-tiv\ *adj* [ME, fr. LL *putativus,* fr. L *putatus,* pp. of *putare* to think] (15c) **1** : commonly accepted or supposed **2** : assumed to exist or to have existed — **pu•ta•tive•ly** *adv*

put away *vt* (14c) **1 a** : DISCARD, RENOUNCE ⟨to *put* grief *away* is disloyal to the memory of the departed —H. A. Overstreet⟩ **b** : DIVORCE **2** : to eat or drink up : CONSUME **3 a** : to confine esp. in a mental institution **b** : BURY **c** : KILL

put by *vt* (15c) **1** *archaic* : REJECT **2** : to lay aside : SAVE

put–down \ˈpu̇t-ˌdau̇n\ *n* (1962) : an act or instance of putting down; *esp* : a humiliating remark

put down *vt* (14c) **1** : to bring to an end : STOP ⟨*put down* a riot⟩ **2 a** : DEPOSE, DEGRADE **b** : DISPARAGE, BELITTLE ⟨mentioned his poetry only to *put* it *down*⟩ **c** : DISAPPROVE, CRITICIZE ⟨was *put down* for the way she dressed⟩ **d** : HUMILIATE, SQUELCH ⟨*put* him *down* with a sharp retort⟩ **3** : to make ineffective : CHECK ⟨*put down* the gossip⟩ **4** : to do away with (as an injured, sick, or aged animal) : DESTROY **5 a** : to put in writing **b** : to enter in a list **6 a** : to place in a category ⟨I *put* him *down* as a hypochondriac —O. S. J. Gogarty⟩ **b** : ATTRIBUTE ⟨*put* it *down* to inexperience⟩ **7** : to pack or preserve for future use **8** : CONSUME ⟨*putting down* helping after helping —Carson McCullers⟩ — **put down roots** : to establish a permanent residence

put in *vt* (15c) **1 :** to make a formal offer or declaration of ⟨*put in* a plea of guilty⟩ **2 :** to come in with : INTERPOSE ⟨*put in* a word for his brother⟩ **3 :** to spend (time) esp. at some occupation or job ⟨*put in* six hours at the office⟩ **4 :** PLANT ⟨*put in* a crop⟩ ~ *vi* **1 :** to call at or enter a place; *esp* : to enter a harbor or port **2 :** to make an application, request, or offer — often used with *for* ⟨had to retire and *put in* for a pension —Seymour Nagan⟩

put·log \ˈpu̇t-ˌlȯg, ˈpət-, -ˌläg\ *n* [prob. alter. of earlier *putlock,* perh. fr. [3]*put* + [2]*lock*] (1645) : one of the short timbers that support the flooring of a scaffold

put off *vt* (14c) **1 a :** DISCONCERT **b :** REPEL **2 a :** to hold back to a later time **b :** to induce to wait ⟨*put* the bill collector *off*⟩ **3 :** to rid oneself of : TAKE OFF **4 :** to sell or pass fraudulently

[1]**put–on** \ˈpu̇t-ˌȯn, -ˌän\ *adj* (ca. 1625) : PRETENDED, ASSUMED

[2]**put–on** \ˈpu̇t-ˌȯn, -ˌän\ *n* (1919) **1 :** an instance of putting someone on ⟨conversational ~*s* are related to old-fashioned joshing —Jacob Brackman⟩ **2 :** PARODY, SPOOF ⟨a kind of ~ of every pretentious film ever made —C. A. Ridley⟩

put on *vt* (15c) **1 a :** to dress oneself in : DON **b :** to make part of one's appearance or behavior **c :** FEIGN ⟨*put* a saintly manner *on*⟩ **2 :** to cause to act or operate : APPLY ⟨*put on* more speed⟩ **3 a :** ADD ⟨*put on* weight⟩ **b :** EXAGGERATE, OVERSTATE **4 :** PERFORM, PRODUCE ⟨*put on* a play⟩ **5 a :** to mislead deliberately esp. for amusement ⟨the interviewer . . . must be put down — or possibly, *put on* —Melvin Maddocks⟩ **b :** KID 1 ⟨you're *putting* me *on*⟩

put·out \ˈpu̇t-ˌau̇t\ *n* (1882) : the retiring of a base runner or batter by a defensive player in baseball

put out *vt* (14c) **1 :** EXTINGUISH ⟨*put* the fire *out*⟩ **2 :** EXERT, USE ⟨*put out* considerable effort⟩ **3 :** PUBLISH, ISSUE **4 :** to produce for sale **5 a :** DISCONCERT, EMBARRASS **b :** ANNOY, IRRITATE **c :** INCONVENIENCE ⟨don't *put* yourself *out* for us⟩ **6 :** to cause to be out (as in baseball or cricket) ~ *vi* **1 :** to set out from shore **2 :** to make an effort **3 :** to engage in sexual intercourse esp. promiscuously

put over *vt* (15c) **1 :** POSTPONE, DELAY **2 :** PUT ACROSS 2 **3 :** to achieve or carry through by deceit or trickery ⟨*put* one *over* on me⟩

pu·tre·fac·tion \ˌpyü-trə-ˈfak-shən\ *n* [ME *putrefaccion,* fr. LL *putrefaction-, putrefactio,* fr. L *putrefacere*] (14c) **1 :** the decomposition of organic matter; *esp* : the typically anaerobic splitting of proteins by bacteria and fungi with the formation of foul-smelling incompletely oxidized products **2 :** the state of being putrefied : CORRUPTION — **pu·tre·fac·tive** \-ˈfak-tiv\ *adj*

pu·tre·fy \ˈpyü-trə-ˌfī\ *vb* **-fied; -fy·ing** [ME *putrefien,* fr. MF & L; MF *putrefier,* fr. L *putrefacere,* fr. *putrēre* to be rotten + *facere* to make — more at DO] *vt* (14c) : to make putrid ~ *vi* : to undergo putrefaction *syn* see DECAY

pu·tres·cence \pyü-ˈtre-sᵊn(t)s\ *n* (1646) : the state of being putrescent

pu·tres·cent \-sᵊnt\ *adj* [L *putrescent-, putrescens,* prp. of *putrescere* to grow rotten, incho. of *putrēre*] (1624) **1 :** undergoing putrefaction : becoming putrid **2 :** of or relating to putrefaction

pu·tres·ci·ble \-ˈtre-sə-bəl\ *adj* (1753) : liable to become putrid

pu·tres·cine \-ˈtre-ˌsēn\ *n* [ISV, fr. L *putrescere*] (1887) : a crystalline slightly poisonous ptomaine $C_4H_{12}N_2$ that occurs in small amounts in virtually all living things

pu·trid \ˈpyü-trəd\ *adj* [L *putridus,* fr. *putrēre* to be rotten, fr. *puter, putris* rotten; akin to L *putēre* to stink — more at FOUL] (15c) **1 a :** being in a state of putrefaction : ROTTEN **b :** of, relating to, or characteristic of putrefaction : FOUL ⟨a ~ odor⟩ **2 a :** morally corrupt **b :** totally objectionable *syn* see MALODOROUS — **pu·trid·i·ty** \pyü-ˈtri-də-tē\ *n* — **pu·trid·ly** \ˈpyü-trəd-lē\ *adv*

putsch \ˈpu̇ch\ *n* [G] (1919) : a secretly plotted and suddenly executed attempt to overthrow a government

putsch·ist \ˈpu̇-chist\ *n* (1898) : one who takes part in a putsch

putt \ˈpət\ *n* [Sc, lit., shove, gentle push, fr. *putt, put* to put] (ca. 1754) : a golf stroke made on a putting green to cause the ball to roll into or near the hole — **putt** *vb*

put·ta·nes·ca \ˌpü-tä-ˈnes-kä\ *adj* [It, short for *alla puttanesca,* lit., in the style of a prostitute] (1969) : served with or being a pungent tomato sauce typically containing olives, garlic, capers, hot pepper, and sometimes anchovies — usu. used postpositively ⟨pasta ~⟩

put·tee \ˌpə-ˈtē, pu-; ˈpə-tē\ *n* [Hindi & Urdu *paṭṭī* strip of cloth, fr. Skt *paṭṭikā*] (1882) **1 :** a cloth strip wrapped around the leg from ankle to knee **2 :** a usu. leather legging secured by a strap or catch or by laces

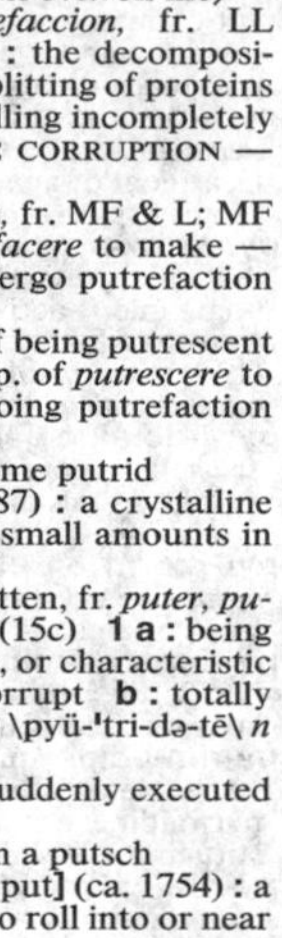

puttees

[1]**put·ter** \ˈpu̇-tər\ *n* (14c) : one that puts ⟨a ~ of questions⟩

[2]**putt·er** \ˈpə-tər\ *n* (1743) **1 :** a golf club used in putting **2 :** one who putts

[3]**put·ter** \ˈpə-tər\ *vi* [alter. of *potter*] (1827) **1 :** to move or act aimlessly or idly **2 :** to work at random : TINKER — **put·ter·er** \-tər-ər\ *n*

put through *vt* (1888) **1 :** to carry to a successful conclusion ⟨*put through* a number of reforms⟩ **2 a :** to make a telephone connection for **b :** to obtain a connection for (a telephone call)

putt·ing green \ˈpə-tiŋ-\ *n* (1805) : a smooth grassy area at the end of a golf fairway containing the hole; *also* : a similar area usu. with many holes that is used for practice

put·to \ˈpü-(ˌ)tō\ *n, pl* **put·ti** \-(ˌ)tē\ [It, lit., boy, fr. VL **puttus,* alter. of L *putus;* akin to L *puer* boy — more at PUERILE] (ca. 1660) : a figure of an infant boy esp. in European art of the Renaissance — usu. used in pl.

Putt–Putt \ˈpət-ˌpət\ *trademark* — used for an entertainment and recreation complex usu. featuring miniature golf

[1]**put·ty** \ˈpə-tē\ *n, pl* **putties** [F *potée* potter's glaze, lit., potful, fr. OF, fr. *pot* pot — more at POTTAGE] (1665) **1 a :** a doughlike material typically made of whiting and linseed oil that is used esp. to fasten glass in window frames and to fill crevices in woodwork **b :** any of various substances resembling putty in appearance, consistency, or use **2 :** a light brownish-gray to light grayish-brown color **3 :** one who is easily manipulated ⟨is ~ in her hands⟩ — **put·ty·less** *adj* — **put·ty·like** *adj*

[2]**putty** *vt* **put·tied; put·ty·ing** (1719) : to use putty on or apply putty to

putty knife *n* (1841) : an implement with a broad flat metal blade used esp. for applying putty and for scraping

put·ty·root \ˈpə-tē-ˌrüt, -ˌru̇t\ *n* (ca. 1818) : a No. American orchid (*Aplectrum hyemale*) having a corm filled with glutinous matter and producing a solitary leaf and a scape bearing a raceme of brownish flowers

put–up \ˈpu̇t-ˈəp\ *adj* (1810) : arranged secretly beforehand ⟨a ~ job⟩

put up *vt* (14c) **1 a :** to place in a container or receptacle ⟨*put* his lunch *up* in a bag⟩ **b :** to put away (a sword) in a scabbard : SHEATHE **c :** to prepare so as to preserve for later use : CAN **d :** to put in storage **2 :** to start (game animals) from cover **3 :** to nominate for election **4 :** to offer up (as a prayer) **5 :** SET 16 **6 :** to make available; *esp* : to offer for public sale ⟨*put* their possessions *up* for auction⟩ **7 :** to give food and shelter to : ACCOMMODATE **8 :** to arrange (as a plot or scheme) with others ⟨*put up* a job to steal the jewels⟩ **9 :** BUILD, ERECT **10 a :** to make a display of ⟨*put up* a brave front⟩ **b :** to engage in ⟨*put up* a struggle⟩ **11 a :** CONTRIBUTE, PAY ⟨*put up* bail money⟩ **b :** to offer as a prize or stake **12** *chiefly Brit* : to increase the amount of : RAISE **13 :** to succeed in producing or achieving ⟨an athlete who has *put up* big numbers⟩; *also* : SCORE 4a(1) ⟨*put up* 20 points⟩ ~ *vi* **1 :** LODGE **2 :** to take direct action — used in the phrase *put up or shut up* — **put one up to :** to incite one to (a course of action) ⟨they *put* him *up to* playing the prank⟩ — **put up with :** to endure or tolerate without complaint or attempt at reprisal

put–up·on \ˈpu̇t-ə-ˌpȯn, -ˌpän\ *adj* (1866) : imposed upon : taken advantage of

[1]**puz·zle** \ˈpə-zəl\ *vb* **puz·zled; puz·zling** \ˈpə-zə-liŋ, ˈpəz-liŋ\ [origin unknown] *vt* (1582) **1 :** to offer or represent to (as a person) a problem difficult to solve or a situation difficult to resolve : challenge mentally; *also* : to exert (as oneself) over such a problem or situation ⟨they *puzzled* their wits to find a solution⟩ **2** *archaic* : COMPLICATE, ENTANGLE **3 :** to solve with difficulty or ingenuity ⟨~ out an answer to a riddle⟩ ~ *vi* **1 :** to be uncertain as to action or choice **2 :** to attempt a solution of a puzzle by guesswork or experiment ⟨~ over the mystery⟩ — **puz·zler** \ˈpə-zə-lər, ˈpəz-lər\ *n*

syn PUZZLE, PERPLEX, BEWILDER, DISTRACT, NONPLUS, CONFOUND, DUMBFOUND mean to baffle and disturb mentally. PUZZLE implies existence of a problem difficult to solve ⟨the persistent fever *puzzled* the doctor⟩. PERPLEX adds a suggestion of worry and uncertainty esp. about making a necessary decision ⟨a behavior that *perplexed* her friends⟩. BEWILDER stresses a confusion of mind that hampers clear and decisive thinking ⟨a *bewildering* number of possibilities⟩. DISTRACT implies agitation or uncertainty induced by conflicting preoccupations or interests ⟨*distracted* by personal problems⟩. NONPLUS implies a bafflement that makes orderly planning or deciding impossible ⟨the remark left us utterly *nonplussed*⟩. CONFOUND implies temporary mental paralysis caused by astonishment or profound abasement ⟨the tragic news *confounded* us all⟩. DUMBFOUND suggests intense but momentary confounding; often the idea of astonishment is so stressed that it becomes a near synonym of *astound* ⟨was at first too *dumbfounded* to reply⟩.

[2]**puzzle** *n* (1599) **1 :** the state of being puzzled : PERPLEXITY **2 a :** something that puzzles **b :** a question, problem, or contrivance designed for testing ingenuity *syn* see MYSTERY

puz·zle·head·ed \ˈpə-zəl-ˌhe-dəd\ *adj* (1729) : having or based on confused attitudes or ideas — **puz·zle·head·ed·ness** *n*

puz·zle·ment \ˈpə-zəl-mənt\ *n* (1731) **1 :** the state of being puzzled : PERPLEXITY **2 :** PUZZLE

puzzling *adj* (ca. 1659) : difficult to understand or solve ⟨~ symptoms⟩ — **puz·zling·ly** *adv*

PV *abbr* **1** photovoltaic **2** polyvinyl

PVA *abbr* polyvinyl acetate

P value *n* [probability] (1947) : the probability of an event or outcome in a statistical experiment; *specif* : LEVEL OF SIGNIFICANCE

PVC *abbr* polyvinyl chloride

PVO *abbr* private voluntary organization

PVS *abbr* persistent vegetative state

pvt *abbr* private

PVT *abbr* pressure, volume, temperature

PW *abbr* prisoner of war

PWA *abbr* people with AIDS; person with AIDS

P–wave \ˈpē-ˌwāv\ *n* [by shortening] (1929) : PRESSURE WAVE

PWC *abbr* personal watercraft

pwr *abbr* power

pwt *abbr* pennyweight

PX *abbr* post exchange

py- *or* **pyo-** *comb form* [Gk, fr. *pyon* pus — more at FOUL] : pus ⟨*py*emia⟩ ⟨*pyo*rrhea⟩

pya \ˈpyä, pē-ˈä\ *n* [Burmese] (1952) — see *kyat* at MONEY table

pyc·nid·i·um \pik-ˈni-dē-əm\ *n, pl* **-ia** \-dē-ə\ [NL, fr. Gk *pyknos* dense] (1857) : a flask-shaped fruiting body bearing conidiophores and conidia on the interior and occurring in various imperfect fungi and ascomycetes — **pyc·nid·i·al** \-dē-əl\ *adj*

pyc·no·go·nid \pik-ˈnä-gə-nəd, ˌpik-nə-ˈgä-nəd\ *n* [ultim. fr. Gk *pyknos* + *gony* knee — more at KNEE] (1869) : SEA SPIDER

pyc·nom·e·ter \pik-ˈnä-mə-tər\ *n* [Gk *pyknos* + ISV *-meter*] (1858) : a standard vessel often provided with a thermometer for measuring and comparing the densities of liquids or solids

pye–dog \ˈpī-ˌdȯg\ *n* [perh. fr. Hindi *pāhī* outsider] (1864) : a half-wild dog common about Asian villages

pyel- *or* **pyelo-** *comb form* [NL, pelvis, fr. Gk *pyelos* basin; akin to Gk *plynein* to wash, *plein* to sail — more at FLOW] : renal pelvis ⟨*pyel*itis⟩

py·eli·tis \ˌpī-ə-ˈlī-təs\ *n* [NL] (1839) : inflammation of the lining of the renal pelvis

py·elo·ne·phri·tis \ˌpī-(ə-)lō-ni-ˈfrī-təs\ *n* [NL] (1839) : inflammation of both the lining of the pelvis and the parenchyma of the kidney — **py·elo·ne·phrit·ic** \-ˈfri-tik\ *adj*

py·emia \pī-ˈē-mē-ə\ *n* [NL] (ca. 1850) : septicemia caused by pus-forming bacteria and accompanied by multiple abscesses

\ə\ **abut** \ᵊ\ **kitten, F table** \ər\ **further** \a\ **ash** \ā\ **ace** \ä\ **mop, mar** \au̇\ **out** \ch\ **chin** \e\ **bet** \ē\ **easy** \g\ **go** \i\ **hit** \ī\ **ice** \j\ **job** \ŋ\ **sing** \ō\ **go** \ȯ\ **law** \ȯi\ **boy** \th\ **thin** \t͟h\ **the** \ü\ **loot** \u̇\ **foot** \y\ **yet** \zh\ **vision, beige** \k̲, ⁿ, œ, ue, ʸ\ *see* Guide to Pronunciation

py·gid·i·um \pī-ˈji-dē-əm\ *n, pl* **-gid·ia** \-ˈji-dē-ə\ [NL, fr. Gk *pygidion,* dim. of *pygē* rump] (1848) **:** a caudal structure or the terminal body region of various invertebrates — **py·gid·i·al** \-dē-əl\ *adj*

pyg·mae·an *or* **pyg·me·an** \pig-ˈmē-ən, ˈpig-mē-\ *adj* [L *pygmaeus*] (ca. 1540) **:** PYGMY

Pyg·ma·lion \pig-ˈmāl-yən, -ˈmā-lē-ən\ *n* [L, fr. Gk *Pygmaliōn*] (14c) **:** a king of Cyprus who makes a female figure of ivory that is brought to life for him by Aphrodite

pyg·moid \ˈpig-ˌmȯid\ *adj* (1906) **:** resembling or having the characteristics of the Pygmies

pyg·my *also* **pig·my** \ˈpig-mē\ *n, pl* **pygmies** *also* **pigmies** [ME *pigmei,* fr. L *pygmaeus* of a pygmy, dwarfish, fr. Gk *pygmaios,* fr. *pygmē* fist, measure of length — more at PUNGENT] (14c) **1** *often cap* **:** any of a race of dwarfs described by ancient Greek authors **2** *cap* **:** any of a small people of equatorial Africa ranging under five feet (1.5 meters) in height **3 a** (1) **:** an unusually small person (2) **:** an insignificant or unimpressive person ⟨an intellectual ~⟩ **b :** something very small of its kind — **pygmy** *adj*

pygmy chimpanzee *n* (1933) **:** BONOBO

py·ja·mas \pə-ˈjä-məz\ *chiefly Brit var of* PAJAMAS

pyk·nic \ˈpik-nik\ *adj* [ISV, fr. Gk *pyknos* dense, stocky] (1925) **:** characterized by shortness of stature, broadness of girth, and powerful muscularity **:** ENDOMORPHIC 2 — **pyknic** *n*

py·lon \ˈpī-ˌlän, -lən\ *n* [Gk *pylōn,* fr. *pylē* gate] (1817) **1 a :** a usu. massive gateway **b :** an ancient Egyptian gateway building in a truncated pyramidal form **c :** a monumental mass flanking an entranceway or an approach to a bridge **2 a** *chiefly Brit* **:** a tower for supporting either end of usu. a number of wires over a long span **b :** any of various towerlike structures **3 a :** a post or tower marking a prescribed course of flight for an airplane **b :** TRAFFIC CONE **c :** one of the flexible upright markers positioned on a football field at the corners of the end zone **4 :** a rigid structure on the outside of an aircraft for supporting something (as an engine or missile) — see AIRPLANE illustration

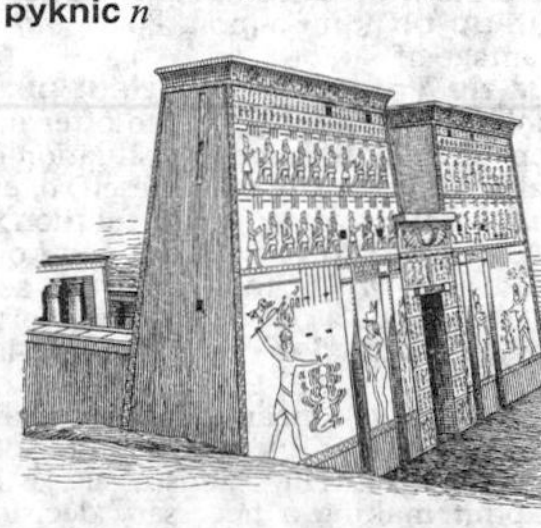

pylon 1b

py·lo·ric \pī-ˈlȯr-ik, pə-\ *adj* (1689) **:** of or relating to the pylorus; *also* **:** of, relating to, or situated in or near the posterior part of the stomach

py·lo·rus \-əs\ *n, pl* **py·lo·ri** \-ˈlȯr-ˌī, -(ˌ)ē\ [LL, fr. Gk *pylōros,* lit., gatekeeper, fr. *pylē*] (1565) **:** the muscular opening from the vertebrate stomach into the intestine

PYO *abbr* pick your own

pyo·der·ma \ˌpī-ə-ˈdər-mə\ *n* [NL] (1930) **:** a bacterial skin inflammation marked by pus-filled lesions

pyo·gen·ic \-ˈje-nik\ *adj* [ISV] (1834) **:** producing pus ⟨~ bacteria⟩; *also* **:** marked by pus production ⟨~ meningitis⟩

py·or·rhea \ˌpī-ə-ˈrē-ə\ *n* [NL] (1878) **:** purulent inflammation of the sockets of the teeth leading usu. to loosening of the teeth

pyr- *or* **pyro-** *comb form* [Gk, fr. *pyr* — more at FIRE] **1 :** fire **:** heat ⟨*pyro*meter⟩ ⟨*pyr*heliometer⟩ **2 a :** produced by or as if by the action of heat ⟨*pyro*electricity⟩ **b :** derived from a corresponding ortho acid by loss usu. of one molecule of water from two molecules of acid ⟨*pyro*phosphoric acid⟩ **3 :** fever ⟨*pyro*genic⟩

pyr·acan·tha \ˌpī-rə-ˈkan(t)-thə\ *n* [NL, fr. Gk *pyrakantha,* a tree, fr. *pyr-* + *akantha* thorn] (1633) **:** any of a small genus (*Pyracantha*) of ornamental Eurasian thorny evergreen or semievergreen shrubs of the rose family with alternate leaves, corymbs of white flowers, and small red or orange pomes — called also *firethorn*

py·ral·id \pī-ˈra-ləd\ *n* [ultim. fr. L *pyralis,* fly fabled as living in fire, fr. Gk, fr. *pyr* fire] (1870) **:** any of a very large heterogeneous family (Pyralidae) of mostly small slender long-legged moths — **pyralid** *adj*

[1]**pyr·a·mid** \ˈpir-ə-ˌmid\ *n* [L *pyramid-, pyramis,* fr. Gk] (1549) **1 a :** an ancient massive structure found esp. in Egypt having typically a square ground plan, outside walls in the form of four triangles that meet in a point at the top, and inner sepulchral chambers **b :** a structure or object of similar form **2 :** a polyhedron having for its base a polygon and for faces triangles with a common vertex — see VOLUME table **3 :** a crystalline form each face of which intersects the vertical axis and either two lateral axes or in the tetragonal system one lateral axis **4 :** an anatomical structure resembling a pyramid: as **a :** any of the conical masses that project from the renal medulla into the kidney pelvis **b :** either of two large bundles of motor fibers from the cerebral cortex that reach the medulla oblongata and are continuous with the pyramidal tracts of the spinal cord **5 :** an immaterial structure built on a broad supporting base and narrowing gradually to an apex ⟨the socioeconomic ~⟩ — **py·ra·mi·dal** \pə-ˈra-mə-dᵊl, ˌpir-ə-ˈmi-\ *adj* — **py·ra·mi·dal·ly** *adv* — **pyr·a·mid·i·cal** \ˌpir-ə-ˈmi-di-kəl\ *adj*

[2]**pyramid** *vi* (ca. 1900) **1 :** to speculate (as on a security or commodity exchange) by using paper profits as margin for additional transactions **2 :** to increase rapidly and progressively step by step on a broad base ~ *vt* **1 :** to arrange or build up as if on the base of a pyramid **2 :** to use (as profits) in speculative pyramiding **3 :** to increase the impact of (as a tax assessed at the production level) on the ultimate consumer by treating as a cost subject to markup

pyramidal tract *n* (1857) **:** any of four columns of motor fibers that run in pairs on each side of the spinal cord and are continuations of the pyramids of the medulla oblongata

pyr·a·mid·ol·o·gy \ˌpir-ə-(ˌ)mi-ˈdä-lə-jē\ *n* (1924) **:** the study of or theory about mathematical or occult significance in measurements of the Great Pyramid of Egypt — **pyr·a·mid·ol·o·gist** \-jist\ *n*

pyramid scheme *n* (1949) **:** a usu. illegal operation in which participants pay to join and profit mainly from payments made by subsequent participants

Pyr·a·mus \ˈpir-ə-məs\ *n* [L, fr. Gk *Pyramos*] (14c) **:** a legendary youth of Babylon who dies for love of Thisbe

py·ran \ˈpī-ˌran\ *n* [ISV] (1904) **:** either of two cyclic compounds C_5H_6O that contain five carbon atoms and one oxygen atom in the ring

py·ra·nose \ˈpī-rə-ˌnōs, -ˌnōz\ *n* [ISV] (1927) **:** a monosaccharide in the form of a cyclic hemiacetal containing a pyran ring

py·ran·o·side \pī-ˈra-nə-ˌsīd\ *n* (1930) **:** a glycoside containing the pyran ring

pyre \ˈpī(-ə)r\ *n* [L *pyra,* fr. Gk, fr. *pyr* fire — more at FIRE] (1587) **:** a combustible heap for burning a dead body as a funeral rite; *broadly* **:** a pile of material to be burned ⟨a ~ of dead leaves⟩

py·re·noid \pī-ˈrē-ˌnȯid, ˈpī-rə-\ *n* [ISV, fr. NL *pyrena* stone of a fruit, fr. Gk *pyrēn;* akin to Gk *pyros* wheat grain, wheat — more at FURZE] (ca. 1875) **:** a protein body in the chloroplasts of algae and hornworts that is involved in carbon fixation and starch formation and storage

py·re·thrin \pī-ˈrē-thrən, -ˈre-\ *n* [ISV, fr. L *pyrethrum*] (1882) **:** either of two oily liquid esters $C_{21}H_{28}O_3$ and $C_{22}H_{28}O_5$ having insecticidal properties and occurring esp. in the flowers of pyrethrum

py·re·throid \-ˈrē-ˌthrȯid, -ˈre-\ *n* [*pyreth*rin + *-oid*] (1949) **:** any of various synthetic compounds that are related to the pyrethrins and resemble them in insecticidal properties — **pyrethroid** *adj*

py·re·thrum \pī-ˈrē-thrəm, -ˈre-\ *n* [L, pellitory, fr. Gk *pyrethron,* fr. *pyr* fire] (ca. 1543) **1 :** any of several chrysanthemums with finely divided often aromatic leaves including ornamentals as well as important sources of insecticides **2 :** an insecticide made from the dried heads of any of several Old World chrysanthemums (esp. *Chrysanthemum cinerariaefolium*)

py·ret·ic \pī-ˈre-tik\ *adj* [NL *pyreticus,* fr. Gk *pyretikos,* fr. *pyretos* fever, fr. *pyr*] (1850) **:** of or relating to fever **:** FEBRILE

Py·rex \ˈpī-ˌreks\ *trademark* — used for borosilicate glass and glassware resistant to heat, chemicals, and electricity

py·rex·ia \pī-ˈrek-sē-ə\ *n* [NL, fr. Gk *pyressein* to be feverish, fr. *pyretos*] (1777) **:** abnormal elevation of body temperature **:** FEVER — **py·rex·i·al** \-sē-əl\ *adj* — **py·rex·ic** \-sik\ *adj*

pyr·he·li·om·e·ter \ˌpī(-ə)r-ˌhē-lē-ˈä-mə-tər, ˌpir-\ *n* [ISV] (1841) **:** an instrument for measuring the sun's radiant energy as received at the earth — **pyr·he·lio·met·ric** \-lē-ə-ˈme-trik\ *adj*

pyr·i·dine \ˈpir-ə-ˌdēn\ *n* [*pyr-* + *-ide* + [2]*-ine*] (1851) **:** a toxic water-soluble flammable liquid base C_5H_5N of pungent odor that is the parent of many naturally occurring organic compounds and is used as a solvent and as a denaturant for alcohol and in the manufacture of pharmaceuticals and waterproofing agents

pyr·i·do·stig·mine bromide \ˌpir-ə-dō-ˈstig-ˌmēn-\ *n* [ISV *pyrid*ine + *neostigmine*] (1961) **:** a cholinergic drug $C_9H_{13}BrN_2O_2$ used esp. in the treatment of myasthenia gravis and as a prophylactic against the effects of nerve gas — called also *pyridostigmine*

pyr·i·dox·al \ˌpir-ə-ˈdäk-ˌsal\ *n* [ISV, fr. *pyridoxine*] (1944) **:** a crystalline aldehyde $C_8H_9NO_3$ of the vitamin B_6 group that occurs as a phosphate and is active as a coenzyme

pyr·i·dox·amine \ˌpir-ə-ˈdäk-sə-ˌmēn\ *n* [ISV *pyridox*ine + *amine*] (1944) **:** a crystalline amine $C_8H_{12}N_2O_2$ of the vitamin B_6 group that occurs as a phosphate and is active as a coenzyme

pyr·i·dox·ine \ˌpir-ə-ˈdäk-ˌsēn, -sən\ *n* [*pyrid*ine + *ox-* + [2]*-ine*] (1939) **:** a crystalline phenolic alcohol $C_8H_{11}NO_3$ of the vitamin B_6 group found esp. in cereals and convertible in the organism into pyridoxal and pyridoxamine

pyr·i·form *or* **pir·i·form** \ˈpir-ə-ˌfȯrm\ *adj* [NL *pyriformis,* fr. ML *pyrum* pear (alter. of L *pirum*) + L *-iformis* -iform] (1741) **:** having the form of a pear

py·ri·meth·amine \ˌpī-rə-ˈme-thə-ˌmēn\ *n* [*pyrimi*dine + *eth*yl + *amine*] (1952) **:** a folic acid antagonist $C_{12}H_{13}ClN_4$ used in the chemoprophylaxis or treatment of malaria and in the treatment of toxoplasmosis

py·rim·i·dine \pī-ˈri-mə-ˌdēn, pə-\ *n* [ISV, alter. of *pyridine*] (1885) **1 :** a feeble organic base $C_4H_4N_2$ of penetrating odor **2 :** a derivative of pyrimidine; *esp* **:** a base (as cytosine, thymine, or uracil) that is a constituent of DNA or RNA

py·rite \ˈpī-ˌrīt\ *n* [L *pyrites*] (1741) **:** a common mineral that consists of iron disulfide, has a pale brass-yellow color and metallic luster, and is burned in making sulfur dioxide and sulfuric acid

py·rites \pə-ˈrī-tēz, pī-; ˈpī-ˌrīts\ *n, pl* **pyrites** [L, flint, fr. Gk *pyritēs* of or in fire, fr. *pyr* fire] (bef. 12c) **:** any of various metallic-looking sulfides of which pyrite is the commonest — **py·rit·ic** \-ˈri-tik\ *adj*

py·ro·cat·e·chol \ˌpī-rō-ˈka-tə-ˌkȯl, -ˌkōl\ *n* [ISV] (1881) **:** CATECHOL 2

py·ro·clas·tic \-ˈklas-tik\ *adj* (1862) **:** formed by or involving fragmentation as a result of volcanic or igneous action

py·ro·elec·tric·i·ty \ˈpī-ˌrō-ə-ˌlek-ˈtri-sə-tē, -ˈtris-tē\ *n* [ISV] (1824) **:** a state of electrical polarization produced (as in a crystal) by a change of temperature — **py·ro·elec·tric** \-ˈlek-trik\ *adj*

py·ro·gal·lol \ˌpī-rō-ˈga-ˌlȯl, -ˌlōl; -ˈgȯ-\ *n* [ISV *pyro-* + *gal*lic (acid) + [1]*-ol*] (1868) **:** a poisonous bitter crystalline phenol $C_6H_6O_3$ with weak acid properties that is usu. obtained by pyrolysis of gallic acid and used esp. as a mild reducing agent (as in photographic developing)

py·ro·gen \ˈpī-rə-jən\ *n* [ISV] (1875) **:** a fever-producing substance

py·ro·gen·ic \ˌpī-rō-ˈje-nik\ *adj* [ISV] (1823) **1 :** of or relating to igneous origin **2 :** producing or produced by heat or fever — **py·ro·ge·nic·i·ty** \ˌpī-rō-jə-ˈni-sə-tē\ *n*

py·ro·la \pī-ˈrō-lə\ *n* [NL, prob. fr. L *pirum* pear] (1527) **:** WINTERGREEN 1

py·ro·lig·ne·ous acid \ˌpī-rō-ˈlig-nē-əs-\ *n* [F *pyroligneux,* fr. *pyr-* + *ligneux* woody, fr. L *lignosus,* fr. *lignum* wood — more at LIGNEOUS] (1788) **:** an acid reddish-brown aqueous liquid containing chiefly acetic acid, methanol, wood oils, and tars that is obtained by destructive distillation of wood

py·ro·lu·site \ˌpī-rō-ˈlü-ˌsīt\ *n* [G *Pyrolusit,* fr. Gk *pyr-* + *lousis* washing, fr. *louein* to wash — more at LYE] (1828) **:** a soft black or steel-gray mineral of metallic luster consisting of manganese dioxide that is the most important ore of manganese

py·rol·y·sate \pī-ˈrä-lə-ˌzāt, -ˌsāt\ *or* **py·rol·y·zate** \-ˌzāt\ *n* (1944) **:** a product of pyrolysis

py·rol·y·sis \pī-ˈrä-lə-səs\ *n* [NL] (ca. 1890) **:** chemical change brought about by the action of heat — **py·ro·lyt·ic** \ˌpī-rə-ˈli-tik\ *adj* — **py·ro·lyt·i·cal·ly** \-ti-k(ə-)lē\ *adv*

py·ro·lyze *also* **py·ro·lize** \ˈpī-rə-ˌlīz\ *vt* **-lyzed** *also* **-lized; -lyz·ing** *also* **-liz·ing** (1919) **:** to subject to pyrolysis — **py·ro·lyz·able** \ˌpī-rə-ˈlī-zə-bəl\ *adj* — **py·ro·lyz·er** *n*

py·ro·man·cy \-ˌman(t)-sē\ *n* [ME *piromancie,* fr. MF, fr. LL *pyromantia,* fr. Gk *pyromanteia,* fr. *pyr* fire + *manteia* divination — more at -MANCY] (14c) **:** divination by means of fire or flames

py·ro·ma·nia \ˌpī-rō-'mā-nē-ə, -nyə\ *n* [NL] (ca. 1842) : an irresistible impulse to start fires — **py·ro·ma·ni·ac** \-nē-ˌak\ *n* — **py·ro·ma·ni·a·cal** \-mə-'nī-ə-kəl\ *adj*

py·ro·met·al·lur·gy \-'me-tə-ˌlər-jē, *esp Brit* -mə-'ta-lər-\ *n* [ISV] (1908) : chemical metallurgy depending on heat action (as roasting and smelting) — **py·ro·met·al·lur·gi·cal** \-ˌme-tə-'lər-ji-kəl\ *adj*

py·rom·e·ter \pī-'rä-mə-tər\ *n* [ISV] (1796) : an instrument for measuring temperatures esp. when beyond the range of mercurial thermometers — **py·ro·met·ric** \ˌpī-rə-'me-trik\ *adj* — **py·ro·met·ri·cal·ly** \-tri-k(ə-)lē\ *adv* — **py·rom·e·try** \pī-'rä-mə-trē\ *n*

py·ro·mor·phite \ˌpī-rə-'mȯr-ˌfīt\ *n* [G *Pyromorphit,* fr. Gk *pyr-* + *morphē* form] (ca. 1814) : a mineral consisting essentially of a chloride and phosphate of lead

py·ro·nine \'pī-rə-ˌnēn\ *n* [ISV, irreg. fr. *pyr-* + *²-ine*] (1895) : any of several basic xanthene dyes used chiefly as biological stains

py·rope \'pī-ˌrōp\ *n* [ME *pirope,* a red gem, fr. MF, fr. L *pyropus,* a red bronze, fr. Gk *pyrōpos,* lit., fiery-eyed, fr. *pyr-* + *ōp-, ōps* eye — more at EYE] (1804) : a magnesium-aluminum garnet that is deep red in color and is frequently used as a gem

py·ro·phor·ic \ˌpī-rō-'fȯr-ik, -'fär-\ *adj* [NL *pyrophorus,* fr. Gk *pyrophoros* fire-bearing, fr. *pyr-* + *-phoros* carrying — more at -PHORE] (1836) **1** : igniting spontaneously **2** : emitting sparks when scratched or struck esp. with steel

py·ro·phos·phate \-'fäs-ˌfāt\ *n* (1833) : a salt or ester of pyrophosphoric acid

py·ro·phos·pho·ric acid \-ˌfäs-'fȯr-ik-, -'fär-; -'fäs-f(ə-)rik-\ *n* [ISV] (1832) : a crystalline acid $H_4P_2O_7$ formed when orthophosphoric acid is heated or prepared in the form of salts by heating acid salts of orthophosphoric acid

py·ro·phyl·lite \ˌpī-rō-'fi-ˌlīt, pī-'rä-fə-ˌlīt\ *n* [G *Pyrophyllit,* fr. Gk *pyr-* + *phyllon* leaf — more at BLADE] (1830) : a soft usu. white or greenish mineral that is a hydrous aluminum silicate, resembles talc, occurs in a foliated form or in compact masses, and is used esp. in ceramic wares

py·ro·sis \pī-'rō-səs\ *n* [NL, fr. Gk *pyrōsis* burning, fr. *pyroun* to burn, fr. *pyr* fire — more at FIRE] (1789) : HEARTBURN

¹py·ro·tech·nic \ˌpī-rə-'tek-nik\ *also* **py·ro·tech·ni·cal** \-ni-kəl\ *adj* [F *pyrotechnique,* fr. Gk *pyr* fire + *technē* art — more at TECHNICAL] (1755) : of or relating to pyrotechnics — **py·ro·tech·ni·cal·ly** \-ni-k(ə-)lē\ *adv*

²pyrotechnic *n* (1840) **1 a** : FIREWORK **b** : any of various similar devices (as for igniting a rocket or producing an explosion) **2** : a combustible substance used in a firework

py·ro·tech·nics \ˌpī-rə-'tek-niks\ *n pl* (1729) **1** *sing or pl in constr* : the art of making or the manufacture and use of fireworks **2 a** : a display of fireworks **b** : a spectacular display (as of extreme virtuosity) ⟨verbal ∼⟩ ⟨keyboard ∼⟩ — **py·ro·tech·ni·cian** \-ˌtek-'ni-shən\ *n* — **py·ro·tech·nist** \-'tek-nist\ *n*

py·rox·ene \pī-'räk-ˌsēn, pə-\ *n* [F *pyroxène,* fr. Gk *pyr-* + *xenos* stranger] (1800) : any of a group of igneous-rock-forming silicate minerals that contain calcium, sodium, magnesium, iron, or aluminum, usu. occur in short prismatic crystals or massive form, are often laminated, and vary in color from white to dark green or black — **py·rox·e·nic** \ˌpī-ˌräk-'sē-nik, pə-, -'se-\ *adj* — **py·rox·e·noid** \pī-'räk-sə-ˌnȯid, pə-\ *adj or n*

py·rox·e·nite \pī-'räk-sə-ˌnīt, pə-\ *n* (1850) : an igneous rock that is free from olivine and is composed essentially of pyroxene — **py·rox·e·nit·ic** \-ˌräk-sə-'ni-tik\ *adj*

py·rox·y·lin \pī-'räk-sə-lən, pə-\ *n* [ISV *pyr-* + Gk *xylon* wood] (ca. 1847) **1** : a flammable mixture of nitrocelluloses used esp. in making plastics and water-repellent coatings (as lacquers) **2** : a pyroxylin product

Pyr·rha \'pir-ə\ *n* [L, fr. Gk] (1560) : the wife of Deucalion

pyr·rhic \'pir-ik\ *n* [L *pyrrhichius,* fr. Gk (*pous*) *pyrrhichios,* fr. *pyrrhichē,* a kind of dance] (1626) : a metrical foot consisting of two short or unaccented syllables

Pyr·rhic \'pir-ik\ *adj* [*Pyrrhus,* king of Epirus who sustained heavy losses in defeating the Romans] (1838) : achieved at excessive cost ⟨a ∼ victory⟩; *also* : costly to the point of negating or outweighing expected benefits ⟨a great but ∼ act of ingenuity⟩

Pyr·rho·nism \'pir-ə-ˌni-zəm\ *n* [F *pyrrhonisme,* fr. *Pyrrhon* Pyrrho, 4th cent. B.C. Gk. philosopher, fr. Gk *Pyrrhōn*] (ca. 1670) **1** : the doctrines of a school of ancient extreme skeptics who suspended judgment on every proposition — compare ACADEMICISM **2** : total or radical skepticism — **Pyr·rho·nist** \-nist\ *n*

pyr·rho·tite \'pir-ə-ˌtīt\ *n* [modif. of G *Pyrrhotin,* fr. Gk *pyrrhotēs* redness, fr. *pyrrhos* red, fr. *pyr* fire — more at FIRE] (1868) : a bronze-colored mineral of metallic luster that consists of ferrous sulfide and is attracted by a magnet

Pyr·rhus \'pir-əs\ *n* [L, fr. Gk *Pyrrhos*] (14c) : a son of Achilles and slayer of Priam at the taking of Troy

pyr·role \'pir-ˌōl\ *n* [Gk *pyrrhos*] (1835) : a toxic liquid heterocyclic compound C_4H_5N that has a ring consisting of four carbon atoms and one nitrogen atom, polymerizes readily in air, and is the parent compound of many biologically important substances (as bile pigments, porphyrins, and chlorophyll); *broadly* : a derivative of pyrrole — **pyr·rol·ic** \pi-'rō-lik\ *adj*

py·ru·vate \pī-'rü-ˌvāt\ *n* (1855) : a salt or ester of pyruvic acid

py·ru·vic acid \pī-'rü-vik-\ *n* [ISV *pyr-* + L *uva* grapes; fr. its importance in fermentation — more at UVULA] (1838) : a 3-carbon acid $C_3H_4O_3$ that in carbohydrate metabolism is an important intermediate product formed esp. during glycolysis

¹Py·thag·o·re·an \pə-ˌtha-gə-'rē-ən, (ˌ)pī-\ *n* (1550) : any of a group professing to be followers of the Greek philosopher Pythagoras

²Pythagorean *adj* (ca. 1580) : of, relating to, or associated with the Greek philosopher Pythagoras, his philosophy, or the Pythagoreans

Py·thag·o·re·an·ism \-'rē-ə-ˌni-zəm\ *n* (ca. 1727) : the doctrines and theories of Pythagoras and the Pythagoreans who developed some basic principles of mathematics and astronomy, originated the doctrine of the harmony of the spheres, and believed in metempsychosis, the eternal recurrence of things, and the mystical significance of numbers

Pythagorean theorem *n* (1743) : a theorem in geometry: the square of the length of the hypotenuse of a right triangle equals the sum of the squares of the lengths of the other two sides

Pyth·i·ad \'pi-thē-ˌad, -əd\ *n* [Gk *Pythia,* the Pythian games, fr. neut. pl. of *pythios*] (1753) : the 4-year period between celebrations of the Pythian games in ancient Greece

¹Pyth·i·an \'pi-thē-ən\ *adj* [L *pythius* of Delphi, fr. Gk *pythios,* fr. *Pythō* Pytho, name for Delphi, Greece] (1603) **1** : of or relating to games celebrated at Delphi every four years **2** : of or relating to Delphi or its oracle of Apollo

²Pythian *n* (1903) : KNIGHT OF PYTHIAS

Pyth·i·as \'pi-thē-əs\ *n* [Gk] (1557) : a friend of Damon condemned to death by Dionysius of Syracuse

py·thon \'pī-ˌthän, -thən\ *n* [L, monstrous serpent killed by Apollo, fr. Gk *Pythōn,* fr. *Pythō* Delphi] (1836) : any of various large constricting snakes (as a boa); *esp* : any of the large oviparous snakes (subfamily Pythoninae of the family Boidae) of Africa, Asia, Australia, and adjacent islands that include some of the largest existing snakes

py·tho·ness \'pī-thə-nəs, 'pi-\ *n* [ME *Phitonesse,* fr. MF *pithonisse,* fr. LL *pythonissa,* fr. Gk *Pythōn,* spirit of divination, perh. fr. *Pythō,* seat of the Delphic oracle] (14c) **1** : a woman who practices divination **2** : a prophetic priestess of Apollo — **py·thon·ic** \pī-'thä-nik\ *adj*

python

py·uria \pī-'yu̇r-ē-ə\ *n* [NL] (ca. 1811) : pus in the urine; *also* : a condition characterized by pus in the urine

pyx \'piks\ *n* [ME, fr. ML *pyxis,* fr. L, box, fr. Gk, fr. *pyxos* box (shrub)] (15c) **1** : a container for the reserved host; *esp* : a small round metal receptacle used to carry the Eucharist to the sick **2** : a box used in a mint for deposit of sample coins reserved for testing weight and fineness

pyx·ie \'pik-sē\ *n* [by shortening & alter. fr. NL *Pyxidanthera*] (1882) : a creeping evergreen dicotyledonous shrub (*Pyxidanthera barbulata* of the family Diapensiaceae) of the sandy pine barrens of the Atlantic coast of the U.S. that has white or pink pentamerous flowers

pyx·is \'pik-səs\ *n, pl* **pyx·i·des** \-sə-ˌdēz\ [NL, fr. L, box] (1845) : a capsular fruit that dehisces so that the upper part falls off like a cap

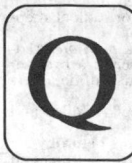

Q

1**q** \ˈkyü\ *n, pl* **q's** *or* **qs** \ˈkyüz\ *often cap, often attrib* (bef. 12c) **1 a :** the 17th letter of the English alphabet **b :** a graphic representation of this letter **c :** a speech counterpart of orthographic *q* **2 :** a graphic device for reproducing the letter *q* **3 :** one designated *q* esp. as the 17th in order or class **4 :** something shaped like the letter Q
2**q** *abbr* **1** quart **2** quartile **3** quarto **4** queen **5** query **6** question **7** quetzal **8** quire
QA *abbr* quality assurance
qat *var of* KHAT
QB *abbr* **1** quarterback **2** Queen's Bench
Q–boat \ˈkyü-ˌbōt\ *n* (1918) **:** Q-SHIP
QC *abbr* **1** quality control **2** Queen's Counsel **3** Quebec
QCD *abbr* quantum chromodynamics
qd *abbr* [L *quaque die*] every day
QED *abbr* **1** quantum electrodynamics **2** [L *quod erat demonstrandum*] which was to be demonstrated
QF *abbr* quick-firing
Q fever *n* [*query*] (1937) **:** a disease characterized by high fever, chills, muscular pains, headache, and sometimes pneumonia that is caused by a bacterium (*Coxiella burnetii* of the family Coxiellaceae) of which domestic animals serve as reservoirs and that is transmitted to humans esp. by inhalation of infective airborne bacteria
qi *var of* 2CHI
qid *abbr* [L *quater in die*] four times a day
qi·gong \ˈchē-ˈgüŋ\ *n, often cap* [Ch (Beijing) *qìgōng,* fr. *qì* chi + *gōng* achievement, skill] (1974) **:** an ancient Chinese healing art involving meditation, controlled breathing, and movement exercises
qin·dar \kyin-ˈdär, kin-\ *n, pl* **qin·dar·ka** \-ˈdär-kə\ [Alb] (ca. 1929) — see *lek* at MONEY table
qi·vi·ut \ˈkē-vē-ət, -vē-ˌüt\ *n* [Inuit] (1958) **:** the wool of the undercoat of the musk ox
Qld *abbr* Queensland
QM *abbr* **1** quantum mechanics **2** quartermaster
QMC *abbr* quartermaster corps
QMG *abbr* quartermaster general
qoph *or* **koph** \ˈkōf\ *n* [Heb *qōph*] (ca. 1567) **:** the 19th letter of the Hebrew alphabet — see ALPHABET table
qp *abbr* [L *quantum placet*] as much as you please
qq v *abbr* [L *quae vide*] which *(pl)* see
qr *abbr* quarter
Q rating *n* [*quotient*] (1977) **:** a scale measuring the popularity of a person or thing typically based on dividing an assessment of familiarity by an assessment of favorable opinion; *also* **:** position on such a scale
qs *abbr* [L *quantum sufficit*] as much as suffices
Q–ship \ˈkyü-ˌship\ *n* (1919) **:** an armed ship disguised as a merchant or fishing ship to decoy enemy submarines into gun range
qt *abbr* **1** quantity **2** quart
q.t. \ˌkyü-ˈtē\ *n, often cap Q&T* [abbr.] (1884) **:** QUIET — usu. used in the phrase *on the q.t.*
qtd *abbr* **1** quartered **2** quoted
Q–tips \ˈkyü-ˌtips\ *trademark* — used for cotton-tipped swabs
qty *abbr* quantity
qu *or* **ques** *abbr* question
qua \ˈkwä *also* ˈkwā\ *prep* [L, which way, as, fr. abl. sing. fem. of *qui* who — more at WHO] (1647) **:** in the capacity or character of **:** AS ⟨discussing the story ~ story⟩
quaa·lude \ˈkwā-ˌlüd\ *n* [fr. *Quaalude,* a trademark] (1966) **:** a tablet or capsule of methaqualone
1**quack** \ˈkwak\ *vi* [alter. of *queck* to quack, fr. ME *queken,* fr. *queke,* interj., of imit. origin] (14c) **:** to make the characteristic cry of a duck
2**quack** *n* (1798) **:** a noise made by quacking
3**quack** *vi* [4*quack*] (1628) **:** to act like a quack
4**quack** *n* [short for *quacksalver*] (1638) **1 :** CHARLATAN 2 **2 :** a pretender to medical skill — **quack·ish** \ˈkwa-kish\ *adj*
5**quack** *adj* (1653) **:** of, relating to, or used by quacks ⟨~ cancer cures⟩
quack·ery \ˈkwa-k(ə-)rē\ *n* (ca. 1711) **:** the practices or pretensions of a quack
quack grass \ˈkwak-\ *n* [alter. of *quick* (grass), alter. of *quitch* (grass)] (ca. 1818) **:** a European grass (*Elytrigia repens* syn. *Agropyron repens*) that is naturalized throughout No. America and spreads by creeping rhizomes — called also *couch grass, quitch, twitch, witchgrass*
quack·sal·ver \ˈkwak-ˌsal-vər\ *n* [obs. D (now *kwakzalver*)] (1579) **:** CHARLATAN, QUACK
1**quad** \ˈkwäd\ *n* (1820) **:** QUADRANGLE
2**quad** *n* [short for *quadrat*] (ca. 1879) **:** a type-metal space that is one en or more in width
3**quad** *vt* **quad·ded; quad·ding** (ca. 1888) **:** to fill out (as a typeset line) with blank space
4**quad** *n* (1896) **1 :** QUADRUPLET **2 :** a ski lift that holds four people **3 :** a quadruple toe loop in competitive figure skating
5**quad** *adj* (1970) **:** QUADRAPHONIC
6**quad** *n* (1971) **:** quadraphonic sound
7**quad** *n* [short for *quadrillion*] (1974) **:** a unit of energy equal to one quadrillion British thermal units
8**quad** *n* (1954) **:** QUADRICEPS — usu. used in pl.
quad·ran·gle \ˈkwä-ˌdraŋ-gəl\ *n* [ME, fr. MF, fr. LL *quadriangulum,* fr. L, neut. of *quadriangulus* quadrangular, fr. *quadri-* + *angulus* angle] (15c) **1 :** QUADRILATERAL **2 a :** a 4-sided enclosure esp. when surrounded by buildings **b :** the buildings enclosing a quadrangle **3 :** a tract of country represented by one of a series of map sheets — **qua·dran·gu·lar** \kwä-ˈdraŋ-gyə-lər\ *adj*
quad·rant \ˈkwä-drənt\ *n* [ME, fr. L *quadrant-, quadrans* fourth part; akin to L *quattuor* four — more at FOUR] (15c) **1 a :** an instrument for measuring altitudes consisting commonly of a graduated arc of 90 degrees with an index or vernier and usu. having a plumb line or spirit level for fixing the vertical or horizontal direction **b :** a device or mechanical part shaped like or suggestive of the quadrant of a circle **2 a :** an arc of 90 degrees that is one quarter of a circle **b :** the area bounded by a quadrant and two radii **3 a :** any of the four parts into which a plane is divided by rectangular coordinate axes lying in that plane **b :** any of the four quarters into which something is divided by two real or imaginary lines that intersect each other at right angles — **qua·dran·tal** \kwä-ˈdran-tᵊl\ *adj*

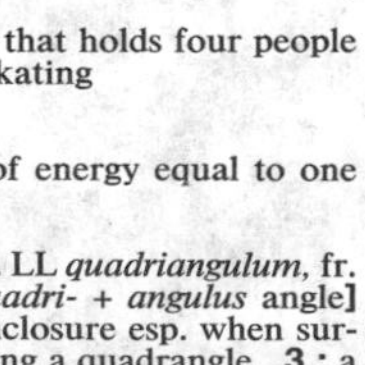

quadrant 2

Qua·dran·tid \kwä-ˈdran-təd\ *n* [NL *Quadrant-, Quadrans* (*Muralis*) mural quadrant, a group of stars in the constellation Draco from which the shower appears to radiate] (1876) **:** any of a group of meteors that appear annually about January 3
quad·ra·phon·ic *also* **quad·ri·phon·ic** \ˌkwä-drə-ˈfä-nik\ *adj* [irreg. fr. *quadri-* + *-phonic* (as in *stereophonic*)] (1969) **:** of, relating to, or using four channels for the transmission, recording, or reproduction of sound — **quad·ra·phon·ics** *or* **quad·ri·phon·ics** \-niks\ *n pl but sing in constr*
quad·rat \ˈkwä-drət, -ˌdrat\ *n* [alter. of 2*quadrate*] (1683) **1 :** 2QUAD **2 :** a usu. rectangular plot used for ecological or population studies
1**quad·rate** \ˈkwä-ˌdrāt, -drət\ *adj* [ME, fr. L *quadratus,* pp. of *quadrare* to make square, fit, fr. *quadrum* square; akin to L *quattuor* four] (14c) **1 :** being square or approximately square **2** *of a heraldic cross* **:** expanded into a square at the junction of the arms — see CROSS illustration **3 :** of, relating to, or constituting a bony or cartilaginous element of each side of the skull to which the lower jaw is articulated in most vertebrates below mammals
2**quadrate** *n* (15c) **1 :** an approximately square or cubical area, space, or body **2 :** a quadrate bone
qua·drat·ic \kwä-ˈdra-tik\ *adj* (1668) **:** involving terms of the second degree at most ⟨~ function⟩ ⟨~ equations⟩ — **quadratic** *n* — **qua·drat·i·cal·ly** \-ti-k(ə-)lē\ *adv*
quadratic form *n* (1853) **:** a homogeneous polynomial (as $x^2 + 5xy + y^2$) of the second degree
quad·ra·ture \ˈkwä-drə-ˌchu̇r, -chər, -ˌtyu̇r, -ˌtu̇r\ *n* (1591) **1 :** a configuration in which two celestial bodies (as the moon and the sun) have an angular separation of 90 degrees as seen from the earth **2 :** the process of finding a square equal in area to a given area
qua·dren·ni·al \kwä-ˈdre-nē-əl\ *adj* (ca. 1656) **1 :** consisting of or lasting for four years **2 :** occurring or being done every four years — **quadrennial** *n* — **qua·dren·ni·al·ly** \-nē-ə-lē\ *adv*
qua·dren·ni·um \-nē-əm\ *n, pl* **-ni·ums** *or* **-nia** \-nē-ə\ [L *quadriennium,* fr. *quadri-* + *annus* year — more at ANNUAL] (1754) **:** a period of four years
quadri- *or* **quadr-** *or* **quadru-** *comb form* [L; akin to L *quattuor* four] **1 a :** four ⟨*quadri*lateral⟩ ⟨*quadru*manous⟩ **b :** square ⟨*quadr*ic⟩ **2 :** fourth ⟨*quadri*centennial⟩
quad·ric \ˈkwä-drik\ *adj* [ISV] (1856) **:** QUADRATIC ⟨~ surface⟩ — used where there are more than two variables — **quadric** *n*
quad·ri·cen·ten·ni·al \ˌkwä-drə-sen-ˈte-nē-əl\ *n* (1882) **:** a 400th anniversary or its celebration
quad·ri·ceps \ˈkwä-drə-ˌseps\ *n, pl* **quadriceps** *also* **quadriceps·es** [NL *quadricipit-, quadriceps,* fr. *quadri-* + *-cipit-, -ceps* (as in *bicipit-, biceps* biceps)] (1840) **:** the greater extensor muscle of the front of the thigh that is divided into four parts
qua·dri·ga \kwä-ˈdrē-gə\ *n, pl* **-gae** \-ˌgī\ [L, sing. of *quadrigae* team of four, contr. of *quadrijugae,* fem. pl. of *quadrijugus* yoked four abreast, fr. *quadri-* + *jungere* to yoke, join — more at YOKE] (ca. 1741) **:** a chariot drawn by four horses abreast
1**quad·ri·lat·er·al** \ˌkwä-drə-ˈla-t(ə-)rəl\ *n* [L *quadrilaterus* four-sided, fr. *quadri-* + *later-, latus* side] (1650) **:** a polygon of four sides
2**quadrilateral** *adj* (1656) **:** having four sides
1**qua·drille** \kwä-ˈdril, kwə-, kə-\ *n* [F, group of knights engaged in a carousel, fr. Sp *cuadrilla* troop, fr. dim. of *cuadra* square, fr. L *quadra, quadrum*] (1726) **1 :** a four-handed variant of ombre popular esp. in the 18th century **2 :** a square dance for four couples made up of five or six figures chiefly in ⁶⁄₈ and ²⁄₄ time; *also* **:** music for this dance
2**quadrille** *adj* [F *quadrillé*] (1856) **:** marked with squares or rectangles
qua·dril·lion \kwä-ˈdril-yən\ *n* [F, fr. MF, fr. *quadri-* + *-illion* (as in *million*)] (ca. 1690) — see NUMBER table — **quadrillion** *adj* — **qua·dril·lionth** \-yən(t)th\ *adj or n*
quad·ri·par·tite \ˌkwä-drə-ˈpär-ˌtīt\ *adj* [ME, fr. L *quadripartitus,* fr. *quadri-* + *partitus,* pp. of *partire* to divide, fr. *part-, pars* part] (15c) **1 :** consisting of or divided into four parts **2 :** shared or participated in by four parties or persons ⟨a ~ agreement⟩
quad·ri·ple·gic \ˌkwä-drə-ˈplē-jik\ *n* [*quadriplegia,* fr. NL] (1921) **:** one affected with paralysis of both arms and both legs — **quad·ri·ple·gia** \-j(ē-)ə\ *n*
1**quad·ri·va·lent** \ˌkwä-drə-ˈvā-lənt, *in sense 2* kwä-ˈdri-və-lənt\ *adj* [ISV] (1865) **1 :** TETRAVALENT **2 :** composed of four homologous chromosomes synapsed in meiotic prophase
2**quadrivalent** *n* (1923) **:** a quadrivalent chromosomal group
qua·driv·i·al \kwä-ˈdri-vē-əl\ *adj* (15c) **1 :** of or relating to the quadrivium **2 :** having four ways or roads meeting in a point
qua·driv·i·um \-vē-əm\ *n* [LL, fr. L, crossroads, fr. *quadri-* + *via* way — more at WAY] (1804) **:** a group of studies consisting of arithmetic, music, geometry, and astronomy and forming the upper division of the seven liberal arts in medieval universities — compare TRIVIUM
qua·droon \kwä-ˈdrün\ *n* [modif. of Sp *cuarterón,* fr. *cuarto* fourth, fr. L *quartus* — more at QUART] (1707) **:** a person of one-quarter black ancestry
qua·dru·ma·nous \kwä-ˈdrü-mə-nəs\ *adj* [ultim. fr. L *quadri-* + *manus* hand — more at MANUAL] (1819) **:** having feet adapted for grasping
qua·drum·vir \kwä-ˈdrəm-vər\ *n* [back-formation fr. *quadrumvirate*] (1790) **:** a member of a quadrumvirate
qua·drum·vi·rate \-və-rət\ *n* [*quadri-* + *-umvirate* (as in *triumvirate*)] (1752) **:** a group or association of four
quad·ru·ped \ˈkwä-drə-ˌped\ *n* [L *quadruped-, quadrupes,* fr. *quadruped-, quadrupes,* adj., having four feet, fr. *quadri-* + *ped-, pes* foot — more at FOOT] (1646) **:** an animal having four feet — **quadruped** *adj* — **qua·dru·pe·dal** \kwä-ˈdrü-pə-dᵊl, ˌkwä-drə-ˈpe-\ *adj*
1**qua·dru·ple** \kwä-ˈdrü-pəl, -ˈdrə-; ˈkwä-drə-\ *vb* **qua·dru·pled; qua·dru·pling** \-p(ə-)liŋ\ [ME (Sc), fr. L *quadruplare,* fr. *quadruplus*] *vt* (14c) **:** to make four times as great or as many ~ *vi* **:** to become four times as great or as numerous
2**quadruple** *n* [ME, fr. AF, fr. L *quadruplum,* fr. neut. of *quadruplus* four times as great, fr. *quadri-* + *-plus* multiplied by — more at -FOLD] (15c) **:** a sum four times as great as another

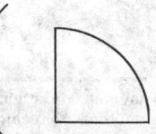

[3]**quadruple** *adj* (1557) **1 :** having four units or members **2 :** being four times as great or as many **3 :** marked by four beats per measure ⟨~ meter⟩ — **qua·dru·ply** \-ˈdrü-plē, -ˈdrə-, -drə-\ *adv* — **qua·dru·plic·i·ty** \ˌkwä-drü-ˈpli-sə-tē\ *n*

qua·dru·plet \kwä-ˈdrü-plət, -ˈdrə-; ˈkwä-drə-plət\ *n* (1709) **1 :** a combination of four of a kind **2 :** one of four offspring born at one birth **3 :** a group of four musical notes to be performed in the time ordinarily given to three of the same kind

[1]**qua·dru·pli·cate** \kwä-ˈdrü-pli-kət\ *adj* [L *quadruplicatus,* pp. of *quadruplicare* to quadruple, fr. *quadruplic-, quadruplex* fourfold, fr. *quadri-* + *-plic-, -plex* fold — more at -FOLD] (1656) **1 :** consisting of or existing in four corresponding or identical parts or examples ⟨~ invoices⟩ **2 :** being the fourth of four things exactly alike

[2]**qua·dru·pli·cate** \-plə-ˌkāt\ *vt* **-cat·ed; -cat·ing** (ca. 1661) **1 :** to make quadruple or fourfold **2 :** to prepare in quadruplicate — **qua·dru·pli·ca·tion** \-ˌdrü-plə-ˈkā-shən\ *n*

[3]**qua·dru·pli·cate** \kwä-ˈdrü-pli-kət\ *n* (1790) **1 :** four copies all alike — used with *in* ⟨typed in ~⟩ **2 :** one of four things exactly alike; *specif* **:** one of four identical copies

quad·ru·pole \ˈkwä-drə-ˌpōl\ *n* [ISV *quadri-* + *pole*] (1922) **:** a system composed of two dipoles of equal but oppositely directed moment

quae·re \ˈkwir-ē, ˈkwer-\ *n* [L, imper. of *quaerere* to seek, question] (1589) *archaic* **:** QUERY

quaes·tor *also* **ques·tor** \ˈkwe-stər, ˈkwē-\ *n* [ME *questor,* fr. L *quaestor,* fr. *quaerere*] (14c) **:** one of numerous ancient Roman officials concerned chiefly with financial administration

quaff \ˈkwäf, ˈkwaf\ *vb* [origin unknown] *vi* (1523) **:** to drink deeply ~ *vt* **:** to drink (a beverage) deeply — **quaff** *n* — **quaff·er** *n*

quag \ˈkwag, ˈkwäg\ *n* [origin unknown] (1589) **:** MARSH, BOG

quag·ga \ˈkwa-gə, ˈkwä-\ *n* [obs. Afrik (now *kwagga*), fr. Khoikhoi *quácha*] (1785) **:** an extinct mammal (*Equus quagga*) of southern Africa that resembled and was related to the zebras

quag·gy \ˈkwa-gē, ˈkwä-\ *adj* (1610) **1 :** MARSHY **2 :** FLABBY

quag·mire \ˈkwag-ˌmī(-ə)r, ˈkwäg-\ *n* (ca. 1576) **1 :** soft miry land that shakes or yields under the foot **2 :** a difficult, precarious, or entrapping position **:** PREDICAMENT

qua·hog *also* **qua·haug** \ˈkō-ˌhȯg, ˈkwȯ-, ˈkwō-, -ˌhäg\ *n* [modif. of Narragansett *poquaûhock*] (1753) **:** a thick-shelled edible clam (*Mercenaria mercenaria*) of the U.S.

quai \ˈkā\ *n* [F, fr. MF *cai* — more at QUAY] (1862) **:** QUAY

quaich *or* **quaigh** \ˈkwāk\ *n* [ScGael *cuach*] (1546) *chiefly Scot* **:** a small shallow drinking vessel with ears for use as handles

[1]**quail** \ˈkwāl\ *n, pl* **quail** *or* **quails** [ME *quaile,* fr. AF, fr. ML *quaccula,* of imit. origin] (14c) **:** any of numerous small gallinaceous birds: as **a :** an Old World migratory game bird (*Coturnix coturnix*) **b :** BOBWHITE

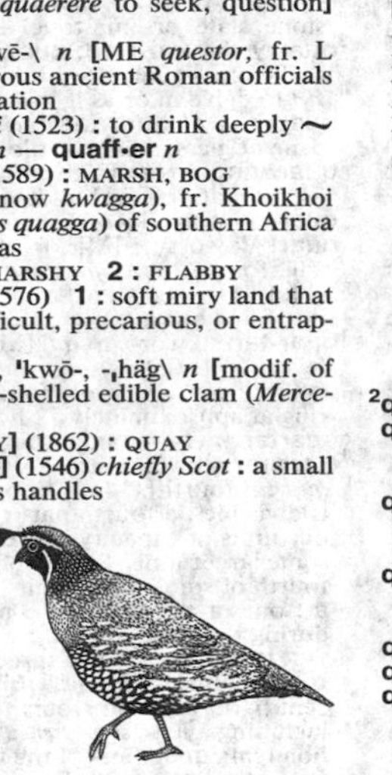
quail

[2]**quail** *vb* [ME, fr. MD *quelen*] *vi* (15c) **1** **a** *chiefly dial* **:** WITHER, DECLINE **b :** to give way **:** FALTER ⟨his courage never ~*ed*⟩ **2 :** to recoil in dread or terror **:** COWER ⟨the strongest ~ before financial ruin —Samuel Butler †1902⟩ ~ *vt, archaic* **:** to make fearful ***syn*** see RECOIL

quaint \ˈkwānt\ *adj* [ME *queinte, cointe,* fr. AF, clever, expert, fr. L *cognitus,* pp. of *cognoscere* to know — more at COGNITION] (13c) **1** *obs* **:** EXPERT, SKILLED **2 a :** marked by skillful design ⟨~ with many a device in India ink —Herman Melville⟩ **b :** marked by beauty or elegance **3 a :** unusual or different in character or appearance **:** ODD **b :** pleasingly or strikingly old-fashioned or unfamiliar ⟨a ~ phrase⟩ ***syn*** see STRANGE — **quaint·ly** *adv* — **quaint·ness** *n*

[1]**quake** \ˈkwāk\ *vi* **quaked; quak·ing** [ME, fr. OE *cwacian*] (bef. 12c) **1 :** to shake or vibrate usu. from shock or instability **2 :** to tremble or shudder usu. from cold or fear

[2]**quake** *n* (14c) **:** an instance of shaking or trembling (as of the earth or moon); *esp* **:** EARTHQUAKE

quak·er \ˈkwā-kər\ *n* (1597) **1 :** one that quakes **2** *cap* **:** FRIEND 5 — **Quak·er·ish** \ˈkwā-k(ə-)rish\ *adj* — **Quak·er·ism** \-kə-ˌri-zəm\ *n* — **Quak·er·ly** \-kər-lē\ *adj*

Quaker gun *n* [fr. opposition to war as a basic Quaker tenet] (1809) **:** a dummy piece of artillery usu. made of wood

quak·er–la·dies \ˌkwā-kər-ˈlā-dēz\ *n pl* (1871) **:** BLUETS

quaking aspen *n* (1812) **:** an aspen (*Populus tremuloides*) chiefly of the U.S. and Canada with small nearly circular leaves that have flattened petioles and finely serrate margins and that flutter in the slightest breeze

qual *abbr* quality

qua·le \ˈkwä-lē, -ˌlā\ *n, pl* **qua·lia** \ˈkwä-lē-ə\ [L, neut. of *qualis* of what kind] (1675) **1 :** a property (as redness) considered apart from things having the property **:** UNIVERSAL **2 :** a property as it is experienced as distinct from any source it might have in a physical object

qual·i·fi·able \ˌkwä-lə-ˈfī-ə-bəl\ *adj* (1611) **:** capable of qualifying or being qualified

qual·i·fi·ca·tion \ˌkwä-lə-fə-ˈkā-shən\ *n* (1538) **1 :** a restriction in meaning or application **:** a limiting modification ⟨this statement stands without ~⟩ **2 a** *obs* **:** NATURE **b** *archaic* **:** CHARACTERISTIC **3 a :** a quality or skill that fits a person (as for an office) ⟨the applicant with the best ~*s*⟩ **b :** a condition or standard that must be complied with (as for the attainment of a privilege) ⟨a ~ for membership⟩

qual·i·fied \ˈkwä-lə-ˌfīd\ *adj* (1558) **1 a :** fitted (as by training or experience) for a given purpose **:** COMPETENT **b :** having complied with the specific requirements or precedent conditions (as for an office or employment) **:** ELIGIBLE **2 :** limited or modified in some way ⟨~ approval⟩ — **qual·i·fied·ly** \-ˌfī(-ə)d-lē\ *adv*

qual·i·fi·er \-ˌfī(-ə)r\ *n* (1561) **:** one that qualifies: as **a :** one that satisfies requirements or meets a specified standard **b :** a word (as an adjective) or word group that limits or modifies the meaning of another word (as a noun) or word group

qual·i·fy \ˈkwä-lə-ˌfī\ *vb* **-fied; -fy·ing** [MF *qualifier,* fr. ML *qualificare,* fr. L *qualis*] *vt* (1533) **1 a :** to reduce from a general to a particular or restricted form **:** MODIFY **b :** to make less harsh or strict **:** MODERATE **c :** to alter the strength or flavor of **d :** to limit or modify the meaning of (as a noun) **2 :** to characterize by naming an attribute **:** DESCRIBE ⟨cannot ~ it as . . . either glad or sorry —T. S. Eliot⟩ **3 a :** to fit by training, skill, or ability for a special purpose **b (1) :** to declare competent or adequate **:** CERTIFY **(2) :** to invest with legal capacity **:** LICENSE ~ *vi* **1 :** to be or become fit (as for an office) **:** meet the required standard **2 :** to acquire legal or competent power or capacity ⟨has just *qualified* as a lawyer⟩ **3 a :** to exhibit a required degree of ability in a preliminary contest ⟨*qualified* for the finals⟩ **b :** to shoot well enough to earn a marksmanship badge

qual·i·ta·tive \ˈkwä-lə-ˌtā-tiv\ *adj* (1607) **:** of, relating to, or involving quality or kind — **qual·i·ta·tive·ly** *adv*

qualitative analysis *n* (1842) **:** chemical analysis designed to identify the components of a substance or mixture

[1]**qual·i·ty** \ˈkwä-lə-tē\ *n, pl* **-ties** [ME *qualite,* fr. AF *qualité,* fr. L *qualitat-, qualitas,* fr. *qualis* of what kind; akin to L *qui* who — more at WHO] (14c) **1 a :** peculiar and essential character **:** NATURE ⟨her ethereal ~ —Gay Talese⟩ **b :** an inherent feature **:** PROPERTY ⟨had a ~ of stridence, dissonance —Roald Dahl⟩ **c :** CAPACITY, ROLE ⟨in the ~ of reader and companion —Joseph Conrad⟩ **2 a :** degree of excellence **:** GRADE ⟨the ~ of competing air service —*Current Biog.*⟩ **b :** superiority in kind ⟨merchandise of ~⟩ **3 a :** social status **:** RANK **b :** ARISTOCRACY **4 a :** a distinguishing attribute **:** CHARACTERISTIC ⟨possesses many fine *qualities*⟩ **b** *archaic* **:** an acquired skill **:** ACCOMPLISHMENT **5 :** the character in a logical proposition of being affirmative or negative **6 :** vividness of hue **7 a :** TIMBRE **b :** the identifying character of a vowel sound determined chiefly by the resonance of the vocal chambers in uttering it **8 :** the attribute of an elementary sensation that makes it fundamentally unlike any other sensation

syn QUALITY, PROPERTY, CHARACTER, ATTRIBUTE mean an intelligible feature by which a thing may be identified. QUALITY is a general term applicable to any trait or characteristic whether individual or generic ⟨material with a silky *quality*⟩. PROPERTY implies a characteristic that belongs to a thing's essential nature and may be used to describe a type or species ⟨the *property* of not conducting heat⟩. CHARACTER applies to a peculiar and distinctive quality of a thing or a class ⟨remarks of an unseemly *character*⟩. ATTRIBUTE implies a quality ascribed to a thing or a being ⟨the *attributes* of a military hero⟩.

[2]**quality** *adj* (1936) **:** being of high quality

quality assurance *n* (1973) **:** a program for the systematic monitoring and evaluation of the various aspects of a project, service, or facility to ensure that standards of quality are being met

quality circle *n* (1979) **:** a group of employees who volunteer to meet regularly to discuss and propose solutions to problems (as of quality or productivity) in the workplace

quality control *n* (1935) **:** an aggregate of activities (as design analysis and inspection for defects) designed to ensure adequate quality esp. in manufactured products — **quality controller** *n*

quality point *n* (1948) **:** GRADE POINT

quality point average *n* (ca. 1972) **:** GRADE POINT AVERAGE

qualm \ˈkwäm *also* ˈkwȯm *or* ˈkwälm\ *n* [origin unknown] (ca. 1530) **1 :** a sudden attack of illness, faintness, or nausea **2 :** a sudden access of usu. disturbing emotion (as doubt or fear) **3 :** a feeling of uneasiness about a point esp. of conscience or propriety — **qualmy** *adj*

syn QUALM, SCRUPLE, COMPUNCTION, DEMUR mean a misgiving about what one is doing or going to do. QUALM implies an uneasy fear that one is not following one's conscience or better judgment ⟨no *qualms* about plagiarizing⟩. SCRUPLE implies doubt of the rightness of an act on grounds of principle ⟨no *scruples* against buying stolen goods⟩. COMPUNCTION implies a spontaneous feeling of responsibility or compassion for a potential victim ⟨had *compunctions* about lying⟩. DEMUR implies hesitation caused by objection to an outside suggestion or influence ⟨accepted her decision without *demur*⟩.

qualm·ish \ˈkwä-mish *also* ˈkwȯ- *or* ˈkwäl-\ *adj* (1548) **1 a :** feeling qualms **:** NAUSEATED **b :** overly scrupulous **:** SQUEAMISH **2 :** of, relating to, or producing qualms — **qualm·ish·ly** *adv* — **qualm·ish·ness** *n*

quamash *var of* CAMAS

quan·da·ry \ˈkwän-d(ə-)rē\ *n, pl* **-ries** [origin unknown] (1579) **:** a state of perplexity or doubt

quan·go \ˈkwaŋ-ˌgō\ *n, pl* **quangos** [*qu*asi-*n*on*g*overnmental *o*rganization] (1973) *Brit* **:** a partly autonomous regulatory agency; *esp* **:** one in Britain organized outside the civil service but financed and appointed by the government

quant \ˈkwänt\ *n* [short for *quantitative (analyst)*] (1979) **:** an expert at analyzing and managing quantitative data

quan·tal \ˈkwän-tᵊl\ *adj* (1933) **1** [L *quanti* how many, pl. of *quantus*] **:** of, relating to, or having only two experimental alternatives (as dead or alive, all or none) **2** [*quantum*] **:** of or relating to a quantum

quan·ti·fi·ca·tion \ˌkwän-tə-fə-ˈkā-shən\ *n* (ca. 1840) **:** the operation of quantifying — **quan·ti·fi·ca·tion·al** \-shnəl, -shə-nᵊl\ *adj* — **quan·ti·fi·ca·tion·al·ly** *adv*

quan·ti·fi·er \ˈkwän-tə-ˌfī(-ə)r\ *n* (1876) **:** one that quantifies: as **a :** a prefixed operator that binds the variables in a logical formula by specifying their quantity **b :** a limiting noun modifier (as *five* in "the five young men") expressive of quantity and characterized by occurrence before the descriptive adjectives in a noun phrase

quan·ti·fy \-ˌfī\ *vt* **-fied; -fy·ing** [ML *quantificare,* fr. L *quantus* how much] (ca. 1840) **1 a (1) :** to limit by a quantifier **(2) :** to bind by prefixing a quantifier **b :** to make explicit the logical quantity of **2 :** to determine, express, or measure the quantity of — **quan·ti·fi·able** \ˌkwän-tə-ˈfī-ə-bəl\ *adj*

quan·ti·tate \ˈkwän-tə-ˌtāt\ *vt* **-tat·ed; -tat·ing** [back-formation fr. *quantitative*] (1927) **1 :** to measure or estimate the quantity of; *esp* **:** to measure or determine precisely **2 :** to express in quantitative terms — **quan·ti·ta·tion** \ˌkwän-tə-ˈtā-shən\ *n*

quan·ti·ta·tive \ˈkwän-tə-ˌtā-tiv\ *adj* [ML *quantitativus,* fr. L *quantitat-, quantitas* quantity] (1581) **1 :** of, relating to, or expressible in terms of quantity **2 :** of, relating to, or involving the measurement of quantity or amount **3 :** based on quantity; *specif, of classical verse* **:** based on temporal quantity or duration of sounds — **quan·ti·ta·tive·ly** *adv* — **quan·ti·ta·tive·ness** *n*

quantitative analysis *n* (ca. 1847) **:** chemical analysis designed to determine the amounts or proportions of the components of a substance

quantitative inheritance *n* (ca. 1929) **:** genetic inheritance of a character (as human skin color) controlled by polygenes

quan·ti·ty \ˈkwän-tə-tē\ *n, pl* **-ties** [ME *quantite,* fr. AF *quantité,* fr. L *quantitat-, quantitas,* fr. *quantus* how much, how large; akin to L *quam* how, as, *quando* when, *qui* who — more at WHO] (14c) **1 a :** an indefinite amount or number **b :** a determinate or estimated amount **c :** total amount or number **d :** a considerable amount or number — often used in pl. ⟨generous *quantities* of luck —H. E. Putsch⟩ **2 a :** the aspect in which a thing is measurable in terms of greater, less, or equal or of increasing or decreasing magnitude **b :** the subject of a mathematical operation **c :** an individual considered with respect to a given situation ⟨an unknown ~ . . . as attorney general —Tom Wicker⟩ **3 a :** duration and intensity of speech sounds as distinct from their individual quality or phonemic character; *specif* **:** the relative length or brevity of a prosodic syllable in some languages (as Greek and Latin) **b :** the relative duration or time length of a speech sound or sound sequence **4 :** the character of a logical proposition as being universal, particular, or singular

quantity theory *n* (1888) **:** a theory in economics: changes in the price level tend to vary directly with the amount of money in circulation and the rate of its circulation

quan·tize \ˈkwän-ˌtīz\ *vt* **quan·tized; quan·tiz·ing** [*quantum*] (1922) **1 :** to subdivide (as energy) into small but measurable increments **2 :** to calculate or express in terms of quantum mechanics — **quan·ti·za·tion** \ˌkwän-tə-ˈzā-shən\ *n* — **quan·tiz·er** \ˈkwän-ˌtī-zər\ *n*

[1]**quan·tum** \ˈkwän-təm\ *n, pl* **quan·ta** \ˈkwän-tə\ [L, neut. of *quantus* how much] (1567) **1 a :** QUANTITY, AMOUNT **b :** PORTION, PART **c :** gross quantity **:** BULK **2 a :** any of the very small increments or parcels into which many forms of energy are subdivided **b :** any of the small subdivisions of a quantized physical magnitude (as magnetic moment)

[2]**quantum** *adj* (1942) **1 :** LARGE, SIGNIFICANT ⟨a ~ improvement⟩ **2 :** of, relating to, or employing the principles of quantum mechanics ⟨~ physics⟩

quantum chromodynamics *n pl but sing in constr* (1975) **:** a theory of fundamental particles based on the assumption that quarks are distinguished by differences in color and are held together (as in hadrons) by an exchange of gluons

quantum electrodynamics *n pl but usu sing in constr* (1927) **:** quantum mechanics applied to electrical interactions (as between nuclear particles)

quantum field theory *n* (1948) **:** a theory in physics: the interaction of two separate physical systems (as particles) is attributed to a field that extends from one to the other and is manifested in a particle exchange between the two systems

quantum jump *n* (1926) **1 :** an abrupt transition (as of an electron, an atom, or a molecule) from one discrete energy state to another **2 :** QUANTUM LEAP

quantum leap *n* (1956) **:** an abrupt change, sudden increase, or dramatic advance

quantum mechanics *n pl but sing or pl in constr* (1922) **:** a theory of matter that is based on the concept of the possession of wave properties by elementary particles, that affords a mathematical interpretation of the structure and interactions of matter on the basis of these properties, and that incorporates within it quantum theory and the uncertainty principle — called also *wave mechanics* — **quantum mechanical** *adj* — **quantum mechanically** *adv*

quantum number *n* (1902) **:** any of a set of numbers that indicate the magnitude of various discrete quantities (as electric charge) of a particle or system and that serve to define its state

quantum theory *n* (1912) **1 :** a theory in physics based on the concept of the subdivision of radiant energy into finite quanta and applied to numerous processes involving transference or transformation of energy in an atomic or molecular scale **2 :** QUANTUM MECHANICS

quar *abbr* quarterly

[1]**quar·an·tine** \ˈkwȯr-ən-ˌtēn, ˈkwär-\ *n* [partly modif. of F *quarantaine,* fr. OF, fr. *quarante* forty, fr. L *quadraginta,* fr. *quadra-* (akin to *quattuor* four) + *-ginta* (akin to *viginti* twenty); partly modif. of It *quarantena* quarantine of a ship, fr. *quaranta* forty, fr. L *quadraginta* — more at FOUR, VIGESIMAL] (1609) **1 :** a period of 40 days **2 a :** a term during which a ship arriving in port and suspected of carrying contagious disease is held in isolation from the shore **b :** a regulation placing a ship in quarantine **c :** a place where a ship is detained during quarantine **3 a :** a restraint upon the activities or communication of persons or the transport of goods designed to prevent the spread of disease or pests **b :** a place in which those under quarantine are kept **4 :** a state of enforced isolation

[2]**quarantine** *vb* **-tined; -tin·ing** *vt* (1804) **1 :** to detain in or exclude by quarantine **2 :** to isolate from normal relations or communication ⟨~ an aggressor⟩ ~ *vi* **:** to establish or declare a quarantine

quare \ˈkwer, ˈkwär\ *dial var of* [1]QUEER

quark \ˈkwȯrk, ˈkwärk\ *n* [coined by Murray Gell-Mann] (1964) **:** any of several elementary particles that are postulated to come in pairs (as in the up and down varieties) of similar mass with one member having a charge of +⅔ and the other a charge of −⅓ and are held to make up hadrons

[1]**quar·rel** \ˈkwȯr(-ə)l, ˈkwär(-ə)l\ *n* [ME, fr. AF, square block of stone, bolt, fr. VL **quadrellum,* dim. of L *quadrum* square — more at QUADRATE] (13c) **:** a square-headed bolt or arrow esp. for a crossbow

[2]**quarrel** *n* [ME *querele,* fr. AF, fr. L *querela* grievance, complaint, fr. *queri* to complain] (14c) **1 :** a ground of dispute or complaint ⟨have no ~ with a different approach⟩ **2 :** a usu. verbal conflict between antagonists **:** ALTERCATION

syn QUARREL, WRANGLE, ALTERCATION, SQUABBLE mean a noisy dispute usu. marked by anger. QUARREL implies heated verbal contention, stressing strained or severed relations which may persist beyond the contention ⟨a *quarrel* nearly destroyed the relationship⟩. WRANGLE suggests undignified and often futile disputation with a noisy insistence on differing opinions ⟨*wrangle* interminably about small issues⟩. ALTERCATION implies fighting with words as the chief weapon, although it may also connote blows ⟨a loud public *altercation*⟩. SQUABBLE stresses childish and unseemly dispute over petty matters, but it need not imply bitterness or anger ⟨a brief *squabble* over what to do next⟩.

[3]**quarrel** *vi* **-reled** *or* **-relled; -rel·ing** *or* **-rel·ling** (14c) **1 :** to find fault ⟨many people ~ with the idea —*Johns Hopkins Mag.*⟩ **2 :** to contend or dispute actively ⟨~*ed* frequently with his superiors —*London Calling*⟩ — **quar·rel·er** *or* **quar·rel·ler** *n*

quar·rel·some \ˈkwȯr(-ə)l-səm, ˈkwär(-ə)l-\ *adj* (1596) **:** apt or disposed to quarrel in an often petty manner **:** CONTENTIOUS ***syn*** see BELLIGERENT — **quar·rel·some·ly** *adv* — **quar·rel·some·ness** *n*

quar·ri·er \ˈkwȯr-ē-ər, ˈkwär-\ *n* (14c) **:** a worker in a stone quarry

[1]**quar·ry** \ˈkwȯr-ē, ˈkwär-\ *n, pl* **quarries** [ME *quirre, querre* entrails of game given to the hounds, fr. AF *cureie, quereie,* fr. *quir, cuir* skin, hide (on which the entrails were placed), fr. L *corium* — more at CUIRASS] (14c) **1** *obs* **:** a heap of the game killed in a hunt **2 :** GAME; *specif* **:** game hunted with hawks **3 :** one that is sought or pursued **:** PREY

[2]**quarry** *n, pl* **quarries** [ME *quarey,* alter. of *quarrere,* fr. AF, fr. VL **quadraria,* fr. LL *quadrus* hewn (lit., squared) stone, fr. L *quadrum* square] (14c) **1 :** an open excavation usu. for obtaining building stone, slate, or limestone **2 :** a rich source

[3]**quarry** *vb* **quar·ried; quar·ry·ing** *vt* (1774) **1 :** to dig or take from or as if from a quarry ⟨~ marble⟩ **2 :** to make a quarry in ⟨~ a hill⟩ ~ *vi* **:** to delve in or as if in a quarry

[4]**quarry** *n, pl* **quarries** [alter. of [1]*quarrel*] (1555) **:** a diamond-shaped pane of glass, stone, or tile

quarrying *n* (ca. 1828) **:** the business, occupation, or act of extracting useful material (as building stone) from quarries

quar·ry·man \ˈkwȯr-ē-mən, ˈkwär-\ *n* (15c) **:** QUARRIER

quart \ˈkwȯrt\ *n* [ME, fr. AF *quarte* quarter, quart, fr. fem. of *quart,* adj., fourth, fr. L *quartus;* akin to L *quattuor* four — more at FOUR] (14c) **1** — see WEIGHT table **2 :** a vessel or measure having a capacity of one quart

[1]**quar·tan** \ˈkwȯr-tᵊn\ *adj* [ME *quarteyn,* fr. AF *(fevre) quartaine* quartan fever, fr. L *(febris) quartana,* fr. *quartanus* of the fourth, fr. *quartus*] (14c) **:** occurring every fourth day reckoning inclusively; *specif* **:** recurring at approximately 72-hour intervals ⟨a ~ ague⟩

[2]**quartan** *n* (14c) **:** a quartan fever

[1]**quar·ter** \ˈkwȯ(r)-tər *also* ˈkȯ(r)-\ *n* [ME, fr. AF, fr. L *quartarius,* fr. *quartus* fourth] (14c) **1 :** one of four equal parts into which something is divisible **:** a fourth part ⟨in the top ~ of his class⟩ **2 :** any of various units of capacity or weight equal to or derived from one fourth of some larger unit **3 :** any of various units of length or area equal to one fourth of some larger unit **4 :** the fourth part of a measure of time: as **a :** one of a set of four 3-month divisions of a year ⟨business was up during the third ~⟩ **b :** a school term of about 12 weeks **c :** QUARTER HOUR ⟨a ~ after three⟩ **5 a :** a coin worth a quarter of a dollar **b :** the sum of 25 cents **6 a :** one limb of a quadruped with the adjacent parts; *esp* **:** one fourth part of the carcass of a slaughtered animal including a leg **b** *pl, Brit* **:** HINDQUARTER 2 **7 a :** the region or direction lying under any of the four divisions of the horizon **b :** one of the four parts into which the horizon is divided or the cardinal point corresponding to it **c :** a compass point or direction other than the cardinal points **d** (1) **:** an unspecified person or group ⟨financial help from many ~*s* —*Current Biog.*⟩ (2) **:** a point, direction, or place not definitely identified ⟨the view to the rear ~ —*Consumer Reports*⟩ **8 a :** a division or district of a town or city ⟨he describes the immigrant ~ —Alfred Kazin⟩ **b :** the inhabitants of such a quarter **9 a :** an assigned station or post **b** *pl* **:** an assembly of a ship's company for ceremony, drill, or emergency **c** *pl* **:** living accommodations **:** LODGINGS ⟨show you to your ~*s*⟩ **10 :** merciful consideration of an opponent ⟨a team that gave no ~ during the championship game⟩; *specif* **:** the clemency of not killing a defeated enemy **11 :** a fourth part of the moon's period **12 :** the side of a horse's hoof between the toe and the heel — see HOOF illustration **13 a :** any of the four parts into which a heraldic field is divided **b :** a bearing or charge occupying the first fourth part of a heraldic field **14 :** the stern area of a ship's side **15 :** one side of the upper of a shoe or boot from heel to vamp **16 :** one of the four equal periods into which the playing time of some games is divided

[2]**quarter** *vt* (14c) **1 a :** to cut or divide into four equal or nearly equal parts ⟨~ an apple⟩ ⟨condemned to be hanged, drawn, and ~*ed*⟩ **b** *archaic* **:** DIVIDE **2 :** to provide with lodging or shelter **3 :** to crisscross (an area) in many directions **4 a :** to arrange or bear (as different coats of arms) quarterly on one escutcheon **b :** to add (a coat of arms) to others on one escutcheon **c :** to divide (a shield) into distinct sections (as by stripes) ~ *vi* **1 :** LODGE, DWELL **2 :** to crisscross a district **3 :** to change from one quarter to another ⟨the moon ~*s*⟩ **4 :** to strike on a ship's quarter ⟨the wind was ~*ing*⟩

[3]**quarter** *adj* (14c) **:** consisting of or equal to a quarter

quar·ter·age \ˈkwȯ(r)-tə-rij\ *n* (14c) **:** a quarterly payment, tax, wage, or allowance

[1]**quar·ter·back** \ˈkwȯ(r)-tər-ˌbak\ *n* (1879) **1 :** an offensive back in football who usu. lines up behind the center, calls the signals, and directs the offensive play of the team **2 :** one who directs and leads

[2]**quarterback** *vt* (1944) **1 :** to direct the offensive play of (as a football team) **2 :** to give executive direction to **:** BOSS ⟨~*ed* the original buying syndicate —*Time*⟩ ~ *vi* **:** to play quarterback

quarterback sneak *n* (ca. 1923) **:** a usu. quick run with the ball by a quarterback into the middle of the offensive line

quar·ter–bound \ˈkwȯ(r)-tər-ˈbau̇nd\ *adj* (ca. 1888) *of a book* **:** bound in material of two qualities with the material of better quality on the spine only — **quarter binding** *n*

quarter day *n* (15c) *chiefly Brit* **:** the day which begins a quarter of the year and on which a quarterly payment often falls due

quar·ter·deck \ˈkwȯ(r)-tər-ˌdek\ *n* (1627) **1 :** the stern area of a ship's upper deck **2 :** a part of a deck on a naval vessel set aside by the captain for ceremonial and official use

[1]**quar·ter·fi·nal** \ˌkwȯ(r)-tər-ˈfī-nᵊl\ *n* (1927) **1** *pl* **:** a quarterfinal round **2 :** a quarterfinal match — **quar·ter·fi·nal·ist** \-nᵊl-ist\ *n*

[2]**quarterfinal** *adj* (ca. 1934) **1 :** immediately preceding the semifinal in an elimination tournament **2 :** of or participating in a quarterfinal

quarter horse *n* [fr. its high speed for distances up to a quarter of a mile] (1834) : any of a breed of compact muscular saddle horses developed in the U.S. and characterized by great endurance and by high speed for short distances

quarter hour *n* (1766) **1 :** fifteen minutes **2 :** any of the quarter points of an hour **3 :** a unit of academic credit representing an hour of class (as lecture class) or three hours of laboratory work each week for an academic quarter

[1]**quar·ter·ing** \ˈkwȯ(r)-tə-riŋ\ *n* (15c) **1 a :** the division of an escutcheon containing different coats of arms into four or more compartments **b :** a quarter of an escutcheon or the coat of arms on it **2 :** a line of usu. noble or distinguished ancestry

[2]**quartering** *adj* (ca. 1692) **1 :** coming from a point well abaft the beam of a ship but not directly astern ⟨~ waves⟩ **2 :** lying at right angles

[1]**quar·ter·ly** \ˈkwȯ(r)-tər-lē\ *adv* (14c) **1 :** in heraldic quarters or quarterings **2 :** at 3-month intervals

[2]**quarterly** *adj* (15c) **1 :** computed for or payable at 3-month intervals ⟨a ~ premium⟩ **2 :** recurring, issued, or spaced at 3-month intervals **3 :** divided into heraldic quarters or compartments

[3]**quarterly** *n, pl* **-lies** (1830) : a periodical published four times a year

Quarterly Meeting *n* (1675) : an organizational unit of the Society of Friends usu. composed of several Monthly Meetings

quar·ter·mas·ter \ˈkwȯ(r)-tər-ˌmas-tər\ *n* (15c) **1 :** a petty officer who attends to a ship's helm, binnacle, and signals **2 :** an army officer who provides clothing and subsistence for a body of troops

quar·tern \ˈkwȯ(r)-tərn\ *n* [ME *quarteron,* fr. AF, quarter of a hundred, fr. *quarter* quarter] (14c) : a fourth part (as of a unit of measurement)

quarter note *n* (1763) : a musical note with the time value of ¼ of a whole note — see NOTE illustration

quarter rest *n* (ca. 1890) : a musical rest corresponding in time value to a quarter note

quar·ter·sawn \ˈkwȯ(r)-tər-ˈsȯn\ *also* **quar·ter·sawed** \-ˈsȯd\ *adj* (ca. 1890) : sawed from quartered logs so that the annual rings are nearly at right angles to the wide face — used of boards and planks

quarter section *n* (1804) : a tract of land that is half a mile square and contains 160 acres in the U.S. government system of land surveying

quarter sessions *n pl* (1566) : a former English local court with limited original and appellate criminal and sometimes civil jurisdiction and often administrative functions held quarterly usu. by two justices of the peace in a county or by a recorder in a borough

quar·ter·staff \ˈkwȯ(r)-tər-ˌstaf\ *n, pl* **-staves** \-ˌstavz, -ˌstāvz\ (ca. 1550) : a long stout staff formerly used as a weapon and wielded with one hand in the middle and the other between the middle and the end

quarter tone *n* (ca. 1776) **1 :** a musical interval of one half a semitone **2 :** a tone at an interval of one quarter

quar·tet *also* **quar·tette** \kwȯr-ˈtet\ *n* [It *quartetto,* fr. *quarto* fourth, fr. L *quartus* — more at QUART] (1773) **1 :** a musical composition for four instruments or voices **2 :** a group or set of four; *esp* **:** the performers of a quartet

quar·tic \ˈkwȯr-tik\ *adj* [L *quartus* fourth] (1861) : of the fourth degree ⟨~ equation⟩ — **quartic** *n*

quar·tier \kär-ˈtyā\ *n* [F, lit., quarter] (1828) : a district or neighborhood esp. in a French city

quar·tile \ˈkwȯr-ˌtī(-ə)l, -tᵊl\ *n* [ISV, fr. L *quartus*] (1879) : any of the three values that divide the items of a frequency distribution into four classes with each containing one fourth of the total population; *also* **:** any one of the four classes

quar·to \ˈkwȯr-(ˌ)tō\ *n, pl* **quartos** [L, abl. of *quartus* fourth] (1589) **1 :** the size of a piece of paper cut four from a sheet; *also* **:** paper or a page of this size **2 :** a book printed on quarto pages

quartz \ˈkwȯrts\ *n* [G *Quarz*] (ca. 1631) **1 :** a mineral consisting of silicon dioxide occurring in colorless and transparent or colored hexagonal crystals or in crystalline masses **2 :** a quartz crystal that when placed in an electric field oscillates at a constant frequency and is used to control devices which require precise regulation ⟨a ~ watch⟩ — **quartz·ose** \ˈkwȯrt-ˌsōs\ *adj*

quartz glass *n* (1903) : vitreous silica prepared from pure quartz and noted for its transparency to ultraviolet radiation

quartz heater *n* (1979) : a portable electric radiant heater that has heating elements sealed in quartz-glass tubes producing infrared radiation in front of a reflective backing

quartz–iodine lamp *n* (ca. 1964) : a lightbulb consisting of a quartz bulb and a tungsten filament with the bulb containing iodine which reacts with the vaporized tungsten to prevent excessive blackening of the bulb

quartz·ite \ˈkwȯrt-ˌsīt\ *n* [ISV] (ca. 1847) : a compact granular rock composed of quartz and derived from sandstone by metamorphism — **quartz·it·ic** \kwȯrt-ˈsi-tik\ *adj*

qua·sar \ˈkwā-ˌzär *also* -ˌsär\ *n* [*quasi*-stell*ar*] (1964) : any of a class of celestial objects that resemble stars but whose large redshift and apparent brightness imply extreme distance and huge energy output

[1]**quash** \ˈkwäsh, ˈkwȯsh\ *vt* [ME *quashen* to smash, fr. AF *quasser, casser,* fr. L *quassare* to shake violently, shatter, freq. of *quatere* to shake] (13c) : to suppress or extinguish summarily and completely ⟨~ a rebellion⟩

[2]**quash** *vt* [ME *quassen,* fr. AF *casser, quasser* to annul, fr. LL *cassare,* fr. L *cassus* void] (14c) : to nullify esp. by judicial action ⟨~ an indictment⟩

qua·si \ˈkwā-ˌzī, -ˌsī; ˈkwä-zē, -sē\ *adj* [*quasi-*] (1642) **1 :** having some resemblance usu. by possession of certain attributes ⟨a ~ corporation⟩ **2 :** having a legal status only by operation or construction of law and without reference to intent ⟨a ~ contract⟩

quasi- *comb form* [L *quasi* as if, as it were, approximately, fr. *quam* as + *si* if — more at QUANTITY, SO] **1 :** in some sense or degree ⟨*quasi*periodic⟩ ⟨*quasi*-judicial⟩ **2 :** resembling in some degree ⟨*quasi*particle⟩

qua·si·crys·tal \ˈkwā-ˌzī-ˌkris-tᵊl, -sī-, ˈkwä-zē-, -sē-\ *n* (1982) : a body of solid material that resembles a crystal in being composed of repeating structural units but that incorporates two or more unit cells into a quasiperiodic structure — **qua·si·crys·tal·line** \-ˈkris-tə-lən *also* -ˌlīn, -ˌlēn\ *adj*

qua·si–gov·ern·men·tal \-ˌgə-vər(n)-ˈmen-tᵊl\ *adj* (1948) : supported by the government but managed privately ⟨a ~ health-care agency⟩

qua·si–ju·di·cial \ˌkwā-ˌzī-jü-ˈdi-shəl, -ˌsī-, ˌkwä-zē-, -sē-\ *adj* (1836) **1 :** having a partly judicial character by possession of the right to hold hearings on and conduct investigations into disputed claims and alleged infractions of rules and regulations and to make decisions in the general manner of courts ⟨~ bodies⟩ **2 :** essentially judicial in character but not within the judicial power or function esp. as constitutionally defined ⟨~ review⟩ — **qua·si–ju·di·cial·ly** \-ˈdi-sh(ə-)lē\ *adv*

qua·si–leg·is·la·tive \-ˈle-jəs-ˌlā-tiv\ *adj* (ca. 1934) **1 :** having a partly legislative character by possession of the right to make rules and regulations having the force of law ⟨a ~ agency⟩ **2 :** essentially legislative in character but not within the legislative power or function esp. as constitutionally defined ⟨~ powers⟩

Qua·si·mo·do \ˌkwä-si-ˈmō-(ˌ)dō, ˌkwä-zi-\ *n* [ML *quasi modo geniti infantes* as newborn babes (words of the introit for Low Sunday)] (ca. 1847) : LOW SUNDAY

qua·si·par·ti·cle \ˌkwā-ˌzī-ˈpär-ti-kəl, -ˌsī-, ˌkwä-zē-, -sē-\ *n* (1957) : a composite entity (as a vibration in a solid) that is analogous in its behavior to a single particle

qua·si·pe·ri·od·ic \-ˌpir-ē-ˈä-dik\ *adj* (ca. 1890) : almost but not quite periodic; *esp* **:** periodic on a small scale but unpredictable at some larger scale — **qua·si·pe·ri·od·ic·i·ty** \-ˌpir-ē-ə-ˈdi-sə-tē\ *n*

qua·si–pub·lic \-ˈpə-blik\ *adj* (1888) : essentially public (as in services rendered) although under private ownership or control

qua·si–stel·lar object \-ˈste-lər-\ *n* (1964) : QUASAR

quas·sia \ˈkwä-shə\ *n* [NL, genus name of a So. American tree, fr. *Quassi* 18th cent. Surinam slave who discovered the medicinal value of quassia] (1770) : a drug from the heartwood and bark of various tropical trees of the ailanthus family used esp. as a bitter tonic and remedy for roundworms in children and as an insecticide

qua·ter·cen·te·na·ry \ˌkwä-tər-sen-ˈte-nə-rē, -ˈsen-tə-ˌner-ē, -sen-ˈtē-nə-rē\ *n* [L *quater* four times + E *centenary* — more at QUATERNION] (1883) : a 400th anniversary or its celebration

[1]**qua·ter·na·ry** \ˈkwä-tə(r)-ˌner-ē, kwə-ˈtər-nə-rē\ *adj* [L *quaternarius,* fr. *quaterni* four each] (1605) **1 a :** of, relating to, or consisting of four units or members **b :** of, relating to, or being a number system with a base of four **2** *cap* **:** of, relating to, or being the geological period from the end of the Tertiary to the present time or the corresponding system of rocks — see GEOLOGIC TIME table **3 :** consisting of, containing, or being an atom bonded to four other atoms

[2]**quaternary** *n, pl* **-ries** (1880) **1** *cap* **:** the Quaternary period or system of rocks **2 :** a member of a group fourth in order or rank

quaternary ammonium compound *n* (ca. 1934) : any of numerous strong bases and their salts derived from ammonium by replacement of the hydrogen atoms with organic radicals and important esp. as surface-active agents, disinfectants, and drugs

qua·ter·ni·on \kwə-ˈtər-nē-ən, kwä-\ *n* [ME *quaternyoun,* fr. LL *quaternion-, quaternio,* fr. L *quaterni* four each, fr. *quater* four times; akin to L *quattuor* four — more at FOUR] (14c) **1 :** a set of four parts, things, or persons **2 :** any of a set of numbers that comprise a four-dimensional vector space with a basis consisting of the real number 1 and three imaginary units *i, j, k,* that follow special rules of multiplication, and that are used esp. in computer graphics, robotics, and animation to rotate objects in three dimensions

qua·ter·ni·ty \kwə-ˈtər-nə-tē, kwä-\ *n, pl* **-ties** [LL *quaternitas,* fr. L *quaterni* four each] (1529) : a union of a group or set of four

qua·train \ˈkwä-ˌtrān, kwä-ˈ\ *n* [MF, fr. *quatre* four, fr. L *quattuor*] (1585) : a unit or group of four lines of verse

qua·tre·foil \ˈka-tər-ˌfȯi(-ə)l, ˈka-trə-\ *n* [ME *quaterfoil* set of four leaves, fr. AF *quatre* + ME *-foil* (as in *trefoil*)] (15c) **1 :** a conventionalized representation of a flower with four petals or of a leaf with four leaflets **2 :** a 4-lobed foliation in architecture

quat·tro·cen·to \ˌkwä-trō-ˈchen-(ˌ)tō\ *n, often cap* [It, lit., four hundred, fr. *quattro* four (fr. L *quattuor*) + *cento* hundred — more at CINQUECENTO] (ca. 1854) : the 15th century esp. with reference to Italian literature and art

quat·tu·or·de·cil·lion \ˌkwä-tə-ˌwȯr-di-ˈsil-yən\ *n, often attrib* [L *quattuordecim* fourteen (fr. *quattuor* four + *decem* ten) + E *-illion* (as in *million*) — more at TEN] (ca. 1903) — see NUMBER table

quatrefoil 2

[1]**qua·ver** \ˈkwā-vər\ *vb* **qua·vered; qua·ver·ing** \ˈkwā-və-riŋ, ˈkwāv-riŋ\ [ME, freq. of *quaven* to tremble] *vi* (15c) **1 :** TREMBLE **2 :** TRILL **3 :** to utter sound in tremulous tones ~ *vt* **:** to utter quaveringly — **qua·ver·ing·ly** *adv* — **qua·very** \ˈkwā-və-rē, ˈkwāv-rē\ *adj*

[2]**quaver** *n* (1570) **1 :** EIGHTH NOTE **2 :** TRILL 1 **3 :** a tremulous sound

quay \ˈkē, ˈkā, ˈkwā\ *n* [alter. of earlier *key,* fr. ME, fr. MF dial. (Picard) *kay,* prob. of Celt origin; akin to Bret *kae* hedge, enclosure; akin to OE *hecg* hedge] (ca. 1635) : a structure built parallel to the bank of a waterway for use as a landing place

quay·age \-ij\ *n* (ca. 1756) **1 :** a charge for use of a quay **2 :** room on or for quays **3 :** a system of quays

quay·side \-ˌsīd\ *n* (1829) : land bordering a quay

Que *abbr* Quebec

quean \ˈkwēn, ˈkwān\ *n* [ME *quene,* fr. OE *cwene;* akin to OE *cwēn* woman, queen] (bef. 12c) **1 :** a disreputable woman; *specif* **:** PROSTITUTE **2** *chiefly Scot* **:** WOMAN; *esp* **:** one that is young or unmarried

quea·sy *also* **quea·zy** \ˈkwē-zē\ *adj* **quea·si·er; -est** [ME *coysy, qwesye*] (15c) **1 a :** causing nausea ⟨~ motion⟩ **b :** suffering from nausea **:** NAUSEATED **2 :** full of doubt **:** HAZARDOUS **3 a :** causing uneasiness **b** (1) **:** DELICATE, SQUEAMISH (2) **:** ill at ease — **quea·si·ly** \-zə-lē\ *adv* — **quea·si·ness** \-zē-nəs\ *n*

Que·bec \kwi-ˈbek *also* ki-\ (1952) — a communications code word for the letter *q*

Que·be·cois *or* **Qué·bé·cois** *or* **Qué·be·cois** \ˌkā-bə-ˈkwä, -ˌbe-\ *n, pl* **Quebecois** *or* **Québécois** *or* **Québecois** \-ˈkwä(z)\ [F *québecois, québécois,* fr. *Québec* Quebec] (1873) : a native or inhabitant of Quebec; *specif* **:** a French-speaking native or inhabitant of Quebec — **Quebecois** *or* **Québécois** *or* **Québecois** *adj*

que·bra·cho \kā-ˈbrä-(ˌ)chō, ki-\ *n* [AmerSp, alter. of *quiebracha,* fr. Sp *quiebra* it breaks + *hacha* ax] (ca. 1881) **1 :** any of several trees of southern So. America with hard wood: as **a :** a tree (*Aspidosperma quebracho*) of the dogbane family which occurs chiefly in Argentina and Chile and whose dried bark is used as a respiratory sedative in dyspnea and in asthma **b :** a chiefly Argentine tree (*Schinopsis lorentzii*) of the cashew family with dense wood rich in tannins **2 a :** the wood of a quebracho **b :** a tannin-rich extract of the Argentine quebracho used in tanning leather

Que·chua \ˈke-chə-wə, ˈkech-wə\ *n, pl* **Quechua** *or* **Quechuas** [Sp, prob. fr. Southern Peruvian Quechua *qheswa* (*simi*), lit., valley speech] (1840) **1 :** a family of languages spoken by Indian peoples of Peru, Bolivia, Ecuador, Chile, and Argentina **2 a :** a member of an Indian people of central Peru **b :** a group of peoples forming the dominant element of the Inca Empire — **Que·chu·an** \-wən\ *adj or n*

1**queen** \ˈkwēn\ *n* [ME *quene,* fr. OE *cwēn* woman, wife, queen; akin to Goth *qens* wife, Gk *gynē* woman, Skt *jani*] (bef. 12c) **1 a :** the wife or widow of a king **b :** the wife or widow of a tribal chief **2 a :** a female monarch **b :** a female chieftain **3 a :** a woman eminent in rank, power, or attractions ⟨a movie ~⟩ **b :** a goddess or a thing personified as female and having supremacy in a specified realm **c :** an attractive girl or woman; *esp* **:** a beauty contest winner **4 :** the most privileged piece of each color in a set of chessmen having the power to move in any direction across any number of unoccupied squares **5 :** a playing card marked with a stylized figure of a queen **6 :** the fertile fully developed female of social bees, ants, and termites whose function is to lay eggs **7 :** a mature female cat kept esp. for breeding **8** *often disparaging* **:** a male homosexual; *esp* **:** an effeminate one

2**queen** *vi* (1611) **1 :** to act like a queen; *esp* **:** to put on airs — usu. used with *it* ⟨~s it over her friends⟩ **2 :** to become a queen in chess ⟨the pawn ~s⟩ ~ *vt* **:** to promote (a pawn) to a queen in chess

Queen Anne \-ˈan\ *adj* [*Queen Anne* of England] (1863) **1 :** of, relating to, or having the characteristics of a style of furniture originating in England under Dutch influence esp. during the first half of the 18th century that is marked by extensive use of upholstery, marquetry, and Asian fabrics **2 :** of, relating to, or having the characteristics of a style of English building of the early 18th century characterized by modified classic ornament and the use of red brickwork in which even relief ornament is carved

Queen Anne's lace *n* (1895) **:** a widely naturalized Eurasian biennial herb (*Daucus carota*) which has a whitish acrid taproot and flat lacelike clusters of tiny white flowers and from which the cultivated carrot originated — called also *wild carrot*

queen consort *n, pl* **queens consort** (1765) **:** the wife of a reigning king

queen·ly \ˈkwēn-lē\ *adj* **queen·li·er; -est** (15c) **1 :** of, relating to, or befitting a queen **2 :** having royal rank **3 :** MONARCHICAL — **queen·li·ness** *n* — **queenly** *adv*

queen mother *n* (1577) **:** a queen dowager who is mother of the reigning sovereign

queen post *n* (1823) **:** one of two vertical tie posts in a truss (as of a roof)

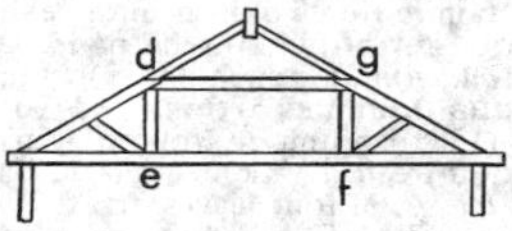

de gf queen posts

queen regnant *n, pl* **queens regnant** (ca. 1639) **:** a queen reigning in her own right

Queen's Bench *n* (1707) **:** a division of the English superior courts system that hears civil and criminal court cases — used during the reign of a queen

Queen's Counsel *n* (1850) **:** a barrister selected to serve as counsel to the British crown — used during the reign of a queen

queen·ship \ˈkwēn-ˌship\ *n* (1536) **1 :** the rank, dignity, or state of being a queen **2 :** a regal quality like that of a queen

queen·side \-ˌsīd\ *n* (1897) **:** the side of a chessboard containing the file on which the queen sits at the beginning of the game

queen–size *adj* (1959) **1 :** having dimensions of approximately 60 by 80 inches (about 1.5 by 2.0 meters) — used of a bed; compare FULL-SIZE, KING-SIZE, TWIN-SIZE **2 :** of a size that fits a queen-size bed ⟨a ~ sheet⟩

queen substance *n* (1954) **:** a pheromone secreted by queen bees that is consumed by worker bees and inhibits ovary development

1**queer** \ˈkwir\ *adj* [origin unknown] (1508) **1 a :** WORTHLESS, COUNTERFEIT ⟨~ money⟩ **b :** QUESTIONABLE, SUSPICIOUS **2 a :** differing in some odd way from what is usual or normal **b (1) :** ECCENTRIC, UNCONVENTIONAL **(2) :** mildly insane **:** TOUCHED **c :** absorbed or interested to an extreme or unreasonable degree **:** OBSESSED **d (1)** *often disparaging* **:** HOMOSEXUAL **(2)** *sometimes offensive* **:** GAY 4b **3 :** not quite well — **queer·ish** \-ish\ *adj* — **queer·ly** *adv* — **queer·ness** *n*

usage Over the past two decades, an important change has occurred in the use of *queer* in sense 2d. The older, strongly pejorative use has certainly not vanished, but a use by some gay people and some academics as a neutral or even positive term has established itself. This development is most noticeable in the adjective but is reflected in the corresponding noun as well. The newer use is sometimes taken to be offensive, esp. by older gay men who fostered the acceptance of *gay* in these uses and still have a strong preference for it.

2**queer** *vt* (ca. 1812) **1 :** to spoil the effect or success of ⟨~ one's plans⟩ **2 :** to put or get into an embarrassing or disadvantageous situation

3**queer** *n* (ca. 1812) **:** one that is queer; *esp, often disparaging* **:** HOMOSEXUAL ***usage*** see 1QUEER

queer theory *n* (1988) **:** an approach to literary and cultural study that rejects traditional categories of gender and sexuality

1**quell** \ˈkwel\ *vt* [ME, to kill, quell, fr. OE *cwellan* to kill; akin to OHG *quellen* to torture, kill, *quāla* torment, Lith *gelti* to hurt] (13c) **1 :** to thoroughly overwhelm and reduce to submission or passivity ⟨~ a riot⟩ **2 :** QUIET, PACIFY ⟨~ fears⟩ — **quell·er** *n*

2**quell** *n* [ME, fr. *quellen* to kill] (15c) **1** *obs* **:** SLAUGHTER **2** *archaic* **:** the power of quelling

quench \ˈkwench\ *vb* [ME, fr. OE *-cwencan;* akin to OE *-cwincan* to vanish, OFris *quinka*] *vt* (12c) **1 a :** PUT OUT, EXTINGUISH **b :** to put out the light or fire of ⟨~ glowing coals with water⟩ **c :** to cool (as heated metal) suddenly by immersion (as in oil or water) **d :** to cause to lose heat or warmth ⟨you have ~*ed* the warmth of France toward you —Alfred Tennyson⟩ **2 a :** to bring (something immaterial) to an end typically by satisfying, damping, cooling, or decreasing ⟨a rational understanding of the laws of nature can ~ impossible desires —Lucius Garvin⟩ ⟨the praise that ~*es* all desire to read the book —T. S. Eliot⟩ **b :** to terminate by or as if by destroying **:** ELIMINATE ⟨the Commonwealth party ~*ed* a whole generation of play-acting —Margery Bailey⟩ ⟨~ a rebellion⟩ **c :** to relieve or satisfy with liquid ⟨~*ed* his thirst at a wayside spring⟩ ~ *vi* **1 :** to become extinguished **:** COOL **2 :** to become calm **:** SUBSIDE — **quench·able** \ˈkwen-chə-bəl\ *adj* — **quench·er** *n* — **quench·less** \ˈkwench-ləs\ *adj*

que·nelle \kə-ˈnel\ *n* [F, fr. G *Knödel* dumpling, fr. MHG; akin to OHG *knoto* knot — more at KNOT] (1845) **:** a poached oval dumpling of pureed forcemeat (as of pike) often served in a cream sauce

quer·ce·tin \ˈkwər-sə-tən\ *n* [ISV, fr. L *quercetum* oak forest, fr. *quercus* oak — more at FIR] (1857) **:** a yellow crystalline pigment $C_{15}H_{10}O_7$ occurring usu. in the form of glycosides in various plants

quer·cit·ron \ˈkwər-ˌsi-trən, ˌkwər-ˈ\ *n* [blend of NL *Quercus* and ISV *citron*] (1794) **1 :** a large timber oak (*Quercus velutina*) chiefly of the eastern and central U.S. **2 :** the bark of the quercitron that is rich in tannin and a dye containing quercetin; *also* **:** the dye

que·rist \ˈkwir-əst, ˈkwer-\ *n* [L *quaerere* to ask] (1633) **:** one who inquires

quern \ˈkwərn\ *n* [ME, fr. OE *cweorn;* akin to OHG *quirn* hand mill, OCS *žrŭny*] (bef. 12c) **:** a primitive hand mill for grinding grain

quer·u·lous \ˈkwer-yə-ləs, -ə-ləs *also* ˈkwir-\ *adj* [ME *querelose,* fr. L *querulus,* fr. *queri* to complain] (15c) **1 :** habitually complaining **2 :** FRETFUL, WHINING ⟨a ~ voice⟩ — **quer·u·lous·ly** *adv* — **quer·u·lous·ness** *n*

1**que·ry** \ˈkwir-ē, ˈkwer-\ *n, pl* **queries** [alter. of earlier *quere,* fr. L *quaere,* imper. of *quaerere* to ask] (ca. 1635) **1 :** QUESTION, INQUIRY **2 :** a question in the mind **:** DOUBT **3 :** QUESTION MARK 2

2**query** *vt* **que·ried; que·ry·ing** (1654) **1 :** to ask questions of esp. with a desire for authoritative information **2 :** to ask questions about esp. in order to resolve a doubt **3 :** to put as a question **4 :** to mark with a query ***syn*** see ASK — **que·ri·er** *n*

que·sa·dil·la \ˌkā-sə-ˈdē-ə *also* -ˈthē- *or* -ˈthēl-yə\ *n* [MexSp, fr. Sp, cheese pastry, dim. of *quesada,* fr. *queso* cheese, fr. L *caseus*] (1935) **:** a tortilla filled with a savory mixture, folded, and usu. fried

1**quest** \ˈkwest\ *n* [ME, fr. AF *queste,* VL **quaesta,* fr. L, fem. of *quaestus,* pp. of *quaerere*] (14c) **1 a :** a jury of inquest **b :** INVESTIGATION **2 :** an act or instance of seeking: **a :** PURSUIT, SEARCH **b :** a chivalrous enterprise in medieval romance usu. involving an adventurous journey **3** *obs* **:** a person or group of persons who search or make inquiry

2**quest** *vi* (14c) **1** *of a dog* **a :** to search a trail **b :** BAY **2 :** to go on a quest ~ *vt* **1 :** to search for **2 :** to ask for — **quest·er** *n*

1**ques·tion** \ˈkwes-chən, ˈkwesh-\ *n* [ME, fr. AF, fr. L *quaestion-, quaestio,* fr. *quaerere* to seek, ask] (14c) **1 a (1) :** an interrogative expression often used to test knowledge **(2) :** an interrogative sentence or clause **b :** a subject or aspect in dispute or open for discussion **:** ISSUE; *broadly* **:** PROBLEM, MATTER **c (1) :** a subject or point of debate or a proposition to be voted on in a meeting **(2) :** the bringing of such to a vote **d :** the specific point at issue **2 a :** an act or instance of asking **:** INQUIRY **b :** INTERROGATION; *also* **:** a judicial or official investigation **c :** torture as part of an examination **d (1) :** OBJECTION, DISPUTE ⟨true beyond ~⟩ **(2) :** room for doubt or objection ⟨little ~ of his skill⟩ **(3) :** CHANCE, POSSIBILITY ⟨no ~ of escape⟩

2**question** *vt* (15c) **1 :** to ask a question of or about **2 :** to interrogate intensively **:** CROSS-EXAMINE **3 a :** DOUBT, DISPUTE **b :** to subject to analysis **:** EXAMINE ~ *vi* **:** to ask questions **:** INQUIRE ***syn*** see ASK — **ques·tion·er** *n*

ques·tion·able \ˈkwes-chə-nə-bəl, ˈkwesh-, *in rapid speech* ˈkwesh-nə-\ *adj* (1580) **1** *obs* **:** inviting inquiry **2** *obs* **:** liable to judicial inquiry or action **3 :** affording reason for being doubted, questioned, or challenged **:** not certain or exact **:** PROBLEMATIC ⟨milk of ~ purity⟩ ⟨a ~ decision⟩ **4 :** attended by well-grounded suspicions of being immoral, crude, false, or unsound **:** DUBIOUS ⟨~ motives⟩ ***syn*** see DOUBTFUL — **ques·tion·able·ness** *n* — **ques·tion·ably** \-blē\ *adv*

ques·tion·ary \ˈkwes-chə-ˌner-ē, ˈkwesh-\ *n, pl* **-ar·ies** (1887) **:** QUESTIONNAIRE

ques·tion·less \ˈkwes-chən-ləs, ˈkwesh-\ *adj* (1532) **1 :** INDUBITABLE, UNQUESTIONABLE **2 :** UNQUESTIONING

question mark *n* (1869) **1 a :** something unknown, unknowable, or uncertain **b :** someone (as an athlete) whose condition, talent, or potential for success is in doubt **2 :** a mark ? used in writing and printing at the conclusion of a sentence to indicate a direct question

ques·tion·naire \ˌkwes-chə-ˈner, ˌkwesh-\ *n* [F, fr. *questionner* to question, fr. MF, fr. *question,* n.] (1899) **1 :** a set of questions for obtaining statistically useful or personal information from individuals **2 :** a written or printed questionnaire often with spaces for answers **3 :** a survey made by the use of a questionnaire

question time *n* (1884) **:** a period in a session of a British parliamentary body during which members may put questions to ministers on matters concerning their departments

questor *var of* QUAESTOR

quet·zal \ket-ˈsäl, -ˈsal\ *n, pl* **quetzals** *or* **quet·za·les** \-ˈsä-(ˌ)lās, -ˈsa-\ [AmerSp, fr. Nahuatl *quetzalli* tail coverts of the quetzal] (1827) **1 :** a Central American trogon (*Pharomachrus mocinno*) that has brilliant green plumage above, a red breast, and in the male long upper tail coverts **2** *pl* *quetzales* — see MONEY table

Quet·zal·co·a·tl \ˌkwet-səl-kə-ˈwä-tᵊl, ˌket-, -səl-ˈkwä-; ket-ˌsäl-, -ˌsal-\ *n* [Nahuatl *Quetzalcōātl*] (1578) **:** a chief Toltec and Aztec god identified with the wind and air and represented by a feathered serpent

1**queue** \ˈkyü\ *n* [F, lit., tail, fr. OF *cue, coe,* L *cauda, coda*] (1748) **1 :** a braid of hair usu. worn hanging at the back of the head **2 :** a waiting line esp. of persons or vehicles **3 a :** a sequence of messages or jobs held in temporary storage awaiting transmission or processing **b :** a data structure that consists of a list of records such that records are added at one end and removed from the other

2**queue** *vb* **queued; queu·ing** *or* **queue·ing** *vt* (1777) **:** to arrange or form in a queue ~ *vi* **:** to line up or wait in a queue — often used with *up* — **queu·er** *n*

[1]**quib·ble** \ˈkwi-bəl\ *vb* **quib·bled; quib·bling** \-b(ə-)liŋ\ *vi* (1656) **1** : to evade the point of an argument by caviling about words **2 a** : CAVIL, CARP **b** : BICKER ~ *vt* : to subject to quibbles — **quib·bler** \-b(ə-)lər\ *n*

[2]**quibble** *n* [prob. dim. of obs. *quib* quibble] (1664) **1** : an evasion of or shift from the point **2** : a minor objection or criticism

quiche \ˈkēsh\ *n* [F, fr. F dial. (Lorraine)] (1933) : an unsweetened custard pie usu. having a savory filling (as spinach, mushrooms, or ham)

quiche lor·raine \-lə-ˈrān, -lō-\ *n, often cap L* [F, quiche of Lorraine] (1926) : a quiche containing cheese and bacon bits

[1]**quick** \ˈkwik\ *adj* [ME *quik,* fr. OE *cwic;* akin to ON *kvikr* living, L *vivus* living, *vivere* to live, Gk *bios, zōē* life] (bef. 12c) **1** : not dead : LIVING, ALIVE **2** : acting or capable of acting with speed: as **a** (1) : fast in understanding, thinking, or learning : mentally agile ⟨a ~ wit⟩ ⟨~ thinking⟩ (2) : reacting to stimuli with speed and keen sensitivity (3) : aroused immediately and intensely ⟨~ tempers⟩ **b** (1) : fast in development or occurrence ⟨a ~ succession of events⟩ (2) : done or taking place with rapidity ⟨gave them a ~ look⟩ **c** : marked by speed, readiness, or promptness of physical movement ⟨walked with ~ steps⟩ **d** : inclined to hastiness (as in action or response) ⟨~ to criticize⟩ **e** : capable of being easily and speedily prepared ⟨a ~ and tasty dinner⟩ **3 a** *archaic* : not stagnant : RUNNING, FLOWING **b** : MOVING, SHIFTING ⟨~ mud⟩ **4** *archaic* : FIERY, GLOWING **5** *obs* **a** : PUNGENT **b** : CAUSTIC **6** *archaic* : PREGNANT **7** : having a sharp angle ⟨a ~ turn in the road⟩ — **quick·ly** *adv* — **quick·ness** *n*

syn QUICK, PROMPT, READY, APT mean able to respond without delay or hesitation or indicative of such ability. QUICK stresses instancy of response and is likely to connote native rather than acquired power ⟨*quick* reflexes⟩ ⟨a keen *quick* mind⟩. PROMPT is more likely to connote training and discipline that fits one for instant response ⟨*prompt* emergency medical care⟩. READY suggests facility or fluency in response ⟨backed by a pair of *ready* assistants⟩. APT stresses the possession of qualities (as intelligence, a particular talent, or a strong bent) that makes quick effective response possible ⟨an *apt* student⟩ ⟨her answer was *apt* and to the point⟩. ***syn*** see in addition FAST

[2]**quick** *n* (bef. 12c) **1 quick** *pl* : living beings **2** [prob. of Scand origin; akin to ON *kvika* sensitive flesh, fr. *kvikr* living] **a** : a painfully sensitive spot or area of flesh (as that underlying a fingernail or toenail) **b** : the inmost sensibilities ⟨hurt to the ~ by the remark⟩ **c** : the very center of something : HEART **3** *archaic* : LIFE 11

[3]**quick** *adv* (14c) : in a quick manner

quick assets *n pl* (1891) : cash, accounts receivable, and other current assets excluding inventories

quick bread *n* (1918) : bread made with a leavening agent (as baking powder or baking soda) that permits immediate baking of the dough or batter mixture

quick·en \ˈkwi-kən\ *vb* **quick·ened; quick·en·ing** \ˈkwi-kə-niŋ, ˈkwik-niŋ\ *vt* (14c) **1 a** : to make alive : REVIVE **b** : to cause to be enlivened : STIMULATE **2** *archaic* **a** : KINDLE **b** : to cause to burn more intensely **3** : to make more rapid : HASTEN, ACCELERATE ⟨~*ed* her steps⟩ **4 a** : to make (a curve) sharper **b** : to make (a slope) steeper ~ *vi* **1** : to quicken something **2** : to come to life; *esp* : to enter into a phase of active growth and development ⟨seeds ~*ing* in the soil⟩ **3** : to reach the stage of gestation at which fetal motion is felt **4** : to shine more brightly ⟨watched the dawn ~*ing* in the east⟩ **5** : to become more rapid ⟨her pulse ~*ed* at the sight⟩ — **quick·en·er** \ˈkwi-kə-nər, ˈkwik-nər\ *n*

syn QUICKEN, ANIMATE, ENLIVEN, VIVIFY mean to make alive or lively. QUICKEN stresses a sudden renewal of life or activity esp. in something inert ⟨the arrival of spring *quickens* the earth⟩. ANIMATE emphasizes the imparting of motion or vitality to what is or might be mechanical or artificial ⟨happiness *animated* his conversation⟩. ENLIVEN suggests a stimulus that arouses from dullness or torpidity ⟨*enlivened* her lectures with humorous anecdotes⟩. VIVIFY implies a freshening or energizing through renewal of vitality ⟨new blood needed to *vivify* the dying club⟩. ***syn*** see in addition PROVOKE

quick fix *n* (1966) : an expedient usu. temporary or inadequate solution to a problem

quick–freeze \ˈkwik-ˈfrēz\ *vt* **-froze** \-ˈfrōz\; **-fro·zen** \-ˈfrō-zᵊn\; **-freez·ing** (1930) : to freeze (food) for preservation so rapidly that ice crystals formed are too small to rupture the cells and the natural juices and flavor are preserved

quick·ie \ˈkwi-kē\ *n, often attrib* (ca. 1926) : something done or made in a hurry: as **a** : a quickly and usu. cheaply produced work (as a motion picture or book) **b** : a hastily performed act of sexual intercourse

quick kick *n* (ca. 1940) : a punt in football esp. on first, second, or third down made from a running or passing formation and designed to take the opposing team by surprise

quick·lime \ˈkwik-ˌlīm\ *n* (14c) : [1]LIME 2a

quick·sand \ˈkwik-ˌsand\ *n* (14c) **1** : sand readily yielding to pressure; *esp* : a deep mass of loose sand mixed with water into which heavy objects readily sink **2** : something that entraps or frustrates ⟨lead poor people into consumerist ~ —Robert Wright⟩

quick·set \-ˌset\ *n* (15c) *chiefly Brit* : plant cuttings set in the ground to grow esp. in a hedgerow; *also* : a hedge or thicket esp. of hawthorn grown from quickset

[1]**quick·sil·ver** \-ˌsil-vər\ *n* (bef. 12c) : MERCURY 2a

[2]**quicksilver** *adj* (1655) : resembling or suggestive of quicksilver; *esp* : MERCURIAL 3

quick·step \-ˌstep\ *n* (ca. 1811) : a spirited march tune usu. accompanying a march in quick time

quick–tem·pered \-ˈtem-pərd\ *adj* (1830) : easily angered : IRASCIBLE

quick time *n* (ca. 1802) : a rate of marching in which 120 steps each 30 inches in length are taken in one minute

quick–wit·ted \ˈkwik-ˈwi-təd\ *adj* (1530) : quick in perception and understanding : mentally alert ***syn*** see INTELLIGENT — **quick–wit·ted·ly** *adv* — **quick–wit·ted·ness** *n*

[1]**quid** \ˈkwid\ *n, pl* **quid** *also* **quids** [origin unknown] (1688) *Brit* : a pound sterling

[2]**quid** *n* [E dial., cud, fr. ME *quide,* fr. OE *cwidu, cwudu* — more at CUD] (ca. 1727) : a cut or wad of something chewable

quid·di·ty \ˈkwi-də-tē\ *n, pl* **-ties** [ME *quidite,* fr. ML *quidditat-, quidditas* essence, fr. L *quid* what, neut. of *quis* who — more at WHO] (14c) **1** : whatever makes something the type that it is : ESSENCE **2 a** : a trifling point : QUIBBLE **b** : CROTCHET, ECCENTRICITY

quid·nunc \ˈkwid-ˌnəŋk\ *n* [L *quid nunc* what now?] (1709) : a person who seeks to know all the latest news or gossip : BUSYBODY

quid pro quo \ˌkwid-ˌprō-ˈkwō\ *n* [NL, something for something] (1582) : something given or received for something else; *also* : a deal arranging a quid pro quo

qui·es·cence \kwī-ˈe-sᵊn(t)s, kwē-\ *n* (ca. 1631) : the quality or state of being quiescent

qui·es·cent \-sᵊnt\ *adj* [L *quiescent-, quiescens,* prp. of *quiescere* to become quiet, rest, fr. *quies*] (1605) **1** : marked by inactivity or repose : tranquilly at rest **2** : causing no trouble or symptoms ⟨~ gallstones⟩ ***syn*** see LATENT — **qui·es·cent·ly** *adv*

[1]**qui·et** \ˈkwī-ət\ *n* [ME, fr. AF *quiete,* L *quiet-, quies* rest, quiet — more at WHILE] (14c) : the quality or state of being quiet : TRANQUILLITY — **on the quiet** : in a secretive manner : in secret

[2]**quiet** *adj* [ME, fr. MF *quiete,* fr. L *quietus,* fr. pp. of *quiescere*] (14c) **1 a** : marked by little or no motion or activity : CALM ⟨a ~ sea⟩ **b** : GENTLE, EASYGOING ⟨a ~ temperament⟩ **c** : not interfered with ⟨~ reading⟩ **d** : enjoyed in peace and relaxation ⟨a ~ cup of tea⟩ **2 a** : free from noise or uproar : STILL **b** : UNOBTRUSIVE, CONSERVATIVE ⟨~ clothes⟩ **3** : SECLUDED ⟨a ~ nook⟩ — **qui·et·ly** *adv* — **qui·et·ness** *n*

[3]**quiet** *adv* (1573) : in a quiet manner ⟨an engine that runs ~⟩

[4]**quiet** *vb* [ME, fr. LL *quietare* to set free, to calm, fr. L *quietus*] *vt* (14c) **1** : to cause to be quiet : CALM **2** : to make secure by freeing from dispute or question ⟨~ title to a property⟩ ~ *vi* : to become quiet — usu. used with *down* — **qui·et·er** *n*

qui·et·en \ˈkwī-ə-tən\ *vb* **qui·et·ened; qui·et·en·ing** \ˈkwī-ət-niŋ, ˈkwī-ə-tᵊn-iŋ\ (ca. 1828) *chiefly Brit* : QUIET

qui·et·ism \ˈkwī-ə-ˌti-zəm\ *n* (1687) **1 a** : a system of religious mysticism teaching that perfection and spiritual peace are attained by annihilation of the will and passive absorption in contemplation of God and divine things **b** : a passive withdrawn attitude or policy toward the world or worldly affairs **2** : a state of calmness or passivity — **qui·et·ist** \-tist\ *adj or n* — **qui·et·ist·ic** \ˌkwī-ə-ˈtis-tik\ *adj*

qui·etude \ˈkwī-ə-ˌtüd, -ˌtyüd\ *n* [MF, fr. LL *quietudo,* fr. L *quietus*] (1597) : a quiet state : REPOSE

qui·etus \kwī-ˈē-təs, -ˈā-\ *n* [ME *quietus est,* fr. ML, he is quit, formula of discharge from obligation] (1540) **1** : final settlement (as of a debt) **2** : removal from activity; *esp* : DEATH **3** : something that quiets or represses ⟨put the ~ on their celebration⟩

quiff \ˈkwif\ *n* [origin unknown] (ca. 1890) *Brit* : a prominent forelock

[1]**quill** \ˈkwil\ *n* [ME *quil* hollow reed, bobbin; akin to MHG *kil* large feather] (15c) **1 a** (1) : a bobbin, spool, or spindle on which filling yarn is wound (2) : a hollow shaft often surrounding another shaft and used in various mechanical devices **b** : a roll of dried bark ⟨cinnamon ~*s*⟩ **2 a** (1) : the hollow horny shaft of a feather — see FEATHER illustration (2) : FEATHER; *esp* : one of the large stiff feathers of the wing or tail **b** : one of the hollow sharp spines of a porcupine or hedgehog **c** : [3]PEN 3 **3** : something made from or resembling the quill of a feather; *esp* : a pen for writing **4** : a float for a fishing line

[2]**quill** *vt* (1783) **1** : to pierce with quills **2 a** : to wind (thread or yarn) on a quill **b** : to make a series of small rounded ridges in (cloth)

quill·back \ˈkwil-ˌbak\ *n, pl* **quill·back** *or* **quillbacks** (1882) : any of several suckers; *esp* : a small fish (*Carpiodes cyprinus*) of central and eastern No. America with a much elongated first ray of the dorsal fin

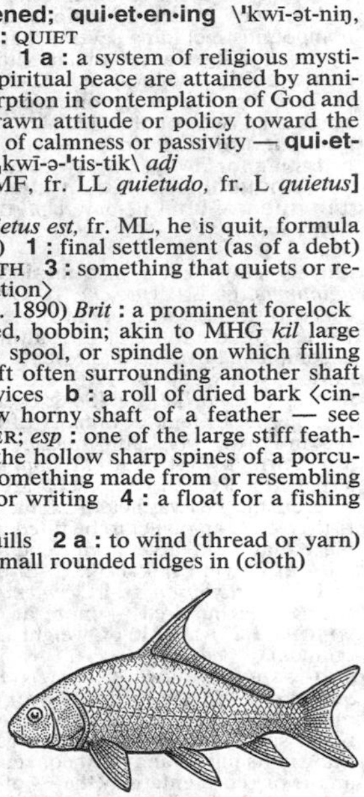

quillback

quill·work \-ˌwərk\ *n* (1843) : ornamental work in porcupine or bird quills

[1]**quilt** \ˈkwilt\ *n* [ME *quilte* mattress, quilt, fr. AF *coilte,* fr. L *culcita* mattress] (14c) **1 a** : a bed coverlet of two layers of cloth filled with padding (as down or batting) held in place by ties or stitched designs **b** : PATCHWORK QUILT 1 **2** : something that is quilted or resembles a quilt ⟨a ~ of houses and parks⟩

[2]**quilt** *vt* (1555) **1 a** : to fill, pad, or line like a quilt **b** (1) : to stitch, sew, or cover with lines or patterns like those used in quilts (2) : to stitch (designs) through layers of cloth **c** : to fasten between two pieces of material **2** : to stitch or sew in layers with padding in between ~ *vi* **1** : to make quilts **2** : to do quilted work — **quilt·er** *n*

quilt·ing \ˈkwil-tiŋ\ *n* (1598) **1** : material that is quilted or used for making quilts **2** : the process of quilting

quin·a·crine \ˈkwi-nə-ˌkrēn\ *n* [*quinine* + *acridine*] (ca. 1934) : an antimalarial drug derived from acridine and used esp. in the form of its dihydrochloride $C_{23}H_{30}ClN_3O \cdot 2HCl \cdot 2H_2O$

quince \ˈkwin(t)s\ *n* [ME *quynce* quinces, pl. of *coyn, quyn* quince, fr. AF *coign,* fr. L *cotoneum,* alter. *cydonium,* fr. Gk *kydōnion*] (14c) **1** : the fruit of a central Asian tree (*Cydonia oblonga*) of the rose family that resembles a hard-fleshed yellow apple and is used esp. in preserves **2** : a tree that bears quinces — compare JAPANESE QUINCE

quin·cen·te·na·ry \ˌkwin-sen-ˈte-nə-rē, -ˈsen-tə-ˌner-ē, *esp Brit* -sen-ˈtē-nə-rē\ *n* [L *quinque* five + E *centenary*] (1879) : a 500th anniversary or its celebration — **quincentenary** *adj*

quin·centen·ni·al \-sen-ˈte-nē-əl\ *n* [L *quinque* five + E *centennial*] (1884) : QUINCENTENARY — **quincentennial** *adj*

quin·cunx \ˈkwin-ˌkəŋ(k)s\ *n* [L *quincunc-, quincunx,* lit., five twelfths, fr. *quinque* five + *uncia* twelfth part — more at FIVE, OUNCE] (1545) : an arrangement of five things in a square or rectangle with one at each corner and one in the middle — **quin·cun·cial** \kwin-ˈkən(t)-shəl\ *or* **quin·cunx·ial** \-ˈkəŋk-sē-əl\ *adj*

quin·de·cil·lion \ˌkwin-di-ˈsil-yən\ *n, often attrib* [L *quindec*im fifteen (fr. *quinque* five + *decem* ten) + E *-illion* (as in *million*) — more at TEN] (1857) — see NUMBER table

quin·i·dine \ˈkwi-nə-ˌdēn\ *n* [ISV, fr. *quinine*] (1836) : an alkaloid $C_{20}H_{24}N_2O_2$ that is stereoisomeric with quinine and is used in the form of its sulfate or gluconate to treat cardiac rhythm irregularities

qui·nie·la \kwin-ˈye-lə\ *or* **qui·nel·la** \kwi-ˈne-lə\ *n* [AmerSp *quiniela,* a game of chance resembling a lottery] (1905) : a bet in which the bettor picks the first and second place finishers but need not designate their order of finish in order to win — compare PERFECTA

qui·nine \ˈkwī-ˌnīn *also* ˈkwi- *or* kwi-ˈnīn *or* ki-ˈnēn *or* kwi-ˈnēn\ *n* [Sp *quina* cinchona, fr. Quechua *kina* bark] (1825) **1 :** a bitter crystalline alkaloid $C_{20}H_{24}N_2O_2$ from cinchona bark used in medicine **2 :** a salt of quinine used esp. as an antipyretic, antimalarial, and bitter tonic

quinine water *n* (1953) : TONIC WATER

qui·noa \ˈkēn-ˌwä, kē-ˈnō-ə\ *n* [Sp, fr. Quechua *kinua*] (1625) : an annual herb (*Chenopodium quinoa*) of the goosefoot family that is native to the Andean highlands and is cultivated for its starchy seeds which are used as food and ground into flour; *also* : its seeds

quin·o·line \ˈkwi-nə-ˌlēn\ *n* [ISV *quin*ine + [3]*-ol* + [2]*-ine*] (1845) **1 :** a pungent oily nitrogenous base C_9H_7N obtained usu. by distillation of coal tar or by synthesis from aniline that is the parent compound of many alkaloids, drugs, and dyes **2 :** a derivative of quinoline

quin·o·lone \ˈkwi-nə-ˌlōn\ *n* [*quinol*ine + *-one*] (1936) : any of a class of synthetic antibacterial drugs that are derivatives of hydroxylated quinolines and inhibit the replication of bacterial DNA

qui·none \kwi-ˈnōn, ˈkwi-ˌ\ *n* [ISV *quin*ine + *-one*] (1853) **1 :** either of two isomeric cyclic crystalline compounds $C_6H_4O_2$ that are derivatives of benzene **2 :** any of various usu. yellow, orange, or red quinonoid compounds including several that are biologically important as coenzymes, hydrogen acceptors, or vitamins

qui·no·noid \kwi-ˈnō-ˌnȯid, ˈkwi-nə-\ *or* **quin·oid** \ˈkwi-ˌnȯid\ *adj* (1878) : resembling quinone esp. in having a 6-membered carbon ring containing two double bonds

quin·quen·ni·al \kwin-ˈkwe-nē-əl, kwiŋ-\ *adj* (15c) **1 :** consisting of or lasting for five years **2 :** occurring or being done every five years — **quinquennial** *n* — **quin·quen·ni·al·ly** \-nē-ə-lē\ *adv*

quin·quen·ni·um \-nē-əm\ *n, pl* **-ni·ums** *or* **-nia** \-nē-ə\ [L, fr. *quinque* five + *annus* year — more at FIVE, ANNUAL] (1621) : a period of five years

quin·sy \ˈkwin-zē\ *n, pl* **quinsies** [ME *quinesie,* fr. AF *esquinauncy, quinancie,* fr. LL *cynanche,* fr. Gk *kynanchē,* fr. *kyn-, kyōn* dog + *anchein* to strangle — more at HOUND, ANGER] (14c) : an abscess in the tissue around a tonsil usu. resulting from bacterial infection and often accompanied by pain and fever

quint \ˈkwint\ *n* (1934) : QUINTUPLET

quin·ta \ˈkin-tə, ˈkēn-\ *n* [Sp & Pg, quinta, farm rented at one fifth of its income, fr. L, fem. of *quintus* fifth] (1754) : a country villa or estate esp. in Portugal or Latin America

quin·tain \ˈkwin-tᵊn\ *n* [ME *quintaine,* fr. AF, perh. fr. L *quintana* street in a Roman camp separating the fifth maniple from the sixth where a market was held, fr. fem. of *quintanus* fifth in rank, fr. *quintus* fifth] (15c) : an object to be tilted at; *esp* : a post with a revolving crosspiece that has a target at one end and a sandbag at the other end

quin·tal \ˈkwin-tᵊl, ˈkan-\ *n* [ME, fr. AF, fr. ML *quintale,* fr. Ar *qinṭār,* fr. LGk *kentēnarion,* fr. LL *centenarium,* fr. L, neut. of *centenarius* consisting of a hundred — more at CENTENARY] (15c) **1 :** HUNDREDWEIGHT **2 :** a unit of weight equal to 100 kilograms (about 220 pounds)

quin·tes·sence \kwin-ˈte-sᵊn(t)s\ *n* [ME, fr. MF *quinte essence,* fr. ML *quinta essentia,* lit., fifth essence] (15c) **1 :** the fifth and highest element in ancient and medieval philosophy that permeates all nature and is the substance composing the celestial bodies **2 :** the essence of a thing in its purest and most concentrated form **3 :** the most typical example or representative ⟨the ~ of calm⟩ — **quin·tes·sen·tial** \ˌkwin-tə-ˈsen(t)-shəl\ *adj* — **quin·tes·sen·tial·ly** *adv*

quin·tet \kwin-ˈtet\ *n* [*quintet* fr. It *quintetto,* fr. *quinto* fifth, fr. L *quintus; quintette* fr. F, fr. It *quintetto*] (1811) **1 :** a musical composition or movement for five instruments or voices **2 :** a group or set of five: as **a :** the performers of a quintet **b :** a basketball team

[1]**quin·tic** \ˈkwin-tik\ *adj* [L *quintus* fifth] (1853) : of the fifth degree

[2]**quintic** *n* (1856) : a polynomial or a polynomial equation of the fifth degree

quin·tile \ˈkwin-ˌtī(-ə)l\ *n* [L *quintus* + E [2]*-ile*] (1922) : any of the four values that divide the items of a frequency distribution into five classes with each containing one fifth of the total population; *also* : any one of the five classes

quin·til·lion \kwin-ˈtil-yən\ *n* [L *quintus* + E *-illion* (as in *million*)] (1674) — see NUMBER table — **quintillion** *adj* — **quin·til·lionth** \-yən(t)th\ *adj or n*

[1]**quin·tu·ple** \kwin-ˈtü-pəl, -ˈtyü-, -ˈtə-; ˈkwin-tə-\ *adj* [MF, fr. ML *quintuplus,* fr. L *quintus* fifth + *-plus* -fold; akin to L *quinque* five — more at FIVE, -FOLD] (1570) **1 :** being five times as great or as many **2 :** having five units or members **3 :** marked by five beats per measure ⟨~ meter⟩ — **quintuple** *n*

[2]**quintuple** *vb* **quin·tu·pled; quin·tu·pling** \-p(ə-)liŋ\ *vt* (1639) : to make five times as great or as many ~ *vi* : to become five times as much or as numerous

quin·tu·plet \kwin-ˈtə-plət, -ˈtü-, -ˈtyü-; ˈkwin-tə-\ *n* (1873) **1 :** a combination of five of a kind **2 :** one of five offspring born at one birth

[1]**quin·tu·pli·cate** \kwin-ˈtü-pli-kət, -ˈtyü-\ *adj* [ML *quintuplicatus,* pp. of *quintuplicare* to quintuple, fr. *quintuplus* quintuple] (1656) **1 :** consisting of or existing in five corresponding or identical parts or examples ⟨~ invoices⟩ **2 :** being the fifth of five things exactly alike ⟨file the ~ copy⟩

[2]**quintuplicate** *n* (1851) **1 :** one of five things exactly alike; *specif* : one of five identical copies **2 :** five copies all alike — used with *in* ⟨typed in ~⟩

[3]**quin·tu·pli·cate** \-plə-ˌkāt\ *vt* **-cat·ed; -cat·ing** (ca. 1889) **1 :** to make quintuple or fivefold **2 :** to prepare in quintuplicate

[1]**quip** \ˈkwip\ *n* [earlier *quippy,* perh. fr. L *quippe* indeed, to be sure (often ironic), fr. *quid* what — more at QUIDDITY] (1532) **1 a :** a clever usu. taunting remark : GIBE **b :** a witty or funny observation or response usu. made on the spur of the moment **2 :** QUIBBLE, EQUIVOCATION **3 :** something strange, droll, curious, or eccentric : ODDITY — **quip·py** \ˈkwi-pē\ *adj*

[2]**quip** *vb* **quipped; quip·ping** *vi* (1579) : to make quips : GIBE ~ *vt* : to jest or gibe at — **quip·per** \ˈkwi-pər\ *n*

quip·ster \ˈkwip-stər\ *n* (1876) : one who is given to quipping

qui·pu \ˈkē-(ˌ)pü\ *n* [Sp *quipo,* fr. Quechua *khipu*] (1704) : a device made of a main cord with smaller varicolored cords attached and knotted and used by the ancient Peruvians (as for calculating)

[1]**quire** \ˈkwī(-ə)r\ *n* [ME *quair* four sheets of paper folded once, collection of sheets, fr. AF *quaier,* fr. VL **quaternum* set of four, fr. L *quaterni* four each, set of four — more at QUATERNION] (15c) : a collection of 24 or sometimes 25 sheets of paper of the same size and quality : one twentieth of a ream

[2]**quire** *archaic var of* CHOIR

Qui·ri·nus \kwə-ˈrī-nəs, -ˈrē-\ *n* [L] (14c) : an early state god of the Romans later identified with Romulus

[1]**quirk** \ˈkwərk\ *n* [origin unknown] (1565) **1 a :** an abrupt twist or curve **b :** a peculiar trait : IDIOSYNCRASY **c :** ACCIDENT, VAGARY ⟨a ~ of fate⟩ **2 :** a groove separating a bead or other molding from adjoining members — **quirk·i·ly** \ˈkwər-kə-lē\ *adv* — **quirk·i·ness** \-kē-nəs\ *n* — **quirk·ish** \ˈkwər-kish\ *adj* — **quirky** \-kē\ *adj*

[2]**quirk** *vb* (1878) : CURVE, TWIST ⟨~*ed* his eyebrows⟩

[1]**quirt** \ˈkwərt\ *n* [MexSp *cuarta*] (1845) : a riding whip with a short handle and a rawhide lash

[2]**quirt** *vt* (1887) : to strike or drive with a quirt

quis·ling \ˈkwiz-liŋ\ *n, often attrib* [Vidkun *Quisling* †1945 Norw. politician who collaborated with the Nazis] (1940) : TRAITOR 2, COLLABORATOR — **quis·ling·ism** \-liŋ-ˌi-zəm\ *n*

[1]**quit** \ˈkwit\ *adj* [ME *quite, quit,* fr. AF] (13c) : released from obligation, charge, or penalty; *esp* : FREE

[2]**quit** *vb* **quit** *also* **quit·ted; quit·ting** [ME *quiten, quitten,* fr. AF *quiter,* fr. *quite* free of, released, fr. L *quietus* quiet, at rest] *vt* (13c) **1 :** to make full payment of : PAY UP ⟨~ a debt⟩ **2 :** to set free : RELIEVE, RELEASE ⟨~ oneself of fear⟩ **3 :** CONDUCT, ACQUIT ⟨the youths ~ themselves like men⟩ **4 a :** to depart from or out of **b :** to leave the company of **c :** GIVE UP 1 ⟨~ a job⟩ **d :** GIVE UP 2 ⟨~ smoking⟩ ~ *vi* **1 :** to cease normal, expected, or necessary action ⟨the engine ~⟩ **2 :** to give up employment **3 :** to admit defeat : GIVE UP ***syn*** see STOP

[3]**quit** *n* (ca. 1923) : the act or an instance of quitting a job

quitch \ˈkwich\ *n* [ME **quicche,* fr. OE *cwice;* akin to OHG *quecca* couch grass] (bef. 12c) : QUACK GRASS

quit·claim \ˈkwit-ˌklām\ *vt* (14c) : to release or relinquish a legal claim to; *esp* : to release a claim to or convey by a quitclaim deed — **quitclaim** *n*

quitclaim deed *n* (1755) : a legal instrument used to release one person's right, title, or interest to another without providing a guarantee or warranty of title

quite \ˈkwīt\ *adv* [ME, fr. *quite,* adj., quit] (14c) **1 :** WHOLLY, COMPLETELY ⟨not ~ finished⟩ **2 :** to an extreme : POSITIVELY ⟨~ sure⟩ — often used as an intensifier with *a* ⟨~ a swell guy⟩ ⟨~ a beauty⟩ **3 :** to a considerable extent : RATHER ⟨~ near⟩ ***usage*** see PLENTY — **quite a bit :** a considerable amount — **quite a few :** MANY

quit·rent \ˈkwit-ˌrent\ *n* (15c) : a fixed rent payable to a feudal superior in commutation of services; *specif* : a fixed rent due from a socage tenant

quits \ˈkwits\ *adj* [ME, quit, prob. fr. ML *quittus,* alter. of L *quietus* at rest] (1663) : being on even terms by repayment or requital

quit·tance \ˈkwi-tᵊn(t)s\ *n* (14c) **1 a :** discharge from a debt or an obligation **b :** a document evidencing quittance **2 :** RECOMPENSE, REQUITAL

quit·ter \ˈkwi-tər\ *n* (1611) : one that quits; *esp* : one that gives up too easily : DEFEATIST

quit·tor \ˈkwi-tər\ *n* [ME *quiture* pus, discharge, fr. AF] (1703) : a purulent inflammation of the feet esp. of horses and donkeys

[1]**quiv·er** \ˈkwi-vər\ *n* [ME, fr. AF *quivre,* of Gmc origin; akin to OE *cocer* quiver, OHG *kohhari*] (14c) **1 :** a case for carrying or holding arrows **2 :** the arrows in a quiver

[2]**quiver** *vi* **quiv·ered; quiv·er·ing** \ˈkwi-və-riŋ, ˈkwiv-riŋ\ [ME, prob. fr. *quiver* agile, quick; akin to OE *cwiferlice* zealously] (15c) : to shake or move with a slight trembling motion — **quiv·er·ing·ly** *adv*

[3]**quiver** *n* (1786) : the act or action of quivering : TREMOR

qui vive \kē-ˈvēv\ *n* [F *qui-vive,* fr. *qui vive?* long live who?, challenge of a French sentry] (1726) : ALERT, LOOKOUT — used in the phrase *on the qui vive*

qui·xote \ˈkwik-sət, kē-ˈhō-tē, -ˈō-\ *n, often cap* [Don *Quixote,* hero of the novel *Don Quixote de la Mancha* (1605, 1615) by Cervantes] (1648) : a quixotic person — **quix·o·tism** \ˈkwik-sə-ˌti-zəm\ *n* — **quix·o·try** \-sə-trē\ *n*

quix·ot·ic \kwik-ˈsä-tik\ *adj* [Don *Quixote*] (1718) **1 :** foolishly impractical esp. in the pursuit of ideals; *esp* : marked by rash lofty romantic ideas or extravagantly chivalrous action **2 :** CAPRICIOUS, UNPREDICTABLE ***syn*** see IMAGINARY — **quix·ot·i·cal** \-ti-kəl\ *adj* — **quix·ot·i·cal·ly** \-ti-k(ə-)lē\ *adv*

[1]**quiz** \ˈkwiz\ *n, pl* **quiz·zes** [origin unknown] (1749) **1 :** an eccentric person **2 :** PRACTICAL JOKE **3 :** the act or action of quizzing; *specif* : a short oral or written test

[2]**quiz** *vt* **quizzed; quiz·zing** (1794) **1 :** to make fun of : MOCK **2 :** to look at inquisitively **3 :** to question closely — **quiz·zer** *n*

quiz·mas·ter \ˈkwiz-ˌmas-tər\ *n* (1943) : one who puts the questions to contestants in a quiz show

quiz show *n* (1944) : an entertainment program (as on radio or television) in which contestants answer questions — called also *quiz program*

quiz·zi·cal \ˈkwi-zi-kəl\ *adj* (1797) **1 :** comically quaint ⟨a ~ old man⟩ **2 :** mildly teasing or mocking ⟨a ~ remark⟩ **3 :** expressive of puzzlement, curiosity, or disbelief ⟨raised a ~ eyebrow⟩ — **quiz·zi·cal·i·ty** \ˌkwi-zə-ˈka-lə-tē\ *n* — **quiz·zi·cal·ly** \ˈkwi-zi-k(ə-)lē\ *adv*

quod \ˈkwäd\ *n* [origin unknown] (ca. 1700) *slang Brit* : PRISON

quod·li·bet \ˈkwäd-lə-ˌbet\ *n* [ME, fr. ML *quodlibetum,* fr. L *quodlibet,* neut. of *quilibet* any whatever, fr. *qui* who, what + *libet* it pleases, fr. *libēre* to please — more at WHO, LOVE] (14c) **1 :** a philosophical or theological point proposed for disputation; *also* : a disputation on such a point **2** : a whimsical combination of familiar melodies or texts

¹**quoin** \'koin, 'kwoin\ *n* [alter. of ¹*coin*] (1532) **1 a** : a solid exterior angle (as of a building) **b** : one of the members (as a block) forming a quoin and usu. differentiated from the adjoining walls by material, texture, color, size, or projection **2** : the keystone or a voussoir of an arch **3** : a wooden or expandable metal block used by printers to lock up a form within a chase

quoin 1b

²**quoin** *vt* (1683) **1** : to equip (a type form) with quoins **2** : to provide with quoins ⟨~ed walls⟩

¹**quoit** \'koit, 'kwoit, 'kwät\ *n* [ME *coite*] (15c) **1** : a flattened ring of iron or circle of rope used in a throwing game **2** *pl but sing in constr* : a game in which the quoits are thrown at an upright pin in an attempt to ring the pin or come as near to it as possible

²**quoit** *vt* (1597) : to throw like a quoit

quok·ka \'kwä-kə\ *n* [Nyungar (Australian aboriginal language of southwest Western Australia) *gwaga*] (1830) : a stocky herbivorous marsupial (*Setonix brachyurus* of the family Macropodidae) of southwestern Australia that has a short tail

quoll \'kwäl\ *n* [short for *je-quoll*, fr. Guugu Yimidhirr (Australian aboriginal language of northern Queensland) *dhigul*] (1770) : any of a genus (*Dasyurus*) of small spotted carnivorous marsupials of Australia and New Guinea

quon·dam \'kwän-dəm, -,dam\ *adj* [L, at one time, formerly, fr. *quom, cum* when; akin to L *qui* who — more at WHO] (1539) : FORMER, SOMETIME ⟨~ a friend⟩

Quon·set \'kwän(t)-sət, 'kwän-zət\ *trademark* — used for a prefabricated shelter having a semicircular arching roof of corrugated metal

quo·rum \'kwór-əm\ *n* [ME, quorum of justices of the peace, fr. L, of whom, gen. pl. of *qui* who; fr. the wording of the commission formerly issued to justices of the peace] (1602) **1** : a select group **2** : the number (as a majority) of officers or members of a body that when duly assembled is legally competent to transact business **3** : a Mormon body comprising those in the same grade of priesthood

quorum sensing *n* (1994) : a regulatory mechanism of bacteria that involves the release of molecules which when present at threshold concentrations signal the expression of bacterial genes controlling specific group actions (as the formation of biofilms)

quot *abbr* quotation

quo·ta \'kwō-tə\ *n* [ML, fr. L *quota pars* how great a part] (1618) **1** : a proportional part or share; *esp* : the share or proportion assigned to each in a division or to each member of a body **2** : the number or amount constituting a proportional share **3** : a fixed number or percentage of minority group members or women needed to meet the requirements of affirmative action

quot·able \'kwō-tə-bəl *also* -kō-\ *adj* (1811) : fit for or worth quoting — **quot·abil·i·ty** \,kwō-tə-'bi-lə-tē *also* ,kō-\ *n*

quo·ta·tion \kwō-'tā-shən *also* kō-\ *n* (1607) **1** : something that is quoted; *esp* : a passage referred to, repeated, or adduced **2 a** : the act or process of quoting **b** (1) : the naming or publishing of current bids and offers or prices of securities or commodities (2) : the bids, offers, or prices so named or published; *esp* : the highest bid and lowest offer

for a particular security in a given market at a given time

quotation mark *n* (ca. 1859) : one of a pair of punctuation marks " " or ' ' used chiefly to indicate the beginning and the end of a quotation in which the exact phraseology of another or of a text is directly cited

quo·ta·tive \'kwō-tə-tiv\ *n* (1893) : a function word used in informal contexts to introduce a quotation ⟨"like" is a ~ in "He was like, 'Oh, no! not again!'"⟩ — **quotative** *adj*

¹**quote** \'kwōt *also* 'kōt\ *vb* **quot·ed; quot·ing** [ML *quotare* to mark the number of, number references, fr. L *quotus* of what number or quantity, fr. *quot* how many, as many as; akin to L *qui* who — more at WHO] *vt* (1582) **1 a** : to speak or write (a passage) from another usu. with credit acknowledgment **b** : to repeat a passage from esp. in substantiation or illustration **c** : BORROW 2a ⟨*quoting* the motifs of past artists⟩ **2** : to cite in illustration ⟨~ a similar case⟩ **3 a** : to state (the current price or bid-offer spread) for a commodity, stock, or bond **b** : to give exact information on **4** : to set off by quotation marks ~ *vi* : to inform a hearer or reader that matter following is quoted — **quot·er** *n*

²**quote** *n* (1888) **1** : QUOTATION **2** : QUOTATION MARK — often used orally to indicate the beginning of a direct quotation

quoth \'kwōth *also* 'kōth\ *vb past* [ME, past of *quethen* to say, fr. OE *cwethan;* akin to OHG *quedan* to say] (bef. 12c) *archaic* : SAID — used chiefly in the first and third persons with a postpositive subject

quotha \'kwō-thə\ *interj* [alter. of *quoth he*] (1519) *archaic* — used esp. to express surprise or contempt

quo·tid·i·an \kwō-'ti-dē-ən\ *adj* [ME *cotidian*, fr. AF, fr. L *quotidianus, cotidianus,* fr. *quotidie* every day, fr. *quot* (as many) as + *dies* day — more at DEITY] (14c) **1** : occurring every day ⟨~ fever⟩ **2 a** : belonging to each day : EVERYDAY ⟨~ routine⟩ **b** : COMMONPLACE, ORDINARY ⟨~ drabness⟩ — **quotidian** *n*

quo·tient \'kwō-shənt\ *n* [ME *quocient*, modif. of L *quotiens* how many times, fr. *quot* how many] (15c) **1** : the number resulting from the division of one number by another **2** : the numerical ratio usu. multiplied by 100 between a test score and a standard value **3** : QUOTA, SHARE **4** : the magnitude of a specified characteristic or quality ⟨the celebrity's likability ~ is high⟩

quotient group *n* (1893) : a group whose elements are the cosets of a normal subgroup of a given group — called also *factor group*

quotient ring *n* (ca. 1958) : a ring whose elements are the cosets of an ideal in a given ring

quo war·ran·to \,kwō-wə-'rän-(,)tō, -'ran-; -'wór-ən-,tō, -'wär-\ *n* [ME *quo waranto,* fr. ML *quo warranto* by what warrant; fr. the wording of the writ] (15c) **1 a** : an English writ formerly requiring a person to show by what authority he exercises a public office, franchise, or liberty **b** : a legal proceeding for a like purpose begun by an information **2** : the legal action begun by a quo warranto

Quran *or* **Qur'an** *var of* KORAN

qv *abbr* [L *quod vide*] which see

QWER·TY \'kwər-tē, 'kwer-\ *n, often not cap* [fr. the first six letters in the second row of the keyboard] (1929) : a standard typewriter or computer keyboard — called also *QWERTY keyboard*

qy *abbr* query

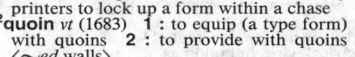

R

¹**r** \'är\ *n, pl* **r's** *or* **rs** \'ärz\ *often cap, often attrib* (bef. 12c) **1 a** : the 18th letter of the English alphabet **b** : a graphic representation of this letter **c** : a speech counterpart of orthographic *r* **2** : a graphic device for reproducing the letter *r* **3** : one designated *r* esp. as the 18th in order or class **4** : something shaped like the letter R

²**r** *abbr* **1** radius **2** rain **3** range **4** rare **5** real **6** recto **7** red **8** repeat **9** rerun **10** resistance **11** right **12** roentgen **13** rook **14** rough **15** run

¹**R** *abbr* **1** rabbi **2** radial **3** radical — used esp. of a monovalent hydrocarbon radical **4** Rankine **5** Reaumur **6** recipe **7** registered trademark — often enclosed in a circle **8** regular **9** Republican **10** river **11** R-value

²**R** *certification mark* — used to certify that a motion picture is of such a nature that admission is restricted to persons over a specified age (as 17) unless accompanied by a parent or guardian; compare G, NC-17, PG, PG-13

ra *abbr* range

¹**Ra** \'rä\ *n* [Egypt *r'*] (1877) : the Egyptian sun god and chief deity

²**Ra** *symbol* radium

RA *abbr* **1** regular army **2** right ascension **3** Royal Academician; Royal Academy **4** residence assistant; resident assistant **5** research assistant

RAAF *abbr* Royal Australian Air Force

¹**rab·bet** \'ra-bət\ *n* [ME *rabet,* perh. fr. MF *rabat* act of forcing down, fr. OF *rabattre* to beat down, fold over, reduce — more at REBATE] (14c) : a channel, groove, or recess cut out of the edge or face of a surface; *esp* : one intended to receive another member (as a panel)

²**rabbet** *vt* (15c) **1** : to unite the edges of in a rabbet joint **2** : to cut a rabbet in ~ *vi* : to become joined by a rabbet

rabbet joint *n* (ca. 1828) : a joint formed by fitting together rabbeted boards or timbers

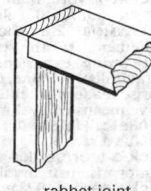
rabbet joint

rab·bi \'ra-,bī\ *n* [ME, fr. OE, fr. LL, fr. Gk *rhabbi,* fr. Heb *rabbī* my master, fr. *rabh* master + *-ī* my] (bef. 12c) **1** : MASTER, TEACHER — used by Jews as a term of address **2** : a Jew qualified to expound and apply the halacha and other Jewish law **3** : a Jew trained and ordained for professional religious leadership; *specif* : the official leader of a Jewish congregation

rab·bin \'ra-bən\ *n* [F] (1579) : RABBI

rab·bin·ate \'ra-bə-nət, -,nāt\ *n* (1702) **1** : the office or tenure of a rabbi **2** : the whole body of rabbis

rab·bin·ic \rə-'bi-nik, ra-\ *or* **rab·bin·i·cal** \-ni-kəl\ *adj* (1612) **1** : of or relating to rabbis or their writings **2** : of or preparing for the rabbinate **3** : comprising or belonging to any of several sets of Hebrew characters simpler than the square Hebrew letters — **rab·bin·i·cal·ly** \-ni-k(ə-)lē\ *adv*

Rabbinic Hebrew *n* (ca. 1909) : the Hebrew used esp. by medieval rabbis

rab·bin·ism \'ra-bə-,ni-zəm\ *n* (1652) : rabbinic teachings and traditions

¹**rab·bit** \'ra-bət\ *n, pl* **rabbit** *or* **rabbits** *often attrib* [ME *rabet,* prob. fr. MF dial. (Walloon) *robett,* fr. obs. or dial. D *robbe, robbeken;* akin to MLG *robbe* seal, East Fris *rubben* to scratch, rub — more at RUB] (14c) **1** : any of a family (Leporidae) of long-eared short-tailed lagomorph mammals with long hind legs **a** : any of various lagomorphs that are born furless, blind, and helpless, that are sometimes gregarious, and that include esp. the cottontails of the New World and a small Old World mammal (*Oryctolagus cuniculus*) that is the source of various domestic breeds **b** : HARE **2** : the pelt of a rabbit **3** : WELSH RABBIT **4 a** : a figure of a rabbit sped mechanically along the edge of a dog track as an object of pursuit **b** : a runner in a long-distance race who sets a fast pace for the field in the first part of the race — **rab·bity** \-bə-tē\ *adj*

\ə\ abut \ᵊ\ kitten, F table \ər\ further \a\ ash \ā\ ace \ä\ mop, mar \aù\ out \ch\ chin \e\ bet \ē\ easy \g\ go \i\ hit \ī\ ice \j\ job \ŋ\ sing \ō\ go \ò\ law \òi\ boy \th\ thin \th\ the \ü\ loot \ù\ foot \y\ yet \zh\ vision, beige \k̲, ⁿ, œ, ᵫ, ᵟ\ see Guide to Pronunciation

[2]**rabbit** *vi* (1846) **:** to hunt rabbits — **rab·bit·er** *n*
rab·bit·brush \ˈra-bət-ˌbrəsh\ *n* (ca. 1890) **:** any of several low branching composite shrubs (genus *Chrysothamnus* and esp. *C. nauseosus*) of the alkali plains of western No. America that are characterized by linear entire leaves and clusters of golden-yellow or white flowers
rabbit–eared bandicoot *n* (1865) **:** BILBY
rabbit ears *n pl* (1952) **:** an indoor dipole television antenna consisting of two usu. extensible rods connected to a base to form a V shape
rabbit fever *n* (1925) **:** TULAREMIA
rabbit hole *n* [fr. the rabbit hole that Alice enters in Lewis Carroll's *Alice in Wonderland*] (1980) **:** a bizarre or difficult state or situation — usu. used in the phrase *down the rabbit hole*
rabbit punch *n* (1915) **:** a short chopping blow delivered to the back of the neck or the base of the skull — **rabbit–punch** *vt*
rab·bit·ry \ˈra-bə-trē\ *n, pl* **-ries** (1838) **:** a place where domestic rabbits are kept; *also* **:** a rabbit-raising enterprise
rabbit warren *n* (1766) **1 :** WARREN 2a **2 :** WARREN 3b
[1]**rab·ble** \ˈra-bəl\ *n* [ME *rabel* pack of animals] (14c) **1 :** a disorganized or confused collection of things **2 a :** a disorganized or disorderly crowd of people **:** MOB **b :** the lowest class of people
[2]**rabble** *vt* **rab·bled; rab·bling** \-b(ə-)liŋ\ (1644) **:** to insult or assault by or as a mob
rab·ble·ment \ˈra-bəl-mənt\ *n* (1548) **1 :** RABBLE **2 :** DISTURBANCE
rab·ble–rous·er \ˈra-bəl-ˌrau̇-zər\ *n* (1843) **:** one that stirs up (as to hatred or violence) the masses of the people **:** DEMAGOGUE — **rab·ble–rous·ing** \-ziŋ\ *n or adj*
Ra·be·lai·sian \ˌra-bə-ˈlā-zhən, -zē-ən\ *adj* (1817) **1 :** of, relating to, or characteristic of Rabelais or his works **2 :** marked by gross robust humor, extravagance of caricature, or bold naturalism
Ra·bi \ˈrə-bē\ *n* [Ar *rabīʿ*] (ca. 1769) **:** either of two months of the Islamic year: **a :** RABI AL-AWWAL **b :** RABI AL-THANI
Ra·bi al–Aw·wal \ˈrə-bē-äl-ə-ˈwäl\ *n* [Ar *rabīʿ al-awwal,* lit., first Rabi] (1979) **:** the third month of the Islamic year — see MONTH table
Ra·bi al–Tha·ni \-äl-tä-ˈnē\ *n* [Ar *rabīʿ al-thānī,* lit., second Rabi] (1983) **:** the fourth month of the Islamic year — see MONTH table
ra·bic \ˈrā-bik\ *adj* (1885) **:** of or relating to rabies
ra·bid \ˈra-bəd *also* ˈrā-\ *adj* [L *rabidus* mad, fr. *rabere*] (1594) **1 a :** extremely violent **:** FURIOUS **b :** going to extreme lengths in expressing or pursuing a feeling, interest, or opinion ⟨~ editorials⟩ ⟨a ~ supporter⟩ **2 :** affected with rabies — **ra·bid·i·ty** \rə-ˈbi-də-tē, ra-, rā-\ *n* — **ra·bid·ly** \ˈra-bəd-lē *also* ˈrā-\ *adv* — **ra·bid·ness** *n*
ra·bies \ˈrā-bēz\ *n, pl* **rabies** [NL, fr. L, madness, fr. *rabere* to rave — more at RAGE] (ca. 1598) **:** an acute virus disease of the nervous system of mammals that is caused by a rhabdovirus (species *Rabies virus* of the genus *Lyssavirus*) usu. transmitted through the bite of a rabid animal and that is characterized typically by increased salivation, abnormal behavior, and eventual paralysis and death when untreated
rac·coon *also* **ra·coon** \ra-ˈkün *also* rə-\ *n, pl* **raccoon** *or* **raccoons** *also* **racoon** *or* **racoons** [Virginia Algonquian *raugroughcun, arocoun*] (1608) **1 a :** a small nocturnal carnivore (*Procyon lotor*) of No. America that is chiefly gray, has a black mask and bushy ringed tail, lives chiefly in trees, and has a varied diet including small animals, fruits, and nuts **b :** the pelt of this animal **2 :** any of several animals resembling or related to the raccoon
raccoon dog *n* (1868) **:** a small omnivorous canid (*Nyctereutes procyonoides*) of eastern Asia having a long yellowish-brown coat and facial markings resembling that of a raccoon — called also *tanuki*
[1]**race** \ˈrās\ *n* [ME *ras,* fr. ON *rās;* akin to OE *rǣs* rush] (14c) **1** *chiefly Scot* **:** the act of running **2 a :** a strong or rapid current of water flowing through a narrow channel **b :** a watercourse used industrially **c :** the current flowing in such a course **3 a :** a set course or duration of time **b :** the course of life **4 a :** a contest of speed **b** *pl* **:** a meeting in which several races (as for horses) are run **c :** a contest or rivalry involving progress toward a goal ⟨pennant ~⟩ **5 :** a track or channel in which something rolls or slides; *specif* **:** a groove (as for the balls) in a bearing — see ROLLER BEARING illustration
[2]**race** *vb* **raced; rac·ing** *vi* (15c) **1 :** to compete in a race **2 :** to go, move, or function at top speed or out of control ⟨people *racing* for safety⟩ ⟨struggled to sleep as his mind *raced*⟩ **3 :** to revolve too fast under a diminished load ~ *vt* **1 :** to engage in a race with **2 a :** to enter in a race **b :** to drive or ride at high speed **c :** to transport or propel at maximum speed **3 :** to speed (as an engine) without a working load or with the transmission disengaged
[3]**race** *n* [MF, generation, fr. OIt *razza*] (1580) **1 :** a breeding stock of animals **2 a :** a family, tribe, people, or nation belonging to the same stock **b :** a class or kind of people unified by shared interests, habits, or characteristics **3 a :** an actually or potentially interbreeding group within a species; *also* **:** a taxonomic category (as a subspecies) representing such a group **b :** BREED **c :** a category of humankind that shares certain distinctive physical traits **4** *obs* **:** inherited temperament or disposition **5 :** distinctive flavor, taste, or strength
race–bait·ing \ˈrās-ˌbā-tiŋ\ *n, often attrib* (ca. 1961) **:** the making of verbal attacks against members of a racial group
race·course \ˈrās-ˌkȯrs\ *n* (1764) **1 :** a course for racing **2 :** RACEWAY 1
race·horse \-ˌhȯrs\ *n* (ca. 1626) **:** a horse bred or kept for racing
ra·ce·mate \rā-ˈsē-ˌmāt, rə-; ˈra-sə-\ *n* (1907) **:** a racemic compound or mixture
ra·ceme \rā-ˈsēm, rə-\ *n* [L *racemus* bunch of grapes; prob. akin to Gk *rhag-, rhax* grape] (1785) **:** a simple inflorescence (as in the lily of the valley) in which the flowers are borne on short stalks of about equal length at equal distances along an elongated axis and open in succession toward the apex — see INFLORESCENCE illustration
ra·ce·mic \-ˈsē-mik\ *adj* [*racemic acid,* a compound with such a structure obtained from grape juice, ultim. fr. L *racemus*] (1892) **:** of, relating to, or constituting a compound or mixture that is composed of equal amounts of dextrorotatory and levorotatory forms of the same compound and is not optically active
ra·ce·mi·za·tion \rā-ˌsē-mə-ˈzā-shən, rə-; ˌra-sə-mə-\ *n* (1895) **:** the action or process of changing from an optically active compound into a racemic compound or mixture — **ra·ce·mize** \rā-ˈsē-ˌmīz, rə-; ˈra-sə-\ *vb*
ra·ce·mose \ˈra-sə-ˌmōs; rā-ˈsē-, rə-\ *adj* [L *racemosus* full of clusters, fr. *racemus*] (1698) **:** having or growing in the form of a raceme
rac·er \ˈrā-sər\ *n* (1648) **1 :** one that races or is used for racing **2 :** any of various active American colubrid snakes (genus *Coluber* and *Mastigophis*): as **a :** BLACK RACER **b :** BLUE RACER
race riot *n* (1890) **:** a riot caused by racial dissensions or hatreds
race runner *n* (1910) **:** a swift No. American lizard (*Cnemidophorus sexlineatus*) that has six narrow stripes down the back
race·track \ˈrās-ˌtrak\ *n* (ca. 1835) **:** a usu. oval course for racing
race·track·er \-ˌtra-kər\ *n* (1953) **:** one who frequents a racetrack
race·walk·ing \-ˌwȯ-kiŋ\ *n* (1954) **:** the competitive sport of racing at a fast walk while maintaining continuous foot contact with the ground and keeping the supporting leg straight — **race·walk** \-ˌwȯk\ *vi* — **race·walk·er** \-ˌwȯ-kər\ *n*
race·way \-ˌwā\ *n* (1828) **1 :** a canal for a current of water **2 :** a channel for loosely holding electrical wires in buildings **3 :** [1]RACE 5 **4 :** a course for racing
Ra·chel \ˈrā-chəl\ *n* (13c) **:** a wife of Jacob and the mother of Joseph and Benjamin
rachet *var of* RATCHET
ra·chis \ˈrā-kəs, ˈra-\ *n, pl* **ra·chis·es** *also* **ra·chi·des** \ˈra-kə-ˌdēz, ˈrā-\ [NL *rachid-, rachis,* fr. Gk *rhachis;* akin to Gk *rhachos* thorn, Lith *ražas* dry twig, tine] (1785) **1 :** an axial structure: as **a (1) :** the elongated axis of an inflorescence **(2) :** an extension of the petiole of a compound leaf that bears the leaflets **b :** the distal part of the shaft of a feather that bears the web **2 :** SPINAL COLUMN
ra·chit·ic \rə-ˈki-tik\ *adj* [NL *rachitis* rickets, fr. Gk *rhachitis* spinal disease, fr. *rhachis*] (1797) **:** RICKETY
ra·cial \ˈrā-shəl\ *adj* (1855) **1 :** of, relating to, or based on a race ⟨a ~ minority⟩ **2 :** existing or occurring between races ⟨~ equality⟩ — **ra·cial·ly** \-shə-lē\ *adv*
ra·cial·ism \ˈrā-shə-ˌli-zəm\ *n* (1906) **:** a theory that race determines human traits and capacities; *also* **:** RACISM — **ra·cial·ist** \-list\ *n or adj* — **ra·cial·is·tic** \ˌrā-shə-ˈlis-tik\ *adj*
ra·cial·ize \ˈrā-shə-ˌlīz\ *vt* **-ized; -iz·ing** (1930) **:** to give a racial character to
racing *n* (1630) **:** the sport or profession of engaging in or holding races
racing form *n* (1910) **:** an information sheet giving details of past performance (as for racehorses) for use by bettors
ra·ci·no \rə-ˈsē-(ˌ)nō\ *n, pl* **-nos** [blend of *racetrack* and *casino*] (1995) **:** a racetrack at which slot machines are available for gamblers
rac·ism \ˈrā-ˌsi-zəm *also* -ˌshi-\ *n* (1933) **1 :** a belief that race is the primary determinant of human traits and capacities and that racial differences produce an inherent superiority of a particular race **2 :** racial prejudice or discrimination — **rac·ist** \-sist *also* -shist\ *n or adj*
[1]**rack** \ˈrak\ *n* [ME *rak* rain cloud, rapid movement] (14c) **:** a wind-driven mass of high often broken clouds
[2]**rack** *vi* (1590) **:** to fly or scud in high wind
[3]**rack** *n* [ME, prob. fr. MD *rec* framework; akin to OE *reccan* to stretch, Gk *oregein* — more at RIGHT] (14c) **1 :** a framework for holding fodder for livestock **2 :** an instrument of torture on which a body is stretched **3 a (1) :** a cause of anguish or pain **(2) :** acute suffering **b :** the action of straining or wrenching **4 :** a framework, stand, or grating on or in which articles are placed **5 a :** a bar with teeth on one face for gearing with a pinion or worm gear to transform rotary motion to linear motion or vice versa (as in an automobile steering mechanism) **b :** a notched bar used as a ratchet to engage with a pawl, click, or detent **6 :** a pair of antlers **7 :** a triangular frame used to set up the balls in a pool game; *also* **:** the balls as set up **8 :** BED, SACK — **rack·ful** \-ˌfu̇l\ *n* — **on the rack :** under great emotional stress
[4]**rack** *vt* (15c) **1 :** to torture on the rack **2 :** to cause to suffer torture, pain, anguish, or ruin ⟨~*ed* with jealousy⟩ ⟨a company ~*ed* by infighting⟩ **3 a :** to stretch or strain violently ⟨~*ed* his brains⟩ **b :** to raise (rents) oppressively **c :** to harass or oppress with high rents or extortions **4 :** to work or treat (material) on a rack **5 :** to work by a rack and pinion or worm so as to extend or contract ⟨~ a camera⟩ **6 :** to seize (as parallel ropes of a tackle) together **7 :** to place (as pool balls) in a rack ~ *vi* **:** to become forced out of shape or out of plumb *syn* see AFFLICT — **rack·er** *n* — **rack·ing·ly** \ˈra-kiŋ-lē\ *adv*
[5]**rack** *vt* [ME *rakken,* fr. OF (Norman & Picard dial.) *reequier,* prob. fr. LL *reaedificare* to rebuild, repair, improve, fr. L *re-* + *aedificare* to build — more at EDIFY] (15c) **:** to draw off (as wine) from the lees
[6]**rack** *vi* [prob. alter. of [1]*rock*] (1530) *of a horse* **:** to go at a rack
[7]**rack** *n* (1580) **:** either of two gaits of a horse: **a :** PACE 4b **b :** a fast showy 4-beat gait
[8]**rack** *n* [perh. fr. [3]*rack*] (1570) **1 :** the neck and spine of a forequarter of veal, pork, or esp. mutton **2 :** the rib section of a lamb's forequarters used for chops or as a roast — see LAMB illustration
[9]**rack** *n* [alter. of *wrack*] (1592) **:** DESTRUCTION ⟨~ and ruin⟩
[1]**rack·et** *or* **rac·quet** \ˈra-kət\ *n* [MF *raquette,* ultim. fr. ML *rasceta* wrist, carpus, modif. of Ar *rusgh* wrist] (ca. 1520) **1 :** a lightweight implement that consists of a netting (as of nylon) stretched in a usu. oval open frame with a handle attached and that is used for striking the ball or shuttlecock in various games (as tennis, racquets, or badminton) **2** *usu* **racquets** *pl but sing in constr* **:** a game for two or four players with ball and racket on a 4-walled court

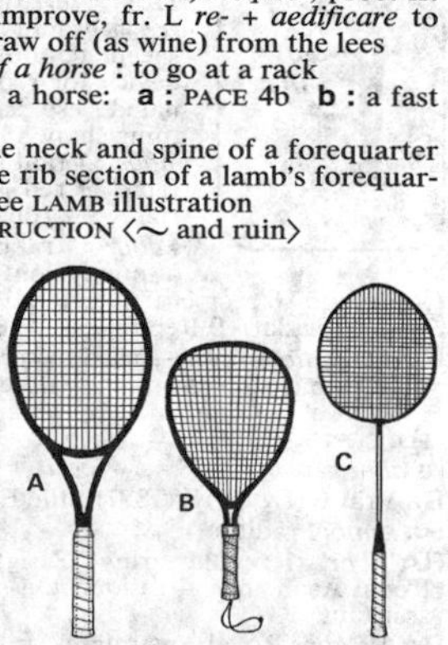

[1]racket 1: *A* tennis, *B* racquetball, *C* badminton

[2]**racket** *n* [origin unknown] (1565) **1 :** confused clattering noise **:** CLAMOR **2 a :** social whirl or excitement **b :** the strain of exciting or trying experiences **3 a :** a fraudulent scheme, enterprise, or activity **b :** a usu. illegitimate enterprise made workable by bribery or intimidation **c :** an easy and lucrative means of livelihood **d** *slang* **:** OCCUPATION, BUSINESS
[3]**racket** *vi* (1609) **1 :** to engage in active social life **2 :** to move with or make a racket
[1]**rack·e·teer** \ˌra-kə-ˈtir\ *n* (1924) **:** one who obtains money by an illegal enterprise usu. involving intimidation
[2]**racketeer** *vi* (1928) **:** to carry on a racket ~ *vt* **:** to extort money from

rack·ety \ˈra-kə-tē\ *adj* (1773) **1** : NOISY **2** : ROWDY **3** : RICKETY
rack railway *n* (1884) : a railway having between its rails a rack that meshes with a gear wheel or pinion of the locomotive for traction on steep grades
rack–rent *vt* (1621) : to subject to rack rent
rack rent *n* [⁴*rack*] (1743) **1** : an excessive or unreasonably high rent **2** *Brit* : the highest rent that can be earned on a property
rack–rent·er \ˈrak-ˌren-tər\ *n* (1680) : one that pays or exacts rack rent
rack up *vt* (1949) : ACHIEVE, GAIN ⟨*racked up* their 10th victory⟩
ra·clette \ra-ˈklet, rä-\ *n* [F, lit., scraper, fr. *racler* to scrape, fr. MF, fr. Old Occitan *rasclar,* fr. VL **rasiculare,* fr. L *rasus,* pp. of *radere* to scrape — more at RODENT] (ca. 1949) : a Swiss dish consisting of cheese melted over a fire and then scraped onto bread or boiled potatoes; *also* : the cheese used in this dish
ra·con \ˈrā-ˌkän\ *n* [*ra*dar bea*con*] (1945) : RADAR BEACON
ra·con·teur \ˌra-ˌkän-ˈtər, -kən-\ *n* [F, fr. MF, fr. *raconter* to tell, fr. OF, fr. *re-* + *aconter, acompter* to tell, count — more at ACCOUNT] (1828) : a person who excels in telling anecdotes
racoon *var of* RACCOON
rac·quet·ball \ˈra-kət-ˌbȯl\ *n* (1965) : a game similar to handball that is played on a 4-walled court with a short-handled racket and a larger ball; *also* : the ball used in this game
¹**racy** \ˈrā-sē\ *adj* **rac·i·er; -est** [³*race*] (ca. 1650) **1 a** : full of zest or vigor **b** : having a strongly marked quality : PIQUANT ⟨a ~ flavor⟩ **c** : RISQUÉ, SUGGESTIVE ⟨~ jokes⟩ **2** : having the distinctive quality of something in its original or most characteristic form ***syn*** see PUNGENT — **rac·i·ly** \ˈrā-sə-lē\ *adv* — **rac·i·ness** \-sē-nəs\ *n*
²**racy** *adj* **rac·i·er; -est** [¹*race*] (1841) : having a body or shape that is suited for racing ⟨a ~ dog⟩ ⟨a car with ~ lines⟩
¹**rad** \ˈrad\ *n* [*r*adiation *a*bsorbed *d*ose] (ca. 1953) : a unit of absorbed dose of ionizing radiation equal to an energy of 100 ergs per gram of irradiated material
²**rad** *adj* (1982) *slang* : COOL 7, RADICAL
³**rad** *abbr* **1** radian **2** radius **3** radix
ra·dar \ˈrā-ˌdär\ *n, often attrib* [*ra*dio *d*etecting *a*nd *r*anging] (1941) **1** : a device or system consisting usu. of a synchronized radio transmitter and receiver that emits radio waves and processes their reflections for display and is used esp. for detecting and locating objects (as aircraft) or surface features (as of a planet) **2** : range of notice ⟨fell off the ~ after losing their first three games⟩
radar astronomy *n* (1959) : astronomy in which celestial bodies in the solar system are studied by analyzing the return of radio waves directed at them
radar beacon *n* (1945) : a radar transmitter that upon receiving a radar signal emits a signal which reinforces the normal reflected signal or which introduces a code into the reflected signal (as for identification)
radar gun *n* (1977) : a handheld device that uses radar to measure the speed of a moving object
ra·dar·scope \ˈrā-ˌdär-ˌskōp\ *n* [*radar* + oscillo*scope*] (1945) : the oscilloscope or screen serving as the visual indicator in a radar receiver
¹**rad·dle** \ˈra-dᵊl\ *n* [ME *radel,* fr. dim. of *rad-, red* red] (14c) : RED OCHER
²**raddle** *vt* **rad·dled; rad·dling** \ˈrad-liŋ, ˈra-dᵊl-iŋ\ (1631) : to mark or paint with raddle
³**raddle** *vt* **rad·dled; rad·dling** [E dial. *raddle* supple stick interwoven with others as in making a fence] (1671) : to twist together : INTERWEAVE
raddled *adj* [origin unknown] (1694) **1** : being in a state of confusion : lacking composure **2** : BROKEN-DOWN, WORN
radi- *or* **radio-** *comb form* [F, fr. L *radius* ray] **1** : radiant energy : radiation ⟨*radio*active⟩ ⟨*radio*paque⟩ **2** : radioactive ⟨*radio*element⟩ **3** : radium : X-rays ⟨*radio*therapy⟩ **4** : radioactive isotopes esp. as produced artificially ⟨*radio*carbon⟩ **5** : radio ⟨*radio*telegraphy⟩ **6** : radius bone ⟨*radio*-ulna⟩
¹**ra·di·al** \ˈrā-dē-əl\ *adj* [ML *radialis,* fr. L *radius* ray] (1570) **1** : arranged or having parts arranged like rays **2 a** : relating to, placed like, or moving along a radius **b** : characterized by divergence from a center **3** : of, relating to, or adjacent to a bodily radius **4** : developing uniformly around a central axis — **ra·di·al·ly** \-ə-lē\ *adv*
²**radial** *n* (1872) **1 a** : a radial part **b** : RAY **2** : a body part (as an artery) lying near or following the course of the radius **3** : a pneumatic tire in which the ply cords that extend to the beads are laid at approximately 90 degrees to the centerline of the tread — called also *radial-ply tire, radial tire*
radial cleavage *n* (1973) : holoblastic cleavage that is typical of deuterostomes and that is characterized by arrangement of the blastomeres of each upper tier directly over those of the next lower tier resulting in radial symmetry around the pole to pole axis of the embryo — compare SPIRAL CLEAVAGE
radial engine *n* (1909) : a usu. internal combustion engine with cylinders arranged radially like the spokes of a wheel
radial ker·a·tot·o·my \-ˌker-ə-ˈtä-tə-mē\ *n* (1980) : a surgical operation on the cornea for the correction of myopia that involves flattening it by making a series of incisions in a radial pattern resembling the spokes of a wheel — compare PHOTOREFRACTIVE KERATOTOMY
radial symmetry *n* (1872) : the condition of having similar parts regularly arranged around a central axis — **radially symmetrical** *adj*
ra·di·an \ˈrā-dē-ən\ *n* (1879) : a unit of plane angular measurement that is equal to the angle at the center of a circle subtended by an arc whose length equals the radius or approximately 57.3 degrees
ra·di·ance \ˈrā-dē-ən(t)s\ *n* (1600) **1** : the quality or state of being radiant **2** : a deep pink **3** : the flux density of radiant energy per unit solid angle and per unit projected area of radiating surface
ra·di·an·cy \-ən(t)-sē\ *n* (1602) : RADIANCE
¹**ra·di·ant** \ˈrā-dē-ənt\ *adj* (15c) **1 a** : radiating rays or reflecting beams of light **b** : vividly bright and shining : GLOWING **2** : marked by or expressive of love, confidence, or happiness ⟨a ~ smile⟩ **3 a** : emitted or transmitted by radiation **b** : emitting or relating to radiant heat ***syn*** see BRIGHT — **ra·di·ant·ly** *adv*
²**radiant** *n* (ca. 1741) : something that radiates: as **a** : a point in the heavens at which the visible paths of meteors appear to meet when traced backward **b** : the part of a gas or electric heater that becomes incandescent
radiant energy *n* (1870) : energy traveling as electromagnetic waves
radiant flux *n* (1917) : the rate of emission or transmission of radiant energy
radiant heat *n* (1621) : heat transmitted by radiation as contrasted with that transmitted by conduction or convection
¹**ra·di·ate** \ˈrā-dē-ˌāt\ *vb* **-at·ed; -at·ing** [L *radiatus,* pp. of *radiare,* fr. *radius* ray] *vi* (ca. 1619) **1** : to proceed in a direct line from or toward a center **2** : to send out rays : shine brightly **3 a** : to issue in or as if in rays **b** : to evolve by adaptive radiation ~ *vt* **1** : to send out in or as if in rays **2** : IRRADIATE, ILLUMINATE **3** : to spread abroad or around as if from a center
²**ra·di·ate** \ˈrā-dē-ət, -ˌāt\ *adj* (1668) : having rays or radial parts: as **a** : having ray flowers **b** : characterized by radial symmetry : radially symmetrical — **ra·di·ate·ly** *adv*
ra·di·a·tion \ˌrā-dē-ˈā-shən\ *n* (15c) **1 a** : the action or process of radiating **b** : the process of emitting radiant energy in the form of waves or particles **c (1)** : the combined processes of emission, transmission, and absorption of radiant energy **(2)** : the transfer of heat by radiation — compare CONDUCTION, CONVECTION **2 a** : something that is radiated **b** : energy radiated in the form of waves or particles **3** : radial arrangement **4** : ADAPTIVE RADIATION — **ra·di·a·tion·al** \-shnəl, -shə-nᵊl\ *adj* — **ra·di·a·tion·less** \-shən-ləs\ *adj* — **ra·di·a·tive** \ˈrā-dē-ˌā-tiv\ *adj*
radiation sickness *n* (1924) : sickness that results from exposure to radiation and is commonly marked by fatigue, nausea, vomiting, loss of teeth and hair, and in more severe cases by damage to blood-forming tissue with decrease in red and white blood cells and with bleeding
radiation therapy *n* (1922) : RADIOTHERAPY
ra·di·a·tor \ˈrā-dē-ˌā-tər, *dial* ˈra-\ *n* (1836) : one that radiates: as **a** : any of various devices (as a series of pipes or tubes) for transferring heat from a fluid within to an area or object outside **b** : a transmitting antenna
¹**rad·i·cal** \ˈra-di-kəl\ *adj* [ME, fr. LL *radicalis,* fr. L *radic-, radix* root — more at ROOT] (14c) **1** : of, relating to, or proceeding from a root: as **a (1)** : of or growing from the root of a plant ⟨~ tubers⟩ **(2)** : growing from the base of a stem, from a rootlike stem, or from a stem that does not rise above the ground ⟨~ leaves⟩ **b** : of, relating to, or constituting a linguistic root **c** : of or relating to a mathematical root **d** : designed to remove the root of a disease or all diseased and potentially diseased tissue ⟨~ surgery⟩ ⟨~ mastectomy⟩ **2** : of or relating to the origin : FUNDAMENTAL **3 a** : very different from the usual or traditional : EXTREME **b** : favoring extreme changes in existing views, habits, conditions, or institutions **c** : associated with political views, practices, and policies of extreme change **d** : advocating extreme measures to retain or restore a political state of affairs ⟨the ~ right⟩ **4** *slang* : EXCELLENT, COOL — **rad·i·cal·ness** *n*
²**radical** *n* (1641) **1 a** : a root part **b** : a basic principle : FOUNDATION **2 a** : ROOT 6 **b** : a sound or letter belonging to a radical **3** : one who is radical **4** : FREE RADICAL; *also* : a group of atoms bonded together that is considered an entity in various kinds of reactions or as a subunit of a larger molecule **5 a** : a mathematical expression indicating a root by means of a radical sign **b** : RADICAL SIGN
radical chic *n* (1970) : a fashionable practice among socially prominent people of associating with radicals or members of minority groups
rad·i·cal·ise *Brit var of* RADICALIZE
rad·i·cal·ism \ˈra-di-kə-ˌli-zəm\ *n* (1817) **1** : the quality or state of being radical **2** : the doctrines or principles of radicals
rad·i·cal·ize \-kə-ˌlīz\ *vt* **-ized; -iz·ing** (1830) : to make radical esp. in politics — **rad·i·cal·i·za·tion** \ˌra-di-kə-lə-ˈzā-shən\ *n*
rad·i·cal·ly \ˈra-di-k(ə-)lē\ *adv* (15c) **1** : in origin or essence **2** : in a radical or extreme manner
radical sign *n* (1668) : the sign $\sqrt{\ }$ or √ placed before an expression to denote that the square root is to be extracted or that the root marked by an index (as in $\sqrt[3]{\ }$ or ∛ for the cube root) is to be extracted
rad·i·cand \ˌra-də-ˈkand\ *n* [L *radicandum,* neut. of *radicandus,* gerundive of *radicari*] (1889) : the quantity under a radical sign
ra·dic·chio \ra-ˈdi-kē-ō\ *n, pl* **-chios** [It, chicory, fr. VL **radiculus,* alter. of L *radicula*] (1968) : a chicory of a red variety with variegated leaves that is used as a salad green
radices *pl of* RADIX
rad·i·cle \ˈra-di-kəl\ *n* [L *radicula,* dim. of *radic-, radix*] (1671) **1** : the lower part of the axis of a plant embryo or seedling: **a** : the embryonic root of a seedling **b** : HYPOCOTYL **c** : the hypocotyl and the root together **2** : RADICAL 4
ra·dic·u·lar \rə-ˈdi-kyə-lər, ra-\ *adj* (1830) **1** : of or relating to a plant radicle **2** : of, relating to, or involving a nerve root ⟨~ pain⟩
ra·dic·u·lop·a·thy \rə-ˌdi-kyə-ˈlä-pə-thē\ *n* [L *radicula* + E *-o-* + *-pathy*] (1942) : irritation of or injury to a nerve root (as from being compressed) that typically causes pain, numbness, or weakness in the part of the body which is supplied with nerves from that root
radii *pl of* RADIUS
¹**ra·dio** \ˈrā-dē-ˌō\ *adj* [²*radio* or *radio-*] (1887) **1** : of, relating to, or operated by radiant energy **2** : of or relating to electric currents or phenomena (as electromagnetic radiation) of frequencies between about 3000 hertz and 300 gigahertz **3 a** : of, relating to, or used in radio or a radio set **b** : specializing in radio or associated with the radio industry **c (1)** : transmitted by radio **(2)** : making or participating in radio broadcasts **d** : controlled or directed by radio
²**radio** *n, pl* **ra·di·os** [short for *radiotelegraphy*] (1903) **1 a** : the wireless transmission and reception of electric impulses or signals by means of electromagnetic waves **b** : the use of these waves for the wireless transmission of electric impulses into which sound is converted **2** : a radio message **3** : a radio receiving set **4 a** : a radio transmitting station **b** : a radio broadcasting organization **c** : the radio broadcasting industry **d** : communication by radio
³**radio** *vt* (1913) **1** : to send or communicate by radio **2** : to send a radio message to ~ *vi* : to send or communicate something by radio
radio- — see RADI-

\ə\ **abut** \ᵊ\ kitten, F table \ər\ **fur**ther \a\ **a**sh \ā\ **a**ce \ä\ m**o**p, m**a**r
\au̇\ **ou**t \ch\ **ch**in \e\ b**e**t \ē\ **ea**sy \g\ **g**o \i\ h**i**t \ī\ **i**ce \j\ **j**ob
\ŋ\ si**ng** \ō\ g**o** \ȯ\ l**aw** \ȯi\ b**oy** \th\ **th**in \t͟h\ **th**e \ü\ l**oo**t \u̇\ f**oo**t
\y\ **y**et \zh\ vi**s**ion, beige \k̲, ⁿ, œ, ue, ʸ\ *see* Guide to Pronunciation

ra·dio·ac·tive \ˌrā-dē-ō-ˈak-tiv\ *adj* [ISV] (1898) **:** of, caused by, or exhibiting radioactivity — **ra·dio·ac·tive·ly** *adv*
ra·dio·ac·tiv·i·ty \-ak-ˈti-və-tē\ *n* [ISV] (1899) **:** the property possessed by some elements (as uranium) or isotopes (as carbon 14) of spontaneously emitting energetic particles (as electrons or alpha particles) by the disintegration of their atomic nuclei; *also* **:** the rays emitted
ra·dio·al·ler·go·sor·bent \ˌrā-dē-ō-ə-ˌlər-gō-ˈsȯr-bənt\ *adj* [*radi-* + *allergen* + *-o-* + *sorbent*] (1967) **:** relating to or being a blood analysis that tests for allergen-specific antibodies of the immunoglobulin class IgE and is used to detect allergic reactions
radio astronomy *n* (1948) **:** astronomy dealing with radio waves received from outside the earth's atmosphere — **radio astronomer** *n* — **radio astronomical** *adj*
ra·dio·au·to·graph \ˌrā-dē-ō-ˈȯ-tə-ˌgraf\ *n* (1941) **:** AUTORADIOGRAPH — **ra·dio·au·to·graph·ic** \-ˌȯ-tə-ˈgra-fik\ *adj* — **ra·dio·au·tog·ra·phy** \-ȯ-ˈtä-grə-fē\ *n*
radio beacon *n* (1919) **:** a radio transmitting station that transmits special radio signals for use (as on a landing field) in determining the direction or position of those receiving them
ra·dio·bi·ol·o·gy \ˌrā-dē-ō-bī-ˈä-lə-jē\ *n* (1919) **:** a branch of biology dealing with the effects of radiation or radioactive materials on biological systems — **ra·dio·bi·o·log·i·cal** \-ˌbī-ə-ˈlä-ji-kəl\ *also* **ra·dio·bi·o·log·ic** \-jik\ *adj* — **ra·dio·bi·o·log·i·cal·ly** \-ji-k(ə-)lē\ *adv* — **ra·dio·bi·ol·o·gist** \-bī-ˈä-lə-jist\ *n*
radio car *n* (1925) **:** an automobile equipped with radio communication
ra·dio·car·bon \ˌrā-dē-ō-ˈkär-bən\ *n, often attrib* [ISV] (1939) **:** radioactive carbon; *esp* **:** CARBON 14
radiocarbon dating *n* (1951) **:** CARBON DATING — **radiocarbon–date** \-ˈdāt\ *vt*
ra·dio·chem·is·try \ˌrā-dē-ō-ˈke-mə-strē\ *n* (1904) **:** a branch of chemistry dealing with radioactive substances and phenomena including tracer studies — **ra·dio·chem·i·cal** \-ˈke-mi-kəl\ *adj* — **ra·dio·chem·i·cal·ly** \-k(ə-)lē\ *adv* — **ra·dio·chem·ist** \-ˈke-mist\ *n*
ra·dio·chro·mato·gram \-krō-ˈma-tə-ˌgram, -krə-\ *n* (1951) **:** a chromatogram revealing one or more radioactive substances
radio collar *n* (1977) **:** a collar with an attached radio transmitter that is put on an animal so that its movements in its natural habitat can be remotely monitored — **radio–collar** *vt*
radio compass *n* (1918) **:** a direction finder used in navigation
ra·dio·ecol·o·gy \ˌrā-dē-ō-i-ˈkä-lə-jē\ *n* (1956) **:** the study of the effects of radiation and radioactive substances on ecological communities
ra·dio·el·e·ment \-ˈe-lə-mənt\ *n* [ISV] (1903) **:** a radioactive element
radio frequency *n* (1915) **:** any of the electromagnetic wave frequencies that lie in the range extending from below 3 kilohertz to about 300 gigahertz and that include the frequencies used for communications signals (as for radio and television broadcasting and cell-phone and satellite transmissions) or radar signals

RADIO FREQUENCIES

CLASS	ABBREVIATION	RANGE
extremely low frequency	ELF	below 3 kilohertz
very low frequency	VLF	3 to 30 kilohertz
low frequency	LF	30 to 300 kilohertz
medium frequency	MF	300 to 3000 kilohertz
high frequency	HF	3 to 30 megahertz
very high frequency	VHF	30 to 300 megahertz
ultrahigh frequency	UHF	300 to 3000 megahertz
superhigh frequency	SHF	3 to 30 gigahertz
extremely high frequency	EHF	30 to 300 gigahertz

radio galaxy *n* (1960) **:** a galaxy that is a powerful source of radio waves
ra·dio·gen·ic \ˌrā-dē-ō-ˈje-nik\ *adj* (1935) **:** produced by or determined from radioactivity ⟨~ isotopes⟩ ⟨~ tumors⟩
ra·dio·gram \ˈrā-dē-ō-ˌgram\ *n* (1896) **1 :** RADIOGRAPH **2 :** a message transmitted by radiotelegraphy **3** [short for *radiogramophone*] *Brit* **:** a combined radio receiver and record player
[1]**ra·dio·graph** \-ˌgraf\ *n* (1896) **:** a picture produced on a sensitive surface by a form of radiation other than visible light; *specif* **:** an X-ray or gamma ray photograph — **ra·dio·graph·ic** \ˌrā-dē-ō-ˈgra-fik\ *adj* — **ra·dio·graph·i·cal·ly** \-fi-k(ə-)lē\ *adv*
[2]**radiograph** *vt* (1896) **:** to make a radiograph of — **ra·di·og·ra·pher** \ˌrā-dē-ˈä-grə-fər\ *n*
ra·di·og·ra·phy \ˌrā-dē-ˈä-grə-fē\ *n* [ISV] (1896) **:** the art, act, or process of making radiographs
ra·dio·im·mu·no·as·say \ˌrā-dē-ˌō-i-myə-nō-ˈa-ˌsā, -i-ˌmyü-, -a-ˈsā\ *n* (1961) **:** immunoassay of a substance that has been radioactively labeled — **ra·dio·im·mu·no·as·say·able** \-ə-bəl\ *adj*
ra·dio·iso·tope \ˌrā-dē-ō-ˈī-sə-ˌtōp\ *n* [ISV] (1946) **:** a radioactive isotope — **ra·dio·iso·to·pic** \-ˌī-sə-ˈtä-pik, -ˈtō-\ *adj* — **ra·dio·iso·to·pi·cal·ly** \-pi-k(ə-)lē\ *adv*
ra·dio·la·bel \-ˈlā-bəl\ *vt* (1953) **:** to label with a radioactive atom or substance
ra·di·o·lar·ia \ˌrā-dē-ō-ˈler-ē-ə\ *n pl* [NL, fr. LL *radiolus* small sunbeam, fr. dim. of L *radius* ray — more at RAY] (1872) **:** protozoans that are radiolarians
ra·di·o·lar·i·an \ˌrā-dē-ō-ˈler-ē-ən\ *n* (1875) **:** any of three classes (Acantharia, Polycystina, and Phaeodaria) of usu. spherical chiefly planktonic marine protozoans having radiating threadlike pseudopodia and often a siliceous skeleton of spicules — **radiolarian** *adj*

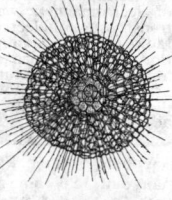

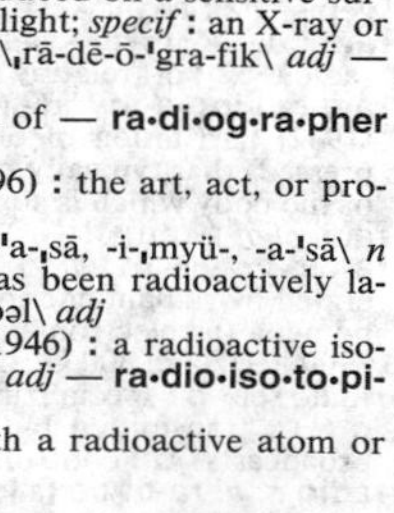
radiolarian

ra·dio·log·i·cal \ˌrā-dē-ə-ˈlä-ji-kəl\ *or* **ra·dio·log·ic** \-jik\ *adj* (1909) **1 :** of or relating to radiology **2 :** of or relating to nuclear radiation — **ra·dio·log·i·cal·ly** \-k(ə-)lē\ *adv*
ra·di·ol·o·gist \ˌrā-dē-ˈä-lə-jist\ *n* (1906) **:** a physician specializing in medical radiology
ra·di·ol·o·gy \-jē\ *n* (1900) **1 :** a branch of medicine concerned with the use of radiant energy (as X-rays) or radioactive material in the diagnosis and treatment of disease **2 :** the science of radioactive substances and high-energy radiations
ra·dio·lu·cent \ˌrā-dē-ō-ˈlü-sᵊnt\ *adj* (1917) **:** partly or wholly permeable to radiation ⟨~ tissues⟩ — **ra·dio·lu·cen·cy** \-sᵊn(t)-sē\ *n*
ra·di·ol·y·sis \ˌrā-dē-ˈä-lə-səs\ *n* [NL] (1948) **:** chemical decomposition by the action of radiation — **ra·dio·lyt·ic** \-dē-ə-ˈli-tik\ *adj*
ra·dio·man \ˈrā-dē-ō-ˌman\ *n* (1921) **:** a radio operator or technician
ra·di·om·e·ter \ˌrā-dē-ˈä-mə-tər\ *n* (1875) **:** an instrument for detecting and usu. for measuring the intensity of radiant energy — **ra·di·om·e·try** \-mə-trē\ *n*
ra·dio·met·ric \ˌrā-dē-ō-ˈme-trik\ *adj* [ISV] (1877) **1 :** relating to, using, or measured by a radiometer **2 :** of or relating to the measurement of geologic time by means of the rate of disintegration of radioactive elements — **ra·dio·met·ri·cal·ly** \-tri-k(ə-)lē\ *adv*
ra·dio·mi·met·ic \-mə-ˈme-tik, -mī-\ *adj* [ISV] (1947) **:** producing effects similar to those of radiation ⟨a ~ antibiotic⟩
ra·dio·nu·clide \ˌrā-dē-ō-ˈnü-ˌklīd, -ˈnyü-\ *n* (1947) **:** a radioactive nuclide
ra·di·opaque \ˌrā-dē-ō-ˈpāk\ *adj* (ca. 1923) **:** being opaque to various forms of radiation (as X-rays)
ra·dio·phar·ma·ceu·ti·cal \ˌrā-dē-ō-ˌfär-mə-ˈsü-ti-kəl\ *n* (1952) **:** a radioactive drug used for diagnostic or therapeutic purposes — **radiopharmaceutical** *adj*
ra·dio·phone \ˈrā-dē-ə-ˌfōn\ *n* (1919) **:** RADIOTELEPHONE
ra·dio·pho·to \ˌrā-dē-ō-ˈfō-(ˌ)tō\ *n* (1929) **:** a picture transmitted by radio
ra·dio·pro·tec·tive \-prə-ˈtek-tiv\ *adj* (1956) **:** serving to protect or aiding in protecting against the injurious effect of radiations ⟨~ drugs⟩ — **ra·dio·pro·tec·tion** \-ˈtek-shən\ *n*
radio range *n* (1929) **:** a radio facility for aircraft navigation
ra·dio·sen·si·tive \ˌrā-dē-ō-ˈsen(t)-sə-tiv, -ˈsen(t)-stiv\ *adj* (1920) **:** sensitive to the effects of radiant energy ⟨~ cancer cells⟩ — **ra·dio·sen·si·tiv·i·ty** \-ˌsen(t)-sə-ˈti-və-tē\ *n*
ra·dio·sonde \ˈrā-dē-ō-ˌsänd\ *n* [ISV] (1937) **:** a miniature radio transmitter that is carried aloft (as by an unmanned balloon) with instruments for sensing and broadcasting atmospheric conditions
radio spectrum *n* (1929) **:** the region of the electromagnetic spectrum spanning the radio frequency range
radio star *n* (1948) **:** a cosmic radio source; *esp* **:** a point source of radio emissions
ra·dio·sur·gery \ˌrā-dē-ō-ˈsərj-rē, -ˈsər-jə-rē\ *n* (1933) **:** surgery using precisely targeted radiation to destroy tissue without cutting
ra·dio–tag \ˈrā-dē-ō-ˌtag\ *vt* (1951) **:** to attach a radio transmitter to (an animal) ⟨tracked the movements of a *radio-tagged* owl⟩
ra·dio·tele·graph \ˌrā-dē-ō-ˈte-lə-ˌgraf\ *n* [ISV] (1903) **:** WIRELESS TELEGRAPHY — **ra·dio·te·leg·ra·phy** \-tə-ˈle-grə-fē\ *n*
ra·dio·te·lem·e·try \-tə-ˈle-mə-trē\ *n* (1951) **1 :** TELEMETRY **2 :** BIOTELEMETRY — **ra·dio·tele·met·ric** \-ˌte-lə-ˈme-trik\ *adj*
ra·dio·tele·phone \-ˈte-lə-ˌfōn\ *n* [ISV] (1904) **:** an apparatus for carrying on wireless telephony by radio waves — **ra·dio·te·le·pho·ny** \-tə-ˈle-fə-nē, -ˈte-lə-ˌfō-nē\ *n*
radio telescope *n* (1929) **:** a radio receiver-antenna combination used for observation in radio astronomy
ra·dio·ther·a·py \ˌrā-dē-ō-ˈther-ə-pē\ *n* [ISV] (1903) **:** the treatment of disease with radiation (as X-rays) — **ra·dio·ther·a·pist** \-pist\ *n*
ra·dio·tho·ri·um \-ˈthȯr-ē-əm\ *n* [NL] (1905) **:** a radioactive isotope of thorium with the mass number 228
ra·dio·trac·er \ˈrā-dē-ō-ˌtrā-sər\ *n* (1946) **:** a radioactive tracer
ra·dio–ul·na \ˌrā-dē-ō-ˈəl-nə\ *n* [NL] (1960) **:** a single bone in the forelimb of an amphibian (as a frog) that represents fusion of the separate radius and ulna of higher vertebrate forms
radio wave *n* (1916) **:** an electromagnetic wave with radio frequency
rad·ish \ˈra-dish *also* ˈre-\ *n* [ME, alter. of OE *rædic,* fr. L *radic-, radix* root, radish — more at ROOT] (15c) **:** the pungent usu. crisp root of a widely cultivated Eurasian plant (*Raphanus sativus*) of the mustard family usu. eaten raw; *also* **:** a plant that produces radishes
ra·di·um \ˈrā-dē-əm\ *n, often attrib* [NL, fr. L *radius* ray] (1899) **:** an intensely radioactive brilliant white metallic element that resembles barium chemically, occurs in combination in minute quantities in minerals (as pitchblende or carnotite), emits alpha particles and gamma rays to form radon, and is used chiefly in luminous materials and in the treatment of cancer — see ELEMENT table
radium therapy *n* (1904) **:** RADIOTHERAPY
ra·di·us \ˈrā-dē-əs\ *n, pl* **ra·dii** \-dē-ˌī\ *also* **ra·di·us·es** [L, ray, radius] (ca. 1611) **1 :** a line segment extending from the center of a circle or sphere to the circumference or bounding surface **2 a :** the bone on the thumb side of the human forearm; *also* **:** a corresponding part of vertebrates above fishes **b :** the third and usu. largest vein of an insect's wing **3 a :** the length of a radius ⟨a truck with a short turning ~⟩ **b :** the circular area defined by a stated radius **c :** a bounded or circumscribed area **4 :** a radial part **5 :** the distance from a center line or point to an axis of rotation
radius of curvature (ca. 1753) **:** the reciprocal of the curvature of a curve
radius vector *n* (ca. 1753) **1 a :** the line segment or its length from a fixed point to a variable point **b :** the linear polar coordinate of a variable point **2 :** a straight line joining the center of an attracting body (as the sun) with that of a body (as a planet) in orbit around it
ra·dix \ˈrā-diks\ *n, pl* **ra·di·ces** \ˈrā-də-ˌsēz, ˈra-\ *or* **ra·dix·es** \ˈrā-dik-səz\ [L, root — more at ROOT] (1798) **1 :** the base of a number system or of logarithms **2 :** the primary source
RADM *abbr* rear admiral
ra·dome \ˈrā-ˌdōm\ *n* [*radar dome*] (ca. 1944) **:** a plastic housing sheltering the antenna assembly of a radar set esp. on an airplane
ra·don \ˈrā-ˌdän\ *n* [ISV, fr. *radium*] (1918) **:** a heavy radioactive gaseous element formed by the decay of radium — see ELEMENT table
rad·u·la \ˈra-jə-lə\ *n, pl* **-lae** \-ˌlē, -ˌlī\ *also* **-las** [NL, fr. L, scraper, fr. *radere* to scrape — more at RODENT] (ca. 1859) **:** a horny band or ribbon in mollusks other than bivalves that bears minute chitinous teeth on its dorsal surface and scrapes or tears off food and draws it into the mouth — **rad·u·lar** \-lər\ *adj*

rad·waste \ˈrad-ˌwāst\ *n, often attrib* [by shortening] (1973) **:** radioactive waste
RAF *abbr* Royal Air Force
raff \ˈraf\ *n* [ME *raf* rubbish] (14c) **:** RIFFRAFF
raf·fia \ˈra-fē-ə\ *n* [Malagasy *rafia*] (1882) **:** the fiber of the raffia palm used esp. as cord for tying and weaving
raffia palm *n* (1872) **:** a large pinnate-leaved palm (*Raphia farinifera* syn. *R. ruffia*) of Madagascar and tropical Africa valued for the fiber obtained from its petiole
raf·fi·nose \ˈra-fə-ˌnōs, -ˌnōz\ *n* [F, fr. *raffiner* to refine, fr. *re-* + *affiner* to make fine, fr. *a-* ad- (fr. L *ad-*) + *fin* fine] (1876) **:** a crystalline slightly sweet sugar $C_{18}H_{32}O_{16}$ obtained commercially from cottonseed meal and present in many plant products
raff·ish \ˈra-fish\ *adj* (1796) **1 :** marked by or suggestive of flashy vulgarity or crudeness **2 :** marked by a careless unconventionality **:** RAKISH — **raff·ish·ly** *adv* — **raff·ish·ness** *n*
[1]**raf·fle** \ˈra-fəl\ *vb* **raf·fled; raf·fling** \ˈra-f(ə-)liŋ\ *vi* (ca. 1680) **:** to engage in a raffle ~ *vt* **:** to dispose of by means of a raffle ⟨~ off a turkey⟩
[2]**raffle** *n* [ME *rafle,* a dice game, fr. MF, dice game in which all the stakes can be won in a throw, lit., rake for a fire, fr. MHG *raffel* rake for a fire, fr. *raffen* to snatch, gather] (1766) **:** a lottery in which the prize is won by one of numerous persons buying chances
[3]**raffle** *n* [prob. fr. F *rafle* act of snatching, sweeping, fr. MF, rake for a fire] (1881) **:** RUBBISH; *esp* **:** a jumble or tangle of nautical equipment
raf·fle·sia \rə-ˈflē-zh(ē-)ə, ra-\ *n* [NL, fr. Sir Stamford *Raffles* †1826 Eng. colonial administrator] (1830) **:** any of a genus (*Rafflesia* of the family Rafflesiaceae) of Malaysian dicotyledonous plants that are parasitic in other plants and have fleshy usu. foul-smelling apetalous flowers emerging from the host, imbricated scales in place of leaves, and no stems
[1]**raft** \ˈraft\ *n* [ME *rafte* rafter, raft, fr. ON *raptr* rafter] (15c) **1 a :** a collection of logs or timber fastened together for conveyance by water **b :** a flat structure for support or transportation on water **2 :** a floating cohesive mass **3 :** an aggregation of animals (as waterfowl) resting on the water
[2]**raft** *vt* (1706) **1 :** to transport in the form of or by means of a raft; *also* **:** to convey (as pebbles) in floating ice or masses of organic material **2 :** to make into a raft ~ *vi* **:** to travel by raft
[3]**raft** *n* [alter. of *raff* jumble] (1830) **:** a large collection or number
[1]**raf·ter** \ˈraf-tər\ *n* [ME, fr. OE *ræfter;* akin to ON *raptr* rafter] (bef. 12c) **:** any of the parallel beams that support a roof — **raf·tered** \-tərd\ *adj*
[2]**raft·er** \ˈraf-tər\ *n* [[2]*raft*] (1809) **1 :** one who maneuvers logs into position and binds them into rafts **2 :** one who travels by raft
rafts·man \ˈraf(t)s-mən\ *n* (1776) **:** a man engaged in rafting
[1]**rag** \ˈrag\ *n* [ME *ragge,* fr. OE **ragg,* fr. ON *rǫgg* tuft, shagginess] (14c) **1 a :** a waste piece of cloth **b** *pl* **:** clothes usu. in poor or ragged condition **c :** CLOTHING ⟨the ~ trade⟩ **2 :** something resembling a rag **3 :** NEWSPAPER; *esp* **:** a sleazy newspaper
[2]**rag** *n* [ME *ragge*] (14c) **1 :** any of various hard rocks **2 :** a large roofing slate that is rough on one side
[3]**rag** *vt* **ragged** \ˈragd\; **rag·ging** [origin unknown] (1739) **1 :** to rail at **:** SCOLD **2 :** TORMENT, TEASE — **rag on :** to make fun of
[4]**rag** *n* (1864) *chiefly Brit* **:** an outburst of boisterous fun; *also* **:** PRANK
[5]**rag** *n* [short for *ragtime*] (1897) **:** a composition in ragtime
ra·ga \ˈrä-gə\ *n* [Skt *rāga,* lit., color, tone; akin to Skt *rajyati* it reddens, Gk *rhezein* to dye] (1788) **1 :** one of the ancient traditional melodic patterns or modes in Indian music **2 :** an improvisation based on a traditional raga — compare TALA
rag·a·muf·fin \ˈra-gə-ˌmə-fən\ *n* [ME *Ragamuffyn,* name for a ragged, oafish person] (1581) **:** a ragged often disreputable person; *esp* **:** a poorly clothed often dirty child
rag·bag \ˈrag-ˌbag\ *n* (1820) **1 :** a bag for scraps **2 :** a miscellaneous collection
rag doll *n* (1850) **:** a stuffed usu. painted cloth doll
[1]**rage** \ˈrāj\ *n* [ME, fr. AF, fr. LL *rabia,* fr. L *rabies* rage, madness, fr. *rabere* to be mad; akin to Skt *rabhas* violence] (14c) **1 a :** violent and uncontrolled anger **b :** a fit of violent wrath **c** *archaic* **:** INSANITY **2 :** violent action (as of wind or sea) **3 :** an intense feeling **:** PASSION **4 :** a fad pursued with intense enthusiasm ⟨was all the ~⟩ ***syn*** see ANGER, FASHION
[2]**rage** *vi* **raged; rag·ing** (14c) **1 :** to be in a rage **2 :** to be in tumult **3 :** to prevail uncontrollably
rag·ged \ˈra-gəd\ *adj* (14c) **1 :** roughly unkempt **2 :** having an irregular edge or outline **3 a :** torn or worn to tatters **b :** worn-out from stress and strain ⟨ran herself ~⟩ **4 :** wearing tattered clothes **5 a :** STRAGGLY **b :** executed in an irregular or uneven manner **c** *of a sound* **:** HARSH, DISSONANT — **rag·ged·ly** *adv* — **rag·ged·ness** *n*
ragged robin *n* (1741) **:** a perennial herb (*Lychnis flos-cuculi*) of the pink family cultivated for its pink flowers with narrow-lobed petals
rag·gedy \ˈra-gə-dē\ *adj* **-ged·i·er; -est** (1881) **:** RAGGED
rag·gle–tag·gle \ˈra-gəl-ˌta-gəl\ *adj* [irreg. fr. *ragtag*] (1904) **:** MOTLEY
ra·gi \ˈra-gē, ˈrä-\ *n* [perh. fr. Deccan Hindi *rāgī*] (1792) **:** an Old World cereal grass (*Eleusine coracana*) yielding a staple food crop esp. in India and Africa; *also* **:** the seeds of ragi used for food
raging *adj* (15c) **1 :** causing great pain or distress **2 :** VIOLENT, WILD ⟨a ~ fire⟩ **3 :** EXTRAORDINARY, TREMENDOUS ⟨a ~ success⟩
rag·lan \ˈra-glən\ *n* [F.J.H. Somerset, Baron *Raglan* †1855 Brit. field marshal] (ca. 1859) **:** a loose overcoat with raglan sleeves
raglan sleeve *n* (1923) **:** a sleeve that extends to the neckline with slanted seams from the underarm to the neck
rag·man \ˈrag-ˌman\ *n* (1586) **:** a man who collects or deals in rags
Rag·na·rok \ˈrag-nə-ˌräk, -rək\ *n* [ON *Ragnarǫk,* lit., fate of the gods, fr. *ragna,* gen. pl. of *regin* gods + *rǫk* fate, course (later rendered as *Ragnarøkkr,* lit., twilight of the gods)] (1770) **:** the final destruction of the world in the conflict between the Aesir and the powers of Hel led by Loki — called also *Twilight of the Gods*
ra·gout \ra-ˈgü\ *n* [F *ragoût,* fr. *ragoûter* to revive the taste, fr. MF *ragouster,* fr. *re-* + *a-* ad- (fr. L *ad-*) + *goust* taste, fr. L *gustus;* akin to L *gustare* to taste — more at CHOOSE] (ca. 1657) **1 :** well-seasoned meat and vegetables cooked in a thick sauce **2 :** MIXTURE, MÉLANGE
rag·pick·er \ˈrag-ˌpi-kər\ *n* (1842) **:** one who collects rags and refuse for a livelihood
rag·tag \ˈrag-ˌtag\ *adj* [*ragtag and bobtail*] (1865) **1 :** RAGGED, UNKEMPT **2 :** MOTLEY 2 ⟨a ~ bunch of misfits⟩
ragtag and bobtail *n* [[1]*rag* + [1]*tag*] (1820) **:** RABBLE
rag·time \ˈrag-ˌtīm\ *n* [prob. fr. *ragged* + *time*] (1897) **1 :** rhythm characterized by strong syncopation in the melody with a regularly accented accompaniment in stride-piano style **2 :** music having ragtime rhythm
rag·top \-ˌtäp\ *n* (1953) **:** a convertible automobile
rag·weed \-ˌwēd\ *n* (1790) **:** any of various chiefly No. American weedy composite herbs (genus *Ambrosia*) that produce highly allergenic pollen

ragweed

rag·wort \-ˌwərt, -ˌwȯrt\ *n* (14c) **:** any of several senecios; *esp* **:** TANSY RAGWORT
rah \ˈrä, ˈrȯ\ *interj* (1870) **:** HOORAY — used esp. to cheer on a team
rah–rah \ˈrä-(ˌ)rä, ˈrȯ-(ˌ)rȯ\ *adj* [redupl. of *rah*] (1911) **:** marked by the enthusiastic expression of college spirit ⟨~ cheerleaders⟩
[1]**raid** \ˈrād\ *n* [ME (Sc) *rade,* fr. OE *rād* ride, raid — more at ROAD] (15c) **1 a :** a hostile or predatory incursion **b :** a surprise attack by a small force **2 a :** a brief foray outside one's usual sphere **b :** a sudden invasion by officers of the law **c :** a daring operation against a competitor **d :** the recruiting of personnel (as faculty, executives, or athletes) from competing organizations **3 :** the act of mulcting public money **4 :** an attempt by professional operators to depress stock prices by concerted selling
[2]**raid** *vi* (1865) **:** to conduct or take part in a raid ~ *vt* **:** to make a raid on
raid·er \ˈrā-dər\ *n* (1863) **:** one that raids: as **a :** a fast lightly armed ship operating against merchant shipping **b :** a soldier specially trained for close-range fighting **c :** one that attempts a usu. hostile takeover of a business corporation ⟨corporate ~*s*⟩
[1]**rail** \ˈrāl\ *n* [ME *raile,* fr. AF *raille, reille* bar, rule, fr. L *regula* straightedge, rule — more at RULE] (14c) **1 a :** a bar extending from one post or support to another and serving as a guard or barrier **b :** a structural member or support **2 a :** RAILING 1 **b :** a light structure serving as a guard at the outer edge of a ship's deck **c :** a fence bounding a racetrack **3 a :** a bar of rolled steel forming a track for wheeled vehicles **b :** TRACK **c :** RAILROAD
[2]**rail** *vt* (14c) **:** to provide with a railing **:** FENCE
[3]**rail** *n, pl* **rail** *or* **rails** [ME *raile,* fr. MF *raalle*] (15c) **:** any of numerous wading birds (family Rallidae, the rail family) that are of small or medium size and have short rounded wings, a short tail, and usu. very long toes which enable them to run on the soft mud of marshes
[4]**rail** *vi* [ME, fr. MF *railler* to mock, prob. fr. OF *reillier* to growl, mutter, fr. VL **ragulare* to bray, fr. LL *ragere* to neigh] (15c) **:** to revile or scold in harsh, insolent, or abusive language ***syn*** see SCOLD — **rail·er** *n*
rail·bird \ˈrāl-ˌbərd\ *n* (1892) **:** a racing enthusiast who sits on or near the track rail to watch a race or workout
rail·bus \-ˌbəs\ *n* (1933) **:** a passenger car with an automotive engine for operation on rails
rail·car \-ˌkär\ *n* (1834) **1 :** a railroad car **2 :** a self-propelled railroad car
rail·head \ˈrāl-ˌhed\ *n* (1896) **:** a point on a railroad at which traffic may originate or terminate
rail·ing \ˈrā-liŋ\ *n* (15c) **1 :** a barrier consisting of a rail and supports **2 :** RAILS; *also* **:** material for making rails
rail·lery \ˈrā-lə-rē\ *n, pl* **-ler·ies** [F *raillerie,* fr. MF, fr. *railler* to mock] (1653) **1 :** good-natured ridicule **:** BANTER **2 :** JEST
[1]**rail·road** \ˈrāl-ˌrōd, ˈrel-; ˈre-ˌrōd\ *n* (1825) **:** a permanent road having a line of rails fixed to ties and laid on a roadbed and providing a track for cars or equipment drawn by locomotives or propelled by self-contained motors; *also* **:** such a road and its assets constituting a single property
[2]**railroad** *vt* (1877) **1 a :** to convict with undue haste and by means of false charges or insufficient evidence **b :** to push through hastily or without due consideration **2 :** to transport by railroad ~ *vi* **:** to work for a railroad company — **rail·road·er** *n*
railroad flat *n* (1947) **:** an apartment having a series of narrow rooms arranged in line
rail·road·ing \ˈrāl-ˌrō-diŋ\ *n* (1862) **:** construction or operation of a railroad
railroad worm *n* (1909) **1** [prob. fr. its dissemination by railroad] **:** APPLE MAGGOT **2** [fr. the rows of luminescent spots along its sides making it resemble a lighted train] **:** the larva or wingless female of any of several So. American beetles (genus *Phrixothrix* of the family Cantharidae)
rail–split·ter \ˈrāl-ˌspli-tər\ *n* (1860) **:** one that makes logs into fence rails
rail·way \-ˌwā\ *n* (1812) **:** RAILROAD; *esp* **:** a railroad operating with light equipment or within a small area
rai·ment \ˈrā-mənt\ *n* [ME *rayment,* short for *arrayment,* fr. *arrayen* to array] (15c) **:** CLOTHING, GARMENTS
[1]**rain** \ˈrān\ *n, often attrib* [ME *reyn,* fr. OE *regn, rēn;* akin to OHG *regan* rain] (bef. 12c) **1 a :** water falling in drops condensed from vapor in the atmosphere **b :** the descent of this water **c :** water that has fallen as rain **:** RAINWATER **2 a :** a fall of rain **:** RAINSTORM **b** *pl* **:** the rainy season **3 :** rainy weather **4 :** a heavy fall ⟨a ~ of arrows⟩
[2]**rain** *vi* (bef. 12c) **1 :** to send down rain **2 :** to fall as water in drops from the clouds **3 :** to fall like rain ⟨soot and ash ~*ed* down⟩ ~ *vt* **1 :** to pour down **2 :** to give or administer abundantly ⟨~*ed* blows on his head⟩ — **rain cats and dogs :** to rain heavily
rain·bird \ˈrān-ˌbərd\ *n* (1555) **:** any of various birds (esp. of the family Cuculidae) whose cries are popularly believed to forecast rain
[1]**rain·bow** \-ˌbō\ *n* (bef. 12c) **1 :** an arc or circle that exhibits in concentric bands the colors of the spectrum and that is formed opposite the sun by the refraction and reflection of the sun's rays in raindrops,

\ə\ **abut** \ᵊ\ kitten, F table \ər\ **further** \a\ **ash** \ā\ **ace** \ä\ **mop, mar**
\au̇\ **out** \ch\ **chin** \e\ **bet** \ē\ **easy** \g\ **go** \i\ **hit** \ī\ **ice** \j\ **job**
\ŋ\ **sing** \ō\ **go** \ȯ\ **law** \ȯi\ **boy** \th\ **thin** \t͟h\ **the** \ü\ **loot** \u̇\ **foot**
\y\ **yet** \zh\ **vision, beige** \k, ⁿ, œ, ue, ʸ\ *see* Guide to Pronunciation

spray, or mist **2 a :** a multicolored array **b :** a wide assortment or range ⟨a ~ of flavors⟩ **3** [fr. the impossibility of reaching the rainbow, at whose foot a pot of gold is said to be buried] **:** an illusory goal or hope **4 :** RAINBOW TROUT — **rain•bow•like** *adj*

[2]**rainbow** *adj* (1652) **1 :** having many colors **2 :** of, relating to, or being people of different races or cultural backgrounds ⟨a ~ coalition⟩

rainbow fish *n* (1722) **:** any of numerous brilliantly colored fishes (as a wrasse, parrot fish, or guppy)

rainbow runner *n* (1940) **:** a large brilliantly colored carangid food and sport fish (*Elagatis bipinnulata*) that is common in warm seas and is blue or dark green above and yellowish white below

rainbow trout *n* (1882) **:** a large stout-bodied salmonid fish (*Oncorhynchus mykiss* syn. *Salmo gairdneri*) of western No. America that is related to the Pacific salmon and is typically greenish above and white on the belly with a pink, red, or lavender stripe along each side of the body and with profuse black dots — compare STEELHEAD

rain check *n* (1884) **1 :** a ticket stub good for a later performance when the scheduled one is rained out **2 :** an assurance of a deferred extension of an offer; *esp* **:** a document assuring that a customer can take advantage of a sale later if the item or service offered is not available (as by being sold out)

rain•coat \ˈrān-ˌkōt\ *n* (1830) **:** a waterproof or water-resistant coat

rain date *n* (1954) **:** an alternative date set aside for use if a scheduled event must be postponed due to rain

rain•drop \-ˌdräp\ *n* (bef. 12c) **:** a drop of rain

rain•fall \-ˌfȯl\ *n* (1854) **1 :** the amount of precipitation usu. measured by the depth in inches **2 :** RAIN 2a

rain forest *n* (1903) **1 :** a tropical woodland with an annual rainfall of at least 100 inches (254 centimeters) and marked by lofty broad-leaved evergreen trees forming a continuous canopy — called also *tropical rain forest* **2 :** TEMPERATE RAIN FOREST

rain gauge *n* (1769) **:** an instrument for measuring the quantity of precipitation

rain•mak•er \ˈrān-ˌmā-kər\ *n* (1775) **1 :** a person who produces or attempts to produce rain by artificial means **2 :** a person (as a partner in a law firm) who brings in new business; *also* **:** a person whose influence can initiate progress or ensure success — **rain•mak•ing** \-ˌmā-ˈkiŋ\ *n*

rain out *vt* (1928) **:** to interrupt or prevent (as a sports event) by rain — **rain•out** \ˈrān-ˌau̇t\ *n*

rain•proof \ˈrān-ˌprüf\ *adj* (1831) **:** impervious to rain

rain shadow *n* (1902) **:** a region of reduced rainfall on the lee side of high mountains

rain•spout \-ˌspau̇t\ *n* (1878) **:** GUTTER 1a; *also* **:** DOWNSPOUT

rain•squall \-ˌskwȯl\ *n* (1838) **:** a squall accompanied by rain

rain•storm \-ˌstȯrm\ *n* (1816) **:** a storm of or with rain

rain tree *n* (ca. 1890) **:** MONKEYPOD

rain•wash \ˈrān-ˌwȯsh, -ˌwäsh\ *n* (1876) **:** the washing away of material by rain; *also* **:** the material so washed away

rain•wa•ter \-ˌwȯ-tər, -ˌwä-\ *n* (bef. 12c) **:** water fallen as rain that has not collected soluble matter from the soil and is therefore soft

rain•wear \-ˌwer\ *n* (1939) **:** waterproof or water-resistant clothing — called also *rain gear*

rainy \ˈrā-nē\ *adj* **rain•i•er; -est** (bef. 12c) **:** marked by, abounding with, or bringing rain ⟨~ weather⟩

rainy day *n* (ca. 1580) **:** a period of want or need ⟨saving for a *rainy day*⟩ — **rainy–day** *adj*

[1]**raise** \ˈrāz\ *vb* **raised; rais•ing** [ME *reisen, raisen,* fr. ON *reisa* — more at REAR] *vt* (13c) **1 :** to cause or help to rise to a standing position **2 a :** AWAKEN, AROUSE **b :** to stir up **:** INCITE ⟨~ a rebellion⟩ **c :** to flush (game) from cover **d :** to recall from or as if from death **3 a :** to set upright by lifting or building ⟨~ a monument⟩ **b :** to lift up ⟨~ your hand⟩ ⟨~ sunken treasure⟩ **c :** to place higher in rank or dignity **:** ELEVATE **d :** HEIGHTEN, INVIGORATE ⟨~ the spirits⟩ **e :** to end or suspend the operation or validity of ⟨~ a siege⟩ **4 :** to get together for a purpose **:** COLLECT ⟨~ funds⟩ **5 a :** GROW, CULTIVATE ⟨~ cotton⟩ **b :** to bring to maturity **:** REAR ⟨~ a child⟩ **c :** to breed and bring (an animal) to maturity **6 a :** to give rise to **:** PROVOKE ⟨~ a commotion⟩ **b :** to give voice to ⟨~ a cheer⟩ **7 :** to bring up for consideration or debate ⟨~ an issue⟩ **8 a :** to increase the strength, intensity, or pitch of ⟨don't ~ your voice⟩ **b :** to increase the degree of **c :** to cause to rise in level or amount ⟨~ the rent⟩ **d** (1) **:** to increase the amount of (a poker bet) (2) **:** to bet more than (a previous bettor) **e** (1) **:** to make a higher bridge bid in (a partner's suit) (2) **:** to increase the bid of (one's partner) **9 :** to make light and porous ⟨~ dough⟩ **10 :** to cause to ascend ⟨~ the dust⟩ **11 :** to multiply (a quantity) by itself a specified number of times ⟨~ two to the fourth power⟩ **12 :** to bring in sight on the horizon by approaching ⟨~ land⟩ **13 a :** to bring up the nap of (cloth) **b :** to cause (as a blister) to form on the skin **14 :** to increase the nominal value of fraudulently ⟨~ a check⟩ **15 :** to articulate (a sound) with the tongue in a higher position **16 :** to establish radio communication with ~ *vi* **1** *dial* **:** RISE **2 :** to increase a bet or bid *syn* see LIFT — **rais•er** *n* — **raise Cain** *or* **raise hell 1 :** to act wildly **:** create a disturbance **2 :** to scold or upbraid someone esp. loudly ⟨*raised hell* with the umpire⟩ — **raise eyebrows :** to cause surprise or mild disapproval — **raise the bar :** to set a higher standard ⟨new software that *raises the bar* for competitors⟩

[2]**raise** *n* (1538) **1 :** an act of raising or lifting **2 :** a rising stretch of road **:** an upward grade **:** RISE **3 :** an increase in amount: as **a :** an increase of a bet or bid **b :** an increase in wages or salary **4 :** a vertical or inclined opening or passageway connecting one mine working area with another at a higher level

raised *adj* (1599) **1 a :** done in relief **b :** having a nap **2 :** leavened with yeast rather than with baking powder or baking soda

raised ranch *n* (1962) **:** BI-LEVEL

rai•sin \ˈrā-zᵊn\ *n* [ME, fr. AF, grape, raisin, fr. L *racemus* cluster of grapes or berries — more at RACEME] (14c) **:** a grape of any of several varieties that has been dried in the sun or by artificial heat

rai•son d'être *also* **rai•son d'etre** \ˌrā-ˌzōⁿ-ˈdetrᵊ\ *n, pl* **rai•sons d'être** *also* **rai•sons d'etre** \-ˌzōⁿz-\ [F] (1864) **:** reason or justification for existence

raj \ˈräj\ *n* [Hindi & Urdu *rāj,* fr. Skt *rājya;* akin to Skt *rājan* king] (1800) **1 :** RULE; *esp, often cap* **:** the former British rule of the Indian subcontinent **2 :** the period of British rule in India

ra•ja *or* **ra•jah** \ˈrä-jə, -(ˌ)jä, -zhə, -(ˌ)zhä\ *n* [Hindi & Urdu *rājā,* fr. Skt *rājan* king — more at ROYAL] (1555) **1 :** an Indian or Malay prince or chief **2 :** the bearer of a title of nobility among the Hindus

Ra•jab \rə-ˈjab\ *n* [Ar] (ca. 1771) **:** the seventh month of the Islamic year — see MONTH table

Ra•jas•tha•ni \ˌrä-jə-ˈstä-nē, ˌrä-zhə-\ *n* [Hindi & Urdu *Rājasthānī,* fr. *Rājasthān* Rajasthan] (1901) **:** the Indo-Aryan dialects of Rajasthan

Raj•put *or* **Raj•poot** \ˈräj-ˌpu̇t, ˈräzh-\ *n* [Hindi & Urdu *rājpūt,* fr. Skt *rājaputra* king's son, fr. *rājan* king + *putra* son — more at FEW] (1598) **:** a member of a dominant military caste of northern India

[1]**rake** \ˈrāk\ *n* [ME, fr. OE *racu;* akin to OHG *rehho* rake] (bef. 12c) **1 a :** an implement equipped with projecting prongs to gather material (as leaves) or for loosening or smoothing the surface of the ground **b :** a machine for gathering hay **2 :** an implement like a rake

[2]**rake** *vt* **raked; rak•ing** (13c) **1 :** to gather, loosen, or smooth with or as if with a rake ⟨~ leaves into a pile⟩ **2 :** to gain rapidly or in abundance — usu. used with *in* ⟨~ in a fortune⟩ **3 a :** to touch in passing over lightly **b :** SCRATCH, SCRAPE **4 :** to censure severely **5 :** to search through **:** RANSACK **6 :** to sweep the length of esp. with gunfire **:** ENFILADE **7 :** to glance over rapidly — **rak•er** *n*

[3]**rake** *n* [origin unknown] (1626) **1 :** inclination from the perpendicular; *esp* **:** the overhang of a ship's bow or stern **2 :** inclination from the horizontal **:** SLOPE **3 :** the angle between the top cutting surface of a tool and a plane perpendicular to the surface of the work

[4]**rake** *vi* **raked; rak•ing** (1691) **:** to incline from the perpendicular

[5]**rake** *n* [short for *rakehell*] (1653) **:** a dissolute person **:** LIBERTINE

rake•hell \ˈrāk-ˌhel\ *n* (1554) **:** LIBERTINE 2 — **rakehell** *or* **rake•helly** \-ˌhe-lē\ *adj*

rake–off \ˈrāk-ˌȯf\ *n* [*rake off,* v.; fr. the use of a rake by a croupier to collect the operator's profits in a gambling casino] (1888) **:** a percentage or cut taken (as by an operator)

rake up *vt* (1581) **:** to make known or public **:** UNCOVER ⟨*rake up* a scandal⟩

ra•ki \rə-ˈkē; ˈra-kē, ˈrä-\ *n* [Turk, fr. Ar *'araqī,* lit., of liquor, fr. *'araq* liquor, arrack] (1675) **:** a Turkish liqueur flavored with aniseed

[1]**rak•ish** \ˈrā-kish\ *adj* [[5]*rake*] (1706) **:** of, relating to, or characteristic of a rake **:** DISSOLUTE

[2]**rakish** *adj* [prob. fr. [4]*rake;* fr. the raking masts of pirate ships] (1824) **1 :** having a trim or streamlined appearance suggestive of speed ⟨a ~ ship⟩ **2 :** dashingly or carelessly unconventional **:** JAUNTY ⟨~ clothes⟩

rak•ish•ly *adv* (1838) **:** in a rakish manner

rak•ish•ness *n* (ca. 1828) **:** the quality or state of being rakish

ra•ku \ˈrä-(ˌ)kü\ *n, often attrib* [Jp, lit., pleasure; fr. the use of the character for this word on a seal given to the family of the potter who introduced the style] (1875) **1 :** Japanese hand-modeled pottery that is fired at a low temperature and rapidly cooled **2 :** a process by which pottery is fired at a relatively low temperature and then moved while hot to a closed container with combustible materials (as paper or sawdust) that ignite and cause a reaction creating colors and patterns in the pottery's surface; *also* **:** pottery produced using this process

rale \ˈral, ˈräl\ *n* [F *râle,* fr. *râler* to make a rattling sound in the throat] (1828) **:** an abnormal sound heard accompanying the normal respiratory sounds on auscultation of the chest

ral•len•tan•do \ˌrä-lən-ˈtän-(ˌ)dō\ *adv or adj* [It, lit., slowing down, verbal of *rallentare* to slow down again, fr. *re-* + *allentare* to slow down, fr. LL, fr. L *al-* ad- + *lentus* slow, pliant — more at LITHE] (1800) **:** RITARDANDO

[1]**ral•ly** \ˈra-lē\ *vb* **ral•lied; ral•ly•ing** [F *rallier,* fr. OF *ralier,* fr. *re-* + *alier* to unite — more at ALLY] *vt* (1603) **1 a :** to muster for a common purpose **b :** to recall to order **2 a :** to arouse for action **b :** to rouse from depression or weakness ~ *vi* **1 :** to come together again to renew an effort **2 :** to join in a common cause **3 :** RECOVER, REBOUND ⟨*rallied* briefly from his illness⟩ **4 :** to engage in a rally

[2]**rally** *n, pl* **rallies** (1651) **1 a :** a mustering of scattered forces to renew an effort **b :** a summoning up of strength or courage after weakness or dejection **c :** a recovery of price after a decline **d :** a renewed offensive **2 :** a mass meeting intended to arouse group enthusiasm **3 :** a series of shots interchanged between players (as in tennis) before a point is won **4** *also* **ral•lye** [F *rallye,* fr. E [1]*rally*] **:** an automobile competition using public roads and ordinary traffic rules with the object of maintaining a specified average speed between checkpoints over a route unknown to the participants until the start of the event

[3]**rally** *vt* **ral•lied; ral•ly•ing** [F *railler* to mock, rally — more at RAIL] (1668) **:** to attack with raillery **:** BANTER

rallying *n* (1957) **:** the sport of driving in automobile rallies

rallying cry *n* (1798) **:** WAR CRY

ral•ox•i•fene \ra-ˈläk-sə-ˌfēn\ *n* [*ral-* (of unknown origin) + *-oxifene,* alter. of *-oxifen* (as in *tamoxifen*)] (1993) **:** a drug used orally in the form of its hydrochloride $C_{28}H_{27}NO_4S{\cdot}HCl$ as prophylaxis against osteoporosis after menopause

[1]**ram** \ˈram\ *n* [ME, fr. OE *ramm;* akin to OHG *ram*] (bef. 12c) **1 a :** a male sheep **b** *cap* **:** ARIES **2 a :** BATTERING RAM **b :** a warship with a heavy beak at the prow for piercing an enemy ship **3 :** any of various guided pieces for exerting pressure or for driving or forcing something by impact: as **a :** the plunger of a hydrostatic press or force pump **b :** the weight that strikes the blow in a pile driver

[2]**ram** *vb* **rammed; ram•ming** [ME *rammen,* prob. fr. *ram,* n.] *vi* (14c) **1 :** to strike with violence **:** CRASH **2 :** to move with extreme rapidity ~ *vt* **1 :** to force in by or as if by driving **2 a :** to make compact (as by pounding) **b :** CRAM, CROWD **3 :** to force passage or acceptance of ⟨~ home an idea⟩ **4 :** to strike against violently — **ram•mer** *n*

RAM \ˈram\ *n* [*r*andom-*a*ccess *m*emory] (1957) **:** a computer memory on which data can be both read and written and on which the location of data does not affect the speed of its retrieval; *esp* **:** RAM that acts as the main storage available to the user for programs and data — called also *random-access memory;* compare ROM

Ra•ma \ˈrä-mə\ *n* [Skt *Rāma*] (1819) **:** a deity or deified hero of later Hinduism worshipped as an avatar of Vishnu

ra•ma•da \rə-ˈmä-də\ *n* [AmerSp, fr. Sp, arbor, fr. *rama* branch, alter. of *ramo,* fr. L *ramus* — more at RAMIFY] (1853) *Southwest* **:** a roofed shelter with usu. open sides

Ram•a•dan \ˈrä-mə-ˌdän, ˌrä-mə-ˈ\ *n* [Ar *Ramaḍān*] (ca. 1595) **:** the ninth month of the Islamic year observed as sacred with fasting practiced daily from dawn to sunset — see MONTH table

ra•mate \ˈrā-ˌmāt\ *adj* [L *ramus* branch — more at RAMIFY] (1897) **:** RAMOSE

^{1}**ram•ble** \ˈram-bəl\ *vb* **ram•bled; ram•bling** \-b(ə-)liŋ\ [ME, prob. alter. of *romblen,* freq. of *romen* to roam] *vi* (15c) **1 a :** to move aimlessly from place to place **b :** to explore idly **2 :** to talk or write in a desultory or long-winded wandering fashion **3 :** to grow or extend irregularly ~ *vt* **:** to wander over **:** ROAM ***syn*** see WANDER — **ram•bling•ly** \-b(ə-)liŋ-lē\ *adv*

^{2}**ramble** *n* (1654) **1 :** a leisurely excursion for pleasure; *esp* **:** an aimless walk **2 :** a rambling story or discussion

ram•bler \ˈram-blər\ *n* (1624) **1 :** one that rambles **2 :** any of various climbing roses with long flexible canes and rather small often double flowers in large clusters **3 :** RANCH HOUSE

ram•bouil•let \ˌram-bə-ˈlā, -bü-ˈyā\ *n, often cap* [*Rambouillet,* France] (1847) **:** any of a breed of large sturdy sheep developed in France

ram•bunc•tious \ram-ˈbəŋk-shəs\ *adj* [prob. alter. of *rumbustious*] (1830) **:** marked by uncontrollable exuberance **:** UNRULY — **ram•bunc•tious•ly** *adv* — **ram•bunc•tious•ness** *n*

ram•bu•tan \ram-ˈbü-tᵊn\ *n* [Malay] (1707) **:** a bright red spiny Malayan fruit closely related to the lychee; *also* **:** a tree (*Nephelium lappaceum*) of the soapberry family that bears this fruit

ram•e•kin *also* **ram•e•quin** \ˈram-kən, ˈra-mi-\ *n* [F *ramequin,* fr. LG *ramken,* dim. of *ram* cream] (ca. 1706) **1 :** a preparation of cheese esp. with bread crumbs or eggs baked in a mold or shell **2 :** an individual baking dish

ra•men \ˈrä-mən\ *n* [Jp *rāmen*] (1972) **:** quick-cooking egg noodles usu. served in a broth with bits of meat and vegetables

ra•met \ˈrā-ˌmet\ *n* [L *ramus* branch] (1929) **:** an independent member of a clone

ra•mie \ˈrā-mē, ˈra-\ *n* [Malay *rami*] (1832) **1 :** an Asian perennial plant (*Boehmeria nivea*) of the nettle family **2 a :** the strong lustrous bast fiber of ramie capable of being spun or woven **b :** fabric made of ramie often resembling linen or silk

ram•i•fi•ca•tion \ˌra-mə-fə-ˈkā-shən\ *n* (1665) **1 a :** BRANCH, OFFSHOOT **b :** a branched structure **2 a :** the act or process of branching **b :** arrangement of branches (as on a plant) **3 :** CONSEQUENCE, OUTGROWTH ⟨the ~*s* of the decision⟩

ram•i•fy \ˈra-mə-ˌfī\ *vb* **-fied; -fy•ing** [ME *ramifien,* fr. AF *ramifier,* fr. ML *ramificare,* fr. L *ramus* branch; akin to L *radix* root — more at ROOT] *vi* (15c) **1 :** to split up into branches or constituent parts **2 :** to send forth branches or extensions ~ *vt* **1 :** to cause to branch **2 :** to separate into divisions

Ra•mism \ˈrā-ˌmi-zəm\ *n* [Petrus *Ramus* †1572 Fr. philosopher] (1710) **:** the doctrines of Ramus based on opposition to Aristotelianism and advocacy of a new logic blended with rhetoric — **Ra•mist** \-mist\ *n or adj*

ram•jet \ˈram-ˌjet\ *n* (1942) **:** a jet engine that consists essentially of a hollow tube without mechanical components and depends on the aircraft's speed of flight to compress the air which is supplied to a burner from which hot gases are discharged rearward

ra•mose \ˈrā-ˌmōs\ *adj* [L *ramosus,* fr. *ramus* branch] (1689) **:** consisting of or having branches ⟨a ~ sponge⟩

^{1}**ramp** \ˈramp\ *vb* [ME, fr. AF *ramper* to crawl, climb, rear, of Gmc origin; akin to OHG *rimpfan* to bend, wrinkle — more at RUMPLE] *vi* (14c) **1 a :** to stand or advance menacingly with forelegs or with arms raised **b :** to move or act furiously **2 :** to creep up — used esp. of plants **3 :** to speed up, expand, or increase esp. quickly or at a constant rate — used with *up* ⟨~*ing* up to full speed⟩ ~ *vt* [^{4}*ramp* (electrical waveform)] **:** to increase, expand, or decrease esp. quickly or at a constant rate — usu. used with *up* or *down* ⟨~ up production⟩

^{2}**ramp** *n* (1671) **:** the act or an instance of ramping

^{3}**ramp** *n* [back-formation fr. *ramps,* alter. of *rams,* fr. ME, fr. OE *hramsa;* akin to OHG *ramusia* ramp, Gk *krommyon* onion] (1826) **:** any of various alliums used for food

^{4}**ramp** *n* [F *rampe,* fr. *ramper,* fr. MF] (1779) **1 :** a sloping way or plane: as **a :** a sloping floor, walk, or roadway leading from one level to another **b :** a slope for launching boats **2 :** APRON 2h

^{1}**ram•page** \ˈram-ˌpāj, (ˌ)ram-ˈ\ *vi* **ram•paged; ram•pag•ing** [Sc] (1808) **:** to rush wildly about

^{2}**ram•page** \ˈram-ˌpāj\ *n* (1861) **:** a course of violent, riotous, or reckless action or behavior — **ram•pa•geous** \ram-ˈpā-jəs\ *adj* — **ram•pa•geous•ly** *adv* — **ram•pa•geous•ness** *n*

ram•pan•cy \ˈram-pən(t)-sē\ *n* (1664) **:** the quality or state of being rampant

ram•pant \ˈram-pənt *also* -ˌpant\ *adj* [ME, fr. AF, prp. of *ramper*] (14c) **1 a :** rearing upon the hind legs with forelegs extended **b :** standing on one hind foot with one foreleg raised above the other and the head in profile — used of a heraldic animal **2 a :** marked by a menacing wildness, extravagance, or absence of restraint ⟨~ rumors⟩ **b :** profusely widespread ⟨~ weeds⟩ — **ram•pant•ly** *adv*

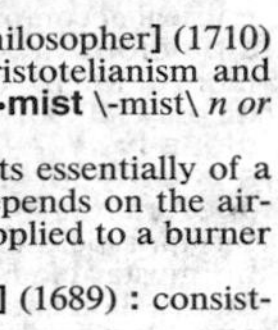

rampant 1b: a lion rampant

ram•part \ˈram-ˌpärt, -pərt\ *n* [MF, fr. *ramparer* to fortify, fr. *re-* + *emparer* to defend, fr. Old Occitan *emparar,* fr. VL **imparare,* fr. L *in-* ^{2}in- + *parare* to prepare — more at PARE] (1536) **1 :** a protective barrier **:** BULWARK **2 :** a broad embankment raised as a fortification and usu. surmounted by a parapet **3 :** a wall-like ridge (as of rock fragments, earth, or debris)

ram•pike \-ˌpīk\ *n* [origin unknown] (1853) **:** an erect broken or dead tree

ramp–up \ˈramp-ˌəp\ *n* (1980) **:** BUILDUP, INCREASE

^{1}**ram•rod** \ˈram-ˌräd\ *n* (1757) **1 :** a rod for ramming home the charge in a muzzle-loading firearm **2 :** a cleaning rod for small arms **3 :** BOSS, OVERSEER

^{2}**ramrod** *adj* (1850) **:** marked by rigidity, severity, or stiffness

^{3}**ramrod** *vt* (ca. 1940) **:** to direct, supervise, and control

^{4}**ramrod** *adv* (1954) **:** in a fully upright position **:** RIGIDLY ⟨sat ~ straight⟩

ram•shack•le \ˈram-ˌsha-kəl\ *adj* [alter. of earlier *ransackled,* fr. pp. of obs. *ransackle,* freq. of *ransack*] (1830) **1 :** appearing ready to collapse **:** RICKETY **2 :** carelessly or loosely constructed ⟨a ~ plot⟩

rams•horn \ˈramz-ˌhȯrn\ *n* (1901) **:** any of various snails (as genera *Planorbis, Helisoma,* and *Planorbarius*) often used as aquarium scavengers

ra•mus \ˈrā-məs\ *n, pl* **ra•mi** \-ˌmī\ [NL, fr. L, branch — more at RAMIFY] (1733) **:** a projecting part, elongated process, or branch: as **a :** the posterior more or less vertical part on each side of the lower jaw that articulates with the skull **b :** a branch of a nerve

ran *past of* RUN

^{1}**ranch** \ˈranch\ *n* [MexSp *rancho* small ranch, fr. Sp, camp, hut & Sp dial., small farm, fr. OSp *ranchearse* to take up quarters, fr. MF *se ranger* to take up a position, fr. *ranger* to set in a row — more at RANGE] (1831) **1 :** a large farm for raising horses, beef cattle, or sheep **2 :** a farm or area devoted to a particular specialty **3 :** RANCH HOUSE

^{2}**ranch** *vi* (1866) **:** to live or work on a ranch ~ *vt* **1 :** to work as a rancher on **2 :** to raise on a ranch

ranch dressing *n* (1981) **:** a creamy salad dressing usu. containing milk or buttermilk and mayonnaise

ranch•er \ˈran-chər\ *n* (1836) **:** one who owns or works on a ranch

ran•che•ro \ran-ˈcher-(ˌ)ō, rän-\ *n, pl* **-ros** [MexSp, fr. *rancho*] (1826) **:** RANCHER; *also* **:** RANCH 1

ranch house *n* (1862) **1 :** the main dwelling house on a ranch **2 :** a one-story house typically with a low-pitched roof and an open plan

ranch•man \ˈranch-mən\ *n* (1856) **:** RANCHER

ran•cho \ˈran-(ˌ)chō, ˈrän-\ *n, pl* **ranchos** [MexSp, small ranch] (1840) **:** RANCH 1

ran•cid \ˈran(t)-səd\ *adj* [L *rancidus,* fr. *rancēre* to be rancid] (1646) **1 :** having a rank smell or taste **2 :** OFFENSIVE — **ran•cid•i•ty** \ran-ˈsi-də-tē\ *n* — **ran•cid•ness** \ˈran(t)-səd-nəs\ *n*

ran•cor \ˈraŋ-kər, -ˌkȯr\ *n* [ME *rancour,* fr. AF *rancur,* fr. LL *rancor* rancidity, rancor, fr. L *rancēre*] (14c) **:** bitter deep-seated ill will ***syn*** see ENMITY

ran•cor•ous \ˈraŋ-k(ə-)rəs\ *adj* (ca. 1570) **:** marked by rancor **:** deeply malevolent ⟨~ envy⟩ — **ran•cor•ous•ly** *adv*

ran•cour *Brit var of* RANCOR

rand \ˈrand, ˈränd, ˈränt\ *n, pl* **rand** [the *Rand,* So. Africa] (1961) **1 —** see MONEY table **2 :** a former monetary unit of Botswana, Lesotho, and Swaziland

R & B *abbr* rhythm and blues

R & D *abbr* research and development

^{1}**ran•dom** \ˈran-dəm\ *n* [ME, succession, surge, fr. AF *randun,* fr. OF *randir* to run, of Gmc origin; akin to OHG *rinnan* to run — more at RUN] (1561) **:** a haphazard course — **at random :** without definite aim, direction, rule, or method ⟨subjects chosen *at random*⟩

^{2}**random** *adj* (1632) **1 a :** lacking a definite plan, purpose, or pattern **b :** made, done, or chosen at random ⟨read ~ passages from the book⟩ **2 a :** relating to, having, or being elements or events with definite probability of occurrence ⟨~ processes⟩ **b :** being or relating to a set or to an element of a set each of whose elements has equal probability of occurrence ⟨a ~ sample⟩; *also* **:** characterized by procedures designed to obtain such sets or elements ⟨~ sampling⟩ — **ran•dom•ly** *adv* — **ran•dom•ness** *n*

syn RANDOM, HAPHAZARD, CASUAL mean determined by accident rather than design. RANDOM stresses lack of definite aim, fixed goal, or regular procedure ⟨a *random* selection of books⟩. HAPHAZARD applies to what is done without regard for regularity or fitness or ultimate consequence ⟨a *haphazard* collection of rocks⟩. CASUAL suggests working or acting without deliberation, intention, or purpose ⟨a *casual* collector⟩.

^{3}**random** *adv* (1618) **:** in a random manner

random–access *adj* (1953) **:** permitting access to stored data in any order the user desires

random–access memory *n* (1955) **:** RAM

ran•dom•ize \ˈran-də-ˌmīz\ *vt* **-ized; -iz•ing** (1926) **:** to select, assign, or arrange in a random way — **ran•dom•i•za•tion** \ˌran-də-mə-ˈzā-shən\ *n* — **ran•dom•iz•er** *n*

randomized block *n* (1926) **:** an experimental design (as in horticulture) in which different treatments are distributed in random order in a block or plot — called also *randomized block design*

random variable *n* (1937) **:** a variable that is itself a function of the result of a statistical experiment in which each outcome has a definite probability of occurrence — called also *variate*

random walk *n* (1905) **:** a process (as Brownian motion or genetic drift) consisting of a sequence of steps (as movements or changes in gene frequency) each of whose characteristics (as magnitude and direction) is determined by chance

R & R *abbr* rest and recreation; rest and recuperation; rest and relaxation

^{1}**randy** \ˈran-dē\ *adj* [prob. fr. obs. *rand* to rant] (1698) **1** *chiefly Scot* **:** having a coarse manner **2 :** LUSTFUL, LECHEROUS — **randi•ness** *n*

^{2}**randy** *n, pl* **rand•ies** (1762) *chiefly Scot* **:** a scolding or dissolute woman

rang *past of* RING

^{1}**range** \ˈrānj\ *n, often attrib* [ME, row of persons, fr. AF *range, renge,* fr. *renger* to range] (14c) **1 a** (1) **:** a series of things in a line **:** ROW (2) **:** a series of mountains (3) **:** one of the north-south rows of townships in a U.S. public-land survey that are numbered east and west from the principal meridian of the survey **b :** an aggregate of individuals in one order **c :** a direction line **2 :** a cooking stove that has an oven and a flat top with burners or heating elements **3 a :** a place that may be ranged over **b :** an open region over which animals (as livestock) may roam and feed **c :** the region throughout which a kind of organism or ecological community naturally lives or occurs **4 :** the act of ranging about **5 a** (1) **:** the horizontal distance to which a projectile can be propelled (2) **:** the horizontal distance between a weapon and target **b :** the maximum distance a vehicle or craft can travel without refuel-

\ə\ **abut** \ᵊ\ kitten, F table \ər\ **fur**ther \a\ **a**sh \ā\ **a**ce \ä\ m**o**p, m**a**r \au̇\ **ou**t \ch\ **ch**in \e\ b**e**t \ē\ **ea**sy \g\ **g**o \i\ h**i**t \ī\ **i**ce \j\ **j**ob \ŋ\ si**ng** \ō\ g**o** \ȯ\ l**aw** \ȯi\ b**oy** \th\ **th**in \t͟h\ **th**e \ü\ l**oo**t \u̇\ f**oo**t \y\ **y**et \zh\ vi**s**ion, bei**ge** \k, ⁿ, œ, ue, ʸ\ *see* Guide to Pronunciation

ing **c** (1) : a place where shooting is practiced (2) : DRIVING RANGE **6 a** : the space or extent included, covered, or used : SCOPE **b** : the extent of pitch covered by a melody or lying within the capacity of a voice or instrument **7 a** : a sequence, series, or scale between limits ⟨a wide ~ of patterns⟩ **b** : the limits of a series : the distance or extent between possible extremes **c** : the difference between the least and greatest values of an attribute or of the variable of a frequency distribution **8 a** : the set of values a function may take on **b** : the class of admissible values of a variable **9** : LINE 11

syn RANGE, GAMUT, COMPASS, SWEEP, SCOPE, ORBIT mean the extent that lies within the powers of something (as to cover or control). RANGE is a general term indicating the extent of one's perception or the extent of powers, capacities, or possibilities ⟨the entire *range* of human experience⟩. GAMUT suggests a graduated series running from one possible extreme to another ⟨a performance that ran the *gamut* of emotions⟩. COMPASS implies a sometimes limited extent of perception, knowledge, or activity ⟨your concerns lie beyond the narrow *compass* of this study⟩. SWEEP suggests extent, often circular or arc-shaped, of motion or activity ⟨the book covers the entire *sweep* of criminal activity⟩. SCOPE is applicable to an area of activity, predetermined and limited, but somewhat flexible ⟨as time went on, the *scope* of the investigation widened⟩. ORBIT suggests an often circumscribed range of activity or influence within which forces work toward accommodation ⟨within that restricted *orbit* they tried to effect social change⟩.

[2]**range** *vb* **ranged; rang•ing** [ME, fr. AF *renger*, fr. *renc, reng* line, place, row — more at RANK] *vt* (14c) **1 a** : to set in a row or in the proper order **b** : to place among others in a position or situation **c** : to assign to a category : CLASSIFY **2 a** : to rove over or through **b** : to sail or pass along **3** : to arrange (an anchor cable) on deck **4** : to graze (livestock) on a range ~ *vi* **1 a** : to roam at large or freely **b** : to move over an area so as to explore it **2** : to take a position **3 a** : to correspond in direction or line : ALIGN **b** : to extend in a particular direction **4** : to have range **5** : to change or differ within limits **6** *of an organism* : to live or occur in or be native to a region

range finder *n* (1872) **1** : an instrument used in gunnery to determine the distance of a target **2** : a surveying instrument (as a transit) for determining quickly the distances, bearings, and elevations of distant objects **3** : a usu. built-in adjustable optical device for focusing a camera that automatically indicates the correct focus (as when two parts of a split image are brought together)

range•land \ˈrānj-ˌland\ *n* (1931) : land used or suitable for range

rang•er \ˈrān-jər\ *n* (14c) **1 a** : the keeper of a British royal park or forest **b** : FOREST RANGER **2** : one that ranges **3 a** : one of a body of organized armed men who range over a region esp. to enforce the law **b** : a soldier specially trained in close-range fighting and in raiding tactics

rangy \ˈrān-jē\ *adj* **rang•i•er; -est** (1868) **1** : able to range for considerable distances **2 a** : long-limbed and long-bodied ⟨~ cattle⟩ **b** : tall and slender **3** : having room for ranging **4** : having great scope — **rang•i•ness** *n*

ra•ni *or* **ra•nee** \rä-ˈnē, ˈrä-ˌnē\ *n* [Hindi & Urdu *rānī*, fr. Skt *rājñī*, fem. of *rājan* king — more at ROYAL] (1673) : a Hindu queen : a rajah's wife

ra•nid \ˈra-nəd, ˈrā-\ *n* [ultim. fr. L *rana* frog] (1888) : any of a large family (Ranidae) of long-legged frogs distinguished by extensively webbed hind feet, horizontal pupils, and a bony sternum

ra•nit•i•dine \ra-ˈni-tə-ˌdēn\ *n* [prob. fr. *ranit-* (blend of *furan* and *nitr-*) + *-idine* (as in *cimetidine*)] (1979) : a histamine blocker $C_{13}H_{22}N_4O_3S$ that is administered in the form of its hydrochloride to inhibit gastric acid secretion

[1]**rank** \ˈraŋk\ *adj* [ME, fr. OE *ranc* overbearing, strong; akin to ON *rakkr* erect and perh. to OE *riht* right — more at RIGHT] (13c) **1** : luxuriantly or excessively vigorous in growth **2** : offensively gross or coarse : FOUL **3** *obs* : grown too large **4 a** : shockingly conspicuous ⟨must lecture him on his ~ disloyalty —David Walden⟩ **b** : OUTRIGHT — used as an intensive ⟨~ beginners⟩ **5** *archaic* : LUSTFUL, RUTTISH **6** : offensive in odor or flavor; *esp* : RANCID **7** : PUTRID, FESTERING **8** : high in amount or degree : FRAUGHT ***syn*** see MALODOROUS, FLAGRANT — **rank•ly** *adv* — **rank•ness** *n*

[2]**rank** *n* [ME, fr. AF *renc, reng*, of Gmc origin; akin to OHG *hring* ring — more at RING] (14c) **1 a** : ROW, SERIES **b** : a row of people **c** (1) : a line of soldiers ranged side by side in close order (2) *pl* : ARMED FORCES (3) *pl* : the body of enlisted personnel **d** : any of the rows of squares that extend across a chessboard perpendicular to the files **e** *Brit* : STAND 6 **2 a** : relative standing or position **b** : a degree or position of dignity, eminence, or excellence : DISTINCTION ⟨soon took ~ as a leading attorney —J. D. Hicks⟩ **c** : high social position ⟨the privileges of ~⟩ **d** : a grade of official standing in a hierarchy **3** : an orderly arrangement : FORMATION **4** : an aggregate of individuals classed together — usu. used in pl. **5** : the order according to some statistical characteristic (as the score on a test) **6** : any of a series of classes of coal based on increasing alteration of the parent vegetable matter, increasing carbon content, and increasing fuel value **7** : the number of linearly independent rows or columns in a matrix

[3]**rank** *vt* (1573) **1** : to arrange in lines or in a regular formation **2** : to determine the relative position of : RATE ⟨a highly ~*ed* prospect⟩ **3** : to take precedence of ~ *vi* **1** : to form or move in ranks **2** : to take or have a position in relation to others ⟨~*s* first in her class⟩

rank and file *n* (1598) **1** : the enlisted personnel of an armed force **2** : the individuals who constitute the body of an organization, society, or nation as distinguished from the leaders — **rank–and–file** \ˌraŋk-ᵊn-ˈfī(-ə)l\ *adj* — **rank and fil•er** \-ˈfī-lər\ *n*

rank correlation *n* (1907) : a measure of correlation depending on rank

rank•er \ˈraŋ-kər\ *n* (1878) : one who serves or has served in the ranks; *esp* : a commissioned officer promoted from the ranks

Ran•kine \ˈraŋ-kən\ *adj* [William J. M. *Rankine* †1872 Scot. engineer & physicist] (ca. 1926) : being, according to, or relating to an absolute temperature scale on which the unit of measurement equals a Fahrenheit degree and on which the freezing point of water is 491.67° and the boiling point 671.67°

rank•ing \ˈraŋ-kiŋ\ *adj* (1847) : having a high position: as **a** : of the highest rank ⟨the ~ officer⟩ **b** : being next to the chairman in seniority ⟨~ committee member⟩

ran•kle \ˈraŋ-kəl\ *vb* **ran•kled; ran•kling** \-k(ə-)liŋ\ [ME *ranclen* to fester, fr. AF *rancler*, fr. OF *draoncler, rancler*, fr. *draoncle, raoncle* festering sore, fr. ML *dracunculus*, fr. L, dim. of *draco* serpent — more at DRAGON] *vi* (1606) **1** : to cause anger, irritation, or deep bitterness **2** : to feel anger and irritation ~ *vt* : to cause irritation or bitterness in

ran•sack \ˈran-ˌsak, (ˌ)ran-ˈ\ *vt* [ME *ransaken*, fr. ON *rannsaka*, fr. *rann* house + *-saka* (akin to OE *sēcan* to seek) — more at SEEK] (13c) **1 a** : to search thoroughly **b** : to examine closely and carefully **2** : to search through to commit robbery : PLUNDER — **ran•sack•er** *n*

[1]**ran•som** \ˈran(t)-səm\ *n* [ME *ransoun*, fr. AF *rançun*, fr. L *redemption-, redemptio* — more at REDEMPTION] (13c) **1** : a consideration paid or demanded for the release of someone or something from captivity **2** : the act of ransoming

[2]**ransom** *vt* (14c) **1** : to deliver esp. from sin or its penalty **2** : to free from captivity or punishment by paying a price ***syn*** see RESCUE — **ran•som•er** *n*

[1]**rant** \ˈrant\ *vb* [obs. D *ranten, randen*] *vi* (1601) **1** : to talk in a noisy, excited, or declamatory manner **2** : to scold vehemently ~ *vt* : to utter in a bombastic declamatory fashion — **rant•er** *n* — **rant•ing•ly** \ˈran-tiŋ-lē\ *adv*

[2]**rant** *n* (1649) **1 a** : a bombastic extravagant speech **b** : bombastic extravagant language **2** *dial Brit* : a rousing good time

ran•u•la \ˈran-yə-lə\ *n* [NL, fr. L, swelling on the tongue of cattle, fr. dim. of *rana* frog] (15c) : a cyst formed under the tongue by obstruction of a gland duct

ra•nun•cu•lus \rə-ˈnəŋ-kyə-ləs\ *n, pl* **ranunculus** *or* **ra•nun•cu•lus•es** *or* **ra•nun•cu•li** \-ˌlī, -ˌlē\ [NL, fr. L, fr. dim. of *rana* frog] (1543) : BUTTERCUP

[1]**rap** \ˈrap\ *n* [ME *rappe*] (14c) **1** : a sharp blow or knock **2 a** : a sharp rebuke or criticism **b** : a negative and often undeserved reputation or charge — often used with *bum* or *bad* ⟨given a bum ~ by the press⟩ **3 a** : the responsibility for or adverse consequences of an action ⟨refused to take the ~⟩ **b** : a criminal charge **c** : a prison sentence

[2]**rap** *vb* **rapped; rap•ping** *vt* (14c) **1** : to strike with a sharp blow **2** : to utter suddenly and forcibly **3** : to cause to be or come by raps ⟨~ the meeting to order⟩ **4** : to criticize sharply ~ *vi* **1** : to strike a quick sharp blow **2** : to make a short sharp sound

[3]**rap** *vt* **rapped** *also* **rapt** \ˈrapt\; **rap•ping** [back-formation fr. *rapt*] (1599) **1** : to snatch away or upward **2** : ENRAPTURE

[4]**rap** *n* [perh. fr. [1]*rap*] (1834) : a minimum amount or degree (as of care or consideration) : the least bit ⟨doesn't care a ~⟩

[5]**rap** *vi* **rapped; rap•ping** [perh. fr. [1]*rap*] (1929) **1** : to talk freely and frankly **2** : to perform rap music

[6]**rap** *n* (1967) **1** : TALK, CONVERSATION; *also* : a line of talk : PATTER **2 a** : a rhythmic chanting often in unison of usu. rhymed couplets to a musical accompaniment **b** : a piece so performed

ra•pa•cious \rə-ˈpā-shəs\ *adj* [L *rapac-, rapax*, fr. *rapere* to seize — more at RAPID] (1651) **1** : excessively grasping or covetous **2** : living on prey **3** : RAVENOUS ⟨a ~ appetite⟩ ***syn*** see VORACIOUS — **ra•pa•cious•ly** *adv* — **ra•pa•cious•ness** *n*

ra•pac•i•ty \rə-ˈpa-sə-tē\ *n* (1543) : the quality of being rapacious

[1]**rape** \ˈrāp\ *n* [ME, fr. L *rapa, rapum* turnip, rape; akin to OHG *rāba* turnip, rape, Lith *ropė*] (14c) : an Old World herb (*Brassica napus*) of the mustard family grown as a forage crop and for its seeds which yield rapeseed oil and are a bird food — compare CANOLA

[2]**rape** *vt* **raped; rap•ing** [ME, fr. L *rapere*] (14c) **1 a** *archaic* : to seize and take away by force **b** : DESPOIL **2** : to commit rape on — **rap•er** *n* — **rap•ist** \ˈrā-pist\ *n*

[3]**rape** *n* (14c) **1** : an act or instance of robbing or despoiling or carrying away a person by force **2** : unlawful sexual activity and usu. sexual intercourse carried out forcibly or under threat of injury against the will usu. of a female or with a person who is beneath a certain age or incapable of valid consent — compare SEXUAL ASSAULT, STATUTORY RAPE **3** : an outrageous violation

[4]**rape** *n* [F *râpe* grape stalk] (1657) : grape pomace

rape•seed \ˈrāp-ˌsēd\ *n* (15c) : the seed of the rape plant; *also* : [1]RAPE

rapeseed oil *n* (1816) : a nondrying or semidrying oil obtained from rapeseed and turnip seed and used chiefly as a lubricant, illuminant, and food — called also *rape oil*; compare CANOLA OIL

Ra•pha•el \ˈra-fē-əl, ˈrā-, -ˌel\ *n* [LL, fr. Gk *Rhaphaēl*, fr. Heb *Rĕphā'ēl*] (14c) : one of the four archangels named in Hebrew tradition

ra•phe \ˈrā-(ˌ)fē\ *n* [NL, fr. Gk *rhaphē* seam, fr. *rhaptein* to sew] (ca. 1753) **1** : the seamlike union of the two lateral halves of a part or organ (as the tongue) having externally a ridge or furrow **2 a** : the part of the stalk of an anatropous ovary that is united in growth to the outside covering and forms a ridge along the body of the ovule **b** : the median line or slit of the valve of certain diatoms

ra•phia \ˈrā-fē-ə, ˈra-\ *n* [NL, genus of palms, fr. Malagasy *rafia* raffia] (ca. 1866) : RAFFIA

raph•ide \ˈra-ˌfīd\ *n, pl* **raph•ides** \ˈra-ˌfīdz, ˈra-fə-ˌdēz\ [F & NL; F *raphide*, fr. NL *raphides*, pl., fr. Gk *rhaphides*, pl. of *rhaphid-, rhaphis* needle, fr. *rhaptein*] (ca. 1842) : any of the needle-shaped crystals usu. of calcium oxalate that develop as metabolic by-products in plant cells

[1]**rap•id** \ˈra-pəd\ *adj* [L *rapidus* seizing, sweeping, rapid, fr. *rapere* to seize, sweep away; akin to Lith *aprėpti* to embrace] (1634) : marked by a fast rate of motion, activity, succession, or occurrence ***syn*** see FAST — **rap•id•ly** *adv* — **rap•id•ness** *n*

[2]**rapid** *n* (1765) : a part of a river where the current is fast and the surface is usu. broken by obstructions — usu. used in pl. but sing. or pl. in constr.

rapid eye movement *n* (1916) : a rapid conjugate movement of the eyes associated esp. with REM sleep

rapid eye movement sleep *n* (1965) : REM SLEEP

rap•id–fire \ˌra-pəd-ˈfī(-ə)r\ *adj* (1890) **1** : firing or adapted for firing shots in rapid succession **2** : marked by rapidity, liveliness, or sharpness ⟨a comedian with a ~ delivery⟩

ra•pid•i•ty \rə-ˈpi-də-tē, ra-\ *n* (1654) : the quality or state of being rapid

rapid transit *n* (1873) : fast passenger transportation (as by subway) in urban areas

[1]**ra•pi•er** \ˈrā-pē-ər\ *n* [MF (*espee*) *rapiere*] (1553) : a straight 2-edged sword with a narrow pointed blade

[2]**rapier** *adj* (1824) : extremely sharp or keen ⟨a ~ wit⟩

rap•ine \ˈra-pən, -ˌpīn\ *n* [ME *rapyne*, fr. AF *rapine*, fr. L *rapina*, fr. *rapere* to seize, rob] (15c) : PILLAGE, PLUNDER

ra·pi·ni *also* **rap·pi·ni** \ra-ˈpē-nē\ *n* [It *rapini,* pl. of *rapino,* dim. of *rapo* turnip, fr. L *rapum* — more at RAPE] (1942) **:** BROCCOLI RABE

rap·pa·ree \ˌra-pə-ˈrē\ *n* [Ir *rapaire, ropaire,* lit., thruster, stabber, fr. *rop* thrust, stab] (1690) **1 :** an Irish irregular soldier or bandit **2 :** VAGABOND, PLUNDERER

rap·pee \ra-ˈpē\ *n* [F (*tabac*) *râpé,* lit., grated tobacco] (ca. 1740) **:** a pungent snuff made from dark tobacco leaves

rap·pel \rə-ˈpel, ra-\ *vi* **-pelled** *also* **-peled; -pel·ling** *also* **-pel·ing** [F, lit., recall, fr. OF *rapel,* fr. *rapeler* to recall, fr. *re-* + *apeler* to appeal, call — more at APPEAL] (1944) **:** to descend (as from a cliff) by sliding down a rope passed under one thigh, across the body, and over the opposite shoulder or through a special friction device — **rappel** *n*

rap·pen \ˈrä-pən\ *n, pl* **rappen** [G, fr. G dial., lit., raven] (1838) **:** the centime of Switzerland

rap·per \ˈra-pər\ *n* (1640) **:** one that raps or is used for rapping: as **a :** a door knocker **b :** a performer of rap music

rap·port \ra-ˈpȯr, rə-\ *n* [F, fr. *rapporter* to bring back, refer, fr. OF *raporter* to bring back, fr. *re-* + *aporter* to bring, fr. L *apportare,* fr. *ad-* ad- + *portare* to carry — more at FARE] (ca. 1661) **:** RELATION; *esp* **:** relation marked by harmony, conformity, accord, or affinity

rap·por·teur \ˌra-ˌpȯr-ˈtər\ *n* [MF, fr. *rapporter* to bring back, report] (ca. 1500) **:** a person who gives reports (as at a meeting of a learned society)

rap·proche·ment \ˌra-ˌprōsh-ˈmä^{n}, -ˌprȯsh-; ra-ˈprōsh-ˌ\ *n* [F, fr. *rapprocher* to bring together, fr. MF, fr. *re-* + *approcher* to approach, fr. OF *aprochier,* fr. LL *appropiare* — more at APPROACH] (1809) **:** establishment of or state of having cordial relations

rap·scal·lion \rap-ˈskal-yən\ *n* [alter. of earlier *rascallion,* irreg. fr. *rascal*] (1699) **:** RASCAL, NE'ER-DO-WELL

rap sheet *n* (1960) **:** a police arrest record esp. for an individual

rapt \ˈrapt\ *adj* [ME, fr. L *raptus,* pp. of *rapere* to seize — more at RAPID] (14c) **1 :** lifted up and carried away **2 :** transported with emotion **:** ENRAPTURED **3 :** wholly absorbed **:** ENGROSSED — **rapt·ly** \ˈrap(t)-lē\ *adv* — **rapt·ness** \ˈrap(t)-nəs\ *n*

rap·tor \ˈrap-tər, -ˌtȯr\ *n* [NL *Raptores,* former order name, fr. L, pl. of *raptor* plunderer, fr. *rapere*] (1873) **1 :** BIRD OF PREY **2** [NL *-raptor* (as in *velociraptor*)] **:** a usu. small-to-medium-sized predatory dinosaur (as a velociraptor or deinonychus)

rap·to·ri·al \rap-ˈtȯr-ē-əl\ *adj* (1825) **1 :** PREDACEOUS 1 **2 :** adapted to seize prey **3 :** of, relating to, or being a bird of prey

[1]**rap·ture** \ˈrap-chər\ *n* [L *raptus*] (1594) **1 :** an expression or manifestation of ecstasy or passion **2 a :** a state or experience of being carried away by overwhelming emotion **b :** a mystical experience in which the spirit is exalted to a knowledge of divine things **3** *often cap* **:** the final assumption of Christians into heaven during the end-time according to Christian theology ***syn*** see ECSTASY — **rap·tur·ous** \ˈrap-chə-rəs, ˈrap-shrəs\ *adj* — **rap·tur·ous·ly** *adv* — **rap·tur·ous·ness** *n*

[2]**rapture** *vt* **rap·tured; rap·tur·ing** (1637) **:** ENRAPTURE

rapture of the deep (1953) **:** NITROGEN NARCOSIS

ra·ra avis \ˌrer-ə-ˈā-vəs, ˌrär-ə-ˈä-wəs\ *n, pl* **ra·ra avis·es** \-ˈā-və-səz\ *or* **ra·rae aves** \ˌrär-ˌī-ˈä-ˌwās\ [L, rare bird] (1607) **:** RARITY 2

[1]**rare** \ˈrer\ *adj* **rar·er; rar·est** [ME, fr. L *rarus*] (14c) **1 :** marked by wide separation of component particles **:** THIN ⟨~ air⟩ **2 a :** marked by unusual quality, merit, or appeal **:** DISTINCTIVE **b :** superlative or extreme of its kind **3 :** seldom occurring or found **:** UNCOMMON ***syn*** see CHOICE, INFREQUENT — **rare·ness** *n*

[2]**rare** *adj* **rar·er; rar·est** [alter. of earlier *rere,* fr. ME, fr. OE *hrēre* boiled lightly; akin to OE *hrēran* to stir, OHG *hruoren*] (1784) **:** cooked so that the inside is still red ⟨~ roast beef⟩

rare bird *n* (1631) **:** RARITY 2, RARA AVIS

rare·bit \ˈrer-bət\ *n* [(*Welsh*) *rarebit*] (ca. 1785) **:** WELSH RABBIT

rare earth *n* (1875) **1 :** any of a group of similar oxides of metals or a mixture of such oxides occurring together in widely distributed but relatively scarce minerals **2 :** RARE EARTH ELEMENT

rare earth element *n* (1924) **:** any of a series of metallic elements of which the oxides are classed as rare earths and which include the elements of the lanthanide series and sometimes yttrium and scandium — called also *rare earth metal*

rar·ee–show \ˈrer-ē-ˌshō\ *n* [alter. of *rare show*] (1684) **:** a small display or scene viewed in a box **:** PEEP SHOW; *broadly* **:** an unusual or amazing show or spectacle

rar·e·fac·tion \ˌrer-ə-ˈfak-shən\ *n* [F or ML; F *raréfaction,* fr. ML *rarefaction-, rarefactio,* fr. L *rarefacere* to rarefy] (1572) **1 :** the action or process of rarefying **2 :** the quality or state of being rarefied **3 :** a state or region of minimum pressure in a medium traversed by compressional waves (as sound waves) — **rar·e·fac·tion·al** \-shnəl, -shə-n^{ə}l\ *adj*

rarefied *also* **rarified** *adj* (14c) **1 :** being less dense **2 :** of, relating to, or interesting to a select group **:** ESOTERIC **3 :** very high

rar·e·fy *also* **rar·i·fy** \ˈrer-ə-ˌfī\ *vb* **-fied; -fy·ing** [ME *rarefien, rarifien,* modif. of L *rarefacere,* fr. *rarus* rare + *facere* to make — more at DO] *vt* (14c) **1 :** to make rare, thin, porous, or less dense **:** to expand without the addition of matter **2 :** to make more spiritual, refined, or abstruse ~ *vi* **:** to become less dense

rare·ly \ˈrer-lē\ *adv* (1549) **1 :** not often **:** SELDOM **2 :** with rare skill **:** EXCELLENTLY **3 :** in an extreme or exceptional manner

rare·ripe \ˈrer-ˌrīp\ *n* [E dial. *rare* early + E *ripe*] (1722) **1 :** an early ripening fruit or vegetable **2** *dial* **:** GREEN ONION

rar·ing \ˈrer-ən, -iŋ\ *adj* [fr. prp. of E dial. *rare* to rear, alter. of E *rear*] (1909) **:** full of enthusiasm or eagerness ⟨ready and ~ to go⟩

rar·i·ty \ˈrer-ə-tē\ *n, pl* **-ties** (1542) **1 :** the quality, state, or fact of being rare **2 :** one that is rare

ras \ˈras\ *n, often attrib* [prob. fr [1]*rat* + *sarcoma;* fr. the isolation of such genes in rat sarcomas] (1982) **:** any of a family of genes that undergo mutation to oncogenes and esp. to some commonly linked to human cancers (as of the colon, lung, and pancreas)

ras·bo·ra \raz-ˈbȯr-ə\ *n* [NL] (1931) **:** any of a genus (*Rasbora*) of tiny brilliantly colored cyprinid freshwater fishes often kept in tropical aquariums

ras·cal \ˈras-kəl\ *n* [ME *rascaile* foot soldiers, commoners, worthless person, fr. AF *rascaille,* fr. OF dial. (Norman & Picard) **rasquer* to scrape, clean off, fr. VL **rasicare*] (15c) **1 :** a mean, unprincipled, or dishonest person **2 :** a mischievous person or animal — **rascal** *adj*

ras·cal·i·ty \ra-ˈska-lə-tē\ *n, pl* **-ties** (ca. 1577) **1 :** RABBLE **2 a :** the character or actions of a rascal **:** KNAVERY **b :** a rascally act

ras·cal·ly \ˈras-kə-lē\ *adj* (1594) **:** of or characteristic of a rascal — **rascally** *adv*

rase \ˈrāz\ *vt* **rased; ras·ing** [ME, fr. AF *raser,* fr. VL **rasare,* freq. of L *radere* to scrape, shave — more at RODENT] (14c) **1** *archaic* **:** ERASE **2** *archaic* **:** RAZE 2

[1]**rash** \ˈrash\ *adv* [ME (northern dial.) *rasch* quickly; akin to OHG *rasc* fast] (15c) *archaic* **:** in a rash manner

[2]**rash** *adj* (1509) **1 :** marked by or proceeding from undue haste or lack of deliberation or caution ⟨a ~ promise⟩ **2** *obs* **:** quickly effective ***syn*** see ADVENTUROUS — **rash·ly** *adv* — **rash·ness** *n*

[3]**rash** *n* [obs. F *rache* scurf, fr. OF *raiche,* fr. VL **rasica,* fr. **rasicare* to scratch, fr. L *rasus,* pp. of *radere*] (1709) **1 :** an eruption on the body **2 :** a large number of instances in a short period ⟨a ~ of complaints⟩

rash·er \ˈra-shər\ *n* [perh. fr. obs. *rash* to cut, fr. ME *rashen*] (1591) **:** a thin slice of bacon or ham broiled or fried; *also* **:** a portion consisting of several such slices

[1]**rasp** \ˈrasp\ *vb* [ME, fr. AF **rasper,* of Gmc origin; akin to OHG *raspōn* to scrape together] *vt* (14c) **1 :** to rub with something rough; *specif* **:** to abrade with a rasp **2 :** to grate upon **:** IRRITATE **3 :** to utter in a raspy tone ~ *vi* **1 :** SCRAPE **2 :** to produce a grating sound — **rasp·er** *n* — **rasp·ing·ly** \ˈras-piŋ-lē\ *adv*

[2]**rasp** *n* (ca. 1512) **1 :** a coarse file with cutting points instead of lines **2 :** something used for rasping **3 a :** an act of rasping **b :** a rasping sound, sensation, or effect

rasp·ber·ry \ˈraz-ˌber-ē, -b(ə-)rē\ *n* [E dial. *rasp* raspberry + E *berry*] (ca. 1616) **1 a :** any of various usu. black or red edible berries that are aggregate fruits consisting of numerous small drupes on a fleshy receptacle and that are usu. rounder and smaller than the closely related blackberries **b :** a perennial plant (genus *Rubus*) of the rose family that bears raspberries **2** [short for *raspberry tart,* rhyming slang for *fart*] **:** a sound of contempt made by protruding the tongue between the lips and expelling air forcibly to produce a vibration; *broadly* **:** an expression of disapproval or contempt

raspberry

raspy \ˈras-pē\ *adj* **rasp·i·er; -est** (1838) **1 :** HARSH, GRATING **2 :** IRRITABLE

ras·sle \ˈra-səl\ *vi* [by alter.] (1758) **:** WRESTLE

Ras·ta \ˈras-tə, ˈräs-\ *n* (1955) **:** RASTAFARIAN — **Rasta** *adj*

Ras·ta·far·i·an \ˌras-tə-ˈfer-ē-ən, ˌräs-tə-ˈfär-\ *n* [*Ras Tafari,* precoronation name of Haile Selassie] (1955) **:** an adherent of Rastafarianism — **Rastafarian** *adj*

Ras·ta·far·i·an·ism \-ē-ə-ˌni-zəm\ *n* (1968) **:** a religious movement among black Jamaicans that teaches the eventual redemption of blacks and their return to Africa, employs the ritualistic use of marijuana, forbids the cutting of hair, and venerates Haile Selassie as a god

ras·ter \ˈras-tər\ *n* [G, fr. L *raster, rastrum* rake, fr. *radere* to scrape] (1934) **:** a scan pattern (as of the electron beam in a cathode-ray tube) in which an area is scanned from side to side in lines from top to bottom; *also* **:** a pattern of closely spaced rows of dots that form an image (as on the cathode-ray tube of a television or computer display)

ra·sure \ˈrā-shər, -zhər\ *n* [MF, fr. L *rasura,* fr. *rasus,* pp. of *radere*] (1508) **:** ERASURE, OBLITERATION

[1]**rat** \ˈrat\ *n* [ME, fr. OE *ræt;* akin to OHG *ratta* rat and perh. to L *rodere* to gnaw — more at RODENT] (bef. 12c) **1 a :** any of numerous rodents (*Rattus* and related genera) differing from the related mice esp. by considerably larger size **b :** any of various similar rodents **2 :** a contemptible person: as **a :** one who betrays or deserts friends or associates **b :** SCAB 3b **c :** INFORMER 2 **3 :** a pad over which a woman's hair is arranged **4 :** a person who spends much time in a specified place ⟨a mall ~⟩ — **rat·like** \-ˌlīk\ *adj*

[2]**rat** *vb* **rat·ted; rat·ting** *vi* (1812) **1 :** to betray, desert, or inform on one's associates — usu. used with *on* **2 :** to catch or hunt rats **3 :** to work as a scab ~ *vt* **1 :** to give (hair) the effect of greater quantity (as by use of a rat) **2 :** to inform on **:** TURN IN — usu. used with *out* ⟨*ratted* out his accomplice⟩

rat·able *or* **rate·able** \ˈrā-tə-bəl\ *adj* (1503) **:** capable of being rated, estimated, or apportioned — **rat·ably** \-blē\ *adv*

rat·a·fia \ˌra-tə-ˈfē-ə\ *n* [F] (1699) **1 :** a liqueur made from an infusion of macerated fruit or fruit juice in a liquor (as brandy) and often flavored with almonds **2 :** a sweet biscuit made of almond paste

rat·a·plan \ˈra-tə-ˌplan\ *n* [F, of imit. origin] (ca. 1848) **:** the iterative sound of beating ⟨a rolling ~ of drums —*Time*⟩

rat–a–tat \ˈra-tə-ˌtat\ *or* **rat–a–tat–tat** \ˌra-tə-ˌta(t)-ˈtat\ *n* [imit.] (1681) **:** a rapid succession of knocking, tapping, or cracking sounds

ra·ta·tou·ille \ˌra-ˌta-ˈtwē, ˌrä-ˌtä-, -ˈtü-ē\ *n* [F, fr. blend of *ratouiller* to disturb, shake and *tatouiller* to stir] (ca. 1877) **:** a seasoned stew made of eggplant, tomatoes, green peppers, squash, and sometimes meat

rat·bag \ˈrat-ˌbag\ *n* (1890) *chiefly Austral* **:** a stupid, eccentric, or disagreeable person

rat–bite fever *n* (1910) **:** either of two febrile bacterial diseases of humans usu. transmitted by the bite of a rat

rat cheese *n* (1939) **:** CHEDDAR

[1]**ratch·et** *also* **rach·et** \ˈra-chət\ *n* [alter. of earlier *rochet,* fr. F, alter. of MF *rocquet* ratchet, bobbin, of Gmc origin; akin to OHG *rocko* distaff — more at ROCK] (1654) **1 :** a mechanism that consists of a bar or wheel having inclined teeth into which a pawl drops so that motion can be imparted to the wheel or bar, governed, or prevented and that is used in a hand tool (as a wrench or screwdriver) to allow effective motion in one direction only **2 :** a pawl or detent for holding or propelling a toothed wheel

\ə\ **a**but \$^{ə}$\ kitten, F table \ər\ **fur**ther \a\ **a**sh \ā\ **a**ce \ä\ mop, mar
\au̇\ **ou**t \ch\ **ch**in \e\ bet \ē\ **ea**sy \g\ **g**o \i\ **hi**t \ī\ **i**ce \j\ **j**ob
\ŋ\ si**ng** \ō\ g**o** \ȯ\ **law** \ȯi\ b**oy** \th\ **th**in \t͟h\ **th**e \ü\ l**oo**t \u̇\ f**oo**t
\y\ yet \zh\ vi**si**on, bei**ge** \k, ^{n}, œ, ue, ^{y}\ *see* Guide to Pronunciation

[2]**ratchet** *also* **rachet** *vt* (1972) : to cause to move by steps or degrees — usu. used with *up* or *down* ⟨tried to ~ down the debt⟩ ~ *vi* : to proceed by steps or degrees

[1]**rate** \ˈrāt\ *vb* **rat·ed; rat·ing** [ME] *vt* (14c) **1** : to rebuke angrily or violently **2** *obs* : to drive away by scolding ~ *vi* : to voice angry reprimands

[2]**rate** *n* [ME, fr. AF, fr. ML *rata*, fr. L (*pro*) *rata* (*parte*) according to a fixed proportion] (15c) **1 a** : reckoned value : VALUATION **b** *obs* : ESTIMATION **2** *obs* : a fixed quantity **3 a** : a fixed ratio between two things **b** : a charge, payment, or price fixed according to a ratio, scale, or standard: as (1) : a charge per unit of a public-service commodity (2) : a charge per unit of freight or passenger service (3) : a unit charge or ratio used in assessing property taxes (4) *Brit* : a local tax **4 a** : a quantity, amount, or degree of something measured per unit of something else ⟨her typing ~ was 80 words per minute⟩ **b** : an amount of payment or charge based on another amount; *specif* : the amount of premium per unit of insurance **5** : relative condition or quality : CLASS — **at any rate** : in any case : ANYWAY

[3]**rate** *vb* **rat·ed; rat·ing** *vt* (15c) **1** *obs* : ALLOT **2 a** : to set an estimate on : VALUE, ESTEEM ⟨black is *rated* very high this season⟩ **b** : to determine or assign the relative rank or class of : GRADE ⟨~ a seaman⟩ **c** : to estimate the normal capacity or power of **3** : CONSIDER, REGARD ⟨was *rated* an excellent pianist⟩ **4** : to fix the amount of premium to be charged per unit of insurance on **5** : to have a right to : DESERVE ⟨she *rated* special privileges⟩ ~ *vi* : to enjoy a status of special privilege ⟨really ~s with the boss⟩ ***syn*** see ESTIMATE

ra·tel \ˈrā-tᵊl, ˈrä-\ *n* [Afrik, lit., rattle, fr. D, fr. MD — more at RATTLE] (1777) : an African or Asian nocturnal omnivorous mammal (*Mellivora capensis*) of the weasel family that resembles a badger

rate·me·ter \ˈrāt-ˌmē-tər\ *n* (1949) : an instrument that indicates the counting rate of an electronic counter

rate of change (1876) : a value that results from dividing the change in a function of a variable by the change in the variable ⟨velocity is the *rate of change* in distance with respect to time⟩

rate of exchange (ca. 1741) : the amount of one currency that will buy a given amount of another

rate·pay·er \ˈrāt-ˌpā-ər\ *n* (1845) **1** *Brit* : TAXPAYER **2** : one who pays for a utility service and esp. electricity according to established rates

rat·er \ˈrā-tər\ *n* (1611) **1** : one that rates; *specif* : a person who estimates or determines a rating **2** : one having a specified rating or class — usu. used in combination ⟨first-*rater*⟩

rat fink *n* (1964) : FINK, INFORMER

rat·fish \ˈrat-ˌfish\ *n* (1882) : CHIMAERA; *esp* : a silvery iridescent white-spotted chimaera (*Hydrolagus colliei*) of cold deep waters of the Pacific coast of No. America

rathe \ˈrāth, ˈrath\ *adj* [ME, quick, fr. OE *hræth*, alter. of *hræd;* akin to OHG *hrad* quick] (14c) *archaic* : EARLY ⟨bring the ~ primrose that forsaken dies —John Milton⟩

rath·er \ˈra-thər, ˈrä-, ˈrə- *also* ˈre-; *interjectionally* ˈra-ˈthər, ˈrä-, ˈrə-\ *adv* [ME, fr. OE *hrathor*, compar. of *hrathe* quickly; akin to OHG *rado* quickly, OE *hræd* quick] (bef. 12c) **1** : with better reason or more propriety : more properly ⟨this you should pity ~ than despise —Shak.⟩ **2** : more readily or willingly : PREFERABLY ⟨I'd ~ not go⟩ ⟨would ~ read than watch television⟩ — often used interjectionally to express affirmation **3** : more correctly speaking ⟨my father, or ~ my stepfather⟩ **4** : to the contrary : INSTEAD ⟨was no better but ~ grew worse —Mk 5:26 (RSV)⟩ **5** : in some degree : SOMEWHAT ⟨it's ~ warm⟩ — often used as a mild intensive ⟨spent ~ a lot of money⟩ — **the rather** *archaic* : the more quickly or readily

[1]**rather than** *conj* (14c) **1** — used with the infinitive form of a verb to indicate negation as a contrary choice or wish ⟨*rather than* continue the argument, he walked away⟩ ⟨chose to sing *rather than* play violin⟩ **2** : and not ⟨obscures *rather than* resolves the problem⟩ ⟨why do one thing *rather than* another?⟩ ⟨happy *rather than* sad⟩

[2]**rather than** *prep* (1595) : INSTEAD OF ⟨*rather than* being pleased, she was angry⟩

raths·kel·ler \ˈrät-ˌske-lər, ˈrat-, ˈrath-\ *n* [obs. G (now *Ratskeller*), city-hall basement restaurant, fr. *Rat* council + *Keller* cellar] (1766) : a usu. basement tavern or restaurant

rat·i·cide \ˈra-tə-ˌsīd\ *n* (1908) : a substance for killing rats

rat·i·fy \ˈra-tə-ˌfī\ *vt* **-fied; -fy·ing** [ME *ratifien*, fr. AF *ratifier*, fr. ML *ratificare*, fr. L *ratus* determined, fr. pp. of *reri* to calculate — more at REASON] (14c) : to approve and sanction formally : CONFIRM ⟨~ a treaty⟩ — **rat·i·fi·ca·tion** \ˌra-tə-fə-ˈkā-shən\ *n* — **rat·i·fi·er** \ˈra-tə-ˌfī(-ə)r\ *n*

ra·ti·né \ˌra-tə-ˈnā\ *or* **ra·tine** \ˌra-tə-ˈnā, ra-ˈtēn\ *n* [F *ratiné*] (ca. 1914) **1** : a rough bulky fabric usu. woven loosely in plain weave from ratiné yarns **2** : a nubby ply yarn of various fibers made by twisting under tension a thick and a thin yarn

rating *n* (1702) **1** : a classification according to grade; *specif* : a military or naval specialist classification **2** *chiefly Brit* : a naval enlisted man **3 a** : relative estimate or evaluation : STANDING ⟨the school has a good academic ~⟩ **b** : an estimate of an individual's or business's credit and responsibility **c** : an estimate of the percentage of the public listening to or viewing a particular radio or television program **4** : a stated operating limit of a machine expressible in power units (as kilowatts of a direct-current generator) or in characteristics (as voltage)

ra·tio \ˈrā-(ˌ)shō, -shē-ˌō\ *n, pl* **ra·tios** [L, computation, reason — more at REASON] (1660) **1 a** : the indicated quotient of two mathematical expressions **b** : the relationship in quantity, amount, or size between two or more things : PROPORTION **2** : the expression of the relative values of gold and silver as determined by a country's currency laws

ra·ti·o·ci·nate \ˌra-tē-ˈō-sə-ˌnāt, ˌra-shē-, -ˈä-\ *vi* **-nat·ed; -nat·ing** [L *ratiocinatus*, pp. of *ratiocinari* to reckon, fr. *ratio* + *-cinari* (as in *vaticinari* to prophesy) — more at VATICINATE] (1643) : REASON — **ra·ti·o·ci·na·tor** \-ˌā-tər\ *n*

ra·ti·o·ci·na·tion \-ˌō-sə-ˈnā-shən, -ˌnä-\ *n* (ca. 1530) **1** : the process of exact thinking : REASONING **2** : a reasoned train of thought — **ra·ti·o·ci·na·tive** \-ˈō-sə-ˌnā-tiv, -ˈnä-\ *adj*

[1]**ra·tion** \ˈra-shən, ˈrā-\ *n* [F, fr. L *ration-, ratio* computation, reason] (ca. 1711) **1 a** : a food allowance for one day **b** *pl* : FOOD, PROVISIONS **2** : a share esp. as determined by supply

[2]**ration** *vt* **ra·tioned; ra·tion·ing** \ˈra-sh(ə-)niŋ, ˈrā-\ (1859) **1** : to supply with or put on rations **2 a** : to distribute as rations — often used with *out* **b** : to distribute equitably **c** : to use sparingly

[1]**ra·tio·nal** \ˈrash-nəl, ˈra-shə-nᵊl\ *adj* [ME *racional*, fr. AF *racionel*, fr. L *rationalis*, fr. *ration-, ratio*] (14c) **1 a** : having reason or understanding **b** : relating to, based on, or agreeable to reason : REASONABLE ⟨a ~ explanation⟩ ⟨~ behavior⟩ **2** : involving only multiplication, division, addition, and subtraction and only a finite number of times **3** : relating to, consisting of, or being one or more rational numbers ⟨a ~ root of an equation⟩ — **ra·tio·nal·ly** *adv* — **ra·tio·nal·ness** *n*

[2]**rational** *n* (1606) : something rational; *specif* : RATIONAL NUMBER

ra·tio·nale \ˌra-shə-ˈnal\ *n* [L, neut. of *rationalis*] (1657) **1** : an explanation of controlling principles of opinion, belief, practice, or phenomena **2** : an underlying reason : BASIS

rational function *n* (1859) : a function that is the quotient of two polynomials; *also* : POLYNOMIAL

ra·tio·nal·ise *Brit var of* RATIONALIZE

ra·tio·nal·ism \ˈrash-nə-ˌli-zəm, ˈra-shə-nə-ˌli-\ *n* (1827) **1** : reliance on reason as the basis for establishment of religious truth **2 a** : a theory that reason is in itself a source of knowledge superior to and independent of sense perceptions **b** : a view that reason and experience rather than the nonrational are the fundamental criteria in the solution of problems **3** : FUNCTIONALISM 2 — **ra·tio·nal·ist** \-nə-list\ *n* — **rationalist** *or* **ra·tio·nal·is·tic** \ˌrash-nə-ˈlis-tik, ˌra-shə-nə-ˈlis-\ *adj* — **ra·tio·nal·is·ti·cal·ly** \-ti-k(ə-)lē\ *adv*

ra·tio·nal·i·ty \ˌra-shə-ˈna-lə-tē\ *n, pl* **-ties** (1628) **1** : the quality or state of being rational **2** : the quality or state of being agreeable to reason : REASONABLENESS **3** : a rational opinion, belief, or practice — usu. used in pl.

ra·tio·nal·ize \ˈrash-nə-ˌlīz, ˈra-shə-nə-ˌlīz\ *vb* **-ized; -iz·ing** *vt* (1803) **1** : to bring into accord with reason or cause something to seem reasonable: as **a** : to substitute a natural for a supernatural explanation of ⟨~ a myth⟩ **b** : to attribute (one's actions) to rational and creditable motives without analysis of true and esp. unconscious motives ⟨*rationalized* his dislike of his brother⟩; *broadly* : to create an excuse or more attractive explanation for ⟨~ the problem⟩ **2** : to free (a mathematical expression) from irrational parts ⟨~ a denominator⟩ **3** : to apply the principles of scientific management to (as an industry or its operations) for a desired result (as increased efficiency) ~ *vi* : to provide plausible but untrue reasons for conduct — **ra·tio·nal·iz·able** \ˌrash-nə-ˈlī-zə-bəl, ˌra-shə-nə-ˈlī-\ *adj* — **ra·tio·nal·i·za·tion** \ˌrash-nə-lə-ˈzā-shən, ˌra-shə-nə-lə-\ *n* — **ra·tio·nal·iz·er** \ˈrash-nə-ˌlī-zər, ˈra-shə-nə-ˌlī-\ *n*

rational number *n* (1879) : a number that can be expressed as an integer or the quotient of an integer divided by a nonzero integer

rat·ite \ˈra-ˌtīt\ *n* [ultim. fr. L *ratitus* marked with the figure of a raft, fr. *ratis* raft] (1877) : a bird with a flat breastbone; *esp* : any of various mostly flightless birds (as an ostrich, rhea, emu, moa, or kiwi) with small or rudimentary wings and no keel on the sternum that are prob. of polyphyletic origin and are assigned to a number of different orders — **ratite** *adj*

rat·line \ˈrat-lən\ *n* [ME *radelyng*] (15c) : any of the small transverse ropes attached to the shrouds of a ship so as to form the steps of a rope ladder — usu. used in pl.

[1]**ra·toon** \ra-ˈtün\ *n* [Sp *retoño*, fr. *retoñar* to sprout, fr. *re-* (fr. L) + *otoñar* to grow in autumn, fr. *otoño* autumn, fr. L *autumnus*] (1631) **1** : a shoot of a perennial plant (as sugarcane) **2** : a crop (as of bananas) produced on ratoons

[2]**ratoon** *vi* (1756) : to sprout or spring up from the root ~ *vt* : to grow or produce (a crop) from or on ratoons

rat race *n* (1939) : strenuous, wearisome, and usu. competitive activity or rush

rats \ˈrats\ *interj* (1886) — used to express disappointment, frustration, or disgust

rat snake *n* (1860) : any of various large harmless chiefly rat-eating colubrid snakes (esp. genus *Elaphe*) — called also *chicken snake*

rat·tail \ˈrat-ˌtāl\ *n* (1705) **1** : a horse's tail with little or no hair **2** : GRENADIER 2

rattail cactus *n* (1900) : a commonly cultivated tropical American cactus (*Aporocactus flagelliformis*) with showy crimson flowers

rat–tail file *n* (1744) : a round slender tapered file

rat·tan \ra-ˈtan, rə-\ *n* [Malay *rotan*] (1660) **1** : a rattan cane or switch **2 a** : a climbing palm (esp. of the genera *Calamus* and *Daemonorops*) with very long tough stems **b** : a part of the jointed stem of a rattan used esp. for furniture, wickerwork, and walking sticks

rat·teen \ra-ˈtēn\ *n* [F *ratine*] (1685) *archaic* : a coarse woolen fabric

rat·ter \ˈra-tər\ *n* (1857) : one that catches rats; *specif* : a rat-catching dog or cat

[1]**rat·tle** \ˈra-tᵊl\ *vb* **rat·tled; rat·tling** \ˈrat-liŋ, ˈra-tᵊl-iŋ\ [ME *ratelen;* akin to MD *ratel* rattle] *vi* (14c) **1** : to make a rapid succession of short sharp noises ⟨the windows *rattled* in the wind⟩ **2** : to chatter incessantly and aimlessly **3** : to move with a clatter or rattle; *also* : to be or move about in a place or station too large or grand ⟨*rattled* around the big old house⟩ ~ *vt* **1** : to say, perform, or affect in a brisk lively fashion ⟨*rattled* off four magnificent backhands —Kim Chapin⟩ **2** : to cause to make a rattling sound **3** : ROUSE; *specif* : to beat (a cover) for game **4** : to upset esp. to the point of loss of poise and composure : DISTURB ***syn*** see EMBARRASS

[2]**rattle** *n* (1519) **1 a** : a device that produces a rattle; *specif* : a case containing pellets used as a baby's toy **b** : the sound-producing organ on a rattlesnake's tail **2 a** : a rapid succession of sharp clattering sounds **b** : NOISE, RACKET **3** : DEATH RATTLE

[3]**rattle** *vt* **rat·tled; rat·tling** \ˈrat-liŋ, ˈra-tᵊl-iŋ\ [irreg. fr. *ratline*] (1729) : to furnish with ratlines

rat·tle·brain \ˈra-tᵊl-ˌbrān\ *n* (1709) : a flighty or thoughtless person — **rat·tle·brained** \-ˌbrānd\ *adj*

rat·tler \ˈrat-lər, ˈra-tᵊl-ər\ *n* (15c) **1** : one that rattles **2** : RATTLESNAKE

rat·tle·snake \ˈra-tᵊl-ˌsnāk\ *n* (1630) : any of several American pit vipers (genera *Crotalus* and *Sistrurus*) that have horny interlocking joints at the end of the tail which make a sharp rattling sound when shaken

rattlesnake master *n* (1843) : BUTTON SNAKEROOT 2

rattlesnake plantain *n* (1778) : any of a genus (*Goodyera*) of orchids with variegated leaves and small flowers in a twisted spike
rattlesnake root *n* (1682) : any of various plants formerly believed to be distasteful to rattlesnakes or effective against their venom: as **a** : any of a genus (*Prenanthes,* esp. *P. altissima*) of composite plants with small heads of drooping ligulate flowers **b** : SENECA SNAKEROOT
rattlesnake weed *n* (1760) : a hawkweed (*Hieracium venosum*) of eastern No. America with purple-veined leaves
rat·tle·trap \ˈra-tᵊl-ˌtrap\ *n* (1822) : something rattly or rickety; *esp* : an old car — **rattletrap** *adj*

rattlesnake

[1]**rat·tling** \ˈrat-liŋ\ *adj* (1560) **1** : LIVELY, BRISK ⟨moved at a ~ pace⟩ **2** : extraordinarily good : SPLENDID — **rat·tling·ly** \-liŋ-lē\ *adv*
[2]**rattling** *adv* (1829) : to an extreme degree : VERY ⟨a ~ good story⟩
rat·tly \ˈrat-lē, ˈra-tᵊl-ē\ *adj* (1881) : likely to rattle : making a rattle
rat·ton \ˈra-tᵊn, ˈrä-\ *n* [ME *ratoun,* fr. AF, dim. of *rat,* prob. of Gmc origin; akin to OE *ræt* rat] (14c) *chiefly dial* : RAT
rat·trap \ˈra(t)-ˌtrap\ *n* (15c) **1** : a trap for rats **2** : a dirty dilapidated structure **3** : a hopeless situation
rat trap cheese *n* (1927) : CHEDDAR
rat·ty \ˈra-tē\ *adj* **rat·ti·er; -est** (1865) **1 a** : infested with rats **b** : of, relating to, or suggestive of a rat **2** : SHABBY, UNKEMPT ⟨a ~ brown overcoat —John Lardner⟩ **3 a** : DESPICABLE, TREACHEROUS **b** : IRRITABLE ⟨feeling ~ as hell —Richard Bissell⟩
rau·cous \ˈrȯ-kəs\ *adj* [L *raucus* hoarse; akin to L *ravis* hoarseness] (1769) **1** : disagreeably harsh or strident : HOARSE ⟨~ voices⟩ **2** : boisterously disorderly ⟨a . . . ~ frontier town —Truman Capote⟩ ***syn*** see LOUD — **rau·cous·ly** *adv* — **rau·cous·ness** *n*
raunch \ˈrȯnch, ˈränch\ *n* [back-formation fr. *raunchy*] (1964) : VULGARITY, LEWDNESS
raun·chy \ˈrȯn-chē, ˈrän-\ *adj* **raun·chi·er; -est** [origin unknown] (1939) **1** : SLOVENLY, DIRTY ⟨a ~ panhandler⟩; *also* : very smelly ⟨~ sneakers⟩ **2** : OBSCENE, SMUTTY ⟨~ jokes⟩ — **raun·chi·ly** \ˈrȯn-chə-lē, ˈrän-\ *adv* — **raun·chi·ness** \-chē-nəs\ *n*
rau·wol·fia \rau̇-ˈwu̇l-fē-ə, rȯ-\ *n* [NL, fr. Leonhard *Rauwolf* †1596 Ger. botanist] (1752) **1** : any of a genus (*Rauvolfia* syn. *Rauwolfia*) of pantropical trees and shrubs of the dogbane family that yield medicinal alkaloids (as reserpine) **2** : the dried root or an extract from the root of a rauwolfia (esp. *Rauvolfia serpentina* of Asia) used chiefly in the treatment of hypertension
[1]**rav·age** \ˈra-vij\ *n* [F, fr. MF, fr. *ravir* to ravish — more at RAVISH] (ca. 1611) **1** : an act or practice of ravaging **2** : damage resulting from ravaging : violently destructive effect ⟨the ~*s* of time⟩
[2]**ravage** *vb* **rav·aged; rav·ag·ing** *vt* (ca. 1611) : to wreak havoc on : affect destructively ⟨a land *ravaged* by war⟩ ~ *vi* : to commit destructive actions — **rav·age·ment** \-vij-mənt\ *n* — **rav·ag·er** *n*
syn RAVAGE, DEVASTATE, WASTE, SACK, PILLAGE, DESPOIL mean to lay waste by plundering or destroying. RAVAGE implies violent often cumulative depredation and destruction ⟨a hurricane *ravaged* the coast⟩. DEVASTATE implies the complete ruin and desolation of a wide area ⟨an earthquake *devastated* the city⟩. WASTE may imply producing the same result by a slow process rather than sudden and violent action ⟨years of drought had *wasted* the area⟩. SACK implies carrying off all valuable possessions from a place ⟨barbarians *sacked* ancient Rome⟩. PILLAGE implies ruthless plundering at will but without the completeness suggested by SACK ⟨settlements *pillaged* by Vikings⟩. DESPOIL applies to looting or robbing without suggesting accompanying destruction ⟨the Nazis *despoiled* the art museums⟩.
[1]**rave** \ˈrāv\ *vb* **raved; rav·ing** [ME] *vi* (14c) **1 a** : to talk irrationally in or as if in delirium **b** : to speak out wildly **c** : to talk with extreme enthusiasm ⟨*raved* about its beauty⟩ **2** : to move or advance violently : STORM ⟨the iced gusts still ~ and beat —John Keats⟩ ~ *vt* : to utter in madness or frenzy
[2]**rave** *n* (1598) **1** : an act or instance of raving **2** : an extravagantly favorable criticism ⟨the play received the critics' ~*s*⟩ **3** : a large overnight dance party featuring techno music and usu. involving the taking of mind-altering drugs
[1]**rav·el** \ˈra-vəl\ *vb* **-eled** *or* **-elled; -el·ing** *or* **-el·ling** \ˈrav-liŋ, ˈra-və-\ [D *rafelen,* fr. *rafel* loose thread] *vt* (1582) **1 a** : to separate or undo the texture of : UNRAVEL **b** : to undo the intricacies of : DISENTANGLE **2** : ENTANGLE, CONFUSE ~ *vi* **1** *obs* : to become entangled or confused **2** : to become unwoven, untwisted, or unwound : FRAY **3** : BREAK UP, CRUMBLE — **rav·el·er** \ˈrav-lər, ˈra-və-\ *n* — **rav·el·ment** \ˈra-vəl-mənt\ *n*
[2]**ravel** *n* (1634) : an act or result of raveling: as **a** : something tangled **b** : something raveled out; *specif* : a loose thread
raveling *or* **ravelling** *n* (1658) : RAVEL b
[1]**ra·ven** \ˈrā-vən\ *n* [ME, fr. OE *hræfn;* akin to OHG *hraban* raven, L *corvus,* Gk *korax*] (bef. 12c) : a large glossy black corvine bird (*Corvus corax*) of Europe, Asia, northern Africa, and America
[2]**raven** *adj* (1588) : shiny and black like a raven's feathers ⟨~ hair⟩
[3]**rav·en** \ˈra-vən\ *vb* **rav·ened; rav·en·ing** \ˈra-və-niŋ, ˈrav-niŋ\ [MF *raviner* to rush, take by force, fr. *ravine* rapine] *vi* (1530) **1** : to feed greedily **2** : to prowl for food : PREY **3** : PLUNDER ~ *vt* **1** : to devour greedily **2** : DESPOIL ⟨men . . . ~ the earth, destroying its resources —*New Yorker*⟩ — **rav·en·er** \ˈra-və-nər, ˈrav-nər\ *n*

raven

rav·en·ous \ˈra-və-nəs, ˈrav-nəs\ *adj* (15c) **1** : RAPACIOUS ⟨~ wolves⟩ **2** : very eager or greedy for food, satisfaction, or gratification ⟨a ~ appetite⟩ ***syn*** see VORACIOUS — **rav·en·ous·ly** *adv* — **rav·en·ous·ness** *n*
rav·er \ˈrā-vər\ *n* (15c) **1** : one that raves **2** : a person who frequents raves
rav·in \ˈra-vən\ *n* [ME, fr. AF *ravine*] (14c) **1** : PLUNDER, PILLAGE **2 a** : an act or habit of preying **b** : something seized as prey
ra·vine \rə-ˈvēn\ *n* [F, fr. MF, rapine, rush, fr. L *rapina* rapine] (ca. 1772) : a small narrow steep-sided valley that is larger than a gully and smaller than a canyon and that is usu. worn by running water
rav·ined \ˈra-vənd\ *adj* (1606) *obs* : RAPACIOUS, RAVENOUS
[1]**raving** *n* (14c) : irrational, incoherent, wild, or extravagant utterance or declamation — usu. used in pl.
[2]**raving** *adj* (15c) **1** : talking wildly or irrationally ⟨a ~ lunatic⟩ **2** : RAVISHING ⟨a ~ beauty⟩
rav·i·o·li \ˌra-vē-ˈō-lē, ˌrä-\ *n, pl* **ravioli** *also* **rav·i·o·lis** \-lēz\ [It, fr. It dial., pl. of *raviolo,* lit., little turnip, dim. of *rava* turnip, fr. L *rapa* — more at RAPE] (1841) : pasta in the form of little cases of dough containing a savory filling (as of meat or cheese)
rav·ish \ˈra-vish\ *vt* [ME *ravisshen,* fr. AF *raviss-,* stem of *ravir,* fr. VL **rapire,* alter. of L *rapere* to seize, rob — more at RAPID] (14c) **1 a** : to seize and take away by violence **b** : to overcome with emotion (as joy or delight) ⟨~*ed* by the scenic beauty⟩ **c** : RAPE 2 **2** : PLUNDER, ROB — **rav·ish·er** *n* — **rav·ish·ment** \-mənt\ *n*
rav·ish·ing \ˈra-vi-shiŋ\ *adj* (14c) : unusually attractive, pleasing, or striking — **rav·ish·ing·ly** \-shiŋ-lē\ *adv*
[1]**raw** \ˈrȯ\ *adj* **raw·er** \ˈrȯ(-ə)r\; **raw·est** \ˈrȯ-əst\ [ME, fr. OE *hrēaw;* akin to OHG *hrō* raw, L *crudus* raw, *cruor* blood, Gk *kreas* flesh] (bef. 12c) **1** : not cooked **2 a (1)** : being in or nearly in the natural state : not processed or purified ⟨~ fibers⟩ ⟨~ sewage⟩ **(2)** : not diluted or blended ⟨~ spirits⟩ **b** : unprepared or imperfectly prepared for use **c** : not being in polished, finished, or processed form ⟨~ data⟩ ⟨a ~ draft of a thesis⟩ **3 a (1)** : having the surface abraded or chafed **(2)** : very irritated ⟨a ~ sore throat⟩ **b** : lacking covering : NAKED **c** : not protected : susceptible to hurt ⟨~ emotions⟩ **4 a** : lacking experience or understanding : GREEN ⟨a ~ recruit⟩ **b (1)** : marked by absence of refinements **(2)** : VULGAR, COARSE ⟨~ language⟩ **c** : not tempered : UNBRIDLED ⟨~ power⟩ **5** : disagreeably damp or cold ⟨a ~ winter day⟩ ***syn*** see RUDE — **raw·ly** *adv* — **raw·ness** *n*
[2]**raw** *n* (1823) : a raw place or state — **in the raw 1** : in a natural, unrefined, or crude state **2** : NAKED ⟨slept *in the raw*⟩
raw bar *n* (1943) : a counter (as in a restaurant) that serves raw shellfish
raw·boned \ˈrȯ-ˌbōnd\ *adj* (1591) : relatively thin with prominent bone structure; *also* : heavy-framed and rugged but not attractively built ***syn*** see LEAN
raw deal *n* (1911) : an instance of unfair treatment
[1]**raw·hide** \ˈrȯ-ˌhīd\ *n* (1829) **1** : a whip of untanned hide **2** : untanned cattle skin
[2]**rawhide** *vt* **raw·hid·ed; raw·hid·ing** (1858) **1** : to whip or drive with or as if with a rawhide **2** : CHASTISE 2
ra·win·sonde \ˈrā-wən-ˌsänd\ *n* [*ra*dar + *win*d + radio*sonde*] (1946) : a radiosonde tracked by a radio direction-finding device to determine the velocity of winds aloft
raw material *n* (1796) : crude or processed material that can be converted by manufacture, processing, or combination into a new and useful product ⟨wheat . . . is *raw material* for the flour mill —C. A. Koepke⟩; *broadly* : something with a potential for improvement, development, or elaboration ⟨perplexities are often the *raw material* of discoveries —Agnes M. Clerke⟩
raw score *n* (1920) : an individual's actual achievement score (as on a test) before being adjusted for relative position in the test group
rax \ˈraks\ *vb* [ME (northern dial.) *raxen,* fr. OE *raxan;* akin to OE *reccan* to stretch — more at RACK] (bef. 12c) *chiefly Scot* : STRETCH
[1]**ray** \ˈrā\ *n* [ME *raye,* fr. AF *raie,* fr. L *raia*] (14c) : any of an order (Rajiformes) of usu. marine cartilaginous fishes (as stingrays and skates) having the body flattened dorsoventrally, the eyes on the upper surface, and enlarged pectoral fins fused with the head
[2]**ray** *n* [ME, fr. AF *rai,* fr. L *radius* rod, ray] (14c) **1 a** : any of the lines of light that appear to radiate from a bright object **b** : a beam of radiant energy (as light) of small cross section **c (1)** : a stream of material particles traveling in the same line (as in radioactive phenomena) **(2)** : a single particle of such a stream **2 a** : light cast by rays : RADIANCE **b** : a moral or intellectual light **3** : a thin line suggesting a ray: as **a** : any of a group of lines diverging from a common center **b** : HALF LINE **4 a** : one of the bony rods that extend and support the membrane in the fin of a fish **b** : one of the radiating divisions of the body of a radiate animal (as a starfish) **5 a** : a branch or flower stalk of an umbel **b (1)** : MEDULLARY RAY **(2)** : VASCULAR RAY **c** : RAY FLOWER 1 **6** : PARTICLE, TRACE ⟨a ~ of hope⟩ — **rayed** \ˈrād\ *adj*
[3]**ray** *vi* (1598) **1 a** : to shine in or as if in rays **b** : to issue as rays **2** : to extend like the radii of a circle : RADIATE ~ *vt* **1** : to emit in rays **2** : to furnish or mark with rays
ray flower *n* (1839) **1** : one of the marginal flowers of the head in a composite plant (as the aster) that also has disk flowers **2** : the entire head in a plant (as chicory) that lacks disk flowers
Ray·leigh scattering \ˈrā-lē-\ *n* [John W. S. *Rayleigh*] (1937) : scattering of light by particles small enough to render the effect selective so that different colors are deflected through different angles
ray·less \ˈrā-ləs\ *adj* (1747) : having, admitting, or emitting no rays; *esp* : DARK — **ray·less·ness** *n*
rayless goldenrod *n* (1923) : a shrubby to herbaceous composite plant (*Haplopappus heterophyllus* syn. *Isocoma wrightii*) esp. of open saline ground from Texas to Arizona and northern Mexico that lacks ray flowers and causes trembles in cattle
ray·on \ˈrā-ˌän\ *n* [irreg. fr. [2]*ray*] (1924) **1** : any of a group of smooth textile fibers made from regenerated cellulose by extrusion through minute holes **2** : a rayon yarn, thread, or fabric

---

\ə\ **abut** \ᵊ\ kitten, F table \ər\ **further** \a\ **ash** \ā\ **ace** \ä\ mop, mar
\au̇\ **out** \ch\ **chin** \e\ **bet** \ē\ **easy** \g\ **go** \i\ **hit** \ī\ **ice** \j\ **job**
\ŋ\ **sing** \ō\ **go** \ȯ\ **law** \ȯi\ **boy** \th\ **thin** \t͟h\ **the** \ü\ **loot** \u̇\ **foot**
\y\ **yet** \zh\ **vision, beige** \k, ⁿ, œ, ue, ʸ\ *see* Guide to Pronunciation

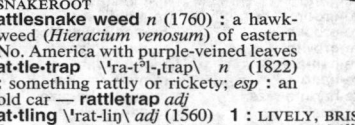

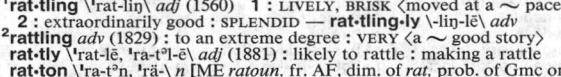

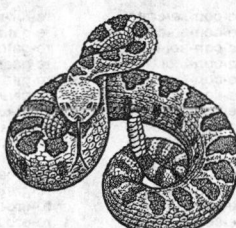

raze \'rāz\ *vt* **razed; raz·ing** [alter. of *rase*] (1536) **1 a** *archaic* : ERASE **b** : to scrape, cut, or shave off **2** : to destroy to the ground : DEMOLISH ⟨∼ an old building⟩ — **raz·er** *n*
ra·zee \rä-'zē\ *n* [F (*vaisseau*) *rasé*, lit., cut-off ship] (1794) : a wooden warship with the upper deck cut away
ra·zor \'rā-zər\ *n* [ME *rasour*, fr. AF *rasur*, fr. *raser* to raze, shave — more at RASE] (14c) : a keen-edged cutting instrument for shaving or cutting hair
ra·zor·back \'rā-zər-ˌbak\ *n* (1849) : a thin-bodied long-legged feral hog chiefly of the southeastern U.S.
ra·zor–backed \-ˌbakt\ *or* **ra·zor·back** \-ˌbak\ *adj* (1829) : having a sharp narrow back ⟨a ∼ horse⟩
ra·zor·bill \-ˌbil\ *n* (1674) : a No. Atlantic auk (*Alca torda*) with the plumage black above and white below and a compressed sharp-edged bill — called also *razor-billed auk*
razor clam *n* (ca. 1882) : any of a family (Solenidae) of marine lamellibranch mollusks having a long narrow thin shell
razor wire *n* (1977) : coiled wire fitted with sharp razor edges and used as an obstacle or barrier; *also* : CONCERTINA WIRE
¹razz \'raz\ *n* [short for *razzberry* sound of contempt, alter. of *raspberry*] (ca. 1919) : RASPBERRY 2
²razz *vt* (1918) : HECKLE, DERIDE ⟨the fans ∼ed the visiting players⟩
razz·a·ma·tazz \ˌra-zə-mə-'taz\ *chiefly Brit var of* RAZZMATAZZ
raz·zle–daz·zle \ˌra-zəl-'da-zəl\ *n* [redupl. of *dazzle*] (1889) **1** : a state of confusion or hilarity **2** : a complex maneuver (as in sports) designed to confuse an opponent **3** : a confusing or colorful often gaudy action or display — **razzle–dazzle** *adj*
razz·ma·tazz \ˌraz-mə-'taz\ *n* [prob. alter. of *razzle-dazzle*] (1942) **1** : RAZZLE-DAZZLE 3 **2** : DOUBLE-TALK 2 **3** : VIM, ZING
Rb *symbol* rubidium
RBC *abbr* red blood cells
RBI \ˌär-(ˌ)bē-'ī, 'ri-bē\ *n, pl* **RBIs** *or* **RBI** [*run batted in*] (1948) : a run in baseball that is driven in by a batter; *also* : official credit to a batter for driving in a run ⟨led the league in ∼s⟩
RC *abbr* **1** Red Cross **2** resistance-capacitance **3** Roman Catholic
RCAF *abbr* Royal Canadian Air Force
RCMP *abbr* Royal Canadian Mounted Police
RCN *abbr* Royal Canadian Navy
r–color *n* (1935) : an acoustic effect of a simultaneously articulated \r\ imparted to a vowel by retroflexion or constriction of the tongue — **r–col·ored** \'är-ˌkə-lərd\ *adj*
rd *abbr* **1** road **2** rod **3** round
RD *abbr* **1** registered dietitian **2** rural delivery
-rd *symbol* — used after the figure 3 to indicate the ordinal number *third* ⟨3rd⟩ ⟨83rd⟩
RDA *abbr* **1** recommended daily allowance **2** recommended dietary allowance
RDF *abbr* **1** radio direction finder; radio direction finding **2** Rapid Deployment Force **3** refuse-derived fuel
¹re \'rā\ *n* [ML, fr. the syllable sung to this note in a medieval hymn to St. John the Baptist] (14c) : the second tone of the diatonic scale in solmization
²re \'rā, 'rē\ *prep* [L, abl. of *res* thing — more at REAL] (1707) : with regard to \ : IN RE
Re *symbol* rhenium
re- *prefix* [ME, fr. AF, fr. L *re-, red-* back, again, against] **1** : again : anew ⟨retell⟩ **2** : back : backward ⟨recall⟩

re·ab·sorp·tion
re·ac·cel·er·ate
re·ac·cept
re·ac·ces·sion
re·ac·cli·ma·tize
re·ac·cred·it
re·ac·cred·i·ta·tion
re·ac·quaint
re·ac·quire
re·ac·qui·si·tion
re·ac·ti·vate
re·ac·ti·va·tion
re·ad·dress
re·ad·just
re·ad·just·ment
re·ad·mis·sion
re·ad·mit
re·adopt
re·af·firm
re·af·fir·ma·tion
re·af·fix
re·al·lo·cate
re·al·lo·ca·tion
re·anal·y·sis
re·an·a·lyze
re·an·i·mate
re·an·i·ma·tion
re·an·nex
re·an·nex·a·tion
re·ap·pear
re·ap·pear·ance
re·ap·pli·ca·tion
re·ap·ply
re·ap·point
re·ap·point·ment
re·ap·prais·al
re·ap·praise
re·ap·pro·pri·ate
re·ap·prove
re·ar·gue
re·ar·gu·ment
re·arous·al
re·arouse
re·ar·range
re·ar·range·ment
re·ar·rest

re·ar·tic·u·late
re·as·cend
re·as·cent
re·as·sem·blage
re·as·sem·ble
re·as·sem·bly
re·as·sert
re·as·ser·tion
re·as·sess
re·as·sess·ment
re·as·sign
re·as·sign·ment
re·as·sume
re·at·tach
re·at·tach·ment
re·at·tain
re·at·tempt
re·at·tri·bute
re·at·tri·bu·tion
re·au·tho·ri·za·tion
re·au·tho·rize
re·awak·en
re·bait
re·bal·ance
re·bap·tism
re·bap·tize
re·be·gin
re·bid
re·bind
re·blend
re·bloom
re·board
re·boil
re·book
re·boot
re·bore
re·bot·tle
re·breed
re·buri·al
re·bury
re·buy
re·cal·cu·late
re·cal·cu·la·tion
re·cal·i·brate
re·cal·i·bra·tion
re·cat·e·go·rize

re·cen·tral·i·za·tion
re·cen·tri·fuge
re·cer·ti·fi·ca·tion
re·cer·ti·fy
re·chal·lenge
re·chan·nel
re·char·ter
re·check
re·cho·reo·graph
re·chris·ten
re–Chris·tian·ize
re·chro·ma·to·graph
re·chro·ma·tog·ra·phy
re·cir·cu·late
re·cir·cu·la·tion
re·clad
re·clas·si·fi·ca·tion
re·clas·si·fy
re·clothe
re·cock
re·cod·i·fi·ca·tion
re·cod·i·fy
re·col·o·ni·za·tion
re·col·o·nize
re·col·or
re·com·mence
re·com·mence·ment
re·com·mis·sion
re·com·pi·la·tion
re·com·pile
re·com·pu·ta·tion
re·com·pute
re·con·ceive
re·con·cen·trate
re·con·cen·tra·tion
re·con·cep·tion
re·con·cep·tu·al·i·za·tion
re·con·cep·tu·al·ize
re·con·dense
re·con·fig·u·ra·tion
re·con·fig·ure
re·con·nect
re·con·nec·tion
re·con·quer
re·con·quest

re·con·se·crate
re·con·se·cra·tion
re·con·sol·i·date
re·con·tact
re·con·tam·i·nate
re·con·tam·i·na·tion
re·con·tour
re·con·vene
re·con·ver·sion
re·con·vert
re·con·vict
re·con·vic·tion
re·con·vince
re·copy
re·cork
re·cross
re·cul·ti·vate
re·ded·i·cate
re·ded·i·ca·tion
re·de·fect
re·de·liv·er
re·de·liv·ery
re·de·pos·it
re·de·ter·mi·na·tion
re·de·ter·mine
re·di·ges·tion
re·dis·cov·er
re·dis·cov·ery
re·dis·cuss
re·dis·play
re·dis·pose
re·dis·po·si·tion
re·dis·solve
re·dis·till
re·dis·til·la·tion
re·di·vide
re·di·vi·sion
re·don
re·draft
re·draw
re·dream
re·drill
re·dub
re·el·i·gi·bil·i·ty
re·el·i·gi·ble
re·emerge
re·emer·gence
re·emit
re·em·pha·sis
re·em·pha·size
re·em·ploy
re·em·ploy·ment
re·en·coun·ter
re·en·dow
re·en·er·gize
re·en·gage
re·en·gage·ment
re·en·grave
re·en·list
re·en·list·ment
re·en·roll
re·en·throne
re·en·vi·sion
re·equip
re·equip·ment
re·erect
re·es·ca·late
re·es·ca·la·tion
re·es·tab·lish
re·es·tab·lish·ment
re·es·ti·mate
re·eval·u·ate
re·eval·u·a·tion
re·ex·am·i·na·tion
re·ex·am·ine
re·ex·pe·ri·ence
re·ex·plore
re·ex·port
re·ex·por·ta·tion
re·ex·pose
re·ex·po·sure
re·ex·press
re·face
re·feed
re·feel
re·fight
re·file
re·find
re·fire
re·fix
re·float
re·fold
re·forge
re·for·mat
re·for·mu·late
re·for·mu·la·tion
re·for·ti·fi·ca·tion
re·for·ti·fy
re·found
re·foun·da·tion
re·frame
re·freeze
re·fry

re·fur·nish
re·gain
re·gath·er
re·gear
re·gild
re·give
re·glaze
re·grade
re·graft
re·grant
re·green
re·grind
re·groom
re·groove
re·growth
re·han·dle
re·hang
re·har·mo·nize
re·heat
re·hinge
re·hire
re·hos·pi·tal·i·za·tion
re·hos·pi·tal·ize
re·hu·man·ize
re·iden·ti·fy
re·ig·nite
re·ig·ni·tion
re·im·age
re·im·merse
re·im·plant
re·im·plan·ta·tion
re·im·port
re·im·por·ta·tion
re·im·pose
re·im·po·si·tion
re·in·cor·po·rate
re·in·cor·po·ra·tion
re·in·dict
re·in·dict·ment
re·in·fes·ta·tion
re·in·flate
re·in·fla·tion
re·in·hab·it
re·ini·tiate
re·in·ject
re·in·jec·tion
re·in·jure
re·in·ju·ry
re·ink
re·in·ner·vate
re·in·ner·va·tion
re·in·oc·u·late
re·in·oc·u·la·tion
re·in·sert
re·in·ser·tion
re·in·spect
re·in·spec·tion
re·in·spire
re·in·stall
re·in·stal·la·tion
re·in·sti·tute
re·in·sti·tu·tion·al·i·za·tion
re·in·ter
re·in·ter·ment
re·in·ter·view
re·in·tro·duce
re·in·tro·duc·tion
re·in·vade
re·in·va·sion
re·in·ves·ti·gate
re·in·ves·ti·ga·tion
re·in·vig·o·rate
re·in·vig·o·ra·tion
re·in·vig·o·ra·tor
re·jack·et
re·judge
re·jug·gle
re·key
re·key·board
re·kin·dle
re·knit
re·la·bel
re·lac·quer
re·land·scape
re·launch
re·learn
re·le·git·i·mize
re·lend
re·li·cense
re·li·cen·sure
re·light
re·link
re·liq·ue·fy
re·load
re·load·able
re·lock
re·look
re·lu·bri·cate
re·lu·bri·ca·tion
re·mar·ket
re·mar·riage
re·mar·ry
re·mate

re·ma·te·ri·al·ize
re·mea·sure
re·mea·sure·ment
re·meet
re·melt
re·merge
re·mi·gra·tion
re·mil·i·ta·ri·za·tion
re·mil·i·ta·rize
re·mo·bi·li·za·tion
re·mo·bi·lize
re·moist·en
re·mold
re·mon·e·ti·za·tion
re·mon·e·tize
re·mo·ti·vate
re·mo·ti·va·tion
re·my·thol·o·gize
re·nail
re·name
re·na·tion·al·i·za·tion
re·na·tion·al·ize
re·nest
re·num·ber
re·ob·serve
re·oc·cu·pa·tion
re·oc·cu·py
re·oc·cur
re·oc·cur·rence
re·oil
re·op·er·ate
re·op·er·a·tion
re·or·ches·trate
re·or·ches·tra·tion
re·ori·ent
re·ori·en·tate
re·ori·en·ta·tion
re·out·fit
re·ox·i·da·tion
re·ox·i·dize
re·ox·y·gen·ate
re·ox·y·gen·a·tion
re·pack
re·paint
re·park
re·patch
re·pat·tern
re·pave
re·peg
re·peo·ple
re·pho·to·graph
re·phrase
re·plan
re·plas·ter
re·plate
re·pledge
re·plot
re·plumb
re·pol·ish
re·poll
re·pop·u·lar·ize
re·pop·u·late
re·pop·u·la·tion
re·pot
re·pres·sur·ize
re·price
re·pri·vat·i·za·tion
re·pri·vat·ize
re·pro·vi·sion
re·pump
re·punc·tu·a·tion
re·pur·chase
re·pu·ri·fy
re·rack
re·raise
re·read
re·read·ing
re·re·cord
re·reg·is·ter
re·reg·is·tra·tion
re·reg·u·late
re·reg·u·la·tion
re·re·lease
re·re·view
re·rig
re·roll
re·roof
re·route
re·sail
re·sam·ple
re·saw
re·school
re·score
re·screen
re·sculpt
re·seal
re·seal·able
re·sea·son
re·seat
re·se·cure
re·see
re·seg·re·gate
re·seg·re·ga·tion
re·sell

re·sell·er
re·sen·si·tize
re·sen·tence
re·ser·vice
re·set·tle
re·set·tle·ment
re·sew
re·shin·gle
re·shoe
re·shoot
re·show
re·sight
re·sil·ver
re·site
re·size
re·slate
re·soak
re·so·cial·i·za·tion
re·so·cial·ize
re·sod
re·sol·der
re·sole
re·so·lid·i·fi·ca·tion
re·so·lid·i·fy
re·sow
re·spool
re·spot
re·spray
re·sprout
re·sta·bi·lize
re·stack
re·stage
re·stamp

re·stim·u·late
re·stim·u·la·tion
re·stock
re·stoke
re·strength·en
re·stress
re·study
re·stuff
re·style
re·sub·mis·sion
re·sub·mit
re·sum·mon
re·sup·ply
re·sur·vey
re·sus·pend
re·sus·pen·sion
re·syn·the·sis
re·syn·the·size
re·tack·le
re·tag
re·tar·get
re·taste
re·teach
re·team
re·test
re·tex·ture
re·the·o·ri·za·tion
re·the·o·rize
re·thread
re·tie
re·tight·en
re·tile
re·time

re·trace
re·trans·fer
re·trans·form
re·trans·for·ma·tion
re·trans·mis·sion
re·trans·mit
re·try
re·tune
re·type
re·uni·fi·ca·tion
re·uni·fy
re·up·hol·ster
re·uti·li·za·tion
re·uti·lize
re·vac·ci·nate
re·vac·ci·na·tion
re·val·i·date
re·val·i·da·tion
re·val·o·ri·za·tion
re·val·o·rize
re·vic·tim·ize
re·vict·ual
re·vi·su·al·i·za·tion
re·vote
re·warm
re·wash
re·weave
re·weigh
re·wet
re·wire
re·wrap
re·zone

're \(ə)r\ *vb* (1591) : ARE ⟨you*'re* right⟩
REA *abbr* Rural Electrification Administration
re·ab·sorb \,rē-əb-'sȯrb, -'zȯrb\ *vt* (ca. 1774) : to take up (something previously secreted or emitted) ⟨sugars ~*ed* in the kidney⟩; *also* : RE-SORB 2
'reach \'rēch\ *vb* [ME *rechen*, fr. OE *rǣcan*; akin to OHG *reichen* to reach, Lith *raižytis* to stretch oneself] *vt* (bef. 12c) **1 a** : to stretch out : EXTEND **b** : THRUST **2 a** : to touch or grasp by extending a part of the body (as a hand) or an object ⟨couldn't ~ the apple⟩ **b** : to pick up and draw toward one : TAKE **c** (1) : to extend to ⟨the shadow ~*ed* the wall⟩ (2) : to get up to or as far as : come to ⟨your letter ~*ed* me yesterday⟩ ⟨his voice ~*ed* the last rows⟩ ⟨they hoped to ~ an agreement⟩ **d** (1) : ENCOMPASS (2) : to make an impression on (3) : to communicate with : hand over : PASS ~ *vi* **1 a** : to make a stretch with or as if with one's hand **b** : to strain after something **2 a** : PROJECT, EXTEND ⟨his land ~*es* to the river⟩ **b** : to arrive at or come to something ⟨as far as the eye could ~⟩ **3** : to sail on a reach — **reach·able** \'rē-chə-bəl\ *adj* — **reach·er** *n*
'reach *n* (1536) **1** : a continuous stretch or expanse; *esp* : a straight portion of a stream or river **2 a** (1) : the action or an act of reaching (2) : an individual part of a progression or journey **b** (1) : a reachable distance ⟨within ~⟩ (2) : ability to reach ⟨had a long ~⟩ **c** : an extent or range esp. of knowledge or comprehension **3** : a bearing shaft or coupling pole; *esp* : the rod joining the hind axle to the forward bolster of a wagon **4** : the tack sailed by a ship with the wind coming just forward of the beam or with the wind directly abeam or abaft the beam **5** : ECHELON, LEVEL — usu. used in pl. ⟨the upper ~*es* of academia⟩
reach–me–down \'rēch-mē-,daun\ *adj or n* (1862) *chiefly Brit* : HAND=ME-DOWN
re·act \rē-'akt\ *vb* [NL *reactus*, pp. of *reagere*, fr. L *re-* + *agere* to act — more at AGENT] *vi* (1644) **1** : to exert a reciprocal or counteracting force or influence — often used with *on* or *upon* **2** : to change in response to a stimulus **3** : to act in opposition to a force or influence — usu. used with *against* **4** : to move or tend in a reverse direction **5** : to undergo chemical reaction ~ *vt* : to cause to react
re·ac·tance \rē-'ak-tən(t)s\ *n* (ca. 1893) : the part of the impedance of an alternating-current circuit that is due to capacitance or inductance or both and that is expressed in ohms
re·ac·tant \-tənt\ *n* (ca. 1920) : a substance that enters into and is altered in the course of a chemical reaction
re·ac·tion \rē-'ak-shən\ *n* (ca. 1611) **1 a** : the act or process or an instance of reacting **b** : resistance or opposition to a force, influence, or movement; *esp* : tendency toward a former and usu. outmoded political or social order or policy **2 a** : a response to some treatment, situation, or stimulus ⟨her stunned ~ to the news⟩; *also* : such a response expressed verbally ⟨critical ~ to the play⟩ **3** : bodily response to or activity aroused by a stimulus: **a** : an action induced by vital resistance to another action; *esp* : the response of tissues to a foreign substance (as an antigen or infective agent) **b** : depression or exhaustion due to excessive exertion or stimulation **c** : heightened activity and overaction succeeding depression or shock **d** : a mental or emotional disorder forming an individual's response to his or her life situation **4** : the force that a body subjected to the action of a force from another body exerts in the opposite direction **5 a** (1) : chemical transformation or change : the interaction of chemical entities (2) : the state resulting from such a reaction **b** : a process involving change in atomic nuclei
re·ac·tion·ary \rē-'ak-shə-,ner-ē\ *adj* (1840) : relating to, marked by, or favoring reaction; *esp* : ultraconservative in politics — **reactionary** *n* — **re·ac·tion·ary·ism** \-,i-zəm\ *n*
re·ac·tive \rē-'ak-tiv\ *adj* (1794) **1** : of, relating to, or marked by reaction or reactance **2** : readily responsive to a stimulus **3** : occurring as a result of stress or emotional upset ⟨~ depression⟩ — **re·ac·tive·ly** *adv* — **re·ac·tive·ness** *n* — **re·ac·tiv·i·ty** \(,)rē-,ak-'ti-və-tē\ *n*
re·ac·tor \rē-'ak-tər\ *n* (1890) **1** : one that reacts **2** : a device (as a coil, winding, or conductor of small resistance) used to introduce reactance into an alternating-current circuit **3 a** : a vat for an industrial chemical reaction **b** : a device for the controlled release of nuclear energy (as for producing heat)

'read \'rēd\ *vb* **read** \'red\; **read·ing** \'rē-diŋ\ [ME *reden* to advise, interpret, read, fr. OE *rǣdan*; akin to OHG *rātan* to advise, Skt *rādhnoti* he achieves, prepares] *vt* (bef. 12c) **1** : to receive or take in the sense of (as letters or symbols) esp. by sight or touch (2) : to study the movements of (as lips) with mental formulation of the communication expressed (3) : to utter aloud the printed or written words of ⟨~ them a story⟩ **b** : to learn from what one has seen or found in writing or printing **c** : to deliver aloud by or as if by reading; *specif* : to utter interpretively **d** (1) : to become acquainted with or look over the contents of (as a book) (2) : to make a study of ⟨~ law⟩ (3) : to read the works of **e** : to check (as copy or proof) for errors **f** (1) : to receive and understand (a voice message) by radio (2) : UNDERSTAND, COMPREHEND ⟨do I ~ you correctly⟩; *esp* : to interpret the meaning or significance of ⟨~ palms⟩ **b** : FORETELL, PREDICT ⟨able to ~ his fortune⟩ **3** : to recognize or interpret as if by reading: as **a** : to learn the nature of by observing outward expression or signs ⟨~*s* him like a book⟩ **b** : to note the action or characteristics of in order to anticipate what will happen ⟨a good canoeist ~*s* the rapids⟩ ⟨a golfer ~*ing* a green⟩; *also* : to predict the movement of (a putt) by reading a green **c** : to anticipate by observation of an opponent's position or movement ⟨~ a blitz⟩ **4 a** : to attribute a meaning to (as something read) : INTERPRET ⟨how do you ~ this passage⟩ **b** : to attribute (a meaning) to something read or considered ⟨~ a nonexistent meaning into her words⟩ **5** : to use as a substitute for or in preference to another word or phrase in a particular passage, text, or version ⟨~ *hurry* for *harry*⟩ — often used to introduce a clarifying substitute for a euphemistic or misleading word or phrase ⟨a friendly, ~ nosy, coworker⟩ **6** : INDICATE ⟨the thermometer ~*s* zero⟩ **7** : to interpret (a musical work) in performance **8 a** : to acquire (information) from storage; *esp* : to sense the meaning of (data) in recorded and coded form — used of a computer or data processor **b** : to read the coded information on (as a floppy disk) ~ *vi* **1 a** : to perform the act of reading words : read something **b** (1) : to learn something by reading (2) : to pursue a course of study **2 a** : to yield a particular meaning or impression when read **b** : to be readable or read in a particular manner or to a particular degree ⟨this book ~*s* smoothly⟩ **3** : to consist of specific words, phrases, or other similar elements ⟨a passage that ~*s* differently in older versions⟩ — **read between the lines** : to understand more than is directly stated — **read the riot act 1** : to order a mob to disperse **2 a** : to order or warn to cease something **b** : to protest vehemently **c** : to reprimand severely
²read *adj* (1586) : instructed by or informed through reading
³read \'rēd\ *n* (1825) **1** *chiefly Brit* : a period of reading ⟨it was a night ... for a ~ and a long sleep —William Sansom⟩ **2** : something (as a book) that is read ⟨a novel that's a good ~⟩ **3** : the action or an instance of reading
read·able \'rē-də-bəl\ *adj* (15c) : able to be read easily: as **a** : LEGIBLE **b** : interesting to read ⟨a highly ~ novel⟩ — **read·abil·i·ty** \,rē-də-'bi-lə-tē\ *n* — **read·able·ness** \'rē-də-bəl-nəs\ *n* — **read·ably** \-blē\ *adv*
read·er \'rē-dər\ *n* (bef. 12c) **1 a** : one that reads : one appointed to read to others: as (1) : LECTOR (2) : one chosen to read aloud selected material in a Christian Science church or society **b** : PROOF-READER (2) : one who evaluates manuscripts (3) : one who reads periodical literature to discover items of special interest or value **d** : an employee who reads and records the indications of meters **e** : a teacher's assistant who reads and marks student papers **2** *Brit* : one who reads lectures or expounds subjects to students **3 a** : a device for projecting a readable image of a transparency **b** : a unit that scans material recorded (as on punch cards) for storage or computation **4 a** : a book for instruction and practice esp. in reading **b** : ANTHOLOGY
read·er·ly \-lē\ *adj* (1959) : of, relating to, or typical of a reader
read·er·ship \-,ship\ *n* (1719) **1 a** : the office or position of a reader **b** : the quality or state of being a reader **2** : the mass or a particular group of readers ⟨a magazine's ~⟩
read·i·ly \'re-də-lē\ *adv* (14c) : in a ready manner: as **a** : without hesitating : WILLINGLY ⟨~ accepted advice⟩ **b** : without much difficulty : EASILY ⟨for reasons that anyone could ~ understand⟩
reading *n* (bef. 12c) **1** : the act of reading **2 a** : material read or for reading **b** : extent of material read **3 a** : a particular version **b** : data indicated by an instrument **4 a** : a particular interpretation of something (as a law) **b** : a particular performance of something (as a musical work) **5** : an indication of a certain state of affairs ⟨a study to get some ~ of shoppers' preferences⟩
reading desk *n* (1703) : LECTERN
reading frame *n* (1965) : a sequence of nucleotide triplets that is potentially translatable into a polypeptide and that is determined by the placement of a codon that initiates translation
read–only memory *n* (1961) : ROM
read·out \'rēd-,aut\ *n* (1652) **1** : the process of reading **2 a** : the process of removing information from an automatic device (as an electronic computer) and displaying it in an understandable form **b** : the information removed from such a device and displayed or recorded (as by magnetic tape or printing device) **c** : an electronic device that presents information in visual form **3** : the radio transmission of data or pictures from a space vehicle
read out *vt* (1600) **1 a** : to read aloud **b** : to produce a readout of **2** : to expel from an organization or group
'ready \'re-dē\ *adj* **read·i·er; -est** [ME *redy*; akin to OE *gerǣde* ready, Goth *garaiths* arranged] (13c) **1 a** : prepared mentally or physically for some experience or action **b** : prepared for immediate use ⟨dinner is ~⟩ **2 a** : willingly disposed : INCLINED ⟨~ to agree to his proposal⟩ **b** : likely to do something indicated ⟨a house that looks ~ to collapse⟩ **3** : displayed readily and spontaneously ⟨a ~ wit⟩ **4** : immediately available ⟨have ~ money⟩ *syn* see QUICK — **read·i·ness** *n* — **at the ready** : ready for immediate use ⟨kept guns *at the ready*⟩
²ready *vt* **read·ied; ready·ing** (14c) : to make ready
ready box *n* (1942) : a box placed near a gun (as on a ship) to hold ammunition kept ready for immediate use

\ə\ **abut** \ᵊ\ **kitten, F table** \ər\ **further** \a\ **ash** \ā\ **ace** \ä\ **mop, mar** \au̇\ **out** \ch\ **chin** \e\ **bet** \ē\ **easy** \g\ **go** \i\ **hit** \ī\ **ice** \j\ **job** \ŋ\ **sing** \ō\ **go** \ȯ\ **law** \ȯi\ **boy** \th\ **thin** \t̲h̲\ **the** \ü\ **loot** \u̇\ **foot** \y\ **yet** \zh\ **vision, beige** \k̲, ⁿ, œ, ⱷ, �ⁱ\ *see* Guide to Pronunciation

1**ready–made** \ˌre-dē-ˈmād\ *adj* (15c) **1 :** made beforehand esp. for general sale ⟨~ suits⟩ **2 :** lacking originality or individuality **3 :** readily available ⟨her illness provided a ~ excuse⟩
2**ready–made** *n* (1882) **1 :** something (as a garment) that is ready-made **2** *usu* **ready•made** [F *ready-made,* fr. E] **:** a commonplace artifact (as a comb or ice tongs) selected and shown as a work of art
ready room *n* (1941) **:** a room in which pilots or astronauts are briefed and await orders
ready–to–wear *adj* (1895) **1** *of clothing* **:** READY-MADE **2 :** dealing in ready-made clothes ⟨~ stores⟩ — **ready–to–wear** *n*
ready–wit•ted \ˌre-dē-ˈwi-təd\ *adj* (1581) **:** QUICK-WITTED
re•af•for•es•ta•tion \ˌrē-ə-ˌfȯr-ə-ˈstā-shən, -ˌfär-\ *n* (1884) *chiefly Brit* **:** REFORESTATION — **re•af•for•est** \-ˈfȯr-əst, -ˈfär-\ *vt, chiefly Brit*
re•agent \rē-ˈā-jənt\ *n* [NL *reagent-, reagens,* prp. of *reagere* to react — more at REACT] (1797) **:** a substance used (as in detecting or measuring a component, in preparing a product, or in developing photographs) because of its chemical or biological activity
re•ag•gre•gate \(ˌ)rē-ˈa-gri-ˌgāt\ *vt* (1862) **:** to cause to re-form into an aggregate or a whole — **re•ag•gre•gate** \-gət\ *n* — **re•ag•gre•ga•tion** \-ˌa-gri-ˈgā-shən\ *n*
re•agin \rē-ˈā-jən, -gən\ *n* [ISV, fr. *reagent*] (ca. 1911) **1 :** a substance in the blood of persons with syphilis responsible for positive serological reactions for syphilis **2 :** an antibody (as IgE in humans) that mediates hypersensitive allergic reactions of rapid onset — **re•agin•ic** \ˌrē-ə-ˈji-nik, -ˈgi-\ *adj*
1**re•al** \ˈrē(-ə)l\ *adj* [ME, real, relating to things (in law), fr. AF, fr. ML & LL; ML *realis* relating to things (in law), fr. LL, real, fr. L *res* thing, fact; akin to Skt *rayi* property] (14c) **1 :** of or relating to fixed, permanent, or immovable things (as lands or tenements) **2 a :** not artificial, fraudulent, or illusory **:** GENUINE ⟨~ gold⟩; *also* **:** being precisely what the name implies ⟨a ~ professional⟩ **b** (1) **:** occurring or existing in actuality ⟨saw a ~ live celebrity⟩ ⟨a story of ~ life⟩ (2) **:** of or relating to practical or everyday concerns or activities ⟨left school to live in the ~ world⟩ (3) **:** existing as a physical entity and having properties that deviate from an ideal, law, or standard ⟨a ~ gas⟩ — compare IDEAL 3b **c :** having objective independent existence ⟨unable to believe that what he saw was ~⟩ **d :** FUNDAMENTAL, ESSENTIAL **e** (1) **:** belonging to or having elements or components that belong to the set of real numbers ⟨the ~ roots of an equation⟩ ⟨a ~ matrix⟩ (2) **:** concerned with or containing real numbers ⟨~ analysis⟩ (3) **:** REAL-VALUED ⟨~ variable⟩ **f :** measured by purchasing power ⟨~ income⟩ ⟨~ dollars⟩ **g :** COMPLETE, UTTER ⟨a ~ fiasco⟩ **3** *of a particle* **:** capable of being detected — compare VIRTUAL 3 — **re•al•ness** *n* — **for real 1 :** in earnest **:** SERIOUSLY ⟨fighting *for real*⟩ **2 :** GENUINE ⟨couldn't believe the threats were *for real*⟩ **3 :** genuinely good or capable of success (as in competition) ⟨not yet sure if this team is *for real*⟩
2**real** *n* (ca. 1626) **:** a real thing; *esp* **:** a mathematically real quantity
3**real** *adv* (1718) **:** VERY ⟨he was ~ cool —H. M. McLuhan⟩
usage Most handbooks consider the adverb *real* to be informal and more suitable to speech than writing. Our evidence shows these observations to be true in the main, but *real* is becoming more common in writing of an informal, conversational style. It is used as an intensifier only and is not interchangeable with *really* except in that use.
4**re•al** \rā-ˈäl\ *n, pl* **reals** *or* **re•ales** \-ˈä-(ˌ)lās\ [Sp, fr. *real* royal, fr. L *regalis* — more at ROYAL] (1555) **:** a former monetary unit and coin of Spain and its possessions
5**re•al** \rā-ˈäl\ *n, pl* **reals** *or* **reis** \ˈrāsh, ˈrās, ˈrāzh, ˈrāz\ [Pg, fr. *real* royal, fr. L *regalis*] (1951) **1 :** a former monetary unit and coin of Portugal **2** — see MONEY table
real estate *n* (1666) **1 :** property in buildings and land **2 :** SPACE, CAPACITY ⟨desktop *real estate*⟩ ⟨the limited *real estate* on hard drives —Leonard Wiener⟩
real focus *n* (1909) **:** a point at which rays (as of light) converge or from which they diverge
re•al•gar \rē-ˈal-ˌgär, -gər\ *n* [ME, fr. ML, fr. Catal, fr. Ar *rahj al-ghār* powder of the mine] (15c) **:** an orange-red mineral consisting of arsenic sulfide and having a resinous luster
re•a•lia \rē-ˈa-lē-ə, -ˈā-\ *n pl* [LL, neut. pl. of *realis* real] (1937) **:** objects or activities used to relate classroom teaching to the real life esp. of peoples studied
re•align \ˌrē-ə-ˈlīn\ *vt* (1899) **:** to align again; *esp* **:** to reorganize or make new groupings of — **re•align•ment** \-mənt\ *n*
real image *n* (1882) **:** an optical image formed of real foci
re•al•i•sa•tion, re•al•ise *chiefly Brit var of* REALIZATION, REALIZE
re•al•ism \ˈrē-ə-ˌli-zəm\ *n* (1817) **1 :** concern for fact or reality and rejection of the impractical and visionary **2 a :** a doctrine that universals exist outside the mind; *specif* **:** the conception that an abstract term names an independent and unitary reality **b :** a theory that objects of sense perception or cognition exist independently of the mind — compare NOMINALISM **3 :** the theory or practice of fidelity in art and literature to nature or to real life and to accurate representation without idealization — **re•al•ist** \-list\ *adj or n* — **re•al•is•tic** \ˌrē-ə-ˈlis-tik\ *adj* — **re•al•is•ti•cal•ly** \-ti-k(ə-)lē\ *adv*
re•al•i•ty \rē-ˈa-lə-tē\ *n, pl* **-ties** (1550) **1 :** the quality or state of being real **2 a** (1) **:** a real event, entity, or state of affairs ⟨his dream became a ~⟩ (2) **:** the totality of real things and events ⟨trying to escape from ~⟩ **b :** something that is neither derivative nor dependent but exists necessarily **3 :** television programming that features videos of actual occurrences (as a police chase, stunt, or natural disaster) — often used attributively ⟨~ TV⟩ — **in reality :** in actual fact
reality check *n* (1960) **:** something that clarifies or serves as a reminder of reality often by correcting a misconception
re•al•i•za•tion \ˌrē-ə-lə-ˈzā-shən\ *n* (ca. 1611) **1 :** the action of realizing **:** the state of being realized **2 :** something realized
re•al•ize \ˈrē-ə-ˌlīz\ *vt* **-ized; -iz•ing** [F *réaliser,* fr. MF *realiser,* fr. *real* real] (ca. 1611) **1 a :** to bring into concrete existence **:** ACCOMPLISH ⟨finally *realized* her goal⟩ **b :** to cause to seem real **:** make appear real ⟨a book in which the characters are carefully *realized*⟩ **2 a :** to convert into actual money ⟨*realized* assets⟩ **b :** to bring or get by sale, investment, or effort **:** GAIN ⟨*realized* a large profit⟩ **3 :** to conceive vividly as real **:** be fully aware of ⟨did not ~ the risk she was taking⟩ ***syn*** see THINK — **re•al•iz•able** \ˌrē-ə-ˈlī-zə-bəl\ *adj* — **re•al•iz•er** *n*
real–life *adj* (1838) **:** existing or occurring in reality **:** drawn from or drawing on actual events or situations ⟨~ problems⟩ ⟨~ drama⟩
re•al•ly \ˈrē-(ə-)lē\ *adv* (15c) **1 a :** in reality **:** ACTUALLY ⟨things as they ~ are⟩ ⟨there was nothing peculiar about her doing this, ~ —Peter Taylor⟩ **b :** TRULY, UNQUESTIONABLY — used as an intensifier ⟨a ~ beautiful day⟩ **c :** VERY 2 ⟨look ~ close⟩ ⟨he runs ~ fast⟩ **2** — used to emphasize an assertion ⟨you ~ should read Yeats⟩ ⟨~, you're being ridiculous⟩
realm \ˈrelm\ *n* [ME *realme,* fr. AF, alter. of OF *reiame,* fr. L *regimen* control — more at REGIMEN] (13c) **1 :** KINGDOM 2 **2 :** SPHERE, DOMAIN ⟨within the ~ of possibility⟩ **3 :** a primary marine or terrestrial biogeographic division of the earth's surface
real number *n* (ca. 1909) **:** a number that has no imaginary part ⟨the set of all *real numbers* comprises the rationals and the irrationals⟩
real part *n* (1949) **:** the term in a complex number (as 2 in 2 + 3*i*) that does not contain the imaginary unit as a factor
re•al•po•li•tik \rā-ˈäl-ˌpō-li-ˌtēk\ *n, often cap* [G, fr. *real* actual + *Politik* politics] (1914) **:** politics based on practical and material factors rather than on theoretical or ethical objectives
real presence *n, often cap R&P* (1554) **:** the doctrine that Christ is actually present in the Eucharist
real time *n* (1953) **:** the actual time during which something takes place ⟨the computer may partly analyze the data in *real time* (as it comes in) —R. H. March⟩ ⟨chatted online in *real time*⟩ — **real–time** *adj*
Re•al•tor \ˈrē(-ə)l-tər, -ˌtȯr, ÷ˈrē-lə-tər *also* rē-ˈal-tər\ *collective mark* — used for a real estate agent who is a member of the National Association of Realtors
re•al•ty \ˈrē(-ə)l-tē\ *n* [*real* + *-ty* (as in *property*)] (1670) **:** REAL ESTATE 1
real–valued *adj* (1965) **:** taking on only real numbers for values
real–world *adj* (1963) **:** REAL-LIFE ⟨a ~ example⟩
1**ream** \ˈrēm\ *n* [ME *reme,* fr. AF, ultim. fr. Ar *rizma,* lit., bundle] (14c) **1 :** a quantity of paper being 20 quires or variously 480, 500, or 516 sheets **2 :** a great amount — usu. used in pl. ⟨~*s* of information⟩
2**ream** *vt* [perh. fr. ME **remen* to open up, fr. OE *rēman;* akin to OE *rȳman* to open up, *rūm* space — more at ROOM] (1815) **1 a :** to widen the opening of (a hole) **:** COUNTERSINK **b** (1) **:** to enlarge, shape, or smooth out (a hole) with a reamer (2) **:** to enlarge the bore of (as a gun) in this way **c :** to remove by reaming **2 a :** to press out with a reamer **b :** to press out the juice of (as an orange) with a reamer **3 :** CHEAT, VICTIMIZE **4 :** REPRIMAND — often used with *out* ⟨~*s* out his players so severely —Alexander Wolff⟩
ream•er \ˈrē-mər\ *n* (1825) **:** one that reams: as **a :** a rotating finishing tool with cutting edges used to enlarge or shape a hole **b :** a fruit juice extractor with a ridged and pointed center rising from a shallow dish

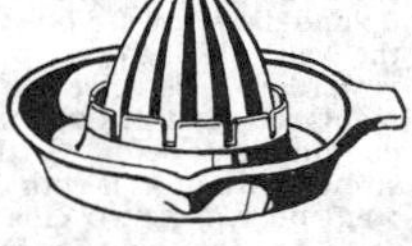
reamer b

reap \ˈrēp\ *vb* [ME *repen,* fr. OE *reopan*] *vt* (bef. 12c) **1 a** (1) **:** to cut with a sickle, scythe, or reaping machine (2) **:** to clear of a crop by reaping **b :** to gather by reaping **:** HARVEST **2 :** OBTAIN, WIN ~ *vi* **:** to reap something
reap•er \ˈrē-pər\ *n* (bef. 12c) **:** one that reaps; *esp* **:** any of various machines for reaping grain
reap•hook \ˈrēp-ˌhu̇k\ *n* (ca. 1591) **:** a hand implement with a hook-shaped blade used in reaping
re•ap•por•tion \ˌrē-ə-ˈpȯr-shən\ *vt* (ca. 1828) **:** to apportion (as a house of representatives) anew ~ *vi* **:** to make a new apportionment — **re•ap•por•tion•ment** \-shən-mənt\ *n*
1**rear** \ˈrir, *vt4 & vi2 are also* ˈrer\ *vb* [ME *reren,* fr. OE *rǣran;* akin to ON *reisa* to raise, OE *rīsan* to rise] *vt* (bef. 12c) **1 :** to erect by building **:** CONSTRUCT **2 :** to raise upright **3 a** (1) **:** to breed and raise (an animal) for use or market (2) **:** to bring to maturity or self-sufficiency usu. through nurturing care ⟨~*ed* five children⟩ ⟨birds ~*ing* their young⟩ **b :** to cause (as plants) to grow **4 :** to cause (a horse) to rise up on the hind legs ~ *vi* **1 :** to rise high **2** *of a horse* **:** to rise up on the hind legs ***syn*** see LIFT — **rear•er** *n*
2**rear** \ˈrir\ *n* [ME *rere,* short for *rerewarde* rearward] (14c) **1 :** the back part of something: as **a :** the unit (as of an army) or area farthest from the enemy **b :** the part of something located opposite its front ⟨the ~ of a house⟩ **c :** BUTTOCKS **2 :** the space or position at the back ⟨moved to the ~⟩
3**rear** \ˈrir\ *adj* [ME *rere-,* fr. AF *rere* backward, behind, fr. L *retro-* — more at RETRO] (14c) **:** being at the back ⟨the ~ entrance⟩
4**rear** \ˈrir\ *adv* (1855) **:** toward or from the rear — usu. used in combination ⟨a *rear*-driven car⟩
rear admiral *n* (1589) **:** a commissioned officer in the navy or coast guard having either of two ranks: **a :** one who ranks above a captain — called also *rear admiral (lower half)* **b :** one who ranks above a rear admiral (lower half) and below a vice admiral — called also *rear admiral (upper half)*
rear echelon *n* (ca. 1934) **:** an element of a military headquarters or unit located at a considerable distance from the front and concerned esp. with administrative and supply duties
rear–end \ˈrir-ˈend, -ˌend\ *vt* (1957) **:** to crash into the back of (as an automobile)
rear end *n* (ca. 1930) **:** BUTTOCKS
rear•guard \ˈrir-ˌgärd\ *adj* (1898) **:** of or relating to resistance esp. to sweeping social forces ⟨fought a ~ action against automation⟩
rear guard \-ˈgärd, -ˌgärd\ *n* [MF *reregarde,* fr. OF, fr. *rere* + *garde* guard] (1659) **:** a military detachment detailed to bring up and protect the rear of a main body or force
re•arm \(ˌ)rē-ˈärm\ *vt* (1750) **:** to arm (as a nation or a military force) again with new or better weapons ~ *vi* **:** to become armed again — **re•ar•ma•ment** \-ˈär-mə-mənt\ *n*
rear•most \ˈrir-ˌmōst\ *adj* (1718) **:** farthest in the rear **:** LAST
rear•view mirror \ˈrir-ˌvyü-\ *n* (1926) **:** a mirror (as in an automobile) that gives a view of the area behind a vehicle
1**rear•ward** \ˈrir-ˌwȯrd\ *n* [ME *rerewarde,* fr. AF *rereguard, rerewarde* rear guard] (14c) **:** REAR; *esp* **:** the rear division (as of an army)
2**rear•ward** \-wərd\ *adj* [4*rear* + *-ward*] (1598) **1 :** located at, near, or toward the rear **2 :** directed toward the rear ⟨a ~ glance⟩
3**rear•ward** \-wərd\ *also* **rear•wards** \-wərdz\ *adv* (1625) **:** at, near, or toward the rear **:** BACKWARD ⟨looking ~⟩

reas *abbr* reasonable
[1]**rea·son** \ˈrē-zᵊn\ *n* [ME *resoun,* fr. AF *raisun,* fr. L *ration-, ratio* reason, computation, fr. *reri* to calculate, think; prob. akin to Goth *rathjo* account, explanation] (13c) **1 a :** a statement offered in explanation or justification ⟨gave ~*s* that were quite satisfactory⟩ **b :** a rational ground or motive ⟨a good ~ to act soon⟩ **c :** a sufficient ground of explanation or of logical defense; *esp* **:** something (as a principle or law) that supports a conclusion or explains a fact ⟨the ~*s* behind her client's action⟩ **d :** the thing that makes some fact intelligible **:** CAUSE ⟨the ~ for earthquakes⟩ ⟨the real ~ why he wanted me to stay —Graham Greene⟩ **2 a** (1) **:** the power of comprehending, inferring, or thinking esp. in orderly rational ways **:** INTELLIGENCE (2) **:** proper exercise of the mind (3) **:** SANITY **b :** the sum of the intellectual powers **3** *archaic* **:** treatment that affords satisfaction — **in reason :** RIGHTLY, JUSTIFIABLY — **within reason :** within reasonable limits — **with reason :** with good cause
[2]**reason** *vb* **rea·soned; rea·son·ing** \ˈrēz-niŋ, ˈrē-zᵊn-iŋ\ *vi* (15c) **1 a** *obs* **:** to take part in conversation, discussion, or argument **b :** to talk with another so as to influence actions or opinions ⟨can't ~ with them⟩ **2 :** to use the faculty of reason so as to arrive at conclusions ~ *vt* **1** *archaic* **:** to justify or support with reasons **2 :** to persuade or influence by the use of reason **3 :** to discover, formulate, or conclude by the use of reason ⟨a carefully ~*ed* analysis⟩ ***syn*** see THINK — **rea·son·er** \ˈrēz-nər, ˈrē-zᵊn-ər\ *n*
rea·son·able \ˈrēz-nə-bəl, ˈrē-zᵊn-ə-bəl\ *adj* (14c) **1 a :** being in accordance with reason ⟨a ~ theory⟩ **b :** not extreme or excessive ⟨~ requests⟩ **c :** MODERATE, FAIR ⟨a ~ chance⟩ ⟨a ~ price⟩ **d :** INEXPENSIVE **2 a :** having the faculty of reason **b :** possessing sound judgment ⟨a ~ man⟩ — **rea·son·abil·i·ty** \ˌrēz-nə-ˈbi-lə-tē, ˌrē-zᵊn-ə-\ *n* — **rea·son·able·ness** \ˈrēz-nə-bəl-nəs, ˈrē-zᵊn-ə-\ *n* — **rea·son·ably** \-blē\ *adv*
reasoning *n* (14c) **1 :** the use of reason; *esp* **:** the drawing of inferences or conclusions through the use of reason **2 :** an instance of the use of reason **:** ARGUMENT
rea·son·less \ˈrē-zᵊn-ləs\ *adj* (14c) **1 :** not having the faculty of reason ⟨a ~ brute⟩ **2 :** not reasoned **:** SENSELESS ⟨~ hostility⟩ **3 :** not based on or supported by reasons ⟨a ~ accusation⟩ — **rea·son·less·ly** *adv*
re·as·sur·ance \ˌrē-ə-ˈshu̇r-ən(t)s\ *n* (ca. 1611) **1 :** the action of reassuring **:** the state of being reassured **2 :** REINSURANCE
re·as·sure \ˌrē-ə-ˈshu̇r\ *vt* (1594) **1 :** to assure anew ⟨*reassured* him that the work was on schedule⟩ **2 :** to restore to confidence ⟨felt *reassured* by their earnest promise to do better⟩ **3 :** REINSURE — **re·as·sur·ing·ly** \-ˈshu̇r-iŋ-lē\ *adv*
re·ata \rē-ˈa-tə, -ˈä-\ *n* [AmerSp — more at LARIAT] (1846) **:** LARIAT
Re·au·mur \ˌrā-ō-ˈmyu̇r, ˈrā-ō-ˌ\ *adj* [René Antoine Ferchault de *Réaumur*] (1799) **:** relating to or conforming to a thermometric scale on which the boiling point of water is at 80° above the zero of the scale and the freezing point is at zero
reave \ˈrēv\ *vb* **reaved** *or* **reft** \ˈreft\; **reav·ing** [ME *reven,* fr. OE *rēafian;* akin to OHG *roubōn* to rob, L *rumpere* to break] *vi* (bef. 12c) **:** PLUNDER, ROB ~ *vt* **1** *archaic* **a** (1) **:** ROB, DESPOIL (2) **:** to deprive one of **b :** SEIZE **2** *archaic* **:** to carry or tear away — **reav·er** *n*
reb \ˈreb\ *n* [short for *rebel*] (1862) **:** JOHNNY REB
Reb \ˈreb\ *n* [Yiddish, fr. Heb *rabbī* my master, rabbi] (1858) **:** RABBI, MISTER — used as a title
re·bar \ˈrē-ˌbär\ *n, pl* **rebar** *or* **rebars** [*re*inforcing *bar*] (1953) **:** a steel rod with ridges for use in reinforced concrete
re·bar·ba·tive \ri-ˈbär-bə-tiv\ *adj* [F *rébarbatif,* fr. MF, fr. *rebarber* to be repellent, fr. *re-* + *barbe* beard, fr. L *barba* — more at BEARD] (1892) **:** REPELLENT, IRRITATING — **re·bar·ba·tive·ly** *adv*
[1]**re·bate** \ˈrē-ˌbāt, ri-ˈ\ *vb* **re·bat·ed; re·bat·ing** [ME, fr. AF *rebatre, rabatre* to beat back, deduct, fr. *re-* + *abatre* to strike down, fr. *a-* (fr. L *ad-*) + *batre* to beat, fr. L *battuere*] *vt* (14c) **1 :** to reduce the force or activity of **:** DIMINISH **2 :** to reduce the sharpness of **:** BLUNT **3 a :** to make a rebate of **b :** to give a rebate to ~ *vi* **:** to give rebates — **re·bat·er** *n*
[2]**re·bate** \ˈrē-ˌbāt\ *n* (1656) **:** a return of a part of a payment
[3]**re·bate** \ˈra-bət, ˈrē-ˌbāt\ *chiefly Brit var of* RABBET
re·ba·to \ri-ˈbä-(ˌ)tō\ *n* [modif. of MF *rabat,* lit., act of folding over — more at RABBET] (1591) **:** a wide lace-edged collar of the early 17th century often stiffened to stand high at the back
reb·be \ˈre-bə\ *n* [Yiddish *rebe,* fr. Heb *rabbī* rabbi] (1881) **:** a Jewish spiritual leader or teacher **:** RABBI
re·bec *or* **re·beck** \ˈrē-ˌbek, ˈre-(ˌ)bek\ *n* [ME *rebecke,* fr. MF *rebec,* alter. of OF *rebebe,* fr. Old Occitan *rebeb,* fr. Ar *rabāb*] (15c) **:** an ancient bowed usu. 3-stringed musical instrument with a pear-shaped body and slender neck
Re·bek·ah \ri-ˈbe-kə\ *n* [Heb *Ribhqāh*] (bef. 12c) **:** the wife of Isaac
[1]**reb·el** \ˈre-bəl\ *adj* [ME, fr. AF, fr. L *rebellis,* fr. *re-* + *bellum* war, fr. OL *duellum*] (14c) **1 a :** opposing or taking arms against a government or ruler **b :** of or relating to rebels ⟨the ~ camp⟩ **2 :** DISOBEDIENT, REBELLIOUS
[2]**rebel** *n* (14c) **:** one who rebels or participates in a rebellion
[3]**re·bel** \ri-ˈbel\ *vi* **re·belled; re·bel·ling** (14c) **1 a :** to oppose or disobey one in authority or control **b :** to renounce and resist by force the authority of one's government **2 a :** to act in or show opposition or disobedience ⟨*rebelled* against the conventions of polite society⟩ **b :** to feel or exhibit anger or revulsion ⟨*rebelled* at the injustice of life⟩
re·bel·lion \ri-ˈbel-yən\ *n* (14c) **1 :** opposition to one in authority or dominance **2 a :** open, armed, and usu. unsuccessful defiance of or resistance to an established government **b :** an instance of such defiance or resistance

syn REBELLION, REVOLUTION, UPRISING, REVOLT, INSURRECTION, MUTINY mean an outbreak against authority. REBELLION implies an open formidable resistance that is often unsuccessful ⟨open *rebellion* against the officers⟩. REVOLUTION applies to a successful rebellion resulting in a major change (as in government) ⟨a political *revolution* that toppled the monarchy⟩. UPRISING implies a brief, limited, and often immediately ineffective rebellion ⟨quickly put down the *uprising*⟩. REVOLT and INSURRECTION imply an armed uprising that quickly fails or succeeds ⟨a *revolt* by the Young Turks that surprised party leaders⟩ ⟨an *insurrection* of oppressed laborers⟩. MUTINY applies to group insubordination or insurrection esp. against naval authority ⟨a *mutiny* led by the ship's cook⟩.

re·bel·lious \-yəs\ *adj* (15c) **1 a :** given to or engaged in rebellion ⟨~ troops⟩ **b :** of, relating to, or characteristic of a rebel or rebellion ⟨a ~ speech⟩ **2 :** resisting treatment or management **:** REFRACTORY — **re·bel·lious·ly** *adv* — **re·bel·lious·ness** *n*
rebel yell *n* (1862) **:** a prolonged high-pitched yell often uttered by Confederate soldiers in the American Civil War
re·birth \(ˌ)rē-ˈbərth, ˈrē-ˌ\ *n* (1837) **1 a :** a new or second birth **:** METEMPSYCHOSIS **b :** spiritual regeneration **2 :** RENAISSANCE, REVIVAL ⟨a ~ of nationalism⟩
Re·blo·chon \rə-blȯ-ˈshōⁿ\ *n* [F *reblochon,* fr. F dial. (Savoy)] (1908) **:** a semisoft creamy mild-flavored French cheese
reb·o·ant \ˈre-bə-wənt\ *adj* [L *reboant-, reboans,* prp. of *reboare* to resound, fr. *re-* + *boare* to cry aloud, roar, fr. Gk *boan,* of imit. origin] (1830) **:** marked by reverberation
re·born \(ˌ)rē-ˈbȯrn\ *adj* (1598) **:** born again **:** REGENERATED, REVIVED
[1]**re·bound** \ˈrē-ˌbau̇nd, ri-ˈ\ *vb* [ME, fr. AF *rebundir,* fr. *re-* + OF *bondir* to bound — more at BOUND] *vi* (14c) **1 a :** to spring back on or as if on collision or impact with another body **b :** to recover from setback or frustration **2 :** REECHO **3 :** to gain possession of a rebound in basketball ~ *vt* **:** to cause to rebound — **re·bound·er** \ˈrē-ˌbau̇n-dər, ri-ˈ\ *n*
[2]**re·bound** \ˈrē-ˌbau̇nd, ri-ˈ\ *n* (1530) **1 a :** the action of rebounding **:** RECOIL **b :** an upward leap or movement **:** RECOVERY ⟨a sharp ~ in prices⟩ **2 a :** a basketball or hockey puck that rebounds **b :** the act or an instance of gaining possession of a basketball rebound ⟨leads the league in ~*s*⟩ **3 :** a reaction to setback, frustration, or crisis ⟨on the ~ from an unhappy love affair⟩
re·bo·zo \ri-ˈbō-(ˌ)zō, -(ˌ)sō\ *n, pl* **-zos** [Sp, shawl, fr. *rebozar* to muffle, alter. of *embozar* to muffle, prob. fr. VL **imbucciare,* fr. L *in-* + *bucca* cheek] (1807) **:** a long scarf worn chiefly by Mexican women
re·branch \(ˌ)rē-ˈbranch\ *vi* (1888) **:** to form secondary branches
re·broad·cast \(ˌ)rē-ˈbrȯd-ˌkast\ *vt* **-cast; -cast·ing** (1923) **1 :** to broadcast again (a radio or television program being simultaneously received from another source) **2 :** to repeat (a broadcast) at a later time — **rebroadcast** *n*
re·buff \ri-ˈbəf\ *vt* [MF *rebuffer,* fr. OIt *ribuffare* to reprimand, fr. *ribuffo* reprimand] (ca. 1586) **:** to reject or criticize sharply **:** SNUB — **rebuff** *n*
re·build \(ˌ)rē-ˈbild\ *vb* **-built** \-ˈbilt\; **-build·ing** *vt* (1537) **1 a :** to make extensive repairs to **:** RECONSTRUCT ⟨~ a war-torn city⟩ **b :** to restore to a previous state ⟨~ inventories⟩ **2 :** to make extensive changes in **:** REMODEL ⟨~ society⟩ ~ *vi* **:** to build again ⟨planned to ~ after the fire⟩ ***syn*** see MEND
[1]**re·buke** \ri-ˈbyük\ *vt* **re·buked; re·buk·ing** [ME, fr. AF *rebucher, rebouker* to blunt, check, reprimand] (14c) **1 a :** to criticize sharply **:** REPRIMAND **b :** to serve as a rebuke to **2 :** to turn back or keep down **:** CHECK ***syn*** see REPROVE — **re·buk·er** *n*
[2]**rebuke** *n* (15c) **:** an expression of strong disapproval **:** REPRIMAND
re·bus \ˈrē-bəs\ *n* [L, by things, abl. pl. of *res* thing — more at REAL] (1605) **:** a representation of words or syllables by pictures of objects or by symbols whose names resemble the intended words or syllables in sound; *also* **:** a riddle made up of such pictures or symbols
re·but \ri-ˈbət\ *vb* **re·but·ted; re·but·ting** [ME, fr. AF *reboter,* fr. *re-* + *boter* to butt — more at BUTT] *vt* (14c) **1 :** to drive or beat back **:** REPEL **2 a :** to contradict or oppose by formal legal argument, plea, or countervailing proof **b :** to expose the falsity of **:** REFUTE ~ *vi* **:** to make or furnish an answer or counter proof — **re·but·ta·ble** \-ˈbə-tə-bəl\ *adj*
re·but·tal \ri-ˈbə-tᵊl\ *n* (1830) **:** the act of rebutting esp. in a legal suit; *also* **:** argument or proof that rebuts
[1]**re·but·ter** \-ˈbə-tər\ *n* [AF *rebuter, reboter,* fr. *reboter,* v.] (1540) **:** the answer of a defendant in matter of fact to a plaintiff's surrejoinder
[2]**rebutter** *n* (1794) **:** one that rebuts
rec *abbr* **1** received **2** receipt **3** record; recording **4** recreation; recreational
re·cal·ci·trance \ri-ˈkal-sə-trən(t)s\ *n* (1856) **:** the state of being recalcitrant
re·cal·ci·tran·cy \-trən(t)-sē\ *n* (1869) **:** RECALCITRANCE
re·cal·ci·trant \-trənt\ *adj* [LL *recalcitrant-, recalcitrans,* prp. of *recalcitrare* to be stubbornly disobedient, fr. L, to kick back, fr. *re-* + *calcitrare* to kick, fr. *calc-, calx* heel] (1843) **1 :** obstinately defiant of authority or restraint **2 a :** difficult to manage or operate **b :** not responsive to treatment **c :** RESISTANT ⟨this subject is ~ both to observation and to experiment —G. G. Simpson⟩ ***syn*** see UNRULY — **recalcitrant** *n*
[1]**re·call** \ri-ˈkȯl\ *vt* (15c) **1 :** CANCEL, REVOKE **2 a :** to call back ⟨was ~*ed* to active duty⟩ ⟨a pitcher ~*ed* from the minors⟩ **b :** to bring back to mind ⟨~*ed* seeing her somewhere before⟩ **c :** to remind one of **:** RESEMBLE ⟨a playwright who ~*s* the Elizabethan dramatists⟩ **3 :** RESTORE, REVIVE ***syn*** see REMEMBER — **re·call·abil·i·ty** \-ˌkȯ-lə-ˈbi-lə-tē\ *n* — **re·call·able** \-ˈkȯ-lə-bəl\ *adj* — **re·call·er** *n*
[2]**re·call** \ri-ˈkȯl, ˈrē-ˌ\ *n* (1611) **1 :** a call to return ⟨a ~ of workers after a layoff⟩ **2 :** the right or procedure by which an official may be removed by vote of the people **3 :** remembrance of what has been learned or experienced **4 :** the act of revoking **5 :** a public call by a manufacturer for the return of a product that may be defective or contaminated
re·ca·mier \ˌrā-käm-ˈyā\ *n* [fr. its appearance in a portrait of Mme. Récamier by Jacques-Louis David] (1924) **:** a sometimes backless couch with a high curved headrest and low footrest

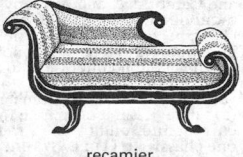

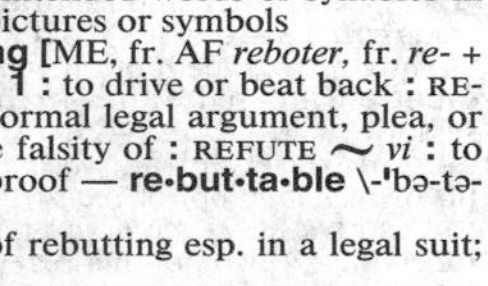
recamier

re·can·a·li·za·tion \(ˌ)rē-ˌka-nə-lə-ˈzā-shən\ *n* (1953) **:** the process of restoring flow to or reuniting an interrupted channel of a bodily tube (as a blood vessel or vas deferens) — **re·can·a·lize** \-kə-ˈna-ˌlīz, -ˈka-nə-ˌlīz\ *vt*

re·cant \ri-ˈkant\ *vb* [L *recantare,* fr. *re-* + *cantare* to sing — more at CHANT] *vt* (1535) **1 :** to withdraw or repudiate (a statement or belief) formally and publicly **:** RENOUNCE **2 :** REVOKE ~ *vi* **:** to make an open confession of error ***syn*** see ABJURE — **re·can·ta·tion** \ˌrē-ˌkan-ˈtā-shən\ *n*

[1]**re·cap** \ˈrē-ˌkap\ *n* [by shortening] (ca. 1926) **:** RECAPITULATION

[2]**re·cap** \ˈrē-ˌkap, ri-ˈ\ *vb* **re·capped; re·cap·ping** (1945) **:** RECAPITULATE

[3]**re·cap** \ˈrē-ˌkap\ *n* [[4]*recap*] (1940) **:** RETREAD 1

[4]**re·cap** \(ˌ)rē-ˈkap\ *vt* **re·capped; re·cap·ping** [*re-* + [1]*cap*] (1941) **:** RETREAD — **re·cap·pa·ble** \-ˈka-pə-bəl\ *adj*

re·cap·i·tal·i·za·tion \(ˌ)rē-ˌka-pə-tə-lə-ˈzā-shən, -ˌkap-tə-\ *n* (1920) **:** a revision of the capital structure of a corporation

re·cap·i·tal·ize \(ˌ)rē-ˈka-pə-tə-ˌlīz, -ˈkap-tə-\ *vt* (1904) **:** to change the capital structure of

re·ca·pit·u·late \ˌrē-kə-ˈpi-chə-ˌlāt\ *vb* **-lat·ed; -lat·ing** [LL *recapitulatus,* pp. of *recapitulare* to restate by heads, sum up, fr. L *re-* + *capitulum* division of a book — more at CHAPTER] *vt* (1556) **1 a :** to restate briefly **:** SUMMARIZE **b :** to give new form or expression to **2 :** to repeat the principal stages or phases of ⟨the view that ontogeny ~*s* phylogeny⟩ ~ *vi* **:** SUM UP

re·ca·pit·u·la·tion \-ˌpi-chə-ˈlā-shən\ *n* (14c) **1 :** a concise summary **2 :** the hypothetical occurrence in an individual organism's development of successive stages resembling the series of ancestral types from which it has descended so that the ontogeny of the individual retraces the phylogeny of its group **3 :** the third section of a sonata form

[1]**re·cap·ture** \(ˌ)rē-ˈkap-chər\ *n* (1752) **1 a :** the act of retaking **b :** an instance of being retaken **2 :** the retaking of a prize or goods under international law **3 :** a government seizure under law of earnings or profits beyond a fixed amount

[2]**recapture** *vt* (1799) **1 a :** to capture again **b :** to experience again ⟨by no effort of the imagination could she ~ the ecstasy —Ellen Glasgow⟩ **2 :** to take (as a portion of earnings or profits above a fixed amount) by law or through negotiations under law

re·cast \(ˌ)rē-ˈkast\ *vt* **-cast; -cast·ing** (1603) **:** to cast again ⟨~ a gun⟩ ⟨~ a play⟩; *also* **:** REMODEL, REFASHION ⟨~*s* his political image to fit the times⟩ — **re·cast** \ˈrē-ˌkast, (ˌ)rē-ˈ\ *n*

rec·ce \ˈre-kē\ *n, often attrib* [by shortening & alter.] (1941) **:** RECONNAISSANCE

rec'd *abbr* received

[1]**re·cede** \ri-ˈsēd\ *vi* **re·ced·ed; re·ced·ing** [ME, fr. L *recedere* to go back, fr. *re-* + *cedere* to go] (15c) **1 a :** to move back or away **:** WITHDRAW ⟨a *receding* hairline⟩ **b :** to slant backward **2 :** to grow less or smaller **:** DIMINISH, DECREASE ⟨a *receding* deficit⟩

syn RECEDE, RETREAT, RETRACT, BACK mean to move backward. RECEDE implies a gradual withdrawing from a forward or high fixed point in time or space ⟨the flood waters gradually *receded*⟩. RETREAT implies withdrawal from a point or position reached ⟨*retreating* soldiers⟩. RETRACT implies drawing back from an extended position ⟨a cat *retracting* its claws⟩. BACK is used with *up, down, out,* or *off* to refer to any retrograde motion ⟨*backed* off on the throttle⟩.

[2]**re·cede** \(ˌ)rē-ˈsēd\ *vt* [*re-* + *cede*] (1771) **:** to cede back to a former possessor

[1]**re·ceipt** \ri-ˈsēt\ *n* [ME *receite,* fr. AF, fr. ML *recepta,* prob. fr. L, neut. pl. of *receptus,* pp. of *recipere* to receive] (14c) **1 :** RECIPE **2 a** *obs* **:** RECEPTACLE **b** *archaic* **:** a revenue office **3 :** the act or process of receiving **4 :** something received — usu. used in pl. **5 :** a writing acknowledging the receiving of goods or money

[2]**receipt** *vt* (1787) **1 :** to give a receipt for or acknowledge the receipt of **2 :** to mark as paid

re·ceiv·able \ri-ˈsē-və-bəl\ *adj* (14c) **1 :** capable of being received **2 :** subject to call for payment ⟨notes ~⟩

re·ceiv·ables \-bəlz\ *n pl* (1863) **:** amounts of money receivable

re·ceive \ri-ˈsēv\ *vb* **re·ceived; re·ceiv·ing** [ME, fr. AF *receivre,* fr. L *recipere,* fr. *re-* + *capere* to take — more at HEAVE] *vt* (14c) **1 :** to come into possession of **:** ACQUIRE ⟨~ a gift⟩ **2 a :** to act as a receptacle or container for ⟨the cistern ~*s* water from the roof⟩ **b :** to assimilate through the mind or senses ⟨~ new ideas⟩ **3 a :** to permit to enter **:** ADMIT **b :** WELCOME, GREET **c :** to react to in a specified manner **4 :** to accept as authoritative, true, or accurate **:** BELIEVE **5 a :** to support the weight or pressure of **:** BEAR **b :** to take (a mark or impression) from the weight of something ⟨some clay ~*s* clear impressions⟩ **c :** ACQUIRE, EXPERIENCE ⟨*received* his early schooling at home⟩ **d :** to suffer the hurt or injury of ⟨*received* a broken nose⟩ ~ *vi* **1 :** to be a recipient **2 :** to be at home to visitors ⟨~*s* on Tuesdays⟩ **3 :** to convert incoming radio waves into perceptible signals **4 :** to prepare to take possession of the ball from a kick in football

received *adj* (15c) **:** generally accepted **:** COMMON ⟨a healthy skepticism about ~ explanations —B. K. Lewalski⟩

Received Pronunciation *n* (1869) **:** the pronunciation of Received Standard

Received Standard *n* (1913) **:** a traditionally prestigious form of English spoken at the English public schools, at the universities of Oxford and Cambridge, and by many educated British people elsewhere

re·ceiv·er \ri-ˈsē-vər\ *n* (14c) **:** one that receives: as **a :** TREASURER **b** (1) **:** a person appointed to hold in trust and administer property under litigation (2) **:** a person appointed to settle the affairs of a business involving a public interest or to manage a corporation during reorganization **c :** one that receives stolen goods **:** FENCE **d :** a device for converting signals (as electromagnetic waves) into audio or visual form: as (1) **:** a device in a telephone for converting electric impulses or varying current into sound (2) **:** a radio receiver with a tuner and amplifier on one chassis **e** (1) **:** CATCHER (2) **:** a member of the offensive team in football eligible to catch a forward pass

receiver general *n, pl* **receivers general** (15c) **:** a public officer in charge of the treasury (as of Massachusetts)

re·ceiv·er·ship \ri-ˈsē-vər-ˌship\ *n* (15c) **1 :** the office or function of a receiver **2 :** the state of being in the hands of a receiver

receiving blanket *n* (1926) **:** a small lightweight blanket used to wrap an infant (as after bathing)

receiving end *n* (1937) **:** the position of being a recipient or esp. a victim — usu. used in the phrase *on the receiving end*

receiving line *n* (1933) **:** a group of people who stand in a line and individually welcome guests (as at a wedding reception)

re·cen·cy \ˈrē-sᵊn(t)-sē\ *n* (1612) **:** the quality or state of being recent

re·cen·sion \ri-ˈsen(t)-shən\ *n* [L *recension-, recensio* enumeration, fr. *recensēre* to review, fr. *re-* + *censēre* to assess, tax — more at CENSOR] (ca. 1828) **1 :** a critical revision of a text **2 :** a text established by critical revision

re·cent \ˈrē-sᵊnt\ *adj* [ME, fr. L *recent-, recens;* perh. akin to Gk *kainos* new] (15c) **1 a :** having lately come into existence **:** NEW, FRESH **b :** of or relating to a time not long past **2** *cap* **:** HOLOCENE — **re·cent·ness** *n*

re·cent·ly *adv* (1533) **:** during a recent period of time **:** LATELY

re·cep·ta·cle \ri-ˈsep-ti-kəl\ *n* [ME, fr. AF, fr. L *receptaculum,* fr. *receptare* to receive, freq. of *recipere* to receive] (15c) **1 :** one that receives and contains something **:** CONTAINER **2** [NL *receptaculum,* fr. L] **a :** the end of the flower stalk upon which the floral organs are borne **b :** a structure or tissue (as of a fungus or fern) bearing spores or sporangia **3 :** a mounted female electrical fitting that contains the live parts of the circuit

re·cep·tion \ri-ˈsep-shən\ *n* [ME *recepcion,* fr. AF or L; AF *reception,* fr. L *reception-, receptio,* fr. *recipere*] (15c) **1 :** the act or action or an instance of receiving: as **a :** RECEIPT ⟨the ~ and distribution of funds⟩ **b :** ADMISSION ⟨~ into the church⟩ **c :** RESPONSE, REACTION ⟨the play met with a mixed ~⟩ **d :** the receiving of a radio or television broadcast **e :** the catching of a forward pass by a receiver **2 :** a social gathering often for the purpose of extending a formal welcome

re·cep·tion·ist \-sh(ə-)nist\ *n* (1901) **:** a person employed to greet telephone callers, visitors, patients, or clients

re·cep·tive \ri-ˈsep-tiv\ *adj* (15c) **1 :** able or inclined to receive; *esp* **:** open and responsive to ideas, impressions, or suggestions **2 a** *of a sensory end organ* **:** fit to receive and transmit stimuli **b :** SENSORY **3** *of a female animal* **:** willing to copulate with a male ⟨a ~ mare⟩ — **re·cep·tive·ly** *adv* — **re·cep·tive·ness** *n* — **re·cep·tiv·i·ty** \ˌrē-ˌsep-ˈti-və-tē, ri-\ *n*

re·cep·tor \ri-ˈsep-tər\ *n* (1898) **:** RECEIVER: as **a :** a cell or group of cells that receives stimuli **:** SENSE ORGAN **b :** a chemical group or molecule (as a protein) on the cell surface or in the cell interior that has an affinity for a specific chemical group, molecule, or virus

[1]**re·cess** \ˈrē-ˌses, ri-ˈ\ *n* [L *recessus,* fr. *recedere* to recede] (1531) **1 :** the action of receding **:** RECESSION **2 :** a hidden, secret, or secluded place or part **3 a :** INDENTATION, CLEFT ⟨a deep ~ in the hill⟩ **b :** ALCOVE ⟨a ~ lined with books⟩ **4 :** a suspension of business or procedure often for rest or relaxation ⟨children playing at ~⟩

[2]**recess** *vt* (1809) **1 :** to put into a recess ⟨~*ed* lighting⟩ **2 :** to make a recess in **3 :** to interrupt for a recess ~ *vi* **:** to take a recess

[1]**re·ces·sion** \ri-ˈse-shən\ *n* (ca. 1652) **1 :** the act or action of receding **:** WITHDRAWAL **2 :** a departing procession (as of clergy and choir at the end of a church service) **3 :** a period of reduced economic activity — **re·ces·sion·ary** \-shə-ˌner-ē\ *adj*

[2]**re·ces·sion** \(ˌ)rē-ˈse-shən\ *n* [*re-* + *cession*] (1828) **:** the act of ceding back to a former possessor

[1]**re·ces·sion·al** \ri-ˈsesh-nəl, -ˈse-shə-nᵊl\ *adj* (1867) **:** of or relating to a withdrawal

[2]**recessional** *n* (1867) **1 :** a hymn or musical piece at the conclusion of a service or program **2 :** [1]RECESSION 2

[1]**re·ces·sive** \ri-ˈse-siv\ *adj* (ca. 1673) **1 a :** tending to recede **b :** WITHDRAWN 2 **2 a :** producing little or no phenotypic effect when occurring in heterozygous condition with a contrasting allele ⟨~ genes⟩ **b :** expressed only when the determining gene is in the homozygous condition ⟨~ traits⟩ ⟨a ~ disease⟩ — **re·ces·sive·ly** *adv* — **re·ces·sive·ness** *n*

[2]**recessive** *n* (1900) **1 :** an organism possessing one or more recessive characters **2 :** a recessive character or gene

re·charge \(ˌ)rē-ˈchärj\ *vi* (1598) **1 :** to make a new attack **2 :** to regain energy or spirit ~ *vt* **1 :** to charge again; *esp* **:** to restore anew the active materials in (a storage battery) **2 :** to inspire or invigorate afresh **:** RENEW — **re·charge** \(ˌ)rē-ˈchärj, ˈrē-ˌ\ *n* — **re·charge·able** \(ˌ)rē-ˈchär-jə-bəl\ *adj* — **re·charg·er** \-jər\ *n*

ré·chauf·fé \ˌrā-shō-ˈfā, -ˈshō-ˌ\ *n* [F, fr. *réchauffé* warmed-over, fr. pp. of *réchauffer* to warm over, fr. *ré-* re- + *chauffer* to warm, fr. MF *chaufer* — more at CHAFE] (1805) **1 :** REHASH **2 :** a warmed-over dish of food

re·cheat \ri-ˈchēt\ *n* [ME *rechate,* fr. *rechaten* to blow the recheat, fr. AF *rechater,* fr. VL **recaptare* to gather, assemble, fr. L *re-* + *captare* to catch at, chase — more at CATCH] (15c) **:** a hunting call sounded on a horn to assemble the hounds

re·cher·ché \rə-ˌsher-ˈshā, -ˈsher-ˌ\ *adj* [F, fr. pp. of *rechercher* to seek out, alter. of *recercher,* fr. MF — more at RESEARCH] (1722) **1 a :** EXQUISITE, CHOICE **b :** EXOTIC, RARE **2 :** excessively refined **:** AFFECTED **3 :** PRETENTIOUS, OVERBLOWN

re·cid·i·vism \ri-ˈsi-də-ˌvi-zəm\ *n* (1886) **:** a tendency to relapse into a previous condition or mode of behavior; *esp* **:** relapse into criminal behavior

re·cid·i·vist \-vist\ *n* [F *récidiviste,* fr. *récidiver* to relapse, fr. MF, fr. ML *recidivare,* fr. L *recidivus* recurring, fr. *recidere* to fall back, fr. *re-* + *cadere* to fall — more at CHANCE] (1880) **:** one who relapses; *specif* **:** a habitual criminal — **recidivist** *adj* — **re·cid·i·vis·tic** \-ˌsi-də-ˈvis-tik\ *adj*

rec·i·pe \ˈre-sə-(ˌ)pē\ *n* [L, take, imper. of *recipere* to take, receive — more at RECEIVE] (1584) **1 :** PRESCRIPTION 4a **2 :** a set of instructions for making something from various ingredients **3 :** a formula or procedure for doing or attaining something ⟨a ~ for success⟩

re·cip·i·ent \ri-ˈsi-pē-ənt\ *n* [L *recipient-, recipiens,* prp. of *recipere*] (1558) **:** one that receives **:** RECEIVER — **recipient** *adj*

[1]**re·cip·ro·cal** \ri-ˈsi-prə-kəl\ *adj* [L *reciprocus* returning the same way, alternating] (1570) **1 a :** inversely related **:** OPPOSITE **b :** of, constituting, or resulting from paired crosses in which the kind that supplies the male parent of the first cross supplies the female parent of the second cross and vice versa **2 :** shared, felt, or shown by both sides **3 :** serving to reciprocate **:** consisting of or functioning as a return in kind ⟨the ~ devastation of nuclear war⟩ **4 a :** mutually corresponding ⟨agreed to extend ~ privileges to each other's citizens⟩ **b**

: marked by or based on reciprocity ⟨~ trade agreements⟩ — **re·cip·ro·cal·ly** \-k(ə-)lē\ *adv*

[2]**reciprocal** *n* (1570) **1** : something in a reciprocal relationship to another **2** : either of a pair of numbers (as ⅔ and 3/2 or 9 and 1/9) whose product is one; *broadly* : MULTIPLICATIVE INVERSE

reciprocal pronoun *n* (1755) : a pronoun (as *each other*) used when its referents are predicated to bear the same relationship to one another

re·cip·ro·cate \ri-ˈsi-prə-ˌkāt\ *vb* **-cat·ed; -cat·ing** *vt* (1607) **1** : to give and take mutually **2** : to return in kind or degree ⟨~ a compliment gracefully⟩ ~ *vi* **1** : to make a return for something ⟨we hope to ~ for your kindness⟩ **2** : to move forward and backward alternately ⟨a *reciprocating* valve⟩ — **re·cip·ro·ca·tor** \-ˌkā-tər\ *n*

syn RECIPROCATE, RETALIATE, REQUITE, RETURN mean to give back usu. in kind or in quantity. RECIPROCATE implies a mutual or equivalent exchange or a paying back of what one has received ⟨*reciprocated* their hospitality by inviting them for a visit⟩. RETALIATE usu. implies a paying back of injury in exact kind, often vengefully ⟨the enemy *retaliated* by executing their prisoners⟩. REQUITE implies a paying back according to one's preference and often not equivalently ⟨*requited* her love with cold indifference⟩. RETURN implies a paying or giving back ⟨*returned* their call⟩ ⟨*return* good for evil⟩.

reciprocating engine *n* (1822) : an engine in which the to-and-fro motion of one or more pistons is transformed into the rotary motion of a crankshaft

re·cip·ro·ca·tion \ri-ˌsi-prə-ˈkā-shən\ *n* (1561) **1 a** : a mutual exchange **b** : a return in kind or of like value **2** : an alternating motion — **re·cip·ro·ca·tive** \-ˈsi-prə-ˌkā-tiv, -kə-\ *adj*

rec·i·proc·i·ty \ˌre-sə-ˈprä-s(ə-)tē\ *n, pl* **-ties** (1766) **1** : the quality or state of being reciprocal : mutual dependence, action, or influence **2** : a mutual exchange of privileges; *specif* : a recognition by one of two countries or institutions of the validity of licenses or privileges granted by the other

re·ci·sion \ri-ˈsi-zhən\ *n* [F, fr. MF, alter. of *rescision,* fr. LL *rescission-, rescissio* rescission] (1611) : an act of rescinding : CANCELLATION

re·cit·al \ri-ˈsī-tᵊl\ *n* (1536) **1 a** : a detailed account : ENUMERATION ⟨a ~ of names and dates⟩ **b** : the act or process or an instance of reciting **c** : DISCOURSE, NARRATION ⟨a colorful ~ of a night on the town⟩ **2 a** : a concert given by an individual musician or dancer or by a dance troupe **b** : a public exhibition of skill given by music or dance pupils — **re·cit·al·ist** \-tᵊl-ist\ *n*

rec·i·ta·tion \ˌre-sə-ˈtā-shən\ *n* (15c) **1** : the act of enumerating ⟨a ~ of relevant details⟩ **2** : the act or an instance of reading or repeating aloud esp. publicly **3 a** : a student's oral reply to questions **b** : a class period esp. in association with and for review of a lecture

rec·i·ta·tive \ˌre-sə-tə-ˈtēv, ˌres-tə-\ *n* [It *recitativo,* fr. *recitare* to recite, fr. L] (1656) **1** : a rhythmically free vocal style that imitates the natural inflections of speech and that is used for dialogue and narrative in operas and oratorios; *also* : a passage to be delivered in this style **2** : RECITATION 2 — **recitative** *adj*

rec·i·ta·ti·vo \-ˈtē-(ˌ)vō\ *n, pl* **-vi** \-(ˌ)vē\ *or* **-vos** [It] (1645) : RECITATIVE 1

re·cite \ri-ˈsīt\ *vb* **re·cit·ed; re·cit·ing** [ME, to relate, state, fr. AF or L; AF *reciter,* fr. L *recitare* to recite, fr. *re-* + *citare* to summon — more at CITE] *vt* (15c) **1** : to repeat from memory or read aloud publicly **2 a** : to relate in full ⟨~*s* dull anecdotes⟩ **b** : to give a recital of : DETAIL ⟨*recited* a catalog of offenses⟩ **3** : to repeat or answer questions about (a lesson) ~ *vi* **1** : to repeat or read aloud something memorized or prepared **2** : to reply to a teacher's question on a lesson — **re·cit·er** *n*

reck \ˈrek\ *vb* [ME, to take heed, fr. OE *reccan;* akin to OHG *ruohhen* to take heed] *vi* (bef. 12c) **1** : WORRY, CARE **2** *archaic* : to be of account or interest : MATTER ~ *vt* **1** *archaic* : to care for : REGARD **2** *archaic* : to matter to : CONCERN

reck·less \ˈre-kləs\ *adj* (bef. 12c) **1** : marked by lack of proper caution : careless of consequences **2** : IRRESPONSIBLE ⟨~ charges⟩ ***syn*** see ADVENTUROUS — **reck·less·ly** *adv* — **reck·less·ness** *n*

reck·on \ˈre-kən\ *vb* **reck·oned; reck·on·ing** \ˈre-kə-niŋ, ˈrek-niŋ\ [ME *rekenen,* fr. OE *-recenian* (as in *gerecenian* to narrate); akin to OE *reccan*] *vt* (13c) **1 a** : COUNT ⟨~ the days till Christmas⟩ **b** : ESTIMATE, COMPUTE ⟨~ the height of a building⟩ **c** : to determine by reference to a fixed basis ⟨the existence of the U.S. is ~*ed* from the Declaration of Independence⟩ **2** : to regard or think of as : CONSIDER **3** *chiefly dial* : THINK, SUPPOSE ⟨I ~ I've outlived my time —Ellen Glasgow⟩ ~ *vi* **1** : to settle accounts **2** : to make a calculation **3 a** : JUDGE **b** *chiefly dial* : SUPPOSE, THINK **4** : to accept something as certain : place reliance ⟨I ~ on your promise to help⟩ — **reckon with** : to take into consideration — **reckon without** : to fail to consider : IGNORE

reckoning *n* (14c) **1** : the act or an instance of reckoning: as **a** : ACCOUNT, BILL **b** : COMPUTATION **c** : calculation of a ship's position **2** : a settling of accounts ⟨day of ~⟩ **3** : a summing up

re·claim \ri-ˈklām\ *vt* [ME *reclamen,* fr. AF *reclamer,* fr. L *reclamare* to cry out, protest, fr. *re-* + *clamare* to cry out — more at CLAIM] (14c) **1 a** : to recall from wrong or improper conduct : REFORM **b** : TAME, SUBDUE **2 a** : to rescue from an undesirable state; *also* : to restore to a previous natural state ⟨~ mining sites⟩ **b** : to make available for human use by changing natural conditions ⟨~ swampland⟩ **3** : to obtain from a waste product or by-product : RECOVER ⟨~*ed* plastic⟩ **4 a** : to demand or obtain the return of **b** : to regain possession of ***syn*** see RESCUE — **re·claim·able** \-ˈklā-mə-bəl\ *adj*

rec·la·ma·tion \ˌre-klə-ˈmā-shən\ *n* [F *réclamation,* fr. L *reclamation-, reclamatio,* fr. *reclamare*] (1633) : the act or process of reclaiming: as **a** : REFORMATION, REHABILITATION **b** : restoration to use : RECOVERY

ré·clame \rā-ˈkläm\ *n* [F, advertising, fr. *réclamer* to appeal, fr. MF *reclamer*] (1883) **1** : a gift for dramatization or publicity : SHOWMANSHIP **2** : public acclaim ⟨the play won critical ~⟩

re·cline \ri-ˈklīn\ *vb* **re·clined; re·clin·ing** [ME, fr. AF or L; AF *recliner,* fr. L *reclinare,* fr. *re-* + *clinare* to bend — more at LEAN] *vt* (15c) : to cause or permit to incline backwards ~ *vi* **1** : to lean or incline backwards **2** : REPOSE, LIE

re·clin·er \-ˈklī-nər\ *n* (1928) : a chair with an adjustable back and footrest

re·clos·able \(ˌ)rē-ˈklō-zə-bəl\ *adj* (1965) : capable of being tightly closed again after opening ⟨~ packages of bacon⟩

[1]**re·cluse** \ˈre-ˌklüs, ri-ˈklüs, ˈre-ˌklüz\ *adj* [ME, fr. AF *reclus,* lit., shut away, fr. LL *reclusus,* pp. of *recludere* to shut up, fr. L *re-* + *claudere* to close — more at CLOSE] (13c) : marked by withdrawal from society : SOLITARY — **re·clu·sive** \ri-ˈklü-siv, -ziv\ *adj* — **re·clu·sive·ly** *adv* — **re·clu·sive·ness** *n*

[2]**recluse** *n* (13c) : a person who leads a secluded or solitary life

re·clu·sion \ri-ˈklü-zhən\ *n* (15c) : the state of being recluse

rec·og·nise *chiefly Brit var of* RECOGNIZE

rec·og·ni·tion \ˌre-kig-ˈni-shən, -kəg-\ *n* [ME *recognicion,* fr. AF *recognition,* fr. L *recognition-, recognitio,* fr. *recognoscere*] (15c) **1** : the action of recognizing : the state of being recognized: as **a** : ACKNOWLEDGMENT; *esp* : formal acknowledgment of the political existence of a government or nation **b** : knowledge or feeling that someone or something present has been encountered before **2** : special notice or attention **3** : the sensing and encoding of printed or written data by a machine ⟨optical character ~⟩ ⟨magnetic ink character ~⟩

re·cog·ni·zance \ri-ˈkäg-nə-zən(t)s, -ˈkä-nə-\ *n* [ME *recognissance,* alter. of *reconissaunce,* fr. AF, fr. *reconoistre* to recognize] (14c) **1 a** : an obligation of record entered into before a court or magistrate requiring the performance of an act (as appearance in court) usu. under penalty of a money forfeiture ⟨released on his own ~⟩ **b** : the sum liable to forfeiture upon such an obligation **2** *archaic* : TOKEN, PLEDGE

rec·og·nize \ˈre-kig-ˌnīz, -kəg-\ *vt* **-nized; -niz·ing** [modif. of AF *reconois-,* stem of *reconoistre,* fr. L *recognoscere,* fr. *re-* + *cognoscere* to know — more at COGNITION] (ca. 1532) **1** : to acknowledge formally: as **a** : to admit as being lord or sovereign **b** : to admit as being of a particular status **c** : to admit as being one entitled to be heard : give the floor to **d** : to acknowledge the de facto existence or the independence of **2** : to acknowledge or take notice of in some definite way: as **a** : to acknowledge with a show of appreciation ⟨~ an act of bravery with the award of a medal⟩ **b** : to acknowledge acquaintance with ⟨~ a neighbor with a nod⟩ **3 a** : to perceive to be something or someone previously known ⟨*recognized* the word⟩ **b** : to perceive clearly : REALIZE — **rec·og·niz·abil·i·ty** \ˌre-kig-ˌnī-zə-ˈbi-lə-tē, -kəg-\ *n* — **rec·og·niz·able** \ˈre-kəg-ˌnī-zə-bəl, -kig-\ *adj* — **rec·og·niz·ably** \-blē\ *adv* — **rec·og·niz·er** *n*

[1]**re·coil** \ri-ˈkȯi(-ə)l\ *vi* [ME *reculen, recoilen,* fr. AF *reculer, reculier,* fr. *re-* + *cul* backside — more at CULET] (14c) **1 a** : to fall back under pressure **b** : to shrink back physically or emotionally **2** : to spring back to or as if to a starting point : REBOUND **3** *obs* : DEGENERATE

syn RECOIL, SHRINK, FLINCH, WINCE, BLENCH, QUAIL mean to draw back in fear or distaste. RECOIL implies a start or movement away through shock, fear, or disgust ⟨*recoiled* at the suggestion of stealing⟩. SHRINK suggests an instinctive recoil through sensitiveness, scrupulousness, or cowardice ⟨*shrank* from the unpleasant truth⟩. FLINCH implies a failure to endure pain or face something dangerous or frightening with resolution ⟨faced her accusers without *flinching*⟩. WINCE suggests a slight involuntary physical reaction (as a start or recoiling) ⟨*winced* in pain⟩. BLENCH implies fainthearted flinching ⟨stood their ground without *blenching*⟩. QUAIL suggests shrinking and cowering in fear ⟨*quailed* before the apparition⟩.

[2]**re·coil** \ˈrē-ˌkȯi(-ə)l, ri-ˈkȯi(-ə)l\ *n* (14c) **1** : the act or action of recoiling; *esp* : the kickback of a gun upon firing **2** : REACTION ⟨the ~ from the rigors of Calvinism —Edmund Wilson⟩

re·coil·less \-ˌkȯi(-ə)l-ləs, -ˈkȯi(-ə)l-\ *adj* (1943) : venting expanding propellant gas before recoil is produced ⟨~ rifle⟩ ⟨~ airgun⟩

recoil–operated *adj* (1942) *of a firearm* : utilizing the movement of parts in recoil to operate the action

re·coin \(ˌ)rē-ˈkȯin\ *vt* (1663) : to coin again or anew; *esp* : REMINT — **re·coin·age** \-ˈkȯi-nij\ *n*

rec·ol·lect \ˌre-kə-ˈlekt\ *vb* [ML *recollectus,* pp. of *recolligere,* fr. L, to gather again] *vt* (1559) **1** : to bring back to the level of conscious awareness : REMEMBER ⟨trying to ~ the name⟩ **2** : to remind (oneself) of something temporarily forgotten ~ *vi* : to call something to mind ***syn*** see REMEMBER

re–col·lect \ˌrē-kə-ˈlekt\ *vt* [partly fr. L *recollectus,* pp. of *recolligere,* fr. *re-* + *colligere* to collect; partly fr. *re-* + *collect*] (1604) : to collect again; *esp* : RALLY, RECOVER

rec·ol·lect·ed \ˌrē-kə-ˈlek-təd\ *adj* (1627) : COMPOSED, CALM

rec·ol·lec·tion \ˌre-kə-ˈlek-shən\ *n* (1624) **1 a** : tranquillity of mind **b** : religious contemplation **2 a** : the action or power of recalling to mind **b** : something recalled to the mind ***syn*** see MEMORY

re·com·bi·nant \(ˌ)rē-ˈkäm-bə-nənt\ *adj* (1942) **1** : relating to or exhibiting genetic recombination ⟨~ progeny⟩ **2 a** : relating to or containing genetically engineered DNA **b** : produced by genetic engineering ⟨~ bovine growth hormone⟩ — **recombinant** *n*

recombinant DNA *n* (1975) : genetically engineered DNA usu. incorporating DNA from more than one species of organism

re·com·bi·na·tion \ˌrē-ˌkäm-bə-ˈnā-shən\ *n* (1903) : the formation by the processes of crossing-over and independent assortment of new combinations of genes in progeny that did not occur in the parents — **re·com·bi·na·tion·al** \-shnəl, -shə-nᵊl\ *adj*

re·com·bine \ˌrē-kəm-ˈbīn\ *vt* (1619) **1** : to combine again or anew **2** : to cause to undergo recombination ~ *vi* : to undergo recombination

rec·om·mend \ˌre-kə-ˈmend\ *vt* [ME, fr. AF *recommender,* fr. ML *recommendare,* fr. L *re-* + *commendare* to commend] (14c) **1 a** : to present as worthy of acceptance or trial ⟨~*ed* the medicine⟩ **b** : to endorse as fit, worthy, or competent ⟨~*s* her for the position⟩ **2** : ENTRUST, COMMIT ⟨~*ed* his soul to God⟩ **3** : to make acceptable ⟨has other points to ~ it⟩ **4** : ADVISE ⟨~ that the matter be dropped⟩ — **rec·om·mend·able** \-ˈmen-də-bəl\ *adj* — **rec·om·men·da·to·ry** \-də-ˌtȯr-ē\ *adj* — **rec·om·mend·er** *n*

rec·om·men·da·tion \ˌre-kə-mən-ˈdā-shən, -ˌmen-\ *n* (15c) **1 a** : the act of recommending **b** : something (as a procedure) recommended **2** : something that recommends or expresses commendation

re·com·mit \ˌrē-kə-ˈmit\ *vt* (1621) **1** : to refer (as a bill) back to a committee **2** : to entrust or consign again — **re·com·mit·ment** \-mənt\ *n* — **re·com·mit·tal** \-ˈmi-tᵊl\ *n*

[1]**rec·om·pense** \ˈre-kəm-ˌpen(t)s\ *vt* **-pensed; -pens·ing** [ME, fr. AF *recompenser,* fr. LL *recompensare,* fr. L *re-* + *compensare* to compensate] (15c) **1 a** : to give something to by way of compensation (as for a service rendered or damage incurred) **b** : to pay for **2** : to return in kind : REQUITE ***syn*** see PAY

[2]**recompense** *n* (15c) : an equivalent or a return for something done, suffered, or given : COMPENSATION ⟨offered in ~ for injuries⟩

re·com·pose \ˌrē-kəm-ˈpōz\ *vt* (1611) **1** : to compose again : REARRANGE **2** : to restore to composure — **re·com·po·si·tion** \(ˌ)rē-ˌkäm-pə-ˈzi-shən\ *n*

re·con \ri-ˈkän, ˈrē-ˌkän\ *n* (1918) : RECONNAISSANCE

rec·on·cile \ˈre-kən-ˌsī(-ə)l\ *vb* **-ciled; -cil·ing** [ME, fr. AF or L; AF *reconciler,* fr. L *reconciliare,* fr. *re-* + *conciliare* to conciliate] *vt* (14c) **1 a** : to restore to friendship or harmony ⟨*reconciled* the factions⟩ **b** : SETTLE, RESOLVE ⟨~ differences⟩ **2** : to make consistent or congruous ⟨~ an ideal with reality⟩ **3** : to cause to submit to or accept something unpleasant ⟨was *reconciled* to hardship⟩ **4 a** : to check (a financial account) against another for accuracy **b** : to account for ~ *vi* : to become reconciled ***syn*** see ADAPT — **rec·on·cil·abil·i·ty** \ˌre-kən-ˌsī-lə-ˈbi-lə-tē\ *n* — **rec·on·cil·able** \ˌre-kən-ˈsī-lə-bəl, ˈre-kən-ˌ\ *adj* — **rec·on·cile·ment** \ˈre-kən-ˌsī(-ə)l-mənt\ *n* — **rec·on·cil·er** *n*

rec·on·cil·i·a·tion \ˌre-kən-ˌsi-lē-ˈā-shən\ *n* [ME *reconsiliacioun,* fr. AF, fr. L *reconciliation-, reconciliatio,* fr. *reconciliare*] (14c) **1** : the action of reconciling : the state of being reconciled **2** : the Roman Catholic sacrament of penance — **rec·on·cil·ia·to·ry** \-ˈsil-yə-ˌtȯr-ē, -ˈsi-lē-ə-\ *adj*

re·con·dite \ˈre-kən-ˌdīt, ri-ˈkän-\ *adj* [L *reconditus,* pp. of *recondere* to conceal, fr. *re-* + *condere* to store up, fr. *com-* + *-dere* to put — more at COM-, DO] (1649) **1** : hidden from sight : CONCEALED **2** : difficult or impossible for one of ordinary understanding or knowledge to comprehend : DEEP ⟨a ~ subject⟩ **3** : of, relating to, or dealing with something little known or obscure ⟨~ fact about the origin of the holiday —Floyd Dell⟩ — **re·con·dite·ly** *adv* — **re·con·dite·ness** *n*

re·con·di·tion \ˌrē-kən-ˈdi-shən\ *vt* (1920) **1** : to restore to good condition (as by replacing parts) **2** : to condition (as a person or a person's attitudes) anew; *also* : to reinstate (a response) in an organism

re·con·firm \ˌrē-kən-ˈfərm\ *vt* (1611) : to confirm again; *also* : to establish more strongly — **re·con·fir·ma·tion** \(ˌ)rē-ˌkän-fər-ˈmā-shən\ *n*

re·con·nais·sance \ri-ˈkä-nə-zən(t)s, -sən(t)s\ *n* [F, lit., recognition, fr. MF *reconoissance,* fr. OF *reconoistre* to recognize] (1810) : a preliminary survey to gain information; *esp* : an exploratory military survey of enemy territory

re·con·noi·ter *or* **re·con·noi·tre** \ˌrē-kə-ˈnȯi-tər, ˌre-kə-\ *vb* **-noi·tered** *or* **-noi·tred; -noi·ter·ing** *or* **-noi·tring** \-ˈnȯi-tə-riŋ, -ˈnȯi-triŋ\ [obs. F *reconnoître,* lit., to recognize, fr. OF *reconoistre* — more at RECOGNIZE] *vt* (1707) : to make a reconnaissance of ~ *vi* : to engage in reconnaissance

re·con·sid·er \ˌrē-kən-ˈsi-dər\ *vt* (1571) : to consider again esp. with a view to changing or reversing ~ *vi* : to consider something again — **re·con·sid·er·a·tion** \-ˌsi-də-ˈrā-shən\ *n*

re·con·sti·tute \(ˌ)rē-ˈkän(t)-stə-ˌtüt, -ˌtyüt\ *vt* (1812) : to constitute again or anew; *esp* : to restore to a former condition by adding water — **re·con·sti·tu·tion** \(ˌ)rē-ˌkän(t)-stə-ˈtü-shən, -ˈtyü-\ *n*

re·con·struct \ˌrē-kən-ˈstrəkt\ *vt* (1768) : to construct again: as **a** : to establish or assemble again **b** : to subject (an organ or part) to surgery to re-form its structure or correct a defect **c** : to build up mentally : RECREATE ⟨~*ing* a lost civilization⟩ — **re·con·struct·ible** \-ˈstrək-tə-bəl\ *adj* — **re·con·struc·tive** \-tiv\ *adj* — **re·con·struc·tor** \-tər\ *n*

re·con·struc·tion \ˌrē-kən-ˈstrək-shən\ *n* (1791) **1 a** : the action of reconstructing : the state of being reconstructed **b** *often cap* : the reorganization and reestablishment of the seceded states in the Union after the American Civil War **2** : something reconstructed

re·con·struc·tion·ism \-shə-ˌni-zəm\ *n, often cap* (1942) **1** : a movement in 20th century American Judaism that advocates a creative adjustment to contemporary conditions through the cultivation of traditions and folkways shared by all Jews **2** : advocacy of post-Civil War reconstruction — **re·con·struc·tion·ist** \-sh(ə-)nist\ *adj or n, often cap*

reconstructive surgery *n* (1943) : surgery to restore function or normal appearance by reconstructing defective organs or parts

re·con·tex·tu·al·ize \ˌrē-kən-ˈteks-chə-wə-ˌlīz, -chə-ˌlīz\ *vt* (1978) : to place (as a literary or artistic work) in a different context

re·con·vey \ˌrē-kən-ˈvā\ *vt* (1506) : to convey back to a previous position or owner — **re·con·vey·ance** \-ˈvā-ən(t)s\ *n*

[1]**re·cord** \ri-ˈkȯrd\ *vb* [ME, lit., to recall, fr. AF *recorder,* fr. L *recordari,* fr. *re-* + *cord-, cor* heart — more at HEART] *vt* (14c) **1 a (1)** : to set down in writing : furnish written evidence of **(2)** : to deposit an authentic official copy of ⟨~ a deed⟩ **b** : to state for or as if for the record ⟨voted in favor but ~*ed* certain reservations⟩ **c (1)** : to register permanently by mechanical means ⟨earthquake shocks ~*ed* by a seismograph⟩ **(2)** : INDICATE, READ ⟨the thermometer ~*ed* 90°⟩ **2** : to give evidence of **3** : to cause (as sound, visual images, or data) to be registered on something (as a disc or magnetic tape) in reproducible form ~ *vi* : to record something — **re·cord·able** \-ˈkȯr-də-bəl\ *adj*

[2]**rec·ord** \ˈre-kərd *also* -ˌkȯrd\ *n* (14c) **1** : the state or fact of being recorded **2** : something that records: as **a** : something that recalls or relates past events **b** : an official document that records the acts of a public body or officer **c** : an authentic official copy of a document deposited with a legally designated officer **d** : the official copy of the papers used in a law case **3 a (1)** : a body of known or recorded facts about something or someone esp. with reference to a particular sphere of activity that often forms a discernible pattern ⟨a good academic ~⟩ ⟨a liberal voting ~⟩ **(2)** : a collection of related items of information (as in a database) treated as a unit **b (1)** : an attested top performance **(2)** : an unsurpassed statistic **4** : something on which sound or visual images have been recorded; *specif* : a disc with a spiral groove carrying recorded sound for phonograph reproduction — **for the record** : for public knowledge : on the record — **off the record** : not for publication ⟨spoke *off the record*⟩ ⟨remarks that were *off the record*⟩ — **of record 1** : being documented or attested ⟨a partner *of record* in several firms⟩ **2** : being authoritative or sanctioned ⟨a newspaper *of record*⟩ — **on record 1** : in the position of having publicly declared oneself ⟨went *on record* as opposed to higher taxes⟩ **2** : being known, published, or documented ⟨the judge's opinion is *on record*⟩ — **on the record** : for publication

[3]**record** *same as* [2]\ *adj* (1884) : of, relating to, or being one that is extraordinary among or surpasses others of its kind

[4]**re·cord** \ri-ˈkȯrd\ *n* (1946) : a function of an electronic device that causes it to record

re·cor·da·tion \ˌre-ˌkȯr-ˈdā-shən; ˌrē-, ri-\ *n* (ca. 1812) : the action or process of recording

re·cord·er \ri-ˈkȯr-dər\ *n* (15c) **1 a** : the chief judicial magistrate of some British cities and boroughs **b** : a municipal judge with criminal jurisdiction of first instance and sometimes limited civil jurisdiction **2** : one that records **3** : any of a group of wind instruments ranging from soprano to bass that are characterized by a conical tube, a whistle mouthpiece, and eight finger holes

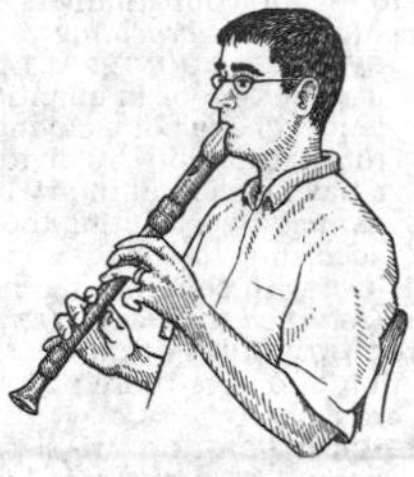

recorder 3

re·cord·ing \ri-ˈkȯr-diŋ\ *n* (1932) : RECORD 4

re·cord·ist \ri-ˈkȯr-dist\ *n* (ca. 1930) : one who records sound (as on magnetic tape)

[1]**re·count** \ri-ˈkau̇nt\ *vt* [ME, fr. AF *recunter,* fr. *re-* + *cunter* to count, relate — more at COUNT] (15c) : to relate in detail : NARRATE — **re·count·er** *n*

[2]**re·count** \(ˌ)rē-ˈkau̇nt\ *vt* [*re-* + *count*] (1764) : to count again

[3]**re·count** \ˈrē-ˌkau̇nt, (ˌ)rē-ˈ\ *n* (1884) : a second or fresh count

re·coup \ri-ˈküp\ *vb* [F *recouper* to cut back, fr. OF, fr. *re-* + *couper* to cut — more at COPE] *vt* (1628) **1 a** : to get an equivalent for (as losses) : make up for **b** : REIMBURSE, COMPENSATE ⟨~ a person for losses⟩ **2** : REGAIN ⟨an attempt to ~ his fortune⟩ ~ *vi* : to make good or make up for something lost; *also* : RECUPERATE — **re·coup·able** \-ˈkü-pə-bəl\ *adj* — **re·coup·ment** \-ˈküp-mənt\ *n*

re·course \ˈrē-ˌkȯrs, ri-ˈ\ *n* [ME *recours,* fr. AF *recurs,* fr. LL *recursus,* fr. L, act of running back, fr. *recurrere* to run back — more at RECUR] (14c) **1 a** : a turning to someone or something for help or protection ⟨settled the matter without ~ to law⟩ **b** : a source of help or strength : RESORT ⟨had no ~ left⟩ **2** : the right to demand payment from the maker or endorser of a negotiable instrument (as a check)

re·cov·er \ri-ˈkə-vər\ *vb* **re·cov·ered; re·cov·er·ing** \-ˈkə-və-riŋ, -ˈkəv-riŋ\ [ME, fr. AF *recoverer,* fr. L *recuperare, fr. re-* + **caperare,* fr. L *capere* to take — more at HEAVE] *vt* (14c) **1** : to get back : REGAIN **2 a** : to bring back to normal position or condition ⟨stumbled, then ~*ed* himself⟩ **b** *archaic* : RESCUE **3 a** : to make up for ⟨~ increased costs through higher prices⟩ **b** : to gain by legal process **4** *archaic* : REACH **5** : to find or identify again ⟨~ a comet⟩ **6 a** : to obtain from an ore, a waste product, or a by-product **b** : to save from loss and restore to usefulness : RECLAIM ~ *vi* **1** : to regain a normal position or condition (as of health) ⟨~*ing* from a cold⟩ **2** : to obtain a final legal judgment in one's favor — **re·cov·er·abil·i·ty** \-ˌkə-və-rə-ˈbi-lə-tē, -ˌkəv-rə-\ *n* — **re·cov·er·able** \-ˈkə-və-rə-bəl, -ˈkəv-rə-\ *adj* — **re·cov·er·er** \-ˈkə-vər-ər\ *n*

re–cov·er \(ˌ)rē-ˈkə-vər\ *vt* (15c) : to cover again or anew

recovered memory *n* (1941) : a memory of a traumatic event (as sexual abuse) experienced typically during childhood that is forgotten and then recalled many years later that is sometimes held to be an invalid or false remembrance generated by outside influence

recovering *adj* (1977) : being in the process of overcoming a disorder or shortcoming ⟨a ~ alcoholic⟩ ⟨a still-bookish ~ academic with a tendency to live in his head —Jon Spayde⟩

re·cov·ery \ri-ˈkə-və-rē, -ˈkəv-rē\ *n, pl* **-er·ies** (15c) **1** : the act, process, or an instance of recovering; *esp* : an economic upturn (as after a depression) **2** : the process of combating a disorder (as alcoholism) or a real or perceived problem

recovery room *n* (1916) : a hospital room equipped for meeting postoperative emergencies

[1]**rec·re·ant** \ˈre-krē-ənt\ *adj* [ME, fr. AF, fr. prp. of (*se*) *recreire* to give up, yield, fr. ML (*se*) *recredere* to resign oneself (to a judgment), fr. L *re-* + *credere* to believe — more at CREED] (14c) **1** : crying for mercy : COWARDLY **2** : unfaithful to duty or allegiance

[2]**recreant** *n* (15c) **1** : COWARD **2** : APOSTATE, DESERTER

rec·re·ate \ˈre-krē-ˌāt\ *vb* **-at·ed; -at·ing** [L *recreatus,* pp. of *recreare*] *vt* (15c) : to give new life or freshness to : REFRESH ~ *vi* : to take recreation — **rec·re·a·tive** \-ˌā-tiv\ *adj*

re–cre·ate \ˌrē-krē-ˈāt\ *vt* (1587) : to create again; *esp* : to form anew in the imagination — **re–cre·at·able** \-ˈā-tə-bəl\ *adj* — **re–cre·a·tion** \-ˈā-shən\ *n* — **re–cre·a·tive** \-ˈā-tiv\ *adj* — **re–cre·a·tor** \-ˈā-tər\ *n*

rec·re·a·tion \ˌre-krē-ˈā-shən\ *n* [ME *recreacion,* fr. AF, fr. L *recreation-, recreatio* restoration to health, fr. *recreare* to create anew, restore, refresh, fr. *re-* + *creare* to create] (15c) : refreshment of strength and spirits after work; *also* : a means of refreshment or diversion : HOBBY

rec·re·a·tion·al \ˌre-krē-ˈā-shnəl, -shə-nᵊl\ *adj* (1656) **1** : of, relating to, or characteristic of recreation **2** : of or relating to recreational drugs or their use

recreational drug *n* (1976) : a drug (as cocaine, marijuana, or methamphetamine) used without medical justification for its psychoactive effects often in the belief that occasional use of such a substance is not habit-forming or addictive

recreational vehicle *n* (1966) : a vehicle designed for recreational use (as in camping); *esp* : MOTOR HOME

rec·re·a·tion·ist \-sh(ə-)nist\ *n* (1904) : a person who seeks recreation esp. in the outdoors

recreation room *n* (1854) **1** : a room (as a rumpus room) used for recreation and relaxation — called also *rec room* **2** : a public room (as in a hospital) for recreation and social activities

re·crim·i·na·tion \ri-ˌkri-mə-ˈnā-shən\ *n* [ML *recrimination-, recriminatio,* fr. *recriminare* to make a retaliatory charge, fr. L *re-* + *criminari* to accuse — more at CRIMINATE] (ca. 1611) : a retaliatory accusation; *also* : the making of such accusations ⟨endless ~⟩ — **re·crim·i·nate** \-ˈkri-mə-ˌnāt\ *vi* — **re·crim·i·na·tive** \-ˌnā-tiv\ *adj* — **re·crim·i·na·to·ry** \-ˈkri-mə-nə-ˌtȯr-ē, -ˈkrim-nə-\ *adj*

re·cru·desce \ˌrē-krü-ˈdes\ *vi* **-desced; -desc·ing** [L *recrudescere* to become raw again, fr. *re-* + *crudescere* to become raw, fr. *crudus* raw — more at RAW] (1713) : to break out or become active again

re·cru·des·cence \-ˈde-sᵊn(t)s\ *n* (1665) : a new outbreak after a period of abatement or inactivity : RENEWAL ⟨a ~ of the symptoms⟩ ⟨a ~ of guerrilla warfare⟩

re·cru·des·cent \-sᵊnt\ *adj* (1722) : breaking out again : RENEWING

[1]**re·cruit** \ri-ˈkrüt\ *vt* (1642) **1 a** (1) : to fill up the number of (as an army) with new members : REINFORCE (2) : to enlist as a member of an armed service **b** : to increase or maintain the number of ⟨America ~*ed* her population from Europe⟩ **c** : to secure the services of : ENGAGE, HIRE **d** : to seek to enroll ⟨~ prospective students⟩ **2** : REPLENISH **3** : to restore or increase the health, vigor, or intensity of ~ *vi* : to enlist new members — **re·cruit·er** *n*

[2]**recruit** *n* [F *recrute, recrue* fresh growth, new levy of soldiers, fr. MF, fr. *recroistre* to grow up again, fr. L *recrescere,* fr. *re-* + *crescere* to grow — more at CRESCENT] (1645) **1** : a fresh or additional supply **2** : a newcomer to a field or activity; *specif* : a newly enlisted or drafted member of the armed forces **3** : a former enlisted man of the lowest rank in the army

re·cruit·ment \ri-ˈkrüt-mənt\ *n* (1793) **1** : the action or process of recruiting **2** : the process of adding new individuals to a population or subpopulation (as of breeding or legally catchable individuals) by growth, reproduction, immigration, and stocking; *also* : a measure (as in numbers or biomass) of recruitment

re·crys·tal·lize \(ˌ)rē-ˈkris-tə-ˌlīz\ *vb* (1724) : to crystallize again or repeatedly — **re·crys·tal·li·za·tion** \(ˌ)rē-ˌkris-tə-lə-ˈzā-shən\ *n*

rec·tal \ˈrek-tᵊl\ *adj* (1826) : relating to, affecting, or being near the rectum ⟨~ walls⟩ ⟨~ cancer⟩ — **rec·tal·ly** *adv*

rect·an·gle \ˈrek-ˌtaŋ-gəl\ *n* [ML *rectangulus* having a right angle, fr. L *rectus* right + *angulus* angle — more at RIGHT, ANGLE] (ca. 1560) : a parallelogram all of whose angles are right angles; *esp* : one with adjacent sides of unequal length

rect·an·gu·lar \rek-ˈtaŋ-gyə-lər\ *adj* (ca. 1560) **1** : shaped like a rectangle ⟨a ~ area⟩ **2 a** : crossing, lying, or meeting at a right angle ⟨~ axes⟩ **b** : having edges, surfaces, or faces that meet at right angles : having faces or surfaces shaped like rectangles ⟨~ parallelepipeds⟩ ⟨a ~ solid⟩ — **rect·an·gu·lar·i·ty** \(ˌ)rek-ˌtaŋ-gyə-ˈla-rə-tē\ *n* — **rect·an·gu·lar·ly** \rek-ˈtaŋ-gyə-lər-lē\ *adv*

rectangular coordinate *n* (1805) : a Cartesian coordinate of a Cartesian coordinate system whose straight-line axes or coordinate planes are perpendicular

rec·ti·fi·able \ˈrek-tə-ˌfī-ə-bəl\ *adj* [*rectify* (to determine the length of an arc)] (1629) : capable of being rectified; *esp* : having finite length ⟨a ~ curve⟩ — **rec·ti·fi·abil·i·ty** \ˌrek-tə-ˌfī-ə-ˈbi-lə-tē\ *n*

rec·ti·fi·er \ˈrek-tə-ˌfī(-ə)r\ *n* (1607) : one that rectifies; *specif* : a device for converting alternating current into direct current

rec·ti·fy \ˈrek-tə-ˌfī\ *vt* **-fied; -fy·ing** [ME *rectifien,* fr. AF *rectifier,* fr. ML *rectificare,* fr. L *rectus* right — more at RIGHT] (ca. 1529) **1** : to set right : REMEDY **2** : to purify (as alcohol) esp. by repeated or fractional distillation **3** : to correct by removing errors : ADJUST ⟨~ the calendar⟩ **4** : to make (an alternating current) unidirectional ***syn*** see CORRECT — **rec·ti·fi·ca·tion** \ˌrek-tə-fə-ˈkā-shən\ *n*

rec·ti·lin·e·ar \ˌrek-tə-ˈli-nē-ər\ *adj* [LL *rectilineus,* fr. L *rectus* + *linea* line] (1651) **1** : moving in or forming a straight line ⟨~ motion⟩ **2** : characterized by straight lines ⟨the ~ skyline of a modern city⟩ **3** : PERPENDICULAR 3 — **rec·ti·lin·e·ar·i·ty** \-ˌli-nē-ˈa-rə-tē\ *n* — **rec·ti·lin·e·ar·ly** *adv*

rec·ti·tude \ˈrek-tə-ˌtüd, -ˌtyüd\ *n* [ME, fr. MF, fr. LL *rectitudo,* fr. L *rectus* straight, right] (15c) **1** : the quality or state of being straight **2** : moral integrity : RIGHTEOUSNESS **3** : the quality or state of being correct in judgment or procedure

rec·ti·tu·di·nous \ˌrek-tə-ˈtüd-nəs, -ˈtyüd-; -ˈtü-də-nəs, -ˈtyü-\ *adj* [LL *rectitudin-, rectitudo* rectitude] (1897) **1** : characterized by rectitude **2** : piously self-righteous

rec·to \ˈrek-(ˌ)tō\ *n, pl* **rectos** [NL *recto (folio)* on the right-hand leaf] (1810) **1** : the side of a leaf (as of a manuscript) that is to be read first **2** : a right-hand page — compare VERSO

rec·tor \ˈrek-tər\ *n* [ME, fr. L, fr. *regere* to direct — more at RIGHT] (14c) **1** : one that directs : LEADER **2 a** : a member of the clergy (as of the Protestant Episcopal Church) in charge of a parish **b** : an incumbent of a Church of England benefice in full possession of its rights **c** : a Roman Catholic priest directing a church with no pastor or one whose pastor has other duties **3** : the head of a university or school — **rec·tor·ate** \-t(ə-)rət\ *n* — **rec·to·ri·al** \rek-ˈtȯr-ē-əl\ *adj* — **rec·tor·ship** \ˈrek-tər-ˌship\ *n*

rec·to·ry \ˈrek-t(ə-)rē\ *n, pl* **-ries** (15c) **1** : a benefice held by a rector **2** : a residence of a rector or a parish priest

rec·trix \ˈrek-triks\ *n, pl* **rec·tri·ces** \ˈrek-trə-ˌsēz, rek-ˈtrī-(ˌ)sēz\ [NL, fr. L, fem. of *rector* one that directs] (1813) : any of the quill feathers of a bird's tail that are important in controlling flight direction — see BIRD illustration

rec·tum \ˈrek-təm\ *n, pl* **rectums** *or* **rec·ta** \-tə\ [ME, fr. ML, fr. *rectum intestinum,* lit., straight intestine] (15c) : the terminal part of the intestine from the sigmoid colon to the anus

rec·tus \ˈrek-təs\ *n, pl* **rec·ti** \-ˌtī, -ˌtē\ [NL, fr. *rectus musculus* straight muscle] (1615) : any of several straight muscles (as of the abdomen)

re·cum·ben·cy \ri-ˈkəm-bən(t)-sē\ *n, pl* **-cies** (1646) : the state of leaning, resting, or reclining : REPOSE; *also* : a recumbent position

re·cum·bent \-bənt\ *adj* [L *recumbent-, recumbens,* prp. of *recumbere* to lie down, fr. *re-* + *-cumbere* to lie down; akin to L *cubare* to lie] (1664) **1 a** : suggestive of repose : LEANING, RESTING **b** : lying down **2** : representing a person lying down ⟨a ~ statue⟩ ***syn*** see PRONE

re·cu·per·ate \ri-ˈkü-pə-ˌrāt, -ˈkyü-\ *vb* **-at·ed; -at·ing** [L *recuperatus,* pp. of *recuperare* — more at RECOVER] *vt* (1542) **1** : to get back : REGAIN **2** : to bring back into use or currency : REVIVE ⟨~ old traditions⟩ ~ *vi* : to regain a former state or condition; *esp* : to recover health or strength — **re·cu·per·a·tion** \-ˌkü-pə-ˈrā-shən, -ˌkyü-\ *n*

re·cu·per·a·tive \-ˈkü-pə-ˌrā-tiv, -ˈkyü-, -p(ə-)rə-tiv\ *adj* (1650) **1** : of or relating to recuperation ⟨~ powers⟩ **2** : aiding in recuperation : RESTORATIVE

re·cur \ri-ˈkər\ *vi* **re·curred; re·cur·ring** [ME *recurren* to return, fr. L *recurrere,* lit., to run back, fr. *re-* + *currere* to run — more at CAR] (ca. 1512) **1** : to have recourse : RESORT **2** : to go back in thought or discourse ⟨on *recurring* to my letters of that date —Thomas Jefferson⟩ **3 a** : to come up again for consideration **b** : to come again to mind **4** : to occur again after an interval : occur time after time ⟨the cancer *recurred*⟩ — **re·cur·rence** \-ˈkər-ən(t)s, -ˈkə-rən(t)s\ *n*

re·cur·rent \-ˈkər-ənt, -ˈkə-rənt\ *adj* [L *recurrent-, recurrens,* prp. of *recurrere*] (1578) **1** : running or turning back in a direction opposite to a former course — used of various nerves and branches of vessels in the arms and legs **2** : returning or happening time after time ⟨~ complaints⟩ — **re·cur·rent·ly** *adv*

recurring decimal *n* (1748) : REPEATING DECIMAL

re·cur·sion \ri-ˈkər-zhən\ *n* [LL *recursion-, recursio,* fr. *recurrere*] (1790) **1** : RETURN 1 **2** : the determination of a succession of elements (as numbers or functions) by operation on one or more preceding elements according to a rule or formula involving a finite number of steps **3** : a computer programming technique involving the use of a procedure, subroutine, function, or algorithm that calls itself one or more times until a specified condition is met at which time the rest of each repetition is processed from the last one called to the first — compare ITERATION

re·cur·sive \ri-ˈkər-siv\ *adj* (1934) **1** : of, relating to, or involving recursion ⟨a ~ function in a computer program⟩ **2** : of, relating to, or constituting a procedure that can repeat itself indefinitely ⟨a ~ rule in a grammar⟩ — **re·cur·sive·ly** *adv* — **re·cur·sive·ness** *n*

re·curve \ˈrē-ˌkərv\ *n* (1956) : an archery bow whose tips are curved toward the back

re·curved \(ˌ)rē-ˈkərvd\ *adj* (1598) : curved backward or inward ⟨~ claws⟩ ⟨~ petals⟩

re·cu·san·cy \ˈre-kyə-zən(t)-sē, ri-ˈkyü-\ *n* (1575) : the act or state of being a recusant

re·cu·sant \-zənt\ *n* [L *recusant-, recusans,* prp. of *recusare* to reject, oppose, fr. *re-* + *causari* to give a reason, fr. *causa* cause, reason] (ca. 1553) **1** : an English Roman Catholic of the time from about 1570 to 1791 who refused to attend services of the Church of England and thereby committed a statutory offense **2** : one who refuses to accept or obey established authority — **recusant** *adj*

re·cuse \ri-ˈkyüz\ *vt* **re·cused; re·cus·ing** [ME, to refuse, reject, fr. AF *recuser,* fr. L *recusare*] (1829) : to disqualify (oneself) as judge in a particular case; *broadly* : to remove (oneself) from participation to avoid a conflict of interest — **re·cus·al** \-ˈkyü-zəl\ *n*

re·cut \(ˌ)rē-ˈkət, ˈrē-ˌ\ *vt* (1664) **1** : to cut again **2** : to edit (as a film) anew

[1]**re·cy·cle** \(ˌ)rē-ˈsī-kəl\ *vt* (1925) **1** : to pass again through a series of changes or treatments: as **a** : to process (as liquid body waste, glass, or cans) in order to regain material for human use **b** : RECOVER 6 **c** : to reuse or make (a substance) available for reuse for biological activities through natural processes of biochemical degradation or modification ⟨green plants *recycling* the residue of forest fires⟩ ⟨~ ADP back to ATP⟩ **2** : to adapt to a new use : ALTER **3** : to bring back : REUSE ⟨~*s* a number of good anecdotes —Larry McMurtry⟩ **4** : to make ready for reuse ⟨a plan to ~ vacant tenements⟩ ~ *vi* **1** : to return to an earlier point in a countdown **2** : to return to an original condition so that operation can begin again — used of an electronic device — **re·cy·cla·bil·i·ty** \-ˌsī-k(ə-)lə-ˈbi-lə-tē\ *n* — **re·cy·cla·ble** \-ˈsī-k(ə-)lə-bəl\ *adj or n* — **re·cy·cler** \-k(ə-)lər\ *n*

[2]**recycle** *n* (1926) : the process of recycling

[1]**red** \ˈred\ *adj* **red·der; red·dest** [ME, fr. OE *rēad;* akin to OHG *rōt* red, L *ruber & rufus,* Gk *erythros*] (bef. 12c) **1 a** : of the color red **b** : having red as a distinguishing color **2 a** (1) : flushed esp. with anger or embarrassment (2) : RUDDY, FLORID (3) : being or having skin of a coppery hue **b** : BLOODSHOT ⟨eyes ~ from crying⟩ **c** : being in the color range between a moderate orange and russet or bay **d** : tinged with red : REDDISH **3** : heated to redness : GLOWING **4 a** : inciting or endorsing radical social or political change esp. by force **b** *often cap* : COMMUNIST **c** *often cap* : of or relating to a communist country and esp. to the U.S.S.R. **5** : tending to support Republicans in a general election ⟨~ states⟩ — **red in tooth and claw** : characterized by or displaying brutal emotion or violent behavior

[2]**red** *n* (bef. 12c) **1** : a color whose hue resembles that of blood or of the ruby or is that of the long-wave extreme of the visible spectrum **2** : red clothing ⟨the lady in ~⟩ **3** : one that is of a red or reddish color: as **a** : RED WINE **b** : an animal with a red or reddish coat **4 a** : a pigment or dye that colors red **b** : a shade or tint of red **5 a** : one who advocates the violent overthrow of an existing social or political order **b** *cap* : COMMUNIST **6** [fr. the bookkeeping practice of entering debit items in red ink] : the condition of showing a loss — usu. used with *the* ⟨in the ~⟩; compare BLACK

red *abbr* reduce; reduction

re·dact \ri-ˈdakt\ *vt* [ME, fr. L *redactus,* pp. of *redigere*] (15c) **1** : to put in writing : FRAME **2** : to select or adapt (as by obscuring or removing sensitive information) for publication or release; *broadly* : EDIT **3** : to obscure or remove (text) from a document prior to publication or release

re·dac·tion \-ˈdak-shən\ *n* [F *rédaction,* fr. LL *redaction-, redactio* act of reducing, compressing, fr. L *redigere* to bring back, reduce, fr. *re-, red-* re- + *agere* to lead — more at AGENT] (1785) **1** : an act or instance of redacting something **2** : a work that has been redacted : EDITION, VERSION — **re·dac·tion·al** \-shnəl, -shə-nᵊl\ *adj*

re·dac·tor \-ˈdak-tər\ *n* (1816) : one who redacts a work; *esp* : EDITOR

red admiral *n* (1798) : a nymphalid butterfly (*Vanessa atalanta*) that is common in both Europe and America, has broad orange-red bands on the forewings, and feeds chiefly on nettles in the larval stage

red alert *n* (1941) : the final stage of alert in which enemy attack appears imminent; *broadly* : a state of alert brought on by impending danger

red alga *n* (1834) : any of a division (Rhodophyta) of chiefly marine algae that have predominantly red pigmentation

red ant *n* (1667) : any of various reddish ants (as the pharaoh ant)

red·ar·gue \ri-ˈdär-(ˌ)gyü\ *vt* **-gued; -gu·ing** [ME, fr. L *redarguere,* fr. *red-* + *arguere* to demonstrate, prove — more at ARGUE] (1627) *archaic* : CONFUTE, DISPROVE
re·date \(ˌ)rē-ˈdāt\ *vt* (1611) **1** : to date again or anew **2** : to change the date of : give a different date to
red–bait \ˈred-ˌbāt\ *vb, often cap R, vt* (1940) : to subject (as a person or group) to red-baiting ~ *vi* : to engage in red-baiting — **red–bait·er** *n, often cap R*
red–bait·ing *n, often cap R* (1928) : the act of attacking or persecuting as a Communist or as communistic
red bay *n* (ca. 1730) : a southern U.S. tree (*Persea borbonia*) of the laurel family having aromatic evergreen leaves and dark red heartwood
red bean *n* (1859) **1** : a red kidney bean and esp. one that is small and round **2** : a small dark red seed of the adzuki bean that is often combined with sugar to produce a sweet paste used in cooking
red·bel·ly dace \ˈred-ˈbe-lē-\ *n* (1948) : either of two small brightly marked No. American cyprinid fishes (*Phoxinus eos* and *P. erythrogaster*) — called also *red-bel·lied dace* \-lēd-\
red·bird \ˈred-ˌbərd\ *n* (1669) : any of several birds (as a cardinal or scarlet tanager) with predominantly red plumage
red blood cell *n* (1910) : any of the hemoglobin-containing cells that carry oxygen to the tissues and are responsible for the red color of vertebrate blood — called also *erythrocyte, red blood corpuscle, red cell, red corpuscle*
red–blood·ed \ˈred-ˈblə-dəd\ *adj* (1860) : VIGOROUS, LUSTY
red·bone \ˈred-ˌbōn\ *n* (1916) : any of a breed of agile speedy coonhounds of U.S. origin having a usu. solid dark red coat
red·breast \ˈred-ˌbrest\ *n* (15c) **1** : a bird (as a robin) with a reddish breast **2** : a reddish-bellied sunfish (*Lepomis auritus*) of the eastern U.S. — called also *red-breasted bream*
red·brick \-ˌbrik\ *adj* (1835) **1** : built of red brick **2** *often cap* [fr. the common use of red brick in constructing the buildings of recently founded universities] : of, relating to, or being the British universities founded in the 19th or early 20th century — compare OXBRIDGE, PLATEGLASS
red·bud \-ˌbəd\ *n* (1705) : any of several deciduous shrubs or trees (genus *Cercis*) of the legume family with usu. pale rosy-pink flowers
red bug *n* (1804) *Southern & Midland* : CHIGGER 2
red·cap \ˈred-ˌkap\ *n* (1918) : a baggage porter (as at a railroad station) — compare SKYCAP
red–carpet *adj* [fr. the traditional laying down of a red carpet for important guests to walk on] (1952) : marked by ceremonial courtesy ⟨~ treatment⟩
red carpet *n* (1934) : a greeting or reception marked by ceremonial courtesy — usu. used in the phrase *roll out the red carpet*
red cedar *n* (1682) **1** : a common juniper (*Juniperus virginiana*) chiefly of the eastern U.S. that has dark green closely imbricated scalelike leaves; *also* : a related tree (*J. silicicola*) of the southeastern U.S. **2** : WESTERN RED CEDAR 1 **3** : the red or reddish-brown wood of a red cedar
red cent *n* (ca. 1839) : PENNY — used for emphasis in negative constructions
red clover *n* (bef. 12c) : a European clover (*Trifolium pratense*) that has globose heads of reddish-purple flowers, is widely cultivated as a hay, forage, and cover crop, and is naturalized in the U.S.
red·coat \ˈred-ˌkōt\ *n* (1520) : a British soldier esp. in America during the Revolutionary War
red–cockaded woodpecker *n* (1810) : an endangered chiefly black-and-white woodpecker (*Picoides borealis*) of the southeastern U.S. having a barred back, white cheek patches, and in the male a small tuft of red feathers on each side of the head
red coral *n* (14c) : a gorgonian (*Corallium rubrum*) of the Mediterranean and adjacent parts of the Atlantic having a hard stony skeleton of a delicate red or pink color used for ornaments and jewelry
Red Cross *n* (1863) : a red Greek cross on a white background used as the emblem of the International Red Cross
red currant *n* (1620) : either of two Old World currants (*Ribes sativum* and *R. rubrum*) often cultivated for their fruit; *also* : the fruit

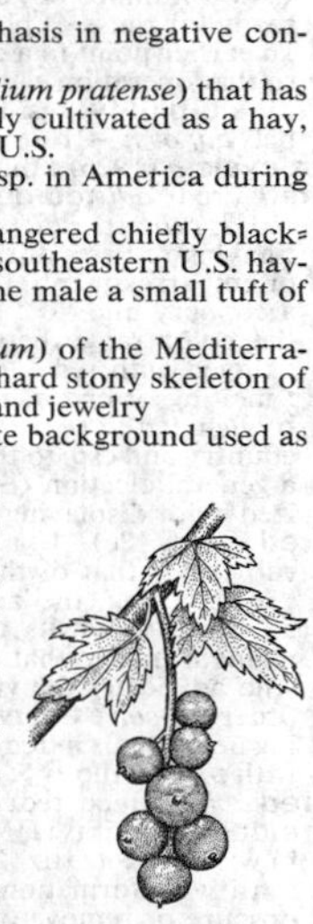
red currant

1**redd** \ˈred\ *vb* **redd·ed** *or* **redd; redd·ing** [ME (Sc), to clear, perh. alter. of *ridden* — more at RID] *vt* (ca. 1520) *chiefly dial* : to set in order — usu. used with *up* or *out* ~ *vi, chiefly dial* : to make things tidy — usu. used with *up*
2**redd** *n* [origin unknown] (1808) : the spawning ground or nest of various fishes
red deer *n* (15c) : ELK 1b — used for one of the Old World
Red Delicious *n* (1933) : a usu. large apple with sweet crisp juicy flesh and dark red skin
red·den \ˈre-dᵊn\ *vb* **red·dened; red·den·ing** \ˈred-niŋ, ˈre-dᵊn-iŋ\ *vt* (ca. 1611) : to make red or reddish ~ *vi* : to become red; *esp* : BLUSH
red·dish \ˈre-dish\ *adj* (14c) : tinged with red — **red·dish·ness** *n*
red dog *n* (1962) : BLITZ 2b — **red dog** *vb*
red drum *n* (1709) : a large coppery drum (*Sciaenops ocellatus*) chiefly of the Gulf of Mexico and the Atlantic coast of No. America that has a black spot at the base of the tail and is an important game and food fish — called also *channel bass, redfish*
red dwarf *n* (1926) : a star having substantially lower surface temperature, intrinsic luminosity, mass, and size than the sun
1**rede** \ˈrēd\ *vt* [ME — more at READ] (bef. 12c) **1** *archaic* : to give counsel to : ADVISE **2** *archaic* : INTERPRET, EXPLAIN
2**rede** *n* (bef. 12c) **1** *archaic* : COUNSEL, ADVICE **2** *archaic* : ACCOUNT, STORY
red·ear \ˈred-ˌir\ *n* (ca. 1948) : a common sunfish (*Lepomis microlophus*) of the southern and eastern U.S. that resembles the bluegill but has the back part of the operculum bright orange red and that feeds esp. on snails — called also *shellcracker*
re·dec·o·rate \(ˌ)rē-ˈde-kə-ˌrāt\ *vt* (ca. 1611) : to freshen or change in appearance : REFURBISH ~ *vi* : to freshen or change a decorative scheme — **re·dec·o·ra·tion** \(ˌ)rē-ˌde-kə-ˈrā-shən\ *n* — **re·dec·o·ra·tor** \(ˌ)rē-ˈde-kə-ˌrā-tər\ *n*
re·deem \ri-ˈdēm\ *vt* [ME *redemen,* fr. AF *redemer,* modif. of L *redimere,* fr. *re-, red-* re- + *emere* to take, buy; akin to Lith *imti* to take] (15c) **1 a** : to buy back : REPURCHASE **b** : to get or win back **2** : to free from what distresses or harms: as **a** : to free from captivity by payment of ransom **b** : to extricate from or help to overcome something detrimental **c** : to release from blame or debt : CLEAR **d** : to free from the consequences of sin **3** : to change for the better : REFORM **4** : REPAIR, RESTORE **5 a** : to free from a lien by payment of an amount secured thereby **b** (1) : to remove the obligation of by payment ⟨the U.S. Treasury ~*s* savings bonds on demand⟩ (2) : to exchange for something of value ⟨~ trading stamps⟩ **c** : to make good : FULFILL **6 a** : to atone for : EXPIATE ⟨~ an error⟩ **b** (1) : to offset the bad effect of (2) : to make worthwhile : RETRIEVE ***syn*** see RESCUE — **re·deem·able** \-ˈdē-mə-bəl\ *adj*
re·deem·er \-ˈdē-mər\ *n* (15c) : a person who redeems; *esp, cap* : JESUS
re·deem·ing \-ˈdē-miŋ\ *adj* (1631) : serving to offset or compensate for a defect ⟨her performance is the film's ~ feature⟩
re·de·fine \ˌrē-di-ˈfīn\ *vt* (1848) **1** : to define (as a concept) again : REFORMULATE ⟨had to ~ their terms⟩ **2 a** : to reexamine or reevaluate esp. with a view to change **b** : TRANSFORM 1c — **re·def·i·ni·tion** \(ˌ)rē-ˌde-fə-ˈni-shən\ *n*
re·demp·tion \ri-ˈdem(p)-shən\ *n* [ME *redempcioun,* fr. AF *redempcion,* fr. L *redemption-, redemptio,* fr. *redimere* to redeem] (14c) : the act, process, or an instance of redeeming
re·demp·tion·er \-sh(ə-)nər\ *n* (1771) : an immigrant to America in the 18th and 19th centuries who obtained passage by becoming an indentured servant
re·demp·tive \-ˈdem(p)-tiv\ *adj* (15c) : of, relating to, or bringing about redemption ⟨~ suffering⟩
Re·demp·tor·ist \ri-ˈdem(p)-t(ə-)rist\ *n* [F *rédemptoriste,* fr. LL *redemptor* redeemer, fr. L, contractor, fr. *redimere*] (1835) : a member of the Congregation of the Most Holy Redeemer founded by St. Alphonsus Liguori in Scala, Italy, in 1732 and devoted to preaching
re·demp·to·ry \ri-ˈdem(p)-t(ə-)rē\ *adj* (1602) : serving to redeem
re·de·ploy \ˌrē-di-ˈplȯi\ *vt* (1945) : to transfer from one area or activity to another ~ *vi* : to relocate men or equipment — **re·de·ploy·ment** \-mənt\ *n*
re·de·scribe \ˌrē-di-ˈskrīb\ *vt* (1858) : to describe anew or again; *esp* : to give a new and more complete description to (a biological taxon)
re·de·scrip·tion \-ˈskrip-shən\ *n* (1884) : a new and more complete description esp. of a biological taxon
re·de·sign \ˌrē-di-ˈzīn\ *vt* (1856) : to revise in appearance, function, or content — **redesign** *n*
re·de·vel·op \ˌrē-di-ˈve-ləp\ *vt* (1841) : to develop again; *esp* : REDESIGN, REBUILD — **re·de·vel·op·er** *n*
re·de·vel·op·ment \-mənt\ *n* (1848) : the act or process of redeveloping; *esp* : renovation of a blighted area ⟨urban ~⟩
red–eye \ˈred-ˌī\ *n* (1819) **1** : cheap whiskey **2** : the phenomenon of a subject's eyes appearing red in a color photograph taken with a flash **3** : a late night or overnight flight
red–eyed vireo *n* (1839) : a No. American vireo (*Vireo olivaceus*) having an olive-green back, white underparts, and red irises
red·eye gravy \ˈred-ˌī-\ *n* (1947) : gravy made from the juices of ham and often flavored with coffee
red fescue *n* (1900) : a perennial pasture and turf fescue (*Festuca rubra*) of Eurasia and No. America that has creeping rootstocks and reddish lemmas and sheaths
red·fish \ˈred-ˌfish\ *n* (15c) : any of various reddish fishes: as **a** (1) : a marine scorpaenid food fish (*Sebastes marinus*) of the northern Atlantic coasts of Europe and No. America that is usu. bright rose red or orange red when mature — called also *rosefish* (2) : a fish (*Sebastes mentella*) related to the redfish **b** : RED DRUM
red flag *n* (1777) **1** : a warning signal **2** : something that attracts usu. irritated attention
red flannel hash *n* (ca. 1907) : hash made esp. from beef, potatoes, and beets
red fox *n* (1761) : a usu. orange-red to reddish-brown Holarctic fox (*Vulpes vulpes*) that has a white-tipped tail — compare SILVER FOX
red giant *n* (1929) : a star that has low surface temperature and a diameter that is large relative to the sun
red–green blindness *n* (1888) : deficiency of color vision ranging from imperfect perception of red and green to an ability to see only tones of yellow, blue, and gray — called also *red-green color blindness*
Red Guard *n* (1966) : a member of a paramilitary youth organization in China in the 1960s
red gum *n* (1788) **1 a** : any of several Australian eucalyptus trees including one (*Eucalyptus camaldulensis*) naturalized esp. in California **b** : the reddish-brown gum of a eucalyptus **2** : SWEET GUM
red–hand·ed \ˈred-ˈhan-dəd\ *adv or adj* (1819) : in the act of committing a crime or misdeed ⟨caught ~⟩
red·head \ˈred-ˌhed\ *n* (1664) **1** : a person having red hair **2** : a No. American duck (*Aythya americana*) resembling the related canvasback but having a shorter bill with a black tip and in the male a brighter reddish head
red·head·ed \-ˌhe-dəd\ *adj* (1565) : having red hair or a red head
red heat *n* (1665) : the state of being red-hot; *also* : the temperature at which a substance is red-hot
red herring *n* (15c) **1** : a herring cured by salting and slow smoking to a dark brown color **2** [fr. the practice of drawing a red herring across a trail to confuse hunting dogs] : something that distracts attention from the real issue
red·horse \ˈred-ˌhȯrs\ *n* (1796) : any of various large suckers (genus *Moxostoma*) of No. American rivers and lakes with the males having red tail fins esp. in the breeding season
red–hot \ˈred-ˈhät\ *adj* (14c) : extremely hot: as **a** : glowing with heat **b** : exhibiting or marked by intense emotion, enthusiasm, or violence ⟨a ~ campaign⟩ **c** : FRESH, NEW ⟨~ news⟩ **d** : extremely popular
red hot *n* (1835) **1** : one who shows intense emotion or partisanship **2** : HOT DOG 1 **3** : a small red candy strongly flavored with cinnamon
red–hot poker *n* (1884) : a south African herb (*Kniphofia uvaria*) of the lily family having long linear leaves and tall spikes of bright red, orange-red, or yellow flowers
re·dia \ˈrē-dē-ə\ *n, pl* **re·di·ae** \-dē-ˌē\ *also* **re·di·as** [NL, fr. Francesco *Redi* †1698? Ital. naturalist] (1877) : a larva produced within the sporo-

cyst of many trematodes that produces another generation of rediae or develops into a cercaria — **re·di·al** \-dē-əl\ *adj*

re·dial \ˈrē-ˌdī(-ə)l, rē-ˈ\ *n* (1980) **:** a function on a telephone that automatically repeats the dialing of the last number called; *also* **:** a button that invokes this function — **re·dial** *vb*

Red Indian *n* (1831) *chiefly Brit* **:** AMERICAN INDIAN

red·in·gote \ˈre-diŋ-ˌgōt\ *n* [F, modif. of E *riding coat*] (1793) **:** a fitted outer garment: as **a :** a double-breasted coat with wide flat cuffs and collar worn by men in the 18th century **b :** a woman's lightweight coat open at the front **c :** a dress with a front gore of contrasting material

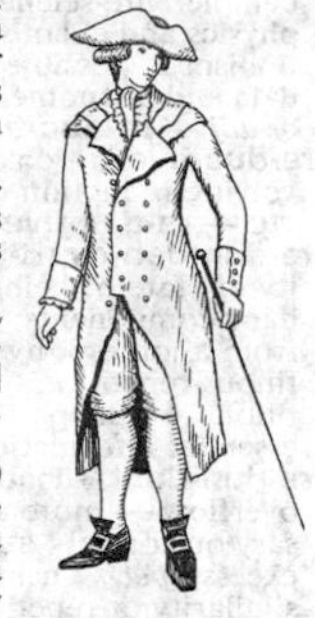
redingote a

red ink *n* [fr. the use of red ink in financial statements to indicate a loss] (1926) **1 :** a business loss **:** DEFICIT **2 :** the condition of showing a business loss

red·in·te·grate \ri-ˈdin-tə-ˌgrāt, re-\ *vt* [ME, fr. L *redintegratus,* pp. of *redintegrare,* fr. *re-, red-* re- + *integrare* to make complete — more at INTEGRATE] (15c) *archaic* **:** to restore to a former and esp. sound state

red·in·te·gra·tion \ri-ˌdin-tə-ˈgrā-shən, re-\ *n* (15c) **1** *archaic* **:** restoration to a former state **2 a :** revival of the whole of a previous mental state when a phase of it recurs **b :** arousal of any response by a part of the complex of stimuli that originally aroused that response — **red·in·te·gra·tive** \-ˈdin-tə-ˌgrā-tiv\ *adj*

re·di·rect \ˌrē-də-ˈrekt, ˌrē-(ˌ)dī-\ *vt* (1650) **:** to change the course or direction of — **re·di·rec·tion** \-ˈrek-shən\ *n*

[1]**re·dis·count** \(ˌ)rē-ˈdis-ˌkau̇nt, ˌrē-dis-ˈ\ *vt* (1838) **:** to discount again (as commercial paper) — **re·dis·count·able** \-ˌkau̇n-tə-bəl, -ˈkau̇n-\ *adj*

[2]**re·dis·count** \(ˌ)rē-ˈdis-ˌkau̇nt\ *n* (1892) **1 :** the act or process of rediscounting **2 :** negotiable paper that is rediscounted

re·dis·trib·ute \ˌrē-də-ˈstri-ˌbyüt *also* -byət\ *vt* (1611) **1 :** to alter the distribution of **:** REALLOCATE **2 :** to spread to other areas — **re·dis·tri·bu·tion** \(ˌ)rē-ˌdis-trə-ˈbyü-shən\ *n* — **re·dis·tri·bu·tion·al** \-shnəl, -shə-nᵊl\ *adj* — **re·dis·trib·u·tive** \ˌrē-də-ˈstri-byü-tiv, -byə-\ *adj*

re·dis·tri·bu·tion·ist \(ˌ)rē-ˌdis-trə-ˈbyü-sh(ə-)nist\ *n* (1961) **:** one who believes in or advocates a welfare state — **redistributionist** *adj*

re·dis·trict \(ˌ)rē-ˈdis-(ˌ)trikt\ *vt* (1850) **:** to divide anew into districts; *specif* **:** to revise the legislative districts of ~ *vi* **:** to revise legislative districts

red·i·vi·vus \ˌre-də-ˈvī-vəs, -ˈvē-\ *adj* [LL, fr. L, reused] (1675) **:** brought back to life **:** REBORN — used postpositively

red kangaroo *n* (1820) **:** a large kangaroo (*Macropus rufus*) of the dry plains of inland Australia with the male having a reddish-brown coat

red lead *n* (15c) **:** an orange-red to brick-red lead oxide Pb_3O_4 used in storage-battery plates, in glass and ceramics, and as a paint pigment

red leaf *n* (1909) **:** any of several plant diseases characterized by reddening of the foliage

red·leg \ˈred-ˌleg, -ˌlāg\ *n* (1900) **:** ARTILLERYMAN

red–legged grasshopper *n* (1867) **:** a widely distributed and sometimes highly destructive small No. American grasshopper (*Melanoplus femur-rubrum*) with red hind legs — called also *red-legged locust*

red–let·ter \ˈred-ˌle-tər\ *adj* [fr. the practice of marking holy days in red letters in church calendars] (1704) **:** of special significance

red–light *adj* (1900) **:** having numerous houses of prostitution ⟨a ~ district⟩

red light *n* (1849) **:** a warning signal; *esp* **:** a red traffic signal

[1]**red·line** \ˈred-ˈlīn\ *n* (1952) **:** a recommended safety limit **:** the fastest, farthest, or highest point or degree considered safe; *also* **:** the red line which marks this point on a gauge

[2]**red·line** \ˈred-ˌlīn, -ˈlīn\ *vi* (1968) **:** to withhold home-loan funds or insurance from neighborhoods considered poor economic risks ~ *vt* **:** to discriminate against in housing or insurance

red·ly \ˈred-lē\ *adv* (1611) **:** in a red manner **:** with red color

red man *n* (1725) **1 :** AMERICAN INDIAN **2** *cap R&M* [Improved Order of *Red Men*] **:** a member of a major benevolent and fraternal order

red maple *n* (1770) **:** a common tree (*Acer rubrum*) of eastern and central No. America that grows chiefly in moist soils, has reddish twigs and flowers, and yields a lighter and softer wood than the sugar maple

red marrow *n* (1900) **:** BONE MARROW b

red mass *n, often cap R&M* (1889) **:** a votive mass of the Holy Spirit celebrated in red vestments esp. at the opening of courts and congresses

red meat *n* (1792) **1 :** meat (as beef) that is red when raw **2 :** something substantial that can satisfy a basic need or appetite ⟨hungry for the *red meat* of passionate partisanship —William Safire⟩

red mite *n* (1894) **:** any of several mites having a red color: as **a :** EUROPEAN RED MITE **b :** CITRUS RED MITE

red mulberry *n* (1717) **:** a mulberry (*Morus rubra*) of No. American forests with toothed leaves and soft durable wood; *also* **:** its edible usu. purple fruit

red mullet *n* (1761) **:** GOATFISH; *esp* **:** either of two red or reddish food fishes (*Mullus surmuletus* and *M. barbatus*) of the Mediterranean Sea and the warmer Atlantic coasts of Europe and northern Africa that are noted for their ability to change color

red·neck \ˈred-ˌnek\ *n* (1830) **1** *sometimes disparaging* **:** a white member of the Southern rural laboring class **2** *often disparaging* **:** a person whose behavior and opinions are similar to those attributed to rednecks — **redneck** *also* **red·necked** \-ˌnekt\ *adj*

red·ness \-nəs\ *n* (bef. 12c) **:** the quality or state of being red or red-hot

re·do \(ˌ)rē-ˈdü\ *vt* **-did** \-ˈdid\; **-done** \-ˈdən\; **-do·ing** \-ˈdü-iŋ\; **-does** \-ˈdəz\ (1597) **1 :** to do over or again **2 :** REDECORATE — **re·do** \ˈrē-ˌdü, ˌrē-ˈdü\ *n*

red oak *n* (1634) **1 :** any of various No. American oaks (as *Quercus rubra* and *Quercus falcata*) that have acorns with the inner surface of the shell lined with woolly hairs, the acorn cap covered with thin scales, and leaf veins that usu. run beyond the margin of the leaf to form bristles **2 :** the wood of a red oak

red ocher *n* (1572) **:** a red earthy hematite used as a pigment

red·o·lence \ˈre-də-lən(t)s\ *n* (15c) **1 :** an often pungent or agreeable odor **2 :** the quality or state of being redolent *syn* see FRAGRANCE

red·o·lent \-lənt\ *adj* [ME, fr. MF, fr. L *redolent-, redolens,* prp. of *redolēre* to emit a scent, fr. *re-, red-* + *olēre* to smell — more at ODOR] (15c) **1 :** exuding fragrance **:** AROMATIC **2 a :** full of a specified fragrance **:** SCENTED ⟨air ~ of seaweed⟩ **b :** EVOCATIVE, SUGGESTIVE ⟨a city ~ of antiquity⟩ *syn* see ODOROUS — **red·o·lent·ly** *adv*

red osier *n* (1807) **:** a common shrubby No. American dogwood (*Cornus stolonifera* syn. *C. sericea*) with reddish-purple twigs, small white flowers, and globose blue or whitish fruit

re·dou·ble \(ˌ)rē-ˈdə-bəl\ *vt* (15c) **1 :** to make twice as great in size or amount; *broadly* **:** INTENSIFY, STRENGTHEN **2 a** *obs* **:** to echo back **b** *archaic* **:** REPEAT ~ *vi* **1 :** to become redoubled **2** *archaic* **:** RESOUND **3 :** to double an opponent's double in bridge — **redouble** *n*

re·doubt \ri-ˈdau̇t\ *n* [F *redoute,* fr. It *ridotto,* fr. ML *reductus* secret place, fr. L, withdrawn, fr. pp. of *reducere* to lead back — more at REDUCE] (ca. 1608) **1 a :** a small usu. temporary enclosed defensive work **b :** a defended position **:** protective barrier **2 :** a secure retreat **:** STRONGHOLD

re·doubt·able \ri-ˈdau̇-tə-bəl\ *adj* [ME *redoutable,* fr. AF, fr. *reduter* to dread, fr. *re-* + *duter* to doubt] (15c) **1 :** causing fear or alarm **:** FORMIDABLE **2 :** ILLUSTRIOUS, EMINENT; *broadly* **:** worthy of respect — **re·doubt·ably** \-blē\ *adv*

re·dound \ri-ˈdau̇nd\ *vi* [ME, fr. MF *redunder,* fr. L *redundare,* fr. *re-, red-* re- + *unda* wave — more at WATER] (14c) **1** *archaic* **:** to become swollen **:** OVERFLOW **2 :** to have an effect for good or ill ⟨new power alignments which may or may not ~ to the faculty's benefit —G. W. Bonham⟩ **3 :** to become transferred or added **:** ACCRUE **4 :** REBOUND, REFLECT

red·out \ˈred-ˌau̇t\ *n* (1942) **:** a condition in which centripetal acceleration (as that created when an aircraft abruptly enters a dive) drives blood to the head and causes reddening of the visual field and headache

re·dox \ˈrē-ˌdäks\ *adj* [*red*uction + *ox*idation] (1928) **:** of or relating to oxidation-reduction

red panda *n* (1955) **:** a long-tailed largely herbivorous mammal (*Ailurus fulgens*) that is related to and resembles the American raccoon, has long rusty or chestnut fur, and is found from the Himalayas to China — called also *lesser panda*

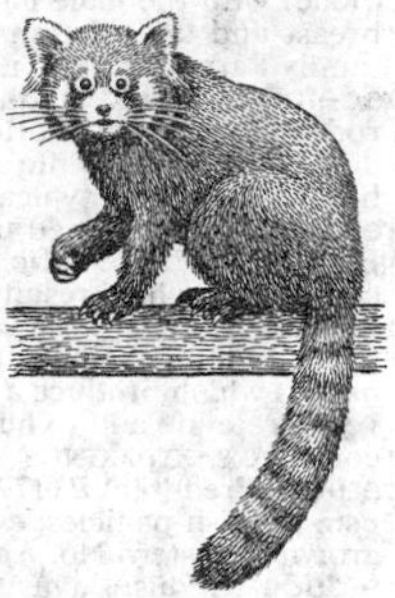
red panda

red–pen·cil \ˈred-ˌpen(t)-səl\ *vt* (1946) **1 :** CENSOR **2 :** CORRECT, REVISE

red pepper *n* (ca. 1591) **1 :** a mature red capsicum fruit (as a sweet pepper or hot pepper) **2 :** CAYENNE PEPPER 1

red pine *n* (1809) **1 :** a No. American pine (*Pinus resinosa*) that has reddish bark and two long needles in each cluster **2 :** the relatively hard wood of the red pine that consists chiefly of sapwood

red·poll \ˈred-ˌpōl\ *n* (1738) **:** either of two small finches (genus *Carduelis* syn. *Acanthis* of the family Fringillidae) having brownish streaked plumage and a red or rosy crown; *esp* **:** one (*C. flammea*) found in northern regions of both the New and Old World

red poll *n, often cap R&P* [alter. of *red polled*] (1891) **:** any of a breed of large hornless red beef cattle of English origin

[1]**re·dress** \ri-ˈdres\ *vt* [ME, fr. AF *redresser* to set upright, restore, redress, fr. *re-* + *dresser* to set straight — more at DRESS] (14c) **1 a** (1) **:** to set right **:** REMEDY ⟨looked to charity, not to legislation, to ~ social wrongs —W. R. Inge⟩ (2) **:** to make up for **:** COMPENSATE **b :** to remove the cause of (a grievance or complaint) **c :** to exact reparation for **:** AVENGE **2** *archaic* **a :** to requite (a person) for a wrong or loss **b :** HEAL *syn* see CORRECT — **re·dress·er** *n*

[2]**re·dress** \ri-ˈdres, ˈrē-ˌ\ *n* (14c) **1 a :** relief from distress **b :** means or possibility of seeking a remedy ⟨without ~⟩ **2 :** compensation for wrong or loss **:** REPARATION **3 a :** an act or instance of redressing **b :** RETRIBUTION, CORRECTION

red ribbon *n* (1927) **:** a red ribbon usu. with appropriate words or markings awarded the second-place winner in a competition

red·root \ˈred-ˌrüt, -ˌru̇t\ *n* (1709) **1 :** a perennial herb (*Lachnanthes caroliniana* syn. *L. tinctoria*) of the eastern U.S. whose red root is the source of a dye **2 :** NEW JERSEY TEA **3 :** BLOODROOT **4 :** a pigweed (*Amaranthus retroflexus*) that bears greenish flowers in dense spikes with bracts almost twice as long as the sepals

red rust *n* (1846) **1 :** the uredinial stage of a rust **2 :** the diseased condition produced by red rust

red salmon *n* (1761) **:** SOCKEYE SALMON

red–shaft·ed flicker \ˈred-ˈshaf-təd-\ *n* (1846) **:** a flicker of western No. America with light red on the underside of the tail and wings, a gray nape with no red, and in the male red on each cheek

red·shank \ˈred-ˌshaŋk\ *n* (1525) **:** a common Old World sandpiper (*Tringa totanus*) with pale red legs and feet

red·shift \ˈred-ˈshift\ *n* (1923) **:** a displacement of the spectrum of a celestial body toward longer wavelengths that is a consequence of the Doppler effect or the gravitational field of the source; *also* **:** a measurement of a celestial body's redshift equal to the ratio of the displacement of a spectral line to its known unshifted wavelength and used esp. to calculate the body's distance from earth — **red·shift·ed** *adj*

red·shirt \ˈred-ˌshərt\ *n* [fr. the red jersey commonly worn by such a player in practice scrimmages against the regulars] (1955) **:** a college athlete who is kept out of varsity competition for a year in order to extend eligibility — **redshirt** *vb*

red–shoul·dered hawk \-ˌshōl-dərd-\ *n* (1812) **:** a common No. American hawk (*Buteo lineatus*) that has a banded tail and a light spot on the underside of the wings toward the tips

red sin·dhi \-ˈsin-dē\ *n* [¹*red* + *sindhi* one belonging to Sind, Pakistan] (1946) : any of a breed of humped rather small red dairy cattle developed in southwestern Asia and extensively used for crossbreeding with European stock in tropical areas

red siskin *n* (1948) : a finch (*Carduelis cucullata* of the family Fringillidae) of northern So. America that is scarlet with black head, wings, and tail

red·skin \ˈred-ˌskin\ *n* (1699) *usu offensive* : AMERICAN INDIAN

red snapper *n* (1755) : any of various reddish fishes (as of the genera *Lutjanus* and *Sebastes*) including several food fishes

red snow *n* (1678) : snow colored by various airborne dusts or by a growth of algae (as of the genus *Chlamydomonas*) that contain red pigment and live in the upper layer of snow; *also* : an alga causing red snow

red soil *n* (1889) : any of a group of zonal soils that develop in a warm temperate moist climate under deciduous or mixed forests and that have thin organic and organic-mineral layers overlying a yellowish-brown leached layer resting on a red horizon marked by illuviation — called also *red podzolic soil*

red spider *n* (1646) : SPIDER MITE; *esp* : TWO-SPOTTED SPIDER MITE

red spruce *n* (1777) : a spruce (*Picea rubens*) of the eastern U.S. and Canada that has pubescent twigs and yellowish-green needles and is an important source of lumber and pulpwood

red squill *n* (1738) **1** : a squill having a bulb with red outer scales; *broadly* : SQUILL 1a **2** : a rat poison derived from the bulb of red squill

red squirrel *n* (1682) : a common and widely distributed No. American squirrel (*Tamiasciurus hudsonicus*) that has reddish upper parts and is smaller than the gray squirrel

red star *n* (1849) : a star having a very low surface temperature and a red color

red·start \ˈred-ˌstärt\ *n* [*red* + obs. *start* handle, tail] (ca. 1570) **1** : a small Old World songbird (*Phoenicurus phoenicurus* of the family Turdidae) with the male having a white brow, black throat, and chestnut breast and tail **2** : an American warbler (*Setophaga ruticilla* of the family Parulidae) with a black and orange male

red–tailed hawk \ˈred-ˌtāld-\ *n* (1805) : a widely distributed chiefly rodent-eating New World hawk (*Buteo jamaicensis*) that is usu. mottled dusky above and white streaked dusky and tinged with buff below and has a rather short typically reddish tail — called also *redtail*

red tape *n* [fr. the red tape formerly used to bind legal documents in England] (1736) : official routine or procedure marked by excessive complexity which results in delay or inaction

red tide *n* (1904) : seawater discolored by the presence of large numbers of dinoflagellates (esp. of the genera *Gonyaulax* and *Gymnodinium*) which produce a toxin poisonous esp. to many forms of marine vertebrate life and to humans who consume contaminated shellfish — compare SAXITOXIN

red·top \ˈred-ˌtäp\ *n* (1790) : any of several grasses (genus *Agrostis*) with usu. reddish panicles; *esp* : a Eurasian grass (*A. alba* syn. *A. gigantea*) grown in eastern No. America as forage and lawn grass

re·duce \ri-ˈdüs, -ˈdyüs\ *vb* **re·duced; re·duc·ing** [ME, to lead back, fr. L *reducere*, fr. *re-* + *ducere* to lead — more at TOW] *vt* (14c) **1 a** : to draw together or cause to converge : CONSOLIDATE ⟨~ all the questions to one⟩ **b (1)** : to diminish in size, amount, extent, or number ⟨~ taxes⟩ ⟨~ the likelihood of war⟩ **(2)** : to decrease the volume and concentrate the flavor of by boiling ⟨add the wine and ~ the sauce for two minutes⟩ **c** : to narrow down : RESTRICT ⟨the Indians were *reduced* to small reservations⟩ **d** : to make shorter : ABRIDGE **2** *archaic* : to restore to righteousness : SAVE **3** : to bring to a specified state or condition ⟨the impact of the movie *reduced* them to tears⟩ **4 a** : to force to capitulate **b** : FORCE, COMPEL **5 a** : to bring to a systematic form or character ⟨~ natural events to laws⟩ **b** : to put down in written or printed form ⟨~ an agreement to writing⟩ **6** : to correct (as a fracture) by bringing displaced or broken parts back into their normal positions **7 a** : to lower in grade or rank : DEMOTE **b** : to lower in condition or status : DOWNGRADE **8 a** : to diminish in strength or density **b** : to diminish in value **9 a (1)** : to change the denominations or form of without changing the value **(2)** : to construct a geometrical figure similar to but smaller than (a given figure) **b** : to transpose from one form into another : CONVERT **c** : to change (an expression) to an equivalent but more fundamental expression ⟨~ a fraction⟩ **10** : to break down (as by crushing or grinding) : PULVERIZE **11 a** : to bring to the metallic state by removal of nonmetallic elements ⟨~ an ore by heat⟩ **b** : DEOXIDIZE **c** : to combine with or subject to the action of hydrogen **d (1)** : to change (an element or ion) from a higher to a lower oxidation state **(2)** : to add one or more electrons to (an atom or ion or molecule) **12** : to change (a stressed vowel) to an unstressed vowel ~ *vi* **1 a (1)** : to become diminished or lessened; *esp* : to lose weight by dieting **(2)** : to become reduced ⟨ferric iron ~*s* to ferrous iron⟩ **b** : to become concentrated or consolidated **c** : to undergo meiosis **2** : to become converted or equated ***syn*** see DECREASE, CONQUER — **re·duc·er** *n* — **re·duc·ibil·i·ty** \-ˌdü-sə-ˈbi-lə-tē, -ˌdyü-\ *n* — **re·duc·ible** \-ˈdü-sə-bəl, -ˈdyü-\ *adj* — **re·duc·ibly** \-blē\ *adv*

reducing agent *n* (ca. 1817) : a substance that reduces a chemical compound usu. by donating electrons

re·duc·tant \ri-ˈdək-tənt\ *n* (1925) : REDUCING AGENT

re·duc·tase \-ˌtās, -ˌtāz\ *n* (1902) : an enzyme that catalyzes reduction

re·duc·tio ad ab·sur·dum \ri-ˈdək-tē-ˌō-ˌad-əb-ˈsər-dəm, -ˈdək-sē-ō-, -shē-, -ˈzər-\ *n* [LL, lit., reduction to the absurd] (1741) **1** : disproof of a proposition by showing an absurdity to which it leads when carried to its logical conclusion **2** : the carrying of something to an absurd extreme

re·duc·tion \ri-ˈdək-shən\ *n* [ME *reduccion* restoration, fr. MF *reduction*, fr. LL & L; LL *reduction-, reductio* reduction (in a syllogism), fr. L, restoration, fr. *reducere*] (15c) **1** : the act or process of reducing : the state of being reduced **2 a** : something made by reducing **b** : the amount by which something is reduced **3** [Sp *reducción*, fr. L *reduction-, reductio*] : a So. American Indian settlement directed by Jesuit missionaries **4** : MEIOSIS 2; *specif* : production of the gametic chromosome number in the first meiotic division — **re·duc·tion·al** \-shnəl, -shə-nᵊl\ *adj*

reduction division *n* (1891) : the usu. first division of meiosis in which chromosome reduction occurs; *also* : MEIOSIS 2

reduction gear *n* (1894) : a combination of gears used to reduce the input speed (as of a marine turbine) to a lower output speed (as of a ship's propeller)

re·duc·tion·ism \ri-ˈdək-shə-ˌni-zəm\ *n* (1943) **1** : explanation of complex life-science processes and phenomena in terms of the laws of physics and chemistry; *also* : a theory or doctrine that complete reductionism is possible **2** : a procedure or theory that reduces complex data and phenomena to simple terms — **re·duc·tion·ist** \-sh(ə-)nist\ *n or adj* — **re·duc·tion·is·tic** \-ˌdək-shə-ˈnis-tik\ *adj*

re·duc·tive \ri-ˈdək-tiv\ *adj* (1633) **1** : of, relating to, causing, or involving reduction **2** : of or relating to reductionism : REDUCTIONISTIC — **re·duc·tive·ly** *adv* — **re·duc·tive·ness** *n*

re·dun·dan·cy \ri-ˈdən-dən(t)-sē\ *n, pl* **-cies** (ca. 1602) **1 a** : the quality or state of being redundant : SUPERFLUITY **b** : the use of redundant components; *also* : such components **c** *chiefly Brit* : dismissal from a job esp. by layoff **2** : PROFUSION, ABUNDANCE **3 a** : superfluous repetition : PROLIXITY **b** : an act or instance of needless repetition **4** : the part of a message that can be eliminated without loss of essential information

re·dun·dant \-dənt\ *adj* [L *redundant-, redundans*, prp. of *redundare* to overflow — more at REDOUND] (1594) **1 a** : exceeding what is necessary or normal : SUPERFLUOUS **b** : characterized by or containing an excess; *specif* : using more words than necessary **c** : characterized by similarity or repetition ⟨a group of particularly ~ brick buildings⟩ **d** *chiefly Brit* : no longer needed for a job and hence laid off **2** : PROFUSE, LAVISH **3** : serving as a duplicate for preventing failure of an entire system (as a spacecraft) upon failure of a single component — **re·dun·dant·ly** *adv*

re·du·pli·cate \ri-ˈdü-pli-ˌkāt, ˈrē-, -ˈdyü-\ *vt* [LL *reduplicatus*, pp. of *reduplicare*, fr. L *re-* + *duplicare* to double — more at DUPLICATE] (ca. 1570) **1** : to make or perform again : COPY, REPEAT **2** : to form (a word) by reduplication — **re·du·pli·cate** \-kət\ *adj*

re·du·pli·ca·tion \ri-ˌdü-pli-ˈkā-shən, ˌrē-, -ˈdyü-\ *n* (1555) **1** : an act or instance of doubling or reiterating **2 a** : an often grammatically functional repetition of a radical element or a part of it occurring usu. at the beginning of a word and often accompanied by change of the radical vowel **b (1)** : a word or form produced by reduplication **(2)** : the repeated element in such a word or form **3** : ANADIPLOSIS — **re·du·pli·ca·tive** \ri-ˈdü-pli-ˌkā-tiv, ˈrē-, -ˈdyü-\ *adj* — **re·du·pli·ca·tive·ly** *adv*

re·du·vi·id \ri-ˈdü-vē-əd, -ˈdyü-\ *n* [ultim. fr. L *reduvia* hangnail] (1888) : ASSASSIN BUG — **reduviid** *adj*

re·dux \(ˌ)rē-ˈdəks, ˈrē-ˌ\ *adj* [L, returning, fr. *reducere* to lead back] (1860) : brought back — used postpositively

red·ware \ˈred-ˌwer\ *n* (1699) : earthenware pottery made of clay containing considerable iron oxide

red water *n* (1594) : any of several cattle diseases (as Texas fever) characterized by hematuria

red wheat *n* (1523) : a wheat that has red grains

red wine *n* (15c) : a wine with a predominantly red color derived during fermentation from the natural pigment in the skins of dark-colored grapes

red·wing \ˈred-ˌwiŋ\ *n* (1657) **1** : a European thrush (*Turdus iliacus* syn. *T. musicus*) having the underwing coverts red **2** : RED-WINGED BLACKBIRD

red–winged blackbird \ˈred-ˌwiŋd-\ *n* (1797) : a No. American blackbird (*Agelaius phoeniceus*) of which the adult male is black with a patch of bright scarlet at the bend of the wings bordered behind with yellow or buff — called also *redwing blackbird*

red wolf *n* (1840) : a wolf (*Canis rufus* syn. *C. niger*) orig. of the southeastern U.S. that has been extirpated from most of its natural range

red·wood \ˈred-ˌwu̇d\ *n* (ca. 1585) **1** : any of various woods (as brazilwood) yielding a red dye **2** : a tree that yields a red dyewood or produces red or reddish wood **3 a** : a very tall coniferous tree (*Sequoia sempervirens*) of the bald cypress family that grows chiefly in coastal California, sometimes reaches a height of 360 feet (110 meters), and is a commercially important timber tree — called also *coast redwood*; see CONE illustration **b** : its brownish-red durable wood

red worm *n* (15c) : BLOODWORM

red zone *n* (1983) : the area of a football field inside an opponent's 20-yard line

re·echo \(ˌ)rē-ˈe-(ˌ)kō\ *vi* (1590) : to repeat or return an echo : echo again or repeatedly : REVERBERATE ~ *vt* : to echo back : REPEAT

¹**reed** \ˈrēd\ *n* [ME *rede*, fr. OE *hrēod*; akin to OHG *hriot* reed] (bef. 12c) **1 a** : any of various tall grasses with slender often prominently jointed stems that grow esp. in wet areas **b** : a stem of a reed **c** : a person or thing too weak to rely on : one easily swayed or overcome **2** : a growth or mass of reeds; *specif* : reeds for thatching **3** : ARROW **4** : a wind instrument made from the hollow joint of a plant **5** : an ancient Hebrew unit of length equal to six cubits **6 a** : a thin elastic tongue (as of cane, wood, metal, or plastic) fastened at one end over an air opening in a wind instrument (as a clarinet, organ pipe, or accordion) and set in vibration by an air current **b** : a woodwind instrument that produces sound by the vibrating of a reed against the mouthpiece ⟨the ~*s* of an orchestra⟩ **7** : a device on a loom resembling a comb and used to space warp yarns evenly **8** : REEDING 1a — **reed·like** \-ˌlīk\ *adj*

²**reed** *vt* (1951) : MILL 2

reed·buck \ˈrēd-ˌbək\ *n, pl* **reedbuck** *also* **reedbucks** (1834) : any of a genus (*Redunca*) of fawn-colored African antelopes in which the males have curved and ridged horns

reed·ed \ˈrē-dəd\ *adj* (1823) : decorated with reeds or reeding ⟨a bed with ~ posts⟩

re·ed·i·fy \(ˌ)rē-ˈe-də-ˌfī\ *vt* **-fied; -fy·ing** [ME *reedifien*, fr. AF *reedifier*, fr. LL *reaedificare*, fr. L *re-* + *aedificare* to build — more at EDIFY] (15c) *Brit* : REBUILD

reed·ing \ˈrē-diŋ\ *n* (1815) **1 a** : a small convex molding — see MOLDING illustration **b** : decoration by series of reedings **2** : MILLING

re·edit \(ˌ)rē-ˈe-dət\ *vt* (1797) : to edit again : make a new edition of — **re·edi·tion** \ˌrē-ə-ˈdi-shən\ *n*

reed·man \ˈrēd-ˌman\ *n* (1872) : one who plays a reed instrument

reed organ *n* (1851) : a keyboard wind instrument in which the wind acts on a set of free reeds

reed pipe *n* (ca. 1741) **:** a pipe-organ pipe producing its tone by vibration of a beating reed in a current of air

re·ed·u·cate \(ˌ)rē-ˈe-jə-ˌkāt\ *vt* (1808) **:** to train again; *esp* **:** to rehabilitate through education — **re·ed·u·ca·tion** \(ˌ)rē-ˌe-jə-ˈkā-shən\ *n* — **re·ed·u·ca·tive** \(ˌ)rē-ˈe-jə-ˌkā-tiv\ *adj*

reedy \ˈrē-dē\ *adj* **reed·i·er; -est** (14c) **1 :** abounding in or covered with reeds **2 :** made of or resembling reeds; *esp* **:** SLENDER, FRAIL **3 :** having the tone quality of a reed instrument — **reed·i·ness** \-nəs\ *n*

[1]**reef** \ˈrēf\ *n* [ME *riff,* fr. ON *rif;* prob. akin to ON *rīfa* to rend — more at RIVE] (14c) **1 :** a part of a sail taken in or let out in regulating size **2 :** reduction in sail area by reefing

[2]**reef** *vt* (1667) **1 :** to reduce the area of (a sail) by rolling or folding a portion **2 :** to lower or bring inboard (a spar) wholly or partially ∼ *vi* **:** to reduce a sail by taking in a reef — **reef·able** \ˈrē-fə-bəl\ *adj*

[3]**reef** *n* [D *rif,* fr. MD, fr. ON, lit. rib; akin to OE *ribb* rib — more at RIB] (1584) **1 a :** a chain of rocks or coral or a ridge of sand at or near the surface of water — compare ATOLL, BARRIER REEF **b :** a hazardous obstruction **2 :** LODE, VEIN — **reefy** \ˈrē-fē\ *adj*

[1]**reef·er** \ˈrē-fər\ *n* (1818) **1 :** one that reefs **2 :** a close-fitting usu. double-breasted jacket or coat of thick cloth

[2]**ree·fer** \ˈrē-fər\ *n* [by shortening & alter.] (1914) **1 :** REFRIGERATOR **2 :** a refrigerator car, truck, trailer, or ship

[3]**ree·fer** *n* [prob. modif. of MexSp *grifa*] (1927) **:** MARIJUANA 2; *also* **:** a marijuana cigarette

reef knot *n* (1841) **:** a square knot used in reefing a sail

[1]**reek** \ˈrēk\ *n* [ME *rek,* fr. OE *rēc;* akin to OHG *rouh* smoke] (bef. 12c) **1** *chiefly dial* **:** SMOKE **2 :** VAPOR, FOG **3 :** a strong or disagreeable fume or odor

[2]**reek** *vi* (bef. 12c) **1 :** to emit smoke or vapor **2 a :** to give off or become permeated with a strong or offensive odor ⟨a room ∼*ing* of incense⟩ **b :** to give a strong impression of some constituent quality or feature ⟨a neighborhood that ∼*s* of poverty⟩ **3 :** EMANATE ∼ *vt* **1 :** to subject to the action of smoke or vapor **2 :** EXUDE, GIVE OFF ⟨a politician who ∼*s* charm⟩ — **reek·er** *n* — **reeky** \ˈrē-kē\ *adj*

[1]**reel** \ˈrēl\ *n* [ME, fr. OE *hrēol;* akin to ON *hræll* weaver's reed, Gk *krekein* to weave] (bef. 12c) **1 :** a revolvable device on which something flexible is wound: as **a :** a small windlass at the butt of a fishing rod for the line **b** *chiefly Brit* **:** a spool or bobbin for sewing thread **c :** a flanged spool for photographic film; *esp* **:** one for motion pictures **2 :** a quantity of something wound on a reel

[2]**reel** *vt* (14c) **1 :** to wind on or as if on a reel **2 :** to draw by reeling a line ⟨∼ a fish in⟩ ∼ *vi* **:** to turn a reel — **reel·able** \ˈrē-lə-bəl\ *adj*

[3]**reel** *vb* [ME *relen,* prob. fr. *reel,* n.] *vi* (14c) **1 a :** to turn or move round and round **b :** to be in a whirl **2 :** to behave in a violent disorderly manner **3 :** to waver or fall back (as from a blow) **4 :** to walk or move unsteadily ∼ *vt* **:** to cause to reel

[4]**reel** *n* (1572) **:** a reeling motion

[5]**reel** *n* [prob. fr. [4]*reel*] (ca. 1585) **1 :** a lively Scottish-Highland dance; *also* **:** the music for this dance **2 :** VIRGINIA REEL

re·elect \ˌrē-ə-ˈlekt\ *vt* (1601) **:** to elect for another term in office — **re·elec·tion** \-ˈlek-shən\ *n*

reel·er \ˈrē-lər\ *n* (ca. 1598) **1 :** one that reels **2 :** a motion picture having a specified number of reels ⟨a two-*reeler*⟩

reel off *vt* (1837) **1 :** to tell or recite readily and usu. at length ⟨*reel off* a few jokes to break the ice⟩ **2 :** to chalk up usu. as a series

reel–to–reel *adj* (1961) **:** of, relating to, or utilizing magnetic tape that requires threading on a take-up reel ⟨a ∼ tape recorder⟩

re·em·broi·der \ˌrē-əm-ˈbrȯi-dər\ *vt* (1927) **:** to outline a design (as on lace) with embroidery stitching

re·en·act \ˌrē-ə-ˈnakt\ *vt* (ca. 1676) **1 :** to enact (as a law) again **2 :** to act or perform again **3 :** to repeat the actions of (an earlier event or incident) — **re·en·act·ment** \-ˈnak(t)-mənt\ *n*

re·en·act·or \ˌrē-ə-ˈnak-tər\ *n* (1980) **:** a person who participates in reenactments of historical events

reenforce *var of* REINFORCE

re·en·gi·neer \(ˌ)rē-ˌen-jə-ˈnir\ *vt* (1944) **1 :** to engineer again or anew **:** REDESIGN ⟨∼*ed* the chassis⟩ **2 :** to reorganize the operations of (an organization) so as to improve efficiency

re·en·ter \(ˌ)rē-ˈen-tər\ *vt* (15c) **1 :** to enter (something) again **2 :** to return to and enter ∼ *vi* **:** to enter again

re·en·trance \(ˌ)rē-ˈen-trən(t)s\ *n* (1594) **:** REENTRY

[1]**re·en·trant** \-trənt\ *adj* (1781) **:** directed inward

[2]**reentrant** *n* (1899) **1 :** one that reenters **2 :** one that is reentrant **3 :** an indentation in a landform

re·en·try \(ˌ)rē-ˈen-trē\ *n* (15c) **1 :** a retaking possession; *esp* **:** entry by a lessor on leased premises on the tenant's failure to perform the conditions of the lease **2 :** a second or new entry **3 :** a playing card that will enable a player to regain the lead **4 :** the action of reentering the earth's atmosphere after travel in space

reest \ˈrēst\ *vi* [prob. short for Sc *arreest* to arrest, fr. ME (Sc) *arreisten,* fr. AF *arester* — more at ARREST] (1786) *chiefly Scot* **:** BALK

[1]**reeve** \ˈrēv\ *n* [ME *reve,* fr. OE *gerēfa,* fr. *ge-* (associative prefix) + *-rēfa* (akin to OE *-rōf* number, OHG *ruova*) — more at CO-] (bef. 12c) **1 :** a local administrative agent of an Anglo-Saxon king **2 :** a medieval English manor officer responsible chiefly for overseeing the discharge of feudal obligations **3 a :** the council president in some Canadian municipalities **b :** a local official charged with enforcement of specific regulations ⟨deer ∼⟩

[2]**reeve** *vb* **rove** \ˈrōv\ *or* **reeved; reev·ing** [origin unknown] *vt* (1627) **1 :** to pass (as a rope) through a hole or opening **2 :** to fasten by passing through a hole or around something **3 :** to pass a rope through ∼ *vi, of a rope* **:** to pass through a block or similar device

[3]**reeve** *n* [origin unknown] (1634) **:** the female of the ruff (sandpiper)

[1]**ref** \ˈref\ *n* (1899) **:** a referee in a game or sport

[2]**ref** *abbr* **1** reference **2** refunding

re·fash·ion \(ˌ)rē-ˈfa-shən\ *vt* (1628) **:** REMAKE, ALTER

re·fect \ri-ˈfekt\ *vt* [L *refectus,* pp. of *reficere*] (14c) *archaic* **:** to refresh with food or drink

re·fec·tion \ri-ˈfek-shən\ *n* [ME *refeccioun,* fr. AF *refectiun,* fr. L *refection-, refectio,* fr. *reficere* to restore, fr. *re-* + *facere* to make — more at DO] (14c) **1 :** refreshment of mind, spirit, or body; *esp* **:** NOURISHMENT **2 a :** the taking of refreshment **b :** food and drink together **:** REPAST

re·fec·to·ry \ri-ˈfek-t(ə-)rē\ *n, pl* **-ries** [ME, fr. AF *refectorie,* fr. LL *refectorium,* fr. L *reficere*] (15c) **:** a dining hall (as in a monastery or college)

refectory table *n* (1857) **:** a long table with heavy legs

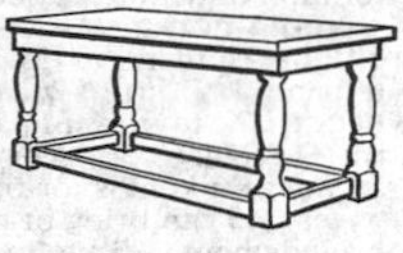
refectory table

re·fel \ri-ˈfel\ *vt* **re·felled; re·fel·ling** [L *refellere* to prove false, refute, fr. *re-* + *fallere* to deceive] (1530) *obs* **:** REJECT, REPULSE

re·fer \ri-ˈfər\ *vb* **re·ferred; re·fer·ring** [ME *referren,* fr. AF *referer, referir,* fr. L *referre* to bring back, report, refer, fr. *re-* + *ferre* to carry — more at BEAR] *vt* (14c) **1 a (1) :** to think of, regard, or classify within a general category or group **(2) :** to explain in terms of a general cause **b :** to allot to a particular place, stage, or period **c :** to regard as coming from or located in a specific area **2 a :** to send or direct for treatment, aid, information, or decision ⟨∼ a patient to a specialist⟩ ⟨∼ a bill back to a committee⟩ **b :** to direct for testimony or guaranty as to character or ability ∼ *vi* **1 a :** to have relation or connection **:** RELATE **b :** to direct attention usu. by clear and specific mention ⟨no one *referred* to yesterday's quarrel⟩ **2 :** to have recourse **:** glance briefly ⟨*referred* frequently to his notes while speaking⟩ — **re·fer·able** \ˈre-f(ə-)rə-bəl, ri-ˈfər-ə-\ *adj* — **re·fer·rer** \ri-ˈfər-ər\ *n*

[1]**ref·er·ee** \ˌre-fə-ˈrē\ *n* (1621) **1 :** one to whom a thing is referred: as **a :** a person to whom a legal matter is referred for investigation and report or for settlement **b :** a person who reviews a paper and esp. a technical paper and recommends that it should or should not be published **c** *chiefly Brit* **:** REFERENCE 4a **2 :** a sports official usu. having final authority in administering a game

[2]**referee** *vb* **-eed; -ee·ing** *vt* (1889) **1 :** to conduct (as a match or game) as referee **2 a :** to arbitrate (as a legal matter) as a judge or third party **b :** to review (as a technical paper) before publication ∼ *vi* **:** to act as a referee

[1]**ref·er·ence** \ˈre-fərn(t)s, ˈre-f(ə-)rən(t)s\ *n* (1589) **1 :** the act of referring or consulting **2 :** a bearing on a matter **:** RELATION ⟨in ∼ to your recent letter⟩ **3 :** something that refers: as **a :** ALLUSION, MENTION **b :** something (as a sign or indication) that refers a reader or consulter to another source of information (as a book or passage) **c :** consultation of sources of information **4 :** one referred to or consulted: as **a :** a person to whom inquiries as to character or ability can be made **b :** a statement of the qualifications of a person seeking employment or appointment given by someone familiar with the person **c (1) :** a source of information (as a book or passage) to which a reader or consulter is referred **(2) :** a work (as a dictionary or encyclopedia) containing useful facts or information **d :** DENOTATION, MEANING

[2]**reference** *adj* (1856) **:** used or usable for reference; *esp* **:** constituting a standard for measuring or constructing

[3]**reference** *vt* **-enced; -enc·ing** (1891) **1 a :** to supply with references **b :** to cite in or as a reference **2 :** to put in a form (as a table) adapted to easy reference

reference mark *n* (1856) **:** a conventional mark (as *, †, or ‡) placed in written or printed text to direct the reader's attention esp. to a footnote

ref·er·en·dum \ˌre-fə-ˈren-dəm\ *n, pl* **-da** \-də\ *or* **-dums** [NL, fr. L, neut. of *referendus,* gerundive of *referre* to refer] (1847) **1 a :** the principle or practice of submitting to popular vote a measure passed on or proposed by a legislative body or by popular initiative **b :** a vote on a measure so submitted **2 :** a diplomatic agent's note asking for government instructions

ref·er·ent \ˈre-f(ə-)rənt\ *n* [L *referent-, referens,* prp. of *referre*] (1844) **:** one that refers or is referred to; *esp* **:** the thing that a symbol (as a word or sign) stands for — **referent** *adj*

ref·er·en·tial \ˌre-fə-ˈren(t)-shəl\ *adj* (1660) **:** of, containing, or constituting a reference; *esp* **:** pointing to or involving a referent ⟨∼ language⟩ ⟨∼ meaning⟩ — **ref·er·en·tial·i·ty** \-ˌren(t)-shē-ˈa-lə-tē\ *n* — **ref·er·en·tial·ly** \-ˈren(t)-sh(ə-)lē\ *adv*

re·fer·ral \ri-ˈfər-əl\ *n* (1927) **1 :** the act, action, or an instance of referring ⟨gave the patient a ∼ to a specialist⟩ **2 :** one that is referred

re·fig·ure \(ˌ)rē-ˈfi-gyər\ *vt* (14c) **1 :** to figure again or anew **2 :** to give new meaning or use to ⟨∼ classic texts⟩

[1]**re·fill** \(ˌ)rē-ˈfil\ *vt* (1615) **:** to fill again **:** REPLENISH ∼ *vi* **:** to become filled again — **re·fill·able** \-ˈfi-lə-bəl\ *adj*

[2]**re·fill** \ˈrē-ˌfil\ *n* (1886) **1 :** a product or a container and a product used to refill the exhausted supply of a device **2 :** something provided again; *esp* **:** a second or later filling of a medical prescription

re·fi·nance \ˌrē-fə-ˈnan(t)s, (ˌ)rē-ˈfī-ˌ, ˌrē-(ˌ)fī-ˈ\ *vt* (1908) **:** to renew or reorganize the financing of ∼ *vi* **:** to finance something anew

re·fine \ri-ˈfīn\ *vb* **re·fined; re·fin·ing** *vt* (1582) **1 :** to free (as metal, sugar, or oil) from impurities or unwanted material **2 :** to free from moral imperfection **:** ELEVATE **3 :** to improve or perfect by pruning or polishing ⟨∼ a poetic style⟩ **4 :** to reduce in vigor or intensity **5 :** to free from what is coarse, vulgar, or uncouth ∼ *vi* **1 :** to become pure or perfected **2 :** to make improvement by introducing subtleties or distinctions — **re·fin·er** *n*

refined *adj* (1582) **1 :** free from impurities **2 :** FASTIDIOUS, CULTIVATED **3 :** PRECISE, EXACT ⟨a ∼ test for radioactivity⟩

re·fine·ment \ri-ˈfīn-mənt\ *n* (ca. 1611) **1 :** the action or process of refining **2 :** the quality or state of being refined **:** CULTIVATION **3 a :** a refined feature or method **b :** a highly refined distinction **:** SUBTLETY **c :** a contrivance or device intended to improve or perfect

re·fin·ery \ri-ˈfī-nə-rē, -ˈfīn-rē\ *n, pl* **-er·ies** (ca. 1741) **:** a building and equipment for refining or processing (as oil or sugar)

re·fin·ish \(ˌ)rē-ˈfi-nish\ *vt* (1886) **:** to give (as furniture) a new surface ∼ *vi* **:** to refinish furniture — **re·fin·ish·er** *n*

[1]**re·fit** \(ˌ)rē-ˈfit\ *vt* (1666) **:** to fit out or supply again ∼ *vi* **:** to obtain repairs or fresh supplies or equipment

[2]**re·fit** \ˈrē-ˌfit, (ˌ)rē-ˈ\ *n* (1799) **:** the action of refitting; *esp* **:** a refitting and renovating of a ship

re·fla·tion \(ˌ)rē-ˈflā-shən\ *n* [*re-* + *-flation* (as in *deflation*)] (1932) **:** restoration of deflated prices to a desirable level — **re·flate** \(ˌ)rē-ˈflāt\ *vb* — **re·fla·tion·ary** \-shə-ˌner-ē\ *adj*

re·flect \ri-ˈflekt\ *vb* [ME, fr. L *reflectere* to bend back, fr. *re-* + *flectere* to bend] *vt* (15c) **1** *archaic* **:** to turn into or away from a course **:** DEFLECT **2 :** to prevent passage of and cause to change direction ⟨a mirror ~*s* light⟩ **3 :** to bend or fold back **4 :** to give back or exhibit as an image, likeness, or outline **:** MIRROR ⟨the clouds were ~*ed* in the water⟩ **5 :** to bring or cast as a result ⟨his attitude ~*s* little credit on his judgment⟩ **6 :** to make manifest or apparent **:** SHOW ⟨the painting ~*s* his artistic vision⟩ ⟨the pulse ~*s* the condition of the heart⟩ **7 :** REALIZE, CONSIDER ~ *vi* **1 :** to throw back light or sound **2 a :** to think quietly and calmly **b :** to express a thought or opinion resulting from reflection **3 a :** to tend to bring reproach or discredit ⟨an investigation that ~*s* on all the members of the department⟩ **b :** to bring about a specified appearance or characterization ⟨an act which ~*s* well on her⟩ **c :** to have a bearing or influence ***syn*** see THINK

re·flec·tance \ri-ˈflek-tən(t)s\ *n* (1926) **:** the fraction of the total radiant flux incident upon a surface that is reflected and that varies according to the wavelength distribution of the incident radiation — called also *re·flec·tiv·i·ty* \ˌrē-ˌflek-ˈti-və-tē, ri-\

reflecting telescope *n* (ca. 1704) **:** REFLECTOR 2

re·flec·tion \ri-ˈflek-shən\ *n* [ME, alter. of *reflexion,* fr. LL *reflexion-, reflexio* act of bending back, fr. L *reflectere*] (14c) **1 :** an instance of reflecting; *esp* **:** the return of light or sound waves from a surface **2 :** the production of an image by or as if by a mirror **3 a :** the action of bending or folding back **b :** a reflected part **:** FOLD **4 :** something produced by reflecting: as **a :** an image given back by a reflecting surface **b :** an effect produced by an influence ⟨the high crime rate is a ~ of our violent society⟩ **5 :** an often obscure or indirect criticism **:** REPROACH ⟨a ~ on his character⟩ **6 :** a thought, idea, or opinion formed or a remark made as a result of meditation **7 :** consideration of some subject matter, idea, or purpose **8** *obs* **:** turning back **:** RETURN **9 a :** a transformation of a figure in which each point is replaced by a point symmetric with respect to a line or plane **b :** a transformation that involves reflection in more than one axis of a rectangular coordinate system — **re·flec·tion·al** \-shnəl, -shə-nᵊl\ *adj*

re·flec·tive \ri-ˈflek-tiv\ *adj* (1627) **1 :** capable of reflecting light, images, or sound waves **2 :** marked by reflection **:** THOUGHTFUL, DELIBERATIVE **3 :** of, relating to, or caused by reflection ⟨~ glare⟩ **4 :** REFLEXIVE 3 **5 :** reflecting something **:** INDICATIVE ⟨how fashion is ~ of society —Glenda Bailey⟩ — **re·flec·tive·ly** *adv* — **re·flec·tive·ness** *n* — **re·flec·tiv·i·ty** *n*

re·flec·tom·e·ter \ˌrē-ˌflek-ˈtä-mə-tər, ri-\ *n* (1891) **:** a device for measuring reflectance — **re·flec·tom·e·try** \-mə-trē\ *n*

re·flec·tor \ri-ˈflek-tər\ *n* (1665) **1 :** one that reflects; *esp* **:** a polished surface for reflecting light or other radiation **2 :** a telescope in which the principal focusing element is a mirror

re·flec·tor·ize \-tə-ˌrīz\ *vt* **-ized; -iz·ing** (1940) **1 :** to make reflecting **2 :** to provide with reflectors

[1]**re·flex** \ˈrē-ˌfleks\ *n* [L *reflexus,* pp. of *reflectere* to reflect] (1508) **1 a** *archaic* **:** reflected heat, light, or color **b :** a mirrored image **c :** a copy exact in essential or peculiar features **2 a :** an automatic and often inborn response to a stimulus that involves a nerve impulse passing inward from a receptor to a nerve center and thence outward to an effector (as a muscle or gland) without reaching the level of consciousness — compare HABIT 7 **b :** the process that culminates in a reflex and comprises reception, transmission, and reaction — called also *reflex action* **c** *pl* **:** the power of acting or responding with adequate speed **d :** a way of thinking or behaving **3 :** a linguistic element (as a word or sound) or system (as writing) that is derived from a prior and esp. an older element or system ⟨*boat* is the ~ of Old English *bāt*⟩

[2]**reflex** *adj* [L *reflexus*] (1649) **1 :** directed back on the mind or its operations **:** INTROSPECTIVE **2 :** REFLEXED **3 :** produced or carried out in reaction, resistance, or return **4** *of an angle* **:** being between 180° and 360° **5 :** of, relating to, or produced by a reflex without intervention of consciousness — **re·flex·ly** *adv*

reflex arc *n* (1882) **:** the complete nervous path involved in a reflex

re·flexed \ˈrē-ˌflekst, ri-ˈ\ *adj* [L *reflexus* + E [1]*-ed*] (1733) **:** bent or curved backward or downward ⟨~ petals⟩ ⟨~ leaves⟩

re·flex·ion *chiefly Brit var of* REFLECTION

[1]**re·flex·ive** \ri-ˈflek-siv\ *adj* [ML *reflexivus,* fr. L *reflexus*] (1640) **1 a :** directed or turned back on itself; *also* **:** overtly and usu. ironically reflecting conventions of genre or form ⟨a ~ novel⟩ **b :** marked by or capable of reflection **:** REFLECTIVE **2 :** of, relating to, characterized by, or being a relation that exists between an entity and itself ⟨the relation "is equal to" is ~ but the relation "is the father of" is not⟩ **3 :** of, relating to, or constituting an action (as in "he perjured himself") directed back on the agent or the grammatical subject **4 :** characterized by habitual and unthinking behavior — **re·flex·ive·ly** *adv* — **re·flex·ive·ness** *n* — **re·flex·iv·i·ty** \ˌrē-ˌflek-ˈsi-və-tē, ri-\ *n*

[2]**reflexive** *n* (1866) **:** REFLEXIVE PRONOUN

reflexive pronoun *n* (1867) **:** a pronoun referring to the subject of the sentence, clause, or verbal phrase in which it stands; *specif* **:** a personal pronoun compounded with *-self*

re·flex·ol·o·gy \ˌrē-ˌflek-ˈsä-lə-jē\ *n* [ISV] (1923) **1 :** the study and interpretation of behavior in terms of simple and complex reflexes **2 :** massage of the hands or feet based on the belief that pressure applied to specific points on these extremities benefits other parts of the body — **re·flex·ol·o·gist** \-ˈsä-lə-jist\ *n*

re·flow \(ˌ)rē-ˈflō\ *vi* (14c) **1 :** to flow back **:** EBB **2 :** to flow in again — **re·flow** \ˈrē-ˌflō\ *n*

ref·lu·ence \ˈre-ˌflü-ən(t)s, re-ˈflü-\ *n* (15c) *archaic* **:** REFLUX 1a

re·flu·ent \-ənt\ *adj* [ME, fr. L *refluent-, refluens,* prp. of *refluere* to flow back, fr. *re-* + *fluere* to flow — more at FLUID] (15c) **:** flowing back

[1]**re·flux** \ˈrē-ˌfləks\ *n* [ME, fr. ML *refluxus,* fr. L *re-* + *fluxus* flow — more at FLUX] (15c) **1 a :** a flowing back **b :** GASTROESOPHAGEAL REFLUX **2 :** a process of refluxing or condition of being refluxed

[2]**re·flux** \ri-ˈfləks, ˈrē-ˌ\ *vt* (1926) **:** to cause to flow back or return; *esp* **:** to heat such that the vapors formed condense and return to be heated again ~ *vi* **:** to flow back

re·fo·cus \(ˌ)rē-ˈfō-kəs\ *vt* (ca. 1865) **1 :** to focus again **2 :** to change the emphasis or direction of ⟨had ~*ed* his life⟩ ~ *vi* **1 :** to focus something again **2 :** to change emphasis or direction

re·for·es·ta·tion \(ˌ)rē-ˌfȯr-ə-ˈstā-shən, -ˌfär-\ *n* (1887) **:** the action of renewing forest cover (as by natural seeding or by the artificial planting of seeds or young trees) — **re·for·est** \(ˌ)rē-ˈfȯr-əst, -ˈfär-\ *vt*

[1]**re·form** \ri-ˈfȯrm\ *vb* [ME, fr. AF *refurmer,* fr. L *reformare,* fr. *re-* + *formare* to form, fr. *forma* form] *vt* (14c) **1 a :** to put or change into an improved form or condition **b :** to amend or improve by change of form or removal of faults or abuses **2 :** to put an end to (an evil) by enforcing or introducing a better method or course of action **3 :** to induce or cause to abandon evil ways ⟨~ a drunkard⟩ **4 a :** to subject (hydrocarbons) to cracking **b :** to produce (as gasoline or gas) by cracking ~ *vi* **:** to become changed for the better ***syn*** see CORRECT — **re·form·abil·i·ty** \-ˌfȯr-mə-ˈbi-lə-tē\ *n* — **re·form·able** \-ˈfȯr-mə-bəl\ *adj*

[2]**reform** *n* (1663) **1 :** amendment of what is defective, vicious, corrupt, or depraved **2 :** a removal or correction of an abuse, a wrong, or errors **3** *cap* **:** REFORM JUDAISM

[3]**reform** *adj* (1819) **:** relating to or favoring reform

re–form \(ˌ)rē-ˈfȯrm\ *vt* (14c) **:** to form again ~ *vi* **:** to take form again ⟨the ice ~*ed* on the lake⟩

re·for·mate \ri-ˈfȯr-ˌmāt, -mət\ *n* (1949) **:** a product of hydrocarbon reforming

ref·or·ma·tion \ˌre-fər-ˈmā-shən\ *n* (15c) **1 :** the act of reforming **:** the state of being reformed **2** *cap* **:** a 16th century religious movement marked ultimately by rejection or modification of some Roman Catholic doctrine and practice and establishment of the Protestant churches — **ref·or·ma·tion·al** \-shnəl, -shə-nᵊl\ *adj*

re·for·ma·tive \ri-ˈfȯr-mə-tiv\ *adj* (1593) **:** intended or tending to reform

[1]**re·for·ma·to·ry** \ri-ˈfȯr-mə-ˌtȯr-ē\ *adj* (1589) **:** REFORMATIVE

[2]**reformatory** *n, pl* **-ries** (1834) **:** a penal institution to which esp. young or first offenders are committed for training and reformation

re·formed \ri-ˈfȯrmd\ *adj* (1563) **1 :** changed for the better **2** *cap* **:** PROTESTANT; *specif* **:** of or relating to the chiefly Calvinist Protestant churches formed in various continental European countries

reformed spelling *n* (1879) **:** any of several methods of spelling English words that use letters with more phonetic consistency than conventional spelling and that usu. discard some silent letters (as in *pedagog* for *pedagogue*)

re·form·er \ri-ˈfȯr-mər\ *n* (1526) **1 :** one that works for or urges reform **2** *cap* **:** a leader of the Protestant Reformation **3 :** an apparatus for cracking oils or gases to form specialized products

re·form·ism \ri-ˈfȯr-ˌmi-zəm\ *n* (1904) **:** a doctrine, policy, or movement of reform — **re·form·ist** \-mist\ *n or adj*

Reform Judaism *n* (ca. 1905) **:** Judaism marked by a liberal approach in nonobservance of much legal tradition regarded as irrelevant to the present and in shortening and simplification of traditional ritual — compare CONSERVATIVE JUDAISM, ORTHODOX JUDAISM

reform school *n* (ca. 1859) **:** a reformatory for boys or girls

refr *abbr* refraction

re·fract \ri-ˈfrakt\ *vt* [L *refractus,* pp. of *refringere* to break open, break up, fr. *re-* + *frangere* to break — more at BREAK] (1612) **1 a :** to subject (as a ray of light) to refraction **b :** to alter or distort as if by refraction ⟨to ~ that familiar world through the mind and heart of a romantic . . . woman —Anton Myrer⟩ **2 :** to determine the refracting power of

re·frac·tile \-ˈfrak-tᵊl, -ˌtī(-ə)l\ *adj* (ca. 1849) **:** capable of refracting **:** REFRACTIVE

refracting telescope *n* (1764) **:** REFRACTOR

re·frac·tion \ri-ˈfrak-shən\ *n* (1603) **1 :** deflection from a straight path undergone by a light ray or energy wave in passing obliquely from one medium (as air) into another (as glass) in which its velocity is different **2 :** the change in the apparent position of a celestial body due to bending of the light rays emanating from it as they pass through the atmosphere; *also* **:** the correction to be applied to the apparent position of a body because of this bending **3 :** the action of distorting an image by viewing through a medium; *also* **:** an instance of this

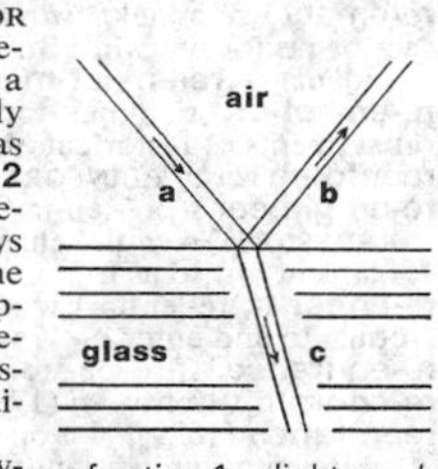

refraction 1: *a* light ray, *b* reflected ray, *c* refracted ray

re·frac·tive \ri-ˈfrak-tiv\ *adj* (1673) **1 :** having power to refract **2 :** relating or due to refraction — **re·frac·tive·ly** *adv* — **re·frac·tive·ness** *n* — **re·frac·tiv·i·ty** \ˌrē-ˌfrak-ˈti-və-tē, ri-\ *n*

refractive index *n* (1839) **:** the ratio of the speed of radiation (as light) in one medium (as air, glass, or a vacuum) to that in another medium

re·frac·tom·e·ter \ˌrē-ˌfrak-ˈtä-mə-tər, ri-\ *n* [ISV] (ca. 1859) **:** an instrument for measuring refractive indices (as for identification or the determination of sugar content) — **re·frac·to·met·ric** \ri-ˌfrak-tə-ˈme-trik\ *adj* — **re·frac·tom·e·try** \ˌrē-ˌfrak-ˈtä-mə-trē, ri-\ *n*

re·frac·tor \ri-ˈfrak-tər\ *n* (1769) **:** a telescope whose principal focusing element is a lens

[1]**re·frac·to·ry** \ri-ˈfrak-t(ə-)rē\ *adj* [alter. of *refractary,* fr. L *refractarius,* irreg. fr. *refragari* to oppose, fr. *re-* + *-fragari* (as in *suffragari* to support with one's vote)] (1606) **1 :** resisting control or authority **:** STUBBORN, UNMANAGEABLE **2 a :** resistant to treatment or cure ⟨a ~ lesion⟩ **b :** unresponsive to stimulus **c :** IMMUNE, INSUSCEPTIBLE ⟨after recovery they were ~ to infection⟩ **3 :** difficult to fuse, corrode, or draw out; *esp* **:** capable of enduring high temperature ***syn*** see UNRULY — **re·frac·to·ri·ly** \-t(ə-)rə-lē; ˌrē-ˌfrak-ˈtȯr-ə-lē, ri-\ *adv* — **re·frac·to·ri·ness** \ri-ˈfrak-t(ə-)rē-nəs\ *n*

[2]**refractory** *n, pl* **-ries** (1627) **:** a refractory person or thing; *esp* **:** a heat-resisting ceramic material

refractory period *n* (ca. 1880) **:** the brief period immediately following the response esp. of a muscle or nerve before it recovers the capacity to make a second response — called also *refractory phase*

[1]**re·frain** \ri-ˈfrān\ *vb* [ME *refreynen,* fr. AF *refreiner, refreindre,* fr. L *refrenare,* fr. *re-* + *frenum* bridle — more at FRENUM] *vt* (14c) *archaic* **:** CURB, RESTRAIN ~ *vi* **:** to keep oneself from doing, feeling, or in-

dulging in something and esp. from following a passing impulse ⟨~*ed* from having dessert⟩ — **re·frain·ment** \-mənt\ *n*

[2]**refrain** *n* [ME *refreyn,* fr. MF *refrain,* alter. of OF *refrait* melody, response, fr. pp. of *refraindre* to break up, moderate, fr. VL **refrangere,* alter. of L *refringere* — more at REFRACT] (14c) **:** a regularly recurring phrase or verse esp. at the end of each stanza or division of a poem or song **:** CHORUS; *also* **:** the musical setting of a refrain

re·fran·gi·ble \ri-ˈfran-jə-bəl\ *adj* [irreg. fr. L *refringere* to break up] (1673) **:** capable of being refracted — **re·fran·gi·bil·i·ty** \-ˌfran-jə-ˈbi-lə-tē\ *n* — **re·fran·gi·ble·ness** \-ˈfran-jə-bəl-nəs\ *n*

re·fresh \ri-ˈfresh\ *vb* [ME *refresshen,* fr. AF *refreschir,* fr. *re-* + *fresch* fresh — more at FRESH] *vt* (14c) **1 :** to restore strength and animation to **:** REVIVE **2 :** to freshen up **:** RENOVATE **3 a :** to restore or maintain by renewing supply **:** REPLENISH **b :** AROUSE, STIMULATE ⟨let me ~ your memory⟩ **4 :** to run water over or restore water to **5 :** to update or renew (as an image, a display screen, or the contents of a computer memory) esp. by sending a new signal ~ *vi* **1 :** to become refreshed **2 :** to take refreshment **3 :** to lay in fresh provisions ***syn*** see RENEW — **refresh** *n*

re·fresh·en \ri-ˈfre-shən, ˌrē-\ *vt* [*re-* + *freshen*] (1782) **:** REFRESH

re·fresh·er \ri-ˈfre-shər\ *n* (15c) **1 :** something (as a drink) that refreshes **2 :** REMINDER **3 :** review or instruction designed esp. to keep one abreast of professional developments ⟨~ course⟩

re·fresh·ing \-shiŋ\ *adj* (ca. 1580) **:** serving to refresh; *esp* **:** agreeably stimulating because of freshness or newness ⟨a ~ change of pace⟩ — **re·fresh·ing·ly** \-shiŋ-lē\ *adv*

re·fresh·ment \ri-ˈfresh-mənt\ *n* (14c) **1 :** the act of refreshing **:** the state of being refreshed **2 a :** something (as food or drink) that refreshes **b** *pl* (1) **:** a light meal (2) **:** assorted light foods

re·fried beans \ˈrē-ˌfrīd-\ *n pl* (1957) **:** beans cooked with seasonings, fried, then mashed and fried again

refrig *abbr* refrigerator

[1]**re·frig·er·ant** \ri-ˈfri-jə-rənt, -ˈfrij-rənt\ *adj* (1599) **:** allaying heat or fever

[2]**refrigerant** *n* (1676) **:** a refrigerant agent or agency: as **a :** a medication for reducing body heat **b :** a substance used in refrigeration

re·frig·er·ate \ri-ˈfri-jə-ˌrāt\ *vt* **-at·ed; -at·ing** [L *refrigeratus,* pp. of *refrigerare,* fr. *re-* + *frigerare* to cool, fr. *frigor-, frigus* cold — more at FRIGID] (1534) **:** to make or keep cold or cool; *specif* **:** to freeze or chill (as food) for preservation — **re·frig·er·a·tion** \-ˌfri-jə-ˈrā-shən\ *n*

re·frig·er·a·tor \ri-ˈfri-jə-ˌrā-tər\ *n* (1611) **:** something that refrigerates; *esp* **:** a room or appliance for keeping food or other items cool

reft *past of* REAVE

re·fu·el \(ˌ)rē-ˈfyü(-ə)l\ *vt* (1811) **:** to provide with additional fuel ~ *vi* **:** to take on additional fuel

[1]**ref·uge** \ˈre-(ˌ)fyüj *also* -(ˌ)fyüzh\ *n* [ME, fr. AF, fr. L *refugium,* fr. *refugere* to escape, fr. *re-* + *fugere* to flee — more at FUGITIVE] (14c) **1 :** shelter or protection from danger or distress **2 :** a place that provides shelter or protection **3 :** something to which one has recourse in difficulty

[2]**refuge** *vb* **ref·uged; ref·ug·ing** *vt* (1594) **:** to give refuge to ~ *vi* **:** to seek or take refuge

ref·u·gee \ˌre-fyu̇-ˈjē, ˈre-fyu̇-ˌ\ *n* [F *réfugié,* pp. of (*se*) *réfugier* to take refuge, fr. MF *refugier,* fr. L *refugium*] (1685) **:** one that flees; *esp* **:** a person who flees to a foreign country or power to escape danger or persecution — **ref·u·gee·ism** \-ˌi-zəm\ *n*

re·fu·gi·um \ri-ˈfyü-jē-əm\ *n, pl* **-gia** \-jē-ə\ [NL, fr. L, refuge] (1943) **:** an area of relatively unaltered climate that is inhabited by plants and animals during a period of continental climatic change (as a glaciation) and remains as a center of relict forms from which a new dispersion and speciation may take place after climatic readjustment

re·ful·gence \ri-ˈfu̇l-jən(t)s, -ˈfəl-\ *n* [L *refulgentia,* fr. *refulgent-, refulgens,* prp. of *refulgēre* to shine brightly, fr. *re-* + *fulgēre* to shine — more at FULGENT] (1634) **:** a radiant or resplendent quality or state **:** BRILLIANCE — **re·ful·gent** \-jənt\ *adj*

[1]**re·fund** \ri-ˈfənd, ˈrē-ˌ\ *vt* [ME *refounden,* fr. AF & L; AF *refunder,* fr. L *refundere,* lit., to pour back, fr. *re-* + *fundere* to pour — more at FOUND] (15c) **1 :** to give or put back **2 :** to return (money) in restitution, repayment, or balancing of accounts — **re·fund·abil·i·ty** \ri-ˌfən-də-ˈbi-lə-tē, (ˌ)rē-\ *n* — **re·fund·able** \-ˈfən-də-bəl\ *adj*

[2]**re·fund** \ˈrē-ˌfənd\ *n* (1866) **1 :** the act of refunding **2 :** a sum refunded

[3]**re·fund** \(ˌ)rē-ˈfənd\ *vt* [*re-* + [2]*fund*] (ca. 1860) **:** to fund again

re·fur·bish \ri-ˈfər-bish\ *vt* (1611) **:** to brighten or freshen up **:** RENOVATE — **re·fur·bish·er** *n* — **re·fur·bish·ment** \-bish-mənt\ *n*

re·fus·al \ri-ˈfyü-zəl\ *n* (15c) **1 :** the act of refusing or denying **2 :** the opportunity or right of refusing or taking before others

[1]**re·fuse** \ri-ˈfyüz\ *vb* **re·fused; re·fus·ing** [ME, fr. AF *refuser,* fr. VL **refusare,* perh. blend of L *refutare* to refute and *recusare* to demur — more at RECUSE] *vt* (14c) **1 :** to express oneself as unwilling to accept ⟨~ a gift⟩ ⟨~ a promotion⟩ **2 a :** to show or express unwillingness to do or comply with ⟨*refused* to answer the question⟩ **b :** DENY ⟨they were *refused* admittance to the game⟩ **3** *obs* **:** GIVE UP, RENOUNCE ⟨deny thy father and ~ thy name —Shak.⟩ **4** *of a horse* **:** to decline to jump or leap over ~ *vi* **:** to withhold acceptance, compliance, or permission ***syn*** see DECLINE — **re·fus·er** *n*

[2]**ref·use** \ˈre-ˌfyüs, -ˌfyüz\ *n* [ME, fr. AF, fr. *refuser*] (14c) **1 :** the worthless or useless part of something **:** LEAVINGS **2 :** TRASH, GARBAGE

[3]**ref·use** \ˈre-ˌfyüs, -ˌfyüz\ *adj* (15c) **:** thrown aside or left as worthless

re·fuse·nik *also* **re·fus·nik** \ri-ˈfyüz-(ˌ)nik\ *n* [part trans. of Russ *otkaznik,* fr. *otkaz* refusal] (1974) **1 :** a Soviet citizen and esp. a Jew refused permission to emigrate **2 :** a person who refuses or declines something

ref·u·ta·tion \ˌre-fyu̇-ˈtā-shən\ *n* (ca. 1548) **:** the act or process of refuting

re·fute \ri-ˈfyüt\ *vt* **re·fut·ed; re·fut·ing** [L *refutare* to check, suppress, refute] (1545) **1 :** to prove wrong by argument or evidence **:** show to be false or erroneous **2 :** to deny the truth or accuracy of ⟨*refuted* the allegations⟩ — **re·fut·able** \-ˈfyü-tə-bəl\ *adj* — **re·fut·ably** \-blē\ *adv* — **re·fut·er** *n*

[1]**reg** \ˈreg\ *n* [by shortening] (1904) **:** REGULATION ⟨federal ~*s*⟩

[2]**reg** *abbr* **1** region **2** register; registered; registration **3** regular

re·gal \ˈrē-gəl\ *adj* [ME, fr. AF or L; AF, fr. L *regalis* — more at ROYAL] (14c) **1 :** of, relating to, or suitable for a king **2 :** of notable excellence or magnificence **:** SPLENDID — **re·gal·i·ty** \ri-ˈga-lə-tē\ *n* — **re·gal·ly** \ˈrē-gə-lē\ *adv*

[1]**re·gale** \ri-ˈgāl\ *vb* **re·galed; re·gal·ing** [F *régaler,* fr. MF, fr. *regale,* n.] *vt* (ca. 1656) **1 :** to entertain sumptuously **:** feast with delicacies **2 :** to give pleasure or amusement to ⟨*regaled* us with tall tales⟩ ~ *vi* **:** to feast oneself **:** FEED

[2]**regale** *n* [F *régal,* fr. MF *regale,* fr. *re-* + *galer* to have a good time — more at GALLANT] (1670) **1 :** a sumptuous feast **2 :** a choice piece esp. of food

re·ga·lia \ri-ˈgāl-yə\ *n pl* [ML, fr. L, neut. pl. of *regalis*] (ca. 1540) **1 :** royal rights or prerogatives **2 a :** the emblems, symbols, or paraphernalia indicative of royalty **b :** decorations or insignia indicative of an office or membership **3 :** special dress; *esp* **:** FINERY

[1]**re·gard** \ri-ˈgärd\ *n* [ME, fr. AF, fr. *regarder*] (14c) **1** *archaic* **:** APPEARANCE **2 a :** ATTENTION, CONSIDERATION ⟨due ~ should be given to all facets of the question⟩ **b :** a protective interest **:** CARE ⟨has no ~ for her health⟩ **3 :** LOOK, GAZE **4 a :** the worth or estimation in which something or someone is held ⟨a man of small ~⟩ **b** (1) **:** a feeling of respect and affection **:** ESTEEM ⟨she soon won the ~ of her colleagues⟩ (2) *pl* **:** friendly greetings implying such feeling ⟨give him my ~*s*⟩ **5 :** a basis of action or opinion **:** MOTIVE **6 :** an aspect to be taken into consideration **:** RESPECT ⟨is a small school, and is fortunate in this ~⟩ **7** *obs* **:** INTENTION — **in regard to :** with respect to **:** CONCERNING — **with regard to :** in regard to

[2]**regard** *vb* [ME, fr. AF *regarder* to look back at, regard, fr. *re-* + *garder* to guard, look at — more at GUARD] *vt* (14c) **1 :** to consider and appraise usu. from a particular point of view ⟨is highly ~*ed* as a mechanic⟩ **2 :** to pay attention to **:** take into consideration or account **3 a :** to show respect or consideration for **b :** to hold in high esteem **4 :** to look at **5** *archaic* **:** to relate to ~ *vi* **1 :** to look attentively **:** GAZE **2 :** to pay attention **:** HEED

syn REGARD, RESPECT, ESTEEM, ADMIRE mean to recognize the worth of a person or thing. REGARD is a general term that is usu. qualified ⟨he is highly *regarded* in the profession⟩. RESPECT implies a considered evaluation or estimation ⟨after many years they came to *respect* her views⟩. ESTEEM implies greater warmth of feeling accompanying a high valuation ⟨no citizen of the town was more highly *esteemed*⟩. ADMIRE suggests usu. enthusiastic appreciation and often deep affection ⟨a friend that I truly *admire*⟩.

re·gar·dant \ri-ˈgär-dᵊnt\ *adj* [ME *regardand,* fr. AF *regardant,* prp. of *regarder*] (15c) **:** looking backward over the shoulder — used of a heraldic animal

re·gard·ful \ri-ˈgärd-fəl\ *adj* (ca. 1586) **1 :** HEEDFUL, OBSERVANT **2 :** full or expressive of regard or respect **:** RESPECTFUL — **re·gard·ful·ly** \-fə-lē\ *adv* — **re·gard·ful·ness** *n*

re·gard·ing *prep* (1802) **:** with respect to **:** CONCERNING

[1]**re·gard·less** \ri-ˈgärd-ləs\ *adj* (1591) **:** HEEDLESS, CARELESS — **re·gard·less·ly** *adv* — **re·gard·less·ness** *n*

[2]**regardless** *adv* (1872) **:** despite everything ⟨went ahead with their plans ~⟩ ***usage*** see IRREGARDLESS

regardless of *prep* (1784) **:** without taking into account ⟨accepts all *regardless of* age⟩; *also* **:** in spite of ⟨*regardless of* our mistakes⟩

re·gat·ta \ri-ˈgä-tə, -ˈga-\ *n* [It *regata*] (1652) **:** a rowing, speedboat, or sailing race or a series of such races

re·gen·cy \ˈrē-jən(t)-sē\ *n, pl* **-cies** (15c) **1 :** the office, jurisdiction, or government of a regent or body of regents **2 :** a body of regents **3 :** the period of rule of a regent or body of regents

Regency *adj* (1880) **:** of, relating to, or characteristic of the styles of George IV's regency as Prince of Wales during the period 1811–20

re·gen·er·a·cy \ri-ˈje-nə-rə-sē, -ˈjen-rə-\ *n* (1626) **:** the state of being regenerated

[1]**re·gen·er·ate** \-rət\ *adj* [ME *regenerat,* fr. L *regeneratus,* pp. of *regenerare* to regenerate, fr. *re-* + *generare* to beget — more at GENERATE] (15c) **1 :** formed or created again **2 :** spiritually reborn or converted **3 :** restored to a better, higher, or more worthy state — **re·gen·er·ate·ly** *adv* — **re·gen·er·ate·ness** *n*

[2]**re·gen·er·ate** \ri-ˈje-nə-ˌrāt\ *vi* (1541) **1 :** to become formed again **2 :** to become regenerate **:** REFORM **3 :** to undergo regeneration ~ *vt* **1 a :** to subject to spiritual regeneration **b :** to change radically and for the better **2 a :** to generate or produce anew; *esp* **:** to replace (a body part) by a new growth of tissue **b :** to produce again chemically sometimes in a physically changed form **3 :** to restore to original strength or properties — **re·gen·er·a·ble** \-ˈje-nə-rə-bəl, -ˈjen-rə-\ *adj*

[3]**re·gen·er·ate** *same as* [1]\ *n* (ca. 1569) **:** one that is regenerated: as **a :** an individual who is spiritually reborn **b** (1) **:** an organism that has undergone regeneration (2) **:** a regenerated body part

regenerated cellulose *n* (1904) **:** cellulose obtained in a changed form by chemical treatment (as of a cellulose solution or derivative)

re·gen·er·a·tion \ri-ˌje-nə-ˈrā-shən, ˌrē-\ *n* (14c) **1 :** an act or the process of regenerating **:** the state of being regenerated **2 :** spiritual renewal or revival **3 :** renewal or restoration of a body, bodily part, or biological system (as a forest) after injury or as a normal process **4 :** utilization by special devices of heat or other products that would ordinarily be lost

re·gen·er·a·tive \ri-ˈje-nə-ˌrā-tiv, -ˈje-nə-rə-, -ˈjen-rə-\ *adj* (14c) **1 :** of, relating to, or marked by regeneration **2 :** tending to regenerate

re·gen·er·a·tor \ri-ˈje-nə-ˌrā-tər\ *n* (ca. 1550) **1 :** one that regenerates **2 :** a device used esp. with hot-air engines or gas furnaces in which incoming air or gas is heated by contact with masses (as of brick) previously heated by outgoing hot air or gas

re·gent \ˈrē-jənt\ *n* [ME, fr. AF or ML; AF, fr. ML *regent-, regens,* fr. L, prp. of *regere* to direct — more at RIGHT] (15c) **1 :** a person who governs a kingdom in the minority, absence, or disability of the sovereign **2 :** a person who rules or reigns **:** GOVERNOR **3 :** a member of a governing board (as of a state university) — **regent** *adj* — **re·gent·al** \-jən-tᵊl\ *adj*

\ə\ **abut** \ᵊ\ kitten, F table \ər\ **further** \a\ **ash** \ā\ **ace** \ä\ **mop, mar**
\au̇\ **out** \ch\ **chin** \e\ **bet** \ē\ **easy** \g\ **go** \i\ **hit** \ī\ **ice** \j\ **job**
\ŋ\ **sing** \ō\ **go** \ȯ\ **law** \ȯi\ **boy** \th\ **thin** \t͟h\ **the** \ü\ **loot** \u̇\ **foot**
\y\ **yet** \zh\ **vision, beige** \k̲, ⁿ, œ, ue, ʸ\ *see* Guide to Pronunciation

reg·gae \ˈre-(ˌ)gā, ˈrā-\ *n* [origin unknown] (1968) **:** popular music of Jamaican origin that combines native styles with elements of rock and soul music and is performed at moderate tempos with the accent on the offbeat

reg·gae·ton \ˌre-gā-ˈtōn, ˌrā-\ *n* [AmerSp *reggaetón,* fr. *reggae* reggae + *-ton* (as in Sp *maratón* marathon)] (2002) **:** popular music of Puerto Rican origin that combines rap with Caribbean rhythms

reg·i·cide \ˈre-jə-ˌsīd\ *n* [L *reg-, rex* king + E *-cide* — more at ROYAL] (ca. 1548) **1 :** a person who kills a king **2 :** the killing of a king — **reg·i·ci·dal** \ˌre-jə-ˈsī-dᵊl\ *adj*

re·gift \(ˌ)rē-ˈgift\ *vi* (1995) **:** to give someone a gift that was previously received from someone else ~ *vt* **:** to give (a previously received gift) to someone else — **re·gift·er** *n*

re·gime *also* **ré·gime** \rā-ˈzhēm, ri- *also* ri-ˈjēm\ *n* [F *régime,* fr. OF *regimen, regime,* fr. LL *regimin-, regimen*] (1776) **1 a :** REGIMEN 1 **b :** a regular pattern of occurrence or action (as of seasonal rainfall) **c :** the characteristic behavior or orderly procedure of a natural phenomenon or process **2 a :** mode of rule or management **b :** a form of government ⟨a socialist ~⟩ **c :** a government in power **d :** a period of rule

reg·i·men \ˈre-jə-mən *also* ˈre-zhə-\ *n* [ME, fr. ML *regimin-, regimen* position of authority, direction, set of rules, fr. L, steering, control, fr. *regere* to direct] (14c) **1 a :** a systematic plan (as of diet, therapy, or medication) esp. when designed to improve and maintain the health of a patient **b :** a regular course of action and esp. of strenuous training ⟨the daily ~ of athletes⟩ **2 :** GOVERNMENT, RULE **3 :** REGIME 1c

[1]**reg·i·ment** \ˈre-jə-mənt, ˈrej-mənt\ *n* [ME, fr. MF, fr. LL *regimentum,* alter. of L *regimen*] (14c) **1** *archaic* **:** governmental rule **2 :** a military unit consisting usu. of a number of battalions

[2]**reg·i·ment** \ˈre-jə-ˌment\ *vt* (1617) **1 :** to form into or assign to a regiment **2 a :** to organize rigidly esp. for the sake of regulation or control ⟨~ an entire country⟩ **b :** to subject to order or uniformity — **reg·i·men·ta·tion** \ˌre-jə-mən-ˈtā-shən, -ˌmen-\ *n*

reg·i·men·tal \ˌre-jə-ˈmen-tᵊl\ *adj* (1659) **1 :** of or relating to a regiment **2 :** AUTHORITATIVE, DICTATORIAL

reg·i·men·tals \-tᵊlz\ *n pl* (1742) **1 :** a regimental uniform **2 :** military dress

re·gion \ˈrē-jən\ *n* [ME *regioun,* fr. AF *regiun,* fr. L *region-, regio* line, direction, area, fr. *regere* to direct] (14c) **1 :** an administrative area, division, or district; *esp* **:** the basic administrative unit for local government in Scotland **2 a :** an indefinite area of the world or universe **b :** a broad geographic area distinguished by similar features **c** (1) **:** a major world area that supports a characteristic fauna (2) **:** an area characterized by the prevalence of one or more vegetational climax types **3 a :** any of the major subdivisions into which the body or one of its parts is divisible **b :** an indefinite area surrounding a specified body part ⟨a pain in the ~ of the heart⟩ **4 :** a sphere of activity or interest **:** FIELD **5 :** any of the zones into which the atmosphere is divided according to height or the sea according to depth **6 :** an open connected set together with none, some, or all of the points on its boundary ⟨a simple closed curve divides a plane into two ~*s*⟩

[1]**re·gion·al** \ˈrēj-nəl, ˈrē-jə-nᵊl\ *adj* (15c) **1 :** affecting a particular region **:** LOCALIZED **2 :** of, relating to, characteristic of, or serving a region ⟨a ~ high school⟩ **3 :** marked by regionalism ⟨~ art⟩

[2]**regional** *n* (1936) **:** something (as a branch of an organization or an edition of a magazine) that serves a region

re·gion·al·ism \ˈrēj-nə-ˌli-zəm, ˈrē-jə-nə-ˌli-\ *n* (1881) **1 a :** consciousness of and loyalty to a distinct region with a homogeneous population **b :** development of a political or social system based on one or more such areas **2 :** emphasis on regional locale and characteristics in art or literature **3 :** a characteristic feature (as of speech) of a geographic area — **re·gion·al·ist** \-list\ *n or adj* — **re·gion·al·is·tic** \ˌrēj-nə-ˈlis-tik, ˌrē-jə-nə-ˈlis-\ *adj*

re·gion·al·ize \ˈrēj-nə-ˌlīz, ˈrē-jə-nə-ˌlīz\ *vt* **-ized; -iz·ing** (1921) **:** to divide into regions or administrative districts **:** arrange regionally — **re·gion·al·i·za·tion** \ˌrēj-nə-lə-ˈzā-shən, ˌrē-jə-nə-lə-\ *n*

re·gion·al·ly \ˈrēj-nə-lē, ˈrē-jə-nᵊl-ē\ *adv* (1879) **:** on a regional basis

re·gis·seur *or* **ré·gis·seur** \ˌrā-zhi-ˈsər\ *n* [F *régisseur,* fr. *régir* to direct, fr. OF *regir, reger,* L *regere* to rule] (1828) **:** a director responsible for staging a theatrical work (as a ballet)

[1]**reg·is·ter** \ˈre-jə-stər\ *n* [ME *registre,* fr. AF, fr. ML *registrum,* alter. of LL *regesta,* pl., register, fr. L, neut. pl. of *regestus,* pp. of *regerere* to bring back, pile up, collect, fr. *re-* + *gerere* to bear] (14c) **1 :** a written record containing regular entries of items or details **2 a :** a book or system of public records **b :** a roster of qualified or available individuals ⟨a civil service ~⟩ **3 :** an entry in a register **4 a :** a set of organ pipes of like quality **:** STOP **b** (1) **:** the range of a human voice or a musical instrument (2) **:** a portion of such a range similarly produced or of the same quality **c :** any of the varieties of a language that a speaker uses in a particular social context **5 :** a grille often with shutters for admitting heated air or for ventilation **6 :** REGISTRATION, REGISTRY **7 a :** an automatic device registering a number or a quantity **b :** a number or quantity so registered **c :** CASH REGISTER **8 :** a condition of correct alignment or proper relative position **9 :** a device (as in a computer) for storing small amounts of data; *esp* **:** one in which data can be both stored and operated on

[2]**register** *vb* **reg·is·tered; reg·is·ter·ing** \-st(ə-)riŋ\ *vt* (14c) **1 a :** to make or secure official entry of in a register **b :** to enroll formally esp. as a voter or student **c :** to record automatically **:** INDICATE **d :** to make a record of **:** NOTE **e :** PERCEIVE; *also* **:** COMPREHEND **2 :** to make or adjust so as to correspond exactly **3 :** to secure special protection for (a piece of mail) by prepayment of a fee **4 :** to convey an impression of **:** EXPRESS **5 :** ACHIEVE ⟨~*ed* an impressive victory⟩ ~ *vi* **1 a :** to enroll one's name in a register ⟨~*ed* at the hotel⟩ **b :** to enroll one's name officially as a prerequisite for voting **c :** to enroll formally as a student **2 a :** to correspond exactly **b :** to be in correct alignment or register **3 :** to make or convey an impression

[3]**register** *n* [ME, prob. alter. of *registrer*] (ca. 1532) **:** REGISTRAR

registered *adj* (1861) **1 a :** having the owner's name entered in a register ⟨~ security⟩ **b :** recorded as the owner of a security **2 :** recorded on the basis of pedigree or breed characteristics in the studbook of a breed association **3 :** qualified formally or officially

registered mail *n* (1886) **:** mail recorded in the post office of mailing and at each successive point of transmission and guaranteed special care in delivery

registered nurse *n* (1896) **:** a graduate trained nurse who has been licensed by a state authority after qualifying for registration

register ton *n* (ca. 1909) **:** TON 1a

reg·is·tra·ble \ˈre-jə-strə-bəl\ *also* **reg·is·ter·able** \-st(ə-)rə-bəl\ *adj* (1765) **:** capable of being registered

reg·is·trant \ˈre-jə-strənt\ *n* (ca. 1890) **:** one that registers or is registered

reg·is·trar \ˈre-jə-ˌsträr\ *n* [alter. of ME *registrer,* fr. *registren* to register, fr. AF *registrer,* fr. ML *registrare,* fr. *registrum*] (1675) **:** an official recorder or keeper of records: as **a :** an officer of an educational institution responsible for registering students, keeping academic records, and corresponding with applicants and evaluating their credentials **b :** an admitting officer at a hospital **c** *chiefly Brit* **:** RESIDENT 3

reg·is·tra·tion \ˌre-jə-ˈstrā-shən\ *n* (ca. 1566) **1 :** the act of registering **2 :** an entry in a register **3 :** the number of individuals registered **:** ENROLLMENT **4 a :** the art or act of selecting and adjusting pipe organ stops **b :** the combination of stops selected for performing a particular organ work **5 :** a document certifying an act of registering

reg·is·try \ˈre-jə-strē\ *n, pl* **-tries** (1589) **1 :** REGISTRATION, ENROLLMENT **2 :** the nationality of a ship according to its entry in a register **:** FLAG **3 :** a place of registration **4 a :** an official record book **b :** an entry in a registry

re·gius professor \ˈrē-j(ē-)əs-\ *n* [NL, royal professor] (1621) **:** a holder of a professorship founded by royal subsidy at a British university

reg·let \ˈre-glət\ *n* [F *réglet,* fr. MF *reglet* straightedge, fr. *regle* rule, fr. L *regula* — more at RULE] (1664) **1 :** a flat narrow architectural molding **2 :** a strip of wood used like a lead between lines of type

reg·nal \ˈreg-nᵊl\ *adj* [ML *regnalis,* fr. L *regnum* reign — more at REIGN] (1612) **:** of or relating to a king or his reign; *specif* **:** calculated from a monarch's accession to the throne ⟨in his eighth ~ year⟩

reg·nant \ˈreg-nənt\ *adj* [L *regnant-, regnans,* prp. of *regnare* to reign, fr. *regnum*] (1600) **1 :** exercising rule **:** REIGNING **2 a :** having the chief power **:** DOMINANT **b :** of common or widespread occurrence

reg·num \ˈreg-nəm\ *n, pl* **reg·na** \-nə\ [L] (ca. 1890) **:** KINGDOM

reg·o·lith \ˈre-gə-ˌlith\ *n* [Gk *rhēgos* blanket + E *-lith;* akin to Gk *rhezein* to dye — more at RAGA] (1897) **:** unconsolidated residual or transported material that overlies the solid rock on the earth, moon, or a planet

reg·o·sol \ˈre-gə-ˌsäl, -ˌsȯl\ *n* [*rego-* (as in *regolith*) + L *solum* soil — more at SOLE] (1949) **:** any of a group of azonal soils consisting chiefly of imperfectly consolidated material and having no clear-cut and specific morphology

re·greet \(ˌ)rē-ˈgrēt\ *vt* (1593) *archaic* **:** to greet in return

regreets *n pl* (1596) *obs* **:** GREETINGS

[1]**re·gress** \ˈrē-ˌgres\ *n* [ME *regresse,* fr. AF, fr. L *regressus,* fr. *regredi* to go back, fr. *re-* + *gradi* to go — more at GRADE] (14c) **1 a :** an act or the privilege of going or coming back **b :** REENTRY 1 **2 :** movement backward to a previous and esp. worse or more primitive state or condition **3 :** the act of reasoning backward

[2]**re·gress** \ri-ˈgres\ *vi* (1552) **1 a :** to make or undergo regress **:** RETROGRADE **b :** to be subject to or exhibit regression **2 :** to tend to approach or revert to a mean ~ *vt* **:** to induce a state of psychological regression in — **re·gres·sor** \-ˈgre-sər\ *n*

re·gres·sion \ri-ˈgre-shən\ *n* (1597) **1 :** the act or an instance of regressing **2 :** a trend or shift toward a lower or less perfect state: as **a :** progressive decline of a manifestation of disease **b** (1) **:** gradual loss of differentiation and function by a body part esp. as a physiological change accompanying aging (2) **:** gradual loss of memories and acquired skills **c :** reversion to an earlier mental or behavioral level **d :** a functional relationship between two or more correlated variables that is often empirically determined from data and is used esp. to predict values of one variable when given values of the others ⟨the ~ of *y* on *x* is linear⟩; *specif* **:** a function that yields the mean value of a random variable under the condition that one or more independent variables have specified values **3 :** retrograde motion

re·gres·sive \ri-ˈgre-siv\ *adj* (1634) **1 :** tending to regress or produce regression **2 :** being, characterized by, or developing in the course of an evolutionary process involving increasing simplification of bodily structure **3 :** decreasing in rate as the base increases ⟨a ~ tax⟩ — **re·gres·sive·ly** *adv* — **re·gres·sive·ness** *n* — **re·gres·siv·i·ty** \ˌrē-ˌgre-ˈsi-və-tē\ *n*

[1]**re·gret** \ri-ˈgret\ *vb* **re·gret·ted; re·gret·ting** [ME *regretten,* fr. AF *regreter,* fr. *re-* + *-greter* (perh. of Gmc origin; akin to ON *grāta* to weep) — more at GREET] *vt* (14c) **1 a :** to mourn the loss or death of **b :** to miss very much **2 :** to be very sorry for ⟨~*s* his mistakes⟩ ~ *vi* **:** to experience regret — **re·gret·ter** *n*

[2]**regret** *n* (1590) **1 :** sorrow aroused by circumstances beyond one's control or power to repair **2 a :** an expression of distressing emotion (as sorrow) **b** *pl* **:** a note politely declining an invitation ***syn*** see SORROW — **re·gret·ful** \-ˈgret-fəl\ *adj* — **re·gret·ful·ness** *n*

re·gret·ful·ly \ri-ˈgret-fə-lē\ *adv* (1682) **1 :** with regret **2 :** it is to be regretted

re·gret·ta·ble \ri-ˈgre-tə-bəl\ *adj* (1603) **:** deserving regret

re·gret·ta·bly \-blē\ *adv* (1866) **1 :** to a regrettable extent ⟨a ~ steep decline in wages⟩ **2 :** it is to be regretted ⟨~, they could not attend⟩

re·group \(ˌ)rē-ˈgrüp\ *vt* (1885) **:** to form into a new grouping ⟨~ military forces⟩ ~ *vi* **1 :** to reorganize (as after a setback) for renewed activity **2 :** to alter the tactical formation of a military force

re·grow \(ˌ)rē-ˈgrō\ *vb* **-grew** \-ˈgrü\; **-grown** \-ˈgrōn\; **-grow·ing** *vt* (1872) **:** to grow (as a missing part) anew ~ *vi* **:** to continue growth after interruption or injury

regt *abbr* regiment

[1]**reg·u·lar** \ˈre-gyə-lər, ˈre-g(ə-)lər *also* ˈrā-\ *adj* [ME *reguler,* fr. AF, fr. LL *regularis* regular, fr. L, of a bar, fr. *regula* rule — more at RULE] (14c) **1 :** belonging to a religious order **2 a :** formed, built, arranged, or ordered according to some established rule, law, principle, or type **b** (1) **:** both equilateral and equiangular ⟨a ~ polygon⟩ (2) **:** having faces that are congruent regular polygons and all the polyhedral angles congruent ⟨a ~ polyhedron⟩ **c** *of a flower* **:** having the arrangement of floral parts exhibiting radial symmetry with members of the same whorl similar in form **3 a :** ORDERLY, METHODICAL ⟨~ habits⟩ **b :** recurring, attending, or functioning at fixed, uniform, or normal intervals ⟨a ~ income⟩ ⟨a ~ churchgoer⟩ ⟨~ bowel movements⟩ **4 a :** constituted, conducted, scheduled, or done in conformity with estab-

lished or prescribed usages, rules, or discipline **b :** NORMAL, STANDARD: as (1) **:** ABSOLUTE, COMPLETE ‹a ~ fool› ‹the office seemed like a ~ madhouse› (2) **:** thinking or behaving in an acceptable, normal, or agreeable manner ‹was a ~ guy› **c** (1) **:** conforming to the normal or usual manner of inflection (2) **:** WEAK 7 **d** *of a postage stamp* **:** issued in large numbers over a long period for general use in prepayment of postage **5 :** of, relating to, or constituting the permanent standing military force of a state ‹the ~ army› ‹~ soldiers›
syn REGULAR, NORMAL, TYPICAL, NATURAL mean being of the sort or kind that is expected as usual, ordinary, or average. REGULAR stresses conformity to a rule, standard, or pattern ‹the club's *regular* monthly meeting›. NORMAL implies lack of deviation from what has been discovered or established as the most usual or expected ‹*normal* behavior for a two-year-old›. TYPICAL implies showing all important traits of a type, class, or group and may suggest lack of strong individuality ‹a *typical* small town›. NATURAL applies to what conforms to a thing's essential nature, function, or mode of being ‹the *natural* love of a mother for her child›.

[2]**regular** *n* (15c) **1 :** one who is regular: as **a :** one of the regular clergy **b :** a soldier in a regular army **c :** one who can be trusted or depended on ‹a party ~› **d :** a player on an athletic team who usu. starts every game **e :** one who is usu. present or participating; *esp* **:** a long-standing regular customer **2 :** something of average or medium size; *esp* **:** a clothing size designed to fit a person of average height

reg·u·lar·i·ty \ˌre-gyə-ˈla-rə-tē *also* ˌrā-\ *n, pl* **-ties** (1603) **1 :** the quality or state of being regular **2 :** something that is regular

reg·u·lar·ize \ˈre-gyə-lə-ˌrīz *also* ˈrā-\ *vt* **-ized; -iz·ing** (1623) **:** to make regular by conformance to law, rules, or custom — **reg·u·lar·i·za·tion** \ˌre-gyə-lə-rə-ˈzā-shən *also* ˌrā-\ *n*

reg·u·lar·ly \ˈre-gyə-lər-lē, ˈre-gyə(r)-lē *also* ˈrā-\ *adv* (14c) **1 :** in a regular manner **2 :** on a regular basis **:** at regular intervals

regular solid *n* (1785) **:** any of the five possible regular polyhedrons that include the regular forms of the tetrahedron, hexahedron, octahedron, dodecahedron, and icosahedron

reg·u·late \ˈre-gyə-ˌlāt *also* ˈrā-\ *vt* **-lat·ed; -lat·ing** [ME, fr. LL *regulatus,* pp. of *regulare,* fr. L *regula* rule] (15c) **1 a :** to govern or direct according to rule **b** (1) **:** to bring under the control of law or constituted authority (2) **:** to make regulations for or concerning ‹~ the industries of a country› **2 :** to bring order, method, or uniformity to ‹~ one's habits› **3 :** to fix or adjust the time, amount, degree, or rate of ‹~ the pressure of a tire› — **reg·u·la·tive** \-ˌlā-tiv\ *adj* — **reg·u·la·to·ry** \-lə-ˌtȯr-ē\ *adj*

[1]**reg·u·la·tion** \ˌre-gyə-ˈlā-shən, ˌre-gə- *also* ˌrā-\ *n* (1665) **1 :** the act of regulating **:** the state of being regulated **2 a :** an authoritative rule dealing with details or procedure ‹safety ~s› **b :** a rule or order issued by an executive authority or regulatory agency of a government and having the force of law **3 a :** the process of redistributing material (as in an embryo) to restore a damaged or lost part independent of new tissue growth **b :** the mechanism by which an early embryo maintains normal development ***syn*** see LAW

[2]**regulation** *adj* (ca. 1839) **:** conforming to regulations **:** OFFICIAL

reg·u·la·tor \ˈre-gyə-ˌlā-tər *also* ˈrā-\ *n* (1655) **1 :** one that regulates **2 :** REGULATORY GENE

regulatory gene *or* **regulator gene** *n* (1961) **:** a gene that regulates the expression of one or more structural genes by controlling the production of a protein (as a genetic repressor) which regulates their rate of transcription

reg·u·lus \ˈre-gyə-ləs\ *n* [NL, fr. L, petty king, fr. *reg-, rex* king — more at ROYAL] (1559) **1** *cap* **:** a first-magnitude star in the constellation Leo **2** [ML, metallic antimony, fr. L] **:** the more or less impure mass of metal formed beneath the slag in smelting and reducing ores

re·gur·gi·tate \(ˌ)rē-ˈgər-jə-ˌtāt\ *vb* **-tat·ed; -tat·ing** [ML *regurgitatus,* pp. of *regurgitare,* fr. L *re-* + LL *gurgitare* to engulf, fr. L *gurgit-, gurges* whirlpool — more at VORACIOUS] *vi* (1653) **:** to become thrown or poured back ~ *vt* **:** to throw or pour back or out from or as if from a cavity ‹~ food› ‹memorized facts to ~ on the exam›

re·gur·gi·ta·tion \(ˌ)rē-ˌgər-jə-ˈtā-shən\ *n* (1601) **:** an act of regurgitating: as **a :** the casting up of incompletely digested food (as by some birds in feeding their young) **b :** the backward flow of blood through a defective heart valve

re·hab \ˈrē-ˌhab\ *n, often attrib* [short for *rehabilitation* or *rehabilitate*] (1941) **1 :** the action or process of rehabilitating **:** REHABILITATION; *esp* **:** a program for rehabilitating esp. drug or alcohol abusers **2 :** a rehabilitated building or dwelling — **rehab** *vb* — **re·hab·ber** \-ˌha-bər\ *n*

re·ha·bil·i·tant \ˌrē-ə-ˈbi-lə-tənt, ˌrē-hə-\ *n* (1961) **:** a disabled person undergoing rehabilitation

re·ha·bil·i·tate \ˌrē-ə-ˈbi-lə-ˌtāt, ˌrē-hə-\ *vt* **-tat·ed; -tat·ing** [ML *rehabilitatus,* pp. of *rehabilitare,* fr. L *re-* + LL *habilitare* to habilitate] (ca. 1581) **1 a :** to restore to a former capacity **:** REINSTATE **b :** to restore to good repute **:** reestablish the good name of **2 a :** to restore to a former state (as of efficiency, good management, or solvency) ‹~ slum areas› **b :** to restore or bring to a condition of health or useful and constructive activity — **re·ha·bil·i·ta·tion** \-ˌbi-lə-ˈtā-shən\ *n* — **re·ha·bil·i·ta·tive** \-ˈbi-lə-ˌtā-tiv\ *adj* — **re·ha·bil·i·ta·tor** \-ˌtā-tər\ *n*

[1]**re·hash** \(ˌ)rē-ˈhash\ *vt* (ca. 1822) **1 :** to talk over or discuss again **2 :** to present or use again in another form without substantial change or improvement

[2]**re·hash** \ˈrē-ˌhash\ *n* (1849) **1 :** something that is rehashed **2 :** the action or process of rehashing

re·hear \(ˌ)rē-ˈhir\ *vt* **-heard** \-ˈhərd\; **-hear·ing** \-ˈhir-iŋ\ (1756) **:** to hear again or anew esp. judicially

rehearing *n* (1686) **:** a second or new hearing by the same tribunal

re·hears·al \ri-ˈhər-səl\ *n* (14c) **1 :** something recounted or told again **:** RECITAL **2 a :** a private performance or practice session preparatory to a public appearance **b :** a practice exercise **:** TRIAL

re·hearse \ri-ˈhərs\ *vb* **re·hearsed; re·hears·ing** [ME *rehersen,* fr. AF *rehercer,* fr. *re-* + *hercer* to harrow, fr. *herce* harrow — more at HEARSE] *vt* (14c) **1 a :** to say again **:** REPEAT **b :** to recite aloud in a formal manner **2 :** to present an account of **:** RELATE ‹~ a familiar story› **3 :** to recount in order **:** ENUMERATE ‹*rehearsed* their demands› **4 a :** to give a rehearsal of **b :** to train or make proficient by rehearsal **5 :** to perform or practice as if in a rehearsal ~ *vi* **:** to engage in a rehearsal — **re·hears·er** *n*

re·house \(ˌ)rē-ˈhau̇z\ *vt* (1820) **:** to house again or anew; *esp* **:** to establish in a new or different housing unit of a better quality

re·hy·drate \(ˌ)rē-ˈhī-ˌdrāt\ *vt* (1943) **:** to restore fluid to (something dehydrated) — **re·hy·drat·able** \-ˌdrā-tə-bəl\ *adj* — **re·hy·dra·tion** \ˌrē-ˌhī-ˈdrā-shən\ *n*

reichs·mark \ˈrīks-ˌmärk\ *n, pl* **reichsmarks** *also* **reichsmark** [G, fr. *Reich* empire, kingdom + *Mark* mark] (1924) **:** the German mark from 1925 to 1948

re·ifi·ca·tion \ˌrā-ə-fə-ˈkā-shən, ˌrē-\ *n* (1846) **:** the process or result of reifying

re·ify \ˈrā-ə-ˌfī, ˈrē-\ *vt* **re·ified; re·ify·ing** [L *res* thing — more at REAL] (1854) **:** to regard (something abstract) as a material or concrete thing

[1]**reign** \ˈrān\ *n* [ME *regne,* fr. AF, fr. L *regnum,* fr. *reg-, rex* king — more at ROYAL] (13c) **1 a :** royal authority **:** SOVEREIGNTY ‹under the ~ of the Stuart kings› **b :** the dominion, sway, or influence of one resembling a monarch ‹the ~ of the Puritan ministers› **2 :** the time during which one (as a sovereign) reigns

[2]**reign** *vi* (14c) **1 a :** to possess or exercise sovereign power **:** RULE **b :** to hold office as chief of state although possessing little governing power ‹in England the sovereign ~s but does not rule› **2 :** to exercise authority in the manner of a monarch **3 :** to be predominant or prevalent ‹chaos ~*ed* in the classroom›

reign of terror [*Reign of Terror,* a period of the French Revolution that was conspicuous for mass executions of political suspects] (1798) **:** a state or a period of time marked by violence often committed by those in power that produces widespread terror

Rei·ki \ˈrā-ˌkē\ *n* [Jp, lit., spirit, fr. *rei* spirit, soul + *ki* vital force, mind] (1985) **:** a system of touching with the hands based on the belief that such touching by an experienced practitioner produces beneficial effects by strengthening and normalizing certain vital energy fields held to exist within the body

re·imag·ine \ˌrē-i-ˈma-jən\ *vt* (ca. 1934) **:** to imagine again or anew; *esp* **:** to form a new conception of **:** RE-CREATE

re·im·burse \ˌrē-əm-ˈbərs\ *vt* **-bursed; -burs·ing** [*re-* + obs. E *imburse* to put in the pocket, pay, fr. ML *imbursare,* fr. L *in-* in- + ML *bursa* purse — more at PURSE] (ca. 1611) **1 :** to pay back to someone **:** REPAY ‹~ travel expenses› **2 :** to make restoration or payment of an equivalent to ‹~ him for his traveling expenses› ***syn*** see PAY — **re·im·burs·able** \-ˈbər-sə-bəl\ *adj* — **re·im·burse·ment** \-ˈbərs-mənt\ *n*

re·im·pres·sion \ˌrē-əm-ˈpre-shən\ *n* (1616) **:** REPRINT a

[1]**rein** \ˈrān\ *n* [ME *reine,* fr. AF *resne, reine,* fr. VL **retina,* fr. L *retinēre* to restrain — more at RETAIN] (14c) **1 :** a strap fastened to a bit by which a rider or driver controls an animal — usu. used in pl. **2 a :** a restraining influence **:** CHECK ‹kept a tight ~ on the proceedings› **b :** controlling or guiding power — usu. used in pl. ‹the ~s of government› **3 :** opportunity for unhampered activity or use ‹gave full ~ to her imagination›

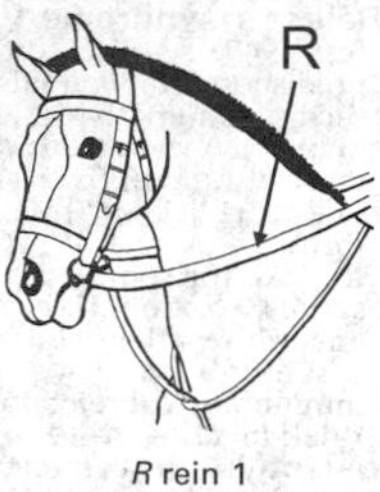

R rein 1

[2]**rein** *vt* (15c) **1 :** to control or direct with or as if with reins **2 :** to check or stop by or as if by a pull at the reins ‹~*ed* in her horse› ‹couldn't ~ his impatience› ~ *vi* **1** *archaic* **:** to submit to the use of reins **2 :** to stop or slow up one's horse or oneself by or as if by pulling the reins

re·in·car·nate \ˌrē-ən-ˈkär-ˌnāt, (ˌ)rē-ˈin-ˌ\ *vt* (1858) **:** to incarnate again

re·in·car·na·tion \ˌrē-(ˌ)in-(ˌ)kär-ˈnā-shən\ *n* (1845) **1 a :** the action of reincarnating **:** the state of being reincarnated **b :** rebirth in new bodies or forms of life; *esp* **:** a rebirth of a soul in a new human body **2 :** a fresh embodiment

rein·deer \ˈrān-ˌdir\ *n* [ME *reindere,* fr. ON *hreinn* reindeer + ME *deer* animal, deer] (14c) **:** CARIBOU — used esp. for one of the Old World

reindeer moss *n* (ca. 1753) **:** a gray, erect, tufted, and much-branched lichen (*Cladonia rangiferina*) that forms extensive patches in arctic and north-temperate regions, constitutes a large part of the food of caribou, and is sometimes eaten by humans — called also *reindeer lichen*

re·in·dus·tri·al·i·za·tion \ˌrē-in-ˌdəs-trē-ə-lə-ˈzā-shən\ *n* (1968) **:** a policy of stimulating economic growth esp. through government aid to revitalize and modernize aging industries and encourage growth of new ones — **re·in·dus·tri·al·ize** \-ˈdəs-trē-ə-ˌlīz\ *vb*

re·in·fec·tion \ˌrē-ən-ˈfek-shən\ *n* (1882) **:** infection following recovery from or superimposed on infection of the same type

re·in·force *also* **re·en·force** \ˌrē-ən-ˈfȯrs\ *vb* [*re-* + *inforce,* alter. of *enforce*] *vt* (1567) **1 :** to strengthen by additional assistance, material, or support **:** make stronger or more pronounced ‹~ levees› ‹~ the elbows of a jacket› ‹~ ideas› **2 :** to strengthen or increase by fresh additions ‹~ our troops› ‹were *reinforcing* their pitching staff› **3 :** to stimulate (as an experimental animal or a student) with a reinforcer; *also* **:** to encourage (a response) with a reinforcer ~ *vi* **:** to seek or get reinforcements — **re·in·force·able** \-ˈfȯr-sə-bəl\ *adj*

reinforced concrete *n* (1902) **:** concrete in which metal (as steel) is embedded so that the two materials act together in resisting forces

re·in·force·ment \ˌrē-ən-ˈfȯrs-mənt\ *n* (1602) **1 :** the action of reinforcing **:** the state of being reinforced **2 :** something that reinforces

re·in·forc·er \-ˈfȯr-sər\ *n* (1955) **:** a stimulus (as a reward or the removal of an electric shock) that increases the probability of a desired response in operant conditioning by being applied or effected following the desired response

re·in·fuse \ˌrē-in-ˈfyüz\ *vt* (1963) **:** to return (as blood or lymphocytes) to the body by infusion after previous withdrawal — **re·in·fu·sion** \-ˈfyü-zhən\ *n*

reins \ˈrānz\ *n pl* [ME, fr. AF, fr. L *renes*] (14c) **1 a :** KIDNEYS **b :** the region of the kidneys **:** LOINS **2 :** the seat of the feelings or passions

re·in·scribe \ˌrē-ən-ˈskrīb\ *vt* (1878) **:** to reestablish or rename in a new and esp. stronger form or context ‹how do contemporary writers re-

\ə\ **abut** \ᵊ\ kitten, F table \ər\ **fur**ther \a\ **ash** \ā\ **ace** \ä\ mop, mar
\au̇\ **out** \ch\ **chin** \e\ bet \ē\ **easy** \g\ **go** \i\ **hit** \ī\ **ice** \j\ **job**
\ŋ\ **sing** \ō\ **go** \ȯ\ **law** \ȯi\ **boy** \th\ **thin** \t͟h\ **the** \ü\ **loot** \u̇\ **foot**
\y\ yet \zh\ vision, beige \k, ⁿ, œ, ue, ʸ\ *see* Guide to Pronunciation

imagine or ~ the culturally laden figure of the aging woman? —Ruth O. Saxton⟩
reins·man \ˈrānz-mən\ *n* (1855) : a skilled driver or rider of horses
re·in·state \ˌrē-ən-ˈstāt\ *vt* **-stat·ed; -stat·ing** (1599) **1** : to place again (as in possession or in a former position) **2** : to restore to a previous effective state — **re·in·state·ment** \-ˈstāt-mənt\ *n*
re·in·sur·ance \ˌrē-ən-ˈshu̇r-ən(t)s *also* (ˌ)rē-ˈin-ˌ\ *n* (1755) : insurance by another insurer of all or a part of a risk previously assumed by an insurance company
re·in·sure \ˌrē-ən-ˈshu̇r\ *vt* (1755) **1** : to insure again by transferring to another insurance company all or a part of a liability assumed **2** : to insure again by assuming all or a part of the liability of an insurance company already covering a risk ~ *vi* : to provide increased insurance — **re·in·sur·er** *n*
re·in·te·grate \(ˌ)rē-ˈin-tə-ˌgrāt\ *vt* [ML *reintegratus,* pp. of *reintegrare* to renew, reinstate, fr. L *re-* + *integrare* to integrate] (1626) : to integrate again into an entity : restore to unity — **re·in·te·gra·tion** \(ˌ)rē-ˌin-tə-ˈgrā-shən\ *n* — **re·in·te·gra·tive** \(ˌ)rē-ˈin-tə-ˌgrā-tiv\ *adj*
re·in·ter·pret \ˌrē-ən-ˈtər-prət, -pət\ *vt* (ca. 1611) : to interpret again; *specif* : to give a new or different interpretation to — **re·in·ter·pre·ta·tion** \-ˌtər-prə-ˈtā-shən, -pə-\ *n*
re·in·vent \ˌrē-ən-ˈvent\ *vt* (1686) **1** : to make as if for the first time something already invented ⟨~ the wheel⟩ **2** : to remake or redo completely **3** : to bring into use again — **re·in·ven·tion** \-ˈven(t)-shən\ *n*
re·in·vest \ˌrē-ən-ˈvest\ *vt* (ca. 1611) **1** : to invest again or anew **2 a** : to invest (as income from investments) in additional securities **b** : to invest (as earnings) in a business rather than distribute as dividends or profits
re·in·vest·ment \-ˈves(t)-mənt\ *n* (ca. 1611) **1** : the action of reinvesting : the state of being reinvested **2** : a second or repeated investment
reis *pl of* REAL
re·is·sue \(ˌ)rē-ˈi-(ˌ)shü, *chiefly Brit* -ˈis-(ˌ)yü\ *vi* (ca. 1618) : to come forth again ~ *vt* : to issue again; *esp* : to cause to become available again — **reissue** *n*
REIT *abbr* real estate investment trust
re·it·er·ate \rē-ˈi-tə-ˌrāt\ *vt* **-at·ed; -at·ing** [ME, fr. L *reiteratus,* pp. of *reiterare* to repeat, fr. *re-* + *iterare* to iterate] (15c) : to state or do over again or repeatedly sometimes with wearying effect — **re·it·er·a·tion** \(ˌ)rē-ˌi-tə-ˈrā-shən\ *n* — **re·it·er·a·tive** \rē-ˈi-tə-ˌrā-tiv, -t(ə-)rə-tiv\ *adj* — **re·it·er·a·tive·ly** *adv*
Rei·ter's syndrome \ˈrī-tərz-\ *n* [Hans *Reiter* †1969 Ger. physician] (ca. 1947) : a disease that is usu. initiated by infection in genetically predisposed individuals and is characterized usu. by recurrence of arthritis, conjunctivitis, and urethritis — called also *Reiter's disease*
reive \ˈrēv\ *vb* **reived; reiv·ing** [ME (Sc) *reifen,* fr. OE *rēafian* to rob — more at REAVE] (bef. 12c) *Scot* : RAID — **reiv·er** *n, Scot*
1**re·ject** \ri-ˈjekt\ *vt* [ME, fr. L *rejectus,* pp. of *reicere,* fr. *re-* + *jacere* to throw — more at JET] (15c) **1 a** : to refuse to accept, consider, submit to, take for some purpose, or use ⟨~*ed* the suggestion⟩ ⟨~ a manuscript⟩ **b** : to refuse to hear, receive, or admit : REBUFF, REPEL ⟨parents who ~ their children⟩ **c** : to refuse as lover or spouse **2** *obs* : to cast off **3** : THROW BACK, REPULSE **4** : to spew out **5** : to subject to immunological rejection ***syn*** see DECLINE — **re·ject·er** *or* **re·jec·tor** \-ˈjek-tər\ *n* — **re·ject·ing·ly** \-tiŋ-lē\ *adv* — **re·jec·tive** \-ˈjek-tiv\ *adj*
2**re·ject** \ˈrē-ˌjekt\ *n* (ca. 1555) : a rejected person or thing; *esp* : one rejected as not wanted, unsatisfactory, or not fulfilling requirements
re·ject·ee \ri-ˌjek-ˈtē, ˌrē-\ *n* (1941) : one that is rejected; *esp* : a person rejected as unfit for military service
re·jec·tion \ri-ˈjek-shən\ *n* (ca. 1552) **1 a** : the action of rejecting : the state of being rejected **b** : an immune response in which foreign tissue (as of a skin graft or transplanted organ) is attacked by immune system components of the recipient organism **2** : something rejected
rejection slip *n* (1906) : a printed slip enclosed with a rejected manuscript returned by an editor to an author
re·jig \(ˌ)rē-ˈjig\ *vt* **re·jigged; re·jig·ging** (1948) *chiefly Brit* : REJIGGER
re·jig·ger \(ˌ)rē-ˈji-gər\ *vt* [*re-* + 3*jigger*] (1942) : ALTER, REARRANGE
re·joice \ri-ˈjȯis\ *vb* **re·joiced; re·joic·ing** [ME, fr. AF *rejois-,* stem of *rejoier, rejoir,* fr. *re-* + *joir* to welcome, enjoy, fr. L *gaudēre* to be glad — more at JOY] *vt* (14c) : to give joy to : GLADDEN ~ *vi* : to feel joy or great delight — **re·joic·er** *n* — **re·joic·ing·ly** \-ˈjȯi-siŋ-lē\ *adv* — **rejoice in** : HAVE, POSSESS
rejoicing *n* (14c) **1** : the action of one that rejoices **2** : an instance, occasion, or expression of joy : FESTIVITY
re·join \ri-ˈjȯin, *vt 1 is* (ˌ)rē-\ *vb* [ME, fr. AF *rejoindre,* fr. *re-* + *joindre* to join — more at JOIN] *vi* (15c) : to answer the replication of the plaintiff ~ *vt* **1** : to join again **2** : to say often sharply or critically in response esp. as a reply to a reply
re·join·der \ri-ˈjȯin-dər\ *n* [ME *rejoiner,* fr. AF *rejoinder,* fr. *rejoinder,* v.] (15c) **1** : the defendant's answer to the plaintiff's replication **2** : REPLY; *specif* : an answer to a reply ***syn*** see ANSWER
re·ju·ve·nate \ri-ˈjü-və-ˌnāt\ *vb* **-nat·ed; -nat·ing** [*re-* + L *juvenis* young — more at YOUNG] *vt* (1789) **1 a** : to make young or youthful again : give new vigor to **b** : to restore to an original or new state ⟨~ old cars⟩ **2 a** : to stimulate (a stream) to renewed erosive activity esp. by uplift **b** : to develop youthful features of topography in ~ *vi* : to cause or undergo rejuvenescence ***syn*** see RENEW — **re·ju·ve·na·tion** \ri-ˌjü-və-ˈnā-shən, ˌrē-\ *n* — **re·ju·ve·na·tor** \ri-ˈjü-və-ˌnā-tər\ *n*
re·ju·ve·nes·cence \ri-ˌjü-və-ˈne-sən(t)s, ˌrē-\ *n* [ML *rejuvenescere* to become young again, fr. L *re-* + *juvenescere* to become young, fr. *juvenis*] (ca. 1631) : a renewal of youthfulness or vigor : REJUVENATION — **re·ju·ve·nes·cent** \-sᵊnt\ *adj*
rel *abbr* **1** released **2** religion; religious
1**re·lapse** \ri-ˈlaps, ˈrē-ˌ\ *n* [ME, fr. ML *relapsus,* fr. L *relabi* to slide back, fr. *re-* + *labi* to slide — more at SLEEP] (15c) **1** : the act or an instance of backsliding, worsening, or subsiding **2** : a recurrence of symptoms of a disease after a period of improvement
2**re·lapse** \ri-ˈlaps\ *vi* **re·lapsed; re·laps·ing** (ca. 1534) **1** : to slip or fall back into a former worse state **2** : SINK, SUBSIDE ⟨~ into deep thought⟩ — **re·laps·er** *n*
relapsing fever *n* (1849) : a variable acute epidemic disease that is marked by recurring high fever usu. lasting three to seven days and is caused by a spirochete (genus *Borrelia*) transmitted by the bites of lice and ticks
re·late \ri-ˈlāt\ *vb* **re·lat·ed; re·lat·ing** [L *relatus* (pp. of *referre* to carry back), fr. *re-* + *latus,* pp. of *ferre* to carry — more at TOLERATE, BEAR] *vt* (15c) **1** : to give an account of : TELL **2** : to show or establish logical or causal connection between ⟨seeks to ~ crime to poverty⟩ ~ *vi* **1** : to apply or take effect retroactively — usu. used with *back* ⟨the law ~*s* back to the initial date of decision⟩ **2** : to have relationship or connection ⟨the readings ~ to his lectures⟩ **3** : to have or establish a relationship : INTERACT ⟨the way a child ~*s* to a teacher⟩ **4** : to respond esp. favorably ⟨can't ~ to that kind of music⟩ — **re·lat·able** \-ˈlā-tə-bəl\ *adj* — **re·lat·er** *or* **re·la·tor** \-ˈlā-tər\ *n*
related *adj* (ca. 1663) **1** : connected by reason of an established or discoverable relation **2** : connected by common ancestry or sometimes by marriage **3** : having close harmonic connection — used of tones, chords, or tonalities — **re·lat·ed·ly** *adv* — **re·lat·ed·ness** *n*
re·la·tion \ri-ˈlā-shən\ *n* [ME *relacion,* fr. AF, fr. L *relation-, relatio,* fr. *referre* (pp. *relatus*) to carry back] (14c) **1** : the act of telling or recounting : ACCOUNT **2** : an aspect or quality (as resemblance) that connects two or more things or parts as being or belonging or working together or as being of the same kind ⟨the ~ of time and space⟩; *specif* : a property (as one expressed by *is equal to, is less than,* or *is the brother of*) that holds between an ordered pair of objects **3** : the referring by a legal fiction of an act to a prior date as the time of its taking effect — usu. used with *back* **4 a** (1) : a person connected by consanguinity or affinity : RELATIVE (2) : a person legally entitled to a share of the property of an intestate **b** : relationship by consanguinity or affinity : KINSHIP **5** : REFERENCE, RESPECT ⟨in ~ to⟩ **6** : the attitude or stance which two or more persons or groups assume toward one another ⟨race ~*s*⟩ **7 a** : the state of being mutually or reciprocally interested (as in social or commercial matters) **b** *pl* (1) : DEALINGS, INTERCOURSE ⟨foreign ~*s*⟩ (2) : SEXUAL INTERCOURSE
re·la·tion·al \-shnəl, -shə-nᵊl\ *adj* (1662) **1** : of or relating to kinship **2** : characterized or constituted by relations **3** : having the function chiefly of indicating a relation of syntax ⟨*has* is notional in *he has luck,* ~ in *he has gone*⟩ **4** : relating to, using, or being a method of organizing data in a database so that it is perceived by the user as a set of tables — **re·la·tion·al·ly** *adv*
relational grammar *n* (1982) : a grammar based on a theory in which grammatical relations (as subject or object) are primitives in terms of which syntactic operations are defined
re·la·tion·ship \-shən-ˌship\ *n* (1741) **1** : the state of being related or interrelated ⟨studied the ~ between the variables⟩ **2** : the relation connecting or binding participants in a relationship: as **a** : KINSHIP **b** : a specific instance or type of kinship **3 a** : a state of affairs existing between those having relations or dealings ⟨had a good ~ with his family⟩ **b** : a romantic or passionate attachment
1**rel·a·tive** \ˈre-lə-tiv\ *n* (14c) **1** : a word referring grammatically to an antecedent **2** : a thing having a relation to or connection with or necessary dependence on another thing **3 a** : a person connected with another by blood or affinity **b** : an animal or plant related to another by common descent **4** : a relative term
2**relative** *adj* (15c) **1** : introducing a subordinate clause qualifying an expressed or implied antecedent ⟨a ~ pronoun⟩; *also* : introduced by such a connective ⟨a ~ clause⟩ **2** : RELEVANT, PERTINENT ⟨matters ~ to world peace⟩ **3** : not absolute or independent : COMPARATIVE ⟨the ~ isolation of life in the country⟩ **4** : having the same key signature — used of major and minor keys and scales **5** : expressed as the ratio of the specified quantity (as an error in measuring) to the total magnitude (as the value of a measured quantity) or to the mean of all the quantities involved
relative humidity *n* (1820) : the ratio of the amount of water vapor actually present in the air to the greatest amount possible at the same temperature
rel·a·tive·ly *adv* (1561) : to a relative degree or extent : SOMEWHAT
relatively prime *adj* (ca. 1890) *of integers* : having no common factors except ±1 ⟨12 and 25 are *relatively prime*⟩
relative to *prep* (1649) : with regard to : in connection with
relative wind *n* (1915) : the motion of the air relative to a body in it
rel·a·tiv·ism \ˈre-lə-ti-ˌvi-zəm\ *n* (1865) **1 a** : a theory that knowledge is relative to the limited nature of the mind and the conditions of knowing **b** : a view that ethical truths depend on the individuals and groups holding them **2** : RELATIVITY — **rel·a·tiv·ist** \-vist\ *n*
rel·a·tiv·is·tic \ˌre-lə-ti-ˈvis-tik\ *adj* (1886) **1** : of, relating to, or characterized by relativity or relativism **2** : moving at a velocity such that there is a significant change in properties (as mass) in accordance with the theory of relativity ⟨a ~ electron⟩ — **rel·a·tiv·is·ti·cal·ly** \-ˈvis-ti-k(ə-)lē\ *adv*
rel·a·tiv·i·ty \ˌre-lə-ˈti-və-tē\ *n, pl* **-ties** (ca. 1834) **1 a** : the quality or state of being relative **b** : something that is relative **2** : the state of being dependent for existence on or determined in nature, value, or quality by relation to something else **3 a** : a theory which is based on the two postulates (1) that the speed of light in a vacuum is constant and independent of the source or observer and (2) that the mathematical forms of the laws of physics are invariant in all inertial systems and which leads to the assertion of the equivalence of mass and energy and of change in mass, dimension, and time with increased velocity — called also *special relativity, special theory of relativity* **b** : an extension of the theory to include gravitation and related acceleration phenomena — called also *general relativity, general theory of relativity* **4** : RELATIVISM 1b
rel·a·tiv·ize \ˈre-lə-tə-ˌvīz\ *vt* **-ized; -iz·ing** (1935) : to treat or describe as relative
re·lax \ri-ˈlaks\ *vb* [ME, fr. L *relaxare,* fr. *re-* + *laxare* to loosen, fr. *laxus* loose — more at SLACK] *vt* (15c) **1** : to make less tense or rigid : SLACKEN ⟨~*ed* his grip⟩ **2** : to make less severe or stringent : MODIFY ⟨~ immigration laws⟩ **3** : to deprive of energy, zeal, or strength of purpose **4** : to relieve from nervous tension **5** : to treat (hair) chemically in order to relax curls ~ *vi* **1** : to become lax, weak, or loose : REST **2** : to become less intense or severe ⟨hoped the committee would ~ in its opposition⟩ **3** *of a muscle or muscle fiber* : to become inactive and lengthen **4** : to cast off social restraint, nervous tension, or anxiety ⟨couldn't ~ in crowds⟩ **5** : to seek rest or recreation ⟨~ at the seashore⟩ **6** : to relieve constipation **7** : to attain equilibrium following the abrupt removal of some influence (as light, high temperature, or stress) — **re·lax·er** *n*

1re·lax·ant \ri-ˈlak-sənt\ *adj* (1771) **:** of, relating to, or producing relaxation ⟨an anesthetic and ~ agent⟩

2relaxant *n* (ca. 1847) **:** a substance (as a drug) that relaxes; *specif* **:** one that relieves muscular tension

re·lax·a·tion \ˌrē-ˌlak-ˈsā-shən, ri-ˌlak-, *esp Brit* ˌre-lək-\ *n* (1548) **1 :** the act of relaxing or state of being relaxed **2 :** a relaxing or recreative state, activity, or pastime **:** DIVERSION **3 :** the lengthening that characterizes inactive muscle fibers or muscles

re·laxed \ri-ˈlakst\ *adj* (1623) **1 :** freed from or lacking in precision or stringency **2 :** set or being at rest or at ease **3 :** easy of manner **:** INFORMAL **4 :** somewhat loose-fitting and usu. casual in style ⟨~ jeans⟩ — **re·laxed·ly** \-ˈlak-səd-lē, -ˈlakst-lē\ *adv* — **re·laxed·ness** \-ˈlak-səd-nəs, -ˈlaks(t)-nəs\ *n*

re·lax·in \ri-ˈlak-sən\ *n* (1930) **:** a sex hormone of the corpus luteum that facilitates birth by causing relaxation of the pelvic ligaments

1re·lay \ˈrē-ˌlā\ *n* [ME, set of fresh hounds, fr. *relayen*] (1651) **1 a :** a supply (as of horses) arranged beforehand for successive relief **b :** a number of persons who relieve others in some work ⟨worked in ~*s* around the clock⟩ **2 a :** a race between teams in which each team member successively covers a specified portion of the course **b :** one of the divisions of a relay **3 :** an electromagnetic device for remote or automatic control that is actuated by variation in conditions of an electric circuit and that operates in turn other devices (as switches) in the same or a different circuit **4 :** SERVOMOTOR **5 :** the act of passing along (as a message or ball) by stages; *also* **:** one of such stages

2re·lay \ˈrē-ˌlā, ri-ˈlā\ *vt* **re·layed; re·lay·ing** [ME, to release a set of fresh hounds, take a fresh horse, fr. MF *relaier,* fr. re- + *laier* to let go, leave — more at DELAY] (1788) **1 a :** to place or dispose in relays **b :** to provide with relays **2 :** to pass along by relays ⟨news was ~*ed* to distant points⟩ **3 :** to control or operate by a relay

3re·lay \(ˌ)rē-ˈlā\ *vt* **-laid** \-ˈlād\; **-lay·ing** [*re-* + *1lay*] (1757) **:** to lay again ⟨~ track⟩

1re·lease \ri-ˈlēs\ *vb* **re·leased; re·leas·ing** [ME *relesen,* fr. AF *relesser,* fr. L *relaxare* to relax] *vt* (14c) **1 :** to set free from restraint, confinement, or servitude ⟨~ hostages⟩ ⟨~ pent-up emotions⟩ ⟨~ the brakes⟩; *also* **:** to let go **:** DISMISS ⟨*released* from her job⟩ **2 :** to relieve from something that confines, burdens, or oppresses ⟨was *released* from her promise⟩ **3 :** to give up in favor of another **:** RELINQUISH ⟨~ a claim to property⟩ **4 :** to give permission for publication, performance, exhibition, or sale of; *also* **:** to make available to the public ⟨the commission *released* its findings⟩ ⟨~ a new movie⟩ ~ *vi* **:** to move from one's normal position (as in football or basketball) in order to assume another position or to perform a second assignment ***syn*** see FREE — **re·leas·able** \-ˈlē-sə-bəl\ *adj*

2release *n* [ME *reles,* fr. AF, fr. *relesser*] (14c) **1 :** relief or deliverance from sorrow, suffering, or trouble **2 a :** discharge from obligation or responsibility **b** (1) **:** relinquishment of a right or claim (2) **:** an act by which a legal right is discharged; *specif* **:** a conveyance of a right in lands or tenements to another having an estate in possession **3 a :** the act or an instance of liberating or freeing (as from restraint) **b :** the act or manner of concluding a musical tone or phrase **c :** the act or manner of ending a sound **:** the movement of one or more vocal organs in quitting the position for a speech sound **d :** the action or manner of throwing a ball ⟨has a quick ~⟩ **4 :** an instrument effecting a legal release **5 :** the state of being freed **6 :** a device adapted to hold or release a mechanism as required **7 a :** the act of permitting performance or publication; *also* **:** PERFORMANCE, PUBLICATION ⟨became a best seller on its ~⟩ **b :** the matter released; *esp* **:** a statement prepared for the press

re–lease \(ˌ)rē-ˈlēs\ *vt* (1828) **:** to lease again

released time *n* (1941) **:** time off from regularly scheduled activities (as school) given to take part in some other specified activity

release print *n* (1937) **:** a motion-picture film released for public showing

re·leas·er \ri-ˈlē-sər\ *n* (15c) **:** one that releases; *specif* **:** a stimulus that serves as the initiator of complex reflex behavior

rel·e·gate \ˈre-lə-ˌgāt\ *vt* **-gat·ed; -gat·ing** [L *relegatus,* pp. of *relegare,* fr. *re-* + *legare* to send with a commission — more at LEGATE] (1599) **1 :** to send into exile **:** BANISH **2 :** ASSIGN: as **a :** to assign to a place of insignificance or of oblivion **:** put out of sight or mind **b :** to assign to an appropriate place or situation on the basis of classification or appraisal **c :** to submit to someone or something for appropriate action **:** DELEGATE **d :** to transfer (a sports team) to a lower ranking division ***syn*** see COMMIT — **rel·e·ga·tion** \ˌre-lə-ˈgā-shən\ *n*

re·lent \ri-ˈlent\ *vb* [ME, to melt, soften, fr. AF *relenter,* fr. *re-* + L *lentare* to bend, fr. *lentus* soft, pliant, slow — more at LITHE] *vi* (1526) **1 a :** to become less severe, harsh, or strict usu. from reasons of humanity **b :** to cease resistance **:** GIVE IN **2 :** LET UP, SLACKEN ~ *vt, obs* **:** SOFTEN, MOLLIFY ***syn*** see YIELD

re·lent·less \-ləs\ *adj* (ca. 1592) **:** showing or promising no abatement of severity, intensity, strength, or pace **:** UNRELENTING ⟨~ pressure⟩ ⟨a ~ campaign⟩ — **re·lent·less·ly** *adv* — **re·lent·less·ness** *n*

rel·e·vance \ˈre-lə-vən(t)s\ *n* (1733) **1 a :** relation to the matter at hand **b :** practical and esp. social applicability **:** PERTINENCE ⟨giving ~ to college courses⟩ **2 :** the ability (as of an information retrieval system) to retrieve material that satisfies the needs of the user

rel·e·van·cy \-vən(t)-sē\ *n, pl* **-cies** (1561) **:** RELEVANCE; *also* **:** something relevant

rel·e·vant \ˈre-lə-vənt\ *adj* [ML *relevant-, relevans,* fr. L, prp. of *relevare* to raise up — more at RELIEVE] (1560) **1 a :** having significant and demonstrable bearing on the matter at hand **b :** affording evidence tending to prove or disprove the matter at issue or under discussion ⟨~ testimony⟩ **c :** having social relevance **2 :** PROPORTIONAL, RELATIVE — **rel·e·vant·ly** *adv*

syn RELEVANT, GERMANE, MATERIAL, PERTINENT, APPOSITE, APPLICABLE, APROPOS mean relating to or bearing upon the matter in hand. RELEVANT implies a traceable, significant, logical connection ⟨found material *relevant* to her case⟩. GERMANE may additionally imply a fitness for or appropriateness to the situation or occasion ⟨a point not *germane* to the discussion⟩. MATERIAL implies so close a relationship that it cannot be dispensed with without serious alteration of the case ⟨facts *material* to the investigation⟩. PERTINENT stresses a clear and decisive relevance ⟨a *pertinent* observation⟩. APPOSITE suggests a felicitous relevance ⟨add an *apposite* quotation to the definition⟩. APPLICABLE suggests the fitness of bringing a general rule or principle to bear upon a particular case ⟨the rule is not *applicable* in this case⟩. APROPOS suggests being both relevant and opportune ⟨the quip was *apropos*⟩.

re·li·abil·i·ty \ri-ˌlī-ə-ˈbi-lə-tē\ *n* (1816) **1 :** the quality or state of being reliable **2 :** the extent to which an experiment, test, or measuring procedure yields the same results on repeated trials

1re·li·able \ri-ˈlī-ə-bəl\ *adj* (1569) **1 :** suitable or fit to be relied on **:** DEPENDABLE **2 :** giving the same result on successive trials — **re·li·able·ness** *n* — **re·li·ably** \-blē\ *adv*

2reliable *n* (1852) **:** one that is reliable

re·li·ance \ri-ˈlī-ən(t)s\ *n* (1607) **1 :** the act of relying **:** the state of being reliant **2 :** something or someone relied on

re·li·ant \-ənt\ *adj* (1849) **:** having reliance on something or someone **:** DEPENDENT — **re·li·ant·ly** *adv*

rel·ic \ˈre-lik\ *n* [ME *relik,* fr. AF *relike,* fr. ML *reliquia,* fr. LL *reliquiae,* pl., remains of a martyr, fr. L, remains, fr. *relinquere* to leave behind — more at RELINQUISH] (13c) **1 a :** an object esteemed and venerated because of association with a saint or martyr **b :** SOUVENIR, MEMENTO **2** *pl* **:** REMAINS, CORPSE **3 :** a survivor or remnant left after decay, disintegration, or disappearance **4 :** a trace of some past or outmoded practice, custom, or belief

1rel·ict \ˈre-likt\ *n* [in sense 1, fr. ME *relicte,* fr. LL *relicta,* fr. L, fem. of *relictus,* pp. of *relinquere;* in senses 2 & 3, fr. *relict* residual, adj., fr. L *relictus*] (15c) **1 :** WIDOW **2 :** a surviving species of an otherwise extinct group of organisms; *also* **:** a remnant of a formerly widespread species that persists in an isolated area **3 a :** a relief feature or rock remaining after other parts have disappeared **b :** something left unchanged

2relict *adj* (15c) **:** of, relating to, or being a relict ⟨~ populations⟩

re·lic·tion \ri-ˈlik-shən\ *n* [L *reliction-, relictio* act of leaving behind, fr. *relinquere*] (ca. 1676) **1 :** the gradual recession of water leaving land permanently uncovered **2 :** land uncovered by reliction

1re·lief \ri-ˈlēf\ *n* [ME *relef, relief,* fr. AF fr. *relever* to relieve] (14c) **1 :** a payment made by a male feudal tenant to his lord on succeeding to an inherited estate **2 a :** removal or lightening of something oppressive, painful, or distressing **b :** WELFARE 2a **c :** military assistance to an endangered post or force **d :** means of breaking or avoiding monotony or boredom **:** DIVERSION **3 :** release from a post or from the performance of duty **4 :** one that takes the place of another on duty **5 :** legal remedy or redress **6** [F, fr. MF, fr. It *rilievo* relievo] **a :** a mode of sculpture in which forms and figures are distinguished from a surrounding plane surface **b :** sculpture or a sculptural form executed in this mode **c :** projecting detail, ornament, or figures **7 a :** sharpness of outline due to contrast ⟨a roof in bold ~ against the sky⟩ **b :** the state of being distinguished by contrast ⟨throws the two opinions into bold ~⟩ **8 :** the elevations or inequalities of a land surface **9 :** the pitching done by a relief pitcher ⟨two innings of hitless ~⟩

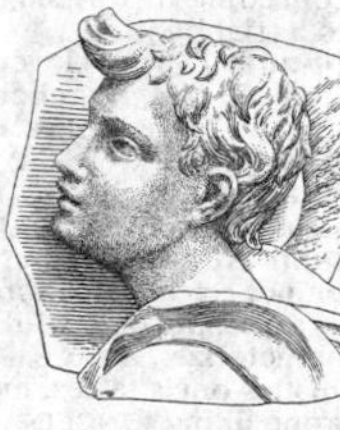

relief 6b

2relief *adj* (1838) **1 :** providing relief **2 :** characterized by surface inequalities **3 :** of or used in letterpress

relief map *n* (1876) **:** a map representing topographic relief

relief pitcher *n* (1906) **:** a baseball pitcher who takes over for another during a game

relief printing *n* (1875) **:** LETTERPRESS 1

re·lieve \ri-ˈlēv\ *vb* **re·lieved; re·liev·ing** [ME *releven,* fr. AF *relever* to raise, relieve, fr. L *relevare,* fr. *re-* + *levare* to raise — more at LEVER] *vt* (14c) **1 a :** to free from a burden **:** give aid or help to **b :** to set free from an obligation, condition, or restriction **c :** to ease of a burden, wrong, or oppression by judicial or legislative interposition **2 a :** to bring about the removal or alleviation of **:** MITIGATE ⟨helps ~ stress⟩ **b :** ROB, DEPRIVE ⟨*relieved* us of our belongings⟩ **3 a :** to release from a post, station, or duty **b :** to take the place of ⟨will ~ the starting pitcher⟩ **4 :** to remove or lessen the monotony of ⟨a park ~*s* the urban landscape⟩ **5 a :** to set off by contrast **b :** to raise in relief **6 :** to discharge the bladder or bowels of (oneself) ~ *vi* **1 :** to bring or give relief **2 :** to stand out in relief **3 :** to serve as a relief pitcher — **re·liev·able** \-ˈlē-və-bəl\ *adj*

syn RELIEVE, ALLEVIATE, LIGHTEN, ASSUAGE, MITIGATE, ALLAY mean to make something less grievous. RELIEVE implies a lifting of enough of a burden to make it tolerable ⟨took an aspirin to *relieve* the pain⟩. ALLEVIATE implies temporary or partial lessening of pain or distress ⟨the lotion *alleviated* the itching⟩. LIGHTEN implies reducing a burdensome or depressing weight ⟨good news would *lighten* our worries⟩. ASSUAGE implies softening or sweetening what is harsh or disagreeable ⟨ocean breezes *assuaged* the intense heat⟩. MITIGATE suggests a moderating or countering of the effect of something violent or painful ⟨the need to *mitigate* barbaric laws⟩. ALLAY implies an effective calming or soothing of fears or alarms ⟨*allayed* their fears⟩.

relieved *adj* (1850) **:** experiencing or showing relief esp. from anxiety or pent-up emotions — **re·liev·ed·ly** \-ˈlē-vəd-lē\ *adv*

re·liev·er \ri-ˈlē-vər\ *n* (15c) **:** one that relieves; *esp* **:** RELIEF PITCHER

re·lie·vo \ri-ˈlē-(ˌ)vō, rēl-ˈyā-(ˌ)vō\ *n, pl* **-vos** [It *rilievo,* fr. *rilevare* to raise, fr. L *relevare*] (1625) **:** RELIEF 6

relig *abbr* religion

re·li·gio- \ri-ˈli-j(ē-)ō\ *comb form* **:** religion and ⟨*religio*-political⟩

re·li·gion \ri-ˈli-jən\ *n* [ME *religioun,* fr. AF *religiun,* L *religion-, religio* supernatural constraint, sanction, religious practice, perh. fr. *religare* to restrain, tie back — more at RELY] (13c) **1 a :** the state of a religious ⟨a nun in her 20th year of ~⟩ **b** (1) **:** the service and worship of God or the supernatural (2) **:** commitment or devotion to religious faith or observance **2 :** a personal set or institutionalized system of religious attitudes, beliefs, and practices **3** *archaic* **:** scrupulous conformity **:** CONSCIENTIOUSNESS **4 :** a cause, principle, or system of beliefs held to with ardor and faith — **re·li·gion·less** *adj*

re·li·gion·ist \-ˈli-jə-nist, -ˈlij-nist\ *n* (1653) **:** a person adhering to a religion; *esp* **:** a religious zealot

re·li·gi·ose \ri-ˈli-jē-ˌōs\ *adj* [*religion* + 1-*ose*] (1853) **:** RELIGIOUS; *esp* **:** excessively, obtrusively, or sentimentally religious — **re·li·gi·os·i·ty** \-ˌli-jē-ˈä-sə-tē\ *n*

1**re·li·gious** \ri-ˈli-jəs\ *adj* [ME, fr. AF *religius,* fr. L *religiosus,* fr. *religio*] (13c) **1 :** relating to or manifesting faithful devotion to an acknowledged ultimate reality or deity ⟨a ~ person⟩ ⟨~ attitudes⟩ **2 :** of, relating to, or devoted to religious beliefs or observances ⟨joined a ~ order⟩ **3 a :** scrupulously and conscientiously faithful **b :** FERVENT, ZEALOUS — **re·li·gious·ly** *adv* — **re·li·gious·ness** *n*

2**religious** *n, pl* **religious** [ME, fr. AF *religius,* fr. *religius,* adj.] (13c) **:** a member of a religious order under monastic vows

re·line \(ˌ)rē-ˈlīn\ *vt* (1838) **:** to put new lines on or a new lining in

re·lin·quish \ri-ˈliŋ-kwish, -ˈlin-\ *vt* [ME *relinquisshen,* fr. AF *relinquiss-,* stem of *relinquir,* fr. L *relinquere* to leave behind, fr. *re-* + *linquere* to leave — more at LOAN] (15c) **1 :** to withdraw or retreat from **:** leave behind **2 :** GIVE UP ⟨~ a title⟩ **3 a :** to stop holding physically **:** RELEASE ⟨slowly ~*ed* his grip on the bar⟩ **b :** to give over possession or control of **:** YIELD ⟨few leaders willingly ~ power⟩ — **re·lin·quish·ment** \-mənt\ *n*

syn RELINQUISH, YIELD, RESIGN, SURRENDER, ABANDON, WAIVE mean to give up completely. RELINQUISH usu. does not imply strong feeling but may suggest some regret, reluctance, or weakness ⟨*relinquished* her crown⟩. YIELD implies concession or compliance or submission to force ⟨the troops *yielded* ground grudgingly⟩. RESIGN emphasizes voluntary relinquishment or sacrifice without struggle ⟨*resigned* her position⟩. SURRENDER implies a giving up after a struggle to retain or resist ⟨*surrendered* their claims⟩. ABANDON stresses finality and completeness in giving up ⟨*abandoned* all hope⟩. WAIVE implies conceding or forgoing with little or no compulsion ⟨*waived* the right to a trial by jury⟩.

rel·i·quary \ˈre-lə-ˌkwer-ē\ *n, pl* **-quar·ies** [F *reliquaire,* fr. ML *reliquiarium,* fr. *reliquia* relic — more at RELIC] (1652) **:** a container or shrine in which sacred relics are kept

re·lique \ri-ˈlēk, ˈre-lik\ *archaic var of* RELIC

re·liq·ui·ae \ri-ˈli-kwē-ˌī, -kwē-ˌē\ *n pl* [L — more at RELIC] (1654) **:** remains of the dead **:** RELICS

1**rel·ish** \ˈre-lish\ *n* [alter. of ME *reles* odor, taste, fr. MF, something left behind, release — more at RELEASE] (1530) **1 :** characteristic flavor; *esp* **:** pleasing or zestful flavor **2 :** a quantity just sufficient to flavor or characterize **:** TRACE **3 a :** enjoyment of or delight in something that satisfies one's tastes, inclinations, or desires ⟨eat with great ~⟩ **b :** a strong liking **:** INCLINATION ⟨has little ~ for sports⟩ **4 a :** something adding a zestful flavor; *esp* **:** a condiment (as of pickles or green tomatoes) eaten with other food to add flavor **b :** APPETIZER, HORS D'OEUVRE

2**relish** *vt* (1586) **1 :** to add relish to **2 :** to be pleased or gratified by **:** ENJOY **3 :** to eat or drink with pleasure **4 :** to appreciate with taste and discernment ~ *vi* **:** to have a characteristic or pleasing taste — **rel·ish·able** \ˈre-li-shə-bəl\ *adj*

re·live \(ˌ)rē-ˈliv\ *vi* (1548) **:** to live again ~ *vt* **:** to live over again; *esp* **:** to experience again in the imagination

re·lo·cate \(ˌ)rē-ˈlō-ˌkāt, ˌrē-lō-ˈ\ *vt* (1834) **:** to locate again **:** establish or lay out in a new place ~ *vi* **:** to move to a new location — **re·lo·cat·able** \-ˈlō-ˌkā-tə-bəl, -ˌlō-ˈkā-\ *adj* — **re·lo·ca·tion** \ˌrē-lō-ˈkā-shən\ *n*

re·lo·cat·ee \ˌrē-lə-ˌkā-ˈtē, ˌrē-ˌlō-kə-ˈtē\ *n* (1954) **:** one who moves to a new location **:** one that is relocated

re·lu·cent \ri-ˈlü-sᵊnt\ *adj* [L *relucent-, relucens,* pp. of *relucēre* to shine back, fr. *re-* + *lucēre* to shine — more at LIGHT] (15c) **:** reflecting light **:** SHINING

re·luct \ri-ˈləkt\ *vi* [L *reluctari*] (1547) **:** to show reluctance

re·luc·tance \ri-ˈlək-tən(t)s\ *n* (1629) **1 :** the quality or state of being reluctant **2 :** the opposition offered in a magnetic circuit to magnetic flux; *specif* **:** the ratio of the magnetic potential difference to the corresponding flux

re·luc·tan·cy \-tən(t)-sē\ *n* (1634) **:** RELUCTANCE

re·luc·tant \ri-ˈlək-tənt\ *adj* [L *reluctant-, reluctans,* prp. of *reluctari* to struggle against, fr. *re-* + *luctari* to struggle] (1667) **:** feeling or showing aversion, hesitation, or unwillingness ⟨~ to get involved⟩; *also* **:** having or assuming a specified role unwillingly ⟨a ~ hero⟩ ***syn*** see DISINCLINED — **re·luc·tant·ly** *adv*

re·lume \(ˌ)rē-ˈlüm\ *vt* **re·lumed; re·lum·ing** [irreg. fr. LL *reluminare,* fr. L *re-* + *luminare* to light up — more at ILLUMINATE] (1604) *archaic* **:** to light or light up again **:** REKINDLE

re·ly \ri-ˈlī\ *vi* **re·lied; re·ly·ing** [ME *relien* to rally, fr. AF *relier* to retie, gather, rally, fr. L *religare* to tie out of the way, fr. *re-* + *ligare* to tie — more at LIGATURE] (1574) **1 :** to be dependent ⟨the system on which we ~ for water⟩ **2 :** to have confidence based on experience ⟨someone you can ~ on⟩ — **re·li·er** \-ˈlī(-ə)r\ *n*

rem \ˈrem\ *n* [*r*oentgen *e*quivalent *m*an] (1947) **:** the dosage of an ionizing radiation that will cause the same biological effect as one roentgen of X-ray or gamma-ray exposure

REM \ˈrem\ *n* (1957) **:** RAPID EYE MOVEMENT

1**re·main** \ri-ˈmān\ *vi* [ME, fr. AF *remaindre,* fr. L *remanēre,* fr. *re-* + *manēre* to remain — more at MANSION] (14c) **1 a :** to be a part not destroyed, taken, or used up ⟨only a few ruins ~⟩ **b :** to be something yet to be shown, done, or treated ⟨it ~*s* to be seen⟩ **2 :** to stay in the same place or with the same person or group; *esp* **:** to stay behind **3 :** to continue unchanged ⟨the fact ~*s* that we can't go⟩

2**remain** *n* (15c) **1** *obs* **:** STAY **2 :** a remaining part or trace — usu. used in pl. **3** *pl* **:** a dead body

1**re·main·der** \ri-ˈmān-dər\ *n* [ME, fr. AF, fr. *remaindre,* v.] (14c) **1 :** an interest or estate in property that follows and is dependent on the termination of a prior intervening possessory estate created at the same time by the same instrument **2 a :** a remaining group, part, or trace **b (1) :** the number left after a subtraction **(2) :** the final undivided part after division that is less or of lower degree than the divisor **3 :** a book sold at a reduced price by the publisher after sales have slowed

2**remainder** *adj* (1567) **:** LEFTOVER, REMAINING

3**remainder** *vt* **-dered; -der·ing** \-d(ə-)riŋ\ (1904) **:** to dispose of as remainders

remainder theorem *n* (1886) **:** a theorem in algebra: if $f(x)$ is a polynomial in x then the remainder on dividing $f(x)$ by $x - a$ is $f(a)$

1**re·make** \(ˌ)rē-ˈmāk\ *vt* **-made** \-ˈmād\; **-mak·ing** (ca. 1635) **:** to make anew or in a different form — **re·mak·er** \-ˈmā-kər\ *n*

2**re·make** \ˈrē-ˌmāk\ *n* (1936) **:** one that is remade; *esp* **:** a new version of a motion picture

re·man \(ˌ)rē-ˈman\ *vt* (1666) **1 :** to man again or anew **2 :** to imbue with courage again

re·mand \ri-ˈmand\ *vt* [ME *remaunden,* fr. AF *remander,* fr. LL *remandare* to send back word, fr. L *re-* + *mandare* to order — more at MANDATE] (15c) **:** to order back: as **a :** to send back (a case) to another court or agency for further action **b :** to return to custody pending trial or for further detention — **remand** *n*

rem·a·nence \ˈre-mə-nən(t)s, ri-ˈmā-\ *n* (ca. 1880) **:** the magnetic induction remaining in a magnetized substance no longer under external magnetic influence

rem·a·nent \-nənt\ *adj* [ME, fr. AF *remanant* — more at REMNANT] (15c) **1 :** RESIDUAL, REMAINING **2 :** of, relating to, or characterized by remanence

re·man·u·fac·ture \(ˌ)rē-ˌma-nyə-ˈfak-chər, -ˌma-nə-\ *vt* (1825) **:** to manufacture into a new product — **remanufacture** *n* — **re·man·u·fac·tur·er** \-chər-ər\ *n*

re·map \(ˌ)rē-ˈmap\ *vt* (1931) **:** to map again; *also* **:** to lay out in a new pattern

1**re·mark** \ri-ˈmärk\ *n* [F *remarque,* fr. MF, fr. *remarquer* to remark, fr. *re-* re- + *marquer* to mark — more at MARQUE] (1660) **1 :** the act of remarking **:** NOTICE **2 :** an expression of opinion or judgment **3 :** mention of that which deserves attention or notice

2**remark** *vt* (1675) **1 :** to take notice of **:** OBSERVE **2 :** to express as an observation or comment **:** SAY ~ *vi* **:** to notice something and comment thereon — used with *on* or *upon*

re·mark·able \ri-ˈmär-kə-bəl\ *adj* (ca. 1604) **:** worthy of being or likely to be noticed esp. as being uncommon or extraordinary ***syn*** see NOTICEABLE — **re·mark·able·ness** *n*

re·mark·ably \-blē\ *adv* (1638) **1 :** in a remarkable manner ⟨~ talented⟩ **2 :** as is remarkable ⟨~, no one was hurt⟩

re·marque \ri-ˈmärk\ *n* [F *remarque* remark, note, fr. MF, fr. *remarquer*] (1882) **1 :** a drawn, etched, or incised scribble or sketch done on the margin of a plate or stone and removed before the regular printing **2 :** a proof taken before remarques have been removed

re·mas·ter \(ˌ)rē-ˈmas-tər\ *vt* (1964) **:** to create a new master of esp. by altering or enhancing the sound quality of an older recording

re·match \ˈrē-ˌmach, (ˌ)rē-ˈ\ *n* (1941) **:** a second match between the same contestants or teams

re·me·di·a·ble \ri-ˈmē-dē-ə-bəl\ *adj* (15c) **:** capable of being remedied — **re·me·di·abil·i·ty** \ri-ˌmē-dē-ə-ˈbi-lə-tē\ *n*

re·me·di·al \ri-ˈmē-dē-əl\ *adj* (1651) **1 :** intended as a remedy **2 :** concerned with the correction of faulty study habits and the raising of a pupil's general competence ⟨~ reading courses⟩; *also* **:** receiving or requiring remedial instruction ⟨~ students⟩ — **re·me·di·al·ly** \-ə-lē\ *adv*

re·me·di·ate \ri-ˈmē-dē-ət\ *adj* (1605) *archaic* **:** REMEDIAL

re·me·di·a·tion \ri-ˌmē-dē-ˈā-shən\ *n* (1818) **:** the act or process of remedying ⟨~ of reading problems⟩ — **re·me·di·ate** \-ˈmē-dē-ˌāt\ *vt*

1**rem·e·dy** \ˈre-mə-dē\ *n, pl* **-dies** [ME *remedie,* fr. AF, fr. L *remedium,* fr. *re-* + *mederi* to heal — more at MEDICAL] (13c) **1 :** a medicine, application, or treatment that relieves or cures a disease **2 :** something that corrects or counteracts **3 :** the legal means to recover a right or to prevent or obtain redress for a wrong — **rem·e·di·less** *adj*

2**remedy** *vt* **-died; -dy·ing** (15c) **:** to provide or serve as a remedy for **:** RELIEVE ⟨~ a social evil⟩ ***syn*** see CORRECT

re·mem·ber \ri-ˈmem-bər\ *vb* **-bered; -ber·ing** \-b(ə-)riŋ\ [ME *remembren,* fr. AF *remembrer,* fr. LL *rememorari,* fr. L *re-* + LL *memorari* to be mindful of, fr. L *memor* mindful — more at MEMORY] *vt* (14c) **1 :** to bring to mind or think of again ⟨~*s* the old days⟩ **2** *archaic* **a :** BETHINK 1b **b :** REMIND **3 a :** to keep in mind for attention or consideration ⟨~*s* friends at Christmas⟩ **b :** REWARD ⟨was ~*ed* in the will⟩ **4 :** to retain in the memory ⟨~ the facts until the test is over⟩ **5 :** to convey greetings from ⟨~ me to her⟩ **6 :** RECORD, COMMEMORATE ~ *vi* **1 :** to exercise or have the power of memory **2 :** to have a recollection or remembrance — **re·mem·ber·abil·i·ty** \-ˌmem-b(ə-)rə-ˈbi-lə-tē\ *n* — **re·mem·ber·able** \-ˈmem-b(ə-)rə-bəl\ *adj* — **re·mem·ber·er** \-bər-ər\ *n*

syn REMEMBER, RECOLLECT, RECALL, REMIND, REMINISCE mean to bring an image or idea from the past into the mind. REMEMBER implies a keeping in memory that may be effortless or unwilled ⟨*remembers* that day as though it were yesterday⟩. RECOLLECT implies a bringing back to mind what is lost or scattered ⟨as near as I can *recollect*⟩. RECALL suggests an effort to bring back to mind and often to re-create in speech ⟨can't *recall* the words of the song⟩. REMIND suggests a jogging of one's memory by an association or similarity ⟨that *reminds* me of a story⟩. REMINISCE implies a casual often nostalgic recalling of experiences long past and gone ⟨old college friends like to *reminisce*⟩.

re·mem·brance \ri-ˈmem-brən(t)s *also* -bə-rən(t)s\ *n* (14c) **1 :** the state of bearing in mind **2 a :** the ability to remember **:** MEMORY **b :** the period over which one's memory extends **3 :** an act of recalling to mind **4 :** a memory of a person, thing, or event **5 a :** something that serves to keep in or bring to mind **:** REMINDER **b :** COMMEMORATION, MEMORIAL **c :** a greeting or gift recalling or expressing friendship or affection ***syn*** see MEMORY

Remembrance Day *n* (1918) **:** November 11 set aside in commemoration of the end of hostilities in 1918 and 1945 and observed as a legal holiday in Canada; *also* **:** REMEMBRANCE SUNDAY

re·mem·branc·er \ri-ˈmem-brən(t)-sər\ *n* (15c) **1 :** any of several English officials **2 :** one that reminds

Remembrance Sunday *n* (1942) **:** a Sunday that is usu. closest to November 11 and that in Great Britain is set aside in commemoration of the end of hostilities in 1918 and 1945

re·mind \ri-ˈmīnd\ *vt* (1660) **:** to put in mind of something **:** cause to remember ***syn*** see REMEMBER — **re·mind·er** *n*

re·mind·ful \-ˈmīn(d)-fəl\ *adj* (1810) **1 :** MINDFUL **2 :** tending to remind **:** SUGGESTIVE, EVOCATIVE

rem·i·nisce \ˌre-mə-ˈnis\ *vi* **-nisced; -nisc·ing** [back-formation fr. *reminiscence*] (1829) **:** to indulge in reminiscence ***syn*** see REMEMBER — **rem·i·nis·cer** \-ˈni-sər\ *n*

rem·i·nis·cence \-ˈni-sᵊn(t)s\ *n* (1589) **1 :** apprehension of a Platonic idea as if it had been known in a previous existence **2 a :** recall to mind of a long-forgotten experience or fact **b :** the process or practice of thinking or telling about past experiences **3 a :** a remembered experience **b :** an account of a memorable experience — often used in pl. **4 :** something so like another as to be regarded as an unconscious repetition, imitation, or survival ***syn*** see MEMORY

rem·i·nis·cent \-sᵊnt\ *adj* [L *reminiscent-, reminiscens,* prp. of *reminisci* to remember, fr. *re-* + *-minisci* (akin to L *ment-, mens* mind) — more at MIND] (1765) **1 :** of the character of or relating to reminiscence **2 :** marked by or given to reminiscence **3 :** tending to remind **:** SUGGESTIVE — **rem·i·nis·cent·ly** *adv*

rem·i·nis·cen·tial \ˌre-mə-(ˌ)ni-ˈsen(t)-shəl\ *adj* (1646) **:** REMINISCENT

re·mint \(ˌ)rē-ˈmint\ *vt* (1823) **:** to melt down (old or worn coin) and make into new coin

re·mise \ri-ˈmīz\ *vt* **re·mised; re·mis·ing** [ME, fr. AF *remis,* pp. of *remettre* to put back, fr. L *remittere* to send back] (15c) **:** to give, grant, or release a claim to **:** DEED

re·miss \ri-ˈmis\ *adj* [ME, fr. AF *remis,* L *remissus,* fr. pp. of *remittere* to send back, relax] (15c) **1 :** negligent in the performance of work or duty **:** CARELESS **2 :** showing neglect or inattention **:** LAX ***syn*** see NEGLIGENT — **re·miss·ly** *adv* — **re·miss·ness** *n*

re·mis·si·ble \ri-ˈmi-sə-bəl\ *adj* (1577) **:** capable of being forgiven ⟨~ sins⟩ — **re·mis·si·bly** \-blē\ *adv*

re·mis·sion \ri-ˈmi-shən\ *n* (13c) **1 :** the act or process of remitting **2 :** a state or period during which something is remitted

[1]**re·mit** \ri-ˈmit\ *vb* **re·mit·ted; re·mit·ting** [ME *remitten,* fr. L *remittere* to send back, fr. *re-* + *mittere* to send] *vt* (14c) **1 a :** to lay aside (a mood or disposition) partly or wholly **b :** to desist from (an activity) **c :** to let (as attention or diligence) slacken **:** RELAX **2 a :** to release from the guilt or penalty of ⟨~ sins⟩ **b :** to refrain from exacting ⟨~ a tax⟩ **c :** to cancel or refrain from inflicting ⟨~ the penalty⟩ **d :** to give relief from (suffering) **3 :** to submit or refer for consideration, judgment, decision, or action; *specif* **:** REMAND **4 :** to restore or consign to a former status or condition **5 :** POSTPONE, DEFER **6 :** to send (money) to a person or place esp. in payment of a demand, account, or draft ~ *vi* **1 a :** to abate in force or intensity **:** MODERATE **b :** to abate symptoms (as of a disease) for a period **2 :** to send money (as in payment) — **re·mit·ment** \-ˈmit-mənt\ *n* — **re·mit·ta·ble** \-ˈmi-tə-bəl\ *adj* — **re·mit·ter** *n*

[2]**re·mit** \ri-ˈmit, ˈrē-ˌ\ *n* (15c) **1 :** an act of remitting **2 :** something remitted to another person or authority

re·mit·tal \ri-ˈmi-tᵊl\ *n* (1596) **:** REMISSION

re·mit·tance \ri-ˈmi-tᵊn(t)s\ *n* (1705) **1 a :** a sum of money remitted **b :** an instrument by which money is remitted **2 :** transmittal of money (as to a distant place)

remittance man *n* (1886) **:** one living abroad on remittances from home

re·mit·tent \ri-ˈmi-tᵊnt\ *adj* [L *remittent-, remittens,* prp. of *remittere*] (1693) *of a disease* **:** marked by alternating periods of abatement and increase of symptoms ⟨~ fever⟩

[1]**re·mix** \(ˈ)rē-ˈmiks\ *vt* (1662) **:** to mix again

[2]**re·mix** \ˈrē-ˌmiks\ *n* (1980) **:** a variant of an original recording (as of a song) made by rearranging or adding to the original

[1]**rem·nant** \ˈrem-nənt\ *n* [ME, contr. of *remenant,* fr. AF *remanant,* fr. prp. of *remaindre* to remain — more at REMAIN] (14c) **1 a :** a usu. small part, member, or trace remaining **b :** a small surviving group — often used in pl. **2 :** an unsold or unused end of piece goods

[2]**remnant** *adj* (1550) **:** still remaining

re·mod·el \(ˌ)rē-ˈmä-dᵊl\ *vt* (1789) **:** to alter the structure of **:** REMAKE

re·mon·strance \ri-ˈmän(t)-strən(t)s\ *n* (1585) **1 :** an earnest presentation of reasons for opposition or grievance; *esp* **:** a document formally stating such points **2 :** an act or instance of remonstrating

re·mon·strant \-strənt\ *adj* (1641) **:** vigorously objecting or opposing — **remonstrant** *n* — **re·mon·strant·ly** *adv*

re·mon·strate \ˈre-mən-ˌstrāt, ri-ˈmän-\ *vb* **-strat·ed; -strat·ing** [ML *remonstratus,* pp. of *remonstrare* to demonstrate, fr. L *re-* + *monstrare* to show — more at MUSTER] *vi* (1695) **:** to present and urge reasons in opposition **:** EXPOSTULATE — usu. used with *with* ~ *vt* **:** to say or plead in protest, reproof, or opposition — **re·mon·stra·tion** \ˌre-mən-ˈstrā-shən, ri-ˌman-\ *n* — **re·mon·stra·tive** \ri-ˈmän(t)-strə-tiv\ *adj* — **re·mon·stra·tive·ly** *adv* — **re·mon·stra·tor** \ˈre-mən-ˌstrā-tər, ri-ˈmän-\ *n*

rem·o·ra \ri-ˈmȯr-ə *also* ˈre-mə-rə\ *n* [LL, fr. L, delay, fr. *remorari* to delay, fr. *re-* + *morari* to delay — more at MORATORIUM] (1567) **1 :** any of a family (Echeneidae) of marine bony fishes that have the anterior dorsal fin modified into a suctorial disk on the head by means of which they adhere esp. to other fishes **2 :** HINDRANCE, DRAG

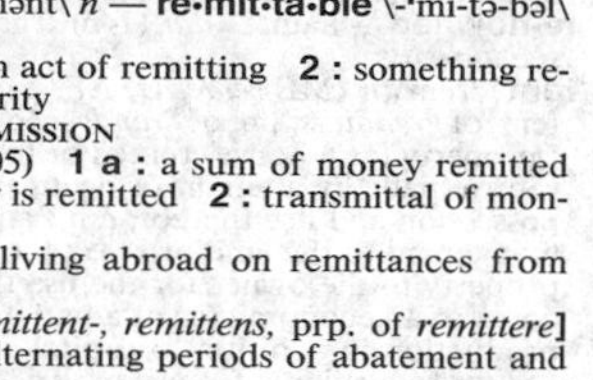
remora 1

re·morse \ri-ˈmȯrs\ *n* [ME, fr. AF *remors,* fr. ML *remorsus,* fr. LL, act of biting again, fr. L *remordēre* to bite again, fr. *re-* + *mordēre* to bite — more at MORDANT] (14c) **1 :** a gnawing distress arising from a sense of guilt for past wrongs **:** SELF-REPROACH **2** *obs* **:** COMPASSION ***syn*** see PENITENCE

re·morse·ful \-ˈmȯrs-fəl\ *adj* (1592) **:** motivated or marked by remorse — **re·morse·ful·ly** \-fə-lē\ *adv* — **re·morse·ful·ness** *n*

re·morse·less \-ləs\ *adj* (1593) **1 :** having no remorse **:** MERCILESS **2 :** RELENTLESS — **re·morse·less·ly** *adv* — **re·morse·less·ness** *n*

[1]**re·mote** \ri-ˈmōt\ *adj* **re·mot·er; -est** [ME, fr. L *remotus,* fr. pp. of *removēre* to remove] (15c) **1 :** separated by an interval or space greater than usual ⟨an involucre ~ from the flower⟩ **2 :** far removed in space, time, or relation **:** DIVERGENT ⟨the ~ past⟩ ⟨comments ~ from the truth⟩ **3 :** OUT-OF-THE-WAY, SECLUDED ⟨a ~ cabin in the hills⟩ **4 :** acting, acted on, or controlled indirectly or from a distance ⟨~ computer operation⟩; *also* **:** relating to the acquisition of information about a distant object (as by radar or photography) without coming into physical contact with it ⟨~ sensing⟩ **5 :** not arising from a primary or proximate action **6 :** small in degree **:** SLIGHT ⟨a ~ possibility⟩ ⟨hadn't the *remotest* idea of what was going on⟩ **7 :** distant in manner **:** ALOOF — **re·mote·ly** *adv* — **re·mote·ness** *n*

[2]**remote** *n* (1937) **1 :** a radio or television program or a portion of a program originating outside the studio **2 :** REMOTE CONTROL 2

remote control *n* (1904) **1 :** control (as by radio signal) of operation from a point at some distance removed **2 :** a device or mechanism for controlling something from a distance

re·mo·tion \ri-ˈmō-shən\ *n* (15c) **1 :** the quality or state of being remote **2 :** the act of removing **:** REMOVAL **3** *obs* **:** DEPARTURE

ré·mou·lade *or* **re·mou·lade** \ˌrā-mə-ˈläd, -mü-\ *n* [F *rémoulade*] (1845) **:** a pungent sauce or dressing resembling mayonnaise and usu. including savory herbs and condiments

[1]**re·mount** \(ˌ)rē-ˈmau̇nt\ *vb* [ME, partly fr. *re-* + *mounten* to mount, partly fr. AF *remunter,* fr. *re-* + *munter* to mount] *vt* (15c) **1 :** to mount (something) again ⟨~ a picture⟩ **2 :** to furnish remounts to ~ *vi* **1 :** to mount again **2 :** REVERT

[2]**re·mount** \ˈrē-ˌmau̇nt, (ˌ)rē-ˈ\ *n* (1781) **:** a fresh horse to replace one no longer available

re·mov·al \ri-ˈmü-vəl\ *n* (1597) **:** the act or process of removing **:** the fact of being removed

[1]**re·move** \ri-ˈmüv\ *vb* **re·moved; re·mov·ing** [ME *remeven, removen,* fr. AF *remuver, removeir,* fr. L *removēre,* fr. *re-* + *movēre* to move] *vt* (14c) **1 a :** to change the location, position, station, or residence of ⟨~ soldiers to the front⟩ **b :** to transfer (a legal proceeding) from one court to another **2 :** to move by lifting, pushing aside, or taking away or off ⟨~ your hat⟩ **3 :** to dismiss from office **4 :** to get rid of **:** ELIMINATE ⟨~ a tumor surgically⟩ ~ *vi* **1 :** to change location, station, or residence ⟨*removing* from the city to the suburbs⟩ **2 :** to go away **3 :** to be capable of being removed — **re·mov·abil·i·ty** \-ˌmü-və-ˈbi-lə-tē\ *n* — **re·mov·able** *also* **re·move·able** \ri-ˈmü-və-bəl\ *adj* — **re·mov·able·ness** \-ˈmü-və-bəl-nəs\ *n* — **re·mov·ably** \-blē\ *adv* — **re·mov·er** *n*

[2]**remove** *n* (1553) **1 :** REMOVAL; *specif* **:** MOVE 2c **2 a :** a distance or interval separating one person or thing from another **b :** a degree or stage of separation

removed *adj* (ca. 1548) **1 a :** distant in degree of relationship **b :** of a younger or older generation ⟨a second cousin's child is a second cousin once ~⟩ **2 :** separate or remote in space, time, or character

REM sleep *n* (1965) **:** a state of sleep that recurs cyclically several times during a normal period of sleep and that is characterized esp. by increased neuronal activity of the forebrain and midbrain, depressed muscle tone, dreaming, and rapid eye movements — called also *paradoxical sleep, rapid eye movement sleep*; compare SLOW-WAVE SLEEP

re·mu·da \ri-ˈmü-də, -ˈmyü-\ *n* [AmerSp, relay of horses, fr. Sp, exchange, fr. *remudar* to exchange, fr. *re-* + *mudar* to change, fr. L *mutare* — more at MUTABLE] (ca. 1892) **:** the herd of horses from which those to be used for the day are chosen

re·mu·ner·ate \ri-ˈmyü-nə-ˌrāt\ *vt* **-at·ed; -at·ing** [L *remuneratus,* pp. of *remunerare* to recompense, fr. *re-* + *munerare* to give, fr. *muner-, munus* gift — more at MEAN] (1523) **1 :** to pay an equivalent for ⟨their services were generously *remunerated*⟩ **2 :** to pay an equivalent to for a service, loss, or expense **:** RECOMPENSE ***syn*** see PAY — **re·mu·ner·a·tor** \-ˌrā-tər\ *n* — **re·mu·ner·a·to·ry** \-rə-ˌtȯr-ē\ *adj*

re·mu·ner·a·tion \ri-ˌmyü-nə-ˈrā-shən\ *n* (15c) **1 :** something that remunerates **:** RECOMPENSE, PAY **2 :** an act or fact of remunerating

re·mu·ner·a·tive \ri-ˈmyü-nə-rə-tiv, -ˌrā-\ *adj* (ca. 1677) **1 :** serving to remunerate **2 :** providing remuneration **:** PROFITABLE — **re·mu·ner·a·tive·ly** *adv* — **re·mu·ner·a·tive·ness** *n*

Re·mus \ˈrē-məs\ *n* [L] (13c) **:** a son of Mars slain by his twin brother Romulus

re·nais·sance \ˌre-nə-ˈsän(t)s, -ˈzän(t)s, -ˈsäⁿs, -ˈzäⁿs, ˈre-nə-ˌ, *chiefly Brit* ri-ˈnā-sᵊn(t)s\ *n, often attrib* [F, fr. MF, rebirth, fr. OF *renaistre* to be born again, fr. L *renasci,* fr. *re-* + *nasci* to be born — more at NATION] (1845) **1** *cap* **a :** the transitional movement in Europe between medieval and modern times beginning in the 14th century in Italy, lasting into the 17th century, and marked by a humanistic revival of classical influence expressed in a flowering of the arts and literature and by the beginnings of modern science **b :** the period of the Renaissance **c :** the neoclassic style of architecture prevailing during the Renaissance **2** *often cap* **:** a movement or period of vigorous artistic and intellectual activity **3 :** REBIRTH, REVIVAL

Renaissance man *n* (1906) **:** a person who has wide interests and is expert in several areas

re·nal \ˈrē-nᵊl\ *adj* [F or LL; F *rénal,* fr. LL *renalis,* fr. L *renes* kidneys] (ca. 1656) **:** relating to, involving, or located in the region of the kidneys **:** NEPHRITIC ⟨~ disease⟩ ⟨~ failure⟩

renal clearance *n* (1948) **:** CLEARANCE 3

re·na·scence \ri-ˈna-sᵊn(t)s, -ˈnā-\ *n, often cap* (1727) **:** RENAISSANCE

re·na·scent \-sᵊnt\ *adj* [L *renascent-, renascens,* prp. of *renasci*] (ca. 1727) **:** rising again into being or vigor

re·na·ture \(ˌ)rē-ˈnā-chər\ *vt* **re·na·tured; re·na·tur·ing** \-ˈnā-chə-riŋ, -ˈnāch-riŋ\ [*re-* + *denature*] (1926) **:** to restore (as a denatured protein) to an original or normal condition — **re·na·tur·ation** \(ˌ)rē-ˌnā-chə-ˈrā-shən\ *n*

ren·con·tre \räⁿ-ˈkōⁿtrᵊ, ren-ˈkän-tər\ *or* **ren·coun·ter** \ren-ˈkau̇n-tər\ *n* [*rencounter* fr. MF *rencontre,* fr. *rencontrer; rencontre* fr. F] (1523) **1 :** a hostile meeting or a contest between forces or individuals **:** COMBAT **2 :** a casual meeting

ren·coun·ter \ren-ˈkau̇n-tər\ *vt* [MF *rencontrer* to meet by chance or in hostility, fr. *re-* + *encontrer* to encounter] (1549) *archaic* **:** to meet casually

\ə\ **abut** \ᵊ\ kitten, F table \ər\ **further** \a\ **ash** \ā\ **ace** \ä\ **mop, mar** \au̇\ **out** \ch\ **chin** \e\ **bet** \ē\ **easy** \g\ **go** \i\ **hit** \ī\ **ice** \j\ **job** \ŋ\ **sing** \ō\ **go** \ȯ\ **law** \ȯi\ **boy** \th\ **thin** \t͟h\ **the** \ü\ **loot** \u̇\ **foot** \y\ **yet** \zh\ **vision, beige** \k, ⁿ, œ, ue, ʸ\ *see* Guide to Pronunciation

rend \ˈrend\ *vb* **rent** \ˈrent\ *also* **rend·ed** \ˈren-dəd\; **rend·ing** [ME, fr. OE *rendan;* akin to OFris *renda* to tear and perh. to Skt *randhra* hole] *vt* (bef. 12c) **1 :** to remove from place by violence : WREST **2 :** to split or tear apart or in pieces by violence **3 :** to tear (the hair or clothing) as a sign of anger, grief, or despair **4 a :** to lacerate mentally or emotionally **b :** to pierce with sound **c :** to divide (as a nation) into contesting factions ~ *vi* **1 :** to perform an act of tearing or splitting **2 :** to become torn or split ***syn*** see TEAR

[1]**ren·der** \ˈren-dər\ *vb* **ren·dered; ren·der·ing** \-d(ə-)riŋ\ [ME *rendren,* fr. AF *rendre* to give back, surrender, fr. VL **rendere,* alter. of L *reddere,* partly fr. *re-* + *dare* to give & partly fr. *re-* + *-dere* to put — more at DATE, DO] *vt* (14c) **1 a :** to melt down ⟨~ suet⟩; *also* **:** to extract by melting ⟨~ lard⟩ **b :** to treat so as to convert into industrial fats and oils or fertilizer **2 a :** to transmit to another : DELIVER **b :** GIVE UP, YIELD **c :** to furnish for consideration, approval, or information: as (1) **:** to hand down (a legal judgment) (2) **:** to agree on and report (a verdict) **3 a :** to give in return or retribution **b** (1) **:** GIVE BACK, RESTORE (2) **:** REFLECT, ECHO **c :** to give in acknowledgment of dependence or obligation : PAY **d :** to do (a service) for another **4 a** (1) **:** to cause to be or become : MAKE ⟨enough rainfall . . . to ~ irrigation unnecessary —P. E. James⟩ ⟨~*ed* him helpless⟩ (2) **:** IMPART **b** (1) **:** to reproduce or represent by artistic or verbal means : DEPICT (2) **:** to give a performance of (3) **:** to produce a copy or version of ⟨the documents are ~*ed* in the original French⟩ (4) **:** to execute the motions of ⟨~ a salute⟩ **c :** TRANSLATE **5 :** to direct the execution of : ADMINISTER ⟨~ justice⟩ **6 :** to apply a coat of plaster or cement directly to ~ *vi* **:** to give recompense — **ren·der·able** \-d(ə-)rə-bəl\ *adj* — **ren·der·er** \-dər-ər\ *n*

[2]**render** *n* (1647) **:** a return esp. in goods or services due from a feudal tenant to his lord

[1]**ren·dez·vous** \ˈrän-di-ˌvü, -dā-\ *n, pl* **ren·dez·vous** \-ˌvüz\ [MF, fr. *rendez vous* present yourselves] (1582) **1 a :** a place appointed for assembling or meeting **b :** a place of popular resort : HAUNT **2 :** a meeting at an appointed place and time **3 :** the process of bringing two spacecraft together

[2]**rendezvous** *vb* **-voused** \-ˌvüd\; **-vous·ing** \-ˌvü-iŋ\; **-vouses** \-ˌvüz\ *vi* (1645) **:** to come together at a rendezvous ~ *vt* **1 :** to bring together at a rendezvous **2 :** to meet at a rendezvous

ren·di·tion \ren-ˈdi-shən\ *n* [obs. F, fr. MF, alter. of *reddition,* fr. LL *reddition-, redditio,* fr. L *reddere* to return] (1601) **:** the act or result of rendering: as **a :** SURRENDER **b :** TRANSLATION **c :** PERFORMANCE, INTERPRETATION

ren·dzi·na \ren-ˈjē-nə\ *n* [Pol *rędzina* rich limy soil] (1922) **:** any of a group of dark grayish-brown intrazonal soils developed in grassy regions of high to moderate humidity from soft calcareous marl or chalk

[1]**ren·e·gade** \ˈre-ni-ˌgād\ *n* [Sp *renegado,* fr. ML *renegatus,* fr. pp. of *renegare* to deny, fr. L *re-* + *negare* to deny — more at NEGATE] (1583) **1 :** a deserter from one faith, cause, or allegiance to another **2 :** an individual who rejects lawful or conventional behavior

[2]**renegade** *vi* **-gad·ed; -gad·ing** (ca. 1611) **:** to become a renegade

[3]**renegade** *adj* (1705) **1 :** having deserted a faith, cause, or religion for a hostile one **2 :** having rejected tradition : UNCONVENTIONAL

re·nege \ri-ˈneg *also* -ˈnāg, -ˈnig; rē-\ *vb* **re·neged; re·neg·ing** [ML *renegare*] *vt* (1548) **:** DENY, RENOUNCE ~ *vi* **1** *obs* **:** to make a denial **2 :** REVOKE **3 :** to go back on a promise or commitment — **re·neg·er** *n*

re·ne·go·tia·ble \ˌrē-ni-ˈgō-sh(ē-)ə-bəl\ *adj* (1943) **:** subject to renegotiation ⟨~ mortgages⟩ ⟨~ rates⟩

re·ne·go·ti·ate \ˌrē-ni-ˈgō-shē-ˌāt\ *vt* (ca. 1934) **:** to negotiate again (as to adjust interest rates or repayments or to get more money) ⟨~ a loan⟩ ⟨~ a contract⟩ — **re·ne·go·ti·a·tion** \ˌrē-ni-ˌgō-shē-ˈā-shən, -sē-ˈā-\ *n*

re·new \ri-ˈnü, -ˈnyü\ *vt* (14c) **1 :** to make like new : restore to freshness, vigor, or perfection ⟨as we ~ our strength in sleep⟩ **2 :** to make new spiritually : REGENERATE **3 a :** to restore to existence : REVIVE **b :** to make extensive changes in : REBUILD **4 :** to do again : REPEAT **5 :** to begin again : RESUME **6 :** REPLACE, REPLENISH ⟨~ water in a tank⟩ **7 a :** to grant or obtain an extension of or on ⟨~ a license⟩ **b :** to grant or obtain an extension on the loan of ⟨~ a library book⟩ ~ *vi* **1 :** to become new or as new **2 :** to begin again : RESUME **3 :** to make a renewal (as of a lease) — **re·new·er** *n*

syn RENEW, RESTORE, REFRESH, RENOVATE, REJUVENATE mean to make like new. RENEW implies a restoration of what had become faded or disintegrated so that it seems like new ⟨efforts to *renew* the splendor of the old castle⟩. RESTORE implies a return to an original state after depletion or loss ⟨*restored* a fine piece of furniture⟩. REFRESH implies the supplying of something necessary to restore lost strength, animation, or power ⟨a *refreshing* drink⟩. RENOVATE suggests a renewing by cleansing, repairing, or rebuilding ⟨the apartment has been entirely *renovated*⟩. REJUVENATE suggests the restoration of youthful vigor, powers, or appearance ⟨the change in jobs *rejuvenated* her spirits⟩.

re·new·able \-ˈnü-ə-bəl, -ˈnyü-\ *adj* (1727) **1 :** capable of being renewed ⟨~ contracts⟩ **2 :** capable of being replaced by natural ecological cycles or sound management practices ⟨~ resources⟩ — **re·new·abil·i·ty** \-ˌnü-ə-ˈbi-lə-tē, -ˌnyü-\ *n* — **renewable** *n* — **re·new·ably** \-ˈnü-ə-blē, -ˈnyü-\ *adv*

re·new·al \ri-ˈnü-əl, -ˈnyü-\ *n* (ca. 1686) **1 :** the act or process of renewing : REPETITION **2 :** the quality or state of being renewed **3 :** something (as a subscription to a magazine) renewed **4 :** something used for renewing; *specif* **:** an expenditure that betters existing fixed assets **5 :** the rebuilding of a large area (as of a city) by a public authority

reni- *or* **reno-** *comb form* [L *renes* kidneys] **:** kidney ⟨*reniform*⟩

re·ni·form \ˈrē-nə-ˌfȯrm, ˈre-\ *adj* [NL *reniformis,* fr. *reni-* + *-formis* -form] (ca. 1753) **:** suggesting a kidney in outline ⟨a ~ nucleus of a cell⟩ — see LEAF illustration

re·nin \ˈrē-nən, ˈre-\ *n* [ISV, fr. L *renes*] (1906) **:** a proteolytic enzyme of the kidney that plays a major role in the release of angiotensin

re·ni·ten·cy \ˈre-nə-tən(t)-sē, ri-ˈnī-tᵊn(t)-\ *n* (1613) **:** RESISTANCE, OPPOSITION

re·ni·tent \ˈre-nə-tənt, ri-ˈnī-tᵊnt\ *adj* [F or L; F *rénitent,* fr. L *renitent-, renitens,* prp. of *reniti* to resist, fr. *re-* + *niti* to strive — more at NISUS] (1701) **1 :** resisting physical pressure **2 :** resisting constraint or compulsion : RECALCITRANT

ren·min·bi \ˈren-ˈmin-ˈbē\ *n pl* [Chin (Beijing) *rénmínbì,* fr. *rénmín* people + *bì* currency] (1957) **:** the currency of the People's Republic of China consisting of yuan

ren·net \ˈre-nət\ *n* [ME, fr. ME **rennen* to cause to coagulate, fr. OE *gerennan,* fr. *ge-* together + **rennan* to cause to run; akin to OHG *rennen* to cause to run, OE *rinnan* to run — more at CO-, RUN] (15c) **1 a :** the contents of the stomach of an unweaned animal and esp. a calf **b :** the lining membrane of a stomach or one of its compartments (as the fourth of a ruminant) used for curdling milk; *also* **:** a preparation of the stomach of animals used for this purpose **2 a :** RENNIN **b :** a substitute for rennin

ren·nin \ˈre-nən\ *n* [*rennet* + [1]*-in*] (1897) **:** an enzyme that coagulates milk and is used in making cheese and junkets; *esp* **:** one from the mucous membrane of the stomach of a calf

re·no·gram \ˈrē-nə-ˌgram\ *n* (1952) **:** a photographic depiction of the course of renal excretion of a radiolabeled substance — **re·no·graph·ic** \ˌrē-nə-ˈgra-fik\ *adj* — **re·nog·ra·phy** \rē-ˈnä-grə-fē\ *n*

re·nom·i·nate \(ˌ)rē-ˈnä-mə-ˌnāt\ *vt* (1864) **:** to nominate again esp. for a succeeding term — **re·nom·i·na·tion** \(ˌ)rē-ˌnä-mə-ˈnā-shən\ *n*

re·nounce \ri-ˈnau̇n(t)s\ *vb* **re·nounced; re·nounc·ing** [ME, fr. AF *renuncer,* fr. L *renuntiare,* fr. *re-* + *nuntiare* to report, fr. *nuntius* messenger] *vt* (14c) **1 :** to give up, refuse, or resign usu. by formal declaration ⟨~ his errors⟩ **2 :** to refuse to follow, obey, or recognize any further : REPUDIATE ⟨~ the authority of the church⟩ ~ *vi* **1 :** to make a renunciation **2 :** to fail to follow suit in a card game ***syn*** see ABDICATE, ABJURE — **re·nounce·ment** \-ˈnau̇n(t)s-mənt\ *n* — **re·nounc·er** *n*

re·no·vas·cu·lar \ˌrē-nō-ˈvas-kyə-lər\ *adj* (1961) **:** of, relating to, or involving the blood vessels of the kidneys ⟨~ hypertension⟩

ren·o·vate \ˈre-nə-ˌvāt\ *vt* **-vat·ed; -vat·ing** [L *renovatus,* pp. of *renovare,* fr. *re-* + *novare* to make new, fr. *novus* new — more at NEW] (ca. 1522) **1 :** to restore to a former better state (as by cleaning, repairing, or rebuilding) **2 :** to restore to life, vigor, or activity : REVIVE ⟨the church was *renovated* by a new ecumenical spirit⟩ ***syn*** see RENEW — **ren·o·va·tion** \ˌre-nə-ˈvā-shən\ *n* — **ren·o·va·tive** \ˈre-nə-ˌvā-tiv\ *adj* — **ren·o·va·tor** \-ˌvā-tər\ *n*

[1]**re·nown** \ri-ˈnau̇n\ *n* [ME *renoun,* fr. AF *renum, renoun,* fr. *renomer* to report, speak of, fr. *re-* + *nomer* to name, fr. L *nominare,* fr. *nomin-, nomen* name — more at NAME] (14c) **1 :** a state of being widely acclaimed and highly honored : FAME **2** *obs* **:** REPORT, RUMOR

[2]**renown** *vt* (15c) **:** to give renown to

re·nowned \-ˈnau̇nd\ *adj* (14c) **:** having renown : CELEBRATED ***syn*** see FAMOUS

[1]**rent** \ˈrent\ *n* [ME *rente,* fr. AF, payment, income, fr. VL **rendita,* fr. fem. of **renditus,* pp. of **rendere* to yield — more at RENDER] (12c) **1 :** property (as a house) rented or for rent **2 a :** a usu. fixed periodical return made by a tenant or occupant of property to the owner for the possession and use thereof; *esp* **:** an agreed sum paid at fixed intervals by a tenant to the landlord **b :** the amount paid by a hirer of personal property to the owner for the use thereof **3 a :** the portion of the income of an economy (as of a nation) attributable to land as a factor of production in addition to capital and labor **b :** ECONOMIC RENT — **for rent :** available for use or service in return for payment

[2]**rent** *vt* (15c) **1 :** to grant the possession and enjoyment of in exchange for rent **2 :** to take and hold under an agreement to pay rent ~ *vi* **1 :** to be for rent **2 a :** to obtain the possession and use of a place or article in exchange for rent **b :** to allow the possession and use of property in exchange for rent ***syn*** see HIRE — **rent·abil·i·ty** \ˌren-tə-ˈbi-lə-tē\ *n* — **rent·able** \ˈren-tə-bəl\ *adj*

[3]**rent** *past and past part of* REND

[4]**rent** *n* [E dial. *rent* to rend, fr. ME, alter. of *renden* — more at REND] (1535) **1 :** an opening made by or as if by rending **2 :** a split in a party or organized group : SCHISM **3 :** an act or instance of rending

rent–a–car \ˈrent-ə-ˌkär\ *n* (1935) **:** a rented car

rent–a–cop *n* (1971) *often disparaging* **:** a security worker (as a guard) who is not a police officer

[1]**rent·al** \ˈren-tᵊl\ *n* (14c) **1 :** an amount paid or collected as rent **2 :** something that is rented **3 :** an act of renting **4 :** a business that rents something

[2]**rental** *adj* (15c) **1 a :** of or relating to rent **b :** available for rent **2 :** dealing in rental property ⟨a ~ agency⟩

rental library *n* (1928) **:** a commercially operated library (as in a store) that lends books at a fixed charge per book per day — called also *lending library*

rent control *n* (1931) **:** government regulation of the amount charged as rent for housing and often also of eviction — **rent–controlled** *adj*

rente \ˈrä^{n}(n)t\ *n* [F] (1873) **:** a government security (as in France) paying interest; *also* **:** the interest paid

rent·er \ˈren-tər\ *n* (1655) **:** one that rents; *specif* **:** the lessee or tenant of property

ren·tier \rä^{n}-ˈtyā\ *n* [F, fr. OF, fr. *rente*] (ca. 1847) **:** a person who lives on income from property or securities

rent strike *n* (1964) **:** a refusal by a group of tenants to pay rent (as in protest against high rates)

re·nun·ci·a·tion \ri-ˌnən(t)-sē-ˈā-shən\ *n* [ME *renunciacion,* fr. AF, fr. L *renuntiation-, renuntiatio,* fr. *renuntiare* to renounce] (14c) **:** the act or practice of renouncing : REPUDIATION; *specif* **:** ascetic self-denial — **re·nun·ci·a·tive** \ri-ˈnən(t)-sē-ˌā-tiv\ *adj* — **re·nun·ci·a·to·ry** \-sē-ə-ˌtȯr-ē\ *adj*

re·of·fer \(ˌ)rē-ˈȯ-fər, -ˈä-\ *vt* (1920) **:** to offer (a security issue) for public sale

re·open \(ˌ)rē-ˈō-pən, -ˈō-pᵊm\ *vt* (1733) **1 :** to open again **2 a :** to take up again : RESUME ⟨~ discussion⟩ **b :** to resume discussion or consideration of ⟨~ a contract⟩ **3 :** to begin again ~ *vi* **:** to open again ⟨school ~*s* in September⟩

[1]**re·or·der** \(ˌ)rē-ˈȯr-dər\ *vt* (1656) **1 :** to arrange in a different way **2 :** to give a reorder for ~ *vi* **:** to place a reorder

[2]**reorder** *n* (1901) **:** an order like a previous order placed with the same supplier

re·or·ga·ni·za·tion \(ˌ)rē-ˌȯr-gə-nə-ˈzā-shən, -ˌȯrg-nə-\ *n* (1813) **:** the act or process of reorganizing : the state of being reorganized; *esp* **:** the financial reconstruction of a business concern — **re·or·ga·ni·za·tion·al** \-shnəl, -shə-nᵊl\ *adj*

re·or·ga·nize \(ˌ)rē-ˈȯr-gə-ˌnīz\ *vt* (ca. 1686) **:** to organize again or anew ~ *vi* **:** to reorganize something — **re·or·ga·niz·er** *n*

reo·vi·rus \ˌrē-ō-ˈvī-rəs\ *n* [*r*espiratory *e*nteric *o*rphan (i.e., unidentified) *virus*] (1959) **:** any of a family (*Reoviridae*) of double-stranded RNA viruses that have a virion with icosahedral structural symmetry but may appear spherical, that have a capsid with one to three concentric protein layers, and that include many plant or animal pathogens (as the rotaviruses and the causative agent of bluetongue)

[1]**rep** \ˈrep\ *n* (ca. 1705) *slang* **:** REPUTATION; *esp* **:** status in a group (as a gang)

[2]**rep** *n* (1848) **:** REPRESENTATIVE ⟨sales ~*s*⟩

[3]**rep** *or* **repp** \ˈrep\ *n* [F *reps,* modif. of E *ribs,* pl. of *rib*] (1860) **:** a plain-weave fabric with prominent rounded crosswise ribs

[4]**rep** *n* (1925) **1 :** REPERTORY 2b **2 :** REPERTORY 3

[5]**rep** *vt* **repped; rep·ping** (1939) **:** REPRESENT 6

[6]**rep** *n* [*r*oentgen *e*quivalent *p*hysical] (1947) **:** the dosage of an ionizing radiation that will develop the same amount of energy upon absorption in human tissue as one roentgen of X-ray or gamma-ray exposure

[7]**rep** *n* [short for *repetition*] (1953) **:** REPETITION 1b

[8]**rep** *abbr* **1** repair **2** repeat **3** report; reporter **4** republic

Rep *abbr* Republican

re·pack·age \(ˌ)rē-ˈpa-kij\ *vt* (1899) **:** to package again or anew; *specif* **:** to put into a more efficient or attractive form — **re·pack·ag·er** *n*

[1]**re·pair** \ri-ˈper\ *vi* [ME, fr. AF *repairer* to go back, return fr. LL *repatriare* to go home again, fr. L *re-* + *patria* native country — more at EXPATRIATE] (14c) **1 a :** to betake oneself **:** GO ⟨~*ed* to the judge's chambers⟩ **b :** to come together **:** RALLY **2** *obs* **:** RETURN

[2]**repair** *n* (14c) **1 :** the act of repairing **:** RESORT **2 :** a popular gathering place

[3]**repair** *vb* [ME, fr. AF *reparer,* fr. L *reparare,* fr. *re-* + *parare* to prepare — more at PARE] *vt* (14c) **1 a :** to restore by replacing a part or putting together what is torn or broken **:** FIX ⟨~ a shoe⟩ **b :** to restore to a sound or healthy state **:** RENEW ⟨~ his strength⟩ **2 :** to make good **:** compensate for **:** REMEDY ⟨~ a gap in my reading⟩ ~ *vi* **:** to make repairs ***syn*** see MEND — **re·pair·abil·i·ty** \-ˌper-ə-ˈbi-lə-tē\ *n* — **re·pair·able** \-ˈper-ə-bəl\ *adj* — **re·pair·er** \-ˈper-ər\ *n*

[4]**repair** *n* (15c) **1 a :** an instance or result of repairing **b :** the act or process of repairing **c :** the replacement of destroyed cells or tissues by new formations **2 a :** relative condition with respect to soundness or need of repairing **b :** the state of being in good or sound condition

re·pair·man \ri-ˈper-ˌman, -mən\ *n* (1871) **:** one who repairs; *specif* **:** one whose occupation is to make repairs in a mechanism

re·pand \ri-ˈpand\ *adj* [L *repandus* spread out, fr. *repandere* to open wide, fr. *re-* + *pandere* to spread — more at FATHOM] (ca. 1760) **:** having a slightly undulating margin ⟨a ~ leaf⟩ ⟨a ~ colony of bacteria⟩

rep·a·ra·ble \ˈre-p(ə-)rə-bəl\ *adj* (1570) **:** capable of being repaired

rep·a·ra·tion \ˌre-pə-ˈrā-shən\ *n* [ME *reparacion,* fr. AF, fr. LL *reparation-, reparatio,* fr. L *reparare*] (14c) **1 a :** a repairing or keeping in repair **b** *pl* **:** REPAIRS **2 a :** the act of making amends, offering expiation, or giving satisfaction for a wrong or injury **b :** something done or given as amends or satisfaction **3 :** the payment of damages **:** INDEMNIFICATION; *specif* **:** compensation in money or materials payable by a defeated nation for damages to or expenditures sustained by another nation as a result of hostilities with the defeated nation — usu. used in pl.

re·par·a·tive \ri-ˈpa-rə-tiv\ *adj* (1656) **1 :** of, relating to, or effecting repair **2 :** serving to make amends

rep·ar·tee \ˌre-pər-ˈtē, -ˌpär-, -ˈtā\ *n* [F *repartie,* fr. *repartir* to retort, fr. MF, fr. *re-* + *partir* to divide — more at PART] (ca. 1645) **1 a :** a quick and witty reply **b :** a succession or interchange of clever retorts **:** amusing and usu. light sparring with words **2 :** adroitness and cleverness in reply **:** skill in repartee ***syn*** see WIT

[1]**re·par·ti·tion** \ˌre-ˌpär-ˈti-shən, ˌrē-\ *n* [prob. fr. Sp *repartición,* fr. *repartir* to distribute, fr. *re-* + *partir* to divide, fr. L *partire* — more at PART] (1555) **:** DISTRIBUTION

[2]**re·par·ti·tion** \ˌrē-ˌpär-ˈti-shən\ *n* [*re-* + *partition*] (1835) **:** a second or additional dividing or distribution

re·pass \(ˌ)rē-ˈpas\ *vb* [ME, fr. AF *repasser,* fr. re- + *passer* to pass] *vi* (15c) **:** to pass again esp. in the opposite direction **:** RETURN ~ *vt* **1 :** to pass through, over, or by again ⟨~ the house⟩ **2 :** to cause to pass again **3 :** to adopt again ⟨~*ed* the resolution⟩ — **re·pas·sage** \-ˈpa-sij\ *n*

[1]**re·past** \ri-ˈpast, ˈrē-ˌ\ *n* [ME, fr. AF, fr. (*soi*) *repaistre* to feed upon, fr. *re-* + *pestre, paistre* to feed, fr. L *pascere* — more at FOOD] (14c) **1 :** something taken as food **:** MEAL **2 :** the act or time of taking food

[2]**re·past** \ri-ˈpast\ *vt* (15c) *obs* **:** FEED ~ *vi* **:** to take food **:** FEAST

re·pa·tri·ate \(ˌ)rē-ˈpā-trē-ˌāt, -ˈpa-\ *vt* **-at·ed; -at·ing** [LL *repatriatus,* pp. of *repatriare* to go home again — more at REPAIR] (1611) **:** to restore or return to the country of origin, allegiance, or citizenship ⟨~ prisoners of war⟩ — **re·pa·tri·ate** \-trē-ət, -trē-ˌāt\ *n* — **re·pa·tri·a·tion** \(ˌ)rē-ˌpā-trē-ˈā-shən, -ˌpa-\ *n*

re·pay \(ˌ)rē-ˈpā\ *vb* **-paid** \-ˈpād\; **-pay·ing** *vt* (15c) **1 a :** to pay back ⟨~ a loan⟩ **b :** to give or inflict in return or requital ⟨~ evil for evil⟩ **2 :** to make a return payment to **:** COMPENSATE, REQUITE **3 :** to make requital for **:** RECOMPENSE ⟨the success that ~*s* hard work⟩ ~ *vi* **:** to make return payment or requital ***syn*** see PAY — **re·pay·able** \-ˈpā-ə-bəl\ *adj* — **re·pay·ment** \-ˈpā-mənt\ *n*

re·peal \ri-ˈpēl\ *vt* [ME *repelen,* fr. AF *repeler,* lit., to call back, fr. *re-* + *apeler* to appeal, call] (14c) **1 :** to rescind or annul by authoritative act; *esp* **:** to revoke or abrogate by legislative enactment **2 :** ABANDON, RENOUNCE **3** *obs* **:** to summon to return **:** RECALL — **repeal** *n* — **re·peal·able** \-ˈpē-lə-bəl\ *adj*

re·peal·er \ri-ˈpē-lər\ *n* (1765) **:** one that repeals; *specif* **:** a legislative act that abrogates an earlier act

[1]**re·peat** \ri-ˈpēt\ *vb* [ME *repeten,* fr. MF & L; MF *repeter,* fr. OF, fr. L *repetere* to return to, repeat, fr. *re-* + *petere* to go to, seek — more at FEATHER] *vt* (14c) **1 a :** to say or state again **b :** to say over from memory **:** RECITE **c :** to say after another **2 a :** to make, do, or perform again ⟨~ an experiment⟩ **b :** to make appear again ⟨the curtains ~ the wallpaper pattern⟩ ⟨will ~ the program tomorrow⟩ **c :** to go through or experience again ⟨had to ~ third grade⟩ **3 :** to express or present (oneself) again in the same words, terms, or form ~ *vi* **:** to say, do, or accomplish something again; *esp* **:** to win (as a sports championship) another time in succession — **re·peat·abil·i·ty** \-ˌpē-tə-ˈbi-lə-tē\ *n* — **re·peat·able** \-ˈpē-tə-bəl\ *adj*

[2]**re·peat** \ri-ˈpēt, ˈrē-ˌ\ *n* (15c) **1 a :** something repeated **:** REPETITION **b :** a musical passage to be repeated in performance; *also* **:** a sign placed before and after such a passage **c :** a usu. transcribed repetition of a radio or television program **d :** a duplication of genetic material (as a sequence of nucleotides) in which the duplicated parts are adjacent to each other along the chromosome **2 :** the act of repeating

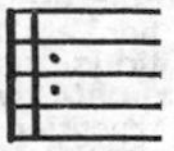

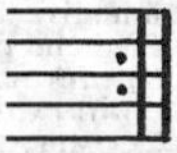

repeat 1b

[3]**re·peat** \ri-ˈpēt\ *adj* (1888) **:** of, relating to, or being one that repeats an offense, achievement, or action ⟨a ~ burglar⟩ ⟨a ~ customer⟩

re·peat·ed \ri-ˈpē-təd\ *adj* (1611) **1 :** renewed or recurring again and again ⟨~ changes of plan⟩ **2 :** said, done, or presented again

re·peat·ed·ly *adv* (ca. 1718) **:** AGAIN AND AGAIN

re·peat·er \ri-ˈpē-tər\ *n* (1598) **:** one that repeats: as **a :** one who relates or recites **b :** a watch or clock with a striking mechanism that upon pressure of a spring will indicate the time in hours or quarters and sometimes minutes **c :** a firearm having a magazine that holds a number of cartridges loaded one at a time into the chamber by the action of the piece **d :** a habitual violator of the laws **e :** one who votes illegally by casting more than one ballot in an election **f :** a student enrolled in a class or course for a second or subsequent time **g :** a device for receiving communication signals and delivering corresponding amplified ones

re·peat·ing \ri-ˈpē-tiŋ\ *adj* (1824) *of a firearm* **:** designed to load cartridges from a magazine

repeating decimal *n* (1773) **:** a decimal in which after a certain point a particular digit or sequence of digits repeats itself indefinitely — compare TERMINATING DECIMAL

re·pe·chage \ˌre-pə-ˈshäzh, ˈre-pə-ˌ\ *n* [F *repêchage* second chance, reexamination for a candidate who has failed, fr. *repêcher* to fish out, rescue, fr. *re-* + *pêcher* to fish, fr. L *piscari* — more at PISCATORY] (1928) **:** a trial heat (as in rowing) in which first-round losers are given another chance to qualify for the semifinals

re·pel \ri-ˈpel\ *vb* **re·pelled; re·pel·ling** [ME *repellen,* fr. MF *repeller,* fr. L *repellere,* fr. *re-* + *pellere* to drive — more at FELT] *vt* (15c) **1 a :** to drive back **:** REPULSE **b :** to fight against **:** RESIST **2 :** TURN AWAY, REJECT ⟨*repelled* the insinuation⟩ **3 a :** to drive away **:** DISCOURAGE ⟨foul words and frowns must not ~ a lover —Shak.⟩ **b :** to be incapable of adhering to, mixing with, taking up, or holding **c :** to force away or apart or tend to do so by mutual action at a distance **4 :** to cause aversion in **:** DISGUST ~ *vi* **:** to cause aversion — **re·pel·ler** *n*

re·pel·len·cy \ri-ˈpe-lən(t)-sē\ *n* (1747) **:** the quality or capacity of repelling

[1]**re·pel·lent** *also* **re·pel·lant** \ri-ˈpe-lənt\ *adj* [L *repellent-, repellens,* prp. of *repellere*] (1643) **1 :** serving or tending to drive away or ward off — often used in combination ⟨a mosquito-*repellent* spray⟩ **2 :** arousing aversion or disgust **:** REPULSIVE — **re·pel·lent·ly** *adv*

[2]**repellent** *also* **repellant** *n* (1661) **:** something that repels; *esp* **:** a substance that repels insects

[1]**re·pent** \ri-ˈpent\ *vb* [ME, fr. AF *repentir,* fr. ML *repoenitēre,* fr. L *re-* + LL *poenitēre* to feel regret, alter. of L *paenitēre* — more at PENITENT] *vi* (14c) **1 :** to turn from sin and dedicate oneself to the amendment of one's life **2 a :** to feel regret or contrition **b :** to change one's mind ~ *vt* **1 :** to cause to feel regret or contrition **2 :** to feel sorrow, regret, or contrition for — **re·pent·er** *n*

[2]**re·pent** \ˈrē-pənt\ *adj* [L *repent-, repens,* prp. of *repere* to creep — more at REPTILE] (1669) **:** CREEPING, PROSTRATE ⟨~ stems⟩

re·pen·tance \ri-ˈpen-tᵊn(t)s\ *n* (14c) **:** the action or process of repenting esp. for misdeeds or moral shortcomings ***syn*** see PENITENCE

re·pen·tant \-tᵊnt\ *adj* (13c) **1 :** experiencing repentance **:** PENITENT **2 :** expressive of repentance — **re·pen·tant·ly** *adv*

re·per·cus·sion \ˌrē-pər-ˈkə-shən, ˌre-\ *n* [L *repercussion-, repercussio,* fr. *repercutere* to drive back, fr. *re-* + *percutere* to beat — more at PERCUSSION] (1536) **1 :** REFLECTION, REVERBERATION **2 a :** an action or effect given or exerted in return **:** a reciprocal action or effect **b :** a widespread, indirect, or unforeseen effect of an act, action, or event — usu. used in pl. — **re·per·cus·sive** \-ˈkə-siv\ *adj*

re·per·fu·sion \ˌrē-pər-ˈfyü-zhən\ *n* (1966) **:** restoration of the flow of blood to a previously ischemic tissue or organ

rep·er·toire \ˈre-pə(r)-ˌtwär\ *n* [F *répertoire,* fr. LL *repertorium*] (1847) **1 a :** a list or supply of dramas, operas, pieces, or parts that a company or person is prepared to perform **b :** a supply of skills, devices, or expedients ⟨part of the ~ of a quarterback⟩; *broadly* **:** AMOUNT, SUPPLY ⟨an endless ~ of summer clothes⟩ **c :** a list or supply of capabilities ⟨the instruction ~ of a computer⟩ **2 a :** the complete list or supply of dramas, operas, or musical works available for performance ⟨our modern orchestral ~⟩ **b :** the complete list or supply of skills, devices, or ingredients used in a particular field, occupation, or practice ⟨the ~ of literary criticism⟩

rep·er·to·ry \ˈre-pə(r)-ˌtȯr-ē\ *n, pl* **-ries** [LL *repertorium* list, fr. L *reperire* to find, fr. *re-* + *parere* to produce — more at PARE] (1593) **1 :** a place where something may be found **:** REPOSITORY **2 a :** REPERTOIRE **b :** a company that presents several different plays, operas, or pieces usu. alternately in the course of a season at one theater **c :** a theater housing such a company **3 :** the production and presentation of plays by a repertory company ⟨acting in ~⟩

rep·e·tend \ˈre-pə-ˌtend\ *n* [L *repetendus* to be repeated, gerundive of *repetere* to repeat] (1874) **:** a repeated sound, word, or phrase; *specif* **:** REFRAIN

rep·e·ti·tion \ˌre-pə-ˈti-shən\ *n* [ME *repeticion,* fr. MF, fr. L *repetition-, repetitio,* fr. *repetere* to repeat] (15c) **1 a :** the act or an instance of repeating or being repeated **b** : a motion or exercise (as a push-up) that is repeated and usu. counted **2** : MENTION, RECITAL — **rep·e·ti·tion·al** \-ˈtish-nəl, -ˈti-shə-nᵊl\ *adj*

rep·e·ti·tious \-ˈti-shəs\ *adj* (1675) : characterized or marked by repetition; *esp* : tediously repeating — **rep·e·ti·tious·ly** *adv* — **rep·e·ti·tious·ness** *n*

re·pet·i·tive \ri-ˈpe-tə-tiv\ *adj* (1839) **1** : REPETITIOUS **2** : containing repetition — **re·pet·i·tive·ly** *adv* — **re·pet·i·tive·ness** *n*

repetitive strain injury *n* (1983) : any of various painful musculoskeletal disorders (as carpal tunnel syndrome or tendinitis) caused by cumulative damage to muscles, tendons, ligaments, nerves, or joints (as of the hand or shoulder) from highly repetitive movements — called also *repetitive stress injury*

re·pine \ri-ˈpīn\ *vi* (1530) **1** : to feel or express dejection or discontent : COMPLAIN **2** : to long for something — **re·pin·er** *n*

repl *abbr* replace; replacement; replacing

re·place \ri-ˈplās\ *vt* (1595) **1** : to restore to a former place or position ⟨~ cards in a file⟩ **2** : to take the place of esp. as a substitute or successor **3** : to put something new in the place of ⟨~ a worn carpet⟩ — **re·place·able** \-ˈplā-sə-bəl\ *adj* — **re·plac·er** *n*

syn REPLACE, DISPLACE, SUPPLANT, SUPERSEDE mean to put out of a usual or proper place or into the place of another. REPLACE implies a filling of a place once occupied by something lost, destroyed, or no longer usable or adequate ⟨*replaced* the broken window⟩. DISPLACE implies an ousting or dislodging ⟨war had *displaced* thousands⟩. SUPPLANT implies either a dispossessing or usurping of another's place, possessions, or privileges or an uprooting of something and its replacement with something else ⟨was abruptly *supplanted* in her affections by another⟩. SUPERSEDE implies replacing a person or thing that has become superannuated, obsolete, or otherwise inferior ⟨the new edition *supersedes* all previous ones⟩.

re·place·ment \ri-ˈplās-mənt\ *n* (ca. 1790) **1** : the action or process of replacing : the state of being replaced **2** : one that replaces another esp. in a job or function

replacement set *n* (1959) : a set of elements any one of which may be used to replace a given variable or placeholder in a mathematical sentence or expression (as an equation)

replacement therapy *n* (1944) : therapy involving the supply of a substance (as a hormone or nutrient) lacking in or lost from the body — compare ESTROGEN REPLACEMENT THERAPY, HORMONE REPLACEMENT THERAPY

re·plant \(ˌ)rē-ˈplant\ *vt* (1575) **1** : to plant again or anew **2** : to provide with new plants **3** : to subject to replantation

re·plan·ta·tion \ˌrē-(ˌ)plan-ˈtā-shən\ *n* (1870) : reattachment or reinsertion of a bodily part (as a limb or tooth) after separation from the body

1**re·play** \(ˌ)rē-ˈplā\ *vt* (1884) : to play again or over

2**re·play** \ˈrē-ˌplā\ *n* (1895) **1 a** : an act or instance of replaying **b** : the playing of a tape (as a videotape) **2** : REPETITION, REENACTMENT ⟨don't want a ~ of our old mistakes⟩

re·plead·er \(ˌ)rē-ˈplē-dər\ *n* [*replead* to plead again + *-er* (as in *misnomer*)] (1607) **1** : a second legal pleading **2** : the right of pleading again granted usu. when the issue raised is immaterial or insufficient

re·plen·ish \ri-ˈple-nish\ *vb* [ME *replenisshen,* fr. AF *repleniss-*, stem of *replenir* to fill, fr. *re-* + *plein* full, fr. L *plenus* — more at FULL] *vt* (14c) **1 a** : to fill with persons or animals : STOCK **b** *archaic* : to supply fully : PERFECT **c** : to fill with inspiration or power : NOURISH **2 a** : to fill or build up again ⟨~*ed* his glass⟩ **b** : to make good : REPLACE ~ *vi* : to become full : fill up again — **re·plen·ish·able** \-ni-shə-bəl\ *adj* — **re·plen·ish·er** *n* — **re·plen·ish·ment** \-nish-mənt\ *n*

re·plete \ri-ˈplēt\ *adj* [ME, fr. MF & L; MF *replet,* fr. L *repletus,* pp. of *replēre* to fill up, fr. *re-* + *plēre* to fill — more at FULL] (14c) **1** : fully or abundantly provided or filled ⟨a book ~ with . . . delicious details —William Safire⟩ **2 a** : abundantly fed **b** : FAT, STOUT **3** : COMPLETE ***syn*** see FULL — **re·plete·ness** *n*

re·ple·tion \ri-ˈplē-shən\ *n* (14c) **1** : the act of eating to excess : the state of being fed to excess : SURFEIT **2** : the condition of being filled up or overcrowded **3** : fulfillment of a need or desire : SATISFACTION

1**re·plev·in** \ri-ˈple-vən\ *n* [ME, fr. AF, fr. *replevir* to give security, fr. *re-* + *plevir* to pledge, fr. LL *plebere — more at PLEDGE] (15c) **1** : the recovery by a person of goods or chattels claimed to be wrongfully taken or detained upon the person's giving security to try the matter in court and return the goods if defeated in the action **2** : the writ or the common-law action whereby goods and chattels are replevied

2**replevin** *vt* (1678) : REPLEVY

1**re·plevy** \ri-ˈple-vē\ *n, pl* **re·plev·ies** [ME, fr. AF *replevir,* v.] (15c) : REPLEVIN

2**replevy** *vt* **re·plev·ied; re·plevy·ing** (1596) : to take or get back by a writ for replevin — **re·plevi·able** \-vē-ə-bəl\ *adj*

rep·li·ca \ˈre-pli-kə\ *n* [It, repetition, fr. *replicare* to repeat, fr. LL, fr. L, to fold back — more at REPLY] (1824) **1** : an exact reproduction (as of a painting) executed by the original artist ⟨a ~ of this was painted . . . this year —Constance Strachey⟩ **2** : a copy exact in all details ⟨DNA makes a ~ of itself⟩ ⟨sailed a ~ of the Viking ship⟩; *broadly* : COPY ⟨this faithful, pathetic ~ of a Midwestern suburb —G. F. Kennan⟩ ***syn*** see REPRODUCTION

rep·li·ca·ble \ˈre-plə-kə-bəl\ *adj* (1950) : capable of replication ⟨~ experimental results⟩ — **rep·li·ca·bil·i·ty** \ˌre-plə-kə-ˈbi-lə-tē\ *n*

rep·li·case \ˈre-pli-ˌkās, -ˌkāz\ *n* [*replic*ation + *-ase*] (1963) : a polymerase of viruses that promotes synthesis of a particular RNA in the presence of a template of RNA

1**rep·li·cate** \ˈre-plə-ˌkāt\ *vb* **-cat·ed; -cat·ing** [ME, fr. LL *replicatus,* pp. of *replicare*] *vt* (15c) : DUPLICATE, REPEAT ⟨~ a statistical experiment⟩ ⟨*replicated* his mentor's writing style⟩ ~ *vi* : to undergo replication : produce a replica of itself ⟨virus particles *replicating* in cells⟩

2**rep·li·cate** \-kət\ *adj* (1922) : MANIFOLD, REPEATED

3**rep·li·cate** \-kət\ *n* (1929) : one of several identical experiments, procedures, or samples

rep·li·ca·tion \ˌre-plə-ˈkā-shən\ *n* (14c) **1 a** : ANSWER, REPLY **b** (1) : an answer to a reply : REJOINDER (2) : a plaintiff's reply to a defendant's plea, answer, or counterclaim **2** : ECHO, REVERBERATION **3 a** : COPY, REPRODUCTION **b** : the action or process of reproducing or duplicating ⟨~ of DNA⟩ ⟨viral ~⟩ **4** : performance of an experiment or procedure more than once

rep·li·ca·tive \ˈre-pli-ˌkā-tiv\ *adj* (ca. 1890) : of, relating to, involved in, or characterized by replication ⟨the ~ form of tobacco mosaic virus⟩

rep·li·con \ˈre-pli-ˌkän\ *n* [*replicate* + 2*-on*] (1963) : a linear or circular section of DNA or RNA which replicates sequentially as a unit

1**re·ply** \ri-ˈplī\ *vb* **re·plied; re·ply·ing** [ME *replien* to fold back, oppose, respond, fr. AF *replier,* fr. L *replicare* to fold back, make a legal replication, fr. *re-* + *plicare* to fold — more at PLY] *vi* (14c) **1 a** : to respond in words or writing **b** : ECHO, RESOUND **c** : to make a legal replication **2** : to do something in response; *specif* : to return gunfire or an attack ~ *vt* : to give as an answer — **re·pli·er** \-ˈplī(-ə)r\ *n*

2**reply** *n, pl* **replies** (1560) **1** : something said, written, or done in answer or response **2** : REPLICATION 1b(2) ***syn*** see ANSWER

1**re·po** \ˈrē-ˌpō\ *adj* [short for *repossession*] (1954) : of, relating to, or being in the business of repossessing property (as a car) from buyers who have defaulted on payments ⟨a ~ company⟩

2**repo** *n, pl* **repos** [by shortening & alter.] (1962) : REPURCHASE AGREEMENT

re·po·lar·i·za·tion \ˌrē-ˌpō-lə-rə-ˈzā-shən\ *n* (1922) : restoration of the difference in charge between the inside and outside of the cell membrane following depolarization — **re·po·lar·ize** \(ˌ)rē-ˈpō-lə-ˌrīz\ *vb*

1**re·port** \ri-ˈpȯrt\ *n* [ME, fr. AF, fr. *reporter* to bring back, report, fr. L *reportare,* fr. *re-* + *portare* to carry — more at FARE] (14c) **1 a** : common talk or an account spread by common talk : RUMOR **b** : quality of reputation ⟨a witness of good ~⟩ **2 a** : a usu. detailed account or statement ⟨a news ~⟩ **b** : an account or statement of a judicial opinion or decision **c** : a usu. formal record of the proceedings of a meeting or session **3** : an explosive noise — **on report** : subject to disciplinary action ⟨was put *on report* for the violation⟩

2**report** *vt* (14c) **1 a** : to give an account of : RELATE **b** : to describe as being in a specified state ⟨~*ed* him much improved⟩ **2 a** : to serve as carrier of (a message) **b** : to relate the words or sense of (something said) **c** : to make a written record or summary of **d** (1) : to watch for and write about the newsworthy aspects or developments of : COVER (2) : to prepare or present an account of for broadcast **3 a** (1) : to give a formal or official account or statement of ⟨the treasurer ~*ed* a balance of ten dollars⟩ (2) : to return or present (a matter referred for consideration) with conclusions or recommendations **b** : to announce or relate as the result of investigation ⟨~*ed* no sign of disease⟩ **c** : to announce the presence, arrival, or sighting of **d** : to make known to the proper authorities ⟨~ a fire⟩ **e** : to make a charge of misconduct against ~ *vi* **1 a** : to give an account : TELL **b** : to present oneself ⟨~*ed* to the front desk⟩ **c** : to account for oneself ⟨~*ed* sick on Friday⟩ **d** : to work as a subordinate ⟨~*s* to the vice president⟩ **2** : to make, issue, or submit a report **3** : to act in the capacity of a reporter

re·port·able \ri-ˈpȯr-tə-bəl\ *adj* (1858) **1** : worth reporting ⟨~ news⟩ **2** : required by law to be reported ⟨~ income⟩ ⟨~ diseases⟩

re·port·age \ri-ˈpȯr-tij, *esp for 2* ˌre-pər-ˈtäzh, ˌre-ˌpȯr-ˈ\ *n* [F, fr. *reporter* to report] (ca. 1864) **1 a** : the act or process of reporting news **b** : something (as news) that is reported **2** : writing intended to give an account of observed or documented events

report card *n* (1920) **1** : a report on a student that is periodically submitted by a school to the student's parents or guardian **2** : an evaluation of performance

re·port·ed·ly \ri-ˈpȯr-təd-lē\ *adv* (1901) : according to report

re·port·er \ri-ˈpȯr-tər\ *n* (14c) : one that reports: as **a** : a person who makes authorized statements of law decisions or legislative proceedings **b** : a person who makes a shorthand record of a speech or proceeding **c** (1) : a person employed by a newspaper, magazine, or television company to gather and report news (2) : a person who broadcasts news — **re·por·to·ri·al** \ˌre-pə(r)-ˈtȯr-ē-əl, ˌrē-\ *adj* — **re·por·to·ri·al·ly** \-ē-ə-lē\ *adv*

report out *vt* (1907) : to return after consideration and often with revisions to a legislative body for action ⟨after much debate the committee *reported* the bill *out*⟩

report stage *n* (ca. 1906) : the stage in the British legislative process preceding the third reading and concerned esp. with amendments and details

re·pos·al \ri-ˈpō-zəl\ *n* (1605) *obs* : the act of reposing

1**re·pose** \ri-ˈpōz\ *vb* **re·posed; re·pos·ing** [ME, fr. AF *reposer,* fr. LL *repausare,* fr. L *re-* + LL *pausare* to stop, fr. L *pausa* pause] *vt* (15c) : to lay at rest ~ *vi* **1 a** : to lie at rest **b** : to lie dead ⟨*reposing* in state⟩ **c** : to remain still or concealed **2** : to take a rest **3** *archaic* : RELY **4** : to rest for support : LIE

2**repose** *n* (1509) **1 a** : a state of resting after exertion or strain; *esp* : rest in sleep **b** : eternal or heavenly rest ⟨pray for the ~ of a soul⟩ **2 a** : a place of rest **b** : PEACE, TRANQUILLITY ⟨the ~ of the bayous⟩ **c** : a harmony in the arrangement of parts and colors that is restful to the eye **3 a** : lack of activity : QUIESCENCE **b** : cessation or absence of activity, movement, or animation ⟨the face in ~ is grave and thoughtful⟩ **4** : composure of manner : POISE

3**re·pose** *vt* **re·posed; re·pos·ing** [ME, to replace, fr. L *reponere* (perf. indic. *reposui*)] (15c) **1** *archaic* : to put away or set down : DEPOSIT **2 a** : to place (as confidence or trust) in someone or something **b** : to place for control, management, or use

re·pose·ful \ri-ˈpōz-fəl\ *adj* (1852) : of a kind to induce ease and relaxation — **re·pose·ful·ly** \-fə-lē\ *adv* — **re·pose·ful·ness** *n*

re·pos·it *vt* **re·pos·it·ed** \-ˈpä-zə-təd, -ˈpäz-təd\; **re·pos·it·ing** \-ˈpä-zə-tiŋ, -ˈpäz-tiŋ\ [L *repositus,* pp. of *reponere* to replace, fr. *re-* + *ponere* to place — more at POSITION] (ca. 1641) **1** \ri-ˈpä-zət\ : DEPOSIT, STORE **2** \(ˌ)rē-\ : to put back in place : REPLACE

1**re·po·si·tion** \ˌrē-pə-ˈzi-shən, ˌre-\ *n* (1588) : the act of repositing : the state of being reposited

2**re·po·si·tion** \ˌrē-pə-ˈzi-shən\ *vt* (ca. 1859) **1** : to change the position of **2** : to revise the marketing strategy for (a product or a company) so as to increase sales

1**re·pos·i·to·ry** \ri-ˈpä-zə-ˌtȯr-ē\ *n, pl* **-ries** (15c) **1** : a place, room, or container where something is deposited or stored : DEPOSITORY **2** : a side altar in a Roman Catholic church where the consecrated Host is reserved from Maundy Thursday until Good Friday **3** : one that contains or stores something nonmaterial ⟨considered the book a ~ of knowledge⟩ **4** : a place or region richly supplied with a natural resource **5** : a person to whom something is confided or entrusted

2**repository** *adj* (1950) *of a drug* : designed to act over a prolonged period ⟨~ penicillin⟩

re·pos·sess \ˌrē-pə-ˈzes *also* -ˈses\ *vt* (15c) **1 a :** to regain possession of **b :** to take possession of (something bought) from a buyer in default of the payment of installments due **2 :** to restore to possession — **re·pos·ses·sion** \-ˈze-shən *also* -ˈse-\ *n* — **re·pos·sess·or** \-ˈze-sər *also* -ˈse-\ *n*

[1]**re·pous·sé** \rə-ˌpü-ˈsā, -ˈpü-ˌ\ *adj* [F, lit., pushed back] (1858) **1 :** shaped or ornamented with patterns in relief made by hammering or pressing on the reverse side — used esp. of metal **2 :** formed in relief

[2]**repoussé** *n* (1858) **1 :** repoussé work **2 :** repoussé decoration

re·pow·er \(ˌ)rē-ˈpau̇(-ə)r\ *vt* (1954) **:** to provide again or anew with power; *esp* **:** to provide (as a boat) with a new engine

repp *var of* REP

repped *past and past part of* [5]REP

repping *pres part of* [5]REP

rep·re·hend \ˌre-pri-ˈhend\ *vt* [ME, fr. L *reprehendere,* lit., to hold back, fr. *re-* + *prehendere* to grasp — more at GET] (14c) **:** to voice disapproval of **:** CENSURE ***syn*** see CRITICIZE

rep·re·hen·si·ble \ˌre-pri-ˈhen(t)-sə-bəl\ *adj* (14c) **:** worthy of or deserving reprehension **:** CULPABLE — **rep·re·hen·si·bil·i·ty** \-ˌhen(t)-sə-ˈbi-lə-tē\ *n* — **rep·re·hen·si·ble·ness** \-ˈhen(t)-sə-bəl-nəs\ *n* — **rep·re·hen·si·bly** \-blē\ *adv*

rep·re·hen·sion \-ˈhen(t)-shən\ *n* [ME *reprehensioun,* fr. AF or L; AF *reprehension,* fr. L *reprehension-, reprehensio,* fr. *reprehendere*] (14c) **:** the act of reprehending **:** CENSURE

rep·re·hen·sive \-ˈhen(t)-siv\ *adj* (1589) **:** serving to reprehend **:** conveying reprehension or reproof

rep·re·sent \ˌre-pri-ˈzent\ *vb* [ME, fr. AF *representer,* fr. L *repraesentare,* fr. *re-* + *praesentare* to present] *vt* (14c) **1 :** to bring clearly before the mind **:** PRESENT ⟨a book which ~*s* the character of early America⟩ **2 :** to serve as a sign or symbol of ⟨the flag ~*s* our country⟩ **3 :** to portray or exhibit in art **:** DEPICT **4 :** to serve as the counterpart or image of **:** TYPIFY ⟨a movie hero who ~*s* the ideals of the culture⟩ **5 a :** to produce on the stage **b :** to act the part or role of **6 a** (1) **:** to take the place of in some respect (2) **:** to act in the place of or for usu. by legal right (3) **:** to manage the legal and business affairs of ⟨athletes ~*ed* by top lawyers and agents⟩ **b :** to serve esp. in a legislative body by delegated authority usu. resulting from election **7 :** to describe as having a specified character or quality ⟨~*s* himself as a friend⟩ **8 a :** to give one's impression and judgment of **:** state in a manner intended to affect action or judgment **b :** to point out in protest or remonstrance **9 :** to serve as a specimen, example, or instance of **10 a :** to form an image or representation of in the mind **b** (1) **:** to apprehend (an object) by means of an idea (2) **:** to recall in memory **11 :** to correspond to in essence **:** CONSTITUTE ~ *vi* **1 :** to make representations against something **:** PROTEST **2** *slang* **:** to perform a task or duty admirably **:** serve as an outstanding example — **rep·re·sent·able** \-ˈzen-tə-bəl\ *adj* — **rep·re·sent·er** *n*

re–pre·sent \ˌrē-pri-ˈzent\ *vt* (1564) **:** to present again or anew — **re–pre·sen·ta·tion** \ˌrē-ˌprē-ˌzen-ˈtā-shən, -ˌpre-zᵊn-, -ˌprē-zᵊn-\ *n*

rep·re·sen·ta·tion \ˌre-pri-ˌzen-ˈtā-shən, -zən-\ *n* (15c) **1 :** one that represents: as **a :** an artistic likeness or image **b** (1) **:** a statement or account made to influence opinion or action (2) **:** an incidental or collateral statement of fact on the faith of which a contract is entered into **c :** a dramatic production or performance **d** (1) **:** a usu. formal statement made against something or to effect a change (2) **:** a usu. formal protest **2 :** the act or action of representing **:** the state of being represented: as **a :** REPRESENTATIONALISM 2 **b** (1) **:** the action or fact of one person standing for another so as to have the rights and obligations of the person represented (2) **:** the substitution of an individual or class in place of a person (as a child for a deceased parent) **c :** the action of representing or the fact of being represented esp. in a legislative body **3 :** the body of persons representing a constituency — **rep·re·sen·ta·tion·al** \-shnəl, -shə-nᵊl\ *adj* — **rep·re·sen·ta·tion·al·ly** *adv*

rep·re·sen·ta·tion·al·ism \-shnə-ˌli-zəm, -shə-nᵊl-ˌi-\ *n* (1842) **1 :** the doctrine that the immediate object of knowledge is an idea in the mind distinct from the external object which is the occasion of perception **2 :** the theory or practice of realistic representation in art — **rep·re·sen·ta·tion·al·ist** \-list, -ist\ *n*

[1]**rep·re·sen·ta·tive** \ˌre-pri-ˈzen-tə-tiv\ *adj* (14c) **1 :** serving to represent **2 a :** standing or acting for another esp. through delegated authority **b :** of, based on, or constituting a government in which the many are represented by persons chosen from among them usu. by election **3 :** serving as a typical or characteristic example ⟨a ~ moviegoer⟩ **4 :** of or relating to representation or representationalism — **rep·re·sen·ta·tive·ly** *adv* — **rep·re·sen·ta·tive·ness** *n* — **rep·re·sen·ta·tiv·i·ty** \-ˌzen-tə-ˈti-və-tē\ *n*

[2]**representative** *n* (1635) **1 :** one that represents another or others: as **a** (1) **:** one that represents a constituency as a member of a legislative body (2) **:** a member of the house of representatives of the U.S. Congress or a state legislature **b :** one that represents another as agent, deputy, substitute, or delegate usu. being invested with the authority of the principal **c :** one that represents a business organization **d :** one that represents another as successor or heir **2 :** a typical example of a group, class, or quality **:** SPECIMEN

re·press \ri-ˈpres\ *vb* [ME, fr. AF *represser,* fr. L *repressus,* pp. of *reprimere* to check, fr. *re-* + *premere* to press — more at PRESS] *vt* (14c) **1 a :** to check by or as if by pressure **:** CURB ⟨injustice was ~*ed*⟩ **b :** to put down by force **:** SUBDUE ⟨~ a disturbance⟩ **2 a :** to hold in by self-control ⟨~*ed* a laugh⟩ **b :** to prevent the natural or normal expression, activity, or development of ⟨~*ed* her anger⟩ **3 :** to exclude from consciousness ⟨~*ed* the memory of abuse⟩ **4 :** to inactivate (a gene or formation of a gene product) by allosteric combination at a DNA binding site ~ *vi* **:** to take repressive action — **re·press·ibil·i·ty** \-ˌpre-sə-ˈbi-lə-tē\ *n* — **re·press·ible** \-ˈpre-sə-bəl\ *adj* — **re·pres·sive** \-ˈpre-siv\ *adj* — **re·pres·sive·ly** *adv* — **re·pres·sive·ness** *n*

re–press \(ˌ)rē-ˈpres\ *vt* (14c) **:** to press again ⟨~ a record⟩

re·pressed \ri-ˈprest\ *adj* (1665) **1 :** subjected to or marked by repression **2 :** characterized by restraint

re·pres·sion \ri-ˈpre-shən\ *n* (1533) **1 a :** the action or process of repressing **:** the state of being repressed ⟨~ of unpopular opinions⟩ **b :** an instance of repressing ⟨racial ~*s*⟩ **2 a :** a mental process by which distressing thoughts, memories, or impulses that may give rise to anxiety are excluded from consciousness and left to operate in the unconscious **b :** an item so excluded — **re·pres·sion·ist** \-sh(ə-)nist\ *adj*

re·pres·sor \ri-ˈpre-sər\ *n* [NL] (1611) **:** one that represses; *esp* **:** a protein that is determined by a regulatory gene, binds to a genetic operator, and inhibits the initiation of transcription of messenger RNA

re·priev·al \ri-ˈprē-vəl\ *n* (ca. 1586) *archaic* **:** REPRIEVE

[1]**re·prieve** \ri-ˈprēv\ *vt* **re·prieved; re·priev·ing** [prob. blend of obs. *repreve* to reprove (fr. ME) and obs. *repry* to remand, postpone, fr. AF *repri-,* past stem of *reprendre* to take back] (1596) **1 :** to delay the punishment of (as a condemned prisoner) **2 :** to give relief or deliverance to for a time

[2]**reprieve** *n* (1592) **1 a :** the act of reprieving **:** the state of being reprieved **b :** a formal temporary suspension of the execution of a sentence esp. of death **2 :** an order or warrant for a reprieve **3 :** a temporary respite (as from pain or trouble)

[1]**rep·ri·mand** \ˈre-prə-ˌmand\ *n* [F *réprimande,* fr. L *reprimenda,* fem. of *reprimendus,* gerundive of *reprimere* to check — more at REPRESS] (1636) **:** a severe or formal reproof

[2]**reprimand** *vt* (1681) **:** to reprove sharply or censure formally usu. from a position of authority ***syn*** see REPROVE

[1]**re·print** \(ˌ)rē-ˈprint\ *vt* (1551) **:** to print again **:** make a reprint of

[2]**re·print** \ˈrē-ˌprint, (ˌ)rē-ˈ\ *n* (1611) **:** a reproduction of printed matter: as **a :** a subsequent printing of a book already published that preserves the identical text of the previous printing **b :** OFFPRINT **c :** matter (as an article) that has appeared in print before

re·print·er \(ˌ)rē-ˈprin-tər\ *n* (1689) **:** one that publishes a reprint

re·pri·sal \ri-ˈprī-zəl\ *n* [ME *reprisail,* fr. AF *reprisaile,* fr. ML *represalia,* fr. OIt *rappresaglia,* ultim. fr. *ripreso,* pp. of *riprendere* to take back, fr. *ri-* re- (fr. L *re-*) + *prendere* to take, fr. L *prehendere* — more at GET] (15c) **1 a :** the act or practice in international law of resorting to force short of war in retaliation for damage or loss suffered **b :** an instance of such action **2** *obs* **:** PRIZE **3 :** the regaining of something (as by recapture) **4 :** something (as a sum of money) given or paid in restitution — usu. used in pl. **5 :** a retaliatory act

[1]**re·prise** \ri-ˈprēz, *1 is also* -ˈprīz\ *n* [ME, fr. AF, seizure, repossession, expense, fr. fem. pp. of *reprendre* to take back, fr. *re-* + *prendre* to take, fr. L *prehendere*] (15c) **1 :** a deduction or charge made yearly out of a manor or estate — usu. used in pl. **2 :** a recurrence, renewal, or resumption of an action **3** [F, fr. MF] **a :** a musical repetition: (1) **:** the repetition of the exposition preceding the development (2) **:** RECAPITULATION 3 **b :** a repeated performance **:** REPETITION

[2]**re·prise** \ri-ˈprīz, *3 is* -ˈprēz\ *vt* **re·prised; re·pris·ing** [ME, fr. MF *repris,* pp. of *reprendre*] (15c) **1** *archaic* **:** TAKE BACK; *esp* **:** to recover by force **2** *archaic* **:** COMPENSATE **3 a :** to repeat the performance of **b :** to repeat the principal points or stages of **:** RECAPITULATE

re·pris·ti·nate \(ˌ)rē-ˈpris-tə-ˌnāt\ *vt* **-nat·ed; -nat·ing** [*re-* + *pristine* + [4]*-ate*] (1659) **:** to restore to an original state or condition — **re·pris·ti·na·tion** \(ˌ)rē-ˌpris-tə-ˈnā-shən\ *n*

re·pro \ˈrē-(ˌ)prō\ *n, pl* **repros** [short for *reproduction*] (1946) **1 :** a clear sharp proof made esp. from a letterpress printing surface to serve as photographic copy for a printing plate **2 :** REPRODUCTION 2

[1]**re·proach** \ri-ˈprōch\ *n* [ME *reproche,* fr. AF, fr. *reprocher* to reproach, fr. VL **repropiare* to bring close, show, fr. L *re-* + *prope* near — more at APPROACH] (14c) **1 :** an expression of rebuke or disapproval **2 :** the act or action of reproaching or disapproving ⟨was beyond ~⟩ **3 a :** a cause or occasion of blame, discredit, or disgrace **b :** DISCREDIT, DISGRACE **4** *obs* **:** one subjected to censure or scorn — **re·proach·ful** \-fəl\ *adj* — **re·proach·ful·ly** \-fə-lē\ *adv* — **re·proach·ful·ness** *n*

[2]**reproach** *vt* (14c) **1 :** to express disappointment in or displeasure with (a person) for conduct that is blameworthy or in need of amendment **2 :** to make (something) a matter of reproach **3 :** to bring into discredit ***syn*** see REPROVE — **re·proach·able** \-ˈprō-chə-bəl\ *adj* — **re·proach·er** *n* — **re·proach·ing·ly** \-ˈprō-chiŋ-lē\ *adv*

rep·ro·bance \ˈre-prə-bən(t)s\ *n* (1604) *archaic* **:** REPROBATION

[1]**rep·ro·bate** \ˈre-prə-ˌbāt\ *vt* **-bat·ed; -bat·ing** [ME, fr. LL *reprobatus,* pp. of *reprobare* — more at REPROVE] (15c) **1 :** to condemn strongly as unworthy, unacceptable, or evil ⟨*reprobating* the laxity of the age⟩ **2 :** to foreordain to damnation **3 :** to refuse to accept **:** REJECT ***syn*** see CRITICIZE — **rep·ro·ba·tive** \ˈre-prə-ˌbā-tiv\ *adj* — **rep·ro·ba·to·ry** \-bə-ˌtȯr-ē\ *adj*

[2]**reprobate** *adj* (15c) **1** *archaic* **:** rejected as worthless or not standing a test **:** CONDEMNED **2 a :** foreordained to damnation **b :** morally corrupt **:** DEPRAVED **3 :** expressing or involving reprobation **4 :** of, relating to, or characteristic of a reprobate

[3]**reprobate** *n* (1545) **:** a reprobate person

rep·ro·ba·tion \ˌre-prə-ˈbā-shən\ *n* (14c) **:** the act of reprobating **:** the state of being reprobated

re·pro·cess \(ˌ)rē-ˈprä-ˌses, -ˈprō-, -səs\ *vt* (1921) **:** to subject to a special process or treatment in preparation for reuse; *esp* **:** to extract uranium and plutonium from (the spent fuel rods of a nuclear reactor) for use again as fuel

re·pro·duce \ˌrē-prə-ˈdüs, -ˈdyüs\ *vt* (ca. 1611) **:** to produce again: as **a :** to produce (new individuals of the same kind) by a sexual or asexual process **b :** to cause to exist again or anew ⟨~ water from steam⟩ **c :** to imitate closely ⟨sound-effects can ~ the sound of thunder⟩ **d :** to present again **e :** to make a representation (as an image or copy) of ⟨~ a face on canvas⟩ **f :** to revive mentally **:** RECALL **g :** to translate (a recording) into sound ~ *vi* **1 :** to undergo reproduction **2 :** to produce offspring — **re·pro·duc·er** *n* — **re·pro·duc·ibil·i·ty** \-ˌdü-sə-ˈbi-lə-tē, -ˌdyü-\ *n* — **re·pro·duc·ible** \-ˈdü-sə-bəl, -ˈdyü-\ *adj or n* — **re·pro·duc·ibly** \-blē\ *adv*

re·pro·duc·tion \ˌrē-prə-ˈdək-shən\ *n* (1659) **1 :** the act or process of reproducing; *specif* **:** the process by which plants and animals give rise to offspring and which fundamentally consists of the segregation of a portion of the parental body by a sexual or an asexual process and its subsequent growth and differentiation into a new individual **2 :** something reproduced **:** COPY **3 :** young seedling trees in a forest

syn REPRODUCTION, DUPLICATE, COPY, FACSIMILE, REPLICA mean a thing made to closely resemble another. REPRODUCTION implies an exact or close imitation of an existing thing ⟨*reproductions* from the museum's furniture collection⟩. DUPLICATE implies a double or counterpart exactly corresponding to another thing ⟨a *duplicate* of a house key⟩. COPY applies esp. to one of a number of things reproduced mechanically ⟨printed 1000 *copies* of the lithograph⟩. FACSIMILE suggests a close reproduction often of graphic matter that may differ in scale ⟨a *facsimile* of a rare book⟩. REPLICA implies the exact reproduction of a particular item in all details ⟨a *replica* of the Mayflower⟩ but not always in the same scale ⟨miniature *replicas* of classic cars⟩.

reproduction proof *n* (1945) : REPRO 1

1re·pro·duc·tive \ˌrē-prə-ˈdək-tiv\ *adj* (1753) : of, relating to, or capable of reproduction ⟨highly ~ wild geese⟩ — **re·pro·duc·tive·ly** *adv*

2reproductive *n* (1934) : an actual or potential parent; *specif* : a sexually functional social insect

reproductive isolation *n* (1949) : the inability of a species to breed successfully with related species due to geographical, behavioral, physiological, or genetic barriers or differences

re·pro·gram \(ˌ)rē-ˈprō-ˌgram, -grəm\ *vt* (1959) : to program anew; *esp* : to revise or write a new program for (as a computer) ~ *vi* : to rewrite or revise a program esp. of a computer — **re·pro·gram·ma·ble** \-ˈprō-ˌgra-mə-bəl, -ˌprō-ˈgra-\ *adj*

re·prog·ra·phy \ri-ˈprä-grə-fē\ *n* [*repro*duction + *-graphy*] (1956) : facsimile reproduction (as by photocopying) of graphic matter — **re·prog·ra·pher** \-grə-fər\ *n* — **re·pro·graph·ic** \ˌrē-prə-ˈgra-fik, ˌre-\ *adj* — **re·pro·graph·ics** \-fiks\ *n pl*

re·proof \ri-ˈprüf\ *n* [ME *repref, reprofe,* fr. AF *reproefe,* fr. *reprover*] (14c) : criticism for a fault : REBUKE

re·prove \ri-ˈprüv\ *vb* **re·proved; re·prov·ing** [ME *repreven, reproven,* fr. AF *reprover,* fr. LL *reprobare* to disapprove, condemn, fr. L *re-* + *probare* to test, approve — more at PROVE] *vt* (14c) **1** : to scold or correct usu. gently or with kindly intent **2** : to express disapproval of : CENSURE ⟨it is not for me to ~ popular taste —D. W. Brogan⟩ **3** *obs* : DISPROVE, REFUTE **4** *obs* : CONVINCE, CONVICT ~ *vi* : to express rebuke or reproof — **re·prov·er** *n* — **re·prov·ing·ly** \-ˈprü-viŋ-lē\ *adv*

syn REPROVE, REBUKE, REPRIMAND, ADMONISH, REPROACH, CHIDE mean to criticize adversely. REPROVE implies an often kindly intent to correct a fault ⟨gently *reproved* my table manners⟩. REBUKE suggests a sharp or stern reproof ⟨the papal letter *rebuked* dissenting clerics⟩. REPRIMAND implies a severe, formal, often public or official rebuke ⟨*reprimanded* by the ethics committee⟩. ADMONISH suggests earnest or friendly warning and counsel ⟨*admonished* by my parents to control expenses⟩. REPROACH and CHIDE suggest displeasure or disappointment expressed in mild reproof or scolding ⟨*reproached* him for tardiness⟩ ⟨*chided* by their mother for untidiness⟩.

rept *abbr* report

1rep·tile \ˈrep-ˌtī(-ə)l, -tᵊl\ *n* [ME *reptil,* fr. MF or LL; MF *reptile* (fem.), fr. LL *reptile* (neut.), fr. neut. of *reptilis* creeping, fr. L *reptus,* pp. of *repere* to crawl; akin to Lith *rėplioti* to crawl] (14c) **1** : an animal that crawls or moves on its belly (as a snake) or on small short legs (as a lizard) **2** : any of a class (Reptilia) of air-breathing vertebrates that include the alligators and crocodiles, lizards, snakes, turtles, and extinct related forms (as dinosaurs and pterosaurs) and are characterized by a completely ossified skeleton with a single occipital condyle, a distinct quadrate bone usu. immovably articulated with the skull, ribs attached to the sternum, and a body usu. covered with scales or bony plates **3** : a groveling or despised person

2reptile *adj* (1607) : characteristic of a reptile : REPTILIAN

1rep·til·ian \rep-ˈti-lē-ən, -ˈtil-yən\ *adj* (1833) **1** : resembling or having the characteristics of the reptiles **2** : of or relating to the reptiles **3** : cold-bloodedly treacherous ⟨a ~ villain —Theodore Dreiser⟩

2reptilian *n* (ca. 1847) : REPTILE 2

re·pub·lic \ri-ˈpə-blik\ *n* [F *république,* fr. MF *republique,* fr. L *respublica,* fr. *res* thing, wealth + *publica,* fem. of *publicus* public — more at REAL, PUBLIC] (1604) **1 a (1)** : a government having a chief of state who is not a monarch and who in modern times is usu. a president **(2)** : a political unit (as a nation) having such a form of government **b (1)** : a government in which supreme power resides in a body of citizens entitled to vote and is exercised by elected officers and representatives responsible to them and governing according to law **(2)** : a political unit (as a nation) having such a form of government **c** : a usu. specified republican government of a political unit ⟨the French Fourth *Republic*⟩ **2** : a body of persons freely engaged in a specified activity ⟨the ~ of letters⟩ **3** : a constituent political and territorial unit of the former nations of Czechoslovakia, the U.S.S.R., or Yugoslavia

1re·pub·li·can \ri-ˈpə-bli-kən\ *n* (1699) **1** : one that favors or supports a republican form of government **2** *cap* **a** : a member of a political party advocating republicanism **b** : a member of the Democratic-Republican party or of the Republican party of the U.S.

2republican *adj* (1690) **1 a** : of, relating to, or having the characteristics of a republic **b** : favoring, supporting, or advocating a republic **c** : belonging or appropriate to one living in or supporting a republic ⟨~ simplicity⟩ **2** *cap* **a** : DEMOCRATIC-REPUBLICAN **b** : of, relating to, or constituting the one of the two major political parties evolving in the U.S. in the mid-19th century that is usu. primarily associated with business, financial, and some agricultural interests and is held to favor a restricted governmental role in economic life

re·pub·li·can·ism \ri-ˈpə-bli-kə-ˌni-zəm\ *n* (1689) **1** : adherence to or sympathy for a republican form of government **2** : the principles or theory of republican government **3** *cap* **a** : the principles, policy, or practices of the Republican party of the U.S. **b** : the Republican party or its members

re·pub·li·can·ize \-kə-ˌnīz\ *vt* **-ized; -iz·ing** (1797) : to make republican in character, form, or principle

re·pub·li·ca·tion \(ˌ)rē-ˌpə-blə-ˈkā-shən\ *n* (1789) **1** : the act or action of republishing : the state of being republished **2** : something that has been republished

re·pub·lish \(ˌ)rē-ˈpə-blish\ *vt* (1592) **1** : to publish again or anew **2** : to execute (a will) anew — **re·pub·lish·er** *n*

re·pu·di·ate \ri-ˈpyü-dē-ˌāt\ *vt* **-at·ed; -at·ing** [L *repudiatus,* pp. of *repudiare,* fr. *repudium* rejection of a prospective spouse, divorce, prob. fr. *re-* + *pudēre* to shame] (1545) **1** : to divorce or separate formally from (a woman) **2** : to refuse to have anything to do with : DISOWN **3 a** : to refuse to accept; *esp* : to reject as unauthorized or as having no binding force ⟨~ a contract⟩ **b** : to reject as untrue or unjust ⟨~ a charge⟩ **4** : to refuse to acknowledge or pay ⟨~ a debt⟩ ***syn*** see DECLINE — **re·pu·di·a·tor** \-ˌā-tər\ *n*

re·pu·di·a·tion \ri-ˌpyü-dē-ˈā-shən\ *n* (1545) : the act of repudiating : the state of being repudiated; *esp* : the refusal of public authorities to acknowledge or pay a debt — **re·pu·di·a·tion·ist** \-sh(ə-)nist\ *n*

re·pugn \ri-ˈpyün\ *vb* [ME, fr. AF & L; AF *repugner,* fr. L *repugnare*] *vi* (14c) *archaic* : to offer opposition, objection, or resistance ~ *vt* : to contend against : OPPOSE

re·pug·nance \ri-ˈpəg-nən(t)s\ *n* (15c) **1 a** : the quality or fact of being contradictory or inconsistent **b** : an instance of such contradiction or inconsistency **2** : strong dislike, distaste, or antagonism

re·pug·nan·cy \-nən(t)-sē\ *n, pl* **-cies** (15c) : REPUGNANCE

re·pug·nant \-nənt\ *adj* [ME, opposed, contradictory, incompatible, fr. AF, fr. L *repugnant-, repugnans,* prp. of *repugnare* to fight against, fr. *re-* + *pugnare* to fight — more at PUNGENT] (15c) **1** : INCOMPATIBLE, INCONSISTENT **2** *archaic* : HOSTILE **3** : exciting distaste or aversion ⟨~ language⟩ ⟨a morally ~ practice⟩ — **re·pug·nant·ly** *adv*

1re·pulse \ri-ˈpəls\ *vt* **re·pulsed; re·puls·ing** [L *repulsus,* pp. of *repellere* to repel] (15c) **1** : to drive or beat back : REPEL **2** : to repel by discourtesy, coldness, or denial **3** : to cause repulsion in

2repulse *n* (1533) **1** : REBUFF, REJECTION **2** : the action of repelling an attacker : the fact of being repelled

re·pul·sion \ri-ˈpəl-shən\ *n* (15c) **1** : the action of repulsing : the state of being repulsed **2** : the action of repelling : the force with which bodies, particles, or like forces repel one another **3** : a feeling of aversion : REPUGNANCE

re·pul·sive \-siv\ *adj* (1594) **1** : serving or able to repulse ⟨~ force⟩ **2** : tending to repel or reject : COLD, FORBIDDING **3** : arousing aversion or disgust ⟨~ crimes⟩ — **re·pul·sive·ly** *adv* — **re·pul·sive·ness** *n*

re·pur·chase agreement \(ˌ)rē-ˈpər-chəs-\ *n* (1924) : a contract giving the seller of securities (as treasury bills) the right to repurchase after a stated period and the buyer the right to retain interest earnings

re·pur·pose \(ˌ)rē-ˈpər-pəs\ *vt* (1984) : to give a new purpose or use to ⟨~ the company's Web site⟩ ⟨~ the archived material⟩

rep·u·ta·ble \ˈre-pyə-tə-bəl\ *adj* (1662) **1** : enjoying good repute : held in esteem **2** : employed widely or sanctioned by good writers — **rep·u·ta·bil·i·ty** \ˌre-pyə-tə-ˈbi-lə-tē\ *n* — **rep·u·ta·bly** \ˈre-pyə-tə-blē\ *adv*

rep·u·ta·tion \ˌre-pyə-ˈtā-shən\ *n* [ME *reputacion,* fr. AF, fr. L *reputation-, reputatio* consideration, fr. *reputare*] (14c) **1 a** : overall quality or character as seen or judged by people in general **b** : recognition by other people of some characteristic or ability ⟨has the ~ of being clever⟩ **2** : a place in public esteem or regard : good name ⟨trying to protect his ~⟩ — **rep·u·ta·tion·al** \-shnəl, -shə-nᵊl\ *adj*

1re·pute \ri-ˈpyüt\ *vt* **re·put·ed; re·put·ing** [ME, fr. AF *reputer,* fr. L *reputare* to reckon up, think over, fr. *re-* + *putare* to reckon] (15c) : BELIEVE, CONSIDER

2repute *n* (1539) **1** : the character or status commonly ascribed to one : REPUTATION **2** : the state of being favorably known, spoken of, or esteemed

reputed *adj* (1549) **1** : having a good repute : REPUTABLE **2** : being such according to reputation or general belief ⟨a ~ mobster⟩

re·put·ed·ly *adv* (1687) : according to reputation or general belief

req *abbr* **1** request **2** require; required **3** requistion

reqd *abbr* required

1re·quest \ri-ˈkwest\ *n* [ME *requeste,* fr. AF, fr. VL **requaesta,* fr. fem. of *requaestus,* pp. of *requaerere* to require] (14c) **1** : the act or an instance of asking for something **2** : something asked for ⟨granted her ~⟩ **3** : the condition or fact of being requested ⟨available on ~⟩ **4** : the state of being sought after : DEMAND

2request *vt* (1533) **1** : to make a request to or of ⟨~*ed* her to write a paper⟩ **2** : to ask as a favor or privilege ⟨~*s* to be excused⟩ **3** *obs* : to ask (a person) to come or go to a thing or place **4** : to ask for ⟨~*ed* a brief delay⟩ ***syn*** see ASK — **re·quest·er** *or* **re·quest·or** \-ˈkwes-tər\ *n*

re·qui·em \ˈre-kwē-əm *also* ˈrā- *or* ˈrē-\ *n* [ME, fr. L (first word of the introit of the requiem mass), acc. of *requies* rest, fr. *re-* + *quies* quiet, rest — more at WHILE] (14c) **1** : a mass for the dead **2 a** : a solemn chant (as a dirge) for the repose of the dead **b** : something that resembles such a solemn chant **3 a** : a musical setting of the mass for the dead **b** : a musical composition in honor of the dead

requiem shark *n* [obs. F *requiem* shark, alter. of F *requin*] (1900) : any of a family (Carcharhinidae) of sharks (as the tiger shark) that includes some dangerous to humans

re·qui·es·cat \ˌre-kwē-ˈes-ˌkät, -ˌkat; ˌrā-kwē-ˈes-ˌkät\ *n* [L, may he (or she) rest, fr. *requiescere* to rest, fr. *re-* + *quiescere* to be quiet, fr. *quies*] (1824) : a prayer for the repose of a dead person

re·quire \ri-ˈkwī(-ə)r\ *vb* **re·quired; re·quir·ing** [ME *requeren,* fr. AF *requere,* fr. VL **requaerere* to seek for, need, require, alter. of L *requirere,* fr. *re-* + *quaerere* to seek, ask] *vt* (14c) **1 a** : to claim or ask for by right and authority **b** *archaic* : REQUEST **2 a** : to call for as suitable or appropriate ⟨the occasion ~*s* formal dress⟩ **b** : to demand as necessary or essential : have a compelling need for ⟨all living beings ~ food⟩ **3** : to impose a compulsion or command on : COMPEL **4** *chiefly Brit* : to feel or be obliged — used with a following infinitive ⟨one does not ~ to be a specialist —Elizabeth Bowen⟩ ~ *vi, archaic* : ASK ***syn*** see DEMAND

re·quire·ment \-ˈkwī(-ə)r-mənt\ *n* (1662) : something required: **a** : something wanted or needed : NECESSITY ⟨production was not sufficient to satisfy military ~*s*⟩ **b** : something essential to the existence or occurrence of something else : CONDITION ⟨failed to meet the school's ~*s* for graduation⟩

req·ui·site \ˈre-kwə-zət\ *adj* [ME, fr. L *requisitus,* pp. of *requirere*] (15c) : ESSENTIAL, NECESSARY — **requisite** *n* — **req·ui·site·ness** *n*

req·ui·si·tion \ˌre-kwə-ˈzi-shən\ *n* [ME *requisicion,* fr. MF or ML; MF *requisition,* fr. ML *requisition-, requisitio,* fr. L, act of searching, fr. *requirere*] (15c) **1 a** : the act of formally requiring or calling upon someone to perform an action **b** : a formal demand made by one nation upon another for the surrender or extradition of a fugitive from justice **2 a** : the act of requiring something to be furnished **b** : a demand or application made usu. with authority: as **(1)** : a demand made by military authorities upon civilians for supplies or other needs (2) : a written request for something authorized but not made available automatically **3** : the state of being in demand or use — **requisition** *vt*

re·quit·al \ri-ˈkwī-tᵊl\ *n* (1567) **1** : something given in return, compensation, or retaliation **2** : the act or action of requiting : the state of being requited

re·quite \ri-ˈkwīt\ *vt* **re·quit·ed; re·quit·ing** [*re-* + obs. *quite* to quit, pay, fr. ME *quiten* — more at QUIT] (1529) **1 a** : to make return for : REPAY **b** : to make retaliation for : AVENGE **2** : to make suitable return to for a benefit or service or for an injury ***syn*** see RECIPROCATE — **re·quit·er** *n*

re·ra·di·ate \(ˌ)rē-ˈrā-dē-ˌāt\ *vt* (1913) : to radiate again or anew; *esp* : to emit (energy) in the form of radiation after absorbing incident radiation — **re·ra·di·a·tion** \(ˌ)rē-ˌrā-dē-ˈā-shən\ *n*

rere·dos \ˈrer-ə-ˌdäs *also* ˈrir-ə-ˌdäs *or* ˈrir-ˌdäs\ *n* [ME, fr. AF *reredors, areredos,* fr. *arere* behind + *dos* back, fr. L *dorsum* — more at ARREAR] (14c) : a usu. ornamental wood or stone screen or partition wall behind an altar

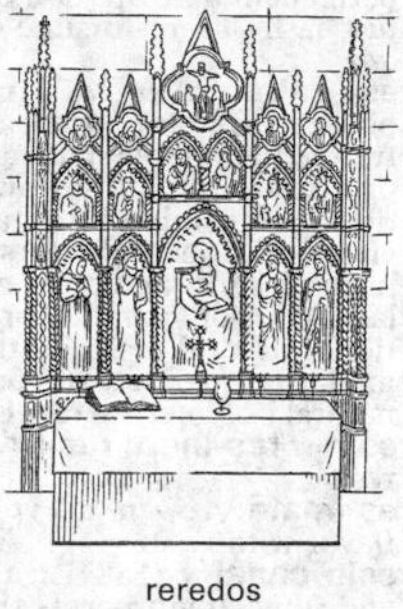

reredos

rere·ward *n* [ME *rerewarde,* fr. AF, fr. *rere, arere* behind + *warde, gard* guard] (14c) *obs* : REAR GUARD

[1]**re·run** \(ˌ)rē-ˈrən\ *vt* **-ran** \-ˈran\; **-run; -run·ning** (1804) : to run again or anew

[2]**re·run** \ˈrē-ˌrən, (ˌ)rē-ˈ\ *n* (ca. 1934) : the act or action or an instance of rerunning : REPETITION; *esp* : a movie or television show that is rerun

[1]**res** \ˈrās, ˈrēz\ *n, pl* **res** [L — more at REAL] (1851) : a particular thing : MATTER — used esp. in legal phrases

[2]**res** *abbr* **1** research **2** reservation **3** reserve **4** reservoir **5** residence; resident **6** resolution

res ad·ju·di·ca·ta \ˈrēz-ə-ˌjü-di-ˈkä-tə\ *n* [LL] (1849) : RES JUDICATA

re·sal·able \(ˌ)rē-ˈsā-lə-bəl\ *adj* (1866) : fit for resale

re·sale \ˈrē-ˌsāl, (ˌ)rē-ˈsāl\ *n* (1625) **1** : the act of selling again usu. to a new party **2 a** : a secondhand sale **b** : an additional sale to the same buyer

re·scale \(ˌ)rē-ˈskāl\ *vt* (1944) : to plan, establish, or formulate on a new and usu. smaller scale

re·sched·ule \(ˌ)rē-ˈske-(ˌ)jül, -jəl, *Canad also* -ˈshe-, *Brit usu* -ˈshe-(ˌ)dyül\ *vt* (1965) : to schedule or plan again according to a different timetable; *esp* : to defer required payment of (a debt or loan)

re·scind \ri-ˈsind\ *vt* [L *rescindere* to annul, fr. *re-* + *scindere* to cut — more at SHED] (1579) **1** : to take away : REMOVE **2 a** : TAKE BACK, CANCEL ⟨refused to ~ the order⟩ **b** : to abrogate (a contract) and restore the parties to the positions they would have occupied had there been no contract **3** : to make void (as an act) by action of the enacting authority or a superior authority : REPEAL — **re·scind·er** *n* — **re·scind·ment** \-ˈsin(d)-mənt\ *n*

re·scis·sion \ri-ˈsi-zhən\ *n* [LL *rescission-, rescissio,* fr. L *rescindere*] (1651) : an act of rescinding

re·scis·so·ry \-ˈsi-zə-rē, -ˈsi-sə-\ *adj* (1605) : relating to, tending to, or having the effect of rescission

re·script \ˈrē-ˌskript\ *n* [ME *rescripte,* fr. L *rescriptum,* fr. neut. of *rescriptus,* pp. of *rescribere* to write in reply, fr. *re-* + *scribere* to write — more at SCRIBE] (15c) **1** : a written answer of a Roman emperor or of a pope to a legal inquiry or petition **2** : an official or authoritative order, decree, edict, or announcement **3** : an act or instance of rewriting

res·cue \ˈres-(ˌ)kyü\ *vt* **res·cued; res·cu·ing** [ME *rescouen, rescuen,* fr. AF *rescure,* fr. *re-* + *escure* to shake off, fr. L *excutere,* fr. *ex-* + *quatere* to shake] (14c) : to free from confinement, danger, or evil : SAVE, DELIVER: as **a** : to take (as a prisoner) forcibly from custody **b** : to recover (as a prize) by force **c** : to deliver (as a place under siege) by armed force — **res·cu·able** \-ə-bəl\ *adj* — **rescue** *n* — **res·cu·er** *n*

syn RESCUE, DELIVER, REDEEM, RANSOM, RECLAIM, SAVE mean to set free from confinement or danger. RESCUE implies freeing from imminent danger by prompt or vigorous action ⟨*rescued* the crew of a sinking ship⟩. DELIVER implies release usu. of a person from confinement, temptation, slavery, or suffering ⟨*delivered* his people from bondage⟩. REDEEM implies releasing from bondage or penalties by giving what is demanded or necessary ⟨job training designed to *redeem* school dropouts from chronic unemployment⟩. RANSOM specif. applies to buying out of captivity ⟨tried to *ransom* the kidnap victim⟩. RECLAIM suggests a bringing back to a former state or condition of someone or something abandoned or debased ⟨*reclaimed* long-abandoned farms⟩. SAVE may replace any of the foregoing terms; it may further imply a preserving or maintaining for usefulness or continued existence ⟨an operation that *saved* my life⟩.

rescue mission *n* (1902) : a city religious mission seeking to convert and rehabilitate the down-and-out

[1]**re·search** \ri-ˈsərch, ˈrē-ˌ\ *n* [MF *recerche,* fr. *recercher* to go about seeking, fr. OF *recerchier,* fr. *re-* + *cerchier, sercher* to search — more at SEARCH] (1577) **1** : careful or diligent search **2** : studious inquiry or examination; *esp* : investigation or experimentation aimed at the discovery and interpretation of facts, revision of accepted theories or laws in the light of new facts, or practical application of such new or revised theories or laws **3** : the collecting of information about a particular subject

[2]**research** *vt* (1593) **1** : to search or investigate exhaustively ⟨~ a problem⟩ **2** : to do research for ⟨~ a book⟩ ~ *vi* : to engage in research — **re·search·able** \ri-ˈsər-chə-bəl, ˈrē-ˌ\ *adj* — **re·search·er** *n*

re·search·ist \ri-ˈsər-chist, ˈrē-ˌsər-\ *n* (1923) : one engaged in research

re·seau \rā-ˈzō, ri-\ *n, pl* **re·seaux** \-ˈzō(z)\ [F *réseau,* lit., network, fr. OF *resel,* dim. of *rais* net, fr. L *retis, rete*] (1578) **1** : a net ground or foundation in lace **2** : a grid photographed by a separate exposure onto a plate containing star images to facilitate astronomical measurements

re·sect \ri-ˈsekt\ *vt* [L *resectus,* pp. of *resecare* to cut off, fr. *re-* + *secare* to cut — more at SAW] (1846) : to perform resection on — **re·sect·abil·i·ty** \-ˌsek-tə-ˈbi-lə-tē\ *n* — **re·sect·able** \-ˈsek-tə-bəl\ *adj*

re·sec·tion \ri-ˈsek-shən\ *n* (1775) : the surgical removal of part of an organ or structure

re·se·da \ˈrā-zə-ˌdä\ *n* [F *réséda,* fr. *réséda,* a mignonette] (1873) : a grayish-green color

re·seed \(ˌ)rē-ˈsēd\ *vt* (1888) **1** : to sow seed on again or anew **2** : to maintain (itself) by self-sown seed ~ *vi* : to maintain itself by self-sown seed

re·sem·blance \ri-ˈzem-blən(t)s\ *n* (14c) **1 a** : the quality or state of resembling; *esp* : correspondence in appearance or superficial qualities **b** : a point of likeness : SIMILARITY **2** : REPRESENTATION, IMAGE **3** *archaic* : characteristic appearance **4** *obs* : PROBABILITY ***syn*** see LIKENESS

re·sem·blant \-blənt\ *adj* (14c) : marked by or showing resemblance

re·sem·ble \ri-ˈzem-bəl\ *vt* **re·sem·bled; re·sem·bling** \-b(ə-)liŋ\ [ME, fr. AF *resembler,* fr. *re-* + *sembler* to be like, seem, fr. L *similare* to copy, fr. *similis* like — more at SAME] (14c) **1** : to be like or similar to ⟨he ~*s* his father⟩ **2** *archaic* : to represent as like

re·send \(ˈ)rē-ˈsend\ *vt* **-sent** \-ˈsent\; **-send·ing** (1534) : to send again or back

re·sent \ri-ˈzent\ *vt* [MF *resentir* to be emotionally sensible of, fr. OF, fr. *re-* + *sentir* to feel, fr. L *sentire* — more at SENSE] (1596) : to feel or express annoyance or ill will at ⟨~*ed* the implication⟩

re·sent·ful \-fəl\ *adj* (1656) **1** : full of resentment : inclined to resent ⟨felt ~ of her success⟩ **2** : caused or marked by resentment ⟨~ anger⟩ — **re·sent·ful·ly** \-fə-lē\ *adv* — **re·sent·ful·ness** *n*

re·sent·ment \ri-ˈzent-mənt\ *n* (1619) : a feeling of indignant displeasure or persistent ill will at something regarded as a wrong, insult, or injury ***syn*** see OFFENSE

re·ser·pine \ri-ˈsər-ˌpēn, -pən\ *n* [G *Reserpin,* prob. irreg. fr. NL *Rauwolfia serpentina,* a species of rauwolfia] (1952) : an alkaloid $C_{33}H_{40}N_2O_9$ extracted esp. from the root of rauwolfias and used as a tranquilizer esp. in psychotic states (as schizophrenia) and as an antihypertensive

res·er·va·tion \ˌre-zər-ˈvā-shən\ *n* (15c) **1** : an act of reserving something: as **a** (1) : the act or fact of a grantor's reserving some newly created thing out of the thing granted (2) : the right or interest so reserved **b** : the setting of limiting conditions or withholding from complete exposition ⟨answered without ~⟩ **c** : an arrangement to have something (as a hotel room) held for one's use; *also* : a promise, guarantee, or record of such engagement **2 a** : a limiting condition ⟨agreed, but with ~*s*⟩ **b** : DOUBT, MISGIVING ⟨had serious ~*s* about marriage⟩ **3** : something reserved: as **a** : a tract of public land set aside (as for use by American Indians) **b** : an area in which hunting is not permitted; *esp* : one set aside as a secure breeding place — **res·er·va·tion·ist** \-sh(ə-)nist\ *n*

[1]**re·serve** \ri-ˈzərv\ *vt* **re·served; re·serv·ing** [ME, fr. AF *reserver,* fr. L *reservare,* lit., to keep back, fr. *re-* + *servare* to keep — more at CONSERVE] (14c) **1 a** : to hold in reserve : keep back ⟨~ grain for seed⟩ **b** : to set aside (part of the consecrated elements) at the Eucharist for future use **c** : to retain or hold over to a future time or place : DEFER ⟨~ one's judgment on a plan⟩ **d** : to make legal reservation of **2** : to set or have set aside or apart ⟨~ a hotel room⟩ ***syn*** see KEEP — **re·serv·able** \-ˈzər-və-bəl\ *adj*

[2]**reserve** *n, often attrib* (1648) **1** : something reserved or set aside for a particular purpose, use, or reason: as **a** (1) : a military force withheld from action for later decisive use — usu. used in pl. (2) : forces not in the field but available (3) : the military forces of a country not part of the regular services; *also* : RESERVIST **b** : a tract (as of public land) set apart : RESERVATION **2** : something stored or kept available for future use or need : STOCK **3** : an act of reserving : QUALIFICATION **4 a** : restraint, closeness, or caution in one's words and actions **b** : forbearance from making a full explanation, complete disclosure, or free expression of one's mind **5** *archaic* : SECRET **6 a** : money or its equivalent kept in hand or set apart usu. to meet liabilities **b** : the liquid resources of a nation for meeting international payments **7** : SUBSTITUTE **8** : RESERVE PRICE **9** : a wine made from select grapes, bottled on the maker's premises, and aged differently from the maker's other wines of the same vintage — **in reserve** : held back for future or special use

reserve bank *n* (1905) : a central bank holding reserves of other banks

reserve clause *n* (1890) : a clause formerly placed in a professional athlete's contract that reserved for the club the exclusive right automatically to renew the contract and that bound the athlete to the club until retirement or until the athlete was traded or released

re·served \ri-ˈzərvd\ *adj* (1601) **1** : restrained in words and actions **2** : kept or set apart or aside for future or special use ***syn*** see SILENT — **re·serv·ed·ly** \-ˈzər-vəd-lē\ *adv* — **re·serv·ed·ness** \-ˈzər-vəd-nəs\ *n*

reserved power *n* (1838) : a political power reserved by a constitution to the exclusive jurisdiction of a specified political authority

reserve price *n* (1919) : a price announced at an auction as the lowest that will be considered

re·serv·ist \ri-ˈzər-vist\ *n* (1876) : a member of a military reserve

res·er·voir \ˈre-zə-ˌvwär, -zər-, -ˌvwȯr *also* -ˌvȯi\ *n* [F *réservoir,* fr. MF, fr. *reserver*] (1690) **1** : a place where something is kept in store: as **a** : an artificial lake where water is collected and kept in quantity for use **b** : a part of an apparatus in which a liquid is held **c** : SUPPLY, STORE ⟨a large ~ of educated people⟩ **2** : an extra supply : RESERVE **3** : an organism in which a parasite that is pathogenic for some other species lives and multiplies usu. without damaging its host

re·set \(ˌ)rē-ˈset\ *vt* **-set; -set·ting** (1628) **1** : to set again or anew ⟨~ type⟩ ⟨~ a diamond⟩ ⟨~ a circuit breaker⟩ **2** : to change the reading of often to zero ⟨~ an odometer⟩ — **re·set** \ˈrē-ˌset\ *n* — **re·set·table** \-ˈse-tə-bəl\ *adj*

res ges·tae \ˈrās-ˈges-ˌtī, ˈrēz-ˈjes-(ˌ)tē\ *n pl* [L] (1616) : things done; *esp* : the facts that form the environment of a litigated issue and are admissible in evidence

resh \ˈrāsh\ *n* [Heb *rēsh*] (ca. 1823) : the 20th letter of the Hebrew alphabet — see ALPHABET table

re·shape \(ˌ)rē-ˈshāp\ *vt* (1827) : to give a new form or orientation to : REORGANIZE — **re·shap·er** *n*

re·shuf·fle \(ˌ)rē-ˈshə-fəl\ *vt* (1830) **1** : to shuffle (as cards) again **2** : to reorganize usu. by the redistribution of existing elements ⟨the cabinet was *reshuffled* by the prime minister⟩ — **reshuffle** *n*

re·sid \ri-ˈzid\ *n* (1967) : RESIDUAL OIL

re·side \ri-ˈzīd\ *vi* **re·sid·ed; re·sid·ing** [ME, fr. MF or L; MF *resider,* fr. L *residēre* to sit back, remain, abide, fr. *re-* + *sedēre* to sit — more at SIT] (15c) **1 a** : to be in residence as the incumbent of a benefice or office **b** : to dwell permanently or continuously : occupy a place as one's legal domicile **2 a** : to be present as an element or quality **b** : to be vested as a right — **re·sid·er** *n*

res·i·dence \ˈre-zə-dən(t)s, ˈrez-dən(t)s, ˈre-zə-ˌden(t)s\ *n* (14c) **1 a** : the act or fact of dwelling in a place for some time **b** : the act or fact of living or regularly staying at or in some place for the discharge of a duty or the enjoyment of a benefit **2 a (1)** : the place where one actually lives as distinguished from one's domicile or a place of temporary sojourn **(2)** : DOMICILE 2a **b** : the place where a corporation is actually or officially established **c** : the status of a legal resident **3 a** : a building used as a home : DWELLING **b** : housing or a unit of housing provided for students **4 a** : the period or duration of abode in a place **b** : a period of active and esp. full-time study, research, or teaching at a college or university — **in residence** : engaged to live and work at a particular place often for a specified time ⟨poet *in residence* at a university⟩

residence time *n* (1954) : the duration of persistence of a mass or substance in a medium or place (as the atmosphere)

res·i·den·cy \ˈre-zə-dən(t)-sē, ˈrez-dən(t)-, ˈre-zə-ˌden(t)-\ *n, pl* **-cies** (1579) **1 a** : a usu. official place of residence **b** : a state or period of residence ⟨a 20-year ∼ in the city⟩; *also* : RESIDENCE 2c **2** : a territory in a protected state in which the powers of the protecting state are executed by a resident agent **3 a** : a period of advanced training in a medical specialty that normally follows graduation from medical school and licensing to practice medicine **b** : RESIDENCE 4b **c** : a period as an artist in residence

[1]res·i·dent \ˈre-zə-dənt, ˈrez-dənt, ˈre-zə-ˌdent\ *adj* [ME, fr. AF, fr. L *resident-, residens,* prp. of *residēre*] (14c) **1 a** : living in a place for some length of time : RESIDING **b** : serving in a regular or full-time capacity ⟨the ∼ engineer for a highway department⟩; *also* : being in residence **2** : PRESENT, INHERENT **3** : not migratory ⟨∼ species⟩

[2]resident *n* (15c) **1** : one who resides in a place **2** : a diplomatic agent residing at a foreign court or seat of government; *esp* : one exercising authority in a protected state as representative of the protecting power **3** : a physician serving a residency

resident commissioner *n* (1902) **1** : a nonvoting representative of a dependency in the U.S. House of Representatives **2** : a resident administrator in a British colony or possession

res·i·den·tial \ˌre-zə-ˈden(t)-shəl, ˌrez-ˈden(t)-\ *adj* (1654) **1 a** : used as a residence or by residents **b** : providing living accommodations for students ⟨a ∼ prep school⟩ **2** : restricted to or occupied by residences ⟨a ∼ neighborhood⟩ **3** : of or relating to residence or residences **4** : provided to patients residing in a facility ⟨∼ drug treatment⟩; *also* : being a facility providing such treatment ⟨a ∼ treatment center⟩ — **res·i·den·tial·ly** \-ˈden(t)-sh(ə-)lē\ *adv*

residential college *n* (1991) : COLLEGE 3a

[1]re·sid·u·al \ri-ˈzi-jə-wəl, -jəl; -ˈzij-wəl\ *n* [L *residuum* residue] (1557) **1** : REMAINDER, RESIDUUM: as **a** : the difference between results obtained by observation and by computation from a formula or between the mean of several observations and any one of them **b** : a residual product or substance **c** : an internal aftereffect of experience or activity that influences later behavior; *esp* : a disability remaining from a disease or operation **2** : a payment (as to an actor or writer) for each rerun after an initial showing (as of a TV show)

[2]residual *adj* (1570) **1** : of, relating to, or constituting a residue **2** : leaving a residue that remains effective for some time ⟨a ∼ pesticide⟩ — **re·sid·u·al·ly** *adv*

residual oil *n* (ca. 1948) : fuel oil that remains after the removal of valuable distillates (as gasoline) from petroleum and that is used esp. by industry — called also *resid*

residual power *n* (1919) : power held to remain at the disposal of a governmental authority after an enumeration or delegation of specified powers to other authorities

re·sid·u·ary \ri-ˈzi-jə-ˌwer-ē\ *adj* (1726) : of, relating to, or constituting a residue ⟨∼ estate⟩

res·i·due \ˈre-zə-ˌdü, -ˌdyü\ *n* [ME, fr. AF, fr. L *residuum,* fr. neut. of *residuus* left over, fr. *residēre* to remain] (14c) : something that remains after a part is taken, separated, or designated or after the completion of a process : REMNANT, REMAINDER: as **a** : the part of a testator's estate remaining after the satisfaction of all debts, charges, allowances, and previous devises and bequests **b** : the remainder after subtracting a multiple of a modulus from an integer or a power of the integer that can appear as the second of the two terms in an appropriate congruence ⟨2 and 7 are ∼*s* of 12 modulo 5⟩ **c** : a constituent structural unit (as a group or monomer) of a usu. complex molecule ⟨amino acid ∼*s* from hydrolysis of protein⟩

residue class *n* (1948) : the set of elements (as integers) that leave the same remainder when divided by a given modulus

re·sid·u·um \ri-ˈzi-jə-wəm\ *n, pl* **re·sid·ua** \-wə\ [L] (1672) : something residual: as **a** : RESIDUE a **b** : a residual product (as from the distillation of petroleum)

re·sign \ri-ˈzīn\ *vb* [ME, fr. AF *resigner,* fr. L *resignare,* lit., to unseal, cancel, fr. *re-* + *signare* to sign, seal — more at SIGN] *vt* (14c) **1** : RELEGATE, CONSIGN; *esp* : to give (oneself) over without resistance ⟨∼*ed* herself to her fate⟩ **2** : to give up deliberately; *esp* : to renounce (as a right or position) by a formal act ∼ *vi* **1** : to give up one's office or position : QUIT **2** : to accept something as inevitable : SUBMIT ***syn*** see RELINQUISH, ABDICATE — **re·sign·ed·ly** \-ˈzī-nəd-lē\ *adv* — **re·sign·ed·ness** \-ˈzī-nəd-nəs\ *n* — **re·sign·er** \-ˈzī-nər\ *n*

re–sign \(ˌ)rē-ˈsīn\ *vt* (1805) : to sign again; *esp* : to rehire (as an athlete) by means of a signed contract ∼ *vi* : to sign up again

res·ig·na·tion \ˌre-zig-ˈnā-shən\ *n* (14c) **1 a** : an act or instance of resigning something : SURRENDER **b** : a formal notification of resigning **2** : the quality or state of being resigned : SUBMISSIVENESS

re·sile \ri-ˈzī(-ə)l\ *vi* **re·siled; re·sil·ing** [LL & L; LL *resilire* to withdraw, fr. L, to recoil] (1529) : RECOIL, RETRACT; *esp* : to return to a prior position ⟨∼ from an agreement⟩

re·sil·ience \ri-ˈzil-yən(t)s\ *n* (1824) **1** : the capability of a strained body to recover its size and shape after deformation caused esp. by compressive stress **2** : an ability to recover from or adjust easily to misfortune or change

re·sil·ien·cy \-yən(t)-sē\ *n* (ca. 1836) : RESILIENCE

re·sil·ient \-yənt\ *adj* [L *resilient-, resiliens,* prp. of *resilire* to jump back, recoil, fr. *re-* + *salire* to leap — more at SALLY] (1674) : characterized or marked by resilience: as **a** : capable of withstanding shock without permanent deformation or rupture **b** : tending to recover from or adjust easily to misfortune or change ***syn*** see ELASTIC — **re·sil·ient·ly** *adv*

[1]res·in \ˈre-zᵊn\ *n* [ME, fr. AF *reisine,* fr. L *resina;* akin to Gk *rhētinē* pine resin] (14c) **1 a** : any of various solid or semisolid amorphous fusible flammable natural organic substances that are usu. transparent or translucent and yellowish to brown, are formed esp. in plant secretions, are soluble in organic solvents (as ether) but not in water, are electrical nonconductors, and are used chiefly in varnishes, printing inks, plastics, and sizes and in medicine **b** : ROSIN **2 a** : any of a large class of synthetic products that have some of the physical properties of natural resins but are different chemically and are used chiefly in plastics **b** : any of various products made from a natural resin or a natural polymer — **res·in·ous** \ˈre-zᵊn-əs, ˈrez-nəs\ *adj*

[2]resin *vt* **res·ined; res·in·ing** \ˈre-zᵊn-iŋ, ˈrez-niŋ\ (1865) : to treat with resin

res·in·ate \ˈre-zᵊn-ˌāt\ *vt* **-at·ed; -at·ing** (ca. 1890) : to impregnate or flavor with resin

resin canal *n* (1884) : a tubular intercellular space in gymnosperms and some angiosperms that is lined with epithelial cells which secrete resin — called also *resin duct*

res·in·oid \ˈre-zᵊn-ˌȯid\ *n* (1880) : GUM RESIN

[1]re·sist \ri-ˈzist\ *vb* [ME, fr. AF or L; AF *resister,* fr. L *resistere,* fr. *re-* + *sistere* to take a stand; akin to L *stare* to stand — more at STAND] *vi* (14c) : to exert force in opposition ∼ *vt* **1** : to exert oneself so as to counteract or defeat ⟨he ∼*ed* temptation⟩ **2** : to withstand the force or effect of ⟨material that ∼*s* heat⟩ ***syn*** see OPPOSE

[2]resist *n, often attrib* (1836) : something (as a coating) that protects against a chemical, electrical, or physical action

[1]re·sis·tance \ri-ˈzis-tən(t)s\ *n* (14c) **1 a** : an act or instance of resisting : OPPOSITION **b** : a means of resisting **2** : the power or capacity to resist: as **a** : the inherent ability of an organism to resist harmful influences (as disease, toxic agents, or infection) **b** : the capacity of a species or strain of microorganism to survive exposure to a toxic agent (as a drug) formerly effective against it **3** : an opposing or retarding force **4 a** : the opposition offered by a body or substance to the passage through it of a steady electric current **b** : a source of resistance **5** : a psychological defense mechanism wherein a patient rejects, denies, or otherwise opposes the therapeutic efforts of a psychotherapist **6** *often cap* : an underground organization of a conquered or nearly conquered country engaging in sabotage and secret operations against occupation forces and collaborators

[2]resistance *adj* (1976) : of, relating to, or being exercise involving pushing against a source of resistance (as a weight) to increase strength ⟨∼ training⟩

[1]re·sis·tant \-tənt\ *adj* (15c) : giving, capable of, or exhibiting resistance — often used in combination ⟨wrinkle-*resistant* clothes⟩ ⟨a drug-*resistant* strain of virus⟩

[2]resistant *n* (1580) : one that resists : RESISTER

re·sist·er \ri-ˈzis-tər\ *n* (14c) : one that resists; *esp* : one who actively opposes the policies of a government

re·sist·ibil·i·ty \ri-ˌzis-tə-ˈbi-lə-tē\ *n* (1617) **1** : the quality or state of being resistible **2** : ability to resist

re·sist·ible \ri-ˈzis-tə-bəl\ *adj* (1608) : capable of being resisted

re·sis·tive \ri-ˈzis-tiv\ *adj* (1603) : marked by resistance — often used in combination ⟨fire-*resistive* material⟩ — **re·sis·tive·ly** *adv* — **re·sis·tive·ness** *n*

re·sis·tiv·i·ty \ri-ˌzis-ˈti-və-tē, ˌrē-\ *n, pl* **-ties** (1885) **1** : the longitudinal electrical resistance of a uniform rod of unit length and unit cross-sectional area : the reciprocal of conductivity **2** : capacity for resisting : RESISTANCE

re·sist·less \ri-ˈzist-ləs\ *adj* (1586) **1** : too strong to be resisted ⟨a ∼ power⟩ **2** : offering no resistance ⟨∼ prey⟩ — **re·sist·less·ly** *adv* — **re·sist·less·ness** *n*

re·sis·tor \ri-ˈzis-tər\ *n* (1905) : a device that has electrical resistance and that is used in an electric circuit for protection, operation, or current control

re·sit·ting \(ˌ)rē-ˈsi-tiŋ\ *n* (1661) : a sitting (as of a legislature) for a second time : another sitting

res ju·di·ca·ta \ˈrēz-ˌjü-di-ˈkä-tə\ *n* [L, judged matter] (1693) : a matter finally decided on its merits by a court having competent jurisdiction and not subject to litigation again between the same parties

res·meth·rin \(ˌ)rez-ˈmeth-rin, -ˈmēth-\ *n* [*res-* (prob. transposed fr. *ester*) + *-methrin,* blend of *methyl* and *-ethrin* (as in *pyrethrin*)] (1971) : a nonpersistent synthetic insecticide $C_{22}H_{26}O_3$ that is a derivative of pyrethrin and is used in aerosols

re·sol·u·ble \ri-ˈzäl-yə-bəl\ *adj* [LL *resolubilis,* fr. L *resolvere* to resolve, unloose] (1602) : capable of being resolved ⟨a difficult but ∼ problem⟩

[1]res·o·lute \ˈre-zə-ˌlüt, -lət\ *adj* [L *resolutus,* pp. of *resolvere*] (1533) **1** : marked by firm determination : RESOLVED ⟨a ∼ character⟩ **2** : BOLD, STEADY ⟨a ∼ gaze⟩ ***syn*** see FAITHFUL — **res·o·lute·ly** \-ˌlüt-lē, -lət-; ˌre-zə-ˈlüt-\ *adv* — **res·o·lute·ness** \-ˌlüt-nəs, -lət-, -ˈlüt-\ *n*

[2]resolute *n* (1602) : a resolute person

res·o·lu·tion \ˌre-zə-ˈlü-shən\ *n* [ME *resolucioun,* fr. AF or L; AF *resolucion,* fr. L *resolution-, resolutio,* fr. *resolvere*] (14c) **1** : the act or process of resolving: as **a** : the act of analyzing a complex notion into simpler ones **b** : the act of answering : SOLVING **c** : the act of determining **d** : the passing of a voice part from a dissonant to a consonant tone or the progression of a chord from dissonance to consonance **e** : the separating of a chemical compound or mixture into its constituents **f** (1) : the division of a prosodic element into its component parts (2) : the substitution in Greek or Latin prosody of two short syllables for a long syllable **g** : the analysis of a vector into two or more vectors of which it is the sum **2** : the subsidence of a pathological state (as inflammation) **3 a** : something that is resolved ⟨made a ~ to mend my ways⟩ **b** : firmness of resolve **4** : a formal expression of opinion, will, or intent voted by an official body or assembled group **5** : the point in a literary work at which the chief dramatic complication is worked out **6 a** : the process or capability of making distinguishable the individual parts of an object, closely adjacent optical images, or sources of light **b** : a measure of the sharpness of an image or of the fineness with which a device (as a video display, printer, or scanner) can produce or record such an image usu. expressed as the total number or density of pixels in the image ⟨a ~ of 1200 dots per inch⟩ ***syn*** see COURAGE

[1]**re·solve** \ri-ˈzälv, -ˈzȯlv *also* -ˈzäv *or* -ˈzȯv\ *vb* **re·solved; re·solv·ing** [ME, fr. L *resolvere* to unloose, dissolve, fr. *re-* + *solvere* to loosen, release — more at SOLVE] *vt* (14c) **1** *obs* : DISSOLVE, MELT **2 a** : BREAK UP, SEPARATE ⟨the prism *resolved* the light into a play of color⟩; *also* : to change by disintegration **b** : to reduce by analysis ⟨~ the problem into simple elements⟩ **c** : to distinguish between or make independently visible adjacent parts of **d** : to separate (a racemic compound or mixture) into the two components **3** : to cause resolution of (a pathological state) **4 a** : to deal with successfully : clear up ⟨~ doubts⟩ ⟨~ a dispute⟩ **b** : to find an answer to **c** : to make clear or understandable **d** : to find a mathematical solution of **e** : to split up (as a vector) into two or more components esp. in assigned directions **5** : to reach a firm decision about ⟨~ to get more sleep⟩ ⟨~ disputed points in a text⟩ **6 a** : to declare or decide by a formal resolution and vote **b** : to change by resolution or formal vote ⟨the house *resolved* itself into a committee⟩ **7** : to make (as voice parts) progress from dissonance to consonance **8** : to work out the resolution of (as a play) ~ *vi* **1** : to become separated into component parts; *also* : to become reduced by dissolving or analysis **2** : to form a resolution : DETERMINE **3** : CONSULT, DELIBERATE **4** : to progress from dissonance to consonance ***syn*** see DECIDE — **re·solv·able** \-ˈzäl-və-bəl, -ˈzȯl- *also* -ˈzä-və- *or* -ˈzȯ-və-\ *adj* — **re·solv·er** *n*

[2]**resolve** *n* (1591) **1** : fixity of purpose : RESOLUTENESS **2** : something that is resolved **3** : a legal or official determination; *esp* : a formal resolution

re·sol·vent \ri-ˈzäl-vənt, -ˈzȯl-\ *n* (1845) : a means of solving something (as an equation) — **resolvent** *adj*

resolving power *n* (1879) **1** : the ability of an optical system to form distinguishable images of objects separated by small angular distances **2** : the ability of a photographic film or plate to reproduce the fine detail of an optical image

res·o·nance \ˈre-zə-nən(t)s, ˈrez-nən(t)s\ *n* [ME *resonaunce,* fr. MF *resonance,* fr. *resoner* to resound — more at RESOUND] (15c) **1 a** : the quality or state of being resonant **b** (1) : a vibration of large amplitude in a mechanical or electrical system caused by a relatively small periodic stimulus of the same or nearly the same period as the natural vibration period of the system (2) : the state of adjustment that produces resonance in a mechanical or electrical system **2 a** : the intensification and enriching of a musical tone by supplementary vibration **b** : a quality imparted to voiced sounds by vibration in anatomical resonating chambers or cavities (as the mouth or the nasal cavity) **c** : a quality of richness or variety **d** : a quality of evoking response ⟨how much ~ the scandal seems to be having —*U.S. News & World Report*⟩ **3** : the sound elicited on percussion of the chest **4** : the conceptual alternation of a chemical species (as a molecule or ion) between two or more equivalent allowed structural representations differing only in the placement of electrons that aids in understanding the actual state of the species as an amalgamation of its possible structures and the usu. higher-than-expected stability of the species **5 a** : the enhancement of an atomic, nuclear, or particle reaction or a scattering event by excitation of internal motion in the system **b** : MAGNETIC RESONANCE **6** : an extremely short-lived elementary particle **7** : a synchronous gravitational relationship of two celestial bodies (as moons) that orbit a third (as a planet) which can be expressed as a simple ratio of their orbital periods

res·o·nant \ˈre-zə-nənt, ˈrez-nənt\ *adj* (1592) **1** : continuing to sound : ECHOING **2 a** : capable of inducing resonance **b** : relating to or exhibiting resonance **3 a** : intensified and enriched by or as if by resonance ⟨a ~ voice⟩ **b** : marked by grandiloquence — **resonant** *n* — **res·o·nant·ly** *adv*

res·o·nate \ˈre-zə-ˌnāt\ *vb* **-nat·ed; -nat·ing** *vi* (1873) **1** : to produce or exhibit resonance **2** : to respond as if by resonance ⟨~ to the music⟩; *also* : to have a repetitive pattern that resembles resonance **3** : to relate harmoniously : strike a chord ⟨a message that ~*s* with voters⟩ ~ *vt* : to subject to resonating

res·o·na·tor \-ˌnā-tər\ *n* (ca. 1869) : something that resounds or resonates: as **a** : a hollow metallic container for producing microwaves or a piezoelectric crystal put into oscillation by the oscillations of an outside source **b** : a device for increasing the resonance of a musical instrument

re·sorb \(ˌ)rē-ˈsȯrb, -ˈzȯrb\ *vb* [L *resorbēre,* fr. *re-* + *sorbēre* to suck up — more at ABSORB] *vt* (1640) **1** : to swallow or suck in again **2** : to break down and assimilate the components of (as bone) ~ *vi* : to undergo resorption

res·or·cin \rə-ˈzȯr-sᵊn\ *n* [ISV *res-* (fr. L *resina* resin) + *orcin,* a phenol ($C_7H_8O_2$)] (ca. 1868) : RESORCINOL

res·or·cin·ol \rə-ˈzȯr-sə-ˌnȯl, -ˌnōl\ *n* (1880) : a crystalline phenol $C_6H_6O_2$ obtained from various resins or artificially and used esp. in making dyes, pharmaceuticals, and resins

re·sorp·tion \(ˌ)rē-ˈsȯrp-shən, -ˈzȯrp-\ *n* [L *resorbēre*] (ca. 1820) : the action or process of resorbing something — **re·sorp·tive** \-tiv\ *adj*

[1]**re·sort** \ri-ˈzȯrt\ *n* [ME, return, source of aid, fr. AF, fr. *resortir* to rebound, resort, fr. *re-* + OF *sortir* to go out, leave] (14c) **1 a** : one that affords aid or refuge : RESOURCE ⟨went to them as a last ~⟩ **b** : RECOURSE 1a ⟨have ~ to outside help⟩ **2 a** : frequent, habitual, or general visiting ⟨a place of popular ~⟩ **b** : persons who frequent a place : THRONG **c** (1) : a frequently visited place : HAUNT (2) : a place providing recreation and entertainment esp. to vacationers ***syn*** see RESOURCE

[2]**resort** *vi* (15c) **1** : to go esp. frequently or habitually : REPAIR **2** : to have recourse ⟨~ to force⟩

re–sort \(ˌ)rē-ˈsȯrt\ *vt* (1889) : to sort again

re·sort·er \ri-ˈzȯr-tər\ *n* (1917) : a frequenter of resorts

re·sound \ri-ˈzau̇nd *also* -ˈsau̇nd\ *vb* [ME *resounen,* fr. MF *resoner,* fr. L *resonare,* fr. *re-* + *sonare* to sound — more at SOUND] *vi* (14c) **1** : to become filled with sound : REVERBERATE **2 a** : to sound loudly ⟨the gunshot ~*ed*⟩ **b** : to produce a sonorous or echoing sound **3** : to become renowned ~ *vt* **1** : to extol loudly or widely : CELEBRATE **2** : ECHO, REVERBERATE **3** : to sound or utter in full resonant tones

re·sound·ing \-ˈzau̇n-diŋ *also* -ˈsau̇n-\ *adj* (15c) **1** : producing or characterized by resonant sound : RESONATING **2 a** : impressively sonorous **b** : EMPHATIC, UNEQUIVOCAL ⟨a ~ success⟩ — **re·sound·ing·ly** *adv*

re·source \ˈrē-ˌsȯrs, -ˌzȯrs, ri-ˈ\ *n* [F *ressource,* fr. OF *ressourse* relief, resource, fr. *resourdre* to relieve, lit., to rise again, fr. L *resurgere* — more at RESURRECTION] (ca. 1611) **1 a** : a source of supply or support : an available means — usu. used in pl. **b** : a natural source of wealth or revenue — often used in pl. **c** : a natural feature or phenomenon that enhances the quality of human life **d** : computable wealth — usu. used in pl. **e** : a source of information or expertise **2** : something to which one has recourse in difficulty : EXPEDIENT **3** : a possibility of relief or recovery **4** : a means of spending one's leisure time **5** : an ability to meet and handle a situation : RESOURCEFULNESS

syn RESOURCE, RESORT, EXPEDIENT, SHIFT, MAKESHIFT, STOPGAP mean something one turns to in the absence of the usual means or source of supply. RESOURCE and RESORT apply to anything one falls back upon ⟨exhausted all of their *resources*⟩ ⟨a last *resort*⟩. EXPEDIENT may apply to any device or contrivance used when the usual one is not at hand or not possible ⟨a flimsy *expedient*⟩. SHIFT implies a tentative or temporary imperfect expedient ⟨desperate *shifts* to stave off foreclosure⟩. MAKESHIFT implies an inferior expedient adopted because of urgent need or allowed through indifference ⟨old equipment employed as a *makeshift*⟩. STOPGAP applies to something used temporarily as an emergency measure ⟨a new law intended only as a *stopgap*⟩.

re·source·ful \ri-ˈsȯrs-fəl, -ˈzȯrs-\ *adj* (1851) : able to meet situations : capable of devising ways and means ⟨a ~ leader⟩ — **re·source·ful·ly** \-fə-lē\ *adv* — **re·source·ful·ness** *n*

[1]**re·spect** \ri-ˈspekt\ *n* [ME, fr. L *respectus,* lit., act of looking back, fr. *respicere* to look back, regard, fr. *re-* + *specere* to look — more at SPY] (14c) **1** : a relation or reference to a particular thing or situation ⟨remarks having ~ to an earlier plan⟩ **2** : an act of giving particular attention : CONSIDERATION **3 a** : high or special regard : ESTEEM **b** : the quality or state of being esteemed **c** *pl* : expressions of respect or deference ⟨paid our ~*s*⟩ **4** : PARTICULAR, DETAIL ⟨a good plan in some ~*s*⟩ — **in respect of** *chiefly Brit* : with respect to : CONCERNING — **in respect to** : with respect to : CONCERNING — **with respect to** : with reference to : in relation to

[2]**respect** *vt* (1560) **1 a** : to consider worthy of high regard : ESTEEM **b** : to refrain from interfering with ⟨please ~ their privacy⟩ **2** : to have reference to : CONCERN ***syn*** see REGARD — **re·spect·er** *n*

[1]**re·spect·able** \ri-ˈspek-tə-bəl\ *adj* (1599) **1** : worthy of respect : ESTIMABLE **2** : decent or correct in character or behavior : PROPER **3 a** : fair in size or quantity ⟨a ~ amount⟩ **b** : moderately good : TOLERABLE **4** : fit to be seen : PRESENTABLE ⟨~ clothes⟩ — **re·spect·abil·i·ty** \-ˌspek-tə-ˈbi-lə-tē\ *n* — **re·spect·able·ness** \-ˈspek-tə-bəl-nəs\ *n* — **re·spect·ably** \-blē\ *adv*

[2]**respectable** *n* (1814) : a respectable person

re·spect·ful \ri-ˈspekt-fəl\ *adj* (1687) : marked by or showing respect or deference — **re·spect·ful·ly** \-fə-lē\ *adv* — **re·spect·ful·ness** *n*

re·spect·ing *prep* (ca. 1611) **1** : in view of : CONSIDERING **2** : with respect to : CONCERNING

re·spec·tive \ri-ˈspek-tiv\ *adj* (ca. 1595) **1** *obs* : PARTIAL, DISCRIMINATIVE **2** : PARTICULAR, SEPARATE ⟨their ~ homes⟩ — **re·spec·tive·ness** *n*

re·spec·tive·ly *adv* (1602) **1** : in particular : SEPARATELY ⟨could not recognize the solutions as salty or sour, ~⟩ **2** : in the order given ⟨Mary and Anne were ~ 12 and 16 years old⟩

re·spell \(ˌ)rē-ˈspel\ *vt* (1806) : to spell again or in another way; *esp* : to spell out according to a phonetic system — **re·spell·ing** \-ˈspe-liŋ\ *n*

re·spi·ra·ble \ˈres-p(ə-)rə-bəl, ri-ˈspī-rə-\ *adj* (1779) : fit for breathing; *also* : capable of being taken in by breathing ⟨~ particles of ash⟩

res·pi·ra·tion \ˌres-pə-ˈrā-shən\ *n* [ME *respiracioun,* fr. L *respiration-, respiratio,* fr. *respirare*] (15c) **1 a** : the placing of air or dissolved gases in intimate contact with the circulating medium of a multicellular organism (as by breathing) **b** : a single complete act of breathing **2** : the physical and chemical processes by which an organism supplies its cells and tissues with the oxygen needed for metabolism and relieves them of the carbon dioxide formed in energy-producing reactions **3** : any of various energy-yielding oxidative reactions in living matter — **re·spi·ra·to·ry** \ˈres-p(ə-)rə-ˌtȯr-ē, ri-ˈspī-rə-\ *adj*

res·pi·ra·tor \ˈres-pə-ˌrā-tər\ *n* (1836) **1** : a device worn over the mouth and nose to protect the respiratory tract by filtering out dangerous substances (as dusts or fumes) from inhaled air **2** : a device for maintaining artificial respiration

respiratory distress syndrome *n* (1964) : a respiratory disorder chiefly of newborn premature infants that is characterized by deficiency of the surfactant coating the inner surface of the lungs resulting in labored breathing, lung collapse, and hypoxemia

respiratory pigment *n* (1888) : any of various permanently or intermittently colored conjugated proteins and esp. hemoglobin that function in the transfer of oxygen in cellular respiration

---

\ə\ **abut** \ᵊ\ **k**itten, F table \ər\ **fur**ther \a\ **a**sh \ā\ **a**ce \ä\ **m**op, m**a**r \au̇\ **ou**t \ch\ **ch**in \e\ **b**et \ē\ **ea**sy \g\ **g**o \i\ **h**it \ī\ **i**ce \j\ **j**ob \ŋ\ si**ng** \ō\ g**o** \ȯ\ l**aw** \ȯi\ b**oy** \th\ **th**in \t͟h\ **th**e \ü\ l**oo**t \u̇\ f**oo**t \y\ **y**et \zh\ vi**si**on, beige \k, n, œ, ue, y\ *see* Guide to Pronunciation

respiratory quotient *n* (ca. 1890) **:** a ratio indicating the relation of the volume of carbon dioxide given off in respiration to that of the oxygen consumed
respiratory syncytial virus *n* (1961) **:** a paramyxovirus (species *Human respiratory syncytial virus* of the genus *Pneumovirus*) that is responsible for severe respiratory diseases (as bronchopneumonia and bronchiolitis) in children and esp. in infants — abbr. *RSV*
respiratory system *n* (1888) **:** a system of organs functioning in respiration and in humans consisting esp. of the nose, nasal passages, pharynx, larynx, trachea, bronchi, and lungs

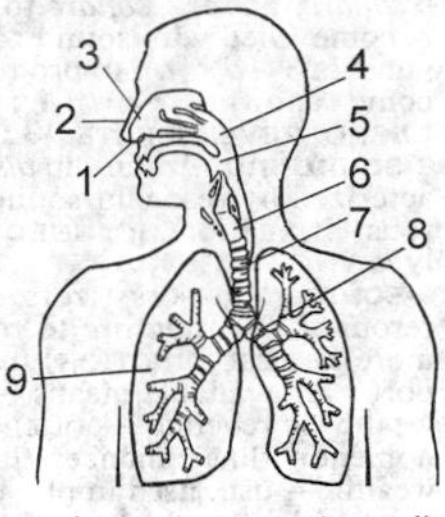

respiratory system: *1* nostril, *2* nose, *3* nasal cavity, *4* nasopharynx, *5* oropharynx, *6* larynx, *7* trachea, *8* bronchus, *9* lung

re·spire \ri-ˈspī(-ə)r\ *vb* **re·spired; re·spir·ing** [ME, fr. L *respirare,* fr. *re-* + *spirare* to blow, breathe] *vi* (15c) **1 :** BREATHE; *specif* **:** to inhale and exhale air successively **2** *of a cell or tissue* **:** to take up oxygen and produce carbon dioxide through oxidation ~ *vt* **:** BREATHE
res·pi·rom·e·ter \ˌres-pə-ˈrä-mə-tər\ *n* (ca. 1883) **:** an instrument for studying the character and extent of respiration — **res·pi·ro·met·ric** \-rō-ˈme-trik\ *adj* — **res·pi·rom·e·try** \-ˈrä-mə-trē\ *n*
[1]**re·spite** \ˈres-pət *also* ri-ˈspīt, *Brit usu* ˈres-ˌpīt\ *n* [ME *respit,* fr. AF, fr. ML *respectus,* fr. L, act of looking back — more at RESPECT] (13c) **1 :** a period of temporary delay **2 :** an interval of rest or relief
[2]**respite** *vt* **re·spit·ed; re·spit·ing** (14c) **1 :** to grant a respite to **2 :** PUT OFF, DELAY
[3]**respite** *adj* (1978) **:** providing or being temporary care in relief of a primary caregiver ⟨~ care⟩ ⟨a ~ worker⟩
re·splen·dence \ri-ˈsplen-dən(t)s\ *n* (15c) **:** the quality or state of being resplendent **:** SPLENDOR
re·splen·den·cy \-dən(t)-sē\ *n* (ca. 1611) **:** RESPLENDENCE
re·splen·dent \-dənt\ *adj* [ME, fr. L *resplendent-, resplendens,* prp. of *resplendēre* to shine back, fr. *re-* + *splendēre* to shine — more at SPLENDID] (15c) **:** shining brilliantly **:** characterized by a glowing splendor ⟨meadows ~ with wildflowers —*Outdoor World*⟩ ***syn*** see SPLENDID — **re·splen·dent·ly** *adv*
[1]**re·spond** \ri-ˈspänd\ *n* [ME *respounde,* lit., reply, fr. AF *respuns, respunt* response] (15c) **:** an engaged pillar supporting an arch or closing a colonnade or arcade
[2]**respond** *vb* [alter. of ME *respounden,* fr. AF *respundre,* fr. L *respondēre* to promise in return, answer, fr. *re-* + *spondēre* to promise — more at SPOUSE] *vi* (1572) **1 :** to say something in return **:** make an answer ⟨~ to criticism⟩ **2 a :** to react in response ⟨~*ed* to a call for help⟩ **b :** to show favorable reaction ⟨~ to surgery⟩ **3 :** to be answerable ⟨~ in damages⟩ ~ *vt* **:** REPLY — **re·spond·er** \-ˈspän-dər\ *n*
[1]**re·spon·dent** \ri-ˈspän-dənt\ *n* [L *respondent-, respondens,* prp. of *respondēre*] (1528) **1 :** one who responds: as **a :** one who maintains a thesis in reply **b** (1) **:** one who answers in various legal proceedings (as in equity cases) (2) **:** the prevailing party in the lower court **c :** a person who responds to a poll **2 :** a reflex that occurs in response to a specific external stimulus — compare OPERANT
[2]**respondent** *adj* (1726) **1 :** making response **:** RESPONSIVE; *esp* **:** being a respondent at law **2 :** relating to or being behavior or responses to a stimulus that are followed by a reward ⟨~ conditioning⟩ — compare OPERANT 3
re·sponse \ri-ˈspän(t)s\ *n* [ME & L; ME *respounce,* fr. AF *respuns, respounce,* fr. L *responsum* reply, fr. neut. of *responsus,* pp. of *respondēre*] (14c) **1 :** an act of responding **2 :** something constituting a reply or a reaction: as **a :** a verse, phrase, or word sung or said by the people or choir after or in reply to the officiant in a liturgical service **b :** the activity or inhibition of previous activity of an organism or any of its parts resulting from stimulation **c :** the output of a transducer or detecting device resulting from a given input ***syn*** see ANSWER
re·spon·si·bil·i·ty \ri-ˌspän(t)-sə-ˈbi-lə-tē\ *n, pl* **-ties** (1737) **1 :** the quality or state of being responsible: as **a :** moral, legal, or mental accountability ⟨take ~ for your actions⟩ **b :** RELIABILITY, TRUSTWORTHINESS **2 :** something for which one is responsible **:** BURDEN ⟨has neglected his *responsibilities*⟩
re·spon·si·ble \ri-ˈspän(t)-sə-bəl\ *adj* [AF *responsable,* fr. *respuns*] (1643) **1 a :** liable to be called on to answer **b** (1) **:** liable to be called to account as the primary cause, motive, or agent ⟨a committee ~ for the job⟩ (2) **:** being the cause or explanation ⟨mechanical defects were ~ for the accident⟩ **c :** liable to legal review or in case of fault to penalties **2 a :** able to answer for one's conduct and obligations **:** TRUSTWORTHY **b :** able to choose for oneself between right and wrong **3 :** marked by or involving responsibility or accountability ⟨~ financial policies⟩ **4 :** politically answerable; *esp* **:** required to submit to the electorate if defeated by the legislature — used esp. of the British cabinet — **re·spon·si·ble·ness** *n* — **re·spon·si·bly** \-blē\ *adv*
syn RESPONSIBLE, ANSWERABLE, ACCOUNTABLE, AMENABLE, LIABLE mean subject to being held to account. RESPONSIBLE implies holding a specific office, duty, or trust ⟨the bureau *responsible* for revenue collection⟩. ANSWERABLE suggests a relation between one having a moral or legal obligation and a court or other authority charged with oversight of its observance ⟨an intelligence agency *answerable* to Congress⟩. ACCOUNTABLE suggests imminence of retribution for unfulfilled trust or violated obligation ⟨elected officials are *accountable* to the voters⟩. AMENABLE and LIABLE stress the fact of subjection to review, censure, or control by a designated authority under certain conditions ⟨laws are *amenable* to judicial review⟩ ⟨not *liable* for the debts of the former spouse⟩.
re·spon·sions \ri-ˈspän(t)-shənz\ *n pl* [ME *responcioun* response, sum to be paid, fr. AF or ML; AF *responsion,* fr. ML *responsion-, responsio,* fr. L, answer, fr. *respondēre*] (1813) **:** an examination formerly required for matriculation as an undergraduate at Oxford
re·spon·sive \ri-ˈspän(t)-siv\ *adj* (15c) **1 :** giving response **:** constituting a response **:** ANSWERING ⟨a ~ glance⟩ ⟨~ aggression⟩ **2 :** quick to respond or react appropriately or sympathetically **:** SENSITIVE **3 :** using responses ⟨a ~ liturgy⟩ — **re·spon·sive·ly** *adv* — **re·spon·sive·ness** *n*
re·spon·so·ry \-ˈspän(t)s-(ə-)rē\ *n, pl* **-ries** [ME, fr. ML *responsorium,* fr. L *respondēre*] (15c) **:** a set of versicles and responses sung or said after or during a lection
re·spon·sum \ri-ˈspän(t)-səm\ *n, pl* **-sa** \-sə\ [NL, fr. L, reply, response] (1896) **:** a written decision from a rabbinic authority in response to a submitted question or problem
res pu·bli·ca \ˈräs-ˈpü-bli-ˌkä\ *n* [L — more at REPUBLIC] (ca. 1898) **1 :** COMMONWEALTH, STATE, REPUBLIC **2 :** COMMONWEAL
res·sen·ti·ment \rə-ˌsäⁿ-tē-ˈmäⁿ\ *n* [F, resentment, fr. *ressentir* to resent, fr. MF *resentir* — more at RESENT] (1941) **:** deep-seated resentment, frustration, and hostility accompanied by a sense of being powerless to express these feelings directly
[1]**rest** \ˈrest\ *n* [ME, fr. OE; akin to OHG *rasta* rest and perh. to OHG *ruowa* calm] (bef. 12c) **1 :** REPOSE, SLEEP; *specif* **:** a bodily state characterized by minimal functional and metabolic activities **2 a :** freedom from activity or labor **b :** a state of motionlessness or inactivity **c :** the repose of death **3 :** a place for resting or lodging **4 :** peace of mind or spirit **5 a** (1) **:** a rhythmic silence in music (2) **:** a character representing such a silence **b :** a brief pause in reading **6 :** something used for support — **at rest 1 :** resting or reposing esp. in sleep or death **2 :** QUIESCENT, MOTIONLESS **3 :** free of anxieties
[2]**rest** *vi* (bef. 12c) **1 a :** to get rest by lying down; *esp* **:** SLEEP **b :** to lie dead **2 :** to cease from action or motion **:** refrain from labor or exertion **3 :** to be free from anxiety or disturbance **4 :** to sit or lie fixed or supported ⟨a column ~*s* on its pedestal⟩ **5 a :** to remain confident **:** TRUST ⟨cannot ~ on that assumption⟩ **b :** to be based or founded ⟨the verdict ~*ed* on several sound precedents⟩ **6 :** to remain for action or accomplishment ⟨the answer ~*s* with you⟩ **7** *of farmland* **:** to remain idle or uncropped **8 :** to bring to an end voluntarily the introduction of evidence in a law case ~ *vt* **1 :** to give rest to **2 :** to set at rest **3 :** to place on or against a support **4 :** to cause to be firmly fixed ⟨~*ed* all hope in his child⟩ **5 :** to desist voluntarily from presenting evidence pertinent to (a case at law) — **rest·er** *n*
[3]**rest** *n* [ME *reste,* lit., stoppage, short for *areste,* fr. AF *arest,* fr. *arester* to arrest] (14c) **:** a projection or attachment on the side of the breastplate of medieval armor for supporting the butt of a lance
[4]**rest** *n* [ME, fr. AF *reste,* fr. *rester* to remain, fr. L *restare,* fr. *re-* + *stare* to stand — more at STAND] (15c) **:** something that remains over **:** REMAINDER ⟨ate the ~ of the candy⟩ — **for the rest :** with regard to remaining issues or needs
rest area *n* (1971) **:** an area adjacent to a highway at which restrooms and refreshments are usu. available
re·start \(ˌ)rē-ˈstärt\ *vt* (1749) **1 :** to start anew **2 :** to resume (as an activity) after interruption ~ *vi* **:** to resume operation — **re·start** \ˈrē-ˌstärt, (ˌ)re-ˈ\ *n* — **re·start·able** \-ˈstär-tə-bəl\ *adj*
re·state \(ˌ)rē-ˈstāt\ *vt* (ca. 1713) **:** to state again or in another way
re·state·ment \-mənt\ *n* (1803) **1 :** something that is restated **2 :** the act of restating
res·tau·rant \ˈres-tə-ˌränt, -tränt *also* -t(ə-)rənt, -tərnt\ *n* [F, fr. prp. of *restaurer* to restore, fr. L *restaurare*] (1819) **:** a business establishment where meals or refreshments may be purchased
res·tau·ra·teur \ˌres-tə-rə-ˈtər\ *also* **res·tau·ran·teur** \-ˌrän-\ *n* [F *restaurateur,* fr. LL *restaurator* restorer, fr. L *restaurare*] (1796) **:** the operator or proprietor of a restaurant
rest·ed \ˈres-təd\ *adj* (15c) **:** having had sufficient rest or sleep
re·ste·no·sis \ˌres-tə-ˈnō-səs, ˌrē-stə-\ *n* [NL] (1954) **:** the reoccurrence of stenosis in a blood vessel or heart valve after it has been treated with apparent success
rest·ful \ˈrest-fəl\ *adj* (14c) **1 :** marked by, affording, or suggesting rest and repose ⟨a ~ color scheme⟩ **2 :** being at rest **:** QUIET ***syn*** see COMFORTABLE — **rest·ful·ly** \-fə-lē\ *adv* — **rest·ful·ness** *n*
rest home *n* (1925) **:** an establishment that provides housing and general care for the aged or the convalescent
rest house *n* (1807) **:** a building used for shelter by travelers
rest·ing \ˈres-tiŋ\ *adj* (14c) **1 :** being or characterized by dormancy **:** QUIESCENT ⟨a ~ spore⟩ ⟨bulbs in the ~ state⟩ **2 :** not undergoing or marked by division **:** VEGETATIVE ⟨a ~ nucleus⟩
res·ti·tute \ˈres-tə-ˌtüt, -ˌtyüt\ *vb* **-tut·ed; -tut·ing** [L *restitutus,* pp. of *restituere*] *vt* (ca. 1500) **1 :** to restore to a former state or position **2 :** GIVE BACK; *esp* **:** REFUND ~ *vi* **:** to undergo restitution
res·ti·tu·tion \ˌres-tə-ˈtü-shən, -ˈtyü-\ *n* [ME *restitucioun,* fr. AF, fr. L *restitution-, restitutio,* fr. *restituere* to restore, fr. *re-* + *statuere* to set up — more at STATUTE] (14c) **1 :** an act of restoring or a condition of being restored: as **a :** a restoration of something to its rightful owner **b :** a making good of or giving an equivalent for some injury **2 :** a legal action serving to cause restoration of a previous state
res·tive \ˈres-tiv\ *adj* [ME *restyf,* fr. AF *restif,* fr. *rester* to stop, resist, remain] (15c) **1 :** stubbornly resisting control **:** BALKY **2 :** marked by impatience or uneasiness **:** FIDGETY ***syn*** see CONTRARY — **res·tive·ly** *adv* — **res·tive·ness** *n*
rest·less \ˈrest-ləs\ *adj* (bef. 12c) **1 :** lacking or denying rest **:** UNEASY ⟨a ~ night⟩ **2 :** continuously moving **:** UNQUIET ⟨the ~ sea⟩ **3 :** characterized by or manifesting unrest esp. of mind ⟨~ pacing⟩; *also* **:** CHANGEFUL, DISCONTENTED — **rest·less·ly** *adv* — **rest·less·ness** *n*
restless legs syndrome *n* (1976) **:** a nervous disorder characterized by aching, crawling, or creeping sensations of the legs that occur esp. at night usu. when lying down (as before sleep) and cause a compelling urge to move the legs — called also *restless legs, restless leg syndrome*
rest mass *n* (1914) **:** the mass of a body exclusive of additional mass the body acquires by its motion according to the theory of relativity
re·stor·able \ri-ˈstȯr-ə-bəl\ *adj* (ca. 1611) **:** fit for restoring or reclaiming
re·stor·al \-əl\ *n* (ca. 1611) **:** RESTORATION
res·to·ra·tion \ˌres-tə-ˈrā-shən\ *n* (14c) **1 :** an act of restoring or the condition of being restored: as **a :** a bringing back to a former position or condition **:** REINSTATEMENT ⟨the ~ of peace⟩ **b :** RESTITUTION **c :** a restoring to an unimpaired or improved condition ⟨the ~ of a painting⟩ **d :** the replacing of missing teeth or crowns **2 :** something that is restored; *esp* **:** a representation or reconstruction of the original form (as of a fossil or a building) **3** *cap* **a :** the reestablishing

of the monarchy in England in 1660 under Charles II **b** : the period in English history usu. held to coincide with the reign of Charles II but sometimes to extend through the reign of James II

1**re·stor·ative** \ri-ˈstȯr-ə-tiv\ *adj* (14c) : of or relating to restoration; *esp* : having power to restore ⟨~ sleep⟩

2**restorative** *n* (15c) : something that serves to restore to consciousness, vigor, or health

re·store \ri-ˈstȯr\ *vt* **re·stored; re·stor·ing** [ME, fr. AF *restorer,* fr. L *restaurare* to renew, rebuild, alter. of *instaurare* to renew] (14c) **1** : GIVE BACK, RETURN **2** : to put or bring back into existence or use **3** : to bring back to or put back into a former or original state : RENEW **4** : to put again in possession of something ***syn*** see RENEW — **re·stor·er** *n*

re·strain \ri-ˈstrān\ *vt* [ME *restraynen,* fr. AF *restreindre,* fr. L *restringere* to restrain, restrict, fr. *re-* + *stringere* to bind tight — more at STRAIN] (14c) **1 a** : to prevent from doing, exhibiting, or expressing something ⟨~*ed* the child from jumping⟩ **b** : to limit, restrict, or keep under control ⟨try to ~ your anger⟩ **2** : to moderate or limit the force, effect, development, or full exercise of ⟨~ trade⟩ **3** : to deprive of liberty; *esp* : to place under arrest or restraint — **re·strain·able** \-ˈstrā-nə-bəl\ *adj* — **re·strain·er** *n*

syn RESTRAIN, CHECK, CURB, BRIDLE mean to hold back from or control in doing something. RESTRAIN suggests holding back by force or persuasion from acting or from going to extremes ⟨*restrained* themselves from laughing⟩. CHECK implies restraining or impeding a progress, activity, or impetus ⟨trying to *check* government spending⟩. CURB suggests an abrupt or drastic checking ⟨learn to *curb* your appetite⟩. BRIDLE implies keeping under control by subduing or holding in ⟨*bridle* an impulse to throw the book down⟩.

re·strained \ri-ˈstrānd\ *adj* (14c) : marked by restraint : not excessive or extravagant — **re·strain·ed·ly** \-ˈstrā-nəd-lē\ *adv*

restraining order *n* (1781) **1** : a preliminary legal order sometimes issued to keep a situation unchanged pending decision upon an application for an injunction **2** : a legal order issued against an individual to restrict or prohibit access or proximity to another specified individual

re·straint \ri-ˈstrānt\ *n* [ME, fr. AF *restreinte,* fr. *restreindre*] (15c) **1 a** : an act of restraining : the state of being restrained **b** (1) : a means of restraining : a restraining force or influence (2) : a device that restricts movement ⟨a ~ for children riding in cars⟩ **2** : a control over the expression of one's emotions or thoughts

re·strict \ri-ˈstrikt\ *vt* [L *restrictus,* pp. of *restringere*] (1535) **1** : to confine within bounds : RESTRAIN **2** : to place under restrictions as to use or distribution ***syn*** see LIMIT

re·strict·ed \ri-ˈstrik-təd\ *adj* (1585) : subject or subjected to restriction: as **a** : not general : LIMITED ⟨the decision had a ~ effect⟩ **b** : available to the use of particular groups or specif. excluding others ⟨a ~ country club⟩ **c** : not intended for general circulation or release ⟨a ~ document⟩ — **re·strict·ed·ly** *adv*

re·stric·tion \ri-ˈstrik-shən\ *n* [ME *restriccioun,* fr. AF *restriction,* fr. LL *restriction-, restrictio,* fr. L *restringere*] (15c) **1** : something that restricts: as **a** : a regulation that restricts or restrains ⟨~*s* for hunters⟩ **b** : a limitation on the use or enjoyment of property or a facility **2** : an act of restricting : the condition of being restricted

restriction enzyme *n* (1965) : any of various enzymes that cleave DNA into fragments at specific sites in the interior of the molecule — called also *restriction endonuclease*

restriction fragment length polymorphism *n* (1982) : variation in the length of a DNA fragment produced by a specific restriction enzyme acting on DNA from different individuals that usu. results from a genetic mutation and that may be used as a genetic marker

re·stric·tion·ism \ri-ˈstrik-shə-ˌni-zəm\ *n* (1937) : a policy or philosophy favoring restriction (as of trade or immigration) — **re·stric·tion·ist** \-sh(ə-)nist\ *adj or n*

re·stric·tive \ri-ˈstrik-tiv\ *adj* (1579) **1 a** : of or relating to restriction **b** : serving or tending to restrict ⟨~ regulations⟩ **2** : limiting the reference of a modified word or phrase **3** : prohibiting further negotiation — **restrictive** *n* — **re·stric·tive·ly** *adv* — **re·stric·tive·ness** *n*

restrictive clause *n* (ca. 1895) : a descriptive clause that is essential to the definiteness of the word it modifies (as *that you ordered* in "the book that you ordered is out of print")

re·strike \(ˌ)rē-ˈstrīk, ˈrē-ˌ\ *n* (1868) : a coin or medal struck from an original die at some time after the original issue

rest·room \ˈrest-ˌrüm, -ˌru̇m\ *n* (1899) : a room or suite of rooms providing toilets and lavatories

re·struc·ture \(ˌ)rē-ˈstrək-chər\ *vt* (1942) : to change the makeup, organization, or pattern of ~ *vi* : to restructure something

1**re·sult** \ri-ˈzəlt\ *vi* [ME, fr. ML *resultare,* fr. L, to rebound, fr. *re-* + *saltare* to leap — more at SALTATION] (15c) **1 a** : to proceed or arise as a consequence, effect, or conclusion ⟨death ~*ed* from the disease⟩ **b** : to have an issue or result ⟨the disease ~*ed* in death⟩ **2** : REVERT 2

2**result** *n* (1610) **1** : something that results as a consequence, issue, or conclusion; *also* : beneficial or tangible effect : FRUIT **2** : something obtained by calculation or investigation — **re·sult·ful** \-fəl\ *adj* — **re·sult·less** \-ləs\ *adj*

1**re·sul·tant** \ri-ˈzəl-tᵊnt\ *adj* (1639) : derived from or resulting from something else — **re·sul·tant·ly** *adv*

2**resultant** *n* (1815) : something that results : OUTCOME; *specif* : the single vector that is the sum of a given set of vectors

re·sume \ri-ˈzüm\ *vb* **re·sumed; re·sum·ing** [ME, fr. AF or L; AF *resumer,* fr. L *resumere,* fr. *re-* + *sumere* to take up, take — more at CONSUME] *vt* (15c) **1** : to assume or take again : REOCCUPY ⟨*resumed* his seat by the fire —Thomas Hardy⟩ **2** : to return to or begin again after interruption ⟨*resumed* her work⟩ **3** : to take back to oneself **4** : to pick up again **5** : REITERATE, SUMMARIZE ~ *vi* : to begin again something interrupted

ré·su·mé *or* **re·su·me** *also* **re·su·mé** \ˈre-zə-ˌmā, ˌre-zə-ˈ *also* ˈrā- *or* ˌrā-\ *n* [F *résumé,* fr. pp. of *résumer* to resume, summarize, fr. MF *resumer*] (1804) **1** : SUMMARY **2** : CURRICULUM VITAE **3** : a set of accomplishments ⟨a musical ~⟩

re·sump·tion \ri-ˈzəm(p)-shən\ *n* [ME, fr. AF or LL; AF, fr. LL *resumption-, resumptio,* fr. L *resumere*] (15c) **1** : an act or instance of resuming : RECOMMENCEMENT **2** : a return to payment in specie

re·su·pi·nate \ri-ˈsü-pə-ˌnāt\ *adj* [L *resupinatus,* pp. of *resupinare* to bend back to a supine position, fr. *re-* + *supinus* supine] (ca. 1776) **1** : inverted in position ⟨~ orchid flowers⟩ **2** : having or being a fruiting body lying flat on the substrate with the hymenium at the periphery or over the whole surface ⟨~ fungi⟩ ⟨~ sporophores⟩

re·sur·face \(ˌ)rē-ˈsər-fəs\ *vt* (1889) : to provide with a new or fresh surface ⟨~ skin by dermabrasion⟩ ~ *vi* : to come again to the surface (as of the water); *broadly* : REAPPEAR — **re·sur·fac·er** \-fə-sər\ *n*

re·surge \ri-ˈsərj\ *vi* **re·surged; re·surg·ing** [L *resurgere*] (1575) : to undergo a resurgence

re·sur·gence \ri-ˈsər-jən(t)s\ *n* (ca. 1834) : a rising again into life, activity, or prominence ⟨a ~ of interest⟩

re·sur·gent \-jənt\ *adj* [L *resurgent-, resurgens,* prp. of *resurgere*] (1805) : undergoing or tending to produce resurgence

res·ur·rect \ˌre-zə-ˈrekt\ *vt* [back-formation fr. *resurrection*] (1772) **1** : to raise from the dead **2** : to bring to view, attention, or use again

res·ur·rec·tion \ˌre-zə-ˈrek-shən\ *n* [ME *resurreccioun,* fr. AF, fr. LL *resurrection-, resurrectio* act of rising from the dead, fr. *resurgere* to rise from the dead, fr. L, to rise again, fr. *re-* + *surgere* to rise — more at SURGE] (14c) **1 a** *cap* : the rising of Christ from the dead **b** *often cap* : the rising again to life of all the human dead before the final judgment **c** : the state of one risen from the dead **2** : RESURGENCE, REVIVAL **3** *Christian Science* : a spiritualization of thought : material belief that yields to spiritual understanding — **res·ur·rec·tion·al** \-shnəl, -shə-nᵊl\ *adj*

res·ur·rec·tion·ist \-sh(ə-)nist\ *n* (1776) **1** : BODY SNATCHER **2** : one who resurrects

re·sus·ci·tate \ri-ˈsə-sə-ˌtāt\ *vb* **-tat·ed; -tat·ing** [L *resuscitatus,* pp. of *resuscitare* to reawaken, fr. *re-* + *suscitare* to rouse, fr. *sub-, sus-* up + *citare* to put in motion, stir — more at SUB-, CITE] *vt* (1532) : to revive from apparent death or from unconsciousness; *also* : REVITALIZE ~ *vi* : COME TO, REVIVE — **re·sus·ci·ta·tion** \ri-ˌsə-sə-ˈtā-shən, ˌrē-\ *n* — **re·sus·ci·ta·tive** \ri-ˈsə-sə-ˌtā-tiv\ *adj*

re·sus·ci·ta·tor \ri-ˈsə-sə-ˌtā-tər\ *n* (1808) : one that resuscitates; *specif* : an apparatus used to restore respiration (as to a partially asphyxiated person)

res·ver·a·trol \rez-ˈvir-ə-ˌtrȯl, -ˌträl, -ˌtrōl\ *n* [prob. fr. *resinous* + *veratr-* (fr. NL *Veratrum grandiflorum,* hellebore in which the substance was found) + 1*-ol*] (1939) : a trihydroxy stilbene derivative $C_{10}H_{12}O_3$ that is found in some plants, fruits, seeds, and grape-derived products (as red wine) and has been linked to a reduced risk of coronary disease and cancer

1**ret** \ˈret\ *vb* **ret·ted; ret·ting** [ME, fr. MD] *vt* (14c) : to soak (as flax) to loosen the fiber from the woody tissue ~ *vi* : to become retted

2**ret** *abbr* retired

re·ta·ble \ˈrē-ˌtā-bəl, rē-ˈ\ *n* [F, fr. MF, modif. of Old Occitan *retaule,* alter. of *reretaule,* ultim. fr. L *retro-* + *tabula* board, tablet] (ca. 1823) : a raised shelf above an altar for the altar cross, lights, and flowers

1**re·tail** \ˈrē-ˌtāl, *esp for 2 also* ri-ˈtāl\ *vt* (15c) **1** : to sell in small quantities directly to the ultimate consumer **2** : TELL, RETELL ~ *vi* : to sell at retail — **re·tail·er** *n*

2**re·tail** \ˈrē-ˌtāl\ *n* [ME, fr. AF *retaille* cutting, deduction, retail, fr. *retailler* to cut out, fr. *re-* + *tailler* to cut — more at TAILOR] (15c) : the sale of commodities or goods in small quantities to ultimate consumers; *also* : the industry of such selling — **at retail 1** : at a retailer's price **2** : 4RETAIL

3**re·tail** \ˈrē-ˌtāl\ *adj* (1601) : of, relating to, or engaged in the sale of commodities at retail ⟨~ trade⟩

4**re·tail** \ˈrē-ˌtāl\ *adv* (1784) : in small quantities : from a retailer

re·tail·ing \ˈrē-ˌtā-liŋ\ *n* (14c) : the activities involved in the selling of goods to ultimate consumers for personal or household consumption

re·tain \ri-ˈtān\ *vt* [ME *reteinen, retainen,* fr. AF *retenir, reteigner,* fr. L *retinēre* to hold back, restrain, fr. *re-* + *tenēre* to hold — more at THIN] (15c) **1 a** : to keep in possession or use **b** : to keep in one's pay or service; *specif* : to employ by paying a retainer **c** : to keep in mind or memory : REMEMBER **2** : to hold secure or intact ***syn*** see KEEP

retained object *n* (ca. 1904) : an object of a verb in the predicate of a passive construction (as *me* in "a book was given me" and *book* in "I was given a book")

1**re·tain·er** \ri-ˈtā-nər\ *n* (1540) **1 a** : a person attached or owing service to a household; *esp* : SERVANT **b** : EMPLOYEE **2** : one that retains **3** : a device or structure that holds something in place: as **a** : the part of a dental replacement (as a bridge) by which it is made fast to adjacent natural teeth **b** : a dental appliance used to hold teeth in correct position esp. following orthodontic treatment

2**retainer** *n* [ME *reteigner,* lit., retention, fr. AF, fr. *reteigner,* v.] (1775) **1** : the act of a client by which the services of a lawyer, counselor, or adviser are engaged **2** : a fee paid to a lawyer or professional adviser for advice or services or for a claim on services when needed

1**re·take** \(ˌ)rē-ˈtāk\ *vt* **-took** \-ˈtu̇k\; **-tak·en** \-ˈtā-kən\; **-tak·ing** (15c) **1** : to take or receive again **2** : RECAPTURE **3** : to photograph again

2**re·take** \ˈrē-ˌtāk\ *n* (1916) : a subsequent filming, photographing, or recording undertaken to improve upon the first; *also* : an instance of this

re·tal·i·ate \ri-ˈta-lē-ˌāt\ *vb* **-at·ed; -at·ing** [LL *retaliatus,* pp. of *retaliare,* fr. L *re-* + *talio* legal retaliation] *vt* (1611) : to repay (as an injury) in kind ~ *vi* : to return like for like; *esp* : to get revenge ***syn*** see RECIPROCATE — **re·tal·i·a·tion** \ri-ˌta-lē-ˈā-shən, ˌrē-\ *n* — **re·tal·i·a·tive** \ri-ˈta-lē-ˌā-tiv\ *adj* — **re·tal·ia·to·ry** \-ˈtal-yə-ˌtȯr-ē, -ˈta-lē-ə-\ *adj*

1**re·tard** \ri-ˈtärd\ *vb* [ME, fr. AF or L; AF *retarder,* fr. L *retardare,* fr. *re-* + *tardus* slow] *vt* (15c) **1** : to slow up esp. by preventing or hindering advance or accomplishment : IMPEDE **2** : to delay academic progress by failure to promote ~ *vi* : to undergo retardation ***syn*** see DELAY — **re·tard·er** *n*

2**re·tard** *n* (1788) **1** \ri-ˈtärd\ : a holding back or slowing down : RETARDATION **2** \ˈrē-ˌtärd\ *often offensive* : a retarded person; *also* : a person held to resemble a retarded person in behavior

re·tar·dant \ri-ˈtär-dᵊnt\ *adj* (1642) : serving or tending to retard ⟨a growth-*retardant* substance⟩ — **retardant** *n*

re·tar·date \-ˈtär-ˌdāt, -dət\ *n* (1915) *often offensive* : a mentally retarded person

re·tar·da·tion \ˌrē-ˌtär-ˈdā-shən, ri-\ *n* (15c) **1** : an act or instance of retarding **2** : the extent to which something is retarded **3** : a musical suspension; *specif* : one that resolves upward **4 a** : an abnormal slowness of thought or action; *esp* : MENTAL RETARDATION **b** : slowness in development or progress

re·tard·ed \ri-ˈtär-dəd\ *adj* (1895) *sometimes offensive* : slow or limited in intellectual or emotional development or academic progress

retch \ˈrech, *esp Brit* ˈrēch\ *vb* [ME **rechen* to spit, retch, fr. OE *hrǣcan* to spit, hawk; akin to ON *hrækja* to spit] *vt* (ca. 1798) : VOMIT 1 ~ *vi* : to make an effort to vomit; *also* : VOMIT — **retch** *n*

retd *abbr* **1** retired **2** returned

re·te \ˈrē-tē, ˈrā-\ *n, pl* **re·tia** \ˈrē-tē-ə, ˈrā-\ [NL, fr. L, net] (1541) **1** : a network esp. of blood vessels or nerves : PLEXUS **2** : an anatomical part resembling or including a network

re·tell \(ˌ)rē-ˈtel\ *vt* **-told** \-ˈtōld\; **-tell·ing** (1593) **1** : to tell again or in another form **2** : to count again

retelling *n* (1883) : a new version of a story ⟨a ~ of a Greek legend⟩

re·ten·tion \ri-ˈten(t)-shən\ *n* [ME *retencioun,* fr. AF, fr. L *retention-, retentio,* fr. *retinēre* to retain — more at RETAIN] (14c) **1 a** : the act of retaining : the state of being retained **b** : abnormal retaining of a fluid or secretion in a body cavity **2 a** : power of retaining : RETENTIVENESS **b** : an ability to retain things in mind; *specif* : a preservation of the aftereffects of experience and learning that makes recall or recognition possible **3** : something retained

re·ten·tive \-ˈten-tiv\ *adj* [ME *retentif,* fr. AF & ML; AF, fr. ML *retentivus,* fr. L *retentus,* pp. of *retinēre*] (14c) : having the power, property, or capacity of retaining ⟨soils ~ of moisture⟩; *esp* : retaining knowledge easily ⟨a ~ memory⟩ — **re·ten·tive·ly** *adv* — **re·ten·tive·ness** *n*

re·ten·tiv·i·ty \ˌrē-ˌten-ˈti-və-tē, ri-\ *n* (1881) : the power of retaining; *specif* : the capacity for retaining magnetism after the action of the magnetizing force has ceased

re·think \(ˌ)rē-ˈthiŋk\ *vb* **-thought** \-ˈthȯt\; **-think·ing** *vt* (1656) : to think about again : RECONSIDER ~ *vi* : to engage in reconsideration — **re·think** \ˈrē-ˌthiŋk, -ˈthiŋk\ *n* — **re·think·er** *n*

ret·i·cence \ˈre-tə-sən(t)s\ *n* (1603) **1** : the quality or state of being reticent : RESERVE, RESTRAINT **2** : an instance of being reticent **3** : RELUCTANCE 1

ret·i·cen·cy \-sən(t)-sē\ *n, pl* **-cies** (ca. 1617) : RETICENCE

ret·i·cent \-sənt\ *adj* [L *reticent-, reticens,* prp. of *reticēre* to keep silent, fr. *re-* + *tacēre* to be silent — more at TACIT] (ca. 1834) **1** : inclined to be silent or uncommunicative in speech : RESERVED **2** : restrained in expression, presentation, or appearance ⟨the room has an aspect of ~ dignity —A. N. Whitehead⟩ **3** : RELUCTANT ***syn*** see SILENT — **ret·i·cent·ly** *adv*

ret·i·cle \ˈre-ti-kəl\ *n* [L *reticulum* small net] (ca. 1731) : a scale on transparent material (as in an optical instrument) used esp. for measuring or aiming

re·tic·u·lar \ri-ˈti-kyə-lər\ *adj* (1597) **1** : RETICULATE 1 ⟨~ connective tissue containing collagen fibers⟩ **2** : INTRICATE

reticular formation *n* (1887) : a mass of nerve cells and fibers situated primarily in the brain stem and functioning upon stimulation esp. in arousal of the organism

[1]**re·tic·u·late** \ri-ˈti-kyə-lət, -ˌlāt\ *adj* [L *reticulatus,* fr. *reticulum*] (1658) **1** : resembling a net or network; *esp* : having veins, fibers, or lines crossing ⟨a ~ leaf⟩ **2** : being or involving evolutionary change dependent on genetic recombination involving diverse interbreeding populations — **re·tic·u·late·ly** *adv*

[2]**re·tic·u·late** \-ˌlāt\ *vb* **-lat·ed; -lat·ing** [back-formation fr. *reticulated,* adj., reticulate] *vt* (ca. 1728) : to divide, mark, or construct so as to form a network ⟨municipalities that ~ electricity to consumers⟩ ~ *vi* : to become reticulated

reticulated giraffe *n* (1953) : a giraffe of a subspecies (*Giraffa camelopardalis reticulata*) found in northeast Africa, Somalia, and northern Kenya that has a deep chestnut-colored coat divided by a network of fine white lines into large geometric patches

re·tic·u·la·tion \ri-ˌti-kyə-ˈlā-shən\ *n* (1671) : a reticulated formation : NETWORK; *also* : something reticulated

ret·i·cule \ˈre-ti-ˌkyül\ *n* [F *réticule,* fr. L *reticulum* small net, mesh bag, fr. dim. of *rete* net] (ca. 1738) **1** : RETICLE **2** : a woman's drawstring bag used esp. as a carryall

re·tic·u·lo·cyte \ri-ˈti-kyə-lō-ˌsīt\ *n* [NL *reticulum* + ISV *-cyte*] (1922) : an immature red blood cell that appears esp. during regeneration of lost blood, lacks a nucleus, and has a fine basophilic reticulum formed of ribosomal remains

re·tic·u·lo·en·do·the·li·al \ri-ˌti-kyə-lō-ˌen-də-ˈthē-lē-əl\ *adj* [NL *reticulum* + *endothelium*] (ca. 1923) : of, relating to, or being the reticuloendothelial system

reticuloendothelial system *n* (ca. 1923) : MONONUCLEAR PHAGOCYTE SYSTEM; *broadly* : the mononuclear phagocyte system plus certain other cells now known to be pinocytic or only weakly phagocytic

re·tic·u·lum \ri-ˈti-kyə-ləm\ *n* [NL, fr. L, small net] (ca. 1658) **1** : the second compartment of the stomach of a ruminant in which folds of the mucous membrane form hexagonal cells — compare ABOMASUM, OMASUM, RUMEN **2** : a reticulate structure : NETWORK

retin- *or* **retino-** *comb form* [*retina*] **1** : retina ⟨*retin*itis⟩ ⟨*retino*scopy⟩ **2** : retinol ⟨*retinoid*⟩

ret·i·na \ˈre-tə-nə, ˈret-nə\ *n, pl* **retinas** *or* **ret·i·nae** \-ˌnē, -ˌnī\ [ME *rethina,* fr. ML *retina,* prob. fr. L *rete* net] (14c) : the sensory membrane that lines the eye, is composed of several layers including one containing the rods and cones, and functions as the immediate instrument of vision by receiving the image formed by the lens and converting it into chemical and nervous signals which reach the brain by way of the optic nerve — see EYE illustration

ret·i·nac·u·lum \ˌre-tə-ˈna-kyə-ləm\ *n, pl* **-la** \-lə\ [NL, fr. L, halter, cable, fr. *retinēre* to hold back — more at RETAIN] (ca. 1825) : any of several fibrous bands of fascia that pass over or under tendons (as at or near the ankle or wrist) and help to keep them in place

[1]**ret·i·nal** \ˈre-tə-nəl, ˈret-nəl\ *adj* (1838) : of, relating to, involving, or being a retina

[2]**ret·i·nal** \ˈre-tə-ˌnal, -ˌnȯl\ *n* [*retin-* + [3]*-al*] (1944) : a yellowish to orange aldehyde $C_{20}H_{28}O$ derived from vitamin A that in combination with proteins forms the visual pigments of the retinal rods and cones

ret·i·nene \ˈre-tə-ˌnēn\ *n* (1934) : RETINAL

ret·i·ni·tis \ˌre-tə-ˈnī-təs\ *n* [NL] (1861) : inflammation of the retina

retinitis pig·men·to·sa \-ˌpig-mən-ˈtō-sə, -(ˌ)men-, -zə\ *n* [NL, pigmented retinitis] (1861) : any of several hereditary progressive degenerative diseases of the eye marked by night blindness in the early stages, atrophy and pigment changes in the retina, constriction of the visual field, and eventual blindness

ret·i·no·blas·to·ma \ˌre-tə-nō-ˌblas-ˈtō-mə\ *n, pl* **-mas** *also* **-ma·ta** \-mə-tə\ [NL, fr. *retin-* + *blast-* + *-oma*] (1924) : a malignant tumor of the retina that develops during childhood, is derived from retinal germ cells, and is associated with a chromosomal abnormality

ret·i·no·ic acid \ˌre-tə-ˈnō-ik-\ *n* (1960) : either of two isomers of an acid $C_{20}H_{28}O_2$ derived from vitamin A and used in the treatment of acne: **a** : TRETINOIN **b** : ISOTRETINOIN

ret·i·noid \ˈre-tə-ˌnȯid\ *n* (1976) : any of various synthetic or naturally occurring analogs of vitamin A

ret·i·nol \ˈre-tə-ˌnȯl, -ˌnōl\ *n* [*retin-* + [1]*-ol;* fr. its being the source of retinal] (1960) : the chief and typical vitamin A $C_{20}H_{29}OH$ that is a highly unsaturated alicyclic alcohol used in various forms in medicine and nutrition

ret·i·nop·a·thy \ˌre-tə-ˈnä-pə-thē\ *n, pl* **-thies** (1932) : any of various noninflammatory disorders of the retina including some that cause blindness

ret·i·nos·co·py \ˌre-tə-ˈnäs-kə-pē\ *n, pl* **pies** (1884) : observation of the retina of the eye esp. to determine the state of refraction

ret·i·no·tec·tal \ˌre-tə-nō-ˈtek-təl\ *adj* [*retin-* + *tect*um + [1]*-al*] (1951) : of, relating to, or being the nerve fibers connecting the retina and the tectum of the midbrain ⟨~ pathways⟩

ret·i·nue \ˈre-tə-ˌnü, -ˌnyü\ *n* [ME *retenue,* fr. AF, fr. fem. of *retenu,* pp. of *retenir* to retain] (14c) : a group of retainers or attendants

re·tin·u·la \re-ˈtin-yə-lə\ *n, pl* **-lae** \-ˌlē, -ˌlī\ *also* **-las** [NL, dim. of ML *retina*] (1878) : the neural receptor of a single facet of an arthropod compound eye — **re·tin·u·lar** \-lər\ *adj*

re·tire \ri-ˈtī(-ə)r\ *vb* **re·tired; re·tir·ing** [MF *retirer,* fr. *re-* + *tirer* to draw] *vi* (1533) **1** : to withdraw from action or danger : RETREAT **2** : to withdraw esp. for privacy ⟨*retired* to her room⟩ **3** : to move back : RECEDE **4** : to withdraw from one's position or occupation : conclude one's working or professional career **5** : to go to bed ~ *vt* **1** : WITHDRAW: as **a** : to march (a military force) away from the enemy **b** : to withdraw from circulation or from the market : RECALL ⟨~ a bond⟩ **c** : to withdraw from usual use or service **2** : to cause to retire from one's position or occupation **3 a** : to put out (a batter or batsman) in baseball or cricket **b** : to cause (a side) to end a turn at bat in baseball **4** : to win permanent possession of (as a trophy) **5** : to pay in full : SETTLE ⟨~ a debt⟩

retired *adj* (1590) **1** : SECLUDED ⟨a ~ village⟩ **2** : withdrawn from one's position or occupation : having concluded one's working or professional career **3** : received by or due to one in retirement — **re·tired·ly** \-ˈtī-rəd-lē, -ˈtī(-ə)rd-\ *adv* — **re·tired·ness** \-ˈtī(-ə)rd-nəs\ *n*

re·tir·ee \ri-ˌtī-ˈrē\ *n* (1945) : a person who has retired from a working or professional career

[1]**re·tire·ment** \ri-ˈtī(-ə)r-mənt\ *n* (1596) **1 a** : an act of retiring : the state of being retired **b** : withdrawal from one's position or occupation or from active working life **c** : the age at which one normally retires ⟨reaches ~ in May⟩ **2** : a place of seclusion or privacy

[2]**retirement** *adj* (1919) : of, relating to, or designed for retired persons

retiring *adj* (1766) : RESERVED, SHY — **re·tir·ing·ly** \-iŋ-lē\ *adv* — **re·tir·ing·ness** *n*

re·tool \(ˌ)rē-ˈtül\ *vt* (1927) **1** : to reequip with tools **2** : REORGANIZE **3** : REVISE, MODIFY ~ *vi* : to make esp. minor changes or improvements ⟨~ for the future⟩

[1]**re·tort** \ri-ˈtȯrt\ *vb* [L *retortus,* pp. of *retorquēre,* lit., to twist back, hurl back, fr. *re-* + *torquēre* to twist — more at TORTURE] *vt* (ca. 1557) **1** : to pay or hurl back : RETURN ⟨~ an insult⟩ **2 a** : to make a reply to **b** : to say in reply **3** : to answer (as an argument) by a counter argument ~ *vi* **1** : to answer back usu. sharply **2** : to return an argument or charge **3** : RETALIATE

[2]**retort** *n* (1600) : a quick, witty, or cutting reply; *esp* : one that turns back or counters the first speaker's words ***syn*** see ANSWER

[3]**re·tort** \ri-ˈtȯrt, ˈrē-ˌ\ *n* [MF *retorte,* fr. ML *retorta,* fr. L, fem. of *retortus;* fr. its shape] (1605) : a vessel or chamber in which substances are distilled or decomposed by heat

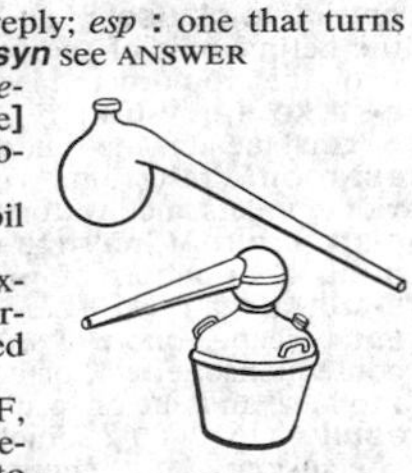

[3]retort

[4]**re·tort** \ri-ˈtȯrt, ˈrē-ˌ\ *vt* (1850) : to treat (as oil shale) by heating in a retort

re·tort pouch \ri-ˈtȯrt-, ˈrē-ˌ\ *n* (1977) : a flexible package in which prepared food is hermetically sealed for long-term unrefrigerated storage

[1]**re·touch** \(ˌ)rē-ˈtəch\ *vb* [F *retoucher,* fr. MF, fr. *re-* + *toucher* to touch] *vt* (1685) **1** : to rework in order to improve : TOUCH UP **2** : to alter (as a photographic negative) to produce a more desirable appearance **3** : to color (new growth of hair) to match previously dyed, tinted, or bleached hair ~ *vi* : to make or give retouches — **re·touch·er** *n*

[2]**re·touch** \ˈrē-ˌtəch, (ˌ)rē-ˈ\ *n* (1703) : the act or process or an instance of retouching; *esp* : the retouching of a new growth of hair

re·tract \ri-ˈtrakt\ *vb* [ME, fr. L *retractus,* pp. of *retrahere* — more at RETREAT] *vt* (15c) **1** : to draw back or in ⟨cats ~ their claws⟩ **2 a** : TAKE BACK, WITHDRAW ⟨~ a confession⟩ **b** : DISAVOW ~ *vi* **1** : to draw or pull back **2** : to recant or disavow something ***syn*** see ABJURE, RECEDE — **re·tract·able** \-ˈtrak-tə-bəl\ *adj*

re·trac·tile \ri-ˈtrak-tᵊl, -ˌtī(-ə)l\ *adj* (1777) : capable of being drawn back or in ⟨~ claws⟩ — **re·trac·til·i·ty** \ˌrē-ˌtrak-ˈti-lə-tē, ri-\ *n*

re·trac·tion \ri-ˈtrak-shən\ *n* (14c) **1** : an act of recanting; *specif* : a statement made by one retracting **2** : an act of retracting : the state of being retracted **3** : the ability to retract

re·trac·tor \ri-ˈtrak-tər\ *n* (1837) : one that retracts: as **a** : a surgical instrument for holding open the edges of a wound **b** : a muscle that draws in an organ or part

re·train \(ˌ)rē-ˈtrān\ *vt* (1898) : to train again or anew ~ *vi* : to become trained again — **re·train·able** \-ˈtrā-nə-bəl\ *adj*

re·trans·late \ˌrē-tran(t)s-ˈlāt, -tranz-\ *vt* (1750) **:** to translate (a translation) into another language; *also* **:** to give a new form to ~ *vi* **:** to retranslate something — **re·trans·la·tion** \-ˈlā-shən\ *n*

[1]**re·tread** \(ˌ)rē-ˈtred\ *vt* **re·tread·ed; re·tread·ing** (1907) **1 :** to bond or vulcanize a new tread to the prepared surface of (a worn tire) **2 :** to make over as if new ⟨~ an old plot⟩

[2]**re·tread** \ˈrē-ˌtred\ *n* (1914) **1 :** a retreaded tire **2 :** something made or done again esp. in slightly altered form **:** REMAKE **3 a :** one (as a retired person) who is recalled or retrained for work **b :** one (as an athlete) who has previously held the same or a similar position

re–tread \(ˌ)rē-ˈtred\ *vt* **-trod** \-ˈträd\; **-trod·den** \-ˈträ-dᵊn\ *or* **-trod; -tread·ing** (1598) **:** to tread again

[1]**re·treat** \ri-ˈtrēt\ *n* [ME *retret,* fr. AF *retrait,* fr. pp. of *retraire* to withdraw, fr. L *retrahere,* fr. *re-* + *trahere* to draw] (14c) **1 a** (1) **:** an act or process of withdrawing esp. from what is difficult, dangerous, or disagreeable (2) **:** the process of receding from a position or state attained ⟨the ~ of a glacier⟩ **b** (1) **:** the usu. forced withdrawal of troops from an enemy or from an advanced position (2) **:** a signal for retreating **c** (1) **:** a signal given by bugle at the beginning of a military flag-lowering ceremony (2) **:** a military flag-lowering ceremony **2 :** a place of privacy or safety **:** REFUGE **3 :** a period of group withdrawal for prayer, meditation, study, or instruction under a director

[2]**retreat** *vi* (15c) **1 :** to make a retreat **:** WITHDRAW **2 :** to slope backward ~ *vt* **:** to draw or lead back **:** REMOVE; *specif* **:** to move (a piece) back in chess ***syn*** see RECEDE — **re·treat·er** *n*

re·treat·ant \-ˈtrē-tᵊnt\ *n* (1880) **:** a person on a religious retreat

re·trench \ri-ˈtrench\ *vb* [obs. F *retrencher* (now *retrancher*), fr. MF *retrenchier,* fr. *re-* + *trenchier* to cut] *vt* (1596) **1 a :** CUT DOWN, REDUCE **b :** to cut out **:** EXCISE **2 :** to pare away **:** REMOVE ~ *vi* **:** to make retrenchments; *specif* **:** ECONOMIZE ***syn*** see SHORTEN

re·trench·ment \-mənt\ *n* (ca. 1600) **:** REDUCTION, CURTAILMENT; *specif* **:** a cutting of expenses

re·tri·al \(ˌ)rē-ˈtrī(-ə)l\ *n* (1852) **:** a second trial, experiment, or test; *specif* **:** a second judicial trial

re·trib·al·i·za·tion \(ˌ)rē-ˌtrī-bə-lə-ˈzā-shən\ *n* (1964) **:** the act of forming or returning to a tribal group or division

ret·ri·bu·tion \ˌre-trə-ˈbyü-shən\ *n* [ME *retribucioun,* fr. AF, fr. LL *retribution-, retributio,* fr. L *retribuere* to pay back, fr. *re-* + *tribuere* to pay — more at TRIBUTE] (14c) **1 :** RECOMPENSE, REWARD **2 :** the dispensing or receiving of reward or punishment esp. in the hereafter **3 :** something given or exacted in recompense; *esp* **:** PUNISHMENT

re·trib·u·tive \ri-ˈtri-byə-tiv\ *adj* (1678) **:** of, relating to, or marked by retribution — **re·trib·u·tive·ly** *adv*

re·trib·u·to·ry \-byə-ˌtȯr-ē\ *adj* (ca. 1615) **:** RETRIBUTIVE

re·triev·al \ri-ˈtrē-vəl\ *n* (ca. 1643) **1 :** an act or process of retrieving **2 :** possibility of being retrieved or of recovering ⟨beyond ~⟩

[1]**re·trieve** \ri-ˈtrēv\ *vb* **re·trieved; re·triev·ing** [ME *retreven,* fr. AF *retrueve-,* pres. stem of *retrover* to find again, fr. *re-* + *trover* to compose, invent, find, fr. VL **tropare* — more at TROUBADOUR] *vt* (15c) **1 :** to locate and bring in (killed or wounded game) **2 :** to call to mind again **3 :** to get back again **:** REGAIN **4 a :** RESCUE, SALVAGE **b :** to return (as a ball or shuttlecock that is difficult to reach) successfully **5 :** RESTORE, REVIVE ⟨his writing ~*s* the past⟩ **6 :** to remedy the evil consequences of **:** CORRECT **7 :** to get and bring back; *esp* **:** to recover (as information) from storage ~ *vi* **:** to bring in game ⟨a dog that ~*s* well⟩; *also* **:** to bring back an object thrown by a person — **re·triev·abil·i·ty** \-ˌtrē-və-ˈbi-lə-tē\ *n* — **re·triev·able** \-ˈtrē-və-bəl\ *adj*

[2]**retrieve** *n* (1697) **1 :** RETRIEVAL **2 :** the successful return of a ball that is difficult to reach or control (as in tennis)

re·triev·er \ri-ˈtrē-vər\ *n* (15c) **:** one that retrieves; *esp* **:** a dog of any of several breeds having a heavy water-resistant coat and used esp. for retrieving game

ret·ro \ˈre-(ˌ)trō\ *adj* [F *rétro,* short for *rétrospectif* retrospective] (1974) **:** relating to, reviving, or being the styles and esp. the fashions of the past **:** fashionably nostalgic or old-fashioned ⟨a ~ look⟩ — **retro** *n*

retro- *prefix* [L, fr. *retro,* fr. *re-* + *-tro* (as in *intro* within) — more at INTRO-] **1 :** backward **:** back ⟨*retro*-rocket⟩ **2 :** situated behind ⟨*retro*peritoneal⟩

ret·ro·ac·tion \ˌre-trō-ˈak-shən\ *n* (ca. 1738) **1** [*retroactive*] **:** retroactive operation (as of a law or tax) **2** [*retro-* + *action*] **:** a reciprocal action **:** REACTION

ret·ro·ac·tive \-ˈak-tiv\ *adj* [F *rétroactif,* fr. L *retroactus,* pp. of *retroagere* to drive back, reverse, fr. *retro-* + *agere* to drive — more at AGENT] (1611) **:** extending in scope or effect to a prior time or to conditions that existed or originated in the past; *esp* **:** made effective as of a date prior to enactment, promulgation, or imposition ⟨~ tax⟩ — **ret·ro·ac·tive·ly** *adv* — **ret·ro·ac·tiv·i·ty** \-ˌak-ˈti-və-tē\ *n*

ret·ro·cede \ˌre-trō-ˈsēd\ *vb* **-ced·ed; -ced·ing** [L *retrocedere,* fr. *retro-* + *cedere* to go, cede] *vi* (1654) **:** to go back **:** RECEDE ~ *vt* [F *rétrocéder,* fr. ML *retrocedere,* fr. L *retro-* + *cedere* to cede] **:** to cede back (as a territory) — **ret·ro·ces·sion** \-ˈse-shən\ *n*

ret·ro·dict \ˌre-trə-ˈdikt\ *vt* [*retro-* + pre*dict*] (1949) **:** to utilize present information or ideas to infer or explain (a past event or state of affairs) — **ret·ro·dic·tion** \-ˈdik-shən\ *n* — **ret·ro·dic·tive** \-ˈdik-tiv\ *adj*

ret·ro·fire \-ˌfī(-ə)r\ *vt* (1961) **:** to cause (a retro-rocket) to become ignited ~ *vi, of a retro-rocket* **:** to become ignited — **retrofire** *n*

ret·ro·fit \ˈre-trō-ˌfit, ˌre-trō-ˈfit\ *vt* (1953) **1 :** to furnish (as a computer, airplane, or building) with new or modified parts or equipment not available or considered necessary at the time of manufacture **2 :** to install (new or modified parts or equipment) in something previously manufactured or constructed **3 :** to adapt to a new purpose or need **:** MODIFY ⟨~ the story for a new audience⟩ — **ret·ro·fit** \ˈre-trō-ˌfit\ *n*

ret·ro·flex \ˈre-trə-ˌfleks\ *adj* [NL *retroflexus,* fr. L *retro-* + *flexus,* pp. of *flectere* to bend] (1776) **1 :** turned or bent abruptly backward **2 :** articulated with the tongue tip turned up or curled back just under the hard palate ⟨~ vowel⟩

ret·ro·flex·ion *or* **ret·ro·flec·tion** \ˌre-trə-ˈflek-shən\ *n* (1845) **1 :** the state of being bent back; *esp* **:** the bending back of an organ (as a uterus) upon itself **2 :** the act or process of bending back **3 :** retroflex articulation

ret·ro·gra·da·tion \ˌre-trō-grā-ˈdā-shən, -grə-\ *n* (ca. 1545) **:** the action or process of retrograding

[1]**ret·ro·grade** \ˈre-trə-ˌgrād\ *adj* [ME, fr. L *retrogradus,* fr. *retrogradi*] (14c) **1 a** (1) **:** having or being motion in a direction contrary to that of the general motion of similar bodies and esp. east to west among the stars ⟨Saturn is ~ for another week⟩ (2) **:** having or being a direction of rotation or revolution that is clockwise as viewed from the north pole of the sky or a planet ⟨a ~ orbit⟩ **b** (1) **:** moving, occurring, or performed in a backward direction (2) **:** occurring or performed in a direction opposite to the normal or forward direction of conduction or flow — compare ANTEROGRADE 1 **c :** contrary to the normal order **:** INVERSE **2 :** tending toward or resulting in a worse or previous state **3** *archaic* **:** CONTRADICTORY, OPPOSED **4 :** characterized by retrogression **5 :** affecting memories of a period prior to a shock or seizure ⟨~ amnesia⟩ **6 :** RETRO ⟨~ fashion⟩ — **ret·ro·grade·ly** *adv*

[2]**retrograde** *adv* (ca. 1619) **:** BACKWARD, REVERSELY

[3]**retrograde** *vb* [L *retrogradi,* fr. *retro-* + *gradi* to go — more at GRADE] *vt* (1582) *archaic* **:** to turn back **:** REVERSE ~ *vi* **1 a :** to go back **:** RETREAT **b :** to go back over or recapitulate something **2 :** to decline to a worse condition

ret·ro·gress \ˌre-trə-ˈgres\ *vi* [L *retrogressus,* pp. of *retrogradi*] (1819) **:** to move backward **:** REVERT

ret·ro·gres·sion \-ˈgre-shən\ *n* (1604) **1 :** REGRESSION 3 **2 :** return to a former and less complex level of development or organization

ret·ro·gres·sive \-ˈgre-siv\ *adj* (1802) **:** characterized by retrogression: as **a :** going or directed backward **b :** declining from a better to a worse state **c :** passing from a higher to a lower level of organization ⟨~ evolution⟩ — **ret·ro·gres·sive·ly** *adv*

ret·ro·nym \ˈre-trō-ˌnim\ *n* [*retro-* + *-onym*] (1980) **:** a term consisting of a noun and a modifier which specifies the original meaning of the noun ⟨"film camera" is a ~⟩

ret·ro·pack \ˈre-trō-ˌpak\ *n* (1962) **:** a system of retro-rockets on a spacecraft

ret·ro·per·i·to·ne·al \ˌre-trō-ˌper-ə-tə-ˈnē-əl\ *adj* (1874) **:** situated behind the peritoneum — **ret·ro·per·i·to·ne·al·ly** \-ə-lē\ *adv*

ret·ro·re·flec·tion \ˌre-trō-ri-ˈflek-shən\ *n* (ca. 1965) **:** the action or use of a retroreflector — **ret·ro·re·flec·tive** \-ˈflek-tiv\ *adj*

ret·ro·re·flec·tor \-ˈflek-tər\ *n* (1946) **:** a device that reflects radiation (as light) so that the paths of the reflected rays are parallel to those of the incident rays

ret·ro–rock·et \ˈre-trō-ˌrä-kət\ *n* (1957) **:** an auxiliary rocket engine (as on a spacecraft) used in decelerating

re·trorse \ˈrē-ˌtrȯrs\ *adj* [L *retrorsus,* contr. of *retroversus*] (ca. 1825) **:** bent backward or downward

[1]**ret·ro·spect** \ˈre-trə-ˌspekt\ *n* [prob. fr. *retro-* + pro*spect*] (1602) **1** *archaic* **:** reference to or regard of a precedent or authority **2 :** a review of or meditation on past events — **in retrospect :** in considering the past or a past event

[2]**retrospect** *adj* (1709) **:** RETROSPECTIVE

[3]**retrospect** *vi* (1659) **1 :** to engage in retrospection **2 :** to refer back **:** REFLECT ~ *vt* **:** to go back over in thought

ret·ro·spec·tion \ˌre-trə-ˈspek-shən\ *n* (1674) **:** the act or process or an instance of surveying the past

[1]**ret·ro·spec·tive** \-ˈspek-tiv\ *adj* (1664) **1 a** (1) **:** of, relating to, or given to retrospection (2) **:** based on memory ⟨a ~ report⟩ **b :** being a retrospective ⟨a ~ exhibition⟩ **2 :** affecting things past **:** RETROACTIVE ⟨~ laws⟩ **3 :** relating to or being a study (as of a disease) that starts with the present condition of a population of individuals and collects data about their past history to explain their present condition — **ret·ro·spec·tive·ly** *adv*

[2]**retrospective** *n* (1932) **:** a generally comprehensive exhibition, compilation, or performance of the work of an artist over a span of years; *broadly* **:** REVIEW 7a ⟨a ~ of 20th century haute couture⟩

re·trous·sé \rə-ˌtrü-ˈsā, rə-ˈtrü-ˌ, ˌre-trü-ˈ\ *adj* [F, fr. pp. of *retrousser* to tuck up, fr. MF, fr. *re-* + *trousser* to truss, tuck up — more at TRUSS] (1837) **:** turned up ⟨~ nose⟩

ret·ro·ver·sion \ˌre-trō-ˈvər-zhən *also* -shən\ *n* [L *retroversus* turned backward, fr. *retro-* + *versus,* pp. of *vertere* to turn — more at WORTH] (1776) **1 :** the bending backward of the uterus and cervix **2 :** the act or process of turning back or regressing

ret·ro·vi·rol·o·gy \ˌre-trō-vī-ˈrä-lə-jē\ *n* (1982) **:** virology concerned with the study of retroviruses — **ret·ro·vi·rol·o·gist** \-jist\ *n*

ret·ro·vi·rus \ˈre-trō-ˌvī-rəs\ *n* [NL] (1975) **:** any of a family (*Retroviridae*) of single-stranded RNA viruses that produce reverse transcriptase by means of which DNA is produced using their RNA as a template and incorporated into the genome of infected cells, that are often tumorigenic, and that include the lentiviruses (as the HIVs) and the causative agent of Rous sarcoma — **ret·ro·vi·ral** \-rəl\ *adj*

ret·si·na \ret-ˈsē-nə\ *n* [ModGk, perh. fr. It *resina* resin, fr. L — more at RESIN] (1940) **:** a resin-flavored Greek wine

[1]**re·turn** \ri-ˈtərn\ *vb* [ME, fr. AF *returner,* fr. *re-* + *turner, tourner* to turn — more at TURN] *vi* (14c) **1 a :** to go back or come back again ⟨~ home⟩ **b :** to go back in thought, practice, or condition **:** REVERT **2 :** to pass back to an earlier possessor **3 :** REPLY, RETORT ~ *vt* **1 a :** to give (as an official account) to a superior **b** *Brit* **:** to elect (a candidate) as attested by official report or returns **c :** to bring back (as a writ or verdict) to an office or tribunal **2 a :** to bring, send, or put back to a former or proper place **b :** to restore to a former or to a normal state **3 a :** to send back **:** VISIT — usu. used with *on* or *upon* **b** *obs* **:** RETORT **4 :** to bring in (as profit) **:** YIELD **5 a :** to give or perform in return **:** REPAY ⟨~ a compliment⟩; *also* **:** to respond to in kind ⟨~*ed* his calls⟩ **b :** to give back to the owner **c :** REFLECT ⟨~ an echo⟩ **6 :** to cause (as a wall) to continue in a different direction (as at a right angle) **7 :** to lead (a specified suit or specified card of a suit) in response to a partner's earlier lead **8 a :** to hit back (a ball or shuttlecock) **b :** to run with (a football) after a change of possession (as by a punt or a fumble) ***syn*** see RECIPROCATE — **re·turn·er** *n*

[2]**return** *n* (14c) **1 a :** the act of coming back to or from a place or condition **b :** a regular or frequent returning **:** RECURRENCE **2 a** (1) **:** the delivery of a legal order (as a writ) to the proper officer or court (2) **:** an endorsed certificate stating an official's action in the execution

\ə\ **a**but \ᵊ\ kitten, F table \ər\ f**ur**ther \a\ **a**sh \ā\ **a**ce \ä\ m**o**p, m**ar** \au̇\ **ou**t \ch\ **ch**in \e\ b**e**t \ē\ **ea**sy \g\ **g**o \i\ h**i**t \ī\ **i**ce \j\ **j**ob \ŋ\ si**ng** \ō\ g**o** \ȯ\ l**aw** \ȯi\ b**oy** \th\ **th**in \t͟h\ **th**e \ü\ l**oo**t \u̇\ f**oo**t \y\ **y**et \zh\ vi**si**on, bei**ge** \k, ⁿ, œ, ue, ʸ\ *see* Guide to Pronunciation

of such an order (3) : the sending back of a commission with the certificate of the commissioners **b** : an account or formal report **c** (1) : a report of the results of balloting — usu. used in pl. ⟨election ~*s*⟩ (2) : an official declaration of the election of a candidate (3) *chiefly Brit* : ELECTION **d** (1) : a formal statement on a required legal form showing taxable income, allowable deductions and exemptions, and the computation of the tax due (2) : a list of taxable property **3 a** : the continuation usu. at a right angle of the face or of a member of a building or of a molding or group of moldings **b** : a means for conveying something (as water) back to its starting point **4 a** : a quantity of goods, consignment, or cargo coming back in exchange for goods sent out as a mercantile venture **b** : the value of or profit from such venture **c** (1) : the profit from labor, investment, or business : YIELD (2) *pl* : RESULTS **d** : the rate of profit in a process of production per unit of cost **5 a** : the act of returning something to a former place, condition, or ownership : RESTITUTION ⟨the ~ of stolen goods⟩ **b** : something returned; *esp, pl* : unsold publications returned to the publisher for cash or credit **6 a** : something given in repayment or reciprocation ⟨a ~ on their years of hard work⟩ **b** : ANSWER, RETORT **7** : an answering play: as **a** : a lead in a suit previously led by one's partner in a card game **b** : the action or an instance of returning a ball (as in football or tennis) **8** *chiefly Brit* : ROUND-TRIP — **in return** : in reciprocation, compensation, or repayment

[3]**return** *adj* (1676) **1 a** : having or formed by a change of direction ⟨a ~ facade⟩ **b** : doubled on itself ⟨a ~ flue⟩ **2 a** : played, delivered, or given in return ⟨~ fire from the enemy⟩ **b** : taking place for the second time ⟨a ~ meeting for the two champions⟩ **3** : used or taken on returning ⟨the ~ road⟩ **4** : returning or permitting return ⟨a ~ valve⟩ **5** : of, relating to, or causing a return to a place or condition ⟨use the prestamped ~ envelope⟩

[1]**re·turn·able** \ri-ˈtər-nə-bəl\ *adj* (15c) **1** : legally required to be returned, delivered, or argued at a specified time or place ⟨a writ ~ on the date indicated⟩ **2 a** : capable of returning or of being returned (as for reuse) ⟨~ beer bottles⟩ **b** : permitted to be returned ⟨sale items are not ~⟩

[2]**returnable** *n* (1963) : something designed to be returned (as for recycling); *esp* : a returnable beverage container

re·turn·ee \ri-ˌtər-ˈnē\ *n* (1944) : one who returns; *esp* : one returning to the U.S. after military service overseas

re·tuse \ri-ˈtüs, -ˈtyüs\ *adj* [L *retusus* blunted, fr. pp. of *retundere* to pound back, blunt, fr. *re-* + *tundere* to beat, pound — more at CONTUSION] (ca. 1753) : having the apex rounded or obtuse with a slight notch

[1]**Reu·ben** \ˈrü-bən\ *n* [Heb *Rĕʼūbhēn*] : a son of Jacob and the traditional eponymous ancestor of one of the tribes of Israel

[2]**Reuben** *n* [prob. fr. *Reuben* Kulakofsky †1960 Am. grocer] (1956) : a grilled sandwich of corned beef, Swiss cheese, and sauerkraut usu. on rye bread

[3]**Reuben** *n* [*Reuben* L. Goldberg †1970 Am. cartoonist] (1958) : a statuette awarded annually by a professional organization for notable achievement in cartoon artistry

re·union \(ˌ)rē-ˈyün-yən\ *n* (1610) **1** : an act of reuniting : the state of being reunited **2** : a reuniting of persons after separation

re·union·ist \-yə-nist\ *n* (1866) : an advocate of reunion (as of sects or parties) — **re·union·is·tic** \(ˌ)rē-ˌyün-yə-ˈnis-tik\ *adj*

re·unite \ˌrē-yü-ˈnīt\ *vb* [ME, fr. ML *reunitus*, pp. of *reunire*, fr. L *re-* + LL *unire* to unite — more at UNITE] *vt* (15c) : to bring together again ~ *vi* : to come together again : REJOIN

re–up \(ˌ)rē-ˈəp\ *vi* [*re-* + sign *up*] (ca. 1906) : to sign on again ⟨*re-upped* with the team for three more years⟩; *esp* : to enlist again

re·up·take \(ˈ)rē-ˈəp-ˌtāk\ *n* (1968) : the reabsorption by a neuron of a neurotransmitter following the transmission of a nerve impulse across a synapse

re·us·able \(ˌ)rē-ˈyü-zə-bəl\ *adj* (1943) : capable of being used again or repeatedly — **re·us·abil·i·ty** \(ˌ)rē-ˌyü-zə-ˈbi-lə-tē\ *n*

[1]**re·use** \(ˌ)rē-ˈyüz\ *vt* (1843) : to use again esp. in a different way or after reclaiming or reprocessing ⟨the need to ~ scarce resources⟩ ⟨~ packing material as insulation⟩

[2]**reuse** \-ˈyüs\ *n* (1866) : further, different, or repeated use

[1]**rev** \ˈrev\ *n* [short for *revolution*] (ca. 1890) **1** : a revolution of a motor **2** : revolution per minute — usu. used in pl.

[2]**rev** *vb* **revved; rev·ving** *vt* (1920) **1 a** : to step up the number of revolutions per minute of — often used with *up* ⟨~ up the engine⟩ **b** : INCREASE — used with *up* ⟨~ up production⟩ **2** : to drive or operate esp. at high speed — often used with *up* **3** : to make more active or effective — used with *up* ⟨*revving* up the economy⟩ **4** : to stir up : EXCITE — usu. used with *up* ⟨*revved* up the kids before bedtime⟩ ~ *vi* **1** : to operate at an increased speed of revolution — usu. used with *up* **2** : to increase in amount or activity — usu. used with *up* ⟨the campaign *revved* up⟩ **3** : to become more excited esp. in anticipation — usu. used with *up* ⟨the partygoers were *revving* up⟩

[3]**rev** *abbr* **1** revenue **2** reverse **3** review; reviewed **4** revised; revision **5** revolution

Rev *abbr* **1** Revelation **2** reverend

re·val·u·ate \(ˌ)rē-ˈval-yə-ˌwāt\ *vt* [back-formation fr. *revaluation*] (1921) : REVALUE; *specif* : to increase the value of (as currency) — **re·val·u·a·tion** \(ˌ)rē-ˌval-yə-ˈwā-shən\ *n*

re·val·ue \(ˌ)rē-ˈval-(ˌ)yü\ *vt* (1592) **1** : to value (as currency) anew **2** : to make a new valuation of : REAPPRAISE

re·vamp \(ˌ)rē-ˈvamp\ *vt* (1850) **1** : REMAKE, REVISE **2** : RENOVATE, RECONSTRUCT — **re·vamp** \ˈrē-ˌ, ri-ˈ\ *n*

re·vanche \rə-ˈvä^{n}sh\ *n* [F, fr. MF, alter. of *revenche* — more at REVENGE] (1853) : REVENGE; *esp* : a usu. political policy designed to recover lost territory or status — **re·vanch·ism** \-ˈvä^n-ˌshi-zəm\ *n*

[1]**re·vanch·ist** \-ˈvä^n-shist\ *n* (1926) : one who advocates a policy of revanche

[2]**revanchist** *adj* (1948) : of or relating to a policy of revanche

re·vas·cu·lar·i·za·tion \ˌrē-ˌvas-kyə-lə-rə-ˈzā-shən\ *n* (1951) : a surgical procedure for the provision of a new, additional, or augmented blood supply to a body part or organ

Revd *abbr, Brit* reverend

[1]**re·veal** \ri-ˈvēl\ *vt* [ME *revelen*, fr. AF *reveler*, fr. L *revelare* to uncover, reveal, fr. *re-* + *velare* to cover, veil, fr. *velum* veil] (14c) **1** : to make known through divine inspiration **2** : to make (something secret or hidden) publicly or generally known ⟨~ a secret⟩ **3** : to open up to view : DISPLAY ⟨the uncurtained window ~*ed* a cluttered room⟩ — **re·veal·able** \-ˈvē-lə-bəl\ *adj* — **re·veal·er** *n*

syn REVEAL, DISCLOSE, DIVULGE, TELL, BETRAY mean to make known what has been or should be concealed. REVEAL may apply to supernatural or inspired revelation of truths beyond the range of ordinary human vision or reason ⟨divine will as *revealed* in sacred writings⟩. DISCLOSE may imply a discovering but more often an imparting of information previously kept secret ⟨candidates must *disclose* their financial assets⟩. DIVULGE implies a disclosure involving some impropriety or breach of confidence ⟨refused to *divulge* an anonymous source⟩. TELL implies an imparting of necessary or useful information ⟨*told* them what he had overheard⟩. BETRAY implies a divulging that represents a breach of faith or an involuntary or unconscious disclosure ⟨a blush that *betrayed* her embarrassment⟩.

[2]**reveal** *n* [alter. of earlier *revale*, prob. ultim. fr. MF *ravaler* to reduce the depth of (masonry or wood), lit., to take back down, fr. OF, fr. *re-* + *avaler* to let fall — more at VAIL] (1688) : the side of an opening (as for a window) between a frame and the outer surface of a wall; *also* : JAMB

re·veal·ing \-ˈvē-liŋ\ *adj* (ca. 1925) : allowing a look at or an understanding of something inner or hidden ⟨a ~ confession⟩; *also* : tending to expose more typically hidden parts of the body ⟨a ~ halter top⟩ — **re·veal·ing·ly** *adv*

re·veal·ment \ri-ˈvēl-mənt\ *n* (1584) : an act of revealing

re·veg·e·tate \(ˌ)rē-ˈve-jə-ˌtāt\ *vt* (1804) : to provide (barren or denuded land) with a new vegetative cover — **re·veg·e·ta·tion** \(ˌ)rē-ˌve-jə-ˈtā-shən\ *n*

rev·eil·le \ˈre-və-lē, *Brit* ri-ˈva-li *or* -ˈve-\ *n* [modif. of F *réveillez*, imper. pl. of *réveiller* to awaken, fr. MF *reveiller*, fr. *re-* + *eveiller* to awaken, fr. VL **exvigilare*, fr. L *ex-* + *vigilare* to keep watch, stay awake — more at VIGILANT] (1644) **1** : a signal to get up mornings **2** : a bugle call at about sunrise signaling the first military formation of the day; *also* : the formation so signaled

[1]**rev·el** \ˈre-vəl\ *vi* **-eled** *or* **-elled; -el·ing** *or* **-el·ling** \ˈre-və-liŋ, ˈrev-liŋ\ [ME, fr. AF *reveler*, lit., to rebel, fr. L *rebellare*] (14c) **1** : to take part in a revel : CAROUSE **2** : to take intense pleasure or satisfaction ⟨~*ed* in the quiet after everyone had gone⟩

[2]**revel** *n* (14c) : a usu. wild party or celebration

rev·e·la·tion \ˌre-və-ˈlā-shən\ *n* [ME *revelacioun*, fr. AF, fr. LL *revelation-, revelatio*, fr. L *revelare* to reveal] (14c) **1 a** : an act of revealing or communicating divine truth **b** : something that is revealed by God to humans **2 a** : an act of revealing to view or making known **b** : something that is revealed; *esp* : an enlightening or astonishing disclosure ⟨shocking ~*s*⟩ **c** : a pleasant often enlightening surprise ⟨her talent was a ~⟩ **3** *cap* : an apocalyptic writing addressed to early Christians of Asia Minor and included as a book in the New Testament — called also *Apocalypse*; see BIBLE table

Rev·e·la·tions \-shənz\ *n pl but sing in constr* (1729) : REVELATION 3

rev·e·la·tor \ˈre-və-ˌlā-tər\ *n* (1764) : one that reveals; *esp* : one that reveals the will of God

re·ve·la·to·ry \ˈre-və-lə-ˌtȯr-ē, ri-ˈve-lə-\ *adj* (1882) : of or relating to revelation : serving to reveal something

rev·el·er *or* **rev·el·ler** \ˈre-və-lər, ˈrev-lər\ *n* (14c) : one who engages in revelry

rev·el·ry \ˈre-vəl-rē\ *n* (15c) : noisy partying or merrymaking

rev·e·nant \ˈre-və-ˌnä^n, -nənt\ *n* [F, fr. prp. of *revenir* to return] (1818) : one that returns after death or a long absence — **revenant** *adj*

[1]**re·venge** \ri-ˈvenj\ *vt* **re·venged; re·veng·ing** [ME, fr. AF *revenger, revengier*, fr. *re-* + *venger* to avenge — more at VENGEANCE] (14c) **1** : to avenge (as oneself) usu. by retaliating in kind or degree **2** : to inflict injury in return for ⟨~ an insult⟩ — **re·veng·er** *n*

[2]**revenge** *n* [MF *revenge, revenche*, fr. *revengier, revenchier* to revenge] (ca. 1547) **1** : a desire for revenge ⟨motivated by ~⟩ **2** : an act or instance of retaliating in order to get even ⟨plotted her ~⟩ **3** : an opportunity for getting satisfaction ⟨sought ~ through a rematch⟩

re·venge·ful \ri-ˈvenj-fəl\ *adj* (1570) : full of or prone to revenge : determined to get even — **re·venge·ful·ly** \-fə-lē\ *adv* — **re·venge·ful·ness** *n*

rev·e·nue \ˈre-və-ˌnü, -ˌnyü\ *n, often attrib* [ME, return, revenue, fr. AF, fr. *revenir* to return, fr. L *revenire*, fr. *re-* + *venire* to come — more at COME] (15c) **1** : the total income produced by a given source ⟨a property expected to yield a large annual ~⟩ **2** : the gross income returned by an investment **3** : the yield of sources of income (as taxes) that a political unit (as a nation or state) collects and receives into the treasury for public use **4** : a government department concerned with the collection of the national revenue

revenue bond *n* (1856) : a bond issued by a public agency authorized to build, acquire, or improve a revenue-producing property (as a toll road) and payable out of revenue derived from such property

revenue cutter *n* (1790) : an armed government vessel employed esp. to enforce revenue laws

rev·e·nu·er \ˈre-və-ˌnü-ər, -ˌnyü-\ *n* (1880) : a revenue department officer

revenue stamp *n* (1862) : a stamp (as on a cigar box) for use as evidence of payment of a tax

revenue tariff *n* (1820) : a tariff intended wholly or primarily to produce public revenue — compare PROTECTIVE TARIFF

re·verb \ri-ˈvərb, ˈrē-ˌ\ *n* [short for *reverberation*] (1953) : an electronically produced echo effect in recorded music; *also* : a device for producing reverb

re·ver·ber·ant \ri-ˈvər-b(ə-)rənt\ *adj* (1781) **1** : tending to reverberate **2** : marked by reverberation : RESONANT — **re·ver·ber·ant·ly** *adv*

[1]**re·ver·ber·ate** \-bə-ˌrāt\ *vb* **-at·ed; -at·ing** [L *reverberatus*, pp. of *reverberare*, fr. *re-* + *verberare* to lash, fr. *verber* rod — more at VERVAIN] *vt* (15c) **1** : REFLECT **2** : REPEL **3** : ECHO ~ *vi* **1 a** : to become driven back **b** : to become reflected **2** : to continue in or as if in a series of echoes : RESOUND ⟨an historic event that still ~*s* today⟩

[2]**re·ver·ber·ate** \-b(ə-)rət\ *adj* (1603) : REVERBERANT

re·ver·ber·a·tion \ri-ˌvər-bə-ˈrā-shən\ *n* (14c) **1** : an act of reverberating : the state of being reverberated **2 a** : something that is reverberated **b** : an effect or impact that resembles an echo

re·ver·ber·a·tive \ri-ˈvər-bə-ˌrā-tiv, -b(ə-)rə-\ *adj* (1716) **1** : constituting reverberation **2** : tending to reverberate : REVERBERANT

re·ver·ber·a·to·ry \ri-ˈvər-b(ə-)rə-ˌtȯr-ē, -bə-ˌtȯr-\ *adj* (1605) : acting by reverberation
reverberatory furnace *n* (1672) : a furnace in which heat is radiated from the roof onto the material treated
[1]**re·vere** \ri-ˈvir\ *vt* **re·vered; re·ver·ing** [L *revereri,* fr. *re-* + *vereri* to fear, respect — more at WARY] (1615) : to show devoted deferential honor to : regard as worthy of great honor ⟨~ the aged⟩ ⟨~ tradition⟩
syn REVERE, REVERENCE, VENERATE, WORSHIP, ADORE mean to honor and admire profoundly and respectfully. REVERE stresses deference and tenderness of feeling ⟨a professor *revered* by her students⟩. REVERENCE presupposes an intrinsic merit and inviolability in the one honored and a similar depth of feeling in the one honoring ⟨*reverenced* the academy's code of honor⟩. VENERATE implies a holding as holy or sacrosanct because of character, association, or age ⟨heroes still *venerated*⟩. WORSHIP implies homage usu. expressed in words or ceremony ⟨*worships* their memory⟩. ADORE implies love and stresses the notion of an individual and personal attachment ⟨we *adored* our doctor⟩.
[2]**revere** *n* [by alter.] (1899) : REVERS
[1]**rev·er·ence** \ˈrev-rən(t)s, ˈre-və-; ˈre-vərn(t)s\ *n* [ME, fr. AF, fr. L *reverentia,* fr. *reverent-, reverens* respectful, reverent] (14c) **1 :** honor or respect felt or shown : DEFERENCE; *esp* : profound adoring awed respect **2 :** a gesture of respect (as a bow) **3 :** the state of being revered **4 :** one held in reverence — used as a title for a clergyman ***syn*** see HONOR
[2]**reverence** *vt* **-enced; -enc·ing** (14c) : to regard or treat with reverence ***syn*** see REVERE — **rev·er·enc·er** *n*
[1]**rev·er·end** \ˈrev-rənd, ˈre-və-; ˈre-vərnd\ *adj* [ME, fr. AF, fr. L *reverendus,* gerundive of *revereri*] (15c) **1 :** worthy of reverence : REVERED **2 a :** of or relating to the clergy **b :** being a member of the clergy — used as a title ⟨the *Reverend* Mr. Doe⟩ ⟨the *Reverend* John Doe⟩ ⟨the *Reverend* Mrs. Jane Doe⟩
[2]**reverend** *n* (1608) : a member of the clergy — sometimes used in pl. as a title
rev·er·ent \ˈrev-rənt, ˈre-və-; ˈre-vərnt\ *adj* [ME, fr. AF, fr. L *reverent-, reverens,* prp. of *revereri*] (14c) : expressing or characterized by reverence : WORSHIPFUL — **rev·er·ent·ly** *adv*
rev·er·en·tial \ˌre-və-ˈren(t)-shəl\ *adj* (ca. 1555) **1 :** expressing or having a quality of reverence ⟨~ awe⟩ **2 :** inspiring reverence — **rev·er·en·tial·ly** \-ˈren(t)-sh(ə-)lē\ *adv*
rev·er·ie *also* **rev·ery** \ˈre-və-rē, ˈrev-rē\ *n, pl* **rev·er·ies** [F *rêverie,* fr. MF, delirium, fr. *resver, rever* to wander, be delirious] (1654) **1 :** DAYDREAM **2 :** the condition of being lost in thought
re·vers \ri-ˈvir, -ˈver\ *n, pl* **re·vers** \-ˈvirz, -ˈverz\ [F, lit., reverse, fr. MF, fr. *revers,* adj.] (1831) : a lapel esp. on a woman's garment
re·ver·sal \ri-ˈvər-səl\ *n* (15c) **1 :** an act or the process of reversing **2 :** a conversion of a photographic positive into a negative or vice versa **3 :** a change (as of fortune) often for the worse
[1]**re·verse** \ri-ˈvərs\ *adj* [ME *revers,* fr. AF, fr. L *reversus,* pp. of *revertere* to turn back — more at REVERT] (14c) **1 a :** opposite or contrary to a previous or normal condition ⟨~ order⟩ **b (1) :** having the back presented to the observer or opponent **(2) :** made with one's back to the basketball net ⟨a ~ layup⟩ **2 :** coming from the rear of a military force **3 :** acting, operating, or arranged in a manner contrary to the usual **4 :** effecting reverse movement ⟨~ gear⟩ **5 :** so made that the part which normally prints in color appears white against a colored background — **re·verse·ly** *adv*
[2]**reverse** *vb* **re·versed; re·vers·ing** *vt* (14c) **1 a :** to turn completely about in position or direction **b :** to turn upside down : INVERT **c :** to cause to take an opposite point of view ⟨*reversed* herself on the issue⟩ **2 :** NEGATE, UNDO: as **a :** to overthrow, set aside, or make void (a legal decision) by a contrary decision **b :** to change to the contrary ⟨~ a policy⟩ **c :** to undo or negate the effect of (as a condition or surgical operation) ⟨had his vasectomy *reversed*⟩ **3 :** to cause to go in the opposite direction; *esp* : to cause (as an engine) to perform its action in the opposite direction ~ *vi* **1 :** to turn or move in the opposite direction ⟨the count's waltzing . . . consisted . . . of *reversing* at top speed —Agatha Christie⟩ **2 :** to put a mechanism (as an engine) in reverse — **re·vers·er** *n* — **reverse field** *or* **reverse one's field** : to make a sudden reversal in direction or opinion
syn REVERSE, TRANSPOSE, INVERT mean to change to the opposite position. REVERSE is the most general term and may imply change in order, side, direction, meaning ⟨*reversed* his position on the trade agreement⟩. TRANSPOSE implies a change in order or relative position of units often through exchange of position ⟨*transposed* the letters to form an anagram⟩. INVERT applies chiefly to turning upside down or inside out ⟨a stamp with an *inverted* picture of an airplane⟩.
[3]**reverse** *n* (14c) **1 :** something directly contrary to something else : OPPOSITE **2 :** an act or instance of reversing; *esp* : DEFEAT, SETBACK ⟨suffered financial ~*s*⟩ **3 :** the back part of something; *esp* : the side of a coin or currency note that is opposite the obverse **4 a (1) :** a gear that reverses something; *also* : the whole mechanism brought into play when such a gear is used **(2) :** movement in reverse **b :** an offensive play in football in which a back moving in one direction gives the ball to a player moving in the opposite direction — **in reverse** : in an opposite manner or direction
reverse discrimination *n* (1964) : discrimination against whites or males (as in employment or education)
reverse engineer *vt* (1973) : to disassemble and examine or analyze in detail (as a product or device) to discover the concepts involved in manufacture usu. in order to produce something similar — **reverse engineering** *n*
reverse mortgage *n* (1977) : a mortgage that allows esp. an elderly person to convert home equity into available funds through a line of credit, cash advance, or periodic disbursements to be repaid with interest usu. when the borrower dies, moves, or sells the home
reverse osmosis *n* (1955) : the movement of freshwater through a semipermeable membrane when pressure is applied to a solution (as seawater) on one side of it
reverse Polish notation *n* (1975) : a system of representing mathematical and logical operations in which the operands precede the operator and which does not require the use of parentheses ⟨(3 + 5) – (2 + 1) in *reverse Polish notation* is expressed as 3 5 + 2 1 + –⟩ — called also *postfix notation*
reverse tran·scrip·tase \-ˌtran-ˈskrip-(ˌ)tās, -(ˌ)tāz\ *n* (1971) : a polymerase esp. of retroviruses that catalyzes the formation of DNA using RNA as a template
reverse transcription *n* (1971) : the process of synthesizing DNA using RNA as a template and reverse transcriptase as a catalyst
[1]**re·vers·ible** \ri-ˈvər-sə-bəl\ *adj* (1648) : capable of being reversed or of reversing: as **a :** capable of going through a series of actions (as changes) either backward or forward ⟨a ~ chemical reaction⟩ **b :** having two finished usable sides ⟨~ fabric⟩ **c :** wearable with either side out ⟨a ~ coat⟩ — **re·vers·ibil·i·ty** \-ˌvər-sə-ˈbi-lə-tē\ *n* — **re·vers·ibly** \-ˈvər-sə-blē\ *adv*
[2]**reversible** *n* (1863) : a reversible cloth or article of clothing
re·ver·sion \ri-ˈvər-zhən, -shən\ *n* [ME, fr. AF, fr. L *reversion-, reversio* act of returning, fr. *revertere*] (15c) **1 a :** the part of a simple estate remaining in the control of its owner after the owner has granted therefrom a lesser particular estate **b :** a future interest in property left in the control of a grantor or the grantor's successor **2 :** the right of succession or future possession or enjoyment **3 a :** an act or the process of returning (as to a former condition) **b :** a return toward an ancestral type or condition : reappearance of an ancestral character **4 :** an act or instance of turning the opposite way : the state of being so turned **5 :** a product of reversion; *specif* : an organism with an atavistic character : THROWBACK
re·ver·sion·al \-ˈvərzh-nəl, -ˈvərsh-; -ˈvər-zhə-nᵊl, -shə-\ *adj* (1675) : REVERSIONARY
re·ver·sion·ary \-ˈvər-zhə-ˌner-ē, -shə-\ *adj* (1720) : of, relating to, constituting, or involving esp. a legal reversion
re·ver·sion·er \-ˈvərzh-nər, -ˈvərsh-; -ˈvər-zhə-nər, -shə-\ *n* (1614) : one that has or is entitled to a reversion; *broadly* : one having a vested right to a future estate
re·vert \ri-ˈvərt\ *vi* [ME, fr. AF *revertir,* fr. L *revertere,* v.t., to turn back & *reverti,* v.i., to return, come back, fr. *re-* + *vertere, verti* to turn — more at WORTH] (15c) **1 :** to come or go back (as to a former condition, period, or subject) **2 :** to return to the proprietor or his or her heirs at the end of a reversion **3 :** to return to an ancestral type — **re·vert·er** *n* — **re·vert·ible** \-ˈvər-tə-bəl\ *adj*
re·ver·tant \ri-ˈvər-tᵊnt\ *n* (1955) : a mutant gene, individual, or strain that regains a former capability (as the production of a particular protein) by undergoing further mutation ⟨yeast ~*s*⟩ — **revertant** *adj*
re·vest \(ˌ)rē-ˈvest\ *vt* (1561) : REINSTATE, REINVEST
re·vet \ri-ˈvet\ *vt* **re·vet·ted; re·vet·ting** [F *revêtir,* lit., to clothe, put on, fr. OF *revestir,* fr. L *revestire,* fr. *re-* + *vestire* to clothe — more at VEST] (1812) : to face (as an embankment) with a revetment
re·vet·ment \ri-ˈvet-mənt\ *n* (1779) **1 :** a facing (as of stone or concrete) to sustain an embankment **2 :** EMBANKMENT; *esp* : a barricade to provide shelter (as against bomb fragments or strafing)
[1]**re·view** \ri-ˈvyü\ *n* [ME *reveue,* fr. MF, fr. fem. pp. of *revoir* to see again, reexamine, fr. OF *reveoir,* fr. *re-* + *veoir, veeir* to see — more at VIEW] (15c) **1 a :** a formal military inspection **b :** a military ceremony honoring a person or an event **2 :** REVISION 1a **3 :** a general survey (as of the events of a period) **4 :** an act or the process of reviewing **5 :** judicial reexamination (as of the proceedings of a lower tribunal by a higher) **6 a :** a critical evaluation (as of a book or play) **b :** a magazine devoted chiefly to reviews and essays **7 a :** a retrospective view or survey (as of one's life) **b (1) :** renewed study of material previously studied **(2) :** an exercise facilitating such study **8 :** REVUE
[2]**re·view** \ri-ˈvyü\ *vb* [in sense 1 of v.t., fr. *re-* + *view;* in other senses, fr. [1]*review*] *vt* (1576) **1** *also* ˈrē-ˌvyü\ **:** to view or see again **2 :** to examine or study again; *esp* : to reexamine judicially **3 :** to look back on : take a retrospective view of ⟨~ the past⟩ **4 a :** to go over or examine critically or deliberately ⟨~*ed* the results of the study⟩ **b :** to give a critical evaluation of ⟨~ a novel⟩ **5 :** to hold a review of ⟨~ troops⟩ ~ *vi* **1 :** to study material again : make a review ⟨~ for a test⟩ **2 :** to write reviews — **re·view·able** \ri-ˈvyü-ə-bəl\ *adj*
re·view·er \ri-ˈvyü-ər\ *n* (1651) : one that reviews; *esp* : a writer of critical reviews
re·vile \ri-ˈvī(-ə)l\ *vb* **re·viled; re·vil·ing** [ME, fr. AF *reviler* to despise, fr. *re-* + *vil* vile] *vt* (14c) : to subject to verbal abuse : VITUPERATE ~ *vi* : to use abusive language : RAIL ***syn*** see SCOLD — **re·vile·ment** \-ˈvī(-ə)l-mənt\ *n* — **re·vil·er** *n*
re·vis·al \ri-ˈvī-zəl\ *n* (1608) : an act of revising : REVISION
[1]**re·vise** \ˈrē-ˌvīz, ri-ˈ\ *n* (1591) **1 :** an act of revising : REVISION **2 :** a printing proof that incorporates changes marked in a previous proof
[2]**re·vise** \ri-ˈvīz\ *vb* **re·vised; re·vis·ing** [MF *reviser,* fr. L *revisere* to look at again, freq. of *revidēre* to see again, fr. *re-* + *vidēre* to see — more at WIT] *vt* (1596) **1 a :** to look over again in order to correct or improve ⟨~ a manuscript⟩ **b** *Brit* : to study again : REVIEW **2 a :** to make a new, amended, improved, or up-to-date version of ⟨~ a dictionary⟩ **b :** to provide with a new taxonomic arrangement ⟨*revising* the alpine ferns⟩ ~ *vi, Brit* : REVIEW 1 ***syn*** see CORRECT — **re·vis·able** \-ˈvī-zə-bəl\ *adj* — **re·vis·er** *or* **re·vi·sor** \-ˈvī-zər\ *n*
Revised Standard Version *n* (1946) : a revision of the American Standard Version of the Bible published in 1946 and 1952
Revised Version *n* (1837) : a British revision of the Authorized Version of the Bible published in 1881 and 1885
re·vi·sion \ri-ˈvi-zhən\ *n* (1611) **1 a :** an act of revising **b :** a result of revising : ALTERATION **2 :** a revised version — **re·vi·sion·ary** \-zhə-ˌner-ē\ *adj*
re·vi·sion·ism \ri-ˈvi-zhə-ˌni-zəm\ *n* (1903) **1 :** a movement in revolutionary Marxian socialism favoring an evolutionary rather than a revolutionary spirit **2 :** advocacy of revision (as of a doctrine or policy or in historical analysis) — **re·vi·sion·ist** \-nist\ *n or adj*
[1]**re·vis·it** \(ˌ)rē-ˈvi-zət\ *vt* (15c) : to visit again : return to ⟨~ the old neighborhood⟩; *also* : to consider or take up again ⟨reluctant to ~ past disputes⟩

[2]**revisit** *n* (1623) : a second or subsequent visit

re•vi•so•ry \ri-ˈvī-zə-rē, -ˈvīz-rē\ *adj* (ca. 1841) : having the power or purpose to revise ⟨a ~ committee⟩ ⟨a ~ function⟩

re•vi•tal•ise *Brit var of* REVITALIZE

re•vi•tal•ize \(ˌ)rē-ˈvī-tə-ˌlīz\ *vt* **-ized; -iz•ing** (1869) : to give new life or vigor to — **re•vi•tal•i•za•tion** \(ˌ)rē-ˌvī-tə-lə-ˈzā-shən\ *n*

re•viv•al \ri-ˈvī-vəl\ *n* (1651) **1** : an act or instance of reviving : the state of being revived: as **a** : renewed attention to or interest in something **b** : a new presentation or publication of something old **c** (1) : a period of renewed religious interest (2) : an often highly emotional evangelistic meeting or series of meetings **2** : restoration of force, validity, or effect (as to a contract)

re•viv•al•ism \-ˈvī-və-ˌli-zəm\ *n* (1815) **1** : the spirit or methods characteristic of religious revivals **2** : a tendency or desire to revive or restore

re•viv•al•ist \-ˈvī-və-list, -ˈvīv-list\ *n* (1820) **1** : one who conducts religious revivals; *specif* : a member of the clergy who travels about to conduct revivals **2** : one who revives or restores something disused — **revivalist** *adj* — **re•viv•al•is•tic** \-ˌvī-və-ˈlis-tik\ *adj*

re•vive \ri-ˈvīv\ *vb* **re•vived; re•viv•ing** [ME, fr. AF *revivre,* fr. L *revivere* to live again, fr. *re-* + *vivere* to live — more at QUICK] *vi* (15c) : to return to consciousness or life : become active or flourishing again ~ *vt* **1** : to restore to consciousness or life **2** : to restore from a depressed, inactive, or unused state : bring back **3** : to renew in the mind or memory — **re•viv•able** \-ˈvī-və-bəl\ *adj* — **re•viv•er** *n*

re•viv•i•fy \rē-ˈvi-və-ˌfī\ *vt* [F *révivifier,* fr. LL *revivificare,* fr. L *re-* + LL *vivificare* to vivify] (1675) : to give new life to : REVIVE — **re•viv•i•fi•ca•tion** \-ˌvi-və-fə-ˈkā-shən\ *n*

re•vi•vis•cence \ˌrē-ˌvī-ˈvi-sᵊn(t)s, ri-\ *n* [L *reviviscere* to come to life again, fr. *re-* + *viviscere* to come to life, fr. *vivus* alive, living — more at QUICK] (1626) : an act of reviving : the state of being revived — **re•vi•vis•cent** \-sᵊnt\ *adj*

rev•o•ca•ble \ˈre-və-kə-bəl *also* ri-ˈvō-\ *also* **re•vok•able** \ri-ˈvō-kə-bəl\ *adj* [ME, fr. AF, fr. L *revocabilis,* fr. *revocare*] (15c) : capable of being revoked ⟨a ~ privilege⟩

rev•o•ca•tion \ˌre-və-ˈkā-shən; ri-ˌvō-, ˌrē-\ *n* [ME, fr. AF, fr. L *revocation-, revocatio,* fr. *revocare*] (15c) : an act or instance of revoking

[1]**re•voke** \ri-ˈvōk\ *vb* **re•voked; re•vok•ing** [ME, fr. AF *revocer, revoquer,* fr. L *revocare,* fr. *re-* + *vocare* to call, fr. *voc-, vox* voice — more at VOICE] *vt* (14c) **1** : to annul by recalling or taking back : RESCIND ⟨~ a will⟩ **2** : to bring or call back ~ *vi* : to fail to follow suit when able in a card game in violation of the rules — **re•vok•er** *n*

[2]**revoke** *n* (1709) : an act or instance of revoking in a card game

[1]**re•volt** \ri-ˈvōlt *also* -ˈvȯlt\ *vb* [MF *revolter,* fr. OIt *rivoltare* to overthrow, fr. VL **revolvitare,* freq. of L *revolvere* to revolve, roll back] *vi* (1539) **1** : to renounce allegiance or subjection (as to a government) : REBEL **2 a** : to experience disgust or shock **b** : to turn away with disgust ~ *vt* : to cause to turn away or shrink with disgust or abhorrence — **re•volt•er** *n*

[2]**revolt** *n* (1560) **1** : a renouncing of allegiance (as to a government or party); *esp* : a determined armed uprising **2** : a movement or expression of vigorous dissent ***syn*** see REBELLION

re•volt•ing \ri-ˈvōl-tiŋ *also* -ˈvȯl-\ *adj* (1806) : extremely offensive ⟨~ behavior⟩ ⟨a ~ odor⟩ — **re•volt•ing•ly** *adv*

rev•o•lute \ˈre-və-ˌlüt\ *adj* [L *revolutus,* pp. of *revolvere*] (ca. 1753) : rolled backward or downward ⟨a leaf with ~ margins⟩

rev•o•lu•tion \ˌre-və-ˈlü-shən\ *n* [ME *revolucioun,* fr. MF *revolution,* fr. LL *revolution-, revolutio,* fr. L *revolvere* to revolve] (14c) **1 a** (1) : the action by a celestial body of going round in an orbit or elliptical course; *also* : apparent movement of such a body round the earth (2) : the time taken by a celestial body to make a complete round in its orbit (3) : the rotation of a celestial body on its axis **b** : completion of a course (as of years); *also* : the period made by the regular succession of a measure of time or by a succession of similar events **c** (1) : a progressive motion of a body around an axis so that any line of the body parallel to the axis returns to its initial position while remaining parallel to the axis in transit and usu. at a constant distance from it (2) : motion of any figure about a center or axis ⟨~ of a right triangle about one of its legs generates a cone⟩ (3) : ROTATION 1b **2 a** : a sudden, radical, or complete change **b** : a fundamental change in political organization; *esp* : the overthrow or renunciation of one government or ruler and the substitution of another by the governed **c** : activity or movement designed to effect fundamental changes in the socioeconomic situation **d** : a fundamental change in the way of thinking about or visualizing something : a change of paradigm ⟨the Copernican ~⟩ **e** : a changeover in use or preference esp. in technology ⟨the computer ~⟩ ⟨the foreign car ~⟩ ***syn*** see REBELLION

[1]**rev•o•lu•tion•ary** \-shə-ˌner-ē\ *adj* (1774) **1 a** : of, relating to, or constituting a revolution ⟨~ war⟩ **b** : tending to or promoting revolution **c** : constituting or bringing about a major or fundamental change ⟨a ~ new product⟩ **2** *cap* : of or relating to the American Revolution or to the period in which it occurred — **rev•o•lu•tion•ar•i•ly** \-ˌlü-shə-ˈner-ə-lē\ *adv* — **rev•o•lu•tion•ar•i•ness** \-ˈlü-shə-ˌner-ē-nəs\ *n*

[2]**revolutionary** *n, pl* **-ar•ies** (1850) **1** : one engaged in a revolution **2** : an advocate or adherent of revolutionary doctrines

rev•o•lu•tion•ise *Brit var of* REVOLUTIONIZE

rev•o•lu•tion•ist \ˌre-və-ˈlü-sh(ə-)nist\ *n* (1710) : REVOLUTIONARY — **revolutionist** *adj*

rev•o•lu•tion•ize \-shə-ˌnīz\ *vb* **-ized; -iz•ing** *vt* (1797) **1** : to overthrow the established government of **2** : to imbue with revolutionary doctrines **3** : to change fundamentally or completely ⟨~ an industry⟩ ~ *vi* : to engage in revolution — **rev•o•lu•tion•iz•er** *n*

re•volve \ri-ˈvälv, -ˈvȯlv *also* -ˈväv *or* -ˈvȯv\ *vb* **re•volved; re•volv•ing** [ME, fr. L *revolvere* to roll back, cause to return, fr. *re-* + *volvere* to roll — more at VOLUBLE] *vt* (15c) **1** : to turn over at length in the mind : PONDER ⟨~ a scheme⟩ **2 a** *obs* : to cause to go round in an orbit **b** : ROTATE 1 ~ *vi* **1** : RECUR **2 a** : to ponder something **b** : to remain under consideration ⟨ideas *revolved* in his mind⟩ **3 a** : to move in a curved path round a center or axis **b** : to turn or roll round on an axis **4** : to have or come to a specified focus : CENTER — usu. used with *around* ⟨the dispute *revolved* around wages⟩ — **re•volv•able** \-ˈväl-və-bəl, -ˈvȯl- *also* -ˈvä-və- *or* -ˈvȯ-və-\ *adj*

re•volv•er \ri-ˈväl-vər, -ˈvȯl- *also* -ˈvä-vər *or* -ˈvȯ-vər\ *n* (ca. 1835) **1** : one that revolves **2** : a handgun with a cylinder of several chambers brought successively into line with the barrel and discharged with the same hammer

revolving *adj* (1599) **1 a** : tending to revolve or recur; *esp* : recurrently available **b** : of, relating to, or being credit that may be used repeatedly up to the specified limit and is usu. repaid in regular proportional installments **2** : turning around on or as if on an axis ⟨a ~ platform⟩

revolving–door *adj* (1973) : characterized by a frequent succession (as of personnel) or a cycle of leaving and returning ⟨~ governments⟩

revolving door *n* (1973) : a revolving-door system or process

revolving fund *n* (1920) : a fund set up for specified purposes with the proviso that repayments to the fund may be used again for these purposes

re•vue \ri-ˈvyü\ *n* [F, fr. MF *reveue* review — more at REVIEW] (1872) : a theatrical production consisting typically of brief loosely connected often satirical skits, songs, and dances

re•vulsed \ri-ˈvəlst\ *adj* [L *revulsus,* pp. of *revellere* + E *-ed*] (ca. 1934) : affected with or having undergone revulsion

re•vul•sion \ri-ˈvəl-shən\ *n* [L *revulsion-, revulsio* act of tearing away, fr. *revellere* to pluck away, fr. *re-* + *vellere* to pluck — more at VULNERABLE] (1609) **1** : a strong pulling or drawing away : WITHDRAWAL **2 a** : a sudden or strong reaction or change **b** : a sense of utter distaste or repugnance — **re•vul•sive** \-ˈvəl-siv\ *adj*

revved *past and past part of* REV

revving *pres part of* REV

re•wake \(ˌ)rē-ˈwāk\ *vb* **-waked** *or* **-woke** \-ˈwōk\; **-waked** *or* **-wo•ken** \-ˈwō-kən\ *or* **-woke; -wak•ing** *vt* (1593) : to waken again or anew ~ *vi* : to become awake again

re•wak•en \(ˌ)rē-ˈwā-kən\ *vb* (1638) : REWAKE

[1]**re•ward** \ri-ˈwȯrd\ *vt* [ME, fr. AF *regarder, rewarder* to look back at, regard, care for, recompense — more at REGARD] (14c) **1** : to give a reward to or for **2** : RECOMPENSE — **re•ward•able** \-ˈwȯr-də-bəl\ *adj* — **re•ward•er** *n*

[2]**reward** *n* (14c) **1** : something that is given in return for good or evil done or received or that is offered or given for some service or attainment ⟨the police offered a ~ for his capture⟩ **2** : a stimulus administered to an organism following a correct or desired response that increases the probability of occurrence of the response

re•ward•ing \-ˈwȯr-diŋ\ *adj* (1697) **1** : yielding or likely to yield a reward : VALUABLE, SATISFYING ⟨a ~ experience⟩ **2** : serving as a reward ⟨a ~ smile of thanks⟩ — **re•ward•ing•ly** *adv*

[1]**re•wind** \(ˌ)rē-ˈwīnd\ *vt* **-wound** \-ˈwau̇nd\; **-wind•ing** (1717) : to wind again; *esp* : to reverse the winding of (as film)

[2]**re•wind** \ˈrē-ˌwīnd, (ˌ)rē-ˈ\ *n* (1926) **1** : something that rewinds or is rewound **2** : an act of rewinding **3** : a function of an electronic device that reverses a recording to a previous portion

re•word \(ˌ)rē-ˈwərd\ *vt* (1602) **1** : to repeat in the same words **2** : to alter the wording of; *also* : to restate in other words

re•work \(ˌ)rē-ˈwərk\ *vt* (1842) : to work again or anew: as **a** : REVISE **b** : to reprocess (as used material) for further use

[1]**re•write** \(ˌ)rē-ˈrīt\ *vb* **-wrote** \-ˈrōt\; **-writ•ten** \-ˈri-tᵊn\; **-writ•ing** \-ˈrī-tiŋ\ *vt* (1567) **1** : to write in reply **2** : to make a revision of (as a story) : cause to be revised: as **a** : to put (contributed material) into form for publication **b** : to alter (previously published material) for use in another publication ~ *vi* : to revise something previously written — **re•writ•er** *n*

[2]**re•write** \ˈrē-ˌrīt\ *n* (1914) **1** : a piece of writing (as a news story) constructed by rewriting **2** : an act or instance of rewriting

re•write man \ˈrē-ˌrīt-ˌman\ *n* (1901) : a newspaperman who specializes in rewriting

re•write rule \ˈrē-ˌrīt-\ *n* (1960) : a rule in a grammar which specifies the constituents of a single symbol

rex \ˈreks\ *n, pl* **rex•es** *or* **rex** [modif. of F *castorrex, castorex,* a variety of rabbit, perh. fr. L *castor* beaver + *rex* king — more at CASTOR, ROYAL] (1920) : an animal (as a domestic rabbit or cat) showing a genetic recessive variation in which the guard hairs are very short, sparse, or entirely lacking — compare CORNISH REX, DEVON REX

rex sole *n* [prob. modif. of NL *Errex* genus name] (ca. 1954) : a flounder (*Errex zachirus* syn. *Glyptocephalus zachirus*) with both eyes on the right side that is an important food fish occurring from the Bering Sea to Baja California

Reye's syndrome \ˈrīz-, ˈrāz-\ *n* [R.D.K. *Reye* †1977 Austral. pathologist] (1965) : an often fatal encephalopathy esp. of childhood characterized by fever, vomiting, fatty infiltration of the liver, and swelling of the kidneys and brain — called also *Reye syndrome*

rey•nard \ˈrā-nərd, ˈre-, -ˌnär(d)\ *n, often cap* [ME *Renard,* name of the fox who is hero of the Fr. beast epic *Roman de Renart,* fr. MF *Renart, Renard*] (14c) : FOX

Rey•nolds number \ˈre-nᵊldz-\ *n* [Osborne *Reynolds* †1912 Eng. physicist] (1910) : a number characteristic of the flow of a fluid in a pipe or past an obstruction

Rf *symbol* rutherfordium

RF *abbr* radio frequency

RFD *abbr* rural free delivery

R factor \ˈär-\ *n* [resistance] (1962) : a group of genes present in some bacteria that provide a basis for resistance to antibiotics and can be transferred from cell to cell by conjugation

RFID *abbr* radio-frequency identification

RFLP *abbr* restriction fragment length polymorphism

RFP *abbr* request for proposal

Rg *symbol* roentgenium

[1]**Rh** \ˌär-ˈāch\ *adj* (1940) : of, relating to, or being an Rh factor ⟨~ antigens⟩ ⟨~ sensitization in pregnancy⟩

[2]**Rh** *symbol* rhodium

RH *abbr* **1** relative humidity **2** right hand; right hander

rhabdo- *comb form* [LGk, fr. Gk *rhabdos* rod — more at VERVAIN] : rodlike structure ⟨*rhabdo*virus⟩

rhab•do•coele \ˈrab-də-ˌsēl\ *n* [NL *Rhabdocoela,* fr. *rhabdo-* + NL *-coela* -coele] (1883) : a turbellarian worm (order Rhabdocoela) with an unbranched intestine

rhab•dom \ˈrab-ˌdäm, -dəm\ *or* **rhab•dome** \-ˌdōm\ *n* [NL, fr. LGk *rhabdōma* bundle of rods, fr. Gk *rhabdos* rod] (1878) : one of the minute rodlike structures in the retinulae in the compound eyes of arthropods

rhab·do·man·cy \ˈrab-də-ˌman(t)-sē\ *n* [LGk *rhabdomanteia,* fr. Gk *rhabdos* rod + *-manteia* -mancy] (1646) **:** divination by rods or wands — **rhab·do·man·cer** \-ˌman(t)-sər\ *n*

rhab·do·mere \-ˌmir\ *n* (1883) **:** a division of a rhabdom

rhab·do·my·ol·y·sis \ˌrab-dō-mī-ˈä-lə-səs\ *n* [NL, fr. *rhabdo-* + *my-* + *-lysis*] (1956) **:** the destruction or degeneration of muscle tissue (as from traumatic injury, excessive exertion, or stroke) accompanied by the release of breakdown products into the bloodstream and sometimes leading to acute renal failure

rhab·do·myo·sar·co·ma \ˈrab-(ˌ)dō-ˌmī-ə-sär-ˈkō-mə\ *n* [NL, fr. *rhabdo-* + *my-* + *sarcoma*] (1898) **:** a malignant tumor composed of striated muscle fibers

rhab·do·vi·rus \-ˌvī-rəs\ *n* [NL] (1966) **:** any of a family (*Rhabdoviridae*) of rod- or bullet-shaped single-stranded RNA viruses found in plants and animals and including the causative agents of rabies and vesicular stomatitis

rhad·a·man·thine \ˌra-də-ˈman(t)-thən, -ˈman-ˌthīn\ *adj, often cap* [*Rhadamanthus*] (1840) **:** rigorously strict or just

Rhad·a·man·thus \ˌra-də-ˈman(t)-thəs\ *n* (15c) **:** a judge of the underworld in Greek mythology

Rhae·to–Ro·mance \ˌrē-tō-rō-ˈman(t)s, -tō-rə-; -ˈrō-ˌman(t)s\ *also* **Rhae·to–Ro·man·ic** \-rō-ˈma-nik\ *n* [L *Rhaetus* of Rhaetia, ancient Roman province] (1867) **:** a group of Romance languages spoken in eastern Switzerland and northeastern Italy

rham·nose \ˈram-ˌnōs, -ˌnōz\ *n* [ISV, fr. NL *Rhamnus,* genus of the buckthorn; fr. its being produced from a plant of this genus] (1888) **:** a crystalline sugar $C_6H_{12}O_5$ that occurs usu. in the form of a glycoside in many plants and is obtained in the common dextrorotatory L form

rhap·sode \ˈrap-ˌsōd\ *n* [F, fr. Gk *rhapsōidos*] (1834) **:** RHAPSODIST

rhap·sod·ic \rap-ˈsä-dik\ *also* **rhap·sod·i·cal** \-di-kəl\ *adj* (1782) **1 :** extravagantly emotional **:** RAPTUROUS **2 :** resembling or characteristic of a rhapsody — **rhap·sod·i·cal·ly** \-di-k(ə-)lē\ *adv*

rhap·so·dist \ˈrap-sə-dist\ *n* (ca. 1656) **1 :** a professional reciter of epic poems **2 :** one who writes or speaks rhapsodically

rhap·so·dize \-sə-ˌdīz\ *vi* **-dized; -diz·ing** (1806) **:** to speak or write in a rhapsodic manner ⟨~ about a new book⟩

rhap·so·dy \ˈrap-sə-dē\ *n, pl* **-dies** [L *rhapsodia,* fr. Gk *rhapsōidia* recitation of selections from epic poetry, rhapsody, fr. *rhapsōidos* rhapsodist, fr. *rhaptein* to sew, stitch together + *aidein* to sing — more at ODE] (1542) **1 :** a portion of an epic poem adapted for recitation **2** *archaic* **:** a miscellaneous collection **3 a** (1) **:** a highly emotional utterance (2) **:** a highly emotional literary work (3) **:** effusively rapturous or extravagant discourse **b :** RAPTURE, ECSTASY **4 :** a musical composition of irregular form having an improvisatory character

rhea \ˈrē-ə\ *n* [NL, genus of birds, prob. fr. L *Rhea,* mother of Zeus, fr. Gk] (1797) **:** either of two So. American ratite birds (*Rhea americana* and *Pterocnemia pennata* of the family Rheidae) that resemble but are smaller than the African ostrich and that have three toes, a fully feathered head and neck, an undeveloped tail, and pale gray to brownish feathers that droop over the rump and back

rhe·bok \ˈrē-ˌbäk\ *n* [Afrik *reebok,* fr. D, male roe deer, fr. *ree* roe + *boc* buck] (1813) **:** a brownish-gray antelope (*Pelea capreolus*) of southern Africa

rhe·ni·um \ˈrē-nē-əm\ *n* [NL, fr. L *Rhenus* Rhine River] (1925) **:** a rare heavy metallic element that is obtained either as a gray powder or as a silver-white hard metal, is usu. extracted as a by-product of molybdenum smelting, and is used esp. in catalysts and alloys — see ELEMENT table

rheo- *comb form* [Gk *rhein* to flow — more at STREAM] **:** flow **:** current ⟨*rheo*stat⟩

rhe·ol·o·gy \rē-ˈä-lə-jē\ *n* [ISV] (1929) **:** a science dealing with the deformation and flow of matter; *also* **:** the ability to flow or be deformed — **rhe·o·log·i·cal** \ˌrē-ə-ˈlä-ji-kəl\ *also* **rheo·log·ic** \-jik\ *adj* — **rhe·o·log·i·cal·ly** \-ji-k(ə-)lē\ *adv* — **rhe·ol·o·gist** \rē-ˈä-lə-jist\ *n*

rhe·om·e·ter \rē-ˈä-mə-tər\ *n* [ISV] (ca. 1859) **:** an instrument for measuring flow (as of viscous substances)

rheo·stat \ˈrē-ə-ˌstat\ *n* (1843) **:** a resistor for regulating a current by means of variable resistances — **rheo·stat·ic** \ˌrē-ə-ˈsta-tik\ *adj*

rhe·sus monkey \ˈrē-səs-\ *n* [NL *Rhesus,* genus of monkeys, fr. L, a mythical king of Thrace, fr. Gk *Rhēsos*] (1841) **:** a pale brown Asian macaque (*Macaca mulatta*) often used in medical research — called also *rhesus, rhesus macaque*

rhet *abbr* rhetoric

rhe·tor \ˈrē-ˌtȯr, ˈre-; ˈrē-tər, ˈre-\ *n* [ME *rethor,* fr. L *rhetor,* fr. Gk *rhētōr*] (14c) **:** RHETORICIAN 1

rhet·o·ric \ˈre-tə-rik\ *n* [ME *rethorik,* fr. AF *rethorique,* fr. L *rhetorica,* fr. Gk *rhētorikē,* lit., art of oratory, fr. fem. of *rhētorikos* of an orator, fr. *rhētōr* orator, rhetorician, fr. *eirein* to say, speak — more at WORD] (14c) **1 :** the art of speaking or writing effectively: as **a :** the study of principles and rules of composition formulated by critics of ancient times **b :** the study of writing or speaking as a means of communication or persuasion **2 a :** skill in the effective use of speech **b :** a type or mode of language or speech; *also* **:** insincere or grandiloquent language **3 :** verbal communication **:** DISCOURSE

rhe·tor·i·cal \ri-ˈtȯr-i-kəl, -ˈtär-\ *also* **rhe·tor·ic** \ri-ˈtȯr-ik, -ˈtär-\ *adj* (15c) **1 a :** of, relating to, or concerned with rhetoric **b :** employed for rhetorical effect; *esp* **:** asked merely for effect with no answer expected ⟨a ~ question⟩ **2 a :** given to rhetoric **:** GRANDILOQUENT **b :** VERBAL — **rhe·tor·i·cal·ly** \-i-k(ə-)lē\ *adv*

rhet·o·ri·cian \ˌre-tə-ˈri-shən\ *n* (15c) **1 a :** a master or teacher of rhetoric **b :** ORATOR **2 :** an eloquent or grandiloquent writer or speaker

rheum \ˈrüm\ *n* [ME *reume,* fr. AF, fr. L *rheuma,* fr. Gk, lit., flow, flux, fr. *rhein* to flow — more at STREAM] (14c) **1 :** a watery discharge from the mucous membranes esp. of the eyes or nose **2** *archaic* **:** TEARS — **rheumy** \ˈrü-mē\ *adj*

[1]**rheu·mat·ic** \ru̇-ˈma-tik\ *adj* [ME *rewmatik* subject to rheum, fr. AF *reumatike,* fr. L *rheumaticus,* fr. Gk *rheumatikos,* fr. *rheumat-, rheuma*] (1711) **:** of, relating to, characteristic of, or affected with rheumatism — **rheu·mat·i·cal·ly** \-ti-k(ə-)lē\ *adv*

[2]**rheumatic** *n* (1846) **:** one affected with rheumatism

rheumatic fever *n* (1782) **:** an acute disease that occurs chiefly in children and young adults and is characterized by fever, by inflammation and pain in and around the joints, and by inflammatory involvement of the pericardium and heart valves

rheu·ma·tism \ˈrü-mə-ˌti-zəm, ˈru̇-\ *n* [L *rheumatismus* flux, rheum, fr. Gk *rheumatismos,* fr. *rheumatizesthai* to suffer from a flux, fr. *rheumat-, rheuma* flux] (1677) **1 :** any of various conditions characterized by inflammation or pain in muscles, joints, or fibrous tissue ⟨muscular ~⟩ **2 :** RHEUMATOID ARTHRITIS

rheu·ma·toid \-ˌtȯid\ *adj* [ISV, fr. *rheumatism*] (1869) **:** characteristic of or affected with rheumatoid arthritis

rheumatoid arthritis *n* (1859) **:** a usu. chronic autoimmune disease that is characterized esp. by pain, stiffness, inflammation, swelling, and sometimes destruction of joints

rheumatoid factor *n* (1949) **:** an autoantibody of high molecular weight that reacts against IgG immunoglobulins and is often present in rheumatoid arthritis

rheu·ma·tol·o·gy \ˌrü-mə-ˈtä-lə-jē, ˌru̇-\ *n* (ca. 1941) **:** a medical science dealing with rheumatic diseases — **rheu·ma·to·log·ic** \-tə-ˈlä-jik\ *or* **rheu·ma·to·log·i·cal** \-ji-kəl\ *adj* — **rheu·ma·tol·o·gist** \-ˈtä-lə-jist\ *n*

Rh factor \ˌär-ˈāch-\ *n* [*rh*esus monkey (in which it was first detected)] (1942) **:** any of one or more genetically determined antigens present in the red blood cells of most persons and of higher animals and capable of inducing intense immunogenic reactions

rhin- *or* **rhino-** *comb form* [NL, fr. Gk, fr. *rhin-, rhis*] **:** nose ⟨*rhino*plasty⟩

rhi·nal \ˈrī-nᵊl\ *adj* (ca. 1859) **:** of or relating to the nose **:** NASAL

rhin·en·ceph·a·lon \ˌrī-(ˌ)nen-ˈse-fə-ˌlän, -lən\ *n* [NL] (1846) **:** the chiefly olfactory part of the forebrain — **rhin·en·ce·phal·ic** \ˌrī-ˌnen-sə-ˈfa-lik\ *adj*

rhine·stone \ˈrīn-ˌstōn\ *n* [*Rhine* River] (ca. 1888) **:** a colorless imitation stone of high luster made of glass, paste, or gem quartz — **rhine·stoned** \-ˌstōnd\ *adj*

Rhine wine \ˈrīn-\ *n* (1843) **1 :** a usu. white wine produced in the Rhine valley **2 :** a wine similar to Rhine wine produced elsewhere

rhi·ni·tis \rī-ˈnī-təs\ *n* [NL] (ca. 1884) **:** inflammation of the mucous membrane of the nose

[1]**rhi·no** \ˈrī-(ˌ)nō\ *n* [origin unknown] (1670) **:** MONEY, CASH

[2]**rhino** *n, pl* **rhinos** *also* **rhino** (1884) **:** RHINOCEROS

rhi·noc·er·os \rī-ˈnä-sə-rəs, rə-, -ˈnä-sə-\ *n, pl* **-noc·er·os·es** *also* **-noc·er·os** *or* **-noc·eri** \-ˈnä-sə-ˌrī\ [ME *rinoceros,* fr. AF, fr. L *rhinocerot-, rhinoceros,* fr. Gk *rhinokerōt-, rhinokerōs,* fr. *rhin-* + *keras* horn — more at HORN] (14c) **:** any of a family (Rhinocerotidae) of large heavyset herbivorous perissodactyl mammals of Africa and Asia that have one or two upright keratinous horns on the snout and thick gray to brown skin with little hair

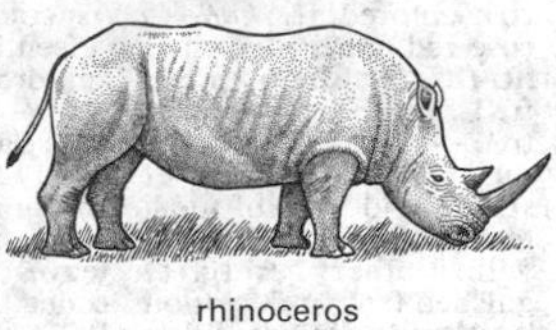

rhinoceros

rhinoceros beetle *n* (1681) **:** any of various large chiefly tropical scarab beetles (subfamily Dynastinae) having projecting horns on thorax and head

rhi·no·plas·ty \ˈrī-nō-ˌplas-tē\ *n, pl* **-ties** (1842) **:** plastic surgery on the nose usu. for cosmetic purposes

rhi·nos·co·py \rī-ˈnäs-kə-pē\ *n* [ISV] (1861) **:** examination of the nasal passages

rhi·no·vi·rus \ˌrī-nō-ˈvī-rəs\ *n* [NL] (1961) **:** any of a genus (*Rhinovirus*) of picornaviruses including two (species *Human rhinovirus A* and *Human rhinovirus B*) having numerous serotypes causing respiratory infections (as the common cold) in humans

rhiz- *or* **rhizo-** *comb form* [NL, fr. Gk, fr. *rhiza* — more at ROOT] **:** root ⟨*rhizo*plane⟩

-rhiza *or* **-rrhiza** *n comb form, pl* **-zae** *or* **-zas** [NL, fr. Gk *rhiza*] **:** root **:** part resembling or connected with a root ⟨coleo*rhiza*⟩ ⟨mycor*rhiza*⟩

rhi·zo·bi·um \rī-ˈzō-bē-əm\ *n, pl* **-bia** \-bē-ə\ [NL, fr. *rhiz-* + Gk *bios* life — more at QUICK] (1921) **:** any of a genus (*Rhizobium*) of small heterotrophic soil bacteria capable of forming symbiotic nodules on the roots of leguminous plants and of there becoming bacteroids that fix atmospheric nitrogen — **rhi·zo·bi·al** \-bē-əl\ *adj*

rhi·zoc·to·nia \ˌrī-ˌzäk-ˈtō-nē-ə\ *n* [NL, fr. *rhiz-* + Gk *-ktonos* killing, fr. *kteinein* to kill; akin to Skt *kṣaṇoti* he wounds] (1897) **:** any of a form genus (*Rhizoctonia*) of imperfect fungi that includes major plant pathogens

rhi·zoid \ˈrī-ˌzȯid\ *n* (1875) **:** a rootlike structure — **rhi·zoi·dal** \rī-ˈzȯi-dᵊl\ *adj*

rhi·zo·ma·tous \rī-ˈzō-mə-təs\ *adj* [ISV, fr. NL *rhizomat-, rhizoma*] (1847) **:** having, resembling, or being a rhizome ⟨a ~ perennial grass⟩

rhi·zome \ˈrī-ˌzōm\ *n* [NL *rhizomat-, rhizoma,* fr. Gk *rhizōmat-, rhizōma* mass of roots, fr. *rhizoun* to cause to take root, fr. *rhiza* root — more at ROOT] (1845) **:** a somewhat elongate usu. horizontal subterranean plant stem that is often thickened by deposits of reserve food material, produces shoots above and roots below, and is distinguished from a true root in possessing buds, nodes, and usu. scalelike leaves — **rhi·zo·mic** \rī-ˈzō-mik, -ˈzä-\ *adj*

rhi·zo·plane \ˈrī-zə-ˌplān\ *n* (1949) **:** the external surface of roots together with closely adhering soil particles and debris

rhi·zo·pod \ˈrī-zə-ˌpäd\ *n* [NL *Rhizopoda,* fr. *rhiz-* + *-poda* -pod] (1851) **:** any of a superclass (Rhizopoda) of usu. creeping protozoans (as an amoeba or a foraminifer) having lobate or rootlike pseudopodia

rhi·zo·pus \ˈrī-zə-pəs, -ˌpu̇s\ *n* [NL, fr. *rhiz-* + Gk *pous* foot — more at FOOT] (1887) **:** any of a genus (*Rhizopus*) of mold fungi including some economically valuable forms and some plant or animal pathogens (as a bread mold)

rhi·zo·sphere \-ˌsfir\ *n* [ISV] (1929) **:** soil that surrounds and is influenced by the roots of a plant

rhi·zot·o·my \rī-ˈzä-tə-mē\ *n, pl* **-mies** [ISV] (1911) : the operation of cutting the anterior or posterior spinal nerve roots

Rh–neg·a·tive \ˌär-ˌāch-ˈne-gə-tiv\ *adj* (1945) : lacking Rh factor in the blood

rho \ˈrō\ *n* [Gk *rhō,* of Sem origin; akin to Heb *rēsh* resh] (15c) : the 17th letter of the Greek alphabet — see ALPHABET table

rhod- *or* **rhodo-** *comb form* [NL, fr. L, fr. Gk, fr. *rhodon* rose — more at ROSE] : rose : red ⟨*rhodo*lite⟩

rho·da·mine \ˈrō-də-ˌmēn\ *n, often cap* [ISV] (1888) : any of a group of yellowish-red to blue fluorescent dyes; *esp* : a brilliant bluish-red dye made by fusing an amino derivative of phenol with phthalic anhydride and used esp. in coloring paper and as a biological stain

Rhode Island Red *n* [*Rhode Island,* U.S. state] (1896) : any of an American breed of general-purpose domestic chickens having a long heavy body, smooth yellow or reddish legs, and rich brownish-red plumage

Rhode Island White *n* (ca. 1923) : any of an American breed of domestic chickens resembling Rhode Island Reds but having pure white plumage

Rhodes grass \ˈrōdz-\ *n* [Cecil J. *Rhodes*] (1915) : an African perennial grass (*Chloris gayana*) widely cultivated as a forage grass esp. in dry regions

Rho·de·sian man \rō-ˈdē-zh(ē-)ən-\ *n* [Northern *Rhodesia,* Africa] (1921) : an extinct African hominid (*Homo sapiens rhodesiensis*) having long limb bones and a cranial capacity like those of modern humans but with more prominent brow ridges and a larger face and palate

Rhodesian ridge·back \-ˈrij-ˌbak\ *n, often cap 2d R* (1925) : any of an African breed of powerful long-bodied hunting dogs having a dense harsh short tan coat with a characteristic crest of reversed hair along the spine

Rhodes scholar \ˈrōd(z)-\ *n* (1902) : a holder of one of numerous scholarships founded under the will of Cecil J. Rhodes that can be used at Oxford University for two or three years and are open to candidates from the Commonwealth of Nations and the U.S.

rho·di·um \ˈrō-dē-əm\ *n* [NL, fr. Gk *rhodon* rose] (1804) : a rare silvery-white hard ductile metallic element that is resistant to acids, occurs native but is usu. obtained from nickel ores, and is used esp. as a catalyst and in platinum alloys — see ELEMENT table

rho·do·chro·site \ˌrō-də-ˈkrō-ˌsīt\ *n* [G *Rhodocrosit,* fr. Gk *rhodochrōs* rose-colored, fr. *rhod-* + *chrōs* color — more at CHROMATIC] (1836) : a rose-red mineral consisting essentially of manganese carbonate

rho·do·den·dron \ˌrō-də-ˈden-drən\ *n* [NL, fr. L, oleander, fr. Gk, fr. *rhod-* + *dendron* tree — more at DENDR-] (1664) : any of a genus (*Rhododendron*) of widely cultivated shrubs and trees of the heath family with alternate leaves and showy flowers; *esp* : one with leathery evergreen leaves as distinguished from a deciduous azalea

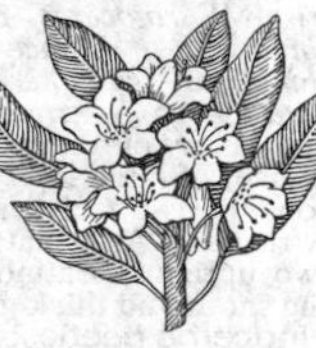
rhododendron

rho·do·lite \ˈrō-də-ˌlīt\ *n* (1897) : a pink or purple garnet used as a gem

rhodomontade *var of* RODOMONTADE

rho·do·nite \ˈrō-də-ˌnīt\ *n* [G *Rhodonit,* fr. Gk *rhodon* rose] (1823) : a pale red triclinic mineral that consists essentially of manganese silicate and is used as an ornamental stone

rho·dop·sin \rō-ˈdäp-sən\ *n* [ISV *rhod-* + Gk *opsis* sight, vision + ISV [1]*-in* — more at OPTIC] (1886) : a red photosensitive pigment in the retinal rods of the eye of most vertebrates that is important in vision in dim light — called also *visual purple*

rho·do·ra \rō-ˈdȯr-ə\ *n* [NL, alter. of L *rodarum,* a plant] (ca. 1731) : an azalea (*Rhododendron canadense*) of northeastern No. America that has spring-flowering pink blossoms

rhomb \ˈräm(b)\ *n, pl* **rhombs** \ˈrämz\ [MF *rhombe,* fr. L *rhombus*] (ca. 1578) **1** : RHOMBUS **2** : RHOMBOHEDRON

rhomb- *or* **rhombo-** *comb form* [NL, fr. Gk *rhombos*] : rhombus ⟨*rhomb*encephalon⟩

rhomb·en·ceph·a·lon \ˌräm-(ˌ)ben-ˈse-fə-ˌlän, -lən\ *n* [NL] (1897) : HINDBRAIN 1

rhom·bic \ˈräm-bik\ *adj* (1701) **1** : having the form of a rhombus **2** : ORTHORHOMBIC

rhom·bo·he·dron \ˌräm-bō-ˈhē-drən\ *n, pl* **-drons** *or* **-dra** \-drə\ [NL] (1836) : a parallelepiped whose faces are rhombuses — **rhom·bo·he·dral** \-drəl\ *adj*

[1]**rhom·boid** \ˈräm-ˌbȯid\ *n* [MF *rhomboïde,* fr. L *rhomboides,* fr. Gk *rhomboeidēs* resembling a rhombus, fr. *rhombos*] (1570) : a parallelogram with no right angles and with adjacent sides of unequal length

[2]**rhom·boid** \ˈräm-ˌbȯid\ *or* **rhom·boi·dal** \räm-ˈbȯi-dᵊl\ *adj* (ca. 1693) : shaped somewhat like a rhombus or rhomboid

rhom·boi·de·us \räm-ˈbȯi-dē-əs\ *n, pl* **-dei** \-dē-ˌī\ [NL, fr. L *rhomboides* rhomboid] (ca. 1836) : either of two muscles that lie beneath the trapezius muscle and connect the spinous processes of various vertebrae with the medial border of the scapula

rhom·bus \ˈräm-bəs\ *n, pl* **rhom·bus·es** *or* **rhom·bi** \-ˌbī, -ˌbē\ [L, fr. Gk *rhombos* piece of wood whirled on a string, lozenge, fr. *rhembein* to whirl] (ca. 1567) : a parallelogram with four equal sides and sometimes one with no right angles

rhon·chus \ˈräŋ-kəs\ *n, pl* **rhon·chi** \ˈräŋ-ˌkī\ [LGk, fr. *rhenchein* to snore, wheeze; prob. akin to OIr *sreinnid* he snores] (1829) : a whistling or snoring sound heard on auscultation of the chest when the air channels are partly obstructed

Rh–pos·i·tive \ˌär-ˌāch-ˈpä-zə-tiv, -ˈpäz-tiv\ *adj* (1942) : containing Rh factor in the red blood cells

rhu·barb \ˈrü-ˌbärb\ *n* [ME *rubarbe,* fr. AF *reubarbe,* fr. ML *reubarbarum,* alter. of *rha barbarum,* lit., barbarian rhubarb] (15c) **1** : any of a genus (*Rheum*) of Asian plants of the buckwheat family having large leaves with thick succulent petioles often used as food; *also* : the petioles of rhubarb **2** : the dried rhizome and roots of any of several rhubarbs (as *Rheum officinale* and *R. palmatum*) grown in China and Tibet and used as a purgative and stomachic **3** : a heated dispute or controversy

rhumb \ˈrəm(b)\ *n, pl* **rhumbs** \ˈrəmz\ [Sp *rumbo* rhumb, rhumb line] (1578) **1** : a line or course on a single bearing **2** : any of the points of the mariner's compass

rhumba *var of* RUMBA

rhumb line *n* [Sp *rumbo*] (1669) : a line on the surface of the earth that follows a single compass bearing and makes equal oblique angles with all meridians — called also *loxodrome*

rhus \ˈrüs\ *n, pl* **rhus·es** *or* **rhus** [NL, fr. L, sumac, fr. Gk *rhous*] (ca. 1611) : SUMAC 2

[1]**rhyme** *also* **rime** \ˈrīm\ *n* [ME *rime,* fr. AF] (13c) **1 a** (1) : rhyming verse (2) : POETRY **b** : a composition in verse that rhymes **2 a** : correspondence in terminal sounds of units of composition or utterance (as two or more words or lines of verse) **b** : one of two or more words thus corresponding in sound **c** : correspondence of other than terminal word sounds: as (1) : ALLITERATION (2) : INTERNAL RHYME **3** : RHYTHM, MEASURE — **rhyme·less** *adj*

[2]**rhyme** *also* **rime** *vb* **rhymed** *also* **rimed; rhym·ing** *also* **rim·ing** *vt* (14c) **1** : to relate or praise in rhyming verse **2 a** : to put into rhyme **b** : to compose (verse) in rhyme **c** : to cause to rhyme : use as rhyme ∼ *vi* **1** : to make rhymes; *also* : to compose rhyming verse **2** *of a word or verse* : to end in syllables that are rhymes **3** : to be in accord : HARMONIZE — **rhym·er** *n*

rhyme or reason *n* (15c) : good sense or reason

rhyme royal \-ˈrȯi(-ə)l\ *n* (ca. 1841) : a stanza of seven lines in iambic pentameter with a rhyme scheme of *ababbcc*

rhyme scheme *n* (1917) : the arrangement of rhymes in a stanza or a poem

rhyme·ster *also* **rime·ster** \ˈrīm(p)-stər\ *n* (1589) : an inferior poet

rhyming slang *n* (1859) : slang in which the word intended is replaced by a word or phrase that rhymes with it (as *loaf of bread* for *head*) or the first part of the phrase (as *loaf* for *head*)

rhyn·cho·ce·pha·lian \ˌriŋ-kō-sə-ˈfāl-yən\ *n* [ultim. fr. Gk *rhynchos* beak, snout + *kephalē* head — more at CEPHALIC] (1886) : any of an order (Rhynchocephalia) of reptiles resembling lizards that includes the tuatara as the only living member — **rhynchocephalian** *adj*

rhy·o·lite \ˈrī-ə-ˌlīt\ *n* [G *Rhyolith,* fr. Gk *rhyax* stream, stream of lava (fr. *rhein*) + G *-lith* -lite] (1868) : a very acid volcanic rock that is the lava form of granite — **rhy·o·lit·ic** \ˌrī-ə-ˈli-tik\ *adj*

rhythm \ˈri-thəm\ *n* [MF & L; MF *rhythme,* fr. L *rhythmus,* fr. Gk *rhythmos,* prob. fr. *rhein* to flow — more at STREAM] (1560) **1 a** : an ordered recurrent alternation of strong and weak elements in the flow of sound and silence in speech **b** : a particular example or form of rhythm ⟨iambic ∼⟩ **2 a** : the aspect of music comprising all the elements (as accent, meter, and tempo) that relate to forward movement **b** : a characteristic rhythmic pattern ⟨rumba ∼⟩; *also* : [1]METER 2 **c** : the group of instruments in a band supplying the rhythm — called also *rhythm section* **3 a** : movement, fluctuation, or variation marked by the regular recurrence or natural flow of related elements ⟨the ∼*s* of country life⟩ **b** : the repetition in a literary work of phrase, incident, character type, or symbol **4** : a regularly recurrent quantitative change in a variable biological process ⟨a circadian ∼⟩ — compare BIORHYTHM **5** : the effect created by the elements in a play, movie, or novel that relate to the temporal development of the action **6** : RHYTHM METHOD

rhythm and blues *n* (1949) : popular music typically including elements of blues and African-American folk music and marked by a strong beat and simple chord structure

rhythm band *n* (ca. 1943) : a band usu. composed of schoolchildren who play simple percussion instruments (as rhythm sticks, sleigh bells, or tambourines) to learn fundamentals of coordination and music

rhyth·mic \ˈrith-mik\ *or* **rhyth·mi·cal** \-mi-kəl\ *adj* (1589) **1** : marked by or moving in pronounced rhythm **2** : of, relating to, or involving rhythm — **rhyth·mi·cal·ly** \-mi-k(ə-)lē\ *adv*

rhyth·mic·i·ty \rith-ˈmi-sə-tē\ *n* (1901) : the state of being rhythmic or of responding rhythmically

rhyth·mics \ˈrith-miks\ *n pl but sing or pl in constr* (ca. 1859) : the science or theory of rhythms

rhyth·mist \ˈri-thə-mist, ˈrith-mist\ *n* (1864) : one who studies or has a feeling for rhythm

rhyth·mize \-ˌmīz\ *vt* **-mized; -miz·ing** (1885) : to order or compose rhythmically — **rhyth·mi·za·tion** \ˌri-thə-mə-ˈzā-shən, ˌrith-mə-\ *n*

rhythm method *n* (1940) : a method of birth control involving abstinence during the period in which ovulation is most likely to occur

rhythm stick *n* (1952) : one of a pair of plain or notched wood sticks that are struck or rubbed together to produce various percussive sounds and are used esp. by young children in rhythm bands

rhyt·i·dome \ˈri-tə-ˌdōm, ˈrī-\ *n* [Gk *rhytidōma* wrinkle, fr. *rhytidoun* to wrinkle, fr. *rhytid-, rhytis* wrinkle] (1881) : the bark external to the last formed periderm

rhy·ton \ˈrī-ˌtän\ *n* [Gk, neut. of *rhytos* flowing, fr. *rhein* to flow — more at STREAM] (1850) : any of various ornate drinking vessels of ancient times typically shaped in part like an animal or animal's head

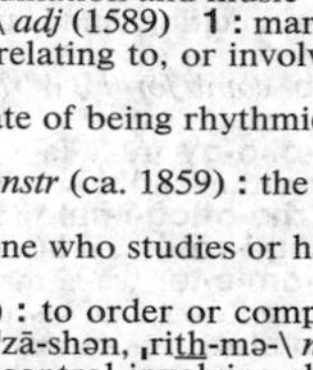
rhyton

RI *abbr* **1** refractive index **2** Rhode Island

RIA *abbr* radioimmunoassay

[1]**ri·al** *also* **ri·yal** \rē-ˈȯl, -ˈäl\ *n* [Pers, fr. Ar *riyāl* riyal] (1932) — see MONEY table

[2]**rial** *var of* RIYAL

ri·al·to \rē-ˈal-(ˌ)tō\ *n, pl* **-tos** [*Rialto,* island and district in Venice] (1549) **1** : EXCHANGE, MARKETPLACE **2** : a theater district

ri·ant \ˈrī-ənt, ˈrē-; rē-ˈäⁿ\ *adj* [MF, prp. of *rire* to laugh, fr. L *ridēre*] (1567) : GAY, MIRTHFUL — **ri·ant·ly** \ˈrī-ənt-lē, ˈrē-\ *adv*

ri·a·ta \rē-ˈa-tə, -ˈä-\ *n* [modif. of AmerSp *reata*] (1846) : LARIAT

[1]**rib** \ˈrib\ *n* [ME, fr. OE *ribb;* akin to OHG *rippi* rib, OCS *rebro,* and prob. to Gk *erephein* to roof over] (bef. 12c) **1 a** : any of the paired curved bony or partly cartilaginous rods that stiffen the walls of the body of most vertebrates and protect the viscera **b** (1) : a cut of meat including a rib — see BEEF illustration (2) : a boneless cut of meat (as beef or pork) from a rib section **c** [fr. the account of Eve's creation from Adam's rib in Gen 2:21–22] : WIFE **2** : something resembling a rib in shape or function: as **a** (1) : a traverse member of the frame of a ship that runs from keel to deck (2) : a light fore-and-aft member in an airplane's wing **b** : one of the stiff strips supporting an umbrella's fabric **c** : one of the arches in Romanesque and Gothic vaulting meet-

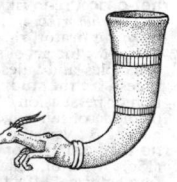

ing and crossing one another and dividing the whole vaulted space into triangles **3 :** an elongated ridge: as **a** (1) **:** a vein of an insect's wing (2) **:** one of the primary veins of a leaf **b :** one of the ridges in a knitted or woven fabric

[2]**rib** *vt* **ribbed; rib·bing** (ca. 1547) **1 :** to furnish or enclose with ribs **2 :** to knit so as to form vertical ridges in — **rib·ber** *n*

[3]**rib** *n* [[4]*rib*] (1929) **1 :** JOKE **2 :** PARODY

[4]**rib** *vt* **ribbed; rib·bing** [prob. fr. [1]*rib;* fr. the tickling of the ribs to cause laughter] (1930) **:** to poke fun at **:** KID — **rib·ber** *n*

[1]**rib·ald** \ˈri-bəld *also* ˈri-ˌbȯld, ˈrī-ˌbȯld\ *n* [ME *ribaud* person of low status, scoundrel, lecher, fr. AF, fr. OF *riber* to be debauched, of Gmc origin; akin to OHG *rīban* to be in heat, copulate, lit., to rub] (13c) **:** a ribald person

[2]**ribald** *adj* (1508) **1 :** CRUDE, OFFENSIVE ⟨~ language⟩ **2 :** characterized by or using coarse indecent humor ***syn*** see COARSE

rib·ald·ry \ˈri-bəl-drē *also* ˈrī-\ *n, pl* **-ries** (14c) **1 :** a ribald quality or element **2 a :** ribald language or humor **b :** an instance of ribald language or humor

rib·and \ˈri-bənd\ *n* [ME, alter. of *riban*] (15c) **:** a ribbon used esp. as a decoration

ri·ba·vi·rin \ˌrī-bə-ˈvī-rən\ *n* [perh. fr. *ribo*nucleic *a*cid + *vir*us + [1]*-in*] (1976) **:** a synthetic broad-spectrum antiviral nucleoside $C_8H_{12}N_4O_5$

rib·band \ˈri(b)-ˌband, ˈri-bən(d)\ *n* [[1]*rib* + [1]*band*] (1711) **:** a long narrow strip or bar used in shipbuilding; *esp* **:** one bent and bolted longitudinally to the frames to hold them in position during construction

ribbing *n* (1564) **:** an arrangement of ribs

[1]**rib·bon** \ˈri-bən\ *n* [ME *riban,* fr. AF *ribane, rubane*] (14c) **1 a :** a flat or tubular narrow closely woven fabric (as of silk or rayon) used for trimmings or knitting **b :** a narrow fabric used for tying packages **c :** a piece of usu. multicolored ribbon worn as a military decoration or in place of a medal **d :** a strip of colored satin given for winning a place in a competition **2 :** a strip of inked fabric (as in a typewriter) **3** *pl* **:** reins for controlling an animal **4 :** TATTER, SHRED — usu. used in pl. ⟨a sheet cut to ~*s*⟩ **5 :** RIBBAND — **rib·bon·like** \-ˌlīk\ *adj*

[2]**ribbon** *vt* (1716) **1 a :** to adorn with ribbons **b :** to divide into ribbons **c :** to cover with or as if with ribbons **2 :** to rip to shreds

ribbon development *n* (1927) **:** a system of buildings built side by side along a road

rib·bon·fish \ˈri-bən-ˌfish\ *n* (ca. 1798) **:** any of a family (Trachipteridae) of elongate greatly compressed marine bony fishes (as a dealfish) with a long ribbonlike dorsal fin arising from behind the head

ribbon worm *n* (1855) **:** NEMERTEAN

rib·by \ˈri-bē\ *adj* (1849) **:** showing or marked by ribs

rib cage *n* (1909) **:** the bony enclosing wall of the chest consisting chiefly of the ribs and the structures connecting them

ri·bes \ˈrī-(ˌ)bēz\ *n, pl* **ribes** [NL, fr. ML, currant, fr. Ar *rībās* rhubarb] (1543) **:** any of a genus (*Ribes*) of shrubs (as a currant or a gooseberry) placed either in the saxifrage or gooseberry family that have small racemose variously colored flowers and pulpy 2-seeded to many-seeded berries

rib eye *n* (1926) **:** the large piece of meat that lies along the outer side of the rib (as of a steer); *also* **:** a serving of this

rib·grass \ˈrib-ˌgras\ *n* (ca. 1500) **:** [1]PLANTAIN; *esp* **:** an Old World plantain (*Plantago lanceolata*) with long narrow ribbed leaves

rib·let \ˈri-blət\ *n* (1943) **:** one of the rib ends in the strip of breast of lamb or veal — see LAMB illustration

ribo- *comb form* [*ribose*] **1 :** ribose ⟨*ribo*flavin⟩ **2 :** ribonucleic acid ⟨*ribo*some⟩

ri·bo·fla·vin \ˌrī-bə-ˈflā-vən, ˈrī-bə-ˌ\ *n* [ISV *ribo-* + L *flavus* yellow — more at BLUE] (1935) **:** a yellow crystalline compound $C_{17}H_{20}N_4O_6$ of the vitamin B complex that occurs both free (as in milk) and combined (as in liver) as a component of coenzymes (as FMN) which are essential to normal metabolism — called also *vitamin B_2*

ri·bo·nu·cle·ase \ˌrī-bō-ˈnü-klē-ˌās, -ˈnyü-, -ˌāz\ *n* (1938) **:** an enzyme that catalyzes the hydrolysis of RNA — called also *RNase*

ri·bo·nu·cle·ic acid \ˌrī-bō-nu̇-ˈklē-ik-, -nyu̇-, -ˌklā-\ *n* (1931) **:** RNA

ri·bo·nu·cleo·pro·tein \-ˌnü-klē-ō-ˈprō-ˌtēn, -ˈprō-tē-ən\ *n* (1940) **:** a nucleoprotein that contains RNA

ri·bo·nu·cle·o·side \-ˈnü-klē-ə-ˌsīd, -ˈnyü-\ *n* (1931) **:** a nucleoside that contains ribose

ri·bo·nu·cle·o·tide \-ˌtīd\ *n* (1929) **:** a nucleotide that contains ribose and occurs esp. as a constituent of RNA

ri·bose \ˈrī-ˌbōs, -ˌbōz\ *n* [ISV, fr. *ribonic acid* an acid $C_5H_{10}O_6$ obtained by oxidation of ribose] (1892) **:** a pentose $C_5H_{10}O_5$ found esp. in the dextrorotatory form as a component of many nucleosides (as adenosine and guanosine) esp. in RNA

ribosomal RNA *n* (1961) **:** RNA that is a fundamental structural element of ribosomes — called also *rRNA*

ri·bo·some \ˈrī-bə-ˌsōm\ *n* (1958) **:** any of the RNA-rich cytoplasmic granules that are sites of protein synthesis — see CELL illustration — **ri·bo·som·al** \ˌrī-bə-ˈsō-məl\ *adj*

ri·bo·zyme \ˈrī-bə-ˌzīm\ *n* [*ribo*nucleic acid + en*zyme*] (1982) **:** a molecule of RNA that functions as an enzyme (as by catalyzing the cleavage of other RNA molecules)

rib roast *n* (ca. 1890) **:** a cut of meat containing the large piece that lies along the outer side of the rib — see BEEF illustration

rib·wort \ˈrib-ˌwərt, -ˌwȯrt\ *n* (14c) **:** RIBGRASS

rice \ˈrīs\ *n* [ME *rys,* fr. AF *ris,* fr. OIt *riso,* fr. Gk *oryza, oryzon,* of Iranian origin; akin to Pashto *wriže* rice; akin to Skt *vrīhi* rice] (13c) **:** the starchy seeds of an annual southeast Asian cereal grass (*Oryza sativa*) that are cooked and used for food; *also* **:** this cereal grass that is widely cultivated in warm climates for its seeds and by-products — compare WILD RICE

RICE *abbr* rest, ice, compression, elevation

rice·bird \ˈrīs-ˌbərd\ *n* (1731) **:** any of several small birds common in rice fields; *esp* **:** BOBOLINK

rice paper *n* [fr. its resemblance to paper made from rice straw] (1822) **:** a thin papery material made from the pith of a small Asian tree or shrub (*Tetrapanax papyriferum*) of the ginseng family

rice polishings *n pl* (1920) **:** the inner bran layer of rice rubbed off in milling

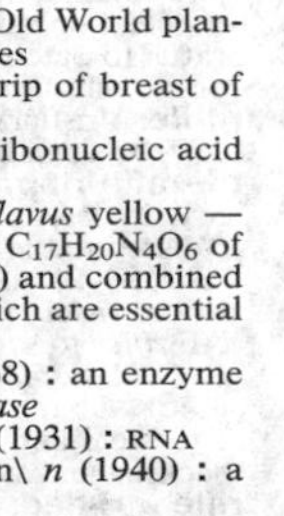

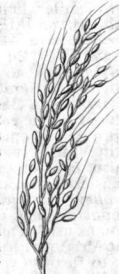

rice

ric·er \ˈrī-sər\ *n* (1896) **:** a kitchen utensil in which soft foods are pressed through a perforated container to produce strings

ri·cer·car \ˌrē-(ˌ)chər-ˈkär\ *or* **ri·cer·ca·re** \-ˈkä-(ˌ)rā\ *n, pl* **ricercars** *or* **ri·cer·ca·ri** \-ˈkä-(ˌ)rē\ [It, fr. *ricercare* to seek again, seek out, fr. *ri-* re- (fr. L *re-*) + *cercare* to seek, fr. LL *circare* to go about — more at SEARCH] (1789) **:** any of various usu. keyboard musical forms esp. of the 16th and 17th centuries in either quasi-improvisatory toccata style or strict polyphonic fugal style

rich \ˈrich\ *adj* [ME *riche,* fr. OE *rīce;* akin to OHG *rīhhi* rich, OE *rīce* kingdom, OHG *rīhhi,* n.; all fr. prehistoric Gmc words borrowed fr. Celt words akin to OIr *rí* (gen. *ríg*) king — more at ROYAL] (bef. 12c) **1 :** having abundant possessions and esp. material wealth **2 a :** having high value or quality **b :** well supplied or endowed ⟨a city ~ in traditions⟩ **3 :** magnificently impressive **:** SUMPTUOUS **4 a :** vivid and deep in color ⟨a ~ red⟩ **b :** full and mellow in tone and quality ⟨a ~ voice⟩ **c :** having a strong fragrance ⟨~ perfumes⟩ **5 :** highly productive or remunerative ⟨a ~ mine⟩ **6 a :** having abundant plant nutrients ⟨~ soil⟩ **b :** highly seasoned, fatty, oily, or sweet ⟨~ foods⟩ **c :** high in the combustible component ⟨a ~ fuel mixture⟩ **d :** high in some component ⟨cholesterol-*rich* foods⟩ **7 a :** ENTERTAINING; *also* **:** LAUGHABLE **b :** MEANINGFUL, SIGNIFICANT ⟨~ allusions⟩ **c :** LUSH ⟨~ meadows⟩ **8 :** pure or nearly pure ⟨~ lime⟩ — **rich·ness** *n*

syn RICH, WEALTHY, AFFLUENT, OPULENT mean having goods, property, and money in abundance. RICH implies having more than enough to gratify normal needs or desires ⟨became *rich* through shrewd investing⟩. WEALTHY stresses the possession of property and intrinsically valuable things ⟨*wealthy* landowners⟩. AFFLUENT suggests prosperity and an increasing wealth ⟨an *affluent* society⟩. OPULENT suggests lavish expenditure and display of great wealth, more often applying to things than people ⟨an *opulent* mansion⟩.

Rich·ard Roe \ˌrich-ərd-ˈrō\ *n* (ca. 1659) **:** a party to legal proceedings whose true name is unknown — compare JOHN DOE

rich·en \ˈri-chən\ *vt* **rich·ened; rich·en·ing** \ˈri-chə-niŋ, ˈrich-niŋ\ (1878) **:** to make rich or richer

rich·es \ˈri-chəz\ *n pl* [ME, sing. or pl., fr. *richesse* wealth, fr. AF *richesce,* fr. *riche* rich, of Gmc origin; akin to OE *rīce* rich] (13c) **:** things that make one rich **:** WEALTH

rich·ly \ˈrich-lē\ *adv* [ME *richely,* fr. OE *rīclīce,* fr. *rīce* rich] (bef. 12c) **1 :** in a rich manner **2 :** in full measure **:** AMPLY ⟨praise ~ deserved⟩

Rich·ter scale \ˈrik-tər-\ *n* [Charles F. *Richter*] (1938) **:** an open-ended logarithmic scale for expressing the magnitude of a seismic disturbance (as an earthquake) in terms of the energy dissipated in it with 1.5 indicating the smallest earthquake that can be felt, 4.5 an earthquake causing slight damage, and 8.5 a very devastating earthquake

ri·cin \ˈrī-sᵊn, ˈri-\ *n* [L *ricinus* castor-oil plant] (1896) **:** a poisonous protein in the castor bean

ri·cin·ole·ic acid \ˌrī-sə-nō-ˈlē-ik-, ˌri-, -ˈlā-\ *n* [L *ricinus* + E *oleic acid*] (1848) **:** an oily unsaturated hydroxy fatty acid $C_{18}H_{34}O_3$ that occurs in castor oil as a glyceride and yields esters important as plasticizers

[1]**rick** \ˈrik\ *n* [ME *reek,* fr. OE *hrēac;* akin to ON *hraukr* rick] (bef. 12c) **1 :** a stack (as of hay) in the open air **2 :** a pile of material (as cordwood) split from short logs

[2]**rick** *vt* (1623) **:** to pile (as hay) in ricks

[3]**rick** *vt* [perh. fr. ME *wrikken* to move unsteadily] (1798) *chiefly Brit* **:** WRENCH, SPRAIN

rick·ets \ˈri-kəts\ *n pl but sing in constr* [origin unknown] (1634) **:** a deficiency disease that affects the young during the period of skeletal growth, is characterized esp. by soft and deformed bones, and is caused by failure to assimilate and use calcium and phosphorus normally due to inadequate sunlight or vitamin D

rick·ett·sia \ri-ˈket-sē-ə\ *n, pl* **-si·as** *or* **-si·ae** \-sē-ˌē, -ˌī\ *also* **-sia** [NL, genus name, fr. Howard T. *Ricketts* †1910 Am. pathologist] (1919) **:** any of a family (Rickettsiaceae) of rod-shaped, coccoid, or diplococcus-shaped, often pleomorphic gram-negative bacteria that are intracellular parasites of arthropods (as lice or ticks) and when transmitted to humans cause various diseases (as typhus) — **rick·ett·si·al** \-sē-əl\ *adj*

rick·ety \ˈri-kə-tē\ *adj* (1683) **1 :** affected with rickets **2 a :** lacking stability or firmness **:** SHAKY 2a ⟨a ~ coalition⟩ **b :** in unsound physical condition ⟨~ veterans⟩ ⟨~ stairs⟩

rick·ey \ˈri-kē\ *n, pl* **rickeys** [prob. fr. the name *Rickey*] (1895) **:** a drink containing liquor, lime juice, sugar, and soda water; *also* **:** a similar drink without liquor

rick·rack *or* **ric·rac** \ˈrik-ˌrak\ *n* [redupl. of [4]*rack*] (1884) **:** a flat braid woven to form zigzags and used esp. as trimming on clothing

rick·shaw *also* **rick·sha** \ˈrik-ˌshȯ\ *n* [alter. of *jinrikisha*] (1887) **:** a small covered 2-wheeled vehicle usu. for one passenger that is pulled by one man and that was used orig. in Japan

RICO *abbr* Racketeer Influenced and Corrupt Organizations (Act)

[1]**ric·o·chet** \ˈri-kə-ˌshā, *Brit also* -ˌshet\ *n* [F] (1769) **:** a glancing rebound (as of a projectile off a flat surface); *also* **:** an object that ricochets

[2]**ricochet** *vi* **-cheted** \-ˌshād\ *also* **-chet·ted** \-ˌshe-təd\; **-chet·ing** \-ˌshā-iŋ\ *also* **-chet·ting** \-ˌshe-tiŋ\ (1828) **:** to bounce or skip with or as if with a glancing rebound

ri·cot·ta \ri-ˈkä-tə, -ˈkȯ-\ *n* [It, fr. fem. of pp. of *ricuocere* to cook again, fr. L *recoquere,* fr. *re-* + *coquere* to cook — more at COOK] (1877) **:** a white unripened whey cheese of Italy that resembles cottage cheese; *also* **:** a similar cheese made in the U.S. from whole or skim milk

ric·tal \ˈrik-tᵊl\ *adj* (1825) **:** of or relating to the rictus

ric·tus \ˈrik-təs\ *n* [NL, fr. L, open mouth, fr. *ringi* to open the mouth; akin to OCS *rǫgŭ* mockery] (1827) **1 :** the gape of a bird's mouth **2 a :** the mouth orifice **b :** a gaping grin or grimace

rid \ˈrid\ *vt* **rid** *also* **rid·ded; rid·ding** [ME *ridden* to clear, prob. fr. OE **ryddan;* akin to OHG *riutan* to clear land, ON *rythja*] (13c) **1** *archaic* **:** SAVE, RESCUE **2 :** to make free **:** RELIEVE, DISENCUMBER ⟨~ the complexion of blemishes⟩ ⟨be ~ of worries⟩ ⟨get ~ of that junk⟩

\ə\ **abut** \ᵊ\ **kitten**, F table \ər\ **further** \a\ **ash** \ā\ **ace** \ä\ **mop, mar** \au̇\ **out** \ch\ **chin** \e\ **bet** \ē\ **easy** \g\ **go** \i\ **hit** \ī\ **ice** \j\ **job** \ŋ\ **sing** \ō\ **go** \ȯ\ **law** \ȯi\ **boy** \th\ **thin** \t͟h\ **the** \ü\ **loot** \u̇\ **foot** \y\ **yet** \zh\ **vision, beige** \k̲, ⁿ, œ, ue, ʸ\ *see* Guide to Pronunciation

rid·dance \ˈri-dᵊn(t)s\ *n* (1533) **1 :** an act of ridding **2 :** DELIVERANCE, RELIEF — often used in the phrase *good riddance* esp. to express relief that someone or something has gone

rid·den \ˈri-dᵊn\ *adj* (1653) **1 :** harassed, oppressed, or obsessed by — usu. used in combination ⟨guilt-*ridden*⟩ ⟨debt-*ridden*⟩ **2 :** excessively full of or supplied with — usu. used in combination ⟨slum-*ridden*⟩

1**rid·dle** \ˈri-dᵊl\ *n* [ME *redels, ridel,* fr. OE *rǣdelse* opinion, conjecture, riddle; akin to OE *rǣdan* to interpret — more at READ] (bef. 12c) **1 :** a mystifying, misleading, or puzzling question posed as a problem to be solved or guessed : CONUNDRUM, ENIGMA **2 :** something or someone difficult to understand ***syn*** see MYSTERY

2**riddle** *vb* **rid·dled; rid·dling** \ˈrid-liŋ, ˈri-dᵊl-iŋ\ *vi* (1571) **:** to speak in or propound riddles ~ *vt* **1 :** to find the solution of : EXPLAIN **2 :** to set a riddle for : PUZZLE — **rid·dler** \ˈrid-lər, ˈri-dᵊl-ər\ *n*

3**riddle** *n* [ME *riddil,* fr. OE *hriddel;* akin to L *cribrum* sieve, *cernere* to sift — more at CERTAIN] (bef. 12c) **:** a coarse sieve

4**riddle** *vt* **rid·dled; rid·dling** \ˈrid-liŋ, ˈri-dᵊl-iŋ\ (13c) **1 :** to separate (as grain from chaff) with a riddle : SCREEN **2 :** to pierce with many holes ⟨*riddled* the car with bullets⟩ **3 :** to spread through : PERMEATE ⟨a book *riddled* with errors⟩

riddling *adj* (1591) **:** containing or presenting riddles

1**ride** \ˈrīd\ *vb* **rode** \ˈrōd\ *or chiefly dial* **rid** \ˈrid\; **rid·den** \ˈri-dᵊn\ *or chiefly dial* **rid** *or* **rode; rid·ing** \ˈrī-diŋ\ [ME, fr. OE *rīdan;* akin to OHG *rītan* to ride, MIr *réidid* he rides] *vi* (bef. 12c) **1 a :** to sit and travel on the back of an animal that one directs **b :** to travel in or on a conveyance **2 :** to travel as if on a conveyance : be borne ⟨*rode* on a wave of popularity⟩ **3 a :** to lie moored or anchored ⟨a ship ~*s* at anchor⟩ **b :** SAIL **c :** to move like a floating object ⟨the moon *rode* in the sky⟩ **4 :** to become supported on a point or surface **5 a :** to travel over a surface ⟨the car ~*s* well⟩ **b :** to move on the body ⟨shorts that ~ up⟩ **6 :** to continue without interference ⟨let it ~⟩ **7 a :** to be contingent : DEPEND ⟨plans on which the future ~*s*⟩ **b :** to become bet ⟨a lot of money *riding* on the favorite⟩ ~ *vt* **1 a :** to travel on ⟨~ a bike⟩ ⟨~ the bus⟩ **b :** to move with like a rider ⟨~ the waves⟩ **2 a :** to traverse by conveyance ⟨*rode* 500 miles⟩ **b :** to ride a horse in ⟨~ a race⟩ **3 :** SURVIVE, OUTLAST — usu. used with *out* ⟨*rode* out the gale⟩ **4 :** to traverse on horseback to inspect or maintain ⟨~ fence⟩ **5 :** to mount in copulation — used of a male animal **6 a :** OBSESS, OPPRESS ⟨*ridden* by anxiety⟩ **b :** to harass persistently : NAG **c :** TEASE, RIB **7 :** CARRY, CONVEY **8 :** to project over : OVERLAP **9 :** to give with (a punch) to soften the impact **10 :** to keep in partial engagement by resting a foot continuously on the pedal ⟨~ the brakes⟩ — **ride·able** *also* **rid·able** \ˈrī-də-bəl\ *adj* — **ride circuit :** to hold court in the various towns of a judicial circuit — **ride for a fall :** to court disaster — **ride herd on :** to keep a check on : SUPERVISE — **ride high :** to experience success — **ride shotgun :** to ride in the front passenger seat of a vehicle

2**ride** *n* (1759) **1 :** an act of riding; *esp* **:** a trip on horseback or by vehicle **2 :** a way (as a road or path) suitable for riding **3 :** any of various mechanical devices (as at an amusement park) for riding on **4 a :** a trip on which gangsters take a victim to murder him **b :** something likened to such a trip ⟨take the taxpayers for a ~⟩ **5 :** a means of transportation **6 :** the qualities of travel comfort in a vehicle

rid·er \ˈrī-dər\ *n* (14c) **1 :** one that rides **2 a :** an addition to a document (as an insurance policy) often attached on a separate piece of paper **b :** a clause appended to a legislative bill to secure a usu. distinct object **3 :** something used to overlie another or to move along on another piece — **rid·er·less** \-ləs\ *adj*

rid·er·ship \ˈrī-dər-ˌship\ *n* (1968) **:** the number of persons who ride a system of public transportation

1**ridge** \ˈrij\ *n* [ME *rigge,* fr. OE *hrycg;* akin to OHG *hrukki* ridge, back] (bef. 12c) **1 :** an elevated body part or structure **2 a :** a range of hills or mountains **b :** an elongate elevation on an ocean bottom **3 :** an elongate crest or a linear series of crests **4 :** a raised strip (as of plowed ground) **5 :** the line of intersection at the top between the opposite slopes or sides of a roof — **ridged** \ˈrijd\ *adj*

2**ridge** *vb* **ridged; ridg·ing** *vt* (1523) **:** to form into a ridge ~ *vi* **:** to extend in ridges

ridge·line \ˈrij-ˌlīn\ *n* (1856) **:** a line marking or following a ridgetop

ridge·ling *or* **ridg·ling** \ˈrij-liŋ\ *n* [perh. fr. 1*ridge;* fr. the supposition that the undescended testis remains near the animal's back] (1555) **1 :** a partially castrated male animal **2 :** a male animal in which one or both testes have not descended into the scrotum

ridge·pole \ˈrij-ˌpōl\ *n* (1774) **1 :** the highest horizontal timber in a roof against which the upper ends of the rafters are fixed **2 :** the horizontal pole at the top of a tent

ridge·top \ˈrij-ˌtäp\ *n* (1847) **:** the crest of a ridge

ridgy \ˈri-jē\ *adj* (1608) **:** having or rising in ridges

1**rid·i·cule** \ˈri-də-ˌkyül\ *n* [F or L; F, fr. L *ridiculum* jest] (1690) **:** the act of ridiculing : DERISION, MOCKERY

2**ridicule** *vt* **-culed; -cul·ing** (ca. 1700) **:** to make fun of — **rid·i·cul·er** *n*

syn RIDICULE, DERIDE, MOCK, TAUNT mean to make an object of laughter of. RIDICULE implies a deliberate often malicious belittling ⟨consistently *ridiculed* everything she said⟩. DERIDE suggests contemptuous and often bitter ridicule ⟨*derided* their efforts to start their own business⟩. MOCK implies scorn often ironically expressed as by mimicry or sham deference ⟨youngsters began to *mock* the helpless wino⟩. TAUNT suggests jeeringly provoking insult or challenge ⟨hometown fans *taunted* the visiting team⟩.

ri·dic·u·lous \rə-ˈdi-kyə-ləs\ *adj* [L *ridiculosus* (fr. *ridiculum* jest, fr. neut. of *ridiculus*) or *ridiculus,* lit., laughable, fr. *ridēre* to laugh] (1550) **:** arousing or deserving ridicule : ABSURD, PREPOSTEROUS ***syn*** see LAUGHABLE — **ri·dic·u·lous·ly** *adv* — **ri·dic·u·lous·ness** *n*

1**riding** *n* (14c) **:** the action or state of one that rides

2**riding** *adj* (15c) **1 :** used for or when riding ⟨a ~ horse⟩ ⟨~ boots⟩ **2 :** operated by a rider ⟨a ~ mower⟩

3**ri·ding** \ˈrī-diŋ\ *n* [ME *-redyng* or *trithing,* alter. of OE **thriding,* fr. ON *thrithjungr* third part, fr. *thrithi* third; akin to OE *thridda* third — more at THIRD] (15c) **1 :** one of the three administrative jurisdictions into which Yorkshire, England, was formerly divided **2 :** an administrative jurisdiction or electoral district in a British dominion (as Canada)

rid·ley \ˈrid-lē\ *n* [origin unknown] (1926) **:** either of two sea turtles (genus *Lepidochelys* of the family Cheloniidae): **a :** KEMP'S RIDLEY **b :** OLIVE RIDLEY

ri·dot·to \ri-ˈdä-(ˌ)tō\ *n, pl* **-tos** [It, retreat, place of entertainment, redoubt — more at REDOUBT] (1722) **:** a public entertainment consisting of music and dancing often in masquerade popular in 18th century England

ri·el \rē-ˈel\ *n* [Khmer *riəl*] (1956) — see MONEY table

Rie·mann·ian geometry \rē-ˈmä-nē-ən-\ *n* [G. F. B. *Riemann*] (1896) **:** a non-Euclidean geometry in which straight lines are geodesics and in which the parallel postulate is replaced by the postulate that every pair of straight lines intersects

Rie·mann integral \ˈrē-ˌmän-, -mən-\ *n* (1914) **:** a definite integral defined as the limit of sums found by partitioning the interval comprising the domain of definition into subintervals, by finding the sum of products each of which consists of the width of a subinterval multiplied by the value of the function at some point in it, and by letting the maximum width of the subintervals approach zero

Ries·ling \ˈrēz-liŋ, ˈrēs-\ *n* [G] (1833) **:** a white wine that ranges from dry to very sweet and is made from a single variety of grape orig. grown in Germany; *also* **:** the grape

RIF *abbr* reduction in force

ri·fam·pin \rī-ˈfam-pən\ *or* **ri·fam·pi·cin** \rī-ˈfam-pə-sən\ *n* [ISV, alter. of *rifamycin,* antibiotic derived from *Streptomyces mediterranei*] (1966) **:** a semisynthetic antibiotic $C_{43}H_{58}N_4O_{12}$ used esp. in the treatment of tuberculosis and to treat asymptomatic carriers of meningococci

rife \ˈrīf\ *adj* [ME *ryfe,* fr. OE *rȳfe;* akin to ON *rifr* abundant] (12c) **1 :** prevalent esp. to an increasing degree ⟨suspicion and cruelty were ~ —W. E. B. DuBois⟩ **2 :** ABUNDANT, COMMON **3 :** copiously supplied : ABOUNDING — usu. used with *with* ⟨~ with rumors⟩ — **rife** *adv* — **rife·ly** *adv*

1**riff** \ˈrif\ *n* [prob. by shortening & alter. fr. *refrain*] (1935) **1 :** an ostinato phrase (as in jazz) typically supporting a solo improvisation; *also* **:** a piece based on such a phrase **2 :** a rapid energetic often improvised verbal outpouring; *esp* **:** one that is part of a comic performance **3 :** a succinct usu. witty comment **4 :** a distinct variation : TAKE ⟨a disturbing . . . ~ on the Cinderella story —Daria Donnelly⟩

2**riff** *vi* (1948) **:** to perform, deliver, or make use of a riff

3**riff** *vb* [short for *riffle*] (1952) **:** RIFFLE, SKIM ⟨~ pages⟩

1**rif·fle** \ˈri-fəl\ *vb* **rif·fled; rif·fling** \ˈri-f(ə-)liŋ\ [2*riffle*] *vi* (1754) **1 :** to form, flow over, or move in riffles **2 :** to flip cursorily : THUMB ⟨~ through the catalog⟩ ~ *vt* **1 :** to ruffle slightly : RIPPLE **2 a :** to leaf through hastily; *specif* **:** to leaf (as a stack of paper) by sliding a thumb along the edge of the leaves **b :** to shuffle (playing cards) by separating the deck into two parts and riffling with the thumbs so the cards intermix **3 :** to manipulate (small objects) idly between the fingers

2**riffle** *n* [perh. alter. of *ruffle*] (1785) **1 a :** a shallow extending across a streambed and causing broken water **b :** a stretch of water flowing over a riffle **2 :** a small wave or succession of small waves : RIPPLE **3 a :** any of various contrivances (as blocks or rails) laid on the bottom of a sluice or launder to make a series of grooves or interstices to catch and retain a mineral (as gold) **b :** a groove or interstice so formed **4 :** a cleat or bar fastened to an inclined surface in a gold-washing apparatus to catch and hold mineral grains **5** [1*riffle*] **a :** the act or process of shuffling (as cards) **b :** the sound made while doing this

rif·fler \ˈri-flər\ *n* [F *rifloir,* fr. *rifler* to file, rifle] (ca. 1797) **:** a small filing or scraping tool

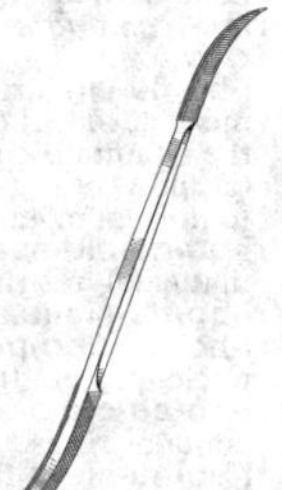
riffler

riff·raff \ˈrif-ˌraf\ *n* [ME *ryffe raffe,* fr. *rif and raf* every single one, fr. AF *rif e raf* altogether] (15c) **1 a :** disreputable persons **b :** RABBLE **c :** one of the riffraff **2 :** REFUSE, RUBBISH — **riffraff** *adj*

1**ri·fle** \ˈrī-fəl\ *vb* **ri·fled; ri·fling** \-f(ə-)liŋ\ [ME, fr. AF *rifler* to scrape off, plunder, of Gmc origin; akin to OHG *riffilōn* to saw, obs. D *rijffelen* to scrape] *vt* (14c) **1 :** to ransack esp. with the intent to steal **2 :** to steal and carry away ~ *vi* **:** to engage in ransacking and stealing — **ri·fler** \-f(ə-)lər\ *n*

2**rifle** *vt* **ri·fled; ri·fling** \-f(ə-)liŋ\ [perh. fr. F *rifler* to scratch, file, fr. MF, to scrape, plunder] (1635) **:** to cut spiral grooves into the bore of ⟨*rifled* arms⟩ ⟨*rifled* pipe⟩

3**rifle** *n* (1770) **1 a :** a shoulder weapon with a rifled bore **b :** a rifled artillery piece **2** *pl* **:** soldiers armed with rifles

4**rifle** *vt* **ri·fled; ri·fling** \-f(ə-)liŋ\ [3*rifle*] (1937) **:** to propel (as a ball) with great force or speed

ri·fle·bird \ˈrī-fəl-ˌbərd\ *n* (1831) **:** any of several birds of paradise (genus *Ptiloris*)

ri·fle·man \-mən\ *n* (1775) **1 :** a soldier armed with a rifle **2 :** one skilled in shooting with a rifle

ri·fle·ry \ˈrī-fəl-rē\ *n* (1935) **:** the practice of shooting at targets with a rifle

rifling *n* (1797) **1 :** the act or process of making spiral grooves **2 :** a system of spiral grooves in the surface of the bore of a gun causing a projectile when fired to rotate about its longer axis

1**rift** \ˈrift\ *n* [ME, of Scand origin; akin to Dan & Norw *rift* fissure, ON *rīfa* to rive — more at RIVE] (14c) **1 a :** FISSURE, CREVASSE **b :** FAULT 5 **2 :** a clear space or interval **3 :** BREACH, ESTRANGEMENT

2**rift** *vi* (14c) **:** to burst open ~ *vt* **1 :** CLEAVE, DIVIDE ⟨hills were ~*ed* by the earthquake⟩ **2 :** PENETRATE

rift valley *n* (1894) **:** an elongated valley formed by the depression of a block of the earth's crust between two faults or groups of faults of approximately parallel orientation

Rift Valley fever *n* [(Great) *Rift Valley,* Africa] (ca. 1931) **:** an acute usu. epizootic mosquito-borne disease of domestic animals chiefly of eastern and southern Africa that is caused by a bunyavirus (species *Rift valley fever virus* of the genus *Phlebovirus*), is marked esp. by fever, abortion, and death of newborns, and is sometimes transmitted to humans usu. in a less severe form

1**rig** \ˈrig\ *vt* **rigged; rig·ging** [prob. back-formation fr. *rigging*] (15c) **1 :** to fit out (as a ship) with rigging **2 :** CLOTHE, DRESS — usu. used with *out* **3 :** to furnish with special gear : EQUIP **4 a :** to put in condition or position for use : ADJUST, ARRANGE ⟨a car *rigged* for manual control⟩ **b :** CONSTRUCT ⟨~ up a temporary shelter⟩

[2]**rig** *n* (1822) **1 :** the distinctive shape, number, and arrangement of sails and masts of a ship **2 :** EQUIPAGE; *esp* **:** a carriage with its horse **3 :** CLOTHING, DRESS **4 :** tackle, equipment, or machinery fitted for a specified purpose ⟨an oil-drilling ~⟩ **5 :** a tractor-trailer combination

[3]**rig** *vt* **rigged; rig·ging** [*rig*, n., a swindle] (1851) **1 :** to manipulate or control usu. by deceptive or dishonest means ⟨~ an election⟩ **2 :** to fix in advance for a desired result ⟨~ the contest⟩

rig·a·doon \ˌri-gə-ˈdün\ *or* **ri·gau·don** \rē-gō-ˈdōⁿ\ *n* [F *rigaudon*] (1691) **:** a lively dance of the 17th and 18th centuries; *also* **:** the music for a rigadoon

rigamarole *var of* RIGMAROLE

rig·a·to·ni \ˌri-gə-ˈtō-nē\ *n* [It, pl., fr. *rigato* furrowed, fluted, fr. pp. of *rigare* to furrow, flute, fr. *riga* line, of Gmc origin; akin to OHG *rīga* line — more at ROW] (ca. 1923) **:** pasta made in short wide fluted tubes

Ri·gel \ˈrī-jəl, -gəl; ˈri-jəl\ *n* [Ar *Rijl*, lit., foot] (1592) **:** a first-magnitude star in the left foot of the constellation Orion

rig·ger \ˈri-gər\ *n* (ca. 1611) **1 :** one that rigs **2 :** a long slender pointed sable paintbrush

rig·ging \ˈri-giŋ, -gən\ *n* [ME *ragging, riggyng* fitting out of a ship] (1594) **1 a :** lines and chains used aboard a ship esp. in working sail and supporting masts and spars **b :** a similar network (as in theater scenery) used for support and manipulation **2 :** CLOTHING

[1]**right** \ˈrīt\ *adj* [ME, fr. OE *riht*; akin to OHG *reht* right, L *rectus* straight, right, *regere* to lead straight, direct, rule, *rogare* to ask, Gk *oregein* to stretch out] (bef. 12c) **1 :** RIGHTEOUS, UPRIGHT **2 :** being in accordance with what is just, good, or proper ⟨~ conduct⟩ **3 :** conforming to facts or truth **:** CORRECT ⟨the ~ answer⟩ **4 :** SUITABLE, APPROPRIATE ⟨the ~ man for the job⟩ **5 :** STRAIGHT ⟨a ~ line⟩ **6 :** GENUINE, REAL **7 a :** of, relating to, situated on, or being the side of the body which is away from the side on which the heart is mostly located **b :** located nearer to the right hand than to the left **c :** located to the right of an observer facing the object specified or directed as the right arm would point when raised out to the side **d (1) :** located on the right of an observer facing in the same direction as the object specified ⟨stage ~⟩ **(2) :** located on the right when facing downstream ⟨the ~ bank of a river⟩ **e :** done with the right hand ⟨a ~ hook to the jaw⟩ **8 :** having the axis perpendicular to the base ⟨~ cone⟩ **9 :** of, relating to, or constituting the principal or more prominent side of an object ⟨made sure the socks were ~ side out⟩ **10 :** acting or judging in accordance with truth or fact ⟨time proved her ~⟩ **11 a :** being in good physical or mental health or order ⟨not in his ~ mind⟩ **b :** being in a correct or proper state ⟨put things ~⟩ **12 :** most favorable or desired **:** PREFERABLE; *also* **:** socially acceptable ⟨knew all the ~ people⟩ **13** *often cap* **:** of, adhering to, or constituted by the Right esp. in politics ***syn*** see CORRECT — **right·ness** *n*

[2]**right** *n* [ME, fr. OE *riht*, fr. *riht*, adj.] (bef. 12c) **1 :** qualities (as adherence to duty or obedience to lawful authority) that together constitute the ideal of moral propriety or merit moral approval **2 :** something to which one has a just claim: as **a :** the power or privilege to which one is justly entitled ⟨voting ~*s*⟩ ⟨his ~ to decide⟩ **b (1) :** the interest that one has in a piece of property — often used in pl. ⟨mineral ~*s*⟩ **(2)** *pl* **:** the property interest possessed under law or custom and agreement in an intangible thing esp. of a literary and artistic nature ⟨film ~*s* of the novel⟩ **3 :** something that one may properly claim as due ⟨knowing the truth is her ~⟩ **4 :** the cause of truth or justice **5 a :** RIGHT HAND 1a; *also* **:** a blow struck with this hand ⟨gave him a hard ~ on the jaw⟩ **b :** the location or direction of the right side ⟨woods on his ~⟩ **c :** the part on the right side **d :** RIGHT FIELD **e :** a turn to the right ⟨take a ~ at the stop sign⟩ **6 a :** the true account or correct interpretation **b :** the quality or state of being factually correct **7** *often cap* **a :** the part of a legislative chamber located to the right of the presiding officer **b :** the members of a continental European legislative body occupying the right as a result of holding more conservative political views than other members **8 a** *often cap* **:** individuals professing support of the established order and favoring traditional attitudes and practices and conservative governmental policies **b** *often cap* **:** a conservative position **9 a :** a privilege given stockholders to subscribe pro rata to a new issue of securities generally below market price **b :** the negotiable certificate evidencing such privilege — usu. used in pl. — **right·most** \-ˌmōst\ *adj* — **by rights** *also* **by all rights :** with reason or justice **:** PROPERLY — **in one's own right :** by virtue of one's own qualifications or properties — **of right 1 :** as an absolute right **2 :** legally or morally exactable — **to rights :** into proper order

[3]**right** *adv* (bef. 12c) **1 :** according to right ⟨live ~⟩ **2 :** in the exact location, position, or moment **:** PRECISELY ⟨~ at his fingertips⟩ ⟨quit ~ then and there⟩ **3 :** in a suitable, proper, or desired manner ⟨knew he wasn't doing it ~⟩ **4 :** in a direct line, course, or manner **:** DIRECTLY, STRAIGHT ⟨go ~ home⟩ ⟨came ~ out and said it⟩ **5 :** according to fact or truth **:** TRULY ⟨guessed ~⟩ **6 a :** all the way ⟨windows ~ to the floor⟩ **b :** in a complete manner ⟨felt ~ at home⟩ **7 :** without delay **:** IMMEDIATELY ⟨~ after lunch⟩ **8 :** to a great degree **:** VERY ⟨a ~ pleasant day⟩ **9 :** on or to the right ⟨looked left and ~⟩

[4]**right** *vt* (bef. 12c) **1 a :** to do justice to **:** redress the injuries of ⟨so just is God to ~ the innocent —Shak.⟩ **b :** JUSTIFY, VINDICATE ⟨felt the need to ~ himself in court⟩ **2 :** AVENGE ⟨vows to ~ the injustice done to his family⟩ **3 a :** to adjust or restore to the proper state or condition ⟨~ the economy⟩ **b :** to bring or restore to an upright position ⟨~ a capsized boat⟩ ~ *vi* **:** to become upright — **right·er** *n*

right and left *adv* (1735) **:** on both or all sides **:** in every direction **:** EVERYWHERE

right angle *n* (15c) **:** the angle bounded by two lines perpendicular to each other **:** an angle of 90° or $\frac{1}{2}\pi$ radians — **right–an·gled** \ˈrīt-ˈaŋ-gəld\ *or* **right–an·gle** \-gəl\ *adj*

right ascension *n* (15c) **:** the arc of the celestial equator between the vernal equinox and the point where the hour circle through a given body intersects the equator reckoned eastward commonly in terms of the corresponding interval of sidereal time in hours, minutes, and seconds

right away *adv* (1749) **:** without delay or hesitation **:** IMMEDIATELY

right brain *n* (1970) **:** the right cerebral hemisphere of the human brain esp. when viewed in terms of its predominant thought processes (as creativity and intuitive thinking) — **right–brained** \ˈrīt-ˈbrānd\ *adj*

right circular cone *n* (1840) **:** CONE 1a

right circular cylinder *n* (1877) **:** a cylinder with the bases circular and with the axis joining the two centers of the bases perpendicular to the planes of the two bases

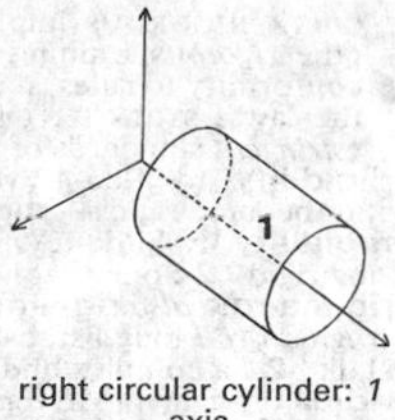

right circular cylinder: *1* axis

righ·teous \ˈrī-chəs\ *adj* [alter. of earlier *rightuous*, alter. of ME *rightwise, rightwos*, fr. OE *rihtwīs*, fr. *riht*, n., right + *wīs* wise] (1530) **1 :** acting in accord with divine or moral law **:** free from guilt or sin **2 a :** morally right or justifiable ⟨a ~ decision⟩ **b :** arising from an outraged sense of justice or morality ⟨~ indignation⟩ **3** *slang* **:** GENUINE, EXCELLENT ***syn*** see MORAL — **righ·teous·ly** *adv* — **righ·teous·ness** *n*

right field *n* (1857) **1 :** the part of the baseball outfield to the right looking out from home plate **2 :** the position of the player defending right field — **right fielder** *n*

right·ful \ˈrīt-fəl\ *adj* (14c) **1 :** JUST, EQUITABLE **2 a :** having a just or legally established claim **:** LEGITIMATE ⟨the ~ owner⟩ **b :** held by right or just claim **:** LEGAL ⟨~ authority⟩ **3 :** PROPER, FITTING ⟨assured of his ~ place in history —Brian Duff⟩ — **right·ful·ly** \-fə-lē\ *adv* — **right·ful·ness** *n*

right–hand \ˈrīt-ˌhand\ *adj* (1567) **1 :** situated on the right **2 :** RIGHT-HANDED **3 :** chiefly relied on ⟨his ~ man⟩

right hand *n* (bef. 12c) **1 a :** the hand on a person's right side **b :** an indispensable person **2 a :** the right side **b :** a place of honor

right–hand·ed \-ˈhan-dəd\ *adj* (14c) **1 :** using the right hand habitually or more easily than the left; *also* **:** swinging from right to left ⟨a ~ batter⟩ **2 :** relating to, designed for, or done with the right hand **3 a :** having the same direction or course as the movement of the hands of a watch viewed from in front **:** CLOCKWISE **b :** having a spiral structure or form that ascends or advances to the right ⟨a ~ screw⟩ **4** *of a door* **:** opening to the right away from one — **right–handed** *adv* — **right–hand·ed·ly** *adv* — **right–hand·ed·ness** *n*

right–hand·er \-ˈhan-dər\ *n* (1846) **1 :** a blow struck with the right hand **2 :** a right-handed person; *esp* **:** a right-handed pitcher

right·ism \ˈrī-ˌti-zəm\ *n, often cap* (1939) **1 :** the principles and views of the Right **2 :** advocacy of or adherence to the doctrines of the Right — **right·ist** \ˈrī-tist\ *n or adj, often cap*

right·ly \ˈrīt-lē\ *adv* (bef. 12c) **1 :** in accordance with right conduct **:** FAIRLY, JUSTLY **2 :** in the right or proper manner **:** PROPERLY, FITTINGLY **3 :** according to truth or fact **:** CORRECTLY, EXACTLY

right–mind·ed \-ˈmīn-dəd\ *adj* (ca. 1586) **:** having a right or honest mind ⟨a ~ citizen⟩ — **right–mind·ed·ness** *n*

right now *adv* (14c) **1 :** RIGHT AWAY **2 :** at present

righto \ˌrī-ˈtō, ˈrī-(ˌ)tō\ *interj* (1896) — used to express cheerful concurrence, assent, or understanding

right off *adv* (1771) **:** RIGHT AWAY

right–of–way \ˌrīt-ə(v)-ˈwā\ *n, pl* **rights–of–way** *also* **right–of–ways** (1768) **1 :** a legal right of passage over another person's ground **2 a :** the area over which a right-of-way exists **b :** the strip of land over which is built a public road **c :** the land occupied by a railroad esp. for its main line **d :** the land used by a public utility (as for a transmission line) **3 a :** a precedence in passing accorded to one vehicle over another by custom, decision, or statute **b :** the right of traffic to take precedence **c :** the right to take precedence over others ⟨gave the bill the ~ in the Senate⟩

right on *adj* (1925) **1 :** exactly correct — often used interjectionally to express agreement **2** *usu* **right–on :** attuned to the spirit of the times

Right Reverend (15c) — used as a title for high ecclesiastical officials

right shoulder arms *n* (1902) **:** a position in the manual of arms in which the butt of the rifle is held in the right hand with the barrel resting on the right shoulder; *also* **:** a command to assume this position

right·size \ˈrīt-ˌsīz\ *vt* (1989) **:** to reduce (as a workforce) to an optimal size ~ *vi* **:** to undergo a reduction to an optimal size

right–to–life \ˈrīt-tə-ˈlīf\ *adj* (1973) **:** opposed to abortion — **right–to–lif·er** \-ˈlī-fər\ *n*

right–to–work *adj* (1949) **:** opposing or banning the closed shop and the union shop

right triangle *n* (1675) **:** a triangle having a right angle — see TRIANGLE illustration

right·ward \ˈrīt-wərd\ *adj or adv* (1733) **:** being at, toward, or to the right

right whale *n* (1725) **:** any of a family (Balaenidae) of large baleen whales having very long baleen, a large head on a stocky body, a smooth throat, and short broad rounded flippers

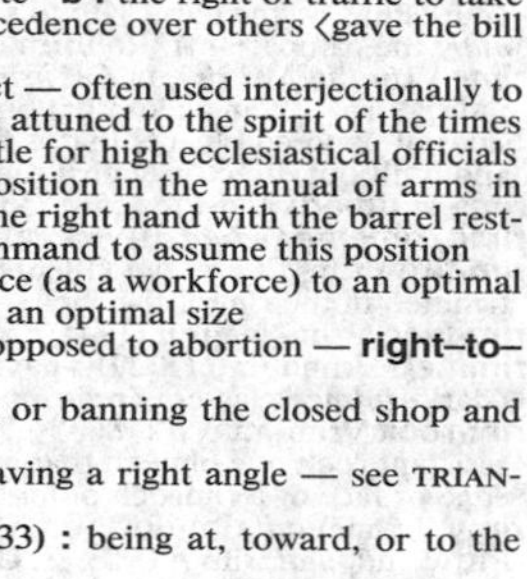
right whale

right wing *n* (1856) **1 :** the rightist division of a group or party **2 :** RIGHT 8 — **right–wing** \ˈrīt-ˈwiŋ, -ˌwiŋ\ *adj* — **right–wing·er** \ˈrīt-ˈwiŋ-ər, ˌrīt-\ *n*

righty \ˈrī-tē\ *n, pl* **right·ies** (1949) **:** RIGHT-HANDER 2

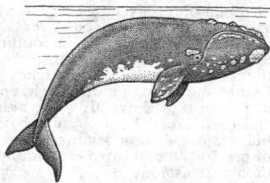

rig·id \ˈri-jəd\ *adj* [ME *rigide*, fr. L *rigidus*, fr. *rigēre* to be stiff] (15c) **1 a :** deficient in or devoid of flexibility ⟨~ price controls⟩ ⟨a ~ bar of metal⟩ **b :** appearing stiff and unyielding ⟨his face ~ with pain⟩ **2 a :** inflexibly set in opinion **b :** strictly observed ⟨adheres to a ~ schedule⟩ **3 :** firmly inflexible rather than lax or indulgent ⟨a ~ disciplinarian⟩ **4 :** precise and accurate in procedure ⟨~ control of the manufacturing process⟩ **5** *of an airship* **:** having the outer shape maintained by a fixed framework — **rig·id·ly** *adv* — **rig·id·ness** *n*

syn RIGID, RIGOROUS, STRICT, STRINGENT mean extremely severe or stern. RIGID implies uncompromising inflexibility ⟨*rigid* rules of conduct⟩. RIGOROUS implies the imposition of hardship and difficulty ⟨the *rigorous* training of recruits⟩. STRICT emphasizes undeviating conformity to rules, standards, or requirements ⟨*strict* enforcement of the law⟩. STRINGENT suggests severe, tight restriction or limitation ⟨*stringent* standards of admission⟩. ***syn*** see in addition STIFF

ri·gid·i·fy \rə-ˈji-də-ˌfī\ *vb* **-fied; -fy·ing** *vt* (1842) : to make rigid ~ *vi* : to become rigid — **ri·gid·i·fi·ca·tion** \-ˌji-də-fə-ˈkā-shən\ *n*

ri·gid·i·ty \rə-ˈji-də-tē\ *n, pl* **-ties** (1624) **1** : the quality or state of being rigid **2** : one that is rigid (as in form or conduct)

rig·ma·role *also* **rig·a·ma·role** \ˈri-gə-mə-ˌrōl, ˈrig-mə-\ *n* [alter. of obs. *ragman roll* long list, catalog] (ca. 1736) **1** : confused or meaningless talk **2** : a complex and sometimes ritualistic procedure

rig·or \ˈri-gər\ *n* [ME *rigour,* fr. AF, fr. L *rigor,* lit., stiffness, fr. *rigēre* to be stiff] (14c) **1 a** (1) : harsh inflexibility in opinion, temper, or judgment : SEVERITY (2) : the quality of being unyielding or inflexible : STRICTNESS (3) : severity of life : AUSTERITY **b** : an act or instance of strictness, severity, or cruelty **2** : a tremor caused by a chill **3** : a condition that makes life difficult, challenging, or uncomfortable; *esp* : extremity of cold **4** : strict precision : EXACTNESS ⟨logical ~⟩ **5 a** *obs* : RIGIDITY, STIFFNESS **b** : rigidness or torpor of organs or tissue that prevents response to stimuli **c** : RIGOR MORTIS

rig·or·ism \ˈri-gə-ˌri-zəm\ *n* (1704) : rigidity in principle or practice — **rig·or·ist** \-rist\ *n or adj* — **rig·or·is·tic** \ˌri-gə-ˈris-tik\ *adj*

rig·or mor·tis \ˌri-gər-ˈmȯr-təs *also chiefly Brit* ˌrī-ˌgȯr-\ *n* [NL, stiffness of death] (1847) : temporary rigidity of muscles occurring after death

rig·or·ous \ˈri-g(ə-)rəs\ *adj* (15c) **1** : manifesting, exercising, or favoring rigor : very strict **2 a** : marked by extremes of temperature or climate : HARSH, SEVERE **3** : scrupulously accurate : PRECISE ***syn*** see RIGID — **rig·or·ous·ly** *adv* — **rig·or·ous·ness** *n*

rig·our *chiefly Brit var of* RIGOR

rijst·ta·fel \ˈrīs-ˌtä-fəl\ *n* [D, fr. *rijst* rice + *tafel* table] (1889) : an Indonesian meal consisting of rice and a variety of accompanying dishes (as meat, seafood, and vegetables)

Riks·mål *or* **Riks·maal** \ˈriks-ˌmȯl, ˈrēks-\ *n* [Norw, fr. *rik* kingdom + *mål* speech] (1913) : BOKMÅL

rile \ˈrī(-ə)l\ *vt* **riled; ril·ing** [var. of *roil*] (1624) **1** : to make agitated and angry : UPSET **2** : ROIL 1 ***syn*** see IRRITATE

ril·ey \ˈrī-lē\ *adj* (1805) **1** : TURBID **2** : ANGRY

1**rill** \ˈril\ *n* [D *ril* or LG *rille;* akin to OE *rīth* rivulet] (1538) : a very small brook

2**rill** *vi* (1610) : to flow like a rill

3**rill** \ˈril\ *or* **rille** \ˈril, ˈri-lə\ *n* [G *Rille,* lit., channel made by a small stream, fr. LG, rill] (1868) : any of several long narrow valleys on the moon's surface

rill·et \ˈri-lət\ *n* (1538) : a little rill

ril·lettes \ri-ˈlets, -ˈyet\ *n pl* [F, pl., dim. of *rille,* sing., piece of pork, fr. MF, dial. var. of *reille* board, lath, fr. L *regula* straightedge — more at RULE] (1889) : cooked shredded meat (as pork or duck) or fish preserved in fat

1**rim** \ˈrim\ *n* [ME, fr. OE *rima;* akin to ON *rimi* strip of land] (13c) **1 a** : BRINK **b** : the outer often curved or circular edge or border of something **2 a** : the outer part of a wheel joined to the hub usu. by spokes **b** : a removable outer metal band on an automobile wheel to which the tire is attached **3** : FRAME 4c(1) — **rim·less** \-ləs\ *adj*

2**rim** *vb* **rimmed; rim·ming** *vt* (1621) **1** : to run around the rim of ⟨putts that ~ the cup⟩ **2** : to serve as a rim for : BORDER ⟨cliffs *rimming* the camp⟩ ~ *vi* : to form or show a rim

1**rime** \ˈrīm\ *n* [ME *rim,* fr. OE *hrīm;* akin to ON *hrīm* frost] (bef. 12c) **1** : FROST 1b **2** : an accumulation of granular ice tufts on the windward sides of exposed objects that is formed from supercooled fog or cloud and built out directly against the wind **3** : CRUST, INCRUSTATION

2**rime** *vt* **rimed; rim·ing** (ca. 1755) : to cover with or as if with rime

3**rime, rimester** *var of* RHYME, RHYMESTER

rim–fire \ˈrim-ˌfī(-ə)r\ *adj* (1866) *of a cartridge* : having the priming distributed in the rim of the shell — **rimfire** *n*

rim·land \ˈrim-ˌland\ *n* (1944) : a region on the edge of the heartland

rimmed \ˈrimd\ *adj* (1729) : having a rim — usu. used in combination ⟨dark-*rimmed* glasses⟩ ⟨red-*rimmed* eyes⟩

rim·rock \ˈrim-ˌräk\ *n* (1860) **1** : a top stratum or overlying strata of resistant rock of a plateau that outcrops to form a vertical face **2** : the edge or face of a rimrock outcrop

rimy \ˈrī-mē\ *adj* **rim·i·er; -est** (bef. 12c) : covered with rime : FROSTY

rind \ˈrīnd, *dial* ˈrīn\ *n* [ME, fr. OE; akin to OHG *rinda* bark, and prob. to OE *rendan* to rend] (bef. 12c) **1** : the bark of a tree **2** : a usu. hard or tough outer layer : PEEL, CRUST — **rind·ed** \ˈrīn-dəd\ *adj*

rin·der·pest \ˈrin-dər-ˌpest\ *n* [G, fr. *Rinder,* pl., cattle + *Pest* pestilence] (1865) : an acute infectious disease of ruminant mammals (as cattle) that is caused by a morbillivirus (species *Rinderpest virus*) and that is marked by fever, diarrhea, and inflammation of mucous membranes and by high mortality in epidemics

1**ring** \ˈriŋ\ *n* [ME, fr. OE *hring;* akin to OHG *hring* ring, OCS *krǫgŭ* circle] (bef. 12c) **1** : a circular band for holding, connecting, hanging, pulling, packing, or sealing ⟨a key ~⟩ ⟨a towel ~⟩ **2** : a circlet usu. of precious metal worn esp. on the finger **3 a** : a circular line, figure, or object ⟨smoke ~⟩ **b** : an encircling arrangement ⟨a ~ of suburbs⟩ **c** : a circular or spiral course — often used figuratively in pl. in the phrase *run rings around* to describe surpassing an opponent decisively **4 a** (1) : an often circular space esp. for exhibitions or competitions; *esp* : such a space at a circus (2) : a structure containing such a ring **b** : a square enclosure in which a fighting contest (as a boxing or wrestling match) takes place **5** : a band of small objects revolving around a planet (as Saturn) and composed of dust and icy or rocky fragments **6** : ANNUAL RING **7 a** : an exclusive combination of persons for a selfish and often corrupt purpose (as to control a market) ⟨a wheat ~⟩ **b** : GANG **8** : the field of a political contest : RACE **9** : food in the shape of a circle **10** : an arrangement of atoms represented in formulas or models in a cyclic manner — called also *cycle* **11** : a set of mathematical elements that is closed under two binary operations of which the first forms a commutative group with the set and the second is associative over the set and is distributive with respect to the first operation **12** *pl* **a** : a pair of usu. rubber-covered metal rings suspended from a ceiling or crossbar to a height of approximately eight feet above the floor and used for hanging, swinging, and balancing feats in gymnastics **b** : an event in gymnastics competition in which the rings are used **13** : 1BOXING ⟨ended his ~ career⟩ — **ring·like** \ˈriŋ-ˌlīk\ *adj*

2**ring** *vb* **ringed; ring·ing** \ˈriŋ-iŋ\ *vt* (14c) **1** : to provide with a ring **2** : to place or form a ring around : ENCIRCLE ⟨police ~*ed* the building⟩ **3** : GIRDLE 2 **4** : to throw a ringer over (the peg) in a game (as horseshoes or quoits) ~ *vi* **1 a** : to move in a ring **b** : to rise in the air spirally **2** : to form or take the shape of a ring

3**ring** *vb* **rang** \ˈraŋ\; **rung** \ˈrəŋ\; **ring·ing** \ˈriŋ-iŋ\ [ME, fr. OE *hringan;* akin to ON *hringja* to ring] *vi* (bef. 12c) **1** : to sound resonantly or sonorously ⟨the doorbell *rang*⟩ ⟨cheers *rang* out⟩ **2 a** : to be filled with a reverberating sound : RESOUND ⟨the halls *rang* with laughter⟩ **b** : to have the sensation of being filled with a humming sound ⟨his ears *rang*⟩ **3** : to cause something to ring ⟨~ for the butler⟩ **4 a** : to be filled with talk or report ⟨the whole land *rang* with her fame⟩ **b** : to have great renown **c** : to sound repetitiously ⟨their praise *rang* in his ears⟩ **5** : to have a sound or character expressive of some quality ⟨a story that ~*s* true⟩ **6** *chiefly Brit* : to make a telephone call — usu. used with *up* ~ *vt* **1** : to cause to sound esp. by striking **2** : to make (a sound) by or as if by ringing a bell **3** : to announce by or as if by ringing **4** : to repeat often, loudly, or earnestly **5 a** : to summon esp. by bell **b** *chiefly Brit* : TELEPHONE — usu. used with *up* — **ring a bell** : to arouse a response ⟨that name *rings a bell*⟩ — **ring down the curtain** : to conclude a performance or an action — **ring off the hook** : to ring frequently or constantly with incoming calls ⟨the telephone was *ringing off the hook*⟩ — **ring the changes** *or* **ring changes** : to run through the range of possible variations — **ring up the curtain** : to begin a performance or an action

4**ring** *n* (1549) **1** : a set of bells **2** : a clear resonant sound made by or resembling that made by vibrating metal **3** : resonant tone : SONORITY **4** : a loud sound continued, repeated, or reverberated **5** : a sound or character expressive of some particular quality ⟨the story had a familiar ~⟩ **6 a** : the act or an instance of ringing **b** : a telephone call

ring–a–le·vio \ˌriŋ-ə-ˈlē-vē-ˌō\ *or* **ring–a–lie·vo** \-ˈlē-(ˌ)vō\ *n* [alter. of earlier *ring relievo,* fr. 1*ring* + *relieve*] (ca. 1901) : a game in which players on one team are given time to hide and are then sought out by members of the other team who try to capture them, keep them in a place of confinement, and keep them from being released by their teammates

ring–around–the–rosy \ˌriŋ-ə-ˌrau̇n(d)-thə-ˈrō-zē\ *also* **ring–around–a–rosy** \-ˌrau̇n-də-\ *n* (1878) : a children's singing game in which players dance around in a circle and at a given signal drop to the ground — called also *ring-a-rosy* \ˌriŋ-ə-ˈrō-zē\

ring·bark \ˈriŋ-ˌbärk\ *vt* (1884) : GIRDLE 2

ring–billed gull \ˈriŋ-ˌbild-\ *n* (1844) : a No. American gull (*Larus delawarensis*) that as an adult is largely white with a gray mantle, dark wing tips, yellowish feet and legs, and a yellow bill with a black ring towards the tip

ring binder *n* (1929) : a loose-leaf binder in which split rings attached to a back hold the perforated sheets of paper

ring·bolt \ˈriŋ-ˌbōlt\ *n* (1599) : an eyebolt with a ring through its eye

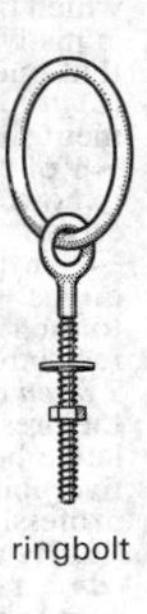

ringbolt

ring·bone \-ˌbōn\ *n* (1523) : a bony outgrowth on or near the articulating surface of the pastern or coffin bone of a horse that typically results from injury and usu. produces lameness

ring dance *n* (1600) : ROUND DANCE 1

ring·dove \ˈriŋ-ˌdəv\ *n* (1538) **1** : WOOD PIGEON **2** : RINGED TURTLE DOVE

ringed *adj* (1513) **1** : encircled or marked with or as if with rings **2** : composed or formed of rings

ringed turtle dove *n* (1983) : a small pale dove (*Streptopelia risoria*) that has a black ring around the sides and back of the neck, exists chiefly in domestication as a cage bird, and is prob. of African origin

1**ring·er** \ˈriŋ-ər\ *n* (15c) **1** : one that sounds esp. by ringing **2 a** (1) : one that enters a competition under false representations (2) : IMPOSTER, FAKE **b** : one that strongly resembles another — often used with *dead* ⟨he's a dead ~ for the senator⟩

2**ringer** *n* (1863) : one that encircles or puts a ring around (as a quoit or horseshoe that lodges so as to surround the peg)

Ring·er's solution \ˈriŋ-ərz-\ *n* [Sidney *Ringer* †1910 Eng. physician] (1893) : an aqueous solution of calcium chloride, sodium chloride, and potassium chloride that provides a medium essentially isotonic to many animal tissues and is used topically to irrigate tissues or intravenously to replenish fluids and electrolytes — called also *Ringer solution*

ring·ette \riŋ-ˈet\ *n* (1974) : a game of Canadian origin for women and girls that is played on ice with two teams of six players on skates whose object is to drive a rubber or plastic ring into the opponents' goal with a straight stick

ring finger *n* (bef. 12c) : the third finger esp. of the left hand counting the index finger as the first

ring·git \ˈriŋ-git\ *n, pl* **ringgit** *or* **ringgits** [Malay, lit., serration, coin with milled edge] (1967) — see MONEY table

ringing *adj* (14c) **1** : clear and full in tone : RESOUNDING ⟨a ~ baritone⟩ **2** : vigorously unequivocal : DECISIVE ⟨a ~ condemnation of immorality⟩ — **ring·ing·ly** \-iŋ-lē\ *adv*

ring·lead·er \ˈriŋ-ˌlē-dər\ *n* (1503) : a leader of a ring of individuals engaged esp. in improper or unlawful activities

ring·let \ˈriŋ-lət\ *n* (1555) **1** : a small ring or circle **2** : CURL; *esp* : a long curl of hair

ring·mas·ter \ˈriŋ-ˌmas-tər\ *n* (1859) : one in charge of performances in a ring (as of a circus); *broadly* : a supervisor or moderator esp. of a performance or presentation ⟨the ~ of a talk show⟩

ring·neck \-ˌnek\ *n* (1791) : a ring-necked animal

ring–necked \ˈriŋ-ˌnekt\ *or* **ring–neck** \ˈriŋ-ˌnek\ *adj* (1817) : having a ring of color about the neck

ring–necked duck *n* (1831) : a No. American duck (*Aythya collaris*) that has a white ring around the bill and in the male a faint narrow chestnut ring encircling the neck

ring–necked pheasant *n* (1834) : a Eurasian pheasant (*Phasianus colchicus*) that has been widely introduced as a game bird in No. America and in which the males have a white neck ring and an iridescent green and purplish head with red wattles around the eyes

ring off *vi* (1882) *chiefly Brit* : HANG UP 1

ring ouzel *n* (ca. 1674) : a dark Old World thrush (*Turdus torquatus*) with the male having a white breast band
ring–po·rous \ˈriŋ-ˌpȯr-əs\ *adj* (1902) : having vessels more numerous and usu. larger in cross section in the springwood with a resulting more or less distinct line between the springwood and the last season's wood — compare DIFFUSE-POROUS
ring road *n* (1928) *chiefly Brit* : a highway skirting an urban area
[1]**ring·side** \ˈriŋ-ˌsīd\ *n* (1866) **1** : the area just outside a ring esp. in which a contest occurs **2** : a place that affords a close view
[2]**ringside** *adj* (1896) : being at the ringside ⟨a ~ seat⟩
ring spot *n* (1923) **1** : any of various plant diseases caused by viruses (genus *Nepovirus* of the family *Comoviridae*) and marked by circular lesions of usu. chlorotic or necrotic tissue **2** : a turf disease caused by an ascomycetous fungus (*Leptosphaeria korrae* syn. *Ophiosphaerella korrae*) and marked by circular patches or rings of dead grass
ring stand *n* (ca. 1865) : a metal stand consisting of a long upright rod attached to a heavy rectangular base that is used with rings and clamps for supporting laboratory apparatus
ring·straked \ˈriŋ-ˌstrākt\ *adj* (1611) *archaic* : marked with circular stripes
ring·tail \-ˌtāl\ *n* (1844) **1** : RACCOON **2** : a carnivore (*Bassariscus astutus*) of the western U.S. and Mexico that is related to and resembles the raccoon — called also *cacomistle, civet cat, ringtail cat, ringtailed cat* **3** : CAPUCHIN 3
ring–tailed \-ˌtāld\ *adj* (1729) **1** : having a tail marked with rings of differing colors **2** : having a tail carried in a form approximating a circle ⟨a ~ Afghan hound⟩
ring·taw \-ˌtȯ\ *n* (1828) : a game of marbles in which marbles are placed in a circle on the ground and shot at from the edge of the circle with the object being to knock them out of the circle
ring·tone \-ˌtōn\ *n* (1983) : the sound made by a cell phone to signal an incoming call
ring·toss \-ˌtȯs, -ˌtäs\ *n* (1871) : a game in which the object is to toss a ring so that it will fall over an upright stick
ring up *vt* (1937) **1** : to total and record esp. by means of a cash register ⟨*ring up* a sale⟩ **2** : ACHIEVE ⟨*rang up* many social triumphs⟩
ring·worm \ˈriŋ-ˌwərm\ *n* (15c) : any of several contagious fungal diseases of the skin, hair, or nails of humans and domestic animals that are characterized by ring-shaped discolored skin patches covered with vesicles and scales
rink \ˈriŋk\ *n* [ME (Sc) *rinc* area in which a contest takes place, fr. AF *renc* row, lists — more at RANK] (1787) **1 a** : a smooth extent of ice marked off for curling or ice hockey **b** : a surface of ice for ice-skating; *also* : a building containing such a rink **c** : an enclosure for roller-skating **2** : an alley for lawn bowling **3** : a team in bowls or curling
rinky–dink \ˈriŋ-kē-ˌdiŋk\ *adj* [origin unknown] (1913) **1** : SMALL-TIME **2** : OLD-FASHIONED
[1]**rinse** \ˈrin(t)s, *esp dial* ˈrench\ *vt* **rinsed; rins·ing** [ME *rincen*, fr. AF *rincer*, alter. of OF *recincier*, fr. VL *recentiare, fr. L *recent-, recens* fresh, recent] (14c) **1** : to cleanse by flushing with liquid (as water) — often used with *out* ⟨~ out the mouth⟩ **2 a** : to cleanse (as of soap) by clear water **b** : to treat (hair) with a rinse **3** : to remove (dirt or impurities) by washing lightly or in water only — **rins·er** *n*
[2]**rinse** *n* (1837) **1** : the act or process of rinsing **2 a** : liquid used for rinsing **b** : a solution that temporarily tints hair
rinsing *n* (1818) **1** : DREGS, RESIDUE — usu. used in pl. **2** : water that has been used for rinsing — usu. used in pl.
RIO *abbr* radar intercept officer
rio·ja \rē-ˈō-(ˌ)hä\ *n, often cap* (1907) : a wine from the Rioja region of Spain; *esp* : a dry red wine from this region
[1]**ri·ot** \ˈrī-ət\ *n* [ME, fr. AF *riote* rash action, noise, disorder] (13c) **1** *archaic* **a** : profligate behavior : DEBAUCHERY **b** : unrestrained revelry **c** : noise, uproar, or disturbance made by revelers **2 a** : public violence, tumult, or disorder **b** : a violent public disorder; *specif* : a tumultuous disturbance of the public peace by three or more persons assembled together and acting with a common intent **3** : a random or disorderly profusion ⟨the woods were a ~ of color⟩ **4** : one that is wildly amusing ⟨the new comedy is a ~⟩
[2]**riot** *vi* (14c) **1** : to indulge in revelry or wantonness **2** : to create or engage in a riot — **ri·ot·er** *n*
riot act *n* [the *Riot Act*, English law of 1715 providing for the dispersal of riots upon command of legal authority] (1819) : a vigorous reprimand or warning — used in the phrase *read the riot act*
riot gun *n* (1916) : a small arm used to disperse rioters rather than to inflict serious injury or death; *esp* : a short-barreled shotgun
ri·ot·ous \ˈrī-ə-təs\ *adj* (15c) **1 a** : of the nature of a riot : TURBULENT **b** : participating in riot **2** : ABUNDANT, EXUBERANT ⟨the garden was ~ with flowers⟩ — **ri·ot·ous·ly** *adv* — **ri·ot·ous·ness** *n*
[1]**rip** \ˈrip\ *vb* **ripped; rip·ping** [ME *rippen*, fr. or akin to MD *reppen, rippen* to pull, jerk] *vt* (15c) **1 a** : to tear or split apart or open **b** : to saw or split (wood) with the grain **2** : to slash or slit with or as if with a sharp blade **3** : to hit sharply ⟨*ripped* a double to left field⟩ **4** : to utter violently : spit out ⟨*ripped* out an oath⟩ **5** : CRITICIZE, DISPARAGE ~ *vi* **1** : to become ripped : REND **2** : to rush headlong ⟨*ripped* past second base⟩ ***syn*** see TEAR — **rip into** : to tear into : ATTACK
[2]**rip** *n* (1711) **1** : a rent made by ripping : TEAR **2** : CUT 5b
[3]**rip** *n* [perh. fr. [2]*rip*] (1775) **1** : a body of water made rough by the meeting of opposing tides, currents, or winds **2** : a current of water roughened by passing over an irregular bottom **3** : RIP CURRENT
[4]**rip** *n* [perh. by shortening & alter. fr. *reprobate*] (1797) : a dissolute person : LIBERTINE
RIP *abbr* [L *requiescat in pace*] may he rest in peace, may she rest in peace; [L *requiescant in pace*] may they rest in peace
ri·par·i·an \rə-ˈper-ē-ən, rī-\ *adj* [L *riparius* — more at RIVER] (ca. 1841) : relating to or living or located on the bank of a natural watercourse (as a river) or sometimes of a lake or a tidewater ⟨~ trees⟩
riparian right *n* (ca. 1860) : a right (as access to or use of the shore, bed, and water) of one owning riparian land
rip cord *n* (1907) **1** : a cord by which the gasbag of a balloon may be ripped open for a limited distance to release the gas quickly and so cause immediate descent **2** : a cord or wire pulled in making a descent to release a parachute out of its container
rip current *n* (1936) : a strong usu. narrow surface current flowing outward from a shore that results from the return flow of waves and wind-driven water
ripe \ˈrīp\ *adj* **rip·er; rip·est** [ME, fr. OE *rīpe*; akin to OE *rīpan, reopan* to reap] (bef. 12c) **1** : fully grown and developed : MATURE ⟨~ fruit⟩ ⟨~ wheat⟩ **2** : having mature knowledge, understanding, or judgment **3** : of advanced years : LATE ⟨a ~ old age⟩ **4 a** : SUITABLE, APPROPRIATE ⟨the time was ~ for the attempt⟩ **b** : fully prepared : READY ⟨the colonies were ~ for revolution⟩ **5 a** : brought by aging to full flavor or the best state : MELLOW ⟨~ cheese⟩ **b** : SMELLY, STINKING **6** : ruddy, plump, or full like ripened fruit ⟨a ~ figure⟩ **7** : INDECENT ⟨~ language⟩ — **ripe·ly** *adv* — **ripe·ness** *n*
rip·en \ˈrī-pən, ˈrī-p^{ə}m\ *vb* **rip·ened; rip·en·ing** \ˈrī-pə-niŋ, ˈrīp-niŋ\ *vi* (1561) : to grow or become ripe ~ *vt* **1** : to make ripe **2 a** : to bring to completeness or perfection **b** : to age or cure (cheese) to develop characteristic flavor, odor, body, texture, and color **c** : to improve flavor and tenderness of (beef or game) by aging under refrigeration — **rip·en·er** \ˈrī-pə-nər, ˈrīp-nər\ *n*
ri·pie·no \ri-ˈpyā-(ˌ)nō, -ˈpye-\ *n, pl* **-ni** \-(ˌ)nē\ *or* **-nos** [It, lit., filled up] (ca. 1930) : TUTTI
rip–off \ˈrip-ˌȯf\ *n* (1969) **1** : an act or instance of stealing : THEFT; *also* : a financial exploitation **2** : a usu. cheap exploitive imitation
rip off *vt* (1967) **1 a** : ROB; *also* : CHEAT, DEFRAUD **b** : STEAL **2** : to copy or imitate blatantly or unscrupulously **3** : to perform, achieve, or score quickly or easily ⟨*ripped off* 10 straight points⟩
ri·poste \ri-ˈpōst\ *n* [F, modif. of It *risposta*, lit., answer, fr. *rispondere* to respond, fr. L *respondēre*] (1707) **1** : a fencer's quick return thrust following a parry **2** : a retaliatory verbal sally : RETORT **3** : a retaliatory maneuver or measure — **riposte** *vb*
ripped *adj* (1970) **1** *slang* : being under the influence of alcohol or drugs : HIGH, STONED **2** : having high muscle definition ⟨~ abs⟩
rip·per \ˈri-pər\ *n* (1611) **1** : one that rips; *esp* : a machine used to break up solid material (as rock or ore) **2** : an excellent example or instance of its kind
ripping *adj* [prob. fr. prp. of [1]*rip*] (1846) *chiefly Brit* : EXCELLENT, DELIGHTFUL ⟨I've had a ~ time here —W. S. Maugham⟩
[1]**rip·ple** \ˈri-pəl\ *vb* **rip·pled; rip·pling** \-p(ə-)liŋ\ [perh. freq. of [1]*rip*] *vi* (ca. 1671) **1 a** : to become lightly ruffled or covered with small waves **b** : to flow in small waves **c** : to fall in soft undulating folds ⟨the scarf *rippled* to the floor⟩ **2** : to flow with a light rise and fall of sound or inflection ⟨laughter *rippled* over the audience⟩ **3** : to move with an undulating motion or so as to cause ripples ⟨the canoe *rippled* through the water⟩ **4** : to have or produce a ripple effect : SPREAD ⟨the news *rippled* outwards⟩ ~ *vt* **1** : to stir up small waves on **2** : to impart a wavy motion or appearance to ⟨*rippling* his arm muscles⟩ **3** : to utter or play with a slight rise and fall of sound — **rip·pler** \-p(ə-)lər\ *n*
[2]**ripple** *n* (1755) **1 a** : a shallow stretch of rough water in a stream **b** (1) : the ruffling of the surface of water (2) : a small wave **2 a** : RIPPLE MARK **b** : a sound like that of rippling water ⟨a ~ of laughter⟩ **c** : a usu. slight noticeable effect or reaction — **rip·ply** \ˈri-p(ə-)lē\ *adj*
ripple effect *n* (1966) : a spreading, pervasive, and usu. unintentional effect or influence ⟨the automotive industry has a *ripple effect* on many other industries⟩ — compare DOMINO EFFECT
ripple mark *n* (1833) **1** : one of a series of small ridges produced esp. on sand by the action of wind, a current of water, or waves **2** : a striation across the grain of wood esp. on the tangential surface — **ripple–marked** \ˈri-pəl-ˌmärkt\ *adj*
[1]**rip·rap** \ˈrip-ˌrap\ *n* [obs. *riprap* sound of rapping] (1833) **1** : a foundation or sustaining wall of stones or chunks of concrete thrown together without order (as in deep water); *also* : a layer of this or similar material on an embankment slope to prevent erosion **2** : material used for riprap
[2]**riprap** *vt* (1848) **1** : to form a riprap in or upon **2** : to strengthen or support with a riprap
rip–roar·ing \ˈrip-ˈrȯr-iŋ\ *adj* (1834) : noisily excited or exciting
rip·saw \ˈrip-ˌsȯ\ *n* (1846) : a coarse-toothed saw used to cut wood in the direction of the grain — compare CROSSCUT SAW
rip·snort·er \ˈrip-ˈsnȯr-tər\ *n* (1840) : something extraordinary : HUMDINGER ⟨the finale was a ~⟩ — **rip·snort·ing** \-tiŋ\ *adj*
rip·stop \ˈrip-ˌstäp\ *adj* (1949) : of, relating to, or being a fabric woven with a double thread at regular intervals so that small tears do not spread ⟨~ nylon⟩ — **ripstop** *n*
rip·tide \ˈrip-ˌtīd\ *n* (1862) : RIP CURRENT
Rip·u·ar·i·an \ˌri-pyə-ˈwer-ē-ən\ *adj* [ML *Ripuarius*] (1781) : of, relating to, or constituting a group of Franks settling in the fourth century on the Rhine near Cologne
Rip van Win·kle \ˌrip-(ˌ)van-ˈwiŋ-kəl, -vən-\ *n* (ca. 1820) : a ne'er-do-well in a story in Washington Irving's *Sketch Book* who sleeps for 20 years
RISC *abbr* reduced instruction-set computer; reduced instruction-set computing
[1]**rise** \ˈrīz\ *vi* **rose** \ˈrōz\; **ris·en** \ˈri-z^{ə}n\; **ris·ing** \ˈrī-ziŋ\ [ME, fr. OE *rīsan*; akin to OHG *rīsan* to rise] (bef. 12c) **1 a** : to assume an upright position esp. from lying, kneeling, or sitting **b** : to get up from sleep or from one's bed **2** : to return from death **3** : to take up arms ⟨~ in rebellion⟩ **4** : to respond warmly : APPLAUD — usu. used with *to* ⟨the audience *rose* to her verve and wit⟩ **5** *chiefly Brit* : to end a session : ADJOURN **6** : to appear above the horizon ⟨the sun ~s at six⟩ **7 a** : to move upward : ASCEND **b** : to increase in height, size, volume, or pitch **8** : to extend above other objects ⟨mountain peaks *rose* to the west⟩ **9 a** : to become heartened or elated ⟨his spirits *rose*⟩ **b** : to increase in fervor or intensity ⟨my anger *rose* as I thought about the insult⟩ **10 a** : to attain a higher level or rank ⟨officers who *rose* from the ranks⟩ **b** : to increase in quantity or number **11 a** : to take place : HAPPEN **b** : to come into being : ORIGINATE **12** : to follow as a consequence : RESULT **13** : to exert oneself to meet a challenge ⟨~ to the occasion⟩ ***syn*** see SPRING

\ə\ **abut** \$^{ə}$\ kitten, F table \ər\ **further** \a\ **ash** \ā\ **ace** \ä\ **mop, mar**
\au̇\ **out** \ch\ **chin** \e\ **bet** \ē\ **easy** \g\ **go** \i\ **hit** \ī\ **ice** \j\ **job**
\ŋ\ **sing** \ō\ **go** \ȯ\ **law** \ȯi\ **boy** \th\ **thin** \t͟h\ **the** \ü\ **loot** \u̇\ **foot**
\y\ **yet** \zh\ **vision, beige** \k̲, ^{n}, œ, ue, ^{y}\ *see* Guide to Pronunciation

[2]**rise** \'rīz *also* 'rīs\ *n* (15c) **1 a :** a spot higher than surrounding ground : HILLTOP **b :** an upward slope ⟨a ~ in the road⟩ **2 :** an act of rising or a state of being risen: as **a :** a movement upward : ASCENT **b :** emergence (as of the sun) above the horizon **c :** the upward movement of a fish to seize food or bait **3 :** BEGINNING, ORIGIN ⟨the river had its ~ in the mountain⟩ **4 :** the distance or elevation of one point above another **5 a :** an increase esp. in amount, number, or volume **b** *chiefly Brit* : RAISE 3b **c :** an increase in price, value, rate, or sum ⟨a ~ in the cost of living⟩ **6 :** an angry reaction ⟨got a ~ out of him⟩ **7 :** the distance from the crotch to the waistline on pants

ris·er \'rī-zər\ *n* (15c) **1 :** one that rises (as from sleep) **2 :** the upright member between two stair treads **3 :** a stage platform on which performers are placed for greater visibility **4 :** a vertical pipe (as for water or gas) or a vertical portion of an electric wiring system **5 :** one of the straps that connects a parachutist's harness with the shroud lines

ris·i·bil·i·ty \ˌri-zə-'bi-lə-tē\ *n, pl* **-ties** (1620) **1 :** LAUGHTER **2 :** the ability or inclination to laugh — often used in pl. ⟨our *risibilities* support us as we skim over the surface of a deep issue —J. A. Pike⟩

ris·i·ble \'ri-zə-bəl\ *adj* [LL *risibilis,* fr. L *risus,* pp. of *ridēre* to laugh] (1557) **1 a :** capable of laughing **b :** disposed to laugh **2 :** arousing or provoking laughter; *esp* : LAUGHABLE **3 :** associated with, relating to, or used in laughter ⟨~ muscles⟩ — **ris·i·bly** \-blē\ *adv*

ris·i·bles \-bəlz\ *n pl* (1785) : sense of the ridiculous : sense of humor

[1]**rising** *n* (14c) : INSURRECTION, UPRISING

[2]**rising** *adv* (ca. 1772) : approaching a stated age : NEARLY ⟨a red cow ~ four years old —*Lancaster (Pa.) Jour.*⟩

rising diphthong *n* (1888) : a diphthong in which the second element is more sonorous than the first (as \wi\ in \'kwit\ *quit*)

rising rhythm *n* (1881) : rhythm with stress occurring regularly on the last syllable of each foot — compare FALLING RHYTHM

rising star *n* (1767) : a person or thing that is growing quickly in popularity or importance in a particular field ⟨a *rising star* in politics⟩

[1]**risk** \'risk\ *n* [F *risque,* fr. It *risco*] (ca. 1661) **1 :** possibility of loss or injury : PERIL **2 :** someone or something that creates or suggests a hazard **3 a :** the chance of loss or the perils to the subject matter of an insurance contract; *also* : the degree of probability of such loss **b :** a person or thing that is a specified hazard to an insurer **c :** an insurance hazard from a specified cause or source ⟨war ~⟩ **4 :** the chance that an investment (as a stock or commodity) will lose value — **risk·less** \'ris-kləs\ *adj* — **at risk :** in a state or condition marked by a high level of risk or susceptibility ⟨patients *at risk* of infection⟩

[2]**risk** *vt* (ca. 1687) **1 :** to expose to hazard or danger ⟨~*ed* her life⟩ **2 :** to incur the risk or danger of ⟨~*ed* breaking his neck⟩ — **risk·er** *n*

risk capital *n* (1944) : VENTURE CAPITAL

risk factor *n* (1949) : something that increases risk or susceptibility

risky \'ris-kē\ *adj* **risk·i·er; -est** (1827) : attended with risk or danger : HAZARDOUS ***syn*** see DANGEROUS — **risk·i·ness** *n*

ri·sor·gi·men·to \(ˌ)rē-ˌzȯr-ji-'men-(ˌ)tō, -ˌsȯr-\ *n, pl* **-tos** [It, lit., rising again, fr. *risorgere* to rise again, fr. L *resurgere* — more at RESURRECTION] (1902) **1** *often cap* : the 19th century movement for Italian political unity **2 :** a time of renewal or renaissance : REVIVAL

ri·sot·to \ri-'sȯ-(ˌ)tō, -'zȯ-\ *n, pl* **-tos** [It, fr. *riso* rice — more at RICE] (1855) : rice cooked usu. in meat or seafood stock and seasoned (as with Parmesan cheese or saffron)

ris·per·i·done \ri-'sper-ə-ˌdōn\ *n* [perh. fr. fluo*r-* + *is-* + pi*peridine* + *-one*] (1988) : an antipsychotic drug $C_{28}H_{27}FN_4O_2$ used esp. to treat schizophrenia

ris·qué \ri-'skā\ *adj* [F, fr. pp. of *risquer* to risk, fr. *risque*] (1867) : verging on impropriety or indecency : OFF-COLOR ⟨a ~ joke⟩

rit *abbr* ritardando

Rit·a·lin \'ri-tə-lən\ *trademark* — used for a preparation of methylphenidate

ri·tard \ri-'tärd\ *n* (ca. 1890) : RITARDANDO

[1]**ri·tar·dan·do** \ri-ˌtär-'dän-(ˌ)dō, ˌrē-\ *adv or adj* [It, fr. L *retardandum,* gerund of *retardare* to retard] (ca. 1811) : with a gradual slackening in tempo — used as a direction in music

[2]**ritardando** *n, pl* **-dos** (1889) : a ritardando passage

rite \'rīt\ *n* [ME, fr. L *ritus;* akin to Gk *arithmos* number — more at ARITHMETIC] (14c) **1 a :** a prescribed form or manner governing the words or actions for a ceremony **b :** the ceremonial practices of a church or group of churches **2 :** a ceremonial act or action ⟨initiation ~*s*⟩ **3 :** a division of the Christian church using a distinctive liturgy

rite of passage (1909) : a ritual associated with a crisis or a change of status (as marriage, illness, or death) for an individual

ri·to·na·vir \ˌrī-'tō-nə-ˌvir, -'tä-, ri-\ *n* [*rito-* (perh. by shortening & alter. fr. *protease*) + *-navir* (as in *saquinavir*)] (1995) : an antiviral protease inhibitor $C_{37}H_{48}N_6O_5S_2$ administered orally to treat HIV infection and AIDS

ri·tor·nel·lo \ˌri-tər-'ne-(ˌ)lō, ˌri-ˌtȯr-\ *n, pl* **-nel·li** \-'ne-(ˌ)lē\ *or* **-nellos** [It, dim. of *ritorno* return, fr. *ritornare* to return, fr. *ri-* re- + *tornare* to turn, fr. L, to turn on a lathe — more at TURN] (1675) **1 a :** a short recurrent instrumental passage in a vocal composition **b :** an instrumental interlude in early opera **2 :** a tutti passage in a concerto or rondo refrain

[1]**rit·u·al** \'ri-chə-wəl, -chəl; 'rich-wəl\ *adj* [L *ritualis,* fr. *ritus* rite] (1570) **1 :** of or relating to rites or a ritual : CEREMONIAL ⟨a ~ dance⟩ **2 :** according to religious law ⟨~ purity⟩ **3 :** done in accordance with social custom or normal protocol ⟨~ handshakes⟩ ⟨~ background checks⟩ — **rit·u·al·ly** *adv*

[2]**ritual** *n* (1649) **1 :** the established form for a ceremony; *specif* : the order of words prescribed for a religious ceremony **2 a :** ritual observance; *specif* : a system of rites **b :** a ceremonial act or action **c :** an act or series of acts regularly repeated in a set precise manner

rit·u·al·ism \'ri-chə-wə-ˌli-zəm, -chə-ˌli-; 'rich-wə-\ *n* (1843) **1 :** the use of ritual **2 :** excessive devotion to ritual — **rit·u·al·ist** \-list\ *n* — **rit·u·al·is·tic** \ˌri-chə-wə-'lis-tik, -chə-'lis-; ˌrich-wə-\ *adj* — **rit·u·al·is·ti·cal·ly** \-ti-k(ə-)lē\ *adv*

rit·u·al·ize \-ˌlīz\ *vb* **-ized; -iz·ing** *vi* (1842) : to practice ritualism ~ *vt* **1 :** to make a ritual of **2 :** to impose a ritual on — **rit·u·al·i·za·tion** \ˌri-chə-wə-lə-'zā-shən, -chə-lə-; ˌrich-wə-\ *n*

ritzy \'rit-sē\ *adj* **ritz·i·er; -est** [*Ritz* hotels, noted for their opulence] (1920) **1 :** SNOBBISH **2 :** impressively or ostentatiously fancy or stylish : FASHIONABLE, POSH ⟨a ~ nightclub⟩ — **ritz·i·ness** *n*

riv *abbr* river

[1]**ri·val** \'rī-vəl\ *n* [MF or L; MF, fr. L *rivalis* one using the same stream as another, rival in love, fr. *rivalis* of a stream, fr. *rivus* stream — more at RUN] (1577) **1 a :** one of two or more striving to reach or obtain something that only one can possess **b :** one striving for competitive advantage **2** *obs* : COMPANION, ASSOCIATE **3 :** EQUAL, PEER

[2]**rival** *adj* (1590) : having the same pretensions or claims : COMPETING

[3]**rival** *vb* **ri·valed** *or* **ri·valled; ri·val·ing** *or* **ri·val·ling** \'rīv-(ə-)liŋ\ *vi* (1605) : to act as a rival : COMPETE ~ *vt* **1 :** to be in competition with **2 :** to strive to equal or excel : EMULATE **3 :** to possess qualities or aptitudes that approach or equal (those of another)

ri·val·rous \'rī-vəl-rəs\ *adj* (1812) : given to rivalry : COMPETITIVE

ri·val·ry \'rī-vəl-rē\ *n, pl* **-ries** (1598) : the act of rivaling : the state of being a rival : COMPETITION

rive \'rīv\ *vb* **rived** \'rīvd\; **riv·en** \'ri-vən\ *also* **rived; riv·ing** \'rī-viŋ\ [ME, fr. ON *rīfa;* akin to Gk *ereipein* to tear down] *vt* (14c) **1 a :** to wrench open or tear apart or to pieces : REND **b :** to split with force or violence **2 a :** to divide into pieces ⟨nations *riven* by civil war⟩ **b :** FRACTURE ~ *vi* : to become split : CRACK ***syn*** see TEAR

riv·er \'ri-vər\ *n, often attrib* [ME *rivere,* fr. AF, fr. VL **riparia,* fr. L, fem. of *riparius* riparian, fr. *ripa* bank, shore; perh. akin to Gk *ereipein* to tear down] (14c) **1 a :** a natural stream of water of usu. considerable volume **b :** WATERCOURSE **2 a :** something resembling a river ⟨a ~ of lava⟩ **b** *pl* : large or overwhelming quantities ⟨drank ~*s* of coffee⟩ — **up the river :** to or in prison ⟨was sent *up the river*⟩

riv·er·bank \'ri-vər-ˌbaŋk\ *n* (1565) : the bank of a river

riv·er·bed \-ˌbed\ *n* (1833) : the channel occupied by a river

river blindness *n* (1953) : ONCHOCERCIASIS

riv·er·boat \-ˌbōt\ *n* (1565) : a boat for use on a river

river duck *n* (1837) : DABBLER b

riv·er·front \-ˌfrənt\ *n* (1855) : the land or area along a river

river horse *n* (1563) : HIPPOPOTAMUS

riv·er·ine \'ri-və-ˌrīn, -ˌrēn\ *adj* (1860) **1 :** relating to, formed by, or resembling a river **2 :** living or situated on the banks of a river

river otter *n* (1801) : any of various Old and New World otters (esp. genera *Lutra* and *Lontra*); *esp* : one (*Lontra canadensis*) of Alaska, Canada, and the conterminous U.S. found in aquatic environments from marine coastal regions to high mountains

riv·er·side \'ri-vər-ˌsīd\ *n* (14c) : the side or bank of a river

riv·er·ward \-wərd\ *or* **riv·er·wards** \-wərdz\ *adv or adj* (1833) : toward a river

[1]**riv·et** \'ri-vət\ *n* [ME, clinch on a nail, rivet, fr. OF, fr. *river* to attach, rivet, prob. fr. *rive* border, edge, bank, fr. L *ripa*] (15c) : a headed pin or bolt of metal used for uniting two or more pieces by passing the shank through a hole in each piece and then beating or pressing down the plain end so as to make a second head

[2]**rivet** *vt* (15c) **1 :** to fasten with or as if with rivets **2 :** to upset the end or point of (as a metallic pin, rod, or bolt) by beating or pressing so as to form a head **3 :** to fasten or fix firmly ⟨stood ~*ed* by fright⟩ **4 :** to attract and hold (as the attention) completely — **riv·et·er** *n*

riv·et·ing \'ri-və-tiŋ\ *adj* (1677) : having the power to fix the attention : ENGROSSING, FASCINATING ⟨a ~ story⟩ — **riv·et·ing·ly** \-lē\ *adv*

ri·vi·era \ˌri-vē-'er-ə, ri-'vyer-\ *n, often cap* [fr. the *Riviera,* region in southeastern France and northwestern Italy] (1766) : a coastal region frequented as a resort area and usu. marked by a mild climate

ri·vi·ère \ˌri-vē-'er, ri-'vyer\ *n* [F, lit., river, fr. OF *rivere*] (1879) : a necklace of precious stones (as diamonds)

riv·u·let \'ri-vyə-lət, -və-\ *n* [It *rivoletto,* dim. of *rivolo,* fr. L *rivulus,* dim. of *rivus* stream — more at RUN] (1587) : a small stream

[1]**ri·yal** *also* **ri·al** \rē-'yäl, -'yal\ *n* [Ar *riyāl,* fr. Sp *real* real] (1856) — see MONEY table

[2]**riyal** *var of* RIAL

rm *abbr* room

rms *abbr* root-mean-square

Rn *symbol* radon

[1]**RN** \ˌär-'en\ *n* (1903) : REGISTERED NURSE

[2]**RN** *abbr* Royal Navy

RNA \ˌär-(ˌ)en-'ā\ *n* [*ribonucleic acid*] (1948) : any of various nucleic acids that contain ribose and uracil as structural components and are associated with the control of cellular chemical activities — compare MESSENGER RNA, RIBOSOMAL RNA, TRANSFER RNA

RNAi \ˌär-ˌen-ˌā-ˈī\ *n* (1998) : RNA INTERFERENCE

RNA interference *n* (1998) : a posttranscriptional genetic mechanism that suppresses gene expression and in which double-stranded RNA cleaved into small fragments initiates the degradation of a complementary messenger RNA; *also* : a technique that artificially induces RNA interference

RNA polymerase *n* (ca. 1962) : any of a group of enzymes that promote the synthesis of RNA using DNA or RNA as a template

RN·ase \ˌär-'en-ˌās, -ˌāz\ *also* **RNA·ase** \ˌär-(ˌ)en-'ā-ˌās, -'ā-ˌāz\ *n* [*RNA* + *-ase*] (1957) : RIBONUCLEASE

RNA virus *n* (1963) : a virus (as a paramyxovirus or a retrovirus) whose genome consists of RNA

rnd *abbr* round

[1]**roach** \'rōch\ *n, pl* **roach** *also* **roach·es** [ME *roche,* fr. AF *roche, rosse*] (13c) **1 :** a silver-green European freshwater cyprinid fish (*Rutilus rutilus*); *also* : any of various related fishes (as some shiners) **2 :** any of several American freshwater sunfishes (family Centrarchidae)

[2]**roach** *n* [origin unknown] (1794) **1 :** a curved cut in the edge of a sail to prevent chafing or to secure a better fit **2 :** a roll of hair brushed straight back from the forehead or side of the head

[3]**roach** *vt* (1818) **1 :** to cut (as a horse's mane) so that the remainder stands upright **2 :** to cause to arch; *specif* : to brush (the hair) in a roach — often used with *up*

[4]**roach** *n* [by shortening] (1845) **1 :** COCKROACH **2 :** the butt of a marijuana cigarette

roach back *n* (1874) : an arched back (as of a dog)

roach clip *n* (1968) : a metal clip that resembles tweezers and is used by marijuana smokers to hold a roach

road \'rōd\ *n* [ME *rode,* fr. OE *rād* ride, journey; akin to OE *rīdan* to ride] (14c) **1 :** ROADSTEAD — often used in pl. **2 a :** an open way for vehicles, persons, and animals; *esp* : one lying outside of an urban district : HIGHWAY **b :** ROADBED 2b **3 :** a route or way to an end, conclusion, or circumstance ⟨on the ~ to success⟩ **4 :** RAILWAY **5 :** a series of scheduled visits or appearances (as games or performances) in several locations or the travel necessary to make these visits ⟨the team is on the ~⟩ ⟨on tour with the musical's ~ company⟩ — **road·less** \ˈrōd-ləs\ *adj* — **down the road** : in or into the future

road·abil·i·ty \ˌrō-də-ˈbi-lə-tē\ *n* (ca. 1914) : the qualities (as steadiness and balance) desirable in an automobile on the road

road agent *n* (1863) : a highwayman who formerly operated esp. on stage routes in unsettled districts

road·bed \ˈrōd-ˌbed\ *n* (ca. 1840) **1 a** : the bed on which the ties, rails, and ballast of a railroad rest **b** : the ballast or the upper surface of the ballast on which the ties rest **2 a** : the earth foundation of a road prepared for surfacing **b** : the part of the surface of a road traveled by vehicles

road·block \-ˌbläk\ *n* (1940) **1 a** : a barricade often with traps or mines for holding up an enemy at a point on a road covered by fire **b** : a road barricade set up esp. by law enforcement officers **2** : an obstruction in a road **3** : something that blocks progress or prevents accomplishment of an objective — **roadblock** *vt*

road hog *n* (1891) : a driver of an automotive vehicle who obstructs others esp. by occupying part of another's traffic lane

road·hold·ing \ˈrōd-ˌhōl-diŋ\ *n* (1932) *chiefly Brit* : the qualities of an automobile that tend to make it respond precisely to the driver's steering

road·house \ˈrōd-ˌhau̇s\ *n* (1857) : an inn or tavern usu. outside city limits providing liquor and usu. meals, dancing, and often gambling

road·ie \ˈrō-dē\ *n* [*road* + *-ie*] (1969) : a person who works (as by moving heavy equipment) for traveling entertainers

road·kill \ˈrōd-ˌkil\ *n* (1972) **1** : the remains of an animal that has been killed on a road by a motor vehicle **2** : one that falls victim to intense competition ⟨political ~⟩ — **road–killed** \-ˌkild\ *adj*

road map *n* (1883) **1** : a map showing roads esp. for automobile travel **2 a** : a detailed plan to guide progress toward a goal **b** : a detailed explanation

road metal *n* (1818) : broken stone or cinders used in making and repairing roads or ballasting railroads

road racing *n* (1828) : racing over public roads; *esp* : automobile racing over roads or over a closed course designed to simulate public roads — **road race** *n*

road rage *n* (1988) : a motorist's uncontrolled anger that is usu. provoked by another motorist's irritating act and is expressed in aggressive or violent behavior

road rash *n* (1976) : mild to severe skin abrasion resulting from a fall (as from a bicycle or motorcycle) which usu. involves sliding on a hard rough surface

road roller *n* (ca. 1876) : one that rolls roadways; *specif* : a machine with heavy wide smooth rollers for compacting roadbeds

road·run·ner \ˈrōd-ˌrə-nər\ *n* (1856) : a largely terrestrial bird (*Geococcyx californianus*) of the cuckoo family that has a long tail and a crest, is a speedy runner, and inhabits arid regions from the southwestern U.S. to Mexico; *also* : a closely related bird (*G. velox*) of Mexico and Central America

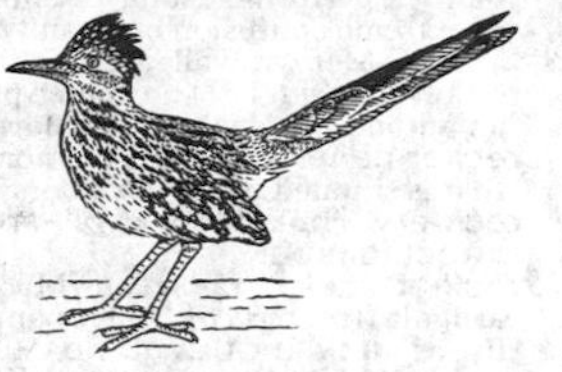

roadrunner

road show *n* (1908) **1** : a theatrical performance given by a troupe on tour **2** : a special engagement of a new motion picture usu. at increased prices **3** : a promotional presentation or meeting conducted in a series of locations

road·side \ˈrōd-ˌsīd\ *n* (1744) : the strip of land along a road : the side of a road — **roadside** *adj*

road·stead \ˈrōd-ˌsted\ *n* (1556) : a place less enclosed than a harbor where ships may ride at anchor

road·ster \ˈrōd-stər\ *n* (ca. 1812) **1 a** : a horse suitable for riding or driving on roads **b** : a utility saddle horse of the hackney type **2 a** : a light carriage : BUGGY **b** : an automobile with an open body that seats two and has a folding fabric top and often a luggage compartment or rumble seat in the rear

road test *n* (1906) **1** : a test of a vehicle under practical operating conditions on the road **2** : a test on the road of a person's driving ability as a requirement for a driver's license — **road test** *vt*

road trip *n* (1953) **1** : a trip taken by a sports team to play one or more away games **2** : an extended trip in a motor vehicle — **road–trip** *vi*

road warrior *n* (1982) : a person who travels frequently esp. on business

road·way \ˈrōd-ˌwā\ *n* (1598) **1 a** : the strip of land over which a road passes **b** : ROAD; *specif* : ROADBED 2b **2** : the part of a bridge used by vehicles

road·work \-ˌwərk\ *n* (1802) **1** : work done in constructing or repairing roads **2** : conditioning for an athletic contest (as a boxing match) consisting mainly of long runs

road·wor·thy \-ˌwər-thē\ *adj* (1819) : fit for use on the road ⟨a ~ vehicle⟩ — **road·wor·thi·ness** *n*

roam \ˈrōm\ *vb* [ME *romen*] *vi* (14c) **1** : to go from place to place without purpose or direction : WANDER **2** : to travel purposefully unhindered through a wide area ⟨cattle ~*ing* in search of water⟩ **3** : to use a cellular phone outside one's local calling area ⟨~*ing* charges⟩ ~ *vt* : to range or wander over ***syn*** see WANDER — **roam** *n* — **roam·er** *n*

[1]**roan** \ˈrōn *also* ˈrō-ən\ *adj* [MF, fr. OSp *roano*] (1530) : having the base color (as red, black, or brown) muted and lightened by admixture of white hairs ⟨a ~ horse⟩ ⟨a ~ calf⟩

[2]**roan** *n* (1580) **1** : an animal (as a horse) with a roan coat — usu. used of a red roan when unqualified **2** : the color of a roan horse — used esp. when the base color is red

[3]**roan** *n* [origin unknown] (1818) : sheepskin tanned with sumac and colored and finished to imitate morocco

[1]**roar** \ˈrȯr\ *vb* [ME *roren,* fr. OE *rārian;* akin to OHG *rērēn* to bleat] *vi* (bef. 12c) **1 a** : to utter or emit a full loud prolonged sound **b** : to sing or shout with full force **2 a** : to make or emit a loud confused sound (as background reverberation or rumbling) **b** : to laugh loudly **3 a** : to be boisterous or disorderly **b** : to proceed or rush with great noise or commotion **4** : to make a loud noise during inhalation (as that of a horse affected with roaring) ~ *vt* **1** : to utter or proclaim with a roar **2** : to cause to roar

[2]**roar** *n* (14c) **1** : the deep cry of a wild animal (as a lion) **2** : a loud deep cry (as of pain or anger) **3** : a loud continuous confused sound ⟨the ~ of the crowd⟩ **4** : a boisterous outcry

roar·er \ˈrȯr-ər\ *n* (14c) **1** : one that roars **2** : a horse subject to roaring

[1]**roar·ing** \ˈrȯr-iŋ\ *adj* (14c) **1** : making or characterized by a sound resembling a roar : LOUD ⟨~ applause⟩ **2** : marked by prosperity esp. of a temporary nature : BOOMING **3** : great in intensity or degree ⟨in the ~ heat⟩ ⟨a ~ success⟩ — **roar·ing·ly** *adv*

[2]**roaring** *adv* (1697) : EXTREMELY ⟨was ~ hungry —Herman Wouk⟩

[3]**roaring** *n* (ca. 1823) : noisy inhalation in a horse esp. upon exercising that is caused by paralysis and muscular atrophy of part of the larynx

roaring boy *n* (ca. 1590) : a noisy street bully esp. of Elizabethan and Jacobean England who intimidated passersby

roaring forties *n, often cap R&F* (1883) : a tract of ocean between roughly 40 and 50 degrees latitude south characterized by strong westerly winds and rough seas; *also* : these winds

[1]**roast** \ˈrōst\ *vb* [ME *rosten,* fr. AF *rostir,* of Gmc origin; akin to OHG *rōsten* to roast] *vt* (13c) **1 a** : to cook by exposing to dry heat (as in an oven or before a fire) or by surrounding with hot embers, sand, or stones ⟨~ a potato in ashes⟩ **b** : to dry and parch by exposure to heat ⟨~ coffee beans⟩ **2** : to heat (inorganic material) with access of air and without fusing to effect change (as expulsion of volatile matter, oxidation, or removal of sulfur from sulfide ores) **3** : to heat to excess ⟨~*ed* by the summer sun⟩ **4** : to subject to severe criticism or ridicule ⟨films have been ~*ed* by most critics —H. J. Seldes⟩ **5** : to honor (a person) at a roast ~ *vi* **1** : to cook food by heat **2** : to undergo being roasted

[2]**roast** *n* (14c) **1** : a piece of meat suitable for roasting **2** : a gathering at which food is roasted before an open fire or in hot ashes or sand **3** : an act or process of roasting; *specif* : severe banter or criticism **4** : a banquet honoring a person (as a celebrity) who is subjected to humorous tongue-in-cheek ridicule by friends

[3]**roast** *adj* (14c) : that has been roasted ⟨~ beef⟩

roast·er \ˈrōs-tər\ *n* (15c) **1** : one that roasts **2** : a device for roasting **3** : something adapted to roasting: as **a** : a suckling pig **b** : a bird fit for roasting; *esp* : a young chicken larger than a broiler

roast·ing ear \ˈrōs-tiŋ-ˌir, *sense 2 usu* ˈrō-sᵊn-ˌir *or* ˈrōs-ˌnir\ *n* (1650) **1** : an ear of young corn roasted or suitable for roasting usu. in the husk **2** *chiefly Southern & Midland* : an ear of corn suitable for boiling or steaming

rob \ˈräb\ *vb* **robbed; rob·bing** [ME *robben,* fr. AF *rober,* of Gmc origin; akin to OHG *roubōn* to rob — more at REAVE] *vt* (13c) **1 a** (1) : to take something away from by force : steal from (2) : to take personal property from by violence or threat **b** (1) : to remove valuables without right from (a place) (2) : to take the contents of (a receptacle) **c** : to take away as loot : STEAL ⟨~ jewelry⟩ **2 a** : to deprive of something due, expected, or desired **b** : to withhold unjustly or injuriously ~ *vi* : to commit robbery — **rob·ber** *n*

usage Sense *vt* 1c, in which the direct object is the thing stolen, is sometimes considered to be wrong, or perhaps archaic. The sense has been in use since the 13th century and is found in earlier literature ⟨contrive to *rob* the honey and subvert the hive —John Dryden⟩. It is still in use though not as common as other senses ⟨then *robbed* $100 after the clerk fled —*Springfield (Mass.) Morning Union*⟩.

ro·ba·lo \rō-ˈbä-(ˌ)lō\ *n, pl* **-los** *or* **-lo** [Sp] (1857) : SNOOK 1

ro·band \ˈrō-ˌband, -bənd\ *n* [ME *robend, robond,* prob. fr. ON *rāband,* fr. *rā* sail yard + *band* band] (14c) : a piece of spun yarn or marline used to fasten the head of a sail to a spar

robber baron *n* (1878) **1** : an American capitalist of the latter part of the 19th century who became wealthy through exploitation (as of natural resources, governmental influence, or low wage scales) **2** : a business owner or executive who acquires wealth through ethically questionable tactics

robber fly *n* (1871) : any of a family (Asilidae) of predaceous dipteran flies including some resembling bumblebees

rob·bery \ˈrä-b(ə-)rē\ *n, pl* **-ber·ies** (13c) : the act or practice of robbing; *specif* : larceny from the person or presence of another by violence or threat

[1]**robe** \ˈrōb\ *n* [ME, fr. AF, booty, clothing, robe, of Gmc origin; akin to OHG *roubōn* to rob] (13c) **1 a** : a long flowing outer garment; *esp* : one used for ceremonial occasions or as a symbol of office or profession **b** : a loose garment (as a bathrobe) for informal wear esp. at home **2** : COVERING, MANTLE ⟨peaks on the axis of the range in their ~*s* of snow and light —John Muir⟩ **3** : a covering of pelts or fabric for the lower body used while driving or at outdoor events

[2]**robe** *vb* **robed; rob·ing** *vt* (14c) : to clothe or cover with or as if with a robe ~ *vi* **1** : to put on a robe **2** : DRESS

robe de cham·bre \ˌrōb-də-ˈshäⁿbrᵊ, -ˈshäm-brə\ *n, pl* **robes de chambre** \ˌrōb(z)-\ [F] (1731) : DRESSING GOWN

rob·in \ˈrä-bən\ *n* [akin to D dial. *robijntje* linnet, Fris *robyntsje*] (1549) **1 a** : a small chiefly European thrush (*Erithacus rubecula*) resembling a warbler and having a brownish-olive back and orangish face and breast **b** : any of various Old World songbirds that are related to or resemble the European robin **2** : a large No. American thrush (*Turdus migratorius*) with olivaceous to slate-gray upperparts, blackish head and tail, black and whitish streaked throat, and dull reddish breast and underparts

Rob·in Good·fel·low \ˈrä-bən-ˈgu̇d-ˌfe-(ˌ)lō\ *n* (1531) : a mischievous sprite in English folklore

Robin Hood \-ˌhu̇d\ *n* [*Robin Hood,* legendary Eng. outlaw who gave to the poor what he stole from the rich] (1597) : a person or group likened to a heroic outlaw; *esp* : one that robs the rich and gives to the poor

robin red·breast \-ˈred-ˌbrest\ *n* [ME (Sc) *Robyn redbrest*] (15c) : ROBIN

Rob•in•son Cru•soe \ˈrä-bə(n)-sən-ˈkrü-(ˌ)sō\ *n* (1719) **:** a shipwrecked sailor in Daniel Defoe's *Robinson Crusoe* who lives for many years on a desert island
Rob•in•son projection \ˈrä-bən-sən-\ *n* [Arthur H. *Robinson b*1915 Am. geographer] (1978) **:** a compromise map projection showing the poles as lines rather than points and more accurately portraying high latitude lands and water to land ratio
ro•ble \ˈrō-(ˌ)blā\ *n* [AmerSp, fr. Sp, oak, fr. L *robur*] (1864) **:** any of several oaks of California and Mexico
ro•bo•call \ˈrō-bō-ˌkȯl\ *n* [*robot* + *-o-* + [2]*call*] (1993) **:** a telephone call from an automated source that delivers a prerecorded message to a large number of people
ro•bot \ˈrō-ˌbät, -bət\ *n* [Czech, fr. *robota* compulsory labor; akin to OHG *arabeit* trouble, L *orbus* orphaned — more at ORPHAN] (1922) **1 a :** a machine that looks like a human being and performs various complex acts (as walking or talking) of a human being; *also* **:** a similar but fictional machine whose lack of capacity for human emotions is often emphasized **b :** an efficient insensitive person who functions automatically **2 :** a device that automatically performs complicated often repetitive tasks **3 :** a mechanism guided by automatic controls — **ro•bot•ism** \ˈrō-ˌbä-ˌti-zəm, -bə-\ *n*
ro•bot•ic \rō-ˈbä-tik, rə-\ *adj* (1941) **1 :** of or relating to mechanical robots **2 :** having the characteristics of a robot ⟨performs with ~ consistency⟩ — **ro•bot•i•cal•ly** \-ti-k(ə-)lē\ *adv*
ro•bot•ics \rō-ˈbä-tiks\ *n pl but sing in constr* (1941) **:** technology dealing with the design, construction, and operation of robots in automation — **ro•bot•i•cist** \-tə-sist\ *n*
ro•bot•i•za•tion \ˌrō-ˌbä-tə-ˈzā-shən, -bə-\ *n* (1927) **1 :** AUTOMATION **2 :** the process of turning a human being into a robot
ro•bot•ize \ˈrō-ˌbä-ˌtīz, -bə-\ *vt* **-ized; -iz•ing** (1927) **1 :** to make automatic **:** equip with robots **2 :** to turn (a human being) into a robot
Rob Roy \ˈräb-ˈrȯi\ *n* [*Rob Roy*, nickname of Robert McGregor †1734 Scot. freebooter] (1919) **:** a manhattan made with Scotch whisky
ro•bust \rō-ˈbəst, ˈrō-(ˌ)bəst\ *adj* [L *robustus* oaken, strong, fr. *robor-, robur* oak, strength] (1533) **1 a :** having or exhibiting strength or vigorous health **b :** having or showing vigor, strength, or firmness ⟨a ~ debate⟩ ⟨a ~ faith⟩ **c :** strongly formed or constructed **:** STURDY ⟨a ~ plastic⟩ **d :** capable of performing without failure under a wide range of conditions ⟨~ software⟩ **2 :** ROUGH, RUDE ⟨stories . . . laden with ~, down-home imagery —*Playboy*⟩ **3 :** requiring strength or vigor ⟨~ work⟩ **4 :** FULL-BODIED ⟨~ coffee⟩; *also* **:** HEARTY ⟨a ~ dinner⟩ **5 :** of, relating to, resembling, or being a relatively large, heavyset australopithecine (esp. *Australopithecus robustus* and *A. boisei*) characterized esp. by heavy molars and small incisors adapted to a vegetarian diet — compare GRACILE 3 ***syn*** see HEALTHY — **ro•bust•ly** *adv* — **ro•bust•ness** \-ˈbəs(t)-nəs, -(ˌ)bəs(t)-\ *n*
ro•bus•ta \rō-ˈbəs-tə\ *n, often attrib* [NL *robusta*, specific epithet of *Coffea robusta*, syn. of *Coffea canephora*] (1909) **1 :** a hardy shrub or tree (*Coffea canephora*) that is indigenous to central Africa but has been introduced elsewhere (as in Java) and yields seeds that form a usu. lower quality coffee of commerce than that of arabica **2 :** the seeds of robusta esp. roasted and often ground
ro•bus•tious \rō-ˈbəs-chəs\ *adj* (ca. 1548) **1 :** ROBUST **2 :** vigorous in a rough or unrefined way **:** BOISTEROUS — **ro•bus•tious•ly** *adv* — **ro•bus•tious•ness** *n*
roc \ˈräk\ *n* [ultim. fr. Ar *rukhkh*] (1579) **:** a legendary bird of great size and strength believed to inhabit the Indian Ocean area
ROC *abbr* Republic of China (Taiwan)
ro•caille \rō-ˈkī, rä-\ *n* [F, lit., stone debris, fr. MF *roquailles*, pl., rocky terrain, fr. *roc* rock, alter. of *roche*, fr. VL **rocca*] (1856) **1 :** a style of ornament developed in the 18th century and characterized by sinuous foliate forms **2 :** ROCOCO
Roche limit \ˈrōsh-, ˈrōsh-\ *n* [E. A. *Roche* †1883 Fr. mathematician] (1889) **:** the distance from a planet's center within which a satellite can neither approach nor reside without being disrupted by tidal forces
Ro•chelle salt \rō-ˈshel-\ *n* [La *Rochelle*, France] (1753) **:** a crystalline salt $KNaC_4H_4O_6 \cdot 4H_2O$ that is a mild purgative
roche mou•ton•née \ˈrōsh-ˌmü-tə-ˈnā, ˈrōsh-\ *n, pl* **roches mou•ton•nées** *same or* -ˈnāz\ [F, lit., fleecy rock] (1843) **:** an elongate rounded ice-sculptured hillock of bedrock
roch•et \ˈrä-chət\ *n* [ME, fr. AF, fr. OF **roc* coat, of Gmc origin; akin to OHG *roc* coat] (13c) **:** a white linen vestment resembling a surplice with close-fitting sleeves worn esp. by bishops and privileged prelates
[1]**rock** \ˈräk\ *vb* [ME *rokken*, fr. OE *roccian;* akin to OHG *rucken* to cause to move] *vt* (12c) **1 :** to move back and forth in or as if in a cradle **2 a :** to cause to sway back and forth ⟨a boat *~ed* by the waves⟩ **b** (1) **:** to cause to shake violently (2) **:** to daze with or as if with a vigorous blow ⟨a hard right *~ed* the contender⟩ (3) **:** to astonish or disturb greatly ⟨the scandal *~ed* the community⟩ **3 :** to rouse to excitement (as by performing rock music) ⟨*~ed* the crowd⟩ *~ vi* **1 :** to become moved backward and forward under often violent impact; *also* **:** to move gently back and forth **2 :** to move forward at a steady pace; *also* **:** to move forward at a high speed ⟨the train *~ed* through the countryside⟩ **3 :** to sing, dance to, or play rock music **4** *slang* **:** to be extremely enjoyable, pleasing, or effective ⟨her new car *~s*⟩ ***syn*** see SHAKE — **rock the boat :** to do something that disturbs the equilibrium of a situation
[2]**rock** *n, often attrib* (1823) **1 :** a rocking movement **2 :** popular music usu. played on electronically amplified instruments and characterized by a persistent heavily accented beat, repetition of simple phrases, and often country, folk, and blues elements
[3]**rock** *n* [ME *roc*, fr. MD *rocke;* akin to OHG *rocko* distaff] (14c) **1 :** DISTAFF **2 :** the wool or flax on a distaff
[4]**rock** *n* [ME *rokke*, fr. OF dial. (Norman & Picard) *roke*, fr. VL **rocca*] (14c) **1 :** a large mass of stone forming a cliff, promontory, or peak **2 :** a concreted mass of stony material; *also* **:** broken pieces of such masses **3 :** consolidated or unconsolidated solid mineral matter; *also* **:** a particular mass of it **4 a :** something like a rock in firmness: (1) **:** FOUNDATION, SUPPORT (2) **:** REFUGE ⟨a ~ of independent thought . . . in an ocean of parochialism —Thomas Molnar⟩ **b :** something that threatens or causes disaster — often used in pl. **5 a :** a flavored stick candy with color running through **b :** ROCK CANDY 1 **6** *slang* **a :** GEM **b :** DIAMOND **7 a :** a small crystallized mass of crack cocaine **b :** CRACK 9 **8 :** the ball used in basketball — **rock** *adj* — **rock•like** \ˈräk-ˌlīk\ *adj* — **between a rock and a hard place** *also* **between the rock and the hard place :** in a difficult or uncomfortable position with no attractive way out — **on the rocks 1 :** in or into a state of destruction or wreckage ⟨their marriage is *on the rocks*⟩ **2 :** on ice cubes ⟨bourbon *on the rocks*⟩
rock•a•bil•ly \ˈrä-kə-ˌbi-lē\ *n* [[2]*rock* + *-a-* (as in *rock-a-bye*, phrase used to put a child to sleep) + hill*billy*] (1956) **:** popular music marked by features of rock and country music
rock and roll *or* **rock 'n' roll** *n* (1954) **:** [2]ROCK 2 — **rock–and–roll** *or* **rock 'n' roll** *adj*
rock and roller *or* **rock 'n' roller** *n* (1956) **:** ROCKER 3
rock•a•way \ˈrä-kə-ˌwā\ *n* [perh. fr. *Rockaway*, New Jersey] (1846) **:** a light low four-wheel carriage with a fixed top and open sides
rock bass *n* (1811) **:** a brown spotted sunfish (*Ambloplites rupestris*) found esp. in the upper Mississippi River valley and Great Lakes region
rock–bottom *adj* (1884) **:** being the very lowest ⟨~ prices⟩; *also* **:** FUNDAMENTAL ⟨the ~ question⟩
rock bottom *n* (1890) **:** the lowest or most fundamental part or level
rock•bound \ˈräk-ˌbau̇nd\ *adj* (1826) **:** fringed, surrounded, or covered with rocks **:** ROCKY
rock brake *n* (ca. 1850) **:** any of several ferns that grow chiefly on or among rocks
rock candy *n* (ca. 1706) **1 :** boiled sugar crystallized in large masses on string **2 :** [4]ROCK 5a
rock climbing *n* (1875) **:** mountain climbing on rocky cliffs — **rock climb** *vi* — **rock climber** *n*
rock cod *n* (1634) **:** ROCKFISH a
Rock Cornish hen *n* (1956) **:** a domestic chicken produced by interbreeding Cornish and white Plymouth Rock chickens and used esp. for small roasters — called also *Rock Cornish, Rock Cornish game hen*
rock crystal *n* (1666) **:** CRYSTAL 1
rock dove *n* (1655) **:** a bluish-gray dove (*Columba livia*) that is indigenous to Eurasia but has been widely established elsewhere including most of No. America and that is the ancestor of many domesticated pigeons and of the feral pigeons found in cities and towns throughout most of the world — called also *rock pigeon*
rock•er \ˈrä-kər\ *n* (1760) **1 a :** either of two curving pieces of wood or metal on which an object (as a cradle) rocks **b :** any of various objects (as a rocking chair or an infant's toy having a seat placed between side pieces) that rock on rockers **c :** any of various objects in the form of a rocker or with parts resembling a rocker (as a skate with a curved blade) **d** (1) **:** any of the curved stripes at the lower part of a chevron worn by a noncommissioned officer above the rank of sergeant (2) **:** the curved stripe at the upper part of a chevron worn by a chief petty officer **2 :** any of various devices that work with a rocking motion **3 :** a rock performer, song, or enthusiast — **off one's rocker :** in a state of extreme confusion or insanity ⟨went *off her rocker*, and had to be put away —Mervyn Wall⟩
rocker arm *n* (1851) **:** a center-pivoted lever actuated by a cam to push an automotive engine valve down
rocker panel *n* (1921) **:** the portion of the body paneling of a vehicle that is situated below the doorsills of the passenger compartment
rock•ery \ˈrä-k(ə-)rē\ *n, pl* **-er•ies** [[4]*rock* + *-ery*] (1845) *chiefly Brit* **:** ROCK GARDEN
[1]**rock•et** \ˈrä-kət, rä-ˈket\ *n* [MF *roquette*, fr. OIt *rochetta*, dim. of *ruca* arugula, fr. L *eruca*] (1530) **:** any of several plants of the mustard family: as **a :** ARUGULA **b :** DAME'S ROCKET
[2]**rock•et** \ˈrä-kət\ *n, often attrib* [It *rocchetta*, lit., small distaff, fr. dim. of *rocca* distaff, of Gmc origin; akin to OHG *rocko* distaff] (1611) **1 a :** a firework consisting of a case partly filled with a combustible composition fastened to a guiding stick and propelled through the air by the rearward discharge of the gases liberated by combustion **b :** a similar device used as an incendiary weapon or as a propelling unit (as for a lifesaving line) **2 :** a jet engine that operates on the same principle as the firework rocket, consists essentially of a combustion chamber and an exhaust nozzle, carries either liquid or solid propellants which provide the fuel and oxygen needed for combustion and thus make the engine independent of the oxygen of the air, and is used esp. for the propulsion of a missile (as a bomb or shell) or a vehicle (as an airplane) **3 :** a rocket-propelled bomb, missile, projectile, or vehicle
[3]**rock•et** \ˈrä-kət\ *vt* (1837) **:** to convey or propel by means of or as if by a rocket *~ vi* **1 :** to rise up swiftly, spectacularly, and with force ⟨*~ed* to the top of the list⟩ **2 :** to travel rapidly in or as if in a rocket
rock•e•teer \ˌrä-kə-ˈtir\ *n* (1832) **1 :** one who fires, pilots, or rides in a rocket **2 :** a scientist who specializes in rocketry
rocket plane *n* (1928) **:** an airplane propelled by rockets
rock•et•ry \ˈrä-kə-trē\ *n* (1930) **:** the study of, experimentation with, or use of rockets
rocket ship *n* (1927) **:** a rocket-propelled spaceship
rocket sled *n* (1954) **:** a rocket-propelled vehicle that runs usu. on a single rail and that is used esp. in aeronautical experimentation
rock•fall \ˈräk-ˌfȯl\ *n* (1901) **:** a mass of falling or fallen rocks
rock•fish \-ˌfish\ *n* (1598) **:** any of various fishes that live among rocks or on rocky bottoms: as **a :** any of a genus (*Sebastes*) of scorpaenid fishes including many important food fishes **b :** STRIPED BASS **c :** any of several groupers

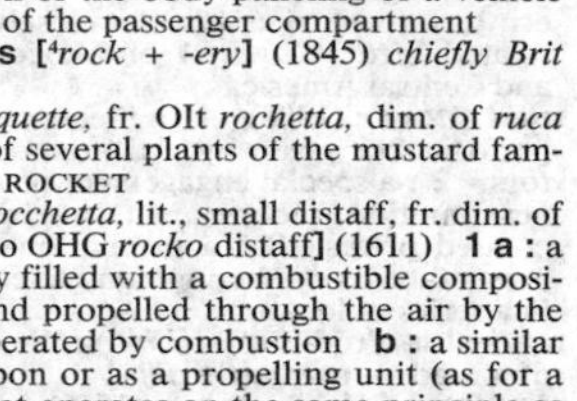
rockfish a

rock garden *n* (1836) **:** a garden laid out among rocks or decorated with rocks and adapted for the growth of particular kinds of plants (as alpines)
rock hind *n* (ca. 1867) **:** a red-spotted tan to olive-brown grouper (*Epinephelus adscensionis*) of the western Atlantic esp. from Massachusetts to southeastern Brazil
rock•hop•per \ˈräk-ˌhä-pər\ *n* (1875) **:** a small penguin (*Eudyptes chrysocome*) with a short thick bill and a yellow crest
rock hound *n* (1915) **1 :** a specialist in geology **2 :** an amateur rock and mineral collector — **rock•hound•ing** \ˈräk-ˌhau̇n-diŋ\ *n*
rock•i•ness \ˈrä-kē-nəs\ *n* (1611) **:** the quality or state of being rocky
rocking chair *n* (1766) **:** a chair mounted on rockers

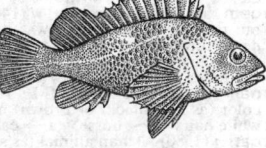

rocking horse *n* (1724) : a toy horse mounted on rockers — called also *hobbyhorse*

rock·ling \ˈrä-kliŋ\ *n* (1602) : any of several small rather elongate marine bony fishes (esp. genera *Enchelyopus* and *Gaidropsarus*) of the cod family

rock lobster *n* (1884) : SPINY LOBSTER

rock maple *n* (1775) : SUGAR MAPLE 1

rock 'n' roll, rock 'n' roller *var of* ROCK AND ROLL, ROCK AND ROLLER

rock oil *n* (1668) : PETROLEUM

rock pigeon *n* (1611) : ROCK DOVE

rock rabbit *n* (1840) **1** : HYRAX **2** : PIKA

rock–ribbed \ˈräk-ˈribd\ *adj* (1776) **1** : 1ROCKY 1 **2** : firm and inflexible in doctrine or integrity ⟨a ~ conservative community —John Hale⟩

rock·rose \ˈräk-ˌrōz\ *n* (1731) : any of a genus (*Cistus* of the family Cistaceae, the rockrose family) of shrubs or woody herbs of the Mediterranean region with simple entire leaves, roselike flowers, and a capsular fruit

rock salt *n* (1693) : common salt occurring in solid form as a mineral; *also* : salt artificially prepared in large crystals or masses

rock·shaft \ˈräk-ˌshaft\ *n* (ca. 1864) : a shaft that oscillates on its journals instead of revolving

rock shrimp *n* (1973) : any of several hard-shelled warm-water shrimp (genus *Sicyonia,* esp. *S. brevirostris*) that are harvested chiefly in the Gulf of Mexico and widely sold as food

rock tripe *n* (1854) : any of various dark leathery umbilicate foliose lichens (as of the genus *Umbilicaria*) that are widely distributed on rocks in boreal and alpine areas and are sometimes used as food

rock wallaby *n* (1841) : any of various medium-sized kangaroos (genus *Petrogale*) having a gray or brown coat usu. with distinctive markings

rock·weed \ˈräk-ˌwēd\ *n* (1583) : any of various coarse brown algae (order Fucales, esp. genera *Fucus, Ascophyllum,* and *Sargassum*) growing in marine environments free-floating or attached to rocks

rock wool *n* (ca. 1909) : mineral wool made by blowing a jet of steam through molten rock (as limestone or siliceous rock) or through slag and used chiefly for heat and sound insulation

1**rocky** \ˈrä-kē\ *adj* **rock·i·er; -est** [ME *rokky,* fr. *rokke* rock] (15c) **1** : abounding in or consisting of rocks **2** : difficult to impress or affect : INSENSITIVE **3** : firmly held : STEADFAST

2**rocky** *adj* **rock·i·er; -est** [1*rock*] (1737) **1** : UNSTABLE, WOBBLY **2** : physically upset or mentally confused (as from drinking excessively) **3** : marked by obstacles or problems : DIFFICULT, ROUGH ⟨a financially ~ year —Michael Murray⟩

Rocky Mountain sheep *n* [*Rocky Mountains,* No. America] (1817) : BIGHORN SHEEP

Rocky Mountain spotted fever *n* (1905) : an acute disease that is characterized by chills, fever, prostration, pains in muscles and joints, and a red to purple eruption and that is caused by a rickettsia (*Rickettsia rickettsii*) usu. transmitted by an ixodid tick and esp. either the American dog tick or a wood tick (*Dermacentor andersoni*)

1**ro·co·co** \rə-ˈkō-(ˌ)kō, rō-kə-ˈkō\ *n* (1840) : rococo work or style

2**rococo** *adj* [F, irreg. fr. *rocaille* rocaille] (1841) **1 a** : of or relating to an artistic style esp. of the 18th century characterized by fanciful curved asymmetrical forms and elaborate ornamentation **b** : of or relating to an 18th century musical style marked by light gay ornamentation and departure from thorough-bass and polyphony **2** : excessively ornate or intricate

rod \ˈräd\ *n* [ME, fr. OE *rodd;* akin to ON *rudda* club] (bef. 12c) **1 a** (1) : a straight slender stick growing on or cut from a tree or bush (2) : OSIER (3) : a stick or bundle of twigs used to punish; *also* : PUNISHMENT (4) : a shepherd's cudgel (5) : a pole with a line and usu. a reel attached for fishing **b** (1) : a slender bar (as of wood or metal) (2) : a bar or staff for measuring (3) : SCEPTER; *also* : a wand or staff carried as a badge of office (as of marshal) **2 a** : a unit of length — see WEIGHT table **b** : a square rod **3** : any of the long rod-shaped photosensitive receptors in the retina responsive to faint light — compare CONE 3a **4** : a rod-shaped bacterium **5** *slang* : HANDGUN — **rod·less** \-ləs\ *adj* — **rod·like** \-ˌlīk\ *adj*

1**rode** *past and chiefly dial past part of* RIDE

2**rode** \ˈrōd\ *n* [origin unknown] (1679) : a line (as of rope or chain) used to attach an anchor to a boat

ro·dent \ˈrō-dᵊnt\ *n* [ultim. fr. L *rodent-, rodens,* prp. of *rodere* to gnaw; akin to L *radere* to scrape, scratch, Skt *radati* he gnaws] (1835) **1** : any of an order (Rodentia) of relatively small gnawing mammals (as a mouse, squirrel, or beaver) that have in both jaws a single pair of incisors with a chisel-shaped edge **2** : a small mammal (as a rabbit or a shrew) other than a true rodent — **rodent** *adj*

ro·den·ti·cide \rō-ˈden-tə-ˌsīd\ *n* (ca. 1935) : an agent that kills, repels, or controls rodents

rodent ulcer *n* [L *rodent-, rodens* gnawing] (1853) : a chronic persisting ulcer of the exposed skin and esp. of the face that is destructive locally, spreads slowly, and is usu. a carcinoma derived from basal cells

1**ro·deo** \ˈrō-dē-ˌō, rə-ˈdā-(ˌ)ō\ *n, pl* **ro·de·os** [Sp, fr. *rodear* to surround, fr. *rueda* wheel, fr. L *rota* — more at ROLL] (1834) **1** : ROUNDUP **2 a** : a public performance featuring bronco riding, calf roping, steer wrestling, and Brahma bull riding **b** : a contest resembling a rodeo

2**rodeo** *vi* (1951) : to participate in a rodeo

rod·man \ˈräd-mən, -ˌman\ *n* (1853) : a surveyor's assistant who holds the leveling rod

ro·do·mon·tade *also* **rho·do·mon·tade** \ˌrä-də-mən-ˈtād, ˌrō-, -ˈtäd\ *n* [F, fr. MF, fr. *rodomont* blusterer, fr. It *Rodomonte,* character in *Orlando Innamorato* by Matteo M. Boiardo] (1612) **1** : a bragging speech **2** : vain boasting or bluster : RANT

1**roe** \ˈrō\ *n, pl* **roe** *or* **roes** [ME *ro,* fr. OE *rā;* akin to OHG *rēh* roe] (bef. 12c) : DOE

2**roe** *n* [ME *roof, roughe, row;* akin to ON *hrogn* roe and prob. to Lith *kurkulai* frog's eggs] (15c) **1** : the eggs of a fish esp. when still enclosed in the ovarian membrane **2** : the eggs or ovaries of an invertebrate (as the coral of a lobster)

roe·buck \ˈrō-ˌbək\ *n, pl* **roebuck** *or* **roebucks** (14c) : ROE DEER; *esp* : the male roe deer

roe deer *n* (1575) : either of two small European or Asian deer (*Capreolus capreolus* and *C. pygarus*) that have short erect antlers forked at the summit, are reddish-brown in summer and grayish in winter, have a white rump patch, and are noted for their nimbleness and grace

1**roent·gen** \ˈrent-gən, ˈrənt-, -jən, -shən\ *adj* [ISV, fr. Wilhelm *Röntgen*] (1896) : of or relating to X-rays ⟨~ examinations⟩

2**roentgen** *n* (1922) : the international unit of x-radiation or gamma radiation equal to the amount of radiation that produces in one cubic centimeter of dry air at 0°C and standard atmospheric pressure ionization of either sign equal to one electrostatic unit of charge

roent·gen·i·um \rent-ˈge-nē-əm, rənt-, -ˈje-\ *n* [NL; fr. the fact that the element was synthesized on the centennial of Röntgen's discovery of X-rays] (2004) : a short-lived radioactive element produced artificially — see ELEMENT table

roent·gen·o·gram \ˈrent-gə-nə-ˌgram, ˈrənt-, -jə-, -shə-\ *n* [ISV] (ca. 1904) : RADIOGRAPH

roent·gen·og·ra·phy \ˌrent-gə-ˈnä-grə-fē, ˌrənt-, -jə-, -shə-\ *n* [ISV] (1905) : RADIOGRAPHY — **roent·gen·o·graph·ic** \-nə-ˈgra-fik\ *adj* — **roent·gen·o·graph·i·cal·ly** \-fi-k(ə-)lē\ *adv*

roent·gen·ol·o·gy \-ˈnä-lə-jē\ *n* [ISV] (1905) : RADIOLOGY — **roent·gen·o·log·ic** \-nə-ˈlä-jik\ *or* **roent·gen·o·log·i·cal** \-ji-kəl\ *adj* — **roent·gen·o·log·i·cal·ly** \-ji-k(ə-)lē\ *adv* — **roent·gen·ol·o·gist** \-ˈnä-lə-jist\ *n*

roentgen ray *n, often cap 1st R* (ca. 1890) : X-RAY

ro·ga·tion \rō-ˈgā-shən\ *n* [ME *rogacion,* fr. LL *rogation-, rogatio,* fr. L, questioning, fr. *rogare* to ask — more at RIGHT] (14c) **1** : LITANY, SUPPLICATION **2** : the religious observance of the Rogation Days — often used in pl.

Rogation Day *n* (15c) : any of the days of prayer esp. for the harvest observed on the three days before Ascension Day and by Roman Catholics also on April 25

rog·er \ˈrä-jər\ *interj* [fr. *Roger,* former communications code word for the letter *r*] (ca. 1941) — used esp. in radio and signaling to indicate that a message has been received and understood — **roger** *vt*

1**rogue** \ˈrōg\ *n* [origin unknown] (1561) **1** : VAGRANT, TRAMP **2** : a dishonest or worthless person : SCOUNDREL **3** : a mischievous person : SCAMP **4** : a horse inclined to shirk or misbehave **5** : an individual exhibiting a chance and usu. inferior biological variation — **rogu·ish** \ˈrō-gish\ *adj* — **rogu·ish·ly** *adv* — **rogu·ish·ness** *n*

2**rogue** *vi* **rogued; rogu·ing** *or* **rogue·ing** (1766) : to weed out inferior, diseased, or nontypical individuals from a crop plant or a field

3**rogue** *adj* (1872) **1** : resembling or suggesting a rogue elephant esp. in being isolated, aberrant, dangerous, or uncontrollable **2** : CORRUPT, DISHONEST ⟨~ cops⟩ **3** : of or being a nation whose leaders defy international law or norms of international behavior ⟨~ states⟩

rogue elephant *n* (1859) **1** : a vicious elephant that separates from the herd and roams alone **2** : one whose behavior resembles that of a rogue elephant in being aberrant or independent

rogu·ery \ˈrō-g(ə-)rē\ *n, pl* **-er·ies** (1592) **1** : an act or behavior characteristic of a rogue **2** : mischievous play

rogues' gallery *n* (1859) : a collection of pictures of persons arrested as criminals; *also* : a collection or list likened to a rogues' gallery

ROI *abbr* return on investment

roil \ˈrȯi(-ə)l, *vt 2 is also* ˈrī(-ə)l\ *vb* [origin unknown] *vt* (1590) **1 a** : to make turbid by stirring up the sediment or dregs of **b** : to stir up : DISTURB, DISORDER **2** : RILE 1 ~ *vi* : to move turbulently : be in a state of turbulence or agitation ⟨conflicting emotions ~*ing* inside her⟩

roily \ˈrȯi-lē\ *adj* (1823) **1** : full of sediment or dregs : MUDDY **2** : TURBULENT ⟨~ waters⟩

1**rois·ter** \ˈrȯi-stər\ *n* [MF *rustre* lout, alter. of *ruste,* fr. *ruste,* adj., rude, rough, fr. L *rusticus* rural — more at RUSTIC] (1551) *archaic* : one that roisters : ROISTERER

2**roister** *vi* **rois·tered; rois·ter·ing** \-st(ə-)riŋ\ (1582) : to engage in noisy revelry : CAROUSE ⟨dressed and ready for a ~*ing* night in town —Sherwood Anderson⟩ — **rois·ter·er** \-stər-ər\ *n* — **rois·ter·ous** \-st(ə-)rəs\ *adj* — **rois·ter·ous·ly** *adv*

ROK *abbr* Republic of Korea (South Korea)

Ro·land \ˈrō-lənd\ *n* [F] (14c) : a stalwart defender of the Christians against the Saracens in the Charlemagne legends who is killed at Roncesvalles

role *also* **rôle** \ˈrōl\ *n* [F *rôle,* lit., roll, fr. OF *rolle*] (1605) **1 a** (1) : a character assigned or assumed ⟨had to take on the ~ of both father and mother⟩ (2) : a socially expected behavior pattern usu. determined by an individual's status in a particular society **b** : a part played by an actor or singer **2** : a function or part performed esp. in a particular operation or process ⟨played a major ~ in the negotiations⟩

role model *n* (1957) : a person whose behavior in a particular role is imitated by others

role–play \ˈrōl-ˌplā, -ˈplā\ *vt* (1949) **1** : to act out the role of **2** : to represent in action ⟨students were asked to ~ the thoughts and feelings of each character —R. G. Lambert⟩ ~ *vi* : to play a role

rolf \ˈrȯlf *also* ˈrȯf\ *vt, often cap* (1970) : to practice Rolfing on

Rolf·ing \ˈrȯl-fiŋ *also* ˈrȯ-\ *service mark* — used for the practice of manipulating the body's deep connective tissues for structural alignment

1**roll** \ˈrōl\ *n* [ME *rolle,* fr. AF *roule, rolle,* fr. ML *rolla,* alter. of *rotula,* fr. L, dim. of *rota* wheel; akin to OHG *rad* wheel, W *rhod,* Skt *ratha* wagon] (13c) **1 a** (1) : a written document that may be rolled up : SCROLL; *specif* : a document containing an official or formal record ⟨the ~*s* of parliament⟩ (2) : a manuscript book **b** : a list of names or related items : CATALOG **c** : an official list ⟨the voter ~*s*⟩: as (1) : MUSTER ROLL (2) : a list of members of a school or class or of members of a legislative body **2** : something that is rolled up into a cylinder or ball or rounded as if rolled ⟨~*s* of fat⟩: as **a** : a quantity (as of fabric or paper) rolled up to form a single package **b** : a hairdo in which some or all of the hair is rolled or curled up or under **c** : any of various food preparations rolled up for cooking or serving ⟨cabbage ~*s*⟩; *esp* : a small piece of baked yeast dough **d** : a cylindrical twist of tobacco **e** : a roll of paper on which music for a player piano is recorded in perforations which actuate the keys **f** : a flexible case (as of

\ə\ **abut** \ᵊ\ kitten, F table \ər\ **further** \a\ **ash** \ā\ **ace** \ä\ **mop, mar** \au̇\ **out** \ch\ **chin** \e\ **bet** \ē\ **easy** \g\ **go** \i\ **hit** \ī\ **ice** \j\ **job** \ŋ\ **sing** \ō\ **go** \ȯ\ **law** \ȯi\ **boy** \th\ **thin** \t͟h\ **the** \ü\ **loot** \u̇\ **foot** \y\ **yet** \zh\ **vision, beige** \k̟, ⁿ, œ, ue, ʸ\ *see* Guide to Pronunciation

leather) in which articles may be rolled and fastened by straps or clasps ⟨jewelry ~⟩ **g** (1) **:** paper money folded or rolled into a wad (2) *slang* **:** BANKROLL **3 :** something that performs a rolling action or movement **:** ROLLER **4 :** a wheel for making decorative lines on book covers; *also* **:** a design impressed by such a tool

[2]**roll** *vb* [ME, fr. AF *rouler, roller,* fr. *roele* wheel, rowel & *roule* roll] *vt* (14c) **1 a :** to impel forward by causing to turn over and over on a surface **b :** to cause to revolve by turning over and over on or as if on an axis **c :** to cause to move in a circular manner ⟨they ~*ed* their eyes at the absurdity⟩ **d :** to form into a mass by turning over and over **e :** to impel forward with an easy continuous motion **f :** to cause to move in a given direction by or as if by turning a crank ⟨~*ed* down the window⟩ **2 a :** to put a wrapping around **:** ENFOLD, ENVELOP **b :** to wrap round on itself **:** shape into a ball or roll ⟨~*ed* up the newspaper⟩; *also* **:** to produce by such shaping ⟨~*ed* his own cigarettes⟩ **3 :** to press, spread, or level with a roller **:** make smooth, even, or compact ⟨hulled and ~*ed* oats⟩ ⟨~ paint⟩ — often used with *out* ⟨~*ed* out the dough⟩ **4 a :** to move on rollers or wheels ⟨~*ed* the patient into the operating room⟩ **b :** to cause to begin operating or moving ⟨~ the cameras⟩ **5 a :** to sound with a full reverberating tone ⟨~*ed* out the words⟩ **b :** to make a continuous beating sound upon **:** sound a roll upon ⟨~*ed* their drums⟩ **c :** to utter with a trill ⟨~*ed* his *r's*⟩ **d :** to play (a chord) in arpeggio style **6 :** to combine so as to comprise one entity — usu. used in the phrase *rolled into one* ⟨a shopping center, amusement park, and nightclub all ~*ed* into one⟩ **7 :** to rob (a drunk, sleeping, or unconscious person) usu. by going through the pockets; *broadly* **:** ROB **8 :** BOWL 1 ~ *vi* **1 a :** to move along a surface by rotation without sliding **b** (1) **:** to turn over and over ⟨the children ~*ed* in the grass⟩ (2) **:** to luxuriate in an abundant supply **:** WALLOW ⟨fairly ~*ing* in money⟩ **2 a :** to move onward or around as if by completing a revolution **:** ELAPSE, PASS ⟨the months ~ on⟩ **b :** to shift the gaze continually ⟨eyes ~*ing* in terror⟩ **c :** to revolve on an axis **3 :** to move about **:** ROAM, WANDER **4 a :** to go forward in an easy, gentle, or undulating manner ⟨the waves ~*ed* in⟩ **b :** to flow in a continuous stream **:** POUR ⟨money was ~*ing* in⟩ **c :** to flow as part of a stream of words or sounds ⟨the names ~ off your tongue⟩ **d :** to have an undulating contour ⟨~*ing* prairie⟩ **e :** to lie extended **:** STRETCH **5 a :** to travel in a vehicle ⟨~*ing* north on the highway⟩ **b :** to become carried on a stream **c :** to move on wheels **6 a :** to make a deep reverberating sound ⟨the thunder ~*s*⟩ **b :** TRILL **7 a :** to swing from side to side ⟨the ship heaved and ~*ed*⟩ **b :** to walk with a swinging gait **:** SWAY **8 a :** to take the form of a cylinder or ball **b :** to respond to rolling in a specified way **9 a :** to get under way **:** begin to move or operate **b :** to move forward **:** develop and maintain impetus ⟨the project finally got ~*ing*⟩; *esp* **:** to proceed or progress with notable ease or success ⟨the team was ~*ing*⟩ **10 :** to execute a somersault **11** *of a football quarterback* **:** to run toward one flank usu. parallel to the line of scrimmage esp. before throwing a pass — often used with *out* — **roll the bones :** to shoot craps — **roll the dice :** to assume a risk by taking action ⟨*rolled the dice* when they bought those stocks⟩ — **roll with the punches 1 :** to move so as to lessen the impact of blows **2 :** to adjust to things as they happen

[3]**roll** *n* (1688) **1 a :** a sound produced by rapid strokes on a drum **b :** a sonorous and often rhythmical flow of speech **c :** a heavy reverberatory sound ⟨the ~ of cannon⟩ **2 :** a rolling movement or an action or process involving such movement ⟨a ~ of the dice⟩ ⟨an airplane's takeoff ~⟩: as **a :** a swaying movement of the body **b :** a side-to-side movement (as of a ship or train) **c** (1) **:** a flight maneuver in which a complete revolution about the longitudinal axis of an airplane is made with the horizontal direction of flight being approximately maintained (2) **:** the motion of an aircraft or spacecraft about its longitudinal axis **d :** a somersault executed in contact with the ground — **on a roll :** in the midst of a series of successes **:** on a hot streak — sometimes used with a modifier ⟨has been *on a* brilliant *roll*⟩

roll·back \ˈrōl-ˌbak\ *n* (1937) **:** the act or an instance of rolling back ⟨a government-ordered ~ of gasoline prices⟩

roll back *vt* (1942) **1 :** to reduce (as a commodity price) to or toward a previous level on a national scale **2 :** to cause to retreat or withdraw **:** push back **3 :** RESCIND ⟨attempted to *roll back* antipollution standards⟩

roll bar *n* (ca. 1952) **:** an overhead metal bar on an automobile that is designed to protect the occupant in case of a rollover

roll cage *n* (1966) **:** a protective framework of metal bars encasing the driver of a vehicle (as a racing car)

roll call *n* (1775) **1 :** the act or an instance of calling off a list of names (as for checking attendance); *also* **:** a time for a roll call **2 :** [8]LIST

[1]**roll·er** \ˈrō-lər\ *n* (13c) **1 a :** a revolving cylinder over or on which something is moved or which is used to press, shape, spread, or smooth something **b :** a cylinder or rod on which something (as a shade) is rolled up **2 a :** a long heavy ocean wave **b :** TUMBLER 1b **3 :** one that rolls or performs a rolling operation **4 :** a slowly rolling ground ball

[2]**rol·ler** \ˈrō-lər\ *n* [G, fr. *rollen* to roll, reverberate, fr. MF *roller* — more at ROLL] (1678) **1 :** any of various mostly brightly colored nonpasserine Old World birds (family Coraciidae) that perform rolling aerial dives during courtship displays **2 :** a canary having a song in which the notes are soft and run together

roller bearing *n* (1857) **:** a bearing in which the journal rotates in peripheral contact with a number of rollers usu. contained in a cage

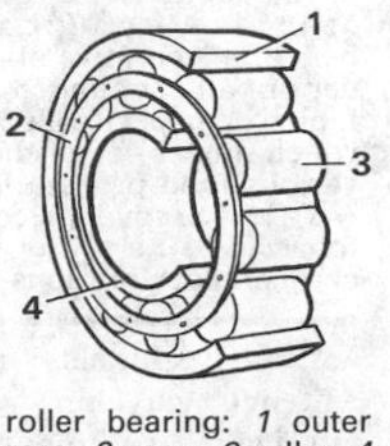

roller bearing: *1* outer race, *2* cage, *3* roller, *4* inner race

Roll·er·blade \ˈrō-lər-ˌblād\ *trademark* — used for an in-line skate

roll·er–coast·er \ˈrō-lər-ˌkō-stər, ˈrō-lə-ˌkō-\ *adj* (1940) **:** marked by numerous ups and downs ⟨an entertainer's ~ career⟩

roll·er coast·er \ˈrō-lər-ˌkō-stər, ˈrō-lē-ˌkō-\ *n* (1884) **1 :** an elevated railway (as in an amusement park) constructed with sharp curves and steep inclines on which cars roll **2 :** something resembling a roller coaster; *esp* **:** behavior, events, or experiences characterized by sudden and extreme changes ⟨an emotional *roller coaster*⟩

Roller Derby *service mark* — used for an entertainment involving a contest between two roller-skating teams on an oval track

roller rink *n* (1885) **:** RINK 1c

roller skate *n* (1863) **:** a shoe with a set of wheels attached for skating over a flat surface; *also* **:** a metal frame with wheels attached that can be fitted to the sole of a shoe — **roller–skate** *vi* — **roller skater** *n*

roller towel *n* (1836) **:** an endless towel hung from a roller

Rolle's theorem \ˈrȯlz-, ˈrōlz-\ *n* [Michel *Rolle* †1719 Fr. mathematician] (ca. 1891) **:** a theorem in mathematics: if a curve is continuous, crosses the x-axis at two points, and has a tangent at every point between the two intercepts, its tangent is parallel to the x-axis at some point between the intercepts

roll film *n* (1895) **:** a strip of film for still camera use wound on a spool

rol·lick \ˈrä-lik\ *vi* [origin unknown] (1826) **:** to move or behave in a carefree joyous manner **:** FROLIC — **rollick** *n*

rol·lick·ing \ˈrä-li-kiŋ\ *adj* (1811) **:** boisterously carefree, joyful, or high-spirited ⟨a ~ adventure film⟩

rolling hitch *n* (ca. 1769) **:** a hitch knot for fastening a line to a spar or to the standing part of another line that will not slip when the pull is parallel to the spar or line — see KNOT illustration

rolling mill *n* (1787) **:** an establishment where metal is rolled into plates and bars

rolling pin *n* (1563) **:** a long cylinder for rolling out dough

rolling stock *n* (1853) **:** the wheeled vehicles owned and used by a railroad or motor carrier

roll–neck \ˈrōl-ˌnek\ *n, often attrib* (1943) *Brit* **:** TURTLENECK — **roll–necked** \-ˌnekt\ *adj*

roll–off \ˈrōl-ˌȯf\ *n* (1947) **:** a play-off match in bowling

roll·out \ˈrōl-ˌau̇t\ *n* (1952) **1 :** the public introduction of a new aircraft; *broadly* **:** the widespread public introduction of a new product **2 :** a football play in which the quarterback rolls to the left or right

roll out *vi* (1884) **:** to get out of bed ~ *vt* **:** to introduce (as a new product) esp. for widespread sale to the public

roll·over \ˈrōl-ˌō-vər\ *n* (1945) **1 :** the act or process of rolling over **2 :** a motor vehicle accident in which the vehicle overturns

roll over *vt* (1949) **1 a :** to defer payment of (an obligation) **b :** to renegotiate the terms of (a financial agreement) **2 :** to place (invested funds) in a new investment of the same kind ⟨*roll over* IRA funds⟩

roll–over arm *n* (ca. 1925) **:** a fully upholstered chair or sofa arm curving outward from the seat

roll·top desk \ˈrōl-ˈtäp-\ *n* (1887) **:** a writing desk with a sliding cover often of parallel slats fastened to a flexible backing

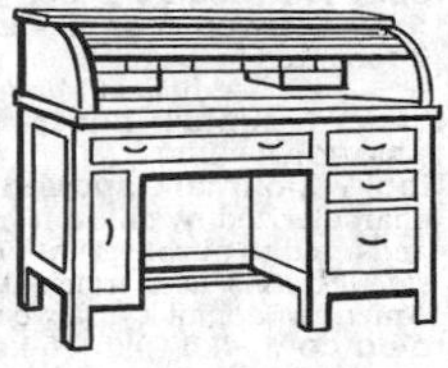
rolltop desk

roll up *vt* (1859) **:** to increase or acquire by successive accumulations **:** ACCUMULATE ⟨*rolled up* a large majority⟩ ~ *vi* **1 :** to become larger by successive accumulations **2 :** to arrive in a vehicle

[1]**ro·ly–po·ly** \ˌrō-lē-ˈpō-lē\ *adj* [redupl. of *roly,* fr. [2]*roll*] (1820) **:** being short and pudgy **:** ROTUND

[2]**roly–poly** *n, pl* **-lies** (1836) **1 :** a roly-poly person or thing **2** *Brit* **:** a sweet dough spread with a filling, rolled, and baked or steamed — called also *roly-poly pudding*

[1]**Rom** \ˈrōm\ *n, pl* **Rom** *also* **Roma** \ˈrō-mə\ [Romany, married man, husband, male Gypsy, fr. Skt *ḍomba, ḍoma* low caste male musician] (1841) **:** GYPSY 1

[2]**Rom** *abbr* **1** Romania **2** Romans

ROM \ˈräm\ *n* (1966) **:** a usu. small computer memory that contains special-purpose information (as a program) which cannot be altered — compare RAM

Ro·ma·ic \rō-ˈmā-ik\ *n* [ModGk *Rhōmaiikos,* fr. Gk *Rhōmaïkos* Roman, fr. *Rhōmē* Rome] (1810) **:** the modern Greek vernacular — **Romaic** *adj*

ro·maine \rō-ˈmān, ˈrō-ˌ\ *n* [F, fr. fem. of *romain* Roman, fr. OF, fr. L *Romanus*] (1907) **:** a lettuce that belongs to a cultivar of garden lettuce (*Lactuca sativa*) and has long crisp leaves and columnar heads — called also *cos lettuce*

ro·man \rō-ˈmäⁿ\ *n* [F, fr. OF *romans* romance] (1765) **:** a metrical romance

[1]**Ro·man** \ˈrō-mən\ *n* [partly fr. ME, fr. OE, fr. L *Romanus,* adj. & n., fr. *Roma* Rome; partly fr. ME *Romain,* fr. AF, fr. L *Romanus*] (bef. 12c) **1 a :** a native or resident of Rome **b :** a citizen of ancient Rome or of the Roman Empire **2** *often offensive* **:** ROMAN CATHOLIC **3** *not cap* **:** roman letters or type

[2]**Roman** *adj* (14c) **1 :** of or relating to Rome or the people of Rome; *specif* **:** characteristic of the ancient Romans ⟨~ fortitude⟩ **2 a :** LATIN 1a **b :** of or relating to the Latin alphabet **3** *not cap* **:** of or relating to a type style with upright characters — compare ITALIC **4 :** of or relating to the see of Rome or the Roman Catholic Church **5 :** having a semicircular intrados ⟨~ arch⟩ **6 :** having a prominent slightly aquiline bridge ⟨a ~ nose⟩

ro·man à clef \rō-ˌmä(ⁿ)n-(ˌ)ä-ˈklā\ *n, pl* **romans à clef** \-ˌmäⁿ-(ˌ)zä-\ [F, lit., novel with a key] (1893) **:** a novel in which real persons or actual events figure under disguise

Roman candle *n* (1833) **:** a cylindrical firework that discharges at intervals balls or stars of fire

[1]**Roman Catholic** *n* (1581) **:** a member of the Roman Catholic Church

[2]**Roman Catholic** *adj* (1614) **:** of, relating to, or being a Christian church having a hierarchy of priests and bishops under the pope, a liturgy centered in the Mass, veneration of the Virgin Mary and saints, clerical celibacy, and a body of dogma including transubstantiation and papal infallibility

Roman Catholicism *n* (ca. 1823) **:** the faith, doctrine, or polity of the Roman Catholic Church

[1]**ro·mance** \rō-ˈman(t)s, rə-; ˈrō-ˌ\ *n* [ME *romauns,* fr. AF *romanz* French, narrative in French, fr. ML *Romanice* in a vernacular (as opposed to Latin), fr. LL *Romanus* Gallo-Romance speaker (as opposed to a Frank), fr. L, Roman] (14c) **1 a** (1) **:** a medieval tale based on legend, chivalric love and adventure, or the supernatural (2) **:** a prose narrative treating imaginary characters involved in events remote in time or place and usu. heroic, adventurous, or mysterious (3) **:** a love

story esp. in the form of a novel **b** : a class of such literature **2** : something (as an extravagant story or account) that lacks basis in fact **3** : an emotional attraction or aura belonging to an esp. heroic era, adventure, or activity **4** : LOVE AFFAIR **5** *cap* : the Romance languages

[2]**romance** *vb* **ro·manced; ro·manc·ing** *vi* (1655) **1** : to exaggerate or invent detail or incident **2** : to entertain romantic thoughts or ideas ~ *vt* **1** : to try to influence or curry favor with esp. by lavishing personal attention, gifts, or flattery **2** : to carry on a love affair with

[3]**romance** *n* [G *Romanze* & F *romance,* both ultim. fr. Sp *romance* romance, ballad, fr. Old Occitan & OF *romanz*] (ca. 1854) : a short instrumental piece in ballad style

Ro·mance \rō-ˈman(t)s, rə-; ˈrō-ˌ\ *adj* (1690) : of, relating to, or being any of the languages developed from Latin (as Italian, French, and Spanish)

ro·manc·er \rō-ˈman(t)-sər, rə-; ˈrō-ˌ\ *n* (1654) **1** : a writer of romance **2** : one that romances

Roman collar *n* (ca. 1890) : CLERICAL COLLAR

Ro·man·esque \ˌrō-mə-ˈnesk\ *adj* (1763) : of or relating to a style of architecture developed in Italy and western Europe between the Roman and the Gothic styles and characterized in its development after 1000 by the use of the round arch and vault, substitution of piers for columns, decorative use of arcades, and profuse ornament — **Romanesque** *n*

ro·man–fleuve \rō-ˌmäⁿ-ˈflœv, -ˈflə(r)v\ *n, pl* **ro·mans–fleuves** \-ˌmäⁿ-ˈflœv, ˈflə(r)v(z)\ [F, lit., river novel] (1935) : a novel in the form of a long usu. easygoing chronicle of a social group (as a family or a community)

Roman holiday *n* (1886) **1** : a time of debauchery or of sadistic enjoyment **2** : a destructive or tumultuous disturbance : RIOT

Ro·ma·nian \ru̇-ˈmā-nē-ən, rō-, -nyən\ *also* **Ru·ma·nian** *or* **Rou·ma·nian** \ru̇-\ *n* (1868) **1** : a native or inhabitant of Romania **2** : the Romance language of the Romanians — **Romanian** *also* **Rumanian** *or* **Roumanian** *adj*

Ro·man·ic \rō-ˈma-nik\ *adj* (1708) : ROMANCE — **Romanic** *n*

ro·man·ise *Brit var of* ROMANIZE

Ro·man·ism \ˈrō-mə-ˌni-zəm\ *n* (1674) *often offensive* : ROMAN CATHOLICISM

Ro·man·ist \-nist\ *n* (1523) **1** *often offensive* : ROMAN CATHOLIC **2** : a specialist in the language, culture, or law of ancient Rome — **Romanist** *or* **Ro·man·is·tic** \ˌrō-mə-ˈnis-tik\ *adj*

ro·man·ize \ˈrō-mə-ˌnīz\ *vt* **-ized; -iz·ing** (1607) **1** *often cap* : to make Roman in character **2** : to write or print (as a language) in the Latin alphabet ⟨~ Chinese⟩ **3** *cap* **a** : to convert to Roman Catholicism **b** : to give a Roman Catholic character to — **ro·man·i·za·tion** \ˌrō-mə-nə-ˈzā-shən\ *n, often cap*

roman law *n, often cap R* (1639) : the legal system of the ancient Romans that includes written and unwritten law, is based on the traditional law and the legislation of the city of Rome, and in form comprises legislation of the assemblies, resolves of the senate, enactments of the emperors, edicts of the praetors, writings of the jurisconsults, and the codes of the later emperors

Roman numeral *n* (1735) : a numeral in a system of notation that is based on the ancient Roman system — see NUMBER table

Ro·ma·no \rə-ˈmä-(ˌ)nō, rō-\ *n* [It, Roman, fr. L *Romanus*] (1908) : a hard sharp cheese of Italian origin that is often served grated

Ro·mans \ˈrō-mənz\ *n pl but sing in constr* : a letter on doctrine written by St. Paul to the Christians of Rome and included as a book in the New Testament — see BIBLE table

Ro·mansh *or* **Ro·mansch** \rō-ˈmänch, -ˈmanch\ *n* [Romansh *romonsch*] (1663) : the Rhaeto-Romance dialects spoken in the Grisons, Switzerland

[1]**ro·man·tic** \rō-ˈman-tik, rə-\ *adj* [F *romantique,* fr. obs. *romant* romance, fr. OF *romanz*] (1650) **1** : consisting of or resembling a romance **2** : having no basis in fact : IMAGINARY **3** : impractical in conception or plan : VISIONARY **4 a** : marked by the imaginative or emotional appeal of what is heroic, adventurous, remote, mysterious, or idealized **b** *often cap* : of, relating to, or having the characteristics of romanticism **c** : of or relating to music of the 19th century characterized by an emphasis on subjective emotional qualities and freedom of form; *also* : of or relating to a composer of this music **5 a** : having an inclination for romance : responsive to the appeal of what is idealized, heroic, or adventurous **b** : marked by expressions of love or affection **c** : conducive to or suitable for lovemaking **6** : of, relating to, or constituting the part of the hero esp. in a light comedy — **ro·man·ti·cal·ly** \-ti-k(ə-)lē\ *adv*

[2]**romantic** *n* (1679) **1** : a romantic person, trait, or component **2** *cap* : a romantic writer, artist, or composer

ro·man·ti·cise *Brit var of* ROMANTICIZE

ro·man·ti·cism \rō-ˈman-tə-ˌsi-zəm, rə-\ *n* (1823) **1** *often cap* **a** (1) : a literary, artistic, and philosophical movement originating in the 18th century, characterized chiefly by a reaction against neoclassicism and an emphasis on the imagination and emotions, and marked esp. in English literature by sensibility and the use of autobiographical material, an exaltation of the primitive and the common man, an appreciation of external nature, an interest in the remote, a predilection for melancholy, and the use in poetry of older verse forms (2) : an aspect of romanticism **b** : adherence to a romantic attitude or style **2** : the quality or state of being romantic — **ro·man·ti·cist** \-sist\ *n, often cap*

ro·man·ti·cize \-ˈman-tə-ˌsīz\ *vb* **-cized; -ciz·ing** *vt* (1818) : to make romantic : treat as idealized or heroic ⟨~ the past⟩ ~ *vi* **1** : to hold romantic ideas **2** : to present details, incidents, or people in a romantic way — **ro·man·ti·ci·za·tion** \-ˌman-tə-sə-ˈzā-shən\ *n*

Ro·ma·ny *also* **Ro·ma·ni** \ˈrä-mə-nē, ˈrō-\ *n, pl* **Romanies** *also* **Romanis** [Romany *romani,* fem. of *romano,* adj., Gypsy, fr. *rom* Gypsy man — more at ROM] (ca. 1812) **1** : GYPSY 1 **2** : the Indo-Aryan language of the Gypsies — **Romany** *adj*

ro·maunt \rō-ˈmȯnt, -ˈmänt\ *n* [ME, fr. AF *romant*] (1530) *archaic* : ROMANCE 1a(1)

Rome Beauty \ˈrōm-\ *n* [prob. fr. *Rome,* village in Adams County, Ohio] (1856) : a round red apple that has firm slightly tart flesh and is used esp. for baking — called also *Rome*

rom·el·dale \ˈrä-məl-ˌdāl\ *n, often cap* [blend of *Romney, Rambouillet,* and *Corriedale*] (ca. 1948) : any of a U.S. breed of sheep yielding a heavy fleece of fine wool and producing a quickly maturing high-grade market lamb

[1]**Ro·meo** \ˈrō-mē-ˌō, *in Shak also* ˈrōm-(ˌ)yō\ *n, pl* **Ro·me·os** (ca. 1595) **1** : the hero of Shakespeare's *Romeo and Juliet* who dies for love of Juliet **2** : a male lover

[2]**Romeo** (1952) — a communications code word for the letter *r*

Rom·ish \ˈrō-mish\ *adj* (1531) *usu disparaging* : ROMAN CATHOLIC — **Rom·ish·ly** *adv, usu disparaging* — **Rom·ish·ness** *n, usu disparaging*

Rom·ney \ˈräm-nē, ˈrəm-\ *n* [*Romney* Marsh, pasture tract in England] (1837) : any of a British breed of hardy long-wooled sheep esp. adapted to damp or marshy regions and raised for both mutton and wool — called also *Romney Marsh*

[1]**romp** \ˈrämp, ˈrȯmp\ *n* [partly alter. of [2]*ramp;* partly alter. of *ramp* bold woman] (1691) **1** : one that romps; *esp* : a romping girl or woman **2 a** : high-spirited, carefree, and boisterous play **b** : something suggestive of such play: as (1) : a light fast-paced narrative, dramatic, or musical work usu. in a comic mood (2) : an episode of lovemaking **3** : an easy winning pace; *also* : RUNAWAY 3

[2]**romp** *vi* [alter. of [1]*ramp*] (1662) **1** : to run or play in a lively, carefree, or boisterous manner **2** : to move or proceed in a brisk, easy, or playful manner **3** : to win a contest easily

romp·er \ˈräm-pər, ˈrȯm-\ *n* (1836) **1** : one that romps **2** : JUMPSUIT 2; *esp* : a jumpsuit for infants — often used in pl.

Rom·u·lus \ˈräm-yə-ləs\ *n* [L] (bef. 12c) : a son of Mars and legendary founder of Rome

ron·deau \ˈrän-(ˌ)dō, rän-ˈdō\ *n, pl* **ron·deaux** \-(ˌ)dōz, -ˈdōz\ [MF *rondel, rondeau*] (1525) **1 a** : a fixed form of verse based on two rhyme sounds and consisting usu. of 13 lines in three stanzas with the opening words of the first line of the first stanza used as an independent refrain after the second and third stanzas **b** : a poem in this form **2** : a monophonic trouvère song with a 2-part refrain

ron·del \ˈrän-dᵊl, rän-ˈdel\ *or* **ron·delle** \rän-ˈdel\ *n* [ME *rondel, roundel* — more at ROUNDEL] (14c) **1** *usu rondelle* : a circular object; *esp* : a circular jewel or jeweled ring **2 a** *usu rondel* : a fixed form of verse based on two rhyme sounds and consisting usu. of 14 lines in three stanzas in which the first two lines of the first stanza are repeated as the refrain of the second and third stanzas **b** : a poem in this form **c** : RONDEAU 1

ron·de·let \ˌrän-də-ˈlet, -ˈlā\ *n* (15c) : a modified rondeau consisting usu. of seven lines in which the first line of four syllables is repeated as the third line and as the final line or refrain and the remaining lines are made up of eight syllables each

ron·do \ˈrän-(ˌ)dō, rän-ˈdō\ *n, pl* **rondos** [It *rondò,* fr. MF *rondeau*] (1797) **1** : an instrumental composition typically with a refrain recurring four times in the tonic and with three couplets in contrasting keys **2** : the musical form of a rondo used esp. for a movement in a concerto or sonata

ron·dure \ˈrän-jər, -(ˌ)dyu̇r, -(ˌ)du̇r\ *n* [F *rondeur* roundness, fr. MF, fr. *rond* round, fr. OF *reont, reund* — more at ROUND] (ca. 1600) **1** : ROUND 1a **2** : gracefully rounded curvature

ron·yon \ˈrən-yən, ˈrän-\ *n* [perh. modif. of MF *rogne* scab] (1598) *obs* : a mangy or scabby creature

rood \ˈrüd\ *n* [ME, fr. OE *rōd* rod, rood; akin to OHG *ruota* rod and perh. to ORuss *ratište* lance] (bef. 12c) **1** : a cross or crucifix symbolizing the cross on which Jesus Christ died; *specif* : a large crucifix on a beam or screen at the entrance to the chancel of a church **2 a** : any of various units of land area; *esp* : a British unit equal to ¼ acre **b** : any of various units of length; *esp* : a British unit equal to seven or eight yards or sometimes a rod

[1]**roof** \ˈrüf, ˈru̇f\ *n, pl* **roofs** \ˈrüfs, ˈru̇fs *also* ˈrüvz, ˈru̇vz\ [ME, fr. OE *hrōf;* akin to ON *hrōf* roof of a boathouse and perh. to OCS *stropŭ* roof] (bef. 12c) **1 a** (1) : the cover of a building (2) : material used for a roof : ROOFING **b** : the roof of a dwelling conventionally designating the home itself ⟨didn't have a ~ over my head⟩ ⟨they share the same ~⟩ **2 a** : the highest point : SUMMIT **b** : an upper limit : CEILING **3 a** : the vaulted upper boundary of the mouth **b** : a covering structure of any of various parts of the body ⟨~ of the skull⟩ **4** : something suggesting a roof: as **a** : a canopy of leaves and branches **b** : the top over the passenger section of a vehicle — **roofed** \ˈrüft, ˈru̇ft\ *adj* — **roof·less** \ˈrü-fləs, ˈru̇-\ *adj* — **roof·like** \-ˌlīk\ *adj* — **through the roof** : to an extremely or excessively high level ⟨prices went *through the roof*⟩

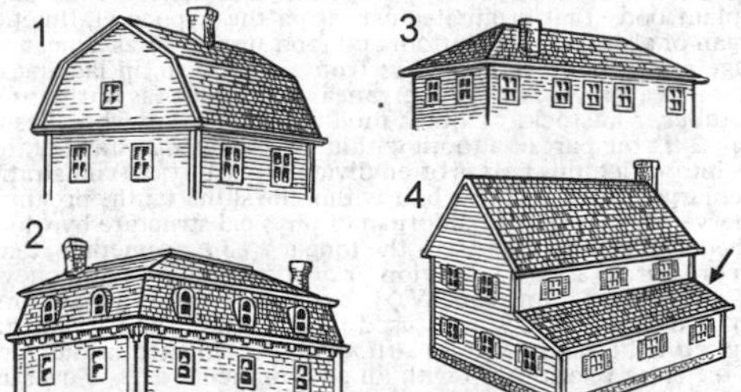

roof 1a(1): *1* gambrel, *2* mansard, *3* hip, *4* lean-to

[2]**roof** *vt* (15c) **1 a** : to cover with or as if with a roof **b** : to provide with a particular kind of roof or roofing — often used in combination ⟨slate-*roofed* houses⟩ **2** : to constitute a roof over — **roof·er** *n*

roof garden *n* (1893) : a restaurant or nightclub at the top of a building often in connection with or decorated to suggest an outdoor garden

\ə\ **abut** \ᵊ\ **kitten,** F **table** \ər\ **further** \a\ **ash** \ā\ **ace** \ä\ **mop, mar** \au̇\ **out** \ch\ **chin** \e\ **bet** \ē\ **easy** \g\ **go** \i\ **hit** \ī\ **ice** \j\ **job** \ŋ\ **sing** \ō\ **go** \ȯ\ **law** \ȯi\ **boy** \th\ **thin** \t͟h\ **the** \ü\ **loot** \u̇\ **foot** \y\ **yet** \zh\ **vision, beige** \k̲, ⁿ, œ, ue, ʸ\ *see* Guide to Pronunciation

roof·ie \ˈrü-fē\ *n* [prob. by shortening & alter. fr. *Rohypnol,* a trademark name for the drug] (1994) *slang* : a tablet of a powerful benzodiazepine sedative and hypnotic drug $C_{16}H_{12}FN_3O_3$ that is not licensed for medical use in the U.S. but is used illicitly
roof·ing \ˈrü-fiŋ, ˈru̇-\ *n* (15c) : material for a roof
roof·line \ˈrüf-ˌlīn, ˈru̇f-\ *n* (1857) : the profile of a roof (as of a house)
roof·top \-ˌtäp\ *n, often attrib* (1611) : ROOF; *esp* : the outer surface of a roof
roof·tree \ˈrüf-ˌtrē, ˈru̇f-\ *n* (14c) : RIDGEPOLE 1
1**rook** \ˈru̇k\ *n* [ME, fr. OE *hrōc;* akin to OHG *hruoch* rook] (bef. 12c) : a common Old World gregarious crow (*Corvus frugilegus*) that nests and roosts in usu. treetop colonies
2**rook** *vt* (ca. 1590) : to defraud by cheating or swindling
3**rook** *n* [ME *rok,* fr. AF *roc,* fr. Ar *rukhkh,* fr. Pers *rukh*] (14c) : either of two pieces of each color in a set of chessmen having the power to move along the ranks or files across any number of unoccupied squares — called also *castle*
4**rook** *n* (1905) : ROOKIE
rook·ery \ˈru̇-kə-rē\ *n, pl* **-er·ies** (ca. 1712) **1 a** : the nests or breeding place of a colony of rooks; *also* : a colony of rooks **b** : a breeding ground or haunt esp. of gregarious birds or mammals (as penguins or seals); *also* : a colony of such birds or mammals **2** : a crowded dilapidated tenement or group of dwellings
rook·ie \ˈru̇-kē\ *n* [perh. alter. of *recruit*] (1892) **1** : RECRUIT; *also* : NOVICE **2** : a first-year participant in a major professional sport
rooky \ˈru̇-kē\ *adj* (1605) : full of or containing rooks
1**room** \ˈrüm, ˈru̇m\ *n* [ME, fr. OE *rūm;* akin to OHG *rūm* room, L *rur-, rus* open land] (bef. 12c) **1** : an extent of space occupied by or sufficient or available for something ⟨~ to run and play⟩ **2 a** *obs* : an appropriate or designated position, post, or station **b** : PLACE, STEAD ⟨in whose ~ I am now assuming the pen —Sir Walter Scott⟩ **3 a** : a partitioned part of the inside of a building; *esp* : such a part used as a lodging **b** : the people in a room **4** : a suitable or fit occasion or opportunity : CHANCE ⟨no ~ for doubt⟩ — **roomed** \ˈrümd, ˈru̇md\ *adj*
2**room** *vi* (1817) : to occupy or share a room esp. as a lodger ~ *vt* : to accommodate with lodgings
room and board *n* (1955) : lodging and food usu. furnished for a set price or as part of wages
room·er \ˈrü-mər, ˈru̇-\ *n* (ca. 1871) : one who occupies a rented room in another's house
room·ette \rü-ˈmet, ru̇-\ *n* (1937) : a small private single room on a railroad sleeping car
room·ful \ˈrüm-ˌfu̇l, ˈru̇m-\ *n* (1671) : as much or as many as a room will hold; *also* : the persons or objects in a room
room·ing house \ˈrü-miŋ-, ˈru̇-\ *n* (1893) : a house where lodgings are provided for rent
rooming–in \ˈrü-miŋ-ˈin, ˈru̇-\ *n* (1943) : an arrangement in a hospital whereby a newborn infant is kept in a crib at the mother's bedside instead of in a nursery
room·mate \ˈrüm-ˌmāt, ˈru̇m-\ *n* (1770) : one of two or more persons sharing the same room or living quarters — called also *room·ie* \ˈrü-mē, ˈru̇-\
room service *n* (1930) : service provided to hotel guests in their rooms; *also* : the hotel department responsible for such service ⟨ordered a meal from *room service*⟩
roomy \ˈrü-mē, ˈru̇-\ *adj* **room·i·er; -est** (1581) **1** : having ample room : SPACIOUS **2** *of a female mammal* : having a large or well-proportioned body suited for breeding — **room·i·ness** *n*
roor·back \ˈru̇r-ˌbak\ *n* [fr. an attack on James K. Polk in 1844 purporting to quote from an invented book by a Baron von *Roorback*] (1855) : a defamatory falsehood published for political effect
roose \ˈrüz\ *vt* [ME *rosen,* fr. ON *hrōsa*] (14c) *chiefly dial* : PRAISE
1**roost** \ˈrüst\ *n* [ME, fr. OE *hrōst;* akin to OS *hrōst* attic] (bef. 12c) **1 a** : a support on which birds rest **b** : a place where winged animals and esp. birds customarily roost **2** : a group of birds roosting together
2**roost** *vi* (1530) **1** : to settle down for rest or sleep : PERCH **2** : to settle oneself as if on a roost ~ *vt* : to supply a roost for or put to roost
roost·er \ˈrüs-tər *also* ˈru̇s-\ *n* (1772) **1 a** : an adult male domestic chicken : COCK **b** : an adult male of various birds other than the domestic chicken **2** : a cocky or vain man
rooster tail *n* (1946) : a high arching spray (as of water, dust, or snow) thrown up behind a fast-moving motorboat, motor vehicle, or skier
1**root** \ˈrüt, ˈru̇t\ *n, often attrib* [ME, fr. OE *rōt,* fr. ON; akin to OE *wyrt* root, L *radix,* Gk *rhiza*] (12c) **1 a** : the usu. underground part of a seed plant body that originates usu. from the hypocotyl, functions as an organ of absorption, aeration, and food storage or as a means of anchorage and support, and differs from a stem esp. in lacking nodes, buds, and leaves **b** : any subterranean plant part (as a true root or a bulb, tuber, rootstock, or other modified stem) esp. when fleshy and edible **2 a** : the part of a tooth within the socket; *also* : any of the processes into which this part is often divided — see TOOTH illustration **b** : the enlarged basal part of a hair within the skin **c** : the proximal end of a nerve **d** : the part of an organ or physical structure by which it is attached to the body ⟨the ~ of the tongue⟩ **3 a** : something that is an origin or source (as of a condition or quality) ⟨the love of money is the ~ of all evil —1 Tim 6:10(AV)⟩ **b** : one or more progenitors of a group of descendants — usu. used in pl. **c** : an underlying support : BASIS **d** : the essential core : HEART — often used in the phrase *at root* **e** : close relationship with an environment : TIE — usu. used in pl. ⟨they put down ~*s* in a farming community⟩ **4 a** : a quantity taken an indicated number of times as an equal factor ⟨2 is a fourth ~ of 16⟩ **b** : a number that reduces an equation to an identity when it is substituted for one variable **5 a** : the lower part : BASE **b** : the part by which an object is attached to something else **6** : the simple element inferred as the basis from which a word is derived by phonetic change or by extension (as composition or the addition of an affix or inflectional ending) **7** : the lowest tone of a chord (as C in a C minor chord) when the tones are arranged in ascending thirds ***syn*** see ORIGIN — **root·ed** \ˈrü-təd, ˈru̇-\ *adj* — **root·ed·ness** *n* — **root·less** \ˈrüt-ləs, ˈru̇t-\ *adj* — **root·less·ness** *n* — **root·like** \-ˌlīk\ *adj*
2**root** *vt* (14c) **1 a** : to furnish with or enable to develop roots **b** : to fix or implant by or as if by roots **2** : to remove altogether by or as if by pulling out by the roots — usu. used with *out* ⟨~ out dissenters⟩ ~ *vi* **1** : to grow roots or take root **2** : to have an origin or base
3**root** *vb* [alter. of *wroot,* fr. ME *wroten,* fr. OE *wrōtan;* akin to OHG *ruozzan* to root] *vi* (1532) **1** : to turn up or dig in the earth with the snout : GRUB **2** : to poke or dig about ~ *vt* : to turn over, dig up, or discover and bring to light — usu. used with *out* ⟨~ out the cause of the problem⟩
4**root** \ˈrüt *also* ˈru̇t\ *vi* [perh. alter. of *2rout*] (1889) **1** : to noisily applaud or encourage a contestant or team : CHEER **2** : to wish the success of or lend support to someone or something — **root·er** *n*
root·age \ˈrü-tij, ˈru̇-\ *n* (ca. 1895) **1** : a developed system of roots **2** : ROOT 3a
root ball \ˈrüt-ˌbȯl *also* ˈru̇t-\ *n* (1930) : the compact mass of roots and soil formed by a plant esp. in a container
root beer *n* (1840) : a sweetened carbonated beverage flavored with extracts of roots (as sarsaparilla) and herbs
root–bound \ˈrüt-ˌbau̇nd *also* ˈru̇t-\ *adj* (1885) : POT-BOUND
root canal *n* (1893) : the part of the pulp cavity lying in the root of a tooth; *also* : a dental operation to save a tooth by removing the contents of its root canal and filling the cavity with a protective substance
root cap *n* (1875) : a protective cap of parenchyma cells that covers the terminal meristem in most root tips
root cellar *n* (1810) : a pit used for the storage esp. of root crops
root crop *n* (1834) : a crop (as turnips) grown for its enlarged roots
root hair *n* (1853) : a filamentous extension of an epidermal cell near the tip of a rootlet that functions in absorption of water and minerals
root·hold \ˈrüt-ˌhōld, ˈru̇t-\ *n* (1839) **1** : the anchorage of a plant to soil through the growing and spreading of roots **2** : a place where plants may obtain a roothold
root knot *n* (1889) : a plant disease caused by nematodes that produce enlargements on the roots and stunt the growth of the plant
root–knot nematode *n* (1922) : any of several small plant-parasitic nematodes (genus *Meloidogyne*) that cause root knot
roo·tle \ˈrü-tᵊl\ *vi* **roo·tled; roo·tling** \ˈrüt-liŋ, ˈrü-tᵊl-iŋ\ [freq. of *3root*] (1809) : 3ROOT
root·let \ˈrüt-lət, ˈru̇t-\ *n* (ca. 1793) : a small root
root–mean–square *n* (1895) : the square root of the arithmetic mean of the squares of a set of numbers
root pressure *n* (1875) : the chiefly osmotic pressure by which water rises into the stems of plants from the roots
root rot *n* (1883) : any of various plant diseases characterized by decay of the roots and caused esp. by fungi
root·stock \ˈrüt-ˌstäk, ˈru̇t-\ *n* (1832) **1** : a rhizomatous underground part of a plant **2** : a stock for grafting consisting of a root or a piece of root; *broadly* : STOCK 3b
rooty \ˈrü-tē, ˈru̇-\ *adj* (15c) : full or consisting of roots ⟨~ soil⟩
1**rope** \ˈrōp\ *n* [ME, fr. OE *rāp;* akin to OHG *reif* hoop] (bef. 12c) **1 a** : a large stout cord of strands of fibers or wire twisted or braided together **b** : a long slender strip of material used as rope ⟨rawhide ~⟩ **c** : a hangman's noose **d** : LARIAT **2** : a row or string consisting of things united by or as if by braiding, twining, or threading **3** *pl* : special or basic techniques or procedures ⟨show him the ~*s*⟩ **4** : LINE DRIVE — **rope·like** \-ˌlīk\ *adj* — **on the ropes** : in a defensive and often helpless position
2**rope** *vb* **roped; rop·ing** *vt* (14c) **1 a** : to bind, fasten, or tie with a rope or cord **b** : to partition, separate, or divide by a rope ⟨~ off the street⟩ **c** : LASSO **2** : to draw as if with a rope : LURE ~ *vi* : to take the form of or twist in the manner of rope — **rop·er** *n*
rope·danc·er \ˈrōp-ˌdan(t)-sər\ *n* (1648) : one that dances, walks, or performs acrobatic feats on a rope high in the air — **rope·danc·ing** \-siŋ\ *n*
rop·ery \ˈrō-p(ə-)rē\ *n* [prob. fr. the thought that the perpetrator deserved the gallows] (1592) *archaic* : roguish tricks or banter
rope tow *n* (1948) : SKI TOW 1
rope·walk \ˈrōp-ˌwȯk\ *n* (1672) : a long covered walk, building, or room where ropes are manufactured
rope·walk·er \-ˌwȯ-kər\ *n* (1615) : an acrobat who walks on a rope high in the air
rope·way \-ˌwā\ *n* (1889) **1** : an endless aerial cable moved by a stationary engine and used to transport freight (as logs and ore) **2** : a fixed cable or a pair of fixed cables between supporting towers serving as a track for suspended passenger or freight carriers
ropy *also* **rop·ey** \ˈrō-pē\ *adj* **rop·i·er; -est** (15c) **1 a** : capable of being drawn into a thread : VISCOUS; *also* : tending to adhere in stringy masses **b** : having a gelatinous or slimy quality from bacterial or fungal contamination ⟨~ milk⟩ ⟨~ flour⟩ **2 a** : resembling rope **b** : MUSCULAR, SINEWY **3** *slang* : POOR, LOUSY — **rop·i·ness** *n*
roque \ˈrōk\ *n* [alter. of *croquet*] (1899) : croquet played on a hard-surfaced court with a raised border
Roque·fort \ˈrōk-fərt\ *trademark* — used for a pungent French blue cheese made from sheep's milk
ro·que·laure \ˌrō-kə-ˈlȯr, ˌrä-\ *n* [F, fr. the Duc de *Roquelaure* †1738 Fr. marshal] (1716) : a knee-length cloak worn esp. in the 18th and 19th centuries
ro·quette \rō-ˈket\ *n* [F, fr. MF — more at ROCKET] (1900) : ARUGULA
Ro–Ro \ˈrō-ˌrō\ *n* [*r*oll on, *r*oll off] (1969) : a ship designed and equipped to allow vehicles (as automobiles or tanks) to be driven on or off
ror·qual \ˈrȯr-kwəl, -ˌkwȯl\ *n* [F, fr. Norw *rørhval,* fr. ON *reytharhvalr,* fr. *reythr* rorqual + *hvalr* whale] (1827) : any of a family (Balaenopteridae) of large baleen whales (as a blue whale or humpback whale) having the skin of the throat marked with deep longitudinal furrows
Ror·schach \ˈrȯr-ˌshäk\ *adj* (1927) : of, relating to, used in connection with, or resulting from the Rorschach test
Rorschach test *n* [Hermann *Rorschach* †1922 Swiss psychiatrist] (1927) : a personality and intelligence test in which a subject interprets inkblot designs in terms that reveal intellectual and emotional factors — called also *Rorschach, Rorschach inkblot test*
ro·sa·cea \rō-ˈzā-sh(ē-)ə\ *n* [short for NL *acne rosacea* rose-colored acne] (1876) : a chronic inflammatory disorder involving esp. the skin of the nose, forehead, and cheeks that is characterized by congestion, flushing, telangiectasia, and marked nodular swelling of tissues esp. of the nose — called also *acne rosacea*
ro·sa·ceous \rō-ˈzā-shəs\ *adj* [ultim. fr. L *rosa*] (1731) : of or relating to roses or the rose family ⟨a faint ~ aroma⟩ ⟨~ genera⟩
ro·sar·i·an \rō-ˈzer-ē-ən\ *n* (1864) : a cultivator of roses

ro·sa·ry \ˈrō-zə-rē, ˈrōz-rē\ *n, pl* **-ries** [ML *rosarium,* fr. L, rose garden, fr. neut. of *rosarius* of roses, fr. *rosa* rose] (1547) **1** *often cap* **:** a Roman Catholic devotion consisting of meditation on usu. five sacred mysteries during recitation of five decades of Hail Marys of which each begins with an Our Father and ends with a Gloria Patri **2 :** a string of beads used in counting prayers esp. of the Roman Catholic rosary

rosary pea *n* (ca. 1866) **1 :** a tropical twining herb (*Abrus precatorius*) of the legume family that bears jequirity beans and has a root used as a substitute for licorice — called also *Indian licorice, jequirity bean* **2 :** JEQUIRITY BEAN 1

ros·coe \ˈräs-(ˌ)kō\ *n* [prob. fr. the name *Roscoe*] (ca. 1914) *slang* **:** HANDGUN

[1]**rose** *past of* RISE

[2]**rose** \ˈrōz\ *n* [ME, fr. OE, fr. L *rosa;* akin to Gk *rhodon* rose, Pers *gul*] (bef. 12c) **1 a :** any of a genus (*Rosa* of the family Rosaceae, the rose family) of usu. prickly shrubs with pinnate leaves and showy flowers having five petals in the wild state but being often double or partly double under cultivation **b :** the flower of a rose **2 :** something resembling a rose in form: as **a** (1) **:** COMPASS CARD (2) **:** a circular card with radiating lines used in other instruments **b :** a rosette esp. on a shoe **c :** ROSE CUT **3** *pl* **:** an easy or pleasant situation or task ⟨it was not all sunshine and ~*s* —Anthony Lewis⟩ **4 :** a moderate purplish red **5 :** a plane curve which consists of three or more loops meeting at the origin and whose equation in polar coordinates is of the form $\rho = a \sin n\theta$ or $\rho = a \cos n\theta$ where n is an integer greater than zero — **rose·like** \-ˌlīk\ *adj* — **under the rose :** SUB ROSA

[3]**rose** *adj* (14c) **1 a :** containing or used for roses **b :** of or relating to a rose **c :** flavored, scented, or colored with or like roses **2 :** of the color rose

ro·sé \rō-ˈzā\ *n* [F] (1897) **:** a light pink table wine made from red grapes by removing the skins after fermentation has begun

ro·se·ate \ˈrō-zē-ət, -zē-ˌāt\ *adj* [L *roseus* rosy, fr. *rosa*] (1589) **1 :** resembling a rose esp. in color **2 :** overly optimistic **:** viewed favorably — **ro·se·ate·ly** *adv*

roseate spoonbill *n* (ca. 1785) **:** a spoonbill (*Ajaia ajaja*) that is found from the southern U.S. to Patagonia and has chiefly pink plumage

roseate tern *n* (ca. 1813) **:** a medium-sized tern (*Sterna dougallii*) that is widespread at sea and in coastal areas of the Atlantic, Pacific, and Indian oceans and that has a faint roseate tinge to the breast in the breeding season

rose·bay \ˈrōz-ˌbā\ *n* (1760) **1 :** RHODODENDRON; *esp* **:** GREAT LAUREL **2 :** FIREWEED b

rosebay rhododendron *n* (ca. 1949) **:** GREAT LAUREL

rose–breast·ed grosbeak \ˈrōz-ˌbres-təd-\ *n* (1810) **:** a grosbeak (*Pheucticus ludovicianus*) chiefly of eastern No. America that is related to the cardinal and in the male is chiefly black and white with a rose-red breast and in the female is grayish brown with a streaked breast

rose·bud \ˈrōz-ˌbəd\ *n* (15c) **:** the bud of a rose

rose·bush \-ˌbu̇sh\ *n* (1587) **:** a shrub that produces roses

rose chafer *n* (1704) **:** a common No. American scarab beetle (*Macrodactylus subspinosus*) that feeds on plant roots as a larva and on leaves and flowers (as of rose or grapevines) as an adult — called also *rose bug*

rose–col·ored \ˈrōz-ˌkə-lərd\ *adj* (1526) **1 :** having a rose color **2 :** seeing or seen in a promising light **:** OPTIMISTIC

rose–colored glasses *n pl* (1926) **:** favorably disposed opinions **:** optimistic eyes ⟨views the world through *rose-colored glasses*⟩

rose cut *n* (ca. 1842) **:** a form in which gems (as diamonds) are cut that usu. has a flat circular base and facets in two ranges rising to a point — **rose–cut** *adj*

rose fever *n* (1851) **:** hay fever occurring in the spring or early summer — called also *rose cold*

rose·fish \ˈrōz-ˌfish\ *n* (1731) **:** REDFISH a(1)

rose geranium *n* (1832) **:** any of several pelargoniums grown for their fragrant 3- to 5-lobed leaves and small pink flowers

rose hip *n* (1857) **:** the ripened usu. red or orange accessory fruit of a rose that consists of a fleshy receptacle enclosing numerous achenes

ro·se·ma·ling \ˈrō-zə-ˌmä-liŋ, -sə-\ *n* [Norw, fr. *rose* rose + *maling* painting] (1942) **:** painted or sometimes carved decoration (as on furniture, walls, or wooden dinnerware) in Scandinavian peasant style that consists esp. of floral designs and inscriptions

rose mallow *n* (1857) **:** any of several hibiscuses with large usu. rose-colored flowers; *esp* **:** a showy perennial (*Hibiscus moscheutos*) of the salt marshes of the eastern U.S.

rose·mary \ˈrōz-ˌmer-ē\ *n, pl* **-mar·ies** [ME *rosmarine,* fr. AF *rosemarin,* fr. L *rosmarinus,* fr. *ror-, ros* dew + *marinus* of the sea; akin to Skt *rasa* sap, juice — more at MARINE] (14c) **:** a fragrant shrubby Mediterranean mint (*Rosmarinus officinalis*) having grayish-green needlelike leaves used as a seasoning; *also* **:** the leaves of rosemary

rose of Jer·i·cho \-ˈjer-i-ˌkō\ [ME, fr. *Jericho,* ancient city in Palestine] (15c) **:** an annual herb (*Anastatica hierochuntica*) of the mustard family found from northern Africa to Iran that rolls up when dry and expands when moistened

rose of Shar·on \-ˈsher-ən\ [Plain of *Sharon,* Palestine] (ca. 1847) **:** a commonly cultivated Asian shrub or small tree (*Hibiscus syriacus*) having showy bell-shaped rose, purple, or white flowers

rose oil *n* (1552) **:** a fragrant essential oil obtained from roses and used chiefly in perfumery and in flavoring

ro·se·o·la \ˌrō-zē-ˈō-lə, rō-ˈzē-ə-lə\ *n* [NL, fr. L *roseus* rosy, fr. *rosa* rose] (ca. 1818) **:** a rose-colored eruption in spots or a disease marked by such an eruption; *esp* **:** ROSEOLA INFANTUM — **ro·se·o·lar** \-lər\ *adj*

roseola in·fan·tum \-in-ˈfan-təm\ *n* [NL, infant roseola] (ca. 1935) **:** a mild virus disease of infants and children marked by fever lasting usu. three days followed by an eruption of rose-colored spots and caused by a herpesvirus (species *Human herpesvirus 6* of the genus *Roseolovirus*)

rose pink *n* (1849) **:** a moderate pink

rose slug *n* (1877) **:** the green larva of either of two sawflies (*Cladius difformis* and *Endelomyia aethiops*) that feed on the parenchyma of and skeletonize the leaves of roses

ro·set \ˈrō-zət\ *n* [ME, alter. of *rosin*] (14c) *chiefly Scot* **:** RESIN

Ro·set·ta stone \rō-ˈze-tə-\ *n* [*Rosetta,* Egypt] (1822) **1 :** a black basalt stone found in 1799 that bears an inscription in hieroglyphics, demotic characters, and Greek and is celebrated for having given the first clue to the decipherment of Egyptian hieroglyphics **2 :** one that gives a clue to understanding

ro·sette \rō-ˈzet\ *n* [F, lit., small rose, fr. OF, fr. *rose,* fr. L *rosa*] (1790) **1 :** an ornament usu. made of material gathered or pleated so as to resemble a rose and worn as a badge of office, as evidence of having won a decoration (as the Medal of Honor), or as trimming **2 :** a disk of foliage or a floral design usu. in relief used as a decorative motif **3 :** a structure or color marking on an animal suggestive of a rosette; *esp* **:** one of the groups of spots on a leopard **4 :** a cluster of leaves in crowded circles or spirals arising basally from a crown (as in the dandelion) or apically from an axis with greatly shortened internodes (as in many tropical palms) **5 :** a food decoration or garnish in the shape of a rose ⟨icing ~*s*⟩ ⟨carrot ~*s*⟩

rose·wa·ter \ˈrōz-ˌwȯ-tər, -ˌwä-\ *adj* (1840) **1 :** affectedly nice or delicate **2 :** having the odor of rose water

rose water *n* (14c) **:** a watery solution of the odoriferous constituents of the rose used as a perfume or a flavoring

rose window *n* (1773) **:** a circular window filled with tracery

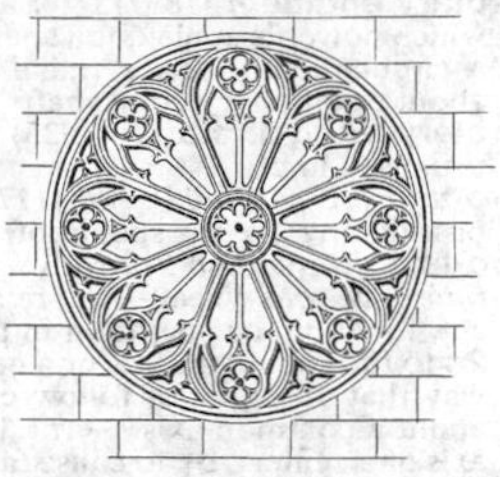
rose window

rose·wood \ˈrōz-ˌwu̇d\ *n* (1660) **:** any of various tropical trees (esp. genus *Dalbergia*) yielding valuable cabinet woods of a usu. dark red or purplish color streaked and variegated with black; *also* **:** the wood

Rosh Ha·sha·nah \ˌräsh-(h)ə-ˈshä-nə, ˌrōsh-, -ˈshō-\ *n* [LHeb *rōsh hashshānāh,* lit., beginning of the year] (1843) **:** the Jewish New Year observed on the first day and by Orthodox and Conservative Jews also on the second day of Tishri

Ro·si·cru·cian \ˌrō-zə-ˈkrü-shən, ˌrä-\ *n* [Christian *Rosenkreutz* (NL *Rosae Crucis*) reputed 15th cent. founder of the movement] (1624) **1 :** an adherent of a 17th and 18th century movement professing esoteric and occult wisdom with emphasis on mysticism and spiritual enlightenment **2 :** a member of one of several organizations held to be descended from the Rosicrucians — **Rosicrucian** *adj* — **Ro·si·cru·cian·ism** \-shə-ˌni-zəm\ *n*

ros·i·ly \ˈrō-zə-lē\ *adv* (1809) **1 :** in an optimistic manner **2 :** with a rosy color or tinge

[1]**ros·in** \ˈrä-zᵊn, ˈrȯ-, *dial* ˈrȯ-zəm\ *n* [ME, fr. AF *reisine, rosine* resin] (13c) **:** a translucent amber-colored to almost black brittle friable resin that is obtained from the oleoresin or deadwood of pine trees or from tall oil and used esp. in making varnish

[2]**rosin** *vt* **ros·ined; ros·in·ing** \ˈräz-niŋ, ˈrȯz-; ˈrä-zᵊn-iŋ, ˈrȯ-\ (15c) **:** to rub or treat (as the bow of a violin) with rosin

ros·in·weed \ˈrä-zᵊn-ˌwēd, ˈrȯ-\ *n* (1831) **:** any of several American plants (as the compass plant) having resinous foliage or a resinous odor

ros·tel·lum \rä-ˈste-ləm\ *n* [NL, fr. L, dim. of *rostrum* beak] (ca. 1826) **:** a small process resembling a beak **:** a diminutive rostrum: as **a :** an extension of the stigma of an orchid flower **b :** an anterior prolongation of the head of a tapeworm bearing hooks — **ros·tel·lar** \rä-ˈste-lər\ *adj*

ros·ter \ˈräs-tər *also* ˈrȯs- *or* ˈrōs-\ *n* [D *rooster,* lit., gridiron; fr. the parallel lines] (1727) **1 a :** a roll or list of personnel **b :** such a list giving the order in which a duty is to be performed ⟨a duty ~⟩ **c :** the persons listed on a roster **2 :** an itemized list

ros·tral \ˈräs-trəl *also* ˈrȯs-\ *adj* [NL *rostralis,* fr. L *rostrum*] (1709) **1 :** of or relating to a rostrum **2 :** situated toward the oral or nasal region: as **a** *of a part of the spinal cord* **:** SUPERIOR 6a **b** *of a part of the brain* **:** ANTERIOR, VENTRAL — **ros·tral·ly** \-trə-lē\ *adv*

ros·trate \ˈräs-ˌtrāt, -trət *also* ˈrȯs-\ *adj* (ca. 1819) **:** having a rostrum

ros·trum \ˈräs-trəm *also* ˈrȯs-\ *n, pl* **ros·tra** \-trə\ *or* **rostrums** [L, beak, ship's beak, fr. *rodere* to gnaw — more at RODENT] (1542) **1** [L *Rostra,* pl., a platform for speakers in the Roman Forum decorated with the beaks of captured ships, fr. pl. of *rostrum*] **a :** an ancient Roman platform for public orators **b :** a stage for public speaking **c :** a raised platform on a stage **2 :** the curved end of a ship's prow; *esp* **:** the beak of a war galley **3 :** a bodily part or process suggesting a bird's bill: as **a :** the beak, snout, or proboscis of any of various insects or arachnids **b :** the often spinelike anterior median prolongation of the carapace of a crustacean (as a crayfish or lobster)

rosy \ˈrō-zē\ *adj* **ros·i·er; -est** (14c) **1 a :** of the color rose **b :** having a pinkish usu. healthy-looking complexion **:** BLOOMING **c :** marked by blushes **2 :** characterized by or tending to promote optimism ⟨a ~ outlook⟩ — **ros·i·ness** *n*

rosy periwinkle *n* (1982) **:** a commonly cultivated subshrub (*Catharanthus roseus* syn. *Vinca rosea*) of the dogbane family that is native to the Old World tropics and is the source of several antineoplastic drugs — called also *Madagascar periwinkle, periwinkle*

[1]**rot** \ˈrät\ *vb* **rot·ted; rot·ting** [ME *roten,* fr. OE *rotian;* akin to OHG *rōzzēn* to rot] *vi* (bef. 12c) **1 a :** to undergo decomposition from the action of bacteria or fungi **b :** to become unsound or weak (as from use or chemical action) **2 a :** to go to ruin **:** DETERIORATE **b :** to become morally corrupt **:** DEGENERATE ~ *vt* **:** to cause to decompose or deteriorate with or as if with rot ***syn*** see DECAY

[2]**rot** *n* (14c) **1 a :** the process of rotting **:** the state of being rotten **:** DECAY **b :** something rotten or rotting **2 a** *archaic* **:** a wasting putrescent disease **b :** any of several parasitic diseases esp. of sheep marked by necrosis and wasting **c :** plant disease marked by breakdown of tissues and caused esp. by fungi or bacteria **3 :** NONSENSE — often used interjectionally

ro·ta \ˈrō-tə\ *n* [L, wheel — more at ROLL] (1619) **1** *cap* [ML, fr. L] **:** a tribunal of the papal curia exercising jurisdiction esp. in matrimonial cases appealed from diocesan courts **2** *chiefly Brit* **a :** a fixed order of rotation (as of persons or duties) **b** : a roll or list of persons : ROSTER

ro·ta·me·ter \ˈrō-tə-ˌmē-tər, rō-ˈta-mə-tər\ *n* [L *rota* + E *-meter*] (1907) : a gauge that consists of a graduated glass tube containing a free float for measuring the flow of a fluid

Ro·tar·i·an \rō-ˈter-ē-ən\ *n* [*Rotary (club)*] (1911) : a member of a major national and international service club

1**ro·ta·ry** \ˈrō-tə-rē\ *adj* [ML *rotarius,* fr. L *rota* wheel] (ca. 1731) **1 a** : turning on an axis like a wheel **b** : taking place about an axis ⟨~ motion⟩ **2** : having an important part that turns on an axis ⟨~ cutter⟩ **3** : characterized by rotation **4** : of, relating to, or being a press in which paper is printed by rotation in contact with a curved printing surface attached to a cylinder

2**rotary** *n, pl* **-ries** (ca. 1888) **1** : a rotary machine **2** : a road junction formed around a central circle about which traffic moves in one direction only — called also *circle, traffic circle*

rotary cultivator *n* (1926) : ROTOTILLER

rotary engine *n* (1837) **1** : any of various engines (as a turbine) in which power is applied to vanes or similar parts constrained to move in a circular path **2** : a radial engine in which the cylinders revolve about a stationary crankshaft

rotary–wing aircraft *n* (1935) : ROTORCRAFT; *specif* : HELICOPTER — usu. used in pl.

1**ro·tate** \ˈrō-ˌtāt\ *adj* [L *rota*] (1785) : having the parts flat and spreading or radiating like the spokes of a wheel ⟨~ blue flowers⟩

2**ro·tate** \ˈrō-ˌtāt, *esp Brit* rō-ˈ\ *vb* **ro·tat·ed; ro·tat·ing** [L *rotatus,* pp. of *rotare,* fr. *rota* wheel — more at ROLL] *vi* (1785) **1 a** : to perform an act, function, or operation in turn **b** : to pass or alternate in a series **2** : to turn about an axis or a center : REVOLVE; *esp* : to move in such a way that all particles follow circles with a common angular velocity about a common axis ~ *vt* **1 a** : to cause to turn or move about an axis or a center **b** : to cause (a plane region or line) to sweep out a volume or surface by moving around an axis so that each of its points remains at a constant distance from the axis ⟨generate a torus by *rotating* a circle about an external line⟩ **2** : to cause to grow in rotation ⟨~ crops⟩ **3** : to cause to pass or act in a series : ALTERNATE **4** : to exchange (individuals or units) with others — **ro·tat·able** \ˈrō-ˌtā-tə-bəl *also* rō-ˈ\ *adj*

ro·ta·tion \rō-ˈtā-shən\ *n* (1555) **1 a** (1) : the action or process of rotating on or as if on an axis or center (2) : the act or an instance of rotating something **b** : one complete turn : the angular displacement required to return a rotating body or figure to its original orientation **2 a** : return or succession in a series ⟨~ of the seasons⟩ **b** : CROP ROTATION **3** : the turning of a body part about its long axis as if on a pivot **4** : a game of pool in which all 15 object balls are shot in numerical order **5** : the series of pitchers on a baseball team who regularly start successive games in turn — **ro·ta·tion·al** \-shnəl, -shə-nᵊl\ *adj*

ro·ta·tive \ˈrō-ˌtā-tiv *also* rō-ˈ\ *adj* (1778) **1** : turning like a wheel : ROTARY **2** : relating to, occurring in, or characterized by rotation — **ro·ta·tive·ly** *adv*

ro·ta·tor \ˈrō-ˌtā-tər *also* rō-ˈ\ *n* (1676) : one that rotates or causes rotation; *esp, pl* **-tors** *or* **-tor·es** \ˌrō-tə-ˈtȯr-ˌēz\ : a muscle that partially rotates a part on its axis

rotator cuff *n* (1961) : a supporting and strengthening structure of the shoulder joint that is made up of the capsule of the shoulder joint blended with tendons and muscles as they pass to the capsule or across it to insert on the head of the humerus

ro·ta·to·ry \ˈrō-tə-ˌtȯr-ē, *Brit* -t(ə-)ri *also* rō-ˈtā-tə-ri\ *adj* (1741) **1** : of, relating to, or producing rotation **2** : occurring in rotation

ro·ta·vi·rus \ˈrō-tə-ˌvī-rəs\ *n* [NL, fr. L *rota* wheel + NL *virus*] (1974) : any of a genus (*Rotavirus*) of reoviruses that have a three-layered protein capsid with no outer lipid envelope when mature and that include one (species *Rotavirus A*) causing epidemics of severe and sometimes fatal diarrhea in infants and young children

ROTC *abbr* Reserve Officers' Training Corps

1**rote** \ˈrōt\ *n* [ME, fr. AF, of Gmc origin; akin to OHG *hruozza* crowd] (14c) : 3CROWD 1

2**rote** *n* [ME] (14c) **1** : the use of memory usu. with little intelligence ⟨learn by ~⟩ **2** : mechanical or unthinking routine or repetition ⟨a joyless sense of order, ~, and commercial hustle —L. L. King⟩

3**rote** *adj* (1641) **1** : learned or memorized by rote **2** : MECHANICAL 3a

4**rote** *n* [perh. of Scand origin; akin to ON *rauta* to roar — more at ROUT] (1610) : the noise of surf on the shore

ro·te·none \ˈrō-tə-ˌnōn\ *n* [ISV, fr. Jp *roten* derris plant] (1924) : a crystalline insecticide $C_{23}H_{22}O_6$ obtained from the roots of several tropical plants (as a derris) that is highly toxic to fish but is of low toxicity to warm-blooded animals and is used esp. in home gardens

rot·gut \ˈrät-ˌgət\ *n* (1633) : cheap or inferior liquor

ro·ti \ˈrō-tē\ *n* [Hindi & Urdu *roṭī* bread; akin to Skt *roṭika,* kind of bread] (1919) : a round soft flat unleavened bread; *also* : such a bread wrapped around a filling and eaten as a sandwich

ro·ti·fer \ˈrō-tə-fər\ *n* [ultim. fr. L *rota* + *-fer*] (1793) : any of a class (Rotifera of the phylum Aschelminthes) of minute usu. microscopic but many-celled chiefly freshwater aquatic invertebrates having the anterior end modified into a retractile disk bearing circles of strong cilia that often give the appearance of rapidly revolving wheels

1**ro·tis·ser·ie** \rō-ˈtis-rē, -ˈti-sə-\ *n* [F *rôtisserie,* fr. MF *rostisserie,* fr. *rostir* to roast — more at ROAST] (ca. 1920) **1** : a restaurant specializing in broiled and barbecued meats **2** : an appliance fitted with a spit on which food is rotated before or over a source of heat

2**rotisserie** *adj, often cap* [fr. La *Rotisserie* Française, restaurant in New York City where a group of fans began the organization of a fantasy baseball league in 1979] (1980) : of, relating to, or being a sports league consisting of imaginary teams whose performance is based on the statistics of actual players ⟨a ~ baseball league⟩

ro·to \ˈrō-(ˌ)tō\ *n, pl* **rotos** (1926) : ROTOGRAVURE

ro·to·gra·vure \ˌrō-tə-grə-ˈvyu̇r\ *n* [G *Rotogravur,* blend of L *rota* wheel and G *Photogravur* photogravure] (1913) **1** : PHOTOGRAVURE **2** : a section of a newspaper devoted to rotogravure pictures

ro·tor \ˈrō-tər\ *n* [contr. of *rotator*] (1903) **1 a** : a part that revolves in a stationary part ⟨a brake ~⟩ **b** : the rotating member of an electrical machine **2** : an assembly of rotating blades that supplies lift or stability for a rotorcraft

ro·tor·craft \-ˌkraft\ *n, pl* **rotorcraft** (1940) : an aircraft (as a helicopter) whose lift is derived principally from rotating airfoils

ro·to·till \ˈrō-tə-ˌtil\ *vt* [back-formation fr. *rototiller*] (1939) : to till or plow (soil) with a rototiller

ro·to·till·er \-ˌti-lər\ *n* [fr. *Rototiller,* a trademark] (1923) : a landscaping implement with engine-powered rotating blades used to lift and turn over soil

1**rot·ten** \ˈrä-tᵊn\ *adj* [ME *roten,* fr. ON *rotinn;* akin to OE *rotian* to rot] (13c) **1** : having rotted : PUTRID **2** : morally corrupt **3** : extremely unpleasant or inferior ⟨a ~ day⟩ ⟨a ~ job⟩ **4** : very uncomfortable ⟨feeling ~⟩ **5** : of very poor quality : LOUSY, ABOMINABLE ⟨a ~ show⟩ ⟨what ~ luck⟩ — **rot·ten·ly** *adv* — **rot·ten·ness** \-tᵊn-(n)əs\ *n*

2**rotten** *adv* (1880) : to an extreme degree ⟨spoiled ~⟩

rotten borough *n* (1784) : an election district that has many fewer inhabitants than other election districts with the same voting power

rot·ten·stone \ˈrä-tᵊn-ˌstōn\ *n* (1677) : a decomposed siliceous limestone used for polishing

rot·ter \ˈrä-tər\ *n* (1893) : a thoroughly objectionable person

rott·wei·ler \ˈrät-ˌwī-lər, ˈrȯt-ˌvī-\ *n, often cap* [G, fr. *Rottweil,* city in Germany] (1907) : any of a breed of tall powerful black-and-tan short-haired dogs of German origin that are commonly used as guard dogs

ro·tund \rō-ˈtənd, ˈrō-ˌ\ *adj* [L *rotundus,* prob. alter. of OL **retundus;* akin to L *rota* wheel — more at ROLL] (1665) **1** : marked by roundness : ROUNDED **2** : marked by fullness of sound or cadence : OROTUND, SONOROUS ⟨a master of ~ diction⟩ **3** : notably plump : CHUBBY — **ro·tun·di·ty** \rō-ˈtən-də-tē\ *n* — **ro·tund·ly** \-ˈtənd-lē, ˈrō-ˌ\ *adv* — **ro·tund·ness** \rō-ˈtən(d)-nəs, ˈrō-ˌ\ *n*

ro·tun·da \rō-ˈtən-də\ *n* [It *rotonda,* fr. L *rotunda,* fem. of *rotundus*] (1645) **1** : a round building; *esp* : one covered by a dome **2 a** : a large round room **b** : a large central area (as in a hotel)

ro·tu·ri·er \rō-ˈtu̇r-ē-ˌā, -ˈtyu̇r-\ *n* [MF] (1586) : a person not of noble birth

rouble *var of* RUBLE

roué \rü-ˈā\ *n* [F, lit., broken on the wheel, fr. pp. of *rouer* to break on the wheel, fr. ML *rotare,* fr. L, to rotate; fr. the feeling that such a person deserves this punishment] (1800) : a man devoted to a life of sensual pleasure : RAKE

1**rouge** \ˈrüzh, *esp Southern* ˈrüj\ *n* [F, fr. MF, fr. *rouge* red, fr. L *rubeus* reddish — more at RUBY] (1751) **1** : any of various cosmetics for coloring the cheeks or lips red **2** : a red powder consisting essentially of ferric oxide used in polishing glass, metal, or gems and as a pigment

2**rouge** *vb* **rouged; roug·ing** *vt* (1777) **1** : to apply rouge to **2** : to cause to redden ~ *vi* : to use rouge

1**rough** \ˈrəf\ *adj* **rough·er; rough·est** [ME, fr. OE *rūh;* akin to OHG *rūh* rough, Lith *raukas* wrinkle] (bef. 12c) **1 a** : marked by inequalities, ridges, or projections on the surface : COARSE **b** : covered with or made up of coarse and often shaggy hair ⟨*rough*-coated collie⟩ — compare SMOOTH, WIREHAIRED **c** (1) : having a broken, uneven, or bumpy surface ⟨~ terrain⟩ (2) : difficult to travel through or penetrate : WILD ⟨into the ~ woods —P. B. Shelley⟩ **2 a** : TURBULENT, TEMPESTUOUS ⟨~ seas⟩ **b** (1) : characterized by harshness, violence, or force (2) : presenting a challenge : DIFFICULT ⟨~ to deal with —R. M. McAlmon⟩ **3** : coarse or rugged in character or appearance: as **a** : harsh to the ear **b** : crude in style or expression **c** : INDELICATE **d** : marked by a lack of refinement or grace : UNCOUTH **4 a** : CRUDE, UNFINISHED ⟨~ carpentry⟩ **b** : executed or ventured hastily, tentatively, or imperfectly ⟨a ~ draft⟩ ⟨~ estimate⟩; *also* : APPROXIMATE ⟨a ~ idea⟩ — **rough·ish** \ˈrə-fish\ *adj* — **rough·ness** \ˈrəf-nəs\ *n*

syn ROUGH, HARSH, UNEVEN, RUGGED, SCABROUS mean not smooth or even. ROUGH implies points, bristles, ridges, or projections on the surface ⟨a *rough* wooden board⟩. HARSH implies a surface or texture distinctly unpleasant to the touch ⟨a *harsh* fabric that chafes the skin⟩. UNEVEN implies a lack of uniformity in height, breadth, or quality ⟨an old house with *uneven* floors⟩. RUGGED implies irregularity or roughness of land surface and connotes difficulty of travel ⟨a *rugged* landscape⟩. SCABROUS implies scaliness or prickliness of surface ⟨a *scabrous* leaf⟩. ***syn*** see in addition RUDE

2**rough** *adv* (14c) **1** : ROUGHLY 1 **2** *Brit* : without usual conveniences; *esp* : without proper shelter ⟨become homeless and have to sleep ~ —*London Times*⟩

3**rough** *n* (15c) **1** : uneven ground covered with high grass, brush, and stones; *specif* : such ground bordering a golf fairway **2** : the rugged or disagreeable side or aspect ⟨hiking-camping admirers of nature in the ~ —Eleanor Stirling⟩ **3 a** : something in a crude, unfinished, or preliminary state **b** : broad outline : general terms ⟨the question . . . has been discussed in ~ —*Manchester Guardian Weekly*⟩ **c** : a hasty preliminary drawing or layout **4** : ROWDY

4**rough** *vt* (1763) **1** : ROUGHEN **2 a** : to subject to abuse : MANHANDLE, BEAT — usu. used with *up* **b** : to subject to unnecessary and intentional violence in a sport ⟨a penalty for ~*ing* the passer⟩ **c** : SHELL 3 — used with *up* ⟨was ~*ed* up for six runs⟩ **3** : to calk or otherwise roughen (a horse's shoes) to prevent slipping **4 a** : to shape, make, or dress in a rough or preliminary way **b** : to indicate the chief lines of ⟨~ out the structure of a building⟩ — **rough·er** *n* — **rough it** : to live under harsh or primitive conditions

rough·age \ˈrə-fij\ *n* (1864) : FIBER 1d; *also* : food containing much indigestible material acting as fiber

rough–and–ready \ˌrə-fən-ˈre-dē\ *adj* (1810) : crude in nature, method, or manner but effective in action or use ⟨a ~ solution⟩

1**rough–and–tum·ble** \-ˈtəm-bəl\ *n* (1792) : rough disorderly unrestrained fighting or struggling; *also* : INFIGHTING

2**rough–and–tumble** *adj* (1832) **1** : marked by rough-and-tumble ⟨grew up in a ~ atmosphere —E. J. Kahn⟩; *also* : ROUGH-AND-READY **2** : put together haphazardly : MAKESHIFT ⟨a ~ fence⟩

rough bluegrass *n* (ca. 1925) : a forage grass (*Poa trivialis*) of Eurasia and northern Africa that is naturalized in No. America

rough breathing *n* (1746) **1** : a mark ʽ used in Greek over some initial vowels to show that they are aspirated or over ρ to show that it is voiceless **2** : the sound indicated by a mark ʽ over a Greek vowel or ρ

1**rough·cast** \ˈrəf-ˌkast, *for 2 also* -ˈkast\ *vt* **-cast; -cast·ing** (ca. 1501) **1** : to plaster (as a wall) with roughcast **2** : to shape or form roughly

[2]**rough·cast** \-ˌkast\ *n* (1579) **1 :** a rough model **2 :** a plaster of lime mixed with shells or pebbles used for covering buildings **3 :** a rough surface finish (as of a plaster wall)

rough cut *n* (1937) **:** a print of an incompletely edited motion picture

[1]**rough–dry** \ˈrəf-ˈdrī\ *vt* (1778) **:** to dry (laundry) without smoothing or ironing

[2]**rough–dry** *adj* (1854) **:** being dry after laundering but not ironed or smoothed over ⟨~ clothes⟩

rough–edged \ˈrəf-ˈejd\ *adj* (1942) **:** lacking refinement or polish ⟨a ~ writing style⟩

rough·en \ˈrə-fən\ *vb* **rough·ened; rough·en·ing** \ˈrə-fə-niŋ, ˈrəf-niŋ\ *vt* (1582) **:** to make rough or rougher ⟨her hands were ~*ed* by work —Ellen Glasgow⟩ ~ *vi* **:** to become rough

rough endoplasmic reticulum *n* (1972) **:** endoplasmic reticulum studded with ribosomes

rough fish *n* (1843) **:** a usu. freshwater fish (as a buffalo or freshwater drum) considered undesirable as a food or sport fish and often viewed as a competitor of more desirable fishes

rough–hew \ˈrəf-ˈhyü\ *vt* **-hewed; -hewn** \-ˈhyün\; **-hew·ing** (1530) **1 :** to hew (as timber) coarsely without smoothing or finishing **2 :** to form crudely

rough–hewn \-ˈhyün\ *adj* (1530) **1 :** being in a rough, unsmoothed, or unfinished state **:** crudely formed ⟨~ beams⟩ **2 :** lacking refinement ⟨he was rather attractive, in a ~ kind of way —Jan Speas⟩

[1]**rough·house** \ˈrəf-ˌhau̇s\ *n* (1887) **:** violence or rough boisterous play

[2]**rough·house** \-ˌhau̇s, -ˌhau̇z\ *vb* **rough·housed; rough·hous·ing** *vt* (1902) **:** to treat in a boisterously rough manner ~ *vi* **:** to engage in roughhouse

rough·leg \ˈrəf-ˌleg, -ˌlāg\ *n* (1895) **:** ROUGH-LEGGED HAWK

rough–legged hawk *n* (1811) **:** a large circumpolar arctic hawk (*Buteo lagopus*) that winters southward and typically has a white tail with a wide black band or bands at the tip

rough lemon *n* (1900) **1 :** a hybrid lemon that forms a large spreading thorny tree, bears rough-skinned fruit, and is important chiefly as a rootstock for other citrus trees **2 :** the fruit of a rough lemon

rough·ly \ˈrə-flē\ *adv* (14c) **1 :** in a rough manner: as **a :** with harshness or violence ⟨treated the prisoner ~⟩ **b :** in crude fashion **:** IMPERFECTLY ⟨~ dressed lumber⟩ **2 :** without completeness or exactness **:** APPROXIMATELY ⟨~ 20 percent⟩

[1]**rough·neck** \ˈrəf-ˌnek\ *n* (1836) **1 a :** a rough or uncouth person **b :** ROWDY, TOUGH **2 :** a worker of an oil-well-drilling crew other than the driller

[2]**roughneck** *adj* (1916) **:** having the characteristics of or suitable for a roughneck

rough·ri·der \ˈrəf-ˈrī-dər\ *n* (1733) **1 :** one who is accustomed to riding unbroken or little-trained horses **2** *usu* **Rough Rider :** a member of the first U.S. Volunteer Cavalry regiment in the Spanish-American War commanded by Theodore Roosevelt

[1]**rough·shod** \-ˌshäd\ *adj* (ca. 1688) **1 :** shod with calked shoes **2 :** marked by tyrannical force ⟨~ rule⟩

[2]**roughshod** *adv* (1813) **:** in a roughly forceful manner ⟨rode ~ over the opposition⟩

rough trade *n* (ca. 1935) **:** male homosexuals who are or affect to be rugged and potentially violent; *also* **:** such a homosexual

rouille \rü-ē\ *n* [F, lit., rust; fr. its color] (1951) **:** a peppery garlic sauce

rou·lade \rü-ˈläd\ *n* [F, lit., act of rolling] (ca. 1706) **1 :** a florid vocal embellishment sung to one syllable **2 :** a slice of usu. stuffed meat that is rolled, browned, and steamed or braised

rou·leau \rü-ˈlō\ *n, pl* **rou·leaux** \-ˈlōz\ [F] (1693) **:** a little roll; *esp* **:** a roll of coins put up in paper

[1]**rou·lette** \rü-ˈlet\ *n* [F, lit., small wheel, fr. OF *roelete,* dim. of *roele* wheel, rowel, fr. LL *rotella,* dim. of L *rota* wheel — more at ROLL] (1745) **1 a :** a gambling game in which players bet on which compartment of a revolving wheel a small ball will come to rest in **b :** something involving a high degree of chance and unpredictability **2 a :** any of various toothed wheels or disks (as for producing rows of dots on engraved plates or for making short consecutive incisions in paper to facilitate subsequent division) **b :** tiny slits between rows of stamps in a sheet that are made by a roulette and serve as an aid in separation — compare PERFORATION

[2]**roulette** *vt* **rou·lett·ed; rou·lett·ing** (1867) **:** to make roulettes in

Roumanian *var of* ROMANIAN

[1]**round** \ˈrau̇nd\ *adj* [ME, fr. AF *rund, reund,* fr. L *rotundus* — more at ROTUND] (14c) **1 a** (1) **:** having every part of the surface or circumference equidistant from the center (2) **:** CYLINDRICAL ⟨a ~ peg⟩ **b :** approximately round ⟨a ~ face⟩ **2 :** well filled out **:** PLUMP, SHAPELY **3 a :** COMPLETE, FULL ⟨a ~ dozen⟩ ⟨a ~ ton⟩ **b :** approximately correct; *esp* **:** exact only to a specific decimal or place ⟨use the ~ number 1400 for the exact figure 1411⟩ **c :** substantial in amount **:** AMPLE ⟨a good ~ price —T. B. Costain⟩ **4 :** direct in utterance **:** OUTSPOKEN ⟨a ~ denunciation⟩ **5 :** moving in or forming a circle **6 a :** brought to completion or perfection **:** FINISHED **b :** presented with lifelike fullness or vividness **7 :** delivered with a swing of the arm ⟨a ~ blow⟩ **8 a :** having full or unimpeded resonance or tone **:** SONOROUS **b :** pronounced with rounded lips **:** LABIALIZED **9 :** of or relating to handwriting predominantly curved rather than angular — **round·ness** \ˈrau̇n(d)-nəs\ *n*

[2]**round** *adv* (14c) **:** AROUND

[3]**round** *n* (14c) **1 a :** something (as a circle, globe, or ring) that is round **b** (1) **:** a knot of people (2) **:** a circle of things **2 :** ROUND DANCE 1 **3 :** a musical canon in which each part begins on the same note and is continuously repeated **4 a :** a rung of a ladder or a chair **b :** a rounded molding **5 a :** a circling or circuitous path or course **b :** motion in a circle or a curving path **6 a :** a route or circuit habitually covered (as by a security guard or police officer) **b :** a series of similar or customary calls or stops ⟨making the ~*s* of his friends —*Current Biog.*⟩; *esp* **:** a series of regularly scheduled professional calls on hospital patients made by a doctor or nurse — usu. used in pl. **7 :** a drink of liquor apiece served at one time to each person in a group ⟨I'll buy the next ~⟩ **8 :** a sequence of recurring routine or repetitive actions or events ⟨went about my ~ of chores⟩ ⟨the newest ~ of talks⟩ **9 :** a period of time that recurs in a fixed pattern ⟨the daily ~⟩ **10 a :** one shot fired by a weapon or by each man in a military unit **b :** a unit of ammunition consisting of the parts necessary to fire one shot **11 a :** a unit of action in a contest or game which comprises a stated period, covers a prescribed distance, includes a specified number of plays, or gives each player one turn **b :** a division of a tournament in which each contestant plays an opponent **12 :** a prolonged burst (as of applause) **13 a :** a cut of meat (as beef) esp. between the rump and the lower leg — see BEEF illustration **b :** a slice of food ⟨a ~ of bread⟩ **14 :** a rounded or curved part — **in the round 1 :** in full sculptured form unattached to a background **2 :** with an inclusive or comprehensive view or representation **3 :** with a center stage surrounded by an audience ⟨a play presented *in the round*⟩

[4]**round** *vt* (14c) **1 a :** to make round **b** (1) **:** to make (the lips) round and protruded (as in the pronunciation of \ü\) (2) **:** to pronounce with lip rounding **:** LABIALIZE **2 a :** GO AROUND **b :** to pass part of the way around **3 :** ENCIRCLE, ENCOMPASS **4 :** to bring to completion or perfection — often used with *off* or *out* **5 :** to express as a round number — often used with *off* ⟨11.3572 ~*ed* off to two decimal places becomes 11.36⟩ ~ *vi* **1 a :** to become round, plump, or shapely **b :** to reach fullness or completion **2 :** to follow a winding course **:** BEND — **round on :** to turn against **:** ASSAIL

[5]**round** *prep* (1602) **1 :** AROUND **2 :** all during **:** THROUGHOUT ⟨~ the year⟩

[6]**round** *vt* [alter. of ME *rounen,* fr. OE *rūnian;* akin to OE *rūn* mystery — more at RUNE] (ca. 1529) **1** *archaic* **:** WHISPER **2** *archaic* **:** to speak to in a whisper

[1]**round·about** \ˈrau̇n-də-ˌbau̇t\ *adj* (1608) **:** CIRCUITOUS, INDIRECT ⟨had to take a ~ route⟩ — **round·about·ness** *n*

[2]**roundabout** *n* (1755) **1 :** a circuitous route **:** DETOUR **2** *Brit* **:** MERRY-GO-ROUND **3 :** a short close-fitting jacket worn by men and boys esp. in the 19th century **4** *Brit* **:** ROTARY 2

round angle *n* (ca. 1934) **:** an angle of 360° or 2π radians

round·ball \ˈrau̇nd-ˌbȯl\ *n* (1971) **:** BASKETBALL

round clam *n* (ca. 1843) **:** QUAHOG

round dance *n* (1683) **1 :** a folk dance in which participants form a ring and move in a prescribed direction **2 :** a ballroom dance in which couples progress around the room **3 :** a series of movements performed by a bee to indicate that a source of food is nearby

round·ed \ˈrau̇n-dəd\ *adj* (1587) **1 :** made round **:** flowing rather than jagged or angular **2 :** fully developed — **round·ed·ness** *n*

roun·del \ˈrau̇n-dᵊl\ *n* [ME, fr. AF *rondel, roundel,* fr. *rund* round — more at ROUND] (14c) **1 :** a round figure or object (as a circular panel, window, or niche) **2 a :** RONDEL 2a **b :** an English modified rondeau

roun·de·lay \ˈrau̇n-də-ˌlā\ *n* [ME, modif. of MF *rondelet,* dim. of *rondel*] (15c) **1 :** a simple song with a refrain **2 :** a poem with a refrain recurring frequently or at fixed intervals as in a rondel

round·er \ˈrau̇n-dər\ *n* (1828) **1** *pl but sing in constr* **:** a game of English origin that is played with ball and bat and that somewhat resembles baseball **2 :** a dissolute person **:** WASTREL **3 :** one that rounds by hand or by machine **4 :** a boxing match lasting a specified number of rounds — usu. used in combination ⟨a 10-*rounder*⟩

Round·head \ˈrau̇nd-ˌhed\ *n* [fr. the Puritans' cropping their hair short in contrast to the Cavaliers] (1641) **1 :** a member of the parliamentary party in England at the time of Charles I and Oliver Cromwell **2 :** PURITAN 1

round·head·ed \-ˈhe-dəd\ *adj* (1729) **:** having a round head

round·house \ˈrau̇nd-ˌhau̇s\ *n* (1589) **1** *archaic* **:** LOCKUP **2 :** a circular building for housing and repairing locomotives **3 :** a blow delivered with a wide swing — **roundhouse** *adj*

round·ish \ˈrau̇n-dish\ *adj* (1545) **:** somewhat round

round lot *n* (ca. 1902) **:** the standard unit of trading in a security market usu. amounting to 100 shares of stock

round·ly \ˈrau̇n(d)-lē\ *adv* (15c) **1 a :** in a complete or thorough manner **:** THOROUGHLY ⟨~ disliked⟩ ⟨~ satisfying⟩ **b :** by nearly everyone **:** WIDELY ⟨~ praised⟩ **2 :** in a plainspoken manner **:** BLUNTLY ⟨told them ~ they would get no help⟩ **3 :** with vigor or asperity ⟨~ attacked the plan⟩

round–rob·in \ˈrau̇nd-ˌrä-bən\ *n* [fr. the name *Robin*] (ca. 1730) **1 a :** a written petition, memorial, or protest to which the signatures are affixed in a circle so as not to indicate who signed first **b :** a statement signed by several persons **c :** something (as a letter) sent in turn to the members of a group each of whom signs and forwards it sometimes after adding comment **2 :** ROUND TABLE 2 **3 :** a tournament in which every contestant meets every other contestant in turn **4 :** SERIES, ROUND

round–shoul·dered \ˈrau̇n(d)-ˌshōl-dərd\ *adj* (1586) **:** having the shoulders stooping or rounded

rounds·man \ˈrau̇n(d)z-mən\ *n* (1795) **1 :** one that makes rounds **2 :** a supervisory police officer of the grade of sergeant or just below

round steak *n* (1864) **:** a steak cut from the round of beef — see BEEF illustration

round ta·ble \ˈrau̇n(d)-ˌtā-bəl\ *n* (14c) **1 a** *cap R&T* **:** the large circular table of King Arthur and his knights **b :** the knights of King Arthur **2** *usu* **round·ta·ble :** a conference for discussion or deliberation by several participants; *also* **:** the participants in such a conference

round–the–clock *adj* (1937) **:** AROUND-THE-CLOCK

round–trip \ˈrau̇n(d)-ˌtrip\ *n, often attrib* (1851) **:** a trip to a place and back usu. over the same route

round·up \ˈrau̇nd-ˌəp\ *n* (1873) **1 a** (1) **:** the act or process of collecting animals (as cattle) by riding around them and driving them in (2) **:** the cowboys and ranch personnel engaged in a cattle roundup **b :** a gathering in of scattered persons or things ⟨a ~ of all suspects⟩ **2 :** a summary of information ⟨a ~ of the news⟩

round up *vt* (1847) **1 :** to collect (as cattle) by means of a roundup **2 :** to gather in or bring together from various quarters

round window *n* (1718) **:** a round opening between the middle ear and the cochlea

\ə\ **abut** \ᵊ\ **kitten, F table** \ər\ **further** \a\ **ash** \ā\ **ace** \ä\ **mop, mar** \au̇\ **out** \ch\ **chin** \e\ **bet** \ē\ **easy** \g\ **go** \i\ **hit** \ī\ **ice** \j\ **job** \ŋ\ **sing** \ō\ **go** \ȯ\ **law** \ȯi\ **boy** \th\ **thin** \t͟h\ **the** \ü\ **loot** \u̇\ **foot** \y\ **yet** \zh\ **vision, beige** \ḵ, ⁿ, œ, ue, ʸ\ *see* Guide to Pronunciation

round·wood \ˈrau̇nd-ˌwu̇d\ *n* (1782) : timber used (as for poles) without being squared by sawing or hewing
round·worm \ˈrau̇nd-ˌwərm\ *n* (1565) : NEMATODE; *also* : a related round-bodied unsegmented worm (as a spiny-headed worm) as distinguished from a flatworm
roup \ˈrüp, ˈrau̇p\ *n* [origin unknown] (ca. 1808) : any of various respiratory disorders of poultry
[1]**rouse** \ˈrau̇z\ *vb* **roused; rous·ing** [ME, to shake the feathers] *vt* (1531) **1** *archaic* : to cause to break from cover **2 a** : to stir up : EXCITE ⟨was *roused* to fury⟩ **b** : to arouse from or as if from sleep or repose : AWAKEN ~ *vi* **1** : to become aroused : AWAKEN **2** : to become stirred — **rouse·ment** \ˈrau̇z-mənt\ *n* — **rous·er** *n*
[2]**rouse** *n* (1824) : an act or instance of rousing; *esp* : an excited stir
[3]**rouse** *n* [alter. (fr. misdivision of *to drink carouse*) of *carouse*] (ca. 1601) **1** *obs* : DRINK, TOAST **2** *archaic* : CAROUSAL
rouse·about \ˈrau̇-zə-ˌbau̇t\ *n* (1861) *Austral* : an unskilled worker
rousing *adj* (1640) **1 a** : giving rise to excitement : STIRRING ⟨a ~ speech⟩ **b** : BRISK, LIVELY **2** : EXCEPTIONAL, SUPERLATIVE ⟨a ~ success⟩ — **rous·ing·ly** *adv*
Rous sarcoma \ˈrau̇s-\ *n* [F. Peyton *Rous* †1970 Am. physician] (ca. 1911) : a sarcoma of chickens caused by a retrovirus (species *Rous sarcoma virus* of the genus *Alpharetrovirus*)
Rous·seau·ism \ru̇-ˈsō-ˌi-zəm\ *n* (1865) **1** : the philosophical, educational, and political doctrines of Jean Jacques Rousseau **2** : the return to or glorification of a simpler and more primitive way of life — **Rousseau·ist** \-ist\ *n* — **Rous·seau·is·tic** \ˌrü-ˌsō-ˈis-tik, ru̇-\ *adj*
roust \ˈrau̇st\ *vt* [alter. of [1]*rouse*] (1658) : to drive (as from bed) roughly or unceremoniously
roust·about \ˈrau̇s-tə-ˌbau̇t\ *n* (1868) **1 a** : DECKHAND **b** : LONGSHOREMAN **2** : an unskilled or semiskilled laborer esp. in an oil field or refinery **3** : a circus worker who erects and dismantles tents, cares for the grounds, and handles animals and equipment **4** : a person with no permanent home or regular occupation; *also* : one who stirs up trouble
roust·er \ˈrau̇s-tər\ *n* (1883) **1** : DECKHAND **2** : LONGSHOREMAN
[1]**rout** \ˈrau̇t\ *n* [ME *route* band, company of soldiers, crowd, fr. AF *rute* band, fr. VL **rupta,* fr. L, fem. of *ruptus,* pp. of *rumpere* to break — more at REAVE] (13c) **1** : a crowd of people; *specif* : RABBLE 2b **2 a** : DISTURBANCE **b** *archaic* : FUSS **3** : a fashionable gathering
[2]**rout** \ˈrōt, ˈrüt\ *vi* [ME *rowten,* fr. ON *rauta;* akin to OE *rēotan* to weep, L *rudere* to roar] (14c) *dial chiefly Brit* : to low loudly : BELLOW — used of cattle
[3]**rout** \ˈrau̇t\ *vb* [alter. of [3]*root*] *vi* (ca. 1564) **1** : to poke around with the snout : ROOT ⟨pigs ~*ing* in the earth⟩ **2** : to search haphazardly ~ *vt* **1 a** *archaic* : to dig up with the snout **b** : to gouge out or make a furrow in (as wood or metal) **2 a** : to force out as if by digging — usu. used with *out* **b** : to cause to emerge esp. from bed **3** : to come up with : UNCOVER ⟨scouts . . . ~*ing* out new talent —Carrie Donovan⟩
[4]**rout** \ˈrau̇t\ *n* [MF *route* defeat, perh. fr. *mettre en route* to set going, put into motion] (1598) **1** : a state of wild confusion or disorderly retreat **2 a** : a disastrous defeat : DEBACLE **b** : a precipitate flight
[5]**rout** \ˈrau̇t\ *vt* (ca. 1600) **1 a** : to disorganize completely : DEMORALIZE **b** : to put to precipitate flight **c** : to defeat decisively or disastrously ⟨the discomfiture of seeing their party ~*ed* at the polls —A. N. Holcombe⟩ **2** : to drive out : DISPEL
[1]**route** \ˈrüt, ˈrau̇t\ *n* [ME, fr. AF *rute,* fr. VL **rupta (via),* lit., broken way, fr. L *rupta,* fem. of *ruptus,* pp.] (13c) **1 a** : a traveled way : HIGHWAY ⟨the main ~ north⟩ **b** : a means of access : CHANNEL ⟨the ~ to social mobility —T. F. O'Dea⟩ **2** : a line of travel : COURSE **3 a** : an established or selected course of travel or action **b** : an assigned territory to be systematically covered ⟨a newspaper ~⟩
[2]**route** *vt* **rout·ed; rout·ing** (1832) **1** : to send by a selected route : DIRECT ⟨was *routed* along the scenic shore road⟩ **2** : to divert in a specified direction
route·man \ˈrüt-mən, ˈrau̇t-ˌman\ *n* (1918) : a person who is responsible for making sales or deliveries on an assigned route
[1]**rout·er** \ˈrau̇-tər\ *n* (1818) : one that routs: as **a** : a routing plane **b** : a machine with a revolving vertical spindle and cutter for milling out the surface of wood or metal
[2]**rout·er** \ˈrü-tər, ˈrau̇-\ *n* (1903) : one that routes; *esp* : a device that mediates the transmission routes of data packets over an electronic communications network (as the Internet)
[3]**rout·er** \ˈrü-tər, ˈrau̇-\ *n* [*route* (race of a mile or more)] (ca. 1951) : a horse trained for distance races
route step *n* (1861) : a style of marching in which troops maintain prescribed intervals but are not required to keep in step or to maintain silence — called also *route march*
route·way \ˈrüt-ˌwā, ˈrau̇t-\ *n* (1946) *chiefly Brit* : ROUTE 3a
routh \ˈrau̇th, ˈrüth\ *n* [origin unknown] (1668) *chiefly Scot* : PLENTY
[1]**rou·tine** \rü-ˈtēn\ *n* [F, fr. MF, fr. *route* traveled way] (1676) **1 a** : a regular course of procedure ⟨if resort to legal action becomes a campus ~ —J. A. Perkins⟩ **b** : habitual or mechanical performance of an established procedure ⟨the ~ of factory work⟩ **2** : a reiterated speech or formula ⟨the old "After you" ~ —Ray Russell⟩ **3** : a worked-out part (as of an entertainment or sports contest) that may be often repeated ⟨a dance ~⟩; *esp* : a theatrical number **4** : a sequence of computer instructions for performing a particular task
[2]**rou·tine** \rü-ˈtēn, ˈrü-ˌ\ *adj* (1817) **1** : of a commonplace or repetitious character : ORDINARY ⟨~ problems⟩ **2** : of, relating to, or being in accordance with established procedure ⟨~ business⟩ — **rou·tine·ly** *adv*
rou·tin·ize \rü-ˈtē-ˌnīz, ˈrü-tə-ˌnīz\ *vt* **-ized; -iz·ing** (1921) : to discipline in or reduce to a routine — **rou·tin·i·za·tion** \(ˌ)rü-ˌtē-nə-ˈzā-shən, ˌrü-tə-nə-\ *n*
roux \ˈrü\ *n, pl* **roux** \ˈrüz\ [F, fr. *beurre roux* brown butter] (1813) : a cooked mixture of flour and fat used as a thickening agent in a soup or a sauce
[1]**rove** \ˈrōv\ *vb* **roved; rov·ing** [earlier, to shoot at random, wander, of unknown origin] *vi* (1536) : to move aimlessly : ROAM ~ *vt* : to wander through or over ***syn*** see WANDER
[2]**rove** *n* (1606) : an act or instance of wandering
[3]**rove** *past and past part of* REEVE
[4]**rove** *vt* **roved; rov·ing** [origin unknown] (1789) : to join (textile fibers) with a slight twist and draw out into roving
[5]**rove** *n* (1789) : ROVING
rove beetle *n* [perh. fr. [1]*rove*] (ca. 1771) : any of a family (Staphylinidae) of often predatory active beetles having a long body and very short wing covers beneath which the wings are folded transversely — called also *staphylinid*

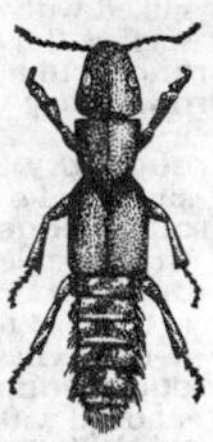
rove beetle

[1]**ro·ver** \ˈrō-vər\ *n* [ME, fr. MD, fr. *roven* to rob; akin to OE *rēafian* to reave — more at REAVE] (14c) : PIRATE
[2]**rov·er** \ˈrō-vər\ *n* (1531) **1** : a random or long-distance mark in archery — usu. used in pl. **2** : WANDERER, ROAMER **3** : a player who is not assigned to a specific position on a team and who plays wherever needed **4** : a vehicle for exploring the surface of an extraterrestrial body (as the moon or Mars)
[1]**roving** *adj* [[1]*rove*] (1590) **1 a** : not restricted as to location or area of concern **b** : capable of being shifted from place to place : MOBILE **2** : inclined to ramble or stray ⟨a ~ fancy⟩
[2]**roving** *n* [[4]*rove*] (1802) : a slightly twisted roll or strand of usu. textile fibers
[1]**row** \ˈrō\ *vb* [ME, fr. OE *rōwan;* akin to MHG *rüejen* to row, L *remus* oar] *vi* (bef. 12c) **1** : to propel a boat by means of oars **2** : to move by or as if by the propulsion of oars ~ *vt* **1 a** : to propel with or as if with oars **b** (1) : to participate in (a rowing match) (2) : to compete against in rowing (3) : to pull (an oar) in a crew **2** : to transport in an oar-propelled boat — **row·er** \ˈrō-ər\ *n*
[2]**row** *n* (1832) : an act or instance of rowing
[3]**row** *n* [ME *rawe;* akin to OE *rǣw* row, OHG *rīga* line, and perh. to Skt *rikhati* he scratches] (13c) **1** : a number of objects arranged in a usu. straight line ⟨a ~ of bottles⟩; *also* : the line along which such objects are arranged ⟨planted the corn in parallel ~*s*⟩ **2 a** : WAY, STREET **b** : a street or area dominated by a specific kind of enterprise or occupancy ⟨doctors' ~⟩ **3** : TWELVE-TONE ROW **4 a** : a continuous strip usu. running horizontally or parallel to a baseline **b** : a horizontal arrangement of items — **in a row** : one after another : SUCCESSIVELY
[4]**row** *vt* (1657) : to form into rows
[5]**row** \ˈrau̇\ *n* [origin unknown] (1746) : a noisy disturbance or quarrel
[6]**row** \ˈrau̇\ *vi* (1797) : to engage in a row : have a quarrel
row·an \ˈrau̇-ən, ˈrō-ən\ *n* [of Scand origin; akin to Norw dial. *raun* rowan; akin to OE *rēad* red — more at RED] (1801) **1** : either of two mountain ashes with flat corymbs of white flowers followed by small red pomes: **a** : one (*Sorbus aucuparia*) native to Eurasia that has become naturalized in the U.S. and Canada **b** : one (*S. americana*) native to the eastern U.S and Canada **2** : the fruit of a rowan
row·an·ber·ry \-ˌber-ē\ *n* (1814) : ROWAN 2
row·boat \ˈrō-ˌbōt\ *n* (1538) : a small boat designed to be rowed
[1]**row·dy** \ˈrau̇-dē\ *adj* **row·di·er; -est** [perh. irreg. fr. [5]*row*] (1819) : coarse or boisterous in behavior : ROUGH; *also* : characterized by such behavior ⟨~ local bars⟩ — **row·di·ly** \ˈrau̇-dᵊl-ē\ *adv* — **row·diness** \ˈrau̇-dē-nəs\ *n* — **row·dy·ish** \-ish\ *adj*
[2]**rowdy** *n, pl* **rowdies** (1808) : a rowdy person : TOUGH
row·dy·ism \ˈrau̇-dē-ˌi-zəm\ *n* (1842) : rowdy character or behavior
[1]**row·el** \ˈrau̇(-ə)l\ *n* [ME *rowelle,* fr. AF *roele* small wheel — more at ROULETTE] (15c) : a revolving disk with sharp marginal points at the end of a spur
[2]**rowel** *vt* **-eled** *or* **-elled; -el·ing** *or* **-el·ling** (1580) **1** : to goad with or as if with a rowel **2** : VEX, TROUBLE
row·en \ˈrau̇-ən\ *n* [ME *rowein,* fr. AF *regain, rewain,* fr. *re-* + *gain, waine* arable land, produce, profit — more at GAIN] (15c) : AFTERMATH 1
row house \ˈrō-\ *n* (1921) : one of a series of houses connected by common sidewalls and forming a continuous group
row·ing \ˈrō-iŋ\ *n* (bef. 12c) **1** : the propelling of a boat by means of oars : the action of one that rows **2** : the sport of racing in shells
rowing boat *n* (1820) *chiefly Brit* : ROWBOAT
rowing machine *n* (1848) : an exercise machine that simulates the action of rowing
row·lock \ˈrä-lək, ˈrə-; ˈrō-ˌläk\ *n* [prob. by alter.] (ca. 1750) *chiefly Brit* : OARLOCK
[1]**roy·al** \ˈrȯi(-ə)l\ *adj* [ME *roial,* fr. AF *real, roial,* fr. L *regalis,* fr. *reg-, rex* king; akin to OIr *rī* (gen. *rīg*) king, Skt *rājan,* L *regere* to rule — more at RIGHT] (14c) **1 a** : of kingly ancestry ⟨the ~ family⟩ **b** : of, relating to, or subject to the crown ⟨the ~ estates⟩ **c** : being in the crown's service ⟨*Royal* Air Force⟩ **2 a** : suitable for royalty : MAGNIFICENT **b** : requiring no exertion : EASY ⟨there is no ~ road to logic —Justus Buchler⟩ **3 a** : of superior size, magnitude, or quality ⟨a patronage of ~ dimensions —J. H. Plumb⟩ — often used as an intensive ⟨a ~ pain⟩ **b** : established or chartered by the crown **4** : of, relating to, or being a part (as a mast, sail, or yard) next above the topgallant — **roy·al·ly** \ˈrȯi-ə-lē\ *adv*
[2]**royal** *n* (14c) **1** : a person of royal blood **2** : a small sail on the royal mast immediately above the topgallant sail **3** : a stag of 8 years or more having antlers with at least 12 points
royal antler *n* (ca. 1727) : the third tine above the base of a stag's antler
royal blue *n* (1789) : a vivid purplish blue
royal flush *n* (ca. 1868) : a straight flush having an ace as the highest card — see POKER illustration
roy·al·ism \ˈrȯi-ə-ˌli-zəm\ *n* (1793) : MONARCHISM
roy·al·ist \-list\ *n* (1640) **1** *often cap* : an adherent of a king or of monarchical government: as **a** : CAVALIER 3 **b** : TORY 4 **2** : a reactionary business tycoon — **royalist** *adj*
royal jelly *n* (1817) : a highly nutritious secretion of the pharyngeal glands of the honeybee that is fed to the very young larvae in a colony and to all queen larvae
royal palm *n* (ca. 1861) : any of a genus (*Roystonea*) of palms chiefly of the Caribbean region; *esp* : a tall graceful pinnate-leaved palm (*R. regia*) native to Cuba that is widely planted for ornament
royal poinciana *n* (ca. 1900) : a showy Madagascan tree (*Delonix regia* syn. *Poinciana regia*) widely planted for its immense racemes of scarlet and orange flowers — called also *flamboyant, peacock flower*
royal purple *n* (1661) : a dark reddish purple
roy·al·ty \ˈrȯi(-ə)l-tē\ *n, pl* **-ties** [ME *roialte,* fr. AF *realté, roialté,* fr. *real*] (14c) **1 a** : royal status or power : SOVEREIGNTY **b** : a right or perquisite of a sovereign (as a percentage paid to the crown of gold or

silver taken from mines) **2 :** regal character or bearing : NOBILITY **3 a :** persons of royal lineage **b :** a person of royal rank ⟨how to address *royalties* —George Santayana⟩ **c :** an elite class **4 :** a right of jurisdiction granted to an individual or corporation by a sovereign **5 a :** a share of the product or profit reserved by the grantor esp. of an oil or mining lease **b :** a payment to an author or composer for each copy of a work sold or to an inventor for each item sold under a patent

roz·zer \ˈrä-zər\ *n* [origin unknown] (1893) *slang Brit* : POLICE OFFICER

RP *abbr* **1** Received Pronunciation **2** relief pitcher **3** reprint; reprinting **4** Republic of the Philippines

[1]**RPG** \ˌär-(ˌ)pē-ˈjē\ *n* [*r*eport *p*rogram *g*enerator] (1966) : a computer language that generates programs from the user's specifications esp. to produce business reports

[2]**RPG** *abbr* **1** rocket-propelled grenade **2** role-playing game

RPh *abbr* registered pharmacist

rpm *abbr* revolutions per minute

rps *abbr* revolutions per second

RPT *abbr* registered physical therapist

RPV \ˌär-(ˌ)pē-ˈvē\ *n* [*r*emotely *p*iloted *v*ehicle] (1970) : an unmanned aircraft flown by remote control and used esp. for reconnaissance

RQ *abbr* respiratory quotient

RR *abbr* **1** railroad **2** rural route

-rrhagia *n comb form* [NL, fr. Gk, fr. *rhēgnynai* to break, burst; prob. akin to Lith *rėžti* to cut] : abnormal or excessive discharge or flow ⟨metro*rrhagia*⟩

-rrhea *n comb form* [ME *-ria,* fr. LL *-rrhoea,* fr. Gk *-rrhoia,* fr. *rhoia,* fr. *rhein* to flow — more at STREAM] : flow : discharge ⟨leuko*rrhea*⟩

-rrhiza — see -RHIZA

-rrhoea *chiefly Brit var of* -RRHEA

rRNA \ˌär-(ˌ)är-(ˌ)en-ˈā\ *n* (ca. 1965) : RIBOSOMAL RNA

RRT *abbr* registered respiratory therapist

RS *abbr* **1** Received Standard **2** recording secretary **3** revised statutes **4** Royal Society

RSA *abbr* Republic of South Africa

RSFSR *abbr* [Russ *Rossiĭskaya Sovetskaya Federativnaya Sotsialisticheskaya Respublika*] Russian Soviet Federated Socialist Republic

RSI *abbr* repetitive strain injury; repetitive stress injury

RSS \ˌär-ˌes-ˈes\ *n* [*R*DF (Resource Description Framework) *S*ite *S*ummary (later explained by its developers as *R*ich *S*ite *S*ummary and *R*eally *S*imple *S*yndication)] (2000) : a computer document format that enables updates to Web sites to be easily distributed

RSV *abbr* **1** Revised Standard Version **2** respiratory syncytial virus

[1]**RSVP** \ˌär-ˌes-ˌvē-ˈpē\ *vi* **RSVP'd** *or* **RSVPed; RSVP'·ing** *or* **RSVP·ing** (1953) : to respond to an invitation

[2]**RSVP** *abbr* [F *répondez s'il vous plaît*] please reply

rt *abbr* **1** right **2** route

RT *abbr* **1** respiratory therapist; respiratory therapy **2** room temperature **3** round-trip

rte *abbr* route

rtw *abbr* ready-to-wear

Ru *symbol* ruthenium

ru·a·na \rü-ˈä-nə\ *n* [AmerSp, fr. Sp, woolen fabric] (ca. 1903) : a woolen covering resembling a poncho

[1]**rub** \ˈrəb\ *vb* **rubbed; rub·bing** [ME *rubben;* akin to East Fris *rubben* to rub, scrape, Icel *rubba* to scrape] *vi* (14c) **1 a :** to move along the surface of a body with pressure : GRATE **b** (1) **:** to fret or chafe with or as if with friction (2) **:** to cause discontent, irritation, or anger **2 :** to continue in a situation usu. with slight difficulty ⟨in spite of financial difficulties, he is *rubbing* along⟩ **3 :** to admit of being rubbed (as for erasure or obliteration) ∼ *vt* **1 a :** to subject to or as if to the action of something moving esp. back and forth with pressure and friction **b** (1) **:** to cause (a body) to move with pressure and friction along a surface (2) **:** to treat in any of various ways by rubbing **c :** to bring into reciprocal back-and-forth or rotary contact **2 :** ANNOY, IRRITATE — **rub elbows** *or* **rub shoulders :** to associate closely : MINGLE — **rub one's nose in :** to bring forcefully or repeatedly to one's attention — **rub the wrong way :** ANTAGONIZE, IRRITATE

[2]**rub** *n* (1586) **1 a :** an unevenness of surface (as of the ground in lawn bowling) **b :** OBSTRUCTION, DIFFICULTY ⟨the ∼ is that so few of the scholars have any sense of this truth themselves —Benjamin Farrington⟩ **c :** something grating to the feelings (as a gibe or harsh criticism) **d :** something that mars serenity **2 :** the application of friction with pressure ⟨an alcohol ∼⟩

Ru·bai·yat stanza \ˈrü-bē-ˌät-, -ˌbī-, -ˌat-\ *n* [*The Rubáiyát of Omar Khayyám,* quatrains translated by Edward FitzGerald (1859)] (1940) : an iambic pentameter quatrain with a rhyme scheme *aaba*

ru·ba·to \rü-ˈbä-(ˌ)tō\ *n, pl* **-tos** [It, lit., robbed] (ca. 1883) : a fluctuation of tempo within a musical phrase often against a rhythmically steady accompaniment

[1]**rub·ber** \ˈrə-bər\ *n* (1536) **1 a :** one that rubs **b :** an instrument or object (as a rubber eraser) used in rubbing, polishing, scraping, or cleaning **c :** something that prevents rubbing or chafing **2** [fr. its use in erasers] **a :** an elastic substance that is obtained by coagulating the milky juice of any of various tropical plants (as of the genera *Hevea* and *Ficus*), is essentially a polymer of isoprene, and is prepared as sheets and then dried — called also *caoutchouc, india rubber* **b :** any of various synthetic rubberlike substances **c :** natural or synthetic rubber modified by chemical treatment to increase its useful properties (as toughness and resistance to wear) and used esp. in tires, electrical insulation, and waterproof materials **3 :** something made of or resembling rubber: as **a :** a rubber overshoe **b** (1) **:** a rubber tire (2) **:** the set of tires on a vehicle **c :** a rectangular slab of white rubber in the middle of a baseball infield on which a pitcher stands while pitching **d :** CONDOM 1 — **rubber** *adj*

[2]**rubber** *n* [origin unknown] (1599) **1 :** a contest consisting of an odd number of games won by the side that takes a majority (as two out of three) **2 :** an odd game played to determine the winner of a tie

rubber band *n* (1886) : a continuous band of rubber used in various ways (as for holding together a sheaf of papers)

rubber bridge *n* (1936) : a form of contract bridge in which settlement is made at the end of each rubber

rubber cement *n* (1886) : an adhesive consisting typically of a dispersion of vulcanized rubber in an organic solvent

rubber check *n* [fr. its coming back like a bouncing rubber ball] (1921) : a check returned by a bank because of insufficient funds in the payer's account

rub·ber–chick·en \ˈrə-bər-ˈchi-kən\ *adj* [fr. the low quality of the food stereotypically served at such events] (1972) : of, relating to, or being a series of social gatherings (as fund-raising dinners) at which speeches are given ⟨the ∼ circuit⟩

rub·ber·ized \ˈrə-bə-ˌrīzd\ *adj* (1908) : coated or saturated with rubber or a rubber solution

rub·ber·like \ˈrə-bər-ˌlīk\ *adj* (1922) : resembling rubber esp. in physical properties (as elasticity and toughness)

[1]**rub·ber·neck** \-ˌnek\ *n* (ca. 1896) **1 :** an overly inquisitive person **2 :** TOURIST; *esp* : one on a guided tour

[2]**rubberneck** *vi* (1896) **1 :** to look about or stare with exaggerated curiosity ⟨drivers passing the accident slowed down to ∼⟩ **2 :** to go on a tour : SIGHTSEE — **rub·ber·neck·er** \-ˌne-kər\ *n*

rubber plant *n* (1888) : a plant that yields rubber; *esp* : a tall tropical widely cultivated Asian tree (*Ficus elastica*) of the mulberry family that is frequently dwarfed as a houseplant

rubber–stamp *vt* (1918) **1 :** to approve, endorse, or dispose of as a matter of routine or at the command of another **2 :** to mark with a rubber stamp

rubber stamp *n* (1881) **1 :** a stamp of rubber for making imprints **2 a :** a person who echoes or imitates others **b :** a mostly powerless yet officially recognized body or person that approves or endorses programs and policies initiated usu. by a single specified source ⟨the parliament was a *rubber stamp* for the dictator⟩ **3 a :** a stereotyped copy or expression ⟨the usual *rubber stamps* of criticism —H. L. Mencken⟩ **b :** a routine endorsement or approval — **rubber–stamp** *adj*

rubber tree *n* (1847) : a tree that yields rubber; *esp* : a So. American tree (*Hevea brasiliensis*) of the spurge family that is cultivated in plantations and is a chief source of rubber

rub·bery \ˈrə-b(ə-)rē\ *adj* (1907) : resembling rubber (as in elasticity, consistency, or texture) ⟨∼ legs⟩ ⟨∼ cheese⟩

rubbing *n* (1845) : an image of a raised, incised, or textured surface obtained by placing paper over it and rubbing the paper with a colored substance

rubbing alcohol *n* (ca. 1931) : a cooling and soothing liquid for external application that contains approximately 70 percent denatured ethanol or isopropanol

rub·bish \ˈrə-bish, *dial* -bij\ *n* [ME *robous*] (15c) **1 :** useless waste or rejected matter : TRASH **2 :** something that is worthless or nonsensical ⟨few real masterpieces are forgotten and not much ∼ survives —William Bridges-Adams⟩ — **rub·bishy** \-bə-shē\ *adj*

[1]**rub·ble** \ˈrə-bəl\ *n* [ME *robyl*] (14c) **1 a :** broken fragments (as of rock) resulting from the decay or destruction of a building ⟨fortifications knocked into ∼ —C. S. Forester⟩ **b :** a miscellaneous confused mass or group of usu. broken or worthless things **2 :** waterworn or rough broken stones or bricks used in coarse masonry or in filling courses of walls **3 :** rough stone as it comes from the quarry

[2]**rubble** *vt* **rub·bled; rub·bling** \-b(ə-)liŋ\ (1926) : to reduce to rubble

rub·board \ˈrəb-ˌbȯrd\ *n* (1864) : WASHBOARD 3a

rub·down \ˈrəb-ˌdau̇n\ *n* (1896) : a brisk rubbing of the body (as to relax fatigued muscles)

rube \ˈrüb\ *n* [*Rube,* nickname for *Reuben*] (1891) **1 :** an awkward unsophisticated person : RUSTIC **2 :** a naive or inexperienced person

[1]**ru·be·fa·cient** \ˌrü-bə-ˈfā-shənt\ *adj* [L *rubefacient-, rubefaciens,* prp. of *rubefacere* to make red, fr. *rubeus* reddish + *facere* to make — more at RUBY, DO] (1804) : causing redness (as of the skin)

[2]**rubefacient** *n* (1805) : a substance for external application that produces redness of the skin

Rube Gold·berg \ˈrüb-ˈgōl(d)-ˌbərg\ *also* **Rube Gold·berg·i·an** \-ˌbər-gē-ən, -ˌbərg-yən\ *adj* [Reuben (*Rube*) L. *Goldberg* †1970 Am. cartoonist] (1931) : accomplishing by complex means what seemingly could be done simply ⟨a kind of *Rube Goldberg* contraption . . . with five hundred moving parts —L. T. Grant⟩; *also* : characterized by such complex means

ru·bel *or* **ru·ble** \ˈrü-bəl\ *n* [Belarusian *rubel'*] (1992) — see MONEY table

ru·bel·la \rü-ˈbe-lə\ *n* [NL, fr. L, fem. of *rubellus* reddish, fr. *ruber* red — more at RED] (1883) : GERMAN MEASLES

ru·bel·lite \rü-ˈbe-ˌlīt, ˈrü-bə-ˌlīt\ *n* [L *rubellus*] (ca. 1796) : a red tourmaline used as a gem

Ru·ben·esque \ˌrü-bə-ˈnesk\ *adj* (1913) : of, relating to, or suggestive of the painter Rubens or his works; *esp* : plump or rounded usu. in a pleasing or attractive way ⟨a ∼ figure⟩

ru·be·o·la \ˌrü-bē-ˈō-lə, rü-ˈbē-ə-lə\ *n* [NL, fr. neut. pl. of *rubeolus* reddish, fr. L *rubeus*] (1803) : MEASLES 1a

Ru·bi·con \ˈrü-bi-ˌkän\ *n* [L *Rubicon-, Rubico,* river of northern Italy forming part of the boundary between Cisalpine Gaul and Italy whose crossing by Julius Caesar in 49 B.C. was regarded by the Senate as an act of war] (1626) : a bounding or limiting line; *esp* : one that when crossed commits a person irrevocably

ru·bi·cund \ˈrü-bi-(ˌ)kənd\ *adj* [ME *rubicunde,* fr. L *rubicundus,* fr. *rubēre* to be red; akin to L *rubeus*] (15c) : RUDDY — **ru·bi·cun·di·ty** \ˌrü-bi-ˈkən-də-tē\ *n*

ru·bid·i·um \rü-ˈbi-dē-əm\ *n* [NL, fr. L *rubidus* red, fr. *rubēre*] (1861) : a soft silvery metallic element of the alkali metal group that reacts violently with water and bursts into flame spontaneously in air — see ELEMENT table

rub in *vt* (1851) : to harp on (as something unpleasant) : EMPHASIZE

ru·bi·ous \ˈrü-bē-əs\ *adj* (1601) : RED, RUBY

ru·ble *also* **rou·ble** \ˈrü-bəl\ *n* [Russ *rubl'*] (1554) — see MONEY table

rub off *vi* (1950) : to become transferred ⟨bad habits *rubbed off* on them⟩ ⟨carbon *rubs off* on your hands⟩ — **rub–off** \ˈrəb-ˌȯf\ *n*

rub out *vt* (14c) **1 :** to obliterate by or as if by rubbing **2 :** to destroy completely; *specif* : KILL, MURDER ⟨somebody *rubbed* him *out* . . . with a twenty-two —Raymond Chandler⟩ — **rub·out** \ˈrəb-ˌau̇t\ *n*

ru·bric \ˈrü-brik, -ˌbrik\ *n* [ME *rubrike* red ocher, heading in red letters of part of a book, fr. AF, fr. L *rubrica,* fr. *rubr-, ruber* red] (14c) **1 a** : an authoritative rule; *esp* : a rule for conduct of a liturgical service **b** (1) : NAME, TITLE; *specif* : the title of a statute (2) : something under which a thing is classed : CATEGORY ⟨the sensations falling under the general ~, "pressure" —F. A. Geldard⟩ **c** : an explanatory or introductory commentary : GLOSS; *specif* : an editorial interpolation **2** : a heading of a part of a book or manuscript done or underlined in a color (as red) different from the rest **3** : an established rule, tradition, or custom **4** : a guide listing specific criteria for grading or scoring academic papers, projects, or tests — **rubric** *or* **ru·bri·cal** \-bri-kəl\ *adj* — **ru·bri·cal·ly** \-bri-k(ə-)lē\ *adv*

ru·bri·cate \ˈrü-bri-ˌkāt\ *vt* **-cat·ed; -cat·ing** (1570) **1** : to write or print as a rubric **2** : to provide with a rubric — **ru·bri·ca·tion** \ˌrü-bri-ˈkā-shən\ *n* — **ru·bri·ca·tor** \ˈrü-bri-ˌkā-tər\ *n*

rub up *vt* (1572) **1** : to revive or refresh knowledge of : RECALL **2** : to improve the keenness of (a mental faculty)

ru·bus \ˈrü-bəs\ *n, pl* **rubus** [NL, fr. L, blackberry] (15c) : any of a genus (*Rubus*) of plants (as a blackberry or a raspberry) of the rose family with leaves that typically have three to seven leaflets or that are simple and lobed, white or pink flowers, usu. prickly stems, and a mass of carpels ripening into an aggregate fruit composed of many drupelets

[1]**ru·by** \ˈrü-bē\ *n, pl* **rubies** [ME, fr. AF *rubi, rubin,* fr. ML *rubinus,* fr. L *rubeus* reddish; akin to L *ruber* red — more at RED] (14c) **1 a** : a precious stone that is a red corundum **b** : something (as a watch bearing) made of ruby **2 a** : the dark red color of the ruby **b** : something resembling a ruby in color

[2]**ruby** *adj* (1508) : of the color ruby

ruby glass *n* (1797) : glass of a deep red color containing selenium, an oxide of copper, or a chloride of gold

ruby spinel *n* (1839) : a usu. red spinel used as a gem

ru·by·throat \ˈrü-bē-ˌthrōt\ *n* (ca. 1783) : RUBY-THROATED HUMMINGBIRD

ru·by–throat·ed hummingbird \ˈrü-bē-ˌthrō-təd-\ *n* (ca. 1782) : a hummingbird (*Archilochus colubris*) of eastern No. America having a bright metallic green back, whitish underparts, and in the adult male a red throat

ruche \ˈrüsh\ *or* **ruch·ing** \ˈrü-shiŋ\ *n* [F *ruche* lit., beehive, fr. ML *rusca* bark] (1827) : a pleated, fluted, or gathered strip of fabric used for trimming — **ruched** \ˈrüsht\ *adj*

[1]**ruck** \ˈrək\ *n* [ME, heap, pile, of Scand origin; akin to ON *hraukr* rick — more at RICK] (15c) **1 a** : the usual run of persons or things : GENERALITY ⟨trying to rise above the ~ —Richard Holt⟩ **b** : an indistinguishable gathering : JUMBLE **2** : the persons or things following the vanguard ⟨finished the race in the ~⟩

[2]**ruck** *vb* [*ruck,* n., wrinkle] (1812) : PUCKER, WRINKLE

ruck·sack \ˈrək-ˌsak, ˈru̇k-\ *n* [G, fr. G dial., fr. *Rucken* back + *Sack* sack] (1879) : KNAPSACK

ruck·us \ˈrə-kəs *also* ˈrü- *or* ˈru̇-\ *n* [prob. blend of *ruction* and *rumpus*] (ca. 1890) : ROW, DISTURBANCE ⟨raise a ~⟩

ruc·tion \ˈrək-shən\ *n* [perh. by shortening & alter. fr. *insurrection*] (ca. 1825) **1** : a noisy fight **2** : DISTURBANCE, UPROAR

rud·beck·ia \ˌrəd-ˈbe-kē-ə, rüd-\ *n* [NL, fr. Olof *Rudbeck* †1702 Swed. scientist] (ca. 1759) : any of a genus (*Rudbeckia*) of No. American chiefly perennial composite herbs having showy flower heads with mostly yellow ray flowers and a usu. conical scaly receptacle

rudd \ˈrəd, ˈru̇d\ *n* [prob. fr. *rud* redness, red ocher, fr. ME *rude,* fr. OE *rudu* — more at RUDDY] (1526) : a freshwater Eurasian cyprinid fish (*Scardinius erythrophthalmus*) resembling the golden shiner

rud·der \ˈrə-dər\ *n* [ME *rother,* fr. OE *rōther* paddle; akin to OE *rōwan* to row] (14c) **1** : an underwater blade that is positioned at the stern of a boat or ship and controlled by its helm and that when turned causes the vessel's head to turn in the same direction **2** : a movable auxiliary airfoil on an airplane usu. attached at the rear end that serves to control direction of flight in the horizontal plane — see AIRPLANE illustration **3** : a guiding force or strategy — **rud·der·less** \-ləs\ *adj*

rud·der·post \-ˌpōst\ *n* (1691) **1** : the shaft of a rudder **2** : an additional sternpost in a ship with a single screw propeller to which the rudder is attached

[1]**rud·dle** \ˈrə-dᵊl\ *n* [dim. of *rud* red ocher] (1538) : RED OCHER

[2]**ruddle** *vt* **rud·dled; rud·dling** \ˈrəd-liŋ, ˈrə-dᵊl-iŋ\ (1718) : to color with or as if with red ocher : REDDEN

rud·dock \ˈrə-dək, ˈru̇-\ *n* [ME *ruddok,* fr. OE *rudduc;* akin to OE *rudu*] (bef. 12c) *archaic* : ROBIN 1a

rud·dy \ˈrə-dē\ *adj* **rud·di·er; -est** [ME *rudi,* fr. OE *rudig,* fr. *rudu* redness; akin to OE *rēad* red — more at RED] (bef. 12c) **1** : having a healthy reddish color **2** : RED, REDDISH **3** *Brit* — used as an intensive ⟨bellowed like a ~ bull when she wanted food —Doreen Tovey⟩ — **rud·di·ly** \ˈrə-dᵊl-ē\ *adv* — **rud·di·ness** \ˈrə-dē-nəs\ *n*

ruddy duck *n* (1814) : an American duck (*Oxyura jamaicensis*) with a long tail of stiff feathers, a broad bill, and in the breeding male a brownish-red back and sides and a blue bill

rude \ˈrüd\ *adj* **rud·er; rud·est** [ME, fr. AF, fr. L *rudis;* prob. akin to L *rudus* rubble] (14c) **1 a** : being in a rough or unfinished state : CRUDE **b** : NATURAL, RAW ⟨~ cotton⟩ **c** : PRIMITIVE, UNDEVELOPED ⟨peasants use ~ wooden plows —Jack Raymond⟩ **d** : SIMPLE, ELEMENTAL **2** : lacking refinement or delicacy: **a** : IGNORANT, UNLEARNED **b** : INELEGANT, UNCOUTH **c** : offensive in manner or action : DISCOURTEOUS **d** : UNCIVILIZED, SAVAGE **e** : COARSE, VULGAR **3** : marked by or suggestive of lack of training or skill : INEXPERIENCED ⟨~ workmanship⟩ **4** : ROBUST, STURDY ⟨in ~ health⟩ **5** : occurring abruptly and disconcertingly ⟨a ~ awakening⟩ — **rude·ly** *adv*

syn RUDE, ROUGH, CRUDE, RAW mean lacking in social refinement. RUDE implies ignorance of or indifference to good form; it may suggest intentional discourtesy ⟨*rude* behavior⟩. ROUGH is likely to stress lack of polish and gentleness ⟨*rough* manners⟩. CRUDE may apply to thought or behavior limited to the gross, the obvious, or the primitive ⟨a *crude* joke⟩. RAW suggests being untested, inexperienced, or unfinished ⟨turning *raw* youths into polished performers⟩.

rude·ness *n* (14c) **1** : the quality or state of being rude **2** : a rude action

[1]**ru·der·al** \ˈrü-də-rəl\ *adj* [NL *ruderalis,* fr. L *ruder-, rudus* rubble] (ca. 1858) : growing where the natural vegetational cover has been disturbed by humans ⟨~ weeds of old fields and roadsides⟩

[2]**ruderal** *n* (ca. 1928) : a weedy and commonly introduced plant growing where the vegetational cover has been interrupted

ru·di·ment \ˈrü-də-mənt\ *n* [L *rudimentum* beginning, fr. *rudis* raw, rude] (1548) **1** : a basic principle or element or a fundamental skill — usu. used in pl. ⟨teaching themselves the ~*s* of rational government —G. B. Galanti⟩ **2 a** : something unformed or undeveloped : BEGINNING — usu. used in pl. ⟨the ~*s* of a plan⟩ **b** (1) : a body part so deficient in size or structure as to be entirely unable to perform its normal function (2) : an organ just beginning to develop : ANLAGE — **ru·di·men·tal** \ˌrü-də-ˈmen-tᵊl\ *adj*

ru·di·men·ta·ry \ˌrü-də-ˈmen-tə-rē, -ˈmen-trē\ *adj* (1839) **1** : consisting in first principles : FUNDAMENTAL ⟨had only a ~ formal education —D. J. Boorstin⟩ **2** : of a primitive kind ⟨the equipment of these past empire-builders was ~ —A. J. Toynbee⟩ **3** : very imperfectly developed or represented only by a vestige ⟨the ~ tail of a hyrax⟩ — **ru·di·men·tar·i·ly** \-ˌmen-ˈter-ə-lē, -ˈmen-trə-lē\ *adv* — **ru·di·men·ta·ri·ness** \-ˈmen-tə-rē-nəs, -ˈmen-trē-\ *n*

[1]**rue** \ˈrü\ *n* [ME *rewe,* fr. OE *hrēow;* akin to OHG *hriuwa* sorrow] (bef. 12c) : REGRET, SORROW ⟨with ~ my heart is laden —A. E. Housman⟩

[2]**rue** *vb* **rued; ru·ing** *vt* (12c) : to feel penitence, remorse, or regret for ~ *vi* : to feel sorrow, remorse, or regret

[3]**rue** *n* [ME, fr. AF, fr. L *ruta,* fr. Gk *rhytē*] (13c) : a European strong-scented perennial woody herb (*Ruta graveolens* of the family Rutaceae, the rue family) that has bitter leaves used medicinally

rue anemone *n* (ca. 1818) : a delicate vernal No. American herb (*Anemonella thalictroides*) of the buttercup family that has white flowers resembling those of the wood anemone and basal leaves

rue·ful \ˈrü-fəl\ *adj* (13c) **1** : exciting pity or sympathy : PITIABLE ⟨~ squalid poverty . . . by every wayside —John Morley⟩ **2** : MOURNFUL, REGRETFUL ⟨troubled her with a ~ disquiet —W. M. Thackeray⟩ — **rue·ful·ly** \-fə-lē\ *adv* — **rue·ful·ness** *n*

ru·fes·cent \rü-ˈfe-sᵊnt\ *adj* [L *rufescent-, rufescens,* prp. of *rufescere* to become reddish, fr. *rufus* red — more at RED] (1817) : REDDISH

[1]**ruff** *or* **ruffe** \ˈrəf\ *n* [ME *ruf*] (15c) : a small freshwater European perch (*Acerina cernua*)

[2]**ruff** *n* [prob. back-formation fr. *ruffle*] (1555) **1** : a large round collar of pleated muslin or linen worn by men and women of the late 16th and early 17th centuries **2** : a fringe or frill of long hairs or feathers growing around or on the neck of an animal **3** : a common Eurasian sandpiper (*Philomachus pugnax*) whose male during the breeding season has a large ruff of erectile feathers on the neck — **ruffed** \ˈrəft\ *adj*

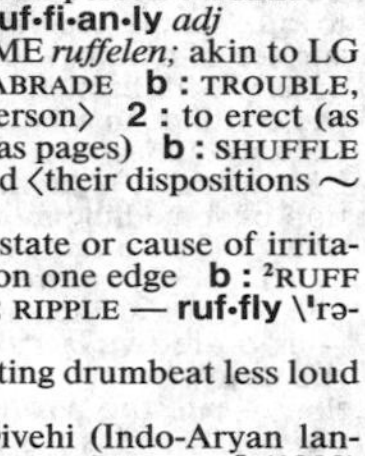

ruff 1

[3]**ruff** *vb* [MF *roffler*] *vi* (1598) : to take a trick with a trump ~ *vt* : to play a trump on (a card previously led or played)

[4]**ruff** *n* (ca. 1828) : the act of trumping

ruffed grouse *n* (ca. 1782) : a grouse (*Bonasa umbellus*) of U.S. and Canadian forests of which the male erects a ruff of black feathers and fans out a broad black-banded tail during breeding displays

ruf·fi·an \ˈrə-fē-ən\ *n* [MF *rufian*] (1531) : a brutal person : BULLY — **ruffian** *adj* — **ruf·fi·an·ism** \-ə-ˌni-zəm\ *n* — **ruf·fi·an·ly** *adj*

[1]**ruf·fle** \ˈrə-fəl\ *vb* **ruf·fled; ruf·fling** \-f(ə-)liŋ\ [ME *ruffelen;* akin to LG *ruffelen* to crumple] *vt* (14c) **1 a** : ROUGHEN, ABRADE **b** : TROUBLE, VEX ⟨is not *ruffled* by such barbs —Bruce Anderson⟩ **2** : to erect (as feathers) in or like a ruff **3 a** : to flip through (as pages) **b** : SHUFFLE **4** : to make into a ruffle ~ *vi* : to become ruffled ⟨their dispositions ~ perceptibly —*Life*⟩

[2]**ruffle** *n* (1534) **1** : COMMOTION, BRAWL **2** : a state or cause of irritation **3 a** : a strip of fabric gathered or pleated on one edge **b** : [2]RUFF 2 **4** : an unevenness or disturbance of surface : RIPPLE — **ruf·fly** \ˈrə-f(ə-)lē\ *adj*

[3]**ruffle** *n* [*ruff* a drumbeat] (ca. 1802) : a low vibrating drumbeat less loud than a roll

ru·fi·yaa \ˈrü-fē-ˌyä\ *n, pl* **rufiyaa** [prob. fr. Divehi (Indo-Aryan language of the Maldive Islands), fr. Hindi *rupīyā, rūpaiyā* rupee] (1982) — see MONEY table

RU-486 \ˈär-ˌyü-ˌfȯr-ˌā-tē-ˈsiks\ *n* [*R*oussel-*U*CLAF, the drug's Fr. manufacturer + *486,* laboratory serial number] (1983) : a drug $C_{29}H_{35}NO_2$ taken orally to induce abortion esp. early in pregnancy by blocking the body's use of progesterone — called also *mifepristone*

ru·fous \ˈrü-fəs\ *adj* [L *rufus* red — more at RED] (1782) : REDDISH

rug \ˈrəg\ *n* [ME **rug* rag, tuft, prob. of Scand origin; akin to Norw dial. *rugga* coarse rug, ON *rǫgg* tuft] (1591) **1** : LAP ROBE **2** : a piece of thick heavy fabric that usu. has a nap or pile and is used as a floor covering **3** : a floor mat of an animal pelt ⟨a bearskin ~⟩ **4** *slang* : TOUPEE 2 **5** *Brit* : a blanket for an animal (as a horse or dog)

ru·ga \ˈrü-gə\ *n, pl* **ru·gae** \-ˌgī, -ˌgē, -ˌjē\ [NL, fr. L, wrinkle — more at CORRUGATE] (1775) : an anatomical fold or wrinkle (as of the gastric mucous membranes) — usu. used in pl.

rug·by \ˈrəg-bē\ *n, often cap* [*Rugby* School, Rugby, England] (1864) : a football game in which play is continuous without time-outs or substitutions, interference and forward passing are not permitted, and kicking, dribbling, lateral passing, and tackling are featured

rug·e·lach *also* **rug·a·lach** \ˈrü-gə-lək\ *n, pl* **-lach** [Yiddish *rugelekh, rogelekh,* pl. of *rugele, rogele,* dim. of *rog* corner, of Slav origin; akin to Pol *róg* horn, corner] (1941) : a pastry made with cream-cheese dough that is rolled around a filling (as nuts, jam, or chocolate) and baked

rug·ged \ˈrə-gəd\ *adj* [ME, fr. ME **rug*] (14c) **1** *obs* : SHAGGY, HAIRY **2** : having a rough uneven surface : JAGGED ⟨~ mountains⟩ **3** : TURBULENT, STORMY ⟨~ weather⟩ **4 a** : seamed with wrinkles and furrows : WEATHERED — used of a human face **b** : showing facial signs of strength ⟨~ good looks⟩ **5 a** : AUSTERE, STERN **b** : COARSE, RUDE **c** : rough and strong in character **6 a** : presenting a severe test of ability, stamina, or resolution **b** : strongly built or constituted : ROBUST ⟨those that survive are stalwart, ~ men —L. D. Stamp⟩ ***syn*** see ROUGH — **rug·ged·ly** *adv* — **rug·ged·ness** *n*

rug·ged·ize \ˈrə-gə-ˌdīz\ *vt* **-ized; -iz·ing** (1950) : to strengthen (as a machine) for better resistance to wear, stress, and abuse ⟨a *ruggedized* camera⟩ — **rug·ged·i·za·tion** \ˌrə-gə-də-ˈzā-shən\ *n*

rug·ger \ˈrə-gər\ *n* [by alter.] (1893) *Brit* : RUGBY; *also* : a rugby player

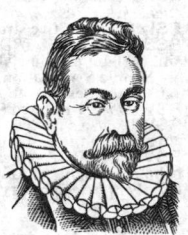

ru·go·la \ˈrü-gə-lə\ *n* [prob. fr. It dial.; akin to It dial. *ruga* arugula, It *ruca* — more at ROCKET] (1973) : ARUGULA
ru·go·sa rose \rü-ˈgō-sə-, -zə-\ *n* [NL *rugosa,* specific epithet of *Rosa rugosa* rugose rose] (1892) : any of various hardy thorny garden roses descended from a rose (*Rosa rugosa*) introduced from China and Japan — called also *rugosa*
ru·gose \ˈrü-ˌgōs\ *adj* [L *rugosus,* fr. *ruga*] (1676) **1** : full of wrinkles ⟨~ cheeks⟩ **2** : having the veinlets sunken and the spaces between elevated ⟨~ leaves of the sage⟩ — **ru·gos·i·ty** \rü-ˈgä-sə-tē\ *n*
rug rat *n* (1975) *slang* : a child not yet old enough for school
ru·gu·lose \ˈrü-gyə-ˌlōs\ *adj* [NL *rugula,* dim. of L *ruga*] (ca. 1819) : having small rugae : finely wrinkled
[1]**ru·in** \ˈrü-ən, -ˌin; ˈrün\ *n* [ME *ruine,* fr. AF, fr. L *ruina,* fr. *ruere* to rush headlong, fall, collapse] (12c) **1 a** *archaic* : a falling down : COLLAPSE ⟨from age to age . . . the crash of ~ fitfully resounds —William Wordsworth⟩ **b** : physical, moral, economic, or social collapse **2 a** : the state of being ruined — archaic except in pl. ⟨the city lay in ~*s*⟩ **b** : the remains of something destroyed — usu. used in pl. ⟨the ~*s* of an ancient temple⟩ ⟨the ~*s* of his life⟩ **3** : a cause of destruction **4 a** : the action of destroying, laying waste, or wrecking **b** : DAMAGE, INJURY **5** : a ruined building, person, or object — **ru·in·ate** \ˈrü-ə-ˌnāt, -nət\ *adj* — **ruinate** \-ˌnāt\ *vt*
[2]**ruin** *vt* (1585) **1** : to reduce to ruins : DEVASTATE **2 a** : to damage irreparably **b** : BANKRUPT, IMPOVERISH ⟨~*ed* by stock speculation⟩ **3** : to subject to frustration, failure, or disaster ⟨will ~ your chances of promotion⟩ ~ *vi* : to become ruined — **ru·in·er** *n*
ru·in·a·tion \ˌrü-ə-ˈnā-shən\ *n* (1664) : RUIN, DESTRUCTION
ru·in·ous \ˈrü-ə-nəs\ *adj* (14c) **1** : DILAPIDATED, RUINED **2** : causing or tending to cause ruin — **ru·in·ous·ly** *adv* — **ru·in·ous·ness** *n*
[1]**rule** \ˈrül\ *n* [ME *reule,* fr. AF, fr. L *regula* straightedge, rule, fr. *regere* to keep straight, direct — more at RIGHT] (13c) **1 a** : a prescribed guide for conduct or action **b** : the laws or regulations prescribed by the founder of a religious order for observance by its members **c** : an accepted procedure, custom, or habit **d (1)** : a usu. written order or direction made by a court regulating court practice or the action of parties **(2)** : a legal precept or doctrine **e** : a regulation or bylaw governing procedure or controlling conduct **2 a (1)** : a usu. valid generalization **(2)** : a generally prevailing quality, state, or mode ⟨fair weather was the ~ yesterday —*N.Y. Times*⟩ **b** : a standard of judgment : CRITERION **c** : a regulating principle **d** : a determinate method for performing a mathematical operation and obtaining a certain result **3 a** : the exercise of authority or control : DOMINION **b** : a period during which a specified ruler or government exercises control **4 a** : a strip of material marked off in units used esp. for measuring : RULER 3, TAPE MEASURE **b** : a metal strip with a type-high face that prints a linear design; *also* : a linear design produced by or as if by such a strip ***syn*** see LAW — **as a rule** : for the most part : GENERALLY
[2]**rule** *vb* **ruled; rul·ing** *vt* (13c) **1 a** : to exert control, direction, or influence on ⟨the passions that ~ our minds⟩ **b** : to exercise control over esp. by curbing or restraining ⟨~ a fractious horse⟩ ⟨*ruled* his appetites firmly⟩ **2 a** : to exercise authority or power over often harshly or arbitrarily ⟨the speaker *ruled* the legislature with an iron hand⟩ **b** : to be preeminent in : DOMINATE **3** : to determine and declare authoritatively; *esp* : to command or determine judicially **4 a (1)** : to mark with lines drawn along or as if along the straight edge of a ruler **(2)** : to mark (a line) on a paper with a ruler **b** : to arrange in a line ~ *vi* **1 a** : to exercise supreme authority **b** : to be first in importance or prominence : PREDOMINATE ⟨the physical did not ~ in her nature —Sherwood Anderson⟩ **2** : to exist in a specified state or condition **3** : to lay down a legal rule **4** *slang* : to be extremely cool or popular — used as a generalized term of praise or approval ⟨for a little attitude at the right price, sneakers ~ —Tish Hamilton⟩ ***syn*** see DECIDE
ruled surface *n* (1862) : a surface generated by a moving straight line with the result that through every point on the surface a line can be drawn lying wholly in the surface
rule·less \ˈrül-ləs\ *adj* (15c) : not restrained or regulated by law
rule of the road (1871) : a customary practice (as driving always on a particular side of the road or yielding the right of way) developed in the interest of safety and often subsequently reinforced by law; *esp* : any of the rules making up a code governing ships in matters relating to mutual safety
rule of thumb (1692) **1** : a method of procedure based on experience and common sense **2** : a general principle regarded as roughly correct but not intended to be scientifically accurate
rule out *vt* (1869) **1** : EXCLUDE, ELIMINATE **2** : to make impossible : PREVENT ⟨heavy rain *ruled out* the picnic⟩
rul·er \ˈrü-lər\ *n* (14c) **1** : one that rules; *specif* : SOVEREIGN **2** : a worker or a machine that rules paper **3** : a smooth-edged strip (as of wood or metal) that is usu. marked off in units (as inches) and is used as a straightedge or for measuring — **rul·er·ship** \-ˌship\ *n*
[1]**ruling** *n* (15c) : an official or authoritative decision, decree, statement, or interpretation (as by a judge on a point of law)
[2]**ruling** *adj* (1593) **1 a** : exerting power or authority ⟨the ~ party⟩ **b** : CHIEF, PREDOMINATING ⟨a ~ passion⟩ **2** : generally prevailing
ruly \ˈrü-lē\ *adj* [back-formation fr. *unruly*] (1837) : OBEDIENT, ORDERLY ⟨a ~ crowd⟩
[1]**rum** \ˈrəm\ *n* [prob. short for obs. *rumbullion* rum] (1654) **1** : an alcoholic beverage distilled from a fermented cane product (as molasses) **2** : alcoholic liquor ⟨the demon ~⟩
[2]**rum** *adj* **rum·mer; rum·mest** [origin unknown] (1752) **1** *chiefly Brit* : QUEER, ODD ⟨writing is a ~ trade —Angela Thirkell⟩ **2** *chiefly Brit* : DIFFICULT, DANGEROUS
Rumanian *var of* ROMANIAN
rum·ba *also* **rhum·ba** \ˈrəm-bə, ˈrüm-, ˈrüm-\ *n* [AmerSp] (1916) : a ballroom dance of Cuban origin in 2/4 or 4/4 time with a basic pattern of step-close-step and marked by a delayed transfer of weight and pronounced hip movements; *also* : the music for this dance
[1]**rum·ble** \ˈrəm-bəl\ *vb* **rum·bled; rum·bling** \-b(ə-)liŋ\ [ME; akin to MHG *rummeln* to rumble] *vi* (14c) **1** : to make a low heavy rolling sound ⟨thunder *rumbling* in the distance⟩ **2** : to travel with a low reverberating sound ⟨wagons *rumbled* into town⟩ **3** : to speak in a low rolling tone **4** : to engage in a rumble ~ *vt* **1** : to utter or emit in a low rolling voice **2** *Brit* : to reveal or discover the true character of — **rum·bler** \-b(ə-)lər\ *n*
[2]**rumble** *n* (14c) **1 a** : a low heavy continuous reverberating often muffled sound (as of thunder) **b** : low frequency noise in phonographic playback caused by the transmission of mechanical vibrations by the turntable to the pickup **2** : a seat for servants behind the body of a carriage **3 a** : widespread expression of dissatisfaction or unrest **b** : a street fight esp. among gangs
rumble seat *n* (1912) : a folding seat in the back of an automobile (as a coupe or roadster) not covered by the top
rumble strip *n* (1962) : a strip of corrugated pavement (as along the edge of a highway) that causes rumbling and vibration when driven over
rumbling *n* (14c) **1** : RUMBLE **2** : general but unofficial talk or opinion often of dissatisfaction — usu. used in pl. ⟨~*s* of political trouble —Anthony Burgess⟩
rum·bly \ˈrəm-b(ə-)lē\ *adj* (1874) : tending to rumble or rattle
rum·bus·tious \ˌrəm-ˈbəs-chəs\ *adj* [alter. of *robustious*] (1778) *chiefly Brit* : RAMBUNCTIOUS — **rum·bus·tious·ly** *adv, chiefly Brit* — **rum·bus·tious·ness** *n, chiefly Brit*
ru·men \ˈrü-mən\ *n, pl* **ru·mi·na** \-mə-nə\ *or* **rumens** [NL *rumin-, rumen,* fr. L] (ca. 1728) : the large first compartment of the stomach of a ruminant in which cellulose is broken down by the action of symbiotic microorganisms — compare ABOMASUM, OMASUM, RETICULUM — **ru·mi·nal** \-mə-nᵊl\ *adj*
[1]**ru·mi·nant** \ˈrü-mə-nənt\ *n* (1661) : a ruminant mammal
[2]**ruminant** *adj* (1691) **1 a (1)** : chewing the cud **(2)** : characterized by chewing again what has been swallowed **b** : of or relating to two suborders (Ruminantia and Tylopoda) of herbivorous even-toed hoofed mammals (as sheep, oxen, deer, and camels) that chew the cud and have a complex 3- or 4-chambered stomach **2** : given to or engaged in contemplation : MEDITATIVE ⟨stood there . . . in this attitude of ~ relish —Thomas Wolfe⟩ — **ru·mi·nant·ly** *adv*
ru·mi·nate \ˈrü-mə-ˌnāt\ *vb* **-nat·ed; -nat·ing** [L *ruminatus,* pp. of *ruminari* to chew the cud, muse upon, fr. *rumin-, rumen* rumen; perh. akin to Skt *romantha* act of chewing the cud] *vt* (1533) **1** : to go over in the mind repeatedly and often casually or slowly **2** : to chew repeatedly for an extended period ~ *vi* **1** : to chew again what has been chewed slightly and swallowed : chew the cud **2** : to engage in contemplation : REFLECT ***syn*** see PONDER — **ru·mi·na·tion** \ˌrü-mə-ˈnā-shən\ *n* — **ru·mi·na·tive** \ˈrü-mə-ˌnā-tiv\ *adj* — **ru·mi·na·tive·ly** *adv* — **ru·mi·na·tor** \-ˌnā-tər\ *n*
[1]**rum·mage** \ˈrə-mij\ *vb* **rum·maged; rum·mag·ing** [[2]*rummage*] *vi* (1582) **1** : to make a thorough search or investigation **2** : to engage in an undirected or haphazard search ~ *vt* **1** : to make a thorough search through : RANSACK ⟨*rummaged* the attic⟩ **2** : to examine minutely and completely **3** : to discover by searching — **rum·mag·er** *n*
[2]**rummage** *n* [obs. E *romage* act of stowing cargo, modif. of MF *arrimage,* fr. *arrimer* to stow, fr. *a-* (fr. L *ad-*) + *-rimer,* fr. ME *rimen* to open up, make room for, fr. OE *rȳman* — more at REAM] (1598) **1 a** : a confused miscellaneous collection **b** : items for sale at a rummage sale **2** : a thorough search esp. among a confusion of objects
rummage sale *n* (ca. 1858) : a usu. informal sale of miscellaneous goods; *esp* : a sale of donated articles conducted by a nonprofit organization (as a church or charity) to help support its programs
rum·mer \ˈrə-mər\ *n* [G or D; G *Römer,* fr. D *roemer*] (1654) : a large-bowled footed drinking glass often elaborately etched or engraved
[1]**rum·my** \ˈrə-mē\ *adj* **rum·mi·er; -est** [[2]*rum*] (1828) : QUEER, ODD ⟨feeling a little ~ from our trip up the escalator —*New Yorker*⟩
[2]**rummy** *n, pl* **rummies** [[1]*rum*] (1851) : DRUNKARD
[3]**rummy** *n* [perh. fr. [1]*rummy*] (1915) : any of several card games for two or more players in which each player tries to assemble groups of three or more cards of the same rank or suit and to be the first to meld them all
[1]**ru·mor** \ˈrü-mər\ *n* [ME *rumour,* fr. AF, fr. L *rumor* clamor, gossip; akin to OE *rēon* to lament, Skt *rauti* he roars] (14c) **1** : talk or opinion widely disseminated with no discernible source **2** : a statement or report current without known authority for its truth **3** *archaic* : talk or report of a notable person or event **4** : a soft low indistinct sound : MURMUR
[2]**rumor** *vt* **ru·mored; ru·mor·ing** (1594) : to tell or spread by rumor
ru·mor·mon·ger \-ˌməŋ-gər, -ˌmäŋ-\ *n* (1884) : a person who spreads rumors — **ru·mor·mon·ger·ing** \-gər-iŋ\ *n*
ru·mour \ˈrü-mər\ *chiefly Brit var of* RUMOR
rump \ˈrəmp\ *n* [ME, of Scand origin; akin to Dan *rumpe* rump; akin to MHG *rumph* torso] (15c) **1 a** : the upper rounded part of the hindquarters of a quadruped mammal **b** : BUTTOCKS **c** : the sacral or dorsal part of the posterior end of a bird **2** : a cut of meat (as beef) between the loin and round — see BEEF illustration **3** : a small or inferior remnant or offshoot; *esp* : a group (as a parliament) carrying on in the name of the original body after the departure or expulsion of a large number of its members
[1]**rum·ple** \ˈrəm-pəl\ *n* (ca. 1520) : FOLD, WRINKLE
[2]**rumple** *vb* **rum·pled; rum·pling** \-p(ə-)liŋ\ [D *rompelen;* akin to OHG *rimpfan* to wrinkle] *vt* (1603) **1** : WRINKLE, CRUMPLE **2** : to make unkempt : TOUSLE ~ *vi* : to become rumpled
rum·ply \ˈrəm-p(ə-)lē\ *adj* **rum·pli·er; -est** (1833) : having rumples
rum·pus \ˈrəm-pəs\ *n* [origin unknown] (1764) : a usu. noisy commotion
rumpus room *n* (1939) : a room usu. in the basement of a home that is used for games, parties, and recreation
rum·run·ner \ˈrəm-ˌrə-nər\ *n* (1920) : a person or ship engaged in bringing prohibited liquor ashore or across a border — **rum–run·ning** \-ˌrə-niŋ\ *adj or n*
[1]**run** \ˈrən\ *vb* **ran** \ˈran\ *also chiefly dial* **run; run; run·ning** [ME *ronnen,* alter. of *rinnen,* v.i. (fr. OE *iernan, rinnan* & ON *rinna*) & of *rennen,* v.t., fr. ON *renna;* akin to OHG *rinnan,* v.i., to run, Skt *riṇāti* he causes to flow, and prob. to L *rivus* stream] *vi* (bef. 12c) **1 a** : to go faster than a walk; *specif* : to go steadily by springing steps so that both

feet leave the ground for an instant in each step **b** *of a horse* : to move at a fast gallop **c** : FLEE, RETREAT, ESCAPE ⟨dropped the gun and *ran*⟩ **d** : to utilize a running play on offense — used of a football team **2 a** : to go without restraint : move freely about at will ⟨let chickens ~ loose⟩ **b** : to keep company : CONSORT ⟨a ram *running* with ewes⟩ ⟨*ran* with a wild crowd when he was young⟩ **c** : to sail before the wind in distinction from reaching or sailing close-hauled **d** : ROAM, ROVE ⟨*running* about with no overcoat⟩ **3 a** : to go rapidly or hurriedly : HASTEN ⟨~ and fetch the doctor⟩ **b** : to go in urgency or distress : RESORT ⟨~*s* to mother at every little difficulty⟩ **c** : to make a quick, easy, or casual trip or visit ⟨*ran* over to borrow some sugar⟩ **4 a** : to contend in a race **b** : to enter into an election contest ⟨will ~ for mayor⟩ **5 a** : to move on or as if on wheels : GLIDE ⟨file drawers *running* on ball bearings⟩ **b** : to roll forward rapidly or freely **c** : to pass or slide freely ⟨a rope ~*s* through the pulley⟩ **d** : to ravel lengthwise ⟨stockings guaranteed not to ~⟩ **6** : to sing or play a musical passage quickly ⟨~ up the scale⟩ **7 a** : to go back and forth : PLY ⟨the train ~*s* between New York and Washington⟩ **b** *of fish* : to migrate or move in considerable numbers; *esp* : to move up or down a river to spawn **8 a** : TURN, ROTATE ⟨a swiftly *running* grindstone⟩ **b** : FUNCTION, OPERATE ⟨the engine ~*s* on gasoline⟩ ⟨software that ~*s* on her computer⟩ **9 a** (1) : to continue in force, operation, or production ⟨the contract has two more years to ~⟩ ⟨the play *ran* for six months⟩ (2) : to have a specified duration, extent, or length ⟨the manuscript ~*s* nearly 500 pages⟩ **b** : to accompany as a valid obligation or right ⟨a right-of-way that ~*s* with the land⟩ **c** : to continue to accrue or become payable ⟨interest on the loan ~*s* from July 1⟩ **10** : to pass from one state to another ⟨~ into debt⟩ **11 a** : to flow rapidly or under pressure **b** : MELT, FUSE **c** : SPREAD, DISSOLVE ⟨colors guaranteed not to ~⟩ **d** : to discharge liquid (as pus or serum) ⟨a *running* sore⟩ **12 a** : to develop rapidly in some specific direction; *esp* : to throw out an elongated shoot of growth **b** : to tend to produce or develop a specified quality or feature ⟨they ~ to big noses in that family⟩ **13 a** : to lie in or take a certain direction ⟨the boundary line ~*s* east⟩ **b** : to lie or extend in relation to something **c** : to go back : REACH **d** (1) : to be in a certain form or expression ⟨the letter ~*s* as follows⟩ (2) : to be in a certain order of succession **14 a** : to occur persistently ⟨musical talent ~*s* in the family⟩ **b** (1) : to remain of a specified size, amount, character, or quality ⟨profits were *running* high⟩ (2) : to have or maintain a relative position or condition (as in a race) ⟨*ran* third⟩ ⟨*running* late⟩ **c** : to exist or occur in a continuous range of variation ⟨shades ~ from white to dark gray⟩ **15 a** : to spread or pass quickly from point to point ⟨chills *ran* up her spine⟩ **b** : to be current : CIRCULATE ⟨speculation *ran* rife⟩ ~ *vt* **1 a** : to cause (an animal) to go rapidly : ride or drive fast **b** : to bring to a specified condition by or as if by running ⟨*ran* himself to death⟩ **c** : to go in pursuit of : HUNT, CHASE ⟨dogs that ~ deer⟩ **d** : to follow the trail of backward : TRACE ⟨*ran* the rumor to its source⟩ **e** : to enter, register, or enroll as a contestant in a race **f** : to put forward as a candidate for office **g** : to carry (the football) on a running play **2 a** : to drive (livestock) esp. to a grazing place **b** : to provide pasturage for (livestock) **c** : to keep or maintain (livestock) on or as if on pasturage **3 a** (1) : to pass over or traverse with speed (2) : to run on or over in athletic competition ⟨~*s* the bases well⟩ ⟨~ the floor⟩ **b** : to accomplish or perform by or as if by running ⟨*ran* a great race⟩ ⟨~ errands⟩ **c** : to slip or go through or past ⟨~ a blockade⟩ ⟨~ a red light⟩ **d** : to travel on (as a river) in a boat ⟨~ the rapids⟩ **4 a** : to cause to penetrate or enter : THRUST ⟨*ran* a splinter into her toe⟩ **b** : STITCH **c** : to cause to pass : LEAD ⟨~ a wire in from the antenna⟩ **d** : to cause to collide ⟨*ran* his head into a post⟩ **e** : SMUGGLE ⟨~ guns⟩ **5** : to cause to pass lightly or quickly over, along, or into something ⟨*ran* her eye down the list⟩ **6 a** : to cause or allow (as a vehicle or a vessel) to go in a specified manner or direction ⟨*ran* the car off the road⟩ **b** : OPERATE ⟨~ a lathe⟩ **c** : to direct the business or activities of : MANAGE, CONDUCT ⟨~ a factory⟩ **d** : to employ or supervise in espionage ⟨~ an agent⟩ **7 a** : to be full of or drenched with ⟨streets *ran* blood⟩ **b** : CONTAIN, ASSAY **8 a** : to cause to move or flow in a specified way or into a specified position ⟨~ cards into a file⟩ **b** : to cause to produce a flow (as of water) ⟨~ the faucet⟩; *also* : to prepare by running a faucet ⟨~ a hot bath⟩ **9 a** : to melt and cast in a mold ⟨~ bullets⟩ **b** : TREAT, PROCESS, REFINE ⟨~ oil in a still⟩ ⟨~ a problem through a computer⟩ **10** : to make oneself liable to : INCUR ⟨*ran* the risk of discovery⟩ **11** : to mark out : DRAW ⟨~ a contour line on a map⟩ **12 a** : to permit (as charges) to accumulate before settling ⟨~ a tab at the bar⟩ — often used with *up* ⟨*ran* up a large phone bill⟩ **b** : COST 1 ⟨rooms that ~ $50 a night⟩ **13 a** : to produce by or as if by printing — usu. used with *off* ⟨*ran* off 10,000 copies of the first edition⟩ **b** : to carry in a printed medium : PRINT ⟨every newspaper *ran* the story⟩ **14 a** : to make (a series of counts) without a miss ⟨~ 19 in an inning in billiards⟩ **b** : to lead winning cards of (a suit) successively **c** : to alter by addition ⟨*ran* his record to six wins and four losses⟩ **15** : to make (a golf ball) roll forward after alighting — **run across** : to meet with or discover by chance — **run a fever** *or* **run a temperature** : to have a fever — **run after 1** : PURSUE, CHASE; *esp* : to seek the company of **2** : to take up with : FOLLOW ⟨*run after* new theories⟩ — **run against 1** : to meet suddenly or unexpectedly **2** : to work or take effect unfavorably to : DISFAVOR, OPPOSE — **run a tight ship** : to have strict and exacting standards in controlling or managing something (as a business) — **run by** *or* **run past** : to present to (as for evaluation) ⟨*ran* some ideas *by* her⟩ — **run circles around** *or* **run rings around** : to show marked superiority over : defeat decisively or overwhelmingly — **run dry 1** : to use up an available supply **2** : to become exhausted or spent ⟨his inspiration had *run dry*⟩ — **run interference** : to provide assistance by or as if by clearing a path through obstructions ⟨*ran interference* for me with the press⟩ — **run into 1 a** : to change or transform into : BECOME **b** : to merge with **c** : to mount up to ⟨their yearly income often *runs into* six figures⟩ **2 a** : to collide with **b** : to meet by chance ⟨*ran into* an old classmate the other day⟩ — **run low on** : to approach running out of ⟨*running low on* options⟩ — **run one's mouth** : to talk excessively or foolishly — **run riot 1** : to act wildly or without restraint **2** : to occur in profusion ⟨daffodils *running riot*⟩ — **run short** : to become insufficient — **run short of** : to use up : run low on — **run the numbers** : to perform calculations — **run the table 1** : to sink all remaining shots without missing in pool **2** : to win all remaining contests — **run to** : to mount up to ⟨the book *runs to* 500 pages⟩ — **run upon** : to run across : meet with — **run with 1** : to use or exploit fully : make the most of ⟨took the idea and *ran with* it⟩ **2** : to publicize widely ⟨the press *ran with* the quote⟩

usage The past tense *run* still survives in speech in southern England and in the speech esp. of older people in some parts of the U.S. It was formerly used in literature, and was a standard variant in our dictionaries from 1828 until 1934. Grammarians have generally opposed it, and many people consider it nonstandard. Just about everybody uses *ran* in writing now.

[2]**run** *n* (14c) **1 a** : an act or the action of running : continued rapid movement **b** : a quickened gallop **c** : a migration of fish (as up or down a river) esp. to spawn; *also* : such fish in the process of migration **d** : a running race ⟨a mile ~⟩ **e** : a score made in baseball by a runner reaching home plate safely **f** : strength or ability to run **g** : a gain of a usu. specified distance made on a running play in football ⟨scored on a 25-yard ~⟩; *also* : a running play **h** : a sustained usu. aggressive effort (as to win or obtain something) ⟨making a ~ at the championship⟩ **2 a** *chiefly Midland* : CREEK 2 **b** : something that flows in the course of an operation or during a particular time ⟨the first ~ of sap in sugar maples⟩ **3 a** : the stern of the underwater body of a ship from where it begins to curve or slope upward and inward **b** : the direction in which a vein of ore lies **c** : a direction of secondary or minor cleavage : GRAIN ⟨the ~ of a mass of granite⟩ **d** : a horizontal distance (as that covered by a flight of steps) **e** : general tendency or direction **4** : a continuous period or series esp. of things of identical or similar sort ⟨a ~ of bad luck⟩: as **a** : a rapid passage up or down a scale in vocal or instrumental music **b** : a number of rapid small dance steps executed in even tempo **c** : the act of making successively a number of successful shots or strokes; *also* : the score thus made ⟨a ~ of 20 in billiards⟩ **d** : an unbroken course of performances or showings ⟨a long ~ on Broadway⟩ **e** : a set of consecutive measurements, readings, or observations **f** : persistent and heavy demands from depositors, creditors, or customers ⟨a ~ on a bank⟩ **g** : SEQUENCE 2b **5** : the quantity of work turned out in a continuous operation ⟨a press ~ of 10,000 copies⟩ **6** : the usual or normal kind, character, type, or group ⟨the average ~ of students⟩ **7 a** : the distance covered in a period of continuous traveling or sailing **b** : a course or trip esp. if mapped out and traveled with regularity **c** : a news reporter's regular territory : BEAT **d** : freedom of movement in or access to a place or area ⟨has the ~ of the house⟩ **8 a** : the period during which a machine or plant is in continuous operation **b** : the use of machinery for a single set of processing procedures ⟨a computer ~⟩ **9 a** : a way, track, or path frequented by animals **b** : an enclosure for domestic animals where they may feed or exercise **c** *Austral* (1) : a large area of land used for grazing ⟨a sheep ~⟩ (2) : RANCH, STATION ⟨*run*-holder⟩ **d** : an inclined passageway **10 a** : an inclined course (as for skiing or bobsledding) **b** : a support (as a track, pipe, or trough) on which something runs **11 a** : a ravel in a knitted fabric (as in hosiery) caused by the breaking of stitches **b** : a paint defect caused by excessive flow **12** *pl but sing or pl in constr* : DIARRHEA — used with *the* — **run·less** \-ləs\ *adj* — **on the run 1** : in haste : without pausing ⟨ate lunch *on the run*⟩ **2** : in retreat : in flight (as from the law) ⟨an escaped convict *on the run*⟩ — **run for one's money** : a serious challenge to one's supremacy ⟨is expected to give the incumbent a good *run for his money*⟩

[3]**run** *adj* (1774) **1 a** : being in a melted state ⟨~ butter⟩ **b** : made from molten material : cast in a mold ⟨~ metal⟩ **2** *of fish* : having made a migration or spawning run ⟨a fresh ~ salmon⟩ **3** : exhausted or winded from running

run·about \ˈrə-nə-ˌbau̇t\ *n* (1549) **1** : one who wanders about : STRAY **2** : a light usu. open wagon, car, or motorboat

run·a·gate \ˈrə-nə-ˌgāt\ *n* [alter. of *renegate,* fr. ML *renegatus* — more at RENEGADE] (1547) **1** : VAGABOND **2** : FUGITIVE, RUNAWAY

run along *vi* (1902) : to go away : be on one's way : DEPART

run–and–gun *adj* (1977) : relating to or being a fast, freewheeling style of play in basketball that de-emphasizes set plays and defense

run–and–shoot *n, often attrib* (1977) : a freewheeling style of offense in football that emphasizes passing

run·around \ˈrə-nə-ˌrau̇nd\ *n* (1915) **1** : deceptive or delaying action esp. in response to a request ⟨tired of getting the ~⟩ **2** : matter typeset in shortened measure to run around something (as a cut)

[1]**run·away** \ˈrə-nə-ˌwā\ *n* (1547) **1** : one that runs away from danger, duty, or restraint : FUGITIVE **2** : the act of running away out of control; *also* : something (as a horse) that is running out of control **3** : a one-sided or overwhelming victory

[2]**runaway** *adj* (1548) **1 a** : running away : FUGITIVE **b** : leaving to gain special advantages (as lower wages) or avoid disadvantages (as governmental or union restrictions) ⟨~ shipping firms⟩ ⟨a ~ shop⟩ **2** : accomplished by elopement or during flight **3** : won by or having a long lead ⟨a ~ success⟩; *also* : extremely successful ⟨a ~ best seller⟩ **4** : subject to uncontrolled changes ⟨~ inflation⟩ **5** : being or operating out of control ⟨a ~ oil well⟩ ⟨a ~ nuclear reactor⟩

run away *vi* (13c) **1 a** : to leave quickly in order to avoid or escape something **b** : to leave home; *esp* : ELOPE **2** : to run out of control : STAMPEDE, BOLT **3** : to gain a substantial lead : win by a large margin — **run away with 1** : to take away in haste or secretly; *esp* : STEAL **2** : to outshine the others in (as a theatrical performance) **3** : to carry or drive beyond prudent or reasonable limits ⟨your imagination *ran away with* you⟩

run·back \ˈrən-ˌbak\ *n* (1929) : a run made in football after catching an opponent's kick or intercepting a pass

run·ci·ble spoon \ˈrən(t)-sə-bəl-\ *n* [coined with an obscure meaning by Edward Lear] (1871) : a sharp-edged fork with three broad curved prongs

run·ci·nate \ˈrən(t)-sə-ˌnāt\ *adj* [L *runcinatus,* pp. of *runcinare* to plane off, fr. *runcina* plane] (1776) : pinnately cut with the lobes pointing downward ⟨~ leaves of the dandelion⟩ — see LEAF illustration

run·dle \ˈrən-dᵊl\ *n* [ME *roundel* circle — more at ROUNDEL] (1565) **1** : a step of a ladder : RUNG **2** : the drum of a windlass or capstan

rund·let *or* **run·let** \ˈrən(d)-lət\ *n* [ME *roundelet,* fr. AF *rondelet* — more at ROUNDELAY] (14c) : a small barrel : KEG

run·down \ˈrən-ˌdau̇n\ *n* (1908) **1** : a play in baseball in which a base runner who is caught off base is chased by two or more opposing players who throw the ball from one to another in an attempt to tag the runner out **2 :** an item-by-item report or review : SUMMARY

run–down \ˈrən-ˈdau̇n\ *adj* (ca. 1821) **1 :** WORN-OUT, EXHAUSTED **2 :** completely unwound **3 :** being in poor repair : DILAPIDATED

run down *vt* (ca. 1578) **1 a :** to collide with and knock down **b :** to run against and cause to sink **2 a :** to chase to exhaustion or until captured **b :** to trace the source of **c :** to tag out (a base runner) between bases on a rundown **3 :** DISPARAGE **~** *vi* **1 :** to cease to operate because of the exhaustion of motive power ⟨the clock *ran down*⟩ **2 :** to decline in physical condition or vigor

rune \ˈrün\ *n* [ON & OE *rūn* mystery, runic character, writing; akin to OHG *rūna* secret discussion, OIr *rún* mystery] (1690) **1 :** any of the characters of any of several alphabets used by the Germanic peoples from about the 3d to the 13th centuries **2 :** MYSTERY, MAGIC **3** [Finn *runo,* of Gmc origin; akin to ON *rūn*] **a :** a Finnish or Old Norse poem **b :** POEM, SONG — **ru·nic** \ˈrü-nik\ *adj*

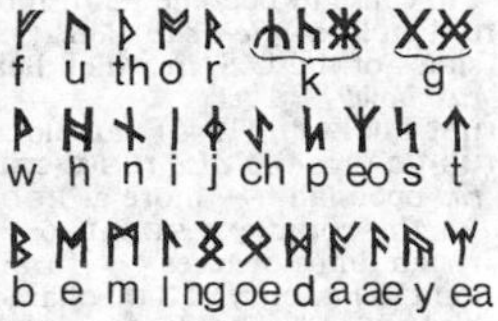
f u th o r k g
w h n i j ch p eo s t
b e m l ng oe d a ae y ea
rune 1: Anglo-Saxon runic alphabet

¹rung *past part of* RING

²rung \ˈrəŋ\ *n* [ME, fr. OE *hrung* crossbar; akin to Goth *hrunga* staff and perh. to OE *hring* ring — more at RING] (14c) **1 a :** a rounded crosspiece between the legs of a chair **b :** one of the crosspieces of a ladder **2** *Scot* **:** a heavy staff or cudgel **3 :** a spoke of a wheel **4 :** a level in a hierarchy ⟨rise a few **~***s* on the social scale —H. W. Van Loon⟩

run–in \ˈrən-ˌin\ *n* (1857) **1** *Brit* **:** the final part of a race or racetrack **2 :** ALTERCATION, QUARREL **3 :** something inserted as a substantial addition in copy or typeset matter

run in *vt* (1817) **1 a :** to insert as additional matter **b :** to make (typeset matter) continuous without a paragraph or other break **2 :** to arrest for a usu. minor offense **3** *chiefly Brit* **:** to break in (a new machine) gradually by careful operation **~** *vi* **:** to pay a casual visit

run·let \ˈrən-lət\ *n* (ca. 1755) : RIVULET, STREAMLET

run·nel \ˈrə-nᵊl\ *n* [alter. of ME *rinel,* fr. OE *rynel;* akin to OE *rinnan* to run — more at RUN] (bef. 12c) : RIVULET, STREAMLET

run·ner \ˈrə-nər\ *n* (14c) **1 a :** one that runs : RACER **b :** BASE RUNNER **c :** BALLCARRIER **2 a :** MESSENGER **b :** one that smuggles or distributes illicit or contraband goods (as drugs, liquor, or guns) **3 :** any of several large vigorous carangid fishes **4 a :** either of the longitudinal pieces on which a sled or sleigh slides **b :** the part of a skate that slides on the ice : BLADE **c :** the support of a drawer or a sliding door **5 a :** an elongated horizontal stem arising from the base of a plant; *esp* : STOLON 1a **b :** a plant (as a strawberry) that forms or spreads by means of runners **c :** a twining vine (as a scarlet runner bean) **6 a :** a long narrow carpet for a hall or staircase **b :** a narrow decorative cloth cover for a table or dresser top **7 :** an adjustable backstay running from mast to rail on a sail boat or ship **8 :** a running shot in basketball

runner bean *n* (1882) *chiefly Brit* : SCARLET RUNNER BEAN

runner's high *n* (1978) **:** a feeling of euphoria that is experienced by some individuals engaged in strenuous running and that is held to be associated with a release of endorphins by the brain

run·ner–up \ˈrə-nə-ˌrəp, ˌrə-nə-ˈ\ *n, pl* **run·ners–up** \-nər-ˌzəp, -ˈzəp\ *also* **runner–ups** (1842) **:** the competitor that does not win first place in a contest; *esp* **:** one that finishes in second place

¹running *n* (bef. 12c) **1 a :** the action of running **b :** RACE **2 :** physical condition for running **3 :** MANAGEMENT, CARE — **in the running 1 :** competing in a contest **2 :** having a chance to win a contest — **out of the running 1 :** not competing in a contest **2 :** having no chance of winning a contest

²running *adj* (14c) **1 :** CURSIVE, FLOWING **2 :** FLUID, RUNNY **3 a :** INCESSANT, CONTINUOUS ⟨a **~** battle⟩ **b :** made during the course of a process or activity ⟨a **~** commentary on the game⟩ **4 :** measured in a straight line ⟨cost of lumber per **~** foot⟩ **5 a :** initiated or performed while running or with a running start ⟨a **~** catch⟩ ⟨a **~** jump⟩ **b :** of, relating to, or being a football play in which the ball is advanced by running rather than by passing ⟨their **~** game was off⟩ **c :** designed for use by runners ⟨a **~** track⟩ ⟨**~** shoes⟩ **6 :** fitted or trained for running rather than walking, trotting, or jumping ⟨a **~** horse⟩

³running *adv* (1719) **:** in succession : CONSECUTIVELY ⟨three days **~**⟩

running back *n* (1924) **:** a football back (as a halfback or fullback) who carries the ball on running plays

running board *n* (1860) **:** a footboard esp. at the side of an automobile

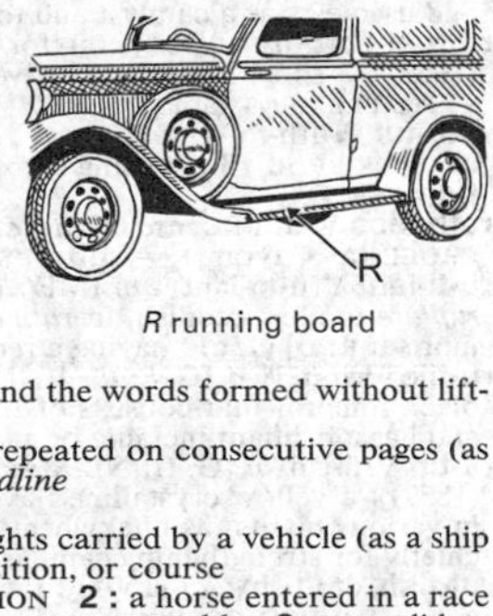
R
R running board

running dog *n* (1927) **:** one who blindly follows someone else's orders : LACKEY

running gear *n* (1662) **1 :** the working and carrying parts of a machine (as a locomotive) **2 :** the parts of an automobile chassis not used in developing, transmitting, and controlling power

running hand *n* (1576) **:** handwriting in which the letters are usu. slanted and the words formed without lifting the pen

running head *n* (1839) **:** a headline repeated on consecutive pages (as of a book) — called also *running headline*

running knot *n* (1611) : SLIPKNOT

running light *n* (1881) **:** any of the lights carried by a vehicle (as a ship or automobile) that indicate size, position, or course

running mate *n* (1727) **1 :** COMPANION **2 :** a horse entered in a race to set the pace for a horse of the same owner or stable **3 :** a candidate running for a subordinate place on a ticket; *esp* **:** the candidate for vice-president

running start *n* (1926) : FLYING START

running stitch *n* (1844) **:** a small even stitch run in and out in cloth

running time *n* (1939) **:** the duration of a motion picture, a theatrical performance, or a recording

running title *n* (1668) **:** the title or abbreviated title of a volume printed at the top of left-hand text pages or sometimes of all text pages

running water *n* (1872) **:** water distributed through pipes and fixtures ⟨a cabin with hot and cold *running water*⟩

run·ny \ˈrə-nē\ *adj* (1817) **:** having a tendency to run: as **a :** extremely or excessively soft and liquid ⟨a **~** dough⟩ **b :** secreting a thin flow of mucus ⟨a **~** nose⟩

run·off \ˈrən-ˌȯf\ *n* (1873) **1 :** a final race, contest, or election to decide an earlier one that has not resulted in a decision in favor of any one competitor **2 :** the portion of precipitation on land that ultimately reaches streams often with dissolved or suspended material

run off *vt* (1683) **1 a :** to recite, compose, or produce rapidly **b :** to cause to be run or played to a finish **c :** to decide (as a race) by a run-off **d :** CARRY OUT **2 :** to drain off : DRAW OFF **3 a :** to drive off (as trespassers) **b :** to steal (as cattle) by driving away **~** *vi* **:** RUN AWAY 1 — **run off with :** to carry off : STEAL ⟨*ran off with* the money⟩

run–of–paper \ˌrən-əv-ˈpā-pər\ *adj* (ca. 1923) **:** to be placed anywhere in a newspaper at the option of the editor ⟨**~** advertisement⟩

run–of–the–mill \ˌrən-ə(v)-t͟hə-ˈmil\ *adj* (1930) **:** not outstanding in quality or rarity : AVERAGE, ORDINARY

run–of–the–mine \-ˈmīn\ *or* **run–of–mine** \-əv-ˈmīn\ *adj* (1903) **1 :** not graded ⟨**~** coal⟩ **2 :** RUN-OF-THE-MILL

¹run–on \ˈrən-ˈȯn, -ˈän\ *adj* (1877) **:** continuing without rhetorical pause from one line of verse into another

²run–on \-ˌȯn, -ˌän\ *n* (ca. 1909) **1 :** something (as a dictionary entry) that is run on **2 :** RUN-ON SENTENCE

run on *vi* (15c) **1 :** to talk or narrate at length **2 :** to keep going : CONTINUE **~** *vt* **1 :** to continue (matter in type) without a break or a new paragraph : RUN IN **2 :** to place or add (as an entry in a dictionary) at the end of a paragraphed item

run–on sentence *n* (1914) **:** a sentence containing two or more clauses not connected by the correct conjunction or punctuation

run out *vi* (14c) **1 a :** to come to an end : EXPIRE ⟨time *ran out*⟩ **b :** to become exhausted or used up ⟨the gasoline *ran out*⟩ **2 :** to jut out **~** *vt* **1 a :** to finish out (as a course, series, or contest) : COMPLETE **b** *of a baseball batter* **:** to run hard to first base after hitting (a batted ball) ⟨*ran out* the grounder⟩ **2 a :** to fill out (a typeset line) with quads, leaders, or ornaments **b :** to set (as the first line of a paragraph) with a hanging indention **3 :** to exhaust (oneself) in running **4 :** to cause to leave by force or coercion : EXPEL — **run out of :** to use up the available supply of ⟨*ran out of* time⟩ — **run out on :** DESERT

run·over \ˈrən-ˌō-vər\ *n* (1927) **:** matter for publication that exceeds the space allotted

run–over \ˈrən-ˈō-vər\ *adj* (ca. 1934) **:** extending beyond the allotted space

run over *vi* (15c) **1 :** to exceed a limit **2 :** OVERFLOW **~** *vt* **1 :** to go over, examine, repeat, or rehearse quickly **2 :** to collide with, knock down, and often drive over ⟨*ran over* a dog⟩

runt \ˈrənt\ *n* [origin unknown] (1501) **1** *chiefly Scot* **:** a hardened stalk or stem of a plant **2 :** an animal unusually small of its kind; *esp* **:** the smallest of a litter of pigs **3 :** a person of small stature — **runt·i·ness** \ˈrən-tē-nəs\ *n* — **runt·ish** \-tish\ *adj* — **runty** \-tē\ *adj*

run–through \ˈrən-ˌthrü\ *n* (1923) **:** a usu. cursory reading, summary, or rehearsal

run through *vt* (15c) **1 :** PIERCE **2 :** to spend or consume wastefully and rapidly **3 :** to read or rehearse without pausing **4 a :** CARRY OUT, DO **b :** to subject to a process

run–up \ˈrən-ˌəp\ *n* (1834) **1 :** the act of running up something **2 :** a usu. sudden increase in volume or price **3** *chiefly Brit* **:** a period immediately preceding an action or event

run up *vi* (1664) **:** to grow rapidly : shoot up **~** *vt* **1 :** BID UP **2 :** to stitch together quickly **3 :** to erect hastily **4 :** to achieve by accumulating ⟨*ran up* a big lead⟩

run·way \ˈrən-ˌwā\ *n* (1833) **1 a :** a beaten path made by animals **b :** a passageway for animals **2 :** a paved strip of ground on a landing field for the landing and takeoff of aircraft **3 a :** a narrow platform from a stage into an auditorium **b :** a platform along which models walk in a fashion show **4 :** RUN 10b **5 :** the area or path along which a jumper, pole vaulter, or javelin thrower runs

ru·pee \rü-ˈpē, ˈrü-ˌpē\ *n* [Hindi & Urdu *rūpaiyā,* fr. Skt *rūpya* coined silver] (1610) — see MONEY table

ru·pi·ah \rü-ˈpē-ə\ *n, pl* **rupiah** *or* **rupiahs** [Malay, fr. Hindi & Urdu *rūpaiyā* rupee] (1947) — see MONEY table

¹rup·ture \ˈrəp(t)-shər\ *n* [ME *ruptur,* fr. AF or L; AF *rupture,* fr. L *ruptura* fracture, fr. *ruptus,* pp. of *rumpere* to break — more at REAVE] (15c) **1 :** breach of peace or concord; *specif* **:** open hostility or war between nations **2 a :** the tearing apart of a tissue ⟨**~** of the heart muscle⟩ ⟨**~** of an intervertebral disk⟩ **b :** HERNIA **3 :** a breaking apart or the state of being broken apart

²rupture *vb* **rup·tured; rup·tur·ing** \-sh(ə-)riŋ\ *vt* (1739) **1 a :** to part by violence : BREAK, BURST **b :** to create or induce a breach of **2 :** to produce a rupture in **~** *vi* **:** to have or undergo a rupture

ru·ral \ˈru̇r-əl\ *adj* [ME, fr. MF, fr. L *ruralis,* fr. *rur-, rus* open land — more at ROOM] (15c) **:** of or relating to the country, country people or life, or agriculture — **ru·ral·i·ty** \ru̇-ˈra-lə-tē\ *n* — **ru·ral·ly** \ˈru̇r-ə-lē\ *adv*

rural dean *n* (ca. 1628) : DEAN 1b

rural free delivery *n* (1892) **:** free delivery of mail to a rural area — called also *rural delivery*

ru·ral·ist \ˈru̇r-ə-list\ *n* (1739) **:** one who lives in a rural area

rural route *n* (1898) **:** a mail-delivery route in a rural free delivery area

rur·ban \ˈrər-bən, ˈru̇r-\ *adj* [blend of *rural* and *urban*] (1918) **:** of, relating to, or constituting an area which is chiefly residential but where some farming is carried on

Ru·ri·tan \ˈru̇r-ə-tən\ *n* [*Ruritan National,* a service club] (1968) **:** a member of a major national service club

Ru·ri·ta·ni·an \ˌru̇r-ə-ˈtā-nē-ən, ˌru̇r-ə-ˈ\ *adj* [*Ruritania,* fictional kingdom in the novel *Prisoner of Zenda* (1894) by Anthony Hope] (1896)

: of, relating to, or having the characteristics of an imaginary place of high romance

ruse \ˈrüs, ˈrüz\ *n* [F, fr. OF, roundabout path taken by fleeing game, trickery, fr. *reuser*] (1625) : a wily subterfuge ***syn*** see TRICK

[1]**rush** \ˈrəsh\ *n* [ME, fr. OE *rysc;* akin to MHG *rusch* rush, Lith *regzti* to knit] (bef. 12c) : any of various monocotyledonous often tufted marsh plants (as of the genera *Juncus* and *Luzula* of the family Juncaceae, the rush family) with cylindrical often hollow stems which are used in bottoming chairs and plaiting mats — **rushy** \ˈrə-shē\ *adj*

[2]**rush** *vb* [ME *russhen,* fr. AF *reuser, ruser, russher* to drive back, repulse, fr. L *recusare* to oppose — more at RECUSANT] *vi* (14c) **1 :** to move forward, progress, or act with haste or eagerness or without preparation **2 :** to advance a football by running plays ⟨∼*ed* for a total of 150 yards⟩ ∼ *vt* **1 :** to push or impel on or forward with speed, impetuosity, or violence **2 :** to perform in a short time or at high speed **3 :** to urge to an unnatural or extreme speed ⟨don't ∼ me⟩ **4 :** to run toward or against in attack : CHARGE **5 a :** to carry (a ball) forward in a running play **b :** to move in quickly on (a kicker or passer) to hinder, prevent, or block a kick or pass — used esp. of defensive linemen **6 a :** to lavish attention on : COURT **b :** to try to secure a pledge of membership (as in a fraternity) from

[3]**rush** *n* (14c) **1 a :** a violent forward motion **b :** ATTACK, ONSET **c :** a surging of emotion **2 a :** a burst of activity, productivity, or speed **b :** a sudden insistent demand **3 :** a thronging of people usu. to a new place in search of wealth ⟨a gold ∼⟩ **4 a :** the act of carrying a football during a game : running play **b :** the action or an instance of rushing a passer or kicker in football ⟨a pass ∼⟩ **5 a :** a round of attention usu. involving extensive social activity **b :** a drive by a fraternity or sorority to recruit new members **6 :** a print of a motion-picture scene processed directly after the shooting for review by the director or producer — usu. used in pl. **7 a :** the immediate pleasurable feeling produced by a drug (as heroin or amphetamine) — called also *flash* **b :** a sudden feeling of intense pleasure or euphoria : THRILL

[4]**rush** *adj* (1879) : requiring or marked by special speed or urgency ⟨∼ orders⟩ ⟨the ∼ season⟩ ⟨a ∼ job⟩

rush candle *n* (1591) : RUSHLIGHT

rush·ee \ˌrə-ˈshē\ *n* (ca. 1916) : a college or university student who is being rushed by a fraternity or sorority

rush·er \ˈrə-shər\ *n* (1654) : one that rushes; *esp* : BALLCARRIER

rush hour *n* (1890) : a period of the day when the demands esp. of traffic or business are at a peak

rush·ing \ˈrə-shiŋ\ *n* (1883) : the act of advancing a football by running plays : the use of running plays; *also* : yardage gained by running plays

rush·light \ˈrəsh-ˌlīt\ *n* (1710) : a candle that consists of the pith of a rush dipped in grease

rusk \ˈrəsk\ *n* [modif. of Sp & Pg *rosca* coil, twisted roll] (1595) **1 :** hard crisp bread orig. used as ship's stores **2 :** a sweet or plain bread baked, sliced, and baked again until dry and crisp

Russ \ˈrəs, ˈrüs, ˈru̇s\ *n, pl* **Russ** *or* **Russ·es** [ultim. fr. ORuss *Rus'* the East Slavic-speaking lands] (1537) : RUSSIAN — **Russ** *adj*

[1]**rus·set** \ˈrə-sət\ *n* [ME, fr. AF, fr. *russet,* adj., russet, fr. *rus, rous* red, fr. L *russus;* akin to L *ruber* red — more at RED] (13c) **1 :** coarse homespun usu. reddish-brown cloth **2 :** a reddish brown **3 :** any of various apples having rough russet-colored skins **4 :** a usu. large elongated potato esp. suited for baking

[2]**russet** *adj* (15c) : of the color russet

rus·set·ing *also* **rus·set·ting** \ˈrə-sə-tiŋ\ *n* (1912) : a brownish roughened area on the skin of fruit (as apples) caused by injury

Rus·sia leather \ˈrə-shə-\ *n* [*Russia,* Europe] (1658) : leather made by tanning various skins with willow, birch, or oak and then rubbing the flesh side with a phenolic oil distilled from a European birch — called also *Russia calf*

Rus·sian \ˈrə-shən\ *n* (1538) **1 a :** a native or inhabitant of Russia **b :** a member of the dominant Slavic-speaking ethnic group of Russia **c :** a person of Russian descent **2 :** a Slavic language of the Russian people spoken as a second language by many non-Russian ethnic groups of the Soviet Union and its successor states — **Russian** *adj* — **Rus·sian·ness** \-nəs\ *n*

Russian blue *n, often cap B* (1889) : any of a breed of slender long-bodied large-eared domestic cats with short silky bluish-gray fur

Russian dressing *n* (1915) : a dressing (as of mayonnaise or oil and vinegar) with added chili sauce, chopped pickles, or pimientos

Rus·sian·ize \ˈrə-shə-ˌnīz\ *vt* **-ized; -iz·ing** (1831) : to make Russian — **Rus·sian·i·za·tion** \ˌrə-shə-nə-ˈzā-shən\ *n*

Russian olive *n* (1913) : a Eurasian large shrub or small tree (*Elaeagnus angustifolia*) of the oleaster family that has silvery foliage and is widely cultivated esp. as an ornamental or as a shelterbelt plant

Russian roulette *n* (1937) **1 :** an act of bravado consisting of spinning the cylinder of a revolver loaded with one cartridge, pointing the muzzle at one's own head, and pulling the trigger **2 :** something resembling Russian roulette in its potential for disaster ⟨taking cocaine is playing *Russian roulette* —Jonathan Nicholas⟩

Russian sage *n* (1940) : an upright Asian subshrub (*Perovskia atriplicifolia*) of the mint family that is grown as an ornamental for its long narrow panicles of violet-blue flowers and grayish-green stems and leaves

Russian thistle *n* (1894) : a prickly European saltwort (*Salsola kali*) that is a serious weed in No. America — called also *Russian tumbleweed*

Russian wolfhound *n* (1872) : BORZOI

Rus·si·fy \ˈrə-sə-ˌfī\ *vt* **-fied; -fy·ing** (1865) : RUSSIANIZE — **Rus·si·fi·ca·tion** \ˌrə-sə-fə-ˈkā-shən\ *n*

Russ·ki *or* **Russ·ky** *or* **Russ·kie** \ˈrəs-kē, ˈru̇s-, ˈrüs-\ *n, pl* **Russkies** *or* **Russkis** [Russ *russkiĭ,* adj. & n., Russian, fr. ORuss, fr. *Rus'*] (1858) : RUSSIAN 1

Rus·so- \ˈrə-(ˌ)sō, ˈrü-, -(ˌ)shō\ *comb form* [*Russia & Russian*] : Russian and ⟨the *Russo*-Japanese war⟩

[1]**rust** \ˈrəst\ *n* [ME, fr. OE *rūst;* akin to OE *rēad* red — more at RED] (bef. 12c) **1 a :** the reddish brittle coating formed on iron esp. when chemically attacked by moist air and composed essentially of hydrated ferric oxide **b :** a comparable coating produced on a metal other than iron by corrosion **c :** something resembling rust : ACCRETION **2 :** corrosive or injurious influence or effect **3 :** any of numerous destructive diseases of plants produced by fungi (order Uredinales) and characterized by usu. reddish-brown pustular lesions; *also* : a fungus causing this **4 :** a strong reddish brown

[2]**rust** *vi* (13c) **1 :** to form rust : become oxidized ⟨iron ∼*s*⟩ **2 :** to degenerate esp. from inaction, lack of use, or passage of time ⟨most men would . . . have allowed their faculties to ∼ —T. B. Macaulay⟩ **3 :** to become reddish brown as if with rust ⟨the leaves slowly ∼*ed*⟩ **4 :** to be affected with a rust fungus ∼ *vt* **1 :** to cause (a metal) to form rust ⟨keep up your bright swords, for the dew will ∼ them —Shak.⟩ **2 :** to impair or corrode by or as if by time, inactivity, or deleterious use **3 :** to cause to become reddish brown : turn the color of rust

rust belt *n, often cap R&B* (1983) : the northeastern and midwestern states of the U.S. in which heavy industry has declined — called also *rust bowl*

rust bucket *n* (1945) : an old and dilapidated ship

[1]**rus·tic** \ˈrəs-tik\ *also* **rus·ti·cal** \-ti-kəl\ *adj* [ME *rustik,* fr. L *rusticus,* fr. *rus* open land — more at ROOM] (15c) **1 :** of, relating to, or suitable for the country : RURAL ⟨∼ rolling farmland⟩ **2 a :** made of the rough limbs of trees ⟨∼ furniture⟩ **b :** finished by rusticating ⟨a ∼ joint in masonry⟩ **3 a :** characteristic of or resembling country people **b :** lacking in social graces or polish **4 :** appropriate to the country (as in plainness or sturdiness) ⟨heavy ∼ boots⟩ — **rus·ti·cal·ly** \-ti-k(ə-)lē\ *adv* — **rus·tic·i·ty** \ˌrəs-ˈti-sə-tē\ *n*

[2]**rustic** *n* (ca. 1550) **1 :** an inhabitant of a rural area **2 a :** an awkward coarse person **b :** an unsophisticated rural person

rus·ti·cate \ˈrəs-ti-ˌkāt\ *vb* **-cat·ed; -cat·ing** *vi* (1660) : to go into or reside in the country : follow a rustic life ∼ *vt* **1** *chiefly Brit* : to suspend from school or college **2 :** to build or face with usu. rough-surfaced masonry blocks having beveled or rebated edges producing pronounced joints ⟨a *rusticated* facade⟩ **3 a :** to compel to reside in the country **b :** to cause to become rustic : implant rustic mannerisms in — **rus·ti·ca·tion** \ˌrəs-ti-ˈkā-shən\ *n* — **rus·ti·ca·tor** \ˈrəs-ti-ˌkā-tər\ *n*

[1]**rus·tle** \ˈrə-səl\ *vb* **rus·tled; rus·tling** \ˈrə-s(ə-)liŋ\ [ME *rustelen*] *vi* (14c) **1 :** to make or cause a rustle **2 a :** to act or move with energy or speed **b :** to forage food **3 :** to steal cattle ∼ *vt* **1 :** to cause to rustle **2 a :** to obtain by one's own exertions — often used with *up* ⟨able to ∼ up $5,000 bail —Jack McCallum⟩ **b :** FORAGE **3 :** to steal (as livestock) esp. from a farm or ranch — **rus·tler** \-s(ə-)lər\ *n*

[2]**rustle** *n* (1759) : a quick succession or confusion of small sounds

rust mite *n* (1884) : any of various small eriophyid mites that burrow in the surface of leaves or fruits usu. producing brown or reddish patches

rust·proof \ˈrəst-ˌprüf\ *adj* (1691) : incapable of rusting

[1]**rusty** \ˈrəs-tē\ *adj* **rust·i·er; -est** (bef. 12c) **1 :** affected by or as if by rust; *esp* : stiff with or as if with rust **2 :** inept and slow through lack of practice or old age **3 a :** of the color rust **b :** dulled in color or appearance by age and use ⟨∼ old boots⟩ **4 :** OUTMODED **5 :** HOARSE, GRATING — **rust·i·ly** \-tə-lē\ *adv* — **rust·i·ness** \-tē-nəs\ *n*

[2]**rus·ty** \ˈrəs-tē\ *adj* **rus·ti·er; -est** [alter. of *restive*] (1625) *chiefly dial* : ILL-NATURED, SURLY

[1]**rut** \ˈrət\ *n* [ME *rutte,* fr. MF *ruit* rut, disturbance, fr. LL *rugitus* roar, fr. L *rugire* to roar; akin to MIr *rucht* roar, OCS *rŭžati* to neigh] (15c) **1 :** an annually recurrent state of sexual excitement in the male deer; *broadly* : sexual excitement in a mammal esp. when periodic **2 :** the period during which rut normally occurs — often used with *the*

[2]**rut** *vi* **rut·ted; rut·ting** (ca. 1625) : to be in or enter into a state of rut

[3]**rut** *n* [perh. modif. of MF *route* way, route] (1552) **1 a :** a track worn by a wheel or by habitual passage **b :** a groove in which something runs **c :** CHANNEL, FURROW **2 :** a usual or fixed practice; *esp* : a monotonous routine ⟨fall easily into a conversational ∼⟩

[4]**rut** *vt* **rut·ted; rut·ting** (1607) : to make a rut in : FURROW

ru·ta·ba·ga \ˌrü-tə-ˈbā-gə, ˌru̇-, -ˈbe-; ˈrü-tə-ˌ, ˈru̇-\ *n* [Sw dial. *rotabagge,* fr. *rot* root + *bagge* bag] (ca. 1791) : a turnip (*Brassica napus napobrassica*) that usu. produces a large yellowish root that is eaten as a vegetable; *also* : the root

ruth \ˈrüth\ *n* [ME *ruthe,* fr. *ruen* to rue] (13c) **1 :** compassion for the misery of another **2 :** sorrow for one's own faults : REMORSE

Ruth \ˈrüth\ *n* [Heb *Rūth*] (14c) **1 :** a Moabite woman who accompanied Naomi to Bethlehem and became the ancestress of David **2 :** a short narrative book of canonical Jewish and Christian Scriptures — see BIBLE table

ru·the·ni·um \rü-ˈthē-nē-əm\ *n* [NL, fr. ML *Ruthenia* Ruthenia] (1848) : a rare hard silvery-white metallic element occurring in platinum ores and used esp. as a catalyst and to harden alloys — see ELEMENT table

ruth·er·ford·ium \ˌrə-th̲ə(r)-ˈfȯr-dē-əm\ *n* [NL, fr. Ernest *Rutherford*] (1969) : a short-lived radioactive element that is produced artificially — see ELEMENT table

ruth·ful \ˈrüth-fəl\ *adj* (13c) **1 :** full of ruth : TENDER **2 :** full of sorrow : WOEFUL **3 :** causing sorrow — **ruth·ful·ly** \-fə-lē\ *adv* — **ruth·ful·ness** *n*

ruth·less \ˈrüth-ləs *also* ˈru̇th-\ *adj* (14c) : having no pity : MERCILESS, CRUEL ⟨a ∼ tyrant⟩ — **ruth·less·ly** *adv* — **ruth·less·ness** *n*

ru·ti·lant \ˈrü-tə-lənt\ *adj* [ME *rutilaunt,* fr. L *rutilant-, rutilans,* pp. of *rutilare* to glow reddish, fr. *rutilus* ruddy; prob. akin to L *ruber* red — more at RED] (15c) : having a reddish glow

ru·tile \ˈrü-ˌtēl\ *n* [G *Rutil,* fr. L *rutilus*] (1803) : a reddish-brown to black mineral that consists of titanium dioxide usu. with a little iron and has a brilliant metallic or adamantine luster

ru·tin \ˈrü-tᵊn\ *n* [G, fr. NL *Ruta,* genus that includes rue + G *-in* [1]-in] (1857) : a yellow crystalline flavonol glycoside $C_{27}H_{30}O_{16}$ that occurs in various plants (as buckwheat and tobacco) and is used in medicine chiefly for strengthening capillary walls

rut·tish \ˈrə-tish\ *adj* (1601) : inclined to rut : LUSTFUL — **rut·tish·ly** *adv* — **rut·tish·ness** *n*

rut·ty \ˈrə-tē\ *adj* **rut·ti·er; -est** (1596) : full of ruts

[1]**RV** \ˌär-ˈvē\ *n* (1967) : RECREATIONAL VEHICLE

[2]**RV** *abbr* Revised Version

R–value \ˈär-ˌval-(ˌ)yü\ *n* [prob. fr. thermal *resistance*] (1948) : a measure of resistance to the flow of heat through a given thickness of a material (as insulation) with higher numbers indicating better insulating properties — compare U-VALUE

RW *abbr* **1** radiological warfare; radiological weapon **2** right worthy

rwy or **ry** abbr railway

Rx \ˌär-ˈeks\ n [alter. of ℞, symbol used at the beginning of a prescription, abbr. for L recipe, lit., take — more at RECIPE] (1926) : PRESCRIPTION 4a, c

-ry n suffix [ME -rie, fr. AF, short for -erie -ery] : -ERY ⟨wizardry⟩ ⟨citizenry⟩ ⟨ancientry⟩

rya \ˈrē-ə\ n [Rya, village in southwest Sweden] (1945) : a Scandinavian handwoven rug with a deep resilient comparatively flat pile; also : the weave typical of this rug

¹**rye** \ˈrī\ n [ME, fr. OE ryge; akin to OHG rocko rye, Lith rugys] (bef. 12c) 1 : a hardy annual grass (Secale cereale) that is widely grown for grain and as a cover crop 2 : the seeds of rye 3 : RYE BREAD 4 : RYE WHISKEY

²**rye** n [Romany rai gentleman, master, fr. Skt rājan king — more at ROYAL] (1851) : a male Gypsy

rye bread n (1547) : bread made wholly or in part of rye flour; esp : a light bread often with caraway seeds

rye·grass \ˈrī-ˌgras\ n (1712) : any of several grasses (genus Lolium); esp : either of two grasses (L. perenne and L. multiflorum) that are used as lawn and pasture grasses and as cover crops

rye whiskey n (1785) : a whiskey distilled from rye or from rye and malt

S

¹**s** \ˈes\ n, pl **s's** or **ss** \ˈe-səz\ often cap, often attrib (bef. 12c) 1 a : the 19th letter of the English alphabet b : a graphic representation of this letter c : a speech counterpart of orthographic s 2 : a graphic device for reproducing the letter s 3 : one designated s esp. as the 19th in order or class 4 [abbr. for satisfactory] a : a grade rating a student's work as satisfactory b : one graded or rated with an S 5 : something shaped like the letter S

²**s** abbr 1 sabbath 2 saint 3 schilling 4 scruple 5 second; secondary 6 section 7 senate 8 series 9 shilling 10 [L signa] label 11 siemens 12 signor 13 sine 14 singular 15 small 16 smooth 17 snow 18 society 19 son 20 sou 21 subject 22 symmetrical

¹**S** abbr 1 satisfactory 2 short 3 standard deviation of a sample 4 svedberg

²**S** symbol sulfur

¹**-s** \s after a voiceless consonant, z after a voiced consonant or a vowel\ n pl suffix [ME -es, -s, fr. OE -as, nom. & acc. pl. ending of some masc. nouns; akin to OS -os] — used to form the plural of most nouns that do not end in s, z, sh, ch, or postconsonantal y ⟨heads⟩ ⟨books⟩ ⟨boys⟩ ⟨beliefs⟩, to form the plural of proper nouns that end in postconsonantal y ⟨Marys⟩, and with or without a preceding apostrophe to form the plural of abbreviations, numbers, letters, and symbols used as nouns ⟨MCs⟩ ⟨PhDs⟩ ⟨4s⟩ ⟨the 1940's⟩ ⟨$s⟩ ⟨B's⟩; compare ¹-ES

²**-s** adv suffix [ME -es, -s, pl. ending of nouns, fr. -es, gen. sing. ending of nouns (functioning adverbially), fr. OE -es] — used to form adverbs denoting usual or repeated action or state ⟨always at home Sundays⟩

³**-s** vb suffix [ME (Northern & North Midland dial.) -es, fr. OE (Northumbrian dial.) -es, -as, prob. fr. OE -es, -as, 2d sing. pres. indic. ending — more at -EST] — used to form the third person singular present of most verbs that do not end in s, z, sh, ch, or postconsonantal y ⟨falls⟩ ⟨takes⟩; compare ²-ES

¹**'s** \same as -'s\ vb [contr. of is, has, does] (1584) 1 a : IS ⟨she's here⟩ b : WAS ⟨when's the last time you ate?⟩ 2 : HAS ⟨he's seen them⟩ 3 : DOES ⟨what's he want?⟩

²**'s** \s\ pron [by contr.] (1588) : US — used with let ⟨let's⟩

-'s \s after voiceless consonants other than s, sh, ch; z after vowels and voiced consonants other than z, zh, j; əz after s, sh, ch, z, zh, j\ n suffix or pron suffix [ME -es, -s, gen. sing. ending, fr. OE -es; akin to OHG -es, gen. sing. ending, Gk -oio, -ou, Skt -asya] — used to form the possessive of singular nouns ⟨boy's⟩, of plural nouns not ending in s ⟨children's⟩, of some pronouns ⟨anyone's⟩, and of word groups functioning as nouns ⟨the man in the corner's hat⟩ or pronouns ⟨someone else's⟩

Sa abbr Saturday

SA abbr 1 Salvation Army 2 seaman apprentice 3 sex appeal 4 [L sine anno without year] without date 5 South Africa 6 South America 7 subject to approval

Saami var of SAMI

Saa·nen \ˈsä-nən, ˈzä-\ n [Saanen, locality in southwest Switzerland] (1906) : any of a Swiss breed of usu. white and hornless short-haired dairy goats

sab·a·dil·la \ˌsa-bə-ˈdi-lə, -ˈdē-yə\ n [Sp cebadilla] (1812) : a Mexican plant (Schoenocaulon officinale) of the lily family; also : its seeds that are used as a source of veratrine and in insecticides

sa·ba·yon \ˌsä-bä-yōⁿ\ n [F, modif. of It zabaione] (1906) 1 : ZABAGLIONE 2 : a sauce of egg yolks, wine, and savory seasonings (as mustard or pepper)

sab·bat \ˈsa-bət\ n, often cap [F, lit., sabbath, fr. L sabbatum] (1652) 1 : WITCHES' SABBATH 2 : any of eight neo-pagan religious festivals commemorating phases of the changing seasons

¹**Sab·ba·tar·i·an** \ˌsa-bə-ˈter-ē-ən\ n [L sabbatarius, fr. sabbatum sabbath] (1613) 1 : one who observes the Sabbath on Saturday in conformity with the letter of the fourth commandment 2 : an adherent of Sabbatarianism

²**Sabbatarian** adj (ca. 1631) 1 : of or relating to the Sabbath 2 : of or relating to the Sabbatarians or Sabbatarianism

Sab·ba·tar·i·an·ism \ˌsa-bə-ˈter-ē-ə-ˌni-zəm\ n (ca. 1674) : strict and often rigorous observance of the Sabbath

Sab·bath \ˈsa-bəth\ n [ME sabat, fr. AF & OE, fr. L sabbatum, fr. Gk sabbaton, fr. Heb shabbāth, lit., rest] (bef. 12c) 1 a : the seventh day of the week observed from Friday evening to Saturday evening as a day of rest and worship by Jews and some Christians b : Sunday observed among Christians as a day of rest and worship 2 : a time of rest

¹**sab·bat·i·cal** \sə-ˈba-ti-kəl\ or **sab·bat·ic** \-tik\ adj [LL sabbaticus, fr. Gk sabbatikos, fr. sabbaton] (1599) 1 : of or relating to a sabbatical year 2 : of or relating to the sabbath ⟨~ laws⟩

²**sabbatical** n (1903) 1 : SABBATICAL YEAR 2 2 : LEAVE 1b 3 : a break or change from a normal routine (as of employment)

sabbatical year n (1599) 1 often cap S : a year of rest for the land observed every seventh year in ancient Judea 2 : a leave often with pay granted usu. every seventh year (as to a college professor) for rest, travel, or research — called also sabbatical leave

Sa·bel·li·an \sə-ˈbe-lē-ən\ n [L Sabellus Sabine] (1601) 1 : a member of one of a group of early Italian peoples including Sabines and Samnites 2 : one or all of several little known languages or dialects of ancient Italy presumably closely related to Oscan and Umbrian — **Sabellian** adj

¹**sa·ber** or **sa·bre** \ˈsā-bər\ n [F sabre, modif. of G dial. Sabel, fr. MHG, prob. of Slav origin; akin to Russ sablya saber] (1680) 1 : a cavalry sword with a curved blade, thick back, and guard 2 a : a light fencing or dueling sword having an arched guard that covers the back of the hand and a tapering flexible blade with a full cutting edge along one side and a partial cutting edge on the back at the tip — compare ÉPÉE, FOIL b : the sport of fencing with the saber

²**saber** or **sabre** vt **sa·bered** or **sa·bred; sa·ber·ing** or **sa·bring** \-b(ə-)riŋ\ (1790) : to strike, cut, or kill with a saber

sa·ber·met·rics \ˌsā-bər-ˈme-triks\ n pl but sing in constr [saber- (fr. Society for American Baseball Research) + -metrics (as in econometrics)] (1982) : the statistical analysis of baseball data — **sa·ber·me·tri·cian** \ˌsā-bər-mə-ˈtri-shən\ n

saber rattling n (1922) : ostentatious display of military power

saber saw n (1953) : a light portable electric saw with a pointed reciprocating blade; esp : JIGSAW 2

sa·ber–toothed \ˈsā-bər-ˌtütht\ adj (1849) : having long sharp canine teeth

saber–toothed tiger n (1849) : any of numerous extinct cats (as genus Smilodon) widely distributed from the Oligocene through the Pleistocene and characterized by long curving upper canines — called also saber-toothed cat

sa·bin \ˈsā-bən\ n [Wallace C. W. Sabine †1919 Am. physicist] (1934) : a unit of acoustic absorption equivalent to the absorption by one square foot of a perfect absorber

Sa·bine \ˈsā-ˌbīn, esp Brit ˈsa-\ n [ME Sabin, fr. L Sabinus] (14c) 1 : a member of an ancient people of the Apennines northeast of Latium 2 : the Italic language of the Sabine people — **Sabine** adj

¹**sa·ble** \ˈsā-bəl\ n, pl **sables** [ME, fr. AF, fr. MLG sabel sable or its fur, fr. MHG zobel, of Slav origin; akin to Russ sobolʹ sable or its fur] (14c) 1 a : the color black b : black clothing worn in mourning — usu. used in pl. 2 a or pl **sable** (1) : a carnivorous mammal (Martes zibellina) of the weasel family that occurs chiefly in northern Asia (2) : any of various animals related to the sable b : the fur or pelt of a sable 3 : the usu. dark brown color of the fur of the sable

²**sable** adj (15c) 1 : of the color black 2 : DARK, GLOOMY

sa·ble·fish \ˈsā-bəl-ˌfish\ n (1917) : BLACK COD

sa·bot \sa-ˈbō, ˈsa-ˌ(ˌ)bō, for 1b also \ˈsa-bət\ n [F] (1607) 1 a : a wooden shoe worn in various European countries b (1) : a strap across the instep in a shoe esp. of the sandal type (2) : a shoe having a sabot strap 2 a : a thrust-transmitting carrier that positions a missile in a gun barrel or launching tube and that prevents the escape of gas ahead of the missile 3 : SHOE 6

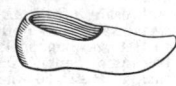

sabot 1a

¹**sab·o·tage** \ˈsa-bə-ˌtäzh\ n [F, fr. saboter to clatter with sabots, botch, sabotage, fr. sabot] (1910) 1 : destruction of an employer's property (as tools or materials) or the hindering of manufacturing by discontented workers 2 : destructive or obstructive action carried on by a civilian or enemy agent to hinder a nation's war effort a : an act or process tending to hamper or hurt b : deliberate subversion

²**sabotage** vt **-taged; -tag·ing** (1918) : to practice sabotage on

sab·o·teur \ˌsa-bə-ˈtər, -ˈtu̇r, -ˈtyu̇r\ n [F, fr. saboter] (1921) : one that practices sabotage

sa·bra \ˈsä-brə\ n, often cap [ModHeb ṣabhār, lit., prickly pear] (1945) : a native-born Israeli

\ə\ abut \ˈ ᵊ\ kitten, F table \ər\ further \a\ ash \ā\ ace \ä\ mop, mar \au̇\ out \ch\ chin \e\ bet \ē\ easy \g\ go \i\ hit \ī\ ice \j\ job \ŋ\ sing \ō\ go \ȯ\ law \ȯi\ boy \th\ thin \t͟h\ the \ü\ loot \u̇\ foot \y\ yet \zh\ vision, beige \k, ⁿ, œ, ᵫ, ᵊ\ see Guide to Pronunciation

1094 **sac • sad**

[1]**sac** \ˈsak\ *n* [F, lit., bag, fr. L *saccus* — more at SACK] (1741) : a pouch within an animal or plant often containing a fluid ⟨a synovial ~⟩ — **sac·like** \-ˌlīk\ *adj*

[2]**sac** *abbr* sacrifice

Sac *var of* SAUK

SAC *abbr* **1** special agent in charge **2** Strategic Air Command

sa·ca·huis·te \ˌsa-kə-ˈwis-tə, ˌsä-, -tē\ *or* **sa·ca·huis·ta** \-tə\ *n* [MexSp *zacahuiscle,* fr. Nahuatl **zacahuitztli,* fr. *zacatl* grass, hay + *huitztli* thorn] (1896) : a bear grass (*Nolina texana*) of the southwestern U.S. and Mexico that may cause poisoning in some livestock

sac·a·ton \ˈsa-kə-ˌtōn\ *n* [AmerSp *zacatón,* fr. *zacate* coarse grass, fr. Nahuatl *zacatl*] (1846) : a coarse perennial grass (*Sporobolus wrightii*) of the southwestern U.S. that is used for forage esp. in alkaline soils

sac·cade \sa-ˈkäd\ *n* [F, twitch, jerk, fr. MF, fr. *saquer* to pull, draw] (1938) : a small rapid jerky movement of the eye esp. as it jumps from fixation on one point to another (as in reading) — **sac·cad·ic** \-ˈkä-dik\ *adj*

sac·cate \ˈsa-ˌkāt\ *adj* [NL *saccatus,* fr. L *saccus*] (1830) : having the form of a sac or pouch ⟨~ pollen grains⟩

sacchar- *or* **sacchari-** *or* **saccharo-** *comb form* [L *saccharum,* fr. Gk *sakcharon,* fr. Prakrit *sakkharā,* fr. Skt *śarkarā* gravel, sugar] : sugar ⟨*sacchari*fy⟩ ⟨*saccharo*meter⟩

sac·cha·rase \ˈsa-kə-ˌrās, -ˌrāz\ *n* [ISV] (1920) : INVERTASE

sac·cha·ride \ˈsa-kə-ˌrīd\ *n* (1895) : a monosaccharide sugar or combination of sugars : CARBOHYDRATE

sac·char·i·fi·ca·tion \sə-ˌka-rə-fə-ˈkā-shən\ *n* (1839) : the process of breaking a complex carbohydrate (as starch or cellulose) into its monosaccharide components — **sac·char·i·fy** \sə-ˈka-rə-ˌfī, sa-\ *vt*

sac·cha·rim·e·ter \ˌsa-kə-ˈri-mə-tər\ *n* [ISV] (1869) : a device for measuring the amount of sugar in a solution; *specif* : a polarimeter so used

sac·cha·rin \ˈsa-k(ə-)rən\ *n* [ISV] (1885) : a crystalline compound $C_7H_5NO_3S$ that is unrelated to the carbohydrates, is several hundred times sweeter than sucrose, and is used as a calorie-free sweetener

sac·cha·rine \ˈsa-k(ə-)rən, -kə-ˌrēn, -kə-ˌrīn\ *adj* [L *saccharum*] (ca. 1674) **1 a** : of, relating to, or resembling that of sugar ⟨~ taste⟩ **b** : yielding or containing sugar ⟨~ vegetables⟩ **2** : overly or sickishly sweet ⟨~ flavor⟩ **3** : ingratiatingly or affectedly agreeable or friendly **4** : overly sentimental : MAWKISH ⟨a ~ love story⟩ — **sac·cha·rin·i·ty** \ˌsa-kə-ˈri-nə-tē\ *n*

sac·cha·roi·dal \ˌsa-kə-ˈrȯi-dᵊl\ *adj* (1838) : having or being a fine granular texture like that of sugar lumps ⟨~ marble⟩

sac·cha·rom·e·ter \-ˈrä-mə-tər\ *n* (1784) : SACCHARIMETER; *esp* : a hydrometer with a special scale

sac·cha·ro·my·ces \-rō-ˈmī-(ˌ)sēz\ *n* [NL, fr. *sacchar-* + *-myces* fungus, fr. Gk *mykēs* — more at MYC-] (1873) : any of a genus (*Saccharomyces* of the family Saccharomycetaceae) of usu. unicellular yeasts (as a brewer's yeast) that are distinguished by their sparse or absent mycelium and by their facility in reproducing asexually by budding

sac·cu·lar \ˈsa-kyə-lər\ *adj* (ca. 1859) : resembling a sac ⟨a ~ aneurysm⟩

sac·cu·lat·ed \-ˌlā-təd\ *also* **sac·cu·late** \-ˌlāt, -lət\ *adj* (ca. 1836) : having or formed of a series of saccular expansions — **sac·cu·la·tion** \ˌsa-kyə-ˈlā-shən\ *n*

sac·cule \ˈsa-(ˌ)kyül\ *n* [NL *sacculus,* fr. L, dim. of *saccus* bag — more at SACK] (ca. 1839) : a little sac; *specif* : the smaller chamber of the membranous labyrinth of the ear

sac·cu·lus \ˈsa-kyə-ləs\ *n, pl* **-li** \-ˌlī, -ˌlē\ [NL] (1728) : SACCULE

sac·er·do·tal \ˌsa-sər-ˈdō-tᵊl, ˌsa-kər-\ *adj* [ME, fr. MF, fr. L *sacerdotalis,* fr. *sacerdot-, sacerdos* priest, fr. *sacer* sacred + *-dot-, -dos* (akin to *facere* to make) — more at SACRED, DO] (15c) **1** : of or relating to priests or a priesthood : PRIESTLY ⟨~ robes⟩ ⟨~ authority⟩ **2** : of, relating to, or suggesting sacerdotalism — **sac·er·do·tal·ly** \-tᵊl-ē\ *adv*

sac·er·do·tal·ism \-tə-ˌli-zəm\ *n* (1856) : religious belief emphasizing the powers of priests as essential mediators between God and humankind — **sac·er·do·tal·ist** \-tᵊl-ist\ *n*

sac fungus *n* (ca. 1929) : ASCOMYCETE

sa·chem \ˈsā-chəm, ˈsa-\ *n* [Narraganset *sâchim*] (1622) **1** : a No. American Indian chief; *esp* : the chief of a confederation of the Algonquian tribes of the No. Atlantic coast **2** : a Tammany leader — **sa·chem·ic** \sā-ˈche-mik, sa-\ *adj*

Sa·cher torte \ˈsä-kər-, ˈzä-\ *n* [G *Sachertorte,* fr. *Sacher* (name of a family of 19th and 20th cent. Austrian restaurant proprietors) + G *Torte* torte] (1906) : a rich chocolate torte with an apricot jam filling

sa·chet \sa-ˈshā\ *n* [MF, fr. OF, dim. of *sac* bag — more at SAC] (15c) **1** : a small bag or packet **2** : a small bag containing a perfumed powder or potpourri used to scent clothes and linens — **sa·cheted** \-ˈshād\ *adj*

[1]**sack** \ˈsak\ *n* [ME *sak* bag, sackcloth, fr. OE *sacc,* fr. L *saccus* bag & LL *saccus* sackcloth, both fr. Gk *sakkos* bag, sackcloth, of Sem origin; akin to Heb *śaq* bag, sackcloth] (bef. 12c) **1** : a usu. rectangular-shaped bag (as of paper, burlap, or canvas) **2** : the amount contained in a sack; *esp* : a fixed amount of a commodity used as a unit of measure **3 a** : a woman's loose-fitting dress **b** : a short usu. loose-fitting coat for women and children **c** : SACQUE 2 **4** : DISMISSAL ⟨gave him the ~⟩ **5 a** : HAMMOCK, BUNK **b** : BED **6** : a base in baseball **7** : an instance of sacking the quarterback in football — **sack·ful** \-ˌfu̇l\ *n*

[2]**sack** *vt* (14c) **1** : to put in or as if in a sack **2** : to dismiss esp. summarily **3** : to tackle (the quarterback) behind the line of scrimmage in football — **sack·er** *n*

[3]**sack** *n* [modif. of MF *sec* dry, fr. L *siccus;* prob. akin to OHG *sīhan* to filter, Skt *siñcati* he pours] (ca. 1532) : any of several white wines imported to England from Spain and the Canary Islands during the 16th and 17th centuries

[4]**sack** *vt* [[5]*sack*] (ca. 1547) **1** : to plunder (as a town) esp. after capture **2** : to strip of valuables : LOOT ***syn*** see RAVAGE — **sack·er** *n*

[5]**sack** *n* [MF *sac,* fr. OIt *sacco,* lit., bag, fr. L *saccus*] (1549) : the plundering of a captured town

sack·but \ˈsak-(ˌ)bət\ *n* [MF *saqueboute* hooked lance, sackbut, fr. *saquer* to pull + *boter* to push — more at BUTT] (1533) : the medieval and Renaissance trombone

sack·cloth \ˈsa(k)-ˌklȯth\ *n* [[1]*sack*] (13c) **1** : a coarse cloth of goat or camel's hair or of flax, hemp, or cotton **2** : a garment of sackcloth worn as a sign of mourning or penitence

sack coat *n* (1847) : a man's jacket with a straight back

sack·ing \ˈsa-kiŋ\ *n* (1707) : material for sacks; *esp* : a coarse fabric (as burlap)

sack out *vi* [[1]*sack*] (1946) : to go to bed : go to sleep

sack race *n* (1859) : a jumping race in which each contestant's legs are enclosed in a sack

sacque \ˈsak\ *n* [alter. of [1]*sack*] (1762) **1** : SACK 3a, b **2** : an infant's usu. short jacket that fastens at the neck

[1]**sa·cral** \ˈsa-krəl, ˈsā-\ *adj* (1767) : of, relating to, or lying near the sacrum ⟨the ~ region of the spinal cord⟩

[2]**sa·cral** \ˈsā-krəl, ˈsa-\ *adj* [L *sacr-, sacer* — more at SACRED] (1882) : HOLY, SACRED ⟨~ authority⟩

sa·cral·ize \ˈsa-krə-ˌlīz, ˈsā-\ *vt* **-ized; -iz·ing** (1933) : to treat as or make sacred — **sa·cral·i·za·tion** \ˌsa-krə-lə-ˈzā-shən, ˌsā-, -ˌlī-\ *n*

sac·ra·ment \ˈsa-krə-mənt\ *n* [ME *sacrement, sacrament,* fr. AF & LL; AF, fr. LL *sacramentum,* fr. L, oath of allegiance, obligation, fr. *sacrare* to consecrate] (13c) **1 a** : a Christian rite (as baptism or the Eucharist) that is believed to have been ordained by Christ and that is held to be a means of divine grace or to be a sign or symbol of a spiritual reality **b** : a religious rite or observance comparable to a Christian sacrament **2** *cap* **a** : COMMUNION 2a **b** : BLESSED SACRAMENT **3** : something likened to a religious sacrament ⟨saw voting as a ~ of democracy⟩

[1]**sac·ra·men·tal** \ˌsa-krə-ˈmen-tᵊl\ *adj* (15c) **1** : of, relating to, or having the character of a sacrament ⟨~ wine⟩ **2** : suggesting a sacrament (as in sacredness) — **sac·ra·men·tal·ly** \-tᵊl-ē\ *adv*

[2]**sacramental** *n* (15c) : an action or object (as the rosary) of ecclesiastical origin that serves to express or increase devotion

sac·ra·men·tal·ism \-tə-ˌli-zəm\ *n* (1861) : belief in or use of sacramental rites, acts, or objects; *specif* : belief that the sacraments are inherently efficacious and necessary for salvation — **sac·ra·men·tal·ist** \-tə-list\ *n*

sa·crar·i·um \sə-ˈkrer-ē-əm, sa-, sā-\ *n, pl* **-ia** \-ē-ə\ [ML, fr. L, shrine, fr. *sacr-, sacer* sacred] (1727) **1 a** : SANCTUARY 1b **b** : SACRISTY **c** : PISCINA **2** : an ancient Roman shrine or sanctuary in a temple or a home holding sacred objects

sa·cred \ˈsā-krəd\ *adj* [ME, fr. pp. of *sacren* to consecrate, fr. AF *sacrer,* fr. L *sacrare,* fr. *sacr-, sacer* sacred; akin to L *sancire* to make sacred, Hitt *šaklāi-* rite] (14c) **1 a** : dedicated or set apart for the service or worship of a deity ⟨a tree ~ to the gods⟩ **b** : devoted exclusively to one service or use (as of a person or purpose) ⟨a fund ~ to charity⟩ **2 a** : worthy of religious veneration : HOLY **b** : entitled to reverence and respect **3** : of or relating to religion : not secular or profane ⟨~ music⟩ **4** *archaic* : ACCURSED **5 a** : UNASSAILABLE, INVIOLABLE **b** : highly valued and important ⟨a ~ responsibility⟩ — **sa·cred·ly** *adv* — **sa·cred·ness** *n*

sacred baboon *n* [fr. its veneration by the ancient Egyptians] (ca. 1889) : HAMADRYAS BABOON

sacred cow *n* [fr. the veneration of the cow by Hindus] (1910) : one that is often unreasonably immune from criticism or opposition

sacred mushroom *n* (1930) **1** : MAGIC MUSHROOM **2** : PEYOTE BUTTON

[1]**sac·ri·fice** \ˈsa-krə-ˌfīs, *also* -fəs *or* -ˌfīz\ *n* [ME, fr. AF, fr. L *sacrificium,* fr. *sacr-, sacer* + *facere* to make — more at DO] (13c) **1** : an act of offering to a deity something precious; *esp* : the killing of a victim on an altar **2** : something offered in sacrifice **3 a** : destruction or surrender of something for the sake of something else **b** : something given up or lost ⟨the ~*s* made by parents⟩ **4** : LOSS ⟨goods sold at a ~⟩ **5** : SACRIFICE HIT

[2]**sacrifice** *vb* **-ficed; -fic·ing** *vt* (14c) **1** : to offer as a sacrifice **2** : to suffer loss of, give up, renounce, injure, or destroy esp. for an ideal, belief, or end **3** : to sell at a loss **4** : to advance (a base runner) by means of a sacrifice hit **5** : to kill (an animal) as part of a scientific experiment ~ *vi* **1** : to make or perform the rites of a sacrifice **2** : to make a sacrifice hit in baseball — **sac·ri·fic·er** *n*

sacrifice fly *n* (1944) : an outfield fly in baseball caught by a fielder after which a runner scores

sacrifice hit *n* (1880) : a bunt in baseball that allows a runner to advance one base while the batter is put out

sac·ri·fi·cial \ˌsa-krə-ˈfi-shəl\ *adj* (1607) **1** : of, relating to, of the nature of, or involving sacrifice **2** : of or relating to a metal that serves as an anode which is electrolytically consumed instead of another metal that is present — **sac·ri·fi·cial·ly** \-shə-lē\ *adv*

sac·ri·lege \ˈsa-krə-lij\ *n* [ME, fr. AF, fr. L *sacrilegium,* fr. *sacrilegus* one who robs sacred property, fr. *sacr-, sacer* + *legere* to gather, steal — more at LEGEND] (14c) **1** : a technical and not necessarily intrinsically outrageous violation (as improper reception of a sacrament) of what is sacred because consecrated to God **2** : gross irreverence toward a hallowed person, place, or thing — **sac·ri·le·gious** \ˌsa-krə-ˈli-jəs *also* -ˈlē-\ *adj* — **sac·ri·le·gious·ly** *adv* — **sac·ri·le·gious·ness** *n*

sac·ris·tan \ˈsa-krə-stən\ *n* [ME, fr. ML *sacristanus,* fr. L *sacr-, sacer*] (14c) : a person in charge of the sacristy and ceremonial equipment; *also* : SEXTON

sac·ris·ty \ˈsa-krə-stē\ *n, pl* **-ties** [ME *sacristie,* fr. ML *sacristia,* fr. *sacrista* sacristan, fr. L *sacr-, sacer*] (15c) : a room in a church where sacred vessels and vestments are kept and where the clergy vests

[1]**sa·cro·il·i·ac** \ˌsa-krō-ˈi-lē-ˌak, ˌsā-\ *adj* [prob. fr. F *sacro-iliaque,* fr. NL *sacrum* + F *iliaque* iliac] (1831) : of, relating to, or being the region of juncture of the sacrum and ilium

[2]**sacroiliac** *n* (1936) : the sacroiliac region; *also* : its firm fibrous cartilage

sac·ro·sanct \ˈsa-krō-ˌsaŋ(k)t\ *adj* [L *sacrosanctus,* prob. fr. *sacro sanctus* hallowed by a sacred rite] (1601) **1** : most sacred or holy : INVIOLABLE **2** : treated as if holy : immune from criticism or violation ⟨politically ~ programs⟩ — **sac·ro·sanc·ti·ty** \ˌsa-krō-ˈsaŋ(k)-tə-tē\ *n*

sa·crum \ˈsa-krəm, ˈsā-\ *n, pl* **sa·cra** \ˈsa-krə, ˈsā-\ [NL, fr. LL *os sacrum* last bone of the spine, lit., holy bone, trans. of Gk *hieron osteon*] (1753) : the part of the vertebral column that is directly connected with or forms a part of the pelvis and in humans consists of five fused vertebrae

sad \ˈsad\ *adj* **sad·der; sad·dest** [ME, fr. OE *sæd* sated; akin to OHG *sat* sated, L *satis* enough] (13c) **1 a** : affected with or expressive of grief or unhappiness : DOWNCAST **b** (1) : causing or associated with grief or unhappiness : DEPRESSING ⟨~ news⟩ (2) : REGRETTABLE,

DEPLORABLE ⟨a ~ relaxation of morals —C. W. Cunnington⟩ **c** : of little worth **2** : of a dull somber color — **sad·ly** *adv* — **sad·ness** *n*
SAD *abbr* seasonal affective disorder
sad·den \'sa-dᵊn\ *vb* **sad·dened; sad·den·ing** \-niŋ, 'sad-dᵊn-iŋ\ (1628) : to make sad ~ *vi* : to become sad
¹**sad·dle** \'sa-dᵊl\ *n, often attrib* [ME *sadel*, fr. OE *sadol*; akin to OHG *satul* saddle (bef. 12c) **1 a** (1) : a girthed usu. padded and leather-covered seat for the rider of an animal (as a horse) (2) : a part of a driving harness comparable to a saddle that is used to keep the breeching in place **b** : a seat to be straddled by the rider of a vehicle (as a bicycle) **2** : a device mounted as a support and often shaped to fit the object held **3 a** : a ridge connecting two higher elevations **b** : a pass in a mountain range **4 a** : both sides of the unsplit back of a carcass including both loins **b** : a colored marking on the back of an animal **c** : the rear part of a male fowl's back extending to the tail — see DUCK illustration **5** : the central part of the spine of the binding of a book **6** : a piece of leather across the instep of a shoe — **sad·dle·less** \-dᵊl-(l)əs\ *adj* — **in the saddle** : in control
²**saddle** *vb* **sad·dled; sad·dling** \'sad-liŋ, 'sa-dᵊl-iŋ\ *vt* (bef. 12c) **1** : to put a saddle on **2 a** : to place under a burden or encumbrance **b** : to place (an onerous responsibility) on a person or group ~ *vi* : to mount a saddled horse
sad·dle·bag \'sa-dᵊl-,bag\ *n* (1742) **1** : one of a pair of covered pouches laid across the back of a horse behind the saddle or hanging over the rear wheel of a bicycle or motorcycle **2** : a bulge of lumpy fat in the outer area of the upper thighs
saddle blanket *n* (1737) : a folded blanket or pad under a saddle to prevent galling the horse
sad·dle·bow \'sa-dᵊl-,bō\ *n* (bef. 12c) : the arch in or the pieces forming the front of a saddle
sad·dle·bred \-,bred\ *n* (1948) : AMERICAN SADDLEBRED
sad·dle·cloth \-,klȯth\ *n* (15c) : a cloth placed under or over a saddle
saddled prominent *n* [fr. the hump or prominence on the back of the larva] (1910) : a moth (*Heterocampa guttivitta*) whose larva is a defoliator of hardwood trees in the eastern and midwestern U.S.
saddle horn *n* (1856) : a hornlike prolongation of the pommel of a stock saddle
saddle horse *n* (1662) : a horse suited for or trained for riding
saddle leather *n* (1771) : leather made of cowhide that is usu. tanned with vegetable tannins and is used esp. for saddlery; *also* : smooth polished leather simulating this
sad·dler \'sad-lər\ *n* (14c) : one that makes, repairs, or sells saddles and other furnishings for horses
sad·dlery \'sad-lə-rē, 'sa-dᵊl-rē\ *n, pl* **-dler·ies** (15c) : the trade, articles of trade, or shop of a saddler
saddle seat *n* (1925) : a slightly concave chair seat (as of a Windsor chair) with sometimes a thickened ridge at the center front
saddle shoe *n* (1939) : an oxford-style shoe having a saddle of contrasting color or leather — called also *saddle oxford*
saddle soap *n* (1889) : a mild soap used for cleansing and conditioning leather
saddle sore *n* (1946) **1** : a gall or open sore developing on the back of a horse at points of pressure from an ill-fitting or ill-adjusted saddle **2** : an irritation or sore on parts of the rider chafed by the saddle
sad·dle·tree \'sa-dᵊl-,trē\ *n* (15c) : the frame of a saddle
Sad·du·ce·an \,sa-jə-'sē-ən, ,sa-dyə-\ *adj* (1593) : of or relating to the Sadducees
Sad·du·cee \'sa-jə-,sē, 'sa-dyə-\ *n* [ME *saducee*, fr. OE *sadduce*, fr. LL *sadducaeus*, fr. Gk *saddoukaios*, fr. LHeb *ṣǎddûqî*] (bef. 12c) : a member of a Jewish party of the intertestamental period consisting of a traditional ruling class of priests and rejecting doctrines not in the Law (as resurrection, retribution in a future life, and the existence of angels) — **Sad·du·cee·ism** \-,i-zəm\ *n*
sa·dhe *or* **tsa·de** \'t)sä-,dē, -dē\ *n* [Heb *ṣādhē*] (ca. 1899) : the 18th letter of the Hebrew alphabet — see ALPHABET table
sa·dhu *also* **sad·dhu** \'sä-(,)dü\ *n* [Skt *sādhu*] (1835) : a usu. Hindu mendicant ascetic
sad·iron \'sad-,ī(-ə)rn\ *n* [*sad* (compact, heavy) + *iron*] (1738) : a flat-iron pointed at both ends and having a removable handle
sa·dism \'sā-,di-zəm, 'sa-\ *n* [ISV, fr. Marquis de *Sade*] (1888) **1** : a sexual perversion in which gratification is obtained by the infliction of physical or mental pain on others (as on a love object) — compare MASOCHISM **2 a** : delight in cruelty **b** : excessive cruelty — **sa·dist** \'sā-dist, 'sa-\ *n* — **sa·dis·tic** \sə-'dis-tik *also* sā- *or* sa-\ *adj* — **sa·dis·ti·cal·ly** \-ti-k(ə-)lē\ *adv*
sa·do·mas·och·ism \,sā-(,)dō-'ma-sə-,ki-zəm, ,sa-, -'ma-zə-\ *n* [ISV *sadism + -o- + masochism*] (1922) : the derivation of pleasure from the infliction of physical or mental pain either on others or on oneself — **sa·do·mas·och·ist** \-kist\ *n or adj* — **sa·do·mas·och·is·tic** \-,ma-sə-'kis-tik, -,ma-zə-\ *adj*
sad sack *n* (1943) : an inept person; *esp* : an inept soldier — **sad–sack** *adj*
SAE *abbr* **1** self-addressed envelope **2** Society of Automotive Engineers **3** stamped addressed envelope
Sa·far \sə-'fär\ *n* [Ar *safar*] (ca. 1771) : the second month of the Islamic year — see MONTH table
sa·fa·ri \sə-'fär-ē, -'far-ē\ *n* [Swahili, journey, fr. Ar *safarī* a journey] (1868) **1** : the caravan and equipment of a hunting expedition esp. in eastern Africa; *also* : such a hunting expedition **2** : JOURNEY, EXPEDITION ⟨an arctic ~⟩ — **safari** *vi*
safari jacket *n* (1951) : a usu. belted shirt jacket with pleated expansible pockets
safari suit *n* (1967) : a safari jacket with matching pants
¹**safe** \'sāf\ *adj* **saf·er; saf·est** [ME *sauf*, fr. AF *salf, sauf*, fr. L *salvus* safe, healthy; akin to L *solidus* solid, Gk *holos* whole, safe, Skt *sarva* entire] (14c) **1** : free from harm or risk : UNHURT **2 a** : secure from threat of danger, harm, or loss **b** : successful at getting to a base in baseball without being put out **3** : affording safety or security from danger, risk, or difficulty **4** *obs, of mental or moral faculties* : HEALTHY, SOUND **5 a** : not threatening danger : HARMLESS **b** : unlikely to produce controversy or contradiction **6 a** : not likely to take risks : CAUTIOUS **b** : TRUSTWORTHY, RELIABLE — **safe** *or* **safe·ly** *adv* — **safe·ness** *n*

²**safe** *n* (15c) **1** : a place or receptacle to keep articles (as valuables) safe **2** : CONDOM **1**
safe–con·duct \'sāf-'kän-(,)dəkt\ *n* [ME *sauf conduit*, fr. AF, safe conduct] (14c) **1** : protection given a person passing through a military zone or occupied area **2** : a document authorizing safe-conduct
safe·crack·er \'sāf-,kra-kər\ *n* (ca. 1825) : one that breaks open safes to steal — **safe·crack·ing** \-kiŋ\ *n*
safe–deposit box *n* (1874) : a box (as in the vault of a bank) for safe storage of valuables — called also *safety-deposit box*
¹**safe–guard** \'sāf-,gärd\ *n* [ME *saufgarde*, fr. AF, fr. *sauf* safe + *garde* guard] (14c) **1 a** : PASS, SAFE-CONDUCT **b** : CONVOY, ESCORT **2 a** : a precautionary measure, stipulation, or device **b** : a technical contrivance to prevent accident
²**safeguard** *vt* (15c) **1** : to provide a safeguard for **2** : to make safe : PROTECT *syn* see DEFEND
safe house *n* (1946) : a place where one may engage in secret activities or take refuge
safe·keep·ing \'sāf-'kē-piŋ\ *n* (15c) **1** : the act or process of preserving in safety **2** : the state of being preserved in safety
safe·light \'sāf-,līt\ *n* (1903) : a darkroom lamp with a filter to screen out rays that are harmful to sensitive film or paper
safe sex *n* (1983) : sexual activity and esp. sexual intercourse in which various measures (as the use of latex condoms or the practice of monogamy) are taken to avoid disease (as AIDS) transmitted by sexual contact — called also *safer sex*
¹**safe·ty** \'sāf-tē\ *n, pl* **safeties** [ME *saufte*, fr. AF *salveté, saufté*, fr. *salf* safe] (14c) **1** : the condition of being safe from undergoing or causing hurt, injury, or loss **2** : a device (as on a weapon or a machine) designed to prevent inadvertent or hazardous operation **3 a** (1) : a situation in football in which a member of the offensive team is tackled behind its own goal line that counts two points for the defensive team — compare TOUCHBACK (2) : a member of a defensive backfield in football who occupies the deepest position in order to receive a kick, defend against a forward pass, or stop a ballcarrier **b** : a billiard shot made with no attempt to score or so as to leave the balls in an unfavorable position for the opponent **c** : BASE HIT
²**safety** *vt* **safe·tied; safe·ty·ing** (1927) : to protect against failure, breakage, or accident ⟨~ a rifle⟩
safety belt *n* (1844) : a belt fastening a person to an object (as a car seat) to prevent falling or injury
safety glass *n* (1919) : transparent material that is made by laminating a sheet of transparent plastic between sheets of clear glass and is used esp. for windows (as of automobiles) likely to be subjected to shock or impact
safety lamp *n* (1816) : a miner's lamp constructed to avoid explosion in an atmosphere containing flammable gas usu. by enclosing the flame in fine wire gauze
safe·ty·man \'sāf-tē-,man\ *n* (1927) : SAFETY 3a(2)
safety match *n* (1857) : a match capable of being struck and ignited only on a specially prepared friction surface
safety net *n* (1953) : something that provides security against misfortune or difficulty
safety pin *n* (1847) : a pin in the form of a clasp with a guard covering its point when fastened
safety razor *n* (ca. 1877) : a razor provided with a guard for the blade to prevent deep cuts in the skin
safety valve *n* (1813) **1** : an automatic escape or relief valve (as for a steam boiler) **2** : an outlet for pent-up energy or emotion **3** : something that relieves the pressure of overcrowding
saf·flow·er \'sa-,flau(-ə)r\ *n* [MF *saffleur*, fr. OIt *saffiore*, fr. Ar *'aṣfar, 'uṣfur*] (ca. 1660) **1** : a widely cultivated Old World composite herb (*Carthamus tinctorius*) with large usu. orange or red flower heads and seeds rich in oil; *also* : a red dyestuff prepared from the flower heads
safflower oil *n* (ca. 1857) : an edible drying oil obtained from the seeds of the safflower
saf·fron \'sa-frän, -frən\ *n* [ME, fr. AF *saffron, safren*, fr. ML *safranum*, fr. Ar *za'farān*] (13c) **1 a** : the deep orange aromatic pungent dried stigmas of a purple-flowered crocus (*Crocus sativus*) used to color and flavor foods and formerly as a dyestuff and in medicine **b** : the crocus supplying saffron **2** : a moderate orange to orange yellow
saf·ra·nine \'sa-frə-,nēn, -nən\ *or* **saf·ra·nin** \-nən\ *n* [ISV, fr. F or G *safran* saffron] (1868) **1** : any of various usu. red synthetic dyes that are amino derivatives of bases **2** : any of various mixtures of safranine salts used in dyeing and as biological stains
saf·role \'sa-,frōl\ *n* [ISV, fr. *sassafras* + *-ole*] (1869) : a poisonous oily cyclic ether $C_{10}H_{10}O_2$ that is the principal component of sassafras oil and is used chiefly in perfumery
¹**sag** \'sag\ *vb* **sagged; sag·ging** [ME *saggen;* akin to MLG *sacken* to sink, Norw dial. *sakka*] (14c) **1** : to droop, sink, or settle from or as if from pressure or loss of tautness **2 a** : to lose firmness, resiliency, or vigor ⟨spirits *sagging* from overwork⟩ **b** : to decline esp. from a thriving state **3** : DRIFT **4** : to fail to stimulate or retain interest ~ *vt* : to cause to sag : leave slack in
²**sag** *n* (1580) **1** : a tendency to drift (as of a ship to leeward) **2 a** : a sagging part ⟨the ~ in a rope⟩ **b** : a drop or depression below the surrounding area **c** : an instance or amount of sagging **3** : a temporary decline (as in the price of a commodity)
SAG *abbr* Screen Actors Guild
sa·ga \'sä-gə *also* 'sa-kə\ *n* [ON — more at SAW] (1709) **1** : a prose narrative recorded in Iceland in the 12th and 13th centuries of historic or legendary figures and events of the heroic age of Norway and Iceland **2** : a modern heroic narrative resembling the Icelandic saga **3** : a long detailed account ⟨a ~ of the Old South⟩
sa·ga·cious \sə-'gā-shəs, si-\ *adj* [L *sagac-, sagax*, fr. *sagire* to perceive keenly; akin to L *sagus* prophetic — more at SEEK] (1607) **1** *obs* : keen in sense perception **2 a** : of keen and farsighted penetration and judgment : DISCERNING ⟨~ judge of character⟩ **b** : caused by or

\ə\ abut \ᵊ\ kitten, F table \ər\ further \a\ ash \ā\ ace \ä\ mop, mar \au̇\ out \ch\ chin \e\ bet \ē\ easy \g\ go \i\ hit \ī\ ice \j\ job \ŋ\ sing \ō\ go \ȯ\ law \ȯi\ boy \th\ thin \th\ the \ü\ loot \u̇\ foot \y\ yet \zh\ vision, beige \k, ⁿ, œ, ʊ, �-y\ *see* Guide to Pronunciation

indicating acute discernment ⟨~ purchase of stock⟩ ***syn*** see SHREWD — **sa·ga·cious·ly** *adv* — **sa·ga·cious·ness** *n*

sa·gac·i·ty \sə-ˈga-sə-tē, si-\ *n* (15c) **:** the quality of being sagacious

sag·a·more \ˈsa-gə-ˌmȯr\ *n* [Eastern Abenaki *sɑ̀kəmɑ*] (1613) **1 :** a subordinate chief of the Algonquian Indians of the No. Atlantic coast **2 :** SACHEM 1

saga novel *n* (ca. 1938) **:** ROMAN-FLEUVE

[1]**sage** \ˈsāj\ *adj* **sag·er; sag·est** [ME, fr. AF, fr. VL **sapius,* fr. L *sapere* to taste, have good taste, be wise; akin to Oscan *sipus* knowing, OS *ansebbian* to perceive] (14c) **1 a :** wise through reflection and experience **b** *archaic* **:** GRAVE, SOLEMN **2 :** proceeding from or characterized by wisdom, prudence, and good judgment ⟨~ advice⟩ ***syn*** see WISE — **sage·ly** *adv* — **sage·ness** *n*

[2]**sage** *n* (14c) **1 :** one (as a profound philosopher) distinguished for wisdom **2 :** a mature or venerable man of sound judgment

[3]**sage** *n* [ME, fr. AF *sage, salge,* fr. L *salvia,* fr. *salvus* healthy; fr. its use as a medicinal herb — more at SAFE] (14c) **1 a :** a European perennial mint (*Salvia officinalis*) with grayish-green aromatic leaves used esp. in flavoring meats; *broadly* **:** SALVIA **b :** the fresh or dried leaves of sage **2 :** SAGEBRUSH **3 :** a light grayish green

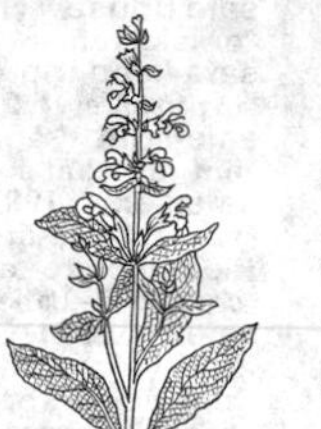

[3]sage 1a

sage·brush \ˈsāj-ˌbrəsh\ *n* (1850) **:** any of several No. American hoary composite subshrubs (genus *Artemisia*); *esp* **:** one (*A. tridentata*) having a bitter juice and an odor resembling sage and often covering vast tracts of alkaline plains in the western U.S.

sage cheese *n* (1699) **:** a cheese similar to mild cheddar flecked with green and flavored with sage

sage grouse *n* (1876) **:** either of two large grouses (*Centrocercus urophasianus* and *C. minimus*) of the dry sagebrush plains of western No. America that have mottled gray and buff plumage above with a contrasting black belly

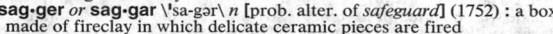

sag·ger *or* **sag·gar** \ˈsa-gər\ *n* [prob. alter. of *safeguard*] (1752) **:** a box made of fireclay in which delicate ceramic pieces are fired

sag·gy \ˈsa-gē\ *adj* (1853) **:** BAGGY; *also* **:** FLACCID 1a

sag·it·tal \ˈsa-jə-t^{ə}l\ *adj* [ME *sagittale,* fr. ML *sagittalis,* fr. L *sagitta* arrow] (14c) **1 :** of or relating to the suture between the parietal bones of the skull **2 :** of, relating to, situated in, or being the median plane of the body or any plane parallel to it — **sag·it·tal·ly** \-t^{ə}l-ē\ *adv*

Sag·it·tar·i·an \ˌsa-jə-ˈter-ē-ən\ *n* (1911) **:** SAGITTARIUS 2b

Sag·it·tar·i·us \-ē-əs\ *n* [L (gen. *Sagittarii*), lit., archer, fr. *sagitta*] (14c) **1 :** a southern zodiacal constellation pictured as a centaur shooting an arrow and containing the point in the sky where the center of the Milky Way galaxy is located **2 a :** the ninth sign of the zodiac in astrology — see ZODIAC table **b :** one born under the sign of Sagittarius

sag·it·tate \ˈsa-jə-ˌtāt\ *adj* [L *sagitta*] (1760) **:** shaped like an arrowhead; *specif* **:** elongated, triangular, and having the two basal lobes prolonged downward ⟨a ~ leaf⟩ — see LEAF illustration

sa·go \ˈsā-(ˌ)gō\ *n, pl* **sagos** [Malay *sagu* sago palm] (ca. 1580) **:** a dry granulated or powdered starch prepared from the pith of a sago palm and used in foods and as textile stiffening

sago palm *n* (1769) **:** a plant that yields sago; *esp* **:** any of various lofty pinnate-leaved Malaysian palms (genus *Metroxylon*)

sa·gua·ro \sə-ˈwär-ə, -ˈgwär-, -ō\ *n, pl* **-ros** [MexSp, prob. fr. Ópata (Uto-Aztecan language of Sonora, Mexico)] (1856) **:** a tall columnar usu. sparsely-branched cactus (*Carnegiea gigantea*) of dry areas of the southwestern U.S. and Mexico that bears white flowers and a scaly reddish edible fruit and that may attain a height of up to 50 feet (16 meters) — called also *giant cactus*

Sa·hap·tin \sə-ˈhap-tən\ *n* [Salish (Columbia River dialects) *ṣ̌ḥáptnəχʷ* Nez Percé] (1836) **:** a language spoken in a number of dialects by American Indian peoples (as the Yakama) of the interior of northern Oregon and southern Washington; *also* **:** a member of a Sahaptin-speaking people

sa·hib \ˈsä-ˌ(h)ib, -ˌ(h)ēb, ˌsä-ˈ\ *n* [Hindi *sāhab* & Urdu *ṣāḥib, ṣāḥab* companion, master, fr. Ar *ṣāḥib*] (1673) **:** SIR, MASTER — used esp. among the native inhabitants of colonial India when addressing or speaking of a European of some social or official status

[1]**said** *past and past part of* SAY

[2]**said** \ˈsed\ *adj* [pp. of *say*] (14c) **:** AFOREMENTIONED

[1]**sail** \ˈsāl, *as last element in compounds often* səl\ *n* [ME, fr. OE *segl;* akin to OHG *segal* sail] (bef. 12c) **1 a** (1) **:** an extent of fabric (as canvas) by means of which wind is used to propel a ship through water (2) **:** the sails of a ship **b** *pl usu* **sail :** a ship equipped with sails **2 :** an extent of fabric used in propelling a wind-driven vehicle (as an iceboat) **3 :** something that resembles a sail; *esp* **:** a streamlined conning tower on a submarine **4 :** a passage by a sailing craft **:** CRUISE — **sailed** \ˈsāld\ *adj* — **under sail :** in motion with sails set

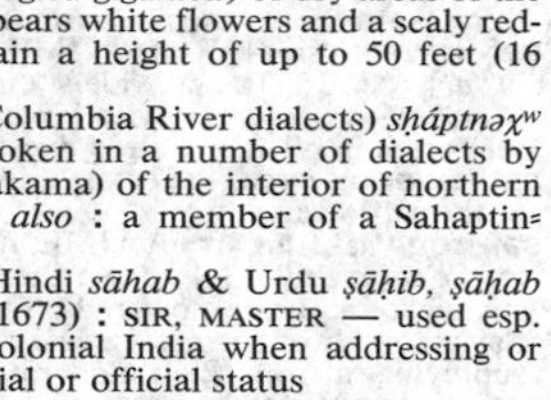

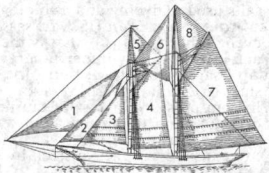

sail 1a (of a schooner): *1* flying jib, *2* jib, *3* forestaysail, *4* foresail, *5* fore gaff-topsail, *6* main-topmast staysail, *7* mainsail, *8* main gaff-topsail

[2]**sail** *vi* (bef. 12c) **1 a :** to travel on water in a ship **b :** YACHT **2 a :** to travel on water by the action of wind upon sails or by other means **b :** to move or proceed easily, gracefully, nonchalantly, or without resistance ⟨~*s* through all sorts of contradictions —Vicki Hearne⟩ ⟨the bill ~*ed* through the legislature⟩ **c :** to move through the air ⟨the ball ~*ed* over his head⟩ **3 :** to begin a water voyage ⟨~ with the tide⟩ ~ *vt* **1 a :** to travel on (water) by means of motive power (as sail) **b :** to glide through **2 :** to direct or manage the motion of (as a ship) — **sail·able** \ˈsā-lə-bəl\ *adj* — **sail into :** to attack vigorously or sharply ⟨*sailed into* me for being late⟩

sail·board \ˈsāl-ˌbȯrd\ *n* (1962) **:** a modified surfboard having a mast mounted on a universal joint and sailed by one person standing up — **sail·board·er** \-ˌbȯr-dər\ *n* — **sail·board·ing** \-diŋ\ *n*

sail·boat \ˈsāl-ˌbōt\ *n* (1752) **:** a boat usu. propelled by sail — **sail·boat·er** \-ˌbō-tər\ *n* — **sail·boat·ing** *n*

sail·cloth \-ˌklȯth\ *n* (13c) **:** a heavy canvas used for sails, tents, or upholstery; *also* **:** a lightweight canvas used for clothing

sail·er \ˈsā-lər\ *n* (15c) **:** a ship or boat esp. having specified sailing qualities

sail·fish \ˈsāl-ˌfish\ *n* (1879) **:** any of a genus (*Istiophorus,* esp. *I. platypterus*) of billfishes having a very large dorsal fin

sail·ing \ˈsā-liŋ\ *n* (bef. 12c) **1 a :** the technical skill of managing a ship **:** NAVIGATION **b :** the method of determining the course to be followed to reach a given point **2 a :** the sport of handling or riding in a sailboat **b :** a departure from a port

sail·mak·er \ˈsāl-ˌmā-kər\ *n* (1596) **:** a person or company that cuts, assembles, and sews sails and canvas parts for boats

sail·or \ˈsā-lər\ *n* [alter. of *sailer*] (1577) **1 a :** one that sails; *esp* **:** MARINER **b** (1) **:** a member of a ship's crew (2) **:** SEAMAN 2b **2 :** a traveler by water **3 :** a stiff straw hat with a low flat crown and straight circular brim

sailor collar *n* (1866) **:** a broad collar having a square flap across the back and tapering to a V in the front

sail·or's–choice \ˌsā-lərz-ˈchȯis\ *n* (1850) **:** any of several small grunts of the Western Atlantic: as **a :** PINFISH **b :** PIGFISH

sail·plane \ˈsāl-ˌplān\ *n* (1922) **:** a glider of such design that it is able to rise in an upward air current — **sailplane** *vi* — **sail·plan·er** *n*

sai·min \ˈsī-ˈmin\ *n* [prob. fr. Chin (Guangdong) *sai mihn* fine noodles] (1949) **:** a Hawaiian noodle soup

sain \ˈsān\ *vt* [ME, fr. OE *segnian,* fr. LL *signare,* fr. L, to mark — more at SIGN] (bef. 12c) **1** *dial Brit* **:** to make the sign of the cross on (oneself) **2** *dial Brit* **:** BLESS

sain·foin \ˈsān-ˌfȯin, ˈsan-\ *n* [F, fr. MF, fr. *sain* healthy (fr. L *sanus*) + *foin* hay, fr. L *fenum*] (1626) **:** a pink-flowered Eurasian perennial leguminous herb (*Onobrychis viciifolia* syn. *O. viciaefolia*) grown for forage

[1]**saint** \ˈsānt, *before a name* (ˌ)sānt *or* sənt\ *n* [ME, fr. AF *seint, saint,* fr. LL *sanctus,* fr. L, sacred, fr. pp. of *sancire* to make sacred — more at SACRED] (13c) **1 :** one officially recognized esp. through canonization as preeminent for holiness **2 a :** one of the spirits of the departed in heaven **b :** ANGEL 1a **3 a :** one of God's chosen and usu. Christian people **b** *cap* **:** a member of any of various Christian bodies; *specif* **:** LATTER-DAY SAINT **4 :** one eminent for piety or virtue **5 :** an illustrious predecessor — **saint·dom** \ˈsānt-dəm\ *n* — **saint·like** \ˈsānt-ˌlīk\ *adj*

[2]**saint** \ˈsānt\ *vt* (13c) **:** to recognize or designate as a saint; *specif* **:** CANONIZE

Saint Ag·nes' Eve \-ˈag-nə-səz-, -ˈag-nəs-\ *n* [*St. Agnes*] (1820) **:** the night of January 20 when a woman is traditionally held to have a revelation of her future husband

Saint An·drew's cross \-ˈan-ˌdrüz-\ *n* [*St. Andrew* †*ab* A.D. 60, apostle who, according to tradition, was crucified on a cross of this type] (1615) **:** a figure of a cross that has the form of two intersecting oblique bars — see CROSS illustration

Saint An·tho·ny's cross \-ˈan(t)-thə-nēz-, *chiefly Brit* -ˈan-tə-\ *n* [*St. Anthony*] (1885) **:** TAU CROSS

Saint Anthony's fire *n* (14c) **:** any of several inflammations or gangrenous conditions (as erysipelas or ergotism) of the skin

Saint Au·gus·tine grass \-ˈȯ-gə-ˌstēn-\ *n* [prob. fr. *St. Augustine,* Fla.] (1900) **:** a tropical perennial grass (*Stenotaphrum secundatum*) that has much-branched creeping stems and is used as a lawn grass and sand binder esp. in the southern U.S.

Saint Ber·nard \-bər-ˈnärd\ *n* [the hospice of Grand *St. Bernard,* where such dogs were first bred] (1839) **:** any of a Swiss alpine breed of tall powerful working dogs used esp. formerly in aiding lost travelers

saint·ed \ˈsān-təd\ *adj* (1593) **1 :** SAINTLY, PIOUS **2 :** befitting or relating to a saint **3 :** entered into heaven **:** DEAD **4 :** much admired **:** IDOLIZED

Saint El·mo's fire \ˈsānt-ˈel-(ˌ)mōz-\ *n* [*St. Elmo* (*Erasmus*) †303 Ital. bishop & patron saint of sailors] (1753) **:** a flaming phenomenon sometimes seen in stormy weather at prominent points on an airplane or ship and on land that is of the nature of a brush discharge of electricity — called also *Saint Elmo's light*

Saint Emi·lion \ˌsaⁿ-tā-mēl-ˈyōⁿ\ *n* [*Saint-Émilion,* village in SW France] (1833) **:** a red Bordeaux wine

saint·hood \ˈsānt-ˌhu̇d\ *n* (1550) **1 :** the quality or state of being a saint **2 :** saints as a group

Saint John's bread \-ˈjänz-ˌbred\ *n* (1591) **:** CAROB 2

Saint–John's–wort \-ˌwərt, -ˌwȯrt\ *n* [*St. John* the Baptist] (15c) **1 :** any of a large genus (*Hypericum* of the family Guttiferae, the Saint-John's-wort family) of cosmopolitan herbs and shrubs with showy pentamerous yellow flowers **2 :** the dried aerial parts of a Saint-John's-wort (*Hypericum perforatum*) that are held to relieve depression and are used in herbal remedies and dietary supplements

Saint Lou·is encephalitis \-ˈlü-əs-\ *n* [*St. Louis,* Mo.] (1934) **:** a No. American encephalitis that is caused by a flavivirus (species *St. Louis encephalitis virus* of the genus *Flavivirus*) transmitted by several culex mosquitoes

saint·ly \ˈsānt-lē\ *adj* **saint·li·er; -est** (1534) **:** relating to, resembling, or befitting a saint **:** HOLY — **saint·li·ness** *n*

Saint Mar·tin's summer \-ˈmär-t^{ə}nz-\ *n* [*Saint Martin's* Day, November 11] (1591) **:** Indian summer when occurring in November

Saint Pat·rick's Day \-ˈpa-triks-\ *n* (1726) **:** March 17 observed by the Roman Catholic Church in honor of St. Patrick and celebrated in Ireland in commemoration of his death

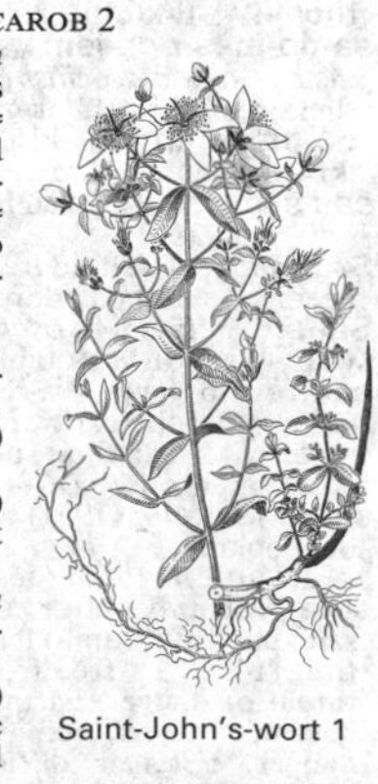

Saint-John's-wort 1

saint's day *n* (15c) **:** a day in a church calendar on which a saint is commemorated

saint·ship \ˈsānt-ˌship\ *n* (1631) **:** SAINTHOOD 1

Saint Valentine's Day *n* [*St. Valentine* †*ab*270 Ital. priest] (14c) : VALENTINE'S DAY
Saint Vi·tus' dance \-ˈvī-təs-, -ˈvī-tə-səz-\ *n* [*St. Vitus,* 3d cent. Christian child martyr] (1621) : CHOREA — called also *Saint Vitus's dance* *same*\
saith \ˈseth, ˈsā-əth\ *archaic pres 3d sing of* SAY
saithe \ˈsāth, ˈsā*th*\ *n, pl* **saithe** [of Scand origin; akin to ON *seithr* coalfish] (1632) : POLLACK 1
Sai·va \ˈsī-və, ˈshī-\ *n* [Skt *Śaiva,* fr. *Śiva* Shiva] (1810) : a member of a major Hindu sect devoted to the cult of Shiva — **Sai·vism** \-ˌvi-zəm\ *n*
[1]**sake** \ˈsāk\ *n* [ME, dispute, guilt, purpose, fr. OE *sacu* guilt, action at law; akin to OHG *sahha* action at law, cause, OE *sēcan* to seek — more at SEEK] (13c) **1** : END, PURPOSE ⟨for the ~ of argument⟩ **2 a** : the good, advantage, or enhancement of some entity (as an ideal) ⟨free to pursue learning for its own ~ —M. S. Eisenhower⟩ **b** : personal or social welfare, safety, or benefit
[2]**sa·ke** *or* **sa·ki** \ˈsä-kē\ *n* [Jp *sake*] (1682) : a Japanese alcoholic beverage of fermented rice often served hot
sa·ker \ˈsā-kər\ *n* [ME *sacre,* fr. AF, fr. Ar *ṣaqr*] (15c) : a grayish-brown Old World falcon (*Falco cherrug*) that is used in falconry
Sakti, Saktism *var of* SHAKTI, SHAKTISM
sal \ˈsal\ *n* [ME, fr. L — more at SALT] (14c) : SALT
[1]**sa·laam** \sə-ˈläm\ *n* [Ar *salām,* lit., peace] (1611) **1** : an obeisance performed by bowing very low and placing the right palm on the forehead **2** : a salutation or ceremonial greeting in the East
[2]**salaam** *vt* (1693) : to greet or pay homage to with a salaam ~ *vi* : to perform a salaam
sal·able *or* **sale·able** \ˈsā-lə-bəl\ *adj* (1530) : capable of being or fit to be sold : MARKETABLE — **sal·abil·i·ty** \ˌsā-lə-ˈbi-lə-tē\ *n*
sa·la·cious \sə-ˈlā-shəs\ *adj* [L *salac-, salax,* fr. *salire* to move spasmodically, leap — more at SALLY] (ca. 1645) **1** : arousing or appealing to sexual desire or imagination : LASCIVIOUS **2** : LECHEROUS, LUSTFUL — **sa·la·cious·ly** *adv* — **sa·la·cious·ness** *n*
sal·ad \ˈsa-ləd\ *n* [ME *salade,* fr. MF, fr. OIt (northern dialects) *salata, salada,* fr. *salar* to salt, fr. *sal* salt, fr. L] (14c) **1** : any of various usu. cold dishes: as **a** : raw greens (as lettuce) often combined with other vegetables and toppings and served esp. with dressing **b** : small pieces of food (as pasta, meat, fruit, or vegetables) usu. mixed with a dressing (as mayonnaise) or set in gelatin **2** : a green vegetable or herb grown for salad; *esp* : LETTUCE **3** : a usu. incongruous mixture : HODGEPODGE
salad bar *n* (1937) : a self-service counter (as in a restaurant) featuring an array of salad makings and dressings
salad days *n pl* (1606) : time of youthful inexperience or indiscretion ⟨my *salad days* when I was green in judgment —Shak.⟩; *also* : an early flourishing period : HEYDAY
salad oil *n* (1537) : an edible vegetable oil suitable for use in salad dressings
sa·lal \sə-ˈlal, sa-\ *n* [Chinook Jargon, fr. Lower Chinook *sálal*] (1825) : a small evergreen shrub (*Gaultheria shallon*) of the heath family found on the Pacific coast of No. America and bearing edible grape-sized dark purple berries
sal·a·man·der \ˈsa-lə-ˌman-dər *also* ˌsa-lə-ˈ\ *n* [ME *salamandre,* fr. AF, fr. L *salamandra,* fr. Gk] (14c) **1** : a mythical animal having the power to endure fire without harm **2** : an elemental being in the theory of Paracelsus inhabiting fire **3** : any of numerous amphibians (order Caudata) superficially resembling lizards but scaleless and covered with a soft moist skin and breathing by gills in the larval stage **4** : an article used in connection with fire: as **a** : a cooking utensil for browning a food (as pastry or pudding) **b** : a portable stove **c** : a cooking device with an overhead heat source like a broiler — **sal·a·man·drine** \ˌsa-lə-ˈman-drən\ *adj*
sa·la·mi \sə-ˈlä-mē\ *n* [It, pl. of *salame* salami, fr. *salare* to salt, fr. *sale* salt, fr. L *sal* — more at SALT] (1850) : a highly seasoned sausage of pork and beef either dried or fresh
sal ammoniac *n* [ME *sal armoniak,* fr. L *sal ammoniacus,* lit., salt of Ammon] (14c) : AMMONIUM CHLORIDE
sa·lar·i·at \sə-ˈler-ē-ət\ *n* [F, fr. *sal*aire salary (fr. L *salarium*) + *-ariat* (as in *prolétariat* proletariat)] (1917) : the class or body of salaried persons usu. as distinguished from wage earners
sal·a·ry \ˈsal-rē, ˈsa-lə-\ *n, pl* **-ries** [ME *salarie,* fr. AF, fr. L *salarium* pension, salary, fr. neut. of *salarius* of salt, fr. *sal* salt — more at SALT] (13c) : fixed compensation paid regularly for services — **sal·a·ried** \-rēd\ *adj*
sal·a·ry·man \-ˌman\ *n* [Jp *sararī-man,* fr. E *salary* + *man*] (1962) : a Japanese white-collar businessman
sal·chow \ˈsal-ˌkau̇, -ˌkȯv, -(ˌ)kō\ *n, often cap* [Ulrich *Salchow* †1949 Swed. figure skater] (1921) : a figure-skating jump with a takeoff from the back inside edge of one skate followed by one or more full turns in the air and a landing on the back outside edge of the opposite skate
sale \ˈsāl\ *n* [ME, fr. OE *sala;* akin to OHG *sala* transfer, OE *sellan* to sell — more at SELL] (bef. 12c) **1** : the act of selling; *specif* : the transfer of ownership of and title to property from one person to another for a price **2 a** : opportunity of selling or being sold : DEMAND **b** : distribution by selling **3** : public disposal to the highest bidder : AUCTION **4** : a selling of goods at bargain prices **5** *pl* **a** : operations and activities involved in promoting and selling goods or services ⟨vice-president in charge of ~*s*⟩ **b** : gross receipts — **for sale** : available for purchase — **on sale** **1** : for sale **2** : available for purchase at a reduced price
sa·lep \ˈsa-ləp, sə-ˈlep\ *n* [F or Sp, both fr. Ar dial. *saḥlab,* perh. alter. of Ar (*khuṣy al-*)*thaʿlab,* lit., testicles of the fox] (1736) : the starchy or mucilaginous dried tubers of various Old World orchids (esp. genus *Orchis*) used for food or in medicine
sal·e·ra·tus \ˌsa-lə-ˈrā-təs\ *n* [NL *sal aeratus* aerated salt] (1837) : a leavening agent consisting of potassium or sodium bicarbonate
sale·room \ˈsāl-ˌrüm, -ˌru̇m\ *chiefly Brit var of* SALESROOM
sales \ˈsālz\ *adj* (1840) : of, relating to, or used in selling
sales·clerk \ˈsālz-ˌklərk\ *n* (1926) : a salesperson in a store
sales·girl \-ˌgər(-ə)l\ *n* (1887) : SALESWOMAN
Sa·le·sian \sə-ˈlē-zhən, sā-\ *n* (1884) : a member of the Society of St. Francis de Sales founded by St. John Bosco in Turin, Italy in the 19th century and devoted chiefly to education
sales·la·dy \ˈsālz-ˌlā-dē\ *n* (1856) : SALESWOMAN
sales·man \ˈsālz-mən\ *n* (1523) : one who sells in a given territory, in a store, or by telephone
sales·man·ship \-ˌship\ *n* (1880) **1** : the skill or art of selling **2** : ability or effectiveness in selling or in presenting persuasively ⟨political ~⟩
sales·peo·ple \-ˌpē-pəl\ *n pl* (1876) : persons employed to sell goods or services
sales·per·son \-ˌpər-sᵊn\ *n* (1901) : a salesman or saleswoman
sales·room \ˈsālz-ˌrüm, -ˌru̇m\ *n* (1840) : a place where goods are displayed for sale; *esp* : an auction room
sales slip *n* (1926) : a receipt for a purchase
sales tax *n* (1921) : a tax levied on the sale of goods and services that is usu. calculated as a percentage of the purchase price and collected by the seller
sales·wom·an \ˈsālz-ˌwu̇-mən\ *n* (1704) : a woman who sells in a given territory, in a store, or by telephone
sal·ic \ˈsa-lik\ *adj* [by alter.] (1902) : SIALIC
Sa·lic \ˈsā-lik, ˈsa-\ *also* **Sa·lique** \ˈsā-lik, ˈsa-; sa-ˈlēk, sā-\ *adj* [MF or ML; MF *salique,* fr. ML *Salicus,* fr. LL *Salii* Salic Franks] (ca. 1548) : of, relating to, or being a Frankish people that settled on the IJssel River early in the fourth century
sal·i·cin \ˈsa-lə-sən\ *n* [F *salicine,* fr. L *salic-, salix* willow — more at SALLOW] (1830) : a bitter white crystalline glucoside $C_{13}H_{18}O_7$ found in the bark and leaves of several willows and poplars and used in medicine like salicylic acid
Salic law *n* (1599) **1** : a rule held to derive from the legal code of the Salic Franks excluding females from the line of succession to a throne **2** : the legal code of the Salic Franks
sa·lic·y·late \sə-ˈli-sə-ˌlāt\ *n* (1842) : a salt or ester of salicylic acid
sal·i·cyl·ic acid \ˌsa-lə-ˈsi-lik-\ *n* [F *salicylique,* fr. *salicyle,* the group HOC_6H_4CO, fr. *salicine* salicin + *-yle* -yl] (1840) : a crystalline phenolic acid $C_7H_6O_3$ that is used medicinally esp. as an exfoliant and in the form of salts and other derivatives as an analgesic and antipyretic — compare ASPIRIN
sa·lience \ˈsā-lyən(t)s, -lē-ən(t)s\ *n* (1836) **1** : the quality or state of being salient **2** : a striking point or feature : HIGHLIGHT
sa·lien·cy \-lyən(t)-sē, -lē-ən(t)-\ *n, pl* **-cies** (1664) : SALIENCE
[1]**sa·lient** \ˈsā-lyənt, -lē-ənt\ *adj* [L *salient-, saliens,* prp. of *salire* to leap — more at SALLY] (1646) **1** : moving by leaps or springs : JUMPING **2** : jetting upward ⟨a ~ fountain⟩ **3 a** : projecting beyond a line, surface, or level **b** : standing out conspicuously : PROMINENT; *esp* : of notable significance ⟨similar to . . . Prohibition, but there are a couple of ~ differences —Tony Gibbs⟩ ***syn*** see NOTICEABLE — **sa·lient·ly** *adv*
[2]**salient** *n* (1828) : something (as a promontory) that projects outward or upward from its surroundings; *esp* : an outwardly projecting part of a fortification, trench system, or line of defense
[1]**sa·line** \ˈsā-ˌlēn, -ˌlīn\ *adj* [ME, fr. AF *salin,* fr. L *salinus,* fr. *sal* salt — more at SALT] (15c) **1** : consisting of or containing salt ⟨a ~ solution⟩ **2** : of, relating to, or resembling salt : SALTY ⟨a ~ taste⟩ **3** : consisting of or relating to the salts of the alkali metals or of magnesium ⟨a ~ cathartic⟩ — **sa·lin·i·ty** \sā-ˈli-nə-tē, sə-\ *n*
[2]**saline** *n* (1662) **1** : a metallic salt; *esp* : a salt of potassium, sodium, or magnesium with a cathartic action **2** : a saline solution; *esp* : one isosmotic with body fluids
sa·li·nize \ˈsa-lə-ˌnīz *also* ˈsā-\ *vt* **-nized; -niz·ing** (1926) : to treat or impregnate with salt — **sa·li·ni·za·tion** \ˌsa-lə-nə-ˈzā-shən *also* ˌsā-\ *n*
sa·li·nom·e·ter \ˌsa-lə-ˈnä-mə-tər, ˌsā-\ *n* [ISV *saline* + *-o-* + *-meter*] (1844) : an instrument (as a hydrometer) for measuring the amount of salt in a solution
Salique *var of* SALIC
Salis·bury steak \ˈsȯlz-ˌber-ē-, ˈsalz-, -b(ə-)rē-\ *n* [James Henry *Salisbury* †1905 Am. physician] (1897) : ground beef mixed with egg, milk, bread crumbs, and seasonings and formed into a large patty and cooked
Sa·lish \ˈsā-lish\ *n* [Flathead dial. of Interior Salish *séliš,* a self-designation] (1831) **1** : a group of American Indian peoples of British Columbia and the northwestern U.S. **2** : the family of languages spoken by the Salish peoples — **Sa·lish·an** \-li-shən\ *adj or n*
sa·li·va \sə-ˈlī-və\ *n* [L] (15c) : a slightly alkaline secretion of water, mucin, protein, salts, and often a starch-splitting enzyme (as ptyalin) that is secreted into the mouth by salivary glands, lubricates ingested food, and often begins the breakdown of starches
sal·i·vary \ˈsa-lə-ˌver-ē\ *adj* (1709) : of or relating to saliva or the glands that secrete it; *esp* : producing or carrying saliva
sal·i·vate \ˈsa-lə-ˌvāt\ *vi* **-vat·ed; -vat·ing** (ca. 1706) **1** : to have a flow of saliva esp. in excess **2** : to show great desire or anticipation : DROOL — **sal·i·va·tion** \ˌsa-lə-ˈvā-shən\ *n* — **sal·i·va·tor** \ˈsa-lə-ˌvā-tər\ *n*
Salk vaccine \ˈsȯk-, ˈsȯlk-\ *n* [Jonas *Salk*] (1954) : a vaccine consisting of poliomyelitis virus inactivated with formaldehyde
sal·let \ˈsa-lət\ *n* [ME, fr. MF *sallade*] (15c) : a light 15th century helmet with or without a visor and with a projection over the neck
[1]**sal·low** \ˈsa-(ˌ)lō\ *n* [ME, fr. OE *sealh;* akin to OHG *salha* sallow, L *salix* willow] (bef. 12c) : any of several Old World broad-leaved willows (as *Salix caprea*) including important sources of charcoal and tanbark
[2]**sallow** *adj* [ME *salowe,* fr. OE *salu;* akin to OHG *salo* murky, Russ *solovyĭ* yellowish gray] (bef. 12c) : of a grayish greenish yellow color — **sal·low·ish** \ˈsa-lə-wish\ *adj* — **sal·low·ness** \ˈsa-lō-nəs, -lə-\ *n*
[1]**sal·ly** \ˈsa-lē\ *n, pl* **sallies** [MF *saillie,* fr. OF, fr. *saillir* to rush forward, fr. L *salire* to leap; akin to Gk *hallesthai* to leap] (1560) **1** : an action of rushing or bursting forth; *esp* : a sortie of troops from a defensive position to attack the enemy **2 a** : a brief outbreak : OUTBURST **b** : a witty or imaginative saying : QUIP **3** : a venture or excursion usu. off the beaten track : JAUNT
[2]**sally** *vi* **sal·lied; sal·ly·ing** (1560) **1** : to leap out or burst forth suddenly **2** : SET OUT, DEPART — often used with *forth*

Sal·ly Lunn \ˌsa-lē-ˈlən\ *n* [*Sally Lunn*, 18th cent. Eng. baker] (1780) **:** a slightly sweetened yeast-leavened bread

sally port *n* (1649) **1 :** a gate or passage in a fortified place for use by troops making a sortie **2 :** a secure entryway (as at a prison) that consists of a series of doors or gates

sal·ma·gun·di \ˌsal-mə-ˈgən-dē\ *n* [F *salmigondis*] (ca. 1674) **1 :** a salad plate of chopped meats, anchovies, eggs, and vegetables arranged in rows for contrast and dressed with a salad dressing **2 :** a heterogeneous mixture **:** POTPOURRI

sal·mi \ˈsal-mē\ *n* [F *salmis*, short for *salmigondis*] (1759) **:** a ragout of partly roasted game stewed in a rich sauce

salm·on \ˈsa-mən\ *n, pl* **salmon** *also* **salmons** [ME *samon*, fr. AF *salmon, samon*, fr. L *salmon-, salmo*] (13c) **1 a :** a large anadromous salmonid fish (*Salmo salar*) of the No. Atlantic noted as a game and food fish — called also *Atlantic salmon* **b :** any of various anadromous salmonid fishes other than the salmon; *esp* **:** PACIFIC SALMON **c :** a fish (as a barramundi) resembling a salmon **2 :** the variable color of salmon's flesh averaging a strong yellowish pink

salm·on·ber·ry \-ˌber-ē\ *n* (1844) **:** a showy red-flowered raspberry (*Rubus spectabilis*) of the Pacific coast of No. America; *also* **:** its edible salmon-colored fruit

sal·mo·nel·la \ˌsal-mə-ˈne-lə\ *n, pl* **-nel·lae** \-ˈne-(ˌ)lē, -ˌlī\ *or* **-nellas** *or* **-nella** [NL, fr. Daniel E. *Salmon* †1914 Am. veterinarian] (1913) **:** any of a genus (*Salmonella*) of usu. motile enterobacteria that are pathogenic for humans and other warm-blooded animals and cause food poisoning, gastrointestinal inflammation, typhoid fever, or septicemia

sal·mo·nel·lo·sis \ˌsal-mə-(ˌ)ne-ˈlō-səs\ *n, pl* **-lo·ses** \-ˌsēz\ [NL] (ca. 1913) **:** infection with or disease caused by salmonellae

sal·mo·nid \ˈsa-mə-nid, ˈsal-\ *n* [NL *Salmonidae*, fr. *Salmon-, Salmo*, genus name, fr. L *salmo* salmon] (1868) **:** any of a family (Salmonidae) of elongate bony fishes (as a salmon or trout) that have the last three vertebrae upturned — **salmonid** *adj*

salm·on·oid \ˈsa-mə-ˌnȯid\ *n* (ca. 1842) **:** SALMONID; *also* **:** a related fish — **salmonoid** *adj*

salmon pink *n* (1882) **:** a strong yellowish pink

Sa·lo·me \sə-ˈlō-mē, ˈsa-lə-(ˌ)mā\ *n* [LL, fr. Gk *Salōmē*] (1623) **:** a niece of Herod Antipas given the head of John the Baptist as a reward for her dancing

sa·lom·e·ter \sā-ˈlä-mə-tər, sə-\ *n* [L *sal* salt + E *-o-* + *-meter*] (1860) **:** a hydrometer for indicating the percentage of salt in a solution

sa·lon \sə-ˈlän, ˈsa-ˌlän, sa-ˈlōⁿ\ *n* [F] (1699) **1 :** an elegant apartment or living room (as in a fashionable home) **2 :** a fashionable assemblage of notables (as literary figures, artists, or statesmen) held by custom at the home of a prominent person **3 a :** a hall for exhibition of art **b** *cap* **:** an annual exhibition of works of art **4 :** a stylish business establishment or shop ⟨a beauty ~⟩

sa·loon \sə-ˈlün\ *n* [F *salon*, fr. It *salone*, aug. of *sala* hall, of Gmc origin; akin to OHG *sal* hall; akin to Lith *sala* village] (1728) **1 a** *chiefly Brit* **:** SALON 1 **b** *chiefly Brit* **:** an often elaborately decorated public hall **c (1) :** a usu. large public cabin on a ship (as for dining) **(2) :** the living area on a yacht **d** *chiefly Brit* **:** SALON 4 **e :** BARROOM **2 :** SALON 2 **3** *Brit* **a :** PARLOR CAR **b :** SEDAN 2a — called also *saloon car*

salp \ˈsalp\ *also* **sal·pa** \ˈsal-pə\ *n* [NL, fr. L, a kind of deep-sea fish, fr. Gk *salpē*] (1835) **:** any of various transparent barrel-shaped or fusiform free-swimming tunicates (class Thaliacea) abundant in warm seas

sal·pi·glos·sis \ˌsal-pə-ˈglä-səs\ *n* [NL, irreg. fr. Gk *salpinx* trumpet + *glōssa* tongue — more at GLOSS] (1827) **:** any of a small genus (*Salpiglossis*) of Chilean herbs of the nightshade family with large funnel-shaped varicolored flowers often strikingly marked

sal·pin·gi·tis \ˌsal-pən-ˈjī-təs\ *n* [NL, fr. *salping-, salpinx* fallopian or eustachian tube, fr. Gk, trumpet] (1860) **:** inflammation of a fallopian or eustachian tube

sal·sa \ˈsȯl-sə, ˈsäl-\ *n* [Sp, lit., sauce, fr. L, fem. of *salsus* salted — more at SAUCE] (ca. 1962) **1 :** a spicy sauce of tomatoes, onions, and hot peppers **2 :** popular music of Latin American origin that has absorbed characteristics of rhythm and blues, jazz, and rock

sal·si·fy \ˈsal-sə-fē, -ˌfī\ *n, pl* **-fies** [F *salsifis*, fr. It *salsefica, sassefrica*] (ca. 1706) **:** a European biennial composite herb (*Tragopogon porrifolius*) with a long fusiform edible root — called also *oyster plant, vegetable oyster*

[1]salt \ˈsȯlt\ *n* [ME, fr. OE *sealt*; akin to OHG *salz* salt, Lith *saldus* sweet, L *sal* salt, Gk *hals* salt, sea] (bef. 12c) **1 a :** a crystalline compound NaCl that consists of sodium chloride, is abundant in nature, and is used esp. to season or preserve food or in industry — called also *common salt* **b :** a substance (as Glauber's salt) resembling common salt **c** *pl* **(1) :** a mineral or saline mixture (as Epsom salts) used as an aperient or cathartic **(2) :** SMELLING SALTS **d :** any of various compounds that result from replacement of part or all of the acid hydrogen of an acid by a metal or a group acting like a metal **:** an ionic crystalline compound **2 :** a container for salt at table — often used in the phrases *above the salt* and *below the salt* alluding to the former custom of seating persons of higher rank above and those of lower rank below a saltcellar placed in the middle of a long table **3 a :** an ingredient that gives savor, piquancy, or zest **:** FLAVOR ⟨a people . . . full of life, vigor, and the ~ of personality —Clifton Fadiman⟩ **b :** sharpness of wit **:** PUNGENCY **c :** COMMON SENSE **d :** RESERVE, SKEPTICISM — usu. used in the phrases *with a grain of salt* and *with a pinch of salt* **e :** a dependable steadfast person or group of people — usu. used in the phrase *salt of the earth* **4 :** SAILOR ⟨a tale worthy of an old ~⟩ **5 :** KEEP 3 — usu. used in the phrase *worth one's salt* — **salt·like** \-ˌlīk\ *adj*

[2]salt *vt* (bef. 12c) **1 a :** to treat, provide, or season with common salt **b :** to preserve (food) with salt or in brine **c :** to supply (as an animal) with salt **2 :** to give flavor or piquancy to (as a story) **3 a :** to enrich (as a mine) artificially by secretly placing valuable mineral in some of the working places **b :** to add something to secretly ⟨~*ed* the files with forged papers⟩; *also* **:** to insert or place secretly ⟨~*ed* the mines along the road⟩ **4 a :** to sprinkle with or as if with a salt **b :** SCATTER, INTERSPERSE — **salt·er** \ˈsȯl-tər\ *n*

[3]salt *adj* (bef. 12c) **1 a :** SALINE, SALTY **b :** being or inducing the one of the four basic taste sensations that is suggestive of seawater — compare BITTER, SOUR, SWEET **2 :** cured or seasoned with salt **:** SALTED ⟨~ cod⟩ **3 :** overflowed with salt water ⟨a ~ pond⟩ **4 :** SHARP, PUNGENT — **salt·ness** *n*

[4]salt *adj* [by shortening & alter. fr. *assaut*, fr. ME, fr. AF *en saut* in rut] (1598) *obs* **:** LUSTFUL, LASCIVIOUS

SALT *abbr* Strategic Arms Limitation Talks

salt–and–pepper *adj* (1915) **:** having black-and-white or dark and light color intermingled in small flecks ⟨a ~ suit⟩ ⟨a ~ beard⟩

sal·ta·rel·lo \ˌsal-tə-ˈre-(ˌ)lō, ˌsäl-\ *n, pl* **-los** [It, fr. *saltare* to jump, fr. L] (ca. 1724) **:** an Italian dance with a lively hop step beginning each measure

sal·ta·tion \sal-ˈtā-shən, sȯl-\ *n* [L *saltation-, saltatio*, fr. *saltare* to leap, dance, freq. of *salire* to leap — more at SALLY] (1646) **1 a :** the action or process of leaping or jumping **b :** DANCE **2 a :** the origin of a new species or a higher taxon in essentially a single evolutionary step that in some esp. former theories is held to be due to a major mutation or to unknown causes — compare DARWINISM, NEO-DARWINISM, PUNCTUATED EQUILIBRIUM **b :** MUTATION — used esp. of bacteria and fungi

sal·ta·to·ri·al \ˌsal-tə-ˈtȯr-ē-əl, ˌsȯl-\ *adj* (1789) **:** relating to, marked by, or adapted for leaping ⟨~ legs of a grasshopper⟩

sal·ta·to·ry \ˈsal-tə-ˌtȯr-ē, ˈsȯl-\ *adj* (1656) **1** *archaic* **:** of or relating to dancing **2 :** proceeding by leaps rather than by gradual transitions **:** DISCONTINUOUS

salt away *vt* (ca. 1890) **:** to lay away (as money) safely **:** SAVE

salt·box \ˈsȯlt-ˌbäks\ *n* (1876) **:** a frame dwelling with two stories in front and one behind and a roof with a long rear slope

salt·bush \-ˌbu̇sh\ *n* (1863) **:** any of various shrubby plants of the goosefoot family that thrive in dry alkaline soil; *esp* **:** any of numerous oraches that are important browse plants in dry regions

salt cedar *n* (1881) **:** TAMARISK

salt·cel·lar \ˈsȯlt-ˌse-lər\ *n* [ME *salt saler*, fr. *salt* + *saler* saltcellar, fr. AF, fr. L *salarius* of salt — more at SALARY] (14c) **:** a small container for holding salt at the table

salt dome *n* (1908) **:** a domical anticline in sedimentary rock that has a mass of rock salt as its core

salt flat *n* (1816) **:** a salt-encrusted flat area resulting from evaporation of a former body of water

salt gland *n* (1950) **:** a gland (as of a marine bird or a plant) capable of excreting a concentrated salt solution

salt grass *n* (1704) **:** a grass (esp. *Distichlis spicata*) native to an alkaline habitat (as a salt marsh)

sal·tim·boc·ca \ˌsȯl-təm-ˈbä-kə\ *n* [It, fr. *saltare* to jump + *in* in + *bocca* mouth] (1937) **:** scallops of veal prepared with sage, slices of ham, and sometimes cheese and served with a wine sauce

sal·tine \sȯl-ˈtēn\ *n* (1907) **:** a thin crisp cracker usu. sprinkled with salt

salt·ing \ˈsȯl-tiŋ\ *n* (1712) *chiefly Brit* **:** land flooded regularly by tides — usu. used in pl.

sal·tire \ˈsȯl-ˌtī(-ə)r, ˈsal-\ *n* [ME *sautire*, fr. AF *sautour*] (14c) **:** a heraldic charge consisting of a cross formed by a bend and a bend sinister crossing in the center

salt lake *n* (1763) **:** a landlocked body of water that has become salty through evaporation

salt·less \ˈsȯlt-ləs\ *adj* (14c) **1 :** having no salt **2 :** INSIPID

salt lick *n* (1751) **:** LICK 3

salt marsh *n* (bef. 12c) **:** flat land subject to overflow by salt water

salt out *vt* (1857) **:** to precipitate, coagulate, or separate (as a dissolved substance) esp. from a solution by the addition of salt ~ *vi* **:** to become salted out

salt pan *n* (15c) **:** an undrained natural depression in which water gathers and leaves a deposit of salt on evaporation

salt·pe·ter \ˈsȯlt-ˈpē-tər\ *n* [ME *salt petre*, alter. of *salpetre*, fr. ML *sal petrae*, lit., salt of the rock] (14c) **1 :** POTASSIUM NITRATE **2 :** SODIUM NITRATE

salt pork *n* (1708) **:** fat pork cured in salt or brine

salt·shak·er \ˈsȯlt-ˌshā-kər\ *n* (1895) **:** a container with a perforated top for sprinkling salt

salt·wa·ter \ˈsȯlt-ˌwȯ-tər, -ˌwä-\ *adj* (bef. 12c) **:** relating to, living in, located near, or consisting of salt water ⟨~ fish⟩

salt·works \ˈsȯlt-ˌwərks\ *n pl but sing or pl in constr* (1565) **:** a plant where salt is prepared commercially

salt·wort \-ˌwərt, -ˌwȯrt\ *n* (1568) **1 :** any of a genus (*Salsola*) of plants (as the Russian thistle) of the goosefoot family of which some have been used in making soda ash **2 :** a low-growing strong-smelling succulent coastal shrub (*Batis maritima* of the family Bataceae) of warm parts of the New World

salty \ˈsȯl-tē\ *adj* **salt·i·er; -est** (15c) **1 :** of, seasoned with, or containing salt **2 :** smacking of the sea or nautical life **3 a :** PIQUANT **b :** EARTHY, CRUDE ⟨~ language⟩ — **salt·i·ly** \-tə-lē\ *adv* — **salt·i·ness** \-tē-nəs\ *n*

sa·lu·bri·ous \sə-ˈlü-brē-əs\ *adj* [L *salubris*; akin to *salvus* safe, healthy — more at SAFE] (1547) **:** favorable to or promoting health or well-being ⟨~ habits⟩ ***syn*** see HEALTHFUL — **sa·lu·bri·ous·ly** *adv* — **sa·lu·bri·ous·ness** *n* — **sa·lu·bri·ty** \-brə-tē\ *n*

sa·lu·ki \sə-ˈlü-kē\ *n* [Ar *salūqī* of Saluq, fr. *Salūq* Saluq, ancient city in Arabia] (1809) **:** any of an ancient northern African and Asian breed of tall swift slender hunting dogs having long narrow heads, long silky ears, and a smooth silky coat

sal·u·tary \ˈsal-yə-ˌter-ē\ *adj* [MF *salutaire*, fr. L *salutaris*, fr. *salut-, salus* health] (15c) **1 :** producing a beneficial effect **:** REMEDIAL ⟨~ influences⟩ **2 :** promoting health **:** CURATIVE ***syn*** see HEALTHFUL — **sal·u·tar·i·ly** \ˌsal-yə-ˈter-ə-lē\ *adv* — **sal·u·tar·i·ness** \ˈsal-yə-ˌter-ē-nəs\ *n*

sal·u·ta·tion \ˌsal-yə-ˈtā-shən\ *n* (14c) **1 a :** an expression of greeting, goodwill, or courtesy by word, gesture, or ceremony **b** *pl* **:** REGARDS **2 :** the word or phrase of greeting (as *Gentlemen* or *Dear Sir* or *Madam*) that conventionally comes immediately before the body of a letter — **sal·u·ta·tion·al** \-shnəl, -shə-nᵊl\ *adj*

sa·lu·ta·to·ri·an \sə-ˌlü-tə-ˈtȯr-ē-ən\ *n* (ca. 1847) **:** the student usu. having the second highest rank in a graduating class who delivers the salutatory address at the commencement exercises

[1]sa·lu·ta·to·ry \sə-ˈlü-tə-ˌtȯr-ē\ *adj* (1702) **:** of or relating to a salutation **:** expressing or containing a welcome or greeting

[2]salutatory *n, pl* **-ries** (1779) **:** an address or statement of welcome or greeting

[1]sa·lute \sə-ˈlüt\ *vb* **sa·lut·ed; sa·lut·ing** [ME, fr. L *salutare*, fr. *salut-, salus* health, safety, greeting, fr. *salvus* safe, healthy — more at SAFE] *vt* (14c) **1 a :** to address with expressions of kind wishes, courtesy, or honor **b :** to give a sign of respect, courtesy, or goodwill to : GREET **2 :** to become apparent to (one of the senses) **3 a :** to honor (as a person, nation, or event) by a conventional military or naval ceremony **b :** to show respect and recognition to (a military superior) by assuming a prescribed position **c :** to express commendation of : PRAISE ~ *vi* : to make a salute — **sa·lut·er** *n*

[2]**salute** *n* (14c) **1 :** GREETING, SALUTATION **2 a :** a sign, token, or ceremony expressing goodwill, compliment, or respect ⟨the festival was a ~ to the arts⟩ **b :** the position (as of the hand) or the entire attitude of a person saluting a superior **3 :** FIRECRACKER

sal·u·tif·er·ous \ˌsal-yə-ˈti-f(ə-)rəs\ *adj* [L *salutifer,* fr. *salut-, salus* + *-i-* + *-fer* -ferous] (ca. 1540) : SALUTARY

salv·able \ˈsal-və-bəl\ *adj* [LL *salvare* to save — more at SAVE] (1667) : capable of being saved or salvaged

[1]**sal·vage** \ˈsal-vij\ *n* [F, fr. MF, fr. *salver* to save — more at SAVE] (1645) **1 a :** compensation paid for saving a ship or its cargo from the perils of the sea or for the lives and property rescued in a wreck **b :** the act of saving or rescuing a ship or its cargo **c :** the act of saving or rescuing property in danger (as from fire) **2 a :** property saved from destruction in a calamity (as a wreck or fire) **b :** something extracted (as from rubbish) as valuable or useful

[2]**salvage** *vt* **sal·vaged; sal·vag·ing** (1889) : to rescue or save esp. from wreckage or ruin — **sal·vage·abil·i·ty** \ˌsal-vi-jə-ˈbi-lə-tē\ *n* — **sal·vage·able** \ˈsal-vi-jə-bəl\ *adj* — **sal·vag·er** *n*

sal·var·san \ˈsal-vər-ˌsan\ *n* [fr. *Salvarsan,* a trademark] (1909) : ARSPHENAMINE

sal·va·tion \sal-ˈvā-shən\ *n* [ME *salvacion,* fr. AF, fr. LL *salvation-, salvatio,* fr. *salvare* to save — more at SAVE] (13c) **1 a :** deliverance from the power and effects of sin **b :** the agent or means that effects salvation **c** *Christian Science* **:** the realization of the supremacy of infinite Mind over all bringing with it the destruction of the illusion of sin, sickness, and death **2 :** liberation from ignorance or illusion **3 a :** preservation from destruction or failure **b :** deliverance from danger or difficulty — **sal·va·tion·al** \-shnəl, -shə-nᵊl\ *adj*

Salvation Army *n* (1878) : an international religious and charitable group organized on military lines and founded in 1865 by William Booth for evangelizing and social betterment (as of the poor)

sal·va·tion·ism \sal-ˈvā-shə-ˌni-zəm\ *n* (1883) : religious teaching emphasizing the saving of the soul

Sal·va·tion·ist \-sh(ə-)nist\ *n* (1882) **1 :** a soldier or officer of the Salvation Army **2** *often not cap* **:** EVANGELIST 2 — **salvationist** *adj, often cap*

[1]**salve** \ˈsav, ˈsäv, ˈsalv, ˈsälv\ *n* [ME, fr. OE *sealf;* akin to OHG *salba* salve, Gk *olpē* oil flask] (bef. 12c) **1 :** an unctuous adhesive substance for application to wounds or sores **2 :** a remedial or soothing influence or agency ⟨a ~ to their hurt feelings⟩

[2]**salve** *vt* **salved; salv·ing** (bef. 12c) **1 :** to remedy (as disease) with or as if with a salve **2 :** QUIET, ASSUAGE ⟨give him a raise in salary to ~ his feelings —Upton Sinclair⟩

[3]**salve** \ˈsalv\ *vt* **salved; salv·ing** [back-formation fr. *salvage*] (ca. 1706) : SALVAGE — **sal·vor** \ˈsal-vər, -ˌvȯr\ *n*

sal·ver \ˈsal-vər\ *n* [modif. of F *salve,* fr. Sp *salva* sampling of food to detect poison, tray, fr. *salvar* to save, sample food to detect poison, fr. LL *salvare* to save — more at SAVE] (ca. 1661) : a tray esp. for serving food or beverages

sal·ver·form \ˈsal-vər-ˌfȯrm\ *adj* (1821) : composed of united petals forming a tube that spreads at the open end ⟨the ~ corolla of phlox⟩

sal·via \ˈsal-vē-ə\ *n* [NL, fr. L, sage — more at SAGE] (1601) : any of a large and widely distributed genus (*Salvia*) of herbs and shrubs of the mint family having a 2-lipped open calyx and two anthers; *esp* : one (*S. splendens*) with scarlet flowers

sal·vif·ic \sal-ˈvi-fik\ *adj* [LL *salvificus,* fr. L *salvus* safe + *-ficus* -fic] (1591) : having the intent or power to save or redeem ⟨the ~ life and death of Christ —E. A. Walsh⟩

[1]**sal·vo** \ˈsal-(ˌ)vō\ *n, pl* **salvos** *or* **salvoes** [It *salva,* fr. F *salve,* fr. L, hail!, fr. *salvus* healthy — more at SAFE] (1591) **1 a :** a simultaneous discharge of two or more guns in military action or as a salute **b :** the release all at one time of a rack of bombs or rockets (as from an airplane) **c :** a series of shots by an artillery battery with each gun firing one round in turn after a prescribed interval **d :** the bombs or projectiles released in a salvo **2 :** something suggestive of a salvo: as **a :** a sudden burst ⟨a ~ of cheers⟩ **b :** a spirited attack ⟨the first ~ of a political campaign⟩

[2]**salvo** *vt* (1839) : to release a salvo of ~ *vi* : to fire a salvo

[3]**salvo** *n, pl* **salvos** [ML *salvo jure* with the right reserved] (1621) **1 :** a mental reservation : PROVISO **2 :** a means of safeguarding one's name or honor or allaying one's conscience : SALVE

sal vo·la·ti·le \ˌsal-və-ˈla-tə-lē\ *n* [NL, lit., volatile salt] (1654) : SMELLING SALTS

Sam *abbr* Samuel

SAM \ˈsam, ˌes-(ˌ)ā-ˈem\ *n* (1950) : a surface-to-air missile

sa·ma·ra \ˈsa-mə-rə; sə-ˈma-rə, -ˈmär-ə\ *n* [NL, fr. L, seed of the elm] (1577) : a dry indehiscent usu. one-seeded winged fruit (as of an ash or elm tree) — called also *key*

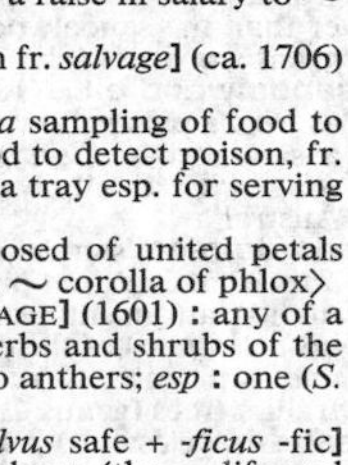
samara

Sa·mar·i·tan \sə-ˈmer-ə-tən\ *n* [ME, fr. OE, fr. LL *samaritanus,* n. & adj., fr. Gk *samaritēs* inhabitant of Samaria, fr. *Samaria*] (bef. 12c) **1 :** a native or inhabitant of Samaria **2** [fr. the parable of the good Samaritan in Lk 10:30–37] **:** a person who is generous in helping those in distress — **samaritan** *adj, often cap*

sa·mar·i·um \sə-ˈmer-ē-əm\ *n* [NL, fr. F *samarskite*] (1879) : a silvery-white lustrous metallic element of the rare-earth group that is used esp. in permanent magnets — see ELEMENT table

sa·mar·skite \sə-ˈmär-ˌskīt, ˈsa-mər-\ *n* [G *Samarskit,* fr. V. E. *Samarskiĭ*-Bykhovets †1870 Russ. mining engineer] (1849) : a black or brownish-black orthorhombic mineral that is a complex oxide of rare earths, uranium, iron, lead, thorium, niobium, tantalum, titanium, and tin

sam·ba \ˈsam-bə, ˈsäm-\ *n* [Pg] (1885) : a Brazilian dance of African origin with a basic pattern of step-close-step-close and characterized by a dip and spring upward at each beat of the music; *also* : the music for this dance — **samba** *vi*

sam·bar *also* **sam·bur** \ˈsäm-bər, ˈsam-\ *n* [Hindi & Urdu *sā̃bar,* fr. Skt *śambara*] (1698) : a large Asian deer (*Cervus unicolor*) with the male having strong 3-pointed antlers and long coarse hair on the throat

sam·bo \ˈsam-(ˌ)bō, ˈsäm-\ *n* [Russ, fr. *samozashchita bez oruzhiya* self-defense without weapons] (1972) : an international style of wrestling employing judo techniques

Sam Browne belt \ˈsam-ˈbrau̇n-\ *n* [Sir *Sam*uel James *Browne* †1901 Brit. army officer] (1915) : a leather belt for a dress uniform supported by a light strap passing over the right shoulder — called also *Sam Browne*

[1]**same** \ˈsām\ *adj* [ME, fr. ON *samr;* akin to OHG *sama* same, L *simulis* like, *simul* together, at the same time, *similis* like, *sem-* one, Gk *homos* same, *hama* together, *hen-, heis* one] (13c) **1 a :** resembling in every relevant respect **b :** conforming in every respect — used with *as* **2 a :** being one without addition, change, or discontinuance : IDENTICAL **b :** being the one under discussion or already referred to **3 :** corresponding so closely as to be indistinguishable **4 :** equal in size, shape, value, or importance — usu. used with *the* or a demonstrative (as *that, those*) in all senses

syn SAME, SELFSAME, VERY, IDENTICAL, EQUIVALENT, EQUAL mean not different or not differing from one another. SAME may imply and SELFSAME always implies that the things under consideration are one thing and not two or more things ⟨took the *same* route⟩ ⟨derived from the *selfsame* source⟩. VERY, like SELFSAME, may imply identity, or, like SAME, may imply likeness in kind ⟨the *very* point I was trying to make⟩. IDENTICAL may imply selfsameness or suggest absolute agreement in all details ⟨*identical* results⟩. EQUIVALENT implies amounting to the same thing in worth or significance ⟨two houses *equivalent* in market value⟩. EQUAL implies being identical in value, magnitude, or some specified quality ⟨*equal* shares in the business⟩.

[2]**same** *pron* (14c) **1 :** something identical with or similar to another **2 :** something or someone previously mentioned or described — often used with *the* or a demonstrative (as *that, those*) in both senses — **all the same** *or* **just the same :** despite everything : NEVERTHELESS

[3]**same** *adv* (1766) : in the same manner — used with *the* or a demonstrative (as *that, those*)

sa·mekh \ˈsä-ˌmek\ *n* [Heb *sāmekh*] (1823) : the 15th letter of the Hebrew alphabet — see ALPHABET table

same·ness \ˈsām-nəs\ *n* (1581) **1 :** the quality or state of being the same : IDENTITY, SIMILARITY **2 :** MONOTONY, UNIFORMITY

Sa·mi *also* **Saa·mi** \ˈsä-mē\ *n, pl* **Sami** *or* **Samis** *also* **Saami** *or* **Saamis** [of Sami origin; akin to North Sami *sápmi,* gen. *sámi* the Sami homeland, language, or way of life] (1842) **1 :** a member of a people of northern Scandinavia, Finland, and the Kola Peninsula of northern Russia who are traditionally fishermen, nomadic herders of caribou, and hunters of sea mammals **2 :** any or all of the closely related Finno-Ugric languages of the Sami people

sam·i·sen \ˈsa-mə-ˌsen\ *or* **sham·i·sen** \ˈsha-\ *n* [Jp] (1864) : a 3-stringed Japanese musical instrument resembling a banjo

sa·mite \ˈsa-ˌmīt, ˈsā-\ *n* [ME *samit,* fr. AF, fr. ML *examitum, samitum,* fr. MGk *hexamiton,* fr. Gk, neut. of *hexamitos* of six threads, fr. *hexa-* + *mitos* thread of the warp] (13c) : a rich medieval silk fabric interwoven with gold or silver

sa·miz·dat \ˈsä-mēz-ˌdät\ *n* [Russ, fr. *sam-* self- + *izdat*el'stvo publishing house] (1967) : a system in the U.S.S.R. and countries within its orbit by which government-suppressed literature was clandestinely printed and distributed; *also* : such literature

sam·let \ˈsam-lət\ *n* [irreg. fr. *salmon* + *-let*] (1655) : PARR

Sam·mar·i·nese \(ˌ)sa(m)-ˌma-rə-ˈnēz, -ˈnēs\ *n, pl* **-ne·si** \-ˈnā-zē\ [It, fr. *San Marino*] (1938) : a native or inhabitant of San Marino

Sam·nite \ˈsam-ˌnīt\ *n* [*Samnium,* Italy] (14c) : a member of an ancient people of central Italy

Sa·mo·an \sə-ˈmō-ən\ *n* (1839) **1 :** a native or inhabitant of Samoa **2 :** the Polynesian language of the Samoans — **Samoan** *adj*

Samoa time *n* (1983) : the time of the 11th time zone west of Greenwich that includes American Samoa

sa·mo·sa \sə-ˈmō-sə\ *n* [Hindi *samosā* & Urdu *samosa, sambūsa,* fr. Pers *sambūsa*] (1932) : a small triangular pastry filled with spiced meat or vegetables and fried in ghee or oil

sam·o·var \ˈsa-mə-ˌvär\ *n* [Russ, fr. *samo-* self + *varit'* to boil] (1830) **1 :** an urn with a spigot at its base used esp. in Russia to boil water for tea **2 :** an urn similar to a Russian samovar with a device for heating the contents

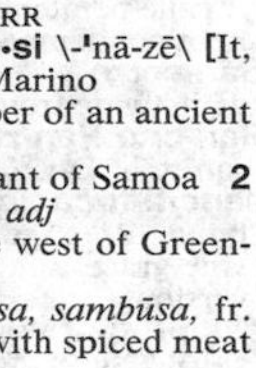
samovar 1

Sam·o·yed *also* **Sam·o·yede** \ˈsa-mə-ˌyed, -ˌmȯi-\ *n* [Russ *samoed,* fr. ORuss *samoyadi,* of Sami origin; akin to North Sami *sápmi* (gen. *sámi*) Sami homeland & *eatnam-, eana* land] (1589) **1 :** a member of any of a group of peoples inhabiting the far north of European Russia and parts of northwestern Siberia **2 :** the family of Uralic languages spoken by the Samoyed people **3 :** any of a Siberian breed of medium-sized white or cream-colored sled dogs — **Samoyed** *adj* — **Sam·o·yed·ic** \ˌsa-mə-ˈye-dik, -ˌmȯi-\ *adj*

samp \ˈsamp\ *n* [modif. of Narragansett *nasàump* corn mush] (1643) : coarse hominy or a boiled cereal made from it

sam·pan \ˈsam-ˌpan\ *n* [Chin (Guangdong) *sàambáan,* fr. *sàam* three + *báan* board, plank] (1620) : a flat-bottomed skiff used in eastern Asia and usu. propelled by two short oars

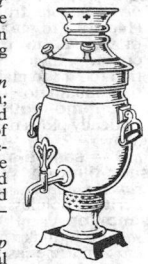

sam·phire \ˈsam-ˌfī(-ə)r\ *n* [alter. of earlier *sampiere,* fr. MF (*herbe de*) *Saint Pierre,* lit., St. Peter's herb] (1545) **1 :** a fleshy European seacoast plant (*Crithmum maritimum*) of the carrot family that is some-

\ə\ **abut** \ᵊ\ kitten, F table \ər\ **further** \a\ **ash** \ā\ **ace** \ä\ **mop, mar** \au̇\ **out** \ch\ **chin** \e\ **bet** \ē\ **easy** \g\ **go** \i\ **hit** \ī\ **ice** \j\ **job** \ŋ\ **sing** \ō\ **go** \ȯ\ **law** \ȯi\ **boy** \th\ **thin** \t͟h\ **the** \ü\ **loot** \u̇\ **foot** \y\ **yet** \zh\ **vision, beige** \k̲, ⁿ, œ, ue, ʸ\ *see* Guide to Pronunciation

times pickled **2 :** a common glasswort (*Salicornia europaea*) that is sometimes pickled

[1]**sam·ple** \ˈsam-pəl\ *n* [ME, fr. AF *sample, essample,* fr. L *exemplum* — more at EXAMPLE] (15c) **1 :** a representative part or a single item from a larger whole or group esp. when presented for inspection or shown as evidence of quality : SPECIMEN **2 :** a finite part of a statistical population whose properties are studied to gain information about the whole **3 :** an excerpt from a musical recording that is used in another artist's recording ***syn*** see INSTANCE

[2]**sample** *vt* **sam·pled; sam·pling** \-p(ə-)liŋ\ (1767) **1 :** to take a sample of or from; *esp* **:** to judge the quality of by a sample : TEST ⟨*sampled* his output for defects⟩ ⟨~ a wine⟩ **2 :** to use a segment of (another's musical recording) as part of one's own recording

[3]**sample** *adj* (1820) **:** serving as an illustration or example ⟨~ questions⟩

[1]**sam·pler** \ˈsam-plər\ *n* (1523) **:** a decorative piece of needlework typically having letters or verses embroidered on it in various stitches as an example of skill

[2]**sam·pler** \-p(ə-)lər\ *n* (1778) **1 :** one that collects, prepares, or examines samples **2 :** something containing representative specimens or selections ⟨a ~ of nineteen poets —K. E. Judd⟩; *also* **:** ASSORTMENT

sample space *n* (1951) **:** a set in which all of the possible outcomes of a statistical experiment are represented as points

sam·pling \ˈsam-pliŋ, *for 1 & 3* -p(ə-)liŋ\ *n* (1778) **1 :** the act, process, or technique of selecting a suitable sample; *specif* **:** the act, process, or technique of selecting a representative part of a population for the purpose of determining parameters or characteristics of the whole population **2 :** a small part selected as a sample for inspection or analysis ⟨ask a ~ of people which candidate they favor⟩ **3 :** the introduction or promotion of a product by distributing trial packages of it

sam·sa·ra \səm-ˈsär-ə\ *n* [Skt *saṁsāra,* lit., passing through] (1886) **:** the indefinitely repeated cycles of birth, misery, and death caused by karma

Sam·son \ˈsam(p)-sən\ *n* [LL, fr. Gk *Sampsōn,* fr. Heb *Shimshōn*] (14c) **:** a Hebrew hero who wreaked havoc among the Philistines by means of his great strength

Sam·so·ni·an \sam(p)-ˈsō-nē-ən\ *adj* [*Samson*] (ca. 1623) **:** of heroic strength or proportions : MIGHTY

Sam·u·el \ˈsam-yə-wəl, -yəl\ *n* [LL, fr. Gk *Samouel,* fr. Heb *Shĕmūʼēl*] (14c) **1 :** the early Hebrew judge who successively anointed Saul and David king **2 :** either of two narrative and historical books of canonical Jewish and Christian Scriptures — see BIBLE table

sam·u·rai \ˈsa-mə-ˌrī, ˈsam-yə-\ *n, pl* **samurai** [Jp] (1727) **1 :** a military retainer of a Japanese daimyo practicing the code of conduct of Bushido **2 :** the warrior aristocracy of Japan

San \ˈsän\ *n* [Khoikhoi] (1876) **1** *pl in constr* **:** BUSHMEN **2 :** BUSHMAN 2

san·a·tive \ˈsa-nə-tiv\ *adj* [ME *sanatif,* fr. AF, fr. LL *sanativus,* fr. L *sanatus,* pp. of *sanare* to cure, fr. *sanus* healthy] (15c) **:** having the power to cure or heal : CURATIVE, RESTORATIVE

san·a·to·ri·um \ˌsa-nə-ˈtȯr-ē-əm\ *n, pl* **-riums** *or* **-ria** \-ē-ə\ [NL, fr. LL, neut. of *sanatorius* curative, fr. *sanare*] (1839) **1 :** an establishment that provides therapy combined with a regimen (as of diet and exercise) for treatment or rehabilitation **2 a :** an institution for rest and recuperation (as of convalescents) **b :** an establishment for the treatment of the chronically ill

san·be·ni·to \ˌsan-bə-ˈnē-(ˌ)tō, ˌsam-\ *n, pl* **-tos** [Sp *sambenito,* fr. *San Benito* St. Benedict of Nursia] (ca. 1560) **1 :** a sackcloth coat worn by penitents on being reconciled to the church **2 :** a Spanish Inquisition garment resembling a scapular and being either yellow with red crosses for the penitent or black with painted devils and flames for the impenitent condemned to an auto-da-fé

San·cerre \säⁿ-ˈser\ *n* [*Sancerre,* village in France] (ca. 1946) **:** a dry white wine from the Loire valley of France

San·cho Pan·za \ˌsan-chō-ˈpan-zə, ˌsän-chō-ˈpän-\ *n* [Sp] (1762) **:** the squire of Don Quixote in Cervantes' *Don Quixote*

sanc·ti·fi·ca·tion \ˌsaŋ(k)-tə-fə-ˈkā-shən\ *n* (14c) **1 :** an act of sanctifying **2 a :** the state of being sanctified **b :** the state of growing in divine grace as a result of Christian commitment after baptism or conversion

sanc·ti·fi·er \ˈsaŋ(k)-tə-ˌfī(-ə)r\ *n* (1548) **:** one that sanctifies; *specif, cap* **:** HOLY SPIRIT

sanc·ti·fy \-ˌfī\ *vt* **-fied; -fy·ing** [ME *seintefien, sanctifien,* fr. AF *seintefier, sanctifier,* fr. LL *sanctificare,* fr. L *sanctus* sacred — more at SAINT] (14c) **1 :** to set apart to a sacred purpose or to religious use : CONSECRATE **2 :** to free from sin : PURIFY **3 a :** to impart or impute sacredness, inviolability, or respect to **b :** to give moral or social sanction to **4 :** to make productive of holiness or piety ⟨observe the day of the sabbath, to ~ it —Deut 5:12(DV)⟩

sanc·ti·mo·nious \ˌsaŋ(k)-tə-ˈmō-nē-əs, -nyəs\ *adj* (1603) **1 :** hypocritically pious or devout ⟨a ~ moralist⟩ ⟨the king's ~ rebuke —G. B. Shaw⟩ **2** *obs* **:** possessing sanctity : HOLY — **sanc·ti·mo·nious·ly** *adv* — **sanc·ti·mo·nious·ness** *n*

sanc·ti·mo·ny \ˈsaŋ(k)-tə-ˌmō-nē\ *n, pl* **-nies** [MF *sanctimonie,* fr. L *sanctimonia,* fr. *sanctus*] (1534) **1** *obs* **:** HOLINESS **2 :** affected or hypocritical holiness

[1]**sanc·tion** \ˈsaŋ(k)-shən\ *n* [MF or L; MF, fr. L *sanction-, sanctio,* fr. *sancire* to make holy — more at SACRED] (15c) **1 :** a formal decree; *esp* **:** an ecclesiastical decree **2 a** *obs* **:** a solemn agreement : OATH **b :** something that makes an oath binding **3 :** the detriment, loss of reward, or coercive intervention annexed to a violation of a law as a means of enforcing the law **4 a :** a consideration, principle, or influence (as of conscience) that impels to moral action or determines moral judgment **b :** a mechanism of social control for enforcing a society's standards **c :** explicit or official approval, permission, or ratification : APPROBATION **5 :** an economic or military coercive measure adopted usu. by several nations in concert for forcing a nation violating international law to desist or yield to adjudication

[2]**sanction** *vt* **sanc·tioned; sanc·tion·ing** \-sh(ə-)niŋ\ (1778) **1 :** to make valid or binding usu. by a formal procedure (as ratification) **2 :** to give effective or authoritative approval or consent to ***syn*** see APPROVE — **sanc·tion·able** \-sh(ə-)nə-bəl\ *adj*

sanc·ti·ty \ˈsaŋ(k)-tə-tē\ *n, pl* **-ties** [ME *saunctite,* fr. AF *sainteté,* fr. L *sanctitat-, sanctitas,* fr. *sanctus* sacred] (14c) **1 :** holiness of life and character : GODLINESS **2 a :** the quality or state of being holy or sacred : INVIOLABILITY **b** *pl* **:** sacred objects, obligations, or rights

sanc·tu·ary \ˈsaŋ(k)-chə-ˌwer-ē\ *n, pl* **-ar·ies** [ME *seintuarie, sanctuarie,* fr. AF, fr. LL *sanctuarium,* fr. L *sanctus*] (14c) **1 :** a consecrated place: as **a :** the ancient Hebrew temple at Jerusalem or its holy of holies **b (1) :** the most sacred part of a religious building (as the part of a Christian church in which the altar is placed) **(2) :** the room in which general worship services are held **(3) :** a place (as a church or a temple) for worship **2 a (1) :** a place of refuge and protection **(2) :** a refuge for wildlife where predators are controlled and hunting is illegal **b :** the immunity from law attached to a sanctuary

sanc·tum \ˈsaŋ(k)-təm\ *n, pl* **sanctums** *also* **sanc·ta** \-tə\ [LL, fr. L, neut. of *sanctus* sacred] (1577) **1 :** a sacred place **2 :** a place where one is free from intrusion ⟨an editor's ~⟩ ⟨the inner ~s of research⟩

sanc·tum sanc·to·rum \ˌsaŋ(k)-təm-ˌsaŋ(k)-ˈtȯr-əm\ *n* [LL] (1558) **1 :** HOLY OF HOLIES **2 :** SANCTUM 2

Sanc·tus \ˈsaŋ(k)-təs; ˈsäŋ(k)-təs, -ˌtüs\ *n* [ME, fr. LL *Sanctus, sanctus, sanctus* Holy, holy, holy, opening of a hymn sung by the angels in Isa 6:3] (15c) **:** an ancient Christian hymn of adoration sung or said immediately before the prayer of consecration in traditional liturgies

Sanctus bell *n* (15c) **:** a bell rung by the server at several points (as at the Sanctus) during the mass

[1]**sand** \ˈsand\ *n* [ME, fr. OE; akin to OHG *sant* sand, L *sabulum,* Gk *psammos*] (bef. 12c) **1 a :** a loose granular material that results from the disintegration of rocks, consists of particles smaller than gravel but coarser than silt, and is used in mortar, glass, abrasives, and foundry molds **b :** soil containing 85 percent or more of sand and a maximum of 10 percent of clay; *broadly* **:** sandy soil **2 a :** a tract of sand : BEACH **b :** a sandbank or sandbar **3 :** the sand in an hourglass; *also* **:** the moments of a lifetime — usu. used in pl. ⟨the ~s of this government run out very rapidly —H. J. Laski⟩ **4 :** an oil-producing formation of sandstone or unconsolidated sand **5 :** firm resolution **6 :** a yellowish-gray color

[2]**sand** *vt* (14c) **1 :** to sprinkle or dust with or as if with sand **2 :** to cover or fill with sand **3 :** to smooth or dress by grinding or rubbing with an abrasive (as sandpaper)

san·dal \ˈsan-dᵊl\ *n* [ME, fr. AF, fr. L *sandalium,* fr. Gk *sandalion,* dim. of *sandalon* sandal] (14c) **1 :** a shoe consisting of a sole strapped to the foot **2 :** a low-cut shoe that fastens by an ankle strap **3 :** a strap to hold on a slipper or low shoe **4 :** a rubber overshoe cut very low — **san·daled** *also* **san·dalled** \ˈsan-dᵊld\ *adj*

san·dal·wood \-ˌwu̇d\ *n* [*sandal* sandalwood (fr. ME, fr. AF *sandali,* fr. ML *sandalum,* fr. LGk *santalon,* ultim. fr. Skt *candana,* of Dravidian origin; akin to Tamil *cāntu* sandalwood tree) + [2]*wood*] (ca. 1511) **1 :** the compact close-grained fragrant yellowish heartwood of a parasitic tree (*Santalum album* of the family Santalaceae, the sandalwood family) of southern Asia much used in ornamental carving and cabinetwork; *also* **:** the tree that yields this wood **2 :** any of various trees other than the sandalwood some of which yield dyewoods; *also* **:** the fragrant wood of such a tree

sandalwood oil *n* (1851) **:** an essential oil obtained from sandalwood: as **a :** a pale yellow somewhat viscous aromatic liquid obtained from a sandalwood (*Santalum album*) and used chiefly in perfumes and soaps **b :** an oil obtained from a sandalwood (*Santalum spicatum*) of Australia

san·da·rac \ˈsan-də-ˌrak\ *n* [L *sandaraca* red coloring, fr. Gk *sandarakē* realgar, red pigment from realgar] (1543) **:** a brittle faintly aromatic translucent resin obtained from a northern African tree (*Tetraclinis articulata*) of the cypress family and used chiefly in making varnish and as incense; *also* **:** a similar resin obtained from any of several Australian trees (genus *Callitris*) of the same family

[1]**sand·bag** \ˈsan(d)-ˌbag\ *n* (1590) **:** a bag filled with sand and used in fortifications, as ballast, or as a weapon

[2]**sandbag** *vt* (1860) **1 :** to bank, stop up, or weight with sandbags **2 a :** to hit or stun with or as if with a sandbag **b :** to treat unfairly or harshly **c :** to coerce by crude means ⟨are raiding the Treasury and *sandbagging* the government —C. W. Ferguson⟩ **d :** to conceal or misrepresent one's true position, potential, or intent esp. in order to take advantage of ~ *vi* **:** to hide the truth about oneself so as to gain an advantage over another — **sand·bag·ger** *n*

sand·bank \ˈsan(d)-ˌbaŋk\ *n* (15c) **:** a large deposit of sand forming a mound, hillside, bar, or shoal

sand·bar \-ˌbär\ *n* (1766) **:** a ridge of sand built up by currents esp. in a river or in coastal waters

[1]**sand·blast** \-ˌblast\ *n* (1871) **:** a stream of sand projected by compressed air (as for engraving, cutting, or cleaning glass or stone)

[2]**sandblast** *vt* (1888) **:** to affect or treat with or as if with a sandblast — **sand·blast·er** *n*

sand–blind \ˈsan(d)-ˌblīnd\ *adj* [ME, prob. alter. of **samblind,* fr. OE *sam-* half (akin to OHG *sāmi-* half) + *blind* — more at SEMI-] (15c) **:** having poor eyesight : PURBLIND

sand bluestem *n* (ca. 1946) **:** a tall rhizomatous No. American grass (*Andropogon hallii* syn. *A. gerardii* var. *paucipilus*) that is a dominant grass of the orig. tallgrass prairies and is used for forage and as a soil binder — compare BLUESTEM 1

sand·box \ˈsan(d)-ˌbäks\ *n* (1572) **:** a box or receptacle containing loose sand: as **a :** a shaker for sprinkling sand on wet ink **b :** a box that contains sand for children to play in

sand·bur \ˈsan(d)-ˌbər\ *n* (1830) **:** any of a genus (*Cenchrus*) of grasses producing spikelets enclosed in ovoid spiny involucres that form burs; *also* **:** one of these burs

sand–cast \-ˌkast\ *vt* **-cast; -cast·ing** (1928) **:** to make (a casting) by pouring metal in a sand mold

sand casting *n* (1926) **:** a casting made in a mold of sand

sand crack *n* (1754) **:** a fissure in the wall of a horse's hoof often causing lameness

sand dab *n* (1789) **:** any of several Pacific flounders (genus *Citharichthys* of the family Bothidae); *esp* **:** a common food fish (*C. sordidus*)

sand dollar *n* (1884) **:** any of numerous flat circular sea urchins (order Clypeasteroida) that live chiefly in shallow water on sandy bottoms

sand·er \ˈsan-dər\ *n* (1627) **:** one that sands: as **a :** a device for spreading sand on newly surfaced or icy roads; *also* **:** the device together with the truck that bears it **b :** a device that smooths, polishes, or scours by means of abrasive material — called also *sanding machine*

sand·er·ling \ˈsan-dər-liŋ\ *n* [*sand* + *-erling,* perh. fr. OE *yrthling,* kind of bird found in fields, lit., plowman, fr. *yrth, earth* plowing, fr. *erian* to plow — more at ARABLE] (1602) : a small widely distributed sandpiper (*Calidris alba*) with pale gray and white plumage in winter

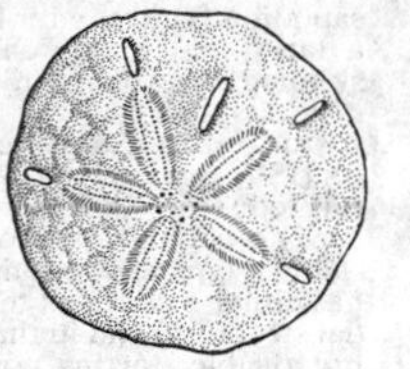

sand dollar

sand flea *n* (1796) **1** : a flea (as a chigoe) found in sandy places **2** : any of numerous amphipod crustaceans (family Talitridae) living on ocean beaches and leaping like fleas — called also *beach flea*
sand fly *n* (1736) : any of various small biting dipteran flies (esp. genus *Phlebotomus* of the family Psychodidae)
sand·fly fever \ˈsan(d)-ˌflī-\ *n* (1910) : a virus disease of brief duration that is characterized by fever, headache, eye pain, malaise, and leukopenia and that is caused by either of two bunyaviruses (species *Sandfly fever Naples virus* and *Sandfly fever Sicilian virus* assigned or tentatively assigned to the genus *Phlebovirus*) transmitted by the bite of a sand fly (esp. *Phlebotomus papatasii*) — called also *phlebotomus fever*
sand·glass \ˈsan(d)-ˌglas\ *n* (1556) : an instrument (as an hourglass) for measuring time by the running of sand
sand·grouse \-ˌgrau̇s\ *n* (1783) : any of numerous birds (family Pteroclididae) of arid parts of southern Europe, Asia, and Africa that have precocial downy young and are related to the shorebirds and the pigeons
S&H *abbr* shipping and handling
san·dhi \ˈsan-dē, ˈsän-, ˈsən-\ *n* [Skt *saṁdhi,* lit., placing together] (1806) : modification of the sound of a morpheme (as a word or affix) conditioned by syntactic context in which it is uttered (as pronunciation of *-ed* as \d\ in *glazed* and as \t\ in *paced* or occurrence of *a* in *a cow* and of *an* in *an old cow*)
sand·hill crane \ˈsand-ˌhil-\ *n* (1805) : a crane (*Grus canadensis*) of No. America and Siberia that has a red crown and is chiefly bluish gray tinged with a sandy yellow
sand·hog \ˈsand-ˌhȯg, -ˌhäg\ *n* (1897) : a laborer who works in a caisson in driving underwater tunnels
San·di·nis·ta \ˌsan-də-ˈnēs-tə, ˌsän-\ *n* [AmerSp, fr. Augusto César *Sandino* †1933 Nicaraguan rebel leader] (1974) : a member of a military and political coalition holding power in Nicaragua from 1979 to 1990
S and L *n* (1951) : SAVINGS AND LOAN ASSOCIATION
sand lance *n* (1776) : any of several small elongate marine bony fishes (genus *Ammodytes* of the family Ammodytidae) that associate in large schools and remain buried in sandy beaches at ebb tide — called also *sand eel, sand launce*
sand lily *n* (ca. 1900) : a western U.S. low-growing spring herb (*Leucocrinum montanum*) of the lily family with narrow linear leaves and fragrant white salverform flowers
sand·lot \ˈsan(d)-ˌlät\ *n* (1878) : a vacant lot esp. when used for usu. unorganized sports — **sandlot** *adj* — **sand·lot·ter** \-ˌlä-tər\ *n*
S and M *n* (ca. 1965) : SADOMASOCHISM
sand·man \ˈsan(d)-ˌman\ *n* (1835) : a genie in folklore who makes children sleepy by sprinkling sand in their eyes — often used to personify sleep ⟨trying to fight off the ~⟩
sand myrtle *n* (1814) : a usu. low-branching evergreen southeastern U.S. shrub (*Leiophyllum buxifolium*) of the heath family
sand·paint·ing \ˈsan(d)-ˌpān-tiŋ\ *n* (1900) : a ceremonial design (as of the Navajo Indians) made usu. of colored sands on a flat surface; *also* : the art of creating such designs
1**sand·pa·per** \-ˌpā-pər\ *n* (1755) : paper covered on one side with abrasive material (as sand) glued fast and used for smoothing and polishing — **sand·pa·pery** \-p(ə-)rē\ *adj*
2**sandpaper** *vt* (1846) : to rub with or as if with sandpaper
sand·pile \ˈsan(d)-ˌpī(-ə)l\ *n* (1901) : a pile of sand; *esp* : sand for children to play in
sand·pip·er \-ˌpī-pər\ *n* (1674) : any of various small shorebirds (family Scolopacidae, the sandpiper family) distinguished from the related plovers chiefly by the longer and soft-tipped bill
sand·pit \-ˌpit\ *n* (1898) *Brit* : SANDBOX b
sand·shoe \-ˌshü\ *n* (1855) *chiefly Austral & NewZeal* : TENNIS SHOE
sand·soap \ˈsan(d)-ˌsōp\ *n* (1853) : a gritty soap for heavy cleaning
sand·spur \-ˌspər\ *n* (ca. 1898) : SANDBUR
sand·stone \-ˌstōn\ *n* (1609) : a sedimentary rock consisting of usu. quartz sand united by some cement (as silica or calcium carbonate)
sand·storm \-ˌstȯrm\ *n* (1774) : a windstorm (as in a desert) driving clouds of sand before it
sand table *n* (1812) **1** : a table holding sand for children to mold **2** : a table bearing a relief model of a terrain built to scale for study or demonstration esp. of military tactics
sand trap *n* (1922) : an artificial hazard on a golf course consisting of a depression containing sand
sand verbena *n* (1898) : any of various western No. American trailing or low-growing herbs (genus *Abronia*) of the four-o'clock family with flowers like the verbena
1**sand·wich** \ˈsan(d)-ˌwich, ˈsam-; *dial* ˈsaŋ-\ *n* [John Montagu, 4th Earl of *Sandwich* †1792 Eng. diplomat] (1762) **1 a** : two or more slices of bread or a split roll having a filling in between **b** : one slice of bread covered with food **2** : something resembling a sandwich; *esp* : composite structural material consisting of layers often of high-strength facings bonded to a low strength central core
2**sandwich** *vt* (1861) **1** : to make into or as if into a sandwich; *esp* : to insert or enclose between usu. two things of another quality or character **2** : to make a place for — often used with *in* or *between*
sandwich board *n* (1897) : two usu. hinged boards designed for hanging from the shoulders with one board before and one behind and used esp. for advertising or picketing
sandwich coin *n* (1965) : a clad coin
sandwich generation *n* (1987) : a generation of people who are caring for their aging parents while supporting their own children
sandwich man *n* (1864) : one who wears a sandwich board
sand·worm \ˈsan(d)-ˌwərm\ *n* (1776) : any of various sand-dwelling polychaete worms: as **a** : any of several large burrowing worms (esp. genus *Nereis*) often used as bait **b** : LUGWORM
sand·wort \ˈsan(d)-ˌwərt, -ˌwȯrt\ *n* (1597) : any of a genus (*Arenaria*) of low tufted herbs of the pink family growing usu. in dry sandy regions
sandy \ˈsan-dē\ *adj* **sand·i·er; -est** (bef. 12c) **1 a** : consisting of or containing sand : full of sand **b** : sprinkled with sand **2** : of the color sand — **sand·i·ness** *n*
sane \ˈsān\ *adj* **san·er; san·est** [L *sanus* healthy, sane] (1628) **1** : proceeding from a sound mind : RATIONAL **2** : mentally sound; *esp* : able to anticipate and appraise the effect of one's actions **3** : healthy in body ***syn*** see WISE — **sane·ly** *adv* — **sane·ness** \ˈsān-nəs\ *n*
San·for·ized \ˈsan-fə-ˌrīzd\ *collective mark* — used for fabrics that are preshrunk by a mechanical process
sang *past of* SING
san·ga·ree \ˌsaŋ-gə-ˈrē\ *n* [Sp *sangría,* lit., act of bleeding, fr. *sangre* blood, fr. L *sanguin-, sanguis*] (1736) **1** : a sweetened iced drink of wine or sometimes of ale, beer, or liquor garnished with nutmeg **2** : SANGRIA
sang·froid \ˈsäⁿ-ˈf(r)wä\ *n* [F *sang-froid,* lit., cold blood] (1750) : self-possession or imperturbability esp. under strain ***syn*** see EQUANIMITY
San·gio·vese \ˌsän-jō-ˈvā-zā, -ˈvez, -ˈvēs\ *n* [It] (1943) : a dry red Italian wine made from a single variety of red grape; *also* : a similar wine made elsewhere
San·greal \ˈsan-ˈgrāl, ˈsaŋ-\ *n* [ME *Sangrayll,* fr. MF *Saint Graal* Holy Grail] (15c) : GRAIL
san·gria \saŋ-ˈgrē-ə, san-\ *n* [Sp] (1951) : a usu. iced punch typically made of red wine, fruit or fruit juice, and soda water
san·gui·nar·ia \ˌsaŋ-gwə-ˈner-ē-ə\ *n* [NL, fr. L, an herb that stanches blood, fr. fem. of *sanguinarius* sanguinary] (1808) **1** : BLOODROOT **2** : the rhizome and roots of a bloodroot or an extract of these having expectorant, emetic, and antimicrobial properties
san·gui·nary \ˈsaŋ-gwə-ˌner-ē\ *adj* [L *sanguinarius,* fr. *sanguin-, sanguis* blood] (ca. 1623) **1** : BLOODTHIRSTY, MURDEROUS ⟨~ hatred⟩ **2** : attended by bloodshed : BLOODY ⟨this bitter and ~ war —T. H. D. Mahoney⟩ **3** : consisting of blood ⟨a ~ stream⟩ ***syn*** see BLOODY — **san·gui·nar·i·ly** \ˌsaŋ-gwə-ˈner-ə-lē\ *adv*
1**san·guine** \ˈsaŋ-gwən\ *adj* [ME *sanguin,* fr. AF, fr. L *sanguineus,* fr. *sanguin-, sanguis*] (14c) **1** : BLOODRED **2 a** : consisting of or relating to blood **b** : BLOODTHIRSTY, SANGUINARY **c** *of the complexion* : RUDDY **3** : having blood as the predominating bodily humor; *also* : having the bodily conformation and temperament held characteristic of such predominance and marked by sturdiness, high color, and cheerfulness **4** : CONFIDENT, OPTIMISTIC — **san·guine·ly** *adv* — **san·guine·ness** \-gwən-nəs\ *n* — **san·guin·i·ty** \saŋ-ˈgwi-nə-tē, san-\ *n*
2**sanguine** *n* (15c) : a moderate to strong red
san·guin·e·ous \san-ˈgwi-nē-əs, saŋ-\ *adj* [L *sanguineus*] (ca. 1520) **1** : BLOODRED **2** : of, relating to, or involving bloodshed : BLOODTHIRSTY **3** : of, relating to, or containing blood
San·he·drin \san-ˈhe-drən, sän-; san-ˈhē-, ˈsa-nə-\ *n* [LHeb *sanhedhrīn* (*gĕdhōlāh*) (great) Sanhedrin, fr. Gk *synedrion* council, fr. *synedros* sitting in council, fr. *syn-* + *hedra* seat — more at SIT] (1588) : the supreme council and tribunal of the Jews during postexilic times headed by a High Priest and having religious, civil, and criminal jurisdiction
san·i·cle \ˈsa-ni-kəl\ *n* [ME, fr. AF, fr. ML *sanicula*] (14c) : any of several plants sometimes held to have healing powers; *esp* : a plant (genus *Sanicula*) of the carrot family with a root used in folk medicine as an anodyne or astringent
san·i·tar·i·an \ˌsa-nə-ˈter-ē-ən\ *n* (1859) : a specialist in sanitary science and public health ⟨milk ~⟩
san·i·tar·i·um \ˌsa-nə-ˈter-ē-əm\ *n, pl* **-i·ums** *or* **-ia** \-ē-ə\ [NL, fr. L *sanitat-, sanitas* health] (1851) : SANATORIUM
san·i·tary \ˈsa-nə-ˌter-ē\ *adj* [F *sanitaire,* fr. L *sanitas*] (1838) **1** : of or relating to health ⟨~ measures⟩ **2** : of, relating to, or used in the disposal esp. of domestic waterborne waste ⟨a ~ sewer system⟩ **3** : characterized by or readily kept in cleanliness ⟨~ packages⟩ — **san·i·tar·i·ly** \ˌsa-nə-ˈter-ə-lē\ *adv*
sanitary landfill *n* (1968) : LANDFILL
sanitary napkin *n* (1915) : a disposable absorbent pad used (as during menstruation) to absorb the uterine flow
sanitary ware *n* (1872) : ceramic plumbing fixtures (as sinks, lavatories, or toilet bowls)
san·i·tate \ˈsa-nə-ˌtāt\ *vt* **-tat·ed; -tat·ing** [back-formation fr. *sanitation*] (1882) : to make sanitary esp. by providing with sanitary appliances or facilities
san·i·ta·tion \ˌsa-nə-ˈtā-shən\ *n* (1848) **1** : the act or process of making sanitary **2** : the promotion of hygiene and prevention of disease by maintenance of sanitary conditions (as by removal of sewage and trash) — often used attributively ⟨a ~ truck⟩ ⟨~ workers⟩
san·i·tize \ˈsa-nə-ˌtīz\ *vt* **-tized; -tiz·ing** [L *sanitas*] (1836) **1** : to make sanitary (as by cleaning or sterilizing) **2** : to make more acceptable by removing unpleasant or undesired features ⟨attempts to ~ historical accounts⟩ — **san·i·ti·za·tion** \ˌsa-nə-tə-ˈzā-shən\ *n*
san·i·to·ri·um \ˌsa-nə-ˈtȯr-ē-əm\ *n, pl* **-ri·ums** *or* **-ria** \-ē-ə\ [by alter. (influenced by *sanitarium*)] (1917) : SANATORIUM
san·i·ty \ˈsa-nə-tē\ *n* [ME *sanite,* fr. AF *sanité,* fr. L *sanitat-, sanitas* health, sanity, fr. *sanus* healthy, sane] (15c) : the quality or state of being sane; *esp* : soundness or health of mind
San Ja·cin·to Day \ˌsan-jə-ˈsin-tə-, -hə-ˌsin-\ *n* (1907) : April 21 observed as a legal holiday in Texas in commemoration of the battle of San Jacinto in 1836 by which independence from Mexico was won
San Jo·se scale \ˌsa-nə-ˈzā-, ˌsan-(h)ō-\ *n* [*San Jose,* Calif.] (1887) : a scale insect (*Quadraspidiotus perniciosus*) prob. of Asian origin that is naturalized in the U.S. and is destructive to fruit trees
sank *past of* SINK
San·khya \ˈsäŋ-kyə\ *n* [Skt *sāṁkhya,* lit., based on calculation] (1788) : an orthodox Hindu philosophy teaching salvation through knowledge of the dualism of matter and souls
sann hemp \ˈsən-, ˈsän-\ *n* [Hindi & Urdu *san*] (1939) : SUNN

\ə\ **abut** \ᵊ\ kitten, F table \ər\ **further** \a\ **ash** \ā\ **ace** \ä\ mop, mar
\au̇\ **out** \ch\ **chin** \e\ **bet** \ē\ **easy** \g\ **go** \i\ **hit** \ī\ **ice** \j\ **job**
\ŋ\ **sing** \ō\ **go** \ȯ\ **law** \ȯi\ **boy** \th\ **thin** \t͟h\ **the** \ü\ **loot** \u̇\ **foot**
\y\ yet \zh\ vision, beige \k̲, ⁿ, œ, ue, ʸ\ *see* Guide to Pronunciation

san·nup \ˈsa-ˌnəp\ *n* [Eastern Abenaki *sénɑpe* man, male human] (1628) **:** a married male American Indian

sann·ya·si \(ˌ)sən-ˈyä-sē\ *or* **sann·ya·sin** \-ˈyä-sᵊn\ *n* [Hindi *sannyāsī,* fr. Skt *sannyāsin*] (1613) **:** a Hindu mendicant ascetic

[1]**sans** \ˈsanz\ *prep* [ME *saun, sans,* fr. AF *san, sanz,* modif. of L *sine* without — more at SUNDER] (14c) **:** WITHOUT ⟨my love to thee is sound, ∼ crack or flaw —Shak.⟩

[2]**sans** \ˈsanz\ *n, pl* **sans** (ca. 1909) **:** SANS SERIF

sans·cu·lotte \ˌsanz-kü-ˈlät, -kyü-\ *n* [F *sans-culotte,* lit., without breeches] (1790) **1 :** an extreme radical republican in France at the time of the French Revolution **2 :** a radical or violent extremist in politics — **sans·cu·lott·ic** \-ˈlä-tik\ *adj* — **sans·cu·lott·ish** \-tish\ *adj* — **sans·cu·lott·ism** \-ˌti-zəm\ *n*

san·sei \ˌsän-ˈsā, ˈsän-ˌ\ *n, pl* **sansei** *often cap* [Jp *san* third + *sei* generation] (1940) **:** a son or daughter of nisei parents who is born and educated in America and esp. in the U.S.

san·se·vie·ria \ˌsan(t)-sə-ˈvir-ē-ə\ *n* [NL, fr. Raimondo di Sangro, prince of *San Severo* †1774 Ital. scholar] (1804) **:** any of a genus (*Sansevieria*) of tropical perennial herbs of the agave family with showy mottled sword-shaped leaves usu. yielding a strong fiber

San·skrit \ˈsan-ˌskrit, ˈsan(t)-skrət\ *n* [Skt *saṁskṛta,* lit., perfected, fr. *sam* together + *karoti* he makes] (1696) **1 :** an ancient Indo-Aryan language that is the classical language of India and of Hinduism **2 :** classical Sanskrit together with the older Vedic and various later modifications of classical Sanskrit — see INDO-EUROPEAN LANGUAGES table — **Sanskrit** *adj* — **San·skrit·ic** \san-ˈskri-tik\ *adj* — **San·skrit·ist** \-ˌskri-tist\ *n*

sans ser·if *or* **san·ser·if** \san-ˈser-əf, ˈsanz-\ *n* [prob. fr. *sans* + modif. of D *schreef* stroke — more at SERIF] (1830) **:** a letter or typeface with no serifs

sans serif

sans serif

San·ta Ana \ˌsan-tə-ˈa-nə\ *n* [*Santa Ana* Mountains in southern Calif.] (1880) **:** a strong hot dry foehn wind from the north, northeast, or east in southern California

San·ta Claus \ˈsan-tə-ˌklȯz *also* ˈsan-tē-\ *n* [modif. of D *Sinterklaas,* alter. of *Sint Nikolaas* Saint Nicholas] (1773) **:** a plump white-bearded and red-suited old man in modern folklore who delivers presents to good children at Christmastime — called also *Santa*

San·ta Ger·tru·dis \ˌsan-tə-(ˌ)gər-ˈtrü-dəs\ *n* [*Santa Gertrudis,* section of the King Ranch, Kingsville, Texas] (1942) **:** any of a U.S. breed of red beef cattle developed from a Brahman-shorthorn cross and valued for their hardiness in hot climates

San·te·ria *also* **San·te·ría** \ˌsan-tə-ˈrē-ə, ˌsän-\ *n* [AmerSp *santería,* fr. *santero* practitioner of Santeria, fr. *santo* Yoruba deity, lit., saint's image, saint, fr. Sp] (1950) **:** a religion practiced orig. in Cuba in which Yoruba deities are identified with Roman Catholic saints

san·tims \ˈsän-ˌtims\ *n, pl* **san·ti·mi** \-ti-mē\ *or* **san·ti·mu** \-ti-mü\ [Latvian (nom. pl. *santimi,* gen. pl. *santimu*), fr. F *centime* centime] (1924) — see *lats* at MONEY table

san·tir \san-ˈtir\ *or* **san·tour** \-ˈtu̇r\ *n* [Ar *santīr, santūr,* ultim. fr. Gk *psaltērion* psaltery] (1853) **:** a Persian dulcimer

san·to \ˈsän-(ˌ)tō\ *n, pl* **santos** [Sp, lit., saint, fr. LL *sanctus* — more at SAINT] (1834) **:** a painted or carved wooden image of a saint common esp. in Mexico and the southwestern U.S.

san·to·li·na \ˌsan-tə-ˈlē-nə\ *n, pl* **-nas** *or* **-na** [NL, alter. of L *santonica,* an herb, fem. of *santonicus* of the Santoni, fr. *Santoni,* a people of Aquitania] (1578) **:** any of a genus (*Santolina*) of aromatic Mediterranean composite subshrubs that have dissected evergreen leaves and clustered flower heads lacking ray flowers

san·to·nin \ˈsan-tə-nən, san-ˈtä-nən\ *n* [ISV, fr. NL *santonica,* fr. L] (1836) **:** a poisonous slightly bitter crystalline compound $C_{15}H_{18}O_3$ found esp. in the unopened flower heads of several artemisias (esp. *Artemisia maritima*) and used as an anthelmintic

[1]**sap** \ˈsap\ *n* [ME, fr. OE *sæp;* akin to OHG *saf* sap] (bef. 12c) **1 a :** the fluid part of a plant; *specif* **:** a watery solution that circulates through a plant's vascular system **b (1) :** a body fluid (as blood) essential to life, health, or vigor **(2) :** bodily health and vigor **2 :** a foolish gullible person **3** [prob. short for *sapling*] **:** BLACKJACK, BLUDGEON — **sap·less** \ˈsa-pləs\ *adj* — **sap·less·ness** \-nəs\ *n*

[2]**sap** *vt* **sapped; sap·ping** (1725) **1 :** to drain or deprive of sap **2 :** to knock out with a sap

[3]**sap** *vb* **sapped; sap·ping** [MF *sapper,* fr. OIt *zappare,* fr. *zappa* hoe] *vi* (1598) **:** to proceed by digging a sap ∼ *vt* **1 :** to subvert by digging or eroding the substratum or foundation **:** UNDERMINE **2 a :** to gradually diminish the supply or intensity of ⟨*sapped* her strength⟩ **b :** to weaken or exhaust the energy or vitality of ⟨the illness *sapped* him of his stamina⟩ **3 :** to operate against or pierce by a sap ***syn*** see WEAKEN

[4]**sap** *n* [F *sape,* fr. *saper*] (1642) **:** the extension of a trench to a point beneath an enemy's fortifications

sap green *n* (1578) **:** a strong yellow green

sap·head \ˈsap-ˌhed\ *n* (1691) **:** a weak-minded stupid person **:** SAP — **sap·head·ed** \-ˈhe-dəd\ *adj*

sa·phe·nous \sə-ˈfē-nəs, ˈsa-fə-nəs\ *adj* [*saphena* saphenous vein, fr. ME, fr. ML, fr. Ar *ṣāfin*] (1840) **:** of, relating to, associated with, or being either of the two chief superficial veins of the leg ⟨∼ nerve⟩

sap·id \ˈsa-pəd\ *adj* [L *sapidus* tasty, fr. *sapere* to taste — more at SAGE] (1623) **1 :** having flavor **:** FLAVORFUL **2** *archaic* **:** agreeable to the mind — **sa·pid·i·ty** \sa-ˈpi-də-tē\ *n, archaic*

sa·pi·ence \ˈsā-pē-ən(t)s, ˈsa-\ *n* [ME, fr. AF, fr. L *sapientia,* fr. *sapient-, sapiens,* prp.] (14c) **:** WISDOM, SAGACITY

sa·pi·ens \ˈsa-pē-ənz, ˈsā-, -ˌenz\ *adj* [NL (specific epithet of *Homo sapiens*), fr. L, prp. of *sapere*] (1939) **:** of, relating to, or being recent humans (*Homo sapiens*) as distinguished from various fossil hominids

sa·pi·ent \ˈsā-pē-ənt, ˈsa-\ *adj* [ME, fr. MF, fr. L *sapient-, sapiens,* fr. prp. of *sapere* to taste, be wise — more at SAGE] (15c) **:** possessing or expressing great sagacity ***syn*** see WISE — **sa·pi·ent·ly** *adv*

sap·ling \ˈsa-pliŋ, -plən\ *n* (14c) **1 :** a young tree; *specif* **:** one not over four inches in diameter at breast height **2 :** YOUTH 2a

sap·o·dil·la \ˌsa-pə-ˈdi-lə, -ˈdē-yə\ *n* [Sp *zapotillo,* dim. of *zapote* sapodilla fruit, fr. Nahuatl *tzapotl*] (1697) **:** a tropical American evergreen tree (*Manilkara zapota* syn. *Achras zapota* of the family Sapotaceae, the sapodilla family) with hard reddish wood, a latex that yields chicle, and a rough-skinned brownish fruit with sweet flesh; *also* **:** its fruit

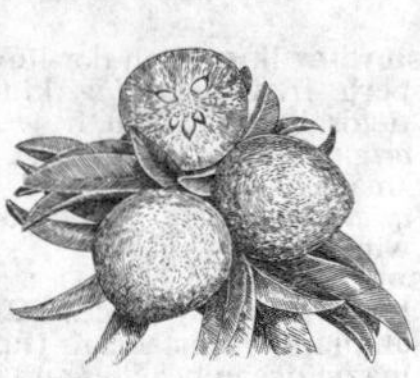
sapodilla

sa·po·ge·nin \ˌsa-pə-ˈje-nən, sə-ˈpä-jə-nən\ *n* [ISV *sapo*nin + *-genin* (compound formed from another compound)] (ca. 1862) **:** a nonsugar portion of a saponin that is typically obtained by hydrolysis, has either a complex terpenoid or a steroidal structure, and in the latter case forms a practicable starting point in the synthesis of steroid hormones

sap·o·na·ceous \ˌsa-pə-ˈnā-shəs\ *adj* [NL *saponaceus,* fr. L *sapon-, sapo* soap, of Gmc origin; akin to OE *sāpe* soap] (1710) **:** resembling or having the qualities of soap — **sap·o·na·ceous·ness** *n*

sa·pon·i·fy \sə-ˈpä-nə-ˌfī\ *vb* **-fied; -fy·ing** [F *saponifier,* fr. L *sapon-, sapo*] *vt* (1821) **:** to convert (as fat) into soap; *specif* **:** to hydrolyze (a fat) with alkali to form a soap and glycerol ∼ *vi* **:** to undergo saponifying — **sa·pon·i·fi·able** \-ˌfi-ə-bəl\ *adj* — **sa·pon·i·fi·ca·tion** \-ˌpä-nə-fə-ˈkā-shən\ *n* — **sa·pon·i·fi·er** \-ˈpä-nə-ˌfī(-ə)r\ *n*

sa·po·nin \ˈsa-pə-nən, sə-ˈpō-\ *n* [F *saponine,* fr. L *sapon-, sapo*] (1831) **:** any of various mostly toxic glucosides that occur in plants (as soapwort or soapbark) and are characterized by the property of producing a soapy lather; *esp* **:** a hygroscopic amorphous saponin mixture used esp. as a foaming and emulsifying agent and detergent

sap·o·nite \ˈsa-pə-ˌnīt\ *n* [Sw *saponit,* fr. L *sapon-, sapo* soap] (ca. 1849) **:** a hydrous magnesium aluminum silicate occurring in soft soapy amorphous masses and filling veins and cavities (as in serpentine)

sa·po·te \sə-ˈpō-tē\ *n* [Sp *zapote* sapodilla fruit] (1572) **:** any of several roundish or ovoid sweet soft-fleshed fruits of Mexican and Central American trees: as **a :** the green- or yellow-skinned fruit of a tree (*Casimiroa edulis*) of the rue family with white or yellow flesh **b :** the green-skinned fruit of a persimmon (*Diospyros digyna*) with brown or blackish flesh **c :** the coarse brown-skinned fruit of a tree (*Pouteria sapota* syn. *Calocarpum sapota*) of the sapodilla family with orange or reddish flesh

sap·per \ˈsa-pər\ *n* (1626) **1 :** a military specialist in field fortification work (as sapping) **2 :** a military demolitions specialist

[1]**sap·phic** \ˈsa-fik\ *adj* (1501) **1** *cap* **:** of or relating to the Greek lyric poet Sappho **2 :** of, relating to, or consisting of a 4-line strophe made up of chiefly trochaic and dactylic feet **3 :** LESBIAN 2

[2]**sapphic** *n* (1586) **1 :** a verse having the metrical pattern of one of the first three lines of a sapphic strophe **2 :** a sapphic strophe

sap·phire \ˈsa-ˌfīr\ *n* [ME *safir,* fr. AF, fr. L *sapphirus,* fr. Gk *sappheiros,* perh. of Sem origin; akin to Heb *sappīr* sapphire] (13c) **1 a :** a gem variety of corundum in transparent or translucent crystals of a color other than red; *esp* **:** one of a transparent rich blue **b :** a gem of such corundum **2 :** a deep purplish-blue color — **sapphire** *adj*

sap·phi·rine \ˈsa-fə-ˌrīn, ˈsa-ˌfīr-ˌēn, sa-ˈfī-rən\ *adj* (15c) **1 :** made of sapphire **2 :** resembling sapphire esp. in color

sap·phism \ˈsa-ˌfi-zəm\ *n* [*Sappho* + *-ism;* fr. the belief that Sappho was homosexual] (ca. 1890) **:** LESBIANISM

sap·pi·ness \ˈsa-pē-nəs\ *n* (1552) **1 :** the state of being full of or smelling of sap **2 :** the quality or state of being sappy **:** FOOLISHNESS

sap·py \ˈsa-pē\ *adj* **sap·pi·er; -est** (12c) **1 :** abounding with sap **2 :** resembling or consisting largely of sapwood **3 a :** overly sweet or sentimental **b :** lacking in good sense **:** SILLY

sapr- *or* **sapro-** *comb form* [NL, fr. Gk *sapros* rotten] **1 :** dead or decaying organic matter ⟨*sapro*phyte⟩ **2 :** decay **:** putrefaction ⟨*sapro*genic⟩

sap·ro·gen·ic \ˌsa-prə-ˈje-nik\ *adj* (1876) **:** of, causing, or resulting from putrefaction — **sap·ro·ge·nic·i·ty** \-jə-ˈni-sə-tē\ *n*

sap·ro·lite \ˈsa-prə-ˌlīt\ *n* (1894) **:** disintegrated rock that lies in its original place

sa·proph·a·gous \sa-ˈprä-fə-gəs\ *adj* [NL *saprophagus,* fr. *sapr-* + *-phagus* -phagous] (1819) **:** feeding on decaying matter

sap·ro·phyte \ˈsa-prə-ˌfīt\ *n* [ISV] (1870) **:** a saprophytic organism

sap·ro·phyt·ic \ˌsa-prə-ˈfi-tik\ *adj* (1882) **:** obtaining food by absorbing dissolved organic material; *esp* **:** obtaining nourishment from the products of organic breakdown and decay ⟨∼ fungi⟩ — **sap·ro·phyt·i·cal·ly** \-ti-k(ə-)lē\ *adv*

sap·ro·zo·ic \ˌsa-prə-ˈzō-ik\ *adj* (ca. 1920) **:** SAPROPHYTIC — used of animals (as protozoans)

sap·sa·go \sap-ˈsā-(ˌ)gō, ˈsap-sə-ˌgō\ *n* [modif. of G *Schabziger*] (ca. 1846) **:** a very hard green skim-milk cheese flavored with the powdered leaves of an aromatic European legume (*Trigonella caerulea*)

sap·suck·er \ˈsap-ˌsə-kər\ *n* (1805) **:** any of a genus (*Sphyrapicus*) of No. American woodpeckers that drill holes in trees in order to obtain sap and insects for food

sap·wood \-ˌwu̇d\ *n* (1791) **:** the younger softer living or physiologically active outer portion of wood that lies between the cambium and the heartwood and is more permeable, less durable, and usu. lighter in color than the heartwood

sa·quin·a·vir \sə-ˈkwi-nə-ˌvir\ *n* [*sa-* (perh. backward spelling of protease) + *quin*oline + *-avir,* alter. of *-ovir* (as in *acyclovir*)] (1994) **:** a protease inhibitor $C_{38}H_{50}N_6O_5$ that is administered in the form of its methylated sulfonic salt esp. in combination with other antiretroviral agents to treat HIV infection

SAR *abbr* search and rescue

sar·a·band *or* **sar·a·bande** \ˈsa-rə-ˌband\ *n* [F *sarabande,* fr. Sp *zarabanda*] (1616) **1 :** a stately court dance of the 17th and 18th centuries resembling the minuet **2 :** the music for the saraband in slow triple time with accent on the second beat

Sar·a·cen \ˈsa-rə-sən\ *n* [ME, fr. OE, fr. LL *Saracenus,* fr. LGk *Sarakēnos*] (bef. 12c) **:** a member of a nomadic people of the deserts between Syria and Arabia; *broadly* **:** ARAB — **Saracen** *adj* — **Sar·a·cen·ic** \ˌsa-rə-ˈse-nik\ *adj*

Sa·rah \ˈser-ə, ˈsa-rə\ *n* [Heb *Śārāh*] (bef. 12c) **1 :** the wife of Abraham and mother of Isaac **2 :** a kinswoman of Tobias married to him

sa·ran \sə-ˈran\ *n* [fr. *Saran,* a trademark] (1940) **:** a tough flexible thermoplastic resin

sarape *var of* SERAPE

Sar·a·to·ga trunk \ˌsa-rə-ˈtō-gə-\ *n* [*Saratoga* Springs, N.Y.] (1858) : a large traveling trunk usu. with a rounded top

sarc- *or* **sarco-** *comb form* [Gk *sark-, sarko-,* fr. *sark-, sarx*] **1** : flesh ⟨*sarc*oid⟩ **2** : striated muscle ⟨*sarco*lemma⟩

sar·casm \ˈsär-ˌka-zəm\ *n* [F or LL; F *sarcasme,* fr. LL *sarcasmos,* fr. Gk *sarkasmos,* fr. *sarkazein* to tear flesh, bite the lips in rage, sneer, fr. *sark-, sarx* flesh; prob. akin to Av *thwarəs-* to cut] (1550) **1** : a sharp and often satirical or ironic utterance designed to cut or give pain **2 a** : a mode of satirical wit depending for its effect on bitter, caustic, and often ironic language that is usu. directed against an individual **b** : the use or language of sarcasm ***syn*** see WIT

sar·cas·tic \sär-ˈkas-tik\ *adj* (1695) **1** : having the character of sarcasm ⟨~ criticism⟩ **2** : given to the use of sarcasm : CAUSTIC ⟨a ~ critic⟩ — **sar·cas·ti·cal·ly** \-ti-k(ə-)lē\ *adv*

syn SARCASTIC, SATIRIC, IRONIC, SARDONIC mean marked by bitterness and a power or will to cut or sting. SARCASTIC implies an intentional inflicting of pain by deriding, taunting, or ridiculing ⟨a critic known for his *sarcastic* remarks⟩. SATIRIC implies that the intent of the ridiculing is censure and reprobation ⟨a *satiric* look at contemporary society⟩. IRONIC implies an attempt to be amusing or provocative by saying usu. the opposite of what is meant ⟨made the *ironic* observation that the government could always be trusted⟩. SARDONIC implies scorn, mockery, or derision that is manifested by either verbal or facial expression ⟨surveyed the scene with a *sardonic* smile⟩.

[1]**sarce·net** *or* **sarse·net** \ˈsär-snət\ *n* [ME *sarsynet,* fr. AF *sarzinett*] (15c) : a soft silk in plain or twill weaves; *also* : a garment made of this

[2]**sarcenet** *or* **sarsenet** *adj* (1521) **1** *archaic* : made of sarcenet **2** *archaic* : soft like sarcenet

sar·coid \ˈsär-ˌkȯid\ *n* (1899) **1** : any of various diseases characterized esp. by the formation of nodules in the skin **2** : a nodule characteristic of sarcoid or of sarcoidosis

sar·coid·o·sis \ˌsär-ˌkȯi-ˈdō-səs\ *n, pl* **-o·ses** \-ˌsēz\ [NL] (1936) : a chronic disease of unknown cause that is characterized by the formation of nodules esp. in the lymph nodes, lungs, bones, and skin

sar·co·lem·ma \ˌsär-kə-ˈle-mə\ *n* [NL, fr. *sarc-* + Gk *lemma* husk — more at LEMMA] (1840) : the membrane enclosing a striated muscle fiber — **sar·co·lem·mal** \-məl\ *adj*

sar·co·ma \sär-ˈkō-mə\ *n, pl* **-mas** *also* **-ma·ta** \-mə-tə\ [NL, fr. Gk *sarkōmat-, sarkōma* fleshy growth, fr. *sarkoun* to grow flesh, fr. *sark-, sarx*] (1804) : a malignant tumor arising in tissue (as connective tissue, bone, cartilage, or striated muscle) of mesodermal origin — **sar·co·ma·tous** \sär-ˈkō-mə-təs\ *adj*

sar·co·ma·to·sis \(ˌ)sär-ˌkō-mə-ˈtō-səs\ *n, pl* **-to·ses** \-ˌsēz\ [NL] (ca. 1890) : a disease characterized by the presence and spread of sarcomas

sar·co·mere \ˈsär-kə-ˌmir\ *n* (1891) : any of the repeating structural units of striated muscle fibrils

sar·coph·a·gus \sär-ˈkä-fə-gəs\ *n, pl* **-gi** \-ˌgī, -ˌjī, -ˌgē\ *also* **-gus·es** [L *sarcophagus* (*lapis*) limestone used for coffins, fr. Gk (*lithos*) *sarkophagos,* lit., flesh-eating stone, fr. *sark-* sarc- + *phagein* to eat — more at BAKSHEESH] (1619) : a stone coffin; *broadly* : COFFIN

sar·co·plasm \ˈsär-kə-ˌpla-zəm\ *n* [NL *sarcoplasma*] (1899) : the cytoplasm of a striated muscle fiber — **sar·co·plas·mic** \-ˈplaz-mik\ *adj*

sarcoplasmic reticulum *n* (1953) : the specialized endoplasmic reticulum of cardiac muscle and skeletal striated muscle that functions esp. as a storage and release area for calcium

sar·cop·tic mange \(ˌ)sär-ˈkäp-tik-\ *n* [NL *Sarcoptes,* fr. *sarc-* + Gk *koptein* to cut — more at CAPON] (1886) : mange caused by mites (genus *Sarcoptes*) burrowing in the skin esp. of the head and face

sar·co·some \ˈsär-kə-ˌsōm\ *n* [NL *sarcosoma,* fr. *sarc-* + *-soma* -some] (1899) : a mitochondrion of a striated muscle fiber — **sar·co·som·al** \ˌsär-kə-ˈsō-məl\ *adj*

sard \ˈsärd\ *n* [ME *sarde,* fr. AF, fr. L *sarda*] (14c) : a reddish-brown variety of chalcedony sometimes classified as a variety of carnelian

sardar *var of* SIRDAR

sar·dine \sär-ˈdēn\ *n, pl* **sardines** *also* **sardine** [ME *sardeine,* fr. AF, fr. L *sardina*] (14c) **1** : any of several small or immature fishes of the herring family; *esp* : the European pilchard (*Sardina pilchardus*) esp. when young and of a size suitable for preserving for food **2** : any of various small fishes (as an anchovy) resembling the true sardines or similarly preserved for food

Sar·din·ian \sär-ˈdi-nē-ən, -ˈdin-yən\ *n* (1598) **1** : a native or inhabitant of Sardinia **2** : the Romance language of central and southern Sardinia — **Sardinian** *adj*

sar·don·ic \sär-ˈdä-nik\ *adj* [F *sardonique,* fr. Gk *sardonios*] (1638) : disdainfully or skeptically humorous : derisively mocking ⟨a ~ comment⟩ ***syn*** see SARCASTIC — **sar·don·i·cal·ly** \-ni-k(ə-)lē\ *adv*

sar·don·i·cism \sär-ˈdä-nə-ˌsi-zəm\ *n* (1926) : sardonic quality or humor

sar·don·yx \sär-ˈdä-niks *also* ˈsär-də-niks\ *n* [ME *sardonix,* fr. L *sardonyx,* fr. Gk] (14c) : an onyx having parallel layers of sard

sar·gas·so \sär-ˈga-(ˌ)sō\ *n, pl* **-sos** [Pg *sargaço*] (1598) **1** : GULFWEED, SARGASSUM **2** : a mass of floating vegetation and esp. sargassums

sar·gas·sum \sär-ˈga-səm\ *n* [NL, genus name, fr. ISV *sargasso*] (ca. 1890) : any of a genus (*Sargassum*) of brown algae that have a branching thallus with lateral outgrowths differentiated as leafy segments, air bladders, or spore-bearing structures : GULFWEED

sarge \ˈsärj\ *n* [by shortening & alter.] (1867) : SERGEANT

sa·ri *also* **sa·ree** \ˈsär-ē\ *n* [Hindi & Urdu *sāṛī,* fr. Skt *śāṭī* strip of cloth] (1785) : a garment of southern Asian women that consists of several yards of lightweight cloth draped so that one end forms a skirt and the other a head or shoulder covering

sa·rin \ˈsär-ən, ˈser-; zä-ˈrēn\ *n* [G] (1951) : an extremely toxic chemical weapon $C_4H_{10}FO_2P$ that is used as a lethal nerve gas — called also *GB*

sark \ˈsärk\ *n* [ME (Sc) *serk,* fr. OE *serc;* akin to ON *serkr* shirt] (bef. 12c) *dial chiefly Brit* : SHIRT

sa·rod *also* **sa·rode** \sə-ˈrōd\ *n* [Hindi & Urdu *sarod,* fr. Pers] (1865) : a lute of northern India — **sa·rod·ist** \-ˈrō-dist\ *n*

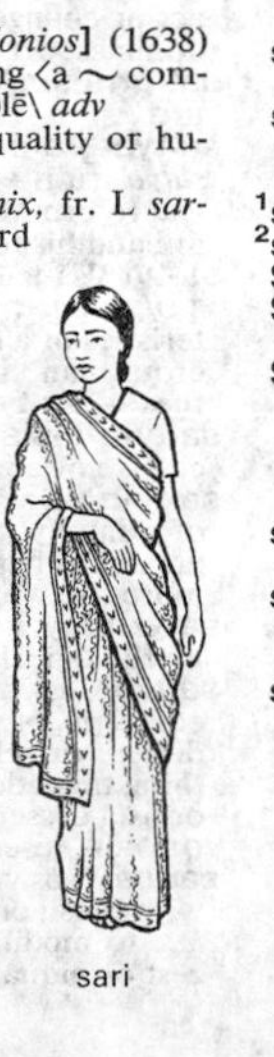

sari

sa·rong \sə-ˈrȯŋ, -ˈräŋ\ *n* [Malay] (1830) : a loose garment made of a long strip of cloth wrapped around the body that is worn by men and women chiefly of the Malay Archipelago and the Pacific islands

Sar·pe·don \sär-ˈpē-dᵊn\ *n* [L, fr. Gk *Sarpēdōn*] (14c) : a son of Zeus and Europa and king of Lycia killed in the Trojan War

sar·ra·ce·nia \ˌsa-rə-ˈsē-nē-ə, -ˈse-\ *n* [NL, fr. Michel *Sarrazin* †1734 Fr. physician & naturalist] (1884) : any of a genus (*Sarracenia*) of eastern No. American insectivorous perennial herbs of the pitcher-plant family

SARS \ˈsärz\ *n* [*s*evere *a*cute *r*espiratory *s*yndrome] (2003) : a severe respiratory illness that is caused by a coronavirus (species *Severe acute respiratory syndrome virus* of the genus *Coronavirus*), is transmitted esp. by contact with infectious material (as respiratory droplets or body fluids), and is characterized by fever, headache, body aches, a dry cough, hypoxia, and usu. pneumonia

sar·sa·pa·ril·la \ˌsas-pə-ˈri-lə, ˌsärs-, -ˈre-; ˌsa-sə-, ˌsär-sə-\ *n* [Sp *zarzaparrilla,* fr. *zarza* bush + *parilla,* dim. of *parra* vine] (1577) **1 a** : any of various tropical American greenbriers **b** : the dried roots of a sarsaparilla used esp. as a flavoring **2** : any of various plants (as wild sarsaparilla) that resemble or are used as a substitute for sarsaparilla **3** : a sweetened carbonated beverage flavored with sassafras and oil distilled from a European birch

sarsenet *var of* SARCENET

sar·to·ri·al \sär-ˈtȯr-ē-əl, sə(r)-\ *adj* [ML *sartor*] (1823) : of or relating to a tailor or tailored clothes; *broadly* : of or relating to clothes ⟨poor ~ taste⟩ — **sar·to·ri·al·ly** \-ē-ə-lē\ *adv*

sar·to·ri·us \sär-ˈtȯr-ē-əs\ *n, pl* **-rii** \-ē-ˌī, -ē-ˌē\ [NL, fr. ML *sartor* tailor, fr. L *sarcire* to mend] (1704) : a muscle that crosses the front of the thigh obliquely, assists in rotating the leg to the cross-legged position in which the knees are spread wide apart, and in humans is the longest muscle

Sar·um \ˈser-əm\ *adj* [*Sarum,* old borough near Salisbury, England] (1570) : of or relating to the Roman rite as modified in Salisbury and used in England, Wales, and Ireland before the Reformation

SASE *abbr* self-addressed stamped envelope

[1]**sash** \ˈsash\ *n* [Ar *shāsh* muslin] (ca. 1678) : a band worn about the waist or over one shoulder and used as a dress accessory or the emblem of an honorary or military order — **sashed** \ˈsasht\ *adj*

[2]**sash** *n, pl* **sash** *also* **sash·es** [prob. modif. of F *châssis* chassis (taken as pl.)] (1681) : the framework in which panes of glass are set in a window or door; *also* : such a framework together with its panes forming a usu. movable part of a window

[1]**sa·shay** \sa-ˈshā *also* sī-\ *vi* [alter. of *chassé*] (1836) **1** : to make a chassé **2 a** : WALK, GLIDE, GO **b** : to strut or move about in an ostentatious or conspicuous manner **c** : to proceed or move in a diagonal or sideways manner

[2]**sashay** *n* (1900) **1** : TRIP, EXCURSION **2** : a square-dance figure in which partners sidestep in a circle around each other with the man moving behind the woman **3** : CHASSÉ

sa·shi·mi \sä-shə-mē, sä-ˈshē-\ *n* [Jp] (1876) : a Japanese dish of thinly sliced raw fish

Sask *abbr* Saskatchewan

sas·ka·toon \ˌsas-kə-ˈtün\ *n* [modif. of Cree *misa·skwato·min* serviceberry fruit] (1810) **1** : SERVICEBERRY 2; *esp* : a serviceberry (*Amelanchier alnifolia*) chiefly of the northwestern U.S. and western Canada **2** : the fruit of a saskatoon

Sas·quatch \ˈsas-ˌkwach, -ˌkwäch\ *n* [Halkomelem (Salishan language of southwestern British Columbia) *sésq̓ac*] (1929) : a hairy creature like a human being reported to exist in the northwestern U.S. and western Canada and said to be a primate between 6 and 15 feet (1.8 and 4.6 meters) tall — called also *bigfoot*

[1]**sass** \ˈsas\ *n* [alter. of [1]*sauce*] (1835) : impudent speech

[2]**sass** *vt* (1856) : to talk impudently or disrespectfully to

sas·sa·fras \ˈsa-sə-ˌfras\ *n* [Sp *sasafrás*] (1577) **1** : an eastern No. American tree (*Sassafras albidum*) of the laurel family having both ovate and lobed aromatic leaves **2** : the carcinogenic dried root bark of the sassafras used formerly as a diaphoretic or flavoring agent

[1]**Sas·sa·ni·an** *or* **Sa·sa·ni·an** \sə-ˈsā-nē-ən, sa-ˈsā-\ *adj* (1788) : of, relating to, or having the characteristics of the Sassanid dynasty of ancient Persia or its art or architecture

[2]**Sassanian** *or* **Sasanian** *n* (1855) : SASSANID

Sas·sa·nid *or* **Sa·sa·nid** \sə-ˈsä-nəd, -ˈsa-; ˈsa-sə-nəd\ *n* [NL *Sassanidae* Sassanids, fr. *Sassan,* founder of the dynasty] (1776) : a member of a dynasty of Persian kings of the third to seventh centuries — **Sassanid** *or* **Sasanid** *adj*

sassy \ˈsa-sē\ *adj* **sass·i·er; -est** [alter. of *saucy*] (1833) **1** : IMPUDENT 2 **2** : VIGOROUS, LIVELY **3** : distinctively smart and stylish

sas·tru·ga \ˈsas-trə-gə, ˈsäs-; ˌsas-ˈtrü-gə, ˌsäs-\ *n, pl* **sas·tru·gi** \-(ˌ)gē\ [G, fr. Russ dial. (Siberia) *zastruga*] (1840) : a wavelike ridge of hard snow formed by the wind — usu. used in pl.

[1]**sat** *past and past part of* SIT

[2]**sat** *abbr* **1** satellite **2** saturated

Sat *abbr* Saturday

SAT \ˌes-ˌā-ˈtē\ *trademark* — used for a standardized test used to evaluate suitability for college admission

Sa·tan \ˈsā-tᵊn\ *n* [ME, fr. OE, fr. LL, fr. Gk, fr. Heb *śāṭān* adversary] (bef. 12c) **1** : the angel who in Jewish belief is commanded by God to tempt humans to sin, to accuse the sinners, and to carry out God's punishment **2** : the rebellious angel who in Christian belief is the adversary of God and lord of evil

sa·tang \sə-ˈtäŋ\ *n, pl* **satang** *or* **satangs** [Thai *sataŋ*] (ca. 1915) — see *baht* at MONEY table

sa·tan·ic \sə-ˈta-nik, sā-\ *adj* (1667) **1** : of, relating to, or characteristic of Satan or satanism ⟨~ pride⟩ ⟨~ rites⟩ **2** : characterized by extreme cruelty or viciousness — **sa·tan·i·cal·ly** \-ni-k(ə-)lē\ *adv*

sa·tan·ism \ˈsā-tə-ˌni-zəm\ *n, often cap* (1565) **1** : innate wickedness **2** : obsession with or affinity for evil; *specif* : worship of Satan marked by the travesty of Christian rites — **sa·tan·ist** \-ist\ *n, often cap*

\ə\ **abut** \ᵊ\ **kitten**, F table \ər\ **further** \a\ **ash** \ā\ **ace** \ä\ **mop, mar** \au̇\ **out** \ch\ **chin** \e\ **bet** \ē\ **easy** \g\ **go** \i\ **hit** \ī\ **ice** \j\ **job** \ŋ\ **sing** \ō\ **go** \ȯ\ **law** \ȯi\ **boy** \th\ **thin** \th\ **the** \ü\ **loot** \u̇\ **foot** \y\ **yet** \zh\ **vision, beige** \k, ⁿ, œ, ue, ʸ\ *see* Guide to Pronunciation

satch·el \ˈsa-chəl\ *n* [ME *sachel,* fr. AF *sachel, sacel,* fr. LL *saccellum,* dim. of L *sacculus,* dim. of *saccus* bag — more at SACK] (14c) : a small bag often with a shoulder strap — **satch·el·ful** \-ˌfu̇l\ *n*

1**sate** \ˈsāt, ˈsat\ *archaic past of* SIT

2**sate** \ˈsāt\ *vt* **sat·ed; sat·ing** [prob. by shortening & alter. fr. *satiate*] (1579) **1 :** to cloy with overabundance : GLUT **2 :** to appease (as a thirst) by indulging to the full ***syn*** see SATIATE

sa·teen \sa-ˈtēn, sə-\ *n* [alter. of *satin*] (ca. 1878) : a smooth durable lustrous fabric usu. made of cotton in satin weave

sat·el·lite \ˈsa-tə-ˌlīt\ *n* [MF, fr. L *satellit-, satelles* attendant] (ca. 1548) **1 :** a hired agent or obsequious follower : MINION, SYCOPHANT **2 a :** a celestial body orbiting another of larger size **b :** a manufactured object or vehicle intended to orbit the earth, the moon, or another celestial body **3 :** someone or something attendant, subordinate, or dependent; *esp* : a country politically and economically dominated or controlled by another more powerful country **4 :** a usu. independent urban community situated near but not immediately adjacent to a large city **5 :** DIRECT BROADCAST SATELLITE — **satellite** *adj*

satellite dish *n* (1978) : a microwave dish for receiving usu. television transmissions from an orbiting satellite

satellite DNA *n* (1969) : a fraction of a eukaryotic organism's DNA that differs in density from most of its DNA as determined by centrifugation, that consists of short repetitive nucleotide sequences, that does not undergo transcription, and that is often found in centromeric regions

satellite television *n* (1971) : DIRECT BROADCAST SATELLITE

sa·tem \ˈsä-təm\ *adj* [Av *satəm* hundred; fr. the fact that its initial sound (derived fr. an alveolar fricative) is the representative of an IE palatal stop — more at HUNDRED] (1901) : of, relating to, or constituting an Indo-European language group in which the palatal stops became in prehistoric times palatal or alveolar fricatives — compare CENTUM

sati *var of* SUTTEE

sa·tia·ble \ˈsā-shə-bəl\ *adj* (1570) : capable of being appeased or satisfied ⟨~ curiosity⟩

1**sa·tiate** \ˈsā-sh(ē-)ət\ *adj* (15c) : filled to satiety

2**sa·ti·ate** \ˈsā-shē-ˌāt\ *vt* **-at·ed; -at·ing** [L *satiatus,* pp. of *satiare,* fr. *satis* enough — more at SAD] (15c) : to satisfy (as a need or desire) fully or to excess — **sa·ti·a·tion** \ˌsā-shē-ˈā-shən, ˌsā-sē-\ *n*

syn SATIATE, SATE, SURFEIT, CLOY, PALL, GLUT, GORGE mean to fill to repletion. SATIATE and SATE may sometimes imply only complete satisfaction but more often suggest repletion that has destroyed interest or desire ⟨years of globe-trotting had *satiated* their interest in travel⟩ ⟨readers were *sated* with sensationalistic stories⟩. SURFEIT implies a nauseating repletion ⟨*surfeited* themselves with junk food⟩. CLOY stresses the disgust or boredom resulting from such surfeiting ⟨sentimental pictures that *cloy* after a while⟩. PALL emphasizes the loss of ability to stimulate interest or appetite ⟨a life of leisure eventually begins to *pall*⟩. GLUT implies excess in feeding or supplying ⟨a market *glutted* with diet books⟩. GORGE suggests glutting to the point of bursting or choking ⟨*gorged* themselves with chocolate⟩.

sa·ti·ety \sə-ˈtī-ə-tē *also* ˈsā-sh(ē-)ə-\ *n* [MF *satieté,* fr. L *satietat-, satietas,* fr. *satis*] (1541) **1 :** the quality or state of being fed or gratified to or beyond capacity : SURFEIT, FULLNESS **2 :** the revulsion or disgust caused by overindulgence or excess

1**sat·in** \ˈsa-tᵊn\ *n* [ME, fr. AF, prob. fr. Ar *zaytūnī,* lit., of Zaytūn, seaport in China during the Middle Ages] (14c) : a fabric (as of silk) in satin weave with lustrous face and dull back

2**satin** *adj* (15c) **1 :** made of or covered with satin **2 :** suggestive of satin in esp. in smooth lustrous appearance or sleekness to touch

sat·in·et \ˌsa-tə-ˈnet\ *n* (1703) **1 :** a thin silk satin or imitation satin **2 :** a variation of satin weave used in making satinet

satin stitch *n* (1664) : an embroidery stitch worked in parallel lines so closely and evenly as to resemble satin

satin weave *n* (ca. 1883) : a weave in which warp threads interlace with filling threads to produce a smooth-faced fabric

sat·in·wood \ˈsa-tᵊn-ˌwu̇d\ *n* (1792) **1 a :** a tree (*Chloroxylon swietenia*) of the rue family native to India and Sri Lanka that yields a lustrous yellowish-brown wood **b :** a tree (as the West Indian *Zanthoxylum flavum* of the rue family) with wood resembling true satinwood **2 :** the wood of a satinwood

sat·iny \ˈsat-nē, ˈsa-tᵊn-ē\ *adj* (1786) : having or resembling the soft usu. lustrous smoothness of satin ⟨a ~ finish⟩

sat·ire \ˈsa-ˌtī(-ə)r\ *n* [MF or L; MF, fr. L *satura, satira,* perh. fr. (*lanx*) *satura* dish of mixed ingredients, fr. fem. of *satur* well-fed; akin to L *satis* enough — more at SAD] (1501) **1 :** a literary work holding up human vices and follies to ridicule or scorn **2 :** trenchant wit, irony, or sarcasm used to expose and discredit vice or folly ***syn*** see WIT

sa·tir·ic \sə-ˈtir-ik\ *or* **sa·tir·i·cal** \-i-kəl\ *adj* (1509) **1 :** of, relating to, or constituting satire ⟨~ writers⟩ **2 :** manifesting or given to satire ***syn*** see SARCASTIC — **sa·tir·i·cal·ly** \-i-k(ə-)lē\ *adv*

sat·i·rise *Brit var of* SATIRIZE

sat·i·rist \ˈsa-tə-rist\ *n* (1589) : one that satirizes; *esp* : a writer of satire

sat·i·rize \-ˌrīz\ *vb* **-rized; -riz·ing** *vi* (ca. 1598) : to utter or write satire ~ *vt* : to censure or ridicule by means of satire — **sat·i·ri·za·ble** \ˌsa-tə-ˈrī-zə-bəl\ *adj*

sat·is·fac·tion \ˌsa-təs-ˈfak-shən\ *n* [ME, fr. AF, fr. LL *satisfaction-, satisfactio,* fr. L, reparation, amends, fr. *satisfacere* to satisfy] (14c) **1 a :** the payment through penance of the temporal punishment incurred by a sin **b :** reparation for sin that meets the demands of divine justice **2 a :** fulfillment of a need or want **b :** the quality or state of being satisfied : CONTENTMENT **c :** a source or means of enjoyment : GRATIFICATION **3 a :** compensation for a loss or injury : ATONEMENT, RESTITUTION **b :** the discharge of a legal obligation or claim **c :** VINDICATION **4 :** convinced assurance or certainty ⟨proved to the ~ of the court⟩

sat·is·fac·to·ry \ˌsa-təs-ˈfak-t(ə-)rē\ *adj* (15c) : giving satisfaction : ADEQUATE ⟨a ~ performance⟩ — **sat·is·fac·to·ri·ly** \-t(ə-)rə-lē\ *adv* — **sat·is·fac·to·ri·ness** *n*

sat·is·fi·able \ˈsa-təs-ˌfī-ə-bəl\ *adj* (1638) : capable of being satisfied

sat·is·fy \ˈsa-təs-ˌfī\ *vb* **-fied; -fy·ing** [ME *satisfien,* fr. AF *satisfier,* modif. of L *satisfacere,* fr. *satis* enough + *facere* to do, make — more at SAD, DO] *vt* (15c) **1 a :** to carry out the terms of (as a contract) : DISCHARGE **b :** to meet a financial obligation to **2 :** to make reparation to (an injured party) : INDEMNIFY **3 a :** to make happy : PLEASE **b :** to gratify to the full : APPEASE **4 a :** CONVINCE **b :** to put an end to (doubt or uncertainty) : DISPEL **5 a :** to conform to (as specifications) : be adequate to (an end in view) **b :** to make true by fulfilling a condition ⟨values that ~ an equation⟩ ⟨~ a hypothesis⟩ ~ *vi* : to be adequate : SUFFICE; *also* : PLEASE ***syn*** see PAY — **sat·is·fy·ing·ly** \-iŋ-lē\ *adv*

sa·to·ri \sə-ˈtȯr-ē, sä-\ *n* [Jp] (1727) : sudden enlightenment and a state of consciousness attained by intuitive illumination representing the spiritual goal of Zen Buddhism

sa·trap \ˈsā-ˌtrap *also* ˈsa-ˌtrap *or* ˈsa-trəp\ *n* [ME, fr. L *satrapes,* fr. Gk *satrapēs,* fr. OPers *khshathrapāvan,* lit., protector of the dominion] (14c) **1 :** the governor of a province in ancient Persia **2 a :** RULER **b :** a subordinate official : HENCHMAN

sa·tra·py \ˈsā-trə-pē, ˈsa-, -ˌtra-pē\ *n, pl* **-pies** (1603) : the territory or jurisdiction of a satrap

sat·su·ma \sat-ˈsü-mə, ˈsat-sə-\ *n* [*Satsuma,* former province in Kyushu, Japan] (1882) **1 :** any of several cultivated cold-tolerant mandarin trees that bear medium-sized largely seedless fruits with thin smooth skin **2 :** the fruit of a satsuma

sat·u·ra·ble \ˈsach-rə-bəl, ˈsa-chə-\ *adj* (1570) : capable of being saturated

sat·u·rant \-rənt\ *n* (ca. 1775) : something that saturates

1**sat·u·rate** \ˈsa-chə-ˌrāt\ *vt* **-rat·ed; -rat·ing** [L *saturatus,* pp. of *saturare,* fr. *satur* well-fed — more at SATIRE] (1538) **1 :** to satisfy fully : SATIATE **2 :** to treat, furnish, or charge with something to the point where no more can be absorbed, dissolved, or retained ⟨water *saturated* with salt⟩ **3 a :** to fill completely with something that permeates or pervades ⟨book is *saturated* with Hollywood —Newgate Callendar⟩ **b :** to load to capacity **4 :** to cause to combine until there is no further tendency to combine ***syn*** see SOAK — **sat·u·ra·tor** \-ˌrā-tər\ *n*

2**sat·u·rate** \ˈsach-rət, ˈsa-chə-\ *adj* (1782) : SATURATED

saturated *adj* (1741) **1 :** full of moisture : made thoroughly wet **2 a :** being a solution that is unable to absorb or dissolve any more of a solute at a given temperature and pressure **b :** being an organic compound having no double or triple bonds between carbon atoms ⟨~ fats⟩ **3** *of a color* : having high saturation : PURE

sat·u·ra·tion \ˌsa-chə-ˈrā-shən\ *n* (ca. 1554) **1 a :** the act of saturating : the state of being saturated **b :** SATIETY, SURFEIT **2 :** conversion of an unsaturated to a saturated chemical compound (as by hydrogenation) **3 :** a state of maximum impregnation: as **a :** complete infiltration : PERMEATION **b :** the presence in air of the most water possible under existent pressure and temperature **c :** magnetization to the point beyond which a further increase in the intensity of the magnetizing force will produce no further magnetization **4 a :** chromatic purity : freedom from dilution with white **b (1) :** degree of difference from the gray having the same lightness — used of an object color **(2) :** degree of difference from the achromatic light-source color of the same brightness — used of a light-source color; compare HUE 2c **5 :** the supplying of a market with as much of a product as it will absorb **6 :** an overwhelming concentration of military forces or firepower

Sat·ur·day \ˈsa-tər-(ˌ)dā, -dē\ *n* [ME *saterday,* fr. OE *sæterndæg* (akin to OFris *sāterdei*), fr. L *Saturnus* Saturn + OE *dæg* day] (bef. 12c) : the seventh day of the week — **Sat·ur·days** \-dēz, -(ˌ)dāz\ *adv*

Saturday night special *n* (1968) : a cheap easily concealed handgun

Sat·urn \ˈsa-tərn\ *n* [L *Saturnus*] (bef. 12c) **1 :** a Roman god of agriculture and father by Ops of Jupiter **2 :** the planet sixth in order from the sun — see PLANET table

sat·ur·na·lia \ˌsa-tər-ˈnāl-yə, -ˈnā-lē-ə\ *n pl but sing or pl in constr* [L, fr. neut. pl. of *saturnalis* of Saturn, fr. *Saturnus*] (1591) **1** *cap* : the festival of Saturn in ancient Rome beginning on Dec. 17 **2** *sing, pl* **saturnalias** *also* **saturnalia a :** an unrestrained often licentious celebration : ORGY **b :** EXCESS, EXTRAVAGANCE — **sat·ur·na·lian** \-ˈnāl-yən, -ˈnā-lē-ən\ *adj* — **sat·ur·na·lian·ly** *adv*

Sa·tur·ni·an \sa-ˈtər-nē-ən, sə-\ *adj* (1557) **1 :** of, relating to, or influenced by the planet Saturn **2** *archaic* : of or relating to the god Saturn or the golden age of his reign

sa·tur·ni·id \-nē-əd\ *n* [NL *Saturniidae,* fr. *Saturnia,* genus of moths, fr. L, daughter of the god Saturn] (ca. 1909) : any of a family (Saturniidae) of usu. large stout strong-winged moths (as a luna moth or a cecropia moth) with hairy bodies — **saturniid** *adj*

sat·ur·nine \ˈsa-tər-ˌnīn\ *adj* (15c) **1 :** born under or influenced astrologically by the planet Saturn **2 a :** cold and steady in mood : slow to act or change **b :** of a gloomy or surly disposition **c :** having a sardonic aspect ⟨a ~ smile⟩ ***syn*** see SULLEN

sat·urn·ism \ˈsa-tər-ˌni-zəm\ *n* [*saturn* lead] (ca. 1855) : LEAD POISONING

sa·tya·gra·ha \(ˌ)sə-ˈtyä-grə-hə, ˈsə-tyə-\ *n* [New Skt *satyāgraha,* fr. Skt *satya* truth + *āgraha* persistence] (1920) : pressure for social and political reform through friendly passive resistance practiced by M. K. Gandhi and his followers in India

sa·tyr \ˈsā-tər, *chiefly Brit* ˈsa-\ *n* [ME, fr. L *satyrus,* fr. Gk *satyros*] (14c) **1** *often cap* : a sylvan deity in Greek mythology having certain characteristics of a horse or goat and fond of Dionysian revelry **2 a :** a lecherous man **b :** one having satyriasis **3 :** any of various satyrid butterflies — **sa·tyr·ic** \sā-ˈtir-ik, sə-, sa-\ *adj*

sa·ty·ri·a·sis \ˌsā-tə-ˈrī-ə-səs, ˌsa-\ *n* [LL, fr. Gk, fr. *satyros*] (15c) : excessive or abnormal sexual craving in the male

sa·ty·rid \sə-ˈtī-rəd\ *n* [NL *Satyridae,* ultim. fr. Gk *satyros*] (1901) : any of a family (Satyridae) of usu. brown or gray butterflies that feed on grasses as larvae, typically have eyespots on the wings, and have one or more forewing veins swollen basally — **satyrid** *adj*

satyr play *n* (1929) : a comic play of ancient Greece burlesquing a mythological subject and having a chorus representing satyrs

1**sauce** \ˈsȯs, *usu* ˈsas *for 4*\ *n* [ME, fr. AF, fr. L *salsa,* fem. of *salsus* salted, fr. pp. of *sallere* to salt, fr. *sal* salt — more at SALT] (14c) **1 :** a condiment or relish for food; *esp* : a fluid dressing or topping **2 :** something that adds zest or piquancy **3 :** stewed fruit eaten with other food or as a dessert **4 :** pert or impudent language or actions **5** *slang* : LIQUOR — used with *the*

2**sauce** \ˈsȯs, *usu* ˈsas *for 3*\ *vt* **sauced; sauc·ing** (15c) **1 a :** to dress with relish or seasoning **b :** to cover or serve with a sauce **2 a** *archaic* : to modify the harsh or unpleasant characteristics of **b :** to give zest or piquancy to **3 :** to be rude or impudent to

sauce·boat \ˈsȯs-ˌbōt\ *n* (1747) **:** a low boat-shaped pitcher for serving sauces and gravies
sauce·box \ˈsȯs-ˌbäks, ˈsas-\ *n* (1588) **:** a saucy impudent person
sauce·pan \ˈsȯs-ˌpan, *esp Brit* -pən\ *n* (1686) **:** a small deep cooking pan with a handle
sau·cer \ˈsȯ-sər\ *n* [ME, plate containing a condiment, fr. AF, fr. *sauce*] (ca. 1702) **1 :** a small shallow dish in which a cup is set at table **2 :** something resembling a saucer esp. in shape; *esp* **:** FLYING SAUCER — **sau·cer·like** \-ˌlīk\ *adj*
saucy \ˈsȯ-sē, ˈsa-\ *adj* **sauc·i·er; -est** (1508) **1 :** served with or having the consistency of sauce **2 a :** impertinently bold and impudent **b :** amusingly forward and flippant **:** IRREPRESSIBLE **3 :** SMART, TRIM ⟨a ~ little hat⟩ — **sauc·i·ly** \-sə-lē\ *adv* — **sauc·i·ness** \-sē-nəs\ *n*
sau·er·bra·ten \ˈsau̇(-ə)r-ˌbrä-tᵊn\ *n* [G, fr. *sauer* sour + *Braten* roast meat] (1889) **:** oven-roasted or pot-roasted beef marinated before cooking in vinegar with peppercorns, garlic, onions, and bay leaves
sau·er·kraut \ˈsau̇(-ə)r-ˌkrau̇t\ *n* [G, fr. *sauer* sour + *Kraut* greens] (1617) **:** cabbage cut fine and fermented in a brine made of its own juice with salt
sau·ger \ˈsȯ-gər\ *n* [origin unknown] (1882) **:** a pike perch (*Stizostedion canadense*) of Canada and the U.S. similar to the walleye but smaller
saugh *or* **sauch** \ˈsäk, ˈsȯk\ *n* [ME (Sc) *sauch,* fr. OE *salh,* alter. of *sealh* — more at SALLOW] (bef. 12c) *chiefly Scot* **:** SALLOW
Sauk \ˈsȯk\ *or* **Sac** \ˈsak, ˈsȯk\ *n, pl* **Sauk** *or* **Sauks** *or* **Sac** *or* **Sacs** [short for *Saukie, Saki,* fr. AmerF *saki,* fr. Ojibwa *osa·ki·,* or a cognate Algonquian word] (1722) **:** a member of an American Indian people formerly living in what is now Wisconsin
Saul \ˈsȯl, ˈsäl\ *n* [LL *Saulus,* fr. Gk *Saulos,* fr. Heb *Shāʼūl*] (bef. 12c) **1 :** the first king of Israel **2 :** the apostle Paul — called also *Saul of Tarsus*
sau·na \ˈsȯ-nə, ˈsau̇-nə\ *n* [Finn] (1881) **1 :** a Finnish steam bath in which the steam is provided by water thrown on hot stones; *also* **:** a bathhouse or room used for such a bath **2 :** a dry heat bath; *also* **:** a room or cabinet used for such a bath
saun·ter \ˈsȯn-tər, ˈsän-\ *vi* [prob. fr. ME *santren* to muse] (ca. 1667) **:** to walk about in an idle or leisurely manner **:** STROLL ⟨~*ed* slowly down the street⟩ — **saunter** *n* — **saun·ter·er** \-tər-ər\ *n*
sau·rel \sȯ-ˈrel\ *n* [F, fr. LL *saurus* horse mackerel, fr. Gk *sauros* horse mackerel, lizard] (1882) **:** JACK MACKEREL
sau·ri·an \ˈsȯr-ē-ən\ *n* [NL *Sauria,* fr. NL *saurus* lizard, fr. Gk *sauros*] (1824) **:** any of a suborder (Sauria) of reptiles including the lizards and in older classifications the crocodiles and various extinct forms (as the dinosaurs and ichthyosaurs) that resemble lizards — **saurian** *adj*
saur·is·chi·an \(ˌ)sȯ-ˈris-kē-ən\ *n* [NL *Saurischia,* ultim. fr. Gk *sauros* lizard + NL *ischium* ischium] (ca. 1889) **:** any of an order (Saurischia) of herbivorous or carnivorous dinosaurs that have the pubis of the pelvis typically pointed downward and forward and that include the sauropods and theropods — compare ORNITHISCHIAN — **saurischian** *adj*
sau·ro·pod \ˈsȯr-ə-ˌpäd\ *n* [NL *Sauropoda,* fr. Gk *sauros* lizard + NL *-poda*] (ca. 1889) **:** any of a suborder (Sauropoda) of quadrupedal herbivorous saurischian dinosaurs (as a brontosaurus) of the Jurassic and Cretaceous having a long neck and tail, small head, and 5-toed limbs on which they tended to walk in a digitigrade fashion — **sauropod** *adj*
sau·ry \ˈsȯr-ē\ *n, pl* **sauries** [NL *saurus* lizard] (ca. 1771) **:** a widely distributed fish (*Scombresox saurus*) of temperate waters of the Atlantic that resembles the related needlefishes; *also* **:** a similar widely distributed fish (*C. saira*) of temperate waters of the Pacific

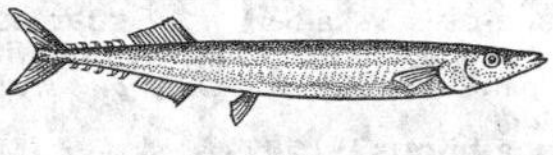
saury

sau·sage \ˈsȯ-sij\ *n* [ME *sausige,* fr. AF *sauseche, saucis,* fr. LL *salsicia,* fr. L *salsus* salted — more at SAUCE] (15c) **:** a highly seasoned minced meat (as pork) usu. stuffed in casings of prepared animal intestine; *also* **:** a link or patty of sausage
1**sau·té** *also* **sau·te** \sȯ-ˈtā, sō-\ *n* [F, fr. pp. of *sauter* to jump, fr. OF, fr. L *saltare* — more at SALTATION] (1813) **:** a sautéed dish — **sauté** *adj*
2**sauté** *also* **saute** *vt* **sau·téed** *also* **sau·teed; sau·té·ing** *also* **sau·te·ing** (1859) **:** to fry in a small amount of fat
sau·ternes \sō-ˈtərn, sȯ-, -ˈtern\ *n* [F, fr. *Sauternes,* commune in France] (1711) **1** *cap* **:** a full-bodied sweet white wine from the Bordeaux region of France **2** *usu* **sauterne :** a semidry to semisweet American white wine that is a blend of several grapes
sau·vi·gnon blanc \ˌsō-vēn-ˈyō^{n}-ˈblä^{n}\ *n* [F, white sauvignon (variety of grape)] (1941) **:** a dry white wine made from a grape orig. grown in Bordeaux and the Loire valley
1**sav·age** \ˈsa-vij\ *adj* [ME, fr. AF *salvage, savage,* fr. LL *salvaticus,* alter. of L *silvaticus* of the woods, wild, fr. *silva* wood, forest] (13c) **1 a :** not domesticated or under human control **:** UNTAMED ⟨~ beasts⟩ **b :** lacking the restraints normal to civilized human beings **:** FIERCE, FEROCIOUS ⟨a ~ criminal⟩ **2 :** WILD, UNCULTIVATED ⟨seldom have I seen such ~ scenery —Douglas Carruthers⟩ **3 a :** BOORISH, RUDE ⟨the ~ bad manners of most motorists —M. P. O'Connor⟩ **b :** MALICIOUS **4 :** lacking complex or advanced culture **:** UNCIVILIZED ⟨a ~ country⟩ ***syn*** see FIERCE — **sav·age·ly** *adv* — **sav·age·ness** *n*
2**savage** *n* (15c) **1 :** a person belonging to a primitive society **2 :** a brutal person **3 :** a rude or unmannerly person
3**savage** *vt* **sav·aged; sav·ag·ing** (1880) **:** to attack or treat brutally
sav·age·ry \ˈsa-vij-rē, -vi-jə-\ *n, pl* **-ries** (1597) **1 a :** the quality of being savage **b :** an act of cruelty or violence **2 :** an uncivilized state
sav·ag·ism \ˈsa-vi-ˌji-zəm\ *n* (1796) **:** SAVAGERY
sa·van·na *also* **sa·van·nah** \sə-ˈva-nə\ *n* [Sp *zavana,* fr. Taino *zabana*] (1555) **1 :** a treeless plain esp. in Florida **2 a :** a tropical or subtropical grassland (as of eastern Africa or northern So. America) containing scattered trees and drought-resistant undergrowth **b :** a temperate grassland with scattered trees (as oaks)
sa·vant \sa-ˈvänt, sə-, -ˈvä^{n}; sə-ˈvant, ˈsa-vənt\ *n* [F, fr. MF, fr. prp. of *savoir* to know, fr. L *sapere* to be wise — more at SAGE] (1719) **1 :** a person of learning; *esp* **:** one with detailed knowledge in some specialized field (as of science or literature) **2 :** IDIOT SAVANT 1
sav·a·rin \ˈsa-və-rən\ *n* [F, fr. Anthelme Brillat-*Savarin* †1826 Fr. politician, writer, and gourmet] (1877) **:** a rich yeast cake baked in a ring mold and soaked in a rum or kirsch syrup
sa·vate \sə-ˈvät, sa-, -ˈvat\ *n* [F, lit., old shoe] (1862) **:** a form of boxing in which blows are delivered with either the hands or the feet
1**save** \ˈsāv\ *vb* **saved; sav·ing** [ME, fr. AF *salver,* fr. LL *salvare,* fr. L *salvus* safe — more at SAFE] *vt* (13c) **1 a :** to deliver from sin **b :** to rescue or deliver from danger or harm **c :** to preserve or guard from injury, destruction, or loss **d :** to store (data) in a computer or on a storage device (as a floppy disk or CD) **2 a :** to put aside as a store or reserve **:** ACCUMULATE ⟨*saving* money for emergencies⟩ **b :** to spend less by ⟨~ 25 percent⟩ **3 a :** to make unnecessary **:** AVOID ⟨it ~*s* an hour's driving⟩ **b** (1) **:** to keep from being lost to an opponent (2) **:** to prevent an opponent from scoring or winning **4 :** MAINTAIN, PRESERVE ⟨~ appearances⟩ ~ *vi* **1 :** to rescue or deliver someone **2 a :** to put aside money **b :** to avoid unnecessary waste or expense **:** ECONOMIZE **c :** to spend less money **3 :** to make a save ***syn*** see RESCUE — **sav·able** *or* **save·able** \ˈsā-və-bəl\ *adj* — **sav·er** *n*
2**save** *n* (1890) **1 :** a play that prevents an opponent from scoring or winning **2 :** the action of a relief pitcher in baseball in successfully protecting a team's lead; *also* **:** official credit for a save
3**save** *prep* [ME *sauf,* fr. AF *sauve,* fr. *sauf,* adj., safe — more at SAFE] (14c) **:** other than **:** BUT, EXCEPT ⟨no hope ~ one⟩
4**save** *conj* (14c) **1 :** except for the fact that **:** ONLY — used with *that* ⟨of his earlier years little is known, ~ that he studied violin —J. N. Burk⟩ **2 :** BUT, EXCEPT — used before a word often taken to be the subject of a clause ⟨no one knows about it ~ she⟩
save–all \ˈsā-ˌvȯl\ *n* (ca. 1645) **:** something that prevents waste, loss, or damage (as a receptacle for catching waste products for further use)
sav·e·loy \ˈsa-və-ˌlȯi\ *n* [modif. of F *cervelas,* fr. MF, fr. OIt *cervellata,* lit., pig's brains, fr. *cervello* brain, fr. L *cerebellum* — more at CEREBELLUM] (1837) *Brit* **:** a highly seasoned dry sausage
sav·in \ˈsa-vən\ *n* [ME, fr. AF, fr. L (*herba*) *sabina,* lit., Sabine plant] (14c) **1 :** a Eurasian juniper (*Juniperus sabina*) with dark berrylike cones and foliage **2 :** RED CEDAR 1
1**saving** *n* [ME, fr. gerund of *saven* to save] (14c) **1 :** preservation from danger or destruction **:** DELIVERANCE **2 :** the act or an instance of economizing **3 a** *pl* **:** money put by **b :** the excess of income over consumption expenditures — often used in pl. **c :** a usu. specified lower cost — often used in pl. ⟨a ~*s* of 50 percent⟩
2**saving** *prep* [ME, fr. prp. of *saven*] (14c) **1 :** EXCEPT, SAVE **2 :** without disrespect to
3**saving** *conj* (15c) **:** EXCEPT, SAVE
saving grace *n* (1597) **:** a redeeming quality or factor
savings account *n* (1911) **:** an account (as in a bank) on which interest is usu. paid and from which withdrawals can be made usu. only by presentation of a passbook or by written authorization on a prescribed form
savings and loan association *n* (1884) **:** a cooperative association organized to hold savings of members in the form of dividend-bearing shares and to invest chiefly in home mortgage loans — called also *savings and loan*
savings bank *n* (1817) **:** a bank organized to hold funds of individual depositors in interest-bearing accounts and to make long-term investments (as in home mortgage loans)
savings bond *n* (1948) **:** a nontransferable registered U.S. bond issued in denominations of $50 to $10,000
sav·ior *or* **sav·iour** \ˈsāv-yər *also* -ˌyȯr\ *n* [ME *saveour,* fr. AF, fr. LL *salvator,* fr. *salvare* to save] (14c) **1 :** one that saves from danger or destruction **2 :** one who brings salvation; *specif, cap* **:** JESUS 1
sa·voir faire \ˌsav-ˌwär-ˈfer\ *n* [F *savoir-faire,* lit., knowing how to do] (1815) **:** capacity for appropriate action; *esp* **:** a polished sureness in social behavior ***syn*** see TACT
1**sa·vor** *also* **sa·vour** \ˈsā-vər\ *n* [ME, fr. AF *savur,* fr. L *sapor,* fr. *sapere* to taste — more at SAGE] (13c) **1 :** the taste or smell of something **2 :** a particular flavor or smell **3 :** a distinctive quality — **sa·vor·less** \-ləs\ *adj* — **sa·vor·ous** \ˈsā-vər-əs, ˈsāv-rəs\ *adj*
2**savor** *also* **savour** *vb* **sa·vored** *also* **sa·voured; sa·vor·ing** *also* **sa·vour·ing** \ˈsā-vər-iŋ, ˈsāv-riŋ\ *vi* (14c) **:** to have a specified smell or quality **:** SMACK ~ *vt* **1 :** to give flavor to **:** SEASON **2 a :** to have experience of **:** TASTE **b :** to taste or smell with pleasure **:** RELISH **c :** to delight in **:** ENJOY ⟨~*ing* the moment⟩ — **sa·vor·er** \ˈsā-vər-ər\ *n*
1**sa·vory** *also* **sa·voury** \ˈsā-və-rē, ˈsāv-rē\ *adj* (13c) **:** having savor: as **a :** piquantly pleasant to the mind ⟨a ~ triumph⟩ **b :** morally exemplary **:** EDIFYING **c :** pleasing to the sense of taste esp. by reason of effective seasoning **d :** pungently flavorful without sweetness ***syn*** see PALATABLE — **sa·vor·i·ly** \-rə-lē\ *adv* — **sa·vor·i·ness** \-rē-nəs\ *n*
2**savory** *also* **savoury** *n, pl* **sa·vor·ies** *also* **sa·vour·ies** (1661) *Brit* **:** a dish of stimulating flavor served usu. at the end of dinner but sometimes as an appetizer
3**sa·vo·ry** \ˈsā-və-rē, ˈsāv-rē\ *n, pl* **-ries** [ME *saverey*] (14c) **:** either of two aromatic mints: **a :** SUMMER SAVORY **b :** WINTER SAVORY
Sa·voy·ard \sə-ˈvȯi-ˌärd, ˌsa-ˌvȯi-ˈärd, ˌsav-ˌwä-ˈyär(d)\ *n* [*Savoy* Theater, London, built for the presentation of Gilbert and Sullivan operas] (1890) **:** a devotee, performer, or producer of the comic operas of W. S. Gilbert and A. S. Sullivan
sa·voy cabbage \sə-ˈvȯi-, ˈsa-ˌvȯi-\ *n, often cap S* [trans. of F *chou de Savoie* cabbage of Savoy] (1707) **:** a cabbage with compact heads of wrinkled and curled leaves
1**sav·vy** \ˈsa-vē\ *vb* **sav·vied; sav·vy·ing** [alter. of *sabi* know (in English-based creoles and pidgins), fr. Pg *sabe* he knows, fr. *saber* to know, fr. L *sapere* to be wise — more at SAGE] (1785) **:** UNDERSTAND
2**savvy** *n* (ca. 1785) **:** practical know-how ⟨political ~⟩
3**savvy** *adj* **sav·vi·er; sav·vi·est** (1905) **:** having or showing perception, comprehension, or shrewdness esp. in practical matters — **sav·vi·ly** *adv* — **sav·vi·ness** *n*
1**saw** *past of* SEE
2**saw** \ˈsȯ\ *n* [ME *sawe,* fr. OE *sagu;* akin to OHG *sega* saw, L *secare* to cut] (bef. 12c) **:** a hand or power tool or a machine used to cut hard material (as wood, metal, or bone) and equipped usu. with a toothed blade or disk — **saw·like** \-ˌlīk\ *adj*

[3]**saw** *vb* **sawed** \ˈsȯd\; **sawed** *or* **sawn** \ˈsȯn\; **saw·ing** \ˈsȯ(-)iŋ\ *vt* (13c) **1** : to cut with a saw **2** : to produce or form by cutting with a saw **3** : to slash as though with a saw ~ *vi* **1 a** : to use a saw **b** : to cut with or as if with a saw **2** : to undergo cutting with a saw **3** : to make motions as though using a saw ⟨~*ed* at the reins⟩ — **saw·er** \ˈsȯ(-ə)r\ *n*
[4]**saw** *n* [ME *sawe,* fr. OE *sagu* discourse; akin to OHG & ON *saga* tale, OE *secgan* to say — more at SAY] (bef. 12c) : MAXIM, PROVERB
saw·bones \ˈsȯ-ˌbōnz\ *n, pl* **sawbones** *or* **saw·bones·es** (1837) *slang* : PHYSICIAN, SURGEON
saw·buck \ˈsȯ-ˌbək\ *n* (1850) **1** *slang* : a 10-dollar bill **2** : SAWHORSE; *esp* : one with X-shaped ends
saw·dust \ˈsȯ-(ˌ)dəst\ *n* (ca. 1528) : fine particles (as of wood) made by a saw in cutting
sawed–off \ˈsȯd-ˌȯf\ *adj* (1869) **1** : having an end sawed off ⟨a ~ shotgun⟩ **2** : of less than average height
saw·fish \ˈsȯ-ˌfish\ *n* (1635) : any of a family (Pristidae) of large elongate rays that resemble sharks but have a long flattened snout with a row of serrate structures along each edge and that live in tropical and subtropical shallow seas and in or near the mouths of rivers
saw·fly \-ˌflī\ *n* (1773) : any of numerous hymenopterous insects (superfamily Tenthredinoidea and esp. family Tenthredinidae) with the female usu. having a sawlike ovipositor and with the larva resembling a plant-feeding caterpillar
saw grass *n* (1822) : any of various sedges (as of the genus *Cladium*) having the edges of the leaves set with minute sharp teeth
saw·horse \ˈsȯ-ˌhȯrs\ *n* (1778) : a frame on which wood is laid for sawing by hand : HORSE 2b
saw·log \-ˌlȯg, -ˌläg\ *n* (1756) : a log of suitable size for sawing into lumber
saw·mill \-ˌmil\ *n* (1553) : a mill or machine for sawing logs
saw palmetto *n* (1797) **1** : any of several shrubby palms chiefly of the southern U.S. and West Indies that have spiny-toothed petioles; *esp* : a common palm (*Serenoa repens*) of the southeastern U.S. with a usu. creeping stem **2** : a preparation derived from the berrylike fruit of a saw palmetto (*Serenoa repens*) that is held to have a therapeutic effect on the prostate gland and is used in dietary supplements and herbal remedies
saw set *n* (1846) : an instrument used to set the teeth of saws
saw·tim·ber \ˈsȯ-ˌtim-bər\ *n* (1901) : timber suitable for sawing into lumber
saw·tooth \-ˌtüth\ *adj* (ca. 1859) : having serrations : arranged or having parts arranged like the teeth of a saw ⟨a ~ roof⟩
saw–toothed \-ˈtütht\ *adj* (ca. 1857) **1** : having teeth like those of a saw ⟨a ~ shark⟩ **2** : SAWTOOTH
saw–whet owl \ˈsȯ-ˌhwet-, -ˌwet-\ *n* [fr. the supposed resemblance of its cry to the sound made in filing a saw] (1834) : a very small harsh-voiced No. American owl (*Aegolius acadicus*) that is largely dark brown above and chestnut streaked with white beneath — called also *saw-whet*
saw·yer \ˈsȯ-yər, ˈsȯi-ər\ *n* (13c) **1** : one that saws **2** : any of several large longicorn beetles whose larvae bore large holes in timber or dead wood **3** : a tree fast in the bed of a stream with its branches projecting to the surface and bobbing up and down with the current
sax \ˈsaks\ *n* (ca. 1923) : SAXOPHONE
sax·horn \ˈsaks-ˌhȯrn\ *n* [Antoine *Sax* †1894 Belgian instrument maker + E *horn*] (1844) : any of a group of valved brass instruments ranging from soprano to bass and characterized by a conical tube, oval shape, and cup-shaped mouthpiece
sax·ic·o·lous \sak-ˈsi-kə-ləs\ *adj* [L *saxum* rock (akin to L *secare* to cut) + E *-colous* — more at SAW] (1856) : inhabiting or growing among rocks ⟨~ lichens⟩
sax·i·frage \ˈsak-sə-frij, -ˌfrāj\ *n* [ME, fr. AF, fr. LL *saxifraga,* fr. L, fem. of *saxifragus* breaking rocks, fr. *saxum* rock + *frangere* to break — more at BREAK] (14c) : any of a genus (*Saxifraga* of the family Saxifragaceae, the saxifrage family) of chiefly perennial herbs with showy pentamerous flowers and often with basal tufted leaves
sax·i·tox·in \ˌsak-sə-ˈtäk-sən\ *n* [*saxi-* (fr. NL *Saxidomus giganteus,* species of butter clam from which it is isolated) + *toxin*] (1962) : a potent nonprotein neurotoxin $C_{10}H_{17}N_7O_4 \cdot 2HCl$ that originates esp. in dinoflagellates (genera *Alexandrium, Gymnodinium,* and *Pyrodinium*) found in red tides and that sometimes occurs in and renders toxic normally edible mollusks which feed on them
Sax·on \ˈsak-sən\ *n* [ME, fr. LL *Saxones* Saxons, of Gmc origin; akin to OE *Seaxan* Saxons] (13c) **1 a (1)** : a member of a Germanic people that entered and conquered England with the Angles and Jutes in the fifth century A.D. and merged with them to form the Anglo-Saxon people **(2)** : an Englishman or lowlander as distinguished from a Welshman, Irishman, or Highlander **b** : a native or inhabitant of Saxony **2 a** : the Germanic language or dialect of any of the Saxon peoples **b** : the Germanic element in the English language esp. as distinguished from the French and Latin — **Saxon** *adj*
sax·o·ny \ˈsak-s(ə-)nē\ *n, pl* **-nies** *often cap* [*Saxony,* Germany] (1837) **1 a** : a fine soft woolen fabric **b** : a fine closely twisted knitting yarn **2** : a Wilton jacquard carpet
sax·o·phone \ˈsak-sə-ˌfōn\ *n* [F, fr. Antoine *Sax* †1894 Belgian instrument maker + F *-phone*] (1851) : one of a group of single-reed woodwind instruments usu. ranging from soprano to bass and characterized by a conical metal tube and finger keys — **sax·o·phon·ic** \ˌsak-sə-ˈfō-nik, -ˈfä-\ *adj* — **sax·o·phon·ist**, *esp Brit* sak-ˈsä-fə-\ *n*
sax·tu·ba \ˈsaks-ˌtü-bə, -ˌtyü-\ *n* [Antoine *Sax* + E *tuba*] (1856) : a bass saxhorn

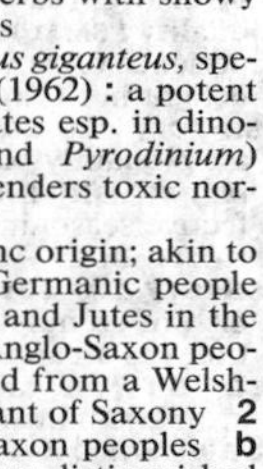
saxophone

[1]**say** \ˈsā, *Southern also* ˈse\ *vb* **said** \ˈsed, *esp when subject follows* səd\; **say·ing** \ˈsā-iŋ\; **says** \ˈsez, *sometimes* ˈsāz, *esp when subject follows* səz\ [ME, fr. OE *secgan;* akin to OHG *sagēn* to say, Lith *sakyti,* Gk en*nepein* to speak, tell] *vt* (bef. 12c) **1 a** : to express in words : STATE **b** : to state as opinion or belief : DECLARE **2 a** : UTTER, PRONOUNCE **b** : RECITE, REPEAT ⟨~ your prayers⟩ **3 a** : INDICATE, SHOW ⟨the clock ~*s* five minutes after twelve⟩ **b** : to give expression to : COMMUNICATE ⟨a glance that *said* all that was necessary⟩ **4** : SUPPOSE, ASSUME ⟨let's ~ you're right⟩ ~ *vi* : to express oneself : SPEAK — **say·er** \ˈsā-ər, ˈser\ *n* — **say uncle** : to admit defeat — **that is to say** : in other words : in effect — **to say nothing of** : not to mention : and notably in addition ⟨will need more time, *to say nothing of* money⟩
[2]**say** *n, pl* **says** \ˈsāz, *Southern also* ˈsez\ (1571) **1** *archaic* : something that is said : STATEMENT **2** : an expression of opinion ⟨had my ~⟩ **3** : a right or power to influence action or decision; *esp* : the authority to make final decisions
[3]**say** *adv* [fr. imper. of [1]*say*] (ca. 1596) **1** : ABOUT, APPROXIMATELY ⟨the property is worth, ~, four million dollars⟩ **2** : for example : AS ⟨if we compress any gas, ~ oxygen⟩
say·able \ˈsā-ə-bəl, ˈse-\ *adj* (1856) **1** : capable of being said **2** : capable of being spoken effectively or easily ⟨readings in ~ Chinese —*Linguistic Reporter*⟩
say·est \ˈsā-əst\ *archaic 2d person sing of* SAY
saying *n* (14c) : something said; *esp* : ADAGE
sa·yo·na·ra \ˌsī-ə-ˈnär-ə, ˌsä-yə-\ *n* [Jp *sayōnara*] (1887) : GOOD-BYE
say–so \ˈsā-(ˌ)sō, ˈse-\ *n* (1637) **1 a** : one's unsupported assertion or assurance **b** : an authoritative pronouncement ⟨left the hospital on the ~ of his doctor⟩ **2** : a right of final decision : SAY ⟨has the ultimate ~ on what will be taught⟩
say·yid \ˈsī-yəd, ˈsā-; ˈsīd, ˈsād\ *n* [Ar] (1788) **1** : an Islamic chief or leader **2** : LORD, SIR — used as a courtesy title for a Muslim of rank or lineage
sb *abbr* substantive
Sb *symbol* [L *stibium*] antimony
SB *abbr* **1** [NL *scientiae baccalaureus*] bachelor of science **2** southbound
SBA *abbr* Small Business Administration
SBN *abbr* Standard Book Number
sc *abbr* **1** scene **2** science **3** scilicet **4** [L *sculpsit*] he carved it; she carved it; he engraved it; she engraved it
[1]**Sc** *abbr* stratocumulus
[2]**Sc** *symbol* scandium
SC *abbr* **1** small capitals **2** South Carolina **3** supercalendered **4** supreme court
[1]**scab** \ˈskab\ *n* [ME, of Scand origin; akin to OSw *skabbr* scab; akin to OE *sceabb* scab, L *scabere* to scratch — more at SHAVE] (13c) **1** : scabies of domestic animals **2** : a crust of hardened blood and serum over a wound **3 a** : a contemptible person **b (1)** : a worker who refuses to join a labor union **(2)** : a union member who refuses to strike or returns to work before a strike has ended **(3)** : a worker who accepts employment or replaces a union worker during a strike **(4)** : one who works for less than union wages or on nonunion terms **4** : any of various bacterial or fungus diseases of plants characterized by crustaceous spots; *also* : one of the spots
[2]**scab** *vi* **scabbed; scab·bing** (1683) **1** : to become covered with a scab **2** : to act as a scab
scab·bard \ˈska-bərd\ *n* [ME *scauberc, scaubert,* fr. AF *escalberc*] (13c) : a sheath for a sword, dagger, or bayonet — **scabbard** *vt*
scab·by \ˈska-bē\ *adj* **scab·bi·er; -est** (15c) **1 a** : covered with or full of scabs ⟨~ skin⟩ **b** : diseased with scab ⟨a ~ animal⟩ ⟨~ potatoes⟩ **2** : MEAN, CONTEMPTIBLE ⟨a ~ trick⟩
sca·bies \ˈskā-bēz\ *n, pl* **scabies** [L, fr. *scabere* to scratch] (1814) : contagious itch or mange esp. with exudative crusts that is caused by parasitic mites (esp. *Sarcoptes scabiei*) — **sca·bi·et·ic** \ˌskā-bē-ˈe-tik\ *adj*
[1]**sca·bi·ous** \ˈskā-bē-əs, ˈska-\ *n* [ME *scabiose,* fr. AF, fr. ML *scabiosa,* fr. L, fem. of *scabiosus,* adj.] (14c) : any of a genus (*Scabiosa*) of Old World herbs of the teasel family with terminal flower heads subtended by a leafy involucre
[2]**scabious** *adj* [L *scabiosus,* fr. *scabies*] (1603) **1** : SCABBY **2** : of, relating to, or resembling scabies ⟨~ eruptions⟩
scab·land \ˈskab-ˌland\ *n* (1904) : a region characterized by elevated tracts of rocky land with little or no soil cover and traversed or isolated by postglacial dry stream channels — usu. used in pl.
sca·brous \ˈska-brəs *also* ˈskā-\ *adj* [L *scabr-, scaber* rough, scurfy; akin to L *scabere* to scratch — more at SCAB] (1646) **1** : DIFFICULT, KNOTTY ⟨a ~ problem⟩ **2** : rough to the touch: as **a** : having small raised dots, scales, or points ⟨a ~ leaf⟩ **b** : covered with raised, roughened, or unwholesome patches ⟨~ paint⟩ ⟨~ skin⟩ **3** : dealing with suggestive, indecent, or scandalous themes : SALACIOUS; *also* : SQUALID ***syn*** see ROUGH — **sca·brous·ly** *adv* — **sca·brous·ness** *n*
[1]**scad** \ˈskad\ *n, pl* **scad** *also* **scads** [origin unknown] (1602) : any of several carangid fishes (esp. of the genus *Decapterus*)
[2]**scad** *n* [prob. alter. of E dial. *scald* a multitude] (1869) : a large number or quantity — usu. used in pl. ⟨~*s* of money⟩
scaf·fold \ˈska-fəld *also* -ˌfōld\ *n* [ME, fr. AF *scaffald,* alter. of OF *eschaafauz, escafaut,* alter. of *chaafaut,* fr. VL **catafalicum* — more at CATAFALQUE] (14c) **1 a** : a temporary or movable platform for workers (as bricklayers, painters, or miners) to stand or sit on when working at a height above the floor or ground **b** : a platform on which a criminal is executed (as by hanging or beheading) **c** : a platform at a height above ground or floor level **2** : a supporting framework
scaf·fold·ing \-fəl-diŋ, -ˌfōl-\ *n* (14c) : a system of scaffolds; *also* : material for scaffolds
scag *also* **skag** \ˈskag\ *n* [origin unknown] (1967) *slang* : HEROIN
sca·glio·la \skal-ˈyō-lə, -ˈyȯ-\ *n, often attrib* [It, lit., little chip] (1747) : an imitation marble used for floors, columns, and ornamental interior work
scal·able \ˈskā-lə-bəl\ *adj* (ca. 1580) **1** : capable of being scaled **2** : capable of being easily expanded or upgraded on demand ⟨a ~ computer network⟩ — **scal·abil·i·ty** \ˌskā-lə-ˈbi-lə-tē\ *n*
sca·lade \skə-ˈlād, -ˈläd\ *or* **sca·la·do** \-ˈlā-(ˌ)dō, -ˈlä-\ *n, pl* **-lades** *or* **-la·dos** [obs. It *scalada,* fr. *scalare* to scale, fr. *scala* ladder, staircase, fr. LL — more at SCALE] (1591) *archaic* : ESCALADE
[1]**sca·lar** \ˈskā-lər, -ˌlär\ *adj* [L *scalaris,* fr. *scalae* stairs, ladder — more at SCALE] (ca. 1656) **1** : having an uninterrupted series of steps : GRADUATED ⟨~ chain of authority⟩ ⟨~ cells⟩ **2 a** : capable of being represented by a point on a scale ⟨~ quantity⟩ **b** : of or relating to a scalar or scalar product ⟨~ multiplication⟩

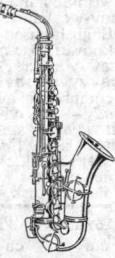

[2]**scalar** *n* (1846) **1 :** a real number rather than a vector **2 :** a quantity (as mass or time) that has a magnitude describable by a real number and no direction

sca·la·re \skə-ˈler-ē, -ˈlär-\ *n* [NL, specific epithet, fr. L, neut. of *scalaris;* fr. the barred pattern on its body] (1928) **:** ANGELFISH 2

sca·lar·i·form \skə-ˈla-rə-ˌfȯrm\ *adj* [NL *scalariformis,* fr. L *scalaris* + *-iformis* -iform] (1836) **:** resembling a ladder esp. in having transverse bars or markings like the rungs of a ladder ⟨~ cells in plants⟩ — **sca·lar·i·form·ly** *adv*

scalar product *n* (1878) **:** a real number that is the product of the lengths of two vectors and the cosine of the angle between them — called also *dot product, inner product*

scal·a·wag *or* **scal·ly·wag** \ˈska-li-ˌwag\ *n* [origin unknown] (ca. 1848) **1 :** SCAMP, REPROBATE **2 :** a white Southerner acting in support of the reconstruction governments after the American Civil War often for private gain

[1]**scald** \ˈskȯld\ *vb* [ME, fr. AF **escalder, eschauder,* fr. LL *excaldare* to wash in warm water, fr. L *ex-* + *calida, calda* warm water, fr. fem. of *calidus* warm, fr. *calēre* to be warm — more at LEE] *vt* (13c) **1 :** to burn with or as if with hot liquid or steam **2 a :** to subject to the action of boiling water or steam **b :** to bring to a temperature just below the boiling point ⟨~ milk⟩ **3 :** SCORCH ~ *vi* **1 :** to scald something **2 :** to become scalded

[2]**scald** *n* (1601) **1 :** an injury to the body caused by scalding **2 :** an act or process of scalding **3 :** any of various conditions or diseases of plants or fruits marked esp. by a usu. brownish discoloration of tissue

[3]**scald** *adj* [*scall* + [1]*-ed*] (1529) **1** *archaic* **:** SCABBY, SCURFY **2** *archaic* **:** SHABBY, CONTEMPTIBLE

[4]**scald** *var of* SKALD

[5]**scald** \ˈskȯld\ *adj* [alter. of *scalded*] (1791) **:** subjected to scalding ⟨coffee . . . with ~ cream —Charles Kingsley⟩

scald·ing \ˈskȯl-diŋ\ *adj* (13c) **1 :** hot enough to scald ⟨~ water⟩ **2 a :** having or producing the feeling of being burned ⟨~ sun⟩ ⟨~ sand⟩ **b :** SCATHING ⟨~ criticism⟩

[1]**scale** \ˈskāl\ *n* [ME *scole, scale* bowl, scale of a balance, fr. ON *skāl;* akin to ON *skel* shell — more at SHELL] (14c) **1 a :** either pan or tray of a balance **b :** a beam that is supported freely in the center and has two pans of equal weight suspended from its ends — usu. used in pl. **2 :** an instrument or machine for weighing

[2]**scale** *vb* **scaled; scal·ing** *vt* (1691) **:** to weigh in scales ~ *vi* **:** to have a specified weight on scales

[3]**scale** *n* [ME, fr. AF *escale, eschale,* of Gmc origin; akin to OE *scealu* shell, husk — more at SHELL] (14c) **1 a :** a small, flattened, rigid, and definitely circumscribed plate forming part of the external body covering esp. of a fish **b :** a small thin plate suggesting a fish scale ⟨~*s* of mica⟩ ⟨the ~*s* on a moth's wing⟩ **c :** the scaly covering of a scaled animal **2 :** a small thin dry lamina shed (as in many skin diseases) from the skin **3 :** a thin coating, layer, or incrustation: as **a :** a usu. black scaly coating of oxide forming on the surface of a metal (as iron) when it is heated for processing **b :** a hard incrustation usu. rich in sulfate of calcium that is deposited on the inside of a vessel (as a boiler) in which water is heated **4 a :** a modified leaf protecting a seed plant bud before expansion **b :** a thin, membranous, chaffy, or woody bract **5 a :** any of the small overlapping usu. metal pieces forming the outer surface of scale armor **b :** SCALE ARMOR **6 a :** SCALE INSECT **b :** infestation with or disease caused by scale insects — **scaled** \ˈskā(ə)ld\ *adj* — **scale·less** \ˈskāl-ləs\ *adj*

[4]**scale** *vb* **scaled; scal·ing** *vt* (15c) **1 :** to remove the scale or scales from (as by scraping) ⟨~ a fish⟩ **2 :** to take off in thin layers or scales ⟨~ tartar from the teeth⟩ **3 :** to throw (as a thin flat stone) so that the edge cuts the air or so that it skips on water **:** SKIM ~ *vi* **1 :** to separate and come off in scales **:** FLAKE **2 :** to shed scales ⟨*scaling* skin⟩

[5]**scale** *vb* **scaled; scal·ing** [ME, fr. [6]*scale*] *vt* (14c) **1 a :** to attack with or take by means of scaling ladders ⟨~ a castle wall⟩ **b :** to climb up or reach by means of a ladder **c :** to reach the highest point of **:** SURMOUNT ⟨~ a mountain⟩ **2 a :** to arrange in a graduated series **b (1) :** to measure by or as if by a scale **(2) :** to measure or estimate the sound content of (as logs) **c :** to pattern, make, regulate, set, or estimate according to some rate or standard **:** ADJUST ⟨a production schedule *scaled* to actual need⟩ — often used with *back, down,* or *up* ⟨~ down imports⟩ ~ *vi* **1 :** to climb by or as if by a ladder **2 :** to rise in a graduated series **3 :** MEASURE

[6]**scale** *n* [ME, fr. LL *scala* ladder, staircase, fr. L *scalae,* pl., stairs, rungs, ladder; akin to L *scandere* to climb — more at SCAN] (15c) **1 a** *obs* **:** LADDER **b** *archaic* **:** a means of ascent **2 :** a graduated series of musical tones ascending or descending in order of pitch according to a specified scheme of their intervals **3 :** something graduated esp. when used as a measure or rule: as **a :** a series of marks or points at known intervals used to measure distances (as the height of the mercury in a thermometer) **b :** an indication of the relationship between the distances on a map and the corresponding actual distances **c :** RULER 3 **4 a :** a graduated series or scheme of rank or order ⟨a ~ of taxation⟩ **b :** MINIMUM WAGE 2 **5 a :** a proportion between two sets of dimensions (as between those of a drawing and its original) **b :** a distinctive relative size, extent, or degree ⟨projects done on a large ~⟩ **6 :** a graded series of tests or of performances used in rating individual intelligence or achievement — **scale** *adj* — **to scale :** according to the proportions of an established scale of measurement ⟨floor plans drawn *to scale*⟩

[7]**scale** *n* [[5]*scale*] (ca. 1587) **1** *obs* **:** ESCALADE **2 :** an estimate of the amount of sound lumber in logs or standing timber

scale armor *n* (1842) **:** armor of small metallic scales on leather or cloth

scale–down \ˈskāl-ˌdau̇n\ *n* (1931) **:** a reduction according to a fixed ratio ⟨a ~ of debts⟩

scale insect *n* (1840) **:** any of numerous small prolific homopterous insects (superfamily Coccoidea) that have winged males, wingless scale-covered females attached to the host plant, and young that suck the juices of plants and some of which are serious pests

scale·like \ˈskāl-ˌlīk\ *adj* (1611) **:** resembling a scale ⟨~ design⟩; *specif* **:** reduced to a minute appressed element resembling a scale

sca·lene \ˈskā-ˌlēn, skā-ˈ\ *adj* [LL *scalenus,* fr. Gk *skalēnos,* lit., uneven; perh. akin to Gk *skolios* crooked, *skelos* leg — more at ISOSCELES] (1734) *of a triangle* **:** having the three sides of unequal length — see TRIANGLE illustration

scal·er \ˈskā-lər\ *n* (1557) **1 :** one that scales **2 :** a dental instrument for removing tartar from teeth

scale–up \ˈskāl-ˌəp\ *n* (1945) **:** an increase according to a fixed ratio

scall \ˈskȯl\ *n* [ME] (14c) *archaic* **:** a scurf or scabby disorder (as of the scalp)

scal·lion \ˈskal-yən\ *n* [ME *scaloun,* fr. AF *scalun, escaloin,* fr. VL **escalonia,* fr. L *ascalonia (caepa)* onion of Ascalon, fr. fem. of *ascalonius* of Ascalon, fr. *Ascalon-, Ascalo* Ascalon, seaport in southern Palestine] (14c) **1 :** SHALLOT **2 :** LEEK **3 :** an onion forming a thick basal portion without a bulb; *also* **:** GREEN ONION

[1]**scal·lop** \ˈskä-ləp, ˈska-, ˈskȯ-\ *also* **scol·lop** \ˈskä-, ˈskȯ-\ *n* [ME *scalop,* fr. AF *escalope* shell, of Gmc origin; akin to MD *schelpe* shell] (15c) **1 a :** any of numerous marine bivalve lamellibranch mollusks (family Pectinidae) that have a radially ribbed shell with the edge undulated and that swim by opening and closing the valves **b :** the adductor muscle of a scallop as an article of food **2 a :** a valve or shell of a scallop **b :** a baking dish shaped like a valve of a scallop **3 :** one of a continuous series of circle segments or angular projections forming a border (as on cloth or metal) **4 :** PATTYPAN **5** [F *escalope,* prob. fr. MF, shell] **:** a thin slice of boneless meat or fish ⟨veal ~*s*⟩ — called also *escalope*

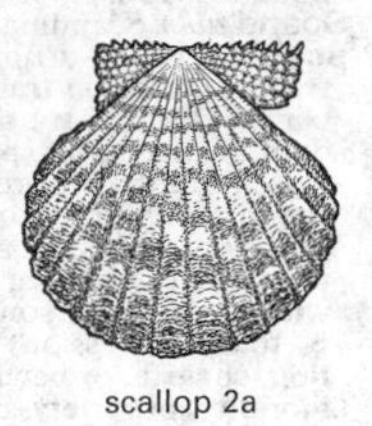

scallop 2a

[2]**scallop** *also* **scollop** *vt* (1682) **1 a :** to shape, cut, or finish in scallops **b :** to form scallops in **2** [fr. the use of a scallop shell as a baking dish] **:** to bake in a sauce usu. covered with seasoned bread or cracker crumbs ⟨~*ed* potatoes⟩ ~ *vi* **:** to gather or dredge scallops

scal·lop·er \-lə-pər\ *n* (ca. 1881) **1 :** a person who dredges for or gathers scallops **2 :** a boat equipped and used to dredge for scallops

scallywag *var of* SCALAWAG

sca·lo·gram \ˈskā-lə-ˌgram\ *n* [[6]*scale* + *-o-* + *-gram*] (1944) **:** an arrangement of items (as problems on a test or features of speech) in ascending order so that the presence or accomplishment of an item at one level implies the presence of or the capability to accomplish items at all lower levels

sca·lop·pi·ne *also* **scal·lo·pi·ni** \ˌskä-lə-ˈpē-nē, ˌska-\ *n* [It *scaloppine,* ultim. fr. F *escalope* thin slice of meat, prob. fr. MF, shell] (1946) **:** thin slices of meat (as veal) sautéed or coated with flour and fried

[1]**scalp** \ˈskalp\ *n* [ME, crown of the head, perh. of Scand origin; akin to ON *skālpr* sheath; akin to MD *schelpe* shell] (14c) **1 a :** the part of the integument of the human head usu. covered with hair in both sexes **b :** the part of an animal (as a wolf or fox) corresponding to the human scalp **2 a :** a part of the human scalp with attached hair cut or torn from an enemy as a token of victory **b :** a trophy of victory or accomplishment **3** *chiefly Scot* **:** a projecting mass of bare ground or rock

[2]**scalp** *vt* (1676) **1 a :** to deprive of the scalp **b :** to remove an upper part from **2 :** to remove a desired constituent from and discard the rest **3 :** to buy and sell so as to make small quick profits ⟨~ stocks⟩ ⟨~ grain⟩; *esp* **:** to resell at greatly increased prices ⟨~ theater tickets⟩ ~ *vi* **1 :** to take scalps **2 :** to profit by slight market fluctuations — **scalp·er** *n*

scal·pel \ˈskal-pəl *also* skal-ˈpel\ *n* [L *scalpellus, scalpellum,* dim. of *scalper, scalprum* chisel, knife, fr. *scalpere* to scratch, carve] (1742) **:** a small straight thin-bladed knife used esp. in surgery

scalp lock *n* (1826) **:** a long tuft of hair on the crown of the otherwise shaved head esp. of a warrior of some American Indian tribes

scaly \ˈskā-lē\ *adj* **scal·i·er; -est** (14c) **1 a :** covered with, composed of, or rich in scale or scales **b :** FLAKY **2 :** of or relating to scaly animals **3 :** DESPICABLE, POOR ⟨a regular ~ old shop —Charles Dickens⟩ **4 :** infested with scale insects ⟨~ fruit⟩ — **scal·i·ness** *n*

scaly anteater *n* (1840) **:** PANGOLIN

[1]**scam** \ˈskam\ *n* [origin unknown] (1963) **:** a fraudulent or deceptive act or operation ⟨an insurance ~⟩

[2]**scam** *vt* **scammed; scam·ming** (1963) **1 :** DECEIVE, DEFRAUD **2 :** to obtain (as money) by a scam — **scam·mer** *n*

scam·mo·ny \ˈska-mə-nē\ *n, pl* **-nies** [ME *scamonie,* fr. OE & AF; OE *scammoniam,* fr. L *scammonia,* fr. Gk *skammōnia;* AF *scamonie,* fr. L] (bef. 12c) **1 :** a twining convolvulus (*Convolvulus scammonia*) of Asia Minor with a large thick root **2 a :** the dried root of scammony **b :** a cathartic resin obtained from scammony

[1]**scamp** \ˈskamp\ *n* [obs. *scamp* to roam about idly] (1808) **1 :** RASCAL, ROGUE **2 :** an impish or playful young person — **scamp·ish** \ˈskam-pish\ *adj*

[2]**scamp** *vt* [origin unknown] (1837) **:** to perform or deal with in a hasty, neglectful, or imperfect manner

[1]**scam·per** \ˈskam-pər\ *vi* **scam·pered; scam·per·ing** \-p(ə-)riŋ\ [prob. fr. obs. D *schampen* to flee, fr. MF *escamper,* fr. It *scampare,* fr. VL **excampare* to decamp, fr. L *ex-* + *campus* field] (1685) **:** to run nimbly and usu. playfully about

[2]**scamper** *n* (1697) **:** a playful or hurried run or movement

scam·pi \ˈskam-pē, ˈskäm-\ *n, pl* **scampi** [It, pl. of *scampo,* a European lobster] (1925) **:** a usu. large shrimp; *also* **:** large shrimp prepared with a garlic-flavored sauce

scam·ster \ˈskam(p)-stər\ *n* (1984) **:** one that scams **:** SCAMMER

[1]**scan** \ˈskan\ *vb* **scanned; scan·ning** [ME *scannen,* fr. LL *scandere,* fr. L, to climb; akin to MIr *sceinnid* he springs, Skt *skandati* he leaps] *vt* (14c) **1 :** to read or mark so as to show metrical structure ⟨~ poetry⟩ **2 :** to examine by point-by-point observation or checking: **a :** to investigate thoroughly by checking point by point and often repeatedly ⟨a fire lookout *scanning* the hills with binoculars⟩ **b :** to glance from point to point of often hastily, casually, or in search of a particular item ⟨~ the want ads looking for a job⟩ **3 a :** to examine systematically (as by passing a beam of radiation over or through) in order to ob-

tain data esp. for display or storage ⟨*scanned* the patient's heart⟩ ⟨radar ~*s* the horizon⟩ ⟨~ the photos into the computer⟩ **b :** to pass over in the formation of an image ⟨the electron beam ~*s* the picture tube⟩ ~ *vi* **1 :** to scan verse **2 :** to conform to a metrical pattern ⟨this poem ~*s* well⟩ ***syn*** see SCRUTINIZE — **scan·na·ble** \ˈska-nə-bəl\ *adj*

[2]**scan** *n* (1706) **1 :** the act or process of scanning **2 :** a radar or television trace **3 :** an image formed by scanning something: as **a :** a depiction (as a photograph) of the distribution of a radioactive material in something (as a bodily organ) **b :** an image of a bodily part produced (as by computer) by combining ultrasonic or radiographic data obtained from several angles or sections

Scand *abbr* Scandinavia

[1]**scan·dal** \ˈskan-dᵊl\ *n* [ME, fr. LL *scandalum* stumbling block, offense, fr. Gk *skandalon* trap, stumbling block, offense; akin to L *scandere* to climb] (13c) **1 a :** discredit brought upon religion by unseemly conduct in a religious person **b :** conduct that causes or encourages a lapse of faith or of religious obedience in another **2 :** loss of or damage to reputation caused by actual or apparent violation of morality or propriety **:** DISGRACE **3 a :** a circumstance or action that offends propriety or established moral conceptions or disgraces those associated with it **b :** a person whose conduct offends propriety or morality ⟨a ~ to the profession⟩ **4 :** malicious or defamatory gossip **5 :** indignation, chagrin, or bewilderment brought about by a flagrant violation of morality, propriety, or religious opinion ***syn*** see OFFENSE

[2]**scandal** *vt* (1592) **1** *obs* **:** DISGRACE **2** *chiefly dial* **:** DEFAME, SLANDER

scan·dal·ise *chiefly Brit var of* SCANDALIZE

scan·dal·ize \ˈskan-də-ˌlīz\ *vt* **-ized; -iz·ing** (1566) **1** *archaic* **:** to speak falsely or maliciously of **2** *archaic* **:** to bring into reproach **3 :** to offend the moral sense of **:** SHOCK ⟨she was *scandalized* by his behavior⟩

scan·dal·mon·ger \ˈskan-dᵊl-ˌməŋ-gər, -ˌmäŋ-\ *n* (1714) **:** a person who circulates scandal — **scan·dal·mon·ger·ing** \-g(ə-)riŋ\ *n*

scan·dal·ous \ˈskan-də-ləs\ *adj* (1575) **1 :** LIBELOUS, DEFAMATORY ⟨~ allegations⟩ **2 :** offensive to propriety or morality **:** SHOCKING ⟨~ behavior⟩ — **scan·dal·ous·ly** *adv* — **scan·dal·ous·ness** *n*

scandal sheet *n* (1904) **:** a newspaper or periodical dealing to a large extent in scandal and gossip

scan·dent \ˈskan-dənt\ *adj* [L *scandent-, scandens,* prp. of *scandere* to climb — more at SCAN] (ca. 1682) **:** characterized by a climbing mode of growth ⟨~ stems⟩ ⟨~ vines⟩

Scan·di·an \ˈskan-dē-ən\ *adj* [L *Scandia*] (1668) **1 :** SCANDINAVIAN **2 :** of or relating to the languages of Scandinavia — **Scandian** *n*

Scan·di·na·vian \ˌskan-də-ˈnā-vē-ən, -vyən\ *n* (1766) **1 :** the North Germanic languages **2 a :** a native or inhabitant of Scandinavia **b :** a person of Scandinavian descent — **Scandinavian** *adj*

scan·di·um \ˈskan-dē-əm\ *n* [NL, fr. L *Scandia,* ancient name of southern Scandinavian peninsula] (1879) **:** a silvery-white metallic element found widely esp. in association with rare earth elements and used esp. in alloys and in high-intensity electric lamps — see ELEMENT table

scan·ner \ˈska-nər\ *n* (1556) **:** one that scans: as **a :** a device for sensing recorded data (as in a bar code) ⟨a supermarket ~⟩ **b :** a radio receiver that sequentially scans a range of frequencies for a signal **c :** a device that scans an image (as a photograph) or document (as a page of text) esp. for use or storage on a computer **d :** a medical device for scanning a living body to collect diagnostic information — compare CAT SCANNER

scanning electron microscope *n* (1953) **:** an electron microscope in which a beam of focused electrons moves across the object with the secondary electrons produced by the object and the electrons scattered by the object being collected to form a three-dimensional image on a display screen — called also *scanning microscope* — **scanning electron microscopy** *n*

scanning tunneling microscope *n* (1983) **:** a microscope that makes use of the phenomenon of tunneling electrons to map the positions of individual atoms in a surface or to move atoms around on a surface — **scanning tunneling microscopy** *n*

scan·sion \ˈskan(t)-shən\ *n* [LL *scansion-, scansio,* fr. L, act of climbing, fr. *scandere*] (1671) **:** the analysis of verse to show its meter

[1]**scant** \ˈskant\ *adj* [ME, fr. ON *skamt,* neut. of *skammr* short] (14c) **1** *dial* **a :** excessively frugal **b :** not prodigal **:** CHARY **2 a :** barely or scarcely sufficient; *esp* **:** not quite coming up to a stated measure ⟨a ~ teaspoon⟩ **b :** lacking in amplitude or quantity ⟨~ growth⟩ **3 :** having a small or insufficient supply ⟨he's fat, and ~ of breath —Shak.⟩ ***syn*** see MEAGER — **scant·ly** *adv* — **scant·ness** *n*

[2]**scant** *adv* (15c) *dial* **:** SCARCELY, HARDLY

[3]**scant** *vt* (ca. 1580) **1 :** to provide an incomplete supply of **2 :** to make small, narrow, or meager **3 :** to give scant attention to **:** SLIGHT **4 :** to provide with a meager or inadequate portion or supply **:** STINT

scant·ies \ˈskan-tēz\ *n pl* [blend of [1]*scant* and *panties*] (1929) **:** abbreviated panties for women

scant·ling \ˈskant-liŋ, -lən\ *n* [alter. of ME *scantilon,* mason's or carpenter's measure, fr. AF *escauntiloun, eschantillon*] (1555) **1 a :** the dimensions of timber and stone used in building **b :** the dimensions of a structural element used in shipbuilding — often used in pl. **2 :** a small quantity, amount, or proportion **:** MODICUM **3 :** a small piece of lumber (as an upright piece in house framing)

scanty \ˈskan-tē\ *adj* **scant·i·er; -est** [E dial. *scant* scanty supply, fr. ME, fr. ON *skamt,* fr. neut. of *skammr* short] (1600) **:** limited or less than sufficient in degree, quantity, or extent ***syn*** see MEAGER — **scant·i·ly** \ˈskan-tə-lē\ *adv* — **scant·i·ness** \ˈskan-tē-nəs\ *n*

[1]**scape** \ˈskāp\ *vb* **scaped; scap·ing** [ME, short for *escapen*] (13c) **:** ESCAPE ⟨some innocents ~ not the thunderbolt —Shak.⟩

[2]**scape** *n* [L *scapus* shaft, stalk — more at SHAFT] (1601) **1 :** a peduncle arising at or beneath the surface of the ground in an acaulescent plant (as the tulip); *broadly* **:** a flower stalk **2 :** the shaft of an animal part (as an antenna or feather)

[3]**scape** *n* [*landscape*] (1773) **:** a view or picture of a scene — usu. used in combination ⟨city*scape*⟩

[1]**scape·goat** \ˈskāp-ˌgōt\ *n* [[1]*scape;* intended as trans. of Heb *ʿazāzēl* (prob. name of a demon), as if *ʿēz ʾōzēl* goat that departs—Lev 16:8(AV)] (1530) **1 :** a goat upon whose head are symbolically placed the sins of the people after which he is sent into the wilderness in the biblical ceremony for Yom Kippur **2 a :** one that bears the blame for others **b :** one that is the object of irrational hostility

[2]**scapegoat** *vt* (1943) **:** to make a scapegoat of — **scape·goat·ism** \-ˌgō-ˌti-zəm\ *n*

scape·grace \ˈskāp-ˌgrās\ *n* [[1]*scape*] (1763) **:** an incorrigible rascal

scaph·oid \ˈska-ˌfȯid\ *n* [NL *scaphoides,* fr. Gk *skaphoeidēs,* fr. *skaphos* boat] (1831) **1 :** NAVICULAR a **2 :** the bone of the thumb side of the carpus that is the largest in the proximal row; *also* **:** the navicular bone of the tarsus — **scaphoid** *adj*

scap·o·lite \ˈska-pə-ˌlīt\ *n* [F, fr. L *scapus* shaft + F *-o-* + *-lite;* fr. the prismatic shape of its crystals] (1802) **:** any of a group of minerals that are essentially complex silicates of aluminum, calcium, and sodium and that include some used as semiprecious stones

scap·u·la \ˈska-pyə-lə\ *n, pl* **-lae** \-ˌlē, -ˌlī\ *or* **-las** [NL, fr. L, shoulder blade, shoulder] (1578) **:** either of a pair of large triangular bones lying one in each dorsal lateral part of the thorax, being the principal bone of the corresponding half of the shoulder girdle, and articulating with the corresponding clavicle or coracoid — called also *shoulder blade*

[1]**scap·u·lar** \-lər\ *n* [ME *scapulare,* fr. LL, fr. L *scapula* shoulder] (15c) **1 a :** a long wide band of cloth with an opening for the head worn front and back over the shoulders as part of a monastic habit **b :** a pair of small cloth squares joined by shoulder tapes and worn under the clothing on the breast and back as a sacramental and often also as a badge of a third order or confraternity **2 a :** SCAPULA **b :** one of the feathers covering the base of a bird's wing — see BIRD illustration

[2]**scapular** *adj* [NL *scapularis,* fr. *scapula*] (1713) **:** of or relating to the shoulder, the scapula, or scapulars

scapular medal *n* (1912) **:** a medal worn in place of a sacramental scapular

[1]**scar** \ˈskär\ *n* [ME *skere,* fr. ON *sker* skerry; prob. akin to ON *skera* to cut — more at SHEAR] (14c) **1 :** an isolated or protruding rock **2 :** a steep rocky eminence **:** a bare place on the side of a mountain

[2]**scar** *n* [ME *escare, scar,* fr. MF *escare* scab, fr. LL *eschara,* fr. Gk, hearth, brazier, scab] (14c) **1 :** a mark left (as in the skin) by the healing of injured tissue **2 a :** a mark left on a stem or branch by a fallen leaf or harvested fruit **b :** CICATRIX 2 **3 :** a mark or indentation resulting from damage or wear **4 :** a lasting moral or emotional injury ⟨one of his men had been killed . . . in a manner that left a ~ upon his mind —H. G. Wells⟩ — **scar·less** \-ləs\ *adj*

[3]**scar** *vb* **scarred; scar·ring** *vt* (1555) **1 :** to mark with a scar **2 :** to do lasting injury to ~ *vi* **1 :** to form a scar **2 :** to become scarred

scar·ab \ˈska-rəb\ *n* [MF *scarabee,* fr. L *scarabaeus*] (1579) **1 :** any of a family (Scarabaeidae) of stout-bodied beetles (as a dung beetle) with lamellate or fan-shaped antennae **2 :** a stone or faience beetle used in ancient Egypt as a talisman, ornament, and a symbol of resurrection

scar·a·bae·us \ˌska-rə-ˈbē-əs\ *n* [L] (1664) **:** SCARAB 2

scar·a·mouch *or* **scar·a·mouche** \ˈskar-ə-ˌmüsh, -ˌmüch, -ˌmau̇ch\ *n* [F *Scaramouche,* fr. It *Scaramuccia,* fr. *scaramuccia* skirmish] (1662) **1** *cap* **:** a stock character in the Italian commedia dell'arte that burlesques the Spanish don and is characterized by boastfulness and cowardliness **2 a :** a cowardly buffoon **b :** RASCAL, SCAMP

[1]**scarce** \ˈskers\ *adj* **scarc·er; scarc·est** [ME *scars,* fr. AF *eschars, escars* narrow, stingy, deficient, fr. VL **excarpsus,* lit., plucked out, pp. of L *excerpere* to pluck out — more at EXCERPT] (14c) **1 :** deficient in quantity or number compared with the demand **:** not plentiful or abundant **2 :** intentionally absent ⟨made himself ~ at inspection time⟩ ***syn*** see INFREQUENT — **scarce·ness** *n*

[2]**scarce** *adv* (15c) **:** SCARCELY, HARDLY ⟨~ was independence half a century old, when a . . . split occurred —John McPhee⟩

scarce·ly *adv* (14c) **1 a :** by a narrow margin **:** only just ⟨had ~ rung the bell when the door flew open —Agnes S. Turnbull⟩ **b :** almost not ⟨could ~ see for the fog⟩ **2 a :** certainly not ⟨could ~ interfere⟩ **b :** probably not ⟨there could ~ have been found a leader better equipped —V. L. Parrington⟩

scar·ci·ty \ˈsker-sə-tē, -stē\ *n, pl* **-ties** (14c) **:** the quality or state of being scarce; *esp* **:** want of provisions for the support of life

[1]**scare** \ˈsker\ *vb* **scared; scar·ing** [ME *skerren,* fr. ON *skirra,* fr. *skjarr* shy, timid] *vt* (13c) **:** to frighten esp. suddenly **:** ALARM ~ *vi* **:** to become scared — **scar·er** *n*

[2]**scare** *n* (ca. 1548) **1 :** a sudden fright **2 :** a widespread state of alarm **:** PANIC — **scare** *adj*

scare·crow \ˈsker-ˌkrō\ *n* (1573) **1 a :** an object usu. suggesting a human figure that is set up to frighten birds away from crops **b :** something frightening but harmless **2 :** a skinny or ragged person

scared *adj* (1579) **:** thrown into or being in a state of fear, fright, or panic ⟨~ of snakes⟩ ⟨~ to go out⟩

scaredy–cat \ˈsker-dē-ˌkat\ *n* [*scared* (pp. of *scare*) + [1]*-y* + *cat*] (1948) **:** an unduly fearful person

scare·head \ˈsker-ˌhed\ *n* (1887) **:** a big, sensational, or alarming newspaper headline

scare·mon·ger \-ˌməŋ-gər, -ˌmäŋ-\ *n* (1888) **:** one inclined to raise or excite alarms esp. needlessly — **scare·mon·ger·ing** \-g(ə-)riŋ\ *n*

scare quotes *n pl* (1960) **:** quotation marks used to express esp. skepticism or derision concerning the use of the enclosed word or phrase

scare up *vt* (1841) **:** to find or get together with considerable labor or difficulty **:** scrape up ⟨managed to *scare up* the money⟩

[1]**scarf** \ˈskärf\ *n, pl* **scarfs** [ME *skarf,* prob. fr. ON *skarfr* butt end of a plank] (15c) **1 :** either of the chamfered or cutaway ends that fit together to form a scarf joint **2 :** an in-line joint made by chamfering, halving, or notching two pieces to correspond and lapping them

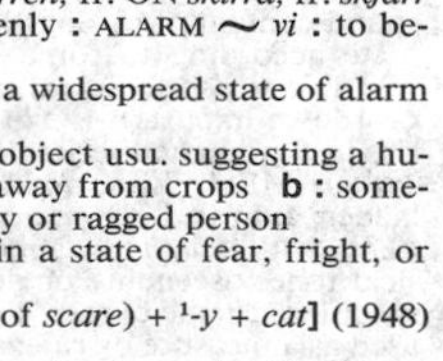

[1]scarf 2

[2]**scarf** *also* **scarph** \ˈskärf\ *vt* (1627) **1 :** to unite by a scarf joint **2 :** to form a scarf on

[3]**scarf** *n, pl* **scarves** \ˈskärvz\ *or* **scarfs** [prob. modif. of MF dial. (Norman) *escreppe,* MF *escherpe* sash, sling, fr. OF, pilgrim's shoulder bag, fr. ML *scrippum*] (1555) **1 :** a military or official sash usu. indicative of rank **b** *archaic* **:** TIPPET 3 **2 :** a broad band of cloth worn about the shoulders, around the neck, or over the head **3 :** RUNNER 6b

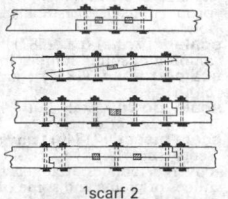

[4]**scarf** *vt* (1598) **1 :** to wrap, cover, or adorn with or as if with a scarf **2 :** to wrap or throw on (a scarf or mantle) loosely

[5]**scarf** *vt* [by alter.] (ca. 1960) **1 :** SCOFF 1 ⟨~*ed* down my sandwich⟩ **2 :** SNAP 2 ⟨~*ed* up the best seats⟩

scarf•pin \ˈskärf-ˌpin\ *n* (1858) **:** TIEPIN

scarf•skin \ˈskärf-ˌskin\ *n* [[3]*scarf*] (1615) **:** EPIDERMIS; *esp* **:** that forming the cuticle of a nail

scar•i•fi•ca•tion \ˌsker-ə-fə-ˈkā-shən\ *n* (14c) **1 :** the act or process of scarifying **2 :** a mark or marks made by scarifying

[1]**scar•i•fy** \ˈsker-ə-ˌfī\ *vt* **-fied; -fy•ing** [ME *scarifien*, fr. MF *scarefier*, fr. LL *scarificare*, alter. of L *scarifare*, fr. Gk *skariphasthai* to scratch an outline, sketch — more at SCRIBE] (14c) **1 :** to make scratches or small cuts in (as the skin) ⟨~ an area for vaccination⟩ **2 :** to lacerate the feelings of **3 :** to break up, loosen, or roughen the surface of (as a field or road) **4 :** to cut or soften the wall of (a hard seed) to hasten germination — **scar•i•fi•er** \-ˌfī(-ə)r\ *n*

[2]**scarify** *vt* **-fied; -fy•ing** (1785) **:** SCARE, FRIGHTEN — **scar•i•fy•ing•ly** \-ˌfī-iŋ-lē\ *adv*

scar•i•ous \ˈsker-ē-əs\ *adj* [NL *scariosus*] (ca. 1806) **:** dry and membranous in texture ⟨a ~ bract⟩

scar•la•ti•na \ˌskär-lə-ˈtē-nə\ *n* [NL, fr. ML *scarlata* scarlet] (1771) **:** SCARLET FEVER — **scar•la•ti•nal** \-ˈtē-nᵊl\ *adj*

[1]**scar•let** \ˈskär-lət\ *n* [ME *scarlat, scarlet*, fr. AF *escarlet*, fr. ML *scarlata*, fr. Pers *saqalāt*, a kind of rich cloth] (13c) **1 :** scarlet cloth or clothes **2 :** any of various bright reds

[2]**scarlet** *adj* (14c) **1 :** of the color scarlet **2 a :** grossly and glaringly offensive ⟨sinning in flagrant and ~ fashion —G. W. Johnson⟩ **b** [fr. the use of the word in Isa 1:18 & Rev 17:1–6(AV)] **:** of, characterized by, or associated with sexual immorality ⟨a ~ woman⟩

scarlet fever *n* (1676) **:** an acute contagious febrile disease caused by hemolytic Group A streptococci and characterized by inflammation of the nose, throat, and mouth, generalized toxemia, and a red rash

scarlet letter *n* [fr. such a letter in the novel *The Scarlet Letter* (1850) by Nathaniel Hawthorne] (1850) **:** a scarlet A worn as a punitive mark of adultery

scarlet pimpernel *n* (1835) **1 :** a European pimpernel (*Anagallis arvensis*) naturalized in No. America and having scarlet, white, or purplish flowers that close in cloudy weather **2** [*Scarlet Pimpernel*, assumed name of the hero of *The Scarlet Pimpernel* (1905), novel by Baroness Orczy] **:** a person who rescues others from mortal danger by smuggling them across a border

scarlet runner bean *n* (1899) **:** a tropical American high-climbing bean (*Phaseolus coccineus*) that has large bright red flowers and red and black seeds and is grown widely as an ornamental and as a food bean — called also *scarlet runner*

scarlet sage *n* (1863) **:** a salvia (*Salvia splendens*) of Brazil that is widely cultivated for its long racemes of typically scarlet flowers; *also* **:** a related salvia (*S. coccinea*) of tropical and subtropical America

scarlet tanager *n* (1810) **:** a common American tanager (*Piranga olivacea*) with the male having scarlet plumage and black wings during the breeding season and the female having chiefly olive plumage

scarp \ˈskärp\ *n* [It *scarpa*] (1589) **1 :** the inner side of a ditch below the parapet of a fortification **2 a :** a line of cliffs produced by faulting or erosion — see FAULT illustration **b :** a low steep slope along a beach caused by wave erosion — **scarped** *adj*

scar•per \ˈskär-pər\ *vi* [prob. ultim. fr. It *scappare*, fr. VL **excappare* — more at ESCAPE] (ca. 1846) *Brit* **:** FLEE, RUN AWAY; *broadly* **:** LEAVE, DEPART

scar•ry \ˈskär-ē\ *adj* [[2]*scar*] (1653) **:** bearing marks of wounds **:** SCARRED

scar tissue *n* (1875) **:** the connective tissue forming a scar and composed chiefly of fibroblasts in recent scars and largely of dense collagenous fibers in old scars

scary \ˈsker-ē\ *adj* **scar•i•er; -est** (1582) **1 :** causing fright **:** ALARMING ⟨a ~ story⟩ **2 :** easily scared **:** TIMID **3 :** feeling alarm or fright **:** FRIGHTENED — **scar•i•ly** \ˈsker-ə-lē\ *adv*

[1]**scat** \ˈskat\ *vi* **scat•ted; scat•ting** [*scat*, interj. used to drive away a cat] (1838) **1 :** to go away quickly **2 :** to move fast **:** SCOOT

[2]**scat** *n* [perh. fr. Gk *skat-*, *skōr* excrement — more at SCATOLOGY] (1927) **:** an animal fecal dropping

[3]**scat** *n* [origin unknown] (1929) **:** jazz singing with nonsense syllables

[4]**scat** *vi* **scat•ted; scat•ting** (1935) **:** to improvise nonsense syllables usu. to an instrumental accompaniment **:** sing scat

SCAT *abbr* **1** School and College Ability Test **2** supersonic commercial air transport

scat•back \ˈskat-ˌbak\ *n* [[1]*scat* + *back*] (1945) **:** an offensive back in football who is an esp. fast and elusive ballcarrier

[1]**scathe** \ˈskāth, ˈskāth\ *n* [ME *skathe*, fr. ON *skathi;* akin to OE *sceatha* injury, Gk *askēthēs* unharmed] (13c) **:** HARM, INJURY — **scathe•less** \-ləs\ *adj*

[2]**scathe** \ˈskāth\ *vt* **scathed; scath•ing** (13c) **1 :** to do harm to; *specif* **:** SCORCH, SEAR **2 :** to assail with withering denunciation

scathing *adj* (1794) **:** bitterly severe ⟨a ~ condemnation⟩ *syn* see CAUSTIC — **scathingly** *adv*

sca•tol•o•gy \ska-ˈtä-lə-jē, skə-\ *n* [Gk *skat-*, *skōr* excrement; akin to OE *scearn* dung, L *muscerdae* mouse droppings] (1876) **1 :** interest in or treatment of obscene matters esp. in literature **2 :** the biologically oriented study of excrement (as for taxonomic purposes or for the determination of diet) — **scat•o•log•i•cal** \ˌska-tᵊl-ˈä-ji-kəl\ *adj*

scatt \ˈskat\ *n* [ME *scat*, fr. ON *skattr;* akin to OE *sceat* property, money, a small coin, OCS *skotŭ* domestic animal] (13c) *archaic* **:** TAX, TRIBUTE

[1]**scat•ter** \ˈska-tər\ *vb* [ME *scateren, schateren* to disperse, break up, destroy; akin to MD *schaderen* to scatter] *vt* (14c) **1 a :** to cause to separate widely **b :** to cause to vanish **2** *archaic* **:** to fling away heedlessly **:** SQUANDER **3 :** to distribute irregularly **4 :** to sow by casting in all directions **:** STREW **5 a :** to reflect irregularly and diffusely **b :** to cause (a beam of radiation) to diffuse or disperse **6 :** to divide into ineffectual small portions ~ *vi* **1 :** to separate and go in various directions **:** DISPERSE **2 :** to occur or fall irregularly or at random — **scat•ter•er** \-tər-ər\ *n*

syn SCATTER, DISPERSE, DISSIPATE, DISPEL mean to cause to separate or break up. SCATTER implies a force that drives parts or units irregularly in many directions ⟨the bowling ball *scattered* the pins⟩. DISPERSE implies a wider separation and a complete breaking up of a mass or group ⟨police *dispersed* the crowd⟩. DISSIPATE stresses complete disintegration or dissolution and final disappearance ⟨the fog was *dissipated* by the morning sun⟩. DISPEL stresses a driving away or getting rid of as if by scattering ⟨an authoritative statement that *dispelled* all doubt⟩.

[2]**scatter** *n* (1642) **1 :** the act of scattering **2 :** a small quantity or number irregularly distributed or strewn about **:** SCATTERING **3 :** the state or extent of being scattered; *esp* **:** DISPERSION

scat•ter•ation \ˌska-tə-ˈrā-shən\ *n* (1776) **1 :** the act or process of scattering **:** the state of being scattered **2 :** the movement of people and industry away from the city; *also* **:** the resulting regional urbanization **3 :** a policy of distributing funds and energies in too many ineffectively small units

scat•ter•brain \ˈska-tər-ˌbrān\ *n* (1659) **:** a giddy heedless person

scat•ter•brained \-ˌbrānd\ *adj* (1747) **:** having the characteristics of a scatterbrain

scatter diagram *n* (1925) **:** a two-dimensional graph in rectangular coordinates consisting of points whose coordinates represent values of two variables under study

scat•ter•good \ˈska-tər-ˌgu̇d\ *n* (1577) **:** a wasteful person **:** SPENDTHRIFT

scat•ter•gram \-ˌgram\ *n* (1938) **:** SCATTER DIAGRAM

scat•ter•gun \-ˌgən\ *n or adj* (1836) **:** SHOTGUN

[1]**scat•ter•ing** \ˈska-tə-riŋ\ *n* (14c) **1 :** an act or process in which something scatters or is scattered **2 :** something scattered: as **a :** a small number or quantity interspersed here and there ⟨a ~ of visitors⟩ **b :** the random change in direction of the particles constituting a beam or wave front due to collision with particles of the medium traversed

[2]**scattering** *adj* (15c) **1 :** going in various directions **2 :** found or placed far apart and in no order **3 :** divided among many or several ⟨~ votes⟩ — **scat•ter•ing•ly** \ˈska-tə-riŋ-lē\ *adv*

scatter rug *n* (1926) **:** THROW RUG

scat•ter•shot \ˈska-tər-ˌshät\ *adj* (1951) **:** broadly and often randomly inclusive **:** SHOTGUN ⟨~ advice⟩ ⟨~ planning⟩

scat•ty \ˈska-tē\ *adj* **scat•ti•er; -est** [prob. fr. *scatter*brain + [1]-*y*] (1911) *chiefly Brit* **:** CRAZY

scaup \ˈskȯp\ *n, pl* **scaup** *or* **scaups** [short for *scaup duck; scaup* prob. alter. of *scalp* bed of shellfish] (1797) **:** either of two diving ducks (*Aythya affinis* or *A. marila*) with the male having a glossy purplish or greenish head and a black breast and tail

scav•enge \ˈska-vənj, -vinj\ *vb* **scav•enged; scav•eng•ing** [back-formation fr. *scavenger*] *vt* (ca. 1644) **1 a** (1) **:** to remove (as dirt or refuse) from an area (2) **:** to clean away dirt or refuse from **:** CLEANSE ⟨~ a street⟩ **b :** to feed on (carrion or refuse) **2 a :** to remove (burned gases) from the cylinder of an internal combustion engine after a working stroke **b :** to remove (as an undesirable constituent) from a substance or region by chemical or physical means **c :** to clean and purify (molten metal) by taking up foreign elements in chemical union **3 :** to salvage from discarded or refuse material; *also* **:** to salvage usable material from ~ *vi* **:** to work or act as a scavenger

scav•en•ger \ˈska-vən-jər\ *n* [alter. of earlier *scavager*, fr. AF *scawageour* collector of scavage (duty collected from non-resident street merchants), fr. *skawage* scavage, fr. MF dial. (Flanders) *escauver* to inspect, fr. MD *scouwen*; akin to OE *scēawian* to look at — more at SHOW] (1530) **1** *chiefly Brit* **:** a person employed to remove dirt and refuse from streets **2 :** one that scavenges: as **a :** a garbage collector **b :** a junk collector **c :** a chemically active substance acting to make innocuous or remove an undesirable substance **3 :** an organism that typically feeds on refuse or carrion

scavenger hunt *n* (1936) **:** a game in which players try to acquire without buying specified items within a time limit

ScD *abbr* doctor of science

sce•na \ˈshā-(ˌ)nä\ *n* [It, lit., scene, fr. L] (1819) **:** an elaborate solo vocal composition that consists of a recitative usu. followed by one or more aria sections

sce•nar•io \sə-ˈner-ē-ˌō, *US also and esp Brit* -ˈnär-\ *n, pl* **-i•os** [It, fr. L *scaenarium* place for erecting stages, fr. *scaena* stage] (1875) **1 a :** an outline or synopsis of a play; *esp* **:** a plot outline used by actors of the commedia dell'arte **b :** the libretto of an opera **2 a :** SCREENPLAY **b :** SHOOTING SCRIPT **3 :** a sequence of events esp. when imagined; *esp* **:** an account or synopsis of a possible course of action or events ⟨his ~ for a settlement envisages . . . reunification —Selig Harrison⟩

sce•nar•ist \-ˈner-ist\ *n* (1920) **:** a writer of scenarios

scend \ˈsend\ *n* [perh. short for *ascend*] (1726) **1 :** the lift of a wave **:** SEND **2 :** the upward movement of a pitching ship

scene \ˈsēn\ *n* [MF, stage, fr. L *scena, scaena* stage, scene, prob. fr. Etruscan, fr. Gk *skēnē* shelter, tent, building forming the background for a dramatic performance, stage; perh. akin to Gk *skia* shadow — more at SHINE] (ca. 1520) **1 :** one of the subdivisions of a play: as **a :** a division of an act presenting continuous action in one place **b :** a single situation or unit of dialogue in a play ⟨the love ~⟩ **c :** a motion-picture or television episode or sequence **2 a :** a stage setting **b :** a real or imaginary prospect suggesting a stage setting ⟨a sylvan ~⟩ **3 :** the place of an occurrence or action **:** LOCALE ⟨~ of the crime⟩ **4 :** an exhibition of anger or indecorous behavior ⟨make a ~⟩ **5 a :** sphere of activity ⟨the drug ~⟩ **b :** SITUATION ⟨a bad ~⟩ — **behind the scenes 1 :** out of public view; *also* **:** in secret **2 :** in a position to see the hidden workings ⟨taken *behind the scenes* and told just how in fact the actual government . . . has operated —William Clark⟩

scen•ery \ˈsē-nə-rē, ˈsēn-rē\ *n, pl* **-er•ies** (1770) **1 :** the painted scenes or hangings and accessories used on a theater stage **2 :** a picturesque view or landscape **3 :** one's usual surroundings ⟨needed a change of ~⟩

scene•shift•er \ˈsēn-ˌshif-tər\ *n* (1749) **:** a worker who moves the scenes in a theater

\ə\ **abut** \ᵊ\ **kitten**, F **table** \ər\ **further** \a\ **ash** \ā\ **ace** \ä\ **mop, mar**
\au̇\ **out** \ch\ **chin** \e\ **bet** \ē\ **easy** \g\ **go** \i\ **hit** \ī\ **ice** \j\ **job**
\ŋ\ **sing** \ō\ **go** \ȯ\ **law** \ȯi\ **boy** \th\ **thin** \th\ **the** \ü\ **loot** \u̇\ **foot**
\y\ **yet** \zh\ **vision, beige** \k, ⁿ, œ, ue, ʸ\ *see* Guide to Pronunciation

scene–steal·er \-ˌstē-lər\ *n* (1949) : an actor who attracts attention when another is intended to be the center of attention
sce·nic \ˈsē-nik *also* ˈse-\ *also* **sce·ni·cal** \-ni-kəl\ *adj* (1623) **1** : of or relating to the stage, a stage setting, or stage representation **2** : of or relating to natural scenery ⟨a ~ view⟩ **3** : representing an action, event, or episode ⟨a ~ bas-relief⟩ — **sce·ni·cal·ly** \-ni-k(ə-)lē\ *adv*
scenic railway *n* (1894) *chiefly Brit* : a miniature railway (as in an amusement park) with artificial scenery along the way
sce·nog·ra·phy \sē-ˈnä-grə-fē\ *n* [Gk *skēnographia* painting of scenery, fr. *skēnē* + *-graphia* -graphy] (1645) : the art of perspective representation esp. as applied to the design and painting of stage scenery — **sce·nog·ra·pher** \-grə-fər\ *n* — **sce·no·graph·ic** \ˌsē-nə-ˈgra-fik\ *adj*
[1]**scent** \ˈsent\ *n* [ME *sent,* fr. AF *sente,* fr. *sentir*] (14c) **1** : effluvia from a substance that affect the sense of smell: as **a** : an odor left by an animal on a surface passed over **b** : a characteristic or particular odor; *esp* : one that is agreeable **2 a** : power of smelling : sense of smell ⟨a keen ~⟩ **b** : power of detection : NOSE ⟨a ~ for heresy⟩ **3** : a course of pursuit or discovery ⟨throw one off the ~⟩ **4** : INKLING, INTIMATION ⟨a ~ of trouble⟩ **5** : PERFUME 2 **6** : bits of paper dropped in the game of hare and hounds **7** : a mixture prepared for use as a lure in hunting or fishing ***syn*** see FRAGRANCE, SMELL — **scent·less** \ˈsent-ləs\ *adj*
[2]**scent** *vb* [ME *senten,* fr. AF *sentir* to feel, smell, fr. L *sentire* to perceive, feel — more at SENSE] *vt* (15c) **1 a** : to perceive by the olfactory organs : SMELL **b** : to get or have an inkling of ⟨~ trouble⟩ **2** : to imbue or fill with odor ⟨~*ed* the air with perfume⟩ ~ *vi* **1** : to yield an odor of some specified kind ⟨this ~*s* of sulfur⟩; *also* : to bear indication or suggestions **2** : to use the nose in seeking or tracking prey
scent·ed \ˈsen-təd\ *adj* (1602) : having scent: as **a** : having a perfumed smell **b** : having the sense of smell **c** : having or exhaling an odor
scent hound *n* (1976) : a hound (as a bloodhound) that hunts and pursues game by scent rather than by sight — compare SIGHT HOUND
[1]**scep·ter** \ˈsep-tər\ *n* [ME *sceptre,* fr. AF *septre,* fr. L *sceptrum,* fr. Gk *skēptron* staff, scepter, fr. *skēptesthai* to prop oneself — more at SHAFT] (14c) **1** : a staff or baton borne by a sovereign as an emblem of authority **2** : royal or imperial authority : SOVEREIGNTY
[2]**scepter** *vt* **scep·tered; scep·ter·ing** \-t(ə-)riŋ\ (1526) : to invest with the scepter in token of royal authority
sceptered *adj* (1513) **1** : invested with a scepter or sovereign authority **2** : of or relating to a sovereign or to royalty
scep·tic, scep·ti·cal, scep·ti·cism *chiefly Brit var of* SKEPTIC, SKEPTICAL, SKEPTICISM
scep·tre *Brit var of* SCEPTER
sch *abbr* school
scha·den·freu·de \ˈshä-dᵊn-ˌfrȯi-də\ *n, often cap* [G, fr. *Schaden* damage + *Freude* joy] (1895) : enjoyment obtained from the troubles of others
[1]**sched·ule** \ˈske-(ˌ)jül, -jəl, *Canad also* ˈshe-, *Brit usu* ˈshe-(ˌ)dyül\ *n* [ME, fr. ML *scedula* slip, page, charter, fr. LL *schedula* slip of paper, dim. of L **scheda* strip of papyrus, prob. back-formation fr. L *schedium* impromptu speech, fr. Gk *schedion,* fr. neut. of *schedios* casual; akin to Gk *schedon* near at hand, *echein* to seize, have] (14c) **1 a** *obs* : a written document **b** : a statement of supplementary details appended to a legal or legislative document **2** : a written or printed list, catalog, or inventory; *also* : TIMETABLE 1 **3** : PROGRAM; *esp* : a procedural plan that indicates the time and sequence of each operation ⟨finished on ~⟩ **4** : a body of items to be dealt with : AGENDA **5** *often cap* : a governmental list of drugs all subject to the same legal restrictions and controls — usu. used with a Roman numeral I to V indicating decreasing potential for abuse or addiction

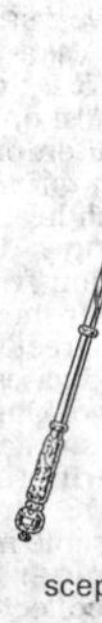
scepter 1

[2]**schedule** *vt* **sched·uled; sched·ul·ing** (1843) **1** : to appoint, assign, or designate for a fixed time **2 a** : to place in a schedule **b** : to make a schedule of — **sched·ul·er** *n*
schee·lite \ˈshā-ˌlīt\ *n* [G *Scheelit,* fr. Karl W. *Scheele* †1786 Swed. chemist] (ca. 1837) : a mineral consisting of the tungstate of calcium that is an ore of tungsten
schef·flera \ˈshe-flə-rə\ *n* [NL, fr. Jacob Christoph *Scheffler* †1742 Ger. physician] (1953) : any of a genus (*Schefflera*) of chiefly tropical and subtropical shrubs and trees of the ginseng family having usu. palmately compound leaves and including some (as *S. actinophylla* syn. *Brassaia actinophylla*) grown indoors and in gardens
Sche·her·a·zade \shə-ˌher-ə-ˈzäd; -ˈzä-də, -dē\ *n* [G *Scheherezade,* fr. Pers *Shīrazād*] (1801) : the fictional wife of a sultan and the narrator of the tales in the *Arabian Nights' Entertainments*
sche·ma \ˈskē-mə\ *n, pl* **sche·ma·ta** \-mə-tə\ *also* **schemas** [Gk *schēmat-, schēma*] (ca. 1890) **1** : a diagrammatic presentation; *broadly* : a structured framework or plan : OUTLINE **2** : a mental codification of experience that includes a particular organized way of perceiving cognitively and responding to a complex situation or set of stimuli
[1]**sche·mat·ic** \ski-ˈma-tik\ *adj* [NL *schematicus,* fr. Gk *schēmat-, schēma*] (1701) : of or relating to a scheme or schema — **sche·mat·i·cal·ly** \-ti-k(ə-)lē\ *adv*
[2]**schematic** *n* (1929) : a schematic drawing or diagram
sche·ma·tism \ˈskē-mə-ˌti-zəm\ *n* (1660) : the disposition of constituents in a pattern or according to a scheme : DESIGN; *also* : a particular systematic disposition of parts
sche·ma·tize \ˈskē-mə-ˌtīz\ *vt* **-tized; -tiz·ing** [Gk *schēmatizein,* fr. *schēmat-, schēma*] (1828) **1** : to form or to form into a scheme or systematic arrangement **2** : to express or depict schematically — **sche·ma·ti·za·tion** \ˌskē-mə-tə-ˈzā-shən\ *n*
[1]**scheme** \ˈskēm\ *n* [L *schemat-, schema* arrangement, figure, fr. Gk *schēmat-, schēma,* fr. *echein* to have, hold, be in (such) a condition; akin to OE *sige* victory, Skt *sahate* he prevails] (ca. 1595) **1 a** *archaic* (1) : a mathematical or astronomical diagram (2) : a representation of the astrological aspects of the planets at a particular time **b** : a graphic sketch or outline **2** : a concise statement or table : EPITOME **3** : a plan or program of action; *esp* : a crafty or secret one **4** : a systematic or organized configuration : DESIGN ⟨color ~⟩ ***syn*** see PLAN
[2]**scheme** *vb* **schemed; schem·ing** *vt* (1749) : to form a scheme for ~ *vi* : to form plans; *also* : PLOT, INTRIGUE — **schem·er** *n*
scheming *adj* (1741) : given to forming schemes; *esp* : DEVIOUS
[1]**scher·zan·do** \skert-ˈsän-(ˌ)dō\ *adv or adj* [It, fr. verbal of *scherzare* to joke, of Gmc origin; akin to MHG *scherzen* to leap for joy, joke; perh. akin to Gk *skairein* to gambol] (ca. 1811) : in sportive manner : PLAYFULLY — used as a direction in music indicating style and tempo ⟨allegretto ~⟩
[2]**scherzando** *n, pl* **-dos** (ca. 1876) : a passage or movement in scherzando style
scher·zo \ˈskert-(ˌ)sō\ *n, pl* **scherzos** *or* **scher·zi** \-(ˌ)sē\ [It, lit., joke, fr. *scherzare*] (1852) : a sprightly humorous instrumental musical composition or movement commonly in quick triple time
Schick test \ˈshik-\ *n* [Béla *Schick*] (1916) : a test for susceptibility to diphtheria by cutaneous injection of a diluted diphtheria toxin that causes an area of reddening and induration in susceptible individuals
Schiff's reagent \ˈshifs-\ *n* [Hugo *Schiff* †1915 Ger. chemist] (1897) : a solution of fuchsine decolorized by treatment with sulfur dioxide that gives a useful test for aldehydes because they restore the dye's color — called also *Schiff reagent* \ˈshif-\; compare FEULGEN REACTION
schil·ler \ˈshi-lər\ *n* [G] (1885) : a bronzy iridescent luster (as of a mineral)
schil·ling \ˈshi-liŋ\ *n* [G, fr. OHG *skilling,* a gold coin — more at SHILLING] (1753) : the basic monetary unit of Austria until 2002
schip·per·ke \ˈski-pər-kē, ˈshi-, -kə; -pərk\ *n* [Flem, dim. of *schipper* skipper; fr. its use as a watchdog on boats — more at SKIPPER] (1887) : any of a Belgian breed of small stocky black tailless dogs with foxy head and heavy coat
schism \ˈsi-zəm, ˈski- *also* ˈshi-; *among clergy usu* ˈsi-\ *n* [ME *scisme,* fr. AF *scisme, cisme,* fr. LL *schismat-, schisma,* fr. Gk, cleft, division, fr. *schizein* to split — more at SHED] (14c) **1** : DIVISION, SEPARATION; *also* : DISCORD, DISHARMONY ⟨a ~ between political parties⟩ **2 a** : formal division in or separation from a church or religious body **b** : the offense of promoting schism
[1]**schis·mat·ic** \siz-ˈma-tik, ski-\ *n* (14c) : one who creates or takes part in schism
[2]**schismatic** *also* **schis·mat·i·cal** \-ti-kəl\ *adj* (15c) : of, relating to, or guilty of schism — **schis·mat·i·cal·ly** \-ti-k(ə-)lē\ *adv*
schis·ma·tize \ˈsiz-mə-ˌtīz, ˈskiz-\ *vb* **-tized; -tiz·ing** *vi* (1601) : to take part in schism; *esp* : to make a breach of union (as in the church) ~ *vt* : to induce into schism
schist \ˈshist\ *n* [F *schiste,* fr. L *schistos (lapis),* lit., fissile stone, fr. Gk *schistos* that may be split, fr. *schizein*] (ca. 1782) : a metamorphic crystalline rock that has a closely foliated structure and can be split along approximately parallel planes
schis·tose \ˈshis-ˌtōs\ *adj* (1794) : of or relating to schist : having the character or structure of a schist — **schis·tos·i·ty** \shis-ˈtä-sə-tē\ *n*
schis·to·some \ˈshis-tə-ˌsōm\ *n* [NL *Schistosoma,* fr. Gk *schistos* + *sōma* body] (1905) : any of a genus (*Schistosoma*) of elongated trematode worms with the sexes separate that parasitize the blood vessels of birds and mammals and cause a destructive human schistosomiasis; *broadly* : a worm of the family (Schistosomatidae) that includes this genus — **schis·to·som·al** \ˌshis-tə-ˈsō-məl\ *adj* — **schistosome** *adj*
schis·to·so·mi·a·sis \ˌshis-tə-sō-ˈmī-ə-səs\ *n, pl* **-a·ses** \-ˌsēz\ [NL, fr. *Schistosoma*] (1906) : infestation with or disease caused by schistosomes; *specif* : a severe endemic disease of humans in Africa and parts of Asia and So. America that is contracted when cercariae released into freshwaters (as rivers) by a snail intermediate host penetrate the skin and that is marked esp. by blood loss and tissue damage — called also *snail fever*
schiz- *or* **schizo-** *comb form* [NL, fr. Gk *schizo-,* fr. *schizein* to split — more at SHED] **1** : split : cleft ⟨*schizo*carp⟩ **2** : characterized by or involving cleavage ⟨*schizo*gony⟩ **3** : schizophrenia ⟨*schizo*id⟩
schizo \ˈskit-(ˌ)sō\ *n, pl* **schiz·os** (1945) : a schizophrenic individual — **schizo** *adj*
schizo·carp \ˈski-zə-ˌkärp, ˈskit-sə-\ *n* [ISV] (1870) : a dry compound fruit that splits at maturity into several indehiscent one-seeded carpels
schi·zog·o·ny \ski-ˈzä-gə-nē, skit-ˈsä-\ *n* [NL *schizogonia,* fr. *schiz-* + L *-gonia* -gony] (1887) : asexual reproduction by multiple segmentation characteristic of sporozoans (as the malaria parasite) — **schizo·gon·ic** \ˌski-zə-ˈgä-nik, ˌskit-sə-\ *adj*
schiz·oid \ˈskit-ˌsȯid\ *adj* [ISV] (1924) : characterized by, resulting from, tending toward, or suggestive of schizophrenia — **schizoid** *n*
schiz·ont \ˈski-ˌzänt, ˈskit-ˌsänt\ *n* [ISV] (1900) : a multinucleate sporozoan that reproduces by schizogony
schizo·phrene \ˈskit-sə-ˌfrēn\ *n* [ISV, prob. back-formation fr. NL *schizophrenia*] (1925) : one affected with schizophrenia : SCHIZOPHRENIC
schizo·phre·nia \ˌskit-sə-ˈfrē-nē-ə\ *n* [NL] (1912) **1** : a psychotic disorder characterized by loss of contact with the environment, by noticeable deterioration in the level of functioning in everyday life, and by disintegration of personality expressed as disorder of feeling, thought (as delusions), perception (as hallucinations), and behavior — called also *dementia praecox*; compare PARANOID SCHIZOPHRENIA **2** : contradictory or antagonistic qualities or attitudes ⟨both parties . . . have exhibited ~ over the desired outcome —Elizabeth Drew⟩ — **schizo·phren·ic** \-ˈfre-nik\ *adj or n* — **schizo·phren·i·cal·ly** \-ni-k(ə-)lē\ *adv*
schizy *or* **schiz·zy** \ˈskit-sē\ *adj* [by shortening & alter.] (1927) : SCHIZOID
schle·miel *also* **shle·miel** \shlə-ˈmēl\ *n* [Yiddish *shlemil*] (1892) : an unlucky bungler : CHUMP
schlep *or* **schlepp** *also* **shlep** *or* **shlepp** \ˈshlep\ *vb* **schlepped** *also* **shlepped; schlep·ping** *also* **shlep·ping** [Yiddish *shlepn,* fr. MHG *sleppen,* fr. MLG *slēpen*] *vt* (1922) : DRAG, HAUL ~ *vi* : to proceed or move esp. slowly, tediously, awkwardly, or carelessly
schlie·ren \ˈshlir-ən\ *n pl* [G] (1898) **1** : small masses or streaks in an igneous rock that differ in composition from the main body **2** : regions of varying refraction in a transparent medium often caused by pressure or temperature differences and detectable esp. by photographing the passage of a beam of light — **schlie·ric** \ˈshlir-ik\ *adj*
schlock \ˈshläk\ *or* **schlocky** \ˈshlä-kē\ *also* **shlock** *or* **shlocky** *adj* [perh. fr. Yiddish *shlak* evil, nuisance, lit., blow] (1916) : of low quality or value — **schlock** *n*
schlub *also* **shlub** \ˈshləb\ *n* [Yiddish *zhlob, zhlub* yokel, boor] (1950) *slang* : a stupid, worthless, or unattractive person
schlump \ˈshləmp\ *n* [Yiddish *shlump* sloppy or dowdy person] (1948) *slang* : SCHLUB — **schlumpy** \ˈshləm-pē\ *adj*

schm- *or* **shm-** \shm\ *prefix* [Yiddish *shm-*] — used to form a rhyming term of derision by replacing the initial consonant or consonant cluster of a word or by preceding the initial vowel ⟨fancy, *schm*ancy, I prefer plain⟩ ⟨Godfather-*shm*odfather—enough already —Judith Crist⟩
schmaltz *also* **schmalz** \ˈshmȯlts, ˈshmälts\ *n* [Yiddish *shmalts,* lit., rendered fat] (1935) **1 :** sentimental or florid music or art **2 :** SENTIMENTALITY — **schmaltzy** \ˈshmȯlt-sē, ˈshmält-\ *adj*
schmear *or* **schmeer** \ˈshmir\ *n* [Yiddish *shmir* smear] (1965) **:** an aggregate of related things ⟨the whole ∼⟩
Schmidt camera \ˈshmit-\ *n* [B. *Schmidt* †1935 Ger. optical scientist] (1936) **:** a photographic telescope with specialized optics that correct for spherical aberration and coma — called also *Schmidt telescope*
schmo *or* **schmoe** \ˈshmō\ *n, pl* **schmoes** [origin unknown] (1947) *slang* **:** JERK 4a
[1]**schmooze** *or* **shmooze** \ˈshmüz\ *vb* **schmoozed** *or* **shmoozed; schmooz·ing** *or* **shmooz·ing** [Yiddish *shmuesn,* fr. *schmues* talk, fr. Heb *shĕmu'ōth* news, rumor] *vi* (1884) **:** to converse informally **:** CHAT; *also* **:** to chat in a friendly and persuasive manner esp. so as to gain favor, business, or connections ∼ *vt* **:** to engage in schmoozing with ⟨she *schmoozed* her professors⟩ — **schmooz·er** \ˈshmü-zər\ *n*
[2]**schmooze** *n* (1949) **1 :** a gathering or time devoted to schmoozing **2 :** casual talk that is often gossipy or ingratiating
schmoozy \ˈshmü-zē\ *adj* (1980) **:** of, relating to, characterized by, or given to schmoozing ⟨a ∼ salesclerk⟩
schmuck \ˈshmək\ *n* [Yiddish *shmok,* lit., penis] (1892) *slang* **:** JERK 4b
schmutz \ˈshmu̇ts\ *n* [Yiddish *shmuts* & G *Schmutz,* fr. MHG *smutzen* to soil, damage] (1940) **:** DIRT, GRIME
schnapps \ˈshnaps\ *n, pl* **schnapps** [G *Schnaps,* lit., dram of liquor, fr. LG *snaps* dram, mouthful, fr. *snappen* to snap] (1796) **:** any of various liquors of high alcoholic content; *esp* **:** strong Holland gin
schnau·zer \ˈshnau̇-zər, ˈshnau̇t-sər\ *n* [G, fr. *Schnauze* snout — more at SNOUT] (1923) **:** a dog of any of three breeds that originated in Germany and are characterized by a wiry coat, long head, pointed ears, heavy eyebrows, and long hair on the muzzle: **a :** STANDARD SCHNAUZER **b :** GIANT SCHNAUZER **c :** MINIATURE SCHNAUZER
schnit·zel \ˈshnit-səl\ *n* [G, lit., shaving, chip, dim. of *Schnitz* slice, fr. MHG *snitz;* akin to OHG *snīdan* to cut, OE *snīthan,* and perh. to Czech *snět* bough] (1854) **:** a seasoned and garnished veal cutlet
schnook \ˈshnu̇k\ *n* [origin unknown] (1940) *slang* **:** a stupid or unimportant person **:** DOLT
schnor·rer \ˈshnȯr-ər\ *n* [Yiddish *shnorer*] (1892) **:** BEGGAR; *esp* **:** one who wheedles others into supplying his wants
schnoz *or* **schnozz** \ˈshnäz\ *n* (1940) *slang* **:** NOSE; *specif* **:** a large nose
schnoz·zle \ˈshnä-zəl\ *n* [prob. modif. of Yiddish *shnoitsl,* dim. of *shnoits* snout] (1937) *slang* **:** SCHNOZ
scho·la can·to·rum \ˌskō-lə-kan-ˈtȯr-əm\ *n, pl* **scho·lae can·torum** \-ˌlē-, -ˌlā-, -ˌlī-\ [ML, school of singers] (1782) **1 :** a singing school esp. for church choristers; *specif* **:** the choir or choir school of a monastery or of a cathedral **2 :** an enclosure designed for a choir and located in the center of the nave in early church buildings
schol·ar \ˈskä-lər\ *n* [ME *scoler,* fr. OE *scolere* & AF *escoler,* fr. ML *scholaris,* fr. LL, of a school, fr. L *schola* school] (bef. 12c) **1 :** a person who attends a school or studies under a teacher **:** PUPIL **2 a :** a person who has done advanced study in a special field **b :** a learned person **3 :** a holder of a scholarship
schol·ar·ly \-lē\ *adj* (1638) **:** of, characteristic of, or suitable to learned persons **:** LEARNED, ACADEMIC
schol·ar·ship \-ˌship\ *n* (ca. 1536) **1 :** a grant-in-aid to a student (as by a college or foundation) **2 :** the character, qualities, activity, or attainments of a scholar **:** LEARNING **3 :** a fund of knowledge and learning ⟨drawing on the ∼ of the ancients⟩ ***syn*** see KNOWLEDGE
Scholarship level *n* (1947) **:** S LEVEL
[1]**scho·las·tic** \skə-ˈlas-tik\ *adj* [ML & L; ML *scholasticus* of the schoolmen, fr. L, of a school, fr. Gk *scholastikos,* fr. *scholazein* to keep a school, fr. *scholē* school] (1596) **1 a** *often cap* **:** of or relating to Scholasticism ⟨∼ theology⟩ ⟨∼ philosophy⟩ **b :** suggestive or characteristic of a scholastic esp. in subtlety or aridity **:** PEDANTIC ⟨dull ∼ reports⟩ **2 :** of or relating to schools or scholars; *esp* **:** of or relating to high school or secondary school — **scho·las·ti·cal·ly** \-ti-k(ə-)lē\ *adv*
[2]**scholastic** *n* (1644) **1 a** *cap* **:** a Scholastic philosopher **b :** PEDANT, FORMALIST **2** [NL *scholasticus,* fr. L *scholasticus,* adj.] **:** a student in a scholasticate **3 :** a person who adopts academic or traditional methods in art
scho·las·ti·cate \skə-ˈlas-tə-ˌkāt, -ti-kət\ *n* [NL *scholasticatus,* fr. *scholasticus* student in a scholasticate] (1853) **:** a college-level school of general study for those preparing for membership in a Roman Catholic religious order
scho·las·ti·cism \skə-ˈlas-tə-ˌsi-zəm\ *n* (1706) **1** *cap* **a :** a philosophical movement dominant in western Christian civilization from the 9th until the 17th century and combining religious dogma with the mystical and intuitional tradition of patristic philosophy esp. of St. Augustine and later with Aristotelianism **b :** NEO-SCHOLASTICISM **2 a :** close adherence to the traditional teachings or methods of a school or sect **b :** pedantic adherence to scholarly methods
scho·li·ast \ˈskō-lē-ˌast, -lē-əst\ *n* [MGk *scholiastēs,* fr. *scholiazein* to write scholia on, fr. Gk *scholion*] (1583) **:** a maker of scholia **:** COMMENTATOR, ANNOTATOR — **scho·li·as·tic** \ˌskō-lē-ˈas-tik\ *adj*
scho·li·um \ˈskō-lē-əm\ *n, pl* **-lia** \-lē-ə\ *or* **-li·ums** [NL, fr. Gk *scholion* comment, scholium, fr. dim. of *scholē* lecture] (1535) **1 :** a marginal annotation or comment (as on the text of a classic by an early grammarian) **2 :** a remark or observation subjoined but not essential to a demonstration or a train of reasoning
[1]**school** \ˈskül\ *n* [ME *scole,* fr. OE *scōl,* fr. L *schola,* fr. Gk *scholē* leisure, discussion, lecture, school; perh. akin to Gk *echein* to hold — more at SCHEME] (bef. 12c) **1 :** an organization that provides instruction: as **a :** an institution for the teaching of children **b :** COLLEGE, UNIVERSITY **c** (1) **:** a group of scholars and teachers pursuing knowledge together that with similar groups constituted a medieval university (2) **:** one of the four faculties of a medieval university (3) **:** an institution for specialized higher education often associated with a university ⟨the ∼ of engineering⟩ **d :** an establishment offering specialized instruction ⟨a secretarial ∼⟩ ⟨driving ∼*s*⟩ **2 a** (1) **:** the process of teaching or learning esp. at a school (2) **:** attendance at a school (3) **:** a session of a school **b :** a school building **c :** the students attending a school; *also* **:** its teachers and students **3 :** a source of knowledge ⟨experience was his ∼⟩ **4 a :** a group of persons who hold a common doctrine or follow the same teacher (as in philosophy, theology, or medicine) ⟨the Aristotelian ∼⟩; *also* **:** the doctrine or practice of such a group **b :** a group of artists under a common influence **c :** a group of persons of similar opinions or behavior; *also* **:** the shared opinions or behavior of such a group ⟨other ∼*s* of thought⟩ **5 :** the regulations governing military drill of individuals or units; *also* **:** the exercises carried out ⟨the ∼ of the soldier⟩
[2]**school** *vt* (15c) **1 a :** to teach or drill in a specific knowledge or skill ⟨well ∼*ed* in languages⟩ **b :** to discipline or habituate to something ⟨∼ oneself in patience⟩ **2 :** to educate in an institution of learning ***syn*** see TEACH
[3]**school** *n* [ME *scole,* fr. MD *schole;* akin to OE *scolu* multitude and prob. to OE *scylian* to separate — more at SKILL] (15c) **:** a large number of fish or aquatic animals of one kind swimming together
[4]**school** *vi* (1597) **:** to swim or feed in a school ⟨bluefish are ∼*ing*⟩
school–age *adj* (1741) **:** old enough to go to school ⟨∼ children⟩
school·bag \ˈskül-ˌbag\ *n* (1841) **:** a bag for carrying schoolbooks and school supplies
school board *n* (1836) **:** a board in charge of local public schools
school·book \-ˌbu̇k\ *n* (1634) **:** a school textbook
[1]**school·boy** \-ˌbȯi\ *n* (1588) **:** a boy attending school
[2]**schoolboy** *adj* (1645) **1 :** of, relating to, or characteristic of a schoolboy ⟨∼ pranks⟩ **2 :** of, relating to, or being a sport for high school or prep school boys; *also* **:** being one who participates in such sports
school·boy·ish \-ˌbȯi-ish\ *adj* (1831) **:** SCHOOLBOY 1
school bus *n* (1908) **:** a vehicle used for transporting children to or from school or on activities connected with school
school·child \ˈskül-ˌchī(-ə)ld\ *n* (1801) **:** a child attending school
school committee *n* (1787) **:** SCHOOL BOARD
school district *n* (1809) **:** a unit for administration of a public-school system often comprising several towns within a state
school·fel·low \ˈskül-ˌfe-(ˌ)lō\ *n* (15c) **:** SCHOOLMATE
school·girl \-ˌgər(-ə)l\ *n* (1678) **:** a girl attending school
school·house \-ˌhau̇s\ *n* (14c) **:** a building used as a school and esp. as an elementary school
school·ing *n* (15c) **1 a :** instruction in school **:** EDUCATION **b :** training, guidance, or discipline derived from experience **2** *archaic* **:** REPROOF **3 :** the cost of instruction and maintenance at school **4 :** the training of a horse for service; *esp* **:** the teaching and exercising of horse and rider in the formal techniques of equitation
school·kid \ˈskül-ˌkid\ *n* (1934) **:** a child or teenager attending school
school–leav·er \ˈskül-ˌlē-vər\ *n* (1925) *Brit* **:** one who has left school usu. after completing a course of study
school·man \ˈskül-mən, -ˌman\ *n* (ca. 1533) **1 a :** one skilled in academic disputation **b** *cap* **:** SCHOLASTIC 1a **2 a :** EDUCATOR 1 **b :** EDUCATOR 2b
school·marm \-ˌmä(r)m\ *or* **school·ma'am** \-ˌmäm, -ˌmam\ *n* [*school* + *marm,* alter. of *ma'am*] (1831) **1 :** a woman who is a schoolteacher esp. in a rural or small-town school **2 :** a person who exhibits characteristics attributed to schoolteachers (as strict adherence to arbitrary rules) — **school·marm·ish** \-ˌmä(r)-mish\ *adj*
school·mas·ter \-ˌmas-tər\ *n* (13c) **1 :** a man who teaches school **2 :** one that disciplines or directs **3 :** a reddish-brown edible snapper (*Lutjanus apodus*) of the tropical Atlantic and the Gulf of Mexico — **school·mas·ter·ish** \-tə-rish\ *adj* — **school·mas·ter·ly** *adj*
school·mate \-ˌmāt\ *n* (1563) **:** a companion at school
school·mis·tress \-ˌmis-trəs\ *n* (15c) **:** a woman who teaches school — **school·mis·tressy** \-trə-sē\ *adj*
school·room \-ˌrüm, -ˌru̇m\ *n* (1752) **:** CLASSROOM
school·teach·er \-ˌtē-chər\ *n* (1751) **:** one who teaches school
school·time \-ˌtīm\ *n* (1740) **1 :** the time for beginning a session of school or during which school is held **2 :** the period of life spent in school or in study
school·work \-ˌwərk\ *n* (1846) **:** lessons done in class or assigned to be done at home
schoo·ner \ˈskü-nər\ *n* [origin unknown] (1716) **1 :** a typically 2-masted fore-and-aft rigged vessel with a foremast and a mainmast stepped nearly amidships **2 :** a larger-than-usual drinking glass (as for beer)
schooner rig *n* (1828) **:** FORE-AND-AFT RIG — **schoo·ner–rigged** \ˈskü-nə(r)-ˈrigd\ *adj*
schorl \ˈshȯr(-ə)l\ *n* [G *Schörl*] (1779) **:** TOURMALINE; *esp* **:** tourmaline of the black variety
schot·tische \ˈshä-tish, shä-ˈtēsh\ *n* [G, fr. *schottisch* Scottish, fr. *Schotte* Scotsman; akin to OE *Scottas* Scots] (1849) **1 :** a round dance resembling a slow polka **2 :** music for the schottische
schrod *var of* SCROD
Schrö·ding·er equation \ˈshrā-diŋ-ər, ˈshrœ-, ˈshrə(r)-\ *n* [Erwin *Schrödinger*] (1936) **:** an equation that describes the wave nature of elementary particles and is fundamental to the description of the properties of all matter
schtick *var of* SHTICK
schuss \ˈshu̇s, ˈshüs\ *vi* [*schuss,* n., fr. G *Schuss,* lit., shot, fr. OHG *scuz* — more at SHOT] (1940) **:** to ski directly down a slope at high speed — **schuss** *n* — **schuss·er** *n*
schuss·boom·er \-ˌbü-mər\ *n* (1953) **:** a skier who schusses
schwa \ˈshwä\ *n* [G, fr. Heb *shĕwā*] (1895) **1 :** an unstressed mid-central vowel (as the usual sound of the first and last vowels of the English word *America*) **2 :** the symbol ə used for the schwa sound and less widely for a similarly articulated stressed vowel (as in *cut*)
Schwann cell \ˈshwän-\ *n* [Theodor *Schwann* †1882 Ger. naturalist] (ca. 1909) **:** the myelin-secreting cell surrounding a myelinated nerve fiber between two nodes of Ranvier
schwar·me·rei \ˌshver-mə-ˈrī\ *n* [G *Schwärmerei,* fr. *schwärmen* to be enthusiastic, lit., to swarm] (1845) **:** excessive sentiment

\ə\ **abut** \ᵊ\ **kitten, F table** \ər\ **further** \a\ **ash** \ā\ **ace** \ä\ **mop, mar**
\au̇\ **out** \ch\ **chin** \e\ **bet** \ē\ **easy** \g\ **go** \i\ **hit** \ī\ **ice** \j\ **job**
\ŋ\ **sing** \ō\ **go** \ȯ\ **law** \ȯi\ **boy** \th\ **thin** \t͟h\ **the** \ü\ **loot** \u̇\ **foot**
\y\ **yet** \zh\ **vision, beige** \k, ⁿ, œ, ue, ʸ\ *see* Guide to Pronunciation

sci *abbr* science; scientific

sci·at·ic \sī-ˈa-tik\ *adj* [MF *sciatique,* fr. LL *sciaticus,* alter. of L *ischiadicus* of sciatica, fr. Gk *ischiadikos,* fr. *ischiad-, ischias* sciatica, fr. *ischion* ischium] (1586) **1 :** of, relating to, or situated near the hip **2 :** of, relating to, or caused by sciatica ⟨~ pains⟩

sci·at·i·ca \sī-ˈa-ti-kə\ *n* [ME, fr. ML, fr. LL, fem. of *sciaticus*] (14c) **:** pain along the course of a sciatic nerve esp. in the back of the thigh; *broadly* **:** pain in the lower back, buttocks, hips, or adjacent parts

sciatic nerve *n* (1741) **:** either of the pair of largest nerves in the body that arise one on each side from the nerve plexus supplying the posterior limb and pelvic region and that pass out of the pelvis and down the back of the thigh

SCID *abbr* severe combined immune deficiency; severe combined immunodeficiency

sci·ence \ˈsī-ən(t)s\ *n* [ME, fr. AF, fr. L *scientia,* fr. *scient-, sciens* having knowledge, fr. prp. of *scire* to know; perh. akin to Skt *chyati* he cuts off, L *scindere* to split — more at SHED] (14c) **1 :** the state of knowing **:** knowledge as distinguished from ignorance or misunderstanding **2 a :** a department of systematized knowledge as an object of study ⟨the ~ of theology⟩ **b :** something (as a sport or technique) that may be studied or learned like systematized knowledge ⟨have it down to a ~⟩ **3 a :** knowledge or a system of knowledge covering general truths or the operation of general laws esp. as obtained and tested through scientific method **b :** such knowledge or such a system of knowledge concerned with the physical world and its phenomena **:** NATURAL SCIENCE **4 :** a system or method reconciling practical ends with scientific laws ⟨cooking is both a ~ and an art⟩ **5** *cap* **:** CHRISTIAN SCIENCE

science fair *n* (1962) **:** a competitive exhibition of science projects usu. carried out by schoolchildren

science fiction *n* (1851) **:** fiction dealing principally with the impact of actual or imagined science on society or individuals or having a scientific factor as an essential orienting component — **sci·ence–fic·tion·al** \ˈsī-ən(t)s-ˈfik-shnəl, -shə-n^{ə}l\ *adj*

sci·en·tial \sī-ˈen(t)-shəl\ *adj* (15c) **1 :** relating to or producing knowledge or science **2 :** having efficient knowledge **:** CAPABLE

sci·en·tif·ic \ˌsī-ən-ˈti-fik\ *adj* [ML *scientificus* producing knowledge, fr. L *scient-, sciens* + *-i-* + *-ficus* -fic] (1589) **:** of, relating to, or exhibiting the methods or principles of science — **sci·en·tif·i·cal·ly** \-fi-k(ə-)lē\ *adv*

scientific creationism *n* (1979) **:** a doctrine holding that the biblical account of creation is supported by scientific evidence

scientific method *n* (ca. 1810) **:** principles and procedures for the systematic pursuit of knowledge involving the recognition and formulation of a problem, the collection of data through observation and experiment, and the formulation and testing of hypotheses

scientific notation *n* (ca. 1934) **:** a widely used floating-point system in which numbers are expressed as products consisting of a number between 1 and 10 multiplied by an appropriate power of 10 (as in 1.591 × $(10)^{-20}$ or 1.591 × 10 – 20)

sci·en·tism \ˈsī-ən-ˌti-zəm\ *n* (1870) **1 :** methods and attitudes typical of or attributed to the natural scientist **2 :** an exaggerated trust in the efficacy of the methods of natural science applied to all areas of investigation (as in philosophy, the social sciences, and the humanities) — **sci·en·tis·tic** \ˌsī-ən-ˈtis-tik\ *adj*

sci·en·tist \ˈsī-ən-tist\ *n* [L *scientia*] (1834) **1 :** a person learned in science and esp. natural science **:** a scientific investigator **2** *cap* **:** CHRISTIAN SCIENTIST

sci·en·tize \ˈsī-ən-ˌtīz\ *vt* **-tized; -tiz·ing** (1890) **:** to treat with a scientific approach ⟨the attempt to ~ reality, to name it and classify it —John Fowles⟩

sci–fi \ˈsī-ˈfī\ *adj* [*science fiction*] (1955) **:** of, relating to, or being science fiction ⟨a ~ film⟩ — **sci–fi** *n*

sci·li·cet \ˈskē-li-ˌket; ˈsī-lə-ˌset, ˈsi-\ *adv* [ME, fr. L, surely, to wit, fr. *scire* to know + *licet* it is permitted, fr. *licēre* to be permitted — more at LICENSE] (14c) **:** TO WIT, NAMELY

scil·la \ˈsi-lə, ˈski-\ *n* [NL, fr. L, squill — more at SQUILL] (1824) **:** any of a genus (*Scilla*) of Old World bulbous herbs of the lily family with narrow basal leaves and purple, blue, or white racemose flowers

scim·i·tar \ˈsi-mə-tər, -ˌtär\ *n* [It *scimitarra*] (1562) **:** a saber having a curved blade with the edge on the convex side and used chiefly by Arabs and Turks

scin·tig·ra·phy \sin-ˈti-grə-fē\ *n* [*scintillation + -graphy;* fr. the scintillation counter used to record radiation on the picture] (1958) **:** a diagnostic technique in which a two-dimensional picture of internal body tissue is produced through the detection of radiation emitted by a radioactive substance administered into the body — **scin·ti·graph·ic** \ˌsin-tə-ˈgra-fik\ *adj*

scin·til·la \sin-ˈti-lə\ *n* [L] (1661) **:** SPARK, TRACE ⟨not a ~ of doubt⟩

scin·til·lant \ˈsin-tə-lənt\ *adj* (1610) **:** that scintillates **:** SPARKLING — **scin·til·lant·ly** *adv*

scin·til·late \ˈsin-tə-ˌlāt\ *vb* **-lat·ed; -lat·ing** [L *scintillatus,* pp. of *scintillare* to sparkle, fr. *scintilla* spark] *vi* (ca. 1623) **1 :** to emit sparks **:** SPARK **2 :** to emit quick flashes as if throwing off sparks **:** SPARKLE ⟨stars ~ in the sky⟩ ~ *vt* **:** to throw off as a spark or as sparkling flashes ⟨~ witticisms⟩ — **scin·til·la·tor** \-ˌlā-tər\ *n*

scintillating *adj* (1846) **:** brilliantly lively, stimulating, or witty ⟨a ~ conversation⟩

scin·til·la·tion \ˌsin-tə-ˈlā-shən\ *n* (ca. 1623) **1 :** an act or instance of scintillating; *esp* **:** rapid changes in the brightness of a celestial body **2 a :** a spark or flash emitted in scintillating **b :** a flash of light produced in a phosphor by an ionizing event **3 :** a brilliant outburst (as of wit) **4 :** a flash of the eye

scintillation counter *n* (1948) **:** a device for detecting and registering individual scintillations (as in radioactive emission)

scin·til·lom·e·ter \ˌsin-tə-ˈlä-mə-tər\ *n* [L *scintilla* + ISV *-o-* + *-meter*] (1877) **:** SCINTILLATION COUNTER

sci·o·lism \ˈsī-ə-ˌli-zəm\ *n* [LL *sciolus* smatterer, fr. dim. of L *scius* knowing, fr. *scire* to know — more at SCIENCE] (1816) **:** a superficial show of learning — **sci·o·list** \-list\ *n* — **sci·o·lis·tic** \ˌsī-ə-ˈlis-tik\ *adj*

sci·on \ˈsī-ən\ *n* [ME *sioun,* fr. OF *cion,* of Gmc origin; akin to OE *cīth* sprout, shoot, OHG *kīdi*] (13c) **1 :** a detached living portion of a plant (as a bud or shoot) joined to a stock in grafting and usu. supplying solely aerial parts to a graft **2 a :** DESCENDANT, CHILD; *esp* **:** a descendant of a wealthy, aristocratic, or influential family **b :** HEIR 1 ⟨~ of a railroad empire⟩

sci·re fa·cias \ˌsī-rē-ˈfā-sh(ē-)əs\ *n* [ME, fr. ML, you should cause to know] (15c) **1 :** a judicial writ founded on some matter of record and requiring the party proceeded against to show cause why the record should not be enforced, annulled, or vacated **2 :** a legal proceeding instituted by a scire facias

scirocco *var of* SIROCCO

scir·rhous \ˈsir-əs, ˈskir-\ *adj* [NL *scirrhosus,* fr. *scirrhus* scirrhous tumor, fr. Gk *skiros, skirrhos* overgrown land, hardened tumor] (1563) **:** of, relating to, or being a hard slow-growing malignant tumor having a preponderance of fibrous tissue

scis·sile \ˈsi-səl, -ˌsī(-ə)l\ *adj* [F, fr. L *scissilis,* fr. *scissus,* pp. of *scindere* to split — more at SHED] (1621) **:** capable of being cut smoothly or split easily ⟨a ~ peptide bond⟩

scis·sion \ˈsi-zhən\ *n* [ME (Sc) *scissione,* fr. LL *scission-, scissio,* fr. L *scindere*] (15c) **1 :** a division or split in a group or union **:** SCHISM **2 :** an action or process of cutting, dividing, or splitting **:** the state of being cut, divided, or split

[1]**scis·sor** \ˈsi-zər\ *n* (15c) **:** SCISSORS

[2]**scissor** *vt* **scis·sored; scis·sor·ing** \ˈsi-zə-riŋ, ˈsiz-riŋ\ (1612) **:** to cut, cut up, or cut off with scissors or shears ⟨~*ed* the paper into strips⟩

scis·sors \ˈsi-zərz\ *n pl but sing or pl in constr* [ME *cisours, sisoures,* fr. MF *cisoires,* fr. VL **caesorium* (sing.) cutting instrument, fr. L *caedere* to cut] (14c) **1 :** a cutting instrument having two blades whose cutting edges slide past each other **2 a :** a gymnastic feat in which the leg movements suggest the opening and closing of scissors **b :** SCISSORS HOLD

scissors–and–paste *adj* (1902) **:** being a compilation rather than an effort of original and independent investigation

scissors hold *n* (1909) **:** a wrestling hold in which the legs are locked around the head or body of an opponent

scissors kick *n* (ca. 1930) **:** a swimming kick used esp. in sidestrokes in which the legs move like scissors

scis·sor–tailed flycatcher \ˈsi-zər-ˌtāld-\ *n* (ca. 1909) **:** a flycatcher (*Tyrannus forficatus*) of the southern U.S., Mexico, and Central America that has a long deeply forked tail — called also *scissortail*

sclaff \ˈsklaf\ *vi* [Sc, fr. *sclaff,* n., lit., blow with the palm; prob. of imit. origin] (1893) **:** to scrape the ground instead of hitting the ball cleanly on a golf stroke — **sclaff** *n* — **sclaff·er** *n*

SCLC *abbr* Southern Christian Leadership Conference

scler- *or* **sclero-** *comb form* [NL, fr. Gk *sklēr-, sklēro-,* fr. *sklēros* — more at SKELETON] **1 :** hard ⟨*scler*ite⟩ ⟨*sclero*derma⟩ **2 :** hardness ⟨*sclero*meter⟩

sclera \ˈskler-ə\ *n* [NL, fr. Gk *sklēros*] (1888) **:** the dense fibrous opaque white outer coat enclosing the eyeball except the part covered by the cornea — see EYE illustration — **scler·al** \-əl\ *adj*

scler·e·id \ˈskler-ē-əd\ *n* [ISV, irreg. fr. Gk *sklēros*] (1896) **:** a variably shaped sclerenchymatous cell of a higher plant

scle·ren·chy·ma \sklə-ˈreŋ-kə-mə\ *n* [NL] (1875) **:** a protective or supporting tissue in higher plants composed of cells with walls thickened and often lignified — **scler·en·chy·ma·tous** \ˌskler-ən-ˈki-mə-təs, -ˈkī-\ *adj*

scler·ite \ˈskler-ˌīt\ *n* [ISV] (1861) **:** a hard chitinous or calcareous plate, piece, or spicule (as of the arthropod integument)

sclero·der·ma \ˌskler-ə-ˈdər-mə\ *n* [NL] (ca. 1860) **:** a usu. slowly progressive disease marked by the deposition of fibrous connective tissue in the skin and often in internal organs and structures

scle·rom·e·ter \sklə-ˈrä-mə-tər\ *n* [ISV] (ca. 1879) **:** an instrument for determining the relative hardnesses of materials

sclero·pro·tein \ˌskler-ō-ˈprō-ˌtēn, -ˈprō-tē-ən\ *n* [ISV] (1907) **:** any of various fibrous proteins esp. from connective and skeletal tissues

scle·ros·ing \sklə-ˈrō-siŋ, -ziŋ\ *adj* [NL *sclerosis* + E [1]*-ing*] (1885) **:** causing or characterized by sclerosis ⟨~ agents⟩

scle·ro·sis \sklə-ˈrō-səs\ *n* [ME *sclirosis* tumor, fr. ML, fr. Gk *sklērōsis* hardening, fr. *sklēroun* to harden, fr. *sklēros*] (1846) **1 :** pathological hardening of tissue esp. from overgrowth of fibrous tissue or increase in interstitial tissue; *also* **:** a disease characterized by sclerosis **2 :** an inability or reluctance to adapt or compromise ⟨political ~⟩

sclero·ther·a·py \ˌskler-ō-ˈther-ə-pē\ *n* (1944) **:** the injection of a sclerosing agent (as saline) into a varicose vein to produce inflammation and scarring which closes the lumen and is followed by shrinkage

[1]**scle·rot·ic** \sklə-ˈrä-tik\ *adj* (1543) **1 :** being or relating to the sclera **2 :** of, relating to, or affected with sclerosis

[2]**sclerotic** *n* [ML *sclerotica,* fr. Gk **sklērōtos,* verbal of Gk *sklēroun* to harden] (1690) **:** SCLERA

sclerotic coat *n* (1741) **:** SCLERA

scler·o·tin \ˈskler-ə-tən, sklə-ˈrō-t^{ə}n\ *n* [prob. *scler-* + *-tin* (as in *chitin*)] (1940) **:** an insoluble tanned protein permeating and stiffening the chitin of the cuticle of arthropods

scle·ro·tium \sklə-ˈrō-sh(ē-)əm\ *n, pl* **-tia** \-sh(ē-)ə\ [NL, fr. Gk **sklērōtos*] (1871) **:** a compact mass of hardened mycelium stored with reserve food material that in some higher fungi becomes detached and remains dormant until a favorable opportunity for growth occurs — **scle·ro·tial** \-ˈrō-shəl\ *adj*

scler·o·tized \ˈskler-ə-ˌtīzd\ *adj* [ˈ*sclerotic* + *-ize* + [1]*-ed*] (ca. 1890) **:** hardened esp. by the formation of sclerotin ⟨~ insect cuticle⟩ — **scler·o·ti·za·tion** \ˌskler-e-tə-ˈzā-shən\ *n*

[1]**scoff** \ˈskäf, ˈskȯf\ *n* [ME *scof,* perh. of Scand origin; akin to obs. Dan *skof* jest; akin to OFris *skof* mockery] (14c) **1 :** an expression of scorn, derision, or contempt **:** GIBE **2 :** an object of scorn, mockery, or derision

[2]**scoff** *vi* (14c) **:** to show contempt by derisive acts or language ⟨~*ed* at the idea⟩ ~ *vt* **:** to treat or address with derision **:** MOCK — **scoff·er** *n*

syn SCOFF, JEER, GIBE, FLEER, SNEER, FLOUT mean to show one's contempt in derision or mockery. SCOFF stresses insolence, disrespect, or incredulity as motivating the derision ⟨*scoffed* at their concerns⟩. JEER suggests a coarser more undiscriminating derision ⟨the crowd *jeered* at the prisoners⟩. GIBE implies taunting either good-naturedly or in sarcastic derision ⟨hooted and *gibed* at the umpire⟩. FLEER suggests grinning or grimacing derisively ⟨the saucy jackanapes *fleered* at my credulity⟩. SNEER stresses insulting by contemptuous facial expression, phrasing, or tone of voice ⟨*sneered* at anything romantic⟩.

FLOUT stresses contempt shown by refusal to heed ⟨*flouted* the conventions of polite society⟩.

[3]**scoff** *vb* [alter. of dial. *scaff* to eat greedily] *vt* (1846) **1 :** to eat greedily ⟨~*ed* dinner⟩ **2 :** SEIZE — often used with *up* ⟨~*ed* up the free gifts⟩ ~ *vi* **:** to eat something greedily

scoff·law \-ˌlȯ\ *n* (1924) **:** a contemptuous law violator

[1]**scold** \ˈskōld\ *n* [ME *scald, scold,* perh. of Scand origin; akin to ON *skāld* poet, skald, Icel *skālda* to make scurrilous verse] (12c) **1 a :** one who scolds habitually or persistently **b :** a woman who disturbs the public peace by noisy and quarrelsome or abusive behavior **2 :** SCOLDING

[2]**scold** *vi* (14c) **1** *obs* **:** to quarrel noisily **2 :** to find fault noisily or angrily ~ *vt* **:** to censure severely or angrily **:** REBUKE — **scold·er** *n*

syn SCOLD, UPBRAID, BERATE, RAIL, REVILE, VITUPERATE mean to reproach angrily and abusively. SCOLD implies rebuking in irritation or ill temper justly or unjustly ⟨angrily *scolding* the children⟩. UPBRAID implies censuring on definite and usu. justifiable grounds ⟨*upbraided* her assistants for poor research⟩. BERATE suggests prolonged and often abusive scolding ⟨*berated* continually by an overbearing boss⟩. RAIL (*at* or *against*) stresses an unrestrained berating ⟨*railed* loudly at their insolence⟩. REVILE implies a scurrilous, abusive attack prompted by anger or hatred ⟨an alleged killer *reviled* in the press⟩. VITUPERATE suggests a violent reviling ⟨was *vituperated* for betraying his friends⟩.

scold·ing \ˈskōl-diŋ\ *n* (1547) **1 :** the action of one who scolds **2 :** a harsh reproof ⟨gave the child a sharp ~ for running into the road⟩

sco·le·cite \ˈskä-lə-ˌsīt, ˈskō-\ *n* [G *Skolezit,* fr. Gk *skōlēk-, skōlēx* worm; fr. the motion of some forms when heated] (ca. 1823) **:** a usu. fibrous zeolite mineral that is a hydrous calcium aluminum silicate

sco·lex \ˈskō-ˌleks\ *n, pl* **sco·li·ces** \-lə-ˌsēz\ *also* **sco·le·ces** \ˈskō-lə-ˌsēz, ˈskä-\ [NL *scolic-, scolex,* fr. Gk *skōlēk-, skōlēx* worm; akin to Gk *skolios* crooked, *skelos* leg — more at ISOSCELES] (1855) **:** the head of a tapeworm either in the larva or adult stage

sco·li·o·sis \ˌskō-lē-ˈō-səs\ *n, pl* **-o·ses** \-ˌsēz\ [NL, fr. Gk *skoliōsis* crookedness of a bodily part, fr. *skolios*] (ca. 1706) **:** a lateral curvature of the spine — **sco·li·ot·ic** \-ˈä-tik\ *adj*

scollop *var of* SCALLOP

scol·o·pen·dra \ˌskä-lə-ˈpen-drə\ *n* [NL, genus of centipedes, fr. L, a kind of millipede, fr. Gk *skolopendra*] (1608) **:** CENTIPEDE

scom·broid \ˈskäm-ˌbrȯid\ *n* [ultim. fr. Gk *skombros* mackerel] (1852) **:** any of a suborder (Scombroidei) of marine bony fishes (as mackerels, tunas, albacores, bonitos, and swordfishes) of great economic importance as food fishes — **scombroid** *adj*

[1]**sconce** \ˈskän(t)s\ *n* [ME, fr. AF *sconce,* **esconse* screened candle or lantern, fr. *escunser* to hide, obscure, fr. OF *escons,* pp. of *escondre* to hide, fr. VL **excondere,* alter. of L *abscondere* — more at ABSCOND] (15c) **1 :** a bracket candlestick or group of candlesticks; *also* **:** an electric light fixture patterned on a candle sconce **2 :** HEAD, SKULL

[2]**sconce** *n* [D *schans,* fr. G *Schanze*] (1571) **:** a detached defensive work

scone \ˈskōn, ˈskän\ *n* [perh. fr. D *schoonbrood* fine white bread, fr. *schoon* pure, clean + *brood* bread] (1513) **:** a rich quick bread cut into usu. triangular shapes and cooked on a griddle or baked on a sheet

[1]**scoop** \ˈskūp\ *n* [ME *scope,* fr. MD *schope;* akin to OHG *skepfen* to shape — more at SHAPE] (14c) **1 a :** a large ladle **b :** a deep shovel or similar implement for digging, dipping, or shoveling **c :** a usu. hemispherical utensil for dipping food **d :** a small spoon-shaped utensil or instrument for cutting or gouging **2 a :** the action of scooping **b :** the amount contained by a scoop **3 a :** a hollow place **:** CAVITY **b :** a part forming or surrounding an opening for channeling a fluid (as air) into a desired path **4 a :** information esp. of immediate interest **b :** BEAT 5b **5 :** a rounded and usu. low-cut neckline on a woman's garment — called also *scoop neck* — **scoop·ful** \-ˌfu̇l\ *n*

[2]**scoop** *vt* (14c) **1 a :** to take out or up with or as if with a scoop **:** DIP **b :** to pick up quickly or surreptitiously with or as if with a sweep of the hand — often used with *up* ⟨~ up the treat⟩ **2 :** to empty by ladling out the contents **3 :** to make hollow **:** DIG OUT **4 :** BEAT 5a(2) ⟨~*ed* the rival newspaper⟩ — **scoop·able** \ˈskü-pə-bəl\ *adj* — **scoop·er** *n*

scoot \ˈsküt\ *vi* [perh. alter. of earlier *scout,* of unknown origin] (1758) **1 :** to move swiftly **2 :** to slide esp. while seated ⟨~ over and let me sit down⟩ — **scoot** *n*

scoot·er \ˈskü-tər\ *n* (1916) **1 :** a child's foot-operated vehicle consisting of a narrow footboard mounted between two wheels tandem with an upright steering handle attached to the front wheel **2 :** MOTOR SCOOTER

scop \ˈshōp, ˈskōp, ˈskäp\ *n* [OE; akin to OHG *schof* poet] (bef. 12c) **:** an Old English bard or poet

[1]**scope** \ˈskōp\ *n* [It *scopo* purpose, goal, fr. Gk *skopos;* akin to Gk *skeptesthai* to watch, look at — more at SPY] (ca. 1555) **1 :** INTENTION, OBJECT **2 :** space or opportunity for unhampered motion, activity, or thought **3 :** extent of treatment, activity, or influence **4 :** range of operation: as **a :** the range of a logical operator **:** a string in predicate calculus that is governed by a quantifier **b :** a grammatical constituent that determines the interpretation of a predicate or quantifier ***syn*** see RANGE

[2]**scope** *n* [*-scope*] (1872) **1 :** any of various instruments for viewing: as **a :** MICROSCOPE **b :** TELESCOPE **c :** a telescope mounted on a firearm for use as a sight **2 :** HOROSCOPE

[3]**scope** *vt* **scoped; scop·ing** [perh. fr. [2]*scope*] (1974) **:** to look at esp. for the purpose of evaluation — often used with *out* ⟨*scoped* her out from across the room —Tim Allis⟩

-scope *n comb form* [NL *-scopium,* fr. Gk *-skopion;* akin to Gk *skeptesthai*] **:** means (as an instrument) for viewing or observing ⟨endo*scope*⟩ ⟨spectro*scope*⟩

sco·pol·amine \skō-ˈpä-lə-ˌmēn, -mən\ *n* [G *Scopolamin,* fr. NL *Scopolia,* genus of plants + G *Amin* amine] (1892) **:** a poisonous alkaloid $C_{17}H_{21}NO_4$ similar to atropine that is found in various solanaceous plants and is used for its anticholinergic effects (as preventing nausea in motion sickness and inducing mydriasis) — called also *hyoscine*

-scopy *n comb form* [Gk *-skopia,* fr. *skeptesthai*] **:** viewing **:** observation ⟨spectro*scopy*⟩

scor·bu·tic \skȯr-ˈbyü-tik\ *adj* [NL *scorbuticus,* fr. *scorbutus* scurvy, prob. of Gmc origin; akin to OE *scurf* scurf] (1655) **:** of, relating to, producing, or affected with scurvy

[1]**scorch** \ˈskȯrch\ *vb* [ME; prob. akin to ME *scorcnen* to become singed, *scorklen* to parch] *vt* (14c) **1 :** to burn a surface of so as to change its color and texture **2 a :** to dry or shrivel with or as if with intense heat **:** PARCH **b :** to afflict painfully with censure or sarcasm **3 :** DEVASTATE; *esp* **:** to destroy (as property of possible use to an advancing enemy) before abandoning — used in the phrase *scorched earth* ~ *vi* **1 :** to become scorched **2 :** to travel at great and usu. excessive speed **3 :** to cause intense heat or mental anguish ⟨~*ing* sun⟩ ⟨~*ing* fury⟩ — **scorch·ing·ly** \ˈskȯr-chiŋ-lē\ *adv*

[2]**scorch** *n* (15c) **1 :** a result of scorching **2 :** a browning of plant tissues usu. from disease or heat

[3]**scorch** *vt* [ME, perh. blend of *scoren* to score and *scocchen* to scotch] (14c) *dial Brit* **:** CUT, SLASH

scorched *adj* (1566) **:** parched or discolored by scorching

scorched–earth \ˈskȯrcht-ˈərth\ *adj* (1937) **1 :** relating to or being a military policy involving deliberate and usu. widespread destruction of property and resources (as housing and factories) so that an invading enemy cannot use them **2 :** directed toward victory or supremacy at all costs **:** RUTHLESS ⟨~ rhetoric⟩

scorch·er \ˈskȯr-chər\ *n* (1733) **:** one that scorches; *esp* **:** a very hot day

[1]**score** \ˈskȯr\ *n, pl* **scores** [ME *scor,* fr. ON *skor* notch, tally, twenty; akin to OE *scieran* to cut — more at SHEAR] (14c) **1** *or pl* **score a :** TWENTY **b :** a group of 20 things — often used in combination with a cardinal number ⟨four*score*⟩ **c :** an indefinitely large number **2 a :** a line (as a scratch or incision) made with or as if with a sharp instrument **b (1) :** a mark used as a starting point or goal **(2) :** a mark used for keeping account **3 a :** an account or reckoning orig. kept by making marks on a tally **b :** amount due **:** INDEBTEDNESS **4 :** GRUDGE ⟨a ~ to settle⟩ **5 a :** REASON, GROUND ⟨was accepted on the ~ of high academic achievement⟩ **b :** SUBJECT, TOPIC ⟨has nothing to say on that ~⟩ **6 a :** the copy of a musical composition in written or printed notation **b :** a musical composition; *specif* **:** the music for a movie or theatrical production **c :** a complete description of a dance composition in choreographic notation **7 a :** a number that expresses accomplishment (as in a game or test) or excellence (as in quality) either absolutely in points gained or by comparison to a standard **b :** an act (as a goal, run, or touchdown) in any of various games or contests that gains points **8 :** success in obtaining something (as money or drugs) esp. through illegal or irregular means **9 :** the stark inescapable facts of a situation ⟨knows the ~⟩

[2]**score** *vb* **scored; scor·ing** *vt* (14c) **1 a :** to keep a record or account of by or as if by notches on a tally **:** RECORD **b :** to enter in a record **c :** to mark with significant lines or notches (as in keeping account) **2 :** to mark with lines, grooves, scratches, or notches **3 :** BERATE, SCOLD; *also* **:** DENOUNCE **4 a (1) :** to make (a score) in a game or contest ⟨*scored* a touchdown⟩ ⟨*scored* three points⟩ **(2) :** to enable (a base runner) to make a score **(3) :** to have as a value in a game or contest **:** COUNT ⟨a touchdown ~*s* six points⟩ **b (1) :** ACHIEVE, ATTAIN ⟨*scored* a dazzling success⟩ **(2) :** ACQUIRE ⟨help a traveler ~ local drugs —Poitor Koper⟩ **(3) :** WIN 1 ⟨*scored* free tickets over the radio⟩ **5 :** to determine the merit of **:** GRADE **6 a :** to write or arrange (music) for a specific performance medium **b :** to make an orchestration of **c :** to compose a score for (a movie) ~ *vi* **1 :** to keep score in a game or contest **2 :** to make a score in a game or contest **3 a :** to gain or have the advantage **b :** to be successful: as **(1) :** to succeed in having sexual intercourse **(2) :** to manage to obtain illicit drugs **c :** [3]RATE — **scor·er** *n* — **score points :** to gain favor, status, or advantage

score·board \ˈskȯr-ˌbȯrd\ *n* (1826) **:** a large board for displaying the score of a game or match

score·card \-ˌkärd\ *n* (ca. 1877) **1 :** a card for recording the score of a game **2 :** a report or indication of the status, condition, or success of something or someone

score·keep·er \-ˌkē-pər\ *n* (1880) **:** one that keeps score; *specif* **:** an official who records the score during a game or contest

score·less \-ləs\ *adj* (1885) **:** having no score

sco·ria \ˈskȯr-ē-ə\ *n, pl* **-ri·ae** \-ē-ˌē, -ē-ˌī\ [ME, fr. L, fr. Gk *skōria,* fr. *skōr* excrement — more at SCATOLOGY] (14c) **1 :** the refuse from melting of metals or reduction of ores **:** SLAG **2 :** rough vesicular cindery lava — **sco·ri·a·ceous** \ˌskȯr-ē-ˈā-shəs\ *adj*

[1]**scorn** \ˈskȯrn\ *n* [ME, fr. AF *escharne, escar,* of Gmc origin; akin to OHG *scern* jest] (13c) **1 :** open dislike and disrespect or derision often mixed with indignation **2 :** an expression of contempt or derision **3 :** an object of extreme disdain, contempt, or derision **:** something contemptible

[2]**scorn** *vt* (13c) **:** to treat with scorn **:** reject or dismiss as contemptible or unworthy ⟨~*ed* local traditions⟩ ⟨~*ed* to reply to the charge⟩ ~ *vi* **:** to show disdain or derision **:** SCOFF ***syn*** see DESPISE — **scorn·er** *n*

scorn·ful \ˈskȯrn-fəl\ *adj* (14c) **:** full of scorn **:** CONTEMPTUOUS — **scorn·ful·ly** \-fə-lē\ *adv* — **scorn·ful·ness** *n*

scor·pae·nid \skȯr-ˈpē-nəd\ *n* [ultim. fr. Gk *skorpaina,* a kind of fish] (1885) **:** any of a family (Scorpaenidae) of marine bony fishes possessing usu. venomous spines on the fins that includes the scorpion fishes, lionfishes, and rockfishes — **scorpaenid** *adj*

Scor·pio \ˈskȯr-pē-ˌō\ *n* [L (gen. *Scorpionis*), fr. Gk *Skorpios,* lit., scorpion] (14c) **1 :** SCORPIUS **2 a :** the eighth sign of the zodiac in astrology — see ZODIAC table **b :** one born under this sign

scor·pi·on \ˈskȯr-pē-ən\ *n* [ME, fr. AF *eskorpiun,* fr. L *scorpion-, scorpio,* fr. Gk *skorpios*] (12c) **1 a :** any of an order (Scorpionida) of nocturnal arachnids that have an elongated body and a

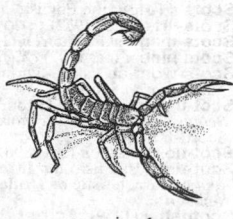

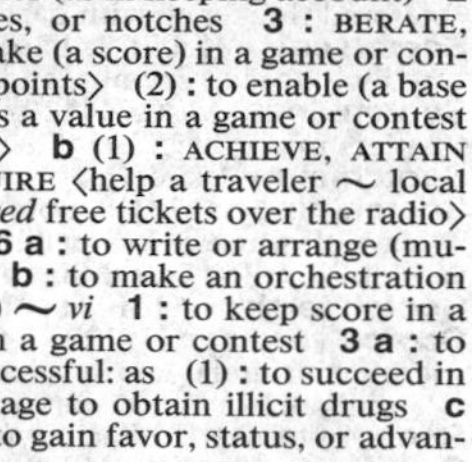
scorpion 1a

narrow segmented tail bearing a venomous stinger at the tip **b** *cap* : SCORPIO **2** : a scourge prob. studded with metal **3** : something that incites to action like the sting of an insect ‹the ~*s* of absolute necessity —Arnold Bennett›
scorpion fish *n* (1661) : any of various scorpaenid fishes (esp. genus *Scorpaena*)
scorpion fly *n* (1668) : any of a family (Panorpidae) of insects that have cylindrical bodies, a long beak with biting mouthparts, and the male genitalia enlarged into a swollen bulb; *broadly* : an insect of the order (Mecoptera) that includes this family
Scor·pi·us \ˈskȯr-pē-əs\ *n* [L (gen. *Scorpii*), fr. Gk *Skorpios*, lit., scorpion] (bef. 12c) : a southern zodiacal constellation partly in the Milky Way and between Libra and Sagittarius
scot \ˈskät\ *n* [ME, fr. ON *skot* shot, contribution — more at SHOT] (14c) : money assessed or paid
Scot \ˈskät\ *n* [ME *Scottes* Scots, fr. OE *Scottas* fr. LL *Scotus*] (bef. 12c) **1** : a member of a Celtic people of northern Ireland settling in Scotland about A.D. 500 **2 a** : a native or inhabitant of Scotland **b** : a person of Scottish descent
scot and lot *n* (15c) **1** : a parish assessment formerly laid on subjects in Great Britain according to their ability to pay **2** : obligations of all kinds taken as a whole
[1]**scotch** \ˈskäch\ *vt* [ME *scocchen* to gash, fr. AF *escocher, eschocher* to pierce] (15c) **1** *archaic* : CUT, GASH, SCORE; *also* : WOUND ‹we have ~*ed* the snake, not killed it —Shak.› **2** : to put an end to ‹~*ed* rumors of a military takeover›
[2]**scotch** *n* (15c) : a superficial cut : SCORE
[3]**scotch** *n* [origin unknown] (1639) : a chock to prevent rolling or slipping
[4]**scotch** *vt* (1642) **1** : to block with a chock **2** : HINDER, THWART
[1]**Scotch** \ˈskäch\ *adj* [contr. of *Scottish*] (1591) **1** : SCOTTISH **2** : inclined to frugality
[2]**Scotch** *n* (ca. 1700) **1** : SCOTS **2** *pl in constr* : the people of Scotland **3** *often not cap* : whiskey distilled in Scotland esp. from malted barley — called also *Scotch whisky*
[3]**Scotch** *trademark* — used for adhesive tape
Scotch bonnet *n* (1986) : a small roundish very hot chili pepper esp. of the Caribbean that is usu. red or yellow when mature
Scotch broom *n* (ca. 1818) : a deciduous broom (*Cytisus scoparius*) of western Europe that is widely cultivated for its bright yellow or partly red flowers and that has become naturalized in No. America
Scotch broth *n* (1818) : a soup made from beef or mutton and vegetables and thickened with barley
Scotch egg *n* (1809) : a hard-boiled egg wrapped in sausage meat, covered with bread crumbs, and fried
Scotch–Irish *adj* (1744) : of, relating to, or descended from Scottish settlers in northern Ireland
Scotch·man \ˈskäch-mən\ *n* (15c) : SCOTSMAN
Scotch pine *n* (1731) : a pine (*Pinus sylvestris*) of northern Europe and Asia with spreading or pendulous branches, short rigid twisted needles, and hard yellow wood that provides valuable timber
Scotch terrier *n* (1810) : SCOTTISH TERRIER
Scotch verdict *n* (1912) **1** : a verdict of not proven that is allowed by Scottish criminal law in some cases instead of a verdict of not guilty **2** : an inconclusive decision or pronouncement
Scotch·wom·an \ˈskäch-ˌwu̇-mən\ *n* (1663) : SCOTSWOMAN
Scotch woodcock *n* (1879) : buttered toast spread with anchovy paste and scrambled egg
sco·ter \ˈskō-tər\ *n, pl* **scoters** *or* **scoter** [origin unknown] (ca. 1674) : any of a genus (*Melanitta*) of sea ducks of chiefly coastal Eurasia, Canada, and the U.S. that have males with chiefly black plumage
scot–free \ˈskät-ˈfrē\ *adj* [*scot*] (1528) : completely free from obligation, harm, or penalty
sco·tia \ˈskō-sh(ē-)ə, -tē-ə\ *n* [L, fr. Gk *skotia*, fr. fem. of *skotios* dark, shadowy, fr. *skotos* darkness — more at SHADE] (1563) : a concave molding used esp. in classical architecture in the bases of columns
Scot·ic \ˈskä-tik\ *adj* (1661) : of or relating to the ancient Scots
Sco·tism \ˈskō-ˌti-zəm\ *n* (ca. 1871) : the doctrines of Duns Scotus — **Sco·tist** \ˈskō-tist\ *n*
Scot·land Yard \ˌskät-lən(d)-ˈyärd\ *n* [*Scotland Yard*, street in London, formerly the headquarters of the metropolitan police] (1864) : the detective department of the London metropolitan police
sco·to·ma \skə-ˈtō-mə\ *n, pl* **-mas** *or* **-ma·ta** \-mə-tə\ [NL, fr. ML, dimness of vision, fr. Gk *skotōmat-, skotōma*, fr. *skotoun* to darken, fr. *skotos*] (1875) : a spot in the visual field in which vision is absent or deficient
sco·to·pic \skə-ˈtō-pik, -ˈtä-\ *adj* [NL *scotopia* scotopic vision, fr. Gk *skotos* darkness + NL *-opia*] (1915) : relating to or being vision in dim light with dark-adapted eyes which involves only the retinal rods as light receptors
[1]**Scots** \ˈskäts\ *adj* [ME *Scottis*, alter. of *Scottish*] (14c) : SCOTTISH — used esp. of the people and language and in legal context
[2]**Scots** *n* (14c) : the English language of Scotland
Scots–Irish *adj* (1972) : SCOTCH-IRISH
Scots·man \ˈskäts-mən\ *n* (14c) : a native or inhabitant of Scotland
Scots pine *n* (ca. 1797) *chiefly Brit* : SCOTCH PINE
Scots·wom·an \ˈskäts-ˌwu̇-mən\ *n* (1818) : a woman who is a native or inhabitant of Scotland
Scot·ti·cism \ˈskä-tə-ˌsi-zəm\ *n* [LL *scotticus* of the ancient Scots, fr. *Scotus* Scot] (1706) : a word, phrase, or expression characteristic of Scottish English
Scot·tie \ˈskä-tē\ *n* (ca. 1896) **1** : SCOTSMAN **2** : SCOTTISH TERRIER
[1]**Scot·tish** \ˈskä-tish\ *adj* [ME, fr. *Scottes* Scotsmen] (13c) : of, relating to, or characteristic of Scotland, Scots, or the Scots — **Scot·tish·ness** \-nəs\ *n*
[2]**Scottish** *n* (1759) : SCOTS
Scottish deerhound *n* (1891) : any of an old breed of dogs of Scottish origin that have the general form of a greyhound but are larger and taller with a shaggy harsh coat
Scottish Gaelic *n* (1897) : the Gaelic language of Scotland
Scottish rite *n* (1903) **1** : a ceremonial observed by one of the Masonic systems **2** : a system or organization that observes the Scottish rite and confers the 4th through the 33d degrees
Scottish terrier *n* (1837) : any of an old Scottish breed of terrier that has short legs, a long head with small erect ears and a powerful muzzle, a broad deep chest, and a very hard coat of wiry hair
scoun·drel \ˈskau̇n-drəl\ *n* [origin unknown] (1589) : a disreputable person : RASCAL — **scoundrel** *adj* — **scoun·drel·ly** \-drə-lē\ *adj*
[1]**scour** \ˈskau̇(-ə)r\ *vb* [ME, prob. fr. MD *schuren*, fr. OF *escurer*, fr. LL *excurare* to clean off, fr. L, to take good care of, fr. *ex-* + *curare* to care for, fr. *cura* care] *vt* (14c) **1 a** : to rub hard esp. with a rough material for cleansing **b** : to remove by rubbing hard and washing **2** *archaic* : to clear (a region) of enemies or outlaws **3** : to clean by purging : PURGE **4** : to remove dirt and debris from (as a pipe or ditch) **5** : to free from foreign matter or impurities by or as if by washing ‹~ wool› **6** : to clear, dig, or remove by or as if by a powerful current of water ~ *vi* **1** : to perform a process of scouring **2** : to suffer from diarrhea or dysentery **3** : to become clean and bright by rubbing — **scour·er** *n*
[2]**scour** *n* (1681) **1** : a place scoured by running water **2** : scouring action (as of a glacier) **3** : DIARRHEA, DYSENTERY — usu. used in pl. but sing. or pl. in constr. **4** : SCOURING 1; *also* : damage done by scouring action
[3]**scour** *vb* [ME *scuren, skouren*, prob. fr. *scour*, n., (in phrase *god scour* quickly), perh. fr. ON *skūr* shower; akin to OE *scūr* shower — more at SHOWER] *vi* (13c) : to move about quickly esp. in search ~ *vt* : to go through or range over in or as if in a search
[1]**scourge** \ˈskərj *also* ˈskōrj, ˈskȯrj, ˈsku̇rj\ *n* [ME, fr. AF *escorge*, fr. *escorger* to whip, fr. VL **excorrigiare*, fr. L *ex-* + *corrigia* thong, whip] (13c) **1** : WHIP; *esp* : one used to inflict pain or punishment **2** : an instrument of punishment or criticism **3** : a cause of wide or great affliction
[2]**scourge** *vt* **scourged; scourg·ing** (14c) **1** : FLOG, WHIP **2 a** : to punish severely **b** : AFFLICT **c** : to drive as if by blows of a whip **d** : CHASTISE — **scourg·er** *n*
scour·ing \ˈskau̇(-ə)r-iŋ\ *n* (1588) **1** : material removed by scouring or cleaning **2** : the lowest rank of society — usu. used in pl.
scouring rush *n* (ca. 1818) : HORSETAIL; *esp* : one (*Equisetum hyemale*) with strongly siliceous stems formerly used for scouring
scouse \ˈskau̇s\ *n* (1840) **1** : LOBSCOUSE **2** *cap* **a** : SCOUSER **b** : a dialect of English spoken in Liverpool
Scous·er \ˈskau̇-sər\ *n* (1959) : a native or inhabitant of Liverpool, England
[1]**scout** \ˈskau̇t\ *vb* [ME, fr. AF *escuter* to listen, fr. L *auscultare* — more at AUSCULTATION] *vi* (14c) **1** : to explore an area to obtain information (as about an enemy) **2 a** : to make a search **b** : to work as a talent scout ~ *vt* **1** : to observe in order to obtain information or evaluate **2** : to explore in order to obtain information **3** : to find by making a search
[2]**scout** *n* (1534) **1 a** : one sent to obtain information; *esp* : a soldier, ship, or plane sent out in war to reconnoiter **b** : WATCHMAN, LOOKOUT **c** : TALENT SCOUT **2 a** : the act of scouting **b** : a scouting expedition : RECONNAISSANCE **3** *often cap* : a member of any of various scouting movements: as **a** : BOY SCOUT **b** : GIRL SCOUT **4** : INDIVIDUAL, PERSON — used chiefly in the phrase *good scout*
[3]**scout** *vb* [prob. of Scand origin; akin to ON *skūti* taunt; akin to OE *scēotan* to shoot — more at SHOOT] *vt* (1605) **1** : MOCK **2** : to reject scornfully ‹~*ed* his explanation as a shabby falsehood —Mark Twain› ~ *vi* : SCOFF
scout car *n* (1933) **1** : a military reconnaissance vehicle **2** : SQUAD CAR
scout·craft \ˈskau̇t-ˌkraft\ *n* (1908) : the craft, skill, or practice of a scout
scout·er \ˈskau̇-tər\ *n* (1642) **1** : one that scouts **2** *often cap* : an adult leader in the Boy Scouts of America
scouth \ˈsküth, ˈskau̇th\ *n* [origin unknown] (1591) *Scot* : PLENTY
scout·ing \ˈskau̇-tiŋ\ *n* (1590) **1** : the action of one that scouts **2** *often cap* : the activities of various national and worldwide organizations for youth directed to developing character, citizenship, and individual skills
scout·mas·ter \ˈskau̇t-ˌmas-tər\ *n* (1579) : the leader of a band of scouts; *specif* : the adult leader of a troop of Boy Scouts
scow \ˈskau̇\ *n* [D *schouw;* akin to OHG *scalta* punt pole] (1669) : a large flat-bottomed boat with broad square ends used chiefly for transporting bulk material (as ore, sand, or refuse)
[1]**scowl** \ˈskau̇(-ə)l\ *vb* [ME *skoulen*, prob. of Scand origin; akin to Dan *skule* to scowl] *vi* (14c) **1** : to contract the brow in an expression of displeasure **2** : to exhibit a threatening aspect ~ *vt* : to express with a scowl — **scowl·er** *n* — **scowl·ing·ly** \ˈskau̇-liŋ-lē\ *adv*
[2]**scowl** *n* (ca. 1520) : a facial expression of displeasure : FROWN
SCPO *abbr* senior chief petty officer
[1]**scrab·ble** \ˈskra-bəl\ *vb* **scrab·bled; scrab·bling** \-b(ə-)liŋ\ [D *schrabbelen* to scratch] *vi* (1537) **1** : SCRAWL, SCRIBBLE **2** : to scratch, claw, or grope about clumsily or frantically **3 a** : SCRAMBLE, CLAMBER **b** : to struggle by or as if by scraping or scratching ‹~ for survival› ~ *vt* **1** : SCRAMBLE **2** : SCRIBBLE — **scrab·bler** \-b(ə-)lər\ *n*
[2]**scrabble** *n* (1794) **1** : SCRAMBLE **2** : SCRIBBLE **3** : a repeated scratching or clawing
scrab·bly \ˈskra-b(ə-)lē\ *adj* (1945) **1** : SCRATCHY, RASPY **2** : SPARSE, SCRUBBY
[1]**scrag** \ˈskrag\ *n* [perh. alter. of [2]*crag*] (1542) **1** : a rawboned or scrawny person or animal **2 a** : the lean end of a neck of mutton or veal — called also *scrag end* **b** : NECK
[2]**scrag** *vt* **scragged; scrag·ging** (1752) **1 a** : to execute by hanging or garroting **b** : to wring the neck of **2 a** : CHOKE **b** : MANHANDLE **1 c** : KILL, MURDER
scrag·gly \ˈskra-g(ə-)lē\ *adj* [alter. of *scraggling*, preh. irreg. fr. [2]*scraggy*] (1869) : irregular in form or growth ‹~ hills› ‹a ~ beard›; *also* : UNKEMPT
[1]**scrag·gy** \ˈskra-gē\ *adj* **scrag·gi·er; -est** [ME *scraggi;* akin to E dial. *scrag* tree stump, uneven ground, ME *scrogge* bush] (13c) : ROUGH, JAGGED; *also* : SCRAGGLY
[2]**scraggy** *adj* **scrag·gi·er; -est** [[1]*scrag*] (ca. 1611) : being lean and long : SCRAWNY
[1]**scram** \ˈskram\ *vi* **scrammed; scram·ming** [short for *scramble*] (ca. 1928) : to go away at once ‹~, you're not wanted›

[2]**scram** *n* (1953) : a rapid emergency shutdown of a nuclear reactor

[1]**scram·ble** \ˈskram-bəl\ *vb* **scram·bled; scram·bling** \-b(ə-)liŋ\ [perh. alter. of [1]*scrabble*] *vi* (1568) **1 a :** to move with urgency or panic **b :** to move or climb hastily on all fours **2 a :** to struggle eagerly or unceremoniously for possession of something ⟨~ for front seats⟩ **b :** to get or gather something with difficulty or in irregular ways ⟨~ for a living⟩ **3 :** to spread or grow irregularly : SPRAWL, STRAGGLE **4 :** to take off quickly in response to an alert **5** *of a football quarterback* **:** to run with the ball after the pass protection breaks down ~ *vt* **1 :** to collect by scrambling **2 a :** to toss or mix together : JUMBLE **b :** to prepare (eggs) by stirring during frying **3 :** to cause or order (a fighter-interceptor group) to scramble **4 :** to disarrange the elements of a transmission (as a telephone or television signal) in order to make unintelligible to interception — **scram·bler** \-b(ə-)lər\ *n*

[2]**scramble** *n* (1648) **1 :** the act or an instance of scrambling **2 :** a disordered mass : JUMBLE ⟨a . . . ~ of patterns and textures —*Vogue*⟩ **3 :** a rapid emergency takeoff of fighter-interceptor planes

scran·nel \ˈskra-nᵊl\ *adj* [origin unknown] (1637) : HARSH, UNMELODIOUS

[1]**scrap** \ˈskrap\ *n, often attrib* [ME, fr. ON *skrap* scraps; akin to ON *skrapa* to scrape] (14c) **1** *pl* **:** fragments of discarded or leftover food **2 a :** a small detached piece ⟨a ~ of paper⟩ **b :** a fragment of something written, printed, or spoken ⟨~*s* of conversation⟩ **c :** the least bit ⟨not a ~ of evidence⟩ **3** *pl* **:** CRACKLINGS **4 a :** fragments of stock removed in manufacturing **b :** manufactured articles or parts rejected or discarded and useful only as material for reprocessing; *esp* **:** waste and discarded metal

[2]**scrap** *vt* **scrapped; scrap·ping** (ca. 1891) **1 :** to convert into scrap **2 :** to abandon or get rid of as no longer of enough worth or effectiveness to retain ⟨~ outworn methods⟩ ***syn*** see DISCARD

[3]**scrap** *n* [origin unknown] (1846) : FIGHT

[4]**scrap** *vi* **scrapped; scrap·ping** (ca. 1874) : QUARREL, FIGHT

scrap·book \ˈskrap-ˌbu̇k\ *n* (1825) : a blank book in which various items (as newspaper clippings or pictures) are collected and preserved

[1]**scrape** \ˈskrāp\ *vb* **scraped; scrap·ing** [ME, fr. ON *skrapa;* akin to OE *scrapian* to scrape, L *scrobis* ditch, Russ *skresti* to scrape] *vt* (14c) **1 a :** to remove from a surface by usu. repeated strokes of an edged instrument **b :** to make (a surface) smooth or clean with strokes of an edged instrument or an abrasive **2 a :** to grate harshly over or against **b :** to damage or injure the surface of by contact with a rough surface **c :** to draw roughly or noisily over a surface **3 :** to collect by or as if by scraping — often used with *up* or *together* ⟨~ up the price of a ticket⟩ ~ *vi* **1 :** to move in sliding contact with a rough surface **2 :** to accumulate money by small economies **3 :** to draw back the foot along the ground in making a bow **4 :** to make one's way with difficulty : barely manage or succeed ⟨just *scraped* through at school⟩ ⟨working two jobs and barely *scraping* by⟩ — **scrap·er** *n*

[2]**scrape** *n* (15c) **1 a :** the act or process of scraping **b :** a sound made by scraping **c :** a mark or injury caused by scraping : ABRASION ⟨bumps and ~*s*⟩ **2 a :** the nest of a bird consisting of a usu. shallow depression in the ground **b :** a cleared area on the forest floor made by a male deer during breeding season to attract a doe **3 :** a bow made with a drawing back of the foot along the ground **4 a :** a distressing encounter ⟨a ~ with death⟩ **b :** ALTERCATION, FIGHT

scrap heap *n* (1838) **1 :** a pile of discarded metal **2 :** the place where useless things are discarded

scra·pie \ˈskrā-pē\ *n* [[1]*scrape*] (1910) : a usu. fatal prion disease of sheep and goats characterized by twitching, excitability, intense itching, excessive thirst, emaciation, weakness, and finally paralysis

scrap·page \ˈskra-pij\ *n* (ca. 1909) **1 :** the scrapping of discarded objects (as automobiles) **2 :** the rate at which objects are scrapped

scrap·per \ˈskra-pər\ *n* (1874) : FIGHTER, QUARRELER; *also* **:** a fierce competitor

scrap·pi·ly \ˈskra-pə-lē\ *adv* (1886) : in a scrappy manner

scrap·pi·ness \ˈskra-pē-nəs\ *n* (1867) : the quality or state of being scrappy

scrap·ple \ˈskra-pəl\ *n* [dim. of [1]*scrap*] (1852) : a seasoned mixture of ground meat (as pork) and cornmeal set in a mold and served sliced and fried

[1]**scrap·py** \ˈskra-pē\ *adj* **scrap·pi·er; -est** [[1]*scrap*] (1837) : consisting of scraps ⟨~ meals⟩

[2]**scrappy** *adj* **scrap·pi·er; -est** [[3]*scrap*] (1895) **1 :** QUARRELSOME **2 :** having an aggressive and determined spirit : FEISTY

[1]**scratch** \ˈskrach\ *vb* [ME *scracchen,* prob. blend of *scratten* to scratch and *cracchen* to scratch] *vt* (15c) **1 :** to scrape or dig with the claws or nails **2 :** to rub and tear or mark the surface of with something sharp or jagged **3 a :** to scrape or rub lightly (as to relieve itching) **b :** to act on (a desire) — used with *itch* ⟨~ the itch to travel⟩ **4 :** to scrape together : collect with difficulty or by effort ⟨~ out a living⟩ **5 :** to write or draw on a surface **6 a :** to cancel or erase by or as if by drawing a line through **b :** to withdraw (an entry) from competition **7 :** SCRIBBLE, SCRAWL **8 :** to scrape along a rough surface ⟨~ a match⟩ ~ *vi* **1 :** to use the claws or nails in digging, tearing, or wounding **2 :** to scrape or rub oneself lightly (as to relieve itching) **3 :** to gather money or make a living by hard work and esp. through irregular means and sacrifice ⟨had to ~ and save for college⟩ **4 a :** to make a thin grating sound **b :** to produce a rhythmic scratching sound by moving a phonograph record back and forth under a phonograph needle **5 :** to withdraw from a contest or engagement **6 :** to make a scratch in billiards or pool — **scratch·er** *n* — **scratch one's back :** to accommodate with a favor esp. in expectation of like return — **scratch one's head :** to be or become confused or perplexed — **scratch the surface :** to make a modest effort or start

[2]**scratch** *n* (ca. 1586) **1 :** a mark or injury produced by scratching; *also* **:** a slight wound **2 :** SCRAWL, SCRIBBLE **3 :** the sound made by scratching **4 :** the starting line in a race **5 a :** a test of courage **b :** satisfactory condition, level, or performance ⟨not up to ~⟩ **6 :** a contestant whose name is withdrawn **7 :** poultry feed (as mixed grains) scattered on the litter or ground esp. to induce birds to exercise — called also *scratch feed* **8 a :** a shot in billiards or pool that ends a player's turn; *specif* **:** a shot in pool in which the cue ball falls into the pocket **b :** a shot that scores by chance : FLUKE **9** *slang* **:** MONEY, FUNDS — **from scratch 1 :** from a point at which nothing has been done ahead of time ⟨build a school system *from scratch*⟩ **2 :** without using a prepared mixture of ingredients ⟨bake a cake *from scratch*⟩

[3]**scratch** *adj* (1851) **1 :** arranged or put together with little selection : HAPHAZARD ⟨a ~ team⟩ **2 :** made as or used for a tentative effort **3 :** made or done by chance and not as intended ⟨a ~ shot⟩ **4 :** having no handicap or allowance ⟨a ~ golfer⟩ **5 :** made from scratch : made with basic ingredients ⟨a ~ cake⟩

scratch·board \ˈskrach-ˌbȯrd\ *n* (ca. 1908) : a black-surfaced cardboard having an undercoat of white clay on which an effect resembling engraving is achieved by scratching away portions of the surface to produce white lines

scratch card *n* (1982) : a card (as a lottery ticket) having a small area covered by an opaque coating which may be scraped away to reveal hidden information — called also *scratch ticket*

scratch hit *n* (1903) : a base hit resulting from a poorly hit ball

scratch pad *n* (1895) : a pad of scratch paper

scratch paper *n* (1899) : paper that may be used for casual writing

scratch sheet *n* (1939) : a racing publication listing competitors scratched from races and giving odds

scratch test *n* (1937) : a test for allergic susceptibility made by rubbing an extract of an allergen into small breaks or scratches in the skin

scratchy \ˈskra-chē\ *adj* **scratch·i·er; -est** (1827) **1 :** marked or made with scratches ⟨~ drawing⟩ ⟨~ handwriting⟩ **2 :** likely to scratch : PRICKLY ⟨~ undergrowth⟩ **3 :** making a scratching noise **4 :** uneven in quality : RAGGED **5 :** causing tingling or itching : IRRITATING ⟨~ wool⟩ **6 :** somewhat inflamed and sore ⟨a ~ throat⟩ — **scratch·i·ly** \-chə-lē\ *adv* — **scratch·i·ness** \-chē-nəs\ *n*

scrawl \ˈskrȯl\ *vb* [origin unknown] *vt* (1612) : to write or draw awkwardly, hastily, or carelessly ⟨~*ed* his name⟩ ~ *vi* **:** to write awkwardly or carelessly — **scrawl** *n* — **scrawl·er** *n* — **scrawly** \ˈskrȯ-lē\ *adj*

scraw·ny \ˈskrȯ-nē\ *adj* **scraw·ni·er; -est** [origin unknown] (1833) : exceptionally thin and slight or meager in body or size ⟨~ scrub cattle⟩ ***syn*** see LEAN — **scraw·ni·ness** *n*

screak \ˈskrēk\ *vi* [of Scand origin; akin to ON *skrækja* to screech] (ca. 1500) : to make a harsh shrill noise : SCREECH — **screak** *n* — **screaky** \ˈskrē-kē\ *adj*

[1]**scream** \ˈskrēm\ *vb* [ME *scremen;* akin to MD *schreem* scream] *vi* (12c) **1 a** (1) **:** to voice a sudden sharp loud cry (2) **:** to produce harsh high tones **b :** to make a noise resembling a scream ⟨the siren ~*ed*⟩ **c :** to move with great rapidity **2 a :** to speak or write with intense or hysterical emotion **b :** to protest, demand, or complain vehemently **c :** to laugh hysterically **3 :** to produce a vivid startling effect ~ *vt* **:** to utter with or as if with a scream

[2]**scream** *n* (1605) **1 :** a loud sharp penetrating cry or noise **2 :** a very funny person or thing

scream·er \ˈskrē-mər\ *n* (1712) **1 :** one that screams **2 :** any of a small family (Anhimidae) of So. American wetland birds having a large body, long legs, and spurred wings **3 :** a sensationally startling headline

scream·ing \ˈskrē-miŋ\ *adj* (1848) **1 :** so striking or conspicuous as to attract notice as if by screaming ⟨~ headlines⟩ ⟨dressed in ~ red⟩ **2 :** so funny as to provoke screams of laughter ⟨a ~ farce⟩ **3 :** extremely fast or powerful ⟨a ~ line drive⟩ — **scream·ing·ly** *adv*

screaming mee·mies \-ˈmē-mēz\ *n pl but sing in constr* [origin unknown] (1942) : nervous hysteria : JITTERS

scree \ˈskrē\ *n* [Sc & northern E dial., of Scand origin; akin to ON *skritha* landslide, fr. *skrītha* to creep; akin to OHG *scrītan* to go, Lith *skriesti* to turn] (ca. 1781) : an accumulation of loose stones or rocky debris lying on a slope or at the base of a hill or cliff : TALUS

[1]**screech** \ˈskrēch\ *n* (1560) **1 :** a high shrill piercing cry usu. expressing pain or terror **2 :** a sound resembling a screech

[2]**screech** *vb* [alter. of earlier *scritch,* fr. ME *scrichen;* akin to ON *skrækja* to screech] *vi* (1577) **1 :** to utter a high shrill piercing cry : make an outcry usu. in terror or pain **2 :** to make a shrill high-pitched sound resembling a screech; *also* **:** to move with such a sound ⟨the car ~*ed* to a stop⟩ ~ *vt* **:** to utter with or as if with a screech — **screech·er** *n*

screech·ing \ˈskrē-chiŋ\ *adj* (1953) : ABRUPT, SUDDEN ⟨her career came to a ~ halt⟩

screech owl *n* (1593) **1 :** BARN OWL **2 :** any of various New World owls (genus *Otus*); *esp* **:** either of two small owls (*O. asio* of eastern No. America and *O. kennicottii* of western No. America) with a pair of tufts of lengthened feathers on the head resembling ears

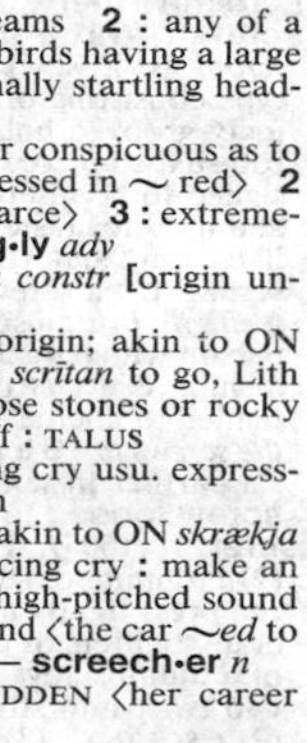

screech owl 2

screechy \ˈskrē-chē\ *adj* (ca. 1830) : producing a screech

screed \ˈskrēd\ *n* [ME *screde* fragment, alter. of OE *scrēade* — more at SHRED] (ca. 1789) **1 a :** a lengthy discourse **b :** an informal piece of writing (as a personal letter) **c :** a ranting piece of writing **2 :** a strip (as of a plaster of the thickness planned for the coat) laid on as a guide **3 :** a leveling device drawn over freshly poured concrete

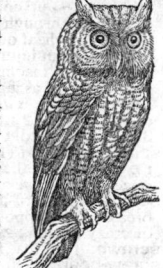

[1]**screen** \ˈskrēn\ *n* [ME *screne,* fr. AF *escren,* fr. MD *scherm;* akin to OHG *skirm* shield; prob. akin to Skt *carman* skin, *kr̥ṇāti* he injures — more at SHEAR] (14c) **1 :** a protective or ornamental device (as a movable partition) shielding an area from heat or drafts or from view **2 :** something that shelters, protects, or hides: as **a :** a growth or stand of trees, shrubs, or plants **b :** a protective formation of troops, ships, or planes **c :** something that covers or disguises the true nature (as of an activity or feeling) ⟨his geniality is just a ~⟩ **d** (1) **:** a maneuver in various sports (as basketball or ice hockey) whereby an opponent is legally impeded or the opponent's view of the play is momentarily blocked (2) **:** SCREEN PASS **3 a :** a perforated plate or cylinder or a meshed wire or cloth fabric usu. mounted and used to separate coarser from finer parts **b :** a system for examining and separating

into different groups **c** : a piece of apparatus designed to prevent agencies in one part from affecting other parts ⟨an optical ~⟩ **d** : a frame holding a usu. metallic netting used esp. in a window or door to exclude pests (as insects) **4 a** : a flat surface on which a picture or series of pictures is projected or reflected **b** : the surface on which the image appears in an electronic display (as in a television set, radar receiver, or computer terminal); *also* : the information displayed on a computer screen at one time **5** : a glass plate ruled with crossing opaque lines through which an image is photographed in making a halftone **6** : the motion-picture medium or industry

[2]**screen** *vt* (15c) **1** : to guard from injury or danger **2 a** : to give shelter or protection to with or as if with a screen **b** : to separate with or as if with a screen; *also* : to shield (an opponent) from a play or from view of a play **3 a** : to pass (as coal, gravel, or ashes) through a screen to separate the fine part from the coarse; *also* : to remove by a screen **b** (1) : to examine usu. methodically in order to make a separation into different groups (2) : to select or eliminate by a screening process (3) : to test or examine for the presence of something (as a disease) ⟨patients were ~*ed* for hepatitis⟩ **4** : to provide with a screen to keep out pests (as insects) **5 a** (1) : to present (as a motion picture) for viewing on a screen (2) : to view the presentation of (as a motion picture) **b** : to present in a motion picture ~ *vi* **1** : to appear on a motion-picture screen **2** : to provide a screen in a game or sport ***syn*** see HIDE — **screen·able** \ˈskrē-nə-bəl\ *adj* — **screen·er** *n*

screen·ful \ˈskrēn-ˌfu̇l\ *n* (1966) : the amount of information visible at one time on a display screen

screen·ing \ˈskrē-niŋ\ *n* (1725) **1** : the act or process of one that screens **2** *pl but sing or pl in constr* : material (as waste or fine coal) separated out by means of a screen **3** : metal or plastic mesh (as for window screens) **4** : a showing of a motion picture

screen·land \ˈskrēn-ˌland\ *n* (1925) : FILMDOM

screen memory *n* (1923) : a recollection of early childhood that may be falsely recalled or magnified in importance and that masks another memory of deep emotional significance

screen pass *n* (ca. 1949) : a forward pass in football to a receiver at or behind the line of scrimmage who is protected by a screen of blockers

screen·play \ˈskrēn-ˌplā\ *n* (1916) : the script and often shooting directions of a story prepared for motion-picture production

screen saver *n* (1982) : a computer program that usu. displays various images on the screen of a computer that is on but not in use

screen·shot \ˈskrēn-ˌshät\ *n* (1983) : an image that shows the contents of a computer display

screen test *n* (1927) : a short film sequence for assessing the ability or suitability of a person for a motion-picture role — **screen–test** *vt*

screen·writ·er \ˈskrēn-ˌrī-tər\ *n* (1921) : a writer of screenplays

[1]**screw** \ˈskrü\ *n* [ME *scrue,* fr. MF *escroe* female screw, nut, fr. ML *scrofa,* fr. L, sow] (15c) **1 a** : a simple machine of the inclined plane type consisting of a spirally grooved solid cylinder and a correspondingly grooved hollow cylinder into which it fits **b** : a nail-shaped or rod-shaped piece with a spiral groove and a slotted or recessed head designed to be inserted into material by rotating (as with a screwdriver) and used for fastening pieces of solid material together **2 a** : a screwlike form : SPIRAL **b** : a turn of a screw; *also* : a twist like the turn of a screw **c** : a screwlike device (as a corkscrew) **3** : a worn-out horse **4** *chiefly Brit* : a small packet (as of tobacco) **5** : a prison guard **6** : a person who bargains shrewdly; *also* : SKINFLINT **7** : a propeller esp. of a ship **8 a** : THUMBSCREW 1 **b** : pressure or punitive measures intended to coerce — used chiefly in the phrase *put the screws on* or *put the screws to* **9 a** *usu vulgar* : an act of sexual intercourse **b** *usu vulgar* : a partner in sexual intercourse — **screw·like** \-ˌlīk\ *adj* — **have a screw loose** : to be mentally unbalanced

[2]**screw** *vt* (1605) **1 a** (1) : to attach, fasten, or close by means of a screw (2) : to unite or separate by means of a screw or a twisting motion (3) : to press tightly in a device (as a vise) operated by a screw (4) : to operate, tighten, or adjust by means of a screw (5) : to torture by means of a thumbscrew **b** : to cause to rotate spirally about an axis **2 a** (1) : to twist into strained configurations : CONTORT ⟨~*ed* up his face⟩ (2) : SQUINT (3) : CRUMPLE **b** : to furnish with a spiral groove or ridge : THREAD **3** : to increase the intensity, quantity, or capability of ⟨trying to ~ up courage to confess —Will Scott⟩ **4 a** (1) : to mistreat or exploit through extortion, trickery, or unfair actions; *esp* : to deprive of or cheat out of something due or expected (2) : to treat so as to bring about injury or loss (as to a person's reputation) ⟨use the available Federal machinery to ~ our political enemies —J. W. Dean III⟩ — often used as a generalized curse ⟨~ you!⟩ **b** : to extract by pressure or threat **5** *usu vulgar* : to copulate with ~ *vi* **1** : to rotate like or as a screw **2** : to turn or move with a twisting or writhing motion **3** *usu vulgar* : COPULATE — **screw·er** *n*

screw around *vi* (1939) **1** : to waste time with unproductive activity : DALLY **2** : to have sexual relations with someone outside of a marriage or steady relationship : be sexually promiscuous

[1]**screw·ball** \ˈskrü-ˌbȯl\ *n* (1908) **1** : a baseball pitch that spins and breaks in the opposite direction to a curve **2** : a whimsical, eccentric, or crazy person : ZANY

[2]**screwball** *adj* (ca. 1936) : crazily eccentric or whimsical : ZANY

screw·bean \ˈskrü-ˌbēn\ *n* (1866) **1** : a leguminous shrub or small tree (*Prosopis pubescens*) of the southwestern U.S. and northern Mexico having spirally twisted pods with sweet pulp — called also *screwbean mesquite* **2** : the pod of the screwbean

screw·driv·er \ˈskrü-ˌdrī-vər\ *n* (1779) **1** : a tool for turning screws **2** : vodka and orange juice served with ice

screw eye *n* (1873) : a wood screw with a head in the form of a loop

screw jack *n* (1719) : a screw-operated jack for lifting, exerting pressure, or adjusting position (as of a machine part)

screw pine *n* (1836) : any of a genus (*Pandanus* of the family Pandanaceae, the screw-pine family) of tropical monocotyledonous Old World trees or shrubs with slender palmlike stems, often huge prop roots, and terminal crowns of swordlike leaves

screw propeller *n* (1839) : PROPELLER

screw thread *n* (ca. 1812) **1** : the projecting helical rib of a screw **2** : one complete turn of a screw thread

screw·up \ˈskrü-ˌəp\ *n* (ca. 1960) **1** : one who screws up **2** : BOTCH, BLUNDER

screw up *vt* (1680) **1** : to tighten, fasten, or lock by or as if by a screw **2 a** : BUNGLE, BOTCH **b** : to cause to act or function in a crazy or confused way : CONFOUND, DISTURB ~ *vi* : to botch an activity or undertaking

screw·worm \ˈskrü-ˌwərm\ *n* (1879) **1** : a blowfly (*Cochliomyia hominivorax*) of the warmer parts of America whose larva develops in sores or wounds or in the nostrils of mammals including humans with serious or sometimes fatal results; *esp* : its larva **2** : any of several flies other than the screwworm and esp. their larvae which parasitize the flesh of mammals

screwy \ˈskrü-ē\ *adj* **screw·i·er; -est** (1887) **1** : crazily absurd, eccentric, or unusual **2** : CRAZY, INSANE — **screw·i·ness** *n*

scrib·al \ˈskrī-bəl\ *adj* (1857) : of, relating to, or due to a scribe

scrib·ble \ˈskri-bəl\ *vb* **scrib·bled; scrib·bling** \-b(ə-)liŋ\ [ME *scriblen,* fr. ML *scribillare,* fr. L *scribere* to write] *vt* (15c) **1** : to write hastily or carelessly without regard to legibility or form **2** : to cover with careless or worthless writings or drawings ~ *vi* : to write or draw hastily and carelessly — **scribble** *n*

scrib·bler \ˈskri-b(ə-)lər\ *n* (ca. 1553) **1** : one that scribbles **2** : a minor or insignificant author

[1]**scribe** \ˈskrīb\ *n* [ME, fr. L *scriba* official writer, fr. *scribere* to write; akin to Gk *skariphasthai* to scratch an outline] (14c) **1** : a member of a learned class in ancient Israel through New Testament times studying the Scriptures and serving as copyists, editors, teachers, and jurists **2 a** : an official or public secretary or clerk **b** : a copier of manuscripts **3** : WRITER; *specif* : JOURNALIST

[2]**scribe** *vi* **scribed; scrib·ing** (1782) : to work as a scribe : WRITE

[3]**scribe** *vt* **scribed; scrib·ing** [prob. short for *describe*] (1678) **1** : to mark a line on by cutting or scratching with a pointed instrument **2** : to make by cutting or scratching

[4]**scribe** *n* (1812) : SCRIBER

scrib·er \ˈskrī-bər\ *n* (ca. 1836) : a sharp-pointed tool for making marks and esp. for marking off material (as wood or metal) to be cut

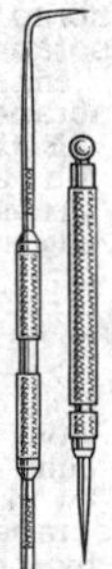

scriber

scrieve \ˈskrēv\ *vi* [perh. of Scand origin; akin to ON *skrefa* to stride] (1785) *Scot* : to move along swiftly and smoothly

scrim \ˈskrim\ *n* [origin unknown] (1792) **1** : a durable plain-woven usu. cotton fabric for use in clothing, curtains, building, and industry **2** : a theater drop that appears opaque when a scene in front is lighted and transparent or translucent when a scene in back is lighted **3** : something likened to a theater scrim

[1]**scrim·mage** \ˈskri-mij\ *n* [ME *scrymmage,* alter. of *skyrmissh* skirmish] (15c) **1 a** : a minor battle : SKIRMISH **b** : a confused fight : SCUFFLE **2 a** : the interplay between two football teams that begins with the snap of the ball and continues until the ball is dead **b** : practice play (as in football or basketball) between two squads

[2]**scrimmage** *vb* **scrim·maged; scrim·mag·ing** *vi* (ca. 1825) : to take part in a scrimmage ~ *vt* : to play a scrimmage against — **scrim·mag·er** *n*

scrimmage line *n* (1909) : LINE OF SCRIMMAGE

scrimp \ˈskrimp\ *vb* [perh. of Scand origin; akin to Sw *skrympa* to shrink, MLG *schrempen* to contract — more at SHRIMP] *vt* (ca. 1774) **1** : to be stingy in providing for **2** : to make too small, short, or scanty ~ *vi* : to be frugal or stingy — **scrimpy** \ˈskrim-pē\ *adj*

scrim·shan·der \ˈskrim-ˌshan-dər\ *n* [origin unknown] (1851) **1** : SCRIMSHAW **2** : a person who creates scrimshaw

[1]**scrim·shaw** \ˈskrim-ˌshȯ\ *vb* [origin unknown] *vt* (ca. 1826) : to carve or engrave into scrimshaw ~ *vi* : to produce scrimshaw

[2]**scrimshaw** *n* (ca. 1864) **1** : any of various carved or engraved articles made orig. by American whalers usu. from baleen or whale ivory **2** : scrimshawed work **3** : the art, practice, or technique of producing scrimshaw

[1]**scrip** \ˈskrip\ *n* [ME *scrippe,* fr. ML *scrippum* pilgrim's knapsack] (13c) *archaic* : a small bag or wallet

[2]**scrip** *n* [alter. of *script*] (1590) **1** : a short writing (as a certificate, schedule, or list) **2** : a small piece **3 a** : any of various documents used as evidence that the holder or bearer is entitled to receive something (as a fractional share of stock or an allotment of land) **b** : paper currency or a token issued for temporary use in an emergency

[3]**scrip** *n* (1966) : PRESCRIPTION 4a

[1]**script** \ˈskript\ *n* [ME, fr. L *scriptum* thing written, fr. neut. of *scriptus,* pp. of *scribere* to write — more at SCRIBE] (14c) **1 a** : something written : TEXT **b** : an original or principal instrument or document **c** (1) : MANUSCRIPT 1 (2) : the written text of a stage play, screenplay, or broadcast; *specif* : the one used in production or performance **2 a** : a style of printed letters that resembles handwriting **b** : written characters : HANDWRITING **c** : ALPHABET **3** : a plan of action

[2]**script** *vt* (1935) **1** : to prepare a script for or from **2** : to provide carefully considered details for (as a plan of action) ⟨an event carefully ~*ed* to attract attention⟩

[3]**script** *n* (1951) : PRESCRIPTION 4a

script·er \ˈskrip-tər\ *n* (1939) : SCRIPTWRITER

scrip·to·ri·um \skrip-ˈtȯr-ē-əm\ *n, pl* **-ria** \-ē-ə\ [ML, fr. L *scribere*] (1774) : a copying room for scribes esp. in a medieval monastery

scrip·tur·al \ˈskrip(t)-sh(ə-)rəl\ *adj* (1641) : of, relating to, contained in, or according to a sacred writing; *esp* : BIBLICAL — **scrip·tur·al·ly** *adv*

scrip·ture \ˈskrip(t)-shər\ *n* [ME, fr. LL *scriptura,* fr. L, act or product of writing, fr. *scriptus*] (14c) **1 a** (1) *cap* : the books of the Bible — often used in pl. (2) *often cap* : a passage from the Bible **b** : a body of writings considered sacred or authoritative **2** : something written ⟨the primitive man's awe for any ~ —George Santayana⟩

script·writ·er \ˈskrip(t)-ˌrī-tər\ *n* (1935) : a person who writes scripts

scriv·en·er \ˈskriv-nər, ˈskri-və-\ *n* [ME *scriveiner,* alter. of *scrivein,* fr. AF *escrivein,* fr. VL **scriban-, scriba,* alter. of L *scriba* scribe] (14c) **1** : a professional or public copyist or writer : SCRIBE **2** : NOTARY PUBLIC

scrod *also* **schrod** \ˈskräd\ *n* [prob. fr. Brit. dial. (Cornwall) *scrawed,* pp. of *scraw, scrawl* to split, salt, and lightly dry (young fish)] (1841) : a young fish (as a cod or haddock); *esp* : one split and boned for cooking

scrof·u·la \ˈskrȯ-fyə-lə, ˈskrä-\ *n* [NL, back-formation fr. LL *scrofulae,* pl., swellings of the lymph nodes of the neck, fr. pl. of *scrofula,* dim. of

L *scrofa* breeding sow] (1791) **:** tuberculosis of lymph nodes esp. in the neck

scrof·u·lous \ˈskrȯf-yə-ləs\ *adj* (1612) **1 :** of, relating to, or affected with scrofula **2 a :** having a diseased run-down appearance **b :** morally contaminated ⟨~ characters . . . so quick to smear —John Garrity⟩

^{1}**scroll** \ˈskrōl\ *n* [ME *scrowle,* blend of *rolle* roll and *scrowe* scrap, scroll (fr. AF *escrowe,* of Gmc origin; akin to MD *schrode* piece cut off, OHG *scrōt*) — more at SHRED] (15c) **1 a :** a roll (as of papyrus, leather, or parchment) for writing a document **b** *archaic* **:** a written message **c :** ROSTER, LIST **d :** a riband with rolled ends often inscribed with a motto **2 a :** something resembling a scroll in shape; *esp* **:** a spiral or convoluted form in ornamental design derived from the curves of a loosely or partly rolled parchment scroll **b :** the curved head of a bowed stringed musical instrument — see VIOLIN illustration — **scrolled** \ˈskrōld\ *adj*

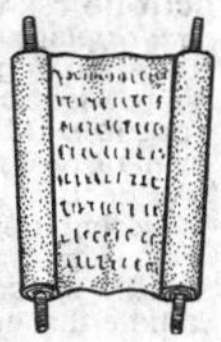

scroll 1a

^{2}**scroll** *vi* (1973) **1 :** to move text or graphics up or down or across a display screen as if by unrolling a scroll **2 :** to progress, move, or be revealed as if by the unrolling of a scroll ⟨watch scenery ~ by large picture windows —David Yeadon⟩ ~ *vt* **:** to cause (text or graphics on a display screen) to move in scrolling

scroll saw *n* (1851) **1 :** FRETSAW **2 :** a machine saw with a table for supporting the material and a narrow vertically reciprocating blade for cutting curved lines or ornamental openwork patterns

scroll·work \ˈskrōl-ˌwərk\ *n* (1739) **:** ornamentation characterized by scrolls; *esp* **:** fancy designs in wood often made with a scroll saw

scrooge \ˈskrüj\ *n, often cap* [Ebenezer *Scrooge,* character in the story *A Christmas Carol* (1843) by Charles Dickens] (1899) **:** a miserly person

scro·tum \ˈskrō-təm\ *n, pl* **scro·ta** \-tə\ *or* **scrotums** [L; akin to L *scrautum* quiver] (1597) **:** the external pouch that in most mammals contains the testes — **scro·tal** \ˈskrō-tᵊl\ *adj*

scrouge \ˈskrau̇j, ˈskrüj\ *vb* **scrouged; scroug·ing** [alter. of E dial. *scruze* to squeeze] (1755) *chiefly dial* **:** CROWD, PRESS

scrounge \ˈskrau̇nj\ *vb* **scrounged; scroung·ing** [alter. of E dial. *scrunge* to wander about idly] *vt* (ca. 1909) **1 :** STEAL, SWIPE **2 a :** to get as needed by or as if by foraging, scavenging, or borrowing ⟨*scrounging* enough money for a bus ticket⟩ **b :** FINAGLE, WHEEDLE — often used with *up* ~ *vi* **:** to search about and turn up something needed from whatever source is available; *also* **:** to actively seek money, work, or sustenance from any available source — **scroung·er** *n*

scroungy \ˈskrau̇n-jē\ *adj* **scroung·i·er; -est** (ca. 1960) **:** being shabby, dirty, or unkempt

^{1}**scrub** \ˈskrəb\ *n, often attrib* [ME, alter. of *schrobbe, schrubbe* shrub — more at SHRUB] (14c) **1 a :** a stunted tree or shrub **b :** vegetation consisting chiefly of scrubs **c :** a tract covered with scrub **2 :** a domestic animal of mixed or unknown parentage and usu. inferior conformation **:** MONGREL **3 :** a person of insignificant size or standing **4 :** a player not belonging to the first string

^{2}**scrub** *vb* **scrubbed; scrub·bing** [of LG or Scand origin; akin to MLG & MD *schrubben* to scrub, Sw *skrubba*] *vt* (ca. 1595) **1 a (1) :** to clean with hard rubbing **:** SCOUR **(2) :** to remove by scrubbing **b :** to subject to friction **:** RUB **2 :** WASH 6c(2) **3 :** CANCEL, ELIMINATE ⟨*scrubbed* the flight because of bad weather⟩ ~ *vi* **1 :** to use hard rubbing in cleaning **2 :** to prepare for performing surgery by scrubbing oneself — **scrub·ba·ble** \ˈskrə-bə-bəl\ *adj*

^{3}**scrub** *n* (1621) **1 :** an act or instance of scrubbing; *esp* **:** CANCELLATION **2 a :** one that scrubs **b :** a powerful and esp. cosmetic cleanser **3** *pl* **:** loose-fitting clothing worn by hospital staff ⟨surgical ~*s*⟩

^{1}**scrubbed** \ˈskrə-bəd\ *adj* [^{1}*scrub*] (1596) *archaic* **:** SCRUBBY 1

^{2}**scrubbed** \ˈskrəbd\ *adj* [fr. pp. of ^{2}*scrub*] (1948) **:** giving the impression of being clean or wholesome as if from scrubbing ⟨days when studios manufactured ~ public images for their stars —Sally Helgesen⟩

scrub·ber \ˈskrə-bər\ *n* (1837) **:** one that scrubs; *esp* **:** an apparatus for removing impurities esp. from gases

scrub brush *n* (1897) **:** a brush with hard bristles for heavy cleaning — called also *scrubbing brush*

scrub·by \ˈskrə-bē\ *adj* **scrub·bi·er; -est** [^{1}*scrub*] (1591) **1 :** inferior in size or quality **:** STUNTED ⟨~ cattle⟩ **2 :** covered with or consisting of scrub **3 :** SHABBY, PALTRY

scrub jay *n* (1923) **:** either of two crestless jays (*Aphelocoma californica* of the western U.S. and Mexico and *A. coerulescens* of Florida) typically of scrub or chaparral that have a blue head, tail, and wings and a brownish back

scrub·land \ˈskrəb-ˌland\ *n* (1779) **:** land covered with scrub

scrub nurse *n* (1927) **:** a nurse who assists the surgeon in an operating room

scrub oak *n* (1766) **:** any of various chiefly American oaks (as *Quercus ilicifolia* of the northeastern U.S.) of small size and usu. shrubby habit

scrub pine *n* (1791) **:** a pine of dwarf, straggly, or scrubby growth usu. by reason of environmental conditions; *specif* **:** a pine tree unsuitable for lumber by reason of inferior or defective growth

scrub typhus *n* (1929) **:** an acute febrile bacterial disease that is caused by a rickettsia (*Orientia tsutsugamushi* syn. *Rickettsia tsutsugamushi*) transmitted by mite larvae, resembles typhus transmitted by lice, and is widespread in the western Pacific area — called also *tsutsugamushi disease*

scrub·wom·an \ˈskrəb-ˌwu̇-mən\ *n* (1873) **:** CHARWOMAN

scruff \ˈskrəf\ *n* [alter. of earlier *scuff,* of unknown origin] (1790) **:** the back of the neck **:** NAPE

scruffy \ˈskrə-fē\ *adj* **scruff·i·er; -est** [E dial. *scruff* something worthless] (1871) **:** UNKEMPT, SLOVENLY, SHAGGY ⟨a ~ neighborhood⟩ ⟨a ~ beard⟩ — **scruff·i·ly** \-fə-lē\ *adv* — **scruff·i·ness** \-fē-nəs\ *n*

scrum \ˈskrəm\ *n* [short for *scrummage,* alter. of *scrimmage*] (1857) **1 a** *or* **scrum·mage** \ˈskrə-mij\ **:** a rugby play in which the forwards of each side come together in a tight formation and struggle to gain possession of the ball using their feet when it is tossed in among them; *also* **:** the arrangement of players in a scrum **b :** a usu. brief and disorderly struggle or fight **:** SCRAPE, SCUFFLE **2 a** *Brit* **:** MADHOUSE 2 **b :** a usu. tightly packed or disorderly crowd **:** THRONG — **scrummage** *vi*

scrump·tious \ˈskrəm(p)-shəs\ *adj* [perh. alter. of *sumptuous*] (1830) **:** DELIGHTFUL, EXCELLENT; *esp* **:** DELICIOUS — **scrump·tious·ly** *adv*

^{1}**scrunch** \ˈskrənch, ˈskru̇nch\ *vb* [alter. of ^{1}*crunch*] *vt* (ca. 1790) **1 :** CRUNCH, CRUSH **2 a :** to draw or squeeze together tightly **b :** CRUMPLE — often used with *up* **c :** to cause (as one's features) to draw together — usu. used with *up* ~ *vi* **1 :** to move with or make a crunching sound **2 :** CROUCH, HUNCH; *also* **:** SQUEEZE

^{2}**scrunch** *n* (1857) **:** a crunching sound

scrunch·ie *or* **scrunchy** \ˈskrən-chē, ˈskru̇n-\ *n, pl* **scrunchies** (1988) **:** a fabric-covered elastic used for holding back hair (as in a ponytail)

^{1}**scru·ple** \ˈskrü-pəl\ *n* [ME *scrupil, scriple,* fr. AF *scruple,* fr. L *scrupulus* a unit of weight, dim. of *scrupus* sharp stone] (14c) **1 —** see WEIGHT table **2 :** a minute part or quantity **:** IOTA

^{2}**scruple** *n* [ME *scripil, scrupill,* fr. AF *scruble,* fr. L *scrupulus,* dim. of *scrupus* source of uneasiness, lit., sharp stone] (15c) **1 :** an ethical consideration or principle that inhibits action **2 :** the quality or state of being scrupulous **3 :** mental reservation ***syn*** see QUALM

^{3}**scruple** *vi* **scru·pled; scru·pling** \-p(ə-)liŋ\ (1627) **1 :** to have scruples **2 :** to show reluctance on grounds of conscience **:** HESITATE

scru·pu·los·i·ty \ˌskrü-pyə-ˈlä-sə-tē\ *n* (1526) **1 :** the quality or state of being scrupulous **2 :** ^{2}SCRUPLE 1

scru·pu·lous \ˈskrü-pyə-ləs\ *adj* [ME, fr. L *scrupulosus,* fr. *scrupulus*] (15c) **1 :** having moral integrity **:** acting in strict regard for what is considered right or proper **2 :** punctiliously exact **:** PAINSTAKING ⟨working with ~ care⟩ ***syn*** see UPRIGHT, CAREFUL — **scru·pu·lous·ly** *adv* — **scru·pu·lous·ness** *n*

scru·ta·ble \ˈskrü-tə-bəl\ *adj* [LL *scrutabilis* searchable, fr. L *scrutari*] (ca. 1600) **:** capable of being deciphered **:** COMPREHENSIBLE

scru·ti·neer \ˌskrü-tə-ˈnir\ *n* (1557) **1 :** one that examines **2** *Brit* **:** one who takes or counts votes

scru·ti·nise *Brit var of* SCRUTINIZE

scru·ti·nize \ˈskrü-tə-ˌnīz\ *vb* **-nized; -niz·ing** *vt* (1671) **:** to examine closely and minutely ~ *vi* **:** to make a scrutiny — **scru·ti·niz·er** *n*

syn SCRUTINIZE, SCAN, INSPECT, EXAMINE mean to look at or over. SCRUTINIZE stresses close attention to minute detail ⟨*scrutinized* the hospital bill⟩. SCAN implies a surveying from point to point often suggesting a cursory overall observation ⟨*scanned* the wine list⟩. INSPECT implies scrutinizing for errors or defects ⟨*inspected* my credentials⟩. EXAMINE suggests a scrutiny in order to determine the nature, condition, or quality of a thing ⟨*examined* the specimens⟩.

scru·ti·ny \ˈskrü-tə-nē, ˈskrüt-nē\ *n, pl* **-nies** [L *scrutinium,* fr. *scrutari* to search, examine, prob. fr. *scruta* trash] (1604) **1 :** a searching study, inquiry, or inspection **:** EXAMINATION **2 :** a searching look **3 :** close watch **:** SURVEILLANCE

SCSI *abbr* small computer system interface

scu·ba \ˈskü-bə\ *n, often attrib* [*s*elf-*c*ontained *u*nderwater *b*reathing *a*pparatus] (1952) **:** an apparatus utilizing a portable supply of compressed gas (as air) supplied at a regulated pressure and used for breathing while swimming underwater

scuba diver *n* (1958) **:** one who swims underwater with the aid of scuba gear — **scuba dive** *vi*

^{1}**scud** \ˈskəd\ *vi* **scud·ded; scud·ding** [perh. fr. MD *schudden* to shake] (1532) **1 :** to move or run swiftly esp. as if driven forward ⟨clouds *scudding* across the sky⟩ **2 :** to run before a gale

^{2}**scud** *n* (1609) **1 :** the action of scudding **:** RUSH **2 a :** loose vapory clouds driven swiftly by the wind **b (1) :** a slight sudden shower **(2) :** mist, rain, snow, or spray driven by the wind **c :** a gust of wind

scu·do \ˈskü-(ˌ)dō\ *n, pl* **scu·di** \-(ˌ)dē\ [It, lit., shield, fr. L *scutum* — more at ESQUIRE] (1644) **1 :** a gold or silver coin formerly used in Italy **2 :** a unit of value equivalent to a scudo

^{1}**scuff** \ˈskəf\ *vb* [origin unknown] *vi* (1768) **1 a :** to walk without lifting the feet **:** SHUFFLE **b :** to poke or shuffle a foot in exploration or embarrassment **2 :** to become scratched, chipped, or roughened by wear ⟨a countertop that won't ~⟩ ~ *vt* **1 :** ^{3}CUFF **2 a :** to scrape (the feet) along a surface while walking or back and forth while standing **b :** to poke at with the toe **3 :** to scratch, gouge, or wear away the surface of ⟨~*ed* my shoes⟩

^{2}**scuff** *n* (1899) **1 a :** a noise of or as if of scuffing **b :** the act or an instance of scuffing **c :** a mark or injury caused by scuffing **2 :** a flat-soled slipper without quarter or heel strap — compare MULE

scuf·fle \ˈskə-fəl\ *vi* **scuf·fled; scuf·fling** \-f(ə-)liŋ\ [perh. freq. of *scuff*] (1590) **1 a :** to struggle at close quarters with disorder and confusion **b :** to struggle (as by working odd jobs) to get by **2 a :** to move with a quick shuffling gait **:** SCURRY **b :** SHUFFLE — **scuffle** *n*

scuffle hoe *n* [D *schoffel* hoe, fr. MD, shovel] (1856) **:** a garden hoe that has both edges sharpened and can be pushed forward or drawn back

^{1}**scull** \ˈskəl\ *n* [ME *skulle*] (14c) **1 a :** an oar used at the stern of a boat to propel it forward with a thwartwise motion **b :** either of a pair of oars usu. less than 10 feet (3 meters) in length and operated by one person **2 :** a racing shell propelled by one or two persons using sculls

^{2}**scull** *vt* (1624) **:** to propel (a boat) by sculls or by a large oar worked thwartwise ~ *vi* **:** to scull a boat — **scull·er** *n*

scul·lery \ˈskə-lə-rē, ˈskəl-rē\ *n, pl* **-ler·ies** [ME *squilerie, sculerie* department of household in charge of dishes, fr. AF *esquilerie,* fr. *escuele, eskel* bowl, fr. L *scutella* drinking bowl — more at SCUTTLE] (15c) **:** a room for cleaning and storing dishes and cooking utensils and for doing messy kitchen work

scul·lion \ˈskəl-yən\ *n* [ME *sculioun*] (15c) **:** a kitchen helper

scul·pin \ˈskəl-pən\ *n, pl* **sculpins** *also* **sculpin** [origin unknown] (1672) **1 :** any of a family (Cottidae) of spiny large-headed usu. bottom-dwelling often scaleless bony fishes with large fanlike pectoral fins **2 :** a scorpion fish (*Scorpaena guttata*) of the southern California coast caught for food and sport

sculpt \ˈskəlpt\ *vb* [F *sculpter,* alter. of obs. *sculper,* fr. L *sculpere*] (1864) **:** CARVE, SCULPTURE

sculpt·ed \ˈskəlp-təd\ *adj* (1984) **:** BUFF 2 ⟨a ~ physique⟩

sculp·tor \ˈskəlp-tər\ *n* [L, fr. *sculpere*] (1634) **:** an artist who makes sculptures

sculp·tress \-trəs\ *n* (1662) **:** a woman who is a sculptor

sculp·tur·al \ˈskəlp-chə-rəl, ˈskəlp-shrəl\ *adj* (1796) **1 :** of or relating to sculpture **2 :** resembling sculpture : SCULPTURESQUE — **sculp·tur·al·ly** *adv*

[1]**sculp·ture** \ˈskəlp-chər\ *n* [ME, fr. L *sculptura,* fr. *sculptus,* pp. of *sculpere* to carve, alter. of *scalpere* to scratch, carve] (14c) **1 a :** the action or art of processing (as by carving, modeling, or welding) plastic or hard materials into works of art **b** (1) **:** work produced by sculpture (2) **:** a three-dimensional work of art (as a statue) **2 :** impressed or raised markings or a pattern of such esp. on a plant or animal part

[2]**sculpture** *vb* **sculp·tured; sculp·tur·ing** \ˈskəlp-chə-riŋ, ˈskəlp-shriŋ\ *vt* (1645) **1 a :** to form an image or representation of from solid material (as wood or stone) **b :** to form into a three-dimensional work of art **2 :** to change (the form of the earth's surface) by natural processes (as erosion and deposition) **3 :** to shape by or as if by carving or molding ~ *vi* **:** to work as a sculptor

sculp·tur·esque \ˌskəlp-chə-ˈresk\ *adj* (1835) **:** done in the manner of or resembling sculpture — **sculp·tur·esque·ly** *adv*

[1]**scum** \ˈskəm\ *n* [ME, fr. MD *schum;* akin to OHG *scūm* foam] (14c) **1 a :** extraneous matter or impurities risen to or formed on the surface of a liquid often as a foul filmy covering — compare POND SCUM 2 **b :** the scoria of metals in a molten state **:** DROSS **c :** a slimy film on a solid or gelatinous object **2 a :** REFUSE **b :** a low, vile, or worthless person or group of people — **scum·my** \ˈskə-mē\ *adj*

[2]**scum** *vi* **scummed; scum·ming** (1661) **:** to become covered with or as if with scum

scum·bag \ˈskəm-ˌbag *also* -ˌbāg\ *n* (1967) *slang* **:** a dirty or despicable person

[1]**scum·ble** \ˈskəm-bəl\ *vt* **scum·bled; scum·bling** \-b(ə-)liŋ\ [perh. freq. of [2]*scum*] (1798) **1 a :** to make (as color or a painting) less brilliant by covering with a thin coat of opaque or semiopaque color applied with a nearly dry brush **b :** to apply (a color) in this manner **2 :** to soften the lines or colors of (a drawing) by rubbing lightly

[2]**scumble** *n* (1834) **1 :** the act or effect of scumbling **2 :** a material used for scumbling

scun·gil·li \skün-ˈjē-lē, -ˈgē-, -ˈji-\ *n* [It dial. (Neapolitan) *scuncigli,* pl. of *scunciglio* conch] (1945) **:** conch used as food

[1]**scun·ner** \ˈskə-nər\ *vi* [ME (Sc) *skunniren*] (14c) *chiefly Scot* **:** to be in a state of disgusted irritation

[2]**scunner** *n* (ca. 1520) **:** an unreasonable or extreme dislike or prejudice

scup \ˈskəp\ *n, pl* **scup** *also* **scups** [short for *scuppaug,* modif. of Narragansett *mishcùppaûog*] (ca. 1848) **:** a porgy (*Stenotomus chrysops*) occurring along the Atlantic coast of the U.S. chiefly from No. Carolina to Maine and used as a panfish

[1]**scup·per** \ˈskə-pər\ *n* [ME *skopper-* (in compounds), perh. fr. AF **escopoir,* fr. *escopir* to spit out] (15c) **1 :** an opening cut through the bulwarks of a ship so that water falling on deck may flow overboard **2 :** an opening in the wall of a building through which water can drain from a floor or flat roof

[2]**scupper** *vt* [origin unknown] (1899) *Brit* **:** to defeat or put an end to **:** DO IN 1a

scup·per·nong \-ˌnȯŋ, -ˌnäŋ\ *n* [*Scuppernong,* river and lake in No. Carolina] (1811) **1 :** MUSCADINE; *esp* **:** a cultivated muscadine with yellowish-green plum-flavored fruits **2 :** a sweet aromatic amber-colored wine made from scuppernongs

scurf \ˈskərf\ *n* [ME, fr. OE, of Scand origin; akin to Icel *skurfa* scurf; akin to OHG *scorf* scurf, OE *sceorfan* to scarify] (bef. 12c) **1 :** thin dry scales detached from the epidermis esp. in an abnormal skin condition; *specif* **:** DANDRUFF **2 a :** something like flakes or scales adhering to a surface **b :** the foul remains of something adherent **3 a :** a scaly deposit or covering on some plant parts; *also* **:** a localized or general darkening and roughening of a plant surface usu. more pronounced than russeting **b :** a plant disease characterized by scurf — **scurfy** \ˈskər-fē\ *adj*

scur·rile *or* **scur·ril** \ˈskər-əl, ˈskə-rəl\ *adj* [MF *scurrile,* fr. L *scurrilis,* fr. *scurra* buffoon] (1567) **:** SCURRILOUS

scur·ril·i·ty \skə-ˈri-lə-tē\ *n, pl* **-ties** (1508) **1 :** the quality or state of being scurrilous **2 a :** scurrilous or abusive language **b :** an offensively rude or abusive remark

scur·ri·lous \ˈskər-ə-ləs, ˈskə-rə-\ *adj* (1576) **1 a :** using or given to coarse language **b :** vulgar and evil ⟨~ imposters who used a religious exterior to rob poor people —Edwin Benson⟩ **2 :** containing obscenities, abuse, or slander ⟨~ accusations⟩ — **scur·ri·lous·ly** *adv* — **scur·ri·lous·ness** *n*

scur·ry \ˈskər-ē, ˈskə-rē\ *vi* **scur·ried; scur·ry·ing** [short for *hurry-scurry,* redupl. of *hurry*] (1810) **1 :** to move in or as if in a brisk pace **:** SCAMPER **2 :** to move around in an agitated, confused, or fluttering manner — **scurry** *n*

[1]**scur·vy** \ˈskər-vē\ *n* [[2]*scurvy*] (ca. 1565) **:** a disease caused by a lack of vitamin C and characterized by spongy gums, loosening of the teeth, and a bleeding into the skin and mucous membranes

[2]**scurvy** *adj* [*scurf*] (1579) **:** arousing disgust or scorn **:** CONTEMPTIBLE, DESPICABLE ⟨a ~ trick⟩ ***syn*** see CONTEMPTIBLE — **scur·vi·ly** \-və-lē\ *adv* — **scur·vi·ness** \-vē-nəs\ *n*

scurvy grass *n* (ca. 1597) **:** a cruciferous herb (as *Cochlearia officinalis*) formerly used in preventing or treating scurvy

scut \ˈskət\ *n* [origin unknown] (ca. 1530) **:** a short erect tail (as of a hare)

scu·tage \ˈskü-tij, ˈskyü-\ *n* [ME, fr. ML *scutagium,* fr. L *scutum* shield — more at ESQUIRE] (15c) **:** a tax levied on a vassal or a knight in lieu of military service

[1]**scutch** \ˈskəch\ *vt* [obs. F *escoucher,* fr. MF *escochier,* fr. VL **excuticare* to beat out, fr. L *excutere,* fr. *ex-* + *quatere* to shake, strike] (1733) **:** to separate the woody fiber from (flax or hemp) by beating

[2]**scutch** *n* (ca. 1791) **1 :** SCUTCHER **2 :** a bricklayer's hammer for cutting, trimming, and dressing bricks

scutch·eon \ˈskə-chən\ *n* [ME *scochon,* fr. MF *escuchon*] (14c) **:** ESCUTCHEON

scutch·er \ˈskə-chər\ *n* (1776) **:** an implement or machine for scutching flax or cotton

scute \ˈsküt, ˈskyüt\ *n* [NL *scutum,* fr. L, shield — more at ESQUIRE] (1848) **:** an external bony or horny plate or large scale

scu·tel·late \skü-ˈte-lət, skyü-; ˈsk(y)ü-tə-ˌlāt\ *or* **scu·tel·lat·ed** \ˈsk(y)ü-tə-ˌlā-təd\ *adj* (1785) **:** having or covered with scutella

scu·tel·lum \skü-ˈte-ləm, skyü-\ *n, pl* **-la** \-lə\ [NL, dim. of L *scutum* shield] (1819) **1 :** a hard plate or scale (as on the thorax of an insect or the tarsus of a bird) **2 :** the shield-shaped cotyledon of a monocotyledon (as a grass) — **scu·tel·lar** \-lər\ *adj*

scut·ter \ˈskə-tər\ *vi* [alter. of [5]*scuttle*] (1781) **:** SCURRY, SCAMPER

[1]**scut·tle** \ˈskə-tᵊl\ *n* [ME *scutel,* fr. L *scutella* drinking bowl, tray, dim. of *scutra* platter] (15c) **1 :** a shallow open basket for carrying something (as grain or garden produce) **2 :** a metal pail that usu. has a bail and a sloped lip and is used esp. for carrying coal

[2]**scuttle** *n* [ME *skottell* lid of a scuttle] (15c) **1 :** a small opening in a wall or roof furnished with a lid: as **a :** a small opening or hatchway in the deck of a ship large enough to admit a person and with a lid for covering it **b :** a small hole in the side or bottom of a ship fitted with a covering or glazed **2 :** a covering that closes a scuttle

[3]**scuttle** *vt* **scut·tled; scut·tling** \ˈskət-liŋ, ˈskə-tᵊl-iŋ\ (1642) **1 :** to cut a hole through the bottom, deck, or side of (a ship); *specif* **:** to sink or attempt to sink by making holes through the bottom **2 :** DESTROY, WRECK; *also* **:** SCRAP 2

[4]**scuttle** *n* [perh. blend of *scud* and *shuttle*] (1623) **1 :** a quick shuffling pace **2 :** a short swift run

[5]**scuttle** *vi* **scut·tled; scut·tling** \ˈskət-liŋ, ˈskə-tᵊl-iŋ\ (1657) **:** SCURRY

scut·tle·butt \ˈskə-tᵊl-ˌbət\ *n* [alter. of *scuttled butt* butt with a hole cut into it] (ca. 1805) **1 a :** a cask on shipboard to contain freshwater for a day's use **b :** a drinking fountain on a ship or at a naval or marine installation **2 :** RUMOR, GOSSIP

scu·tum \ˈskü-təm, ˈskyü-\ *n, pl* **scu·ta** \-tə\ [NL, fr. L, shield — more at ESQUIRE] (1771) **:** a bony, horny, or chitinous plate **:** SCUTE

scut work \ˈskət-\ *n* [prob. fr. medical argot *scut* junior intern] (ca. 1962) **:** routine and often menial labor

scuzz·ball \ˈskəz-ˌbȯl\ *n* [*scuzz-,* back-formation fr. *scuzzy*] (1981) *slang* **:** an unpleasant, dirty, or dangerous person **:** CREEP

scuz·zy \ˈskə-zē\ *adj* **scuz·zi·er; -est** [origin unknown] (1969) *slang* **:** dirty, shabby, or foul in condition or character

Scyl·la \ˈsi-lə\ *n* [L, fr. Gk *Skyllē*] (14c) **:** a nymph changed into a monster in Greek mythology who terrorizes mariners in the Strait of Messina — **between Scylla and Charybdis :** between two equally hazardous alternatives

scy·phis·to·ma \sī-ˈfis-tə-mə\ *n, pl* **-mae** \-(ˌ)mē\ *also* **-mas** [NL, fr. L *scyphus* cup + Gk *stoma* mouth — more at STOMACH] (1861) **:** a sexually produced scyphozoan larva that ultimately repeatedly constricts transversely to form free-swimming medusae

scy·pho·zo·an \ˌsī-fə-ˈzō-ən\ *n* [NL *Scyphozoa,* fr. L *scyphus* + NL *-zoa*] (ca. 1909) **:** any of a class (Scyphozoa) of coelenterates that comprise jellyfishes lacking a true polyp and usu. a velum — **scyphozoan** *adj*

[1]**scythe** \ˈsīth, ˈsī\ *n* [ME *sithe,* fr. OE *sīthe;* akin to OE *sagu* saw — more at SAW] (bef. 12c) **:** an implement used for mowing (as grass) and composed of a long curving blade fastened at an angle to a long handle

[2]**scythe** *vb* **scythed; scyth·ing** *vi* (ca. 1580) **:** to use a scythe ~ *vt* **:** to cut with or as if with a scythe ⟨*scything* cornstalks⟩

Scyth·i·an \ˈsi-thē-ən, -thē-\ *n* [L *Scytha,* fr. Gk *Skythēs*] (15c) **1 :** a member of an ancient nomadic people inhabiting Scythia **2 :** the Iranian language of the Scythians — **Scythian** *adj*

sd *abbr* sine die

SD *abbr* **1** South Dakota **2** special delivery **3** standard deviation

S Dak *abbr* South Dakota

SDI *abbr* Strategic Defense Initiative

SDRAM *abbr* synchronous DRAM

SDRs *abbr* special drawing rights

SDS *abbr* Students for a Democratic Society

Se *symbol* selenium

SE *abbr* **1** self-explanatory **2** southeast **3** special edition **4** Standard English **5** stock exchange **6** straight edge

sea \ˈsē\ *n* [ME *see,* fr. OE *sǣ;* akin to OHG *sē* sea, Goth *saiws*] (bef. 12c) **1 a :** a great body of salt water that covers much of the earth; *broadly* **:** the waters of the earth as distinguished from the land and air **b :** a body of salt water of second rank more or less landlocked ⟨the Mediterranean ~⟩ **c :** OCEAN **d :** an inland body of water — used esp. for names of such bodies ⟨the Caspian *Sea*⟩ **2 a :** surface motion on a large body of water or its direction; *also* **:** a large swell or wave — often used in pl. ⟨heavy ~*s*⟩ **b :** the disturbance of the ocean or other body of water due to the wind **3 :** something likened to the sea esp. in vastness ⟨a ~ of faces⟩ **4 :** the seafaring life **5 :** [3]MARE — **sea** *adj* — **at sea 1 :** on the sea; *specif* **:** on a sea voyage **2 :** LOST, BEWILDERED — **to sea :** to or on the open waters of the sea

sea anchor *n* (1769) **:** a drag typically of canvas thrown overboard to retard the drifting of a ship or seaplane and to keep its head to the wind

sea anemone *n* (1742) **:** any of numerous usu. solitary anthozoan polyps (order Actiniaria) whose form, bright and varied colors, and cluster of tentacles superficially resemble a flower

sea·bag \ˈsē-ˌbag\ *n* (1917) **:** a cylindrical canvas bag used esp. by a sailor for clothes and other gear

sea bass *n* (1765) **1 :** any of numerous marine bony fishes (family Serranidae) that are usu. smaller and more active than the groupers; *esp* **:** a food and sport fish (*Centropristis striata*) of the Atlantic coast of the U.S. **2 :** any of numerous croakers or drums including noted sport and food fishes

sea·bed \-ˌbed\ *n* (1838) **:** the floor of a sea or ocean

Sea·bee \ˈsē-(ˌ)bē\ *n* [alter. of *cee* + *bee;* fr. the initials of *construction battalion*] (1942) **:** a member of one of the U.S. Navy construction battalions for building naval shore facilities in combat zones

sea·bird \ˈsē-ˌbərd\ *n* (1564) **:** a bird (as a gull or an albatross) frequenting the open ocean

sea biscuit *n* (ca. 1690) **:** HARDTACK 1

sea·board \ˈsē-ˌbȯrd\ *n* (1781) **:** SEACOAST; *also* **:** the country bordering a seacoast — **seaboard** *adj*

sea·boot \-ˌbüt\ *n* (1851) **:** a very high waterproof boot used esp. by sailors and fishermen

sea·borg·i·um \sē-ˈbȯr-gē-əm\ *n* [NL, fr. Glenn T. *Seaborg*] (1994) **:** a short-lived radioactive element that is produced artificially — see ELEMENT table

sea·borne \-ˌbȯrn\ *adj* (1823) **1 :** borne over or on the sea ⟨a ~ invasion⟩ **2 :** carried on by oversea shipping ⟨~ trade⟩

sea bream *n* (ca. 1530) **:** BREAM 2a

sea breeze *n* (1661) : a cooling breeze blowing generally in the daytime inland from the sea
sea captain *n* (1612) : the master esp. of a merchant vessel
sea change *n* (1612) **1** *archaic* : a change brought about by the sea **2** : a marked change : TRANSFORMATION ⟨a *sea change* in public policy⟩
sea chest *n* (1613) : a sailor's storage chest for personal property
sea·coast \ˈsē-ˌkōst\ *n* (14c) : the shore or border of the land adjacent to the sea
sea cow *n* (1613) : SIRENIAN
sea·craft \ˈsē-ˌkraft\ *n* (1658) **1** : seagoing ships **2** : skill in navigation
sea crayfish *n* (1601) : SPINY LOBSTER
sea cucumber *n* (1841) : any of a class (Holothurioidea) of echinoderms having a tough muscular elongate body with tentacles surrounding the mouth — called also *holothurian*

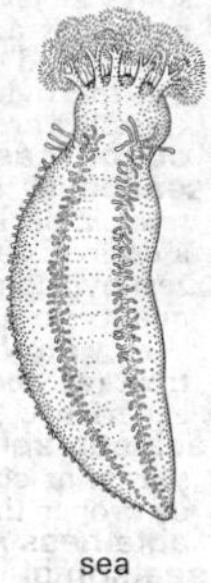
sea cucumber

sea devil *n* (1634) : MANTA RAY
sea dog *n* (1823) : a veteran sailor
sea duck *n* (1753) : a diving duck (as a scoter, merganser, or eider) that frequents the sea
sea duty *n* (1945) : duty in the U.S. Navy performed with a deployable unit (as a ship or aircraft squadron)
sea eagle *n* (1668) : any of various fish-eating eagles (esp. genus *Haliaeetus*)
Sea Explorer *n* (1954) : an Explorer in a scouting program that teaches seamanship
sea fan *n* (1633) : any of various gorgonians (esp. genus *Gorgonia*) with a fan-shaped skeleton; *esp* : either of two (*Gorgonia ventalina* and *G. flabellum*) of Florida and the West Indies
sea·far·er \ˈsē-ˌfer-ər\ *n* [*sea* + 1*fare* + 2*-er*] (1513) : MARINER
sea·far·ing \-ˌfer-iŋ\ *n* (1592) : the use of the sea for travel or transportation — **seafaring** *adj*
sea fire *n* (1814) : marine bioluminescence
sea·floor \ˈsē-ˌflȯr\ *n* (1855) : SEABED
seafloor spreading *n* (1969) : the divergence at mid-ocean ridges of the tectonic plates underlying the oceans that is due to upwelling from the earth's interior of magma which solidifies and adds to the spreading plates
sea·food \-ˌfüd\ *n* (1836) : edible marine fish and shellfish
sea·fowl \-ˌfau̇(-ə)l\ *n* (14c) : SEABIRD
sea·front \-ˌfrənt\ *n* (1878) : the waterfront of a seaside place
sea·girt \ˈsē-ˌgərt\ *adj* (1616) : surrounded by the sea
sea·go·ing \-ˌgō-iŋ, -ˌgȯ(-)iŋ\ *adj* (1828) : OCEANGOING
sea grape *n* (1806) : a tree (*Coccoloba uvifera*) of the buckwheat family that inhabits sandy shores from Florida to So. America, has rounded leaves, and bears clusters of purple to whitish edible berries
sea grass *n* (1578) : any of various grasslike plants that inhabit coastal areas; *esp* : EELGRASS 1
sea green *n* (1598) **1** : a moderate green or bluish green **2** : a moderate yellow green
sea·gull \ˈsē-ˌgəl\ *n* (1542) : a gull frequenting the sea; *broadly* : GULL
sea hare *n* (1593) : any of various large opisthobranch mollusks (esp. genus *Aplysia*) that have an arched back and two anterior tentacles and have the shell much reduced or missing
sea holly *n* (1548) : a European coastal herb (*Eryngium maritimum*) of the carrot family with spiny leaves and pale blue flowers
sea horse *n* (15c) **1** : WALRUS **2** : a mythical creature half horse and half fish **3** : any of a genus (*Hippocampus* of the family Syngnathidae) of small bony fishes that have the head angled downward toward the body which is carried vertically and are equipped with a prehensile tail
sea island cotton *n, often cap S&I* [*Sea Islands,* chain of islands off the southeastern U.S. coast] (1805) : a cotton (*Gossypium barbadense*) with esp. long silky fiber — called also *sea island*
sea kale *n* (1699) : a succulent Eurasian perennial herb (*Crambe maritima*) of the mustard family used as a potherb
sea king *n* (1819) : a Norse pirate chief
1**seal** \ˈsēl\ *n, pl* **seals** *also* **seal** [ME *sele,* fr. OE *seolh;* akin to OHG *selah* seal] (bef. 12c) **1** : any of numerous carnivorous marine mammals (families Phocidae and Otariidae) that live chiefly in cold regions and have limbs modified into webbed flippers adapted primarily to swimming; *esp* : a fur seal or hair seal as opposed to a sea lion **2 a** : the pelt of a fur seal **b** : leather made from the skin of a seal **3** : a dark brown
2**seal** *vi* (1828) : to hunt seals
3**seal** *n* [ME *sele, seel,* fr. AF *seal, sel,* fr. L *sigillum* seal, fr. dim. of *signum* sign, seal — more at SIGN] (13c) **1 a** : something that confirms, ratifies, or makes secure : GUARANTEE, ASSURANCE **b** (1) : a device with a cut or raised emblem, symbol, or word used esp. to certify a signature or authenticate a document (2) : a medallion or ring face bearing such a device incised so that it can be impressed on wax or moist clay; *also* : a piece of wax or a wafer bearing such an impression **c** : an impression, device, or mark given the effect of a common-law seal by statute law or by American local custom recognized by judicial decision **d** : a usu. ornamental adhesive stamp that may be used to close a letter or package; *esp* : one given in a fund-raising campaign **2 a** : something that secures (as a wax seal on a document) **b** : a closure that must be broken to be opened and that thus reveals tampering **c** (1) : a tight and perfect closure (as against the passage of gas or water) (2) : a device to prevent the passage or return of gas or air into a pipe or container **3** : a seal that is a symbol or mark of office — **under seal** : with an authenticating seal affixed
4**seal** *vt* (14c) **1 a** : to confirm or make secure by or as if by a seal ⟨~ the deal⟩ **b** : to solemnize for eternity (as a marriage) by a Mormon rite **2 a** : to set or affix an authenticating seal to; *also* : AUTHENTICATE, RATIFY **b** : to mark with a stamp or seal usu. as an evidence of standard exactness, legal size, weight, or capacity, or merchantable quality **3 a** : to fasten with or as if with a seal to prevent tampering **b** : to close or make secure against access, leakage, or passage by a fastening or coating **c** : to fix in position or close breaks in with a filling (as of plaster) **4** : to determine irrevocably or indisputably ⟨that answer ~*ed* our fate⟩
SEAL *abbr* sea, air, land (team)
sea lamprey *n* (1879) : a large anadromous lamprey (*Petromyzon marinus*) that has a mottled upper surface, is an ectoparasite of fish, and is sometimes used as food
sea–lane \ˈsē-ˌlān\ *n* (1869) : an established sea route
seal·ant \ˈsē-lənt\ *n* (1944) **1** : a sealing agent ⟨a radiator ~⟩ **2** : a plastic material applied to parts of teeth with imperfections (as pits and fissures) to prevent dental decay
sea lavender *n* (1597) : any of a genus (*Limonium*) of chiefly perennial herbs of the plumbago family with small flowers and basal leaves
sea lawyer *n* (1829) : an argumentative captious sailor
sealed–beam \ˈsēl(d)-ˈbēm\ *adj* (1939) : being an electric lamp with a prefocused reflector and lens sealed in the lamp vacuum
sea legs *n pl* (1712) : bodily adjustment to the motion of a ship indicated esp. by ability to walk steadily and by freedom from seasickness
1**seal·er** \ˈsē-lər\ *n* (15c) **1** : an official who attests or certifies conformity to a standard of correctness **2** : a coat (as of size) applied to prevent subsequent coats of paint or varnish from sinking in
2**sealer** *n* (1770) : a person or a ship engaged in hunting seals
sea lettuce *n* (1668) : any of a genus (*Ulva*) of marine green algae with broad fronds sometimes eaten as salad or used in soups
sea level *n* (1806) : the level of the surface of the sea esp. at its mean position midway between mean high and low water
sea·lift \ˈsē-ˌlift\ *n* (1948) : transport of military personnel and esp. equipment by ship — **sealift** *vt*
sea lily *n* (1851) : CRINOID; *esp* : a stalked crinoid
sealing wax *n* (14c) : a resinous composition that is plastic when warm and is used for sealing (as letters, dry cells, or cans)
sea lion *n* (1697) : any of several Pacific eared seals (as genera *Eumetopias* and *Zalophus*) that are usu. larger than the related fur seals and lack a thick underfur
seal off *vt* (1931) : to close tightly
seal point *n* [1*seal* (the color)] (1934) : a coat color of cats characterized by a cream or fawn body with dark brown points; *also* : a Siamese cat with such coloring
seal ring *n* (1608) : a finger ring engraved with a seal : SIGNET RING
seal·skin \ˈsēl-ˌskin\ *n* (14c) **1** : the fur or pelt of a fur seal **2** : a garment (as a jacket, coat, or cape) of sealskin — **sealskin** *adj*
Sea·ly·ham terrier \ˈsē-lē-ˌham-, *esp Brit* -lē-əm-\ *n* [*Sealyham,* Pembrokeshire, Wales] (1907) : any of a breed of short-legged long-headed terriers developed in Wales with a usu. white wiry outer coat and soft dense undercoat
1**seam** \ˈsēm\ *n* [ME *seem,* fr. OE *sēam;* akin to OE *sīwian* to sew — more at SEW] (bef. 12c) **1 a** : the joining of two pieces (as of cloth or leather) by sewing usu. near the edge **b** : the stitching used in such a joining **2** : the space between adjacent planks or strakes of a ship **3 a** : a line, groove, or ridge formed by the abutment of edges **b** : a thin layer or stratum (as of rock) between distinctive layers; *also* : a bed of valuable mineral and esp. coal irrespective of thickness **c** : a line left by a cut or wound; *also* : WRINKLE **4** : a weak or vulnerable area or gap ⟨found a ~ in the zone defense⟩ — **seam·like** \-ˌlīk\ *adj* — **at the seams** : ENTIRELY, COMPLETELY ⟨falling apart *at the seams*⟩
2**seam** *vt* (1582) **1 a** : to join by sewing **b** : to join as if by sewing (as by welding, riveting, or heat-sealing) **2** : to mark with lines suggesting seams ~ *vi* : to become fissured or ridgy — **seam·er** *n*
sea–maid \ˈsē-ˌmād\ *or* **sea–maid·en** \-ˌmā-dᵊn\ *n* (1584) : MERMAID; *also* : a goddess or nymph of the sea
sea·man \ˈsē-mən\ *n* (bef. 12c) **1** : SAILOR, MARINER **2 a** : any of the three ranks below petty officer in the navy or coast guard **b** : an enlisted man in the navy or coast guard ranking above a seaman apprentice and below a petty officer
seaman apprentice *n* (1947) : an enlisted man in the navy or coast guard ranking above a seaman recruit and below a seaman
sea·man·like \ˈsē-mən-ˌlīk\ *adj* (1796) : characteristic of or befitting a competent seaman
sea·man·ly \-lē\ *adj* (1798) : SEAMANLIKE
seaman recruit *n* (1947) : an enlisted man of the lowest rank in the navy or coast guard
sea·man·ship \ˈsē-mən-ˌship\ *n* (1756) : the art or skill of handling, working, and navigating a ship
sea·mark \-ˌmärk\ *n* (15c) **1** : a line on a coast marking the tidal limit **2** : an elevated object serving as a beacon to mariners
sea mew *n* (15c) : SEAGULL; *esp* : a common gull (*Larus canus*) of Eurasia and northwestern No. America
sea mile *n* (1796) : NAUTICAL MILE
seam·less \ˈsēm-ləs\ *adj* (15c) **1** : having no seams **2 a** : having no awkward transitions, interruptions, or indications of disparity ⟨a ~ fusion of beauty and intelligence —Jack Kroll *et al.*⟩ **b** : PERFECT, FLAWLESS ⟨a ~ performance⟩ — **seam·less·ly** \-lē\ *adv* — **seam·less·ness** \-nəs\ *n*
sea monkey *n* (1973) : a brine shrimp (*Artemia salina*) that hatches from dormant encysted eggs and is sometimes raised in aquariums
sea·mount \ˈsē-ˌmau̇nt\ *n* (1941) : a submarine mountain rising above the deep-sea floor
sea mouse *n* (ca. 1520) : any of various large broad marine polychaete worms (esp. genus *Aphrodite*) covered with hairlike setae
seam·ster \ˈsēm(p)-stər *also* ˈsem(p)-\ *n* [ME *semester, semster,* fr. OE *sēamestre* seamstress, tailor, fr. *sēam* seam] (bef. 12c) : a person employed at sewing; *esp* : TAILOR
seam·stress \-strəs\ *n* (1598) : a woman whose occupation is sewing
seamy \ˈsē-mē\ *adj* **seam·i·er; -est** (1605) **1** *archaic* : having the rough side of the seam showing **2 a** : UNPLEASANT **b** : DEGRADED, SORDID ⟨the ~ side of urban life⟩ — **seam·i·ness** *n*
sé·ance \ˈsā-ˌän(t)s, -ˌäⁿs, sā-ˈ\ *n* [F, fr. MF, fr. *seoir* to sit, assemble, fr. OF, fr. L *sedēre* — more at SIT] (1803) **1** : SESSION, SITTING **2** : a spiritualist meeting to receive spirit communications

\ə\ **abut** \ᵊ\ kitten, F table \ər\ **fur**ther \a\ **ash** \ā\ **ace** \ä\ **mop, mar** \au̇\ **out** \ch\ **chin** \e\ **bet** \ē\ **easy** \g\ **go** \i\ **hit** \ī\ **ice** \j\ **job** \ŋ\ **sing** \ō\ **go** \ȯ\ **law** \ȯi\ **boy** \th\ **thin** \t͟h\ **the** \ü\ **loot** \u̇\ **foot** \y\ **yet** \zh\ **vision, beige** \k̲, ⁿ, œ, ue, ʸ\ *see* Guide to Pronunciation

sea nettle *n* (1601) : a stinging jellyfish; *esp* : one (*Chrysaora quinquecirrha*) occurring esp. in Atlantic estuaries from Cape Cod to the West Indies
sea oats *n pl but sing or pl in constr* (1894) : a tall grass (*Uniola paniculata*) that has panicles resembling those of the oat, grows chiefly on the coast of the southern U.S., and is useful as a sand binder; *also* : a related plant (*Chasmanthium latifolium* syn. *U. latifolia*) chiefly of the eastern U.S.
sea onion *n* (14c) : SQUILL 1a
sea otter *n* (1664) : a rare marine otter (*Enhydra lutris*) of the northern Pacific coasts that may attain a length of six feet (two meters), is chiefly brown but with lighter coloration on the back of the head and neck, and feeds largely on shellfish
sea pen *n* (1763) : any of numerous anthozoans (order Pennatulacea) growing in colonies with a feathery form
sea•piece \ˈsē-ˌpēs\ *n* (1656) : SEASCAPE 2
sea pink *n* (1731) **1** : THRIFT 4 **2** : any of several No. American herbs (genus *Sabatia,* esp. *S. stellaris*) of the gentian family with usu. pink or white flowers
sea•plane \-ˌplān\ *n* (1913) : an airplane designed to take off from and land on the water
sea•port \ˈsē-ˌpȯrt\ *n* (ca. 1520) : a port, harbor, or town accessible to seagoing ships
sea power *n* (1849) **1** : a nation having formidable naval strength **2** : naval strength
sea puss \-ˌpu̇s\ *n* [alter. of dial. *seapoose* tidal stream, fr. Unquachog (Algonquian language of Long Island, N.Y.) *seépus* river] (1842) : a swirling or along shore undertow
sea•quake \ˈsē-ˌkwāk\ *n* [*sea* + earth*quake*] (1680) : a submarine earthquake
[1]**sear** *var of* SERE
[2]**sear** \ˈsir\ *vb* [ME *seren,* fr. OE *sēarian* to become dry, fr. *sēar* sere] *vi* (bef. 12c) : to cause withering or drying ~ *vt* **1** : to make withered and dry : PARCH **2 a** : to burn, scorch, mark, or injure with or as if with sudden application of intense heat **b** : to cook the surface of quickly with intense heat ⟨~ a steak⟩
[3]**sear** *n* (1874) : a mark or scar left by searing
[4]**sear** *n* [prob. fr. MF *serre* grasp, fr. *serrer* to press, grasp, fr. OF, fr. LL *serare* to bolt, latch, fr. L *sera* bar for fastening a door] (1596) : the catch that holds the hammer of a gun's lock at cock or half cock
[1]**search** \ˈsərch\ *vb* [ME *cerchen,* fr. AF *cercher, sercher* to travel about, investigate, search, fr. LL *circare* to go about, fr. L *circum* round about — more at CIRCUM-] *vt* (14c) **1** : to look into or over carefully or thoroughly in an effort to find or discover something: as **a** : to examine in seeking something ⟨~*ed* the north field⟩ **b** : to look through or explore by inspecting possible places of concealment or investigating suspicious circumstances **c** : to read thoroughly : CHECK; *esp* : to examine a public record or register for information about ⟨~ land titles⟩ **d** : to examine for articles concealed on the person **e** : to look at as if to discover or penetrate intention or nature **2** : to uncover, find, or come to know by inquiry or scrutiny — usu. used with *out* ~ *vi* **1** : to look or inquire carefully ⟨~*ed* for the papers⟩ **2** : to make painstaking investigation or examination — **search•able** \ˈsər-chə-bəl\ *adj* — **search•er** *n* — **search•ing•ly** \-chiŋ-lē\ *adv*
[2]**search** *n* (15c) **1 a** : an act of searching ⟨a ~ for food⟩ ⟨go in ~ of help⟩ **b** : an act of boarding and inspecting a ship on the high seas in exercise of right of search **2** *obs* : a party that searches **3** : power or range of penetrating; *also* : a penetrating effect
search engine *n* (1984) : computer software used to search data (as text or a database) for specified information; *also* : a site on the World Wide Web that uses such software to locate key words in other sites
search•light \-ˌlīt\ *n* (1883) : an apparatus for projecting a powerful beam of light; *also* : a beam of light projected by it
search warrant *n* (1739) : a warrant authorizing a search (as of a house) for stolen goods, illegal possessions, or incriminating evidence
sear•ing \ˈsir-iŋ\ *adj* (1678) **1** : very hot **2** : marked by extreme intensity, harshness, or emotional power ⟨~ pain⟩ ⟨a ~ review⟩ ⟨a ~ portrayal⟩ — **sear•ing•ly** *adv*
sea robin *n* (1814) : any of a family (Triglidae) of marine bony fishes typically having a spiny armored head and the bottom three rays of the pectoral fin on each side free of membrane and elongated for use as feelers or in crawling — called also *gurnard*
sea room *n* (ca. 1554) : room for maneuver at sea
sea rover *n* (ca. 1580) : one that roves the sea; *specif* : PIRATE
sea–run \ˈsē-ˈrən\ *adj* (1885) : ANADROMOUS ⟨a ~ salmon⟩
sea scallop *n* (ca. 1931) : a large deep-water scallop (*Placopecten magellanicus*) of the Atlantic coast of No. America that is harvested commercially for food
sea•scape \ˈsē-ˌskāp\ *n* (1792) **1** : a view of the sea **2** : a picture representing a scene at sea
sea scorpion *n* (1867) **1** : SCULPIN 1 **2** : EURYPTERID
Sea Scout *n* (1911) : SEA EXPLORER
sea serpent *n* (1774) : a large marine animal resembling a serpent often reported to have been seen but never proved to exist
sea•shell \ˈsē-ˌshel\ *n* (bef. 12c) : the shell of a marine animal and esp. a mollusk
sea•shore \-ˌshȯr\ *n* (1526) **1 a** : land adjacent to the sea : SEACOAST **b** : NATIONAL SEASHORE **2** : all the ground between the ordinary high-water and low-water marks : FORESHORE
sea•sick \-ˌsik\ *adj* (ca. 1566) : affected with or suggestive of seasickness
sea•sick•ness \-nəs\ *n* (1613) : motion sickness experienced on the water
sea•side \ˈsē-ˌsīd\ *n* (13c) : the district or land bordering the sea : country adjacent to the sea : SEASHORE — **seaside** *adj*
sea slug *n* (1779) **1** : SEA CUCUMBER **2** : a naked marine gastropod; *specif* : NUDIBRANCH
sea snake *n* (1755) **1** : SEA SERPENT **2** : any of numerous venomous aquatic chiefly viviparous elapid snakes of warm seas
[1]**sea•son** \ˈsē-zᵊn\ *n* [ME *sesoun,* fr. AF *seison* natural season, appropriate time, fr. L *sation-, satio* action of sowing, fr. *serere* to sow — more at SOW] (14c) **1 a** : a time characterized by a particular circumstance or feature ⟨in a ~ of religious awakening —F. A. Christie⟩ **b** : a suitable or natural time or occasion ⟨when my ~ comes to sit on David's throne —John Milton⟩ **c** : an indefinite period of time : WHILE ⟨sent home again to her father for a ~ —Francis Hackett⟩ **2 a** : a period of the year characterized by or associated with a particular activity or phenomenon ⟨hay fever ~⟩: as (1) : a period associated with some phase or activity of agriculture (as growth or harvesting) (2) : a period in which an animal engages in some activity (as migrating or mating); *also* : ESTRUS, HEAT (3) : the period normally characterized by a particular kind of weather ⟨a long rainy ~⟩ (4) : a period marked by special activity esp. in some field ⟨tourist ~⟩ ⟨hunting ~⟩ (5) : a period in which a place is most frequented **b** : one of the four quarters into which the year is commonly divided **c** : the time of a major holiday **3** : YEAR ⟨a boy of seven ~*s*⟩ **4** [ME *sesoun,* fr. *sesounen* to season] : SEASONING **5** : the schedule of official games played or to be played by a sports team during a playing season ⟨got through the ~ undefeated⟩ **6** : OFF-SEASON ⟨closed for the ~⟩ — **in season 1** : at the right time **2** : at the stage of greatest fitness (as for eating) ⟨peaches are *in season*⟩ **3** : legally available to be hunted or caught — **out of season** : not in season
[2]**season** *vb* **sea•soned; sea•son•ing** \ˈsēz-niŋ, ˈsē-zᵊn-iŋ\ [ME *sesounen,* back-formation fr. *sesounde* flavored, fr. AF *seisoné* brought to a desired state, fr. *seison*] *vt* (14c) **1 a** : to give (food) more flavor or zest by adding seasoning or savory ingredients **b** : to give a distinctive quality to as if by seasoning; *esp* : to make more agreeable ⟨advice ~*ed* with wit⟩ **c** *archaic* : to qualify by admixture : TEMPER **2 a** : to treat (as wood or a skillet) so as to prepare for use **b** : to make fit by experience ⟨a ~*ed* veteran⟩ ~ *vi* : to become seasoned
sea•son•able \ˈsēz-nə-bəl, ˈsē-zᵊn-ə-bəl\ *adj* (14c) **1** : suitable to the season or circumstances : TIMELY ⟨a ~ frost⟩ **2** : occurring in good or proper time : OPPORTUNE ⟨a ~ time for discussion⟩ — **sea•son•able•ness** *n* — **sea•son•ably** \-blē\ *adv*
sea•son•al \ˈsēz-nəl, ˈsē-zᵊn-əl\ *adj* (1838) **1** : of, relating to, or varying in occurrence according to the season ⟨~ storms⟩ **2** : affected or caused by seasonal need or availability ⟨~ industries⟩ — **sea•son•al•i•ty** \ˌsē-zə-ˈna-lə-tē\ *n* — **sea•son•al•ly** \ˈsēz-nə-lē, ˈsē-zᵊn-ə-lē\ *adv*
seasonal affective disorder *n* (1983) : depression that tends to recur as the days grow shorter during the fall and winter — abbr. *SAD*
sea•son•er \ˈsēz-nər, ˈsē-zᵊn-ər\ *n* (1555) : one that seasons: as **a** : a user of seasonings ⟨a heavy ~⟩ **b** : SEASONING
seasoning *n* (1579) : something that serves to season; *esp* : an ingredient (as a condiment, spice, or herb) added to food primarily for the savor that it imparts
sea•son•less \ˈsē-zᵊn-ləs\ *adj* (1816) **1** : exhibiting no seasonal changes **2** : not restricted to a particular season; *esp* : suitable for wearing in any season ⟨~ fabrics⟩
season ticket *n* (1820) : a ticket (as to all of a club's home games or for specified daily transportation) valid during a specified time
sea spider *n* (1855) : any of various small long-legged marine arthropods (class Pycnogonida) that superficially resemble spiders
sea squirt *n* (1850) : ASCIDIAN
sea star *n* (1569) : STARFISH
sea stores *n pl* (1659) : supplies (as of foodstuffs) laid in before starting on a sea voyage
sea•strand \ˈsē-ˌstrand\ *n* (bef. 12c) : SEASHORE
[1]**seat** \ˈsēt\ *n* [ME *sete,* fr. ON *sæti;* akin to OE *gesete* seat, *sittan* to sit] (13c) **1 a** : a special chair of one in eminence; *also* : the status represented by it **b** : a chair, stool, or bench intended to be sat in or on **c** : the particular part of something on which one rests in sitting ⟨the ~ of a chair⟩ ⟨trouser ~⟩ **d** : BUTTOCKS **2 a** : a seating accommodation ⟨a ~ for the game⟩ ⟨a 200-*seat* restaurant⟩ **b** : a right of sitting ⟨lost his ~ in Congress⟩ **c** : membership on an exchange **3 a** : a place where something specified is prevalent : CENTER ⟨a ~ of learning⟩ **b** : a place from which authority is exercised ⟨the county ~⟩ **c** : a bodily part in which some function or condition is centered ⟨the brain as the ~ of the mind⟩ **4** : posture in or way of sitting on horseback **5 a** : a part at or forming the base of something **b** : a part (as a socket) or surface on or in which another part or surface rests — **by the seat of one's pants** : using experience and intuition rather than mechanical aids or formal theory
[2]**seat** *vt* (1586) **1 a** : to install in a seat of dignity or office **b** (1) : to cause to sit or assist in finding a seat (2) : to provide seats for ⟨a theater ~*ing* 1000 persons⟩ **c** : to put in a sitting position **2** : to repair the seat of or provide a new seat for **3** : to fit to or with a seat ⟨~ a valve⟩ ~ *vi* **1** *archaic* : to take one's seat or place **2** : to fit correctly on a seat
seat belt *n* (1932) : an arrangement of straps designed to hold a person steady in a seat (as in an airplane or automobile)
seat•er \ˈsē-tər\ *n* (1693) **1** : one that seats **2** : one that has a specified number of seats — used in combination ⟨a 2-*seater* jet⟩
seat•ing \ˈsē-tiŋ\ *n* (1761) **1 a** : material for covering or upholstering seats **b** : a seat on or in which something rests ⟨a valve ~⟩ **2** : the act of providing with seats
seat•mate \ˈsēt-ˌmāt\ *n* (1859) : one with whom one shares a seat (as in a vehicle with double or paired seats)
SEATO *abbr* Southeast Asia Treaty Organization
seat–of–the–pants *adj* (1942) : employing or based on personal experience, judgment, and effort rather than technological aids or formal theory ⟨~ navigation⟩ ⟨a ~ decision⟩
sea•train \ˈsē-ˌtrān\ *n* (1932) : a seagoing ship equipped for carrying a train of railroad cars
sea trout *n* (1661) **1** : any of various trouts or chars that as adults inhabit the sea but ascend rivers to spawn **2** : any of various marine fishes resembling trouts: as **a** : WEAKFISH 1 **b** : SPOTTED SEA TROUT
sea turtle *n* (1612) : any of two families (Cheloniidae and Dermochelyidae) of widely distributed marine turtles that have the feet modified into paddles and that include the green turtle, leatherback, hawksbill, loggerhead, and ridley
sea urchin *n* (1591) : any of numerous echinoderms (class Echinoidea) that are usu. enclosed in thin brittle globular tests covered with movable spines
sea•wall \ˈsē-ˌwȯl\ *n* (15c) : a wall or embankment to protect the shore from erosion or to act as a breakwater
[1]**sea•ward** \ˈsē-wərd\ *n* (14c) : the direction or side away from land and toward the open sea
[2]**seaward** *also* **sea•wards** \-wərdz\ *adv* (1517) : toward the sea

[3]**seaward** *adj* (ca. 1621) **1 :** directed or situated toward the sea **2 :** coming from the sea ⟨a ~ wind⟩
sea wasp *n* (1910) **:** any of various cube-shaped scyphozoan jellyfishes (order or suborder Cubomedusae) that sting virulently and sometimes fatally — called also *box jellyfish*
sea·wa·ter \ˈsē-ˌwȯ-tər, -ˌwä-\ *n* (bef. 12c) **:** water in or from the sea
sea·way \-ˌwā\ *n* (bef. 12c) **1 :** the sea as a route for travel; *also* **:** an ocean traffic lane **2 :** a moderate or rough sea **3 :** a deep inland waterway that admits ocean shipping
sea·weed \-ˌwēd\ *n* (1577) **1 :** a mass or growth of marine plants **2 :** a plant growing in the sea; *esp* **:** a marine alga (as a kelp)
sea whip *n* (1775) **:** any of various gorgonian corals with elongated flexible unbranched or little-branched whiplike colonies
sea·wor·thy \ˈsē-ˌwər-t͟hē\ *adj* (1798) **:** fit or safe for a sea voyage ⟨a ~ ship⟩ — **sea·wor·thi·ness** \-t͟hē-nəs\ *n*
sea wrack *n* (1551) **:** SEAWEED; *esp* **:** seaweed cast ashore in masses
se·ba·ceous \si-ˈbā-shəs\ *adj* [L *sebaceus* made of tallow, fr. *sebum* tallow] (1728) **1 :** secreting sebum ⟨~ glands⟩ **2 :** of, relating to, or being fatty material **:** FATTY ⟨a ~ exudate⟩
se·bac·ic acid \si-ˈba-sik-, ˌsē-, -ˈbā-\ *n* [F (*acide*) *sébacique,* fr. L *sebaceus*] (1790) **:** a crystalline dicarboxylic acid $C_{10}H_{18}O_4$ used esp. in the manufacture of synthetic resins
seb·or·rhea \ˌse-bə-ˈrē-ə\ *n* [NL, fr. L *sebum* + NL *-rrhea*] (ca. 1860) **:** abnormally increased secretion and discharge of sebum — **seb·or·rhe·ic** \-ˈrē-ik\ *adj*
se·bum \ˈsē-bəm\ *n* [L, tallow, grease] (ca. 1860) **:** fatty lubricant matter secreted by sebaceous glands of the skin
[1]**sec** \ˈsek\ *adj* [F, lit., dry — more at SACK] (1863) *of champagne* **:** moderately dry
[2]**sec** *abbr* **1** secant **2** second; secondary **3** secretary **4** section
SEC *abbr* Securities and Exchange Commission
se·cant \ˈsē-ˌkant, -kənt\ *n* [NL *secant-, secans,* fr. L, prp. of *secare* to cut — more at SAW] (1593) **1 :** a straight line cutting a curve at two or more points **2 :** a straight line drawn from the center of a circle through one end of a circular arc to a tangent drawn from the other end of the arc **3 a :** a trigonometric function that for an acute angle is the ratio of the hypotenuse of a right triangle of which the angle is considered part and the leg adjacent to the angle **b :** a trigonometric function *sec θ* that is the reciprocal of the cosine for all real numbers *θ* for which the cosine is not zero and that is exactly equal to the secant of an angle of measure *θ* in radians
sec·a·teur \ˌse-kə-ˈtər, ˈse-kə-ˌ\ *n* [F *sécateur,* fr. L *secare* to cut] (1881) *chiefly Brit* **:** pruning shears — usu. used in pl.
[1]**sec·co** \ˈse-(ˌ)kō\ *n* [It, fr. *secco* dry, fr. L *siccus* — more at SACK] (1852) **:** the art of painting on dry plaster
[2]**secco** *adj or adv* [It, lit., dry] (ca. 1854) **1 :** short and very staccato — used as a direction in music **2** *of a recitative* **:** accompanied only by the instruments playing the continuo
se·cede \si-ˈsēd\ *vi* **se·ced·ed; se·ced·ing** [L *secedere,* fr. *sed-, se-* apart (fr. *sed, se* without) + *cedere* to go — more at SUICIDE] (1749) **:** to withdraw from an organization (as a religious communion or political party or federation) — **se·ced·er** *n*
se·cern \si-ˈsərn\ *vt* [L *secernere* to separate — more at SECRET] (1604) **:** to discriminate in thought **:** DISTINGUISH
se·ces·sion \si-ˈse-shən\ *n* [L *secession-, secessio,* fr. *secedere*] (1604) **1 :** withdrawal into privacy or solitude **:** RETIREMENT **2 :** formal withdrawal from an organization
se·ces·sion·ist \-ˈse-sh(ə-)nist\ *n* (ca. 1850) **:** one who joins in a secession or maintains that secession is a right — **se·ces·sion·ism** \-shə-ˌni-zəm\ *n* — **secessionist** *adj*
Seck·el \ˈse-kəl, ˈsi-\ *n* [perh. fr. *Seckle* or *Seckel,* surname of a farmer in eastern Pennsylvania] (1817) **:** a small pear with sweet very flavorful firm flesh and yellowish-green skin with a red blush
se·clude \si-ˈklüd\ *vt* **se·clud·ed; se·clud·ing** [ME, to cut off (from), fr. L *secludere* to separate, seclude, fr. *se-* apart + *claudere* to close — more at SECEDE, CLOSE] (ca. 1533) **1** *obs* **:** to exclude from a privilege, rank, or dignity **:** DEBAR **2 :** to remove or separate from intercourse or outside influence **:** ISOLATE **3 :** SHUT OFF, SCREEN
secluded *adj* (1604) **1 :** screened or hidden from view **:** SEQUESTERED ⟨a ~ valley⟩ **2 :** living in seclusion **:** SOLITARY ⟨~ monks⟩ — **se·clud·ed·ly** *adv* — **se·clud·ed·ness** *n*
se·clu·sion \si-ˈklü-zhən\ *n* [ML *seclusion-, seclusio,* fr. L *secludere*] (ca. 1616) **1 :** the act of secluding **:** the condition of being secluded **2 :** a secluded or isolated place ***syn*** see SOLITUDE — **se·clu·sive** \-ˈklü-siv, -ziv\ *adj* — **se·clu·sive·ly** *adv* — **se·clu·sive·ness** *n*
seco·bar·bi·tal \ˌse-kō-ˈbär-bə-ˌtȯl\ *n* [fr. *Seco*nal, a trademark + *barbital*] (1951) **:** a barbiturate $C_{12}H_{18}N_2O_3$ that is used chiefly in the form of its sodium salt as a hypnotic and sedative
Sec·o·nal \ˈse-kə-ˌnȯl, -ˌnal, -nᵊl\ *trademark* — used for a preparation of secobarbital
[1]**sec·ond** \ˈse-kənd *also* -kənt, *esp before a consonant* -kən, -kᵊŋ\ *adj* [ME, fr. AF *secund,* fr. L *secundus* second, following, favorable, fr. *sequi* to follow — more at SUE] (13c) **1 a :** next to the first in place or time ⟨was ~ in line⟩ **b (1) :** next to the first in value, excellence, or degree ⟨his ~ choice of schools⟩ **(2) :** INFERIOR, SUBORDINATE ⟨was ~ to none⟩ **c :** ranking next below the top of a grade or degree in authority or precedence ⟨~ mate⟩ **d :** ALTERNATE, OTHER ⟨elects a mayor every ~ year⟩ **e :** resembling or suggesting a prototype **:** ANOTHER ⟨a ~ Thoreau⟩ **f :** being the forward gear or speed next higher than first in a motor vehicle **2 :** relating to or having a part typically subordinate to and lower in pitch than the first part in concerted or ensemble music — **second** *or* **sec·ond·ly** *adv*
[2]**second** *n* (14c) **1 a** — see NUMBER table **b :** one that is next after the first in rank, position, authority, or precedence ⟨the ~ in line⟩ **2 :** one that assists or supports another; *esp* **:** the assistant of a duelist or boxer **3 a :** the musical interval embracing two diatonic degrees **b :** a tone at this interval; *specif* **:** SUPERTONIC **c :** the harmonic combination of two tones a second apart **4 a** *pl* **:** merchandise that is usu. slightly flawed and does not meet the manufacturer's standard for firsts or irregulars **b :** an article of such merchandise **5 :** the act or declaration by which a parliamentary motion is seconded **6 :** a place next below the first in a competition, examination, or contest **7 :** SECOND BASE **8 :** the second forward gear or speed of a motor vehicle **9** *pl* **:** a second helping of food
[3]**second** *n* [ME *secounde,* fr. ML *secunda,* fr. L, fem. of *secundus* second; fr. its being the second sexagesimal division of a unit, as a minute is the first] (14c) **1 a :** the 60th part of a minute of angular measure **b :** the 60th part of a minute of time **:** 1/86,400 part of the mean solar day; *specif* **:** the base unit of time in the International System of Units that is equal to the duration of 9,192,631,770 periods of the radiation corresponding to the transition between the two hyperfine levels of the ground state of the cesium-133 atom **2 :** an instant of time **:** MOMENT
[4]**second** *vt* [L *secundare,* fr. *secundus* second, favorable] (ca. 1586) **1 a :** to give support or encouragement to **:** ASSIST **b :** to support (a fighting person or group) in combat **:** bring up reinforcements for **2 a :** to support or assist in contention or debate **b :** to endorse (a motion or a nomination) so that debate or voting may begin **3** \si-ˈkänd\ *chiefly Brit* **:** to release (as a military officer) from a regularly assigned position for temporary duty with another unit or organization — **sec·ond·er** *n*
[1]**sec·ond·ary** \ˈse-kən-ˌder-ē\ *adj* (14c) **1 a :** of second rank, importance, or value **b :** of, relating to, or constituting the second strongest of the three or four degrees of stress recognized by most linguists ⟨the fourth syllable of *basketball team* carries ~ stress⟩ **c** *of a tense* **:** expressive of past time **2 a :** immediately derived from something original, primary, or basic **b :** of, relating to, or being the induced current or its circuit in an induction coil or transformer ⟨~ voltage⟩ **c :** characterized by or resulting from the substitution of two atoms or groups in a molecule ⟨a ~ salt⟩; *esp* **:** being, characterized by, or attached to a carbon atom having bonds to two other carbon atoms **d (1) :** not first in order of occurrence or development **(2) :** dependent or consequent on another disease or condition ⟨~ hypertension⟩ **(3) :** produced by activity of formative tissue and esp. cambium other than that at a growing point ⟨~ growth⟩ ⟨~ phloem⟩ **3 a :** of, relating to, or being the second order or stage in a series **b :** of, relating to, or being the second segment of the wing of a bird or the quills of this segment **c :** of or relating to a secondary school ⟨~ education⟩ — **sec·ond·ar·i·ly** \ˌse-kən-ˈder-ə-lē\ *adv* — **sec·ond·ar·i·ness** \ˈse-kən-ˌder-ē-nəs\ *n*
[2]**secondary** *n, pl* **-ar·ies** (15c) **1 :** one occupying a subordinate or auxiliary position rather than that of a principal **2 :** a defensive football backfield **3 :** the coil through which the secondary current passes in an induction coil or transformer — called also *secondary coil* **4 :** any of the quill feathers of the forearm of a bird — see WING illustration
secondary care *n* (1976) **:** medical care provided by a specialist or facility upon referral by a primary care physician — compare PRIMARY CARE, TERTIARY CARE
secondary cell *n* (1885) **:** STORAGE BATTERY
secondary color *n* (1831) **:** a color formed by mixing two primary colors in equal or equivalent quantities
secondary emission *n* (1918) **:** the emission of electrons from a surface that is bombarded by particles (as electrons or ions) from a primary source
secondary radiation *n* (1900) **:** radiation emitted by molecules or atoms after bombardment by a primary radiation
secondary road *n* (1903) **1 :** a road not of primary importance **2 :** a feeder road
secondary root *n* (1861) **:** one of the branches of a primary root
secondary school *n* (1835) **:** a school intermediate between elementary school and college and usu. offering general, technical, vocational, or college-preparatory courses
secondary sex characteristic *n* (1927) **:** a physical characteristic (as the breasts of a female mammal or the breeding plumage of a male bird) that appears in members of one sex at puberty or in seasonal breeders at the breeding season and is not directly concerned with reproduction — called also *secondary sexual characteristic*
secondary syphilis *n* (1861) **:** the second stage of syphilis that appears from 2 to 6 months after primary infection, that is marked by lesions esp. in the skin but also in organs and tissues, and that lasts from 3 to 12 weeks — compare TERTIARY SYPHILIS
second banana *n* (1953) **:** a comedian who plays a supporting role to a top banana; *broadly* **:** a person in a subservient position
second base *n* (1845) **1 :** the base that must be touched second by a base runner in baseball **2 :** the player position for defending the area on the first-base side of second base — **second baseman** *n*
sec·ond–best \ˌse-kən(d)-ˈbest, -kᵊŋ-\ *adj* (14c) **:** next to the best
[1]**second best** *n* (1647) **:** one that is below or after the best
[2]**second best** *adv* (1777) **:** in second place
second blessing *n* (1891) **:** sanctification as a second gift of the Holy Spirit that follows an initial experience of conversion
second childhood *n* (1641) **:** DOTAGE
second–class *adj* (ca. 1838) **1 :** of or relating to a second class **2 :** MEDIOCRE; *also* **:** socially, politically, or economically deprived
second class *n* (1810) **1 :** the second and usu. next to highest group in a classification **2 :** CABIN CLASS **3 :** a class of U.S. or Canadian mail comprising periodicals sent to regular subscribers
Second Coming *n* (1588) **:** the coming of Christ as judge on the last day
second cousin *n* (1660) **:** the child of one's parent's first cousin
second–degree burn *n* (1937) **:** a burn marked by pain, blistering, and superficial destruction of dermis with edema and hyperemia of the tissues beneath the burn
Second Empire *adj* (1873) **:** of, relating to, or characteristic of a style (as of furniture) developed in France under Napoleon III and marked by heavy ornate modification of Empire styles
second estate *n, often cap S&E* (ca. 1935) **:** the second of the traditional political classes; *specif* **:** NOBILITY
second fiddle *n* (1809) **:** one that plays a supporting or subservient role
second growth *n* (1829) **:** forest trees that come up naturally after removal of the first growth by cutting or by fire
sec·ond–guess \ˌse-kᵊŋ-ˈges, -kən(d)-\ *vt* (1941) **1 :** to criticize or question actions or decisions of (someone) often after the results of

\ə\ **abut** \ᵊ\ **kitten, F table** \ər\ **further** \a\ **ash** \ā\ **ace** \ä\ **mop, mar**
\au̇\ **out** \ch\ **chin** \e\ **bet** \ē\ **easy** \g\ **go** \i\ **hit** \ī\ **ice** \j\ **job**
\ŋ\ **sing** \ō\ **go** \ȯ\ **law** \ȯi\ **boy** \th\ **thin** \t͟h\ **the** \ü\ **loot** \u̇\ **foot**
\y\ **yet** \zh\ **vision, beige** \k̲, ⁿ, œ, ue, ʸ\ *see* Guide to Pronunciation

those actions or decisions are known ⟨meet almost every morning and, over coffee, ~ the local coach —Bruce Newman⟩; *also* : to engage in such criticism of (an action or decision) ⟨~ the general's strategy⟩ **2** : to seek to anticipate or predict ⟨lived royally by his ability to ~ the stock market —*Time*⟩ — **sec·ond–guess·er** *n*

[1]**sec·ond·hand** \ˈse-kən(d)-ˈhand\ *adj* (1654) **1 a** : received from or through an intermediary : BORROWED **b** : DERIVATIVE ⟨~ ideas⟩ **2 a** : acquired after being used by another : not new ⟨~ books⟩ **b** : dealing in secondhand merchandise ⟨a ~ bookstore⟩

[2]**secondhand** *adv* (1795) **1** : at second hand : INDIRECTLY ⟨heard about it ~⟩ **2** : as a secondhand item ⟨bought the couch ~⟩

[1]**second hand** \ˌse-kən(d)-ˈhand\ *n* (15c) : an intermediate person or means : INTERMEDIARY — usu. used in the phrase *at second hand*

[2]**second hand** \ˈsek-ən(d)-ˌ\ *n* (1759) : the hand marking seconds on a timepiece

secondhand smoke *n* (1976) : tobacco smoke that is exhaled by smokers or is given off by burning tobacco and is inhaled by persons nearby

second lieutenant *n* (1702) : a commissioned officer of the lowest rank in the army, air force, or marine corps

sec·ond–line \ˈse-kᵊn(d)-ˈlīn\ *adj* (1991) : not being the usual or preferred choice ⟨~ drugs to treat tuberculosis⟩ — compare FIRST-LINE

second mortgage *n* (1912) : a mortgage the lien of which is subordinate to that of a first mortgage

second nature *n* (1582) : an acquired deeply ingrained habit or skill ⟨after a while, using the gearshift becomes *second nature*⟩

se·con·do \si-ˈkōn-(ˌ)dō, -ˈkän-\ *n, pl* **-di** \-(ˌ)dē\ [It, fr. *secondo,* adj., second, fr. L *secundus*] (1792) : the second part in a concerted piece; *esp* : the lower part (as in a piano duet)

second person *n* (1612) **1 a** : a set of linguistic forms (as verb forms, pronouns, and inflectional affixes) referring to the person or thing addressed in the utterance in which they occur **b** : a linguistic form belonging to such a set **2** : reference of a linguistic form to the person or thing addressed in the utterance in which it occurs

sec·ond–rate \ˌse-kən(d)-ˈrāt\ *adj* (1669) : of second or inferior quality or value : MEDIOCRE ⟨a ~ restaurant⟩ — **sec·ond–rate·ness** *n* — **sec·ond–rat·er** \-ˈrā-tər\ *n*

Second Reader *n* (1895) : a member of a Christian Science church or society chosen for a term of office to assist the First Reader in conducting services by reading aloud selections from the Bible

second reading *n* (1647) **1** : the stage in the British legislative process following the first reading and usu. providing for debate on the principal features of a bill before its submission to a committee for consideration of details **2** : the stage in the U.S. legislative process that occurs when a bill has been reported back from committee and that provides an opportunity for full debate and amendment before a vote is taken on the question of a third reading

second sight *n* (1616) : the capacity to see remote or future objects or events : CLAIRVOYANCE, PRECOGNITION

second–story man *n* (1886) : a burglar who enters a house by an upstairs window

sec·ond–string \ˌse-kən(d)-ˈstriŋ, ˌse-kᵊŋ-\ *adj* [fr. the reserve bowstring carried by an archer in case the first breaks] (1922) : being a substitute as distinguished from a regular (as on a ball team)

second thought *n* (1622) : reconsideration or a revised opinion of a previous often hurried decision ⟨began to have *second thoughts*⟩

second wind *n* (1824) : renewed energy or endurance

second world *n, often cap S&W* [after *third world*] (1966) : Communist nations regarded in the latter part of the 20th century as a political and economic bloc

se·cre·cy \ˈsē-krə-sē\ *n, pl* **-cies** [alter. of earlier *secretie,* fr. ME *secretee,* fr. *secret* secret] (1556) **1** : the condition of being hidden or concealed **2** : the habit or practice of keeping secrets or maintaining privacy or concealment

[1]**se·cret** \ˈsē-krət\ *adj* [ME, fr. AF *secré, secret,* fr. L *secretus,* fr. pp. of *secernere* to separate, distinguish, fr. *se-* apart + *cernere* to sift — more at SECEDE, CERTAIN] (14c) **1 a** : kept from knowledge or view : HIDDEN **b** : marked by the habit of discretion : CLOSEMOUTHED **c** : working with hidden aims or methods : UNDERCOVER ⟨a ~ agent⟩ **d** : not acknowledged : UNAVOWED ⟨a ~ bride⟩ **e** : conducted in secret ⟨a ~ trial⟩ **2** : remote from human frequentation or notice : SECLUDED **3** : revealed only to the initiated : ESOTERIC **4** : designed to elude observation or detection ⟨a ~ panel⟩ **5** : containing information whose unauthorized disclosure could endanger national security — compare CONFIDENTIAL, TOP SECRET — **se·cret·ly** *adv*

syn SECRET, COVERT, STEALTHY, FURTIVE, CLANDESTINE, SURREPTITIOUS, UNDERHANDED mean done without attracting observation. SECRET implies concealment on any grounds for any motive ⟨met at a *secret* location⟩. COVERT stresses the fact of not being open or declared ⟨*covert* intelligence operations⟩. STEALTHY suggests taking pains to avoid being seen or heard esp. in some misdoing ⟨the *stealthy* step of a burglar⟩. FURTIVE implies a sly or cautious stealthiness ⟨lovers exchanging *furtive* glances⟩. CLANDESTINE implies secrecy usu. for an evil, illicit, or unauthorized purpose and often emphasizes the fear of being discovered ⟨a *clandestine* meeting of conspirators⟩. SURREPTITIOUS applies to action or behavior done secretly often with skillful avoidance of detection and in violation of custom, law, or authority ⟨the *surreptitious* stockpiling of weapons⟩. UNDERHANDED stresses fraud or deception ⟨an *underhanded* trick⟩.

[2]**secret** *n* (14c) **1 a** : something kept hidden or unexplained : MYSTERY **b** : something kept from the knowledge of others or shared only confidentially with a few **c** : a method, formula, or process used in an art or operation and divulged only to those of one's own company or craft : TRADE SECRET **d** *pl* : the practices or knowledge making up the shared discipline or culture of an esoteric society **2** : a prayer traditionally said inaudibly by the celebrant just before the preface of the mass **3** : something taken to be a specific or key to a desired end ⟨the ~ of longevity⟩ — **in secret** : in a private place or manner

se·cre·ta·gogue \si-ˈkrē-tə-ˌgäg\ *n* [*secretion* + *-agogue*] (1919) : a substance stimulating secretion (as by the stomach or pancreas)

sec·re·tar·i·at \ˌse-krə-ˈter-ē-ət, -ē-ˌat\ *n* [F *secrétariat,* fr. ML *secretariatus,* fr. *secretarius*] (1811) **1** : the office of secretary **2** : a secretarial corps; *specif* : the clerical staff of an organization **3** : the administrative department of a governmental organization

sec·re·tary \ˈse-krə-ˌter-ē, ˈse-kə-ˌter-, *in rapid speech also* ˈsek-ˌter-, *esp Brit* ˈse-k(r)ə-trē\ *n, pl* **-tar·ies** [ME *secretarie,* fr. ML *secretarius,* confidential employee, secretary, fr. L *secretum* secret, fr. neut. of *secretus*] (15c) **1** : one employed to handle correspondence and manage routine and detail work for a superior **2 a** : an officer of a business concern who may keep records of directors' and stockholders' meetings and of stock ownership and transfer and help supervise the company's legal interests **b** : an officer of an organization or society responsible for its records and correspondence **3** : an officer of state who superintends a government administrative department ⟨the ~ of labor⟩ **4 a** : WRITING DESK, ESCRITOIRE **b** : a writing desk with a top section for books — **sec·re·tar·i·al** \ˌse-krə-ˈter-ē-əl\ *adj* — **sec·re·tary·ship** \ˈse-krə-ˌter-ē-ˌship\ *n*

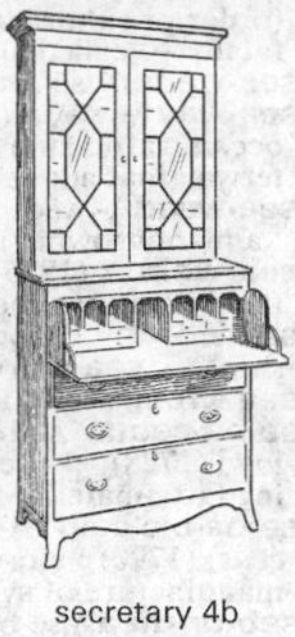

secretary 4b

secretary bird *n* [prob. fr. the resemblance of its crest to a bunch of quill pens stuck behind the ear] (1824) : a large long-legged bird of prey (*Sagittarius serpentarius* of the family Sagittariidae) of sub-Saharan Africa that feeds largely on reptiles

secretary–general *n, pl* **secretaries–general** (1701) : a principal administrative officer ⟨~ of the United Nations⟩

secret ballot *n* (1917) : AUSTRALIAN BALLOT

[1]**se·crete** \si-ˈkrēt\ *vt* **se·cret·ed; se·cret·ing** [back-formation fr. *secretion*] (1693) : to form and give off (a secretion)

[2]**se·crete** \si-ˈkrēt, ˈsē-krət\ *vt* **se·cret·ed; se·cret·ing** [alter. of obs. *secret,* fr. [1]*secret*] (1741) **1** : to deposit or conceal in a hiding place **2** : to appropriate secretly : ABSTRACT ***syn*** see HIDE

se·cre·tin \si-ˈkrē-tᵊn\ *n* [*secretion* + [1]*-in*] (1902) : an intestinal proteinaceous hormone capable of stimulating secretion by the pancreas and liver

se·cre·tion \si-ˈkrē-shən\ *n* [F *sécrétion,* fr. L *secretion-, secretio* separation, fr. *secernere* to separate — more at SECRET] (1646) **1 a** : the process of segregating, elaborating, and releasing some material either functionally specialized (as saliva) or isolated for excretion (as urine) **b** : a product of secretion formed by an animal or plant; *esp* : one performing a specific useful function in the organism **2** [[2]*secrete*] : the act of hiding something : CONCEALMENT — **se·cre·tion·ary** \-shə-ˌner-ē\ *adj*

se·cre·tive \ˈsē-krə-tiv, si-ˈkrē-\ *adj* [back-formation fr. *secretiveness,* part trans. of F *secrétivité*] (1835) : disposed to secrecy : not open or outgoing in speech, activity, or purposes ***syn*** see SILENT — **se·cre·tive·ly** *adv* — **se·cre·tive·ness** *n*

se·cre·tor \si-ˈkrē-tər\ *n* (1941) : an individual of blood group A, B, or AB who secretes the antigens characteristic of these blood groups in bodily fluids (as saliva)

se·cre·to·ry \ˈsē-krə-ˌtȯr-ē, *esp Brit* si-ˈkrē-t(ə-)rē\ *adj* (1692) : of, relating to, or promoting secretion; *also* : produced by secretion

secret partner *n* (1844) : a partner whose membership in a partnership is kept secret from the public

secret police *n* (1823) : a police organization operating for the most part in secrecy and esp. for the political purposes of its government often with terroristic methods

secret service *n* (1706) **1** : a governmental service of a secret nature **2** *cap both Ss* : a division of the U.S. Treasury Department charged chiefly with the suppression of counterfeiting and the protection of the president

secret society *n* (1821) : any of various oath-bound societies often devoted to brotherhood, moral discipline, and mutual assistance

[1]**sect** \ˈsekt\ *n* [ME *secte,* fr. AF & LL & L; AF, group, faction, fr. LL *secta* organized ecclesiastical body, fr. L, course of action, way of life, prob. fr. *sectari* to pursue, freq. of *sequi* to follow — more at SUE] (14c) **1 a** : a dissenting or schismatic religious body; *esp* : one regarded as extreme or heretical **b** : a religious denomination **2** *archaic* : SEX 1 ⟨so is all her ~ —Shak.⟩ **3 a** : a group adhering to a distinctive doctrine or to a leader **b** : PARTY **c** : FACTION

[2]**sect** *abbr* section; sectional

[1]**sec·tar·i·an** \sek-ˈter-ē-ən\ *adj* (1649) **1** : of, relating to, or characteristic of a sect or sectarian **2** : limited in character or scope : PAROCHIAL — **sec·tar·i·an·ism** \-ē-ə-ˌni-zəm\ *n*

[2]**sectarian** *n* (1819) **1** : an adherent of a sect **2** : a narrow or bigoted person

sec·tar·i·an·ize \sek-ˈter-ē-ə-ˌnīz\ *vb* **-ized; -iz·ing** *vi* (1842) : to act as sectarians ~ *vt* : to make sectarian

sec·ta·ry \ˈsek-tə-rē\ *n, pl* **-ries** (1556) : a member of a sect

sec·tile \ˈsek-tᵊl, -ˌtī(-ə)l\ *adj* [L *sectilis,* fr. *sectus,* pp. of *secare*] (1805) : capable of being severed by a knife with a smooth cut ⟨amber is a ~ resin⟩ — **sec·til·i·ty** \sek-ˈti-lə-tē\ *n*

[1]**sec·tion** \ˈsek-shən\ *n* [L *section-, sectio,* fr. *secare* to cut — more at SAW] (1534) **1 a** : the action or an instance of cutting or separating by cutting **b** : a part set off by or as if by cutting **2** : a distinct part or portion of something written (as a chapter, law, or newspaper) **3 a** : the profile of something as it would appear if cut through by an intersecting plane **b** : the plane figure resulting from the cutting of a solid by a plane **4** : a natural subdivision of a taxonomic group **5** : a character § used as a mark for the beginning of a section and as a reference mark **6** : a piece of land one square mile in area forming esp. one of the 36 subdivisions of a township **7** : a distinct part of a territorial or political area, community, or group of people ⟨the historic ~ of the city⟩ **8 a** : a part that may be, is, or is viewed as separated ⟨a board cut into ~*s*⟩ ⟨the northern ~ of the route⟩ **b** : one segment of a fruit : CARPEL **9** : a basic military unit usu. having a special function **10** : a very thin slice (as of tissue) suitable for microscopic examination **11 a** : one of the classes formed by dividing the students taking a course **b** : one of the discussion groups into which a conference or organization is divided **12 a** : a part of a permanent railroad way under the care of a particular crew **b** : one of two or more vehicles or trains which run on the same schedule **13** : one of several component parts

that may be assembled or reassembled ⟨a bookcase in ~*s*⟩ **14 :** a division of an orchestra composed of one class of instruments ⟨the string ~⟩ **15 :** SIGNATURE 3b ***syn*** see PART

[2]**section** *vb* **sec·tioned; sec·tion·ing** \-sh(ə-)niŋ\ *vt* (1819) **1 :** to cut or separate into sections ⟨~ an orange⟩ **2 :** to represent in sections ~ *vi* **:** to become cut or separated into parts

[1]**sec·tion·al** \ˈsek-shnəl, -shə-nᵊl\ *adj* (1806) **1 a :** of or relating to a section **b :** local or regional rather than general in character ⟨~ interests⟩ **2 :** consisting of or divided into sections ⟨~ furniture⟩ — **sec·tion·al·ly** *adv*

[2]**sectional** *n* (1901) **:** a piece of furniture made up of modular units capable of use separately or in various combinations

sec·tion·al·ism \ˈsek-shnə-ˌli-zəm, -shə-nə-ˌli-\ *n* (1847) **:** an exaggerated devotion to the interests of a region

Section Eight *n* [*Section VIII,* Army Regulation 615–360, in effect from December 1922 to July 1944] (1943) **:** a discharge from the U.S. Army for military inaptitude or undesirable habits or traits of character; *also* **:** a soldier receiving such a discharge

section gang *n* (1889) **:** a crew of track workers employed to maintain a railroad section

section hand *n* (1873) **:** a laborer belonging to a section gang

[1]**sec·tor** \ˈsek-tər, -ˌtȯr\ *n* [LL, fr. L, cutter, fr. *secare* to cut — more at SAW] (1570) **1 a :** a geometric figure bounded by two radii and the included arc of a circle **b** (1) **:** a subdivision of a defensive military position (2) **:** a portion of a military front or area of operation **c :** an area or portion resembling a sector ⟨bilingual ~ of town —David Kleinberg⟩ **d :** a sociological, economic, or political subdivision of society ⟨cooperation between the public and private ~*s* —Peter Chapman⟩ **2 :** a mathematical instrument consisting of two rulers connected at one end by a joint and marked with several scales **3 :** a subdivision of a track on a computer disk — **sec·tor·al** \ˈsek-t(ə-)rəl\ *adj*

[2]**sec·tor** \-tər\ *vt* **sec·tored; sec·tor·ing** \-t(ə-)riŋ\ (1884) **:** to divide into or furnish with sectors

sec·to·ri·al \sek-ˈtȯr-ē-əl\ *adj* (1803) **:** of, relating to, or having the shape of a sector of a circle

[1]**sec·u·lar** \ˈse-kyə-lər\ *adj* [ME, fr. AF *seculer,* fr. LL *saecularis,* fr. *saeculum* the present world, fr. L, generation, age, century, world; akin to W *hoedl* lifetime] (14c) **1 a :** of or relating to the worldly or temporal ⟨~ concerns⟩ **b :** not overtly or specif. religious ⟨~ music⟩ **c :** not ecclesiastical or clerical ⟨~ courts⟩ ⟨~ landowners⟩ **2 :** not bound by monastic vows or rules; *specif* **:** of, relating to, or forming clergy not belonging to a religious order or congregation ⟨a ~ priest⟩ **3 a :** occurring once in an age or a century **b :** existing or continuing through ages or centuries **c :** of or relating to a long term of indefinite duration ⟨~ inflation⟩ — **sec·u·lar·i·ty** \ˌse-kyə-ˈla-rə-tē\ *n* — **sec·u·lar·ly** \ˈse-kyə-lər-lē\ *adv*

[2]**secular** *n, pl* **seculars** *or* **secular** (14c) **1 :** a secular ecclesiastic (as a diocesan priest) **2 :** LAYMAN

secular humanism *n* (1933) **:** HUMANISM 3; *esp* **:** humanistic philosophy viewed as a nontheistic religion antagonistic to traditional religion — **secular humanist** *n or adj*

sec·u·lar·ise *Brit var of* SECULARIZE

sec·u·lar·ism \ˈse-kyə-lə-ˌri-zəm\ *n* (1851) **:** indifference to or rejection or exclusion of religion and religious considerations — **sec·u·lar·ist** \-rist\ *n* — **secularist** *also* **sec·u·lar·is·tic** \ˌse-kyə-lə-ˈris-tik\ *adj*

sec·u·lar·ize \ˈse-kyə-lə-ˌrīz\ *vt* **-ized; -iz·ing** (1611) **1 :** to make secular **2 :** to transfer from ecclesiastical to civil or lay use, possession, or control **3 :** to convert to or imbue with secularism — **sec·u·lar·i·za·tion** \ˌse-kyə-lə-rə-ˈzā-shən\ *n* — **sec·u·lar·iz·er** *n*

[1]**se·cure** \si-ˈkyu̇r\ *adj* **se·cur·er; -est** [L *securus* safe, secure, fr. *se* without + *cura* care — more at SUICIDE] (ca. 1533) **1 a** *archaic* **:** unwisely free from fear or distrust **:** OVERCONFIDENT **b :** easy in mind **:** CONFIDENT **c :** assured in opinion or expectation **:** having no doubt **2 a :** free from danger **b :** free from risk of loss **c :** affording safety ⟨a ~ hideaway⟩ **d :** TRUSTWORTHY, DEPENDABLE ⟨a ~ foundation⟩ **3 :** ASSURED 1 ⟨a ~ victory⟩ — **se·cure·ly** *adv* — **se·cure·ness** *n*

[2]**secure** *vb* **se·cured; se·cur·ing** *vt* (1588) **1 a :** to relieve from exposure to danger **:** act to make safe against adverse contingencies ⟨~ a supply line from enemy raids⟩ **b :** to put beyond hazard of losing or of not receiving **:** GUARANTEE ⟨~ the blessings of liberty —*U.S. Constitution*⟩ **c :** to give pledge of payment to (a creditor) or of (an obligation) ⟨~ a note by a pledge of collateral⟩ **2 a :** to take (a person) into custody **:** hold fast **:** PINION **b :** to make fast ⟨~ a door⟩ ⟨~ a bike to a tree⟩ **3 a :** to get secure usu. lasting possession or control of ⟨~ a job⟩ **b :** BRING ABOUT, EFFECT **4 :** to release (naval personnel) from work or duty ~ *vi* **1** *of naval personnel* **:** to stop work **:** go off duty **2** *of a ship* **:** to tie up **:** BERTH ***syn*** see ENSURE — **se·cur·er** *n*

se·cure·ment \si-ˈkyu̇r-mənt\ *n* (1622) **1** *obs* **:** PROTECTION **2 :** the act or process of securing

se·cu·ri·tize \si-ˈkyu̇r-ə-ˌtīz\ *vt* **-tized; -tiz·ing** (1981) **:** to consolidate (as mortgage loans) and sell to other investors for resale to the public in the form of securities — **se·cu·ri·ti·za·tion** \-ˌkyu̇r-ə-tə-ˈzā-shən\ *n*

se·cu·ri·ty \si-ˈkyu̇r-ə-tē\ *n, pl* **-ties** (15c) **1 :** the quality or state of being secure: as **a :** freedom from danger **:** SAFETY **b :** freedom from fear or anxiety **c :** freedom from the prospect of being laid off ⟨job ~⟩ **2 a :** something given, deposited, or pledged to make certain the fulfillment of an obligation **b :** SURETY **3 :** an instrument of investment in the form of a document (as a stock certificate or bond) providing evidence of its ownership **4 a :** something that secures **:** PROTECTION **b** (1) **:** measures taken to guard against espionage or sabotage, crime, attack, or escape (2) **:** an organization or department whose task is security

security blanket *n* (1968) **1 :** a blanket carried by a child as a protection against anxiety **2 :** a usu. familiar object whose presence dispels anxiety

Security Council *n* (1944) **:** a permanent council of the United Nations with primary responsibility for maintaining peace and security

security interest *n* (1951) **:** the rights that a creditor has in the personal property of a debtor that secures an obligation **:** LIEN

security police *n* (1920) **1 :** police engaged in counterespionage **2 :** AIR POLICE

secy *abbr* secretary

sed *abbr* sedimentation

se·dan \si-ˈdan\ *n* [origin unknown] (1635) **1 :** a portable often covered chair that is designed to carry one person and that is borne on poles by two people **2 a :** a 2- or 4-door automobile seating four or more persons and usu. having a permanent top — compare COUPE **b :** a motorboat having one passenger compartment

[1]**se·date** \si-ˈdāt\ *adj* [L *sedatus,* fr. pp. of *sedare* to calm; akin to *sedēre* to sit — more at SIT] (1663) **:** keeping a quiet steady attitude or pace **:** UNRUFFLED ***syn*** see SERIOUS — **se·date·ly** *adv* — **se·date·ness** *n*

[2]**sedate** *vt* **se·dat·ed; se·dat·ing** [back-formation fr. *sedative*] (1945) **:** to dose with sedatives

se·da·tion \si-ˈdā-shən\ *n* (1543) **1 :** the inducing of a relaxed easy state esp. by the use of sedatives **2 :** a state resulting from or as if from sedation

[1]**sed·a·tive** \ˈse-də-tiv\ *adj* [ME, alleviating pain, fr. MF *sedatif,* fr. ML *sedativus,* fr. L *sedatus*] (1779) **:** tending to calm, moderate, or tranquilize nervousness or excitement

[2]**sedative** *n* (1797) **:** a sedative agent or drug

sed·en·tary \ˈse-dᵊn-ˌter-ē\ *adj* [MF *sedentaire,* fr. L *sedentarius,* fr. *sedent-, sedens,* prp. of *sedēre* to sit — more at SIT] (1598) **1 :** not migratory **:** SETTLED ⟨~ birds⟩ ⟨~ civilizations⟩ **2 a :** doing or requiring much sitting ⟨a ~ job⟩ **b :** not physically active ⟨a ~ lifestyle⟩ **3 :** permanently attached ⟨~ barnacles⟩

se·der \ˈsā-dər\ *n, pl* **seders** *also* **se·da·rim** \sə-ˈdär-əm, ˌse-dä-ˈrēm\ *often cap* [Heb *sēdher* order] (1865) **:** a Jewish home or community service including a ceremonial dinner held on the first or first and second evenings of the Passover in commemoration of the exodus from Egypt

se·de·runt \sə-ˈdir-ənt, -ˈder-\ *n* [L, there (they) sat (fr. *sedēre* to sit), word used to introduce list of those attending a session — more at SIT] (1825) **:** a prolonged sitting (as for discussion)

sedge \ˈsej\ *n* [ME *segge,* fr. OE *secg;* akin to MHG *segge* sedge, OE *sagu* saw — more at SAW] (bef. 12c) **:** any of a family (Cyperaceae, the sedge family) of usu. tufted monocotyledonous marsh plants differing from the related grasses in having achenes and solid stems; *esp* **:** any of a cosmopolitan genus (*Carex*) — **sedgy** \ˈse-jē\ *adj*

se·di·lia \sə-ˈdēl-yə, -ˈdil-, *esp Brit* -ˈdī(-ə)l-\ *n pl* [L, pl. of *sedile* seat, fr. *sedēre*] (1793) **:** seats on the south side of the chancel for the celebrant and his assistants

[1]**sed·i·ment** \ˈse-də-mənt\ *n* [L *sedimentum* settling, fr. *sedēre* to sit, sink down] (1547) **1 :** the matter that settles to the bottom of a liquid **2 :** material deposited by water, wind, or glaciers

[2]**sed·i·ment** \-ˌment\ *vt* (1859) **:** to deposit as sediment ~ *vi* **1 :** to settle to the bottom in a liquid **2 :** to deposit sediment

sed·i·ment·able \ˌse-də-ˈmen-tə-bəl\ *adj* (1943) **:** capable of being sedimented by centrifugation ⟨~ ribosomal particles⟩

sed·i·men·ta·ry \ˌse-də-ˈmen-tə-rē, -ˈmen-trē\ *adj* (1830) **1 :** of, relating to, or containing sediment ⟨~ deposits⟩ **2 :** formed by or from deposits of sediment ⟨~ rock⟩

sed·i·men·ta·tion \ˌse-də-mən-ˈtā-shən, -ˌmen-\ *n* (1848) **:** the action or process of forming or depositing sediment **:** SETTLING

sed·i·men·tol·o·gy \ˌse-də-mən-ˈtä-lə-jē, -ˌmen-\ *n* (1932) **:** a branch of science that deals with sedimentary rocks and their inclusions — **sed·i·men·to·log·ic** \-ˌmen-tə-ˈlä-jik\ *or* **sed·i·men·to·log·i·cal** \-ji-kəl\ *adj* — **sed·i·men·to·log·i·cal·ly** \-ji-k(ə-)lē\ *adv* — **sed·i·men·tol·o·gist** \-mən-ˈtä-lə-jist, -ˌmen-\ *n*

se·di·tion \si-ˈdi-shən\ *n* [ME *sedicioun,* fr. AF *sediciun,* fr. L *sedition-, seditio,* lit., separation, fr. *sed-, se-* apart + *ition-, itio* act of going, fr. *ire* to go — more at SECEDE, ISSUE] (14c) **:** incitement of resistance to or insurrection against lawful authority

se·di·tious \si-ˈdi-shəs\ *adj* (15c) **1 :** disposed to arouse or take part in or guilty of sedition **2 :** of, relating to, or tending toward sedition — **se·di·tious·ly** *adv* — **se·di·tious·ness** *n*

se·duce \si-ˈdüs, -ˈdyüs\ *vt* **se·duced; se·duc·ing** [LL *seducere,* fr. L, to lead away, fr. *se-* apart + *ducere* to lead — more at TOW] (15c) **1 :** to persuade to disobedience or disloyalty **2 :** to lead astray usu. by persuasion or false promises **3 :** to carry out the physical seduction of **:** entice to sexual intercourse **4 :** ATTRACT ***syn*** see LURE — **se·duc·er** *n*

se·duce·ment \-mənt\ *n* (1586) **1 :** SEDUCTION **2 :** something that serves to seduce

se·duc·tion \si-ˈdək-shən\ *n* [MF, fr. LL *seduction-, seductio,* fr. L, act of leading aside, fr. *seducere*] (1526) **1 :** the act of seducing; *esp* **:** the enticement of a person to sexual intercourse **2 :** something that seduces **:** TEMPTATION **3 :** something that attracts or charms

se·duc·tive \-ˈdək-tiv\ *adj* (1651) **:** tending to seduce **:** having alluring or tempting qualities ⟨a ~, sometimes disingenuous man —Thatcher Freund⟩ ⟨a ~ aroma⟩ — **se·duc·tive·ly** *adv* — **se·duc·tive·ness** *n*

se·duc·tress \-ˈdək-trəs\ *n* [obs. *seductor* male seducer, fr. LL, fr. *seducere* to seduce] (1802) **:** a woman who seduces

se·du·li·ty \si-ˈdü-lə-tē, -ˈdyü-\ *n* (1542) **:** sedulous activity **:** DILIGENCE

sed·u·lous \ˈse-jə-ləs\ *adj* [L *sedulus,* fr. *sedulo* sincerely, diligently, fr. *sed-, se* without + *dolus* guile — more at SUICIDE] (1540) **1 :** involving or accomplished with careful perseverance ⟨~ craftsmanship⟩ **2 :** diligent in application or pursuit ⟨a ~ student⟩ ***syn*** see BUSY — **sed·u·lous·ly** *adv* — **sed·u·lous·ness** *n*

se·dum \ˈsē-dəm\ *n* [NL, fr. L, houseleek] (1760) **:** any of a genus (*Sedum*) of widely distributed fleshy herbs of the orpine family — compare STONECROP

[1]**see** \ˈsē\ *vb* **saw** \ˈsȯ\; **seen** \ˈsēn\; **see·ing** \ˈsē-iŋ\ [ME *seen,* fr. OE *sēon;* akin to OHG *sehan* to see and perh. to L *sequi* to follow — more at SUE] *vt* (bef. 12c) **1 a :** to perceive by the eye **b :** to perceive or detect as if by sight **2 a :** to have experience of **:** UNDERGO ⟨~ army service⟩ **b :** to come to know **:** DISCOVER **c :** to be the setting or time of ⟨the last fifty years have *seen* a sweeping revolution in science —Barry Commoner⟩ **3 a :** to form a mental picture of **:** VISUALIZE ⟨can still ~ her as she was years ago⟩ **b :** to perceive the meaning or importance of **:** UNDERSTAND **c :** to be aware of **:** RECOGNIZE ⟨~*s* only our faults⟩ **d :** to imagine as a possibility **:** SUPPOSE ⟨couldn't ~

\ə\ **abut** \ᵊ\ **kitten,** F **table** \ər\ **further** \a\ **ash** \ā\ **ace** \ä\ **mop, mar** \au̇\ **out** \ch\ **chin** \e\ **bet** \ē\ **easy** \g\ **go** \i\ **hit** \ī\ **ice** \j\ **job** \ŋ\ **sing** \ō\ **go** \ȯ\ **law** \ȯi\ **boy** \th\ **thin** \t͟h\ **the** \ü\ **loot** \u̇\ **foot** \y\ **yet** \zh\ **vision, beige** \k, ⁿ, œ, ue, ʸ\ *see* Guide to Pronunciation

him as a crook⟩ **4 a** : EXAMINE, WATCH ⟨want to ~ how she handles the problem⟩ **b** (1) : READ (2) : to read of **c** : to attend to as a spectator ⟨~ a play⟩ **5 a** : to take care of : provide for ⟨had enough money to ~ us through⟩ **b** : to make sure ⟨~ that order is kept⟩ **6 a** : to regard as : JUDGE **b** : to prefer to have ⟨I'll ~ him hanged first⟩ ⟨I'll ~ you dead before I accept your terms⟩ **c** : to find acceptable or attractive ⟨can't understand what he ~*s* in her⟩ **7 a** : to call on : VISIT **b** (1) : to keep company with esp. in courtship or dating ⟨had been ~*ing* each other for a year⟩ (2) : to grant an interview to : RECEIVE ⟨the president will ~ you now⟩ **8** : ACCOMPANY, ESCORT ⟨~ the guests to the door⟩ **9** : to meet (a bet) in poker or to equal the bet of (a player) : CALL ~ *vi* **1 a** : to give or pay attention **b** : to look about **2 a** : to have the power of sight **b** : to apprehend objects by sight **c** : to perceive objects as if by sight **3 a** : to grasp something mentally **b** : to acknowledge or consider something being pointed out ⟨~, I told you it would rain⟩ **4** : to make investigation or inquiry — **see·able** \-ə-bəl\ *adj* — **see after** : to attend to : care for — **see eye to eye** : to have a common viewpoint : AGREE — **see red** : to become very angry — **see the light** : to discover or realize a usu. obscured truth — **see the light of day** : to become publicly known or available (as through publication) ⟨manuscripts that will never *see the light of day*⟩ — **see things** : HALLUCINATE — **see through** : to grasp the true nature of ⟨*saw through* the scheme⟩ — **see to** : to attend to : care for

2**see** *n* [ME *se,* fr. AF *sé, see,* fr. L *sedes* seat; akin to L *sedēre* to sit — more at SIT] (14c) **1 a** *archaic* : CATHEDRA **b** : a cathedral town **c** : a seat of a bishop's office, power, or authority **2** : the authority or jurisdiction of a bishop

1**seed** \'sēd\ *n, pl* **seed** *or* **seeds** [ME, fr. OE *sǣd;* akin to OHG *sāt* seed, OE *sāwan* to sow — more at SOW] (bef. 12c) **1 a** (1) : the grains or ripened ovules of plants used for sowing (2) : the fertilized ripened ovule of a flowering plant containing an embryo and capable normally of germination to produce a new plant; *broadly* : a propagative plant structure (as a spore or small dry fruit) **b** : a propagative animal structure: (1) : MILT, SEMEN (2) : a small egg (as of an insect) (3) : a developmental form of a lower animal suitable for transplanting; *specif* : SPAT **c** : the condition or stage of bearing seed ⟨in ~⟩ **2** : PROGENY **3** : a source of development or growth : GERM ⟨sowed the ~*s* of discord⟩ **4** : something (as a tiny particle or a bubble in glass) that resembles a seed in shape or size **5** : a competitor who has been seeded in a tournament ⟨the top ~⟩ — **seed** *adj* — **seed·ed** \'sē-dəd\ *adj* — **seed·less** \'sēd-ləs\ *adj* — **seed·like** \-ˌlīk\ *adj* — **go to seed** *or* **run to seed** **1** : to develop seed **2** : DECAY, DETERIORATE

2**seed** *vi* (14c) **1** : to bear or shed seed **2** : to sow seed : PLANT ~ *vt* **1 a** : to plant seeds in : SOW ⟨~ a lawn with grass⟩ **b** : to furnish with something that causes or stimulates growth or development **c** : INOCULATE **d** : to supply with nuclei (as of crystallization or condensation); *esp* : to treat (a cloud) with solid particles to convert water droplets into ice crystals in an attempt to produce precipitation **e** : to cover or permeate by or as if by scattering something ⟨~*ed* [the] sea-lanes with thousands of magnetic mines —Otto Friedrich⟩ **2** : PLANT 1a **3** : to extract the seeds from (as raisins) **4 a** : to schedule (tournament players or teams) so that superior ones will not meet in early rounds **b** : to rank (a contestant) relative to others in a tournament on the basis of previous record ⟨the top-*seeded* tennis star⟩

seed·bed \'sēd-ˌbed\ *n* (1660) **1** : soil or a bed of soil prepared for planting seed **2** : a place or source of growth or development

seed·cake \-ˌkāk\ *n* (1573) **1** : a cake or cookie containing aromatic seeds (as sesame or caraway) **2** : OIL CAKE

seed coat *n* (1796) : an outer protective covering of a seed

seed·eat·er \'sēd-ˌē-tər\ *n* (ca. 1879) : a bird (as a finch) whose diet consists basically of seeds

seed·er \'sē-dər\ *n* (1853) **1** : an implement for planting or sowing seeds **2** : a device for seeding fruit **3** : one that seeds clouds

seed fern *n* (1927) : any of an order (Pteridospermales) of extinct cycadophytes with foliage like that of ferns and with naked seeds

seed leaf *n* (1686) : COTYLEDON 2

seed·ling \'sēd-liŋ\ *n* (1660) **1** : a young plant grown from seed **2 a** : a young tree before it becomes a sapling **b** : a nursery plant not yet transplanted — **seedling** *adj*

seed money *n* (1943) : money used for setting up a new enterprise

seed oyster *n* (1854) : a young oyster esp. of a size for transplantation

seed pearl *n* (1553) **1** : a very small and often irregular pearl **2** : minute pearls imbedded in some binding material

seed plant *n* (1707) : a plant that bears seeds; *specif* : SPERMATOPHYTE

seed·pod \'sēd-ˌpäd\ *n* (1688) : 2POD 1

seed potato *n* (1742) : a potato tuber grown for its buds which are used to start new plants; *also* : a section of such a tuber with one or more buds

seeds·man \'sēdz-mən\ *n* (1601) **1** : a person who sows seeds **2** : a dealer in seeds

seed stock *n* (1926) : a supply (as of seed) for planting; *broadly* : a source of new individuals ⟨*seed stock* for hardy dairy cattle⟩

seed tick *n* (1705) : the 6-legged larva of a tick

seed·time \'sēd-ˌtīm\ *n* (bef. 12c) **1** : the season of sowing **2** : a period of original development

seedy \'sē-dē\ *adj* **seed·i·er; -est** (1574) **1** : containing or full of seeds ⟨a ~ fruit⟩ **2** : inferior in condition or quality: as **a** : SHABBY, RUN-DOWN ⟨~ clothes⟩ **b** : somewhat disreputable ⟨a ~ district⟩ ⟨a ~ lawyer⟩ **c** : slightly unwell : DEBILITATED ⟨felt ~ and went home early⟩ — **seed·i·ly** \'sē-dᵊl-ē\ *adv* — **seed·i·ness** \'sē-dē-nəs\ *n*

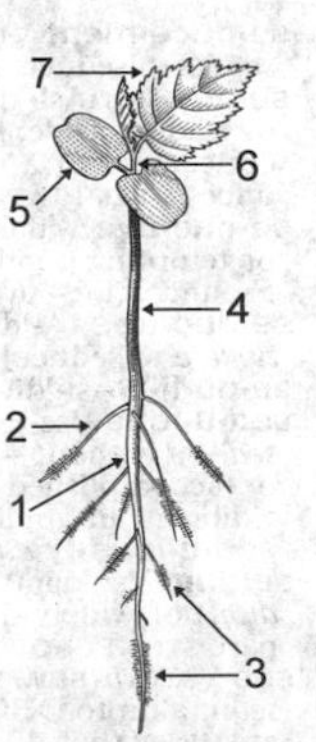

seedling 2a: *1* primary root, *2* rootlet, *3* root hairs, *4* hypocotyl, *5* cotyledon, *6* young stem, *7* true leaf

1**seeing** *conj* (1503) : INASMUCH AS — often used with *as* or *that*

2**seeing** *n* (1903) : the quality of the images of celestial bodies observed telescopically

Seeing Eye *trademark* — used for a guide dog trained to lead the blind

seek \'sēk\ *vb* **sought** \'sȯt\; **seek·ing** [ME *seken,* fr. OE *sēcan;* akin to OHG *suohhen* to seek, L *sagus* prophetic, Gk *hēgeisthai* to lead] *vt* (bef. 12c) **1** : to resort to : go to **2 a** : to go in search of : look for **b** : to try to discover **3** : to ask for : REQUEST ⟨~*s* advice⟩ **4** : to try to acquire or gain : aim at ⟨~ fame⟩ **5** : to make an attempt : TRY — used with *to* and an infinitive ⟨governments . . . ~ to keep the bulk of their people contented —D. M. Potter⟩ ~ *vi* **1** : to make a search or inquiry **2 a** : to be sought **b** : to be lacking ⟨in critical judgment . . . they were sadly to ~ —*Times Lit. Supp.*⟩ — **seek·er** *n*

seel \'sēl\ *vt* [alter. of ME *silen,* fr. AF *ciller,* fr. ML *ciliare,* fr. L *cilium* eyelid] (15c) **1** : to close the eyes of (as a hawk) by drawing threads through the eyelids **2** *archaic* : to close up (one's eyes)

see·ly \'sē-lē\ *adj* [ME *sely* — more at SILLY] (14c) *archaic* : pitiable esp. because of weak physical or mental condition : FRAIL

seem \'sēm\ *vi* [ME *semen* to appear to be, be fitting, of Scand origin; akin to ON *sœma* to honor, *sœmr* fitting, *samr* same — more at SAME] (13c) **1** : to appear to the observation or understanding **2** : to give the impression of being

1**seem·ing** \'sē-miŋ\ *n* (15c) : external appearance as distinguished from true character : LOOK

2**seeming** *adj* (ca. 1557) : outwardly or superficially evident but not true or real ⟨the ~ immortality of our heroes⟩ ***syn*** see APPARENT — **seem·ing·ly** *adv*

seem·ly \'sēm-lē\ *adj* **seem·li·er; -est** [ME *semely,* fr. ON *sœmiligr,* fr. *sœmr* fitting] (13c) **1 a** : GOOD-LOOKING, HANDSOME **b** : agreeably fashioned : ATTRACTIVE **2** : conventionally proper : DECOROUS ⟨not ~ to brag about oneself⟩ **3** : suited to the occasion, purpose, or person : FIT — **seem·li·ness** *n* — **seemly** *adv*

seen *past part of* SEE

1**seep** \'sēp\ *vi* [alter. of earlier *sipe,* fr. ME *sipen,* fr. OE *sipian;* akin to MLG *sipen* to seep] (1790) **1** : to flow or pass slowly through fine pores or small openings : OOZE ⟨water ~*ed* in through a crack⟩ **2 a** : to enter or penetrate slowly ⟨fear of nuclear war had ~*ed* into the national consciousness —Tip O'Neill⟩ **b** : to become diffused or spread ⟨a sadness ~*ed* through his being —Agnes S. Turnbull⟩

2**seep** *n* (1824) **1 a** : a spot where a fluid (as water, oil, or gas) contained in the ground oozes slowly to the surface and often forms a pool **b** : a small spring **2** : SEEPAGE — **seepy** \'sē-pē\ *adj*

seep·age \'sē-pij\ *n* (ca. 1825) **1** : the process of seeping : OOZING **2** : a quantity of fluid that has seeped (as through porous material)

seer \'sir, 'sē-ər\ *n* (14c) **1** : one that sees **2 a** : one that predicts events or developments **b** : a person credited with extraordinary moral and spiritual insight **3** : one that practices divination esp. by concentrating on a glass or crystal globe

seer·ess \'sir-əs, 'sē-ər-əs\ *n* (1845) : a woman who predicts events or developments : PROPHETESS

seer·suck·er \'sir-ˌsə-kər\ *n* [Hindi *sīr-śakkar, sīr-sakkar* & Urdu *shīrshakar,* lit., milk and sugar, fr. Pers *shīr-o-shakar*] (1722) : a light fabric of linen, cotton, or rayon usu. striped and slightly puckered

1**see·saw** \'sē-ˌsȯ\ *n* [prob. fr. redupl. of 3*saw*] (1704) **1** : an alternating up-and-down or backward-and-forward motion or movement; *also* : a contest or struggle in which now one side now the other has the lead **2 a** : a pastime in which two children or groups of children ride on opposite ends of a plank balanced in the middle so that one end goes up as the other goes down **b** : the plank or apparatus so used — **seesaw** *adj*

2**seesaw** *vi* (1712) **1 a** : to move backward and forward or up and down **b** : to play at seesaw **2** : ALTERNATE ⟨~ between two activities⟩ ~ *vt* : to cause to move in seesaw fashion

1**seethe** \'sēth\ *vb* **seethed; seeth·ing** [ME *sethen,* fr. OE *sēothan;* akin to OHG *siodan* to seethe and prob. to Old Lith *siausti* (it) storms, rages] *vt* (bef. 12c) **1** *archaic* : BOIL, STEW **2** : to soak or saturate in a liquid ~ *vi* **1** *archaic* : BOIL **2 a** : to be in a state of rapid agitated movement **b** : to churn or foam as if boiling **3** : to suffer violent internal excitement ⟨~ with jealousy⟩

2**seethe** *n* (1816) : a state of seething : EBULLITION

seething *adj* (14c) **1** : intensely hot : BOILING ⟨a ~ inferno⟩ **2** : constantly moving or active : AGITATED

see–through \'sē-ˌthrü\ *adj* (1945) : TRANSPARENT 1

1**seg·ment** \'seg-mənt\ *n* [L *segmentum,* fr. *secare* to cut — more at SAW] (1570) **1** : a portion cut off from a geometric figure by one or more points, lines, or planes: as **a** : the area of a circle bounded by a chord and an arc of that circle **b** : the part of a sphere cut off by a plane or included between two parallel planes **c** : the finite part of a line between two points in the line **2 a** : a separate piece of something : BIT, FRAGMENT ⟨chop the stalks into short ~*s*⟩ **b** : one of the constituent parts into which a body, entity, or quantity is divided or marked off by or as if by natural boundaries ⟨all ~*s* of the population agree⟩ ***syn*** see PART — **seg·men·tary** \-mən-ˌter-ē\ *adj*

2**seg·ment** \'seg-ˌment\ *vt* (1859) : to separate into segments : give off as segments

seg·men·tal \seg-'men-tᵊl\ *adj* (1816) **1** : of, relating to, or having the form of a segment and esp. the sector of a circle ⟨~ fanlight⟩ **2** : of, relating to, or composed of somites or metameres : METAMERIC **3 a** : divided into segments ⟨~ knowledge⟩ **b** : PARTIAL, INCOMPLETE **c** : resulting from segmentation — **seg·men·tal·ly** \-tᵊl-ē\ *adv*

seg·men·ta·tion \ˌseg-mən-'tā-shən, -ˌmen-\ *n* (1851) : the process of dividing into segments; *esp* : the formation of many cells from a single cell (as in a developing egg)

segmentation cavity *n* (1883) : BLASTOCOEL

seg·ment·ed \'seg-ˌmen-təd, seg-'\ *adj* (1854) : divided into or composed of segments or sections ⟨~ worms⟩

se·gno \'sān-(ˌ)yō\ *n, pl* **segnos** [It, sign, fr. L *signum* — more at SIGN] (1908) : a notational sign; *specif* : the sign that marks the beginning or end of a musical repeat

se·go lily \'sē-(ˌ)gō-\ *n* [*sego* the bulb of the sego lily, fr. Southern Paiute *siyoʔo*] (1913) : a mariposa lily (*Calochortus nuttallii*) of western No. America having mostly white or in some areas mostly yellow flowers mottled with a darker color

seg·re·gant \'se-gri-gənt\ *n* (1926) : a genetic segregate

1**seg·re·gate** \'se-gri-ˌgāt\ *vb* **-gat·ed; -gat·ing** [L *segregatus,* pp. of *segregare,* fr. *se-* apart + *greg-, grex* herd — more at SECEDE] *vt* (1542) **1** : to separate or set apart from others or from the general mass : ISOLATE **2** : to cause or force the separation of (as from the rest of society) ~ *vi* **1** : SEPARATE, WITHDRAW **2** : to practice or enforce a policy of segregation **3** : to undergo genetic segregation — **seg·re·ga·tive** \ˈ-ˌgā-tiv\ *adj*

2**seg·re·gate** \ˈse-gri-gət, -ˌgāt\ *n* (1871) : one that is in some respect segregated; *esp* : one that differs genetically from the parental line because of genetic segregation

segregated *adj* (1652) **1 a** : set apart or separated from others of the same kind or group ⟨a ~ account in a bank⟩ **b** : divided in facilities or administered separately for members of different groups or races ⟨~ education⟩ **c** : restricted to members of one group or one race by a policy of segregation ⟨~ schools⟩ **2** : practicing or maintaining segregation esp. of races ⟨~ states⟩

seg·re·ga·tion \ˌse-gri-ˈgā-shən\ *n* (1555) **1** : the act or process of segregating : the state of being segregated **2 a** : the separation or isolation of a race, class, or ethnic group by enforced or voluntary residence in a restricted area, by barriers to social intercourse, by separate educational facilities, or by other discriminatory means **b** : the separation for special treatment or observation of individuals or items from a larger group ⟨~ of gifted children into accelerated classes⟩ **3** : the separation of allelic genes that occurs typically during meiosis

seg·re·ga·tion·ist \-sh(ə-)nist\ *n* (1913) : a person who believes in or practices segregation esp. of races — **segregationist** *adj*

1**se·gue** \ˈse-(ˌ)gwā, ˈsā-\ *vb imper* [It, there follows, fr. *seguire* to follow, fr. L *sequi* — more at SUE] (ca. 1740) **1** : proceed to what follows without pause — used as a direction in music **2** : perform the music that follows like that which has preceded — used as a direction in music

2**segue** *vi* **se·gued; se·gue·ing** (ca. 1913) **1** : to proceed without pause from one musical number or theme to another **2** : to make a transition without interruption from one activity, topic, scene, or part to another ⟨*segued* smoothly into the next story⟩

3**segue** *n* (ca. 1937) : the act or an instance of segueing

se·gui·di·lla \ˌse-gə-ˈdē-yə, -ˈdēl-yə\ *n* [Sp, dim. of *seguida*, a dance, lit., sequence, fr. *seguido*, pp. of *seguir* to follow, fr. L *sequi*] (1763) **1 a** : a Spanish dance with many regional variations **b** : the music for such a dance **2** : a Spanish stanza of four or seven short partly assonant verses

sei·cen·to \sā-ˈchen-(ˌ)tō\ *n* [It, lit., six-hundred, fr. *sei* six (fr. L *sex*) + *cento* hundred — more at SIX, CINQUECENTO] (ca. 1902) : the 17th century; *specif* : the 17th century period in Italian literature and art

seiche \ˈsāsh, ˈsēch\ *n* [F] (ca. 1839) : an oscillation of the surface of a landlocked body of water (as a lake) that varies in period from a few minutes to several hours

sei·del \ˈsī-dᵊl, ˈzī-\ *n* [G, fr. MHG *sīdel*, fr. L *situla* bucket] (1908) : a large glass for beer

Seid·litz powders \ˈsed-ləts-\ *n pl* [*Sedlitz* (Sedlčany), village in Bohemia; fr. the similarity of their effect to that of the water of the village] (1815) : effervescing salts consisting of one powder of sodium bicarbonate and Rochelle salt and another of tartaric acid that are mixed in water and drunk as a mild cathartic

sei·gneur \sān-ˈyər\ *n, often cap* [MF, fr. ML *senior*, fr. L, adj., elder — more at SENIOR] (1592) **1** : a man of rank or authority; *esp* : the feudal lord of a manor **2** : a member of the landed gentry of Canada

sei·gneur·ial \-ˈyu̇r-ē-əl, -ˈyər-\ *adj* (1656) : of, relating to, or befitting a seigneur

sei·gneury \ˈsān-yə-rē\ *n, pl* **-gneur·ies** (1630) **1 a** : the territory under the government of a feudal lord **b** : a landed estate held in Canada by feudal tenure until 1854 **2** : the manor house of a Canadian seigneur

sei·gnior \sān-ˈyȯr, ˈsān-ˌ\ *n* [ME *seygnour*, fr. AF *seignur*, fr. ML *senior*] (14c) : SEIGNEUR 1

sei·gnior·age *or* **sei·gnor·age** \ˈsān-yə-rij\ *n* [ME *seigneurage*, fr. AF *seignurage* right of the lord (esp. to coin money), fr. *seignur*] (15c) : a government revenue from the manufacture of coins calculated as the difference between the face value and the metal value of the coins

sei·gniory *or* **sei·gnory** \ˈsān-yə-rē\ *n, pl* **-gnior·ies** *or* **-gnor·ies** (14c) **1** : LORDSHIP, DOMINION; *specif* : the power or authority of a feudal lord **2** : the territory over which a lord holds jurisdiction

sei·gno·ri·al \sān-ˈyȯr-ē-əl\ *adj* (1796) : of, relating to, or befitting a seignior : MANORIAL

1**seine** \ˈsān\ *n* [ME, fr. OE *segne*, fr. L *sagena*, fr. Gk *sagēnē*] (bef. 12c) : a large net with sinkers on one edge and floats on the other that hangs vertically in the water and is used to enclose and catch fish when its ends are pulled together or are drawn ashore

2**seine** *vb* **seined; sein·ing** *vi* (1836) : to fish with or catch fish with a seine ~ *vt* : to fish for or in with a seine

sein·er \ˈsā-nər\ *n* (1602) **1** : one who fishes with a seine **2** : a boat used for seining

sei·sin *or* **sei·zin** \ˈsē-zᵊn\ *n* [ME *seisine*, fr. AF, fr. *seisir* to seize — more at SEIZE] (14c) **1** : the possession of land or chattels **2** : the possession of a freehold estate in land by one having title thereto

seis·mic \ˈsīz-mik, ˈsīs-\ *adj* [Gk *seismos* shock, earthquake, fr. *seiein* to shake; prob. akin to Av *thwaēshō* fear] (1858) **1** : of, subject to, or caused by an earthquake; *also* : of or relating to an earth vibration caused by something else (as an explosion or the impact of a meteorite) **2** : of or relating to a vibration on a celestial body (as the moon) comparable to a seismic event on earth **3** : having a strong or widespread impact : EARTHSHAKING ⟨~ social changes⟩ — **seis·mi·cal·ly** \-mi-k(ə-)lē\ *adv*

seis·mic·i·ty \sīz-ˈmi-sə-tē, sīs-\ *n* (1902) : the relative frequency and distribution of earthquakes

seismo- *comb form* [Gk, fr. *seismos*] : earthquake : vibration ⟨*seismometer*⟩

seis·mo·gram \ˈsīz-mə-ˌgram, ˈsīs-\ *n* [ISV] (ca. 1891) : the record of an earth tremor by a seismograph

seis·mo·graph \-ˌgraf\ *n* [ISV] (1858) : an apparatus to measure and record vibrations within the earth and of the ground — **seis·mog·ra·pher** \sīz-ˈmä-grə-fər, sīs-\ *n* — **seis·mo·graph·ic** \ˌsīz-mə-ˈgra-fik, ˌsīs-\ *adj* — **seis·mog·ra·phy** \sīz-ˈmä-grə-fē, sīs-\ *n*

seis·mol·o·gy \sīz-ˈmä-lə-jē, sīs-\ *n* [ISV] (1858) : a science that deals with earthquakes and with artificially produced vibrations of the earth — **seis·mo·log·i·cal** \ˌsīz-mə-ˈlä-ji-kəl, ˌsīs-\ *also* **seis·mo·log·ic** \-jik\ *adj* — **seis·mol·o·gist** \sīz-ˈmä-lə-jist, sīs-\ *n*

seis·mom·e·ter \sīz-ˈmä-mə-tər, sīs-\ *n* (1841) : a seismograph measuring the actual movements of the ground (as on the earth or the moon) — **seis·mo·met·ric** \ˌsīz-mə-ˈme-trik, ˌsīs-\ *adj*

seis·mom·e·try \sīz-ˈmä-mə-trē, sīs-\ *n* [ISV] (1858) : the scientific study of earthquakes

sei·tan \ˈsā-ˌtan, -ˌtän\ *n* [origin unknown] (1974) : flavored wheat gluten often used as a meat analogue

sei whale \ˈsā-, ˈsī-\ *n* [part trans. of Norw *seihval*, fr. *sei* coalfish + *hval* whale] (1912) : a widely distributed dark gray baleen whale (*Balaenoptera borealis*) that has a ridge on the top of the head and may reach a length of nearly 60 feet (18 meters) — called also *sei*

seize \ˈsēz\ *vb* **seized; seiz·ing** [ME *saisen*, fr. AF *seisir*, fr. ML *sacire*, of Gmc origin; perh. akin to OHG *sezzen* to set — more at SET] *vt* (14c) **1 a** *usu* **seise** \ˈsēz\ : to vest ownership of a freehold estate in **b** *often* **seise** : to put in possession of something ⟨the biographer will be *seized* of all pertinent papers⟩ **2 a** : to take possession of : CONFISCATE **b** : to take possession of by legal process **3 a** : to possess or take by force : CAPTURE **b** : to take prisoner : ARREST **4 a** : to take hold of : CLUTCH **b** : to possess oneself of : GRASP **c** : to understand fully and distinctly : APPREHEND **5 a** : to attack or overwhelm physically : AFFLICT ⟨*seized* with chest pains⟩ **b** : to possess (as one's mind) completely or overwhelmingly ⟨*seized* the popular imagination —Basil Davenport⟩ **6** : to bind or fasten together with a lashing of small stuff (as yarn, marline, or fine wire) ~ *vi* **1** : to take or lay hold suddenly or forcibly **2 a** : to cohere to a relatively moving part through excessive pressure, temperature, or friction — used esp. of machine parts (as bearings, brakes, or pistons) **b** : to fail to operate due to the seizing of a part — used of an engine ***syn*** see TAKE — **seiz·er** *n*

seizing *n* (14c) **1 a** : the cord or lashing used in binding or fastening **b** : the fastening so made — see KNOT illustration **2** : the operation of fastening together or lashing with tarred small stuff

sei·zure \ˈsē-zhər\ *n* (15c) **1 a** : the act, action, or process of seizing : the state of being seized **b** : the taking possession of person or property by legal process **2 a** : a sudden attack (as of disease); *esp* : the physical manifestations (as convulsions, sensory disturbances, or loss of consciousness) resulting from abnormal electrical discharges in the brain (as in epilepsy) **b** : an abnormal electrical discharge in the brain

se·jant \ˈsē-jənt\ *adj* [modif. of MF *seant*, prp. of *seoir* to sit, fr. L *sedēre* — more at SIT] (ca. 1500) : SITTING — used of a heraldic animal

1**sel** \ˈsel\ *chiefly Scot var of* SELF

2**sel** *abbr* select; selected; selection

se·la·chi·an \sə-ˈlā-kē-ən\ *n* [ultim. fr. Gk *selachos* cartilaginous phosphorescent fish; akin to Gk *selas* brightness] (1835) : any of a variously classified group (Selachii) of cartilaginous fishes that includes the existing sharks and typically most related elasmobranchs (as rays) — **selachian** *adj*

se·lag·i·nel·la \sə-ˌla-jə-ˈne-lə\ *n* [NL, fr. L *selagin-*, *selago*, a plant resembling the savin] (1891) : any of a genus (*Selaginella*) of mosslike lower tracheophytes that are related to or grouped with the club mosses and have scalelike leaves and produce one-celled sporangia containing both megaspores and microspores

se·lah \ˈsē-lə, -ˌlä\ *interj* [Heb *selāh*] (ca. 1530) — a term of uncertain meaning found in the Hebrew text of the Psalms and Habakkuk carried over untranslated into some English versions

sel·couth \ˈsel-ˌküth\ *adj* [ME, fr. OE *seldcūth*, fr. *seldan* seldom + *cūth* known — more at UNCOUTH] (bef. 12c) *archaic* : UNUSUAL, STRANGE

1**sel·dom** \ˈsel-dəm\ *adv* [ME, fr. OE *seldan*; akin to OHG *seltan* seldom] (bef. 12c) : in few instances : RARELY, INFREQUENTLY

2**seldom** *adj* (13c) : RARE, INFREQUENT

1**se·lect** \sə-ˈlekt\ *adj* [L *selectus*, pp. of *seligere* to select, fr. *se-* apart (fr. *sed, se* without) + *legere* to gather, select — more at SUICIDE, LEGEND] (ca. 1555) **1** : chosen from a number or group by fitness or preference **2 a** : of special value or excellence : SUPERIOR, CHOICE **b** : exclusively or fastidiously chosen often with regard to social, economic, or cultural characteristics **3** : judicious or restrictive in choice : DISCRIMINATING ⟨pleased with the ~ appreciation of his books —Osbert Sitwell⟩ — **se·lect·able** \sə-ˈlek-tə-bəl\ *adj* — **se·lect·ness** \sə-ˈlek(t)-nəs\ *n* — **se·lec·tor** \sə-ˈlek-tər\ *n*

2**select** *vt* (1566) : to choose (as by fitness or excellence) from a number or group : pick out ~ *vi* : to make a choice

3**select** *n* (1610) : one that is select — often used in pl.

se·lect·ed \sə-ˈlek-təd\ *adj* (1590) : SELECT; *specif* : of a higher grade or quality than the ordinary

se·lect·ee \sə-ˌlek-ˈtē\ *n* (1940) **1** : a person inducted into military service under selective service **2** : a person who is chosen from a group by fitness or preference

se·lec·tion \sə-ˈlek-shən\ *n* (ca. 1623) **1** : the act or process of selecting : the state of being selected **2** : one that is selected : CHOICE; *also* : a collection of selected things **3** : a natural or artificial process that results or tends to result in the survival and propagation of some individuals or organisms but not of others with the result that the inherited traits of the survivors are perpetuated — compare DARWINISM, NATURAL SELECTION ***syn*** see CHOICE

se·lec·tion·ist \-sh(ə-)nist\ *n* (1892) : one who considers natural selection a fundamental factor in evolution — **selectionist** *adj*

se·lec·tive \sə-ˈlek-tiv\ *adj* (1625) **1** : of, relating to, or characterized by selection : selecting or tending to select **2** : highly specific in activity or effect ⟨~ pesticides⟩ ⟨~ absorption⟩ — **se·lec·tive·ly** *adv* — **se·lec·tive·ness** *n* — **se·lec·tiv·i·ty** \sə-ˌlek-ˈti-və-tē, ˌsē-\ *n*

selective serotonin reuptake inhibitor *n* (1987) : SSRI

selective service *n* (1917) : a system under which men are called up for military service : DRAFT

se·lect·man \si-ˈlek(t)-ˌman, -ˌlek(t)-ˈman, -ˈlek(t)-mən; ˈsē-ˌlek(t)-ˌman\ *n* (1635) : one of a board of officials elected in towns of all New England states except Rhode Island to serve as the chief administrative authority of the town

1**selen-** *or* **seleno-** *comb form* [L *selen-*, fr. Gk *selēn-*, fr. *selēnē* — more at SELENIUM] : moon ⟨*selen*ium⟩ ⟨*seleno*logy⟩

\ə\ **abut** \ᵊ\ **kitten,** F **table** \ər\ **further** \a\ **ash** \ā\ **ace** \ä\ **mop, mar**
\au̇\ **out** \ch\ **chin** \e\ **bet** \ē\ **easy** \g\ **go** \i\ **hit** \ī\ **ice** \j\ **job**
\ŋ\ **sing** \ō\ **go** \ȯ\ **law** \ȯi\ **boy** \th\ **thin** \th̲\ **the** \ü\ **loot** \u̇\ **foot**
\y\ **yet** \zh\ **vision, beige** \k̲, ⁿ, œ, ue, ʸ\ *see* Guide to Pronunciation

[2]**selen-** *or* **seleni-** *comb form* [Sw, fr. NL *selenium*] : selenium ⟨*selenif*erous⟩
sel·e·nate \ˈse-lə-ˌnāt\ *n* [Sw *selenat,* fr. *selen* of or containing selenium, fr. NL *selenium*] (1818) : a salt containing the anion $SeO_4{}^{2-}$
Se·le·ne \sə-ˈlē-nē\ *n* (1845) : the Greek goddess of the moon
sel·e·nide \ˈse-lə-ˌnīd\ *n* (1849) : a binary compound of selenium with a more electropositive element or group
sel·e·nif·er·ous \ˌse-lə-ˈni-f(ə-)rəs\ *adj* (1823) : containing or yielding selenium ⟨∼ vegetation⟩ ⟨∼ soils⟩
sel·e·nite \ˈse-lə-ˌnīt\ *n* [ME *selinete,* fr. L *selenites,* fr. Gk *selēnitēs* (*lithos*), lit., stone of the moon, fr. *selēnē;* fr. the belief that it waxed and waned with the moon] (15c) : a variety of gypsum occurring in transparent crystals or crystalline masses
se·le·ni·um \sə-ˈlē-nē-əm\ *n* [NL, fr. Gk *selēnē* moon, fr. *selas* brightness] (1818) : a photosensitive element that occurs in both crystalline and amorphous forms, is obtained chiefly as a by-product in copper refining, and is used esp. in glass, semiconductor devices, and alloys — see ELEMENT table
selenium cell *n* (1880) : an insulated strip of selenium mounted with electrodes and used as a photoconductive element
se·le·no·cen·tric \sə-ˌlē-nə-ˈsen-trik\ *adj* [ISV] (ca. 1852) : of or relating to the center of the moon; *also* : referred to or involving the moon as a center
sel·e·nol·o·gy \ˌse-lə-ˈnä-lə-jē\ *n* (1821) : a branch of astronomy that deals with the moon — **se·le·no·log·i·cal** \ˌse-lə-nō-ˈlä-ji-kəl, sə-ˌlē-nə-ˈlä-\ *adj* — **sel·e·nol·o·gist** \ˌse-lə-ˈnä-lə-jist\ *n*
Se·leu·cid \sə-ˈlü-səd, səl-ˈyü-\ *n* [NL *seleucides,* fr. *Seleucus I*] (1851) : a member of a Greek dynasty ruling Syria and at various times other Asian territories from 312 B.C. to 64 B.C. — **Seleucid** *adj*
[1]**self** \ˈself, *Southern also* ˈsef\ *pron* [ME (intensive pron.), fr. OE; akin to OHG *selb,* intensive pron., and prob. to L *suus* one's own — more at SUICIDE] (bef. 12c) : MYSELF, HIMSELF, HERSELF ⟨a check payable to ∼⟩
[2]**self** *adj* (bef. 12c) **1** *obs* : IDENTICAL, SAME **2** *obs* : belonging to oneself : OWN **3 a** : having a single character or quality throughout; *specif* : having one color only ⟨a ∼ flower⟩ **b** : of the same kind (as in color, material, or pattern) as something with which it is used ⟨∼ trimming⟩
[3]**self** *n, pl* **selves** \ˈselvz, *Southern also* ˈsevz\ (13c) **1 a** : the entire person of an individual **b** : the realization or embodiment of an abstraction **2 a** (1) : an individual's typical character or behavior ⟨her true ∼ was revealed⟩ (2) : an individual's temporary behavior or character ⟨his better ∼⟩ **b** : a person in prime condition ⟨feel like my old ∼ today⟩ **3** : the union of elements (as body, emotions, thoughts, and sensations) that constitute the individuality and identity of a person **4** : personal interest or advantage **5** : material that is part of an individual organism ⟨ability of the immune system to distinguish ∼ from nonself⟩
[4]**self** *vt* (1905) **1** : INBREED **2** : to pollinate with pollen from the same flower or plant ∼ *vi* : to undergo self-pollination
self- *comb form* [ME, fr. OE, fr. *self*] **1 a** : oneself or itself ⟨*self*-supporting⟩ **b** : of oneself or itself ⟨*self*-abasement⟩ **c** : by oneself or itself ⟨*self*-propelled⟩ ⟨*self*-acting⟩ **2 a** : to, with, for, or toward oneself or itself ⟨*self*-consistent⟩ ⟨*self*-addressed⟩ ⟨*self*-love⟩ **b** : of or in oneself or itself inherently ⟨*self*-evident⟩ **c** : from or by means of oneself or itself ⟨*self*-fertile⟩

self–abase·ment
self–ab·ne·gat·ing
self–ab·ne·ga·tion
self–ac·cel·er·at·ing
self–ac·cep·tance
self–ac·cu·sa·tion
self–ac·cu·sa·to·ry
self–ac·cus·ing
self–ac·knowl·edged
self–ad·just·ing
self–ad·min·is·ter
self–ad·min·is·tra·tion
self–ad·mit·ted
self–ad·mit·ted·ly
self–ad·u·la·to·ry
self–ad·vance·ment
self–ad·ver·tise·ment
self–ad·ver·tis·er
self–af·fir·ma·tion
self–ag·gran·dize·ment
self–ag·gran·diz·ing
self–alien·ation
self–anoint·ed
self–ap·prais·al
self–ap·pro·ba·tion
self–as·sess·ment
self–as·sign·ment
self–au·then·ti·cat·ing
self–avowed
self–bet·ter·ment
self–can·cel
self–care
self–car·i·ca·ture
self–cas·ti·gate
self–cas·ti·ga·tion
self–cen·sor·ship
self–char·ac·ter·i·za·tion
self–clas·si·fi·ca·tion
self–clean·ing
self–com·mand
self–com·mun·ing
self–com·mu·nion
self–com·pla·cen·cy
self–com·pla·cent
self–con·dem·na·tion
self–con·demned
self–con·firm·ing
self–con·se·cra·tion
self–con·sti·tut·ed
self–con·sum·ing
self–con·tem·pla·tion
self–con·tempt
self–cre·at·ed
self–cre·a·tion
self–crit·i·cal
self–crit·i·cism
self–cri·tique
self–cul·ti·va·tion
self–cul·ture
self–damn·ing
self–de·base·ment
self–de·ceit
self–de·ceive
self–de·cep·tion
self–de·feat·ing
self–de·lud·ed
self–de·lud·ing
self–de·lu·sion
self–den·i·grat·ing
self–den·i·gra·tion
self–de·pen·dence
self–de·pen·dent
self–dep·re·cat·ing
self–dep·re·cat·ing·ly
self–dep·re·ca·tion
self–dep·re·ca·to·ry
self–de·pre·ci·a·tion
self–de·scribed
self–de·scrip·tion
self–de·scrip·tive
self–de·stroy·er
self–de·vel·op·ment
self–de·vour·ing
self–dif·fer·en·ti·a·tion
self–di·rect·ed
self–di·rect·ing
self–di·rec·tion
self–di·rec·tive
self–dis·gust
self–dis·play
self–dis·sat·is·fac·tion
self–doubt
self–ed·u·cat·ed
self–ed·u·cat·ing
self–ed·u·ca·tion
self–ef·face·ment
self–ef·fac·ing
self–eman·ci·pa·tion
self–emas·cu·la·tion
self–en·closed
self–en·grossed
self–en·hance·ment
self–eval·u·ate
self–eval·u·a·tion
self–ex·clu·sion
self–ex·cul·pa·tion
self–ex·hi·bi·tion
self–ex·is·tence
self–ex·is·tent
self–ex·plain·ing
self–ex·tinc·tion
self–fi·nance
self–formed
self–gen·er·ate
self–giv·ing
self–guid·ed
self–hate
self–hat·ing
self–ha·tred
self–heal·ing
self–hum·bling
self–hu·mil·i·a·tion
self–hyp·no·sis
self–idol·a·try
self–im·posed
self–im·prove·ment
self–im·prov·er
self–in·duced
self–in·fat·u·at·ed
self–in·fla·tion
self–in·flict·ed
self–ini·ti·at·ed
self–in·struct·ed
self–in·struc·tion
self–in·struc·tion·al
self–in·ter·view
self–in·vent·ed
self–in·ven·tion
self–iso·la·tion
self–la·beled
self–lac·er·at·ing
self–lac·er·a·tion
self–loath·ing
self–lock·ing
self–lu·bri·cat·ing
self–lu·mi·nous
self–main·te·nance
self–man·age·ment
self–mas·tery
self–med·i·ca·tion
self–mock·ery
self–mock·ing
self–mor·ti·fi·ca·tion
self–mo·ti·vat·ed
self–mu·ti·lat·ing
self–mu·ti·la·tion
self–ne·gat·ing
self–ob·sessed
self–op·er·at·ing
self–or·dained
self–ori·ent·ed
self–par·o·dist
self–par·o·dy
self–penned
self–per·pet·u·at·ing
self–per·pet·u·a·tion
self–pla·gia·rism
self–pleas·ing
self–po·lic·ing
self–praise
self–pre·oc·cu·pa·tion
self–pre·oc·cu·pied
self–pre·serv·ing
self–pro·duced
self–pro·mot·er
self–pro·mot·ing
self–pro·mo·tion
self–pro·tec·tion
self–pro·tec·tive
self–pro·tec·tive·ness
self–pun·ish·ing
self–pun·ish·ment
self–raised
self–re·crim·i·na·tion
self–ref·er·ence
self–ref·er·en·tial
self–re·fer·ring
self–ref·or·ma·tion
self–reg·u·la·tion
self–reg·u·la·tive
self–reg·u·la·to·ry
self–re·in·forc·ing
self–re·new·al
self–re·new·ing
self–re·nounc·ing
self–re·nun·ci·a·tion
self–re·proach
self–re·proach·ful
self–re·proof
self–re·prov·ing
self–re·straint
self–rid·i·cule
self–sat·i·riz·ing
self–se·lect·ed
self–se·lec·tion
self–set
self–sur·ren·der
self–sus·tained
self–ther·a·py
self–tor·ment
self–tor·men·tor
self–tor·ture
self–tran·scen·dence
self–trans·for·ma·tion
self–un·der·stand·ing
self–val·i·dat·ing
self–wor·ship
self–wor·ship·er

self–aban·doned \ˌself-ə-ˈban-dənd\ *adj* (1791) : abandoned by oneself; *esp* : given up to one's impulses
self–aban·don·ment \-dən-mənt\ *n* (1809) **1** : a lack of self-restraint **2** : a surrender of one's selfish interests or desires
self–ab·sorbed \-əb-ˈsȯrbd, -ˈzȯrbd\ *adj* (1796) : absorbed in one's own thoughts, activities, or interests
self–ab·sorp·tion \-ˈsȯrp-shən, -ˈzȯrp-\ *n* (1835) : preoccupation with oneself
self–abuse \-ə-ˈbyüs\ *n* (1605) **1** : reproach of oneself **2** : MASTURBATION **3** : abuse of one's body or health
self–act·ing \-ˈak-tiŋ\ *adj* (ca. 1680) : acting or capable of acting of or by itself : AUTOMATIC
self–ac·tiv·i·ty \-ˌak-ˈti-və-tē\ *n* (1644) : independent and esp. self-determined activity
self–ac·tu·al·ize \-ˈak-ch(ə-w)ə-ˌlīz, -sh(ə-w)ə-ˌlīz\ *vi* (1874) : to realize fully one's potential — **self–ac·tu·al·i·za·tion** \-ˌak-ch(ə-w)ə-lə-ˈzā-shən, -sh(ə-w)ə-lə-\ *n*
self–ad·dressed \-ə-ˈdrest, -ˈa-ˌdrest\ *adj* (1904) : addressed for return to the sender ⟨a ∼ envelope⟩
self–ad·he·sive \-əd-ˈhē-siv, -ziv\ *adj* (1958) : having a side coated with an adhesive that sticks without wetting ⟨∼ labels⟩
self–ad·just·ment \-ə-ˈjəs(t)-mənt\ *n* (1848) : adjustment to oneself or one's environment
self–ad·mi·ra·tion \-ˌad-mə-ˈrā-shən\ *n* (1661) : SELF-CONCEIT
self–af·fect·ed \-ə-ˈfek-təd\ *adj* (1606) : CONCEITED, SELF-LOVING
self–anal·y·sis \-ə-ˈna-lə-səs\ *n* (1821) : a systematic attempt by an individual to understand his or her own personality without the aid of another person
self–an·a·lyt·i·cal \-ˌa-nə-ˈli-ti-kəl\ *also* **self–an·a·lyt·ic** *adj* (1943) : relating to or using self-analysis
self–an·ni·hi·la·tion \-ə-ˌnī-ə-ˈlā-shən\ *n* (1647) : annihilation of the self (as in mystical contemplation of God)
self–ap·plaud·ing \-ə-ˈplȯ-diŋ\ *adj* (1654) : marked by self-applause
self–ap·plause \-ˈplȯz\ *n* (1678) : an expression or feeling of approval of oneself
self–ap·point·ed \-ə-ˈpȯin-təd\ *adj* (1792) : appointed by oneself : SELF-PROCLAIMED
self–as·sem·bly \-ə-ˈsem-blē\ *n* (1966) : the process by which a complex macromolecule (as collagen) or a supramolecular system (as a virus) spontaneously assembles itself from its components — **self–as·sem·ble** \-ə-ˈsem-bəl\ *vi*
self–as·sert·ing \-ə-ˈsər-tiŋ\ *adj* (1837) **1** : asserting oneself or one's own rights, claims, or opinions **2 a** : SELF-ASSURED, CONFIDENT **b** : ARROGANT — **self–as·sert·ing·ly** \-tiŋ-lē\ *adv*
self–as·ser·tion \-ə-ˈsər-shən\ *n* (1806) **1** : the act of asserting oneself or one's own rights, claims, or opinions **2** : the act of asserting one's superiority over others
self–as·ser·tive \-ˈsər-tiv\ *adj* (1862) : given to or characterized by self-assertion *syn* see AGGRESSIVE — **self–as·ser·tive·ly** *adv* — **self–as·ser·tive·ness** *n*
self–as·sump·tion \-ə-ˈsəm(p)-shən\ *n* (1606) : SELF-CONCEIT
self–as·sur·ance \-ə-ˈshu̇r-ən(t)s\ *n* (1594) : SELF-CONFIDENCE
self–as·sured \-ˈshu̇rd\ *adj* (1711) : sure of oneself : SELF-CONFIDENT — **self–as·sured·ly** \-ˈshu̇r-əd-lē, -ˈshu̇rd-\ *adv* — **self–as·sured·ness** \-ˈshu̇r-əd-nəs, -ˈshu̇rd-\ *n*
self–aware \-ə-ˈwer\ *adj* (1924) : characterized by self-awareness
self–aware·ness *n* (1880) : an awareness of one's own personality or individuality
self–belt \ˈself-ˈbelt\ *n* (1960) : a belt made of the same material as the garment with which it is worn — **self–belt·ed** \-ˈbel-təd\ *adj*
self–be·tray·al \ˌself-bi-ˈtrā(-ə)l\ *n* (1822) : SELF-REVELATION
self–born \-ˈbȯrn\ *adj* (1587) **1** : arising within the self ⟨∼ sorrows⟩ **2** : springing from a prior self ⟨phoenix rising ∼ from the fire⟩
self–ca·ter·ing \-ˈkā-tər-iŋ\ *adj* (1970) *Brit* : provided with lodging and cooking facilities but not meals ⟨∼ holiday cottages⟩
self–cen·tered \-ˈsen-tərd\ *adj* (ca. 1764) **1** : independent of outside force or influence : SELF-SUFFICIENT **2** : concerned solely with one's own desires, needs, or interests — **self–cen·tered·ly** *adv* — **self–cen·tered·ness** *n*
self–clos·ing \-ˈklō-ziŋ\ *adj* (ca. 1875) : closing or shutting automatically after being opened
self–cock·ing \-ˈkä-kiŋ\ *adj* (1847) *of a firearm* : cocked by the operation of some part of the action ⟨∼ on pushing the bolt forward⟩
self–col·lect·ed \-kə-ˈlek-təd\ *adj* (ca. 1711) : SELF-POSSESSED
self–col·ored \-ˈkə-lərd\ *adj* (1759) : of a single color ⟨a ∼ flower⟩

self–com·pat·i·ble \-kəm-ˈpa-tə-bəl\ *adj* (1922) **:** capable of effective self-pollination that results in the production of seeds and fruits — **self–com·pat·i·bil·i·ty** \-ˌpa-tə-ˈbi-lə-tē\ *n*

self–com·posed \-kəm-ˈpōzd\ *adj* (1838) **:** having control over one's emotions **:** CALM — **self–com·pos·ed·ly** \-ˈpō-zəd-lē\ *adv* — **self–com·posed·ness** \-ˈpō-zəd-nəs, -ˈpōz(d)-nəs\ *n*

self–con·ceit \-kən-ˈsēt\ *n* (1577) **:** an exaggerated opinion of one's own qualities or abilities **:** VANITY — **self–con·ceit·ed** \-ˈsē-təd\ *adj*

self–con·cept \ˈself-ˈkän-ˌsept\ *n* (1925) **:** the mental image one has of oneself

self–con·cep·tion \ˌself-kən-ˈsep-shən\ *n* (1875) **:** SELF-CONCEPT

self–con·cern \-ˈsərn\ *n* (1681) **:** a selfish or morbid concern for one-self — **self–con·cerned** \-ˈsərnd\ *adj*

self–con·fessed \-ˈfest\ *adj* (1746) **:** openly acknowledged by oneself **:** AVOWED — **self–con·fess·ed·ly** \-ˈfe-səd-lē, -ˈfest-lē\ *adv*

self–con·fes·sion \-ˈfe-shən\ *n* (1707) **:** open acknowledgment **:** AVOWAL

self–con·fi·dence \-ˈkän-fə-dən(t)s, -ˌden(t)s\ *n* (1609) **:** confidence in oneself and in one's powers and abilities — **self–con·fi·dent** \-fə-dənt, -ˌdent\ *adj* — **self–con·fi·dent·ly** *adv*

self–con·fron·ta·tion \-ˌkän-(ˌ)frən-ˈtā-shən\ *n* (1961) **:** SELF-ANALYSIS

self–con·grat·u·la·tion \-kən-ˌgra-chə-ˈlā-shən, -ˌgra-jə-\ *n* (1712) **:** congratulation of oneself; *esp* **:** a complacent acknowledgment of one's own superiority or good fortune

self–con·grat·u·la·to·ry \-ˈgra-chə-lə-ˌtȯr-ē, -ˌgra-jə-\ *adj* (1833) **:** expressive of self-congratulation ⟨∼ memoirs⟩

self–con·scious \-ˈkän(t)-shəs\ *adj* (ca. 1680) **1 a :** conscious of one's own acts or states as belonging to or originating in oneself **:** aware of oneself as an individual **b :** intensely aware of oneself **:** CONSCIOUS ⟨a rising and ∼ social class⟩; *also* **:** produced or done with such awareness ⟨∼ art⟩ **2 :** uncomfortably conscious of oneself as an object of the observation of others **:** ILL AT EASE — **self–con·scious·ly** *adv* — **self–con·scious·ness** *n*

self–con·se·quence \-ˈkän(t)-sə-ˌkwen(t)s, -si-kwən(t)s\ *n* (1751) **:** SELF-IMPORTANCE

self–con·sis·ten·cy \-kən-ˈsis-tən(t)-sē\ *n* (1692) **:** the quality or state of being self-consistent

self–con·sis·tent \-tənt\ *adj* (1683) **:** having each part logically consistent with the rest

self–con·tained \-kən-ˈtānd\ *adj* (1591) **1 a :** complete in itself **:** INDEPENDENT ⟨a ∼ machine⟩ ⟨a ∼ program of study⟩ **b :** BUILT-IN ⟨a lectern with a ∼ light fixture⟩ **2 a :** showing self-control **b :** formal and reserved in manner — **self–con·tained·ly** \-ˈtā-nəd-lē, -ˈtānd-lē\ *adv* — **self–con·tained·ness** \-ˈtā-nəd-nəs, -ˈtān(d)-nəs\ *n* — **self–con·tain·ment** \-ˈtān-mənt\ *n*

self–con·tam·i·na·tion \-kən-ˌta-mə-ˈnā-shən\ *n* (1955) **1 :** contamination by oneself **2 :** contamination from within

self–con·tent \-kən-ˈtent\ *n* (1654) **:** SELF-SATISFACTION

self–con·tent·ed \-ˈten-təd\ *adj* (1818) **:** SELF-SATISFIED — **self–con·tent·ed·ly** *adv* — **self–con·tent·ed·ness** *n*

self–con·tent·ment \-ˈtent-mənt\ *n* (1815) **:** SELF-SATISFACTION

self–con·tra·dic·tion \-ˌkän-trə-ˈdik-shən\ *n* (1658) **1 :** contradiction of oneself **2 :** a self-contradictory statement or proposition

self–con·tra·dic·to·ry \-ˈdik-t(ə-)rē\ *adj* (1657) **:** consisting of two contradictory members or parts

self–con·trol \-kən-ˈtrōl\ *n* (1711) **:** restraint exercised over one's own impulses, emotions, or desires — **self–con·trolled** \-ˈtrōld\ *adj*

self–cor·rect·ing \-kə-ˈrek-tiŋ\ *adj* (1805) **:** correcting or compensating for one's own errors or weaknesses

self–cor·rec·tive \-ˈrek-tiv\ *adj* (ca. 1925) **:** SELF-CORRECTING

self–deal·ing \ˈself-ˈdē-liŋ\ *n* (1940) **:** financial dealing that is not at arm's length; *esp* **:** borrowing from or lending to a company by a controlling individual primarily to the individual's own advantage

self–de·fense \ˌself-di-ˈfen(t)s\ *n* (1651) **1 :** a plea of justification for the use of force or for homicide **2 :** the act of defending oneself, one's property, or a close relative

self–de·fen·sive \-ˈfen(t)-siv\ *adj* (1809) **:** of, relating to, or given to self-defense ⟨a ∼ person⟩ ⟨a ∼ attitude⟩

self–def·i·ni·tion \-ˌde-fə-ˈni-shən\ *n* (1957) **:** the evaluation by oneself of one's worth as an individual in distinction from one's interpersonal or social roles

self–de·ni·al \-di-ˈnī(-ə)l\ *n* (1642) **:** a restraint or limitation of one's own desires or interests

self–de·ny·ing \-ˈnī-iŋ\ *adj* (1632) **:** showing self-denial — **self–de·ny·ing·ly** \-iŋ-lē\ *adv*

self–des·ig·na·tion \-ˌde-zig-ˈnā-shən\ *n* (1848) **:** a name or title that an animate entity (as a person or body of people) uses usu. by choice to refer to itself

self–de·spair \-di-ˈsper\ *n* (1652) **:** despair of oneself **:** HOPELESSNESS

self–de·stroy·ing \-ˈstrȯi-iŋ\ *adj* (1645) **:** SELF-DESTRUCTIVE

self–de·struct \-di-ˈstrəkt\ *vi* (1968) **:** to destroy oneself or itself — **self–destruct** *adj*

self–de·struc·tion \-ˈstrək-shən\ *n* (ca. 1586) **:** destruction of oneself; *esp* **:** SUICIDE

self–de·struc·tive \-ˈstrək-tiv\ *adj* (1641) **:** acting or tending to harm or destroy oneself ⟨∼ behavior⟩; *also* **:** SUICIDAL ⟨a ∼ impulse⟩ — **self–de·struc·tive·ness** *n*

self–de·ter·mi·na·tion \-di-ˌtər-mə-ˈnā-shən\ *n* (ca. 1670) **1 :** free choice of one's own acts or states without external compulsion **2 :** determination by the people of a territorial unit of their own future political status

self–de·ter·mined \-ˈtər-mənd\ *adj* (ca. 1670) **:** determined by oneself

self–de·ter·min·ing \-ˈtər-mə-niŋ, -ˈtərm-niŋ\ *adj* (1662) **:** capable of determining one's or its own acts

self–de·ter·min·ism \-ˈtər-mə-ˌni-zəm\ *n* (1936) **:** a doctrine that the actions of a self are determined by itself

self–de·vot·ed \-di-ˈvō-təd\ *adj* (1713) **:** characterized by total devotion of oneself (as to a cause) — **self–de·vot·ed·ness** *n*

self–dis·ci·pline \-ˈdi-sə-plən\ *n* (1838) **:** correction or regulation of oneself for the sake of improvement

self–dis·ci·plined \-plənd\ *adj* (1828) **:** capable of or subject to self-discipline

self–dis·cov·ery \-dis-ˈkə-v(ə-)rē\ *n* (1924) **:** the act or process of achieving self-knowledge

self–dis·trust \-ˈtrəst\ *n* (1789) **:** a lack of confidence in oneself **:** DIFFIDENCE — **self–dis·trust·ful** \-fəl\ *adj*

self–dra·ma·ti·za·tion \ˌself-ˌdra-mə-tə-ˈzā-shən, -ˌdrä-\ *n* (1933) **:** the act or an instance of dramatizing oneself — **self–dra·ma·tiz·er** \-ˈdra-mə-ˌtī-zər, -ˈdrä-\ *n*

self–dra·ma·tiz·ing \-ˈdra-mə-ˌtī-ziŋ, -ˈdrä-\ *adj* (1938) **:** seeing and presenting oneself as an important or dramatic figure

self–drive \ˈself-ˈdrīv\ *adj* (1929) *chiefly Brit* **:** being a rental car

self–elect·ed \ˌself-ə-ˈlek-təd\ *adj* (1799) **:** SELF-APPOINTED

self–em·ployed \-im-ˈplȯid\ *adj* (1916) **:** earning income directly from one's own business, trade, or profession rather than as a specified salary or wages from an employer — **self–employed** *n*

self–em·ploy·ment \-ˈplȯi-mənt\ *n* (1745) **:** the state of being self-employed

self–en·er·giz·ing \-ˈe-nər-ˌjī-ziŋ\ *adj* (1931) **:** containing means for augmentation of power within itself ⟨a ∼ brake⟩

self–en·forc·ing \-in-ˈfȯr-siŋ\ *adj* (1952) **:** containing in itself the authority or means that provide for its enforcement

self–en·rich·ment \-in-ˈrich-mənt\ *n* (1920) **:** the act or process of increasing one's intellectual or spiritual resources

self–es·teem \-ə-ˈstēm\ *n* (1657) **1 :** a confidence and satisfaction in oneself **:** SELF-RESPECT **2 :** SELF-CONCEIT

self–ev·i·dence \-ˈe-və-dən(t)s, -ˌden(t)s\ *n* (1671) **:** the quality or state of being self-evident

self–ev·i·dent \-dənt, -ˌdent\ *adj* (1671) **:** evident without proof or reasoning — **self–ev·i·dent·ly** *adv*

self–ex·am \-ig-ˈzam\ *n* (1978) **:** SELF-EXAMINATION

self–ex·am·i·na·tion \-ig-ˌza-mə-ˈnā-shən\ *n* (1647) **1 :** a reflective examination (as of one's beliefs or motives) **:** INTROSPECTION **2 :** examination of one's body esp. for evidence of disease

self–ex·cit·ed \-ik-ˈsī-təd\ *adj* (1882) **:** excited by a current produced by the generator itself ⟨∼ generators⟩

self–ex·e·cut·ing \-ˈek-sə-ˌkyü-tiŋ\ *adj* (1857) **:** taking effect immediately without implementing legislation ⟨a ∼ treaty⟩

self–ex·iled \-ˈeg-ˌzī(-ə)ld, -ˈek-ˌsī(-ə)ld\ *adj* (1737) **:** exiled by one's own wish or decision

self–ex·plan·a·to·ry \ik-ˈspla-nə-ˌtȯr-ē\ *adj* (1848) **:** explaining itself **:** capable of being understood without explanation

self–ex·plo·ra·tion \-ˌek-splə-ˈrā-shən, -ˌsplȯ-\ *n* (1954) **:** the examination and analysis of one's own unrealized spiritual or intellectual capacities

self–ex·pres·sion \-ik-ˈspre-shən\ *n* (1892) **:** the expression of one's own personality **:** assertion of one's individual traits — **self–ex·pres·sive** \-ˈspre-siv\ *adj*

self–feed \ˈself-ˈfēd\ *vt* **-fed** \-ˈfed\; **-feed·ing** (ca. 1924) **:** to provide rations to (animals) in bulk so as to permit feeding as wanted

self–feed·er \-ˈfē-dər\ *n* (1924) **:** a device for providing feed to livestock that is equipped with a feed hopper that automatically supplies a trough below

self–feel·ing \ˈself-ˈfē-liŋ\ *n* (1879) **:** self-centered emotion

self–fer·tile \ˌself-ˈfər-t^{ə}l\ *adj* (1865) **:** fertile by means of its own pollen or sperm — **self–fer·til·i·ty** \-(ˌ)fər-ˈti-lə-tē\ *n*

self–fer·til·i·za·tion \-ˌfər-tə-lə-ˈzā-shən\ *n* (1859) **:** fertilization effected by union of ova with pollen or sperm from the same individual — **self–fer·til·ize** \-ˈfər-tə-ˌlīz\ *vb*

self–flag·el·la·tion \-ˌfla-jə-ˈlā-shən\ *n* (1925) **:** extreme criticism of oneself — **self–flag·el·late** \-ˈfla-jə-ˌlāt\ *vb*

self–flat·ter·ing \-ˈfla-tə-riŋ\ *adj* (ca. 1586) **:** given to self-flattery

self–flat·tery \-tə-rē\ *n* (1657) **:** the glossing over of one's own weaknesses or mistakes and the exaggeration of one's own good qualities and achievements

self–for·get·ful \-fər-ˈget-fəl\ *adj* (1822) **:** having or showing no thought of self or selfish interests — **self–for·get·ful·ly** \-fə-lē\ *adv* — **self–for·get·ful·ness** *n*

self–for·get·ting \-ˈge-tiŋ\ *adj* (1824) **:** SELF-FORGETFUL — **self–for·get·ting·ly** \-tiŋ-lē\ *adv*

self–fruit·ful \ˈself-ˈfrüt-fəl\ *adj* (1940) **:** capable of setting a crop of self-pollinated fruit — **self–fruit·ful·ness** *n*

self–ful·fill·ing \ˌself-fül-ˈfi-liŋ\ *adj* (1876) **1 :** becoming real or true by virtue of having been predicted or expected ⟨a ∼ prophecy⟩ **2 :** marked by or achieving self-fulfillment

self–ful·fill·ment \-ˈfil-mənt\ *n* (ca. 1864) **:** fulfillment of oneself

self–giv·en \-ˈgi-vən\ *adj* (1662) **1 :** given by oneself ⟨∼ authority⟩ **2 :** derived from itself ⟨a ∼ entity⟩

self–glo·ri·fi·ca·tion \-ˌglȯr-ə-fə-ˈkā-shən\ *n* (1834) **:** a feeling or expression of one's own superiority

self–glo·ri·fy·ing \-ˈglȯr-ə-ˌfī-iŋ\ *adj* (1840) **:** given to or marked by boasting **:** BOASTFUL

self–glo·ry \-ˈglȯr-ē\ *n* (1647) **:** personal vanity **:** PRIDE

self–gov·er·nance \-ˈgə-vər-nən(t)s\ *n* (1839) **:** SELF-GOVERNMENT 2

self–gov·erned \-ˈgə-vərnd\ *adj* (1709) **1 :** not influenced or controlled by others **2 :** exercising self-control

self–gov·ern·ing \-ˈgə-vər-niŋ\ *adj* (1778) **:** having control or rule over oneself; *specif* **:** having self-government **:** AUTONOMOUS

self–gov·ern·ment \-ˈgə-vər(n)-mənt, -ˈgə-v^{ə}m-ənt\ *n* (1654) **1 :** SELF-CONTROL, SELF-COMMAND **2 :** government under the control and direction of the inhabitants of a political unit rather than by an outside authority; *broadly* **:** control of one's own affairs

self–grat·i·fi·ca·tion \-ˌgra-tə-fə-ˈkā-shən\ *n* (1677) **:** the act of pleasing oneself or of satisfying one's desires; *esp* **:** the satisfying of one's own sexual urges

self–grat·u·la·tion \-ˌgra-chə-ˈlā-shən\ *n* (1771) **:** SELF-CONGRATULATION

\ə\ **abut** \$^{ə}$\ kitten, F table \ər\ **further** \a\ **ash** \ā\ **ace** \ä\ **mop, mar** \au̇\ **out** \ch\ **chin** \e\ **bet** \ē\ **easy** \g\ **go** \i\ **hit** \ī\ **ice** \j\ **job** \ŋ\ **sing** \ō\ **go** \ȯ\ **law** \ȯi\ **boy** \th\ **thin** \t͟h\ **the** \ü\ **loot** \u̇\ **foot** \y\ **yet** \zh\ **vision, beige** \k̲, ^{n}, œ, ue, ^{y}\ *see* Guide to Pronunciation

self–grat·u·la·to·ry \-ˈgra-chə-lə-ˌtȯr-ē\ *adj* (ca. 1841) : SELF-CONGRATULATORY

self–heal \ˈself-ˌhēl\ *n* (14c) : a blue-flowered Eurasian mint (*Prunella vulgaris*) that is naturalized throughout No. America and is held to have medicinal properties useful in herbal medicine

self–help \ˈself-ˈhelp; *Southern also* ˈhep\ *n* (1831) : the action or process of bettering oneself or overcoming one's problems without the aid of others; *esp* : the coping with one's personal or emotional problems without professional help — **self–help** *adj*

self·hood \-ˌhu̇d\ *n* (1649) **1** : INDIVIDUALITY **2** : the quality or state of being selfish

self–iden·ti·cal \ˌself-ī-ˈden-ti-kəl, -ə-ˈden-\ *adj* (1877) : having self-identity

self–iden·ti·fi·ca·tion \-ˌden-tə-fə-ˈkā-shən\ *n* (1941) : identification with someone or something outside oneself

self–iden·ti·ty \-ˈden-tə-tē, -ˈde-nə-tē\ *n* (1835) **1** : sameness of a thing with itself **2** : INDIVIDUALITY ⟨self-understanding is the necessary condition of a sense of ~ —J. C. Murray⟩

self·ie \ˈsel-fē\ *n* (2002) : an image of oneself taken by oneself using a digital camera esp. for posting on social networks

self–ig·nite \-ig-ˈnīt\ *vi* (1835) : to become ignited without flame or spark (as under high compression) — **self–ig·ni·tion** \-ˈni-shən\ *n*

self–im·age \ˈself-ˈi-mij\ *n* (1939) : one's conception of oneself or of one's role

self–im·mo·la·tion \ˌself-ˌi-mə-ˈlā-shən\ *n* (1799) : a deliberate and willing sacrifice of oneself often by fire — **self–im·mo·late** \-ˈi-mə-ˌlāt\ *vb*

self–im·por·tance \-im-ˈpȯr-tᵊn(t)s, -tən(t)s\ *n* (1754) **1** : an exaggerated estimate of one's own importance : SELF-CONCEIT **2** : arrogant or pompous behavior

self–important \-tᵊnt, -tənt\ *adj* (1766) : having or showing self-importance — **self–im·por·tant·ly** *adv*

self–in·clu·sive \-in-ˈklü-siv, -ziv\ *adj* (1877) **1** : enclosing itself **2** : complete in itself

self–in·com·pat·i·ble \-ˌin-kəm-ˈpa-tə-bəl\ *adj* (1922) : incapable of effective self-pollination — **self–in·com·pat·i·bil·i·ty** \-ˌpa-tə-ˈbi-lə-tē\ *n*

self–in·crim·i·nat·ing \-in-ˈkri-mə-ˌnā-tiŋ\ *adj* (1925) : serving or tending to incriminate oneself

self–in·crim·i·na·tion \-ˌkri-mə-ˈnā-shən\ *n* (1911) : incrimination of oneself; *specif* : the giving of testimony which will likely subject one to criminal prosecution

self–in·duc·tance \-ˈdək-tən(t)s\ *n* (1888) : inductance in which an electromotive force is produced by self-induction

self–in·duc·tion \-ˈdək-shən\ *n* (1865) : induction of an electromotive force in a circuit by a varying current in the same circuit

self–in·dul·gence \-ˈdəl-jən(t)s\ *n* (1711) : excessive or unrestrained gratification of one's own appetites, desires, or whims — **self–in·dul·gent** \-jənt\ *adj* — **self–in·dul·gent·ly** *adv*

self–in·sur·ance \in-ˈshu̇r-ən(t)s, -ˈin-ˌ\ *n* (ca. 1897) : insurance of oneself or of one's own interests by the setting aside of money at regular intervals to provide a fund to cover possible losses

self–insure \-in-ˈshu̇r\ *vb* (1932) : to insure oneself; *esp* : to practice self-insurance — **self–insurer** \-ˈshu̇r-ər\ *n*

self–in·ter·est \-ˈin-t(ə-)rəst; -ˈin-tə-ˌrest, -ˌtrest; -ˈin-tərst\ *n* (1649) **1** : a concern for one's own advantage and well-being ⟨acted out of ~ and fear⟩ **2** : one's own interest or advantage ⟨~ requires that we be generous in foreign aid⟩ — **self–in·ter·est·ed** *adj* — **self–in·ter·est·ed·ly** *adv* — **self–in·ter·est·ed·ness** *n*

self–in·volved \-in-ˈvälvd, -ˈvȯlvd *also* -ˈvävd *or* ˈvȯvd\ *adj* (1823) : SELF-ABSORBED

self–involvement \-ˈvälv-mənt, -ˈvȯlv-\ *n* (1971) : SELF-ABSORPTION

self·ish \ˈsel-fish\ *adj* (1640) **1** : concerned excessively or exclusively with oneself : seeking or concentrating on one's own advantage, pleasure, or well-being without regard for others **2** : arising from concern with one's own welfare or advantage in disregard of others ⟨a ~ act⟩ **3** : being an actively replicating repetitive sequence of nucleic acid that serves no known function ⟨~ DNA⟩; *also* : being genetic material solely concerned with its own replication ⟨~ genes⟩ — **self·ish·ly** *adv* — **self·ish·ness** *n*

self–jus·ti·fi·ca·tion \ˌself-ˌjəs-tə-fə-ˈkā-shən\ *n* (ca. 1775) : the act or an instance of making excuses for oneself

self–jus·ti·fy·ing \-ˈjəs-tə-ˌfī-iŋ\ *adj* (1740) : seeking to justify oneself

self–know·ing \-ˈnō-iŋ\ *adj* (1601) : having self-knowledge

self–knowl·edge \-ˈnä-lij\ *n* (1564) : knowledge or understanding of one's own capabilities, character, feelings, or motivations

self·less \ˈsel-fləs\ *adj* (1821) : having no concern for self : UNSELFISH — **self·less·ly** *adv* — **self·less·ness** *n*

self–lim·it·ed \ˌself-ˈli-mə-təd\ *adj* (1845) : limited by one's or its own nature; *specif* : running a definite and limited course ⟨a ~ disease⟩

self–lim·it·ing \-tiŋ\ *adj* (1863) : limiting oneself or itself; *esp, of a disease* : SELF-LIMITED

self–liq·ui·dat·ing \-ˈli-kwə-ˌdā-tiŋ\ *adj* (1915) **1** : of or relating to a commercial transaction in which goods are converted into cash in a short time **2** : generating funds from its own operations to repay the investment made to create it ⟨a ~ housing project⟩

self–load·er \-ˈlō-dər\ *n* (ca. 1936) : a semiautomatic firearm

self–load·ing \-diŋ\ *adj* (1899) *of a firearm* : SEMIAUTOMATIC

self–love \ˈself-ˈləv\ *n* (1563) : love of self: **a** : CONCEIT **b** : regard for one's own happiness or advantage — **self–lov·ing** \-ˈlə-viŋ\ *adj*

self–made \ˈself-ˈmād\ *adj* (1615) : made such by one's own actions; *esp* : having achieved success or prominence by one's own efforts ⟨a ~ man⟩

self–mail·er \-ˈmā-lər\ *n* (ca. 1942) : a folder that can be sent by mail without enclosure in an envelope by use of a gummed sticker or a precanceled stamp to hold the leaves together

self–mail·ing \-liŋ\ *adj* (ca. 1948) : capable of being mailed without being enclosed in an envelope

self–moved \ˈself-ˈmüvd\ *adj* (ca. 1670) : moved by inherent power

self–mur·der \-ˈmər-dər\ *n* (1583) : SELF-DESTRUCTION, SUICIDE

self·ness \ˈself-nəs\ *n* (ca. 1586) **1** : EGOISM, SELFISHNESS **2** : PERSONALITY, SELFHOOD

self–ob·ser·va·tion \ˌself-ˌäb-sər-ˈvā-shən, -zər-\ *n* (1827) **1** : INTROSPECTION **2** : observation of one's own appearance

self–opin·ion \-ə-ˈpin-yən\ *n* (ca. 1580) : high or exaggerated opinion of oneself : SELF-CONCEIT

self–opin·ion·at·ed \-yə-ˌnā-təd\ *adj* (1656) **1** : CONCEITED **2** : stubbornly holding to one's own opinion : OPINIONATED — **self–opin·ion·at·ed·ness** *n*

self–or·ga·ni·za·tion \-ˌȯr-gə-nə-ˈzā-shən, -ˌȯrg-nə-\ *n* (1898) **1** : organization of oneself or itself **2** : the act or process of forming or joining an organization (as a labor union)

self–paced \ˈself-ˈpāst\ *adj* (1962) : designed to permit learning at the student's own pace ⟨~ math course⟩

self–par·tial·i·ty \ˌself-ˌpär-shē-ˈa-lə-tē, -ˌpär-ˈsha-\ *n* (1628) **1** : an excessive estimate of oneself as compared with others **2** : a prejudice in favor of one's own claims or interests

self–per·cep·tion \-pər-ˈsep-shən\ *n* (1678) : perception of oneself; *esp* : SELF-CONCEPT

self–pity \ˈself-ˈpi-tē\ *n* (1621) : pity for oneself; *esp* : a self-indulgent dwelling on one's own sorrows or misfortunes — **self–pity·ing** \-tē-iŋ\ *adj* — **self–pity·ing·ly** \-iŋ-lē\ *adv*

self–pleased \-ˈplēzd\ *adj* (1748) : SELF-SATISFIED

self–poise \-ˈpȯiz\ *n* (1854) : the quality or state of being self-poised

self–poised \-ˈpȯizd\ *adj* (1621) : having poise through self-command

self–pol·li·nate \ˈself-ˈpä-lə-ˌnāt\ *vt* (1890) : SELF 2 ~ *vi* : to undergo self-pollination

self–pol·li·na·tion \ˌself-ˌpä-lə-ˈnā-shən\ *n* (1872) : the transfer of pollen from the anther of a flower to the stigma of the same flower or sometimes to that of a genetically identical flower (as of the same plant or clone)

self–por·trait \-ˈpȯr-trət, -ˌtrāt\ *n* (1831) : a portrait of oneself done by oneself

self–pos·sessed \-pə-ˈzest *also* -ˈsest\ *adj* (1795) : having or showing self-possession : composed in mind or manner : CALM — **self–pos·sessed·ly** \-ˈze-səd-lē, -ˈse-; -ˈzest-lē, -ˈsest-\ *adv*

self–pos·ses·sion \-pə-ˈze-shən *also* -ˈse-\ *n* (1745) : control of one's emotions or reactions esp. when under stress : PRESENCE OF MIND, COMPOSURE **syn** see CONFIDENCE

self–pres·er·va·tion \-ˌpre-zər-ˈvā-shən\ *n* (ca. 1614) **1** : preservation of oneself from destruction or harm **2** : a natural or instinctive tendency to act so as to preserve one's own existence

self–pride \ˈself-ˈprīd\ *n* (ca. 1586) : pride in oneself or in that which relates to oneself

self–pro·claimed \-prō-ˈklāmd, -prə-\ *adj* (1835) : based on one's own assertion ⟨a ~ genius⟩

self–pro·fessed \-prə-ˈfest, -prō-\ *adj* (1967) : SELF-PROCLAIMED

self–pro·pelled \ˌself-prə-ˈpeld\ *adj* (1869) **1** : containing within itself the means for its own propulsion ⟨a ~ vehicle⟩ **2** : mounted on or fired from a moving vehicle ⟨a ~ gun⟩

self–pro·pel·ling \-ˈpe-liŋ\ *adj* (1845) : SELF-PROPELLED 1

self–pro·pul·sion \-ˈpəl-shən\ *n* (1874) : propulsion by one's own power

self–pub·lish \-ˈpə-blish\ *vt* (1979) : to publish (a book) using the author's own resources

self–pu·ri·fi·ca·tion \-ˌpyu̇r-ə-fə-ˈkā-shən\ *n* (1919) **1** : purification by natural process ⟨~ of water⟩ **2** : purification of oneself

self–ques·tion \ˈself-ˈkwes-chən, -ˈkwesh-\ *n* (1917) : a question asked of oneself by oneself

self–ques·tion·ing \-chə-niŋ\ *n* (1805) : examination of one's own actions and motives

self–rat·ing \-ˈrā-tiŋ\ *n* (1925) : determination of one's own rating with reference to a standard scale

self–re·al·i·za·tion \ˌself-ˌrē-ə-lə-ˈzā-shən\ *n* (1874) : fulfillment by oneself of the possibilities of one's character or personality

self–rec·og·ni·tion \-ˌre-kig-ˈni-shən, -kəg-\ *n* (1946) **1** : recognition of one's own self **2** : the process by which the immune system of an organism distinguishes between the body's own chemicals, cells, and tissues and those of foreign organisms and agents

self–re·cord·ing \-ri-ˈkȯr-diŋ\ *adj* (1865) : making an automatic record ⟨~ instruments⟩

self–re·flec·tion \-ri-ˈflek-shən\ *n* (1652) : SELF-EXAMINATION 1

self–re·flec·tive \-ri-ˈflek-tiv\ *adj* (1858) : marked by or engaging in self-reflection

self–re·flex·ive \-ri-ˈflek-siv\ *adj* (1933) : marked by or making reference to its own artificiality or contrivance ⟨~ fiction⟩ — **self–re·flex·ive·ly** *adv* — **self–re·flex·ive·ness** *n* — **self–re·flex·iv·i·ty** \-ˌrē-ˌflek-ˈsi-və-tē, -ri-\ *n*

self–re·gard \-ri-ˈgärd\ *n* (1595) : regard for or consideration of oneself or one's own interests

self–re·gard·ing \-ri-ˈgär-diŋ\ *adj* (1789) : concerned with oneself or one's own interests

self–reg·u·lat·ing \-ˈre-gyə-ˌlā-tiŋ\ *adj* (1745) : regulating oneself or itself; *esp* : AUTOMATIC ⟨a ~ mechanism⟩

self–re·li·ance \-ri-ˈlī-ənts\ *n* (1815) : reliance on one's own efforts and abilities

self–re·li·ant \-ənt\ *adj* (1848) : having confidence in and exercising one's own powers or judgment

self–rep·li·cat·ing \-ˈre-plə-ˌkā-tiŋ\ *adj* (1946) : reproducing itself autonomously ⟨DNA is a ~ molecule⟩ — **self–rep·li·ca·tion** \-ˌre-plə-ˈkā-shən\ *n*

self–re·port \-ri-ˈpȯrt\ *n* (1970) : a report about one's behavior provided esp. by one who is a subject of research — **self–re·port·ed** \-ˈpȯr-təd\ *adj*

self–re·spect \-ri-ˈspekt\ *n* (1765) **1** : a proper respect for oneself as a human being **2** : regard for one's own standing or position

self–re·spect·ing \-ri-ˈspek-tiŋ\ *adj* (1786) : having or characterized by self-respect

self–re·veal·ing \-ri-ˈvē-liŋ\ *adj* (1839) : marked by self-revelation

self–rev·e·la·tion \-ˌre-və-ˈlā-shən\ *n* (1852) : revelation of one's own thoughts, feelings, and attitudes esp. without deliberate intent

self–re·ward·ing \-ri-ˈwȯr-diŋ\ *adj* (1740) : containing or producing its own reward ⟨virtue is ~⟩

self–righ·teous \-ˈrī-chəs\ *adj* (ca. 1680) : convinced of one's own righteousness esp. in contrast with the actions and beliefs of others : narrow-mindedly moralistic — **self–righ·teous·ly** *adv* — **self–righ·teous·ness** *n*

self–ris·ing flour \ˈself-ˈrī-ziŋ-\ *n* (1854) **:** a commercially prepared mixture of flour, salt, and a leavening agent — called also *self-raising flour*
self–rule \ˈself-ˈrül\ *n* (1660) **:** SELF-GOVERNMENT
self–rul·ing \-ˈrü-liŋ\ *adj* (ca. 1680) **:** SELF-GOVERNING
self–sac·ri·fice \ˈself-ˈsa-krə-ˌfīs *also* -fəs *or* -ˌfīz\ *n* (1591) **:** sacrifice of oneself or one's interest for others or for a cause or ideal
self–sa·cri·fic·ing \-ˌfī-siŋ *also* -fə- *or* -ˌfī-\ *adj* (1817) **:** sacrificing oneself for others — **self–sac·ri·fic·ing·ly** *adv*
self·same \ˈself-ˌsām\ *adj* (15c) **:** being the one mentioned or in question **:** IDENTICAL ⟨left the ~ day⟩ ***syn*** see SAME — **self·same·ness** \-ˌsām-nəs, -ˈsām-\ *n*
self–sat·is·fac·tion \ˌself-ˌsa-təs-ˈfak-shən\ *n* (1661) **:** a usu. smug satisfaction with oneself or one's position or achievements
self–sat·is·fied \ˈself-ˈsa-təs-ˌfīd\ *adj* (1734) **:** feeling or showing self-satisfaction
self–scru·ti·ny \ˈself-ˈskrü-tə-nē, -ˈskrüt-nē\ *n* (ca. 1711) **:** SELF-EXAMINATION
self–seal·ing \ˈself-ˈsē-liŋ\ *adj* (1851) **1 :** capable of being sealed by pressure without the addition of moisture ⟨~ envelopes⟩ **2 :** capable of sealing itself (as after puncture) ⟨a ~ tire⟩
self–search·ing \-ˈsər-chiŋ\ *n* (1681) **:** SELF-QUESTIONING
self–seek·er \-ˈsē-kər\ *n* (1632) **:** a self-seeking person
[1]**self–seek·ing** \-kiŋ\ *n* (ca. 1586) **:** the act or practice of selfishly advancing one's own ends
[2]**self–seeking** *adj* (ca. 1628) **:** seeking only to further one's own interests
self–serve \ˈself-ˈsərv\ *adj* (1926) **:** permitting self-service
self–ser·vice \ˈself-ˈsər-vəs\ *n* (1919) **:** the serving of oneself (as in a restaurant or gas station) with goods or services to be paid for at a cashier's desk or by using a coin-operated mechanism or a credit or debit card — **self–service** *adj*
self–serv·ing \-ˈsər-viŋ\ *adj* (1621) **:** serving one's own interests often in disregard of the truth or the interests of others — **self–serv·ing·ly** *adv*
self–sim·i·lar·i·ty \-ˌsi-mə-ˈla-rə-tē\ *n* (1967) **:** the quality or state of having an appearance that is invariant upon being scaled larger or smaller ⟨magnify the fractal and you can see the ~ of its edge⟩ — **self–sim·i·lar** \-ˈsi-mə-lər, -ˈsim-lər\ *adj*
self–slaugh·ter \-ˈslȯ-tər\ *n* (ca. 1601) **:** SUICIDE 1a
self–slaugh·tered \-tərd\ *adj* (1594) **:** killed by oneself
self–sow \ˈself-ˈsō\ *vi* **-sowed** \-ˈsōd\; **-sown** \-ˈsōn\ *or* **-sowed; -sow·ing** (1608) **:** to sow itself by dropping seeds or by natural action (as of wind or water)
self–start·er \ˌself-ˈstär-tər\ *n* (1894) **1 :** STARTER 3a **2 :** a person who has initiative
self–start·ing \-ˈstär-tiŋ\ *adj* (1866) **:** capable of starting by oneself or itself
self–ster·ile \-ˈster-əl\ *adj* (1876) **:** sterile to its own pollen or sperm — **self–ste·ril·i·ty** \-stə-ˈri-lə-tē\ *n*
self–stick \ˈself-ˈstik\ *adj* (1947) **:** capable of adhering to a surface by application of pressure without the addition of moisture
self–stim·u·la·tion \ˌself-ˌstim-yə-ˈlā-shən\ *n* (1947) **:** stimulation of oneself as a result of one's own activity or behavior ⟨electrical ~ of the brain⟩; *esp* **:** MASTURBATION — **self–stim·u·la·to·ry** \-ˈstim-yə-lə-ˌtȯr-ē, -ˌtȯr-\ *adj*
self–study \ˈself-ˈstə-dē\ *n* (1683) **:** study of oneself; *also* **:** a record of observations from such study
self–styled \-ˈstī(-ə)ld\ *adj* (1822) **:** SELF-PROCLAIMED ⟨~ experts⟩
self–sub·sis·tent \ˌself-səb-ˈsis-tənt\ *adj* (1647) **:** subsisting independently of anything external to itself — **self–sub·sis·tence** \-tən(t)s\ *n*
self–sub·sist·ing \-ˈsis-tiŋ\ *adj* (1646) **:** SELF-SUBSISTENT
self–suf·fi·cien·cy \-sə-ˈfi-shən(t)-sē\ *n* (1623) **:** the quality or state of being self-sufficient
self–suf·fi·cient \-ˈfi-shənt\ *adj* (1592) **1 :** able to maintain oneself or itself without outside aid **:** capable of providing for one's own needs ⟨a ~ farm⟩ **2 :** having an extreme confidence in one's own ability or worth **:** HAUGHTY, OVERBEARING
self–suf·fic·ing \-ˈfī-siŋ *also* -ziŋ\ *adj* (1647) **:** SELF-SUFFICIENT — **self–suf·fic·ing·ly** *adv* — **self–suf·fic·ing·ness** *n*
self–sug·ges·tion \-səg-ˈjes-chən, -sə-ˈ, -ˈjesh-\ *n* (1892) **:** AUTOSUGGESTION
self–sup·port \ˌself-sə-ˈpȯrt\ *n* (1774) **:** independent support of oneself or itself — **self–sup·port·ed** *adj*
self–sup·port·ing \-ˈpȯr-tiŋ\ *adj* (1722) **:** characterized by self-support: as **a :** meeting one's needs by one's own efforts or output **b :** supporting itself or its own weight ⟨a ~ wall⟩
self–sus·tain·ing \-sə-ˈstā-niŋ\ *adj* (1799) **1 :** maintaining or able to maintain oneself or itself by independent effort ⟨a ~ community⟩ **2 :** maintaining or able to maintain itself once commenced ⟨a ~ nuclear reaction⟩
self–tan·ner \ˈself-ˈta-nər\ *n* (1980) **:** a product (as one containing dihydroxyacetone) that when applied to the skin reacts chemically with its surface layer to give the appearance of a suntan
self–taught \ˈself-ˈtȯt\ *adj* (1725) **1 :** having knowledge or skills acquired by one's own efforts without formal instruction ⟨a ~ musician⟩ **2 :** learned by oneself ⟨~ knowledge⟩
self–tol·er·ance \-ˈtä-lə-rən(t)s, -ˈtäl-rən(t)s\ *n* (1964) **:** the physiological state that exists in an organism when its immune system has proceeded far enough in the process of self-recognition to lose the capacity to attack and destroy its own bodily constituents
self–treat·ment \-ˈtrēt-mənt\ *n* (1878) **:** medication of oneself or treatment of one's own disease or condition without medical supervision or prescription
self–trust \-ˈtrəst\ *n* (1583) **:** SELF-CONFIDENCE
self–will \-ˈwil\ *n* (14c) **:** stubborn or willful adherence to one's own desires or ideas **:** OBSTINACY
self–willed \-ˈwild\ *adj* (14c) **:** governed by one's own will **:** not yielding to the wishes of others **:** OBSTINATE — **self–willed·ly** \-ˈwild-lē\ *adv* — **self–willed·ness** \-ˈwild-nəs\ *n*
self–wind·ing \-ˈwīn-diŋ\ *adj* (1825) **:** not needing to be wound by hand ⟨a ~ watch⟩
self–worth \-ˈwərth\ *n* (1944) **:** SELF-ESTEEM
Sel·juk \ˈsel-ˌjük, sel-ˈ\ *or* **Sel·ju·ki·an** \sel-ˈjü-kē-ən\ *adj* [Turk *Selçuk*, eponymous ancestor of the dynasties] (1603) **1 :** of or relating to any of several Turkish dynasties ruling over a great part of western Asia in the 11th, 12th, and 13th centuries **2 :** of, relating to, or characteristic of a Turkish people ruled over by a Seljuk dynasty — **Seljuk** *or* **Seljukian** *n*
[1]**sell** \ˈsel\ *vb* **sold** \ˈsōld\; **sell·ing** [ME, fr. OE *sellan;* akin to OHG *sellen* to sell, Gk *helein* to take] *vt* (bef. 12c) **1 :** to deliver or give up in violation of duty, trust, or loyalty and esp. for personal gain **:** BETRAY — often used with *out* ⟨~ out their country⟩ **2 a (1) :** to give up (property) to another for something of value (as money) **(2) :** to offer for sale **b :** to give up in return for something else esp. foolishly or dishonorably ⟨*sold* his birthright for a mess of pottage⟩ **c :** to exact a price for ⟨*sold* their lives dearly⟩ **3 a :** to deliver into slavery for money **b :** to give into the power of another ⟨*sold* his soul to the devil⟩ **c :** to deliver the personal services of for money **4 :** to dispose of or manage for profit instead of in accordance with conscience, justice, or duty ⟨*sold* their votes⟩ **5 a :** to develop a belief in the truth, value, or desirability of **:** gain acceptance for ⟨trying to ~ a program to the Congress⟩ **b :** to persuade or influence to a course of action or to the acceptance of something ⟨~ children on reading⟩ **6 :** to impose on **:** CHEAT **7 a :** to cause or promote the sale of ⟨using television advertising to ~ cereal⟩ **b :** to make or attempt to make sales to **c :** to influence or induce to make a purchase **8 :** to achieve a sale of ⟨*sold* a million copies⟩ ~ *vi* **1 :** to dispose of something by sale ⟨thinks now is a good time to ~⟩ **2 :** to achieve a sale; *also* **:** to achieve satisfactory sales ⟨hoped that the new line would ~⟩ **3 :** to have a specified price — **sell·able** \ˈse-lə-bəl\ *adj* — **sell down the river :** to betray the faith of — **sell short 1 :** to make a short sale **2 :** to fail to value properly **:** UNDERESTIMATE
[2]**sell** *n* (1838) **1 :** a deliberate deception **:** HOAX **2 :** the act or an instance of selling **3 :** something to be sold or caused to be accepted ⟨the new mystery novel was an easy ~⟩; *also* **:** someone to whom something is sold ⟨the new purchasing agent was a tough ~⟩
[3]**sell** *or* **selle** \ˈsel\ *n* [ME *selle,* fr. AF *sele,* fr. L *sella* — more at SETTLE] (15c) *archaic* **:** SADDLE
[4]**sell** *chiefly Scot var of* SELF
sell·er \ˈse-lər\ *n* (13c) **1 :** one that offers for sale **2 :** a marketed product that sells well, to a specified extent, or in a specified manner ⟨a million-copy ~⟩ ⟨a poor ~⟩
seller's market *n* (1932) **:** a market in which goods are scarce, buyers have a limited range of choice, and prices are high — compare BUYER'S MARKET
selling climax *n* (ca. 1949) **:** a sharp decline in stock prices for a short time on very heavy trading volume followed by a rally
sell·ing–plat·er \ˈse-liŋ-ˌplā-tər\ *n* (1886) **:** a horse that runs in selling races
selling point *n* (1923) **:** an aspect or detail of something that is emphasized (as in selling or promoting)
selling race *n* (1867) **:** a claiming race in which the winning horse is put up for auction
sell–off \ˈsel-ˌȯf\ *n* (1976) **:** a usu. sudden sharp decline in security prices accompanied by increased volume of trading
sell off *vi* (1976) **:** to suffer a drop in prices
sell·out \ˈsel-ˌau̇t\ *n* (1859) **1 :** the act or an instance of selling out **2 :** something sold out; *esp* **:** something (as a concert or contest) for which all tickets are sold **3 :** one who sells out
sell out *vt* (1796) **1 :** to sell the goods of (a debtor) in order to satisfy creditors **2 :** to sell security or commodity holdings of usu. to satisfy an uncovered margin **3 a :** to sell all the available tickets for ⟨*sold out* the concert⟩ **b :** to sell all of ⟨the merchandise was quickly *sold out*⟩ ~ *vi* **1 :** to dispose of one's goods by sale; *esp* **:** to sell one's business **2 :** to betray one's cause or associates esp. for personal gain **3 :** to be or achieve a sellout
selt·zer \ˈselt-sər\ *n* [modif. of G *Selterser* (*Wasser*) water of Selters, fr. Nieder *Selters,* Germany] (1775) **:** artificially carbonated water
sel·vage *or* **sel·vedge** \ˈsel-vij\ *n* [ME *selfegge, selvage,* fr. *self* self + *egge* edge (after MD *selfegghe*)] (15c) **1 a :** the edge on either side of a woven or flat-knitted fabric so finished as to prevent raveling; *specif* **:** a narrow border often of different or heavier threads than the fabric and sometimes in a different weave **b :** an edge (as of fabric or paper) meant to be cut off and discarded **2 :** an outer or peripheral part **:** BORDER, EDGE — **sel·vaged** *or* **sel·vedged** \-vijd\ *adj*
selves *pl of* SELF
sem *abbr* seminar
SEM *abbr* scanning electron microscope; scanning electron microscopy
se·man·tic \si-ˈman-tik\ *also* **se·man·ti·cal** \-ti-kəl\ *adj* [Gk *sēmantikos* significant, fr. *sēmainein* to signify, mean, fr. *sēma* sign, token] (1894) **1 :** of or relating to meaning in language **2 :** of or relating to semantics — **se·man·ti·cal·ly** \-ti-k(ə-)lē\ *adv*
se·man·ti·cist \-ˈman-tə-sist\ *n* (1902) **:** a specialist in semantics
se·man·tics \si-ˈman-tiks\ *n pl but sing or pl in constr* (1893) **1 :** the study of meanings: **a :** the historical and psychological study and the classification of changes in the signification of words or forms viewed as factors in linguistic development **b (1) :** SEMIOTICS **(2) :** a branch of semiotic dealing with the relations between signs and what they refer to and including theories of denotation, extension, naming, and truth **2 :** GENERAL SEMANTICS **3 a :** the meaning or relationship of meanings of a sign or set of signs; *esp* **:** connotative meaning **b :** the language used (as in advertising or political propaganda) to achieve a desired effect on an audience esp. through the use of words with novel or dual meanings
[1]**sem·a·phore** \ˈse-mə-ˌfȯr\ *n* [Gk *sēma* sign, signal + ISV *-phore*] (1816) **1 :** an apparatus for visual signaling (as by the position of one or more

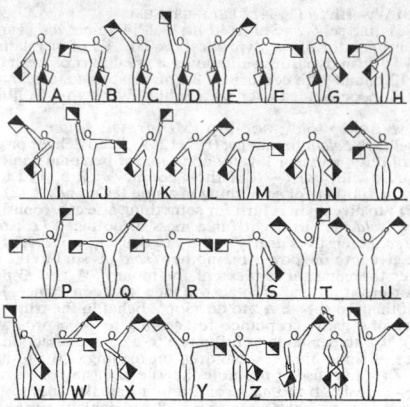

semaphore 2: alphabet; 3 positions following Z: error, end of word, numerals follow; numerals 1, 2, 3, 4, 5, 6, 7, 8, 9, 0 same as A through J

movable arms)   **2** : a system of visual signaling by two flags held one in each hand
²semaphore *vb* **-phored; -phor·ing** *vt* (1893) : to convey (information) by or as if by semaphore ～ *vi* : to send signals by or as if by semaphore
se·ma·si·ol·o·gy \si-ˌmä-sē-ˈä-lə-jē, -ˌmä-zē-\ *n* [ISV, fr. Gk *sēmasia* meaning, fr. *sēmainein* to mean] (1847) : SEMANTICS 1 — **se·ma·si·o·log·i·cal** \-sē-ə-ˈlä-ji-kəl, -zē-\ *adj*
¹sem·bla·ble \ˈsem-blə-bəl\ *adj* [ME, fr. AF fr. *sembler* to be like, seem] (14c)   **1** : SIMILAR   **2** : SUITABLE   **3** : APPARENT, SEEMING — **sem·bla·bly** \-blə-blē\ *adv*
²semblable *n* (15c)   **1** *archaic* : something similar : LIKE   **2** : one that is like oneself : one's fellow
sem·blance \ˈsem-blən(t)s\ *n* [ME, fr. AF, fr. *sembler* to be like, seem — more at RESEMBLE] (14c)   **1 a** : outward and often specious appearance or show : FORM ⟨wrapped in a ～ of composure —Harry Hervey⟩   **b** : MODICUM ⟨has been struggling to get some ～ of justice for his people —Bayard Rustin⟩   **2** : ASPECT, COUNTENANCE   **3 a** : a phantasmal form : APPARITION   **b** : IMAGE, LIKENESS   **4** : actual or apparent resemblance ⟨her story bears some ～ to the truth⟩
seme \ˈsēm\ *n* [Gk *sēma* sign] (ca. 1866)   **1** : a linguistic sign   **2** : any of the basic components of the meaning of a morpheme
Sem·e·le \ˈse-mə-ˌlē\ *n* [L, fr. Gk *Semelē*] (1527) : a daughter of Cadmus consumed by flames when visited by Zeus in his divine splendor
sem·el·pa·rous \ˌse-ˈmel-pə-rəs\ *adj* [L *semel* once (akin to L *simul* at the same time) + E *-parous* — more at SAME] (1954) : reproducing or breeding only once in a lifetime ⟨～ salmon⟩
sem·eme \ˈse-ˌmēm\ *n* [ISV, fr. Gk *sēma* + ISV *-eme*] (1913)   **1** : the meaning of a morpheme   **2 a** : SEME 2   **b** : a class of related semes — **se·me·mic** \sə-ˈmē-mik\ *adj*
se·men \ˈsē-mən\ *n* [ME, fr. L, seed, semen; akin to OHG *sāmo* seed, L *serere* to sow — more at SOW] (14c) : a viscid whitish fluid of the male reproductive tract consisting of spermatozoa suspended in secretions of accessory glands (as of the prostate and Cowper's glands)
se·mes·ter \sə-ˈmes-tər\ *n* [G, fr. L *semestris* half-yearly, fr. *sex* six + *mensis* month — more at SIX, MOON] (1827)   **1** : either of the two usu. 18-week periods of instruction into which an academic year is often divided   **2** : a period of six months — **se·mes·tral** \-trəl\ *or* **se·mes·tri·al** \-trē-əl\ *adj*
semester hour *n* (1922) : a unit of academic credit representing an hour of class (as lecture class) or three hours of laboratory work each week for an academic semester
¹semi \ˈse-ˌmī *also* -ˌmē\ *n, pl* **sem·is** [short for *semidetached*] (1912) *chiefly Brit* : a semidetached house
²semi \ˈse-ˌmī *also* -mē\ *n, pl* **sem·is** (1942) : SEMITRAILER
³semi *same as* ²\ *n, pl* **sem·is** (1942) : SEMIFINAL — often used in pl.
semi- \ˌse-ˌmē, -ˌmī, -mi\ *prefix* [ME, fr. L; akin to OHG *sāmi-* half, Gk *hēmi-*]   **1 a** : precisely half of: (1) : forming a bisection of ⟨*semi*diameter⟩   (2) : being a usu. vertically bisected form of (a specified architectural feature) ⟨*semi*dome⟩   **b** : half in quantity or value : half of or occurring halfway through a specified period of time ⟨*semi*annual⟩ ⟨*semi*monthly⟩ — compare BI-   **2** : to some extent : partly : incompletely ⟨*semi*civilized⟩ ⟨*semi*independent⟩ ⟨*semi*dry⟩ — compare DEMI-, HEMI-   **3 a** : partial : incomplete ⟨*semi*consciousness⟩ ⟨*semi*darkness⟩   **b** : having some of the characteristics of ⟨*semi*porcelain⟩ ⟨*semi*monastic⟩   **c** : QUASI- ⟨*semi*governmental⟩ ⟨*semi*monastic⟩
semi·ab·stract \-ab-ˈstrakt, -ˈab-ˌ\ *adj* (1871) : having subject matter that is easily recognizable although the form is stylized ⟨～ art⟩ — **semi·ab·strac·tion** \-ab-ˈstrak-shən\ *n*
semi·an·nu·al \-ˈan-yə-wəl\ *adj* (1791) : occurring every six months or twice a year — **semi·an·nu·al·ly** *adv*
semi·an·tique \-an-ˈtēk\ *adj* (ca. 1930) : being approximately 50 to 100 years old ⟨a ～ carpet⟩ — **semi–antique** *n*
semi·aquat·ic \-ə-ˈkwä-tik, -ˈkwa-\ *adj* (1833) : growing equally well in or adjacent to water; *also* : frequenting but not living wholly in water
semi·ar·bo·re·al \-är-ˈbȯr-ē-əl\ *adj* (1938) : often inhabiting and frequenting trees but not completely arboreal ⟨～ snakes⟩
semi·ar·id \-ˈa-rəd\ *adj* (1880) : characterized by light rainfall; *esp* : having from about 10 to 20 inches (25 to 51 centimeters) of annual precipitation — **semi·arid·i·ty** \-ə-ˈri-də-tē, -a-ˈri-\ *n*
semi·au·to·bio·graph·i·cal \-ˌȯ-tə-ˌbī-ə-ˈgra-fi-kəl\ *adj* (1939) : partly autobiographical ⟨a ～ comedy⟩
semi·au·to·mat·ic \-ˌȯ-tə-ˈma-tik\ *adj* (1853) : not fully automatic: as   **a** : operated partly automatically and partly by hand   **b** *of a firearm* : able to fire repeatedly but requiring release and another pressure of

the trigger for each successive shot — **semiautomatic** *n* — **semi·au·to·mat·i·cal·ly** \-ti-k(ə-)lē\ *adv*
semi·au·ton·o·mous \-ȯ-ˈtä-nə-məs\ *adj* (1893) : largely self-governing within a larger political or organizational entity
semi·breve \ˈse-mē-ˌbrēv, ˈse-ˌmī-, -mi-, -ˌbrev\ *n* (15c) : WHOLE NOTE
semi·cen·ten·ni·al \-ˌsen-ˈte-nē-əl\ *n* (1859) : a 50th anniversary or its celebration — **semicentennial** *adj*
semi·cir·cle \ˈse-mē-ˌsər-kəl, ˈse-ˌmī-, -mi-\ *n* [L *semicirculus*, fr. *semi-* + *circulus* circle] (1526)   **1** : a half of a circle   **2** : an object or arrangement of objects in the form of a half circle — **semi·cir·cu·lar** \ˌse-mē-ˈsər-kyə-lər\ *adj*
semicircular canal *n* (1748) : any of the loop-shaped tubular parts of the labyrinth of the ear that together constitute a sensory organ associated with the maintenance of bodily equilibrium — see EAR illustration
semi·civ·i·lized \ˌse-mē-ˈsi-və-ˌlīzd, ˌse-ˌmī-, -mi-\ *adj* (1806) : partly civilized
semi·clas·sic \-ˈkla-sik\ *n* (1843) : a semiclassical work
semi·clas·si·cal \-si-kəl\ *adj* (1847) : of, relating to, or being a musical composition that is intermediate in style between classical and popular music
semi·co·lon \ˈse-mē-ˌkō-lən, ˈse-ˌmī-, -mi-\ *n* (1644) : a punctuation mark ; used chiefly in a coordinating function between major sentence elements (as independent clauses of a compound sentence)
semi·co·lo·nial \ˌse-mē-kə-ˈlō-nyəl, ˌse-ˌmī-, -mi-, -nē-əl\ *adj* (1932)   **1** : nominally independent but actually under foreign domination   **2** : dependent on foreign nations as suppliers of manufactured goods and as purchasers of raw materials — **semi·co·lo·nial·ism** \-nyə-ˌli-zəm, -nē-ə-\ *n*
semi·col·o·ny \-ˈkä-lə-nē\ *n* (1945) : a semicolonial state
semi·com·mer·cial \-kə-ˈmər-shəl\ *adj* (1926) : of, relating to, adapted to, or characterized by limited marketing of an experimental product
semi·con·duct·ing \ˌse-mē-kən-ˈdək-tiŋ, ˌse-ˌmī-, -mi-\ *adj* (1782) : of, relating to, or having the characteristics of a semiconductor
semi·con·duc·tor \-ˈdək-tər\ *n* (1838) : any of a class of solids (as germanium or silicon) whose electrical conductivity is between that of a conductor and that of an insulator in being nearly as great as that of a metal at high temperatures and nearly absent at low temperatures
semi·con·scious \-ˈkän(t)-shəs\ *adj* (1839) : incompletely conscious : imperfectly aware or responsive — **semi·con·scious·ness** *n*
semi·con·ser·va·tive \-kən-ˈsər-və-tiv\ *adj* (1957) : relating to or being genetic replication in which a double-stranded molecule of nucleic acid separates into two single strands each of which serves as a template for the formation of a complementary strand that together with the template forms a complete molecule — **semi·con·ser·va·tive·ly** *adv*
semi·crys·tal·line \-ˈkris-tə-lən\ *adj* (1816) : incompletely or imperfectly crystalline
semi·cy·lin·dri·cal \-sə-ˈlin-dri-kəl\ *adj* (ca. 1731) : having the shape of a longitudinal half of a cylinder
semi·dark·ness \-ˈdärk-nəs\ *n* (1849) : partial darkness
semi·de·ify \-ˈdē-ə-ˌfī, -ˈdā-\ *vt* (1953) : to regard as somewhat godlike
semi·des·ert \-ˈde-zərt\ *n* (1845) : an arid area that has some of the characteristics of a desert but has greater annual precipitation
semi·de·tached \-di-ˈtacht\ *adj* (1856) : forming one of a pair of residences joined into one building by a common sidewall
semi·di·am·e·ter \-ˌdī-ˈa-mə-tər\ *n* (14c) : RADIUS; *specif* : the apparent radius of a generally spherical celestial body
semi·di·ur·nal \-ˌdī-ˈər-nᵊl\ *adj* (1594)   **1** : relating to or accomplished in half a day   **2** : occurring twice a day   **3** : occurring approximately every half day ⟨the ～ tides⟩
semi·di·vine \-də-ˈvīn\ *adj* (1600) : more than mortal but not fully divine
semi·doc·u·men·ta·ry \-ˌdä-kyə-ˈmen-tə-rē, -ˈmen-trē\ *n* (1939) : a motion picture that uses many details taken from actual events or situations in presenting a fictional story — **semidocumentary** *adj*
semi·dome \ˈse-mē-ˌdōm, ˈse-ˌmī-, -mi-\ *n* (1788) : a roof or ceiling covering a semicircular or nearly semicircular room or recess — **semi·domed** \-ˌdōmd\ *adj*
semi·do·mes·ti·ca·tion \ˌse-mē-də-ˌmes-ti-ˈkā-shən, ˌse-ˌmī-, -mi-\ *n* (ca. 1835) : a captive state of a wild animal in which its living conditions and often its breeding are controlled by humans — **semi·do·mes·ti·cat·ed** \-də-ˈmes-ti-ˌkā-təd\ *adj*
semi·dom·i·nant \-ˈdä-mə-nənt, -ˈdäm-nənt\ *adj* (1942) : producing an intermediate phenotype in the heterozygous condition ⟨a ～ gene⟩
semi·dry \-ˈdrī\ *adj* (1871) : moderately dry ⟨a ～ wine⟩
semi·dry·ing \-ˈdrī-iŋ\ *adj* (1905) : that dries imperfectly or slowly — used of some oils (as cottonseed oil)
semi·dwarf \-ˈdwȯrf\ *adj* (1959) : of or being a plant of a variety that is undersized but larger than a dwarf ⟨～ wheats⟩ — **semidwarf** *n*
semi·em·pir·i·cal \-im-ˈpir-ə-kəl, -em-\ *adj* (1935) : partly empirical; *esp* : involving assumptions, approximations, or generalizations designed to simplify calculation or to yield a result in accord with observation
semi·erect \-ə-ˈrekt\ *adj* (1822)   **1** : incompletely upright in bodily posture ⟨～ primates⟩   **2** : erect for half the length ⟨～ stems⟩
semi·ev·er·green \-ˈe-vər-ˌgrēn\ *adj* (1900)   **1** : having functional and persistent foliage during part of the winter or dry season   **2** : tending to be evergreen in a mild climate but deciduous in a rigorous climate
semi·feu·dal \-ˈfyü-dᵊl\ *adj* (1898) : having some characteristics of feudalism
¹semi·fi·nal \-ˈfī-nᵊl\ *adj* (1884)   **1** : being next to the last in an elimination tournament   **2** : of or participating in a semifinal
²semi·fi·nal \ˈse-mē-ˌfī-nᵊl, ˈse-ˌmī-, -mi-\ *n* (1895)   **1** : a semifinal match   **2** : a semifinal round — **semi·fi·nal·ist** \ˌse-mē-ˈfī-nᵊl-ist, ˌse-ˌmī-, -mi-\ *n*
semi·fin·ished \ˌse-mē-ˈfi-nisht, ˌse-ˌmī-, -mi-\ *adj* (1902) : partially finished or processed; *esp, of steel* : rolled from ingots into shapes (as bars, billets, or plates) suitable for further processing
semi·fit·ted \-ˈfi-təd\ *adj* (ca. 1950) : conforming somewhat to the lines of the body
semi·flex·i·ble \-ˈflek-sə-bəl\ *adj* (1925)   **1** : somewhat flexible   **2** *of a book cover* : having a thin board stiffener under the covering material
semi·flu·id \-ˈflü-əd\ *adj* (ca. 1735) : having the qualities of both a fluid and a solid : VISCOUS ⟨fluid and ～ lubricants⟩ — **semifluid** *n*

semi·for·mal \-ˈfȯr-məl\ *adj* (1906) **:** being or suitable for an occasion of moderate formality ⟨a ~ dinner⟩ ⟨~ gowns⟩
semi·gloss \ˈse-mē-ˌgläs, ˈse-ˌmī-, -mi-, -ˌglȯs\ *adj* (1937) **:** having a low luster; *specif* **:** producing a finish midway between glossy and flat
semi·gov·ern·men·tal \ˌse-mē-ˌgəv-ər(n)-ˈmen-tᵊl, ˌse-ˌmī-, -mi-, -ˌgə-vᵊm-ˈen-\ *adj* (1919) **:** having some governmental functions and powers
semi·group \ˈse-mē-ˌgrüp, ˈse-ˌmī-, -mi-\ *n* (1904) **:** a mathematical set that is closed under an associative binary operation
semi–in·de·pen·dent \-ˌin-də-ˈpen-dənt\ *adj* (1853) **:** partially independent; *specif* **:** SEMIAUTONOMOUS
semi·leg·end·ary \-ˈle-jən-ˌder-ē\ *adj* (1866) **:** having historical foundation but elaborated in legend
semi·le·thal \-ˈlē-thəl\ *n* (1919) **:** a mutation that in the homozygous condition produces more than 50 percent mortality but not complete mortality — **semilethal** *adj*
semi·liq·uid \-ˈli-kwəd\ *adj* (1684) **:** having the qualities of both a liquid and a solid **:** SEMIFLUID ⟨~ manure⟩ — **semiliquid** *n*
semi·lit·er·ate \-ˈli-tə-rət *also* -ˈli-trət\ *adj* (1927) **1 a :** able to read and write on an elementary level **b :** able to read but unable to write **2 :** having limited knowledge or understanding — **semiliterate** *n*
semi·log \-ˈlȯg, -ˈläg\ *adj* (1921) **:** SEMILOGARITHMIC
semi·log·a·rith·mic \-ˌlȯ-gə-ˈrith-mik, -ˌlä-\ *adj* (1919) **:** having one scale logarithmic and the other arithmetic — used of graph paper or of a graph on such paper
semi·lu·nar \-ˈlü-nər\ *adj* [NL *semilunaris,* fr. L *semi-* + *lunaris* lunar] (1597) **:** LUNATE
semilunar valve *n* (ca. 1719) **:** any of the crescent-shaped cusps that occur as a set of three between the heart and the aorta and another of three between the heart and the pulmonary artery, are forced apart by pressure in the ventricles during systole and pushed together by pressure in the arteries during diastole, and prevent regurgitation of blood into the ventricles; *also* **:** either set of three cusps
semi·lus·trous \-ˈləs-trəs\ *adj* (1894) **:** slightly lustrous
semi·ma·jor axis \-ˈmā-jər-\ *n* (1818) **:** one half of the major axis of an ellipse (as that formed by the orbit of a planet)
semi·matte *also* **semi·mat** *or* **semi·matt** \-ˈmat\ *adj* [*semi-* + [2]*matte*] (1937) **:** having a slight luster
semi·met·al \-ˈme-tᵊl\ *n* (1661) **:** an element (as arsenic) possessing metallic properties in an inferior degree and not malleable — **semi·me·tal·lic** \-mə-ˈta-lik\ *adj*
semi·mi·cro \-ˈmī-(ˌ)krō\ *adj* (1935) **:** of, relating to, or dealing with quantities intermediate between those treated as micro and macro ⟨~ analysis for chlorine⟩ ⟨a ~ balance⟩
semi·mi·nor axis \-ˈmī-nər-\ *n* (1909) **:** one half of the minor axis of an ellipse (as that formed by the orbit of a planet)
semi·moist \-ˈmȯist\ *adj* (1903) **:** slightly moist
semi·mo·nas·tic \-mə-ˈnas-tik\ *adj* (1911) **:** having some features characteristic of a monastic order
[1]**semimonthly** *adv* (1829) **:** twice a month
[2]**semimonthly** *adj* (1829) **:** occurring twice a month
[3]**semi·month·ly** \-ˈmən(t)th-lē\ *n* (1843) **:** a semimonthly publication
semi·mys·ti·cal \-ˈmis-ti-kəl\ *adj* (1878) **:** having some of the qualities of mysticism
sem·i·nal \ˈse-mə-nᵊl\ *adj* [ME, fr. L *seminalis,* fr. *semin-, semen* seed — more at SEMEN] (14c) **1 :** of, relating to, or consisting of seed or semen **2 :** containing or contributing the seeds of later development **:** CREATIVE, ORIGINAL ⟨a ~ book⟩ — **sem·i·nal·ly** \-nᵊl-ē\ *adv*
seminal duct *n* (1882) **:** a tube or passage serving esp. or exclusively as an efferent duct of the testis and in the human male being made up of the epididymis, the vas deferens, and the ejaculatory duct
seminal fluid *n* (ca. 1929) **1 :** SEMEN **2 :** the part of the semen that is produced by various accessory glands (as the prostate gland and seminal vesicles) **:** semen excepting the spermatozoa
seminal vesicle *n* (ca. 1890) **:** either of a pair of glandular pouches that lie one on either side of the male reproductive tract and in the human male secrete a sugar- and protein-containing fluid into the ejaculatory duct
sem·i·nar \ˈse-mə-ˌnär\ *n* [G, fr. L *seminarium* nursery] (1863) **1 :** a group of advanced students studying under a professor with each doing original research and all exchanging results through reports and discussions **2 a (1) :** a course of study pursued by a seminar **(2) :** an advanced or graduate course often featuring informality and discussion **b :** a scheduled meeting of a seminar or a room for such meetings **3 :** a meeting for giving and discussing information
sem·i·nar·i·an \ˌse-mə-ˈner-ē-ən\ *n* (1794) **:** a student in a seminary esp. of the Roman Catholic Church
sem·i·na·rist \ˈse-mə-nə-rist\ *n* (1835) **:** SEMINARIAN
sem·i·nary \ˈse-mə-ˌner-ē\ *n, pl* **-nar·ies** [ME, seedbed, nursery, fr. L *seminarium,* fr. *semin-, semen* seed] (1542) **1 :** an environment in which something originates and from which it is propagated ⟨a ~ of vice and crime⟩ **2 a :** an institution of secondary or higher education **b :** an institution for the training of candidates for the priesthood, ministry, or rabbinate
semi·nat·u·ral \ˌse-mē-ˈna-chə-rəl, ˌse-ˌmī-, -mi-, -ˈnach-rəl\ *adj* (1948) **:** modified by human influence but retaining many natural features ⟨a ~ park⟩
sem·i·nif·er·ous \ˌse-mə-ˈni-f(ə-)rəs\ *adj* [L *semin-, semen* seed + E *-iferous*] (1692) **:** producing or bearing seed or semen
seminiferous tubule *n* (1860) **:** any of the coiled threadlike tubules that make up the bulk of the testis and are lined with a layer of epithelial cells from which the spermatozoa are produced
Sem·i·nole \ˈse-mə-ˌnōl\ *n, pl* **Seminoles** *or* **Seminole** [Creek *simanó·li* untamed, wild, alter. of *simaló·ni,* fr. AmerSp *cimarrón* wild] (1771) **:** a member of any of the groups of American Indians that emigrated to Florida from Georgia and Alabama in the 18th and 19th centuries and that are now located in southern Florida and Oklahoma
semi·no·mad \ˌse-mē-ˈnō-ˌmad, ˌse-ˌmī-, -mi-\ *n* (ca. 1934) **:** a member of a people living usu. in portable or temporary dwellings and practicing seasonal migration but having a base camp at which some crops are cultivated — **semi·no·mad·ic** \-nō-ˈma-dik\ *adj*
semi·nude \-ˈnüd, -ˈnyüd\ *adj* (1829) **:** partially nude — **semi·nu·di·ty** \-ˈnü-də-tē, -ˈnyü-\ *n*
semi·of·fi·cial \-ə-ˈfi-shəl\ *adj* (1806) **:** having some official authority or standing — **semi·of·fi·cial·ly** \-ˈfi-sh(ə-)lē\ *adv*
se·mi·ol·o·gy \ˌsē-mē-ˈä-lə-jē, ˌse-mē-, ˌsē-ˌmī-\ *n* [Gk *sēmeion* sign] (ca. 1890) **:** the study of signs; *esp* **:** SEMIOTICS — **se·mi·o·log·i·cal** \(ˌ)sē-ˌmī-ə-ˈlä-ji-kəl, ˌse-mē-ə-\ *adj* — **se·mi·o·log·i·cal·ly** \-ə-ˈlä-ji-k(ə-)lē\ *adv* — **se·mi·ol·o·gist** \-ˈä-lə-jist\ *n*
semi·opaque \ˌse-mē-ō-ˈpāk, ˌse-ˌmī-, -mi-\ *adj* (1691) **:** nearly opaque
se·mi·o·sis \ˌsē-mē-ˈō-səs, ˌse-mē-, ˌsē-ˌmī-\ *n* [NL, fr. Gk *sēmeiōsis* observation of signs, fr. *sēmeioun* to observe signs, fr. *sēmeion*] (ca. 1907) **:** a process in which something functions as a sign to an organism
se·mi·ot·ics \-ˈä-tiks\ *or* **se·mi·ot·ic** \-tik\ *n, pl* **semiotics** [Gk *sēmeiōtikos* observant of signs, fr. *sēmeiousthai* to interpret signs, fr. *sēmeion* sign, fr. *sēma* sign] (1880) **:** a general philosophical theory of signs and symbols that deals esp. with their function in both artificially constructed and natural languages and comprises syntactics, semantics, and pragmatics — **semiotic** *adj* — **se·mi·o·ti·cian** \-ə-ˈti-shən\ *n* — **se·mi·ot·i·cist** \-ˈä-tə-sist\ *n*
semi·pal·mat·ed \ˌse-mē-ˈpal-ˌmā-təd, ˌse-ˌmī-, -mi-, -ˈpäl-, -ˈpä-\ *adj* (1785) **:** having the toes joined only part way down with a web ⟨a plover with ~ feet⟩
semi·par·a·sit·ic \-ˌpa-rə-ˈsi-tik\ *adj* (ca. 1909) **:** of, relating to, or being a parasitic plant that contains some chlorophyll and is capable of photosynthesis — **semi·par·a·site** \-ˈpa-rə-ˌsīt\ *n*
semi·per·ma·nent \-ˈpər-mə-nənt, -ˈpərm-nənt\ *adj* (1881) **:** lasting or intended to last for a long time but not permanent
semi·per·me·able \-ˈpər-mē-ə-bəl\ *adj* (1888) **:** partially but not freely or wholly permeable; *specif* **:** permeable to some usu. small molecules but not to other usu. larger particles ⟨a ~ membrane⟩ — **semi·per·me·abil·i·ty** \-ˌpər-mē-ə-ˈbi-lə-tē\ *n*
semi·po·lit·i·cal \-pə-ˈli-ti-kəl\ *adj* (1837) **:** of, relating to, or involving some political features or activity
semi·pop·u·lar \-ˈpä-pyə-lər\ *adj* (1860) **:** somewhat popular
semi·por·ce·lain \-ˈpȯr-s(ə-)lən\ *n* (1880) **:** any of several ceramic wares resembling or imitative of porcelain; *esp* **:** a relatively hard-glazed white earthenware widely used for tableware
semi·por·no·graph·ic \-ˌpȯr-nə-ˈgra-fik\ *adj* (1964) **:** somewhat pornographic — **semi·por·nog·ra·phy** \-pȯr-ˈnä-grə-fē\ *n*
semi·post·al \-ˈpōs-tᵊl\ *n* (1927) **:** a postage stamp sold at a premium over its postal value esp. for a humanitarian purpose
semi·pre·cious \-ˈpre-shəs\ *adj* (1858) *of a gemstone* **:** of less commercial value than a precious stone
semi·pri·vate \-ˈprī-vət\ *adj* (1876) **:** of, receiving, or associated with hospital service giving a patient more privileges than a ward patient but fewer than a private patient
semi·pro \ˈse-mē-ˌprō, ˈse-ˌmī-, -mi-\ *adj or n* (1908) **:** SEMIPROFESSIONAL
[1]**semi·pro·fes·sion·al** \ˌse-mē-prə-ˈfesh-nəl, ˌse-ˌmī-, -mi-, -ˈfe-shə-nᵊl\ *n* (1861) **:** one who engages in an activity (as a sport) semiprofessionally
[2]**semiprofessional** *adj* (1900) **1 :** engaging in an activity for pay or gain but not as a full-time occupation **2 :** engaged in by semiprofessional players ⟨~ baseball⟩ — **semi·pro·fes·sion·al·ly** *adv*
semi·pub·lic \-ˈpə-blik\ *adj* (1804) **1 :** open to some persons outside the regular constituency **2 :** having some features of a public institution; *specif* **:** maintained as a public service by a private nonprofit organization
semi·quan·ti·ta·tive \-ˈkwän-tə-ˌtā-tiv\ *adj* (1927) **:** constituting or involving less than quantitative precision — **semi·quan·ti·ta·tive·ly** *adv*
semi·qua·ver \ˈse-mē-ˌkwā-vər, ˈse-ˌmī-, -mi-\ *n* (1576) **:** SIXTEENTH NOTE
semi·re·li·gious \ˌse-mē-ri-ˈli-jəs, ˌse-ˌmī-, -mi-\ *adj* (1832) **:** somewhat religious
semi·re·tired \-ri-ˈtī(-ə)rd\ *adj* (1937) **:** working only part-time esp. because of age or ill health
semi·re·tire·ment \-ˈtī(-ə)r-mənt\ *n* (1923) **:** the state or condition of being semiretired
semi·rig·id \-ˈri-jəd\ *adj* (1906) **1 :** rigid to some degree or in some parts **2** *of an airship* **:** having a flexible cylindrical gas container with an attached stiffening keel that carries the load
semi·rur·al \-ˈrůr-əl\ *adj* (1835) **:** somewhat rural
semi·sa·cred \-ˈsā-krəd\ *adj* (1849) **:** SEMIRELIGIOUS
semi·se·cret \-ˈsē-krət\ *adj* (1852) **:** not publicly announced but widely known nevertheless
semi·sed·en·tary \-ˈse-dᵊn-ˌter-ē\ *adj* (ca. 1930) **:** sedentary during part of the year and nomadic otherwise ⟨~ tribes⟩
semi·shrub·by \ˈse-mē-ˌshrə-bē, ˈse-ˌmī-, -mi-, *esp Southern* -ˌsrə-\ *adj* (1930) **:** resembling or being a subshrub
semi·skilled \ˌse-mē-ˈskild, ˌse-ˌmī-, -mi-\ *adj* (1916) **:** having or requiring less training than skilled labor and more than unskilled labor
semi·soft \-ˈsȯft\ *adj* (1859) **:** moderately soft; *specif* **:** firm but easily cut ⟨~ cheese⟩
semi·sol·id \-ˈsä-ləd\ *adj* (1834) **:** having the qualities of both a solid and a liquid **:** highly viscous — **semisolid** *n*
semi·sub·mers·ible \-səb-ˈmər-sə-bəl\ *adj* (1962) **:** being a floating deepwater drilling platform that is towed to a desired location and then partially flooded for stabilization and usu. anchored — **semisubmersible** *n*
semi·sweet \-ˈswēt\ *adj* (1943) **:** slightly sweetened ⟨~ chocolate⟩
semi·syn·thet·ic \-sin-ˈthe-tik\ *adj* (1937) **1 :** produced by chemical alteration of a natural starting material ⟨~ penicillins⟩ **2 :** containing both chemically identified and complex natural ingredients ⟨a ~ diet⟩
Sem·ite \ˈse-ˌmīt, *esp Brit* ˈsē-ˌmīt\ *n* [F *sémite,* fr. *Sem* Shem, fr. LL, fr. Gk *Sēm,* fr. Heb *Shēm*] (1848) **1 a :** a member of any of a number of peoples of ancient southwestern Asia including the Akkadians, Phoenicians, Hebrews, and Arabs **b :** a descendant of these peoples **2 :** a member of a modern people speaking a Semitic language
semi·ter·res·tri·al \ˌse-mē-tə-ˈres-trē-əl, ˌse-ˌmī-, -mi-, -ˈres-chəl, -ˈresh-\ *adj* (1919) **1 :** growing on boggy ground **2 :** frequenting but not living wholly on land

\ə\ **abut** \ᵊ\ **kitten**, F **table** \ər\ **further** \a\ **ash** \ā\ **ace** \ä\ **mop, mar** \au̇\ **out** \ch\ **chin** \e\ **bet** \ē\ **easy** \g\ **go** \i\ **hit** \ī\ **ice** \j\ **job** \ŋ\ **sing** \ō\ **go** \ȯ\ **law** \ȯi\ **boy** \th\ **thin** \th\ **the** \ü\ **loot** \u̇\ **foot** \y\ **yet** \zh\ **vision, beige** \k, ⁿ, œ, ue, ʸ\ *see* Guide to Pronunciation

[1]**Se·mit·ic** \sə-ˈmi-tik *also* -ˈme-\ *adj* [G *semitisch,* fr. *Semit, Semite* Semite, prob. fr. NL *Semita,* fr. LL *Sem* Shem] (1813) **1 :** of, relating to, or constituting a subfamily of the Afro-Asiatic language family that includes Hebrew, Aramaic, Arabic, and Amharic **2 :** of, relating to, or characteristic of the Semites **3 :** JEWISH
[2]**Semitic** *n* (1831) **:** any or all of the Semitic languages
Se·mit·i·cist \sə-ˈmi-tə-sist\ *n* (1956) **:** SEMITIST
Se·mit·ics \-ˈmi-tiks\ *n pl but sing in constr* (1888) **:** the study of the language, literature, and history of Semitic peoples; *specif* **:** Semitic philology
Sem·i·tism \ˈse-mə-ˌti-zəm\ *n* (1851) **1 a :** Semitic character or qualities **b :** a characteristic feature of a Semitic language occurring in another language **2 :** policy or predisposition favorable to Jews
Sem·i·tist \-tist\ *n* (1881) **1 :** a scholar of the Semitic languages, cultures, or histories **2** *often not cap* **:** a person favoring or disposed to favor the Jews
semi·ton·al \ˌse-mē-ˈtō-nᵊl, ˌse-ˌmī-, -mi-\ *adj* (1863) **:** CHROMATIC 3a, SEMITONIC — **semi·ton·al·ly** *adv*
semi·tone \ˈse-mē-ˌtōn, ˈse-ˌmī-, -mi-\ *n* (15c) **:** the tone at a half step; *also* **:** HALF STEP — **semi·ton·ic** \ˌse-mē-ˈtä-nik, ˌse-ˌmī-, -mi-\ *adj* — **semi·ton·i·cal·ly** \-ni-k(ə-)lē\ *adv*
semi·trail·er \ˈse-ˌmī-ˌtrā-lər, ˈse-mē-, -mi-\ *n* (1919) **1 :** a freight trailer that when attached is supported at its forward end by the fifth wheel device of the truck tractor **2 :** a trucking rig made up of a tractor and a semitrailer
semi·trans·lu·cent \ˌse-mē-ˌtran(t)s-ˈlü-sᵊnt, ˌse-ˌmī-, -mi-, -ˌtranz-\ *adj* (1832) **:** somewhat translucent
semi·trans·par·ent \-ˌtran(t)s-ˈper-ənt\ *adj* (1731) **:** imperfectly transparent
semi·trop·i·cal \-ˈträ-pi-kəl\ *also* **semi·trop·ic** \-pik\ *adj* (1845) **:** SUBTROPICAL
semi·trop·ics \-piks\ *n pl* (1908) **:** SUBTROPICS
semi·truck \ˈse-ˌmī-ˌtrək\ *n* (1969) **:** SEMITRAILER 2
semi·vow·el \ˈse-mē-ˌvau̇(-ə)l, ˈse-ˌmī-, -mi-\ *n* (1530) **1 :** a speech sound (as \y\, \w\, or \r\) that has the articulation of a vowel but that is shorter in duration and is treated as a consonant in syllabication **2 :** a letter representing a semivowel
[1]**semi·week·ly** \ˌse-mē-ˈwē-klē, ˌse-ˌmī-, -mi-\ *adj* (1791) **:** occurring twice a week — **semiweekly** *adv*
[2]**semiweekly** *n* (1833) **:** a semiweekly publication
semi·works \ˈse-mē-ˌwərks, ˈse-ˌmī-, -mi-\ *n pl, often attrib* (1926) **:** a manufacturing plant operating on a limited commercial scale to provide final tests of a new product or process
semi·year·ly \ˌse-mē-ˈyir-lē, ˌse-ˌmī-, -mi-\ *adj* (1845) **:** occurring twice a year
sem·o·li·na \ˌse-mə-ˈlē-nə\ *n* [It *semolino,* dim. of *semola* bran, fr. L *simila* wheat flour] (1797) **:** the purified middlings of hard wheat (as durum) used esp. for pasta (as macaroni or spaghetti)
sem·per·vi·vum \ˌsem-pər-ˈvī-vəm\ *n* [NL, fr. L, neuter of *sempervivus* ever-living, fr. *semper* ever + *vivus* living — more at QUICK] (1591) **:** any of a genus (*Sempervivum*) of Old World fleshy perennial herbs of the orpine family often grown as ornamentals
sem·pi·ter·nal \ˌsem-pi-ˈtər-nᵊl\ *adj* [ME, fr. LL *sempiternalis,* fr. L *sempiternus,* fr. *semper* ever, always, fr. *sem-* one, same (akin to ON *samr* same) + *per* through — more at SAME, FOR] (15c) **:** of never-ending duration **:** ETERNAL — **sem·pi·ter·nal·ly** *adv*
sem·pi·ter·ni·ty \-ˈtər-nə-tē\ *n* (1599) **:** ETERNITY
sem·ple \ˈsem-pəl\ *adj* [alter. of *simple*] (ca. 1520) *Scot* **:** of humble birth
sem·pli·ce \ˈsem-pli-ˌchā\ *adj or adv* [It, fr. L *simplic-, simplex* — more at SIMPLE] (ca. 1740) **:** SIMPLE — used as a direction in music
sem·pre \ˈsem-(ˌ)prā\ *adv* [It, fr. L *semper*] (ca. 1801) **:** ALWAYS — used in music directions ⟨~ legato⟩
[1]**sen** \ˈsen\ *n, pl* **sen** [Jp] (1875) — see *yen* at MONEY table
[2]**sen** *n, pl* **sen** [Malay, prob. fr. E *cent*] (1952) — see *dollar, ringgit, rupiah* at MONEY table
[3]**sen** *n, pl* **sen** [Khmer *sein,* prob. fr. F *cent.,* abbr. of *centime* centime] (1964) — see *riel* at MONEY table
[4]**sen** *abbr* **1** senate; senator **2** senior
se·nar·i·us \si-ˈner-ē-əs\ *n, pl* **se·nar·ii** \-ē-ˌī, -ē-ˌē\ [L, fr. *senarius* consisting of six each, fr. *seni* six each, fr. *sex* six — more at SIX] (1540) **:** a verse consisting of six feet esp. in Latin prosody
se·na·ry \ˈse-nə-rē, ˈsē-\ *adj* [L *senarius* consisting of six] (1661) **:** of, based on, or characterized by six **:** compounded of six things or six parts ⟨a ~ scale⟩ ⟨~ division⟩
sen·ate \ˈse-nət\ *n* [ME *senat,* fr. AF, fr. L *senatus,* fr. *sen-, senex* old, old man — more at SENIOR] (13c) **1 :** an assembly or council usu. possessing high deliberative and legislative functions: as **a :** the supreme council of the ancient Roman republic and empire **b :** the second chamber in the bicameral legislature of a major political unit (as a nation, state, or province) **2 :** the hall or chamber in which a senate meets **3 :** a governing body of some universities charged with maintaining academic standards and regulations and usu. composed of the principal or representative members of the faculty
sen·a·tor \ˈse-nə-tər\ *n* [ME *senatour,* fr. AF *senatur,* fr. L *senator,* fr. *senatus*] (13c) **:** a member of a senate — **sen·a·tor·ship** \-ˌship\ *n*
sen·a·to·ri·al \ˌse-nə-ˈtȯr-ē-əl\ *adj* (1740) **:** of, relating to, or befitting a senator or a senate ⟨~ office⟩ ⟨~ rank⟩
senatorial courtesy *n* (1884) **:** a custom of the U.S. Senate of refusing to confirm a presidential appointment of an official in or from a state when the appointment is opposed by the senators or senior senator of the president's party from that state
senatorial district *n* (1785) **:** a territorial division from which a senator is elected — compare CONGRESSIONAL DISTRICT
sen·a·to·ri·an \ˌse-nə-ˈtȯr-ē-ən\ *adj* (1614) **:** SENATORIAL; *specif* **:** of or relating to the ancient Roman senate
se·na·tus con·sul·tum \sə-ˌnä-təs-kən-ˈsəl-təm, -ˈsu̇l-\ *n, pl* **senatus con·sul·ta** \-tə\ [L, decree of the senate] (1696) **:** a decree of the ancient Roman senate
[1]**send** \ˈsend\ *vb* **sent** \ˈsent\; **send·ing** [ME, fr. OE *sendan;* akin to OHG *sendan* to send, OE *sith* road, journey, OIr *sét* path, way] *vt* (bef. 12c) **1 :** to cause to go: as **a :** to propel or throw in a particular direction **b :** DELIVER ⟨*sent* a blow to the chin⟩ **c :** DRIVE ⟨*sent* the ball between the goalposts⟩ **2 :** to cause to happen ⟨whatever fate may ~⟩ **3 :** to dispatch by a means of communication **4 a :** to direct, order, or request to go **b :** to permit or enable to attend a term or session ⟨~ a daughter to college⟩ **c :** to direct by advice or reference **d :** to cause or order to depart **:** DISMISS **5 a :** to force to go **:** drive away **b :** to cause to assume a specified state ⟨*sent* them into a rage⟩ **6 :** to cause to issue: as **a :** to pour out **:** DISCHARGE ⟨clouds ~*ing* forth rain⟩ **b :** UTTER ⟨~ forth a cry⟩ **c :** EMIT ⟨*sent* out waves of perfume⟩ **d :** to grow out (parts) in the course of development ⟨a plant ~*ing* forth shoots⟩ **7 :** to cause to be carried to a destination; *esp* **:** to consign to death or a place of punishment **8 :** to convey or cause to be conveyed or transmitted by an agent ⟨*sent* out invitations⟩ **9 :** to strike or thrust so as to impel violently ⟨*sent* him sprawling⟩ **10 :** DELIGHT, THRILL ~ *vi* **1 a :** to dispatch someone to convey a message or do an errand — often used with *out* ⟨~ out for pizza⟩ **b :** to dispatch a request or order — often used with *away* **2 :** TRANSMIT — **send·er** *n* — **send for :** to request by message to come **:** SUMMON — **send packing :** to send off or dismiss roughly or in disgrace
[2]**send** *n* (1726) **:** the lift of a wave **:** SCEND
send down *vt* (1848) *Brit* **:** to suspend or expel from a university
send in *vt* (1616) **1 :** to cause to be delivered ⟨*send in* a letter of complaint⟩ **2 :** to give (one's name or card) to a servant when making a call **3 :** to send (a player) into an athletic contest
send–off \ˈsend-ˌȯf\ *n* (1872) **:** a demonstration of goodwill and enthusiasm for the beginning of a new venture (as a trip)
send–up \-ˌəp\ *n* (1958) **:** PARODY, TAKEOFF
send up *vt* (1852) **1 :** to send to jail **2 :** to make fun of **:** PARODY
se·ne \ˈsā-(ˌ)nā\ *n, pl* **sene** [Samoan, fr. E *cent*] (1967) — see *tala* at MONEY table
Sen·e·ca \ˈse-ni-kə\ *n, pl* **Seneca** *or* **Senecas** [D *Sennecaas,* pl., the Iroquois living west of the Mohawks] (ca. 1616) **1 :** a member of an American Indian people of what is now western New York **2 :** the Iroquoian language of the Seneca people
seneca snakeroot *n* (1789) **:** a milkwort (*Polygala senega*) of eastern No. America having racemes of small white flowers — called also *rattlesnake root, senega root;* compare SENEGA

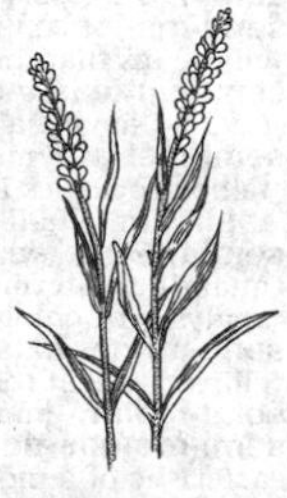

seneca snakeroot

se·ne·cio \si-ˈnē-sh(ē-ˌ)ō\ *n, pl* **-cios** [NL, fr. L, old man, groundsel (fr. its hoary pappus), fr. *sen-, senic-, senex* old man] (1562) **:** any of a large genus (*Senecio*) of widely distributed composite plants that have alternate or basal leaves and flower heads usu. with yellow ray flowers
se·nec·ti·tude \si-ˈnek-tə-ˌtüd, -ˌtyüd\ *n* [ML *senectitudo,* alter. of L *senectus* old age, fr. *sen-, senic-, senex* old, old man — more at SENIOR] (1796) **:** the final stage of the normal life span
sen·e·ga \ˈse-ni-gə\ *n* (1748) **:** the dried root of seneca snakeroot that contains an irritating saponin and is used as an expectorant
senega root *n* [alter. of *Seneca root;* fr. its use by the Seneca as a remedy for snakebite] (ca. 1846) **1 :** SENECA SNAKEROOT **2 :** SENEGA
se·nes·cence \si-ˈne-sᵊn(t)s\ *n* [*senescent,* fr. L *senescent-, senescens,* prp. of *senescere* to grow old, fr. *sen-, senex* old] (1695) **1 :** the state of being old **:** the process of becoming old **2 :** the growth phase in a plant or plant part (as a leaf) from full maturity to death — **se·nes·cent** \-sᵊnt\ *adj*
sen·e·schal \ˈse-nə-shəl\ *n* [ME, fr. AF, of Gmc origin; akin to Goth *sineigs* old and to OHG *scalc* servant — more at SENIOR] (14c) **:** an agent or steward in charge of a lord's estate in feudal times
se·nhor \si-ˈnyȯr\ *n, pl* **senhors** *or* **se·nho·res** \-ˈnyȯr-ēsh, -ēzh, -ēs, -ēz\ [Pg, fr. ML *senior* superior, lord, fr. L, adj., elder] (1795) **:** a Portuguese or Brazilian man — used as a title equivalent to *Mr.*
se·nho·ra \-ˈnyȯr-ə\ *n* [Pg, fem. of *senhor*] (1802) **:** a married Portuguese or Brazilian woman — used as a title equivalent to *Mrs.*
se·nho·ri·ta \ˌsē-nyə-ˈrē-tə\ *n* [Pg, fr. dim. of *senhora*] (1874) **:** an unmarried Portuguese or Brazilian girl or woman — used as a title equivalent to *Miss*
se·nile \ˈsē-ˌnī(-ə)l *also* ˈse-\ *adj* [L *senilis,* fr. *sen-, senex* old, old man] (1661) **1 :** of, relating to, exhibiting, or characteristic of old age ⟨~ weakness⟩; *esp* **:** exhibiting a loss of cognitive abilities (as memory) associated with old age **2 :** approaching the end of a geological cycle of erosion — **se·nile·ly** \-ˌnī(-ə)l-lē\ *adv*
senile dementia *n* (ca. 1851) **:** dementia of old age esp. of the degenerative type associated with Alzheimer's disease
se·nil·i·ty \si-ˈni-lə-tē *also* se-\ *n* (1791) **:** the quality or state of being senile; *specif* **:** the physical and mental infirmity of old age
[1]**se·nior** \ˈsē-nyər\ *n* [ME, fr. L, fr. *senior,* adj.] (14c) **1 :** a person older than another ⟨five years my ~⟩ **2 a :** a person with higher standing or rank **b :** a senior fellow of a college at an English university **c :** a student in the year preceding graduation from a school of secondary or higher level **3** *cap* **:** a member of a program of the Girl Scouts for girls in the 9th through 12th grades in school **4 :** SENIOR CITIZEN
[2]**senior** *adj* [ME, fr. L, older, elder, compar. of *sen-, senex* old; akin to Goth *sineigs* old, Gk *henos*] (14c) **1 :** of prior birth, establishment, or enrollment — often used to distinguish a father with the same given name as his son **2 :** higher ranking **:** SUPERIOR ⟨~ officers⟩ **3 :** of, relating to, or intended for seniors ⟨a ~ center⟩ **4 :** having a claim on corporate assets and income prior to other securities
senior airman *n* (ca. 1977) **:** an enlisted man in the air force who ranks above an airman first class but who has not been made staff sergeant
senior chief petty officer *n* (ca. 1960) **:** an enlisted man in the navy or coast guard ranking above a chief petty officer and below a master chief petty officer
senior citizen *n* (1938) **:** an elderly person; *esp* **:** one who has retired
senior high school *n* (1909) **:** a school usu. including grades 10 to 12
se·nior·i·tis \ˌsē-nyər-ˈī-təs\ *n* (1957) **:** an ebbing of effort by school seniors as evidenced by tardiness, absences, and lower grades
se·nior·i·ty \sēn-ˈyȯr-ə-tē, -ˈyär-\ *n* (15c) **1 :** the quality or state of being senior **:** PRIORITY **2 :** a privileged status attained by length of continuous service (as in a company)
senior master sergeant *n* (ca. 1962) **:** a noncommissioned officer in the air force ranking above a master sergeant and below a chief master sergeant

senior moment *n* (1996) **:** an instance of momentary forgetfulness or confusion that is attributed to the aging process
sen·i·ti \ˈse-nə-ˌtē\ *n, pl* **seniti** [Tongan, modif. of E *cent*] (1967) — see *pa'anga* at MONEY table
sen·na \ˈse-nə\ *n* [NL, fr. Ar *sanā*] (1543) **1 :** any of a genus (*Cassia* syn. *Senna*) of leguminous herbs, shrubs, and trees native to warm regions; *esp* **:** one used medicinally **2 :** the dried leaflets or pods of various sennas (esp. *C. angustifolia* syn. *Senna alexandrina*) used as a purgative
sen·net \ˈse-nət\ *n* [prob. alter. of obs. *signet* signal] (ca. 1590) **:** a signal call on a trumpet or cornet for entrance or exit on the stage
sen·night *also* **se'n·night** \ˈse-ˌnīt\ *n* [ME, fr. OE *seofon nihta* seven nights] (15c) *archaic* **:** the space of seven nights and days **:** WEEK
sen·nit \ˈse-nət\ *n* [origin unknown] (ca. 1769) **1 :** a braided cord or fabric (as of plaited rope yarns) **2 :** a straw or grass braid for hats
se·nor *or* **se·ñor** \sān-ˈyȯr\ *n, pl* **senors** *or* **se·ño·res** \-ˈyȯr-(ˌ)ās\ [Sp *señor,* fr. ML *senior* superior, lord, fr. L, adj., elder] (1622) **:** a Spanish or Spanish-speaking man — used as a title equivalent to *Mr.*
se·no·ra *or* **se·ño·ra** \sān-ˈyȯr-ə\ *n* [Sp *señora,* fem. of *señor*] (1579) **:** a married Spanish or Spanish-speaking woman — used as a title equivalent to *Mrs.*
se·no·ri·ta *or* **se·ño·ri·ta** \ˌsān-yə-ˈrē-tə\ *n* [Sp *señorita,* fr. dim. of *señora*] (1822) **:** an unmarried Spanish or Spanish-speaking girl or woman — used as a title equivalent to *Miss*
sen·ryu \ˈsen-rē-(ˌ)ü\ *n, pl* **senryu** [Jp] (1938) **:** a 3-line unrhymed Japanese poem structurally similar to haiku but treating human nature usu. in an ironic or satiric vein
sensa *pl of* SENSUM
sen·sate \ˈsen-ˌsāt\ *adj* [ME *sensat,* fr. ML *sensatus,* fr. LL, endowed with sense, fr. L *sensus* sense] (15c) **1 :** relating to or apprehending or apprehended through the senses **2 :** preoccupied with things that can be experienced through a sense modality — **sen·sate·ly** *adv*
sen·sa·tion \sen-ˈsā-shən, sən-\ *n* [ML *sensation-, sensatio,* fr. LL, understanding, idea, fr. L *sensus*] (1615) **1 a :** a mental process (as seeing, hearing, or smelling) resulting from the immediate external stimulation of a sense organ often as distinguished from a conscious awareness of the sensory process — compare PERCEPTION **b :** awareness (as of heat or pain) due to stimulation of a sense organ **c :** a state of consciousness due to internal bodily changes ⟨a ~ of hunger⟩ **d :** an indefinite bodily feeling ⟨a ~ of buoyancy⟩ **2 :** something (as a physical stimulus, sense-datum, or afterimage) that causes or is the object of sensation **3 a :** a state of excited interest or feeling ⟨their elopement caused a ~⟩ **b :** a cause of such excitement ⟨the show was the musical ~ of the season⟩; *esp* **:** one (as a person) in some respect exceptional or outstanding ⟨the rookie hitting ~ of the American League⟩
sen·sa·tion·al \-shnəl, -shə-nᵊl\ *adj* (1840) **1 :** of or relating to sensation or the senses **2 :** arousing or tending to arouse (as by lurid details) a quick, intense, and usu. superficial interest, curiosity, or emotional reaction ⟨~ tabloid news⟩ **3 :** exceedingly or unexpectedly excellent or great ⟨a ~ talent⟩ — **sen·sa·tion·al·ly** *adv*
sen·sa·tion·al·ise *Brit var of* SENSATIONALIZE
sen·sa·tion·al·ism \-shnə-ˌli-zəm, -shə-nə-ˌli-zəm\ *n* (1846) **1 :** empiricism that limits experience as a source of knowledge to sensation or sense perceptions **2 :** the use or effect of sensational subject matter or treatment — **sen·sa·tion·al·ist** \-list\ *adj or n* — **sen·sa·tion·al·is·tic** \-ˌsā-shnə-ˈlis-tik, -shə-nə-ˈlis-tik\ *adj*
sen·sa·tion·al·ize \-ˌlīz\ *vt* **-ized; -iz·ing** (1869) **:** to present in a sensational manner
[1]**sense** \ˈsen(t)s\ *n* [ME, fr. AF or L; AF *sen, sens* sensation, feeling, mechanism of perception, meaning, fr. L *sensus,* fr. *sentire* to perceive, feel; perh. akin to OHG *sinnan* to go, strive, OE *sith* journey — more at SEND] (14c) **1 :** a meaning conveyed or intended **:** IMPORT, SIGNIFICATION; *esp* **:** one of a set of meanings a word or phrase may bear esp. as segregated in a dictionary entry **2 a :** the faculty of perceiving by means of sense organs **b :** a specialized function or mechanism (as sight, hearing, smell, taste, or touch) by which an animal receives and responds to external or internal stimuli **c :** the sensory mechanisms constituting a unit distinct from other functions (as movement or thought) **3 :** conscious awareness or rationality — usu. used in pl. ⟨finally came to his ~*s*⟩ **4 a :** a particular sensation or kind or quality of sensation ⟨a good ~ of balance⟩ **b :** a definite but often vague awareness or impression ⟨felt a ~ of insecurity⟩ ⟨a ~ of danger⟩ **c :** a motivating awareness ⟨a ~ of shame⟩ **d :** a discerning awareness and appreciation ⟨her ~ of humor⟩ **5 :** CONSENSUS ⟨the ~ of the meeting⟩ **6 a :** capacity for effective application of the powers of the mind as a basis for action or response **:** INTELLIGENCE **b :** sound mental capacity and understanding typically marked by shrewdness and practicality; *also* **:** agreement with or satisfaction of such power ⟨this decision makes ~⟩ **7 :** one of two opposite directions esp. of motion (as of a point, line, or surface)
syn SENSE, COMMON SENSE, JUDGMENT, WISDOM mean ability to reach intelligent conclusions. SENSE implies a reliable ability to judge and decide with soundness, prudence, and intelligence ⟨a choice showing good *sense*⟩. COMMON SENSE suggests an average degree of such ability without sophistication or special knowledge ⟨*common sense* tells me it's wrong⟩. JUDGMENT implies sense tempered and refined by experience, training, and maturity ⟨they relied on her *judgment* for guidance⟩. WISDOM implies sense and judgment far above average ⟨a leader of rare *wisdom*⟩.
[2]**sense** *vt* **sensed; sens·ing** (ca. 1531) **1 a :** to perceive by the senses **b :** to be or become conscious of ⟨~ danger⟩ **2 :** GRASP, COMPREHEND **3 :** to detect automatically esp. in response to a physical stimulus (as light or movement)
sense–datum *n, pl* **sense–data** (1882) **:** an immediate unanalyzable private object of sensation
sense·ful \ˈsen(t)s-fəl\ *adj* (1591) **:** REASONABLE, JUDICIOUS
sen·sei \ˈsen-ˌsā\ *n, pl* **sensei** *or* **senseis** [Jp, teacher, master] (1968) **:** a teacher or instructor usu. of Japanese martial arts (as karate or judo)
sense·less \ˈsen(t)s-ləs\ *adj* (1557) **:** destitute of, deficient in, or contrary to sense: as **a :** UNCONSCIOUS ⟨knocked ~⟩ **b :** FOOLISH, STUPID ⟨it was some ~ practical joke —A. Conan Doyle⟩ **c :** MEANINGLESS ⟨a ~ murder⟩ — **sense·less·ly** *adv* — **sense·less·ness** *n*
sense organ *n* (1854) **:** a bodily structure that receives a stimulus and is affected in such a manner as to initiate excitation of associated sensory nerve fibers which convey specific impulses to the central nervous system where they are interpreted as corresponding sensations **:** RECEPTOR
sen·si·bil·ia \ˌsen(t)-sə-ˈbi-lē-ə, -ˈbil-yə\ *n pl* [LL, fr. neut. pl. of L *sensibilis* sensible] (1856) **:** what may be sensed
sen·si·bil·i·ty \ˌsen(t)-sə-ˈbi-lə-tē\ *n, pl* **-ties** (15c) **1 :** ability to receive sensations **:** SENSITIVENESS ⟨tactile ~⟩ **2 :** peculiar susceptibility to a pleasurable or painful impression (as from praise or a slight) — often used in pl. **3 :** awareness of and responsiveness toward something (as emotion in another) **4 :** refined or excessive sensitiveness in emotion and taste with especial responsiveness to the pathetic
[1]**sen·si·ble** \ˈsen(t)-sə-bəl\ *adj* [ME, fr. AF, fr. L *sensibilis,* fr. *sensus,* pp. of *sentire* to feel] (14c) **1 :** of a kind to be felt or perceived: as **a :** perceptible to the senses or to reason or understanding ⟨felt a ~ chill⟩ ⟨her distress was ~ from her manner⟩ **b** *archaic* **:** perceptibly large **:** CONSIDERABLE **c :** perceptible as real or material **:** SUBSTANTIAL ⟨the ~ world in which we live⟩ **2 a :** capable of receiving sensory impressions ⟨~ to pain⟩ **b :** receptive to external influences **:** SENSITIVE ⟨the most ~ reaches of the spirit⟩ **3 a :** perceiving through the senses or mind **:** COGNIZANT ⟨~ of the increasing heat⟩; *also* **:** convinced by perceived evidence **:** SATISFIED ⟨~ of my error⟩ **b :** emotionally aware and responsive ⟨we are ~ of your problems⟩ **c :** CONSCIOUS **4 :** having, containing, or indicative of good sense or reason **:** RATIONAL, REASONABLE ⟨~ people⟩ ⟨made a ~ answer⟩ **5 :** designed for practical ends (as comfort) rather than for appearance ⟨~ shoes⟩ ***syn*** see MATERIAL, PERCEPTIBLE, AWARE, WISE — **sen·si·ble·ness** *n* — **sen·si·bly** \-blē\ *adv*
[2]**sensible** *n* (1589) **:** something that can be sensed
sensible heat *n* (1839) **:** thermal energy whose transfer to or from a substance results in a change of temperature — compare LATENT HEAT
sen·sil·lum \sen-ˈsi-ləm\ *also* **sen·sil·la** \-ˈsi-lə\ *n, pl* **-sil·la** \-ˈsi-lə\ *also* **-sil·lae** \-ˈsi-(ˌ)lē\ [NL *sensillum,* dim. of ML *sensus* sense organ, fr. L, sense] (1925) **:** a simple epithelial sense organ of an invertebrate (as an insect) usu. in the form of a spine, plate, rod, cone, or peg that is composed of one or a few cells with a nerve connection
sen·si·ti·sa·tion, sen·si·tise *Brit var of* SENSITIZATION, SENSITIZE
[1]**sen·si·tive** \ˈsen(t)-sə-tiv, ˈsen(t)s-təv\ *adj* [ME, fr. AF, fr. ML *sensitivus,* prob. alter. of *sensativus,* fr. *sensatus* sensate] (15c) **1 :** SENSORY 2 **2 a :** receptive to sense impressions **b :** capable of being stimulated or excited by external agents (as light, gravity, or contact) ⟨~ cells⟩ **3 :** highly responsive or susceptible: as **a** (1) **:** easily hurt or damaged; *esp* **:** easily hurt emotionally (2) **:** delicately aware of the attitudes and feelings of others **b :** excessively or abnormally susceptible **:** HYPERSENSITIVE ⟨~ to egg protein⟩ **c :** readily fluctuating in price or demand ⟨~ commodities⟩ **d :** capable of indicating minute differences **:** DELICATE ⟨~ scales⟩ **e :** readily affected or changed by various agents (as light or mechanical shock) ⟨a photographic emulsion ~ to red light⟩ **f :** highly radiosensitive **4 a :** concerned with highly classified government information or involving discretionary authority over important policy matters ⟨~ documents⟩ **b :** calling for tact, care, or caution in treatment **:** TOUCHY ⟨a ~ issue like race relations⟩ **5 :** having or showing concern for a specified matter — usu. used in combination ⟨a price-*sensitive* customer⟩ ⟨environmentally ~ policies⟩ ***syn*** see LIABLE — **sen·si·tive·ly** *adv* — **sen·si·tive·ness** *n*
[2]**sensitive** *n* (1838) **1 :** a person having occult or psychical abilities **2 :** a sensitive person
sensitive plant *n* (1659) **:** any of several mimosas (esp. *Mimosa pudica*) with leaves that fold or droop when touched; *broadly* **:** a plant responding to touch with movement
sen·si·tiv·i·ty \ˌsen(t)-sə-ˈti-və-tē\ *n, pl* **-ties** (1803) **:** the quality or state of being sensitive: as **a :** the capacity of an organism or sense organ to respond to stimulation **:** IRRITABILITY **b :** the quality or state of being hypersensitive **c :** the degree to which a radio receiving set responds to incoming waves **d :** the capacity of being easily hurt **e :** awareness of the needs and emotions of others ⟨a book written with just the right mix of empathy and ~ —L. C. Brown⟩
sen·si·ti·za·tion \ˌsen(t)-sə-tə-ˈzā-shən, ˌsen(t)s-tə-ˈzā-\ *n* (1887) **1 :** the action or process of sensitizing **2 :** the quality or state of being sensitized (as to an antigen)
sen·si·tize \ˈsen(t)-sə-ˌtīz\ *vb* **-tized; -tiz·ing** [*sensitive* + *-ize*] *vt* (1856) **:** to make sensitive or hypersensitive ~ *vi* **:** to become sensitive — **sen·si·tiz·er** *n*
sen·si·tom·e·ter \ˌsen(t)-sə-ˈtä-mə-tər\ *n* [ISV *sensit*ive + *-o-* + *-meter*] (1880) **:** an instrument for measuring sensitivity of photographic material — **sen·si·to·met·ric** \ˌsen(t)-sə-tə-ˈme-trik\ *adj* — **sen·si·tom·e·try** \-sə-ˈtä-mə-trē\ *n*
sen·sor \ˈsen-ˌsȯr, ˈsen(t)-sər\ *n* [L *sentire* to perceive + E [1]*-or* — more at SENSE] (ca. 1928) **1 :** a device that responds to a physical stimulus (as heat, light, sound, pressure, magnetism, or a particular motion) and transmits a resulting impulse (as for measurement or operating a control) **2 :** SENSE ORGAN
sen·so·ri·al \sen-ˈsȯr-ē-əl\ *adj* (1768) **:** SENSORY — **sen·so·ri·al·ly** \-ə-lē\ *adv*
sen·so·ri·mo·tor \ˌsen(t)s-rē-ˈmō-tər, ˌsen(t)-sə-\ *adj* [*sensory* + *motor*] (1855) **:** of, relating to, or functioning in both sensory and motor aspects of bodily activity ⟨~ skills⟩
sen·so·ri·neu·ral \-ˈnu̇r-əl, -ˈnyu̇r-\ *adj* (1960) **:** of, relating to, or involving the aspects of sense perception mediated by nerves ⟨~ hearing loss⟩
sen·so·ri·um \sen-ˈsȯr-ē-əm\ *n, pl* **-ri·ums** *or* **-ria** \-ē-ə\ [LL, sense organ, fr. L *sentire*] (1647) **:** the parts of the brain or the mind concerned with the reception and interpretation of sensory stimuli; *broadly* **:** the entire sensory apparatus
sen·so·ry \ˈsen(t)s-rē, ˈsen(t)-sə-rē\ *adj* (1749) **1 :** of or relating to sensation or to the senses ⟨~ stimulation⟩ **2 :** conveying nerve impulses from the sense organs to the nerve centers **:** AFFERENT ⟨~ neurons⟩

\ə\ **abut** \ᵊ\ kitten, F table \ər\ **fur**ther \a\ **ash** \ā\ **ace** \ä\ m**o**p, m**a**r
\au̇\ **out** \ch\ **ch**in \e\ b**e**t \ē\ **ea**sy \g\ **g**o \i\ h**i**t \ī\ **i**ce \j\ **j**ob
\ŋ\ si**ng** \ō\ g**o** \ȯ\ **law** \ȯi\ b**oy** \th\ **th**in \th\ **th**e \ü\ l**oo**t \u̇\ f**oo**t
\y\ **y**et \zh\ vi**s**ion, bei**ge** \k, ⁿ, œ, ue, ʸ\ *see* Guide to Pronunciation

sensory area *n* (1896) : an area of the cerebral cortex that receives afferent nerve fibers from lower sensory or motor areas

sen·su·al \'sen(t)-sh(ə-)wəl, -shəl\ *adj* [ME, fr. LL *sensualis*, fr. L *sensus* sense] (15c) **1 :** relating to or consisting in the gratification of the senses or the indulgence of appetite : FLESHLY **2 :** SENSORY 1 **3 a :** devoted to or preoccupied with the senses or appetites **b :** VOLUPTUOUS **c :** deficient in moral, spiritual, or intellectual interests : WORLDLY; *esp* : IRRELIGIOUS ***syn*** see CARNAL, SENSUOUS — **sen·su·al·i·ty** \,sen(t)-shə-'wa-lə-tē\ *n* — **sen·su·al·ly** \'sen(t)-sh(ə-)wə-lē, 'sen-shə-lē\ *adv*

sen·su·al·ism \'sen(t)-sh(ə-)wə-,li-zəm, 'sen-shə-,li-\ *n* (1813) : persistent or excessive pursuit of sensual pleasures and interests — **sen·su·al·ist** \-list\ *n* — **sen·su·al·is·tic** \,sen(t)-sh(ə-)wə-'lis-tik, ,sen-shə-'lis-\ *adj*

sen·su·al·ize \'sen(t)-sh(ə-)wə-,līz, 'sen-shə-,līz\ *vt* **-ized; -iz·ing** (ca. 1687) : to make sensual — **sen·su·al·i·za·tion** \,sen(t)-sh(ə-)wə-lə-'zā-shən, ,sen-shə-lə-\ *n*

sen·sum \'sen(t)-səm\ *n, pl* **sen·sa** \-sə\ [ML, fr. L, neut. of *sensus*, pp. of *sentire* to feel — more at SENSE] (1868) : SENSE-DATUM

sen·su·ous \'sen(t)-sh(ə-)wəs\ *adj* [L *sensus* sense + E *-ous*] (1640) **1 a :** of or relating to the senses or sensible objects **b :** producing or characterized by gratification of the senses : having strong sensory appeal ⟨~ pleasure⟩ **2 :** characterized by sense impressions or imagery aimed at the senses ⟨~ verse⟩ **3 :** highly susceptible to influence through the senses — **sen·su·os·i·ty** \,sen(t)-shə-'wä-sə-tē\ *n* — **sen·su·ous·ly** \'sen(t)-shə wəs lē\ *adv* — **sen·su·ous·ness** *n*

syn SENSUOUS, SENSUAL, LUXURIOUS, VOLUPTUOUS mean relating to or providing pleasure through gratification of the senses. SENSUOUS implies gratification of the senses for the sake of aesthetic pleasure ⟨the *sensuous* delights of great music⟩. SENSUAL tends to imply the gratification of the senses or the indulgence of the physical appetites as ends in themselves ⟨a life devoted to *sensual* pleasures⟩. LUXURIOUS suggests the indulgence of sensuous pleasure inducing bodily ease and languor ⟨a *luxurious* hotel⟩. VOLUPTUOUS implies more strongly an abandonment esp. to sensual pleasure ⟨a *voluptuous* feast⟩.

sen·su stric·to \'sen-(,)sü-'strik-(,)tō\ *adv* [NL] (1902) : in a narrow or strict sense

[1]**sent** *past and past part of* SEND

[2]**sent** \'sent\ *n, pl* **sen·ti** \'sen-tē\ [Estonian (partitive sing. *senti*), prob. fr. F *centime* or E *cent*] (1930) : a former monetary unit equal to ¹⁄₁₀₀ kroon

sen·te \'sen-tē\ *n, pl* **li·cen·te** *or* **li·sen·te** \li-'sen-tē\ [Sesotho, fr. E *cent*] (1966) — see *loti* at MONEY table

[1]**sen·tence** \'sen-tᵊn(t)s, -tᵊnz\ *n* [ME, fr. AF, fr. L *sententia* feeling, opinion, fr. **sentent-*, **sentens*, irreg. prp. of *sentire* to feel — more at SENSE] (14c) **1** *obs* : OPINION; *esp* : a conclusion given on request or reached after deliberation **2 a :** JUDGMENT 2a; *specif* : one formally pronounced by a court or judge in a criminal proceeding and specifying the punishment to be inflicted upon the convict **b :** the punishment so imposed ⟨serve out a ~⟩ **3** *archaic* : MAXIM, SAW **4 a :** a word, clause, or phrase or a group of clauses or phrases forming a syntactic unit which expresses an assertion, a question, a command, a wish, an exclamation, or the performance of an action, that in writing usu. begins with a capital letter and concludes with appropriate end punctuation, and that in speaking is distinguished by characteristic patterns of stress, pitch, and pauses **b :** a mathematical or logical statement (as an equation or a proposition) in words or symbols **5 :** PERIOD 2b

[2]**sentence** *vt* **sen·tenced; sen·tenc·ing** (1592) **1 :** to impose a sentence on **2 :** to cause to suffer something ⟨*sentenced* these most primitive cultures to extinction —E. W. Count⟩

sentence fragment *n* (1947) : a word, phrase, or clause that usu. has in speech the intonation of a sentence but lacks the grammatical structure usu. found in the sentences of formal and esp. written composition

sentence stress *n* (1884) : the manner in which stresses are distributed on the syllables of words assembled into sentences — called also *sentence accent*

sen·ten·tia \sen-'ten(t)-sh(ē-)ə\ *n, pl* **-ti·ae** \-shē-,ē\ [L, lit., feeling, opinion] (1917) : APHORISM — usu. used in pl.

sen·ten·tial \sen-'ten(t)-shəl\ *adj* (1646) **1 :** of or relating to a sentence ⟨a relative clause with a ~ antecedent⟩ **2 :** of, relating to, or involving a proposition in logic ⟨~ connective⟩

sentential calculus *n* (1937) : PROPOSITIONAL CALCULUS

sentential function *n* (1937) : an expression that contains one or more variables and becomes a declarative sentence when constants are substituted for the variables

sen·ten·tious \sen-'ten(t)-shəs\ *adj* [ME, full of meaning, fr. L *sententiosus*, fr. *sententia* sentence, maxim] (1509) **1 a :** given to or abounding in aphoristic expression **b :** given to or abounding in excessive moralizing **2 :** terse, aphoristic, or moralistic in expression : PITHY, EPIGRAMMATIC — **sen·ten·tious·ly** *adv* — **sen·ten·tious·ness** *n*

sen·tience \'sen(t)-sh(ē-)ən(t)s, 'sen-tē-ən(t)s\ *n* (1839) **1 :** a sentient quality or state **2 :** feeling or sensation as distinguished from perception and thought

sen·tient \'sen(t)-sh(ē-)ənt, 'sen-tē-ənt\ *adj* [L *sentient-*, *sentiens*, prp. of *sentire* to perceive, feel] (1632) **1 :** responsive to or conscious of sense impressions ⟨~ beings⟩ **2 :** AWARE **3 :** finely sensitive in perception or feeling — **sen·tient·ly** *adv*

sen·ti·ment \'sen-tə-mənt\ *n* [F or ML; F, fr. ML *sentimentum*, fr. L *sentire*] (1639) **1 a :** an attitude, thought, or judgment prompted by feeling : PREDILECTION **b :** a specific view or notion : OPINION **2 a :** EMOTION **b :** refined feeling : delicate sensibility esp. as expressed in a work of art **c :** emotional idealism **d :** a romantic or nostalgic feeling verging on sentimentality **3 a :** an idea colored by emotion **b :** the emotional significance of a passage or expression as distinguished from its verbal context ***syn*** see FEELING, OPINION

sen·ti·men·tal \,sen-tə-'men-tᵊl\ *adj* (1741) **1 a :** marked or governed by feeling, sensibility, or emotional idealism **b :** resulting from feeling rather than reason or thought ⟨a ~ attachment⟩ ⟨a ~ favorite⟩ **2 :** having an excess of sentiment or sensibility — **sen·ti·men·tal·ly** *adv*

sen·ti·men·tal·ise *Brit var of* SENTIMENTALIZE

sen·ti·men·tal·ism \,sen-tə-'men-tə-,li-zəm\ *n* (1817) **1 :** the disposition to favor or indulge in sentimentality **2 :** an excessively sentimental conception or statement — **sen·ti·men·tal·ist** \-tə-list\ *n*

sen·ti·men·tal·i·ty \,sen-tə-,men-'ta-lə-tē, -mən-\ *n, pl* **-ties** (1770) **1 :** the quality or state of being sentimental esp. to excess or in affectation **2 :** a sentimental idea or its expression

sen·ti·men·tal·ize \-'men-tə-,līz\ *vb* **-ized; -iz·ing** *vi* (1788) : to indulge in sentiment ~ *vt* : to look upon or imbue with sentiment — **sen·ti·men·tal·i·za·tion** \-,men-tə-lə-'zā-shən\ *n*

sen·ti·mo \sen-'tē-(,)mō\ *n, pl* **-mos** [Tag, fr. Sp *céntimo*] (1968) — see *peso* at MONEY table

[1]**sen·ti·nel** \'sent-nəl, 'sen-tə-nəl\ *n* [MF *sentinelle*, fr. OIt *sentinella*, fr. *sentina* vigilance, fr. *sentire* to perceive, fr. L] (1579) : SENTRY

[2]**sentinel** *vt* **-neled** *or* **-nelled; -nel·ing** *or* **-nel·ling** (1593) **1 :** to watch over as a sentinel **2 :** to furnish with a sentinel **3 :** to post as sentinel

sen·try \'sen-trē\ *n, pl* **sentries** [perh. fr. obs. *sentry* sanctuary, watchtower] (1608) : GUARD, WATCH; *esp* : a soldier standing guard at a point of passage (as a gate)

sentry box *n* (ca. 1728) : a shelter for a sentry on his post

sep *abbr* separate; separated

Sep *abbr* September

SEP *abbr* simplified employee pension

se·pal \'sē-pəl, 'se-\ *n* [NL *sepalum*, fr. *sep-* (irreg. fr. Gk *skepē* covering) + *-alum* (as in *petalum* petal)] (1821) : one of the modified leaves comprising a calyx — see FLOWER illustration

se·pal·oid \-pə-,lȯid\ *adj* (1830) : resembling or functioning as a sepal

sep·a·ra·ble \'se-p(ə-)rə-bəl\ *adj* [ME, fr. L *separabilis*, fr. *separare*] (14c) **1 :** capable of being separated or dissociated ⟨~ parts⟩ **2** *obs* : causing separation — **sep·a·ra·bil·i·ty** \,se-p(ə-)rə-'bi-lə-tē\ *n* — **sep·a·ra·ble·ness** *n*

[1]**sep·a·rate** \'se-p(ə-),rāt\ *vb* **-rat·ed; -rat·ing** [ME, fr. L *separatus*, pp. of *separare*, fr. *se-* apart + *parare* to prepare, procure — more at SECEDE, PARE] *vt* (15c) **1 a :** to set or keep apart : DISCONNECT, SEVER **b :** to make a distinction between : DISCRIMINATE, DISTINGUISH ⟨~ religion from magic⟩ **c :** SORT ⟨~ mail⟩ **d :** to disperse in space or time : SCATTER ⟨widely *separated* homesteads⟩ **2** *archaic* : to set aside for a special purpose : CHOOSE, DEDICATE **3 :** to part by a legal separation: **a :** to sever conjugal ties with **b :** to sever contractual relations with : DISCHARGE ⟨was *separated* from the army⟩ **4 :** to block off : SEGREGATE **5 a :** to isolate from a mixture : EXTRACT ⟨~ cream from milk⟩ **b :** to divide into constituent parts **6 :** to dislocate (as a shoulder) esp. in sports ~ *vi* **1 :** to become divided or detached **2 a :** to sever an association : WITHDRAW **b :** to cease to live together as a married couple **3 :** to go in different directions **4 :** to become isolated from a mixture ⟨the crystals *separated* out⟩

syn SEPARATE, PART, DIVIDE, SEVER, SUNDER, DIVORCE mean to become or cause to become disunited or disjointed. SEPARATE may imply any of several causes such as dispersion, removal of one from others, or presence of an intervening thing ⟨*separated* her personal life from her career⟩. PART implies the separating of things or persons in close union or association ⟨vowed never to *part*⟩. DIVIDE implies separating into pieces or sections by cutting or breaking ⟨civil war *divided* the nation⟩. SEVER implies violence esp. in the removal of a part or member ⟨a *severed* limb⟩. SUNDER suggests violent rending or wrenching apart ⟨a city *sundered* by racial conflict⟩. DIVORCE implies separating two things that commonly interact and belong together ⟨cannot *divorce* scientific research from moral responsibility⟩.

[2]**sep·a·rate** \'se-p(ə-)rət\ *adj* (15c) **1 a :** set or kept apart : DETACHED **b** *archaic* : SOLITARY, SECLUDED **c :** IMMATERIAL, DISEMBODIED **2 a :** not shared with another : INDIVIDUAL ⟨~ rooms⟩ **b** *often cap* : estranged from a parent body ⟨~ churches⟩ **3 a :** existing by itself : AUTONOMOUS ⟨a ~ country⟩ **b :** dissimilar in nature or identity ⟨consulted five ~ authorities⟩ ***syn*** see DISTINCT — **sep·a·rate·ly** \-p(ə-)rət-lē, 'se-pərt-lē\ *adv* — **sep·a·rate·ness** \-nəs\ *n*

[3]**sep·a·rate** \'se-p(ə-)rət\ *n* (1886) **1 :** OFFPRINT **2 :** an article of dress designed to be worn interchangeably with others to form various costume combinations — usu. used in pl.

sep·a·ra·tion \,se-pə-'rā-shən\ *n* (14c) **1 :** the act or process of separating : the state of being separated **2 a :** a point, line, or means of division **b :** an intervening space : GAP ⟨the ~ between wheel spokes⟩ **3 a :** cessation of cohabitation between a married couple by mutual agreement or judicial decree **b :** termination of a contractual relationship (as employment or military service)

separation anxiety *n* (1943) : a form of anxiety experienced by a young child and caused by separation from a significant nurturant figure and typically a parent or from familiar surroundings

sep·a·ra·tion·ist \-sh(ə-)nist\ *n* (1831) : SEPARATIST

sep·a·rat·ism \'se-p(ə-)rə-,ti-zəm\ *n* (1628) : a belief in, movement for, or state of separation (as schism, secession, or segregation)

sep·a·rat·ist \'se-p(ə-)rə-tist, 'se-pə-,rā-\ *n* (1608) : one that favors separatism: as **a** *cap* : one of a group of 16th and 17th century English Protestants preferring to separate from rather than to reform the Church of England **b :** an advocate of independence or autonomy for a part of a political unit (as a nation) **c :** an advocate of racial or cultural separation — **separatist** *adj* — **sep·a·ra·tis·tic** \,se-p(ə-)rə-'tis-tik\ *adj*

sep·a·ra·tive \'se-pə-,rā-tiv, 'se-p(ə-)rə-\ *adj* (1592) : tending toward, causing, or expressing separation

sep·a·ra·tor \'se-p(ə-),rā-tər\ *n* (1607) : one that separates; *esp* : a device for separating liquids of different specific gravities (as cream from milk) or liquids from solids

Se·phar·di \sə-'fär-dē\ *n, pl* **Se·phar·dim** \-'fär-dəm\ [LHeb *sĕphāradhī*, fr. *sĕphāradh* Spain, fr. Heb, region where Jews were once exiled (Obad 1:20)] (1851) : a member of the occidental branch of European Jews settling in Spain and Portugal and later in the Balkans, the Levant, England, the Netherlands, and the Americas; *also* : one of their descendants — compare ASHKENAZI — **Se·phar·dic** \-'fär-dik\ *adj*

[1]**se·pia** \'sē-pē-ə\ *n* [L, cuttlefish, ink, fr. Gk *sēpia*] (1821) **1 a :** a brown melanin-containing pigment from the ink of cuttlefishes **b :** the inky secretion of a cuttlefish **2 :** a print or photograph of a brown color resembling sepia **3 :** a brownish-gray to dark olive-brown color

[2]**sepia** *adj* (1827) **1 :** made of or done in sepia **2 :** of the color sepia

se·pi·o·lite \'sē-pē-ə-,līt\ *n* [G *Sepiolith*, fr. Gk *sēpion* cuttlebone (fr. *sēpia*) + G *-lith* -lite] (1854) : MEERSCHAUM 1

se·poy \ˈsē-ˌpȯi\ *n* [Pg *sipai,* fr. Hindi & Urdu *sipāhī,* fr. Pers. cavalryman] (ca. 1718) **:** a native of India employed as a soldier by a European power

sep·pu·ku \se-ˈpü-(ˌ)kü, ˈse-pə-ˌkü\ *n* [Jp] (1871) **:** HARA-KIRI 1

sep·sis \ˈsep-səs\ *n, pl* **sep·ses** \ˈsep-ˌsēz\ [NL, fr. Gk *sēpsis* decay, fr. *sēpein* to putrefy] (1876) **:** a toxic condition resulting from the spread of bacteria or their toxins from a focus of infection; *esp* **:** SEPTICEMIA

sept \ˈsept\ *n* [perh. fr. L *septum, saeptum* enclosure, fold — more at SEPTUM] (1517) **:** a branch of a family; *esp* **:** CLAN

Sept *abbr* September

sep·tal \ˈsep-tᵊl\ *adj* (ca. 1847) **:** of or relating to a septum

sep·tate \ˈsep-ˌtāt\ *adj* (1846) **:** divided by or having a septum

Sep·tem·ber \sep-ˈtem-bər, səp-\ *n* [ME *Septembre,* fr. AF & OE, both fr. L *September* (seventh month), fr. *septem* seven — more at SEVEN] (bef. 12c) **:** the ninth month of the Gregorian calendar

sep·ten·de·cil·lion \(ˌ)sep-ˌten-di-ˈsil-yən\ *n, often attrib* [L *septendecim* seventeen (fr. *septem* seven + *decem* ten) + E *-illion* (as in *million*) — more at TEN] (1848) — see NUMBER table

sep·ten·ni·al \sep-ˈte-nē-əl\ *adj* [LL *septennium* period of seven years, fr. L *septem* + *-ennium* (as in *biennium*)] (1640) **1 :** occurring or being done every seven years **2 :** consisting of or lasting for seven years — **sep·ten·ni·al·ly** \-ə-lē\ *adv*

sep·ten·tri·on \sep-ˈten-trē-ˌän, -trē-ən\ *n* [ME, fr. AF, fr. L *septentriones,* pl., the seven stars of Ursa Major or Ursa Minor, fr. *septem* seven + *triones* plowing oxen] (14c) *obs* **:** the northern regions **:** NORTH

sep·ten·tri·o·nal \-trē-ə-nᵊl\ *adj* (14c) **:** NORTHERN

sep·tet \sep-ˈtet\ *n* [G, fr. L *septem*] (1828) **1 :** a musical composition for seven instruments or voices **2 :** a group or set of seven; *esp* **:** the performers of a septet

sep·tic \ˈsep-tik\ *adj* [L *septicus,* fr. Gk *sēptikos,* fr. *sēpein* to putrefy] (1605) **1 :** of, relating to, or causing putrefaction **2 :** relating to, involving, caused by, or affected with sepsis ⟨~ patients⟩ **3 :** used for sewage treatment and disposal ⟨a ~ system⟩; *also* **:** of or relating to a septic system ⟨~ effluents⟩

sep·ti·ce·mia \ˌsep-tə-ˈsē-mē-ə\ *n* [NL, fr. L *septicus* + NL *-emia*] (ca. 1860) **:** invasion of the bloodstream by virulent microorganisms and esp. bacteria along with their toxins from a local seat of infection accompanied esp. by chills, fever, and prostration — called also *blood poisoning*; compare SEPSIS — **sep·ti·ce·mic** \-ˈsē-mik\ *adj*

sep·ti·ci·dal \ˌsep-tə-ˈsī-dᵊl\ *adj* [NL *septum* + L *-cidere* to cut, fr. *caedere*] (1819) **:** dehiscent longitudinally along a septum ⟨a ~ fruit⟩

septic shock *n* (1966) **:** a life-threatening form of sepsis that usu. results from the presence of gram-negative bacteria and their toxins in the bloodstream and that is characterized esp. by decreased blood flow to organs and tissues, hypotension, organ dysfunction (as of the heart, kidneys, or lungs), impaired mental state, and often multiple organ failure

septic sore throat *n* (1924) **:** STREP THROAT

septic tank *n* (ca. 1902) **:** a tank in which the solid matter of continuously flowing sewage is disintegrated by bacteria

sep·til·lion \sep-ˈtil-yən\ *n, often attrib* [F, fr. L *septem* + F *-illion* (as in *million*) — more at SEVEN] (1690) — see NUMBER table

sep·tu·a·ge·nar·i·an \(ˌ)sep-ˌtü-ə-jə-ˈner-ē-ən, -ˌtyü-, -ˌchü-\ *n* [LL *septuagenarius* seventy years old, fr. L, of or containing seventy, fr. *septuageni* seventy each, fr. *septuaginta*] (1805) **:** a person whose age is in the seventies — **septuagenarian** *adj*

Sep·tu·a·ge·si·ma \ˌsep-tə-wə-ˈje-sə-mə, -ˈjā-zə-\ *n* [ME, fr. LL, fr. L, fem. of *septuagesimus* seventieth, fr. *septuaginta* seventy; fr. its being approximately seventy days before Easter] (14c) **:** the third Sunday before Lent

Sep·tu·a·gint \sep-ˈtü-ə-jənt, -ˈtyü-; ˈsep-tə-wə-ˌjint\ *n* [LL *Septuaginta,* fr. L, seventy, irreg. fr. *septem* seven + *-ginta* (akin to L *viginti* twenty); fr. the approximate number of its translators — more at SEVEN, VIGESIMAL] (1633) **:** a Greek version of the Jewish Scriptures redacted in the third and second centuries B.C. by Jewish scholars and adopted by Greek-speaking Christians — **Sep·tu·a·gin·tal** \(ˌ)sep-ˌtü-ə-ˈjin-tᵊl, -ˌtyü-; ˌsep-tə-wə-\ *adj*

sep·tum \ˈsep-təm\ *n, pl* **sep·ta** \-tə\ [NL, fr. L *saeptum* enclosure, fence, wall, fr. *saepire* to fence in, fr. *saepes* fence, hedge] (1698) **:** a dividing wall or membrane esp. between bodily spaces or masses of soft tissue — compare DISSEPIMENT

se·pul·chral \sə-ˈpəl-krəl *also* -ˈpu̇l-\ *adj* (1615) **1 :** of or relating to a sepulchre ⟨~ inscriptions⟩ **2 :** suited to or suggestive of a sepulchre **:** FUNEREAL ⟨spoke in ~ whispers⟩ — **se·pul·chral·ly** \-krə-lē\ *adv*

[1]**sep·ul·chre** *or* **sep·ul·cher** \ˈse-pəl-kər\ *n* [ME *sepulcre,* fr. AF, fr. L *sepulcrum, sepulchrum,* fr. *sepelire* to bury; akin to Gk *hepein* to care for, Skt *saparyati* he honors] (13c) **1 :** a place of burial **:** TOMB **2 :** a receptacle for religious relics esp. in an altar

[2]**sepulchre** *or* **sepulcher** *vt* **-chred** *or* **-chered; -chring** *or* **-chering** \-k(ə-)riŋ\ (1591) **1** *archaic* **:** to place in or as if in a sepulchre **:** BURY **2** *archaic* **:** to serve as a sepulchre for

sep·ul·ture \ˈse-pəl-ˌchu̇r\ *n* [ME, fr. AF, fr. L *sepultura,* fr. *sepultus,* pp. of *sepelire*] (14c) **1 :** BURIAL **2 :** SEPULCHRE

se·qua·cious \si-ˈkwā-shəs\ *adj* [L *sequac-, sequax* inclined to follow, fr. *sequi*] (1643) **1** *archaic* **:** SUBSERVIENT, TRACTABLE **2 :** intellectually servile — **se·qua·cious·ly** *adv* — **se·quac·i·ty** \-ˈkwa-sə-tē\ *n*

se·quel \ˈsē-kwəl *also* -ˌkwel\ *n* [ME, fr. AF *sequele,* fr. L *sequela,* fr. *sequi* to follow — more at SUE] (15c) **1 :** CONSEQUENCE, RESULT **2 a :** subsequent development **b :** the next installment (as of a speech or story); *esp* **:** a literary, cinematic, or televised work continuing the course of a story begun in a preceding one

se·quela \si-ˈkwe-lə\ *n, pl* **se·quel·ae** \-ˈkwe-(ˌ)lē\ [NL, fr. L, sequel] (ca. 1793) **1 :** an aftereffect of a disease, condition, or injury **2 :** a secondary result

[1]**se·quence** \ˈsē-kwən(t)s, -ˌkwen(t)s\ *n* [ME, fr. AF, fr. ML *sequentia,* fr. LL, sequel, lit., act of following, fr. L *sequent-, sequens,* prp. of *sequi*] (14c) **1 :** a hymn in irregular meter between the gradual and Gospel in masses for special occasions (as Easter) **2 :** a continuous or connected series: as **a :** an extended series of poems united by a single theme ⟨a sonnet ~⟩ **b :** three or more playing cards usu. of the same suit in consecutive order of rank **c :** a succession of repetitions of a melodic phrase or harmonic pattern each in a new position **d :** a set of elements ordered so that they can be labeled with the positive integers **e :** the exact order of bases in a nucleic acid or of amino acids in a protein **f** (1) **:** a succession of related shots or scenes developing a single subject or phase of a film story (2) **:** EPISODE **3 a :** order of succession **b :** an arrangement of the tenses of successive verbs in a sentence designed to express a coherent relationship esp. between main and subordinate parts **4 a :** CONSEQUENCE, RESULT **b :** a subsequent development **5 :** continuity of progression ⟨the narrative ~⟩

[2]**sequence** *vt* **se·quenced; se·quenc·ing** (1941) **1 :** to arrange in a sequence **2 :** to determine the sequence of chemical constituents (as amino-acid residues or nucleic-acid bases) in

se·quenc·er \ˈsē-kwən(t)-sər, -ˌkwen(t)-\ *n* (1949) **:** one that sequences: as **a :** a device for arranging things (as events in the ignition of a rocket) in a sequence **b :** a device for determining the order of occurrence of amino acids in a protein or of bases in a nucleic acid

se·quen·cy \ˈsē-kwən(t)-sē\ *n* [LL *sequentia*] (1818) **:** SEQUENCE 3a, 5

se·quent \ˈsē-kwənt\ *adj* [L *sequent-, sequens,* prp.] (1601) **1 :** CONSECUTIVE, SUCCEEDING **2 :** CONSEQUENT, RESULTANT

se·quen·tial \si-ˈkwen(t)-shəl\ *adj* (1844) **1 :** of, relating to, or arranged in a sequence **:** SERIAL ⟨~ file systems⟩ **2 :** following in sequence **3 :** relating to or based on a method of testing a statistical hypothesis that involves examination of a sequence of samples for each of which the decision is made to accept or reject the hypothesis or to continue sampling — **se·quen·tial·ly** \-ˈkwen(t)-sh(ə-)lē\ *adv*

[1]**se·ques·ter** \si-ˈkwes-tər\ *vt* **-tered; -ter·ing** \-t(ə-)riŋ\ [ME *sequestren,* fr. AF *sequestrer,* fr. L *sequestrare* to hand over to a trustee, fr. *sequester* third party to whom disputed property is entrusted, agent, fr. *secus* beside, otherwise; akin to L *sequi* to follow] (14c) **1 a :** to set apart **:** SEGREGATE ⟨~ a jury⟩ **b :** SECLUDE, WITHDRAW ⟨widely spaced homes are forbiddingly grand and ~*ed* —Don Asher⟩ **2 a :** to seize esp. by a writ of sequestration **b :** to place (property) in custody esp. in sequestration **3 :** to hold (as a metallic ion) in solution usu. by inclusion in an appropriate coordination complex

[2]**sequester** *n* (1604) **1** *obs* **:** SEPARATION, ISOLATION **2 :** the imposition of automatic government spending reductions in accordnace with sequestration

se·ques·trate \ˈsē-kwəs-ˌtrāt, ˈse-; si-ˈkwes-\ *vt* **-trat·ed; -trat·ing** [L *sequestratus,* pp. of *sequestrare*] (15c) **:** SEQUESTER; *esp* **:** SEQUESTER 2 — **se·ques·tra·tor** \ˈsē-kwəs-ˌtrā-tər, si-ˈkwes-\ *n*

se·ques·tra·tion \ˌsē-kwəs-ˈtrā-shən, ˌse-; (ˌ)sē-ˌkwes-\ *n* (15c) **1 :** the act of sequestering **:** the state of being sequestered ⟨a jury in ~⟩ **2 a :** a legal writ authorizing a sheriff or commissioner to take into custody the property of a defendant who is in contempt until the orders of a court are complied with **b :** a deposit whereby a neutral depositary agrees to hold property in litigation and to restore it to the party to whom it is adjudged to belong **3 :** the practice of imposing automatic government spending reductions by withholding appropriations by a fixed percentage that applies uniformly to all government programs except those exempted

se·ques·trum \si-ˈkwes-trəm\ *n, pl* **-trums** *also* **-tra** \-trə\ [NL, fr. L, legal sequestration, fr. *sequester*] (1831) **:** a fragment of dead bone detached from adjoining sound bone

se·quin \ˈsē-kwən\ *n* [F, fr. It *zecchino,* fr. *zecca* mint, fr. Ar (*dār al-*) *sikka,* lit., house of the minting die] (1617) **1 :** an old gold coin of Italy and Turkey **2 :** a small plate of shining metal or plastic used for ornamentation esp. on clothing

se·quined *or* **se·quinned** \-kwənd\ *adj* (1894) **:** ornamented with or as if with sequins

se·qui·tur \ˈse-kwə-tər, -ˌtu̇r\ *n* [L, it follows, 3d pers. sing. pres. indic. of *sequi* to follow — more at SUE] (1836) **:** the conclusion of an inference **:** CONSEQUENCE

se·quoia \si-ˈkwȯi-ə\ *n* [NL, genus name, fr. *Sequoya* (George Guess)] (ca. 1866) **:** either of two huge coniferous California trees of the bald cypress family that may reach a height of over 300 feet (90 meters): **a :** GIANT SEQUOIA **b :** REDWOOD 3a

ser *abbr* **1** serial **2** series **3** service

sera *pl of* SERUM

se·rac \sə-ˈrak, sā-\ *n* [F *sérac,* lit., a kind of white cheese, fr. ML *seracium* whey, fr. L *serum* whey — more at SERUM] (1860) **:** a pinnacle, sharp ridge, or block of ice among the crevasses of a glacier

se·ra·glio \sə-ˈral-(ˌ)yō, -ˈräl-\ *n, pl* **-glios** [It *serraglio,* modif. of Turk *saray* palace] (1581) **1 :** HAREM 1a **2 :** a palace of a sultan

se·rai \sə-ˈrī\ *n* [Turk & Pers; Turk *saray* mansion, palace, fr. Pers *sarāī* mansion, inn] (1609) **1 :** CARAVANSARY **2 :** SERAGLIO 2

ser·al \ˈsir-əl\ *adj* (1916) **:** of, relating to, or being an ecological sere

se·ra·pe *also* **sa·ra·pe** \sə-ˈrä-pē, -ˈra-\ *n* [MexSp *sarape*] (1834) **:** a colorful woolen shawl worn over the shoulders esp. by Mexican men

ser·aph \ˈser-əf\ *n, pl* **ser·a·phim** \-ə-ˌfim, -ˌfēm\ *or* **seraphs** [assumed sing. of Heb *śĕrāphīm*] (1667) **:** SERAPHIM 2

ser·a·phim \ˈser-ə-ˌfim, -ˌfēm\ *n pl* [LL *seraphim,* pl., seraphs, fr. Heb *śĕrāphīm*] (12c) **1 :** an order of angels — see CELESTIAL HIERARCHY **2** *sing, pl* **seraphim :** one of the 6-winged angels standing in the presence of God — **se·raph·ic** \sə-ˈra-fik\ *adj* — **se·raph·i·cal·ly** \-fi-k(ə-)lē\ *adv*

Se·ra·pis \sə-ˈrā-pəs\ *n* [L, fr. Gk *Sarapis*] (1587) **:** an Egyptian god combining attributes of Osiris and Apis and having a widespread cult in Ptolemaic Egypt and ancient Greece

Serb \ˈsərb\ *n* [ultim. fr. Serbian & Croatian *Srbin* (pl. *Srbi*)] (1860) **1 :** a native or inhabitant of Serbia **2 :** SERBIAN 2 — **Serb** *adj*

Ser·bi·an \ˈsər-bē-ən\ *n* (1848) **1 :** SERB 1 **2 :** a south Slavic language spoken by the Serbian people — **Serbian** *adj*

Ser·bo–Cro·a·tian \ˌsər-(ˌ)bō-krō-ˈā-shən\ *n* (1883) **1 :** the Serbian and Croatian languages together with the Slavic speech of Bosnia, Herzegovina, and Montenegro taken as a single language with regional variants **2 :** a person whose native language is Serbo-Croatian — **Serbo–Croatian** *adj*

[1]**sere** *also* **sear** \ˈsir\ *adj* [ME, fr. OE *sēar* dry; akin to OHG *sōrēn* to wither, Gk *hauos* dry, Lith *sausas*] (bef. 12c) **1 :** being dried and withered **2** *archaic* **:** THREADBARE

\ə\ **abut** \ᵊ\ **kitten,** F **table** \ər\ **further** \a\ **ash** \ā\ **ace** \ä\ **mop, mar** \au̇\ **out** \ch\ **chin** \e\ **bet** \ē\ **easy** \g\ **go** \i\ **hit** \ī\ **ice** \j\ **job** \ŋ\ **sing** \ō\ **go** \ȯ\ **law** \ȯi\ **boy** \th\ **thin** \t͟h\ **the** \ü\ **loot** \u̇\ **foot** \y\ **yet** \zh\ **vision, beige** \k̲, ⁿ, œ, ue, ʸ\ *see* Guide to Pronunciation

[2]**sere** *n* [L *series* series] (1916) **:** a series of ecological communities formed in ecological succession

[1]**ser·e·nade** \ˌser-ə-ˈnād\ *n* [F *sérénade,* fr. It *serenata,* fr. *sereno* clear, calm (of weather), fr. L *serenus* serene] (1649) **1 a :** a complimentary vocal or instrumental performance; *esp* **:** one given outdoors at night for a woman being courted **b :** a work so performed **2 :** an instrumental composition in several movements, written for a small ensemble, and midway between the suite and the symphony in style

[2]**serenade** *vb* **-nad·ed; -nad·ing** *vi* (1668) **:** to play a serenade ~ *vt* **:** to perform a serenade in honor of — **ser·e·nad·er** *n*

ser·e·na·ta \ˌser-ə-ˈnä-tə\ *n* [It, serenade] (ca. 1724) **:** an 18th century secular cantata of a dramatic character usu. composed in honor of an individual or event

ser·en·dip·i·tous \ˌser-ən-ˈdi-pə-təs\ *adj* (1943) **:** obtained or characterized by serendipity ⟨~ discoveries⟩ — **ser·en·dip·i·tous·ly** *adv*

ser·en·dip·i·ty \-ˈdi-pə-tē\ *n* [fr. its possession by the heroes of the Pers fairy tale *The Three Princes of Serendip*] (1754) **:** the faculty or phenomenon of finding valuable or agreeable things not sought for; *also* **:** an instance of this

[1]**se·rene** \sə-ˈrēn\ *adj* [ME, fr. L *serenus* clear, cloudless, untroubled] (15c) **1 a :** clear and free of storms or unpleasant change ⟨~ skies⟩ **b :** shining bright and steady ⟨the moon, ~ in glory —Alexander Pope⟩ **2 :** AUGUST — used as part of a title ⟨His *Serene* Highness⟩ **3 :** marked by or suggestive of utter calm and unruffled repose or quietude ⟨a ~ smile⟩ ***syn*** see CALM — **se·rene·ly** *adv* — **se·rene·ness** \-ˈrēn-nəs\ *n*

[2]**serene** *n* (1644) **1** *archaic* **:** a serene condition or expanse (as of sky, sea, or light) **2** *archaic* **:** SERENITY, TRANQUILITY

se·ren·i·ty \sə-ˈre-nə-tē\ *n* (15c) **:** the quality or state of being serene

serf \ˈsərf\ *n* [F, fr. OF, fr. L *servus* slave] (1611) **:** a member of a servile feudal class bound to the land and subject to the will of its owner — **serf·age** \ˈsər-fij\ *n* — **serf·dom** \ˈsərf-dəm, -təm\ *n*

serge \ˈsərj\ *n* [ME *sarge,* fr. AF, fr. VL **sarica,* alter. of L *serica,* fem. of *sericus* silken — more at SERICEOUS] (14c) **:** a durable twilled fabric having a smooth clear face and a pronounced diagonal rib on the front and the back

ser·gean·cy \ˈsär-jən(t)-sē\ *n* (ca. 1670) **:** the function, office, or rank of a sergeant

ser·geant \ˈsär-jənt\ *n* [ME, servant, attendant, sergeant, fr. AF *sergant, serjant,* fr. L *servient-, serviens,* prp. of *servire* to serve] (13c) **1 :** SERGEANT AT ARMS **2** *obs* **:** an officer who enforces the judgments of a court or the commands of one in authority **3 :** a noncommissioned officer ranking in the army and marine corps above a corporal and below a staff sergeant; *broadly* **:** NONCOMMISSIONED OFFICER **4 :** an officer in a police force ranking in the U.S. just below captain or sometimes lieutenant and in England just below inspector

sergeant at arms (14c) **:** an officer of an organization (as a legislative body or court of law) who preserves order and executes commands

sergeant first class *n* (1948) **:** a noncommissioned officer in the army ranking above a staff sergeant and below a master sergeant

sergeant fish *n* (1873) **1 :** COBIA **2 :** SNOOK 1

sergeant major *n, pl* **sergeants major** *or* **sergeant majors** (1797) **1 :** a noncommissioned officer in the army or marine corps serving as chief administrative assistant in a headquarters **2 :** a noncommissioned officer in the marine corps ranking above a first sergeant **3 :** a bluish-green to yellow bony fish (*Abudefduf saxatilis* of the family Pomacentridae) with black vertical stripes on the sides that is widely distributed in the western tropical Atlantic Ocean

sergeant major of the army (1966) **:** the ranking noncommissioned officer of the army serving as adviser to the chief of staff

sergeant major of the marine corps (ca. 1971) **:** the ranking noncommissioned officer of the marine corps serving as adviser to the commandant

ser·geanty \ˈsär-jən-tē\ *n, pl* **-geant·ies** [ME *sergeantie,* fr. AF *sergantie, sergeantie,* fr. *sergant* sergeant] (15c) **:** any of numerous feudal services of a personal nature by which an estate is held of the king or other lord distinct from military tenure and from socage tenure

serg·ing \ˈsər-jiŋ\ *n* [*serge*] (ca. 1909) **:** the process of overcasting the raw edges of a piece of fabric (as a carpet) to prevent raveling

sergt *abbr* sergeant

[1]**se·ri·al** \ˈsir-ē-əl\ *adj* (1840) **1 :** of, relating to, consisting of, or arranged in a series, rank, or row ⟨~ order⟩ **2 :** appearing in successive parts or numbers ⟨a ~ story⟩ **3 :** belonging to a series maturing periodically rather than on a single date ⟨~ bonds⟩ **4 :** of, relating to, or being music based on a series of tones in a chosen pattern without regard for traditional tonality **5 a :** performing a series of similar acts over a period of time ⟨a ~ killer⟩ **b :** occurring in or involving such a series ⟨a ~ murder⟩ **6 :** relating to or being a connection in a computer system in which the bits of a byte are transmitted sequentially over a single wire — compare PARALLEL — **se·ri·al·ly** \-ə-lē\ *adv*

[2]**serial** *n* (1846) **1 a :** a work appearing (as in a magazine or on television) in parts at intervals **b :** one part of a serial work **:** INSTALLMENT **2 :** a publication (as a newspaper or journal) issued as one of a consecutively numbered and indefinitely continued series

se·ri·al·ise *Brit var of* SERIALIZE

se·ri·al·ism \ˈsir-ē-ə-ˌli-zəm\ *n* (1958) **:** serial music; *also* **:** the theory or practice of composing serial music

se·ri·al·ist \-list\ *n* (1846) **1 :** a writer of serials **2 :** a composer of serial music

se·ri·al·ize \-ˌlīz\ *vt* **-ized; -iz·ing** (1857) **:** to arrange or publish in serial form ⟨~ a novel⟩ — **se·ri·al·i·za·tion** \ˌsir-ē-ə-lə-ˈzā-shən\ *n*

serial number *n* (1896) **:** a number indicating place in a series and used as a means of identification

[1]**se·ri·ate** \ˈsir-ē-ˌāt\ *vt* **-at·ed; -at·ing** (1617) **:** to arrange in a series

[2]**se·ri·ate** \ˈsir-ē-ˌāt, -ē-ət\ *adj* [L *series*] (1846) **:** arranged in a series or succession — **se·ri·ate·ly** *adv*

[1]**se·ri·a·tim** \ˌsir-ē-ˈā-təm, -ˈa-\ *adv* [ML, fr. L *series*] (1680) **:** in a series

[2]**seriatim** *adj* (1871) **:** following seriatim

se·ri·ceous \sə-ˈri-shəs\ *adj* [LL *sericeus* silken, fr. L *sericum* silk garment, silk, fr. neut. of *sericus* silken, fr. Gk *sērikos,* fr. *Sēres,* an eastern Asian people, prob. the Chinese] (ca. 1777) **:** covered with fine silky hair ⟨~ leaf⟩

ser·i·cin \ˈser-ə-sən\ *n* [ISV, fr. L *sericum* silk] (ca. 1868) **:** a gelatinous protein that cements the two fibroin filaments in a silk fiber

seri·cul·ture \ˈser-ə-ˌkəl-chər\ *n* [L *seri*cum silk + E *culture*] (ca. 1854) **:** the production of raw silk by raising silkworms — **seri·cul·tur·al** \-ˈkəl-chə-rəl, -ˈkəlch-rəl\ *adj* — **seri·cul·tur·ist** \-rist\ *n*

se·ries \ˈsir-(ˌ)ēz\ *n, pl* **series** *often attrib* [L, fr. *serere* to join, link together; akin to Gk *eirein* to string together, *hormos* chain, necklace, and perh. to L *sort-, sors* lot] (1611) **1 a :** a number of things or events of the same class coming one after another in spatial or temporal succession ⟨a concert ~⟩ ⟨the hall opened into a ~ of small rooms⟩ **b :** a set of regularly presented television programs each of which is complete in itself **2 :** the indicated sum of a usu. infinite sequence of numbers **3 a :** the coins or currency of a particular country and period **b :** a group of postage stamps in different denominations **4 :** a succession of volumes or issues published with related subjects or authors, similar format and price, or continuous numbering **5 :** a division of rock formations that is smaller than a system and comprises rocks deposited during an epoch **6 :** a group of chemical compounds related in composition and structure **7 :** an arrangement of the parts of or elements in an electric circuit whereby the whole current passes through each part or element without branching — compare PARALLEL **8 :** a set of vowels connected by ablaut (as *i, a, u* in *ring, rang, rung*) **9 :** a number of games (as of baseball) played usu. on consecutive days between two teams ⟨in town for a 3-game ~⟩ **10 :** a group of successive coordinate sentence elements joined together **11 :** SOIL SERIES **12 :** three consecutive games in bowling — **in series :** in a serial or series arrangement

ser·if \ˈser-əf\ *n* [prob. fr. D *schreef* stroke, line, fr. MD, fr. *schriven* to write, fr. L *scribere* — more at SCRIBE] (1841) **:** any of the short lines stemming from and at an angle to the upper and lower ends of the strokes of a letter — **ser·ifed** *or* **ser·iffed** \-əft\ *adj*

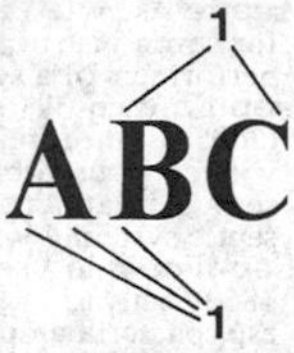

1 serif

seri·graph \ˈser-ə-ˌgraf\ *n* [L *seri*cum silk + Gk *graphein* to write, draw — more at CARVE] (1940) **:** an original silk-screen color print — **se·rig·ra·pher** \sə-ˈri-grə-fər\ *n* — **se·rig·ra·phy** \-fē\ *n*

se·rin \sə-ˈra^{n}\ *n* [F] (ca. 1672) **:** a small yellow and grayish Old World finch (*Serinus serinus* of the family Fringillidae) that is related to the canary

ser·ine \ˈser-ˌēn\ *n* [ISV *sericin* + [2]*-ine*] (1880) **:** a crystalline nonessential amino acid $C_3H_7NO_3$ that occurs as a residue in many proteins

se·rio·com·ic \ˌsir-ē-ō-ˈkä-mik\ *adj* [*serious* + *-o-* + *comic*] (1783) **:** having a mixture of the serious and the comic ⟨a ~ novel⟩ — **se·rio·com·i·cal·ly** \-mi-k(ə-)lē\ *adv*

se·ri·ous \ˈsir-ē-əs\ *adj* [ME *seryows,* fr. AF or LL; AF *serious,* fr. LL *seriosus,* alter. of L *serius* weighty, serious; prob. akin to OE *swǣr* heavy, sad] (15c) **1 :** thoughtful or subdued in appearance or manner **:** SOBER ⟨a quiet, ~ girl⟩ **2 a :** requiring much thought or work ⟨~ study⟩ **b :** of or relating to a matter of importance ⟨a ~ play⟩ **3 a :** not joking or trifling **:** being in earnest ⟨a ~ question⟩ **b** *archaic* **:** PIOUS **c :** deeply interested **:** DEVOTED ⟨a ~ musician⟩ **4 a :** not easily answered or solved ⟨~ objections⟩ **b :** having important or dangerous possible consequences ⟨a ~ injury⟩ **5 :** excessive or impressive in quality, quantity, extent, or degree ⟨~ stereo equipment⟩ ⟨making ~ money⟩ ⟨~ drinking⟩ — **se·ri·ous·ness** *n*

syn SERIOUS, GRAVE, SOLEMN, SEDATE, STAID, SOBER, EARNEST mean not light or frivolous. SERIOUS implies a concern for what really matters ⟨a *serious* play about social injustice⟩. GRAVE implies both seriousness and dignity in expression or attitude ⟨read the proclamation in a *grave* voice⟩. SOLEMN suggests an impressive gravity utterly free from levity ⟨a sad and *solemn* occasion⟩. SEDATE implies a composed and decorous seriousness ⟨remained *sedate* amid the commotion⟩. STAID suggests a settled, accustomed sedateness and prim self-restraint ⟨a quiet and *staid* community⟩. SOBER stresses seriousness of purpose and absence of levity or frivolity ⟨a *sober* look at the state of our schools⟩. EARNEST suggests sincerity or often zealousness of purpose ⟨an *earnest* reformer⟩.

se·ri·ous·ly *adv* (1509) **1 :** in a sincere manner **:** EARNESTLY ⟨speaking ~⟩ **2 :** to a serious extent **:** SEVERELY, EXTREMELY ⟨~ injured⟩

se·ri·ous–mind·ed \ˌsir-ē-əs-ˈmīn-dəd\ *adj* (1845) **:** having a serious disposition or trend of thought — **se·ri·ous–mind·ed·ly** *adv* — **se·ri·ous–mind·ed·ness** *n*

ser·jeant, ser·jeanty *Brit var of* SERGEANT, SERGEANTY

ser·jeant–at–law \ˌsär-jənt-ət-ˈlȯ\ *n, pl* **ser·jeants–at–law** (1503) *Brit* **:** a member of a former class of barristers of the highest rank

ser·mon \ˈsər-mən\ *n* [ME, fr. AF *sermun,* fr. ML *sermon-, sermo,* fr. L, speech, conversation, fr. *serere* to link together — more at SERIES] (13c) **1 :** a religious discourse delivered in public usu. by a clergyman as a part of a worship service **2 :** a speech on conduct or duty — **ser·mon·ic** \ˌsər-ˈmä-nik\ *adj*

ser·mon·ette \ˌsər-mə-ˈnet\ *n* (1814) **:** a short sermon

ser·mon·ize \ˈsər-mə-ˌnīz\ *vb* **-ized; -iz·ing** *vi* (1635) **1 :** to compose or deliver a sermon **2 :** to speak didactically or dogmatically ~ *vt* **:** to preach to or on at length — **ser·mon·iz·er** *n*

Sermon on the Mount : an ethical discourse delivered by Jesus and recorded in Matthew 5–7 and paralleled briefly in Luke 6:20–49

sero- *comb form* [L *serum*] **:** serum ⟨serology⟩

se·ro·con·ver·sion \ˌsir-ō-kən-ˈvər-zhən, -shən\ *n* (1963) **:** the production of antibodies in response to an antigen — **se·ro·con·vert** \-ˈvərt\ *vi*

se·rol·o·gy \sə-ˈrä-lə-jē, si-\ *n* [ISV] (1909) **:** a medical science dealing with blood serum esp. in regard to its reactions and properties — **se·ro·log·i·cal** \ˌsir-ə-ˈlä-ji-kəl\ *or* **se·ro·log·ic** \-jik\ *adj* — **se·ro·log·i·cal·ly** \-ji-k(ə-)lē\ *adv* — **se·rol·o·gist** \sə-ˈrä-lə-jist, si-\ *n*

se·ro·neg·a·tive \ˌsir-ō-ˈne-gə-tiv\ *adj* (1927) **:** having or being a negative serum reaction esp. in a test for the presence of an antibody — **se·ro·neg·a·tiv·i·ty** \-ˌne-gə-ˈti-və-tē\ *n*

se·ro·pos·i·tive \-ˈpä-zə-tiv, -ˈpäz-tiv\ *adj* (ca. 1930) **:** having or being a positive serum reaction esp. in a test for the presence of an antibody — **se·ro·pos·i·tiv·i·ty** \-ˌpä-zə-ˈti-və-tē\ *n*

se·ro·prev·a·lence \-ˈpre-və-lən(t)s, -ˈprev-lən(t)s\ *n* (1977) **:** the frequency of individuals in a population that have a particular element (as antibodies to HIV) in their blood serum

se·ro·pu·ru·lent \-ˈpyu̇r-ə-lənt, ˌser-, -ˈpyu̇r-yə-\ *adj* (ca. 1836) : consisting of a mixture of serum and pus ⟨a ~ exudate⟩
se·ro·sa \sə-ˈrō-zə\ *n* [NL, fr. fem. of *serosus* serous, fr. L *serum*] (ca. 1890) : a usu. enclosing serous membrane — **se·ro·sal** \-zəl\ *adj*
se·ro·ti·nal \sə-ˈrät-nəl, -ˈrä-tə-; ˌser-ə-ˈtī-nᵊl\ *adj* [L *serotinus* coming late] (1898) : of or relating to the latter and usu. drier part of summer
se·rot·i·nous \sə-ˈrät-nəs, -ˈrä-tə-; ˌser-ə-ˈtī-nəs\ *adj* [L *serotinus* coming late, fr. *sero* late — more at SOIREE] (ca. 1656) : remaining closed on the tree with seed dissemination delayed or occurring gradually ⟨~ cones⟩ — **se·rot·i·ny** \sə-ˈrät-nē, -ˈrä-tə-\ *n*
se·ro·to·ner·gic \ˌsir-ə-tə-ˈnər-jik\ *also* **se·ro·to·nin·er·gic** \ˌsir-ə-ˌtō-nə-ˈnər-jik\ *adj* [*serotonin* + *-ergic*] (1957) : liberating, activated by, or involving serotonin in the transmission of nerve impulses ⟨a ~ neuron⟩ ⟨~ pathways⟩
se·ro·to·nin \ˌsir-ə-ˈtō-nən, ˌser-\ *n* [*sero-* + *tonic* + [1]*-in*] (1948) : a phenolic amine neurotransmitter $C_{10}H_{12}N_2O$ that is a powerful vasoconstrictor and is found esp. in the brain, blood serum, and gastric mucous membrane of mammals
se·ro·type \ˈsir-ə-ˌtīp, ˈser-\ *n* (1946) : a group of intimately related microorganisms distinguished by a common set of antigens; *also* : the set of antigens characteristic of such a group
se·rous \ˈsir-əs\ *adj* [ME, fr. ML *serosus,* fr. L *serum*] (15c) : of, relating to, or resembling serum; *esp* : of thin watery constitution ⟨a ~ exudate⟩
serous membrane *n* (1813) : a thin membrane (as the peritoneum) with cells that secrete a serous fluid; *esp* : SEROSA
se·row \sə-ˈrō\ *n* [Lepcha *să-ro* long-haired Tibetan goat] (1847) : any of several goatlike artiodactyl mammals (genus *Capricornis*) of eastern Asia that are usu. rather dark and heavily built and some of which have distinct manes
ser·pent \ˈsər-pənt\ *n* [ME, fr. AF, fr. L *serpent-, serpens,* fr. prp. of *serpere* to creep; akin to Gk *herpein* to creep, Skt *sarpati* he creeps] (13c) **1 a** *archaic* : a noxious creature that creeps, hisses, or stings **b** : SNAKE **2** : DEVIL 1 **3** : a treacherous person
[1]**ser·pen·tine** \ˈsər-pən-ˌtēn, -ˌtīn\ *adj* [ME, fr. AF *serpentin,* fr. LL *serpentinus,* fr. L *serpent-, serpens*] (15c) **1** : of or resembling a serpent (as in form or movement) **2** : subtly wily or tempting **3 a** : winding or turning one way and another ⟨a ~ road⟩ **b** : having a compound curve whose central curve is convex — **ser·pen·tine·ly** *adv*
[2]**serpentine** *n* (1519) : something that winds sinuously
[3]**ser·pen·tine** \-ˌtēn\ *n* [ME, fr. AF *serpentin,* ML *serpentina, serpentinum,* fr. LL, fem. & neut. of *serpentinus* resembling a serpent] (15c) : a mineral or rock consisting essentially of a hydrous magnesium silicate usu. having a dull green color and often a mottled appearance
ser·pig·i·nous \(ˌ)sər-ˈpi-jə-nəs\ *adj* [ME *serpiginose,* fr. ML *serpiginosus,* fr. *serpigin-, serpigo* creeping skin disease, fr. L *serpere* to creep] (15c) : CREEPING, SPREADING; *esp* : healing over in one portion while continuing to advance in another ⟨~ ulcers⟩ — **ser·pig·i·nous·ly** *adv*
ser·ra·nid \sə-ˈra-nəd, ˈser-ə-nəd\ *n* [ultim. fr. L *serra* saw] (ca. 1900) : any of a large family (Serranidae) of carnivorous marine bony fishes which have an oblong compressed body covered with usu. ctenoid scales and many of which are important food and sport fishes (as the sea basses) esp. of warm seas — **serranid** *adj*
ser·ra·no \sə-ˈrä-(ˌ)nō, si-\ *n, pl* **-nos** [MexSp, fr. Sp *serrano,* adj., montane, highland, fr. *sierra* mountain range — more at SIERRA] (ca. 1972) : a small very hot chili pepper that is red when mature
[1]**ser·rate** \ˈser-ˌāt, sə-ˈrāt\ *adj* [L *serratus,* fr. *serra* saw] (1668) : notched or toothed on the edge; *specif* : having marginal teeth pointing forward or toward the apex ⟨a ~ leaf⟩
[2]**ser·rate** \sə-ˈrāt, ˈser-ˌāt\ *vt* **ser·rat·ed; ser·rat·ing** [LL *serratus,* pp. of *serrare* to saw, fr. L *serra*] (1750) : to mark or make with serrations ⟨a *serrated* knife⟩
ser·ra·tion \sə-ˈrā-shən, se-\ *n* (1842) **1** : the condition of being serrate **2** : a formation resembling the toothed edge of a saw **3** : one of the teeth in a serrate margin
ser·ried \ˈser-ēd\ *adj* (1667) **1** : crowded or pressed together : COMPACT ⟨the crowd collected in a ~ mass —W. S. Maugham⟩ **2** [by alter.] : marked by ridges : SERRATE ⟨the ~ contours of the . . . mountains —*Amer. Guide Series: Oregon*⟩ — **ser·ried·ly** *adv* — **ser·ried·ness** *n*
ser·ry \ˈser-ē\ *vb* **ser·ried; ser·ry·ing** [MF *serré,* pp. of *serrer* to press, crowd — more at SEAR] *vi* (1581) *archaic* : to press together esp. in ranks ~ *vt* : to crowd together
Ser·to·li cell \ˌsər-ˈtō-lē-\ *n* [Enrico *Sertoli* †1910 Ital. histologist] (1888) : one of the elongated striated cells lining the seminiferous tubules that support and apparently nourish the spermatids
Ser·to·man \(ˌ)sər-ˈtō-mən\ *n* [*Sertoma* (Club)] (1956) : a member of a major international service club
ser·tra·line \ˈsər-trə-ˌlēn\ *n* [perh. fr. *se*rotonin + *tetra*hydro (combined with four atoms of hydrogen) + naphtha*lene* + am*ine*] (1983) : an antidepressant drug $C_{17}H_{17}NCl_2$ administered in the form of its hydrochloride and acting to enhance serotonin activity
[1]**se·rum** \ˈsir-əm\ *n, pl* **serums** *or* **se·ra** \-ə\ [L, whey, wheylike fluid; akin to Gk *oros* whey] (1665) **1** : the watery portion of an animal fluid remaining after coagulation: **a (1)** : BLOOD SERUM **(2)** : ANTISERUM **b** : WHEY **c** : a normal or pathological serous fluid (as in a blister) **2** : the watery part of a plant fluid
[2]**serum** *adj* (1876) : occurring or found in the blood serum ⟨~ cholesterol⟩ ⟨~ antibodies⟩
serum albumin *n* (1879) : a crystallizable albumin or mixture of albumins that normally constitutes more than half of the protein in blood serum and serves to maintain the osmotic pressure of the blood
serum globulin *n* (ca. 1890) : a globulin or mixture of globulins occurring in blood serum and containing most of the antibodies of the blood
serum hepatitis *n* (1932) : HEPATITIS B
serum sickness *n* (ca. 1913) : an allergic reaction to the injection of foreign serum manifested by hives, swelling, eruption, arthritis, and fever
serv *abbr* service
ser·val \ˈsər-vəl, (ˌ)sər-ˈval\ *n* [F, fr. Pg *lobo cerval* lynx, fr. ML *lupus cervalis,* lit., deerlike wolf] (1771) : a long-legged African wildcat (*Felis serval*) having large ears and a tawny black-spotted coat

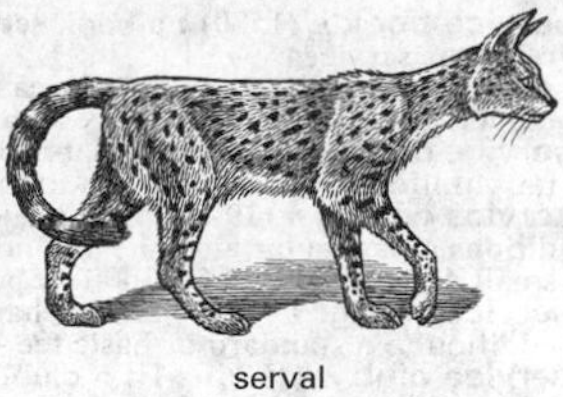
serval

ser·vant \ˈsər-vənt\ *n* [ME, fr. AF, fr. prp. of *servir*] (13c) : one that serves others ⟨a public ~⟩; *esp* : one that performs duties about the person or home of a master or personal employer — **ser·vant·hood** \-ˌhu̇d\ *n* — **ser·vant·less** *adj*
[1]**serve** \ˈsərv\ *vb* **served; serv·ing** [ME, fr. AF *servir,* fr. L *servire* to be a slave, serve, fr. *servus* slave, servant] *vi* (13c) **1 a** : to be a servant **b** : to do military or naval service **2** : to assist a celebrant as server at mass **3 a** : to be of use ⟨in a day when few people could write, seals *served* as signatures —Elizabeth W. King⟩ **b** : to be favorable, opportune, or convenient **c** : to be worthy of reliance or trust ⟨if memory ~*s*⟩ **d** : to hold an office : discharge a duty or function ⟨~ on a jury⟩ **4** : to prove adequate or satisfactory : SUFFICE ⟨it will ~ for this task⟩ **5** : to help persons to food: as **a** : to wait at table **b** : to set out portions of food or drink **6** : to wait on customers **7** : to put the ball or shuttlecock in play in various games (as tennis, volleyball, or badminton) ~ *vt* **1 a** : to be a servant to : ATTEND **b** : to give the service and respect due to (a superior) **c** : to comply with the commands or demands of : GRATIFY **d** : to give military or naval service to **e** : to perform the duties of (an office or post) **2** : to act as server at (mass) **3** *archaic* : to pay a lover's or suitor's court to (a lady) ⟨that gentle lady, whom I love and ~ —Edmund Spenser⟩ **4 a** : to work through (a term of service) **b** : to put in (a term of imprisonment) **5 a** : to wait on at table **b** : to bring (food) to a diner **c** : PRESENT, PROVIDE — usu. used with *up* ⟨the novel *served* up many laughs⟩ **6 a** : to furnish or supply with something needed or desired **b** : to wait on (a customer) in a store **c** : to furnish professional service to **7 a** : to answer the needs of **b** : to be enough for : SUFFICE **c** : to contribute or conduce to : PROMOTE **8** : to treat or act toward in a specified way ⟨he *served* me ill⟩ **9 a** : to bring to notice, deliver, or execute as required by law **b** : to make legal service upon (a person named in a process) **10** *of a male animal* : to copulate with **11** : to wind yarn or wire tightly around (a rope or stay) for protection **12** : to provide services that benefit or help **13** : to put (the ball or shuttlecock) in play (as in tennis or badminton) — **serve one right** : to be deserved
[2]**serve** *n* (1688) : the act or action of putting the ball or shuttlecock in play in various games (as volleyball, badminton, or tennis); *also* : a turn to serve ⟨it's your serve⟩
serv·er \ˈsər-vər\ *n* (15c) **1** : one that serves food or drink **2** : the player who serves (as in tennis) **3** : something used in serving food or drink **4** : one that serves legal processes upon another **5** : the celebrant's assistant at mass **6** : a computer in a network that is used to provide services (as access to files or shared peripherals or the routing of e-mail) to other computers in the network
[1]**ser·vice** \ˈsər-vəs\ *n* [ME, fr. AF *servise,* fr. L *servitium* condition of a slave, body of slaves, fr. *servus* slave] (13c) **1 a** : the occupation or function of serving ⟨in active ~⟩ **b** : employment as a servant ⟨entered his ~⟩ **2 a** : the work performed by one that serves ⟨good ~⟩ **b** : HELP, USE, BENEFIT ⟨glad to be of ~⟩ **c** : contribution to the welfare of others **d** : disposal for use ⟨I'm entirely at your ~⟩ **3 a** : a form followed in worship or in a religious ceremony ⟨the burial ~⟩ **b** : a meeting for worship — often used in pl. ⟨held evening ~*s*⟩ **4** : the act of serving: as **a** : a helpful act ⟨did him a ~⟩ **b** : useful labor that does not produce a tangible commodity — usu. used in pl. ⟨charge for professional ~*s*⟩ **c** : SERVE **5** : a set of articles for a particular use ⟨a silver tea ~⟩ **6 a** : an administrative division (as of a government or business) ⟨the consular ~⟩ **b** : one of a nation's military forces (as the army or navy) **7 a** : a facility supplying some public demand ⟨telephone ~⟩ ⟨bus ~⟩ **b** : a facility providing maintenance and repair ⟨television ~⟩ **8** : the materials (as spun yarn, small lines, or canvas) used for serving a rope **9** : the act of bringing a legal writ, process, or summons to notice as prescribed by law **10** : the act of a male animal copulating with a female animal **11** : a branch of a hospital medical staff devoted to a particular specialty ⟨obstetrical ~⟩
[2]**service** *vt* **ser·viced; ser·vic·ing** (1528) : to perform services for: as **a** : to repair or provide maintenance for ⟨*serviced* the furnace⟩ **b** : to meet interest and sinking fund payments on (as government debt) **c** : to perform any of the business functions auxiliary to production or distribution of **d** *of a male animal* : SERVE 10 — **ser·vic·er** *n*
[3]**service** *adj* (1837) **1** : of or relating to the armed services **2** : used in serving or supplying ⟨delivery men use the ~ entrance⟩ **3** : intended for hard or everyday use **4 a** : providing services ⟨the ~ trades—from filling stations to universities —John Fischer⟩ **b** : offering repair, maintenance, or incidental services
[4]**ser·vice** \ˈsər-vəs\ *n* [ME *serves,* pl. of *serve* fruit of the service tree, service tree, fr. OE *syrfe,* fr. VL **sorbea,* fr. L *sorbus* service tree] (1530) : an Old World tree (*Sorbus domestica*) resembling the related mountain ashes but having larger flowers and larger edible fruit; *also* : a related Old World tree (*S. torminalis*) with bitter fruits
ser·vice·able \ˈsər-və-sə-bəl\ *adj* (14c) **1** : HELPFUL, USEFUL **2** : fit for use ⟨a ~ design⟩; *also* : of adequate quality ⟨her ~ but not exceptional voice —Irving Kolodin⟩ — **ser·vice·abil·i·ty** \ˌsər-və-sə-ˈbi-lə-tē\ *n* — **ser·vice·able·ness** \ˈsər-və-sə-bəl-nəs\ *n* — **ser·vice·ably** \-blē\ *adv*
ser·vice·ber·ry \ˈsər-vəs-ˌber-ē *also* ˈsär-\ *n* [[4]*service*] (1784) **1** : the edible purple or red fruit of any of various No. American trees or shrubs (genus *Amelanchier*) of the rose family **2** : a tree or shrub that produces serviceberries and has showy white flowers in the spring — called also *Juneberry, shadblow, shadbush*

service book *n* (1580) : a book setting forth forms of worship used in religious services
service box *n* (ca. 1898) : the area in which a player stands while serving in various court games (as squash or handball)
service cap *n* (ca. 1908) : a flat-topped visor cap worn as part of a military uniform — compare GARRISON CAP
service ceiling *n* (1920) : the altitude at which under standard air conditions a particular airplane can no longer rise at a rate greater than a small designated rate (as 100 feet per minute)
service charge *n* (1917) : a fee charged for a particular service often in addition to a standard or basic fee — called also *service fee*
service club *n* (1926) **1 :** a club of business or professional men or women organized for their common benefit and active in community service **2 :** a recreation center for enlisted personnel provided by one of the armed services
service court *n* (ca. 1878) : a part of the court into which the ball or shuttlecock must be served
service line *n* (1875) : a line marked on a court in various games (as handball or tennis) parallel to the front wall or to the net to mark a boundary of the service area or service court
ser·vice·man \ˈsər-vəs-ˌman, -mən\ *n* (1899) **1 :** a male member of the armed forces **2 :** a man employed to repair or maintain equipment **3 :** a gas station attendant
service mark *n* (1945) : a mark or device used to identify a service (as transportation or insurance) offered to customers
service medal *n* (1914) : a medal awarded to an individual for military service in a specified war or campaign
service module *n* (1961) : a space vehicle module that contains oxygen, water, fuel cells, propellant tanks, and the main rocket engine
service road *n* (1921) : FRONTAGE ROAD
service station *n* (1916) **1 :** GAS STATION **2 :** a place at which some service is offered
service stripe *n* (ca. 1920) : a stripe worn on an enlisted man's left sleeve to indicate three years of service in the army or four years in the navy
service tree *n* (1600) : ⁴SERVICE
ser·vice·wom·an \ˈsər-vəs-ˌwu̇-mən\ *n* (1943) : a woman who is a member of the armed forces
ser·vi·ette \ˌsər-vē-ˈet\ *n* [F, fr. MF, fr. *servir* to serve] (1818) *chiefly Brit* : a table napkin
ser·vile \ˈsər-vəl, -ˌvī(-ə)l\ *adj* [ME, fr. AF *servil,* fr. L *servilis,* fr. *servus* slave] (15c) **1 :** of or befitting a slave or a menial position **2 :** meanly or cravenly submissive : ABJECT ***syn*** see SUBSERVIENT — **ser·vile·ly** \-və(l)-lē, -ˌvī(-ə)l-lē\ *adv* — **ser·vile·ness** \-vəl-nəs, -ˌvī(-ə)l-\ *n* — **ser·vil·i·ty** \(ˌ)sər-ˈvi-lə-tē\ *n*
serving *n* (1864) : a helping of food or drink
Ser·vite \ˈsər-ˌvīt\ *n* [ML *Servitae,* pl., Servites, fr. L *servus*] (ca. 1550) : a member of the mendicant Order of Servants of Mary founded in Florence, Italy, in 1233 — **Servite** *adj*
ser·vi·tor \ˈsər-və-tər, -ˌtȯr\ *n* [ME *servitour,* fr. AF, fr. LL *servitor,* fr. L *servire* to serve] (14c) : a male servant
ser·vi·tude \ˈsər-və-ˌtüd, -ˌtyüd\ *n* [ME, fr. AF *servitute,* fr. L *servitudo* slavery, fr. *servus* slave] (15c) **1 :** a condition in which one lacks liberty esp. to determine one's course of action or way of life **2 :** a right by which something (as a piece of land) owned by one person is subject to a specified use or enjoyment by another
ser·vo \ˈsər-(ˌ)vō\ *n, pl* **servos** (1947) **1 :** SERVOMOTOR **2 :** SERVOMECHANISM
ser·vo·mech·a·nism \ˈsər-vō-ˌme-kə-ˌni-zəm\ *n* [*servo-* (as in *servomotor*) + *mechanism*] (1926) : an automatic device for controlling large amounts of power by means of very small amounts of power and automatically correcting the performance of a mechanism
ser·vo·mo·tor \ˈsər-vō-ˌmō-tər\ *n* [F *servo-moteur,* fr. L *servus* slave, servant + F *-o-* + *moteur* motor, fr. L *motor* one that moves — more at MOTOR] (1889) : a power-driven mechanism that supplements a primary control operated by a comparatively feeble force (as in a servomechanism)
SES *abbr* socioeconomic status
-ses *pl of* -SIS
ses·a·me \ˈse-sə-mē *also* ˈse-zə-\ *n* [alter. of earlier *sesam, sesama,* fr. L *sesamum, sesama,* fr. Gk *sēsamon, sēsamē,* of Sem origin; akin to Akkadian *šamaššamu* sesame] (15c) **1 :** a widely cultivated chiefly tropical or subtropical annual erect herb (*Sesamum indicum* of the family Pedaliaceae); *also* : its small seeds used esp. as a source of oil and a flavoring agent **2 :** OPEN SESAME
sesame oil *n* (1870) : a pale yellow bland semidrying fatty oil obtained from sesame seeds and used chiefly as an edible oil, as a vehicle for various pharmaceuticals, and in cosmetics and soaps
ses·a·moid \ˈse-sə-ˌmȯid\ *n* [Gk *sēsamoeidēs,* lit., resembling sesame seed, fr. *sēsamon*] (ca. 1696) : a nodular mass of bone (as the patella) or cartilage in a tendon esp. at a joint or bony prominence — **sesamoid** *adj*
Se·so·tho \se-ˈsō-(ˌ)thō, -(ˌ)tō\ *n* [Sesotho] (1846) : the Bantu language of the Basotho people
sesqui- *comb form* [L, one and a half, half again, lit., and a half, fr. *semis* half of an as, one half (prob. fr. *semi-* + *as* as) + *-que* (enclitic) and; akin to Gk *te* and, Skt *ca,* Goth *-h, -uh*] **1 :** one and a half times ⟨*sesqui*centennial⟩ **2 :** containing half again as many atoms ⟨*sesqui*terpene⟩ **3 :** intermediate : combination ⟨*sesqui*carbonate⟩
ses·qui·car·bon·ate \ˌses-kwi-ˈkär-bə-ˌnāt, -nət\ *n* (1825) : a salt (as $Na_2CO_3 \cdot NaHCO_3 \cdot 2H_2O$) that is neither a simple normal carbonate nor a simple bicarbonate but often a combination of the two
ses·qui·cen·te·na·ry \-kwi-sen-ˈte-nə-rē, -ˈsen-tə-ˌner-ē, -sen-ˈtē-nə-rē\ *n* (1954) : SESQUICENTENNIAL
ses·qui·cen·ten·ni·al \-sen-ˈte-nē-əl\ *n* (1880) : a 150th anniversary or its celebration — **sesquicentennial** *adj*
ses·qui·pe·da·lian \ˌses-kwə-pə-ˈdāl-yən\ *adj* [L *sesquipedalis,* lit., a foot and a half long, fr. *sesqui-* + *ped-, pes* foot — more at FOOT] (1656) **1 :** having many syllables : LONG ⟨∼ terms⟩ **2 :** given to or characterized by the use of long words ⟨a ∼ television commentator⟩
ses·qui·ter·pene \ˌses-kwə-ˈtər-ˌpēn\ *n* (ca. 1888) : any of a class of terpenes $C_{15}H_{24}$; *also* : a derivative of such a terpene
sess *abbr* session
ses·sile \ˈse-ˌsī(-ə)l, -səl\ *adj* [L *sessilis* of or fit for sitting, low, dwarf (of plants), fr. *sessus,* pp. of *sedēre*] (ca. 1753) **1 :** attached directly by the base : not raised upon a stalk or peduncle ⟨a ∼ leaf⟩ ⟨∼ bubbles⟩ **2 :** permanently attached or established : not free to move about ⟨∼ sponges and coral polyps⟩
¹**ses·sion** \ˈse-shən\ *n* [ME, fr. AF, fr. L *session-, sessio,* lit., act of sitting, fr. *sedēre* to sit — more at SIT] (14c) **1 :** a meeting or series of meetings of a body (as a court or legislature) for the transaction of business ⟨morning ∼⟩ **2** *pl* **a** (1) **:** a sitting of English justices of peace in execution of the powers conferred by their commissions (2) **:** an English court holding such sessions **b :** any of various courts similar to the English sessions **3 :** the period between the first meeting of a legislative or judicial body and the prorogation or final adjournment **4 :** the ruling body of a Presbyterian congregation consisting of the elders in active service **5 :** the period during the year or day in which a school conducts classes **6 :** a meeting or period devoted to a particular activity ⟨a recording ∼⟩ — **ses·sion·al** \ˈsesh-nəl, ˈse-shə-nᵊl\ *adj*
²**session** *adj* (1958) : employed to perform at recording sessions ⟨a ∼ drummer⟩
ses·terce \ˈses-ˌtərs\ *n* [L *sestertius,* fr. *sestertius* two and a half times as great (fr. its being equal orig. to two and a half asses), fr. *semis* half of an as, one half + *tertius* third — more at SESQUI-, THIRD] (1598) : an ancient Roman coin equal to ¼ denarius
ses·ter·tium \se-ˈstər-sh(ē-)əm\ *n, pl* **-tia** \-sh(ē-)ə\ [L, fr. gen. pl. of *sestertius* (in the phrase *milia sestertium* thousands of sesterces)] (1540) : a unit of value in ancient Rome equal to 1000 sesterces
ses·tet \ses-ˈtet\ *n* [It *sestetto,* fr. *sesto* sixth, fr. L *sextus* — more at SEXT] (ca. 1859) : a stanza or a poem of six lines; *specif* : the last six lines of an Italian sonnet
ses·ti·na \se-ˈstē-nə\ *n* [It, fr. *sesto* sixth] (ca. 1586) : a lyrical fixed form consisting of six 6-line usu. unrhymed stanzas in which the end words of the first stanza recur as end words of the following five stanzas in a successively rotating order and as the middle and end words of the three verses of the concluding tercet
¹**set** \ˈset\ *vb* **set; set·ting** [ME *setten,* fr. OE *settan;* akin to OHG *sezzen* to set, OE *sittan* to sit] *vt* (bef. 12c) **1 :** to cause to sit : place in or on a seat **2 a :** to put (a fowl) on eggs to hatch them **b :** to put (eggs) for hatching under a fowl or into an incubator **3 :** to place (oneself) in position to start running in a race **4 a :** to place with care or deliberate purpose and with relative stability ⟨∼ a ladder against the wall⟩ ⟨∼ a stone on the grave⟩ **b :** TRANSPLANT 1 ⟨∼ seedlings⟩ **c** (1) **:** to make (as a trap) ready to catch prey (2) **:** to fix (a hook) firmly into the jaw of a fish **d :** to put aside (as dough containing yeast) for fermenting **5 :** to direct with fixed attention ⟨∼ your mind to it⟩ **6 a :** to cause to assume a specified condition, relation, or occupation ⟨slaves were ∼ free⟩ ⟨∼ the house on fire⟩ **b :** to cause the start of ⟨∼ a fire⟩ **7 a :** to appoint or assign to an office or duty **b :** POST, STATION **8 :** to cause to assume a specified posture or position ⟨∼ the door ajar⟩ **9 a :** to fix as a distinguishing imprint, sign, or appearance ⟨the years have ∼ their mark on him⟩ **b :** AFFIX **c :** APPLY ⟨∼ a match to kindling⟩ **10 :** to fix or decide on as a time, limit, or regulation : PRESCRIBE ⟨∼ a wedding day⟩ ⟨∼ the rules for the game⟩ **11 a :** to establish as the highest level or best performance ⟨∼ a record for the half mile⟩ **b :** to furnish as a pattern or model ⟨∼ an example of generosity⟩ **c :** to allot as a task ⟨*setting* lessons for the children to work upon at home —*Manchester Examiner*⟩ **12 a :** to adjust (a device and esp. a measuring device) to a desired position ⟨∼ the alarm for 7:00⟩ ⟨∼ a thermostat at 68⟩; *also* : to adjust (as a clock) in conformity with a standard **b :** to restore to normal position or connection when dislocated or fractured ⟨∼ a broken bone⟩ **c :** to spread to the wind ⟨∼ the sails⟩ **13 a :** to put in order for use ⟨∼ a place for a guest⟩ **b :** to make scenically ready for a performance ⟨∼ the stage⟩ **c** (1) **:** to arrange (type) for printing ⟨∼ type by hand⟩ (2) **:** to put into type or its equivalent (as on film) ⟨∼ the first word in italic⟩ **14 a :** to put a fine edge on by grinding or honing ⟨∼ a razor⟩ **b :** to bend slightly the tooth points of (a saw) alternately in opposite directions **c :** to sink (the head of a nail) below the surface **15 :** to fix in a desired position (as by heating or stretching) **16 :** to arrange (hair) in a desired style by using implements (as curlers, rollers, or clips) and gels or lotions **17 a :** to adorn with something affixed or infixed : STUD, DOT ⟨clear sky ∼ with stars⟩ **b :** to fix (as a precious stone) in a border of metal : place in a setting **c :** to place in a specified literary or dramatic setting ⟨a story ∼ in Paris⟩ **18 a :** to hold something in regard or esteem at the rate of ⟨∼*s* a great deal by daily exercise⟩ **b :** to place in a relative rank or category ⟨∼ duty before pleasure⟩ **c :** to fix at a certain amount ⟨∼ bail at $500⟩ **d :** VALUE, RATE ⟨their promises were ∼ at naught⟩ **e :** to place as an estimate of worth ⟨∼ a high value on life⟩ **19 :** to place in relation for comparison or balance ⟨theory ∼ against practice⟩ **20 a :** to direct to action **b :** to incite to attack or antagonism ⟨war ∼*s* brother against brother⟩ **21 a :** to place by transporting ⟨was ∼ ashore on the island⟩ **b :** to put in motion **c :** to put and fix in a direction ⟨∼ our faces toward home once more⟩ **d** *of a dog* : to point out the position of (game) by holding a fixed attitude **22 :** to defeat (an opponent or a contract) in bridge **23 a :** to fix firmly : make immobile : give rigid form or condition to ⟨∼ her jaw in determination⟩ **b :** to make unyielding or obstinate **24 :** to cause to become firm or solid ⟨∼ milk for cheese⟩ **25 :** to cause (as fruit or seed) to develop ∼ *vi* **1** *chiefly dial* : SIT **2 :** to be becoming : be suitable : FIT ⟨the coat ∼*s* well⟩ **3 :** to cover and warm eggs to hatch them **4 a :** to affect one with or as if with weight ⟨the pudding ∼*s* heavily on my stomach⟩ **b :** to place oneself in position in preparation for an action (as running) **5** *of a plant part* : to undergo development usu. as a result of pollination **6 a :** to pass below the horizon : go down ⟨the sun ∼*s*⟩ **b :** to come to an end ⟨this century ∼*s* with little mirth —Thomas Fuller⟩ **7 :** to apply oneself to some activity ⟨∼ to work⟩ **8 :** to have a specified direction in motion : FLOW, TEND ⟨the wind was *setting* from Pine Hill to the farm —Esther Forbes⟩ **9** *of a dog* : to indicate the position of game by crouching or pointing **10 :** to dance face to face with another in a square dance ⟨∼ to your partner and turn⟩ **11 a :** to become solid or thickened by chemical or physical alteration ⟨the cement ∼*s* rapidly⟩ **b** *of a dye or color* : to become permanent **c** *of a bone* : to become whole by growing together — **set about :** to begin to do — **set apart 1 :** to reserve to a particular use **2 :** to make noticeable or outstanding — **set**

aside **1** : to put to one side : DISCARD **2** : to reserve for a purpose : SAVE **3** : DISMISS **4** : ANNUL, OVERRULE — **set at** : to mount an attack on : ASSAIL ⟨would go although . . . devils should *set at* me —Charlotte Yonge⟩ — **set eyes on** : to catch sight of — **set foot in** : ENTER — **set foot on** : to step onto — **set forth** **1** : to give an account or statement of **2** : to start out on a journey — **set forward** **1** : FURTHER **2** : to start out on a journey — **set in motion** : to give impulse to ⟨*sets* the story *in motion* vividly —Howard Thompson⟩ — **set one's hand to** : to become engaged in — **set one's heart on** : RESOLVE *vt* 5 ⟨she *set her heart on* going to medical school⟩ — **set one's house in order** : to organize one's affairs — **set one's sights on** : to determine to pursue — **set one's teeth on edge** : IRRITATE, ANNOY — **set one straight** : to correct someone by providing accurate information — **set sail** : to start out on a course; *esp* : to begin a voyage ⟨*set sail* for Bermuda⟩ — **set store by** *or* **set store on** : to consider valuable, trustworthy, or worthwhile — **set the stage** : to provide the basis or background ⟨this trend will *set the stage* for higher earnings⟩ — **set to music** : to provide music or instrumental accompaniment for (a text) — **set upon** : to attack usu. with violence ⟨the dogs *set upon* the trespassers⟩

[2]**set** *n* (14c) **1 a** : the act or action of setting **b** : the condition of being set **2** : a number of things of the same kind that belong or are used together ⟨an electric train ~⟩ **3 a** : mental inclination, tendency, or habit : BENT ⟨a ~ toward mathematics⟩ **b** : a state of psychological preparedness to perceive or respond to an anticipated stimulus or situation **4** : direction of flow ⟨the ~ of the wind⟩ **5** : form or carriage of the body or of its parts ⟨her face took on a cynical ~ —Raymond Kennedy⟩ **6** : the manner of fitting or of being placed or suspended ⟨in order to give the skirt a pretty ~ —Mary J. Howell⟩ **7** : amount of deflection from a straight line ⟨~ of a saw's teeth⟩ **8** : permanent change of form (as of metal) due to repeated or excessive stress **9** : the act or result of arranging hair by curling or waving **10** *also* **sett** \ˈset\ **a** : a young plant or rooted cutting ready for transplanting **b** : a small bulb, corm, or tuber or a piece of tuber used for propagation ⟨onion ~*s*⟩ **c** : the blossoms of a plant that have set fruit as a result of fertilization **11** *or* **sett** : the burrow of a badger **12** : the width of the body of a piece of type **13** : an artificial setting for a scene of a theatrical or film production **14** *also* **sett** : a rectangular paving stone of sandstone or granite **15** : a division of a tennis match won by the side that wins at least six games beating the opponent by two games or by winning a tiebreaker **16** : a collection of books or periodicals forming a unit **17** : a clutch of eggs **18** : the basic formation in a country-dance or square dance **19** : a session of music (as jazz or dance music) usu. followed by an intermission; *also* : the music played at one session **20** : a group of persons associated by common interests **21** : a collection of elements and esp. mathematical ones (as numbers or points) — called also *class* **22** : an apparatus of electronic components assembled so as to function as a unit ⟨a television ~⟩ **23** : a usu. offensive formation in football or basketball **24** : a group of a specific number of repetitions of a particular exercise

[3]**set** *adj* [ME *sett,* fr. OE *gesett,* pp. of *settan*] (14c) **1** : INTENT, DETERMINED ⟨~ upon going⟩ **2** : INTENTIONAL, PREMEDITATED ⟨did it of ~ purpose⟩ **3** : fixed by authority or appointment : PRESCRIBED, SPECIFIED ⟨~ hours of study⟩ **4** : reluctant to change ⟨~ in their ways⟩ **5 a** : IMMOVABLE, RIGID ⟨~ frown⟩ **b** : BUILT-IN ⟨a ~ tub⟩ **6** : SETTLED, PERSISTENT ⟨~ defiance⟩ **7** : being in readiness : PREPARED ⟨~ for an early morning start⟩

se•ta \ˈsē-tə\ *n, pl* **se•tae** \ˈsē-ˌtē\ [NL, fr. L *saeta, seta* bristle] (ca. 1793) : a slender usu. rigid or bristly and springy organ or part of an animal or plant — **se•tal** \ˈsē-tᵊl\ *adj*

se•ta•ceous \si-ˈtā-shəs\ *adj* [L *saeta, seta*] (1664) **1** : set with or consisting of bristles **2** : resembling a bristle in form or texture

set–aside \ˈset-ə-ˌsīd\ *n* (1943) **1** : something (as a portion of receipts or production) that is set aside for a specified purpose **2** : a program requiring a percentage of opportunities (as for jobs or funding) to be reserved for an underrepresented group

set•back \ˈset-ˌbak\ *n* (1674) **1** : a checking of progress **2** : DEFEAT, REVERSE **3** : [4]PITCH 7 **4** : a placing of a face of a building on a line some distance to the rear of the building line or of the wall below; *also* : the area produced by a setback **5** : automatic scheduled adjustment to a lower temperature setting of a thermostat **6** : the distance of a structure or other feature (as a well or septic system) from the property line or other feature

set back *vt* (1600) **1** : to slow the progress of : HINDER, DELAY **2** : COST ⟨a new suit will *set* you *back* $200⟩

set by *vt* (ca. 1601) : to set apart for future use

set down *vt* (15c) **1** : to cause to sit down : SEAT **2** : to place at rest on a surface or on the ground **3** : to suspend (a jockey) from racing **4** : to cause or allow to get off a vehicle : DELIVER **5** : to land (an airplane) on the ground or water **6 a** : ORDAIN, ESTABLISH **b** : to put in writing **7 a** : REGARD, CONSIDER ⟨*set* him *down* as a liar⟩ **b** : ATTRIBUTE

se te•nant \sə-ˈte-nənt, sē-; ˌse-tə-ˈnäⁿ\ *adj* [F, lit., holding one another] (ca. 1911) *of postage stamps* : joined together as in the original sheet but differing in design, overprint, color, or perforation

Seth \ˈseth\ *n* [Heb *Shēth*] (bef. 12c) : a son of Adam and Eve

[1]**set–in** \ˈset-ˈin\ *adj* (1534) **1** : placed, located, or built as a part of some other construction ⟨a ~ bookcase⟩ ⟨a ~ washbasin⟩ **2** : cut separately and stitched in ⟨~ sleeves⟩

[2]**set–in** \ˈset-ˌin\ *n* (1953) : INSERT

set in *vt* (15c) : INSERT; *esp* : to stitch (a small part) within a large article ⟨*set in* a sleeve of a dress⟩ ~ *vi* : to become established

set•line \ˈset-ˌlīn\ *n* (1865) : a long heavy fishing line to which several hooks are attached in series

set•off \ˈset-ˌȯf\ *n* (1621) **1** : something that is set off against another thing: **a** : DECORATION, ORNAMENT **b** : COMPENSATION, COUNTERBALANCE **2** : the reduction or discharge of a debt or claim by setting against it a distinct claim in favor of the debtor or party who is the object of the first claim (as in a lawsuit); *also* : the offsetting claim itself **3** : OFFSET 7a

set off *vt* (ca. 1598) **1 a** : to put in relief : show up by contrast **b** : ADORN, EMBELLISH **c** : to set apart : make distinct or outstanding **2 a** : OFFSET, COMPENSATE ⟨more variety in the Lancashire weather to *set off* its most disagreeable phases —*Geog. Jour.*⟩ **b** : to make a setoff of ⟨the respective totals shall be *set off* against one another —O. R. Hobson⟩ **3 a** : to set in motion : cause to begin **b** : to cause to explode **4** : to measure off on a surface ~ *vi* : to start out on a course or a journey ⟨*set off* for home⟩

set on *vt* (14c) **1** : ATTACK **2 a** *obs* : PROMOTE **b** : to urge (as a dog) to attack or pursue **c** : to incite to action : INSTIGATE **d** : to set to work ~ *vi* : GO ON, ADVANCE

se•tose \ˈsē-ˌtōs\ *adj* [L *saetosus,* fr. *saeta*] (1661) : SETACEOUS, BRISTLY

set•out \ˈset-ˌau̇t\ *n* (ca. 1807) **1 a** (1) : ARRAY, DISPLAY (2) : ARRANGEMENT, LAYOUT **b** : BUFFET, SPREAD **c** : TURNOUT 5 **2** : PARTY, ENTERTAINMENT **3** : BEGINNING, OUTSET

set out *vt* (14c) **1 a** : to arrange and present graphically or systematically **b** : to mark out (as a design) : lay out the plan of **2** : to state, describe, or recite at length ⟨distributed copies of a pamphlet *setting out* his ideas in full —S. F. Mason⟩ **3** : to begin with a definite purpose : INTEND, UNDERTAKE ~ *vi* : to start out on a course, a journey, or a career ⟨*set out* across the country⟩

set piece *n* (1834) **1 a** : a composition (as in literature, art, or music) executed in a fixed or ideal form often with studied artistry and brilliant effect **b** : a scene, depiction, speech, or event that is obviously designed to have an imposing effect **2** : a realistic piece of stage scenery standing by itself **3** : a precisely planned and conducted military operation ⟨an offensive *set piece* that caught the enemy off guard⟩ — **set–piece** *adj*

set point *n* (1928) **1** : a situation (as in tennis) in which one player will win the set by winning the next point; *also* : the point won **2** : the level or point at which a variable physiological state (as body temperature or weight) tends to stabilize

set•screw \ˈset-ˌskrü\ *n* (1849) **1** : a screw screwed through one part tightly upon or into another part to prevent relative movement **2** : a screw for regulating a valve opening or a spring tension

set shot *n* (1937) : a two-handed shot in basketball taken from a stationary position

sett *var of* SET

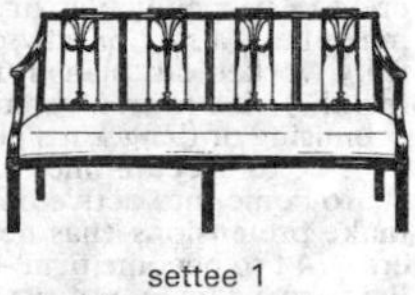
settee 1

set•tee \se-ˈtē\ *n* [alter. of *settle*] (1716) **1** : a long seat with a back **2** : a medium-sized sofa with arms and a back

set•ter \ˈse-tər\ *n* (15c) **1** : one that sets **2** : a large bird dog (as an Irish setter) of a type trained to point on finding game

set theory *n* (1936) : a branch of mathematics or of symbolic logic that deals with the nature and relations of sets — **set theoretic** *adj*

setting *n* (14c) **1** : the manner, position, or direction in which something is set **2** : the frame or bed in which a gem is set; *also* : style of mounting **3 a** : the time, place, and circumstances in which something occurs or develops **b** : the time and place of the action of a literary, dramatic, or cinematic work **c** : the scenery used in a theatrical or film production **4** : the music composed for a text (as a poem) **5** : the articles of tableware for setting a place at table ⟨two ~*s* of sterling silver⟩ **6** : a batch of eggs for incubation ***syn*** see BACKGROUND

setting circle *n* (1869) : a graduated scale or wheel on the mounting of an equatorial telescope for indicating right ascension or declination

setting–up exercise *n* (ca. 1900) : any of a series of gymnastic exercises used to give an erect carriage, supple muscles, and easy control of the limbs

[1]**set•tle** \ˈse-tᵊl\ *vb* **set•tled; set•tling** \ˈset-liŋ, ˈse-tᵊl-iŋ\ [ME, to seat, bring to rest, come to rest, fr. OE *setlan,* fr. *setl* seat] *vt* (1515) **1** : to place so as to stay **2 a** : to establish in residence **b** : to furnish with inhabitants : COLONIZE **3 a** : to cause to pack down **b** : to clarify by causing dregs or impurities to sink **4** : to make quiet or orderly **5 a** : to fix or resolve conclusively ⟨~ the question⟩ **b** : to establish or secure permanently ⟨~ the order of royal succession⟩ **c** : to conclude (a lawsuit) by agreement between parties usu. out of court **d** : to close (as an account) by payment often of less than is due **6** : to arrange in a desired position **7** : to make or arrange for final disposition of ⟨*settled* his affairs⟩ **8** *of an animal* : IMPREGNATE ~ *vi* **1** : to come to rest **2 a** : to sink gradually or to the bottom **b** : to become clear by the deposit of sediment or scum **c** : to become compact by sinking **3 a** : to become fixed, resolved, or established ⟨a cold *settled* in his chest⟩ **b** : to establish a residence or colony ⟨*settled* in Wisconsin⟩ — often used with *down* **4 a** : to become quiet or orderly **b** : to take up an ordered or stable life — often used with *down* ⟨marry and ~ down⟩ **5 a** : to adjust differences or accounts **b** : to come to a decision — used with *on* or *upon* ⟨*settled* on a new plan⟩ **c** : to conclude a lawsuit by agreement out of court **6** *of an animal* : CONCEIVE ***syn*** see DECIDE — **set•tle•able** \ˈse-tᵊl-ə-bəl, ˈset-lə-bəl\ *adj* — **settle for** : to be content with — **settle one's hash** : to silence or subdue someone by decisive action — **settle the stomach** : to remove or relieve the distress or nausea of indigestion

[2]**settle** *n* [ME, place for sitting, seat, chair, fr. OE *setl;* akin to OHG *sezzal* seat, L *sella* seat, chair, OE *sittan* to sit] (1553) : a wooden bench with arms, a high solid back, and an enclosed foundation which can be used as a chest

set•tle•ment \ˈse-tᵊl-mənt\ *n* (1648) **1** : the act or process of settling **2 a** : an act of bestowing or giving possession under legal sanction **b** : the sum, estate, or income secured to one by such a settlement **3 a** : occupation by settlers **b** : a place or region newly settled **c** : a small village **4** : SETTLEMENT HOUSE **5** : an agreement composing differences **6** : payment or adjustment of an account

settlement house *n* (1907) : an institution providing various community services esp. to large city populations

set•tler \ˈset-lər, ˈse-tᵊl-ər\ *n* (1696) : one that settles (as a new region)

settling *n* (1594) : SEDIMENT, DREGS — usu. used in pl.

\ə\ **abut** \ᵊ\ **kitten**, F **table** \ər\ **further** \a\ **ash** \ā\ **ace** \ä\ **mop, mar**
\au̇\ **out** \ch\ **chin** \e\ **bet** \ē\ **easy** \g\ **go** \i\ **hit** \ī\ **ice** \j\ **job**
\ŋ\ **sing** \ō\ **go** \ȯ\ **law** \ȯi\ **boy** \th\ **thin** \t͟h\ **the** \ü\ **loot** \u̇\ **foot**
\y\ **yet** \zh\ **vision, beige** \k, ⁿ, œ, ue, ʸ\ *see* Guide to Pronunciation

set·tlor \ˈset-ˌlȯr, ˈse-tᵊl-ˌȯr\ *n* (1818) **:** one that makes a settlement or creates a trust of property
set–to \ˈset-ˌtü\ *n, pl* **set–tos** (1743) **:** a usu. brief and vigorous fight or debate
set to *vi* (ca. 1525) **1 :** to begin actively and earnestly **2 :** to begin fighting
set·up \ˈset-ˌəp\ *n* (1890) **1 a :** carriage of the body; *esp* **:** erect and soldierly bearing **b :** CONSTITUTION, MAKEUP **2 a :** the assembly and arrangement of the tools and apparatus required for the performance of an operation **b :** the preparation and adjustment of machines for an assigned task **3 a :** a table setting **b :** glass, ice, and mixer served to patrons who supply their own liquor **4 a :** a camera position from which a scene is filmed; *also* **:** the footage taken from one camera position **b :** the final arrangement of the scenery and properties for a scene of a theatrical or cinematic production **5 a :** a position of the balls in billiards or pool from which it is easy to score **b :** a task or contest purposely made easy **c :** something easy to get or accomplish **d :** something (as a plot) that has been constructed or contrived **e :** the execution of a planned scoring play in sports **6 a :** the manner in which the elements or components of a machine, apparatus, or system are arranged, designed, or assembled **b :** the patterns within which political, social, or administrative forces operate **:** customary or established practice **7 :** PROJECT, PLAN **8 :** something done by deceit or trickery in order to compromise or frame someone
set up *vt* (13c) **1 a :** to raise to and place in a high position **b :** to place in view **:** POST **c :** to put forward (as a plan) for acceptance **2 a :** to place upright **:** ERECT ⟨*set up* a statue⟩ **b :** to assemble the parts of and erect in position **c :** to put (a machine) in readiness or adjustment for an operation **3 a :** CAUSE, CREATE ⟨*set up* a clamor⟩ **b :** BRING ABOUT **4 :** to place in power or in office ⟨*set up* the general as dictator⟩ **5 a :** to raise from depression **:** ELATE, GRATIFY **b :** to make proud or vain **6 a :** to put forward or extol as a model **b :** to claim oneself to be ⟨*sets* himself *up* as an authority⟩ **7 :** FOUND, INAUGURATE **8 a :** to provide with means of making a living ⟨*set* him *up* in business⟩ **b :** to bring or restore to normal health **c :** to cause (one) to take on a soldierly or athletic appearance esp. through drill **9 :** to erect (a perpendicular or a figure) on a base in a drawing **10 a :** to make taut (a stay or hawser) **b :** to tighten firmly **11 :** to make carefully worked out plans for ⟨*set up* a bank robbery⟩ **12 a :** to pay for (drinks) **b :** to treat (someone) to something **13 a :** to put in a compromising or dangerous position usu. by trickery or deceit **b :** FRAME 3 **14 :** to execute one or more plays in preparation for scoring ~ *vi* **1 :** to come into active operation or use **2 :** to begin business **3 :** to make pretensions ⟨has never *set up* to be a wise man —Thomas Rogers⟩ **4 :** to become firm — **set up housekeeping :** to establish one's living quarters — **set up shop :** to establish one's business
sev·en \ˈse-vən, ˈse-bᵊm\ *n* [ME, fr. *seven,* adj., fr. OE *seofon;* akin to OHG *sibun* seven, L *septem,* Gk *hepta*] (bef. 12c) **1** — see NUMBER table **2 :** the seventh in a set or series ⟨the ~ of clubs⟩ **3 :** something having seven units or members — **seven** *adj* — **seven** *pron, pl in constr*
sev·en·fold \-ˌfōld\ *adj* (bef. 12c) **1 :** having seven units or members **2 :** being seven times as great or as many — **sevenfold** *adv*
seven seas *n pl* (1872) **:** all the waters or oceans of the world
sev·en·teen \ˌse-vən-ˈtēn, ˌse-bᵊm-\ *n* [*seventeen,* adj., fr. ME *seventene,* fr. OE *seofontēne;* akin to OE *tīen* ten] (14c) — see NUMBER table — **seventeen** *adj* — **seventeen** *pron, pl in constr* — **sev·en·teenth** \-ˈtēn(t)th\ *adj or n*
seventeen–year locust *n* (1817) **:** a cicada (*Magicicada septendecim*) of the U.S. that has in the North a life of seventeen years and in the South of thirteen years of which most is spent underground as a nymph and only a few weeks as a winged adult
sev·enth \ˈse-vən(t)th, ˈse-bᵊm(t)th\ *n, pl* **sevenths** \ˈse-vən(t)s, -vən(t)ths; ˈse-bᵊm(t)s, -bᵊm(t)ths\ (12c) **1** — see NUMBER table **2 a :** a musical interval embracing seven diatonic degrees **b :** a tone at this interval; *specif* **:** LEADING TONE **c :** the harmonic combination of two tones a seventh apart — **seventh** *adj or adv*
seventh chord *n* (ca. 1909) **:** a chord comprising a fundamental tone with its third, fifth, and seventh
Seventh–Day *adj* (1684) **:** advocating or practicing observance of Saturday as the Sabbath
seventh heaven *n* [fr. the seventh being the highest of the seven heavens of Islamic and cabalist doctrine] (1818) **:** a state of extreme joy
sev·en·ty \ˈse-vən-tē, ˈse-bᵊm-, -dē\ *n, pl* **-ties** [*seventy,* adj., fr. ME, fr. OE *seofontig,* short for *hundseofontig,* fr. *hundseofontig,* n., group of seventy, fr. *hund* hundred + *seofon* seven + *-tig* group of ten; akin to OE *tīen* ten] (13c) **1** — see NUMBER table **2** *pl* **:** the numbers 70 to 79; *specif* **:** the years 70 to 79 in a lifetime or century **3** *cap* **:** a Mormon elder ordained for missionary work under the apostles — **sev·en·ti·eth** \-tē-əth, -dē-\ *adj or n* — **seventy** *adj* — **seventy** *pron, pl in constr*
sev·en·ty–eight \ˌse-vən-tē-ˈāt, ˌse-bᵊm-, -dē-ˈāt\ *n* (1631) **1** — see NUMBER table **2 :** a phonograph record designed to be played at 78 revolutions per minute — usu. written 78 — **seventy–eight** *adj* — **seventy–eight** *pron, pl in constr*
sev·en–up \ˌse-və-ˈnəp, ˌse-bᵊm-ˈəp\ *n* (1830) **:** an American variety of all fours in which a total of seven points constitutes game
sev·er \ˈse-vər\ *vb* **sev·ered; sev·er·ing** \ˈsev-riŋ, ˈse-və-\ [ME, fr. AF *severer,* fr. L *separare* — more at SEPARATE] *vt* (14c) **:** to put or keep apart **:** DIVIDE; *esp* **:** to remove (as a part) by or as if by cutting ~ *vi* **:** to become separated ***syn*** see SEPARATE
sev·er·able \ˈsev-rə-bəl, ˈse-və-\ *adj* (1548) **:** capable of being severed; *esp* **:** capable of being divided into legally independent rights or obligations — **sev·er·abil·i·ty** \ˌsev-rə-ˈbi-lə-tē, ˌse-və-\ *n*
1**sev·er·al** \ˈsev-rəl, ˈse-və-\ *adj* [ME, fr. AF, fr. ML *separalis,* fr. L *separ* separate, back-formation fr. *separare* to separate] (15c) **1 a :** separate or distinct from one another ⟨federal union of the ~ states⟩ **b (1) :** individually owned or controlled **:** EXCLUSIVE ⟨a ~ fishery⟩ — compare COMMON **(2) :** of or relating separately to each individual involved ⟨a ~ judgment⟩ **c :** being separate and distinctive **:** RESPECTIVE ⟨specialists in their ~ fields⟩ **2 a :** more than one ⟨~ pleas⟩ **b :** more than two but fewer than many ⟨moved ~ inches⟩ **c** *chiefly dial* **:** being a great many
2**several** *pron, pl in constr* (1639) **:** an indefinite number more than two and fewer than many ⟨~ of the guests⟩
sev·er·al·fold \ˌsev-rəl-ˈfōld, ˌse-və-\ *adj* (1738) **1 :** having several parts or aspects **2 :** being several times as large, as great, or as many as some understood size, degree, or amount — **severalfold** *adv*
sev·er·al·ly \ˈsev-rə-lē, ˈse-və-\ *adv* (14c) **1 :** one at a time **:** each by itself **:** SEPARATELY **2 :** apart from others **:** INDEPENDENTLY
sev·er·al·ty \ˈsev-rəl-tē, ˈse-və-\ *n* [ME *severalte,* fr. AF *severalté,* fr. *several*] (15c) **1 :** the quality or state of being several **:** DISTINCTNESS, SEPARATENESS **2 a :** a sole, separate, and exclusive possession, dominion, or ownership **:** one's own right without a joint interest in any other person ⟨tenants in ~⟩ **b :** the quality or state of being individual or particular **3 a :** land owned in severalty **b :** the quality or state of being held in severalty
sev·er·ance \ˈsev-rən(t)s, ˈse-və-\ *n* (15c) **:** the act or process of severing **:** the state of being severed
severance pay *n* (1943) **:** an allowance usu. based on length of service that is payable to an employee on termination of employment
severance tax *n* (1928) **:** a tax levied by a state on the extractor of oil, gas, or minerals intended for consumption in other states — compare ROYALTY 5a
se·vere \sə-ˈvir\ *adj* **se·ver·er; -est** [MF or L; MF, fr. L *severus*] (1548) **1 a :** strict in judgment, discipline, or government **b :** of a strict or stern bearing or manner **:** AUSTERE **2 :** rigorous in restraint, punishment, or requirement **:** STRINGENT **3 :** strongly critical or condemnatory ⟨a ~ critic⟩ **4 a :** maintaining a scrupulously exacting standard of behavior or self-discipline **b :** establishing exacting standards of accuracy and integrity in intellectual processes ⟨a ~ logician⟩ **5 :** sober or restrained in decoration or manner **:** PLAIN ⟨a ~ dress⟩ **6 a :** causing discomfort or hardship **:** HARSH ⟨~ winters⟩ **b :** very painful or harmful ⟨a ~ wound⟩ **7 :** requiring great effort **:** ARDUOUS ⟨a ~ test⟩ **8 :** of a great degree ⟨~ depression⟩ — **se·vere·ly** *adv* — **se·vere·ness** *n* — **se·ver·i·ty** \sə-ˈver-ə-tē\ *n*
syn SEVERE, STERN, AUSTERE, ASCETIC mean given to or marked by strict discipline and firm restraint. SEVERE implies standards enforced without indulgence or laxity and may suggest harshness ⟨*severe* military discipline⟩. STERN stresses inflexibility and inexorability of temper or character ⟨*stern* arbiters of public morality⟩. AUSTERE stresses absence of warmth, color, or feeling and may apply to rigorous restraint, simplicity, or self-denial ⟨living an *austere* life in the country⟩. ASCETIC implies abstention from pleasure and comfort or self-indulgence as spiritual discipline ⟨the *ascetic* life of the monks⟩.
severe acute respiratory syndrome *n* (2003) **:** SARS
severe combined immunodeficiency *n* (1973) **:** a rare congenital disorder of the immune system that is characterized by inability to produce a normal complement of antibodies and T cells and that usu. results in early death — called also *severe combined immune deficiency*
se·vi·che \sə-ˈvē-(ˌ)chā, -chē\ *n* [AmerSp] (1939) **:** a dish of raw fish marinated in lime or lemon juice often with oil, onions, peppers, and seasonings and served esp. as an appetizer
Sevres *or* **Sèvres** \ˈsev-rə, ˈsev(rᵊ)\ *n* [*Sèvres,* France] (1786) **:** an often elaborately decorated French porcelain
sev·ru·ga \sə-ˈvrü-gə, se-\ *n* [Russ *sevryuga,* a species of sturgeon] (1591) **:** a gray caviar from a sturgeon (*Acipenser sevru*) of the Caspian Sea with roe that is smaller than that of osetra; *also* **:** the fish
sew \ˈsō\ *vb* **sewed; sewn** \ˈsōn\ *or* **sewed; sew·ing** [ME, fr. OE *sīwian;* akin to OHG *siuwen* to sew, L *suere*] *vt* (bef. 12c) **1 :** to unite or fasten by stitches **2 :** to close or enclose by sewing ⟨~ the money in a bag⟩ ~ *vi* **:** to practice or engage in sewing — **sew·abil·i·ty** \ˌsō-ə-ˈbi-lə-tē\ *n* — **sew·able** \ˈsō-ə-bəl\ *adj*
sew·age \ˈsü-ij\ *n* [3*sewer*] (1834) **:** refuse liquids or waste matter usu. carried off by sewers
1**sew·er** \ˈsü-ər, ˈsu̇r\ *n* [ME, fr. AF *asseour,* lit., seater, fr. AF *asseer* to seat — more at ASSIZE] (14c) **:** a medieval household officer often of high rank in charge of serving the dishes at table and sometimes of seating and tasting
2**sew·er** \ˈsō-ər\ *n* (14c) **:** one that sews
3**sew·er** \ˈsü-ər, ˈsu̇r\ *n* [ME, fr. AF, fr. *assewer, essiver* to drain, fr. VL **exaquare,* fr. L *ex-* + *aqua* water — more at ISLAND] (15c) **:** an artificial usu. subterranean conduit to carry off sewage and sometimes surface water (as from rainfall)
sew·er·age \ˈsü-ə-rij, ˈsu̇r-ij\ *n* (1834) **1 :** the removal and disposal of sewage and surface water by sewers **2 :** a system of sewers **3 :** SEWAGE
sewing *n* (14c) **1 :** the act, method, or occupation of one that sews **2 :** material that has been or is to be sewed
sew up *vt* (15c) **1 :** to mend completely by sewing **2 :** to get exclusive use or control of **3 :** to make certain of **:** be assured of ⟨the team *sewed up* the division title⟩
1**sex** \ˈseks\ *n* [ME, fr. L *sexus*] (14c) **1 :** either of the two major forms of individuals that occur in many species and that are distinguished respectively as female or male esp. on the basis of their reproductive organs and structures **2 :** the sum of the structural, functional, and behavioral characteristics of organisms that are involved in reproduction marked by the union of gametes and that distinguish males and females **3 a :** sexually motivated phenomena or behavior **b :** SEXUAL INTERCOURSE **4 :** GENITALIA
2**sex** *vt* (1884) **1 :** to identify the sex of ⟨~ newborn chicks⟩ **2 a :** to increase the sexual appeal of — often used with *up* **b :** to arouse the sexual desires of
sex act *n* (1918) **1 :** COITUS — used with *the* **2 :** an act performed with another for sexual gratification
sex·a·ge·nar·i·an \ˌsek-sə-jə-ˈner-ē-ən\ *n* [L *sexagenarius* of or containing sixty, sixty years old, fr. *sexageni* sixty each, fr. *sexaginta* sixty, fr. *sex* six + *-ginta* (akin to L *viginti* twenty) — more at SIX, VIGESIMAL] (1738) **:** a person whose age is in the sixties — **sexagenarian** *adj*
1**sex·a·ges·i·mal** \-ˈje-sə-məl\ *adj* [L *sexagesimus* sixtieth, fr. *sexaginta* sixty] (1685) **:** of, relating to, or based on the number 60
2**sexagesimal** *n* (1685) **:** a sexagesimal fraction
sex appeal *n* (1912) **1 :** personal appeal or physical attractiveness esp. for members of the opposite sex **2 :** stimulating attractiveness
sex cell *n* (1889) **:** GAMETE; *also* **:** its cellular precursor
sex chromatin *n* (1952) **:** BARR BODY
sex chromosome *n* (1906) **:** a chromosome that is inherited differently in the two sexes, that is concerned directly with the inheritance of sex, and that is the seat of factors governing the inheritance of various

sex-linked and sex-limited characters — compare X CHROMOSOME, Y CHROMOSOME

sex·de·cil·lion \ˌseks-di-ˈsil-yən\ *n, often attrib* [L *sedecim, sexdecim* sixteen (fr. *sex* six + *decem* ten) + E *-illion* (as in *million*) — more at TEN] (1848) — see NUMBER table

sexed \ˈsekst\ *adj* (1621) **1 :** having sex or sexual instincts **2 :** having sex appeal

sex gland *n* (1916) **:** GONAD

sex hormone *n* (1917) **:** a steroid hormone (as estrogen or testosterone) that is produced esp. by the ovaries, testes, or adrenal cortex and affects the growth or function of the reproductive organs or the development of secondary sex characteristics

sex·ism \ˈsek-ˌsi-zəm\ *n* [*sex* + *-ism* (as in *racism*)] (1968) **1 :** prejudice or discrimination based on sex; *esp* **:** discrimination against women **2 :** behavior, conditions, or attitudes that foster stereotypes of social roles based on sex — **sex·ist** \ˈsek-sist\ *adj or n*

sex kitten *n* (1958) **:** a young woman with conspicuous sex appeal

sex·less \ˈseks-ləs\ *adj* (1598) **1 :** lacking sex **:** NEUTER **2 :** devoid of sexual interest or activity — **sex·less·ly** *adv* — **sex·less·ness** *n*

sex–lim·it·ed \ˈseks-ˈli-mə-təd\ *adj* (1923) **:** expressed in the phenotype of only one sex

sex–link·age \-ˌliŋ-kij\ *n* (1912) **:** the quality or state of being sex-linked

sex–linked \-ˌliŋ(k)t\ *adj* (1912) **1 :** located on a sex chromosome ⟨a ~ gene⟩ **2 :** mediated by a sex-linked gene ⟨a ~ character⟩

sex object *n* (1911) **:** a person regarded esp. exclusively as an object of sexual interest

sex offender *n* (1911) **:** a person who has been convicted of a crime involving sex

sex·ol·o·gy \sek-ˈsä-lə-jē\ *n* (1867) **:** the study of sex or of the interaction of the sexes esp. among human beings — **sex·ol·o·gist** \-jist\ *n*

sex·ploi·ta·tion \ˌseks-ˌplȯi-ˈtā-shən\ *n* [blend of *sex* and *exploitation*] (ca. 1942) **:** the exploitation of sex in the media and esp. in film

sex·pot \ˈseks-ˌpät\ *n* (1948) **:** a conspicuously sexy woman

sex symbol *n* (ca. 1911) **:** a usu. renowned person (as an entertainer) noted and admired for conspicuous sex appeal

sext \ˈsekst\ *n, often cap* [ME *sexte,* fr. LL *sexta,* fr. L, sixth hour of the day, fr. fem. of *sextus* sixth, fr. *sex* six] (15c) **:** the fourth of the canonical hours

Sex·tans \ˈseks-ˌtanz\ *n* [NL (gen. *Sextantis*), lit., sextant] (1795) **:** a constellation on the equator south of Leo

sex·tant \ˈseks-tənt\ *n* [NL *sextant-, sextans* sixth part of a circle, fr. L, sixth part, fr. *sextus* sixth] (1628) **:** an instrument for measuring angular distances used esp. in navigation to observe altitudes of celestial bodies (as in ascertaining latitude and longitude)

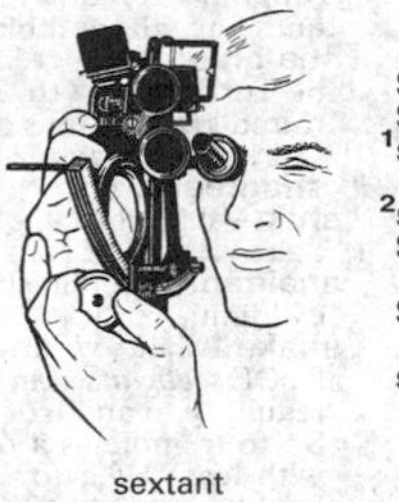
sextant

sex·tet \seks-ˈtet\ *n* [alter. of *sestet*] (1841) **1 :** a musical composition for six instruments or voices **2 :** a group or set of six: as **a :** the performers of a sextet **b :** a hockey team

sex·til·lion \seks-ˈtil-yən\ *n, often attrib* [F, irreg. fr. *sex-* (fr. L *sex*) + *-illion* (as in *million*)] (1690) — see NUMBER table

sex·ting \ˈsek-stiŋ\ *n* [blend of *sex* and *texting*] (2007) **:** the sending of sexually explicit messages or images by cell phone

sex·to \ˈseks-(ˌ)tō\ *n, pl* **sextos** [L *sexto,* abl. of *sextus* sixth] (1847) **:** SIXMO

sex·to·dec·i·mo \ˌseks-tə-ˈde-sə-ˌmō\ *n, pl* **-mos** [L, abl. of *sextus decimus* sixteenth, fr. *sextus* sixth + *decimus* tenth — more at DIME] (1688) **:** SIXTEENMO

sex·ton \ˈseks-tən\ *n* [ME *secresteyn, sexteyn,* fr. AF *segrestein,* fr. ML *sacristanus* — more at SACRISTAN] (14c) **:** a church officer or employee who takes care of the church property and performs related minor duties (as ringing the bell for services and digging graves)

1**sex·tu·ple** \seks-ˈtü-pəl, -ˈtyü-, -ˈtə-; ˈseks-tə-\ *adj* [prob. fr. ML *sextuplus,* fr. L *sextus* sixth + *-plus* multiplied by; akin to L *-plex* -plex — more at -FOLD] (1626) **1 :** having six units or members **2 :** being six times as great or as many **3 :** marked by six beats per measure of music ⟨~ time⟩ — **sextuple** *n*

2**sextuple** *vb* **sex·tu·pled; sex·tu·pling** \-p(ə-)liŋ\ *vt* (1632) **:** to make six times as much or as many ~ *vi* **:** to become six times as much or as numerous

sex·tu·plet \seks-ˈtə-plət, -ˈtü-; -ˈtyü-; ˈseks-t(y)ə-\ *n* (1852) **1 :** a combination of six of a kind **2 :** one of six offspring born at one birth **3 :** a group of six equal musical notes performed in the time ordinarily given to four of the same value

1**sex·tu·pli·cate** \seks-ˈtü-pli-kət, -ˈtyü-\ *adj* [blend of *sextuple* and *-plicate* (as in *duplicate*)] (1657) **1 :** repeated six times **2 :** SIXTH ⟨file the ~ copy⟩ — **sextuplicate** *n*

2**sex·tu·pli·cate** \-plə-ˌkāt\ *vt* **-cat·ed; -cat·ing** (ca. 1934) **1 :** SEXTUPLE **2 :** to provide in sextuplicate

sex·u·al \ˈsek-sh(ə-)wəl, ˈsek-shəl\ *adj* [LL *sexualis,* fr. L *sexus* sex] (1651) **1 :** of, relating to, or associated with sex or the sexes ⟨~ differentiation⟩ ⟨~ conflict⟩ **2 :** having or involving sex ⟨~ reproduction⟩ — **sex·u·al·ly** \ˈsek-sh(ə-)wə-lē, ˈsek-sh(ə-)lē\ *adv*

sexual assault *n* (1971) **:** illegal sexual contact that usu. involves force upon a person without consent or is inflicted upon a person who is incapable of giving consent (as because of age or physical or mental incapacity) or who places the assailant (as a doctor) in a position of trust or authority

sexual generation *n* (1880) **:** the generation of an organism with alternation of generations that reproduces sexually

sexual harassment *n* (1973) **:** uninvited and unwelcome verbal or physical behavior of a sexual nature esp. by a person in authority toward a subordinate (as an employee or student)

sexual intercourse *n* (1799) **1 :** heterosexual intercourse involving penetration of the vagina by the penis **:** COITUS **2 :** intercourse (as anal or oral intercourse) that does not involve penetration of the vagina by the penis

sex·u·al·i·ty \ˌsek-shə-ˈwa-lə-tē\ *n* (1797) **:** the quality or state of being sexual: **a :** the condition of having sex **b :** sexual activity **c :** expression of sexual receptivity or interest esp. when excessive

sex·u·al·ize \ˈsek-sh(ə-)wə-ˌlīz, ˈsek-shə-ˌlīz\ *vt* **-ized; -iz·ing** (1839) **:** to make sexual **:** endow with a sexual character or cast

sexual predator *n* (1985) **:** a person who has committed a sexually violent offense and esp. one who is likely to commit more sexual offenses

sexual relations *n pl* (1890) **:** SEXUAL INTERCOURSE

sexual selection *n* (1859) **:** natural selection for characters that confer success in competition for a mate as distinguished from competition with other species; *also* **:** the choice of a mate based on a preference for certain characteristics (as color or bird song)

sex worker *n* (1971) **:** a person whose work involves sexually explicit behavior; *esp* **:** PROSTITUTE 1

sexy \ˈsek-sē\ *adj* **sex·i·er; -est** (1912) **1 :** sexually suggestive or stimulating **:** EROTIC **2 :** generally attractive or interesting **:** APPEALING ⟨a ~ stock⟩ — **sex·i·ly** \-sə-lē\ *adv* — **sex·i·ness** \-sē-nəs\ *n*

Sey·fert galaxy \ˈsē-fərt- *also* ˈsī-\ *n* [Carl K. *Seyfert* †1960 Am. astronomer] (1959) **:** any of a class of spiral galaxies that have small compact bright nuclei characterized by variability in light intensity, emission of radio waves, and spectra — called also *Seyfert*

sf *or* **sfz** *abbr* sforzando

SF *abbr* **1** sacrifice fly **2** science fiction **3** sinking fund **4** square feet; square foot

SFC *abbr* sergeant first class

sfer·ics \ˈsfir-iks, ˈsfer-\ *n pl* [by shortening & alter.] (1945) **:** ATMOSPHERICS

1**sfor·zan·do** \sfȯrt-ˈsän-(ˌ)dō, -ˈsan-\ *adj or adv* [It, verbal of *sforzare* to force] (ca. 1801) **:** played with prominent stress or accent — used as a direction in music

2**sforzando** *n, pl* **-dos** *or* **-di** \-(ˌ)dē\ (1890) **:** an accented tone or chord

sfu·ma·to \sfü-ˈmä-(ˌ)tō\ *n* [It, fr. pp. of *sfumare* to evaporate] (1909) **:** the definition of form in painting without abrupt outline by the blending of one tone into another

Sg *symbol* seaborgium

SG *abbr* **1** sergeant **2** solicitor general **3** *often not cap* specific gravity **4** surgeon general

sgd *abbr* signed

SGML \ˌes-(ˌ)jē-(ˌ)em-ˈel\ *n* [*s*tandard *g*eneralized *m*arkup *l*anguage] (1983) **:** a markup language used to define the structure of and manage documents in electronic form — compare HTML

sgraf·fi·to \zgra-ˈfē-(ˌ)tō, skra-\ *n, pl* **-ti** \-(ˌ)tē\ [It, fr. pp. of *sgraffire* to scratch, produce sgraffito] (ca. 1730) **1 :** decoration by cutting away parts of a surface layer (as of plaster or clay) to expose a different colored ground — compare GRAFFITO **2 :** something (as traditional Pennsylvania Dutch pottery) decorated with sgraffito

Sgt *abbr* sergeant

Sgt Maj *abbr* sergeant major

1**sh** \sh *often prolonged*\ *interj* (1847) — used often in prolonged or rapidly repeated form to urge or command silence or less noise

2**sh** *abbr* share

Sha·ban \shə-ˈbän\ *n* [Ar *shaʿbān*] (ca. 1771) **:** the eighth month of the Islamic year — see MONTH table

Shab·bat \shə-ˈbät, ˈshä-bəs\ *n* [Heb *shabbāth*] (ca. 1905) **:** the Jewish Sabbath

shab·by \ˈsha-bē\ *adj* **shab·bi·er; -est** [obs. E *shab* a low fellow] (1669) **1 :** clothed with worn or seedy garments ⟨a ~ hobo⟩ **2 a :** threadbare and faded from wear ⟨a ~ sofa⟩ **b :** ill-kept **:** DILAPIDATED ⟨a ~ neighborhood⟩ **3 a :** MEAN, DESPICABLE, CONTEMPTIBLE ⟨must feel ~ . . . because of his compromises —Nat Hentoff⟩ **b :** UNGENEROUS, UNFAIR ⟨laments the ~ way in which this country often treated a poet —Paul Engle⟩ **c :** inferior in quality ⟨~ reasoning⟩ — **shab·bi·ly** \ˈsha-bə-lē\ *adv* — **shab·bi·ness** \ˈsha-bē-nəs\ *n*

Shabuoth *var of* SHAVUOT

sha·bu–sha·bu \ˈshä-bü-ˈshä-bü\ *n* [Jp, of imit. origin] (1967) **:** a Japanese dish consisting of thinly sliced beef and vegetables cooked briefly in simmering broth at the table

shack \ˈshak\ *n* [prob. back-formation fr. E dial. *shackly* rickety] (1878) **1 :** HUT, SHANTY **2 :** a room or similar enclosed structure for a particular person or use ⟨a guard ~⟩

1**shack·le** \ˈsha-kəl\ *n* [ME *schakel,* fr. OE *sceacul;* akin to ON *skǫkull* pole of a cart] (bef. 12c) **1 :** something (as a manacle or fetter) that confines the legs or arms **2 :** something that checks or prevents free action as if by fetters — usu. used in pl. **3 :** a usu. U-shaped fastening device secured by a bolt or pin through holes in the end of the two arms **4 :** a length of cable or anchor chain of usu. 15 fathoms

2**shackle** *vt* **shack·led; shack·ling** \-k(ə-)liŋ\ (15c) **1 a :** to bind with shackles **:** FETTER **b :** to make fast with or as if with a shackle **2 :** to deprive of freedom esp. of action by means of restrictions or handicaps **:** IMPEDE *syn* see HAMPER — **shack·ler** \-k(ə-)lər\ *n*

shack·le·bone \ˈsha-kəl-ˌbōn, ˈshā-\ *n* (1571) *Scot* **:** WRIST

shack up *vi* (1935) **:** to sleep or live together as unmarried sexual partners

shad \ˈshad\ *n, pl* **shad** [ME **shad,* fr. OE *sceadd*] (bef. 12c) **:** any of several fishes (esp. genus *Alosa*) of the herring family that differ from the typical herrings (genus *Clupeus*) in having a relatively deep body and in being anadromous and that include some important food fishes of Europe and No. America

shad·ber·ry \-ˌber-ē\ *n* (1847) **:** SERVICEBERRY

shad·blow \ˈshad-ˌblō\ *n* (1846) **:** SERVICEBERRY 2

shad·bush \-ˌbu̇sh\ *n* (ca. 1818) **:** SERVICEBERRY 2

shad·dock \ˈsha-dək\ *n* [Captain *Shaddock,* 17th cent. Eng. ship commander] (1696) **:** POMELO 2

1**shade** \ˈshād\ *n* [ME, fr. OE *sceadu;* akin to OHG *scato* shadow, Gk *skotos* darkness] (bef. 12c) **1 a :** comparative darkness or obscurity owing to interception of the rays of light **b :** relative obscurity or retirement **2 a :** shelter (as by foliage) from the heat and glare of sunlight **b :** a place sheltered from the sun **3 :** an evanescent or unreal appearance **4** *pl* **a :** the shadows that gather as darkness comes on b : NETHERWORLD, HADES 5 a : a disembodied spirit : GHOST b — used to signal the similarity between a previously encountered person or situation and one at hand; usu. used in pl. ⟨~*s* of my childhood⟩ 6 : something that intercepts or shelters from light, sun, or heat: as a : a device partially covering a lamp so as to reduce glare b : a flexible screen usu. mounted on a roller for regulating the light or the view through a window c *pl* : SUNGLASSES 7 a : the reproduction of the effect of shade in painting or drawing b : a subdued or somber feature 8 a : a color produced by a pigment or dye mixture having some black in it b : a color slightly different from the one under consideration 9 a : a minute difference or variation : NUANCE b : a minute degree or quantity 10 : a facial expression of sadness or displeasure — **shade·less** \-ləs\ *adj*

[2]**shade** *vb* **shad·ed; shad·ing** *vt* (14c) 1 a : to shelter or screen by intercepting radiated light or heat b : to cover with a shade 2 : to hide partly by or as if by a shadow 3 : to darken with or as if with a shadow 4 : to better or exceed by a shade 5 a : to represent the effect of shade or shadow on b : to add shading to c : to color so that the shades pass gradually from one to another 6 : to change by gradual transition or qualification 7 : to reduce slightly (as a price) 8 : SLANT, BIAS ~ *vi* 1 : to pass by slight changes or imperceptible degrees 2 : to undergo or exhibit minute difference or variation — **shad·er** *n*

shade–grown \'shād-ˌgrōn\ *adj* (1922) : grown in the shade; *specif* : grown under cloth ⟨~ tobacco⟩

shade tree *n* (1806) : a tree grown primarily to produce shade

shading *n* (1663) 1 : the use of marking made within outlines to suggest three-dimensionality, shadow, or degrees of light and dark in a picture or drawing 2 : an interpretative effect in music gained esp. by subtle changes in dynamics

sha·doof *also* **sha·duf** \shə-'düf, sha-\ *n* [Ar *shādūf*] (1836) : a counterbalanced sweep used since ancient times esp. in Egypt for raising water (as for irrigation)

[1]**shad·ow** \'sha-(ˌ)dō\ *n* [ME *shadwe,* fr. OE *sceaduw-, sceadu* shade] (bef. 12c) 1 : partial darkness or obscurity within a part of space from which rays from a source of light are cut off by an interposed opaque body 2 : a reflected image 3 : shelter from danger or observation 4 a : an imperfect and faint representation b : an imitation of something : COPY 5 : the dark figure cast upon a surface by a body intercepting the rays from a source of light 6 : PHANTOM 7 *pl* : DARK 1a 8 : a shaded or darker portion of a picture 9 : an attenuated form or a vestigial remnant 10 a : an inseparable companion or follower b : one (as a spy or detective) that shadows 11 : a small degree or portion : TRACE 12 : a source of gloom or unhappiness 13 a : an area near an object : VICINITY b : pervasive and dominant influence 14 : a state of ignominy or obscurity — **shad·ow·less** \'sha-dō-ləs, -də-ləs\ *adj* — **shad·ow·like** \-ˌlīk\ *adj*

[2]**shadow** *vt* (bef. 12c) 1 *archaic* : SHELTER, PROTECT 2 : to cast a shadow upon : CLOUD 3 *obs* : to shelter from the sun 4 *obs* : CONCEAL 5 : to represent or indicate obscurely or faintly — often used with *forth* or *out* 6 a : to follow esp. secretly : TRAIL b : to accompany and observe esp. in a professional setting 7 *archaic* : SHADE 5 ~ *vi* 1 : to pass gradually or by degrees 2 : to become overcast with or as if with shadows — **shad·ow·er** \-dō-ər, -də-wər\ *n*

[3]**shadow** *adj* (1906) 1 : of, relating to, or resembling a shadow cabinet ⟨~ minister of defense⟩ 2 a : having an indistinct pattern ⟨~ plaid⟩ b : having darker sections of design ⟨~ lace⟩

shad·ow·box \'sha-dō-ˌbäks, -də-ˌbäks\ *vi* (1924) : to box with an imaginary opponent esp. as a form of training

shadow box *n* (1891) : a shallow enclosing case usu. with a glass front in which something is set for protection and display

shadow cabinet *n* (1906) : a group of leaders of a parliamentary opposition who constitute the probable membership of the cabinet when their party is returned to power

shadow dance *n* (ca. 1909) : a dance shown by throwing the shadows of dancers on a screen

shad·ow·graph \'sha-dō-ˌgraf, -də-ˌgraf\ *n* (1886) 1 : SHADOW PLAY 2 : a photographic image resembling a shadow — **shad·ow·graphy** \-ˌgra-fē\ *n*

shadow mask *n* (1951) : a metal plate in a color cathode-ray tube that contains minute apertures permitting passage of electron beams to specific phosphors on the screen during a scan

shadow play *n* (ca. 1890) : a drama exhibited by throwing shadows of puppets or actors on a screen — called also *shadow show*

shad·owy \'sha-dō-ē, -də-wē\ *adj* (14c) 1 a : of the nature of or resembling a shadow b : faintly perceptible : INDISTINCT 2 : being in or obscured by shadow ⟨deep ~ interiors⟩ 3 a : SHADY 1 b : SHADY 3 — **shad·ow·i·ly** \-wə-lē\ *adv* — **shad·ow·i·ness** \-wē-nəs\ *n*

shady \'shā-dē\ *adj* **shad·i·er; -est** (1579) 1 : producing or affording shade 2 : sheltered from the sun's rays 3 a : of questionable merit : UNCERTAIN, UNRELIABLE b : DISREPUTABLE — **shad·i·ly** \'shā-dᵊl-ē\ *adv* — **shad·i·ness** \'shā-dē-nəs\ *n*

[1]**shaft** \'shaft\ *n, pl* **shafts** \'shaf(t)s, *for 1b usu* 'shavz\ [ME, fr. OE *sceaft;* akin to OHG *scaft* shaft, L *scapus* shaft, stalk, Gk *skēptesthai* to prop oneself, lean] (bef. 12c) 1 a (1) : the long handle of a spear or similar weapon (2) : SPEAR, LANCE b *or pl* **shaves** \'shavz\ : POLE; *specif* : either of two long pieces of wood between which a horse is hitched to a vehicle c (1) : an arrow esp. for a longbow (2) : the body or stem of an arrow extending from the nock to the head 2 : a sharply delineated beam of light shining through an opening 3 : something suggestive of the shaft of a spear or arrow esp. in long slender cylindrical form: as a : the trunk of a tree b : the cylindrical pillar between the capital and the base c : the handle of a tool or instrument (as a golf club) d : a commonly cylindrical bar used to support rotating pieces or to transmit power or motion by rotation e : the stem or central axis of a feather f : the upright member of a cross esp. below the arms g : the cylindrical part of a long bone between the enlarged ends h : a small architectural column (as at each side of a doorway) i : a column, obelisk, or other spire-shaped or columnar monument j : a vertical or inclined opening of uniform and limited cross section made for finding or mining ore, raising water, or ventilating underground workings (as in a cave) k : the part of a hair that is visible above the surface of the skin l : a vertical opening or passage through the floors of a building 4 a : a projectile thrown like a spear or shot like an arrow b : a scornful, satirical, or pithily critical remark or attack c : harsh or unfair treatment — usu. used with *the* ⟨gave them the ~⟩

[2]**shaft** *vt* (1611) 1 : to fit with a shaft 2 : to treat unfairly or harshly

shaft horsepower *n* (1908) : horsepower transmitted by an engine shaft

shaft·ing \'shaf-tiŋ\ *n* (1825) : shafts or material for shafts

[1]**shag** \'shag\ *n* [ME **shagge,* fr. OE *sceacga;* akin to ON *skegg* beard, *skaga* to project] (bef. 12c) 1 a : a shaggy tangled mass or covering (as of hair) b : long coarse or matted fiber, nap, or pile c : a layered haircut of uneven length 2 : tobacco cut into fine shreds 3 : any of various waterbirds related to the cormorants; *also* : CORMORANT 1

[2]**shag** *adj* (1581) : SHAGGY

[3]**shag** *vb* **shagged; shag·ging** *vi* (1596) : to fall or hang in shaggy masses ~ *vt* : to make rough or shaggy

[4]**shag** *vt* **shagged shag·ging** [earlier argot, prob. ultim. fr. ME *shoggen, shaggen* to shake — more at SHOG] (1788) *chiefly Brit, usu vulgar* : to have sexual intercourse with

[5]**shag** *vt* **shagged; shag·ging** [origin unknown] (1896) 1 a : to chase after; *esp* : to chase after and return (a ball) hit usu. out of play b : to catch (a fly) in baseball practice 2 : to chase away

[6]**shag** *vi* **shagged; shag·ging** [var. of *shog*] (1914) 1 : to move or lope along 2 : to dance the shag

[7]**shag** *n* (1932) : a dance step executed by hopping livelily on each foot in turn

shag·bark \'shag-ˌbärk\ *n* (1777) : SHAGBARK HICKORY

shagbark hickory *n* (1751) : a hickory (*Carya ovata*) of eastern No. America with sweet edible nuts and a gray shaggy outer bark that peels off in long strips; *also* : its wood

shag·gy \'sha-gē\ *adj* **shag·gi·er; -est** (1581) 1 a : covered with or consisting of long, coarse, or matted hair b : covered with or consisting of thick, tangled, or unkempt vegetation c : having a rough nap, texture, or surface d : having hairlike processes 2 a : UNKEMPT b : confused or unclear in conception or thinking ⟨~ ideas⟩ ⟨a ~ argument⟩ — **shag·gi·ly** \'sha-gə-lē\ *adv* — **shag·gi·ness** \'sha-gē-nəs\ *n*

shag·gy–dog \ˌsha-gē-'dȯg\ *adj* (1946) : of, relating to, or being a long-drawn-out circumstantial story concerning an inconsequential happening that impresses the teller as humorous or interesting but the hearer as boring and pointless; *also* : of, relating to, or being a similar humorous story whose humor lies in the pointlessness or irrelevance of the punch line ⟨a ~ comedy⟩

shag·gy·mane \'sha-gē-ˌmān\ *n* (1895) : a common edible white mushroom (*Coprinus comatus*) having an elongated shaggy white pileus with deliquescing gills and black spores — called also *shaggy cap*

sha·green \sha-'grēn, shə-\ *n* [by folk etymology fr. F *chagrin,* modif. of Turk *sağrı*] (1677) 1 : an untanned leather covered with small round granulations and usu. dyed green 2 : the rough skin of various sharks and rays when covered with small close-set tubercles — **shagreen** *adj*

shah \'shä, 'shȯ\ *n, often cap* [Pers *shāh* king — more at CHECK] (1566) : a sovereign of Iran — **shah·dom** \'shä-dəm, 'shȯ-\ *n*

shai·tan \shā-'tän, shī-\ *n* [Ar *shayṭān*] (1638) : an evil spirit; *specif* : an evil jinni

[1]**shake** \'shāk\ *vb* **shook** \'shu̇k\; **shak·en** \'shā-kən\; **shak·ing** [ME, fr. OE *sceacan;* akin to ON *skaka* to shake] *vi* (bef. 12c) 1 : to move irregularly to and fro 2 : to vibrate esp. as the result of a blow or shock 3 : to tremble as a result of physical or emotional disturbance ⟨*shook* with fear⟩ 4 : to experience a state of instability : TOTTER 5 : to briskly move something to and fro or up and down esp. in order to mix 6 : to clasp hands 7 : [3]TRILL ~ *vt* 1 : to brandish, wave, or flourish often in a threatening manner ⟨protesters *shaking* their fists⟩ 2 : to cause to move to and fro, up and down, or from side to side esp. in a repetitive, rhythmic, or quick jerky manner ⟨*shook* his head in disapproval⟩ 3 : to cause to quake, quiver, or tremble 4 a : to free oneself from ⟨~ a habit⟩ ⟨~ off a cold⟩ b : to get away from : get rid of ⟨can you ~ your friend? I want to talk to you alone —Elmer Davis⟩ 5 : to lessen the stability of : WEAKEN ⟨~ one's faith⟩ 6 : to bring to a specified condition by or as if by repeated quick jerky movements ⟨*shook* himself loose from the man's grasp⟩ 7 : to dislodge or eject by quick jerky movements of the support or container ⟨*shook* the dust from the cloth⟩ 8 : to clasp (hands) in greeting or farewell or as a sign of goodwill or agreement 9 : to stir the feelings of : UPSET, AGITATE ⟨*shook* her up⟩ 10 : [3]TRILL — **shak·able** *or* **shake·able** \'shā-kə-bəl\ *adj* — **shake a leg** 1 : DANCE 2 : to hurry up — **shake a stick at** : to form a conception of (as by counting or imagining) : CONCEIVE — usu. used in the phrase *more than one can shake a stick at*

syn SHAKE, AGITATE, ROCK, CONVULSE mean to move up and down or to and fro with some violence. SHAKE often carries a further implication of a particular purpose ⟨*shake* well before using⟩. AGITATE suggests a violent and prolonged tossing or stirring ⟨an ocean *agitated* by storms⟩. ROCK suggests a swinging or swaying motion resulting from violent impact or upheaval ⟨the whole city was *rocked* by the explosion⟩. CONVULSE suggests a violent pulling or wrenching as of a body in a paroxysm ⟨spectators were *convulsed* with laughter⟩.

[2]**shake** *n* (1581) 1 : an act of shaking: as a : an act of shaking hands b : an act of shaking oneself 2 a : a blow or shock that upsets the equilibrium or disturbs the balance of something b : EARTHQUAKE 3 *pl* a : a condition of trembling or nervousness; *specif* : DELIRIUM TREMENS b : MALARIA 2a 4 : something produced by shaking: as a : a fissure separating annual rings of growth in timber b (1) : MILK SHAKE (2) : a beverage resembling a milk shake but made without milk 5 : a wavering, quivering, or alternating motion caused by a blow or shock 6 : TRILL 7 : a very brief period of time ⟨I'll be there in two ~*s*⟩ 8 *pl* : one that is exceptional esp. in importance, ability, or merit — usu. used in the phrase *no great shakes* 9 : a shingle split from a piece of log usu. three or four feet (about one meter) long 10 : [3]DEAL 3 ⟨a fair ~⟩

shake·down \'shāk-ˌdau̇n\ *n* (ca. 1730) 1 : an improvised bed (as one made up on the floor) 2 : a boisterous dance 3 : an act or instance of shaking someone down; *esp* : EXTORTION 4 : a thorough search 5 : a process or period of adjustment 6 : a testing under operating conditions of something new (as a ship) for possible faults and defects and for familiarizing the operators with it

shake down *vi* (ca. 1859) 1 a : to take up temporary quarters b : to occupy an improvised or makeshift bed 2 a : to become accustomed esp. to new surroundings or duties **b :** to settle down ~ *vt* **1 :** to obtain money from in a deceitful, contemptible, or illegal manner ⟨racketeers *shaking down* store owners for protection⟩ **2 :** to make a thorough search of **3 :** to bring about a reduction of **4 :** to give a shakedown test to ⟨*shook down* the vessel before its maiden voyage⟩

shake·out \ˈshāk-ˌau̇t\ *n* (1895) **1 :** the failure or retrenchment of a significant number of firms in the economy or a sector or an industry that usu. results in a depressed market **2 :** a period or process in which the relatively weak or unessential are eliminated

shake out *vi* (1982) **:** to prove to be in the end **:** TURN OUT ⟨wait to see how things *shake out*⟩

shak·er \ˈshā-kər\ *n* (15c) **1 :** one that shakes: as **a :** a utensil or machine used in shaking ⟨cocktail ~⟩ **b :** one that incites, promotes, or directs action ⟨a mover and ~⟩ **2** *cap* [fr. a dance with shaking movements performed as part of worship] **:** a member of a millenarian sect originating in England in 1747 and practicing celibacy and an ascetic communal life — **Shaker** *adj* — **Shak·er·ism** \-kə-ˌri-zəm\ *n*

[1]**Shake·spear·ean** *or* **Shake·spear·ian** *also* **Shak·sper·ean** *or* **Shak·sper·ian** \shāk-ˈspir-ē-ən\ *adj* (1755) **1 :** of, relating to, or having the characteristics of Shakespeare or his writings **2 :** evocative of a theme, setting, or event from a work of Shakespeare ⟨~ pageantry⟩

[2]**Shakespearean** *or* **Shakespearian** *also* **Shaksperean** *or* **Shaksperian** *n* (1837) **:** an authority on or devotee of Shakespeare

Shake·spear·eana *or* **Shake·spear·iana** \(ˌ)shāk-ˌspir-ē-ˈa-nə, -ˈä-, -ˈā-\ *n pl* (1718) **:** collected items by, about, or relating to Shakespeare

Shakespearean sonnet *n* (1903) **:** ENGLISH SONNET

shake–up \ˈshāk-ˌəp\ *n* (1847) **:** an act or instance of shaking up; *specif* **:** an extensive and often drastic reorganization

shake up *vt* (1538) **1** *obs* **:** CHIDE, SCOLD **2 :** to jar by or as if by a physical shock ⟨the collision *shook up* both drivers⟩ **3 :** to effect an extensive and often drastic reorganization of

shaking palsy *n* (1817) **:** PARKINSON'S DISEASE

sha·ko \ˈsha-(ˌ)kō, ˈshā-, ˈshä-\ *n, pl* **shakos** *or* **shakoes** [F, fr. Hung *csákó*] (1793) **:** a stiff military hat with a high crown and plume

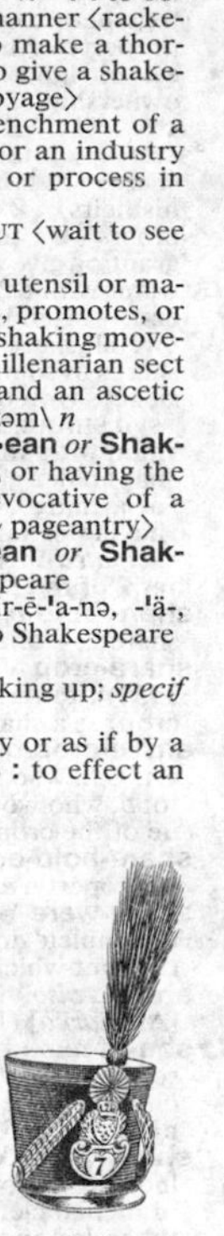

shako

Shak·ta *also* **Sak·ta** \ˈshäk-tə, ˈsäk-\ *n or adj* [Skt *śākta*, fr. *Śakti*] (1810) **:** an adherent of Shaktism

Shak·ti *also* **Sak·ti** \-tē\ *n* [Skt *Śakti*] (1810) **:** the dynamic energy of a Hindu god personified as his female consort; *broadly* **:** cosmic energy as conceived in Hindu thought

Shak·tism *also* **Sak·tism** \-ˌti-zəm\ *n* (1877) **:** a Hindu sect worshipping Shakti under various names (as Kali or Durga) in a cult of devotion to the female principle often with magical or orgiastic rites

shaky \ˈshā-kē\ *adj* **shak·i·er; -est** (1703) **1 :** characterized by shakes ⟨~ timber⟩ **2 a :** lacking stability **:** PRECARIOUS ⟨a ~ economy⟩ ⟨performed well after a ~ start⟩ **b :** lacking in firmness (as of beliefs or principles) **c :** lacking in authority or reliability **:** QUESTIONABLE ⟨~ experimental procedures⟩ ⟨~ data⟩ **3 a :** somewhat unsound in health **b :** characterized by shaking **4 :** likely to give way or break down — **shak·i·ly** \-kə-lē\ *adv* — **shak·i·ness** \-kē-nəs\ *n*

shale \ˈshāl\ *n* [prob. fr. obs. or dial. *shale* scale, shell, fr. ME, fr. OE *scealu* — more at SHELL] (1747) **:** a fissile rock that is formed by the consolidation of clay, mud, or silt, has a finely stratified or laminated structure, and is composed of minerals essentially unaltered since deposition — **shal·ey** *also* **shaly** \ˈshā-lē\ *adj*

shale oil *n* (1857) **:** a crude dark oil obtained from oil shale by heating

shall \shəl, ˈshal\ *vb, past* **should** \shəd, ˈshu̇d\; *pres sing & pl* **shall** [ME *shal* (1st & 3d sing. pres. indic.), fr. OE *sceal;* akin to OHG *scal* (1st & 3d sing. pres. indic.) ought to, must, Lith *skola* debt] *verbal auxiliary* (bef. 12c) **1** *archaic* **a :** will have to **:** MUST **b :** will be able to **:** CAN **2 a** — used to express a command or exhortation ⟨you ~ go⟩ **b** — used in laws, regulations, or directives to express what is mandatory ⟨it ~ be unlawful to carry firearms⟩ **3 a** — used to express what is inevitable or seems likely to happen in the future ⟨we ~ have to be ready⟩ ⟨we ~ see⟩ **b** — used to express simple futurity ⟨when ~ we expect you⟩ **4** — used to express determination ⟨they ~ not pass⟩ ~ *vi, archaic* **:** will go ⟨he to England ~ along with you —Shak.⟩

usage From the reams of pronouncements written about the distinction between *shall* and *will*—dating back as far as the 17th century—it is clear that the rules laid down have never very accurately reflected actual usage. The nationalistic statements of 18th and 19th century British grammarians, who commonly cited the misuses of the Irish, the Scots, and occas. the Americans, suggest that the traditional rules may have come closest to the usage of southern England. Some modern commentators believe that English usage is still the closest to the traditionally prescribed norms. Most modern commentators allow that *will* is more common in nearly all uses. The entries for *shall* and *will* in this dictionary show current usage.

shal·loon \shə-ˈlün, sha-\ *n* [*Châlons*-sur-Marne, France] (1665) **:** a lightweight twilled fabric of wool or worsted

shal·lop \ˈsha-ləp\ *n* [MF *chaloupe*] (ca. 1578) **1 :** a usu. 2-masted ship with lugsails **2 :** a small open boat propelled by oars or sails and used chiefly in shallow waters

shal·lot \shə-ˈlät *also* ˈsha-lət\ *n* [modif. of F *échalote*, fr. MF *eschalotte*, alter. of *eschaloigne*, fr. VL **escalonia* — more at SCALLION] (1664) **1 :** a bulbous perennial onion (*Allium cepa aggregatum*) that produces small clustered bulbs which resemble those of garlic and are used in seasoning; *also* **:** its bulb **2 :** GREEN ONION

[1]**shal·low** \ˈsha-(ˌ)lō\ *adj* [ME *schalowe;* prob. akin to OE *sceald* shallow — more at SKELETON] (14c) **1 :** having little depth ⟨~ water⟩ **2 :** having little extension inward or backward ⟨office buildings have taken the form of ~ slabs —Lewis Mumford⟩ **3 a :** penetrating only the easily or quickly perceived ⟨~ generalizations⟩ **b :** lacking in depth of knowledge, thought, or feeling ⟨a ~ demagogue⟩ **4 :** displacing comparatively little air **:** WEAK ⟨~ breathing⟩ ***syn*** see SUPERFICIAL — **shal·low·ly** \-lō-lē, -lə-lē\ *adv* — **shal·low·ness** *n*

[2]**shallow** *vt* (1510) **:** to make shallow ~ *vi* **:** to become shallow

[3]**shallow** *n* (1569) **:** a shallow place or area in a body of water — usu. used in pl. but sing. or pl. in constr.

sha·lom *also* **sho·lom** \shä-ˈlōm, shə-\ *interj* [Heb *shālōm* peace] (1904) — used as a Jewish greeting and farewell

shalt \shəlt, ˈshalt\ *archaic pres 2d sing of* SHALL

[1]**sham** \ˈsham\ *n* [perh. fr. E dial. *sham* shame, alter. of E *shame*] (1677) **1 :** a trick that deludes **:** HOAX ⟨feared that the deal was a ~⟩ **2 :** cheap falseness **:** HYPOCRISY ⟨saw through the hollowness, the ~, the silliness of the empty pageant —Oscar Wilde⟩ **3 :** an ornamental covering for a pillow **4 :** an imitation or counterfeit purporting to be genuine **5 :** a person who shams ***syn*** see IMPOSTURE

[2]**sham** *adj* (1681) **1 :** not genuine **:** FALSE, FEIGNED **2 :** having such poor quality as to seem false

[3]**sham** *vb* **shammed; sham·ming** *vt* (1739) **:** to go through the external motions necessary to counterfeit ~ *vi* **:** to act intentionally so as to give a false impression **:** FEIGN ***syn*** see ASSUME — **sham·mer** \ˈsha-mər\ *n*

sha·man \ˈshä-mən, ˈshā- *also* shə-ˈmän\ *n, pl* **shamans** [ultim. fr. Evenki (Tungusic language of Siberia) *šamān*] (1698) **1 :** a priest or priestess who uses magic for the purpose of curing the sick, divining the hidden, and controlling events **2 :** one who resembles a shaman; *esp* **:** HIGH PRIEST 3 — **sha·man·ic** \shə-ˈma-nik, -ˈmä-\ *adj*

sha·man·ism \-ˌni-zəm\ *n* (1780) **:** a religion practiced by indigenous peoples of far northern Europe and Siberia that is characterized by belief in an unseen world of gods, demons, and ancestral spirits responsive only to the shamans; *also* **:** any similar religion — **sha·man·ist** \-nist\ *n* — **sha·man·is·tic** \ˌshä-mə-ˈnis-tik, ˌshā-mə-\ *adj*

sham·ble \ˈsham-bəl\ *vi* **sham·bled; sham·bling** \-b(ə-)liŋ\ [*shamble* bowed, malformed] (1717) **:** to walk awkwardly with dragging feet **:** SHUFFLE — **shamble** *n*

sham·bles \ˈsham-bəlz\ *n pl but sing or pl in constr* [ME *shameles*, pl. of *schamel* vendor's table, footstool, fr. OE *sceamol* stool, fr. L *scamillum*, dim. of *scamnum* stool, bench; perh. akin to Skt *skambha* pillar] (15c) **1** *archaic* **:** a meat market **2 :** SLAUGHTERHOUSE **3 a :** a place of mass slaughter or bloodshed ⟨the battlefield became a ~⟩ **b :** a scene or a state of great destruction **:** WRECKAGE ⟨the city was a ~ after the bombing⟩ **c (1) :** a scene or a state of great disorder or confusion ⟨an economy in ~⟩ **(2) :** great confusion **:** MESS

shambling *adj* (1592) **:** characterized by slow awkward movement

sham·bol·ic \sham-ˈbä-lik\ *adj* [prob. fr. *shambles*] (1970) *chiefly Brit* **:** obviously disorganized or confused

[1]**shame** \ˈshām\ *n* [ME, fr. OE *scamu;* akin to OHG *scama* shame] (bef. 12c) **1 a :** a painful emotion caused by consciousness of guilt, shortcoming, or impropriety **b :** the susceptibility to such emotion ⟨have you no ~?⟩ **2 :** a condition of humiliating disgrace or disrepute **:** IGNOMINY ⟨the ~ of being arrested⟩ **3 a :** something that brings censure or reproach; *also* **:** something to be regretted **:** PITY ⟨it's a ~ you can't go⟩ **b :** a cause of feeling shame

[2]**shame** *vt* **shamed; sham·ing** (13c) **1 :** to bring shame to **:** DISGRACE ⟨*shamed* the family name⟩ **2 :** to put to shame by outdoing **3 :** to cause to feel shame **4 :** to force by causing to feel guilty ⟨*shamed* into confessing⟩

shame·faced \ˈshām-ˌfāst\ *adj* [alter. of *shamefast*] (1593) **1 :** showing modesty **:** BASHFUL **2 :** showing shame **:** ASHAMED — **shame·faced·ly** \-ˌfā-səd-lē, -ˌfāst-lē\ *adv* — **shame·faced·ness** \-ˌfā-səd-nəs, -ˌfās(t)-nəs\ *n*

shame·fast \ˈshām-ˌfast\ *adj* [ME, fr. OE *scamfæst*, fr. *scamu* + *fæst* fixed, fast] (bef. 12c) *archaic* **:** SHAMEFACED

shame·ful \ˈshām-fəl\ *adj* (13c) **1 a :** bringing shame **:** DISGRACEFUL **b :** arousing the feeling of shame **2** *archaic* **:** full of the feeling of shame **:** ASHAMED — **shame·ful·ly** \-fə-lē\ *adv* — **shame·ful·ness** *n*

shame·less \ˈshām-ləs\ *adj* (bef. 12c) **1 :** having no shame **:** insensible to disgrace ⟨a ~ braggart⟩ **2 :** showing lack of shame ⟨the ~ exploitation of the natives⟩ — **shame·less·ly** *adv* — **shame·less·ness** *n*

shamisen *var of* SAMISEN

sham·mes \ˈshä-məs\ *n, pl* **sham·mo·sim** \shä-ˈmo̅-səm\ [Yiddish *shames*, fr. LHeb *shāmmāsh*] (1650) **1 :** the sexton of a synagogue **2 :** the candle or taper used to light the other candles in a Hanukkah menorah

shammy *var of* CHAMOIS

[1]**sham·poo** \sham-ˈpü\ *vt* [Hindi & Urdu *cā̃po*, imper. of *cā̃pnā* to press, massage] (1762) **1** *archaic* **:** MASSAGE **2 a :** to wash (as the hair) with soap and water or with a special preparation **b :** to wash the hair of — **sham·poo·er** *n*

[2]**shampoo** *n, pl* **shampoos** (1838) **1 :** an act or instance of shampooing **2 :** a preparation used in shampooing

sham·rock \ˈsham-ˌräk\ *n* [Ir *seamróg*, dim. of *seamar* clover] (1577) **:** a trifoliate plant used as a floral emblem by the Irish: as **a :** a yellow-flowered Old World clover (*Trifolium dubium*) often regarded as the true shamrock **b :** WOOD SORREL **c :** WHITE CLOVER

sha·mus \ˈshä-məs, ˈshā-\ *n* [perh. fr. Yiddish *shames* shammes; fr. a jocular comparison of the duties of a sexton and those of a store detective] (1925) **1** *slang* **:** POLICE OFFICER **2** *slang* **:** PRIVATE INVESTIGATOR

Shan \ˈshän, ˈshan\ *n, pl* **Shan** *or* **Shans** [Burmese *Shàn*] (1795) **1 :** a member of a people living primarily in Myanmar and southern China **2 :** the Thai language of the Shan

shan·dy \ˈshan-dē\ *n, pl* **shandies** (1888) **1 :** SHANDYGAFF **2 :** a drink consisting of beer and lemonade

shan·dy·gaff \ˈshan-dē-ˌgaf\ *n* [origin unknown] (1853) **:** beer diluted with a nonalcoholic drink (as ginger beer)

Shang \ˈshäŋ\ *n* [Chin (Beijing) *Shāng*] (1669) **:** a Chinese dynasty traditionally dated 1766–1122 B.C. and known esp. for bronze work

shang·hai \shaŋ-ˌhī, shaŋ-ˈhī\ *vt* **shang·haied; shang·hai·ing** [*Shanghai*, China; fr. the former use of this method to secure sailors for voyages to eastern Asia] (1871) **1 a :** to put aboard a ship by force often with the help of liquor or a drug **b :** to put by force or threat of force into or as if into a place of detention **2 :** to put by trickery into an undesirable position — **shang·hai·er** \-ˈhī(-ə)r\ *n*

Shan·gri–la \ˌshaŋ-gri-ˈlä\ *n* [*Shangri-La*, imaginary land depicted in the novel *Lost Horizon* (1933) by James Hilton] (1937) **1 :** a remote beautiful imaginary place where life approaches perfection : UTOPIA **2** : a remote usu. idyllic hideaway

[1]**shank** \ˈshaŋk\ *n* [ME *shanke,* fr. OE *scanca;* akin to ON *skakkr* crooked, Gk *skazein* to limp] (bef. 12c) **1 a :** the part of the leg between the knee and the ankle in humans or the corresponding part in various other vertebrates **b :** LEG **c :** a cut of beef, veal, mutton, or lamb from the upper or the lower part of the leg : SHIN — see BEEF illustration **2 :** a straight narrow usu. essential part of an object: as **a :** the straight part of a nail or pin **b :** a straight part of a plant : STEM, STALK **c :** the part of an anchor between the ring and the crown — see ANCHOR illustration **d :** the part of a fishhook between the eye and the bend **e :** the part of a key between the handle and the bit **f :** the stem of a tobacco pipe or the part between the stem and the bowl **g :** TANG 1 **h (1) :** the narrow part of the sole of a shoe beneath the instep **(2) :** SHANKPIECE **3 :** a part of an object by which it can be attached: as **a (1) :** a projection on the back of a solid button **(2) :** a short stem of thread that holds a sewn button away from the cloth **b :** the end (as of a drill bit) that is gripped in a chuck **4 a :** the latter part of a period of time **b :** the early or main part of a period of time ⟨11 p.m. on the East coast is merely the ~ of the evening on the West coast⟩ **5** *slang* **:** an often homemade knife — **shanked** \ˈshaŋ(k)t\ *adj*

[2]**shank** *vt* (1927) **:** to hit (a golf ball or shot) with the extreme heel of the club so that the ball goes off in an unintended direction; *also* **:** to kick (a football) in an unintended direction

shank•piece \ˈshaŋk-ˌpēs\ *n* (1885) **:** a support for the arch of the foot inserted in the shank of a shoe

shank's mare *n* (ca. 1795) **:** one's own legs ⟨traveling by *shank's mare*⟩

shan't \ˈshant, ˈshänt\ (1664) **:** shall not

shan•tung \(ˌ)shan-ˈtəŋ\ *n* [*Shantung* (Shandong), China] (ca. 1882) **:** a fabric in plain weave having a slightly irregular surface due to uneven slubbed filling yarns

[1]**shanty** *var of* CHANTEY

[2]**shanty** *n, pl* **shanties** [prob. fr. CanF *chantier* lumber camp, hut, fr. F, builder's yard, ways, support for barrels, fr. OF *chantier, gantier* support — more at GANTRY] (1820) **:** a small crudely built dwelling or shelter usu. of wood

shan•ty•man \-mən, -ˌman\ *n* (1824) **:** LOGGER

shan•ty•town \-ˌtau̇n\ *n* (1876) **:** a usu. poor town or section of a town consisting mostly of shanties

shap•able *or* **shape•able** \ˈshā-pə-bəl\ *adj* (1647) **1 :** capable of being shaped **2 :** SHAPELY

[1]**shape** \ˈshāp\ *vb* **shaped; shap•ing** [ME, fr. OE *sceapen, gescapen,* pp. of *scieppan;* akin to OHG *skepfen* to shape] *vt* (bef. 12c) **1 :** FORM, CREATE; *esp* **:** to give a particular form or shape to **2** *obs* **:** ORDAIN, DECREE **3 :** to adapt in shape so as to fit neatly and closely ⟨a dress *shaped* to her figure⟩ **4 a :** DEVISE, PLAN ⟨~ a policy⟩ **b :** to embody in definite form ⟨*shaping* a folktale into an epic⟩ **5 a :** to make fit for (as a particular use or purpose) **:** ADAPT ⟨~ the questions to fit the answers⟩ **b :** to determine or direct the course or character of ⟨events that *shaped* history⟩ **c :** to modify (behavior) by rewarding changes that tend toward a desired response ~ *vi* **1 :** to come to pass **:** HAPPEN ⟨it's *shaping* up that I am known now for my husbands —Leslie Marmon Silko⟩ **2 :** to take on or approach a mature or definite form — often used with *up* ⟨the summer is *shaping* up to be one of the hottest on record⟩ — **shap•er** *n*

[2]**shape** *n* (bef. 12c) **1 a :** the visible makeup characteristic of a particular item or kind of item ⟨a cake in the ~ of a Christmas tree⟩ **b (1) :** spatial form or contour ⟨the clouds kept changing ~⟩ **(2) :** a standard or universally recognized spatial form ⟨a stain in the ~ of a perfect circle⟩ **2 :** the appearance of the body as distinguished from that of the face **:** FIGURE **3 a :** PHANTOM, APPARITION ⟨eerie ~*s* floating in the mist⟩ **b :** assumed appearance **:** GUISE ⟨a trick-or-treater in the ~ of a pumpkin⟩ **4 :** form of embodiment ⟨our plans are taking ~⟩ **5 :** a mode of existence or form of being having identifying features **6 :** a molded dessert; *esp* **:** BLANCMANGE **7 :** the condition in which someone or something exists at a particular time ⟨the car was in fine ~⟩ — **shaped** \ˌshāpt\ *adj* — **in shape :** in an original, normal, or fit condition ⟨exercises to keep *in shape*⟩

shaped charge *n* (1946) **:** an explosive charge the energy of which is focused in one direction so that it usu. achieves an armor-penetrating effect

shape•less \ˈshā-pləs\ *adj* (14c) **1 :** having no definite shape **2 a :** deprived of usual or normal shape **:** MISSHAPEN ⟨a ~ old hat⟩ **b :** not shapely — **shape•less•ly** *adv* — **shape•less•ness** *n*

shape•ly \ˈshā-plē\ *adj* **shape•li•er; -est** (14c) **1 :** having a regular or pleasing shape **2 :** orderly and consistent in arrangement or plan ⟨~ essays⟩ — **shape•li•ness** *n*

shap•en \ˈshā-pən\ *adj* [ME, fr. pp. of *shapen* to shape] (14c) **:** fashioned in or provided with a definite shape — usu. used in combination ⟨an ill-*shapen* body⟩

shape note *n* (1932) **:** one of a system of seven notes showing the musical scale degree by the shape of the note head

shape–shift•er \ˈshāp-ˌshif-tər\ *n* (1887) **:** one that seems able to change form or identity at will; *esp* **:** a mythical figure that can assume different forms (as of animals) — **shape–shift** \-ˌshift\ *vi*

shape–up \ˈshāp-ˌəp\ *n* (1940) **:** a system of hiring workers and esp. longshoremen by the day or shift by having applicants gather for each day's selection; *also* **:** an instance of such hiring practice

shape up *vi* (ca. 1920) **:** to improve to a good or acceptable condition or standard of behavior ⟨*shaping up* at the gym⟩ ~ *vt* **:** to bring to a good or acceptable condition or standard of behavior

shard \ˈshärd\ *n* [ME, fr. OE *sceard;* akin to OE *scieran* to cut — more at SHEAR] (bef. 12c) **1 a :** a piece or fragment of a brittle substance ⟨~*s* of glass⟩; *broadly* **:** a small piece or part **:** SCRAP ⟨little ~*s* of time and space recorded by the camera's lens —Rosalind Krauss⟩ **b :** SHELL, SCALE; *esp* **:** ELYTRON **2** *or* **sherd** \ˈshərd\ **:** fragments of pottery vessels found on sites and in refuse deposits where pottery-making peoples have lived **3 :** highly angular curved glass fragments of tuffaceous sediments

[1]**share** \ˈsher\ *n* [ME *schare,* fr. OE *scear;* akin to OHG *scaro* plowshare, OE *scieran* to cut — more at SHEAR] (bef. 12c) **:** PLOWSHARE

[2]**share** *n* [ME, fr. OE *scearu* cutting, tonsure; akin to OE *scieran* to cut] (14c) **1 a :** a portion belonging to, due to, or contributed by an individual or group **b :** one's full or fair portion ⟨has had his ~ of bad luck⟩ **2 a :** the part allotted or belonging to one of a number owning together property or interest **b :** any of the equal portions into which property or invested capital is divided; *specif* **:** any of the equal interests or rights into which the entire stock of a corporation is divided and ownership of which is regularly evidenced by one or more certificates **c** *pl, chiefly Brit* **:** STOCK 7c(1)

[3]**share** *vb* **shared; shar•ing** *vt* (1590) **1 :** to divide and distribute in shares **:** APPORTION — usu. used with *out* ⟨*shared* out the land among his heirs⟩ **2 a :** to partake of, use, experience, occupy, or enjoy with others **b :** to have in common ⟨they ~ a passion for opera⟩ **3 :** to grant or give a share in — often used with *with* ⟨*shared* the last of her water with us⟩ **4 :** to tell (as thoughts, feelings, or experiences) to others — often used with *with* ~ *vi* **1 :** to have a share — used with *in* ⟨we all *shared* in the fruits of our labor⟩ **2 :** to apportion and take shares of something **3 :** to talk about one's thoughts, feelings, or experiences with others — **shar•er** *n*

syn SHARE, PARTICIPATE, PARTAKE mean to have, get, or use in common with another or others. SHARE usu. implies that one as the original holder grants to another the partial use, enjoyment, or possession of a thing ⟨*shared* my toys with the others⟩. PARTICIPATE implies a having or taking part in an undertaking, activity, or discussion ⟨*participated* in sports⟩. PARTAKE implies accepting or acquiring a share esp. of food or drink ⟨*partook* freely of the refreshments⟩.

share•able *or* **shar•able** \ˈsher-ə-bəl\ *adj* (1920) **:** capable of being shared — **share•abil•i•ty** \ˌsher-ə-ˈbi-lə-tē\ *n*

share•crop \ˈsher-ˌkräp\ *vb* [back-formation fr. *sharecropper*] *vi* (ca. 1930) **:** to farm as a sharecropper ~ *vt* **:** to farm (land) or produce (a crop) as a sharecropper

share•crop•per \-ˌkrä-pər\ *n* (1923) **:** a tenant farmer esp. in the southern U.S. who is provided with credit for seed, tools, living quarters, and food, who works the land, and who receives an agreed share of the value of the crop minus charges

share•hold•er \-ˌhōl-dər\ *n* (ca. 1832) **:** one that holds or owns a share in property; *esp* **:** STOCKHOLDER — **share•hold•ing** \-ˌhōl-diŋ\ *n*

share•ware \-ˌwer\ *n* (1983) **:** software with usu. limited capability or incomplete documentation which is available for trial use at little or no cost but which can be upgraded upon payment of a fee to the author

sha•ria *also* **sha•ri'a** *or* **sha•ri•ah** *or* **sha•ri•'ah** \shə-ˈrē-ə\ *n, often cap* [Ar *sharīʿa*] (1855) **:** Islamic law based on the Koran

sha•rif *also* **she•rif** \shə-ˈrēf\ *n* [Ar *sharīf,* lit., illustrious] (1599) **:** a descendant of the prophet Muhammad through his daughter Fatima; *broadly* **:** one of noble ancestry or political preeminence in predominantly Islamic countries — **sha•rif•ian** \-ˈrē-fē-ən\ *adj*

[1]**shark** \ˈshärk\ *n* [ME] (15c) **:** any of numerous mostly marine cartilaginous fishes of medium to large size that have a fusiform body, lateral branchial clefts, and a tough usu. dull gray skin roughened by minute tubercles and are typically active predators sometimes dangerous to humans — **shark•like** \ˈshärk-ˌlīk\ *adj*

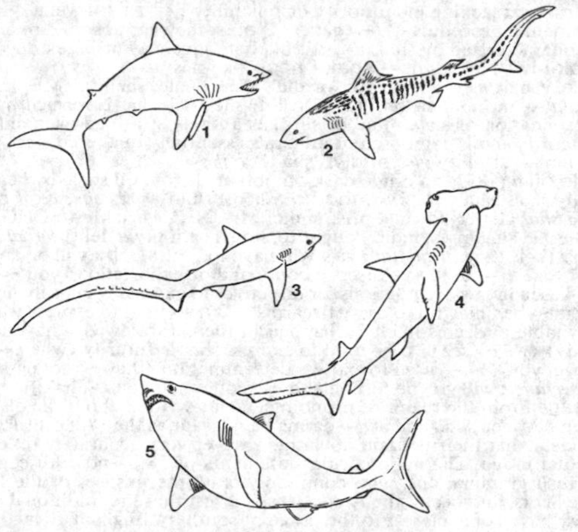

shark: *1* mako, *2* tiger, *3* thresher, *4* hammerhead, *5* great white

[2]**shark** *n* [prob. modif. of G *Schurke* scoundrel] (1599) **1 :** a rapacious crafty person who takes advantage of others often through usury, extortion, or devious means ⟨loan ~*s*⟩ **2 :** one who excels greatly esp. in a particular field

[3]**shark** *vt* (1602) **1** *archaic* **:** to gather hastily **2** *archaic* **:** to obtain by some irregular means ~ *vi* **1** *archaic* **:** to practice fraud or trickery **2** *archaic* **:** SNEAK

shark repellent *n* (1977) **:** any of various measures that a company uses to fend off unwanted takeover attempts

shark•skin \ˈshärk-ˌskin\ *n* (1851) **1 :** the hide of a shark or leather made from it **2 a :** a smooth durable woolen or worsted suiting in twill or basket weave with small woven designs **b :** a smooth crisp fabric with a dull finish made usu. of rayon in basket weave

shark sucker *n* (ca. 1850) **:** REMORA 1

[1]**sharp** \ˈshärp\ *adj* [ME, fr. OE *scearp;* akin to OHG *scarf* sharp and perh. to OE *scrapian* to scrape — more at SCRAPE] (bef. 12c) **1 :** adapted to cutting or piercing: as **a :** having a thin keen edge or fine point **b :** briskly or bitingly cold **:** NIPPING ⟨a ~ wind⟩ **2 a :** keen in intellect **:** QUICK-WITTED **b :** keen in perception **:** ACUTE ⟨~ sight⟩ **c :** keen in attention **:** VIGILANT ⟨keep a ~ lookout⟩ **d :** keen in attention to one's own interest sometimes to the point of being unethical ⟨a ~ trader⟩; *also* **:** CORRUPT, UNETHICAL ⟨~ business practices⟩ **3 :** keen in spirit or action: as **a :** full of activity or energy **:** BRISK ⟨~ blows⟩ **b :** capable of acting or reacting strongly; *esp* **:** CAUSTIC **4 :** SEVERE, HARSH: as **a :** inclined to or marked by irritability or anger

⟨a ~ temper⟩ **b :** causing intense mental or physical distress ⟨a ~ pain⟩ **c :** cutting in language or import ⟨a ~ rebuke⟩ **5 :** affecting the senses or sense organs intensely: as **a** (1) **:** having a strong odor or flavor ⟨~ cheese⟩ (2) **:** ACRID **b :** having a strong piercing sound **c :** having the effect of or involving a sudden brilliant display of light ⟨a ~ flash⟩ **6 a :** terminating in a point or edge ⟨~ features⟩ **b :** involving an abrupt or marked change esp. in direction ⟨a ~ turn⟩ **c :** clear in outline or detail **:** DISTINCT ⟨a ~ image⟩ **d :** set forth with clarity and distinctness ⟨~ contrast⟩ **7 a** *of a tone* **:** raised a half step in pitch **b :** higher than the proper pitch **c :** MAJOR, AUGMENTED — used of an interval in music **8 :** STYLISH, DRESSY — **sharp·ly** *adv* — **sharp·ness** *n*

syn SHARP, KEEN, ACUTE mean having or showing alert competence and clear understanding. SHARP implies quick perception, clever resourcefulness, or sometimes questionable trickiness ⟨*sharp* enough to spot a confidence game⟩. KEEN suggests quickness, enthusiasm, and a penetrating mind ⟨a *keen* observer of the political scene⟩. ACUTE implies a power to penetrate and may suggest subtlety and sharpness of discrimination ⟨an *acute* sense of style⟩.

2**sharp** *adv* (bef. 12c) **1 :** in a sharp manner **2 :** EXACTLY ⟨1:15 ~⟩

3**sharp** *n* (14c) **:** one that is sharp: as **a :** a sharp edge or point **b** (1) **:** a musical note or tone one half step higher than a note or tone named (2) **:** a character ♯ on a line or space of the musical staff indicating a pitch a half step higher than the degree would indicate without it **c :** a needle with a small eye for sewing by hand **d :** a real or self-proclaimed expert; *also* **:** SHARPER

4**sharp** *vt* (1662) **:** to raise (as a musical tone) in pitch; *esp* **:** to raise in pitch by a half step ~ *vi* **:** to sing or play above the proper pitch

shar–pei \ˌshä-ˈpā, ˌshär-\ *n, pl* **shar–peis** *often cap S&P* [Chin (Guangdong) *sà* sand + *péi* fur] (1975) **:** any of an ancient breed of dogs originating in China that have loose wrinkled skin esp. when young, a short bristly coat, blue-black tongue, and wide blunt muzzle

sharp·en \ˈshär-pən\ *vb* **sharp·ened; sharp·en·ing** \ˈshärp-niŋ, ˈshär-pə-\ *vt* (15c) **:** to make sharp or sharper; *esp* **:** HONE ~ *vi* **:** to become sharp or sharper — **sharp·en·er** \ˈshärp-nər, ˈshär-pə-\ *n*

sharp·er \ˈshär-pər\ *n* (1681) **:** CHEAT 2; *esp* **:** a cheating gambler

sharp–eyed \ˈshärp-ˈīd\ *adj* (1670) **:** having keen sight; *also* **:** keen in observing or penetrating

sharp·ie *or* **sharpy** \ˈshär-pē\ *n, pl* **sharp·ies** (ca. 1859) **1 :** a long narrow shallow-draft boat with flat or slightly V-shaped bottom and one or two masts each carrying a triangular sail **2 a :** SHARPER **b :** an exceptionally keen or alert person

sharp–nosed \ˈshärp-ˈnōzd\ *adj* (1561) **1 :** keen in smelling **2 :** having a pointed nose or snout

sharp practice *n* (1836) **:** the act of dealing in which advantage is taken or sought unscrupulously

sharp–set \ˈshärp-ˈset\ *adj* (1540) *archaic* **:** eager in appetite or desire

sharp–shinned hawk \ˈshärp-ˈshind-\ *n* (ca. 1812) **:** a common widely distributed American accipiter (*Accipiter striatus*) that is grayish above, has a chestnut breast, short rounded wings, and a tail with a notched or square tip when folded — called also *sharp-shin*

sharp·shoot·er \ˈshärp-ˌshü-tər\ *n* (1802) **1 :** a proficient marksman **2 :** a consistently accurate shooter (as in basketball)

sharp·shoot·ing \-ˌshü-tiŋ\ *n* (1806) **1 :** shooting with great precision **2 :** accurate and usu. unexpected attack (as in words)

sharp–sight·ed \-ˈsī-təd\ *adj* (1571) **1 :** having acute sight **2 :** mentally keen or alert — **sharp–sight·ed·ness** *n*

sharp–tongued \-ˈtəŋd\ *adj* (1837) **:** having a sharp tongue **:** harsh or bitter in speech or language

sharp–wit·ted \-ˈwi-təd\ *adj* (ca. 1586) **:** having an acute mind

shash·lik *also* **shas·lik** \shäsh-ˈlik, ˈshäsh-lik\ *n* [Russ *shashlyk*, prob. modif. of Crimean Tatar *šišlik*, fr. *šiš* skewer] (1876) **:** KEBAB

Shas·ta daisy \ˈshas-tə-\ *n* [Mount *Shasta*, California] (ca. 1893) **:** a large-flowered hybrid garden daisy (*Chrysanthemum* x *superbum* syn. *Leucanthemum* x *superbum*) that resembles the oxeye daisy

shat *past and past part of* SHIT

1**shat·ter** \ˈsha-tər\ *vb* [ME *schateren* — more at SCATTER] *vt* (14c) **1 :** to cause to drop or be dispersed **2 a :** to break at once into pieces **b :** to damage badly **:** RUIN **3 :** to cause the disruption or annihilation of **:** DEMOLISH ~ *vi* **1 :** to break apart **:** DISINTEGRATE **2 :** to drop off parts (as leaves, petals, or fruit) — **shat·ter·ing·ly** \-tə-riŋ-lē\ *adv*

2**shatter** *n* (ca. 1640) **1 :** FRAGMENT, SHRED — usu. used in pl. ⟨the broken vase lay in ~*s*⟩ **2 :** an act of shattering **:** the state of being shattered **3 :** a result of shattering **:** SHOWER

shatter cone *n* (1933) **:** a conical fragment of rock that has striations radiating from the apex and that is formed by high pressure (as from volcanism or meteorite impact)

shat·ter·proof \ˈsha-tər-ˌprüf\ *adj* (1930) **:** proof against shattering

1**shave** \ˈshāv\ *vb* **shaved; shaved** *or* **shav·en** \ˈshā-vən\; **shav·ing** [ME, fr. OE *scafan*; akin to Lith *skobti* to pluck, L *scabere* to scratch, and perh. to Gk *koptein* to cut — more at CAPON] *vt* (bef. 12c) **1 a :** to remove a thin layer from **b :** to cut off in thin layers or shreds **:** SLICE **c :** to cut off closely **2 a :** to sever the hair from (the head or another part of the body) close to the roots **b :** to cut off (hair or beard) close to the skin **3 a :** to discount (a note) at an exorbitant rate **b :** DEDUCT, REDUCE **c :** to conspire to score fewer (points) than one is capable of (as to affect gambling outcomes) **4 :** to come close to or touch lightly in passing ~ *vi* **1 :** to cut off hair or beard close to the skin **2 :** to proceed with difficulty **:** SCRAPE

2**shave** *n* (bef. 12c) **1 :** SHAVER 3 **2 :** a thin slice **:** SHAVING **3 :** an act or the process of shaving

shave·ling \ˈshāv-liŋ\ *n* (1529) **1** *usu disparaging* **:** a tonsured clergyman **:** PRIEST **2 :** YOUTH, STRIPLING

shav·er \ˈshā-vər\ *n* (15c) **1 :** a person who shaves **2** *archaic* **:** one who swindles **3 :** a tool or machine for shaving; *esp* **:** an electric razor **4 :** BOY, YOUNGSTER

shaves *pl of* SHAFT

shave·tail \ˈshāv-ˌtāl\ *n* [fr. the practice of shaving the tails of newly broken mules to distinguish them from seasoned ones] (1846) **1 :** a pack mule esp. when newly broken in **2** *usu disparaging* **:** SECOND LIEUTENANT

Sha·vi·an \ˈshā-vē-ən\ *n* [NL *Shavius*, latinized form of George Bernard *Shaw*] (1905) **:** an admirer or devotee of G. B. Shaw, his writings, or his social and political theories — **Shavian** *adj*

shav·ie \ˈshā-vē\ *n* [*shave* (swindle) + *-ie*] (1737) *Scot* **:** PRANK

shaving *n* (14c) **1 :** the act of one that shaves **2 :** something shaved off ⟨wood ~*s*⟩

Sha·vu·ot *also* **Sha·vu·oth** *or* **Sha·bu·oth** \shə-ˈvü-ˌōt, -ˌōth, -ˌōs, -əs\ *n* [Heb *shābhūʿōth*, pl. of *shābhūaʿ* week] (1846) **:** a Jewish holiday observed on the sixth and seventh of Sivan in commemoration of the revelation of the Ten Commandments at Mt. Sinai — called also *Pentecost*

1**shaw** \ˈshȯ\ *n* [ME, fr. OE *sceaga*; akin to ON *skegg* beard — more at SHAG] (bef. 12c) *dial* **:** COPPICE, THICKET

2**shaw** *n* [prob. alter. of *show*] (1726) *chiefly Brit* **:** the tops and stalks of a cultivated crop (as potatoes or turnips)

sha·war·ma \shä-ˈwȯr-mə, ˈshwȯr-mə\ *n* [Levantine Ar *shāwurma* sliced lamb on a skewer, fr. Turk *çevirme*, lit., turn, rotation, fr. *çevir-* turn] (1953) **:** a sandwich esp. of sliced lamb or chicken, vegetables, and often tahini wrapped in pita bread

1**shawl** \ˈshȯl\ *n* [Pers *shāl*] (1662) **:** a square or oblong usu. fabric garment or wrapper used esp. as a covering for the head or shoulders

2**shawl** *vt* (1812) **:** to wrap in or as if in a shawl

shawl collar *n* (ca. 1908) **:** a turned-over collar of a garment that combines with lapels forming an unbroken curving line

shawm \ˈshȯm\ *n* [ME (Sc) *schalme*, alter. of ME *shalemie*, fr. MF *chalemie*, ultim. fr. L *calamus* reed — more at CALAMUS] (15c) **:** an early double-reed woodwind instrument

Shaw·nee \shȯ-ˈnē, shä-\ *n, pl* **Shawnee** *or* **Shawnees** [back-formation fr. obs. E *Shawnese*, ultim. fr. Shawnee *ša·wano·ki*, lit., southerners] (1728) **1 :** a member of an American Indian people orig. of the central Ohio valley **2 :** the Algonquian language of the Shawnee people

Shaw·wal \shə-ˈwäl\ *n* [Ar *shawwāl*] (ca. 1771) **:** the 10th month of the Islamic year — see MONTH table

shay \ˈshā\ *n* [back-formation fr. *chaise*, taken as pl.] (1717) *chiefly dial* **:** CHAISE 1

shd *abbr* should

1**she** \ˈshē\ *pron* [ME, prob. alter. of *hye*, alter. of OE *hēo* she — more at HE] (12c) **1 :** that female one who is neither speaker nor hearer ⟨~ is my wife⟩ — compare HE, HER, HERS, IT, THEY **2 —** used to refer to one regarded as feminine (as by personification) ⟨~ was a fine ship⟩ **3 —** used as an alternative to *he* to refer to a person of unspecified gender ⟨allow anyone to do whatever ~ wants —D. J. Callahan⟩

2**she** *n* (14c) **:** a female person or animal — often used in combination ⟨*she*-cat⟩ ⟨*she*-cousin⟩

s/he \ˈshē-ˈhē; ˈshē-ər-ˈhē; ˈshē-ˌslash-ˈhē\ *pron* (1973) **:** she or he — used in writing as a pronoun of common gender

shea butter \ˈshē-, ˈshā-\ *n* (1847) **:** a pale solid fat from the seeds of the shea tree used in food, soap, and candles

sheaf \ˈshēf\ *n, pl* **sheaves** \ˈshēvz\ [ME *sheef*, fr. OE *scēaf*; akin to OHG *scoub* sheaf, Russ *chub* forelock] (bef. 12c) **1 :** a quantity of the stalks and ears of a cereal grass or sometimes other plant material bound together **2 :** something resembling a sheaf of grain ⟨a ~ of papers⟩ **3 :** a large amount or number — **sheaf·like** \ˈshēf-ˌlīk\ *adj*

shea nut *n* (1919) **:** the seed of the shea tree

1**shear** \ˈshir\ *vb* **sheared; sheared** *or* **shorn** \ˈshȯrn\; **shear·ing** [ME *sheren*, fr. OE *scieran*; akin to ON *skera* to cut, L *curtus* mutilated, curtailed, Gk *keirein* to cut, shear, Skt *kṛnāti* he injures] *vt* (bef. 12c) **1 a :** to cut off the hair from **b :** to cut or clip (as hair or wool) from someone or something; *also* **:** to cut something from ⟨~ a lawn⟩ **c** *chiefly Scot* **:** to reap with a sickle **d :** to cut or trim with shears or a similar instrument **2 :** to cut with something sharp **3 :** to deprive of something as if by cutting ⟨lives *shorn* of any hope —M. W. Browne⟩ **4 a :** to subject to a shear force **b :** to cause (as a rock mass) to move along the plane of contact ~ *vi* **1 :** to cut through something with or as if with a sharp instrument **2** *chiefly Scot* **:** to reap crops with a sickle **3 :** to become divided under the action of a shear — **shear·er** *n*

2**shear** *n* (bef. 12c) **1 a** (1) **:** a cutting implement similar or identical to a pair of scissors but typically larger — usu. used in pl. (2) **:** one blade of a pair of shears **b :** any of various cutting tools or machines operating by the action of opposed cutting edges of metal — usu. used in pl. **c** (1) **:** something resembling a shear or a pair of shears (2) **:** a hoisting apparatus consisting of two or sometimes more upright spars fastened together at their upper ends and having tackle for masting or dismasting ships or lifting heavy loads (as guns) — usu. used in pl. but sing. or pl. in constr. **2** *chiefly Brit* **:** the action or process or an instance of shearing — used in combination to indicate the approximate age of sheep in terms of shearings undergone **3 a :** internal force tangential to the section on which it acts — called also *shearing force* **b :** an action or stress resulting from applied forces that causes or tends to cause two contiguous parts of a body to slide relatively to each other in a direction parallel to their plane of contact

sheared *adj* (1616) **:** formed or finished by shearing; *esp* **:** cut to uniform length ⟨a ~ rug⟩

shear·ling \ˈshir-liŋ\ *n* (14c) **:** skin from a recently sheared sheep or lamb that has been tanned and dressed with the wool left on

shear pin *n* (ca. 1931) **:** an easily replaceable pin inserted at a critical point in a machine and designed to break when stressed to excess

shear·wa·ter \ˈshir-ˌwȯ-tər, -ˌwä-\ *n* (ca. 1671) **:** any of numerous oceanic birds (esp. genus *Puffinus*) that are related to the petrels and usu. skim close to the waves in flight

sheath \ˈshēth\ *n, pl* **sheaths** \ˈshē*th*z, ˈshēths\ [ME *shethe*, fr. OE *scēath*; akin to OHG *sceida* sheath and perh. to L *scindere* to split — more at SHED] (bef. 12c) **1 :** a case for a blade (as of a knife) **2 :** an investing cover or case of a plant or animal body or body part: as **a :** the tubular fold of skin into which the penis of many mammals is retracted **b** (1) **:** the lower part of a leaf when surrounding the stem (2) **:** an ensheathing spathe **3 :** any of various covering or supporting structures that resemble in appearance or function the sheath of a blade: as **a :** SHEATHING 2 **b :** a woman's close-fitting dress that is usu. worn without a belt **c** *Brit* **:** CONDOM 1

\ə\ **abut** \ᵊ\ **kitten**, F **table** \ər\ **further** \a\ **ash** \ā\ **ace** \ä\ **mop, mar**
\au̇\ **out** \ch\ **chin** \e\ **bet** \ē\ **easy** \g\ **go** \i\ **hit** \ī\ **ice** \j\ **job**
\ŋ\ **sing** \ō\ **go** \ȯ\ **law** \ȯi\ **boy** \th\ **thin** *th*\ **the** \ü\ **loot** \u̇\ **foot**
\y\ **yet** \zh\ **vision, beige** \ḵ, ⁿ, œ, ue, ʸ\ *see* Guide to Pronunciation

sheath·bill \ˈshēth-ˌbil\ *n* (ca. 1781) **:** either of two white shorebirds (*Chionis alba* and *C. minor* of the family Chionididae) of colder parts of the southern hemisphere that have a horny sheath over the base of the upper mandible and suggest the pigeons in general appearance

sheathe \ˈshēth\ *also* **sheath** \ˈshēth\ *vt* **sheathed; sheath·ing** [ME *shethen,* fr. *shethe* sheath] (15c) **1 :** to put into or furnish with a sheath **2 :** to plunge or bury (as a sword) in flesh **3 :** to withdraw (a claw) into a sheath **4 :** to case or cover with something (as sheets of metal) that protects — **sheath·er** \ˈshē-thər, -thər\ *n*

sheath·ing \ˈshē-thiŋ, -thiŋ\ *n* (15c) **1 :** the action of one that sheathes something **2 :** material used to sheathe something; *esp* **:** the first covering of boards or of waterproof material on the outside wall of a frame house or on a timber roof

sheath knife *n* (1837) **:** a knife having a fixed blade and designed to be carried in a sheath

shea tree \ˈshē-, ˈshā-\ *n* [Bambara *si*] (1799) **:** a tropical African tree (*Vitellaria paradoxa* syn. *Butyrospermum parkii*) of the sapodilla family with fatty nuts that yield shea butter

[1]**sheave** \ˈshiv, ˈshēv\ *n* [ME *sheve;* akin to OHG *scība* disk] (14c) **:** a grooved wheel or pulley (as of a pulley block)

[2]**sheave** \ˈshēv\ *vt* **sheaved; sheav·ing** [*sheaf*] (1598) **:** to gather and bind into a sheaf

she·bang \shi-ˈbaŋ\ *n* [origin unknown] (1869) **:** everything involved in what is under consideration — usu. used in the phrase *the whole shebang*

She·bat \shə-ˈbät, -ˈvät\ *n* [Heb *shĕbhāṭ*] (1535) **:** the 5th month of the civil year or the 11th month of the ecclesiastical year in the Jewish calendar — see MONTH table

she·been \shə-ˈbēn\ *n* [Ir *síbín* illicit whiskey, shebeen] (ca. 1787) *chiefly Irish & SoAfr* **:** an unlicensed or illegally operated drinking establishment

She·chi·nah *or* **She·ki·nah** \shə-ˈkē-nə, -ˈkē-nə, -ˈkī-nə\ *n* [Heb *shĕkhīnāh*] (1663) **:** the presence of God in the world as conceived in Jewish theology

she–crab \ˈshē-ˈkrab\ *n* (1967) **:** an immature female blue crab

[1]**shed** \ˈshed\ *vb* **shed; shed·ding** [ME, to divide, separate, fr. OE *scēadan;* akin to OHG *skeidan* to separate, L *scindere* to split, cleave, Gk *schizein* to split] *vt* (bef. 12c) **1** *chiefly dial* **:** to set apart **:** SEGREGATE **2 :** to cause to be dispersed without penetrating ⟨duck's plumage ~*s* water⟩ **3 a :** to cause (blood) to flow by cutting or wounding **b :** to pour forth in drops ⟨~ tears⟩ **c :** to give off or out ⟨~*s* some light on the subject⟩ **4 :** to give off, discharge, or expel from the body of a plant or animal: as **a :** to eject, slough off, or lose as part of the normal processes of life ⟨a caterpillar *shedding* its skin⟩ ⟨a cat *shedding* hair⟩ ⟨a deciduous tree ~*s* its leaves in the fall⟩ **b :** to discharge usu. gradually esp. as part of a pathological process ⟨~ a virus in the feces⟩ **5 :** to rid oneself of temporarily or permanently as superfluous or unwanted ⟨~ her inhibitions⟩ ⟨the company ~ 100 jobs⟩ ~ *vi* **1 :** to pour out **:** SPILL **2 :** to become dispersed **:** SCATTER **3 :** to cast off some natural covering (as fur or skin) ⟨the cat is *shedding*⟩ ***syn*** see DISCARD — **shed blood :** to cause death by violence

[2]**shed** *n* (12c) **1** *obs* **:** DISTINCTION, DIFFERENCE **2 :** something (as the skin of a snake) that is discarded in shedding **3 :** a divide of land

[3]**shed** *n* [alter. of earlier *shadde,* prob. fr. ME *shade* shade] (1557) **1 a :** a slight structure built for shelter or storage; *esp* **:** a single-storied building with one or more sides unenclosed **b :** a building that resembles a shed **2** *archaic* **:** HUT — **shed·like** \-ˌlīk\ *adj*

[4]**shed** *vt* **shed·ded; shed·ding** (1850) **:** to put or house in a shed

she'd \ˈshēd\ (1609) **:** she had **:** she would

shed·der \ˈshe-dər\ *n* (14c) **:** one that sheds something: as **a :** a crab or lobster about to molt **b :** a newly molted crab

shed dormer *n* (1948) **:** a dormer with a roof sloping in the same direction as the roof from which the dormer projects

[1]**sheen** \ˈshēn\ *adj* [ME *shene,* fr. OE *sciene;* akin to OE *scēawian* to look — more at SHOW] (bef. 12c) **1** *archaic* **:** BEAUTIFUL **2** *archaic* **:** SHINING, RESPLENDENT

[2]**sheen** *vi* (14c) **:** to be bright **:** show a sheen

[3]**sheen** *n* (1600) **1 a :** a bright or shining condition **:** BRIGHTNESS **b :** a subdued glitter approaching but short of optical reflection **c :** a lustrous surface imparted to textiles through finishing processes or use of shiny yarns **2 :** a textile exhibiting notable sheen — **sheeny** \ˈshē-nē\ *adj*

sheep \ˈshēp\ *n, pl* **sheep** *often attrib* [ME, fr. OE *scēap;* akin to OHG *scāf* sheep] (bef. 12c) **1 :** any of various hollow-horned typically gregarious ruminant mammals (genus *Ovis*) related to the goats but stockier and lacking a beard in the male; *specif* **:** one (*O. aries*) long domesticated esp. for its flesh and wool **2 a :** a timid defenseless creature **b :** a timid docile person; *esp* **:** one easily influenced or led **3 :** leather prepared from the skins of sheep **:** SHEEPSKIN

sheep·cote \-ˌkōt, -ˌkät\ *n* (15c) *chiefly Brit* **:** SHEEPFOLD

sheep·dog \-ˌdȯg\ *n* (ca. 1774) **:** a dog (as a border collie) used to tend, drive, or guard sheep

sheep fescue *n* (1945) **:** a hardy fine-foliaged fescue (*Festuca ovina*) widely used as a pasture grass — called also *sheep's fescue*

sheep·fold \ˈshēp-ˌfōld\ *n* (bef. 12c) **:** a pen or shelter for sheep

sheep·herd·er \ˈshēp-ˌhər-dər\ *n* (1871) **:** a worker in charge of sheep esp. on open range

sheep·herd·ing \-ˌhər-diŋ\ *n* (1836) **:** the activities of a worker engaged in tending sheep

sheep·ish \ˈshē-pish\ *adj* (13c) **1 :** resembling a sheep in meekness, stupidity, or timidity **2 :** affected by or showing embarrassment caused by consciousness of a fault ⟨a ~ grin⟩ — **sheep·ish·ly** *adv* — **sheep·ish·ness** *n*

sheep ked \ˈshēp-ˌked\ *n* [*sheep* + *ked* sheep ked, of unknown origin] (1925) **:** a wingless bloodsucking dipteran fly (*Melophagus ovinus*) that feeds chiefly on sheep and is a vector of sheep trypanosomiasis — called also *sheep tick*

sheep laurel *n* (1810) **:** a dwarf shrub (*Kalmia angustifolia*) of the heath family that is native to northeastern No. America and is poisonous to livestock and that resembles mountain laurel but has narrower leaves and smaller bright red flowers — called also *lambkill*

sheep's eye *n* (ca. 1529) **:** a shy longing usu. amorous glance — usu. used in pl.

sheep·shank \ˈshēp-ˌshaŋk\ *n* (1627) **1 :** a knot for shortening a line — see KNOT illustration **2** *Scot* **:** something of no worth or importance

sheeps·head \ˈshēps-ˌhed\ *n* (1643) **1 :** a marine bony fish (*Archosargus probatocephalus* of the family Sparidae) of the Atlantic and Gulf coasts of the U.S. that has broad front teeth and is used for food **2 :** FRESHWATER DRUM **3 :** a largely red or rose-colored wrasse (*Semicossyphus pulcher*) of the California coast

sheep·shear·er \ˈshēp-ˌshir-ər\ *n* (1539) **:** one that shears sheep

sheep·shear·ing \ˈshēp-ˌshir-iŋ\ *n* (1580) **1 :** the act of shearing sheep **2 :** the time or season for shearing sheep

sheep·skin \-ˌskin\ *n* (13c) **1 a :** the skin of a sheep; *also* **:** leather prepared from it **b :** PARCHMENT **c :** a garment made of or lined with sheepskin **2 :** DIPLOMA

sheep sorrel *n* (1806) **:** a small dock (*Rumex acetosella*) of acidic soils

sheep walk *n* (1586) *chiefly Brit* **:** a pasture or range for sheep

[1]**sheer** \ˈshir\ *vb* [perh. alter. of [1]*shear*] *vi* (1539) **:** to deviate from a course **:** SWERVE ~ *vt* **:** to cause to sheer

[2]**sheer** *n* (1670) **1 :** a turn, deviation, or change in a course (as of a ship) **2 :** the position of a ship riding to a single anchor and heading toward it

[3]**sheer** *adj* [ME *schere* freed from guilt, prob. alter. of *skere,* fr. ON *skærr* pure; akin to OE *scīnan* to shine] (ca. 1568) **1** *obs* **:** BRIGHT, SHINING **2 :** of very thin or transparent texture **:** DIAPHANOUS **3 a :** UNQUALIFIED, UTTER ⟨~ folly⟩ ⟨~ ignorance⟩ **b :** being free from an adulterant **:** PURE, UNMIXED **c :** viewed or acting in dissociation from all else ⟨in terms of ~ numbers⟩ **4 :** marked by great and continuous steepness ***syn*** see STEEP — **sheer·ly** *adv* — **sheer·ness** *n*

[4]**sheer** *adv* (1599) **1 :** in a complete manner **:** ALTOGETHER **2 :** straight up or down without a break **:** PERPENDICULARLY

[5]**sheer** *n* (ca. 1920) **:** a sheer fabric; *also* **:** an article of such a fabric

[6]**sheer** *n* [perh. alter. of [2]*shear*] (1691) **:** the fore-and-aft curvature from bow to stern of a ship's deck as shown in side elevation

sheer·legs \ˈshir-ˌlegz, -ˌlāgz\ *n pl but sing or pl in constr* (ca. 1860) **:** SHEAR 1c(2)

sheesh \ˈshēsh\ *interj* (1972) — used to express disappointment, annoyance, or surprise

[1]**sheet** \ˈshēt\ *n* [ME *shete,* fr. OE *scēte, sciete;* akin to OE *scēat* edge, OHG *scōz* flap, skirt] (bef. 12c) **1 a :** a broad piece of cloth; *esp* **:** BEDSHEET **b :** SAIL 1a(1) **2 a** (1) **:** a usu. rectangular piece of paper; *esp* **:** one manufactured for printing (2) **:** a rectangular piece of heavy paper with a plant specimen mounted on it ⟨an herbarium of 100,000 ~*s*⟩ **b :** a printed signature for a book esp. before it has been folded, cut, or bound — usu. used in pl. **c :** a newspaper, periodical, or occasional publication ⟨a gossip ~⟩ **d :** the unseparated postage stamps printed by one impression of a plate on a single piece of paper; *also* **:** a pane of stamps **3 :** a broad stretch or surface of something ⟨a ~ of ice⟩ **4 :** a suspended or moving expanse (as of fire or rain) **5 a :** a portion of something that is thin in comparison to its length and breadth **b :** a flat baking pan of tinned metal ⟨a cookie ~⟩ **6 :** a surface or part of a surface in which it is possible to pass from any one point of it to any other without leaving the surface ⟨a hyperboloid of two ~*s*⟩ — **sheet·like** \-ˌlīk\ *adj*

[2]**sheet** *adj* (1582) **1 :** rolled or spread out in a sheet **2 :** of, relating to, or concerned with the making of sheet metal

[3]**sheet** *vt* (1606) **1 :** to cover with a sheet ⟨floors ~*ed* with dust⟩ **2 :** to furnish with sheets **3 :** to form into sheets ~ *vi* **:** to fall, spread, or flow in a sheet ⟨the rain ~*ed* against the windows⟩ — **sheet·er** *n*

[4]**sheet** *n* [ME *shete,* fr. OE *scēata* lower corner of a sail; akin to OE *scӯte* sheet] (13c) **1 :** a rope or chain that regulates the angle at which a sail is set in relation to the wind **2** *pl* **:** the spaces at either end of an open boat not occupied by thwarts **:** foresheets and stern sheets together — **three sheets in the wind** *or* **three sheets to the wind :** DRUNK 1a

[5]**sheet** *vt* (1925) **:** to move or set (a sail) by manipulation of a sheet — **sheet home 1 :** to extend (a sail) and set as flat as possible by hauling upon the sheets **2 :** to fix the responsibility for **:** bring home to one

sheet anchor *n* [alter. of earlier *shoot anchor,* fr. ME *shute anker*] (1626) **1 :** a large strong anchor formerly carried in the waist of a ship and used as a spare in an emergency **2 :** something that constitutes a main support or dependence esp. in danger

sheet bend *n* (ca. 1823) **:** a bend or hitch used for temporarily fastening a rope to the bight of another rope or to an eye — see KNOT illustration

sheet·fed \ˈshēt-ˌfed\ *adj* (1926) **:** of, relating to, being, or printed by a press that prints on paper in sheet form

sheet glass *n* (1768) **:** glass made in large sheets directly from the furnace or by making a cylinder and then flattening it

sheet·ing \ˈshē-tiŋ\ *n* (1711) **1 :** material in the form of sheets or suitable for forming into sheets: as **a :** a sturdy plain-woven cloth usu. of cotton used esp. for bedsheets **b :** material (as a plastic) in the form of a continuous film **2 :** a lining (as wood or steel) used to support an embankment or the walls of an excavation

sheet lightning *n* (1794) **:** lightning in diffused or sheet form due to reflection and diffusion by the clouds and sky

sheet metal *n* (1852) **:** metal in the form of a sheet

sheet music *n* (1852) **:** music printed on large unbound sheets of paper

Sheet·rock \ˈshēt-ˌräk\ *trademark* — used for drywall

sheikh *or* **sheik** \ˈshēk, *also* ˈshāk *for 1*\ *n* [Ar *shaykh*] (1577) **1 :** an Arab chief **2** *usu sheik* **:** a man held to be irresistibly attractive to romantic young women

sheikh·dom *or* **sheik·dom** \-dəm, -təm\ *n* (1860) **:** a region under the rule of a sheikh

shei·la \ˈshē-lə\ *n* [prob. fr. *Sheila,* female given name] (ca. 1914) *Austral & NewZeal* **:** a girl or young woman

shek·el *also* **sheq·el** \ˈshe-kəl\ *n, pl* **shekels** *also* **sheqels** *or* **shek·alim** \shē-ˈkä-lim\ *or* **shek·a·lim** *or* **sheq·a·lim** \she-ˈkä-lim\ [Heb *sheqel*] (15c) **1 a :** any of various ancient units of weight; *esp* **:** a Hebrew unit equal to about 252 grains troy **b :** a unit of value based on a shekel weight of gold or silver **2 :** a coin weighing one shekel **3** *pl* **:** MONEY **4** — see MONEY table

Shekinah *var of* SHECHINAH

shel·drake \ˈshel-ˌdrāk\ *n* [ME, fr. *sheld-* (akin to MD *schillede* particolored) + *drake*] (14c) **1 :** SHELDUCK **2 :** MERGANSER

shel•duck \-ˌdək\ *n* [*shel-* (as in *sheldrake*) + *duck*] (1707) **:** any of various Old World ducks (genus *Tadorna*); *esp* **:** a common mostly black-and-white duck (*T. tadorna*) slightly larger than the mallard

shelf \ˈshelf\ *n, pl* **shelves** \ˈshelvz\ [ME, prob. fr. OE *scylfe;* akin to ON hlīth*skjalf* Odin's seat] (14c) **1 a :** a thin flat usu. long and narrow piece of material (as wood) fastened horizontally (as on a wall) at a distance from the floor to hold objects **b :** one of several similar pieces in a closet, bookcase, or similar structure **c :** the contents of a shelf ⟨the author of a ~ of best sellers⟩ **2 :** something resembling a shelf in form or position: as **a :** a sandbank or ledge of rocks usu. partially submerged **b :** a flat projecting layer of rock **c :** the submerged gradually sloping border of a continent or island **:** CONTINENTAL SHELF — **shelf•ful** \ˈshelf-ˌfu̇l\ *n* — **shelf•like** \ˈshelf-ˌlīk\ *adj* — **off the shelf :** available from stock **:** not made to order ⟨*off the shelf* equipment⟩ — **on the shelf :** in a state of inactivity or uselessness

shelf fungus *n* (ca. 1903) **:** BRACKET FUNGUS

shelf ice *n* (1910) **:** an extensive ice sheet originating on land but continuing out to sea beyond the depths at which it rests on the sea bottom

shelf life *n* (1927) **:** the period of time during which a material may be stored and remain suitable for use; *broadly* **:** the period of time during which something lasts or remains popular

[1]**shell** \ˈshel\ *n* [ME, fr. OE *sciell;* akin to OE *scealu* shell, ON *skel,* Lith *skelti* to split, Gk *skallein* to hoe] (bef. 12c) **1 a :** a hard rigid usu. largely calcareous covering or support of an animal **b :** the hard or tough often thin outer covering of an egg (as of a bird or reptile) — see EGG illustration **2 :** the covering or outside part of a fruit or seed esp. when hard or fibrous **3 :** shell material (as of mollusks or turtles) or their substance **4 :** something that resembles a shell: as **a :** a framework or exterior structure; *esp* **:** a building with an unfinished interior **b** (1) **:** an external case or outside covering ⟨the ~ of a ship⟩ (2) **:** a thin usu. spherical layer or surface enclosing a space or surrounding an object ⟨an expanding ~ of gas around a neutron star⟩ **c :** a casing without substance ⟨mere effigies and ~s of men —Thomas Carlyle⟩ **d :** an edible crust for holding a filling ⟨a pastry ~⟩ ⟨a taco salad in a tortilla ~⟩ **e :** BAND SHELL **f :** a small beer glass **g :** an unlined article of outerwear **5 :** a shell-bearing mollusk **6 :** an impersonal attitude or manner that conceals the presence or absence of feeling ⟨he retreated into his ~⟩ **7 :** a narrow light racing boat propelled by one or more persons pulling oars or sculls **8 :** any of the regions occupied by the orbits of a group of electrons of approximately equal energy surrounding the nucleus of an atom **9 a :** a projectile for cannon containing an explosive bursting charge **b :** a metal or paper case which holds the charge of powder and shot or bullet used with breech-loading small arms **10 :** a plain usu. sleeveless blouse or sweater **11 :** a company or corporation that exists without assets or independent operations as a legal entity through which another company or corporation can conduct various dealings — **shell** *adj*

[2]**shell** *vt* (1562) **1 a :** to take out of a natural enclosing cover (as a shell, husk, pod, or capsule) ⟨~ peanuts⟩ **b :** to separate the kernels of (as an ear of Indian corn, wheat, or oats) from the cob, ear, or husk **2 :** to throw shells at, upon, or into **:** BOMBARD **3 :** to score heavily against (as an opposing pitcher in baseball) ~ *vi* **1 :** to fall or scale off in thin pieces **2 :** to cast the shell or exterior covering **:** fall out of the pod or husk ⟨nuts which ~ in falling⟩ **3 :** to gather shells (as from a beach)

she'll \ˈshēl, ˈshil\ (ca. 1590) **:** she will **:** she shall

[1]**shel•lac** \shə-ˈlak\ *n* [[1]*shell* + *lac*] (1704) **1 :** purified lac usu. prepared in thin orange or yellow flakes by heating and filtering and often bleached white **2 :** a preparation of lac dissolved usu. in alcohol and used chiefly as a wood filler and finish **3 a :** a composition containing shellac formerly used for making phonograph records **b :** an old 78 rpm phonograph record

[2]**shellac** *vt* **shel•lacked; shel•lack•ing** (1876) **1 :** to coat or otherwise treat with shellac or a shellac varnish **2 :** to defeat decisively

shellacking *n* (1931) **:** a decisive defeat **:** DRUBBING

shell•back \ˈshel-ˌbak\ *n* (1853) **1 :** an old or veteran sailor **2 :** a person who has crossed the equator and been initiated in the traditional ceremony

shell bean *n* (1868) **1 :** a bean grown primarily for its edible seeds — compare SNAP BEAN **2 :** the edible seed of a bean

shell•crack•er \ˈshel-ˌkra-kər\ *n* (ca. 1889) **:** REDEAR

shelled \ˈsheld\ *adj* (15c) **1 :** having a shell esp. of a specified kind — often used in combination ⟨pink-*shelled*⟩ ⟨thick-*shelled*⟩ **2 a :** having the shell removed ⟨~ nuts⟩ **b :** removed from the cob ⟨~ corn⟩

shell•er \ˈshe-lər\ *n* (1694) **1 :** one that shells ⟨a peanut ~⟩ **2 :** a person who collects seashells

shell•fish \-ˌfish\ *n* (bef. 12c) **:** an aquatic invertebrate animal with a shell; *esp* **:** an edible mollusk or crustacean

shell•fish•ery \-ˌfi-shə-rē, -ˌfish-rē\ *n* (1885) **:** a commercially exploited population of shellfish

shell game *n* (1890) **1 :** thimblerig played esp. with three walnut shells **2 :** FRAUD; *esp* **:** a swindle involving the substitution of something of little or no value for a valuable item

shell jacket *n* (1840) **1 :** a short tight military jacket worn buttoned up the front **2 :** MESS JACKET

shell out *vb* (1801) **:** PAY

shell pink *n* (1887) **:** a light yellowish pink

shell•proof \ˈshel-ˌprüf\ *adj* (ca. 1859) **:** capable of resisting shells or bombs

shell shock *n* (1915) **:** COMBAT FATIGUE

shell–shocked *adj* (1916) **1 :** affected with combat fatigue **2 :** mentally confused, upset, or exhausted as a result of excessive stress

shell steak *n* (ca. 1968) **:** the part of a short loin of beef that contains no tenderloin

shell•work \ˈshel-ˌwərk\ *n* (1592) **:** work adorned with shells or composed of a pattern of shells

shelly \ˈshe-lē\ *adj* **shell•i•er; -est** (1555) **1 :** abounding in or covered with shells ⟨a ~ shore⟩ **2 :** of, relating to, or resembling a shell

[1]**shel•ter** \ˈshel-tər\ *n* [origin unknown] (1585) **1 a :** something that covers or affords protection ⟨a bomb ~⟩ **b :** an establishment providing food and shelter (as to the homeless) **c :** an establishment that houses and feeds stray animals **2 :** a position or the state of being covered and protected ⟨took ~⟩ — **shel•ter•less** \-ləs\ *adj*

[2]**shelter** *vb* **shel•tered; shel•ter•ing** \-t(ə-)riŋ\ *vt* (1590) **1 :** to constitute or provide a shelter for **:** PROTECT ⟨has led a ~*ed* life⟩ **2 :** to place under shelter or protection ⟨~*ed* himself in a mountain cave⟩ **3 :** to protect (income) from taxation ~ *vi* **:** to take shelter — **shel•ter•er** \-tər-ər\ *n*

shel•ter•belt \ˈshel-tər-ˌbelt\ *n* (1868) **:** a barrier of trees and shrubs that protects (as crops) from wind and storm and lessens erosion

shelter half *n* (1911) **:** one of the halves of a shelter tent

shelter tent *n* (1862) **:** a small tent usu. consisting of two interchangeable pieces **:** PUP TENT

shel•tie *or* **shel•ty** \ˈshel-tē\ *n, pl* **shelties** [prob. fr. ON *Hjalti* Shetlander] (1650) **1 :** SHETLAND PONY **2 :** SHETLAND SHEEPDOG

shelve \ˈshelv\ *vb* **shelved; shelv•ing** [*shelf*] *vt* (1598) **1 :** to furnish with shelves **2 :** to place on a shelf ⟨~ books⟩ **3 a :** to remove from active service **b :** to put off or aside ⟨~ a project⟩ ~ *vi* **:** to slope in a formation like a shelf — **shelv•er** *n*

[1]**shelving** *n* (1678) **1 :** a sloping surface or place **2 :** the state or degree of sloping

[2]**shelving** *n* (1817) **1 :** material for shelves **2 :** SHELVES

Shem \ˈshem\ *n* [Heb *Shēm*] (bef. 12c) **:** the eldest son of Noah held to be the progenitor of the Semitic peoples

She•ma \shə-ˈmä\ *n* [Heb *shĕmaʿ* hear, first word of Deut 6:4] (1706) **:** the Jewish confession of faith made up of Deut 6:4–9 and 11:13–21 and Num 15:37–41

She•mi•ni Atze•reth \shə-ˈmē-nē-ät-ˈser-ət, -əth, -əs\ *n* [LHeb *shĕmīnī ʿăṣereth,* fr. Heb *shĕmīnī* eighth + *ʿăṣereth* assembly] (ca. 1905) **:** a Jewish festival following the seventh day of Sukkoth and marked by a special prayer for seasonal rain

Shem•ite \ˈshe-ˌmīt\ *n* [*Shem*] (1659) *archaic* **:** SEMITE — **She•mit•ic** \shə-ˈmi-tik\ *or* **Shem•it•ish** \ˈshe-ˌmī-tish\ *adj, archaic*

she•nan•i•gan \shə-ˈna-ni-gən\ *n* [origin unknown] (1855) **1 :** a devious trick used esp. for an underhand purpose **2 a :** tricky or questionable practices or conduct — usu. used in pl. **b :** high-spirited or mischievous activity — usu. used in pl.

shend \ˈshend\ *vt* **shent** \ˈshent\; **shend•ing** [ME, fr. OE *scendan;* akin to OE *scamu* shame — more at SHAME] (bef. 12c) **1** *archaic* **:** to put to shame or confusion **2** *archaic* **:** REPROVE, REVILE **3** *chiefly dial* **a :** INJURE, MAR **b :** RUIN, DESTROY

she–oak \ˈshē-ˌōk\ *n* (1792) **:** any of various casuarinas

She•ol \shē-ˈōl, ˈshē-ˌ\ *n* [Heb *Shĕʾōl*] (1597) **:** the abode of the dead in early Hebrew thought

[1]**shep•herd** \ˈshe-pərd\ *n* [ME *sheepherde,* fr. OE *scēaphyrde,* fr. *scēap* sheep + *hierde* herdsman; akin to OE *heord* herd] (bef. 12c) **1 :** a person who tends sheep **2 :** PASTOR **3 :** GERMAN SHEPHERD

[2]**shepherd** *vt* (1790) **1 :** to tend as a shepherd **2 :** to guide or guard in the manner of a shepherd ⟨~*ed* the bill through Congress⟩

shepherd dog *n* (15c) **:** SHEEPDOG

shep•herd•ess \ˈshe-pər-dəs\ *n* (14c) **:** a woman or girl who tends sheep; *also* **:** a rural girl or woman

shepherd's check *n* (1863) **:** a pattern of small even black-and-white checks; *also* **:** a fabric woven in this pattern — called also *shepherd's plaid*

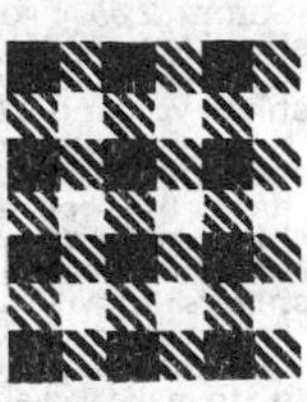

shepherd's check

shepherd's pie *n* (1877) **:** a meat pie with a mashed potato crust

shepherd's purse *n* (15c) **:** a white-flowered weedy annual herb (*Capsella bursa-pastoris*) of the mustard family with flat heart-shaped pods

sheqel *var of* SHEKEL

Sher•a•ton \ˈsher-ə-tən\ *adj* [Thomas *Sheraton*] (1883) **:** of, relating to, or being a style of furniture that originated in England around 1800 and is characterized by straight lines and graceful proportions

sher•bet \ˈshər-bət\ *also* **sher•bert** \-bərt\ *n* [Turk & Pers; Turk *şerbet,* fr. Pers *sharbat,* fr. Ar *sharba* drink] (1603) **1 :** a cold drink of sweetened and diluted fruit juice **2 :** an ice with milk, egg white, or gelatin added

sherd *var of* SHARD 2

sher•got•tite \ˈshər-gə-ˌtīt\ *n* [*Shergotty* (Sherghati), town in India] (ca. 1911) **:** any of a class of achondritic geologically young meteorites of feldspar and pyroxene

sherif *var of* SHARIF

sher•iff \ˈsher-əf\ *n* [ME *shirreve,* fr. OE *scīrgerēfa,* fr. *scīr* shire + *gerēfa* reeve — more at SHIRE, REEVE] (bef. 12c) **:** an important official of a shire or county charged primarily with judicial duties (as executing the processes and orders of courts and judges) — **sher•iff•dom** \-əf-dəm, -təm\ *n*

sher•lock \ˈshər-ˌläk, -lək\ *n, often cap* [*Sherlock* Holmes, detective in stories by Sir Arthur Conan Doyle] (1903) **:** DETECTIVE

she•ro \ˈshir-(ˌ)ō\ *n, pl* **sheroes** [blend of *she* and *hero*] (1982) **:** a woman regarded as a hero

Sher•pa \ˈsher-pə, ˈshər-\ *n* [of Tibetan origin; akin to Tibetan (Central dialects) *shār̥ba, shār̥po* easterner, Sherpa] (1847) **:** a member of a Tibetan people living on the high southern slopes of the Himalayas in eastern Nepal and known for providing support for foreign trekkers and mountain climbers

sher•ris \ˈsher-is\ *archaic var of* SHERRY

sher•ry \ˈsher-ē\ *n, pl* **sherries** [alter. of earlier *sherris* (taken as pl.), fr. *Xeres* (now *Jerez*), Spain] (1584) **:** a Spanish fortified wine with a distinctive nutty flavor; *also* **:** a similar wine produced elsewhere

she's \ˈshēz\ (1588) **:** she is **:** she has

Shet•land \ˈshet-lənd\ *n* (1836) **1 a :** SHETLAND PONY **b :** SHETLAND SHEEPDOG **2** *often not cap* **a :** a lightweight loosely twisted yarn of Shetland wool used for knitting and weaving **b :** a fabric or a garment made from Shetland wool

Shetland pony *n* (1801) **:** any of a breed of small stocky hardy ponies that originated in the Shetland Islands

Shetland sheepdog *n* (1909) **:** any of a breed of small heavy-coated dogs developed in the Shetland Islands that resemble miniature collies

\ə\ **abut** \ᵊ\ **kitten, F table** \ər\ **further** \a\ **ash** \ā\ **ace** \ä\ **mop, mar**
\au̇\ **out** \ch\ **chin** \e\ **bet** \ē\ **easy** \g\ **go** \i\ **hit** \ī\ **ice** \j\ **job**
\ŋ\ **sing** \ō\ **go** \ȯ\ **law** \ȯi\ **boy** \th\ **thin** \t͟h\ **the** \ü\ **loot** \u̇\ **foot**
\y\ **yet** \zh\ **vision, beige** \ḵ, ⁿ, œ, ue, ʸ\ *see* **Guide to Pronunciation**

Shetland wool *n* (1790) : fine wool from sheep raised in the Shetland Islands; *also* : yarn spun from this

sheugh \ˈshük\ *n* [ME *sogh* swamp; akin to MLG *sō* gutter] (1501) *chiefly Scot* : DITCH, TRENCH

shew \ˈshō\ *Brit var of* SHOW

shew·bread *or* **show·bread** \ˈshō-ˌbred\ *n* [trans. of G *Schaubrot*] (1526) : consecrated unleavened bread ritually placed by the Jewish priests of ancient Israel on a table in the sanctuary of the Tabernacle on the Sabbath

SHF *abbr* superhigh frequency

Shia \ˈshē-(ˌ)ä\ *n* [Ar *shīʿa* followers, faction, sect] (1626) **1** : the Muslims of the branch of Islam comprising sects believing in Ali and the Imams as the only rightful successors of Muhammad and in the concealment and messianic return of the last recognized Imam — compare SUNNI **2** : SHIITE **3** : the branch of Islam formed by the Shia

shi·at·su *also* **shi·at·zu** \shē-ˈät-(ˌ)sü\ *n, often cap* [short for Jp *shiatsu-ryōhō,* fr. *shi-* finger + *-atsu* pressure + *ryōhō* treatment] (1967) : ACUPRESSURE; *esp* : a form of acupressure that originated in Japan

Shi·ba Inu \ˈshē-bä-ˈē-nü\ *n* [Jp *shiba-inu,* fr. *shiba* brushwood + *inu* dog] (1982) : any of a breed of small thick-coated agile dogs developed in Japan

shib·bo·leth \ˈshi-bə-ləth *also* -ˌleth\ *n* [Heb *shibbōleth* stream; fr. the use of this word in Judg 12:6 as a test to distinguish Gileadites from Ephraimites] (1638) **1 a** : a word or saying used by adherents of a party, sect, or belief and usu. regarded by others as empty of real meaning ⟨the old ~*s* come rolling off their lips —Joseph Epstein⟩ **b** : a widely held belief ⟨today this book publishing ~ is a myth —L. A. Wood⟩ **c** : TRUISM, PLATITUDE ⟨some truth in the ~ that crime does not pay —Lee Rogow⟩ **2 a** : a use of language regarded as distinctive of a particular group ⟨accent was . . . a ~ of social class —Vivian Ducat⟩ **b** : a custom or usage regarded as distinguishing one group from others ⟨for most of the well-to-do in the town, dinner was a ~, its hour dividing mankind —Osbert Sitwell⟩

shiel \ˈshēl\ *n* [ME (northern dial.) *schele;* prob. akin to OFris *skiāle* stable, ON *skjōl* shelter] (13c) *chiefly Scot* : SHIELING

1shield \ˈshēld\ *n* [ME *sheld,* fr. OE *scield;* akin to OHG *scilt* shield and prob. to OE *sciell* shell] (bef. 12c) **1** : a broad piece of defensive armor carried on the arm **2** : one that protects or defends : DEFENSE **3** : DRESS SHIELD **4 a** : a device or part that serves as a protective cover or barrier **b** : a protective structure (as a carapace, scale, or plate) of some animals **5** : ESCUTCHEON; *esp* : one that is wide at the top and rounds to a point at the bottom **6** : the Precambrian nuclear mass of a continent that is surrounded and sometimes covered by sedimentary rocks **7** : something resembling a shield: as **a** : APOTHECIUM **b** : a police officer's badge **c** : a decorative or identifying emblem

2shield *vt* (bef. 12c) **1 a** : to protect with or as if with a shield : provide with a protective cover or shelter **b** : to cut off from observation : HIDE **2** *obs* : FORBID ***syn*** see DEFEND — **shield·er** *n*

shield law *n* (1971) : a law that protects journalists from forced disclosure of confidential news sources

shield volcano *n* (1911) : a broad rounded volcano that is built up by successive outpourings of very fluid lava

shiel·ing \ˈshē-lən, -liŋ\ *n* (1568) **1** *Brit* : a mountain hut used as a shelter by shepherds **2** *dial Brit* : a summer pasture in the mountains

shier *comparative of* SHY

shiest *superlative of* SHY

1shift \ˈshift\ *vb* [ME, fr. OE *sciftan* to divide, arrange; akin to ON *skipa* to arrange, assign] *vt* (13c) **1** : to exchange for or replace by another : CHANGE **2 a** : to change the place, position, or direction of : MOVE **b** : to make a change in (place) **3** : to change phonetically ~ *vi* **1 a** : to change place or position **b** : to change direction ⟨the wind ~*ed*⟩ **c** : to change gears **d** : to depress the shift key (as on a typewriter) **2 a** : to assume responsibility ⟨had to ~ for themselves⟩ **b** : to resort to expedients **3 a** : to go through a change ⟨she ~*ed* in her approach⟩ **b** : to change one's clothes **c** : to become changed phonetically — **shift·able** \ˈshif-tə-bəl\ *adj* — **shift gears** : to make a change

2shift *n* (1523) **1 a** : a means or device for effecting an end **b** (1) : a deceitful or underhand scheme : DODGE (2) : an effort or expedient exerted or tried in difficult circumstances : EXTREMITY ⟨was put to hard ~*s* for a living —Benjamin Franklin⟩ **2 a** *chiefly dial* : a change of clothes **b** (1) *chiefly dial* : SHIRT (2) : a woman's slip or chemise (3) : a usu. loose-fitting or semifitted dress **3 a** : a change in direction ⟨a ~ in the wind⟩ **b** : a change in emphasis, judgment, or attitude **4 a** : a group of people who work or occupy themselves in turn with other groups **b** (1) : a change of one group of people (as workers) for another in regular alternation (2) : a scheduled period of work or duty ⟨works the night ~⟩ **5** : a change in place or position: as **a** : a change in the position of the hand on a fingerboard (as of a violin) **b** (1) : FAULT 5 (2) : the relative displacement of rock masses on opposite sides of a fault or fault zone **c** (1) : a simultaneous change of position in football by two or more players from one side of the line to the other (2) : a change of positions made by one or more players in baseball to provide better defense against a particular hitter **d** : a change in frequency resulting in a change in position of a spectral line or band — compare DOPPLER EFFECT **e** : a movement of bits in a computer register a specified number of places to the right or left **6** : a removal from one person or thing to another : TRANSFER **7** : CONSONANT SHIFT **8** : a bid in bridge in a suit other than the suit one's partner has bid — compare JUMP **9** : GEARSHIFT ***syn*** see RESOURCE

shift·er \ˈshif-tər\ *n* (1920) : one that shifts; *esp* : GEARSHIFT

shift key *n* (1893) : a key on a keyboard that when pressed enables an alternate set of characters to be produced by the other keys

shift·less \ˈshif(t)-ləs\ *adj* [*shift* (resourcefulness)] (1584) **1** : lacking in resourcefulness : INEFFICIENT **2** : lacking in ambition or incentive : LAZY ⟨~ freeloaders⟩ — **shift·less·ly** *adv* — **shift·less·ness** *n*

shifty \ˈshif-tē\ *adj* **shift·i·er; -est** (ca. 1570) **1** : full of or ready with expedients : RESOURCEFUL **2 a** : given to deception, evasion, or fraud : TRICKY **b** : capable of evasive movement : ELUSIVE ⟨a ~ boxer⟩ **3** : indicative of a tricky nature ⟨~ eyes⟩ — **shift·i·ly** \-tə-lē\ *adv* — **shift·i·ness** \-tē-nəs\ *n*

shi·gel·la \shi-ˈge-lə\ *n, pl* **-gel·lae** \-ˈge-(ˌ)lē, -(ˌ)lī\ *also* **-gellas** [NL, fr. Kiyoshi *Shiga* †1957 Jp. bacteriologist] (1937) **1** : any of a genus (*Shigella*) of nonmotile rod-shaped bacteria that cause dysenteries in animals and esp. humans **2** : SHIGELLOSIS

shig·el·lo·sis \ˌshi-gə-ˈlō-səs\ *n, pl* **-lo·ses** \-ˈlō-ˌsēz\ [NL] (1944) : dysentery caused by shigellae

shih tzu \ˈshēd-ˈzü, ˈshēt-ˈsü\ *n, pl* **shih tzus** *also* **shih tzu** *often cap S&T* [Chin (Beijing) *shīzi* (*gǒu*), fr. *shīzi* lion + *gǒu* dog] (1921) : any of an old Chinese breed of toy dogs that have a square short unwrinkled muzzle, short muscular legs, and a long dense flowing coat

Shi'i \shē-ˈē, ˈshē-ē\ *n* [Ar *shīʿī,* fr. *shīʿa*] (1728) : SHIITE — **Shi'i** *adj*

Shi·ism \ˈshē-ˌi-zəm\ *n* (ca. 1883) : Islam as taught by the Shia

shii·ta·ke *also* **shi·ta·ke** \shē-ˈtä-kē\ *n* [Jp, fr. *shii,* the Japanese chinquapin + *take* mushroom] (1877) : a dark Asian mushroom (*Lentinus edodes* of the family Agaricaceae) widely cultivated esp. on woods of the beech family for its edible flavorful tan to brown cap

Shi·ite \ˈshē-ˌīt\ *n* (1728) : a Muslim of the Shia branch of Islam — **Shi·ite** *adj*

shi·ka·ri \shi-ˈkär-ē, -ˈka-rē\ *n* [Hindi & Urdu *shikārī,* fr. Pers, fr. *shikār* hunt] (1827) *India* : a big game hunter; *esp* : a professional hunter or guide

shik·sa *or* **shik·se** \ˈshik-sə\ *n* [Yiddish *shikse,* fem. of *sheygets* non-Jewish boy, fr. Heb *sheqeṣ* blemish, abomination] (1872) **1** *often disparaging* : a non-Jewish girl or woman **2** : a Jewish girl or woman who does not observe Jewish precepts — used esp. by Orthodox Jews

1shill \ˈshil\ *vi* [*2shill*] (ca. 1914) **1** : to act as a shill **2** : to act as a spokesperson or promoter ⟨the eminent Shakespearean producer . . . is now ~*ing* for a brokerage house —Andy Rooney⟩

2shill *n* [perh. short for *shillaber,* of unknown origin] (ca. 1916) **1 a** : one who acts as a decoy (as for a pitchman or gambler) **b** : one who makes a sales pitch or serves as a promoter **2** : PITCH 8a

shil·le·lagh *also* **shil·la·lah** \shə-ˈlā-lē\ *n* [*Shillelagh,* town in Ireland] (1772) : CUDGEL

shil·ling \ˈshi-liŋ\ *n* [ME, fr. OE *scilling;* akin to OHG *skilling,* a gold coin] (bef. 12c) **1 a** : a former monetary unit of the United Kingdom equal to 12 pence or 1/20 pound **b** : a former monetary unit equal to 1/20 pound of any of various countries in or formerly in the Commonwealth of Nations **2** : a coin representing one shilling **3** : any of several early American coins **4** — see MONEY table

Shil·luk \shi-ˈlük\ *n, pl* **Shilluk** *or* **Shilluks** [prob. fr. dial. Ar, fr. Shilluk *cɔlɔ,* a self-designation] (1790) **1** : a member of a Nilotic people of the Sudan dwelling mainly on the west bank of the White Nile **2** : the language of the Shilluk people

1shilly–shally \ˈshi-lē-ˌsha-lē\ *adv* [irreg. redupl. of *shall I*] (1700) : in an irresolute, undecided, or hesitating manner

2shilly–shally *adj* (1734) : IRRESOLUTE, VACILLATING

3shilly–shally *vi* **shilly–shall·ied; shilly–shally·ing** (1754) **1** : to show hesitation or lack of decisiveness or resolution **2** : DAWDLE

4shilly–shally *n* (1755) : INDECISION, IRRESOLUTION

shil·pit \ˈshil-pət\ *adj* [origin unknown] (1812) **1** *Scot* : pinched and starved in appearance **2** *Scot* : WEAK, INSIPID — used of drink

1shim \ˈshim\ *n* [origin unknown] (1860) : a thin often tapered piece of material (as wood, metal, or stone) used to fill in space between things (as for support, leveling, or adjustment of fit)

2shim *vt* **shimmed; shim·ming** (ca. 1890) : to fill out or level up by the use of a shim

1shim·mer \ˈshi-mər\ *vb* **shim·mered; shim·mer·ing** \ˈshi-mə-riŋ, ˈshim-riŋ\ [ME *schimeren,* fr. OE *scimerian;* akin to OE *scīnan* to shine — more at SHINE] *vi* (bef. 12c) **1** : to shine with a soft tremulous or fitful light : GLIMMER **2** : to reflect a wavering sometimes distorted visual image ~ *vt* : to cause to shimmer ***syn*** see FLASH

2shimmer *n* (1821) **1** : a light that shimmers : subdued sparkle or sheen : GLIMMER **2** : a wavering sometimes distorted visual image usu. resulting from heat-induced changes in atmospheric refraction — **shim·mery** \ˈshi-mə-rē, ˈshim-rē\ *adj*

1shim·my \ˈshi-mē\ *n, pl* **shimmies** (1837) **1** [by alter.] : CHEMISE **2** [short for *shimmy-shake*] : a jazz dance characterized by a shaking of the body from the shoulders down **3** : an abnormal vibration esp. in the front wheels of a motor vehicle

2shimmy *vi* **shim·mied; shim·my·ing** (1919) **1** : to shake, quiver, or tremble in or as if in dancing a shimmy **2** : to vibrate abnormally — used esp. of automobiles **3** : SHINNY

1shin \ˈshin\ *n* [ME *shine,* fr. OE *scinu;* akin to OHG *scina* shin, OE *scīa* shin, leg] (bef. 12c) : the front part of the vertebrate leg below the knee

2shin *vb* **shinned; shin·ning** *vi* (1829) **1** : SHINNY **2** : to move forward rapidly on foot ~ *vt* **1** : to kick or strike on the shins **2** : to climb by shinnying

3shin \ˈshēn, ˈshin\ *n* [Heb *shīn*] (ca. 1823) : the 22d letter of the Hebrew alphabet — see ALPHABET table

Shin \ˈshin, ˈshēn\ *n* [Jp, lit., truth] (1877) : a major Japanese Buddhist sect that emphasizes salvation by faith in exclusive worship of Amida Buddha

Shi·na \ˈshē-nə\ *n* [Shina *ṣiṇā',* fr. *ṣiṇ* speaker of Shina] (1854) : an Indo-Aryan language spoken in Gilgit in northern Kashmir

shin·bone \ˈshin-ˌbōn\ *n* (bef. 12c) : TIBIA 1

shin·dig \ˈshin-ˌdig\ *n* [prob. alter. of *shindy*] (1842) **1 a** : a social gathering with dancing **b** : a usu. large or lavish party **2** : SHINDY 2

shin·dy \ˈshin-dē\ *n, pl* **shindys** *or* **shindies** [prob. alter. of *1shinny*] (1814) **1** : SHINDIG 1 **2** : FRACAS, UPROAR

1shine \ˈshīn\ *vb* **shone** \ˈshōn, *esp Canad & Brit* ˈshän\ *or* **shined; shin·ing** [ME, fr. OE *scīnan;* akin to OHG *skīnan* to shine and perh. to Gk *skia* shadow] *vi* (bef. 12c) **1** : to emit rays of light **2** : to be bright by reflection of light **3 a** : to be eminent, conspicuous, or distinguished ⟨~*s* in math⟩ **b** : to perform extremely well ⟨when will stocks really ~ again? —Temma Ehrenfeld⟩ **4** : to have a bright glowing appearance ⟨his face *shone* with enthusiasm⟩ **5** : to be conspicuously evident or clear ~ *vt* **1 a** : to cause to emit light **b** : to throw or direct the light of **2** *past & past part* **shined** : to make bright by polishing ⟨*shined* his shoes⟩

2shine *n* (15c) **1** : brightness caused by the emission of light **2** : brightness caused by the reflection of light : LUSTER ⟨the ~ of polished silver⟩ **3** : BRILLIANCE, SPLENDOR ⟨still has a ~ about her⟩ **4** : fair weather : SUNSHINE ⟨rain or ~⟩ **5** : TRICK, CAPER — usu. used in pl. **6** : LIKING, FANCY ⟨took a ~ to him⟩ **7 a** : a polish or gloss given to shoes **b** : a single polishing of a pair of shoes

shin·er \ˈshī-nər\ *n* (14c) **1** : one that shines **2** : a silvery fish; *esp* : any of numerous small freshwater American cyprinid fishes (esp. genus *Notropis*) — compare GOLDEN SHINER **3** : BLACK EYE 1

[1]**shin·gle** \'shiŋ-gəl\ *n* [ME *schingel,* alter. of OE *scindel,* fr. ML *scindula,* alter. of L *scandula*] (13c) **1 :** a small thin piece of building material often with one end thicker than the other for laying in overlapping rows as a covering for the roof or sides of a building **2 :** a small signboard esp. designating a professional office — used chiefly in the phrase *hang out one's shingle* **3 :** a woman's haircut with the hair trimmed short from the back of the head to the nape

[2]**shingle** *vt* **shin·gled; shin·gling** \-g(ə-)liŋ\ (1562) **1 :** to cover with or as if with shingles **2 :** to bob and shape (the hair) in a shingle **3 :** to lay out or arrange so as to overlap — **shin·gler** \-g(ə-)lər\ *n*

[3]**shingle** *n* [ME *chyngell;* akin to MLG *singel* seashore gravel] (15c) **1 :** coarse rounded detritus or alluvial material esp. on the seashore that differs from ordinary gravel only in the larger size of the stones **2 :** a place strewn with shingle — **shin·gly** \-g(ə-)lē\ *adj*

shin·gles \'shiŋ-gəlz\ *n pl but sing in constr* [ME *schingles,* by folk etymology fr. ML *cingulus,* fr. L *cingulum* girdle — more at CINGULUM] (14c) **:** an acute viral inflammation of the sensory ganglia of spinal and cranial nerves that is associated with a vesicular eruption and neuralgic pains and is caused by reactivation of the herpesvirus causing chicken pox — called also *herpes zoster, zoster*

Shin·gon \'shin-ˌgän, 'shēn-\ *n* [Jp] (1727) **:** an esoteric Japanese Buddhist sect claiming the achievement of Buddhahood in this life through prescribed rituals

shining *adj* (bef. 12c) **1 :** emitting or reflecting light **2 :** bright and often splendid in appearance **:** RESPLENDENT **3 :** possessing a distinguished quality **:** ILLUSTRIOUS **4 :** full of sunshine

shin·leaf \'shin-ˌlēf\ *n, pl* **shinleafs** (ca. 1818) **:** any of several wintergreens (esp. *Pyrola elliptica*) with lustrous evergreen basal leaves and racemose white or pinkish flowers

shin·nery \'shi-nə-rē\ *n, pl* **-ner·ies** [modif. of LaF *chênière,* fr. F *chêne* oak] (1901) **:** a dense growth of small trees or an area of such growth; *esp* **:** one of scrub oak in the West and Southwest

[1]**shin·ny** *also* **shin·ney** \'shi-nē\ *n* [perh. fr. [1]*shin*] (1672) **:** a variation of hockey played by children with a curved stick and a ball or block of wood; *also* **:** the stick used

[2]**shinny** *vi* **shin·nied; shin·ny·ing** [alter. of [2]*shin*] (1851) **:** to move oneself up or down something vertical (as a pole) esp. by alternately hugging it with the arms or hands and the legs

shin·plas·ter \'shin-ˌplas-tər\ *n* (1824) **1 :** a piece of privately issued paper currency; *esp* **:** one poorly secured and depreciated in value **2 :** a piece of fractional currency

shin splints *n pl but sing or pl in constr* (ca. 1930) **:** injury to and inflammation of the tibial and toe extensor muscles or their fasciae caused by repeated minimal traumas (as by running)

Shin·to \'shin-(ˌ)tō\ *n* [Jp *shintō*] (1727) **:** the indigenous religion of Japan consisting chiefly in the cultic devotion to deities of natural forces and veneration of the Emperor as a descendant of the sun goddess — **Shinto** *adj* — **Shin·to·ism** \-(ˌ)tō-ˌi-zəm\ *n* — **Shin·to·ist** \-ˌtō-ist\ *n or adj* — **Shin·to·is·tic** \ˌshin-tō-'is-tik\ *adj*

shiny \'shī-nē\ *adj* **shin·i·er; -est** (1558) **1 :** having a smooth glossy surface ⟨∼ new shoes⟩ **2 a :** bright with the rays of the sun **:** SUNSHINY **b :** filled with light **3 :** rubbed or worn smooth **4 :** lustrous with natural secretions ⟨a ∼ nose⟩ — **shin·i·ness** *n*

[1]**ship** \'ship\ *n, often attrib* [ME, fr. OE *scip;* akin to OHG *skif* ship] (bef. 12c) **1 a :** a large seagoing vessel **b :** a sailing vessel having a bowsprit and usu. three masts each composed of a lower mast, a topmast, and a topgallant mast **2 :** BOAT; *esp* **:** one propelled by power or sail **3 :** a ship's crew **4 :** FORTUNE 3 ⟨when their ∼ comes in they'll be able to live in better style⟩ **5 :** AIRSHIP, AIRPLANE, SPACECRAFT

[2]**ship** *vb* **shipped; ship·ping** *vt* (14c) **1 a :** to place or receive on board a ship for transportation by water **b :** to cause to be transported ⟨*shipped* him off to prep school⟩ **2** *obs* **:** to provide with a ship **3 :** to put in place for use ⟨∼ the tiller⟩ **4 :** to take into a ship or boat ⟨∼ the gangplank⟩ **5 :** to engage for service on a ship **6 :** to take (as water) over the side — used of a boat or a ship ∼ *vi* **1 :** to embark on a ship **2 a :** to go or travel by ship — often used with *out* **b :** to proceed by ship or other means under military orders — often used with *out* **3 :** to engage to serve on shipboard **4 :** to be sent for delivery ⟨the order will ∼ soon⟩ — **ship·pa·ble** \'shi-pə-bəl\ *adj*

-ship *n suffix* [ME, fr. OE *-scipe;* akin to OHG *-scaft* -ship, OE *scieppan* to shape — more at SHAPE] **1 :** state **:** condition **:** quality ⟨friend*ship*⟩ **2 :** office **:** dignity **:** profession ⟨clerk*ship*⟩ **3 :** art **:** skill ⟨horseman*ship*⟩ **4 :** something showing, exhibiting, or embodying a quality or state ⟨town*ship*⟩ ⟨fellow*ship*⟩ **5 :** one entitled to a (specified) rank, title, or appellation ⟨his Lord*ship*⟩ **6 :** the body of persons participating in a specified activity ⟨reader*ship*⟩ ⟨listener*ship*⟩

ship biscuit *n* (1797) **:** HARDTACK — called also *ship bread*

[1]**ship·board** \'ship-ˌbȯrd\ *n* (13c) **1 :** the side of a ship **2 :** SHIP ⟨met on ∼⟩

[2]**shipboard** *adj* (1857) **:** existing or taking place on board a ship

ship·borne \'ship-ˌbȯrn\ *adj* (ca. 1835) **:** transported or designed to be transported by ship ⟨∼ aircraft⟩

ship·build·er \'ship-ˌbil-dər\ *n* (ca. 1700) **:** one who designs or constructs ships — **ship·build·ing** \-diŋ\ *n*

ship·fit·ter \'ship-ˌfi-tər\ *n* (1941) **1 :** one that fits together the structural members of ships and puts them into position for riveting or welding **2 :** a naval enlisted man who works in sheet metal and performs the work of a plumber aboard ship

ship·lap \-ˌlap\ *n* (1895) **:** wooden sheathing in which the boards are rabbeted so that the edges of each board lap over the edges of adjacent boards to make a flush joint

ship·load \-'lōd, -ˌlōd\ *n* (1639) **1 :** as much or as many as will fill or load a ship **2 :** an indefinitely large amount or number

ship·man \-mən\ *n* (bef. 12c) **1 :** SAILOR, SEAMAN **2 :** SHIPMASTER

ship·mas·ter \-ˌmas-tər\ *n* (14c) **:** the master or commander of a ship other than a warship

ship·mate \-ˌmāt\ *n* (1748) **:** a fellow sailor

ship·ment \-mənt\ *n* (1799) **1 :** the act or process of shipping **2 :** the goods shipped

ship of state (1615) **:** the affairs of a state symbolized as a ship on a course

ship of the line (1706) **:** a large warship; *specif* **:** a square-rigged warship having at least two gun decks and designed to be positioned for battle in a line with other such ships

ship·own·er \'ship-ˌō-nər\ *n* (ca. 1530) **:** the owner of a ship

ship·per \'shi-pər\ *n* (1755) **:** one that sends goods by any form of conveyance

shipping *n* (14c) **1 a :** passage on a ship **b :** SHIPS **c :** the body of ships in one place or belonging to one port or country **2 :** the act or business of one that ships

shipping clerk *n* (ca. 1858) **:** one who is employed in a shipping room to assemble, pack, and send out or receive goods

ship·shape \ˌship-'shāp, 'ship-ˌ\ *adj* [short for earlier *shipshapen,* fr. *ship* + *shapen,* archaic pp. of *shape*] (1769) **:** TRIM, TIDY

ship·side \'ship-ˌsīd\ *n* (15c) **:** the area adjacent to a ship; *specif* **:** a dock at which a ship loads or unloads passengers and freight

ship's papers *n pl* (1830) **:** the papers a ship is legally required to carry for due inspection to show the character of the ship and cargo

ship·way \'ship-ˌwā\ *n* (1834) **:** the ways on which a ship is built

ship·worm \-ˌwərm\ *n* (ca. 1778) **:** any of various marine clams (esp. family Teredinidae) that have a shell used for burrowing in submerged wood and a wormlike body and that cause damage to wharf piles and wooden ships

[1]**ship·wreck** \-ˌrek\ *n* [alter. of earlier *shipwrack,* fr. ME *schipwrak,* fr. OE *scipwræc,* fr. *scip* ship + *wræc* something driven by the sea — more at WRACK] (12c) **1 :** a wrecked ship or its parts **2 :** the destruction or loss of a ship **3 :** an irretrievable loss or failure

[2]**shipwreck** *vt* (1589) **1 a :** to cause to experience shipwreck **b :** RUIN **2 :** to destroy (a ship) by grounding or foundering

ship·wright \'ship-ˌrīt\ *n* (bef. 12c) **:** a carpenter skilled in ship construction and repair

ship·yard \-ˌyärd\ *n* (1647) **:** a yard, place, or enclosure where ships are built or repaired

Shi·raz \shi-'räz\ *n* [prob. fr. F *chiraz,* alter. (influenced by *Shiraz,* city in Persia) of *syrah, syrac* Syrah] (1927) **:** SYRAH

shire \'shī(-ə)r, *in place-name compounds* ˌshir, shər\ *n* [ME, fr. OE *scīr* office, shire; akin to OHG *scīra* care] (bef. 12c) **1 :** an administrative subdivision; *esp* **:** a county in England **2 :** any of an old breed of large heavy draft horses of British origin having heavily feathered legs

shire town *n* (15c) **1** *Brit* **:** a town that is the seat of the government of a shire **2** *NewEng* **:** a town where a court of superior jurisdiction (as a circuit court or a court with a jury) sits

shirk \'shərk\ *vb* [origin unknown] *vi* (1681) **1 :** to go stealthily **:** SNEAK **2 :** to evade the performance of an obligation ∼ *vt* **:** AVOID, EVADE ⟨∼ one's duty⟩ — **shirk·er** *n*

Shir·ley poppy \'shər-lē-\ *n* [*Shirley* vicarage, Croydon, England] (1886) **:** a cultivated corn poppy with brightly colored usu. white, pink, or red single or double flowers

shirr \'shər\ *vt* [origin unknown] (1891) **1 :** to draw (as cloth) together in a shirring **2 :** to bake (eggs removed from the shell) until set

shirr·ing \'shər-iŋ\ *n* (ca. 1882) **:** a decorative gathering (as of cloth) made by drawing up the material along two or more parallel lines of stitching

shirt \'shərt\ *n* [ME *shirte,* fr. OE *scyrte;* akin to ON *skyrta* shirt, OE *scort* short] (bef. 12c) **1 :** a garment for the upper part of the body: as **a :** a cloth garment usu. having a collar, sleeves, a front opening, and a tail long enough to be tucked inside trousers or a skirt **b :** UNDERSHIRT **2 :** all or a large part of one's money or resources ⟨lost his ∼ on that business deal⟩ — **shirt·less** \-ləs\ *adj*

shirt·dress \-ˌdres\ *n* (1943) **:** a tailored dress patterned after a shirt and having buttons down the front

shirt·front \-ˌfrənt\ *n* (1838) **:** the front of a shirt; *also* **:** the part of a man's shirt not covered by coat or vest

shirt·ing \'shər-tiŋ\ *n* (1604) **:** fabric suitable for shirts

shirt jacket *n* (1879) **:** a jacket designed in the style of a shirt — called also *shirt-jac*

shirt·mak·er \'shərt-ˌmā-kər\ *n* (ca. 1858) **:** one that makes shirts

[1]**shirt·sleeve** \-ˌslēv\ *n* (ca. 1566) **:** the sleeve of a shirt — **in one's shirtsleeves** *or* **in shirtsleeves :** wearing a shirt but no coat

[2]**shirtsleeve** *also* **shirt·sleeves** \-ˌslēvz\ *or* **shirt·sleeved** \-ˌslēvd\ *adj* (1842) **1 a :** being without a coat ⟨a ∼ spectator⟩ **b :** calling for the removal of coats for the sake of comfort or efficiency ⟨∼ weather⟩ **2 :** marked by informality and directness ⟨∼ diplomacy⟩

[1]**shirt·tail** \'shərt-ˌtāl\ *n* (1809) **1 :** the part of a shirt that reaches below the waist esp. in the back **2 :** something small or inadequate

[2]**shirttail** *adj* (1845) **1 :** very young **:** IMMATURE ⟨∼ boys fishing in the creek⟩ **2 :** distantly and indefinitely related ⟨a ∼ cousin on her father's side⟩ **3 :** small, trivial, or short typically to the point of inadequacy ⟨has a gullied ∼ ranch in the hills⟩

shirt·waist \'shərt-ˌwāst\ *n* (1879) **:** a woman's tailored garment (as a blouse or dress) with details copied from men's shirts

shirty \'shər-tē\ *adj* (1846) *chiefly Brit* **:** ANGRY, IRRITATED

shish ke·bab \'shish-kə-ˌbäb\ *n* [Turk *şişkebabı,* fr. *şiş* spit + *kebap* roast meat] (1913) **:** kebab cooked on skewers

[1]**shit** \'shit, *interjectionally also* 'shē-ət\ *n* [ME **shit,* fr. OE *scite;* akin to OE *-scītan* to defecate] (ca. 1526) **1** *usu vulgar* **:** FECES **2** *usu vulgar* **:** an act of defecation **3** *usu vulgar* **:** NONSENSE, CRAP **4** *usu vulgar* **:** any of several intoxicating or narcotic drugs; *esp* **:** HEROIN **5** *usu vulgar* **:** DAMN 2 **6** *usu vulgar* **:** a worthless, offensive, or detestable person **7** *usu vulgar* **a —** used as an interjection **b —** used as an intensive usu. with *the* — **shit·ty** \'shi-tē\ *adj, usu vulgar*

[2]**shit** \'shit\ *vb* **shit** *or* **shat** \'shat\; **shit·ting** [alter. of earlier *shite,* fr. ME *shiten,* fr. OE *-scītan;* akin to OHG *scīzan* to defecate and prob. to OE *scēadan* to separate — more at SHED] *vi* (14c) *usu vulgar* **:** DEFECATE ∼ *vt* **1** *usu vulgar* **:** to defecate in **2** *usu vulgar* **:** to attempt to deceive **:** BULLSHIT

shitake *var of* SHIITAKE

shit·less \'shit-ləs\ *adv* (1936) *usu vulgar* **:** to an extreme degree — used as an intensive esp. with *scare*

shit·load \'shit-ˌlōd\ *n* (1973) *usu vulgar* **:** a very large amount **:** LOT

shit·tah \'shi-tə\ *n, pl* **shittahs** *or* **shit·tim** \'shi-təm\ [Heb *shiṭṭāh*]

(1611) : a tree of uncertain identity but prob. an acacia (as *Acacia seyal*) from the wood of which the ark and fittings of the Hebrew tabernacle were made

shit·tim·wood \ˈshi-təm-ˌwu̇d\ *n* [Heb *shiṭṭīm* (pl. of *shiṭṭāh*) + E *wood*] (1588) **1** : the wood of the shittah tree **2** : any of several trees (genus *Bumelia*, esp. *B. lanuginosa*) of the sapodilla family of the southern U.S.; *also* : their hard heavy dense wood

shiv \ˈshiv\ *n* [alter. of *chiv*, of unknown origin] (1915) *slang* : KNIFE

Shi·va \ˈshi-və, ˈshē-\ *also* **Si·va** \ˈsi-və, ˈshi-, ˈsē-, ˈshē-\ *n* [Skt *Śiva*] (1788) : the god of destruction and regeneration in the Hindu sacred triad — compare BRAHMA, VISHNU

shi·vah *or* **shi·va** *also* **shi·ve** \ˈshi-və\ *n* [Heb *shibhʿāh* seven (days)] (1875) : a traditional seven-day period of mourning the dead that is observed in Jewish homes — often used in the phrase *sit shivah*

shiv·a·ree \ˌshi-və-ˈrē, ˈshi-və-ˌ\ *n* [modif. of F *charivari* — more at CHARIVARI] (1843) : a noisy mock serenade to a newly married couple — **shivaree** *vt*

[1]**shiv·er** \ˈshi-vər\ *n* [ME; akin to OHG *scivaro* splinter] (13c) : one of the small pieces into which a brittle thing is broken by sudden violence

[2]**shiver** *vb* **shiv·ered; shiv·er·ing** \ˈshi-və-riŋ, ˈshiv-riŋ\ (13c) : to break into many small pieces : SHATTER

[3]**shiver** *vb* **shiv·ered; shiv·er·ing** \ˈshi-və-riŋ, ˈshiv-riŋ\ [ME, alter. of *chiveren*] *vi* (15c) **1** : to undergo trembling : QUIVER **2** : to tremble in the wind as it strikes first one and then the other side (of a sail) ~ *vt* : to cause (a sail) to shiver by steering close to the wind

[4]**shiver** *n* (1727) **1** : an instance of shivering : TREMBLE **2** : an intense shivery sensation esp. of fear — often used in pl. with *the* ⟨horror movies give him the ~*s*⟩ **3** : a hard blow (as with a forearm) esp. to the head or neck

[1]**shiv·ery** \ˈshi-və-rē, ˈshiv-rē\ *adj* (1683) : easily broken into shivers

[2]**shivery** *adj* (1747) **1** : characterized by shivers **2** : causing shivers

shlemiel *var of* SCHLEMIEL

shlep *var of* SCHLEP

shlock *var of* SCHLOCK

shlub *var of* SCHLUB

shm- — see SCHM-

Sho·ah \ˈshō-ə, -ˌä\ *n* [ModHeb *shōʾāh*, lit., catastrophe, fr. Heb] (1967) : HOLOCAUST 3a

[1]**shoal** \ˈshōl\ *adj* [alter. of ME *shold*, fr. OE *sceald* — more at SKELETON] (ca. 1554) : SHALLOW

[2]**shoal** *n* (1555) **1** : SHALLOW **2** : a sandbank or sandbar that makes the water shallow

[3]**shoal** *vi* (1574) : to become shallow ~ *vt* **1** : to come to a shallow or less deep part of **2** : to cause to become shallow or less deep

[4]**shoal** *n* [ME *shole, fr. OE *scolu* multitude — more at SCHOOL] (1579) : a large group or number : CROWD ⟨a ~ of fish⟩

[5]**shoal** *vi* (1610) : THRONG, SCHOOL

shoat \ˈshōt\ *n* [ME *schot*, *shote* projectile, young branch, young weaned pig — more at SHOOT] (15c) : a young hog and esp. one that has been weaned

[1]**shock** \ˈshäk\ *n* [ME; akin to MHG *schoc* heap] (14c) : a pile of sheaves of grain or stalks of Indian corn set up in a field with the butt ends down

[2]**shock** *vt* (15c) : to collect into shocks

[3]**shock** *n, often attrib* [MF *choc*, fr. *choquer* to strike against, fr. OF *choquier*, prob. of Gmc origin; akin to MD *schocken* to jolt] (1565) **1** : the impact or encounter of individuals or groups in combat **2 a** : a violent shake or jar : CONCUSSION **b** : an effect of such violence **3 a** (1) : a disturbance in the equilibrium or permanence of something (2) : a sudden or violent mental or emotional disturbance **b** : something that causes such disturbance ⟨the loss came as a ~⟩ **c** : a state of being so disturbed ⟨were in ~ after they heard the news⟩ **4** : a state of profound depression of the vital processes associated with reduced blood volume and pressure and caused usu. by severe esp. crushing injuries, hemorrhage, or burns **5** : sudden stimulation of the nerves and convulsive contraction of the muscles caused by the discharge of electricity through the animal body **6 a** : STROKE 5 **b** : CORONARY THROMBOSIS **7** : SHOCK ABSORBER ***syn*** see IMPACT

[4]**shock** *vt* (1656) **1 a** : to strike with surprise, terror, horror, or disgust **b** : to cause to undergo a physical or nervous shock **c** : to subject to the action of an electrical discharge **2** : to drive by or as if by a shock ~ *vi* **1** : to meet with a shock : COLLIDE **2** : to cause surprise or shock ⟨an exhibit meant to ~⟩ — **shock·able** \ˈshä-kə-bəl\ *adj*

[5]**shock** *adj* [perh. fr. [1]*shock*] (1681) : BUSHY, SHAGGY

[6]**shock** *n* (1819) : a thick bushy mass (as of hair)

shock absorber *n* (1906) : any of several devices for absorbing the energy of sudden impulses or shocks in machinery or structures

shock·er \ˈshä-kər\ *n* (ca. 1824) : one that shocks; *esp* : something horrifying or offensive (as a sensational film or work of fiction)

shock front *n* (1949) : the advancing edge of a shock wave

shock·ing \ˈshä-kiŋ\ *adj* (1655) : extremely startling, distressing, or offensive ⟨~ news⟩ — **shock·ing·ly** \-kiŋ-lē\ *adv*

shocking pink *n* (1938) : a striking, vivid, bright, or intense pink

shock jock *n* (1986) : a radio personality noted for provocative or inflammatory commentary

shock·proof \ˈshäk-ˌprüf\ *adj* (1911) **1** : incapable of being shocked **2 a** : resistant to damage by shock **b** : unlikely to cause shock : protectively insulated ⟨a ~ switch⟩

shock therapy *n* (1917) : the treatment of mental disorder by the artificial induction of coma or convulsions through use of drugs or electric current — called also *shock treatment*

shock troops *n pl* (1917) **1** : troops esp. suited and chosen for offensive work because of their high morale, training, and discipline **2** : a group of people militant in pressing for a cause

shock tube *n* (1949) : a usu. enclosed tube in which experimental shock waves are produced as a result of the rupturing of a diaphragm separating two chambers containing a gas or gases at differential pressure

shock wave *n* (1907) **1** : a compressional wave of high amplitude caused by a shock (as from an earthquake or explosion) to the medium through which the wave travels **2** : a violent often pulsating disturbance or reaction ⟨*shock waves* of rebellion⟩

shod \ˈshäd\ *adj* [ME, fr. pp. of *shoen* to shoe, fr. OE *scōgan*, fr. *scōh* shoe — more at SHOE] (13c) **1 a** : wearing footgear (as shoes) **b** : equipped with tires **2** : furnished or equipped with a shoe

[1]**shod·dy** \ˈshä-dē\ *n* [origin unknown] (1832) **1 a** : a reclaimed wool from materials that are not felted that is of better quality and longer staple than mungo **b** : a fabric often of inferior quality manufactured wholly or partly from reclaimed wool **2 a** : inferior, imitative, or pretentious articles or matter **b** : pretentious vulgarity

[2]**shoddy** *adj* **shod·di·er; -est** (1847) **1** : made wholly or partly of shoddy **2 a** : cheaply imitative : vulgarly pretentious ⟨~ merchandise⟩ **b** : hastily or poorly done : INFERIOR ⟨~ workmanship⟩ **c** : SHABBY, DISREPUTABLE ⟨~ business deals⟩ — **shod·di·ly** \ˈshä-də-lē\ *adv* — **shod·di·ness** \ˈshä-dē-nəs\ *n*

[1]**shoe** \ˈshü\ *n* [ME *shoo*, fr. OE *scōh*; akin to OHG *scuoh* shoe] (bef. 12c) **1 a** : an outer covering for the human foot typically having a thick or stiff sole with an attached heel and an upper part of lighter material (as leather) **b** : a metal plate or rim for the hoof of an animal **2** : something resembling a shoe in function or placement **3** *pl* : another's place, function, or viewpoint ⟨steps from assistant stage manager into the star's ~*s* —Steven Fuller⟩ **4** : a device that retards, stops, or controls the motion of an object; *esp* : the part of a brake that presses on the brake drum **5 a** : any of various devices that are inserted in or run along a track or groove to guide a movement, provide a contact or friction grip, or protect against wear, damage, or slipping **b** : a device (as a clip or track) on a camera that permits attachment of an accessory item (as a flash unit) **6** : a dealing box designed to hold several decks of playing cards — **shoe·less** *adj*

[2]**shoe** *vt* **shod** \ˈshäd\ *also* **shoed** \ˈshüd\; **shoe·ing** \ˈshü-iŋ\ (bef. 12c) **1** : to furnish with a shoe **2** : to cover for protection, strength, or ornament

shoe·bill \ˈshü-ˌbil\ *n* (1861) : a large gray wading bird (*Balaeniceps rex*) related to the storks and herons that inhabits wetlands of eastern Africa and has a thick broad bill

shoe·black \-ˌblak\ *n* (1751) : BOOTBLACK

[1]**shoe·horn** \-ˌhȯrn\ *n* (1589) : a curved piece (as of horn, wood, or metal) used in putting on a shoe

[2]**shoehorn** *vt* (1859) **1** : to force to be included or admitted ⟨~*ed* irrelevant arguments into his essay⟩ **2** : to force or compress into an insufficient space or period of time : SQUEEZE ⟨~ the past, present, and future into about 500 pages —Otis Port⟩

shoe·lace \ˈshü-ˌlās\ *n* (ca. 1647) : a lace or string for fastening a shoe

shoe–leath·er \ˈshü-ˌle-t͟hər\ *adj* (1951) : involving or using basic, direct, or old-fashioned methods ⟨~ journalism⟩

shoe·mak·er \-ˌmā-kər\ *n* (14c) : a person whose occupation is making or repairing shoes

shoe·pac *or* **shoe·pack** \ˈshü-ˌpak\ *n* [by folk etymology fr. Delaware Jargon (Delaware-based pidgin) *seppock* shoe, fr. Delaware (Unami dial.) *čípahkɔ* shoes] (1731) : a waterproof laced boot worn esp. over heavy socks in cold weather

[1]**shoe·string** \ˈshü-ˌstriŋ\ *n* (1616) **1** : SHOELACE **2** [fr. shoestrings being a typical item sold by itinerant vendors] : a small sum of money : capital inadequate or barely adequate to the needs of a transaction ⟨started the business on a ~⟩

[2]**shoestring** *adj* (1878) **1** : narrow and long like a shoestring ⟨~ french fries⟩ **2** : operating on, accomplished by, or consisting of a small amount of money or capital ⟨a ~ budget⟩

shoestring catch *n* (1926) : a catch (as in baseball) made very close to the feet

shoe tree *n* (1827) : a foot-shaped device for inserting in a shoe to preserve its shape

sho·far \ˈshō-ˌfär, -fər\ *n, pl* **sho·froth** \shō-ˈfrōt, -ˈfrōth, -ˈfrōs\ [Heb *shōphār*] (1833) : a ram's-horn trumpet blown by the ancient Hebrews in battle and during religious observances and used in modern Judaism esp. during Rosh Hashanah and at the end of Yom Kippur

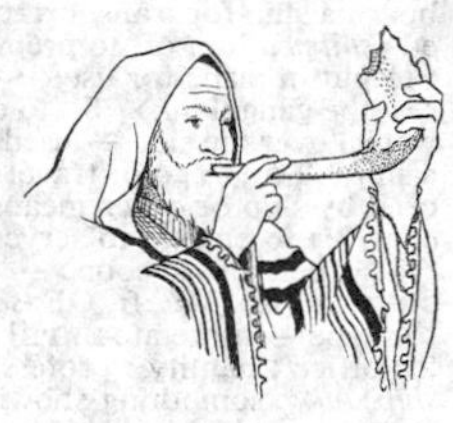
shofar

[1]**shog** \ˈshäg\ *vb* **shogged; shog·ging** [ME *shoggen*, *shaggen*; prob. akin to MD *schocken* to shake, jolt] *vt* (15c) **1** *chiefly dial* : JOLT, SHAKE ~ *vi* **1** *chiefly dial* : to move in a jerky manner **2** *chiefly dial* : to move along

[2]**shog** *n* (1584) *chiefly dial* : SHAKE, JOLT

sho·gun \ˈshō-gən\ *n* [Jp *shōgun*] (1727) : one of a line of military governors ruling Japan until the revolution of 1867–68 — **sho·gun·al** \ˈshō-gə-nəl\ *adj* — **sho·gun·ate** \ˈshō-gə-nət, -ˌnāt\ *n*

sho·ji \ˈshō-(ˌ)jē\ *n, pl* **shoji** *also* **shojis** [Jp *shōji*] (1880) : a paper screen serving as a wall, partition, or sliding door

sho·jo \ˈshō-(ˌ)jō\ *n, pl* **shojo** [Jp *shōjo manga*, lit., girl manga] (1994) : manga intended primarily for girls

sholom *var of* SHALOM

Sho·na \ˈshō-nə\ *n, pl* **Shona** *or* **Shonas** (ca. 1895) **1** : a member of any of a group of Bantu peoples of Zimbabwe and southern Mozambique **2** : the group of languages spoken by the Shona

shone *past and past part of* SHINE

[1]**shoo** \ˈshü\ *interj* [ME *schowe*] (15c) — used esp. in driving away an unwanted animal

[2]**shoo** *vt* (ca. 1798) : to scare, drive, or send away by or as if by crying *shoo* ⟨~*ed* us away from the kitchen⟩

shoo·fly \ˈshü-ˌflī\ *n* [[1]*shoo* + *fly*] (1886) **1** : a child's rocker having the seat built on or usu. between supports representing an animal figure **2** : any of several plants held to repel flies

shoofly pie *n* (1924) : a rich pie of Pennsylvania Dutch origin made of molasses or brown sugar sprinkled with a crumbly mixture of flour, sugar, and butter

shoo–in \ˈshü-ˌin\ *n* (1937) : one that is a certain and easy winner

[1]**shook** *past or chiefly dial past part of* SHAKE

[2]**shook** \ˈshu̇k\ *n* [origin unknown] (1796) **1 a** : a set of staves and headings for one hogshead, cask, or barrel **b** : a bundle of parts (as of boxes) ready to be put together **2** : [1]SHOCK

shook–up \ˌshu̇k-ˈəp\ *adj* (1897) : nervously upset : AGITATED

shoon \ˈshün, ˈshōn\ *chiefly dial pl of* SHOE

[1]**shoot** \'shüt\ *vb* **shot** \'shät\; **shoot·ing** [ME *sheten, shoten, shuten,* fr. OE *scēotan;* akin to ON *skjōta* to shoot] *vt* (bef. 12c) **1 a** (1) : to eject or impel or cause to be ejected or impelled by a sudden release of tension (as of a bowstring or slingshot or by a flick of a finger) ⟨~ an arrow⟩ ⟨~ a spitball⟩ ⟨~ a marble⟩ (2) : to drive forth or cause to be driven forth by an explosion (as of a powder charge in a firearm or of ignited fuel in a rocket) (3) : to drive forth or cause to be driven forth by a sudden release of gas or air ⟨~ darts from a blowgun⟩ ⟨a steam catapult ~*s* planes from a carrier⟩ (4) : to propel (as a ball or puck) toward a goal by striking or pushing with part of the body (as the hand or foot) or with an implement; *also* : to score by so doing ⟨~ the winning goal⟩ ⟨~ a basket⟩ (5) : to throw or cast off or out often with force ⟨~ dice⟩ ⟨the horse *shot* his rider out of the saddle⟩ **b** : to cause (as a gun or bow) to propel a missile **c** (1) : to utter (as words or sounds) rapidly or suddenly or with force ⟨~ out a stream of invective⟩ (2) : to emit (as light, flame, or fumes) suddenly and rapidly (3) : to send forth with suddenness or intensity ⟨*shot* a look of anger at them⟩ **d** : to discharge, dump, or empty esp. by overturning, upending, or directing into a slide **2** : to affect by shooting: as **a** : to strike with a missile esp. from a bow or gun; *esp* : to wound or kill with a missile discharged from a bow or firearm **b** : to remove or destroy by use of firearms ⟨*shot* out the light⟩; *also* : WRECK, EXPLODE **3 a** : to push or slide (as the bolt of a door or lock) into or out of a fastening **b** : to push or thrust forward : stick out ⟨toads ~*ing* out their tongues⟩ **c** : to put forth in growing **d** : to place, send, or bring into position abruptly **4 a** (1) : to engage in (a sport or game or a portion of a game that involves shooting) : PLAY ⟨~ pool⟩ ⟨~ a round of golf⟩ ⟨~ craps⟩ (2) : to achieve (a particular score) in a game that involves shooting ⟨~ 80 in golf⟩ **b** (1) : to place or offer (a bet) on the result of casting dice ⟨~ $5⟩ (2) : to use up by or as if by betting : EXHAUST ⟨*shot* his annual bonus on a shady deal⟩ **5 a** : to engage in the hunting and killing of (as game) with firearms esp. as a sport ⟨~ woodcock⟩ **b** : to hunt over ⟨~ a tract of woodland⟩ **6 a** : to cause to move suddenly or swiftly forward ⟨*shot* the car onto the highway⟩ **b** : to send or carry quickly : DISPATCH ⟨~ the letter on to me as soon as you receive it⟩ **7** : to variegate as if by sprinkling color in streaks, flecks, or patches **8** : to pass swiftly by, past, or along ⟨~*ing* rapids⟩ **9** : to plane (as the edge of a board) straight or true **10 a** : SET OFF, DETONATE, IGNITE ⟨~ a charge of dynamite⟩ **b** : to effect by blasting **11** : to determine the altitude of **12** : to take a picture or series of pictures or television images of : PHOTOGRAPH, FILM **13 a** : to give an injection to **b** : to inject (an illicit drug) esp. into the bloodstream ~ *vi* **1 a** : to go or pass rapidly and precipitately ⟨sparks ~*ing* all over⟩ ⟨his feet *shot* out from under him⟩ **b** : to move ahead by force of momentum **c** : to stream out suddenly : SPURT **d** : to dart in or as if in rays from a source of light **e** : to dart with a piercing sensation ⟨pain *shot* up my arm⟩ **2 a** : to cause an engine or weapon to discharge a missile **b** : to use a firearm or bow esp. for sport (as in hunting) **3** : to propel a missile ⟨guns that ~ many miles⟩ **4** : PROTRUDE, PROJECT **5 a** : to grow or sprout by or as if by putting forth shoots **b** : DEVELOP, MATURE **c** : to spring or rise rapidly or suddenly — often used with *up* ⟨in a burst of growth he *shot* up to six feet tall⟩ ⟨prices *shot* up⟩ **6 a** : to propel an object (as a ball) in a particular way **b** : to drive the ball or puck toward a goal **7** : to cast dice **8** : to slide into or out of a fastening ⟨a bolt that ~*s* in either direction⟩ **9** : to record something (as on film or videotape) with a camera **10** : to begin to speak — usu. used as an imperative ⟨OK, ~, what do you have to say⟩ — **shoot at** *or* **shoot for** : to aim at : strive for — **shoot from the hip** : to act or speak hastily without consideration of the consequences — **shoot one's bolt** : to exhaust one's capabilities and resources — **shoot one's cuffs** : to tug one's shirt cuffs below those of one's coat — **shoot oneself in the foot** : to act against one's own best interests — **shoot the breeze** : to converse idly : GOSSIP — **shoot the shit** *usu vulgar* : to shoot the breeze — **shoot the works 1** : to venture all one's capital on one play **2** : to put forth all one's efforts

[2]**shoot** *n* [ME *schot, schote* projectile, new growth, in part fr. *shoten,* v., in part fr. OE *sceot* shot] (15c) **1** : a sending out of new growth or the growth sent out: as **a** : a stem or branch with its leaves and appendages esp. when not yet mature **b** : OFFSHOOT **2 a** : an act of shooting (as with a bow or a firearm): (1) : SHOT (2) : the firing of a missile esp. by artillery **b** (1) : a hunting trip or party (2) : the right to shoot game in a particular area or land over which it is held **c** (1) : a shooting match ⟨skeet ~⟩ (2) : a round of shots in a shooting match **d** : the action or an instance of shooting with a camera : a session or a series of sessions of photographing or filming ⟨a movie ~⟩ **3 a** : a motion or movement of rapid thrusting: as (1) : a sudden or rapid advance (2) : a momentary darting sensation : TWINGE (3) : THRUST 2b (4) : the pace between strokes in rowing **b** : a bar of rays : BEAM ⟨a ~ of sunlight⟩ **4** [prob. by folk etymology fr. F *chute* — more at CHUTE] **a** : a rush of water down a steep or rapid **b** : a place where a stream runs or descends swiftly

[3]**shoot** *interj* [euphemism for *shit*] (1876) — used to express annoyance or surprise

shoot·around \'shüt-ə-ˌrau̇nd\ *n* (1978) : a usu. informal basketball practice session

shoot down *vt* (1657) **1** : to cause to fall by shooting ⟨*shot down* the helicopter⟩; *esp* : to kill in this way ⟨was *shot down* in cold blood⟩ **2** : to put an end to : DEFEAT, REJECT ⟨*shoot down* legislation⟩ **3** : DEFLATE, RIDICULE **4** : DISCREDIT 2 ⟨*shoot down* a theory⟩

shoot–'em–up \'shüt-əm-ˌəp\ *n* (1947) : a movie, television show, or computer game with much shooting and bloodshed

shoot·er \'shü-tər\ *n* (13c) **1** : one that shoots: as **a** : a person who fires a missile-discharging device (as a rifle or bow) **b** : the person who is shooting or whose turn it is to shoot **c** : PHOTOGRAPHER **2** : something that is used in shooting: as **a** : a marble shot from the hand **b** : REVOLVER — usu. used in combination ⟨six-*shooter*⟩ **3** : a shot of hard liquor (as whiskey or tequila) often diluted with something (as soda); *also* : a bit of food (as a raw oyster) served in a shot glass

shooting gallery *n* (1836) **1** : a usu. covered range equipped with targets for practice with firearms **2** *slang* : a place where one can obtain narcotics and shoot up

shooting guard *n* (1977) : a guard in basketball whose chief role is as an outside shooter

shooting iron *n* (1775) : FIREARM; *esp* : HANDGUN

shooting script *n* (ca. 1929) **1** : the final completely detailed version of a motion-picture script in which scenes are grouped in the order most convenient for shooting **2** : the final version of a television script used in the production of a program

shooting star *n* (1593) **1** : a visual meteor appearing as a temporary streak of light in the night sky **2** : any of several No. American perennial herbs (genus *Dodecatheon,* esp. *D. meadia*) of the primrose family that have entire oblong leaves and showy flowers with reflexed petals **3** : one resembling a shooting star esp. in sudden and temporary brilliance

shooting stick *n* (1926) : a spiked stick with a top that opens into a seat

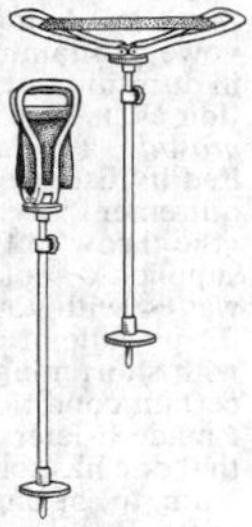

shooting stick

shoot–out \'shüt-ˌau̇t\ *n* (1948) **1** : a battle fought with handguns or rifles **2** : something resembling a shoot-out; *broadly* : SHOWDOWN **3** : a shooting competition in overtime that is used to determine the winner of a game (as in soccer or hockey) tied at the end of regular play

shoot–the–chutes \ˌshüt-thə-'shüts\ *n pl but sing in constr* (1920) : an amusement ride consisting of a steep incline down which boats slide into a pool at the bottom

shoot up *vt* (1890) **1** : to shoot or shoot at esp. recklessly ⟨cowboys *shooting up* the town⟩ **2** : to inject (a narcotic drug) into a vein ~ *vi* : to inject a narcotic into a vein — **shoot–up** \'shüt-ˌəp\ *n*

[1]**shop** \'shäp\ *n, often attrib* [ME *shoppe,* fr. OE *sceoppa* booth; akin to OHG *scopf* shed] (14c) **1** : a handicraft establishment : ATELIER **2 a** : a building or room stocked with merchandise for sale : STORE **b** *also* **shoppe** \'shäp\ : a small retail establishment or a department in a large one offering a specified line of goods or services ⟨a millinery ~⟩ ⟨a sandwich ~⟩ **3** : a commercial establishment for the making or repair of goods or machinery ⟨machine ~⟩ ⟨repair ~⟩ **4 a** : a school laboratory equipped for industrial arts education **b** : the art or science of working with tools and machinery **5 a** : a business establishment : OFFICE ⟨a public relations ~⟩ **b** : SHOPTALK ⟨talking ~⟩

[2]**shop** *vb* **shopped; shop·ping** *vi* (1764) **1 a** : to examine goods or services with intent to buy **b** : to hunt through a market in search of the best buy **2** : to make a search : HUNT ⟨*shopping* around for a better idea⟩ ~ *vt* **1** *Brit* : to inform on : BETRAY **2** : to examine the stock or offerings of ⟨~ the stores for Christmas gift ideas⟩ **3** : to offer for consideration or acceptance; *esp* : to offer for sale or in a trade — often used with *around* ⟨*shopping* the manuscript around⟩

shop·a·hol·ic \ˌshä-pə-'hȯ-lik, -'hä-\ *n* (1983) : one who is extremely or excessively fond of shopping

shop·girl \'shäp-ˌgər(-ə)l\ *n* (1798) : a woman employed to sell merchandise esp. in a store

shop·keep·er \'shäp-ˌkē-pər\ *n* (1530) : STOREKEEPER 2

shop·lift \-ˌlift\ *vb* [back-formation fr. *shoplifter*] *vi* (1820) : to steal displayed goods from a store ~ *vt* : to steal (displayed goods) from a store

shop·lift·er \-ˌlif-tər\ *n* (1680) : one who shoplifts

shop·per \'shä-pər\ *n* (1860) **1** : one who shops **2** : one whose occupation is shopping as an agent for customers or for an employer **3** : a usu. free paper carrying advertising and sometimes local news

shopping bag *n* (1886) : a bag (as of strong paper) that has handles and is intended for carrying purchases

shopping center *n* (1898) : a group of retail stores and service establishments usu. with ample parking facilities and usu. designed to serve a community or neighborhood — called also *shopping plaza*

shopping list *n* (1913) : a list of items to be purchased; *broadly* : a list of related items ⟨the biggest possible *shopping list* of budget cuts —Leonard Silk⟩

shopping mall *n* (1959) : MALL 3

shop–soiled \'shäp-ˌsȯi(-ə)ld\ *adj* (1898) *Brit* : SHOPWORN

shop steward *n* (1904) : a union member elected as the union representative of a shop or department in dealings with the management

shop·talk \'shäp-ˌtȯk\ *n* (1881) : the jargon or subject matter peculiar to an occupation or a special area of interest

shop·win·dow \-ˌwin-(ˌ)dō\ *n* (15c) : a display window of a store

shop·worn \-ˌwȯrn\ *adj* (1838) **1** : faded, soiled, or otherwise impaired by remaining too long in a store **2** : stale from excessive use or familiarity ⟨~ clichés⟩ **3** : WORN-OUT ⟨a ~ veteran⟩

[1]**shore** \'shȯr\ *n, often attrib* [ME, fr. OE **scor;* akin to MLG *schōr* foreland and perh. to OE *scieran* to cut — more at SHEAR] (14c) **1** : the land bordering a usu. large body of water; *specif* : COAST **2** : a boundary (as of a country) or an area within a boundary — usu. used in pl. ⟨immigrated to these ~*s*⟩ **3** : land as distinguished from the sea ⟨shipboard and ~ duty⟩

[2]**shore** *n* [ME; akin to MD *scōre* prop, MLG *schōre*] (14c) : a prop for preventing sinking or sagging

[3]**shore** *vt* **shored; shor·ing** (14c) **1** : to support by a shore : PROP **2** : to give support to : BRACE — usu. used with *up* ⟨trying to ~ up his claim⟩

shore·bird \'shȯr-ˌbərd\ *n* (ca. 1672) : any of a suborder (Charadrii) of birds (as a plover or sandpiper) that frequent the seashore

shore dinner *n* (1892) : a dinner consisting chiefly of seafoods

shore·front \-ˌfrənt\ *n* (1919) : land along a shore; *specif* : BEACHFRONT

shore leave *n* (1888) : a leave of absence to go on shore granted to a sailor or naval officer

shore·line \-ˌlīn\ *n* (1852) **1** : the line where a body of water and the shore meet **2** : the strip of land along the shoreline

shore patrol *n* (1917) **1** : a branch of a navy that exercises guard and police functions — compare MILITARY POLICE **2** : petty officers detailed to perform police duty while a ship is in port

shore·side \-ˌsīd\ *adj* (1883) : situated at or near a shore

shore•ward \-wərd\ *or* **shore•wards** \-wərdz\ *adv* (ca. 1691) : toward the shore

shoring *n* (15c) **1** : the act of supporting with or as if with a prop **2** : a system or group of shores

shorn *past part of* SHEAR

[1]**short** \ˈshȯrt\ *adj* [ME, fr. OE *sceort;* akin to OHG *scurz* short, ON *skortr* lack] (bef. 12c) **1 a** : having little length **b** : not tall or high : LOW **2 a** : not extended in time : BRIEF ⟨a ~ vacation⟩ **b** : not retentive ⟨a ~ memory⟩ **c** : EXPEDITIOUS, QUICK ⟨made ~ work of the problem⟩ **d** : seeming to pass quickly ⟨made great progress in just a few ~ years⟩ **3 a** *of a speech sound* : having a relatively short duration **b** : being the member of a pair of similarly spelled vowel or vowel-containing sounds that is descended from a vowel that was short in duration but is no longer so and that does not necessarily have duration as its chief distinguishing feature ⟨~ *i* in *sin*⟩ **c** *of a syllable in prosody* (1) : of relatively brief duration (2) : UNSTRESSED **4** : limited in distance ⟨a ~ trip⟩ **5 a** : not coming up to a measure or requirement : INSUFFICIENT ⟨in ~ supply⟩ **b** : not reaching far enough ⟨the throw to first was ~⟩ **c** : enduring privation **d** : insufficiently supplied ⟨~ of cash⟩ ⟨~ on brains⟩ **6 a** : ABRUPT, CURT ⟨I'm sorry I was ~ with you⟩ **b** : quickly provoked ⟨a ~ temper⟩ **7** : CHOPPY 2 **8** : payable at an early date ⟨a ~ loan⟩ **9 a** : containing or cooked with shortening; *also* : FLAKY ⟨~ pastry⟩ **b** *of metal* : brittle under certain conditions **10 a** : not lengthy or drawn out ⟨a ~ speech⟩ **b** : made briefer : ABBREVIATED **11 a** : not having goods or property that one has sold in anticipation of a fall in prices **b** : consisting of, relating to, or engaging in the sale of securities or commodities that the seller does not possess or has not contracted for at the time of the sale ⟨~ sale⟩ ⟨a ~ seller⟩ **12** : near the end of a tour of duty — **short•ish** \ˈshȯr-tish\ *adj* — **short•ness** \ˈshȯrt-nəs\ *n* — **in short order** : with dispatch : QUICKLY

[2]**short** *adv* (14c) **1** : in a curt manner **2** : for or during a brief time ⟨*short*-lasting⟩ **3** : at a disadvantage : UNAWARES ⟨caught ~⟩ **4** : in an abrupt manner : SUDDENLY ⟨the car stopped ~⟩ **5** : at some point or degree before a goal or limit aimed at or under consideration ⟨the bombs fell ~⟩ ⟨quit a month ~ of graduation⟩ **6** : clean across ⟨the axle was snapped ~⟩ **7** : by or as if by a short sale

[3]**short** *n* (ca. 1586) **1** : the sum and substance : UPSHOT **2 a** : a short syllable **b** : a short sound or signal **3** *pl* **a** : a by-product of wheat milling that includes the germ, fine bran, and some flour **b** : refuse, clippings, or trimmings discarded in various manufacturing processes **4 a** : knee-length or less than knee-length trousers — usu. used in pl. **b** *pl* : short drawers **c** : a size in clothing for short men **5 a** : one who operates on the short side of the market **b** *pl* : short-term bonds **6** *pl* : DEFICIENCIES **7** : SHORT CIRCUIT **8** : SHORTSTOP **9 a** : SHORT SUBJECT **b** : a brief story or article (as in a newspaper) — **for short** : as an abbreviation ⟨named Katherine or Kate *for short*⟩ — **in short** : by way of summary : BRIEFLY

[4]**short** *vt* (1904) **1** : SHORT-CIRCUIT **2** : SHORTCHANGE, CHEAT **3** : to sell (a security) short in expectation of a fall in prices

short•age \ˈshȯr-tij\ *n* (1868) : LACK, DEFICIT

short ballot *n* (1909) : a ballot limiting the number of elective offices to the most important legislative and executive posts and leaving minor positions to be filled by appointment

short•bread \ˈshȯrt-ˌbred\ *n* (1801) : a thick cookie made of flour, sugar, and a large amount of shortening

short•cake \-ˌkāk\ *n* (1594) **1** : a crisp and often unsweetened biscuit or cookie **2 a** : a dessert made typically of very short baking-powder-biscuit dough spread with sweetened fruit **b** : a dish consisting of a rich biscuit split and covered with a meat mixture

short•change \-ˈchānj\ *vt* (1903) **1** : to give less than the correct amount of change to **2** : to deprive of or give less than something due : CHEAT ⟨was *shortchanged* out of a promotion⟩ — **short•chang•er** *n*

short–cir•cuit *vt* (1867) **1** : to apply a short circuit to or establish a short circuit in **2** : BYPASS 2 **3** : FRUSTRATE, IMPEDE

short circuit *n* (1854) : a connection of comparatively low resistance accidentally or intentionally made between points on a circuit between which the resistance is normally much greater

short•com•ing \ˈshȯrt-ˌkə-miŋ, ˌshȯrt-ˈ\ *n* (15c) : an imperfection or lack that detracts from the whole; *also* : the quality or state of being flawed or lacking

[1]**short•cut** \ˈshȯrt-ˌkət *also* -ˈkət\ *n* (1637) **1** : a route more direct than the one ordinarily taken **2** : a method or means of doing something more directly and quickly than and often not so thoroughly as by ordinary procedure ⟨a ~ to success⟩

[2]**shortcut** *vb* **-cut; -cut•ting** *vt* (1915) : to shorten (as a route or procedure) by use of a shortcut; *also* : CIRCUMVENT ~ *vi* : to take or use a shortcut

short–day \ˈshȯrt-ˌdā\ *adj* (1920) : responding to or relating to a short photoperiod — used esp. of a plant; compare DAY-NEUTRAL, LONG-DAY

short division *n* (1851) : mathematical division in which the successive steps are performed without writing out the remainders

short–eared owl \ˈshȯrt-ˌird-\ *n* (1766) : a medium-sized nearly cosmopolitan owl (*Asio flammeus*) that has very short ear tufts and usu. nests on the ground

short•en \ˈshȯr-tᵊn\ *vb* **short•ened; short•en•ing** \ˈshȯrt-niŋ, ˈshȯr-tᵊn-iŋ\ *vt* (14c) **1 a** : to reduce the length or duration of **b** : to cause to seem short **2 a** : to reduce in power or efficiency ⟨is my hand ~*ed*, that it cannot redeem —Isa 50:2(RSV)⟩ **b** *obs* : to deprive of effect **3** : to add fat to (as pastry dough) in order to make tender and flaky ~ *vi* : to become short or shorter — **short•en•er** \ˈshȯrt-nər, ˈshȯr-tᵊn-ər\ *n*

syn SHORTEN, CURTAIL, ABBREVIATE, ABRIDGE, RETRENCH mean to reduce in extent. SHORTEN implies reduction in length or duration ⟨*shorten* a speech⟩. CURTAIL adds an implication of cutting that in some way deprives of completeness or adequacy ⟨ceremonies *curtailed* because of rain⟩. ABBREVIATE implies a making shorter usu. by omitting some part ⟨using an *abbreviated* title⟩. ABRIDGE implies a reduction in compass or scope with retention of essential elements and a relative completeness in the result ⟨the *abridged* version of the novel⟩. RETRENCH suggests a reduction in extent or costs of something felt to be excessive ⟨declining business forced the company to *retrench*⟩.

shortening *n* (1538) **1** : the action or process of making or becoming short; *specif* : the dropping of the latter part of a word so as to produce a new and shorter word of the same meaning **2** : an edible fat used to shorten baked goods

short•fall \ˈshȯrt-ˌfȯl\ *n* (1895) : a failure to come up to expectation or need ⟨a budget ~⟩; *also* : the amount of such failure ⟨a $2 million ~⟩

short fuse *n* (1958) : a tendency to get angry easily : a quick temper

short–grass prairie \ˈshȯrt-ˌgras-\ *n* (1844) : PRAIRIE 2b

short–hair \-ˌher\ *n* (1903) : a domestic cat with a short thick coat; *esp* : a member of any of several breeds of muscular medium- to large-sized cats with a short plushy coat — **short–haired** *adj*

short•hand \-ˌhand\ *n* (1636) **1** : a method of writing rapidly by substituting characters, abbreviations, or symbols for letters, sounds, words, or phrases : STENOGRAPHY **2** : something likened to shorthand esp. in providing rapid or abbreviated communication or representation ⟨stereotype and cliché serve a purpose as a form of ~ —Stephanie Ericsson⟩ ⟨headline ~⟩ — **shorthand** *adj*

short•hand•ed \ˌshȯrt-ˈhan-dəd\ *adj* (1794) : having, working with, or done with fewer than the regular or necessary number of people

short–haul \ˈshȯrt-ˌhȯl\ *adj* (1895) : traveling or involving a short distance ⟨~ flights⟩

short•horn \-ˌhȯrn\ *n, often cap* (1847) : any of a breed of red, roan, white, or red and white beef cattle originating in northern England and including good milk-producing strains — called also *Durham*

short–horned grasshopper \ˈshȯrt-ˌhȯrn(d)-\ *n* (ca. 1890) : any of a family (Acrididae) of grasshoppers with short antennae

short hundredweight *n* (1924) : HUNDREDWEIGHT 1

short•leaf pine \ˈshȯrt-ˌlēf-\ *n* (1796) : a pine (*Pinus echinata*) chiefly of the southeastern U.S. that has short flexible needles usu. in clusters of two and reddish-brown bark; *also* : its yellow wood

short line *n* (ca. 1917) : a transportation system (as a railroad) operating over a relatively short distance

short list *n* (1927) : a limited list of important items or individuals; *esp* : a list of candidates for final consideration (as for a position or a prize) — **short–list** *vt*

short–lived \ˈshȯrt-ˈlivd *also* -ˈlīvd\ *adj* (1588) : not living or lasting long ⟨~ insects⟩ ⟨~ joy⟩

short loin *n* (ca. 1923) : a portion of the hindquarter of beef immediately behind the ribs that is usu. cut into steaks — see BEEF illustration

short•ly \ˈshȯrt-lē\ *adv* (bef. 12c) **1 a** : in a few words : BRIEFLY **b** : in an abrupt manner **2 a** : in a short time ⟨we will be there ~⟩ **b** : at a short interval ⟨~ after sunset⟩

short–nosed cattle louse \ˈshȯrt-ˌnōz(d)-\ *n* (1942) : a large bluish sucking louse (*Haematopinus eurysternus*) that attacks domestic cattle

short of (1560) *prep* : OTHER THAN; *esp* : of a lesser degree than ⟨had few options *short of* replacing the motor⟩

short–order \ˈshȯrt-ˌȯr-dər, -ˈȯr-\ *adj* (1920) : preparing or serving food that can be cooked quickly to a customer's order ⟨a ~ cook⟩

short–range \ˈshȯrt-ˈrānj\ *adj* (1869) **1** : involving or taking into account a short period of time ⟨~ plans⟩ **2** : relating to or fit for short distances

short ribs *n pl* (1611) : a cut of beef consisting of rib ends between the rib roast and the plate — see BEEF illustration

short run *n* (1879) : a relatively brief period of time — often used in the phrase *in the short run* — **short–run** *adj*

short shrift *n* (1594) **1** : barely adequate time for confession before execution **2 a** : little or no attention or consideration ⟨gave the problem *short shrift*⟩ **b** : quick work — usu. used in the phrase *make short shrift of*

short sight *n* (ca. 1829) : MYOPIA

short•sight•ed \ˈshȯrt-ˌsī-təd\ *adj* (1622) **1** : lacking foresight **2** : NEARSIGHTED — **short•sight•ed•ly** *adv* — **short•sight•ed•ness** *n*

short–spo•ken \-ˌspō-kən\ *adj* (1865) : CURT

short•stop \-ˌstäp\ *n* (1857) **1** : the player position in baseball for defending the infield area on the third-base side of second base **2** : the player stationed in the shortstop position

short–stop \-ˌstäp\ *n* (1936) : STOP BATH

short story *n* (1877) : an invented prose narrative shorter than a novel usu. dealing with a few characters and aiming at unity of effect and often concentrating on the creation of mood rather than plot

short subject *n* (1944) : a brief often documentary or educational film

short–tem•pered \ˌshȯrt-ˈtem-pərd\ *adj* (1877) : having a quick temper

short–term \ˈshȯrt-ˌtərm\ *adj* (1901) **1** : occurring over or involving a relatively short period of time **2 a** : of, relating to, or constituting a financial operation or obligation based on a brief term and esp. one of less than a year **b** : generated by assets held for less than six months

short ton *n* (1881) — see WEIGHT table

short•wave \ˈshȯrt-ˌwāv\ *n, often attrib* (1907) **1** : a radio wave having a wavelength between 10 and 100 meters **2** : a radio transmitter or receiver using shortwaves **3** : electromagnetic radiation having a wavelength equal to or less than that of visible light

short–weight \ˈshȯrt-ˈwāt\ *vt* (1926) : to defraud with short weight

short weight \ˈshȯrt-ˈwāt\ *n* (1789) : weight less than the stated weight or less than one is charged for

short–wind•ed \ˌshȯrt-ˈwin-dəd\ *adj* (15c) **1** : affected with or characterized by shortness of breath **2 a** : BRIEF **b** : broken up into short units

shorty *or* **short•ie** \ˈshȯr-tē\ *n, pl* **short•ies** (1888) : one that is short

Sho•shone \shə-ˈshōn, -ˈshō-nē; ˈshō-ˌshōn\ *or* **Sho•sho•ni** \shə-ˈshō-nē\ *n, pl* **Shoshones** *or* **Shoshoni** *also* **Shoshone** *or* **Shoshonis** [origin unknown] (1805) **1** : a member of a group of American Indian peoples orig. ranging through California, Idaho, Nevada, Utah, and Wyoming **2** : the Uto-Aztecan language of the Shoshones

[1]**shot** \ˈshät\ *n* [ME, fr. OE *sceot, scot;* akin to OHG *scuz,* ON *skot* shot, OE *scēotan* to shoot — more at SHOOT] (bef. 12c) **1 a** : an action of shooting **b** : a directed propelling of a missile; *specif* : a directed discharge of a firearm **c** (1) : a stroke or throw in an attempt to score points in a game (as tennis, pool, or basketball); *also* : HOME RUN (2) : ability to shoot ⟨has the best ~ on the team⟩ **d** : BLAST 5a **e** : a medical or narcotics injection **2 a** *pl* **shot** : something propelled by shooting; *esp* : small lead or steel pellets esp. forming a charge for a shotgun **b** : a metal sphere of iron or brass that is heaved in the shot put **3 a** : the distance that a missile is or can be thrown **b** : RANGE, REACH **4** : a charge to be paid : SCOT **5** : one that shoots; *esp* : MARKSMAN **6 a** : ATTEMPT, TRY ⟨give it a ~⟩ **b** : GUESS, CONJEC-

TURE **c** : CHANCE 4a ⟨a ~ at winning the prize⟩ **d** : a single appearance as an entertainer ⟨did a guest ~ for the program⟩ **7** : an effective remark; *esp* : SWIPE 2 ⟨a parting ~⟩ **8 a** : a single photographic exposure; *esp* : SNAPSHOT **b** : a single sequence of a motion picture or a television program shot by one camera without interruption **9** : a charge of explosives **10 a** : a small measure or serving (as one ounce) of undiluted liquor or other beverage ⟨vodka ~*s*⟩ ⟨a ~ of espresso⟩ **b** : a small amount applied at one time : DOSE ⟨a ~ of fertilizer⟩ ⟨a ~ of humor⟩ **11 shot** *pl* : SPRINKLES, JIMMIES — **a shot** : for each one : APIECE — **like a shot** : very rapidly — **shot in the arm** : STIMULUS, BOOST — **shot in the dark** **1** : a wild guess **2** : an attempt that has little chance of success

²shot *past and past part of* SHOOT

³shot *adj* (1763) **1 a** *of a fabric* : having contrasting and changeable color effects : IRIDESCENT **b** : suffused or streaked with a color ⟨hair ~ with gray⟩ **c** : infused or permeated with a quality or element ⟨~ through with wit⟩ **2** : having the form of pellets resembling shot **3** : reduced to a ruined or useless state ⟨his nerves are ~⟩

shot clock *n* (1973) : a clock in basketball that displays a countdown of the time within which shooting the ball is required

¹shot·gun \ˈshät-ˌgən\ *n* (1776) **1** : a smoothbore shoulder weapon for firing shot at short ranges **2** : an offensive football formation in which the quarterback plays a few yards behind the line of scrimmage and the other backs are scattered as flankers or slotbacks — **shotgun** *vt* — **shot·gun·ner** \-ˌgə-nər\ *n*

²shotgun *adj* (1892) **1** : of, relating to, or using a shotgun **2** : involving coercion **3** : covering a wide field with hit-or-miss effectiveness

shotgun house *n* (1903) : a house in which all the rooms are in direct line with each other usu. front to back — called also *shotgun cottage, shotgun shack*; compare RAILROAD FLAT

shotgun marriage *n* (1929) **1** : a marriage forced or required because of pregnancy — called also *shotgun wedding* **2** : a forced union ⟨a spate of brokerage mergers . . . hastily arranged *shotgun marriages* —John Brooks⟩

shot hole *n* (1875) **1** : a drilled hole in which a charge of dynamite is exploded **2** : the dropping out of small rounded fragments of leaves that produces a shot-riddled appearance and is caused esp. by parasitic action

shot put *n* (1898) : a field event in which a shot is heaved for distance — **shot–put·ter** \ˈshät-ˌpu̇-tər\ *n*

shot·ten \ˈshä-tᵊn\ *adj* [ME *shotyn,* fr. pp. of *sheten* to shoot] (15c) : having ejected the spawn and so of inferior food value ⟨~ herring⟩

should \shəd, ˈshu̇d\ *verbal auxiliary, past of* SHALL [ME *sholde,* fr. OE *sceolde* owed, was obliged to, ought to] (bef. 12c) **1** — used in auxiliary function to express condition ⟨if he ~ leave his father, his father would die —Gen 44:22(RSV)⟩ **2** — used in auxiliary function to express obligation, propriety, or expediency ⟨'tis commanded I ~ do so —Shak.⟩ ⟨this is as it ~ be —H. L. Savage⟩ ⟨you ~ brush your teeth after each meal⟩ **3** — used in auxiliary function to express futurity from a point of view in the past ⟨realized that she ~ have to do most of her farm work before sunrise —Ellen Glasgow⟩ **4** — used in auxiliary function to express what is probable or expected ⟨with an early start, they ~ be here by noon⟩ **5** — used in auxiliary function to express a request in a polite manner or to soften direct statement ⟨I ~ suggest that a guide . . . is the first essential —L. D. Reddick⟩

¹shoul·der \ˈshōl-dər\ *n* [ME *sholder,* fr. OE *sculdor;* akin to OHG *scultra* shoulder] (bef. 12c) **1 a** : the laterally projecting part of the human body formed of the bones and joints with their covering tissue by which the arm is connected with the trunk **b** : the region of the body of nonhuman vertebrates that corresponds to the shoulder but is less projecting **2 a** : the two shoulders and the upper part of the back — usu. used in pl. **b** *pl* : capacity for bearing a task or blame ⟨placed the guilt squarely on his ~*s*⟩ **3** : a cut of meat including the upper joint of the foreleg and adjacent parts — see LAMB illustration **4** : the part of a garment at the wearer's shoulder **5** : an area adjacent to or along the edge of a higher, more prominent, or more important part: as **a** (1) : the part of a hill or mountain near the top (2) : a lateral protrusion or extension of a hill or mountain **b** : either edge of a roadway; *specif* : the part of a roadway outside of the traveled way **6** : a rounded or sloping part (as of a stringed instrument or a bottle) where the neck joins the body — **shoul·dered** \-dərd\ *adj*

²shoulder *vb* **shoul·dered; shoul·der·ing** \-d(ə-)riŋ\ *vt* (14c) **1** : to push or thrust with or as if with the shoulder : JOSTLE ⟨~*ed* his way through the crowd⟩ **2 a** : to place or bear on the shoulder ⟨~*ed* her knapsack⟩ **b** : to assume the burden or responsibility of ⟨~ the blame⟩ ~ *vi* : to push with or as if with the shoulders aggressively

shoulder bag *n* (1912) : a handbag looped over the shoulder by a strap

shoulder belt *n* (1967) : an automobile safety belt worn across the torso and over the shoulder — called also *shoulder harness*

shoulder blade *n* (14c) : SCAPULA

shoulder board *n* (1942) : one of a pair of broad pieces of stiffened cloth worn on the shoulders of a military uniform and carrying insignia

shoulder girdle *n* (1868) : the bony or cartilaginous arch that supports the forelimbs of a vertebrate — called also *pectoral girdle*

shoulder knot *n* (1676) **1** : an ornamental knot of ribbon or lace worn on the shoulder in the 17th and 18th centuries **2** : a detachable ornament of braided wire cord worn on ceremonial occasions on the shoulders of a uniform by a commissioned officer

shoulder patch *n* (1945) : a cloth patch bearing an identifying mark and worn on one sleeve of a uniform below the shoulder

shoulder strap *n* (1688) : a strap that passes across the shoulder and holds up an article or garment

should·est \ˈshu̇-dəst\ *archaic past 2d sing of* SHALL

shouldn't \ˈshu̇-dᵊnt, -dᵊn, *dial also* ˈshu̇-tᵊn(t) *or* ˈshu̇nt\ (1675) : should not

shouldst \shədst, ˈshu̇dst, shətst, ˈshu̇tst\ *archaic past 2d sing of* SHALL

¹shout \ˈshau̇t\ *vb* [ME] *vi* (14c) **1** : to utter a sudden loud cry **2** : to command attention as if by shouting ⟨a quality that ~*s* from good novels —John Gardner⟩ ~ *vt* **1** : to utter in a loud voice **2** : to cause to be, come, or stop by or as if by shouting ⟨~*ed* himself hoarse⟩ ⟨the proponents ~*ed* down the opposition⟩ — **shout·er** *n*

²shout *n* (14c) : a loud cry or call

shouting distance *n* (1930) : a short distance : easy reach — usu. used with *within* ⟨lived within *shouting distance* of her cousins⟩

shout–out \ˈshau̇t-ˌau̇t\ *n* (1990) : a brief expression of greeting or praise given esp. on a broadcast or audio recording

shout song *n* (1925) : a rhythmic song sung at religious services esp. by black Americans and characterized by responsive singing or shouting between leader and congregation

¹shove \ˈshəv\ *vb* **shoved; shov·ing** [ME, fr. OE *scūfan* to thrust away; akin to OHG *scioban* to push and prob. to Lith *skubti* to hurry] *vt* (bef. 12c) **1** : to push along **2** : to push or put in a rough, careless, or hasty manner : THRUST **3** : to force by other than physical means : COMPEL ⟨~ a bill through the legislature⟩ ~ *vi* **1** : to move by forcing a way ⟨bargain hunters *shoving* up to the counter⟩ **2 a** : to move something by exerting force **b** : LEAVE — usu. used with *off* ⟨*shoved* off for home⟩ — **shov·er** *n*

²shove *n* (14c) : an act or instance of shoving : a forcible push

¹shov·el \ˈshə-vəl\ *n* [ME, fr. OE *scofl;* akin to OHG *scūfla* shovel, OE *scūfan* to thrust away] (bef. 12c) **1 a** : a hand implement consisting of a broad scoop or a more or less hollowed out blade with a handle used to lift and throw material **b** : something that resembles a shovel **c** : an excavating machine; *esp* : a hydraulic diesel-engine driven power shovel **2** : SHOVELFUL

²shovel *vb* **-eled** *or* **-elled; -el·ing** *or* **-el·ling** \ˈshə-və-liŋ, ˈshəv-liŋ\ *vt* (15c) **1** : to take up and throw with a shovel **2** : to dig or clean out with a shovel **3** : to throw or convey roughly or in a mass as if with a shovel ⟨~*ed* his food into his mouth⟩ ~ *vi* : to use a shovel

shov·el·er *or* **shov·el·ler** \ˈshə-və-lər, ˈshəv-lər\ *n* (15c) **1** : one that shovels **2** : any of several freshwater ducks (genus *Anas*) that have a large very broad bill and feed by dabbling

shov·el·ful \ˈshə-vəl-ˌfu̇l\ *n, pl* **shovelfuls** \-ˌfu̇lz\ *also* **shov·els·ful** \-vəlz-ˌfu̇l\ (1533) : as much as a shovel will hold

shovel hat *n* (1812) : a shallow-crowned hat with a wide brim curved up at the sides that is worn by some clergymen

shov·el·nose \-ˌnōz\ *n* (1709) : a shovel-nosed animal and esp. a fish

shov·el–nosed \ˈshə-vəl-ˌnōzd\ *adj* (1707) : having a broad flat head, nose, or beak

shovel pass *n* (1940) : a short underhand pass (as in football)

shov·el–ready \ˈshə-vəl-ˌre-dē\ *adj* (1998) *of a construction project or site* : ready for the start of work

¹show \ˈshō\ *vb* **showed** \ˈshōd\; **shown** \ˈshōn\ *or* **showed; showing** [ME *shewen, showen,* fr. OE *scēawian* to look, look at, see; akin to OHG *scouwōn* to look, look at, and prob. to L *cavēre* to be on one's guard] *vt* (12c) **1** : to cause or permit to be seen : EXHIBIT ⟨~*ed* pictures of the baby⟩ **2** : to offer for sale ⟨stores were ~*ing* new spring suits⟩ **3** : to present as a public spectacle : PERFORM **4** : to reveal by one's condition, nature, or behavior ⟨~*ed* themselves to be cowards⟩ **5** : to give indication or record of ⟨an anemometer ~*s* wind speed⟩ **6 a** : to point out : direct attention to ⟨~*ed* the view from the terrace⟩ **b** : CONDUCT, USHER ⟨~*ed* me to an aisle seat⟩ **7** : ACCORD, BESTOW ⟨~*s* them no mercy⟩ **8 a** : to set forth : DECLARE **b** : ALLEGE, PLEAD — used esp. in law ⟨~ cause⟩ **9 a** : to demonstrate or establish by argument or reasoning ⟨~ a plan to be faulty⟩ **b** : INFORM, INSTRUCT ⟨~*ed* me how to solve the problem⟩ **10** : to present (an animal) for judging in a show ~ *vi* **1 a** : to be or come in view ⟨3:15 ~*ed* on the clock⟩ **b** : to put in an appearance ⟨failed to ~⟩ **2 a** : to appear in a particular way ⟨anger ~*ed* in their faces⟩ **b** : SEEM, APPEAR **3 a** : to give a theatrical performance **b** : to be staged or presented **4 a** : to appear as a contestant **b** : to present an animal in a show **5** : to finish third or at least third (as in a horse race) **6** : to exhibit one's artistic work — **show·able** \ˈshō-ə-bəl\ *adj* — **show one's hand** *also* **show one's cards** **1** : to display one's cards faceup **2** : to declare one's intentions or reveal one's resources — **show one the door** : to tell someone to get out; *also* : FIRE 2b

syn SHOW, EXHIBIT, DISPLAY, EXPOSE, PARADE, FLAUNT mean to present so as to invite notice or attention. SHOW implies no more than enabling another to see or examine ⟨*showed* her snapshots to the whole group⟩. EXHIBIT stresses putting forward prominently or openly ⟨*exhibit* paintings at a gallery⟩. DISPLAY emphasizes putting in a position where others may see to advantage ⟨*display* sale items⟩. EXPOSE suggests bringing forth from concealment and displaying ⟨sought to *expose* the hypocrisy of the town fathers⟩. PARADE implies an ostentatious or arrogant displaying ⟨*parading* their piety for all to see⟩. FLAUNT suggests a shameless, boastful, often offensive parading ⟨nouveaux riches *flaunting* their wealth⟩.

syn SHOW, MANIFEST, EVIDENCE, EVINCE, DEMONSTRATE mean to reveal outwardly or make apparent. SHOW is the general term but sometimes implies that what is revealed must be gained by inference from acts, looks, or words ⟨careful not to *show* his true feelings⟩. MANIFEST implies a plainer, more immediate revelation ⟨*manifested* musical ability at an early age⟩. EVIDENCE suggests serving as proof of the actuality or existence of something ⟨a commitment *evidenced* by years of loyal service⟩. EVINCE implies a showing by outward marks or signs ⟨*evinced* not the slightest fear⟩. DEMONSTRATE implies showing by action or by display of feeling ⟨*demonstrated* their approval by loud applause⟩.

²show *n, often attrib* (13c) **1** : a demonstrative display ⟨a ~ of strength⟩ **2 a** *archaic* : outward appearance **b** : a false semblance : PRETENSE ⟨made a ~ of friendship⟩ **c** : a more or less true appearance of something : SIGN **d** : an impressive display ⟨his role as househusband . . . was purely for ~ —John Lahr⟩ **e** : OSTENTATION **3** : CHANCE 2 ⟨gave him a ~ in spite of his background⟩ **4** : something exhibited esp. for wonder or ridicule : SPECTACLE **5 a** : a large display or exhibition arranged to arouse interest or stimulate sales ⟨the national auto ~⟩ **b** : a competitive exhibition of animals (as dogs) to demonstrate quality in breeding **6 a** : a theatrical presentation **b** : a radio or television program **c** : ENTERTAINMENT 3b(1) **7** : ENTERPRISE, AFFAIR ⟨they ran the whole ~⟩ **8** : third place at the finish (as of a horse race) **9** *often cap* : the major leagues in baseball — used with *the*

\ə\ **abut** \ᵊ\ kitten, F table \ər\ **further** \a\ **ash** \ā\ **ace** \ä\ **mop, mar**
\au̇\ **out** \ch\ **chin** \e\ **bet** \ē\ **easy** \g\ **go** \i\ **hit** \ī\ **ice** \j\ **job**
\ŋ\ **sing** \ō\ **go** \ȯ\ **law** \ȯi\ **boy** \th\ **thin** \t͟h\ **the** \ü\ **loot** \u̇\ **foot**
\y\ **yet** \zh\ **vision, beige** \k̲, ⁿ, œ, ue, ʸ\ *see* Guide to Pronunciation

show–and–tell \ˈshō-ən(d)-ˈtel\ *n* (1950) **1 :** a classroom exercise in which children display an item and talk about it **2 :** a public display or demonstration
show bill *n* (1801) : an advertising poster
show·biz \ˈshō-ˌbiz\ *n, often attrib* [by shortening & alter.] (1945) : SHOW BUSINESS; *also* : RAZZLE-DAZZLE, FLASH — **show·biz·zy** \-ˌbi-zē\ *adj*
[1]**show·boat** \ˈshō-ˌbōt\ *n* (1869) **1 :** a river steamship containing a theater and carrying a troupe of actors to give plays at river communities **2 :** one who tries to attract attention by conspicuous behavior
[2]**showboat** *vi* (1951) : to behave in a conspicuous or ostentatious manner : SHOW OFF — **show·boat·er** *n*
showbread *var of* SHEWBREAD
show business *n* (1850) : the arts, occupations, and businesses (as theater, motion pictures, and television) that comprise the entertainment industry
[1]**show·case** \ˈshō-ˌkās\ *n* (1835) **1 :** a glazed case, box, or cabinet for displaying and protecting wares in a store or articles in a museum **2 :** a setting, occasion, or medium for exhibiting something or someone esp. in an attractive or favorable aspect
[2]**showcase** *vt* **show·cased; show·cas·ing** (1945) : to exhibit esp. in an attractive or favorable aspect ⟨~ new talent⟩
show·down \ˈshō-ˌdau̇n\ *n* (1884) **1 :** the placing of poker hands faceup on the table to determine the winner of a pot **2 :** a decisive confrontation or contest
[1]**show·er** \ˈshau̇(-ə)r\ *n* [ME *shour,* fr. OE *scūr;* akin to OHG *scūr* shower, storm, L *caurus* northwest wind] (bef. 12c) **1 a :** a fall of rain of short duration **b :** a similar fall of sleet, hail, or snow **2 :** something resembling a rain shower ⟨a ~ of statistics⟩; *esp* : a fall of meteors which belong to a single group and whose trails appear to originate at the same point in space **3 :** a party given by friends who bring gifts often of a particular kind ⟨a bridal ~⟩ **4 :** a bath in which water is showered on the body; *also* : the apparatus that provides a shower — **show·er·less** \-ləs\ *adj* — **show·ery** \ˈshau̇(-ə)-rē\ *adj* — **to the showers :** out of the ball game ⟨a pitcher sent *to the showers*⟩
[2]**shower** *vi* (15c) **1 :** to rain or fall in or as if in a shower ⟨letters ~*ed* on him in praise and protest⟩ **2 :** to bathe in a shower ~ *vt* **1 a :** to wet (as with water) in a spray, fine stream, or drops **b** (1) : to cause to fall in a shower ⟨factory chimneys ~*ed* soot on the district⟩ (2) : to cause a shower to fall on ⟨~*ed* the newlyweds with rice⟩ **2 :** to give in abundance ⟨~*ed* her with honors⟩ — **show·er·er** \ˈshau̇(-ə)r-ər\ *n*
[3]**show·er** \ˈshō-ər\ *n* (14c) : one that shows : EXHIBITOR
shower bath *n* (1785) : SHOWER 4
show·er·head \ˈshau̇(-ə)r-ˌhed\ *n* (1925) : a fixture for directing the spray of water in a bathroom shower
show·girl \ˈshō-ˌgər(-ə)l\ *n* (1836) : a chorus girl in a musical comedy or nightclub show
showing *n* (bef. 12c) **1 a :** an act or an instance of putting something (as an artist's work) on view : DISPLAY **b :** the presentation of a motion picture **c :** SHOW 5 ⟨fashion ~*s*⟩ **2 :** PERFORMANCE, RECORD ⟨made a good ~ in competition⟩ **3 a :** a statement or presentation of a case **b :** APPEARANCE, EVIDENCE
show jumping *n* (1929) : the competitive riding of horses one at a time over a set course of obstacles in which the winner is judged according to ability and speed — **show jumper** *n*
show·man \ˈshō-mən\ *n* (ca. 1734) **1 :** the producer of a play or theatrical show **2 :** a notably spectacular, dramatic, or effective performer — **show·man·ship** \-ˌship\ *n*
show–me \ˈshō-mē\ *adj* (1909) : insistent on proof or evidence
show–off \ˈshō-ˌȯf\ *n, often attrib* (1843) **1 :** the act of showing off **2 :** one that shows off : EXHIBITIONIST — **show–offy** \-ˌȯ-fē\ *adj*
show off *vt* (ca. 1793) : to display proudly ⟨wanted to *show* our new car *off*⟩ ~ *vi* : to seek to attract attention by conspicuous behavior ⟨boys *showing off* for the girls⟩
show·piece \ˈshō-ˌpēs\ *n* (1847) : a prime or outstanding example used for exhibition
show·place \-ˌplās\ *n* (1794) : a place (as an estate or building) that is regarded as an example of beauty or excellence
show ring *n* (1902) : a ring (as at a cattle show) where animals are displayed
show·room \-ˌrüm, -ˌru̇m\ *n* (1616) : a room where merchandise is exhibited for sale or where samples are displayed
show·stop·per \-ˌstä-pər\ *n* (1926) **1 :** an act, song, or performer that wins applause so prolonged as to interrupt a performance **2 :** something or someone exceptionally arresting or attractive ⟨the gold crown was the ~ of the exhibition⟩ **3 :** one that stops or could stop the progress, operation, or functioning of something — **show·stop·ping** \-ˌstä-piŋ\ *adj*
show·time \ˈshō-ˌtīm\ *n* (1951) : the scheduled or actual time at which a show or something likened to a show begins
show trial *n* (1937) : a trial (as of political opponents) in which the verdict is rigged and a public confession is often extracted
show up *vt* (1826) **1 :** to expose or discredit esp. by revealing faults ⟨*showed* them *up* as frauds⟩ **2 :** to embarrass or cause to look bad esp. by comparison ⟨trying to *show up* the boss⟩ **3 :** REVEAL ⟨*showed up* my ignorance⟩ ~ *vi* **1 :** ARRIVE, APPEAR ⟨*showed up* late for his own wedding⟩ **2 :** to be plainly evident
show window *n* (1826) **1 :** an outside display window in which a store exhibits merchandise **2 :** a sample or setting used to exhibit or illustrate something at its best
showy \ˈshō-ē\ *adj* **show·i·er; -est** (1709) **1 :** making an attractive show : STRIKING ⟨a ~ orchid⟩ **2 :** given to or marked by a flashy often tasteless display — **show·i·ly** \ˈshō-ə-lē\ *adv* — **show·i·ness** \ˈshō-ē-nəs\ *n*

syn SHOWY, PRETENTIOUS, OSTENTATIOUS mean given to excessive outward display. SHOWY implies an imposing or striking appearance but usu. suggests cheapness or poor taste ⟨the performers' *showy* costumes⟩. PRETENTIOUS implies an appearance of importance not justified by the thing's value or the person's standing ⟨a *pretentious* parade of hard words⟩. OSTENTATIOUS stresses vainglorious display or parade ⟨the *ostentatious* summer homes of the rich⟩.

sho·yu \ˈshō-(ˌ)yü\ *n* [Jp *shōyu*] (1727) : SOY 1
shp *abbr* shaft horsepower
shrank *past of* SHRINK
shrap·nel \ˈshrap-nᵊl, *esp Southern* ˈsrap-\ *n, pl* **shrapnel** [Henry *Shrapnel* †1842 Eng. artillery officer] (1806) **1 :** a projectile that consists of a case provided with a powder charge and a large number of usu. lead balls and that is exploded in flight **2 :** bomb, mine, or shell fragments
[1]**shred** \ˈshred, *esp Southern* ˈsred\ *n* [ME *shrede,* fr. OE *scrēade;* akin to OHG *scrōt* piece cut off] (bef. 12c) **1 a :** a long narrow strip cut or torn off **b** *pl* : a shredded, damaged, or ruined condition ⟨a reputation torn to ~*s*⟩ **2 :** PARTICLE, SCRAP ⟨not a ~ of evidence⟩
[2]**shred** *vb* **shred·ded; shred·ding** *vt* (bef. 12c) **1** *archaic* : to cut off **2 :** to cut or tear into shreds ⟨*shredded* the documents⟩ **3 :** DEMOLISH 2 ⟨sharp lawyers *shredding* hapless witnesses —Charles Krauthammer⟩ ~ *vi* : to come apart in or break up into shreds — **shred·der** *n*
shredded wheat *n* (1898) : a breakfast cereal made from cooked partially dried wheat that is shredded and molded into biscuits which are then oven-baked and toasted
[1]**shrew** \ˈshrü, *esp Southern* ˈsrü\ *n* [ME *shrewe* evil or scolding person, fr. OE *scrēawa* shrew (animal)] (bef. 12c) **1 :** any of a family (Soricidae) of small chiefly nocturnal insectivores related to the moles and distinguished by a long pointed snout, very small eyes, and short velvety fur **2 :** an ill-tempered scolding woman — **shrew·like** \-ˌlīk\ *adj*
[2]**shrew** *vt* (14c) *obs* : CURSE
shrewd \ˈshrüd, *esp Southern* ˈsrüd\ *adj* [ME *shrewed,* fr. *shrewe* + [1]*-ed*] (13c) **1** *archaic* : MISCHIEVOUS **2** *obs* : ABUSIVE, SHREWISH **3** *obs* : OMINOUS, DANGEROUS **4 a :** SEVERE, HARD ⟨a ~ knock⟩ **b :** SHARP, PIERCING ⟨a ~ wind⟩ **5 a :** marked by clever discerning awareness and hardheaded acumen ⟨~ common sense⟩ **b :** given to wily and artful ways or dealing ⟨a ~ operator⟩ — **shrewd·ly** *adv* — **shrewd·ness** *n*

syn SHREWD, SAGACIOUS, PERSPICACIOUS, ASTUTE mean acute in perception and sound in judgment. SHREWD stresses practical, hardheaded cleverness and judgment ⟨a *shrewd* judge of character⟩. SAGACIOUS suggests wisdom, penetration, and farsightedness ⟨*sagacious* investors got in on the ground floor⟩. PERSPICACIOUS implies unusual power to see through and understand what is puzzling or hidden ⟨a *perspicacious* counselor saw through the child's facade⟩. ASTUTE suggests shrewdness, perspicacity, and diplomatic skill ⟨an *astute* player of party politics⟩.

shrew·ish \ˈshrü-ish, *esp Southern* ˈsrü-\ *adj* (1565) : ILL-NATURED, INTRACTABLE — **shrew·ish·ly** *adv* — **shrew·ish·ness** *n*
shri *var of* SRI
[1]**shriek** \ˈshrēk, *esp Southern* ˈsrēk\ *vb* [ME *shreken,* prob. irreg. fr. *shriken* to shriek; akin to ON *skrækja* to shriek] *vi* (15c) **1 :** to utter a sharp shrill sound **2 a :** to cry out in a high-pitched voice : SCREECH **b :** to suggest such a cry (as by vividness of expression) ⟨neon colors ~*ed* for attention —Calvin Tomkins⟩ ~ *vt* **1 :** to utter with a shriek ⟨~ an alarm⟩ **2 :** to express in a manner suggestive of a shriek
[2]**shriek** *n* (1567) **1 :** a shrill usu. wild or involuntary cry **2 :** a sound resembling a shriek ⟨the ~ of chalk on the blackboard⟩
shrie·val \ˈshrē-vəl, *esp Southern* ˈsrē-\ *adj* [obs. *shrieve* sheriff, fr. ME *shirreve* — more at SHERIFF] (1681) *chiefly Brit* : of or relating to a sheriff
shrie·val·ty \-vəl-tē\ *n* (1502) *chiefly Brit* : the office, term of office, or jurisdiction of a sheriff
shrieve \ˈshrēv, *esp Southern* ˈsrēv\ *archaic var of* SHRIVE
shrift \ˈshrift, *esp Southern* ˈsrift\ *n* [ME, fr. OE *scrift,* fr. *scrīfan* to shrive — more at SHRIVE] (bef. 12c) **1** *archaic* **a :** a remission of sins pronounced by a priest in the sacrament of reconciliation **b :** the act of shriving : CONFESSION **2** *obs* : CONFESSIONAL
shrike \ˈshrīk, *esp Southern* ˈsrīk\ *n* [perh. fr. ME **shrik,* fr. OE *scrīc* thrush; akin to ME *shriken* to shriek] (1544) : any of numerous usu. largely gray or brownish oscine birds (family Laniidae) that have a hooked bill, feed chiefly on insects, and often impale their prey on thorns

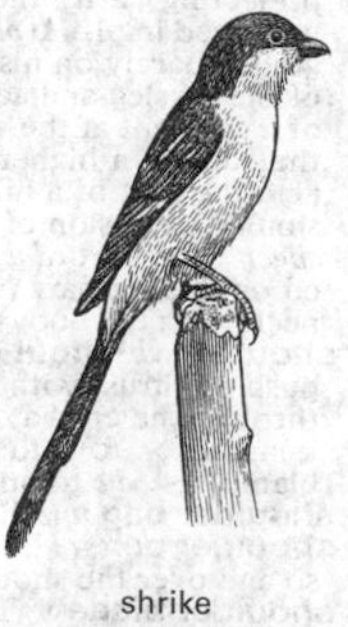
shrike

[1]**shrill** \ˈshril, *esp Southern* ˈsril\ *vb* [ME; prob. akin to OE *scralletan* to resound loudly — more at SKIRL] *vt* (13c) : SCREAM ~ *vi* : to utter or emit an acute piercing sound
[2]**shrill** *adj* (14c) **1 a :** having or emitting a sharp high-pitched tone or sound : PIERCING **b :** accompanied by sharp high-pitched sounds or cries ⟨~ gaiety⟩ **2 :** having a sharp or vivid effect on the senses ⟨~ light⟩ **3 :** STRIDENT, INTEMPERATE ⟨~ anger⟩ ⟨~ criticism⟩ — **shrill** *adv* — **shrill·ness** *n* — **shril·ly** \ˈshril-lē, *esp Southern* ˈsril-\ *adv*
[3]**shrill** *n* (1589) : a shrill sound ⟨the ~ of the ship's whistle⟩
[1]**shrimp** \ˈshrimp, *esp Southern* ˈsrimp\ *n, pl* **shrimps** *or* **shrimp** [ME *shrimpe;* akin to MLG *schrempen* to contract, wrinkle, ON *skorpna* to shrivel up] (14c) **1 :** any of numerous mostly small and marine decapod crustaceans (suborders Dendrobranchiata and Pleocyemata) having a slender elongated body, a compressed abdomen, and a long spiny rostrum and including some (esp. family Penaeidae) that are commercially important as food; *also* : a small crustacean (as an amphipod or a branchiopod) resembling the true shrimps **2 :** a very small or puny person or thing — **shrimp·like** \-ˌlīk\ *adj* — **shrimpy** \ˈshrim-pē, ˈsrim-\ *adj*
[2]**shrimp** *vi* (1808) : to fish for or catch shrimps
shrimp·er \ˈshrim-pər, *esp Southern* ˈsrim-\ *n* (1835) **1 :** a shrimp fisherman **2 :** a boat engaged in shrimping
[1]**shrine** \ˈshrīn, *esp Southern* ˈsrīn\ *n* [ME, fr. OE *scrīn,* fr. L *scrinium* case, chest] (bef. 12c) **1 a :** a case, box, or receptacle; *esp* : one in which sacred relics (as the bones of a saint) are deposited **b :** a place in which devotion is paid to a saint or deity : SANCTUARY **c :** a niche containing a religious image **2 :** a receptacle (as a tomb) for the dead **3 :** a place or object hallowed by its associations
[2]**shrine** *vt* **shrined; shrin·ing** (14c) : ENSHRINE
Shrin·er \ˈshrī-nər, *esp Southern* ˈsrī-\ *n* [Ancient Arabic Order of Nobles of the Mystic *Shrine*] (1886) : a member of a secret fraternal society that is non-Masonic but admits only Master Masons to membership

[1]**shrink** \'shriŋk, *esp Southern* 'sriŋk\ *vb* **shrank** \'shraŋk, 'sraŋk\ *or* **shrunk** \'shrəŋk, 'srəŋk\; **shrunk** *or* **shrunk·en** \'shrəŋ-kən, 'srəŋ-\; **shrink·ing** [ME, fr. OE *scrincan;* akin to MD *schrinken* to draw back] *vi* (bef. 12c) **1** : to contract or curl up the body or part of it : HUDDLE, COWER **2 a** : to contract to less extent or compass **b** : to become smaller or more compacted **c** : to lose substance or weight **d** : to lessen in value : DWINDLE **3 a** : to recoil instinctively (as from something painful or horrible) ⟨*shrank* from the challenge⟩ **b** : to hold oneself back : REFRAIN ⟨did not ~ from telling the truth⟩ ~ *vt* : to cause to contract or shrink; *specif* : to compact (cloth) by causing to contract when subjected to washing, boiling, steaming, or other processes ***syn*** see CONTRACT, RECOIL — **shrink·able** \'shriŋ-kə-bəl, 'sriŋ-\ *adj* — **shrink·er** *n*

[2]**shrink** *n* (1590) **1** : the act of shrinking **2** : SHRINKAGE **3** [short for *headshrinker*] : a clinical psychiatrist or psychologist

shrink·age \'shriŋ-kij, *esp Southern* 'sriŋ-\ *n* (1800) **1** : the act or process of shrinking **2 a** : the loss in weight of livestock during shipment and in the process of preparing the meat for consumption **b** : the loss of goods esp. by theft ⟨inventory ~⟩ **3** : the amount lost by shrinkage

shrinking violet *n* (1915) : a bashful or retiring person

shrink–wrap \'shriŋk-ˌrap, *esp Southern* 'sriŋk-\ *vt* (1959) : to wrap (as a book or meat) in tough clear plastic film that is then shrunk (as by heating) to form a tightly fitting package — **shrink–wrap** *n*

shrive \'shrīv, *esp Southern* 'srīv\ *vb* **shrived** *or* **shrove** \'shrōv, 'srōv\; **shriv·en** \'shri-vən, 'sri-\ *or* **shrived; shriv·ing** [ME, fr. OE *scrīfan* to shrive, prescribe (akin to OHG *scrīban* to write), fr. L *scribere* to write — more at SCRIBE] *vt* (bef. 12c) **1** : to administer the sacrament of reconciliation to **2** : to free from guilt ~ *vi, archaic* : to confess one's sins esp. to a priest

shriv·el \'shri-vəl, *esp Southern* 'sri-\ *vb* **-eled** *or* **-elled; -el·ing** *or* **-el·ling** \'shri-və-liŋ, 'sri-; 'shriv-liŋ, 'sriv-\ [origin unknown] *vi* (1565) **1** : to draw into wrinkles esp. with a loss of moisture **2 a** : to become reduced to inanition, helplessness, or inefficiency **b** : DWINDLE ~ *vt* : to cause to shrivel

shroff \'shräf, 'shrȯf, *esp Southern* 'sräf, 'srȯf\ *n* [Hindi *śarāf* & Urdu *sharāf,* ultim. fr. Ar *ṣarrāf*] (1618) : a banker or money changer in the Far East; *esp* : one who tests and evaluates coin

Shrop·shire \'shräp-ˌshir, -shər, *esp US* -ˌshī(-ə)r, *esp Southern* 'sräp-\ *n* [*Shropshire,* England] (1803) : any of a breed of dark-faced hornless sheep of English origin that are raised for both mutton and wool

[1]**shroud** \'shrau̇d, *esp Southern* 'srau̇d\ *n* [ME, garment, fr. OE *scrūd;* akin to OE *scrēade* shred — more at SHRED] (14c) **1** *obs* : SHELTER, PROTECTION **2** : something that covers, screens, or guards: as **a** : one of two flanges that give peripheral support to turbine or fan bedding **b** : a usu. fiberglass guard that protects a spacecraft from the heat of launching **3** : burial garment : WINDING-SHEET, CEREMENT **4 a** : one of the ropes leading usu. in pairs from a ship's mastheads to give lateral support to the masts **b** : one of the cords that suspend the harness of a parachute from the canopy

[2]**shroud** *vt* (14c) **1 a** *archaic* : to cover for protection **b** *obs* : CONCEAL **2 a** : to cut off from view : OBSCURE ⟨trees ~*ed* by fog⟩ ⟨this point is ~*ed* in uncertainty —Henry James⟩ **b** : to veil under another appearance (as by obscuring or disguising) ⟨~*ed* the decision in a series of formalities⟩ **3** : to dress for burial ~ *vi, archaic* : to seek shelter

Shrove·tide \'shrōv-ˌtīd, *esp Southern* 'srōv-\ *n* [ME *schroftide,* fr. *schrof-* (fr. *shriven* to shrive) + *tide*] (15c) : the period usu. of three days immediately preceding Ash Wednesday

Shrove Tuesday \'shrōv-, *esp Southern* 'srōv-\ *n* [ME *schroftewesday,* fr. *schrof-* (as in *schroftide*) + *tewesday* Tuesday] (15c) : the Tuesday before Ash Wednesday

[1]**shrub** \'shrəb, *esp Southern* 'srəb\ *n* [ME *schrobbe,* fr. OE *scrybb* brushwood; akin to Norw *skrubbebær,* a cornel of a dwarf species] (bef. 12c) : a low usu. several-stemmed woody plant

[2]**shrub** *n* [Ar *sharāb* beverage] (ca. 1706) **1** : an aged blend of fruit juice, sugar, and spirits served chilled and diluted with water **2** : a beverage made by adding acidulated fruit juice to iced water

shrub·bery \'shrə-b(ə-)rē, *esp Southern* 'srə-\ *n, pl* **-ber·ies** (1731) : a planting or growth of shrubs

shrub·by \'shrə-bē, *esp Southern* 'srə-\ *adj* **shrub·bi·er; -est** (1540) **1** : consisting of or covered with shrubs **2** : resembling a shrub

shrub·land \'shrəb-ˌland, *esp Southern* 'srəb-\ *n* (1903) : land on which shrubs are the dominant vegetation

[1]**shrug** \'shrəg, *esp Southern* 'srəg\ *vb* **shrugged; shrug·ging** [ME *schruggen*] *vi* (14c) : to raise or draw in the shoulders esp. to express aloofness, indifference, or uncertainty ~ *vt* : to lift or contract (the shoulders) esp. to express aloofness, indifference, or uncertainty

[2]**shrug** *n* (1594) **1** : an act of shrugging **2** : a woman's small waist-length or shorter jacket

shrug off *vt* (1902) **1** : to shake off ⟨*shrugging off* sleep⟩ **2** : to brush aside : MINIMIZE ⟨*shrugs off* the problem⟩ **3** : to remove (a garment) by wriggling out

shtetl *also* **shte·tel** \'shte-tᵊl, 'shtā-\ *n, pl* **shtet·lach** \'shtet-ˌläk, 'shtāt-\ *also* **shtetels** [Yiddish *shtetl,* fr. MHG *stetel,* dim. of *stat* place, town, city, fr. OHG, place — more at STEAD] (1949) : a small Jewish town or village formerly found in Eastern Europe

shtick *also* **schtick** *or* **shtik** \'shtik\ *n* [Yiddish *shtik* pranks, lit., piece, fr. MHG *stücke,* fr. OHG *stucki;* akin to OE *stycce* piece, OHG *stoc* stick — more at STOCK] (1959) **1** : a usu. comic or repetitious performance or routine : BIT **2** : one's special trait, interest, or activity : BAG ⟨he's alive and well and now doing his ~ out in Hollywood —Robert Daley⟩ — **shticky** \'shti-kē\ *adj*

[1]**shuck** \'shək\ *n* [origin unknown] (ca. 1674) **1** : SHELL, HUSK: as **a** : the outer covering of a nut or of Indian corn **b** : the shell of an oyster or clam **2** : something of little value — usu. used in pl. ⟨not worth ~*s*⟩

[2]**shuck** *vt* (1772) **1** : to strip of shucks **2 a** : to peel off (as clothing) — often used with *off* **b** : to lay aside — often used with *off* ⟨bad habits are being ~*ed* off —A. W. Smith⟩ — **shuck·er** *n*

shucks \'shəks\ *interj* (1847) — used esp. to express mild disappointment or embarrassment ⟨~, it was nothing⟩

[1]**shud·der** \'shə-dər\ *vi* **shud·dered; shud·der·ing** \-d(ə-)riŋ\ [ME *shoddren;* akin to OHG *skutten* to shake and perh. to Lith *kutėti* to shake up] (13c) : to tremble convulsively : SHIVER, QUIVER

[2]**shudder** *n* (1607) : an act of shuddering — **shud·dery** \-d(ə-)rē\ *adj*

[1]**shuf·fle** \'shə-fəl\ *vb* **shuf·fled; shuf·fling** \-f(ə-)liŋ\ [perh. irreg. fr. [1]*shove*] *vt* (1570) **1** : to mix in a mass confusedly : JUMBLE **2** : to put or thrust aside or under cover ⟨*shuffled* the whole matter out of his mind⟩ **3 a** : to rearrange (as playing cards, dominoes, or tiles) to produce a random order **b** : to move about, back and forth, or from one place to another : SHIFT ⟨~ funds among various accounts⟩ **4 a** : to move (as the feet) by sliding along or back and forth without lifting **b** : to perform (as a dance) with a dragging, sliding step ~ *vi* **1** : to work into or out of trickily ⟨*shuffled* out of the difficulty⟩ **2** : to act or speak in a shifty or evasive manner **3 a** : to move or walk in a sliding dragging manner without lifting the feet **b** : to dance in a lazy nonchalant manner with sliding and tapping motions of the feet **c** : to execute in a perfunctory or clumsy manner **4** : to mix playing cards or counters by shuffling — **shuf·fler** \-f(ə-)lər\ *n*

[2]**shuffle** *n* (1628) **1** : an evasion of the issue : EQUIVOCATION **2 a** : an act of shuffling (as of cards) **b** : a right or turn to shuffle ⟨it's your ~⟩ **c** : a confusing jumble (as of papers or events) ⟨lost in the ~⟩ **3 a** : a dragging sliding movement; *specif* : a sliding or scraping step in dancing **b** : a dance characterized by such a step **c** (1) : a rhythm where each beat of the measure is played as a triplet with the first and second parts of the triplet tied and the third part accented (2) : music played in a shuffle rhythm

shuf·fle·board \'shə-fəl-ˌbȯrd\ *n* [alter. of obs. E *shove-board*] (1836) **1** : a game in which players use long-handled cues to shove disks into scoring areas of a diagram marked on a smooth surface **2** : a diagram on which shuffleboard is played

shul \'shu̇l\ *n* [Yiddish, school, synagogue, fr. MHG *schuol* school] (1771) : SYNAGOGUE

shun \'shən\ *vt* **shunned; shun·ning** [ME *shonen, shunnen,* fr. OE *scunian*] (bef. 12c) : to avoid deliberately and esp. habitually ⟨~*s* publicity⟩ ***syn*** see ESCAPE — **shun·ner** *n*

shun·pike \'shən-ˌpīk\ *n* (1862) : a side road used to avoid the toll on or the speed and traffic of a superhighway — **shun·pik·er** \-ˌpī-kər\ *n* — **shun·pik·ing** \-kiŋ\ *n*

[1]**shunt** \'shənt\ *vb* [ME, to move suddenly, turn away, evade, perh. fr. pp. of *shonen*] *vt* (13c) **1 a** : to turn off to one side : SHIFT ⟨was ~*ed* aside⟩ **b** : to switch (as a train) from one track to another **2** : to provide with or divert by means of an electrical shunt **3** : to divert (blood) from one part to another by a surgical shunt **4** : SHUTTLE ⟨~*ed* the missiles from shelter to shelter⟩ ~ *vi* **1** : to move to the side **2** : to travel back and forth ⟨~*ed* between the two towns⟩ — **shunt·er** *n*

[2]**shunt** *n* (1842) **1** : a means or mechanism for turning or thrusting aside: as **a** *chiefly Brit* : a railroad switch **b** : a conductor joining two points in an electrical circuit so as to form a parallel or alternative path through which a portion of the current may pass (as for regulating the amount passing in the main circuit) **c** : a surgical passage created to divert a bodily fluid (as blood) from one vessel or part to another; *also* : a device (as a narrow tube) used to establish a similar passage **2** *chiefly Brit* : an accident (as a collision between two cars) esp. in auto racing

shush \'shəsh, 'shu̇sh\ *vt* [imit.] (1925) : to urge to be quiet : HUSH — **shush** *n*

[1]**shut** \'shət\ *vb* **shut; shut·ting** [ME *shetten, shutten,* fr. OE *scyttan;* akin to MD *schutten* to shut in, OE *scēotan* to shoot — more at SHOOT] *vt* (bef. 12c) **1 a** : to move into position to close an opening ⟨~ the lid⟩ **b** : to prevent entrance to or passage to or from **2** : to confine by or as if by enclosure ⟨~ herself in her study⟩ **3** : to fasten with a lock or bolt **4** : to close by bringing enclosing or covering parts together ⟨~ the eyes⟩ **5** : to cause to cease or suspend an operation or activity — often used with *down* ~ *vi* **1** : to close itself or become closed ⟨flowers that ~ at night⟩ **2** : to cease or suspend an operation or activity — often used with *down*

[2]**shut** *adj* (15c) **1** : closed, fastened, or folded together **2** : RID, CLEAR, FREE — usu. used with *of*

[3]**shut** *n* (1667) : the act of shutting

shut·down \'shət-ˌdau̇n\ *n* (1888) : the cessation or suspension of an operation or activity

shut down *vi* (1779) : to settle so as to obscure vision : CLOSE IN ⟨the night *shut down* early⟩ ~ *vt* : to make ineffective in competition ⟨*shut down* the opposition's offensive line⟩

shute *var of* CHUTE

shut–eye \'shət-ˌī\ *n* (1899) : SLEEP ⟨get some ~⟩

[1]**shut–in** \'shət-ˌin\ *n* (1891) **1** : a person who is confined to home, a room, or bed because of illness or incapacity **2** : a narrow gorge-shaped part of an otherwise wide valley **3** : available oil or gas which is not being produced from an existing well

[2]**shut–in** \'shət-'in\ *adj* (1909) **1** : confined to one's home or an institution by illness or incapacity **2 a** : SECRETIVE, BROODING ⟨a bitter, ~ face —Claudia Cassidy⟩ **b** : tending to avoid social contact : WITHDRAWN ⟨the ~ personality type —S. K. Weinberg⟩

shut in *vt* (14c) **1** : CONFINE, ENCLOSE **2** : to prevent production of (oil or gas) by closing down a well

shut·off \'shət-ˌȯf\ *n* (1847) **1** : something (as a valve) that shuts off **2** : STOPPAGE, INTERRUPTION

shut off *vt* (1818) **1** : to close off : SEPARATE — usu. used with *from* ⟨*shut off* from the rest of the world⟩ **2 a** : to cut off (as flow or passage) : STOP ⟨*shuts off* the oxygen supply⟩ **b** : to stop the operation of (as a machine) ⟨*shut* the motor *off*⟩ ~ *vi* : to cease operating : STOP ⟨*shuts off* automatically⟩

shut·out \'shət-ˌau̇t\ *n* (1889) **1** : a game or contest in which one side fails to score **2** : a preemptive bid in bridge

shut out *vt* (14c) **1** : EXCLUDE **2** : to prevent (an opponent) from scoring in a game or contest **3** : to forestall the bidding of (bridge opponents) by making a high or preemptive bid

[1]**shut·ter** \ˈshə-tər\ *n* (1542) **1 :** one that shuts **2 :** a usu. movable cover or screen for a window or door **3 :** a mechanical device that limits the passage of light; *esp* **:** a camera component that allows light to enter by opening and closing an aperture **4 :** the movable louvers in a pipe organ by which the swell box is opened — **shut·ter·less** \-ləs\ *adj*

[2]**shutter** *vt* (1826) **1 :** to close by or as if by shutters ⟨corporations ~*ing* their production plants⟩ **2 :** to furnish with shutters

shut·ter·bug \ˈshə-tər-ˌbəg\ *n* (1940) **:** a photography enthusiast

[1]**shut·tle** \ˈshə-tᵊl\ *n* [ME *shittle, shutle,* fr. OE *scutel, scytel* dart; akin to ON *skutill* bolt, OE *scēotan* to shoot — more at SHOOT] (14c) **1 a :** a device used in weaving for passing the thread of the weft between the threads of the warp **b :** a spindle-shaped device holding the thread in tatting, knotting, or netting **c :** a sliding thread holder for the lower thread of a sewing machine that carries the lower thread through a loop of the upper thread to make a stitch **2 :** SHUTTLECOCK **3 a :** a going back and forth regularly over an often short route by a vehicle **b** (1) **:** an established route used in a shuttle (2) **:** a vehicle used in a shuttle ⟨a ~ bus⟩ **c :** SPACE SHUTTLE — **shut·tle·less** *adj*

[2]**shuttle** *vb* **shut·tled; shut·tling** \ˈshət-liŋ, ˈshə-tᵊl-iŋ\ *vt* (1550) **1 :** to cause to move or travel back and forth frequently **2 :** to transport in, by, or as if by a shuttle ⟨*shuttled* them to school⟩ ~ *vi* **1 :** to move or travel back and forth frequently **2 :** to move by or as if by a shuttle

[1]**shut·tle·cock** \ˈshə-tᵊl-ˌkäk\ *n* (1522) **:** a lightweight conical object with a rounded often rubber-covered nose that is used in badminton

[2]**shuttlecock** *vt* (1687) **:** to send or toss to and fro **:** BANDY

shuttle diplomacy *n* (1974) **:** negotiations esp. between nations carried on by an intermediary who shuttles back and forth between the disputants

shut up *vt* (1814) **:** to cause (a person) to stop talking ~ *vi* **:** to cease writing or speaking

[1]**shy** \ˈshī\ *adj* **shi·er** *or* **shy·er** \ˈshī(-ə)r\; **shi·est** *or* **shy·est** \ˈshī-əst\ [ME *schey,* fr. OE *scēoh;* akin to OHG *sciuhen* to frighten off] (bef. 12c) **1 :** easily frightened **:** TIMID **2 :** disposed to avoid a person or thing ⟨publicity ~⟩ **3 :** hesitant in committing oneself **:** CIRCUMSPECT **4 :** sensitively diffident or retiring **:** RESERVED; *also* **:** expressive of such a state or nature ⟨a ~ smile⟩ **5 :** SECLUDED, HIDDEN **6 :** having less than the full or specified amount or number **:** SHORT ⟨just ~ of six feet tall⟩ **7 :** DISREPUTABLE ⟨gambling hells and ~ saloons —*Blackwood's*⟩ — **shy·ly** *adv* — **shy·ness** *n*

syn SHY, BASHFUL, DIFFIDENT, MODEST, COY mean not inclined to be forward. SHY implies a timid reserve and a shrinking from familiarity or contact with others ⟨*shy* with strangers⟩. BASHFUL implies a frightened or hesitant shyness characteristic of childhood and adolescence ⟨a *bashful* boy out on his first date⟩. DIFFIDENT stresses a distrust of one's own ability or opinion that causes hesitation in acting or speaking ⟨felt *diffident* about raising an objection⟩. MODEST suggests absence of undue confidence or conceit ⟨*modest* about her success⟩. COY implies a pretended shyness ⟨put off by her *coy* manner⟩.

[2]**shy** *vi* **shied; shy·ing** (1649) **1 :** to develop or show a dislike or distaste — usu. used with *from* or *away from* ⟨an author who *shies* away from publicity⟩ **2 :** to start suddenly aside through fright or alarm

[3]**shy** *n, pl* **shies** (1791) **:** a sudden start aside (as from fright)

[4]**shy** *vb* **shied; shy·ing** [perh. fr. [1]*shy*] *vi* (1787) **:** to make a sudden throw ~ *vt* **:** to throw (an object) with a jerk **:** FLING

[5]**shy** *n, pl* **shies** (1791) **1 :** the act of shying **:** TOSS, THROW **2 :** a verbal fling or attack **3 :** COCKSHY

[1]**shy·lock** \ˈshī-ˌläk\ *n* (ca. 1597) **1** *cap* **:** the Jewish usurer and antagonist of Antonio in Shakespeare's *The Merchant of Venice* **2 :** LOAN SHARK

[2]**shylock** *vi* (ca. 1934) **:** to lend money at high rates of interest ⟨exposé of systematic thievery . . . ~*ing,* and murder —*Current Biog.*⟩

shy·ster \ˈshīs-tər\ *n* [prob. fr. G *Scheisser,* lit., defecator] (1844) **:** a person who is professionally unscrupulous esp. in the practice of law or politics **:** PETTIFOGGER

si \ˈsē\ *n* [It] (1728) **:** [2]TI

Si *symbol* silicon

SI *abbr* [F *Système International d'Unités*] International System of Units

si·al·a·gogue \sī-ˈa-lə-ˌgäg\ *n* [NL *sialagogus* promoting the expulsion of saliva, fr. Gk *sialon* saliva + NL *-agogus* -agogue] (ca. 1783) **:** an agent that promotes the flow of saliva

si·al·ic \sī-ˈa-lik\ *adj* [ISV *si*licon + *al*uminum] (1924) **:** of, relating to, or being relatively light rock that is rich in silica and alumina and is typical of the outer layers of the earth

sialic acid *n* [Gk *sialon* saliva] (1952) **:** any of a group of reducing amido acids that are essentially carbohydrates and are found esp. as components of blood glycoproteins and mucoproteins

si·a·mang \ˈsē-ə-ˌmaŋ, ˈsī-\ *n* [Malay] (1822) **:** a black gibbon (*Hylobates syndactylus*) of Sumatra and the Malay Peninsula that is the largest of the gibbons

[1]**Si·a·mese** \ˌsī-ə-ˈmēz, -ˈmēs\ *adj* [*Siam* (Thailand); in senses 2 & 3, fr. *Siamese twin*] (1693) **1 :** of, relating to, or characteristic of Thailand, the Thais, or their language **2 :** exhibiting great resemblance **:** very like **3** *not cap* **:** connecting two or more pipes or hoses so as to permit discharge in a single stream

[2]**Siamese** *n, pl* **Siamese** (1693) **1 :** THAI 2 **2 :** THAI 3 **3 :** SIAMESE CAT

Siamese cat *n* (1871) **:** any of a breed of slender blue-eyed short-haired domestic cats of Asian origin with pale fawn or gray body and darker ears, paws, tail, and face and a long wedge-shaped head

Siamese fighting fish *n* (1929) **:** a brightly colored betta (*Betta splendens*) that has highly aggressive males and is a popular aquarium fish

Siamese twin *n* [fr. Chang †1874 and Eng †1874 congenitally united twins born in Siam] (1829) **:** one of a pair of congenitally united twins

[1]**sib** \ˈsib\ *adj* [ME, fr. OE *sibb,* fr. *sibb* kinship; akin to OHG *sippa* kinship, family, L *sodalis* comrade, Gk *ēthos* custom, character, L *suus* one's own — more at SUICIDE] (bef. 12c) **:** related by blood **:** AKIN

[2]**sib** *n* (bef. 12c) **1 a :** KINDRED, RELATIVES **b :** a blood relation **:** KINSMAN **2 :** a brother or sister considered irrespective of sex; *broadly* **:** any plant or animal of a group sharing a degree of genetic relationship corresponding to that of human sibs **3 :** a group of persons unilaterally descended from a real or supposed ancestor

Si·be·ri·an husky \sī-ˈbir-ē-ən-\ *n* (1930) **:** any of a breed of medium-sized thick-coated compact dogs that were developed in Siberia for use as sled dogs and that have erect ears and a bushy tail

Siberian tiger *n* (1889) **:** a large endangered tiger (*Panthera tigris altaica*) formerly inhabiting eastern Siberia to Korea but now much restricted in range

sib·i·lance \ˈsi-bə-lən(t)s\ *n* (1823) **:** a sibilant quality or sound

[1]**sib·i·lant** \ˈsi-bə-lənt\ *adj* [L *sibilant-, sibilans,* prp. of *sibilare* to hiss, whistle, of imit. origin] (1669) **:** having, containing, or producing the sound of or a sound resembling that of the *s* or the *sh* in *sash* ⟨a ~ affricate⟩ ⟨a ~ snake⟩ — **sib·i·lant·ly** *adv*

[2]**sibilant** *n* (1788) **:** a sibilant speech sound (as English \s\, \z\, \sh\, \zh\, \ch(=tsh)\, or \j(=dzh)\)

sib·i·late \ˈsi-bə-ˌlāt\ *vb* **-lat·ed; -lat·ing** [L *sibilatus,* pp. of *sibilare*] *vi* (ca. 1656) **1 :** HISS **2 :** to utter an initial sibilant **:** prefix an \s\-sound ~ *vt* **1 :** HISS **2 :** to pronounce with an initial sibilant **:** prefix an \s\-sound to — **sib·i·la·tion** \ˌsi-bə-ˈlā-shən\ *n*

sib·ling \ˈsi-bliŋ\ *n* (bef. 12c) **1 :** SIB 2; *also* **:** one of two or more individuals having one common parent **2 :** one of two or more things related by a common tie or characteristic ⟨the sedan's smaller ~⟩

sibling species *n* (1940) **:** one of two or more species that are nearly indistinguishable morphologically

sib·yl \ˈsi-bəl\ *n, often cap* [ME *sibile, sybylle,* fr. AF & L; AF *sibile,* fr. L *sibylla,* fr. Gk] (14c) **1 :** any of several prophetesses usu. accepted as 10 in number and credited to widely separate parts of the ancient world (as Babylonia, Egypt, Greece, and Italy) **2 a :** PROPHETESS **b :** FORTUNE-TELLER — **si·byl·ic** *or* **si·byl·lic** \sə-ˈbi-lik\ *adj* — **sib·yl·line** \ˈsi-bə-ˌlīn, -ˌlēn\ *adj*

[1]**sic** \ˈsik\ *chiefly Scot var of* SUCH

[2]**sic** *also* **sick** \ˈsik\ *vt* **sicced** *also* **sicked** \ˈsikt\; **sic·cing** *also* **sick·ing** [alter. of *seek*] (1845) **1 :** CHASE, ATTACK — usu. used as a command esp. to a dog ⟨~ 'em⟩ **2 :** to incite or urge to an attack, pursuit, or harassment **:** SET ⟨*sicced* their lawyers on me⟩

[3]**sic** \ˈsik, ˈsēk\ *adv* [L, so, thus — more at SO] (ca. 1859) **:** intentionally so written — used after a printed word or passage to indicate that it is intended exactly as printed or to indicate that it exactly reproduces an original ⟨said he seed [~] it all⟩

Sichuan *var of* SZECHUAN

[1]**sick** \ˈsik\ *adj* [ME *sek, sik,* fr. OE *sēoc;* akin to OHG *sioh* sick] (bef. 12c) **1 a** (1) **:** affected with disease or ill health **:** AILING (2) **:** of, relating to, or intended for use in sickness ⟨~ pay⟩ ⟨a ~ ward⟩ **b :** QUEASY, NAUSEATED ⟨~ to one's stomach⟩ ⟨was ~ in the car⟩ **c :** undergoing menstruation **2 :** spiritually or morally unsound or corrupt **3 a :** sickened by strong emotion ⟨~ with fear⟩ ⟨worried ~⟩ **b :** having a strong distaste from surfeit **:** SATIATED ⟨~ of flattery⟩ **c :** filled with disgust or chagrin ⟨gossip makes me ~⟩ **d :** depressed and longing for something ⟨~ for one's home⟩ **4 a :** mentally or emotionally unsound or disordered **:** MORBID ⟨~ thoughts⟩ **b :** highly distasteful **:** MACABRE, SADISTIC ⟨~ jokes⟩ ⟨a ~ crime⟩ **5 :** lacking vigor **:** SICKLY: as **a :** badly outclassed ⟨made the competition look ~⟩ **b :** incapable of producing profitable yields of a crop ⟨~ soils⟩ — **sick·ly** *adv*

[2]**sick** *n* (1957) *Brit* **:** VOMIT 1

sick and tired *adj* (1775) **:** thoroughly fatigued or bored; *also* **:** FED UP

sick bay *n* (1813) **:** a compartment in a ship used as a dispensary and hospital; *broadly* **:** a place for the care of the sick or injured

sick·bed \ˈsik-ˌbed\ *n* (14c) **:** the bed on which one lies sick

sick building syndrome *n* (1983) **:** a set of symptoms (as headache, fatigue, and eye irritation) typically affecting workers in modern airtight office buildings that is believed to be caused by indoor pollutants (as formaldehyde fumes or microorganisms) — compare MULTIPLE CHEMICAL SENSITIVITY

sick call *n* (1836) **:** a scheduled time at which individuals (as soldiers) may report as sick to the medical officer

sick day *n* (1968) **:** a paid day of sick leave

sick·en \ˈsi-kən\ *vb* **sick·ened; sick·en·ing** \ˈsi-kə-niŋ, ˈsik-niŋ\ *vi* (13c) **1 :** to become sick **2 :** to become weary or satiated ~ *vt* **1 :** to make sick **2 :** to cause revulsion in ⟨their prejudice ~*s* me⟩ — **sick·en·er** \ˈsi-kə-nər, ˈsik-nər\ *n*

sickening *adj* (1789) **:** causing sickness or disgust ⟨a ~ odor⟩ ⟨a ~ display⟩ — **sick·en·ing·ly** \-niŋ-lē\ *adv*

sick·er \ˈsi-kər\ *adj* [ME *siker,* fr. OE *sicor,* fr. L *securus* secure] (bef. 12c) *chiefly Scot* **:** SECURE, SAFE; *also* **:** DEPENDABLE — **sicker** *adv, chiefly Scot* — **sick·er·ly** *adv, chiefly Scot*

sick headache *n* (1778) **:** MIGRAINE

sick·ie \ˈsi-kē\ *n* (1967) **:** SICKO

sick·ish \ˈsi-kish\ *adj* (1581) **1** *archaic* **:** somewhat ill **:** SICKLY **2 :** somewhat nauseated **:** QUEASY **3 :** somewhat sickening ⟨a ~ odor⟩ — **sick·ish·ly** *adv* — **sick·ish·ness** *n*

[1]**sick·le** \ˈsi-kəl\ *n* [ME *sikel,* fr. OE *sicol,* fr. L *secula* sickle, fr. *secare* to cut — more at SAW] (bef. 12c) **1 :** an agricultural implement consisting of a curved metal blade with a short handle fitted on a tang **2 :** the cutting mechanism (as of a reaper, combine, or mower) consisting of a bar with a series of cutting elements

[2]**sickle** *adj* (1688) **:** having the form of a sickle blade **:** having a curve similar to that of a sickle blade ⟨the ~ moon⟩

[3]**sickle** *vb* **sick·led; sick·ling** \ˈsi-k(ə-)liŋ\ *vt* (1922) **1 :** to mow or reap with a sickle **2 :** to change (a red blood cell) into a sickle cell ~ *vi* **:** to change into a sickle cell ⟨the ability of red blood cells to ~⟩

sick leave *n* (1820) **1 :** an absence from work permitted because of illness **2 :** the number of days per year for which an employer agrees to pay employees who are sick

sickle cell *n* (ca. 1923) **:** an abnormal red blood cell of crescent shape

sickle–cell anemia *n* (1922) **:** a chronic inherited anemia that occurs primarily in individuals of African, Mediterranean, or southwest Asian ancestry who are homozygous for the gene controlling hemoglobin S and that is characterized esp. by episodic blocking of small blood vessels by sickle cells — called also *sickle-cell disease*

sickle–cell trait *n* (1928) **:** an inherited usu. asymptomatic blood condition in which some red blood cells tend to sickle but usu. not enough to produce anemia and that occurs primarily in individuals of African, Mediterranean, or southwest Asian ancestry who are heterozygous for the gene controlling hemoglobin S

sick·le·mia \ˌsi-kə-ˈlē-mē-ə\ *n* [NL, fr. E *sickle* (cell) + NL *-emia*] (1932) **:** SICKLE-CELL TRAIT

[1]**sick·ly** \ˈsi-klē\ *adj* (14c) **1 :** somewhat unwell; *also* **:** habitually ailing **2 :** produced by or associated with sickness ⟨a ~ complexion⟩ ⟨a ~

appetite⟩ **3 :** producing or tending to produce disease : UNWHOLESOME ⟨a ~ climate⟩ **4 a :** appearing as if sick **b :** lacking in vigor : WEAK ⟨a ~ plant⟩ **5 :** SICKENING ⟨a ~ odor⟩ — **sick·li·ness** *n*

[2]**sickly** *vt* **sick·lied; sick·ly·ing** (1763) **:** to make sick or sickly

sick·ness \ˈsik-nəs\ *n* (bef. 12c) **1 a :** ill health : ILLNESS **b :** a disordered, weakened, or unsound condition **2 :** a specific disease **3 :** NAUSEA, QUEASINESS

sicko \ˈsi-(ˌ)kō\ *n, pl* **sick·os** (1963) **:** a person who is mentally or morally sick — **sicko** *adj*

sick–out \ˈsik-ˌau̇t\ *n* (1951) **:** an organized absence from work by workers on the pretext of sickness

sick pay *n* (1887) **:** salary or wages paid to an employee while on sick leave

sick·room \ˈsik-ˌrüm, -ˌru̇m\ *n* (1749) **:** a room in which a person is confined by sickness

sic pas·sim \ˈsik-ˈpa-səm, ˈsēk-ˈpä-sim\ *adv* [L] (ca. 1921) **:** so throughout — used of a word or idea to be found throughout a book or a writer's work

SID *abbr* sports information director

sid·dur \ˈsi-dər, -ˌdu̇r\ *n, pl* **sid·du·rim** \sə-ˈdu̇r-əm\ [LHeb *siddūr,* lit., order, arrangement] (ca. 1864) **:** a Jewish prayer book containing liturgies for daily, Sabbath, and holiday observances

[1]**side** \ˈsīd\ *n* [ME, fr. OE *sīde;* akin to OHG *sīta* side, OE *sīd* ample, wide] (bef. 12c) **1 a :** the right or left part of the wall or trunk of the body ⟨a pain in the ~⟩ **b** (1) **:** one of the halves of the animal body on either side of the median plane (2) **:** a cut of meat including that about the ribs of one half of the body — used chiefly of smoked pork products **c :** one longitudinal half of a hide **2 :** a place, space, or direction with respect to a center or to a line of division (as of an aisle, river, or street) **3 a :** one of the longer bounding surfaces or lines of an object esp. contrasted with the ends ⟨the ~ of a barn⟩ **b :** a line or surface forming a border or face of an object ⟨a die has six ~*s*⟩ ⟨the back ~ of the moon⟩ **c :** either surface of a thin object ⟨one ~ of a record⟩ ⟨right ~ of the cloth⟩ **d :** a bounding line of a geometric figure ⟨~ of a triangle⟩ **4 a :** the space beside one ⟨stood by my ~⟩ **b :** an area next to something — usu. used in combination ⟨a pool*side* interview⟩ **5 :** a slope (as of a hill) considered as opposed to another slope ⟨the far ~ of the hill⟩ **6 a :** the attitude or activity of one person or group with respect to another : PART ⟨there was no malice on my ~⟩ **b :** a position that is opposite to or contrasted with another ⟨two ~*s* to every question⟩ ⟨came down on the ~ of law and order⟩ **c :** a body of partisans or contestants ⟨victory for neither ~⟩ **d :** TEAM 4a ⟨11 players on each ~⟩; *also* **:** the players on a baseball team batting in an inning ⟨struck out the ~⟩ **7 :** a line of descent traced through one's parent ⟨grandfather on his mother's ~⟩ **8 :** an aspect or part of something contrasted with some other real or implied aspect or part ⟨the better ~ of his nature⟩ ⟨the sales ~ of the business⟩ ⟨the seasoning is a bit on the heavy ~⟩ **9** *Brit* **:** sideways spin imparted to a billiard or snooker ball **10 :** a sheet containing the lines and cues for a single theatrical role **11 :** a recording of music **12 :** a side order or dish ⟨a ~ of fries⟩ — **on the side 1 :** in addition to the main portion **2 :** in addition to a principal occupation **3 :** secretly outside of one's marriage or romantic relationship ⟨seeing another woman *on the side*⟩ — **this side of :** short of : ALMOST ⟨an attitude just *this side of* scandalous⟩

[2]**side** *adj* (14c) **1 a :** situated on the side ⟨~ window⟩ **b :** of or relating to the side **2 a :** directed toward or from the side ⟨~ thrust⟩ ⟨~ wind⟩ **b :** INCIDENTAL, INDIRECT ⟨~ issue⟩ ⟨~ remark⟩ **c :** made on the side ⟨~ payment⟩ **d :** additional to the main portion ⟨a ~ order of french fries⟩

[3]**side** *vb* **sid·ed; sid·ing** *vt* (1591) **1 :** to agree with : SUPPORT **2 :** to be side by side with **3 :** to set or put aside : clear away ⟨~ the dishes⟩ **4 :** to furnish with sides or siding ⟨~ a house⟩ ~ *vi* **:** to take sides : join or form sides ⟨*sided* with the rebels⟩

[4]**side** *n* [obs. E *side* proud, boastful] (1878) *chiefly Brit* **:** swaggering or arrogant manner : PRETENTIOUSNESS

[1]**side·arm** \ˈsīd-ˌärm\ *n* (1689) **:** a weapon (as a sword, revolver, or bayonet) worn at the side or in the belt

[2]**sidearm** *adj* (1908) **:** of, relating to, using, or being a throw (as in baseball) in which the arm is not raised above the shoulder and the ball is thrown with a sideways sweep of the arm between shoulder and hip ⟨~ delivery⟩ ⟨a ~ pass⟩ — **sidearm** *adv*

side·band \-ˌband\ *n* (1921) **:** the band of frequencies (as of radio waves) on either side of the carrier frequency produced by modulation

side·bar \-ˌbär\ *n* (1945) **1 a :** a short news story or graphic accompanying and presenting sidelights of a major story **b :** something incidental : SIDELIGHT ⟨a ~ to the essay's central theme⟩ **2 :** a conference between the judge, the lawyers, and sometimes the parties to a case that the jury does not hear

side bearing *n* (ca. 1894) **:** the space provided at each side of a typeset letter to prevent its touching adjoining letters

side·board \ˈsīd-ˌbȯrd\ *n* (1671) **1 :** a piece of dining-room furniture having compartments and shelves for holding articles of table service **2 sideboards** *pl, Brit* **:** SIDEBURNS

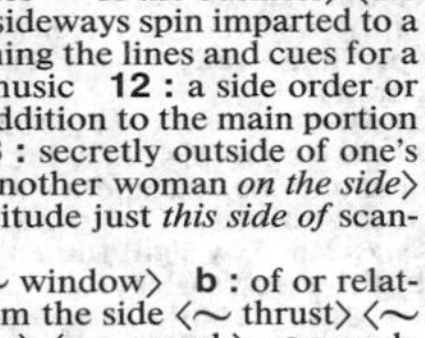

sideboard 1

side·burns \-ˌbərnz\ *n pl* [anagram of *burnsides*] (1887) **1 :** SIDE-WHISKERS **2 :** continuations of the hairline in front of the ears — **side·burned** \-ˌbərnd\ *adj*

side by side *adv* (13c) **1 :** beside one another ⟨walking *side by side*⟩ **2 :** in the same place, time, or circumstance ⟨lived peacefully *side by side* for many years⟩ — **side–by–side** *adj*

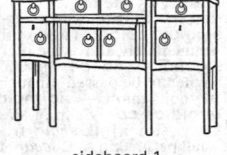

side·car \ˈsīd-ˌkär\ *n* (1903) **1 :** a car attached to the side of a motorcycle for a passenger **2 :** a cocktail consisting of a liqueur with lemon juice and brandy

side chain *n* (1886) **:** a shorter chain or group of atoms attached to a principal chain or to a ring in a molecule

side chair *n* (1905) **:** a chair without arms used usu. in a dining room

sided *adj* (15c) **:** having sides often of a specified number or kind ⟨one-*sided*⟩ ⟨glass-*sided*⟩ — **sid·ed·ness** *n*

side dish *n* (1706) **:** a food served separately along with the main course

side–dress \ˈsīd-ˌdres\ *vt* (ca. 1939) **:** to place plant nutrients on or in the soil near the roots of (a growing crop)

side–dress·ing \-ˌdre-siŋ\ *n* (1935) **:** plant nutrients (as fertilizer) used to side-dress a crop

side drum *n* (ca. 1800) **:** SNARE DRUM

side effect *n* (1884) **:** a secondary and usu. adverse effect (as of a drug) ⟨toxic *side effects*⟩ — called also *side reaction*

side–glance \ˈsīd-ˌglan(t)s\ *n* (ca. 1611) **1 :** a glance directed to the side **2 :** a passing allusion : an indirect or slight reference

side·hill \-ˌhil\ *n* (1674) **:** HILLSIDE — **sidehill** *adj*

side horse *n* (ca. 1934) **:** POMMEL HORSE

side·kick \ˈsīd-ˌkik\ *n* (1906) **:** a person closely associated with another as a subordinate or partner

side·light \-ˌlīt\ *n* (1610) **1 a :** light coming or produced from the side **b :** incidental light or information **2 :** the red light on the port bow or the green light on the starboard bow carried by ships under way at night

[1]**side·line** \-ˌlīn\ *n* (ca. 1862) **1 :** a line at right angles to a goal line or end line and marking a side of a court or field of play for athletic games **2 a :** a line of goods sold in addition to one's principal line **b :** a business or activity pursued in addition to one's regular occupation **3 a :** the space immediately outside the lines along either side of an athletic field or court **b :** a sphere of little or no participation or activity — usu. used in pl.

[2]**sideline** *vt* (1943) **:** to put out of action : put on the sidelines

side·lin·er \ˈsīd-ˌlī-nər\ *n* (1947) **:** one that remains on the sidelines during an activity : one that does not participate

[1]**side·ling** \ˈsīd-liŋ\ *adv* [ME *sidling,* fr. [1]*side* + [2]*-ling*] (14c) *archaic* **:** in a sidelong direction : SIDEWAYS

[2]**sideling** *adj* (ca. 1611) **1** *archaic* **:** directed toward one side : OBLIQUE **2** *archaic* **:** having an inclination : SLOPING ⟨~ ground⟩

[1]**side·long** \ˈsīd-ˌlȯŋ\ *adv* [alter. of [1]*sideling*] (14c) **1 :** SIDEWAYS, OBLIQUELY **2** *archaic* **:** on the side

[2]**sidelong** *adj* (1597) **1 :** lying or inclining to one side : SLANTING **2 a :** directed to one side ⟨~ looks⟩ **b :** indirect rather than straightforward

side·man \ˈsīd-ˌman\ *n* (ca. 1936) **:** a member of a band or orchestra and esp. of a jazz or swing orchestra

side–out \ˈsīd-ˈau̇t\ *n* (1949) **:** the termination of a team's right to serve (as in volleyball)

side·piece \-ˌpēs\ *n* (1648) **:** a piece forming or contained in the side of something ⟨the ~ of a carriage⟩

sider- *or* **sidero-** *comb form* [Gk *sidēr-, sidēro-,* fr. *sidēros*] **:** iron ⟨he*mosider*in⟩ ⟨*sidero*lite⟩

-sid·er \ˈsīd-ər\ *comb form* **:** one placed or living in a usu. specified side (as a section of the city) ⟨an east-*sider*⟩

si·de·re·al \sī-ˈdir-ē-əl, sə-\ *adj* [L *sidereus,* fr. *sider-, sidus* star, constellation] (1647) **:** of, relating to, or expressed in relation to stars or constellations : ASTRAL

sidereal day *n* (1764) **:** the interval between two successive transits of a point on the celestial sphere (as the vernal equinox) over the upper meridian of a place : 23 hours, 56 minutes, 4.1 seconds of mean time

sidereal hour *n* (ca. 1695) **:** the 24th part of a sidereal day

sidereal minute *n* (ca. 1909) **:** the 60th part of a sidereal hour

sidereal month *n* (1868) **:** the mean time of the moon's revolution in its orbit with reference to a star's position : 27 days, 7 hours, 43 minutes, 11.5 seconds of mean time

sidereal second *n* (ca. 1909) **:** the 60th part of a sidereal minute

sidereal time *n* (1764) **1 :** time based on the sidereal day **2 :** the hour angle of the vernal equinox at a place

sidereal year *n* (1681) **:** the time in which the earth completes one revolution in its orbit around the sun measured with respect to the fixed stars : 365 days, 6 hours, 9 minutes, and 9.5 seconds of mean time

[1]**sid·er·ite** \ˈsi-də-ˌrīt\ *n* [G *Siderit,* fr. Gk *sidēros* iron] (1850) **:** a native ferrous carbonate $FeCO_3$ that is a valuable iron ore

[2]**siderite** *n* (1875) **:** a nickel-iron meteorite

side road *n* (1691) **:** a smaller road off a main road

si·de·ro·lite \sī-ˈdir-ə-ˌlīt, ˈsi-də-rə-\ *n* (1863) **:** a stony iron meteorite

side·sad·dle \ˈsīd-ˌsa-dᵊl\ *n* (15c) **:** a saddle for women in which the rider sits with both legs on one side of the horse — **sidesaddle** *adv*

side–scan sonar \-ˌskan-\ *n* (1967) **:** a sonar that scans the ocean floor to the side of a ship's track and is used esp. for mapping the ocean bottom

side·show \-ˌshō\ *n* (1846) **1 :** a minor show offered in addition to a main exhibition (as of a circus) **2 :** an incidental diversion or spectacle

side·slip \-ˌslip\ *vi* (1887) **1 :** to skid or slide sideways **2 :** to slide sideways through the air in a downward direction in an airplane along an inclined lateral axis — **sideslip** *n*

side·spin \-ˌspin\ *n* (1926) **:** a rotary motion that causes a ball to revolve horizontally

side·split·ting \-ˌspli-tiŋ\ *adj* (1846) **:** extremely funny ⟨a ~ comedy⟩ — **side·split·ting·ly** *adv*

side·step \ˈsīd-ˌstep\ *vt* (1900) **1 :** BYPASS, EVADE ⟨~ a question⟩ **2 :** to move out of the way of : AVOID ⟨~ a blow⟩ ~ *vi* **1 :** to take a side step **2 :** to avoid an issue or decision — **side·step·per** *n*

side step *n* (ca. 1789) **1 :** a step aside (as in boxing to avoid a blow) **2 :** a step taken sideways (as when climbing on skis)

side·stream \-ˌstrēm\ *adj* (1951) **:** relating to or being tobacco smoke that is emitted from the lighted end of a cigarette or cigar

side street *n* (1617) **:** a street joining and often terminated by a main thoroughfare

side·stroke \ˈsīd-ˌstrōk\ *n* (1867) **:** a swimming stroke which is executed on the side and in which the arms are swept in separate strokes towards the feet and downward and the legs do a scissors kick

\ə\ **abut** \ᵊ\ kitten, F table \ər\ **fur**ther \a\ ash \ā\ ace \ä\ mop, mar
\au̇\ **out** \ch\ **ch**in \e\ bet \ē\ **ea**sy \g\ **g**o \i\ **hi**t \ī\ **i**ce \j\ **j**ob
\ŋ\ si**ng** \ō\ g**o** \ȯ\ **law** \ȯi\ b**oy** \th\ **th**in \t͟h\ **th**e \ü\ l**oo**t \u̇\ f**oo**t
\y\ **y**et \zh\ vi**si**on, beige \k, ⁿ, œ, ue, ʸ\ *see* Guide to Pronunciation

[1]**side·swipe** \ˈ-ˌswīp\ *vt* (1904) : to strike with a glancing blow along the side ⟨*sideswiped* a parked car⟩

[2]**sideswipe** *n* (1917) **1 a :** the action of sideswiping **b :** an instance of sideswiping : a glancing blow **2 :** an incidental deprecatory remark, allusion, or reference

side table *n* (14c) : a table designed to be placed against a wall

[1]**side·track** \ˈsīd-ˌtrak\ *n* (1835) **1 :** SIDING 2 **2 :** a position or condition of secondary importance to which one may be diverted

[2]**sidetrack** *vt* (1880) **1 :** to shunt aside (as to a railroad siding) **2 a :** to turn aside from a purpose : DEFLECT **b :** to prevent action on by diversionary tactics ⟨~ an issue⟩

side·walk \ˈsīd-ˌwȯk\ *n* (1739) : a usu. paved walk for pedestrians at the side of a street

sidewalk superintendent *n* (1940) : a spectator at a building or demolition job

side·wall \ˈsīd-ˌwȯl\ *n* (14c) **1 :** a wall forming the side of something **2 :** the side of an automotive tire between the tread shoulder and the rim bead

side·ward \ˈsīd-wərd\ *or* **side·wards** \-wərdz\ *adv* (15c) : toward a side

side·way \ˈsīd-ˌwā\ *adv or adj* (1612) : SIDEWAYS

side·ways \-ˌwāz\ *adv or adj* (1577) **1 :** from one side **2 :** with one side forward ⟨turn ~⟩ **3 a :** in a lateral direction or downward to one side ⟨hopped ~⟩ ⟨slump ~⟩ **b :** ASKANCE ⟨look ~ at someone⟩

side–wheel \ˈsīd-ˌhwēl, -ˌwēl\ *adj* (1854) : of or being a steamer having a paddle wheel on each side — **side–wheel·er** \-ˌhwē-lər, -ˌwē-\ *n*

side–whis·kers \ˈsīd-ˌhwis-kərz, -ˌwis-\ *n pl* (1858) : whiskers on the side of the face usu. worn long — **side–whis·kered** \-kərd\ *adj*

side·wind·er \ˈsīd-ˌwīn-dər\ *n* (1840) **1 :** a heavy swinging blow from the side **2 :** a small pale-colored desert rattlesnake (*Crotalus cerastes*) of the southwestern U.S. that moves by thrusting its body diagonally forward in a series of flat S-shaped curves

side·wise \ˈsīd-ˌwīz\ *adv or adj* (1571) : SIDEWAYS

siding *n* (1603) **1** *archaic* : the taking of sides : PARTISANSHIP **2 :** a short railroad track connected with the main track **3 :** material (as boards or metal or plastic pieces) forming the exposed surface of outside walls of frame buildings

si·dle \ˈsī-dᵊl\ *vb* **si·dled; si·dling** \ˈsīd-liŋ, ˈsī-dᵊl-iŋ\ [prob. back-formation fr. [2]*sideling*] *vi* (1577) : to go or move with one side foremost esp. in a furtive advance ~ *vt* : to cause to move or turn sideways — **sidle** *n*

SIDS *abbr* sudden infant death syndrome

siege \ˈsēj *also* ˈsēzh\ *n* [ME *sege,* fr. AF, seat, blockade, fr. OF **siegier* to seat, settle, fr. VL **sedicare,* fr. L *sedēre* to sit — more at SIT] (13c) **1** *obs* : a seat of distinction : THRONE **2 a :** a military blockade of a city or fortified place to compel it to surrender **b :** a persistent or serious attack (as of illness) — **siege** *vt* — **lay siege to 1 :** to besiege militarily **2 :** to pursue diligently or persistently

siege mentality *n* (1953) : a defensive or overly fearful attitude

Siege Perilous *n* (15c) : a seat at King Arthur's Round Table reserved for the knight destined to achieve the quest of the Holy Grail and fatal to any other occupying it

Sieg·fried \ˈsig-ˌfrēd, ˈsēg-\ *n* [G] (1831) : a hero in Germanic legend who slays a dragon guarding a gold hoard and wakes Brunhild from her enchanted sleep

Siegfried line *n* [*Siegfried*] (1918) : a line of German defensive fortifications facing the Maginot Line

sie·mens \ˈsē-mənz, ˈzē-\ *n, pl* **siemens** [Werner von *Siemens* †1892 Ger. electrical engineer] (ca. 1933) : a unit of conductance in the meter-kilogram-second system equivalent to one ampere per volt

si·en·na \sē-ˈe-nə\ *n* [It *terra di Siena,* lit., Siena earth, fr. *Siena,* Italy] (1787) : an earthy substance containing oxides of iron and usu. of manganese that is brownish yellow when raw and orange red or reddish brown when burnt and is used as a pigment

si·er·ra \sē-ˈer-ə\ *n* [Sp, lit., saw, fr. L *serra*] (1600) **1 a :** a range of mountains esp. with a serrated or irregular outline **b :** the country about a sierra **2 :** any of several large scombroid fishes (genus *Scomberomorus*) related to the mackerel

Sierra (1952) — a communications code word for the letter *s*

si·er·ran \sē-ˈer-ən\ *adj* (1873) **1 :** of or relating to a sierra ⟨~ foothills⟩ **2** *cap* : of or relating to the Sierra Nevada Mountains of the western U.S.

Sierran *n* (1906) : a native or inhabitant of the region around the Sierra Nevada Mountains

si·es·ta \sē-ˈes-tə\ *n* [Sp, fr. L *sexta* (*hora*) noon, lit., sixth hour — more at SEXT] (1655) : an afternoon nap or rest

sie·va bean \ˈsē-və-, ˈsi-vē-\ *n* [origin unknown] (1888) : a bean plant (*Phaseolus lunatus*) of tropical America that is closely related to and sometimes classified with the lima bean; *also* : its flat edible seed

[1]**sieve** \ˈsiv\ *n* [ME *sive,* fr. OE *sife;* akin to OHG *sib* sieve] (bef. 12c) : a device with meshes or perforations through which finer particles of a mixture (as of ashes, flour, or sand) of various sizes may be passed to separate them from coarser ones, through which the liquid may be drained from liquid-containing material, or through which soft materials may be forced for reduction to fine particles

[2]**sieve** *vb* **sieved; siev·ing** (15c) : SIFT

sieve of Er·a·tos·the·nes \-ˌer-ə-ˈtäs-thə-ˌnēz\ (1803) : a procedure for finding prime numbers that involves writing down the odd numbers from 2 up in succession and crossing out every third number after 3, every fifth after 5 including those already crossed out, every seventh after 7, and so on with the numbers that are never crossed out being prime

sieve plate *n* (1875) : a perforated wall or part of a wall at the end of one of the individual cells making up a sieve tube

sie·vert \ˈsē-vərt\ *n* [Rolf Maximilian *Sievert* †1966 Swed. radiologist] (1945) : an SI unit for the dosage of ionizing radiation equal to 100 rems

sieve tube *n* (1875) : a tube consisting of an end-to-end series of thin-walled living plant cells characteristic of the phloem and held to function chiefly in translocation of organic solutes

si·faka \sə-ˈfa-kə\ *n* [Malagasy] (1845) : any of several diurnal mostly black-and-white lemurs (genus *Propithecus*) with a long tail and silky fur

sift \ˈsift\ *vb* [ME, fr. OE *siftan;* akin to OE *sife* sieve] *vt* (bef. 12c) **1 a :** to put through a sieve ⟨~ flour⟩ **b :** to separate or separate out by or as if by putting through a sieve **2 :** to go through esp. to sort out what is useful or valuable ⟨~*ed* the evidence⟩ — often used with *through* ⟨~ through a pile of old letters⟩ **3 :** to scatter by or as if by sifting ⟨~ sugar on a cake⟩ ~ *vi* **1 :** to use a sieve **2 :** to pass or fall as if through a sieve — **sift·er** *n*

sift·ing \ˈsif-tiŋ\ *n* (15c) **1 :** the act or process of sifting **2** *pl* : sifted material

sig *abbr* signature

Sig *abbr* signa

SIG *abbr* special interest group

[1]**sigh** \ˈsī\ *vb* [ME *sihen,* alter. of *sichen,* fr. OE *sīcan;* akin to MD *versiken* to sigh] *vi* (13c) **1 :** to take a deep audible breath (as in weariness or relief) **2 :** to make a sound like sighing ⟨wind ~*ing* in the branches⟩ **3 :** GRIEVE, YEARN ⟨~*ing* for days gone by⟩ ~ *vt* **1 :** to express by sighs **2** *archaic* : to utter sighs over : MOURN — **sigh·er** \ˈsī(-ə)r\ *n*

[2]**sigh** *n* (14c) **1 :** an often involuntary act of sighing esp. when expressing an emotion or feeling (as weariness or relief) **2 :** the sound of gently moving or escaping air ⟨~*s* of the summer breeze⟩

[1]**sight** \ˈsīt\ *n* [ME, fr. OE *gesiht* faculty or act of sight, thing seen; akin to OHG *gisiht* sight, OE *sēon* to see] (bef. 12c) **1 :** something that is seen : SPECTACLE **2 a :** a thing regarded as worth seeing — usu. used in pl. ⟨the ~*s* of the city⟩ **b :** something ludicrous or disorderly in appearance ⟨you look a ~⟩ **3 a** *chiefly dial* : a great number or quantity **b :** a good deal : LOT ⟨a far ~ better⟩ ⟨not by a damn ~⟩ **4 a :** the process, power, or function of seeing; *specif* : the physical sense by which light stimuli received by the eye are interpreted by the brain and constructed into a representation of the position, shape, brightness, and usu. color of objects in space **b :** mental or spiritual perception **c :** mental view; *specif* : JUDGMENT **5 a :** the act of looking at or beholding **b :** INSPECTION, PERUSAL **c :** VIEW, GLIMPSE **d :** an observation to determine direction or position (as by a navigator) **6 a :** a perception of an object by or as if by the eye ⟨never lost ~ of the objective⟩ **b :** the range of vision ⟨was nowhere in ~⟩ **7 :** presentation of a note or draft to the maker or draftee : DEMAND **8 a :** a device that aids the eye in aiming or in finding the direction of an object **b** *pl* : ASPIRATION ⟨set her ~*s* on a medical career⟩ — **in sight :** at or within a reasonable distance or time — **on sight :** as soon as seen ⟨ordered to shoot *on sight*⟩ — **out of sight 1 :** beyond comparison **2 :** beyond all expectation or reason **3 —** used as a generalized expression of approval — **sight for sore eyes :** one whose appearance or arrival is an occasion for joy or relief

[2]**sight** *vt* (1602) **1 :** to get or catch sight of ⟨several whales were ~*ed*⟩ **2 :** to look at through or as if through a sight; *esp* : to test for straightness **3 :** to aim by means of sights **4 a :** to equip with sights **b :** to adjust the sights of ~ *vi* **1 :** to take aim **2 :** to look carefully in a particular direction

[3]**sight** *adj* (1801) **1 :** based on recognition or comprehension without previous study ⟨~ translation⟩ **2 :** payable on presentation ⟨a ~ draft⟩

sight·ed \ˈsī-təd\ *adj* (1552) : having sight ⟨clear-*sighted*⟩ ⟨a ~ person⟩

sight gag *n* (1949) : a comic bit or episode whose effect is produced by pantomime or camera shot rather than by words

sight hound *n* (1969) : a hound (as a greyhound) that hunts and pursues game by sight rather than by scent — compare SCENT HOUND

sight·less \ˈsīt-ləs\ *adj* (13c) **1 :** lacking sight : BLIND **2 :** INVISIBLE 1 — **sight·less·ly** *adv* — **sight·less·ness** *n*

sight line *n* (1753) : a line extending from an observer's eye to a viewed object or area (as a stage) ⟨a theater with excellent *sight lines*⟩

sight·ly \-lē\ *adj* (1534) **1 :** pleasing to the sight : ATTRACTIVE **2 :** affording a fine view — **sight·li·ness** *n* — **sightly** *adv*

sight–read \-ˌrēd\ *vb* **-read** \-ˌred\; **-read·ing** \-ˌrē-diŋ\ [back-formation fr. *sight reader*] *vt* (1903) : to read (as a foreign language) or perform (music) without previous preparation or study ~ *vi* : to read at sight; *esp* : to perform music at sight — **sight reader** *n*

sight rhyme *n* (ca. 1936) : EYE RHYME

sight·see \ˈsīt-ˌsē\ *vi, past* **-saw;** *pres part* **-see·ing** [back-formation fr. *sightseeing*] (1824) : to go about seeing sights of interest — **sight·seer** \-ˌsē-ər, -ˌsir\ *n*

sightsee·ing \ˈsīt-ˌsē-iŋ\ *adj* (1827) : devoted to or used for seeing sights — **sightseeing** *n*

sight unseen *adv* (1892) : without inspection or appraisal

sig·il \ˈsi-jil\ *n* [ME *sigulle,* fr. L *sigillum* — more at SEAL] (15c) **1 :** SEAL, SIGNET **2 :** a sign, word, or device held to have occult power in astrology or magic

SIG·INT \ˈsig-ˌint\ *n* [*sig*nals *int*elligence] (1969) : intelligence obtained through the interception of transmission signals

sig·ma \ˈsig-mə\ *n* [Gk] (1584) **1 :** the 18th letter of the Greek alphabet — see ALPHABET table **2 :** STANDARD DEVIATION

sig·moid \ˈsig-ˌmȯid\ *also* **sig·moi·dal** \sig-ˈmȯi-dᵊl\ *adj* [Gk *sigmoeidēs,* fr. *sigma;* fr. a common form of sigma shaped like the Roman letter C] (1670) **1 a :** curved like the letter C **b :** curved in two directions like the letter S **2 :** of, relating to, or being the sigmoid colon — **sig·moi·dal·ly** \sig-ˈmȯi-dᵊl-ē\ *adv*

sigmoid colon *n* (1896) : the contracted and crooked part of the colon immediately above the rectum — called also *sigmoid flexure*

sig·moid·o·scope \sig-ˈmȯi-də-ˌskōp\ *n* (ca. 1900) : an endoscope designed to be passed through the anus for visual examination esp. of the sigmoid colon — **sig·moid·o·scop·ic** \-ˌmȯi-də-ˈskä-pik\ *adj* — **sig·moid·os·co·py** \-ˌmȯi-ˈdäs-kə-pē\ *n*

[1]**sign** \ˈsīn\ *n* [ME *signe,* fr. AF, fr. L *signum* mark, token, sign, image, seal; perh. akin to L *secare* to cut — more at SAW] (13c) **1 a :** a motion or gesture by which a thought is expressed or a command or wish made known **b :** SIGNAL 2a **c :** a fundamental linguistic unit that designates an object or relation or has a purely syntactic function ⟨~*s* include words, morphemes, and punctuation⟩ **d :** one of a set of gestures used to represent language; *also* : SIGN LANGUAGE **2 :** a mark having a conventional meaning and used in place of words or to represent a complex notion **3 :** one of the 12 divisions of the zodiac **4 a** (1) : a character (as a flat or sharp) used in musical notation (2) : SEGNO **b :** a character (as ÷) indicating a mathematical operation; *also* : one of two characters + and − that form part of the symbol of a number and characterize it as positive or negative **5 a :** a display (as a

lettered board or a configuration of neon tubing) used to identify or advertise a place of business or a product **b :** a posted command, warning, or direction **c :** SIGNBOARD **6 a :** something material or external that stands for or signifies something spiritual **b :** something indicating the presence or existence of something else ⟨~*s* of success⟩ ⟨a ~ of the times⟩ **c :** PRESAGE, PORTENT ⟨~*s* of an early spring⟩ **d :** an objective evidence of plant or animal disease **7** *pl usu* **sign :** traces of a usu. wild animal ⟨red fox ~⟩

syn SIGN, MARK, TOKEN, NOTE, SYMPTOM mean a discernible indication of what is not itself directly perceptible. SIGN applies to any indication to be perceived by the senses or the reason ⟨encouraging *signs* for the economy⟩. MARK suggests something impressed on or inherently characteristic of a thing often in contrast to general outward appearance ⟨a *mark* of a good upbringing⟩. TOKEN applies to something that serves as a proof of something intangible ⟨this gift is a *token* of our esteem⟩. NOTE suggests a distinguishing mark or characteristic ⟨a *note* of irony in her writing⟩. SYMPTOM suggests an outward indication of an internal change or condition ⟨rampant crime is a *symptom* of that city's decay⟩.

[2]**sign** *vb* [ME, fr. AF *signer,* fr. L *signare* to mark, sign, seal, fr. *signum*] *vt* (13c) **1 a :** CROSS 2 **b :** to place a sign on or mark by signs ⟨~ a trail⟩ **c :** to represent or indicate by a sign **2 a :** to affix a signature to **:** ratify or attest by hand or seal ⟨~ a bill into law⟩ ⟨~ a confession⟩ **b :** to assign or convey formally ⟨~*ed* over his property to his brother⟩ **c :** to write down (one's name) **d :** to affix one's name to ⟨a ~*ed* review⟩ **3 :** to communicate by making a sign or by sign language **4 :** to engage or hire by securing the signature of on a contract of employment — often used with *up* or *on* ~ *vi* **1 :** to write one's name in token of assent, responsibility, or obligation ⟨~*ed* for the packages⟩ ⟨~*ed* with the team for one season⟩ **2 a :** to make a sign or signal **b :** to use sign language — **sign·ee** \ˌsī-ˈnē\ *n* — **sign·er** \ˈsī-nər\ *n*

sig·na \ˈsig-nə\ *vb imper* [L, indicate, mark, imper. of *signare*] (1896) **:** write on label

sign·age \ˈsī-nij\ *n* (1976) **:** signs (as of identification, warning, or direction) or a system of such signs

[1]**sig·nal** \ˈsig-nᵊl\ *n* [ME, fr. ML *signale,* fr. LL, neut. of *signalis* of a sign, fr. L *signum*] (14c) **1 :** SIGN, INDICATION **2 a :** an act, event, or watchword that has been agreed on as the occasion of concerted action **b :** something that incites to action **3 :** something (as a sound, gesture, or object) that conveys notice or warning **4 a :** an object used to transmit or convey information beyond the range of human voice **b :** the sound or image conveyed in telegraphy, telephony, radio, radar, or television **c :** a detectable physical quantity or impulse (as a voltage, current, or magnetic field strength) by which messages or information can be transmitted

[2]**signal** *vb* **sig·naled** *or* **sig·nalled; sig·nal·ing** *or* **sig·nal·ling** \-nə-liŋ\ *vt* (1805) **1 :** to notify by a signal ⟨~ the fleet to turn back⟩ **2 a :** to communicate or indicate by or as if by signals ⟨~*ed* the end of an era⟩ **b :** to constitute a characteristic feature of (a meaningful linguistic form) ~ *vi* **:** to make or send a signal — **sig·nal·er** *or* **sig·nal·ler** *n*

[3]**signal** *adj* [modif. of F *signalé,* pp. of *signaler* to distinguish, fr. OIt *segnalare* to signal, distinguish, fr. *segnale* signal, fr. ML *signale*] (1627) **:** distinguished from the ordinary **:** NOTABLE ⟨a ~ achievement⟩

sig·nal·ise *Brit var of* SIGNALIZE

sig·nal·ize \ˈsig-nə-ˌlīz\ *vt* **-ized; -iz·ing** (1654) **1 :** to make conspicuous **:** DISTINGUISH, MARK **2 :** to point out carefully or distinctly **3 :** to make signals to **:** SIGNAL; *also* **:** INDICATE ⟨his silence ~*s* approval⟩ **4 :** to place traffic signals at or on — **sig·nal·i·za·tion** \ˌsig-nə-lə-ˈzā-shən\ *n*

sig·nal·ly \ˈsig-nə-lē\ *adv* (1641) **:** in a signal manner **:** NOTABLY

sig·nal·man \ˈsig-nᵊl-mən, -ˌman\ *n* (1737) **:** a person who signals or works with signals (as on a railway)

sig·nal·ment \-mənt\ *n* [F *signalement,* fr. *signaler*] (1778) **:** description by peculiar, appropriate, or characteristic marks; *specif* **:** the systematic description of a person for purposes of identification

sig·na·to·ry \ˈsig-nə-ˌtȯr-ē\ *n, pl* **-ries** [L *signatorius* of sealing, fr. *signare*] (1866) **:** a signer with another or others ⟨*signatories* to a petition⟩; *esp* **:** a government bound with others by a signed convention — **signatory** *adj*

sig·na·ture \ˈsig-nə-ˌchu̇r, -chər, -ˌtyu̇r, -ˌtu̇r\ *n* [MF or ML; MF, fr. ML *signatura,* fr. L *signatus,* pp. of *signare* to sign, seal] (1536) **1 a :** the act of signing one's name to something **b :** the name of a person written with his or her own hand **2 :** a feature in the appearance or qualities of a natural object formerly held to indicate its utility in medicine **3 a :** a letter or figure placed usu. at the bottom of the first page on each sheet of printed pages (as of a book) as a direction to the binder in arranging and gathering the sheets **b :** one unit of a book comprising a group of printed sheets that are folded and stitched together **4 a :** KEY SIGNATURE **b :** TIME SIGNATURE **5 :** the part of a medical prescription that contains the directions to the patient **6 :** something (as a tune, style, or logo) that serves to set apart or identify; *also* **:** a characteristic mark **7 :** FINGERPRINT 2

sign·board \ˈsīn-ˌbȯrd\ *n* (1632) **:** a board bearing a notice or sign

signed \ˈsīnd\ *adj* (1873) **:** having a sign; *esp* **:** having a plus or minus sign ⟨~ numbers like +6 and –4⟩

[1]**sig·net** \ˈsig-nət\ *n* [ME small seal, signet ring, fr. AF, dim. of *signe* sign, seal] (14c) **1 :** a seal used officially to give personal authority to a document in lieu of signature **2 :** the impression made by or as if by a signet **3 :** a small intaglio seal (as in a finger ring)

[2]**signet** *vt* (15c) **:** to stamp or authenticate with a signet

signet ring *n* (1681) **:** a finger ring engraved with a signet, seal, or monogram **:** SEAL RING

sig·nif·i·cance \sig-ˈni-fi-kən(t)s\ *n* (13c) **1 a :** something that is conveyed as a meaning often obscurely or indirectly **b :** the quality of conveying or implying **2 a :** the quality of being important **:** MOMENT **b :** the quality of being statistically significant ***syn*** see IMPORTANCE

significance level *n* (1947) **:** LEVEL OF SIGNIFICANCE

sig·nif·i·can·cy \sig-ˈni-fi-kən(t)-sē\ *n* (ca. 1595) **:** SIGNIFICANCE

sig·nif·i·cant \-kənt\ *adj* [L *significant-, significans,* prp. of *significare* to signify] (1579) **1 :** having meaning; *esp* **:** SUGGESTIVE ⟨a ~ glance⟩ **2 a :** having or likely to have influence or effect **:** IMPORTANT ⟨a ~ piece of legislation⟩; *also* **:** of a noticeably or measurably large amount ⟨a ~ number of layoffs⟩ ⟨producing ~ profits⟩ **b :** probably caused by something other than mere chance ⟨statistically ~ correlation between vitamin deficiency and disease⟩

significant digit *n* (1923) **:** any of the digits of a number beginning with the digit farthest to the left that is not zero and ending with the last digit farthest to the right that is either not zero or that is a zero but is considered to be exact — called also *significant figure*

sig·nif·i·cant·ly \sig-ˈni-fi-kənt-lē\ *adv* (1577) **1 :** in a significant manner **:** to a significant degree ⟨the salaries differed ~⟩ **2 :** it is significant ⟨~, they were on time⟩

significant other *n* (1953) **:** a person who is important to one's well-being; *esp* **:** a spouse or one in a similar relationship

sig·ni·fi·ca·tion \ˌsig-nə-fə-ˈkā-shən\ *n* (14c) **1 a :** the act or process of signifying by signs or other symbolic means **b :** a formal notification **2 :** PURPORT; *esp* **:** the meaning that a term, symbol, or character regularly conveys or is intended to convey **3** *chiefly dial* **:** IMPORTANCE, CONSEQUENCE

sig·nif·i·ca·tive \sig-ˈni-fə-ˌkā-tiv\ *adj* (15c) **1 :** SIGNIFICANT, SUGGESTIVE **2 :** INDICATIVE ⟨symptoms ~ of malaria⟩

sig·nif·ics \sig-ˈni-fiks\ *n pl but sing or pl in constr* [*signify*] (1896) **:** SEMIOTICS, SEMANTICS

signified *n* (1939) **:** a concept or meaning as distinguished from the sign through which it is communicated — compare SIGNIFIER 2

sig·ni·fi·er \ˈsig-nə-ˌfī(-ə)r\ *n* (1532) **1 :** one that signifies **2 :** a symbol, sound, or image (as a word) that represents an underlying concept or meaning — compare SIGNIFIED

sig·ni·fy \ˈsig-nə-ˌfī\ *vb* **-fied; -fy·ing** [ME *signifien,* fr. AF *signifier,* fr. L *significare* to indicate, signify, fr. *signum* sign] *vt* (13c) **1 a :** to be a sign of **:** MEAN **b :** IMPLY **2 :** to show esp. by a conventional token (as word, signal, or gesture) ~ *vi* **1 :** to have significance **:** MATTER ⟨it will not much ~ what one wears —Jane Austen⟩ **2 :** to engage in signifying

signifying *n* (1959) **:** a good-natured needling or goading esp. among urban blacks by means of indirect gibes and clever often preposterous put-downs; *also* **:** DOZENS

sign in *vi* (1930) **:** to make a record of arrival by signing a register or punching a time clock ~ *vt* **:** to record arrival of (a person) or receipt of (an article) by signing

sign language *n* (1839) **1 :** a formal language employing a system of hand gestures for communication (as by the deaf) **2 :** an unsystematic method of communicating chiefly by manual gestures used by people speaking different languages

sign of aggregation (ca. 1942) **:** any of various conventional devices (as braces, brackets, parentheses, or vinculums) used in mathematics to indicate that two or more terms are to be treated as one quantity

sign off *vi* (1923) **1 :** to announce the end of something (as a message or broadcast) **2 :** to approve or acknowledge something by or as if by a signature ⟨*sign off* on a memo⟩ — **sign–off** \ˈsī-ˌnȯf\ *n*

sign of the cross (14c) **:** a gesture of the hand forming a cross esp. on forehead, breast, and shoulders to profess Christian faith or invoke divine protection or blessing

sign on *vi* (1906) **1 :** to engage oneself by or as if by a signature ⟨*signed on* to the new project⟩ **2 :** to announce the start of broadcasting for the day — **sign–on** \ˈsī-ˌnȯn, -ˌnän\ *n*

si·gnor *also* **si·gnior** \sēn-ˈyȯr\ *n, pl* **signors** *or* **si·gno·ri** \sēn-ˈyȯr-(ˌ)ē\ *also* **signiors** [It *signore, signor,* fr. ML *senior* superior, lord — more at SENOR] (1545) **:** an Italian man usu. of rank or gentility — used as a title equivalent to *Mr.*

si·gno·ra \sēn-ˈyȯr-ə\ *n, pl* **signoras** *or* **si·gno·re** \-ˈyȯr-(ˌ)ā\ [It, fem. of *signore, signor*] (1741) **:** a married Italian woman usu. of rank or gentility — used as a title equivalent to *Mrs.*

si·gno·re \sēn-ˈyȯr-(ˌ)ā\ *n, pl* **si·gno·ri** \-ˈyȯr-(ˌ)ē\ [It] (1594) **:** SIGNOR

si·gno·ri·na \ˌsē-nyə-ˈrē-nə\ *n, pl* **-nas** *or* **-ne** \-(ˌ)nā\ [It, fr. dim. of *signora*] (1820) **:** an unmarried Italian woman — used as a title equivalent to *Miss*

si·gnory *or* **si·gniory** \ˈsē-nyə-rē\ *n, pl* **si·gnor·ies** *or* **si·gnior·ies** [ME *signorie,* fr. AF *seignurie*] (14c) **:** SEIGNIORY

sign out *vi* (1948) **:** to indicate departure by signing a register ~ *vt* **:** to record or approve the release or departure of ⟨*signed out* the library books for a week⟩ — **sign–out** \ˈsī-ˌnau̇t\ *n or adj*

[1]**sign·post** \ˈsīn-ˌpōst\ *n* (1620) **1 :** a post (as at the fork of a road) with signs on it to direct travelers **2 :** GUIDE, BEACON **3 :** SIGN, INDICATION

[2]**signpost** *vt* (1895) **:** to provide with or as if with signposts or guides

sign up *vi* (1926) **:** to sign one's name (as to a contract) in order to obtain, do, or join something ⟨*sign up* for insurance⟩ ⟨*sign up* for classes⟩ — **sign–up** \ˈsī-ˌnəp\ *n or adj*

Sig·urd \ˈsi-gu̇rd, -gərd\ *n* [ON *Sigurthr*] (1822) **:** a hero in Norse mythology who slays the dragon Fafnir

si·ka \ˈsē-kə\ *n* [Jp *shika*] (1859) **:** a deer (*Cervus nippon*) of eastern Asia that has a chestnut to brownish coat often spotted with white and that has established populations in other regions (as Europe and the U.S.) as a result of introduction

sike \ˈsīk\ *n* [ME, fr. OE *sīc;* akin to ON *sīk* slow stream, OE *sicerian* to trickle] (bef. 12c) **1** *dial chiefly Brit* **:** a small stream; *esp* **:** one that dries up in summer **2** *dial chiefly Brit* **:** DITCH

[1]**Sikh** \ˈsēk, ˈsik\ *n* [Hindi & Urdu, lit., disciple] (1756) **:** an adherent of a monotheistic religion of India founded about 1500 by Guru Nānak and marked by rejection of idolatry and caste — **Sikh·ism** \ˈsē-ˌki-zəm\ *n*

[2]**Sikh** *adj* (1845) **:** of or relating to Sikhs or Sikhism

si·lage \ˈsī-lij\ *n* [short for *ensilage*] (1884) **:** fodder converted into succulent feed for livestock through processes of anaerobic acid fermentation (as in a silo)

si·lane \ˈsi-ˌlān, ˈsī-\ *n* [ISV *sil*icon + meth*ane*] (1916) **:** any of various compounds of hydrogen and silicon that have the general formula Si_nH_{2n+2} and are analogous to alkanes

Si·las·tic \sə-ˈlas-tik, sī-\ *trademark* — used for a soft pliable plastic

sild \ˈsil(d)\ *n, pl* **sild** *or* **silds** [Norw] (1921) **:** a young herring other than a brisling that is canned as a sardine in Norway

sil·den·a·fil \sil-ˈde-nə-ˌfil\ *n* [perh. by alter. and recombination of letters fr. *sulfonyl, phenyl,* and *pyrimidine*] (1995) **:** a drug used in the form of its citrate $C_{22}H_{30}N_6O_4S \cdot C_6H_8O_7$ to treat erectile dysfunction

[1]**si·lence** \ˈsī-lən(t)s\ *n* [ME, fr. AF, fr. L *silentium,* fr. *silent-, silens*] (13c) **1 :** forbearance from speech or noise **:** MUTENESS — often used interjectionally **2 :** absence of sound or noise **:** STILLNESS ⟨in the ~ of the night⟩ **3 :** absence of mention: **a :** OBLIVION, OBSCURITY **b :** SECRECY ⟨weapons research was conducted in ~⟩

[2]**silence** *vt* **si·lenced; si·lenc·ing** (1598) **1 :** to compel or reduce to silence **:** STILL ⟨*silenced* the crowd⟩ **2 :** SUPPRESS ⟨~ dissent⟩ **3 :** to cause to cease hostile firing or criticism ⟨~ the opposition⟩

si·lenc·er \ˈsī-lən(t)-sər\ *n* (1600) **:** one that silences: as **a** *chiefly Brit* **:** the muffler of an internal combustion engine **b :** a silencing device for small arms

[1]**si·lent** \ˈsī-lənt\ *adj* [ME *sylent,* fr. L *silent-, silens,* fr. prp. of *silēre* to be silent; akin to Goth ana*silan* to cease, grow calm] (15c) **1 a :** making no utterance **:** MUTE, SPEECHLESS **b :** indisposed to speak **:** not loquacious **2 :** free from sound or noise **:** STILL **3 :** performed or borne without utterance **:** UNSPOKEN ⟨~ prayer⟩ ⟨~ grief⟩ **4 a :** making no mention ⟨history is ~ about this person⟩ **b :** not widely or generally known or appreciated ⟨the ~ pressures on a person in public office⟩ **c :** making no protest or outcry ⟨the ~ majority⟩ **5 :** UNPRONOUNCED ⟨the ~ *b* in *doubt*⟩ **6 :** not exhibiting the usual signs or symptoms of presence ⟨a ~ infection⟩ **7 a :** made without spoken dialogue ⟨~ movies⟩ **b :** of or relating to silent movies — **si·lent·ly** *adv* — **si·lent·ness** *n*

syn SILENT, TACITURN, RETICENT, RESERVED, SECRETIVE mean showing restraint in speaking. SILENT implies a habit of saying no more than is needed ⟨the strong, *silent* type⟩. TACITURN implies a temperamental disinclination to speech and usu. connotes unsociability ⟨*taciturn* villagers⟩. RETICENT implies a reluctance to speak out or at length, esp. about one's own affairs ⟨was *reticent* about his plans⟩. RESERVED implies reticence and suggests the restraining influence of caution or formality in checking easy informal conversational exchange ⟨greetings were brief, formal, and *reserved*⟩. SECRETIVE, too, implies reticence but usu. carries a suggestion of deviousness and lack of frankness or of an often ostentatious will to conceal ⟨the *secretive* research and development division⟩.

[2]**silent** *n* (1929) **:** a motion picture made without spoken dialogue — usu. used in pl.

silent auction *n* (1952) **:** an auction in which sealed bids are submitted beforehand

silent butler *n* (1937) **:** a receptacle with hinged lid for collecting table crumbs and the contents of ashtrays

silent partner *n* (1828) **1 :** a partner who is known to the public but has no voice in the conduct of a firm's business **2 :** SECRET PARTNER

silent service *n* (ca. 1929) **1 :** NAVY — used with *the* **2 :** the submarine service — used with *the*

silent treatment *n* (1947) **:** an act of completely ignoring a person or thing by resort to silence esp. as a means of expressing contempt or disapproval

si·le·nus \sī-ˈlē-nəs\ *n, pl* **-ni** \-ˌnī\ *often cap* [L, fr. Gk *silēnos,* fr. *Silēnos* foster father of Dionysus] (1542) **:** a minor woodland deity and companion of Dionysus in Greek mythology with a horse's ears and tail

si·lex \ˈsī-ˌleks\ *n* [L *silic-, silex* hard stone, flint] (ca. 1592) **:** silica or a siliceous material (as powdered tripoli) esp. for use as a filler in paints or wood

[1]**sil·hou·ette** \ˌsi-lə-ˈwet\ *n* [F, fr. Étienne de *Silhouette* †1767 Fr. controller general of finances; perh. fr. his ephemeral tenure] (1783) **1 :** a likeness cut from dark material and mounted on a light ground or one sketched in outline and solidly colored in **2 :** the outline of a body viewed as circumscribing a mass ⟨the ~ of a bird⟩ ***syn*** see OUTLINE

[2]**silhouette** *vt* **-ett·ed; -ett·ing** (1876) **:** to represent by a silhouette; *also* **:** to project on a background like a silhouette — **sil·hou·et·tist** \-ˈwe-tist\ *n*

sil·i·ca \ˈsi-li-kə\ *n* [NL, fr. L *silic-, silex* hard stone, flint] (ca. 1801) **:** the dioxide of silicon SiO_2 occurring in crystalline, amorphous, and impure forms (as in quartz, opal, and sand respectively)

silica gel *n* (1919) **:** colloidal silica resembling coarse white sand in appearance but possessing many fine pores and therefore extremely adsorbent

sil·i·cate \ˈsi-lə-ˌkāt, -kət\ *n* [*silicic (acid)*] (1811) **:** a salt or ester derived from a silicic acid; *esp* **:** any of numerous insoluble often complex metal salts that contain silicon and oxygen in the anion, constitute the largest class of minerals, and are used in building materials (as cement, bricks, and glass)

si·li·ceous *also* **si·li·cious** \sə-ˈli-shəs\ *adj* [L *siliceus* of flint, fr. *silic-, silex* hard stone, flint] (ca. 1656) **:** of, relating to, or containing silica or a silicate ⟨~ limestone⟩

si·lic·ic \sə-ˈli-sik\ *adj* [NL *silica* & NL *silicium* silicon (fr. *silica*)] (1817) **:** of, relating to, or derived from silica or silicon

silicic acid *n* (1817) **:** any of various weakly acid substances obtained as gelatinous masses by treating silicates with acids

sil·i·cide \ˈsi-lə-ˌsīd\ *n* [ISV *silic*on + *-ide*] (ca. 1868) **:** a binary compound of silicon with a more electropositive element or group

si·lic·i·fi·ca·tion \sə-ˌli-sə-fə-ˈkā-shən\ *n* (1830) **:** the action or process of silicifying **:** the state of being silicified

si·lic·i·fy \sə-ˈli-sə-ˌfī\ *vb* **-fied; -fy·ing** *vt* (ca. 1828) **:** to convert into or impregnate with silica ~ *vi* **:** to become silicified

sil·i·con \ˈsi-li-kən, ˈsi-lə-ˌkän\ *n* [NL *silica* + E *-on* (as in *carbon*)] (1817) **:** a tetravalent nonmetallic element that occurs combined as the most abundant element next to oxygen in the earth's crust and is used esp. in ferrosilicon for steelmaking, in other alloys, and in semiconductors — see ELEMENT table

silicon carbide *n* (1893) **:** a very hard dark crystalline compound SiC of silicon and carbon that is used as an abrasive and as a refractory and in electric resistors

silicon dioxide *n* (ca. 1909) **:** SILICA

sil·i·cone \ˈsi-lə-ˌkōn\ *n* [*silicon* + *-one*] (1943) **:** any of various polymeric organic silicon compounds obtained as oils, greases, or plastics and used esp. for water-resistant and heat-resistant lubricants, varnishes, binders, and electric insulators

silicone rubber *n* (1944) **:** rubber made from silicone elastomers and noted for its retention of flexibility, resilience, and tensile strength over a wide temperature range

sil·i·con·ized \ˈsi-lə-kə-ˌnīzd, -ˌkō-\ *adj* (1949) **:** treated or coated with a silicone ⟨~ glassware⟩

silicon nitride *n* (1903) **:** any of several compounds of silicon and nitrogen; *specif* **:** a compound Si_3N_4 that is a hard ceramic used in high-temperature applications and in composites

sil·i·co·sis \ˌsi-lə-ˈkō-səs\ *n* [NL, fr. *silica* + *-osis*] (1881) **:** pneumoconiosis characterized by massive fibrosis of the lungs resulting in shortness of breath and caused by prolonged inhalation of silica dusts — **sil·i·cot·ic** \-ˈkä-tik\ *adj or n*

si·lique \sə-ˈlēk\ *n* [F, fr. NL *siliqua,* fr. L, pod, husk] (1785) **:** a narrow elongated 2-valved usu. many-seeded capsule that is characteristic of the mustard family, opens by sutures at either margin, and has two parietal placentas

[1]**silk** \ˈsilk\ *n, often attrib* [ME, fr. OE *seolc, sioluc,* prob. ultim. fr. Gk *sērikos* silken — more at SERICEOUS] (bef. 12c) **1 :** a fine continuous protein fiber produced by various insect larvae usu. for cocoons; *esp* **:** a lustrous tough elastic fiber produced by silkworms and used for textiles **2 :** thread, yarn, or fabric made from silk filaments **3 a :** a garment of silk **b (1) :** a distinctive silk gown worn by a King's or Queen's Counsel **(2) :** a King's or Queen's Counsel **c** *pl* **:** the colored cap and blouse of a jockey or harness horse driver made in the registered racing color of the employing stable **4 a :** a filament resembling silk; *esp* **:** one produced by a spider **b :** silky material ⟨milkweed ~⟩; *esp* **:** the styles of an ear of Indian corn **5 :** PARACHUTE — **silk·like** \-ˌlīk\ *adj*

[2]**silk** *vi* (1783) *of corn* **:** to develop the silk

silk cotton *n* (1697) **:** the silky or cottony covering of seeds of various silk-cotton trees; *esp* **:** KAPOK

silk–cotton tree *n* (1712) **:** any of various tropical trees (family Bombacaceae, the silk-cotton family) with palmate leaves and large fruits with the seeds enveloped by silk cotton; *esp* **:** CEIBA 1

silk·en \ˈsil-kən\ *adj* (bef. 12c) **1 :** made or consisting of silk **2 :** resembling silk: as **a :** SOFT, LUSTROUS **b (1) :** agreeably smooth **:** HARMONIOUS ⟨a ~ voice⟩ **(2) :** SUAVE, INGRATIATING **3 a :** dressed in silk ⟨~ ankles⟩ **b :** having a richly luxurious quality ⟨the same ~ surroundings encountered at the restaurant's far more expensive evening meal —Elaine Tait⟩

silk gland *n* (1870) **:** a gland that produces a viscid fluid which is extruded in filaments and hardens into silk on exposure to air: as **a :** either of a pair of greatly enlarged and modified salivary glands of an insect larva that produce a compound filament from which a larval or pupal cover (as a cocoon) is spun **b :** any of two or more abdominal glands of a spider that open through spinnerets and produce a filament used chiefly in the spinning of webs

silk hat *n* (ca. 1836) **:** a hat with a tall cylindrical crown and a silk-plush finish worn by men as a dress hat

silk moth *n* (1772) **1 :** the common silkworm (*Bombyx mori*) **2 :** SATURNIID; *esp* **:** one (as the cecropia moth) that produces a cocoon of silk

silk oak *n* (1866) **:** any of various Australian timber trees (esp. genus *Grevillea*) of the protea family that have mottled wood used in cabinetmaking and veneering — called also *silky oak*

silk screen *n* (1930) **:** a stencil process in which coloring matter is forced onto the material to be printed through the meshes of a silk or organdy screen so prepared as to have pervious printing areas and impervious nonprinting areas; *also* **:** a print made by this process — **silk–screen** *vt*

silk–stock·ing \ˈsilk-ˈstä-kiŋ\ *adj* (1798) **1 :** ARISTOCRATIC, WEALTHY ⟨a ~ district⟩ ⟨a ~ law firm⟩ **2 :** fashionably dressed ⟨a ~ audience⟩ **3 :** of or relating to the American Federalist party

silk stocking *n* (1836) **1 :** an aristocratic or wealthy person **2 :** a fashionably dressed person **3 :** FEDERALIST 2

silk tree *n* (ca. 1852) **:** a leguminous Asian tree (*Albizia julibrissin*) naturalized esp. in the southeastern U.S. and having pink flowers with long silky stamens — called also *mimosa*

silk·weed \ˈsilk-ˌwēd\ *n* (1784) **:** MILKWEED

silk·worm \-ˌwərm\ *n* (bef. 12c) **:** a moth whose larva spins a large amount of strong silk in constructing its cocoon; *esp* **:** an Asian moth (*Bombyx mori* of the family Bombycidae) whose rough wrinkled hairless caterpillar produces the silk of commerce

silky \ˈsil-kē\ *adj* **silk·i·er; -est** (1611) **1 a (1) :** SILKEN 1 **(2) :** SILKEN 2 **b :** smooth or fluid in motion ⟨~ dance moves⟩ **2 :** having or covered with fine soft hairs, plumes, or scales — **silk·i·ly** \-kə-lē\ *adv* — **silk·i·ness** \-kē-nəs\ *n*

silky terrier *n* (1959) **:** any of a breed of low-set toy terriers of Australian origin that have a flat silky glossy coat colored blue with tan on the head, chest, and legs — called also *silky*

sill \ˈsil\ *n* [ME *sille,* fr. OE *syll;* akin to OHG *swelli* beam, threshold] (bef. 12c) **1 :** a horizontal piece (as a timber) that forms the lowest member or one of the lowest members of a framework or supporting structure: as **a :** the horizontal member at the base of a window **b :** the threshold of a door **2 :** a tabular body of igneous rock injected while molten between sedimentary or volcanic beds or along foliation planes of metamorphic rocks **3 :** a submerged ridge at relatively shallow depth separating the basins of two bodies of water

sillabub *var of* SYLLABUB

sil·li·man·ite \ˈsi-lə-mə-ˌnīt\ *n* [Benjamin *Silliman* †1864 Am. geologist] (ca. 1830) **:** a brown, grayish, or pale green mineral that consists of an aluminum silicate in orthorhombic crystals often occurring in fibrous or columnar forms

sil·ly \ˈsi-lē\ *adj* **sil·li·er; -est** [ME *sely, silly* happy, innocent, pitiable, feeble, fr. OE *sǣlig,* fr. *sǣl* happiness; akin to OHG *sālig* happy] (14c) **1** *archaic* **:** HELPLESS, WEAK **2 a :** RUSTIC, PLAIN **b** *obs* **:** lowly in station **:** HUMBLE **3 a :** weak in intellect **:** FOOLISH **b :** exhibiting or indicative of a lack of common sense or sound judgment ⟨a very ~ mistake⟩ **c :** TRIFLING, FRIVOLOUS **4 :** being stunned or dazed ⟨scared ~⟩ ⟨knocked me ~⟩ ***syn*** see SIMPLE — **sil·li·ly** \ˈsi-lə-lē\ *adv* — **sil·li·ness** \ˈsi-lē-nəs\ *n* — **silly** *n or adv*

silly season *n* (1861) **1 :** a period (as late summer) when the mass media often focus on trivial or frivolous matters for lack of major news stories **2** : a period marked by frivolous, outlandish, or illogical activity or behavior

si·lo \'sī-(,)lō\ *n, pl* **silos** [Sp] (1856) **1** : a trench, pit, or esp. a tall cylinder (as of wood or concrete) usu. sealed to exclude air and used for making and storing silage **2 a** : a deep bin for storing material (as coal) **b** : an underground structure for housing a guided missile

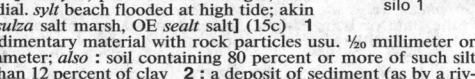

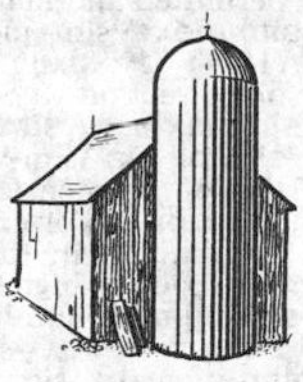

silo 1

si·lox·ane \sə-'läk-,sān, sī-\ *n* [*sil*icon + *ox*ygen + meth*ane*] (1917) : any of various compounds containing alternate silicon and oxygen atoms in either a linear or cyclic arrangement usu. with one or two organic groups attached to each silicon atom

¹**silt** \'silt\ *n* [ME *cylte*, prob. of Scand origin; akin to Norw dial. *sylt* beach flooded at high tide; akin to OHG *sulza* salt marsh, OE *sealt* salt] (15c) **1** : loose sedimentary material with rock particles usu. ½₀ millimeter or less in diameter; *also* : soil containing 80 percent or more of such silt and less than 12 percent of clay **2** : a deposit of sediment (as by a river) — **silty** \'sil-tē\ *adj*

²**silt** *vi* (1799) : to become choked or obstructed with silt — often used with *up* ⟨the channel ~*ed* up⟩ ~ *vt* : to choke, fill, cover, or obstruct with silt or mud — **silt·ta·tion** \sil-'tā-shən\ *n*

silt·stone \'silt-,stōn\ *n* (ca. 1920) : a rock composed chiefly of silt hardened by heat, pressure, or cementation

Sil·u·res \'sil-yə-,rēz\ *n pl* [L] (1581) : a people of ancient Britain described by Tacitus as occupying chiefly southern Wales

Si·lu·ri·an \sī-'lùr-ē-ən, sə-\ *adj* [L *Silures*] (1708) **1** : of or relating to the Silures or their place of habitation **2** : of, relating to, or being a period of the Paleozoic era between the Ordovician and Devonian or the corresponding system of rocks marked by numerous eurypterid crustaceans and the appearance of the first land plants — see GEOLOGIC TIME table — **Silurian** *n*

sil·va \'sil-və\ *n* [NL, fr. L, wood, forest] (ca. 1848) : the forest trees of a region or country

silvan *var of* SYLVAN

¹**sil·ver** \'sil-vər\ *n* [ME, fr. OE *seolfor*; akin to OHG *silbar* silver, Lith *sidabras*] (bef. 12c) **1** : a white ductile very malleable metallic element that is capable of a high degree of polish, is chiefly monovalent in compounds, and has the highest thermal and electric conductivity of any substance — see ELEMENT table **2** : silver as a commodity ⟨the value of ~ has risen⟩ **3** : coin made of silver **4** : articles (as hollowware or table flatware) made of or plated with silver; *also* : similar articles and esp. flatware of other metals (as stainless steel) **5** : a nearly neutral slightly brownish medium gray **6** : COHO **7** : a silver medal awarded as the second prize in a competiton

²**silver** *adj* (bef. 12c) **1** : made of silver **2** : resembling silver: as **a** (1) : having a white lustrous sheen (2) : of or tending towards the color silver ⟨~ fur⟩ ⟨a ~ gray⟩ **b** : giving a soft resonant sound : dulcet in tone **c** : eloquently persuasive **3** : consisting of or yielding silver **4** : of, relating to, or characteristic of silver **5** : advocating the use of silver as a standard of currency **6** : of, relating to, or being a 25th anniversary or its celebration

³**silver** *vt* **sil·vered; sil·ver·ing** \'sil-v(ə-)riŋ\ (14c) **1 a** : to cover with silver (as by electroplating) **b** : to coat with a substance (as a metal) resembling silver **2 a** : to give a silvery luster to **b** : to make white like silver — **sil·ver·er** \'sil-vər-ər\ *n*

silver age *n* (1565) : a historical period of achievement secondary to that of a golden age

sil·ver·back \'sil-vər-,bak\ *n* (1963) : an older adult usu. dominant male gorilla having gray or whitish hair on the back

silver bell *n* (1785) : any of a genus (*Halesia*) of deciduous trees and shrubs of the storax family; *esp* : one (*H. carolina*) of the southeastern U.S. cultivated for its bell-shaped white flowers

sil·ver·ber·ry \'sil-vər-,ber-ē\ *n* (1856) : a No. American shrub (*Elaeagnus commutata*) of the oleaster family with silvery deciduous foliage

silver bromide *n* (1869) : a compound AgBr that is extremely sensitive to light and is much used for photographic materials

silver bullet *n* (1806) : something that acts as a magical weapon; *esp* : one that instantly solves a long-standing problem

silver certificate *n* (1882) : a certificate formerly issued against the deposit of silver coin as legal tender in the U.S. and its possessions

silver chloride *n* (1869) : a compound AgCl that is sensitive to light and is used esp. for photographic materials

silver cord *n* [*The Silver Cord* (1926), play by Sidney Howard] (1942) : the emotional tie between a mother and a child and esp. a son

silver fir *n* (1705) : any of various firs (genus *Abies*) with leaves that are white or silvery white beneath; *esp* : a valuable European timber tree (*A. alba*)

sil·ver·fish \'sil-vər-,fish\ *n* (1703) **1** : any of various silvery fishes (as a tarpon or silverside) **2** : any of various small wingless insects (order Thysanura); *esp* : one (*Lepisma saccharina*) found in houses and sometimes injurious esp. to sized papers or starched clothes

silver fox *n* (ca. 1792) : a genetically determined color phase of the common red fox in which the fur is black tipped with white

silver hake *n* (1873) : a common hake (*Merluccius bilinearis*) of the northern Atlantic coast of the U.S. that is an important food fish

silver iodide *n* (1878) : a compound AgI that darkens on exposure to light and is used in photography, rainmaking, and medicine

silver lining *n* [fr. the phrase "every cloud has a *silver lining*"] (1871) : a consoling or hopeful prospect

sil·ver·ly \'sil-vər-lē\ *adv* (1597) : with silvery appearance or sound

silver maple *n* (1765) **1** : a common maple (*Acer saccharinum*) of eastern No. America with deeply cut 5-lobed leaves that are light green above and silvery white below **2** : the hard close-grained but brittle light brown wood of the silver maple

sil·vern \'sil-vərn\ *adj* (bef. 12c) **1** : made of silver **2** : resembling or characteristic of silver : SILVERY

silver nitrate *n* (1869) : an irritant compound AgNO₃ that in contact with organic matter turns black and is used as a chemical reagent, in photography, and in medicine esp. as an antiseptic and caustic

silver paper *n* (1846) : TIN FOIL

silver perch *n* (1820) : any of various somewhat silvery fishes that re-

semble perch: as **a** : a drum (*Bairdiella chrysoura*) that occurs esp. along the more southern Atlantic coast of the U.S. — called also *mademoiselle, yellowtail* **b** : WHITE PERCH 1

silver plate *n* (1610) **1** : domestic flatware and hollowware of silver or of a silver-plated base metal **2** : a plating of silver

sil·ver·point \'sil-vər-,point\ *n* (1882) : a drawing technique utilizing a pencil of silver usu. on specially prepared paper or parchment

silver protein *n* (1928) : any of several colloidal light-sensitive preparations of silver and protein used in aqueous solution on mucous membranes as antiseptics

silver salmon *n* (1878) : COHO

silver screen *n* (1918) **1** : a motion-picture screen **2** : MOTION PICTURES

sil·ver·side \'sil-vər-,sīd\ *n* (1820) : any of various small chiefly marine bony fishes (family Atherinidae) with a silvery stripe along each side of the body

sil·ver·sides \'sil-vər-,sīdz\ *n pl but sing or pl in constr* (1851) : SILVERSIDE

sil·ver·smith \-,smith\ *n* (bef. 12c) : an artisan who makes articles of silverware — **sil·ver·smith·ing** *n*

silver spoon *n* [fr. the phrase "born with a *silver spoon* in one's mouth" (born wealthy)] (1801) : WEALTH; *esp* : inherited wealth

silver standard *n* (1719) : a monetary standard under which the currency unit is defined by a stated quantity of silver

Silver Star *n* (1932) : a U.S. military decoration awarded for gallantry in action — called also *Silver Star Medal*

sil·ver·sword \'sil-vər-,sórd\ *n* (1856) : a long-lived composite plant (*Argyroxiphium sandwicense*) of Maui and Hawaii that has a rosette of lanceolate leaves covered with silvery hairs and that dies after producing a very tall raceme of numerous usu. purplish or reddish flowers

sil·ver–tongued \'sil-vər-,təŋd\ *adj* (1592) : marked by convincing and eloquent expression ⟨a ~ politician⟩

sil·ver·ware \'sil-vər-,wer\ *n* (1848) **1** : SILVER PLATE 1 **2** : FLATWARE

sil·ver·weed \-,wēd\ *n* (1578) : any of several cinquefoils with leaves silvery or white-tomentose beneath; *esp* : one (*Potentilla anserina*) with silky hairs over the entire plant

sil·very \'sil-v(ə-)rē\ *adj* (14c) **1** : having the luster of silver **2** : having a soft high clear musical tone ⟨a ~ voice⟩ **3** : containing or consisting of silver — **sil·ver·i·ness** *n*

sil·vex \'sil-,veks\ *n* [prob. fr. L *silva* wood + E *exterminator*] (1961) : a toxic selective herbicide C₉H₇Cl₃O₃ formerly used in controlling woody plants

sil·vi·cul·ture \'sil-və-,kəl-chər\ *n* [F, fr. L *silva* + *cultura* culture] (1880) : a branch of forestry dealing with the development and care of forests — **sil·vi·cul·tur·al** \,sil-və-'kəlch-rəl, -'kəl-chə-\ *adj* — **sil·vi·cul·tur·al·ly** \-rə-lē\ *adv* — **sil·vi·cul·tur·ist** \,sil-və-'kəlch-rist, -'kəl-chə-\ *n*

sim *abbr* simulation; simulator

si·ma·zine \'sī-mə-,zēn\ *n* [*sim*- (prob. alter. of *sym*- symmetrical, prefix used in names of organic compounds) + tri*azine*] (1956) : a selective herbicide C₇H₁₂N₅Cl used to control weeds esp. among crop plants

SIM card \'sim\ *n* [*s*ubscriber *i*dentity *m*odule] (1991) : a card that is inserted into a device (as a cell phone) and that is used to store data (as phone numbers or contact information)

Sim·chas To·rah \,sim-kəs-'tòr-ə\ *n* [Heb *śimḥath tōrāh* rejoicing of the Torah] (ca. 1878) : a Jewish holiday observed on the 23d of Tishri in celebration of the completion of the annual reading of the Torah

Sim·e·on \'si-mē-ən\ *n* [LL, fr. Gk *Symeōn*, fr. Heb *Shim'ōn*] (bef. 12c) **1** : a son of Jacob and the traditional eponymous ancestor of one of the tribes of Israel **2** : a devout man of Jerusalem held to have uttered the Nunc Dimittis on seeing the infant Jesus in the temple

¹**sim·i·an** \'si-mē-ən\ *adj* [L *simia* ape, fr. *simus* snub-nosed, fr. Gk *simos*] (1607) : of, relating to, or resembling monkeys or apes

²**simian** *n* (1880) : MONKEY, APE; *also* : any of a suborder (Anthropoidea) of primates that includes monkeys, apes, and humans

simian immunodeficiency virus *n* (1986) : SIV

sim·i·lar \'si-mə-lər, 'sim-lər\ *adj* [F *similaire*, fr. L *similis* like, similar — more at SAME] (1611) **1** : having characteristics in common : strictly comparable **2** : alike in substance or essentials : CORRESPONDING ⟨no two animal habitats are exactly ~ —W. H. Dowdeswell⟩ **3** : not differing in shape but only in size or position — **sim·i·lar·ly** *adv*

syn SIMILAR, ANALOGOUS, PARALLEL mean closely resembling each other. SIMILAR implies the possibility of being mistaken for each other ⟨*similar* houses⟩. ANALOGOUS applies to things belonging in essentially different categories but nevertheless having many similarities ⟨*analogous* political systems⟩. PARALLEL suggests a marked likeness in the development of two things ⟨the *parallel* careers of two movie stars⟩.

sim·i·lar·i·ty \,si-mə-'la-rə-tē\ *n, pl* **-ties** (1664) **1** : the quality or state of being similar : RESEMBLANCE **2** : a comparable aspect : CORRESPONDENCE **syn** see LIKENESS

sim·i·le \'si-mə-(,)lē\ *n* [ME, fr. L, comparison, fr. neut. of *similis*] (14c) : a figure of speech comparing two unlike things that is often introduced by *like* or *as* (as in *cheeks like roses*) — compare METAPHOR

si·mil·i·tude \sə-'mi-lə-,tüd, -,tyüd\ *n* [ME, fr. AF, allegory, analogy, fr. L *similitudo* resemblance, fr. *similis*] (14c) **1 a** : COUNTERPART, DOUBLE **b** : a visible likeness : IMAGE **2** : an imaginative comparison : SIMILE **3** : correspondence in kind or quality **b** : a point of comparison **syn** see LIKENESS

SIMM *abbr* single in-line memory module

Sim·men·tal *also* **Sim·men·thal** \'si-mən-,täl\ *n* [*Simmental*, valley of the Simme River in Switzerland] (1906) : any of a breed of large usu. buff or dull red and white cattle of Swiss origin that are used widely throughout the world for meat and milk

¹**sim·mer** \'si-mər\ *vb* **sim·mered; sim·mer·ing** \'si-mə-riŋ, 'sim-riŋ\ [alter. of E dial. *simper*, fr. ME *simperen*, of imit. origin] *vi* (1653) **1** : to stew gently below or just at the boiling point **2 a** : to be in a state

\ə\ abut \ᵊ\ kitten, F table \ər\ further \a\ ash \ā\ ace \ä\ mop, mar
\aù\ out \ch\ chin \e\ bet \ē\ easy \g\ go \i\ hit \ī\ ice \j\ job
\ŋ\ sing \ō\ go \ò\ law \òi\ boy \th\ thin \t̷h\ the \ü\ loot \ù\ foot
\y\ yet \zh\ vision, beige \k, ⁿ, œ, ᵫ, �\ see Guide to Pronunciation

of incipient development : FERMENT ⟨ideas ∼*ing* in the back of my mind⟩   **b** : to be in inward turmoil : SEETHE ∼ *vt* : to cook slowly in a liquid just below the boiling point
²**simmer** *n* (1809) : the state of simmering
simmer down *vi* (1871)   **1** : to become calm or peaceful   **2** : to become reduced by or as if by simmering
sim·nel \'sim-nⁿl\ *n* [ME *simenel*, fr. AF, ultim. fr. L *simila* wheat flour] (13c)   **1** : a bun or bread of fine wheat flour   **2** *Brit* : a rich fruitcake sometimes coated with almond paste and baked for mid-Lent, Easter, and Christmas
si·mo·le·on \sə-'mō-lē-ən\ *n* [origin unknown] (1896) *slang* : DOLLAR
Si·mon \'sī-mən\ *n* [Gk *Simōn*, fr. Heb *Shim'ōn*] (bef. 12c)   **1** : PETER — called also *Simon Peter*   **2** : one of the twelve disciples of Jesus — called also *Simon the Zealot*   **3** : a kinsman of Jesus   **4** : a Cyrenian constrained to help Jesus bear his cross to his place of crucifixion — called also *Simon the Cyrenian*   **5** : SIMON MAGUS
si·mo·ni·ac \sī-'mō-nē-ˌak, sə-\ *n* [ME, fr. ML *simoniacus*, fr. LL *simonia* simony] (14c) : one who practices simony — **simoniac** *or* **si·mo·ni·a·cal** \ˌsī-mə-'nī-ə-kəl, ˌsi-\ *adj* — **si·mo·ni·a·cal·ly** \-k(ə-)lē\ *adv*
si·mo·nize \'sī-mə-ˌnīz\ *vt* -**nized**; -**niz·ing** [fr. *Simoniz*, a trademark] (1934) : to polish with or as if with wax ⟨∼ a car⟩
Si·mon Le·gree \ˌsī-mən-lə-'grē\ *n* (1853) : a slave owner who has Tom flogged to death in Harriet B. Stowe's novel *Uncle Tom's Cabin*
Simon Ma·gus \-'mā-gəs\ *n* (ca. 1548) : a Samaritan sorcerer converted by the apostle Philip and severely rebuked by Peter for offering money for the gifts of the Holy Spirit
si·mon–pure \ˌsī-mən-'pyùr\ *adj* [fr. *the real Simon Pure*, alluding to a character impersonated by another in the play *A Bold Stroke for a Wife* (1718) by Susannah Centlivre] (1840) : of untainted purity or integrity; *also* : pretentiously or hypocritically pure
si·mo·ny \'sī-mə-nē, 'si-\ *n* [ME *symonie*, fr. AF *simonie*, fr. LL *simonia*, fr. *Simon* Magus, Samaritan sorcerer in Acts 8: 9–24] (13c) : the buying or selling of a church office or ecclesiastical preferment
si·moom \sə-'müm, sī-\ *or* **si·moon** \-'mün\ *n* [Ar *samūm*] (1790) : a hot dry violent dust-laden wind from Asian and African deserts
simp \'simp\ *n* (1903) : SIMPLETON
sim·pa·ti·co \sim-'pä-ti-ˌkō, -'pa-\ *adj* [It *simpatico* & Sp *simpático*, ultim. fr. L *sympathia* sympathy] (1864)   **1** : AGREEABLE, LIKABLE   **2** : being on the same wavelength : CONGENIAL, SYMPATHETIC
¹**sim·per** \'sim-pər\ *vb* **sim·pered**; **sim·per·ing** \-p(ə-)riŋ\ [akin to MD *zimperlijc* elegant, Dan dial. *simper* affected, coy] *vi* (ca. 1563) : to smile in a silly manner ∼ *vt* : to say with a simper ⟨∼*ed* an apology⟩ — **sim·per·er** \-pər-ər\ *n*
²**simper** *n* (1599) : a silly smile : SMIRK
¹**sim·ple** \'sim-pəl\ *adj* **sim·pler** \-p(ə-)lər\; **sim·plest** \-p(ə-)ləst\ [ME, fr. AF, fr. ML *simplus*, alter. of L *simplic-, simplex* single, having one ingredient, plain, fr. *sem-, sim-* one + *-plic-, -plex* -fold — more at SAME, -FOLD] (13c)   **1** : free from guile : INNOCENT   **2 a** : free from vanity : MODEST   **b** : free from ostentation or display ⟨a ∼ outfit⟩   **3** : of humble origin or modest position ⟨a ∼ farmer⟩   **4 a** : lacking in knowledge or expertise ⟨a ∼ amateur of the arts⟩   **b** (1) : STUPID   (2) : mentally retarded   **c** : not socially or culturally sophisticated : NAIVE; *also* : CREDULOUS   **5 a** : SHEER, UNMIXED ⟨∼ honesty⟩   **b** : free of secondary complications ⟨a ∼ vitamin deficiency⟩   **c** (1) : having only one main clause and no subordinate clauses ⟨a ∼ sentence⟩   (2) *of a subject or predicate* : having no modifiers, complements, or objects   **d** : constituting a basic element : FUNDAMENTAL   **e** : not made up of many like units ⟨a ∼ eye⟩   **6** : free from elaboration or figuration ⟨∼ harmony⟩   **7 a** (1) : not subdivided into branches or leaflets ⟨a ∼ stem⟩ ⟨a ∼ leaf⟩   (2) : consisting of a single carpel   (3) : developing from a single ovary ⟨a ∼ fruit⟩   **b** : controlled by a single gene ⟨∼ inherited characters⟩   **8** : not limited or restricted : UNCONDITIONAL ⟨a ∼ obligation⟩   **9** : readily understood or performed ⟨∼ directions⟩ ⟨the adjustment was ∼ to make⟩   **10** *of a statistical hypothesis* : specifying exact values for one or more statistical parameters — compare COMPOSITE 3 — **sim·ple·ness** \-pəl-nəs\ *n*

syn SIMPLE, FOOLISH, SILLY, FATUOUS, ASININE mean actually or apparently deficient in intelligence. SIMPLE implies a degree of intelligence inadequate to cope with anything complex or involving mental effort ⟨considered people *simple* who had trouble with computers⟩. FOOLISH implies the character of being or seeming unable to use judgment, discretion, or good sense ⟨*foolish* stunts⟩. SILLY suggests failure to act as a rational being esp. by ridiculous behavior ⟨the *silly* antics of revelers⟩. FATUOUS implies foolishness, inanity, and disregard of reality ⟨*fatuous* conspiracy theories⟩. ASININE suggests utter and contemptible failure to use normal rationality or perception ⟨an *asinine* plot⟩.   **syn** see in addition EASY

²**simple** *n* (14c)   **1 a** : a person of humble birth : COMMONER ⟨thought very little of anybody, ∼s or gentry —Virginia Woolf⟩   **b** (1) : a rude or credulous person : IGNORAMUS   (2) : a mentally retarded person   **2 a** : a medicinal plant   **b** : a vegetable drug having only one ingredient   **3** : one component of a complex; *specif* : an unanalyzable constituent
simple closed curve *n* (1919) : a closed plane curve (as a circle or an ellipse) that does not intersect itself — called also *Jordan curve*
simple equation *n* (1758) : a linear equation
simple fraction *n* (ca. 1728) : a fraction having whole numbers for the numerator and denominator — compare COMPLEX FRACTION
simple fracture *n* (1597) : a bone fracture that does not form an open wound in the skin — compare COMPOUND FRACTURE
simple interest *n* (1798) : interest paid or computed on the original principal only of a loan or on the amount of an account
simple machine *n* (ca. 1704) : any of various elementary mechanisms formerly considered as the elements of which all machines are composed and including the lever, the wheel and axle, the pulley, the inclined plane, the wedge, and the screw
sim·ple·mind·ed \ˌsim-pəl-'mīn-dəd, 'sim-pəl-ˌ\ *adj* (1601) : devoid of subtlety : UNSOPHISTICATED; *also* : FOOLISH — **sim·ple·mind·ed·ly** *adv* — **sim·ple·mind·ed·ness** *n*
simple protein *n* (1908) : a protein (as a globulin) that yields amino acids as the chief or only products of complete hydrolysis — compare CONJUGATED PROTEIN
simple sugar *n* (1942) : MONOSACCHARIDE
sim·ple·ton \'sim-pəl-tən\ *n* [*simple* + *-ton* (as in surnames such as *Washington*)] (ca. 1630) : a person lacking in common sense

simple vow *n* (1621) : a public vow taken by a religious in the Roman Catholic Church under which retention of property by the individual is permitted and marriage though illicit is valid under canon law
¹**sim·plex** \'sim-ˌpleks\ *adj* [L *simplic-, simplex* — more at SIMPLE] (1594)   **1** : SIMPLE, SINGLE   **2** : allowing telecommunication in only one direction ⟨a ∼ system⟩
²**simplex** *n*, *pl* **sim·plex·es** (1892)   **1** *or pl* **sim·pli·ces** \-plə-ˌsēz\ *or* **sim·pli·cia** \sim-'pli-sh(ē-)ə\ : a simple word   **2** : a spatial configuration of *n* dimensions determined by *n* + 1 points in a space of dimension equal to or greater than *n* ⟨a triangle together with its interior determined by its three vertices is a two-dimensional ∼ in the plane or any space of higher dimension⟩
sim·pli·cial \sim-'pli-shəl\ *adj* (1926) : of or relating to simplexes — **sim·pli·cial·ly** \-shə-lē\ *adv*
sim·plic·i·ty \sim-'pli-sə-tē, -'plis-tē\ *n, pl* -**ties** [ME *simplicite*, fr. AF *simplicité*, fr. L *simplicitat-, simplicitas*, fr. *simplic-, simplex*] (14c)   **1** : the state of being simple, uncomplicated, or uncompounded   **2 a** : lack of subtlety or penetration : INNOCENCE, NAIVETÉ   **b** : FOLLY, SILLINESS   **3** : freedom from pretense or guile : CANDOR   **4 a** : directness of expression : CLARITY   **b** : restraint in ornamentation : AUSTERITY
sim·pli·fy \'sim-plə-ˌfī\ *vt* -**fied**; -**fy·ing** [F *simplifier*, fr. ML *simplificare*, fr. *simplus* simple] (1759) : to make simple or simpler: as   **a** : to reduce to basic essentials   **b** : to diminish in scope or complexity : STREAMLINE ⟨was urged to ∼ management procedures⟩   **c** : to make more intelligible : CLARIFY — **sim·pli·fi·ca·tion** \ˌsim-plə-fə-'kā-shən\ *n* — **sim·pli·fi·er** \'sim-plə-ˌfī(-ə)r\ *n*
sim·plism \'sim-ˌpli-zəm\ *n* (1849) : the act or an instance of oversimplifying; *esp* : the reduction of a problem to a false simplicity by ignoring complicating factors
sim·plis·tic \sim-'plis-tik\ *adj* (ca. 1881)   **1** : SIMPLE   **2** : of, relating to, or characterized by simplism : OVERSIMPLE ⟨adequate, if occasionally ∼, historical background —Harlow Robinson⟩ — **sim·plis·ti·cal·ly** \-ti-k(ə-)lē\ *adv*
sim·ply \'sim-plē, *for 1 also* -pə-lē\ *adv* (14c)   **1 a** : without ambiguity : CLEARLY   **b** : without embellishment : PLAINLY   **c** : DIRECTLY, CANDIDLY   **2 a** : SOLELY, MERELY ⟨eats ∼ to keep alive⟩ ⟨∼ cleaned it up and went to bed —Garrison Keillor⟩   **b** : REALLY, LITERALLY ⟨the concert was ∼ marvelous⟩ — often used as an intensive ⟨∼ crawling with geniuses —F. Scott Fitzgerald⟩
simply connected *adj* (1893) : being or characterized by a surface that is divided into two separate parts by every closed curve it contains
simply ordered *adj* (ca. 1909) : having any two elements connected by a relationship that is reflexive, antisymmetric, and transitive
Simp·son's rule \'sim(p)-sənz-\ *n* [Thomas Simpson †1761 Eng. mathematician] (ca. 1875) : a method for approximating the area under a curve over a given interval that involves partitioning the interval by an odd number *n* + 1 of equally spaced ordinates and adding the areas of the *n*/2 figures formed by pairs of successive odd-numbered ordinates and the parabolas which they determine with their included even-numbered ordinates
sim·u·la·cre \'sim-yə-ˌlā-kər, -ˌla-\ *n* [ME, fr. AF, fr. L *simulacrum*] (14c) *archaic* : SIMULACRUM
sim·u·la·crum \ˌsim-yə-'la-krəm, -'lā-\ *n, pl* -**cra** \-krə\ *also* -**crums** [ME, fr. L, fr. *simulare*] (15c)   **1** : IMAGE, REPRESENTATION ⟨a reasonable ∼ of reality —Martin Mayer⟩   **2** : an insubstantial form or semblance of something : TRACE
¹**sim·u·lar** \'sim-yə-lər, -ˌlär\ *n* [irreg. fr. L *simulare* to simulate] (1526) *archaic* : one that simulates : DISSEMBLER
²**simular** *adj* (ca. 1610) *archaic* : COUNTERFEIT, PRETENDED
sim·u·late \'sim-yə-ˌlāt\ *vt* -**lat·ed**; -**lat·ing** [L *simulatus*, pp. of *simulare* to copy, represent, feign, fr. *similis* like — more at SAME] (1652)   **1** : to give or assume the appearance or effect of often with the intent to deceive : IMITATE   **2** : to make a simulation of (as a physical system)   **syn** see ASSUME — **sim·u·la·tive** \-ˌlā-tiv\ *adj*
simulated *adj* (1622) : made to look genuine : FAKE ⟨∼ pearls⟩
sim·u·la·tion \ˌsim-yə-'lā-shən\ *n* [ME *simulacion*, fr. AF, fr. L *simulation-, simulatio*, fr. *simulare*] (14c)   **1** : the act or process of simulating   **2** : a sham object : COUNTERFEIT   **3 a** : the imitative representation of the functioning of one system or process by means of the functioning of another ⟨a computer ∼ of an industrial process⟩   **b** : examination of a problem often not subject to direct experimentation by means of a simulating device
sim·u·la·tor \'sim-yə-ˌlā-tər\ *n* (1835) : one that simulates; *esp* : a device that enables the operator to reproduce or represent under test conditions phenomena likely to occur in actual performance
si·mul·cast \'sī-məl-ˌkast *also* 'si-\ *vb* [*simul*taneous broad*cast*] *vi* (1948) : to broadcast simultaneously (as by radio and television) ∼ *vt* : to broadcast (a program) by simulcasting — **simulcast** *n*
si·mul·ta·neous \ˌsī-məl-'tā-nē-əs, -nyəs *also* ˌsi-\ *adj* [L *simul* at the same time + E *-taneous* (as in *instantaneous*) — more at SAME] (ca. 1660)   **1** : existing or occurring at the same time : exactly coincident   **2** : satisfied by the same values of the variables ⟨∼ equations⟩   **syn** see CONTEMPORARY — **si·mul·ta·ne·i·ty** \-tə-'nē-ə-tē, -'nā-\ *n* — **si·mul·ta·neous·ly** \-'tā-nē-əs-lē, -nyəs-\ *adv* — **si·mul·ta·neous·ness** *n*
sim·va·stat·in \'sim-və-ˌsta-tⁿn, ˌsim-və-'sta-\ *n* [*sim-* (prob. alter. of *synthetic*) + lova*statin*] (1987) : a semisynthetic drug $C_{25}H_{38}O_5$ that decreases the level of cholesterol in the bloodstream and is derived from a compound produced by a mold (*Aspergillus terreus*)
¹**sin** \'sin\ *n* [ME *sinne*, fr. OE *synn*; akin to OHG *sunta* sin and prob. to L *sont-, sons* guilty, *est* is — more at IS] (bef. 12c)   **1 a** : an offense against religious or moral law   **b** : an action that is or is felt to be highly reprehensible ⟨it's a ∼ to waste food⟩   **c** : an often serious shortcoming : FAULT   **2 a** : transgression of the law of God   **b** : a vitiated state of human nature in which the self is estranged from God   **syn** see OFFENSE
²**sin** *vi* **sinned**; **sin·ning** (bef. 12c)   **1** : to commit a sin   **2** : to commit an offense or fault
³**sin** \'sēn, 'sin\ *n* [Heb *śin*] (ca. 1823) : the 21st letter of the Hebrew alphabet — see ALPHABET table
⁴**sin** *abbr* sine
Sin·bad *or* **Sind·bad** \'sin-ˌbad\ *n* (1789) : a citizen of Baghdad whose adventures at sea are told in the *Arabian Nights' Entertainments*

[1]**since** \ˈsin(t)s\ *adv* [ME *sins,* contr. of *sithens,* fr. *sithen,* fr. OE *siththan,* fr. *sīth tham* after that, fr. *sīth* after, late + *tham,* dat. of *thæt* that; akin to OHG *sīd* later and perh. to L *setius* to a lesser degree] (15c) **1 :** from a definite past time until now ⟨has stayed there ever ~⟩ **2 :** before the present time : AGO ⟨long ~ dead⟩ **3 :** after a time in the past : SUBSEQUENTLY ⟨has ~ become rich⟩

[2]**since** *conj* (15c) **1 :** at a time in the past after or later than ⟨has held two jobs ~ he graduated⟩ : from the time in the past when ⟨ever ~ I was a child⟩ **2** *obs* : WHEN **3 :** in view of the fact that : BECAUSE ⟨~ it was raining she took an umbrella⟩

[3]**since** *prep* (ca. 1530) : in the period after a specified time in the past : from a specified time in the past

sin·cere \sin-ˈsir, sən-\ *adj* **sin·cer·er; sin·cer·est** [MF, fr. L *sincerus* whole, pure, genuine, prob. fr. *sem-* one + *-cerus* (akin to L *crescere* to grow) — more at SAME, CRESCENT] (1533) **1 a :** free of dissimulation : HONEST ⟨a ~ interest⟩ **b :** free from adulteration : PURE ⟨a ~ doctrine⟩ ⟨~ wine⟩ **2 :** marked by genuineness : TRUE — **sin·cere·ly** *adv* — **sin·cere·ness** *n*

syn SINCERE, WHOLEHEARTED, HEARTFELT, HEARTY, UNFEIGNED mean genuine in feeling. SINCERE stresses absence of hypocrisy, feigning, or any falsifying embellishment or exaggeration ⟨a *sincere* apology⟩. WHOLEHEARTED suggests sincerity and earnest devotion without reservation or misgiving ⟨promised our *wholehearted* support⟩. HEARTFELT suggests depth of genuine feeling outwardly expressed ⟨expresses our *heartfelt* gratitude⟩. HEARTY suggests honesty, warmth, and exuberance in displaying feeling ⟨received a *hearty* welcome⟩. UNFEIGNED stresses spontaneity and absence of pretense ⟨her *unfeigned* delight at receiving the award⟩.

sin·cer·i·ty \-ˈser-ə-tē, -ˈsir-\ *n* (15c) : the quality or state of being sincere : honesty of mind : freedom from hypocrisy

sin·cip·i·tal \sin-ˈsi-pə-tᵊl\ *adj* (1653) : of or relating to the sinciput

sin·ci·put \ˈsin(t)-sə-(ˌ)pət\ *n, pl* **sinciputs** *or* **sin·cip·i·ta** \sin-ˈsi-pə-tə\ [L *sincipit-, sinciput,* fr. *semi-* + *caput* head — more at HEAD] (1578) **1 :** FOREHEAD **2 :** the upper half of the skull

Sind·hi \ˈsin-dē\ *n, pl* **Sindhi** *or* **Sindhis** [Hindi & Urdu *sindhī,* fr. *Sindh* Sind] (1815) **1 :** a member of a mostly Muslim people of Sind **2 :** the Indo-Aryan language of the Sindhi people

sine \ˈsīn\ *n* [ML *sinus,* fr. L, curve] (1593) **1 :** the trigonometric function that for an acute angle is the ratio between the leg opposite the angle when it is considered part of a right triangle and the hypotenuse **2 :** a trigonometric function sin θ that for all real numbers θ is exactly equal to the sine of an angle of measure θ in radians and that is given by the sum of the alternating series

$$\sin\theta = \theta - \frac{\theta^3}{3!} + \frac{\theta^5}{5!} - \frac{\theta^7}{7!} + \frac{\theta^9}{9!} - \cdots$$

si·ne·cure \ˈsī-ni-ˌkyu̇r, ˈsi-\ *n* [ML *sine cura* without cure (of souls)] (1662) **1** *archaic* : an ecclesiastical benefice without cure of souls **2 :** an office or position that requires little or no work and that usu. provides an income

sine curve *n* (1893) : the graph in rectangular coordinates of the equation $y=a \sin bx$ where *a* and *b* are constants

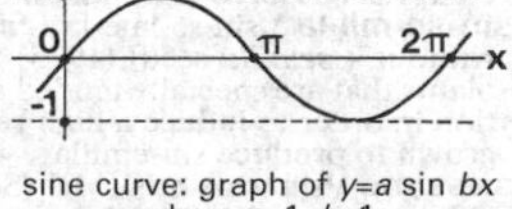

sine curve: graph of $y=a \sin bx$ where $a=1$, $b=1$

si·ne die \ˌsī-ni-ˈdī(-ˌē), ˌsi-nā-ˈdē-ˌā\ *adv* [L, without day] (1607) : without any future date being designated (as for resumption) : INDEFINITELY ⟨the meeting adjourned *sine die*⟩

si·ne qua non \ˌsi-ni-ˌkwä-ˈnän, -ˈnōn *also* ˌsē-; *also* ˌsī-ni-ˌkwā-ˈnän\ *n, pl* **sine qua nons** *also* **sine qui·bus non** \-ˌkwi-(ˌ)bu̇s- *also* -ˌkwī-\ [LL, without which not] (1602) : something absolutely indispensable or essential ⟨reliability is a *sine qua non* for success⟩

[1]**sin·ew** \ˈsin-(ˌ)yü *also* ˈsi-(ˌ)nü\ *n* [ME *sinewe,* fr. OE *seono;* akin to OHG *senawa* sinew, Skt *syati* he binds] (bef. 12c) **1 :** TENDON; *esp* : one dressed for use as a cord or thread **2** *obs* : NERVE **3 a :** solid resilient strength : POWER ⟨astonishing intellectual ~ and clarity —Reynolds Price⟩ **b :** the chief supporting force : MAINSTAY — usu. used in pl. ⟨providing the ~*s* of better living —Sam Pollock⟩

[2]**sinew** *vt* (ca. 1614) : to strengthen as if with sinews

sine wave *n* (1893) : a waveform that represents periodic oscillations in which the amplitude of displacement at each point is proportional to the sine of the phase angle of the displacement and that is visualized as a sine curve : SINE CURVE; *also* : a wave so represented

sin·ewy \ˈsin-yə-wē *also* ˈsi-nə-\ *adj* (14c) **1 :** full of sinews: as **a :** TOUGH, STRINGY ⟨~ meat⟩ **b :** STRONG ⟨~ arms⟩ **2 :** marked by the strength of sinews ⟨a demanding ~ intelligence —Helen Dudar⟩

sin·fo·nia \ˌsin-fə-ˈnē-ə\ *n, pl* **-nie** \-ˈnē-ˌā\ [It, fr. L *symphonia* symphony] (1773) **1 :** an orchestral prelude to a vocal work (as an opera) esp. in the 18th century **2 :** RITORNELLO 1, SYMPHONY 2c

sinfonia con·cer·tante \-ˌkän(t)-sər-ˈtän-tē, -shər-, -ˌtā\ *n* [It, lit., symphony in concerto style] (ca. 1903) : a concerto for more than one solo instrument

sin·fo·niet·ta \ˌsin-fən-ˈye-tə, -fōn-\ *n* [It, dim. of *sinfonia*] (ca. 1907) **1 :** a symphony of less than standard length or for fewer instruments **2 :** a small symphony orchestra; *esp* : an orchestra of strings only

sin·ful \ˈsin-fəl\ *adj* (bef. 12c) **1 :** tainted with, marked by, or full of sin : WICKED **2 :** such as to make one feel guilty ⟨a ~ chocolate cake⟩ — **sin·ful·ly** \-fə-lē\ *adv* — **sin·ful·ness** *n*

[1]**sing** \ˈsiŋ\ *vb* **sang** \ˈsaŋ\ *or* **sung** \ˈsəŋ\; **sung; sing·ing** \ˈsiŋ-iŋ\ [ME, fr. OE *singan;* akin to OHG *singan* to sing, Gk *omphē* voice] *vi* (bef. 12c) **1 a :** to produce musical tones by means of the voice **b :** to utter words in musical tones and with musical inflections and modulations **c :** to deliver songs as a trained or professional singer **2 :** to make a shrill whining or whistling sound **3 a :** to relate or celebrate something in verse **b :** to compose poetry **c :** to create in or through words a feeling or sense of song ⟨prose that ~*s*⟩ **4 :** to produce musical or harmonious sounds ⟨birds ~*ing*⟩ **5 :** BUZZ, RING **6 :** to make a cry : CALL **7 :** to give information or evidence ~ *vt* **1 :** to utter with musical inflections; *esp* : to interpret in musical tones produced by the voice **2 :** to relate or celebrate in verse **3 :** CHANT, INTONE **4 :** to bring or accompany to a place or state by singing ⟨~*s* the child to sleep⟩ — **sing·able** \ˈsiŋ-ə-bəl\ *adj*

[2]**sing** *n* (1850) : a session of group singing

sing–along \ˈsiŋ-ə-ˌlȯŋ\ *n* (1959) : SONGFEST; *also* : a song appropriate for a sing-along

[1]**singe** \ˈsinj\ *vt* **singed; singe·ing** \ˈsin-jiŋ\ [ME *sengen,* fr. OE *sængan, sengan;* akin to OHG *bisengan* to singe, OCS *isęknǫti* to dry up] (bef. 12c) : to burn superficially or lightly : SCORCH; *esp* : to remove the hair, down, or fuzz from usu. by passing rapidly over a flame

[2]**singe** *n* (1658) : a slight burn : SCORCH

[1]**sing·er** \ˈsiŋ-ər\ *n* (14c) : one that sings

[2]**sing·er** \ˈsin-jər\ *n* (ca. 1875) : one that singes

singing game *n* (1865) : a children's game in which the players accompany their actions with the singing of a narrative song

[1]**sin·gle** \ˈsiŋ-gəl\ *adj* [ME *sengle,* fr. AF, fr. L *singulus* one only; akin to L *sem-* one — more at SAME] (14c) **1 a :** not married **b :** of or relating to celibacy **2 :** unaccompanied by others : LONE, SOLE ⟨the ~ survivor of the disaster⟩ **3 a (1) :** consisting of or having only one part, feature, or portion ⟨~ consonants⟩ **(2) :** consisting of one as opposed to or in contrast with many : UNIFORM ⟨a ~ standard for men and women⟩ **(3) :** consisting of only one in number ⟨holds to a ~ ideal⟩ **b :** having but one whorl of petals or ray flowers ⟨a ~ rose⟩ **4 a :** consisting of a separate unique whole : INDIVIDUAL ⟨every ~ citizen⟩ **b :** of, relating to, or involving only one person **5 a :** FRANK, HONEST ⟨a ~ devotion⟩ **b :** exclusively attentive ⟨an eye ~ to the truth⟩ **6 :** UNBROKEN, UNDIVIDED **7 :** having no equal or like : SINGULAR **8 :** designed for the use of one person only ⟨a ~ room⟩ ⟨a ~ bed⟩

[2]**single** *n* (1604) **1 a :** a separate individual person or thing **b :** an unmarried person and esp. one young and socially active — usu. used in pl. **c (1) :** a recording having one short tune on each side **(2) :** a music recording having two or more tracks that is shorter than a full-length album; *also* : a song that is particularly popular independent of other songs on the same album or by the same artist **2 :** a base hit that allows the batter to reach first base **3 a** *pl* : a tennis match or similar game with one player on each side **b :** a golf match between two players — usu. used in pl. **4 :** a room (as in a hotel) for one guest — compare DOUBLE 7

[3]**single** *vb* **sin·gled; sin·gling** \-g(ə-)liŋ\ *vt* (1628) **1 :** to select or distinguish from a number or group — usu. used with *out* **2 a :** to advance or score (a base runner) by a single **b :** to bring about the scoring of (a run) by a single ~ *vi* : to make a single in baseball

sin·gle–ac·tion \ˈsiŋ-gəl-ˈak-shən\ *adj* (1900) *of a revolver* : that can be cocked only by manually retracting the hammer

sin·gle–blind \ˈsiŋ-gəl-ˌblīnd\ *adj* (1963) : of, relating to, or being an experimental procedure in which the experimenters but not the subjects know the makeup of the test and control groups during the actual course of the experiments — compare DOUBLE-BLIND, OPEN-LABEL

single bond *n* (1903) : a chemical bond in which one pair of electrons is shared by two atoms in a molecule esp. when the atoms can share more than one pair of electrons — compare DOUBLE BOND, TRIPLE BOND

sin·gle–breast·ed \ˈsiŋ-gəl-ˈbres-təd\ *adj* (1775) : having a center closing with one row of buttons and no lap ⟨a ~ coat⟩

single combat *n* (1585) : combat between two persons

single cross *n* (1940) : a first-generation hybrid between two selected and usu. inbred lines — compare DOUBLE CROSS 2

single entry *n* (1825) : a method of bookkeeping that recognizes only one side of a business transaction and usu. consists only of a record of cash and personal accounts with debtors and creditors

single file *n* (1609) : a row of persons, animals, or things arranged one behind the other — **single file** *adv*

[1]**sin·gle–foot** \ˈsiŋ-gəl-ˌfu̇t\ *n, pl* **single–foots** (1867) : [7]RACK b

[2]**single–foot** *vi* (1890) *of a horse* : to go at a rack — **sin·gle–foot·er** *n*

[1]**sin·gle–hand·ed** \ˌsiŋ-gəl-ˈhan-dəd\ *adj* (1585) **1 :** managed or done by one person or with one on a side **2 :** working alone or unassisted by others — **sin·gle–hand·ed·ly** *adv*

[2]**single–handed** *adv* (1719) : in a single-handed manner

sin·gle–hand·er \-ˈhan-dər\ *n* (1946) : a person who sails single-handed

sin·gle–heart·ed \ˌsiŋ-gəl-ˈhär-təd\ *adj* (1577) : characterized by sincerity and unity of purpose or dedication — **sin·gle–heart·ed·ly** *adv* — **sin·gle–heart·ed·ness** *n*

single knot *n* (1825) : OVERHAND KNOT

single–lens reflex \ˈsiŋ-gəl-ˈlenz-\ *n* (1940) : a camera having a single lens that forms an image which is reflected to the viewfinder or recorded on film

single malt *n* (1968) : whiskey that is made at one distillery and is not blended with other whiskeys

sin·gle–mind·ed \ˌsiŋ-gəl-ˈmīn-dəd, ˈsiŋ-gəl-ˌ\ *adj* (1836) : having one driving purpose or resolve : DETERMINED, DEDICATED — **sin·gle–mind·ed·ly** *adv* — **sin·gle–mind·ed·ness** *n*

sin·gle·ness \ˈsiŋ-gəl-nəs\ *n* (1560) : the quality or state of being single

sin·gle–pay·er \-ˈpā-ər\ *adj* (1987) : of, relating to, or being a system in which health-care providers are paid for their services by the government rather than by private insurers

sin·gle–phase \ˈsiŋ-gəl-ˈfāz\ *adj* (1895) : of or relating to a circuit energized by a single alternating electromotive force

sin·gle–space \-ˈspās\ *vt* (1928) : to type or print with no blank lines between lines of text

sin·gle·stick \-ˌstik\ *n* (1749) : fighting or fencing with a wooden stick or sword held in one hand; *also* : the weapon used

sin·glet \ˈsiŋ-glət\ *n* (ca. 1746) **1** [fr. its having only one thickness of cloth] *chiefly Brit* : an athletic jersey; *also* : UNDERSHIRT **2 :** an atom or molecule that has no net electronic magnetic moment; *also* : an excited state of an atom or molecule that is a singlet

single tax *n* (1795) **:** a tax to be levied on a single item (as real estate) as the sole source of public revenue

sin·gle·ton \ˈsiŋ-gəl-tən\ *n* [F, fr. E *single*] (1876) **1 :** a card that is the only one of its suit orig. dealt to a player **2 a :** an individual member or thing distinct from others grouped with it **b :** an offspring born singly ⟨~*s* are more common than twins⟩

sin·gle–track \ˈsiŋ-gəl-ˈtrak\ *adj* (1849) **1 :** having only one track **2 :** lacking intellectual range, receptiveness, or flexibility **:** ONE-TRACK ⟨had a ~ mind incapable of adjusting to changes⟩

sin·gle·tree \ˈsiŋ-gəl-(ˌ)trē\ *n* (ca. 1841) **:** WHIFFLETREE

sin·gle–val·ued \ˌsiŋ-gəl-ˈval-(ˌ)yüd\ *adj* (1879) **:** having one and only one value of the range associated with each value of the domain ⟨a ~ function⟩ — compare MULTIPLE-VALUED

single wing *n* (1945) **:** an offensive football formation in which one back plays as a flanker and two backs line up four or five yards behind the line in position to receive a direct snap from center

sin·gly \ˈsiŋ-g(ə-)lē\ *adv* (14c) **1 :** without the company of others **:** INDIVIDUALLY **2 :** SINGLE-HANDED

1sing·song \ˈsiŋ-ˌsȯŋ\ *n* (1609) **1 :** verse with marked and regular rhythm and rhyme **2 :** a voice delivery marked by a narrow range or monotonous pattern of pitch **3** *Brit* **:** SONGFEST — **sing·songy** \-ˌsȯŋ-ē\ *adj*

2singsong *adj* (1734) **:** having a monotonous cadence or rhythm

sing·spiel \ˈsiŋ-ˌspēl, ˈziŋ-ˌshpēl\ *n* [G, fr. *singen* to sing + *Spiel* play] (1876) **:** a musical work popular in Germany esp. in the latter part of the 18th century characterized by spoken dialogue interspersed with songs

1sin·gu·lar \ˈsiŋ-gyə-lər\ *adj* [ME *singuler,* fr. AF, fr. L *singularis,* fr. *singulus* only one — more at SINGLE] (14c) **1 a :** of or relating to a separate person or thing **:** INDIVIDUAL **b :** of, relating to, or being a word form denoting one person, thing, or instance ⟨a ~ noun⟩ **c :** of or relating to a single instance or to something considered by itself **2 :** distinguished by superiority **:** EXCEPTIONAL ⟨an artist of ~ attainments⟩ **3 :** being out of the ordinary **:** UNUSUAL ⟨on the way home we had a ~ adventure⟩ **4 :** departing from general usage or expectation **:** PECULIAR, ODD ⟨the air had a ~ chill⟩ **5 a** *of a matrix* **:** having a determinant equal to zero **b** *of a linear transformation* **:** having the property that the matrix of coefficients of the new variables has a determinant equal to zero ***syn*** see STRANGE — **sin·gu·lar·ly** *adv*

2singular *n* (14c) **1 :** the singular number, the inflectional form denoting it, or a word in that form **2 :** a singular term

sin·gu·lar·i·ty \ˌsiŋ-gyə-ˈla-rə-tē\ *n, pl* **-ties** (14c) **1 :** something that is singular: as **a :** a separate unit **b :** unusual or distinctive manner or behavior **:** PECULIARITY **2 :** the quality or state of being singular **3 :** a point at which the derivative of a given function of a complex variable does not exist but every neighborhood of which contains points for which the derivative does exist **4 :** a point or region of infinite mass density at which space and time are infinitely distorted by gravitational forces and which is held to be the final state of matter falling into a black hole

sin·gu·lar·ize \ˈsiŋ-gyə-lə-ˌrīz\ *vt* **-ized; -iz·ing** (1589) **:** to make singular

singular point *n* (ca. 1856) **:** SINGULARITY 3

Sin·ha·la \sin-ˈhä-lä, siŋ-\ *n* [Skt *Siṁhala* Sri Lanka] (ca. 1954) **:** SINHALESE 2

Sin·ha·lese *or* **Sin·gha·lese** \ˌsiŋ-gə-ˈlēz, ˌsin-(h)ə-, -ˈlēs\ *n, pl* **Sinhalese** *or* **Singhalese** (1598) **1 :** a member of a people that inhabit Sri Lanka and form a major part of its population **2 :** the Indo-Aryan language of the Sinhalese people — **Sinhalese** *or* **Sin·ghalese** *adj*

si·ni·cize \ˈsī-nə-ˌsīz, ˈsi-\ *vt* **-cized; -ciz·ing** *often cap* [ML *sinicus* Chinese, fr. LL *Sinae,* pl., Chinese — more at SINO-] (1889) **:** to modify by Chinese influence

sin·is·ter \ˈsi-nəs-tər, *archaic* sə-ˈnis-\ *adj* [ME *sinistre,* fr. AF *senestre* on the left, fr. L *sinistr-, sinister* on the left side, unlucky, inauspicious] (15c) **1** *archaic* **:** UNFAVORABLE, UNLUCKY **2** *archaic* **:** FRAUDULENT **3 :** singularly evil or productive of evil **4 a :** of, relating to, or situated to the left or on the left side of something; *esp* **:** being or relating to the side of a heraldic shield at the left of the person bearing it **b :** of ill omen by reason of being on the left **5 :** presaging ill fortune or trouble **6 :** accompanied by or leading to disaster — **sin·is·ter·ly** *adv* — **sin·is·ter·ness** *n*

syn SINISTER, BALEFUL, MALIGN mean seriously threatening evil or disaster. SINISTER suggests a general or vague feeling of fear or apprehension on the part of the observer ⟨a *sinister* aura haunts the place⟩. BALEFUL imputes perniciousness or destructiveness to something whether working openly or covertly ⟨exerting a corrupt and *baleful* influence⟩. MALIGN applies to what is inherently evil or harmful ⟨the *malign* effects of racism⟩.

si·nis·tral \ˈsi-nəs-trəl, sə-ˈnis-\ *adj* (1803) **:** of, relating to, or inclined to the left: as **a :** LEFT-HANDED **b** *of a gastropod shell* **:** having the whorls coiling counterclockwise down the spire when viewed with the apex toward the observer and having the aperture situated on the left of the axis when held with the spire uppermost and with the aperture opening toward the observer — compare DEXTRAL b

si·nis·trous \ˈsi-nəs-trəs, sə-ˈnis-\ *adj* (ca. 1575) *archaic* **:** SINISTER

Si·nit·ic \sī-ˈni-tik, sə-\ *adj* [LL *Sinae,* pl., Chinese + E *-itic* (as in *Semitic*) — more at SINO-] (ca. 1895) **:** of or relating to the Chinese, their language, or their culture

1sink \ˈsiŋk\ *vb* **sank** \ˈsaŋk\ *or* **sunk** \ˈsəŋk\; **sunk; sink·ing** [ME, fr. OE *sincan;* akin to OHG *sinkan* to sink] *vi* (bef. 12c) **1 a :** to go to the bottom **:** SUBMERGE **b :** to become partly buried (as in mud) **c :** to become engulfed **2 a** (1) **:** to fall or drop to a lower place or level (2) **:** to flow at a lower depth or level (3) **:** to burn with lower intensity (4) **:** to fall to a lower pitch or volume ⟨his voice *sank* to a whisper⟩ **b :** to subside gradually **:** SETTLE **c :** to disappear from view **d :** to slope gradually **:** DIP **3 a :** to soak or become absorbed **:** PENETRATE **b :** to become impressively known or felt ⟨the lesson had *sunk* in⟩ **4 :** to become deeply absorbed ⟨*sank* into reverie⟩ **5 a :** to go downward in quality, state, or condition **b :** to grow less in amount or worth **6 a :** to fall or drop slowly for lack of strength **b :** to become depressed **c :** to fail in health or strength; *broadly* **:** FAIL ~ *vt* **1 a :** to cause to sink ⟨~ a battleship⟩ **b :** to force down esp. below the earth's surface **c :** to cause (something) to penetrate **2 :** IMMERSE, ABSORB ⟨he *sank* himself into his studies⟩ **3 a :** to dig or bore (a well or shaft) in the earth **:** EXCAVATE **b :** to form by cutting or excising ⟨~ words in stone⟩ **4 :** to cast down or bring to a low condition or state **:** OVERWHELM, DEFEAT **5 :** to lower in standing or reputation **:** ABASE **6 a :** to lessen in value or amount **b :** to lower or soften (the voice) in speaking **7 :** RESTRAIN, SUPPRESS ⟨~*s* her pride and approaches the despised neighbor —Richard Harrison⟩ **8 :** to pay off (as a debt) **:** LIQUIDATE **9 :** INVEST 1 **10 :** DROP 7c ⟨~ a putt⟩ ⟨~ a jump shot⟩ **11** *chiefly Brit* **:** to drink down completely — **sink·able** \ˈsiŋ-kə-bəl\ *adj* — **sink one's teeth into 1 :** to bite into **2 :** to eagerly devote one's attention to ⟨likes to *sink her teeth into* a good book⟩

2sink *n* (15c) **1 a :** a pool or pit for the deposit of waste or sewage **:** CESSPOOL **b :** a ditch or tunnel for carrying off sewage **:** SEWER **c :** a stationary basin connected with a drain and usu. a water supply for washing and drainage **2 :** a place where vice, corruption, or evil collects **3 :** SUMP 3 **4 a :** a depression in the land surface; *esp* **:** one having a saline lake with no outlet **b :** SINKHOLE **5 :** a body or process that acts as a storage device or disposal mechanism: as **a :** HEAT SINK; *broadly* **:** a device that collects or dissipates energy (as radiation) **b :** a reactant with or absorber of a substance ⟨forests are a ~ for carbon dioxide⟩

sink·age \ˈsiŋ-kij\ *n* (1847) **1 :** DEPRESSION, INDENTATION **2 :** the process or degree of sinking **3 :** the distance from the top line of a full page to the first line of lowered matter

sink·er \ˈsiŋ-kər\ *n* (1632) **1 :** one that sinks; *specif* **:** a weight for sinking a fishing line, seine, or sounding line **2 :** DOUGHNUT **3 :** a fastball that sinks as it reaches the plate — called also *sinker ball*

sink·hole \ˈsiŋk-ˌhōl\ *n* (15c) **1 :** a hollow place or depression in which drainage collects **2 :** a hollow in a limestone region that communicates with a cavern or passage **3 :** SINK 2 **4 :** something (as an unprofitable investment) that steadily drains money or resources ⟨a financial ~⟩

sinking fund *n* (1724) **:** a fund set up and accumulated by usu. regular deposits for paying off the principal of a debt when it falls due

sin·less \ˈsin-ləs\ *adj* (bef. 12c) **:** free from sin **:** IMPECCABLE — **sin·less·ly** *adv* — **sin·less·ness** *n*

sin·ner \ˈsi-nər\ *n* (14c) **1 :** one that sins **2 :** REPROBATE, SCAMP

Si·no- \ˌsī-(ˌ)nō, ˈsī-, -nə\ *comb form* [F, fr. LL *Sinae,* pl., Chinese, fr. Gk *Sinai,* prob. of Indo-Aryan origin; akin to Skt *Cīnā,* pl., Chinese] **1 :** Chinese ⟨*sino*logy⟩ **2 :** Chinese and ⟨*Sino*-Tibetan⟩

si·no·atri·al \ˌsī-nō-ˈā-trē-əl\ *adj* [NL *sinus* + *atrium*] (1913) **:** of, involving, or being the sinus node ⟨~ block⟩

sinoatrial node *n* (1913) **:** SINUS NODE

si·no·logue \ˈsī-nə-ˌlȯg, ˈsi-, -ˌläg\ *n, often cap* [F, fr. *sino-* + *-logue*] (1848) **:** a specialist in sinology

si·nol·o·gy \sī-ˈnä-lə-jē, sə-\ *n, often cap* [prob. fr. F *sinologie,* fr. *sino-* + *-logie* -logy] (ca. 1882) **:** the study of the Chinese and esp. their language, literature, history, and culture — **si·no·log·i·cal** \ˌsī-nə-ˈlä-ji-kəl, ˌsi-\ *adj, often cap* — **si·nol·o·gist** \sī-ˈnä-lə-jist, sə-\ *n, often cap*

si·no·pia \sə-ˈnō-pē-ə\ *n, pl* **-pi·as** *or* **-pie** \-pē-ˌā\ [It, fr. L *sinopis,* fr. Gk *sinōpis,* fr. *Sinōpē* Sinop, ancient seaport in Asia Minor] (1844) **1 :** a red to reddish-brown earth pigment used by the ancients that depends for its color on its content of red ferric oxide **2 :** a preliminary drawing for a fresco done in sinopia

Si·no–Ti·bet·an \ˌsī-nō-tə-ˈbe-tᵊn, ˈsī-\ *n* (1920) **:** a language family comprising Tibeto-Burman and Chinese

sin·se·mil·la \ˌsin-sə-ˈmē-lə, -ˈmi-; -ˈmē-yə, -ˈmēl-\ *n* [AmerSp, fr. *sin* without + *semilla* seed] (1975) **:** highly potent marijuana from female plants that are specially tended and kept seedless by preventing pollination in order to induce a high resin content; *also* **:** a female hemp plant grown to produce sinsemilla

sin·syne \ˈsin-ˌsīn\ *adv* [ME (Sc) *sensyne,* fr. *sen* since (contr. of ME *sithen*) + *syne* since — more at SINCE, SYNE] (14c) *chiefly Scot* **:** since that time

sin tax *n* (1964) **:** a tax on substances or activities considered sinful or harmful (as tobacco, alcohol, or gambling)

sin·ter \ˈsin-tər\ *vb* [G *Sinter* slag, cinder, fr. OHG *sintar* — more at CINDER] *vt* (1871) **:** to cause to become a coherent mass by heating without melting ~ *vi* **:** to undergo sintering — **sinter** *n* — **sin·ter·abil·i·ty** \ˌsin-tə-rə-ˈbi-lə-tē\ *n*

sin·u·ate \ˈsin-yə-wət, -ˌwāt\ *adj* [L *sinuatus,* pp. of *sinuare* to bend, fr. *sinus* curve] (1688) **:** having the margin wavy with strong indentations ⟨~ leaves⟩

sin·u·os·i·ty \ˌsin-yə-ˈwä-sə-tē\ *n, pl* **-ties** (1598) **1 :** the quality or state of being sinuous **2 :** something that is sinuous

sin·u·ous \ˈsin-yə-wəs, -yü-əs\ *adj* [L *sinuosus,* fr. *sinus*] (1578) **1 a :** of a serpentine or wavy form **:** WINDING **b :** marked by strong lithe movements **2 :** INTRICATE, COMPLEX — **sin·u·ous·ly** *adv* — **sin·u·ous·ness** *n*

si·nus \ˈsī-nəs\ *n* [ME, fr. ML, fr. L, curve, fold, hollow] (15c) **:** CAVITY, HOLLOW: as **a :** a narrow elongated tract extending from a focus of suppuration and serving for the discharge of pus **b** (1) **:** a cavity in the substance of a bone of the skull that usu. communicates with the nostrils and contains air (2) **:** a channel for venous blood (3) **:** a dilatation in a bodily canal or vessel **c :** a cleft or indentation between adjoining lobes (as of a leaf or corolla)

si·nus·i·tis \ˌsīn-yə-ˈsī-təs, ˌsī-nə-\ *n* (1896) **:** inflammation of a sinus of the skull

sinus node *n* (1937) **:** a small mass of tissue that is embedded in the musculature of the right atrium of higher vertebrates and that originates the impulses stimulating the heartbeat

si·nu·soid \ˈsīn-yə-ˌsȯid, ˈsī-nə-\ *n* [ML *sinus* sine] (1823) **1 :** SINE CURVE, SINE WAVE **2** [NL *sinus*] **:** a minute endothelium-lined space or passage for blood in the tissues of an organ (as the liver)

si·nu·soi·dal \ˌsīn-yə-ˈsȯi-dᵊl, ˌsī-nə-\ *adj* (1878) **:** of, relating to, shaped like, or varying according to a sine curve or sine wave ⟨~ motion⟩ ⟨~ alternating current⟩ ⟨~ grooves⟩ — **si·nu·soi·dal·ly** \-dᵊl-ē\ *adv*

sinusoidal projection *n* (1944) **:** an equal-area map projection capable of showing the entire surface of the earth with all parallels as straight lines evenly spaced, the central meridian as one half the length of the equator, and all other meridians as curved lines

sinus rhythm *n* (1911) **:** the rhythm of the heart produced by impulses from the sinus node ⟨restored the patient to normal *sinus rhythm*⟩

si·nus ve·no·sus \ˈsī-nəs-vi-ˈnō-səs\ *n* [NL, venous sinus] (ca. 1839) **:** an enlarged pouch that adjoins the heart, is formed by the union of the large systemic veins, and is the passage through which venous blood enters the heart in lower vertebrates and in embryos of higher forms

Sion *var of* ZION

Siou·an \ˈsü-ən\ *n* (1885) **1 :** an American Indian language family of central and southeastern No. America **2 :** a member of any of the peoples speaking Siouan languages

Sioux \ˈsü\ *n, pl* **Sioux** \ˈsü, ˈsüz\ [AmerF, short for *Nadouessioux,* fr. Ojibwa *na·towe·ssiw-*] (1762) **1 :** DAKOTA **2 :** SIOUAN

[1]**sip** \ˈsip\ *vb* **sipped; sip·ping** [ME *sippen;* akin to LG *sippen* to sip] *vi* (14c) **:** to take a sip of something esp. repeatedly ~ *vt* **1 :** to drink in small quantities **2 :** to take sips from — **sip·per** *n*

[2]**sip** *n* (15c) **1 :** a small draft taken with the lips **2 :** the act of sipping

[1]**si·phon** *also* **sy·phon** \ˈsī-fən\ *n* [F *siphon,* fr. L *siphon-, sipho* tube, pipe, siphon, fr. Gk *siphōn*] (1659) **1 a :** a tube bent to form two legs of unequal length by which a liquid can be transferred to a lower level over an intermediate elevation by the pressure of the atmosphere in forcing the liquid up the shorter branch of the tube immersed in it while the excess of weight of the liquid in the longer branch when once filled causes a continuous flow **b** *usu* **syphon :** a bottle for holding aerated water that is driven out through a bent tube in its neck by the pressure of the gas when a valve in the tube is opened **2 :** any of various tubular organs in animals and esp. mollusks or arthropods that are used for drawing in or ejecting fluids

[2]**siphon** *also* **syphon** *vb* **si·phoned** *also* **sy·phoned; si·phon·ing** *also* **sy·phon·ing** \ˈsī-fə-niŋ, ˈsīf-niŋ\ *vt* (1859) **:** to convey, draw off, or empty by or as if by a siphon — often used with *off* ~ *vi* **:** to pass by or as if by a siphon

si·pho·no·phore \sī-ˈfä-nə-ˌfȯr, ˈsī-fə-nə-\ *n* [ultim. fr. Gk *siphōn* + *pherein* to carry — more at BEAR] (ca. 1842) **:** any of an order (Siphonophora) of compound free-swimming or floating pelagic hydrozoans that are mostly delicate, transparent, and colored and have specialized zooids

si·pho·no·stele \sī-ˈfä-nə-ˌstēl, ˌsī-fə-nə-ˈstē-lē\ *n* [Gk *siphōn* tube, siphon] (1902) **:** a stele consisting of vascular tissue surrounding a central core of pith parenchyma

sip·pet \ˈsi-pət\ *n* [alter. of *sop*] (1530) *chiefly Brit* **:** a small bit of toast or fried bread esp. for garnishing

sip·py cup \ˈsi-pē-\ *n* [*sip* + [4]*-y*] (1986) **:** a cup that has a detachable lid with a projecting hole designed to help a young child sip liquid from the cup without spilling it

sir \ˈsər\ *n* [ME, fr. *sire*] (13c) **1 a :** a man entitled to be addressed as *sir* — used as a title before the given name of a knight or baronet and formerly sometimes before the given name of a priest **b :** a man of rank or position **2 a** — used as a usu. respectful form of address **b** *cap* — used as a conventional form of address in the salutation of a letter

Si·rach \ˈsī-rak *also* sə-ˈräk\ *n* [Gk *Seirach*] (1976) **:** a didactic book of the Roman Catholic canon of the Old Testament — see BIBLE table

sir·dar *or* **sar·dar** \ˈsər-ˌdär, sər-ˈ\ *n* [Hindi & Urdu *sardār,* fr. Pers] (1595) **1 a :** a person of high rank (as a hereditary noble) esp. in India **b :** the commander of the Anglo-Egyptian army **2 :** one (as a foreman) holding a responsible position esp. in India

[1]**sire** \ˈsī(-ə)r\ *n* [ME, fr. AF, lord, feudal superior, fr. VL **seior,* alter. of L *senior* older — more at SENIOR] (13c) **1 a :** FATHER **b** *archaic* **:** male ancestor **:** FOREFATHER **c :** AUTHOR, ORIGINATOR **2 a** *archaic* **:** a man of rank or authority; *esp* **:** LORD — used formerly as a form of address and as a title **b** *obs* **:** an elderly man **:** SENIOR **3 :** the male parent of an animal and esp. of a domestic animal

[2]**sire** *vt* **sired; sir·ing** (1611) **1 :** BEGET — used esp. of male domestic animals **2 :** to bring into being **:** ORIGINATE

[1]**si·ren** \ˈsī-rən, *for 3 also* sī-ˈrēn\ *n* [ME, fr. MF & L; MF *sereine,* fr. LL *sirena,* fr. L *siren,* fr. Gk *seirēn*] (14c) **1** *often cap* **:** any of a group of female and partly human creatures in Greek mythology that lured mariners to destruction by their singing **2 a :** a woman who sings with enchanting sweetness **b :** TEMPTRESS **c :** TEMPTATION 2 **3 a :** an apparatus producing musical tones esp. in acoustical studies by the rapid interruption of a current of air, steam, or fluid by a perforated rotating disk **b :** a device often electrically operated for producing a penetrating warning sound ⟨an ambulance ~⟩ ⟨an air-raid ~⟩ **4** [NL, fr. L] **:** either of two No. American eel-shaped amphibians that constitute a genus (*Siren*) and have small forelimbs but neither hind legs nor pelvis and have permanent external gills as well as lungs

[2]**si·ren** \ˈsī-rən\ *adj* (1568) **:** resembling that of a siren **:** ENTICING

si·re·ni·an \sī-ˈrē-nē-ən\ *n* [NL *Sirenia,* fr. L *siren*] (1883) **:** any of an order (Sirenia) of aquatic herbivorous mammals (as a manatee, dugong, or Steller's sea cow) that have large forelimbs resembling paddles, no hind limbs, and a flattened tail resembling a fin — **sirenian** *adj*

siren song *n* (1568) **:** an alluring utterance or appeal; *esp* **:** one that is seductive or deceptive

Sir·i·us \ˈsir-ē-əs\ *n* [ME, fr. L, fr. Gk *Seirios*] (14c) **:** a star of the constellation Canis Major that is the brightest star in the heavens — called also *Dog Star*

sir·loin \ˈsər-ˌlȯin\ *n* [alter. of earlier *surloin,* modif. of MF *surlonge,* fr. *sur* over (fr. L *super*) + *loigne, longe* loin — more at OVER, LOIN] (1554) **:** a cut of meat and esp. of beef from the part of the hindquarter just in front of the round — see BEEF illustration

si·roc·co *also* **sci·roc·co** \shə-ˈrä-(ˌ)kō, sə-\ *n, pl* **-cos** [It *scirocco, sirocco,* alter. of OIt *scilocco,* fr. Ar dial. (Maghreb) *šlōq* southeast wind, alter. of Ar *sharūq, shulūq*] (1617) **1 a :** a hot dust-laden wind from the Libyan deserts that blows on the northern Mediterranean coast chiefly in Italy, Malta, and Sicily **b :** a warm moist oppressive southeast wind in the same regions **2 :** a hot or warm wind of cyclonic origin from an arid or heated region

sir·rah *also* **sir·ra** \ˈsir-ə\ *n* [alter. of *sir*] (1526) *obs* — used as a form of address implying inferiority in the person addressed

sir·ree *also* **sir·ee** \(ˌ)sər-ˈē\ *n* [by alter.] (1823) **:** SIR — used as an emphatic form usu. after *yes* or *no*

sir–reverence *n* [prob. alter. of *save-reverence,* trans. of ML *salva reverentia* with all respect, lit., saving (your) reverence] (1575) **1** *obs* — used as an expression of apology before a statement that might be taken as offensive **2** *obs* **:** human feces; *also* **:** a lump of human feces

Sir Rog·er de Cov·er·ley \sə(r)-ˌrä-jər-di-ˈkə-vər-lē\ *n* [alter. of *roger of coverley,* prob. fr. *Roger,* male given name + *of* + *Coverley,* a fictitious place name] (1804) **:** an English country-dance that resembles the Virginia reel

sirup *var of* SYRUP

sir·vente \sir-ˈvänt\ *or* **sir·ven·tes** \-ˈven-təs\ *n, pl* **sir·ventes** \-ˈvänt, -ˈvän(t)s, -ˈven-təs\ [F, fr. Occitan *sirventes,* lit., servant's song, fr. *sirvent* servant, fr. L *servient-, serviens,* prp. of *servire* to serve] (1819) **:** a usu. moral or religious song of the Provençal troubadours satirizing social vices

sis \ˈsis\ *n* (1656) **:** SISTER — usu. used in direct address

SIS *abbr* Secret Intelligence Service (Brit)

-sis *n suffix, pl* **-ses** [L, fr. Gk, fem. suffix of action] **:** process **:** action ⟨peristal*sis*⟩

si·sal \ˈsī-səl, -zəl\ *n* [*Sisal,* port in Yucatán, Mexico] (1842) **1 a :** a strong white fiber used esp. for cordage and twine — called also *sisal hemp* **b :** a widely cultivated Mexican agave (*Agave sisalana*) whose leaves yield sisal **2 :** any of several fibers similar to true sisal

sis·kin \ˈsis-kən\ *n* [G dial. *Sisschen,* dim. of MHG *zīse* siskin, of Slav origin; akin to Czech *čížek* siskin] (1562) **:** a small chiefly greenish and yellowish finch (*Carduelis spinus*) of Europe, Asia, and northern Africa that is related to the goldfinch — compare PINE SISKIN, RED SISKIN

sis·si·fied \ˈsi-si-ˌfīd\ *adj* (ca. 1903) **:** of, relating to, or having the characteristics of a sissy

sis·sy \ˈsi-sē\ *n, pl* **sissies** [*sis*] (1879) **:** an effeminate man or boy; *also* **:** a timid or cowardly person — **sissy** *adj*

sis·ter \ˈsis-tər\ *n* [ME *suster, sister,* partly fr. OE *sweostor* and partly fr. ON *systir* sister; akin to L *soror* sister, Skt *svasṛ*] (bef. 12c) **1 :** a female who has one or both parents in common with another **2** *often cap* **a :** a member of a women's religious order (as of nuns or deaconesses); *esp* **:** one of a Roman Catholic congregation under simple vows **b :** a girl or woman who is a member of a Christian church **3 a :** a girl or woman regarded as a comrade **b :** a girl or woman who shares with another a common national or racial origin; *esp* **:** a black girl or woman **4 :** one that is closely similar to or associated with another ⟨~ cities⟩ **5** *chiefly Brit* **:** NURSE **6 a :** GIRL, WOMAN **b :** PERSON — usu. used in the phrase *weak sister* **7 :** a member of a sorority

sis·ter·hood \-ˌhu̇d\ *n* (14c) **1 a :** the state of being a sister **b :** sisterly relationship **2 :** a community or society of sisters; *esp* **:** a society of women in a religious order **3 :** the solidarity of women based on shared conditions, experiences, or concerns

sis·ter–in–law \ˈsis-t(ə-)rən-ˌlȯ, -tərn-ˌlȯ\ *n, pl* **sis·ters–in–law** \-tər-zən-\ (15c) **1 :** the sister of one's spouse **2 a :** the wife of one's brother **b :** the wife of one's spouse's brother

sis·ter·ly \ˈsis-tər-lē\ *adj* (ca. 1570) **:** of, relating to, or having the characteristics of a sister — **sisterly** *adv*

Sis·tine \ˈsis-ˌtēn, sis-ˈ\ *also* **Six·tine** \ˈsik-ˌstīn, -ˌstēn\ *adj* [It *sistino,* fr. NL *sixtinus,* fr. *Sixtus,* name of some popes] (1771) **1** [fr. Pope *Sixtus* IV †1484] **:** of or relating to the Sistine Chapel in the Vatican **2 :** of or relating to any of the popes named Sixtus

Si·swa·ti *or* **Si·Swa·ti** \sē-ˈswä-tē\ *also* **Swa·zi** \ˈswä-zē\ *n* [Siswati] (1919) **:** the Bantu language of the Swazi people spoken in Swaziland and adjacent countries

Sis·y·phe·an \ˌsi-sə-ˈfē-ən\ *also* **Si·syph·i·an** \si-ˈsi-fē-ən\ *adj* (1635) **:** of, relating to, or suggestive of the labors of Sisyphus ⟨a ~ task⟩

Sis·y·phus \ˈsi-sə-fəs\ *n* [L, fr. Gk *Sisyphos*] (14c) **:** a legendary king of Corinth condemned eternally to repeatedly roll a heavy rock up a hill in Hades only to have it roll down again as it nears the top

[1]**sit** \ˈsit\ *vb* **sat** \ˈsat\; **sit·ting** [ME *sitten,* fr. OE *sittan;* akin to OHG *sizzen* to sit, L *sedēre,* Gk *hezesthai* to sit, *hedra* seat] *vi* (bef. 12c) **1 a :** to rest on the buttocks or haunches ⟨~ in a chair⟩ — often used with *down* **b :** PERCH, ROOST **2 :** to occupy a place as a member of an official body ⟨~ in Congress⟩ **3 :** to hold a session **:** be in session for official business **4 :** to cover eggs for hatching **:** BROOD **5 a :** to take a position for having one's portrait painted or for being photographed **b :** to serve as a model **6** *archaic* **:** to have one's dwelling place **:** DWELL **7 a :** to lie or hang relative to a wearer ⟨the collar ~*s* awkwardly⟩ **b :** to affect one with or as if with weight ⟨the food *sat* heavily on his stomach⟩ **8 :** LIE, REST ⟨a kettle *sitting* on the stove⟩ **9 a :** to have a location ⟨the house ~*s* well back from the road⟩ **b** *of wind* **:** to blow from a certain direction **10 :** to remain inactive or quiescent ⟨the car ~*s* in the garage⟩ **11 :** to take an examination **12 :** BABYSIT **13 :** to please or agree with one — used with *with* and an adverb ⟨the decision did not ~ well with me⟩ ~ *vt* **1 :** to cause to be seated **:** place on or in a seat — often used with *down* **2 :** to sit on (eggs) **3 :** to keep one's seat on ⟨~ a horse⟩ **4 :** to provide seats or seating room for — **sit on 1 :** to hold deliberations concerning **2 :** REPRESS, SQUELCH **3 :** to delay action or decision concerning **4 :** to wait or be ready for (a specific pitch) in baseball — **sit on one's hands 1 :** to withhold applause **:** fail to show approval or enthusiasm **2 :** to fail to take expected or appropriate action — **sit pretty :** to be in a highly favorable situation — **sit tight 1 :** to maintain one's position without change **2 :** to remain quiet in or as if in hiding — **sit under :** to attend religious service under the instruction or ministrations of; *also* **:** to attend the classes or lectures of

[2]**sit** *n* (1776) **1 :** the manner in which a garment fits **2 :** an act or period of sitting

si·tar \si-ˈtär, ˈsi-ˌ\ *n* [Hindi & Urdu *sitār,* fr. Pers, a three-stringed lute, fr. *sih* three + *tār* string, thread] (1828) **:** an Indian lute with a long neck and a varying number of strings — **si·tar·ist** \-ist\ *n*

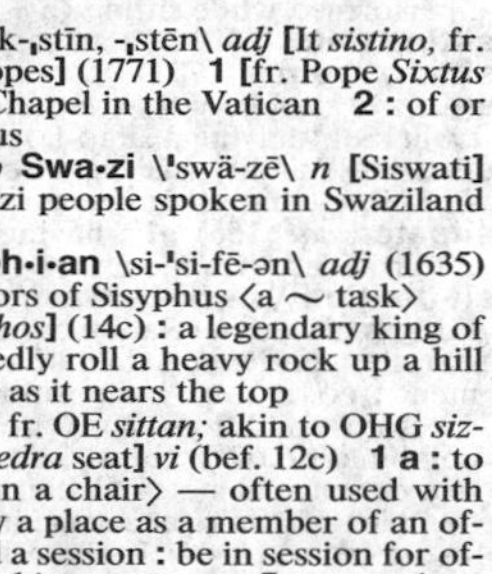

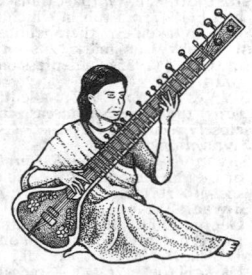

sitar

sit·com \ˈsit-ˌkäm\ *n* [*sit*uation *com*edy] (1951) : SITUATION COMEDY

[1]**sit–down** \ˈsit-ˌdau̇n\ *adj* (1834) : served to seated diners ⟨a ~ dinner⟩; *also* : of, relating to, or serving sit-down meals ⟨a ~ restaurant⟩

[2]**sit–down** \ˈsit-ˌdau̇n\ *n* (1936) **1** : a cessation of work by employees while maintaining continuous occupation of their place of employment as a protest and means toward forcing compliance with demands **2** : a mass obstruction of an activity by sitting down to demonstrate a grievance or to get the activity modified or halted **3** : a meeting held esp. to discuss and resolve problems or conflicts

[1]**site** \ˈsīt\ *n* [ME, place, position, fr. AF or L; AF *sit, site,* fr. L *situs,* fr. *sinere* to leave, allow] (14c) **1 a** : the spatial location of an actual or planned structure or set of structures (as a building, town, or monuments) **b** : a space of ground occupied or to be occupied by a building **2 a** : the place, scene, or point of an occurrence or event ⟨a picnic ~⟩ **b** : one or more Internet addresses at which an individual or organization provides information to others ⟨an FTP ~⟩; *esp* : WEB SITE

[2]**site** *vt* **sit·ed; sit·ing** (15c) : to place on a site or in position : LOCATE

sith \ˈsith\ *or* **sith·ence** \ˈsi-thən(t)s\ *or* **sith·ens** \ˈsi-thənz\ *archaic var of* SINCE

sit–in \ˈsit-ˌin\ *n* (1937) **1** : SIT-DOWN 1 **2 a** : an act of occupying seats in a racially segregated establishment in organized protest against discrimination **b** : an act of sitting in the seats or on the floor of an establishment as a means of organized protest

sit in *vi* (1868) **1** : to take part in or be present at a session of music or discussion as a visitor — often used with *on* ⟨invited to *sit in* on a rehearsal⟩ **2** : to participate in a sit-in

Sit·ka spruce \ˈsit-kə-\ *n* [*Sitka,* Alaska] (1895) : a tall spruce (*Picea sitchensis*) of the northern Pacific coast of No. America that has thin reddish-brown bark, flat needles, and cones with slightly toothed scales — see CONE illustration

si·tos·ter·ol \sī-ˈtäs-tə-ˌrȯl, sə-, -ˌrōl\ *n* [Gk *sitos* grain + E *sterol*] (1898) : any of several sterols that are widespread esp. in plant products (as wheat germ or soybean oil) and are used as starting materials for the synthesis of steroid hormones

sit out *vt* (1578) : to refrain from participating in ⟨*sat out* every dance⟩

sit·ter \ˈsi-tər\ *n* (14c) : one that sits: as **a** : a person who sits for a portrait or a bust **b** : a person who babysits

[1]**sitting** *n* (13c) **1 a** : the act of one that sits **b** : a single occasion of continuous sitting (as for a portrait or meal) **2 a** : a brooding over eggs for hatching **b** : SETTING 6 **3** : SESSION ⟨a ~ of the legislature⟩

[2]**sitting** *adj* (15c) **1** : that is setting ⟨a ~ hen⟩ **2** : occupying a judicial, legislative, or executive seat : being in office **3** : easily hit or played ⟨a ~ target⟩ **4 a** : used in or for sitting ⟨a ~ position⟩ **b** : performed while sitting ⟨a ~ shot⟩

sitting duck *n* (1942) : an easy or defenseless target

sitting room *n* (1771) : LIVING ROOM 1

[1]**sit·u·ate** \ˈsi-chə-wət, -ˌwāt; ˈsich-wət\ *adj* [ME, fr. LL *situatus,* fr. L *situs*] (15c) : having a site : LOCATED

[2]**sit·u·ate** \ˈsi-chə-ˌwāt\ *vt* **-at·ed; -at·ing** (ca. 1532) : to place in a site, situation, context, or category : LOCATE

situated *adj* (15c) **1** : having a site, situation, or location : LOCATED **2** : provided with money or possessions ⟨comfortably ~⟩

sit·u·a·tion \ˌsi-chə-ˈwā-shən\ *n* (15c) **1 a** : the way in which something is placed in relation to its surroundings **b** : SITE **c** *archaic* : LOCALITY **2** *archaic* : state of health **3 a** : position or place of employment : POST, JOB **b** : position in life : STATUS **4** : position with respect to conditions and circumstances **5 a** : relative position or combination of circumstances at a certain moment **b** : a critical, trying, or unusual state of affairs : PROBLEM **c** : a particular or striking complex of affairs at a stage in the action of a narrative or drama

sit·u·a·tion·al \-shnəl, -shə-nᵊl\ *adj* (1903) **1** : of, relating to, or appropriate to a situation **2** : of or relating to situation ethics — **sit·u·a·tion·al·ly** *adv*

situation comedy *n* (1946) : a radio or television comedy series that involves a continuing cast of characters in a succession of episodes

situation ethics *n* (1955) : a system of ethics by which acts are judged within their contexts instead of by categorical principles — called also *situational ethics*

sit–up \ˈsit-ˌəp\ *n* (1938) : a conditioning exercise performed from a supine position by raising the torso to a sitting position and returning to the original position without using the arms or lifting the feet

sit up *vi* (13c) **1 a** : to rise from a lying to a sitting position **b** : to sit with the back erect **2** : to show interest, alertness, or surprise ⟨*sit up* and take notice⟩ **3** : to stay up after the usual time for going to bed

si·tus \ˈsī-təs\ *n* [L — more at SITE] (1701) : the place where something exists or originates; *specif* : the place where something (as a right) is held to be located in law

sitz bath \ˈsits-\ *n* [part trans. of G *Sitzbad,* fr. *Sitz* act of sitting + *Bad* bath] (1847) : a tub in which one bathes in a sitting posture; *also* : a bath so taken esp. therapeutically

sitz·mark \ˈsits-ˌmärk, ˈzits-\ *n* [prob. fr. G *sitzen* to sit + E [1]*mark* (impression)] (1935) : a depression left in the snow by a skier falling backward

SIV \ˌes-ˌī-ˈvē\ *n* (1987) : a lentivirus (species *Simian immunodeficiency virus*) that causes a disease in monkeys similar to AIDS and that is closely related to HIV-2

Siva *var of* SHIVA

Si·van \ˈsi-vən\ *n* [Heb *Sīwān*] (1535) : the ninth month of the civil year or the third month of the ecclesiastical year in the Jewish calendar — see MONTH table

Si·wash \ˈsī-ˌwȯsh, -ˌwäsh\ *n* [*Siwash,* fictional college in stories by George Fitch †1915 Am. author] (1936) : a small usu. inland college that is notably provincial in outlook ⟨cheer for dear old *Siwash*⟩

six \ˈsiks\ *n* [ME, fr. *six,* adj., fr. OE *siex;* akin to OHG *sehs* six, L *sex,* Gk *hex*] (bef. 12c) **1** — see NUMBER table **2** : the sixth in a set or series **3** : something having six units or members: as **a** : an ice-hockey team **b** : a 6-cylinder engine or automobile — **six** *adj* — **six** *pron, pl in constr* — **at sixes and sevens** : in a state of disorder

six·fold \ˈsiks-ˌfōld, -ˈfōld\ *adj* (bef. 12c) **1** : having six units or members **2** : being six times as great or as many — **six·fold** \-ˈfōld\ *adv*

six–gun \ˈsiks-ˌgən\ *n* (1912) : a 6-chambered revolver

six·mo \ˈsiks-(ˌ)mō\ *n, pl* **sixmos** (1924) : the size of a piece of paper cut six from a sheet; *also* : a book, a page, or paper of this size

six–o–six *or* **606** \ˌsiks-ˌō-ˈsiks\ *n* [fr. its having been the 606th compound tested and introduced by Paul Ehrlich †1915] (1910) : ARSPHENAMINE

six–pack \ˈsiks-ˌpak\ *n* (1952) **1** : six bottles or cans (as of beer) packaged and purchased as a unit **2** : the contents of a six-pack

six·pence \ˈsiks-pən(t)s, *US also* -ˌpen(t)s\ *n* (14c) **1** : a former British monetary unit equal to six pennies **2** *pl* **sixpence** *or* **six·penc·es** : a coin worth sixpence

six·pen·ny \ˈsiks-pə-nē, *US also* -ˌpe-nē\ *adj* (15c) : costing or worth sixpence

sixpenny bit *n* (1861) : SIXPENCE 2

six·pen·ny nail \ˈsiks-ˌpe-nē-\ *n* (15c) : a nail about two inches long

six–shoot·er \ˈsik(s)-ˌshü-tər\ *n* (1844) : SIX-GUN

six·teen \ˌsik-ˈstēn, ˈsiks-ˌtēn\ *n* [ME *sixtene,* fr. OE *sixtӯne,* adj., fr. *six* six + *-tӯne* (akin to OE *tīen* ten) — more at TEN] (bef. 12c) — see NUMBER table — **sixteen** *adj* — **sixteen** *pron, pl in constr* — **six·teenth** \-ˈstēn(t)th, -ˌtēn(t)th\ *adj or n*

six·teen·mo \sik-ˈstēn-(ˌ)mō\ *n, pl* **-mos** (1847) : the size of a piece of paper cut 16 from a sheet; *also* : a book, a page, or paper of this size

sixteenth note *n* (ca. 1861) : a musical note with the time value of 1/16 of a whole note — see NOTE illustration

sixteenth rest *n* (ca. 1890) : a musical rest corresponding in time value to a sixteenth note

sixth \ˈsiks(t)th, ˈsiks(t)\ *n, pl* **sixths** \ˈsiks(ts), ˈsiks(t)ths\ (12c) **1** — see NUMBER table **2 a** : a musical interval embracing six diatonic degrees **b** : a tone at this interval; *specif* : SUBMEDIANT **c** : the harmonic combination of two tones a sixth apart — **sixth** *adj or adv* — **sixth·ly** \ˈsiksth-lē, ˈsikst-\ *adv*

sixth chord *n* (ca. 1903) : a musical chord consisting of a tone with its third and its sixth above and usu. being the first inversion of a triad

sixth sense *n* (1761) : a power of perception like but not one of the five senses : a keen intuitive power

Sixtine *var of* SISTINE

six·ty \ˈsiks-tē\ *n, pl* **sixties** [ME, fr. *sixty,* adj., fr. OE *siextig,* n., group of sixty, fr. *siex* six + *-tig* group of ten; akin to OE *tīen* ten] (14c) **1** — see NUMBER table **2** *pl* : the numbers 60 to 69; *specif* : the years 60 to 69 in a lifetime or century — **six·ti·eth** \ˈsiks-tē-əth\ *adj or n* — **sixty** *adj* — **sixty** *pron, pl in constr* — **six·ty·ish** \ˈsiks-tē-ish\ *adj*

sixty–fourth note \ˌsiks-tē-ˈfȯrth-\ *n* (ca. 1890) : a musical note with the time value of 1/64 of a whole note — see NOTE illustration

sixty–fourth rest *n* (ca. 1903) : a musical rest corresponding in time value to a sixty-fourth note

six·ty–nine \ˌsiks-tē-ˈnīn\ *n* (1609) **1** — see NUMBER table **2** : mutual cunnilingus and fellatio : mutual fellatio : mutual cunnilingus

siz·able *or* **size·able** \ˈsī-zə-bəl\ *adj* (1613) : fairly large : CONSIDERABLE ⟨a ~ donation⟩ — **siz·able·ness** *n* — **siz·ably** \-blē\ *adv*

siz·ar *also* **siz·er** \ˈsī-zər\ *n* [*sizar* alter. of *sizer,* fr. [1]*size*] (1588) : a student (as in the university of Cambridge) who receives an allowance toward college expenses and who orig. acted as a servant to other students in return for this allowance

[1]**size** \ˈsīz\ *n* [ME *sise* assize, fr. AF, short for *assise* — more at ASSIZE] (13c) **1** *dial Brit* : ASSIZE 2a — usu. used in pl. **2** *obs* : a fixed portion of food or drink **3 a** : physical magnitude, extent, or bulk : relative or proportionate dimensions **b** : relative aggregate amount or number **c** : considerable proportions : BIGNESS **4** : one of a series of graduated measures esp. of manufactured articles (as of clothing) conventionally identified by numbers or letters ⟨a ~ seven hat⟩ **5** : character, quality, or status of a person or thing esp. with reference to importance, relative merit, or correspondence to needs ⟨try this idea on for ~⟩ **6** : actual state of affairs ⟨that's about the ~ of it⟩

[2]**size** *vb* **sized; siz·ing** *vt* (1609) **1** : to make a particular size : bring to proper or suitable size **2** : to arrange, grade, or classify according to size or bulk ~ *vi* : to equal in size or other particular characteristic : COMPARE — usu. used with *up* and often with *to* or *with*

[3]**size** \ˈsīz, ˌsīz\ *adj* (1848) : SIZED — usu. used in combination

[4]**size** \ˈsīz\ *n* [ME *sise*] (15c) : any of various glutinous materials (as preparations of glue, flour, varnish, or resins) used for filling the pores in surfaces (as of paper, textiles, leather, or plaster) or for applying color or metal leaf (as to book edges or covers)

[5]**size** *vt* **sized; siz·ing** (1667) : to cover, stiffen, or glaze with or as if with size

sized \ˈsīzd, ˌsīzd\ *adj* (1582) **1** : having a specified size or bulk — usu. used in combination ⟨a small-*sized* house⟩ **2** : arranged or adjusted according to size

size up *vt* (1884) : to form a judgment of ⟨*size up* the situation⟩

sizing *n* (1825) : [4]SIZE

[1]**siz·zle** \ˈsi-zəl\ *vb* **siz·zled; siz·zling** \ˈsi-zə-liŋ, ˈsiz-liŋ\ [perh. freq. of *siss* to hiss] *vt* (1603) : to burn up or sear with or as if with a hissing sound ~ *vi* **1** : to make a hissing sound in or as if in burning or frying **2** : to seethe with deep anger or resentment

[2]**sizzle** *n* (ca. 1823) **1** : a hissing sound (as of something frying over a fire) **2** : PIZZAZZ, EXCITEMENT

siz·zler \ˈsi-zə-lər, ˈsiz-lər\ *n* (1848) : one that sizzles; *esp* : SCORCHER

SJ *abbr* Society of Jesus

SK *abbr* Saskatchewan

ska \ˈskä\ *n* [perh. alter. of [3]*scat*] (1964) : popular music of Jamaican origin that combines elements of traditional Caribbean rhythms and jazz

skag *var of* SCAG

skald *or* **scald** \ˈskȯld, ˈskäld\ *n* [ON *skāld*] (1780) : an ancient Scandinavian poet; *broadly* : BARD — **skald·ic** \ˈskȯl-dik, ˈskäl-\ *adj*

[1]**skank** \ˈskaŋk\ *n* [origin unknown] (1964) *slang* : a person and esp. a woman of low or sleazy character

[2]**skank** *n* [Jamaican E] (1964) : a rhythmic dance performed by swinging the arms while bending the knees esp. to reggae or ska; *also* : the music for this dance

[3]**skank** *vi* (1976) : to dance the skank

[4]**skank** *vt* [prob. alter. of [2]*shank*] (1990) *slang* : to bungle (a stroke) in golf

skanky \ˈskaŋ-kē\ *adj* **skank·i·er; -est** [[1]*skank*] (1982) **1** *slang* : repugnantly filthy or squalid **2** *slang* : of low or sleazy character

skat \ˈskät, ˈskat\ *n* [G, modif. of It *scarto* discard, fr. *scartare* to discard, fr. *s-* (fr. L *ex-*) + *carta* card — more at CARD] (1864) **1** : a three-handed card game played with 32 cards in which players bid for the privilege of attempting any of several contracts **2** : a widow of two cards in skat that may be used by the winner of the bid

[1]**skate** \ˈskāt\ *n, pl* **skates** *also* **skate** [ME *scate,* fr. ON *skata*] (14c) : any of a family (Rajidae, esp. genus *Raja*) of rays with the pectoral fins greatly developed giving the fish a flat diamond shape

[2]**skate** *n* [modif. of D *schaats,* fr. MD *schaetse* stilt, fr. OF dial. (Flanders, Hainaut) **escace,* prob. of Gmc origin; akin to OE *sceacan* to shake — more at SHAKE] (1684) **1 a :** a metal frame that can be fitted to the sole of a shoe and to which is attached a runner or a set of wheels for gliding over ice or a surface other than ice **b :** ROLLER SKATE; *esp* **:** IN-LINE SKATE **c :** ICE SKATE **2 :** a period of skating

[3]**skate** *vb* **skat·ed; skat·ing** *vi* (1696) **1 :** to glide along on skates propelled by the alternate action of the legs **2 :** to slip or glide as if on skates **3 :** to proceed in a superficial or blithe manner ~ *vt* **:** to go along or through by skating

[4]**skate** *n* [prob. alter. of E dial. *skite* an offensive person] (1894) **1 :** a thin awkward-looking or decrepit horse **:** NAG **2 :** FELLOW 4c

[1]**skate·board** \ˈskāt-ˌbȯrd\ *n* (1959) **:** a short board mounted on small wheels that is used for coasting and for performing athletic stunts

[2]**skateboard** *vi* (1964) **:** to ride or perform stunts on a skateboard — **skate·board·er** \-ˌbȯr-dər\ *n*

skate park *n* (1970) **:** an outdoor area having structures and surfaces for roller-skating and skateboarding

skat·er \ˈskā-tər\ *n* (1700) **1 :** one that skates **2 :** WATER STRIDER

skating *n* (1723) **:** the act, art, or sport of gliding on skates

ska·tole \ˈska-ˌtōl, ˈskā-\ *also* **ska·tol** \-ˌtȯl, -ˌtōl\ *n* [ISV, fr. Gk *skat-, skōr* excrement — more at SCATOLOGY] (1879) **:** a foul-smelling compound C_9H_9N found in the intestines and feces, in civet, and in several plants or made synthetically and used in perfumes as a fixative

[1]**skean** *or* **skeane** *var of* SKEIN

[2]**skean** *or* **skene** \ˈskē(-ə)n\ *n* [ME *skene,* fr. Ir *scian* & ScGael *sgian,* fr. OIr *scían;* prob. akin to Skt *chyati* he cuts off — more at SCIENCE] (15c) **:** DAGGER, DIRK

ske·dad·dle \ski-ˈda-dᵊl\ *vi* **ske·dad·dled; ske·dad·dling** \-ˈdad-liŋ, -ˈda-dᵊl-iŋ\ [prob. alter. of Brit. dial. *scaddle* to run off in a fright, fr. *scaddle,* adj., wild, timid, skittish, fr. ME *scathel, skadylle* harmful, fierce, wild, of Scand origin; akin to ON *skathi* harm — more at SCATHE] (1860) **:** RUN AWAY, SCRAM; *esp* **:** to flee in a panic — **ske·dad·dler** \-ˈdad-lər, -ˈda-dᵊl-ər\ *n*

skeet \ˈskēt\ *n* [perh. fr. Norw *skyte* to shoot] (1926) **:** trapshooting in which clay pigeons are thrown in such a way as to simulate the angles of flight of birds

[1]**skee·ter** \ˈskē-tər\ *n* [by shortening & alter.] (1839) **1 :** MOSQUITO **2 :** an iceboat 16 feet (5 meters) or more in length having a single sail

[2]**skeet·er** \ˈskē-tər\ *n* (1926) **:** a skeet shooter

skee·vy \ˈskē-vē\ *adj* **skeev·i·er; -est** [It *schifo* disgust & *schifare* to sicken, disgust] (1976) *slang* **:** morally or physically repulsive **:** DISGUSTING, SLEAZY

skeg \ˈskeg\ *also* **skag** \ˈskag\ *n* [ME *skegge,* fr. ON *skegg* cutwater, lit., beard — more at SHAG] (13c) **1 :** the stern of the keel of a ship near the sternpost; *esp* **:** the part connecting the keel with the bottom of the rudderpost in a single-screw ship **2 :** a fin situated on the rear bottom of a surfboard that is used for steering and stability

[1]**skein** \ˈskān\ *n* [ME *skeyne,* fr. MF (Picard) *escagne,* prob. fr. VL **scamnia,* fr. **scamniare* to wind yarn, fr. **scamnium* rack for holding bobbins, fr. L *scamnum* bench, stool — more at SHAMBLES] (14c) **1** *also* **skean** *or* **skeane** \ˈskān\ **:** a loosely coiled length of yarn or thread wound on a reel **2 :** something suggesting the twists or coils of a skein **:** TANGLE **3 :** a flock of wildfowl (as geese or ducks) in flight

[2]**skein** *vt* (ca. 1775) **:** to wind into skeins ⟨~ yarn⟩

skel·e·tal \ˈske-lə-tᵊl\ *adj* (1854) **:** of, relating to, forming, attached to, or resembling a skeleton — **skel·e·tal·ly** \-tᵊl-ē\ *adv*

skeletal muscle *n* (1877) **:** striated muscle that is usu. attached to the skeleton and is usu. under voluntary control

[1]**skel·e·ton** \ˈske-lə-tən\ *n* [NL, fr. Gk, neut. of *skeletos* dried up; akin to Gk *skellein* to dry up, *sklēros* hard and perh. to OE *sceald* shallow] (1578) **1 :** a usu. rigid supportive or protective structure or framework of an organism; *esp* **:** the bony or more or less cartilaginous framework supporting the soft tissues and protecting the internal organs of a vertebrate **2 :** something reduced to its minimum form or essential parts **3 :** an emaciated person or animal **4 a :** something forming a structural framework **b :** the straight or branched chain or ring of atoms that forms the basic structure of an organic molecule **5 :** something shameful and kept secret (as in a family) — often used in the phrase *skeleton in the closet* **6 :** a small sled that is ridden in a prone position and used esp. in competition; *also* **:** the competition itself — **skel·e·ton·ic** \ˌske-lə-ˈtä-nik\ *adj*

[2]**skeleton** *adj* (1778) **:** of, consisting of, or resembling a skeleton

skel·e·ton·ise *Brit var of* SKELETONIZE

skel·e·ton·ize \-ˌīz\ *vt* **-ized; -iz·ing** (1644) **:** to produce in or reduce to skeleton form ⟨~ a leaf⟩

skel·e·ton·iz·er \-ˌī-zər\ *n* (ca. 1891) **:** any of various lepidopteran larvae that eat the parenchyma of leaves reducing them to a skeleton of veins

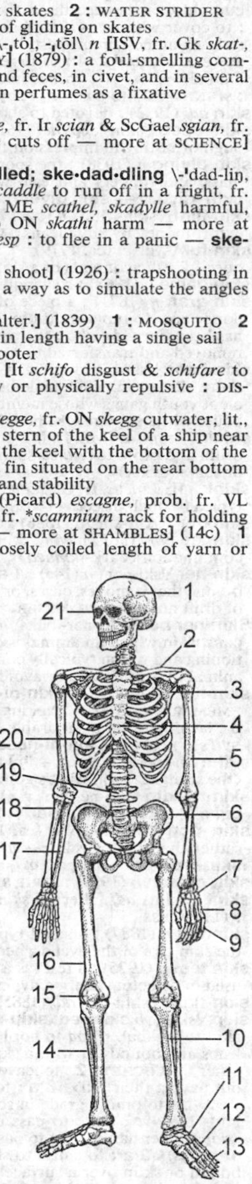

skeleton 1: *1* skull, *2* clavicle, *3* scapula, *4* sternum, *5* humerus, *6* pelvis, *7* carpus, *8* metacarpal bones, *9* phalanges (fingers), *10* tibia, *11* tarsus, *12* metatarsal bones, *13* phalanges (toes), *14* fibula, *15* patella, *16* femur, *17* ulna, *18* radius, *19* spinal column, *20* rib, *21* orbit

skeleton key *n* (1810) **:** a key with a large part of the bit filed away to enable it to open low quality locks as a master key

skel·ter \ˈskel-tər\ *vi* **skel·tered; skel·ter·ing** \-t(ə-)riŋ\ [fr. *-skelter* (in *helter-skelter*)] (1852) **:** SCURRY

Skel·ton·ics \skel-ˈtä-niks\ *n pl* [John *Skelton*] (1898) **:** short verses of an irregular meter and usu. with rhymed couplets

skep \ˈskep\ *n* [ME *skeppe* basket, beehive, fr. OE *sceppe* basket, fr. ON *skeppa* bushel; akin to OHG *sceffil* bushel, *scaf* tub] (15c) **:** HIVE 1; *esp* **:** a domed hive made of twisted straw

skep·sis \ˈskep-səs\ *n* [NL, fr. Gk *skepsis* examination, doubt, skeptical philosophy, fr. *skeptesthai*] (ca. 1864) **:** philosophic doubt as to the objective reality of phenomena; *broadly* **:** a skeptical outlook or attitude

skep·tic \ˈskep-tik\ *n* [L or Gk; L *scepticus,* fr. Gk *skeptikos,* fr. *skeptikos* thoughtful, fr. *skeptesthai* to look, consider — more at SPY] (1587) **1 :** an adherent or advocate of skepticism **2 :** a person disposed to skepticism esp. regarding religion or religious principles

skep·ti·cal \-ti-kəl\ *adj* (1639) **:** relating to, characteristic of, or marked by skepticism ⟨a ~ listener⟩ — **skep·ti·cal·ly** \-k(ə-)lē\ *adv*

skep·ti·cism \ˈskep-tə-ˌsi-zəm\ *n* (1646) **1 :** an attitude of doubt or a disposition to incredulity either in general or toward a particular object **2 a :** the doctrine that true knowledge or knowledge in a particular area is uncertain **b :** the method of suspended judgment, systematic doubt, or criticism characteristic of skeptics **3 :** doubt concerning basic religious principles (as immortality, providence, and revelation) ***syn*** see UNCERTAINTY

sker·ry \ˈsker-ē\ *n, pl* **skerries** [Sc (Shetland and Orkney islands), ultim. fr. ON *skerj-, sker* rocky islet — more at SCAR] (1612) **:** a rocky isle **:** REEF

[1]**sketch** \ˈskech\ *n* [D *schets,* fr. It *schizzo,* lit., splash, fr. *schizzare* to splash, of imit. origin] (1668) **1 a :** a rough drawing representing the chief features of an object or scene and often made as a preliminary study **b :** a tentative draft (as for a literary work) **2 :** a brief description (as of a person) or outline **3 a :** a short literary composition somewhat resembling the short story and the essay but intentionally slight in treatment, discursive in style, and familiar in tone **b :** a short instrumental composition usu. for piano **c :** a slight theatrical piece having a single scene; *esp* **:** a comic variety act

[2]**sketch** *vt* (1694) **:** to make a sketch, rough draft, or outline of ~ *vi* **:** to draw or paint a sketch — **sketch·er** *n*

sketch·book \ˈskech-ˌbu̇k\ *n* (1820) **:** a book of or for sketches

sketchy \ˈske-chē\ *adj* **sketch·i·er; -est** (1805) **1 :** of the nature of a sketch **:** roughly outlined **2 :** wanting in completeness, clearness, or substance **:** SLIGHT, SUPERFICIAL ⟨the details are ~⟩ **3 :** QUESTIONABLE, IFFY ⟨got into a ~ situation⟩ ⟨a ~ character⟩ — **sketch·i·ly** \ˈske-chə-lē\ *adv* — **sketch·i·ness** \ˈske-chē-nəs\ *n*

[1]**skew** \ˈskyü\ *vb* [ME, to escape, run obliquely, fr. AF **eskiuer, eschiver* to escape, avoid — more at ESCHEW] *vi* (15c) **1 :** to take an oblique course **2 :** to look askance ~ *vt* **1 :** to make, set, or cut on the skew **2 :** to distort esp. from a true value or symmetrical form ⟨~*ed* data⟩

[2]**skew** *adj* (1609) **1 :** set, placed, or running obliquely **:** SLANTING **2 :** more developed on one side or in one direction than another **:** not symmetrical

[3]**skew** *n* (1688) **:** a deviation from a straight line **:** SLANT

skew·back \ˈskyü-ˌbak\ *n* (1703) **:** a course of masonry, a stone, or an iron plate having an inclined face against which the voussoirs of an arch abut

[1]**skew·bald** \-ˌbȯld\ *adj* [*skewed* (skewbald) + *bald*] (1654) *of an animal* **:** marked with patches of white and any other color but black

[2]**skewbald** *n* (1863) **:** a skewbald horse

skew curve *n* (ca. 1889) **:** a curve in three-dimensional space that does not lie in a single plane

skew distribution *n* (ca. 1931) **:** an unsymmetrical frequency distribution having the mode at a different value from the mean

[1]**skew·er** \ˈskyü-ər, ˈskyu̇r\ *n* [ME *skeuier*] (15c) **1 :** a pin of wood or metal for fastening meat to keep it in form while roasting or to hold small pieces of meat or vegetables for broiling **2 :** any of various things shaped or used like a meat skewer

[2]**skewer** *vt* (1701) **1 :** to fasten or pierce with or as if with a skewer **2 :** to criticize or ridicule sharply and effectively

skew lines *n pl* (1952) **:** straight lines that do not intersect and are not in the same plane

skew·ness \ˈskyü-nəs\ *n* (1894) **:** lack of straightness or symmetry **:** DISTORTION; *esp* **:** lack of symmetry in a frequency distribution

[1]**ski** \ˈskē, *Brit sometimes* ˈshē\ *n, pl* **skis** *also* **ski** [Norw, fr. ON *skīth* stick of wood, ski; akin to OE *scīd* board, *scēadan* to divide — more at SHED] (1755) **1 a :** one of a pair of narrow strips of wood, metal, or plastic curving upward in front that are used esp. for gliding over snow **b :** WATER SKI **2 :** a piece of material that resembles a ski and is used as a runner on a vehicle

[2]**ski** *vb* **skied** \ˈskēd, ˈshēd\; **ski·ing** *vi* (ca. 1890) **:** to glide on skis in travel or as a sport ~ *vt* **:** to travel or pass over on skis — **ski·able** \ˈskē-ə-bəl\ *adj* — **ski·er** *n*

skia·gram \ˈskī-ə-ˌgram\ *n* [ISV, fr. Gk *skia* shadow + ISV *-gram* — more at SCENE] (1801) **1 :** a figure formed by shading in the outline of a shadow **2 :** RADIOGRAPH

ski boot *n* (1907) **:** a rigid padded shoe that extends just above the ankle, is secured to the foot, and is locked into position in a ski binding

ski cross *n* [[2]*ski* + *-cross* (as in *motocross*)] (2006) **:** a skiing race in which competitors race directly against each other down a sloped course that features jumps and banked curves

[1]**skid** \ˈskid\ *n* [perh. of Scand origin; akin to ON *skīth* stick of wood — more at SKI] (ca. 1610) **1 :** one of a group of objects (as planks or logs) used to support or elevate a structure or object **2 :** a wooden fender hung over a ship's side to protect it in handling cargo **3 :** a usu. iron shoe or clog attached to a chain and placed under a wheel to prevent its turning when descending a steep hill **:** DRAG **4 :** a timber, bar, rail, pole, or log used in pairs or sets to form a slideway (as for an incline

from a truck to the sidewalk) **5 :** the act of skidding : SLIP, SIDESLIP **6 :** a runner used as a member of the landing gear of an airplane or helicopter **7 a** *pl* : a route to defeat or downfall ⟨on the ~*s*⟩ ⟨his career hit the ~*s*⟩ **b :** a losing streak ⟨a 5-game ~⟩ **8 :** a low platform mounted (as on wheels) on which material is set for handling and moving; *also* : PALLET 3 — **skidproof** *adj*

2**skid** *vb* **skid·ded; skid·ding** *vt* (1674) **1 :** to apply a brake or skid to : slow or halt by a skid **2 a :** to haul (as logs) by dragging ⟨cutting and *skidding* firewood⟩ **b :** to haul along, slide, hoist, or store on skids ~ *vi* **1 :** to slide without rotating (as a wheel held from turning while a vehicle moves onward) **2 a :** to fail to grip the roadway; *esp* : to slip sideways on the road **b** *of an airplane* : to slide sideways away from the center of curvature when turning **c :** SLIDE, SLIP **3 :** to fall rapidly, steeply, or far ⟨sales *skidded* last year⟩

skid·der \ˈski-dər\ *n* (1870) **1 :** one that skids or uses a skid **2 :** a tractor used esp. for hauling logs

skid·doo *or* **ski·doo** \ski-ˈdü, skē-\ *vi* [prob. alter. of *skedaddle*] (1903) : to go away : DEPART

skid·dy \ˈski-dē\ *adj* **skid·di·er; -est** (1902) : likely to skid or cause skidding ⟨a wet ~ road⟩

skid road *n* (1880) **1 :** a road along which logs are skidded **2 a** *West* : the part of a town frequented by loggers **b :** SKID ROW

skid row \-ˈrō\ *n* [alter. of *skid road*] (ca. 1931) : a district of cheap saloons and flophouses frequented by vagrants and alcoholics

skiff \ˈskif\ *n* [ME *skif,* fr. MF or OIt; MF *esquif,* fr. OIt *schifo,* of Gmc origin; akin to OE *scip* ship] (15c) : any of various small boats; *esp* : a flat-bottomed rowboat

skif·fle \ˈski-fəl\ *n* [origin unknown] (1926) : American jazz or folk music played entirely or in part on nonstandard instruments (as jugs, washboards, or Jew's harps); *also* : a derivative form of music formerly popular in Great Britain featuring vocals with a simple instrumental accompaniment

skiing *n* (1893) : the art or sport of sliding and jumping on skis

ski·jor·ing \ˈskē-ˌjȯr-iŋ, (ˌ)skē-ˈ\ *n* [modif. of Norw *skikjøring,* fr. *ski* + *kjøring* driving] (1910) : a winter sport in which a person wearing skis is drawn over snow or ice (as by a horse or vehicle)

ski jump *n* (1907) : a jump made by a person wearing skis; *also* : a course or track esp. prepared for such jumping — **ski jump** *vi* — **ski jumper** *n*

skil·ful *chiefly Brit var of* SKILLFUL

ski lift *n* (1939) : a motor-driven conveyor consisting usu. of a series of bars or seats suspended from an overhead moving cable and used for transporting skiers or sightseers up a long slope

1**skill** \ˈskil\ *vi* [ME *skilen,* fr. ON *skilja* to separate, divide; akin to ON *skil* distinction] (13c) *archaic* : to make a difference : MATTER, AVAIL

2**skill** *n* [ME *skil,* fr. ON, distinction, knowledge; prob. akin to OE *scylian* to separate, *sciell* shell — more at SHELL] (13c) **1** *obs* : CAUSE, REASON **2 a :** the ability to use one's knowledge effectively and readily in execution or performance **b :** dexterity or coordination esp. in the execution of learned physical tasks **3 :** a learned power of doing something competently : a developed aptitude or ability ⟨language ~*s*⟩ ***syn*** see ART — **skill–less** *or* **skil·less** \ˈskil-ləs\ *adj* — **skill–less·ness** *or* **skil·less·ness** *n*

skilled \ˈskild\ *adj* (1552) **1 :** having acquired mastery of or skill in something (as a technique or a trade) ⟨~ in the art of negotiation⟩ **2 :** of, relating to, or requiring workers or labor with skill and training in a particular occupation, craft, or trade ***syn*** see PROFICIENT

skil·let \ˈski-lət\ *n* [ME *skelet,* prob. fr. AF **escuelete,* dim. of *escuelle, eskil* bowl — more at SCULLERY] (15c) **1** *chiefly Brit* : a small kettle or pot usu. having three or four often long feet and used for cooking on the hearth **2 :** FRYING PAN

skill·ful \ˈskil-fəl\ *adj* (14c) **1 :** possessed of or displaying skill : EXPERT ⟨a ~ chef⟩ **2 :** accomplished with skill ⟨a ~ treatment⟩ ***syn*** see PROFICIENT — **skill·ful·ly** \-fə-lē\ *adv* — **skill·ful·ness** *n*

1**skim** \ˈskim\ *vb* **skimmed; skim·ming** [ME *skymmen, skemen,* prob. fr. AF *escumer,* fr. *escume* foam, scum, of Gmc origin; akin to MD *schum* scum — more at SCUM] *vt* (14c) **1 a :** to clear (a liquid) of scum or floating substance ⟨~ boiling syrup⟩ **b :** to remove (as film or scum) from the surface of a liquid **c :** to remove cream from by skimming **d :** to remove the best or most easily obtainable contents from **2 :** to read, study, or examine superficially and rapidly; *esp* : to glance through (as a book) for the chief ideas or the plot **3 :** to throw in a gliding path; *esp* : to throw so as to ricochet along the surface of water **4 :** to cover with or as if with a film, scum, or coat **5 :** to pass swiftly or lightly over **6 a :** to remove or conceal (as a portion of casino profits) to avoid payment of taxes **b :** EMBEZZLE ⟨*skimming* money from employee pension plans⟩ ~ *vi* **1 a :** to pass lightly or hastily : glide or skip along, above, or near a surface **b :** to give a cursory glance, consideration, or reading **2 :** to become coated with a thin layer of film or scum **3 :** to put on a finishing coat of plaster **4 :** to embezzle money

2**skim** *n* (14c) **1 :** a thin layer, coating, or film **2 :** the act of skimming **3 :** something skimmed; *specif* : SKIM MILK

3**skim** *adj* (1794) **1 :** having the cream removed by skimming **2 :** made of skim milk ⟨~ cheese⟩

ski mask *n* (1966) : a knit fabric mask that covers the head, has openings for the eyes, mouth, and sometimes the nose, and is worn esp. by skiers for protection from the cold

skim·ble–skam·ble \ˌskim-bəl-ˈskam-bəl\ *adj* [redupl. of E dial. *scamble* to stumble along] (1596) : rambling and confused : SENSELESS

skim·mer \ˈski-mər\ *n* (14c) **1 :** one that skims; *specif* : a flat perforated scoop or spoon used for skimming **2 :** any of a small genus (*Rynchops*) of long-winged marine birds that have the lower mandible longer than the upper **3 :** a usu. straw flat-crowned hat with a wide straight brim **4 :** a fitted sleeveless dress with a usu. flaring skirt

skim milk *n* (1596) : milk from which the cream has been taken — called also *skimmed milk*

skimming *n* (15c) : that which is skimmed from a liquid

ski·mo·bile \ˈskē-mō-ˌbēl\ *n* (1944) : SNOWMOBILE

1**skimp** \ˈskimp\ *adj* [perh. alter. of *scrimp*] (1775) : SKIMPY

2**skimp** *vt* (ca. 1879) : to give insufficient or barely sufficient attention or effort to or funds for ~ *vi* : to save by or as if by skimping

skimpy \ˈskim-pē\ *adj* **skimp·i·er; -est** (1842) : deficient in supply or execution esp. through skimping : SCANTY ***syn*** see MEAGER — **skimp·i·ly** \-pə-lē\ *adv* — **skimp·i·ness** \-pē-nəs\ *n*

1**skin** \ˈskin\ *n, often attrib* [ME, fr. ON *skinn;* akin to OE *scinn* skin, MHG *schint* fruit peel] (13c) **1 a (1) :** the integument of an animal (as a fur-bearing mammal or a bird) separated from the body usu. with its hair or feathers **(2) :** a usu. unmounted specimen of a vertebrate (as in a museum) **b :** the hide or pelt of a game or domestic animal **c (1) :** the pelt of an animal prepared for use as a trimming or in a garment — compare 4HIDE **(2) :** a sheet of parchment or vellum made from a hide **(3) :** BOTTLE 1b **2 a :** the external limiting tissue layer of an animal body; *esp* : the 2-layered covering of a vertebrate body consisting of an outer epidermis and an inner dermis **b :** an outer covering (as a rind or husk) of a fruit or seed **c :** a membranous film or scum (as on boiling milk or drying paint) **3 :** the life or physical well-being of a person ⟨saved his own ~⟩ **4 :** a sheathing or casing forming the outside surface of a structure (as a ship or airplane) — **skin·less** \-ləs\ *adj* — **by the skin of one's teeth :** by a very narrow margin — **under one's skin :** so deeply penetrative as to irritate, stimulate, provoke thought, or otherwise excite — **under the skin :** beneath apparent or surface differences : at heart

2**skin** *vb* **skinned; skin·ning** *vt* (14c) **1 a :** to strip, scrape, or rub off an outer covering (as the skin or rind) of **b :** to strip or peel off **c :** to cut, chip, or damage the surface of ⟨fell and *skinned* my knee⟩ **2 a :** to cover with or as if with skin **b :** to heal over with skin **3 a :** to strip of money or property : FLEECE **b :** to defeat badly **c :** CENSURE, CASTIGATE **4 :** to urge on and direct the course of (as a draft animal) ~ *vi* **1 :** to become covered with or as if with skin **2 a :** SHINNY **b :** to pass or get by with scant room to spare

3**skin** *adj* (1933) : devoted to showing nudes ⟨~ magazines⟩

skin–deep \ˈskin-ˈdēp\ *adj* (1613) **1 :** as deep as the skin **2 :** not thorough or lasting in impression : SUPERFICIAL

skin diving *n* (1938) : the sport of swimming under water with a face mask and flippers and esp. without a portable breathing device — **skin–dive** *vi* — **skin diver** *n*

skin·flint \ˈskin-ˌflint\ *n* (ca. 1700) : a person who would save, gain, or extort money by any means : MISER

skin·ful \-ˌfu̇l\ *n* (ca. 1779) **1 :** a large or satisfying quantity esp. of liquor **2 :** the contents of a skin bottle

skin game *n* (1868) : a swindling game or trick

skin graft *n* (1871) : a piece of skin that is surgically removed from a donor area to replace skin in a defective or denuded area (as one that has been burned); *also* : the procedure by which such a piece of skin is removed and transferred to a new area — **skin grafting** *n*

skin·head \ˈskin-ˌhed\ *n* (ca. 1953) **1 :** a person whose hair is cut very short **2 :** a usu. white male belonging to any of various sometimes violent youth gangs whose members have close-shaven hair and often espouse white-supremacist beliefs

1**skink** \ˈskiŋk\ *vt* [ME, fr. MD *schenken;* akin to OE *scencan* to pour out drink and prob. to *scanca* shank] (15c) *chiefly dial* : to draw, pour out, or serve (drink)

2**skink** *n* [L *scincus,* fr. Gk *skinkos*] (1590) : any of a family (Scincidae) of typically small insectivorous lizards with long tapering bodies

skink·er \ˈskiŋ-kər\ *n* (1586) : one that serves liquor : BARTENDER

skinned *adj* (15c) : having skin esp. of a specified kind — usu. used in combination ⟨dark-*skinned*⟩

skin·ner \ˈski-nər\ *n* (14c) **1 a :** one that deals in skins, pelts, or hides **b :** one that removes, cures, or dresses skins **2 :** SHARPER **3 :** a driver of draft animals : TEAMSTER

Skin·ner box \ˈski-nər-ˌbäks\ *n* [B. F. *Skinner*] (1940) : a laboratory apparatus in which an animal is caged for experiments in operant conditioning and which typically contains a lever that must be pressed by the animal to gain reward or avoid punishment

1**skin·ny** \ˈski-nē\ *adj* **skin·ni·er; -est** (1573) **1 :** resembling skin : MEMBRANOUS **2 a :** lacking sufficient flesh : very thin : EMACIATED **b :** lacking usual or desirable bulk, quantity, qualities, or significance ***syn*** see LEAN — **skin·ni·ness** *n*

2**skinny** *n* [perh. fr. 1*skin* + 4*-y*] (1938) *slang* : inside information : DOPE ⟨the straight ~ on what's going on —John Geary⟩

skin·ny–dip \ˈski-nē-ˌdip\ *vi* (1964) : to swim in the nude — **skinny–dip** *n* — **skin·ny–dip·per** \-ˌdi-pər\ *n*

skin–pop \ˈskin-ˈpäp\ *vi* (ca. 1952) : to inject a drug subcutaneously rather than into a vein ~ *vt* : to inject (a drug) by skin-popping — **skin–pop·per** \-ˌpä-pər\ *n*

skin search *n* (1929) : STRIP SEARCH

skint \ˈskint\ *adj* [alter. of *skinned,* pp. of 2*skin*] (ca. 1925) *chiefly Brit* : PENNILESS

skin tag *n* (1887) : a small typically benign soft pendulous growth on the skin esp. of the eyelids, neck, armpits, or groin

skin test *n* (1925) : a test (as a scratch test) performed on the skin and used in detecting allergic hypersensitivity

skin·tight \ˈskin-ˈtīt\ *adj* (1885) : closely fitted to the figure ⟨~ pants⟩

1**skip** \ˈskip\ *vb* **skipped; skip·ping** [ME *skippen,* perh. of Scand origin; akin to Sw dial. *skopa* to hop] *vi* (14c) **1 a :** to move or proceed with leaps and bounds or with a skip **b :** to bound off one point after another : RICOCHET **2 :** to leave hurriedly or secretly ⟨*skipped* out without paying their bill⟩ **3 a :** to pass over or omit an interval, item, or step **b :** to omit a grade in school in advancing to the next **c :** MISFIRE 1 ~ *vt* **1 a :** to pass over without notice or mention : OMIT ⟨*skipped* her name⟩ **b :** to pass by or leave out (a step in a progression or series) **2 a :** to cause to skip (a grade in school) **b :** to cause to bound or skim over a surface ⟨~ a stone across a pond⟩ **3 :** to leap over lightly and nimbly **4 a :** to depart from quickly and secretly ⟨*skipped* town⟩ **b :** to fail to attend or participate in ⟨~ the tournament⟩ — **skip·pa·ble** \ˈski-pə-bəl\ *adj* — **skip bail :** to jump bail — **skip rope :** to use a jump rope (as for exercise or a game)

2**skip** *n* (15c) **1 a :** a light bounding step **b :** a gait composed of alternating hops and steps **2 :** an act of omission or the thing omitted

3**skip** *n* [short for 2*skipper*] (1830) **1 :** the captain of a side in a game (as curling or lawn bowling) who advises the team as to the play and controls the action **2 :** 2SKIPPER

4**skip** *vt* **skipped; skip·ping** (1900) : to act as skipper of

skip bomb *vt* (1943) **:** to attack by releasing delayed-action bombs from a low-flying airplane so that they skip along a land or water surface and strike a target

skip·jack \ˈskip-ˌjak\ *n, pl* **skipjacks** *or* **skipjack** (1703) **1 :** any of various fishes (as a ladyfish or bluefish) that jump above or are active at the surface of the water; *esp* **:** SKIPJACK TUNA **2 :** a sailboat with vertical sides and a bottom similar to a flat V

skipjack tuna *n* (1950) **:** a relatively small tuna (*Katsuwonus pelamis* syn. *Euthynnus pelamis*) that is bluish above and silvery below with oblique dark stripes on the sides and belly

ski pole *n* (1920) **:** one of a pair of lightweight poles used in skiing that have a handgrip and usu. a wrist strap at one end and an encircling disk set above the point at the other end

[1]**skip·per** \ˈski-pər\ *n* (13c) **1 :** any of various erratically active insects (as a click beetle or a water strider) **2 :** one that skips **3 :** SAURY **4 :** any of a superfamily (Hesperioidea, esp. family Hesperiidae) of lepidopterous insects that visibly differ from the typical butterflies esp. in having stout bodies, smaller wings, and usu. hooked antennae

[2]**skipper** *n* [ME, fr. MD *schipper,* fr. *schip* ship; akin to OE *scip* ship — more at SHIP] (14c) **1 :** the master of a ship; *esp* **:** the master of a fishing, small trading, or pleasure boat **2 :** the captain or first pilot of an airplane **3 :** a person in a position of leadership; *esp* **:** a baseball team's manager

[3]**skipper** *vt* **skip·pered; skip·per·ing** \ˈski-p(ə-)riŋ\ (1893) **1 :** to act as skipper of (as a boat) **2 :** to act as coach of (as a team)

[1]**skirl** \ˈskər(-ə)l, ˈskir(-ə)l\ *vb* [ME (Sc) *skrillen, skirlen* to scream, shriek, of Scand origin; akin to Norw dial. *skræla* to cry aloud; akin to OE *scrallettan* to resound loudly] *vi* (ca. 1665) *of a bagpipe* **:** to emit the high shrill tone of the chanter; *also* **:** to give forth music ~ *vt* **:** to play (music) on the bagpipe

[2]**skirl** *n* (1856) **:** a high shrill sound produced by the chanter of a bagpipe

[1]**skir·mish** \ˈskər-mish\ *n* [ME *skyrmissh,* alter. (influenced by AF *eskermir* to fence (with swords), protect, of Gmc origin; akin to OHG *scirmen* to protect, *scirm* shield) of *skarmuch,* fr. AF *escarmuche,* fr. OIt *scaramuccia* — more at SCREEN] (14c) **1 :** a minor fight in war usu. incidental to larger movements **2 a :** a brisk preliminary verbal conflict **b :** a minor dispute or contest between opposing parties ⟨the debate touched off a ~⟩

[2]**skirmish** *vi* (14c) **1 :** to engage in a skirmish **2 :** to search about (as for supplies) **:** scout around — **skir·mish·er** *n*

skirr \ˈskər, ˈskir\ *vb* [perh. alter. of [3]*scour*] *vi* (ca. 1548) **1 :** to leave hastily **:** FLEE ⟨birds ~*ed* off from the bushes —D. H. Lawrence⟩ **2 :** to run, fly, sail, or move along rapidly ~ *vt* **1 :** to search about in ⟨~ the country round —Shak.⟩ **2 :** to pass rapidly over **:** SKIM

[1]**skirt** \ˈskərt\ *n* [ME, fr. ON *skyrta* shirt, kirtle — more at SHIRT] (14c) **1 a (1) :** a free-hanging part of an outer garment or undergarment extending from the waist down **(2) :** a separate free-hanging outer garment or undergarment usu. worn by women and girls covering some or all of the body from the waist down **b :** either of two usu. leather flaps on a saddle covering the bars on which the stirrups are hung **c :** a cloth facing that hangs from the bottom edge or across the front of a piece of furniture **d :** the lower branches of a tree when near the ground **2 a :** the rim, periphery, or environs of an area **b** *pl* **:** outlying parts (as of a town or city) **3 :** a part or attachment serving as a rim, border, or edging **4** *slang* **:** a girl or woman — **skirt·ed** *adj*

[2]**skirt** *vt* (1602) **1 :** to form or run along the border or edge of **:** BORDER **2 a :** to provide a skirt for **b :** to furnish a border or shield for **3 a :** to go or pass around or about; *specif* **:** to go around or keep away from in order to avoid danger or discovery **b :** to avoid esp. because of difficulty or fear of controversy ⟨~*ed* the issue⟩ **c :** to evade or miss by a narrow margin ⟨having ~*ed* disaster —Edith Wharton⟩ ~ *vi* **:** to be, lie, or move along an edge or border — **skirt·er** *n*

skirt·ing \ˈskər-tiŋ\ *n* (1764) **1 :** something that skirts: as **a :** BORDER, EDGING **b** *chiefly Brit* **:** BASEBOARD — called also *skirting board* **2 :** fabric suitable for skirts

skirt steak *n* (ca. 1909) **:** a boneless strip of beef cut from the plate

ski run *n* (1924) **:** a slope or trail suitable for skiing

skit \ˈskit\ *n* [origin unknown] (ca. 1727) **1 :** a jeering or satirical remark **:** TAUNT **2 a :** a satirical or humorous story or sketch **b (1) :** a brief burlesque or comic sketch included in a dramatic performance (as a revue) **(2) :** a short serious dramatic piece; *esp* **:** one done by amateurs

ski touring *n* (1935) **:** cross-country skiing for pleasure

ski tow *n* (1935) **1 :** a motor-driven conveyor that is used for pulling skiers up a slope and that consists usu. of an endless moving rope which a skier grasps **2 :** SKI LIFT

skit·ter \ˈski-tər\ *vb* [prob. freq. of E dial. (Sc and northern) *skite* to move quickly, prob. fr. ON *skyt-,* stem of *skjōta* to shoot] *vi* (1845) **1 a :** to glide or skip lightly or quickly **b :** to move in or as in a jittery or jerky way ⟨leaves ~*ing* over the sidewalk⟩ **2 :** to twitch the hook of a fishing line through or along the surface of water ~ *vt* **:** to cause to skitter

skit·tery \ˈski-tə-rē\ *adj* (1941) **:** SKITTISH

skit·tish \ˈski-tish\ *adj* [ME, fr. *skit-* (prob. fr. ON *skyt-*) + *-ish*] (15c) **1 a :** lively or frisky in action **:** CAPRICIOUS **b :** VARIABLE, FLUCTUATING **2 :** easily frightened **:** RESTIVE ⟨a ~ horse⟩ **3 a :** COY, BASHFUL **b :** marked by extreme caution **:** WARY ⟨~ investors⟩ — **skit·tish·ly** *adv* — **skit·tish·ness** *n*

skit·tle \ˈski-tᵊl\ *n* [perh. of Scand origin; akin to ON *skutill* harpoon, bolt, Dan *skyttel* shuttle — more at SHUTTLE] (1634) **1** *pl but sing in constr* **:** English ninepins played with a wooden disk or ball **2 :** one of the pins used in skittles

skive \ˈskīv\ *vt* **skived; skiv·ing** [perh. of Scand origin; akin to ON *skīfa* to slice] (ca. 1825) **:** to cut off (as leather or rubber) in thin layers or pieces **:** PARE

skiv·er \ˈskī-vər\ *n* (1800) **1 :** a thin soft leather made of the grain side of a split sheepskin, usu. tanned in sumac and dyed **2 :** one that skives something (as leather)

Skiv·vies \ˈski-vēz\ *trademark* — used for men's underwear

skiv·vy \ˈski-vē\ *n, pl* **skivvies** [origin unknown] (ca. 1902) *Brit* **:** a female domestic servant

ski·wear \ˈskē-ˌwer\ *n* (1961) **:** clothing suitable for wear while skiing

skoal \ˈskōl\ *n* [Dan *skål,* lit., cup; akin to ON *skāl* bowl — more at SCALE] (1600) **:** TOAST, HEALTH — often used interjectionally

skort \ˈskȯrt\ *n* [blend of [1]*skirt* and *shorts*] (1951) **:** a pair of shorts made to resemble a skirt (as with an overlapping front panel)

skosh \ˈskōsh\ *n* [Jp *sukoshi*] (1952) **:** a small amount **:** BIT, SMIDGEN — used adverbially with *a* ⟨just a ~ bit shook —Josiah Bunting⟩

SKU *abbr* stock-keeping unit

skua \ˈskyü-ə\ *n* [NL, fr. Faeroese *skúgvur;* akin to ON *skūfr* tassel, skua, OE *scēaf* sheaf — more at SHEAF] (1678) **:** any of various seabirds (genus *Catharacta*) related to the jaegers: as **a :** GREAT SKUA **b :** a bird (*C. maccormicki*) that resembles but is slightly smaller than the great skua and that breeds in the Antarctic

skul·dug·gery *or* **skull·dug·gery** \ˌskəl-ˈdə-g(ə-)rē, ˈskəl-ˌ\ *n, pl* **-ger·ies** [origin unknown] (1867) **:** underhanded or unscrupulous behavior; *also* **:** a devious device or trick

[1]**skulk** \ˈskəlk\ *vi* [ME, of Scand origin; akin to Norw dial. *skulka* to lie in wait, lurk] (13c) **1 :** to move in a stealthy or furtive manner ⟨~*ed* into her sister's room⟩ **2 a :** to hide or conceal something (as oneself) often out of cowardice or fear or with sinister intent **b** *chiefly Brit* **:** MALINGER ***syn*** see LURK — **skulk·er** *n*

[2]**skulk** *n* (14c) **1 :** one that skulks **2 :** a group of foxes

[1]**skull** \ˈskəl\ *n* [ME *skulle,* of Scand origin; akin to Sw dial. *skulle* skull] (13c) **1 :** the skeleton of the head of a vertebrate forming a bony or cartilaginous case that encloses and protects the brain and chief sense organs and supports the jaws **2 :** the seat of understanding or intelligence **:** MIND — **skulled** \ˈskəld\ *adj*

[2]**skull** *vt* (1945) **1 :** to hit on the head **2 :** to unintentionally hit (a golf ball or shot) with the bottom edge of the clubface

skull and cross·bones \-ˈkrȯs-ˌbōnz\ *n, pl* **skulls and crossbones** (1826) **:** a representation of a human skull over crossbones usu. used as a warning of danger to life

skull·cap \ˈskəl-ˌkap\ *n* (1682) **1 :** a close-fitting cap; *esp* **:** a light brimless cap for indoor wear **2 :** any of various mints (genus *Scutellaria*) having a bell-shaped calyx that when inverted resembles a helmet **3 :** the upper portion of the skull **:** CALVARIUM

skull session *n* (1937) **1 :** a strategy class for an athletic team **2 :** a meeting for consultation, discussion, or the interchange of ideas or information — called also *skull practice*

[1]**skunk** \ˈskəŋk\ *n, pl* **skunks** *also* **skunk** [earlier *squuncke,* fr. a Massachusett reflex of Algonquian **šeka·kwa,* fr. *šek-* urinate + *-a·kw* fox, foxlike animal] (1634) **1 a :** any of various common omnivorous black-and-white New World mammals (esp. genus *Mephitis*) of the weasel family that have a pair of perineal glands from which a secretion of pungent and offensive odor is ejected **b :** the fur of a skunk **2 :** an obnoxious or disliked person

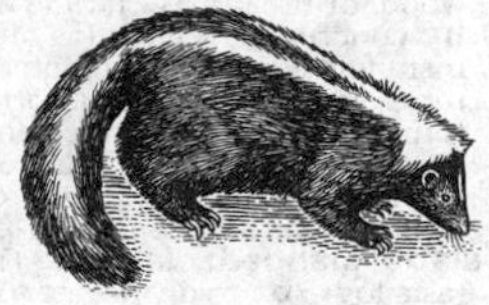
skunk 1a

[2]**skunk** *vt* (1843) **1 a :** DEFEAT **b :** to prevent entirely from scoring or succeeding **:** SHUT OUT **2 :** to fail to pay; *also* **:** CHEAT

skunk·brush \ˈskəŋk-ˌbrəsh\ *n* (1940) **:** SQUAWBUSH

skunk cabbage *n* (1751) **:** either of two No. American perennial herbs of the arum family that occur in shaded wet to swampy areas and have a fetid odor suggestive of a skunk: **a :** one (*Symplocarpus foetidus*) of eastern No. America that sends up in spring a cowl-shaped brownish-purple spathe **b :** one (*Lysichiton americanus*) chiefly of the Pacific coast region that has a large yellow spathe

Skunk Works *service mark* — used for research and development services

skunky \ˈskəŋ-kē\ *adj* **skunk·i·er; -est** (1868) **:** having a rancid smell or taste suggestive of a skunk ⟨~ beer⟩

[1]**sky** \ˈskī\ *n, pl* **skies** [ME, cloud, sky, fr. ON *skȳ* cloud; akin to OE *scēo* cloud] (13c) **1 :** the upper atmosphere or expanse of space that constitutes an apparent great vault or arch over the earth **2 :** HEAVEN 2 **3 a :** weather in the upper atmosphere **b :** CLIMATE ⟨temperate English *skies* —G. G. Coulton⟩

[2]**sky** *vb* **skied** *or* **skyed; sky·ing** *vt* (1802) **1** *chiefly Brit* **:** to throw or toss up **:** FLIP **2 :** to hang (as a painting) above the line of vision **3 :** to hit (a ball) high into the air ~ *vi* **:** to jump high ⟨~ for a rebound⟩

sky blue *n* (1738) **:** a pale to light blue color

sky·borne \ˈskī-ˌbȯrn\ *adj* (1589) **:** AIRBORNE ⟨~ troops⟩

sky·box \-ˌbäks\ *n* (1974) **:** a roofed enclosure of private seats situated high in a sports stadium and typically featuring luxurious amenities

sky·cap \-ˌkap\ *n* [[1]*sky* + *-cap* (as in *redcap*)] (1941) **:** one employed to carry hand luggage at an airport — compare REDCAP

sky·div·ing \-ˌdī-viŋ\ *n* (1957) **:** the sport of jumping from an airplane at a moderate altitude (as 6000 feet) and executing various body maneuvers before pulling the rip cord of a parachute — **sky·dive** \-ˌdīv\ *vi* — **sky·div·er** *n*

Skye terrier \ˈskī-\ *n* [*Skye,* Scotland] (1847) **:** any of a Scottish breed of small short-legged terriers with a long body and long straight coat

sky·ey \ˈskī-ē\ *adj* (1603) **:** of or resembling the sky **:** ETHEREAL

[1]**sky–high** \ˈskī-ˈhī\ *adv* (1818) **1 a :** high into the air **b :** to a high or exorbitant level or degree ⟨lifted my spirit ~ —Elmer Morriss⟩ **2 :** in an enthusiastic manner **3 :** to bits **:** APART ⟨blown ~⟩

[2]**sky–high** *adj* (1945) **1 :** excessively expensive **:** EXORBITANT **2 :** extremely or excessively high ⟨her blood pressure was ~⟩

sky·hook \-ˌhu̇k\ *n* (1915) **:** a hook conceived as being suspended from the sky

sky·jack \ˈskī-ˌjak\ *vt* [[1]*sky* + *-jack* (as in *hijack*)] (1961) **:** to commandeer (an airplane in flight) by the threat of violence — **sky·jack·er** \-ˌja-kər\ *n* — **sky·jack·ing** \-kiŋ\ *n*

[1]**sky·lark** \ˈskī-ˌlärk\ *n* (1686) **1 :** a common largely brown Old World lark (*Alauda arvensis*) noted for its song esp. as uttered in flight **2 :** any of various birds resembling the skylark

[2]skylark *vi* (1809) **1 :** to run up and down the rigging of a ship in sport **2 :** FROLIC, SPORT — **sky·lark·er** *n*

sky·light \ˈskī-ˌlīt\ *n* (1679) **1 :** the diffused and reflected light of the sky **2 :** an opening in a house roof or ship's deck that is covered with translucent or transparent material and that is designed to admit light

sky·light·ed \-ˌlī-təd\ *also* **sky·lit** \-ˌlit\ *adj* (1849) **:** having a skylight

sky·line \-ˌlīn\ *n* (1824) **1 :** the apparent juncture of earth and sky **:** HORIZON **2 :** an outline (as of buildings or a mountain range) against the background of the sky

sky marshal *n* (1968) **:** an armed federal plainclothesman assigned to prevent skyjackings

sky pilot *n* (1883) **:** CLERGYMAN; *specif* **:** CHAPLAIN

[1]sky·rock·et \ˈskī-ˌrä-kət\ *n* (1688) **:** [2]ROCKET 1a

[2]skyrocket *vt* (1851) **1 :** to cause to rise or increase abruptly and rapidly **2 :** CATAPULT ~ *vi* **:** to shoot up abruptly ⟨prices are ~*ing*⟩

sky·sail \ˈskī-ˌsāl, -səl\ *n* (1829) **:** the sail above the royal

sky·scrap·er \-ˌskrā-pər\ *n* (1883) **:** a very tall building

sky·scrap·ing \-ˌskrā-piŋ\ *adj* (1840) **:** extraordinarily tall or high ⟨~ basketball players⟩

sky·surf·ing \-ˌsər-fiŋ\ *n* (1990) **:** skydiving in which the participant performs maneuvers during free fall while riding on a modified surfboard — **sky·surf·er** \-fər\ *n*

sky·walk \-ˌwȯk\ *n* (1953) **:** a usu. enclosed aerial walkway connecting two buildings

sky·ward \-wərd\ *adv* (1582) **1 :** toward the sky **2 :** UPWARD

sky wave *n* (1928) **:** a radio wave that is propagated by means of the ionosphere

sky·way \ˈskī-ˌwā\ *n* (1919) **1 :** a route used by airplanes **:** AIR LANE **2 :** an elevated highway **3 :** SKYWALK

sky·write \-ˌrīt\ *vb* **-wrote** \-ˌrōt\; **-writ·ten** \-ˌri-tᵊn\; **-writ·ing** \-ˌrī-tiŋ\ [back-formation from *skywriting*] *vt* (1926) **:** to letter by skywriting ~ *vi* **:** to do skywriting — **sky·writ·er** *n*

skywriting *n* (1922) **:** writing formed in the sky by means of a visible substance (as smoke) emitted from an airplane

sl *abbr* **1** slightly **2** slip **3** slow

SL *abbr* sea level

[1]slab \ˈslab\ *n* [ME *slabbe*] (14c) **1 :** a thick plate or slice (as of stone, wood, or bread): as **a :** the outside piece cut from a log in squaring it **b :** concrete pavement (as of a road); *specif* **:** a strip of concrete pavement laid as a single unjointed piece **c** (1) **:** a flat rectangular architectural element that is usu. formed of a single piece or mass ⟨a concrete foundation ~⟩ (2) **:** a rectangular building having little width with respect to its length and usu. height **2 :** something that resembles a slab (as in size, shape, or density) ⟨backed up by a solid ~ of reference material —*Times Lit. Supp.*⟩ — **slab·like** \-ˌlīk\ *adj*

[2]slab *vt* **slabbed; slab·bing** (1703) **1 a :** to remove an outer slab from (as a log) **b :** to divide or form into slabs **2 :** to cover or support (as a roadbed or roof) with slabs **3 :** to put on thickly

[3]slab *adj* [akin to ME *slabben* to wallow, obs. Dan *slab* muck] (1605) *dial chiefly Eng* **:** THICK, VISCOUS

slab–sid·ed \ˈslab-ˈsī-dəd\ *adj* (1817) **:** having flat sides; *also* **:** being tall or long and lank

[1]slack \ˈslak\ *adj* [ME *slak,* fr. OE *sleac;* akin to OHG *slah* slack, L *laxus* slack, loose, *languēre* to languish, Gk *lagnos* lustful and perh. to Gk *lēgein* to stop] (bef. 12c) **1 :** not using due diligence, care, or dispatch **:** NEGLIGENT **2 a :** characterized by slowness, sluggishness, or lack of energy ⟨a ~ pace⟩ **b :** moderate in some quality; *esp* **:** moderately warm ⟨a ~ oven⟩ **c :** blowing or flowing at low speed ⟨the tide was ~⟩ **3 a :** not tight or taut ⟨a ~ rope⟩ **b :** lacking in usual or normal firmness and steadiness **:** WEAK ⟨~ muscles⟩ ⟨~ supervision⟩ **4 :** wanting in activity **:** DULL ⟨a ~ market⟩ **5 :** lacking in completeness, finish, or perfection ⟨a very ~ piece of work⟩ ***syn*** see NEGLIGENT — **slack·ly** *adv* — **slack·ness** *n*

[2]slack *vi* (13c) **1 :** to be or become slack **2 :** to shirk or evade work or duty ~ *vt* **1 a :** to be slack or negligent in performing or doing **b :** LESSEN, MODERATE **2 :** to release tension on **:** LOOSEN **3 a :** to cause to abate **b :** SLAKE 3

[3]slack *n* (1756) **1 :** cessation in movement or flow **2 :** a part of something that hangs loose without strain ⟨take up the ~ of a rope⟩ **3 :** trousers esp. for casual wear — usu. used in pl. **4 :** a dull season or period **5 a :** a part that is available but not used ⟨some ~ in the budget⟩ **b :** a portion (as of labor or resources) that is required but lacking ⟨hired a temp to take up the ~⟩ **6 :** additional leeway or relief from pressure — usu. used with *cut* ⟨refused to cut me some ~ on the schedule⟩

[4]slack *n* [ME *slak,* fr. ON *slakki*] (14c) *dial Eng* **:** a pass between hills

[5]slack *n* [earlier *sleck,* prob. fr. MD *slacke, slecke* slag] (1729) **:** the finest screenings of coal produced at a mine unusable as fuel unless cleaned

slack·en \ˈsla-kən\ *vb* **slack·ened; slack·en·ing** \ˈsla-kᵊn-iŋ\ *vt* (14c) **1 :** to make less active **:** slow up ⟨~ speed at a crossing⟩ **2 :** to make slack (as by lessening tension or firmness) ⟨~ sail⟩ ~ *vi* **1 :** to become slack or slow or negligent **:** slow down **2 :** to become less active **:** SLACK ***syn*** see DELAY

slack·er \ˈsla-kər\ *n* (1898) **1 :** a person who shirks work or obligation; *esp* **:** one who evades military service in time of war **2 :** a person and esp. a young person who is perceived to be disaffected, apathetic, cynical, or lacking ambition — **slacker** *adj*

slack water *n* (1764) **:** the period at the turn of the tide when there is little or no horizontal motion of tidal water — called also *slack tide*

[1]slag \ˈslag\ *n* [MLG *slagge*] (1552) **:** the dross or scoria of a metal

[2]slag *n* [earlier argot *slag* coward, worthless person] (ca. 1958) *slang chiefly Brit* **:** a lewd or promiscuous woman

[3]slag *vt* **slagged; slag·ging** [prob. fr. [2]*slag*] (1971) *chiefly Brit* **:** to criticize harshly

slain *past part of* SLAY

slake \ˈslāk, *vi 2 & vt 3 are also* ˈslak\ *vb* **slaked; slak·ing** [ME, fr. OE *slacian,* fr. *sleac* slack] *vi* (14c) **1** *archaic* **:** SUBSIDE, ABATE **2 :** to become slaked **:** CRUMBLE ⟨lime may ~ spontaneously in moist air⟩ ~ *vt* **1** *archaic* **:** to lessen the force of **:** MODERATE **2 :** SATISFY, QUENCH ⟨~ your thirst⟩ ⟨will ~ your curiosity⟩ **3 :** to cause (as lime) to heat and crumble by treatment with water **:** HYDRATE

[1]sla·lom \ˈslä-ləm\ *n, often attrib* [Norw *slalåm,* lit., sloping track] (1921) **1 :** skiing in a zigzag or wavy course between upright obstacles (as flags) **2 :** a timed race (as on skis or in an automobile or kayak) over a winding or zigzag course past a series of flags or markers; *broadly* **:** movement over a zigzag route

[2]slalom *vi* (1932) **:** to move over a zigzag course in or as if in a slalom

[1]slam \ˈslam\ *n* [origin unknown] (1660) **1 :** GRAND SLAM **2 :** LITTLE SLAM

[2]slam *n* [perh. of Scand origin; akin to Norw *slamre* to bang, Sw *slamra* to rattle] (1672) **1 :** a heavy blow or impact **2 a :** a noisy violent closing **b :** a banging noise; *esp* **:** one made by the slam of a door **3 :** a cutting or violent criticism **4 :** SLAMMER **5 :** a poetry competition performed before judges

[3]slam *vb* **slammed; slam·ming** *vt* (ca. 1691) **1 :** to strike or beat hard **:** KNOCK **2 :** to shut forcibly and noisily **:** BANG **3 a :** to set or slap down violently or noisily ⟨*slammed* down the phone⟩ **b :** to propel, thrust, or produce by or as if by striking hard ⟨~ on the brakes⟩ ⟨*slammed* the car into a wall⟩ **4 :** to criticize harshly ~ *vi* **1 :** to make a banging noise **2 :** to function (as in moving) with emphatic and usu. noisy vigor ⟨the hurricane *slammed* into the coast⟩ ⟨*slammed* out of the room⟩ **3 :** to utter verbal abuse or harsh criticism

slam–bang \ˈslam-ˈbaŋ\ *adj* (ca. 1823) **1 :** unduly loud or violent ⟨a ~ clatter⟩ **2 :** having fast-paced often nonstop action ⟨a ~ adventure novel⟩ **3 :** vigorously enthusiastic ⟨made a ~ effort to win⟩

slam dunk *n* (1972) **1 :** DUNK SHOT **2 :** SURE THING ⟨the case is a *slam dunk*⟩ — **slam–dunk** *vb*

slam·mer \ˈsla-mər\ *n* (1952) **:** JAIL, PRISON

[1]slan·der \ˈslan-dər\ *vt* **slan·dered; slan·der·ing** \-d(ə-)riŋ\ (13c) **:** to utter slander against **:** DEFAME ***syn*** see MALIGN — **slan·der·er** \-dər-ər\ *n*

[2]slander *n* [ME *sclaundre, slaundre,* fr. AF *esclandre,* alter. of *escandle,* fr. LL *scandalum* stumbling block, offense — more at SCANDAL] (14c) **1 :** the utterance of false charges or misrepresentations which defame and damage another's reputation **2 :** a false and defamatory oral statement about a person — compare LIBEL — **slan·der·ous** \-d(ə-)rəs\ *adj* — **slan·der·ous·ly** *adv* — **slan·der·ous·ness** *n*

[1]slang \ˈslaŋ\ *n* [origin unknown] (1756) **1 :** language peculiar to a particular group: as **a :** ARGOT **b :** JARGON 2 **2 :** an informal nonstandard vocabulary composed typically of coinages, arbitrarily changed words, and extravagant, forced, or facetious figures of speech — **slang** *adj* — **slang·i·ly** \ˈslaŋ-ə-lē\ *adv* — **slang·i·ness** \ˈslaŋ-ē-nəs\ *n* — **slangy** \ˈslaŋ-ē\ *adj*

[2]slang *vi* (1828) **:** to use slang or vulgar abuse ~ *vt* **:** to abuse with harsh or coarse language

slanging match *n* (1896) *chiefly Brit* **:** a heated exchange of abuse

slan·guage \ˈslaŋ-gwij\ *n* [blend of *slang* and *language*] (1879) **:** slangy speech or writing

[1]slant \ˈslant\ *vb* [ME *slenten* to fall obliquely, of Scand origin; akin to Norw dial. *slenta* to slope, ON *sletta* to throw carelessly] *vi* (1644) **1 :** to take a diagonal course, direction, or path **2 :** to turn or incline from a right line or a level **:** SLOPE ~ *vt* **1 :** to give an oblique or sloping direction to **2 :** to interpret or present in line with a special interest **:** ANGLE ⟨stories ~*ed* toward youth⟩; *esp* **:** to maliciously or dishonestly distort or falsify — **slant·ing·ly** \ˈslan-tiŋ-lē\ *adv*

[2]slant *n* (1655) **1 :** a slanting direction, line, or plane **:** SLOPE **2 a :** something that slants **b :** SLASH 4 **c :** a football running play in which the ballcarrier runs obliquely toward the line of scrimmage **3 a :** a peculiar or personal point of view, attitude, or opinion **b :** a slanting view **:** GLANCE — **slant** *adj* — **slant·ways** \-ˌwāz\ *adv* — **slant·wise** \-ˌwīz\ *adv or adj* — **slanty** \ˈslan-tē\ *adj*

slant height *n* (1798) **1 :** the length of an element of a right circular cone **2 :** the altitude of a side of a regular pyramid

[1]slap \ˈslap\ *n* [ME *slop,* fr. MD; akin to MD *slippen* to slip] (14c) *dial Brit* **:** OPENING, BREACH

[2]slap *vt* **slapped; slap·ping** [akin to LG *slapp,* n. blow] (15c) **1 a :** to strike sharply with or as if with the open hand **b :** to cause to strike with a motion or sound like that of a blow with the open hand **2 :** to put, place, or throw with careless haste or force ⟨*slapped* on a coat of paint⟩ **3 :** to assail verbally **:** INSULT **4 :** to subject to a penalty — usu. used with *with* ⟨*slapped* him with a $10 fine⟩

[3]slap *n* (1606) **1 a :** a quick sharp blow **b :** a blow with the open hand **2 :** a noise like that of a slap **3 :** REBUFF, INSULT — **slap on the wrist :** a gentle usu. ineffectual reprimand

[4]slap *adv* [prob. fr. LG *slapp,* fr. *slapp,* n.] (1672) **:** DIRECTLY, SMACK

slap·dash \ˈslap-ˈdash, -ˌdash\ *adj* (ca. 1792) **:** HAPHAZARD, SLIPSHOD

slap down *vt* (1842) **1 :** to prohibit or restrain usu. abruptly and with censure from acting in a specified way **:** SQUELCH **2 :** to put an abrupt stop to **:** SUPPRESS

slap·hap·py \ˈslap-ˌha-pē\ *adj* (1936) **1 :** PUNCH-DRUNK **2 :** buoyantly or recklessly carefree or foolish **:** HAPPY-GO-LUCKY

slap·jack \-ˌjak\ *n* [[2]*slap* + *-jack* (as in *flapjack*)] (1796) **1 :** PANCAKE **2 :** a card game in which each player tries to be the first to slap a hand on any jack that appears faceup

slap shot *n* (1942) **:** a shot in ice hockey made with a swinging stroke

slap·stick \ˈslap-ˌstik\ *n* (1896) **1 :** a device made of two flat pieces of wood fastened at one end so as to make a loud noise when used by an actor to strike a person **2 :** comedy stressing farce and horseplay; *also* **:** activity resembling slapstick — **slapstick** *adj* — **slap·sticky** \-ˌsti-kē\ *adj*

slap–up \ˈslap-ˌəp\ *adj* (ca. 1823) *chiefly Brit* **:** FIRST-RATE, BANG-UP

[1]slash \ˈslash\ *vb* [origin unknown] *vi* (1548) **:** to lash out, cut, or thrash about with or as if with an edged blade ~ *vt* **1 :** to cut with or as if with rough sweeping strokes **2 :** CANE, LASH **3 :** to cut slits in (as a garment) so as to reveal a color beneath **4 :** to criticize cuttingly **5 :** to reduce sharply **:** CUT

[2]slash *n* (1576) **1 :** the act of slashing; *also* **:** a long cut or stroke made by or as if by slashing **2 :** an ornamental slit in a garment **3 a :** an open tract in a forest strewn with debris (as from logging) **b :** the debris in such a tract **4 :** a mark / used typically to denote "or" (as in *and/or*), "and or" (as in *straggler/deserter*), or "per" (as in *feet/second*) — called also *diagonal, slant, solidus, virgule*

[3]slash *n* [origin unknown] (1652) **:** a low swampy area often overgrown with brush

slash–and–burn *adj* (1939) **1 :** characterized or developed by felling and burning trees to clear land esp. for temporary agriculture **2 :** extremely ruthless and unsparing ⟨~ tactics⟩ ⟨~ criticism⟩

slash·er \ˈsla-shər\ *n, often attrib* (1559) **:** one that slashes; *esp* **:** a person who mutilates or kills with an edged blade ⟨a ~ film⟩

1slash·ing \ˈsla-shiŋ\ *adj* (1593) **1 :** incisively satiric or critical **2 :** DRIVING, PELTING **3 :** VIVID, BRILLIANT — **slash·ing·ly** *adv*

2slashing *n* (1576) **1 :** the act or process of slashing **2 :** an insert or layer of contrasting color revealed by a slash (as in a garment) **3 :** SLASH 3

slash pine *n* [3*slash*] (ca. 1882) **:** a pine (*Pinus elliottii*) of the southeastern U.S. that has two or three needles in a cluster and is a source of turpentine, lumber, and pulpwood

slash pocket *n* (1742) **:** a pocket suspended on the wrong side of a garment from a finished slit on the right side that serves as its opening

1slat \ˈslat\ *vt* **slat·ted; slat·ting** [perh. of Scand origin; akin to ON *sletta* to throw carelessly] (ca. 1587) **1 :** STRIKE, PUMMEL **2 :** to hurl or throw smartly

2slat *n* [ME *sclate, slate* slate] (1764) **1 :** a thin narrow flat strip esp. of wood or metal **2** *pl, slang* **:** RIBS **3 :** an auxiliary airfoil at the leading edge of the wing of an airplane — **slat** *adj* — **slat·ted** \ˈsla-təd\ *adj*

3slat *vt* **slat·ted; slat·ting** (1886) **:** to make or equip with slats

1slate \ˈslāt\ *n* [ME *sclate, slate,* fr. AF **esclat,* fr. *esclater* to splinter, break off, of Gmc origin; akin to OHG *zesleizzen, slīzan* to tear apart — more at SLIT] (14c) **1 :** a piece of construction material (as laminated rock) prepared as a shingle for roofing and siding **2 :** a dense fine-grained metamorphic rock produced by the compression of various sediments (as clay or shale) so as to develop a characteristic cleavage **3 :** a tablet (as of slate) used for writing on **4 a :** a written or unwritten record (as of deeds) ⟨started with a clean ~⟩ **b :** a list of candidates for nomination or election **5 a :** a dark purplish gray **b :** any of various grays similar in color to common roofing slates — **slate** *adj* — **slate·like** \-ˌlīk\ *adj*

2slate *vt* **slat·ed; slat·ing** (15c) **1 :** to cover with slate or a slatelike substance ⟨~ a roof⟩ **2 :** to designate for a specified purpose or action **:** SCHEDULE ⟨was *slated* to direct the play⟩

3slate *vt* **slat·ed; slat·ing** [prob. alter. of 1*slat*] (1825) **1 :** to thrash or pummel severely **2** *chiefly Brit* **:** to criticize or censure severely

slate black *n* (1887) **:** a nearly neutral slightly purplish black

slate blue *n* (1796) **:** a grayish-blue color

slat·er \ˈslā-tər\ *n* (14c) **1 :** one that slates **2** [1*slate;* fr. its color] **a :** WOOD LOUSE **b :** any of various marine isopods

1slath·er \ˈsla-t͟hər\ *n* [origin unknown] (1843) **:** a great quantity — often used in pl.

2slather *vt* **slath·ered; slath·er·ing** \ˈsla-t͟hə-riŋ, ˈslat͟h-riŋ\ (1866) **1 :** to use or spend in a wasteful or lavish manner **:** SQUANDER **2 a :** to spread thickly or lavishly ⟨~*ed* sunscreen on her skin⟩ **b :** to spread something thickly or lavishly on ⟨~*ed* her skin with sunscreen⟩

slating *n* (15c) **:** the work of a slater

1slat·tern \ˈsla-tərn\ *n* [prob. fr. G *schlottern* to hang loosely, slouch; akin to D *slodderen* to hang loosely, *slodder* slut] (ca. 1639) **:** an untidy slovenly woman; *also* **:** SLUT, PROSTITUTE

2slattern *adj* (1684) **:** SLATTERNLY

slat·tern·ly \ˈsla-tərn-lē\ *adj* (1677) **1 :** untidy and dirty through habitual neglect; *also* **:** CARELESS, DISORDERLY **2 :** of, relating to, or characteristic of a slut or prostitute — **slat·tern·li·ness** *n*

slaty *also* **slat·ey** \ˈslā-tē\ *adj* (ca. 1529) **:** of, containing, or characteristic of slate; *also* **:** gray like slate

1slaugh·ter \ˈslȯ-tər\ *n* [ME, of Scand origin; akin to ON *slātra* to slaughter; akin to OE *sleaht* slaughter, *slēan* to slay — more at SLAY] (14c) **1 :** the act of killing; *specif* **:** the butchering of livestock for market **2 :** killing of great numbers of human beings (as in battle or a massacre) **:** CARNAGE

2slaughter *vt* (1535) **1 :** to kill (animals) for food **:** BUTCHER **2 a :** to kill in a bloody or violent manner **:** SLAY **b :** to kill in large numbers **:** MASSACRE **3 :** to discredit, defeat, or demolish completely — **slaugh·ter·er** \-tər-ər\ *n*

slaugh·ter·house \ˈslȯ-tər-ˌhau̇s\ *n* (14c) **:** an establishment where animals are butchered

slaugh·ter·ous \ˈslȯ-tə-rəs\ *adj* (1581) **:** of or relating to slaughter **:** MURDEROUS ⟨a ~ rampage⟩ — **slaugh·ter·ous·ly** *adv*

Slav \ˈsläv, ˈslav\ *n* [ME *Sclav,* fr. ML *Sclavus,* fr. LGk *Sklabos,* fr. *Sklabēnoi* Slavs, of Slav origin; akin to ORuss *Slověne,* an East Slavic tribe] (14c) **:** a person whose native tongue is a Slavic language — **Slav** *adj*

1slave \ˈslāv\ *n* [ME *sclave,* fr. AF or ML; AF *esclave,* fr. ML *sclavus,* fr. *Sclavus* Slav; fr. the frequent enslavement of Slavs in central Europe during the early Middle Ages] (14c) **1 :** a person held in servitude as the chattel of another **2 :** one that is completely subservient to a dominating influence **3 :** a device (as the printer of a computer) that is directly responsive to another **4 :** DRUDGE, TOILER — **slave** *adj*

2slave *vb* **slaved; slav·ing** *vt* (1602) **1** *archaic* **:** ENSLAVE **2 :** to make directly responsive to another mechanism ~ *vi* **1 :** to work like a slave **:** DRUDGE **2 :** to traffic in slaves

slave driver *n* (1792) **1 :** a supervisor of slaves at work **2 :** a harsh taskmaster

slave·hold·er \ˈslāv-ˌhōl-dər\ *n* (1776) **:** an owner of slaves — **slave·hold·ing** \-diŋ\ *adj or n*

slave–mak·ing ant \ˈslāv-ˌmā-kiŋ-\ *n* (1817) **:** an ant that attacks the colonies of ants of other species and carries off the larvae and pupae to be reared in its own nest as slave workers

1sla·ver \ˈsla-vər, ˈslā-, ˈslä-\ *vb* **sla·vered; sla·ver·ing** \-v(ə-)riŋ\ [ME, of Scand origin; akin to ON *slafra* to slaver; akin to MD *slabben* to slaver] *vi* (14c) **:** DROOL, SLOBBER ~ *vt, archaic* **:** to smear with or as if with saliva

2slaver *n* (14c) **:** saliva dribbling from the mouth

3slav·er \ˈslā-vər\ *n* [1*slave*] (1827) **1 a :** a ship used in the slave trade **b :** a person engaged in the slave trade **2 :** WHITE SLAVER

slav·ery \ˈslā-v(ə-)rē\ *n* (1551) **1 :** DRUDGERY, TOIL **2 :** submission to a dominating influence **3 a :** the state of a person who is a chattel of another **b :** the practice of slaveholding

slave state *n* (1809) **1 :** a state of the U.S. in which slavery was legal until the Civil War **2 :** a nation subjected to totalitarian rule

slave trade *n* (1734) **:** traffic in slaves; *esp* **:** the buying and selling of blacks for profit prior to the American Civil War

slav·ey \ˈslā-vē\ *n, pl* **slaveys** (ca. 1812) **:** DRUDGE; *esp* **:** a household servant who does general housework

1Slav·ic \ˈslä-vik, ˈsla-\ *n* (1812) **:** a branch of the Indo-European language family containing Belarusian, Bulgarian, Czech, Polish, Serbian and Croatian, Slovene, Russian, and Ukrainian — see INDO-EUROPEAN LANGUAGES table

2Slavic *adj* (1813) **:** of, relating to, or characteristic of the Slavs or their languages

Slav·i·cist \ˈslä-və-sist, ˈsla-\ *n* (ca. 1930) **:** a specialist in the Slavic languages or literatures

slav·ish \ˈslā-vish *sometimes* ˈsla-\ *adj* (1565) **1 a :** of or characteristic of a slave; *esp* **:** basely or abjectly servile **b** *archaic* **:** DESPICABLE, LOW **2** *archaic* **:** OPPRESSIVE, TYRANNICAL **3 :** copying obsequiously or without originality **:** IMITATIVE ***syn*** see SUBSERVIENT — **slav·ish·ly** *adv* — **slav·ish·ness** *n*

Slav·ist \ˈslä-vist, ˈsla-\ *n* (1863) **:** SLAVICIST

slav·oc·ra·cy \slā-ˈvä-krə-sē\ *n* (1840) **:** a faction of slaveholders and advocates of slavery in the South before the American Civil War

1Sla·von·ic \slə-ˈvä-nik\ *adj* [NL *slavonicus,* fr. ML *Sclavonia, Slavonia,* the Slavic-speaking countries, fr. *Sclavus* Slav] (ca. 1645) **:** SLAVIC

2Slavonic *n* (1668) **1 :** SLAVIC **2 :** OLD CHURCH SLAVONIC

Slav·o·phile \ˈslä-və-ˌfī(-ə)l, ˈsla-\ *or* **Slav·o·phil** \-ˌfil\ *n* (1877) **:** an admirer of the Slavs **:** an advocate of Slavophilism

Slav·oph·i·lism \sla-ˈvä-fə-ˌli-zəm; ˈsla-və-ˌfī-ˌli-, ˈslä-\ *n* (1877) **:** advocacy of Slavic and specif. Russian culture over western European culture esp. as practiced among some members of the Russian intelligentsia in the middle 19th century

slaw \ˈslȯ\ *n* (1861) **:** COLESLAW

slay \ˈslā\ *vb* **slew** \ˈslü\ *also esp in sense 2* **slayed; slain** \ˈslān\; **slay·ing** [ME *slen,* fr. OE *slēan* to strike, slay; akin to OHG *slahan* to strike, MIr *slachta* stricken] *vt* (bef. 12c) **1 :** to kill violently, wantonly, or in great numbers; *broadly* **:** to strike down **:** KILL **2 :** to delight or amuse immensely ⟨~*ed* the audience⟩ ~ *vi* **:** KILL, MURDER ***syn*** see KILL — **slay·er** *n*

SLBM *abbr* submarine-launched ballistic missile

SLE *abbr* systemic lupus erythematosus

1sleave \ˈslēv\ *n* [2*sleave*] (1591) *archaic* **:** SKEIN ⟨sleep that knits up the raveled ~ of care —Shak.⟩

2sleave *vt* [ME **sleven,* fr. OE *-slǣfan* to cut] (ca. 1628) *obs* **:** to separate (silk thread) into filaments

sleave silk *n* (1588) *obs* **:** floss silk that is easily separated into filaments for embroidery

sleaze \ˈslēz *also* ˈslāz\ *n* [back-formation fr. *sleazy*] (1954) **1 :** sleazy quality, appearance, or behavior; *also* **:** sleazy material **2 :** a sleazy person

sleaze·bag \-ˌbag *also* -ˌbāg\ *n* (1981) *slang* **:** a sleazy person

sleaze·ball \-ˌbȯl\ *n* (1981) *slang* **:** a sleazy person

sleazo \ˈslē-(ˌ)zō\ *adj* (1972) *slang* **:** SLEAZY

slea·zy \ˈslē-zē *also* ˈslā-\ *adj* **slea·zi·er; -est** [origin unknown] (ca. 1645) **1 a :** lacking firmness of texture **:** FLIMSY **b :** carelessly made of inferior materials **:** SHODDY **2 a :** marked by low character or quality ⟨~ tabloids⟩ **b :** SQUALID, DILAPIDATED ⟨~ bars⟩ — **slea·zi·ly** \-zə-lē\ *adv* — **slea·zi·ness** \-zē-nəs\ *n*

1sled \ˈsled\ *n* [ME *sledde,* fr. MD; akin to OE *slīdan* to slide] (14c) **1 :** a vehicle usu. on runners for transportation esp. on snow or ice; *esp* **:** a small steerable one used esp. by children for coasting down snow-covered hills **2 :** ROCKET SLED

2sled *vb* **sled·ded; sled·ding** *vt* (1706) **:** SLEDGE ~ *vi* **:** to ride on a sled or sleigh — **sled·der** *n*

sledding *n* (15c) **1 a :** the use of a sled **b :** the conditions under which one may use a sled **2 :** GOING 4 ⟨tough ~⟩

sled dog *n* (1692) **:** a dog trained to draw a sledge esp. in the Arctic regions — called also *sledge dog*

1sledge \ˈslej\ *n* [ME *slegge,* fr. OE *slecg;* akin to ON *sleggja* sledgehammer, OE *slēan* to strike — more at SLAY] (bef. 12c) **:** SLEDGEHAMMER

2sledge *vb* **sledged; sledg·ing** (1654) **:** SLEDGEHAMMER

3sledge *n* [D dial. *sleedse;* akin to MD *sledde* sled] (1617) **1** *Brit* **:** SLEIGH **2 :** a strong heavy sled

4sledge *vb* **sledged; sledg·ing** *vi* (1708) **1 :** to travel with a sledge **2** *Brit* **:** to ride in a sleigh ~ *vt* **:** to transport on a sledge

1sledge·ham·mer \ˈslej-ˌha-mər\ *n* (15c) **:** a large heavy hammer that is wielded with both hands; *also* **:** something that resembles a sledgehammer in action

2sledgehammer *vt* (1834) **:** to strike with or as if with a sledgehammer ~ *vi* **:** to strike blows with or as if with a sledgehammer

3sledgehammer *adj* (1827) **:** marked by heavy-handed directness or hard-hitting force ⟨trusting in ~ warfare —C. J. Rolo⟩

1sleek \ˈslēk\ *vb* [ME *sleken,* alter. of *sliken* — more at SLICK] *vt* (15c) **1 :** SLICK ⟨grooms ~*ing* cooled horses —*Sunset*⟩ **2 :** to cover up **:** gloss over ~ *vi* **:** SLICK

2sleek *adj* [alter. of 2*slick*] (1578) **1 a :** smooth and glossy as if polished ⟨~ dark hair⟩ **b :** having a smooth well-groomed look ⟨~ cattle⟩ **c :** healthy-looking **2 :** smooth in speech or manner; *also* **:** UNCTUOUS **3 a :** having a prosperous air ⟨~ luxury condominiums⟩ **b :** having trim graceful lines ⟨a ~ car⟩ **c :** ELEGANT, STYLISH ⟨a ~ wardrobe⟩ — **sleek·ly** *adv* — **sleek·ness** *n*

syn SLEEK, SLICK, GLOSSY mean having a smooth bright surface or appearance. SLEEK suggests a smoothness or brightness resulting from attentive grooming or physical conditioning ⟨a *sleek* racehorse⟩. SLICK suggests extreme smoothness that results in a slippery surface ⟨slipped and fell on the *slick* floor⟩. GLOSSY suggests a highly reflective surface ⟨photographs having a *glossy* finish⟩.

sleek·en \ˈslē-kən\ *vt* **sleek·ened; sleek·en·ing** \ˈslē-kə-niŋ, ˈslēk-niŋ\ (1621) **:** to make sleek

sleek·it \ˈslē-kət\ *adj* [Sc, fr. pp. of 1*sleek*] (1513) **1** *chiefly Scot* **:** SLEEK, SMOOTH **2** *chiefly Scot* **:** CRAFTY, DECEITFUL

1sleep \ˈslēp\ *n* [ME *slepe,* fr. OE *slǣp;* akin to OHG *slāf* sleep and perh. to L *labi* to slip, slide] (bef. 12c) **1 :** the natural periodic suspension of consciousness during which the powers of the body are restored —

\ə\ **abut** \ᵊ\ **kitten, F table** \ər\ **further** \a\ **ash** \ā\ **ace** \ä\ **mop, mar** \au̇\ **out** \ch\ **chin** \e\ **bet** \ē\ **easy** \g\ **go** \i\ **hit** \ī\ **ice** \j\ **job** \ŋ\ **sing** \ō\ **go** \ȯ\ **law** \ȯi\ **boy** \th\ **thin** \t͟h\ **the** \ü\ **loot** \u̇\ **foot** \y\ **yet** \zh\ **vision, beige** \k̲, ⁿ, œ, ue, ʸ\ *see* Guide to Pronunciation

compare REM SLEEP, SLOW-WAVE SLEEP **2 :** a state resembling sleep: as **a :** a state of torpid inactivity **b :** DEATH ⟨put a pet cat to ~⟩; *also* **:** TRANCE, COMA **c :** the closing of leaves or petals esp. at night **d :** a state marked by a diminution of feeling followed by tingling ⟨my foot's gone to ~⟩ **e :** the state of an animal during hibernation **3 a :** a period spent sleeping **b :** NIGHT **c :** a day's journey **4 :** crusty matter present in the corner of an eye upon awakening — **sleep·like** \-ˌlīk\ *adj*

[2]**sleep** *vb* **slept** \ˈslept\; **sleep·ing** *vi* (bef. 12c) **1 :** to rest in a state of sleep **2 :** to be in a state (as of quiescence or death) resembling sleep **3 :** to have sexual relations — usu. used with *with* ~ *vt* **1 :** to be slumbering in ⟨*slept* the sleep of the dead⟩ **2 :** to get rid of or spend in or by sleep ⟨~ away the hours⟩ ⟨~ off a headache⟩ **3 :** to provide sleeping accommodations for ⟨the boat ~*s* six⟩

sleep apnea *n* (1975) **:** apnea that recurs during sleep and is caused esp. by obstruction of the airway or a disturbance in the brain's respiratory center

sleep around *vi* (1928) **:** to engage in sex promiscuously

sleep·away \ˈslēp-ə-ˌwā\ *adj* (1971) **:** providing accommodations for overnight sleep and extended stay away from home ⟨~ camps⟩

sleep·er \ˈslē-pər\ *n* (12c) **1 :** one that sleeps **2 :** a piece of timber, stone, or steel on or near the ground to support a superstructure, keep railroad rails in place, or receive floor joists **:** STRINGPIECE **3 :** SLEEPING CAR **4 :** someone or something unpromising or unnoticed that suddenly attains prominence or value ⟨the low-budget film became the summer's ~⟩ **5 :** children's pajamas usu. with feet — usu. used in pl. **6** *chiefly Brit* **:** a small earring or stud worn to keep the hole of a pierced ear from closing **7 :** [2]MOLE 4

sleeper cell *n* (1968) **:** a terrorist cell whose members work under cover in an area until sent into action

sleep–in \ˈslēp-ˈin\ *adj* (1951) **:** that lives at the place of employment ⟨a ~ maid⟩

sleep in *vi* (1827) **1 :** to sleep where one is employed **2 a :** OVERSLEEP **b :** to sleep late intentionally

sleeping bag *n* (1850) **:** a bag that is warmly lined or padded for sleeping outdoors or in a camp or tent

Sleeping Beauty *n* (1729) **:** a princess of a fairy tale who is wakened from an enchanted sleep by the kiss of a prince

sleeping car *n* (1839) **:** a railroad passenger car having berths for sleeping

sleeping giant *n* (1970) **:** one that has great but unrealized or newly emerging power

sleeping partner *n* (ca. 1785) *chiefly Brit* **:** SILENT PARTNER

sleeping pill *n* (1664) **:** a drug and esp. a barbiturate that is taken as a tablet or capsule to induce sleep

sleeping porch *n* (1915) **:** a porch or room having open sides or many windows arranged to permit sleeping in the open air

sleeping sickness *n* (1875) **1 :** a serious disease that is prevalent in much of tropical Africa, is marked by fever, headache, lethargy, confusion, and sleep disturbances, and is caused by either of two trypanosomes (*Trypanosoma brucei gambiense* and *T. b. rhodesiense*) transmitted by tsetse flies **2 :** any of various viral encephalitides or encephalomyelitides of which lethargy or somnolence is a prominent feature

sleep·less \ˈslēp-ləs\ *adj* (15c) **1 :** not able to sleep ⟨lay ~ with fever⟩ **2 :** affording no sleep ⟨~ nights⟩ **3 :** unceasingly active or operative ⟨~ casinos⟩ — **sleep·less·ly** *adv* — **sleep·less·ness** *n*

sleep out *vi* (1818) **:** to sleep outdoors

sleep·over \ˈslēp-ō-vər\ *n* (1965) **1 :** an overnight stay (as at another's home) **2 :** an instance of hosting a sleepover in one's home

sleep·walk \ˈslēp-ˌwȯk\ *vi* (1842) **1 :** to walk while or as if while asleep **2 :** to proceed in a passive often lethargic manner ⟨~*ed* through the workday⟩ — **sleepwalk** *n* — **sleep·walk·er** \-ˌwȯ-kər\ *n*

sleep·wear \-ˌwer\ *n* (1935) **:** NIGHTCLOTHES

sleepy \ˈslē-pē\ *adj* **sleep·i·er; -est** (13c) **1 a :** ready to fall asleep **b :** of, relating to, or characteristic of sleep **2 :** sluggish as if from sleep **:** LETHARGIC; *also* **:** having little activity ⟨a ~ coastal village⟩ **3 :** sleep-inducing — **sleep·i·ly** \-pə-lē\ *adv* — **sleep·i·ness** \-pē-nəs\ *n*

sleepy·head \ˈslē-pē-ˌhed\ *n* (1577) **:** a sleepy person

[1]**sleet** \ˈslēt\ *n* [ME *slete;* akin to MHG *slōz* hailstone] (13c) **:** frozen or partly frozen rain — **sleety** \ˈslē-tē\ *adj*

[2]**sleet** *vi* (14c) **:** to shower sleet

sleeve \ˈslēv\ *n* [ME *sleve,* fr. OE *slīefe;* perh. akin to OE *slēfan* to slip (clothes) on, *slūpan* to slip, OHG *sliofan,* L *lubricus* slippery] (bef. 12c) **1 a :** a part of a garment covering an arm **b :** SLEEVELET **2 a :** a tubular part (as a hollow axle or a bushing) designed to fit over another part **b :** an open-ended flat or tubular packaging or cover; *esp* **:** JACKET 3c(2) — **sleeved** \ˈslēvd\ *adj* — **sleeve·less** \ˈslēv-ləs\ *adj* — **on one's sleeve :** in an honest and open manner — used with *wear* ⟨wears his emotions *on his sleeve*⟩ — **up one's sleeve :** held secretly in reserve ⟨has a few tricks *up her sleeve*⟩

sleeve·let \ˈslēv-lət\ *n* (1889) **:** a covering for the forearm to protect clothing from wear or dirt

[1]**sleigh** \ˈslā\ *n* [D *slee,* alter. of *slede;* akin to MD *sledde* sled] (1703) **:** an open usu. horse-drawn vehicle with runners for use on snow or ice

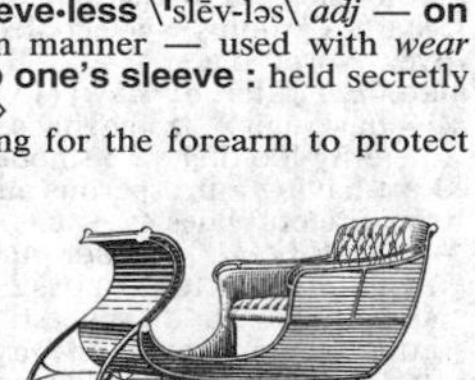
sleigh

[2]**sleigh** *vi* (ca. 1729) **:** to drive or travel in a sleigh

sleigh bed *n* (1902) **:** a bed common esp. in the first half of the 19th century having a solid headboard and footboard that roll outward at the top

sleigh bell *n* (1772) **:** any of various bells commonly attached to a sleigh or to the harness of a horse drawing a sleigh: as **a :** CASCABEL 2 **b :** a hemispherical bell with an attached clapper

sleight \ˈslīt\ *n* [ME, fr. ON *slœgth,* fr. *slœgr* sly — more at SLY] (14c) **1 :** deceitful craftiness; *also* **:** STRATAGEM **2 :** DEXTERITY, SKILL

sleight of hand (1593) **1 a :** a cleverly executed trick or deception **b :** a conjuring trick requiring manual dexterity **2 a :** skill and dexterity in conjuring tricks **b :** adroitness in deception

slen·der \ˈslen-dər\ *adj* [ME *sclendre, slendre,* fr. AF *esclendre*] (14c) **1 a :** spare in frame or flesh; *esp* **:** gracefully slight **b :** small or narrow in circumference or width in proportion to length or height **2 :** limited or inadequate in amount or scope **:** MEAGER ⟨people of ~ means⟩ ***syn*** see THIN — **slen·der·ly** *adv* — **slen·der·ness** *n*

slen·der·ize \-də-ˌrīz\ *vt* **-ized; -iz·ing** (1923) **:** to make slender

slept *past and past part of* SLEEP

[1]**sleuth** \ˈslüth\ *n* [short for *sleuthhound*] (1872) **:** DETECTIVE

[2]**sleuth** *vi* (1900) **:** to act as a detective **:** search for information ~ *vt* **:** to search for and discover

sleuth·hound \ˈslüth-ˌhau̇nd\ *n* [ME (Sc) *sleuth hund,* a kind of bloodhound, fr. ME *sleuth, sloith, sloth* track of an animal or person (fr. ON *slōth*) + *hund* hound] (1850) **:** DETECTIVE

S level *n* (1951) **1 :** the highest of three standardized British examinations in a secondary school subject used as a qualification for university entrance; *also* **:** successful completion of an S-level examination in a particular subject — called also *Scholarship level*; compare A LEVEL, O LEVEL **2 a :** the level of education required to pass an S-level examination **b :** a course leading to an S-level examination

[1]**slew** *past of* SLAY

[2]**slew** *var of* [1]SLOUGH 1b

[3]**slew** *also* **slue** \ˈslü\ *vb* [origin unknown] *vt* (ca. 1769) **1 :** to turn (as a telescope or a ship's spar) about a fixed point that is usu. the axis **2 :** to cause to skid **:** VEER ⟨~ a car around a turn⟩ ~ *vi* **1 :** to turn, twist, or swing about **:** PIVOT **2 :** SKID

[4]**slew** *n* [perh. fr. Ir *slua* army, host, throng, fr. OIr *slúag;* akin to Lith *slaugyti* to tend] (1839) **:** a large number ⟨a ~ of books⟩

[1]**slice** \ˈslīs\ *vb* **sliced; slic·ing** [ME *sklicen,* fr. AF *esclicer* to splinter, of Gmc origin; akin to OHG *slīzan* to tear apart — more at SLIT] *vt* (1551) **1 :** to cut with or as if with a knife **2 :** to stir or spread with a slice **3 :** to hit (a ball) so that a slice results **4 :** INTERPRET, CONSTRUE — used in phrases like *any way you slice it* ~ *vi* **1 :** to slice something **2 :** to move with a cutting action ⟨the ship *sliced* through the waves⟩ — **slice·able** \ˈslī-sə-bəl\ *adj* — **slic·er** *n*

[2]**slice** *n* [ME *sclise, slise,* fr. AF *esclice* splinter, fr. *esclicer*] (1613) **1 a :** a thin flat piece cut from something **b :** a wedge-shaped piece (as of pie or cake) **2 :** a spatula for spreading paint or ink **3 :** a serving knife with wedge-shaped blade ⟨a fish ~⟩ **4 :** a flight of a ball that deviates from a straight course in the direction of the dominant hand of the player propelling it; *also* **:** a ball following such a course — compare HOOK **5 a :** PORTION, SHARE **b :** SEGMENT, SAMPLE

slice–of–life *adj* (ca. 1934) **:** of, relating to, or marked by the accurate transcription (as into drama) of a segment of actual life experience

[1]**slick** \ˈslik\ *vb* [ME *sliken,* fr. OE **slician*; akin to OHG *slīhhan* to glide] *vt* (14c) **:** to make sleek or smooth ~ *vi* **:** SPRUCE — usu. used with *up*

[2]**slick** *adj* [ME *slyke;* akin to OE **slician*] (14c) **1 a :** having a smooth surface **:** SLIPPERY ⟨~ wet leaves⟩ **b :** having surface plausibility or appeal **:** GLOSSY ⟨~ advertising⟩ **c :** based on stereotype **:** TRITE ⟨~ stories soon forgotten⟩ **2** *archaic* **:** SLEEK 1 **3 a :** characterized by subtlety or nimble wit **:** CLEVER; *esp* **:** WILY ⟨a ~ swindler⟩ **b :** DEFT, SKILLFUL ⟨a ~ ballplayer⟩ **4 :** extremely good **:** FIRST-RATE ***syn*** see SLEEK, SLY — **slick** *adv* — **slick·ly** *adv* — **slick·ness** *n*

[3]**slick** *n* (1849) **1 a :** something that is smooth or slippery; *esp* **:** a smooth patch of water covered with a film of oil **b :** a film of oil **2 :** an implement for producing a smooth or slick surface **3 :** a shrewd untrustworthy person **4 :** a popular magazine printed on coated stock and intended to appeal to sophisticated readers **5 :** an automobile tire made without a tread for maximum traction (as in drag racing) **6** *slang* **:** a military helicopter without armaments that is used to transport troops or light cargo

slick–ear \ˈslik-ˌir\ *n* (1914) **:** a range animal lacking an earmark

slick·en·side \ˈsli-kən-ˌsīd\ *n* [E dial. *slicken* smooth (fr. [2]*slick*) + E *side*] (1822) **:** a smooth often striated surface produced on rock by movement along a fault or a subsidiary fracture — usu. used in pl.

slick·er \ˈsli-kər\ *n* (1881) **1** [[2]*slick*] **:** OILSKIN; *broadly* **:** RAINCOAT **2** [*slick* to defraud cleverly] **a** (1) **:** a clever crook **:** SWINDLER (2) **:** SLICKSTER **b :** a city dweller esp. of natty appearance or sophisticated mannerisms

slick·rock \ˈslik-ˌräk\ *n* (1925) **:** smooth wind-polished rock

slick·ster \ˈslik-stər\ *n* (1965) **:** a slick untrustworthy person

[1]**slide** \ˈslīd\ *vb* **slid** \ˈslid\; **slid·ing** \ˈslī-diŋ\ [ME, fr. OE *slīdan;* akin to MHG *slīten* to slide] *vi* (bef. 12c) **1 a :** to move smoothly along a surface **:** SLIP **b :** to coast over snow or ice **c** *of a base runner in baseball* **:** to fall or dive feetfirst or headfirst when approaching a base **2 a :** to slip or fall by loss of footing **b :** to change position or become dislocated **:** SHIFT **3 a :** to slither along the ground **:** CRAWL **b :** to stream along **:** FLOW **4 a :** to move or pass smoothly or easily ⟨*slid* into the prepared speech⟩ **b :** to pass unnoticed or unremarked ⟨let the criticism ~⟩ **5 a :** to pass unobtrusively **:** STEAL **b :** to pass by gradations esp. downward ⟨the economy *slid* from recession to depression⟩ ~ *vt* **1 a :** to cause to glide or slip **b :** to traverse in a sliding manner **2 :** to put unobtrusively or stealthily ⟨*slid* the bill into his hand⟩

[2]**slide** *n* (1570) **1 a :** an act or instance of sliding **b** (1) **:** a musical grace of two or more small notes (2) **:** PORTAMENTO **2 :** a sliding part or mechanism: as **a** (1) **:** a U-shaped section of tube in the trombone that is pushed out and in to produce the tones between the fundamental and its harmonics (2) **:** a short U-shaped section of tube in a brass instrument that is used to adjust the pitch of the instrument or of individual valves **b** (1) **:** a moving piece (as the ram of a punch press) that is guided by a part along which it slides (2) **:** a guiding surface (as a feeding mechanism) along which something slides **c :** SLIDING SEAT **3 a :** the descent of a mass of earth, rock, or snow down a hill or mountainside **b :** a dislocation in which one rock mass in a mining lode has slid on another **:** FAULT **4 a** (1) **:** a slippery surface for coasting (2) **:** a chute with a slippery bed down which children slide in play **b :** a channel or track on which something is slid **c :** a sloping trough down which objects are carried by gravity ⟨a log ~⟩ **5 a :** a flat piece of glass or plastic on which an object is mounted for microscopic examination **b :** a photographic transparency on a small plate or film mounted for projection **6 :** BOTTLENECK 3

slide fastener *n* (1934) **:** ZIPPER

slid·er \ˈslī-dər\ *n* (1530) **1 :** one that slides **2 :** a freshwater turtle (*Trachemys scripta* syn. *Pseudemys scripta*) chiefly of the southeastern U.S.; *esp* **:** one (*T. scripta elegans*) usu. having a red stripe behind each eye and often sold as a pet **3 :** a fast baseball pitch that breaks slightly in the same direction as a curve **4 :** a very small meat sandwich typically served on a bun; *esp* **:** a small hamburger

slide rule *n* (1663) **:** a manual device used for calculation that consists in its simple form of a ruler and a movable middle piece which are graduated with similar logarithmic scales
slide valve *n* (1802) **:** a valve that opens and closes a passageway by sliding over a port; *specif* **:** such a valve often used in steam engines for admitting steam to the piston and releasing it
slide·way \ˈslīd-ˌwā\ *n* (1851) **:** a way along which something slides
sliding scale *n* (1842) **1 :** a wage scale geared to the selling price of the product or to the consumer price index but usu. guaranteeing a minimum below which the wage will not fall **2 a :** a system for raising or lowering tariffs in accord with price changes **b :** a flexible scale (as of fees or subsidies) adjusted to the needs or income of individuals ⟨the *sliding scale* of medical fees⟩
sliding seat *n* (1874) **:** a rower's seat (as in a racing shell) that slides fore and aft — called also *slide*
slier *comparative of* SLY
sliest *superlative of* SLY
[1]**slight** \ˈslīt\ *adj* [ME, smooth, slight, prob. fr. OE *sliht-* (in *eorth-slihtes* level with the ground); akin to OHG *sleht* smooth, *slīhhan* to glide — more at SLICK] (14c) **1 a :** having a slim or delicate build **:** not stout or massive in body **b :** lacking in strength or substance **:** FLIMSY, FRAIL **c :** deficient in weight, solidity, or importance **:** TRIVIAL ⟨a ~ movie⟩ **2 :** small of its kind or in amount ⟨a ~ chance⟩ ⟨a ~ odor of gas⟩ ***syn*** see THIN — **slight·ly** *adv* — **slight·ness** *n*
[2]**slight** *vt* (1586) **1 :** to treat as slight or unimportant **:** make light of **2 :** to treat with disdain or indifference ⟨~ a guest⟩ **3 :** to perform or attend to carelessly and inadequately ⟨don't ~ your work⟩ ***syn*** see NEGLECT
[3]**slight** *n* (1701) **1 :** an act or an instance of slighting **2 :** an instance of being slighted **:** a humiliating discourtesy
slight·ing \ˈslī-tiŋ\ *adj* (1632) **:** characterized by disregard or disrespect **:** DISPARAGING ⟨a ~ remark⟩ — **slight·ing·ly** *adv*
slily *var of* SLYLY
[1]**slim** \ˈslim\ *adj* **slim·mer; slim·mest** [D, bad, inferior, fr. MD *slimp* crooked, bad; akin to MHG *slimp* awry] (1657) **1 :** of small diameter or thickness in proportion to the height or length **:** SLENDER **2 a :** MEAN, WORTHLESS **b :** ADROIT, CRAFTY **3 a :** inferior in quality or amount **:** SLIGHT **b :** SCANTY, SMALL ⟨a ~ chance⟩ ***syn*** see THIN — **slim·ly** *adv* — **slim·ness** *n*
[2]**slim** *vb* **slimmed; slim·ming** *vt* (1862) **:** to make slender **:** decrease the size of ~ *vi* **:** to become slender
[1]**slime** \ˈslīm\ *n* [ME, fr. OE *slīm;* akin to MHG *slīm* slime, L *limus* mud — more at LIME] (bef. 12c) **1 :** soft moist earth or clay; *esp* **:** viscous mud **2 :** a viscous, glutinous, or gelatinous substance: as **a :** a mucous or mucoid secretion of various animals (as slugs and catfishes) **b :** a product of wet crushing consisting of ore ground so fine as to pass a 200-mesh screen **3 :** a repulsive or odious person
[2]**slime** *vb* **slimed; slim·ing** *vt* (1628) **1 :** to smear or cover with slime **2 :** to remove slime from (as fish for canning) ~ *vi* **:** to become slimy
slime·ball \ˈslīm-ˌbȯl\ *n* (1986) *slang* **:** SLIME 3
slime mold *n* (1880) **:** any of a group (Myxomycetes or Mycetozoa) of organisms usu. held to be lower fungi but sometimes considered protozoans that exist vegetatively as mobile plasmodia and reproduce by spores
slim–jim \ˈslim-ˈjim, -ˌjim\ *adj* [[1]*slim* + *Jim,* nickname for *James*] (1889) **:** notably slender
slim·mer \ˈsli-mər\ *n* (1967) *chiefly Brit* **:** a person dieting to lose weight
slim·nas·tics \ˌslim-ˈnas-tiks\ *n pl but sing in constr* [[1]*slim* + gym*nastics*] (1967) **:** exercises designed to reduce one's weight
slim·sy *or* **slimp·sy** \ˈslim-zē, ˈslim(p)-sē\ *adj* [blend of *slim* and *flimsy*] (1845) **:** FLIMSY, FRAIL
slimy \ˈslī-mē\ *adj* **slim·i·er; -est** (14c) **1 :** of, relating to, or resembling slime **:** VISCOUS; *also* **:** covered with or yielding slime **2 :** VILE, OFFENSIVE — **slim·i·ly** \-mə-lē\ *adv* — **slim·i·ness** \-mē-nəs\ *n*
[1]**sling** \ˈsliŋ\ *vt* **slung** \ˈsləŋ\; **sling·ing** \ˈsliŋ-iŋ\ [ME, prob. fr. ON *slyngva* to hurl; akin to OE & OHG *slingan* to worm, twist, Lith *slinkti*] (14c) **1 :** to cast with a sudden and usu. sweeping or swirling motion ⟨*slung* the sack over my shoulder⟩ **2 :** to throw with or as if with a sling ⟨~*ing* punches⟩ ⟨political campaigners ~*ing* mud⟩ **3 :** to serve (food) to a customer ⟨had a job ~*ing* hamburgers⟩ ***syn*** see THROW — **sling·er** \ˈsliŋ-ər\ *n*
[2]**sling** *n* (14c) **1 a :** an instrument for throwing stones that usu. consists of a short strap with strings fastened to its ends and is whirled round to discharge its missile by centrifugal force **b :** SLINGSHOT 1 **2 a :** a usu. looped line (as of strap, chain, or rope) used to hoist, lower, or carry something; *esp* **:** a hanging bandage suspended from the neck to support an arm or hand **b :** a chain or rope attached to a lower yard at the middle and passing around a mast near the masthead to support a yard **c :** a chain hooked at the bow and stern of a boat for lowering or hoisting **d :** a device (as a rope net) for enclosing material to be hoisted by a tackle or crane **3 :** a slinging or hurling of or as if of a missile
[3]**sling** *vt* **slung** \ˈsləŋ\; **sling·ing** \ˈsliŋ-iŋ\ (1522) **1 :** to place in a sling for hoisting or lowering **2 :** to suspend by or as if by a sling
[4]**sling** *n* [origin unknown] (1768) **:** an alcoholic drink that is served hot or cold and that usu. consists of liquor, sugar, lemon juice, and plain or carbonated water ⟨gin ~⟩ ⟨rum ~⟩
slings and arrows *n pl* [fr. the phrase "the slings and arrows of outrageous fortune" in Shakespeare's *Hamlet*] (1963) **:** pointed often acerbic critical attacks ⟨has suffered the *slings and arrows* of detractors —Roland Gelatt⟩
sling·shot \ˈsliŋ-ˌshät\ *n* (1849) **1 :** a forked stick with an elastic band attached for shooting small stones **2 a :** a maneuver in auto racing in which a drafting car accelerates past the car in front by taking advantage of reserve power **b :** a dragster in which the driver sits behind the rear wheels
[1]**slink** \ˈsliŋk\ *vb* **slunk** \ˈsləŋk\ *also* **slinked** \ˈsliŋ(k)t\; **slink·ing** [ME, fr. OE *slincan* to creep; akin to OE *slingan* to worm, twist] *vi* (14c) **1 :** to go or move stealthily or furtively (as in fear or shame) **:** STEAL **2 :** to move in a sinuous provocative manner ~ *vt* **:** to give premature birth to — used esp. of a domestic animal ⟨a cow that ~*s* her calf⟩ ***syn*** see LURK
[2]**slink** *n* (1607) **:** the young of an animal (as a calf) brought forth prematurely; *also* **:** the flesh or skin of such an animal
[3]**slink** *adj* (1750) **:** born prematurely or abortively ⟨a ~ calf⟩
slinky \ˈsliŋ-kē\ *adj* **slink·i·er; -est** (1918) **1 :** characterized by slinking **:** stealthily quiet ⟨~ movements⟩ **2 :** sleek and sinuous in movement or outline; *esp* **:** following the lines of the figure in a gracefully flowing manner ⟨a ~ evening gown⟩ — **slink·i·ly** \-kə-lē\ *adv* — **slink·i·ness** \-kē-nəs\ *n*
[1]**slip** \ˈslip\ *vb* **slipped; slip·ping** [ME *slippen,* fr. MD or MLG; akin to MHG *slipfen* to slide, OHG *slīfan* to smooth, and perh. to Gk *olibros* slippery] *vi* (14c) **1 a :** to move with a smooth sliding motion **b :** to move quietly and cautiously **:** STEAL **c :** ELAPSE, PASS **2 a** (1) **:** to escape from memory or consciousness (2) **:** to become uttered through inadvertence **b :** to pass quickly or easily away **:** become lost ⟨let an opportunity ~⟩ **3 :** to fall into error or fault **:** LAPSE **4 a :** to slide out of place or away from a support or one's grasp **b :** to slide on or down a slippery surface ⟨~ on the stairs⟩ **c :** to flow smoothly **5 :** to get speedily into or out of clothing ⟨*slipped* into his coat⟩ **6 :** to fall off from a standard or accustomed level by degrees **:** DECLINE **7 :** SIDESLIP ~ *vt* **1 :** to cause to move easily and smoothly **:** SLIDE **2 a :** to get away from **:** ELUDE, EVADE ⟨*slipped* his pursuers⟩ **b :** to free oneself from ⟨the dog *slipped* its collar⟩ **c :** to escape from (one's memory or notice) ⟨their names ~ my mind⟩ **3 :** SHED, CAST ⟨the snake *slipped* its skin⟩ **4 :** to put on (a garment) quickly — usu. used with *on* ⟨~ on a coat⟩ **5 a :** to let loose from a restraining leash or grasp **b :** to cause to slip open **:** RELEASE, UNDO ⟨~ a lock⟩ **c :** to let go of **d :** to disengage from (an anchor) instead of hauling **6 a :** to insert, place, or pass quietly or secretly **b :** to give or pay on the sly **7 :** SLINK, ABORT **8 :** DISLOCATE ⟨*slipped* his shoulder⟩ **9 :** to transfer (a stitch) from one needle to another without working a stitch **10 :** to avoid (a punch) by moving the body or head quickly to one side
[2]**slip** *n* (15c) **1 a :** a sloping ramp extending out into the water to serve as a place for landing or repairing ships **b :** a ship's or boat's berth between two piers **2 :** the act or an instance of departing secretly or hurriedly ⟨gave his pursuer the ~⟩ **3 a :** a mistake in judgment, policy, or procedure **b :** an unintentional and trivial mistake or fault **:** LAPSE ⟨a ~ of the tongue⟩ **4 :** a leash so made that it can be quickly slipped **5 a :** the act or an instance of slipping down or out of a place ⟨a ~ on the ice⟩; *also* **:** a sudden mishap **b :** a movement dislocating parts (as of a rock or soil mass); *also* **:** the result of such movement **c :** a fall from some level or standard **:** DECLINE ⟨a ~ in stock prices⟩ **6 a :** an undergarment made in dress length and usu. having shoulder straps; *also* **:** HALF-SLIP **b :** a case into which something is slipped; *specif* **:** PILLOWCASE **7 :** a disposition or tendency to slip easily **8 :** the action of sideslipping **:** an instance of sideslipping ***syn*** see ERROR
[3]**slip** *n* [ME *slippe,* prob. fr. MD or MLG, split, slit, flap] (15c) **1 a :** a small shoot or twig cut for planting or grafting **:** SCION **b :** DESCENDANT, OFFSPRING **2 a :** a long narrow strip of material **b :** a small piece of paper **3 :** a young and slender person ⟨a ~ of a girl⟩ **4 :** a long seat or narrow pew
[4]**slip** *vt* **slipped; slip·ping** (1530) **:** to take cuttings from (a plant) **:** divide into slips ⟨~ a geranium⟩
[5]**slip** *n* [ME *slyp* slime, fr. OE *slypa* slime, paste; akin to OE *slūpan* to slip — more at SLEEVE] (1640) **:** a mixture of finely divided clay and water used esp. by potters (as for casting or decorating wares or in cementing separately formed parts)
slip·case \ˈslip-ˌkās\ *n* (ca. 1925) **:** a protective container for books or magazines that has one open end — **slip·cased** \-ˌkāst\ *adj*
slip·cov·er \ˈslip-ˌkə-vər\ *n* (1856) **:** a cover that may be slipped off and on; *specif* **:** a removable covering for an article of furniture
slip·form \ˈslip-ˌfȯrm\ *vt* (1962) **:** to construct with the use of a slip form
slip form *n* (1949) **:** a form that is moved slowly as concrete is placed during construction (as of a building or pavement)
slip·knot \ˈslip-ˌnät\ *n* (1659) **:** a knot that slips along the rope or line around which it is made; *esp* **:** one made by tying an overhand knot around the standing part of a rope — see KNOT illustration
slip noose *n* (1835) **:** a noose with a slipknot
slip–on \ˈslip-ˌȯn, -ˌän\ *n* (1815) **:** an article of clothing that is easily slipped on or off: as **a :** a glove or shoe without fastenings **b :** a garment (as a girdle) that one steps into and pulls up **c :** PULLOVER
slip·over \-ˌō-vər\ *n* (1917) **:** a garment or cover that slips on and off easily; *specif* **:** a pullover sweater
slip·page \ˈsli-pij\ *n* (1850) **1 :** an act, instance, or process of slipping **2 :** a loss in transmission of power; *also* **:** the difference between theoretical and actual output (as of power)
slipped disk *n* (1942) **:** a protrusion of one of the cartilage disks between vertebrae with pressure on spinal nerves resulting in low back pain or sciatic pain
[1]**slip·per** \ˈsli-pər\ *adj* [ME, fr. OE *slipor;* akin to MLG *slipper* slippery, *slippen* to slip] (bef. 12c) *chiefly dial* **:** SLIPPERY
[2]**slipper** *n* [ME, fr. *slippen* to slip] (15c) **:** a light low-cut shoe that is easily slipped on the foot — **slip·pered** \-pərd\ *adj*
slipper chair *n* (1927) **:** an armless upholstered chair with short legs
slip·pery \ˈsli-p(ə-)rē\ *adj* **slip·per·i·er; -est** [alter. of ME *slipper*] (ca. 1500) **1 a :** causing or tending to cause something to slide or fall ⟨~ roads⟩ **b :** tending to slip from the grasp ⟨a ~ fish⟩ **2 a :** not firmly fixed **:** UNSTABLE **b :** not precise or fixed in meaning **:** AMBIGUOUS, ELUSIVE **3 :** not to be trusted **:** TRICKY — **slip·per·i·ness** *n*
slippery elm *n* (1748) **:** a large-leaved elm (*Ulmus rubra* syn. *U. fulva*) of eastern and central No. America that has hard wood and fragrant mucilaginous inner bark; *also* **:** the bark
slippery slope *n* (1951) **:** a course of action that seems to lead inevitably from one action or result to another with unintended consequences
slip·py \ˈsli-pē\ *adj* **slip·pi·er; -est** (1548) **:** SLIPPERY
slip ring *n* [[2]*slip*] (1898) **:** one of two or more continuous conducting rings from which the brushes take or to which they deliver current in a generator or motor
slip–sheet \ˈslip-ˌshēt\ *vt* (ca. 1909) **:** to insert slip sheets between (newly printed sheets)

slip sheet *n* [[1]*slip*] (1903) : a sheet of paper placed between newly printed sheets to prevent offsetting

slip•shod \'slip-'shäd\ *adj* [[1]*slip*] (1580) **1 a** : wearing loose shoes or slippers **b** : down at the heel : SHABBY **2** : CARELESS, SLOVENLY

slip•slop \-ˌsläp\ *n* [redupl. of [2]*slop*] (1675) **1** *archaic* : watery food : SLOPS **2** *archaic* : shallow talk or writing — **slip–slop** *adj*

slip•sole \-ˌsōl\ *n* (ca. 1908) **1** : a thin insole **2** : a half sole inserted between the insole or welt and the outsole of a shoe to give additional height — called also *slip tap*

slip stitch *n* (ca. 1882) **1** : a concealed stitch for sewing folded edges (as hems) made by alternately running the needle inside the fold and picking up a thread or two from the body of the article **2** : an unworked stitch; *esp* : a knitting stitch that is shifted from one needle to another without knitting it

[1]**slip•stream** \'slip-ˌstrēm\ *n* (1913) **1** : a stream of fluid (as air or water) driven aft by a propeller **2** : an area of reduced air pressure and forward suction immediately behind a rapidly moving vehicle

[2]**slipstream** *vi* (1957) : to drive in the slipstream of a vehicle

slip•up \'slip-ˌəp\ *n* (1854) **1** : MISTAKE **2** : MISCHANCE

slip up *vi* (1909) : to make a mistake : BLUNDER

slip•ware \'slip-ˌwer\ *n* (1883) : pottery coated with slip to improve or decorate the surface

slip•way \-ˌwā\ *n* (1840) : an inclined usu. concrete surface for a ship being built or repaired

[1]**slit** \'slit\ *n* [ME, fr. *slitten*] (12c) : a long narrow cut or opening — **slit** *adj* — **slit•less** \'slit-ləs\ *adj*

[2]**slit** *vt* **slit; slit•ting** [ME *slitten;* akin to MHG *slitzen* to slit, OHG *slīzan* to tear apart, OE *sciell* shell — more at SHELL] (14c) **1 a** : to make a slit in **b** : to cut off or away : SEVER **c** : to form into a slit **2** : to cut into long narrow strips — **slit•ter** *n*

slith•er \'sli-t͟hər\ *vb* [ME *slideren,* fr. OE *slidrian,* freq. of *slīdan* to slide] *vi* (bef. 12c) **1** : to slide on or as if on a loose gravelly surface **2** : to slip or slide like a snake ~ *vt* : to cause to slide

slith•ery \'sli-t͟hə-rē\ *adj* (ca. 1825) : having a slippery surface, texture, or quality

slit trench *n* (1942) : a narrow trench esp. for shelter in battle from bomb and shell fragments

[1]**sliv•er** \'sli-vər, *2 is usu* 'slī-\ *n* [ME *slivere,* fr. *sliven* to slice off, fr. OE *-slīfan;* akin to OE *-slǣfan* to cut] (14c) **1 a** : a long slender piece cut or torn off : SPLINTER **b** : a small and narrow portion ⟨a ~ of land⟩ **c** : PARTICLE, SCRAP ⟨not a ~ of evidence⟩ **2** : an untwisted strand or rope of textile fiber produced by a carding or combing machine and ready for drawing, roving, or spinning

[2]**sliv•er** \'sli-vər\ *vb* **sliv•ered; sliv•er•ing** \'sli-və-riŋ, 'sliv-riŋ\ *vt* (1605) : to cut into slivers : SPLINTER ~ *vi* : to become split into slivers

sliv•o•vitz \'sli-və-ˌvits, 'slē-, -ˌwits\ *n* [Serbian & Croatian *šljivovica,* fr. *šljiva, sliva* plum; akin to Russ *sliva* plum — more at LIVID] (1837) : a dry usu. colorless plum brandy made esp. in the Balkan countries

slob \'släb\ *n* [Ir *slab* mud, ooze, slovenly person] (1861) **1** : a slovenly or boorish person **2** : an ordinary person ⟨just some poor ~⟩ — **slob•bish** \'slä-bish\ *adj* — **slob•by** \-bē\ *adj*

[1]**slob•ber** \'slä-bər\ *vb* **slob•bered; slob•ber•ing** \-b(ə-)riŋ\ [ME *sloberen* to eat in a slovenly manner; akin to LG *slubberen* to sip] *vi* (1607) **1** : to let saliva dribble from the mouth : DROOL **2** : to indulge the feelings effusively and without restraint ~ *vt* : to smear with or as if with dribbling saliva or food — **slob•ber•er** \-bər-ər\ *n*

[2]**slobber** *n* (ca. 1755) **1** : saliva drooled from the mouth **2** : driveling, sloppy, or incoherent utterance — **slob•bery** \'slä-b(ə-)rē\ *adj*

sloe \'slō\ *n* [ME *slo,* fr. OE *slāh;* akin to OHG *slēha* sloe and prob. to Russ *sliva* plum — more at LIVID] (bef. 12c) : the small dark globose astringent fruit of the blackthorn; *also* : BLACKTHORN

sloe–eyed \'slō-ˌīd\ *adj* (1867) **1** : having soft dark bluish- or purplish-black eyes **2** : having slanted eyes

sloe gin *n* (1895) : a sweet reddish liqueur consisting of grain spirits flavored chiefly with sloes

[1]**slog** \'släg\ *vb* **slogged; slog•ging** [origin unknown] *vt* (1824) **1** : to hit hard : BEAT **2** : to plod (one's way) perseveringly esp. against difficulty ~ *vi* **1** : to plod heavily : TRAMP ⟨*slogged* through the snow⟩ **2** : to work hard and steadily : PLUG — **slog•ger** *n*

[2]**slog** *n* (1888) **1 a** : hard persistent work ⟨the endless enervating ~ of war —Michael Gorra⟩ **b** : a prolonged arduous task or effort ⟨reform will be a hard political ~ —M. S. Forbes⟩ **2** : a hard dogged march or journey

slo•gan \'slō-gən\ *n* [alter. of earlier *slogorn,* fr. ScGael *sluagh-ghairm,* fr. *sluagh* army, host + *gairm* cry] (1513) **1 a** : a war cry esp. of a Scottish clan **b** : a word or phrase used to express a characteristic position or stand or a goal to be achieved **2** : a brief attention-getting phrase used in advertising or promotion

slo•gan•eer \ˌslō-gə-'nir\ *n* (1922) : a maker or user of slogans — **sloganeer** *vi*

slo•gan•ize \'slō-gə-ˌnīz\ *vt* **-ized; -iz•ing** (1926) : to express as a slogan

slo–mo \'slō-ˌmō\ *adj* (1972) : SLOW-MOTION — **slo–mo** *n*

sloop \'slüp\ *n* [D *sloep*] (1629) : a fore-and-aft rigged boat with one mast and a single jib

sloop of war (1704) : a small warship with guns on only one deck

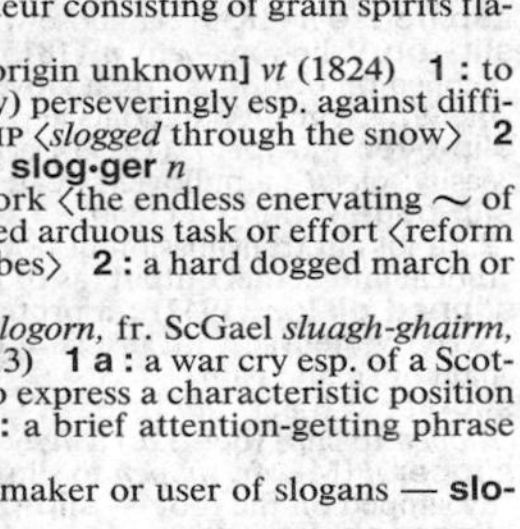

sloop

[1]**slop** \'släp\ *n* [ME *sloppe,* prob. fr. MD *slop;* akin to OE *oferslop* surplice] (14c) **1** : a loose smock or overall **2** *pl* : short full breeches worn by men in the 16th century **3** *pl* : articles (as clothing) sold to sailors

[2]**slop** *n* [ME *sloppes,* prob. fr. OE *-sloppe* (in *cū-sloppe* cowslip, lit., cow dung); akin to OE *slypa* slime — more at SLIP] (15c) **1** : soft mud : SLUSH **2** : thin tasteless drink or liquid food — usu. used in pl. **3** : liquid spilled or splashed **4 a** : food waste (as garbage) fed to animals : SWILL 2a **b** : excreted body waste — usu. used in pl. **c** : a product of little or no value : RUBBISH ⟨watching the usual ~ on TV⟩ **5** : sentimental effusiveness in speech or writing : GUSH

[3]**slop** *vb* **slopped; slop•ping** *vt* (1557) **1 a** : to spill from a container **b** : to splash or spill liquid on **c** : to cause (a liquid) to splash **2** : to dish out messily **3** : to eat or drink greedily or noisily **4** : to feed slop to ⟨~ the hogs⟩ ~ *vi* **1** : to tramp in mud or slush **2** : to become spilled or splashed **3** : to be effusive : GUSH **4** : to pass beyond or exceed a boundary or limit

slop basin *n* (1731) *Brit* : SLOP BOWL

slop bowl *n* (1810) : a bowl for receiving the leavings of tea or coffee cups at table

slop chest *n* [[1]*slop*] (1840) : a store of clothing and personal requisites (as tobacco) carried on merchant ships for issue to the crew usu. as a charge against their wages

[1]**slope** \'slōp\ *adj* [ME *sloop,* prob. fr. *aslope,* adv., at an angle] (15c) : that slants : SLOPING — often used in combination ⟨*slope*-sided⟩

[2]**slope** *vb* **sloped; slop•ing** *vi* (1591) **1** : to take an oblique course **2** : to lie or fall in a slant : INCLINE **3** : GO, TRAVEL ⟨~*s* off into the night —Wolcott Gibbs⟩ ~ *vt* : to cause to incline or slant — **slop•er** *n*

[3]**slope** *n* (ca. 1568) **1** : ground that forms a natural or artificial incline **2** : upward or downward slant or inclination or degree of slant **3** : the part of a continent draining to a particular ocean ⟨Alaska's North *Slope*⟩ **4 a** : the tangent of the angle made by a straight line with the x-axis **b** : the slope of the line tangent to a plane curve at a point

slope–intercept form *n* (ca. 1942) : the equation of a straight line in the form $y = mx + b$ where m is the slope of the line and b is its y-intercept

slo–pitch \'slō-'pich, -ˌpich\ *n, often attrib* [alter. of *slow pitch*] (1967) : SLOW-PITCH

slop jar *n* (1855) : a large pail used as a chamber pot or to receive waste water from a washbowl or the contents of chamber pots

slop pail *n* (1854) : a pail for toilet or household slops

slop•py \'slä-pē\ *adj* **slop•pi•er; -est** (1672) **1 a** : wet so as to spatter easily : SLUSHY ⟨a ~ racetrack⟩ **b** : wet or smeared with or as if with something slopped over **2** : SLOVENLY, CARELESS ⟨a ~ dresser⟩ ⟨did ~ work⟩ **3** : disagreeably effusive ⟨~ sentimentalism⟩ — **slop•pi•ly** \'slä-pə-lē\ *adv* — **slop•pi•ness** *n*

sloppy joe \-'jō\ *n* [prob. fr. the name *Joe,* nickname for *Joseph*] (1942) **1** *often cap S&J* : a loose-fitting sweater esp. for girls **2** : ground beef cooked in a thick spicy sauce and usu. served on a bun

slop•work \'släp-ˌwərk\ *n* (1849) **1** : the manufacture of cheap ready-made clothing **2** : hasty slovenly work

[1]**slosh** \'släsh, 'slȯsh\ *n* [prob. blend of *slop* and *slush*] (1814) **1** : SLUSH 1 **2** : the slap or splash of liquid — **sloshy** \'slä-shē\ *adj*

[2]**slosh** *vi* (1844) **1** : to flounder or splash through water, mud, or slush **2** : to move with a splashing motion ⟨the water ~*ed* around him —Bill Alcine⟩ ~ *vt* **1** : to splash about in liquid **2** : to splash (a liquid) about or on something **3** : to splash with liquid

sloshed \'slăsht, 'slȯsht\ *adj* (ca. 1946) *slang* : DRUNK, INTOXICATED

[1]**slot** \'slät\ *n* [ME, the hollow at the base of the throat above the breastbone, fr. AF *esclot* hoofprint, of Gmc origin; akin to MHG *slag* blow, hoofprint; prob. fr. its resemblance to a hoofprint — more at SCHLOCK] (1523) **1 a** : a narrow opening or groove : SLIT, NOTCH ⟨a mail ~ in a door⟩ **b** : a narrow passage or enclosure **c** : a passage through the wing of an airplane or of a missile that is located usu. near the leading edge and formed between a main and an auxiliary airfoil for improving flow conditions over the wing so as to increase lift and delay stalling of the wing **d** : the area on a hockey rink in front of the crease and between the face-off circles **2** : a place or position in an organization, arrangement, or sequence : NICHE, SPOT **3** : SLOT MACHINE 2 — usu. used in pl. **4** : a gap between an end and a tackle in an offensive football line

[2]**slot** *vb* **slot•ted; slot•ting** *vt* (1747) **1** : to cut a slot in **2** : to place in or assign to a slot ~ *vi* : to fit easily ⟨her ideas ~ neatly into the theory⟩

[3]**slot** *n, pl* **slot** [MF *esclot* track] (1575) : the track of an animal (as a deer)

slot•back \'slät-ˌbak\ *n* (1959) : an offensive football halfback who lines up just behind the slot between an offensive end and tackle

slot car *n* (1966) : an electric toy racing car with a pin underneath that fits into a groove on a track for guidance

sloth \'slȯth, 'släth *also* 'slōth\ *n, pl* **sloths** *with* ths *or* t͟hz\ [ME *slouthe,* fr. *slow* slow] (12c) **1 a** : disinclination to action or labor : INDOLENCE **b** : spiritual apathy and inactivity ⟨the deadly sin of ~⟩ **2** : any of various slow-moving arboreal edentate mammals (genera *Bradypus* and *Choloepus*) that inhabit tropical forests of So. and Central America, hang from the branches back downward, and feed on leaves, shoots, and fruits — compare THREE-TOED SLOTH, TWO-TOED SLOTH

sloth bear *n* (1835) : a forest-dwelling bear (*Melurus ursinus*) of India and adjacent regions that has long black hair, very large claws, and a long snout and that feeds chiefly on insects

sloth•ful \'slȯth-fəl, 'släth- *also* 'slōth-\ *adj* (15c) : inclined to sloth : INDOLENT ***syn*** see LAZY — **sloth•ful•ly** \-fə-lē\ *adv* — **sloth•ful•ness** *n*

slot machine *n* (1891) **1** : a machine whose operation is begun by dropping a coin into a slot **2** : an orig. coin-operated gambling machine that pays off according to the matching of symbols on wheels spun by a handle; *also* : an electronic version of this machine

slot racing *n* (1965) : the racing of slot cars — **slot racer** *n*

slotting fee *n* (1984) : a fee charged by a vendor in exchange for carrying a manufacturer's product — called also *slotting allowance*

[1]**slouch** \'slau̇ch\ *n* [origin unknown] (1515) **1 a** : an awkward fellow : LOUT **b** : one that is unimpressive; *esp* : a lazy or incompetent person — used in negative constructions ⟨was no ~ at cooking⟩ **2 a** : a gait or posture characterized by an ungainly stooping of the head and shoulders or excessive relaxation of body muscles

[2]**slouch** *vi* (1754) **1** : to walk, stand, or sit with a slouch : assume a slouch **2** : DROOP **3** : to go or move slowly or reluctantly ~ *vt* : to cause to droop ⟨~*ed* his shoulders⟩ — **slouch•er** *n*

slouch hat *n* (1837) : a soft usu. felt hat with a wide flexible brim

slouchy \'slau̇-chē\ *adj* **slouch•i•er; -est** (ca. 1693) : lacking erectness or stiffness (as in form or posture) ⟨a ~ sweater⟩ ⟨~ figures waiting in line⟩ — **slouch•i•ly** \-chə-lē\ *adv* — **slouch•i•ness** \-chē-nəs\ *n*

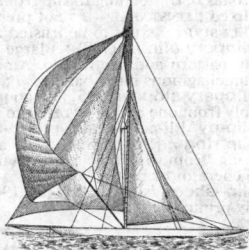

[1]**slough** \ˈslü, ˈslau̇; *in the US* (*exc NewEng*) ˈslü *is usual for sense 1 with those to whom the sense is familiar; Brit usu* ˈslau̇ *for both senses*\ *n* [ME *sloughe, slo,* fr. OE *slōh;* akin to MHG *slouche* ditch] (bef. 12c) **1 a :** a place of deep mud or mire **b** *also* **slew** *or* **slue** \ˈslü\ (1) **:** SWAMP (2) **:** an inlet on a river; *also* **:** BACKWATER (3) **:** a creek in a marsh or tide flat **2 :** a state of moral degradation or spiritual dejection — **sloughy** \-ē\ *adj*

[2]**slough** *vt* (1846) **:** to engulf in a slough ~ *vi* **:** to plod through or as if through mud **:** SLOG

[3]**slough** \ˈsləf\ *also* **sluff** *n* [ME *slughe;* akin to MHG *slūch* snakeskin] (14c) **1 :** the cast-off skin of a snake **2 :** a mass of dead tissue separating from an ulcer **3 :** something that may be shed or cast off

[4]**slough** \ˈsləf\ *also* **sluff** *vi* (1720) **1 a :** to become shed or cast off **b :** to cast off one's skin **c :** to separate in the form of dead tissue from living tissue **2 :** to crumble slowly and fall away ~ *vt* **1 :** to cast off **2 a :** to get rid of or discard as irksome, objectionable, or disadvantageous — usu. used with *off* **b :** to dispose of (a losing card in bridge) by discarding ***syn*** see DISCARD

slough of de·spond \ˌslau̇-əv-di-ˈspänd, ˌslü-\ [fr. the *Slough of Despond,* deep bog into which Christian falls on the way from the City of Destruction and from which Help saves him in the allegory *Pilgrim's Progress* (1678) by John Bunyan] (1776) **:** a state of extreme depression

Slo·vak \ˈslō-ˌväk, -ˌvak\ *n* [Slovak *slovák*] (1829) **1 :** a member of a Slavic people of Slovakia **2 :** the Slavic language of the Slovak people — **Slovak** *adj* — **Slo·va·ki·an** \slō-ˈvä-kē-ən, -ˈva-\ *adj or n*

[1]**slov·en** \ˈslə-vən\ *n* [ME *sloveyn* slut, rascal, perh. fr. MD *slof* negligent] (15c) **:** one habitually negligent of neatness or cleanliness esp. in personal appearance

[2]**sloven** *adj* (1815) **:** SLOVENLY

Slo·vene \ˈslō-ˌvēn\ *n* [G *Slowene* fr. Slovene *Slovenec*] (1876) **1 :** a member of a Slavic people living largely in Slovenia **2 :** the language of the Slovenes — **Slovene** *adj* — **Slo·ve·nian** \slō-ˈvē-nē-ən, -nyən\ *adj or n*

slov·en·ly \ˈslə-vən-lē *also* ˈslä-\ *adj* (ca. 1568) **1 a :** untidy esp. in personal appearance **b :** lazily slipshod ⟨~ in thought⟩ **2 :** characteristic of a sloven ⟨~ habits⟩ — **slo·ven·li·ness** *n* — **slovenly** *adv*

[1]**slow** \ˈslō\ *adj* [ME, fr. OE *slāw;* akin to OHG *slēo* dull] (bef. 12c) **1 a :** mentally dull **:** STUPID ⟨a ~ student⟩ **b :** naturally inert or sluggish **2 a :** lacking in readiness, promptness, or willingness **b :** not hasty or precipitate ⟨was ~ to anger⟩ **3 a :** moving, flowing, or proceeding without speed or at less than usual speed ⟨traffic was ~⟩ **b :** exhibiting or marked by low speed ⟨he moved with ~ deliberation⟩ **c :** not acute ⟨a ~ disease⟩ **d :** LOW, GENTLE ⟨~ fire⟩ **4 :** requiring a long time **:** GRADUAL ⟨a ~ recovery⟩ **5 :** having qualities that hinder rapid progress or action ⟨a ~ track⟩ **6 a :** registering behind or below what is correct ⟨the clock is ~⟩ **b :** less than the time indicated by another method of reckoning **c :** that is behind the time at a specified time or place **7 a :** lacking in life, animation, or gaiety **:** BORING ⟨the first chapter is a bit ~⟩ **b :** marked by reduced activity ⟨business was ~⟩ ⟨a ~ news week⟩ — **slow·ish** \ˈslō-ish\ *adj* — **slow·ness** *n*

[2]**slow** *adv* (15c) **:** SLOWLY

usage Some commentators claim that careful writers avoid the adverb *slow,* in spite of the fact that it has had over four centuries of usage ⟨have a continent forbearance till the speed of his rage goes *slower* —Shak.⟩. In actual practice, *slow* and *slowly* are not used in quite the same way. *Slow* is almost always used with verbs that denote movement or action, and it regularly follows the verb it modifies ⟨beans . . . are best cooked long and *slow* —Louise Prothro⟩. *Slowly* is used before the verb ⟨a sense of outrage, which *slowly* changed to shame —Paul Horgan⟩ and with participial adjectives ⟨a *slowly* dawning awareness . . . of the problem —*Amer. Labor*⟩. *Slowly* is used after verbs where *slow* might also be used ⟨burn *slow* or *slowly*⟩ and after verbs where *slow* would be unidiomatic ⟨the leadership turned *slowly* toward bombing as a means of striking back —David Halberstam⟩.

[3]**slow** *vt* (1557) **:** to make slow or slower **:** slacken the speed of ⟨~ a car⟩ — often used with *down* or *up* ~ *vi* **:** to go or become slower ⟨production of new cars ~*ed* sharply⟩ ***syn*** see DELAY

slow·down \ˈslō-ˌdau̇n\ *n* (1897) **:** a slowing down ⟨a business ~⟩

slow–foot·ed \-ˌfu̇-təd\ *adj* (1642) **:** moving at a very slow pace **:** PLODDING ⟨a ~ novel⟩ ⟨a ~ ship⟩ — **slow–foot·ed·ness** *n*

slow·ly \-lē\ *adv* (13c) **:** in a slow manner **:** not quickly, fast, early, rashly, or readily ***usage*** see SLOW

slow match *n* (ca. 1802) **:** a match or fuse made so as to burn slowly and evenly and used for firing (as of blasting charges)

slow–motion \ˈslō-ˈmō-shən\ *adj* (1923) **:** of, relating to, or being motion-picture or video photography in which the action that has been photographed is made to appear to occur slower than it actually occurred ⟨a ~ replay⟩; *also* **:** slowly moving ⟨a ~ dance⟩

slow motion *n* (1924) **:** slow-motion photography

slow–pitch \ˈslō-ˌpich\ *n* (1967) **:** softball which is played with 10 players on each side and in which each pitch must have an arc 3 to 10 feet high and base stealing is not allowed — compare FAST-PITCH

slow·poke \ˈslō-ˌpōk\ *n* [[1]*slow* + *poke* annoyingly stupid person] (ca. 1848) **:** a very slow person

slow–twitch \ˈslō-ˌtwich\ *adj* (1971) **:** of, relating to, or being muscle fiber that contracts slowly esp. during sustained physical activity requiring endurance — compare FAST-TWITCH

slow virus *n* (1954) **:** any of various infectious agents now usu. considered to be prions that have a long incubation period between infection and the clinical appearance of the associated disease — compare PRION DISEASE

slow–wave sleep *n* (1967) **:** a state of deep usu. dreamless sleep that occurs regularly during a normal period of sleep with intervening periods of REM sleep and that is characterized by delta waves and a low level of autonomic physiological activity

slow–wit·ted \-ˈwi-təd\ *adj* (1571) **:** mentally slow **:** DULL

slow·worm \-ˌwərm\ *n* [ME *sloworm,* fr. OE *slāwyrm,* fr. *slā-* (akin to Sw *slå* earthworm) + *wyrm* worm] (bef. 12c) **:** a burrowing limbless European lizard (*Anguis fragilis*) with small eyes — called also *blindworm*

SLR *abbr* single-lens reflex

[1]**slub** \ˈsləb\ *vt* **slubbed; slub·bing** [back-formation fr. *slubbing*] (1834) **:** to draw out and twist (as slivers of wool) slightly

[2]**slub** *n* (1851) **:** a soft thick uneven section in a yarn or thread

slub·ber \ˈslə-bər\ *vt* **slub·bered; slub·ber·ing** \-b(ə-)riŋ\ [prob. fr. obs. D *slubberen*] (1530) **1** *dial chiefly Eng* **:** STAIN, SULLY **2 :** to perform in a slipshod fashion

slub·bing \ˈslə-biŋ\ *n* [origin unknown] (1786) **:** ROVING

sludge \ˈsləj\ *n* [ME *slugge,* perh. alter. of *slicche* mud, slush; akin to OHG *slīh* mire] (15c) **1 :** MUD, MIRE; *esp* **:** a muddy deposit (as on a riverbed) **:** OOZE **2 :** a muddy or slushy mass, deposit, or sediment: as **a :** precipitated solid matter produced by water and sewage treatment processes **b :** muddy sediment in a steam boiler **c :** a precipitate or settling (as a mixture of impurities and acid) from a mineral oil **3 :** SLUSH 5 — **sludgy** \ˈslə-jē\ *adj*

[1]**slue** *var of* [1]SLOUGH 1b

[2]**slue** *var of* [3]SLEW

[3]**slue** *n* [[2]*slue*] (ca. 1860) **1 :** position or inclination after slewing **2 :** SKID 5

[1]**slug** \ˈsləg\ *n* [ME *slugge,* of Scand origin; akin to Norw dial. *slugga* to walk sluggishly] (15c) **1 :** SLUGGARD **2 :** a lump, disk, or cylinder of material (as plastic or metal): as **a** (1) **:** a musket ball (2) **:** BULLET **b :** a piece of metal roughly shaped for subsequent processing **c :** a $50 gold piece **d :** a disk for insertion in a slot machine; *esp* **:** one used illegally instead of a coin **3 :** any of numerous chiefly terrestrial pulmonate gastropods (order Stylommatophora) that are found in most parts of the world where there is a reasonable supply of moisture and are closely related to the land snails but are long and wormlike and have only a rudimentary shell often buried in the mantle or entirely absent **4 :** a smooth soft larva of a sawfly or moth that creeps like a mollusk **5 a :** a quantity of liquor drunk in one swallow **b :** a detached mass of fluid (as water vapor or oil) that causes impact (as in a circulating system) **6 a :** a strip of metal thicker than a printer's lead **b :** a line of type cast as one piece **c :** a usu. temporary type line serving to instruct or identify **7 :** the gravitational unit of mass in the foot-pound-second system to which a pound force can impart an acceleration of one foot per second per second and which is equal to the mass of an object weighing 32 pounds

[2]**slug** *vt* **slugged; slug·ging** (1912) **1 :** to add a printer's slug to **2 :** to drink in gulps — often used with *down*

[3]**slug** *n* [perh. fr. *slug* to load with slugs] (1830) **:** a heavy blow esp. with the fist

[4]**slug** *vt* **slugged; slug·ging** (ca. 1861) **1 :** to strike heavily with or as if with the fist or a bat **2 :** FIGHT 4b — usu. used in the phrase *slug it out*

slug·abed \ˈslə-gə-ˌbed\ *n* (1592) **:** a person who stays in bed after the usual or proper time to get up; *broadly* **:** SLUGGARD

slug·fest \ˈsləg-ˌfest\ *n* (1916) **:** a fight marked by the exchange of heavy blows; *also* **:** a heated dispute ⟨a vocal ~⟩

[1]**slug·gard** \ˈslə-gərd\ *n* [ME *sluggart*] (14c) **:** a habitually lazy person

[2]**sluggard** *adj* (1557) **:** SLUGGARDLY — **slug·gard·ness** *n*

slug·gard·ly \ˈslə-gərd-lē\ *adj* (1865) **:** lazily inactive

slug·ger \ˈslə-gər\ *n* (1877) **:** one that strikes hard or with heavy blows: as **a :** a prizefighter who punches hard but has usu. little defensive skill **b :** a hard-hitting batter in baseball

slugging percentage *n* (ca. 1949) **:** the ratio (as a rate per thousand) of the total number of bases reached on base hits to official times at bat for a baseball player — called also *slugging average*

slug·gish \ˈslə-gish\ *adj* (15c) **1 :** averse to activity or exertion **:** INDOLENT; *also* **:** TORPID **2 :** slow to respond (as to stimulation or treatment) **3 a :** markedly slow in movement, flow, or growth **b :** economically inactive or slow — **slug·gish·ly** *adv* — **slug·gish·ness** *n*

[1]**sluice** \ˈslüs\ *n* [ME *sluse,* alter. of *scluse,* fr. AF *escluse,* fr. LL *exclusa,* fr. L, fem. of *exclusus,* pp. of *excludere* to exclude] (15c) **1 a :** an artificial passage for water (as in a millstream) fitted with a valve or gate for stopping or regulating flow **b :** a body of water pent up behind a floodgate **2 :** a dock gate **:** FLOODGATE **3 a :** a stream flowing through a floodgate **b :** a channel to drain or carry off surplus water **4 :** a long inclined trough usu. on the ground; *esp* **:** such a contrivance paved usu. with riffles to hold quicksilver for catching gold

[2]**sluice** *vb* **sluiced; sluic·ing** *vt* (1596) **1 :** to draw off by or through a sluice **2 a :** to wash with or in water running through or from a sluice **b :** to drench with a sudden flow **:** FLUSH **3 :** to transport (as logs) in a sluice ~ *vi* **:** to pour as if from a sluice

sluice·way \ˈslüs-ˌwā\ *n* (1779) **:** an artificial channel into which water is let by a sluice

sluicy \ˈslü-sē\ *adj* (1697) **:** falling copiously or in streams **:** STREAMING

[1]**slum** \ˈsləm\ *n, often attrib* [origin unknown] (1825) **:** a densely populated usu. urban area marked by crowding, dirty run-down housing, poverty, and social disorganization

[2]**slum** *vi* **slummed; slum·ming** (1884) **:** to visit slums esp. out of curiosity; *broadly* **:** to go somewhere or do something that might be considered beneath one's station — sometimes used with *it* ⟨*slumming* it in budget hotels⟩ — **slum·mer** *n*

[1]**slum·ber** \ˈsləm-bər\ *vi* **slum·bered; slum·ber·ing** \-b(ə-)riŋ\ [ME *slomren, slombren,* freq. of *slumen* to doze, prob. fr. *slume* slumber, fr. OE *slūma;* akin to MHG *slumen* to slumber] (13c) **1 a :** to sleep lightly **:** DOZE **b :** SLEEP **2 a :** to be in a torpid, slothful, or negligent state **b :** to lie dormant or latent — **slum·ber·er** \-bər-ər\ *n*

[2]**slumber** *n* (14c) **1 a :** SLEEP **b :** a light sleep **2 :** LETHARGY, TORPOR

slum·ber·ous *or* **slum·brous** \ˈsləm-b(ə-)rəs\ *adj* (15c) **1 :** heavy with sleep **:** SLEEPY **2 :** inducing slumber **:** SOPORIFIC **3 :** marked by or suggestive of a state of sleep or lethargy ⟨a ~ state of peace⟩

slumber party *n* (1925) **:** an overnight gathering esp. of teenage girls usu. at one of their homes

slum·bery \ˈsləm-b(ə-)rē\ *adj* (14c) *archaic* **:** SLUMBEROUS

slum·gul·lion \ˈsləm-ˌgəl-yən, ˌsləm-ˈ\ *n* [perh. fr. *slum* slime + E dial. *gullion* mud, cesspool] (1890) **:** a meat stew

slum·lord \ˈsləm-ˌlȯrd\ *n* [[1]*slum* + land*lord*] (1953) **:** a landlord who receives unusually large profits from substandard properties

slum·my \'slə-mē\ *adj* **slum·mi·er; -est** (1873) : of, relating to, or suggestive of a slum ⟨~ streets⟩

[1]**slump** \'sləmp\ *vi* [prob. imit.] (ca. 1677) **1 a :** to fall or sink suddenly **b :** to drop or slide down suddenly : COLLAPSE **2 :** to assume a drooping posture or carriage : SLOUCH **3 :** to go into a slump ⟨sales ~*ed*⟩

[2]**slump** *n* (1887) **1 a :** a marked or sustained decline esp. in economic activity or prices **b :** a period of poor or losing play by a team or individual **2 :** a downward slide of a mass of rock or land

slump·fla·tion \ˌsləmp-'flā-shən\ *n* [[2]*slump* + in*flation*] (1974) : a state or period of combined economic decline and rising inflation

slung *past and past part of* SLING

slung·shot \'sləŋ-ˌshät\ *n* (1842) : a striking weapon consisting of a small mass of metal or stone fixed on a flexible handle or strap

slunk *past and past part of* SLINK

[1]**slur** \'slər\ *n* [obs. E dial. *slur* thin mud, fr. ME *sloor;* akin to MHG *slier* mud] (1609) **1 a :** an insulting or disparaging remark or innuendo : ASPERSION **b :** a shaming or degrading effect : STAIN, STIGMA **2 :** a blurred spot in printed matter : SMUDGE

[2]**slur** *vb* **slurred; slur·ring** *vt* (1660) **1 :** to cast aspersions on : DISPARAGE ⟨*slurred* his reputation⟩ **2 :** to make indistinct : OBSCURE ~ *vi* **:** to slip so as to cause a slur — used of a sheet being printed

[3]**slur** *vb* **slurred; slur·ring** [prob. fr. LG *slurrn* to shuffle; akin to ME *sloor* mud] *vt* (1660) **1 a :** to slide or slip over without due mention, consideration, or emphasis ⟨*slurred* over certain facts⟩ **b :** to perform hurriedly : SKIMP ⟨let him not ~ his lesson —R. W. Emerson⟩ **2 :** to perform (successive tones of different pitch) in a smooth or connected manner **3 a :** to reduce, make a substitution for, or omit (sounds that would normally occur in an utterance) **b :** to utter with such reduction, substitution, or omission of sounds ⟨his speech was *slurred*⟩ ~ *vi* **1** *dial chiefly Eng* **:** SLIP, SLIDE **2 :** DRAG, SHUFFLE

[4]**slur** *n* (ca. 1801) **1 a :** a curved line connecting notes to be sung to the same syllable or performed without a break **b :** the combination of two or more slurred tones **2 :** a slurring manner of speech

slurb \'slərb\ *n* [*sl-* (as in *slovenly, sleazy*) + sub*urb*] (1962) : a suburb of wearisomely uniform and usu. poorly constructed houses

slurp \'slərp\ *vb* [D *slurpen;* akin to MLG *slorpen* to slurp] *vi* (1648) : to make a sucking noise while eating or drinking ~ *vt* **:** to eat or drink noisily or with a sucking sound — **slurp** *n*

[1]**slur·ry** \'slər-ē, 'slə-rē\ *n, pl* **slur·ries** [ME *slory*] (15c) : a watery mixture of insoluble matter (as mud, lime, or plaster of paris)

[2]**slurry** *vt* **slur·ried; slur·ry·ing** (1947) : to convert into a slurry

slurve \'slərv\ *n* [*sl*ider + *curve*] (1973) : a baseball pitch having the characteristics of both a slider and a curve

[1]**slush** \'sləsh\ *n* [perh. of Scand origin; akin to Norw *slusk* slush] (1641) **1 a :** partly melted or watery snow **b :** loose ice crystals formed during the early stages of freezing of salt water **2 :** soft mud : MIRE **3 :** refuse grease and fat from cooking esp. on shipboard **4 :** paper pulp in water suspension **5 :** trashy and usu. cheaply sentimental material **6 :** unsolicited writings submitted (as to a magazine) for publication

[2]**slush** *vt* (1807) : to wet or splash with slush ~ *vi* **1 :** to make one's way through slush **2 :** to make a splashing sound

slush fund *n* (1839) **1 :** a fund raised from the sale of refuse to obtain small luxuries or pleasures for a warship's crew **2 :** a fund for bribing public officials or carrying on corruptive propaganda **3 :** an unregulated fund often used for illicit purposes

slushy \'slə-shē\ *adj* **slush·i·er; -est** (1791) : being, involving, or resembling slush: as **a :** full of or covered with slush ⟨~ streets⟩ **b :** made up of or having the consistency of slush ⟨~ snow⟩ **c :** having a cheaply sentimental quality ⟨a ~ novel⟩ — **slush·i·ness** *n*

slut \'slət\ *n* [ME *slutte*] (15c) **1** *chiefly Brit* **:** a slovenly woman **2 a :** a promiscuous woman; *esp* **:** PROSTITUTE **b :** a saucy girl : MINX — **slut·tish** \'slə-tish\ *adj* — **slut·tish·ly** *adv* — **slut·tish·ness** *n* — **slut·ty** \'slə-tē\ *adj*

sly \'slī\ *adj* **sli·er** *or* **sly·er** \'slī(-ə)r\; **sli·est** *or* **sly·est** \'slī-əst\ [ME *sleighe, sli,* fr. ON *slœgr;* akin to OE *slēan* to strike — more at SLAY] (13c) **1** *chiefly dial* **a :** wise in practical affairs **b :** displaying cleverness : INGENIOUS **2 a :** clever in concealing one's aims or ends : FURTIVE **b :** lacking in straightforwardness and candor : DISSEMBLING **3 :** lightly mischievous : ROGUISH ⟨a ~ jest⟩ — **sly·ly** *also* **sli·ly** *adv* — **sly·ness** *n* — **on the sly :** in a manner intended to avoid notice

syn SLY, CUNNING, CRAFTY, WILY, TRICKY, FOXY, ARTFUL, SLICK mean attaining or seeking to attain one's ends by guileful or devious means. SLY implies furtiveness, lack of candor, and skill in concealing one's aims and methods ⟨a *sly* corporate raider⟩. CUNNING suggests the inventive use of sometimes limited intelligence in overreaching or circumventing ⟨the *cunning* fox avoided the trap⟩. CRAFTY implies cleverness and subtlety of method ⟨a *crafty* lefthander⟩. WILY implies skill and deception in maneuvering ⟨the *wily* fugitive escaped the posse⟩. TRICKY is more likely to suggest shiftiness and unreliability than skill in deception and maneuvering ⟨a *tricky* political operative⟩. FOXY implies a shrewd and wary craftiness usu. involving devious dealing ⟨a *foxy* publicity man planting stories⟩. ARTFUL implies indirectness in dealing and often connotes sophistication or cleverness ⟨elicited the information by *artful* questioning⟩. SLICK emphasizes smoothness and guile ⟨*slick* operators selling time-sharing⟩.

sly·boots \'slī-ˌbüts\ *n pl but sing in constr* (ca. 1700) : a sly tricky person; *esp* **:** one who is cunning or mischievous in an engaging way

sm *abbr* small

Sm *symbol* samarium

SM *abbr* **1** [NL *scientiae magister*] master of science **2** sergeant major **3** service mark **4** stage manager **5** stationmaster

S–M *or* **S/M** *abbr* sadomasochism; sadomasochist

SMA *abbr* sergeant major of the army

[1]**smack** \'smak\ *n* [ME, fr. OE *smæc;* akin to OHG *smac* taste and prob. to Lith *smaguris* sweet tooth] (bef. 12c) **1 :** characteristic taste or flavor; *also* **:** a perceptible taste or tincture **2 :** a small quantity

[2]**smack** *vi* (13c) **1 :** to have a taste or flavor **2 :** to have a trace, vestige, or suggestion ⟨a proposal that ~*s* of treason⟩

[3]**smack** *n* [D *smak* or LG *smack*] (1533) : a sailing ship (as a sloop or cutter) used chiefly in coasting and fishing

[4]**smack** *vb* [akin to MD *smacken* to strike] *vt* (1557) **1 :** to close and open (lips) noisily and often in rapid succession esp. in eating **2 a :** to kiss with or as if with a smack **b :** to strike so as to produce a smack ~ *vi* **:** to make or give a smack

[5]**smack** *n* (1570) **1 :** a quick sharp noise made by rapidly compressing and opening the lips **2 :** a loud kiss **3 :** a sharp slap or blow

[6]**smack** *adv* (1782) : squarely and sharply : DIRECTLY ⟨~ in the middle⟩

[7]**smack** *n* [perh. fr. Yiddish *shmek* sniff, whiff, pinch (of snuff)] (ca. 1960) *slang* **:** HEROIN

smack–dab \'smak-'dab\ *adv* (1892) : EXACTLY, SQUARELY

smack·down \'smak-ˌdau̇n\ *n* (1997) **1 :** the act of knocking down or bringing down an opponent **2 :** a contest in entertainment wrestling **3 :** a decisive defeat **4 :** a confrontation between rivals or competitors

smack·er \'sma-kər\ *n* (1611) **1 :** one that smacks **2** *slang* **:** DOLLAR

smack·ing \'sma-kiŋ\ *adj* (1820) : BRISK, LIVELY ⟨a ~ breeze⟩

smack talk *n* (1992) : TRASH TALK — **smack–talk** *vb*

SMaj *abbr* sergeant major

[1]**small** \'smȯl\ *adj* [ME *smal,* fr. OE *smæl;* akin to OHG *smal* small, Gk *mēlon* small domestic animal] (bef. 12c) **1 a :** having comparatively little size or slight dimensions **b :** LOWERCASE **2 a :** minor in influence, power, or rank **b :** operating on a limited scale **3 :** lacking in strength ⟨a ~ voice⟩ **4 a :** little or close to zero in an objectively measurable aspect (as quantity) **b :** made up of few or little units **5 a :** of little consequence : TRIVIAL **b :** HUMBLE, MODEST **6 :** limited in degree **7 a :** MEAN, PETTY **b :** reduced to a humiliating position — **small·ish** \'smȯ-lish\ *adj* — **small·ness** \'smȯl-nəs\ *n*

syn SMALL, LITTLE, DIMINUTIVE, MINUTE, TINY, MINIATURE mean noticeably below average in size. SMALL and LITTLE are often interchangeable, but SMALL applies more to relative size determined by capacity, value, number ⟨a relatively *small* backyard⟩. LITTLE is more absolute in implication often carrying the idea of petiteness, pettiness, insignificance, or immaturity ⟨your pathetic *little* smile⟩. DIMINUTIVE implies abnormal smallness ⟨*diminutive* bonsai plants⟩. MINUTE implies extreme smallness ⟨a *minute* amount of caffeine in the soda⟩. TINY is an informal equivalent to MINUTE ⟨*tiny* cracks formed in the painting⟩. MINIATURE applies to an exactly proportioned reproduction on a very small scale ⟨a dollhouse with *miniature* furnishings⟩.

[2]**small** *adv* (bef. 12c) **1 :** in or into small pieces **2 :** without force or loudness ⟨speak as ~ as you will —Shak.⟩ **3 :** in a small manner

[3]**small** *n* (14c) **1 :** a part smaller and esp. narrower than the remainder ⟨the ~ of the back⟩ **2 a** *pl* **:** small-sized products **b** *pl, chiefly Brit* **:** SMALLCLOTHES; *esp* **:** UNDERWEAR

small arm *n* (1685) : a handheld firearm (as a handgun or shoulder arm) — usu. used in pl.

small beer *n* (1568) **1 :** weak or inferior beer **2 :** something of small importance : TRIVIA — **small–beer** *adj*

small calorie *n* (ca. 1889) : CALORIE 1a

small capital *n* (1770) : a letter having the form of but smaller than a capital letter (as in THESE WORDS) — called also *small cap*

small–cell lung cancer *n* (1975) : cancer of a highly malignant form that affects the lungs, tends to metastasize to other parts of the body, and is characterized by small round or oval cells which resemble oat grains and have little cytoplasm — called also *small-cell carcinoma*

small change *n* (1819) **1 :** coins of low denomination **2 :** TRIFLE 1

small–claims court *n* (1925) : a special court intended to simplify and expedite the handling of small claims on debts

small·clothes \'smȯl-ˌklō(th)z\ *n pl* (1759) **1 :** small articles of clothing (as underclothing or handkerchiefs) **2 :** close-fitting knee breeches worn in the 18th century

smaller European elm bark beetle *n* (ca. 1945) : ELM BARK BEETLE b

small forward *n* (1977) : a basketball forward who is usu. smaller than a power forward and whose play is characterized by quickness and scoring ability

small–fry \'smȯl-ˌfrī\ *adj* (1817) **1 :** MINOR, UNIMPORTANT ⟨a ~ politician⟩ **2 :** of, relating to, or intended for children : CHILDISH

small·hold·ing \-ˌhōl-diŋ\ *n* (1892) *chiefly Brit* **:** a small farm — **small·hold·er** \-dər\ *n*

small hours *n pl* (ca. 1837) : the early morning hours

small intestine *n* (1767) : the part of the intestine that lies between the stomach and colon, consists of duodenum, jejunum, and ileum, secretes digestive enzymes, and is the chief site of the absorption of digested nutrients

small–mind·ed \'smȯl-'mīn-dəd\ *adj* (1847) **1 :** having narrow interests, sympathies, or outlook **2 :** typical of a small-minded person : marked by pettiness, narrowness, or meanness ⟨~ conduct⟩ — **small–mind·ed·ly** *adv* — **small–mind·ed·ness** *n*

small·mouth bass \'smȯl-ˌmau̇th-\ *n* (1938) : a black bass (*Micropterus dolomieu*) of clear rivers and lakes that is bronzy-green above and lighter below and has the vertex of the angle of the jaw falling below the eye — called also *smallmouth, smallmouth black bass*

small potato *n* (1831) : one that is of trivial importance or worth — usu. used in pl. but sing. or pl. in constr.

small·pox \'smȯl-ˌpäks\ *n* (1518) : an acute contagious febrile disease of humans that is caused by a poxvirus (species *Variola virus* of the genus *Orthopoxvirus*), is characterized by a skin eruption with pustules, sloughing, and scar formation, and is believed to have been eradicated globally by widespread vaccination — called also *variola*

small–scale \-'skāl\ *adj* (1852) **1 :** small in scope; *esp* **:** small in output or operation **2** *of a map* **:** having a scale (as one inch to 25 miles) that permits plotting of comparatively little detail and shows mainly large features

small screen *n* (1956) : TELEVISION

small stuff *n* (1846) : small rope (as spun yarn or marline) usu. identified by the number of threads or yarns which it contains

small·sword \'smȯl-ˌsȯrd\ *n* (1687) : a light tapering sword for thrusting used chiefly in dueling and fencing

small talk *n* (1751) : light or casual conversation : CHITCHAT

small–time \'smȯl-'tīm\ *adj* (1910) : insignificant in performance, scope, or standing : PETTY ⟨~ thieves⟩ — **small–tim·er** \-'tī-mər\ *n*

smalt \'smȯlt\ *n* [MF, fr. OIt *smalto,* of Gmc origin; akin to OHG *smelzan* to melt — more at SMELT] (1558) : a deep blue pigment consisting of a powdered glass that contains oxide of cobalt

smal·to \'smäl-(ˌ)tō, 'smȯl-\ *n, pl* **smal·ti** \-(ˌ)tē\ [It, smalt, smalto] (ca. 1705) : colored glass or enamel or a piece of either used in mosaic work

sma·ragd \smə-'ragd, 'sma-ˌragd\ *n* [ME *smaragde,* fr. L *smaragdus,* fr. Gk *smaragdos,* of Sem origin; akin to Akkadian *barraqtu* gemstone] (13c) : EMERALD — **sma·rag·dine** \smə-'rag-dən, 'sma-rəg-ˌdīn\ *adj*

smarm \ˈsmärm\ *n* [back-formation fr. *smarmy*] (1937) **:** smarmy language or behavior

smarmy \ˈsmär-mē\ *adj* **smarm·i·er; -est** [*smarm* to gush, slobber] (1924) **1 :** revealing or marked by a smug, ingratiating, or false earnestness ⟨a tone of ~ self-satisfaction —*New Yorker*⟩ **2 :** of low sleazy taste or quality ⟨~ eroticism⟩ — **smarm·i·ly** \-mə-lē\ *adv* — **smarm·i·ness** \-mē-nəs\ *n*

[1]**smart** \ˈsmärt\ *adj* [ME *smert* causing pain, fr. OE *smeart*; akin to OE *smeortan*] (bef. 12c) **1 :** making one smart **:** causing a sharp stinging **2 :** marked by often sharp forceful activity or vigorous strength ⟨a ~ pull of the starter cord⟩ **3 :** BRISK, SPIRITED ⟨a ~ pace⟩ **4 a :** mentally alert **:** BRIGHT **b :** KNOWLEDGEABLE **c :** SHREWD ⟨a ~ investment⟩ **5 a :** WITTY, CLEVER ⟨a ~ sitcom⟩ **b :** PERT, SAUCY ⟨don't get ~ with me⟩ **6 a :** NEAT, TRIM ⟨soldiers in ~ uniforms⟩ **b :** stylish or elegant in dress or appearance **c** (1) **:** appealing to sophisticated tastes (2) **:** characteristic of or patronized by fashionable society **7 a :** being a guided missile ⟨a laser-guided ~ bomb⟩ **b :** operating by automation ⟨a ~ machine tool⟩ **c :** INTELLIGENT 3 — **smart·ly** *adv* — **smart·ness** *n*

[2]**smart** *vi* [ME *smerten,* fr. OE *smeortan;* akin to OHG *smerzan* to pain] (13c) **1 :** to cause or be the cause or seat of a sharp stinging pain; *also* **:** to feel or have such a pain **2 a :** to feel or endure distress, remorse, or embarrassment ⟨~*ing* from wounded vanity —W. L. Shirer⟩ **b :** to pay a heavy or stinging penalty ⟨would have to ~ for this foolishness⟩

[3]**smart** *n* (13c) **1 :** a smarting pain; *esp* **:** a stinging local pain **2 :** poignant grief or remorse ⟨was not the sort to get over ~*s* —Sir Winston Churchill⟩ **3** *pl, slang* **:** INTELLIGENCE, KNOW-HOW

[4]**smart** *adv* (13c) **:** in a smart manner **:** SMARTLY

smart al·eck *also* **smart al·ec** \ˈsmärt-ˌa-lik, -ˌe-\ *n* [*Aleck,* nickname for *Alexander*] (1865) **:** an obnoxiously conceited and self-assertive person with pretensions to smartness or cleverness — **smart–aleck** *adj* — **smart–al·ecky** \-ˌa-lə-kē, -ˌe-\ *adj*

smart–ass \-ˌas\ *n* (1964) **:** SMART ALECK — **smart–ass** *adj* — **smart–assed** \-ˌast\ *adj*

smart card *n* (1980) **:** a small plastic card that has a built-in microprocessor to store and process data and records

smart drug *n* (1991) **:** NOOTROPIC

smart·en \ˈsmär-tᵊn\ *vb* **smart·ened; smart·en·ing** \ˈsmärt-niŋ, ˈsmär-tᵊn-iŋ\ *vt* (1793) **:** to make smart or smarter; *esp* **:** SPRUCE — usu. used with *up* ~ *vi* **:** to smarten oneself — used with *up*

[1]**smart money** \ˈsmärt-ˌmə-nē\ *n* [[3]*smart*] (1693) **:** PUNITIVE DAMAGES

[2]**smart money** \-ˈmə-nē, -ˌmə-nē\ *n* [[1]*smart*] (1926) **1 :** money ventured by one having inside information or much experience **2 :** well-informed bettors or speculators

smart–mouthed \ˈsmärt-ˌmau̇tht, -ˌmau̇t͟hd\ *adj* (1976) **:** annoyingly cocky or sarcastic in speech

smart·phone \ˈsmärt-ˌfōn\ *n* (1997) **:** a cell phone that includes additional software functions (as e-mail or an Internet browser)

smart·weed \ˈsmärt-ˌwēd\ *n* (ca. 1787) **:** any of various polygonums with strong acidic juice

smarty *or* **smart·ie** \ˈsmär-tē\ *n, pl* **smart·ies** (1847) **:** SMART ALECK

smarty–pants \-ˌpan(t)s\ *n pl but sing in constr* (1941) **:** SMART ALECK — **smarty–pants** *adj*

[1]**smash** \ˈsmash\ *n* [perh. blend of [4]*smack* and [2]*mash*] (1725) **1 a :** a smashing blow or attack **b :** a hard overhand stroke (as in tennis or badminton) **2 a :** the action or sound of smashing; *esp* **:** a wreck due to collision **:** CRASH **b :** utter collapse **:** RUIN **3 :** a striking success

[2]**smash** *vt* (1764) **1 :** to break or crush by violence **2 a :** to drive or throw violently esp. with a shattering or battering effect; *also* **:** to effect in this way **b :** to hit violently **:** BATTER **c** (1) **:** to hit (as a tennis ball) with a hard overhand stroke (2) **:** to drive (a ball) with a forceful stroke **3 :** to destroy utterly **:** WRECK ~ *vi* **1 :** to move or become propelled with violence or crashing effect ⟨~*ed* into a tree⟩ **2 :** to become wrecked **3 :** to go to pieces suddenly under collision or pressure — **smash·er** *n*

[3]**smash** *adj* (1923) **:** being a smash **:** OUTSTANDING ⟨a ~ hit⟩

smashed \ˈsmasht\ *adj* (ca. 1959) *slang* **:** DRUNK, INTOXICATED

smash·ing \ˈsma-shiŋ\ *adj* (1825) **1 :** that smashes **:** CRUSHING ⟨a ~ defeat⟩ **2 :** extraordinarily impressive or effective ⟨a ~ performance⟩ — **smash·ing·ly** \-shiŋ-lē\ *adv*

smash·mouth \ˈsmash-ˌmau̇th\ *adj* (1984) **:** characterized by brute force without finesse ⟨~ football⟩

smash·up \ˈsmash-ˌəp\ *n* (1856) **1 :** a collision between vehicles **2 :** a complete collapse

[1]**smat·ter** \ˈsma-tər\ *vb* [ME *smateren* to make dirty, talk idly] *vi* (15c) **:** to talk superficially **:** BABBLE ~ *vt* **1 :** to speak with spotty or superficial knowledge ⟨~*s* French⟩ **2 :** to dabble in — **smat·ter·er** \-tər-ər\ *n*

[2]**smatter** *n* (1668) **:** SMATTERING ⟨a ~ of applause⟩

smat·ter·ing \ˈsma-tə-riŋ\ *n* (1538) **1 :** superficial piecemeal knowledge ⟨a ~ of carpentry, house painting, bricklaying —Alva Johnston⟩ **2 :** a small scattered number or amount ⟨a ~ of spectators⟩

[1]**smear** \ˈsmir\ *n* [ME *smere,* fr. OE *smeoru;* akin to OHG *smero* grease and prob. to OIr *smiur* marrow] (bef. 12c) **1 a :** a viscous or sticky substance **b :** a spot made by or as if by an unctuous or adhesive substance **2 :** material smeared on a surface (as of a microscopic slide); *also* **:** a preparation made by smearing material on a surface ⟨a vaginal ~⟩ **3 :** a usu. unsubstantiated charge or accusation against a person or organization — often used attributively ⟨a ~ campaign⟩ ⟨a ~ job⟩

[2]**smear** *vt* (bef. 12c) **1 a :** to overspread with something unctuous, viscous, or adhesive **:** DAUB ⟨~*ed* the paper with glue⟩ **b :** to spread over a surface **2 a :** to stain, smudge, or dirty by or as if by smearing **b :** SULLY, BESMIRCH; *specif* **:** to vilify esp. by secretly and maliciously spreading grave charges and imputations **3 :** to obliterate, obscure, blur, blend, wipe out, or defeat by or as if by smearing — **smear·er** *n*

smear·case *also* **smier·case** \ˈsmir-ˌkās\ *n* [modif. of G *Schmierkäse,* fr. *schmieren* to smear + *Käse* cheese] (1829) *chiefly Midland* **:** COTTAGE CHEESE

smeary \ˈsmir-ē\ *adj* **smear·i·er; -est** (ca. 1529) **1 :** marked by or covered with smears **2 :** liable to cause smears ⟨~ lipstick⟩

smec·tic \ˈsmek-tik\ *adj* [L *smecticus* cleansing, having the properties of soap, fr. Gk *smēktikos,* fr. *smēchein* to clean] (1923) **:** of, relating to, or being the phase of a liquid crystal characterized by arrangement of molecules in layers with the long molecular axes in a given layer being parallel to one another and those of other layers and perpendicular or slightly inclined to the plane of the layer — compare CHOLESTERIC, NEMATIC

smec·tite \ˈsmek-ˌtīt\ *n* [*smectis* fuller's earth, modif. of Gk *smēktris* kind of fuller's earth, fr. *smēchein* to clean] (1811) **:** MONTMORILLONITE — **smec·tit·ic** \(ˌ)smek-ˈti-tik\ *adj*

smeg·ma \ˈsmeg-mə\ *n* [NL, fr. L, detergent, soap, fr. Gk *smēgma,* fr. *smēchein* to wash off, clean] (ca. 1819) **:** the secretion of a sebaceous gland; *specif* **:** the cheesy sebaceous matter that collects between the glans penis and the foreskin or around the clitoris and labia minora

[1]**smell** \ˈsmel\ *vb* **smelled** \ˈsmeld\ *or* **smelt** \ˈsmelt\; **smell·ing** [ME] *vt* (12c) **1 :** to perceive the odor or scent of through stimuli affecting the olfactory nerves **:** get the odor or scent of with the nose **2 :** to detect or become aware of as if by the sense of smell ⟨I ~ trouble⟩ **3 :** to emit the odor of ~ *vi* **1 :** to exercise the sense of smell **2 a** (1) **:** to have an odor or scent (2) **:** to have a characteristic aura or atmosphere **:** SMACK ⟨the accounts . . . seemed to me to ~ of truth —R. S. Bourne⟩; *also* **:** SEEM, APPEAR ⟨the story didn't ~ right⟩ **b** (1) **:** to have an offensive odor **:** STINK (2) **:** to be of bad or questionable quality ⟨all this from the moral point of view ~*s* —A. F. Wills⟩ — **smell·er** *n* — **smell a rat :** to have a suspicion of something wrong — **smell blood :** to sense an opponent's weakness or vulnerability — **smell the roses :** to enjoy or savor life

[2]**smell** *n* (12c) **1 :** the property of a thing that affects the olfactory organs **:** ODOR **2 a :** the process, function, or power of smelling **b :** the sense concerned with the perception of odor **3 a :** a very small amount **:** TRACE ⟨add only a ~ of garlic⟩ **b :** a pervading or characteristic quality **:** AURA ⟨the ~ of affluence, of power —Harry Hervey⟩ **4 :** an act or instance of smelling

syn SMELL, SCENT, ODOR, AROMA mean the quality that makes a thing perceptible to the olfactory sense. SMELL implies solely the sensation without suggestion of quality or character ⟨an odd *smell* permeated the room⟩. SCENT applies to the characteristic smell given off by a substance, an animal, or a plant ⟨the *scent* of lilacs⟩. ODOR may imply a stronger or more readily distinguished scent or it may be equivalent to SMELL ⟨a cheese with a strong *odor*⟩. AROMA suggests a somewhat penetrating usu. pleasant odor ⟨the *aroma* of freshly ground coffee⟩.

smelling salts *n pl but sing or pl in constr* (1837) **:** a usu. scented aromatic preparation of ammonium carbonate and ammonia water used as a stimulant and restorative

smelly \ˈsme-lē\ *adj* **smell·i·er; -est** (1862) **:** having a smell; *esp* **:** MALODOROUS ⟨~ socks⟩

[1]**smelt** \ˈsmelt\ *n, pl* **smelts** *or* **smelt** [ME, fr. OE; akin to Norw *smelte* whiting] (bef. 12c) **:** any of a family (Osmeridae) of small bony fishes that closely resemble the trouts in general structure, live along coasts and ascend rivers to spawn or are landlocked, and have delicate oily flesh with a distinctive odor and taste

[2]**smelt** *vt* [D or LG *smelten;* akin to OHG *smelzan* to melt, OE *meltan* — more at MELT] (1543) **1 :** to melt or fuse (as ore) often with an accompanying chemical change usu. to separate the metal **2 :** REFINE, REDUCE

smelt·er \ˈsmel-tər\ *n* (15c) **:** one that smelts: **a :** a worker who smelts ore **b :** an owner or operator of a smeltery **c** *or* **smelt·ery** \-t(ə-)rē\ **:** an establishment for smelting

smew \ˈsmyü\ *n* [akin to MHG *smiehe* smew] (1674) **:** a small Eurasian merganser (*Mergus albellus*) with the male being white, gray, and black and the female chiefly gray but with a chestnut and white head

smid·gen *also* **smid·geon** *or* **smid·gin** \ˈsmi-jən\ *or* **smidge** \ˈsmij\ *n* [prob. alter. of E dial. *smitch* soiling mark] (1845) **:** a small amount **:** BIT ⟨a ~ of salt⟩ ⟨a ~ of common sense⟩

smi·lax \ˈsmī-ˌlaks\ *n* [L, bindweed, yew, fr. Gk] (1551) **1 :** GREENBRIER **2 :** a tender twining asparagus (*Asparagus asparagoides*) of southern Africa that has ovate bright green cladophylls which are often used in floral arrangements

[1]**smile** \ˈsmī(-ə)l\ *vb* **smiled; smil·ing** [ME; akin to OE *smerian* to laugh, Skt *smayate* he smiles] *vi* (14c) **1 :** to have, produce, or exhibit a smile **2 a :** to look or regard with amusement or ridicule ⟨*smiled* at his own folly —Martin Gardner⟩ **b :** to bestow approval ⟨feeling that Heaven *smiled* on his labors —Sheila Rowlands⟩ **c :** to appear pleasant or agreeable ~ *vt* **1 :** to affect with or by smiling **2 :** to express by a smile — **smil·er** *n* — **smil·ing·ly** \ˈsmī-liŋ-lē\ *adv*

[2]**smile** *n* (15c) **1 :** a facial expression in which the eyes brighten and the corners of the mouth curve slightly upward and which expresses esp. amusement, pleasure, approval, or sometimes scorn **2 :** a pleasant or encouraging appearance — **smile·less** \ˈsmī(-ə)l-ləs\ *adj*

[1]**smil·ey** \ˈsmī-lē\ *adj* (1848) **:** having a smile **:** smiling often ⟨~ kids⟩

[2]**smiley** *n* [short for *smiley face*] (1987) **:** EMOTICON

smiley face *n* (1972) **:** a line drawing of a smiling face

smirch \ˈsmərch\ *vt* [ME *smorchen*] (15c) **1 a :** to make dirty, stained, or discolored **:** SULLY **b :** to smear with something that stains or dirties **2 :** to bring discredit or disgrace on — **smirch** *n*

smirk \ˈsmərk\ *vb* [ME, fr. OE *smearcian* to smile; akin to OE *smerian* to laugh] *vi* (bef. 12c) **:** to smile in an affected or smug manner **:** SIMPER ~ *vt* **:** to say or express with a smirk — **smirk** *n*

smirky \ˈsmər-kē\ *adj* **smirk·i·er; -est** (1728) **:** that smirks **:** SMIRKING

smite \ˈsmīt\ *vb* **smote** \ˈsmōt\; **smit·ten** \ˈsmi-tᵊn\ *or* **smote; smit·ing** \ˈsmī-tiŋ\ [ME, fr. OE *smītan* to smear, defile; akin to OHG bi*smīzan* to defile] *vt* (12c) **1 :** to strike sharply or heavily esp. with the hand or an implement held in the hand **2 a :** to kill or severely injure by smiting **b :** to attack or afflict suddenly and injuriously ⟨*smitten* by disease⟩ **3 :** to cause to strike **4 :** to affect as if by striking ⟨children *smitten* with the fear of hell —V. L. Parrington⟩ **5 :** CAPTIVATE, TAKE ⟨*smitten* with her beauty⟩ ~ *vi* **:** to deliver or deal a blow with or as if with the hand or something held — **smit·er** \ˈsmī-tər\ *n*

smith \ˈsmith\ *n* [ME, fr. OE; akin to OHG *smid* smith and prob. to Gk *smilē* wood-carving knife] (bef. 12c) **1 :** a worker in metals **:** BLACK-

SMITH **2 :** MAKER — often used in combination ⟨gun*smith*⟩ ⟨tune*smith*⟩
smith·er·eens \ˌsmi-thə-ˈrēnz\ *n pl* [perh. fr. Ir *smidiríní*] (1829) **:** FRAGMENTS, BITS ⟨the house was blown to ~ by the explosion⟩
smith·ery \ˈsmi-thə-rē\ *n, pl* **-er·ies** (1611) **1 :** the work, art, or trade of a smith **2 :** SMITHY 1
Smith·field ham \ˈsmith-ˌfēld-\ *n* (1888) **:** a Virginia ham produced in or near Smithfield, Va.
smith·son·ite \ˈsmith-sə-ˌnīt\ *n* [James *Smithson*] (1856) **:** a mineral that is a carbonate of zinc and constitutes a minor ore of zinc
smithy \ˈsmi-thē *also* -thē\ *n, pl* **smith·ies** (13c) **1 :** the workshop of a smith **2 :** BLACKSMITH
[1]**smock** \ˈsmäk\ *n* [ME *smok,* fr. OE *smoc;* akin to OHG *smocco* adornment] (bef. 12c) **1** *archaic* **:** a woman's undergarment; *esp* **:** CHEMISE **2 :** a light loose garment worn esp. for protection of clothing while working
[2]**smock** *vt* (1888) **:** to embroider or shirr with smocking
smock frock *n* (ca. 1800) **:** a loose outer garment worn by workmen esp. in Europe
smock·ing \ˈsmä-kiŋ\ *n* (1888) **:** a decorative embroidery or shirring made by gathering cloth in regularly spaced round tucks
smog \ˈsmäg, ˈsmȯg\ *n* [*sm*oke + f*og*] (1884) **:** a fog made heavier and darker by smoke and chemical fumes; *also* **:** a photochemical haze caused by the action of solar ultraviolet radiation on atmosphere polluted with hydrocarbons and oxides of nitrogen esp. from automobile exhaust — **smog·less** \ˈsmä-gləs, ˈsmȯ-\ *adj*
smog·gy \ˈsmä-gē, ˈsmȯ-\ *adj* **smog·gi·er; -est** (1905) **:** characterized by or abounding in smog ⟨a ~ haze⟩ ⟨~ freeways⟩
smok·able *or* **smoke·able** \ˈsmō-kə-bəl\ *adj* (1839) **:** fit for smoking
[1]**smoke** \ˈsmōk\ *n* [ME, fr. OE *smoca;* akin to OE *smēocan* to emit smoke, MHG *smouch* smoke, and prob. to Gk *smychein* to smolder] (bef. 12c) **1 a :** the gaseous products of burning materials esp. of organic origin made visible by the presence of small particles of carbon **b :** a suspension of particles in a gas **2 a :** a mass or column of smoke **b :** SMUDGE **3 :** fume or vapor often resulting from the action of heat on moisture **4 :** something of little substance, permanence, or value **5 :** something that obscures **6 a** (1) **:** something (as a cigarette) to smoke (2) **:** MARIJUANA 2 **b :** an act of smoking tobacco; *esp* **:** a smoking break **7 a :** a pale blue **b :** any of the colors of smoke **8 :** pitches that are fastballs ⟨if a guy's going to hit you . . . he certainly isn't going to throw a spitter—he gives you ~ —Tony Conigliaro⟩ — **smoke·less** \ˈsmō-kləs\ *adj* — **smoke·like** \ˈsmōk-ˌlīk\ *adj*
[2]**smoke** *vb* **smoked; smok·ing** *vi* (bef. 12c) **1 a :** to emit or exhale smoke **b :** to emit excessive smoke **2** *archaic* **:** to undergo punishment **:** SUFFER **3 :** to spread or rise like smoke **4 :** to inhale and exhale the fumes of burning plant material and esp. tobacco; *esp* **:** to smoke tobacco habitually ~ *vt* **1 a :** FUMIGATE **b :** to drive (as mosquitoes) away by smoke **c :** to blacken or discolor with smoke ⟨*smoked* glasses⟩ **d :** to cure by exposure to smoke ⟨*smoked* ham⟩ **e :** to stupefy (as bees) by smoke **2** *archaic* **:** SUSPECT **3 :** to inhale and exhale the smoke of ⟨~ a cigarette⟩ **4** *archaic* **:** RIDICULE **5** *slang* **:** KILL 1a **6** *slang* **:** to defeat or surpass decisively **7 :** to hit (as a baseball) with great force
smoke and mirrors *n pl* (1979) **:** something intended to disguise or draw attention away from an often embarrassing or unpleasant issue — usu. hyphenated when used attributively
smoke detector *n* (ca. 1927) **:** an alarm that activates automatically when it detects smoke — called also *smoke alarm*
smoke–filled room \ˈsmōk-ˈfild-\ *n* (1920) **:** a room (as in a hotel) in which a small group of politicians carry on negotiations
smoke·house \ˈsmōk-ˌhau̇s\ *n* (1746) **:** a building where meat or fish is cured by means of dense smoke
smoke·jack \-ˌjak\ *n* (1675) **:** a device for turning a spit by a fly or wheel moved by rising gases in a chimney
smoke jumper *n* (1927) **:** a forest firefighter who parachutes to locations otherwise difficult to reach
smokeless powder *n* (1890) **:** any of a class of explosive propellants that produce comparatively little smoke on explosion and consist mostly of gelatinized nitrocellulose
smokeless tobacco *n* (1976) **:** pulverized or shredded tobacco chewed or placed between cheek and gum **:** SNUFF
smoke out *vt* (1593) **1 :** to drive out by or as if by smoke **2 :** to cause to be made public
smok·er \ˈsmō-kər\ *n* (1599) **1 :** one that smokes **2 :** a railroad car or compartment in which smoking is allowed **3 :** an informal social gathering for men
smoke screen *n* (1915) **1 :** a screen of smoke to hinder enemy observation of a military force, area, or activity **2 :** something designed to obscure, confuse, or mislead
[1]**smoke·stack** \ˈsmōk-ˌstak\ *n* (1838) **:** a pipe or funnel through which smoke and gases are discharged
[2]**smokestack** *adj* (1926) **:** of, relating to, being, or characterized by manufacturing and esp. heavy industry ⟨~ industries⟩
smoke tree *n* (1846) **:** either of two small shrubby trees (genus *Cotinus*) of the cashew family with large panicles of minute flowers that suggest a cloud of smoke: **a :** one (*C. coggygria*) of Eurasia that is widely planted in the eastern U.S. **b :** one (*C. obovatus*) of the southeastern U.S. and Texas
smoking gun *n* (1974) **:** something that serves as conclusive evidence or proof (as of a crime or scientific theory)
smoking jacket *n* (1870) **:** a loose-fitting jacket or short robe for wear at home
smoking lamp *n* (ca. 1881) **:** a lamp on a ship kept lighted during the hours when smoking is allowed
smoking room *n* (1689) **:** a room (as in a hotel or club) set apart for smokers
smoky *also* **smok·ey** \ˈsmō-kē\ *adj* **smok·i·er; -est** (14c) **1 :** emitting smoke esp. in large quantities ⟨a ~ fireplace⟩ **2 a :** having the characteristics of or resembling smoke ⟨a ~ haze⟩ **b :** suggestive of smoke esp. in flavor or odor **3 a :** filled with smoke ⟨a ~ room⟩ **b :** made dark or black by or as if by smoke **4 :** having a low throaty quality ⟨a ~ voice⟩ — **smok·i·ly** \-kə-lē\ *adv* — **smok·i·ness** \-kē-nəs\ *n*
smoky quartz *n* (1837) **:** CAIRNGORM
smoky topaz *n* (1797) **:** CAIRNGORM
smol·der *or* **smoul·der** \ˈsmōl-dər\ *vi* **smol·dered** *or* **smoul·dered; smol·der·ing** *or* **smoul·der·ing** \-d(ə-)riŋ\ [ME *smolderen* to smother, fr. *smolder* smoke, smudge; akin to MD *smōlen* to smolder] (1529) **1 a :** to burn sluggishly, without flame, and often with much smoke **b :** to be consumed by smoldering — often used with *out* **2 :** to exist in a state of suppressed activity ⟨hostilities ~*ed* for years⟩ **3 :** to show suppressed anger, hate, or jealousy ⟨eyes ~*ing* with hate⟩
smolt \ˈsmōlt\ *n* [ME (Sc)] (15c) **:** a young salmon or sea trout about two years old that is at the stage of development when it assumes the silvery color of the adult and is ready to migrate to the sea
[1]**smooch** \ˈsmüch\ *vi* [alter. of *smouch* to kiss loudly] (1577) **:** KISS, PET
[2]**smooch** *n* (1578) **:** KISS
[3]**smooch** *vt* [prob. alter. of *smutch,* vb.] (1631) **:** SMUDGE, SMEAR
[4]**smooch** *n* (1825) **:** SMUDGE, SMEAR — **smoochy** \ˈsmü-chē\ *adj*
[1]**smooth** \ˈsmüth\ *adj* [ME *smothe,* fr. OE *smōth;* akin to OS *smōthi* smooth] (bef. 12c) **1 a** (1) **:** having a continuous even surface (2) *of a curve* **:** being the representation of a function with a continuous first derivative (3) **:** having or being a short even coat of hair ⟨a ~ collie⟩ — compare ROUGH, WIREHAIRED **b :** being without hair **c :** GLABROUS ⟨a ~ leaf⟩ **d :** causing no resistance to sliding **2 :** free from difficulties or impediments ⟨the ~ course of his life⟩ **3 :** even and uninterrupted in flow or flight **4 :** excessively and often artfully suave **:** INGRATIATING ⟨a ~ operator⟩ **5 a :** SERENE, EQUABLE ⟨a ~ disposition⟩ **b :** AMIABLE, COURTEOUS **6 a :** not sharp or harsh ⟨a ~ sherry⟩ **b :** free from lumps ***syn*** see LEVEL, EASY, SUAVE — **smooth** *adv* — **smooth·ly** *adv* — **smooth·ness** *n*
[2]**smooth** *vb* **smoothed; smooth·ing; smooths** *also* **smoothes** *vt* (15c) **1 :** to make smooth **2 a :** to free from what is harsh or disagreeable **:** POLISH ⟨~*ed* out his style⟩ **b :** SOOTHE **3 :** to minimize (as a fault) esp. in order to allay anger or ill will ⟨his main job is to ~ over the friction that so often arises —Brian Crozier⟩ **4 :** to free from obstruction or difficulty ⟨conciliation ~*ed* the way to an agreement⟩ **5 a :** to press flat ⟨~*ed* down the folds of her dress⟩ **b :** to remove expression from (one's face) **:** COMPOSE **6 :** to cause to lie evenly and in order **:** PREEN ⟨a bird ~*ing* its feathers⟩ **7 :** to free (as a graph or data) from irregularities ~ *vi* **:** to become smooth — **smooth·er** *n*
[3]**smooth** *n* (15c) **1 :** a smooth part **2 :** the act of smoothing **3 :** a smoothing implement
smooth·bore \ˈsmüth-ˈbȯr\ *adj* (1754) *of a firearm* **:** having a barrel with an unrifled bore — **smoothbore** \-ˌbȯr\ *n*
smooth breathing *n* (ca. 1888) **1 :** a mark ʼ placed over some initial vowels in Greek to show that they are not aspirated (as in ἐκεῖ pronounced \e-ˈkā\) **2 :** the absence of aspiration indicated by a mark ʼ
smooth·en \ˈsmü-thən\ *vb* **smooth·ened; smooth·en·ing** \ˈsmü-thə-niŋ, ˈsmüth-niŋ\ *vt* (1635) **:** to make smooth ~ *vi* **:** to become smooth
smooth fox terrier *n* (1929) **:** any of a breed of fox terriers having a dense smooth chiefly white coat
smooth hound *n* [fr. the absence of a spine in front of the dorsal fin] (1603) **:** any of several dogfishes (genus *Mustelus*) closely related to or included with the requiem sharks
smooth muscle *n* (ca. 1890) **:** muscle tissue that lacks cross striations, is made up of elongated spindle-shaped cells having a central nucleus, and is found esp. in vertebrate hollow organs and structures (as the digestive tract and bladder) as thin sheets performing functions not subject to direct voluntary control and in all or most of the musculature of invertebrates other than arthropods — compare STRIATED MUSCLE

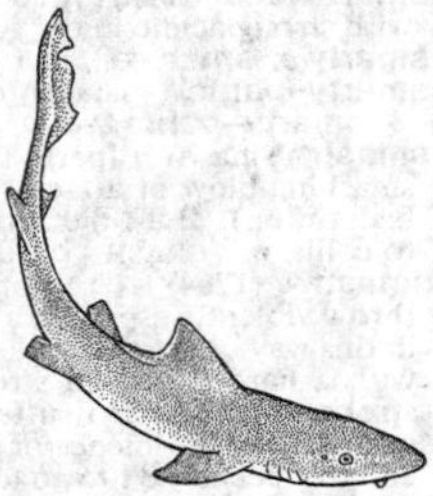
smooth hound

smooth–tongued \ˈsmüth-ˈtəŋd\ *adj* (1579) **:** ingratiating in speech
smoothy *or* **smooth·ie** \ˈsmü-thē\ *n, pl* **smooth·ies** (1904) **1 :** a smooth-tongued person **2 a :** a person with polished manners **b :** one who behaves or performs with deftness, assurance, and easy competence; *esp* **:** a man with an ingratiating manner toward women **3** *smoothie* **:** a creamy beverage made of fruit blended with juice, milk, or yogurt
s'more \ˈsmȯr\ *n* [alter. of *some more*] (1974) **:** a dessert consisting usu. of toasted marshmallow and pieces of chocolate bar sandwiched between two graham crackers
smor·gas·bord \ˈsmȯr-gəs-ˌbȯrd\ *n* [Sw *smörgåsbord,* fr. *smörgås* open sandwich + *bord* table] (1879) **1 :** a luncheon or supper buffet offering a variety of foods and dishes (as hors d'oeuvres, hot and cold meats, smoked and pickled fish, cheeses, salads, and relishes) **2 :** an often large heterogeneous mixture **:** MÉLANGE
smote *past of* SMITE
[1]**smoth·er** \ˈsmə-thər\ *n* [ME, alter. of *smorther,* fr. *smoren* to smother, fr. OE *smorian* to suffocate; akin to MD *smoren* to suffocate] (13c) **1 a :** thick stifling smoke or smudge **b :** a state of being stifled or suppressed **2 :** a dense cloud (as of fog or dust) **3 :** a confused multitude of things **:** WELTER — **smoth·ery** \ˈsmə-thə-rē, ˈsməth-rē\ *adj*
[2]**smother** *vb* **smoth·ered; smoth·er·ing** \ˈsmə-thə-riŋ, ˈsməth-riŋ\ *vi* (ca. 1520) **:** to be overcome or killed through or as if through lack of air ~ *vt* **1 :** to overcome or kill with smoke or fumes **2 a :** to kill by depriving of air **b :** to overcome or discomfit through or as if through lack of air **c :** to suppress (a fire) by excluding oxygen **3 a :** to cause to smolder **b :** to suppress expression or knowledge of ⟨~*ed* his rage⟩ **c :** to stop or prevent the growth or activity of ⟨~ a child with too much care⟩; *also* **:** OVERWHELM **d :** to cover thickly **:** BLANKET ⟨snow ~*ed* the trails⟩ **e :** to overcome or vanquish quickly or decisively **4 :** to cook in a covered pan or pot with little liquid over low heat
SMSA *abbr* Standard Metropolitan Statistical Area
SMSgt *abbr* senior master sergeant
[1]**smudge** \ˈsməj\ *vb* **smudged; smudg·ing** [ME *smogen*] *vt* (15c) **1 a :** to make a smudge on **b :** to soil as if by smudging **2 a :** to rub, daub, or wipe in a smeary manner **b :** to make indistinct **:** BLUR ⟨*smudged* the writing⟩ **3 :** to smoke or protect by means of a smudge ~ *vi* **1 :** to make a smudge **2 :** to become smudged

²**smudge** n (ca. 1774) **1 a** : a blurry spot or streak **b** : an immaterial stain ⟨cleanse him of every last ∼ of impropriety —Richard Hanser⟩ **c** : an indistinct mass : BLUR **2** : a smoldering mass placed on the windward side (as to protect from frost) **3** : a bid of four in pitch that if made wins the game — **smudg·i·ly** \'smə-jə-lē\ adv — **smudg·i·ness** \'smə-jē-nəs\ n — **smudgy** \-jē\ adj

smug \'sməg\ adj **smug·ger; smug·gest** [prob. modif. of LG smuck neat, fr. MLG, fr. smucken to dress; akin to OE smoc smock] (1551) **1** : trim or smart in dress : SPRUCE **2** : scrupulously clean, neat, or correct : TIDY **3** : highly self-satisfied — **smug·ly** adv — **smug·ness** n

smug·gle \'smə-gəl\ vb **smug·gled; smug·gling** \-g(ə-)liŋ\ [LG smuggeln & D smokkelen] vt (1687) **1** : to import or export secretly contrary to the law and esp. without paying duties imposed by law **2** : to convey or introduce surreptitiously ∼ vi : to import or export something in violation of the customs laws — **smug·gler** \'smə-glər\ n

¹**smut** \'smət\ vb **smut·ted; smut·ting** [prob. alter. of earlier smot to stain, fr. ME smotten; akin to MHG smutzen to stain] vt (1587) **1** : to stain or taint with smut **2** : to affect (a crop or plant) with smut ∼ vi : to become affected with smut

²**smut** n (1664) **1** : matter that soils or blackens; specif : a particle of soot **2** : any of various destructive diseases esp. of cereal grasses caused by parasitic basidiomycetous fungi (order Ustilaginales) and marked by transformation of plant parts into dark masses of spores; also : a fungus causing a smut **3** : obscene language or matter

smutch \'sməch\ n [akin to ME smogen to smudge] (1530) : a dark stain : SMUDGE — **smutch** vt — **smutchy** \'smə-chē\ adj

smut·ty \'smə-tē\ adj **smut·ti·er; -est** (1597) **1** : soiled or tainted with smut; esp : affected with smut fungus **2** : OBSCENE, INDECENT ⟨a ∼ joke⟩ **3** : resembling smut in appearance : SOOTY — **smut·ti·ly** \'smə-t²l-ē\ adv — **smut·ti·ness** \'smə-tē-nəs\ n

SMV abbr slow-moving vehicle

Sn Symbol [LL stannum] tin

SN abbr seaman

¹**snack** \'snak\ n [ME snak bite, fr. snaken to bite, perh. fr. MD snacken to snap at — more at SNATCH] (1757) : a light meal : food eaten between regular meals; also : food suitable for snacking

²**snack** vi (1807) : to eat a snack

snack bar n (1930) : a public eating place where snacks are served usu. at a counter

¹**snaf·fle** \'sna-fəl\ n [origin unknown] (1533) : a simple usu. jointed bit for a bridle

²**snaffle** vt **snaf·fled; snaf·fling** \'sna-f(ə-)liŋ\ [origin unknown] (1724) : to obtain esp. by devious or irregular means

¹**sna·fu** \sna-'fü, 'sna-,fü\ n [situation normal all fucked up (fouled up)] (ca. 1941) : a situation marked by errors or confusion : MUDDLE; also : an error causing such a situation ⟨a scheduling ∼⟩

²**snafu** adj (1942) : snarled or stalled in confusion : AWRY

³**snafu** vt (1943) : to bring into a state of confusion

¹**snag** \'snag\ n [perh. of Scand origin; akin to ON snagi clothes peg] (ca. 1587) **1 a** : a tree or branch embedded in a lake or stream bed and constituting a hazard to navigation **b** : a standing dead tree **2** : a rough sharp or jagged projecting part : PROTUBERANCE: as **a** : a projecting tooth; also : a stump of a tooth **b** : one of the secondary branches of an antler **3** : a concealed or unexpected difficulty or obstacle **4 a** : a jagged tear made by or as if by catching on a snag **b** : an irregularity that suggests the result of tearing; esp : a pulled thread in fabric ⟨a ∼ in her stocking⟩ — **snag·gy** \'sna-gē\ adj

²**snag** vt **snagged; snag·ging** (1807) **1 a** : to catch and usu. damage on or as if on a snag **b** : to halt or impede as if by catching on a snag **2** : to hew, trim, or cut roughly or jaggedly **3** : to clear (as a river) of snags **4** : to catch or obtain usu. by quick action or good fortune

snag·gle·tooth \'sna-gəl-,tüth\ n [E dial. snaggle irregularly shaped tooth + E tooth] (ca. 1825) : an irregular, broken, or projecting tooth — **snag·gle·toothed** \-,tütht\ adj

¹**snail** \'snāl\ n [ME, fr. OE snægl; akin to OHG snecko snail, snahhan to creep] (bef. 12c) **1** : a gastropod mollusk esp. when having an external enclosing spiral shell **2** : a slow-moving or sluggish person or thing — **snail·like** \-,līk\ adj

²**snail** vi (1582) : to move, act, or go slowly or lazily

snail darter n (1975) : a darter (Percina tanasi) of the Tennessee River drainage system of eastern Tennessee and northern Georgia

snail fever n [fr. the snails which serve as intermediate hosts to the schistosomes causing the disease] (1947) : SCHISTOSOMIASIS

snail mail n (1983) **1** : mail delivered by a postal system **2** : MAIL 3

snail–paced \'snāl-'pāst\ adj (1594) : moving very slowly

snail's pace n (15c.) : an extremely slow pace

¹**snake** \'snāk\ n [ME, fr. OE snaca; akin to ON snakr snake, OHG snahhan to crawl] (bef. 12c) **1** : any of numerous limbless scaled reptiles (suborder Serpentes syn. Ophidia) with a long tapering body and with salivary glands often modified to produce venom which is injected through grooved or tubular fangs **2** : a worthless or treacherous fellow **3** : something (as a plumber's snake) resembling a snake — **snake·like** \-,līk\ adj

²**snake** vb **snaked; snak·ing** vt (1653) **1** : to wind (as one's way) in the manner of a snake **2** : to move (as logs) by dragging ∼ vi : to crawl, move, or extend silently, secretly, or sinuously

snake·bird \'snāk-,bərd\ n (1791) : ANHINGA

snake·bit \-,bit\ or **snake·bit·ten** \-,bi-t²n\ adj (1957) : having or experiencing failure or bad luck : UNLUCKY

snake·bite \-,bīt\ n (1839) : the bite of a snake and esp. a venomous snake

snake charmer n (1836) : an entertainer who exhibits a professed power to charm or fascinate venomous snakes

snake–dance vi (1922) : to engage in a snake dance

snake dance n (1772) **1** : a ceremonial dance in which snakes or their images are handled, invoked, or symbolically imitated by individual sinuous actions **2** : a group progression in a single-file serpentine path (as in celebration of an athletic victory)

snake doctor n (1862) **1** : DRAGONFLY **2** : HELLGRAMMITE

snake fence n (1805) : WORM FENCE

snake in the grass (1696) : a secretly faithless friend

snake oil n (1917) **1** : any of various substances or mixtures sold (as by a traveling medicine show) as medicine usu. without regard to their medical worth or properties **2** : POPPYCOCK, BUNKUM

snake pit n (1946) **1** : a hospital for mental diseases **2** : a place or state of chaotic disorder and distress

snake·root \'snāk-,rüt, -,rüt\ n (1635) : any of various plants (as seneca snakeroot and Virginia snakeroot) most of which have roots sometimes believed to cure snakebites; also : the root of such a plant

snake·skin \'snāk-,skin\ n (1825) : leather prepared from the skin of a snake

snake·weed \-,wēd\ n (1597) **1** : any of various plants popularly associated with snakes (as in appearance, habitat, or the treatment of snakebite); esp : any of an American genus (Gutierrezia) of composite herbs or low shrubs with clustered yellow flower heads

snaky also **snak·ey** \'snā-kē\ adj (1567) **1** : of, formed of, or entwined with snakes ⟨the Gorgon with ∼ hair —Joseph Addison⟩ **2** : SERPENTINE, SNAKELIKE ⟨∼ coils⟩ **3** : suggestive of a snake (the oiliness and ∼ insinuation of his demeanor —Thomas DeQuincy⟩ **4** : abounding in snakes — **snak·i·ly** \-kə-lē\ adv

¹**snap** \'snap\ vb **snapped; snap·ping** [D or LG snappen; akin to MHG snappen to snap] vi (1530) **1 a** : to make a sudden closing of the jaws : seize something sharply with the mouth ⟨fish snapping at the bait⟩ **b** : to grasp at something eagerly : make a pounce or snatch ⟨∼ at any chance⟩ **2** : to utter sharp biting words : bark out irritable or peevish retorts **3 a** : to break suddenly with a sharp sound ⟨the twig snapped⟩ **b** : to give way suddenly under strain **4** : to make a sharp or crackling sound **5** : to close or fit in place with an abrupt movement or sharp sound ⟨the lock snapped shut⟩ **6 a** : to move briskly or sharply ⟨∼s to attention⟩ **b** : to undergo a sudden and rapid change (as from one condition to another) ⟨∼ out of it⟩ ⟨snapped awake⟩ **7** : SPARKLE, FLASH ⟨eyes snapping with fury⟩ ∼ vt **1** : to seize with or as if with a snap of the jaws **2** : to take possession or advantage of suddenly or eagerly — usu. used with up ⟨shoppers snapping up bargains⟩ **3 a** : to retort to or interrupt curtly and irritably **b** : to utter curtly or abruptly **4** : to break suddenly : break short or in two **5 a** : to cause to make a snapping sound ⟨∼ a whip⟩ **b** : to put into or remove from a particular position by a sudden movement or with a sharp sound ⟨∼ the lock shut⟩ **b** : to project with a snap **b** : to put (a football) in play with a snap **c** (1) : to take photographically ⟨snapping exclusive news pictures —Current Biog.⟩ (2) : to take a snapshot of

²**snap** n (1555) **1** : an abrupt closing (as of the mouth in biting or of scissors in cutting) **2 a** archaic : a share of profits or booty **b** : something that brings quick and easy profit or advantage **c** : something that is easy and presents no problems : CINCH **3** : a small amount : BIT **4 a** : an act or instance of seizing abruptly : a sudden snatching at something **b** : a quick short movement ⟨lithe ∼s of its body —Barbara Taylor⟩ **c** : a sudden sharp breaking **5 a** : a sound made by snapping something ⟨shut the book with a ∼⟩ **b** : a brief sharp and usu. irritable speech or retort **6** : a sudden spell of weather ⟨a cold ∼⟩ **7** : a catch or fastening that closes or locks with a click ⟨the ∼ of a bracelet⟩ **8** : a flat brittle cookie — compare GINGERSNAP **9** : SNAPSHOT **10 a** : the condition of being vigorous in body, mind, or spirit : ALERTNESS, ENERGY **b** : a pleasing vigorous quality **11** : the act of a center's putting the football in play from its position on the ground by quickly passing it between his legs to a teammate (as a quarterback) standing behind him

³**snap** adv (1583) : with a snap

⁴**snap** adj (1739) **1** : done, made, or carried through suddenly or without deliberation ⟨a ∼ judgment⟩ **2** : called or taken without prior warning ⟨a ∼ election⟩ **3** : fastening with a snap ⟨a ∼ lock⟩ **4** : unusually easy or simple ⟨a ∼ course⟩

snap–back \'snap-,bak\ n (1887) **1** : a football snap **2** : a sudden rebound or recovery ⟨a ∼ of prices on the stock exchange⟩

snap back vi (1945) : to make a quick or vigorous recovery

snap bean n (1770) : a bean grown primarily for its long pods that are cooked as a vegetable while young and tender and before the seeds have become enlarged — compare SHELL BEAN

snap–brim \'snap-,brim\ n, often attrib (ca. 1908) : a usu. felt hat with brim turned up in back and down in front and with a dented crown

snap·drag·on \'snap-,dra-gən\ n [fr. the fancied resemblance of the flowers to the face of a dragon] (1573) : any of a genus (Antirrhinum of the family Scrophulariaceae, the snapdragon family) of herbs having showy bilabiate flowers; esp : a widely cultivated one (A. majus) of Mediterranean origin having usu. pink, red, yellow, or white flowers

snap–on \'snap-,ón, -,än\ adj (1925) : designed to snap into position and fit tightly ⟨∼ cuffs⟩

snap pea n (1978) : a cultivated pea that has edible usu. round pods easily snapped like beans and that is classified with the snow pea as a variety (Pisum sativum macrocarpon) — called also sugar snap pea

snap·per \'sna-pər\ n, pl **snappers** (ca. 1587) **1** : one that snaps: as **a** : something (as a remark) that gives new orientation to a situation or utterance **b** (1) : SNAPPING TURTLE (2) : CLICK BEETLE **2** pl also **snapper** **a** : any of numerous active carnivorous fishes (family Lutjanidae) of warm seas important as food and often as sport fishes **b** : any of several immature fishes (as the young of the bluefish) that resemble a snapper

snap–per–back \-,bak\ n (1887) : a football center

snapping turtle n (1784) : either of two large American freshwater turtles (family Chelydridae) with a large head, powerful jaws, a long tail, and a strong musky odor: **a** : one (Chelydra serpentina) that has the head covered with smooth skin, has large plates in a double row on the underside of the tail, and is distributed from eastern Canada to Central America **b** : ALLIGATOR SNAPPING TURTLE

snap·pish \'sna-pish\ adj (1542) **1 a** : given to curt irritable speech **b** : arising from annoyance or irascibility ⟨a ∼ remark⟩ **2** : inclined to bite ⟨a ∼ dog⟩ — **snap·pish·ly** adv — **snap·pish·ness** n

snap·py \'sna-pē\ adj **snap·pi·er; -est** (1746) **1** : SNAPPISH 1 **2 a** : quickly made or done ⟨a ∼ decision⟩ **b** : marked by vigor or liveliness ⟨∼ dialogue⟩ **c** : briskly cold **d** : STYLISH, SMART ⟨a ∼ dresser⟩ — **snap·pi·ly** \'sna-pə-lē\ adv — **snap·pi·ness** \'sna-pē-nəs\ n

---

\ə\ abut \ᵊ\ kitten, F table \ər\ further \a\ ash \ā\ ace \ä\ mop, mar \aú\ out \ch\ chin \e\ bet \ē\ easy \g\ go \i\ hit \ī\ ice \j\ job \ŋ\ sing \ō\ go \ò\ law \òi\ boy \th\ thin \t͟h\ the \ü\ loot \ù\ foot \y\ yet \zh\ vision, beige \k̟, ⁿ, œ, �, ᵁ\ see Guide to Pronunciation

snap roll *n* (ca. 1934) : an airplane maneuver in which a rapid full revolution is completed about the plane's longitudinal axis while an approximately level line of flight is maintained
snap·shoot·er \ˈsnap-ˌshü-tər\ *n* (1896) : a person who takes snapshots
snap·shot \ˈsnap-ˌshät\ *n* (1890) **1** : a casual photograph made typically by an amateur with a small handheld camera **2** : an impression or view of something brief or transitory ⟨a ~ of life back then⟩
[1]**snare** \ˈsner\ *n* [ME, fr. OE *sneare,* prob. fr. ON *snara;* akin to OHG *snuor* cord and perh. to Gk *narkē* numbness] (bef. 12c) **1 a** (1) : a contrivance often consisting of a noose for entangling birds or mammals (2) : TRAP, GIN **b** (1) : something by which one is entangled, involved in difficulties, or impeded (2) : something deceptively attractive **2** [prob. fr. D *snaar,* lit., cord; akin to OHG *snuor*] **a** : one of the catgut strings or metal spirals of a snare drum **b** : SNARE DRUM **3** : a surgical instrument consisting usu. of a wire loop constricted by a mechanism in the handle and used for removing tissue masses (as tonsils)
[2]**snare** *vt* **snared; snar·ing** (14c) **1 a** : to capture by or as if by use of a snare **b** : to win or attain by artful or skillful maneuvers **2** : to entangle or hold as if in a snare ⟨any object that *snared* his eye —*Current Biog.*⟩ *syn* see CATCH — **snar·er** *n*
snare drum *n* (ca. 1859) : a small double-headed drum with one or more snares stretched across its lower head — see DRUM illustration
snarf \ˈsnärf\ *vt* [perh. blend of [2]*snack* and [5]*scarf*] (ca. 1963) : [3]SCOFF 1 ⟨~*ed* down some pizza⟩
snarky \ˈsnär-kē\ *adj* [dial. *snark* to annoy, perh. alter. of *nark* to irritate] (1906) **1** : CROTCHETY, SNAPPISH **2** : sarcastic, impertinent, or irreverent in tone or manner ⟨~ lyrics⟩ — **snark·i·ly** \-kə-lē\ *adv*
[1]**snarl** \ˈsnär(-ə)l\ *vb* [ME, to trap, entangle, prob. freq. of *snaren* to snare] *vt* (14c) **1** : to cause to become knotted and intertwined : TANGLE **2** : to make excessively complicated ~ *vi* : to become snarled — **snarl·er** *n*
[2]**snarl** *n* [ME *snarle* snare, noose, prob. fr. *snarlen,* v.] (1609) **1** : a tangle esp. of hairs or thread : KNOT **2** : a tangled situation ⟨traffic ~*s*⟩ — **snarly** \ˈsnär-lē\ *adj*
[3]**snarl** *vb* [freq. of obs. E *snar* to growl; akin to MLG *snorren* to drone, rattle] *vi* (1589) **1** : to growl with a snapping, gnashing, or display of teeth **2** : to give vent to anger in surly language ~ *vt* : to utter or express with a snarl or by snarling — **snarl·er** *n*
[4]**snarl** *n* (1613) : a surly angry growl — **snarly** \ˈsnär-lē\ *adj*
[1]**snatch** \ˈsnach\ *vb* [ME *snacchen* to snap, seize; akin to MD *snacken* to snap at] *vi* (13c) : to attempt to seize something suddenly ~ *vt* : to take or grasp abruptly or hastily ⟨~ up a pen⟩ ⟨~*ed* the first opportunity⟩; *also* : to seize or take suddenly without permission, ceremony, or right ⟨~*ed* a kiss⟩ *syn* see TAKE — **snatch·er** *n*
[2]**snatch** *n* (1563) **1 a** : a brief period ⟨caught ~*es* of sleep⟩ **b** : a brief, fragmentary, or hurried part : BIT ⟨caught ~*es* of the conversation⟩ **2 a** : a snatching at or of something **b** *slang* : an act or instance of kidnapping **3** : a lift in weight lifting in which the weight is raised from the floor directly to an overhead position in a single motion — compare CLEAN AND JERK, PRESS **4** *usu vulgar* : the female pudenda
snatch block *n* (ca. 1625) : a block that can be opened on one side to receive the bight of a rope
snath \ˈsnath, ˈsneth\ *or* **snathe** \ˈsnāth, ˈsnāth\ *n* [akin to ME *snede* long scythe, fr. OE *snǣd* scythe handle] (1574) : the handle of a scythe
snaz·zy \ˈsna-zē\ *adj* **snaz·zi·er; -est** [origin unknown] (ca. 1932) : conspicuously or flashily attractive : FANCY ⟨~ clothes⟩ ⟨a ~ car⟩
SNCC *abbr* Student Nonviolent Coordinating Committee
[1]**sneak** \ˈsnēk\ *vb* **sneaked** \ˈsnēkt\ *or* **snuck** \ˈsnək\; **sneak·ing** [akin to OE *snīcan* to sneak along, ON *snīkja*] *vi* (1594) **1** : to go stealthily or furtively : SLINK ⟨*snuck* out early⟩ **2** : to act in or as if in a furtive manner **3** : to carry the football on a quarterback sneak ~ *vt* : to put, bring, or take in a furtive or artful manner ⟨~ a smoke⟩ *syn* see LURK — **sneak up on** : to approach or act on stealthily
usage From its earliest appearance in print in the late 19th century as a dialectal and prob. uneducated form, the past and past participle *snuck* has risen to the status of standard and to approximate equality with *sneaked.* It is most common in the U.S. and Canada but has also been spotted in British and Australian English.
[2]**sneak** *n* (ca. 1643) **1** : a person who acts in a stealthy, furtive, or shifty manner **2 a** : a stealthy or furtive move **b** : an unobserved departure or escape **3** : SNEAKER 2 — usu. used in pl. **4** : QUARTERBACK SNEAK
[3]**sneak** *adj* (ca. 1859) **1** : carried on secretly : CLANDESTINE **2** : occurring without warning : SURPRISE ⟨a ~ attack⟩
sneak·er \ˈsnē-kər\ *n* (1598) **1** : one that sneaks **2** : a sports shoe with a pliable rubber sole — **sneak·ered** \-kərd\ *adj*
sneaking *adj* (1582) **1** : MEAN, CONTEMPTIBLE **2** : characteristic of a sneak : FURTIVE, UNDERHANDED **3 a** : not openly expressed or acknowledged ⟨a ~ respect for culture —H. A. Burton⟩ **b** : that is a persistent conjecture ⟨a ~ suspicion⟩ — **sneak·ing·ly** *adv*
sneak preview *n* (ca. 1937) : a special advance showing of a motion picture usu. announced but not named
sneak thief *n* (ca. 1859) : a thief who steals whatever is readily available without using violence or forcibly breaking into buildings
sneaky \ˈsnē-kē\ *adj* **sneak·i·er; -est** (1833) : marked by stealth, furtiveness, or shiftiness ⟨a ~ trick⟩ — **sneak·i·ly** \-kə-lē\ *adv* — **sneak·i·ness** \-kē-nəs\ *n*
[1]**sneap** \ˈsnēp\ *vt* [ME *snaipen* to injure, nip, rebuke, prob. of Scand origin; akin to Icel *sneypa* to scold — more at SNUB] (14c) **1** *archaic* : to blast or blight with cold : NIP **2** *dial Eng* : CHIDE
[2]**sneap** *n* (1597) *archaic* : REBUKE, SNUB
sneck \ˈsnek\ *n* [ME *snekke*] (14c) *chiefly dial* : LATCH
[1]**sneer** \ˈsnir\ *vb* [prob. akin to MHG *snerren* to chatter, gossip — more at SNORE] *vi* (1680) **1** : to smile or laugh with facial contortions that express scorn or contempt **2** : to speak or write in a scornfully jeering manner ~ *vt* : to utter with a sneer *syn* see SCOFF — **sneer·er** *n*
[2]**sneer** *n* (1707) : the act of sneering; *also* : a sneering expression or remark
[1]**sneeze** \ˈsnēz\ *vi* **sneezed; sneez·ing** [ME *snesen,* alter. of *fnesen,* fr. OE *fnēosan;* akin to MHG *pfnūsen* to snort, sneeze, Gk *pnein* to breathe] (14c) : to make a sudden violent spasmodic audible expiration of breath through the nose and mouth esp. as a reflex act — **sneez·er** *n* — **sneeze at** : to make light of ⟨the cost was nothing to *sneeze at*⟩
[2]**sneeze** *n* (1646) : an act or instance of sneezing
sneeze·weed \ˈsnēz-ˌwēd\ *n* (ca. 1837) : any of several composite plants; *esp* : a No. American perennial herb (*Helenium autumnale*) with yellow ray flowers and a darker globose disk
sneezy \ˈsnē-zē\ *adj* (1839) : given to or causing sneezing
[1]**snell** \ˈsnel\ *adj* [ME, fr. OE; akin to OHG *snel* bold, agile] (bef. 12c) **1** *chiefly Scot* : QUICK, ACUTE **2** *chiefly Scot* : KEEN, PIERCING ⟨a ~ wind smote us —*Scotsman*⟩ **3** *chiefly Scot* : GRIEVOUS, SEVERE
[2]**snell** *n* [origin unknown] (1846) : a short line (as of gut) by which a fishhook is attached to a longer line
SNF *abbr* skilled nursing facility
[1]**snick** \ˈsnik\ *vb* [prob. fr. obs. *snick or snee* to engage in cut-and-thrust fighting — more at SNICKERSNEE] *vt* (ca. 1700) **1** *archaic* : to cut through **2** : to cut slightly ~ *vi* : to perform a light cutting action
[2]**snick** *n* (ca. 1775) : a small cut : NICK
[3]**snick** *vb* [imit.] (1828) : CLICK
[4]**snick** *n* (ca. 1886) : a slight often metallic sound : CLICK
[1]**snick·er** \ˈsni-kər\ *vi* **snick·ered; snick·er·ing** \-k(ə-)riŋ\ [origin unknown] (1694) : to laugh in a covert or partly suppressed manner : TITTER — **snick·er·er** \-kər-ər\ *n* — **snick·ery** \-k(ə-)rē\ *adj*
[2]**snicker** *n* (1835) : an act or sound of snickering
snick·er·snee \ˈsni-kə(r)-ˌsnē\ *n* [obs. *snick or snee* to engage in cut-and-thrust fighting, alter. of earlier *steake or snye,* fr. D *steken of snijden* to thrust or cut] (ca. 1775) : a large knife
snide \ˈsnīd\ *adj* [origin unknown] (ca. 1859) **1 a** : FALSE, COUNTERFEIT **b** : practicing deception : DISHONEST ⟨a ~ merchant⟩ **2** : unworthy of esteem : LOW ⟨a ~ trick⟩ **3** : slyly disparaging : INSINUATING ⟨~ remarks⟩ — **snide·ly** *adv* — **snide·ness** *n*
[1]**sniff** \ˈsnif\ *vb* [ME] *vi* (14c) **1** : to draw air audibly up the nose esp. for smelling ⟨~*ed* at the flowers⟩ **2** : to show or express disdain or scorn **3** : SNOOP, NOSE ⟨~*ed* around for clues⟩ ~ *vt* **1** : to smell or take by inhalation through the nose **2** : to utter contemptuously **3** : to recognize or detect by or as if by smelling ⟨~ out trouble⟩
[2]**sniff** *n* (1767) **1** : an act or sound of sniffing **2** : a quantity that is sniffed
sniff·er *n* (1864) : one that sniffs; *esp* : one who takes drugs illicitly by sniffing
sniff·ish \ˈsni-fish\ *adj* (1923) : SNIFFY, SUPERCILIOUS — **sniff·ish·ly** *adv* — **sniff·ish·ness** *n*
[1]**snif·fle** \ˈsni-fəl\ *vi* **snif·fled; snif·fling** \-f(ə-)liŋ\ [freq. of *sniff*] (1632) **1** : to sniff repeatedly : SNUFFLE **2** : to speak with or as if with sniffling — **snif·fler** \-f(ə-)lər\ *n*
[2]**sniffle** *n* (ca. 1825) **1** *pl* : a head cold marked by nasal discharge **2** : an act or sound of sniffling
sniffy \ˈsni-fē\ *adj* **sniff·i·er; -est** (1871) : having or expressing a haughty attitude : DISDAINFUL, SUPERCILIOUS — **sniff·i·ly** \ˈsni-fə-lē\ *adv* — **sniff·i·ness** \ˈsni-fē-nəs\ *n*
snif·ter \ˈsnif-tər\ *n* [E dial., sniff, snort, fr. ME, to sniff, snort] (1844) **1** : a small drink of distilled liquor **2** : a short-stemmed goblet with a bowl narrowing toward the top
[1]**snig·ger** \ˈsni-gər\ *vi* **snig·gered; snig·ger·ing** \-g(ə-)riŋ\ [by alter.] (ca. 1706) : SNICKER — **snig·ger·er** \-gər-ər\ *n*
[2]**snigger** *n* (ca. 1823) : SNICKER
snig·gle \ˈsni-gəl\ *vb* **snig·gled; snig·gling** \-g(ə-)liŋ\ [E dial. *snig* small eel, fr. ME *snygge*] *vi* (1653) : to fish for eels by thrusting a baited hook into their hiding places ~ *vt* : to catch (an eel) by sniggling
[1]**snip** \ˈsnip\ *n* [fr. or akin to D & LG *snip;* akin to MHG *snipfen* to snap the fingers] (1558) **1 a** : a small piece that is snipped off; *also* : FRAGMENT, BIT **b** : a cut or notch made by snipping **c** : an act or sound of snipping **2** : a white or light mark; *esp* : a white spot between the nostrils of a horse **3** : a presumptuous or impertinent person; *esp* : an impertinent or saucy girl **4** *Brit* : BARGAIN, BUY
[2]**snip** *vb* **snipped; snip·ping** *vt* (1586) : to cut or cut off with or as if with shears or scissors ⟨*snipped* the stray threads⟩; *specif* : to clip suddenly or by bits ~ *vi* : to make a short quick cut with or as if with shears or scissors — **snip·per** *n*
[1]**snipe** \ˈsnīp\ *n, pl* **snipes** [ME, prob. of Scand origin; akin to ON *snīpa* snipe; akin to OHG *snepfa* snipe] (14c) **1** *or pl* **snipe** : any of various usu. slender-billed birds of the sandpiper family; *esp* : any of several game birds (esp. genus *Gallinago*) esp. of marshy areas **2** : a contemptible person
[2]**snipe** *vi* **sniped; snip·ing** (1832) **1** : to shoot at exposed individuals (as of an enemy's forces) from a usu. concealed point of vantage **2** : to aim a carping or snide attack — **snip·er** *n*
snip·er·scope \ˈsnī-pər-ˌskōp\ *n* (1941) : an optical device for use esp. with a rifle that allows a person to see targets better in the dark
snip·per·snap·per \ˈsni-pər-ˌsna-pər\ *n* [origin unknown] (ca. 1590) : WHIPPERSNAPPER
snip·pet \ˈsni-pət\ *n* [[1]*snip*] (1664) : a small part, piece, or thing; *esp* : a brief quotable passage
snip·pety \-pə-tē\ *adj* (1864) **1** : made up of snippets **2** [prob. fr. [2]*snip* + *-ety* (as in *pernickety*)] : SNIPPY
snip·py \ˈsni-pē\ *adj* **snip·pi·er; -est** [[2]*snip*] (ca. 1848) **1** : SHORT-TEMPERED, SNAPPISH **2** : unduly brief or curt **3** : putting on airs : SNIFFY — **snip·pi·ly** \ˈsni-pə-lē\ *adv*
snips \ˈsnips\ *n pl but sing or pl in constr* (1846) : hand shears used esp. for cutting sheet metal
snit \ˈsnit\ *n* [origin unknown] (1939) : a state of agitation ⟨in a ~⟩
[1]**snitch** \ˈsnich\ *n* [origin unknown] (ca. 1785) : one who snitches : TATTLETALE
[2]**snitch** *vi* (1801) : INFORM, TATTLE — **snitch·er** *n*
[3]**snitch** *vt* [prob. alter. of *snatch*] (1904) : to take by stealth : PILFER
snit·ty \ˈsni-tē\ *adj* **snit·ti·er; -est** (1978) : disagreeably ill-tempered
[1]**sniv·el** \ˈsni-vəl\ *vi* **-eled** *or* **-elled; -el·ing** *or* **-el·ling** \ˈsni-və-liŋ, ˈsniv-liŋ\ [ME, fr. OE **snyflan;* akin to D *snuffelen* to snuffle, *snuffen* to sniff] (14c) **1** : to run at the nose **2** : to snuff mucus up the nose audibly : SNUFFLE **3** : to cry or whine with snuffling **4** : to speak or act in a whining, sniffling, tearful, or weakly emotional manner — **sniv·el·er** \ˈsni-və-lər, ˈsniv-lər\ *n*
[2]**snivel** *n* (1600) **1** *pl, dial* : HEAD COLD **2** : an act of sniveling
snob \ˈsnäb\ *n* [origin unknown] (1781) **1** *Brit* : COBBLER **2** : one who blatantly imitates, fawningly admires, or vulgarly seeks association with those regarded as social superiors **3 a** : one who tends to rebuff, avoid, or ignore those regarded as inferior **b** : one who has an offensive air of superiority in matters of knowledge or taste

snob appeal *n* (1933) : qualities in a product that appeal to the snobbery in a purchaser
snob·bery \ˈsnä-b(ə-)rē\ *n, pl* **-ber·ies** (1843) **1** : snobbish conduct or character : SNOBBISHNESS **2** : an instance of snobbery
snob·bish \ˈsnä-bish\ *adj* (1840) : being, characteristic of, or befitting a snob ⟨a ~ attitude⟩ — **snob·bish·ly** *adv* — **snob·bish·ness** *n*
snob·bism \ˈsnä-ˌbi-zəm\ *n* (1845) : SNOBBERY
snob·by \ˈsnä-bē\ *adj* **snob·bi·er; -est** (1846) : characterized by snobbery ⟨a ~ brat⟩ ⟨~ neighborhoods⟩
sno–cone *var of* SNOW CONE
[1]**snood** \ˈsnüd\ *n* [ME **snod,* fr. OE *snōd*] (bef. 12c) **1 a** *Scot* : a fillet or band for a woman's hair **b** : a net or fabric bag pinned or tied on at the back of a woman's head for holding the hair **2** : SNELL
[2]**snood** *vt* (1714) : to secure with a snood
[1]**snook** \ˈsnu̇k, ˈsnük\ *n, pl* **snook** *or* **snooks** [D *snoek* pike, snook] (1697) **1** : a large vigorous bony fish (*Centropomus undecimalis* of the family Centropomidae) of coastal and brackish waters that is an important food and sport fish **2** : any of various marine fishes of the same family as the snook
[2]**snook** *n* [origin unknown] (1791) : a gesture of derision made by thumbing the nose
[1]**snook·er** \ˈsnu̇-kər, *chiefly Brit* ˈsnü-\ *n* [origin unknown] (1889) : a variation of pool played with 15 red balls and 6 variously colored balls
[2]**snooker** *vt* (1925) : to make a dupe of : HOODWINK
[1]**snoop** \ˈsnüp\ *vi* [D *snoepen* to buy or eat on the sly; akin to D *snappen* to snap] (1832) : to look or pry esp. in a sneaking or meddlesome manner — **snoop·er** *n*
[2]**snoop** *n* (ca. 1890) : one that snoops
snoopy \ˈsnü-pē\ *adj* **snoop·i·er; -est** (ca. 1895) : given to snooping esp. for personal information about others — **snoop·i·ly** \-pə-lē\ *adv*
[1]**snoot** \ˈsnüt\ *n* [ME *snute*] (1861) **1 a** : SNOUT **b** : NOSE **2** : a grimace expressive of contempt **3** : a snooty person : SNOB
[2]**snoot** *vt* (1928) : to treat with disdain : look down one's nose at
snooty \ˈsnü-tē\ *adj* **snoot·i·er; -est** (1919) **1** : looking down the nose : showing disdain **2** : characterized by snobbery ⟨a ~ store⟩ — **snoot·i·ly** \ˈsnü-tə-lē\ *adv* — **snoot·i·ness** \ˈsnü-tē-nəs\ *n*
[1]**snooze** \ˈsnüz\ *vi* **snoozed; snooz·ing** [origin unknown] (1785) : to take a nap : DOZE
[2]**snooze** *n* (1793) **1** : NAP **2** : something boring or uninspiring
snooze button *n* (1956) : a button on an alarm clock that stops and resets the alarm for a short time later to allow for more rest — called also *snooze alarm*
snooz·er \ˈsnü-zər\ *n* (1837) **1** : one that snoozes **2** : SNOOZE 2
snoo·zle \ˈsnü-zəl\ *vb* **snoo·zled; snoo·zling** \ˈsnü-zə-liŋ, ˈsnüz-liŋ\ [perh. blend of *snooze* and *nuzzle*] (1831) *chiefly dial* : NUZZLE
[1]**snore** \ˈsnȯr\ *vb* **snored; snor·ing** [ME *snoren, fnoren;* akin to OE *fnora* sneezing, *fnǣran* to breathe heavily] *vi* (15c) : to breathe during sleep with a rough hoarse noise due to vibration of the soft palate ~ *vt* : to spend (time) in snoring or sleeping — **snor·er** *n*
[2]**snore** *n* (1605) **1** : an act of snoring **2** : a noise of or as if of snoring
[1]**snor·kel** \ˈsnȯr-kəl\ *n* [G *Schnorchel*] (1944) **1** : a tube housing air intake and exhaust pipes for a submarine's diesel engine that can be extended above the water's surface so that the engines can be operated while the submarine is submerged **2** : any of various devices (as for an underwater swimmer) resembling a snorkel in function
[2]**snorkel** *vi* **snor·keled; snor·kel·ing** \-k(ə-)liŋ\ (1949) : to operate or swim submerged using a snorkel — **snor·kel·er** \-k(ə-)lər\ *n*
[1]**snort** \ˈsnȯrt\ *vb* [ME *snorten, fnorten;* akin to OE *fnora* sneezing] *vi* (14c) **1 a** : to force air violently through the nose with a rough harsh sound **b** : to express scorn, anger, indignation, or surprise by a snort **2** : to emit explosive sounds resembling snorts **3** : to take in a drug by inhalation ~ *vt* **1** : to utter with or express by a snort **2** : to expel or emit with or as if with snorts **3** : to inhale (a drug) through the nose
[2]**snort** *n* (1786) **1** : a drink of usu. straight liquor taken in one draft **2** : an act or sound of snorting
snort·er \ˈsnȯr-tər\ *n* (1601) **1** : one that snorts **2** : something that is extraordinary or prominent : HUMDINGER **3** : SNORT 1
snot \ˈsnät\ *n* [ME, fr. OE *gesnot;* akin to OHG *snuzza* nasal mucus] (15c) **1** : nasal mucus **2** : a snotty person
snot·ty \ˈsnä-tē\ *adj* **snot·ti·er; -est** (ca. 1570) **1** : soiled with nasal mucus ⟨a ~ nose⟩ **2** : annoyingly or spitefully unpleasant; *esp* : SNOOTY — **snot·ti·ly** \ˈsnä-tə-lē\ *adv* — **snot·ti·ness** \ˈsnä-tē-nəs\ *n*
snout \ˈsnau̇t\ *n* [ME *snute;* akin to MD *snūt* snout, G *Schnauze*] (13c) **1 a (1)** : a long projecting nose (as of a swine) **(2)** : an anterior prolongation of the head of various animals (as a weevil) : ROSTRUM **b** : the human nose esp. when large or grotesque **2** : something resembling an animal's snout in position, function, or shape: as **a** : PROW **b** : NOZZLE **c** : the terminal face of a glacier — **snout·ed** \ˈsnau̇-təd\ *adj* — **snout·ish** \-tish\ *adj* — **snouty** \-tē\ *adj*
snout beetle *n* (1781) : WEEVIL
[1]**snow** \ˈsnō\ *n, often attrib* [ME, fr. OE *snāw;* akin to OHG *snēo* snow, L *niv-, nix,* Gk *nipha* (acc.)] (bef. 12c) **1 a** : precipitation in the form of small white ice crystals formed directly from the water vapor of the air at a temperature of less than 32°F (0°C) **b (1)** : a descent or shower of snow crystals **(2)** : a mass of fallen snow crystals **2** : something resembling snow: as **a** : a dessert made of stiffly beaten whites of eggs, sugar, and fruit pulp ⟨apple ~⟩ **b** : a usu. white crystalline substance that condenses from a fluid phase as snow does ⟨ammonia ~⟩ **c** *slang* **(1)** : COCAINE **(2)** : HEROIN **d** : small transient light or dark spots on a television screen — **snow·less** \-ləs\ *adj*
[2]**snow** *vi* (14c) : to fall in or as snow ~ *vt* **1** : to cause to fall like or as snow **2 a** : to cover, shut in, or imprison with or as if with snow **b** : to deceive, persuade, or charm glibly **3** : to whiten like snow
[1]**snow·ball** \ˈsnō-ˌbȯl\ *n* (15c) **1 a** : a round mass of snow pressed or rolled together **b** : SNOW CONE **2** : any of several cultivated shrubby viburnums (genus *Viburnum*) with clusters of white sterile flowers — called also *snowball bush*
[2]**snowball** *vi* (1843) **1** : to engage in throwing snowballs **2** : to increase, accumulate, expand, or multiply at a rapidly accelerating rate ~ *vt* **1** : to throw snowballs at **2** : to cause to increase or multiply at a rapidly accelerating rate
snow·bank \ˈsnō-ˌbaŋk\ *n* (1779) : a mound or slope of snow
snow·belt \-ˌbelt\ *n, often cap* (1874) : a region that receives an appreciable amount of annual snowfall
snow·ber·ry \-ˌber-ē\ *n* (1760) : any of several white-berried shrubs (esp. genus *Symphoricarpos* of the honeysuckle family); *esp* : a low-growing No. American shrub (*S. albus*) with pinkish-white flowers in small axillary clusters
snow·bird \-ˌbərd\ *n* (1674) **1** : any of several birds (as a junco or fieldfare) seen chiefly in winter **2** : one who travels to warm climes for the winter
snow blindness *n* (1748) : inflammation and photophobia caused by exposure of the eyes to ultraviolet rays reflected from snow or ice — **snow–blind** \ˈsnō-ˌblīnd\ *or* **snow–blind·ed** \-ˌblīn-dəd\ *adj*
snow·blow·er \ˈsnō-ˌblō-ər\ *n* (1950) : a machine for removing snow (as from a driveway or sidewalk) in which a rotating spiral blade picks up and propels the snow aside
snow·board \-ˌbȯrd\ *n* (1981) : a board like a wide ski ridden in a surfing position downhill over snow — **snowboard** *vi* — **snow·board·er** *n* — **snow·board·ing** *n*
snow·board·cross \ˈsnō-ˌbȯrd-ˌkrȯs\ *n* [*snowboard* + *-cross* (as in *motocross*)] (1997) : a snowboard race that includes jumps and turns
snow·bound \-ˈbau̇nd\ *adj* (1802) : shut in or blockaded by snow
snow·brush \-ˌbrəsh\ *n* (ca. 1923) : a spreading white-flowered western No. American shrub (*Ceanothus velutinus*) of the buckthorn family
snow bunting *n* (1771) : a white bunting (*Plectrophenax nivalis*) with black or brown markings on the upperparts that breeds in arctic regions and winters in northern parts of No. America and Eurasia
snow·cap \-ˌkap\ *n* (1859) : a covering cap of snow (as on a mountain peak) — **snow·capped** \-ˌkapt\ *adj*
snow·cat \ˈsnō-ˌkat\ *n* (1955) : a tracklaying vehicle for travel on snow
snow cone *or* **sno–cone** \ˈsnō-ˌkōn\ *n* (1941) : granular ice molded into a ball and flavored with a syrup
snow crab *n* (1974) : any of several long-legged crabs (genus *Chionoecetes,* esp. *C. opilio* and *C. bairdi*) of the eastern north Pacific Ocean and esp. Alaska and the western north Atlantic Ocean that are used for food
snow·drift \ˈsnō-ˌdrift\ *n* (14c) : a bank of drifted snow
snow·drop \-ˌdräp\ *n* (1664) : a bulbous European herb (*Galanthus nivalis*) of the amaryllis family bearing nodding white flowers that often appear while the snow is on the ground
snow·fall \-ˌfȯl\ *n* (1821) : a fall of snow; *specif* : the amount of snow that falls in a single storm or in a given period
snow fence *n* (1872) : a usu. slatted fence placed across the path of prevailing winds to protect (as a building, road, or railroad track) from drifting snow by disrupting the flow of wind and causing the snow to be deposited on the lee side of the fence
snow·field \ˈsnō-ˌfēld\ *n* (1830) : a broad level expanse of snow; *esp* : a mass of perennial snow at the head of a glacier
snow·flake \-ˌflāk\ *n* (1734) **1** : a flake or crystal of snow **2** : any of a genus (*Leucojum*) of Old World bulbous plants of the amaryllis family; *esp* : one (*L. vernum*) resembling the snowdrop
snow goose *n* (1771) : a No. American goose (*Chen caerulescens* syn. *Anser caerulescens*) that has a pinkish bill and exists either as a white form with black primaries or as a grayish-black form with a white head
snow–in–summer *n* (1886) : a European creeping perennial herb (*Cerastium tomentosum*) of the pink family with hairy grayish foliage and white flowers that is often used as a ground cover
snow job *n* (1943) : an intensive effort at persuasion or deception
snow leopard *n* (1866) : a large cat (*Panthera uncia* syn. *Uncia uncia*) of upland central Asia with long heavy grayish-white fur irregularly marked with brownish-black spots, rosettes, and rings
snow line *n* (ca. 1835) : the lower margin of a perennial snowfield
snow·mak·er \ˈsnō-ˌmā-kər\ *n* (1954) : a device for making snow
snow·mak·ing \-ˌmā-kiŋ\ *n, often attrib* (1953) : the production of snow usu. for ski slopes
snow·man \-ˌman\ *n* (1827) : snow shaped to resemble a human figure
snow·melt \-ˌmelt\ *n* (ca. 1927) : runoff produced by melting snow
snow·mo·bile \ˈsnō-mō-ˌbēl\ *n* (1923) : any of various automotive vehicles for travel on snow; *specif* : an open vehicle for usu. one or two persons with steerable skis on the front and an endless belt at the rear
snow·mo·bil·ing \-ˌbē-liŋ\ *n* (1964) : the sport of driving a snowmobile — **snow·mo·bil·er** \-lər\ *also* **snow·mo·bil·ist** \-list\ *n*
snow–on–the–mountain *n* (ca. 1873) : a spurge (*Euphorbia marginata*) of the central and western U.S. that has showy white-bracted flower clusters and is grown as an ornamental
snow·pack \ˈsnō-ˌpak\ *n* (ca. 1946) : a seasonal accumulation of slow-melting packed snow
snow pea *n* (1949) : a cultivated pea with flat edible pods that is classified with the snap pea as a variety (*Pisum sativum macrocarpon*)
snow plant *n* (1846) : a fleshy bright-red saprophytic herb (*Sarcodes sanguinea*) of the Indian-pipe family that grows in high-altitude coniferous woods of the western U.S. and often appears before the snow melts
[1]**snow·plow** \ˈsnō-ˌplau̇\ *n* (1792) **1** : any of various devices used for clearing away snow **2** : a stemming with both skis used for coming to a stop, slowing down, or descending slowly
[2]**snowplow** *vi* (1904) : to execute a snowplow ⟨~*ed* to a stop⟩
snow pudding *n* (1876) : a pudding made very fluffy and light by the addition of whipped egg whites and gelatin
snow·scape \ˈsnō-ˌskāp\ *n* (1886) : a landscape covered with snow
snow·shed \-ˌshed\ *n* (1868) : a shelter against snowslides
[1]**snow·shoe** \-ˌshü\ *n* (1666) : a usu. lightweight platform for the foot that is designed to enable a person to walk on soft snow

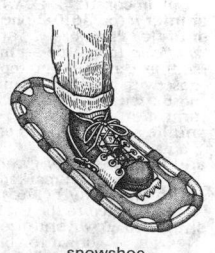

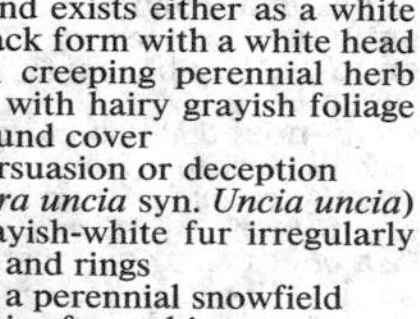
snowshoe

without sinking and that typically consists of an oblong frame crossed with leather thongs or synthetic material

[2]**snowshoe** *vi* **snow·shoed; snow·shoe·ing** (1880) : to travel on snowshoes — **snow·sho·er** \-ˌshü-ər\ *n*

snowshoe hare *n* (ca. 1890) : a hare (*Lepus americanus*) of northern No. America with heavy fur on the hind feet and a coat that in most populations is brown in the summer but usu. white in the winter — called also *snowshoe rabbit, varying hare*

snow·slide \ˈsnō-ˌslīd\ *n* (1841) : an avalanche of snow

snow·storm \-ˌstȯrm\ *n* (1755) : a storm of or with snow

snow·suit \-ˌsüt\ *n* (1935) : a one-piece or two-piece lined garment for winter wear by children

snow thrower *n* (1954) : SNOWBLOWER

snow tire *n* (1943) : an automotive tire with a tread designed to give added traction on snow

snow tube *n* (1982) : a large inflatable ring-shaped tube used for sliding down a snow-covered incline

snow under *vt* (1880) **1** : to overwhelm esp. in excess of capacity to absorb or deal with something **2** : to defeat by a large margin

snow–white \ˈsnō-ˈhwīt, -ˈwīt\ *adj* (bef. 12c) : white as snow

snowy \ˈsnō-ē\ *adj* **snow·i·er; -est** (bef. 12c) **1 a** : composed of snow or melted snow **b** : marked by or covered with snow **2 a** : whitened by snow **b** : SNOW-WHITE — **snow·i·ly** \ˈsnō-ə-lē\ *adv* — **snow·i·ness** \ˈsnō-ē-nəs\ *n*

snowy egret *n* (1859) : a white American egret (*Egretta thula*) having a slender black bill, black legs, and yellow feet

snowy owl *n* (1781) : a large ground-nesting diurnal arctic owl (*Nyctea scandiaca*) that enters the chiefly northern parts of the U.S. in winter and has plumage that is sometimes nearly pure white but usu. with brownish spots or bars

snowy plover *n* (1872) : a small plover (*Charadrius alexandrinus*) of the Gulf coast and the eastern U.S. and Mexico that is light gray above with a black bill, black patches on the head and sides of the neck, and white underparts

SNP \ˈsnip\ *n* [*s*ingle *n*ucleotide *p*olymorphism] (1991) : a variant DNA sequence in which the purine or pyrimidine base (as cytosine) of a single nucleotide has been replaced by another such base (as thymine)

Snr *abbr, Brit* senior

[1]**snub** \ˈsnəb\ *vt* **snubbed; snub·bing** [ME *snibben, snubben,* prob. of Scand origin; akin to ON *snubba* to scold, Sw dial. *snubba* to reproach, cut off] (13c) **1** : to check or stop with a cutting retort : REBUKE **2 a** : to check (as a line) suddenly while running out esp. by turning around a fixed object (as a post or a cleat); *also* : to check the motion of by snubbing a line ⟨~ the anchor⟩ **b** : to restrain the action of : SUPPRESS ⟨~ a vibration⟩ **3** : to treat with contempt or neglect ⟨~ an old acquaintance⟩ **4** : to extinguish by stubbing ⟨~ out a cigarette⟩

[2]**snub** *n* (14c) : an act or an instance of snubbing; *esp* : SLIGHT

[3]**snub** *adj* (1724) **1** *or* **snubbed** \ˈsnəbd\ : BLUNT, STUBBY ⟨a ~ nose⟩ **2** : used in snubbing ⟨~ line⟩ — **snub·ness** *n*

snub·ber \ˈsnə-bər\ *n* (1853) **1** : one that snubs **2** : SHOCK ABSORBER

snub·by \ˈsnə-bē\ *adj* (1779) **1** : SNUB-NOSED **2** : SNUB — **snub·bi·ness** *n*

snub–nosed \ˈsnəb-ˌnōzd\ *adj* (1725) **1** : having a stubby and usu. slightly turned-up nose **2** : having a very short barrel ⟨a ~ revolver⟩

snuck *past and past part of* SNEAK

[1]**snuff** \ˈsnəf\ *n* [ME *snoffe*] (14c) **1** : the charred part of a candlewick **2 a** *obs* : UMBRAGE, OFFENSE **b** *chiefly Scot* : HUFF

[2]**snuff** *vt* (15c) **1** : to crop the snuff of (a candle) by pinching or by the use of snuffers so as to brighten the light **2 a** : to extinguish by or as if by the use of a candlesnuffer — often used with *out* **b** : to make extinct : put an end to — usu. used with *out* ⟨~*ed* out their hopes⟩; *also* : KILL, EXECUTE ⟨~*ed* the bad guys⟩ — **snuff it** *Brit* : DIE

[3]**snuff** *adj* (1971) : characterized by the sensationalistic depiction of violence; *esp* : featuring a real rather than a staged murder ⟨~ movies⟩

[4]**snuff** *vb* [akin to D *snuffen* to sniff, snuff — more at SNIVEL] *vt* (1527) **1** : to draw forcibly through or into the nostrils **2** : SCENT, SMELL **3** : to sniff at in order to examine — used of an animal ~ *vi* **1** : to inhale through the nose noisily and forcibly; *also* : to sniff or smell inquiringly **2** *obs* : to sniff loudly in or as if in disgust **3** : to take snuff

[5]**snuff** *n* (1568) : the act of snuffing : SNIFF

[6]**snuff** *n* [D *snuf,* short for *snuftabak,* fr. *snuffen* to snuff + *tabak* tobacco] (1650) **1** : a preparation of pulverized tobacco to be inhaled through the nostrils, chewed, or placed against the gums **2** : the amount of snuff taken at one time — **up to snuff** : of sufficient quality : meeting an applicable standard

snuff·box \ˈsnəf-ˌbäks\ *n* (ca. 1673) : a small box for holding snuff usu. carried about the person

[1]**snuff·er** \ˈsnə-fər\ *n* (15c) **1** : a device similar to a pair of scissors for cropping and holding the snuff of a candle — usu. used in pl. but sing. or pl. in constr. **2** : CANDLESNUFFER

[2]**snuffer** *n* (ca. 1610) : one that snuffs or sniffs

[1]**snuf·fle** \ˈsnə-fəl\ *vb* **snuf·fled; snuf·fling** \-f(ə-)liŋ\ [akin to D *snuffelen* to snuffle — more at SNIVEL] *vi* (ca. 1600) **1** : to snuff or sniff usu. audibly and repeatedly **2** : to breathe through an obstructed nose with a sniffing sound **3** : to speak through or as if through the nose : WHINE ~ *vt* : to seek or test by or as if by repeated sniffs — **snuf·fler** \-f(ə-)lər\ *n*

[2]**snuffle** *n* (1717) **1** *pl* : SNIFFLES **2** : the act or sound of snuffling **3** : a nasal twang

[1]**snuffy** \ˈsnə-fē\ *adj* [[4]*snuff*] (1678) **1** : quick to become annoyed or take offense **2** : marked by snobbery

[2]**snuffy** *adj* [[6]*snuff*] (1765) **1** : soiled with snuff **2** : resembling snuff **3 a** : addicted to the use of snuff **b** : having unpleasant habits

[1]**snug** \ˈsnəg\ *vb* **snugged; snug·ging** [[2]*snug*] *vi* (1583) : SNUGGLE, NESTLE ⟨~ down for bed⟩ ~ *vt* **1** : to cause to fit closely **2** : to make snug **3** : HIDE 1 **4** : to secure by fastening or lashing down

[2]**snug** *adj* **snug·ger; snug·gest** [perh. of Scand origin; akin to Sw *snygg* tidy] (ca. 1595) **1 a** *of a ship* : manifesting seaworthiness : TAUT **b** : TRIM, NEAT **c** : fitting closely and comfortably ⟨a ~ coat⟩ **2 a** : enjoying or affording warm secure shelter or cover and opportunity for ease and contentment ⟨a ~ cottage⟩ ⟨a ~ haven⟩ **b** : marked by cordiality and secure privacy **3** : affording a degree of comfort and ease ⟨a ~ income⟩ **4** : offering safe concealment ⟨a ~ hideout⟩ ***syn*** see COMFORTABLE — **snug** *adv* — **snug·ly** *adv* — **snug·ness** *n*

[3]**snug** *n* [short for *snuggery*] (1860) *Brit* : a small private room or compartment in a pub

snug·gery \ˈsnə-g(ə-)rē\ *n, pl* **-ger·ies** (1812) *chiefly Brit* : a snug cozy place; *esp* : a small room

snug·gle \ˈsnə-gəl\ *vb* **snug·gled; snug·gling** \-g(ə-)liŋ\ [freq. of [1]*snug*] *vi* (1687) : to curl up comfortably or cozily ~ *vt* **1** : to draw close esp. for comfort or in affection **2** : to make snug — **snuggle** *n*

[1]**so** \ˈsō, *esp before adj or adv followed by "that"* sə\ *adv* [ME, fr. OE *swā;* akin to OHG *sō* so, L *sic* so, thus, *si* if, Gk *hōs* so, thus, L *suus* one's own — more at SUICIDE] (bef. 12c) **1 a** : in a manner or way indicated or suggested ⟨do you really think ~⟩ — often used as a substitute for a preceding clause ⟨are you ready? I think ~⟩ ⟨I didn't like it and I told her ~⟩ **b** : in the same manner or way : ALSO ⟨worked hard and ~ did she⟩ **c** : THUS 1 ⟨for ~ the Lord said —Isa 18:4(AV)⟩ **d** : THEN, SUBSEQUENTLY ⟨and ~ home and to bed⟩ **2 a** : to an indicated or suggested extent or degree ⟨had never been ~ happy⟩ **b** : to a great extent or degree : VERY, EXTREMELY ⟨loves her ~⟩ **c** : to a definite but unspecified extent or degree ⟨can only do ~ much in a day⟩ **d** : most certainly : INDEED ⟨you did ~ do it⟩ **e** : most decidedly : SURELY ⟨I ~ don't believe you⟩ **3** : THEREFORE, CONSEQUENTLY ⟨the witness is biased and ~ unreliable⟩

usage The intensive use of *so* (sense 2b) is widely condemned in college handbooks but is nonetheless standard ⟨why is American television *so* shallow? —Anthony Lewis⟩ ⟨the cephalopod eye is an example of a remarkable evolutionary parallel because it is *so* like the eye of a vertebrate —Sarah F. Robbins⟩ ⟨the kind of sterile over-ingenuity which afflicts *so* many academic efforts —*Times Lit. Supp.*⟩. There is no stigma attached to its use in negative contexts and when qualified by a dependent clause ⟨not *so* long ago⟩ ⟨was *so* good in mathematics that he began to consider engineering —*Current Biog.*⟩. The denotation in these uses is, of course, slightly different (see sense 2a). Another emphatic use of *so* (sense 2e) has developed more recently and occurs mostly in informal contexts.

[2]**so** *conj* (bef. 12c) **1 a** : with the result that ⟨the acoustics are good, ~ every note is clear⟩ **b** : in order that ⟨be quiet ~ he can sleep⟩ **2** *archaic* : provided that **3 a** : for that reason : THEREFORE ⟨don't want to go, ~ I won't⟩ **b** (1) — used as an introductory particle ⟨~ here we are⟩ often to belittle a point under discussion ⟨~ what?⟩ (2) — used interjectionally to indicate awareness of a discovery ⟨~, that's who did it⟩ or surprised dissent — **so as to** : in order to

usage Although occas. condemned, use of *so* to introduce clauses of result (sense 1a) and purpose (sense 1b) is standard. In sense 1b *so that* is more common in formal contexts than *so* alone.

[3]**so** *adj* (bef. 12c) **1** : conforming with actual facts : TRUE ⟨said things that were not ~⟩ **2** : marked by a desired order ⟨his books are always just ~⟩ **3** — used to replace a preceding adjective ⟨was witty by adult standards and of course doubly ~ by mine —Sally Kempton⟩

[4]**so** *pron* (bef. 12c) **1** : such as has been specified or suggested : the same ⟨if you have to file a claim, do ~ as soon as possible⟩ **2** — used in the phrase *or so* to indicate an estimate, approximation, or conjecture ⟨stayed a week or ~⟩ ⟨cost $15 or ~⟩

[5]**so** *var of* SOL

[6]**so** *abbr* south; southern

SO *abbr* **1** seller's option **2** strikeout

[1]**soak** \ˈsōk\ *vb* [ME *soken,* fr. OE *socian;* akin to OE *sūcan* to suck] *vi* (bef. 12c) **1** : to lie immersed in liquid (as water) : become saturated by or as if by immersion **2 a** : to enter or pass through something by or as if by pores or interstices : PERMEATE **b** : to penetrate or affect the mind or feelings — usu. used with *in* or *into* **3** : to drink alcoholic beverages intemperately ~ *vt* **1** : to permeate so as to wet, soften, or fill thoroughly **2** : to place in a surrounding element (as liquid) to wet or permeate thoroughly **3** : to extract by or as if by steeping ⟨~ the dirt out⟩ **4 a** : to draw or take in by or as if by suction or absorption ⟨~*ed* up the sunshine⟩ **b** : to intoxicate (oneself) by drinking alcoholic beverages **5** : to cause to pay an exorbitant amount — **soak·er** *n*

syn SOAK, SATURATE, DRENCH, STEEP, IMPREGNATE mean to permeate or be permeated with a liquid. SOAK implies usu. prolonged immersion as for softening or cleansing ⟨*soak* the garment in soapy water⟩. SATURATE implies a resulting effect of complete absorption until no more liquid can be held ⟨a *saturated* sponge⟩. DRENCH implies a thorough wetting by something that pours down or is poured ⟨clothes *drenched* by a cloudburst⟩. STEEP suggests either the extraction of an essence (as of tea leaves) by the liquid or the imparting of a quality (as a color) to the thing immersed ⟨*steep* the tea for five minutes⟩. IMPREGNATE implies a thorough interpenetration of one thing by another ⟨a cake strongly *impregnated* with brandy⟩.

[2]**soak** *n* (15c) **1 a** : the act or process of soaking : the state of being soaked **b** : that (as liquid) in which something is soaked **2** : DRUNKARD **3** *slang* : [2]PAWN 2

[1]**so–and–so** \ˈsō-ən-ˌsō\ *n, pl* **so–and–sos** *or* **so–and–so's** \-ˌsōz\ (13c) **1** : an unnamed or unspecified person, thing, or action **2** : BASTARD 3

[2]**so–and–so** *adv* (1565) **1** : to an unspecified amount or degree **2** : in an unspecified manner or fashion

[1]**soap** \ˈsōp\ *n* [ME *sope,* fr. OE *sāpe;* akin to OHG *seifa* soap] (bef. 12c) **1 a** : a cleansing and emulsifying agent made usu. by action of alkali on fat or fatty acids and consisting essentially of sodium or potassium salts of such acids **b** : a salt of a fatty acid and a metal **2** : SOAP OPERA

[2]**soap** *vt* (1585) **1** : to rub soap over or into **2** : FLATTER

soap·bark \ˈsōp-ˌbärk\ *n* (1861) : a Chilean tree (*Quillaja saponaria*) of the rose family with glossy leaves and terminal white flowers; *also* : its saponin-rich bark used in cleaning and in emulsifying oils

soap·ber·ry \-ˌber-ē\ *n* (1693) : any of a genus (*Sapindus* of the family Sapindaceae, the soapberry family) of chiefly tropical woody plants; *also* : the fruit of a soapberry and esp. of a tree (*S. saponaria*) that is saponin-rich and used as a soap substitute

soap·box \-ˌbäks\ *n* (1907) : an improvised platform used by a self-appointed, spontaneous, or informal orator; *broadly* : something that provides an outlet for delivering opinions — **soapbox** *adj*

soap bubble *n* (1639) : a hollow iridescent globe formed by blowing a film of soapsuds (as from a pipe)

soap·er \ˈsō-pər\ *n* (1946) : SOAP OPERA

soap opera *n* [fr. its sponsorship by soap manufacturers] (1939) **1 a** : a serial drama performed orig. on a daytime radio or television program and chiefly characterized by tangled interpersonal situations and melodramatic or sentimental treatment **b** : a series of real-life events resembling a soap opera **2** : the melodrama and sentimentality characteristic of a soap opera ⟨even cops need a little *soap opera* in their lives —Joseph Wambaugh⟩; *also* : something (as a novel) having such qualities — **soap–op·er·at·ic** \ˈsōp-ˌä-pə-ˈra-tik\ *adj*

soap plant *n* (1844) : a plant having a part (as a root or fruit) that may be used in place of soap; *esp* : a California plant (*Chlorogalum pomeridianum*) of the lily family

soap·stone \ˈsōp-ˌstōn\ *n* (ca. 1681) : a soft stone having a soapy feel and composed essentially of talc, chlorite, and often some magnetite

soap·suds \-ˌsədz\ *n pl* (ca. 1611) : SUDS 1

soap·wort \-ˌwərt, -ˌwȯrt\ *n* (ca. 1548) : BOUNCING BET

soapy \ˈsō-pē\ *adj* **soap·i·er; -est** (1610) **1** : smeared with soap : LATHERED **2** : containing or combined with soap or saponin **3 a** : having the qualities of soap; *esp* : smooth and slippery **b** : UNCTUOUS, SUAVE **4** : of, relating to, or having the characteristics of a soap opera — **soap·i·ly** \-pə-lē\ *adv* — **soap·i·ness** \-pē-nəs\ *n*

1**soar** \ˈsȯr\ *vi* [ME *soren,* fr. MF *essorer,* fr. OF, fr. VL **exaurare,* fr. L *ex-* + *aura* air — more at AURA] (14c) **1 a** : to fly aloft or about **b** (1) : to sail or hover in the air often at a great height : GLIDE (2) *of a glider* : to fly without engine power and without loss of altitude **2** : to rise or increase dramatically (as in position, value, or price) ⟨stocks ~*ed*⟩ **3** : to ascend to a higher or more exalted level ⟨makes my spirits ~⟩ **4** : to rise to majestic stature — **soar·er** *n*

2**soar** *n* (1596) **1** : the range, distance, or height attained in soaring **2** : the act of soaring : upward flight

soar·ing *n* (15c) : the act or process of soaring; *specif* : the act or sport of flying a heavier-than-air craft without power by utilizing ascending air currents

Soa·ve \ˈswä-(ˌ)vā\ *n* [*Soave,* village near Verona, Italy] (1934) : a dry white Italian wine

1**sob** \ˈsäb\ *vb* **sobbed; sob·bing** [ME *sobben;* akin to MLG *sabben* to drool] *vi* (13c) **1 a** : to catch the breath audibly in a spasmodic contraction of the throat **b** : to cry or weep with convulsive catching of the breath **2** : to make a sound like that of a sob or sobbing ~ *vt* **1** : to bring (as oneself) to a specified state by sobbing ⟨*sobbed* himself to sleep⟩ **2** : to utter with sobs ⟨*sobbed* out her grief⟩

2**sob** *n* (14c) **1** : an act of sobbing **2** : a sound like that of a sob

SOB \ˌes-ˌō-ˈbē\ *n* [*s*on *o*f a *b*itch] (1918) : BASTARD 3, SON OF A BITCH

so·ba \ˈsō-bə\ *n* [Jp] (ca. 1896) : a Japanese noodle made from buckwheat flour

1**so·ber** \ˈsō-bər\ *adj* **so·ber·er** \-bər-ər\; **so·ber·est** \-b(ə-)rəst\ [ME *sobre,* fr. AF, fr. L *sobrius;* akin to L *ebrius* drunk] (14c) **1 a** : sparing in the use of food and drink : ABSTEMIOUS **b** : not addicted to intoxicating drink **c** : not drunk **2** : marked by sedate or gravely or earnestly thoughtful character or demeanor **3** : UNHURRIED, CALM **4** : marked by temperance, moderation, or seriousness ⟨a ~ candlelight vigil⟩ **5** : subdued in tone or color **6** : showing no excessive or extreme qualities of fancy, emotion, or prejudice ***syn*** see SERIOUS — **so·ber·ly** \-bər-lē\ *adv* — **so·ber·ness** *n*

2**sober** *vb* **so·bered; so·ber·ing** \-b(ə-)riŋ\ *vt* (14c) : to make sober ~ *vi* : to become sober — usu. used with *up*

so·ber·ing *adj* (1816) : tending to make one thoughtful or sober

so·ber·sid·ed \ˌsō-bər-ˈsī-dəd\ *adj* (1805) : solemn or serious in nature or appearance — **so·ber·sid·ed·ness** \-nəs\ *n*

so·ber·sides \ˈsō-bər-ˌsīdz\ *n pl but sing or pl in constr* (1705) : a sober-sided person

so·bri·ety \sə-ˈbrī-ə-tē, sō-\ *n* [ME *sobrete,* fr. AF *sobreté,* fr. L *sobrietat-, sobrietas,* fr. *sobrius*] (15c) : the quality or state of being sober

so·bri·quet \ˈsō-bri-ˌkā, -ˌket, ˌsō-bri-ˈ\ *also* **sou·bri·quet** \ˈsō-, ˌsō-, ˈsü-, ˌsü-\ *n* [F] (1646) : a descriptive name or epithet : NICKNAME

sob sister *n* (1912) **1** : a journalist who specializes in writing or editing sob stories or other material of a sentimental type **2** : a sentimental and often impractical person usu. engaged in good works

sob story *n* (1913) : a sentimental story or account intended chiefly to evoke sympathy or sadness

soc *abbr* **1** social **2** society **3** sociology

so·ca \ˈsō-kə, -kä\ *n* [*so*ul music + 2*ca*lypso] (1973) : a blend of soul and calypso music

so·cage \ˈsä-kij, ˈsō-\ *also* **soc·cage** \ˈsä-\ *n* [ME, fr. AF, fr. *soc* soke] (14c) : a tenure of land by agricultural service fixed in amount and kind or by payment of money rent only and not burdened with any military service — **so·cag·er** \-ki-jər\ *n*

so–called \ˈsō-ˈkȯld\ *adj* (15c) **1** : commonly named ⟨the ~ pocket veto⟩ **2** : falsely or improperly so named ⟨deceived by a ~ friend⟩

soc·cer \ˈsä-kər\ *n* [by shortening & alter. fr. *association football*] (1885) : a game played on a field between two teams of 11 players each with the object to propel a round ball into the opponent's goal by kicking or by hitting it with any part of the body except the hands and arms — called also *association football*

soccer mom *n* (1987) : a typically suburban mother who accompanies her children to their soccer games and is considered as part of a significant voting bloc or demographic group

so·cia·bil·i·ty \ˌsō-shə-ˈbi-lə-tē\ *n, pl* **-ties** (15c) : the quality or state of being sociable; *also* : the act or an instance of being sociable

1**so·cia·ble** \ˈsō-shə-bəl\ *adj* [MF or L; MF, fr. L *sociabilis,* fr. *sociare* to join, associate, fr. *socius*] (1511) **1** : inclined by nature to companionship with others of the same species : SOCIAL **2 a** : inclined to seek or enjoy companionship **b** : marked by or conducive to friendliness or pleasant social relations ***syn*** see GRACIOUS — **so·cia·ble·ness** *n* — **so·cia·bly** \-blē\ *adv*

2**sociable** *n* (1750) : an informal social gathering frequently involving a special activity or interest

1**so·cial** \ˈsō-shəl\ *adj* [ME, fr. L *socialis,* fr. *socius* companion, ally, associate; akin to OE *secg* man, companion, L *sequi* to follow — more at SUE] (14c) **1** : involving allies or confederates ⟨the *Social* War between the Athenians and their allies⟩ **2 a** : marked by or passed in pleasant companionship with friends or associates ⟨an active ~ life⟩ **b** : SOCIABLE **c** : of, relating to, or designed for sociability ⟨a ~ club⟩ **3** : of or relating to human society, the interaction of the individual and the group, or the welfare of human beings as members of society ⟨~ institutions⟩ **4 a** : tending to form cooperative and interdependent relationships with others **b** : living and breeding in more or less organized communities ⟨~ insects⟩ **c** *of a plant* : tending to grow in groups or masses so as to form a pure stand **5 a** : of, relating to, or based on rank or status in a particular society ⟨a member of our ~ set⟩ **b** : of, relating to, or characteristic of the upper classes **c** : FORMAL **6** : being such in social situations ⟨a ~ drinker⟩

2**social** *n* (1870) : SOCIABLE

social climber *n* (1911) : one who attempts to gain a higher social position or acceptance in fashionable society — **social climbing** *n*

social contract *n* (1837) : an actual or hypothetical agreement among the members of an organized society or between a community and its ruler that defines and limits the rights and duties of each

social Darwinism *n* (1887) : an extension of Darwinism to social phenomena; *specif* : a sociological theory that sociocultural advance is the product of intergroup conflict and competition and the socially elite classes (as those possessing wealth and power) possess biological superiority in the struggle for existence — **social Darwinist** *n or adj*

social democracy *n* (1850) **1** : a political movement advocating a gradual and peaceful transition from capitalism to socialism by democratic means **2** : a democratic welfare state that incorporates both capitalist and socialist practices — **social democrat** *n* — **social democratic** *adj*

social disease *n* (1891) **1** : VENEREAL DISEASE **2** : a disease (as tuberculosis) whose incidence is directly related to social and economic factors

social engineering *n* (1899) : management of human beings in accordance with their place and function in society : applied social science — **social engineer** *n*

social gospel *n* (1890) **1** : the application of Christian principles to social problems **2** *cap S&G* : a movement in American Protestant Christianity esp. in the first part of the 20th century to bring the social order into conformity with Christian principles

social insurance *n* (1909) : protection of the individual against economic hazards (as unemployment, old age, or disability) in which the government participates or enforces the participation of employers and affected individuals

so·cial·ise *Brit var of* SOCIALIZE

so·cial·ism \ˈsō-shə-ˌli-zəm\ *n* (1837) **1** : any of various economic and political theories advocating collective or governmental ownership and administration of the means of production and distribution of goods **2 a** : a system of society or group living in which there is no private property **b** : a system or condition of society in which the means of production are owned and controlled by the state **3** : a stage of society in Marxist theory transitional between capitalism and communism and distinguished by unequal distribution of goods and pay according to work done

so·cial·ist \ˈsō-sh(ə-)list\ *n* (1827) **1** : one who advocates or practices socialism **2** *cap* : a member of a party or political group advocating socialism — **socialist** *adj, often cap* — **so·cial·is·tic** \ˌsō-shə-ˈlis-tik\ *adj* — **so·cial·is·ti·cal·ly** \-ti-k(ə-)lē\ *adv*

socialist realism *n* (1934) : a Marxist aesthetic theory calling for the didactic use of literature, art, and music to develop social consciousness in an evolving socialist state — **socialist realist** *n or adj*

so·cial·ite \ˈsō-shə-ˌlīt\ *n* (1928) : a socially prominent person

so·ci·al·i·ty \ˌsō-shē-ˈa-lə-tē\ *n, pl* **-ties** (ca. 1649) **1 a** : SOCIABILITY **b** : an instance of social intercourse or sociability **2** : the tendency to associate in or form social groups

so·cial·ize \ˈsō-shə-ˌlīz\ *vb* **-ized; -iz·ing** *vt* (1810) **1** : to make social; *esp* : to fit or train for a social environment **2 a** : to constitute on a socialistic basis ⟨~ industry⟩ **b** : to adapt to social needs or uses **3** : to organize group participation in ⟨~ a recitation⟩ ~ *vi* : to participate actively in a social group — **so·cial·i·za·tion** \ˌsō-sh(ə-)lə-ˈzā-shən\ *n* — **so·cial·iz·er** \ˈsō-shə-ˌlī-zər\ *n*

socialized medicine *n* (1937) : medical and hospital services for the members of a class or population administered by an organized group (as a state agency) and paid for from funds obtained usu. by assessments, philanthropy, or taxation

so·cial·ly \ˈsō-sh(ə-)lē\ *adv* (ca. 1763) **1** : in a social manner **2** : with respect to society **3** : by or through society

social media *n pl but sing or pl in constr* (2004) : forms of electronic communication (as Web sites for social networking and microblogging) through which users create online communities to share information, ideas, personal messages, and other content (as videos)

so·cial–mind·ed \ˌsō-shəl-ˈmīn-dəd\ *adj* (1927) : having an interest in society; *specif* : actively interested in social welfare or the well-being of society as a whole

social networking *n* (1998) : the creation and maintenance of personal and business relationships esp. online

social promotion *n* (1960) : the practice of promoting a student from one grade level to the next on the basis of age rather than academic achievement

social psychology *n* (1880) : the study of the manner in which the personality, attitudes, motivations, and behavior of the individual influence and are influenced by social groups — **social psychologist** *n*

social science *n* (1772) **1** : a branch of science that deals with the institutions and functioning of human society and with the interpersonal relationships of individuals as members of society **2** : a science (as economics or political science) dealing with a particular phase or aspect of human society — **social scientist** *n*

social secretary *n* (1903) : a personal secretary employed to handle social correspondence and appointments

social security *n* (1908) **1** : the principle or practice or a program of public provision (as through social insurance or assistance) for the economic security and social welfare of the individual and his or her family; *esp, cap both Ss* : a U.S. government program established in 1935 to include old-age and survivors insurance, contributions to state unem-

ployment insurance, and old-age assistance **2 :** money paid out through a social security program ⟨began collecting *social security*⟩
social service *n* (1851) **:** an activity designed to promote social well-being; *specif* **:** organized philanthropic assistance (as of the disabled or disadvantaged)
social studies *n pl* (1926) **:** a part of a school or college curriculum concerned with the study of social relationships and the functioning of society and usu. made up of courses in history, government, economics, civics, sociology, geography, and anthropology
social welfare *n* (1917) **:** organized public or private social services for the assistance of disadvantaged groups; *specif* **:** SOCIAL WORK
social work *n* (1890) **:** any of various professional activities or methods concretely concerned with providing social services and esp. with the investigation, treatment, and material aid of the economically, physically, mentally, or socially disadvantaged — **social worker** *n*
so·ci·e·tal \sə-ˈsī-ə-tᵊl\ *adj* (1898) **:** of or relating to society **:** SOCIAL ⟨~ forces⟩ — **so·ci·e·tal·ly** \-tᵊl-ē\ *adv*
[1]**so·ci·e·ty** \sə-ˈsī-ə-tē\ *n, pl* **-ties** [MF *societé,* fr. L *societat-, societas,* fr. *socius* companion — more at SOCIAL] (1531) **1 :** companionship or association with one's fellows **:** friendly or intimate intercourse **:** COMPANY **2 :** a voluntary association of individuals for common ends; *esp* **:** an organized group working together or periodically meeting because of common interests, beliefs, or profession **3 a :** an enduring and cooperating social group whose members have developed organized patterns of relationships through interaction with one another **b :** a community, nation, or broad grouping of people having common traditions, institutions, and collective activities and interests **4 a :** a part of a community that is a unit distinguishable by particular aims or standards of living or conduct **:** a social circle or a group of social circles having a clearly marked identity ⟨literary ~⟩ **b :** a part of the community that sets itself apart as a leisure class and that regards itself as the arbiter of fashion and manners **5 a :** a natural group of plants usu. of a single species or habit within an association **b :** the progeny of a pair of insects when constituting a social unit (as a hive of bees); *broadly* **:** an interdependent system of organisms or biological units
[2]**society** *adj* (1693) **:** of, relating to, or typical of fashionable society
So·cin·i·an \sə-ˈsi-nē-ən, sō-\ *n* [NL *socinianus,* fr. Faustus *Socinus*] (1621) **:** an adherent of a 16th and 17th century theological movement professing belief in God and adherence to the Christian Scriptures but denying the divinity of Christ and consequently denying the Trinity — **Socinian** *adj* — **So·cin·i·an·ism** \-nē-ə-ˌni-zəm\ *n*
socio- *comb form* [F, fr. L *socius* companion] **1 :** society **:** social ⟨*sociogram*⟩ **2 :** social and ⟨*socio*political⟩
so·cio·bi·ol·o·gy \ˌsō-sē-ō-bī-ˈä-lə-jē, ˌsō-shē-\ *n* (1946) **:** the comparative study of social organization and behavior in animals including humans esp. with regard to its genetic basis and evolutionary history — **so·cio·bio·log·i·cal** \-ˌbī-ə-ˈlä-ji-kəl\ *adj* — **so·cio·bi·ol·o·gist** \-bī-ˈä-lə-jist\ *n*
so·cio·cul·tur·al \-ˈkəlch-rəl, -ˈkəl-chə-\ *adj* (1928) **:** of, relating to, or involving a combination of social and cultural factors — **so·cio·cul·tur·al·ly** \-rə-lē\ *adv*
so·cio·eco·nom·ic \-ˌe-kə-ˈnä-mik, -ˌē-kə-\ *adj* (1883) **:** of, relating to, or involving a combination of social and economic factors — **so·cio·eco·nom·i·cal·ly** \-mi-k(ə-)lē\ *adv*
so·cio·gram \ˈsō-sē-ə-ˌgram, ˈsō-shē-\ *n* (1933) **:** a sociometric chart plotting the structure of interpersonal relations in a group situation
so·cio·his·tor·i·cal \ˌsō-sē-ō-his-ˈtȯr-i-kəl, ˌsō-shē-, -ˈtär-\ *adj* (1949) **:** of, relating to, or involving social history or a combination of social and historical factors
so·cio·lin·guis·tic \-liŋ-ˈgwis-tik\ *adj* (1949) **1 :** of or relating to the social aspects of language **2 :** of or relating to sociolinguistics
so·cio·lin·guis·tics \-tiks\ *n pl but sing in constr* (1938) **:** the study of linguistic behavior as determined by sociocultural factors — **so·cio·lin·guist** \-ˈliŋ-gwist\ *n*
so·ci·ol·o·gese \ˌsō-sē-ˌä-lə-ˈjēz, ˌsō-shē-, -ˈjēs\ *n* [*sociology* + [2]*-ese*] (1952) **:** a style of writing held to be characteristic of sociologists
so·cio·log·i·cal \ˌsō-sē-ə-ˈlä-ji-kəl, ˌsō-sh(ē-)ə-\ *also* **so·cio·log·ic** \-jik\ *adj* (1843) **1 :** of or relating to sociology or to the methodological approach of sociology **2 :** oriented or directed toward social needs and problems — **so·cio·log·i·cal·ly** \-ji-k(ə-)lē\ *adv*
so·ci·ol·o·gy \ˌsō-sē-ˈä-lə-jē, ˌsō-shē-\ *n* [F *sociologie,* fr. *socio-* + *-logie* -logy] (1843) **1 :** the science of society, social institutions, and social relationships; *specif* **:** the systematic study of the development, structure, interaction, and collective behavior of organized groups of human beings **2 :** the scientific analysis of a social institution as a functioning whole and as it relates to the rest of society **3 :** SYNECOLOGY — **so·ci·ol·o·gist** \-jist\ *n*
so·ci·om·e·try \-ˈä-mə-trē\ *n* [ISV] (1908) **:** the study and measurement of interpersonal relationships in a group of people — **so·cio·met·ric** \ˌsō-sē-ə-ˈme-trik, ˌsō-shē-\ *adj*
so·cio·path \ˈsō-sē-ə-ˌpath, ˈsō-sh(ē-)ə-\ *n* (1930) **:** a sociopathic individual **:** PSYCHOPATH
so·cio·path·ic \ˌsō-sē-ə-ˈpa-thik, ˌsō-sh(ē-)ə-\ *adj* (1930) **:** of, relating to, or characterized by asocial or antisocial behavior or exhibiting antisocial personality disorder
so·cio·po·lit·i·cal \ˌsō-sē-ō-pə-ˈli-ti-kəl, ˌsō-shē-\ *adj* (1884) **:** of, relating to, or involving a combination of social and political factors
so·cio·psy·cho·log·i·cal \-ˌsī-kə-ˈlä-ji-kəl\ *adj* (1899) **1 :** of, relating to, or involving a combination of social and psychological factors **2 :** of or relating to social psychology
so·cio·re·li·gious \-ri-ˈli-jəs\ *adj* (1871) **:** involving a combination of social and religious factors
so·cio·sex·u·al \-ˈsek-sh(ə-)wəl, -ˈsek-shəl\ *adj* (1932) **:** of or relating to the interpersonal aspects of sexuality
[1]**sock** \ˈsäk\ *n, pl* **socks** [ME *socke,* fr. OE *socc,* fr. L *soccus*] (bef. 12c) **1** *archaic* **:** a low shoe or slipper **2** *also pl* **sox** \ˈsäks\ **:** a knitted or woven covering for the foot usu. worn under shoes and extending above the ankle and sometimes to the knee **3 a :** a shoe worn by actors in Greek and Roman comedy **b :** comic drama — **sock·less** *adj*
[2]**sock** *vb* [origin unknown] *vt* (ca. 1700) **:** to hit, strike, or apply forcefully ⟨~ a home run⟩ ⟨an area ~*ed* by a blizzard⟩ ~ *vi* **:** to deliver a blow **:** HIT — **sock it to** *slang* **:** to subject to or as if to a vigorous assault ⟨they may let you off the first time . . . but the second time they'll *sock it to* you —James Jones⟩
[3]**sock** *n* (ca. 1700) **:** a vigorous or violent blow; *also* **:** [3]PUNCH 3
sock away *vt* [fr. the practice of concealing savings in the toe of a sock] (ca. 1942) **:** to put away (money) as savings or investment
sock·dol·a·ger *or* **sock·dol·o·ger** \säk-ˈdä-li-jər\ *n* [origin unknown] (ca. 1830) **1 :** something that settles a matter **:** a decisive blow or answer **:** FINISHER **2 :** something outstanding or exceptional
[1]**sock·et** \ˈsä-kət\ *n* [ME *soket,* fr. AF, dim. of *soc* plowshare, of Celt origin; akin to MIr *soc* plowshare, snout; akin to OE *sugu* sow — more at SOW] (15c) **:** an opening or hollow that forms a holder for something ⟨an electric bulb ~⟩ ⟨the eye ~⟩
[2]**socket** *vt* (1533) **:** to provide with or support in or by a socket
socket wrench *n* (ca. 1890) **:** a wrench usu. in the form of a bar and removable socket made to fit a bolt or nut

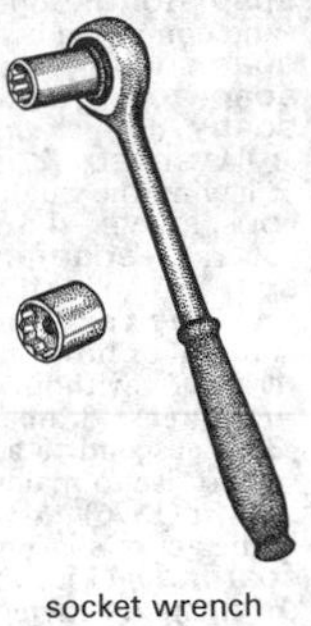
socket wrench

sock·eye salmon \ˈsäk-ˌī-\ *n* [by folk etymology fr. Northern Straits (Salishan language of southern Vancouver Island and nearby islands) *sə́qəy̓*] (1869) **:** a commercially important Pacific salmon (*Oncorhynchus nerka*) that is greenish blue above and silvery below when sexually immature and turns red with a greenish head when ascending rivers to spawn which it does chiefly from the Columbia northward — called also *red salmon, sockeye;* compare KOKANEE
sock in *vt* [*(wind) sock*] (1944) **1 :** to close to takeoffs or landings by aircraft ⟨an airport *socked in* by fog⟩ **2 :** to restrict from flying
socko \ˈsä-(ˌ)kō\ *adj* [[2]*sock*] (1938) **:** strikingly impressive, effective, or successful **:** OUTSTANDING ⟨a ~ performance⟩
sock puppet *n* (1959) **1 :** a hand puppet made with a sock **2 :** a false online identity used for deceptive purposes
so·cle \ˈsō-kəl, ˈsä-\ *n* [F, fr. It *zoccolo* sock, socle, fr. L *socculus,* dim. of *soccus* sock] (ca. 1704) **:** a projecting usu. molded member at the foot of a wall or pier or beneath the base of a column, pedestal, or superstructure
[1]**So·crat·ic** \sə-ˈkra-tik, sō-\ *adj* (1598) **:** of or relating to Socrates, his followers, or his philosophical method of systematic doubt and questioning of another to elicit a clear expression of a truth supposed to be knowable by all rational beings — **So·crat·i·cal·ly** \-ti-k(ə-)lē\ *adv*
[2]**Socratic** *n* (1678) **:** a follower of Socrates
Socratic irony *n* (ca. 1871) **:** IRONY 1
[1]**sod** \ˈsäd\ *n* [ME, fr. MD or MLG *sode;* akin to OFris *sātha* sod] (15c) **1 :** TURF 1; *also* **:** the grass- and forb-covered surface of the ground **2 :** one's native land
[2]**sod** *vt* **sod·ded; sod·ding** (1653) **:** to cover with sod or turfs
[3]**sod** *n* [short for *sodomite*] (1818) *chiefly Brit* **:** BUGGER ⟨if I ever find the ~ I'll kill him —John Le Carré⟩
[4]**sod** *vt* (1904) *chiefly Brit* **:** DAMN 2
so·da \ˈsō-də\ *n* [It, fr. Ar *suwwād,* any of several saltworts from the ashes of which sodium carbonate is obtained] (1558) **1 a :** SODIUM CARBONATE **b :** SODIUM BICARBONATE **c :** SODIUM — often used in combination ⟨*soda*-feldspar⟩ ⟨nitrate of ~⟩ **2 a :** SODA WATER 2a **b :** SODA POP **c :** a sweet drink consisting of soda water, flavoring, and often ice cream **3 :** the faro card that shows faceup in the dealing box before play begins
soda ash *n* (1839) **:** commercial anhydrous sodium carbonate
soda biscuit *n* (1830) **1 :** a biscuit leavened with baking soda and sour milk or buttermilk **2 :** SODA CRACKER
soda bread *n* (1850) **:** a quick bread made esp. with buttermilk and leavened with baking soda
soda cracker *n* (1830) **:** a cracker leavened with bicarbonate of soda and cream of tartar
soda fountain *n* (1824) **1 :** an apparatus with delivery tube and faucets for drawing soda water **2 :** the equipment and counter for the preparation and serving of sodas, sundaes, and ice cream
soda jerk \-ˌjərk\ *n* (1922) **:** a person who dispenses carbonated drinks and ice cream at a soda fountain — called also *soda jerker*
soda lime *n* (1862) **:** a mixture of sodium hydroxide and slaked lime used esp. to absorb moisture and gases
so·da·list \ˈsō-də-list, sō-ˈda-list\ *n* (1794) **:** a member of a sodality
so·da·lite \ˈsō-də-ˌlīt\ *n* [*soda*] (1810) **:** a transparent to translucent mineral that consists of a silicate of sodium and aluminum with some chlorine, has a vitreous or greasy luster, and is found in various igneous rocks
so·dal·i·ty \sō-ˈda-lə-tē\ *n, pl* **-ties** [L *sodalitat-, sodalitas* comradeship, club, fr. *sodalis* comrade — more at SIB] (1600) **1 :** BROTHERHOOD, COMMUNITY **2 :** an organized society or fellowship; *specif* **:** a devotional or charitable association of Roman Catholic laity
soda pop *n* (1863) **:** a beverage consisting of soda water, flavoring, and a sweet syrup
soda water *n* (1802) **1 :** a weak solution of sodium bicarbonate with some acid added to cause effervescence **2 a :** a beverage consisting of water highly charged with carbon dioxide **b :** SODA POP
sod·bust·er \ˈsäd-ˌbəs-tər\ *n* (ca. 1918) **:** one (as a farmer or a plow) that breaks the sod
[1]**sod·den** \ˈsä-dᵊn\ *adj* [ME *soden,* fr. pp. of *sethen* to seethe] (1589) **1 a :** dull or expressionless esp. from continued indulgence in alcoholic beverages ⟨~ features⟩ **b :** TORPID, SLUGGISH ⟨~ minds⟩ **2 a :** heavy with or as if with moisture or water ⟨the ~ ground⟩ **b :** heavy or doughy because of imperfect cooking ⟨~ biscuits⟩ — **sod·den·ly** *adv* — **sod·den·ness** \-dᵊn-(n)əs\ *n*
[2]**sodden** *vb* **sod·dened; sod·den·ing** \ˈsäd-niŋ, ˈsä-dᵊn-iŋ\ *vt* (1812) **:** to make sodden ~ *vi* **:** to become soaked or saturated
so·dic \ˈsō-dik\ *adj* (1859) **:** of, relating to, or containing sodium
so·di·um \ˈsō-dē-əm\ *n* [NL, fr. E *soda*] (1807) **:** a silver-white soft waxy ductile element of the alkali metal group that occurs abundantly in nature in combined form and is very active chemically — see ELEMENT table
sodium azide *n* (ca. 1937) **:** a poisonous crystalline salt NaN_3 used esp. to make lead azide
sodium benzoate *n* (ca. 1900) **:** a crystalline or granular salt $C_7H_5O_2Na$ used chiefly as a food preservative

sodium bicarbonate *n* (1885) : a white crystalline weakly alkaline salt $NaHCO_3$ used esp. in baking powders and fire extinguishers and in medicine as an antacid — called also *baking soda, bicarbonate of soda*

sodium bo·ro·hy·dride \-ˌbȯr-ə-ˈhī-ˌdrīd\ *n* [*sodium* + *boron* + *hydride*] (1946) : a crystalline compound $NaBH_4$ used in various industrial applications and as a reducing agent in organic chemistry

sodium carbonate *n* (1868) : a sodium salt of carbonic acid used esp. in making soaps and chemicals, in water softening, in cleaning and bleaching, and in photography: as **a** : a hygroscopic crystalline anhydrous strongly alkaline salt Na_2CO_3 **b** : the transparent crystalline hydrate $Na_2CO_3 \cdot 10H_2O$ found in nature as natron

sodium chlorate *n* (1885) : a colorless crystalline salt $NaClO_3$ used esp. as an oxidizing agent and weed killer

sodium chloride *n* (1868) : an ionic crystalline chemical compound consisting of equal numbers of sodium and chlorine atoms : SALT 1a

sodium citrate *n* (1919) : a crystalline salt $Na_3C_6H_5O_7$ used chiefly as a buffering agent, as an emulsifier, and in medicine as an expectorant, chelator, alkalinizing agent, and blood anticoagulant

sodium cyanide *n* (1885) : a white deliquescent poisonous salt NaCN used esp. in electroplating, in fumigating, and in treating steel

sodium fluoride *n* (1869) : a poisonous crystalline salt NaF that is used in trace amounts in the fluoridation of drinking water and toothpastes, in metallurgy, as a flux, and as a pesticide

sodium fluo·ro·ac·e·tate \-ˌflu̇r-ō-ˈa-sə-ˌtāt, -ˌflȯr-\ *n* (1945) : a poisonous powdery compound $C_2H_2FNaO_2$ — compare 1080

sodium hydroxide *n* (1885) : a white brittle solid NaOH that is a strong caustic base used esp. in making soap, rayon, and paper

sodium hypochlorite *n* (1885) : an unstable salt NaOCl produced usu. in aqueous solution and used as a bleaching and disinfecting agent

sodium lau·ryl sulfate \-ˈlȯr-əl-, -ˈlär-\ *n* (1885) : the crystalline sodium salt $C_{12}H_{25}NaO_4S$ of sulfated lauryl alcohol; *also* : a mixture of sulfates of sodium consisting principally of this salt and used as a detergent, wetting agent, and emulsifying agent (as in toothpastes, ointments, and shampoos)

sodium meta·sil·i·cate \-ˌme-tə-ˈsi-lə-ˌkāt, -ˈsi-li-kət\ *n* (ca. 1926) : a toxic corrosive crystalline salt Na_2SiO_3 used esp. as a detergent or as a substitute for phosphates in detergent formulations

sodium nitrate *n* (1869) : a deliquescent crystalline salt $NaNO_3$ used as a fertilizer and an oxidizing agent and in curing meat

sodium nitrite *n* (1869) : a salt $NaNO_2$ used esp. in dye manufacture and as a meat preservative

sodium pump *n* (1951) **1** : a molecular mechanism by which sodium ions are transferred across a cell membrane by active transport; *esp* : one that is controlled by a specialized plasma membrane protein by which a high concentration of potassium ions and a low concentration of sodium ions are maintained within a cell **2** : the specialized plasma membrane protein that controls the sodium pump mechanism

sodium salicylate *n* (1885) : a crystalline salt $NaC_7H_5O_3$ that has a sweetish saline taste and is used chiefly as an analgesic, antipyretic, and antirheumatic

sodium sulfate *n* (1869) : a bitter salt Na_2SO_4 used esp. in detergents, in the manufacture of wood pulp and rayon, in dyeing and finishing textiles, and in its hydrated form as a cathartic — compare GLAUBER'S SALT

sodium thiosulfate *n* (1885) : a hygroscopic crystalline salt $Na_2S_2O_3$ used esp. as a photographic fixing agent and a reducing or bleaching agent — called also *fixer, hypo*

sodium tri·poly·phos·phate \-ˌtrī-ˌpä-li-ˈfäs-ˌfāt\ *n* (1945) : a crystalline salt $Na_5P_3O_{10}$ that is used as a food additive and as a component in some detergents and is suspected of contributing to water pollution

sodium–vapor lamp *n* (1933) : an electric lamp that contains sodium vapor and electrodes between which a luminous discharge takes place and that is used esp. for lighting highways

sod off *vi* [[4]*sod*] (1960) *Brit* : SCRAM — usu. used as a command

Sod·om \ˈsä-dəm\ *n* [*Sodom*, ancient city destroyed by God for its wickedness in Gen 19] (1594) : a place notorious for vice or corruption

sod·om·ist \ˈsä-də-mist\ *n* (1873) : SODOMITE

sod·om·ite \-ˌmīt\ *n* (14c) : one who practices sodomy

sod·om·ize \-ˌmīz\ *vt* **-ized; -iz·ing** (1868) : to perform sodomy on

sod·omy \ˈsä-də-mē\ *n* [ME, fr. AF *sodomie*, fr. LL *Sodoma* Sodom; fr. the homosexual proclivities of the men of the city in Gen 19:1–11] (13c) : anal or oral copulation with a member of the same or opposite sex; *also* : copulation with an animal — **sod·om·it·ic** \ˌsä-də-ˈmi-tik\ *or* **sod·om·it·i·cal** \-ti-kəl\ *adj*

so·ev·er \sō-ˈe-vər\ *adv* [*-soever* (as in *howsoever*)] (12c) **1** : to any possible or known extent — used after an adjective preceded by *how* or a superlative preceded by *the* ⟨how fair ~ she may be⟩ ⟨the most selfish ~ in this world⟩ **2** : of any or every kind that may be specified — used after a noun modified esp. by *any, no,* or *what* ⟨gives no information ~⟩

so·fa \ˈsō-fə\ *n* [earlier, raised carpeted floor, fr. It *sofà*, fr. Turk *sofa*, fr. Ar *ṣuffa* carpet, divan] (1717) : a long upholstered seat usu. with arms and a back and often convertible into a bed

sofa bed *n* (1805) : a sofa that can be made to serve as a bed by lowering its hinged upholstered back to horizontal position or by pulling out a concealed mattress

so·far \ˈsō-ˌfär\ *n* [*so*und *f*ixing *a*nd *r*anging] (1946) : a system for locating an underwater explosion at sea by triangulation

so far as *conj* (1530) : INSOFAR AS

sof·fit \ˈsä-fət\ *n* [F *soffite*, fr. It *soffitto*, fr. VL **suffictus*, pp. of L *suffigere* to fasten underneath — more at SUFFIX] (1592) : the underside of a part or member of a building (as of an overhang or staircase); *esp* : the intrados of an arch

[1]**soft** \ˈsȯft\ *adj* [ME, fr. OE *sōfte*, alter. of *sēfte*; akin to OHG *semfti* soft] (bef. 12c) **1 a** : pleasing or agreeable to the senses : bringing ease, comfort, or quiet ⟨the ~ influences of home⟩ **b** : having a bland or mellow rather than a sharp or acid taste **c** (1) : not bright or glaring : SUBDUED (2) : having or producing little contrast or a relatively short range of tones ⟨a ~ photographic print⟩ **d** : quiet in pitch or volume **e** *of the eyes* : having a liquid or gentle appearance **f** : smooth or delicate in texture, grain, or fiber ⟨~ cashmere⟩ ⟨~ fur⟩ **g** (1) : balmy, mild, or clement in weather or temperature (2) : moving or falling with slight force or impact : not violent ⟨~ breezes⟩ **2** : demanding little work or effort : EASY ⟨a ~ job⟩ **3 a** : sounding as in *ace* and *gem* respectively — used of *c* and *g* or their sound **b** *of a consonant* : VOICED **c** : constituting a vowel before which there is a \y\ sound or a \y\-like modification of a consonant or constituting a consonant in whose articulation there is a \y\-like modification or which is followed by a \y\ sound (as in Russian) **4** *archaic* : moving in a leisurely manner **5** : rising gradually ⟨a ~ slope⟩ **6** : having curved or rounded outline : not harsh or jagged ⟨~ hills against the horizon⟩ **7** : marked by a gentleness, kindness, or tenderness: as **a** (1) : not harsh or onerous in character ⟨a policy of ~ competition⟩ (2) : based on negotiation, conciliation, or flexibility rather than on force, threats, or intransigence ⟨took a ~ line during the crisis⟩ (3) : tending to take a soft line — usu. used with *on* ⟨~ on dictators⟩ ⟨~ on law and order⟩ **b** : tending to ingratiate or disarm : ENGAGING, KIND ⟨a ~ answer turns away wrath —Prov 15:1(RSV)⟩ **c** : marked by mildness : UNASSUMING, LOW-KEY **8 a** : emotionally suggestible or responsive : IMPRESSIONABLE **b** : unduly susceptible to influence : COMPLIANT **c** : lacking firmness or strength of character : FEEBLE, UNMANLY **d** : amorously attracted or emotionally involved — used with *on* ⟨has been ~ on her for years⟩ **9 a** : lacking robust strength, stamina, or endurance esp. because of living in ease or luxury ⟨grown ~ and indolent⟩ **b** : weak or deficient mentally ⟨~ in the head⟩ **10 a** : yielding to physical pressure **b** : permitting someone or something to sink in — used of wet ground **c** (1) : of a consistency that may be shaped or molded (2) : capable of being spread **d** : easily magnetized and demagnetized **e** : lacking relatively or comparatively in hardness ⟨~ iron⟩ **11** : deficient in or free from substances (as calcium and magnesium salts) that prevent lathering of soap ⟨~ water⟩ **12** : having relatively low energy ⟨~ X-rays⟩ **13** *of news* : relatively less serious or significant **14** : occurring at such a speed and under such circumstances as to avoid destructive impact ⟨~ landing of a spacecraft on the moon⟩ **15** : not protected against enemy attack ⟨a ~ aboveground launching site⟩ ⟨~ targets⟩ **16** : BIODEGRADABLE ⟨a ~ detergent⟩ ⟨~ pesticides⟩ **17** *of a drug* : considered less detrimental than a hard narcotic **18** : easily polarized — used of acids and bases **19 a** *of currency* : not readily convertible **b** *of a loan* : not secured by collateral **20 a** : being low due to sluggish market conditions ⟨~ prices⟩ **b** : SLUGGISH, SLOW ⟨a ~ market⟩ **21** : not firmly committed ⟨~ unreliable political support⟩ **22** : SOFT-CORE ⟨~ porn⟩ **23 a** : being or based on interpretive or speculative data ⟨~ evidence⟩ **b** : utilizing or based on soft data ⟨~ science⟩ **24** : being or using renewable sources of energy (as solar radiation, wind, or tides) ⟨~ technologies⟩ **25** *of money* : contributed (as by a corporation) to a political party rather than directly to a particular candidate — **soft·ish** \ˈsȯf-tish\ *adj* — **soft·ly** \ˈsȯf(t)-lē\ *adv* — **soft·ness** \ˈsȯf(t)-nəs\ *n*

[2]**soft** *adv* (bef. 12c) : in a soft or gentle manner : SOFTLY

[3]**soft** *n* (15c) : a soft object, material, or part ⟨the ~ of the thumb⟩

soft·back \ˈsȯf(t)-ˌbak\ *adj* (1958) : SOFTCOVER — **softback** *n*

soft·ball \-ˌbȯl\ *n* (1926) **1** : a sport similiar to baseball played on a small diamond with a ball that is larger than a baseball and that is pitched underhand; *also* : the ball used in this game **2** : a question requiring only an easy or simple response — **soft·ball·er** \-ˌbȯ-lər\ *n*

soft–boiled \-ˈbȯi(-ə)ld\ *adj* (1889) **1** *of an egg* : boiled to a soft consistency **2** : SENTIMENTAL

soft·bound \-ˌbau̇nd\ *adj* (1953) : SOFTCOVER

soft chancre *n* (1859) : CHANCROID

soft coal *n* (1789) : BITUMINOUS COAL

soft–coated wheaten terrier *n* (1943) : any of a breed of compact medium-sized terriers developed in Ireland and having a soft abundant light fawn coat

soft–core \ˈsȯf(t)-ˈkȯr\ *adj* [[1]*soft* + hard-*core*] (1966) *of pornography* : containing descriptions or scenes of sex acts that are less explicit than hard-core material

soft·cov·er \-ˌkə-vər\ *adj* (1952) : bound in flexible covers : not bound in hard covers; *specif* : PAPERBACK ⟨~ books⟩ — **softcover** *n*

soft drink *n* (ca. 1880) : a usu. carbonated nonalcoholic beverage; *esp* : SODA POP

soft·en \ˈsȯ-fən\ *vb* **soft·ened; soft·en·ing** \ˈsȯ-fə-niŋ, ˈsȯf-niŋ\ *vt* (14c) **1** : to make soft or softer **2 a** : to weaken the military resistance or the morale of esp. by harassment (as preliminary bombardment) — often used with *up* **b** : to impair the strength or resistance of — often used with *up* ⟨~ up a sales prospect⟩ ~ *vi* : to become soft or softer ⟨her face ~*ed*⟩ — **soft·en·er** \ˈsȯ-fə-nər, ˈsȯf-nər\ *n*

soft–fo·cus \ˈsȯf(t)-ˈfō-kəs\ *adj* (1916) **1** *of a photographic image* : having unsharp outlines **2** *of a lens* : producing an image having unsharp outlines

soft goods *n pl* (1833) : goods that are not durable — used esp. of textile products

soft hail *n* (1881) : GRAUPEL

soft·head \ˈsȯft-ˌhed\ *n* (1650) : a silly or feebleminded person

soft·head·ed \-ˌhe-dəd\ *adj* (1667) : having or indicative of a weak, unrealistic, or uncritical mind ⟨a ~ belief⟩ — **soft·head·ed·ly** *adv* — **soft·head·ed·ness** *n*

soft·heart·ed \-ˌhär-təd\ *adj* (ca. 1592) : emotionally responsive : SYMPATHETIC — **soft·heart·ed·ly** *adv* — **soft·heart·ed·ness** *n*

soft–land \-ˈland\ *vb* [back-formation fr. *soft landing*] *vt* (1960) : to cause to make a soft landing on a celestial body (as the moon) ~ *vi* : to make a soft landing — **soft–lander** *n*

soft–line \-ˈlīn\ *adj* (1973) : advocating or involving a conciliatory or flexible course of action — **soft–lin·er** \-ˈlī-nər\ *n*

soft palate *n* (ca. 1811) : the fold at the back of the hard palate that partially separates the mouth from the pharynx

soft–paste porcelain *n* (1854) : a translucent ceramic ware fired at a low temperature that was produced in Europe during the 16th through 18th centuries in imitation of hard-paste porcelain; *also* : an article of soft-paste porcelain

soft–ped·al \ˈsȯf(t)-ˈpe-dᵊl\ *vt* (1925) **1** : PLAY DOWN, DE-EMPHASIZE ⟨~ the issue⟩ **2** : to use the soft pedal in playing

\ə\ **abut** \ᵊ\ **kitten**, F **table** \ər\ **further** \a\ **ash** \ā\ **ace** \ä\ **mop, mar**
\au̇\ **out** \ch\ **chin** \e\ **bet** \ē\ **easy** \g\ **go** \i\ **hit** \ī\ **ice** \j\ **job**
\ŋ\ **sing** \ō\ **go** \ȯ\ **law** \ȯi\ **boy** \th\ **thin** \t͟h\ **the** \ü\ **loot** \u̇\ **foot**
\y\ **yet** \zh\ **vision, beige** \k̲, ⁿ, œ, ue, ʸ\ *see* Guide to Pronunciation

soft pedal *n* (1847) **1 :** a foot pedal on a piano that reduces the volume of sound **2 :** something that muffles, deadens, or reduces effect
soft rock *n* (1967) **:** rock music that is less driving and gentler sounding than hard rock
soft rot *n* (1897) **:** a mushy, watery, or slimy decay of plants or their parts caused by bacteria or fungi
soft·scape \ˈsȯft-ˌskāp\ *n* (1984) **:** vegetation (as shrubs and flowers) that is incorporated into a landscape — compare HARDSCAPE
soft sell *n* (1954) **:** the use of suggestion or gentle persuasion in selling rather than aggressive pressure — compare HARD SELL
soft–serve \ˈsȯf(t)-ˌsərv\ *n* (1982) **:** smooth semisolid ice cream made in and dispensed from a freezer in which it is aerated and continuously churned
soft·shell \ˈsȯf(t)-ˌshel\ *n* (1771) **:** any of a family (Trionychidae) of freshwater carnivorous turtles that have sharp claws and mandibles and a flat round shell covered with soft leathery skin instead of with horny plates — called also *soft-shelled turtle*

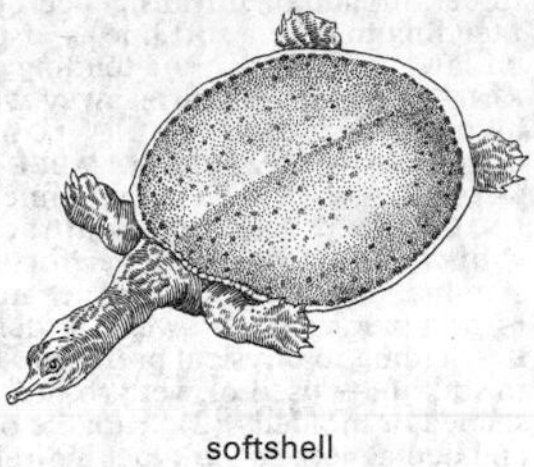
softshell

soft–shell \ˈsȯf(t)-ˌshel\ *or* **soft–shelled** \-ˈsheld\ *adj* (1805) **:** having a soft or fragile shell esp. as a result of recent shedding ⟨~ crabs⟩
soft–shell clam *n* (1796) **:** an elongated clam (*Mya arenaria*) of the east coast of No. America that has a thin friable shell and long siphon and is eaten esp. when steamed — called also *soft-shelled clam, steamer*
soft–shoe \ˈsȯf(t)-ˈshü\ *adj* (1920) **:** of or relating to tap dancing done in soft-soled shoes without metal taps
soft–soap \ˈsȯf(t)-ˈsōp\ *vt* (1840) **:** to soothe or persuade with flattery or blarney *syn* see CAJOLE — **soft–soap·er** \-ˌsō-pər\ *n*
soft soap *n* (1634) **1 :** a semifluid soap made esp. from potassium hydroxide **2 :** FLATTERY
soft–spo·ken \-ˈspō-kən\ *adj* (1609) **:** having a mild or gentle voice; *also* **:** SUAVE
soft spot *n* (1845) **1 :** a sentimental weakness ⟨has a *soft spot* for him⟩ **2 :** a vulnerable point ⟨a *soft spot* in the defense system⟩
soft touch *n* (1939) **:** a person who is easily imposed on or taken advantage of
soft·ware \ˈsȯft-ˌwer\ *n* (1958) **:** something used or associated with and usu. contrasted with hardware: as **a :** the entire set of programs, procedures, and related documentation associated with a system and esp. a computer system; *specif* **:** computer programs **b :** materials for use with audiovisual equipment
soft wheat *n* (1812) **:** a wheat with soft kernels high in starch but usu. low in gluten
[1]**soft·wood** \ˈsȯft-ˌwu̇d\ *n* (1809) **1 :** the wood of a coniferous tree (as a fir or pine) whether hard or soft as distinguished from that of an angiospermous tree **2 :** a tree that yields softwood
[2]**softwood** *adj* (1855) **:** having or made of softwood
soft–wood·ed \ˈsȯft-ˌwu̇-dəd\ *adj* (1827) **1 :** having soft wood that is easy to work or finish **2 :** SOFTWOOD
softy *or* **soft·ie** \ˈsȯf-tē\ *n, pl* **soft·ies** [[1]*soft*] (1863) **1 :** a weak or foolish person **2 :** a softhearted or sentimental person
Sog·di·an \ˈsäg-dē-ən\ *n* [L *Sogdiani,* pl., fr. Gk *Sogdianoi,* fr. OPers *Suguda* Sogdiana] (1553) **1 :** a native or inhabitant of Sogdiana **2 :** an Iranian language of the Sogdians — see INDO-EUROPEAN LANGUAGES table — **Sogdian** *adj*
sog·gy \ˈsä-gē, ˈsȯ-\ *adj* **sog·gi·er; -est** [E dial. *sog* to soak] (1599) **1 :** saturated or heavy with water or moisture: as **a :** WATERLOGGED, SOAKED ⟨a ~ lawn⟩ **b :** heavy or doughy because of imperfect cooking ⟨~ bread⟩ **2 :** heavily dull **:** SPIRITLESS ⟨~ prose⟩ — **sog·gi·ly** \ˈsä-gə-lē, ˈsȯ-\ *adv* — **sog·gi·ness** \ˈsä-gē-nəs, ˈsȯ-\ *n*
soi–di·sant \ˌswä-dē-ˈzäⁿ\ *adj* [F, lit., saying oneself] (1752) **:** SELF-PROCLAIMED, SO-CALLED ⟨threw the ~ epic novel aside in disgust⟩
soi·gné *or* **soi·gnée** \swän-ˈyā\ *adj* [F, pp. of *soigner* to take care of] (1821) **1 :** WELL-GROOMED, SLEEK **2 :** elegantly maintained or designed ⟨a ~ restaurant⟩ ⟨a ~ black dress⟩
[1]**soil** \ˈsȯi(-ə)l\ *vb* [ME, fr. AF *soiller, suiller,* fr. OF *soil* wallow of a wild boar, abyss, fr. L *solium* chair, bathtub; akin to L *sedēre* to sit — more at SIT] *vt* (13c) **1 :** to stain or defile morally **:** CORRUPT **2 :** to make unclean esp. superficially **:** DIRTY **3 :** to blacken or taint (as a person's reputation) by word or deed ~ *vi* **:** to become soiled or dirty
[2]**soil** *n* (1501) **1 a :** SOILAGE, STAIN ⟨protect a dress from ~⟩ **b :** moral defilement **:** CORRUPTION **2 :** something that spoils or pollutes: as **a :** REFUSE **b :** SEWAGE **c :** DUNG, EXCREMENT
[3]**soil** *n* [ME, fr. AF, soil, piece of land, fr. VL **solium,* alter. of L *solea* sole, sandal, foundation timber — more at SOLE] (14c) **1 :** firm land **:** EARTH **2 a :** the upper layer of earth that may be dug or plowed and in which plants grow **b :** the superficial unconsolidated and usu. weathered part of the mantle of a planet and esp. of the earth **3 :** COUNTRY, LAND ⟨our native ~⟩ **4 :** the agricultural life or calling **5 :** a medium in which something takes hold and develops
[4]**soil** *vt* [origin unknown] (1605) **:** to feed (livestock) in the barn or an enclosure with fresh grass or green food; *also* **:** to purge (livestock) by feeding on green food
[1]**soil·age** \ˈsȯi-lij\ *n* [[1]*soil*] (1926) **:** the act of soiling **:** the condition of being soiled
[2]**soilage** *n* [[4]*soil*] (1916) **:** green crops for feeding confined animals
soil·borne \ˈsȯi(-ə)l-ˌbȯrn\ *adj* (1944) **:** transmitted by or in soil
soil·less \ˈsȯi(-ə)l-ləs\ *adj* (1938) **:** having, containing, or utilizing no soil ⟨~ agriculture⟩ ⟨~ media for starting seeds⟩
soil pipe *n* (1833) **:** a pipe for carrying off wastes from toilets
soil science *n* (1915) **:** a science dealing with soils — called also *pedology* — **soil scientist** *n*
soil series *n* (1905) **:** a group of soils with similar profiles developed from similar parent materials under comparable climatic and vegetational conditions
soil·ure \ˈsȯi(-ə)l-yər\ *n* [ME, fr. AF *soilleure,* fr. *soiller* to soil] (13c) **1 :** the act of soiling **:** the condition of being soiled **2 :** STAIN, SMUDGE
soi·ree *or* **soi·rée** \swä-ˈrā\ *n* [F *soirée* evening period, evening party, fr. MF, fr. *soir* evening, fr. L *sero* at a late hour, fr. *serus* late; akin to OIr *sír* long, lasting and perh. to OE *sīth* late — more at SINCE] (1802) **:** a party or reception held in the evening
soi·xante–neuf \ˌswä-ˌsäⁿt-ˈnœf\ *n* [F] (1888) **:** SIXTY-NINE 2
[1]**so·journ** \ˈsō-ˌjərn, sō-ˈ\ *n* [ME *sojorn,* fr. AF *sujur, sujurn,* fr. *sujurner*] (13c) **:** a temporary stay ⟨a ~ in the country⟩
[2]**sojourn** *vi* [ME, fr. AF *sujurner, sejurner,* fr. VL **subdiurnare,* fr. L *sub* under, during + LL *diurnum* day — more at UP, JOURNEY] (14c) **:** to stay as a temporary resident **:** STOP — **so·journ·er** *n*
so·ju \ˈsō-ˌjü\ *n* [Korean] (1978) **:** Korean vodka distilled usu. from rice or sweet potato
soke \ˈsōk\ *n* [ME *soc, soke,* fr. OE *soka,* fr. ML *soca,* fr. OE *sōcn* inquiry, jurisdiction; akin to OE *sēcan* to seek] (12c) **1 :** the right in Anglo-Saxon and early English law to hold court and administer justice with the franchise to receive certain fees or fines arising from it **:** jurisdiction over a territory or over people **2 :** the district included in a soke jurisdiction or franchise
[1]**sol** \ˈsōl\ *also* **so** \ˈsō\ *n* [ML *sol;* fr. the syllable sung to this note in a medieval hymn to St. John the Baptist] (14c) **:** the fifth tone of the diatonic scale in solmization
[2]**sol** \ˈsäl, ˈsȯl\ *n* [MF — more at SOU] (1583) **:** an old French coin equal to 12 deniers; *also* **:** a corresponding unit of value
[3]**sol** \ˈsäl, ˈsȯl\ *n, pl* **so·les** \ˈsō-(ˌ)lās\ [AmerSp, fr. Sp, sun, fr. L] (1883) **:** the basic monetary unit of Peru before 1985 and since 1990 — see MONEY table
[4]**sol** \ˈsäl, ˈsȯl\ *n* [*-sol* (as in *hydrosol*), fr. *solution*] (1899) **:** a fluid colloidal system; *esp* **:** one in which the medium is a liquid
[5]**sol** *abbr* soluble
Sol \ˈsäl\ *n* [ME, fr. L] (15c) **1 :** the Roman god of the sun — compare HELIOS **2 :** SUN
sola *pl of* SOLUM
[1]**so·lace** \ˈsä-ləs *also* ˈsō-\ *vt* **so·laced; so·lac·ing** (13c) **1 :** to give solace to **:** CONSOLE **2 a :** to make cheerful **b :** AMUSE **3 :** ALLAY, SOOTHE ⟨~ grief⟩ — **so·lace·ment** \-mənt\ *n* — **so·lac·er** *n*
[2]**solace** *n* [ME *solas,* fr. AF, fr. L *solacium,* fr. *solari* to console] (14c) **1 :** alleviation of grief or anxiety **2 :** a source of relief or consolation
so·la·na·ceous \ˌsō-lə-ˈnā-shəs\ *adj* [NL *Solanaceae,* family name, fr. *Solanum*] (1804) **:** of or relating to the nightshade family of plants
so·la·nine *also* **so·la·nin** \ˈsō-lə-ˌnēn, -nən\ *n* [F *solanine,* fr. L *solanum*] (1838) **:** a bitter poisonous crystalline alkaloid $C_{45}H_{73}NO_{15}$ found in the parts (as tubers and fruits) of several plants (as potatoes and tomatoes) of the nightshade family
so·la·num \sə-ˈlā-nəm, -ˈlä-, -ˈla-\ *n* [NL, fr. L, nightshade] (1578) **:** NIGHTSHADE 1
so·lar \ˈsō-lər, -ˌlär\ *adj* [ME, fr. L *solaris,* fr. *sol* sun; akin to OE & ON *sōl* sun, Lith *saulė,* Gk *hēlios*] (15c) **1 :** of, derived from, relating to, or caused by the sun **2 :** measured by the earth's course in relation to the sun ⟨a ~ year⟩; *also* **:** relating to or reckoned by solar time **3 a :** produced or operated by the action of the sun's light or heat ⟨~ energy⟩ **b :** utilizing the sun's rays esp. to produce heat or electricity ⟨a ~ house⟩; *also* **:** of or relating to such utilization ⟨~ design⟩
solar battery *n* (1954) **:** an array of solar cells
solar cell *n* (1955) **:** a photovoltaic cell used as a power source
solar collector *n* (1955) **:** any of various devices for the absorption of solar radiation for the heating of water or buildings or the production of electricity
solar constant *n* (1869) **:** the quantity of radiant solar energy received at the outer layer of the earth's atmosphere that has a mean value of 1370 watts per square meter
solar day *n* (1751) **:** the interval between transits of the apparent or mean sun across the meridian at any place
solar eclipse *n* (1695) **:** an eclipse of the sun by the moon — see ECLIPSE illustration
solar flare *n* (1938) **:** a sudden temporary outburst of energy from a small area of the sun's surface — called also *flare*
so·lar·i·um \sō-ˈler-ē-əm, sə-\ *n, pl* **-ia** \-ē-ə\ *also* **-ums** [L, porch exposed to the sun, fr. *sol*] (ca. 1823) **:** a glass-enclosed porch or room; *also* **:** a room (as in a hospital) used esp. for sunbathing or therapeutic exposure to light
so·lar·i·za·tion \ˌsō-lə-rə-ˈzā-shən\ *n* (1853) **1 :** a reversal of gradation in a photographic image obtained by intense or continued exposure **2 :** an act or process of solarizing
so·lar·ize \ˈsō-lə-ˌrīz\ *vt* **-ized; -iz·ing** (1853) **1 a :** to affect by the action of the sun's rays **b :** to expose to sunlight **2 :** to subject (photographic materials) to solarization
solar mass *n* (1941) **:** the mass of the sun used as a unit for the expression of the masses of other celestial objects and equal to about 2×10^{30} kilograms
solar panel *n* (1961) **:** a battery of solar cells (as in a spacecraft)
so·lar plexus \ˈsō-lər-\ *n* [fr. the radiating nerve fibers] (1771) **1 :** a nerve plexus in the abdomen that is situated behind the stomach and in front of the aorta and the crura of the diaphragm and contains several ganglia distributing nerve fibers to the viscera **2 :** the pit of the stomach
solar pond *n* (1961) **:** a pool of salt water heated by the sun and used either as a direct source of heat or to provide power for an electric generator
solar sail *n* (1958) **:** a propulsive device for a spacecraft that consists of a flat material (as aluminized plastic) designed to receive thrust from solar radiation pressure
solar system *n* (ca. 1704) **:** the sun together with the group of celestial bodies that are held by its attraction and revolve around it; *also* **:** a similar system centered on another star
solar wind *n* (1958) **:** plasma continuously ejected from the sun's surface into and through interplanetary space
sol·ation \sä-ˈlā-shən, sȯ-\ *n* (1915) **:** the process of changing to a sol
so·la·ti·um \sō-ˈlā-shē-əm\ *n, pl* **-tia** \-shē-ə\ [LL *solacium, solatium,* fr. L, solace] (1817) **:** a compensation (as money) given as solace for suffering, loss, or injured feelings
sold *past and past part of* SELL
sol·dan \ˈsäl-dən, ˈsōl-\ *n* [ME, fr. AF, fr. Ar *sulṭān*] (14c) *archaic* **:** SULTAN; *esp* **:** the sultan of Egypt
[1]**sol·der** \ˈsä-dər, ˈsȯ-, *Brit also* ˈsäl-dər, ˈsōl-\ *n* [ME *soudure,* fr. AF, fr. *souder* to solder, fr. L *solidare* to make solid, fr. *solidus* solid] (14c) **1**

: a metal or metallic alloy used when melted to join metallic surfaces; *esp* : an alloy of lead and tin so used **2** : something that unites

[2]**solder** *vb* **sol·dered; sol·der·ing** \-d(ə-)riŋ\ *vt* (15c) **1** : to unite or make whole by solder **2** : to bring into or restore to firm union ⟨a friendship ~*ed* by common interests⟩ ~ *vi* **1** : to use solder **2** : to become united or repaired by or as if by solder — **sol·der·abil·i·ty** \ˌsä-də-rə-ˈbi-lə-tē, ˌsȯ-\ *n* — **sol·der·er** \ˈsä-dər-ər, ˈsȯ-\ *n*

soldering iron *n* (1688) : a pointed or wedge-shaped device that is usu. electrically heated and that is used for soldering

[1]**sol·dier** \ˈsōl-jər\ *n* [ME *soudeour,* fr. AF *soudeer, soudeour* mercenary, fr. *soudee* shilling's worth, wage, fr. *sou, soud* shilling, fr. LL *solidus* solidus] (14c) **1 a** : one engaged in military service and esp. in the army **b** : an enlisted man or woman **c** : a skilled warrior **2** : a militant leader, follower, or worker **3 a** : one of a caste of wingless sterile termites usu. differing from workers in larger size and head and long jaws **b** : one of a type of worker ants distinguished by exceptionally large head and jaws **4** \ˈsō-jər, ˈsōl-\ : one who shirks work — **sol·dier·ly** \-lē\ *adj or adv* — **sol·dier·ship** \-ˌship\ *n*

[2]**soldier** *vi* **sol·diered; sol·dier·ing** \ˈsōl-jə-riŋ, ˈsōlj-riŋ\ (1647) **1 a** : to serve as a soldier **b** : to behave in a soldierly manner **c** : to push doggedly forward — usu. used with *on* ⟨~*ed* on to the end⟩ **2** : to make a pretense of working while really loafing

soldiering *n* (1643) : the life, service, or practice of one who soldiers

soldier of fortune (1661) : one who follows a military career wherever there is promise of profit, adventure, or pleasure

soldiers' home *n* (1860) : an institution maintained (as by the federal or a state government) for the care and relief of military veterans

soldier's medal *n* (ca. 1930) : a U.S. military decoration awarded for heroism not involving combat

sol·diery \ˈsōl-jə-rē, ˈsōlj-rē\ *n* (ca. 1570) **1 a** : a body of soldiers **b** : SOLDIERS, MILITARY **2** : the profession or technique of soldiering

sol·do \ˈsȯl-(ˌ)dō\ *n, pl* **sol·di** \-(ˌ)dē\ [It, fr. LL *solidus* solidus] (1599) : an old Italian coin worth five centesimi

sold–out \ˈsōld-ˈau̇t\ *adj* (1903) : having all available tickets or accommodations sold completely and esp. in advance; *also* : of or relating to a sold-out event ⟨a ~ crowd⟩

[1]**sole** \ˈsōl\ *n* [ME, fr. AF, fr. L *solea* sandal, a flatfish] (13c) : any of various flatfishes (family Soleidae) having a small mouth, small or rudimentary fins, and small eyes placed close together and including important food fishes (as the European Dover sole); *also* : any of various mostly market flatfishes (as lemon sole) of other families (as Pleuronectidae)

[2]**sole** *n* [ME, fr. AF *sole, soele,* fr. L *solea* sandal; akin to L *solum* base, ground, soil] (14c) **1 a** : the undersurface of a foot **b** : the part of an item of footwear on which the sole rests and upon which the wearer treads **2** : the usu. flat or flattened bottom or lower part of something or the base on which something rests — **soled** \ˈsōld\ *adj*

[3]**sole** *vt* **soled; sol·ing** (ca. 1570) **1** : to furnish with a sole ⟨~ a shoe⟩ **2** : to place the sole of (a golf club) on the ground

[4]**sole** *adj* [ME, alone, fr. AF *sul, soul, seul,* fr. L *solus*] (14c) **1** : not married — used chiefly of women **2** *archaic* : having no companion : SOLITARY **3 a** : having no sharer **b** : being the only one ⟨she was her mother's ~ support⟩ **4** : functioning independently and without assistance or interference ⟨let conscience be the ~ judge⟩ **5** : belonging exclusively or otherwise limited to one usu. specified individual, unit, or group — **sole·ness** \ˈsōl-nəs\ *n*

so·le·cism \ˈsä-lə-ˌsi-zəm, ˈsō-\ *n* [L *soloecismus,* fr. Gk *soloikismos,* fr. *soloikos* speaking incorrectly, lit., inhabitant of Soloi, fr. *Soloi,* city in ancient Cilicia where a substandard form of Attic was spoken] (ca. 1555) **1** : an ungrammatical combination of words in a sentence; *also* : a minor blunder in speech **2** : something deviating from the proper, normal, or accepted order **3** : a breach of etiquette or decorum — **so·le·cis·tic** \ˌsä-lə-ˈsis-tik, ˌsō-\ *adj*

sole·ly \ˈsō(l)-lē\ *adv* (15c) **1** : without another : SINGLY ⟨went ~ on her way⟩ **2** : to the exclusion of all else ⟨done ~ for money⟩

sol·emn \ˈsä-ləm\ *adj* [ME *solempne,* fr. AF, fr. L *sollemnis* regularly appointed, solemn] (14c) **1** : marked by the invocation of a religious sanction ⟨a ~ oath⟩ **2** : marked by the observance of established form or ceremony; *specif* : celebrated with full liturgical ceremony **3 a** : awe-inspiring : SUBLIME ⟨~ beauty⟩ **b** : marked by grave sedateness and earnest sobriety ⟨a ~ gathering⟩ **c** : SOMBER, GLOOMY ⟨a ~ gray building⟩ ***syn*** see SERIOUS — **sol·emn·ly** *adv* — **sol·emn·ness** *n*

so·lem·ni·fy \sə-ˈlem-nə-ˌfī\ *vt* **-fied; -fy·ing** (1780) : to make solemn

so·lem·ni·ty \sə-ˈlem-nə-tē\ *n, pl* **-ties** (14c) **1** : formal or ceremonious observance of an occasion or event **2** : a solemn event or occasion **3** : a solemn condition or quality ⟨the ~ of his words⟩

sol·em·nize \ˈsä-ləm-ˌnīz\ *vb* **-nized; -niz·ing** *vt* (14c) **1** : to observe or honor with solemnity **2** : to perform with pomp or ceremony; *esp* : to celebrate (a marriage) with religious rites **3** : to make solemn : DIGNIFY ~ *vi* : to speak or act with solemnity — **sol·em·ni·za·tion** \ˌsä-ləm-nə-ˈzā-shən\ *n*

solemn mass *n* (15c) : a mass marked by the use of incense and by the presence of a deacon and a subdeacon in attendance on the celebrant

solemn vow *n* (14c) : an absolute and irrevocable public vow taken by a religious in the Roman Catholic Church under which ownership of property by the individual is prohibited and marriage is invalid under canon law

so·le·noid \ˈsō-lə-ˌnȯid, ˈsä-\ *n* [F *solénoïde,* fr. Gk *sōlēnoeidēs* pipe-shaped, fr. Gk *sōlēn* pipe] (1827) : a coil of wire usu. in cylindrical form that when carrying a current acts like a magnet so that a movable core is drawn into the coil when a current flows and that is used esp. as a switch or control for a mechanical device (as a valve) — **so·le·noi·dal** \ˌsō-lə-ˈnȯi-dᵊl, ˌsä-\ *adj*

sole·plate \ˈsōl-ˌplāt\ *n* (1741) **1** : the lower plate of a studded partition on which the bases of the studs butt **2** : the undersurface of an iron

soles *pl of* SOL

so·le·us \ˈsō-lē-əs\ *n, pl* **so·lei** \-lē-ˌī\ [NL, fr. L *solea* sandal — more at SOLE] (1676) : a broad flat muscle of the calf of the leg lying immediately beneath the gastrocnemius

[1]**sol–fa** \ˌsōl-ˈfä, ˈsōl-ˌ\ *vi* (ca. 1529) : to sing the sol-fa syllables ~ *vt* : to sing (as a melody) to sol-fa syllables

[2]**sol–fa** *n* (1548) **1** : SOL-FA SYLLABLES **2** : SOLMIZATION; *also* : an exercise thus sung **3** : TONIC SOL-FA — **sol–fa·ist** \-ˈfä(-i)st, -ˈfä-ˌist\ *n*

sol–fa syllables *n pl* (1913) : the syllables *do, re, mi, fa, sol, la, ti,* used in singing the tones of the scale

sol·fa·ta·ra \ˌsōl-fə-ˈtär-ə\ *n* [It, sulfur mine, fr. *solfo* sulfur, fr. L *sulfur*] (1777) : a volcanic area or vent that yields only hot vapors and sulfurous gases

sol·fège \säl-ˈfezh\ *n* [F, fr. It *solfeggio*] (ca. 1903) **1** : the application of the sol-fa syllables to a musical scale or to a melody **2** : a singing exercise esp. using sol-fa syllables; *also* : practice in sight-reading vocal music using the sol-fa syllables

sol·feg·gio \säl-ˈfe-j(ē-ˌ)ō\ *n* [It, fr. *sol-fa*] (1774) : SOLFÈGE

sol·gel \ˈsäl-ˌjel, ˈsȯl-\ *adj* (1915) : involving alternation between sol and gel states

soli *pl of* SOLO

so·lic·it \sə-ˈli-sət\ *vb* [ME, to disturb, promote, fr. AF *solliciter,* fr. L *sollicitare* to disturb, fr. *sollicitus* anxious, fr. *sollus* whole (fr. Oscan; akin to Gk *holos* whole) + *citus,* pp. of *ciēre* to move — more at SAFE, -KINESIS] *vt* (15c) **1 a** : to make petition to : ENTREAT **b** : to approach with a request or plea ⟨~*ed* Congress for funding⟩ **2** : to urge (as one's cause) strongly **3 a** : to entice or lure esp. into evil **b** : to proposition (someone) esp. as or in the character of a prostitute **4** : to try to obtain by usu. urgent requests or pleas ⟨~*ed* donations⟩ ~ *vi* **1** : to make solicitation : IMPORTUNE **2** *of a prostitute* : to offer to have sexual relations with someone for money ***syn*** see ASK

so·lic·i·tant \sə-ˈli-sə-tənt\ *n* (ca. 1812) : one who solicits

so·lic·i·ta·tion \sə-ˌli-sə-ˈtā-shən\ *n* (ca. 1520) **1** : the practice or act or an instance of soliciting; *esp* : ENTREATY, IMPORTUNITY **2** : a moving or drawing force : INCITEMENT, ALLUREMENT

so·lic·i·tor \sə-ˈli-sə-tər, -ˈlis-tər\ *n* (15c) **1** : one that solicits; *esp* : an agent that solicits (as contributions to charity) **2** : a British lawyer who advises clients, represents them in the lower courts, and prepares cases for barristers to try in higher courts **3** : the chief law officer of a municipality, county, or government department — **so·lic·i·tor·ship** \-ˌship\ *n*

solicitor general *n, pl* **solicitors general** (1647) : a law officer appointed primarily to assist an attorney general

so·lic·i·tous \sə-ˈli-sə-təs, -ˈlis-təs\ *adj* [L *sollicitus*] (1563) **1** : manifesting or expressing solicitude ⟨a ~ inquiry about his health⟩ **2** : full of concern or fears : APPREHENSIVE ⟨~ about the future⟩ **3** : meticulously careful ⟨~ in matters of dress⟩ **4** : full of desire : EAGER — **so·lic·i·tous·ly** *adv* — **so·lic·i·tous·ness** *n*

so·lic·i·tude \sə-ˈli-sə-ˌtüd, -ˌtyüd\ *n* (15c) **1 a** : the state of being concerned and anxious **b** : attentive care and protectiveness; *also* : an attitude of earnest concern or attention ⟨expressed ~ for his health⟩ **2** : a cause of care or concern — usu. used in pl.

[1]**sol·id** \ˈsä-ləd\ *adj* [ME *solide,* fr. MF, fr. L *solidus;* akin to Gk *holos* whole — more at SAFE] (14c) **1 a** : being without an internal cavity ⟨a ~ ball of rubber⟩ **b (1)** : printed with minimum space between lines **(2)** : joined without a hyphen ⟨a ~ compound⟩ **c** : not interrupted by a break or opening ⟨a ~ wall⟩ **2** : having, involving, or dealing with three dimensions or with solids ⟨a ~ configuration⟩ **3 a** : of uniformly close and coherent texture : not loose or spongy : COMPACT **b** : possessing or characterized by the properties of a solid : neither gaseous nor liquid ⟨~ waste⟩ **4** : of good substantial quality or kind ⟨~ comfort⟩: as **a** : SOUND ⟨~ reasons⟩ **b** : made firmly and well ⟨~ furniture⟩ **c** : RELIABLE ⟨a ~ performer⟩ **5 a** : having no break or interruption ⟨waited three ~ hours⟩ **b** : UNANIMOUS ⟨had the ~ support of the party⟩ **c** : intimately friendly or associated ⟨~ with the boss⟩ **6 a** : PRUDENT; *also* : well established financially **b** : serious in purpose or character **7** : of one substance or character: as **a** : entirely of one metal or containing the minimum of alloy necessary to impart hardness ⟨~ gold⟩ **b** : of a single color — **sol·id·ly** *adv* — **sol·id·ness** *n*

[2]**solid** *n* (15c) **1** : a geometrical figure or element (as a cube or sphere) having three dimensions — see VOLUME table **2 a** : a substance that does not flow perceptibly under moderate stress, has a definite capacity for resisting forces (as compression or tension) which tend to deform it, and under ordinary conditions retains a definite size and shape **b** : the part of a solution or suspension that when freed from solvent or suspending medium has the qualities of a solid — usu. used in pl. ⟨milk ~*s*⟩ **3** : something that is solid: as **a** : a solid color **b** : a compound word whose members are joined together without a hyphen

[3]**solid** *adv* (1651) : in a solid manner; *also* : UNANIMOUSLY

sol·i·da·go \ˌsä-lə-ˈdā-(ˌ)gō, -ˈdä-\ *n, pl* **-gos** [NL, fr. ML *soldago,* an herb reputed to heal wounds, fr. *soldare* to make whole, fr. L *solidare,* fr. *solidus* solid] (ca. 1771) : any of a genus (*Solidago*) of chiefly No. American composite herbs including the typical goldenrods

solid angle *n* (ca. 1704) : the three-dimensional angular spread at the vertex of a cone measured by the area intercepted by the cone on a unit sphere whose center is the vertex of the cone

sol·i·da·rism \ˈsä-lə-də-ˌri-zəm\ *n* (1906) : SOLIDARITY — **sol·i·da·rist** \-rist\ *n* — **sol·i·da·ris·tic** \ˌsä-lə-də-ˈris-tik\ *adj*

sol·i·dar·i·ty \ˌsä-lə-ˈda-rə-tē\ *n* [F *solidarité,* fr. *solidaire* characterized by solidarity, fr. L *solidum* whole sum, fr. neut. of *solidus* solid] (1841) : unity (as of a group or class) that produces or is based on community of interests, objectives, and standards

solid geometry *n* (1733) : a branch of geometry that deals with figures of three-dimensional space

so·lid·i·fy \sə-ˈli-də-ˌfī\ *vb* **-fied; -fy·ing** *vt* (1799) **1** : to make solid, compact, or hard **2** : to make secure, substantial, or firmly fixed ⟨factors that ~ public opinion⟩ ~ *vi* : to become solid, compact, or hard — **so·lid·i·fi·ca·tion** \-ˌli-də-fə-ˈkā-shən\ *n*

so·lid·i·ty \sə-ˈli-də-tē\ *n, pl* **-ties** (14c) **1** : the quality or state of being solid **2** : something solid

sol·id–look·ing \ˌsä-ləd-ˈlu̇k-iŋ\ *adj* (1840) : giving an impression of solid worth or substance ⟨~ citizens⟩

solid of revolution (1816) **:** a mathematical solid conceived as formed by the revolution of a plane figure about an axis in its plane

solid–state *adj* (ca. 1951) **1 :** relating to the properties, structure, or reactivity of solid material; *esp* **:** relating to the arrangement or behavior of ions, molecules, nucleons, electrons, and holes in the crystals of a substance (as a semiconductor) or to the effect of crystal imperfections on the properties of a solid substance ⟨~ physics⟩ **2 a :** utilizing the electric, magnetic, or optical properties of solid materials ⟨~ circuitry⟩ **b :** using semiconductor devices rather than electron tubes ⟨a ~ radio⟩

sol·i·dus \ˈsä-lə-dəs\ *n, pl* **-i·di** \-lə-ˌdī, -ˌdē\ [ME, fr. LL, fr. L, solid] (14c) **1 :** an ancient Roman gold coin introduced by Constantine and used to the fall of the Byzantine Empire **2** [ML, shilling, fr. LL; fr. its use as a symbol for shillings] **:** SLASH 4

so·li·fluc·tion \ˌsō-lə-ˈflək-shən\ *n* [L *solum* soil + *-i-* + *fluction-, fluctio* act of flowing, fr. *fluere* to flow — more at FLUID] (1906) **:** the slow creeping of saturated fragmental material (as soil) down a slope that usu. occurs in regions of perennial frost

so·lil·o·quise *Brit var of* SOLILOQUIZE

so·lil·o·quist \sə-ˈli-lə-kwist\ *n* (1804) **:** one who soliloquizes

so·lil·o·quize \-ˌkwīz\ *vi* **-quized; -quiz·ing** (1759) **:** to utter a soliloquy **:** talk to oneself — **so·lil·o·quiz·er** *n*

so·lil·o·quy \sə-ˈli-lə-kwē\ *n, pl* **-quies** [LL *soliloquium,* fr. L *solus* alone + *loqui* to speak] (ca. 1613) **1 :** the act of talking to oneself **2 :** a dramatic monologue that represents a series of unspoken reflections

so·lip·sism \ˈsō-ləp-ˌsi-zəm, ˈsä-\ *n* [L *solus* alone + *ipse* self] (1874) **:** a theory holding that the self can know nothing but its own modifications and that the self is the only existent thing; *also* **:** extreme egocentrism — **so·lip·sist** \ˈsō-ləp-sist, ˈsä-ləp-, sə-ˈlip-\ *n* — **so·lip·sis·tic** \ˌsō-ləp-ˈsis-tik, ˌsä-\ *adj* — **so·lip·sis·ti·cal·ly** \-ti-k(ə-)lē\ *adv*

sol·i·taire \ˈsä-lə-ˌter\ *n* [F, fr. *solitaire,* adj., solitary, fr. L *solitarius*] (ca. 1727) **1 :** a single gem (as a diamond) set alone **2 :** any of various card games that can be played by one person

[1]**sol·i·tary** \ˈsä-lə-ˌter-ē\ *adj* [ME, *solitarie,* fr. AF, fr. L *solitarius,* fr. *solitas* aloneness, fr. *solus* alone] (14c) **1 a :** being, living, or going alone or without companions **b :** saddened by isolation **2 :** UNFREQUENTED, DESOLATE ⟨a ~ seashore⟩ **3 a :** taken, passed, or performed without companions ⟨a ~ ramble⟩ **b :** keeping a prisoner apart from others ⟨~ confinement⟩ **4 :** being at once single and isolated ⟨a ~ example⟩ **5 a :** occurring singly and not as part of a group or cluster ⟨flowers terminal and ~⟩ **b :** not gregarious, colonial, social, or compound ⟨~ bees⟩ ***syn*** see ALONE — **sol·i·tar·i·ly** \ˌsä-lə-ˈter-ə-lē\ *adv* — **sol·i·tar·i·ness** \ˈsä-lə-ˌter-ē-nəs\ *n*

[2]**solitary** *n, pl* **-tar·ies** (15c) **1 :** one who lives or seeks to live a solitary life **:** RECLUSE **2 :** solitary confinement in prison ⟨put him in ~⟩

sol·i·ton \ˈsä-lə-ˌtän\ *n* [*solitary* + [2]*-on*] (1965) **:** a solitary wave (as in a gaseous plasma) that propagates with little loss of energy and retains its shape and speed after colliding with another such wave

sol·i·tude \ˈsä-lə-ˌtüd, -ˌtyüd\ *n* [ME, fr. MF & L; MF, fr. L *solitudin-, solitudo,* fr. *solus*] (14c) **1 :** the quality or state of being alone or remote from society **:** SECLUSION **2 :** a lonely place (as a desert)

syn SOLITUDE, ISOLATION, SECLUSION mean the state of one who is alone. SOLITUDE may imply a condition of being apart from all human beings or of being cut off by wish or circumstances from one's usual associates ⟨a few quiet hours of *solitude*⟩. ISOLATION stresses detachment from others often involuntarily ⟨the *isolation* of the village in winter⟩. SECLUSION suggests a shutting away or keeping apart from others often connoting deliberate withdrawal from the world or retirement to a quiet life ⟨lived in pastoral *seclusion*⟩.

sol·i·tu·di·nar·i·an \ˌsä-lə-ˌtü-də-ˈner-ē-ən, -ˌtyü-\ *n* [L *solitudin-, solitudo* + E *-arian*] (1691) **:** RECLUSE

sol·ler·et \ˌsä-lə-ˈret\ *n* [F] (1826) **:** a flexible steel shoe forming part of a medieval suit of armor — see ARMOR illustration

sol·mi·za·tion \ˌsäl-mə-ˈzā-shən\ *n* [F *solmisation,* fr. *solmiser* to sol-fa, fr. *sol* (fr. ML) + *mi* (fr. ML) + *-iser* -ize] (1730) **:** the act, practice, or system of using syllables to denote the tones of a musical scale

soln *abbr* solution

[1]**so·lo** \ˈsō-(ˌ)lō\ *n, pl* **solos** [It, fr. *solo* alone, fr. L *solus*] (1695) **1** *or pl* **so·li** \ˈsō-(ˌ)lē\ **a :** a musical composition for a single voice or instrument with or without accompaniment **b :** the featured part of a concerto or similar work **2 :** a performance in which the performer has no partner or associate **:** something undertaken or done alone ⟨a student pilot's first ~⟩ **3 :** any of several card games in which a player elects to play without a partner against the other players

[2]**solo** *adv* (1712) **:** without a companion **:** ALONE ⟨fly ~⟩

[3]**solo** *adj* (1774) **1 :** accommodating one person ⟨a ~ canoe⟩ **2 :** of, relating to, or being a solo ⟨a ~ performance⟩ ⟨a ~ flight⟩ **3 :** hit with no runners on base ⟨a ~ home run⟩

[4]**solo** *vi* **so·loed; so·lo·ing** \-(ˌ)lō-iŋ, -lə-wiŋ\ (1886) **:** to perform by oneself: as **a :** to perform a musical solo **b :** to fly an airplane without one's instructor on board ~ *vt* **1 :** to fly (as an airplane) alone **2 :** to climb (as a mountain) alone

so·lo·ist \ˈsō-lə-wist, -(ˌ)lō-ist\ *n* (1864) **:** one who performs a solo

Sol·o·mon \ˈsä-lə-mən\ *n* [LL, fr. Heb *Shĕlōmōh*] (bef. 12c) **:** a son of David and 10th century B.C. king of Israel proverbial for his wisdom

Sol·o·mon·ic \ˌsä-lə-ˈmä-nik\ *adj* (1857) **:** marked by notable wisdom, reasonableness, or discretion esp. under trying circumstances

Solomon's seal *n* (1543) **1 :** any of a genus (*Polygonatum*) of perennial herbs of the lily family with tubular flowers and gnarled rhizomes **2 :** an emblem consisting of two interlaced triangles forming a 6-pointed star and formerly used as an amulet esp. against fever — compare HEXAGRAM

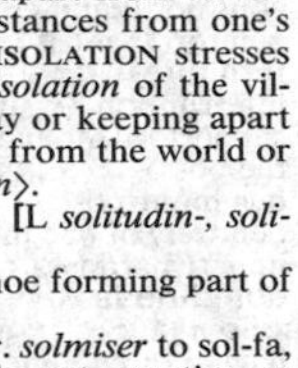

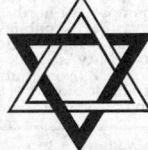

Solomon's seal 2

so·lon \ˈsō-lən, -ˌlän\ *n* [*Solon*] (1625) **1 :** a wise and skillful lawgiver **2 :** a member of a legislative body

so long \sō-ˈlȯŋ, sə-\ *interj* [origin unknown] (1854) — used to express farewell

so long as *conj* (14c) **1 :** during and up to the end of the time that **:** WHILE ⟨*so long as* you are here, I'm fine⟩ **2 :** provided that ⟨you may go, *so long as* you return by dinnertime⟩

sol·stice \ˈsäl-stəs, ˈsōl-, ˈsȯl-\ *n* [ME, fr. L *solstitium,* fr. *sol* sun + *-stit-, -stes* standing; akin to L *stare* to stand — more at SOLAR, STAND] (13c) **1 :** either of the two points on the ecliptic at which its distance from the celestial equator is greatest and which is reached by the sun each year about June 22 and December 22 **2 :** the time of the sun's passing a solstice which occurs about June 22 to begin summer in the northern hemisphere and about December 22 to begin winter in the northern hemisphere

sol·sti·tial \säl-ˈsti-shəl, sōl-, sȯl-\ *adj* [ME *solsticial,* fr. AF & L; AF, fr. L *solstitialis,* fr. *solstitium*] (14c) **1 :** of, relating to, or characteristic of a solstice and esp. the summer solstice **2 :** happening or appearing at or associated with a solstice

sol·u·bi·lise *Brit var of* SOLUBILIZE

sol·u·bil·i·ty \ˌsäl-yə-ˈbi-lə-tē\ *n* (1661) **1 :** the quality or state of being soluble **2 :** the amount of a substance that will dissolve in a given amount of another substance

sol·u·bi·lize \ˈsäl-yə-bə-ˌlīz\ *vt* **-lized; -liz·ing** (ca. 1926) **:** to make soluble or more soluble — **sol·u·bi·li·za·tion** \ˌsäl-yə-bə-lə-ˈzā-shən\ *n*

sol·u·ble \ˈsäl-yə-bəl\ *adj* [ME, fr. AF, digestible, laxative, fr. LL *solubilis,* fr. L *solvere* to loosen, dissolve — more at SOLVE] (15c) **1 :** susceptible of being dissolved in or as if in a liquid and esp. water **2 :** subject to being solved or explained ⟨~ questions⟩

so·lum \ˈsō-ləm\ *n, pl* **so·la** \-lə\ *or* **solums** [NL, fr. L, ground, soil] (1928) **:** the altered layer of soil above the parent material that includes the A and B horizons

so·lus \ˈsō-ləs\ *adv or adj* [L] (1599) **:** ALONE — often used in stage directions

sol·ute \ˈsäl-ˌyüt\ *n* [L *solutus,* pp. of *solvere*] (1893) **:** a dissolved substance

so·lu·tion \sə-ˈlü-shən\ *n* [ME *solucion* explanation, dispersal of bodily humors, fr. AF, fr. L *solution-, solutio,* fr. *solvere* to loosen, solve] (14c) **1 a :** an action or process of solving a problem **b :** an answer to a problem **:** EXPLANATION; *specif* **:** a set of values of the variables that satisfies an equation **2 a :** an act or the process by which a solid, liquid, or gaseous substance is homogeneously mixed with a liquid or sometimes a gas or solid **b :** a homogeneous mixture formed by this process; *esp* **:** a single-phase liquid system **c :** the condition of being dissolved **3 :** a bringing or coming to an end or into a state of discontinuity

solution set *n* (1959) **:** the set of values that satisfy an equation; *also* **:** TRUTH SET

So·lu·tre·an \sə-ˈlü-trē-ən\ *adj* [*Solutré,* village in France] (1888) **:** of or relating to an Upper Paleolithic culture characterized by leaf-shaped finely flaked stone implements

solv·able \ˈsäl-və-bəl, ˈsȯl-\ *adj* (ca. 1676) **:** susceptible of solution or of being solved, resolved, or explained ⟨a ~ problem⟩ — **solv·abil·i·ty** \ˌsäl-və-ˈbi-lə-tē, ˌsȯl-\ *n*

[1]**sol·vate** \ˈsäl-ˌvāt, ˈsȯl-\ *n* [*solvent* + [1]*-ate*] (1904) **:** an aggregate that consists of a solute ion or molecule with one or more solvent molecules; *also* **:** a substance (as a hydrate) containing such ions

[2]**solvate** *vt* **sol·vat·ed; sol·vat·ing** (1909) **:** to make part of a solvate — **sol·va·tion** \säl-ˈvā-shən, sȯl-\ *n*

Sol·vay process \ˈsäl-ˌvā-\ *n* [Ernest *Solvay* †1922 Belg. chemist] (1884) **:** a process for making soda from common salt by passing carbon dioxide into ammoniacal brine resulting in precipitation of sodium bicarbonate which is then calcined to carbonate

solve \ˈsälv, ˈsȯlv\ *vb* **solved; solv·ing** [ME, to loosen, fr. L *solvere* to loosen, solve, dissolve, fr. *sed-, se-* apart + *luere* to release — more at SECEDE, LOSE] *vt* (ca. 1533) **1 :** to find a solution, explanation, or answer for ⟨~ a problem⟩ ⟨*solved* the crime⟩ **2 :** to pay (as a debt) in full ~ *vi* **:** to solve something ⟨substitute and ~ for *x*⟩ — **solv·er** *n*

sol·ven·cy \ˈsäl-vən(t)-sē, ˈsȯl-\ *n* (ca. 1727) **:** the quality or state of being solvent

[1]**sol·vent** \-vənt\ *adj* [L *solvent-, solvens,* prp. of *solvere* to dissolve, pay] (1630) **1 :** able to pay all legal debts ⟨a ~ company⟩ **2 :** that dissolves or can dissolve ⟨~ action of water⟩ — **sol·vent·ly** *adv*

[2]**solvent** *n* (1671) **1 :** a usu. liquid substance capable of dissolving or dispersing one or more other substances **2 :** something that provides a solution **3 :** something that eliminates or attenuates something esp. unwanted — **sol·vent·less** \-ləs\ *adj*

sol·vol·y·sis \säl-ˈvä-lə-səs, sȯl-\ *n* [NL, fr. E *solvent* + NL *-o-* + *-lysis*] (1916) **:** a chemical reaction (as hydrolysis) of a solvent and solute that results in the formation of new compounds — **sol·vo·lyt·ic** \ˌsäl-və-ˈli-tik, ˌsȯl-\ *adj*

[1]**som** \ˈsōm\ *n, pl* **som** [Kyrgyz, crude iron casting, ruble] (1993) — see MONEY table

[2]**som** *n, pl* **som** [Uzbek *so'm* ruble] (1993) **:** the sum of Uzbekistan

Som *abbr* Somersetshire

[1]**so·ma** \ˈsō-mə\ *n* [Skt; akin to Av *haoma,* a Zoroastrian ritual drink, Skt *sunoti* he presses out] (1827) **:** an intoxicating juice from a plant of disputed identity that was used in ancient India as an offering to the gods and as a drink of immortality by worshippers in Vedic ritual and worshipped in personified form as a Vedic god

[2]**soma** *n, pl* **so·ma·ta** \ˈsō-mə-tə\ *or* **somas** [NL *somat-, soma,* fr. Gk *sōmat-, sōma* body] (ca. 1885) **1 :** the body of an organism **2 :** all of an organism except the germ cells **3 :** CELL BODY

So·ma·li \sō-ˈmä-lē, sə-\ *n, pl* **Somali** *or* **Somalis** [fr. or akin to Somali *Soomaali*] (1814) **1 :** a member of a people of Somaliland **2 :** the Cushitic language of the Somali — **Somali** *adj*

so·man \ˈsō-mən\ *n, often cap* [G] (1951) **:** an extremely toxic chemical warfare agent $C_7H_{16}FO_2P$ similar to sarin in action

so many *adj* (1533) **1 :** constituting an unspecified number ⟨can only read *so many* chapters each night⟩ **2 :** constituting a group or pack ⟨behaved like *so many* animals⟩

somat- *or* **somato-** *comb form* [NL, fr. Gk *sōmat-, sōmato-,* fr. *sōmat-, sōma* body] **:** body ⟨*somato*logy⟩

so·mat·ic \sō-ˈma-tik, sə-\ *adj* [Gk *sōmatikos,* fr. *sōmat-, sōma*] (ca. 1775) **1 :** of, relating to, or affecting the body esp. as distinguished from the germplasm or the psyche **2 :** of or relating to the wall of the body **:** PARIETAL — **so·mat·i·cal·ly** \-ti-k(ə-)lē\ *adv*

somatic cell *n* (1888) **:** one of the cells of the body that compose the tissues, organs, and parts of that individual other than the germ cells

so·ma·ti·za·tion \ˌsō-mə-tə-ˈzā-shən\ *n* (1925) **:** conversion of a mental state (as depression or anxiety) into physical symptoms; *also* **:** the existence of physical bodily complaints in the absence of a known medical condition

so·ma·tol·o·gy \ˌsō-mə-ˈtä-lə-jē\ *n* [NL *somatologia,* fr. *somat-* + *-logia* -logy] (ca. 1878) : a branch of anthropology primarily concerned with the comparative study of human evolution, variation, and classification esp. through measurement and observation — **so·ma·to·log·i·cal** \ˌsō-mə-tə-ˈlä-ji-kəl, sō-ˌma-\ *adj*

so·mato·me·din \ˌsō-mə-tō-ˈmē-dᵊn, sō-ˌma-tə-\ *n* [*somat-* + inter*mediary* + ¹*-in*] (1971) : any of several endogenous peptides produced esp. in the liver that are dependent on and prob. mediate growth hormone activity (as in sulfate uptake by epiphyseal cartilage)

so·mato·pleure \sō-ˈma-tə-ˌplu̇r\ *n* [NL *somatopleura,* fr. *somat-* + Gk *pleura* side] (1874) : a complex fold of tissue in the embryo of a craniate vertebrate consisting of an outer layer of mesoderm together with the ectoderm that sheathes it and giving rise to the amnion and chorion

so·mato·sen·so·ry \sō-ˌma-tə-ˈsen(t)s-rē, -ˈsen(t)-sə-rē\ *adj* (1952) : of, relating to, or being sensory activity having its origin elsewhere than in the special sense organs (as eyes and ears) and conveying information about the state of the body proper and its immediate environment; *also* : relating to or being either of two regions in the parietal lobe that receive and process somatosensory stimuli

so·mato·stat·in \sō-ˌma-tə-ˈsta-tᵊn\ *n* [*somat-* + L *status* (pp. of *sistere* to halt, cause to stand) + E ¹*-in;* akin to L *stare* to stand — more at STAND] (1973) : a polypeptide neurohormone that is found esp. in the hypothalamus and inhibits the secretion of several other hormones (as growth hormone, insulin, and gastrin)

so·mato·tro·pic hormone \-ˈtrō-pik-\ *n* [*somat-* + *-tropic*] (1938) : GROWTH HORMONE 1

so·mato·tro·pin \-ˈtrō-pən\ *also* **so·mato·tro·phin** \-fən\ *n* [*somatotropic* + ¹*-in*] (1941) : GROWTH HORMONE 1

so·mato·type \sō-ˈma-tə-ˌtīp\ *n* (1940) : body type : PHYSIQUE

som·ber *or* **som·bre** \ˈsäm-bər\ *adj* [F *sombre*] (1760) **1** : so shaded as to be dark and gloomy **2 a** : of a serious mien : GRAVE ⟨~ dignitaries⟩ **b** : of a dismal or depressing character : MELANCHOLY **c** : conveying gloomy suggestions or ideas **3** : of a dull or heavy cast or shade : dark colored — **som·ber·ly** *adv* — **som·ber·ness** *n*

som·bre·ro \səm-ˈbrer-(ˌ)ō, säm-\ *n, pl* **-ros** [Sp, fr. *sombra* shade] (1599) : an often high-crowned hat of felt or straw with a very wide brim worn esp. in the Southwest and Mexico

som·brous \ˈsäm-brəs\ *adj* [F *sombre*] (1730) *archaic* : SOMBER

¹**some** \ˈsəm, *for 2 without stress*\ *adj* [ME *som,* adj. & pron., fr. OE *sum;* akin to OHG *sum* some, Gk *hamē* somehow, *homos* same — more at SAME] (bef. 12c) **1** : being an unknown, undetermined, or unspecified unit or thing ⟨~ person knocked⟩ **2 a** : being one, a part, or an unspecified number of something (as a class or group) named or implied ⟨~ gems are hard⟩ **b** : being of an unspecified amount or number ⟨give me ~ water⟩ ⟨have ~ apples⟩ **3** : REMARKABLE, STRIKING ⟨that was ~ party⟩ **4** : being at least one — used to indicate that a logical proposition is asserted only of a subclass or certain members of the class denoted by the term which it modifies

²**some** \ˈsəm\ *pron, sing or pl in constr* (bef. 12c) **1** : one indeterminate quantity, portion, or number as distinguished from the rest **2** : an indefinite additional amount ⟨ran a mile and then ~⟩

³**some** \ˈsəm, ˌsəm\ *adv* (bef. 12c) **1** : ABOUT ⟨~ 80 houses⟩ ⟨twenty-*some* people⟩ **2 a** : in some degree : SOMEWHAT ⟨felt ~ better⟩ **b** : to some degree or extent : a little ⟨the cut bled ~⟩ ⟨I need to work on it ~ more⟩ **c** — used as a mild intensive ⟨that's going ~⟩

usage When *some* is used to modify a number, it is almost always a round number ⟨a community of *some* 150,000 inhabitants⟩ but because *some* is slightly more emphatic than *about* or *approximately* it is occas. used with a more exact number in an intensive function ⟨an expert parachutist, he has *some* 115 jumps to his credit —*Current Biog.*⟩. When *some* is used without a number, most commentators feel that *somewhat* is to be preferred. Their advice is an oversimplification, however; only when *some* modifies an adjective, usu. a comparative, will *somewhat* always substitute smoothly. When *some* modifies a verb or adverb, and esp. when it follows a verb, substitution of *somewhat* may prove awkward ⟨Italy forced me to grow up *some* —E. W. Brooke⟩ ⟨I'm not a prude; I've been around *some* in my day —Roy Rogers⟩ ⟨here in Newport, both Southern Cross and Courageous practiced *some* more —W. N. Wallace⟩.

¹**-some** *adj suffix* [ME *-som,* fr. OE *-sum;* akin to OHG *-sam* -some, OE *sum* some] : characterized by a (specified) thing, quality, state, or action ⟨awe*some*⟩ ⟨burden*some*⟩ ⟨cuddle*some*⟩

²**-some** *n suffix* [ME (northern dial.) *-sum,* fr. ME *sum,* pron., one, some] : group of (so many) members and esp. persons ⟨four*some*⟩

³**-some** *n comb form* [NL *-somat-, -soma,* fr. Gk *sōmat-, sōma*] **1** : body ⟨chromo*some*⟩ **2** : chromosome ⟨mono*some*⟩

¹**some·body** \ˈsəm-(ˌ)bə-dē, -ˌbä-\ *pron* (14c) : one or some person of unspecified or indefinite identity ⟨~ will come in⟩

²**somebody** *n* (ca. 1566) : a person of position or importance

some·day \ˈsəm-ˌdā\ *adv* (14c) : at some future time

some·deal \ˈsəm-ˌdēl\ *adv* (bef. 12c) *archaic* : SOMEWHAT

some·how \ˈsəm-ˌhau̇\ *adv* (1664) : in one way or another not known or designated : by some means ⟨we'll manage ~⟩

some·one \-(ˌ)wən\ *pron* (14c) : some person : SOMEBODY

some·place \-ˌplās\ *adv* (1880) : SOMEWHERE

som·er·sault *also* **sum·mer·sault** \ˈsə-mər-ˌsȯlt\ *n* [MF *sombresaut* leap, ultim. fr. L *super* over + *saltus* leap, fr. *salire* to jump — more at OVER, SALLY] (ca. 1530) : a movement (as in gymnastics) in which a person turns forward or backward in a complete revolution along the ground or in the air bringing the feet over the head; *also* : a falling or tumbling head over heels — **somersault** *vi*

som·er·set \-ˌset\ *n or vi* [by alter.] (1591) : SOMERSAULT

¹**some·thing** \ˈsəm(p)-thiŋ, *esp in rapid speech or for 2* ˈsəm-pᵊm\ *pron* (bef. 12c) **1 a** : some indeterminate or unspecified thing **b** : some indeterminate amount more than a specified number — used in combination ⟨twenty-*something* years old⟩ ⟨a group of fifty-*somethings*⟩ **2** : a person or thing of consequence **3** : one having more or less the character, qualities, or nature of something different ⟨is ~ of a bore⟩ — **something else** : something or someone special or extraordinary

²**something** *adv* (13c) **1** : in some degree : SOMEWHAT **2** — used as an intensive giving adverbial force to an adjective ⟨swears ~ awful⟩

¹**some·time** \ˈsəm-ˌtīm\ *adv* (14c) **1** *archaic* : in the past : FORMERLY **2** *archaic* : once in a while : OCCASIONALLY **3** : at some time in the future ⟨I'll do it ~⟩ **4** : at some not specified or definitely known point of time ⟨~ last night⟩

²**sometime** *adj* (14c) **1** : having been formerly : FORMER, LATE **2** : being so occasionally or in only some respects ⟨a ~ father⟩

¹**some·times** \ˈsəm-ˌtīmz *also* (ˌ)səm-ˈ\ *adv* (14c) : at times : now and then : OCCASIONALLY

²**sometimes** *adj* (1593) : SOMETIME

some·way \ˈsəm-ˌwā\ *also* **some·ways** \-ˌwāz\ *adv* (15c) : SOMEHOW

¹**some·what** \-ˌ(h)wät, -ˌ(h)wət, (ˌ)səm-ˈ\ *pron* (13c) : SOMETHING

²**somewhat** *adv* (13c) : in some degree or measure : SLIGHTLY

some·when \ˈsəm-ˌ(h)wen\ *adv* (1833) : SOMETIME

¹**some·where** \-ˌ(h)wer, -(ˌ)(h)wər\ *adv* (13c) **1** : in, at, from, or to a place unknown or unspecified ⟨mentions it ~⟩ **2** : to a place symbolizing positive accomplishment or progress ⟨now we're getting ~⟩ **3** : in the vicinity of : APPROXIMATELY ⟨~ about nine o'clock⟩

²**somewhere** *n* (1647) : an undetermined or unnamed place

some·wheres \-ˌ(h)werz, -(ˌ)(h)wərz\ *adv* (1815) *chiefly dial* : SOMEWHERE

some·whith·er \-ˌ(h)wi-t͟hər\ *adv* (1530) *archaic* : to some place : SOMEWHERE

-somic *adj comb form* [ISV ³*-some* + *-ic*] : having or being a chromosome complement of which one or more but not all members exhibit (such) a degree of reduplication of chromosomes or genomes ⟨mono*somic*⟩

so·mite \ˈsō-ˌmīt\ *n* [ISV, fr. Gk *sōma* body] (1869) : one of the longitudinal series of segments into which the body of many animals is divided : METAMERE

som·me·lier \ˌsə-məl-ˈyā\ *n, pl* **sommeliers** \-ˈyā(z)\ [F, fr. MF *soumelier* official charged with transportation of supplies, fr. OF, pack animal driver, prob. alter. of *sommerier, fr. *somier* pack animal, fr. ML *saugmarius,* fr. LL *sagma* packsaddle — more at SUMPTER] (1829) : a waiter in a restaurant who has charge of wines and their service : a wine steward

somnambul- *comb form* [NL, fr. *somnambulus* somnambulist, fr. L *somnus* sleep + *-ambulus* (as in *funambulus* funambulist) — more at SOMNOLENT] : somnambulism : somnambulist ⟨*somnambul*ant⟩

som·nam·bu·lant \säm-ˈnam-byə-lənt\ *adj* (1866) **1** : walking or having the habit of walking while asleep **2** : resembling or having the characteristics of a sleepwalker : SLUGGISH

som·nam·bu·late \-ˌlāt\ *vi* **-lat·ed; -lat·ing** (1833) : to walk when asleep — **som·nam·bu·la·tion** \(ˌ)säm-ˌnam-byə-ˈlā-shən\ *n*

som·nam·bu·lism \säm-ˈnam-byə-ˌli-zəm\ *n* (1797) **1** : an abnormal condition of sleep in which motor acts (as walking) are performed **2** : actions characteristic of somnambulism — **som·nam·bu·list** \-list\ *n* — **som·nam·bu·lis·tic** \(ˌ)säm-ˌnam-byə-ˈlis-tik\ *adj* — **som·nam·bu·lis·ti·cal·ly** \-ti-k(ə-)lē\ *adv*

som·ni·fa·cient \ˌsäm-nə-ˈfā-shənt\ *adj* [L *somnus* sleep + E *-facient*] (ca. 1890) : HYPNOTIC 1 — **somnifacient** *n*

som·nif·er·ous \säm-ˈni-f(ə-)rəs\ *adj* [L *somnifer* somniferous, fr. *somnus* + *-fer* -ferous] (1602) : SOPORIFIC

som·no·lence \ˈsäm-nə-lən(t)s\ *n* (14c) : the quality or state of being drowsy : SLEEPINESS

som·no·lent \-lənt\ *adj* [ME *sompnolent,* fr. AF, fr. L *somnolentus,* fr. *somnus* sleep; akin to OE *swefn* sleep, Gk *hypnos*] (15c) **1** : of a kind likely to induce sleep ⟨a ~ sermon⟩ **2 a** : inclined to or heavy with sleep : DROWSY **b** : SLEEPY 2 ⟨~ rivers⟩ — **som·no·lent·ly** *adv*

somoni \ˌsō-mō-ˈnē\ *n, pl* **somoni** [Tajik *somonī,* fr. *Ismoil Somonī* (Abū Ibrāhīm Ismāʽīl) †A.D. 907 ruler of an early Muslim dynasty in northern and eastern Iranian lands] (2000) — see MONEY table

¹**so much** *adv* (13c) : by the amount indicated or suggested ⟨if they lose their way, *so much* the better for us⟩

²**so much** *pron* (14c) **1** : something (as an amount or price) unspecified or undetermined ⟨charge *so much* a mile⟩ **2** : all that can be or is to be said or done ⟨*so much* for the history of the case⟩

³**so much** *adj* (1557) — used as an intensive ⟨the house burned like *so much* paper⟩ ⟨sounded like *so much* nonsense⟩

so much as *adv* (15c) : EVEN 2d ⟨scowls if I *so much as* look at him⟩

son \ˈsən\ *n* [ME *sone,* fr. OE *sunu;* akin to OHG *sun* son, Gk *hyios*] (bef. 12c) **1 a** : a human male offspring esp. of human beings **b** : a male adopted child **c** : a human male descendant **2** *cap* : the second person of the Trinity **3** : a person closely associated with or deriving from a formative agent (as a nation, school, or race) — **son·hood** \-ˌhu̇d\ *n*

son- *or* **sono-** *comb form* [L *sonus* sound] : sound ⟨*son*ic⟩ ⟨*sono*gram⟩

so·nant \ˈsō-nənt\ *adj* [L *sonant-, sonans,* prp. of *sonare* to sound — more at SOUND] (1846) **1** : VOICED 2 **2** : SYLLABIC 1a — **sonant** *n*

so·nar \ˈsō-ˌnär\ *n* [*so*und *na*vigation *r*anging] (1945) : a method or device for detecting and locating objects esp. underwater by means of sound waves sent out to be reflected by the objects; *also* : a device for detecting the presence of a vessel (as a submarine) by the sound it emits in water

so·na·ta \sə-ˈnä-tə\ *n* [It, fr. *sonare* to sound, fr. L] (1694) : an instrumental musical composition typically of three or four movements in contrasting forms and keys

sonata form *n* (1858) : a musical form that consists basically of an exposition, a development, and a recapitulation and that is used esp. for the first movement of a sonata

son·a·ti·na \ˌsä-nə-ˈtē-nə\ *n* [It, dim. of *sonata*] (1764) : a short usu. simplified sonata

sonde \ˈsänd\ *n* [F, lit., sounding line — more at SOUND] (1901) : any of various devices for testing physical conditions (as at high altitudes, below the earth's surface, or inside the body)

sone \ˈsōn\ *n* [ISV, fr. L *sonus* sound — more at SOUND] (1948) : a subjective unit of loudness for an average listener equal to the loudness of a 1000-hertz sound that has an intensity 40 decibels above the listener's own threshold of hearing

son et lu·mière \ˌsō^{n}-(n)ä-lüm-ˈyer\ *n* [F, lit., sound and light] (1957) : an outdoor spectacle at a historic site consisting of recorded narration with light and sound effects
song \ˈsȯŋ\ *n* [ME, fr. OE *sang;* akin to OE *singan* to sing] (bef. 12c) **1** : the act or art of singing **2** : poetical composition **3 a** : a short musical composition of words and music **b** : a collection of such compositions **4** : a distinctive or characteristic sound or series of sounds (as of a bird, insect, or whale) **5 a** : a melody for a lyric poem or ballad **b** : a poem easily set to music **6 a** : a habitual or characteristic manner **b** : a violent, abusive, or noisy reaction ⟨put up quite a ~⟩ **7** : a small amount ⟨sold for a ~⟩ — **song·like** \-ˌlīk\ *adj*
song and dance *n* (1870) **1** : a theatrical performance (as a vaudeville performance) combining singing and dancing **2** : a long and often familiar statement or explanation that is usu. not true or pertinent
song·bird \ˈsȯŋ-ˌbərd\ *n* (1683) **1 a** : a bird that utters a succession of musical tones **b** : an oscine bird **2** : a female singer
song·book \-ˈbu̇k\ *n* (bef. 12c) : a collection of songs; *specif* : a book containing vocal music (as hymns)
song cycle *n* (1871) : a group of related songs designed to form a musical entity
song·fest \ˈsȯŋ-ˈfest\ *n* (ca. 1912) : an informal session of group singing of popular or folk songs
song·ful \-fəl\ *adj* (14c) : given to or suggestive of singing : MELODIOUS — **song·ful·ly** \-fə-lē\ *adv* — **song·ful·ness** *n*
song·less \-ləs\ *adj* (ca. 1805) : lacking in, incapable of, or not given to song — **song·less·ly** *adv*
Song of Sol·o·mon \-ˈsä-lə-mən\ [fr. the opening verse: "The song of songs, which is Solomon's"] (1620) : a collection of love poems forming a book in the Protestant canon of the Old Testament — see BIBLE table
Song of Songs [trans. of Heb *shīr hashshīrīm*] (1597) : a collection of love poems forming a book in the canonical Jewish Scriptures and in the Roman Catholic canon of the Old Testament and corresponding to the Song of Solomon in the Protestant canon of the Old Testament — see BIBLE table
song·smith \ˈsȯŋ-ˌsmith\ *n* (1795) : a composer of songs
song sparrow *n* (1810) : a No. American sparrow (*Melospiza melodia* of the family Emberizidae) that is brownish above and white below with brownish streaks on the breast and that has a melodious song
song·ster \ˈsȯŋ(k)-stər\ *n* (14c) **1** : one that sings with skill **2** : SONGBOOK
song·stress \ˈsȯŋ(k)-strəs\ *n* (1684) : a female singer
song thrush *n* (1598) : an Old World thrush (*Turdus philomelos* of the family Turdidae) that is largely brown above with brown-spotted white underparts — called also *mavis, throstle*
song·writ·er \ˈsȯŋ-ˌrī-tər\ *n* (1821) : a person who composes words or music or both esp. for popular songs — **song·writ·ing** \-ˌrī-tiŋ\ *n*
son·ic \ˈsä-nik\ *adj* (1923) **1** : utilizing, produced by, or relating to sound waves ⟨~ altimeter⟩; *broadly* : of or involving sound ⟨~ pollution⟩ **2** : having a frequency within the audibility range of the human ear — used of waves and vibrations **3** : of, relating to, or being the speed of sound in air or about 761 miles per hour (1224 kilometers per hour) at sea level at 59°F (15°C) — **son·i·cal·ly** \-ni-k(ə-)lē\ *adv*
son·i·cate \ˈsä-nə-ˌkāt\ *vt* **-cat·ed; -cat·ing** [*sonic* + [4]*-ate*] (1959) : to disrupt (as bacterial cells) by exposure to high-frequency sound waves — **son·i·ca·tion** \ˌsä-nə-ˈkā-shən\ *n*
sonic barrier *n* (1946) : SOUND BARRIER
sonic boom *n* (1952) : a sound resembling an explosion produced when a shock wave formed at the nose of an aircraft traveling at supersonic speed reaches the ground — called also *sonic bang*
son–in–law \ˈsən-ən-ˌlȯ\ *n, pl* **sons–in–law** (14c) : the husband of one's daughter
son·less \ˈsən-ləs\ *adj* (14c) : not possessing or never having had a son
son·ly \-lē\ *adj* (15c) : FILIAL
son·net \ˈsä-nət\ *n* [It *sonetto,* fr. Old Occitan *sonet* little song, fr. *son* sound, song, fr. L *sonus* sound] (1557) : a fixed verse form of Italian origin consisting of 14 lines that are typically 5-foot iambics rhyming according to a prescribed scheme; *also* : a poem in this pattern
son·ne·teer \ˌsä-nə-ˈtir\ *n* (1665) **1** : a composer of sonnets **2** : a minor or insignificant poet — **son·ne·teer·ing** \-iŋ\ *n*
sonnet sequence *n* (1881) : a series of sonnets often having a unifying theme
son·ny \ˈsə-nē\ *n* (1838) : a young boy — usu. used in address
so·no·buoy \ˈsä-nə-ˌbȯi, -ˌbü-ē\ *n* (1945) : a buoy equipped for detecting underwater sounds and transmitting them by radio
son of a bitch \ˈsən-ə-və-ˌbich *also* ˈsəm-ˌbich; *as an interj* ˌsən-ə-və-ˈbich\ *n, pl* **sons of bitch·es** \ˌsən-zə-ˈbi-chəz\ (1671) *sometimes vulgar* : BASTARD 3 — sometimes used interjectionally to express surprise or disappointment
son of a gun \ˈsən-ə-və-ˌgən; *as an interj* ˌsən-ə-və-ˈgən\ *n, pl* **sons of guns** (1708) — usu. used as a mild or euphemistic alternative to *son of a bitch*; sometimes used interjectionally to express surprise or disappointment
son of God (14c) **1** *often cap S* : a superhuman or divine being (as an angel) **2** *cap S* : MESSIAH 1 **3** : a person established in the love of God by divine promise
son of man (14c) **1** : a human being **2** *often cap S* : God's messiah destined to preside over the final judgment of humankind
sono·gram \ˈsä-nə-ˌgram\ *n* (1956) : an image produced by ultrasound
so·nog·ra·phy \sō-ˈnä-grə-fē\ *n* (1975) : ULTRASOUND 2 — **so·nog·ra·pher** \-fər\ *n* — **sono·graph·ic** \ˌsä-nə-ˈgra-fik\ *adj*
so·nor·i·ty \sə-ˈnȯr-ə-tē, -ˈnär-\ *n, pl* **-ties** (ca. 1623) **1** : the quality or state of being sonorous : RESONANCE **2** : a sonorous tone or speech
so·no·rous \sə-ˈnȯr-əs, ˈsä-nə-rəs\ *adj* [L *sonorus;* akin to L *sonus* sound] (1611) **1** : producing sound (as when struck) **2** : full or loud in sound ⟨a ~ voice⟩ **3** : imposing or impressive in effect or style **4** : having a high or an indicated degree of sonority ⟨~ sounds such as \ä\ and \ȯ\⟩ — **so·no·rous·ly** *adv* — **so·no·rous·ness** *n*
son·ship \ˈsən-ˌship\ *n* (1587) : the relationship of son to father
sonsy *or* **sons·ie** \ˈsän(t)-sē\ *adj* [Sc *sons* health, fr. ScGael *sonas* luck, happiness] (1725) *chiefly dial* : BUXOM, COMELY
soon \ˈsün, *esp NewEng* ˈsu̇n\ *adv* [ME *soone,* fr. OE *sōna;* akin to OHG *sān* immediately] (bef. 12c) **1 a** *obs* : at once : IMMEDIATELY **b** : without undue time lapse : BEFORE LONG ⟨~ after sunrise⟩ **2** : in a prompt manner : SPEEDILY ⟨as ~ as possible⟩ ⟨the ~*er* the better⟩ ⟨no ~*er* said than done⟩ **3** *archaic* : before the usual time **4** : in agreement with one's choice or preference : WILLINGLY ⟨I'd just as ~ walk as drive⟩
soon·er \ˈsü-nər\ *n* [*sooner,* compar. of *soon*] (1890) **1** : a person settling on land in the early West before its official opening to settlement in order to gain the prior claim allowed by law to the first settler after official opening **2** *cap* : a native or resident of Oklahoma — used as a nickname
sooner or later *adv* (1577) : at some uncertain future time : SOMETIME
[1]**soot** \ˈsu̇t, ˈsət, ˈsüt\ *n* [ME, fr. OE *sōt;* akin to OIr *suide* soot, OE *sittan* to sit] (bef. 12c) : a black substance formed by combustion or separated from fuel during combustion, rising in fine particles, and adhering to the sides of the chimney or pipe conveying the smoke; *esp* : the fine powder consisting chiefly of carbon that colors smoke
[2]**soot** *vt* (1602) : to coat or cover with soot
[1]**sooth** \ˈsüth\ *adj* [ME, fr. OE *sōth;* akin to OHG *sand* true, L *esse* to be] (bef. 12c) **1** *archaic* : TRUE **2** *archaic* : SOFT, SWEET
[2]**sooth** *n* (bef. 12c) **1** : TRUTH, REALITY **2** *obs* : BLANDISHMENT
soothe \ˈsüth\ *vb* **soothed; sooth·ing** [ME *sothen* to verify, fr. OE *sōthian,* fr. *sōth*] *vt* (1657) **1** : to please by or as if by attention or concern : PLACATE **2** : RELIEVE, ALLEVIATE ⟨~ a cough⟩ **3** : to bring comfort, solace, or reassurance to ⟨music ~*s* the soul⟩ ~ *vi* : to bring peace, composure, or quietude — **sooth·er** *n*
sooth·fast \ˈsüth-ˌfast\ *adj* (bef. 12c) **1** *archaic* : TRUE **2** *archaic* : TRUTHFUL
soothing *adj* (1700) : tending to soothe; *also* : having a sedative effect ⟨~ syrup⟩ — **sooth·ing·ly** *adv* — **sooth·ing·ness** *n*
sooth·ly \ˈsüth-lē\ *adv* (bef. 12c) *archaic* : in truth : TRULY
sooth·say·er \-ˌsā-ər, -ˌser\ *n* (14c) : a person who predicts the future by magical, intuitive, or more rational means : PROGNOSTICATOR
sooth·say·ing \-ˌsā-iŋ\ *n* (15c) **1** : the act of foretelling events **2** : PREDICTION, PROPHECY — **sooth·say** \-ˌsā\ *vi*
sooty \ˈsu̇-tē, ˈsə-, ˈsü-\ *adj* **soot·i·er; -est** (13c) **1 a** : of, relating to, or producing soot **b** : soiled with soot **2** : of the color of soot — **soot·i·ly** \-tə-lē\ *adv* — **soot·i·ness** \-tē-nəs\ *n*
sooty mold *n* (1901) : a dark growth of fungus mycelium growing in insect honeydew on plants; *also* : any of various ascomycetous fungi (order Dothideales) producing such growth
sooty tern *n* (1785) : a widely distributed tern (*Sterna fuscata*) of tropical oceans that is blackish above and white below — called also *wideawake*
[1]**sop** \ˈsäp\ *n* [ME *soppe,* fr. OE *sopp;* akin to OE *sūpan* to swallow — more at SUP] (bef. 12c) **1** *chiefly dial* : a piece of food dipped or steeped in a liquid **2** : a conciliatory or propitiatory bribe, gift, or gesture
[2]**sop** *vt* **sopped; sop·ping** (ca. 1529) **1 a** : to steep or dip in or as if in liquid **b** : to wet thoroughly : SOAK **2** : MOP 1
SOP *abbr* standard operating procedure; standing operating procedure
so·pai·pil·la \ˌsō-pī-ˈpē-yə, -ˈpēl-yə\ *or* **so·pa·pil·la** \ˈsō-pə-\ *n* [AmerSp *sopaipilla,* dim. of Sp *sopaipa* fritter soaked in honey, fr. *sopa* food soaked in milk, of Gmc origin; akin to OE *sūpan* to swallow] (ca. 1940) : a usu. puffy piece of deep-fried dough often sweetened with honey
soph *abbr* sophomore
soph·ism \ˈsä-ˌfi-zəm\ *n* (15c) **1** : an argument apparently correct in form but actually invalid; *esp* : such an argument used to deceive **2** : SOPHISTRY 1
soph·ist \ˈsä-fist\ *n* [L *sophista,* fr. Gk *sophistēs,* lit., expert, wise man, fr. *sophizesthai* to become wise, deceive, fr. *sophos* clever, wise] (14c) **1** : PHILOSOPHER **2** *cap* : any of a class of ancient Greek teachers of rhetoric, philosophy, and the art of successful living prominent about the middle of the fifth century B.C. for their adroit subtle and allegedly often specious reasoning **3** : a captious or fallacious reasoner
so·phis·tic \sä-ˈfis-tik, sə-\ *or* **so·phis·ti·cal** \-ti-kəl\ *adj* (15c) **1** : of or relating to sophists, sophistry, or the ancient Sophists ⟨~ rhetoric⟩ ⟨~ subtleties⟩ **2** : plausible but fallacious ⟨~ reasoning⟩ — **so·phis·ti·cal·ly** \-ti-k(ə-)lē\ *adv*
[1]**so·phis·ti·cate** \sə-ˈfis-tə-ˌkāt\ *vt* **-cat·ed; -cat·ing** [ME, fr. ML *sophisticatus,* pp. of *sophisticare,* fr. L *sophisticus* sophistic, fr. Gk *sophistikos,* fr. *sophistēs* sophist] (15c) **1** : to alter deceptively; *esp* : ADULTERATE **2** : to deprive of genuineness, naturalness, or simplicity; *esp* : to deprive of naïveté and make worldly-wise : DISILLUSION **3** : to make complicated or complex
[2]**so·phis·ti·cate** \-ti-kət, -tə-ˌkāt\ *n* (1923) : a sophisticated person
so·phis·ti·cat·ed \-tə-ˌkā-təd\ *adj* [ML *sophisticatus*] (1601) **1** : deprived of native or original simplicity: as **a** : highly complicated or developed : COMPLEX ⟨~ electronic devices⟩ **b** : having a refined knowledge of the ways of the world cultivated esp. through wide experience ⟨a ~ lady⟩ **2** : devoid of grossness: as **a** : finely experienced and aware ⟨a ~ columnist⟩ **b** : intellectually appealing ⟨a ~ novel⟩ — **so·phis·ti·cat·ed·ly** *adv*
syn SOPHISTICATED, WORLDLY-WISE, BLASÉ mean experienced in the ways of the world. SOPHISTICATED often implies refinement, urbanity, cleverness, and cultivation ⟨guests at her salon were usually rich and *sophisticated*⟩. WORLDLY-WISE suggests a close and practical knowledge of the affairs and manners of society and an inclination toward materialism ⟨a *worldly-wise* woman with a philosophy of personal independence⟩. BLASÉ implies a lack of responsiveness to common joys as a result of a real or affected surfeit of experience and cultivation ⟨*blasé* travelers who claimed to have been everywhere⟩.
so·phis·ti·ca·tion \sə-ˌfis-tə-ˈkā-shən\ *n* (15c) **1 a** : the use of sophistry : sophistic reasoning **b** : SOPHISM, QUIBBLE **2** : the process or result of becoming cultured, knowledgeable, or disillusioned; *esp* : CULTIVATION, URBANITY **3** : the process or result of becoming more complex, developed, or subtle
soph·ist·ry \ˈsä-fə-strē\ *n* (14c) **1** : subtly deceptive reasoning or argumentation **2** : SOPHISM 1
[1]**soph·o·more** \ˈsäf-ˌmȯr *also* ˈsȯf- *or* ˈsä-fə- *or* ˈsȯ-fə-\ *n* [perh. fr. Gk *sophos* wise + *mōros* foolish] (1688) : a student in the second year at college or a 4-year secondary school
[2]**sophomore** *adj* (1953) : being or associated with the second in a series ⟨their ~ album⟩
soph·o·mor·ic \ˌsäf-ˈmȯr-ik, -ˈmär- *also* ˌsȯf- *or* ˌsä-fə- *or* ˌsȯ-fə-\ *adj* (1813) **1** : conceited and overconfident of knowledge but poorly in-

formed and immature ⟨a ~ argument⟩ **2 :** of, relating to, or characteristic of a sophomore ⟨~ humor⟩

So·pho·ni·as \ˌsä-fə-ˈnī-əs, ˌsō-\ *n* [LL, fr. Gk, fr. Heb *Sĕphanyāh*] (1535) : ZEPHANIAH

so·phy \ˈsō-fē\ *n* [Pers *Safī*] (1534) *archaic* : a sovereign of Persia

-sophy *n comb form* [F *-sophie,* fr. L *-sophia,* fr. Gk, fr. *sophia* wisdom, fr. *sophos*] : knowledge : wisdom : science ⟨anthropo*sophy*⟩

[1]**sop·o·rif·ic** \ˌsä-pə-ˈri-fik\ *adj* [prob. fr. F *soporifique,* fr. L *sopor* deep sleep; akin to L *somnus* sleep — more at SOMNOLENT] (1665) **1 a :** causing or tending to cause sleep ⟨~ drugs⟩ **b :** tending to dull awareness or alertness **2 :** of, relating to, or marked by sleepiness or lethargy

[2]**soporific** *n* (ca. 1727) : a soporific agent; *specif* : HYPNOTIC 1

sopping *adj* (1877) : wet through : SOAKING

sop·py \ˈsä-pē\ *adj* **sop·pi·er; -est** (1631) **1 :** SENTIMENTAL, MAWKISH **2 a :** soaked through : SATURATED **b :** very wet — **sop·pi·ness** \-nəs\ *n*

so·pra·ni·no \ˌsō-prə-ˈnē-(ˌ)nō, ˌsä-\ *n, pl* **-nos** [It, dim. of *soprano*] (1905) : a musical instrument (as a recorder or saxophone) higher in pitch than the soprano

[1]**so·pra·no** \sə-ˈpra-(ˌ)nō, -ˈprä-\ *adj* [It, adj. & n., fr. *sopra* above, fr. L *supra* — more at SUPRA-] (1730) : relating to or having the range or part of a soprano

[2]**soprano** *n, pl* **-nos** (1738) **1 :** the highest singing voice of women or boys and formerly of castrati; *also* : a person having this voice **2 :** the highest voice part in a 4-part chorus **3 :** a member of a family of instruments having the highest range

so·ra \ˈsȯr-ə\ *n* [origin unknown] (1705) : a small short-billed No. American rail (*Porzana carolina*) common in marshes

sorb \ˈsȯrb\ *vt* [back-formation fr. *absorb & adsorb*] (1909) : to take up and hold by either adsorption or absorption — **sorb·abil·i·ty** \ˌsȯr-bə-ˈbi-lə-tē\ *n* — **sorb·able** \ˈsȯr-bə-bəl\ *adj*

Sorb \ˈsȯrb\ *n* [G *Sorbe,* fr. Sorbian *serbje*] (1843) **1 :** WEND **2 :** WENDISH — **Sor·bi·an** \ˈsȯr-bē-ən\ *adj or n*

sor·bate \ˈsȯr-ˌbāt, ˈsȯr-bət\ *n* (ca. 1823) : a salt or ester of sorbic acid — compare POTASSIUM SORBATE

sor·bent \ˈsȯr-bənt\ *n* [L *sorbent-, sorbens,* prp. of *sorbēre* to suck up — more at ABSORB] (ca. 1856) : a substance that sorbs

sor·bet \sȯr-ˈbā *also* ˈsȯr-bət\ *n* [F, fr. MF, sweetened fruit juice, fr. OIt *sorbetto,* fr. Turk *şerbet* — more at SHERBET] (1864) : a usu. fruit-flavored ice served as a dessert or between courses as a palate refresher

sor·bic acid \ˈsȯr-bik-\ *n* [*sorb* fruit of the service or related trees, fr. F *sorbe,* fr. L *sorbum*] (1815) : a crystalline acid $C_6H_8O_2$ obtained from the unripe fruits of the mountain ash or synthesized and used esp. as a fungicide and food preservative

sor·bi·tol \ˈsȯr-bə-ˌtȯl, -ˌtōl\ *n* [*sorb* fruit of the service or related trees + *-itol*] (1895) : a faintly sweet alcohol $C_6H_{14}O_6$ that occurs in some fruits, is made synthetically, and is used esp. as a humectant and softener and in making ascorbic acid

sor·cer·er \ˈsȯr-sə-rər, ˈsȯrs-rər\ *n* (15c) : a person who practices sorcery : WIZARD

sor·cer·ess \-rəs\ *n* (14c) : a woman who is a sorcerer

sor·cer·ous \-rəs\ *adj* (1546) : of or relating to sorcery : MAGICAL

sor·cery \-rē\ *n* [ME *sorcerie,* fr. AF, fr. *sorcer* sorcerer, fr. ML *sortiarius,* fr. L *sort-, sors* chance, lot — more at SERIES] (14c) **1 :** the use of power gained from the assistance or control of evil spirits esp. for divining : NECROMANCY **2 :** MAGIC 2a

sor·did \ˈsȯr-dəd\ *adj* [L *sordidus,* fr. *sordes* dirt — more at SWART] (1606) **1 :** marked by baseness or grossness : VILE ⟨~ motives⟩ **2 a :** DIRTY, FILTHY **b :** WRETCHED, SQUALID **3 :** meanly avaricious : COVETOUS **4 :** of a dull or muddy color ***syn*** see MEAN — **sor·did·ly** *adv* — **sor·did·ness** *n*

sor·di·no \sȯr-ˈdē-(ˌ)nō\ *n, pl* **-di·ni** \-(ˌ)nē\ [It, fr. *sordo* silent, fr. L *surdus*] (ca. 1801) : MUTE 3

[1]**sore** \ˈsȯr\ *adj* **sor·er; sor·est** [ME *sor,* fr. OE *sār;* akin to OHG *sēr* sore and prob. to OIr *saeth* distress] (bef. 12c) **1 a :** causing pain or distress ⟨a ~ subject⟩ **b :** painfully sensitive : TENDER ⟨~ muscles⟩ **c :** hurt or inflamed so as to be or seem painful ⟨~ runny eyes⟩ ⟨a dog limping on a ~ leg⟩ **2 :** attended by difficulties, hardship, or exertion **3 :** ANGRY, IRKED ⟨a ~ loser⟩ — **sore·ness** *n*

[2]**sore** *n* (bef. 12c) **1 :** a localized sore spot on the body; *esp* : one (as an ulcer) with the tissues ruptured or abraded and usu. with infection **2 :** a source of pain or vexation : AFFLICTION

[3]**sore** *adv* (bef. 12c) : SORELY

sore·head \ˈsȯr-ˌhed\ *n* (1848) : a person easily angered or disgruntled — **sorehead** *or* **sore·head·ed** \-ˈhe-dəd\ *adj*

sore·ly \ˈsȯr-lē\ *adv* (bef. 12c) **1 :** in a sore manner : PAINFULLY **2 :** VERY, EXTREMELY ⟨~ needed changes⟩

sore throat *n* (1629) : pain in the throat due to inflammation of the fauces and pharynx

sor·ghum \ˈsȯr-gəm\ *n* [NL, fr. It *sorgo,* fr. VL *Syricum (granum), lit., Syrian grain] (1597) **1 :** any of an economically important genus (*Sorghum*) of Old World tropical grasses similar to corn in habit but with the spikelets in pairs on a hairy rachis; *esp* : any of various cultivars (as grain sorghum or sorgo) derived from a wild form (*S. bicolor* syn. *S. vulgare*) **2 :** syrup from the juice of a sorgo that resembles cane syrup **3 :** something cloyingly sentimental

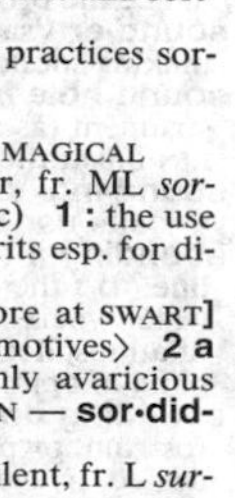

sorghum 1

sor·go \ˈsȯr-(ˌ)gō\ *n* [It] (ca. 1760) : a sorghum cultivated primarily for the sweet juice in its stems from which sugar and syrup are made but also used for fodder and silage — called also *sweet sorghum*

so·ri·tes \sə-ˈrī-(ˌ)tēz\ *n, pl* **sorites** [L, fr. Gk *sōritēs,* fr. *sōros* heap] (1551) : an argument consisting of propositions so arranged that the predicate of any one forms the subject of the next and the conclusion unites the subject of the first proposition with the predicate of the last

So·rop·ti·mist \sə-ˈräp-tə-mist, sȯ-\ *n* [*Soroptimist* (Club)] (1924) : a member of a service club composed of professional women and businesswomen

so·ro·ral \sə-ˈrȯr-əl\ *adj* [L *soror* sister — more at SISTER] (1858) : of, relating to, or characteristic of a sister : SISTERLY

so·ro·rate \sə-ˈrȯr-ət\ *n* [L *soror*] (1910) : the marriage of one man to two or more sisters usu. successively and after the first wife has been found to be barren or after her death

so·ror·i·ty \sə-ˈrȯr-ə-tē, -ˈrär-\ *n, pl* **-ties** [ML *sororitas* sisterhood, fr. L *soror* sister] (1900) : a club of women; *specif* : a women's student organization formed chiefly for social purposes and having a name consisting of Greek letters

sorp·tion \ˈsȯrp-shən\ *n* [back-formation fr. *absorption & adsorption*] (1909) : the process of sorbing : the state of being sorbed — **sorp·tive** \ˈsȯrp-tiv\ *adj*

[1]**sor·rel** \ˈsȯr-əl, ˈsär-\ *n* [ME *sorel,* n. & adj., fr. AF, fr. *sor* red, auburn, prob. of Gmc origin; akin to MD *soor* dry, barren, OE *sēar* dry — more at SERE] (15c) **1 :** a sorrel-colored animal; *esp* : a light bright chestnut horse often with white mane and tail — compare [1]CHESTNUT 4, [2]BAY 1 **2 :** a brownish orange to light brown

[2]**sorrel** *n* [ME *sorel,* fr. AF *surele,* fr. *sur, siur* sour, of Gmc origin; akin to OHG *sūr* sour — more at SOUR] (15c) : any of various plants or plant parts with sour juice: as **a :** any of various docks (as *Rumex acetosa* and *R. acetosella*); *also* : the leaves used as a potherb **b :** WOOD SORREL

sorrel tree *n* (1687) : SOURWOOD

[1]**sor·row** \ˈsär-(ˌ)ō, ˈsȯr-\ *n* [ME *sorow,* fr. OE *sorg;* akin to OHG *sorga* sorrow] (bef. 12c) **1 a :** deep distress, sadness, or regret esp. for the loss of someone or something loved **b :** resultant unhappy or unpleasant state ⟨to their great ~ they could not marry⟩ **2 :** a cause of grief or sadness **3 :** a display of grief or sadness

syn SORROW, GRIEF, ANGUISH, WOE, REGRET mean distress of mind. SORROW implies a sense of loss or a sense of guilt and remorse ⟨a family united in *sorrow* upon the patriarch's death⟩. GRIEF implies poignant sorrow for an immediate cause ⟨the inexpressible *grief* of the bereaved parents⟩. ANGUISH suggests torturing grief or dread ⟨the *anguish* felt by the parents of the kidnapped child⟩. WOE is deep or inconsolable grief or misery ⟨cries of *woe* echoed throughout the bombed city⟩. REGRET implies pain caused by deep disappointment, fruitless longing, or unavailing remorse ⟨nagging *regret* for missed opportunities⟩.

[2]**sorrow** *vi* (bef. 12c) : to feel or express sorrow — **sor·row·er** \ˈsär-ə-wər, ˈsȯr-\ *n*

sor·row·ful \-ō-fəl, -ə-fəl\ *adj* (bef. 12c) **1 :** full of or marked by sorrow ⟨a ~ good-bye⟩ **2 :** expressive of or inducing sorrow ⟨~ eyes⟩ — **sor·row·ful·ly** \-f(ə-)lē\ *adv* — **sor·row·ful·ness** \-fəl-nəs\ *n*

sor·ry \ˈsär-ē, ˈsȯr-\ *adj* **sor·ri·er; -est** [ME *sory,* fr. OE *sārig,* fr. *sār* sore] (bef. 12c) **1 :** feeling sorrow, regret, or penitence **2 :** MOURNFUL, SAD **3 :** inspiring sorrow, pity, scorn, or ridicule : PITIFUL ⟨their affairs were in a ~ state⟩ ***syn*** see CONTEMPTIBLE — **sor·ri·ly** \-ə-lē\ *adv* — **sor·ri·ness** \-ē-nəs\ *n*

[1]**sort** \ˈsȯrt\ *n* [ME, fr. AF, fate, lot, characteristic, fr. L *sort-, sors* lot, share, category — more at SERIES] (14c) **1 a :** a group set up on the basis of any characteristic in common : CLASS, KIND **b :** one approximating the character or qualities of another ⟨a ~ of latter-day Abe Lincoln⟩ **c :** PERSON, INDIVIDUAL ⟨he's not a bad ~⟩ **2** *archaic* : GROUP, COMPANY **3 a** *archaic* : method or manner of acting : WAY, MANNER **b :** CHARACTER, NATURE ⟨people of an evil ~⟩ **4 a :** a letter or character that is one element of a font **b :** a character or piece of type that is not part of a regular font **5 :** an instance of sorting ⟨a numeric ~ of a data file⟩ ***syn*** see TYPE — **after a sort :** in a rough or haphazard way ⟨plays the piano, *after a sort*⟩ — **all sorts of :** many different : all kinds of ⟨knows *all sorts of* people⟩ — **of sorts** *or* **of a sort :** in some respects but not entirely or truly ⟨a vacation *of sorts*⟩ — **out of sorts 1 :** somewhat ill **2 :** GROUCHY, IRRITABLE

[2]**sort** *vt* (14c) **1 a :** to put in a certain place or rank according to kind, class, or nature ⟨~ apples⟩ ⟨~ mail⟩ **b :** to arrange according to characteristics : CLASSIFY — usu. used with *out* ⟨~ out colors⟩ **2** *chiefly Scot* : to put to rights : put in order **3 a :** to examine in order to clarify — used with *out* ⟨~*ing* out his problems⟩ **b :** to free of confusion : CLARIFY — used with *out* ⟨waited until things ~*ed* themselves out⟩ ~ *vi* **1 :** to join or associate with others esp. of the same kind ⟨~ with thieves⟩ **2 :** AGREE, HARMONIZE ⟨his benign view ~*s* badly with reality —Henry Trewhitt⟩ **3 :** SEARCH ⟨~ through some old papers⟩ — **sort·able** \ˈsȯr-tə-bəl\ *adj* — **sort·er** *n*

sor·tie \ˈsȯr-tē, sȯr-ˈtē\ *n* [F, fr. MF, fr. *sortir* to go out, leave] (1778) **1 :** a sudden issuing of troops from a defensive position against the enemy **2 :** one mission or attack by a single plane **3 a :** FORAY, RAID **b :** EXCURSION, EXPEDITION ⟨diving ~*s*⟩ — **sortie** *vi*

sor·ti·lege \ˈsȯr-tə-lij, -ˌlej\ *n* [ME, fr. ML *sortilegium,* fr. L *sortilegus* foretelling, fr. *sort-, sors* lot + *-i-* + *legere* to gather — more at LEGEND] (14c) **1 :** divination by lots **2 :** SORCERY

sor·ti·tion \sȯr-ˈti-shən\ *n* [L *sortition-, sortitio,* fr. *sortiri* to cast or draw lots, fr. *sort-, sors* lot] (1597) : the act or an instance of casting lots

sort of *adv* (1790) : to a moderate degree : SOMEWHAT

so·rus \ˈsȯr-əs\ *n, pl* **so·ri** \ˈsȯr-ˌī, -ˌē\ [NL, fr. Gk *sōros* heap] (1832) : a cluster of plant reproductive bodies: as **a :** a cluster of sporangia on the underside of a fertile fern frond **b :** a mass of spores bursting through the epidermis of the host plant of a parasitic fungus **c :** a cluster of gemmae on the thallus of a lichen

SOS \ˌes-(ˌ)ō-ˈes\ *n* (1910) **1 :** an internationally recognized signal of distress in radio code · · · – – – · · · used esp. by ships calling for help **2 :** a call or request for help or rescue

[1]**so–so** \ˈsō-ˈsō\ *adv* (ca. 1530) : moderately well : TOLERABLY

[2]**so–so** *adj* (1542) : neither very good nor very bad : MIDDLING ⟨a ~ performance⟩

[1]**so·ste·nu·to** \ˌsōs-tə-ˈnü-(ˌ)tō, ˌsȯs-\ *adj or adv* [It, fr. pp. of *sostenere* to sustain, fr. L *sustinēre*] (ca. 1724) : sustained to or beyond the note's full value — used as a direction in music

[2]**sostenuto** *n* (1757) : a movement or passage whose notes are markedly prolonged

sot \ˈsät\ *n* [ME, fool, fr. OE *sott*] (1592) : a habitual drunkard

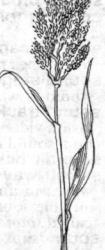

so·te·ri·ol·o·gy \sō-ˌtir-ē-ˈä-lə-jē\ *n* [Gk *sōtērion* salvation (fr. *sōtēr* savior, preserver) + E *-logy* — more at CREOSOTE] (ca. 1774) : theology dealing with salvation esp. as effected by Jesus Christ — **so·te·ri·o·log·i·cal** \-ē-ə-ˈlä-ji-kəl\ *adj*

so that *conj* (bef. 12c) : THAT 2a(1)

So·tho \ˈsō-(ˌ)tō\ *n, pl* **Sotho** *or* **Sothos** (1928) **1 a** : any one of the Sotho languages and esp. Sesotho **b** : a group of closely related Bantu languages of Lesotho, Botswana, and northern So. Africa **2** : a member of a group of southern African peoples whose language is Sotho

so·tol \ˈsō-ˌtōl\ *n* [AmerSp, fr. Nahuatl *zōtōlin* palm tree] (1881) : any of several plants (genus *Dasylirion*) of the agave family of the southwestern U.S. and Mexico that resemble a yucca

sot·tish \ˈsä-tish\ *adj* (1583) : resembling a sot : DRUNKEN; *also* : DOLTISH, STUPID — **sot·tish·ly** *adv* — **sot·tish·ness** *n*

sot·to vo·ce \ˌsä-tō-ˈvō-chē\ *adv or adj* [It *sottovoce*, lit., under the voice] (1737) **1** : under the breath : in an undertone; *also* : in a private manner **2** : very softly — used as a direction in music

sou \ˈsü\ *n, pl* **sous** \ˈsüz\ [F, fr. OF *sol*, fr. LL *solidus* solidus] (1814) **1** : [2]SOL **2** : a 5-centime piece

sou·bise \sü-ˈbēz\ *n* [F, fr. Charles de Rohan, Prince de *Soubise* †1787 Fr. nobleman] (1822) : a garnish or white sauce containing onions or onion purée

sou·brette \sü-ˈbret\ *n* [F, fr. Occitan *soubreto*, fem. of *soubret* coy, fr. *soubra* to surmount, exceed, fr. L *superare* — more at INSUPERABLE] (1753) **1 a** : a coquettish maid or frivolous young woman in comedies **b** : an actress who plays such a part **2** : a soprano who sings supporting roles in comic opera

soubriquet *var of* SOBRIQUET

sou·chong \ˈsü-ˌchȯŋ, -ˌshȯŋ\ *n* [of Chin origin; akin to Chin (Beijing) *xiǎozhǒng*, lit., small sort] (1760) : a tea made from the larger older leaves of the shoot

[1]**souf·flé** \sü-ˈflā, ˈsü-ˌ\ *n* [F, fr. *soufflé*, pp. of *souffler* to blow, puff up, fr. OF *sufler*, fr. L *sufflare*, fr. *sub-* + *flare* to blow — more at BLOW] (1813) : a dish that is made from a sauce, egg yolks, beaten egg whites, and a flavoring or purée (as of seafood, fruit, or vegetables) and baked until puffed up

[2]**soufflé** *or* **souf·fléed** \-ˈflād, -ˌflād\ *adj* (1888) : puffed up by or in cooking

sough \ˈsau̇, ˈsəf\ *vi* [ME *swoughen*, fr. OE *swōgan;* akin to Goth *gaswogjan* to groan, Lith *svagėti* to sound] (bef. 12c) : to make a moaning or sighing sound — **sough** *n*

sought *past and past part of* SEEK

souk *also* **suq** \ˈsük\ *n* [Ar *sūq* market] (1826) : a marketplace in northern Africa or the Middle East; *also* : a stall in such a marketplace

sou·kous \ˈsü-ˌküs\ *n* [African F (of Brazzaville and Kinshasa) *soucous, soukous*, a dance popular in the late 1960s, alter. of F *secousse* jolt, jerk] (1982) : popular guitar-driven dance music created in the Democratic Republic of the Congo under the influence of Cuban rumba

[1]**soul** \ˈsōl\ *n* [ME *soule*, fr. OE *sāwol;* akin to OHG *sēula* soul] (bef. 12c) **1** : the immaterial essence, animating principle, or actuating cause of an individual life **2 a** : the spiritual principle embodied in human beings, all rational and spiritual beings, or the universe **b** *cap, Christian Science* : GOD 1b **3** : a person's total self **4 a** : an active or essential part **b** : a moving spirit : LEADER **5 a** : the moral and emotional nature of human beings **b** : the quality that arouses emotion and sentiment **c** : spiritual or moral force : FERVOR **6** : PERSON ⟨not a ~ in sight⟩ **7** : PERSONIFICATION ⟨she is the ~ of integrity⟩ **8 a** : a strong positive feeling (as of intense sensitivity and emotional fervor) conveyed esp. by black American performers **b** : NEGRITUDE **c** : SOUL MUSIC **d** : SOUL FOOD **e** : SOUL BROTHER

[2]**soul** *adj* (1958) **1** : of, relating to, or characteristic of black Americans or their culture **2** : designed for or controlled by blacks

soul brother *n* (1959) : a black male

souled \ˈsōld\ *adj* (15c) : having a soul : possessing soul and feeling — usu. used in combination ⟨whole-*souled* repentance⟩

soul food *n* (1964) : food (as chitterlings, ham hocks, and collard greens) traditionally eaten by southern black Americans

soul·ful \ˈsōl-fəl\ *adj* (1860) : full of or expressing feeling or emotion ⟨~ music⟩ — **soul·ful·ly** \-fə-lē\ *adv* — **soul·ful·ness** *n*

soul kiss *n* (ca. 1948) : FRENCH KISS

soul·less \ˈsōl-ləs\ *adj* (15c) : having no soul or no greatness or warmth of mind or feeling — **soul·less·ly** *adv* — **soul·less·ness** *n*

soul mate *n* (1822) **1** : a person who is perfectly suited to another in temperament **2** : a person who strongly resembles another in attitudes or beliefs ⟨ideological *soul mates*⟩

soul music *n* (1961) : music that originated in black American gospel singing, is closely related to rhythm and blues, and is characterized by intensity of feeling and earthiness

soul patch *n* (1991) : a small growth of beard under a man's lower lip

soul–search·ing \ˈsōl-ˌsər-chiŋ\ *n* (1924) : examination of one's conscience esp. with regard to motives and values

[1]**sound** \ˈsau̇nd\ *adj* [ME, fr. OE *gesund;* akin to OHG *gisunt* healthy] (13c) **1 a** : free from injury or disease **b** : free from flaw, defect, or decay **2** : SOLID, FIRM; *also* : STABLE **3 a** : free from error, fallacy, or misapprehension ⟨~ reasoning⟩ **b** : exhibiting or based on thorough knowledge and experience ⟨~ scholarship⟩ **c** : legally valid ⟨a ~ title⟩ **d** : logically valid and having true premises **e** : agreeing with accepted views : ORTHODOX **4 a** : THOROUGH **b** : deep and undisturbed ⟨a ~ sleep⟩ **c** : HARD, SEVERE ⟨a ~ whipping⟩ **5** : showing good judgment or sense ⟨~ advice⟩ ***syn*** see HEALTHY, VALID — **sound·ly** \ˈsau̇n(d)-lē\ *adv* — **sound·ness** \ˈsau̇n(d)-nəs\ *n*

[2]**sound** *adv* (14c) : to the full extent : THOROUGHLY ⟨~ asleep⟩

[3]**sound** *n* [ME *soun*, fr. AF *son, sun*, fr. L *sonus*, fr. *sonare* to sound; akin to OE *swinn* melody, Skt *svanati* it sounds] (13c) **1 a** : a particular auditory impression : TONE **b** : the sensation perceived by the sense of hearing **c** : mechanical radiant energy that is transmitted by longitudinal pressure waves in a material medium (as air) and is the objective cause of hearing **2 a** : a speech sound ⟨a peculiar *r-sound*⟩ **b** : value in terms of speech sounds ⟨*-cher* of *teacher* and *-ture* of *creature* have the same ~⟩ **3** *archaic* : RUMOR, FAME **4 a** : meaningless noise **b** *obs* : MEANING **c** : the impression conveyed : IMPORT **5** : hearing distance : EARSHOT ⟨within ~ of your voice⟩ **6** : recorded auditory material **7** : a particular musical style characteristic of an individual, a group, or an area ⟨the Nashville ~⟩

[4]**sound** *vt* (13c) **1 a** : to cause to sound ⟨~ a trumpet⟩ **b** : PRONOUNCE 3a **2** : to put into words : VOICE **3 a** : to make known : PROCLAIM **b** : to order, signal, or indicate by a sound ⟨~ the alarm⟩ **4** : to examine by causing to emit sounds ⟨~ the lungs⟩ **5** *chiefly Brit* : to convey the impression of : sound like ⟨that ~*s* a logical use of resources —*Economist*⟩ ~ *vi* **1 a** : to make a sound **b** : RESOUND **c** : to give a summons by sound ⟨the bugle ~*s* to battle⟩ **2** : to make or convey an impression esp. when heard ⟨it ~*s* good to me⟩ ⟨you ~ just like your mother⟩ — **sound·able** \ˈsau̇n-də-bəl\ *adj*

[5]**sound** *n* [ME, fr. OE *sund* swimming, sea & ON *sund* swimming, strait; akin to OE *swimman* to swim] (14c) **1 a** : a long broad inlet of the ocean generally parallel to the coast **b** : a long passage of water connecting two larger bodies (as a sea with the ocean) or separating a mainland and an island **2** : the air bladder of a fish

[6]**sound** *vb* [ME, fr. MF *sonder*, fr. OF **sonde* sounding line, prob. fr. OE or ME *sund-* (as in OE *sundline* sounding line) fr. *sund* sea] *vt* (15c) **1** : to measure the depth of : FATHOM **2** : to try to find out the views or intentions of : PROBE — often used with *out* **3** : to explore or examine (a body cavity) with a sound ~ *vi* **1 a** : to ascertain the depth of water esp. with a sounding line **b** : to look into or investigate the possibility ⟨sent commissioners . . . to ~ for peace —Thomas Jefferson⟩ **2** : to dive down suddenly — used of a fish or whale

[7]**sound** *n* [F *sonde*, fr. MF, lit., sounding line] (1739) : an elongated instrument for exploring or sounding body cavities

sound·alike \ˈsau̇n-də-ˌlīk\ *n* (1970) : one that sounds like another — **soundalike** *adj*

sound–and–light show *n* (1967) : SON ET LUMIÈRE

sound barrier *n* (1939) : a sudden large increase in aerodynamic drag that occurs as the speed of an aircraft approaches the speed of sound

sound–bite *adj* (1986) : containing or characterized by sound bites ⟨~ politics⟩

sound bite *n* (1972) : a brief recorded statement (as by a public figure) broadcast esp. on a television news program; *also* : a brief catchy comment or saying

sound·board \ˈsau̇n(d)-ˌbȯrd\ *n* (1504) **1** : a thin resonant board (as the belly of a violin) so placed in an instrument as to reinforce its tones by sympathetic vibration — see VIOLIN illustration **2** : SOUNDING BOARD 1a **3** *usu* **sound board** : SOUND CARD

sound bow *n* (1688) : the thick part of a bell against which the clapper strikes

sound box *n* (ca. 1875) **1** : a hollow chamber in a musical instrument for increasing its sonority **2** : a device in an early phonograph for producing sound from a record by using the vibration of a needle to move a diaphragm

sound card *n* (1983) : a circuit board in a computer system designed to produce or reproduce sound

sound effects *n pl* (1909) : effects that are imitative of sounds called for in the script of a dramatic production (as a radio show) and that enhance the production's illusion of reality

sound·er \ˈsau̇n-dər\ *n* (1575) : one that sounds; *specif* : a device for making soundings

sound hole *n* (1611) : an opening in the top surface of a stringed instrument (as a violin) to enhance vibration and resonance — see VIOLIN illustration

[1]**sound·ing** \ˈsau̇n-diŋ\ *adj* (14c) **1** : RESONANT, SONOROUS **2 a** : POMPOUS **b** : IMPOSING — **sound·ing·ly** *adv*

[2]**sounding** *n* (15c) **1 a** : measurement of depth esp. with a sounding line **b** : the depth so ascertained **c** *pl* : a place or part of a body of water where a hand sounding line will reach bottom **2** : measurement of atmospheric conditions at various heights **3** : a probe, test, or sampling of opinion or intention

sounding board *n* (1729) **1 a** : a structure behind or over a pulpit, rostrum, or platform to give distinctness and sonority to sound **b** : a device or agency that helps propagate opinions or utterances **c** : a person or group on whom one tries out an idea or opinion as a means of evaluating it **2** : SOUNDBOARD 1

sounding line *n* (14c) : a line or wire weighted at one end for sounding

sounding rocket *n* (ca. 1945) : a rocket used esp. to obtain information concerning atmospheric conditions at various altitudes

[1]**sound·less** \ˈsau̇n(d)-ləs\ *adj* [[6]*sound*] (ca. 1586) : incapable of being sounded : UNFATHOMABLE

[2]**soundless** *adj* [[3]*sound*] (1601) : making no sound : SILENT — **sound·less·ly** *adv*

sound·man \ˈsau̇n(d)-ˌman\ *n* (1929) : a person who controls the volume and tone of sound picked up by a microphone (as in a recording studio or on a motion-picture set) for recording

sound off *vi* (1909) **1** : to play three chords before and after marching up and down a line of troops during a ceremonial parade or formal guard mount **2** : to count cadence while marching **3 a** : to speak up in a loud voice **b** : to voice one's opinions freely and vigorously

sound pressure *n* (1893) : the difference between the actual pressure at any point in the field of a sound wave at any instant and the average pressure at that point

[1]**sound·proof** \ˈsau̇n(d)-ˌprüf\ *adj* (ca. 1878) : impervious to sound

[2]**soundproof** *vt* (1919) : to insulate so as to obstruct the passage of sound

sound·scape \ˈsau̇n(d)-ˌskāp\ *n* (1964) : a mélange of musical and sometimes nonmusical sounds

sound·stage \ˈsau̇n(d)-ˌstāj\ *n* (1931) : the part of a motion-picture studio in which a production is filmed

sound track *n* (1928) **1** : a track (as on a motion-picture film or television videotape) that carries the sound record **2** : the sound recorded on a sound track; *esp* : the music on a sound track

sound truck *n* (1936) : a truck equipped with a loudspeaker

sound wave *n* (1848) **1** : [3]SOUND 1a **2** *pl* : longitudinal pressure waves in any material medium regardless of whether they constitute audible sound ⟨earthquake waves and ultrasonic waves are sometimes called *sound waves*⟩

soup \ˈsüp\ *n* [ME *soupe*, fr. AF *supe* sop, soup, of Gmc origin; akin to ON *soppa* soup, OE *sopp* — more at SUP] (14c) **1** : a liquid food esp. with a meat, fish, or vegetable stock as a base and often containing pieces of solid food **2** : something (as a heavy fog or nitroglycerine) having or suggesting the consistency or nutrient qualities of soup **3** : an unfortunate predicament ⟨that stunt landed her in the ~⟩

soup·çon \süp-ˈsōⁿ, ˈsüp-ˌsän\ *n* [F, lit., suspicion, fr. OF *sospeçon,* fr. L *suspection-, suspectio,* fr. L *suspicere* to suspect — more at SUSPECT] (1766) **:** a little bit **:** TRACE ⟨a ~ of suspicion⟩

soup du jour \ˌsüp-də-ˈzhu̇r\ *n* [part trans. of F *soupe du jour* soup of the day] (ca. 1945) **:** a soup offered by a restaurant on a particular day

souped–up \ˈsüpt-ˈəp\ *adj* (1931) **:** enhanced or increased in appeal, power, performance, or intensity; *also* **:** ELABORATE, EMBELLISHED

soup kitchen *n* (1831) **:** an establishment dispensing minimum dietary essentials (as soup and bread) to the needy

soup·spoon \ˈsüp-ˌspün\ *n* (1705) **:** a spoon with a large or rounded bowl for eating soup

soup up *vt* [*soup* (drug injected into a racehorse to improve its performance)] (ca. 1933) **:** to increase the power or efficiency of ⟨*soup up* an engine⟩

soupy \ˈsü-pē\ *adj* **soup·i·er; -est** (1869) **1 :** having the consistency of soup **2 :** densely foggy or cloudy **3 :** overly sentimental

[1]**sour** \ˈsau̇(-ə)r\ *adj* [ME, fr. OE *sūr;* akin to OHG *sūr* sour, Lith *sūrus* salty] (bef. 12c) **1 :** causing or characterized by the one of the four basic taste sensations that is produced chiefly by acids ⟨~ pickles⟩ — compare BITTER, SALT, SWEET **2 a** (1) **:** having the acid taste or smell of or as if of fermentation **:** TURNED ⟨~ milk⟩ (2) **:** of or relating to fermentation **b :** smelling or tasting of decay **:** RANCID, ROTTEN ⟨~ breath⟩ **c** (1) **:** BAD, WRONG ⟨a project gone ~⟩ (2) **:** HOSTILE, DISENCHANTED ⟨went ~ on Marxism⟩ **3 a :** UNPLEASANT, DISTASTEFUL **b :** CROSS, SULLEN **c :** not up to the usual, expected, or standard quality or pitch **4 :** acid in reaction — used esp. of soil **5 :** containing malodorous sulfur compounds — used esp. of petroleum products — **sour·ish** \ˈsau̇(-ə)r-ish\ *adj* — **sour·ly** *adv* — **sour·ness** *n*

[2]**sour** *n* (bef. 12c) **1 a :** something sour **b :** the primary taste sensation produced by acid stimuli **2 :** a cocktail consisting of a liquor (as whiskey), lemon or lime juice, sugar, and sometimes ice

[3]**sour** *vi* (14c) **:** to become sour ~ *vt* **:** to make sour

sour ball *n* (ca. 1909) **:** a spherical hard candy having a tart flavor

[1]**source** \ˈsȯrs\ *n* [ME *sours,* fr. AF *surse* spring, source, fr. pp. of *surdre* to rise, spring forth, fr. L *surgere* — more at SURGE] (14c) **1 a :** a generative force **:** CAUSE **b** (1) **:** a point of origin or procurement **:** BEGINNING (2) **:** one that initiates **:** AUTHOR; *also* **:** PROTOTYPE, MODEL (3) **:** one that supplies information **2 a :** the point of origin of a stream of water **:** FOUNTAINHEAD **b** *archaic* **:** SPRING, FOUNT **3 :** a firsthand document or primary reference work **4 :** an electrode in a field-effect transistor that supplies the charge carriers for current flow — compare DRAIN, GATE ***syn*** see ORIGIN — **source·less** \-ləs\ *adj*

[2]**source** *vt* **sourced; sourc·ing** (1957) **1 :** to specify the source of (as quoted material) **2 :** to obtain from a source ⟨metals *sourced* from abroad⟩

[3]**source** *adj* (1959) **:** of, relating to, or being source code ⟨a ~ file⟩

source·book \-ˌbu̇k\ *n* (1899) **:** a fundamental document or record (as of history, literature, art, or religion) on which subsequent writings, compositions, opinions, beliefs, or practices are based; *also* **:** a collection of such documents

source code *n* (1965) **:** a computer program in its original programming language (as FORTRAN or C) before translation into object code usu. by a compiler

source language *n* (1953) **:** a language which is to be translated into another language — compare TARGET LANGUAGE

sour cherry *n* (ca. 1884) **:** a widely cultivated cherry (*Prunus cerasus*) that has a round crown and bright red to almost black soft-fleshed acid fruits; *also* **:** the fruit

sour cream *n* (1776) **:** a soured cream product produced by the action of lactobacilli

sour·dough \ˈsau̇(-ə)r-ˌdō, *1 is also* -ˈdō\ *n* (14c) **1 :** a leaven consisting of dough in which fermentation is active **2** [fr. the use of sourdough for making bread in prospectors' camps] **:** a veteran inhabitant and esp. an old-time prospector of Alaska or northwestern Canada

sour grapes *n pl* [fr. the fable ascribed to Aesop of the fox who after finding himself unable to reach some grapes he had desired disparaged them as sour] (1760) **:** disparagement of something that has proven unattainable ⟨his criticisms are just *sour grapes*⟩

sour grass *n* (1855) **:** SORREL

sour gum *n* (1749) **:** BLACK GUM

sour mash *n* (1877) **:** grain mash for brewing or distilling whose initial acidity has been adjusted to optimum condition for yeast fermentation by mash from a previous run

sour orange *n* (1748) **:** a citrus tree (*Citrus aurantium*) that is used esp. as a stock in grafting citrus; *also* **:** its bitter fruit — called also *bitter orange*

sour·puss \ˈsau̇(-ə)r-ˌpu̇s\ *n* [[2]*puss*] (1930) **:** GROUCH, KILLJOY

sour·sop \ˈsau̇(-ə)r-ˌsäp\ *n* (1667) **:** a small tropical American tree (*Annona muricata*) of the custard-apple family that has spicy odoriferous leaves; *also* **:** its large edible fruit that has fleshy spines and a slightly acid fibrous pulp

sour·wood \-ˌwu̇d\ *n* (1709) **:** a small U.S. tree (*Oxydendrum arboreum*) of the heath family with white flowers and sour-tasting leaves

sous \ˈsü\ *adj* [F, prep., lit., under, fr. OF *suz,* fr. L *subtus,* adv., below, under; akin to L *sub* under — more at UP] (1687) **:** being an assistant — used chiefly in titles ⟨a *sous*-chef⟩

sou·sa·phone \ˈsü-zə-ˌfōn, -sə-\ *n* [John Philip *Sousa*] (1925) **:** a large circular tuba that has a flared adjustable bell — compare HELICON

[1]**souse** \ˈsau̇s\ *vb* **soused; sous·ing** [ME, fr. AF *suz, souce* pickling juice, of Gmc origin; akin to OHG *sulza* brine, OE *sealt* salt] *vt* (14c) **1 :** PICKLE **2 a :** to plunge in liquid **:** IMMERSE **b :** DRENCH, SATURATE **3 :** to make drunk ~ *vi* **:** to become immersed or drenched

[2]**souse** *n* (14c) **1 :** something pickled; *esp* **:** seasoned and chopped pork trimmings, fish, or shellfish **2 :** an act of sousing **:** WETTING **3 a :** a habitual drunkard **b :** a drinking spree **:** BINGE

[3]**souse** *vb* **soused; sous·ing** [ME *souce,* n., start of a bird's flight, alter. of *sours,* prob. fr. AF *surse* source — more at SOURCE] *vi* (1567) *archaic* **:** to swoop down **:** PLUNGE ~ *vt, archaic* **:** to swoop down on

sous vide \ˌsü-ˈvēd\ *adj or adv* [F, lit., under vacuum] (1986) **:** relating to or denoting a method of cooking food slowly in a vacuum-sealed pouch at a low temperature so as to retain most of the juice and aroma

sou·tache \sü-ˈtash\ *n* [F, fr. Hung *sujtás*] (1848) **:** a narrow braid with herringbone pattern used as trimming

sou·tane \sü-ˈtän, -ˈtan\ *n* [F, fr. It *sottana,* lit., undergarment, fr. fem. of *sottano* being underneath, fr. ML *subtanus,* fr. L *subtus* underneath — more at SOUS] (1838) **:** CASSOCK

[1]**south** \ˈsau̇th\ *adv* [ME, fr. OE *sūth;* akin to OHG *sund-* south and prob. to OE *sunne* sun] (bef. 12c) **1 :** to, toward, or in the south ⟨a house facing ~⟩ **2 :** into a state of decline or ruin ⟨causes the sluggish economy to go ~ —G. F. Will⟩

[2]**south** *adj* (12c) **1 :** situated toward or at the south ⟨the ~ entrance⟩ **2 :** coming from the south ⟨a ~ wind⟩

[3]**south** *n* (13c) **1 a :** the direction of the south terrestrial pole **:** the direction to the right of one facing east **b :** the compass point directly opposite to north **2** *cap* **:** regions or countries lying to the south of a specified or implied point of orientation; *esp* **:** the southeastern part of the U.S. **3 :** the right side of a church looking toward the altar from the nave **4** *often cap* **a :** the one of four positions at 90-degree intervals that lies to the south or at the bottom of a diagram **b :** a person (as a bridge player) occupying this position in the course of a specified activity; *specif* **:** the declarer in bridge **5** *often cap* **:** the developing nations of the world **:** THIRD WORLD 3 — compare NORTH 2b

South African *n* (1806) **1 :** a native or inhabitant of the Republic of South Africa **2 :** AFRIKANER — **South African** *adj*

south·bound \ˈsau̇th-ˌbau̇nd\ *adj* (1655) **:** traveling or heading south

south by east (1613) **:** a compass point that is one point east of due south **:** S11°15′E

south by west (1613) **:** a compass point that is one point west of due south **:** S11°15′W

South Dev·on \-ˈde-vən\ *n* [*Devon,* England] (1897) **:** any of a breed of large red cattle of English origin formerly bred for both milk and meat but now increasingly specialized for beef production

South·down \ˈsau̇th-ˌdau̇n\ *n* [*South Downs,* England] (1787) **:** any of a breed of small medium-wooled hornless sheep of English origin

[1]**south·east** \sau̇th-ˈēst, *naut* sau̇-ˈēst\ *adv* (bef. 12c) **:** to, toward, or in the southeast

[2]**southeast** *n* (14c) **1 a :** the general direction between south and east **b :** the point midway between the south and east compass points **2** *cap* **:** regions or countries lying to the southeast of a specified or implied point of orientation

[3]**southeast** *adj* (14c) **1 :** coming from the southeast ⟨a ~ wind⟩ **2 :** situated toward or at the southeast ⟨the ~ corner⟩

southeast by east (ca. 1599) **:** a compass point that is one point east of due southeast **:** S56°15′E

southeast by south (1613) **:** a compass point that is one point south of due southeast **:** S33°45′E

south·east·er \sau̇th-ˈē-stər, sau̇-ˈē-\ *n* (1753) **1 :** a strong southeast wind **2 :** a storm with southeast winds

south·east·er·ly \-stər-lē\ *adv or adj* [[2]*southeast* + *-erly* (as in *easterly*)] (1613) **1 :** from the southeast **2 :** toward the southeast

south·east·ern \-stərn\ *adj* [[2]*southeast* + *-ern* (as in *eastern*)] (1577) **1** *often cap* **:** of, relating to, or characteristic of a region conventionally designated southeast **2 :** lying toward or coming from the southeast — **south·east·ern·most** \-ˌmōst\ *adj*

South·east·ern·er \-stə(r)-nər\ *n* (1919) **:** a native or inhabitant of the Southeast; *esp* **:** a native or resident of the southeastern part of the U.S.

[1]**south·east·ward** \sau̇th-ˈēs-twərd, sau̇-ˈēs-\ *adv or adj* (1528) **:** toward the southeast — **south·east·wards** \-twərdz\ *adv*

[2]**southeastward** *n* (1555) **:** SOUTHEAST

[1]**south·er·ly** \ˈsə-t͟hər-lē\ *adj or adv* [[3]*south* + *-erly* (as in *easterly*)] (1551) **1 :** situated toward or belonging to the south ⟨the ~ shore of the lake⟩ **2 :** coming from the south ⟨a ~ wind⟩

[2]**southerly** *n, pl* **-lies** (1943) **:** a wind from the south

south·ern \ˈsə-t͟hərn\ *adj* [ME *southern, southren,* fr. OE *sūtherne;* akin to OHG *sundrōni* southern, OE *sūth* south] (bef. 12c) **1** *cap* **:** of, relating to, or characteristic of a region conventionally designated South **2 a :** lying toward the south **b :** coming from the south ⟨a ~ wind⟩ — **south·ern·most** \-ˌmōst\ *adj* — **south·ern·ness** \-t͟hərn-nəs\ *n, often cap*

Southern *n* (1935) **:** the dialect of English spoken in most of the Chesapeake Bay area, the coastal plain and the greater part of the upland plateau in Virginia, No. Carolina, So. Carolina, and Georgia, and the Gulf states at least as far west as the valley of the Brazos in Texas and sometimes taken to include the south Midland area

Southern blot *n* [Edwin M. *Southern* b1938 Brit. biologist] (1979) **:** a blot consisting of a nitrocellulose or nylon sheet containing spots of DNA for identification by a suitable molecular probe — compare WESTERN BLOT — **Southern blotting** *n*

southern corn rootworm *n* (1918) **:** SPOTTED CUCUMBER BEETLE

Southern Cross *n* (1681) **:** four bright stars in the southern hemisphere that are situated as if at the extremities of a Latin cross; *also* **:** the constellation of which these four stars are the brightest

Southern English *n* (14c) **1 :** the English spoken esp. by cultivated people native to or educated in the South of England **2 :** SOUTHERN

South·ern·er \ˈsə-t͟hə(r)-nər\ *n* (1827) **:** a native or inhabitant of the South; *esp* **:** a native or resident of the southern part of the U.S.

southern hemisphere *n, often cap S&H* (ca. 1771) **:** the part of the earth that lies south of the equator

South·ern·ism \ˈsə-t͟hər-ˌni-zəm\ *n* (1861) **1 :** an attitude or trait characteristic of the South or Southerners esp. in the U.S. **2 :** a locution or pronunciation characteristic of the southern U.S.

southern lights *n pl* (1775) **:** AURORA AUSTRALIS

south·ern·wood \ˈsə-t͟hərn-ˌwu̇d\ *n* (bef. 12c) **:** a shrubby fragrant European wormwood (*Artemisia abrotanum*) with bitter foliage

south·ing \ˈsau̇-thiŋ, -t͟hiŋ\ *n* (1669) **1 :** difference in latitude to the south from the last preceding point of reckoning **2 :** southerly progress

south·land \ˈsau̇th-ˌland, -lənd\ *n, often cap* (bef. 12c) **:** land in the south **:** the south of a country

south·paw \-ˌpȯ\ *n* (1870) **:** LEFT-HANDER; *esp* **:** a left-handed baseball pitcher — **southpaw** *adj*

\ə\ abut \ᵊ\ kitten, F table \ər\ **further** \a\ **ash** \ā\ **ace** \ä\ **mop, mar**
\au̇\ **out** \ch\ **chin** \e\ **bet** \ē\ **easy** \g\ **go** \i\ **hit** \ī\ **ice** \j\ **job**
\ŋ\ **sing** \ō\ **go** \ȯ\ **law** \ȯi\ **boy** \th\ **thin** \t͟h\ **the** \ü\ **loot** \u̇\ **foot**
\y\ **yet** \zh\ **vision, beige** \k, ⁿ, œ, ue, ʸ\ *see* Guide to Pronunciation

south pole *n* (14c) **1 a** *often cap S&P* **:** the southernmost point of the earth **b :** the zenith of the heavens as viewed from the south terrestrial pole **2** *of a magnet* **:** the pole that points toward the south
[1]**South·ron** \ˈsəth-rən\ *adj* [ME (Sc)] (15c) *chiefly Scot* **:** SOUTHERN; *specif* **:** ENGLISH
[2]**Southron** *n* (15c) **:** SOUTHERNER: as **a** *chiefly Scot* **:** ENGLISHMAN **b** *chiefly Southern* **:** a native or inhabitant of the southern U.S.
south–seeking pole *n* (ca. 1922) **:** SOUTH POLE 2
south–southeast *n* (15c) **:** a compass point that is two points east of due south **:** S22°30′E
south–southwest *n* (1513) **:** a compass point that is two points west of due south **:** S22°30′W
[1]**south·ward** \ˈsau̇th-wərd\ *adv or adj* (bef. 12c) **:** toward the south — **south·wards** \-wərdz\ *adv*
[2]**southward** *n* (14c) **:** southward direction or part ⟨sail to the ~⟩
[1]**south·west** \sau̇th-ˈwest, *naut* sau̇-ˈwest\ *adv* (bef. 12c) **:** to, toward, or in the southwest
[2]**southwest** *n* (12c) **1 a :** the general direction between south and west **b :** the point midway between the south and west compass points **2** *cap* **:** regions or countries lying to the southwest of a specified or implied point of orientation
[3]**southwest** *adj* (14c) **1 :** coming from the southwest ⟨a ~ wind⟩ **2 :** situated toward or at the southwest ⟨the ~ corner⟩
southwest by south (1613) **:** a compass point that is one point south of due southwest **:** S33°45′W
southwest by west (1613) **:** a compass point that is one point west of due southwest **:** S56°15′W
south·west·er \sau̇(th)-ˈwes-tər\ *n* (1833) **1 :** a strong southwest wind **2 :** a storm with southwest winds
south·west·er·ly \-tər-lē\ *adv or adj* [[2]*southwest* + *-erly* (as in *westerly*)] (1708) **1 :** from the southwest **2 :** toward the southwest
south·west·ern \-tərn\ *adj* [ME, fr. OE *sūth-westerne,* fr. *sūth* south + *westerne* western] (bef. 12c) **1 :** lying toward or coming from the southwest **2** *often cap* **:** of, relating to, or characteristic of a region conventionally designated Southwest — **south·west·ern·most** \-ˌmōst\ *adj*
southwestern corn borer *n* (1943) **:** a pyralid moth (*Diatraea grandiosella*) whose larva causes serious damage esp. to corn crops by boring in the stalks
South·west·ern·er \sau̇(th)-ˈwes-tə(r)-nər\ *n* (1860) **:** a native or inhabitant of the Southwest; *esp* **:** a native or resident of the southwestern U.S.
[1]**south·west·ward** \sau̇(th)-ˈwes-twərd\ *adv or adj* (1548) **:** toward the southwest — **south·west·wards** \-twərdz\ *adv*
[2]**southwestward** *n* (1775) **:** SOUTHWEST
sou·ve·nir \ˈsü-və-ˌnir, ˌsü-və-ˈ\ *n* [F, lit., act of remembering, fr. MF, fr. (*se*) *souvenir* to remember, fr. L *subvenire* to come up, come to mind — more at SUBVENTION] (1782) **:** something that serves as a reminder
souvenir sheet *n* (1940) **:** a block or set of postage stamps or a single stamp printed on a single sheet of paper often without gum or perforations and with margins containing lettering or design that identifies some notable event being commemorated
sou·vla·ki \süv-ˈlä-kē\ *also* **sou·vla·kia** \-kē-ə\ *n* [ModGk *soublakia,* pl. of *soublaki,* fr. dim. of *soubla* skewer, fr. MGk, fr. L *subula* awl, fr. *suere* to sew — more at SEW] (1942) **:** SHISH KEBAB
sou'·west·er \sau̇-ˈwes-tər\ *n* (1837) **1 :** a long oilskin coat worn esp. at sea during stormy weather **2 :** a waterproof hat with wide slanting brim longer in back than in front

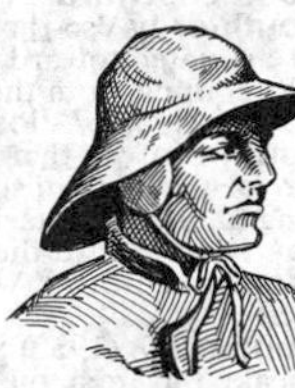

sou'wester 2

[1]**sov·er·eign** *also* **sov·ran** \ˈsä-v(ə-)rən, -vərn *also* ˈsə-\ *n* [ME *soverain,* fr. AF *soverein,* fr. *soverein,* adj.] (13c) **1 a :** one possessing or held to possess sovereignty **b :** one that exercises supreme authority within a limited sphere **c :** an acknowledged leader **:** ARBITER **2 :** any of various gold coins of the United Kingdom
[2]**sovereign** *also* **sovran** *adj* [ME *soverain,* fr. AF *soverein,* fr. VL **superanus,* fr. L *super* over, above — more at OVER] (14c) **1 a :** superlative in quality **:** EXCELLENT **b :** of the most exalted kind **:** SUPREME ⟨~ virtue⟩ **c :** having generalized curative powers ⟨a ~ remedy⟩ **d :** of an unqualified nature **:** UNMITIGATED ⟨~ contempt⟩ **e :** having undisputed ascendancy **:** PARAMOUNT **2 a :** possessed of supreme power ⟨a ~ ruler⟩ **b :** unlimited in extent **:** ABSOLUTE **c :** enjoying autonomy **:** INDEPENDENT ⟨~ states⟩ **3 :** relating to, characteristic of, or befitting a sovereign ***syn*** see FREE — **sov·er·eign·ly** *adv*
sov·er·eign·ty *also* **sov·ran·ty** \-tē\ *n, pl* **-ties** [ME *soverainte,* fr. AF *sovereinté,* fr. *soverein*] (14c) **1** *obs* **:** supreme excellence or an example of it **2 a :** supreme power esp. over a body politic **b :** freedom from external control **:** AUTONOMY **c :** controlling influence **3 :** one that is sovereign; *esp* **:** an autonomous state
so·vi·et \ˈsō-vē-ˌet, ˈsä-, -vē-ət\ *n* [Russ *sovet* council, soviet] (1917) **1 :** an elected governmental council in a Communist country **2** *pl, cap* **a :** BOLSHEVIKS **b :** the people and esp. the political and military leaders of the U.S.S.R. — **soviet** *adj, often cap* — **so·vi·et·ism** \-vē-ə-ˌtizəm\ *n, often cap*
so·vi·et·ize \ˈsō-vē-ˌe-ˌtīz, ˈsä-, -vē-ə-\ *vt* **-ized; -iz·ing** *often cap* (1919) **1 :** to bring under Soviet control **2 :** to force into conformity with Soviet cultural patterns or governmental policies — **so·vi·et·i·za·tion** \ˌsō-vē-ˌe-tə-ˈzā-shən, -vē-ə-\ *n, often cap*
So·vi·et·ol·o·gist \ˌsō-vē-ˌe-ˈtä-lə-jist, ˌsä-, -vē-ə-\ *n* (1955) **:** a specialist in the policies and practices of the Soviet government **:** KREMLINOLOGIST — **So·vi·et·ol·o·gy** \-lə-jē\ *n*
sov·khoz \säf-ˈkȯz, -ˈkȯs\ *n, pl* **sov·kho·zy** \-ˈkȯ-zē\ *or* **sov·khoz·es** [Russ, short for *sovetskoe khozyaĭstvo* soviet farm] (1921) **:** a state-owned farm of the U.S.S.R. paying wages to the workers
[1]**sow** \ˈsau̇\ *n* [ME *sowe,* fr. OE *sugu;* akin to OE & OHG *sū* sow, L *sus* pig, swine, hog, Gk *hys*] (bef. 12c) **1 :** an adult female swine; *also* **:** the adult female of various other animals (as a bear) **2 a :** a channel that conducts molten metal to molds **b :** a mass of metal solidified in such a mold **:** INGOT
[2]**sow** \ˈsō\ *vb* **sowed; sown** \ˈsōn\ *or* **sowed; sow·ing** [ME, fr. OE *sāwan;* akin to OHG *sāwen* to sow, L *serere,* Lith *sėti*] *vi* (bef. 12c) **1 :** to plant seed for growth esp. by scattering **2 :** to set something in motion **:** begin an enterprise ~ *vt* **1 a :** to scatter (as seed) upon the earth for growth; *broadly* **:** PLANT 1a **b :** to strew with or as if with seed **c :** to introduce into a selected environment **:** IMPLANT **2 :** to set in motion **:** FOMENT ⟨~ suspicion⟩ **3 :** to spread abroad **:** DISPERSE — **sow·er** \ˈsō(-ə)r\ *n*
sow·bel·ly \ˈsau̇-ˌbe-lē\ *n* (1867) **:** fat salt pork or bacon
sow bug \ˈsau̇-\ *n* (1750) **:** WOOD LOUSE; *esp* **:** a wood louse capable of curling itself into a ball
sow·ens \ˈsü-ənz, ˈsō-\ *n pl but sing or pl in constr* [ScGael *sùghan*] (1582) **:** porridge from oat husks and siftings
sow thistle \ˈsau̇-\ *n* (13c) **:** any of a genus (*Sonchus*) of spiny weedy Eurasian and African composite herbs including some (as *S. arvensis* and *S. oleraceus*) widely naturalized in No. America
sox *pl of* SOCK
SO$_x$ *symbol* sulfur oxide
soy \ˈsȯi\ *n* [Jp *shōyu*] (1679) **1 :** a brown liquid sauce made by subjecting beans (as soybeans) to long fermentation and to digestion in brine **2** *also* **soya** \ˈsȯi-ə\ **:** SOYBEAN
soy·bean \ˈsȯi-ˌbēn\ *also* **soya bean** \ˈsȯi-ə-\ *n* (1802) **:** a hairy annual Asian legume (*Glycine max*) widely grown for its oil-rich proteinaceous seeds and for forage and soil improvement; *also* **:** its seed
soybean oil *n* (1904) **:** a pale yellow drying or semidrying oil that is obtained from soybeans and is used chiefly as a food, in paints, varnishes, linoleum, printing ink, and soap, and as a source of phospholipids, fatty acids, and sterols — called also *soya oil*
soz·zled \ˈsä-zəld\ *adj* [*sozzle* to splash, intoxicate, alter. of *sossle,* prob. freq. of Brit. dial. *soss* to mess] (ca. 1880) **:** DRUNK, INTOXICATED
sp *abbr* **1** special **2** species **3** specific **4** spelling
Sp *abbr* Spain; Spanish
SP *abbr* **1** shore patrol; shore patrolman; shore police **2** specialist
spa \ˈspä, ˈspȯ\ *n* [*Spa,* watering place in Belgium] (1610) **1 a :** a mineral spring **b :** a resort with mineral springs **2 :** a fashionable resort or hotel **3** *NewEng* **:** SODA FOUNTAIN **4 :** a commercial establishment providing facilities devoted esp. to health, fitness, weight loss, beauty, and relaxation **5 :** a hot tub with a whirlpool device
[1]**space** \ˈspās\ *n, often attrib* [ME, fr. AF *espace, space,* fr. L *spatium* area, room, interval of space or time] (14c) **1 :** a period of time; *also* **:** its duration **2 a :** a limited extent in one, two, or three dimensions **:** DISTANCE, AREA, VOLUME **b :** an extent set apart or available ⟨parking ~⟩ ⟨floor ~⟩ **c :** the distance from other people or things that a person needs in order to remain comfortable ⟨invading my personal ~⟩ **3 :** one of the degrees between or above or below the lines of a musical staff — compare LINE **4 a :** a boundless three-dimensional extent in which objects and events occur and have relative position and direction ⟨infinite ~ and time⟩ **b :** physical space independent of what occupies it — called also *absolute space* **5 :** the region beyond the earth's atmosphere or beyond the solar system **6 a :** a blank area separating words or lines **b :** material used to produce such blank area; *esp* **:** a piece of type less than one en in width **7 :** a set of mathematical elements and esp. of abstractions of all the points on a line, in a plane, or in physical space; *esp* **:** a set of mathematical entities with a set of axioms of geometric character — compare METRIC SPACE, TOPOLOGICAL SPACE, VECTOR SPACE **8 a :** LINAGE **b :** broadcast time available esp. to advertisers **9 :** accommodations on a public vehicle **10 a :** the opportunity to assert or experience one's identity or needs freely **b :** an opportunity for privacy or time to oneself
[2]**space** *vb* **spaced; spac·ing** *vt* (1703) **:** to place at intervals or arrange with space between — often used with *out* ~ *vi* **:** to leave one or more blank spaces (as in a line of typing) — **spac·er** *n*
space–age \ˈspās-ˈāj\ *adj* (1946) **:** of, relating to, or befitting the age of space exploration; *esp* **:** MODERN ⟨~ technology⟩
space cadet *n* (1973) **:** a flaky, lightheaded, or forgetful person
space charge *n* (1913) **:** an electric charge distributed throughout a three-dimensional region
space·craft \ˈspās-ˌkraft\ *n* (1930) **:** a vehicle or device designed for travel or operation outside the earth's atmosphere
spaced–out \ˌspāst-ˈau̇t\ *adj* (1937) **1** *or* **spaced** \ˈspāst\ **:** dazed or stupefied by or as if by a narcotic substance **:** HIGH **2 :** of very strange character **:** WEIRD ⟨a ~ fantasy⟩
space·far·ing \ˈspās-ˌfer-iŋ\ *adj* [[1]*space* + *seafaring*] (1962) **:** having vehicles capable of traveling beyond the earth's atmosphere ⟨~ nations⟩
space·flight \ˈspās-ˌflīt\ *n* (1931) **:** flight beyond the earth's atmosphere
space frame *n* (1912) **:** a usu. open three-dimensional framework of struts and braces (as in buildings and racing cars) which defines a structure and distributes its weight evenly in all directions
space heater *n* (1925) **:** a usu. portable appliance for heating a relatively small area
space heating *n* (1934) **:** heating of spaces esp. for human comfort by any means (as fuel, electricity, or solar radiation) with the heater either within the space or external to it
space lattice *n* (1895) **:** LATTICE 2
space·less \ˈspās-ləs\ *adj* (1606) **1 :** having no limits **:** BOUNDLESS **2 :** occupying no space
space·man \ˈspās-ˌman, -mən\ *n* (1938) **1 :** one who travels outside the earth's atmosphere **2 :** a visitor to earth from outer space
space mark *n* (ca. 1890) **:** the symbol #
space medicine *n* (1949) **:** a branch of medicine that deals with the physiological and biological effects on the human body of spaceflight
space opera *n* (1949) **:** a futuristic melodramatic fantasy involving space travelers and extraterrestrial beings
space out *vi* (1970) **:** to become inattentive, distracted, or mentally remote ⟨*spaced out* halfway through the lecture⟩
space·port \ˈspās-ˌpȯrt\ *n* (1935) **:** an installation for testing and launching spacecraft
space·ship \-ˌship\ *n* (1894) **:** a vehicle used for space travel
space shuttle *n* (1969) **:** a reusable spacecraft designed to transport people and cargo between earth and space
space station *n* (1936) **:** a large artificial satellite designed to be occupied for long periods and to serve as a base (as for scientific observation) — called also *space platform*
space suit *n* (1929) **1 :** a suit equipped with life supporting provisions to make life in space possible for its wearer **2 :** G SUIT

space–time \ˈspās-ˈtīm, ˈspās-ˌ\ *n* (1915) **1 :** a system of one temporal and three spatial coordinates by which any physical object or event can be located — called also *space-time continuum* **2 :** the whole or a portion of physical reality determinable by a usu. four-dimensional coordinate system; *also* **:** the properties characteristic of such an order
space walk *n* (1965) **:** a period of activity spent outside a spacecraft by an astronaut in space — **space•walk** \ˈspās-ˌwȯk\ *vi* — **space•walker** \-ˌwȯ-kər\ *n*
space•ward \ˈspās-wərd\ *adv* (1958) **:** toward space
spac•ey *also* **spacy** \ˈspā-sē\ *adj* **spac•i•er; -est** (1970) **:** SPACED-OUT
spacial *var of* SPATIAL
spacing *n* (1683) **1 a :** the act of providing with spaces or placing at intervals **b :** an arrangement in space **2 a :** a limited extent **:** SPACE **b :** the distance between any two objects in a usu. regularly arranged series
spa•cious \ˈspā-shəs\ *adj* [ME, fr. AF *spacioux,* fr. L *spatiosus,* fr. *spatium* space, room] (14c) **1 :** vast or ample in extent **:** ROOMY ⟨a ~ residence⟩ **2 :** large or magnificent in scale **:** EXPANSIVE ⟨a more ~ and stimulating existence than the farm could offer —H. L. Mencken⟩ — **spa•cious•ly** *adv* — **spa•cious•ness** *n*
syn SPACIOUS, COMMODIOUS, CAPACIOUS, AMPLE mean larger in extent or capacity than the average. SPACIOUS implies great length and breadth ⟨a *spacious* front lawn⟩. COMMODIOUS stresses roominess and comfortableness ⟨a *commodious* and airy penthouse apartment⟩. CAPACIOUS stresses the ability to hold, contain, or retain more than the average ⟨a *capacious* suitcase⟩. AMPLE implies having a greater size, expanse, or amount than that deemed adequate ⟨*ample* closet space⟩.
spack•le \ˈspa-kəl\ *vt* **spack•led; spack•ling** \-k(ə-)liŋ\ [*Spackle*] (ca. 1940) **:** to apply Spackle paste or other crack-filling paste to
Spackle *trademark* — used for a compound that is used as a filler for cracks or holes in a surface
[1]**spade** \ˈspād\ *n* [ME, fr. OE *spadu;* akin to Gk *spathē* blade of a sword or oar] (bef. 12c) **1 :** a digging implement adapted for being pushed into the ground with the foot **2 :** a spade-shaped instrument — **spade•ful** \-ˌfu̇l\ *n*
[2]**spade** *vb* **spad•ed; spad•ing** *vt* (ca. 1647) **:** to dig up or out or shape with or as if with a spade ~ *vi* **:** to use a spade — **spad•er** *n*
[3]**spade** *n* [It *spada* or Sp *espada* broadsword; both fr. L *spatha,* fr. Gk *spathē* blade] (ca. 1598) **1 a** *pl but sing or pl in constr* **:** the suit comprising cards marked with spades **b :** a black figure that resembles a stylized spearhead on each playing card of one of the four suits; *also* **:** a card marked with this figure **2** *usu offensive* **:** BLACK 4 — **in spades :** to an unusually great degree **:** in the extreme
spade beard *n* [[1]*spade*] (1598) **1 :** an oblong beard with square ends **2 :** a beard rounded off at the top and pointed at the bottom — **spade–beard•ed** \ˈspād-ˈbir-dəd\ *adj*
spade•fish \ˈspād-ˌfish\ *n* (1704) **:** a laterally compressed bony fish (*Chaetodipterus faber* of the family Ephippidae) that resembles the angelfishes and is found in the warmer parts of the western Atlantic
spade•foot toad \ˈspād-ˌfu̇t-\ *n* (1867) **:** any of a family (Pelobatidae) of burrowing toads having the inner bone of the tarsus edged with a strong horny sheath with which they dig
spade•work \-ˌwərk\ *n* (1778) **1 :** work done with a spade **2 :** the hard plain preliminary drudgery in an undertaking
spa•dille \spə-ˈdil, -ˈdē\ *n* [F, fr. Sp *espadilla,* dim. of *espada* broadsword, spade (in cards) — more at SPADE] (1728) **:** the highest trump in various card games (as ombre)
spa•dix \ˈspā-diks\ *n, pl* **spa•di•ces** \ˈspā-də-ˌsēz\ [NL *spadic-, spadix,* fr. L, frond torn from a palm tree, fr. Gk *spadik-, spadix,* fr. *span* to draw, pull] (ca. 1752) **:** a floral spike with a fleshy or succulent axis usu. enclosed in a spathe

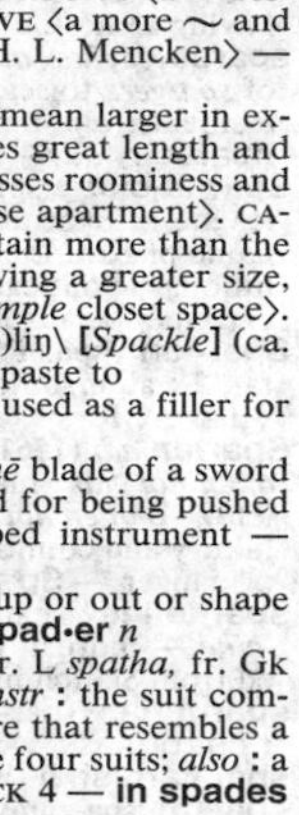

1 spadix

spae \ˈspā\ *vt* **spaed; spae•ing** [ME *span,* fr. ON *spā;* akin to OHG *spehōn* to watch, spy — more at SPY] (14c) *chiefly Scot* **:** FORETELL
spaetz•le *also* **spätz•le** \ˈshpet-slə, -sᵊl, -slē *also* ˈshpāt-\ *n, pl* **spaetzle** *or* **spaetzles** *also* **spätzle** *or* **spätzles** [G *Spätzle,* fr. G dial., dim. of *Spatz* sparrow, dumpling] (1933) **:** a small dumpling cooked by running batter through a colander into boiling water
spa•ghet•ti \spə-ˈge-tē\ *n* [It, fr. pl. of *spaghetto,* dim. of *spago* cord, string, fr. LL *spacus*] (1874) **1 :** pasta made in thin solid strings **2 :** insulating tubing typically of varnished cloth or of plastic for covering bare wire or holding insulated wires together — **spa•ghet•ti•like** \-ˌlīk\ *adj*
spa•ghet•ti•ni \spə-ˌge-ˈtē-nē\ *n* [It, dim. of *spaghetti*] (1923) **:** a pasta thinner than spaghetti but thicker than vermicelli
spaghetti squash *n* (1975) **:** an oval winter squash (*Cucurbita pepo*) with flesh that once cooked is similar in texture to spaghetti
spaghetti strap *n* (1972) **:** a very slender fabric shoulder strap
spaghetti western *n, often cap W* (1967) **:** a western motion picture produced in Italy
spa•hi \ˈspä-ˌhē\ *n* [MF, fr. Turk *sipahi,* fr. Pers *sipāhī* cavalryman] (1562) **1 :** one of a former corps of irregular Turkish cavalry **2 :** one of a former corps of Algerian native cavalry in the French army
spake \ˈspāk\ *archaic past of* SPEAK
[1]**spall** \ˈspȯl\ *n* [ME *spalle*] (15c) **:** a small fragment or chip esp. of stone
[2]**spall** *vt* (1758) **:** to break up or reduce by or as if by chipping with a hammer ~ *vi* **1 :** to break off chips, scales, or slabs **:** EXFOLIATE **2 :** to undergo spallation — **spall•able** \ˈspȯ-lə-bəl\ *adj*
spall•ation \spȯ-ˈlā-shən\ *n* (1947) **1 :** a nuclear reaction in which light particles are ejected as the result of bombardment (as by high-energy protons) **2 :** the process of spalling
spal•peen \spal-ˈpēn, spȯl-\ *n* [Ir *spailpín* seasonal laborer, rascal] (1767) *chiefly Irish* **:** RASCAL
[1]**spam** \ˈspam\ *n* [fr. a skit on the British television series *Monty Python's Flying Circus* in which chanting of the word *Spam* overrides the other dialogue] (1994) **:** unsolicited usu. commercial e-mail sent to a large number of addresses
[2]**spam** *vb* **spammed; spam•ming** *vt* (1994) **:** to send spam to ~ *vi* **:** to send spam — **spam•mer** *n*
Spam *trademark* — used for a canned meat product
[1]**span** \ˈspan\ *archaic past of* SPIN
[2]**span** *n* [ME, fr. OE *spann;* akin to OHG *spanna* span, MD *spannen* to stretch, hitch up] (bef. 12c) **1 :** the distance from the end of the thumb to the end of the little finger of a spread hand; *also* **:** an English unit of length equal to nine inches (22.9 centimeters) **2 :** an extent, stretch, reach, or spread between two limits: as **a :** a limited space (as of time); *esp* **:** an individual's lifetime **b :** the spread or extent between abutments or supports (as of a bridge); *also* **:** a portion thus supported **c :** the maximum distance laterally from tip to tip of an airplane
[3]**span** *vt* **spanned; span•ning** (1560) **1 a :** to measure by or as if by the hand with fingers and thumb extended **b :** MEASURE **2 a :** to extend across ⟨a career that *spanned* four decades⟩ **b :** to form an arch over ⟨a small bridge *spanned* the pond⟩ **c :** to place or construct a span over **3 :** to be capable of expressing any element of under given operations ⟨a set of vectors that ~*s* a vector space⟩
[4]**span** *n* [D, fr. MD, fr. *spannen* to hitch up] (1769) **:** a pair of animals (as mules) usu. matched in appearance and action and driven together
spa•na•ko•pi•ta *also* **spa•no•ko•pi•ta** \ˌspä-nə-ˈkō-pē-tə, -pi-tə\ *n* [ModGk *spanakopēta,* fr. *spanaki* spinach + *pēta, pita* pie] (1950) **:** a traditional Greek pie of spinach, feta cheese, and seasonings baked in phyllo
span•dex \ˈspan-ˌdeks\ *n* [anagram of *expands*] (1959) **:** any of various elastic textile fibers made chiefly of polyurethane; *also* **:** clothing made of this material
span•drel *also* **span•dril** \ˈspan-drəl\ *n* [ME *spandrell,* fr. AF *spaunder,* fr. *espandre* to spread out — more at SPAWN] (15c) **1 :** the sometimes ornamented space between the right or left exterior curve of an arch and an enclosing right angle **2 :** the triangular space beneath the string of a stair

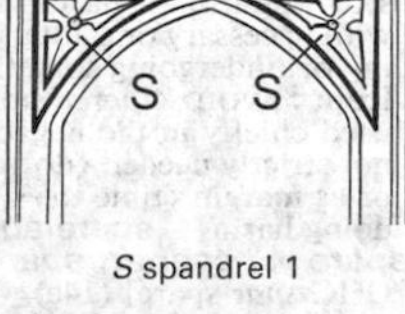

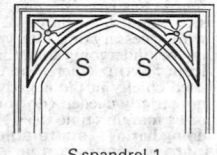

S spandrel 1

spang \ˈspaŋ\ *adv* [Sc *spang* to leap, cast, bang] (1843) **1 :** to a complete degree **2 :** in an exact or direct manner **:** SQUARELY
[1]**span•gle** \ˈspaŋ-gəl\ *n* [ME *spangel,* dim. of *spang* shiny ornament, prob. fr. MD *spange;* akin to OE *spang* buckle, MD *spannen* to stretch] (15c) **1 :** a small plate of shining metal or plastic used for ornamentation esp. on clothing **2 :** a small glittering object or particle
[2]**spangle** *vb* **span•gled; span•gling** \ˈspaŋ-g(ə-)liŋ\ *vt* (ca. 1548) **:** to set or sprinkle with or as if with spangles ~ *vi* **:** to glitter as if covered with spangles **:** SPARKLE
Span•glish \ˈspaŋ-glish, -lish\ *n* [blend of *Spanish* and *English*] (1958) **:** Spanish marked by numerous borrowings from English; *broadly* **:** any of various combinations of Spanish and English
Span•iard \ˈspan-yərd\ *n* [ME *Spaignard,* fr. MF *Espaignard,* fr. *Espaigne* Spain, fr. L *Hispania*] (15c) **:** a native or inhabitant of Spain
span•iel \ˈspan-yəl *also* ˈspa-nᵊl\ *n* [ME *spaynel, spaniell,* fr. AF *espainnel,* alter. of *espaignol* Spaniard, fr. VL **Hispaniolus,* fr. L *Hispania* Spain] (14c) **1 :** a member of any of several breeds of small or medium-sized mostly short-legged dogs usu. having long wavy hair, feathered legs and tail, and large drooping ears **2 :** a fawning servile person
Span•ish \ˈspa-nish\ *n* [*Spanish,* adj., fr. ME *Spainish,* fr. *Spain*] (15c) **1 :** the Romance language of the largest part of Spain and of the countries colonized by Spaniards **2** *pl in constr* **:** the people of Spain — **Spanish** *adj* — **Span•ish•ness** *n*
Spanish American *n* (1770) **1 :** a native or inhabitant of one of the countries of America in which Spanish is the national language **2 :** a resident of the U.S. whose native language is Spanish and whose culture is of Spanish origin — **Spanish–American** *adj*
Spanish bayonet *n* (1843) **:** any of several yuccas; *esp* **:** one (*Yucca aloifolia*) of the southeastern U.S. and West Indies with rigid spine-tipped leaves
Spanish chestnut *n* (1683) **1 :** the sweet edible nut of a large Mediterranean chestnut (*Castanea sativa*) — called also *marron* **2 :** a tree that bears Spanish chestnuts
Spanish fly *n* (ca. 1634) **1 :** a green blister beetle (*Lytta vesicatoria*) of southern Europe **2 :** CANTHARIS 2
Spanish mackerel *n* (1666) **:** a large mackerel (*Scomberomorus maculatus*) that is bluish above with oval brown spots on the sides, is found off the Atlantic coast of No. America from Cape Cod to the Yucatán, and is an important food and game fish
Spanish moss *n* (1823) **:** an epiphytic plant (*Tillandsia usneoides*) of the pineapple family forming pendent tufts of grayish-green filaments on trees from the southern U.S. to Argentina
Spanish needles *n pl but sing or pl in constr* (1743) **:** any of several bur marigolds; *esp* **:** an annual (*Bidens bipinnata*) of No. America and Asia having yellow flowers and dissected leaves
Spanish omelet *n* (1866) **:** an omelet served with a sauce containing chopped green pepper, onion, and tomato
Spanish onion *n* (1706) **:** a large mild-flavored onion typically having yellow or white skin
Spanish rice *n* (1928) **:** rice cooked with onions, green pepper, and tomatoes
[1]**spank** \ˈspaŋk\ *vt* [imit.] (ca. 1712) **:** to strike esp. on the buttocks with the open hand — **spank** *n*
[2]**spank** *vi* [back-formation fr. *spanking*] (1788) **:** to move quickly, dashingly, or spiritedly ⟨~*ing* along in his new car⟩
span•ker \ˈspaŋ-kər\ *n* [origin unknown] (1794) **1 :** the fore-and-aft sail on the mast nearest the stern of a square-rigged ship **2 :** the sail on the mast nearest the stern of a schooner of four or more masts
[1]**spank•ing** \ˈspaŋ-kiŋ\ *adj* [origin unknown] (ca. 1666) **1 :** remarkable of its kind **2 :** being fresh and strong **:** BRISK
[2]**spanking** *adv* (1787) **:** VERY ⟨a ~ clean floor⟩ ⟨~ new⟩

span·ner \ˈspa-nər\ *n* [G, instrument for winding springs, fr. *spannen* to stretch; akin to MD *spannen* to stretch — more at SPAN] (ca. 1790) **1** *chiefly Brit* : WRENCH **2** : a wrench that has a hole, projection, or hook at one or both ends of the head for engaging with a corresponding device on the object that is to be turned

span–new \ˈspan-ˈnü, -ˈnyü\ *adj* [ME, part trans. of ON *spānnȳr,* fr. *spānn* chip of wood + *nȳr* new] (14c) : BRAND-NEW

span·worm \ˈspan-ˌwərm\ *n* [[3]*span*] (1820) : LOOPER 1

[1]**spar** \ˈspär\ *n* [ME *sparre;* akin to OE *spere* spear — more at SPEAR] (14c) **1** : a stout pole **2 a** : a stout rounded usu. wood or metal piece (as a mast, boom, gaff, or yard) used to support rigging **b** : any of the main longitudinal members of the wing of an airplane that carry the ribs

[2]**spar** *vi* **sparred; spar·ring** [ME *sparren* to dart, spring] (1537) **1 a** : BOX; *esp* : to gesture without landing a blow to draw one's opponent or create an opening **b** : to engage in a practice or exhibition bout of boxing **2** : SKIRMISH, WRANGLE **3** : to strike or fight with feet or spurs in the manner of a gamecock

[3]**spar** *n* (1814) **1** : a movement of offense or defense in boxing **2** : a sparring match or session

[4]**spar** *n* [LG; akin to OE *spærstān* gypsum, *spæren* of plaster] (1581) : any of various nonmetallic usu. cleavable and lustrous minerals

SPAR \ˈspär\ *n* [*S*emper *Par*atus, motto of the U.S. Coast Guard, fr. NL, always ready] (1942) : a member of the women's reserve of the U.S. Coast Guard

[1]**spare** \ˈsper\ *vb* **spared; spar·ing** [ME, fr. OE *sparian;* akin to OHG *sparōn* to spare, OE *spær,* adj., scant] *vt* (bef. 12c) **1** : to forbear to destroy, punish, or harm **2** : to refrain from attacking or reprimanding with necessary or salutary severity **3** : to relieve of the necessity of doing or undergoing something ⟨~ yourself the trouble⟩ **4** : to refrain from : AVOID ⟨*spared* no expense⟩ **5** : to use or dispense frugally — used chiefly in the negative ⟨don't ~ the syrup⟩ **6 a** : to give up as not strictly needed ⟨do you have any cash to ~⟩ **b** : to have left over or as margin ⟨time to ~⟩ ~ *vi* **1** : to be frugal **2** : to refrain from doing harm — **spare·able** \-ə-bəl\ *adj* — **spar·er** *n*

[2]**spare** *adj* **spar·er; spar·est** [ME, fr. OE *spær* sparing, scant; akin to OHG *spar* spare] (14c) **1** : not being used; *esp* : held for emergency use ⟨a ~ tire⟩ **2** : being over and above what is needed : SUPERFLUOUS ⟨~ time⟩ **3** : not liberal or profuse : SPARING ⟨a ~ prose style⟩ **4** : healthily lean **5** : not abundant or plentiful ***syn*** see LEAN, MEAGER — **spare·ly** *adv* — **spare·ness** *n*

[3]**spare** *n* (1907) **1 a** : a spare tire **b** : a duplicate (as a key or a machine part) kept in reserve **2** : the knocking down of all 10 pins with the first 2 balls in a frame in bowling

spare·ribs \ˈsper-ˌ(r)ibz, -əbz\ *n pl* [by folk etymology fr. LG *ribbesper* pickled pork ribs roasted on a spit, fr. MLG, fr. *ribbe* rib + *sper* spear, spit] (1596) : a cut of pork ribs separated from the bacon strip

sparge \ˈspärj\ *vt* **sparged; sparg·ing** [prob. fr. MF *espargier,* fr. L *spargere* to scatter] (1569) **1** : SPRINKLE, BESPATTER; *esp* : SPRAY **2** : to agitate (a liquid) by means of compressed air or gas entering through a pipe — **sparge** *n* — **sparg·er** *n*

sparing *adj* (14c) **1** : marked by or practicing careful restraint (as in the use of resources) **2** : MEAGER, BARE ⟨the map is ~ of information⟩ — **spar·ing·ly** *adv*

syn SPARING, FRUGAL, THRIFTY, ECONOMICAL mean careful in the use of one's money or resources. SPARING stresses abstention and restraint ⟨*sparing* in the offering of advice⟩. FRUGAL implies absence of luxury and simplicity of lifestyle ⟨ran a *frugal* household⟩. THRIFTY stresses good management and industry ⟨*thrifty* use of nonrenewable resources⟩. ECONOMICAL stresses prudent management, lack of wastefulness, and use of things to their best advantage ⟨an *economical* health-care plan⟩.

[1]**spark** \ˈspärk\ *n* [ME *sparke,* fr. OE *spearca;* akin to MD *sparke* spark and perh. to L *spargere* to scatter] (bef. 12c) **1 a** : a small particle of a burning substance thrown out by a body in combustion or remaining when combustion is nearly completed **b** : a hot glowing particle struck from a larger mass; *esp* : one heated by friction **2 a** : a luminous disruptive electrical discharge of very short duration between two conductors separated by a gas (as air) **b** : the discharge in a spark plug **c** : the mechanism controlling the discharge in a spark plug **3** : SPARKLE, FLASH **4** : something that sets off a sudden force ⟨provided the ~ that helped the team to rally⟩ **5** : a latent particle capable of growth or developing : GERM ⟨still retains a ~ of decency⟩ **6** *pl but sing in constr* : a radio operator on a ship

[2]**spark** *vi* (13c) **1 a** : to throw out sparks **b** : to flash or fall like sparks **2** : to produce sparks; *specif* : to have the electric ignition working **3** : to respond with enthusiasm ~ *vt* **1** : to set off in a burst of activity : ACTIVATE ⟨the question ~*ed* a lively discussion⟩ — often used with *off* **2** : to stir to activity : INCITE ⟨~*ed* her team to victory⟩ — **spark·er** *n*

[3]**spark** *n* [perh. fr. [1]*spark*] (ca. 1600) **1** : a foppish young man **2** : LOVER, BEAU — **spark·ish** \ˈspär-kish\ *adj*

[4]**spark** *vb* (1787) : WOO, COURT — **spark·er** *n*

spark chamber *n* (1961) : a device usu. used to detect the path of a high-energy particle that consists of a series of charged metal plates or wires separated by a gas (as neon) in which observable electric discharges follow the path of the particle

spark gap *n* (1889) : a space between two high-potential terminals (as of an induction coil or spark plug) through which pass discharges of electricity; *also* : a device having a spark gap

sparking plug *n* (1902) *Brit* : SPARK PLUG

[1]**spar·kle** \ˈspär-kəl\ *vb* **spar·kled; spar·kling** \-k(ə-)liŋ\ [ME, freq. of *sparken* to spark] *vi* (13c) **1 a** : to throw out sparks **b** : to give off or reflect bright moving points of light **c** : to perform brilliantly **2** : EFFERVESCE ⟨wine that ~*s*⟩ **3** : to become lively or animated ⟨the dialogue ~*s* with wit⟩ ⟨eyes *sparkling* with anger⟩ ~ *vt* : to cause to glitter or shine ***syn*** see FLASH — **spar·kly** \-k(ə-)lē\ *adj*

[2]**sparkle** *n* [ME, dim. of *sparke*] (14c) **1** : a little spark : SCINTILLATION **2** : the quality of sparkling **3 a** : ANIMATION, LIVELINESS **b** : the quality or state of being effervescent

spar·kler \ˈspär-klər\ *n* (1713) : one that sparkles: as **a** : DIAMOND **b** : a firework that throws off brilliant sparks on burning **c** : SPARKLING WINE

sparkling wine *n* (1565) : an effervescent table wine

spark plug *n* (1903) **1** : a part that fits into the cylinder head of an internal combustion engine and carries two electrodes separated by an air gap across which the current from the ignition system discharges to form the spark for combustion **2** : one that initiates or gives impetus to an undertaking — **spark-plug** \ˈspärk-ˌpləg\ *vt*

sparky \ˈspär-kē\ *adj* **spark·i·er; -est** (ca. 1865) : marked by animation : LIVELY ⟨~ children⟩ — **spark·i·ly** \-kə-lē\ *adv*

spar·row \ˈspa-(ˌ)rō\ *n* [ME *sparow,* fr. OE *spearwa;* akin to OHG *sparo* sparrow] (bef. 12c) **1** : any of a genus (*Passer* of the family Passeridae) of small chiefly brownish or grayish Old World oscine songbirds that include some which have been widely introduced; *esp* : HOUSE SPARROW **2** : any of numerous finches (family Emberizidae) that are New World birds (as the song sparrow or tree sparrow) resembling the Old World sparrows — **spar·row·like** \-rō-ˌlīk, -rə-ˌlīk\ *adj*

sparrow hawk *n* (15c) : any of various small hawks: as **a** : an Old World accipiter (*Accipiter nisus*) that is dark gray to blackish above with the female having a grayish-brown barred underside and the male having a chestnut barred underside **b** : KESTREL b

sparse \ˈspärs\ *adj* **spars·er; spars·est** [L *sparsus* spread out, fr. pp. of *spargere* to scatter — more at SPARK] (1753) : of few and scattered elements; *esp* : not thickly grown or settled ***syn*** see MEAGER — **sparse·ly** *adv* — **sparse·ness** *n* — **spar·si·ty** \ˈspär-sə-tē\ *n*

Spar·ta·cist \ˈspär-tə-sist\ *n* [G *Spartakist,* fr. *Spartakusbund,* lit., league of Spartakus, a revolutionary organization, fr. *Spartakus,* pen name of Karl Liebknecht, its cofounder] (1919) : a member of a revolutionary political group organized in Germany in 1918 and advocating extreme socialistic doctrines

[1]**Spar·tan** \ˈspär-tᵊn\ *n* (15c) **1** : a native or inhabitant of ancient Sparta **2** : a person of great courage and self-discipline — **Spar·tan·ism** \-ˌi-zəm\ *n*

[2]**Spartan** *adj* (1561) **1** : of or relating to Sparta in ancient Greece **2 a** *often not cap* : marked by strict self-discipline or self-denial ⟨a ~ athlete⟩ **b** *often not cap* : marked by simplicity, frugality, or avoidance of luxury and comfort ⟨a ~ room⟩ **c** : LACONIC **d** : undaunted by pain or danger — **Spar·tan·ly** *adv*

spar·te·ine \ˈspär-tē-ən, ˈspär-ˌtēn\ *n* [L *spartum* esparto, broom + ISV *-eine* — more at ESPARTO] (1851) : a liquid alkaloid $C_{15}H_{26}N_2$ extracted from Scotch broom and used in medicine in the form of its sulfate

spar·ti·na \ˈspär-tə-nə\ *n* [NL, fr. Gk *spartinē* rope, cord] (1836) : CORDGRASS

spar varnish *n* [[1]*spar*] (ca. 1909) : an exterior waterproof varnish

spasm \ˈspa-zəm\ *n* [ME *spasme,* fr. AF *espasme,* fr. L *spasmus,* fr. Gk *spasmos,* fr. *span* to draw, pull] (14c) **1** : an involuntary and abnormal muscular contraction **2** : a sudden violent and temporary effort, emotion, or sensation ⟨a ~ of creativity⟩ ⟨~*s* of pain⟩ — **spasm** *vi*

spas·mod·ic \spaz-ˈmä-dik\ *adj* [NL *spasmodicus,* fr. Gk *spasmōdēs,* fr. *spasmos*] (ca. 1681) **1 a** : relating to or affected or characterized by spasm **b** : resembling a spasm esp. in sudden violence ⟨a ~ jerk⟩ **2** : acting or proceeding fitfully : INTERMITTENT ⟨~ activity⟩ **3** : subject to outbursts of emotional excitement : EXCITABLE ***syn*** see FITFUL — **spas·mod·i·cal·ly** \-di-k(ə-)lē\ *adv*

spas·mo·lyt·ic \ˌspaz-mə-ˈli-tik\ *adj* [ISV *spasmo-* (fr. Gk *spasmos* spasm) + *-lytic*] (ca. 1935) : tending or having the power to relieve spasms or convulsions — **spasmolytic** *n*

[1]**spas·tic** \ˈspas-tik\ *adj* [L *spasticus,* fr. Gk *spastikos* drawing in, fr. *span*] (1753) **1 a** : of, relating to, characterized by, or affected with or as if with spasm ⟨a ~ patient⟩ **b** : characterized by hypertonic muscles ⟨~ cerebral palsy⟩ **2** : SPASMODIC 2 ⟨a ~ influx of data⟩ — **spas·ti·cal·ly** \-ti-k(ə-)lē\ *adv*

[2]**spastic** *n* (1896) : one suffering from spastic paralysis

spastic colon *n* (1973) : IRRITABLE BOWEL SYNDROME; *also* : a colon affected with spasms

spas·tic·i·ty \spa-ˈsti-sə-tē\ *n* (ca. 1827) : a spastic state or condition; *esp* : muscular hypertonicity with increased tendon reflexes

spastic paralysis *n* (1879) : paralysis with tonic spasm of the affected muscles and with increased tendon reflexes

[1]**spat** \ˈspat\ *past and past part of* SPIT

[2]**spat** *n, pl* **spat** *or* **spats** [origin unknown] (1667) : a young bivalve (as an oyster)

[3]**spat** *n* [short for *spatterdash* legging] (ca. 1802) : a cloth or leather gaiter covering the instep and ankle

[4]**spat** *n* [origin unknown] (1729) **1** *chiefly dial* : SLAP **2** : a brief petty quarrel or angry outburst ⟨a lovers' ~⟩ **3** : a sound like that of rain falling in large drops

[5]**spat** *vb* **spat·ted; spat·ting** *vt* (ca. 1832) *chiefly dial* : SLAP ~ *vi* **1** : to quarrel pettily or briefly **2** : to strike with a sound like that of rain falling in large drops

spate \ˈspāt\ *n* [ME] (15c) **1** : FRESHET, FLOOD **2 a** : a large number or amount ⟨a ~ of books on gardening⟩ **b** : a sudden or strong outburst : RUSH ⟨a ~ of anger⟩

spathe \ˈspāth\ *n* [NL *spatha,* fr. L, broadsword — more at SPADE] (1785) : a sheathing bract or pair of bracts partly enclosing an inflorescence and esp. a spadix on the same axis ⟨the ~ of the calla lily⟩

spath·u·late \ˈspath-yə-lət\ *adj* [LL *spathula, spatula* spatula] (1821) : SPATULATE ⟨~ petals of a flower⟩

spa·tial \ˈspā-shəl\ *adj* [L *spatium* space] (1847) **1** : relating to, occupying, or having the character of space **2** : of or relating to facility in perceiving relations (as of objects) in space ⟨tests of ~ ability⟩ — **spa·ti·al·i·ty** \ˌspā-shē-ˈa-lə-tē\ *n* — **spa·tial·ly** \ˈspā-sh(ə-)lē\ *adv*

spatial summation *n* (1968) : sensory summation that involves stimulation of several spatially separated neurons at the same time

spa·tio·tem·po·ral \ˌspā-shē-ō-ˈtem-p(ə-)rəl\ *adj* [L *spatium* + *tempor-, tempus* time] (1900) **1** : having both spatial and temporal qualities **2** : of or relating to space-time — **spa·tio·tem·po·ral·ly** \-p(ə-)rə-lē\ *adv*

[1]**spat·ter** \ˈspa-tər\ *vb* [akin to Fris *spatterje* to spatter, MD be*spatten* to splash] *vi* (1600) : to spurt forth in scattered drops ⟨blood ~*ing* everywhere⟩ ~ *vt* **1** : to splash with or as if with a liquid; *also* : to soil in this way ⟨his coat was ~*ed* with mud⟩ **2** : to scatter by or as if by splashing ⟨~ water⟩ **3** : to cover with or as if with splashes or spots **4** : to cast aspersions on : DEFAME ⟨~*ed* my reputation⟩

[2]**spatter** *n* (1797) **1 a** : the act or process of spattering : the state of being spattered **b** : the noise of spattering **2 a** : a drop or splash spat-

tered on something or a spot or stain due to spattering **b :** a small amount or number : SPRINKLE ⟨a ~ of applause⟩
spat·ter·dock \ˈspa-tər-ˌdäk\ *n* (1813) : any of a genus (*Nuphar*) of water lilies having usu. cordate leaves and typically yellow flowers
spat·u·la \ˈspa-chə-lə, ˈspach-lə\ *n* [LL, spoon, spatula — more at EPAULET] (1525) : a flat thin implement used esp. for spreading or mixing soft substances, scooping, or lifting
spat·u·late \ˈspa-chə-lət\ *adj* (ca. 1760) : shaped like a spatula ⟨a ~ leaf⟩ ⟨~ spines of a caterpillar⟩ ⟨a ~ tool⟩ — see LEAF illustration
spätzle *var of* SPAETZLE
spav·in \ˈspa-vən\ *n* [ME *spavayne,* fr. MF *espavin,* alter. of OF *esparvains,* prob. of Gmc origin; akin to OHG *sparo* sparrow (likened to a lump)] (15c) : SWELLING; *esp* : a bony enlargement of the hock of a horse associated with strain
spav·ined \-vənd\ *adj* (15c) **1 :** affected with spavin **2 :** old and decrepit : OVER-THE-HILL
[1]**spawn** \ˈspȯn, ˈspän\ *vb* [ME, fr. AF *espandre* to spread out, shed, scatter, spawn, fr. L *expandere* to expand] *vi* (15c) **1 :** to deposit or fertilize spawn **2 :** to produce young esp. in large numbers ~ *vt* **1 a :** to produce or deposit (eggs) — used of an aquatic animal **b :** to induce (fish) to spawn **c :** to plant with mushroom spawn **2 :** BRING FORTH, GENERATE ⟨the idea ~*ed* controversy⟩ — **spawn·er** *n*
[2]**spawn** *n* (15c) **1 :** the eggs of aquatic animals (as fishes or oysters) that lay many small eggs **2 :** PRODUCT, OFFSPRING; *also* : offspring in great numbers **3 :** the seed, germ, or source of something **4 :** mycelium esp. prepared (as in bricks) for propagating mushrooms
spay \ˈspā, ÷ ˈspīd\ *vt* **spayed** \ˈspād, ÷ ˈspā-dəd\; **spay·ing** \ˈspā-iŋ, ÷ ˈspā-diŋ\ [ME, fr. AF *espeer* to pierce, castrate, fr. *espee* sword, fr. L *spatha* sword — more at SPADE] (15c) : to remove the ovaries and uterus of (a female animal)
spaz \ˈspaz\ *n, pl* **spaz·zes** [by shortening & alter. fr. *spastic*] (ca. 1965) *slang* : one who is inept : KLUTZ
Spc *abbr* specialist
SPCA *abbr* Society for the Prevention of Cruelty to Animals
SPCC *abbr* Society for the Prevention of Cruelty to Children
speak \ˈspēk\ *vb* **spoke** \ˈspōk\; **spo·ken** \ˈspō-kən\; **speak·ing** [ME *speken,* fr. OE *sprecan, specan;* akin to OHG *sprehhan* to speak, Gk *spharageisthai* to crackle] *vi* (bef. 12c) **1 a :** to utter words or articulate sounds with the ordinary voice : TALK **b** (1) **:** to express thoughts, opinions, or feelings orally (2) **:** to extend a greeting (3) **:** to be friendly enough to engage in conversation ⟨still were not ~*ing* after the dispute⟩ **c** (1) **:** to express oneself before a group (2) **:** to address one's remarks ⟨~ to the issue⟩ **2 a :** to make a written statement ⟨his diaries . . . *spoke* . . . of his entrancement with death —Sy Kahn⟩ **b :** to use such an expression — often used in the phrase *so to speak* ⟨was at the enemy's gates, so to ~ —C. S. Forester⟩ **c :** to serve as spokesperson **3 a :** to express feelings by other than verbal means ⟨actions ~ louder than words⟩ **b :** SIGNAL **c :** to be interesting or attractive : APPEAL ⟨great music . . . ~*s* directly to the emotions —A. N. Whitehead⟩ **4 :** to make a request or claim — used with *for;* usu. used in passive constructions ⟨the seat was already *spoken for*⟩ **5 :** to make a characteristic or natural sound ⟨all at once the thunder *spoke* —George Meredith⟩ **6 a :** TESTIFY **b :** to be indicative or suggestive ⟨his gold . . . *spoke* of riches in the land —Julian Dana⟩ ~ *vt* **1 a** (1) **:** to utter with the speaking voice : PRONOUNCE (2) **:** to give a recitation of : DECLAIM **b :** to express orally : DECLARE ⟨free to ~ their minds⟩ **c :** ADDRESS, ACCOST; *esp* : HAIL **2 :** to make known in writing : STATE **3 :** to use or be able to use in speaking ⟨~*s* Spanish⟩ **4 :** to indicate by other than verbal means **5** *archaic* **:** DESCRIBE, DEPICT — **speak·able** \ˈspē-kə-bəl\ *adj* — **to speak of :** worthy of mention or notice — usu. used in negative constructions ⟨no progress *to speak of*⟩
-speak \ˌspēk\ *n comb form* [*newspeak*] — used to form esp. nonce words denoting a particular kind of jargon ⟨California*speak*⟩
speak·easy \ˈspēk-ˌē-zē\ *n, pl* **-eas·ies** (1889) : a place where alcoholic beverages are illegally sold; *specif* : such a place during the period of prohibition in the U.S.
speak·er \ˈspē-kər\ *n* (14c) **1 a :** one that speaks; *esp* : one who uses a language ⟨native ~*s* of French⟩ **b :** one who makes a public speech **c :** one who acts as a spokesperson **2 :** the presiding officer of a deliberative assembly ⟨*Speaker* of the House of Representatives⟩ **3 :** LOUDSPEAKER — **speak·er·ship** \-ˌship\ *n*
speak·er·phone \ˈspē-kər-ˌfōn\ *n* (1955) : a combination microphone and loudspeaker device for two-way communication by telephone lines
speaking *adj* (13c) **1 a :** that speaks : capable of speech **b :** having a population that speaks a specified language — usu. used in combination ⟨English-*speaking* countries⟩ **c :** that involves talking or giving speeches ⟨a ~ role⟩ ⟨a ~ tour⟩ **2 :** highly significant or expressive : ELOQUENT **3 :** resembling a living being or a real object
speaking tube *n* (1822) : a pipe through which conversation may be conducted (as between different parts of a building)
speak–out \ˈspēk-ˌau̇t\ *n* (1968) : an event in which people publicly share their experiences of or views on an issue
speak out *vi* (14c) **1 :** to speak loud enough to be heard **2 :** to speak boldly : express an opinion frankly ⟨*spoke out* on the issues⟩
speak up *vi* (1681) **1 :** to speak loudly and distinctly **2 :** to express an opinion freely ⟨*speak up* for truth and justice —Clive Bell⟩
spean \ˈspēn\ *vt* [MD *spenen*] (1595) *chiefly Scot* : WEAN
[1]**spear** \ˈspir\ *n* [ME *spere,* fr. OE; akin to OHG *sper* spear, L *sparus* hunting spear] (bef. 12c) **1 :** a thrusting or throwing weapon with long shaft and sharp head or blade **2 :** a sharp-pointed instrument with barbs used in spearing fish **3 :** SPEARMAN
[2]**spear** *vt* (15c) **1 :** to pierce, strike, or take with or as if with a spear ⟨~ salmon⟩ ⟨~*ed* a chop from the platter⟩ **2 :** to catch (as a baseball) with a sudden thrust of the arm ~ *vi* **:** to thrust at or wound something with or as if with a spear — **spear·er** *n*
[3]**spear** *adj* (1861) : PATERNAL 3 ⟨the ~ side of the family⟩ — compare DISTAFF
[4]**spear** *vi* [[5]*spear*] (1573) *of a plant* : to thrust a spear upward
[5]**spear** *n* [alter. of [1]*spire*] (1647) : a usu. young blade, shoot, or sprout (as of grass)
spear–car·ri·er \ˈspir-ˌka-rē-ər\ *n* (1953) **1 a :** a member of an opera chorus **b :** a bit actor in a play **2 :** a person whose actions are of little significance or value in an event or organization
[1]**spear·fish** \-ˌfish\ *n* (ca. 1882) : any of several billfishes (genus *Tetrapturus*) having the anterior part of the first dorsal fin about as high as the body is deep

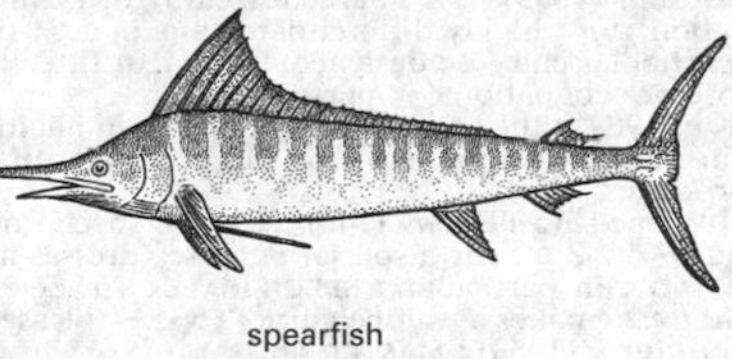
spearfish

[2]**spearfish** *vi* (ca. 1949) : to fish with a spear
spear·gun \ˈspir-ˌgən\ *n* (1951) : a gun that shoots a spear and is used in spearfishing
[1]**spear·head** \-ˌhed\ *n* (14c) **1 :** the sharp-pointed head of a spear **2 :** a leading element, force, or influence in an undertaking or development
[2]**spearhead** *vt* (1937) : to serve as leader or leading element of
spear·man \ˈspir-mən\ *n* (14c) : a person armed with a spear
spear·mint \-ˌmint, -mənt\ *n* (1562) : a common mint (*Mentha spicata*) grown for flavoring and esp. for its aromatic oil
spear–throw·er \-ˌthrō-ər\ *n* (1871) : ATLATL
spear·wort \-ˌwərt, -ˌwȯrt\ *n* (14c) : any of several buttercups (esp. *Ranunculus flammula*) with spear-shaped leaves
[1]**spec** \ˈspek\ *n* [by alter.] (1926) **1 :** SPECIFICATION — usu. used in pl.; *also* : a single quantity (as a dimension or a measure of performance) describing a product esp. as part of a specification **2 :** SPECULATION ⟨built the house on ~⟩
[2]**spec** *vt* **specced** *or* **spec'd** \ˈspekt\; **spec·cing** (1965) : to write specifications for
[3]**spec** *abbr* **1** special; specialist **2** specifically
[1]**spe·cial** \ˈspe-shəl\ *adj* [ME, fr. AF or L; AF *especial,* fr. L *specialis* individual, particular, fr. *species* species] (13c) **1 :** distinguished by some unusual quality; *esp* : being in some way superior ⟨our ~ blend⟩ **2 :** held in particular esteem ⟨a ~ friend⟩ **3 a :** readily distinguishable from others of the same category : UNIQUE ⟨they set it apart as a ~ day of thanksgiving⟩ **b :** of, relating to, or constituting a species : SPECIFIC **4 :** being other than the usual : ADDITIONAL, EXTRA **5 :** designed for a particular purpose or occasion — **spe·cial·ness** *n*
syn SPECIAL, ESPECIAL, SPECIFIC, PARTICULAR, INDIVIDUAL mean of or relating to one thing or class. SPECIAL stresses having a quality, character, identity, or use of its own ⟨*special* ingredients⟩. ESPECIAL may add implications of preeminence or preference ⟨a matter of *especial* importance⟩. SPECIFIC implies a quality or character distinguishing a kind or a species ⟨children with *specific* nutritional needs⟩. PARTICULAR stresses the distinctness of something as an individual ⟨a ballet step of *particular* difficulty⟩. INDIVIDUAL implies unequivocal reference to one of a class or group ⟨valued each *individual* opinion⟩.
[2]**special** *n* (1866) **1 :** one that is used for a special service or occasion ⟨caught the commuter ~ to work⟩ **2 :** something (as a television program) that is not part of a regular series **3 :** a featured dish at a restaurant ⟨the ~*s* of the day⟩
special assessment *n* (1875) : a specific tax levied on private property to meet the cost of public improvements that enhance the value of the property
special delivery *n* (1870) : expedited messenger delivery of mail matter for an extra fee
special district *n* (1950) : a political subdivision of a state established to provide a single public service (as water supply or sanitation) within a specific geographic area
special drawing rights *n* (1967) : a means of exchange used by governments to settle their international indebtedness
special education *n* (1921) : classes or instruction designed for students with special educational needs
special effects *n pl* (1937) : visual or sound effects introduced into a motion picture, video recording, or taped television production
Special Forces *n pl* (1955) : a branch of the U.S. Army composed of soldiers specially trained in guerrilla warfare
special handling *n* (1928) : the handling of parcel-post or mail as first-class but not as special-delivery matter for an extra fee
special interest *n* (1910) : a person or group seeking to influence legislative or government policy to further often narrowly defined interests; *esp* : LOBBY
spe·cial·i·sa·tion, spe·cial·ise, specialised *Brit var of* SPECIALIZATION, SPECIALIZE, SPECIALIZED
spe·cial·ism \ˈspe-shə-ˌli-zəm\ *n* (1856) **1 :** specialization in an occupation or branch of learning **2 :** a field of specialization : SPECIALTY
spe·cial·ist \ˈspe-sh(ə-)list\ *n* (1855) **1 :** one who specializes in a particular occupation, practice, or branch of learning **2 :** an enlisted rank in the U.S. Army corresponding to the grade of corporal; *also* : any of several former enlisted ranks corresponding to the grades of sergeant through sergeant major **3 :** an organism (as a bird) specialized esp. in food or habitat — **specialist** *or* **spe·cial·is·tic** \ˌspe-shə-ˈlis-tik\ *adj*
spe·ci·al·i·ty \ˌspe-shē-ˈa-lə-tē\ *n, pl* **-ties** (15c) **1 :** a special mark or quality **2 :** a special object or class of objects **3 a :** a special aptitude or skill **b :** SPECIALTY 3
spe·cial·i·za·tion \ˌspe-sh(ə-)lə-ˈzā-shən\ *n* (1843) **1 :** a making or becoming specialized **2 a :** structural adaptation of a body part to a particular function or of an organism for life in a particular environment **b :** a body part or an organism adapted by specialization
spe·cial·ize \ˈspe-shə-ˌlīz\ *vb* **-ized; -iz·ing** *vt* (1613) **1 :** to make particular mention of : PARTICULARIZE **2 :** to apply or direct to a specific

\ə\ **abut** \ᵊ\ kitten, F table \ər\ **further** \a\ **ash** \ā\ **ace** \ä\ **mop, mar**
\au̇\ **out** \ch\ **chin** \e\ **bet** \ē\ **easy** \g\ **go** \i\ **hit** \ī\ **ice** \j\ **job**
\ŋ\ **sing** \ō\ **go** \ȯ\ **law** \ȯi\ **boy** \th\ **thin** \th\ **the** \ü\ **loot** \u̇\ **foot**
\y\ **yet** \zh\ **vision, beige** \k, ⁿ, œ, ue, ʸ\ *see* Guide to Pronunciation

end or use ⟨*specialized* their study⟩ ~ *vi* **1 :** to concentrate one's efforts in a special activity, field, or practice **2 :** to undergo specialization; *esp* **:** to change adaptively

specialized *adj* (1853) **1 :** characterized by or exhibiting biological specialization; *esp* **:** highly differentiated esp. in a particular direction or for a particular end **2 :** designed, trained, or fitted for one particular purpose or occupation ⟨~ personnel⟩

Special K *n* (1987) **:** the anesthetic ketamine used illicitly usu. by being inhaled in powdered form esp. for the dreamlike or hallucinogenic state it produces

spe·cial·ly \ˈspe-sh(ə-)lē\ *adv* (14c) **1 :** in a special manner ⟨treated her friends ~⟩ **2 a :** for a special purpose ⟨dresses made ~ for the occasion⟩ **b :** in particular **:** SPECIFICALLY ⟨made ~ for you⟩ **3 :** ESPECIALLY 2 ⟨makes a ~ fine curry⟩ ⟨was ~ pleased with the gift⟩

special master *n* (1953) **:** MASTER 4b

special needs *n pl* (1915) **:** the individual requirements (as for education) of a person with a disadvantaged background or a mental, emotional, or physical disability or a high risk of developing one — **special–needs** *adj*

special pleading *n* (1684) **1 :** the allegation of special or new matter to offset the effect of matter pleaded by the opposite side and admitted, as distinguished from a direct denial of the matter pleaded **2 :** misleading argument that presents one point or phase as if it covered the entire question at issue

special relativity *n* (1937) **:** RELATIVITY 3a

special theory of relativity (1920) **:** RELATIVITY 3a

spe·cial·ty \ˈspe-shəl-tē\ *n, pl* **-ties** *often attrib* [ME *specialte,* fr. AF *especialté,* fr. LL *specialitat-, specialitas,* fr. L *specialis* special] (15c) **1 :** a distinctive mark or quality **2 a :** a special object or class of objects: as **(1) :** a legal agreement embodied in a sealed instrument **(2) :** a product of a special kind or of special excellence ⟨fried chicken is my ~⟩ **b :** the state of being special, distinctive, or peculiar **3 :** something in which one specializes

spe·ci·a·tion \ˌspē-shē-ˈā-shən, -sē-\ *n* (1906) **:** the process of biological species formation — **spe·ci·ate** \ˈspē-shē-ˌāt, -sē-\ *vi* — **spe·ci·a·tion·al** \ˌspē-shē-ˈā-shnəl, -sē-, -shə-nᵊl\ *adj*

[1]**spe·cie** \ˈspē-shē, -sē\ *n* [fr. *in specie,* fr. L, in kind] (1617) **:** money in coin — **in specie :** in the same or like form or kind ⟨ready to return insult *in specie*⟩; *also* **:** in coin

[2]**specie** *n* [back-formation fr. *species* (taken as a pl.)] (1647) *nonstand* **:** SPECIES

[1]**spe·cies** \ˈspē-(ˌ)shēz, -(ˌ)sēz\ *n, pl* **species** [ME, fr. L, appearance, kind, species, fr. *specere* to look — more at SPY] (14c) **1 a :** KIND, SORT **b :** a class of individuals having common attributes and designated by a common name; *specif* **:** a logical division of a genus or more comprehensive class ⟨confessing sins in ~ and in number⟩ **c :** the human race **:** human beings — often used with *the* ⟨survival of the ~ in the nuclear age⟩ **d (1) :** a category of biological classification ranking immediately below the genus or subgenus, comprising related organisms or populations potentially capable of interbreeding, and being designated by a binomial that consists of the name of a genus followed by a Latin or latinized uncapitalized noun or adjective agreeing grammatically with the genus name **(2) :** an individual or kind belonging to a biological species **e :** a particular kind of atomic nucleus, atom, molecule, or ion **2 :** the consecrated eucharistic elements of the Roman Catholic or Eastern Orthodox Eucharist **3 a :** a mental image; *also* **:** a sensible object **b :** an object of thought correlative with a natural object

[2]**species** *adj* (1899) **:** belonging to a biological species as distinguished from a horticultural variety ⟨a ~ rose⟩

spe·cies·ism \ˈspē-shēz-ˌi-zəm, -sēz-\ *n* (1973) **1 :** prejudice or discrimination based on species; *esp* **:** discrimination against animals **2 :** the assumption of human superiority on which speciesism is based

[1]**spe·cif·ic** \spi-ˈsi-fik\ *adj* [LL *specificus,* fr. L *species*] (ca. 1631) **1 a :** constituting or falling into a specifiable category **b :** sharing or being those properties of something that allow it to be referred to a particular category **2 a :** restricted to a particular individual, situation, relation, or effect ⟨a disease ~ to horses⟩ **b :** exerting a distinctive influence (as on a body part or a disease) ⟨~ antibodies⟩ **3 :** free from ambiguity **:** ACCURATE ⟨a ~ statement of faith⟩ **4 :** of, relating to, or constituting a species and esp. a biological species **5 a :** being any of various arbitrary physical constants and esp. one relating a quantitative attribute to unit mass, volume, or area **b :** imposed at a fixed rate per unit (as of weight or count) ⟨~ import duties⟩ — compare AD VALOREM ***syn*** see SPECIAL, EXPLICIT — **spe·cif·i·cal·ly** \-fi-k(ə-)lē\ *adv*

[2]**specific** *n* (1661) **1 a :** something peculiarly adapted to a purpose or use **b :** a drug or remedy having a specific mitigating effect on a disease ⟨used as a ~ against malaria⟩ **2 a :** a characteristic quality or trait **b :** DETAILS, PARTICULARS — usu. used in pl. ⟨haggling over the legal and financial ~*s* of independence —*Time*⟩ **c** *pl* **:** SPECIFICATION 2a

-specific *comb form* [[1]*specific*] **:** relating or applying specifically to or intended specifically for ⟨gender-*specific*⟩

spec·i·fi·ca·tion \ˌspe-sə-fə-ˈkā-shən, ˌspes-fə-\ *n* (1633) **1 :** the act or process of specifying **2 a :** a detailed precise presentation of something or of a plan or proposal for something — usu. used in pl. **b :** a statement of legal particulars (as of charges or of contract terms); *also* **:** a single item of such statement **c :** a written description of an invention for which a patent is sought

specific epithet *n* (1906) **:** the Latin or latinized noun or adjective that follows the genus name in a taxonomic binomial

specific gravity *n* (1660) **:** the ratio of the density of a substance to the density of some substance (as pure water) taken as a standard when both densities are obtained by weighing in air

specific heat *n* (1799) **:** the heat in calories required to raise the temperature of one gram of a substance one degree Celsius

specific impulse *n* (1947) **:** the thrust produced per unit rate of consumption of the propellant that is usu. expressed in pounds of thrust per pound of propellant used per second and that is a measure of the efficiency of a rocket engine

spec·i·fic·i·ty \ˌspe-sə-ˈfi-sə-tē\ *n* (1875) **:** the quality or condition of being specific: as **a :** the condition of being peculiar to a particular individual or group of organisms ⟨host ~ of a parasite⟩ **b :** the condition of participating in or catalyzing only one or a few chemical reactions ⟨the ~ of an enzyme⟩

specific performance *n* (1750) **1 :** the performance of a legal contract strictly or substantially according to its terms **2 :** an equitable remedy enjoining specific performance

spec·i·fy \ˈspe-sə-ˌfī\ *vt* **-fied; -fy·ing** [ME *specifien,* fr. AF *specifier,* fr. LL *specificare,* fr. *specificus*] (14c) **1 :** to name or state explicitly or in detail **2 :** to include as an item in a specification — **spec·i·fi·able** \ˌspe-sə-ˈfī-ə-bəl\ *adj* — **spec·i·fi·er** \ˈspe-sə-ˌfī(-ə)r\ *n*

spec·i·men \ˈspes-mən, ˈspe-sə-\ *n* [L, fr. *specere* to look at, look — more at SPY] (1610) **1 a :** an individual, item, or part considered typical of a group, class, or whole **b :** a portion or quantity of material for use in testing, examination, or study ⟨a urine ~⟩ **2 a :** something that obviously belongs to a particular category but is noticed by reason of an individual distinguishing characteristic **b :** PERSON, INDIVIDUAL ⟨he's a tough ~⟩ **3 :** a plant grown for exhibition or in the open to display its full development ⟨~ trees⟩ ***syn*** see INSTANCE

spe·cious \ˈspē-shəs\ *adj* [ME, visually pleasing, fr. L *speciosus* beautiful, plausible, fr. *species*] (1513) **1** *obs* **:** SHOWY **2 :** having deceptive attraction or allure **3 :** having a false look of truth or genuineness **:** SOPHISTIC ⟨~ reasoning⟩ — **spe·cious·ly** *adv* — **spe·cious·ness** *n*

[1]**speck** \ˈspek\ *n* [ME *specke,* fr. OE *specca*] (bef. 12c) **1 :** a small discoloration or spot esp. from stain or decay **2 :** a very small amount **:** BIT **3 :** something marked or marred with specks — **specked** \ˈspekt\ *adj*

[2]**speck** *vt* (14c) **:** to produce specks on or in

[1]**speck·le** \ˈspe-kəl\ *n* [ME; akin to OE *specca*] (15c) **:** a little speck (as of color)

[2]**speckle** *vt* **speck·led; speck·ling** \-k(ə-)liŋ\ (15c) **1 :** to mark with speckles **2 :** to be distributed in or on like speckles

speckled perch *n* (1856) **:** BLACK CRAPPIE

speckled trout *n* (1765) **1 :** BROOK TROUT **2 :** SPOTTED SEA TROUT

speckle interferometry *n* (1970) **:** a technique for generating a clear composite image of a celestial object blurred by atmospheric turbulence in which a large number of short-exposure photographs are mathematically correlated by a computer

specs \ˈspeks\ *n pl* [contr. of *spectacles*] (1807) **:** GLASSES

spec·ta·cle \ˈspek-ti-kəl *also* -ˌti-kəl\ *n* [ME, fr. AF, fr. L *spectaculum,* fr. *spectare* to watch, freq. of *specere* to look, look at — more at SPY] (14c) **1 a :** something exhibited to view as unusual, notable, or entertaining; *esp* **:** an eye-catching or dramatic public display **b :** an object of curiosity or contempt ⟨made a ~ of herself⟩ **2** *pl* **:** GLASSES **3 :** something (as natural markings on an animal) suggesting a pair of glasses

spec·ta·cled \-kəld\ *adj* (1607) **1 :** having or wearing spectacles **2 :** having markings suggesting a pair of spectacles ⟨a ~ alligator⟩

spectacled bear *n* (1835) **:** a black or dark brown bear (*Tremarctos ornatus*) of the Andes mountains with white markings encircling the eyes

[1]**spec·tac·u·lar** \spek-ˈta-kyə-lər, spək-\ *adj* [L *spectaculum*] (1682) **:** of, relating to, or being a spectacle **:** STRIKING, SENSATIONAL ⟨a ~ display of fireworks⟩ — **spec·tac·u·lar·ly** *adv*

[2]**spectacular** *n* (1873) **:** something that is spectacular; *esp* **:** an elaborate film, television, or theatrical production

spec·tate \ˈspek-ˌtāt\ *vi* **spec·tat·ed; spec·tat·ing** [back-formation fr. *spectator*] (1858) **:** to be present as a spectator (as at a sports event)

spec·ta·tor \ˈspek-ˌtā-tər, spek-ˈ\ *n* [L, fr. *spectare* to watch] (ca. 1586) **1 :** one who looks on or watches **2 :** a woman's pump usu. having contrasting colors with a perforated design at the toe and sometimes heel — **spectator** *adj* — **spec·ta·tor·i·al** \ˌspek-tə-ˈtȯr-ē-əl\ *adj* — **spec·ta·tor·ship** \ˈspek-ˌtā-tər-ˌship, spek-ˈ\ *n*

spec·ter *or* **spec·tre** \ˈspek-tər\ *n* [F *spectre,* fr. L *spectrum* appearance, specter, fr. *specere* to look, look at — more at SPY] (1605) **1 :** a visible disembodied spirit **:** GHOST **2 :** something that haunts or perturbs the mind **:** PHANTASM ⟨the ~ of hunger⟩

spec·ti·no·my·cin \ˌspek-tə-nō-ˈmī-sᵊn\ *n* [*spect-* (fr. NL *spectabilis,* specific epithet of *Streptomyces spectabilis*) + act*inomycin*] (1964) **:** a white crystalline broad-spectrum antibiotic $C_{14}H_{24}N_2O_7$ produced by a bacterium (*Streptomyces spectabilis*) that is used clinically esp. in the form of its hydrochloride to treat gonorrhea

spec·tral \ˈspek-trəl\ *adj* (1769) **1 :** of, relating to, or suggesting a specter **:** GHOSTLY **2 :** of, relating to, or made by a spectrum — **spec·tral·ly** \ˈspek-trə-lē\ *adv*

spectral line *n* (1849) **:** one of a series of linear images formed by a spectrograph or similar instrument and corresponding to a narrow portion of the spectrum of the radiation emitted or absorbed by a particular source

spectro- *comb form* [NL *spectrum*] **:** spectrum ⟨*spectro*scope⟩

spec·tro·flu·o·rom·e·ter \ˌspek-(ˌ)trō-ˌflu̇-ˈrä-mə-tər, -flȯ-\ *also* **spec·tro·flu·o·rim·e·ter** \-ˈri-\ *n* (1957) **:** a device for measuring and recording fluorescence spectra — **spec·tro·flu·o·ro·met·ric** \-ˌflu̇r-ə-ˈme-trik, -ˌflȯr-\ *adj* — **spec·tro·flu·o·rom·e·try** \-flu̇-ˈrä-mə-trē, -ˌflȯ-\ *n*

spec·tro·gram \ˈspek-t(r)ə-ˌgram\ *n* [ISV] (1892) **:** a photograph, image, or diagram of a spectrum

spec·tro·graph \-ˌgraf\ *n* [ISV] (1884) **:** an instrument for dispersing radiation (as electromagnetic radiation or sound waves) into a spectrum and recording or mapping the spectrum — **spec·tro·graph·ic** \ˌspek-t(r)ə-ˈgra-fik\ *adj* — **spec·tro·graph·i·cal·ly** \-fi-k(ə-)lē\ *adv* — **spec·trog·ra·phy** \spek-ˈträ-grə-fē\ *n*

spec·tro·he·lio·gram \ˌspek-trō-ˈhē-lē-ə-ˌgram\ *n* (1905) **:** a photograph of the sun that is made by monochromatic light and shows the sun's faculae and prominences

spec·tro·he·lio·graph \-ˌgraf\ *n* [ISV] (1892) **:** an apparatus for making spectroheliograms — **spec·tro·he·li·og·ra·phy** \-ˌhē-lē-ˈä-grə-fē\ *n*

spec·tro·he·lio·scope \-ˈhē-lē-ə-ˌskōp\ *n* [ISV] (1906) **1 :** SPECTROHELIOGRAPH **2 :** an instrument similar to a spectroheliograph used for visual as distinguished from photographic observations

spec·trom·e·ter \spek-ˈträ-mə-tər\ *n* [ISV] (1874) **1 :** an instrument used for measuring wavelengths of light spectra **2 :** any of various analytical instruments in which an emission (as of particles or radiation) is dispersed according to some property (as mass or energy) of the emission and the amount of dispersion is measured ⟨nuclear magnetic resonance ⁀⟩ — **spec·tro·met·ric** \ˌspek-trə-'me-trik\ *adj* — **spec·trom·e·try** \spek-'trä-mə-trē\ *n*

spec·tro·pho·tom·e·ter \ˌspek-trō-fə-'tä-mə-tər\ *n* [ISV] (1881) : a photometer for measuring the relative intensities of the light in different parts of a spectrum — **spec·tro·pho·to·met·ric** \-trə-ˌfō-tə-'me-trik\ *also* **spec·tro·pho·to·met·ri·cal** \-tri-kəl\ *adj* — **spec·tro·pho·to·met·ri·cal·ly** \-tri-k(ə-)lē\ *adv* — **spec·tro·pho·tom·e·try** \ˌspek-(ˌ)trō-fə-'tä-mə-trē\ *n*

spec·tro·scope \'spek-trə-ˌskōp\ *n* [ISV] (1861) : an instrument for forming and examining spectra esp. in the visible region of the electromagnetic spectrum — **spec·tro·scop·ic** \ˌspek-trə-'skä-pik\ *adj* — **spec·tro·scop·i·cal·ly** \-pi-k(ə-)lē\ *adv* — **spec·tros·co·pist** \spek-'träs-kə-pist\ *n*

spec·tros·co·py \spek-'träs-kə-pē\ *n* (1869) **1** : the process or technique of using a spectroscope or spectrometer **2** : the production and investigation of spectra

spec·trum \'spek-trəm\ *n, pl* **spec·tra** \-trə\ *or* **spectrums** [NL, fr. L, appearance — more at SPECTER] (1671) **1 a** : a continuum of color formed when a beam of white light is dispersed (as by passage through a prism) so that its component wavelengths are arranged in order **b** : any of various continua that resemble a color spectrum in consisting of an ordered arrangement by a particular characteristic (as frequency or energy): as **(1)** : ELECTROMAGNETIC SPECTRUM **(2)** : RADIO SPECTRUM **(3)** : the range of frequencies of sound waves **(4)** : MASS SPECTRUM **c** : the representation (as a plot) of a spectrum **2 a** : a continuous sequence or range ⟨a wide ⁀ of interests⟩ ⟨opposite ends of the political ⁀⟩ **b** : kinds of organisms associated with a particular situation (as an environment) **c** : a range of effectiveness against pathogenic organisms ⟨an antibiotic with a broad ⁀⟩

spec·u·lar \'spe-kyə-lər\ *adj* [L *specularis* of a mirror, fr. *speculum*] (1640) **1** : of, relating to, or having the qualities of a mirror — **spec·u·lar·i·ty** \ˌspe-kyə-'la-rə-tē\ *n* — **spec·u·lar·ly** \'spe-kyə-lər-lē\ *adv*

spec·u·late \'spe-kyə-ˌlāt\ *vb* **-lat·ed; -lat·ing** [L *speculatus*, pp. of *speculari* to spy out, examine, fr. *specula* lookout post, fr. *specere* to look, look at — more at SPY] *vi* (1599) **1 a** : to meditate on or ponder a subject : REFLECT **b** : to review something idly or casually and often inconclusively **2** : to assume a business risk in hope of gain; *esp* : to buy or sell in expectation of profiting from market fluctuations ⁀ *vt* **1** : to take to be true on the basis of insufficient evidence : THEORIZE **2** : to be curious or doubtful about : WONDER ⟨⁀s whether it will rain all vacation⟩ *syn* see THINK — **spec·u·la·tor** \-ˌlā-tər\ *n*

spec·u·la·tion \ˌspe-kyə-'lā-shən\ *n* (14c) : an act or instance of speculating: as **a** : assumption of unusual business risk in hopes of obtaining commensurate gain **b** : a transaction involving such speculation

spec·u·la·tive \'spe-kyə-lə-tiv, -ˌlā-\ *adj* (14c) **1** : involving, based on, or constituting intellectual speculation; *also* : theoretical rather than demonstrable ⟨⁀ knowledge⟩ **2** : marked by questioning curiosity ⟨gave him a ⁀ glance⟩ **3** : of, relating to, or being a financial speculation ⟨⁀ stocks⟩ ⟨⁀ venture⟩ — **spec·u·la·tive·ly** *adv*

spec·u·lum \'spe-kyə-ləm\ *n, pl* **-la** \-lə\ *also* **-lums** [ME, fr. L, mirror, fr. *specere*] (15c) **1** : an instrument inserted into a body passage esp. to facilitate visual inspection or medication **2** : a drawing or table showing the relative positions of all the planets (as in an astrological nativity) **3** : a patch of color on the secondaries of most ducks and some other birds

SpEd *or* **SPED** *abbr* special education

speech \'spēch\ *n* [ME *speche*, fr. OE *sprǣc, spǣc;* akin to OE *sprecan* to speak — more at SPEAK] (bef. 12c) **1 a** : the communication or expression of thoughts in spoken words **b** : exchange of spoken words : CONVERSATION **2 a** : something that is spoken : UTTERANCE **b** : a usu. public discourse : ADDRESS **3 a** : LANGUAGE, DIALECT **b** : an individual manner or style of speaking **4** : the power of expressing or communicating thoughts by speaking

speech community *n* (1894) : a group of people sharing characteristic patterns of vocabulary, grammar, and pronunciation

speech form *n* (1863) : LINGUISTIC FORM

speech·ify \'spē-chə-ˌfī\ *vi* **-ified; -ify·ing** (1723) : to make a speech

speech·less \'spēch-ləs\ *adj* (bef. 12c) **1** : unable to speak : DUMB **2** : not speaking : SILENT **3** : not capable of being expressed in words — **speech·less·ly** *adv* — **speech·less·ness** *n*

speech·writ·er \-ˌrī-tər\ *n* (1834) : a person who writes speeches (as for a politician)

¹**speed** \'spēd\ *n* [ME *spede*, fr. OE *spēd;* akin to OHG *spuot* prosperity, speed, OE *spōwan* to succeed, L *spes* hope, Lith *spéti* to be in time] (bef. 12c) **1** *archaic* : prosperity in an undertaking : SUCCESS **2 a** : the act or state of moving swiftly : SWIFTNESS **b** : rate of motion: as **(1)** : VELOCITY 1 **(2)** : the magnitude of a velocity irrespective of direction **c** : IMPETUS **3** : swiftness or rate of performance or action : VELOCITY 3a **4 a** : the sensitivity of a photographic film, plate, or paper expressed numerically **b** : the light-gathering power of a lens or optical system **c** : the time during which a camera shutter is open **5** : a transmission gear in automotive vehicles or bicycles — usu. used in combination ⟨a ten-*speed* bicycle⟩ **6** : someone or something that appeals to one's taste ⟨just my ⁀⟩ **7** : METHAMPHETAMINE; *also* : a related stimulant drug and esp. an amphetamine *syn* see HASTE — **speed·ster** \'spēd-stər\ *n* — **at speed** *chiefly Brit* : FAST, RAPIDLY — **up to speed** : operating at full effectiveness or potential

²**speed** *vb* **sped** \'sped\ *or* **speed·ed; speed·ing** *vi* (bef. 12c) **1 a** *archaic* : to prosper in an undertaking **b** *archaic* : GET ALONG, FARE **2 a** : to make haste ⟨*sped* to her bedside⟩ **b** : to go or drive at excessive or illegal speed **3** : to move, work, or take place faster : ACCELERATE ⟨the heart ⁀s up⟩ ⁀ *vt* **1 a** *archaic* : to cause or help to prosper : AID **b** : to further the success of **2 a** : to cause to move quickly : HASTEN **b** : to wish Godspeed to **c** : to increase the speed of : ACCELERATE **3** : to send out ⟨⁀ an arrow⟩ — **speed·er** *n*

¹**speed·ball** \'spēd-ˌbȯl\ *n* (1905) **1** *slang* : a dose of cocaine mixed with heroin or morphine or an amphetamine and usu. taken by injection **2** : a game which resembles soccer but in which a ball caught in the air may be passed with the hands and in which a score is made by kicking or heading the ball between the goalposts or by a successful forward pass over the goal line **3** : one that is outstandingly fast

²**speedball** *vi* (1970) *slang* : to take a speedball esp. by injection

speed·boat \-ˌbōt\ *n* (1911) : a fast launch or motorboat — **speed·boat·ing** \-ˌbō-tiŋ\ *n*

speed bump *n* (1972) : a low raised ridge across a roadway (as in a parking lot) to limit vehicle speed

speed dating *n* (2000) : an event at which each participant converses individually with all the prospective partners for a few minutes in order to select those with whom dating is desired

speed dial *n* (1983) : a telephone function by which a selected stored number can be dialed by pressing only one key — **speed–dial** *vb*

speed freak *n* (1967) : one who habitually misuses amphetamines and esp. methamphetamine

speed limit *n* (1902) : the maximum or minimum speed permitted by law in a given area under specified circumstances

speedo \'spē-(ˌ)dō\ *n, pl* **speed·os** [by alter.] (1934) *chiefly Brit* : SPEEDOMETER

speed of light (1823) : a fundamental physical constant that is the speed at which electromagnetic radiation propagates in a vacuum and that has a value fixed by international convention of 299,792,458 meters per second — symbol *c*

speed·om·e·ter \spi-'dä-mə-tər\ *n* (1903) **1** : an instrument for indicating speed : TACHOMETER **2** : an instrument for indicating distance traversed as well as speed of travel; *also* : ODOMETER

speed–read·ing \'spēd-ˌrē-diŋ\ *n* (1962) : a method of reading rapidly by skimming — **speed–read** *vt*

speed shop *n* (1953) : a shop that sells custom automotive equipment esp. to hot-rodders

speed skating *n* (1885) : the sport of racing on skates — **speed skat·er** *n*

speed trap *n* (1925) : a stretch of road policed by often concealed officers or devices (as radar) so as to catch speeders

speed–up \'spēd-ˌəp\ *n* (1921) **1** : ACCELERATION **2** : an employer's demand for accelerated output without increased pay

speed·way \'spēd-ˌwā\ *n* (1894) **1** : a public road on which fast driving is allowed; *specif* : EXPRESSWAY **2** : a racecourse for automobiles or motorcycles **3** : a sprint race for motorcycles

speed·well \'spēd-ˌwel\ *n* (1578) : a perennial European herb (*Veronica officinalis*) of the snapdragon family that is naturalized in No. America and has small bluish flowers in axillary racemes; *broadly* : VERONICA

speedy \'spē-dē\ *adj* **speed·i·er; -est** (14c) : marked by swiftness of motion or action; *also* : PROMPT **2** *syn* see FAST — **speed·i·ly** \'spē-dᵊl-ē\ *adv* — **speed·i·ness** \'spē-dē-nəs\ *n*

speel \'spēl\ *vb* [origin unknown] (1513) *chiefly Scot* : CLIMB

speer *or* **speir** \'spir\ *vb* [ME (Sc) *speren,* fr. OE *spyrian* to seek after; akin to OE *spor* spoor] (bef. 12c) *chiefly Scot* : ASK, INQUIRE

spe·le·ol·o·gy \ˌspē-lē-'ä-lə-jē, ˌspe-\ *n* [L *speleum* cave (fr. Gk *spēlaion*) + ISV *-o- + -logy* — more at SPELUNKER] (1895) : the scientific study or exploration of caves — **spe·le·o·log·i·cal** \ˌspē-lē-ə-'lä-ji-kəl, ˌspe-\ *adj* — **spe·le·ol·o·gist** \ˌspē-lē-'ä-lə-jist, ˌspe-\ *n*

¹**spell** \'spel\ *vb* **spelled** \'speld, 'spelt\; **spell·ing** [ME, to mean, signify, read by spelling out letters, fr. AF *espeleir*, of Gmc origin; akin to OE *spellian* to relate, *spell* talk] *vt* (14c) **1** : to read slowly and with difficulty — often used with *out* **2** : to find out by study : come to understand — often used with *out* ⟨it requires some pains to ⁀ out those decorations —F. J. Mather⟩ **3 a (1)** : to name the letters of in order; *also* : to write or print the letters of in order **(2)** : to write or print the letters of in a particular way **b** : to make up (a word) ⟨what word do these letters ⁀⟩ **c** : WRITE 1b ⟨*ed* as one word⟩ **4** : to add up to : MEAN ⟨crop failure was likely to ⁀ stark famine —Stringfellow Barr⟩ ⁀ *vi* : to form words with letters ⟨teach children to ⁀⟩; *also* : to spell words in a certain way ⟨⁀s the way he speaks⟩

²**spell** *n* [ME, talk, tale, fr. OE; akin to OHG *spel* talk, tale] (1579) **1 a** : a spoken word or form of words held to have magic power **b** : a state of enchantment **2** : a strong compelling influence or attraction

³**spell** \'spel\ *vt* **spelled** \'speld\; **spell·ing** (ca. 1623) : to put under a spell

⁴**spell** *n* [prob. alter. of ME *spale* substitute, fr. OE *spala*] (1593) **1 a** *archaic* : a shift of workers **b** : one's turn at work **2** : a period spent in a job or occupation **b** *chiefly Austral* : a period of rest from work, activity, or use **3 a** : an indeterminate period of time ⟨waited a ⁀ before advancing⟩; *also* : a continuous period of time ⟨did a ⁀ in prison⟩ **b** : a stretch of a specified type of weather **4** : a period of bodily or mental distress or disorder ⟨a ⁀ of coughing⟩ ⟨fainting ⁀s⟩

⁵**spell** *vb* **spelled** \'speld\; **spell·ing** [ME *spelen,* fr. OE *spelian;* akin to OE *spala* substitute] *vt* (1595) **1** : to take the place of for a time : RELIEVE ⟨we ⁀ each other every two hours⟩ **2** : REST ⁀ *vi* **1** : to work in turns **2** *chiefly Austral* : to rest from an activity for a time

spell·bind \'spel-ˌbīnd\ *vt* **-bound** \-ˌbau̇nd\; **-bind·ing** [back-formation fr. *spellbound*] (1808) : to bind or hold by or as if by a spell

spell·bind·er \-ˌbīn-dər\ *n* (1888) : a speaker of compelling eloquence; *also* : one that compels attention

spell·bind·ing \-ˌbīn-diŋ\ *adj* (1827) : holding the attention as if by a spell ⟨a ⁀ story⟩ — **spell·bind·ing·ly** \-diŋ-lē\ *adv*

spell·bound \-ˌbau̇nd\ *adj* (1785) : held by or as if by a spell

spell–checker *n* (1980) : a computer program that identifies possible misspellings in a block of text by comparing the text with a database of accepted spellings — called also *spell-check, spelling checker* — **spell-check** \'spel-ˌchek\ *vb*

spell·er \'spe-lər\ *n* (15c) **1** : a person who spells words esp. in a certain way ⟨a poor ⁀⟩ **2** : a book with exercises for teaching spelling

spell·ing *n* (15c) **1** : the forming of words from letters according to accepted usage : ORTHOGRAPHY **2 a** : a sequence of letters composing a word **b** : the way in which a word is spelled

spelling bee *n* (1871) : a spelling contest in which contestants are eliminated as soon as they misspell a word

spelling pronunciation *n* (1901) : a pronunciation of a word that is based on its spelling alone and often includes the vocalization of silent letters

spell out *vt* (1940) **1** : to make plain ⟨*spelled out* the orders in detail⟩ **2** : to write or print in letters and in full ⟨numbers are to be *spelled out*⟩

\ə\ abut \ᵊ\ kitten, F table \ər\ further \a\ ash \ā\ ace \ä\ mop, mar \au̇\ out \ch\ chin \e\ bet \ē\ easy \g\ go \i\ hit \ī\ ice \j\ job \ŋ\ sing \ō\ go \ȯ\ law \ȯi\ boy \th\ thin \t̠h\ the \ü\ loot \u̇\ foot \y\ yet \zh\ vision, beige \k, ⁿ, œ, ɶ, �\ *see* Guide to Pronunciation

[1]**spelt** \ˈspelt\ *n* [ME, fr. OE, fr. LL *spelta,* of Gmc origin; perh. akin to MHG *spelte* split piece of wood, OHG *spaltan* to split — more at SPLIT] (bef. 12c) **:** an ancient wheat (*Triticum spelta* syn. *T. aestivum spelta*) with spikelets containing two light red grains; *also* **:** the grain of spelt

[2]**spelt** \ˈspelt\ *chiefly Brit past and past part of* SPELL

spel·ter \ˈspel-tər\ *n* [prob. alter. of MD *speauter*] (1661) **:** ZINC; *esp* **:** zinc cast in slabs for commercial use

spe·lunk·er \spi-ˈləŋ-kər, ˈspē-ˌ\ *n* [L *spelunca* cave, fr. Gk *spēlynx;* akin to Gk *spēlaion* cave] (1942) **:** one who makes a hobby of exploring and studying caves

spe·lunk·ing \-kiŋ\ *n* (1944) **:** the hobby or practice of exploring caves

spence \ˈspen(t)s\ *n* [ME, fr. AF *espence, spence,* fr. ML *expensa* victuals, fr. LL, outlay, compulsory supply of food — more at EXPENSE] (14c) *dial chiefly Brit* **:** PANTRY

[1]**spen·cer** \ˈspen(t)-sər\ *n* [George John, 2d earl *Spencer* †1834 Eng. politician] (1795) **:** a short waist-length jacket

[2]**spencer** *n* [prob. fr. the name *Spencer*] (1840) **:** a trysail abaft the foremast or mainmast

Spen·ce·ri·an \spen-ˈsir-ē-ən\ *adj* [Platt R. *Spencer* †1864 Am. calligrapher] (1862) **:** of or relating to a form of slanting handwriting

Spen·ce·ri·an·ism \spen-ˈsir-ē-ə-ˌni-zəm\ *n* (1881) **:** the synthetic philosophy of Herbert Spencer that has as its central idea the mechanistic evolution of the cosmos from relative simplicity to relative complexity

spend \ˈspend\ *vb* **spent** \ˈspent\; **spend·ing** [ME, fr. OE *-spendan,* fr. ML *expendere* to disburse, use up, fr. L, to measure by weight, pay out — more at EXPEND] *vt* (13c) **1 :** to use up or pay out **:** EXPEND **2 a :** EXHAUST, WEAR OUT ⟨the hurricane gradually *spent* itself⟩ **b :** to consume wastefully **:** SQUANDER ⟨the waters are not ours to ~ —J. R. Ellis⟩ **3 :** to cause or permit to elapse **:** PASS ⟨~ the night⟩ **4 :** GIVE UP, SACRIFICE ~ *vi* **1 :** to expend or waste wealth or strength **2 :** to become expended or consumed **3 :** to have an orgasm — **spend·able** \ˈspen-də-bəl\ *adj* — **spend·er** *n*

spending money *n* (15c) **:** POCKET MONEY

spend·thrift \ˈspen(d)-ˌthrift\ *n* (1584) **:** a person who spends improvidently or wastefully — **spendthrift** *adj*

spendy \ˈspen-dē\ *adj* **spend·i·er; -est** (1985) *chiefly Northwest* **:** EXPENSIVE

Spen·gle·ri·an \ˌshpeŋ-ˈglir-ē-ən, ˌspeŋ-, -ˈlir-\ *adj* (1922) **:** of or relating to the theory of world history developed by Oswald Spengler which holds that all major cultures undergo similar cyclical developments from birth to maturity to decay — **Spenglerian** *n*

Spen·se·ri·an stanza \spen-ˈsir-ē-ən-\ *n* [Edmund *Spenser*] (1817) **:** a stanza consisting of eight verses of iambic pentameter and an alexandrine with a rhyme scheme *ababbcbcc*

spent \ˈspent\ *adj* [ME, fr. pp. of *spenden* to spend] (15c) **1 a :** used up **:** CONSUMED **b :** exhausted of active or required components or qualities often for a particular purpose ⟨~ nuclear fuel⟩ **2 :** drained of energy or effectiveness **:** EXHAUSTED **3 :** exhausted of spawn or sperm ⟨~ fishes⟩

sperm \ˈspərm\ *n, pl* **sperm** *or* **sperms** [ME, fr. MF *esperme, sperme,* fr. LL *spermat-, sperma,* fr. Gk, lit., seed, fr. *speirein* to sow; prob. akin to Arm *p'aratem* I dispense] (14c) **1 a :** SEMEN **b :** a male gamete; *esp* **:** SPERMATOZOON 1 **2 :** a product of the sperm whale

sperm- *or* **spermo-** *or* **sperma-** *or* **spermi-** *comb form* [Gk *sperm-, spermo-,* fr. *sperma*] **:** seed **:** germ **:** sperm ⟨*sperma*theca⟩ ⟨*spermi*cide⟩

sper·ma·ce·ti \ˌspər-mə-ˈsē-tē, -ˈse-\ *n* [ME *sperma cete,* fr. ML *sperma ceti* whale sperm] (15c) **:** a waxy solid obtained from the oil of cetaceans and esp. from a closed cavity in the heads of sperm whales and used esp. formerly in ointments, cosmetics, and candles

sper·ma·go·ni·um \ˌspər-mə-ˈgō-nē-əm\ *n, pl* **-nia** \-nē-ə\ [NL] (1861) **:** a flask-shaped or depressed receptacle in which spermatia are produced in some fungi and lichens

sper·ma·ry \ˈspər-mə-rē, ˈspərm-rē\ *n, pl* **-ries** [NL *spermarium,* fr. Gk *sperma*] (ca. 1859) **:** an organ in which male gametes are developed

spermat- *or* **spermato-** *comb form* [Gk, fr. *spermat-, sperma*] **:** seed **:** spermatozoon ⟨*spermat*id⟩ ⟨*spermato*cyte⟩

sper·ma·the·ca \ˌspər-mə-ˈthē-kə\ *n* [NL] (1826) **:** a sac for sperm storage in the female reproductive tract of various lower animals and esp. insects

sper·mat·ic \(ˌ)spər-ˈma-tik\ *adj* (15c) **1 :** relating to sperm or a spermary **2 :** resembling, carrying, or full of sperm

spermatic cord *n* (1783) **:** a cord that suspends the testis within the scrotum and contains the vas deferens and vessels and nerves of the testis

sper·ma·tid \ˈspər-mə-təd\ *n* (1889) **:** one of the haploid cells that are formed by the second division in meiosis of a spermatocyte and that differentiate into spermatozoa

sper·ma·ti·um \(ˌ)spər-ˈmā-sh(ē-)əm\ *n, pl* **-tia** \-sh(ē-)ə\ [NL, fr. Gk *spermation,* dim. of *spermat-, sperma*] (1856) **:** a nonmotile male gamete of a red alga; *also* **:** a nonmotile cell functioning as a male gamete in certain fungi and lichens — **sper·ma·tial** \-sh(ē-)əl\ *adj*

sper·mato·cyte \(ˌ)spər-ˈma-tə-ˌsīt\ *n* (1886) **:** a cell giving rise to sperm cells; *esp* **:** a cell that is derived by mitosis from a spermatogonium and ultimately gives rise by meiosis to four haploid spermatids

sper·mato·gen·e·sis \(ˌ)spər-ˌma-tə-ˈje-nə-səs\ *n* [NL] (1881) **:** the process of male gamete formation including formation of a spermatocyte from a spermatogonium, meiotic division of the spermatocyte, and transformation of the four resulting spermatids into spermatozoa — **sper·mato·gen·ic** \-ˈje-nik\ *adj*

sper·mato·go·ni·um \-ˈgō-nē-əm\ *n, pl* **-nia** \-nē-ə\ [NL] (1861) **:** a primitive male germ cell — **sper·mato·go·ni·al** \-nē-əl\ *adj*

sper·mato·phore \(ˌ)spər-ˈma-tə-ˌfȯr\ *n* [ISV] (ca. 1849) **:** a capsule, packet, or mass enclosing spermatozoa that is extruded by the male of various lower animals (as insects) and is transferred to the reproductive tract of the female

sper·mato·phyte \-ˌfīt\ *n* [ultim. fr. NL *spermat-* + Gk *phyton* plant — more at PHYT-] (1897) **:** any of a group (Spermatophyta) of higher plants comprising those that produce seeds and including the gymnosperms and angiosperms — **sper·mato·phyt·ic** \-ˌma-tə-ˈfi-tik\ *adj*

sper·ma·to·zo·an \(ˌ)spər-ˌma-tə-ˈzō-ən, ˌspər-mə-tə-\ *n* (ca. 1900) **:** SPERMATOZOON — **spermatozoan** *adj*

sper·ma·to·zo·id \-ˈzō-əd\ *n* [ISV, fr. NL *spermatozoon*] (1854) **:** a motile male gamete of a plant usu. produced in an antheridium

sper·ma·to·zo·on \-ˈzō-ˌän, -ˈzō-ən\ *n, pl* **-zoa** \-ˈzō-ə\ [NL] (ca. 1839) **1 :** a motile male gamete of an animal usu. with rounded or elongate head and a long posterior flagellum **2 :** SPERMATOZOID — **sper·ma·to·zo·al** \-ˈzō-əl\ *adj*

sperm cell *n* (1851) **:** SPERM 1b

sper·mi·cide \ˈspər-mə-ˌsīd\ *n* (1929) **:** a preparation or substance (as nonoxynol-9) used to kill sperm — **sper·mi·cid·al** \ˌspər-mə-ˈsī-dəl\ *adj*

sper·mio·gen·e·sis \ˌspər-mē-ō-ˈje-nə-səs\ *n* [NL, fr. *spermium* spermatozoon + *-o-* + L *genesis*] (1916) **:** SPERMATOGENESIS; *specif* **:** transformation of a spermatid into a spermatozoon

sperm nucleus *n* (1887) **:** either of two nuclei that derive from the generative nucleus of a pollen grain and function in the fertilization of a seed plant

sperm oil *n* (1839) **:** a pale yellow oil from the sperm whale

sper·mo·phile \ˈspər-mə-ˌfī(-ə)l\ *n* [ultim. fr. Gk *sperma* seed + *philos* loving] (1824) **:** GROUND SQUIRREL

sperm whale \ˈspərm-\ *n* [short for *spermaceti whale*] (ca. 1700) **:** a large toothed whale (*Physeter macrocephalus* syn. *P. catodon*) with a massive squarish head having a large closed cavity containing a fluid mixture of spermaceti and oil

-spermy *n comb form* [Gk *sperma* seed, sperm] **:** state of exhibiting or resulting from (such) a fertilization ⟨agamo*spermy*⟩

sper·ry·lite \ˈsper-i-ˌlīt\ *n* [Francis L. *Sperry,* †1906 Am. chemist + E *-lite*] (1889) **:** a mineral consisting of an arsenide of platinum

spes·sar·tite \ˈspe-sər-ˌtīt\ *or* **spes·sar·tine** \-ˌtēn\ *n* [F, fr. *Spessart* mountain range, Germany] (1850) **:** a manganese aluminum garnet usu. containing other elements (as iron) in minor amounts

[1]**spew** \ˈspyü\ *vb* [ME, fr. OE *spīwan;* akin to OHG *spīwan* to spit, L *spuere,* Gk *ptyein*] *vi* (bef. 12c) **1 :** VOMIT **2 :** to come forth in a flood or gush **3 :** to ooze out as if under pressure **:** EXUDE ~ *vt* **1 :** VOMIT **2 :** to send or cast forth with vigor or violence or in great quantity ⟨a volcano ~*ing* out ash⟩ — often used with *out* — **spew·er** *n*

[2]**spew** *n* (15c) **1 :** matter that is vomited **:** VOMIT **2 :** material that exudes or is extruded

SPF *abbr* sun protection factor

sp gr *abbr* specific gravity

sphag·nous \ˈsfag-nəs\ *adj* (ca. 1828) **:** of, relating to, or abounding in sphagnum

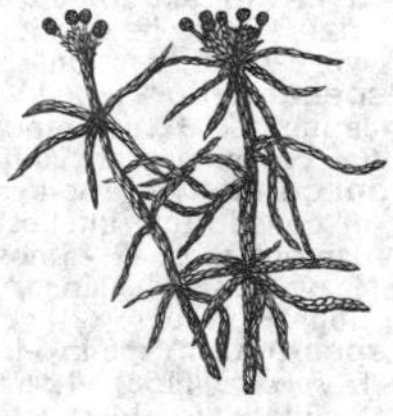
sphagnum 1

sphag·num \ˈsfag-nəm\ *n* [NL, fr. L *sphagnos,* a moss, fr. Gk] (1741) **1 :** any of an order (Sphagnales, containing a single genus *Sphagnum*) of atypical mosses that grow only in wet acid areas where their remains become compacted with other plant debris to form peat **2 :** a mass of sphagnum plants

sphal·er·ite \ˈsfa-lə-ˌrīt\ *n* [G *Sphalerit,* fr. Gk *sphaleros* deceitful, fr. *sphallein* to cause to fall; fr. its often being mistaken for galena — more at SPILL] (ca. 1868) **:** a mineral composed essentially of zinc sulfide that is the most important ore of zinc — called also *zinc blende*

S phase *n* [*s*ynthesis] (1966) **:** the period in the cell cycle during which DNA replication takes place — compare G_1 PHASE, G_2 PHASE, M PHASE

sphene \ˈsfēn\ *n* [F *sphène,* fr. Gk *sphēn* wedge] (1815) **:** a mineral that is a silicate of calcium and titanium and often contains other elements

sphen·odon \ˈsfē-nə-ˌdän, ˈsfe-\ *n* [NL, genus name, fr. Gk *sphēn* wedge + *odōn, odous* tooth — more at TOOTH] (1878) **:** TUATARA — **sphen·odont** \-ˌdänt\ *adj*

[1]**sphe·noid** \ˈsfē-ˌnȯid\ *or* **sphe·noi·dal** \sfi-ˈnȯi-dᵊl\ *adj* [NL *sphenoides,* fr. Gk *sphēnoeidēs* wedge-shaped, fr. *sphēn* wedge] (1732) **1 :** of, relating to, or being a winged compound bone of the base of the cranium **2** *usu sphenoidal* **:** having a wedged shape

[2]**sphenoid** *n* (1828) **:** a sphenoid bone

sphe·nop·sid \sfi-ˈnäp-səd\ *n* [ultim. fr. Gk *sphēn* wedge + NL *-opsis*] (1957) **:** any of a class or division (Sphenopsida or Sphenophyta) of primitive vascular plants characterized by jointed ribbed stems, small leaves usu. in whorls at distinct stem nodes, and sporangia in sporangiophores and made up of the horsetails and extinct related forms

spher- *or* **sphero-** *also* **sphaer-** *or* **sphaero-** *comb form* [NL *sphaer-,* fr. Gk *sphair-, sphairo-,* fr. *sphaira* sphere] **:** sphere ⟨*spher*ule⟩ ⟨*sphero*meter⟩

spher·al \ˈsfir-əl\ *adj* (1545) **1 :** SPHERICAL **2 :** of or relating to the spheres of ancient astronomy

[1]**sphere** \ˈsfir\ *n* [ME *spere* globe, celestial sphere, fr. AF *espere,* fr. L *sphaera,* fr. Gk *sphaira,* lit., ball; perh. akin to Gk *spairein* to quiver — more at SPURN] (14c) **1 a (1) :** the apparent surface of the heavens of which half forms the dome of the visible sky **(2) :** any of the concentric and eccentric revolving spherical transparent shells in which according to ancient astronomy stars, sun, planets, and moon are set **b :** a globe depicting such a sphere; *broadly* **:** GLOBE a **2 a :** a globular body **:** BALL **b :** PLANET, STAR **c (1) :** a solid that is bounded by a surface consisting of all points at a given distance from a point constituting its center — see VOLUME table **(2) :** the bounding surface of a sphere **3 :** natural, normal, or proper place; *esp* **:** social order or rank ⟨not in the same ~ as his moneyed friends⟩ **4 a** *obs* **:** ORBIT **b :** an area or range over or within which someone or something acts, exists, or has influence or significance ⟨the public ~⟩ — **spher·ic** \ˈsfir-ik, ˈsfer-\ *adj, archaic* — **sphe·ric·i·ty** \sfir-ˈi-sə-tē\ *n*

[2]**sphere** *vt* **sphered; spher·ing** (1602) **1 :** to place in a sphere or among the spheres **:** ENSPHERE **2 :** to form into a sphere

sphere of influence (1885) **:** a territorial area within which the political influence or the interests of one nation are held to be more or less paramount

spher·i·cal \ˈsfir-i-kəl, ˈsfer-\ *adj* (15c) **1 :** having the form of a sphere or of one of its segments **2 :** relating to or dealing with a sphere or its properties — **spher·i·cal·ly** \-k(ə-)lē\ *adv*

spherical aberration *n* (1868) **:** aberration that is caused by the spherical form of a lens or mirror and that gives different foci for central and marginal rays

spherical angle *n* (1678) **:** the angle between two intersecting arcs of great circles of a sphere measured by the plane angle formed by the tangents to the arcs at the point of intersection

spherical coordinate *n* (ca. 1864) : one of three coordinates that are used to locate a point in space and that comprise the radius of the sphere on which the point lies in a system of concentric spheres, the angle formed by the point, the center, and a given axis of the sphere, and the angle between the plane of the first angle and a reference plane through the given axis of the sphere

spherical geometry *n* (1728) : the geometry of figures on a sphere

spherical polygon *n* (ca. 1825) : a figure analogous to a plane polygon that is formed on a sphere by arcs of great circles

spherical triangle *n* (1585) : a spherical polygon of three sides

spherical trigonometry *n* (ca. 1728) : trigonometry applied to spherical triangles and polygons

spher·oid \ˈsfir-ˌȯid, ˈsfer-\ *n* (1570) : a figure resembling a sphere; *also* : an object of approximately spherical shape — **sphe·roi·dal** \sfi-ˈrȯi-dᵊl\ *also* **spheroid** *adj* — **sphe·roi·dal·ly** \-dᵊl-ē\ *adv*

sphe·rom·e·ter \sfir-ˈä-mə-tər\ *n* [ISV] (ca. 1828) : an instrument for measuring the curvature of a surface

sphe·ro·plast \ˈsfir-ə-ˌplast, ˈsfer-\ *n* (ca. 1920) : a bacterium or yeast cell that is modified (as by enzymatic action) so that there is partial loss of the cell wall and increased osmotic sensitivity

spher·ule \ˈsfir-ül, ˈsfer-, -ˌyül\ *n* (1665) : a little sphere or spherical body

spher·u·lite \ˈsfir-yə-ˌlīt, ˈsfer-, -ə-ˌlīt\ *n* (1823) : a usu. spherical crystalline body of radiating crystal fibers often found in vitreous volcanic rocks — **spher·u·lit·ic** \ˌsfir-yə-ˈli-tik, ˌsfer-, -ə-ˌli-\ *adj*

sphery \ˈsfir-ē\ *adj* (1596) **1** : of, relating to, or suggestive of the celestial bodies **2** : ROUND, SPHERICAL

sphinc·ter \ˈsfiŋ(k)-tər\ *n* [LL, fr. Gk *sphinktēr,* lit., band, fr. *sphingein* to bind tight] (1578) : an annular muscle surrounding and able to contract or close a bodily opening — **sphinc·ter·ic** \sfiŋ(k)-ˈter-ik\ *adj*

sphin·gid \ˈsfin-jəd\ *n* [ultim. fr. Gk *sphing-, sphinx* sphinx] (ca. 1909) : HAWK MOTH

sphin·go·sine \ˈsfiŋ-gə-ˌsēn\ *n* [Gk *sphingos* (gen. of *sphinx*) + E ²*-ine;* fr. riddles it posed to its first investigators] (1881) : a long-chain unsaturated amino alcohol $C_{18}H_{37}O_2N$ found esp. in nervous tissue and cell membranes

sphinx \ˈsfiŋ(k)s\ *n, pl* **sphinx·es** *or* **sphin·ges** \ˈsfin-ˌjēz\ [L, fr. Gk *Sphinx, Sphix*] (15c) **1 a** *cap* : a winged female monster in Greek mythology having a woman's head and a lion's body and noted for killing anyone unable to answer its riddle **b** : an enigmatic or mysterious person ⟨she is a ~ whose features hold a blank fascination⟩ **2** : an ancient Egyptian image in the form of a recumbent lion having a man's head, a ram's head, or a hawk's head — **sphinx·like** \-ˌlīk\ *adj*

sphinx moth *n* (1839) : HAWK MOTH

sp ht *abbr* specific heat

sphyg·mo·graph \ˈsfig-mə-ˌgraf\ *n* [Gk *sphygmos* pulse + ISV *-graph*] (ca. 1859) : an instrument that records graphically the movements or character of the pulse

sphyg·mo·ma·nom·e·ter \ˌsfig-mō-mə-ˈnä-mə-tər\ *n* [Gk *sphygmos* pulse (fr. *sphyzein* to throb) + ISV *manometer*] (ca. 1889) : an instrument for measuring blood pressure and esp. arterial blood pressure — **sphyg·mo·ma·nom·e·try** \-mə-ˈnä-mə-trē\ *n*

sphynx \ˈsfiŋ(k)s\ *n, pl* **sphynx** *or* **sphynx·es** [prob. alter. of *sphinx;* fr. the cat's appearance] (1970) : any of a breed of large-eared virtually hairless cats that originated as a spontaneous mutation

spic *also* **spick** \ˈspik\ *n* [by shortening & alter. fr. *spiggoty,* of unknown origin] (1916) *usu offensive* : SPANISH AMERICAN

spi·ca \ˈspī-kə\ *n, pl* **spi·cae** \-ˌkē\ *or* **spicas** [L, ear of grain — more at SPINE] (ca. 1731) : a bandage that is applied in successive V-shaped crossings and is used to immobilize a limb esp. at a joint

Spi·ca \ˈspī-kə\ *n* [L, lit., ear of grain] (15c) : a star of the first magnitude in the constellation Virgo

spi·cate \ˈspī-ˌkāt\ *adj* [L *spicatus,* pp. of *spicare* to arrange in the shape of heads of grain, fr. *spica*] (1668) : arranged in the form of a spike ⟨a ~ inflorescence⟩

¹**spic·ca·to** \spi-ˈkä-(ˌ)tō\ *adj* [It, pp. of *spiccare* to detach, pick off] (ca. 1724) : performed with a slight lifting of the bow after each note — used as a direction in music

²**spiccato** *n, pl* **-tos** (ca. 1903) : a spiccato technique, performance, or passage

¹**spice** \ˈspīs\ *n* [ME, fr. AF *espece, espis,* fr. LL *species* product, wares, drugs, spices, fr. L, appearance, species — more at SPECIES] (13c) **1** : any of various aromatic vegetable products (as pepper or nutmeg) used to season or flavor foods **2 a** *archaic* : a small portion, quantity, or admixture : DASH **b** : something that gives zest or relish ⟨variety's the very ~ of life —William Cowper⟩ **3** : a pungent or fragrant odor : PERFUME — **spice·less** \-ləs\ *adj*

²**spice** *vt* **spiced; spic·ing** (14c) **1** : to season with spices **2** : to add zest or relish to ⟨cynicism *spiced* with humor —J. W. Dawson⟩ — often used with *up*

spice·bush \ˈspīs-ˌbu̇sh\ *n* (1770) : an aromatic shrub (*Lindera benzoin*) of the laurel family found chiefly in the eastern U.S. that bears dense clusters of small greenish-yellow flowers followed by usu. scarlet berries

spic·ery \ˈspī-sə-rē, ˈspīs-rē\ *n, pl* **-er·ies** (13c) **1** : SPICES **2** *archaic* : a repository of spices **3** : a spicy quality

spick–and–span *or* **spic–and–span** \ˌspik-ən(d)-ˈspan, ˌspik-ᵊŋ-\ *adj* [short for *spick-and-span-new,* fr. obs. E *spick* spike + E *and* + *span-new*] (1665) **1** : FRESH, BRAND-NEW **2** : spotlessly clean

spic·ule \ˈspi-(ˌ)kyül\ *n* [NL *spicula* & L *spiculum;* NL *spicula,* alter. of L *spiculum* head of a spear or arrow, dim. of *spicum, spica* ear of grain] (1785) **1** : a slender pointed usu. hard body; *esp* : one of the minute calcareous or siliceous bodies that support the tissue of various invertebrates (as sponges) **2** : a spikelike short-lived prominence appearing close to the chromosphere of the solar atmosphere — **spic·u·lar** \ˈspi-kyə-lər\ *adj* — **spic·u·la·tion** \ˌspi-kyə-ˈlā-shən\ *n*

spicy \ˈspī-sē\ *adj* **spic·i·er; -est** (1562) **1** : having the quality, flavor, or fragrance of spice **2** : producing or abounding in spices **3** : LIVELY, SPIRITED **4** : PIQUANT, RACY; *esp* : somewhat scandalous or salacious ⟨~ gossip⟩ — **spic·i·ly** \-sə-lē\ *adv* — **spic·i·ness** \-sē-nəs\ *n*

spi·der \ˈspī-dər\ *n* [ME *spyder,* alter. of *spithre;* akin to OE *spinnan* to spin] (15c) **1** : any of an order (Araneae syn. Araneida) of arachnids having the abdomen usu. unsegmented and constricted at the base, chelicerae modified into poison fangs, and two or more pairs of abdominal spinnerets for spinning threads of silk for various uses (as in making cocoons for their eggs or webs to catch prey) **2** : a cast-iron frying pan orig. made with short feet to stand among coals on the hearth **3** : any of various devices consisting of a frame or skeleton with radiating arms or members — **spi·der·ish** \-də-rish\ *adj* — **spi·der·like** \-dər-ˌlīk\ *adj*

spider crab *n* (ca. 1710) : any of a family (Majidae) of crabs with extremely long legs and nearly triangular bodies which they often cover with kelp

spider mite *n* (1870) : any of various small web-spinning mites (family Tetranychidae) that include destructive pests of plants — called also *red spider*

spider monkey *n* (1764) : any of a genus (*Ateles*) of New World monkeys with long slender limbs, the thumb absent or rudimentary, and a very long prehensile tail

spider plant *n* (1944) : any of several cultivars of a southern African plant (*Chlorophytum comosum*) of the lily family widely grown as houseplants and having long narrow green leaves usu. striped with white or ivory and producing white flowers and tufts of plantlets on long hanging stems

spider vein *n* (1976) : a telangiectasia (as of the legs or face) often appearing as a central area with outward radiations resembling the legs of a spider

spi·der·web \ˈspī-dər-ˌweb\ *n* (ca. 1649) **1** : the network of silken thread spun by most spiders and used as a resting place and as a trap for small prey **2** : something that resembles or suggests a spiderweb

spi·der·wort \-ˌwərt, -ˌwȯrt\ *n* (1629) : any of a genus (*Tradescantia* of the family Commelinaceae, the spiderwort family) of American monocotyledonous plants with ephemeral often blue or violet flowers

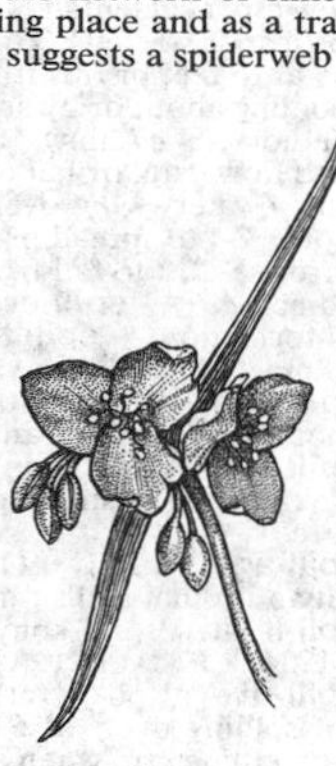

spiderwort

spi·dery \ˈspī-də-rē\ *adj* (1825) **1 a** : resembling a spider in form or manner **b** : resembling a spiderweb ⟨~ handwriting⟩; *esp* : composed of fine threads or lines in a weblike arrangement ⟨~ lace⟩ **2** : infested with spiders

spie·gel·ei·sen \ˈspē-gə-ˌlī-zᵊn\ *also* **spie·gel** \ˈspē-gəl\ *n* [G *Spiegeleisen,* fr. *Spiegel* mirror + *Eisen* iron] (1855) : a composition of iron that contains 15 to 30 percent manganese and 4.5 to 6.5 percent carbon

¹**spiel** \ˈspēl\ *vb* [G *spielen* to play, fr. OHG *spilōn;* akin to OE *spilian* to revel] *vi* (1870) **1** : to play music **2** : to talk volubly or extravagantly ~ *vt* : to utter, express, or describe volubly or extravagantly — **spiel·er** \ˈspē-lər\ *n*

²**spiel** *n* (1896) : a voluble line of often extravagant talk : PITCH

¹**spi·er** \ˈspī(-ə)r\ *n* (13c) : SPY

²**spier** \ˈspir\ *chiefly Scot var of* SPEER

spiff \ˈspif\ *vb* [E dial. *spiff* dandified] (1877) : SPRUCE — usu. used with *up* ⟨~ up your wardrobe⟩ — **spiffed–up** \ˈspift-ˈəp\ *adj*

spiffy \ˈspi-fē\ *adj* **spiff·i·er; -est** (1853) : fine looking : SMART ⟨a ~ sports jacket⟩ — **spiff·i·ly** \-fə-lē\ *adv* — **spiff·i·ness** \-fē-nəs\ *n*

spig·ot \ˈspi-gət, -kət\ *n* [ME] (14c) **1 a** : SPILE 2 **b** : the plug of a faucet or cock **c** : FAUCET **2** : something resembling a spigot esp. in regulating availability or flow (as of money)

¹**spike** \ˈspīk\ *n* [ME, prob. fr. ON *spīk* splinter & *spīkr* spike; akin to MD *spiker* spike — more at SPOKE] (13c) **1** : a very large nail **2 a** : one of a row of pointed irons placed (as on the top of a wall) to prevent passage **b** (1) : one of several metal projections set in the sole and heel of a shoe to improve traction (2) *pl* : a pair of shoes having spikes attached to the soles or soles and heels **c** : SPINDLE 1e **3** : something resembling a spike: as **a** : a young mackerel not over six inches (15.2 centimeters) long **b** : an unbranched antler of a young deer **4** *pl* : SPIKE HEEL 2 **5** : the act or an instance of spiking (as in volleyball) **6 a** : a pointed element in a graph or tracing **b** : an unusually high and sharply defined maximum (as of amplitude in a wave train) **7** *slang* : HYPODERMIC NEEDLE **8** : a momentary sharp increase and fall in electric potential; *also* : ACTION POTENTIAL **9** : an abrupt sharp increase (as in prices or rates) — **spike·like** \-ˌlīk\ *adj*

²**spike** *vb* **spiked; spik·ing** *vt* (1624) **1** : to fasten or furnish with spikes **2 a** : to disable (a muzzle-loading cannon) temporarily by driving a spike into the vent **b** : to suppress or block completely ⟨*spiked* the rumor⟩ **3 a** : to pierce or impale with or on a spike **b** : to reject (as a story) for publication or broadcast for editorial reasons **4 a** : to add an alcoholic beverage to (a drink) ⟨*spiked* the punch⟩ **b** : to add a foreign substance to ⟨~ the coffee with tranquilizers⟩ **c** : to add something highly reactive (as a radioactive tracer) to **d** : to add vitality, zest, or spice to : LIVEN ⟨*spiked* the speech with humor⟩ ⟨~ the broth with peppers⟩ **5** : to drive (as a volleyball) sharply downward with a hard blow; *also* : to throw down sharply ⟨*spiked* the ball in the end zone⟩ **6** : to undergo a sudden sharp increase in (temperature or fever) ⟨the patient *spiked* a fever of 103°⟩ ~ *vi* : to increase sharply ⟨battery sales *spiked* after the storm⟩ — **spik·er** *n*

³**spike** *n* [ME *spik,* fr. L *spica* — more at SPINE] (14c) **1** : an ear of grain **2** : an elongated inflorescence similar to a raceme but having the flowers sessile on the main axis — see INFLORESCENCE illustration

spiked \ˈspīkt, ˈspī-kəd\ *adj* (1601) **1** : having an inflorescence that is a spike **2** : having a sharp projecting point **3** *of hair* : arranged in stiff tufts

spike heel *n* (1926) **1** : a very high tapering heel used on women's shoes **2** *pl* : shoes with spike heels

spike lavender \ˈspīk-\ *n* [alter. of E dial. *spick* lavender] (1607) : a European mint (*Lavandula latifolia*) related to true lavender

spike·let \ˈspī-klət\ *n* (1793) **:** a small or secondary spike; *specif* **:** one of the small few-flowered bracted spikes that make up the compound inflorescence of a grass or sedge

spike·nard \ˈspīk-ˌnärd\ *n* [ME, fr. AF or ML; AF *spicanarde,* fr. ML *spica nardi,* lit., spike of nard] (14c) **1 a :** a fragrant ointment of the ancients **b :** a Himalayan aromatic plant (*Nardostachys jatamansi*) of the valerian family from which spikenard is believed to have been derived **2 :** a No. American perennial herb (*Aralia racemosa*) of the ginseng family with an aromatic root and panicled umbels

spike–tooth harrow \ˈspīk-ˈtüth-\ *n* (1926) **:** a harrow with straight steel teeth set in horizontal bars

spiky *also* **spikey** \ˈspī-kē\ *adj* **spik·i·er; -est** (1578) **1 :** of, relating to, or characterized by spikes ⟨~ barbed wire⟩ **2 :** sharply irritating or acerbic (as in temper or manner) — **spik·i·ly** \-kə-lē\ *adv* — **spik·i·ness** \-kē-nəs\ *n*

[1]**spile** \ˈspī(-ə)l\ *n* [prob. fr. D *spijl* stake] (1513) **1 :** [1]PILE 1 **2 :** a small plug used to stop the vent of a cask **:** BUNG **3 :** a spout inserted in a tree to draw off sap

[2]**spile** *vt* **spiled; spil·ing** (1691) **1 :** to plug with a spile **2 :** to supply with a spile

[1]**spill** \ˈspil\ *vb* **spilled** \ˈspild, ˈspilt\ *also* **spilt** \ˈspilt\; **spill·ing** [ME, fr. OE *spillan;* akin to OE *spildan* to destroy and perh. to L *spolium* animal skin, Gk *sphallein* to cause to fall] *vt* (bef. 12c) **1 a** *archaic* **:** KILL, DESTROY **b :** to cause (blood) to be lost by wounding **2 :** to cause or allow esp. accidentally or unintentionally to fall, flow, or run out so as to be lost or wasted **3 a :** to relieve (a sail) from the pressure of the wind so as to reef or furl it **b :** to relieve the pressure of (wind) on a sail by coming about or by adjusting the sail with lines **4 :** to throw off or out ⟨a horse ~*ed* him⟩ **5 :** to let out **:** DIVULGE ⟨~ a secret⟩ ~ *vi* **1 a :** to flow, run, or fall out, over, or off and become wasted, scattered, or lost ⟨water ~*ing* over the dam⟩ **b :** to cause or allow something to spill **2 :** to spread profusely or beyond bounds ⟨crowds ~*ed* into the streets⟩ **3 :** to fall from one's place (as on a horse) — **spill·able** \ˈspi-lə-bəl\ *adj* — **spill·er** *n* — **spill one's guts :** to divulge esp. personal information — **spill the beans :** to divulge secret or hidden information

[2]**spill** *n* (ca. 1845) **1 :** the act or an instance of spilling; *esp* **:** a fall from a horse or vehicle or an erect position **2 :** something spilled

[3]**spill** *n* [ME *spille;* akin to MLG *spīle* thin stick, peg] (14c) **1 :** a wooden splinter **2 :** a small roll or twist of paper or slip of wood for lighting a fire

spill·age \ˈspi-lij\ *n* (1924) **1 :** the act or process of spilling **2 :** the quantity that spills **:** material lost or scattered by spilling

spil·li·kin \ˈspi-li-kən\ *n* [prob. alter. of obs. D *spelleken* small peg] (1734) **1 :** JACKSTRAW 2 **2** *pl* **:** JACKSTRAW 1

spill·over \ˈspil-ˌō-vər\ *n, often attrib* (1940) **1 :** the act or an instance of spilling over **2 :** a quantity that spills over **3 :** an extension of something esp. when an excess exists ⟨benefiting from a ~ of prosperity from neighboring states⟩

spill·way \-ˌwā\ *n* (1889) **:** a passage for surplus water to run over or around an obstruction (as a dam)

spilth \ˈspilth\ *n* (1608) **1 :** the act or an instance of spilling **2 a :** something spilled **b :** REFUSE, RUBBISH

[1]**spin** \ˈspin\ *vb* **spun** \ˈspən\; **spin·ning** [ME *spinnen,* fr. OE *spinnan;* akin to OHG *spinnan* to spin and perh. to Lith *spęsti* to set (a trap)] *vi* (bef. 12c) **1 :** to draw out and twist fiber into yarn or thread **2 :** to form a thread by extruding a viscous rapidly hardening fluid — used esp. of a spider or insect **3 a :** to revolve rapidly **:** GYRATE **b :** to feel as if in a whirl **:** REEL ⟨my head is *spinning*⟩ **4 :** to move swiftly esp. on or as if on wheels or in a vehicle **5 :** to fish with spinning bait **:** TROLL **6 a** *of an airplane* **:** to fall in a spin **b :** to plunge helplessly and out of control **7 :** to engage in spin control (as in politics) ~ *vt* **1 a :** to draw out and twist into yarns or threads **b :** to produce by drawing out and twisting a fibrous material **2 :** to form (as a web or cocoon) by spinning **3 a :** to stretch out or extend (as a story) lengthily **:** PROTRACT — usu. used with *out* **b :** to evolve, express, or fabricate by processes of mind or imagination ⟨~ a yarn⟩ **4 :** to cause to whirl **:** impart spin to ⟨~ a top⟩ **5 :** to shape into threadlike form in manufacture; *also* **:** to manufacture by a whirling process **6 :** to set (records or compact discs) rotating on a player **:** PLAY ⟨~ some discs⟩ **7 :** to present (as information) with a particular spin ⟨~ the statistics⟩ — **spin one's wheels :** to make futile efforts to achieve progress

[2]**spin** *n* (1831) **1 a :** the act of spinning or twirling something; *also* **:** an instance of spinning or of spinning something ⟨doing axels and ~*s*⟩ ⟨an assortment of ~*s* and lobs⟩ **b :** the whirling motion imparted (as to a ball or top) by spinning **c :** an excursion or ride in a vehicle esp. on wheels ⟨go for a ~⟩ **2 a :** an aerial maneuver or flight condition consisting of a combination of roll and yaw with the longitudinal axis of the airplane inclined steeply downward **b :** a plunging descent or downward spiral **c :** a state of mental confusion ⟨all in a ~⟩ **3 a :** a quantum characteristic of an elementary particle that is visualized as the rotation of the particle on its axis and that is responsible for measurable angular momentum and magnetic moment **b :** the angular momentum associated with such rotation whose magnitude is quantized and which may assume either of two possible directions; *also* **:** the angular momentum of a system of such particles derived from the spins and orbital motions of the particles **4 a :** a usu. ingenious twist ⟨puts an Asian ~ on the pasta dishes⟩ **b** (1) **:** a special point of view, emphasis, or interpretation presented for the purpose of influencing opinion ⟨put the most favorable ~ on the findings⟩ (2) **:** SPIN CONTROL — **spin·less** \ˈspin-ləs\ *adj*

spi·na bi·fi·da \ˌspī-nə-ˈbi-fə-də\ *n* [NL, lit., spine split in two] (1720) **:** a congenital cleft of the spinal column with hernial protrusion of the meninges and sometimes the spinal cord

spin·ach \ˈspi-nich\ *n* [ME *spinache,* fr. AF, alter. of OF *espinaces,* fr. ML *spinachium,* ultim. fr. Ar *isfānākh,* fr. Pers] (15c) **1 :** an Asian herb (*Spinacia oleracea*) of the goosefoot family cultivated for its edible leaves which form in a dense basal rosette; *also* **:** its leaves **2 a :** something unwanted, pretentious, or spurious **b :** an untidy overgrowth — **spin·ach·like** \-nich-ˌlīk\ *adj* — **spin·achy** \-ni-chē\ *adj*

[1]**spi·nal** \ˈspī-nᵊl\ *adj* (1578) **1 :** of, relating to, or situated near the spinal column **2 a :** of, relating to, or affecting the spinal cord ⟨~ reflexes⟩ **b :** having the spinal cord functionally isolated (as by surgical section) from the brain ⟨experiments on ~ animals⟩ **3 :** of, relating to, or resembling a spine

[2]**spinal** *n* (1944) **:** a spinal anesthetic

spinal canal *n* (1801) **:** VERTEBRAL CANAL

spinal column *n* (1831) **:** the axial skeleton of a vertebrate that consists of an articulated series of vertebrae which extend from the neck to the tail and protect the spinal cord — called also *backbone*

spinal cord *n* (1834) **:** the cord of nervous tissue that extends from the brain lengthwise along the back in the vertebral canal, gives off the pairs of spinal nerves, carries impulses to and from the brain, and serves as a center for initiating and coordinating many reflex acts — see BRAIN illustration

spinal ganglion *n* (ca. 1860) **:** a ganglion on the dorsal root of each spinal nerve that is one of a series of ganglia lodging cell bodies of sensory neurons

spi·nal·ly \ˈspī-nᵊl-ē\ *adv* (1885) **:** with respect to or along the spine

spinal nerve *n* (ca. 1793) **:** any of the paired nerves which leave the spinal cord of a craniate vertebrate, supply muscles of the trunk and limbs, and connect with the nerves of the sympathetic nervous system, which arise by a short motor ventral root and a short sensory dorsal root, and of which there are 31 pairs in humans

spinal tap *n* (1947) **:** LUMBAR PUNCTURE

spin control *n* (1984) **:** the act or practice of attempting to manipulate the way an event is interpreted by others ⟨political *spin control*⟩

[1]**spin·dle** \ˈspin-dᵊl\ *n* [ME *spindel,* fr. OE *spinel;* akin to OE *spinnan* to spin] (12c) **1 a :** a round stick with tapered ends used to form and twist the yarn in hand spinning **b :** the long slender pin by which the thread is twisted in a spinning wheel **c :** any of various rods or pins holding a bobbin in a textile machine (as a spinning frame) **d :** the pin in a loom shuttle **e :** a device usu. consisting of a long upright pin in a base on which papers can be stuck for filing — called also *spindle file* **2 :** something shaped like a spindle: as **a :** a spindle-shaped network of chiefly microtubular fibers along which the chromosomes are distributed during mitosis and meiosis **b :** MUSCLE SPINDLE **3 a :** the bar or shaft usu. of square section that carries the knobs and actuates the latch or bolt of a lock **b** (1) **:** a turned often decorative piece (as in a baluster) (2) **:** NEWEL **c** (1) **:** a revolving piece esp. when thinner than a shaft (2) **:** a horizontal or vertical axle revolving on pin or pivot ends **d :** the part of an axle on which a vehicle wheel turns

[2]**spindle** *vb* **spin·dled; spin·dling** \ˈspin(d)-liŋ, ˈspin-dᵊl-iŋ\ *vi* (1577) **1 :** to shoot or grow into a long slender stalk **2 :** to grow to stalk or stem rather than to flower or fruit ~ *vt* **1 :** to impale, thrust, or perforate on the spike of a spindle file **2 :** to make or equip (as a piece of furniture) with spindles — **spin·dler** \ˈspin(d)-lər, ˈspin-dᵊl-ər\ *n*

spindle cell *n* (1878) **:** a fusiform cell (as in some tumors)

spin·dle–legged \ˈspin-dᵊl-ˌ(l)e-gəd *also* -ˌ(l)ā- *or* -ˌ(l)egd\ *adj* (1652) **:** having long slender legs ⟨a ~ table⟩ ⟨~ dogs⟩

spin·dle–shanked \-ˌshaŋ(k)t\ *adj* (1593) **:** SPINDLE-LEGGED

spindle tree *n* (1548) **:** any of various often evergreen shrubs, small trees, or vines (genus *Euonymus*) of the staff-tree family

spin·dling \ˈspin(d)-liŋ, -lən; ˈspin-dᵊl-iŋ, -ən\ *adj* (1750) **:** SPINDLY

spin·dly \ˈspin(d)-lē, ˈspin-dᵊl-ē\ *adj* **spin·dli·er; -est** (1651) **1 :** of a disproportionately tall or long and thin appearance that often suggests physical weakness ⟨~ legs⟩ **2 :** frail or flimsy in appearance or structure ⟨a ~ tower⟩

spin doctor *n* (1984) **:** a person (as a political aide) responsible for ensuring that others interpret an event from a particular point of view — **spin–doctor** *vb*

spin·drift \ˈspin-ˌdrift\ *n* [alter. of Sc *speendrift,* fr. *speen* to drive before a strong wind + E *drift*] (1823) **1 :** sea spray; *esp* **:** spray blown from waves during a gale **2 :** fine wind-borne snow or sand

spine \ˈspīn\ *n* [ME, thorn, spinal column, fr. L *spina;* perh. akin to L *spica* ear of grain] (15c) **1 a :** SPINAL COLUMN **b :** something resembling a spinal column or constituting a central axis or chief support **c :** the part of a book to which the pages are attached and on the cover of which usu. appear the title and author's and publisher's names **2 :** a stiff pointed plant process; *esp* **:** one that is a modified leaf or leaf part **3 :** a sharp rigid process on an animal: as **a :** SPICULE **b :** a stiff unsegmented fin ray of a fish **c :** a pointed prominence on a bone — **spined** \ˈspīnd\ *adj* — **spine·like** \-ˌlīk\ *adj*

spine–chill·ing \-ˌchi-liŋ\ *adj* (1946) **:** alarmingly or eerily frightening

spi·nel *or* **spi·nelle** \spə-ˈnel\ *n* [It *spinella,* dim. of *spina* thorn, fr. L] (1528) **1 :** a hard crystalline mineral consisting of an oxide of magnesium and aluminum that varies from colorless to ruby red to black and is used as a gem **2 :** any of a group of minerals that are essentially oxides of magnesium, ferrous iron, zinc, or manganese

spine·less \ˈspīn-ləs\ *adj* (1827) **1 :** free from spines, thorns, or prickles **2 a :** having no spinal column **:** INVERTEBRATE **b :** lacking strength of character — **spine·less·ly** *adv* — **spine·less·ness** *n*

spin·et \ˈspi-nət *also* spi-ˈnet\ *n* [It *spinetta,* perh. fr. dim. of *spina* thorn, fr. L; fr. the manner of plucking its strings] (1664) **1 :** an early harpsichord having a single keyboard and only one string for each note **2 a :** a compactly built small upright piano **b :** a small electronic organ

spin fishing *n* (1950) **:** SPINNING

spi·ni·fex \ˈspī-nə-ˌfeks\ *n* [NL, fr. L *spina* + *facere* to make — more at DO] (1846) **:** any of several Australian grasses (genera *Spinifex* and *Triodia*) with spiny seeds or stiff sharp leaves

spin·meis·ter \ˈspin-ˌmīs-tər\ *also* **spin·mas·ter** \-ˌmas-\ *n* (1986) **:** SPIN DOCTOR

spin·na·ker \ˈspi-ni-kər\ *n* [origin unknown] (1866) **:** a large triangular sail set on a long light pole and used when running before the wind

spin·ner \ˈspi-nər\ *n* (13c) **1 :** one that spins **2 :** a fisherman's lure consisting of a spoon, blade, or set of wings that revolves when drawn through the water **3 :** a conical sheet metal fairing that is attached to an airplane propeller boss and revolves with it **4 :** a movable arrow that is spun on its dial to indicate the number or kind of moves a player may make in a board game **5 :** SPIN DOCTOR

spinner dolphin *n* (1976) **:** a long-beaked dolphin (*Stenella longirostris*) that is typically dark gray above and white below and that is noted for its habit of spinning in the air when breaching

spin·ner·et \ˌspi-nə-ˈret\ *n* (1826) **1 :** an organ (as of a spider or caterpillar) for producing threads of silk from the secretion of silk glands **2** *or* **spin·ner·ette :** a small metal plate, thimble, or cap with fine holes through which a chemical solution (as of cellulose) is forced in the spinning of man-made filaments (as of rayon or nylon)

spin·ney \ˈspi-nē\ *n, pl* **spinneys** [AF *espinei* thorny thicket, ultim. fr. L *spinetum,* fr. *spina* thorn] (1597) *chiefly Brit* : a small wood with undergrowth

spinning *n* (1855) : a method of fishing in which a lure is cast by use of a light flexible rod, a spinning reel, and a light line

spinning frame *n* (1825) : a machine that draws, twists, and winds yarn

spinning jen·ny \-ˌje-nē\ *n* [*Jenny,* nickname for *Jane*] (1783) : an early multiple-spindle machine for spinning wool or cotton

spinning reel *n* (1950) : a fishing reel with a nonmoving spool on which the line is wound by means of a revolving arm which can be disengaged to allow the line to spiral freely off the spool during casting

spinning rod *n* (1870) : a light flexible fishing rod used with a spinning reel

spinning wheel *n* (15c) : a small domestic hand-driven or foot-driven machine for spinning yarn or thread

spin–off \ˈspin-ˌȯf\ *n* (1950) **1** : the distribution by a business to its stockholders of particular assets and esp. of stock of another company; *also* : the new company created by such a distribution **2** : a collateral or derived product or effect : BY-PRODUCT; *also* : a number of such products ⟨the ~ from the space program⟩ **3** : something that is imitative or derivative of an earlier work, product, or establishment; *esp* : a television show starring a character popular in a secondary role of an earlier show

spin off *vt* (1950) : to establish or produce as a spin-off ⟨the company *spun off* its computer division⟩ ⟨*spin off* a new TV series⟩ ~ *vi* : to establish or become a spin-off

spin·or \ˈspi-nər, -ˌnȯr\ *n* [ISV *spin* + *-or* (as in *vector*)] (1931) : a vector whose components are complex numbers in a two-dimensional or four-dimensional space and which is used esp. in the mathematics of the theory of relativity

spi·nose \ˈspī-ˌnōs\ *adj* (1661) : SPINY 2 ⟨a fly with black ~ legs⟩ — **spi·nos·i·ty** \spī-ˈnä-sə-tē\ *n*

spi·nous \ˈspī-nəs\ *adj* (15c) **1 a** : SPINY 2 ⟨a ~ plant⟩ **b** : SPINY 3 **2** : difficult or unpleasant to handle or meet : THORNY

spin·out \ˈspin-ˌau̇t\ *n* (1955) : a rotational skid by an automobile that usu. causes it to leave the roadway

spin out *vi* (1951) : to make a rotational skid in an automobile

Spi·no·zism \spi-ˈnō-ˌzi-zəm\ *n* (1728) : the philosophy of Baruch Spinoza who taught that reality is one substance with an infinite number of attributes of which only thought and extension are capable of being apprehended by the human mind — **Spi·no·zist** \-zist\ *n* — **Spi·no·zis·tic** \ˌspi-nō-ˈzis-tik\ *adj*

spin·ster \ˈspin(t)-stər\ *n* (14c) **1** : a woman whose occupation is to spin **2 a** *archaic* : an unmarried woman of gentle family **b** : an unmarried woman and esp. one past the common age for marrying **3** : a woman who seems unlikely to marry — **spin·ster·hood** \-ˌhu̇d\ *n* — **spin·ster·ish** \-st(ə-)rish\ *adj* — **spin·ster·ly** *adj*

spin·thar·i·scope \spin-ˈtha-rə-ˌskōp\ *n* [Gk *spintharis* spark + E *-scope*] (1903) : an instrument for visual detection of alpha particles that consists of a fluorescent screen and a magnifying lens system

spin the bottle *n* (1955) : a kissing game in which one has as a partner the person a bottle points to when it stops spinning

spin·to \ˈspēn-(ˌ)tō, ˈspin-\ *n, pl* **spin·tos** [It, lit., pushed, fr. pp. of *spingere* to push, fr. VL **expingere,* fr. L *ex-* + *pangere* to fasten — more at PACT] (1944) : a singing voice having both lyric and dramatic qualities — **spinto** *adj*

spi·nule \ˈspī-(ˌ)nyül\ *n* [L *spinula,* dim. of *spina* thorn — more at SPINE] (1752) : a minute spine — **spi·nu·lose** \ˈspī-nyə-ˌlōs\ *adj*

spiny \ˈspī-nē\ *adj* **spin·i·er; -est** (1586) **1** : abounding with difficulties, obstacles, or annoyances : THORNY ⟨~ problems⟩ **2** : covered or armed with spines; *broadly* : bearing spines, prickles, or thorns **3** : slender and pointed like a spine — **spin·i·ness** *n*

spiny anteater *n* (1827) : ECHIDNA

spiny–head·ed worm \ˈspī-nē-ˌhe-dəd-\ *n* (1946) : any of a small phylum (Acanthocephala) of unsegmented parasitic worms that have a proboscis bearing hooks by which attachment is made to the intestinal wall of the host

spiny lobster *n* (1819) : any of several edible crustaceans (family Palinuridae, esp. genus *Panulirus*) distinguished from true lobsters by the simple unenlarged first pair of legs and claws and the spiny carapace

spi·ra·cle \ˈspir-i-kəl, ˈspī-ri-\ *n* [ME, fr. L *spiraculum,* fr. *spirare* to breathe] (15c) **1** : a breathing hole : VENT **2** : a breathing orifice: as **a** : BLOWHOLE 2 **b** : an external tracheal aperture of a terrestrial arthropod that in an insect is usu. one of a series of small apertures located along each side of the thorax and abdomen — see INSECT illustration — **spi·rac·u·lar** \spə-ˈra-kyə-lər, spī-\ *adj*

1**spi·ral** \ˈspī-rəl\ *adj* [ML *spiralis,* fr. L *spira* coil — more at SPIRE] (1551) **1 a** : winding around a center or pole and gradually receding from or approaching it ⟨the ~ curve of a watch spring⟩ **b** : HELICAL **c** : SPIRAL-BOUND ⟨a ~ notebook⟩ **2** : of or relating to the advancement to higher levels through a series of cyclical movements — **spi·ral·ly** \-rə-lē\ *adv*

2**spiral** *n* (1656) **1 a** : the path of a point in a plane moving around a central point while continuously receding from or approaching it **b** : a three-dimensional curve (as a helix) with one or more turns about an axis **2** : a single turn or coil in a spiral object **3** : something having a spiral form as: **a** : SPIRAL GALAXY **b** (1) : a spiral flight (2) : a kick or pass in which a football rotates on its long axis while moving through the air **4** : a continuously spreading and accelerating increase or decrease ⟨wage ~*s*⟩

3**spiral** *vb* **-raled** *or* **-ralled; -ral·ing** *or* **-ral·ling** *vi* (1834) : to go and esp. to rise or fall in a spiral course ⟨costs ~*ed* upward⟩ ~ *vt* **1** : to form into a spiral **2** : to cause to spiral

spiral binding *n* (1944) : a book or notebook binding in which a continuous spiral wire or plastic strip is passed through holes along one edge

spi·ral–bound \ˈspī-rəl-ˌbau̇nd\ *adj* (1941) : having a spiral binding

spiral cleavage *n* (1892) : holoblastic cleavage that is typical of protostomes and that is characterized by arrangement of the blastomeres of each upper tier over the cell junctions of the next lower tier so that the blastomeres spiral around the pole to pole axis of the embryo — compare RADIAL CLEAVAGE

spiral galaxy *n* (1913) : a galaxy exhibiting a central nucleus or barred structure from which extend curved arms of higher luminosity — called also *spiral nebula*

spiral of Ar·chi·me·des \-ˌär-kə-ˈmē-dēz\ [*Archimedes*] (ca. 1856) : a plane curve that is generated by a point moving away from or toward a fixed point at a constant rate while the radius vector from the fixed point rotates at a constant rate and that has the equation $\rho = a\,\theta$ in polar coordinates

spiral spring *n* (1690) : a spring consisting of a wire coiled usu. in a flat spiral or in a helix

spi·rant \ˈspī-rənt\ *n* [ISV, fr. L *spirant-, spirans,* prp. of *spirare* to breathe] (1862) : a consonant (as \f\, \s\, \sh\) uttered with friction of the breath against some part of the oral passage : FRICATIVE — **spirant** *adj*

1**spire** \ˈspī(-ə)r\ *n* [ME, fr. OE *spīr;* akin to MD *spier* blade of grass] (bef. 12c) **1** : a slender tapering blade or stalk (as of grass) **2** : the upper tapering part of something (as a tree or antler) : PINNACLE **3 a** : a tapering roof or analogous pyramidal construction surmounting a tower **b** : STEEPLE ⟨a church ~⟩

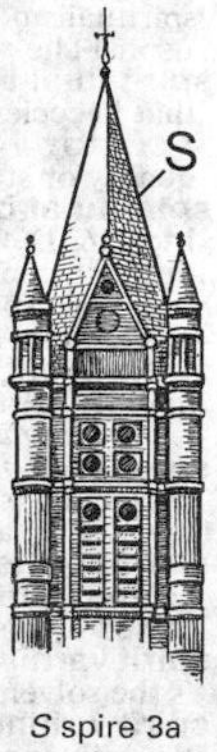

S spire 3a

2**spire** *vi* **spired; spir·ing** (14c) : to rise like a spire

3**spire** *n* [L *spira* coil, fr. Gk *speira;* perh. akin to Gk *sparton* rope, esparto] (1545) **1 a** : SPIRAL **b** : COIL **2** : the inner or upper part of a spiral gastropod shell consisting of all the whorls except the whorl in contact with the body

4**spire** *vi* **spired; spir·ing** (1591) : to rise in or as if in a spiral

spi·rea *or* **spi·raea** \spī-ˈrē-ə\ *n* [NL *Spiraea,* fr. L, a plant, fr. Gk *speiraia*] (1669) **1** : any of a genus (*Spiraea*) of deciduous shrubs of the rose family with small usu. white or pink flowers in dense racemes, corymbs, cymes, or panicles **2** : any of several garden plants resembling spireas; *esp* : a shrub (*Astilbe japonica*) of the saxifrage family

spired *adj* (1610) **1** : having a spire ⟨a ~ church⟩ **2** : tapering usu. to a sharp point ⟨~ cedars⟩

spi·ril·lum \spī-ˈri-ləm\ *n, pl* **-ril·la** \-ˈri-lə\ [NL, fr. dim. of L *spira* coil] (ca. 1875) : any of a genus (*Spirillum*) of curved elongated motile bacteria having tufts of flagella at both poles; *broadly* : a spiral filamentous bacterium (as a spirochete)

1**spir·it** \ˈspir-ət\ *n* [ME, fr. AF or L; AF, *espirit, spirit,* fr. L *spiritus,* lit., breath, fr. *spirare* to blow, breathe] (13c) **1** : an animating or vital principle held to give life to physical organisms **2** : a supernatural being or essence: as **a** *cap* : HOLY SPIRIT **b** : SOUL 2a **c** : an often malevolent being that is bodiless but can become visible; *specif* : GHOST 2 **d** : a malevolent being that enters and possesses a human being **3** : temper or disposition of mind or outlook esp. when vigorous or animated ⟨in high ~*s*⟩ **4** : the immaterial intelligent or sentient part of a person **5 a** : the activating or essential principle influencing a person ⟨acted in a ~ of helpfulness⟩ **b** : an inclination, impulse, or tendency of a specified kind : MOOD **6 a** : a special attitude or frame of mind ⟨the money-making ~ was for a time driven back —J. A. Froude⟩ **b** : the feeling, quality, or disposition characterizing something ⟨undertaken in a ~ of fun⟩ **7** : a lively or brisk quality in a person or a person's actions **8** : a person having a character or disposition of a specified nature **9** : a mental disposition characterized by firmness or assertiveness ⟨denied the charge with ~⟩ **10 a** : DISTILLATE 1: as (1) : the liquid containing ethanol and water that is distilled from an alcoholic liquid or mash — often used in pl. (2) : any of various volatile liquids obtained by distillation or cracking (as of petroleum, shale, or wood) — often used in pl. **b** : a usu. volatile organic solvent (as an alcohol, ester, or hydrocarbon) **11 a** : prevailing tone or tendency ⟨~ of the age⟩ **b** : general intent or real meaning ⟨~ of the law⟩ **12** : an alcoholic solution of a volatile substance ⟨~ of camphor⟩ **13** : enthusiastic loyalty ⟨school ~⟩ **14** *cap, Christian Science* : GOD 1b *syn* see COURAGE

2**spirit** *vt* (1608) **1** : to infuse with spirit; *esp* : ANIMATE ⟨hope and apprehension of feasibleness ~*s* all industry —John Goodman⟩ **2** : to carry off usu. secretly or mysteriously ⟨was hustled into a . . . motorcar and ~*ed* off to the country —W. L. Shirer⟩

spir·it·ed \ˈspir-ə-təd\ *adj* (1599) : full of energy, animation, or courage ⟨a ~ discussion⟩ — **spir·it·ed·ly** *adv* — **spir·it·ed·ness** *n*

spirit gum *n* (1886) : a solution (as of gum arabic in ether) used esp. for attaching false hair to the skin

spir·it·ism \ˈspir-ə-ˌti-zəm\ *n* (1856) : SPIRITUALISM 2a — **spir·it·ist** \-tist\ *n* — **spir·it·is·tic** \ˌspir-ə-ˈtis-tik\ *adj*

spir·it·less \ˈspir-ət-ləs\ *adj* (1598) : lacking animation, cheerfulness, or courage *syn* see LANGUID — **spir·it·less·ly** *adv* — **spir·it·less·ness** *n*

spirit level *n* (1768) : LEVEL 1

spirit of wine (15c) : ALCOHOL 1c

spir·i·to·so \ˌspir-ə-ˈtō-(ˌ)sō, -(ˌ)zō\ *adj* [It, fr. *spirito* spirit, fr. L *spiritus*] (ca. 1724) : ANIMATED — used as a direction in music

spir·it·ous \ˈspir-ə-təs\ *adj* (1605) **1** *archaic* : PURE, REFINED **2** : SPIRITUOUS

spirit rapping *n* (1852) : communication by raps held to be from the spirits of the dead

spirits of turpentine (ca. 1792) : TURPENTINE 2a

spirits of wine (1646) : rectified spirit : ALCOHOL 1c

1**spir·i·tu·al** \ˈspir-i-chə-wəl, -i-chəl, -ich-wəl\ *adj* [ME, fr. AF & LL; AF *espirital, spiritual,* fr. LL *spiritualis,* fr. L, of breathing, of wind, fr. *spiritus*] (14c) **1** : of, relating to, consisting of, or affecting the spirit : INCORPOREAL ⟨~ needs⟩ **2 a** : of or relating to sacred matters ⟨~ songs⟩ **b** : ecclesiastical rather than lay or temporal ⟨~ authority⟩

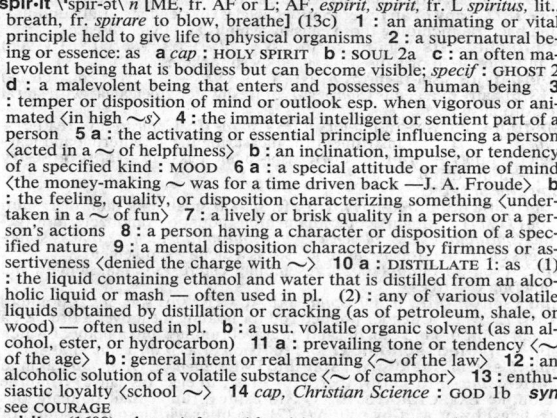

\ə\ abut \ᵊ\ kitten, F table \ər\ further \a\ ash \ā\ ace \ä\ mop, mar \au̇\ out \ch\ chin \e\ bet \ē\ easy \g\ go \i\ hit \ī\ ice \j\ job \ŋ\ sing \ō\ go \ȯ\ law \ȯi\ boy \th\ thin \t͟h\ the \ü\ loot \u̇\ foot \y\ yet \zh\ vision, beige \k̟, ⁿ, œ, ue, ʸ\ see Guide to Pronunciation

⟨lords ~⟩ **3 :** concerned with religious values **4 :** related or joined in spirit ⟨our ~ home⟩ ⟨his ~ heir⟩ **5 a :** of or relating to supernatural beings or phenomena **b :** of, relating to, or involving spiritualism **:** SPIRITUALISTIC — **spir·i·tu·al·ly** *adv* — **spir·i·tu·al·ness** *n*

2**spiritual** *n* (1582) **1** *pl* **:** things of a spiritual, ecclesiastical, or religious nature **2 :** a religious song usu. of a deeply emotional character that was developed esp. among blacks in the southern U.S. **3** *cap* **:** any of a party of 13th and 14th century Franciscans advocating strict observance of a rule of poverty for their order

spiritual bouquet *n* (1926) **:** a card notifying the recipient of a number of devotional acts performed by a Roman Catholic on behalf of a person on special occasions (as name days or anniversaries) or for the soul of someone recently deceased esp. as an expression of sympathy

spir·i·tu·al·ism \ˈspir-i-chə-wə-ˌli-zəm, -i-chə-ˌli-, -ich-wə-ˌli-\ *n* (1796) **1 :** the view that spirit is a prime element of reality **2 a :** a belief that spirits of the dead communicate with the living usu. through a medium **b** *cap* **:** a movement comprising religious organizations emphasizing spiritualism — **spir·i·tu·al·ist** \-list\ *n, often cap* — **spir·i·tu·al·is·tic** \ˌspir-i-chə-wə-ˈlis-tik, -i-chə-ˈlis-, -ich-wə-ˈlis-\ *adj*

spir·i·tu·al·i·ty \ˌspir-i-chə-ˈwa-lə-tē\ *n, pl* **-ties** (15c) **1 :** something that in ecclesiastical law belongs to the church or to a cleric as such **2 :** CLERGY **3 :** sensitivity or attachment to religious values **4 :** the quality or state of being spiritual

spir·i·tu·al·ize \ˈspir-i-chə-wə-ˌlīz, -i-chə-ˌlīz, -ich-wə-ˌlīz\ *vt* **-ized; -iz·ing** (1631) **1 :** to make spiritual; *esp* **:** to purify from the corrupting influences of the world **2 :** to give a spiritual meaning to or understand in a spiritual sense — **spir·i·tu·al·i·za·tion** \ˌspir-i-chə-wə-lə-ˈzā-shən, -i-chə-lə-, -ich-wə-lə-\ *n*

spir·i·tu·al·ty \ˈspir-i-chə-wəl-tē, -i-chəl-tē, -ich-wəl-tē\ *n* [ME *spiritualte,* fr. AF *espiritauté, spiritualté,* fr. ML *spiritualitat-, spiritualitas,* fr. LL *spiritualis* spiritual] (14c) **1 :** SPIRITUALITY 1 **2 :** CLERGY

spi·ri·tu·el *or* **spi·ri·tu·elle** \ˌspir-i-chə-ˈwel, spē-rē-tw(y)el\ *adj* [*spirituel* fr. F, lit., spiritual; *spirituelle* fr. F, fem. of *spirituel*] (1673) **:** having or marked by a refined and esp. sprightly or witty nature

spir·i·tu·ous \ˈspir-i-chə-wəs, -ich-wəs\ *adj* [prob. fr. F *spiritueux,* fr. L *spiritus* spirit] (1662) **:** containing or impregnated with alcohol obtained by distillation ⟨~ liquors⟩

spirit varnish *n* (1758) **:** a varnish in which a volatile liquid (as alcohol) is the solvent

spirit writing *n* (1864) **:** automatic writing held to be produced under the influence of spirits

spi·ro·chet·al \ˌspī-rə-ˈkē-tᵊl\ *adj* (1913) **:** caused by spirochetes

spi·ro·chete *also* **spi·ro·chaete** \ˈspī-rə-ˌkēt\ *n* [NL *Spirochaeta,* genus of bacteria, fr. L *spira* coil + Gk *chaitē* long hair — more at SPIRE] (ca. 1877) **:** any of an order (Spirochaetales) of slender spirally undulating bacteria including those causing syphilis and Lyme disease

spi·ro·chet·osis \ˌspī-rə-ˌkē-ˈtō-səs\ *n, pl* **-oses** \-ˌsēz\ [NL] (1906) **:** infection with or a disease caused by spirochetes

spi·ro·gy·ra \ˌspī-rə-ˈjī-rə\ *n* [NL, fr. L *spira* + Gk *gyros* ring, circle] (1875) **:** any of a genus (*Spirogyra*) of freshwater green algae with spiral chloroplasts

spi·rom·e·ter \spī-ˈrä-mə-tər\ *n* [ISV *spiro-* (fr. L *spirare* to breathe) + *-meter*] (1809) **:** an instrument for measuring the air entering and leaving the lungs — **spi·ro·met·ric** \ˌspī-rə-ˈme-trik\ *adj* — **spi·rom·e·try** \spī-ˈrä-mə-trē\ *n*

spirt *var of* SPURT

spi·ru·lina \ˌspī-rə-ˈlī-nə\ *n* [NL, fr. *spirula* small coil, dim. of L *spira* coil] (1977) **:** a microscopic filamentous aquatic cyanobacterium (genus *Spirulina,* esp. *S. platensis* syn. *Arthrospira platensis*) that is sometimes cultivated for use as food esp. as a dietary supplement

spiry \ˈspī(-ə)r-ē\ *adj* (1602) **:** resembling a spire; *esp* **:** tall, slender, and tapering ⟨~ trees⟩

1**spit** \ˈspit\ *n* [ME, fr. OE *spitu;* akin to OHG *spiz* spit, *spizzi* pointed] (bef. 12c) **1 :** a slender pointed rod for holding meat over a fire **2 :** a small point of land esp. of sand or gravel running into a body of water

2**spit** *vt* **spit·ted; spit·ting** (13c) **:** to fix on or as if on a spit **:** IMPALE

3**spit** *vb* **spit** *or* **spat** \ˈspat\; **spit·ting** [ME *spitten,* fr. OE *spittan;* akin to MHG *spiutzen* to spit] *vt* (bef. 12c) **1 a :** to eject (as saliva) from the mouth **:** EXPECTORATE **b** (1) **:** to express (unpleasant or malicious feelings) by or as if by spitting (2) **:** to utter with a spitting sound or scornful expression ⟨*spat* out his words⟩ **c :** to emit as if by spitting; *esp* **:** to emit (precipitation) in driving particles or in flurries ⟨~ rain⟩ **2 :** to set to burning ⟨~ a fuse⟩ ~ *vi* **1 a** (1) **:** to eject saliva as an expression of aversion or contempt (2) **:** to exhibit contempt **b :** to eject matter (as saliva) from the mouth **:** EXPECTORATE **2 :** to rain or snow slightly or in flurries **3 :** to make a noise suggesting expectoration **:** SPUTTER — **spit it out :** to say what is in the mind without further delay

4**spit** *n* (14c) **1 a** (1) **:** SPITTLE, SALIVA (2) **:** the act or an instance of spitting **b** (1) **:** a frothy secretion exuded by spittlebugs (2) **:** SPITTLEBUG **2 :** perfect likeness **3 :** a sprinkle of rain or flurry of snow

spit·al \ˈspi-tᵊl\ *n* [ME *spitel,* modif. of ML *hospitale* — more at HOSPITAL] (14c) *archaic* **:** LAZARETTO, HOSPITAL

spit and polish *n* [fr. the practice of polishing objects such as shoes by spitting on them and then rubbing them with a cloth] (1895) **:** extreme attention to cleanliness, orderliness, smartness of appearance, and ceremony often at the expense of operational efficiency — **spit–and–polish** *adj*

spit·ball \ˈspit-ˌbȯl\ *n* (1846) **1 :** paper chewed and rolled into a ball to be thrown or shot as a missile **2 :** a baseball pitch delivered after the ball has been moistened with saliva or sweat

spit curl *n* [prob. fr. its being sometimes plastered down with saliva] (1831) **:** a spiral curl that is usu. plastered on the forehead, temple, or cheek

1**spite** \ˈspīt\ *n* [ME, short for *despite*] (14c) **1 :** petty ill will or hatred with the disposition to irritate, annoy, or thwart **2 :** an instance of spite ***syn*** see MALICE — **in spite of :** in defiance or contempt of **:** without being prevented by ⟨succeeded *in spite of* their opposition⟩

2**spite** *vt* **spit·ed; spit·ing** (ca. 1555) **1 a :** ANNOY, OFFEND **b :** to fill with spite **2 :** to treat maliciously (as by shaming or thwarting)

spite·ful \ˈspīt-fəl\ *adj* (15c) **:** filled with or showing spite **:** MALICIOUS — **spite·ful·ly** \-fə-lē\ *adv* — **spite·ful·ness** *n*

spit·fire \ˈspit-ˌfī(-ə)r\ *n* (1656) **:** a quick-tempered or highly emotional person

1**spit·ter** \ˈspi-tər\ *n* (14c) **:** one that spits

2**spitter** *n* (1908) **:** SPITBALL 2

spitting cobra *n* (1910) **:** any of several cobras (as *Naja nigricollis* and *Hemachatus haemachatus* of Africa) that in defense typically eject their venom toward the victim without striking

spitting image *n* [alter. of *spit and image*] (1887) **:** IMAGE 3b

spit·tle \ˈspi-tᵊl\ *n* [ME *spetil,* fr. OE *spǣtl;* akin to OE *spittan* to spit] (bef. 12c) **1 :** SALIVA **2 :** 4SPIT 1b(1)

spit·tle·bug \-ˌbəg\ *n* (1882) **:** any of a family (Cercopidae) of leaping homopterous insects whose nymphal larvae produce a frothy secretion — called also *froghopper*

spittle insect *n* (1891) **:** SPITTLEBUG

spit·toon \spi-ˈtün, spə-\ *n* [4*spit* + *-oon* (as in *balloon*)] (1823) **:** a receptacle for spit — called also *cuspidor*

spit up *vb* (1779) **:** REGURGITATE, VOMIT — **spit–up** *n*

spitz \ˈspits\ *n* [G, fr. *spitz* pointed, fr. OHG *spizzi;* fr. the shape of its ears and muzzle — more at SPIT] (1842) **:** a member of any of several breeds of stocky heavy-coated dogs of northern origin with erect ears and usu. a heavily furred tail carried over the back

spiv \ˈspiv\ *n* [alter. of E dial. *spiff* flashy dresser, fr. *spiff* dandified] (ca. 1934) **1** *Brit* **:** a man who lives by his wits without regular employment **2** *Brit* **:** SLACKER 1 — **spiv·vy** \ˈspi-vē\ *adj, Brit*

splanch·nic \ˈsplaŋk-nik\ *adj* [NL *splanchnicus,* fr. Gk *splanchnikos,* fr. *splanchna,* pl., viscera; akin to Gk *splēn* spleen] (1681) **:** of or relating to the viscera **:** VISCERAL

1**splash** \ˈsplash\ *vb* [alter. of *plash*] *vi* (1715) **1 a :** to strike and dash about a liquid or semiliquid substance **b :** to move in or into a liquid or semiliquid substance and cause it to spatter **2 a** (1) **:** to become spattered about (2) **:** to spread or scatter in the manner of splashed liquid **b :** to fall, strike, or move with a splashing sound ⟨a brook ~*ing* over rocks⟩ ~ *vt* **1 a** (1) **:** to dash a liquid or thinly viscous substance upon or against (2) **:** to soil or stain with splashed liquid **b :** to mark or overlay with patches of contrasting color or texture **c :** to display prominently ⟨a story ~*ed* on the front page⟩ **2 a :** to cause (a liquid or thinly viscous substance) to spatter about esp. with force **b :** to scatter in the manner of a splashed liquid — **splash·er** *n*

2**splash** *n* (1736) **1 a** (1) **:** splashed liquid or semiliquid substance; *also* **:** impounded water released suddenly (2) **:** a spot or daub from or as if from splashed liquid ⟨a mud ~ on the fender⟩ **b :** a colored patch **2 a :** the action of splashing **b :** a short plunge **3 :** a sound produced by or as if by a liquid falling, moving, being hurled, or oscillating **4 a :** a vivid impression created esp. by ostentatious activity or appearance **b :** ostentatious display **5 :** a small amount **:** SPRINKLING

splash·board \ˈsplash-ˌbȯrd\ *n* (1826) **1 :** DASHBOARD 1 **2 :** a panel to protect against splashes

splash·down \ˈsplash-ˌdau̇n\ *n* (1959) **:** the landing of a manned spacecraft in the ocean — **splash down** *vi*

splash guard *n* (1926) **:** a flap suspended behind a rear wheel to prevent tire splash from muddying windshields of following vehicles

splashy \ˈspla-shē\ *adj* **splash·i·er; -est** (1834) **1 :** moving or being moved with a splash or splashing sounds **2 :** tending to or exhibiting ostentatious display **:** making a splash ⟨a ~ movie⟩ ⟨a ~ debut⟩ **3 :** that can be easily splashed about **4 :** consisting of, being, or covered with colored splashes — **splash·i·ly** \ˈspla-shə-lē\ *adv* — **splash·i·ness** \ˈspla-shē-nəs\ *n*

1**splat** \ˈsplat\ *n* [obs. *splat* to spread flat] (1833) **:** a single flat thin often ornamental member of a back of a chair

2**splat** *n* [imit.] (1897) **:** a splattering or slapping sound

1**splat·ter** \ˈspla-tər\ *vb* [prob. blend of *splash* and *spatter*] *vt* (1785) **:** SPATTER ~ *vi* **:** to scatter or fall in or as if in drops

2**splatter** *n* (1819) **:** SPATTER, SPLASH

3**splatter** *adj* (1980) **:** characterized by extreme or excessive gore or violence ⟨a ~ movie⟩

1**splay** \ˈsplā\ *vb* [ME, short for *displayen* — more at DISPLAY] *vt* (15c) **1 :** to cause to spread outward **2 :** to make oblique **:** BEVEL ~ *vi* **1 :** to extend apart or outward esp. in an awkward manner **2 :** SLOPE, SLANT

2**splay** *n* (ca. 1508) **1 :** a slope or bevel esp. of the sides of a door or window **2 :** SPREAD, EXPANSION

3**splay** *adj* (1548) **1 :** turned outward ⟨~ knees⟩ **2 :** AWKWARD, UNGAINLY

splay·foot \ˈsplā-ˌfu̇t\ *n* (1548) **:** a foot abnormally flattened and spread out; *specif* **:** FLATFOOT — **splay·foot·ed** \-ˌfu̇-təd\ *adj*

spleen \ˈsplēn\ *n* [ME *splen,* fr. AF or L; AF *espleen,* fr. L *splen,* fr. Gk *splēn;* akin to L *lien* spleen, Skt *plīhan*] (14c) **1 :** a highly vascular ductless organ that is located in the left abdominal region near the stomach or intestine of most vertebrates and is concerned with final destruction of red blood cells, filtration and storage of blood, and production of lymphocytes **2** *obs* **:** the seat of emotions or passions **3** *archaic* **:** MELANCHOLY **4 :** feelings of anger or ill will often suppressed **5** *obs* **:** a sudden impulse or whim **:** CAPRICE ***syn*** see MALICE

spleen·ful \-fəl\ *adj* (1588) **:** full of or affected with spleen **:** SPLENETIC

spleen·wort \-ˌwərt, -ˌwȯrt\ *n* [fr. the belief in its power to cure disorders of the spleen] (1578) **:** any of a large genus (*Asplenium*) of chiefly evergreen ferns having linear or oblong sori

spleeny \ˈsplē-nē\ *adj* (1604) **1 :** full of or displaying spleen **2** *New Eng* **:** peevish and irritable with hypochondriac inclinations

splen- *or* **spleno-** *comb form* [L, fr. Gk *splēn-, splēno-,* fr. *splēn*] **:** spleen ⟨*splen*ectomy⟩ ⟨*spleno*megaly⟩

splen·dent \ˈsplen-dənt\ *adj* [ME, fr. LL *splendent-, splendens,* fr. L, prp. of *splendēre*] (15c) **1 :** SHINING, GLOSSY ⟨~ luster⟩ **2 :** ILLUSTRIOUS, BRILLIANT ⟨~ genius⟩

splen·did \ˈsplen-dəd\ *adj* [L *splendidus,* fr. *splendēre* to shine; perh. akin to MIr *lainn* bright] (1624) **1 :** possessing or displaying splendor: as **a :** SHINING, BRILLIANT **b :** marked by showy magnificence **2 :** ILLUSTRIOUS, GRAND **3 a :** EXCELLENT ⟨a ~ opportunity⟩ **b :** being out of the ordinary **:** SINGULAR — **splen·did·ly** *adv* — **splen·did·ness** *n*

syn SPLENDID, RESPLENDENT, GORGEOUS, GLORIOUS, SUBLIME, SUPERB mean extraordinarily or transcendently impressive. SPLENDID implies outshining the usual or customary ⟨the wedding was a *splendid* occasion⟩. RESPLENDENT suggests a glowing or blazing splendor ⟨*resplendent* in her jewelry⟩. GORGEOUS implies a rich splendor esp. in display of color ⟨a *gorgeous* red dress⟩. GLORIOUS suggests radiance that heightens beauty or distinction ⟨a *glorious* sunset⟩. SUBLIME implies an exaltation or elevation almost beyond human comprehension ⟨a vision of *sublime* beauty⟩. SUPERB suggests an excellence reaching the highest conceivable degree ⟨her singing was *superb*⟩.

splen·dif·er·ous \splen-ˈdi-f(ə-)rəs\ *adj* [*splendor* + *-i-* + *-ferous*] (1843) : extraordinarily or showily impressive — **splen·dif·er·ous·ly** *adv* — **splen·dif·er·ous·ness** *n*

splen·dor \ˈsplen-dər\ *n* [ME *splendure,* fr. AF *splendur,* fr. L *splendor,* fr. *splendēre*] (15c) **1 a** : great brightness or luster : BRILLIANCY **b** : MAGNIFICENCE, POMP **2** : something splendid ⟨the ~*s* of the past⟩ — **splen·dor·ous** *also* **splen·drous** \-d(ə-)rəs\ *adj*

splen·dour \-dər\ *chiefly Brit var of* SPLENDOR

sple·nec·to·my \spli-ˈnek-tə-mē\ *n, pl* **-mies** [ISV] (ca. 1859) : surgical removal of the spleen — **sple·nec·to·mize** \-ˌmīz\ *vt*

sple·net·ic \spli-ˈne-tik, *archaic* ˈsple-nə-(ˌ)tik\ *adj* [LL *spleneticus,* fr. L *splen* spleen] (1697) **1** *archaic* : given to melancholy **2** : marked by bad temper, malevolence, or spite — **splenetic** *n* — **sple·net·i·cal·ly** \spli-ˈne-ti-k(ə-)lē\ *adv*

splen·ic \ˈsple-nik\ *adj* [L *splenicus,* fr. Gk *splēnikos,* fr. *splēn* spleen] (1619) : of, relating to, or located in the spleen ⟨~ blood flow⟩

sple·ni·us \ˈsplē-nē-əs\ *n, pl* **-nii** \-nē-ˌī\ [NL, fr. L *splenium* plaster, compress, fr. Gk *splēnion,* fr. *splēn*] (1732) : either of two flat oblique muscles on each side of the back of the neck and upper thoracic region

spleno·meg·a·ly \ˌsple-nō-ˈme-gə-lē\ *n, pl* **-lies** [ISV] (ca. 1900) : abnormal enlargement of the spleen

spleu·chan \ˈsplü-kən, ˈsplyü-\ *n* [ScGael *spliùcan* & Ir *spliúchán*] (1785) *Scot & Irish* : a pouch esp. for tobacco or money

[1]**splice** \ˈsplīs\ *vt* **spliced; splic·ing** [obs. D *splissen;* akin to MD *splitten* to split] (ca. 1525) **1 a** : to unite (as two ropes) by interweaving the strands **b** : to unite (as lengths of magnetic tape) by overlapping and securing together two ends **2** : to unite, link, or insert as if by splicing **3** : to combine or insert (as genes) by genetic engineering ⟨*spliced* a human gene for insulin into a bacterium⟩ — **splic·er** *n*

[2]**splice** *n* (1627) **1** : a joining or joint made by splicing something **2** : MARRIAGE, WEDDING

splice 1

spliff \ˈsplif\ *n* [origin unknown] (1936) : JOINT 4

spline \ˈsplīn\ *n* [origin unknown] (1756) **1** : a thin wood or metal strip used in building construction **2** : a key that is fixed to one of two connected mechanical parts and fits into a keyway in the other; *also* : a keyway for such a key **3** : a function that is defined on an interval, is used to approximate a given function, and is composed of pieces of simple functions defined on subintervals and joined at their endpoints with a suitable degree of smoothness

[1]**splint** \ˈsplint\ *also* **splent** \ˈsplent\ *n* [ME, fr. MLG *splinte, splente;* prob. akin to MD *splitten* to split] (14c) **1** : a small plate or strip of metal used in making armor **2 a** : a thin strip of wood suitable for interweaving (as into baskets) **b** : SPLINTER **c** : material or a device used to protect and immobilize a body part (as a broken arm) **3** : a bony enlargement on the upper part of the cannon bone of a horse usu. on the inside of the leg

[2]**splint** *vt* (15c) **1** : to support and immobilize (as a broken bone) with a splint **2** : to brace with or as if with splints

splint bone *n* (1704) : one of the slender rudimentary metacarpal or metatarsal bones on either side of the cannon bone in the limbs of the horse and related animals

[1]**splin·ter** \ˈsplin-tər\ *n* [ME, fr. MD; akin to MLG *splinte* splint] (14c) **1 a** : a thin piece split or broken off lengthwise : SLIVER **b** : a small needlelike particle **2** : a group or faction broken away from a parent body — **splinter** *adj* — **splin·tery** \ˈsplin-tə-rē, -trē\ *adj*

[2]**splinter** *vb* **splin·tered; splin·ter·ing** \ˈsplin-tə-riŋ, -triŋ\ *vt* (1582) **1** : to split or rend into long thin pieces : SHIVER **2** : to split into fragments, parts, or factions ~ *vi* : to become splintered

[1]**split** \ˈsplit\ *vb* **split; split·ting** [D *splitten,* fr. MD; akin to MHG *splīzen* to split and prob. to OHG *spaltan* to split] *vt* (1567) **1 a** : to divide lengthwise usu. along a grain or seam or by layers **b** : to affect as if by cleaving or forcing apart ⟨the river ~*s* the town in two⟩ **2 a (1)** : to tear or rend apart : BURST **(2)** : to subject (an atom or atomic nucleus) to artificial disintegration by fission **b** : to affect as if by breaking up or tearing apart : SHATTER ⟨a roar that ~ the air⟩ **3** : to divide into parts or portions: as **a** : to divide between persons : SHARE **b** : to divide into factions, parties, or groups **c** : to mark (a ballot) or cast or register (a vote) so as to vote for candidates of different parties **d (1)** : to divide or break down (a chemical compound) into constituents ⟨~ a fat into glycerol and fatty acids⟩ **(2)** : to remove by such separation ⟨~ off carbon dioxide⟩ **e** : to divide (stock) by issuing a larger number of shares to existing shareholders usu. without increase in total par value **4** : to separate (the parts of a whole) by interposing something ⟨~ an infinitive⟩ **5** : LEAVE ⟨~ the party⟩ ⟨~ town⟩ ~ *vi* **1 a** : to become split lengthwise or into layers **b** : to break apart : BURST **2 a** : to become divided up or separated off ⟨~ into factions⟩ ⟨~ from the group⟩ **b** : to sever relations or connections : SEPARATE **c** : LEAVE; *esp* : to leave without delay ⟨~ for the coast⟩ **3** *Brit* : to betray confidence : act as an informer — usu. used with *on* **4** : to apportion shares ***syn*** see TEAR — **split hairs** : to make oversubtle or trivial distinctions — **split one's sides** : to laugh heartily — **split the difference** : to arrive at a compromise

[2]**split** *adj* (1593) **1** : DIVIDED, FRACTURED **2** : prepared for use by splitting ⟨~ bamboo⟩ ⟨~ hides⟩ **3** : HETEROZYGOUS — used esp. by breeders of cage birds sometimes with *for*

[3]**split** *n* (1597) **1 a** : a narrow break made by or as if by splitting **b** : an arrangement of bowling pins left standing with space for pins between them **2** : a piece split off or made thin by splitting **3 a** : a division into or between divergent or antagonistic elements or forces ⟨a cultural ~⟩ **b** : a faction formed in this way **4 a** : the act or process of splitting (as the stock of a corporation) **b** : the act of lowering oneself to the floor or leaping into the air with legs extended at right angles to the trunk **5** : a product of division by or as if by splitting **6** : a wine bottle holding one quarter the usual amount or about .1875 liters (6 to 6.5 ounces); *also* : the quantity held by a split **7** : an ice cream sundae served over slices of fruit (as banana) **8** : the recorded time at or for a specific part of a race

split–brain \ˈsplit-ˈbrān\ *adj* (1958) : having the optic chiasma and corpus callosum severed ⟨behavior in ~ animals⟩

split decision *n* (1952) : a decision in a boxing match reflecting a division of opinion among the referee and judges

split end *n* (1955) **1** : an offensive football end who lines up usu. several yards to the side of the formation **2** : a hair tip that has become frayed (as from dryness) — usu. used in pl.

split–fingered fastball \ˈsplit-ˈfiŋ-gərd-\ *n* (1979) : a fastball thrown with the ball gripped as for a forkball so that it drops rapidly as it nears the plate — called also *split-finger, splitter*

split infinitive *n* (1897) : an infinitive with *to* having a modifier between the *to* and the verbal (as in "to really start")

usage The split infinitive was discovered and named in the 19th century. 19th century writers seem to have made greater use of this construction than earlier writers; the frequency of occurrence attracted the disapproving attention of grammarians, many of whom thought it to be a modern corruption. The construction had in fact been in occasional use since the 14th century; only its frequency had changed. Even though there has never been a rational basis for objecting to the split infinitive, the subject has become a fixture of folk belief about grammar. You can hardly publish a sentence containing one without hearing about it from somebody. Modern commentators know the split infinitive is not a vice, but they are loath to drop such a popular subject. They usu. say it's all right to split an infinitive in the interest of clarity. Since clarity is the usual reason for splitting, this advice means merely that you can split them whenever you need to.

split–lev·el \ˈsplit-ˈle-vəl\ *adj* (1946) : divided vertically so that the floor level of rooms in one part is approximately midway between the levels of two successive stories in an adjoining part ⟨a ~ house⟩ — **split–lev·el** \-ˌle-vəl\ *n*

split pea *n* (1736) : a dried hulled pea (as a field pea) in which the cotyledons usu. split apart

split personality *n* (1919) **1 a** : SCHIZOPHRENIA — not used technically **b** : MULTIPLE PERSONALITY DISORDER — not used technically **2** : a dual nature or character ⟨a city with a *split personality*⟩

split rail *n* (1826) : a fence rail split from a log

split screen *n* (1944) : a film or video technique in which the frame is divided into discrete nonoverlapping images; *also* : the visual composition based on this technique

split–second *adj* (1944) **1** : occurring in a split second ⟨a ~ decision⟩ **2** : extremely precise ⟨~ timing⟩

split second *n* (1912) : a fractional part of a second : FLASH

split shift *n* (1943) : a shift of working hours divided into two or more working periods at times (as morning and evening) separated by more than normal periods of time off (as for lunch or rest)

split shot *n, pl* **split shot** (1889) : a small ball-shaped sinker of malleable metal having a slit for the insertion of a fishing line

split·ter \ˈspli-tər\ *n* (1623) **1** : one that splits **2** : one who classifies organisms into numerous named groups based on relatively minor variations or characters — compare LUMPER **3** : SPLIT-FINGERED FASTBALL

split ticket *n* (1836) : a ballot cast by a voter who votes for candidates of more than one party

splitting *adj* (1593) : that splits or causes to split: as **a** : causing a piercing sensation ⟨a ~ headache⟩ **b** : very fast or quick ⟨racing off at a ~ pace —Charles Dickens⟩ **c** : SIDESPLITTING ⟨a ~ laugh⟩

splore \ˈsplȯr\ *n* [origin unknown] (1785) **1** *Scot* : FROLIC, CAROUSAL **2** *Scot* : COMMOTION

[1]**splotch** \ˈspläch\ *n* [perh. blend of *spot* and *blotch*] (1601) : SPOT, BLOTCH — **splotchy** \ˈsplä-chē\ *adj*

[2]**splotch** *vt* (1654) : to mark with a splotch : cover with splotches

[1]**splurge** \ˈsplərj\ *n* [perh. blend of *splash* and *surge*] (1830) : an ostentatious effort, display, or expenditure

[2]**splurge** *vb* **splurged; splurg·ing** *vi* (1843) **1** : to make a splurge **2** : to indulge oneself extravagantly — often used with *on* ⟨~ on a new dress⟩ ~ *vt* : to spend extravagantly or ostentatiously

[1]**splut·ter** \ˈsplə-tər\ *n* [prob. alter. of *sputter*] (1677) **1** : a confused noise (as of hasty speaking) **2** : a splashing or sputtering sound

[2]**splutter** *vt* (1693) : to utter hastily or confusedly : STAMMER ~ *vi* **1** : to make a noise as if spitting **2** : to speak hastily and confusedly — **splut·ter·er** \ˈsplə-tər-ər\ *n*

splut·tery \ˈsplə-tə-rē\ *adj* (1866) : marked by spluttering

Spode \ˈspōd\ *n* (1869) : ceramic ware (as bone china, stone china, or Parian ware) made at the works established by Josiah Spode in 1770 at Stoke in Staffordshire, England

spod·u·mene \ˈspä-jə-ˌmēn\ *n* [prob. fr. F *spodumène,* fr. G *Spodumen,* fr. Gk *spodoumenos,* prp. of *spodousthai* to be burnt to ashes, fr. *spodos* ashes] (1893) : a white to yellowish, purplish, or emerald-green monoclinic mineral that is a silicate of lithium and aluminum and occurs in prismatic crystals often of great size

[1]**spoil** \ˈspȯi(-ə)l\ *n* [ME *spoile,* fr. AF *espuille,* fr. *espuiller*] (14c) **1 a** : plunder taken from an enemy in war or from a victim in robbery : LOOT **b** : public offices made the property of a successful party — usu. used in pl. **c** : something valuable or desirable gained through special effort or opportunism or in return for a favor — usu. used in pl. **2 a** : SPOLIATION, PLUNDERING **b** : the act of damaging : HARM, IMPAIRMENT **3** : an object of plundering : PREY **4** : earth and rock excavated or dredged **5** : an object damaged or flawed in the making

syn SPOIL, PLUNDER, BOOTY, PRIZE, LOOT mean something taken from another by force or craft. SPOIL, more commonly SPOILS, applies to what belongs by right or custom to the victor in war or political contest ⟨the *spoils* of political victory⟩. PLUNDER applies to what is taken not only in war but in robbery, banditry, grafting, or swindling ⟨a bootlegger's *plunder*⟩. BOOTY implies plunder to be shared among confederates ⟨thieves dividing up their *booty*⟩. PRIZE applies to spoils captured on the high seas or territorial waters of the enemy ⟨the wartime right of seizing *prizes* at sea⟩. LOOT applies esp. to what is taken from victims of a catastrophe ⟨picked through the ruins for *loot*⟩.

²**spoil** *vb* **spoiled** \ˈspȯi(-ə)ld, ˈspȯi(-ə)lt\ *also* **spoilt** \ˈspȯi(-ə)lt\; **spoil·ing** [ME, fr. AF *espuiller, espoiller,* fr. L *spoliare* to strip of natural covering, despoil, fr. *spolium* skin, hide — more at SPILL] *vt* (14c) **1 a** *archaic* : DESPOIL, STRIP **b** : PILLAGE, ROB **2** *archaic* : to seize by force **3 a** : to damage seriously : RUIN **b** : to impair the quality or effect of ⟨a quarrel ~*ed* the celebration⟩ **4 a** : to impair the disposition or character of by overindulgence or excessive praise **b** : to pamper excessively : CODDLE ~ *vi* **1** : to practice plunder and robbery **2** : to lose valuable or useful qualities usu. as a result of decay ⟨the fruit ~*ed*⟩ **3** : to have an eager desire ⟨~*ing* for a fight⟩ ***syn*** see DECAY, INDULGE — **spoil·able** \ˈspȯi-lə-bəl\ *adj*

spoil·age \ˈspȯi-lij\ *n* (1597) **1** : the act or process of spoiling; *esp* : the process of decay in foodstuffs **2** : something spoiled or wasted **3** : loss by spoilage

spoil·er \ˈspȯi-lər\ *n* (15c) **1 a** : one that spoils **b** : one (as a political candidate) having little or no chance of winning but capable of depriving a rival of success **2 a** : a long narrow plate along the upper surface of an airplane wing that may be raised for reducing lift and increasing drag — see AIRPLANE illustration **b** : an air deflector on an automobile to reduce the tendency to lift off the road at high speeds **3** : information about the plot of a motion picture or TV program that can spoil a viewer's sense of surprise or suspense; *also* : a person who discloses such information

spoiler alert *n* (1994) : a reviewer's warning that a plot spoiler is about to be revealed

spoils·man \ˈspȯi(-ə)lz-mən\ *n* (1846) : one who serves a party for a share of the spoils; *also* : one who sanctions such practice

spoil·sport \ˈspȯi(-ə)l-ˌspȯrt\ *n* (1785) : one who spoils the sport or pleasure of others

spoils system *n* (1838) : a practice of regarding public offices and their emoluments as plunder for members of the victorious party

¹**spoke** \ˈspōk\ *past & archaic past part of* SPEAK

²**spoke** *n* [ME, fr. OE *spāca;* akin to OHG *speihha* spoke, MD *spike* spike] (bef. 12c) **1 a** : any of the small radiating bars inserted in the hub of a wheel to support the rim **b** : something resembling the spoke of a wheel **2** : any of the projecting handles of a boat's steering wheel

³**spoke** *vt* **spoked; spok·ing** (bef. 12c) : to furnish with spokes

spo·ken \ˈspō-kən\ *adj* [pp. of *speak*] (1560) **1** : delivered by word of mouth : ORAL **2** : characterized by speaking in (such) a manner — used in combination ⟨soft-*spoken*⟩ ⟨plain*spoken*⟩

spoke·shave \ˈspōk-ˌshāv\ *n* [²*spoke*] (1510) : a drawknife or small transverse plane with end handles for planing convex or concave surfaces

spokes·man \ˈspōks-mən\ *n* [prob. irreg. fr. *spoke,* obs. pp. of *speak*] (1537) : a person who speaks as the representative of another or others often in a professional capacity — **spokes·man·ship** \-ˌship\ *n*

spokes·mod·el \-ˌmä-dᵊl\ *n* (1984) : a model who is a spokesman or spokeswoman

spokes·peo·ple \-ˌpē-pəl\ *n pl* (1972) : people serving as spokesmen or spokeswomen

spokes·per·son \-ˌpər-sᵊn\ *n* (1971) : SPOKESMAN

spokes·wom·an \-ˌwu̇-mən\ *n* (1569) : a woman who speaks as the representative of another or others often in a professional capacity

spo·li·ate \ˈspō-lē-ˌāt\ *vt* **-at·ed; -at·ing** [L *spoliatus,* pp. of *spoliare*] (ca. 1727) : DESPOIL — **spo·li·a·tor** \-ˌā-tər\ *n*

spo·li·a·tion \ˌspō-lē-ˈā-shən\ *n* [ME, fr. AF *spoliacion,* L *spoliation-, spoliatio,* fr. *spoliare* to plunder — more at SPOIL] (15c) **1 a** : the act of plundering **b** : the state of having been plundered esp. in war **2** : the act of injuring esp. beyond reclaim

spon·dee \ˈspän-ˌdē\ *n* [ME *sponde,* fr. MF or L; MF *spondee,* fr. L *spondeum,* fr. Gk *spondeios,* fr. *spondeios* of a libation, fr. *spondē* libation, fr. *spendein* to make a libation; fr. its use in music accompanying libations — more at SPOUSE] (14c) : a metrical foot consisting of two long or stressed syllables — **spon·da·ic** \spän-ˈdā-ik\ *adj or n*

spon·dy·li·tis \ˌspän-də-ˈlī-təs\ *n* [NL, fr. Gk *sphondylos, spondylos* vertebra] (ca. 1849) : inflammation of the vertebrae

¹**sponge** \ˈspənj\ *n* [ME, fr. OE, fr. L *spongia,* fr. Gk] (bef. 12c) **1 a** (1) : an elastic porous mass of interlacing horny fibers that forms the internal skeleton of various marine animals (phylum Porifera) and is able when wetted to absorb water (2) : a piece of sponge (as for scrubbing) (3) : a porous rubber or cellulose product used similarly to a sponge **b** : any of a phylum (Porifera) of aquatic chiefly marine simple invertebrate animals that have a double-walled body of loosely aggregated cells with a skeleton supported by spicules or spongin and are filter feeders that are sessile as adults **2** : a pad (as of folded gauze) used in surgery and medicine (as to remove discharge) **3** : one who lives on others **4 a** : a soft mixture of yeast, liquid, and flour that is allowed to rise and then mixed with additional ingredients to create bread dough **b** : a whipped dessert usu. containing whites of eggs or gelatin **c** : a metal (as platinum) obtained in porous form usu. by reduction without fusion ⟨titanium ~⟩ **d** : the egg mass of a crab **5** : an absorbent contraceptive device that is impregnated with spermicide and inserted into the vagina before sexual intercourse to cover the cervix ***syn*** see PARASITE — **sponge·like** \ˈspənj-ˌlīk\ *adj*

²**sponge** *vb* **sponged; spong·ing** *vt* (14c) **1** : to cleanse, wipe, or moisten with or as if with a sponge **2** : to erase or destroy with or as if with a sponge — often used with *out* **3** : to get by sponging on another **4** : to absorb with or as if with or in the manner of a sponge ~ *vi* **1** : to absorb, soak up, or imbibe like a sponge **2** : to get something from or live on another by imposing on hospitality or good nature ⟨*sponged* off of her sister⟩ **3** : to dive or dredge for sponges — **spong·er** *n*

sponge cake *n* (1805) : a light cake made without shortening

sponge rubber *n* (1886) : cellular rubber resembling a natural sponge in structure used esp. for cushions, vibration dampeners, weather stripping, and gaskets

sponge·ware \ˈspənj-ˌwer\ *n* (1943) : a typically 19th century earthenware with background color spattered or dabbed (as with a sponge) and usu. a freehand central design

spon·gi·form encephalopathy \ˈspən-ji-ˌfȯrm-\ *n* [*spongiform* resembling a sponge, fr. L *spongia* + E *-iform*] (1960) : any of various degenerative diseases of the brain characterized by the development of porous spongelike lesions in brain tissue and by deterioration in neurological functioning; *specif* : PRION DISEASE

spon·gin \ˈspən-jən\ *n* [G, fr. L *spongia* sponge] (ca. 1868) : a scleroprotein that is the chief constituent of flexible fibers found in certain sponge skeletons

spongy \ˈspən-jē\ *adj* **spong·i·er; -est** (14c) **1** : resembling a sponge: **a** : soft and full of cavities ⟨~ ice⟩ **b** : elastic, porous, and absorbent **2 a** : not firm or solid **b** : being in the form of a metallic sponge ⟨~ iron⟩ **3** : moist and soft like a sponge full of water ⟨a ~ moor⟩ — **spong·i·ness** *n*

spongy parenchyma *n* (1884) : a spongy layer of irregular chlorophyll-bearing cells interspersed with air spaces that fills the interior part of a leaf below the palisade layer — called also *spongy layer, spongy tissue*

spon·son \ˈspän(t)-sən\ *n* [perh. by shortening & alter. fr. *expansion*] (1835) **1 a** : a projection (as a gun platform) from the side of a ship or a tank **b** : an air chamber along a watercraft (as a canoe) to increase stability and buoyancy **2** : a light air-filled structure or a winglike part protruding from the hull of a seaplane to steady it on water

¹**spon·sor** \ˈspän(t)-sər\ *n* [LL, fr. L, guarantor, surety, fr. *spondēre* to promise — more at SPOUSE] (1651) **1** : one who presents a candidate for baptism or confirmation and undertakes responsibility for the person's religious education or spiritual welfare **2** : one who assumes responsibility for some other person or thing **3** : a person or an organization that pays for or plans and carries out a project or activity; *esp* : one that pays the cost of a radio or television program usu. in return for advertising time during its course — **spon·so·ri·al** \spän-ˈsȯr-ē-əl\ *adj* — **spon·sor·ship** \ˈspän(t)-sər-ˌship\ *n*

²**sponsor** *vt* **spon·sored; spon·sor·ing** \ˈspän(t)s-(ə-)riŋ\ (1869) : to be or stand sponsor for

spon·ta·ne·i·ty \ˌspän-tə-ˈnē-ə-tē, -ˈnā-\ *n* (1651) **1** : the quality or state of being spontaneous **2** : voluntary or undetermined action or movement; *also* : its source

spon·ta·ne·ous \spän-ˈtā-nē-əs\ *adj* [LL *spontaneus,* fr. L *sponte* of one's free will, voluntarily] (1653) **1** : proceeding from natural feeling or native tendency without external constraint **2** : arising from a momentary impulse **3** : controlled and directed internally : SELF-ACTING ⟨~ movement characteristic of living things⟩ **4** : produced without being planted or without human labor : INDIGENOUS **5** : developing or occurring without apparent external influence, force, cause, or treatment **6** : not apparently contrived or manipulated : NATURAL — **spon·ta·ne·ous·ly** *adv* — **spon·ta·ne·ous·ness** *n*

syn SPONTANEOUS, IMPULSIVE, INSTINCTIVE, AUTOMATIC, MECHANICAL mean acting or activated without deliberation. SPONTANEOUS implies lack of prompting and connotes naturalness ⟨a *spontaneous* burst of applause⟩. IMPULSIVE implies acting under stress of emotion or spirit of the moment ⟨*impulsive* acts of violence⟩. INSTINCTIVE stresses action involving neither judgment nor will ⟨blinking is an *instinctive* reaction⟩. AUTOMATIC implies action engaging neither the mind nor the emotions and connotes a predictable response ⟨his denial was *automatic*⟩. MECHANICAL stresses the lifeless, often perfunctory character of the response ⟨a *mechanical* teaching method⟩.

spontaneous combustion *n* (1795) : self-ignition of combustible material through chemical action (as oxidation) of its constituents — called also *spontaneous ignition*

spontaneous generation *n* (1665) : a now discredited notion that living organisms spontaneously originate directly from nonliving matter — called also *abiogenesis*

spontaneous recovery *n* (1943) : reappearance of an extinguished conditioned response without positive reinforcement

spon·toon \spän-ˈtün\ *n* [F *sponton,* fr. It *spuntone,* fr. *punta* sharp point, fr. VL **puncta* — more at POINT] (1598) : a short pike formerly borne by subordinate officers of infantry

¹**spoof** \ˈspüf\ *vt* [*Spoof,* a hoaxing game invented by Arthur Roberts †1933 Eng. comedian] (1889) **1** : DECEIVE, HOAX **2** : to make good-natured fun of

²**spoof** *n* (1889) **1** : HOAX, DECEPTION **2** : a light humorous parody — **spoof·ery** \ˈspü-f(ə-)rē\ *n* — **spoofy** \ˈspü-fē\ *adj*

¹**spook** \ˈspük\ *n* [D; akin to MLG *spōk* ghost] (1801) **1** : GHOST, SPECTER **2** : an undercover agent : SPY — **spook·ish** \ˈspü-kish\ *adj*

²**spook** *vt* (1883) **1** : HAUNT 3 **2** : to make frightened or frantic : SCARE; *esp* : to startle into violent activity (as stampeding) ~ *vi* : to become spooked ⟨cattle ~*ing* at shadows⟩

spook·ery \ˈspü-k(ə-)rē\ *n, pl* **-er·ies** (1893) : the quality of being spooky; *also* : something (as a story) that involves spooks

spooky \ˈspü-kē\ *adj* **spook·i·er; -est** (1854) **1** : relating to, resembling, or suggesting spooks **2** : NERVOUS, SKITTISH ⟨a ~ horse⟩ — **spook·i·ly** \-kə-lē\ *adv* — **spook·i·ness** \-kē-nəs\ *n*

¹**spool** \ˈspül\ *n* [ME *spole,* fr. MD *spoele;* akin to OHG *spuola* spool] (14c) **1** : a cylindrical device which has a rim or ridge at each end and an axial hole for a pin or spindle and on which material (as thread, wire, or tape) is wound **2** : material or the amount of material wound on a spool

²**spool** *vt* (1603) **1** : to wind on a spool **2** : WIND ⟨~ the thread off the bobbin⟩ **3** : to regulate the transmission of by means of a spooler ⟨~ data⟩ ~ *vi* **1** : to wind itself on a spool **2** : to be wound or unwound **3** : to regulate data flow by means of a spooler

spool·er \ˈspü-lər\ *n* (1971) : a computer utility that regulates data flow by receiving data (as from a word processor), queuing the data in a buffer, and then transmitting it (as to a printer) with increased efficiency

¹**spoon** \ˈspün\ *n* [ME, fr. OE *spōn* splinter, chip; akin to OHG *spān* splinter, chip] (14c) **1** : an eating or cooking implement consisting of a small shallow bowl with a relatively long handle **2** : something (as a tool or fishing lure) that resembles a spoon in shape

²**spoon** *vt* (1715) : to take up and usu. transfer in a spoon ~ *vi* [perh. fr. the Welsh custom of an engaged man's presenting his fiancée with an elaborately carved wooden spoon] : to make love by caressing, kissing, and talking amorously : NECK

spoon·bill \ˈspün-ˌbil\ *n* (ca. 1678) **1** : any of several wading birds (family Threskiornithidae) related to the ibises that have an expanded bill that is flattened and rounded at the tip **2** : any of several broad-billed ducks (as the shoveler)

spoonbill cat *n* (ca. 1882) : a paddlefish (*Polyodon spathula*)

spoon–billed \'spün-ˌbild\ *adj* (1668) : having the bill or snout expanded and spatulate at the end
spoon bread *n* (1847) : soft bread made of cornmeal mixed with milk, eggs, and shortening and served with a spoon
spoo•ner•ism \'spü-nə-ˌri-zəm\ *n* [William A. *Spooner* †1930 Eng. clergyman & educator] (1900) : a transposition of usu. initial sounds of two or more words (as in *tons of soil* for *sons of toil*)
spoon–feed \'spün-ˌfēd\ *vt* **-fed** \-ˌfed\; **-feed•ing** (1615) **1** : to feed by means of a spoon **2 a** : to present (information) so completely as to preclude independent thought ⟨~ material to students⟩ **b** : to present information to in this manner
spoon•ful \'spün-ˌfu̇l\ *n, pl* **spoonfuls** \-ˌfu̇lz\ *also* **spoons•ful** \'spünz-ˌfu̇l\ (14c) : as much as a spoon will hold; *specif* : TEASPOONFUL
spoony *or* **spoon•ey** \'spü-nē\ *adj* **spoon•i•er; -est** [E slang *spoon* simpleton] (ca. 1812) **1** : SILLY, FOOLISH; *esp* : unduly sentimental **2** : being sentimentally in love
[1]**spoor** \'spu̇r, 'spȯr\ *n, pl* **spoor** *or* **spoors** [Afrik, fr. D; akin to OE *spor* footprint, spoor, *spurnan* to kick — more at SPURN] (1823) **1** : a track, a trail, a scent, or droppings esp. of a wild animal **2** : a trace by which the progress of someone or something may be followed
[2]**spoor** *vt* (1850) : to track by a spoor ~ *vi* : to track something by its spoor
spor- *or* **spori-** *or* **sporo-** *comb form* [NL *spora*] : seed : spore ⟨*sporo*cyst⟩ ⟨*spor*angium⟩ ⟨*spori*cidal⟩
spo•rad•ic \spə-'ra-dik\ *adj* [ML *sporadicus,* fr. Gk *sporadikos,* fr. *sporadēn* here and there, fr. *sporad-, sporas* scattered; akin to Gk *speirein* to sow — more at SPERM] (ca. 1689) : occurring occasionally, singly, or in irregular or random instances ⟨~ protests⟩ ⟨a ~ disease⟩ ***syn*** see INFREQUENT — **spo•rad•i•cal•ly** \-di-k(ə-)lē\ *adv*
sporadic E layer *n* (1949) : a layer of ionization occurring irregularly within the E region of the ionosphere
spo•ran•gio•phore \spə-'ran-jē-ə-ˌfȯr\ *n* (1875) : a stalk or similar structure bearing sporangia
spo•ran•gi•um \spə-'ran-jē-əm\ *n, pl* **-gia** \-jē-ə\ [NL, fr. *spor-* + Gk *angeion* vessel — more at ANGI-] (1821) : a structure within which spores are produced — **spo•ran•gial** \-j(ē-)əl\ *adj*
[1]**spore** \'spȯr\ *n* [NL *spora* seed, spore, fr. Gk, act of sowing, seed, fr. *speirein* to sow — more at SPERM] (1836) : a primitive usu. unicellular often environmentally resistant dormant or reproductive body produced by plants, fungi, and some microorganisms and capable of development into a new individual either directly or after fusion with another spore — **spored** \'spȯrd\ *adj*
[2]**spore** *vi* **spored; spor•ing** (1866) : to produce or reproduce by spores
spore case *n* (1836) : a case containing spores : SPORANGIUM
spo•ri•cid•al \ˌspȯr-ə-'sī-dᵊl\ *adj* (1939) : tending to kill spores — **spo•ri•cide** \'spȯr-ə-ˌsīd\ *n*
spo•ro•carp \'spȯr-ə-ˌkärp\ *n* [ISV] (1849) : a structure (as in red algae, fungi, or mosses) in or on which spores are produced
spo•ro•cyst \-ˌsist\ *n* [ISV] (1861) **1** : a case or cyst secreted by some sporozoans preliminary to sporogony; *also* : a sporozoan encysted in such a case **2** : a saccular body that is the first asexual reproductive form of a digenetic trematode, develops from a miracidium, and buds off cells from its inner surface which develop into rediae
spo•ro•gen•e•sis \ˌspȯr-ə-'je-nə-səs\ *n* [NL] (ca. 1890) **1** : reproduction by spores **2** : spore formation — **spo•rog•e•nous** \spə-'rä-jə-nəs, spȯ-\ *also* **spo•ro•gen•ic** \ˌspȯr-ə-'je-nik\ *adj*
spo•rog•o•ny \spə-'rä-gə-nē, spȯ-\ *n* [ISV] (1888) : reproduction by spores; *specif* : formation of spores typically containing sporozoites that is characteristic of some sporozoans and that results from the encystment and subsequent division of a zygote — **spo•ro•gon•ic** \ˌspȯr-ə-'gä-nik\ *adj*
spo•ro•phore \'spȯr-ə-ˌfȯr\ *n* [ISV] (1849) : the spore-producing organ of a fungus or slime mold
spo•ro•phyll \-ˌfil\ *n* [ISV] (1888) : a spore-bearing and usu. greatly modified leaf
spo•ro•phyte \-ˌfīt\ *n* [ISV] (1886) : the diploid multicellular individual or generation of a plant with alternation of generations that begins from a diploid zygote and produces haploid spores by meiotic division — compare GAMETOPHYTE — **spo•ro•phyt•ic** \ˌspȯr-ə-'fi-tik\ *adj*
spo•ro•pol•len•in \ˌspȯr-ə-'pä-lə-nən\ *n* [ISV *spor-* + *pollen* + [1]*-in*] (1931) : a relatively chemically inert polymer that makes up the outer layer of pollen grains and some spores
spo•ro•tri•cho•sis \spə-ˌrä-tri-'kō-səs; ˌspȯr-ə-tri-\ *n* [NL, fr. *Sporotrich-, Sporothrix,* genus name, fr. *spor-* + Gk *trich-, thrix* hair] (1908) : infection with or disease caused by a fungus (*Sporothrix schenckii*) that is characterized by often ulcerating or suppurating nodules in the skin, subcutaneous tissues, and nearby lymph nodes and is usu. transmitted by fungal entry through a skin abrasion or wound
-sporous *adj comb form* [NL *spora* spore] : having (such or so many) spores ⟨homo*sporous*⟩
spo•ro•zo•an \ˌspȯr-ə-'zō-ən\ *n* [NL *Sporozoa,* fr. *spor-* + *-zoa*] (1888) : any of a large class (Sporozoa) of strictly parasitic nonmotile protozoans that have a complex life cycle usu. involving both asexual and sexual generations often in different hosts and include important pathogens (as malaria parasites and babesias) — **sporozoan** *adj*
spo•ro•zo•ite \-'zō-ˌīt\ *n* [NL *Sporozoa* + ISV *-ite*] (1888) : a usu. motile infective form of some sporozoans that is a product of sporogony and initiates an asexual cycle in the new host
spor•ran \'spȯr-ən, 'spär-\ *n* [ScGael *sporan* purse] (1752) : a pouch usu. of skin with the hair or fur on that is worn in front of the kilt with Scots Highland dress

1 sporran

[1]**sport** \'spȯrt\ *vb* [ME, to divert, disport, short for *disporten*] *vi* (15c) **1 a** : to amuse oneself : FROLIC ⟨lambs ~*ing* in the meadow⟩ **b** : to engage in a sport **2 a** : to mock or ridicule something **b** : to speak or act in jest : TRIFLE **3** [[2]*sport*] : to deviate or vary abruptly from type (as by bud variation) : MUTATE ~ *vt* **1** : to display or wear usu. ostentatiously : BOAST ⟨~*ing* expensive new shoes⟩ **2** [[2]*sport*] : to put forth as a sport or bud variation
[2]**sport** *n* (15c) **1 a** : a source of diversion : RECREATION **b** : sexual play **c** (1) : physical activity engaged in for pleasure (2) : a particular activity (as an athletic game) so engaged in **2 a** : PLEASANTRY, JEST **b** : often mean-spirited jesting : MOCKERY, DERISION **3 a** : something tossed or driven about in or as if in play **b** : LAUGHINGSTOCK **4 a** : SPORTSMAN **b** : a person considered with respect to living up to the ideals of sportsmanship ⟨a good ~⟩ ⟨a poor ~⟩ **c** : a companionable person **5** : an individual exhibiting a sudden deviation from type beyond the normal limits of individual variation usu. as a result of mutation esp. of somatic tissue ***syn*** see FUN
[3]**sport** *or* **sports** *adj* (1582) : of, relating to, or suitable for sports; *esp* : styled in a manner suitable for casual or informal wear ⟨~ coats⟩
sport fish *n* (1944) : a fish important for the sport it affords anglers
sport•fish•er•man \'spȯrt-ˌfi-shər-mən\ *n* (1954) : a motorboat equipped for sportfishing
sport•fish•ing \-ˌfi-shiŋ\ *n* (1910) : fishing done with a rod and reel for sport or recreation
sport•ful \-fəl\ *adj* (15c) **1 a** : productive of sport or amusement : ENTERTAINING, DIVERTING **b** : PLAYFUL, FROLICSOME **2** : done in sport — **sport•ful•ly** \-fə-lē\ *adv* — **sport•ful•ness** *n*
spor•tif \'spȯr-tif\ *adj* [F, sporting, of sports, fr. *sport* sport, fr. E] (1920) : SPORTY
sport•ing \'spȯr-tiŋ\ *adj* (1799) **1 a** : of, relating to, used, or suitable for sport; *esp* : trained for trapping or retrieving game ⟨~ dogs⟩ **b** : marked by or calling for sportsmanship **c** : involving such risk as a sports contender may expect to take or encounter ⟨a ~ chance⟩ **2** : of or relating to dissipation and esp. gambling **3** : tending to mutate freely — **sport•ing•ly** *adv*
sporting house *n* (1615) : BORDELLO
sport•ive \'spȯr-tiv\ *adj* (1590) **1 a** : FROLICSOME, PLAYFUL **b** : ARDENT, WANTON **2** : of or relating to sports and esp. field sports — **sport•ive•ly** *adv* — **sport•ive•ness** *n*
sports bar *n* (1975) : a bar catering esp. to sports fans and typically containing several televisions and often sports memorabilia
sports car *n* (1928) : a low small usu. 2-passenger automobile designed for quick response, easy maneuverability, and high-speed driving
sports•cast \'spȯrts-ˌkast\ *n* [*sport* + broad*cast*] (1941) : a radio or television broadcast of a sports event or of information about sports — **sports•cast•er** \-ˌkas-tər\ *n*
sports•man \'spȯrts-mən\ *n* (ca. 1707) **1** : a person who engages in sports (as hunting or fishing) **2** : a person who shows sportsmanship — **sports•man•like** \-ˌlīk\ *adj* — **sports•man•ly** \-lē\ *adj*
sports•man•ship \-ˌship\ *n* (1745) : conduct (as fairness, respect for one's opponent, and graciousness in winning or losing) becoming to one participating in a sport
sports medicine *n* (1961) : a field of medicine concerned with the prevention and treatment of injuries and disorders that are related to participation in sports
sports•wear \'spȯrts-ˌwer\ *n* (1912) : clothing suitable for recreation; *broadly* : clothing designed for casual or informal wear
sports•wom•an \-ˌwu̇-mən\ *n* (1754) : a woman who engages in sports
sports•writ•er \'spȯrts-ˌrī-tər\ *n* (1927) : a person who writes about sports esp. for a newspaper — **sports•writ•ing** \-tiŋ\ *n*
sport–util•i•ty vehicle \'spȯrt-yü-'ti-lə-tē-\ *n* (1978) : a rugged automotive vehicle similar to a station wagon but built on a light-truck chassis — called also *sport-ute* \-ˌyüt\, *sport-utility, SUV*
sporty \'spȯr-tē\ *adj* **sport•i•er; -est** (1889) **1** : of, relating to, or typical of sports, sportsmen, sportswomen, or sportswear **2** : resembling a sports car in styling or performance ⟨a ~ sedan⟩ — **sport•i•ly** \'spȯr-tə-lē\ *adv* — **sport•i•ness** \'spȯr-tē-nəs\ *n*
spor•u•late \'spȯr-yə-ˌlāt, -ə-ˌlāt\ *vi* **-lat•ed; -lat•ing** [back-formation fr. *sporulation*] (ca. 1891) : to undergo sporulation
spor•u•la•tion \ˌspȯr-yə-'lā-shən, -ə-'lā-\ *n* [ISV, fr. NL *sporula,* dim. of *spora* spore] (1876) : the formation of spores; *esp* : division into many small spores (as after encystment) — **spor•u•la•tive** \'spȯr-yə-ˌlā-tiv, -ə-ˌlā-\ *adj*
-spory *n comb form* [*-spor*ous + [2]*-y*] : quality or state of having (such) spores ⟨homo*spory*⟩
[1]**spot** \'spät\ *n* [ME; akin to MD *spotte* stain, speck, ON *spotti* small piece] (13c) **1** : a taint on character or reputation : FAULT ⟨the only ~ on the family name⟩ **2 a** : a small area visibly different (as in color, finish, or material) from the surrounding area **b** (1) : an area marred or marked (as by dirt) (2) : a circumscribed surface lesion of disease (as measles) or decay ⟨~*s* of rot⟩ ⟨rust ~*s* on a leaf⟩ **c** : a conventionalized design used on playing cards to distinguish the suits and indicate values **3** : an object having a specified number of spots or a specified numeral on its surface **4** : a small quantity or amount : BIT **5 a** : a particular place, area, or part **b** : a small extent of space **6** *pl usu* **spot** : a small croaker (*Leiostomus xanthurus*) of the Atlantic coast with a black spot behind the opercula **7 a** : a particular position (as in an organization or a hierarchy) **b** : a place or appearance on an entertainment program **8** : SPOTLIGHT **9** : a position usu. of difficulty or embarrassment **10** : a brief announcement or advertisement broadcast between scheduled radio or television programs **11** : a brief segment or report on a broadcast esp. of news — **on the spot** **1** : at once : IMMEDIATELY **2** : at the place of action **3 a** : in a responsible or accountable position **b** : in a difficult or trying situation
[2]**spot** *vb* **spot•ted; spot•ting** *vt* (14c) **1** : to stain the character or reputation of : DISGRACE **2** : to mark in or with a spot : STAIN **3** : to locate or identify by a spot **4 a** : to single out : IDENTIFY; *esp* : to note as a known criminal or a suspicious person **b** : DETECT, NOTICE ⟨~ a mistake⟩ **c** (1) : to locate accurately ⟨~ an enemy position⟩ (2) : to cause to strike accurately ⟨~ the battery's fire⟩ **5 a** : to lie at intervals in or over : STUD **b** : to place at intervals or in a desired spot ⟨~ field telephones⟩ **c** : to fix in or as if in the beam of a spotlight **d** : to

\ə\ **abut** \ᵊ\ **kitten**, F **table** \ər\ **further** \a\ **ash** \ā\ **ace** \ä\ **mop, mar**
\au̇\ **out** \ch\ **chin** \e\ **bet** \ē\ **easy** \g\ **go** \i\ **hit** \ī\ **ice** \j\ **job**
\ŋ\ **sing** \ō\ **go** \ȯ\ **law** \ȯi\ **boy** \th\ **thin** \t͟h\ **the** \ü\ **loot** \u̇\ **foot**
\y\ **yet** \zh\ **vision, beige** \k, ⁿ, œ, ue, ʸ\ *see* Guide to Pronunciation

schedule in a particular spot or at a particular time **6 :** to remove a spot from **7 :** to allow as a handicap ~ *vi* **1 :** to become stained or discolored in spots **2 :** to cause a spot **3 :** to act as a spotter; *esp* **:** to locate targets **4 :** to experience abnormal and sporadic bleeding in small amounts from the uterus — **spot·ta·ble** \'spä-tə-bəl\ *adj*

[3]**spot** *adj* (1881) **1 a :** being, originating, or done on the spot or in or for a particular spot ⟨~ coverage of the news⟩ **b :** available for immediate delivery after sale ⟨~ commodities⟩ **c** (1) **:** paid out upon delivery ⟨~ cash⟩ (2) **:** involving immediate cash payment ⟨a ~ transaction⟩ **d** (1) **:** broadcast between scheduled programs ⟨~ announcements⟩ (2) **:** originating in a local station for a national advertiser **e :** performing occasionally when needed ⟨a ~ starter⟩ **2 :** made at random or restricted to a few places or instances ⟨a ~ check⟩; *also* **:** selected at random or as a sample

spot–check \'spät-ˌchek\ *vt* (1943) **:** to sample or investigate quickly or at random ~ *vi* **:** to make a spot check

spot·less \'spät-ləs\ *adj* (14c) **:** having no spot: **a :** free from impurity **:** IMMACULATE ⟨~ kitchens⟩ **b :** PURE, UNBLEMISHED ⟨a ~ reputation⟩ — **spot·less·ly** *adv* — **spot·less·ness** *n*

[1]**spot·light** \'spät-ˌlīt\ *n* (1904) **1 a :** a projected spot of light used to illuminate brilliantly a person, object, or group on a stage **b :** public notice or attention ⟨held the political ~⟩ **2 a :** a light designed to direct a narrow intense beam of light on a small area **b :** something that illuminates brilliantly

[2]**spotlight** *vt* **-light·ed** *or* **-lit; -light·ing** (1922) **1 :** to illuminate with a spotlight **2 :** to direct attention to **:** HIGHLIGHT

spot–on \'spät-'än\ *adj* (1949) **:** exactly correct ⟨a ~ impersonation⟩

spot pass *n* (1948) **:** a pass (as in football or basketball) made to a predetermined spot on the field or court rather than directly to a player

spotted *adj* (13c) **1 :** marked with spots **2 :** being sullied **:** TARNISHED **3 :** characterized by the appearance of spots

spotted alfalfa aphid *n* (1958) **:** a highly destructive Old World aphid (*Therioaphis maculata*) that is established in the U.S. in warmer areas and causes yellowing and stunting of affected plants

spotted cucumber beetle *n* (1923) **:** a rather slender greenish-yellow beetle (*Diabrotica undecimpunctata howardi*) that feeds as an adult on various ornamental and crop plants and is a vector of wilt disease esp. of cucumbers and melons

spotted dick *n* [dial. *dick* pudding, prob. fr. the name *Dick*] (1849) *Brit* **:** a pudding made with suet and currants or raisins — called also *spotted dog*

spotted fever *n* (1650) **:** any of various eruptive fevers: as **a :** TYPHUS **b :** ROCKY MOUNTAIN SPOTTED FEVER

spotted knapweed *n* (1921) **:** a knapweed (*Centaurea maculosa* syn. *C. biebersteinii*) with usu. pink flowers and deeply cleft leaves that is native to Europe and Asia but is now widespread in the U.S.

spotted owl *n* (1910) **:** a rare large dark brown dark-eyed owl (*Strix occidentalis*) that has barred and spotted underparts and is found in humid old growth forests and thickly wooded canyons from British Columbia to southern California and central Mexico; *esp* **:** NORTHERN SPOTTED OWL

spotted salamander *n* (1922) **:** a common salamander (*Ambystoma maculatum*) of eastern No. America with glossy black skin spotted with yellow or orange on the back

spotted sea trout *n* (1873) **:** a weakfish (*Cynoscion nebulosus*) that is a valuable food and sport fish of the southern Atlantic and Gulf coasts of the U.S. — called also *sea trout, speckled trout, spotted weakfish*

spotted turtle *n* (1868) **:** a freshwater turtle (*Clemmys guttata*) of the eastern U.S. that has a blackish carapace with round yellow spots

spot·ter \'spä-tər\ *n* (1611) **1 :** one that makes or applies a spot (as for identification) **2 :** one that looks or keeps watch: as **a :** one that locates enemy targets **b :** a civilian who watches for approaching airplanes **c :** a person who assists another during exercise (as to prevent injury) **3 :** one that removes spots **4 :** one that places something on or in a desired spot

spot test *n* (1921) **1 :** a test limited to a few key or sample points or a relatively small percentage of random spots **2 :** a test conducted on the spot to yield immediate results

spotting scope *n* (1921) **:** a lightweight portable telescope that is usu. mounted on a tripod and used for viewing wildlife and terrestrial objects and features

spot·ty \'spä-tē\ *adj* **spot·ti·er; -est** (14c) **1 :** marked with spots **:** SPOTTED **2 :** lacking uniformity esp. in quality ⟨the performance was ~⟩; *also* **:** irregularly or sparsely distributed ⟨~ attendance⟩ ⟨~ data⟩ — **spot·ti·ly** \'spä-tə-lē\ *adv* — **spot·ti·ness** \'spä-tē-nəs\ *n*

spou·sal \'spau̇-zəl, -səl\ *n* [ME *spousaile,* fr. AF *spousailles, espusailles* espousal] (14c) **:** NUPTIALS — usu. used in pl.

[1]**spouse** \'spau̇s *also* 'spau̇z\ *n* [ME, fr. AF *espus* (masc.) & *espuse* (fem.), fr. L *sponsus* betrothed man, groom & *sponsa* betrothed woman, bride, both fr. *sponsus,* pp. of *spondēre* to promise, betroth; akin to Gk *spendein* to pour a libation, Hitt *šipant-*] (13c) **:** married person **:** HUSBAND, WIFE — **spou·sal** \'spau̇-zəl, -səl\ *adj*

[2]**spouse** \'spau̇z, 'spau̇s\ *vt* **spoused; spous·ing** (13c) *archaic* **:** WED

[1]**spout** \'spau̇t\ *vb* [ME; akin to MD *spoiten* to spout, OE *spīwan* to spew] *vt* (14c) **1 :** to eject (as liquid) in a stream ⟨wells ~*ing* oil⟩ **2 a :** to speak or utter readily, volubly, and at length **b :** to speak or utter in a pompous or oratorical manner **:** DECLAIM ⟨a candidate ~*ing* empty promises⟩ ~ *vi* **1 :** to issue with force or in a jet **:** SPURT **2 :** to eject material (as liquid) in a jet **3 :** DECLAIM — **spout·er** *n*

[2]**spout** *n* (14c) **1 :** a pipe or conductor through which a liquid is discharged or conveyed in a stream: as **a :** a pipe for carrying rainwater from a roof **b :** a projecting tube or lip from which a liquid (as water) issues **2 :** a discharge or jet of liquid or moisture from or as if from a pipe: as **a :** WATERSPOUT **b :** the blowing of a whale **3** *archaic* **:** PAWNSHOP — **spout·ed** \'spau̇-təd\ *adj*

spp *abbr* species (*pl*)

SPQR *abbr* [L *senatus populusque Romanus*] the senate and the people of Rome

sprach·ge·fühl \'shpräḵ-gə-ˌfu̅e̅l\ *n* [G, fr. *Sprache* language + *Gefühl* feeling] (1894) **1 :** the character of a language **2 :** an intuitive sense of what is linguistically appropriate

sprad·dle \'spra-dᵊl\ *vb* **sprad·dled; sprad·dling** \'sprad-liŋ, 'spra-dᵊl-iŋ\ [perh. blend of *straddle* and *sprawl*] *vi* (1632) **1 :** SPRAWL **2 :** to go or walk with a straddling gait **:** STRADDLE ~ *vt* **1 :** SPRAWL **2 :** to spread (the legs) wide apart ⟨a duck with *spraddled* legs⟩

sprag \'sprag\ *n* [origin unknown] (1902) **:** a pointed stake or steel bar let down from a halted vehicle (as a wagon) to prevent it from rolling

[1]**sprain** \'sprān\ *n* [origin unknown] (1601) **1 :** a sudden or violent twist or wrench of a joint with stretching or tearing of ligaments **2 :** a sprained condition

[2]**sprain** *vt* (1622) **:** to injure by a sudden or severe twist

[1]**sprang** *past of* SPRING

[2]**sprang** \'spraŋ\ *n* [prob. fr. Norw, a kind of embroidery] (1951) **:** a weaving technique in which threads or cords are intertwined and twisted over one another to form an openwork mesh

sprat \'sprat\ *n* [alter. of ME *sprot,* fr. OE *sprott*] (1537) **1 a :** a small European marine fish (*Sprattus sprattus*) of the herring family — called also *brisling* **b :** any of various small or young fish (as an anchovy) related to or resembling the herrings **2 :** a young, small, or insignificant person

[1]**sprawl** \'sprȯl\ *vb* [ME, fr. OE *sprēawlian*] *vi* (bef. 12c) **1 a** *archaic* **:** to lie thrashing or tossing about **b :** to creep or clamber awkwardly **2 :** to lie or sit with arms and legs spread out **3 :** to spread or develop irregularly or without restraint ⟨bushes ~*ing* along the road⟩ ⟨~*ing* suburbs⟩ ⟨a ~*ing* narrative⟩ ~ *vt* **:** to cause to spread out carelessly or awkwardly ⟨~*ed* out her books on the table⟩

[2]**sprawl** *n* (1598) **1 :** the act, posture, or condition of sprawling **2 :** an irregularly spread or scattered group or mass **3 :** URBAN SPRAWL

[1]**spray** \'sprā\ *n* [ME, fr. OE **spræg, spræc*] (13c) **1 :** a usu. flowering branch or shoot **2 :** a decorative flat arrangement of flowers and foliage (as on a coffin) **3 :** something (as a jeweled pin) resembling a spray

[2]**spray** *n* [obs. E *spray* to sprinkle, fr. MD *sprayen*] (1621) **1 :** water flying in small drops or particles blown from waves or thrown up by a waterfall **2 a :** a jet of vapor or finely divided liquid ⟨disinfectant ~*s*⟩ **b :** a device (as an atomizer or sprayer) by which a spray is dispersed or applied **c** (1) **:** an application of a spray or by spraying (2) **:** a substance (as paint) so applied

[3]**spray** *vt* (1527) **1 :** to project spray or something resembling spray on or into ⟨~ the table⟩ ⟨~*ing* the wall with bullets⟩ **2 :** to disperse or apply as a spray ⟨~*ed* some perfume⟩ ~ *vi* **1 :** to break up into spray **2 :** to disperse or apply a spray **3 :** to emit a stream or spray of urine ⟨a cat may ~ to mark its territory⟩ — **spray·er** *n*

spray can *n* (1958) **:** a pressurized container from which aerosols are dispensed

spray gun *n* (1920) **:** an apparatus resembling a gun for applying a substance (as paint or insecticide) in the form of a spray

[1]**spread** \'spred\ *vb* **spread; spread·ing** [ME *spreden,* fr. OE *-sprǣdan;* akin to OHG *spreiten* to spread] *vt* (13c) **1 a :** to open or expand over a larger area ⟨~ out the map⟩ **b :** to stretch out **:** EXTEND ⟨~ its wings for flight⟩ **2 a :** to distribute over an area ⟨~ fertilizer⟩ **b :** to distribute over a period or among a group ⟨~ the work over a few weeks⟩ **c :** to apply on a surface ⟨~ butter on bread⟩ **d** (1) **:** to cover or overlay something with ⟨~ the cloth on the table⟩ (2) *archaic* **:** to cover completely **e** (1) **:** to prepare or furnish for dining **:** SET ⟨~ the table⟩ (2) **:** SERVE ⟨~ the afternoon tea⟩ **3 a :** to make widely known ⟨~ the news⟩ **b :** to extend the range or incidence of ⟨~ a disease⟩ **c :** DIFFUSE, EMIT ⟨flowers ~*ing* their fragrance⟩ **4 :** to push apart by weight or force ~ *vi* **1 a :** to become dispersed, distributed, or scattered **b :** to become known or disseminated ⟨panic ~ rapidly⟩ **2 :** to grow in length or breadth **:** EXPAND **3 :** to move apart (as from pressure or weight) **:** SEPARATE — **spread·abil·i·ty** \ˌspre-də-'bi-lə-tē\ *n* — **spread·able** \'spre-də-bəl\ *adj*

[2]**spread** *n* (1626) **1 a :** the act or process of spreading **b :** extent of spreading **2 :** something spread out: as **a :** a surface area **:** EXPANSE **b** (1) **:** a ranch or homestead esp. in the western U.S. (2) *West* **:** a herd of animals **c** (1) **:** a prominent display in a periodical (2) **:** two facing pages (as of a newspaper) usu. with matter running across the fold; *also* **:** the matter occupying these pages **3 :** something spread on or over a surface: as **a :** a food to be spread (as on bread or crackers) ⟨a cheese ~⟩ **b :** a sumptuous meal **:** FEAST **c :** a cloth cover for a table or bed **4 :** distance between two points **:** GAP **5 :** a commodities market transaction in which a participant hedges with simultaneous long and short options in different commodities or different delivery dates in the same commodity

[1]**spread–ea·gle** \'spred-ˌē-gəl\ *vb* **-ea·gled; -ea·gling** \-ˌē-g(ə-)liŋ\ *vi* (1826) **1 :** to execute a spread eagle (as in skating) **2 :** to stand or move with arms and legs stretched out **:** SPRAWL ~ *vt* **1 :** to stretch out into the position of a spread eagle **2 :** to spread over

[2]**spread–eagle** *adj* [fr. the spread eagle on the Great Seal of the U.S.] (1858) **:** marked by bombast and boastful exaggeration esp. of the greatness of the U.S. ⟨~ oratory⟩

spread eagle *n* (1570) **1 :** a representation of an eagle with wings raised and legs extended **2 :** something resembling or suggestive of a spread eagle; *specif* **:** a skating figure executed with the skates heel to heel in a straight line

spread·er \'spre-dər\ *n* (15c) **:** one that spreads: as **a :** an implement for scattering material **b :** a small knife used esp. for spreading butter **c :** a device (as a bar) holding two linear elements (as lines, guys, rails) apart and usu. taut

spread formation *n* (ca. 1949) **:** an offensive football formation in which the pass receivers are spread out across the field

spreading factor *n* (1932) **:** HYALURONIDASE

spread·sheet \'spred-ˌshēt\ *n* (1982) **:** an accounting program for a computer; *also* **:** the ledger layout modeled by such a program

spree \'sprē\ *n* [origin unknown] (1804) **:** an unrestrained indulgence in or outburst of an activity ⟨a buying ~⟩; *also* **:** a drunken revel **:** BINGE

sprent \'sprent\ *adj* [ME *spreynt,* fr. pp. of *sprengen* to sprinkle] (14c) *archaic* **:** sprinkled over

sprier *comparative of* SPRY

spriest *superlative of* SPRY

[1]**sprig** \'sprig\ *n* [ME *sprigge*] (14c) **1 a :** a small shoot **:** TWIG ⟨a ~ of parsley⟩ **b :** a small division of grass used for propagation **2 a :** HEIR **b :** YOUTH **c :** a small specimen **3 :** an ornament resembling a sprig, stemmed flower, or leaf **4 :** a small headless nail **:** BRAD

[2]**sprig** *vt* **sprigged; sprig·ging** (1713) **1 :** to drive sprigs or brads into **2 :** to mark or adorn with the representation of plant sprigs **3 :** to propagate (a grass) by means of stolons or small divisions

spright·ful \ˈsprīt-fəl\ *adj* [obs. *spright*] (1595) *archaic* : SPRIGHTLY — **spright·ful·ly** \-fə-lē\ *adv* — **spright·ful·ness** *n*

spright·ly \-lē\ *adj* **spright·li·er; -est** [obs. *spright* (sprite), alter. of *sprite*] (1596) **1 :** marked by a gay lightness and vivacity : SPIRITED ⟨a ~ musical⟩ **2 :** having a distinctively piquant taste : ZESTY ⟨a ~ salsa⟩ ***syn*** see LIVELY — **spright·li·ness** *n* — **sprightly** *adv*

[1]**spring** \ˈspriŋ\ *vb* **sprang** \ˈspraŋ\ *or* **sprung** \ˈsprəŋ\; **sprung; spring·ing** \ˈspriŋ-iŋ\ [ME, fr. OE *springan;* akin to OHG *springan* to jump and perh. to Gk *sperchesthai* to hasten] *vi* (bef. 12c) **1 a (1)** : DART, SHOOT ⟨sparks *sprang* out from the fire⟩ **(2) :** to be resilient or elastic; *also* : to move by elastic force ⟨the lid *sprang* shut⟩ **b :** to become warped **2 :** to issue with speed and force or as a stream ⟨tears ~ from our eyes⟩ **3 a :** to grow as a plant **b :** to issue by birth or descent ⟨*sprang* from the upper class⟩ **c :** to come into being : ARISE ⟨towns *sprang* up across the plains⟩ **d** *archaic* : DAWN **e :** to begin to blow — used with *up* ⟨a breeze quickly *sprang* up⟩ **4 a :** to make a leap or series of leaps ⟨*~ing* across the lawn⟩ **b :** to leap or jump up suddenly ⟨*sprang* from their seats⟩ **5 :** to stretch out in height : RISE **6 :** PAY — used with *for* ⟨I'll ~ for the drinks⟩ **~** *vt* **1 :** to cause to spring **2 a :** to undergo or bring about the splitting or cracking of ⟨wind *sprang* the mast⟩ **b :** to undergo the opening of (a leak) **3 a :** to cause to operate suddenly ⟨~ a trap⟩ **b :** to apply or insert by bending **c :** to bend by force **4 :** to leap over **5 :** to produce or disclose suddenly or unexpectedly **6 :** to make lame **7 :** to release or cause to be released from confinement or custody ⟨*sprung* them from jail⟩

syn SPRING, ARISE, RISE, ORIGINATE, DERIVE, FLOW, ISSUE, EMANATE, PROCEED, STEM mean to come up or out of something into existence. SPRING implies rapid or sudden emerging ⟨an idea that *springs* to mind⟩. ARISE and RISE may both convey the fact of coming into existence or notice but RISE often stresses gradual growth or ascent ⟨new questions have *arisen*⟩ ⟨slowly *rose* to prominence⟩. ORIGINATE implies a definite source or starting point ⟨the fire *originated* in the basement⟩. DERIVE implies a prior existence in another form ⟨the holiday *derives* from an ancient Roman feast⟩. FLOW adds to SPRING a suggestion of abundance or ease of inception ⟨words *flowed* easily from her pen⟩. ISSUE suggests emerging from confinement through an outlet ⟨blood *issued* from the cut⟩. EMANATE applies to the coming of something immaterial (as a thought) from a source ⟨reports *emanating* from the capital⟩. PROCEED stresses place of origin, derivation, parentage, or logical cause ⟨advice that *proceeds* from the best of intentions⟩. STEM implies originating by dividing or branching off from something as an outgrowth or subordinate development ⟨industries *stemming* from space research⟩.

[2]**spring** *n, often attrib* (bef. 12c) **1 a :** a source of supply; *esp* : a source of water issuing from the ground **b :** an ultimate source esp. of action or motion **2 :** SPRING TIDE **3 :** a time or season of growth or development; *specif* : the season between winter and summer comprising in the northern hemisphere usu. the months of March, April, and May or as reckoned astronomically extending from the March equinox to the June solstice **4 :** an elastic body or device that recovers its original shape when released after being distorted **5 a :** the act or an instance of leaping up or forward : BOUND **b (1) :** capacity for springing : RESILIENCE **(2) :** ENERGY, BOUNCE **6 :** the point or plane at which an arch or vault curve springs from its impost — **spring·like** \-ˌlīk\ *adj*

[3]**spring** *vt* **sprung** \ˈsprəŋ\; **spring·ing** \ˈspriŋ-iŋ\ (1884) : to fit with springs

spring·ald \ˈspriŋ-əld\ *or* **spring·al** \-əl\ *n* [prob. fr. ME, a kind of catapult, fr. AF *espringal*] (1501) *archaic* : a young man : STRIPLING

spring beauty *n* (1821) : any of a genus (*Claytonia*) of herbs of the purslane family; *esp* : one (*C. virginica*) of No. America that sends up in early spring a usu. 2-leaved stem bearing delicate pink flowers

spring·board \ˈspriŋ-ˌbȯrd\ *n* (1799) **1 :** a flexible board usu. secured at one end and used for gymnastic stunts or diving **2 :** a point of departure : JUMPING-OFF PLACE

spring·bok \ˈspriŋ-ˌbäk\ *n, pl* **springbok** *or* **springboks** [Afrik, fr. *spring* to jump + *bok* male goat] (1775) : a swift and graceful southern African gazelle (*Antidorcas marsupialis*) noted for its habit of springing lightly and suddenly into the air

spring bolt *n* (1634) : a bolt retracted by pressure and shot by a spring when the pressure is released

spring chicken *n* (1879) : a young person ⟨is no *spring chicken*⟩

spring–clean·ing \ˈspriŋ-ˈklē-niŋ\ *n* [[2]*spring*] (1857) : the act or process of doing a thorough cleaning of a place

springe \ˈsprinj\ *n* [ME *sprenge, springe;* akin to OE *springan* to spring] (13c) **1 :** a noose fastened to an elastic body to catch small game **2** : SNARE, TRAP

spring·er \ˈspriŋ-ər\ *n* (1611) **1 :** a stone or other solid laid at the impost of an arch — see ARCH illustration **2 :** one that springs **3** : SPRINGER SPANIEL **4 :** a cow nearly ready to calve

springer spaniel *n* (1885) : a medium-sized sporting dog of either of two breeds that is often used for finding and flushing small game: **a** : ENGLISH SPRINGER SPANIEL **b :** WELSH SPRINGER SPANIEL

spring fever *n* (1843) : a lazy or restless feeling often associated with the onset of spring

Spring·field rifle \ˈspriŋ-ˌfēld-\ *n* [*Springfield*, Mass.] (1888) : a.30 caliber bolt-action rifle used by U.S. troops esp. in World War I

spring·form pan \ˈspriŋ-ˌfȯrm-\ *n* (1927) : a pan or mold with an upright detachable rim fastened to the bottom of the pan with a clamp or spring

spring·head \ˈspriŋ-ˌhed\ *n* (1561) : FOUNTAINHEAD

spring·house \-ˌhau̇s\ *n* (1755) : a small building situated over a spring and used for cool storage (as of dairy products or meat)

springing *n* (1590) **1 :** SPRING 5 **2 :** a point where an arch rises from its support

spring line *n* (1803) : a line led diagonally from the bow or stern of a ship to a point on a wharf and made fast to help keep the ship from moving fore and aft while docked

spring–load \ˈspriŋ-ˈlōd\ *vt* (1944) : to load or secure by means of spring tension or compression

spring onion *n* (1840) : SCALLION 3

spring peeper *n* (1906) : a small brown tree frog (*Pseudacris crucifer* syn. *Hyla crucifer*) of the eastern U.S. and Canada that has a shrill piping call and breeds in ponds and streams in the spring

spring roll *n* (1943) : EGG ROLL; *also* : any of various similar appetizers esp. in Asian cuisine

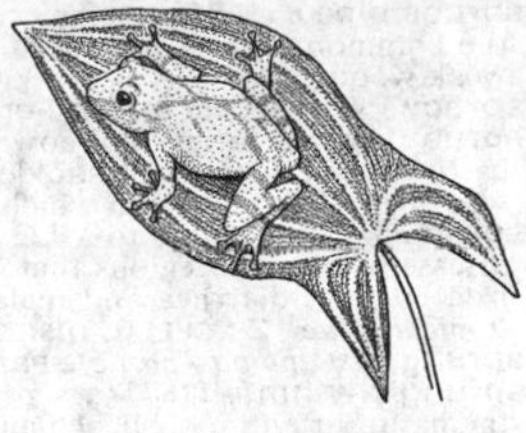

spring peeper

spring·tail \ˈspriŋ-ˌtāl\ *n* (ca. 1797) : any of an order (Collembola) of small primitive wingless insects that exhibit incomplete metamorphosis and usu. possess a furcula used for jumping — called also *collembolan*

spring·tide \-ˌtīd\ *n* (ca. 1530) : SPRINGTIME

spring tide *n* (ca. 1548) : a tide of greater-than-average range around the times of new moon and full moon

spring·time \ˈspriŋ-ˌtīm\ *n* (15c) **1** : the season of spring **2 :** YOUTH 1a **3 :** an early or flourishing stage of development

spring wagon *n* (1794) : a light farm wagon equipped with springs

spring·wa·ter \ˈspriŋ-ˌwȯ-tər, -ˌwä-\ *n* (15c) : water from a spring

spring·wood \-ˌwu̇d\ *n* (1884) : the softer more porous portion of an annual ring of wood that develops early in the growing season — compare SUMMERWOOD

springy \ˈspriŋ-ē\ *adj* **spring·i·er; -est** (1660) **1 :** having an elastic quality : RESILIENT ⟨green ~ wood⟩ **2 :** having or showing a lively and energetic movement ⟨walks with a ~ step⟩ ***syn*** see ELASTIC — **spring·i·ly** \ˈspriŋ-ə-lē\ *adv* — **spring·i·ness** \ˈspriŋ-ē-nəs\ *n*

[1]**sprin·kle** \ˈspriŋ-kəl\ *vb* **sprin·kled; sprin·kling** \-k(ə-)liŋ\ [ME *sprenklen, sprinclen;* akin to MHG *spreckel, sprenkel* spot] *vt* (14c) **1 :** to scatter in drops or particles **2 a :** to scatter over **b :** to scatter at intervals in or among : DOT ⟨*sprinkled* the speech with quips⟩ **c :** to wet lightly **~** *vi* **1 :** to scatter a liquid in fine drops **2 :** to rain lightly in scattered drops — **sprin·kler** \-k(ə-)lər\ *n*

[2]**sprinkle** *n* (1641) **1 :** the act or an instance of sprinkling; *esp* : a light rain **2 :** SPRINKLING **3** *pl* : small particles of candy used as a topping (as on ice cream) : JIMMIES

sprin·klered \ˈspriŋ-klərd\ *adj* (1927) : having a sprinkler system

sprinkler system *n* (ca. 1909) : a system for protecting a building against fire by means of overhead pipes which convey an extinguishing fluid (as water) to heat-activated outlets

sprin·kling \ˈspriŋ-kliŋ\ *n* (1594) **1 :** a limited quantity or amount : MODICUM **2 :** a small quantity falling in scattered drops or particles **3 :** a small number distributed at random : SCATTERING

[1]**sprint** \ˈsprint\ *vi* [ME (Sc) *sprenten* to spring, leap, of Scand origin; akin to Sw dial. *sprinta* to jump, hop; akin to OHG *sprinzan* to jump up] (1889) : to run or go at top speed esp. for a short distance — **sprint·er** *n*

[2]**sprint** *n* (ca. 1865) **1 :** the act or an instance of sprinting **2 a :** DASH 6b **b :** a burst of speed

sprint car *n* (1954) : a rugged racing automobile that is midway in size between midget racers and ordinary racers, has about the same horsepower as the larger racers, and is usu. raced on a dirt track

sprit \ˈsprit\ *n* [ME *spret, sprit,* fr. OE *sprēot* pole, spear; akin to OE *-sprūtan* to sprout] (14c) : a spar that crosses a fore-and-aft sail diagonally

sprite \ˈsprīt\ *n* [ME *sprit,* fr. AF *espriz, esprit* spirit, sprite — more at SPIRIT] (14c) **1 a** *archaic* : SOUL **b :** a disembodied spirit : GHOST **2 a :** ELF, FAIRY **b :** an elfish person

sprit·sail \ˈsprit-ˌsāl, -səl\ *n* (15c) **1 :** a sail extended by a sprit **2 :** a sail formerly set on a yard beneath the bowsprit

spritz \ˈsprits, ˈshprits\ *vb* [G *spritzen* to squirt, spray] *vt* (1902) : SPRAY **~** *vi* : to disperse or apply a spray — **spritz** *n*

spritz·er \ˈsprit-sər, ˈshprit-\ *n* [G, fr. *spritzen*] (1945) : a beverage of usu. white wine and soda water

sprock·et \ˈsprä-kət\ *n* [origin unknown] (1886) **1 :** a toothed wheel whose teeth engage the links of a chain **2 :** a cylinder with teeth around the circumference at either end that project through perforations in something (as motion-picture film) to move it through a mechanism (as a projector)

[1]**sprout** \ˈsprau̇t\ *vb* [ME *spruten,* fr. OE *-sprūtan;* akin to OHG *spriozan* to sprout, Lith *sprausti* to squeeze, thrust] *vi* (13c) **1 :** to grow, spring up, or come forth as or as if a sprout **2 :** to send out new growth **~** *vt* : to send forth or up : cause to develop : GROW

[2]**sprout** *n* (13c) **1 a :** SHOOT 1a; *esp* : a young shoot (as from a seed or root) **b** *pl* **(1)** *chiefly Brit* : BRUSSELS SPROUT 2 **(2) :** edible sprouts esp. from recently germinated seeds (as of alfalfa or mung beans) **2** : something resembling a sprout: as **a :** a young person **b :** SCION 2

sprouting broccoli *n* (1852) : BROCCOLI 2a(2)

[1]**spruce** \ˈsprüs\ *vb* **spruced; spruc·ing** *vt* (1594) : to make spruce — often used with *up* **~** *vi* : to make oneself spruce ⟨~ up a bit⟩

[2]**spruce** *adj* **spruc·er; spruc·est** [perh. fr. obs. E *Spruce leather* leather imported from Prussia] (1599) : neat or smart in appearance : TRIM — **spruce·ly** *adv* — **spruce·ness** *n*

[3]**spruce** *n, pl* **spruc·es** *also* **spruce** [obs. *Spruce* Prussia, fr. ME, alter. of *Pruce,* fr. AF] (1670) **1 a :** any of a genus (*Picea*) of evergreen trees of the pine family with a conical head of dense foliage, flat or 4-sided needles, pendulous cones, and soft light wood **b :** any of several coniferous trees (as Douglas fir) of similar habit **2 :** the wood of a spruce

spruce beer *n* (1744) : a beverage flavored with spruce; *esp* : one made from spruce twigs and leaves boiled with molasses or sugar and fermented with yeast

spruce budworm *n* (1884) : a tortricid moth (*Choristoneura fumiferana*) whose larva feeds on evergreen trees (as spruce and balsam fir) in the northern U.S. and Canada; *also* : a related moth (*C. occidentalis*) of the northwestern U.S. and adjacent Canada

\ə\ **abut** \ᵊ\ **kitten**, F **table** \ər\ **further** \a\ **ash** \ā\ **ace** \ä\ **mop, mar**
\au̇\ **out** \ch\ **chin** \e\ **bet** \ē\ **easy** \g\ **go** \i\ **hit** \ī\ **ice** \j\ **job**
\ŋ\ **sing** \ō\ **go** \ȯ\ **law** \ȯi\ **boy** \th\ **thin** \t͟h\ **the** \ü\ **loot** \u̇\ **foot**
\y\ **yet** \zh\ **vision, beige** \k̲, ⁿ, œ, ue, ʸ\ *see* Guide to Pronunciation

spruce pine *n* (1684) : an American tree (as some pines and spruces or the common eastern hemlock) of the pine family with light, soft, or weak wood

sprucy \ˈsprü-sē\ *adj* **spruc·i·er; -est** (1774) : SPRUCE

[1]**sprue** \ˈsprü\ *n* [origin unknown] (ca. 1875) **1** : the waste piece on a casting (as of metal or plastic) left by the hole through which the mold was filled **2** : the hole in which a sprue forms

[2]**sprue** *n* [D *spruw;* akin to MLG *sprūwe,* a kind of tumor] (1888) **1** : a disease of tropical regions that is of unknown cause and is characterized by fatty diarrhea and malabsorption of nutrients — called also *tropical sprue* **2** : CELIAC DISEASE

sprung *past and past part of* SPRING

sprung rhythm *n* (1877) : a poetic rhythm designed to approximate the natural rhythm of speech and characterized by the frequent juxtaposition of single accented syllables and the occurrence of mixed types of feet

spry \ˈsprī\ *adj* **spri·er** *or* **spry·er** \ˈsprī(-ə)r\; **spri·est** *or* **spry·est** \ˈsprī-əst\ [origin unknown] (1746) : NIMBLE 1 ⟨a ~ 75-year-old⟩ — **spry·ly** *adv* — **spry·ness** *n*

[1]**spud** \ˈspəd\ *vb* **spud·ded; spud·ding** *vt* (1652) **1** : to dig with a spud **2** : to begin to drill (an oil well) ~ *vi* : to use a spud

[2]**spud** *n* [ME *spudde* dagger] (1667) **1** : a tool or device (as for digging, lifting, or cutting) having the characteristics of a spade and a chisel **2** : POTATO 2b

[1]**spume** \ˈspyüm\ *n* [ME, fr. AF, fr. L *spuma* — more at FOAM] (14c) : frothy matter on liquids : FOAM, SCUM ⟨ocean ~⟩ — **spu·mous** \ˈspyü-məs\ *adj* — **spumy** \-mē\ *adj*

[2]**spume** *vi* **spumed; spum·ing** (14c) : FROTH, FOAM

spu·mo·ni *also* **spu·mo·ne** \spu̇-ˈmō-nē\ *n* [It *spumone,* aug. of *spuma* foam, fr. L] (1924) : ice cream in layers of different colors, flavors, and textures often with candied fruits and nuts

spun *past and past part of* SPIN

spun·bond·ed \ˈspən-ˌbän-dəd\ *adj* (1961) : of or relating to a nonwoven polymeric material that resembles cloth or fabric

spun glass *n* (1779) **1** : blown glass that has slender threads of glass incorporated in it **2** : FIBERGLASS

[1]**spunk** \ˈspəŋk\ *n* [ScGael *spong* sponge, tinder, fr. MIr *spongc,* fr. L *spongia* sponge] (1582) **1 a** : a woody tinder : PUNK **b** : any of various fungi used to make tinder **2** : METTLE, PLUCK **3** : SPIRIT, LIVELINESS

[2]**spunk** *vi* (1840) *dial* : to show spirit — usu. used with *up*

spunk·ie \ˈspəŋ-kē\ *n* (1727) *Scot* : IGNIS FATUUS 1

spunky \ˈspəŋ-kē\ *adj* **spunk·i·er; -est** (1786) : full of spunk : SPIRITED — **spunk·i·ly** \-kə-lē\ *adv* — **spunk·i·ness** \-kē-nəs\ *n*

spun sugar *n* (1846) : sugar boiled to long threads and gathered up and shaped or heaped on a stick as a candy

spun yarn *n* (14c) **1** : a textile yarn spun from staple-length fiber **2** : a small rope or stuff formed of two or more rope yarns loosely twisted and used for seizings esp. on board ship

[1]**spur** \ˈspər\ *n* [ME *spure,* fr. OE *spura;* akin to OE *spurnan* to kick — more at SPURN] (bef. 12c) **1 a** : a pointed device secured to a rider's heel and used to urge on the horse **b** *pl* [fr. the acquisition of spurs by a person achieving knighthood] : recognition and reward for achievement ⟨won his academic ~*s* as the holder of a chair in a university —James Mountford⟩ **2** : a goad to action : STIMULUS **3** : something projecting like or suggesting a spur: as **a** : a projecting root or branch of a tree, shrub, or vine **b** (1) : a stiff sharp spine (as on the wings or legs of a bird or insect); *esp* : one on a cock's leg (2) : a gaff for a gamecock **c** : a hollow projecting appendage of a corolla or calyx (as in larkspur or columbine) **d** : a bony outgrowth (as on the heel of the foot) **e** : CLIMBING IRON **4 a** : an angular projection, offshoot, or branch extending out beyond or away from a main body or formation; *esp* : a ridge or lesser elevation that extends laterally from a mountain or mountain range **b** : a railroad track that branches off from a main line **5** : a reinforcing buttress of masonry in a fortification *syn* see MOTIVE — **on the spur of the moment** : on impulse : SUDDENLY

[2]**spur** *vb* **spurred; spur·ring** *vt* (13c) **1** : to urge (a horse) on with spurs **2** : to incite to action or accelerated growth or development : STIMULATE **3** : to put spurs on ~ *vi* : to spur one's horse on

spurge \ˈspərj\ *n* [ME, fr. AF *espurge, spurge,* fr. *espurger* to clean out, purge, fr. L *expurgare* — more at EXPURGATE] (14c) : any of a family (Euphorbiaceae) of widely distributed herbs, shrubs, and trees often with a bitter milky juice; *esp* : EUPHORBIA

spur gear *n* (1823) : a gear wheel with radial teeth parallel to its axis — called also *spur wheel*

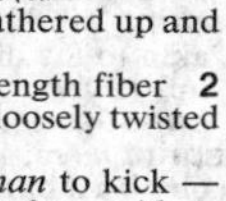

spur gear

spurge laurel *n* (1597) : a low-growing Eurasian shrub (*Daphne laureola*) with oblong evergreen leaves and axillary racemes of yellowish flowers

spu·ri·ous \ˈspyu̇r-ē-əs\ *adj* [LL & L; LL *spurius* false, fr. L, of illegitimate birth, fr. *spurius,* n., bastard] (1598) **1** : of illegitimate birth : BASTARD **2** : outwardly similar or corresponding to something without having its genuine qualities : FALSE ⟨the ~ eminence of the pop celebrity⟩ **3 a** : of falsified or erroneously attributed origin : FORGED **b** : of a deceitful nature or quality ⟨~ excuses⟩ — **spu·ri·ous·ly** *adv* — **spu·ri·ous·ness** *n*

[1]**spurn** \ˈspərn\ *vb* [ME, fr. OE *spurnan;* akin to OHG *spurnan* to kick, L *spernere* to spurn, Gk *spairein* to quiver] *vi* (bef. 12c) **1** *obs* **a** : STUMBLE **b** : KICK 1a **2** *archaic* : to reject something disdainfully ~ *vt* **1** : to tread sharply or heavily upon : TRAMPLE **2** : to reject with disdain or contempt : SCORN *syn* see DECLINE — **spurn·er** *n*

[2]**spurn** *n* (14c) **1 a** : KICK 1a **b** *obs* : STUMBLE **2 a** : disdainful rejection **b** : contemptuous treatment

spur–of–the–moment *adj* (1948) : occurring or developing without premeditation : hastily extemporized ⟨a ~ decision⟩

spurred *adj* (15c) **1** : wearing spurs **2** : having one or more spurs ⟨a ~ violet⟩

spur·rey *or* **spur·ry** \ˈspər-ē, ˈspə-rē\ *n, pl* **spurreys** *or* **spurries** [D *spurrie,* fr. ML *spergula*] (1577) : a white-flowered European annual weedy herb (*Spergula arvensis*) of the pink family with whorled filiform leaves; *also* : any of several related and similar herbs

[1]**spurt** \ˈspərt\ *vb* [perh. akin to MHG *spürzen* to spit, OE *-sprūtan* to sprout — more at SPROUT] *vi* (1570) : to gush forth : SPOUT ~ *vt* : to expel in a stream or jet : SQUIRT ⟨the faucet ~*s* water⟩

[2]**spurt** *n* (1644) : a sudden gush : JET

[3]**spurt** *n* [origin unknown] (ca. 1591) **1** : a short period of time : MOMENT **2 a** : a sudden brief burst of effort, activity, or development ⟨a ~ of work⟩ ⟨a growth ~⟩ **b** : a sharp or sudden increase in business activity

[4]**spurt** *vi* (1664) : to make a spurt

spur·tle \ˈspər-tᵊl\ *n* [origin unknown] (1756) *chiefly Scot* : a wooden stick for stirring porridge

Sput·nik \ˈspu̇t-nik, ˈspət-, ˈspüt-\ *n* [Russ, lit., traveling companion, fr. *s, so* with + *put'* path] (1957) : any of a series of earth-orbiting satellites launched by the Soviet Union beginning in 1957

[1]**sput·ter** \ˈspə-tər\ *vb* [akin to D *sputteren* to sputter] *vt* (1598) **1** : to spit or squirt from the mouth with explosive sounds **2** : to utter hastily or explosively in confusion or excitement ⟨"that's ridiculous!" she ~*ed*⟩ **3** : to dislodge (atoms) from the surface of a material by collision with high energy particles; *also* : to deposit (a metallic film) by such a process ~ *vi* **1** : to spit or squirt particles of food or saliva noisily from the mouth **2** : to speak explosively or confusedly in anger or excitement **3** : to make explosive popping sounds — **sput·ter·er** *n*

[2]**sputter** *n* (1673) **1** : confused and excited speech or discussion **2** : the act or sound of sputtering

spu·tum \ˈspyü-təm, ˈspü-\ *n, pl* **spu·ta** \-tə\ [L, fr. neut. of *sputus,* pp. of *spuere* to spit — more at SPEW] (ca. 1693) : expectorated matter esp. from the air passages in diseases of the lungs, bronchi, or upper respiratory tract

[1]**spy** \ˈspī\ *vb* **spied; spy·ing** [ME *spien,* fr. AF *espier,* of Gmc origin; akin to OHG *spehōn* to spy; akin to L *specere* to look, look at, Gk *skeptesthai & skopein* to watch, look at, consider] *vt* (13c) **1** : to watch secretly usu. for hostile purposes **2** : to catch sight of : SEE **3** : to search or look for intensively — usu. used with *out* ⟨~ out places fit for vending . . . goods —S. E. Morison⟩ ~ *vi* **1** : to observe or search for something : LOOK **2** : to watch secretly as a spy

[2]**spy** *n, pl* **spies** (13c) **1** : one that spies: **a** : one who keeps secret watch on a person or thing to obtain information **b** : a person employed by one nation to secretly convey classified information of strategic importance to another nation; *also* : a person who conveys the trade secrets of one company to another **2** : an act of spying

spy·glass \ˈspī-ˌglas\ *n* (1706) : a small telescope

spy·mas·ter \ˈspī-ˌmas-tər\ *n* (1938) : the head of a ring of spies : a director of intelligence

spy·ware \ˈspī-ˌwer\ *n* (1994) : software that is installed in a computer without the user's knowledge and transmits information about the user's computer activities over the Internet

sq *abbr* **1** squadron **2** square

squab \ˈskwäb\ *n, pl* **squabs** [prob. of Scand origin; akin to Sw dial. *skvabb* loose, fat flesh] (1664) **1 a** : COUCH **b** : a cushion for a chair or couch **2** *or pl* **squab** : a fledgling bird; *specif* : a fledgling pigeon about four weeks old **3** : a short fat person — **squab** *adj*

[1]**squab·ble** \ˈskwä-bəl\ *n* [prob. of Scand origin; akin to Sw dial. *skvabbel* dispute] (1602) : a noisy altercation or quarrel usu. over petty matters *syn* see QUARREL

[2]**squabble** *vi* **squab·bled; squab·bling** \-b(ə-)liŋ\ (1604) : to quarrel noisily and usu. over petty matters — **squab·bler** \-b(ə-)lər\ *n*

[1]**squad** \ˈskwäd\ *n* [MF *esquade,* fr. OSp & OIt; OSp *escuadra* & OIt *squadra,* ultim. fr. VL **exquadrare* to make square — more at SQUARE] (1649) **1** : a small organized group of military personnel; *esp* : a tactical unit that can be easily directed in the field **2** : a small group engaged in a common effort or occupation

[2]**squad** *vt* **squad·ded; squad·ding** (ca. 1802) : to arrange in squads

squad car *n* (1938) : a police automobile connected with headquarters by a two-way radio — called also *black-and-white, cruiser, prowl car*

squad·ron \ˈskwä-drən\ *n* [It *squadrone,* aug. of *squadra* squad, fr. OIt] (1562) **1** : a unit of military organization: as **a** : a cavalry unit higher than a troop and lower than a regiment **b** : a naval unit consisting of two or more divisions and sometimes additional vessels **c** (1) : a unit of the U.S. Air Force higher than a flight and lower than a group (2) : a military flight formation **2** : a large group of people or things ⟨a ~ of limos⟩

squadron leader *n* (1919) : a commissioned officer in the British air force who ranks with a major in the army

squad room *n* (1943) **1** : a room in a barracks used to billet soldiers **2** : a room in a police station where members of the force assemble

squa·lene \ˈskwä-ˌlēn\ *n* [ISV, fr. L *squalus,* a sea fish — more at WHALE] (1916) : an acyclic hydrocarbon $C_{30}H_{50}$ that is widely distributed in nature (as a major component of sebum and in shark-liver oils) and is a precursor of sterols (as cholesterol)

squal·id \ˈskwä-ləd\ *adj* [L *squalidus* rough, dirty, fr. *squalēre* to be covered with scales or dirt, fr. *squalus* dirty; perh. akin to L *squama* scale] (1596) **1** : marked by filthiness and degradation from neglect or poverty **2** : SORDID *syn* see DIRTY — **squal·id·ly** *adv* — **squal·id·ness** *n*

[1]**squall** \ˈskwȯl\ *vb* [prob. of Scand origin; akin to ON *skval* useless chatter] *vi* (ca. 1631) : to cry out raucously : SCREAM ~ *vt* : to utter in a strident voice — **squall·er** *n*

[2]**squall** *n* (1709) : a raucous cry

[3]**squall** *n* [prob. of Scand origin; akin to Sw *skval* rushing water] (1699) **1** : a sudden violent wind often with rain or snow **2** : a short-lived commotion

[4]**squall** *vi* (ca. 1890) : to blow a squall

squally \ˈskwȯ-lē\ *adj* **squall·i·er; -est** (1719) **1** : marked by squalls **2** : GUSTY

squa·lor \ˈskwä-lər *also* ˈskwā- *or* ˈskwȯ-\ *n* [L, fr. *squalēre*] (1621) : the quality or state of being squalid

squa·ma \ˈskwā-mə, ˈskwä-\ *n, pl* **squa·mae** \ˈskwā-ˌmē, ˈskwä-ˌmī\ [L] (ca. 1706) : SCALE; *also* : a structure resembling a scale

squa·mate \ˈskwā-ˌmāt, ˈskwä-\ *n* [ultim. fr. LL *squamatus* scaly, fr. L *squama*] (1968) : any of an order (Squamata) of reptiles including the snakes and lizards and related extinct forms — **squamate** *adj*

[1]**squa·mo·sal** \skwə-ˈmō-səl, -zəl\ *n* (1848) : a squamosal bone

[2]**squamosal** *adj* (ca. 1852) **1** : SQUAMOUS **2** : of, relating to, or being a bone of the skull of many vertebrates corresponding to the squamous portion of the temporal bone of most mammals including humans

squa·mous \ˈskwā-məs *also* ˈskwä-\ *adj* [ME, fr. L *squamosus,* fr. *squama* scale] (15c) **1 a** : covered with or consisting of scales : SCALY **b**

: of, relating to, or being a stratified epithelium that consists at least in its outer layers of small scalelike cells **2 :** of, relating to, or being the anterior upper portion of the temporal bone of most mammals including humans

squamous cell *n* (1907) **:** a cell of or derived from squamous epithelium

squamous cell carcinoma *n* (1907) **:** a carcinoma that is made up of or arises from squamous cells and usu. occurs in areas of the body exposed to strong sunlight over many years

squa·mu·lose \ˈskwā-myə-ˌlōs, ˈskwä-\ *adj* [L *squamula,* dim. of *squama*] (1857) **:** being or having a thallus made up of small leafy lobes ⟨a ~ lichen⟩

[1]**squan·der** \ˈskwän-dər\ *vb* **squan·dered; squan·der·ing** \-d(ə-)riŋ\ [origin unknown] *vt* (1536) **1 :** to spend extravagantly or foolishly **:** DISSIPATE, WASTE ⟨~*ed* a fortune⟩ **2 :** to cause to disperse **:** SCATTER **3 :** to lose (as an advantage or opportunity) through negligence or inaction ~ *vi* **:** DISPERSE, SCATTER — **squan·der·er** \-dər-ər\ *n*

[2]**squander** *n* (1709) **:** an act of squandering

[1]**square** \ˈskwer\ *n* [ME, fr. AF *esquarre,* fr. VL **exquadra,* fr. **exquadrare* to square, fr. L *ex-* + *quadrare* to square — more at QUADRATE] (13c) **1 :** an instrument having at least one right angle and two straight edges used esp. to lay out or test right angles **2 :** a rectangle with all four sides equal **3 :** any of the quadrilateral spaces marked out on a board for playing games **4 :** the product of a number multiplied by itself **5 a :** an open place or area formed at the meeting of two or more streets **b :** BLOCK 6a **6 :** a solid object or piece approximating a cube or having a square as its largest face **7 :** an unopened cotton flower with its enclosing bracts **8 :** a person who is conventional or conservative in taste or way of life **9 :** a square meal ⟨ate three ~*s* a day⟩ — **on the square 1 :** at right angles **2 :** in a fair open manner **:** HONESTLY — **out of square :** not at an exact right angle

[2]**square** *adj* **squar·er; squar·est** (14c) **1 a :** having four equal sides and four right angles **b :** forming a right angle ⟨~ corner⟩ **c :** having a square base ⟨a ~ pyramid⟩ **2 :** raised to the second power **3 a :** being approximately a cube ⟨~ cabinet⟩ **b :** having a shape that is broad for the height and rectangular rather than curving in outline ⟨~ shoulders⟩ ⟨a ~, thick, hard-working man —Maria Edgeworth⟩ **c :** rectangular and equilateral in section ⟨~ tower⟩ **4 a :** being or converted to a unit of area equal in measure to a square each side of which measures one unit of a specified unit of length ⟨a ~ foot⟩ — see METRIC SYSTEM table, WEIGHT table **b :** being of a specified length in each of two equal dimensions ⟨10 feet ~⟩ **5 a :** exactly adjusted **:** precisely constructed or aligned **b :** JUST, FAIR ⟨a ~ deal⟩ ⟨~ in all his dealings⟩ **c :** leaving no balance **:** SETTLED **d :** EVEN, TIED **e :** SUBSTANTIAL, SATISFYING ⟨~ meal⟩ **f :** being unsophisticated, conservative, or conventional **6 :** set at right angles with the mast and keel — used of the yards of a square-rigged ship — **square·ness** *n*

[3]**square** *vb* **squared; squar·ing** *vt* (14c) **1 a :** to make square or rectangular ⟨~ a building stone⟩ **b :** to test for deviation from a right angle, straight line, or plane surface **2 :** to bring approximately to a right angle ⟨*squared* his shoulders⟩ **3 a :** to multiply (a number) by itself **:** raise to the second power **b :** to find a square equal in area to ⟨~ a circle⟩ **4 :** to regulate or adjust by or to some standard or principle ⟨~ our actions by the opinions of others —John Milton⟩ **5 a :** BALANCE, SETTLE ⟨~ an account⟩ **b :** to even the score of **6 :** to mark off into squares **7 a :** to set right **:** bring into agreement ⟨*squared* their goals with their beliefs⟩ **b :** BRIBE, FIX ~ *vi* **1 :** to agree precisely **:** CORRESPOND ⟨your actions should ~ with your words⟩ **2 :** to settle matters; *esp* **:** to pay the bill — **squar·er** *n*

[4]**square** *adv* (ca. 1582) **1 :** in a straightforward or honest manner **2 a :** so as to face or be face-to-face **b :** at right angles **3 :** with nothing intervening **:** DIRECTLY ⟨ran ~ into it⟩ **4 :** in a firm manner ⟨looked her ~ in the eye⟩ **5 :** in a square shape

square away *vi* (1838) **1 :** to square the yards so as to sail before the wind **2 :** to put everything in order or in readiness **3 :** to take up a fighting stance ~ *vt* **:** to put in order or in readiness

square bracket *n* (1872) **:** BRACKET 3a

square dance *n* (1870) **:** a dance for four couples who form the sides of a square — **square–dance** *vi* — **square dancer** *n* — **square dancing** *n*

square knot *n* (ca. 1867) **:** a knot made of two reverse half-knots and typically used to join the ends of two cords — see KNOT illustration

square·ly \ˈskwer-lē\ *adv* (1564) **1 :** in a straightforward or honest manner ⟨we must ~ face the issue⟩ **2 a :** EXACTLY, PRECISELY ⟨~ in the middle⟩ **b :** so as to make solid contact ⟨hit the ball ~⟩ ⟨feet ~ planted⟩ **3 :** in a square form or manner **:** so as to be square ⟨a ~ cut dress⟩ **4 :** in a plain or unequivocal manner ⟨the responsibility lies ~ with us⟩ ⟨align ourselves ~ with our allies⟩

square matrix *n* (1858) **:** a mathematical matrix with the same number of rows and columns

square measure *n* (1728) **:** a unit or system of units for measuring area — see METRIC SYSTEM table, WEIGHT table

square off *vi* (1837) **:** to take a fighting stance **:** prepare to fight; *also* **:** FIGHT

square of opposition (1864) **:** a square figure on which may be demonstrated the logical relationships of contraries, contradictories, subcontraries, and subalterns and superalterns

square one *n* [fr. the use of numbered squares in some board games] (1960) **:** the initial stage or starting point ⟨the failure set us back to *square one*⟩

square rig *n* (ca. 1875) **:** a sailing-ship rig in which the principal sails are extended on yards fastened to the masts horizontally and at their center

square–rigged \ˈskwer-ˈrigd\ *adj* (1769) **:** having or equipped with a square rig

square–rig·ger \-ˌri-gər\ *n* (1855) **:** a square-rigged craft

square root *n* (1557) **:** a factor of a number that when squared gives the number ⟨the *square root* of 9 is ±3⟩

square sail \ˈskwer-ˌsāl, -səl\ *n* (1600) **:** a 4-sided sail extended on a yard suspended at the middle from a mast

square shooter *n* (ca. 1914) **:** a just or honest person

square–toed \-ˈtōd\ *adj* (1785) **1 :** having a toe that is square **2 :** OLD-FASHIONED, CONSERVATIVE

square wave *n* (1932) **:** a waveform that varies periodically and abruptly from one to the other of two uniform values

squar·ish \ˈskwer-ish\ *adj* (1742) **:** somewhat square in form or appearance — **squar·ish·ly** *adv* — **squar·ish·ness** *n*

squark \ˈskwȯrk, ˈskwärk\ *n* [prob. fr. *s*upersymmetric + *quark*] (1982) **:** the hypothetical boson analogue of a quark postulated under the rules of supersymmetry

[1]**squash** \ˈskwäsh, ˈskwȯsh\ *vb* [alter. of ME *squachen* to crush, annul, fr. AF *esquacher,* fr. OF *es-* ex- + *quachier* to hide from view, fr. VL **coacticare* to press together — more at CACHE] *vt* (1565) **1 :** to press or beat into a pulp or a flat mass **:** CRUSH **2 :** PUT DOWN, SUPPRESS ⟨~ a revolt⟩ ~ *vi* **1 :** to flatten out under pressure or impact **2 :** to proceed with a splashing or squelching sound ⟨~ through the mud⟩ **3 :** SQUEEZE, PRESS — **squash·er** *n*

[2]**squash** *n* (1590) **1** *obs* **:** something soft and easily crushed; *specif* **:** an unripe pod of peas **2 :** the sudden fall of a heavy soft body or the sound of such a fall **3 :** SQUELCH 1 **4 :** a crushed mass **5** *Brit* **:** sweetened citrus fruit juice often served with added soda water **6 :** a singles or doubles game played in a 4-wall court with a long-handled racket and a rubber ball that can be hit off any number of walls

[3]**squash** *adv* (1766) **:** with a squash or a squashing sound

[4]**squash** *n, pl* **squash·es** *or* **squash** [by shortening & alter. fr. earlier *isquoutersquash,* fr. Narragansett *askútasquash*] (1634) **:** any of various fruits of plants (genus *Cucurbita*) of the gourd family widely cultivated as vegetables; *also* **:** a plant and esp. a vine that bears squashes — compare SUMMER SQUASH, WINTER SQUASH

squash bug *n* (ca. 1846) **:** a large black American bug (*Anasa tristis* of the family Coreidae) injurious to plants of the gourd family

squash racquets *n pl but sing in constr* (1886) **:** SQUASH 6

squash tennis *n* (1901) **:** a singles racket game resembling squash played with an inflated ball the size of a tennis ball

squashy \ˈskwä-shē, ˈskwȯ-\ *adj* **squash·i·er; -est** (1698) **1 :** easily squashed **2 :** softly wet **:** BOGGY **3 :** soft because overripe ⟨~ melons⟩ — **squash·i·ly** \-shə-lē\ *adv* — **squash·i·ness** \-shē-nəs\ *n*

[1]**squat** \ˈskwät\ *vb* **squat·ted; squat·ting** [ME *squatten* to crush, crouch in hiding, fr. MF (Picard dial.) *esquatir, escuater,* fr. OF *es-* ex- + *quatir* to hide, fr. VL **coactire* to squeeze, alter. of L *coactare* to compel — more at CACHE] *vt* (15c) **1 :** to cause (oneself) to crouch or sit on the ground **2 :** to occupy as a squatter ⟨~ in an abandoned building⟩ ~ *vi* **1 :** to crouch close to the ground as if to escape observation ⟨a hare *squatting* in the grass⟩ **2 :** to assume or maintain a position in which the body is supported on the feet and the knees are bent so that the buttocks rest on or near the heels **3 :** to be or become a squatter

[2]**squat** *adj* **squat·ter; squat·test** (15c) **1 :** sitting with the haunches close above the heels **2 a :** low to the ground **b :** marked by disproportionate shortness or thickness — **squat·ly** *adv* — **squat·ness** *n*

[3]**squat** *n* (1580) **1 a :** the act of squatting **b :** the posture of one that squats **2 a :** a place where one squats **b :** the lair of a small animal ⟨the ~ of a hare⟩ **3 :** a lift in which a standing weight lifter drops to a squatting position and then rises to an upright position while holding a barbell on the shoulders; *also* **:** a competitive event involving this lift **4** *chiefly Brit* **:** an empty house or building that is occupied by squatters **5** *slang* **:** DIDDLY-SQUAT

[1]**squat·ter** \ˈskwä-tər\ *vi* [imit.] (1785) **:** to go along through or as if through water ⟨ducks ~*ing* to the shore⟩

[2]**squatter** *n* (1788) **:** one that squats: as **a :** one that settles on property without right or title or payment of rent **b :** one that settles on public land under government regulation with the purpose of acquiring title

squatter sovereignty *n* (1854) **:** POPULAR SOVEREIGNTY 2

squat·ty \ˈskwä-tē\ *adj* **squat·ti·er; -est** (1881) **1 :** low to the ground **2 :** DUMPY, THICKSET

squaw \ˈskwȯ\ *n* [Massachusett *squa, ussqua* woman] (1634) **1** *often offensive* **:** an American Indian woman **2** *usu disparaging* **:** WOMAN, WIFE

squaw·bush \ˈskwȯ-ˌbu̇sh\ *n* (1906) **:** a strong-scented sumac (*Rhus trilobata*) of western No. America with ternately compound leaves — called also *skunkbrush*

squaw·fish \-ˌfish\ *n* (1881) **:** any of several large cyprinid fishes (genus *Ptychocheilus*) of western No. America — called also *pikeminnow*

[1]**squawk** \ˈskwȯk\ *vi* [prob. blend of *squall* and *squeak*] (1821) **1 :** to utter a harsh abrupt scream **2 :** to complain or protest loudly or vehemently ⟨opponents of the bill ~*ed*⟩ — **squawk·er** *n*

[2]**squawk** *n* (1850) **1 :** a harsh abrupt scream **2 :** a noisy complaint

squawk box *n* (1945) **:** an intercom speaker

squaw man *n* (1866) *often disparaging* **:** a white man married to an American Indian woman and usu. living as one of her tribe

squaw·root \ˈskwȯ-ˌrüt, -ˌru̇t\ *n* (ca. 1848) **:** a No. American scaly herb (*Conopholis americana*) of the broomrape family parasitic esp. on oak roots

[1]**squeak** \ˈskwēk\ *vb* [ME *squeken,* of imit. origin] *vi* (14c) **1 :** to utter or make a short shrill cry or noise **2 :** SQUEAL 2a **3 :** to pass, succeed, or win by a narrow margin ⟨just ~*ed* by in the election⟩ ~ *vt* **:** to utter in a shrill piping tone

[2]**squeak** *n* (1700) **1 :** a sharp shrill cry or sound **2 :** ESCAPE ⟨a close ~⟩ — **squeaky** \ˈskwē-kē\ *adj*

squeak·er \ˈskwē-kər\ *n* (1641) **1 :** one that squeaks **2 :** a contest (as a game or an election) won by a small margin

squeaky–clean *adj* (1968) **1 :** completely clean ⟨~ hair⟩ **2 :** completely free from moral taint of any kind ⟨a ~ reputation⟩

[1]**squeal** \ˈskwēl\ *vb* [ME *squelen,* of imit. origin] *vi* (14c) **1 :** to make a shrill cry or noise **2 a :** to turn informer ⟨~ to the police⟩ **b :** COMPLAIN, PROTEST ~ *vt* **1 :** to express with or as if with a squeal **2 :** to cause to make a loud shrill noise ⟨~*ing* the tires⟩ — **squeal·er** *n*

[2]**squeal** *n* (1747) **:** a shrill sharp cry or noise

squea·mish \ˈskwē-mish\ *adj* [ME *squaymisch,* modif. of AF *escoymous*] (15c) **1 a :** easily nauseated **:** QUEASY **b :** affected with nausea **2 a :** excessively fastidious or scrupulous in conduct or belief **b :** easily offended or disgusted — **squea·mish·ly** *adv* — **squea·mish·ness** *n*

[1]**squee·gee** \'skwē-ˌjē\ *also* **squil·gee** \'skwē-, 'skwil-\ *n* [origin unknown] (1844) **:** a blade of leather or rubber set on a handle and used for spreading, pushing, or wiping liquid material on, across, or off a surface (as a window); *also* **:** a smaller similar device or a small rubber roller with handle used by a photographer or lithographer

[2]**squeegee** *also* **squilgee** *vt* **squee·geed** *also* **squil·geed; squee·gee·ing** *also* **squil·gee·ing** (1883) **:** to smooth, wipe, or treat with a squeegee

[1]**squeeze** \'skwēz\ *vb* **squeezed; squeez·ing** [alter. of obs. E *quease,* fr. ME *queysen,* fr. OE *cwȳsan;* akin to Icel *kveisa* stomach cramps] *vt* (ca. 1601) **1 a :** to exert pressure esp. on opposite sides of **:** COMPRESS **b :** to extract or emit under pressure **c :** to force or thrust by compression **2 a** (1) **:** to get by extortion (2) **:** to deprive by extortion **b :** to cause economic hardship to **c :** to reduce the amount of ⟨~*s* profits⟩ **3 :** to crowd into a limited area **4 :** to gain or win by a narrow margin **5 :** to force (another player) to discard in bridge so as to unguard a suit **6 :** to score by means of a squeeze play ~ *vi* **1 :** to give way before pressure **2 :** to exert pressure; *also* **:** to practice extortion or oppression **3 :** to force one's way ⟨~ through a door⟩ **4 :** to pass, win, or get by narrowly — **squeez·abil·i·ty** \ˌskwē-zə-'bi-lə-tē\ *n* — **squeez·able** \'skwē-zə-bəl\ *adj* — **squeez·er** *n*

[2]**squeeze** *n* (1611) **1 a :** an act or instance of squeezing **:** COMPRESSION **b :** HANDCLASP; *also* **:** EMBRACE **2 a :** a quantity squeezed out from something ⟨a ~ of lemon⟩ **b :** a group crowded together **:** CROWD **3 :** a profit taken by a middleman on goods or transactions **4 :** a financial pressure caused by narrowing margins or by shortages **5 :** a forced discard in bridge **6 :** SQUEEZE PLAY **7** *slang* **:** a romantic partner ⟨she's my main ~⟩

squeeze bottle *n* (1950) **:** a bottle of flexible plastic that dispenses its contents when it is squeezed

squeeze off *vt* (ca. 1949) **:** to fire (a round) by squeezing the trigger ~ *vi* **:** to fire a weapon by squeezing the trigger

squeeze play *n* (1905) **1 :** a baseball play in which a runner on third base starts for home plate as the ball is being pitched and the batter attempts to bunt to give the runner a chance to score **2 :** the exertion of pressure in order to extort a concession or gain a goal

[1]**squelch** \'skwelch\ *vb* [origin unknown] *vt* (1624) **1 a :** to fall or stamp on so as to crush **b** (1) **:** to completely suppress **:** QUELL ⟨~ resistance⟩ (2) **:** SILENCE ⟨~*ed* the protesters⟩ **2 :** to emit or move with a sucking sound ~ *vi* **1 :** to emit a sucking sound **2 :** to splash through water, slush, or mire — **squelch·er** *n*

[2]**squelch** *n* (1895) **1 :** a sound of or as if of semiliquid matter under suction ⟨the ~ of mud⟩ **2 :** the act of suppressing; *esp* **:** a retort that silences an opponent — **squelchy** *adj*

sque·teague \skwi-'tēg\ *n, pl* **squeteague** [of southeast New England Algonquian origin; akin to Mohegan *cheegut* weakfish] (1803) **:** any of several weakfishes (esp. *Cynoscion regalis*)

[1]**squib** \'skwib\ *n* [origin unknown] (ca. 1525) **1 a :** a short humorous or satiric writing or speech **b :** a short news item; *esp* **:** FILLER **2 a :** a small firecracker **b :** a broken firecracker in which the powder burns with a fizz **3 :** a small electric or pyrotechnic device used to ignite a charge

[2]**squib** *vb* **squibbed; squib·bing** *vi* (ca. 1580) **1 :** to speak, write, or publish squibs **2 :** to fire a squib ~ *vt* **1 a :** to utter in an offhand manner **b :** to make squibs against **:** LAMPOON **2 :** to shoot off **:** FIRE **3 :** to kick (a football) on a kickoff so that it bounces along the ground

squib kick *n* (ca. 1956) **:** a kickoff in football in which the ball bounces along the ground

[1]**squid** \'skwid\ *n, pl* **squid** *or* **squids** [origin unknown] (1613) **:** any of an order (Teuthoidea) of cephalopods having eight short arms and two usu. longer tentacles, a long tapered body, a caudal fin on each side, and usu. a slender internal chitinous support

[2]**squid** *vi* **squid·ded; squid·ding** (ca. 1859) **:** to fish with or for squid

SQUID \'skwid\ *n* [*s*uperconducting *qu*antum *i*nterference *d*evice] (1967) **:** an instrument for detecting and measuring very weak magnetic fields

squiffed \'skwift\ *or* **squif·fy** \'skwi-fē\ *adj* [origin unknown] (ca. 1855) **:** INTOXICATED, DRUNK

[1]**squig·gle** \'skwi-gəl\ *vb* **squig·gled; squig·gling** \-g(ə-)liŋ\ [blend of *squirm* and *wriggle*] *vi* (ca. 1816) **1 :** SQUIRM, WRIGGLE ⟨*squiggling* in her seat⟩ **2 :** to write or paint hastily **:** SCRIBBLE ~ *vt* **1 :** SCRIBBLE **2 :** to form or cause to form in squiggles

[2]**squiggle** *n* (1900) **:** a short wavy twist or line **:** CURLICUE; *esp* **:** an illegible scrawl — **squig·gly** \-g(ə-)lē\ *adj*

squilgee *var of* SQUEEGEE

squill \'skwil\ *n* [ME, fr. AF *squille,* L *squilla, scilla,* fr. Gk *skilla*] (14c) **1 a :** a Mediterranean bulbous herb (*Urginea maritima*) of the lily family — called also *sea onion*; compare RED SQUILL 1 **b** (1) **:** the dried sliced bulb scales of a squill used as an expectorant, cardiac stimulant, and diuretic (2) **:** RED SQUILL 2 **2 :** SCILLA

squil·la \'skwi-lə\ *n, pl* **squillas** *or* **squil·lae** \'skwi-ˌlē, -ˌlī\ [NL, fr. L, shrimp, crayfish] (1658) **:** any of various stomatopod crustaceans (esp. genus *Squilla*) that burrow in mud or beneath stones in shallow water along the seashore

[1]**squinch** \'skwinch\ *vb* [prob. blend of *squint* and *pinch*] *vt* (1835) **1 :** to screw up (the eyes or face) **:** SQUINT **2 a :** to make more compact **b :** to cause to crouch down or draw together ~ *vi* **1 :** FLINCH **2 :** to crouch down or draw together **3 :** SQUINT

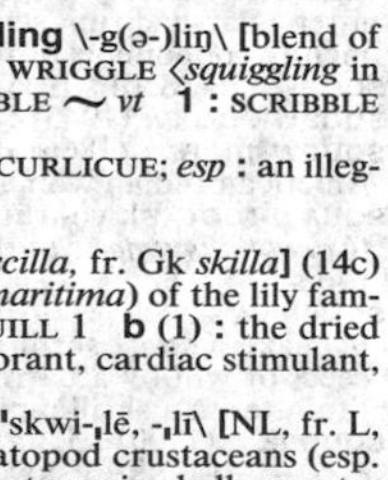

squinch

[2]**squinch** *n* [alter. of earlier *scunch* back part of the side of an opening] (ca. 1840) **:** a support (as an arch, lintel, or corbeling) carried across the corner of a room under a superimposed mass

[1]**squin·ny** \'skwi-nē\ *vb* **squin·nied; squin·ny·ing** [prob. fr. obs. E *squin* asquint, fr. ME *skuin*] (1605) **:** SQUINT

[2]**squinny** *n* (ca. 1881) **:** SQUINT — **squinny** *adj*

[1]**squint** \'skwint\ *adj* [ME *asquint*] (1579) **1** *of an eye* **:** looking or tending to look obliquely or askance (as with envy or disdain) **2** *of the eyes* **:** not having the visual axes parallel **:** CROSSED

[2]**squint** *vi* (1599) **1 a :** to have an indirect bearing, reference, or aim **b :** to deviate from a true line **2 a :** to look in a squint-eyed manner **b :** to be cross-eyed **c :** to look or peer with eyes partly closed ~ *vt* **:** to cause (an eye) to squint — **squint·er** *n* — **squint·ing·ly** \'skwin-tiŋ-lē\ *adv*

[3]**squint** *n* (ca. 1652) **1 :** STRABISMUS **2 :** an instance of squinting **3 :** HAGIOSCOPE — **squinty** \'skwin-tē\ *adj*

squint–eyed \'skwint-ˌīd\ *adj* (1589) **1 :** having eyes that squint; *specif* **:** affected with cross-eye **2 :** looking askance (as in envy)

squinting modifier *n* (1924) **:** a modifier (as *often* in "getting dressed often is a nuisance") so placed in a sentence that it can be interpreted as modifying either what precedes or what follows

[1]**squire** \'skwī(-ə)r\ *n* [ME *squier,* fr. AF *esquier* — more at ESQUIRE] (13c) **1 :** a shield bearer or armor bearer of a knight **2 a :** a male attendant esp. on a great personage **b :** a man who devotedly attends a lady **:** GALLANT **3 a :** a member of the British gentry ranking below a knight and above a gentleman **b :** an owner of a country estate; *esp* **:** the principal landowner in a village or district **c** (1) **:** JUSTICE OF THE PEACE (2) **:** LAWYER (3) **:** JUDGE — **squir·ish** \'skwīr-ish\ *adj*

[2]**squire** *vt* **squired; squir·ing** (14c) **:** to attend as a squire **:** ESCORT

squire·ar·chy *also* **squir·ar·chy** \'skwī(-ə)r-ˌär-kē\ *n, pl* **-chies** (1796) **:** the class of landed gentry or landed proprietors

squirm \'skwərm\ *vi* [origin unknown] (ca. 1691) **:** to twist about like a worm **:** FIDGET — **squirm** *n* — **squirmy** \'skwər-mē\ *adj*

[1]**squir·rel** \'skwər(-ə)l, 'skwə-rəl, *chiefly Brit* 'skwir-əl\ *n, pl* **squirrels** *also* **squirrel** [ME *squirel,* fr. AF *escurel, esquirel,* fr. VL **scuriolus,* dim. of *scurius,* alter. of L **sciurus,* fr. Gk *skiouros,* prob. fr. *skia* shadow + *oura* tail — more at SHINE, ASS] (14c) **1 :** any of various small or medium-sized rodents (family Sciuridae, the squirrel family): as **a :** any of numerous New or Old World arboreal forms having a long bushy tail and strong hind legs **b :** GROUND SQUIRREL **2 :** the fur of a squirrel

[2]**squirrel** *vt* **-reled** *or* **-relled; -rel·ing** *or* **-rel·ling** [fr. the squirrel's habit of storing up gathered nuts and seeds for winter use] (1925) **:** to store up for future use — often used with *away* ⟨~ away some money⟩

squirrel cage *n* (1821) **1 :** a cage for a small animal (as a squirrel) that contains a rotatable cylinder for exercising **2 :** something resembling the working of a squirrel cage in repetitiveness or endlessness

squirrel corn *n* (1843) **:** a No. American herb (*Dicentra canadensis*) of the fumitory family with much-divided leaves and a scapose raceme of cream-colored flowers

squir·rel·fish \'skwər(-ə)l-ˌfish, 'skwə-rəl-\ *n* (1803) **:** any of various small chiefly tropical usu. red bony fishes (family Holocentridae) with large eyes, spiny fins, and rough scales

squir·rel·ly \'skwər(-ə)-lē, 'skwə-rə-\ *adj* (1928) **:** NUTTY 3

squirrel monkey *n* (1773) **:** any of several small soft-haired So. American monkeys (genus *Saimiri,* esp. *S. sciureus* of the family Cebidae) that have a long tail not used for grasping and are colored chiefly yellowish gray with a white face and black muzzle

squirrel rifle *n* [fr. its being suitable only for small game] (1834) **:** a small-caliber rifle — called also *squirrel gun*

[1]**squirt** \'skwərt\ *vb* [ME; akin to LG *swirtjen* to squirt] *vi* (15c) **:** to come forth in a sudden rapid stream from a narrow opening **:** SPURT ~ *vt* **:** to cause to squirt — **squirt·er** *n*

[2]**squirt** *n* (15c) **1 a :** an instrument (as a syringe) for squirting a liquid **b :** a small quick stream **:** JET **c :** the action or an instance of squirting **2 a :** an impudent youngster **b :** KID 3

squirt gun *n* (1803) **:** WATER PISTOL

squirting cucumber *n* (1802) **:** a Mediterranean plant (*Ecballium elaterium*) of the gourd family with oblong fruit that bursts from the peduncle when ripe and forcibly ejects the seeds

squish \'skwish\ *vb* [alter. of *squash*] *vt* (ca. 1647) **1 :** SQUASH ⟨~*ed* the bug⟩ **2 :** SQUELCH, SUCK ~ *vi* **:** SQUELCH, SUCK — **squish** *n*

squishy \'skwi-shē\ *adj* **squish·i·er; -est** (ca. 1847) **1 :** being soft, yielding, and usu. damp **2 :** not firm, steady, or fixed**:** SOFT: as **a :** LENIENT 2 **b :** IMPRECISE ⟨~ estimates⟩ — **squish·i·ness** *n*

squoosh \'skwůsh, 'skwüsh\ *vb* [alter. of [1]*squash*] (1942) **:** SQUASH

squooshy \'skwů-shē\ *adj* **squoosh·i·er; -est** [by alter.] (1981) **:** SQUISHY 1

[1]**Sr** *abbr* **1** senior **2** senor; señor **3** sister

[2]**Sr** *symbol* strontium

SR *abbr* **1** seaman recruit **2** shipping receipt

Sra *abbr* senora; señora

SRAM \'es-ˌram\ *n* [*s*tatic *r*andom-*a*ccess *m*emory] (1982) **:** a type of RAM that must be continuously supplied with power but does not need to be periodically rewritten in order to retain data — compare DRAM

Sra·nan \'srä-nən\ *n* [Sranan, short for *Sranan Tongo,* lit., Suriname tongue] (1953) **:** an English-based creole widely spoken in Suriname — called also *Sranan Tongo* \-'täŋ-(ˌ)gō\

S Res *abbr* Senate resolution

sri \'srē, 'shrē\ *also* **shri** \'shrē, 'srē\ *n* [Skt *śrī,* lit., beauty, majesty; akin to Gk *kreiōn* ruler, master] (1799) — used as a conventional title of respect when addressing or speaking of a distinguished Indian

[1]**SRO** \ˌes-(ˌ)är-'ō\ *n* [*s*ingle-*r*oom *o*ccupancy] (1941) **:** a house, apartment building, or residential hotel in which low-income or welfare tenants live in single rooms

[2]**SRO** *abbr* standing room only

Srta *abbr* senorita; señorita

ss *abbr* **1** scilicet — used in legal documents **2** [L *semis*] one half

[1]**SS** \ˌes-'es\ *n* [G, abbr. for *Schutzstaffel,* lit., protection echelon] (1932) **:** a unit of Nazis created as bodyguard to Hitler and later expanded to take charge of intelligence, central security, policing action, and the mass extermination of those they considered inferior or undesirable

[2]**SS** *abbr* **1** saints **2** Social Security **3** steamship

SSA *abbr* Social Security Administration

SSE *abbr* south-southeast

SSG *or* **SSgt** *abbr* staff sergeant

SSI *abbr* supplemental security income

SSM *abbr* staff sergeant major

SSN *abbr* Social Security number

ssp *abbr* subspecies

SSR *abbr* Soviet Socialist Republic
SSRI \ˌes-(ˌ)es-(ˌ)är-ˈī\ *n* (1991) **:** any of a class of antidepressants (as fluoxetine) that inhibit the inactivation of serotonin by blocking its reuptake by presynaptic neuron endings — called also *selective serotonin reuptake inhibitor*
SSS *abbr* Selective Service System
SST \ˌes-ˌes-ˈtē\ *n* [*s*uper*s*onic *t*ransport] (1961) **:** SUPERSONIC TRANSPORT
SSW *abbr* south-southwest
st *abbr* **1** stanza **2** state **3** stitch **4** stone
St *abbr* **1** saint **2** stratus **3** street
ST *abbr* standard time
1**-st** — see -EST
2**-st** *symbol* — used after the figure 1 to indicate the ordinal number *first* ⟨1*st*⟩ ⟨91*st*⟩
sta *abbr* station
1**stab** \ˈstab\ *n* [ME *stabbe*] (15c) **1 :** a wound produced by a pointed object or weapon **2 a :** a thrust of a pointed weapon **b :** a jerky thrust **3 :** EFFORT, TRY **4 :** a sudden sharp feeling ⟨∼*s* of regret⟩
2**stab** *vb* **stabbed; stab•bing** *vt* (1530) **1 :** to wound or pierce by the thrust of a pointed object or weapon **2 :** THRUST, DRIVE ∼ *vi* **:** to thrust or give a wound with or as if with a pointed weapon — **stab•ber** *n* — **stab in the back :** BETRAY
1**sta•bile** \ˈstā-ˌbī(-ə)l, -ˌbil\ *adj* [L *stabilis* — more at STABLE] (1896) **:** STATIONARY, STABLE
2**sta•bile** \-ˌbēl\ *n* [prob. fr. F, fr. L *stabilis,* adj.] (1937) **:** an abstract sculpture or construction similar in appearance to a mobile but made to be stationary
sta•bi•lise, sta•bi•lis•er *Brit var of* STABILIZE, STABILIZER
sta•bil•i•ty \stə-ˈbi-lə-tē\ *n, pl* **-ties** (14c) **1 :** the quality, state, or degree of being stable: as **a :** the strength to stand or endure **:** FIRMNESS **b :** the property of a body that causes it when disturbed from a condition of equilibrium or steady motion to develop forces or moments that restore the original condition **c :** resistance to chemical change or to physical disintegration **2 :** residence for life in one monastery
sta•bi•lize \ˈstā-bə-ˌlīz\ *vb* **-lized; -liz•ing** *vt* (1861) **1 :** to make stable, steadfast, or firm **2 :** to hold steady: as **a :** to maintain the stability of (as an airplane) by means of a stabilizer **b :** to limit fluctuations of (as prices) **c :** to establish a minimum price for ∼ *vi* **:** to become stable, firm, or steadfast — **sta•bi•li•za•tion** \ˌstā-bə-lə-ˈzā-shən\ *n*
sta•bi•liz•er \ˈstā-bə-ˌlī-zər\ *n* (ca. 1909) **:** one that stabilizes something: as **a :** a substance added to another substance (as an explosive or plastic) or to a system (as an emulsion) to prevent or retard an unwanted alteration of physical state **b :** a gyroscope device to keep ships steady in a heavy sea **c :** an airfoil providing stability for an airplane; *specif* **:** the fixed horizontal member of the tail assembly — see AIRPLANE illustration
1**sta•ble** \ˈstā-bəl\ *n* [ME, fr. AF *estable, stable,* fr. L *stabulum,* fr. *stare* to stand — more at STAND] (13c) **1 :** a building in which domestic animals are sheltered and fed; *esp* **:** such a building having stalls or compartments ⟨a horse ∼⟩ **2 a :** the racehorses of one owner **b :** a group of people (as athletes, writers, or performers) under one management **c :** the racing cars of one owner **d :** GROUP, COLLECTION — **sta•ble•man** \-mən, -ˌman\ *n*
2**stable** *vb* **sta•bled; sta•bling** \-b(ə-)liŋ\ *vt* (14c) **:** to put or keep in a stable ∼ *vi* **:** to dwell in or as if in a stable
3**stable** *adj* **sta•bler** \-b(ə-)lər\; **sta•blest** \-b(ə-)ləst\ [ME, fr. AF *estable, stable,* fr. L *stabilis,* fr. *stare* to stand] (13c) **1 a :** firmly established **:** FIXED, STEADFAST ⟨∼ opinions⟩ **b :** not changing or fluctuating **:** UNVARYING ⟨in ∼ condition⟩ **c :** PERMANENT, ENDURING ⟨∼ civilizations⟩ **2 a :** steady in purpose **:** firm in resolution **b :** not subject to insecurity or emotional illness **:** SANE, RATIONAL ⟨a ∼ personality⟩ **3 a (1) :** placed so as to resist forces tending to cause motion or change of motion **(2) :** designed so as to develop forces that restore the original condition when disturbed from a condition of equilibrium or steady motion **b (1) :** not readily altering in chemical makeup or physical state ⟨∼ emulsions⟩ **(2) :** not spontaneously radioactive ***syn*** see LASTING — **sta•ble•ness** \-bəl-nəs\ *n* — **sta•bly** \-b(ə-)lē\ *adv*
stable fly *n* (1862) **:** a biting dipteran fly (*Stomoxys calcitrans*) that resembles the common housefly and is abundant about stables
sta•ble•mate \ˈstā-bəl-ˌmāt\ *n* (1926) **1 :** an animal stabled with another **2 :** a member of a stable
sta•bler \-b(ə-)lər\ *n* (15c) **:** one who keeps a stable
stabling *n* (15c) **:** accommodation for animals in a building; *also* **:** the building for this
stab•lish \ˈsta-blish\ *vb* [ME, short for *establissen*] (14c) *archaic* **:** ESTABLISH — **stab•lish•ment** \-mənt\ *n, archaic*
stac•ca•to \stə-ˈkä-(ˌ)tō\ *adj* [It, fr. pp. of *staccare* to detach, fr. *s-* ex- (fr. L *ex-*) + *attaccare* to attack, attach, perh. fr. OF *estachier* — more at ATTACH] (ca. 1724) **1 a :** cut short or apart in performing **:** DISCONNECTED ⟨∼ notes⟩ **b :** marked by short clear-cut playing or singing of tones or chords ⟨a ∼ style⟩ **2 :** ABRUPT, DISJOINTED ⟨∼ screams⟩ — **staccato** *adv* — **staccato** *n*
staccato mark *n* (ca. 1903) **:** a pointed vertical stroke or a dot placed over or under a musical note to be produced staccato
1**stack** \ˈstak\ *n* [ME *stak,* fr. ON *stakkr;* akin to Russ *stog* stack and prob. to OE *staca* stake] (14c) **1 :** a large usu. conical pile (as of hay, straw, or grain in the sheaf) left standing in the field for storage **2 a :** an orderly pile or heap **b :** a large quantity or number **3 :** an English unit of measure esp. for firewood that is equal to 108 cubic feet **4 a :** a number of flues embodied in one structure rising above a roof **b :** a vertical pipe (as to carry off smoke) **c :** the exhaust pipe of an internal combustion engine **5 a :** a structure of bookshelves for compact storage of books — usu. used in pl. **b** *pl* **:** a section of a building housing such structures **6 :** a pile of poker chips **7 a :** a memory or a section of memory in a computer for temporary storage in which the last item stored is the first retrieved; *also* **:** a data structure that simulates a stack ⟨a push-down ∼⟩ **b :** a computer memory consisting of arrays of memory elements stacked one on top of another
2**stack** *vt* (14c) **1 a :** to arrange in a stack **:** PILE **b :** to pile in or on ⟨∼*ed* the table with books⟩ ⟨∼ the dishwasher⟩ **2 a :** to arrange secretly for cheating ⟨∼ a deck of cards⟩ **b :** to arrange or fix so as to make a particular result likely ⟨the odds are ∼*ed* against us⟩ ⟨will ∼ juries to suit themselves —Patrice Horn⟩ **3 a :** to assign (an airplane) by radio to a particular altitude and position within a group circling before landing **b :** to put into a waiting line ⟨another dozen rigs are ∼*ed* up and waiting —P. H. Hutchins, Jr.⟩ **4 :** COMPARE — used with *against* ⟨such a crime is nothing when ∼*ed* against a murder —Pete Censky⟩ ∼ *vi* **:** to form a stack — **stack•er** *n*
stack•able \ˈsta-kə-bəl\ *adj* (1958) **:** easily arranged in a stack
stacked \ˈstakt\ *adj* (1942) *of a woman* **:** having large breasts
stack up *vi* (1896) **1 :** to add up **:** TOTAL **2 :** MEASURE UP, COMPARE — usu. used with *against*
stac•te \ˈstak-tē\ *n* [ME *stacten,* fr. L *stacte,* fr. Gk *staktē,* fr. fem. of *staktos* oozing out in drops, fr. *stazein* to drip] (1535) **:** a sweet spice used by the ancient Jews in preparing incense
stad•dle \ˈsta-dᵊl\ *n* [ME *stathel* base, support, bottom of a stack, fr. OE *statho* base; akin to OHG *stān* to stand — more at STAND] (15c) **:** a base (as of piling) for a stack of hay or straw
stade \ˈstād\ *n* [MF *estade,* fr. L *stadium*] (1537) **:** STADIUM 1a
sta•dia \ˈstā-dē-ə\ *n* [perh. fr. F, fr. NL, pl. of *stadium* stage, gradation, fr. L, stadium] (1865) **:** a surveying method for determination of distances and differences of elevation by means of a telescopic instrument having two horizontal lines through which the marks on a graduated rod are observed; *also* **:** the instrument or rod
sta•di•um \ˈstā-dē-əm\ *n, pl* **-dia** \-dē-ə\ *or* **-di•ums** [ME, fr. L, fr. Gk *stadion*] (14c) **1 a :** any of various ancient Greek units of length ranging in value from 607 to 738 feet (about 185 to 225 meters) **b :** an ancient Roman unit of length equal to 607 feet (185 meters) **2 a :** a course for footraces in ancient Greece orig. one stadium in length **b :** a tiered structure with seats for spectators surrounding an ancient Greek running track **c :** a large usu. roofless building with tiers of seats for spectators at sports events **3** [NL, fr. L] **:** a stage in a life history; *esp* **:** one between successive molts of an insect
stadt•hold•er \ˈstat-ˌhōl-dər\ *n* [part trans. of D *stadhouder,* fr. *stad* place + *houder* holder] (1668) **1 :** a viceroy in a province of the Netherlands **2 :** a chief executive officer of the provinces that formed a union leading to establishment of the Netherlands — **stadt•hold•er•ate** \-də-rət\ *n* — **stadt•hold•er•ship** \-dər-ˌship\ *n*
1**staff** \ˈstaf\ *n, pl* **staffs** \ˈstafs, ˈstavz\ *or* **staves** \ˈstavz, ˈstāvz\ [ME *staf,* fr. OE *stæf;* akin to OHG *stab* staff, Skt *stabhnāti* he supports] (bef. 12c) **1 a :** a long stick carried in the hand for support in walking **b :** a supporting rod: as **(1)** *archaic* **:** SHAFT 1a(1) **(2) :** a crosspiece in a ladder or chair **:** RUNG **(3) :** FLAGSTAFF **(4) :** a pivoted arbor **c :** CLUB, CUDGEL **2 a :** CROSIER **b :** a rod carried as a symbol of office or authority **3 :** the horizontal lines with their spaces on which music is written — called also *stave* **4 :** any of various graduated sticks or rules used for measuring **:** ROD **5** *pl* ***staffs*** **a :** the officers chiefly responsible for the internal operations of an institution or business **b :** a group of officers appointed to assist a civil executive or commanding officer **c :** military or naval officers not eligible for operational command **d :** the personnel who assist a director in carrying out an assigned task **e** *pl* **staff :** a member of a staff ⟨employs three full-time ∼⟩ — **staff** *adj*
2**staff** *vt* (1859) **1 :** to supply with a staff or with workers **2 :** to serve as a staff member of ⟨an organization ∼*ed* by volunteers⟩
staff•er \ˈsta-fər\ *n* (1941) **:** a member of a staff (as of a newspaper)
staff officer *n* (1777) **:** a commissioned officer assigned to a military commander's staff — compare LINE OFFICER
staff of life (1638) **:** a staple of diet; *esp* **:** BREAD
Staf•ford•shire bull terrier \ˈsta-fərd-ˌshir-, -shər-\ *n* [*Staffordshire,* England] (1901) **:** any of a breed of compact muscular terriers that have a short stiff glossy coat, were developed in England by crossing bulldogs and terriers, and were orig. bred for dogfighting — compare AMERICAN STAFFORDSHIRE TERRIER
Staffs *abbr* Staffordshire
staff sergeant *n* (1811) **:** a noncommissioned officer ranking in the army above a sergeant and below a platoon sergeant or sergeant first class, in the air force above a sergeant and below a technical sergeant, and in the marine corps above a sergeant and below a gunnery sergeant
staff sergeant major *n* (1967) **:** a noncommissioned officer in the army ranking above a master sergeant
staff tree *n* (ca. 1633) **:** any of a genus (*Celastrus* of the family Celastraceae, the staff-tree family) of mostly twining shrubby plants including the common bittersweet
1**stag** \ˈstag\ *n, pl* **stags** [ME *stagge,* fr. OE *stagga;* akin to ON *andarsteggi* drake] (12c) **1** *or pl* **stag :** an adult male red deer; *also* **:** the male of various other deer (esp. genus *Cervus*) **2** *chiefly Scot* **:** a young horse; *esp* **:** a young unbroken stallion **3 :** a male animal castrated after sexual maturity — compare STEER 1 **4 :** a young adult male domestic chicken or turkey **5 a :** a social gathering of men only **b :** one who attends a dance or party without a companion
2**stag** *vb* **stagged; stag•ging** [*stag* (informer)] *vt* (1796) *Brit* **:** to spy on ∼ *vi* **:** to attend a dance or party without a companion
3**stag** *adj* (1843) **1 a :** restricted to men ⟨a ∼ party⟩ **b :** intended for a male audience; *esp* **:** PORNOGRAPHIC ⟨∼ movies⟩ **2 :** unaccompanied by someone of the opposite sex ⟨∼ women⟩ — **stag** *adv*
stag beetle *n* (1681) **:** any of a family (Lucanidae) of mostly large beetles having males with long and often branched mandibles suggesting the antlers of a stag
1**stage** \ˈstāj\ *n* [ME, fr. AF *estage* abode, story of a building, state, fr. VL **staticum,* fr. L *stare* to stand — more at STAND] (14c) **1 a :** one of a series of positions or stations one above the other **:** STEP **b :** the height of the surface of a river above an arbitrary zero point ⟨flood ∼⟩ **2 a (1) :** a raised platform **(2) :** the part of a theater on which the acting takes place and which often includes the wings **(3) :** the acting profession **:** the theater as an occupation or activity **(4) :** SOUNDSTAGE **b :** a center of attention or scene of action **3 a :** a scaffold for workmen **b :** the small platform of a microscope on which an object is placed for examination **4 a :** a place of rest formerly provided for those traveling by stagecoach **:** STATION **b :** the distance between two

\ə\ **abut** \ᵊ\ **kitten**, F **table** \ər\ **further** \a\ **ash** \ā\ **ace** \ä\ **mop, mar**
\au̇\ **out** \ch\ **chin** \e\ **bet** \ē\ **easy** \g\ **go** \i\ **hit** \ī\ **ice** \j\ **job**
\ŋ\ **sing** \ō\ **go** \ȯ\ **law** \ȯi\ **boy** \th\ **thin** \t͟h\ **the** \ü\ **loot** \u̇\ **foot**
\y\ **yet** \zh\ **vision, beige** \k̲, ⁿ, œ, ue, ʸ\ *see* Guide to Pronunciation

stopping places on a road **c** : STAGECOACH **5 a** : a period or step in a process, activity, or development: as (1) : one of the distinguishable periods of growth and development of a plant or animal ⟨the larval ~ of an insect⟩ (2) : a period or phase in the course of a disease; *also* : the degree of involvement or severity of a disease **b** : one passing through a (specified) stage **6** : an element or part of an electronic device (as an amplifier) **7** : one of two or more sections of a rocket that have their own fuel and engine — **stage·ful** \-ˌfu̇l\ *n* — **stage·like** \-ˌlīk\ *adj* — **on the stage** : in or into the acting profession

[2]**stage** *vt* **staged; stag·ing** (1879) **1** : to produce (as a play) on a stage **2** : to produce or cause to happen for public view or public effect ⟨~ a track meet⟩ ⟨~ a hunger strike⟩ **3** : to determine the phase or severity of (a disease) based on a classification of established symptomatic criteria; *also* : to evaluate (a patient) to determine the phase, severity, or progression of a disease — **stage·able** \ˈstā-jə-bəl\ *adj*

[3]**stage** *adj* (1824) : intended to represent a type or stereotype ⟨a ~ Irishman⟩ ⟨a ~ French accent⟩

stage business *n* (1825) : BUSINESS 6

stage·coach \ˈstāj-ˌkōch\ *n* (1658) : a horse-drawn passenger and mail coach running on a regular schedule between established stops

stage·craft \-ˌkraft\ *n* (1882) : the effective management of theatrical devices or techniques

stage direction *n* (1790) : a description (as of a character or setting) or direction (as to indicate stage business) provided in the text of a play

stage director *n* (1782) **1** : DIRECTOR C **2** : STAGE MANAGER

stage fright *n* (1876) : nervousness felt at appearing before an audience

stage·hand \ˈstāj-ˌhand\ *n* (1885) : a stage worker who handles scenery, properties, or lights

stage left *n* (1931) : the left part of a stage from the viewpoint of one who faces the audience

stage–man·age \-ˌma-nij\ *vt* [back-formation fr. *stage manager*] (1879) **1 a** : to arrange or exhibit so as to achieve a desired effect **b** : to arrange or direct from behind the scenes **2** : to act as stage manager for — **stage management** *n*

stage manager *n* (1805) : one who supervises the physical aspects of a stage production, assists the director during rehearsals, and is in charge of the stage during a performance

stag·er \ˈstā-jər\ *n* (1570) : an experienced person : VETERAN

stage right *n* (1931) : the right part of a stage from the viewpoint of one who faces the audience

stage set *n* (1861) : scenery and properties designed and arranged for a particular scene in a play

stage·struck \ˈstāj-ˌstrək\ *adj* (1813) : fascinated by the stage; *esp* : having an ardent desire to become an actor

stage whisper *n* (1864) **1** : a loud whisper by an actor that is audible to the spectators but is supposed for dramatic effect not to be heard by one or more of the actors **2** : an audible whisper — **stage–whisper** *vb*

stag·fla·tion \ˌstag-ˈflā-shən\ *n* [blend of *stagnation* and *inflation*] (1965) : persistent inflation combined with stagnant consumer demand and relatively high unemployment — **stag·fla·tion·ary** \-shə-ˌner-ē\ *adj*

[1]**stag·ger** \ˈsta-gər\ *vb* **stag·gered; stag·ger·ing** \-g(ə-)riŋ\ [alter. of earlier *stacker,* fr. ME *stakeren,* fr. ON *stakra,* freq. of *staka* to push; perh. akin to OE *staca* stake — more at STAKE] *vi* (15c) **1 a** : to reel from side to side : TOTTER **b** : to move on unsteadily ⟨~*ed* toward the door⟩ **2** : to waver in purpose or action : HESITATE **3** : to rock violently ⟨the ship ~*ed*⟩ ~ *vt* **1** : to cause to doubt or hesitate : PERPLEX **2** : to cause to reel or totter **3** : to arrange in any of various zigzags, alternations, or overlappings of position or time ⟨~ work shifts⟩ ⟨~ teeth on a cutter⟩ — **stag·ger·er** \-gər-ər\ *n*

[2]**stagger** *n* (1577) **1** *pl but sing or pl in constr* : an abnormal condition of domestic animals associated with damage to the central nervous system and marked by incoordination and a reeling unsteady gait **2** : a reeling or unsteady gait or stance **3** : an arrangement in which the leading edge of the upper wing of a biplane is advanced over that of the lower

[3]**stagger** *adj* (1918) : marked by an alternating or overlapping pattern

stag·ger·bush \ˈsta-gər-ˌbu̇sh\ *n* (1847) : a shrubby heath (*Lyonia mariana*) of the eastern U.S. that is poisonous to livestock; *also* : a congeneric heath

staggering *adj* (1565) : so great as to cause one to stagger : ASTONISHING, OVERWHELMING ⟨a ~ feat⟩ ⟨~ medical bills⟩ — **stag·ger·ing·ly** *adv*

stag·gery \ˈsta-g(ə-)rē\ *adj* (1837) : UNSTEADY

stag·gy \ˈsta-gē\ *adj* (1918) : having the appearance of a mature male — used of female or castrated male domestic animals

stag·horn coral \ˈstag-ˌhȯrn-\ *n* (1884) : any of several large branching corals (genus *Acropora,* esp. *A. cervicornis*) that somewhat resemble antlers

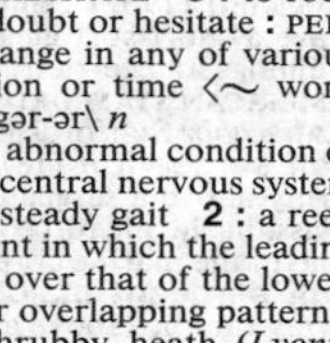

staghorn coral

staghorn sumac *n* (ca. 1868) : a sumac (*Rhus typhina*) of eastern No. America that is a shrub or small tree with velvety-pubescent branches and flower stalks, leaves turning brilliant red in fall, and dense panicles of greenish-yellow flowers followed by hairy crimson fruits

stag·hound \ˈstag-ˌhau̇nd\ *n* (1707) : a hound formerly used in hunting the stag and other large animals; *specif* : a large heavy hound resembling the English foxhound

staging *n* (14c) **1** : SCAFFOLDING **2 a** : the business of running stagecoaches **b** : the act of journeying in stagecoaches **3** : the act of putting on a play **4 a** : the moving of troops or matériel forward in several stages **b** : the assembling of troops or matériel in transit in a particular place

staging area *n* (1943) : an area in which participants in a new esp. military operation or mission are assembled and readied

staging ground *n* (1970) : a place where something is planned or initiated

staging post *n* (1911) : STOPOVER 2

Stag·i·rite \ˈsta-jə-ˌrīt\ *n* [Gk *Stagiritēs,* fr. *Stagira,* city in ancient Macedonia] (1603) : a native or resident of Stagira ⟨Aristotle the ~⟩

stag·nant \ˈstag-nənt\ *adj* (1666) **1 a** : not flowing in a current or stream ⟨~ water⟩ **b** : STALE ⟨long disuse had made the air ~ and foul —Bram Stoker⟩ **2** : not advancing or developing ⟨a ~ economy⟩ — **stag·nan·cy** \-nən(t)-sē\ *n* — **stag·nant·ly** *adv*

stag·nate \ˈstag-ˌnāt\ *vi* **stag·nat·ed; stag·nat·ing** [L *stagnatus,* pp. of *stagnare,* fr. *stagnum* body of standing water] (1661) : to become or remain stagnant — **stag·na·tion** \stag-ˈnā-shən\ *n*

stagy \ˈstā-jē\ *or* **stag·ey** *adj* **stag·i·er; -est** (1856) : of or characteristic of the stage; *esp* : marked by pretense or artificiality : THEATRICAL — **stag·i·ly** \-jə-lē\ *adv* — **stag·i·ness** \-jē-nəs\ *n*

[1]**staid** \ˈstād\ *adj* [fr. pp. of [3]*stay*] (1557) : marked by settled sedateness and often prim self-restraint : SOBER, GRAVE ***syn*** see SERIOUS — **staid·ly** *adv* — **staid·ness** *n*

[2]**staid** *past and past part of* STAY

[1]**stain** \ˈstān\ *vb* [ME *steynen,* partly fr. AF *desteindre* to take away the color from & partly of Scand origin; akin to ON *steina* to paint — more at DISTAIN] *vt* (14c) **1** : to suffuse with color **2** : DISCOLOR, SOIL **3 a** : TAINT 3 ⟨a conscience ~*ed* with guilt⟩ **b** : to bring discredit on ⟨the scandal ~*ed* his reputation⟩ **4** : to color (as wood, glass, or cloth) by processes affecting chemically or otherwise the material itself ~ *vi* : to receive a stain — **stain·able** \ˈstā-nə-bəl\ *adj* — **stain·er** \ˈstā-nər\ *n*

[2]**stain** *n* (1557) **1 a** : a soiled or discolored spot **b** : a natural spot of color contrasting with the ground **2** : a taint of guilt : STIGMA **3** : a preparation (as of dye or pigment) used in staining: as **a** : a dye or pigment capable of penetrating the pores of wood **b** : a dye or mixture of dyes used in microscopy to make visible minute and transparent structures, to differentiate tissue elements, or to produce specific chemical reactions — **stain·proof** \-ˌprüf\ *adj*

stain·abil·i·ty \ˌstā-nə-ˈbi-lə-tē\ *n* (1890) : the capacity of cells and cell parts to stain specifically and consistently with particular dyes and stains

stained glass *n* (1791) : glass colored or stained (as by fusing metallic oxides into it) for decorative applications (as in windows)

[1]**stain·less** \ˈstān-ləs\ *adj* (ca. 1586) **1** : free from stain or stigma ⟨the ~ purity of his boyish life —Oscar Wilde⟩ **2 a** : highly resistant to stain or corrosion **b** : made from materials resistant to stain ⟨~ silverware⟩ — **stain·less·ly** *adv*

[2]**stainless** *n* (1953) : tableware made of stainless steel

stainless steel *n* (1917) : an alloy of steel with chromium and sometimes another element (as nickel or molybdenum) that is practically immune to rusting and ordinary corrosion

stair \ˈster\ *n* [ME *steir,* fr. OE *stǣger;* akin to OE & OHG *stīgan* to rise, Gk *steichein* to walk] (bef. 12c) **1** : a series of steps or flights of steps for passing from one level to another — often used in pl. but sing. or pl. in constr. ⟨a narrow private ~*s* —Lewis Mumford⟩ **2** : a single step of a stairway

stair·case \-ˌkās\ *n* (1624) **1** : the structure containing a stairway **2** : a flight of stairs with the supporting framework, casing, and balusters

stair–climb·er \ˈster-ˈklī-mər\ *n* (1986) : an exercise apparatus that simulates the act of climbing stairs — **stair–climb·ing** \-miŋ\ *n*

stair·way \-ˌwā\ *n* (1767) : one or more flights of stairs usu. with landings to pass from one level to another

stair·well \-ˌwel\ *n* (1920) : a vertical shaft in which stairs are located

[1]**stake** \ˈstāk\ *n* [ME, fr. OE *staca;* akin to MLG *stake* pole, and perh. to L *tignum* beam] (bef. 12c) **1** : a pointed piece of wood or other material driven or to be driven into the ground as a marker or support **2 a** : a post to which a person is bound for execution by burning **b** : execution by burning at a stake **3 a** : something that is staked for gain or loss **b** : the prize in a contest **c** : an interest or share in an undertaking or enterprise **4** : a Mormon territorial jurisdiction comprising a group of wards **5** : GRUBSTAKE **6** : STAKES RACE — usu. used in pl. but sing. or pl. in constr. — **at stake** : at issue : in jeopardy

[2]**stake** *vt* **staked; stak·ing** (14c) **1** : to mark the limits of by or as if by stakes **2** : to tether to a stake **3** : BET, WAGER **4** : to fasten up or support (as plants) with stakes **5** : to back financially **6** : GRUBSTAKE — **stake a claim** : to assert a title or right to something by or as if by placing stakes usu. to satisfy a legal requirement

stake body *n* (1907) : an open motortruck body consisting of a platform with upright sticks inserted along the outside edges to retain a load

stake·hold·er \ˈstāk-ˌhōl-dər\ *n* (1708) **1** : a person entrusted with the stakes of bettors **2** : one that has a stake in an enterprise **3** : one who is involved in or affected by a course of action — **stake·hold·ing** \-diŋ\ *n*

stake·out \ˈstāk-ˌau̇t\ *n* (ca. 1942) : a surveillance maintained by the police of an area or a person suspected of criminal activity

stake out *vt* (1951) **1** : to assign (as a police officer) to an area usu. to conduct a surveillance **2** : to maintain a stakeout of **3** : to claim as one's own

stakes race *n* (1895) : a horse race in which the prize offered is made up at least in part of money (as entry fees) put up by the owners of the horses entered — called also *stake race*

stake truck *n* (1907) : a truck having a stake body — called also *stake-bed truck*

Sta·kha·nov·ite \stə-ˈkä-nə-ˌvīt\ *n* [trans. of Russ *stakhanovets,* fr. Alexei G. *Stakhanov* †1977 Russ. miner] (1935) : a Soviet industrial worker awarded recognition and special privileges for output beyond production norms — **Sta·kha·nov·ism** \-ˌvi-zəm\ *n* — **Stakhanovite** *adj*

sta·lac·tite \stə-ˈlak-ˌtīt *also* ˈsta-lək-\ *n* [NL *stalactites,* fr. Gk *stalaktos* dripping, fr. *stalassein* to let drip] (1677) : a deposit of calcium carbonate (as calcite) resembling an icicle hanging from the roof or sides of a cave — **sta·lac·tit·ic** \ˌsta-(ˌ)lak-ˈti-tik, stə-\ *adj*

sta·lag \ˈstä-ˌläg\ *n* [G, short for *Stammlager* base camp, fr. *Stamm* base + *Lager* camp] (1940) : a German prison camp for noncommissioned officers or enlisted men; *broadly* : PRISON CAMP 2

sta·lag·mite \stə-ˈlag-ˌmīt *also* ˈsta-ləg-\ *n* [NL *stalagmites,* fr. Gk *stalagma* drop or *stalagmos* dripping, fr. *stalassein* to let drip] (1681) : a deposit of calcium carbonate like an inverted stalactite formed on the floor of a cave by the drip of calcareous water — **sta·lag·mit·ic** \ˌsta-(ˌ)lag-ˈmi-tik, stə-\ *adj*

[1]**stale** \ˈstāl\ *adj* **stal·er; stal·est** [ME, settled, clear (of ale), not fresh, fr. AF *estale,* prob. fr. MD *stel* old (of beer)] (15c) **1** : tasteless or unpalatable from age ⟨~ bread⟩ **2** : tedious from familiarity ⟨a ~ routine⟩ **3** : impaired in legal force or effect by reason of being allowed

to rest without timely use, action, or demand ⟨a ~ affidavit⟩ ⟨a ~ debt⟩ **4 :** impaired in vigor or effectiveness — **stale·ly** \ˈstāl-lē\ *adv* — **stale·ness** *n*

[2]**stale** *vb* **staled; stal·ing** *vt* (1599) **1 :** to make stale **2** *archaic* **:** to make common **:** CHEAPEN ~ *vi* **:** to become stale

[3]**stale** *vi* **staled; stal·ing** [ME; akin to MLG *stallen* to urinate, *stal* urine of horses] (15c) **:** URINATE — used chiefly of camels and horses

[4]**stale** *n* (1548) **:** urine of a domestic animal (as a horse)

[1]**stale·mate** \ˈstāl-ˌmāt\ *n* [obs. E *stale* stalemate (fr. ME, fr. AF *estaler* to stalemate, fr. *estal* station, position) + E [1]*mate* — more at INSTALLMENT] (1765) **1 :** a drawing position in chess in which a player is not in checkmate but has no legal move to play **2 :** a drawn contest **:** DEADLOCK; *also* **:** the state of being stalemated

[2]**stalemate** *vt* (1765) **:** to bring into a stalemate

Sta·lin·ism \ˈstä-lə-ˌni-zəm, ˈsta-\ *n* (1927) **:** the political, economic, and social principles and policies associated with Stalin; *esp* **:** the theory and practice of communism developed by Stalin from Marxism-Leninism and marked esp. by rigid authoritarianism, widespread use of terror, and often emphasis on Russian nationalism — **Sta·lin·ist** \-nist\ *n or adj* — **Sta·lin·ize** \-ˌnīz\ *vt* — **Sta·lin·oid** \-ˌnȯid\ *n or adj*

[1]**stalk** \ˈstȯk\ *n* [ME *stalke;* akin to OE *stela* stalk, support] (14c) **1 :** a slender upright object or supporting or connecting part; *esp* **:** PEDUNCLE **2 a :** the main stem of an herbaceous plant often with its dependent parts **b :** a part of a plant (as a petiole or stipe) that supports another — **stalked** \ˈstȯkt\ *adj* — **stalk·less** \ˈstȯ-kləs\ *adj* — **stalky** \ˈstȯ-kē\ *adj*

[2]**stalk** *vb* [ME, fr. OE be*stealcian;* akin to OE *stelan* to steal — more at STEAL] *vi* (14c) **1 :** to pursue quarry or prey stealthily **2 :** to walk stiffly or haughtily ~ *vt* **1 :** to pursue by stalking **2 :** to go through (an area) in search of prey or quarry ⟨~ the woods for deer⟩ **3 :** to pursue obsessively and to the point of harassment — **stalk·er** *n*

[3]**stalk** *n* (14c) **1 :** the act of stalking **2 :** a stalking gait

stalk·e·raz·zo \ˌstȯ-kə-ˈrät-(ˌ)sō\ *n, pl* **-raz·zi** [blend of *stalker* and *paparazzo*] (1995) **:** a freelance photographer or videographer who aggressively stalks celebrities for candid photographs or videos

stalk·ing horse \ˈstȯ-kiŋ-\ *n* (1519) **1 :** a horse or a figure like a horse behind which a hunter stalks game **2 :** something used to mask a purpose **3 :** a candidate put forward to divide the opposition or to conceal someone's real candidacy

[1]**stall** \ˈstȯl\ *n* [ME, fr. OE *steall;* akin to OHG *stal* place, stall and perh. to L *locus* (OL *stlocus*) place] (bef. 12c) **1 a :** a compartment for a domestic animal in a stable or barn **b :** a space marked off for parking a motor vehicle **2 a :** a seat in the chancel of a church with back and sides wholly or partly enclosed **b :** a church pew **c** *chiefly Brit* **:** a front orchestra seat in a theater — usu. used in pl. **3 :** a booth, stand, or counter at which articles are displayed for sale **4 :** a protective sheath for a finger or toe **5 :** a small compartment ⟨a shower ~⟩; *esp* **:** one with a toilet or urinal

[2]**stall** *vt* (14c) **1 :** to put into or keep in a stall **2** *obs* **:** INSTALL 1 **3 a :** to bring to a standstill **:** BLOCK; *esp* **:** MIRE **b :** to cause (an engine) to stop usu. inadvertently **c :** to cause (an aircraft or airfoil) to go into a stall ~ *vi* **1 :** to come to a standstill (as from mired wheels or engine failure) **2 :** to experience a stall in flying

[3]**stall** *n* (1916) **:** the condition of an airfoil or aircraft in which excessive angle of attack causes disruption of airflow with attendant loss of lift

[4]**stall** *n* [alter. of *stale* lure] (1846) **:** a ruse to deceive or delay

[5]**stall** *vi* [[4]*stall*] (1903) **:** to play for time **:** DELAY ~ *vt* **:** to hold off, divert, or delay by evasion or deception

stall–feed \ˈstȯl-ˌfēd\ *vt* **-fed** \-ˌfed\; **-feed·ing** (1554) **:** to feed in a stall esp. so as to fatten ⟨~ an ox⟩

stall·hold·er \-ˌhōl-dər\ *n* (1881) *chiefly Brit* **:** one who manages a stall at which articles are sold

stal·lion \ˈstal-yən\ *n* [ME *staloun, stalion,* fr. AF *estaloun,* of Gmc origin; akin to OHG *stal* stall] (14c) **:** an uncastrated male horse **:** a male horse kept for breeding; *also* **:** a male animal (as a dog or a sheep) kept primarily as a stud

[1]**stal·wart** \ˈstȯl-wərt\ *adj* [ME, alter. of *stalworth,* fr. OE *stǣlwierthe* serviceable] (15c) **:** marked by outstanding strength and vigor of body, mind, or spirit ⟨~ common sense⟩ *syn* see STRONG — **stal·wart·ly** *adv* — **stal·wart·ness** *n*

[2]**stalwart** *n* (15c) **1 :** a stalwart person **2 :** an unwavering partisan

stal·worth \ˈstȯl-(ˌ)wərth\ *archaic var of* STALWART

sta·men \ˈstā-mən\ *n, pl* **stamens** *also* **sta·mi·na** \ˈstā-mə-nə, ˈsta-\ [L, warp, thread, fr. *stare* to stand — more at STAND] (1668) **:** a microsporophyll of a seed plant; *specif* **:** the pollen-producing male organ of a flower that consists of an anther and a filament — see FLOWER illustration

stamin- *comb form* [L *stamin-, stamen*] **:** stamen ⟨*stamin*odium⟩

stam·i·na \ˈsta-mə-nə\ *n* [L, pl. of *stamen* warp, thread of life spun by the Fates] (1726) **:** STAYING POWER, ENDURANCE

sta·mi·nate \ˈstā-mə-nət, ˈsta-, -ˌnāt\ *adj* (ca. 1850) **1 :** having or producing stamens **2** *of a diclinous flower* **:** having stamens but no pistils

sta·mi·no·di·um \ˌstā-mə-ˈnō-dē-əm, ˌsta-\ *n, pl* **-dia** \-dē-ə\ [NL, fr. *stamin-* + *-odium* thing resembling, fr. Gk *-ōdēs* like] (ca. 1821) **:** an abortive or sterile stamen

stam·mel \ˈsta-məl\ *n* [prob. fr. *stamin* a woolen fabric] (1530) **1** *obs* **:** a coarse woolen clothing fabric usu. dyed red and used sometimes for undershirts of penitents **2** *archaic* **:** the bright red color of stammel

stam·mer \ˈsta-mər\ *vb* **stam·mered; stam·mer·ing** \ˈsta-mə-riŋ, ˈstam-riŋ\ [ME *stameren,* fr. OE *stamerian;* akin to OHG *stamalōn* to stammer, ON *stemma* to hinder, damn up — more at STEM] *vi* (bef. 12c) **:** to make involuntary stops and repetitions in speaking ~ *vt* **:** to utter with involuntary stops or repetitions — **stammer** *n* — **stam·mer·er** \-mər-ər\ *n*

[1]**stamp** \ˈstamp; *vt2a & vi2 are also* ˈstämp *or* ˈstȯmp\ *vb* [ME; akin to OHG *stampfōn* to stamp and perh. to Gk *stembein* to shake up] *vt* (13c) **1 :** to pound or crush with a pestle or a heavy instrument **2 a** (1) **:** to strike or beat forcibly with the bottom of the foot (2) **:** to bring down (the foot) forcibly **b :** to extinguish or destroy by or as if by stamping with the foot — usu. used with *out* ⟨~ out cancer⟩ **3 a :** IMPRESS, IMPRINT ⟨~ "paid" on the bill⟩ **b :** to attach a stamp to **4 :** to cut out, bend, or form with a stamp or die **5 a :** to provide with a distinctive character ⟨~*ed* with a dreary, institutionalized look —Bernard Taper⟩ **b :** CHARACTERIZE ⟨~*ed* as honest women —W. M. Thackeray⟩ ~ *vi* **1 :** POUND 1 **2 :** to strike the foot forcibly or noisily downward

[2]**stamp** *n* (15c) **1 :** a device or instrument for stamping **2 :** the impression or mark made by stamping or imprinting **3 a :** a distinctive character, indication, or mark **b :** a lasting imprint **4 :** the act of stamping **5 :** a stamped or printed paper affixed in evidence that a tax has been paid; *also* **:** POSTAGE STAMP — **stamp·less** *adj*

[1]**stam·pede** \(ˌ)stam-ˈpēd\ *n* [AmerSp *estampida,* fr. Sp, crash, fr. *estampar* to stamp, of Gmc origin; akin to OHG *stampfōn* to stamp] (1828) **1 :** a wild headlong rush or flight of frightened animals **2 :** a mass movement of people at a common impulse **3 :** an extended festival combining a rodeo with exhibitions, contests, and social events

[2]**stampede** *vb* **stam·ped·ed; stam·ped·ing** *vt* (1838) **1 :** to cause to run away in headlong panic **2 :** to cause (as a group of people) to act on sudden or rash impulse ~ *vi* **1 :** to flee headlong in panic **2 :** to act on mass impulse — **stam·ped·er** *n*

stamp·er \ˈstam-pər, ˈstäm-, ˈstȯm-; *compare* [1]STAMP\ *n* (14c) **:** one that stamps: as **a :** a worker who performs an industrial stamping operation **b :** an implement for pounding or stamping **c :** any of various stamping machines

stamping ground \ˈstam-piŋ, ˈstäm-, ˈstȯm-\ *n* (1786) **:** STOMPING GROUND

stamp mill \ˈstamp-\ *n* (1749) **:** a mill in which ore is crushed with stamps; *also* **:** a machine for stamping ore

stamp tax *n* (1764) **:** a tax collected by means of a stamp purchased and affixed (as to a deck of playing cards); *specif* **:** such a tax on a document (as a deed or promissory note) — called also *stamp duty*

stance \ˈstan(t)s\ *n* [ME *stance, staunce,* fr. MF *estance* position, posture, stay, fr. OF, fr. VL **stantia,* fr. L *stant-, stans,* prp. of *stare* to stand] (14c) **1** *chiefly Scot* **a :** STATION **b :** SITE **2 a :** a way of standing or being placed **:** POSTURE **b :** intellectual or emotional attitude ⟨took an antiwar ~⟩ **3 a :** the position of the feet of a golfer or batter preparatory to making a swing **b :** the position of both body and feet from which an athlete starts or operates

[1]**stanch** \ˈstȯnch, ˈstänch, ˈstanch\ *or* **staunch** \ˈstȯnch, ˈstänch\ *vt* [ME *staunchen,* fr. AF *estancher,* perh. fr. VL **stanticare,* fr. L *stant-, stans,* prp.] (14c) **1 :** to check or stop the flowing of ⟨~*ed* her tears⟩; *also* **:** to stop the flow of blood from (a wound) **2** *archaic* **:** ALLAY, EXTINGUISH **3 a :** to stop or check in its course ⟨trying to ~ the crime wave⟩ **b :** to make watertight **:** stop up — **stanch·er** *n*

[2]**stanch** *var of* [2]STAUNCH

stan·chion \ˈstan-chən\ *n* [ME *stanchon,* fr. AF **stanchun, stançun,* alter. of OF *estançon,* dim. of *estance* stay, prop] (15c) **1 :** an upright bar, post, or support (as for a roof or a ship's deck) **2 :** a device that fits loosely around the neck of an animal (as a cow) and limits forward and backward motion (as in a stall) — **stan·chioned** \-chənd\ *adj*

[1]**stand** \ˈstand\ *vb* **stood** \ˈstu̇d\; **stand·ing** [ME, fr. OE *standan;* akin to OHG *stantan, stān* to stand, L *stare,* Gk *histanai* to cause to stand, set, *histasthai* to stand, be standing] *vi* (bef. 12c) **1 a :** to support oneself on the feet in an erect position **b :** to be a specified height when fully erect ⟨~*s* six feet two⟩ **c :** to rise to an erect position **2 a :** to take up or maintain a specified position or posture ⟨~ aside⟩ ⟨can you ~ on your head⟩ **b :** to maintain one's position ⟨~ firm⟩ **3 :** to be in a particular state or situation ⟨~*s* accused⟩ **4 :** to hold a course at sea **5** *obs* **:** HESITATE **6 a :** to have or maintain a relative position in or as if in a graded scale ⟨~*s* first in the class⟩ **b :** to be in a position to gain or lose because of an action taken or a commitment made ⟨~*s* to make quite a profit⟩ **7** *chiefly Brit* **:** to be a candidate **:** RUN **8 a :** to rest or remain upright on a base or lower end ⟨a clock *stood* on the mantle⟩ **b :** to occupy a place or location ⟨the house ~*s* on a knoll⟩ **9 a :** to remain stationary or inactive ⟨the car *stood* in the garage for a week⟩ **b :** to gather slowly and remain ⟨tears ~*ing* in her eyes⟩ **10 :** AGREE, ACCORD — used chiefly in the expression *it stands to reason* **11 a :** to exist in a definite written or printed form ⟨copy a passage exactly as it ~*s*⟩ **b :** to remain valid or efficacious ⟨the order given last week still ~*s*⟩ **12** *of a male animal* **:** to be available as a sire — used esp. of horses **13 :** to refuse additional cards (as in blackjack) ~ *vt* **1 a :** to endure or undergo successfully ⟨this book will ~ the test of time⟩ **b :** to tolerate without flinching **:** bear courageously ⟨~*s* pain well⟩ **c :** to endure the presence or personality of ⟨can't ~ the boss⟩ **d :** to derive benefit or enjoyment from ⟨you look like you could ~ a drink⟩ **2 :** to remain firm in the face of ⟨~ a siege⟩ **3 :** to submit to ⟨~ trial⟩ **4 a :** to perform the duty of ⟨~ guard⟩ **b :** to participate in (a military formation) **5 :** to pay the cost of (a treat) **:** pay for ⟨I'll ~ you a dinner⟩ ⟨~ drinks⟩ **6 :** to cause to stand **:** set upright **7 :** to make available for breeding ⟨~ a stallion⟩ *syn* see BEAR — **stand·er** *n* — **stand a chance :** to have a chance — **stand for 1 :** to be a symbol for **:** REPRESENT **2 :** to put up with **:** PERMIT — **stand on 1 :** to depend on **2 :** to insist on ⟨never *stands on* ceremony⟩ — **stand one's ground :** to maintain one's position — **stand on one's own feet :** to think or act independently — **stand tall :** to exhibit courage, strength, or calm esp. in the face of adversity — **stand treat :** to pay the cost of food, drink, or entertainment for others in a group

[2]**stand** *n* (1590) **1 a :** a halt for defense or resistance **b :** an often defensive effort of some duration or degree of success ⟨a goal-line ~⟩ **c** (1) **:** a stop made to give a performance ⟨a 6-game ~ at home⟩ (2) **:** a town where such a stop is made **2 :** an act of stopping or staying in one place **3 a :** a place or post where one stands **b :** a strongly or aggressively held position esp. on a debatable issue ⟨took a ~ against higher taxes⟩ **4 a :** the place taken by a witness for testifying in court **b** *pl* (1) **:** a section of the tiered seats for spectators of a sport or spectacle (2) **:** the occupants of such seats **c :** a raised platform (as for a speaker or hunter) serving as a point of vantage **5 a :** a small often open-air structure for a small retail business ⟨a vegetable ~⟩ ⟨a hot dog ~⟩ **b :** a site fit for business opportunity **6 :** a place where a passenger vehicle stops or parks ⟨a taxi ~⟩ **7 :** HIVE 2 **8 :** a frame on or in which something may be placed for support **9 :** a group of plants growing in a continuous area **10 :** a standing posture

stand–alone \ˈstand-ə-ˈlōn\ *adj* (1966) : SELF-CONTAINED; *esp* : operating or capable of operating independently of a computer system ⟨a ~ word processor⟩

1**stan·dard** \ˈstan-dərd\ *n* [ME, fr. AF *estandard* banner, standard, of Gmc origin; akin to OE *standan* to stand and prob. to OHG *hart* hard] (12c) **1** : a conspicuous object (as a banner) formerly carried at the top of a pole and used to mark a rallying point esp. in battle or to serve as an emblem **2 a** : a long narrow tapering flag that is personal to an individual or corporation and bears heraldic devices **b** : the personal flag of the head of a state or of a member of a royal family **c** : an organization flag carried by a mounted or motorized military unit **d** : BANNER 1 **3** : something established by authority, custom, or general consent as a model or example : CRITERION ⟨quite slow by today's ~*s*⟩ **4** : something set up and established by authority as a rule for the measure of quantity, weight, extent, value, or quality **5 a** : the fineness and legally fixed weight of the metal used in coins **b** : the basis of value in a monetary system ⟨the gold ~⟩ **6** : a structure built for or serving as a base or support **7 a** : a shrub or herb grown with an erect main stem so that it forms or resembles a tree **b** : a fruit tree grafted on a stock that does not induce dwarfing **8 a** : the large odd upper petal of a papilionaceous flower (as of the pea) **b** : one of the three inner usu. erect and incurved petals of an iris **9** : a musical composition (as a song) that has become a part of the standard repertoire — **stan·dard·less** *adj*

syn STANDARD, CRITERION, GAUGE, YARDSTICK, TOUCHSTONE mean a means of determining what a thing should be. STANDARD applies to any definite rule, principle, or measure established by authority ⟨*standards* of behavior⟩. CRITERION may apply to anything used as a test of quality whether formulated as a rule or principle or not ⟨questioned the critic's *criteria* for excellence⟩. GAUGE applies to a means of testing a particular dimension (as thickness, depth, diameter) or figuratively a particular quality or aspect ⟨polls as a *gauge* of voter dissatisfaction⟩. YARDSTICK is an informal substitute for CRITERION that suggests quantity more often than quality ⟨housing construction as a *yardstick* of economic growth⟩. TOUCHSTONE suggests a simple test of the authenticity or value of something intangible ⟨fine service is one *touchstone* of a first-class restaurant⟩.

2**standard** *adj* (1567) **1 a** : constituting or conforming to a standard esp. as established by law or custom ⟨~ weight⟩ **b** : sound and usable but not of top quality ⟨~ beef⟩ **2 a** : regularly and widely used, available, or supplied ⟨~ automobile equipment⟩ **b** : well-established and very familiar ⟨the ~ opera⟩ **3** : having recognized and permanent value ⟨a ~ reference work⟩ **4** : substantially uniform and well established by usage in the speech and writing of the educated and widely recognized as acceptable ⟨~ pronunciation is subject to regional variations⟩ — **stan·dard·ly** *adv*

stan·dard–bear·er \ˈstan-dərd-ˌber-ər\ *n* (15c) **1** : one who bears a standard or banner **2** : one that leads an organization, movement, or party ⟨a ~ for political reform⟩

stan·dard·bred \-ˌbred\ *n, often cap* (1921) : any of a breed of trotting and pacing horses developed in the U.S., noted for speed and stamina, and used esp. in harness racing

standard candle *n* (1879) : CANDELA

standard deviation *n* (1894) **1** : a measure of the dispersion of a frequency distribution that is the square root of the arithmetic mean of the squares of the deviation of each of the class frequencies from the arithmetic mean of the frequency distribution; *also* : a similar quantity found by dividing by one less than the number of squares in the sum of squares instead of taking the arithmetic mean **2** : a parameter that indicates the way in which a probability function or a probability density function is centered around its mean and that is equal to the square root of the moment in which the deviation from the mean is squared

Standard English *n* (1836) : the English that with respect to spelling, grammar, pronunciation, and vocabulary is substantially uniform though not devoid of regional differences, that is well established by usage in the formal and informal speech and writing of the educated, and that is widely recognized as acceptable wherever English is spoken and understood

standard error *n* (1897) : the standard deviation of the probability function or probability density function of a random variable and esp. of a statistic; *specif* : the standard error of the mean of a sample from a population with a normal distribution that is equal to the standard deviation of the normal distribution divided by the square root of the sample size

standard gauge *n* (1871) : a railroad gauge of 4 feet 8½ inches (1435 millimeters)

stan·dard·ise *Brit var of* STANDARDIZE

stan·dard–is·sue \ˈstan-dərd-ˈi-(ˌ)shü\ *adj* (1976) : STANDARD, TYPICAL ⟨a ~ action movie⟩ ⟨a ~ blue suit⟩

stan·dard·ize \ˈstan-dər-ˌdīz\ *vt* **-ized; -iz·ing** (1873) **1** : to compare with a standard **2** : to bring into conformity with a standard — **stan·dard·i·za·tion** \ˌstan-dər-də-ˈzā-shən\ *n*

standard of living (1902) **1** : the necessities, comforts, and luxuries enjoyed or aspired to by an individual or group **2** : a minimum of necessities, comforts, or luxuries held essential to maintaining a person or group in customary or proper status or circumstances

standard operating procedure *n* (1952) : established or prescribed methods to be followed routinely for the performance of designated operations or in designated situations — called also *standing operating procedure*

standard position *n* (1950) : the position of an angle with its vertex at the origin of a rectangular-coordinate system and its initial side coinciding with the positive x-axis

standard schnauzer *n* (ca. 1934) : any of a breed of medium-sized schnauzers that attain a height at the highest point of the shoulder blades of about 18 to 20 inches (46 to 51 centimeters) and have a salt-and-pepper or black coat

standard score *n* (1921) : an individual test score expressed as the deviation from the mean score of the group in units of standard deviation

standard time *n* (1879) : the time of a region or country that is established by law or general usage as civil time; *specif* : the mean solar time of a meridian that is a multiple of 15 arbitrarily applied to a local area or to one of the 24 time zones and designated as a number of hours earlier or later than Greenwich time

stand·away \ˈstan-də-ˌwā\ *adj* (1948) : standing out from the body ⟨a ~ skirt⟩

1**stand·by** \ˈstan(d)-ˌbī\ *n, pl* **stand·bys** \-ˌbīz\ (1796) **1 a** : one to be relied on esp. in emergencies **b** : a favorite or reliable choice or resource **2** : one that is held in reserve ready for use : SUBSTITUTE — **on standby** : ready or available for immediate action or use

2**standby** *adj* (1872) **1** : held near at hand and ready for use ⟨a ~ power plant⟩ ⟨~ equipment⟩ **2** : relating to the act or condition of standing by ⟨~ duty⟩ ⟨a ~ period⟩ **3** : of, relating to, or traveling by an airline service in which the passenger must wait for an available unreserved seat ⟨~ passengers⟩ ⟨a ~ ticket⟩

3**standby** *adv* (1971) : on a standby basis ⟨fly ~⟩

stand by *vi* (13c) **1** : to be present; *also* : to remain apart or aloof **2** : to be or to get ready to act ⟨an ambulance was *standing by*⟩ ~ *vt* : to remain loyal or faithful to : DEFEND ⟨*stood by* his decision⟩

stand–down \ˈstan(d)-ˌdau̇n\ *n* (ca. 1919) : a relaxation of status of a military unit or force from an alert or operational posture

stand down *vi* (1681) **1** : to leave the witness stand **2** *chiefly Brit* **a** : to go off duty **b** : to withdraw from a contest, a position of leadership, or a state of alert or readiness ~ *vt* : to remove (as a military unit) from active duty

stand·ee \stan-ˈdē\ *n* (1856) : a standing person : one who occupies standing room

stand–in \ˈstand-ˌin\ *n* (ca. 1928) **1** : someone employed to occupy an actor's place while lights and camera are readied **2** : SUBSTITUTE

stand in *vi* (1904) : to act as a stand-in — **stand in with** : to be in a specially favored position with

1**stand·ing** \ˈstan-diŋ\ *adj* (14c) **1 a** : not yet cut or harvested ⟨~ timber⟩ ⟨~ grain⟩ **b** : upright on the feet or base : ERECT ⟨the ~ audience⟩ **2** : not flowing : STAGNANT ⟨~ water⟩ **3 a** : remaining at the same level, degree, or amount for an indeterminate period ⟨a ~ offer⟩ **b** : continuing in existence or use indefinitely ⟨a ~ joke⟩ **4** : established by law or custom **5** : not movable **6** : done from a standing position ⟨a ~ jump⟩ ⟨a ~ ovation⟩

2**standing** *n* (15c) **1 a** : a place to stand in : LOCATION **b** : a position from which one may assert or enforce legal rights and duties **2 a** : length of service or experience esp. as determining rank, pay, or privilege **b** : position or condition in society or in a profession; *esp* : good reputation ⟨a member in good ~⟩ **c** : position relative to a standard of achievement or to achievements of competitors; *also, pl* : a listing of the standings of individuals or teams (as in a league) **3** : maintenance of position or condition : DURATION ⟨a custom of long ~⟩

standing army *n* (1603) : a permanent army of paid soldiers

standing committee *n* (ca. 1636) : a permanent committee esp. of a legislative body

standing crop *n* (1861) : the total amount or number of living things or of one kind of living thing (as an uncut farm crop, the fish in a pond, or organisms in an ecosystem) in a particular area at any given time

standing O \-ˈō\ *n* [*o*vation] (1975) : a standing ovation

standing order *n* (1737) : an instruction or prescribed procedure in force permanently or until changed or canceled; *esp* : any of the rules for the guidance and government of parliamentary procedure which endure through successive sessions until vacated or repealed

standing room *n* (1603) : space for standing; *esp* : accommodation available for spectators or passengers after all seats are filled

standing wave *n* (1896) : a single-frequency mode of vibration of a body or physical system in which the amplitude varies from place to place, is constantly zero at fixed points, and has maxima at other points

stan·dish \ˈstan-dish\ *n* [ME *staundys, standyshe*] (14c) : a stand for writing materials : INKSTAND

1**stand·off** \ˈstand-ˌȯf\ *n* (ca. 1835) **1 a** : TIE, DEADLOCK ⟨the two teams played to a ~⟩ **b** : a counterbalancing effect **2** : the act of standing off

2**standoff** *adj* (1837) **1** : STANDOFFISH **2** : used for holding something at a distance from a surface ⟨a ~ insulator⟩

stand off *vi* (1603) **1** : to stay at a distance from something **2** : to sail away from the shore ~ *vt* **1** : to keep from advancing : REPEL **2** : PUT OFF, STALL

stand·off·ish \stand-ˈȯ-fish\ *adj* (1860) : somewhat cold and reserved — **stand·off·ish·ly** *adv* — **stand·off·ish·ness** *n*

stand oil *n* (1908) : a thickened drying oil; *esp* : linseed oil heated to about 600° F (315° C)

stand·out \ˈstand-ˌau̇t\ *n, often attrib* (1928) : one that is prominent or conspicuous esp. because of excellence

stand out *vi* (14c) **1 a** : to appear as if in relief : PROJECT **b** : to be prominent or conspicuous ⟨*stands out* from the crowd⟩ **2** : to steer away from shore **3** : to be stubborn in resolution or resistance

stand·pat \ˈstan(d)-ˈpat\ *adj* (1904) : stubbornly conservative : resisting or opposing change

stand pat *vi* [4*pat*] (1882) **1** : to play one's hand as dealt in draw poker without drawing **2** : to oppose or resist change — **stand·pat·ter** \ˈstan(d)-ˌpa-tər, -ˈpa-tər\ *n* — **stand·pat·tism** \-ˌpa-ˌti-zəm\ *n*

stand·pipe \ˈstan(d)-ˌpīp\ *n* (ca. 1850) : a high vertical pipe or reservoir that is used to secure a uniform pressure in a water-supply system

stand·point \-ˌpȯint\ *n* (1829) : a position from which objects or principles are viewed and according to which they are compared and judged

stand·still \-ˌstil\ *n* (1702) : a state characterized by absence of motion or of progress : STOP ⟨brought traffic to a ~⟩

1**stand–up** \ˈstand-ˌəp\ *adj* (1812) **1 a** : ERECT, UPRIGHT **b** : stiffened to stay upright without folding over ⟨a ~ collar⟩ **2** : performed in, performing in, or requiring a standing position ⟨a ~ bar⟩; *esp* : of, relating to, performing, or being a monologue of jokes, gags, or satirical comments delivered usu. while standing alone on a stage or in front of a camera ⟨~ comedy⟩ ⟨a ~ comedian⟩ **3** : marked by a high degree of personal integrity or loyalty ⟨a ~ guy⟩

2**stand–up** *n* (1971) **1** : stand-up comedy; *also* : a performer of such comedy **2** : a television broadcast in which the reporter or narrator faces the camera with the scene of the story in the background

stand up *vi* (bef. 12c) **1** : to rise to a standing position **2** : to remain sound and intact under stress, attack, or close scrutiny ~ *vt* : to fail to keep an appointment with — **stand up for** : to defend against attack or criticism — **stand up to** **1** : to meet fairly and fully **2** : to face boldly — **stand up with** : to be best man or maid of honor for at a wedding ceremony

stand–up·per \ˈstand-ˈə-pər\ *n* (1973) : STAND-UP 2
stane \ˈstān\ *Scot var of* STONE
Stan·ford–Bi·net test \ˌstan-fərd-bi-ˈnā-\ *n* [*Stanford* University + Alfred *Binet* †1911 Fr. psychologist] (1918) : an intelligence test prepared at Stanford University as a revision of the Binet-Simon scale and commonly used with children — called also *Stanford-Binet*
[1]**stang** \ˈstaŋ\ *vt* [ME, fr. ON *stanga* to prick; akin to ON *stinga* to sting] (14c) *chiefly Scot* : STING
[2]**stang** *n* (1513) *chiefly Scot* : PANG
stan·hope \ˈsta-nəp\ *n* [Fitzroy *Stanhope* †1864 Brit. clergyman] (1821) : a gig, buggy, or phaeton typically having a high seat and closed back
sta·nine \ˈstā-ˌnīn\ *n* [*sta*ndard (score) + *nine*] (1944) : any of the nine classes into which a set of normalized standard scores arranged according to rank in educational testing are divided, which include the bottom 4 percent and the top 4 percent of the scores in the first and ninth classes and the middle 20 percent in the fifth, and which have a standard deviation of 2 and a mean of 5
Sta·ni·slav·ski method \ˌsta-nə-ˈslaf-ski-, -ˈslav-, -ˈsläf-, -ˈsläv-\ *n* [Konstantin *Stanislavsky*] (1941) : a technique in acting by which an actor strives to empathize with the character being portrayed so as to effect a realistic interpretation
[1]**stank** *past of* STINK
[2]**stank** \ˈstaŋk\ *n* [ME, fr. AF *estank, stanc,* fr. *estancher* to dam up, stanch — more at STANCH] (14c) **1** *dial Brit* **a** : POND, POOL **b** : a ditch containing water **2** *Brit* : a small dam : WEIR
stan·na·ry \ˈsta-nə-rē\ *n, pl* **-ries** [ME *stannarie,* fr. ML *stannaria* tin mine, fr. LL *stannum* tin] (15c) : any of the regions in England containing establishments for the working of tin — usu. used in pl.
stan·nic \ˈsta-nik\ *adj* [prob. fr. F *stannique,* fr. LL *stannum* tin, fr. L *stagnum,* an alloy of silver and lead] (1790) : of, relating to, or containing tin esp. with a valence of four
stan·nite \ˈsta-ˌnīt\ *n* [LL *stannum*] (1868) : a metallic black or gray mineral that is a sulfide of copper, iron, and tin
stan·nous \ˈsta-nəs\ *adj* [ISV, fr. LL *stannum*] (1849) : of, relating to, or containing tin esp. with a valence of two
sta·nol \ˈsta-ˌnȯl, ˈstā-\ *n* [*-stane* (as in *cholestane,* a saturated derivative of cholesterol, fr. *cholest*erol + *-ane*) + *sterol*] (1949) : any of the fully saturated phytosterols
stan·za \ˈstan-zə\ *n* [It, stay, abode, room, stanza, fr. VL **stantia* stay — more at STANCE] (1589) : a division of a poem consisting of a series of lines arranged together in a usu. recurring pattern of meter and rhyme : STROPHE — **stan·za·ic** \stan-ˈzā-ik\ *adj*
sta·pe·dec·to·my \ˌstā-pi-ˈdek-tə-mē\ *n, pl* **-mies** [ISV, fr. NL *staped-, stapes*] (1894) : surgical removal and prosthetic replacement of part or all of the stapes to relieve deafness
sta·pe·di·al \stā-ˈpē-dē-əl, stə-\ *adj* (ca. 1859) : of, relating to, or located near the stapes
sta·pe·lia \stə-ˈpēl-yə\ *n* [NL, fr. J. B. van *Stapel* †1636 Du. botanist] (1776) : any of a genus (*Stapelia*) of chiefly African perennial herbs of the milkweed family with succulent typically leafless toothed stems and showy but usu. putrid-smelling star-shaped flowers
sta·pes \ˈstā-(ˌ)pēz\ *n, pl* **stapes** *or* **sta·pe·des** \ˈstā-pə-ˌdēz\ [NL *staped-, stapes,* fr. ML, stirrup, alter. of LL *stapia*] (1615) : the innermost ossicle of the middle ear of mammals — called also *stirrup;* see EAR illustration
staph \ˈstaf\ *n* (ca. 1933) : STAPHYLOCOCCUS
staph·y·li·nid \ˌsta-fə-ˈlī-nəd\ *n* [NL *Staphylinidae,* ultim. fr. Gk *staphylē* bunch of grapes] (1862) : ROVE BEETLE — **staphylinid** *adj*
staph·y·lo·coc·cal \ˌsta-f(ə-)lō-ˈkä-kəl\ *also* **staph·y·lo·coc·cic** \-ˈkä-kik, -ˈkäk-sik\ *adj* (1900) : of, relating to, caused by, or being a staphylococcus
staph·y·lo·coc·cus \-ˈkä-kəs\ *n, pl* **-coc·ci** \-ˈkä-ˌkī, -(ˌ)kē; -ˈkäk-ˌsī, -(ˌ)sē\ [NL, fr. Gk *staphylē* bunch of grapes + NL *-coccus*] (1887) : any of a genus (*Staphylococcus*) of nonmotile gram-positive spherical bacteria that occur singly, in pairs or tetrads, or in irregular clusters and include causative agents of various diseases (as skin infections, food poisoning, and endocarditis)
[1]**sta·ple** \ˈstā-pəl\ *n* [ME *stapel* post, staple, fr. OE *stapol* post; akin to MD *stapel* step, heap, emporium, OE *steppan* to step] (13c) : a usu. U-shaped fastener: as **a** : a metal loop both ends of which are driven into a surface to hold the hook, hasp, or bolt of a lock, secure a rope, or fix a wire in place **b** : a small wire both ends of which are driven through layers of thin and easily penetrable material (as paper) and usu. clinched to hold the layers together **c** : a usu. metal surgical fastener used to hold layers of tissue together (as in the closure of an incision)
[2]**staple** *vt* **sta·pled; sta·pling** \-p(ə-)liŋ\ (14c) : to provide with or secure by staples
[3]**staple** *n* [ME, fr. AF *estaple,* fr. MD *stapel* emporium] (15c) **1** : a town used as a center for the sale or exportation of commodities in bulk **2** : a place of supply : SOURCE **3** : a chief commodity or production of a place **4 a** : a commodity for which the demand is constant **b** : something having widespread and constant use or appeal **c** : the sustaining or principal element : SUBSTANCE **5** : RAW MATERIAL **6 a** : textile fiber (as wool and rayon) of relatively short length that when spun and twisted forms a yarn rather than a filament **b** : the length of a piece of such textile fiber
[4]**staple** *adj* (1615) **1** : used, needed, or enjoyed constantly usu. by many individuals **2** : produced regularly or in large quantities ⟨~ crops such as wheat and rice⟩ **3** : PRINCIPAL, CHIEF
[1]**sta·pler** \ˈstā-p(ə-)lər\ *n* (ca. 1533) : one that deals in staple goods or in staple fiber
[2]**stapler** *n* (ca. 1909) : one that inserts staples; *esp* : a small usu. hand-operated device for inserting wire staples
[1]**star** \ˈstär\ *n, often attrib* [ME *sterre,* fr. OE *steorra;* akin to OHG *sterno* star, L *stella,* Gk *astēr, astron*] (bef. 12c) **1 a** : a natural luminous body visible in the sky esp. at night **b** : a self-luminous gaseous spheroidal celestial body of great mass which produces energy by means of nuclear fusion reactions **2 a** (1) : a planet or a configuration of the planets that is held in astrology to influence one's destiny or fortune — usu. used in pl. (2) : a waxing or waning fortune or fame ⟨her ~ was rising⟩ **b** *obs* : DESTINY **3 a** : a conventional figure with five or more points that represents a star; *esp* : ASTERISK **b** : an often star-shaped ornament or medal worn as a badge of honor, authority, or rank or as the insignia of an order **c** : one of a group of conventional stars used to place something in a scale of value **4** : something resembling a star ⟨was hit on the head and saw ~*s*⟩ **5 a** : the principal member of a theatrical or operatic company who usu. plays the chief roles **b** : a highly publicized theatrical or motion-picture performer **c** : an outstandingly talented performer ⟨a track ~⟩ **d** : a person who is preeminent in a particular field — **star·less** \-ləs\ *adj* — **star·like** \-ˌlīk\ *adj*
[2]**star** *vb* **starred; star·ring** *vt* (1718) **1** : to sprinkle or adorn with stars **2 a** : to mark with a star as being preeminent **b** : to mark with an asterisk **3** : to feature in the most prominent or important role ⟨the movie ~*s* a famous stage personality⟩ ~ *vi* **1** : to play the most prominent or important role **2** : to perform outstandingly
[3]**star** *adj* (1821) **1** : of, relating to, or being a star ⟨received ~ billing⟩ **2** : of outstanding excellence : PREEMINENT ⟨a ~ athlete⟩
star anise *n* (1838) : the small brown star-shaped pungent fruit of a Chinese and Vietnamese tree (*Illicium verum*) that has a flavor similar to but stronger than anise and is dried and used whole or ground as a spice esp. in Chinese cooking
star apple *n* (1683) : a tropical American tree (*Chrysophyllum cainito*) of the sapodilla family grown in warm regions for ornament or fruit; *also* : its usu. green to purple apple-shaped edible fruit that when cut in cross-section reveals a star-shaped pattern formed by the carpels
[1]**star·board** \ˈstär-bərd\ *n* [ME *sterbord,* fr. OE *stēorbord,* fr. *stēor-* steering oar + *bord* ship's side — more at STEER, BOARD] (bef. 12c) : the right side of a ship or aircraft looking forward — compare PORT
[2]**starboard** *adj* (15c) : of, relating to, or situated to starboard
[3]**starboard** *vt* (1598) : to turn or put (a helm or rudder) to the right
star·burst \ˈstär-ˌbərst\ *n* (1959) : something (as a pattern) that resembles diverging rays of light ⟨~*s* of color⟩
[1]**starch** \ˈstärch\ *vt* [ME *sterchen,* prob. fr. OE **stercan* to stiffen; akin to OE *stearc* stiff — more at STARK] (15c) : to stiffen with or as if with starch
[2]**starch** *n* (15c) **1** : a white odorless tasteless granular or powdery complex carbohydrate $(C_6H_{10}O_5)_x$ that is the chief storage form of carbohydrate in plants, is an important foodstuff, and is used also in adhesives and sizes, in laundering, and in pharmacy and medicine **2** : a stiff formal manner : FORMALITY **3** : resolute vigor
star–cham·ber \ˈstär-ˈchām-bər\ *adj* [*Star Chamber,* a court existing in England from the 15th century until 1641] (1788) : characterized by secrecy and often by being irresponsibly arbitrary and oppressive
starchy \ˈstär-chē\ *adj* **starch·i·er; -est** (1802) **1** : containing, consisting of, or resembling starch ⟨~ foods⟩ **2** : FORMAL, STIFF ⟨a ~ lawyer⟩ — **starch·i·ly** \-chə-lē\ *adv* — **starch·i·ness** \-chē-nəs\ *n*
star–crossed \ˈstär-ˌkrȯst\ *adj* (1595) : not favored by the stars : ILL-FATED ⟨a pair of ~ lovers take their life —Shak.⟩
star·dom \ˈstär-dəm\ *n* (1865) : the status or position of a star
star·dust \ˈstär-ˌdəst\ *n* (1927) : a feeling or impression of romance, magic, or ethereality
[1]**stare** \ˈster\ *vb* **stared; star·ing** [ME, fr. OE *starian;* akin to OHG *starēn* to stare, Gk *stereos* solid, Lith *starinti* to stiffen] *vi* (bef. 12c) **1** : to look fixedly often with wide-open eyes **2** : to show oneself conspicuously ⟨the error *stared* from the page⟩ **3** *of hair* : to stand on end : BRISTLE; *also* : to appear rough and lusterless ~ *vt* **1** : to have an effect on by staring **2** : to look at with a searching or earnest gaze — **star·er** *n* — **stare one in the face** : to be undeniably and forcefully evident or apparent
[2]**stare** *n* (15c) : the act or an instance of staring ⟨a blank ~⟩
sta·re de·ci·sis \ˌster-ē-di-ˈsī-səs, ˌstär-\ *n* [L, to stand by decided matters] (1782) : a doctrine or policy of following rules or principles laid down in previous judicial decisions unless they contravene the ordinary principles of justice
stare down *vt* (1925) : to cause to waver or submit by or as if by staring
sta·rets \ˈstär-əts, -yəts\ *n, pl* **star·tsy** \ˈstärt-sē\ [Russ, fr. *staryĭ* old — more at STOUR] (1917) : a spiritual director or religious teacher in the Eastern Orthodox Church; *specif* : a spiritual adviser who is not necessarily a priest, who is recognized for his piety, and who is turned to by monks or laymen for spiritual guidance
star facet *n* (1750) : one of the eight small triangular facets which abut on the table in the bezel of a brilliant
star·fish \ˈstär-ˌfish\ *n* (1538) : any of a class (Asteroidea) of echinoderms that have a body of usu. five arms radially arranged about a central disk and feed largely on mollusks (as oysters) — called also *sea star*
star·flow·er \-ˌflau̇(-ə)r\ *n* (1629) : any of several plants having star-shaped pentamerous flowers; *esp* : any of a genus (*Trientalis,* esp. *T. borealis*) of perennial herbs of the primrose family
star fruit *n* (1965) : CARAMBOLA 1
star·gaze \-ˌgāz\ *vi* [back-formation fr. *stargazer*] (1626) **1** : to gaze at stars **2** : to gaze raptly or contemplatively
star·gaz·er \-ˌgā-zər\ *n* (1560) **1** : one who gazes at the stars: as **a** : ASTROLOGER **b** : ASTRONOMER **2** : any of various marine bony fishes (families Uranoscopidae and Dactyloscopidae) with the eyes on top of a blocky or conical head
star·gaz·ing \-ˌgā-ziŋ\ *n* (1576) **1** : the act or practice of a stargazer **2 a** : absorption in chimerical or impractical ideas : WOOLGATHERING **b** : the quality or state of being absentminded
star grass *n* (1687) **1** : any of a genus (*Hypoxis* of the family Hypoxidaceae) of grasslike perennial herbs with small star-shaped white or yellow flowers **2** : either of two colicroots (*Aletris farinosa* and *A. aurea*)
[1]**stark** \ˈstärk\ *adj* [ME, stiff, strong, fr. OE *stearc;* akin to OHG *starc* strong, Lith *starinti* to stiffen — more at STARE] (bef. 12c) **1 a** : rigid in or as if in death **b** : rigidly conforming (as to a pattern or doctrine) : ABSOLUTE ⟨~ discipline⟩ **2** *archaic* : STRONG, ROBUST **3** : UTTER, SHEER ⟨~ nonsense⟩ **4 a** : BARREN, DESOLATE **b** (1) : having few or no ornaments : BARE ⟨a ~ white room⟩ (2) : HARSH, BLUNT ⟨the ~ realities of death⟩ **5** : sharply delineated ⟨a ~ contrast⟩ — **stark·ly** *adv* — **stark·ness** *n*

[2]**stark** *adv* (13c) **1 :** in a stark manner **2 :** to an absolute or complete degree : WHOLLY ⟨~ naked⟩ ⟨~ mad⟩
stark·ers \ˈstär-kərz\ *adj* [alter. of [1]*stark*] (ca. 1923) *chiefly Brit* : completely unclothed : NAKED
star·let \ˈstär-lət\ *n* (1920) : a young movie actress being coached and publicized for starring roles
star·light \-ˌlīt\ *n* (14c) : the light given by the stars
star·ling \ˈstär-liŋ\ *n* [ME, fr. OE *stærlinc,* fr. *stær* starling + *-ling, -linc* -ling; akin to OHG *stara* starling, L *sturnus*] (bef. 12c) : any of a family (Sturnidae, esp. genus *Sturnus*) of usu. dark gregarious oscine birds; *esp* : a dark brown or in summer glossy greenish-black European bird (*S. vulgaris*) naturalized nearly worldwide and often considered a pest
star·lit \ˈstär-ˌlit\ *adj* (1834) : lighted by the stars
star–nosed mole \ˈstär-ˌnōz(d)-\ *n* (1826) : a common black long-tailed semiaquatic mole (*Condylura cristata*) of the northeastern U.S. and adjacent Canada that has a series of pink fleshy projections surrounding the nostrils
star–of–Beth·le·hem \-ˈbeth-li-ˌhem, -lē-(h)əm\ *n* (1573) : any of various Old World bulbous herbs (genus *Ornithogalum*) of the lily family with basal leaves resembling grass; *esp* : one (*O. umbellatum*) with white star-shaped flowers that is naturalized in the eastern U.S.
star of Bethlehem (1789) : a star which according to Christian tradition guided the Magi to the infant Jesus in Bethlehem
Star of Da·vid \-ˈdā-vəd\ (ca. 1936) : MAGEN DAVID
star route *n* [fr. the asterisk used to designate such routes in postal publications] (1876) : a mail-delivery route in a rural or thinly populated area served by a private carrier under contract who takes mail from one post office to another or from a railroad station to a post office and usu. also delivers mail to private mailboxes along the route
star·ry \ˈstär-ē\ *adj* **star·ri·er; -est** (14c) **1 a :** adorned with stars; *esp* : STAR-STUDDED **b :** of, relating to, or consisting of stars : STELLAR **c :** shining like stars : SPARKLING **d :** having parts arranged like the rays of a star : STELLATE **2 :** as high as or seemingly as high as the stars ⟨~ speculations⟩ **3 :** STARRY-EYED
star·ry–eyed \ˈstär-ē-ˌīd\ *adj* (1904) : regarding an object or a prospect in an overly favorable light; *specif* : characterized by dreamy, impracticable, or utopian thinking : VISIONARY
Stars and Bars *n pl but sing in constr* (1861) : the first flag of the Confederate States of America having three bars of red, white, and red respectively and a blue union with white stars in a circle representing the seceded states
Stars and Stripes *n pl but sing in constr* (1777) : the flag of the United States having 13 alternately red and white horizontal stripes and a blue union with white stars representing the states
star sapphire *n* (1798) : a sapphire that when cut with a convex surface and polished exhibits asterism
star shell *n* (ca. 1876) **1 :** a shell that on bursting releases a shower of brilliant stars and is used for signaling **2 :** a shell with an illuminating projectile
star·ship \ˈstär-ˌship\ *n* (1934) : a spacecraft designed for interstellar travel
star–span·gled \ˈstär-ˌspaŋ-gəld\ *adj* (1591) : STAR-STUDDED
star·struck \-ˌstrək\ *adj* (1968) : particularly taken with celebrities (as movie stars)
star–stud·ded \ˈstär-ˌstə-dəd\ *adj* (1904) : abounding in or covered with stars ⟨a ~ cast⟩ ⟨a ~ uniform⟩
star system *n* (1832) : the practice of casting famous performers in principal roles (as in motion pictures or the theater) esp. in order to capitalize on their popular appeal
[1]**start** \ˈstärt\ *vb* [ME *sterten;* akin to MHG *sterzen* to stand up stiffly, move quickly] *vi* (14c) **1 a :** to move suddenly and violently : SPRING ⟨~*ed* angrily to his feet⟩ **b :** to react with a sudden brief involuntary movement ⟨~*ed* when a shot rang out⟩ **2 a :** to issue with sudden force ⟨blood ~*ing* from the wound⟩ **b :** to come into being, activity, or operation ⟨when does the movie ~⟩ ⟨the rain ~*ed* up again⟩ **3** : to protrude or seem to protrude ⟨eyes ~*ing* from their sockets⟩ **4** : to become loosened or forced out of place ⟨one of the planks has ~*ed*⟩ **5 a :** to begin a course or journey ⟨~*ed* toward the door⟩ ⟨just ~*ing* out⟩ **b :** to range from a specified initial point ⟨the rates ~ at $10⟩ **6 :** to begin an activity or undertaking; *esp* : to begin work **7** : to be a participant in a game or contest; *esp* : to be in the starting lineup ~ *vt* **1 :** to cause to leave a place of concealment : FLUSH ⟨~ a rabbit⟩ **2** *archaic* : STARTLE, ALARM **3 :** to bring up for consideration or discussion **4 :** to bring into being ⟨~ a rumor⟩ **5 :** to cause to become loosened or displaced **6 :** to begin the use of ⟨~ a fresh loaf of bread⟩ **7 a :** to cause to move, act, or operate ⟨~ the motor⟩ **b :** to cause to enter a game or contest; *esp* : to put in the starting lineup **c :** to care for or train during the early stages of growth and development ⟨~*ed* plants⟩ ⟨a well-*started* coonhound⟩ **8 :** to do or experience the first stages or actions of ⟨~*ed* studying music at the age of five⟩ ***syn*** see BEGIN — **start something** *also* **start anything :** to make trouble ⟨always trying to *start something*⟩ ⟨don't *start anything*⟩ — **to start with 1 :** at the beginning : INITIALLY **2 :** in any event
[2]**start** *n* (14c) **1 a :** a sudden involuntary bodily movement or reaction ⟨woke with a ~⟩ **b :** a brief and sudden action or movement **c :** a sudden capricious impulse or outburst **2 :** a beginning of movement, activity, or development ⟨a false ~⟩ ⟨housing ~*s*⟩ **3 :** HEAD START **4 :** a place of beginning **5 :** the act or an instance of being a competitor in a race or a member of a starting lineup in a game ⟨undefeated in six ~*s* —*Current Biog.*⟩
START *abbr* strategic arms reduction talks
[1]**start·er** \ˈstär-tər\ *n* (1622) **1 :** a person who initiates or sets going: as **a :** an official who gives the signal to begin a race **b :** one who dispatches vehicles **2 a :** one that engages in a competition; *esp* : a member of a starting lineup **b :** one that begins to engage in an activity or process **3 :** one that causes something to begin operating: as **a :** a device for starting an engine; *esp* : an electric motor used to start an internal combustion engine **b :** material containing microorganisms (as yeast) used to induce a desired fermentation **4 :** something that is the beginning of a process, activity, or series; *esp* : APPETIZER — **for starters :** to begin with
[2]**starter** *adj* (1946) : of, relating to, or being an item acquired with the expectation that a more elaborate or sophisticated model will be acquired in the future ⟨a ~ home⟩
star thistle *n* (1578) **1 :** a widely naturalized spiny Old World knapweed (*Centaurea calcitrapa*) with purple flowers — called also *caltrops* **2 :** any of various knapweeds related to the star thistle
starting block *n* (1937) **1 :** a device that usu. consists of two blocks mounted on either side of an adjustable frame and that provides a runner with a rigid surface against which to brace the feet at the start of a race **2** : one of a series of boxes or low platforms at one end of a pool on which a competitor stands for the start of a swimming race

starting block 1

starting gate *n* (1898) **1 :** a mechanically operated barrier used as a starting device for a race **2 :** a barrier that when knocked aside by a competitor (as a skier) starts an electronic timing device
[1]**star·tle** \ˈstär-tᵊl\ *vb* **star·tled; star·tling** \ˈstärt-liŋ, ˈstär-tᵊl-iŋ\ [ME *sterten,* freq. of *sterten* to start] *vi* (1530) : to move or jump suddenly (as in surprise or alarm) ⟨the baby ~*s* easily⟩ ~ *vt* : to frighten or surprise suddenly and usu. not seriously — **star·tle·ment** \-mənt\ *n*
[2]**startle** *n* (1714) : a sudden mild shock (as of surprise or alarm)
startling *adj* (1714) : causing momentary fright, surprise, or astonishment ⟨a ~ discovery⟩ — **star·tling·ly** *adv*
startsy *pl of* STARETS
start–up \ˈstärt-ˌəp\ *n, often attrib* (1845) **1 :** the act or an instance of setting in operation or motion **2 :** a fledgling business enterprise
star turn *n* (1898) *chiefly Brit* : the featured skit or number in a theatrical production; *broadly* : the most widely publicized person or item in a group
star·va·tion \stär-ˈvā-shən\ *n* (1778) **1 :** the act or an instance of starving **2 :** the state of being starved
starvation wages *n pl* (1870) : wages insufficient to provide the ordinary necessities of life
starve \ˈstärv\ *vb* **starved; starv·ing** [ME *sterven* to die, starve, fr. OE *steorfan* to die; akin to OHG *sterban* to die, and prob. to Lith *starinti* to stiffen — more at STARE] *vi* (15c) **1 a :** to perish from lack of food **b** : to suffer extreme hunger **2 a** *archaic* : to die of cold **b** *Brit* : to suffer greatly from cold **3 :** to suffer or perish from deprivation ⟨*starved* for affection⟩ ~ *vt* **1 a :** to kill with hunger **b :** to deprive of nourishment **c :** to cause to capitulate by or as if by depriving of nourishment **2 :** to destroy by or cause to suffer from deprivation **3** *archaic* : to kill with cold
[1]**starve·ling** \ˈstärv-liŋ\ *n* (1546) : one that is thin from or as if from lack of food
[2]**starveling** *adj* (1578) : being a starveling; *also* : marked by poverty or inadequacy ⟨~ wages⟩
[1]**stash** \ˈstash\ *vt* [origin unknown] (1797) : to store in a usu. secret place for future use — often used with *away*
[2]**stash** *n* (ca. 1914) **1 :** hiding place : CACHE **2 :** something stored or hidden away ⟨a ~ of narcotics⟩
sta·sis \ˈstā-səs, ˈsta-\ *n, pl* **sta·ses** \ˈstā-ˌsēz, ˈsta-\ [NL, fr. Gk, act or condition of standing, stopping, fr. *histasthai* to stand — more at STAND] (1745) **1 :** a slowing or stoppage of the normal flow of a bodily fluid or semifluid: as **a :** slowing of the current of circulating blood **b :** reduced motility of the intestines with retention of feces **2 a :** a state of static balance or equilibrium : STAGNATION **b :** a state or period of stability during which little or no evolutionary change in a lineage occurs
-stasis *n comb form, pl* **-stases** [NL, fr. Gk *stasis*] **1 :** stoppage : slowing ⟨hemo*stasis*⟩ ⟨bacterio*stasis*⟩ **2 :** stable state ⟨homeo*stasis*⟩
[1]**stat** \ˈstat\ *n* (ca. 1961) : STATISTIC — usu. used in pl.
[2]**stat** *adv* [fr. *stat.,* abbr. for L. *statim*] (1875) : without delay : IMMEDIATELY ⟨get a doctor ~⟩
[3]**stat** *abbr* statute
-stat *n comb form* [NL *-stata,* fr. Gk *-statēs* one that stops or steadies, fr. *histanai* to cause to stand — more at STAND] **1 :** stabilizing agent or device ⟨thermo*stat*⟩ **2 :** instrument for reflecting (something specified) constantly in one direction ⟨helio*stat*⟩ **3 :** agent causing inhibition of growth without destruction ⟨bacterio*stat*⟩
sta·tant \ˈstā-tᵊnt\ *adj* [L *status,* pp. + E *-ant*] (ca. 1500) : standing in profile with all feet on the ground — used of a heraldic animal
[1]**state** \ˈstāt\ *n, often attrib* [ME *stat,* fr. AF & L; AF *estat,* fr. L *status,* fr. *stare* to stand — more at STAND] (13c) **1 a :** mode or condition of being ⟨a ~ of readiness⟩ **b (1) :** condition of mind or temperament ⟨in a highly nervous ~⟩ **(2) :** a condition of abnormal tension or excitement **2 a :** a condition or stage in the physical being of something ⟨insects in the larval ~⟩ ⟨the gaseous ~ of water⟩ **b :** any of various conditions characterized by definite quantities (as of energy, angular momentum, or magnetic moment) in which an atomic system may exist **3 a :** social position; *esp* : high rank **b (1) :** elaborate or luxurious style of living **(2) :** formal dignity : POMP — usu. used with *in* **4 a :** a body of persons constituting a special class in a society : ESTATE 3 **b** *pl* : the members or representatives of the governing classes assembled in a legislative body **c** *obs* : a person of high rank (as a noble) **5 a :** a politically organized body of people usu. occupying a definite territory; *esp* : one that is sovereign **b :** the political organization of such a body of people **c :** a government or politically organized society having a particular character ⟨a police ~⟩ ⟨the welfare ~⟩ **6 :** the operations or concerns of the government of a country **7 a :** one of the constituent units of a nation having a federal government ⟨the fifty ~*s*⟩ **b** *pl, cap* : The United States of America **8 :** the territory of a state
[2]**state** *vt* **stat·ed; stat·ing** (1579) **1 :** to set by regulation or authority **2 :** to express the particulars of esp. in words : REPORT; *broadly* : to express in words — **stat·able** *or* **state·able** \ˈstā-tə-bəl\ *adj*
state aid *n* (1855) : public monies appropriated by a state government for the partial support or improvement of a public local institution
state bank *n* (1815) **1 :** CENTRAL BANK **2 :** a bank chartered by and operating under the laws of a state of the U.S.

state bird *n* (1910) : a bird selected (as by the legislature) as an emblem of a state of the U.S.

state capitalism *n* (1903) : an economic system in which private capitalism is modified by a varying degree of government ownership and control

state church *n, often cap S&C* (1726) : ESTABLISHED CHURCH

state college *n* (1831) : a college that is financially supported by a state government, often specializes in a branch of technical or professional education, and often forms part of the state university

state·craft \ˈstāt-ˌkraft\ *n* (1642) : the art of conducting state affairs

stated *adj* (ca. 1641) **1** : FIXED, REGULAR ⟨the president shall, at ~ times, receive . . . a compensation —*U.S. Constitution*⟩ **2** : set down explicitly : DECLARED ⟨our ~ intention⟩ — **stat·ed·ly** *adv*

stated clerk *n* (ca. 1909) : an executive officer of a Presbyterian general assembly, synod, or presbytery ranking below the moderator

state flower *n* (1898) : a flowering plant selected (as by the legislature) as an emblem of a state of the U.S.

state·hood \ˈstāt-ˌhu̇d\ *n* (1868) : the condition of being a state; *esp* : the status of being one of the states of the U.S.

state·house \-ˌhau̇s\ *n* (1638) : the building in which a state legislature sits

state·less \-ləs\ *adj* (1609) **1** : having no state **2** : lacking the status of a national ⟨a ~ refugee⟩ — **state·less·ness** *n*

state·ly \-lē\ *adj* **state·li·er; -est** (15c) **1 a** : marked by lofty or imposing dignity **b** : HAUGHTY, UNAPPROACHABLE **2** : impressive in size or proportions ***syn*** see GRAND — **state·li·ness** *n* — **stately** *adv*

state·ment \ˈstāt-mənt\ *n* (1702) **1** : something stated: as **a** : a single declaration or remark : ASSERTION **b** : a report of facts or opinions **2** : the act or process of stating or presenting orally or on paper **3** : PROPOSITION 2a **4** : the presentation of a theme in a musical composition **5** : a summary of activity in a financial account over a particular period of time **6** : an opinion, comment, or message conveyed indirectly usu. by nonverbal means ⟨monuments are ~*s* in form and space —O. B. Hardison, Jr.⟩ **7** : an instruction in a computer program

state of the art (1910) : the level of development (as of a device, procedure, process, technique, or science) reached at any particular time usu. as a result of modern methods — **state–of–the–art** *adj*

state of war (1656) **1 a** : a state of actual armed hostilities regardless of a formal declaration of war **b** : a legal state created and ended by official declaration regardless of actual armed hostilities and usu. characterized by operation of the rules of war **2** : the period of time during which a state of war is in effect

sta·ter \ˈstā-tər, stä-ˈter\ *n* [ME, fr. LL, fr. Gk *statēr,* lit., a unit of weight, fr. *histanai* to cause to stand, weigh — more at STAND] (14c) : an ancient gold or silver coin of the Greek city-states

state·room \ˈstāt-ˌrüm, -ˌru̇m\ *n* (1660) **1** : CABIN 1a(1) **2** : a private room on a railroad car with one or more berths and a toilet

state's attorney *n* (1809) : a legal officer (as a district attorney) appointed or elected to represent a state in court proceedings within a district — called also *state attorney*

state's evidence *n, often cap S* (1787) : a participant in a crime or an accomplice who gives evidence for the prosecution esp. in return for a reduced sentence; *also* : the evidence given — used chiefly in the phrase *turn state's evidence*

States General *n pl* (1585) **1** : the assembly of the three orders of clergy, nobility, and third estate in France before the French Revolution **2** : the legislature of the Netherlands from the 15th century to 1796

[1]**state·side** \ˈstāt-ˌsīd\ *adj, often cap* [*(United) States + side*] (1943) : being in, going to, coming from, or characteristic of the 48 conterminous states of the U.S. ⟨transferred from Europe to ~ duty⟩

[2]**stateside** *adv, often cap* (1943) : in or to the continental U.S.

states·man \ˈstāts-mən\ *n* (1592) **1** : one versed in the principles or art of government; *esp* : one actively engaged in conducting the business of a government or in shaping its policies **2** : one who exercises political leadership wisely and without narrow partisanship — **states·man·like** \-ˌlīk\ *adj* — **states·man·ly** \-lē\ *adj* — **states·man·ship** \-ˌship\ *n*

state socialism *n* (1879) : an economic system with limited socialist characteristics that is effected by gradual state action and typically includes public ownership of major industries and remedial measures to benefit the working class

states' right·er \ˈstāts-ˈrī-tər\ *n* (1945) : a person who advocates strict interpretation of the U.S. constitutional guarantee of states' rights

states' rights *n pl* (1839) : all rights not vested by the U.S. Constitution in the federal government nor forbidden by it to the separate states

state tree *n* (1917) : a tree selected (as by the legislature) as an emblem of a state of the U.S.

state university *n* (1785) : a university maintained and administered by one of the states of the U.S. as part of the state public educational system

[1]**state·wide** \ˈstāt-ˈwīd\ *adj* (1911) : affecting or extending throughout all parts of a state

[2]**statewide** *adv* (ca. 1934) : throughout the state

[1]**stat·ic** \ˈsta-tik\ *adj* [NL *staticus,* fr. Gk *statikos* causing to stand, skilled in weighing, fr. *histanai* to cause to stand, weigh — more at STAND] (1638) **1** : exerting force by reason of weight alone without motion **2** : of or relating to bodies at rest or forces in equilibrium **3** : showing little change ⟨a ~ population⟩ **4 a** : characterized by a lack of movement, animation, or progression **b** : producing an effect of repose or quiescence ⟨a ~ design⟩ **5 a** : standing or fixed in one place : STATIONARY **b** *of water* : stored in a tank but not under pressure **6** : of, relating to, or producing stationary charges of electricity : ELECTROSTATIC **7** : of, relating to, or caused by radio static — **stat·i·cal** \-ti-kəl\ *adj* — **stat·i·cal·ly** \-ti-k(ə-)lē\ *adv*

[2]**static** *n* [*static electricity*] (1913) **1** : noise produced in a radio or television receiver by atmospheric or various natural or man-made electrical disturbances; *also* : the electrical disturbances producing this noise **2** : heated opposition or criticism — **stat·icky** \ˈsta-ti-kē\ *adj*

-static *adj comb form* [NL *-staticus,* fr. *staticus*] **1** : of or relating to a position or state ⟨ortho*static*⟩ **2** : inhibiting the growth of ⟨fungi*static*⟩

static cling *n* (1962) : the tendency of a material (as fabric) to adhere to another material or surface because of a buildup of static electricity

stat·i·ce \ˈsta-tə-(ˌ)sē\ *n* [NL, genus of herbs, fr. L, an astringent plant, fr. Gk *statikē,* fr. fem. of *statikos* causing to stand, astringent] (1739) : SEA LAVENDER

static electricity *n* (ca. 1844) : electricity that consists of isolated motionless charges (as those produced by friction)

static line *n* (1930) : a cord attached to a parachute pack and to an airplane to open the parachute after a jumper clears the plane

stat·ics \ˈsta-tiks\ *n pl but sing or pl in constr* (1692) : mechanics dealing with the relations of forces that produce equilibrium among material bodies

static tube *n* (1923) : a tube used for indicating static as distinct from impact pressure in a stream of fluid

stat·in \ˈsta-tᵊn\ *n* [fr. *-statin* (as in *lovastatin*)] (1986) : any of a group of drugs (as lovastatin and simvastatin) that inhibit the synthesis of cholesterol and promote the production of LDL-binding receptors in the liver resulting in a usu. marked decrease in the level of LDL and a modest increase in the level of HDL circulating in blood plasma

[1]**sta·tion** \ˈstā-shən\ *n* [ME *stacioun,* fr. AF *estation, statiun,* fr. L *station-, statio,* fr. *stare* to stand — more at STAND] (14c) **1 a** : the place or position in which something or someone stands or is assigned to stand or remain **b** : any of the places in a manufacturing operation at which one part of the work is done **c** : equipment used usu. by one person for performing a particular job **2** : the act or manner of standing : POSTURE **3** : a stopping place: as **a** (1) : a regular stopping place in a transportation route ⟨a bus ~⟩ (2) : the building connected with such a stopping place : DEPOT 3 **b** : one of the stations of the cross **4 a** : a post or sphere of duty or occupation **b** : a stock farm or ranch esp. of Australia or New Zealand **5** : STANDING, RANK ⟨a woman of high ~⟩ **6** : a place for specialized observation and study of scientific phenomena ⟨a seismological ~⟩ ⟨a marine biological ~⟩ **7** : a place established to provide a public service: as **a** (1) : FIRE STATION (2) : POLICE STATION **b** : a branch post office **8** : GAS STATION **9 a** : a complete assemblage of radio or television equipment for transmitting or receiving **b** : the place in which such a station is located

[2]**station** *vt* **sta·tioned; sta·tion·ing** \ˈstā-sh(ə-)niŋ\ (1742) : to assign to or set in a station or position : POST ⟨~ a guard at the door⟩

sta·tion·al \ˈstā-shnəl, -shə-nᵊl\ *adj* (1902) : of, relating to, or being a mass formerly celebrated by the pope at designated churches in Rome on appointed holy days

sta·tion·ary \ˈstā-shə-ˌner-ē\ *adj* (1626) **1** : fixed in a station, course, or mode : IMMOBILE **2** : unchanging in condition ⟨a ~ population⟩

stationary bicycle *n* (1962) : an exercise apparatus that can be pedaled like a bicycle — called also *stationary bike*

stationary front *n* (ca. 1940) : the boundary between two air masses neither of which is replacing the other

stationary wave *n* (1856) : STANDING WAVE

station break *n* (1937) : a pause in a radio or television broadcast for announcement of the identity of the network or station; *also* : an announcement or advertisement during this pause

sta·tio·ner \ˈstā-sh(ə-)nər\ *n* [ME *stacіouner,* fr. AF *stationer,* fr. ML *stationarius,* fr. *station-, statio* market stall, fr. L, station] (14c) **1** *archaic* **a** : BOOKSELLER **b** : PUBLISHER **2** : one that sells stationery

sta·tio·nery \ˈstā-shə-ˌner-ē\ *n* [*stationer*] (ca. 1688) **1** : materials (as paper, pens, and ink) for writing or typing **2** : letter paper usu. accompanied with matching envelopes

station house *n* (1833) : a house at a post or station; *esp* : POLICE STATION

sta·tion·mas·ter \ˈstā-shən-ˌmas-tər\ *n* (1849) : an official in charge of the operation of a railroad station

stations of the cross *often cap S&C* (ca. 1890) **1** : a series of usu. 14 images or pictures esp. in a church that represent the stages of Christ's passion and death **2** : a devotion involving commemorative meditation before the stations of the cross

station wagon *n* (1904) : an automobile that has a passenger compartment which extends to the back of the vehicle, that has no trunk, that has one or more rear seats which can be folded down to make space for light cargo, and that has a tailgate or liftgate

stat·ism \ˈstā-ˌti-zəm\ *n* (1919) : concentration of economic controls and planning in the hands of a highly centralized government often extending to government ownership of industry

stat·ist \ˈstā-tist\ *n* (1946) : an advocate of statism — **statist** *adj*

sta·tis·tic \stə-ˈtis-tik\ *n* [sing. of *statistics*] (1880) **1** : a single term or datum in a collection of statistics **2 a** : a quantity (as the mean of a sample) that is computed from a sample; *specif* : ESTIMATE 3b **b** : a random variable that takes on the possible values of a statistic

sta·tis·ti·cal \-ti-kəl\ *adj* (1784) : of, relating to, based on, or employing the principles of statistics ⟨~ analysis⟩ — **sta·tis·ti·cal·ly** \-k(ə-)lē\ *adv*

statistical mechanics *n pl but usu sing in constr* (1885) : a branch of mechanics dealing with the application of the principles of statistics to the mechanics of a system consisting of a large number of parts having motions that differ by small steps over a large range

stat·is·ti·cian \ˌsta-tə-ˈsti-shən\ *n* (1821) : one versed in or engaged in compiling statistics

sta·tis·tics \stə-ˈtis-tiks\ *n pl but sing or pl in constr* [G *Statistik* study of political facts and figures, fr. NL *statisticus* of politics, fr. L *status* state] (1770) **1** : a branch of mathematics dealing with the collection, analysis, interpretation, and presentation of masses of numerical data **2** : a collection of quantitative data

sta·tive \ˈstā-tiv\ *adj* (1874) : expressing a state, condition, or relation — compare ACTIVE 3b

stato- *comb form* [ISV, fr. Gk *statos* stationary, fr. *histasthai* to stand — more at STAND] **1** : resting ⟨*stato*blast⟩ **2** : equilibrium ⟨*stato*cyst⟩

stato·blast \ˈsta-tə-ˌblast\ *n* [ISV] (1855) **1** : a bud in a freshwater bryozoan that overwinters in a chitinous envelope and develops into a new individual in spring **2** : GEMMULE b

---

\ə\ **abut** \ᵊ\ **kitten**, F table \ər\ **further** \a\ **ash** \ā\ **ace** \ä\ **mop, mar**
\au̇\ **out** \ch\ **chin** \e\ **bet** \ē\ **easy** \g\ **go** \i\ **hit** \ī\ **ice** \j\ **job**
\ŋ\ **sing** \ō\ **go** \ȯ\ **law** \ȯi\ **boy** \th\ **thin** \t͟h\ **the** \ü\ **loot** \u̇\ **foot**
\y\ **yet** \zh\ **vision, beige** \k̲, ⁿ, œ, ue, ʸ\ *see* Guide to Pronunciation

stato·cyst \-ˌsist\ *n* [ISV] (1902) : an organ of equilibrium found in usu. aquatic invertebrates that is typically a fluid-filled vesicle lined with sensory hairs which detect the position of suspended statoliths

stato·lith \ˈsta-tə-ˌlith\ *n* [ISV] (1900) **1** : any of the usu. calcareous bodies suspended in a statocyst **2** : any of various starch grains or other solid bodies in the plant cytoplasm that are held to be responsible by changes in their position for changes in orientation of a part or organ

sta·tor \ˈstā-tər\ *n* [NL, fr. L, one that stands, fr. *stare* to stand — more at STAND] (1895) : a stationary part in a machine in or about which a rotor revolves

stato·scope \ˈsta-tə-ˌskōp\ *n* [ISV] (ca. 1900) : a sensitive aneroid barometer for recording small changes in atmospheric pressure; *esp* : one used for indicating small changes in the altitude of an aircraft

[1]**stat·u·ary** \ˈsta-chə-ˌwer-ē\ *n, pl* **-ar·ies** (1542) **1** : SCULPTOR **2 a** : the art of making statues **b** : a collection of statues : STATUES

[2]**statuary** *adj* (1627) : of, relating to, or suitable for statues

stat·ue \ˈsta-(ˌ)chü\ *n* [ME, fr. AF *estatue, statue,* fr. L *statua,* fr. *statuere* to set up — more at STATUTE] (14c) : a three-dimensional representation usu. of a person, animal, or mythical being that is produced by sculpturing, modeling, or casting

Statue of Liberty (1887) **1** : a large copper statue of a woman holding a torch aloft in her right hand located on Liberty Island in New York harbor **2** : a trick play in football in which the ballcarrier takes the ball from the raised hand of a teammate who is faking a pass

stat·u·esque \ˌsta-chə-ˈwesk\ *adj* (1834) : resembling a statue esp. in dignity, shapeliness, or stillness; *esp* : having a tall and shapely form ⟨a ~ actress⟩ — **stat·uesque·ly** *adv*

stat·u·ette \ˌsta-chə-ˈwet\ *n* (1840) : a small statue

stat·ure \ˈsta-chər\ *n* [ME, fr. AF *estature, stature,* fr. L *statura,* fr. *status,* pp. of *stare* to stand — more at STAND] (14c) **1** : natural height (as of a person) in an upright position **2** : quality or status gained by growth, development, or achievement

sta·tus \ˈstā-təs, ˈsta-\ *n, pl* **sta·tus·es** *often attrib* [L — more at STATE] (ca. 1630) **1 a** : position or rank in relation to others ⟨the ~ of a father⟩ **b** : relative rank in a hierarchy of prestige; *esp* : high prestige **2** : the condition of a person or thing in the eyes of the law **3** : state or condition with respect to circumstances ⟨the ~ of the negotiations⟩

status offender *n* (1975) : a young offender (as a runaway or a truant) who is under the jurisdiction of a court for repeated offenses that are not crimes

status quo \-ˈkwō\ *n* [L, state in which] (1807) : the existing state of affairs ⟨seeks to preserve the *status quo*⟩

status quo an·te \-ˈan-tē\ *n* [L, state in which previously] (1877) : the state of affairs that existed previously

sta·tusy \ˈstā-tə-sē, ˈsta-\ *adj* (1962) : having, showing, or conferring prestige ⟨a ~ job⟩

stat·ut·able \ˈsta-chə-tə-bəl, ˈsta-ˌchü-\ *adj* (1636) : made, regulated, or imposed by or in conformity to statute : STATUTORY ⟨~ tonnage⟩

stat·ute \ˈsta-(ˌ)chüt, -chət\ *n* [ME, fr. AF *estatut,* fr. LL *statutum* law, regulation, fr. L, neut. of *statutus,* pp. of *statuere* to set up, station, fr. *status* position, state] (14c) **1** : a law enacted by the legislative branch of a government **2** : an act of a corporation or of its founder intended as a permanent rule **3** : an international instrument setting up an agency and regulating its scope or authority ***syn*** see LAW

statute book *n* (1593) : the whole body of legislation of a given jurisdiction whether or not published as a whole — usu. used in pl.

statute mile *n* (1719) : MILE 1a

statute of limitations (1701) : a statute assigning a certain time after which rights cannot be enforced by legal action or offenses cannot be punished

stat·u·to·ry \ˈsta-chə-ˌtȯr-ē\ *adj* (1766) **1** : of or relating to statutes **2** : enacted, created, or regulated by statute ⟨a ~ age limit⟩ — **stat·u·to·ri·ly** \ˌsta-chə-ˈtȯr-ə-lē\ *adv*

statutory rape *n* (1873) : sexual intercourse with a person who is below the statutory age of consent

[1]**staunch** *var of* [1]STANCH

[2]**staunch** \ˈstȯnch, ˈstänch\ *also* **stanch** \ˈstȯnch, ˈstänch, ˈstanch\ *adj* [ME, fr. AF *estanche,* fem. of *estanc,* fr. *estancher* to stanch — more at STANCH] (15c) **1 a** : WATERTIGHT, SOUND **b** : strongly built : SUBSTANTIAL **2** : steadfast in loyalty or principle ⟨a ~ friend⟩ ***syn*** see FAITHFUL — **staunch·ly** *adv* — **staunch·ness** *n*

stau·ro·lite \ˈstȯr-ə-ˌlīt\ *n* [F, fr. Gk *stauros* cross + F *-lite* — more at STEER] (ca. 1815) : a mineral consisting of a basic silicate of iron and aluminum in prismatic orthorhombic crystals often twinned so as to resemble a cross — **stau·ro·lit·ic** \ˌstȯr-ə-ˈli-tik\ *adj*

[1]**stave** \ˈstāv\ *n* [ME, back-formation fr. *staves,* pl. of *staf* staff] (13c) **1** : [1]STAFF 1 **2** : any of the narrow strips of wood or narrow iron plates placed edge to edge to form the sides, covering, or lining of a vessel (as a barrel) or structure **3** : STANZA **4** : [1]STAFF 3

[2]**stave** *vb* **staved** *or* **stove** \ˈstōv\; **stav·ing** *vt* (ca. 1595) **1** : to break in the staves of (a cask) **2** : to smash a hole in ⟨*stove* in the boat⟩; *also* : to crush or break inward ⟨*staved* in several ribs⟩ **3** : to drive or thrust away ~ *vi* **1** *archaic* : to become stove in — used of a boat or ship **2** : to walk or move rapidly

stave off *vt* (1611) **1** : to fend off ⟨*staving off* creditors⟩ **2** : to ward off (as something adverse) : FORESTALL ⟨trying to *stave off* disaster⟩

staves *pl of* STAFF

stav·u·dine \ˈstav-yü-ˌdēn\ *n* [*sta-* (of unknown origin) + *-vudine* (as in *zidovudine*)] (1992) : D4T

[1]**stay** \ˈstā\ *n* [ME, fr. OE *stæg;* akin to ON *stag* stay] (bef. 12c) **1** : a large strong rope usu. of wire used to support a mast **2** : [1]GUY

[2]**stay** *vt* (1627) **1** : to secure upright with or as if with stays **2** : to incline (a mast) forward, aft, or to one side by the stays ~ *vi* : to go about : TACK

[3]**stay** *vb* **stayed** \ˈstād\ *also* **staid** \ˈstād\; **stay·ing** [ME, fr. AF *estei-, estai-,* stem of *ester* to stand, stay, fr. L *stare* — more at STAND] *vi* (15c) **1** : to stop going forward : PAUSE **2** : to stop doing something : CEASE **3** : to continue in a place or condition : REMAIN ⟨~*ed* up all night⟩ ⟨went for a short vacation but ~*ed* on for weeks⟩ ⟨~ put till I come back⟩ **4** : to stand firm **5** : to take up residence : LODGE **6** : to keep even in a contest or rivalry ⟨~ with the leaders⟩ **7** : to call a poker bet without raising **8** *obs* : to be in waiting or attendance ~ *vt* **1** : to wait for : AWAIT **2** : to stick or remain with (as a race or trial of endurance) to the end — usu. used in the phrase *stay the course* **3** : to remain during ⟨~*ed* the whole time⟩ **4 a** : to stop or delay the proceeding or advance of by or as if by interposing an obstacle : HALT **b** : to check the course of (as a disease) **c** : ALLAY, PACIFY ⟨~*ed* tempers⟩ **d** : to quiet the hunger of temporarily ***syn*** see DEFER

[4]**stay** *n* (1536) **1 a** : the action of halting : the state of being stopped **b** : a stopping or suspension of procedure or execution by judicial or executive order **2** *obs* : SELF-CONTROL, MODERATION **3** : a residence or sojourn in a place **4** : capacity for endurance

[5]**stay** *n* [ME, fr. MF *estaie,* of Gmc origin; akin to MD *stake* pole, MLG *stak* post, *stake* pole — more at STAKE] (14c) **1** : one that serves as a prop : SUPPORT **2** : a thin firm strip (as of plastic) used for stiffening a garment or part (as a shirt collar) **3** : a corset stiffened with bones — usu. used in pl.

[6]**stay** *vt* (1548) **1** : to provide physical or moral support for : SUSTAIN **2** : to fix on something as a foundation

stay–at–home \ˈstā-ət-ˈhōm\ *adj* (1806) : remaining in one's residence, locality, or country; *esp* : remaining at home esp. to tend to children and domestic duties while a spouse is at work — **stay–at–home** *n*

stay·ca·tion \ˈstā-ˈkā-shən\ *n* [blend of [3]*stay* and *vacation*] (2005) : a vacation spent at home or nearby — **stay·ca·tion·er** \ˈstā-ˈkā-sh(ə-)nər\ *n*

stay·er \ˈstā-ər\ *n* (ca. 1580) : one that stays; *esp* : one that supports

staying power *n* (1859) : capacity for continuing (as in existence, influence, or popularity) without weakening

stay·sail \ˈstā-ˌsāl, -səl\ *n* (1669) : a fore-and-aft sail hoisted on a stay — see SAIL illustration

STB *abbr* **1** [NL *sacrae theologiae baccalaureus*] bachelor of sacred theology; **2** [NL *scientiae theologicae baccalaureus*] bachelor of theology

std *abbr* standard

[1]**STD** \ˌes-(ˌ)tē-ˈdē\ *n* [*s*exually *t*ransmitted *d*isease] (1974) : any of various diseases or infections (as syphilis, gonorrhea, chlamydia, and genital herpes) that are usu. transmitted by direct sexual contact and that include some (as hepatitis B and AIDS) that may be contracted by other than sexual means

[2]**STD** *abbr* [NL *sacrae theologiae doctor*] doctor of sacred theology

Ste *abbr* [F *sainte*] saint (female)

[1]**stead** \ˈsted\ *n* [ME *stede,* fr. OE; akin to OHG *stat* place, OE *standan* to stand — more at STAND] (bef. 12c) **1** *obs* : LOCALITY, PLACE **2** : ADVANTAGE — used chiefly in the phrase *to stand one in good stead* **3** : the office, place, or function ordinarily occupied or carried out by someone or something else ⟨acted in his brother's ~⟩

[2]**stead** *vt* (13c) : to be of avail to : HELP

stead·fast \ˈsted-ˌfast *also* -fəst\ *adj* [ME *stedefast,* fr. OE *stedefæst,* fr. *stede* + *fæst* fixed, fast] (bef. 12c) **1 a** : firmly fixed in place : IMMOVABLE **b** : not subject to change ⟨the ~ doctrine of original sin —Ellen Glasgow⟩ **2** : firm in belief, determination, or adherence : LOYAL ⟨her followers have remained ~⟩ ***syn*** see FAITHFUL — **stead·fast·ly** *adv* — **stead·fast·ness** \-ˌfas(t)-nəs, -fəs(t)-\ *n*

stead·ing \ˈste-dᵊn, ˈstē-, -diŋ\ *n* [ME *steding,* fr. *stede* place, farm] (15c) **1** : a small farm **2** *chiefly Scot* : the service buildings or area of a farm

[1]**steady** \ˈste-dē\ *adj* **steadi·er; -est** [ME *stedy,* fr. *stede*] (14c) **1 a** : direct or sure in movement : UNFALTERING ⟨a ~ hand⟩ **b** : firm in position : FIXED ⟨held the pole ~⟩ **c** : keeping nearly upright in a seaway ⟨a ~ ship⟩ **2** : showing little variation or fluctuation : STABLE, UNIFORM ⟨a ~ breeze⟩ ⟨~ prices⟩ **3 a** : not easily disturbed or upset ⟨~ nerves⟩ **b (1)** : constant in feeling, principle, purpose, or attachment ⟨~ friends⟩ **(2)** : DEPENDABLE **c** : not given to dissipation : SOBER — **steadi·ly** \ˈste-dᵊl-ē\ *adv* — **steadi·ness** \ˈste-dē-nəs\ *n*

syn STEADY, EVEN, EQUABLE mean not varying throughout a course or extent. STEADY implies lack of fluctuation or interruption of movement ⟨*steady* progress⟩. EVEN suggests a lack of variation in quality or character ⟨an *even* distribution⟩. EQUABLE implies lack of extremes or of sudden sharp changes ⟨maintain an *equable* temper⟩.

[2]**steady** *vb* **stead·ied; steady·ing** *vt* (1530) : to make or keep steady ~ *vi* : to become steady — **steadi·er** *n*

[3]**steady** *adv* (ca. 1605) **1** : in a steady manner : STEADILY **2** : on the course set — used as a direction to the helmsman of a ship

[4]**steady** *n, pl* **stead·ies** (1792) : one that is steady; *specif* : a boyfriend or girlfriend with whom one goes steady

steady state *n* (1885) : a state or condition of a system or process (as one of the energy states of an atom) that does not change in time; *broadly* : a condition that changes only negligibly over a specified time — **steady–state** *adj*

steady state theory *n* (1948) : a theory in astronomy: the universe has always existed and has always been expanding with hydrogen being created continuously — compare BIG BANG THEORY

steak \ˈstāk\ *n* [ME *steke,* fr. ON *steik;* akin to ON *steikja* to roast on a stake, *stik* stick, stake — more at STICK] (15c) **1 a** : a slice of meat cut from a fleshy part of a beef carcass **b** : a similar slice of a specified meat other than beef ⟨ham ~⟩ **c** : a cross-section slice of a large fish ⟨swordfish ~⟩ **2** : ground beef prepared for cooking or for serving in the manner of a steak ⟨hamburger ~⟩

steak house *n* (1762) : a restaurant whose specialty is beefsteak

steak knife *n* (1870) : a table knife with a sharp often serrated blade

steak tar·tare \-tär-ˈtär\ *n* [F *tartare* Tartar] (1911) : highly seasoned ground beef eaten raw

[1]**steal** \ˈstēl\ *vb* **stole** \ˈstōl\; **sto·len** \ˈstō-lən\; **steal·ing** [ME *stelen,* fr. OE *stelan;* akin to OHG *stelan* to steal] *vi* (bef. 12c) **1** : to take the property of another wrongfully and esp. as a habitual or regular practice **2** : to come or go secretly, unobtrusively, gradually, or unexpectedly **3** : to steal or attempt to steal a base ~ *vt* **1 a** : to take or appropriate without right or leave and with intent to keep or make use of wrongfully ⟨*stole* a car⟩ **b** : to take away by force or unjust means ⟨they've *stolen* our liberty⟩ **c** : to take surreptitiously or without permission ⟨~ a kiss⟩ **d** : to appropriate to oneself or beyond one's proper share : make oneself the focus of ⟨~ the show⟩ **2 a** : to move, convey, or introduce secretly : SMUGGLE **b** : to accomplish in a concealed or unobserved manner ⟨~ a visit⟩ **3 a** : to seize, gain, or win by trickery, skill, or daring ⟨a basketball player adept at ~*ing* the ball⟩ ⟨*stole* the election⟩ **b** *of a base runner* : to reach (a base) safely solely by running and usu. catching the opposing team off guard — **steal·able** \ˈstē-lə-bəl\ *adj* — **steal·er** *n* — **steal a march on** : to gain an

advantage on unobserved — **steal one's thunder** : to grab attention from another esp. by anticipating an idea, plan, or presentation; *also* : to claim credit for another's idea

syn STEAL, PILFER, FILCH, PURLOIN mean to take from another without right or without detection. STEAL may apply to any surreptitious taking of something and differs from the other terms by commonly applying to intangibles as well as material things ⟨*steal* jewels⟩ ⟨*stole* a look at the gifts⟩. PILFER implies stealing repeatedly in small amounts ⟨*pilfered* from his employer⟩. FILCH adds a suggestion of snatching quickly and surreptitiously ⟨*filched* an apple from the tray⟩. PURLOIN stresses removing or carrying off for one's own use or purposes ⟨printed a *purloined* document⟩.

2steal *n* (ca. 1825) **1** : the act or an instance of stealing **2** : a fraudulent or questionable political deal **3** : BARGAIN 2 ⟨it's a ~ at that price⟩

1stealth \ˈstelth\ *n* [ME *stelthe;* akin to OE *stelan* to steal] (13c) **1 a** *archaic* : THEFT **b** *obs* : something stolen **2** : the act or action of proceeding furtively, secretly, or imperceptibly ⟨the state moves by ~ to gather information —Nat Hentoff⟩ **3** : the state of being furtive or unobtrusive **4** : an aircraft-design characteristic consisting of oblique angular construction and avoidance of vertical surfaces that is intended to produce a very weak radar return

2stealth *adj* (1987) : intended not to attract attention : STEALTHY ⟨a ~ campaign⟩

stealthy \ˈstel-thē\ *adj* **stealth·i·er; -est** (1565) **1** : slow, deliberate, and secret in action or character **2 a** : intended to escape observation : FURTIVE **b** : designed to produce a very weak radar return ⟨a ~ airplane⟩ ***syn*** see SECRET — **stealth·i·ly** \-thə-lē\ *adv* — **stealth·i·ness** \-thē-nəs\ *n*

1steam \ˈstēm\ *n* [ME *stem,* fr. OE *stēam;* akin to D *stoom* steam] (bef. 12c) **1** : a vapor arising from a heated substance **2 a** : the invisible vapor into which water is converted when heated to the boiling point **b** : the mist formed by the condensation on cooling of water vapor **3 a** : water vapor kept under pressure so as to supply energy for heating, cooking, or mechanical work; *also* : the power so generated **b** : active force : POWER, MOMENTUM ⟨got there under his own ~⟩ ⟨sales began to pick up ~⟩; *also* : normal force ⟨at full ~⟩ **c** : pent-up emotional tension ⟨needed to let off a little ~⟩ **4 a** : STEAMER 2a **b** : travel by or a trip in a steamer

2steam *vt* (15c) **1** : to give out as fumes : EXHALE **2** : to apply steam to; *esp* : to expose to the action of steam (as for softening or cooking) ~ *vi* **1** : to rise or pass off as vapor **2** : to give off steam or vapor **3 a** : to move or travel by the agency of steam **b** : to move or proceed with energy or force **4** : to be angry : BOIL ⟨~*ing* over the insult⟩

steam·boat \ˈstēm-ˌbōt\ *n* (1785) : a boat driven by steam power; *specif* : a shallow-draft vessel used on inland waterways

steamboat Gothic *n* [fr. its use in homes of retired steamboat captains in imitation of the style of river steamboats] (1941) : an elaborately ornamented architectural style used in homes built in the middle 19th century in the Ohio and Mississippi river valleys

steam boiler *n* (1805) : a boiler for producing steam

steam chest *n* (1797) : the chamber from which steam is distributed to a cylinder of a steam engine

steamed \ˈstēmd\ *adj* (1802) **1** : cooked by steam **2** : ANGRY 1 — often used with *up*

steam engine *n* (1751) : an engine driven or worked by steam; *specif* : a reciprocating engine having a piston driven in a closed cylinder by steam

steam·er \ˈstē-mər\ *n* (1802) **1** : a vessel in which articles are subjected to steam **2 a** : a ship propelled by steam **b** : an engine, machine, or vehicle operated or propelled by steam **3** : one that steams **4** : SOFT-SHELL CLAM

steamer rug *n* (1890) : a warm covering for the lap and feet esp. of a person sitting on a ship's deck

steamer trunk *n* (1867) : a trunk suitable for use in a stateroom of a steamer; *esp* : a shallow trunk that may be stowed beneath a berth

steam·fit·ter \ˈstēm-ˌfi-tər\ *n* (1864) : one that installs or repairs equipment (as steam pipes) for heating, ventilating, or refrigerating systems — **steam fitting** *n*

steam iron *n* (ca. 1943) : a pressing iron with a compartment holding water that is converted to steam by the iron's heat and emitted through the soleplate onto the fabric being pressed

steam·punk \ˈstēm-ˌpəŋk\ *n* [1*steam* + cyber*punk*] (1987) : science fiction dealing with 19th-century societies dominated by historical or imagined steam-powered technology

1steam·roll·er \ˈstēm-ˌrō-lər\ *n* (1863) **1** : a steam-driven road roller; *broadly* : ROAD ROLLER **2** : a crushing force esp. when ruthlessly applied to overcome opposition

2steamroller *or* **steam·roll** \-ˌrōl\ *vt* (1879) **1** : to overwhelm usu. by greatly superior force ⟨~ the opposition⟩ **2** : to bring or advance by overwhelming force or pressure ⟨~*ed* the bill through the legislature⟩ ~ *vi* : to move or proceed with irresistible force

steam·ship \ˈstēm-ˌship\ *n* (1790) : STEAMER 2a

steamship round *n* (1964) : a large beef roast consisting of the whole round with rump and heel

steam shovel *n* (1878) : a power shovel operated by steam; *broadly* : POWER SHOVEL

steam table *n* (1849) : a table having openings to hold containers of cooked food over steam or hot water circulating beneath them

steam turbine *n* (1860) : a turbine that is driven by the pressure of steam discharged at high velocity against the turbine vanes

steam up *vt* (1922) : to make angry or excited : AROUSE

steamy \ˈstē-mē\ *adj* **steam·i·er; -est** (1565) **1** : consisting of, characterized by, or full of steam **2** : intensely or uncomfortably hot: as **a** : hot and humid ⟨a ~ afternoon⟩ **b** : sensually hot : EROTIC ⟨a ~ love scene⟩ — **steam·i·ly** \-mə-lē\ *adv* — **steam·i·ness** \-mē-nəs\ *n*

stea·rate \ˈstē-ə-ˌrāt, ˈstir-ˌāt\ *n* (1839) : a salt or ester of stearic acid

stea·ric acid \stē-ˈa-rik-, ˈstir-ik-\ *n* [F *stéarique,* fr. Gk *stear* hard fat] (1830) : a white crystalline fatty acid $C_{18}H_{36}O_2$ obtained by saponifying tallow or other hard fats containing stearin; *also* : a commercial mixture of stearic and palmitic acids

stea·rin \ˈstē-ə-rən, ˈstir-ən\ *n* [F *stéarine,* fr. Gk *stear*] (1817) : an ester of glycerol and stearic acid

ste·a·tite \ˈstē-ə-ˌtīt\ *n* [L *steatitis,* a precious stone, fr. Gk, fr. *steat-, stear*] (1794) **1** : a massive talc having a grayish-green or brown color : SOAPSTONE **2** : an electrically insulating porcelain composed largely of steatite — **ste·a·tit·ic** \ˌstē-ə-ˈti-tik\ *adj*

steato- *comb form* [Gk, fr. *steat-, stear;* perh. akin to Skt *styāyate* it hardens] : fat ⟨*steato*rrhea⟩

ste·a·to·py·gia \ˌstē-a-tə-ˈpi-j(ē-)ə, -ˈpī-\ *n* [NL, fr. *steat-, stear* + Gk *pygē* buttocks] (1879) : an excessive development of fat on the buttocks that occurs chiefly among women of some African peoples and esp. the Khoisan — **ste·a·to·py·gous** \-gəs\ *or* **ste·a·to·py·gic** \ˌstē-ə-ˈtä-pə-jik, -tə-ˈpī-jik\ *adj*

ste·at·or·rhea \(ˌ)stē-ˌa-tə-ˈrē-ə\ *n* [NL] (ca. 1859) : an excess of fat in the stools

ste·at·or·rhoea *chiefly Brit var of* STEATORRHEA

sted·fast *archaic var of* STEADFAST

steed \ˈstēd\ *n* [ME *stede,* fr. OE *stēda* stallion; akin to OE *stōd* stud — more at STUD] (bef. 12c) : HORSE; *esp* : a spirited horse (as for war)

steek \ˈstēk\ *vb* [ME *steken* to pierce, fix, enclose; akin to OE *stician* to pierce — more at STICK] (13c) *chiefly Scot* : SHUT, CLOSE

1steel \ˈstēl\ *n* [ME *stele,* fr. OE *stȳle, stēle;* akin to OHG *stahal* steel and perh. to Skt *stakati* he resists] (bef. 12c) **1** : commercial iron that contains carbon in any amount up to about 1.7 percent as an essential alloying constituent, is malleable when under suitable conditions, and is distinguished from cast iron by its malleability and lower carbon content **2** : an instrument or implement of or characteristically of steel: as **a** : a thrusting or cutting weapon **b** : an instrument (as a fluted round rod with a handle) for sharpening knives **c** : a piece of steel for striking sparks from flint **3** : a quality (as hardness of mind or spirit) that suggests steel ⟨nerves of ~⟩ **4 a** : the steel manufacturing industry **b** *pl* : shares of stock in steel companies

2steel *vt* (13c) **1** : to overlay, point, or edge with steel **2 a** : to cause to resemble steel (as in looks or hardness) **b** : to fill with resolution or determination ⟨~*ed* herself to face the crisis⟩

3steel *adj* (13c) **1** : made of steel **2** : of or relating to the production of steel **3** : resembling steel

steel band *n* (1949) : a band of steel drums

steel blue *n* (1803) **1** : a grayish blue **2** : any of the blue colors assumed by steel at various temperatures in tempering

steel drum *n* (1952) : a musical instrument orig. developed in Trinidad that is played by hammering raised and tuned portions of the bottom of an oil drum

steel engraving *n* (1824) **1** : the art or process of engraving on steel **2** : an impression taken from an engraved steel plate

steel guitar *n* (1925) **1** : HAWAIIAN GUITAR **2** : PEDAL STEEL — **steel guitarist** *n*

steel·head \ˈstēl-ˌhed\ *n, pl* **steelhead** *also* **steelheads** (ca. 1882) : an anadromous rainbow trout — called also *steelhead trout*

steel·ie *also* **steely** \ˈstē-lē\ *n, pl* **steel·ies** (1922) : a playing marble made of steel

steel·mak·er \ˈstēl-ˌmā-kər\ *n* (1774) : a manufacturer of steel — **steel·mak·ing** \-kiŋ\ *n*

steel–trap \ˈstēl-ˈtrap\ *adj* (1945) : QUICK, INCISIVE ⟨a ~ mind⟩

steel wool *n* (1896) : an abrasive material composed of long fine steel shavings and used esp. for scouring and burnishing

steel·work \ˈstēl-ˌwərk\ *n* (1681) **1** : work in steel **2** *pl but sing or pl in constr* : an establishment where steel is made

steel·work·er \-ˌwər-kər\ *n* (1857) : a person who works in steel and esp. in the manufacturing of it

steely \ˈstē-lē\ *adj* **steel·i·er; -est** (1509) **1** : resembling or suggesting steel (as in hardness, color, strength, or coldness) ⟨~ determination⟩ ⟨~ blue⟩ **2** : made of steel — **steel·i·ness** *n*

steel·yard \ˈstēl-ˌyärd, ˈstil-yərd\ *n* [prob. fr. 3*steel* + 4*yard* (rod)] (1639) : a balance in which an object to be weighed is suspended from the shorter arm of a lever and the weight determined by moving a counterpoise along a graduated scale on the longer arm until equilibrium is attained

steen·bok \ˈstēn-ˌbäk, ˈstān-\ *or* **stein·bok** \ˈstīn-, ˈstān-\ *n* [Afrik *steenbok,* fr. D, ibex, fr. MD *steenboc;* akin to OE *stānbucca* ibex, *stān* stone, *bucca* buck] (1775) : a small slender antelope (*Raphicerus campestris*) with long legs that inhabits chiefly grasslands of eastern and southern Africa

1steep \ˈstēp\ *adj* [ME *stepe,* fr. OE *stēap* high, steep, deep; akin to OFris *stāp* steep, MHG *stief* — more at STOOP] (bef. 12c) **1** : LOFTY, HIGH — used chiefly of a sea **2** : making a large angle with the plane of the horizon **3 a** : mounting or falling precipitously ⟨the stairs were very ~⟩ **b** : being or characterized by a rapid and intensive decline or increase **4** : extremely or excessively high ⟨~ prices⟩ — **steep·ish** \ˈstē-pish\ *adj* — **steep·ly** *adv* — **steep·ness** *n*

syn STEEP, ABRUPT, PRECIPITOUS, SHEER mean having an incline approaching the perpendicular. STEEP implies such sharpness of pitch that ascent or descent is very difficult ⟨a *steep* hill⟩ ⟨a *steep* dive⟩. ABRUPT implies a sharper pitch and a sudden break in the level ⟨a beach with an *abrupt* drop-off⟩. PRECIPITOUS applies to an incline approaching the vertical ⟨the river winds through a *precipitous* gorge⟩. SHEER suggests an unbroken perpendicular expanse ⟨*sheer* cliffs that daunted the climbers⟩.

2steep *n* (1555) : a precipitous place

3steep *vb* [ME *stepen*] *vt* (14c) **1** : to soak in a liquid at a temperature under the boiling point (as for softening, bleaching, or extracting an essence) **2** : to cover with or plunge into a liquid (as in bathing, rinsing, or soaking) **3** : to saturate with or subject thoroughly to (some strong or pervading influence) ⟨practices ~*ed* in tradition⟩ ~ *vi* : to undergo the process of soaking in a liquid ***syn*** see SOAK — **steep·er** *n*

4steep *n* (15c) **1** : the state or process of being steeped **2** : a bath or solution in which something is steeped

steep·en \ˈstē-pən, -pᵊm\ *vb* **steep·ened; steep·en·ing** \ˈstē-pə-niŋ, ˈstēp-niŋ\ *vi* (1847) : to become steeper ~ *vt* : to make steeper

stee·ple \ˈstē-pəl\ *n* [ME *stepel,* fr. OE *stēpel* tower; akin to OE *stēap* steep] (bef. 12c) : a tall structure usu. having a small spire at the top and surmounting a church tower; *broadly* : a whole church tower — **stee·pled** \-pəld\ *adj*

stee·ple·bush \ˈstē-pəl-ˌbu̇sh\ *n* (ca. 1818) : HARDHACK

stee·ple·chase \-ˌchās\ *n* [fr. the use of church steeples as landmarks to guide the riders] (1793) **1 a :** a horse race across country **b :** a horse race over a closed course with obstacles (as hedges and walls) **2 :** a footrace of usu. 3000 meters over hurdles and a water jump — **stee·ple·chas·er** \-ˌchā-sər\ *n* — **stee·ple·chas·ing** \-siŋ\ *n*

stee·ple·jack \-ˌjak\ *n* (1852) : a person whose work is building smokestacks, towers, or steeples or climbing up the outside of them to paint and make repairs

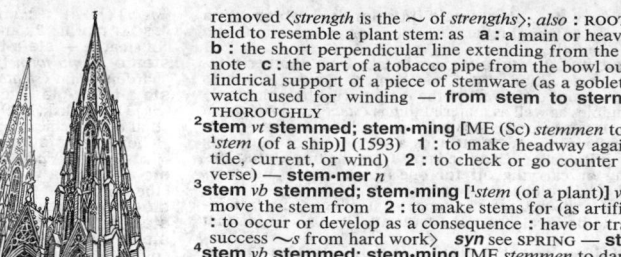

steeple

[1]**steer** \ˈstir\ *n* [ME, fr. OE *stēor* young ox; akin to OHG *stior* young ox] (bef. 12c) **1 :** a male bovine animal and esp. a domestic ox (*Bos taurus*) castrated before sexual maturity — compare STAG 3 **2 :** an ox less than four years old

[2]**steer** *vb* [ME *steren,* fr. OE *stīeran;* akin to OE *stēor-* steering oar, Gk *stauros* stake, cross, *stylos* pillar, Skt *sthavira, sthūra* stout, thick] *vt* (12c) **1 :** to control the course of : DIRECT; *esp* : to guide by mechanical means (as a rudder) **2 :** to set and hold to (a course) ~ *vi* **1 :** to direct the course (as of a ship or automobile) **2 :** to pursue a course of action **3 :** to be subject to steering ⟨the car ~*s* well⟩ ***syn*** see GUIDE — **steer·able** \ˈstir-ə-bəl\ *adj* — **steer·er** *n* — **steer clear :** to keep entirely away — often used with *of* ⟨tries to *steer clear* of debt⟩

[3]**steer** *n* (1894) : a hint as to procedure : TIP

[4]**steer** *dial Brit var of* STIR

steer·age \ˈstir-ij\ *n* (15c) **1 :** the act or practice of steering; *broadly* : DIRECTION **2** [fr. its orig. being located near the rudder] : a section of inferior accommodations in a passenger ship for passengers paying the lowest fares

steer·age·way \-ˌwā\ *n* (1762) : a rate of motion sufficient to make a ship or boat respond to movements of the rudder

steering column *n* (1903) : the column that encloses the connections to the steering gear of a vehicle (as an automobile)

steering committee *n* (1887) : a managing or directing committee; *specif* : a committee that determines the order in which business will be taken up in a U.S. legislative body

steering gear *n* (1851) : a mechanism (as a gear train) by which something is steered

steering wheel *n* (1750) : a handwheel by means of which one steers

steers·man \ˈstirz-mən\ *n* (bef. 12c) : one who steers : HELMSMAN

[1]**steeve** \ˈstēv\ *vt* **steeved; steev·ing** [prob. fr. Sp *estibar* or Pg *estivar* to pack tightly, fr. L *stipare* to press together — more at STIFF] (ca. 1644) *archaic* : to stow esp. in a ship's hold

[2]**steeve** *vb* **steeved; steev·ing** [origin unknown] *vi* (ca. 1644) *of a bowsprit* : to incline upward at an angle with the horizon or the line of the keel ~ *vt* : to set (a bowsprit) at an upward inclination

steg·a·nog·ra·phy \ˌste-gə-ˈnä-grə-fē\ *n* [NL *steganographia,* fr. Gk *steganos* covered, reticent (fr. *stegein* to cover) + L *-graphia* -graphy — more at THATCH] (1569) **1** *archaic* : CRYPTOGRAPHY **2 :** the art or practice of concealing a message, image, or file within another message, image, or file — **steg·a·no·graph·ic** \-nə-ˈgra-fik\ *adj*

stego·saur \ˈste-gə-ˌsȯr\ *n* [NL *Stegosauria,* fr. *Stegosaurus*] (1897) : any of a suborder (Stegosauria) of quadrupedal ornithischian herbivorous dinosaurs chiefly of the Jurassic with strongly developed dorsal plates and spikes

stego·sau·rus \ˌste-gə-ˈsȯr-əs\ *n* [NL, fr. Gk *stegos* roof + *sauros* lizard — more at THATCH] (1892) : any of a genus (*Stegosaurus*) of stegosaurs known from the Upper Jurassic rocks esp. of Colorado and Wyoming

stein \ˈstīn\ *n* [prob. fr. G *Steingut* stoneware, fr. *Stein* stone + *Gut* goods] (1855) : a large mug (as of earthenware) used esp. for beer; *also* : the quantity of beer that a stein holds

ste·la \ˈstē-lə\ *or* **ste·le** \ˈstē-lē\ *n, pl* **ste·lae** \-(ˌ)lē\ *or* **steles** [L & Gk; L *stela,* fr. Gk *stēlē;* akin to OHG *stollo* pillar, Gk *stellein* to set up] (1776) : a usu. carved or inscribed stone slab or pillar used for commemorative purposes

ste·lar \ˈstē-lər, -ˌlär\ *adj* (1901) : of, relating to, or constituting a stele

stele \ˈstēl, ˈstē-lē\ *n* [NL, fr. Gk *stēlē* stela, pillar] (1895) : the usu. cylindrical central vascular portion of the axis of a vascular plant

stel·la \ˈste-lə\ *n* [L, star; fr. the star on the reverse] (1879) : an experimental international coin based on the metric system that was issued by the U.S. in 1879 and 1880 and was worth about four dollars

stel·lar \ˈste-lər\ *adj* [LL *stellaris,* fr. L *stella* star — more at STAR] (ca. 1656) **1 a :** of or relating to the stars : ASTRAL **b :** composed of stars **2 :** of or relating to a theatrical or film star ⟨~ names⟩ **3 a :** PRINCIPAL, LEADING ⟨a ~ role⟩ **b :** OUTSTANDING ⟨a ~ performance⟩

stellar wind *n* (1965) : plasma continuously ejected from a star's surface into surrounding space

stel·late \ˈste-ˌlāt\ *adj* [L *stella*] (1661) : resembling a star (as in shape)

Stel·ler's jay \ˈste-lərz, ˈshte-\ *n* [Georg W. *Steller* †1746 Ger. naturalist] (1828) : a jay (*Cyanocitta stelleri*) of western No. America with a high crest and black and dark blue plumage

Steller's sea cow *n* (1814) : an extinct very large sirenian (*Hydrodamalis gigas*) formerly common near the Asian coast of the Bering Sea

[1]**stem** \ˈstem\ *n* [ME, fr. OE *stefn, stemn* stem of a plant or ship; akin to OHG *stam* plant stem and prob. to Gk *stamnos* wine jar, *histanai* to set — more at STAND] (bef. 12c) **1 a :** the main trunk of a plant; *specif* : a primary plant axis that develops buds and shoots instead of roots **b :** a plant part (as a branch, petiole, or stipe) that supports another (as a leaf or fruit) **c :** the complete fruiting stalk of a banana plant with its bananas **2 a :** the main upright member at the bow of a ship **b :** the bow or prow of a ship — compare STERN **3 :** a line of ancestry : STOCK; *esp* : a fundamental line from which others have arisen **4 :** the part of an inflected word that remains after the inflected part is removed ⟨*strength* is the ~ of *strengths*⟩; *also* : ROOT 6 **5 :** something held to resemble a plant stem: as **a :** a main or heavy stroke of a letter **b :** the short perpendicular line extending from the head of a musical note **c :** the part of a tobacco pipe from the bowl outward **d :** the cylindrical support of a piece of stemware (as a goblet) **e :** a shaft of a watch used for winding — **from stem to stern :** THROUGHOUT, THOROUGHLY

[2]**stem** *vt* **stemmed; stem·ming** [ME (Sc) *stemmen* to keep a course, fr. [1]*stem* (of a ship)] (1593) **1 :** to make headway against (as an adverse tide, current, or wind) **2 :** to check or go counter to (something adverse) — **stem·mer** *n*

[3]**stem** *vb* **stemmed; stem·ming** [[1]*stem* (of a plant)] *vt* (1724) **1 :** to remove the stem from **2 :** to make stems for (as artificial flowers) ~ *vi* : to occur or develop as a consequence : have or trace an origin ⟨her success ~*s* from hard work⟩ ***syn*** see SPRING — **stem·mer** *n*

[4]**stem** *vb* **stemmed; stem·ming** [ME *stemmen* to dam up, fr. ON *stemma;* akin to MHG *stemmen* to dam up and prob. to Lith *stumti* to shove] *vt* (14c) **1 a :** to stop or dam up (as a river) **b :** to stop or check by or as if by damming; *esp* : STANCH ⟨~ a flow of blood⟩ **2 :** to turn (a ski) in stemming ~ *vi* **1 :** to restrain or check oneself; *also* : to become checked or stanched **2 :** to slide the heel of one ski or of both skis outward usu. in making or preparing to make a turn

[5]**stem** *n* (1700) **1 :** CHECK, DAM **2 :** an act or instance of stemming on skis

STEM *abbr* science, technology, engineering, and mathematics

stem cell *n* (1896) : an unspecialized cell that gives rise to differentiated cells ⟨hematopoietic *stem cells* in bone marrow⟩

stem christie *n, often cap C* (1936) : a turn in skiing begun by stemming a ski and completed by bringing the skis parallel into a christie

stem·less \ˈstem-ləs\ *adj* (1753) : having no stem : ACAULESCENT

stem·ma \ˈste-mə\ *n, pl* **stem·ma·ta** \-mə-tə\ [L, wreath, pedigree (fr. the wreaths placed on ancestral images), fr. Gk, wreath, fr. *stephein* to crown, enwreathe] (1826) **1 :** a simple eye present in some insects **2 :** a scroll (as among the ancient Romans) containing a genealogical list **3 :** a tree showing the relationships of the manuscripts of a literary work — **stem·mat·ic** \ste-ˈma-tik, stə-\ *adj*

stemmed *adj* (1576) : having a stem — usu. used in combination ⟨long-*stemmed* roses⟩

stem·my \ˈste-mē\ *adj* **stem·mi·er; -est** (1863) **1 :** abounding in stems **2** *of wine* : having a bitter aftertaste

stem rust *n* (1899) **1 :** a rust attacking the stem of a plant; *esp* : a destructive disease esp. of wheat caused by a rust fungus (*Puccinia graminis*) which produces reddish-brown lesions in the uredospore stage and black lesions in the teliospore stage and has any of several plants of the barberry family as an intermediate host **2 :** the fungus causing stem rust

stem turn *n* (1922) : a skiing turn executed by stemming an outside ski

stem·ware \ˈstem-ˌwer\ *n* (1892) : glass hollowware mounted on a stem

stem–wind·er \-ˌwīn-dər\ *n* (1875) **1 :** a stem-winding watch **2** [fr. the superiority of the stem-winding watch over the older key-wound watch] : one that is first-rate of its kind; *esp* : a stirring speech

stem–wind·ing \-diŋ\ *adj* (1867) : wound by an inside mechanism turned by the knurled knob on the stem ⟨a ~ watch⟩

Sten \ˈsten\ *n* [R. V. *S*hepherd, 20th cent. Eng. army officer + H. J. *T*urpin, 20th cent. Eng. civil servant + *En*field, Eng.] (1942) : a light simple 9-millimeter British submachine gun

sten- *or* **steno-** *comb form* [Gk, fr. *stenos*] : close : narrow : little ⟨*steno*thermal⟩

stench \ˈstench\ *n* [ME, fr. OE *stenc;* akin to OE *stincan* to emit a smell — more at STINK] (bef. 12c) **1 :** STINK **2 :** a characteristic repugnant quality — **stench·ful** \-fəl\ *adj* — **stenchy** \ˈsten-chē\ *adj*

[1]**sten·cil** \ˈsten(t)-səl\ *n* [prob. ultim. fr. ME *stanseld* brightly ornamented, fr. AF *estencelé* spangled, pp. of *estenceler* to sparkle, fr. *estencele* spark, fr. VL **stincilla,* alter. of L *scintilla*] (1707) **1 :** an impervious material (as a sheet of paper, thin wax, or woven fabric) perforated with lettering or a design through which a substance (as ink, paint, or metallic powder) is forced onto a surface to be printed **2 :** something (as a pattern, design, or print) that is produced by means of a stencil **3 :** a printing process that uses a stencil

[2]**stencil** *vt* **sten·ciled** *or* **sten·cilled; sten·cil·ing** *or* **sten·cil·ling** \-s(ə-)liŋ\ (ca. 1828) **1 :** to mark or paint with a stencil **2 :** to produce by stencil — **sten·cil·er** *or* **sten·cil·ler** \-s(ə-)lər\ *n*

steno \ˈste-(ˌ)nō\ *n, pl* **sten·os** (1913) **1 :** STENOGRAPHER **2 :** STENOGRAPHY

ste·nog·ra·pher \stə-ˈnä-grə-fər\ *n* (1809) **1 :** a writer of shorthand **2 :** a person employed chiefly to take and transcribe dictation

ste·nog·ra·phy \-fē\ *n* (1602) **1 :** the art or process of writing in shorthand **2 :** shorthand esp. written from dictation or oral discourse **3 :** the making of shorthand notes and subsequent transcription of them — **steno·graph·ic** \ˌste-nə-ˈgra-fik\ *adj* — **steno·graph·i·cal·ly** \-fi-k(ə-)lē\ *adv*

steno·ha·line \ˌste-nō-ˈhā-ˌlīn, -ˈha-ˌlīn\ *adj* [ISV *sten-* + Gk *halinos* of salt, fr. *hals* salt — more at SALT] (ca. 1920) *of an aquatic organism* : unable to withstand wide variation in salinity of surrounding water

ste·nosed \stə-ˈnōzd, -ˈnōst\ *adj* [fr. pp. of *stenose* to affect with stenosis] (1897) : affected with stenosis

ste·no·sis \stə-ˈnō-səs\ *n, pl* **-no·ses** \-ˌsēz\ [NL, fr. Gk *stenōsis* act of narrowing, fr. *stenoun* to narrow, fr. *stenos* narrow] (ca. 1860) : a narrowing or constriction of the diameter of a bodily passage or orifice — **ste·not·ic** \-ˈnä-tik\ *adj*

steno·ther·mal \ˌste-nə-ˈthər-məl\ *adj* (1881) : capable of surviving over only a narrow range of temperatures ⟨~ fish⟩ — **steno·therm** \ˈste-nə-ˌthərm\ *n*

steno·top·ic \ˌste-nə-ˈtä-pik\ *adj* [prob. fr. G *stenotop* stenotopic, fr. *sten-* + Gk *topos* place] (1945) : having a narrow range of adaptability to changes in environmental conditions

steno·type \ˈste-nə-ˌtīp\ *n* [*steno-* (as in *stenography*) + *type*] (1913) : a small machine somewhat like a typewriter used to record speech by means of phonograms — **stenotype** *vt* — **steno·typ·ist** \-ˌtī-pist\ *n* — **ste·no·ty·py** \-ˌtī-pē\ *n*

stent \ˈstent\ *n* [Charles Thomas *Stent* †1885 Eng. dentist] (1961) : a short narrow metal or plastic tube often in the form of a mesh that is inserted into the lumen of an anatomical vessel (as an artery or a bile duct) esp. to keep a previously blocked passageway open

sten·tor \ˈsten-ˌtȯr, -tər\ *n* [L, fr. Gk *Stentōr* Stentor, a Greek herald in the Trojan War noted for his loud voice] (1609) **1 :** a person having a loud voice **2 :** any of a widely distributed genus (*Stentor*) of ciliate protozoans having a trumpet-shaped body with the mouth at the broad end and with the narrow end often attached to the substrate

sten·to·ri·an \sten-ˈtȯr-ē-ən\ *adj* (1605) **:** extremely loud ⟨~ tones⟩ ***syn*** see LOUD

[1]**step** \ˈstep\ *n* [ME, fr. OE *stæpe;* akin to OHG *stapfo* step, *stampfōn* to stamp] (bef. 12c) **1 :** a rest for the foot in ascending or descending: as **a :** one of a series of structures consisting of a riser and a tread **b :** a ladder rung **2 a** (1) **:** an advance or movement made by raising the foot and bringing it down elsewhere (2) **:** a combination of foot or foot and body movements constituting a unit or a repeated pattern ⟨a dance ~⟩ (3) **:** manner of walking **:** STRIDE **b :** FOOTPRINT 1 **c :** the sound of a footstep **3 a :** the space passed over in one step **b :** a short distance **c :** the height of one stair **4** *pl* **:** COURSE, WAY ⟨directed his ~*s* toward the river⟩ **5 a :** a degree, grade, or rank in a scale **b :** a stage in a process ⟨was guided through every ~ of my career⟩ **6 :** a frame on a ship designed to receive an upright shaft; *esp* **:** a block supporting the heel of a mast **7 :** an action, proceeding, or measure often occurring as one in a series ⟨taking ~*s* to improve the situation⟩ **8 :** a steplike offset or part usu. occurring in a series **9 :** an interval in a musical scale **10 :** STEP AEROBICS **11 :** a slight lead in or as if in a race ⟨has a ~ on the competition⟩ — **step·like** \-ˌlīk\ *adj* — **stepped** \ˈstept\ *adj* — **in step 1 :** with each foot moving to the same time as the corresponding foot of others or in time to music **2 :** in harmony or agreement — **out of step :** not in step ⟨*out of step* with the times⟩

[2]**step** *vb* **stepped; step·ping** *vi* (bef. 12c) **1 a :** to move by raising the foot and bringing it down elsewhere or by moving each foot in succession **b :** DANCE **2 a :** to go on foot **:** WALK **b** *obs* **:** ADVANCE, PROCEED **c :** to be on one's way **:** LEAVE — often used with *along* **d :** to move briskly ⟨kept us *stepping*⟩ **3 :** to press down with the foot ⟨~ on the brake⟩ **4 :** to come as if at a single step ⟨*stepped* into a good job⟩ ~ *vt* **1 :** to take by moving the feet in succession ⟨~ three paces⟩ **2 a :** to move (the foot) in any direction **:** SET ⟨the first man to ~ foot on the moon⟩ **b :** to traverse on foot **3 :** to go through the steps of **:** PERFORM ⟨~ a minuet⟩ **4 :** to make erect by fixing the lower end in a step ⟨~ the mast⟩ **5 :** to measure by steps ⟨~ off 50 yards⟩ **6 a :** to provide with steps **b :** to make steps in ⟨~ a key⟩ **7 :** to construct or arrange in or as if in steps ⟨craggy peaks with terraces *stepped* up the sides —*Time*⟩ — **step on it :** to increase one's speed **:** hurry up

step- *comb form* [ME, fr. OE *stēop-;* akin to OHG *stiof-* step-, OE *astēpan* to deprive, bereave] **:** related by virtue of a remarriage (as of a parent) and not by blood ⟨*step*parent⟩ ⟨*step*sister⟩

step aerobics *n pl but sing or pl in constr* (1985) **:** aerobics that involves repeatedly stepping on and off a raised platform — called also *step training*

step aside *vi* (1949) **:** STEP DOWN

step·broth·er \ˈstep-ˌbrə-t͟hər\ *n* (15c) **:** a son of one's stepparent by a former partner

step–by–step \ˌstep-bī-ˈstep\ *adj or adv* (1581) **:** marked by successive degrees usu. of limited extent **:** GRADUAL

step·child \ˈstep-ˌchī(-ə)ld\ *n* (bef. 12c) **1 :** one that fails to receive proper care or attention ⟨is no longer a ~ in the family of nations —F. R. Smith⟩ **2 :** a child of one's wife or husband by a former partner

step dance *n* (1887) **:** a dance in which steps are emphasized rather than gesture or posture

step·daugh·ter \ˈstep-ˌdȯ-tər\ *n* (bef. 12c) **:** a daughter of one's wife or husband by a former partner

step–down \ˈstep-ˌdau̇n\ *n* (1922) **:** a decrease or reduction in size or amount ⟨a ~ in dosage⟩

step down *vi* (1890) **:** RETIRE, RESIGN ~ *vt* **1 :** to lower (a voltage) by means of a transformer **2 :** to decrease or reduce esp. by one or more steps — **step–down** \ˈstep-ˌdau̇n\ *adj*

step·fam·i·ly \ˈstep-ˌfam-lē, -ˌfa-mə-\ *n* (1873) **:** a family in which there is a stepparent

step·fa·ther \ˈstep-ˌfä-t͟hər\ *n* (bef. 12c) **:** the husband of one's mother when distinct from one's natural or legal father

step function *n* (ca. 1929) **:** a mathematical function of a single real variable that remains constant within each of a series of adjacent intervals but changes in value from one interval to the next

steph·a·no·tis \ˌste-fə-ˈnō-təs\ *n* [NL, fr. Gk *stephanōtis* fit for a crown, fr. *stephanos* crown, fr. *stephein* to crown] (1843) **:** any of a genus (*Stephanotis,* esp. *S. floribunda*) of Old World tropical woody vines of the milkweed family with fragrant white waxy flowers having a tubular corolla terminating in five lobes

step–in \ˈstep-ˌin\ *n* (1921) **:** an article of clothing put on by being stepped into: as **a :** a shoe resembling but usu. having a higher vamp than a pump and having concealed elastic to adjust the fit **b :** short panties for women — usu. used in pl. — **step–in** *adj*

step in *vi* (15c) **1 a :** to intervene in an affair or dispute **b :** to act as a replacement **2 :** to make a brief informal visit

step·lad·der \ˈstep-ˌla-dər\ *n* (1751) **:** a ladder that has broad flat steps and two pairs of legs connected by a hinge at the top and that opens at the bottom to become freestanding

step·moth·er \-ˌmə-t͟hər\ *n* (bef. 12c) **:** the wife of one's father when distinct from one's natural or legal mother

step out *vi* (ca. 1533) **1 :** to go away from a place usu. for a short distance and for a short time **2 :** to go or march at a vigorous or increased pace **3 :** DIE **4 :** to lead an active social life **5 :** to be unfaithful — usu. used with *on* ⟨had been *stepping out* on his wife⟩

step·par·ent \ˈstep-ˌper-ənt\ *n* (1840) **:** a person who is a stepmother or stepfather

step·par·ent·ing \-ən-tiŋ\ *n* (1979) **:** parenting by a stepparent

steppe \ˈstep\ *n* [Russ *step'*] (1671) **1 :** one of the vast usu. level and treeless tracts in southeastern Europe or Asia **2 :** arid land with xerophilous vegetation found usu. in regions of extreme temperature range and loess soil

stepped–up \ˈstept-ˈəp\ *adj* (1902) **:** increased in intensity

step·per \ˈste-pər\ *n* (1835) **:** one (as a fast horse or a dancer) that steps

stepper motor *n* (1961) **:** a motor whose driveshaft rotates in small steps rather than continuously — called also *stepping motor*

step·ping–stone \ˈste-piŋ-ˌstōn\ *n* (14c) **1 :** a stone on which to step (as in crossing a stream) **2 :** a means of progress or advancement

step·sis·ter \ˈstep-ˌsis-tər\ *n* (15c) **:** a daughter of one's stepparent by a former partner

step·son \-ˌsən\ *n* (bef. 12c) **:** a son of one's husband or wife by a former partner

step stool *n* (1946) **:** a stool with one or two steps that often fold away beneath the seat

step turn *n* (1941) **:** a skiing turn executed in a downhill traverse by lifting the upper ski from the ground, placing it in the desired direction, weighting it, and bringing the other ski parallel

step–up \ˈstep-ˌəp\ *n* (1922) **:** an increase or advance in size or amount

step up *vt* (1902) **1 :** to increase (a voltage) by means of a transformer **2 :** to increase, augment, or advance esp. by one or more steps ⟨*step up* production⟩ ~ *vi* **1 a :** to come forward ⟨*stepped up* to claim responsibility⟩ **b :** to succeed in meeting a challenge (as by increased effort or improved performance) **2 :** to undergo an increase ⟨business is *stepping up*⟩ **3 :** to receive a promotion — **step–up** \ˈstep-ˌəp\ *adj*

step·wise \-ˌwīz\ *adj* (1902) **1 :** marked by or proceeding in steps **2 :** moving by step to adjacent musical tones

ster *abbr* sterling

-ster *n comb form* [ME, fr. OE *-estre* female agent; akin to MD *-ster*] **1 :** one that does or handles or operates ⟨spin*ster*⟩ ⟨tap*ster*⟩ ⟨team*ster*⟩ **2 :** one that makes or uses ⟨song*ster*⟩ **3 :** one that is associated with or participates in ⟨game*ster*⟩ ⟨gang*ster*⟩ **4 :** one that is ⟨young*ster*⟩

ster·co·ra·ceous \ˌstər-kə-ˈrā-shəs\ *adj* [L *stercor-, stercus* excrement] (1731) **:** relating to, being, or containing feces

stere- *or* **stereo-** *comb form* [NL, fr. Gk, fr. *stereos* solid — more at STARE] **1 :** solid **:** solid body ⟨*stereo*gram⟩ **2 a :** stereoscopic ⟨*stereo*psis⟩ **b :** having or dealing with three dimensions of space ⟨*stereo*chemistry⟩

[1]**ste·reo** \ˈster-ē-ˌō, ˈstir-\ *n, pl* **ste·re·os** (ca. 1823) **1 :** STEREOTYPE **2** [by shortening] **a :** stereophonic reproduction **b :** a stereophonic sound system

[2]**stereo** *adj* (1876) **1 a :** STEREOSCOPIC **b :** produced by or as if by means of a stereotype **2 :** STEREOPHONIC

ste·reo·chem·is·try \ˌster-ē-ō-ˈke-mə-strē, ˌstir-\ *n* [ISV] (1890) **1 :** a branch of chemistry that deals with the spatial arrangement of atoms and groups in molecules **2 :** the spatial arrangement of atoms and groups in a compound and its relation to the properties of the compound — **ste·reo·chem·i·cal** \-ˈke-mi-kəl\ *adj*

ste·reo·gram \ˈster-ē-ə-ˌgram, ˈstir-\ *n* [ISV] (1868) **1 :** a diagram or picture representing objects with an impression of solidity or relief **2 :** STEREOGRAPH

ste·reo·graph \-ˌgraf\ *n* [ISV] (1859) **:** a pair of stereoscopic pictures or a picture composed of two superposed stereoscopic images that gives a three-dimensional effect when viewed with a stereoscope or special spectacles — **stereograph** *vt*

ste·reo·graph·ic \ˌster-ē-ə-ˈgra-fik\ *adj* (1704) **:** of, relating to, or being a delineation of the form of a solid body (as the earth) on a plane ⟨~ projection⟩ — **ste·re·og·ra·phy** \ˌster-ē-ˈä-grə-fē\ *n*

ste·reo·iso·mer \ˌster-ē-ō-ˈī-sə-mər, ˌstir-\ *n* [ISV] (1894) **:** any of a group of isomers in which atoms are linked in the same order but differ in their spatial arrangement — **ste·reo·iso·mer·ic** \-ˌī-sə-ˈmer-ik\ *adj* — **ste·reo·isom·er·ism** \-ī-ˈsä-mə-ˌri-zəm\ *n*

ste·re·ol·o·gy \ˌster-ē-ˈä-lə-jē, ˌstir-\ *n* [ISV] (1963) **:** a branch of science concerned with inferring the three-dimensional properties of objects or matter ordinarily observed two-dimensionally — **ste·reo·log·i·cal** \-ē-ə-ˈlä-ji-kəl\ *adj* — **ste·reo·log·i·cal·ly** \-ji-k(ə-)lē\ *adv*

ste·reo·mi·cro·scope \-ˈmī-krə-ˌskōp\ *n* (1948) **:** a microscope having a set of optics for each eye to make an object appear in three dimensions — **ste·reo·mi·cro·scop·ic** \-ˌmī-krə-ˈskä-pik\ *adj* — **ste·reo·mi·cro·scop·i·cal·ly** \-pi-k(ə-)lē\ *adv*

ste·reo·phon·ic \ˌster-ē-ə-ˈfä-nik, ˌstir-\ *adj* [ISV] (1927) **:** of, relating to, or constituting sound reproduction involving the use of separated microphones and two transmission channels to achieve the sound separation of a live hearing — **ste·reo·phon·i·cal·ly** \-ni-k(ə-)lē\ *adv* — **ste·reo·pho·ny** \ˌster-ē-ˈä-fə-nē, ˌstir-; ˈster-ē-ə-ˌfō-nē, ˈstir-\ *n*

ste·reo·pho·tog·ra·phy \ˌster-ē-ō-fə-ˈtä-grə-fē, ˌstir-\ *n* [ISV] (1903) **:** stereoscopic photography — **ste·reo·pho·to·graph·ic** \-ˌfō-tə-ˈgra-fik\ *adj*

ste·re·op·sis \ˌster-ē-ˈäp-səs, ˌstir-\ *n* [NL, fr. *stere-* + Gk *opsis* vision, appearance — more at OPTIC] (ca. 1911) **:** stereoscopic vision

ste·re·op·ti·con \-ˈäp-ti-kən\ *n* [NL, fr. *stere-* + Gk *optikon,* neut. of *optikos* optic] (1863) **1 :** a projector for transparent slides often made double so as to produce dissolving views **2 :** STEREOSCOPE

ste·reo·reg·u·lar \ˌster-ē-ō-ˈre-gyə-lər, ˌstir-\ *adj* (1958) **:** of, relating to, or involving stereochemical regularity in the repeating units of a polymeric structure — **ste·reo·reg·u·lar·i·ty** \-ˌre-gyə-ˈla-rə-tē\ *n*

ste·reo·scope \ˈster-ē-ə-ˌskōp, ˈstir-\ *n* (1838) **:** an optical instrument with two eyepieces for helping the observer to combine the images of two pictures taken from points of view a little way apart and thus to get the effect of solidity or depth

ste·reo·scop·ic \ˌster-ē-ə-ˈskä-pik, ˌstir-\ *adj* (1855) **1 :** of or relating to stereoscopy or the stereoscope **2 :** characterized by stereoscopy ⟨~ vision⟩ — **ste·reo·scop·i·cal·ly** \-pi-k(ə-)lē\ *adv*

ste·re·os·co·py \ˌster-ē-ˈäs-kə-pē, ˌstir-; ˈster-ē-ə-ˌskō-pē, ˈstir-\ *n* [ISV] (ca. 1859) **1 :** a science that deals with stereoscopic effects and methods **2 :** the seeing of objects in three dimensions

ste·reo·spe·cif·ic \ˌster-ē-ō-spi-ˈsi-fik, ˌstir-\ *adj* (1949) **:** being, produced by, or involved in a stereochemically specific process ⟨many enzymes act as ~ catalysts⟩ ⟨~ plastics⟩ — **ste·reo·spe·cif·i·cal·ly** \-fi-k(ə-)lē\ *adv* — **ste·reo·spec·i·fic·i·ty** \-ˌspe-sə-ˈfi-sə-tē\ *n*

ste·reo·tac·tic \ˌster-ē-ə-ˈtak-tik, ˌstir-\ *adj* (1950) **:** involving, being, utilizing, or used in a surgical technique for precisely directing the tip of a delicate instrument (as a needle) or beam of radiation in three planes using coordinates provided by medical imaging in order to reach a specific locus in the body — **ste·reo·tac·ti·cal·ly** \-ti-k(ə-)lē\ *adv*

---

ste·reo·tax·ic \ˌster-ē-ə-ˈtak-sik, ˌstir-\ *adj* [NL *stereotaxis* stereotactic technique, fr. *stere-* + *-taxis*] (1908) : STEREOTACTIC — **ste·reo·tax·i·cal·ly** \-si-k(ə-)lē\ *adv*

[1]**ste·reo·type** \ˈster-ē-ə-ˌtīp, ˈstir-\ *vt* (1804) **1** : to make a stereotype from **2 a** : to repeat without variation : make hackneyed **b** : to develop a mental stereotype about — **ste·reo·typ·er** *n*

[2]**stereotype** *n* [F *stéréotype,* fr. *stéré-* stere- + *type*] (1817) **1** : a plate cast from a printing surface **2** : something conforming to a fixed or general pattern; *esp* : a standardized mental picture that is held in common by members of a group and that represents an oversimplified opinion, prejudiced attitude, or uncritical judgment — **ste·reo·typ·i·cal** \ˌster-ē-ə-ˈti-pi-kəl\ *also* **ste·reo·typ·ic** \-pik\ *adj* — **ste·reo·typ·i·cal·ly** \-pi-k(ə-)lē\ *adv*

ste·reo·typed *adj* (1849) : lacking originality or individuality ***syn*** see TRITE

ste·reo·ty·py \ˈster-ē-ə-ˌtī-pē, ˈstir-\ *n, pl* **-pies** (ca. 1889) : frequent almost mechanical repetition of the same posture, movement, or form of speech (as in schizophrenia)

ste·ric \ˈster-ik, ˈstir-\ *adj* [ISV *stere-* + [1]*-ic*] (1898) : relating to or involving the arrangement of atoms in space : SPATIAL — **ste·ri·cal·ly** \ˈster-i-k(ə-)lē, ˈstir-\ *adv*

ste·rig·ma \stə-ˈrig-mə\ *n, pl* **-ma·ta** \-mə-tə\ *also* **-mas** [NL, fr. Gk *stērigma* support, fr. *stērizein* to prop; perh. akin to Gk *stereos* solid — more at STARE] (1874) : one of the slender stalks at the top of the basidium of some fungi from the tips of which the basidiospores are formed; *broadly* : a stalk or filament that bears conidia or spermatia

ster·il·ant \ˈster-ə-lənt\ *n* (1941) : a sterilizing agent

ster·ile \ˈster-əl, *chiefly Brit* -ˌī(-ə)l\ *adj* [ME *steryle,* fr. L *sterilis;* akin to Goth *stairo* barren animal, Skt *starī* sterile cow] (15c) **1 a** : failing to bear or incapable of producing fruit or spores **b** : failing to produce or incapable of producing offspring ⟨a ~ hybrid⟩ **c** : incapable of germinating ⟨~ spores⟩ **d** *of a flower* : neither perfect nor pistillate **2 a** : unproductive of vegetation ⟨a ~ arid region⟩ **b** : free from living organisms and esp. microorganisms ⟨a ~ syringe⟩ **c** : lacking in stimulating emotional or intellectual quality : LIFELESS ⟨a ~ work of art⟩ — **ster·ile·ly** \-ə(l)-lē\ *adv* — **ste·ril·i·ty** \stə-ˈri-lə-tē\ *n*

ster·il·ize \ˈster-ə-ˌlīz\ *vt* **-ized; -iz·ing** (1695) : to make sterile: as **a** : to cause (land) to become unfruitful **b (1)** : to deprive of the power of reproducing ⟨surgically ~ cats and dogs⟩ **(2)** : to make incapable of germination **c** : to make powerless or useless usu. by restraining from a normal function, relation, or participation **d** : to free from living microorganisms — **ster·il·i·za·tion** \ˌster-ə-lə-ˈzā-shən\ *n* — **ster·il·iz·er** \ˈster-ə-ˌlī-zər\ *n*

[1]**ster·ling** \ˈstər-liŋ\ *n* [ME, silver penny, prob. fr. OE *steorling, fr. OE *steorra* star + [1]*-ling* — more at STAR] (14c) **1** : British money **2** : sterling silver or articles of it

[2]**sterling** *adj* (15c) **1 a** : of, relating to, or calculated in terms of British sterling **b** : payable in sterling **2 a** *of silver* : having a fixed standard of purity usu. defined legally as represented by an alloy of 925 parts of silver with 75 parts of copper **b** : made of sterling silver **3** : conforming to the highest standard ⟨~ character⟩ ⟨a ~ record of achievement⟩ — **ster·ling·ly** *adv* — **ster·ling·ness** *n*

sterling area *n* (1932) : a former group of countries with currencies tied to the British pound sterling

[1]**stern** \ˈstərn\ *adj* [ME *sterne,* fr. OE *styrne;* akin to OE *starian* to stare — more at STARE] (bef. 12c) **1 a** : having a definite hardness or severity of nature or manner : AUSTERE **b** : expressive of severe displeasure : HARSH **2** : forbidding or gloomy in appearance **3** : INEXORABLE ⟨~ necessity⟩ **4** : STURDY, STOUT ⟨a ~ resolve⟩ ***syn*** see SEVERE — **stern·ly** *adv* — **stern·ness** \ˈstərn-nəs\ *n*

[2]**stern** *n* [ME, rudder, prob. of Scand origin; akin to ON *stjōrn* steering, rudder; akin to OE *stīeran* to steer — more at STEER] (14c) **1** : the rear end of a boat **2** : a hinder or rear part : the last or latter part

ster·nal \ˈstər-nᵊl\ *adj* (1756) : of or relating to the sternum

stern chase *n* [[2]*stern*] (1627) : a chase in which a pursuing ship follows in the path of another

stern chaser *n* (1815) : a gun so placed as to be able to fire astern at a pursuing ship

ster·nite \ˈstər-ˌnīt\ *n* [ISV, fr. Gk *sternon* chest] (1868) : the ventral part or shield of a somite of an arthropod; *esp* : the chitinous plate that forms the ventral surface of an abdominal or occas. a thoracic segment of an insect

stern·most \ˈstərn-ˌmōst\ *adj* (1622) : farthest astern

ster·no·cos·tal \ˌstər-nō-ˈkäs-tᵊl\ *adj* [NL *sternum* + E *-o-* + *costal*] (1785) : of, relating to, or situated between the sternum and ribs

stern·post \ˈstərn-ˌpōst\ *n* (15c) : the principal member at the stern of a ship extending from keel to deck

stern sheets *n pl* (15c) : the space in the stern of an open boat not occupied by the thwarts

ster·num \ˈstər-nəm\ *n, pl* **sternums** *or* **ster·na** \-nə\ [NL, fr. Gk *sternon* chest, breastbone; akin to OHG *stirna* forehead, L *sternere* to spread out — more at STREW] (1667) : a compound ventral bone or cartilage of most vertebrates other than fishes that connects the ribs or the shoulder girdle or both and in humans consists of the manubrium, gladiolus, and xiphoid process — called also *breastbone*

ster·nu·ta·tion \ˌstər-nyə-ˈtā-shən\ *n* [ME *sternutacion,* fr. L *sternutation-, sternutatio,* fr. *sternutare* to sneeze, freq. of *sternuere* to sneeze; akin to Gk *ptarnysthai* to sneeze] (15c) : the act or noise of sneezing

ster·nu·ta·tor \ˈstər-nyə-ˌtā-tər\ *n* (1922) : an agent that induces sneezing and often lacrimation and vomiting

stern·ward \ˈstərn-wərd\ *or* **stern·wards** \-wərdz\ *adv* (1832) : AFT

stern·way \ˈstərn-ˌwā\ *n* (1769) : movement of a ship backward or with stern foremost

stern–wheel·er \-ˈhwē-lər, -ˈwē-\ *n* (1855) : a steamboat driven by a single paddle wheel at the stern

ste·roid \ˈstir-ˌȯid *also* ˈster-\ *n* [ISV *sterol* + *-oid*] (1926) : any of various compounds containing a 17-carbon 4-ring system and including the sterols and numerous hormones (as anabolic steroids or corticosteroids) and glycosides — **steroid** *or* **ste·roi·dal** \stə-ˈrȯi-dᵊl\ *adj*

ste·roido·gen·e·sis \stə-ˌrȯi-də-ˈje-nə-səs; ˌstir-ˌȯid- *also* ˌster-\ *n* [NL] (1951) : synthesis of steroids — **ste·roido·gen·ic** \-ˈje-nik\ *adj*

ste·rol \ˈstir-ˌȯl, ˈster-, -ˌōl\ *n* [ISV, fr. *-sterol* (as in *cholesterol*)] (1913) : any of various solid steroid alcohols (as cholesterol) widely distributed in animal and plant lipids

-sterone *n comb form* [*sterol* + *-one*] : steroid hormone ⟨andro*sterone*⟩

ster·tor \ˈstər-tər, -ˌtȯr\ *n* [NL, fr. L *stertere* to snore; akin to *sternuere* to sneeze] (1804) : the act of producing a snoring sound : SNORING

ster·to·rous \ˈstər-tə-rəs\ *adj* (1802) : characterized by a harsh snoring or gasping sound — **ster·to·rous·ly** *adv*

stet \ˈstet\ *vt* **stet·ted; stet·ting** [L, let it stand, fr. *stare* to stand — more at STAND] (1875) : to direct retention of (a word or passage previously ordered to be deleted or omitted from a manuscript or printer's proof) by annotating usu. with the word *stet*

stetho·scope \ˈste-thə-ˌskōp *also* -t͟hə-\ *n* [F *stéthoscope,* fr. Gk *stēthos* chest + F *-scope*] (1820) : a medical instrument for detecting sounds produced in the body that are conveyed to the ears of the listener through rubber tubing connected with a piece placed upon the area to be examined — **stetho·scop·ic** \ˌste-thə-ˈskä-pik *also* -t͟hə-\ *adj*

Stet·son \ˈstet-sən\ *trademark* — used for a broad-brimmed high-crowned felt hat

[1]**ste·ve·dore** \ˈstē-və-ˌdȯr *also* ˈstēv-ˌ\ *n* [Sp *estibador,* fr. *estibar* to pack — more at STEEVE] (1788) : one who works at or is responsible for loading and unloading ships in port

[2]**stevedore** *vb* **-dored; -dor·ing** *vt* (1862) : to handle (cargo) as a stevedore; *also* : to load or unload the cargo of (a ship) in port ~ *vi* : to work as a stevedore

stevedore knot *n* (ca. 1863) : a stopper knot similar to a figure eight knot but with one or more extra turns — called also *stevedore's knot;* see KNOT illustration

Ste·ven·graph \ˈstē-vən-ˌgraf\ *or* **Ste·vens·graph** \-vənz-\ *n* [Thomas *Stevens* †1888 Eng. weaver] (1879) : a woven silk picture

ste·via \ˈstē-vē-ə, -vyə\ *n* [NL, fr. Petrus Jacobus *Stevus* (Pedro Jaime Esteve) †1555 Sp. physician and botanist] (1806) **1** : any of a genus (*Stevia*) of composite herbs and shrubs of tropical and subtropical America; *esp* : a white-flowered tender perennial (*S. rebaudiana*) native to Paraguay **2** : a white powder composed of one or more intensely sweet glycosides derived from the leaves of a stevia (*S. rebaudiana*) and used as noncaloric sweetener

[1]**stew** \ˈstü, ˈstyü\ *n* [ME *stewe* heated room for a steam bath, fr. AF *estuve,* fr. VL *extufa — more at STOVE] (13c) **1** *obs* : a utensil used for boiling **2** : a hot bath **3 a** : WHOREHOUSE **b** : a district of bordellos — usu. used in pl. **4 a** : fish or meat usu. with vegetables prepared by stewing **b (1)** : a heterogeneous mixture **(2)** : a state of heat and congestion **5** : a state of excitement, worry, or confusion

[2]**stew** *vt* (14c) : to boil slowly or with simmering heat ~ *vi* **1** : to become cooked by stewing **2** : to swelter esp. from confinement in a hot or stuffy atmosphere **3** : to be in a state of suppressed agitation, worry, or resentment

[3]**stew** *n* [short for *stewardess*] (1970) : FLIGHT ATTENDANT

[1]**stew·ard** \ˈstü-ərd, ˈstyü-; ˈst(y)u̇rd\ *n* [ME, fr. OE *stīweard,* fr. *stī, stig* hall, sty + *weard* ward — more at STY, WARD] (bef. 12c) **1** : one employed in a large household or estate to manage domestic concerns (as the supervision of servants, collection of rents, and keeping of accounts) **2** : SHOP STEWARD **3** : a fiscal agent **4 a** : an employee on a ship, airplane, bus, or train who manages the provisioning of food and attends passengers **b** : one appointed to supervise the provision and distribution of food and drink in an institution **5** : one who actively directs affairs : MANAGER

[2]**steward** *vt* (1621) : to act as a steward for : MANAGE ~ *vi* : to perform the duties of a steward

stew·ard·ess \ˈstü-ər-dəs, ˈstyü-; ˈst(y)u̇r-dəs\ *n* (1631) : a woman who performs the duties of a steward; *esp* : one who attends passengers (as on an airplane)

stew·ard·ship \ˈstü-ərd-ˌship, ˈstyü-; ˈst(y)u̇rd-\ *n* (15c) **1** : the office, duties, and obligations of a steward **2** : the conducting, supervising, or managing of something; *esp* : the careful and responsible management of something entrusted to one's care ⟨~ of natural resources⟩

stewed \ˈstüd\ *adj* (ca. 1737) : DRUNK 1a

stew·pan \ˈstü-ˌpan, ˈstyü-\ *n* (1651) : a pan used for stewing

stg *abbr* sterling

stib·nite \ˈstib-ˌnīt\ *n* [alter. of obs. E *stibine* stibnite, fr. F, fr. L *stibium* antimony, fr. Gk *stibi,* fr. Egypt *stm*] (ca. 1854) : a mineral that consists of the trisulfide of antimony and occurs in orthorhombic lead-gray crystals of metallic luster or in massive form

sticho·myth·ia \ˌsti-kə-ˈmi-thē-ə\ *also* **sti·chom·y·thy** \sti-ˈkä-mə-thē\ *n* [Gk *stichomythia,* fr. *stichomythein* to speak dialogue in alternate lines, fr. *stichos* row, verse + *mythos* speech, myth; akin to Gk *steichein* to walk, go — more at STAIR] (1861) : dialogue esp. of altercation or dispute delivered by two actors in alternating lines (as in classical Greek drama) — **sticho·myth·ic** \ˌsti-kə-ˈmi-thik\ *adj*

[1]**stick** \ˈstik\ *n* [ME *stik,* fr. OE *sticca;* akin to ON *stik* stick, OE *stician* to stick] (bef. 12c) **1** : a woody piece or part of a tree or shrub: as **a** : a usu. dry or dead severed shoot, twig, or slender branch **b** : a cut or broken branch or piece of wood gathered for fuel or construction material **2 a** : a long slender piece of wood or metal: as **(1)** : a club or staff used as a weapon **(2)** : WALKING STICK **b** : an implement used for striking or propelling an object in a game **c** : something used to force compliance **d** : a baton symbolizing an office or dignity; *also* : a person entitled to bear such a baton **3** : a piece of the materials composing something (as a building) **4** : any of various implements resembling a stick in shape, origin, or use: as **a** : COMPOSING STICK **b** : an airplane lever operating the elevators and ailerons **c** : the gearshift lever of an automobile **5** : something prepared (as by cutting, molding, or rolling) in a relatively long and slender often cylindrical form ⟨a ~ of candy⟩ ⟨a ~ of butter⟩ **6 a** : PERSON, CHAP **b** : a dull, inert, stiff, or spiritless person **7** *pl* : remote usu. rural districts regarded esp. as backward, dull, or unsophisticated : BOONDOCKS **8** : an herbaceous stalk resembling a woody stick ⟨celery ~*s*⟩ **9** : [1]MAST 1; *also* : [1]YARD 4 **10** : a piece of furniture **11 a** : a number of bombs arranged for release from a bombing plane in a

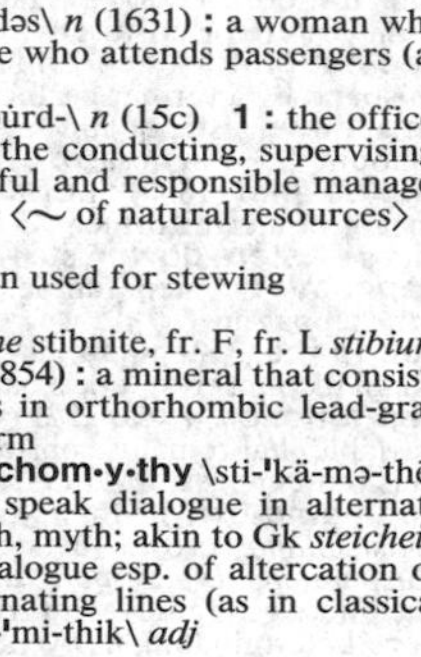

[1]stick 2b: *a* lacrosse, *b* ice hockey, *c* field hockey

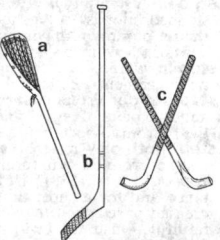

series across a target **b :** a number of parachutists dropping together **12** *slang* **:** a marijuana cigarette **13 a :** punishment or the threat of punishment used to force compliance or cooperation ⟨choosing between the carrot and the ∼⟩ **b** *Brit* **:** CRITICISM, ABUSE — **stick·like** \-ˌlīk\ *adj*

[2]**stick** *vt* (1937) **:** to hit or propel (as a hockey puck) with a stick

[3]**stick** *vb* **stuck** \ˈstək\; **stick·ing** [ME *stikken,* fr. OE *stician;* akin to OHG *sticken* to prick, L *instigare* to urge on, goad, Gk *stizein* to tattoo] *vt* (bef. 12c) **1 a :** to pierce with something pointed **:** STAB **b :** to kill by piercing **2 :** to push or thrust so as or as if to pierce **3 a :** to fasten by thrusting in **b :** IMPALE **c :** PUSH, THRUST **4 :** to put or set in a specified place or position **5 :** to furnish with things fastened on by or as if by piercing **6 :** to attach by or as if by causing to adhere to a surface **7 a :** to compel to pay esp. by trickery ⟨got *stuck* with the bar bill⟩ **b :** OVERCHARGE **8 a :** to halt the movement or action of **b :** BAFFLE, STUMP **9 a :** CHEAT, DEFRAUD **b :** to saddle with something disadvantageous or disagreeable ⟨is still *stuck* with that lousy car⟩ **10 :** to execute (a landing) flawlessly in gymnastics ∼ *vi* **1 :** to hold to something firmly by or as if by adhesion: **a :** to become fixed in place by means of a pointed end **b :** to become fast by or as if by miring or by gluing or plastering ⟨*stuck* in the mud⟩ **2 a :** to remain in a place, situation, or environment **b :** to hold fast or adhere resolutely **:** CLING ⟨she *stuck* to her story⟩ **c :** to remain effective **d :** to keep close in a chase or competition **3 :** to become blocked, wedged, or jammed **4 a :** BALK, SCRUPLE **b :** to find oneself baffled **c :** to be unable to proceed **5 :** PROJECT, PROTRUDE — **stick in one's craw :** to irritate, nag at, or obsess one — **stick it to :** to treat harshly or unfairly — **stick one's neck out :** to make oneself vulnerable by taking a risk — **stick to one's guns :** to maintain one's position esp. in face of opposition — **stuck on :** infatuated with

syn STICK, ADHERE, COHERE, CLING, CLEAVE mean to become closely attached. STICK implies attachment by affixing or by being glued together ⟨couldn't get the label to *stick*⟩. ADHERE is often interchangeable with *stick* but sometimes implies a growing together ⟨antibodies *adhering* to a virus⟩. COHERE suggests a sticking together of parts so that they form a unified mass ⟨eggs will make the mixture *cohere*⟩. CLING implies attachment by hanging on with arms or tendrils ⟨*clinging* to a capsized boat⟩. CLEAVE stresses strength of attachment ⟨the wet shirt *cleaved* to his back⟩.

[4]**stick** *n* (1633) **1 :** a thrust with a pointed instrument **:** STAB **2 a :** DELAY, STOP **b :** IMPEDIMENT **3 :** adhesive quality or substance

stick around *vi* (ca. 1912) **:** to stay or wait about **:** LINGER

stick·ball \ˈstik-ˌbȯl\ *n* (1922) **:** baseball adapted for play in streets or small areas and using a broomstick and a lightweight ball

stick blender *n* (1990) **:** IMMERSION BLENDER

stick·er \ˈsti-kər\ *n* (15c) **1 :** one that pierces with a point **2 a :** one that adheres or causes adhesion **b :** a slip of paper with adhesive back that can be fastened to a surface

sticker price *n* (1969) **:** a manufacturer's suggested retail price that is printed on a sticker and affixed to a new automobile; *broadly* **:** the stated cost of something ⟨a computer with a high *sticker price*⟩

sticker shock *n* (1981) **:** astonishment and dismay experienced on being informed of a product's unexpectedly high price

stick figure *n* (1949) **1 :** a drawing showing the head of a human being or animal as a circle and all other parts as straight lines **2 :** a fictional character lacking depth and believability

stick·han·dle \ˈstik-ˌhan-dᵊl\ *vi* (1929) **:** to maneuver a puck (as in hockey) or a ball (as in lacrosse) with a stick — **stick·han·dler** \-ˌhan(d)-lər, -ˌhan-dᵊl-ər\ *n*

sticking plaster *n* (1655) *chiefly Brit* **:** an adhesive plaster esp. for closing superficial wounds

sticking point *n* (1946) **:** an item (as in negotiations) resulting or likely to result in an impasse

stick insect *n* (1854) **:** any of various usu. wingless phasmid insects (esp. family Phasmatidae) with a long cylindrical body resembling a stick; *broadly* **:** PHASMID

stick–in–the–mud \ˈstik-ən-thə-ˌməd\ *n* (1733) **:** one who is slow, old-fashioned, or unprogressive; *esp* **:** an old fogy

stick·it \ˈsti-kət\ *adj* [Sc, fr. pp. of E [3]*stick*] (1787) **1** *Scot* **:** UNFINISHED **2** *chiefly Scot* **:** having failed esp. in an intended profession

stick·le \ˈsti-kəl\ *vi* **stick·led; stick·ling** \-k(ə-)liŋ\ [alter. of ME *stightlen,* freq. of *stighten* to arrange, fr. OE *stihtan;* akin to ON *stētta* to found, support] (1642) **1 :** to contend esp. stubbornly and usu. on insufficient grounds **2 :** to feel scruples **:** SCRUPLE

stick·le·back \ˈsti-kəl-ˌbak\ *n, pl* **-backs** *also* **-back** [ME *stykylbak,* fr. OE *sticel* goad + ME *bak* back; akin to OE *stician* to stick] (15c) **:** any of a family (Gasterosteidae) of small scaleless bony fishes having two or more free spines in front of the dorsal fin and including marine, anadromous, and freshwater forms

stick·ler \ˈsti-k(ə-)lər\ *n* (1644) **1 :** one who insists on exactness or completeness in the observance of something ⟨a ∼ for the rules⟩ **2 :** something that baffles or puzzles **:** POSER, STICKER

stick·man \ˈstik-ˌman, -mən\ *n* (ca. 1931) **:** one who handles a stick: as **a :** one who supervises the play at a dice table, calls the decisions, and retrieves the dice **b :** a player in any of various games (as hockey or lacrosse) played with a stick

stick out *vi* (1567) **1 a :** to jut out **:** PROJECT **b :** to be prominent or conspicuous **2 :** to be persistent (as in a demand or an opinion) ∼ *vt* **:** ENDURE, LAST — often used with *it* ⟨*stuck* it *out* to the end⟩

stick·pin \ˈstik-ˌpin\ *n* (1895) **:** an ornamental pin esp. for a necktie

stick·seed \-ˌsēd\ *n* (1843) **:** any of various weedy herbs (genera *Lappula* and *Hackelia*) of the borage family with bristly adhesive fruit

stick shift *n* (1959) **:** a manually operated gearshift for a motor vehicle usu. mounted on the floor

stick·tight \ˈstik-ˌtīt\ *n* (ca. 1884) **:** BUR MARIGOLD

stick–to–it·ive·ness \stik-ˈtü-ə-tiv-nəs\ *n* [fr. the phrase *stick to it*] (1867) **:** dogged perseverance **:** TENACITY

stick·um \ˈsti-kəm\ *n* [[3]*stick* + *-um* (prob. alter. of *'em* them)] (ca. 1909) **:** a substance that adheres or causes adhesion

stick·up \ˈstik-ˌəp\ *n* (1904) **:** a robbery at gunpoint **:** HOLDUP

stick up *vi* (15c) **:** to stand upright or on end **:** PROTRUDE ∼ *vt* **:** to rob at gunpoint — **stick up for :** to speak or act in defense of **:** SUPPORT

stick·weed \ˈstik-ˌwēd\ *n* (1743) **:** any of several plants (as a beggar's-lice) with adhesive seeds

stick·work \-ˌwərk\ *n* (1903) **:** the use of one's stick in offensive and defensive techniques (as in hockey)

sticky \ˈsti-kē\ *adj* **stick·i·er; -est** (1731) **1 a :** ADHESIVE **b** (1) **:** VISCOUS, GLUEY (2) **:** coated with a sticky substance **2 :** HUMID, MUGGY; *also* **:** CLAMMY **3 :** tending to stick **4 a :** DISAGREEABLE, UNPLEASANT ⟨came to a ∼ end⟩ **b :** AWKWARD, STIFF **c :** DIFFICULT, PROBLEMATIC ⟨a ∼ situation⟩ **5 :** excessively sentimental **:** CLOYING — **stick·i·ly** \ˈsti-kə-lē\ *adv* — **stick·i·ness** \ˈsti-kē-nəs\ *n*

sticky bun *n* (1909) **:** a spiral-shaped cinnamon roll topped with melted brown sugar and butter

sticky note *n* (1984) **:** a slip of notepaper having an adhesive strip on the back that allows attachment to and removal from a surface

sticky wicket *n* (1882) **:** a difficult or delicate problem or situation

stic·tion \ˈstik-shən\ *n* [*st*atic + fr*iction*] (1946) **:** the force required to cause one body in contact with another to begin to move

[1]**stiff** \ˈstif\ *adj* [ME *stif,* fr. OE *stīf;* akin to MD *stijf* stiff, L *stipare* to press together, Gk *steibein* to tread on] (bef. 12c) **1 a :** not easily bent **:** RIGID ⟨a ∼ collar⟩ **b :** lacking in suppleness or flexibility ⟨∼ muscles⟩ **c :** impeded in movement — used of a mechanism ⟨a truck's ∼ suspension⟩ **d :** DRUNK 1a **2 a :** FIRM, RESOLUTE **b :** STUBBORN, UNYIELDING **c :** PROUD **d** (1) **:** marked by reserve or decorum (2) **:** lacking in ease or grace **:** STILTED **3 :** hard fought ⟨∼ competition⟩ **4 a** (1) **:** exerting great force ⟨a ∼ wind⟩ (2) **:** FORCEFUL, VIGOROUS **b :** POTENT ⟨poured her a ∼ drink⟩ **5 :** of a dense or glutinous consistency **:** THICK **6 a :** HARSH, SEVERE ⟨a ∼ penalty⟩ **b :** ARDUOUS, RUGGED ⟨∼ terrain⟩ **7 :** not easily heeled over by an external force (as the wind) ⟨a ∼ ship⟩ **8 :** EXPENSIVE, STEEP ⟨paid a ∼ price⟩ — **stiff·ish** \ˈsti-fish\ *adj* — **stiff·ly** *adv* — **stiff·ness** *n*

syn STIFF, RIGID, INFLEXIBLE mean difficult to bend. STIFF may apply to any degree of this condition ⟨stretching keeps your muscles from becoming *stiff*⟩. RIGID applies to something so stiff that it cannot be bent without breaking ⟨a *rigid* surfboard⟩. INFLEXIBLE stresses lack of suppleness or pliability ⟨ski boots with *inflexible* soles⟩.

[2]**stiff** *adv* (13c) **1 :** in a stiff manner **:** STIFFLY **2 :** to an extreme degree **:** SEVERELY ⟨scared ∼⟩ ⟨bored ∼⟩ **3 :** close enough to the hole for an easy putt in golf ⟨hit it ∼ and tapped it in for an easy birdie⟩

[3]**stiff** *n* (ca. 1859) **1 :** CORPSE **2 a :** VAGRANT, TRAMP **b :** a member of the working class; *esp* **:** a blue-collar worker **c :** PERSON ⟨a lucky ∼⟩; *esp* **:** a stodgy or excessively decorous person **3 :** FLOP, FAILURE

[4]**stiff** *vt* (1950) **1 a :** to refuse to pay or tip ⟨∼*ed* the waiter⟩ **b :** CHEAT ⟨∼*ed* him in a business deal⟩ **c :** STICK 7a ⟨∼*ed* us with the bar bill⟩ **2 :** SNUB 3 ⟨∼*ed* sportswriters after the game⟩ ∼ *vi* **:** to fail commercially ⟨the movie ∼*ed* at the box office⟩

[1]**stiff–arm** \ˈstif-ˌärm\ *vi* (1909) **:** STRAIGHT-ARM ∼ *vt* **1 :** STRAIGHT-ARM **2 :** to treat with disdain or neglect **:** SLIGHT, SNUB

[2]**stiff–arm** *n* (1927) **:** STRAIGHT-ARM

stiff·en \ˈsti-fən\ *vb* **stiff·ened; stiff·en·ing** \ˈsti-fə-niŋ, ˈstif-niŋ\ *vt* (15c) **:** to make stiff or stiffer ∼ *vi* **:** to become stiff or stiffer — **stiff·en·er** \ˈsti-fə-nər, ˈstif-nər\ *n*

stiff–necked \ˈstif-ˈnekt\ *adj* (1526) **1 :** HAUGHTY, STUBBORN **2 :** FORMAL, STILTED

stiff upper lip *n* [fr. the phrase *keep a stiff upper lip*] (1815) **:** a steady and determined attitude or manner in the face of trouble — **stiff–upper–lip** *adj*

[1]**sti·fle** \ˈstī-fəl\ *n* [ME] (14c) **:** the joint next above the hock in the hind leg of a quadruped (as a horse or dog) corresponding to the human knee — see HORSE illustration

[2]**stifle** *vb* **sti·fled; sti·fling** \-f(ə-)liŋ\ [alter. of ME *stuflen*] *vt* (1513) **1 a :** to kill by depriving of oxygen **:** SUFFOCATE **b** (1) **:** SMOTHER (2) **:** MUFFLE **2 a :** to cut off (as the voice or breath) **b :** to withhold from circulation or expression ⟨*stifled* our anger⟩ **c :** DETER, DISCOURAGE ∼ *vi* **:** to be or become unable to breathe easily ⟨*stifling* in the heat⟩ — **sti·fler** \-f(ə-)lər\ *n* — **sti·fling·ly** \-f(ə-)liŋ-lē\ *adv*

stig·ma \ˈstig-mə\ *n, pl* **stig·ma·ta** \stig-ˈmä-tə, ˈstig-mə-tə\ *or* **stigmas** [L *stigmat-, stigma* mark, brand, fr. Gk, fr. *stizein* to tattoo — more at STICK] (ca. 1593) **1 a** *archaic* **:** a scar left by a hot iron **:** BRAND **b :** a mark of shame or discredit **:** STAIN ⟨bore the ∼ of cowardice⟩ **c :** an identifying mark or characteristic; *specif* **:** a specific diagnostic sign of a disease **2 a** *stigmata pl* **:** bodily marks or pains resembling the wounds of the crucified Jesus and sometimes accompanying religious ecstasy **b :** PETECHIA **3 a :** a small spot, scar, or opening on a plant or animal **b :** the usu. apical part of the pistil of a flower which receives the pollen grains and on which they germinate — see FLOWER illustration — **stig·mal** \ˈstig-məl\ *adj*

stig·mas·ter·ol \stig-ˈmas-tə-ˌrȯl, -ˌrōl\ *n* [NL Physo*stigma* (genus including the Calabar bean, a source of stigmasterol) + ISV *sterol*] (1907) **:** a crystalline sterol $C_{29}H_{48}O$ obtained esp. from soybean oil

[1]**stig·mat·ic** \stig-ˈma-tik\ *n* (1594) **:** one marked with stigmata

[2]**stigmatic** *adj* (1601) **1 :** having or conveying a social stigma **2 :** of or relating to a stigma **3 :** of or relating to supernatural stigmata **4 :** ANASTIGMATIC — used esp. of a bundle of light rays intersecting at a single point — **stig·mat·i·cal·ly** \-ti-k(ə-)lē\ *adv*

stig·ma·tist \ˈstig-mə-tist, stig-ˈmä-\ *n* (1607) **:** STIGMATIC

stig·ma·tize \ˈstig-mə-ˌtīz\ *vt* **-tized; -tiz·ing** (1585) **1 a** *archaic* **:** BRAND **b :** to describe or identify in opprobrious terms **2 :** to mark with stigmata — **stig·ma·ti·za·tion** \ˌstig-mə-tə-ˈzā-shən\ *n*

stil·bene \ˈstil-ˌbēn\ *n* [ISV, fr. Gk *stilbein* to glitter] (ca. 1868) **:** an aromatic hydrocarbon $C_{14}H_{12}$ used as a phosphor and in making dyes; *also* **:** a compound derived from stilbene

stil·bes·trol \stil-ˈbes-ˌtrȯl, -ˌtrōl\ *n* [*stil*bene + *estr*us + [1]*-ol*] (ca. 1939) **:** DIETHYLSTILBESTROL

stil·bite \ˈstil-ˌbīt\ *n* [F, fr. Gk *stilbein*] (1815) **:** a mineral consisting of a hydrous silicate of aluminum, calcium, and sodium and often occurring in sheaflike aggregations of crystals

[1]**stile** \ˈstī(-ə)l\ *n* [ME, fr. OE *stigel;* akin to OE *stǣger* stair — more at STAIR] (bef. 12c) **:** a step or set of steps for passing over a fence or wall; *also* **:** TURNSTILE

\ə\ **abut** \ᵊ\ kitten, F table \ər\ **fur**ther \a\ **ash** \ā\ **ace** \ä\ **mop, mar**
\au̇\ **out** \ch\ **chin** \e\ **bet** \ē\ **easy** \g\ **go** \i\ **hit** \ī\ **ice** \j\ **job**
\ŋ\ **sing** \ō\ **go** \ȯ\ **law** \ȯi\ **boy** \th\ **thin** \th\ **the** \ü\ **loot** \u̇\ **foot**
\y\ **yet** \zh\ **vision, beige** \k, ⁿ, œ, ue, ʸ\ *see* Guide to Pronunciation

[2]**stile** *n* [prob. fr. D *stijl* post] (1678) **:** one of the vertical members in a frame or panel into which the secondary members are fitted

sti·let·to \stə-ˈle-(ˌ)tō\ *n, pl* **-tos** *or* **-toes** [It, dim. of *stilo* stylus, dagger, fr. L *stilus* stylus — more at STYLE] (ca. 1611) **1 :** a slender dagger with a blade thick in proportion to its breadth **2 :** a pointed instrument for piercing holes for eyelets or embroidery **3 :** STILETTO HEEL; *also* **:** a shoe with a stiletto heel

stiletto heel *n* (1953) **:** a high thin heel on women's shoes that is narrower than a spike heel

[1]**still** \ˈstil\ *adj* [ME *stille,* fr. OE; akin to OHG *stilli* still and perh. to OE *steall* stall — more at STALL] (bef. 12c) **1 a :** devoid of or abstaining from motion **b** *archaic* **:** SEDENTARY **c :** not effervescent ⟨~ wine⟩ **d** (1) **:** of, relating to, or being a static photograph as contrasted with a motion picture (2) **:** designed for taking still photographs ⟨a ~ camera⟩ (3) **:** engaged in taking still photographs ⟨a ~ photographer⟩ **2 a :** uttering no sound **:** QUIET **b :** SUBDUED, MUTED **3 a :** CALM, TRANQUIL **b :** free from noise or turbulence — **still·ness** *n*

[2]**still** *vi* (bef. 12c) **:** to become motionless or silent **:** QUIET ~ *vt* **1 a :** ALLAY, CALM ⟨~*ed* their nerves⟩ **b :** to put an end to **:** SETTLE **2 :** to arrest the motion of **3 :** SILENCE

[3]**still** *adv* (bef. 12c) **1 :** without motion ⟨sit ~⟩ **2** *archaic* **a :** ALWAYS, CONTINUALLY **b :** in a progressive manner **:** INCREASINGLY **3 —** used as a function word to indicate the continuance of an action or condition ⟨~ lives there⟩ ⟨drink it while it's ~ hot⟩ **4 :** in spite of that **:** NEVERTHELESS ⟨those who take the greatest care ~ make mistakes⟩ **5 a :** EVEN 2c ⟨a ~ more difficult problem⟩ ⟨heavier ~⟩ **b :** YET 1a ⟨has ~ to be recognized⟩

[4]**still** *n* (13c) **1 :** QUIET, SILENCE **2 :** a static photograph; *specif* **:** a photograph of actors or scenes of a motion picture for publicity or documentary purposes

[5]**still** *vb* [ME *stillen,* short for *distillen* to distill] (13c) **:** DISTILL

[6]**still** *n* (1533) **1 :** DISTILLERY **2 :** apparatus used in distillation comprising either the chamber in which the vaporization is carried out or the entire equipment

still alarm *n* (1875) **:** a fire alarm transmitted (as by telephone call) without sounding the signal apparatus

still and all *adv* (1829) **:** NEVERTHELESS, STILL

still·birth \ˈstil-ˌbərth, -ˈbərth\ *n* (1880) **:** the birth of a dead fetus

still·born \-ˈbȯrn\ *adj* (1593) **1 :** dead at birth **2 :** failing from the start **:** ABORTIVE, UNSUCCESSFUL ⟨a ~ venture⟩ — **still·born** \-ˌbȯrn\ *n*

still–hunt \-ˌhənt\ *vi* (1858) **:** to ambush or stalk a quarry; *esp* **:** to pursue game noiselessly usu. without a dog ~ *vt* **:** to lie in wait for **:** approach by stealth

still hunt *n* (1828) **:** a quiet pursuing or ambushing of game

still less *conj* (1721) **:** MUCH LESS, LET ALONE ⟨no living person . . . seemed to notice him, *still less* to expect him —Thomas Hardy⟩

still life *n, pl* **still lifes** (1695) **1 :** a picture consisting predominantly of inanimate objects **2 :** the category of graphic arts concerned with inanimate subject matter

still·man \ˈstil-mən\ *n* (ca. 1864) **:** one who owns or operates a still

still·room \ˈstil-ˌrüm, -ˌru̇m\ *n* [[6]*still*] (ca. 1710) *Brit* **:** a room connected with the kitchen where liqueurs, preserves, and cakes are kept and beverages (as tea) are prepared

still water *n* (1832) **:** a part of a stream where no current is visible

[1]**stil·ly** \ˈstil-lē\ *adv* (bef. 12c) **:** in a calm manner **:** QUIETLY

[2]**stilly** \ˈsti-lē\ *adj* [[1]*still* + [1]*-y*] (1722) **:** STILL, QUIET

[1]**stilt** \ˈstilt\ *n* [ME *stilte;* akin to OHG *stelza* stilt] (15c) **1 a :** one of two poles each with a rest or strap for the foot used to elevate the wearer above the ground in walking **b :** a pile or post serving as one of the supports of a structure above ground or water level **2** *pl also* **stilt :** any of several very long-legged 3-toed shorebirds (genera *Himantopus* and *Cladorhynchus*) that are related to the avocets, frequent inland ponds and marshes, and nest in small colonies

[2]**stilt** *vt* (1649) **:** to raise on or as if on stilts

stilt·ed \ˈstil-təd\ *adj* (1820) **1 a :** POMPOUS, LOFTY **b :** FORMAL, STIFF **2 :** having the curve beginning at some distance above the impost ⟨a ~ arch⟩ — **stilt·ed·ly** *adv* — **stilt·ed·ness** *n*

Stil·ton \ˈstil-tᵊn\ *n* [*Stilton,* Huntingdonshire, England] (1736) **:** a blue-veined cheese with wrinkled rind made of whole cows' milk enriched with cream

stime \ˈstīm\ *n* [ME (northern dial.)] (14c) *chiefly Scot & Irish* **:** GLIMMER; *also* **:** GLIMPSE

stim·u·lant \ˈstim-yə-lənt\ *n* (ca. 1728) **1 :** an agent (as a drug) that produces a temporary increase of the functional activity or efficiency of an organism or any of its parts **2 :** STIMULUS **3 :** an alcoholic beverage — not used technically — **stimulant** *adj*

stim·u·late \-ˌlāt\ *vb* **-lat·ed; -lat·ing** [L *stimulatus,* pp. of *stimulare,* fr. *stimulus* goad; perh. akin to L *stilus* stem, stylus — more at STYLE] *vt* (1566) **1 :** to excite to activity or growth or to greater activity **:** ANIMATE, AROUSE **2 a :** to function as a physiological stimulus to **b :** to arouse or affect by a stimulant (as a drug) ~ *vi* **:** to act as a stimulant or stimulus ***syn*** see PROVOKE — **stim·u·la·tion** \ˌstim-yə-ˈlā-shən\ *n* — **stim·u·la·tive** \ˈstim-yə-ˌlā-tiv\ *adj* — **stim·u·la·tor** \-ˌlā-tər\ *n* — **stim·u·la·to·ry** \-lə-ˌtȯr-ē\ *adj*

stim·u·lus \ˈstim-yə-ləs\ *n, pl* **-li** \-ˌlī, -ˌlē\ [L] (1684) **:** something that rouses or incites to activity: as **a :** INCENTIVE **b :** STIMULANT 1 **c :** an agent (as an environmental change) that directly influences the activity of a living organism or one of its parts (as by exciting a sensory organ or evoking muscular contraction or glandular secretion)

[1]**sting** \ˈstiŋ\ *vb* **stung** \ˈstəŋ\; **sting·ing** \ˈstiŋ-iŋ\ [ME, fr. OE *stingan;* akin to ON *stinga* to sting and prob. to Gk *stachys* spike of grain, *stochos* target, aim] *vt* (bef. 12c) **1 :** to prick painfully: as **a :** to pierce or wound with a poisonous or irritating process **b :** to affect with sharp quick pain or smart ⟨hail *stung* their faces⟩ **2 :** to cause to suffer acutely ⟨*stung* with remorse⟩ **3 :** OVERCHARGE, CHEAT ~ *vi* **1 :** to wound one with or as if with a sting **2 :** to feel a keen burning pain or smart; *also* **:** to cause such pain — **sting·ing·ly** \-iŋ-lē\ *adv*

[2]**sting** *n* (bef. 12c) **1 a :** the act of stinging; *specif* **:** the thrust of a stinger into the flesh **b :** a wound or pain caused by or as if by stinging **2 :** STINGER 2 **3 :** a sharp or stinging element, force, or quality **4 :** an elaborate confidence game; *specif* **:** such a game worked by undercover police in order to trap criminals

sting·a·ree \ˈstiŋ-ə-rē *also* ˈstiŋ-rē\ *n* [by alter.] (1836) **:** STINGRAY

sting·er \ˈstiŋ-ər\ *n* (ca. 1552) **1 :** one that stings; *specif* **:** a sharp blow or remark **2 :** a sharp organ (as of a bee, scorpion, or stingray) that is usu. connected with a poison gland or otherwise adapted to wound by piercing and injecting a poison **3 :** a cocktail usu. consisting of brandy and white crème de menthe

stinging nettle *n* (1525) **:** NETTLE 1; *esp* **:** a Eurasian nettle (*Urtica dioica*) widely naturalized in No. America that has numerous hairs extremely irritating to the skin

sting·less \ˈstiŋ-ləs\ *adj* (1554) **:** having no sting or stinger

sting·ray \-ˌrā\ *n* (1624) **:** any of numerous rays (as of the family Dasyatidae) with one or more large sharp barbed dorsal spines near the base of the whiplike tail capable of inflicting severe wounds

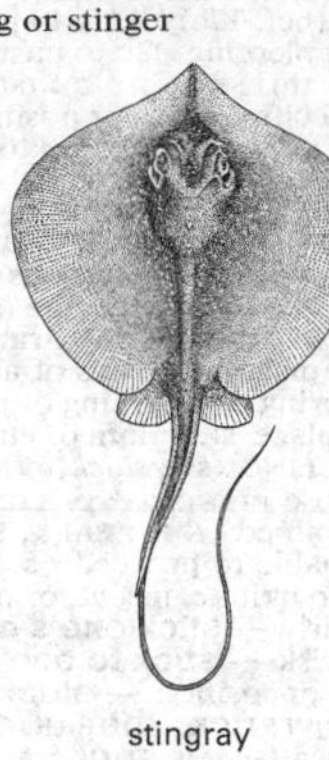
stingray

stin·gy \ˈstin-jē\ *adj* **stin·gi·er; -est** [perh. fr. E dial. **stinge,* n., sting; akin to OE *stingan* to sting] (1659) **1 :** not generous or liberal **:** sparing or scant in using, giving, or spending ⟨~ with the salt⟩ ⟨~ employee benefits⟩ **2 :** meanly scanty or small ⟨~ portions of meat⟩ — **stin·gi·ly** \-jə-lē\ *adv* — **stin·gi·ness** \-jē-nəs\ *n*

syn STINGY, CLOSE, NIGGARDLY, PARSIMONIOUS, PENURIOUS, MISERLY mean being unwilling or showing unwillingness to share with others. STINGY implies a marked lack of generosity ⟨a *stingy* child, not given to sharing⟩. CLOSE suggests keeping a tight grip on one's money and possessions ⟨folks who are very *close* when charity calls⟩. NIGGARDLY implies giving or spending the very smallest amount possible ⟨the *niggardly* amount budgeted for the town library⟩. PARSIMONIOUS suggests a frugality so extreme as to lead to stinginess ⟨a *parsimonious* lifestyle notably lacking in luxuries⟩. PENURIOUS implies niggardliness that gives an appearance of actual poverty ⟨the *penurious* eccentric bequeathed a fortune⟩. MISERLY suggests a sordid avariciousness and a morbid pleasure in hoarding ⟨a *miserly* couple devoid of social conscience⟩.

[1]**stink** \ˈstiŋk\ *vi* **stank** \ˈstaŋk\ *or* **stunk** \ˈstəŋk\; **stunk; stink·ing** [ME, fr. OE *stincan;* akin to OHG *stinkan* to emit a smell] (bef. 12c) **1 :** to emit a strong offensive odor ⟨*stank* of urine⟩ **2 :** to be offensive ⟨the election *stank* of corruption⟩; *also* **:** to be in bad repute **3 :** to possess something to an offensive degree ⟨~*ing* with wealth⟩ **4 :** to be extremely bad or unpleasant ⟨the performance *stank*⟩ ⟨that news really ~*s*⟩ — **stinky** \ˈstiŋ-kē\ *adj*

[2]**stink** *n* (13c) **1 :** a strong offensive odor **:** STENCH **2 :** a public outcry against something **:** FUSS ⟨made a big ~ when asked to leave⟩

stink·ard \ˈstiŋ-kərd\ *n* (ca. 1600) **:** a mean or contemptible person

stink bomb *n* (1915) **:** a small bomb charged usu. with chemicals that gives off a foul odor on bursting

stink·bug \ˈstiŋk-ˌbəg\ *n* (ca. 1877) **:** any of various hemipterous bugs (esp. family Pentatomidae) that emit a disagreeable odor

stink·er \ˈstiŋ-kər\ *n* (1602) **1 a :** an offensive or contemptible person **b :** one that stinks **c :** something of very poor quality; *also* **:** DUD 2a ⟨the movie is a ~⟩ **2 :** any of several large petrels that have an offensive odor **3** *slang* **:** something extremely difficult ⟨the examination was a real ~⟩

stink·horn \ˈstiŋk-ˌhȯrn\ *n* (ca. 1724) **:** any of various fetid basidiomycetous fungi (order Phallales, esp. *Phallus impudicus*) having spores dispersed by insects

[1]**stinking** *adj* (bef. 12c) **1 :** strong and offensive to the sense of smell ⟨~ garbage⟩ **2** *slang* **:** offensively drunk **3 :** CONTEMPTIBLE, LOUSY — often used as an intensive ⟨the whole ~ affair⟩ ***syn*** see MALODOROUS — **stink·ing·ly** *adv*

[2]**stinking** *adv* (1887) **:** to an extreme degree ⟨got ~ drunk⟩

stinking smut *n* (ca. 1891) **:** [4]BUNT

stink·pot \ˈstiŋk-ˌpät\ *n* (1669) **1 :** an earthen jar filled with fetid material and formerly sometimes thrown as a stink bomb on the deck of an enemy ship **2 :** a musk turtle (*Sternotherus odoratus*) of the U.S. and Canada **3 :** STINKER 1 **4** *slang* **:** MOTORBOAT

stink up *vt* (1941) **:** to cause to stink or be filled with a stench

stink·weed \ˈstiŋk-ˌwēd\ *n* (1753) **:** any of various strong-scented or fetid plants: as **a :** PENNYCRESS **b :** JIMSONWEED

stink·wood \-ˌwu̇d\ *n* (1731) **1 :** any of several trees with a wood of unpleasant odor; *esp* **:** a southern African tree (*Ocotea bullata*) of the laurel family yielding a hard strong wood used in cabinetmaking **2 :** the wood of a stinkwood

[1]**stint** \ˈstint\ *vb* [ME, fr. OE *styntan* to blunt, dull; akin to ON *stuttr* scant] *vi* (13c) **1** *archaic* **:** STOP, DESIST **2 :** to be sparing or frugal ⟨not ~*ing* with their praise⟩ ~ *vt* **1** *archaic* **:** to put an end to **:** STOP **2 a** *archaic* **:** to limit within certain boundaries **b :** to restrict with respect to a share or allowance ⟨~*ed* herself of luxuries⟩ — **stint·er** *n*

[2]**stint** *n* (1593) **1 a :** a definite quantity of work assigned **b :** a period of time spent at a particular activity ⟨served a brief ~ as a waiter⟩ **2 :** RESTRAINT, LIMITATION ***syn*** see TASK

[3]**stint** *n, pl* **stints** *also* **stint** [ME *stynte*] (15c) **:** any of several small sandpipers (genus *Calidris*)

stipe \ˈstīp\ *n* [NL *stipes,* fr. L, tree trunk; akin to L *stipare* to press together — more at STIFF] (1785) **:** a usu. short stalk of a plant or fungus: as **a :** the stem supporting the cap of a fungus **b :** a part that is similar to a stipe and connects the holdfast and blade of a frondose alga **c :** the petiole of a fern frond **d :** a prolongation of the receptacle beneath the ovary of a seed plant — **stiped** \ˈstīpt\ *adj*

sti·pend \ˈstī-ˌpend, -pənd\ *n* [ME, alter. of *stipendy,* fr. L *stipendium,* fr. *stip-, stips* gift + *pendere* to weigh, pay] (15c) **:** a fixed sum of money paid periodically for services or to defray expenses

[1]**sti·pen·di·ary** \stī-ˈpen-dē-ˌer-ē\ *n, pl* **-ar·ies** (15c) **:** one who receives a stipend

[2]**stipendiary** *adj* (ca. 1545) **1 :** receiving or compensated by wages or salary ⟨a ~ curate⟩ **2 :** of or relating to a stipend

[1]**stip·ple** \ˈsti-pəl\ *vt* **stip·pled; stip·pling** \-p(ə-)liŋ\ [D *stippelen* to spot, dot] (ca. 1762) **1 :** to engrave by means of dots and flicks **2 a :** to make by small short touches (as of paint or ink) that together pro-

duce an even or softly graded shadow **b** : to apply (as paint) by repeated small touches **3** : SPECKLE, FLECK — **stip·pler** \-p(ə-)lər\ *n*

[2]**stipple** *n* (1837) : production of gradation of light and shade in graphic art by stippling small points, larger dots, or longer strokes; *also* : an effect produced in this way

stip·u·lar \ˈsti-pyə-lər\ *adj* (1793) : of, resembling, or having stipules ⟨~ glands⟩

[1]**stip·u·late** \ˈsti-pyə-ˌlāt\ *vb* **-lat·ed; -lat·ing** [L *stipulatus,* pp. of *stipulari* to demand a guarantee (from a prospective debtor)] *vi* (ca. 1624) **1** : to make an agreement or covenant to do or forbear something : CONTRACT **2** : to demand an express term in an agreement — used with *for* ~ *vt* **1** : to specify as a condition or requirement (as of an agreement or offer) **2** : to give a guarantee of — **stip·u·la·tor** \-ˌlā-tər\ *n*

[2]**stip·u·late** \ˈsti-pyə-lət\ *adj* [NL *stipula*] (ca. 1776) : having stipules

stip·u·la·tion \ˌsti-pyə-ˈlā-shən\ *n* (ca. 1552) **1** : an act of stipulating **2** : something stipulated; *esp* : a condition, requirement, or item specified in a legal instrument — **stip·u·la·to·ry** \ˈsti-pyə-lə-ˌtȯr-ē\ *adj*

stip·ule \ˈsti-(ˌ)pyül\ *n* [NL *stipula,* fr. L, stalk; akin to L *stipes* tree trunk] (ca. 1793) : either of a pair of appendages borne at the base of the petiole in many plants

[1]**stir** \ˈstər\ *vb* **stirred; stir·ring** [ME, fr. OE *styrian;* akin to OHG *stōren* to scatter] *vt* (bef. 12c) **1 a** : to cause an esp. slight movement or change of position of **b** : to disturb the quiet of : AGITATE — often used with *up* ⟨the bear *stirred* up the bees⟩ **2 a** : to disturb the relative position of the particles or parts of esp. by a continued circular movement ⟨~ the pudding⟩ ⟨~ the fire⟩ — often used with *up* ⟨*stirred* up mud from the lake bottom⟩ **b** : to mix by or as if by stirring — often used with *in* ⟨~ in the spices⟩ **3** : BESTIR, EXERT **4** : to bring into notice or debate : RAISE — often used with *up* ⟨~ up sensitive issues⟩ **5 a** : to rouse to activity : evoke strong feelings in ⟨music that ~*s* the emotions⟩ **b** : to call forth (as a memory) : EVOKE **c** : PROVOKE ⟨~ a storm of controversy⟩ ~ *vi* **1 a** : to make a slight movement ⟨the leaves were barely *stirring*⟩ **b** : to begin to move (as in rousing) **c** : to shift to another location : BUDGE ⟨haven't *stirred* since I arrived⟩ **2** : to begin to be active ⟨the factory *stirred* to life⟩ **3** : to be active or busy ⟨not a creature was *stirring* —Clement Moore⟩ **4** : to pass an implement through a substance with a circular movement **5** : to be able to be stirred — **stir·rer** *n*

[2]**stir** *n* (14c) **1 a** : a state of disturbance, agitation, or brisk activity **b** : widespread notice and discussion : IMPRESSION ⟨the book caused quite a ~⟩ **2** : a slight movement **3** : a stirring movement

[3]**stir** *n* [origin unknown] (1851) *slang* : PRISON

stir·about \ˈstər-ə-ˌbau̇t\ *n* (1682) : a porridge of Irish origin consisting of oatmeal or cornmeal boiled in water or milk and stirred

stir–cra·zy \ˈstər-ˈkrā-zē\ *adj* [[3]*stir*] (ca. 1908) *slang* : distraught because of prolonged confinement

[1]**stir–fry** \-ˈfrī\ *vt* (1959) : to fry quickly over high heat in a lightly oiled pan (as a wok) while stirring continuously ~ *vi* : to prepare food by stir-frying it

[2]**stir–fry** \-ˌfrī\ *n* (1959) : a dish of something stir-fried

stirk \ˈstərk\ *n* [ME, fr. OE *stirc;* akin to MLG *sterke* young cow and perh. to Goth *stairo* sterile animal — more at STERILE] (bef. 12c) *Brit* : a young bull or cow esp. between one and two years old

Stir·ling engine \ˈstər-liŋ-\ *n* [Robert *Stirling* †1878 Scot. engineer] (1896) : an external combustion engine having an enclosed working fluid (as helium) that is alternately compressed and expanded to operate a piston

Stir·ling's formula \ˈstər-liŋz-\ *n* [James *Stirling* †1770 Scot. mathematician] (1908) : a formula

$$\sqrt{2\pi n}\, n^n e^{-n}$$

that approximates the value of the factorial of a very large number *n*

stirp \ˈstərp\ *n* [L *stirp-, stirps*] (1502) : a line descending from a common ancestor : STOCK, LINEAGE

[1]**stirring** *adj* (bef. 12c) **1** : ACTIVE, BUSTLING **2** : ROUSING, INSPIRING ⟨a ~ speech⟩

[2]**stirring** *n* (14c) : a beginning of motion or activity : MOVEMENT — often used in pl. ⟨the first ~*s* of revolution⟩

stir·rup \ˈstər-əp *also* ˈstir-əp *or* ˈstə-rəp\ *n* [ME *stirop,* fr. OE *stigrāp,* fr. *stig-* (akin to OHG *stīgan* to go up) + *rāp* rope — more at STAIR, ROPE] (bef. 12c) **1** : either of a pair of small light frames or rings for receiving the foot of a rider that are attached by a strap to a saddle and used to aid in mounting and as a support while riding **2** : a piece resembling a stirrup: as **a** : one used as a support or clamp in carpentry and machinery **b** : a stirrup-shaped footrest **3** : a rope secured to a yard and attached to a thimble in its lower end for supporting a footrope **4** : STAPES

stirrup cup *n* (1681) **1** : a small serving of drink (as wine) taken by a rider about to depart; *also* : the vessel in which it is served **2** : a farewell cup

stirrup leather *n* (14c) : the looped strap suspending a stirrup

stirrup pump *n* (1939) : a portable hand pump held in position by a foot bracket and used for throwing a jet or spray of liquid

[1]**stitch** \ˈstich\ *n* [ME *stiche,* fr. OE *stice;* akin to OE *stician* to stick] (bef. 12c) **1** : a local sharp and sudden pain esp. in the side **2 a** : one in-and-out movement of a threaded needle in sewing, embroidering, or suturing **b** : a portion of thread left in the material or suture left in the tissue after one stitch **3** : a least bit esp. of clothing ⟨didn't have a ~ on⟩ **4** : a single loop of thread or yarn around an implement (as a knitting needle or crochet hook) **5** : a stitch or series of stitches formed in a particular way ⟨a basting ~⟩ — **in stitches** : in a state of uncontrollable laughter ⟨he had us all *in stitches*⟩

[2]**stitch** *vt* (13c) **1 a** : to fasten, join, or close with or as if with stitches ⟨~*ed* a seam⟩ **b** : to make, mend, or decorate with or as if with stitches **2** : to unite by means of staples ~ *vi* : SEW — **stitch·er** *n*

stitch·ery \ˈstich-rē, ˈsti-chə-\ *n* (ca. 1608) : NEEDLEWORK

stitch·wort \ˈstich-ˌwərt, -ˌwȯrt\ *n* (13c) : any of several chickweeds (esp. genus *Stellaria*)

stithy \ˈsti-t͟hē, -thē\ *n, pl* **stith·ies** [ME, fr. ON *stethi;* akin to OE *stede* stead] (13c) **1** *archaic* : ANVIL **2** *archaic* : SMITHY 1

sti·ver \ˈstī-vər\ *n* [D *stuiver*] (1502) **1** : a unit of value and coin of the Netherlands equal to 1/20 gulden **2** : something of little value

stk *abbr* stock

STL *abbr* [NL *sacrae theologiae licentiatus*] licentiate of sacred theology

STM *abbr* **1** [NL *sacrae theologiae magister*] master of sacred theology **2** scanning tunneling microscope; scanning tunneling microscopy

stoa \ˈstō-ə\ *n* [Gk; akin to Gk *stylos* pillar — more at STEER] (1603) : an ancient Greek portico usu. walled at the back with a front colonnade designed to afford a sheltered promenade

stoat \ˈstōt\ *n, pl* **stoats** *also* **stoat** [ME *stote*] (15c) : the common Holarctic ermine (*Mustela erminea*) esp. in its brown summer coat

stob \ˈstäb\ *n* [ME, stump; akin to ME *stubb* stub] (15c) *chiefly dial* : STAKE, POST

stoc·ca·do \stə-ˈkä-(ˌ)dō\ *n, pl* **-dos** [It *stoccata*] (1582) *archaic* : a thrust with a rapier

sto·chas·tic \stə-ˈkas-tik, stō-\ *adj* [Gk *stochastikos* skillful in aiming, fr. *stochazesthai* to aim at, guess at, fr. *stochos* target, aim, guess — more at STING] (1934) **1** : RANDOM; *specif* : involving a random variable ⟨a ~ process⟩ **2** : involving chance or probability : PROBABILISTIC ⟨a ~ model of radiation-induced mutation⟩ — **sto·chas·ti·cal·ly** \-ti-k(ə-)lē\ *adv*

[1]**stock** \ˈstäk\ *n* [ME *stok,* fr. OE *stocc;* akin to OHG *stoc* stick] (bef. 12c) **1 a** *archaic* : STUMP **b** *archaic* : a log or block of wood **c** (1) *archaic* : something without life or consciousness (2) : a dull, stupid, or lifeless person **2** : a supporting framework or structure: as **a** *pl* : the frame or timbers holding a ship during construction **b** *pl* : a device for publicly punishing offenders consisting of a wooden frame with holes in which the feet or feet and hands can be locked **c** (1) : the wooden part by which a shoulder arm is held during firing (2) : the butt of an implement (as a whip or fishing rod) (3) : BITSTOCK, BRACE **d** : a long beam on a field gun forming the third support point in firing **3 a** : the main stem of a plant : TRUNK **b** (1) : a plant or plant part united with a scion in grafting and supplying mostly underground parts to a graft (2) : a plant from which slips or cuttings are taken **4** : the crosspiece of an anchor — see ANCHOR illustration **5 a** : the original (as a person, race, or language) from which others derive : SOURCE **b** (1) : the descendants of one individual : FAMILY, LINEAGE ⟨of European ~⟩ (2) : a compound organism **c** : an infraspecific group usu. having unity of descent **d** (1) : a related group of languages (2) : a language family **6 a** (1) : the equipment, materials, or supplies of an establishment (2) : LIVESTOCK **b** : a store or supply accumulated or available; *esp* : the inventory of goods of a merchant or manufacturer **7 a** *archaic* : a supply of capital : FUNDS; *esp* : money or capital invested or available for investment or trading **b** (1) : the part of a tally formerly given to the creditor in a transaction (2) : a debt or fund due (as from a government) for money loaned at interest; *also, Brit* : capital or a debt or fund bearing interest in perpetuity and not ordinarily redeemable as to principal **c** (1) : the proprietorship element in a corporation usu. divided into shares and represented by transferable certificates (2) : a portion of such stock of one or more companies (3) : STOCK CERTIFICATE **8** : any of a genus (*Matthiola*) of Old World herbs or subshrubs of the mustard family with racemes of usu. sweet-scented flowers **9** : a wide band or scarf worn about the neck esp. by some clergymen **10 a** : liquid in which meat, fish, or vegetables have been simmered that is used as a basis for soup, gravy, or sauce **b** (1) : raw material from which something is manufactured (2) : paper used for printing **c** : the portion of a pack of cards not distributed to the players at the beginning of a game **11 a** (1) : an estimate or evaluation of something ⟨take ~ of the situation⟩ (2) : the estimation in which someone or something is held ⟨his ~ with the electorate remains high —*Newsweek*⟩ **b** : confidence or faith placed in someone or something ⟨put little ~ in his testimony⟩ **12** : the production and presentation of plays by a stock company **13** : STOCK CAR 1 — **in stock** : on hand : in the store and ready for delivery — **out of stock** : having no more on hand : completely sold out

[2]**stock** *vt* (15c) **1** : to make (a domestic animal) pregnant **2** : to fit to or with a stock **3** : to provide with stock or a stock : SUPPLY ⟨~ a stream with trout⟩ **4** : to procure or keep a stock of ⟨our store ~*s* that brand⟩ **5** : to graze (livestock) on land ~ *vi* **1** : to send out new shoots **2** : to put in stock or supplies ⟨~ up on canned goods⟩

[3]**stock** *adj* (1625) **1 a** : kept regularly in stock ⟨comes in ~ sizes⟩ ⟨a ~ model⟩ **b** : commonly used or brought forward : STANDARD ⟨the ~ answer⟩ **2 a** : kept for breeding purposes : BROOD ⟨a ~ mare⟩ **b** : devoted to the breeding and rearing of livestock ⟨a ~ farm⟩ **c** : used or intended for livestock ⟨a ~ train⟩ **d** : used in herding livestock ⟨a ~ horse⟩ ⟨a ~ dog⟩ **3** : of or relating to a stock company **4** : employed in handling, checking, or taking care of the stock of merchandise on hand ⟨a ~ clerk⟩

[1]**stock·ade** \stä-ˈkād\ *n* [Sp *estacada,* fr. *estaca* stake, pale, of Gmc origin; akin to OE *staca* stake] (1614) **1** : a line of stout posts set firmly to form a defense **2 a** : an enclosure or pen made with posts and stakes **b** : an enclosure in which prisoners are kept

[2]**stockade** *vt* **stock·ad·ed; stock·ad·ing** (1677) : to fortify or surround with a stockade

stockade fence *n* (1985) : a solid fence of half-round boards pointed at the top

stock boy *n* (1950) : a boy or man employed to stock shelves

stock·breed·er \ˈstäk-ˌbrē-dər\ *n* (1815) : a person engaged in the breeding and care of livestock for the market, for show purposes, or for racing

stock·bro·ker \-ˌbrō-kər\ *n* (ca. 1706) : a broker who executes orders to buy and sell securities and often also acts as a security dealer — **stock·bro·ker·age** \-k(ə-)rij\ *n* — **stock·brok·ing** \-ˌbrō-kiŋ\ *n*

stock car *n* (1858) **1** : a latticed railroad boxcar for carrying livestock **2** : a racing car having the basic chassis of a commercially produced assembly-line model

stock certificate *n* (1863) : an instrument evidencing ownership of one or more shares of the stock of a corporation

\ə\ **abut** \ᵊ\ kitten, F table \ər\ **fur**ther \a\ **ash** \ā\ **ace** \ä\ mop, mar
\au̇\ **out** \ch\ **chin** \e\ bet \ē\ **easy** \g\ go \i\ **hit** \ī\ **ice** \j\ **job**
\ŋ\ sing \ō\ go \ȯ\ **law** \ȯi\ **boy** \th\ **thin** \t͟h\ **the** \ü\ **loot** \u̇\ **foot**
\y\ yet \zh\ vision, beige \k̲, ⁿ, œ, ue, ʸ\ *see* Guide to Pronunciation

stock company *n* (1827) **1 :** a corporation or joint-stock company of which the capital is represented by stock **2 :** a theatrical company attached to a repertory theater; *esp* : one without outstanding stars

stock dividend *n* (ca. 1902) **1 :** the payment by a corporation of a dividend in the form of shares usu. of its own stock without change in par value — compare STOCK SPLIT **2 :** the stock distributed in a stock dividend

stock·er \ˈstä-kər\ *n* (1881) **1 :** a young animal (as a steer or heifer) suitable for being fed and fattened for market **2 :** an animal (as a heifer) suitable for use in a breeding establishment **3 :** STOCK CAR 2

stock exchange *n* (1773) **1 :** a place where security trading is conducted on an organized system **2 :** an association of people organized to provide an auction market among themselves for the purchase and sale of securities

stock·fish \-ˌfish\ *n* [ME *stokfish,* fr. MD *stocvisch,* fr. *stoc* stick + *visch* fish] (13c) : fish (as cod, haddock, or hake) dried hard in the open air without salt

stock·hold·er \ˈstäk-ˌhōl-dər\ *n* (1753) : an owner of corporate stock

Stock·holm syndrome \ˈstäk-ˌhō(l)m-\ *n* [fr. a 1973 robbery attempt in *Stockholm,* Sweden, during which bank employees held hostage developed sympathetic feelings toward their captors] (1978) : the psychological tendency of a hostage to bond with, identify with, or sympathize with his or her captor

stock·i·nette *or* **stock·i·net** \ˌstä-kə-ˈnet\ *n* [alter. of earlier *stocking net*] (1784) : a soft elastic usu. cotton fabric used esp. for bandages and infants' wear

stock·ing \ˈstä-kiŋ\ *n* [obs. *stock* to cover with a stocking] (1580) **1 a :** a usu. knit close-fitting covering for the foot and leg **b :** SOCK **2 :** something resembling a stocking; *esp* : a ring of distinctive color on the lower part of the leg of an animal — **stock·inged** \-kiŋd\ *adj* — **in one's stocking feet :** with the feet in stockings but not shoes

stocking cap *n* (ca. 1897) : a long knitted cone-shaped cap with a tassel or pom-pom worn esp. for winter sports or play

stocking stuffer *n* (1948) : a small gift suitable for placing in a Christmas stocking

stock–in–trade \ˌstäk-ən-ˈtrād, ˈstäk-ən-ˌ\ *n* (1721) **1 :** the equipment, merchandise, or materials necessary to or used in a trade or business **2 :** something that resembles the standard equipment of a tradesman or business ‹humor was her ~ as a writer›

stock·ish \ˈstä-kish\ *adj* (1596) : like a stock : STUPID

stock·ist \ˈstä-kist\ *n* (1910) *Brit* : one (as a retailer) that stocks goods

stock·job·ber \ˈstäk-ˌjä-bər\ *n* (1604) : one who deals in stocks: as **a :** a member of the London Stock Exchange who deals speculatively with brokers or other jobbers and usu. specializes in one class of securities — called also *jobber* **b** *usu disparaging* : STOCKBROKER

stock·job·bing \-ˌjä-biŋ\ *n* (1692) : speculative exchange dealings

stock·keep·er \ˈstäk-ˌkē-pər\ *n* (1668) **1 :** one that keeps and records stock (as in a warehouse) : one that keeps an inventory of goods on hand, shipped, or received **2 :** one (as a herdsman or shepherd) having the charge or care of livestock

stock·man \-mən, -ˌman\ *n* (1806) : one occupied as an owner or worker in the raising of livestock (as cattle or sheep)

stock market *n* (1809) **1 :** STOCK EXCHANGE 1 **2 a :** a market for particular stocks **b :** the market for stocks throughout a country

stock option *n* (1945) **1 :** an option contract involving stock **2 :** a right granted by a corporation to officers or employees as a form of compensation that allows purchase of corporate stock at a fixed price usu. within a specified period

[1]**stock·pile** \ˈstäk-ˌpī(-ə)l\ *n* (1872) : a storage pile: as **a :** a reserve supply of something essential accumulated within a country for use during a shortage **b :** a gradually accumulated reserve of something ‹avert ~*s* of unsold cars —Bert Pierce›

[2]**stockpile** *vt* (1921) **1 :** to place or store in or on a stockpile **2 :** to accumulate a stockpile of ‹a country suspected of *stockpiling* weapons› — **stock·pil·er** *n*

stock·pot \ˈstäk-ˌpät\ *n* (1835) **1 :** a pot in which soup stock is prepared **2 :** an abundant supply : REPOSITORY

stock·room \-ˌrüm, -ˌru̇m\ *n* (1825) : a storage place for supplies or goods used in a business

stock saddle *n* (1886) : WESTERN SADDLE

stock split *n* (1950) : a division of corporate stock by the issuing to existing shareholders of a specified number of new shares with a corresponding lowering of par value for each outstanding share — compare STOCK DIVIDEND

stock–still \ˈstäk-ˈstil\ *adj* (15c) : very still : MOTIONLESS ‹stood ~›

stock·tak·ing \ˈstäk-ˌtā-kiŋ\ *n* (1851) **1 :** the action of estimating a situation at a given moment **2 :** INVENTORY 4

stocky \ˈstä-kē\ *adj* **stock·i·er; -est** (1622) : compact, sturdy, and relatively thick in build — **stock·i·ly** \ˈstä-kə-lē\ *adv* — **stock·i·ness** \ˈstä-kē-nəs\ *n*

stock·yard \ˈstäk-ˌyärd\ *n* (1756) : a yard for stock; *specif* : one in which transient cattle, sheep, swine, or horses are kept temporarily for slaughter, market, or shipping

[1]**stodge** \ˈstäj\ *vt* **stodged; stodg·ing** [origin unknown] (1674) *Brit* : to stuff full esp. with food

[2]**stodge** *n* (1825) *Brit* : something or someone stodgy

stodgy \ˈstä-jē\ *adj* **stodg·i·er; -est** (1854) **1 :** having a rich filling quality : HEAVY ‹~ bread› **2 :** moving in a slow plodding way esp. as a result of physical bulkiness **3 :** BORING, DULL ‹out on a peaceful rather ~ Sunday boat trip —Edna Ferber› **4 :** extremely old-fashioned : HIDEBOUND ‹received a pompously Victorian letter from his ~ father —E. E. S. Montagu› **5 a :** DRAB **b :** DOWDY — **stodg·i·ly** \ˈstä-jə-lē\ *adv* — **stodg·i·ness** \ˈstä-jē-nəs\ *n*

sto·gie *or* **sto·gy** \ˈstō-gē\ *n, pl* **stogies** [*Conestoga,* Pa.] (1874) **1 :** a stout coarse shoe : BROGAN **2 :** an inexpensive slender cylindrical cigar; *broadly* : CIGAR

[1]**sto·ic** \ˈstō-ik\ *n* [ME, fr. L *stoicus,* fr. Gk *stōïkos,* lit., of the portico, fr. *Stoa* (*Poikilē*) the Painted Portico, portico at Athens where Zeno taught] (14c) **1** *cap* : a member of a school of philosophy founded by Zeno of Citium about 300 B.C. holding that the wise man should be free from passion, unmoved by joy or grief, and submissive to natural law **2 :** one apparently or professedly indifferent to pleasure or pain

[2]**stoic** *or* **sto·i·cal** \-i-kəl\ *adj* (15c) **1** *cap* : of, relating to, or resembling the Stoics or their doctrines ‹*Stoic* logic› **2 :** not affected by or showing passion or feeling; *esp* : firmly restraining response to pain or distress ‹a ~ indifference to cold› ***syn*** see IMPASSIVE — **sto·ical·ly** \-i-k(ə-)lē\ *adv*

stoi·chio·met·ric \ˌstȯi-kē-ō-ˈme-trik\ *adj* (1892) : of, relating to, used in, or marked by stoichiometry — **stoi·chio·met·ri·cal·ly** \-tri-k(ə-)lē\ *adv*

stoi·chi·om·e·try \ˌstȯi-kē-ˈä-mə-trē\ *n* [Gk *stoicheion* element (fr. *stoichos* row) + E *-metry;* akin to Gk *steichein* to walk, go — more at STAIR] (1807) **1 :** a branch of chemistry that deals with the application of the laws of definite proportions and of the conservation of mass and energy to chemical activity **2 a :** the quantitative relationship between constituents in a chemical substance **b :** the quantitative relationship between two or more substances esp. in processes involving physical or chemical change

sto·i·cism \ˈstō-ə-ˌsi-zəm\ *n* (1626) **1** *cap* : the philosophy of the Stoics **2 :** indifference to pleasure or pain : IMPASSIVENESS

stoke \ˈstōk\ *vb* **stoked; stok·ing** [D *stoken;* akin to MD *stuken* to push] *vt* (1683) **1 :** to poke or stir up (as a fire) : supply with fuel **2 :** to feed abundantly **3 :** to increase the activity, intensity, or amount of ‹limiting the number of cars available . . . will help ~ demand for the car —Keith Naughton› ~ *vi* : to stir up or tend a fire (as in a furnace) : supply a furnace with fuel

stoked *adj* (1965) *slang* : being in an enthusiastic or exhilarated state

stoke·hold \ˈstōk-ˌhōld\ *n* (1887) : the boiler room of a ship

stok·er \ˈstō-kər\ *n* (1660) **1 :** one employed to tend a furnace and supply it with fuel; *specif* : one that tends a marine steam boiler **2 :** a machine for feeding a fire

Stokes' aster \ˈstōks-\ *n* [Jonathan *Stokes* †1831 Eng. botanist] (ca. 1890) : a perennial composite herb (*Stokesia laevis*) of the southern U.S. often grown for its large showy heads of usu. blue flowers — called also *sto·ke·sia* \stō-ˈkē-zh(ē-)ə, -zē-ə\

STOL *abbr* short takeoff and landing

[1]**stole** *past of* STEAL

[2]**stole** \ˈstōl\ *n* [ME, fr. OE, fr. L *stola,* fr. Gk *stolē* equipment, robe, fr. *stellein* to set up, make ready] (bef. 12c) **1 :** a long loose garment : ROBE **2 :** an ecclesiastical vestment consisting of a long usu. silk band worn traditionally around the neck by bishops and priests and over the left shoulder by deacons **3 :** a long wide scarf or similar covering worn by women usu. across the shoulders

stolen *past part of* STEAL

stol·id \ˈstä-ləd\ *adj* [L *stolidus* dull, stupid] (ca. 1600) : having or expressing little or no sensibility : UNEMOTIONAL ***syn*** see IMPASSIVE — **sto·lid·i·ty** \stä-ˈli-də-tē, stə-\ *n* — **stol·id·ly** \ˈstä-ləd-lē\ *adv*

stol·len \ˈshtō-lən, ˈshtö-, ˈshtə-, *or with* s *for* sh\ *n, pl* **stollen** *or* **stollens** [G, lit., post, support, fr. OHG *stollo* — more at STELA] (1906) : a sweet yeast bread of German origin containing fruit and nuts

sto·lon \ˈstō-lən, -ˌlän\ *n* [NL *stolon-, stolo,* fr. L, branch, sucker; akin to OE *stela* stalk, Arm *steɫn* branch] (1601) **1 a :** a horizontal branch from the base of a plant that produces new plants from buds at its tip or nodes (as in the strawberry) — called also *runner* **b :** a hypha (as of rhizopus) produced on the surface and connecting a group of conidiophores **2 :** an extension of the body wall (as of a hydrozoan or bryozoan) that develops buds giving rise to new zooids which usu. remain united by the stolon

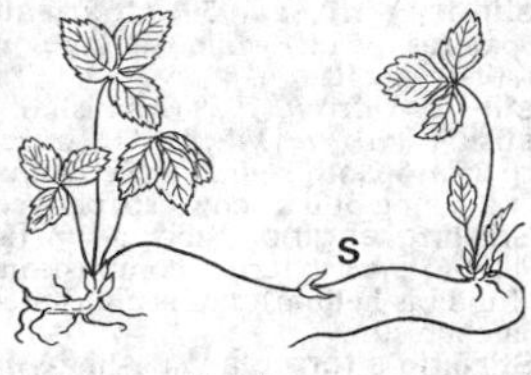

S stolon 1a

sto·lon·if·er·ous \ˌstō-lə-ˈni-f(ə-)rəs\ *adj* (ca. 1777) : bearing or developing stolons ‹~ bamboos›

sto·ma \ˈstō-mə\ *n, pl* **sto·ma·ta** \-mə-tə\ *also* **stomas** [NL, fr. Gk *stomat-, stoma* mouth] (ca. 1684) **1 :** any of various small simple bodily openings esp. in a lower animal **2 :** one of the minute openings in the epidermis of a plant organ (as a leaf) through which gaseous interchange takes place; *also* : the opening with its associated cellular structures **3 :** an artificial permanent opening esp. in the abdominal wall made in surgical procedures

[1]**stom·ach** \ˈstə-mək, -mik\ *n* [ME *stomak,* fr. AF *estomac,* fr. L *stomachus* gullet, esophagus, stomach, fr. Gk *stomachos,* fr. *stoma* mouth; akin to MBret *staffn* mouth, Av *staman-*] (14c) **1 a (1) :** a dilatation of the alimentary canal of a vertebrate communicating anteriorly with the esophagus and posteriorly with the duodenum **(2) :** one of the compartments of a ruminant stomach ‹the abomasum is the fourth ~ of a ruminant› **b :** a cavity in an invertebrate animal that is analogous to a stomach **c :** the part of the body that contains the stomach : BELLY, ABDOMEN **2 a :** desire for food caused by hunger : APPETITE **b :** INCLINATION, DESIRE ‹had no ~ for an argument›; *also* : COURAGE, GUTS **3** *obs* **a :** SPIRIT, VALOR **b :** PRIDE **c :** SPLEEN, RESENTMENT

[2]**stomach** *vt* (1523) **1** *archaic* : to take offense at **2 :** to bear without overt reaction or resentment : put up with ‹couldn't ~ office politics›

stom·ach·ache \-ˌāk\ *n* (1744) : pain in or in the region of the stomach

stom·ach·er \ˈstə-mi-kər, -chər\ *n* (15c) : the center front section of a waist or underwaist or a usu. heavily embroidered or jeweled separate piece for the center front of a bodice worn by men and women in the 15th and 16th centuries and later by women only

[1]**sto·mach·ic** \stə-ˈma-kik\ *adj* (ca. 1656) : of or relating to the stomach ‹~ vessels›

[2]**stomachic** *n* (1735) : a stimulant or tonic for the stomach

stom·achy \ˈstə-mə-kē, -mi-\ *adj* (ca. 1825) **1** *dial Brit* : IRASCIBLE, IRRITABLE **2 :** having a large stomach

sto·mal \ˈstō-məl\ *adj* (ca. 1941) : of, relating to, or situated near a surgical stoma ‹a ~ ulcer›

stomat- *or* **stomato-** *comb form* [NL, fr. Gk, fr. *stomat-, stoma*] : mouth : stoma ‹*stomat*itis›

sto·ma·tal \ˈstō-mə-tᵊl\ *adj* (1861) : of, relating to, or constituting plant stomata ‹~ openings› ‹~ transpiration›

sto·mate \ˈstō-ˌmāt\ *n* [irreg. fr. NL *stomat-, stoma*] (1835) : STOMA 2

sto·ma·ti·tis \ˌstō-mə-ˈtī-təs\ *n, pl* **-tit·i·des** \-ˈti-tə-ˌdēz\ *or* **-ti·tis·es** \-ˈtī-tə-səz\ [NL] (1842) : any of numerous inflammatory diseases of the mouth

sto·mato·pod \stō-ˈma-tə-ˌpäd\ *n* [NL *Stomatopoda,* fr. *stomat-* + Gk *pod-, pous* foot — more at FOOT] (1877) **:** any of an order (Stomatopoda) of marine crustaceans (as a squilla) that have gills on the abdominal appendages — **stomatopod** *adj*

sto·mo·de·um *also* **sto·mo·dae·um** \ˌstō-mə-ˈdē-əm\ *n, pl* **-dea** \-ˈdē-ə\ *also* **-daea** \-ˈdē-ə\ [NL, fr. Gk *stoma* mouth + *hodaion,* neut. of *hodaios* being on the way, fr. *hodos* way] (1876) **:** the embryonic anterior ectodermal part of the alimentary canal or tract — **sto·mo·de·al** *also* **sto·mo·dae·al** \-ˈdē-əl\ *adj*

[1]**stomp** \ˈstämp, ˈstȯmp\ *vb* [by alter.] *vt* (1803) **:** STAMP 2 ~ *vi* **1 :** to walk with a loud heavy step usu. in anger ⟨~*ed* out of the office in a fit⟩ **2 :** STAMP 2 ⟨~*ed* on the brakes⟩

[2]**stomp** *n* (ca. 1899) **1 :** STAMP 4 **2 :** a jazz dance marked by heavy stamping

stomping ground *n* (1854) **:** a favorite or habitual resort; *also* **:** familiar territory

-stomy *n comb form* [ISV, fr. Gk *stoma* mouth, opening] **:** surgical operation establishing a usu. permanent opening into (such) a part ⟨entero*stomy*⟩

[1]**stone** \ˈstōn\ *n* [ME, fr. OE *stān;* akin to OHG *stein* stone, OCS *stěna* wall, and perh. to Skt *styāyate* it hardens — more at STEATO-] (bef. 12c) **1 :** a concretion of earthy or mineral matter: **a** (1) **:** such a concretion of indeterminate size or shape (2) **:** ROCK **b :** a piece of rock for a specified function: as (1) **:** a building block (2) **:** a paving block (3) **:** a precious stone **:** GEM (4) **:** GRAVESTONE (5) **:** GRINDSTONE (6) **:** WHETSTONE (7) **:** a surface upon which a drawing, text, or design to be lithographed is drawn or transferred **2 :** something resembling a small stone: as **a :** CALCULUS 3a **b :** the hard central portion of a drupaceous fruit (as a peach) **c :** a hard stony seed (as of a date) **3** *pl usu* **stone :** any of various units of weight; *esp* **:** an official British unit equal to 14 pounds (6.3 kilograms) **4 a :** CURLING STONE **b :** a round playing piece used in various games (as backgammon or go) **5 :** a stand or table with a smooth flat top on which to impose or set type — **in stone :** in or into a permanent and unchangeable state ⟨plans are not set *in stone*⟩

[2]**stone** *vt* **stoned; ston·ing** (13c) **1 :** to hurl stones at; *esp* **:** to kill by pelting with stones **2** *archaic* **:** to make hard or insensitive to feeling **3 :** to face, pave, or fortify with stones **4 :** to remove the stones or seeds of (a fruit) **5 a :** to rub, scour, or polish with a stone **b :** to sharpen with a whetstone — **ston·er** *n*

[3]**stone** *adv* (13c) **:** ENTIRELY, UTTERLY — used as an intensive; often used in combination ⟨*stone*-broke⟩ ⟨*stone*-cold soup⟩ ⟨*stone*-dead⟩

[4]**stone** *adj* (14c) **1 :** of, relating to, or made of stone **2 :** ABSOLUTE, UTTER ⟨pure ~ craziness —Edwin Shrake⟩

[1]**Stone Age** *n* (1854) **1 :** the first known period of prehistoric human culture characterized by the use of stone tools — compare MESOLITHIC, NEOLITHIC, PALEOLITHIC **2 :** a stage in a human institution or field of endeavor regarded as primitive, outmoded, or obsolete ⟨the *Stone Age* of information handling before computers⟩

[2]**Stone Age** *adj* (1865) **1 :** of, relating to, or resembling the culture of the Stone Age esp. in the use of stone implements ⟨modern *Stone Age* peoples⟩ ⟨our *Stone Age* ancestors⟩ **2 :** primitive, outmoded, or unsophisticated (as in ideas or technology) by currently accepted standards ⟨marauding mercenaries with *Stone Age* political ideas —Robert Moss⟩ ⟨using a *Stone Age* camera⟩

stone–blind \ˈstōn-ˈblīnd\ *adj* (14c) **:** totally blind

stone·boat \-ˌbōt\ *n* (1848) **:** a flat sledge or drag for transporting heavy articles (as stones)

stone canal *n* (1887) **:** a tube in many echinoderms that contains calcareous deposits and leads from the madreporite to the ring of the water-vascular system surrounding the mouth

stone cell *n* (1875) **:** SCLEREID

stone·chat \-ˌchat\ *n* [[2]*chat*] (ca. 1783) **:** an Old World oscine songbird (*Saxicola torquata*) of the thrush family; *also* **:** any of various related birds (genus *Saxicola*)

stone china *n* (1823) **:** a hard dense opaque feldspathic pottery developed in England; *broadly* **:** IRONSTONE CHINA

stone–cold \ˈstōn-ˈkōld\ *adv* (1592) **:** ABSOLUTELY ⟨~ sober⟩

stone crab *n* (1709) **:** a large brownish edible crab (*Menippe mercenaria* of the family Xanthidae) found on the southern coast of the U.S. and in the Caribbean area

stone·crop \ˈstōn-ˌkräp\ *n* (bef. 12c) **1 :** SEDUM; *esp* **:** an Old World creeping evergreen sedum (*Sedum acre*) with pungent fleshy leaves and yellow flowers **2 :** any of various plants of the orpine family related to the sedums

stone·cut·ter \-ˌkə-tər\ *n* (1540) **1 :** one that cuts, carves, or dresses stone **2 :** a machine for dressing stone — **stone·cut·ting** \-ˌkə-tiŋ\ *n*

stoned \ˈstōnd\ *adj* (1952) **1 :** DRUNK 1a **2 :** being under the influence of a drug (as marijuana) taken esp. for pleasure **:** HIGH

stone–deaf \-ˈdef\ *adj* (1762) **:** totally deaf

stone–faced \-ˌfāst\ *adj* (1876) **:** showing no emotion **:** EXPRESSIONLESS

stone·fish \ˈstōn-ˌfish\ *n* (1896) **:** any of several small spiny venomous bony fishes (family Synanceiidae, esp. genus *Synanceja*) common about coral reefs of the tropical Indo-Pacific

stone fly *n* (15c) **:** any of an order (Plecoptera) of insects with an aquatic carnivorous nymph having gills and an adult having long antennae, two pairs of membranous wings, and usu. long cerci

stone fruit *n* (ca. 1534) **:** a fruit with a stony endocarp **:** DRUPE

stone–ground \ˈstōn-ˈgrau̇nd\ *adj* (1905) **:** ground with millstones ⟨~ flour⟩

stone·ma·son \ˈstōn-ˌmā-sᵊn\ *n* (1748) **:** a mason who builds with stone — **stone·ma·son·ry** \-rē\ *n*

ston·er \ˈstō-nər\ *n* [*stoned*] (1979) **:** a person who habitually uses drugs or alcohol

stone roller *n* (1878) **1 :** HOG SUCKER **2 :** a common cyprinid fish (*Campostoma anomalum*) found esp. in clear streams of the central U.S.

stone's throw *n* (1581) **:** a short distance ⟨lives within a *stone's throw* of town⟩

stone·wall \ˈstōn-ˌwȯl\ *vi* (1880) **1** *chiefly Brit* **:** to engage in obstructive parliamentary debate or delaying tactics **2 :** to be uncooperative, obstructive, or evasive ~ *vt* **:** to refuse to comply or cooperate with — **stone·wall·er** *n*

stone wall *n* (bef. 12c) **1 :** a fence made of stones; *esp* **:** one built of rough stones without mortar to enclose a field **2 :** an immovable block or obstruction (as in public affairs)

stone·ware \-ˌwer\ *n* (1683) **:** a strong opaque ceramic ware that is high-fired, well vitrified, and nonporous

stone–washed \-ˌwȯsht, -ˌwäsht *also* -ˌwȯrsht *or* -ˌwärsht\ *adj* (1982) **:** subjected to a washing process during manufacture that includes the use of abrasive stones esp. to create a softer fabric ⟨~ denim jeans⟩

stone·work \-ˌwərk\ *n* (bef. 12c) **1 :** a structure or part built of stone **:** MASONRY **2 :** the shaping, preparation, or setting of stone

stone·wort \-ˌwərt, -ˌwȯrt\ *n* (1816) **:** any of various freshwater green algae (order Charales) that have a thallus differentiated into rhizoids and stems with whorls of branchlets and that are often encrusted with calcareous deposits

stony *also* **ston·ey** \ˈstō-nē\ *adj* **ston·i·er; -est** (bef. 12c) **1 :** abounding in or having the nature of stone **:** ROCKY **2 a :** insensitive to pity or human feeling **:** OBDURATE **b :** manifesting no movement or reaction **:** DUMB, EXPRESSIONLESS **c :** fearfully gripping **:** PETRIFYING **3** *archaic* **:** consisting of or made of stones **4** *Brit* **:** stone broke — **ston·i·ly** \ˈstō-nə-lē\ *adv* — **ston·i·ness** \ˈstō-nē-nəs\ *n*

stony·heart·ed \ˈstō-nē-ˌhär-təd\ *adj* (1569) **:** UNFEELING, CRUEL

stood *past and past part of* STAND

[1]**stooge** \ˈstüj\ *n* [origin unknown] (1913) **1 a :** one who plays a subordinate or compliant role to a principal **b :** PUPPET 3 **2 :** STRAIGHT MAN **3 :** STOOL PIGEON 1

[2]**stooge** *vi* **stooged; stoog·ing** (1939) **:** to act as a stooge ⟨congressmen who ~ for the oil and mineral interests —*New Republic*⟩

stook \ˈstük, ˈstu̇k\ *n* [ME *stouk;* akin to OE *stocc* stock — more at STOCK] (15c) *chiefly Brit* **:** [1]SHOCK — **stook** *vt, chiefly Brit*

[1]**stool** \ˈstül\ *n* [ME, fr. OE *stōl;* akin to OHG *stuol* chair, OCS *stolŭ* seat, throne] (bef. 12c) **1 a :** a seat usu. without back or arms supported by three or four legs or by a central pedestal **b :** a low bench or portable support for the feet or knees **:** FOOTSTOOL **2 :** a seat used as a symbol of office or authority; *also* **:** the rank, dignity, office, or rule of a chieftain **3 a :** a seat used while defecating or urinating **b :** a discharge of fecal matter **4 a :** a stump or group of stumps of a tree esp. when producing suckers **b :** a plant crown from which shoots grow out **c :** a shoot or growth from a stool **5 :** STOOL PIGEON 1

[2]**stool** *vi* (1770) **:** to throw out shoots in the manner of a stool

stool·ie \ˈstü-lē\ *n* (1924) **:** STOOL PIGEON 1

stool pigeon *n* [prob. fr. the early practice of fastening the decoy bird to a stool] (1826) **1 :** a person acting as a decoy or informer; *esp* **:** a spy sent into a group to report (as to the police) on its activities **2 :** a pigeon used as a decoy to draw others within a net

[1]**stoop** \ˈstüp\ *vb* [ME *stoupen,* fr. OE *stūpian;* akin to Sw *stupa* to fall, plunge, OE *stēap* steep, deep] *vi* (bef. 12c) **1 a :** to bend the body or a part of the body forward and downward sometimes simultaneously bending the knees **b :** to stand or walk with a forward inclination of the head, body, or shoulders **2 :** YIELD, SUBMIT **3 a :** to descend from a superior rank, dignity, or status **b :** to lower oneself morally ⟨~*ed* to lying⟩ **4 a** *archaic* **:** to move down from a height **:** ALIGHT **b :** to fly or dive down swiftly usu. to attack prey ~ *vt* **1 :** DEBASE, DEGRADE **2 :** to bend (a part of the body) forward and downward

[2]**stoop** *n* (1571) **1 a :** an act of bending the body forward **b :** a temporary or habitual forward bend of the back and shoulders **2 :** the descent of a bird esp. on its prey **3 :** a lowering of oneself

[3]**stoop** *n* [D *stoep;* akin to OE *stæpe* step — more at STEP] (1755) **:** a porch, platform, entrance stairway, or small veranda at a house door

stoop·ball \ˈstüp-ˌbȯl\ *n* (1941) **:** a variation of baseball in which a player throws a ball against a stoop or building and runs to base while other players attempt to retrieve the rebound and put the runner out

stoop labor *n* (1939) **:** the hard labor done or required to plant, cultivate, and harvest a crop and esp. a crop of vegetables

[1]**stop** \ˈstäp\ *vb* **stopped; stop·ping** [ME *stoppen,* fr. OE *-stoppian,* fr. VL **stuppare* to stop with tow, fr. L *stuppa* tow, fr. Gk *styppē*] *vt* (13c) **1 a :** to close by filling or obstructing **b :** to hinder or prevent the passage of **c :** to get in the way of **:** be wounded or killed by ⟨easy to ~ a bullet along a lonely . . . road —Harvey Fergusson⟩ **2 a :** to close up or block off (an opening) **:** PLUG **b :** to make impassable **:** CHOKE, OBSTRUCT **c :** to cover over or fill in (a hole or crevice) **3 a :** to cause to give up or change a course of action **b :** to keep from carrying out a proposed action **:** RESTRAIN, PREVENT ⟨*stopped* them from leaving⟩ **4 a :** to cause to cease **:** CHECK, SUPPRESS **b :** DISCONTINUE **5 a :** to deduct or withhold (a sum due) **b :** to instruct one's bank to refuse (payment) or refuse payment of (as a check) **6 a :** to arrest the progress or motion of **:** cause to halt ⟨*stopped* the car⟩ **b :** PARRY **c :** to check by means of a weapon **:** BRING DOWN, KILL **d :** to beat in a boxing match by a knockout; *broadly* **:** DEFEAT **e :** BAFFLE, NONPLUS **7 :** to change the pitch of (as a violin string) by pressing with the finger or (as a wind instrument) by closing one or more finger holes or by thrusting the hand or a mute into the bell **8 :** to hold an honor card and enough protecting cards to be able to block (a bridge suit) before an opponent can run many tricks ~ *vi* **1 a :** to cease activity or operation ⟨his heart *stopped*⟩ ⟨the rain *stopped*⟩ **b :** to come to an end esp. suddenly **:** CLOSE, FINISH **2 a :** to cease to move on **:** HALT **b :** PAUSE, HESITATE **3 a :** to break one's journey **:** STAY **b** *chiefly Brit* **:** REMAIN **c :** to make a brief call **:** drop in **4 :** to become choked **:** CLOG ⟨the sink often ~*s* up⟩ — **stop·pa·ble** \ˈstä-pə-bəl\ *adj*

syn STOP, CEASE, QUIT, DISCONTINUE, DESIST mean to suspend or cause to suspend activity. STOP applies to action or progress or to what is operating or progressing and may imply suddenness or definiteness ⟨*stopped* at the red light⟩. CEASE applies to states, conditions, or existence and may add a suggestion of gradualness and a degree of finality ⟨by nightfall the fighting had *ceased*⟩. QUIT may stress either finality or abruptness in stopping or ceasing ⟨the engine faltered, sputtered, then *quit* altogether⟩. DISCONTINUE applies to the stopping of an accustomed activity or practice ⟨we have *discontinued* the manufacture of that item⟩. DESIST implies forbearance or restraint as a motive for stopping or ceasing ⟨*desisted* from further efforts to persuade them⟩.

[2]**stop** *n* (15c) **1 a :** CESSATION, END **b :** a pause or breaking off in speech **2 a** (1) **:** a graduated set of organ pipes of similar design and tone quality (2) **:** a corresponding set of vibrators or reeds of a reed organ (3) **:** STOP KNOB — often used figuratively in phrases like *pull out all the stops* to suggest holding nothing back **b :** a means of regulating the pitch of a musical instrument **3 a :** something that impedes, obstructs, or brings to a halt **:** IMPEDIMENT, OBSTACLE **b :** the aperture of a camera lens; *also* **:** a marking of a series (as of f-numbers) on a camera for indicating settings of the diaphragm **c :** a drain plug **:** STOPPER **4 :** a device for arresting or limiting motion **5 :** the act of stopping **:** the state of being stopped **:** CHECK **6 a :** a halt in a journey **:** STAY ⟨made a brief ~ to refuel⟩ **b :** a stopping place ⟨a bus ~⟩ **7 a** *chiefly Brit* **:** any of several punctuation marks **b** — used in telegrams and cables to indicate a period **c :** a pause or break in a verse that marks the end of a grammatical unit **8 a :** an order stopping payment (as of a check or note) by a bank **b :** STOP ORDER **9 :** a consonant characterized by complete closure of the breath passage in the course of articulation — compare CONTINUANT **10 :** a depression in the face of an animal at the junction of forehead and muzzle **11 :** a function of an electronic device that stops a recording

[3]**stop** *adj* (1594) **:** serving to stop **:** designed to stop ⟨~ line⟩ ⟨~ signal⟩

stop–ac·tion \'stäp-'ak-shən\ *n, often attrib* (1946) **:** STOP-MOTION

stop–and–go \ˌstäp-ən-'gō, -ᵊm-, *attributively* -ˌgō\ *adj* (1925) **:** of, relating to, or involving frequent stops; *esp* **:** controlled or regulated by traffic lights ⟨~ driving⟩

stop bath *n* (1898) **:** an acid bath used to check photographic development of a negative or print

stop·cock \'stäp-ˌkäk\ *n* (1584) **:** a cock for stopping or regulating flow (as through a pipe)

stop down *vt* (ca. 1891) **:** to reduce the effective aperture of (a lens) by means of a diaphragm

stope \'stōp\ *n* [prob. fr. LG *stope,* lit., step; akin to OE *stæpe* step — more at STEP] (1747) **:** a usu. steplike excavation underground for the removal of ore that is formed as the ore is mined in successive layers

stop·gap \'stäp-ˌgap\ *n, often attrib* (1684) **:** something that serves as a temporary expedient **:** MAKESHIFT ⟨~ measures⟩ ***syn*** see RESOURCE

stop knob *n* (1887) **:** one of the handles by which an organist draws or shuts off a particular stop

stop·light \'stäp-ˌlīt\ *n* (1926) **1 :** a light on the rear of a motor vehicle that is illuminated when the driver presses the brake pedal **2 :** TRAFFIC SIGNAL

stop–mo·tion \'stäp-'mō-shən\ *n, often attrib* (1912) **:** a filming technique in which successive positions of objects (as clay models) are photographed to produce the appearance of movement

stop order *n* (1882) **:** an order to a broker to buy or sell respectively at the market when the price of a security advances or declines to a designated level

stop out *vi* [after *drop out*] (1971) **:** to withdraw temporarily from enrollment at a college or university — **stop–out** \'stäp-ˌau̇t\ *n*

stop·over \'stäp-ˌō-vər\ *n* (1885) **1 :** a stop at an intermediate point in one's journey **2 :** a stopping place on a journey

stop·page \'stä-pij\ *n* (15c) **:** the act of stopping **:** the state of being stopped **:** HALT, OBSTRUCTION ⟨a ~ in play⟩

stop payment *n* (ca. 1919) **:** a depositor's order to a bank to refuse to honor a specified check drawn by him or her

[1]**stop·per** \'stä-pər\ *n* (15c) **1 :** one that brings to a halt or causes to stop operating or functioning **:** CHECK: as **a :** a playing card that will stop the running of a suit **b :** a baseball pitcher depended on to win important games or to stop a losing streak; *also* **:** an effective relief pitcher **2 :** one that closes, shuts, or fills up; *specif* **:** something (as a bung or cork) used to plug an opening

[2]**stopper** *vt* **stop·pered; stop·per·ing** \-p(ə-)riŋ\ (ca. 1769) **:** to close or secure with or as if with a stopper ⟨~ the bottle⟩

stopper knot *n* (ca. 1860) **:** a knot used to prevent a rope from passing through a hole or opening

[1]**stop·ple** \'stä-pəl\ *n* [ME *stoppell,* fr. *stoppen* to stop] (14c) **:** something that closes an aperture **:** STOPPER, PLUG

[2]**stopple** *vt* **stop·pled; stop·pling** \-p(ə-)liŋ\ (ca. 1795) **:** STOPPER

stop·watch \'stäp-ˌwäch\ *n* (1737) **:** a watch with a hand or a digital display that can be started and stopped at will for exact timing (as of a race)

stor *abbr* storage

stor·age \'stȯr-ij\ *n* (ca. 1613) **1 a :** space or a place for storing **b :** an amount stored **c :** MEMORY 4 **2 a :** the act of storing **:** the state of being stored; *esp* **:** the safekeeping of goods in a depository (as a warehouse) **b :** the price charged for keeping goods in a storehouse **3 :** the production by means of electric energy of chemical reactions that when allowed to reverse themselves generate electricity again without serious loss

storage battery *n* (1881) **:** a cell or connected group of cells that converts chemical energy into electrical energy by reversible chemical reactions and that may be recharged by passing a current through it in the direction opposite to that of its discharge — called also *storage cell*

sto·rax \'stȯr-ˌaks\ *n* [ME, fr. LL, alter. of L *styrax,* fr. Gk] (14c) **1 a :** a fragrant balsam obtained from the bark of an Asian tree (*Liquidambar orientalis*) of the witch-hazel family that is used as an expectorant and sometimes in perfumery — called also *Levant storax* **b :** a balsam from the sweet gum that is similar to storax **2 :** any of a genus (*Styrax* of the family Styracaceae, the storax family) of trees or shrubs with usu. hairy leaves and white flowers in drooping racemes — compare BENZOIN

[1]**store** \'stȯr\ *vt* **stored; stor·ing** [ME, fr. AF *estorer* to establish, restore, supply, fr. L *instaurare* to resume, restore] (13c) **1 :** LAY AWAY, ACCUMULATE ⟨~ vegetables for winter use⟩ ⟨an organism that absorbs and ~s DDT⟩ **2 :** FURNISH, SUPPLY; *esp* **:** to stock against a future time ⟨~ a ship with provisions⟩ **3 :** to place or leave in a location (as a warehouse, library, or computer memory) for preservation or later use or disposal **4 :** to provide storage room for **:** HOLD ⟨elevators for *storing* surplus wheat⟩ — **stor·able** \'stȯr-ə-bəl\ *adj*

[2]**store** *n* (13c) **1 a :** something that is stored or kept for future use **b** *pl* **:** articles (as of food) accumulated for some specific object and drawn upon as needed **:** STOCK, SUPPLIES **c :** something that is accumulated **d :** a source from which things may be drawn as needed **:** a reserve fund **2 :** STORAGE — usu. used with *in* ⟨when placing eggs in ~ —*Dublin Sunday Independent*⟩ **3 :** VALUE, IMPORTANCE ⟨set great ~ by a partner's opinion⟩ **4 :** a large quantity, supply, or number **:** ABUNDANCE **5 a :** STOREHOUSE, WAREHOUSE **b** *chiefly Brit* **:** MEMORY 4 **6 :** a business establishment where usu. diversified goods are kept for retail sale ⟨a grocery ~⟩ — compare SHOP — **in store :** in readiness **:** in preparation ⟨there's a surprise *in store* for you⟩

[3]**store** *adj* (1574) **1** *or* **stores :** of, relating to, kept in, or used for a store **2 :** purchased from a store as opposed to being natural or homemade **:** MANUFACTURED, READY-MADE ⟨~ clothes⟩ ⟨~ bread⟩

store–bought \'stȯr-ˌbȯt\ *adj* (1876) **:** STORE 2

store cheese *n* [fr. its being a staple article stocked in grocery stores] (1863) **:** CHEDDAR

[1]**store·front** \'stȯr-ˌfrənt\ *n* (1850) **1 :** the front side of a store or store building facing a street **2 :** a building, room, or suite of rooms having a storefront

[2]**storefront** *adj* (1937) **1 :** of, relating to, or characteristic of a storefront church ⟨a ~ evangelist⟩ **2 :** occupying a room or suite of rooms in a store building at street level and immediately behind a storefront ⟨a ~ school⟩ **3 :** of, relating to, or being outreach professional services ⟨~ lawyers⟩ ⟨a ~ clinic⟩

storefront church *n* (1937) **:** a city church that utilizes storefront quarters as a meeting place

store·house \'stȯr-ˌhau̇s\ *n* (14c) **1 :** a building for storing goods (as provisions) **:** MAGAZINE, WAREHOUSE **2 :** an abundant supply or source **:** REPOSITORY ⟨a ~ of information⟩

store·keep·er \-ˌkē-pər\ *n* (1618) **1 :** one that has charge of supplies (as military stores) **2 :** one that operates a retail store

store·room \-ˌrüm, -ˌru̇m\ *n* (1685) **1 :** a room or space for the storing of goods or supplies **2 :** STOREHOUSE 2

store·ship \-ˌship\ *n* (1693) **:** a ship used to carry supplies

store·wide \-'wīd\ *adj* (ca. 1937) **:** including all or most merchandise in a store ⟨a ~ sale⟩

[1]**sto·ried** \'stȯr-ēd\ *adj* (14c) **1 :** decorated with designs representing scenes from story or history ⟨a ~ tapestry⟩ **2 :** having an interesting history **:** celebrated in story or history ⟨a ~ institution⟩

[2]**storied** *or* **sto·reyed** \'stȯr-ēd\ *adj* (1624) **:** having stories — used in combination ⟨a two-*storied* house⟩

stork \'stȯrk\ *n* [ME, fr. OE *storc;* akin to OHG *storah* stork and prob. to OE *stearc* stiff — more at STARK] (bef. 12c) **:** any of various large mostly Old World wading birds (family Ciconiidae) that have long stout bills and are related to the ibises and herons

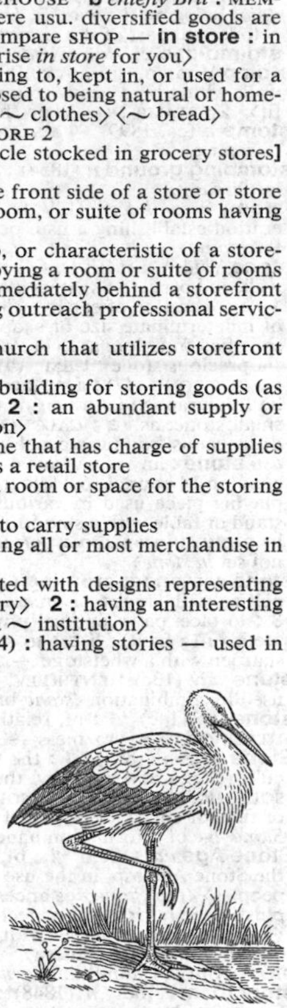
stork

storks·bill \'stȯrks-ˌbil\ *n* (1562) **:** any of several plants of the geranium family with elongate beaked fruits: **a :** PELARGONIUM **b :** any of a genus (*Erodium*) of herbs with small often veined or blotched flowers

[1]**storm** \'stȯrm\ *n, often attrib* [ME, fr. OE; akin to OHG *sturm* storm, OE *styrian* to stir] (bef. 12c) **1 a :** a disturbance of the atmosphere marked by wind and usu. by rain, snow, hail, sleet, or thunder and lightning **b :** a heavy fall of rain, snow, or hail **c** (1) **:** wind having a speed of 64 to 72 miles (103 to 117 kilometers) per hour (2) **:** WHOLE GALE — see BEAUFORT SCALE table **d :** a serious disturbance of any element of nature **2 :** a disturbed or agitated state ⟨~*s* of emotion⟩ **:** a sudden or violent commotion **3 :** a heavy discharge of objects (as missiles) **4 :** a tumultuous outburst ⟨a ~ of protests⟩ **5 a :** PAROXYSM 2 **b :** a sudden heavy influx or onset **6 :** a violent assault on a defended position **7** *pl* **:** STORM WINDOW — **by storm :** by or as if by employing a bold swift frontal movement esp. with the intent of defeating or winning over quickly ⟨took the literary world *by storm*⟩ — **up a storm :** in a remarkable or energetic fashion — used as an intensifier ⟨dancing *up a storm*⟩

[2]**storm** *vi* (15c) **1 a :** to blow with violence **b :** to rain, hail, snow, or sleet vigorously **2 :** to attack by storm ⟨~*ed* ashore at zero hour⟩ **3 :** to be in or to exhibit a violent passion **:** RAGE ⟨~*ing* at the unusual delay⟩ **4 :** to rush about or move impetuously, violently, or angrily ⟨the mob ~*ed* through the streets⟩ ~ *vt* **:** to attack, take, or win over by storm ⟨~ a fort⟩ ***syn*** see ATTACK

storm and stress *n, often cap both Ss* (1827) **:** STURM UND DRANG

storm·bound \'stȯrm-'bau̇nd\ *adj* (1804) **:** cut off from outside communication by a storm or its effects **:** stopped or delayed by storms

storm cellar *n* (ca. 1902) **:** a cellar or covered excavation designed for protection from dangerous windstorms (as tornadoes)

storm door *n* (1878) **:** an additional door placed outside an ordinary outside door for protection against severe weather

storm petrel *n* (ca. 1833) **:** any of various widespread small dark petrels (family Hydrobatidae) that typically return to land only to nest usu. in burrows — called also *Mother Carey's chicken*

storm trooper *n* (1933) **1 :** a member of a private Nazi army notorious for aggressiveness, violence, and brutality **2 :** one that resembles a Nazi storm trooper

storm window *n* (ca. 1888) **:** a sash placed outside an ordinary window as a protection against severe weather — called also *storm sash*

stormy \'stȯr-mē\ *adj* **storm·i·er; -est** (12c) **1 :** relating to, characterized by, or indicative of a storm ⟨a ~ day⟩ ⟨a ~ autumn⟩ **2 :** marked by turmoil or fury ⟨a ~ life⟩ ⟨a ~ conference⟩ — **storm·i·ly** \'stȯr-mə-lē\ *adv* — **storm·i·ness** \-mē-nəs\ *n*

stormy petrel *n* (ca. 1776) **1 :** STORM PETREL **2 a :** one fond of strife **b :** a harbinger of trouble

[1]**sto·ry** \'stȯr-ē\ *n, pl* **stories** [ME *storie,* fr. AF *estoire, estorie,* fr. L *historia* — more at HISTORY] (13c) **1** *archaic* **a :** HISTORY 1 **b :** HISTORY 3 **2 a :** an account of incidents or events **b :** a statement regarding the facts pertinent to a situation in question **c :** ANECDOTE; *esp* **:** an amusing one **3 a :** a fictional narrative shorter than a novel; *specif* **:** SHORT STORY **b :** the intrigue or plot of a narrative or dramat-

ic work **4 :** a widely circulated rumor **5 :** LIE, FALSEHOOD **6 :** LEGEND, ROMANCE **7 :** a news article or broadcast **8 :** MATTER, SITUATION

2story *vt* **sto·ried; sto·ry·ing** (15c) **1** *archaic* **:** to narrate or describe in story **2 :** to adorn with a story or a scene from history

3story *also* **sto·rey** \ˈstȯr-ē\ *n, pl* **stories** *also* **storeys** [ME *storie,* fr. ML *historia* narrative, illustration, story of a building, fr. L, history, tale; prob. fr. narrative friezes on the window level of medieval buildings] (14c) **1 a :** the space in a building between two adjacent floor levels or between a floor and the roof **b :** a set of rooms in such a space **c :** a unit of measure equal to the height of the story of a building ⟨one ~ high⟩ **2 :** a horizontal division of a building's exterior not necessarily corresponding exactly with the stories within

sto·ry·board \-ˌbȯrd\ *n* (1942) **:** a panel or series of panels on which a set of sketches is arranged depicting consecutively the important changes of scene and action in a series of shots (as for a film, television show, or commercial) — **storyboard** *vt*

1sto·ry·book \-ˌbu̇k\ *n* (1711) **:** a book of stories usu. for children

2storybook *adj* (1844) **:** FAIRY-TALE ⟨a ~ romance⟩

story line *n* (1941) **:** the plot of a story or drama

sto·ry·tell·er \ˈstȯr-ē-ˌte-lər\ *n* (1709) **:** a teller of stories: as **a :** a relater of anecdotes **b :** a reciter of tales (as in a children's library) **c :** LIAR, FIBBER **d :** a writer of stories — **sto·ry·tell·ing** \-ˌte-liŋ\ *n*

stoss \ˈstäs, ˈstȯs, ˈstōs, ˈshtōs\ *adj* [G *stoss-,* fr. *stossen* to push, fr. OHG *stōzen;* akin to Goth *stautan* to strike — more at CONTUSION] (1878) **:** facing toward the direction from which an overriding glacier impinges ⟨the ~ slope of a hill⟩

stot *also* **stott** \ˈstät\ *vi* **stot·ted; stot·ting** [Sc & northern dial. *stot* to bounce, rebound] (1801) **:** to bound with a stiff-legged gait ⟨the gazelle *stotted* when alarmed⟩

sto·tin \stō-ˈtēn\ *n, pl* **sto·ti·nov** \stō-ˈtē-ˌnȯv\ [Slovenian (nom. pl. *stotini,* gen. pl. *stotinov*), fr. *sto* hundred] (1991) **:** a former monetary unit equal to 1/100 Slovenian tolar

sto·tin·ka \stō-ˈtiŋ-kə, stə-\ *n, pl* **-tin·ki** \-kē\ [Bulg, fr. *sto* hundred] (ca. 1892) — see *lev* at MONEY table

stound \ˈstau̇nd, ˈstünd\ *n* [ME, fr. OE *stund;* akin to OHG *stunta* time, hour] (bef. 12c) *archaic* **:** TIME, WHILE

stoup \ˈstüp\ *n* [ME *stowp,* prob. of Scand origin; akin to ON *staup* cup; akin to OE *stēap* flagon] (14c) **1 a :** a beverage container (as a glass or tankard) **b :** FLAGON **2 :** a basin for holy water at the entrance of a church

1stour \ˈstu̇r\ *adj* [ME *stor,* fr. OE *stōr;* akin to OHG *stuori* large, Russ *staryĭ* old, OE *standan* to stand] (bef. 12c) **1** *chiefly Scot* **:** STRONG, HARDY **2** *chiefly Scot* **:** STERN, HARSH

2stour *n* [ME, fr. AF *estur, estour,* of Gmc origin; akin to OHG *sturm* storm, battle — more at STORM] (14c) **1 a** *archaic* **:** BATTLE, CONFLICT **b** *dial Brit* **:** TUMULT, UPROAR **2** *chiefly Scot* **:** DUST, POWDER

1stout \ˈstau̇t\ *adj* [ME, fr. AF *estut, estout,* of Gmc origin; akin to OHG *stolz* proud; perh. akin to OHG *stelza* stilt — more at STILT] (14c) **1 :** strong of character: as **a :** BRAVE, BOLD **b :** FIRM, DETERMINED; *also* **:** OBSTINATE, UNCOMPROMISING **2 :** physically or materially strong: **a :** STURDY, VIGOROUS **b :** STAUNCH, ENDURING **c :** sturdily constructed **:** SUBSTANTIAL **3 :** FORCEFUL ⟨a ~ attack⟩; *also* **:** VIOLENT ⟨a ~ wind⟩ **4 :** bulky in body **:** FAT *syn* see STRONG — **stout·ish** \ˈstau̇-tish\ *adj* — **stout·ly** *adv* — **stout·ness** *n*

2stout *n* (1677) **1 :** a very dark full-bodied ale with a distinctive malty flavor **2 a :** a fat person **b :** a clothing size designed for the large figure

stout·en \ˈstau̇-tᵊn\ *vb* **stout·ened; stout·en·ing** \ˈstau̇t-niŋ, ˈstau̇-tᵊn-iŋ\ *vt* (1834) **:** to make stout ⟨~ a resolve⟩ ~ *vi* **:** to become stout

stout·heart·ed \ˈstau̇t-ˌhär-təd\ *adj* (1552) **:** having a stout heart or spirit: **a :** COURAGEOUS **b :** STUBBORN — **stout·heart·ed·ly** *adv* — **stout·heart·ed·ness** *n*

1stove \ˈstōv\ *n* [ME (Sc), heated room, steam bath, fr. MD or MLG, fr. VL **extufa,* ultim. fr. L *ex-* + Gk *typhein* to smoke — more at DEAF] (ca. 1618) **1 a :** a portable or fixed apparatus that burns fuel or uses electricity to provide heat (as for cooking or heating) **b :** a device that generates heat for special purposes (as for heating tools or heating air for a hot blast) **c :** KILN **2** *chiefly Brit* **:** a hothouse esp. for the cultivation of tropical exotics; *broadly* **:** GREENHOUSE

2stove *past and past part of* STAVE

stove·pipe \ˈstōv-ˌpīp\ *n* (1699) **1 :** pipe of large diameter usu. of sheet steel used as a stove chimney or to connect a stove with a flue **2 :** SILK HAT

sto·ver \ˈstō-vər\ *n* [ME, modif. of AF *estovers* necessary supplies, fr. *estover* to be necessary, ultim. fr. L *est opus* there is need] (14c) **1** *dial chiefly Eng* **:** FODDER **2 :** mature cured stalks of corn with the ears removed that are used as feed for livestock

stow \ˈstō\ *vt* [ME, to place, fr. *stowe* place, fr. OE *stōw;* akin to OFris *stō* place, Gk *stylos* pillar — more at STEER] (14c) **1 :** HOUSE, LODGE **2 a :** to put away for future use **:** STORE **b** *obs* **:** to lock up for safekeeping **:** CONFINE **3 a :** to dispose in an orderly fashion **:** ARRANGE, PACK **b :** LOAD **4** *slang* **:** to put aside **:** STOP **5 a** *archaic* **:** CROWD **b :** to eat or drink up — usu. used with *away* ⟨~*ed* away a huge dinner⟩

stow·age \-ij\ *n* (14c) **1 a :** an act or process of stowing **b :** goods in storage or to be stowed **2 a :** storage capacity **b :** a place or receptacle for storage **3 :** the state of being stored

stow·away \ˈstō-ə-ˌwā\ *n* (1848) **:** one that stows away

stow away *vi* (1879) **:** to secrete oneself aboard a vehicle as a means of obtaining transportation

1STP \ˌes-ˌtē-ˈpē\ *n* [prob. fr. *STP,* a trademark for a motor fuel additive] (1967) **:** a hallucinogenic drug chemically related to mescaline and amphetamine

2STP *abbr* **1** shielded twisted pair **2** standard temperature and pressure

str *abbr* steamer

stra·bis·mus \strə-ˈbiz-məs\ *n* [NL, fr. Gk *strabismos* condition of squinting, fr. *strabizein* to squint, fr. *strabos* squint-eyed; akin to Gk *strephein* to twist] (ca. 1684) **:** inability of one eye to attain binocular vision with the other because of imbalance of the muscles of the eyeball — called also *squint;* compare CROSS-EYE — **stra·bis·mic** \-mik\ *adj*

1strad·dle \ˈstra-dᵊl\ *vb* **strad·dled; strad·dling** \ˈstrad-liŋ, ˈstra-dᵊl-iŋ\ [irreg. fr. *stride*] *vi* (1565) **1 :** to stand, sit, or walk with the legs wide apart; *esp* **:** to sit astride **2 :** to spread out irregularly **:** SPRAWL **3 :** to favor or seem to favor two apparently opposite sides **4 :** to execute a commodities market spread ~ *vt* **1 :** to stand, sit, or be astride of ⟨~ a horse⟩ ⟨campsites *straddling* the river⟩ **2 :** to be noncommittal in regard to ⟨~ an issue⟩ **3 :** to belong in part to (each of several categories) ⟨a movie *straddling* genres⟩ — **strad·dler** \ˈstrad-lər, ˈstra-dᵊl-ər\ *n* — **straddle the fence :** to be in a position of neutrality or indecision

2straddle *n* (1611) **1 :** the act or position of one who straddles **2 :** a noncommittal or equivocal position **3 :** SPREAD 5

Stra·di·va·ri \ˌstra-də-ˈvär-ē, -ˈver-\ *n* (1902) **:** STRADIVARIUS

Strad·i·var·i·us \ˌstra-də-ˈver-ē-əs\ *n, pl* **-var·ii** \-ē-ˌī\ [latinized form of *Stradivari*] (1833) **:** a stringed instrument (as a violin) made by Antonio Stradivari of Cremona

strafe \ˈstrāf, *esp Brit* ˈsträf\ *vt* **strafed; straf·ing** [G *Gott strafe England* may God punish England, German propaganda slogan during World War I] (1915) **:** to rake (as ground troops) with fire at close range and esp. with machine-gun fire from low-flying aircraft — **strafe** *n* — **straf·er** *n*

1strag·gle \ˈstra-gəl\ *vi* **strag·gled; strag·gling** \-g(ə-)liŋ\ [ME *straglen*] (15c) **1 :** to wander from the direct course or way **:** ROVE, STRAY **2 :** to trail off from others of its kind ⟨little cabins *straggling* off into the woods⟩ — **strag·gler** \-g(ə-)lər\ *n*

2straggle *n* (1865) **:** a straggling group (as of persons or objects)

strag·gly \ˈstra-g(ə-)lē\ *adj* **strag·gli·er; -est** (1818) **:** spread out or scattered irregularly ⟨a ~ beard⟩

1straight \ˈstrāt\ *adj* [ME *streght, straight,* fr. pp. of *strecchen* to stretch — more at STRETCH] (14c) **1 a :** free from curves, bends, angles, or irregularities ⟨~ hair⟩ ⟨~ timber⟩ **b :** generated by a point moving continuously in the same direction and expressed by a linear equation ⟨a ~ line⟩ ⟨the ~ segment of a curve⟩ **2 a :** lying along or holding to a direct or proper course or method ⟨a ~ thinker⟩ **b :** CANDID, FRANK ⟨a ~ answer⟩ **c :** coming directly from a trustworthy source ⟨a ~ tip on the horses⟩ **d (1) :** having the elements in an order ⟨the ~ sequence of events⟩ **(2) :** CONSECUTIVE ⟨12 ~ days⟩ **e :** having the cylinders arranged in a single straight line ⟨a ~ 8-cylinder engine⟩ **f :** PLUMB, VERTICAL ⟨the picture isn't quite ~⟩ **3 a :** exhibiting honesty and fairness ⟨~ dealing⟩ **b :** properly ordered or arranged ⟨set the kitchen ~⟩ ⟨set us ~ on that issue⟩; *also* **:** CORRECT ⟨get the facts ~⟩ **c :** free from extraneous matter **:** UNMIXED ⟨~ whiskey⟩ **d :** marked by no exceptions or deviations in support of a principle or party ⟨votes a ~ Democratic ticket⟩ **e :** having a fixed price for each regardless of the number sold **f :** not deviating from an indicated pattern ⟨writes ~ humor⟩ ⟨a *straight*-A student⟩ **g (1) :** exhibiting no deviation from what is established or accepted as usual, normal, or proper **:** CONVENTIONAL; *also* **:** SQUARE 5f **(2) :** not using or under the influence of drugs or alcohol **h :** HETEROSEXUAL **4 :** being the only form of remuneration ⟨on ~ commission⟩ — **straight·ish** \ˈstrā-tish\ *adj* — **straight·ly** *adv* — **straight·ness** *n*

2straight *adv* (14c) **:** in a straight manner ⟨came ~ home from work⟩

3straight *vt* (15c) *chiefly Scot* **:** STRAIGHTEN

4straight *n* (1645) **1 :** something that is straight: as **a :** a straight line or arrangement **b :** STRAIGHTAWAY; *esp* **:** HOMESTRETCH **c :** a true or honest report or course **2 a :** a sequence (as of shots, strokes, or moves) resulting in a perfect score in a game or contest **b :** first place at the finish of a horse race **:** WIN **3 :** a poker hand containing five cards in sequence but not of the same suit — see POKER illustration **4 :** a person who adheres to conventional attitudes and mores

straight–ahead \ˈstrāt-ə-ˈhed\ *adj* (1836) **:** relating to or being music performed in an unembellished manner typical of a given idiom or performer; *broadly* **:** STRAIGHTFORWARD

straight and narrow *n* [prob. alter. of *strait and narrow;* fr. the admonition of Mt 7:14(AV), "strait is the gate and narrow is the way which leadeth unto life"] (1930) **:** the way of propriety and rectitude — used with *the*

straight angle *n* (1601) **:** an angle whose sides lie in opposite directions from the vertex in the same straight line and which equals two right angles

straight–arm \ˈstrāt-ˌärm\ *n* (1903) **:** an act or instance of warding off a person or thing by pushing with the palm of the hand with the arm fully extended from the shoulder and the elbow locked — called also *stiff-arm* — **straight–arm** *vb*

straight arrow *n* [fr. the expression *straight as an arrow*] (1969) **:** a person who lives by rigidly proper or conventional standards — **straight–arrow** *adj*

1straight·away \ˌstrāt-ə-ˈwā\ *adv* (1662) **:** without hesitation or delay

2straight·away \ˈstrāt-ə-ˌwā\ *adj* (1874) **1 :** proceeding in a straight line **:** continuous in direction **2 :** IMMEDIATE

3straight·away \ˈstrā-tə-ˌwā\ *n* (1878) **:** a straight course: as **a :** the straight part of a closed racecourse **:** STRETCH **b :** a straight and unimpeded stretch of road or way

straight·bred \ˈstrāt-ˈbred\ *adj* (1898) **:** produced by breeding a single breed, strain, or type ⟨~ cattle⟩ — **straight·bred** \-ˌbred\ *n*

straight chain *n* (1890) **:** an open chain of atoms having no side chains — usu. hyphenated when used attributively

straight·edge \ˈstrāt-ˌej\ *n* (1795) **:** a bar or piece of material (as of wood, metal, or plastic) with a straight edge for testing straight lines and surfaces or for cutting along or drawing straight lines

straight·en \ˈstrā-tᵊn\ *vb* **straight·ened; straight·en·ing** \ˈstrāt-niŋ, ˈstrā-tᵊn-iŋ\ *vt* (1542) **:** to make straight — usu. used with *up* or *out* ~ *vi* **:** to become straight — usu. used with *up* or *out* — **straight·en·er** \ˈstrāt-nər, ˈstrā-tᵊn-ər\ *n*

straight face *n* (1853) **:** a face giving no evidence of emotion and esp. of merriment ⟨lied with a *straight face*⟩ — **straight–faced** \ˈstrāt-ˈfāst\ *adj* — **straight–faced·ly** \-ˈfā-səd-lē, -ˈfāst-lē\ *adv*

straight flush *n* (1864) **:** a poker hand containing five cards of the same suit in sequence — see POKER illustration

[1]straight·for·ward \ˌstrāt-ˈfȯr-wərd, ˈstrāt-ˌ\ *adj* (1790) **1 a :** free from evasiveness or obscurity : EXACT, CANDID ⟨a ~ account⟩ **b :** CLEAR-CUT, PRECISE **2 :** proceeding in a straight course or manner : DIRECT, UNDEVIATING — **straight·for·ward·ly** *adv* — **straight·for·ward·ness** *n*

[2]straightforward *also* **straight·for·wards** \-wərdz\ *adv* (1809) : in a straightforward manner

straight–line \ˈstrāt-ˈlīn\ *adj* (1843) **1 :** being a mechanical linkage or equivalent device designed to produce or copy motion in a straight line **2 :** having the principal parts arranged in a straight line **3 :** marked by a uniform spread and esp. in equal segments over a given term ⟨~ amortization⟩ ⟨~ depreciation⟩ **4 :** occurring, measured, or made in or along a straight line ⟨~ motion⟩ ⟨~ extrapolation⟩

straight–line wind *n* (1849) : a powerful, fast-moving surface wind that lacks a rotational pattern and that can cause widespread damage

straight man *n* (1923) : a member of a comedy team who feeds lines to a partner who in turn replies with usu. humorous quips

straight off *adv* (ca. 1841) : at once : IMMEDIATELY

straight–out \ˈstrāt-ˈau̇t\ *adj* (1840) **1 :** FORTHRIGHT, BLUNT ⟨gave a ~ answer⟩ **2 :** OUTRIGHT, THOROUGHGOING — **straight–out** *adv*

straight poker *n* (1864) : poker in which the players bet on the five cards dealt to them and then have a showdown without drawing — compare DRAW POKER, STUD POKER

straight razor *n* (1917) : a razor with a rigid steel cutting blade hinged to a case that forms a handle when the razor is open for use

straight shooter *n* (1928) : a thoroughly upright straightforward person

straight·way \ˈstrāt-ˈwā, -ˌwā\ *adv* (15c) **1 :** in a direct course : DIRECTLY ⟨fell ~ down the stairs⟩ **2 :** RIGHT AWAY, IMMEDIATELY, STRAIGHTAWAY ⟨~ the clouds began to part⟩

[1]strain \ˈstrān\ *n* [ME *streen* progeny, lineage, fr. OE *strēon* gain, acquisition; akin to OHG *gistriuni* gain, L *struere* to heap up — more at STREW] (13c) **1 a :** LINEAGE, ANCESTRY **b :** a group of presumed common ancestry with clear-cut physiological but usu. not morphological distinctions ⟨a high-yielding ~ of winter wheat⟩; *broadly* : a specified infraspecific group (as a stock, line, or ecotype) **c :** KIND, SORT ⟨discussions of a lofty ~⟩ **2 a :** inherited or inherent character, quality, or disposition ⟨a ~ of madness in the family⟩ **b :** TRACE, STREAK ⟨a ~ of fanaticism⟩ **3 a :** TUNE, AIR **b :** a passage of verbal or musical expression **c :** a stream or outburst of forceful or impassioned speech **4 a :** the tenor, pervading note, burden, or tone of an utterance or of a course of action or conduct **b :** MOOD, TEMPER

[2]strain *vb* [ME, fr. AF *estreindre,* fr. L *stringere* to bind or draw tight, press together; akin to Gk *strang-, stranx* drop squeezed out, *strangalē* halter] *vt* (14c) **1 a :** to draw tight : cause to fit firmly ⟨~ the bandage over the wound⟩ **b :** to stretch to maximum extension and tautness ⟨~ a canvas over a frame⟩ **2 a :** to exert (as oneself) to the utmost **b :** to injure by overuse, misuse, or excessive pressure ⟨~*ed* his back⟩ **c :** to cause a change of form or size in (a body) by application of external force **3 :** to squeeze or clasp tightly: as **a :** HUG **b :** to compress painfully : CONSTRICT **4 a :** to cause to pass through a strainer : FILTER **b :** to remove by straining ⟨~ lumps out of the gravy⟩ **5 :** to stretch beyond a proper limit ⟨that story ~*s* my credulity⟩ **6** *obs* : to squeeze out : EXTORT ~ *vi* **1 a :** to make violent efforts : STRIVE ⟨has to ~ to reach the high notes⟩ **b :** to pull against resistance ⟨a dog ~*ing* at its leash⟩ **c :** to contract the muscles forcefully in attempting to defecate — often used in the phrase *strain at stool* **2 :** to pass through or as if through a strainer ⟨the liquid ~*s* readily⟩ **3 :** to make great difficulty or resistance : BALK — **strain a point :** to go beyond a usual, accepted, or proper limit or rule

[3]strain *n* (1558) **1 :** an act of straining or the condition of being strained: as **a :** bodily injury from excessive tension, effort, or use ⟨heart ~⟩; *esp* : one resulting from a wrench or twist and involving undue stretching of muscles or ligaments ⟨back ~⟩ **b :** excessive or difficult exertion or labor **c :** excessive physical or mental tension; *also* : a force, influence, or factor causing such tension ⟨a ~ on the marriage⟩ **d :** deformation of a material body under the action of applied forces **2 :** an unusual reach, degree, or intensity : PITCH **3** *archaic* : a strained interpretation of something said or written

strained \ˈstrānd\ *adj* (ca. 1542) **1 :** done or produced with excessive effort **2 :** pushed by antagonism near to open conflict ⟨~ relations⟩

strain·er \ˈstrā-nər\ *n* (14c) : one that strains: as **a :** a device (as a sieve) to retain solid pieces while a liquid passes through **b :** any of various devices for stretching or tightening something

strain gauge *n* (1910) : EXTENSOMETER

[1]strait \ˈstrāt\ *adj* [ME, fr. AF *estreit,* fr. L *strictus* strait, strict, fr. pp. of *stringere*] (13c) **1** *archaic* : STRICT, RIGOROUS **2** *archaic* **a :** NARROW **b :** limited in space or time **c :** closely fitting : CONSTRICTED, TIGHT **3 a :** causing distress : DIFFICULT **b :** limited as to means or resources — **strait·ly** *adv* — **strait·ness** *n*

[2]strait *adv* (13c) *obs* : in a close or tight manner

[3]strait *n* (14c) **1 a** *archaic* : a narrow space or passage **b :** a comparatively narrow passageway connecting two large bodies of water — often used in pl. but sing. in constr. **c :** ISTHMUS **2 :** a situation of perplexity or distress — often used in pl. ⟨in dire ~*s*⟩ ***syn*** see JUNCTURE

strait·en \ˈstrā-tᵊn\ *vt* **strait·ened; strait·en·ing** \ˈstrāt-niŋ, ˈstrā-tᵊn-iŋ\ (ca. 1552) **1 a :** to make strait or narrow **b :** to hem in : CONFINE **2** *archaic* : to restrict in freedom or scope : HAMPER **3 :** to subject to distress, privation, or deficiency ⟨in ~*ed* circumstances⟩

[1]strait·jack·et *also* **straight·jack·et** \ˈstrāt-ˌja-kət\ *n* (1814) **1 :** a cover or overgarment of strong material (as canvas) used to bind the body and esp. the arms closely in restraining a violent prisoner or patient **2 :** something that restricts or confines like a straitjacket

[2]straitjacket *also* **straightjacket** *vt* (1863) : to confine in or as if in a straitjacket

strait·laced *or* **straight·laced** \ˈstrāt-ˈlāst\ *adj* (1554) **1 :** excessively strict in manners, morals, or opinion **2 :** wearing or having a bodice or stays tightly laced — **strait·laced·ly** \-ˈlā-səd-lē, -ˈlāst-lē\ *adv* — **strait·laced·ness** \-ˈlās(t)-nəs, -ˈlā-səd-nəs\ *n*

Straits dollar \ˈstrāts-\ *n* [*Straits* Settlements, former British crown colony] (1908) : a dollar formerly issued by British Malaya and used in much of southern and eastern Asia and the East Indies

strake \ˈstrāk\ *n* [ME; akin to OE *streccan* to stretch — more at STRETCH] (14c) **1 :** a continuous band of hull planking or plates on a ship; *also* : the width of such a band **2 :** STREAK, STRIPE

stra·mash \strə-ˈmash\ *n* [origin unknown] (1803) **1** *chiefly Scot* : DISTURBANCE, RACKET **2** *chiefly Scot* : CRASH, SMASHUP

stra·mo·ni·um \strə-ˈmō-nē-əm\ *n* [NL] (1663) **1 :** the dried leaves of the jimsonweed or of a related plant (genus *Datura*) that contain toxic alkaloids (as atropine) used in medicine **2 :** JIMSONWEED

[1]strand \ˈstrand\ *n* [ME, fr. OE; akin to ON *strǫnd* shore] (bef. 12c) : the land bordering a body of water : SHORE, BEACH

[2]strand *vt* (1621) **1 :** to run, drive, or cause to drift onto a strand : run aground **2 :** to leave in a strange or an unfavorable place esp. without funds or means to depart **3 :** to leave (a base runner) on base at the end of an inning in baseball ~ *vi* : to become stranded

[3]strand *n* [ME *stronde, strande*] (13c) **1** *Scot & dial Eng* : STREAM **2** *Scot & dial Eng* : SEA

[4]strand *n* [ME *strond*] (15c) **1 a :** fibers or filaments twisted, plaited, or laid parallel to form a unit for further twisting or plaiting into yarn, thread, rope, or cordage **b :** one of the wires twisted together or laid parallel to form a wire rope or cable **c :** something (as a molecular chain) resembling a strand ⟨a ~ of DNA⟩ **2 :** an element (as a yarn or thread) of a woven or plaited material **3 :** an elongated or twisted and plaited body resembling a rope ⟨a ~ of pearls⟩ **4 :** one of the elements interwoven in a complex whole ⟨one ~ of the novel's plot⟩

[5]strand *vt* (1841) **1 :** to break a strand of (a rope) accidentally **2 a :** to form (as a rope) from strands **b :** to play out, twist, or arrange in a strand

strand·ed \ˈstran-dəd\ *adj* (1769) : having a strand or strands esp. of a specified kind or number — usu. used in combination ⟨double-*stranded* DNA⟩ — **strand·ed·ness** *n*

strand·line \ˈstran(d)-ˌlīn\ *n* (1903) : SHORELINE; *esp* : a shoreline above the present water level

[1]strange \ˈstrānj\ *adj* **strang·er; strang·est** [ME, fr. AF *estrange,* fr. L *extraneus,* lit., external, fr. *extra* outside — more at EXTRA-] (13c) **1 a** *archaic* : of, relating to, or characteristic of another country : FOREIGN **b :** not native to or naturally belonging in a place : of external origin, kind, or character **2 a :** not before known, heard, or seen : UNFAMILIAR **b :** exciting wonder or awe : EXTRAORDINARY **3 a :** discouraging familiarities : RESERVED, DISTANT **b :** ILL AT EASE **4 :** UNACCUSTOMED 2 ⟨she was ~ to his ways⟩ — **strange·ly** *adv*

syn STRANGE, SINGULAR, UNIQUE, PECULIAR, ECCENTRIC, ERRATIC, ODD, QUAINT, OUTLANDISH mean departing from what is ordinary, usual, or to be expected. STRANGE stresses unfamiliarity and may apply to the foreign, the unnatural, the unaccountable ⟨a journey filled with *strange* sights⟩. SINGULAR suggests individuality or puzzling strangeness ⟨a *singular* feeling of impending disaster⟩. UNIQUE implies singularity and the fact of being without a known parallel ⟨a career *unique* in the annals of science⟩. PECULIAR implies a marked distinctiveness ⟨the *peculiar* status of America's first lady⟩. ECCENTRIC suggests a wide divergence from the usual or normal esp. in behavior ⟨the *eccentric* eating habits of preschoolers⟩. ERRATIC stresses a capricious and unpredictable wandering or deviating ⟨a friend's suddenly *erratic* behavior⟩. ODD applies to a departure from the regular or expected ⟨an *odd* sense of humor⟩. QUAINT suggests an old-fashioned but pleasant oddness ⟨a *quaint* fishing village⟩. OUTLANDISH applies to what is uncouth, bizarre, or barbaric ⟨*outlandish* fashions of the time⟩.

[2]strange *n, often attrib* (1974) : a fundamental quark that has an electric charge of $-\frac{1}{3}$ and a measured energy of approximately 150 MeV; *also* : the flavor characterizing this particle

strange·ness \ˈstrānj-nəs\ *n* (14c) **1 :** the quality or state of being strange **2 :** the flavor characterizing a strange quark

[1]strang·er \ˈstrān-jər\ *n* [ME, fr. AF *estrangier* stranger, foreigner, fr. *estrange*] (14c) **1 :** one who is strange: as **a** (1) : FOREIGNER (2) : a resident alien **b :** one in the house of another as a guest, visitor, or intruder **c :** a person or thing that is unknown or with whom one is unacquainted **d :** one who does not belong to or is kept from the activities of a group **e :** one not privy or party to an act, contract, or title : one that interferes without right **2 :** one ignorant of or unacquainted with someone or something

[2]stranger *adj* (15c) : of, relating to, or being a stranger : FOREIGN

[3]stranger *vt* (1606) *obs* : ESTRANGE, ALIENATE

strange woman *n* [fr. the expression frequently used in Prov (AV)] (1535) : PROSTITUTE

stran·gle \ˈstraŋ-gəl\ *vb* **stran·gled; stran·gling** \-g(ə-)liŋ\ [ME, fr. AF *estrangler,* fr. L *strangulare,* fr. Gk *strangalan,* fr. *strangalē* halter — more at STRAIN] *vt* (14c) **1 a :** to choke to death by compressing the throat with something (as a hand or rope) : THROTTLE **b :** to obstruct seriously or fatally the normal breathing of **c :** STIFLE **2 :** to suppress or hinder the rise, expression, or growth of ⟨repression ~*s* free speech⟩ ~ *vi* **1 :** to become strangled **2 :** to die from or as if from interference with breathing — **stran·gler** \-g(ə-)lər\ *n*

stran·gle·hold \ˈstraŋ-gəl-ˌhōld\ *n* (1893) **1 :** an illegal wrestling hold by which one's opponent is choked **2 :** a force or influence that chokes or suppresses freedom of movement or expression

strangler fig *n* (1933) : any of several figs (as *Ficus aurea* of the southeastern U.S.) that start as epiphytes but send down roots to the ground around the host tree; *broadly* : any of various epiphytic vines or trees (as *Clusia rosea* syn. *C. major*) of similar habit

stran·gles \ˈstraŋ-gəlz\ *n pl but sing or pl in constr* [pl. of obs. *strangle* act of strangling] (ca. 1706) : an infectious febrile disease of horses caused by a streptococcus (*Streptococcus equi*) and marked esp. by inflammation and congestion of mucous membranes of the respiratory tract

stran·gu·late \ˈstraŋ-gyə-ˌlāt\ *vb* **-lat·ed; -lat·ing** [L *strangulatus,* pp. of *strangulare*] *vt* (1665) : STRANGLE, CONSTRICT ~ *vi* : to become constricted so as to stop circulation ⟨the hernia will ~⟩

stran·gu·la·tion \ˌstraŋ-gyə-ˈlā-shən\ *n* (1542) **1 :** the action or process of strangling or strangulating **2 :** the state of being strangled or strangulated; *esp* : excessive or pathological constriction or compression of a bodily tube (as a blood vessel or a loop of intestine) that interrupts its ability to act as a passage

stran·gu·ry \ˈstraŋ-gyə-rē, -ˌgyu̇r-ē\ *n, pl* **-ries** [ME, fr. AF *strangerie,* fr. L *stranguria,* fr. Gk *strangouria,* fr. *strang-, stranx* drop squeezed out + *ourein* to urinate, fr. *ouron* urine — more at STRAIN, URINE] (14c) : a slow and painful spasmodic discharge of urine drop by drop

[1]**strap** \ˈstrap\ *n* [alter. of *strop,* fr. ME, band or loop of leather or rope, fr. OE, thong for securing an oar, fr. L *struppus* band, strap, fr. Gk *strophos* twisted band, fr. *strephein* to twist] (1602) **1 a :** a narrow usu. flat strip or thong of a flexible material and esp. leather used for securing, holding together, or wrapping **b :** something made of a strap forming a loop ⟨a boot ~⟩ **c :** a strip of leather used for flogging **d :** STROP **2 :** a band, plate, or loop of metal for binding objects together or for clamping an object in position **3 :** a shoe fastened with a usu. buckled strap **4** *Irish* **:** TROLLOP — **strap·py** \ˈstra-pē\ *adj*

[2]**strap** *vt* **strapped; strap·ping** (1711) **1 a** (1) **:** to secure with or attach by means of a strap (2) **:** to support (as a sprained joint) with overlapping strips of adhesive plaster **b :** BIND, CONSTRICT **2 :** to beat or punish with a strap **3 :** STROP **4 :** to cause to suffer from an extreme scarcity ⟨is often *strapped* for cash⟩

strap·hang·er \ˈstrap-ˌhaŋ-ər\ *n* (1905) **:** a standing passenger in a subway, streetcar, bus, or train who clings for support to one of the short straps or similar devices placed along the aisle — **strap·hang** \-ˌhaŋ\ *vi*

strap·less \-ləs\ *adj* (1846) **:** having no strap; *specif* **:** made or worn without shoulder straps ⟨a ~ evening gown⟩ — **strapless** *n*

strap·pa·do \strə-ˈpā-(ˌ)dō, -ˈpä-\ *n* [modif. of It *strappata,* lit., sharp pull] (1560) **:** a punishment or torture in which the subject is hoisted by rope and allowed to fall its full length; *also* **:** a machine used to inflict this torture

strap·per \ˈstra-pər\ *n* (1675) **:** one that is unusually large or robust

[1]**strapping** *adj* (1657) **:** having a vigorously sturdy constitution

[2]**strapping** *n* (1818) **1 :** material for a strap **2 :** STRAPS

strass \ˈstras\ *n* [F *stras, strass*] (1820) **:** PASTE 3

strat·a·gem \ˈstra-tə-jəm, -ˌjem\ *n* [It *stratagemma,* fr. L *strategema,* fr. Gk *stratēgēma,* fr. *stratēgein* to be a general, maneuver, fr. *stratēgos* general, fr. *stratos* camp, army (akin to L *stratus,* pp., spread out) + *agein* to lead — more at STRATUM, AGENT] (15c) **1 a :** an artifice or trick in war for deceiving and outwitting the enemy **b :** a cleverly contrived trick or scheme for gaining an end **2 :** skill in ruses or trickery ***syn*** see TRICK

stra·te·gic \strə-ˈtē-jik\ *adj* (1825) **1 :** of, relating to, or marked by strategy ⟨a ~ retreat⟩ **2 a :** necessary to or important in the initiation, conduct, or completion of a strategic plan **b :** required for the conduct of war and not available in adequate quantities domestically ⟨~ materials⟩ **c :** of great importance within an integrated whole or to a planned effect ⟨emphasized ~ points⟩ **3 :** designed or trained to strike an enemy at the sources of its military, economic, or political power ⟨a ~ bomber⟩ — **stra·te·gi·cal** \-ji-kəl\ *adj* — **stra·te·gi·cal·ly** \-ji-k(ə-)lē\ *adv*

strat·e·gist \ˈstra-tə-jist\ *n* (1832) **:** a person skilled in strategy

strat·e·gize \-ˌjīz\ *vi* **-gized; -giz·ing** (1921) **:** to devise a strategy or course of action

strat·e·gy \-jē\ *n, pl* **-gies** [Gk *stratēgia* generalship, fr. *stratēgos*] (1810) **1 a** (1) **:** the science and art of employing the political, economic, psychological, and military forces of a nation or group of nations to afford the maximum support to adopted policies in peace or war (2) **:** the science and art of military command exercised to meet the enemy in combat under advantageous conditions **b :** a variety of or instance of the use of strategy **2 a :** a careful plan or method **:** a clever stratagem **b :** the art of devising or employing plans or stratagems toward a goal **3 :** an adaptation or complex of adaptations (as of behavior, metabolism, or structure) that serves or appears to serve an important function in achieving evolutionary success ⟨foraging *strategies* of insects⟩

strath \ˈstrath\ *n* [ScGael *srath*] (1540) **:** a flat wide river valley or the low-lying grassland along it

strath·spey \ˌstrath-ˈspā\ *n, pl* **strathspeys** [*Strath Spey,* district of Scotland] (ca. 1653) **:** a Scottish dance that is similar to but slower than the reel; *also* **:** the music for this dance

strati- *comb form* [NL *stratum*] **:** stratum ⟨*strati*form⟩

strat·i·fi·ca·tion \ˌstra-tə-fə-ˈkā-shən\ *n* (ca. 1617) **1 a :** the act or process of stratifying **b :** the state of being stratified **2 :** a stratified formation

strat·i·fi·ca·tion·al grammar \ˌstra-tə-fə-ˈkā-shnəl-, -shə-nᵊl-\ *n* (1962) **:** a grammar based on the theory that language consists of a series of hierarchically related strata linked together by representational rules

stratified charge engine *n* (1962) **:** an internal-combustion engine in whose cylinders the combustion of fuel in a layer of rich fuel-air mixture promotes ignition in a greater volume of lean mixture

strat·i·form \ˈstra-tə-ˌfȯrm\ *adj* (1805) **:** having a stratified formation

strat·i·fy \ˈstra-tə-ˌfī\ *vb* **-fied; -fy·ing** [NL *stratificare,* fr. *stratum* + L *-ificare* -ify] *vt* (1661) **1 :** to form, deposit, or arrange in strata **2 a :** to divide or arrange into classes, castes, or social strata **b :** to divide into a series of graded statuses ~ *vi* **:** to become arranged in strata

strat·i·graph·ic \ˌstra-tə-ˈgra-fik\ *also* **strat·i·graph·i·cal** \-fi-kəl\ *adj* (1877) **:** of, relating to, or determined by stratigraphy

stra·tig·ra·phy \strə-ˈti-grə-fē\ *n* [ISV] (1865) **1 :** geology that deals with the origin, composition, distribution, and succession of strata **2 :** the arrangement of strata

strato- *comb form* [NL *stratus*] **:** stratus and ⟨*strato*cumulus⟩

stra·to·cu·mu·lus \ˌstrā-tō-ˈkyü-myə-ləs, ˌstra-\ *n* [NL] (1873) **:** stratified low cumulus consisting of large balls or rolls of dark cloud which often cover the whole sky esp. in winter — see CLOUD illustration

strato·sphere \ˈstra-tə-ˌsfir\ *n* [F *stratosphère,* fr. NL *stratum* + *-o-* + F *sphère* sphere, fr. L *sphaera*] (1909) **1 :** the part of the earth's atmosphere which extends from the top of the troposphere to about 30 miles (50 kilometers) above the surface and in which temperature increases gradually to about 32° F (0° C) and clouds rarely form **2 :** a very high or the highest region on or as if on a graded scale ⟨construction costs in the ~⟩ ⟨the celebrity ~⟩ — **strato·spher·ic** \ˌstra-tə-ˈsfir-ik, -ˈsfer-\ *adj* — **strato·spher·i·cal·ly** \-i-k(ə-)lē\ *adv*

stra·to·vol·ca·no \ˌstra-tō-väl-ˈkā-(ˌ)nō, ˌstrā-, -vȯl-\ *n* [NL *strat*um + E *-o-* + *volcano*] (1937) **:** a volcano composed of explosively erupted cinders and ash with occasional lava flows

stra·tum \ˈstrā-təm, ˈstra-\ *n, pl* **stra·ta** \ˈstrā-tə, ˈstra-\ [NL, fr. L, spread, bed, fr. neut. of *stratus,* pp. of *sternere* to spread out — more at STREW] (1599) **1 :** a bed or layer artificially made **2 a :** a sheetlike mass of sedimentary rock or earth of one kind lying between beds of other kinds **b :** a region of the sea or atmosphere that is analogous to a stratum of the earth **c :** a layer of tissue ⟨deep ~ of the skin⟩ **d :** a layer in which archaeological material (as artifacts, skeletons, and dwelling remains) is found on excavation **3 a :** a part of a historical or sociological series representing a period or a stage of development **b :** a socioeconomic level of society comprising persons of the same or similar status esp. with regard to education or culture **4 :** one of a series of layers, levels, or gradations in an ordered system ⟨*strata* of thought⟩ **5 :** a statistical subpopulation

usage The plural *strata* has occas. been used as a singular since the 18th century and is sometimes given the plural *stratas* ⟨there was a *strata* of Paris which mere criticism of books fails to get hold of —Ezra Pound⟩ ⟨a Roman burial ground suggests *stratas* of corruption and decay —Connie Fletcher, *Booklist*⟩. Current evidence shows senses 2, 3b, and 4 so used, with 3b the most common. Singular *strata* is persistent but not frequent. *Strata* may someday establish itself as a singular like *agenda,* but that use is still not established.

stratum cor·ne·um \-ˈkȯr-nē-əm\ *n* [NL, lit., horny layer] (ca. 1860) **:** the outer part of the epidermis consisting chiefly of layers of dead flattened nonnucleated cells filled with keratin

stra·tus \ˈstrā-təs, ˈstra-\ *n, pl* **stra·ti** \ˈstrā-ˌtī, ˈstra-\ [NL, fr. L, pp. of *sternere*] (ca. 1803) **:** a low cloud form extending over a large area at altitudes of usu. 2000 to 7000 feet (600 to 2100 meters) — see CLOUD illustration

stra·vage *or* **stra·vaig** \strə-ˈvāg\ *vi* [prob. by shortening & alter. fr. *extravagate*] (1773) *chiefly Scot* **:** ROAM

[1]**straw** \ˈstrȯ\ *n* [ME, fr. OE *strēaw;* akin to OHG *strō* straw, OE *strewian* to strew] (bef. 12c) **1 a :** stalks of grain after threshing; *broadly* **:** dry stalky plant residue used like grain straw (as for bedding or packing) **b :** a natural or artificial heavy fiber used for weaving, plaiting, or braiding **2 :** a dry coarse stem esp. of a cereal grass **3 a** (1) **:** something of small worth or significance (2) **:** something too insubstantial to provide support or help in a desperate situation ⟨clutching at ~*s*⟩ **b :** CHAFF 2 **4 a :** something (as a hat) made of straw **b :** a tube (as of paper, plastic, or glass) for sucking up a beverage — **strawy** \ˈstrȯ-ē\ *adj* — **straw in the wind :** a slight fact that is an indication of a coming event

[2]**straw** *adj* (15c) **1 :** made of straw ⟨a ~ hat⟩ **2 :** of, relating to, or used for straw ⟨a ~ barn⟩ **3 :** of the color of straw ⟨~ hair⟩ **4 :** of little or no value **:** WORTHLESS **5 :** of, relating to, resembling, or being a straw man **6 :** of, relating to, or concerned with the discovery of preferences by means of a straw vote

straw·ber·ry \ˈstrȯ-ˌber-ē, -b(ə-)rē\ *n, often attrib* [ME, fr. OE *strēawberige,* fr. *strēaw* straw + *berige* berry; perh. fr. the appearance of the achenes on the surface] (bef. 12c) **1 :** the juicy edible usu. red fruit of any of several low-growing temperate herbs (genus *Fragaria*) of the rose family that is technically an enlarged pulpy receptacle bearing numerous achenes on its surface **2 :** a plant whose fruits are strawberries; *esp* **:** a hybrid (*Fragaria ananassa*) that is the source of most cultivated strawberries

[1]**strawberry blonde** *n* (1880) **1 :** a person having reddish-blond hair **2 :** a reddish-blond color

[2]**strawberry blonde** *or* **strawberry blond** *adj* (1884) **:** of a reddish-blond color; *also* **:** having reddish-blond hair ⟨a *strawberry blond* child⟩ — spelled *blond* when used of a boy or man and usu. *blonde* when used of a girl or woman

strawberry bush *n* (ca. 1856) **1 :** a shrubby spindle tree (*Euonymus americanus*) of the eastern U.S. with crimson pods and seeds with a scarlet aril **2 :** [2]WAHOO

strawberry mark *n* (1847) **:** a hemangioma appearing usu. as a red and elevated birthmark

strawberry roan *n* (1759) **:** a roan horse with a light red base color

strawberry tomato *n* (ca. 1847) **:** GROUND-CHERRY; *esp* **:** a stout hairy annual herb (*Physalis pruinosa*) of eastern No. America with sweet globular yellow fruits

strawberry tree *n* (15c) **:** a small European evergreen tree (*Arbutus unedo*) of the heath family with racemose white flowers and fruits resembling strawberries

straw boss *n* (1894) **1 :** an assistant to a foreman in charge of supervising and expediting the work of a small group of workers **2 :** a member of a group of workers who supervises the work of the others in addition to doing his or her own job

straw·flow·er \ˈstrȯ-ˌflau̇(-ə)r\ *n* (ca. 1922) **:** any of several plants having everlasting flowers; *esp* **:** an Australian composite herb (*Helichrysum bracteatum*) widely cultivated for its brightly colored flower heads in which papery bracts resembling ray flowers surround a central disk

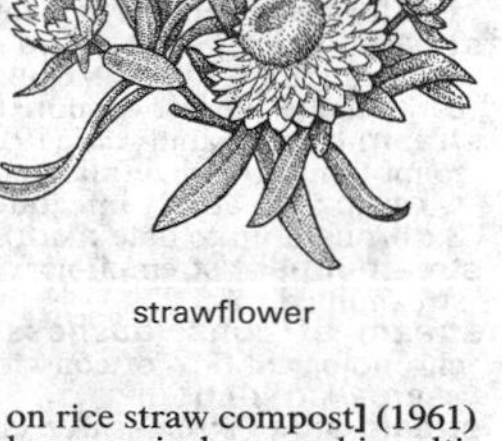

strawflower

straw·hat \ˈstrȯ-ˈhat\ *adj* [fr. the former fashion of wearing straw hats in summer] (1935) **:** of, relating to, or being summer theater

straw man *n* (1886) **1 :** a weak or imaginary opposition (as an argument or adversary) set up only to be easily confuted **2 :** a person set up to serve as a cover for a usu. questionable transaction

straw mushroom *n* [fr. their cultivation on rice straw compost] (1961) **:** a mushroom (*Volvariella volvacea*) that has a conical cap and is cultivated in southeastern Asia and used esp. in Chinese cooking

straw vote *n* (1866) **:** an unofficial vote taken (as at a chance gathering) to indicate the relative strength of opposing candidates or issues — called also *straw poll*

straw wine *n* (1824) **:** a sweet wine produced by partially drying the grapes on beds of straw prior to vinification

straw yellow *n* (ca. 1796) **:** a pale yellow

\ə\ **abut** \ᵊ\ **kitten,** F **table** \ər\ **further** \a\ **ash** \ā\ **ace** \ä\ **mop, mar** \au̇\ **out** \ch\ **chin** \e\ **bet** \ē\ **easy** \g\ **go** \i\ **hit** \ī\ **ice** \j\ **job** \ŋ\ **sing** \ō\ **go** \ȯ\ **law** \ȯi\ **boy** \th\ **thin** \t͟h\ **the** \ü\ **loot** \u̇\ **foot** \y\ **yet** \zh\ **vision, beige** \k͟, ⁿ, œ, ᵫ, ʸ\ *see* **Guide to Pronunciation**

[1]**stray** \ˈstrā\ *n* [ME, fr. AF *estraié,* pp. of *estraier*] (13c) **1 a :** a domestic animal that is wandering at large or is lost **b :** a person or thing that strays **2** [ME, fr. *straien* to stray] *archaic* **:** the act of going astray

[2]**stray** *vi* [ME *straien,* fr. AF *estraier,* fr. VL **extravagare,* fr. L *extra-* outside + *vagari* to wander — more at EXTRA-] (14c) **:** WANDER: as **a :** to wander from company, restraint, or proper limits **b :** to roam about without fixed direction or purpose **c :** to move in a winding course **:** MEANDER **d :** to move without conscious or intentional effort ⟨eyes ~*ing* absently around the room⟩ **e :** to become distracted from an argument or train of thought ⟨~*ed* from the point⟩ **f :** to wander accidentally from a fixed or chosen route **g :** ERR, SIN — **stray·er** *n*

[3]**stray** *adj* (1589) **1 :** having strayed or escaped from a proper or intended place ⟨a ~ dog⟩ **2 :** occurring at random or sporadically ⟨~ thoughts⟩ **3 :** not serving any useful purpose **:** UNWANTED ⟨~ light⟩

[1]**streak** \ˈstrēk\ *n* [ME *streke,* fr. OE *strica;* akin to OHG *strich* line, L *striga* row — more at STRIKE] (bef. 12c) **1 :** a line or mark of a different color or texture from the ground **:** STRIPE **2 a :** the color of the fine powder of a mineral obtained by scratching or rubbing against a hard white surface and constituting an important distinguishing character **b :** inoculum implanted in a line on a solid medium **c :** any of numerous virus diseases of plants (as tobacco and corn) resembling mosaic but usu. producing at least some linear markings **3 a :** a narrow band of light **b :** a lightning bolt **4 a :** a slight admixture **:** TRACE ⟨had a mean ~ in him⟩ **b :** a brief run (as of luck) **c :** a consecutive series ⟨was on a winning ~⟩ **5 :** a narrow layer (as of fat) **6 :** an act or instance of streaking

[2]**streak** *vt* (1576) **:** to make streaks on or in ⟨tears ~*ing* her face⟩ ~ *vi* **1 :** to move swiftly **:** RUSH ⟨a jet ~*ing* across the sky⟩ **2 :** to have a streak (as of winning or outstanding performances) **3 :** to run naked through a public place — **streak·er** *n*

streak camera *n* (1959) **:** a camera for recording very fast or short-lived phenomena (as fluorescence or shock waves)

streaked \ˈstrēkt, ˈstrē-kəd\ *adj* (1576) **1 :** marked with stripes or linear discolorations **2 :** physically or mentally disturbed **:** UPSET

streak·ing \ˈstrē-kiŋ\ *n* (ca. 1964) **:** the lightening (as by chemicals) of a few long strands of hair to produce a streaked effect

streaky \ˈstrē-kē\ *adj* **streak·i·er; -est** (1722) **1 :** marked with streaks ⟨~ bacon⟩ **2 :** APPREHENSIVE ⟨nervous and ~⟩ **3 :** apt to vary (as in effectiveness) **:** UNRELIABLE — **streak·i·ness** *n*

[1]**stream** \ˈstrēm\ *n* [ME *streme,* fr. OE *strēam;* akin to OHG *stroum* stream, Gk *rhein* to flow] (bef. 12c) **1 :** a body of running water (as a river or brook) flowing on the earth; *also* **:** any body of flowing fluid (as water or gas) **2 a :** a steady succession (as of words or events) ⟨kept up an endless ~ of chatter⟩ **b :** a constantly renewed or steady supply ⟨a ~ of revenue⟩ **c :** a continuous moving procession ⟨a ~ of traffic⟩ **3 :** an unbroken flow (as of gas or particles of matter) **4 :** a ray of light **5 a :** a prevailing attitude or group ⟨has always run against the ~ of current fashion⟩ **b :** a dominant influence or line of development ⟨the influence of two ~*s* of inheritance: genetic and cultural —P. B. Baltes⟩ **6** *Brit* **:** TRACK 3c

[2]**stream** *vi* (13c) **1 a :** to flow in or as if in a stream **b :** to leave a bright trail ⟨a meteor ~*ed* through the sky⟩ **2 a :** to exude a bodily fluid profusely ⟨her eyes were ~*ing*⟩ **b :** to become wet with a discharge of bodily fluid ⟨~*ing* with perspiration⟩ **3 :** to trail out at full length ⟨her hair ~*ing* back as she ran⟩ **4 :** to pour in large numbers ⟨complaints came ~*ing* in⟩ ~ *vt* **1 :** to emit freely or in a stream ⟨his eyes ~*ed* tears⟩ **2 :** to display (as a flag) by waving **3 :** to transfer (digital data, such as audio or video material) in a continuous stream esp. for immediate processing or playback

stream·bed \ˈstrēm-ˌbed\ *n* (1857) **:** the channel occupied or formerly occupied by a stream

stream·er \ˈstrē-mər\ *n* (13c) **1 a :** a flag that streams in the wind; *esp* **:** PENNANT **b :** any long narrow wavy strip resembling or suggesting a banner floating in the wind **c :** BANNER 2 **2 a :** a long extension of the solar corona visible only during a total solar eclipse **b** *pl* **:** AURORA BOREALIS

[1]**stream·ing** \ˈstrē-miŋ\ *n* (14c) **1 :** an act or instance of flowing; *specif* **:** CYCLOSIS **2** *Brit* **:** TRACKING

[2]**streaming** *adj* (1980) **:** relating to or being the transfer of data (as audio or video material) in a continuous stream esp. for immediate processing or playback

stream·let \ˈstrēm-lət\ *n* (ca. 1552) **:** a small stream

[1]**stream·line** \ˈstrēm-ˌlīn\ *n* (1868) **1 :** the path of a particle in a fluid relative to a solid body past which the fluid is moving in smooth flow without turbulence **2 a :** a contour designed to minimize resistance to motion through a fluid (as air) **b :** a smooth or flowing line designed as if for decreasing air resistance

[2]**streamline** *vt* (1913) **1 :** to design or construct with a streamline **2 :** to bring up to date **:** MODERNIZE **3 a :** to put in order **:** ORGANIZE **b :** to make simpler or more efficient ⟨a system that ~*s* the process⟩

stream·lined \-ˌlīnd\ *adj* (1913) **1 a :** contoured to reduce resistance to motion through a fluid (as air) **b :** stripped of nonessentials **:** COMPACT **c :** effectively integrated **:** ORGANIZED **2 :** having flowing lines **3 :** brought up to date **:** MODERNIZED

stream·lin·er \ˈstrēm-ˌlī-nər\ *n* (1934) **:** one that is streamlined; *esp* **:** a streamlined train

stream of consciousness (1855) **1 :** the continuous unedited chronological flow of conscious experience through the mind **2 :** INTERIOR MONOLOGUE

stream·side \ˈstrēm-ˌsīd\ *n* (1844) **:** the land bordering on a stream

streek \ˈstrēk\ *vt* [ME (northern dial.) *streken;* akin to OE *streccan* to stretch] (13c) **1** *chiefly Scot* **:** STRETCH, EXTEND **2** *chiefly Scot* **:** to lay out (a dead body)

[1]**streel** \ˈstrēl\ *vi* [Ir *straoill-, sraoill-* to tear apart, trail, trudge, fr. OIr *sroiglid* he scourges, fr. *sroigell* scourge, fr. L *flagellum* — more at FLAGELLATE] (1805) **1** *chiefly Irish* **:** to saunter idly and aimlessly **2** *chiefly Irish* **:** to trail or float in the manner of a streamer

[2]**streel** *n* [Ir *straoill, sraoill,* fr. *straoill-,* v.] (1842) *chiefly Irish* **:** an untidy slovenly person

[1]**street** \ˈstrēt\ *n* [ME *strete,* fr. OE *strǣt,* fr. LL *strata* paved road, fr. L, fem. of *stratus,* pp. — more at STRATUM] (bef. 12c) **1 a :** a thoroughfare esp. in a city, town, or village that is wider than an alley or lane and that usu. includes sidewalks **b :** the part of a street reserved for vehicles **c :** a thoroughfare with abutting property ⟨lives on a fashionable ~⟩ **2 :** the people occupying property on a street ⟨the whole ~ knew about the accident⟩ **3 :** a promising line of development or a channeling of effort ⟨a crafty politician working both sides of the ~⟩ ⟨success through compromise is a two-way ~⟩ **4** *cap* **a :** a district (as Wall Street or Fleet Street) identified with a particular profession **b :** the people who work in such a district ⟨doing better than the *Street* expected⟩ **5 :** an environment (as in a depressed neighborhood or section of a city) of poverty, dereliction, or crime ⟨grew up on the mean ~*s*⟩ — **on the street** *or* **in the street 1 :** idle, homeless, or out of a job **2 :** out of prison **:** at liberty — **up one's street** *or* **down one's street :** suited to one's abilities or taste

[2]**street** *adj* (15c) **1 :** of or relating to the streets: as **a :** adjoining or giving access to a street ⟨the ~ door⟩ **b :** carried on or taking place in the street ⟨~ fighting⟩ **c :** living or working on the streets ⟨a ~ peddler⟩ ⟨~ people⟩ **d :** located in, used for, or serving as a guide to the streets ⟨a ~ map⟩ **e :** performing in or heard on the street ⟨a ~ band⟩ **f** (1) **:** suitable for wear or use on the street ⟨~ clothes⟩ (2) **:** not touching the ground — used of a woman's dress in lengths reaching the knee, calf, or ankle **g :** of, relating to, or characteristic of the street environment ⟨~ drugs⟩ ⟨used . . . his new ~ cred to develop contacts —Dale Keiger⟩ **2 :** RETAIL ⟨the ~ price⟩

street·car \ˈstrēt-ˌkär\ *n* (1860) **:** a vehicle on rails used primarily for transporting passengers and typically operating on city streets

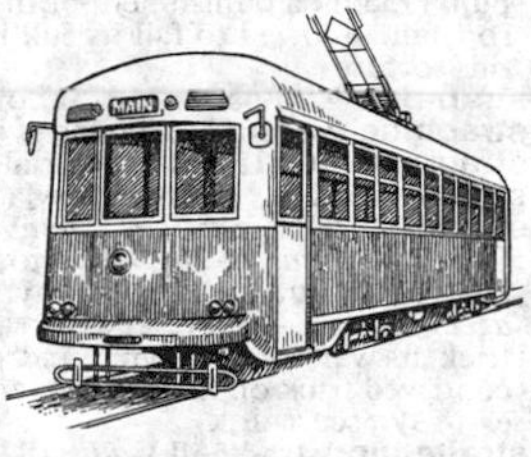

streetcar

street fighter *n* (1970) **:** a tough belligerent person ⟨a political *street fighter*⟩

street hockey *n* (1964) **:** a game resembling ice hockey played on a hard surface by players wearing shoes or roller skates and using hockey sticks and a small ball

street·light \-ˌlīt\ *n* (1906) **:** a light usu. mounted on a pole and constituting one of a series spaced at intervals along a public street or highway — called also *streetlamp*

street railway *n* (1853) **:** a line operating streetcars or buses

streets \ˈstrēts\ *adv* (1898) *chiefly Brit* **:** by a considerable margin ⟨a nice woman, ~ above these other callers —Katherine Mansfield⟩

street·scape \ˈstrēt-ˌskāp\ *n* (1924) **1 :** the appearance or view of a street **2 :** a work of art depicting a view of a street

street–smart \-ˌsmärt\ *adj* (1974) **:** STREETWISE

street smarts *n pl* (1972) **:** the quality of being streetwise

street theater *n* (1967) **:** drama dealing with controversial social and political issues that is usu. performed outdoors

street·walk·er \ˈstrēt-ˌwȯ-kər\ *n* (1592) **:** PROSTITUTE; *esp* **:** one who solicits in the streets — compare CALL GIRL — **street·walk·ing** \-kiŋ\ *n*

street·wise \-ˌwīz\ *adj* (1965) **:** possessing the skills and attitudes necessary to survive in a difficult or dangerous situation or environment

strength \ˈstreŋ(k)th, ˈstren(t)th\ *n, pl* **strengths** \ˈstreŋ(k)ths, ˈstren(t)ths, ˈstreŋks\ [ME *strengthe,* fr. OE *strengthu;* akin to OHG *strengi* strong — more at STRONG] (bef. 12c) **1 :** the quality or state of being strong **:** capacity for exertion or endurance **2 :** power to resist force **:** SOLIDITY, TOUGHNESS **3 :** power of resisting attack **:** IMPREGNABILITY **4 a :** legal, logical, or moral force **b :** a strong attribute or inherent asset ⟨the ~*s* and the weaknesses of the book are evident⟩ **5 a :** degree of potency of effect or of concentration ⟨chili peppers in varying ~*s*⟩ **b :** intensity of light, color, sound, or odor **c :** vigor of expression **6 :** force as measured in numbers **:** effective numbers of any body or organization ⟨an army at full ~⟩ **7 :** one regarded as embodying or affording force or firmness **:** SUPPORT ⟨you are my love and my ~⟩ **8 :** maintenance of or a rising tendency in a price level **:** firmness of prices ⟨the ~ of the dollar⟩ **9 :** BASIS — used in the phrase *on the strength of* ***syn*** see POWER — **from strength to strength :** vigorously forward **:** from one high point to the next

strength·en \ˈstreŋ(k)-thən, ˈstren(t)-\ *vb* **strength·ened; strength·en·ing** \ˈstreŋ(k)th-niŋ, ˈstren(t)th-; ˈstreŋ(k)-thə-, ˈstren(t)-\ *vt* (15c) **:** to make stronger ~ *vi* **:** to become stronger — **strength·en·er** \ˈstreŋ(k)th-nər, ˈstren(t)th-; ˈstreŋ(k)-thə-, ˈstren(t)-\ *n*

stren·u·ous \ˈstren-yə-wəs\ *adj* [L *strenuus*] (1599) **1 a :** vigorously active **:** ENERGETIC **b :** FERVENT, ZEALOUS ⟨his most ~ supporters⟩ **2 :** marked by or calling for energy or stamina **:** ARDUOUS ⟨a ~ hike⟩ ***syn*** see VIGOROUS — **stren·u·os·i·ty** \ˌstren-yə-ˈwä-sə-tē\ *n* — **stren·u·ous·ly** \ˈstren-yə-wəs-lē\ *adv* — **stren·u·ous·ness** *n*

strep \ˈstrep\ *n, often attrib* (1927) **:** STREPTOCOCCUS

strep throat *n* (1927) **:** an inflammatory sore throat caused by hemolytic Group A streptococci and marked by fever, prostration, and toxemia — called also *septic sore throat*

strepto- *comb form* [NL, fr. Gk, fr. *streptos* twisted, fr. *strephein* to twist] **1 :** twisted **:** twisted chain ⟨*strepto*coccus⟩ **2 :** streptococcus ⟨*strepto*kinase⟩

strep·to·ba·cil·lus \ˌstrep-tō-bə-ˈsi-ləs\ *n* [NL] (1897) **:** any of a genus (*Streptobacillus*) of nonmotile gram-negative rod-shaped bacteria in which the individual cells are often joined in a chain; *esp* **:** one (*S. moniliformis*) that is the causative agent of one form of rat-bite fever

strep·to·car·pus \ˌstrep-tə-ˈkär-pəs\ *n, pl* **-carpus·es** *also* **-carpus** [NL, fr. *strepto-* + *-carpus* -carpous] (1828) **:** any of a genus (*Streptocarpus*) of usu. stemless African gesneriads that have showy brightly colored flowers with funnel-shaped corollas

strep·to·coc·cal \ˌstrep-tə-ˈkä-kəl\ *also* **strep·to·coc·cic** \-ˈkä-kik, -ˈkäk-sik\ *adj* (1877) **:** of, relating to, caused by, or being streptococci ⟨a ~ sore throat⟩ ⟨~ organisms⟩

strep·to·coc·cus \-ˈkä-kəs\ *n, pl* **-coc·ci** \-ˈkä-ˌkī, -(ˌ)kē; -ˈkäk-ˌsī, -(ˌ)sē\ [NL] (1877) **:** any of a genus (*Streptococcus*) of spherical or ovoid chiefly nonmotile and parasitic gram-positive bacteria that divide only in one plane, occur in pairs or chains, and include important pathogens of humans and domestic animals; *broadly* **:** a coccus occurring in chains

strep·to·ki·nase \ˌstrep-tō-ˈkī-ˌnās, -ˌnāz\ *n* (1944) **:** a proteolytic enzyme produced by hemolytic streptococci that promotes the dissolution of blood clots by activating plasminogen to produce plasmin

strep·to·ly·sin \ˌstrep-tə-ˈlī-sᵊn\ *n* (1904) **:** an antigenic hemolysin produced by streptococci

strep·to·my·ces \-ˈmī-ˌsēz\ *n, pl* **streptomyces** [NL, fr. *strepto-* + Gk *mykēs* fungus — more at MYC-] (1944) **:** any of a genus (*Streptomyces*) of mostly soil streptomycetes including some that form antibiotics as by-products of their metabolism

strep·to·my·cete \-ˈmī-ˌsēt, -ˌmī-ˈsēt\ *n* [NL *Streptomycet-, Streptomyces,* genus name] (1948) **:** any of a family (Streptomycetaceae) of actinomycetes (as a streptomyces) that form vegetative mycelia which rarely break up into bacillary forms, have conidia borne on sporophores, and are typically aerobic soil saprophytes but include a few parasites of plants and animals

strep·to·my·cin \-ˈmī-sᵊn\ *n* (1944) **:** an antibiotic organic base $C_{21}H_{39}N_7O_{12}$ that is produced by a soil actinomycete (*Streptomyces griseus*), is active against many bacteria, and is used esp. in the treatment of infections (as tuberculosis) by gram-negative bacteria

strep·to·thri·cin \-ˈthrī-sᵊn, -ˈthri-\ *n* [NL *Streptothric-, Streptothrix,* genus of bacteria, fr. *strepto-* + Gk *trich-, thrix* hair] (1926) **:** any of a group of related basic antibiotics produced by a streptomyces (*Streptomyces lavendulae*) and active esp. against bacteria

[1]**stress** \ˈstres\ *n* [ME *stresse* stress, distress, short for *destresse* — more at DISTRESS] (14c) **1 :** constraining force or influence: as **a :** a force exerted when one body or body part presses on, pulls on, pushes against, or tends to compress or twist another body or body part; *esp* **:** the intensity of this mutual force commonly expressed in pounds per square inch **b :** the deformation caused in a body by such a force **c :** a physical, chemical, or emotional factor that causes bodily or mental tension and may be a factor in disease causation **d :** a state resulting from a stress; *esp* **:** one of bodily or mental tension resulting from factors that tend to alter an existent equilibrium ⟨job-related ~⟩ **e :** STRAIN, PRESSURE ⟨the environment is under ~ to the point of collapse —Joseph Shoben⟩ **2 :** EMPHASIS, WEIGHT ⟨lay ~ on a point⟩ **3** *archaic* **:** intense effort or exertion **4 :** intensity of utterance given to a speech sound, syllable, or word producing relative loudness **5 a :** relative force or prominence of sound in verse **b :** a syllable having relative force or prominence **6 :** ACCENT 6a

[2]**stress** *vt* (1545) **1 :** to subject to physical or psychological stress ⟨~*ing* the equipment⟩ ⟨this traffic is ~*ing* me out⟩ **2 :** to subject to phonetic stress **:** ACCENT **3 :** to lay stress on **:** EMPHASIZE ⟨~*ed* the importance of teamwork⟩ ~ *vi* **:** to feel stress ⟨~*ing* about the big exam⟩ — often used with *out*

stressed \ˈstrest\ *adj* (1973) **:** STRESSED-OUT ⟨feeling ~ about work⟩

stressed–out \ˈstrest-ˈau̇t\ *adj* (1983) **:** suffering from high levels of physical or esp. psychological stress

stress fracture *n* (1952) **:** a usu. hairline fracture of a bone that has been subjected to repeated stress

stress·ful \ˈstres-fəl\ *adj* (1853) **:** full of or tending to induce stress — **stress·ful·ly** \-fə-lē\ *adv*

stress incontinence *n* (1935) **:** involuntary leakage of urine from the bladder accompanying physical activity (as laughing or coughing) which places increased pressure on the abdomen — compare URGE INCONTINENCE

stress·less \-ləs\ *adj* (1885) **:** having no stress; *specif* **:** having no accent ⟨a ~ syllable⟩ — **stress·less·ness** *n*

stress mark *n* (1888) **:** a mark used with (as before, after, or over) a written syllable in the respelling of a word to show that this syllable is to be stressed when spoken **:** ACCENT MARK

stress·or \ˈstre-sər, -ˌsȯr\ *n* (1950) **:** a stimulus that causes stress

stress test *n* (1975) **:** an electrocardiographic test of heart function before, during, and after a controlled period of increasingly strenuous exercise (as on a treadmill)

[1]**stretch** \ˈstrech\ *vb* [ME *strecchen,* fr. OE *streccan;* akin to OHG *strecchan* to stretch, OE *stræc* firm, severe] *vt* (bef. 12c) **1 :** to extend (as one's limbs or body) in a reclining position **2 :** to reach out **:** EXTEND ⟨~*ed* out her arms⟩ **3 :** to extend in length ⟨~*ed* his neck to see what was going on⟩ **4 :** to fell with or as if with a blow **5 :** to cause the limbs of (a person) to be pulled esp. in torture **6 :** to draw up (one's body) from a cramped, stooping, or relaxed position **7 :** to pull taut ⟨canvas ~*ed* on a frame⟩ **8 a :** to enlarge or distend esp. by force **b :** to extend or expand as if by physical force ⟨~ one's mind with a good book⟩ **c :** STRAIN ⟨~*ed* his already thin patience⟩ **9 :** to cause to reach or continue (as from one point to another or across a space) ⟨~ a wire between two posts⟩ **10 a :** to amplify or enlarge beyond natural or proper limits ⟨the rules can be ~*ed* this once⟩ **b :** to expand (as by improvisation) to fulfill a larger function ⟨~*ing* a dollar⟩ **11 :** to extend (a hit) to an extra base usu. by fast or daring running ⟨~ a single into a double⟩ ~ *vi* **1 a :** to become extended in length or breadth or both **:** SPREAD ⟨broad plains ~*ing* to the sea⟩ **b :** to extend over a continuous period ⟨the dynasty ~*es* back several centuries⟩ **2 :** to become extended without breaking **3 a :** to extend one's body or limbs ⟨~*ed* before jogging⟩ ⟨wanted to ~ out on the sofa⟩ **b :** to lie down at full length — **stretch·abil·i·ty** \ˌstre-chə-ˈbi-lə-tē\ *n* — **stretch·able** \ˈstre-chə-bəl\ *adj* — **stretchy** \-chē\ *adj* — **stretch a point :** to go beyond what is strictly warranted in making a claim or concession — **stretch one's legs 1 :** to extend the legs **2 :** to take a walk in order to relieve stiffness caused by prolonged sitting

[2]**stretch** *n* (1541) **1 a :** an exercise of something (as the understanding or the imagination) beyond ordinary or normal limits ⟨their conclusion seemed like a bit of a ~⟩ **b :** an extension of the scope or application of something ⟨a ~ of language⟩ **2 :** the extent to which something may be stretched **3 a :** the act of stretching **:** the state of being stretched ⟨a good ~ for legs⟩ **b :** the position of a pitcher standing sideways to home plate so as to keep a runner close to a base ⟨pitching from the ~⟩ **4 a :** an extent in length or area ⟨an open ~ of road⟩ **b :** a continuous period of time ⟨can write for eight hours at a ~⟩ **5 :** a walk to relieve fatigue **6 :** a term of imprisonment ⟨served a 10-year ~⟩ **7 a :** either of the straight sides of a racecourse; *esp* **:** HOMESTRETCH **b :** a final stage (as of a contest or season) ⟨won some crucial games down the ~⟩ **8 :** the capacity for being stretched **:** ELASTICITY ⟨a waistband with lots of ~⟩ **9 :** a stretch limousine

[3]**stretch** *adj* (1954) **1 :** easily stretched **:** ELASTIC ⟨a ~ wig⟩ **2 :** longer than the standard size ⟨a ~ limousine⟩

[1]**stretch·er** \ˈstre-chər\ *n* (15c) **1 a :** one that stretches; *esp* **:** a device or machine for stretching or expanding something **b :** an exaggerated story **:** a tall tale **2 a :** a brick or stone laid with its length parallel to the face of the wall **b :** a timber or rod used esp. when horizontal as a tie in framed work **3 :** a device for carrying a sick, injured, or dead person **4 :** a rod or bar extending between two legs of a chair or table

[2]**stretcher** *vt* (1973) **:** to carry or transport on a stretcher

stretch marks *n pl* (1956) **:** striae on the skin (as of the hips, abdomen, and breasts) from excessive stretching and rupture of elastic fibers esp. due to pregnancy or obesity

stretch–out \ˈstrech-ˌau̇t\ *n* (1930) **1 :** a system of industrial operation in which workers are required to do extra work with slight or with no additional pay **2 :** the act of stretching out **:** the state of being stretched out **3 :** an economizing measure that spreads a limited quantity over a larger field than orig. intended: as **a :** a slackening of production schedules so that a quantity of goods will be produced over a longer period than initially planned **b :** a restructuring of a loan repayment schedule over an extended period of time

stretch receptor *n* (1936) **:** MUSCLE SPINDLE

stretch runner *n* (1922) **:** a racehorse that makes a strong bid in the homestretch

stret·to \ˈstre-(ˌ)tō\ *also* **stret·ta** \-tə\ *n, pl* **stret·ti** \-(ˌ)tē\ *or* **strettos** [*stretto* fr. It, fr. *stretto* narrow, close, fr. L *strictus,* pp.; *stretta* fr. It, fr. fem. of *stretto* — more at STRICT] (ca. 1740) **1 a :** the overlapping of answer with subject in a musical fugue **b :** the part of a fugue characterized by this overlapping **2 :** a concluding passage performed in a quicker tempo

streu·sel \ˈstrü-səl, -zəl, ˈstrȯi-, ˈshtrȯi-\ *n* [G, lit., something strewn, fr. MHG *ströusel,* fr. *ströuwen* to strew, fr. OHG *strewen*] (1909) **:** a crumbly mixture of fat, sugar, and flour and sometimes nuts and spices that is used as topping or filling for cake

strew \ˈstrü\ *vt* **strewed; strewed** *or* **strewn** \ˈstrün\; **strew·ing** [ME *strewen, strowen,* fr. OE *strewian, strēowian;* akin to OHG *strewen* to strew, L *struere* to heap up, *sternere* to spread out, Gk *stornynai*] (bef. 12c) **1 :** to spread by scattering **2 :** to cover by or as if by scattering something ⟨~*ing* the highways with litter⟩ **3 :** to become dispersed over as if scattered **4 :** to spread abroad **:** DISSEMINATE

strew·ment \ˈstrü-mənt\ *n* (1602) *archaic* **:** something (as flowers) strewed or designed for strewing

stria \ˈstrī-ə\ *n, pl* **stri·ae** \ˈstrī-ˌē\ [L, furrow, channel — more at STRIKE] (1563) **1 :** STRIATION 2 **2 :** a stripe or line (as in the skin) distinguished from the surrounding area by color, texture, or elevation — compare STRETCH MARKS

[1]**stri·ate** \ˈstrī-ˌāt\ *vt* **stri·at·ed; stri·at·ing** (1646) **:** to mark with striations or striae

[2]**stri·ate** \ˈstrī-ət, -ˌāt\ *adj* (1670) **:** STRIATED

stri·at·ed \ˈstrī-ˌā-təd\ *adj* (1646) **1 :** marked with striations or striae **2 :** of, relating to, or being striated muscle

striated muscle *n* (1866) **:** muscle tissue that is marked by transverse dark and light bands, is made up of elongated usu. multinucleated fibers, and includes skeletal muscle, cardiac muscle, and most muscle of arthropods — compare SMOOTH MUSCLE, VOLUNTARY MUSCLE

stri·a·tion \strī-ˈā-shən\ *n* (ca. 1847) **1 a :** the fact or state of being striated **b :** arrangement of striations or striae **2 :** a minute groove, scratch, or channel esp. when one of a parallel series **3 :** any of the alternate dark and light cross bands of a myofibril of striated muscle

stri·a·tum \strī-ˈā-təm\ *n, pl* **-ta** \-tə\ (1882) **:** CORPUS STRIATUM; *esp* **:** the part of the corpus striatum consisting of the caudate nucleus and putamen

strick·en \ˈstri-kən\ *adj* [ME *striken,* fr. pp. of *striken* to strike] (14c) **1 a :** afflicted or overwhelmed by or as if by disease, misfortune, or sorrow **b :** made incapable or unfit ⟨rescuers were sent to the ~ ship⟩ **2 :** hit or wounded by or as if by a missile ⟨the deer had been ~ by an arrow⟩

strict \ˈstrikt\ *adj* [ME *stricte,* fr. L *strictus,* fr. pp. of *stringere* to bind tight — more at STRAIN] (15c) **1** *archaic* **a :** TIGHT, CLOSE; *also* **:** INTIMATE **b :** NARROW **2 a :** stringent in requirement or control ⟨under ~ orders⟩ **b :** severe in discipline ⟨a ~ teacher⟩ **3 a :** inflexibly maintained or adhered to ⟨~ secrecy⟩ **b :** rigorously conforming to principle or a norm or condition **4 :** EXACT, PRECISE ⟨in the ~ sense of the word⟩ **5 :** of narrow erect habit of growth ⟨a ~ inflorescence⟩ ***syn*** see RIGID — **strict·ly** \ˈstrik(t)-lē\ *adv* — **strict·ness** \-nəs\ *n*

strict liability *n* (1896) **:** liability imposed without regard to fault

stric·ture \ˈstrik-chər\ *n* [ME, fr. LL *strictura,* fr. L *strictus,* pp.] (14c) **1 a :** an abnormal narrowing of a bodily passage; *also* **:** the narrowed part **b :** a constriction of the breath passage in the production of a speech sound **2 :** something that closely restrains or limits **:** RESTRICTION ⟨moral ~*s*⟩ **3 :** an adverse criticism **:** CENSURE

[1]**stride** \ˈstrīd\ *vb* **strode** \ˈstrōd\; **strid·den** \ˈstri-dᵊn\; **strid·ing** \ˈstrī-diŋ\ [ME, fr. OE *strīdan;* akin to MLG *striden* to straddle, OHG *strītan* to quarrel] *vi* (bef. 12c) **1 :** to stand astride **2 :** to move with or as if with long steps ⟨*strode* across the room⟩ **3 :** to take a very long step ~ *vt* **1 :** BESTRIDE, STRADDLE **2 :** to step over **3 :** to move over or along with or as if with long measured steps ⟨*striding* the boardwalk⟩ — **strid·er** \ˈstrī-dər\ *n*

[2]**stride** *n* (bef. 12c) **1 a :** a cycle of locomotor movements (as of a horse) completed when the feet regain the initial relative positions; *also* **:** the distance traversed in a stride **b :** the most effective natural pace **:** maximum competence or capability — often used in the phrase *hit one's stride* **2 :** a long step **3 :** an act of striding **4 :** a stage of progress **:** ADVANCE ⟨made great ~*s* toward their goal⟩ **5 :** a manner of striding **6 :** STRIDE PIANO — **in stride 1 :** without interference with regular activities **2 :** without emotional reaction ⟨took the news *in stride*⟩

stri·dence \ˈstrī-dᵊn(t)s\ *n* (1890) **:** STRIDENCY

stri·den·cy \ˈstrī-dᵊn(t)-sē\ *n, pl* **-cies** (1865) **:** the quality or state of being strident

stri·dent \ˈstrī-dᵊnt\ *adj* [L *strident-, stridens,* prp. of *stridere, stridēre* to make a harsh noise] (ca. 1656) **:** characterized by harsh, insistent, and

\ə\ **abut** \ᵊ\ **kitten,** F **table** \ər\ **further** \a\ **ash** \ā\ **ace** \ä\ **mop, mar**
\au̇\ **out** \ch\ **chin** \e\ **bet** \ē\ **easy** \g\ **go** \i\ **hit** \ī\ **ice** \j\ **job**
\ŋ\ **sing** \ō\ **go** \ȯ\ **law** \ȯi\ **boy** \th\ **thin** \t͟h\ **the** \ü\ **loot** \u̇\ **foot**
\y\ **yet** \zh\ **vision, beige** \k, ⁿ, œ, ue, ʸ\ *see* Guide to Pronunciation

discordant sound ⟨a ~ voice⟩; *also* : commanding attention by a loud or obtrusive quality ⟨~ slogans⟩ ***syn*** see LOUD, VOCIFEROUS — **stri·dent·ly** *adv*

stride piano *n* [fr. *stride bass* left hand part consisting of large skips] (1952) : a style of jazz piano playing in which the right hand plays the melody while the left hand alternates between a single note and a chord played an octave or more higher

stri·dor \ˈstrī-dər, -ˌdȯr\ *n* [L, fr. *stridere, stridēre*] (1632) **1 :** a harsh, shrill, or creaking noise **2 :** a harsh vibrating sound heard during respiration in cases of obstruction of the air passages

strid·u·late \ˈstri-jə-ˌlāt\ *vi* **-lat·ed; -lat·ing** [back-formation fr. *stridulation,* fr. F, high-pitched sound, fr. L *stridulus* shrill] (1838) : to make a shrill creaking noise by rubbing together special bodily structures — used esp. of male insects (as crickets or grasshoppers) — **strid·u·la·tion** \ˌstri-jə-ˈlā-shən\ *n* — **strid·u·la·to·ry** \ˈstri-jə-lə-ˌtȯr-ē\ *adj*

strid·u·lous \ˈstri-jə-ləs\ *adj* [L *stridulus,* fr. *stridere, stridēre*] (1611) : making a shrill creaking sound — **strid·u·lous·ly** *adv*

strife \ˈstrīf\ *n* [ME *strif,* fr. AF *estrif, estri,* of Gmc origin; akin to MD *striden* to fight, OHG *strītan* to quarrel — more at STRIDE] (13c) **1 a :** bitter sometimes violent conflict or dissension ⟨political ~⟩ **b :** an act of contention : FIGHT, STRUGGLE **2 :** exertion or contention for superiority **3** *archaic* : earnest endeavor ***syn*** see DISCORD — **strife·less** \ˈstrī-fləs\ *adj*

strig·il \ˈstri-jəl\ *n* [L *strigilis;* akin to L *stringere* to touch lightly] (1581) : an instrument used by ancient Greeks and Romans for scraping moisture off the skin after bathing or exercising

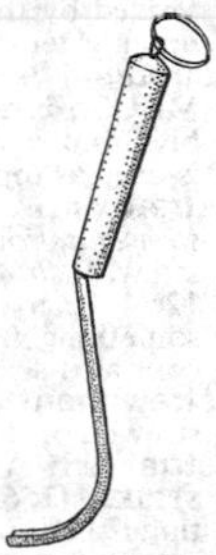
strigil

stri·gose \ˈstrī-ˌgōs\ *adj* [NL *strigosus,* fr. *striga* row of bristles, fr. L, furrow] (1793) : having appressed bristles or scales ⟨a ~ leaf⟩

[1]**strike** \ˈstrīk\ *vb* **struck** \ˈstrək\; **struck** *also* **strick·en** \ˈstri-kən\; **strik·ing** \ˈstrī-kiŋ\ [ME, fr. OE *strīcan* to stroke, go; akin to OHG *strīhhan* to stroke, L *stringere* to touch lightly, *striga, stria* furrow] *vi* (bef. 12c) **1 :** to take a course : GO ⟨*struck* off through the brush⟩ **2 a :** to aim and usu. deliver a blow, stroke, or thrust (as with the hand, a weapon, or a tool) **b :** to arrive with detrimental effect ⟨disaster *struck*⟩ **c :** to attempt to undermine or harm something as if by a blow ⟨*struck* at . . . cherished notions —R. P. Warren⟩ **3 :** to come into contact forcefully ⟨two ships *struck* in mid channel⟩ **4 :** to delete something **5 :** to lower a flag usu. in surrender **6 a :** to become indicated by a clock, bell, or chime ⟨the hour had just *struck*⟩ **b :** to make known the time by sounding ⟨the clock *struck* as they entered⟩ **7 :** PIERCE, PENETRATE ⟨the wind seemed to ~ through our clothes⟩ **8 a :** to engage in battle **b :** to make a military attack **9 :** to become ignited ⟨the match *struck*⟩ **10 :** to discover something ⟨*struck* on a new plan of attack⟩ **11 a :** to pull on a fishing rod in order to set the hook **b** *of a fish* : to seize the bait **12 :** DART, SHOOT **13 a** *of a plant cutting* : to take root **b** *of a seed* : GERMINATE **14 :** to make an impression **15 :** to stop work in order to force an employer to comply with demands **16 :** to make a beginning ⟨the need to ~ vigorously for success⟩ **17 :** to thrust oneself forward ⟨he *struck* into the midst of the argument⟩ **18 :** to work diligently : STRIVE ~ *vt* **1 a :** to strike at : HIT **b :** to drive or remove by or as if by a blow **c :** to attack or seize with a sharp blow (as of fangs or claws) ⟨*struck* by a snake⟩ **d :** INFLICT ⟨~ a blow⟩ **e :** to produce by or as if by a blow or stroke ⟨Moses *struck* water from the rock⟩ **f :** to separate by a sharp blow ⟨~ off flints⟩ **2 a :** to haul down : LOWER ⟨~ the sails⟩ **b :** to dismantle and take away ⟨~ the set⟩ **c :** to strike the tents of (a camp) **3 :** to afflict suddenly ⟨*stricken* by a heart attack⟩ **4 a :** to engage in (a battle) : FIGHT **b :** to make a military attack on **5 :** DELETE, CANCEL ⟨~ the last paragraph⟩ **6 a :** to penetrate painfully : PIERCE **b :** to cause to penetrate ⟨~ the needle⟩ **c :** to send down or out ⟨trees *struck* roots deep into the soil⟩ **7 a :** to level (as a measure of grain) by scraping off what is above the rim **b :** to smooth or form (as a mold) with a tool **8 :** to indicate by sounding ⟨the clock *struck* one⟩ **9 a** (1) **:** to bring into forceful contact ⟨*struck* his head on the doorjamb⟩ (2) **:** to shake (hands) in confirming an agreement (3) **:** to thrust suddenly **b :** to come into contact or collision with ⟨the car *struck* the tree⟩ **c** *of light* : to fall on **d** *of a sound* : to become audible to **10 a :** to affect with a mental or emotional state or a strong emotion ⟨*struck* with horror at the sight⟩ **b :** to affect a person with (a strong emotion) ⟨words that *struck* fear in the listeners⟩ **c :** to cause to become by or as if by a sudden blow ⟨*struck* him dead⟩ **11 a :** to produce by stamping ⟨~ a coin⟩ **b** (1) **:** to produce (as fire) by or as if by striking (2) **:** to cause to ignite by friction ⟨~ a match⟩ **12 :** to make and ratify the terms of ⟨~ a bargain⟩ **13 a :** to play or produce by stroking keys or strings ⟨*struck* a series of chords on the piano⟩ **b :** to produce as if by playing an instrument ⟨his voice *struck* a note of concern⟩ **14 a :** to hook (a fish) by a sharp pull on the line **b** *of a fish* : to snatch at (a bait) **15 a :** to occur to ⟨the answer *struck* me suddenly⟩ **b :** to appear to esp. as a revelation or as remarkable : IMPRESS ⟨it *struck* the crowd as insensitive⟩ **16 :** BEWITCH **17 :** to arrive at by or as if by computation ⟨~ a balance⟩ **18 a :** to come to : ATTAIN **b :** to come upon : DISCOVER ⟨~ gold⟩ **19 :** to engage in a strike against (an employer) **20 :** TAKE ON, ASSUME ⟨~ a pose⟩ **21 a :** to place (a plant cutting) in a medium for growth and rooting **b :** to so propagate (a plant) **22 :** to make one's way along ⟨will ~ the southern coast⟩ **23 :** to cause (an arc) to form (as between electrodes of an arc lamp) **24** *of an insect* : to oviposit on or in ***syn*** see AFFECT — **strike it rich :** to become rich usu. suddenly

[2]**strike** *n* (15c) **1 :** a tool for smoothing a surface (as of a mold) **2 :** an act or instance of striking **3 a :** a work stoppage by a body of workers to enforce compliance with demands made on an employer **b :** a temporary stoppage of activities in protest against an act or condition **4 :** the direction of the line of intersection of a horizontal plane with an uptilted geological stratum **5 a :** a pull on a fishing rod to strike a fish **b :** a pull on a line by a fish in striking **6 :** a stroke of good luck; *esp* : a discovery of a valuable mineral deposit **7 a :** a pitched ball that is in the strike zone or is swung at and is not hit fair **b :** a perfectly thrown ball or pass **8 :** DISADVANTAGE, HANDICAP **9 :** an act or instance of knocking down all the bowling pins with the first bowl **10 :** establishment of roots and plant growth **11 :** cutaneous myiasis (as of sheep) **12 a :** a military attack; *esp* : an air attack on a single objective **b :** a group of airplanes taking part in such an attack

strike·bound \ˈstrīk-ˌbau̇nd\ *adj* (1943) : subjected to a strike

strike·break·er \-ˌbrā-kər\ *n* (1904) : a person hired to replace a striking worker

strike·break·ing \-kiŋ\ *n* (1905) : action designed to break up a strike

strike down *vt* (1779) : ANNUL, NULLIFY ⟨the board *struck down* the appointment⟩; *esp* : to declare (a law) illegal and unenforceable ⟨the Supreme Court *struck down* the law⟩

strike force *n* (1955) **1 :** an armed force equipped to deliver a strong offensive or retaliatory blow **2 :** a team of federal agents assigned to investigate organized crime in a specific area

strike off *vt* (1821) **1 :** to produce in an effortless manner ⟨*strike off* a poem⟩ **2 :** to depict clearly and exactly

strike·out \ˈstrīk-ˌau̇t\ *n* (1887) : an out in baseball resulting from a batter's being charged with three strikes

strike out *vi* (1707) **1 :** to enter upon a course of action **2 :** to set out vigorously **3 :** to make an out in baseball by a strikeout **4 :** to finish bowling a string with consecutive strikes; *specif* : to bowl three strikes in the last frame **5 :** FAIL 2c ~ *vt, of a baseball pitcher* : to retire (as a batter) by a strikeout

strike·over \ˈstrīk-ˌō-vər\ *n* (1938) : an act or instance of striking a typewriter character on a spot occupied by another character

strike price *n* (1972) : an agreed-upon price at which an option contract can be exercised — called also *striking price*

strik·er \ˈstrī-kər\ *n* (1581) **1 :** one that strikes: as **a :** a player in any of several games who is striking or attempting to strike a ball **b :** the hammer of the striking mechanism of a clock or watch **c :** a blacksmith's helper who swings the sledgehammer **d :** a worker on strike **2 :** a junior enlisted man in the U.S. Navy who has declared an occupational specialty **3 :** a forward in soccer

strike–slip \ˈstrīk-ˌslip\ *n, often attrib* (1964) **1 :** a fault about which movement is predominantly horizontal **2 :** a slipping movement along the strike of a fault ⟨~ earthquakes⟩

strike up *vi* (ca. 1562) : to begin to sing or play or to be sung or played ~ *vt* **1 :** to cause to begin singing or playing ⟨*strike up* the band⟩ **2 :** to cause to begin ⟨*strike up* a conversation⟩

strike zone *n* (1948) : the area over home plate through which a pitched baseball must pass to be called a strike

striking *adj* (1725) : attracting attention or notice through unusual or conspicuous qualities ⟨a place of ~ beauty⟩ ***syn*** see NOTICEABLE — **strik·ing·ly** *adv*

striking distance *n* (1751) : a distance from which something can be easily reached or attained ⟨almost within *striking distance* of their goal⟩

[1]**string** \ˈstriŋ\ *n* [ME, fr. OE *streng;* akin to OHG *strang* rope, L *stringere* to bind tight — more at STRAIN] (bef. 12c) **1 a :** a cord usu. used to bind, fasten, or tie — often used attributively ⟨a ~ bag⟩ **b :** something that resembles a string ⟨garnished with potato ~*s*⟩ **2 a** *archaic* : a cord (as a tendon or ligament) of an animal body **b :** a plant fiber (as a leaf vein) **3 a :** the gut, wire, or nylon cord of a musical instrument **b** *pl* (1) **:** the stringed instruments of an orchestra (2) **:** the players of such instruments **4 :** the gut, wire, or cord of a racket or shooting bow **5 a :** a group of objects threaded on a string ⟨a ~ of fish⟩ ⟨a ~ of pearls⟩ **b** (1) **:** a series of things arranged in or as if in a line ⟨a ~ of cars⟩ ⟨a ~ of names⟩ (2) **:** a sequence of like items (as bits, characters, or words) **c :** a group of business properties scattered geographically ⟨a ~ of newspapers⟩ **d :** the animals and esp. horses belonging to or used by one individual **6 a :** a means of recourse : EXPEDIENT **b :** a group of players ranked according to skill or proficiency **7 :** SUCCESSION 3a ⟨a ~ of successes⟩ **8 :** one of the inclined sides of a stair supporting the treads and risers **9 a :** BALKLINE 1 **b :** the action of lagging for break in billiards **10 :** LINE 13 **11** *pl* **a :** contingent conditions or obligations **b :** CONTROL, DOMINATION **12 :** a hypothetical one-dimensional object that is infinitely thin but has a length of 10^{-33} centimeters, that vibrates as it moves through space, and whose mode of vibration manifests itself as a subatomic particle — **string·less** \ˈstriŋ-ləs\ *adj* — **on the string :** subject to one's influences

[2]**string** *vb* **strung** \ˈstrəŋ\; **string·ing** \ˈstriŋ-iŋ\ *vt* (15c) **1 a :** to equip with strings **b :** to tune the strings of **2 :** to make tense : key up **3 a :** to thread on or as if on a string **b :** to thread with objects **c :** to tie, hang, or fasten with string **d :** to put together (as words or ideas) like objects threaded on a string ⟨*strung* her thoughts together⟩ **4 :** to hang by the neck — used with *up* **5 :** to remove the strings of ⟨~ beans⟩ **6 a :** to extend or stretch like a string ⟨~ wires from tree to tree⟩ **b :** to set out in a line or series — often used with *out* ~ *vi* **1 :** to move, progress, or lie in a string **2 :** to form into strings **3 :** LAG 3

[3]**string** *adj* (15c) : of or relating to stringed musical instruments ⟨the ~ section⟩

string along *vt* (1914) **1 :** to keep waiting ⟨*strung* him *along* until the boss was back from lunch⟩ **2 :** DECEIVE, FOOL ⟨~*ing* us along with ruses and red herrings —John Powers⟩ ~ *vi* : GO ALONG, AGREE ⟨held her tongue and *strung along* with the rest of them⟩

string bass *n* (ca. 1927) : DOUBLE BASS

string bean *n* (1754) **1 :** a bean of one of the older varieties of kidney bean that have stringy fibers on the lines of separation of the pods; *broadly* : SNAP BEAN **2 :** a very tall thin person

string bikini *n* (1974) : a scanty bikini with string-like straps

string cheese *n* (1974) : cheese formed usu. into sticks that can be pulled apart in narrow strips

string·course \-ˌkōrs\ *n* (1825) : a horizontal band (as of bricks) in a building forming a part of the design

stringed \ˈstriŋd\ *adj* (bef. 12c) **1 :** having strings ⟨~ instruments⟩ **2 :** produced by strings

strin·gen·cy \ˈstrin-jən(t)-sē\ *n, pl* **-cies** (1844) : the quality or state of being stringent

strin·gen·do \strin-ˈjen-(ˌ)dō\ *adv* [It, verbal of *stringere* to press, fr. L, to bind tight — more at STRAIN] (1853) : with quickening of tempo (as to a climax) — used as a direction in music

strin·gent \ˈstrin-jənt\ *adj* [L *stringent-, stringens,* prp. of *stringere*] (1736) **1 :** TIGHT, CONSTRICTED **2 :** marked by rigor, strictness, or severity esp. with regard to rule or standard ⟨~ decontamination procedures⟩ **3 :** marked by money scarcity and credit strictness ⟨a ~ budget⟩ ***syn*** see RIGID — **strin·gent·ly** *adv*

string·er \ˈstriŋ-ər\ *n* (14c) **1 :** one that strings **2 :** a string, wire, or chain often with snaps on which fish are strung by a fisherman **3 :** a narrow vein or irregular filament of mineral traversing a rock mass of different material **4 a :** a long horizontal timber to connect uprights in a frame or to support a floor **b :** STRING 8 **c :** a tie in a truss **5 a :** a longitudinal member extending from bent to bent of a railroad bridge and carrying the track **b :** a longitudinal member (as in an airplane fuselage or wing) to reinforce the skin **6 a :** a news correspondent who is paid space rates **b :** a reporter who works for a publication or news agency on a part-time basis; *broadly* **:** CORRESPONDENT **7 :** one estimated to be of specified excellence or efficiency — used in combination ⟨first-*stringer*⟩ ⟨second-*stringer*⟩

string·halt \ˈstriŋ-ˌhȯlt\ *n* (ca. 1534) **:** a condition of lameness in a horse's hind legs caused by muscular spasms and resulting in excessive flexion of the hock — **string·halt·ed** \-ˌhȯl-təd\ *adj*

string·ing \ˈstriŋ-iŋ\ *n* (1812) **1 :** lines of inlay in furniture decoration **2 :** the material with which a racket is strung

string line *n* (1867) **:** BALKLINE 1

string·piece \ˈstriŋ-ˌpēs\ *n* (1786) **:** the heavy squared timber lying along the top of the piles forming a dock front or timber pier

string quartet *n* (1875) **1 :** a composition for string quartet **2 :** a quartet of performers on stringed instruments usu. including a first and second violin, a viola, and a cello

string theory *n* (1973) **:** a theory in physics: all elementary particles are manifestations of the vibrations of one-dimensional strings

string tie *n* (1886) **:** a narrow necktie

string trimmer *n* (1976) **:** a machine for cutting grass with a rapidly spinning length of monofilament cord

stringy \ˈstriŋ-ē\ *adj* **string·i·er; -est** (1662) **1 a :** containing, consisting of, or resembling fibrous matter or string ⟨~ hair⟩ **b :** lean and sinewy in build **:** WIRY **2 :** capable of being drawn out to form a string **:** ROPY ⟨a ~ precipitate⟩ — **string·i·ness** *n*

stringy·bark \ˈstriŋ-ē-ˌbärk\ *n* (1799) **1 :** any of several Australian eucalypti with fibrous inner bark **2 :** the bark of a stringybark

[1]**strip** \ˈstrip\ *vb* **stripped** \ˈstript\ *also* **stript; strip·ping** [ME *strepen, strippen,* fr. OE *-strīepan;* akin to OHG *stroufen* to strip] *vt* (13c) **1 a :** to remove clothing, covering, or surface matter from **b :** to deprive of possessions **c :** to divest of honors, privileges, or functions **2 a :** to remove extraneous or superficial matter from ⟨a prose style *stripped* to the bones⟩ **b :** to remove furniture, equipment, or accessories from ⟨~ a ship for action⟩ **3 :** to make bare or clear (as by cutting or grazing) **4 :** to finish a milking of by pressing the last available milk from the teats ⟨~ a cow⟩ **5 a :** to remove cured leaves from the stalks of (tobacco) **b :** to remove the midrib from (tobacco leaves) **6 :** to tear or damage the thread of (a separable part or fitting) **7 :** to separate (components) from a mixture or solution **8 :** to press eggs or milt out of (a fish) **9 :** to remove (a subcutaneous vein) by means of a surgical instrument ~ *vi* **1 a :** to take off clothes **b :** to perform a striptease **2 :** PEEL 1 — **strip·pa·ble** \ˈstri-pə-bəl\ *adj*

[2]**strip** *n* [prob. alter. of [3]*stripe*] (1548) **1 a :** a long narrow piece of a material **b :** a long narrow area of land or water **2 :** AIRSTRIP **3 :** a commercially developed area esp. along a highway **4 :** COMIC STRIP **5 :** STRIPTEASE

strip–chart recorder \ˈstrip-ˌchärt-\ *n* (1950) **:** a device used for the continuous graphic recording of time-dependent data — **strip–chart recording** *n*

strip cropping *n* (1936) **:** the growing of a cultivated crop (as corn) in strips alternating with strips of a sod-forming crop (as hay) arranged to follow an approximate contour of the land and minimize erosion — **strip–crop** \ˈstrip-ˌkräp\ *vb*

[1]**stripe** \ˈstrīp\ *n* [ME, welt, long scar, blow, prob. fr. *stripe* band on a garment] (15c) **:** a stroke or blow with a rod or lash

[2]**stripe** *vt* **striped** \ˈstrīpt\; **strip·ing** [ME, to place bands or edging on (a garment), fr. MD *stripan,* fr. *stripe, strepe* stripe; akin to MHG *strīfe* stripe] (15c) **:** to make stripes on or variegate with stripes

[3]**stripe** *n* [ME, band or stripe on a garment, in part fr. *stripen,* v., in part fr. MD *stripe*] (15c) **1 a :** a line or long narrow section differing in color or texture from parts adjoining **b** (1) **:** a textile design consisting of lines or bands against a plain background (2) **:** a fabric with a striped design **2 :** a narrow strip of braid or embroidery usu. in the shape of a bar, arc, or chevron that is worn (as on the sleeve of a military uniform) to indicate rank or length of service **3 :** a distinct variety or sort **:** TYPE ⟨persons of the same political ~⟩ — **stripe·less** \ˈstrī-pləs\ *adj*

striped \ˈstrīpt, ˈstrī-pəd\ *adj* (1567) **:** having stripes or streaks

striped bass *n* (1818) **:** a large anadromous silvery food and sport fish (*Morone saxatilis* of the family Percichthyidae) with black horizontal stripes on the sides that occurs along the Atlantic coast of the U.S. and has been introduced into inland waters (as lakes and reservoirs) and along the Pacific coast — called also *rockfish*

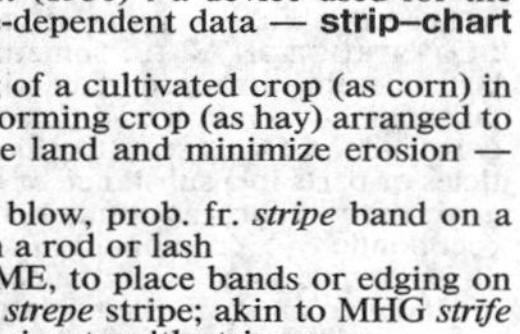

striped bass

striped skunk *n* (1882) **:** a common No. American skunk (*Mephitis mephitis*) usu. with white on the top of the head that extends posteriorly in two narrowly separated stripes

strip·er \ˈstrī-pər\ *n* (1937) **:** STRIPED BASS

striping *n* (1677) **1 a :** the stripes marked or painted on something **b :** a design of stripes **2 :** the act or process of marking with stripes

strip·ling \ˈstri-pliŋ\ *n* [ME] (14c) **:** YOUTH 2a

strip mall *n* (1977) **:** a long usu. one-story building or group of buildings housing several adjacent retail stores or service establishments

strip mine *n* (1926) **:** a mine that is worked from the earth's surface by the stripping of overburden; *esp* **:** a coal mine situated along the outcrop of a flat dipping bed — **strip–mine** *vb* — **strip miner** *n*

stripped–down \ˈstrip(t)-ˈdau̇n\ *adj* (1928) **:** lacking any extra features

strip·per \ˈstri-pər\ *n* (1581) **1 :** one that strips **2 :** STRIPTEASER **3 :** a machine that separates a desired part of an agricultural crop **4 :** an oil well that produces 10 barrels or less per day

strip poker *n* (1912) **:** a poker game in which players pay their losses by removing articles of clothing

strip search *n* (1947) **:** a search for something concealed on a person made after removal of the person's clothing — **strip–search** *vb*

strip·tease \ˈstrip-ˌtēz\ *n* (1932) **:** a burlesque act in which a performer removes clothing piece by piece

strip·teas·er \-ˌtē-zər\ *n* (1930) **:** one who performs a striptease

stripy \ˈstrī-pē\ *adj* **strip·i·er; -est** (1513) **:** marked by stripes or streaks ⟨a ~ cat⟩

strive \ˈstrīv\ *vi* **strove** \ˈstrōv\ *also* **strived** \ˈstrīvd\; **striv·en** \ˈstri-vən\ *or* **strived; striv·ing** \ˈstrī-viŋ\ [ME, to quarrel, contend, fight, endeavor, fr. AF *estriver* to quarrel, fr. *estri, estrif* strife — more at STRIFE] (13c) **1 :** to devote serious effort or energy **:** ENDEAVOR ⟨~ to finish a project⟩ **2 :** to struggle in opposition **:** CONTEND ***syn*** see ATTEMPT — **striv·er** \ˈstrī-vər\ *n*

strobe \ˈstrōb\ *n* [by shortening & alter.] (1942) **1 :** STROBOSCOPE **2 :** a device that utilizes a flashtube for high-speed illumination (as in photography) **3 :** FLASHTUBE

strobe light *n* (1947) **:** STROBE

stro·bi·la \strō-ˈbī-lə, ˈstrō-bə-\ *n, pl* **-lae** \-(ˌ)lē\ [NL, fr. Gk *strobilē* plug of lint shaped like a pinecone, fr. *strobilos* pinecone] (ca. 1864) **:** a linear series of similar animal structures (as the proglottids of a tapeworm) produced by budding

stro·bi·la·tion \ˌstrō-bə-ˈlā-shən\ *n* [NL *strobila*] (1878) **:** asexual reproduction (as in various coelenterates and tapeworms) by transverse division of the body into segments which develop into separate individuals, zooids, or proglottids

stro·bi·lus \strō-ˈbī-ləs, ˈstrō-bə-\ *n, pl* **-li** \-ˌlī\ [NL, fr. LL, pinecone, fr. Gk *strobilos* twisted object, top, pinecone, fr. *strobos* action of whirling; akin to Gk *strephein* to twist] (1771) **1 :** an aggregation of sporophylls resembling a cone (as in the club mosses and horsetails) **2 :** the cone of a gymnosperm

stro·bo·scope \ˈstrō-bə-ˌskōp\ *n* [Gk *strobos* whirling + ISV *-scope*] (1896) **:** an instrument for determining the speed of cyclic motion (as rotation or vibration) that causes the motion to appear slowed or stopped: as **a :** a revolving disk with holes around the edge through which an object is viewed **b :** a device that uses a flashtube to intermittently illuminate a moving object **c :** a cardboard disk with marks to be viewed under intermittent light

stro·bo·scop·ic \ˌstrō-bə-ˈskä-pik\ *adj* (ca. 1846) **:** of, utilizing, or relating to a stroboscope or a strobe — **stro·bo·scop·i·cal·ly** \-pi-k(ə-)lē\ *adv*

strode *past of* STRIDE

[1]**stroke** \ˈstrōk\ *vt* **stroked; strok·ing** [ME, fr. OE *strācian;* akin to OHG *strīhhan* to stroke — more at STRIKE] (bef. 12c) **1 :** to rub gently in one direction; *also* **:** CARESS **2 :** to flatter or pay attention to in a manner designed to reassure or persuade — **strok·er** *n*

[2]**stroke** *n* [ME; akin to OE *strīcan* to stroke — more at STRIKE] (13c) **1 :** the act of striking; *esp* **:** a blow with a weapon or implement **2 :** a single unbroken movement; *esp* **:** one of a series of repeated or to-and-fro movements **3 a :** a controlled swing intended to hit a ball or shuttlecock; *also* **:** a striking of the ball **b :** such a stroke charged to a player as a unit of scoring in golf **4 a :** a sudden action or process producing an impact ⟨a ~ of lightning⟩ **b :** an unexpected result ⟨a ~ of luck⟩ **5 :** sudden diminution or loss of consciousness, sensation, and voluntary motion caused by rupture or obstruction (as by a clot) of a blood vessel of the brain — called also *apoplexy, brain attack, cerebrovascular accident* **6 a :** one of a series of propelling beats or movements against a resisting medium ⟨a ~ of the oar⟩ **b :** a rower who sets the pace for a crew **7 a :** a vigorous or energetic effort by which something is done, produced, or accomplished ⟨a ~ of genius⟩ ⟨a brilliant diplomatic ~⟩ **b :** a delicate or clever touch in a narrative, description, or construction **8 :** HEARTBEAT **9 :** the movement in either direction of a mechanical part (as a piston) having a reciprocating motion; *also* **:** the distance of such movement **10 :** the sound of a bell being struck ⟨at the ~ of twelve⟩; *also* **:** the specific time indicated by or as if by such a sound **11** [[1]*stroke*] **:** an act of stroking or caressing **12 a :** a mark or dash made by a single movement of an implement **b :** one of the lines of a letter of the alphabet — **at a stroke :** all at once ⟨spent her savings *at a stroke*⟩

[3]**stroke** *vb* **stroked; strok·ing** *vt* (1597) **1 a :** to mark with a short line ⟨~ the *t*'s⟩ **b :** to cancel by drawing a line through ⟨*stroked* out his name⟩ **2 :** to set the stroke for (a rowing crew); *also* **:** to set the stroke for the crew of (a rowing boat) **3 :** HIT; *esp* **:** to propel (a ball) with a controlled swinging blow ~ *vi* **1 :** to execute a stroke **2 :** to row at a certain number of strokes a minute

stroke play *n* (1905) **:** golf competition scored by total number of strokes

stroll \ˈstrōl\ *vb* [prob. fr. G dial. *strollen*] *vi* (1668) **1 :** to go from place to place in search of work or profit ⟨~*ing* players⟩ ⟨~*ing* musicians⟩ **2 :** to walk in a leisurely or idle manner **:** RAMBLE ~ *vt* **:** to walk at leisure along or about — **stroll** *n*

stroll·er \ˈstrō-lər\ *n* (1608) **1 a :** an itinerant actor **b :** VAGRANT, TRAMP **2 :** one that strolls **3 :** a collapsible carriage designed as a chair in which a small child may be pushed

stro·ma \ˈstrō-mə\ *n, pl* **stro·ma·ta** \-mə-tə\ [NL *stromat-, stroma,* fr. L, bed covering, fr. Gk *strōmat-, strōma,* fr. *stornynai* to spread out — more at STREW] (ca. 1832) **1 a :** a compact mass of fungal hyphae producing perithecia or pycnidia **b :** the colorless proteinaceous matrix of a chloroplast in which the chlorophyll-containing lamellae are embedded **2 a :** the supporting framework of an animal organ typically consisting of connective tissue **b :** the spongy protoplasmic framework of some cells (as a red blood cell) — **stro·mal** \-məl\ *adj*

stro·mat·o·lite \strō-ˈma-tə-ˌlīt\ *n* [L *stromat-, stroma* bed covering + E *-o-* + *-lite*] (1930) **:** a laminated usu. mounded sedimentary fossil formed from layers of cyanobacteria, calcium carbonate, and trapped sediment — **stro·mat·o·lit·ic** \-ˌma-tə-ˈli-tik\ *adj*

strong \ˈstrȯŋ\ *adj* **stron·ger** \ˈstrȯŋ-gər *also* -ər\; **stron·gest** \ˈstrȯŋ-gəst *also* -əst\ [ME, fr. OE *strang;* akin to OHG *strengi* strong, L *strin-*

gere to bind tight — more at STRAIN] (bef. 12c) **1 :** having or marked by great physical power **2 :** having moral or intellectual power **3 :** having great resources (as of wealth or talent) **4 :** of a specified number ⟨an army ten thousand ~⟩ **5 a :** striking or superior of its kind ⟨a ~ resemblance⟩ **b :** effective or efficient esp. in a specified direction ⟨~ on watching other people work —A. Alvarez⟩ **6 :** FORCEFUL, COGENT ⟨~ evidence⟩ ⟨~ talk⟩ **7 :** not mild or weak **:** EXTREME, INTENSE: as **a :** rich in some active agent ⟨~ beer⟩ **b** *of a color* **:** high in chroma **c :** ionizing freely in solution ⟨~ acids and bases⟩ **d :** magnifying by refracting greatly ⟨a ~ lens⟩ **8** *obs* **:** FLAGRANT **9 :** moving with rapidity or force ⟨a ~ wind⟩ **10 :** ARDENT, ZEALOUS ⟨a ~ supporter⟩ **11 a :** not easily injured or disturbed **:** SOLID **b :** not easily subdued or taken ⟨a ~ fort⟩ **12 :** well established **:** FIRM ⟨~ beliefs⟩ **13 :** not easily upset or nauseated ⟨a ~ stomach⟩ **14 :** having an offensive or intense odor or flavor **:** RANK ⟨~ breath⟩ **15 :** tending to steady or higher prices ⟨a ~ market⟩ **16 :** of, relating to, or being a verb that is inflected by a change in the root vowel (as *strive, strove, striven*) rather than by regular affixation — **strong** *adv* — **strong·ish** \'strȯŋ-ish\ *adj* — **strong·ly** \'strȯŋ-lē\ *adv*
syn STRONG, STOUT, STURDY, STALWART, TOUGH, TENACIOUS mean showing power to resist or to endure. STRONG may imply power derived from muscular vigor, large size, structural soundness, intellectual or spiritual resources ⟨*strong* arms⟩ ⟨the defense has a *strong* case⟩. STOUT suggests an ability to endure stress, pain, or hard use without giving way ⟨*stout* hiking boots⟩. STURDY implies strength derived from vigorous growth, determination of spirit, solidity of construction ⟨a *sturdy* table⟩ ⟨people of *sturdy* independence⟩. STALWART suggests an unshakable dependability ⟨*stalwart* environmentalists⟩. TOUGH implies great firmness and resiliency ⟨a *tough* political opponent⟩. TENACIOUS suggests strength in seizing, retaining, clinging to, or holding together ⟨*tenacious* farmers clinging to an age-old way of life⟩.

strong anthropic principle *n* (1985) **:** ANTHROPIC PRINCIPLE b

1**strong–arm** \'strȯŋ-'ärm\ *adj* (1897) **:** having or using undue force

2**strong–arm** *vt* (1903) **1 a :** to use force on **:** ASSAULT **b :** BULLY, INTIMIDATE **2 :** to rob by force

strong·box \'strȯŋ-ˌbäks\ *n* (1684) **:** a strongly made chest or case for money or valuables

strong breeze *n* (ca. 1867) **:** wind having a speed of 25 to 31 miles (40 to 50 kilometers) per hour — see BEAUFORT SCALE table

strong drink *n* (14c) **:** intoxicating liquor

strong force *n* (1964) **:** a fundamental physical force that acts on hadrons and is responsible for the binding together of protons and neutrons in the atomic nucleus and for processes of particle creation in high-energy collisions and that is the strongest known fundamental physical force but acts only over distances comparable to those between nucleons in an atomic nucleus — called also *strong interaction, strong nuclear force*; compare ELECTROMAGNETISM 2a, GRAVITY 3a(2), WEAK FORCE

strong gale *n* (ca. 1867) **:** wind having a speed of 47 to 54 miles (75 to 87 kilometers) per hour — see BEAUFORT SCALE table

strong·hold \'strȯŋ-ˌhōld\ *n* (15c) **1 :** a fortified place **2 a :** a place of security or survival ⟨one of the last ~*s* of the ancient Gaelic language —George Holmes⟩ **b :** a place dominated by a particular group or marked by a particular characteristic ⟨a Republican ~⟩ ⟨~*s* of snobbery —Lionel Trilling⟩

strong·man \'strȯŋ-ˌman\ *n* (1859) **:** one who leads or controls by force of will and character or by military methods

strong–mind·ed \'strȯŋ-'mīn-dəd\ *adj* (1788) **:** having a vigorous mind; *esp* **:** marked by independence of thought and judgment — **strong–mind·ed·ly** *adv* — **strong–mind·ed·ness** *n*

strong·point \'strȯŋ-ˌpȯint\ *n* (1821) **:** a strongly fortified tactical locality in a defensive position

strong room *n* (1844) **:** a room for money or valuables specially constructed to be fireproof and burglarproof

strong safety *n* (1970) **:** a safety in football who plays opposite the strong side of an offensive formation

strong side *n* (ca. 1951) **:** the side of a football formation having the greater number of players; *specif* **:** the side on which the tight end plays

strong suit *n* (1742) **1 :** a long suit containing high cards **2 :** something in which one excels **:** FORTE ⟨details of legislation have never been my *strong suit* —Tip O'Neill⟩

stron·gyle \'strän-ˌjī(-ə)l, -jəl\ *n* [NL *Strongylus,* genus of worms, fr. Gk *strongylos* round, compact; akin to Gk *stranx* drop squeezed out — more at STRAIN] (1847) **:** any of various nematode worms (family Strongylidae) related to the hookworms and parasitic esp. in the intestines and tissues of horses — compare BLOODWORM 2

stron·gy·loi·di·a·sis \ˌsträn-jə-ˌlȯi-'dī-ə-səs\ *also* **stron·gy·loi·do·sis** \-'dō-səs\ *n* [NL, fr. *Strongyloides,* genus name, fr. *Strongylus*] (1905) **:** infestation with or disease caused by any of a genus (*Strongyloides*) of strongyles that parasitize esp. the intestines of vertebrates including humans

stron·tian·ite \'strän(t)-shə-ˌnīt\ *n* (1794) **:** a mineral consisting of a carbonate of strontium and occurring in various forms and colors

stron·tium \'strän(t)-sh(ē-)əm, 'strän-tē-əm\ *n* [NL, fr. *strontia* strontium oxide, fr. obs. E *strontian,* fr. *Strontian,* village in Scotland] (1808) **:** a soft malleable ductile metallic element of the alkaline-earth group occurring only in combination and used esp. in color TV tubes, in crimson fireworks, and in the production of some ferrites — see ELEMENT table

strontium 90 *n* (1952) **:** a heavy radioactive isotope of strontium of mass number 90 that has a half-life of 29 years, that is present in nuclear waste and fallout, and that is hazardous because like calcium it can be assimilated in biological processes and deposited in the bones of human beings and animals

1**strop** \'sträp\ *n* [ME — more at STRAP] (bef. 12c) **:** STRAP: **a :** a short rope with its ends spliced to form a circle **b :** a usu. leather band for sharpening a razor

2**strop** *vt* **stropped; strop·ping** (1837) **:** to sharpen (a razor) on a strop

stro·phan·thin \strō-'fan(t)-thən\ *n* [ISV, fr. NL *Strophanthus,* fr. Gk *strophos* twisted band (fr. *strephein* to twist) + *anthos* flower — more at ANTHOLOGY] (ca. 1873) **:** any of several glycosides (as ouabain) or mixtures of glycosides from African plants (genera *Strophanthus* and *Acokanthera*) of the dogbane family; *esp* **:** a bitter toxic glycoside $C_{36}H_{54}O_{14}$ from a woody vine (*Strophanthus kombé*) used similarly to digitalis

stro·phe \'strō-(ˌ)fē\ *n* [Gk *strophē,* lit., act of turning, fr. *strephein* to turn, twist] (1603) **1 a :** a rhythmic system composed of two or more lines repeated as a unit; *esp* **:** such a unit recurring in a series of strophic units **b :** STANZA **2 a :** the movement of the classical Greek chorus while turning from one side to the other of the orchestra **b :** the part of a Greek choral ode sung during the strophe of the dance

stro·phic \'strō-fik, 'strä-\ *adj* (1848) **1 :** relating to, containing, or consisting of strophes **2** *of a song* **:** using the same music for successive stanzas — compare THROUGH-COMPOSED

strop·py \'strä-pē\ *adj* [perh. by shortening & alter. fr. *obstreperous*] (1951) *Brit* **:** TOUCHY, BELLIGERENT

stroud \'strau̇d\ *n* [prob. fr. *Stroud,* town in England] (1683) **1** *also* **stroud·ing** \'strau̇-diŋ\ **:** a coarse woolen cloth formerly used in trade with No. American Indians **2 :** a blanket or garment of stroud

strove *past & chiefly dial past part of* STRIVE

strow \'strō\ *vt* **strowed; strown** \'strōn\ *or* **strowed; strow·ing** [ME — more at STREW] (14c) *archaic* **:** SCATTER

stroy *vb* [ME *stroyen,* short for *destroyen*] (13c) *obs* **:** DESTROY

1**struck** *past and past part of* STRIKE

2**struck** *adj* (1894) **:** closed by or subjected to a labor strike ⟨a ~ factory⟩ ⟨a ~ employer⟩

struc·tur·al \'strək-chə-rəl, 'strək-shrəl\ *adj* (ca. 1827) **1 :** of or relating to the physical makeup of a plant or animal body ⟨~ defects of the heart⟩ **2 a :** of, relating to, or affecting structure ⟨~ stability⟩ **b :** used in building structures ⟨~ clay⟩ **c :** involved in or caused by structure esp. of the economy ⟨~ unemployment⟩ **3 :** of, relating to, or resulting from the effects of folding or faulting of the earth's crust **:** TECTONIC **4 :** concerned with or relating to structure rather than history or comparison ⟨~ linguistics⟩ — **struc·tur·al·ly** *adv*

structural formula *n* (ca. 1872) **:** an expanded molecular formula showing the arrangement within the molecule of atoms and of bonds

structural gene *n* (1959) **:** a gene that codes for the amino acid sequence of a protein (as an enzyme) or for a ribosomal RNA or transfer RNA

struc·tur·al·ism \'strək-chə-rə-ˌli-zəm, 'strək-shrə-\ *n* (1907) **1 :** psychology concerned esp. with resolution of the mind into structural elements **2 :** structural linguistics **3 :** an anthropological movement associated esp. with Claude Lévi-Strauss that seeks to analyze social relationships in terms of highly abstract relational structures often expressed in a logical symbolism **4 :** a method of analysis (as of a literary text or a political system) that is related to cultural anthropology and that focuses on recurring patterns of thought and behavior — **struc·tur·al·ist** \-list\ *n or adj*

structural isomer *n* (1926) **:** one of two or more compounds that contain the same number and kinds of atoms but that differ significantly in their geometric arrangement

struc·tur·al·ize \'strək-chə-rə-ˌlīz, 'strək-shrə-ˌlīz\ *vt* **-ized; -iz·ing** (ca. 1931) **:** to organize or incorporate into a structure — **struc·tur·al·i·za·tion** \ˌstrək-chə-rə-lə-'zā-shən, ˌstrək-shrə-\ *n*

structural steel *n* (1884) **1 :** rolled steel in structural shapes **2 :** steel suitable for structural shapes

struc·tur·a·tion \ˌstrək-chə-'rā-shən, -shə-'rā-\ *n* (1925) **:** the interrelation of parts in an organized whole

1**struc·ture** \'strək-chər\ *n* [ME, fr. L *structura,* fr. *structus,* pp. of *struere* to heap up, build — more at STREW] (15c) **1 :** the action of building **:** CONSTRUCTION **2 a :** something (as a building) that is constructed **b :** something arranged in a definite pattern of organization ⟨a rigid totalitarian ~ —J. L. Hess⟩ ⟨leaves and other plant ~*s*⟩ **3 :** manner of construction **:** MAKEUP ⟨Gothic in ~⟩ **4 a :** the arrangement of particles or parts in a substance or body ⟨soil ~⟩ ⟨molecular ~⟩ **b :** organization of parts as dominated by the general character of the whole ⟨economic ~⟩ ⟨personality ~⟩ **c :** coherent form or organization ⟨tried to give some ~ to the children's lives⟩ **5 :** the aggregate of elements of an entity in their relationships to each other ⟨the ~ of a language⟩ — **struc·ture·less** \-ləs\ *adj* — **struc·ture·less·ness** \-nəs\ *n*

2**structure** *vt* **struc·tured; struc·tur·ing** \'strək-chə-riŋ, 'strək-shriŋ\ (ca. 1693) **1 :** to form into or according to a structure **2 :** CONSTRUCT

structured *adj* (1966) **:** of, relating to, or being a method of computer programming in which each step of the solution to a problem is contained in a separate subprogram

stru·del \'strü-dᵊl, 'shtrü-\ *n* [G, lit., whirlpool] (1881) **:** a pastry made from a thin sheet of dough rolled up with filling and baked ⟨apple ~⟩

1**strug·gle** \'strə-gəl\ *vi* **strug·gled; strug·gling** \-g(ə-)liŋ\ [ME *struglen*] (14c) **1 :** to make strenuous or violent efforts in the face of difficulties or opposition ⟨*struggling* with the problem⟩ **2 :** to proceed with difficulty or with great effort ⟨*struggled* through the high grass⟩ ⟨*struggling* to make a living⟩ — **strug·gler** \-g(ə-)lər\ *n*

2**struggle** *n* (1560) **1 :** CONTEST, STRIFE ⟨armed ~⟩ ⟨a power ~⟩ **2 :** a violent effort or exertion **:** an act of strongly motivated striving ⟨a ~ to make ends meet⟩ **3 :** TUSSLE 1 ⟨during the ~ the gun went off⟩

struggle for existence (1832) **:** the automatic competition of members of a natural population for limited vital resources (as food, space, or light) that results in natural selection

1**strum** \'strəm\ *n* [imit.] (1764) **:** an act, instance, or sound of strumming

2**strum** *vb* **strummed; strum·ming** *vt* (1777) **1 a :** to brush the fingers over the strings of (a musical instrument) in playing ⟨~ a guitar⟩; *also* **:** 3THRUM 1 **b :** to play (music) on a stringed instrument ⟨~ a tune⟩ **2 :** to cause to sound vibrantly ⟨winds *strummed* the rigging —H. A. Chippendale⟩ ~ *vi* **1 :** to strum a stringed instrument **2 :** to sound vibrantly — **strum·mer** *n*

stru·ma \'strü-mə\ *n, pl* **stru·mae** \-(ˌ)mē, -ˌmī\ *or* **strumas** [L, swelling of the lymph glands] (1565) **:** GOITER

strum·pet \'strəm-pət\ *n* [ME] (14c) **:** PROSTITUTE 1a

strung *past and past part of* STRING

strung out *adj* (ca. 1959) **1 :** physically debilitated (as from long-term drug addiction) **2 :** addicted to a drug **3 :** intoxicated or stupefied from drug use

strunt \'strənt\ *vi* [by alter.] (1786) *Scot* **:** STRUT

1**strut** \'strət\ *vb* **strut·ted; strut·ting** [ME *strouten,* fr. OE *strūtian* to stand out stiffly, struggle; akin to MHG *strozzen* to be swollen] *vi* (13c)

1 : to become turgid : SWELL **2 a :** to walk with a proud gait **b :** to walk with a pompous and affected air ~ *vt* **:** to parade (as clothes) with a show of pride — **strut·ter** *n* — **strut one's stuff :** to display one's best work : SHOW OFF

[2]**strut** *n* (1587) **1 :** a structural piece designed to resist pressure in the direction of its length **2 :** a pompous step or walk **3 :** arrogant behavior : SWAGGER

[3]**strut** *vt* **strut·ted; strut·ting** (ca. 1828) **:** to provide, stiffen, support, or hold apart with or as if with a strut

stru·thi·ous \ˈstrü-thē-əs, -t͟hē-\ *adj* [LL *struthio* ostrich, irreg. fr. Gk *strouthos*] (1773) **:** of or relating to the ostriches and related birds

strych·nine \ˈstrik-ˌnīn, -nən, -ˌnēn\ *n* [F, fr. NL *Strychnos,* fr. L, nightshade, fr. Gk] (1819) **:** a bitter poisonous alkaloid $C_{21}H_{22}N_2O_2$ that is obtained from nux vomica and related plants (genus *Strychnos*) and is used as a poison (as for rodents) and medicinally as a stimulant of the central nervous system

Stu·art \ˈstü-ərt, ˈstyü-; ˈst(y)u̇rt\ *adj* [Robert *Stewart* (Robert II of Scotland) †1390] (1715) **:** of or relating to the Scottish royal house to which belonged the rulers of Scotland from 1371 to 1603 and of Great Britain from 1603 to 1649 and from 1660 to 1714 — **Stuart** *n*

[1]**stub** \ˈstəb\ *n* [ME *stubb,* fr. OE *stybb;* akin to ON *stūfr* stump, Gk *stypos* stem] (bef. 12c) **1 a :** STUMP 2 **b :** a short piece remaining on a stem or trunk where a branch has been lost **2 :** something made or worn to a short or blunt shape; *esp* **:** a pen with a short blunt nib **3 :** a short blunt part left after a larger part has been broken off or used up ⟨a pencil ~⟩ **4 :** something cut short or stunted **5 a :** a small part of a leaf (as of a checkbook) attached to the spine for memoranda of the contents of the part torn away **b :** the part of a ticket returned to the user

[2]**stub** *vt* **stubbed; stub·bing** (15c) **1 a :** to grub up by the roots **b :** to clear (land) by grubbing out rooted growth **c :** to hew or cut down (a tree) close to the ground **2 :** to extinguish (as a cigarette) by crushing **3 :** to strike (one's foot or toe) against an object

stub·ble \ˈstə-bəl\ *n, often attrib* [ME *stuble,* fr. AF *estuble,* fr. L *stupula* stalk, straw, alter. of *stipula* — more at STIPULE] (14c) **1 :** the basal part of herbaceous plants and esp. cereal grasses remaining attached to the soil after harvest **2 :** a rough surface or growth resembling stubble; *esp* **:** a short growth of beard — **stub·bled** \-bəld\ *adj* — **stub·bly** \-b(ə-)lē\ *adj*

stubble mulch *n* (1942) **:** a lightly tilled mulch of plant residue used to prevent erosion, conserve moisture, and add organic matter to the soil

stub·born \ˈstə-bərn\ *adj* [ME *stibourne, stuborn*] (14c) **1 a** (1) **:** unreasonably or perversely unyielding : MULISH (2) **:** justifiably unyielding : RESOLUTE **b :** suggestive or typical of a strong stubborn nature ⟨a ~ jaw⟩ **2 :** performed or carried on in an unyielding, obstinate, or persistent manner ⟨~ effort⟩ **3 :** difficult to handle, manage, or treat ⟨a ~ cold⟩ **4 :** LASTING ⟨~ facts⟩ ***syn*** see OBSTINATE — **stub·born·ly** *adv* — **stub·born·ness** \-bər(n)-nəs\ *n*

stub·by \ˈstə-bē\ *adj* **stub·bi·er; -est** (15c) **1 :** abounding with stubs **2 a :** resembling a stub : being short and thick ⟨~ fingers⟩ **b :** being short and thickset : SQUAT **c :** being short, broad, or blunt (as from use or wear) ⟨an old ~ pencil⟩

stuc·co \ˈstə-(ˌ)kō\ *n, pl* **stuccos** *or* **stuccoes** [It, of Gmc origin; akin to OHG *stucki* piece, crust, OE *stocc* stock — more at STOCK] (1598) **1 a :** a fine plaster used in decoration and ornamentation (as of interior walls) **b :** a material usu. made of portland cement, sand, and a small percentage of lime and applied in a plastic state to form a hard covering for exterior walls **2 :** STUCCOWORK — **stuc·coed** \-(ˌ)kōd\ *adj*

stuc·co·work \ˈstə-kō-ˌwərk\ *n* (1686) **:** work done in stucco

stuck *past and past part of* STICK

stuck–up \ˈstək-ˈəp\ *adj* (1829) **:** CONCEITED, SNOBBISH

[1]**stud** \ˈstəd\ *n, often attrib* [ME *stod,* fr. OE *stōd;* akin to OCS *stado* flock and prob. to OHG *stān* to stand — more at STAND] (bef. 12c) **1 a :** a group of animals and esp. horses kept primarily for breeding **b :** a place (as a farm) where a stud is kept **2 :** STUDHORSE; *broadly* **:** a male animal kept for breeding **3 a :** a young man : GUY; *esp* **:** one who is virile and promiscuous **b :** a tough person **c :** HUNK 2 — **at stud :** for breeding as a stud ⟨retired racehorses *at stud*⟩

[2]**stud** *n* [ME *stode,* fr. OE *studu;* akin to MHG *stud* prop, ON *stoth* post] (bef. 12c) **1 a :** one of the smaller uprights in the framing of the walls of a building to which sheathing, paneling, or laths are fastened : SCANTLING **b :** height from floor to ceiling **2 a :** a boss, rivet, or nail with a large head used (as on a shield or belt) for ornament or protection **b :** a solid button with a shank or eye on the back inserted (as through an eyelet in a garment) as a fastener or ornament **c :** a small button-like ornament with a post for inserting through a body part (as the earlobe or nostril) and into a clasp **3 a :** any of various infixed pieces (as a rod or pin) projecting from a machine and serving chiefly as a support or axis **b :** one of the metal or rubber cleats projecting from a snow tire to increase traction

[3]**stud** *vt* **stud·ded; stud·ding** (ca. 1506) **1 :** to furnish (as a building or wall) with studs **2 :** to adorn, cover, or protect with studs **3 :** to set, mark, or decorate conspicuously often at intervals ⟨a sky *studded* with stars⟩ ⟨a career *studded* with honors⟩

[4]**stud** *abbr* student

stud·book \ˈstəd-ˌbu̇k\ *n* (1803) **:** an official record (as in a book) of the pedigree of purebred animals (as horses or dogs); *also* **:** a record of the lineage of a wild animal bred in captivity (as at a zoo)

studding *n* (1588) **:** the studs of a building or wall

stud·ding sail \ˈstə-diŋ-ˌsāl, ˈstən(t)-səl\ *n* [origin unknown] (1549) **:** a light sail set at the side of a principal square sail of a ship in free winds

stu·dent \ˈstü-dᵊnt, ˈstyü-, *chiefly Southern* -dənt\ *n, often attrib* [ME, fr. L *student-, studens,* fr. prp. of *studēre* to study — more at STUDY] (14c) **1 :** SCHOLAR, LEARNER; *esp* **:** one who attends a school **2 :** one who studies : an attentive and systematic observer ⟨a ~ of politics⟩

student body *n* (1906) **:** the students at an educational institution

student government *n* (1948) **:** the organization and management of student life by various student organizations

student lamp *n* (1852) **:** a desk reading lamp with a tubular shaft, one or two arms for a shaded light, and orig. an oil reservoir

stu·dent·ship \ˈstü-dᵊnt-ˌship, ˈstyü-, -dənt-\ *n* (ca. 1782) **1** *Brit* **:** a grant for university study **2 :** the state of being a student

stu·dent's t distribution \ˈstü-dᵊn(t)s-, -dən(t)s-\ *n, often cap S* [*Student,* pen name of W. S. Gosset †1937 Brit. statistician] (1929) **:** T DISTRIBUTION

Student's t–test *n* (1935) **:** T-TEST

student teacher *n* (1909) **:** a student who is engaged in practice teaching

student teaching *n* (1929) **:** PRACTICE TEACHING

student union *n* (1949) **:** a building on a college campus that is devoted to student activities and that usu. contains lounges, auditoriums, offices, and game rooms

stud·horse \ˈstəd-ˌhȯrs\ *n* (bef. 12c) **:** a stallion kept esp. for breeding

stud·ied \ˈstə-dēd\ *adj* (15c) **1 :** carefully considered or prepared : THOUGHTFUL ⟨a ~ response⟩ **2 :** KNOWLEDGEABLE, LEARNED ⟨~ in the craft of blacksmithing⟩ **3 :** produced or marked by conscious design or premeditation : CALCULATED ⟨~ indifference⟩ ⟨spoke with a ~ accent⟩ — **stud·ied·ly** *adv* — **stud·ied·ness** *n*

stu·dio \ˈstü-dē-(ˌ)ō, ˈstyü-\ *n, pl* **-dios** [It, lit., study, fr. L *studium*] (1819) **1 a :** the working place of a painter, sculptor, or photographer **b :** a place for the study of an art (as dancing, singing, or acting) **2 a :** a place where motion pictures are made **b :** a company that produces motion pictures **3 :** a place maintained and equipped for the transmission of radio or television programs **4 :** a place where audio recordings are made **5 :** STUDIO APARTMENT

studio apartment *n* (1903) **:** a small apartment consisting typically of a main room, kitchenette, and bathroom

studio couch *n* (1931) **:** an upholstered usu. backless couch that can be made to serve as a double bed by sliding from underneath it the frame of a single cot

stu·di·ous \ˈstü-dē-əs, ˈstyü-\ *adj* (14c) **1 :** assiduous in the pursuit of learning **2 a :** of, relating to, or concerned with study ⟨~ habits⟩ **b :** favorable to study ⟨a ~ environment⟩ **3 a :** diligent or earnest in intent ⟨made a ~ effort⟩ **b :** marked by or suggesting purposefulness or diligence ⟨a ~ expression on his face⟩ **c :** deliberately or consciously planned ⟨~ avoidance of gender-specific pronouns⟩ — **stu·di·ous·ly** *adv* — **stu·di·ous·ness** *n*

stud·ly \ˈstəd-lē\ *adj* [[1]*stud*] (1972) *slang* **:** attractively masculine : HUNKY

stud poker *n* [[1]*stud*] (1864) **:** poker in which each player is dealt the first card facedown and the other four cards faceup with a round of betting taking place after each of the last four rounds of dealing

[1]**study** \ˈstə-dē\ *n, pl* **stud·ies** [ME *studie,* fr. AF *estudie,* fr. L *studium,* fr. *studēre* to devote oneself, study; prob. akin to L *tundere* to beat — more at CONTUSION] (14c) **1 :** a state of contemplation : REVERIE **2 a :** application of the mental faculties to the acquisition of knowledge ⟨years of ~⟩ **b :** such application in a particular field or to a specific subject ⟨the ~ of Latin⟩ **c :** careful or extended consideration ⟨the proposal is under ~⟩ **d** (1) **:** a careful examination or analysis of a phenomenon, development, or question (2) **:** the published report of such a study **3 :** a building or room devoted to study or literary pursuits **4 :** PURPOSE, INTENT ⟨it has been the ~ of my life to avoid those weaknesses —Jane Austen⟩ **5 a :** a branch or department of learning : SUBJECT — often used in pl. ⟨American *studies*⟩ **b :** the activity or work of a student ⟨returning to her *studies* after vacation⟩ **c :** an object of study or deliberation ⟨every gesture a careful ~ —Marcia Davenport⟩ **d :** something attracting close attention or examination **6 :** a person who learns or memorizes something (as a part in a play) — usu. used with a qualifying adjective ⟨he's a quick ~⟩ **7 :** a literary or artistic production intended as a preliminary outline, an experimental interpretation, or an exploratory analysis of specific features or characteristics **8 :** a musical composition for the practice of a point of technique

[2]**study** *vb* **stud·ied; study·ing** *vi* (14c) **1 a :** to engage in study **b :** to undertake formal study of a subject **2** *dial* **:** MEDITATE, REFLECT **3 :** ENDEAVOR, TRY ~ *vt* **1 :** to read in detail esp. with the intention of learning **2 :** to engage in the study of ⟨~ biology⟩ **3 :** PLOT, DESIGN **4 :** to consider attentively or in detail ⟨~*ing* his face for a reaction⟩ ***syn*** see CONSIDER — **stud·i·er** \ˈstə-dē-ər\ *n*

study hall *n* (1836) **1 :** a room in a school set aside for study **2 :** a period in a student's day set aside for study and homework

[1]**stuff** \ˈstəf\ *n* [ME, fr. AF *estuffes* goods, fr. *estuffer* to fill in (with rubble), furnish, equip, of Gmc origin; akin to OHG *stopfōn* to stop up, fr. VL **stuppare* — more at STOP] (14c) **1 :** materials, supplies, or equipment used in various activities: as **a** *obs* **:** military baggage **b :** PERSONAL PROPERTY **2 :** material to be manufactured, wrought, or used in construction ⟨clear half-inch pine ~ —Emily Holt⟩ **3 :** a finished textile suitable for clothing; *esp* **:** wool or worsted material **4 a :** literary or artistic production **b :** writing, discourse, talk, or ideas of little value : TRASH **5 a :** an unspecified material substance or aggregate of matter ⟨volcanic rock is curious ~⟩ **b :** something (as a drug or food) consumed or introduced into the body by humans **c :** a matter to be considered ⟨the truth was heady ~⟩ ⟨long-term policy ~⟩ **d :** a group or scattering of miscellaneous objects or articles ⟨pick that ~ up off the floor⟩; *also* **:** nonphysical unspecified material ⟨conservation and . . . all kinds of good ~ —Eric Korn⟩ **6 a :** fundamental material : SUBSTANCE ⟨the ~ of greatness⟩ **b :** subject matter ⟨a teacher who knows her ~⟩ **7 :** special knowledge or capability ⟨showing their ~⟩ **8 a :** spin imparted to a thrown or hit ball to make it curve or change course **b :** the movement of a baseball pitch out of its apparent line of flight : the liveliness of a pitch ⟨greatest pitcher of my time . . . had tremendous ~ —Ted Williams⟩ **9 :** DUNK SHOT — **stuff·less** *adj*

[2]**stuff** *vt* (15c) **1 a :** to fill by packing things in : CRAM ⟨the boy ~*ed* his pockets with candy⟩ **b :** to fill to satiety : SURFEIT ⟨~*ed* themselves with turkey⟩ **c :** to prepare (meat or vegetables) by filling or lining with a stuffing **d :** to fill (as a cushion) with a soft material **e :** to fill out the skin of (an animal) for mounting **2 a :** to fill by intellectual effort ⟨~*ing* their heads with facts⟩ **b :** to pack full of something immaterial ⟨a book ~*ed* with information⟩ **3 :** to fill or block up (as na-

sal passages) **4 a :** to cause to enter or fill : THRUST ⟨~*ed* a lot of clothing into a laundry bag⟩ **b :** to put (as a ball or puck) into a goal forcefully from close range **5** — used in the imperative to express contempt ⟨if they didn't like it, ~ 'em —Eric Clapton⟩; often used in the phrases *stuff it* and *get stuffed* **6 :** to stop (a ballcarrier) abruptly in a football game ⟨~*ed* the runner just short of a first down⟩

stuffed shirt *n* (1904) **:** a smug, conceited, and usu. pompous person often with an inflexibly conservative or reactionary attitude

stuff·er \ˈstə-fər\ *n* (1611) **1 :** one that stuffs **2 :** an enclosure (as a leaflet) inserted in an envelope in addition to a bill, statement, or notice **3 :** a series of extra threads or yarn running lengthwise in a fabric to add weight and bulk and to form a backing esp. for carpets

stuff·ing \ˈstə-fiŋ\ *n* (15c) **:** material used to stuff; *esp* **:** a seasoned mixture used to stuff food (as meat, vegetables, or eggs)

stuffing box *n* (1798) **:** a device that prevents leakage along a moving part (as a connecting rod) passing through a hole in a vessel (as a cylinder) containing steam, water, or oil and that consists of a box or chamber made by enlarging the hole and a gland to compress the contained packing

stuffy \ˈstə-fē\ *adj* **stuff·i·er; -est** (1798) **1 :** ILL-NATURED, ILL-HUMORED **2 :** lacking in vitality or interest **:** STODGY, DULL **3 a :** oppressive to the breathing **:** CLOSE ⟨a ~ room⟩ **b :** stuffed up ⟨a ~ nose⟩ **4 a :** narrowly inflexible in standards of conduct **:** SELF-RIGHTEOUS **b :** stiffly conventional **:** PRIGGISH ⟨~ formalities⟩ — **stuff·i·ly** \ˈstə-fə-lē\ *adv* — **stuff·i·ness** \ˈstə-fē-nəs\ *n*

stul·ti·fy \ˈstəl-tə-ˌfī\ *vt* **-fied; -fy·ing** [LL *stultificare* to make foolish, fr. L *stultus* foolish; akin to L *stolidus* stolid] (1737) **1** *archaic* **:** to allege or prove to be of unsound mind and hence not responsible **2 :** to cause to appear or be stupid, foolish, or absurdly illogical **3 a :** to impair, invalidate, or make ineffective **:** NEGATE **b :** to have a dulling or inhibiting effect on — **stul·ti·fi·ca·tion** \ˌstəl-tə-fə-ˈkā-shən\ *n*

1stum·ble \ˈstəm-bəl\ *vb* **stum·bled; stum·bling** \-b(ə-)liŋ\ [ME, prob. of Scand origin; akin to Norw dial. *stumle* to stumble] *vi* (14c) **1 a :** to fall into sin or waywardness **b :** to make an error **:** BLUNDER **c :** to come to an obstacle to belief **2 :** to trip in walking or running **3 a :** to walk unsteadily or clumsily **b :** to speak or act in a hesitant or faltering manner **4 a :** to come unexpectedly or by chance ⟨~ onto the truth⟩ **b :** to fall or move carelessly ~ *vt* **1 :** to cause to stumble **:** TRIP **2 :** BEWILDER, CONFOUND — **stum·bler** \-b(ə-)lər\ *n* — **stum·bling·ly** \-b(ə-)liŋ-lē\ *adv*

2stumble *n* (1547) **:** an act or instance of stumbling

stum·ble·bum \ˈstəm-bəl-ˌbəm\ *n* (1932) **:** a clumsy or inept person; *esp* **:** an inept boxer

stum·bling block \ˈstəm-bliŋ-\ *n* (1588) **1 :** an obstacle to progress **2 :** an impediment to belief or understanding **:** PERPLEXITY

1stump \ˈstəmp\ *n* [ME *stumpe;* akin to OHG *stumpf* stump and perh. to ME *stampen* to stamp] (14c) **1 a :** the basal portion of a bodily part remaining after the rest is removed **b :** a rudimentary or vestigial bodily part **2 :** the part of a plant and esp. a tree remaining attached to the root after the trunk is cut **3 :** a remaining part **:** STUB **4 :** one of the pointed rods stuck in the ground to form a cricket wicket **5 :** a place or occasion for public speaking (as for a cause or candidate); *also* **:** the circuit followed by a maker of such speeches — used esp. in the phrase *on the stump*

2stump *vt* (1581) **1 :** to reduce to a stump **:** TRIM **2 a :** DARE, CHALLENGE **b :** to frustrate the progress or efforts of **:** BAFFLE **3 :** to clear (land) of stumps **4 :** to travel over (a region) making political speeches or supporting a cause **5 a :** to walk over heavily or clumsily **b :** STUB 3 ~ *vi* **1 :** to walk heavily or clumsily **2 :** to go about making political speeches or supporting a cause — **stump·er** *n*

3stump *n* [F or D dial.; F *estompe,* fr. D dial *stomp,* lit., stub, fr. MD; akin to OHG *stumpf* stump] (1778) **:** a short thick roll of leather, felt, or paper usu. pointed at both ends and used for shading or blending a drawing in crayon, pencil, charcoal, pastel, or chalk

4stump *vt* (1807) **:** to tone or treat (a drawing) with a stump

stump·age \ˈstəm-pij\ *n* (1835) **1 :** the value of standing timber **2 :** uncut marketable timber; *also* **:** the right to cut it

stump–tailed macaque \ˈstəmp-ˈtāl(d)-\ *n* (1938) **:** a dark reddish-brown naked-faced short-tailed macaque (*Macaca arctoides* syn. *M. speciosa*) of eastern Asia — called also *stump-tailed monkey*

stump work *n* (1904) **:** embroidery with intricate padded designs or scenes in high relief popular esp. in the 17th century

stumpy \ˈstəm-pē\ *adj* **stump·i·er; -est** (1600) **1 :** short and thick **:** STUBBY **2 :** full of stumps

1stun \ˈstən\ *vt* **stunned; stun·ning** [ME *stonen, stunen,* fr. AF *estoner* — more at ASTONISH] (14c) **1 :** to make senseless, groggy, or dizzy by or as if by a blow **:** DAZE **2 :** to shock with noise **3 :** to overcome esp. with paralyzing astonishment or disbelief

2stun *n* (1727) **:** the effect of something that stuns **:** SHOCK

stung *past and past part of* STING

stun gun *n* (1967) **:** a weapon designed to stun or immobilize (as by electric shock) rather than kill or injure the one affected

stunk *past and past part of* STINK

stun·ner \ˈstə-nər\ *n* (1829) **:** one that stuns or is stunning

stunning *adj* (1667) **1 :** causing astonishment or disbelief ⟨~ news⟩ **2 :** strikingly impressive esp. in beauty or excellence ⟨a ~ view⟩ ⟨~ workmanship⟩ — **stun·ning·ly** *adv*

1stunt \ˈstənt\ *vt* [E dial. *stunt* stubborn, stunted, abrupt, prob. of Scand origin; akin to ON *stuttr* scant — more at STINT] (1583) **:** to hinder the normal growth, development, or progress of — **stunt·ed·ness** *n*

2stunt *n* (1725) **1 :** one (as an animal) that is stunted **2 :** a check in growth **3 :** a plant disease in which dwarfing occurs

3stunt *n* [origin unknown] (1878) **1 :** an unusual or difficult feat requiring great skill or daring; *esp* **:** one performed or undertaken chiefly to gain attention or publicity **2 :** a shifting or switching of the positions by defensive players at the line of scrimmage in football to disrupt the opponent's blocking efforts

4stunt *vi* (1917) **:** to perform or engage in a stunt

stunt·man \ˈstənt-ˌman\ *n* (1927) **:** a man who performs stunts; *esp* **:** one who doubles for an actor during the filming of stunts and dangerous scenes

stunt·wom·an \-ˌwu̇-mən\ *n* (1948) **:** a woman who doubles for an actress during the filming of stunts and dangerous scenes

stu·pa \ˈstü-pə\ *n* [Skt *stūpa*] (1876) **:** a usu. dome-shaped structure (as a mound) serving as a Buddhist shrine

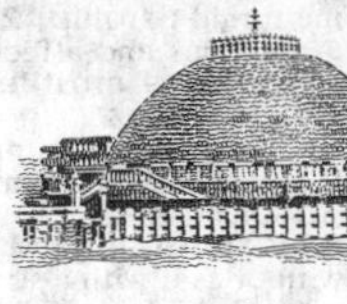

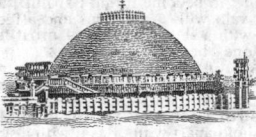

stupa

1stupe \ˈstüp, ˈstyüp\ *n* [ME, fr. AF, lit., tow, fr. L *stuppa* coarse part of flax, tow, fr. Gk *styppē*] (14c) **:** a hot wet often medicated cloth applied externally (as to stimulate circulation)

2stupe *n* [short for *stupid*] (1729) **:** a stupid person **:** DOLT

stu·pe·fac·tion \ˌstü-pə-ˈfak-shən, ˌstyü-\ *n* [ME *stupefaccioun,* fr. ML *stupefaction-, stupefactio,* fr. L *stupefacere*] (15c) **:** the act of stupefying **:** the state of being stupefied

stu·pe·fy \ˈstü-pə-ˌfī, ˈstyü-\ *vt* **-fied; -fy·ing** [ME *stupifien,* modif. of L *stupefacere,* fr. *stupēre* to be astonished + *facere* to make, do — more at DO] (15c) **1 :** to make stupid, groggy, or insensible **2 :** ASTONISH, ASTOUND — **stu·pe·fy·ing·ly** \-iŋ-lē\ *adv*

stu·pen·dous \stu̇-ˈpen-dəs, styu̇-\ *adj* [L *stupendus,* gerundive of *stupēre*] (1640) **1 :** causing astonishment or wonder **:** AWESOME, MARVELOUS **2 :** of amazing size or greatness **:** TREMENDOUS ***syn*** see MONSTROUS — **stu·pen·dous·ly** *adv* — **stu·pen·dous·ness** *n*

1stu·pid \ˈstü-pəd, ˈstyü-\ *adj* [MF *stupide,* fr. L *stupidus,* fr. *stupēre* to be numb, be astonished — more at TYPE] (1541) **1 a :** slow of mind **:** OBTUSE **b :** given to unintelligent decisions or acts **:** acting in an unintelligent or careless manner **c :** lacking intelligence or reason **:** BRUTISH **2 :** dulled in feeling or sensation **:** TORPID ⟨still ~ from the sedative⟩ **3 :** marked by or resulting from unreasoned thinking or acting **:** SENSELESS ⟨a ~ decision⟩ **4 a :** lacking interest or point ⟨a ~ event⟩ **b :** VEXATIOUS, EXASPERATING ⟨the ~ car won't start⟩ — **stu·pid·ly** *adv* — **stu·pid·ness** *n*

syn STUPID, DULL, DENSE, CRASS, DUMB mean lacking in power to absorb ideas or impressions. STUPID implies a slow-witted or dazed state of mind that may be either congenital or temporary ⟨*stupid* students just keeping the seats warm⟩ ⟨*stupid* with drink⟩. DULL suggests a slow or sluggish mind such as results from disease, depression, or shock ⟨monotonous work that leaves the mind *dull*⟩. DENSE implies a thickheaded imperviousness to ideas ⟨too *dense* to take a hint⟩. CRASS suggests a grossness of mind precluding discrimination or delicacy ⟨a *crass,* materialistic people⟩. DUMB applies to an exasperating obtuseness or lack of comprehension ⟨too *dumb* to figure out what's going on⟩.

2stupid *n* (1712) **:** a stupid person

stu·pid·i·ty \stu̇-ˈpi-də-tē, styu̇-\ *n, pl* **-ties** (1541) **1 :** the quality or state of being stupid **2 :** a stupid idea or act

stu·por \ˈstü-pər, ˈstyü-\ *n* [ME, fr. L, fr. *stupēre*] (14c) **1 :** a condition of greatly dulled or completely suspended sense or sensibility ⟨a drunken ~⟩ **2 :** a state of extreme apathy or torpor resulting often from stress or shock **:** DAZE ***syn*** see LETHARGY

stu·por·ous \ˈstü-p(ə-)rəs, ˈstyü-\ *adj* (1877) **:** marked or affected by or as if by stupor ⟨had been taken, gray and ~, to the hospital —Oliver Sacks⟩

stur·dy \ˈstər-dē\ *adj* **stur·di·er; -est** [ME, brave, stubborn, fr. AF *esturdi* stunned, fr. pp. of *esturdir* to stun, fr. VL **exturdire,* fr. L *ex-* + VL **turdus* simpleton, fr. L *turdus* thrush — more at THRUSH] (14c) **1 a :** firmly built or constituted **:** STOUT **b :** HARDY ⟨~ plants⟩ **c :** sound in design or execution **:** SUBSTANTIAL **2 a :** marked by or reflecting physical strength or vigor **b :** FIRM, RESOLUTE **c :** RUGGED, STABLE ***syn*** see STRONG — **stur·di·ly** \ˈstər-də-lē\ *adv* — **stur·di·ness** \ˈstər-dē-nəs\ *n*

stur·geon \ˈstər-jən\ *n* [ME, fr. AF *estourgeoun,* of Gmc origin; akin to OE *styria* sturgeon] (13c) **:** any of a family (Acipenseridae) of usu. large elongate anadromous or freshwater bony fishes which are widely distributed in the north temperate zone and whose roe is made into caviar

Sturm und Drang \ˌshtu̇rm-u̇nt-ˈdräŋ, ˌstu̇rm-, -ənt-\ *n* [G, lit., storm and stress, fr. *Sturm und Drang* (1776), drama by Friedrich von Klinger †1831 Ger. novelist and dramatist] (1845) **1 :** a late 18th century German literary movement characterized by works containing rousing action and high emotionalism that often deal with the individual's revolt against society **2 :** TURMOIL

sturt \ˈstərt\ *n* [ME, contention, alter. of *strut;* akin to OE *strūtian* to struggle — more at STRUT] (14c) *chiefly Scot* **:** CONTENTION

1stut·ter \ˈstə-tər\ *vb* [freq. of E dial. *stut* to stutter, fr. ME *stutten;* akin to D *stotteren* to stutter, Goth *stautan* to strike — more at CONTUSION] *vi* (1566) **1 :** to speak with involuntary disruption or blocking of speech (as by spasmodic repetition or prolongation of vocal sounds) **2 :** to move or act in a halting or spasmodic manner ⟨the old jalopy bucks and ~*s* uphill —William Cleary⟩ ~ *vt* **:** to say, speak, or sound with or as if with a stutter — **stut·ter·er** \-tər-ər\ *n*

2stutter *n* (1651) **1 :** an act or instance of stuttering **2 :** a speech disorder involving stuttering

stutter step *n* (1966) **:** a momentary hesitation or false step by a runner (as in football) done to fake a defender out of position — **stutter–step** *vb*

STV *abbr* subscription television

1sty \ˈstī\ *n, pl* **sties** *also* **styes** [ME, fr. OE *stig* pen; pigpen; akin to ON *svīnsti* pigpen] (bef. 12c) **:** PIGPEN

2sty *vb* **stied** *or* **styed; sty·ing** *vt* (bef. 12c) **:** to lodge or keep in a sty ~ *vi* **:** to live in a sty

3sty *or* **stye** \ˈstī\ *n, pl* **sties** *or* **styes** [short for obs. E *styan,* fr. ME *styanye* eye with a sty, fr. OE *stīgend* sty, fr. *stīgan* to go up, rise — more at STAIR] (1617) **:** an inflamed swelling of a sebaceous gland at the margin of an eyelid

sty·gian \ˈsti-j(ē-)ən\ *adj, often cap* [L *stygius,* fr. Gk *stygios,* fr. *Styg-, Styx* Styx] (1513) **1 :** of or relating to the river Styx **2 :** extremely dark, gloomy, or forbidding ⟨the ~ blackness of the cave⟩

styl- *or* **styli-** *or* **stylo-** *comb form* [L *stilus* spike, stem — more at STYLE] **:** style **:** styloid process ⟨*stylo*podium⟩ ⟨*stylo*graphy⟩

sty·lar \ˈstī-lər, -ˌlär\ *adj* [ˈ*style*] (ca. 1928) **:** of or relating to the style of a plant ovary

1style \ˈstī(-ə)l\ *n* [ME *stile, style,* fr. L *stilus* spike, stem, stylus, style of writing; perh. akin to L *instigare* to goad — more at STICK] (14c) **1 :** DESIGNATION, TITLE **2 a :** a distinctive manner of expression (as in writing or speech) ‹writes with more attention to ~ than to content› ‹the flowery ~ of 18th century prose› **b :** a distinctive manner or custom of behaving or conducting oneself ‹the formal ~ of the court› ‹his ~ is abrasive›; *also* **:** a particular mode of living ‹in high ~› **c :** a particular manner or technique by which something is done, created, or performed ‹a unique ~ of horseback riding› ‹the classical ~ of dance› **3 a :** STYLUS **b :** GNOMON 1b **c :** the filiform usu. elongated part of the pistil bearing a stigma at its apex — see FLOWER illustration **d :** a slender elongated process (as a bristle) on an animal **4 :** a distinctive quality, form, or type of something ‹a new dress ~› ‹the Greek ~ of architecture› **5 a :** the state of being popular **:** FASHION ‹clothes that are always in ~› **b :** fashionable elegance **c :** beauty, grace, or ease of manner or technique ‹an awkward moment she handled with ~› **6 :** a convention with respect to spelling, punctuation, capitalization, and typographic arrangement and display followed in writing or printing ***syn*** see FASHION — **style·less** \ˈstī(-ə)l-ləs\ *adj* — **style·less·ness** *n*

2**style** *vt* **styled; styl·ing** (ca. 1580) **1 :** to call or designate by an identifying term **:** NAME **2 a :** to give a particular style to **b :** to design, make, or arrange in accord with the prevailing mode — **styl·er** *n*

-style *adj or adv comb form* **:** being in the style of ‹a Beaujolais-*style* wine›

style·book *n* (1708) **:** a book explaining, describing, or illustrating a prevailing, accepted, or authorized style

sty·let \stī-ˈlet, ˈstī-lət\ *n* [F, fr. MF *stilet* stiletto, fr. OIt *stiletto* — more at STILETTO] (1697) **1 a :** a slender surgical probe **b :** a thin wire inserted into a catheter to maintain rigidity or into a hollow needle to maintain patency **c :** a pointed instrument (as for graving) **2 :** a relatively rigid elongated organ or appendage (as a piercing mouthpart) of an animal **3 :** STILETTO

sty·li·form \ˈstī-lə-ˌfȯrm\ *adj* [NL *stiliformis,* fr. L *stilus* + *-formis* -form] (1578) **:** resembling a style **:** bristle-shaped ‹a ~ copulatory organ›

styling *n* (1928) **:** the way in which something is styled

styl·ise *Brit var of* STYLIZE

styl·ish \ˈstī-lish\ *adj* (1785) **:** having style; *specif* **:** conforming to current fashion — **styl·ish·ly** *adv* — **styl·ish·ness** *n*

styl·ist \ˈstī-list\ *n* (1795) **1 a :** a master or model of style; *esp* **:** a writer or speaker who is eminent in matters of style **b :** a person (as a writer or singer) noted for a distinctive style **2 a :** a person who develops, designs, or advises on styles **b :** HAIRSTYLIST

sty·lis·tic \stī-ˈlis-tik\ *adj* (1860) **:** of or relating esp. to literary or artistic style — **sty·lis·ti·cal·ly** \-ti-k(ə-)lē\ *adv*

sty·lis·tics \stī-ˈlis-tiks\ *n pl but sing or pl in constr* (ca. 1883) **1 :** an aspect of literary study that emphasizes the analysis of various elements of style (as metaphor and diction) **2 :** the study of the devices in a language that produce expressive value

sty·lite \ˈstī-ˌlīt\ *n* [LGk *stylitēs,* fr. Gk *stylos* pillar — more at STEER] (ca. 1638) **:** a Christian ascetic living atop a pillar — **sty·lit·ic** \stī-ˈlitik\ *adj*

styl·ize \ˈstī(-ə)-ˌlīz\ *vt* **styl·ized; styl·iz·ing** (1898) **:** to conform to a conventional style; *specif* **:** to represent or design according to a style or stylistic pattern rather than according to nature or tradition — **styl·i·za·tion** \ˌstī-lə-ˈzā-shən\ *n*

sty·lo·bate \ˈstī-lə-ˌbāt\ *n* [L *stylobates,* fr. Gk, *stylobatēs,* fr. *stylos* pillar + *bainein* to walk, go — more at COME] (1694) **:** a continuous flat coping or pavement supporting a row of architectural columns

sty·log·ra·phy \stī-ˈlä-grə-fē\ *n* (ca. 1840) **:** a mode of writing or tracing lines by means of a style or similar instrument

sty·loid \ˈstī(-ə)-ˌlȯid\ *adj* (1709) **:** resembling a style **:** STYLIFORM — used esp. of slender pointed skeletal processes (as on the ulna)

sty·lus \ˈstī-ləs\ *n, pl* **sty·li** \ˈstī(-ə)-ˌlī\ *also* **sty·lus·es** \ˈstī-lə-səz\ [L *stylus, stilus* spike, stylus — more at STYLE] (1773) **:** an instrument for writing, marking, or incising: as **a :** an instrument used by the ancients in writing on clay or waxed tablets **b :** a hard-pointed pen-shaped instrument for marking on stencils used in a reproducing machine **c** (1) **:** NEEDLE 3c (2) **:** a cutting tool used to produce an original record groove during disc recording **d :** a pen-shaped pointing device used for entering data (as positional information from a graphics tablet) into a computer

sty·mie \ˈstī-mē\ *vt* **sty·mied; sty·mie·ing** [Sc *stimie, stymie* to obstruct a golf shot by interposition of the opponent's ball] (1902) **:** to present an obstacle to **:** stand in the way of ‹*stymied* by red tape›

styp·tic \ˈstip-tik\ *adj* [ME *stiptik,* fr. AF, fr. L *stypticus,* fr. Gk *styptikos,* fr. *styphein* to contract] (14c) **:** tending to contract or bind **:** ASTRINGENT; *esp* **:** tending to check bleeding — **styptic** *n*

styptic pencil *n* (1908) **:** a stick of a medicated styptic substance for use in shaving to stop the bleeding from small cuts

sty·rax \ˈstī-ˌraks\ *n* [L — more at STORAX] (1555) **:** STORAX

sty·rene \ˈstī-ˌrēn\ *n* [ISV, fr. L *styrax*] (1885) **:** a fragrant liquid unsaturated hydrocarbon C_8H_8 used chiefly in making synthetic rubber, resins, and plastics and in improving drying oils; *also* **:** any of various synthetic plastics made from styrene by polymerization or copolymerization

Sty·ro·foam \ˈstī-rə-ˌfōm\ *trademark* — used for an expanded rigid polystyrene plastic

Styx \ˈstiks\ *n* [L *Styg-, Styx,* fr. Gk] (14c) **:** the principal river of the underworld in Greek mythology

su·able \ˈsü-ə-bəl\ *adj* (ca. 1623) **:** liable to be sued in court — **su·abil·i·ty** \ˌsü-ə-ˈbi-lə-tē\ *n*

sua·sion \ˈswā-zhən\ *n* [ME, fr. L *suasion-, suasio,* fr. *suadēre* to urge, persuade — more at SWEET] (14c) **:** the act of influencing or persuading — **sua·sive** \ˈswā-siv, -ziv\ *adj* — **sua·sive·ly** *adv* — **sua·sive·ness** *n*

suave \ˈswäv\ *adj* **suav·er; -est** [F, fr. MF, pleasant, sweet, fr. L *suavis* — more at SWEET] (1831) **1 :** smoothly though often superficially gracious and sophisticated **2 :** smooth in texture, performance, or style — **suave·ly** *adv* — **suave·ness** *n* — **sua·vi·ty** \ˈswä-və-tē\ *n*

syn SUAVE, URBANE, DIPLOMATIC, BLAND, SMOOTH, POLITIC mean pleasantly tactful and well-mannered. SUAVE suggests a specific ability to deal with others easily and without friction ‹a *suave* public relations coordinator›. URBANE implies high cultivation and poise coming from wide social experience ‹an *urbane* traveler›. DIPLOMATIC stresses an ability to deal with ticklish situations tactfully ‹a *diplomatic* negotiator›. BLAND emphasizes mildness of manner and absence of irritating qualities ‹a *bland* master of ceremonies›. SMOOTH suggests often a deliberately assumed suavity ‹a *smooth* salesman›. POLITIC implies shrewd as well as tactful and suave handling of people ‹a cunningly *politic* manager›.

1**sub** \ˈsəb\ *n* (1830) **:** SUBSTITUTE

2**sub** *vb* **subbed; sub·bing** *vi* (1853) **:** to act as a substitute ~ *vt* **1** *Brit* **:** to read and edit as a copy editor **:** SUBEDIT **2 :** SUBCONTRACT 1

3**sub** *n* (1916) **:** SUBMARINE

4**sub** *abbr* **1** subaltern **2** subscription **3** subsidiary **4** suburb

sub- *prefix* [ME, fr. L, under, below, secretly, from below, near, fr. *sub* under, close to — more at UP] **1 :** under **:** beneath **:** below ‹*sub*soil› ‹*sub*aqueous› **2 a :** subordinate **:** secondary **:** next lower than or inferior to ‹*sub*station› ‹*sub*editor› **b :** subordinate portion of **:** subdivision of ‹*sub*committee› ‹*sub*species› **c :** with repetition (as of a process) so as to form, stress, or deal with subordinate parts or relations ‹*sub*let› ‹*sub*contract› **3 :** less than completely, perfectly, or normally **:** somewhat ‹*sub*acute› ‹*sub*clinical› **4 a :** almost **:** nearly ‹*sub*erect› **b :** falling nearly in the category of and often adjoining **:** bordering on ‹*sub*arctic›

sub·ad·o·les·cent
sub·agen·cy
sub·agent
sub·al·lo·ca·tion
sub·ar·ea
sub·au·di·ble
sub·av·er·age
sub·base·ment
sub·ba·sin
sub·block
sub·branch
sub·caste
sub·cat·e·go·ri·za·tion
sub·cat·e·go·rize
sub·cat·e·go·ry
sub·ceil·ing
sub·cel·lar
sub·chap·ter
sub·chief
sub·clan
sub·clus·ter
sub·code
sub·col·lec·tion
sub·col·lege
sub·col·le·giate
sub·col·o·ny
sub·com·mis·sion
sub·com·po·nent
sub·co·ri·a·ceous
sub·coun·ty
sub·cult
sub·cu·ra·tive
sub·dean
sub·de·ci·sion
sub·de·part·ment
sub·de·vel·op·ment
sub·di·a·lect
sub·di·rec·tor
sub·dis·ci·pline
sub·dis·trict
sub·econ·o·my
sub·fac·ul·ty
sub·file
sub·frag·ment
sub·frame
sub·gen·er·a·tion
sub·genre
sub·goal
sub·gov·ern·ment
sub·hu·mid
sub·in·dus·try
sub·in·hib·i·to·ry
sub·lan·guage
sub·lev·el
sub·li·brar·i·an
sub·li·cense
sub·lit·er·a·cy
sub·lit·er·ate
sub·lot
sub·man·ag·er
sub·mar·ket
sub·max·i·mal
sub·menu
sub·min·i·mal
sub·min·i·mum
sub·min·is·ter
sub·na·tion·al
sub·net·work
sub·niche
sub·op·ti·mal
sub·op·ti·mi·za·tion
sub·op·ti·mize
sub·op·ti·mum
sub·or·ga·ni·za·tion
sub·pan·el
sub·par
sub·para·graph
sub·par·al·lel
sub·part
sub·pe·ri·od
sub·phase
sub·pri·mate
sub·pro·cess
sub·prod·uct
sub·proj·ect
sub·pro·le·tar·i·at
sub·ra·tio·nal
sub·sat·u·rat·ed
sub·sat·u·ra·tion
sub·scale
sub·science
sub·sea
sub·sec·re·tary
sub·sec·tor
sub·seg·ment
sub·sense
sub·sen·tence
sub·se·ries
sub·site
sub·skill
sub·so·ci·ety
sub·spe·cial·ist
sub·spe·cial·ize
sub·spe·cial·ty
sub·state
sub·stel·lar
sub·sys·tem
sub·task
sub·test
sub·theme
sub·ther·a·peu·tic
sub·top·ic
sub·trea·sury
sub·trend
sub·tribe
sub·type
sub·unit
sub·va·ri·ety
sub·vas·sal
sub·vis·i·ble
sub·vi·su·al
sub·world
sub·writ·er
sub·ze·ro
sub·zone

sub·ac·id \ˌsəb-ˈa-səd\ *adj* [L *subacidus,* fr. *sub-* + *acidus* acid] (1760) **:** somewhat acrimonious **:** CUTTING ‹~ comments› — **sub·ac·id·ly** *adv* — **sub·ac·id·ness** *n*

sub·acute \-ə-ˈkyüt\ *adj* (1822) **1 :** having a tapered but not sharply pointed form ‹~ leaves› **2 a :** falling between acute and chronic in character esp. when closer to acute ‹~ endocarditis› **b :** less marked in severity or duration than a corresponding acute state ‹~ pain› — **sub·acute·ly** *adv*

subacute sclerosing pan·en·ceph·a·li·tis \-ˌpan-in-ˌse-fə-ˈlī-təs\ *n* [*panencephalitis* fr. NL, fr. *pan-* + *encephalitis*] (1950) **:** a usu. fatal neurological disease of children and young adults caused by infection of the brain by a previously latent measles virus that is marked esp. by intellectual deterioration, behavioral changes, myoclonic seizures, progressive deterioration of motor and mental functioning, and coma

sub·adult \ˌsəb-ə-ˈdəlt; ˌsəb-ˈa-ˌdəlt\ *n* (1903) **:** an individual that has passed through the juvenile period but not yet attained typical adult characteristics — **subadult** *adj*

sub·aer·i·al \-ˈer-ē-əl, -ā-ˈir-ē-əl\ *adj* (1833) **:** situated, formed, or occurring on or immediately adjacent to the surface of the earth ‹~ erosion› ‹~ roots› — **sub·aer·i·al·ly** \-ē-ə-lē\ *adv*

su·bah·dar *or* **su·ba·dar** \ˌsü-bə-ˈdär\ *n* [Hindi & Urdu *sūbadār, sūbedār,* fr. Pers *ṣūbadār,* fr. *ṣūba* province (fr. Ar) + *-dār* one holding] (1698) **1 :** a governor of a province **2 :** the chief Indian officer of a company of Indian troops in the British army of India

sub·al·pine \ˌsəb-ˈal-ˌpīn\ *adj* (ca. 1656) **1 :** of or relating to the region about the foot and lower slopes of the Alps **2 :** of, relating to, or inhabiting high upland slopes and esp. the zone just below the timberline

subalpine fir *n* (1898) **:** a medium-sized fir (*Abies lasiocarpa*) of subalpine regions of No. America having bluish-green white-lined needles

1**sub·al·tern** \sə-ˈbȯl-tərn, *esp Brit* ˈsə-bəl-tərn\ *adj* [LL *subalternus,* fr. L *sub-* + *alternus* alternate, fr. *alter* other (of two) — more at ALTER] (1570) **1 :** particular with reference to a related universal proposition ‹"some S is P" is a ~ proposition to "all S is P"› **2 :** SUBORDINATE

\ə\ abut \ᵊ\ kitten, F table \ər\ further \a\ ash \ā\ ace \ä\ mop, mar
\au̇\ out \ch\ chin \e\ bet \ē\ easy \g\ go \i\ hit \ī\ ice \j\ job
\ŋ\ sing \ō\ go \ȯ\ law \ȯi\ boy \th\ thin \t͟h\ the \ü\ loot \u̇\ foot
\y\ yet \zh\ vision, beige \k, ⁿ, œ, ue, ʸ\ *see* Guide to Pronunciation

[2]**subaltern** *n* (1605) **1 :** a person holding a subordinate position; *specif* **:** a junior officer (as in the British army) **2 :** a particular proposition that follows immediately from a universal
sub·ant·arc·tic \ˌsəb-ant-ˈärk-tik, -ˈär-tik\ *adj* (1875) **:** of, relating to, characteristic of, or being a region just outside the antarctic circle
sub·api·cal \-ˈā-pi-kəl *also* -ˈa-\ *adj* (1846) **:** situated below or near an apex
sub·aquat·ic \-ə-ˈkwä-tik, -ˈkwa-\ *adj* [ISV] (1844) **:** somewhat aquatic ⟨~ vegetation⟩
sub·aque·ous \-ˈā-kwē-əs, -ˈa-\ *adj* (1677) **:** existing, formed, or taking place in or under water
sub·arach·noid \-ə-ˈrak-ˌnȯid\ *also* **sub·arach·noid·al** \-rak-ˈnȯi-dᵊl\ *adj* (1843) **:** of, relating to, occurring, or situated under the arachnoid membrane ⟨~ hemorrhage⟩
sub·arc·tic \-ˈärk-tik, -ˈär-tik\ *adj* [ISV] (1854) **:** of, relating to, characteristic of, or being regions immediately outside of the arctic circle or regions similar to these in climate or conditions of life — **subarctic** *n*
sub·as·sem·bly \-ə-ˈsem-blē\ *n* (1919) **:** an assembled unit designed to be incorporated with other units in a finished product
sub·at·mo·spher·ic \-ˌat-mə-ˈsfir-ik, -ˈsfer-\ *adj* (1941) **:** less or lower than that of the atmosphere ⟨~ pressure⟩
sub·atom·ic \-ə-ˈtä-mik\ *adj* (1903) **1 :** of or relating to the inside of the atom **2 :** of, relating to, or being particles smaller than atoms
sub·au·di·tion \-ȯ-ˈdi-shən\ *n* [LL *subaudition-, subauditio*, fr. *subaudire* to understand, fr. L *sub-* + *audire* to hear — more at AUDIBLE] (1798) **:** the act of understanding or supplying something not expressed **:** a reading between the lines
sub·base \ˈsəb-ˌbās\ *n* (1826) **:** underlying support placed below what is normally construed as a base: as **a :** the lowest member horizontally of an architectural base or of a baseboard or pedestal **b :** pervious fill (as crushed stone) placed under a roadbed
sub·bi·tu·mi·nous \ˌsəb-bə-ˈtü-mə-nəs, -bī-, -ˈtyü-\ *adj* (1908) **:** of, relating to, or being coal of lower rank than bituminous coal but higher than lignite
sub·cab·i·net \-ˈkab-nit, -ˈka-bə-\ *adj* (1954) **:** of, relating to, or being a high administrative position in the U.S. government that ranks below the cabinet level
sub·cap·su·lar \-ˈkap-sə-lər\ *adj* (1889) **:** situated or occurring beneath or within a capsule ⟨~ cataracts⟩
sub·cel·lu·lar \-ˈsel-yə-lər\ *adj* (1948) **:** of less than cellular scope or level of organization ⟨~ organelles⟩ ⟨~ studies⟩
sub·cen·ter \-ˈsen-tər\ *n* (ca. 1925) **:** a secondary center; *esp* **:** a center (as for shopping) located outside the main business area of a city
sub·cen·tral \-trəl\ *adj* (1822) **1 :** nearly but not quite central **2 :** located under a center — **sub·cen·tral·ly** \-trə-lē\ *adv*
sub·chas·er \ˈsəb-ˌchā-sər\ *n* (ca. 1918) **:** a small maneuverable patrol or escort vessel used for antisubmarine warfare
sub·class \ˈsəb-ˌklas\ *n* (1819) **:** a primary division of a class: as **a :** a category in biological classification ranking below a class and above an order **b :** SUBSET 1
sub·clas·si·fi·ca·tion \ˌsəb-ˌkla-sə-fə-ˈkā-shən\ *n* (1873) **1 :** a primary division of a classification **2 :** arrangement into or assignment to subclassifications — **sub·clas·si·fy** \-ˈkla-sə-ˌfī\ *vt*
[1]**sub·cla·vi·an** \-ˈklā-vē-ən\ *adj* [NL *subclavius*, fr. *sub-* + *clavicula* clavicle] (1646) **:** of, relating to, being, or inserted into a part (as an artery, vein, or nerve) located under the clavicle ⟨~ catheter⟩
[2]**subclavian** *n* (1719) **:** a subclavian part (as an artery, vein, or nerve)
subclavian artery *n* (1688) **:** the proximal part of the main artery of the arm or forelimb
subclavian vein *n* (1704) **:** the proximal part of the main vein of the arm or forelimb
sub·cli·max \ˌsəb-ˈklī-ˌmaks\ *n* (1916) **:** a stage or community in an ecological succession immediately preceding a climax; *esp* **:** one held in relative stability throughout by edaphic or biotic influences or by fire
sub·clin·i·cal \-ˈkli-ni-kəl\ *adj* (ca. 1935) **:** not detectable or producing effects that are not detectable by the usual clinical tests ⟨a ~ infection⟩ ⟨~ cancer⟩ — **sub·clin·i·cal·ly** \-k(ə-)lē\ *adv*
sub·com·mit·tee \ˈsəb-kə-ˌmi-tē, ˌsəb-kə-ˈ\ *n* (ca. 1607) **:** a subdivision of a committee usu. organized for a specific purpose
sub·com·mu·ni·ty \ˌsəb-kə-ˈmyü-nə-tē\ *n* (1966) **:** a distinct grouping within a community
sub·com·pact \ˈsəb-ˈkäm-ˌpakt\ *n* (1967) **:** an automobile smaller than a compact
[1]**sub·con·scious** \ˌsəb-ˈkän(t)-shəs, ˈsəb-\ *adj* (ca. 1834) **:** existing in the mind but not immediately available to consciousness ⟨a ~ motive⟩ — **sub·con·scious·ly** *adv* — **sub·con·scious·ness** *n*
[2]**subconscious** *n* (1886) **:** the mental activities just below the threshold of consciousness
sub·con·ti·nent \ˌsəb-ˈkän-tə-nənt, -ˈkänt-nənt\ *n* (1863) **:** a large landmass smaller than a continent; *esp* **:** a major subdivision of a continent ⟨the Indian ~⟩ — **sub·con·ti·nen·tal** \ˌsəb-ˌkän-tə-ˈnen-tᵊl\ *adj*
[1]**sub·con·tract** \ˌsəb-ˈkän-ˌtrakt\ *n* (1817) **:** a contract between a party to an original contract and a third party; *esp* **:** one to provide all or a specified part of the work or materials required in the original contract
[2]**sub·con·tract** \ˌsəb-ˈkän-ˌtrakt, ˌsəb-kən-ˈ\ *vi* (1842) **:** to let out or undertake work under a subcontract ~ *vt* **1 :** to engage a third party to perform under a subcontract all or part of (work included in an original contract) — sometimes used with *out* **2 :** to undertake (work) under a subcontract
sub·con·trac·tor \ˌsəb-ˈkän-ˌtrak-tər, ˌsəb-kən-ˈ\ *n* (1834) **:** an individual or business firm contracting to perform part or all of another's contract
sub·con·trary \ˌsəb-ˈkän-ˌtrer-ē\ *n* (1685) **:** a proposition so related to another that though both may be true they cannot both be false — **subcontrary** *adj*
sub·cool \-ˈkül\ *vt* (1916) **:** SUPERCOOL
sub·cor·ti·cal \-ˈkȯr-ti-kəl\ *adj* (1899) **:** of, relating to, involving, or being a part of the brain below the cerebral cortex ⟨~ lesions⟩
sub·crit·i·cal \-ˈkri-ti-kəl\ *adj* (1930) **1 :** less or lower than critical in respect to a specified factor **2 a :** of insufficient size to sustain a chain reaction ⟨a ~ mass of fissionable material⟩ **b :** designed for use with fissionable material of subcritical mass ⟨a ~ reactor⟩
sub·crust·al \-ˈkrəs-tᵊl\ *adj* (1897) **:** situated or occurring below a crust and esp. the crust of the earth
sub·cul·ture \ˈsəb-ˌkəl-chər\ *n* (1886) **1 a :** a culture (as of bacteria) derived from another culture **b :** an act or instance of producing a subculture **2 :** an ethnic, regional, economic, or social group exhibiting characteristic patterns of behavior sufficient to distinguish it from others within an embracing culture or society ⟨a criminal ~⟩ — **sub·cul·tur·al** \-ˈkəlch-rəl, -ˈkəl-chə-\ *adj* — **sub·cul·tur·al·ly** *adv* — **subculture** *vt*
sub·cu·ta·ne·ous \ˌsəb-kyu̇-ˈtā-nē-əs\ *adj* [LL *subcutaneus*, fr. L *sub-* + *cutis* skin — more at HIDE] (1651) **:** being, living, occurring, or administered under the skin ⟨~ parasites⟩ ⟨~ tissues⟩ — **sub·cu·ta·ne·ous·ly** *adv*
sub·cu·tis \ˌsəb-ˈkyü-təs\ *n* [NL, fr. LL, beneath the skin, fr. L *sub-* + *cutis*] (1879) **:** the deeper part of the dermis
sub·dea·con \-ˈdē-kən\ *n* [ME *subdecon*, fr. AF *subdiakene*, fr. LL *subdiaconus*, fr. L *sub-* + LL *diaconus* deacon — more at DEACON] (14c) **:** a cleric ranking below a deacon: as **a :** a cleric in the lowest of the former major orders of the Roman Catholic Church **b :** an Eastern Orthodox or Armenian cleric in minor orders **c :** a clergyman performing the liturgical duties of a subdeacon
sub·deb \ˈsəb-ˌdeb\ *n* (1917) **:** SUBDEBUTANTE
sub·deb·u·tante \ˌsəb-ˈde-byu̇-ˌtänt\ *n* (1919) **:** a young girl who is about to become a debutante; *broadly* **:** a girl in her middle teens
sub·der·mal \-ˈdər-məl\ *adj* (1887) **:** SUBCUTANEOUS — **sub·der·mal·ly** \-mə-lē\ *adv*
sub·di·vide \ˌsəb-də-ˈvīd, ˈsəb-də-ˌ\ *vb* [ME, fr. LL *subdividere*, fr. L *sub-* + *dividere* to divide] *vt* (15c) **1 :** to divide the parts of into more parts **2 :** to divide into several parts; *esp* **:** to divide (a tract of land) into building lots ~ *vi* **:** to separate or become separated into subdivisions — **sub·di·vid·able** \-ˈvī-də-bəl, -ˌvī-\ *adj* — **sub·di·vid·er** *n*
sub·di·vi·sion \ˈsəb-də-ˌvi-zhən\ *n* (15c) **1 :** an act or instance of subdividing **2 :** something produced by subdividing: as **a :** a subordinate part of a larger whole ⟨political ~*s*⟩ **b :** a tract of land surveyed and divided into lots for purposes of sale; *esp* **:** one with houses built on it **3 :** a category in botanical classification ranking below a division and above a class
sub·dom·i·nant \ˌsəb-ˈdäm-nənt, -ˈdä-mə-\ *n* (1793) **1 :** the fourth tone of a major or minor scale **2 :** something partly but incompletely dominant; *esp* **:** an ecologically important life form subordinate in influence to the dominants of a community — **subdominant** *adj*
sub·duc·tion \(ˌ)səb-ˈdək-shən\ *n* [F, fr. LL *subduction-, subductio* withdrawal, fr. L *subducere* to withdraw, fr. *sub-* + *ducere* to draw — more at TOW] (1970) **:** the action or process in plate tectonics of the edge of one crustal plate descending below the edge of another — **sub·duct** \(ˌ)səb-ˈdəkt\ *vb*
sub·due \səb-ˈdü, -ˈdyü\ *vt* **sub·dued; sub·du·ing** [ME *sodewen, subduen*, fr. AF *soduire, subdure* to lead astray, overcome, arrest (influenced in form and meaning by L *subdere* to subject), fr. L *subducere* to withdraw, remove stealthily] (14c) **1 :** to conquer and bring into subjection **:** VANQUISH **2 :** to bring under control esp. by an exertion of the will **:** CURB ⟨*subdued* my foolish fears⟩ **3 :** to bring (land) under cultivation **4 :** to reduce the intensity or degree of **:** tone down ***syn*** see CONQUER — **sub·du·er** *n*
sub·dued \-ˈdüd, -ˈdyüd\ *adj* (1796) **:** lacking in vitality, intensity, or strength ⟨~ colors⟩ — **sub·dued·ly** \-ˈdü-(ə)d-lē, -ˈdyü-(ə)d-\ *adv*
sub·dur·al \ˌsəb-ˈdu̇r-əl, -ˈdyu̇r-; ˈsəb-ˌ\ *adj* [*sub-* + *dura (mater)*] (1875) **:** situated or occurring beneath the dura mater or between the dura mater and the arachnoid membrane ⟨~ space⟩ ⟨~ hematomas⟩
sub·dwarf \ˈsəb-ˌdwȯrf\ *n* (1939) **:** a small hot star containing few elements heavier than helium and having lower luminosity than a main-sequence star of similar temperature
sub·ed·i·tor \-ˈe-də-tər\ *n* (1819) *chiefly Brit* **:** COPY EDITOR — **sub·ed·it** \-ˈe-dət\ *vt, chiefly Brit* — **sub·ed·i·to·ri·al** \ˌsəb-ˌe-də-ˈtȯr-ē-əl\ *adj, chiefly Brit*
sub·em·ployed \ˌsəb-im-ˈplȯid\ *adj* (1967) **:** UNDEREMPLOYED
sub·em·ploy·ment \-ˈplȯi-mənt\ *n* (1967) **:** a condition of inadequate employment in a labor force including unemployment and underemployment
sub·en·try \ˈsəb-ˌen-trē\ *n* (1876) **:** an entry (as in a catalog or an account) made under a more general entry
sub·epi·der·mal \ˌsəb-ˌe-pə-ˈdər-məl\ *adj* (1853) **:** lying beneath or constituting the innermost part of the epidermis
su·ber·in \ˈsü-bə-rən\ *n* [F *subérine*, fr. L *suber* cork tree, cork] (1830) **:** a complex fatty substance found esp. in the cell walls of cork
su·ber·i·za·tion \ˌsü-bə-rə-ˈzā-shən\ *n* (1875) **:** conversion of the cell walls into corky tissue by infiltration with suberin — **su·ber·ized** \ˈsü-bə-ˌrīzd\ *adj*
sub·fam·i·ly \ˈsəb-ˌfam-lē, -ˌfa-mə-\ *n* [ISV] (1833) **1 :** a category in biological classification ranking below a family and above a genus **2 :** a subgroup of languages within a language family
sub·field \-ˌfēld\ *n* (1940) **1 :** a subset of a mathematical field that is itself a field **2 :** a subdivision of a field (as of study)
sub·floor \-ˌflȯr\ *n* (1858) **:** a rough floor laid as a base for a finished floor
sub·fos·sil \-ˌfä-səl\ *adj* [ISV] (1832) **:** of less than typical fossil age but partially fossilized ⟨~ bones⟩ — **subfossil** *n*
sub·freez·ing \-ˈfrē-ziŋ\ *adj* (1949) **:** being or marked by temperature below the freezing point (as of water) ⟨~ weather⟩
sub·fusc \(ˌ)səb-ˈfəsk, ˈsəb-ˌ\ *adj* [L *subfuscus* brownish, dusky, fr. *sub-* + *fuscus* dark brown — more at DUSK] (1710) *chiefly Brit* **:** DRAB, DUSKY
sub·ge·nus \ˈsəb-ˌjē-nəs\ *n* [NL] (1813) **:** a category in biological classification ranking below a genus and above a species
sub·gla·cial \ˌsəb-ˈglā-shəl\ *adj* (1820) **:** of or relating to the bottom of a glacier or the area immediately underlying a glacier — **sub·gla·cial·ly** \-shə-lē\ *adv*
sub·grade \ˈsəb-ˌgrād\ *n* (1893) **:** a surface of earth or rock leveled off to receive a foundation (as of a road)
sub·graph \ˈsəb-ˌgraf\ *n* (1931) **:** a graph all of whose points and lines are contained in a larger graph
sub·group \-ˌgrüp\ *n* (1845) **1 :** a subordinate group whose members usu. share some common differential quality **2 :** a subset of a mathematical group that is itself a group

sub·gum \ˈsəb-ˈgəm\ *n* [Chin (Guangdong) *sahp-gâm,* lit., assorted, mixed] (1911) : a dish of Chinese origin prepared with a mixture of vegetables (as peppers, water chestnuts, and mushrooms)
sub·head \-ˌhed\ *n* (1673) **1** : a heading of a subdivision (as in an outline) **2** : a subordinate caption, title, or headline
sub·head·ing \-ˌhe-diŋ\ *n* (1863) : SUBHEAD
[1]**sub·hu·man** \ˌsəb-ˈhyü-mən, -ˈyü-\ *adj* (1793) : less than human: as **a** : failing to attain the level (as of morality or intelligence) associated with normal human beings **b** : unsuitable to or unfit for human beings ⟨~ living conditions⟩ **c** : of or relating to a taxonomic group lower than that of humans ⟨the ~ primates⟩
[2]**subhuman** *n* (1937) : a subhuman being
sub·in·dex \ˌsəb-ˈin-ˌdeks\ *n* (1923) : an index to a division of a main classification
sub·in·feu·da·tion \ˌsəb-ˌin-fyü-ˈdā-shən\ *n* [*sub-* + *infeudation* enfeoffment] (ca. 1730) : the subdivision of a feudal estate by a vassal who in turn becomes feudal lord over his tenants — **sub·in·feu·date** *vt*
sub·in·ter·val \ˌsəb-ˈin-tər-vəl\ *n* (1927) : an interval that is a subdivision or a subset of an interval
sub·ir·ri·ga·tion \-ˌir-ə-ˈgā-shən\ *n* (1875) : irrigation below the surface (as by a periodic rise of the water table or by a system of underground porous pipes) — **sub·ir·ri·gate** \-ˈir-ə-ˌgāt\ *vt*
su·bi·to \ˈsü-bi-ˌtō\ *adv* [It, fr. L, suddenly, fr. *subitus* sudden — more at SUDDEN] (ca. 1724) : IMMEDIATELY, SUDDENLY — used as a direction in music
subj *abbr* subject
sub·ja·cen·cy \ˌsəb-ˈjā-sᵊn(t)-sē\ *n* (ca. 1891) : the quality or state of being subjacent
sub·ja·cent \-sᵊnt\ *adj* [L *subjacent-, subjacens,* prp. of *subjacēre* to lie under, fr. *sub-* + *jacēre* to lie — more at ADJACENT] (1592) : lying under or below; *also* : lower than though not directly below ⟨hills and ~ valleys⟩ — **sub·ja·cent·ly** *adv*
[1]**sub·ject** \ˈsəb-jikt, -(ˌ)jekt\ *n* [ME *suget, subget,* fr. AF, fr. L *subjectus* one under authority & *subjectum* subject of a proposition, fr. masc. & neut. respectively of *subjectus,* pp. of *subicere* to subject, lit., to throw under, fr. *sub-* + *jacere* to throw — more at JET] (14c) **1** : one that is placed under authority or control: as **a** : VASSAL **b** (1) : one subject to a monarch and governed by the monarch's law (2) : one who lives in the territory of, enjoys the protection of, and owes allegiance to a sovereign power or state **2 a** : that of which a quality, attribute, or relation may be affirmed or in which it may inhere **b** : SUBSTRATUM; *esp* : material or essential substance **c** : the mind, ego, or agent of whatever sort that sustains or assumes the form of thought or consciousness **3 a** : a department of knowledge or learning **b** : MOTIVE, CAUSE **c** (1) : one that is acted on ⟨the helpless ~ of their cruelty⟩ (2) : an individual whose reactions or responses are studied (3) : a dead body for anatomical study and dissection **d** (1) : something concerning which something is said or done ⟨the ~ of the essay⟩ (2) : something represented or indicated in a work of art **e** (1) : the term of a logical proposition that denotes the entity of which something is affirmed or denied; *also* : the entity denoted (2) : a word or word group denoting that of which something is predicated **f** : the principal melodic phrase on which a musical composition or movement is based *syn* see CITIZEN — **sub·ject·less** \-ləs\ *adj*
[2]**subject** *adj* (14c) **1** : owing obedience or allegiance to the power or dominion of another **2 a** : suffering a particular liability or exposure ⟨~ to temptation⟩ **b** : having a tendency or inclination : PRONE ⟨~ to colds⟩ **3** : contingent on or under the influence of some later action ⟨the plan is ~ to discussion⟩ *syn* see LIABLE
[3]**sub·ject** \səb-ˈjekt, ˈsəb-ˌjekt\ *vt* (14c) **1 a** : to bring under control or dominion : SUBJUGATE **b** : to make (as oneself) amenable to the discipline and control of a superior **2** : to make liable : PREDISPOSE **3** : to cause or force to undergo or endure (something unpleasant, inconvenient, or trying) ⟨was ~*ed* to constant verbal abuse⟩ — **sub·jec·tion** \səb-ˈjek-shən\ *n*
[1]**sub·jec·tive** \(ˌ)səb-ˈjek-tiv\ *adj* (15c) **1** : of, relating to, or constituting a subject: as **a** *obs* : of, relating to, or characteristic of one that is a subject esp. in lack of freedom of action or in submissiveness **b** : being or relating to a grammatical subject; *esp* : NOMINATIVE **2** : of or relating to the essential being of that which has substance, qualities, attributes, or relations **3 a** : characteristic of or belonging to reality as perceived rather than as independent of mind : PHENOMENAL — compare OBJECTIVE 1b **b** : relating to or being experience or knowledge as conditioned by personal mental characteristics or states **4 a** (1) : peculiar to a particular individual : PERSONAL ⟨~ judgments⟩ (2) : modified or affected by personal views, experience, or background ⟨a ~ account of the incident⟩ **b** : arising from conditions within the brain or sense organs and not directly caused by external stimuli ⟨~ sensations⟩ **c** : arising out of or identified by means of one's perception of one's own states and processes ⟨a ~ symptom of disease⟩ — compare OBJECTIVE 1c **5** : lacking in reality or substance : ILLUSORY — **sub·jec·tive·ly** *adv* — **sub·jec·tive·ness** *n* — **sub·jec·tiv·i·ty** \-ˌjek-ˈti-və-tē\ *n*
[2]**subjective** *n* (1817) : something that is subjective; *also* : NOMINATIVE
subjective complement *n* (1923) : a grammatical complement relating to the subject of an intransitive verb (as *sick* in "he had fallen sick")
sub·jec·tiv·ise *Brit var of* SUBJECTIVIZE
sub·jec·tiv·ism \(ˌ)səb-ˈjek-ti-ˌvi-zəm\ *n* (1856) **1 a** : a theory that limits knowledge to subjective experience **b** : a theory that stresses the subjective elements in experience **2 a** : a doctrine that the supreme good is the realization of a subjective experience or feeling (as pleasure) **b** : a doctrine that individual feeling or apprehension is the ultimate criterion of the good and the right — **sub·jec·tiv·ist** \-vist\ *n* — **sub·jec·tiv·is·tic** \-ˌjek-ti-ˈvis-tik\ *adj*
sub·jec·tiv·ize \-ti-ˌvīz\ *vt* **-ized; -iz·ing** (1868) : to make subjective — **sub·jec·tiv·i·za·tion** \-jek-ti-və-ˈzā-shən\ *n*
subject matter *n* (1657) : matter presented for consideration in discussion, thought, or study
sub·join \(ˌ)səb-ˈjȯin\ *vt* [MF *subjoindre,* fr. L *subjungere* to join beneath, add, fr. *sub-* + *jungere* to join — more at YOKE] (1573) : ANNEX, APPEND ⟨~*ed* a statement of expenses to her report⟩
sub ju·di·ce \ˌsu̇b-ˈyü-di-ˌkā, ˈsəb-ˈjü-də-(ˌ)sē\ *adv* [L] (1613) : before a judge or court : not yet judicially decided
sub·ju·gate \ˈsəb-ji-ˌgāt\ *vt* **-gat·ed; -gat·ing** [ME, fr. L *subjugatus,* pp. of *subjugare,* fr. *sub-* + *jugum* yoke — more at YOKE] (15c) **1** : to bring under control and governance as a subject : CONQUER **2** : to make submissive : SUBDUE — **sub·ju·ga·tion** \ˌsəb-ji-ˈgā-shən\ *n* — **sub·ju·ga·tor** \ˈsəb-ji-ˌgā-tər\ *n*
sub·junc·tion \(ˌ)səb-ˈjəŋ(k)-shən\ *n* (1633) **1** : an act of subjoining or the state of being subjoined **2** : something subjoined
[1]**sub·junc·tive** \səb-ˈjəŋ(k)-tiv\ *adj* [LL *subjunctivus,* fr. L *subjunctus,* pp. of *subjungere* to join beneath, subordinate] (1530) : of, relating to, or constituting a verb form or set of verb forms that represents a denoted act or state not as fact but as contingent or possible or viewed emotionally (as with doubt or desire) ⟨the ~ mood⟩
[2]**subjunctive** *n* (1622) **1** : the subjunctive mood of a language **2** : a form of verb or verbal in the subjunctive mood
sub·king·dom \ˈsəb-ˌkiŋ-dəm\ *n* (1825) : a category in biological classification ranking below a kingdom and above a phylum
sub·late \ˌsə-ˈblāt\ *vt* **sub·lat·ed; sub·lat·ing** [L *sublatus* (pp. of *tollere* to take away, lift up), fr. *sub-* up + *latus,* pp. of *ferre* to carry — more at SUB-, TOLERATE, BEAR] (1838) **1** : NEGATE, DENY **2** : to negate or eliminate (as an element in a dialectic process) but preserve as a partial element in a synthesis — **sub·la·tion** \-ˈblā-shən\ *n*
[1]**sub·lease** \ˈsəb-ˈlēs, -ˌlēs\ *n* (1826) : a lease by a tenant or lessee of part or all of leased premises to another person but with the original tenant retaining some right or interest under the original lease
[2]**sublease** *vt* (ca. 1843) : to make or obtain a sublease of
[1]**sub·let** \ˈsəb-ˈlet\ *vb* **-let; -let·ting** *vt* (1766) **1** : SUBLEASE **2** : SUBCONTRACT 1 ~ *vi* : to lease or rent all or part of a leased or rented property
[2]**sub·let** \-ˌlet\ *n* (1906) : property and esp. housing obtained by or available through a sublease
sub·le·thal \ˌsəb-ˈlē-thəl\ *adj* (1895) : less than but usu. only slightly less than lethal ⟨a ~ dose⟩ — **sub·le·thal·ly** \-thə-lē\ *adv*
sub·lieu·ten·ant \ˌsəb-lü-ˈte-nənt, *Brit* -le(f)-ˈten-\ *n* (1796) : a commissioned officer in the British navy ranking immediately below lieutenant
[1]**sub·li·mate** \ˈsə-blə-ˌmāt\ *vt* **-mat·ed; -mat·ing** [ME, fr. ML *sublimatus,* pp. of *sublimare*] (15c) **1 a** : SUBLIME 1 **b** *archaic* : to improve or refine as if by subliming **2** : to divert the expression of (an instinctual desire or impulse) from its unacceptable form to one that is considered more socially or culturally acceptable — **sub·li·ma·tion** \ˌsə-blə-ˈmā-shən\ *n*
[2]**sub·li·mate** \ˈsə-blə-ˌmāt, -mət\ *n* (ca. 1626) : a chemical product obtained by sublimation
[1]**sub·lime** \sə-ˈblīm\ *vb* **sub·limed; sub·lim·ing** [ME, fr. MF *sublimer,* fr. ML *sublimare* to refine, sublime, fr. L, to elevate, fr. *sublimis*] *vt* (14c) **1** : to cause to pass directly from the solid to the vapor state and condense back to solid form **2** [F *sublimer,* fr. L *sublimare*] **a** (1) : to elevate or exalt esp. in dignity or honor (2) : to render finer (as in purity or excellence) **b** : to convert (something inferior) into something of higher worth ~ *vi* : to pass directly from the solid to the vapor state — **sub·lim·able** \-ˈblī-mə-bəl\ *adj* — **sub·lim·er** *n*
[2]**sublime** *adj* **sub·lim·er; -est** [L *sublimis,* lit., high, elevated] (ca. 1567) **1 a** : lofty, grand, or exalted in thought, expression, or manner **b** : of outstanding spiritual, intellectual, or moral worth **c** : tending to inspire awe usu. because of elevated quality (as of beauty, nobility, or grandeur) or transcendent excellence **2 a** *archaic* : high in place **b** *obs* : lofty of mien : HAUGHTY **c** *cap* : SUPREME — used in a style of address **d** : COMPLETE, UTTER ⟨~ ignorance⟩ *syn* see SPLENDID — **sub·lime·ly** *adv* — **sub·lime·ness** *n*
sub·lim·i·nal \(ˌ)sə-ˈbli-mə-nᵊl\ *adj* [*sub-* + L *limin-, limen* threshold] (1886) **1** : inadequate to produce a sensation or a perception **2** : existing or functioning below the threshold of consciousness ⟨the ~ mind⟩ ⟨~ advertising⟩ — **sub·lim·i·nal·ly** *adv*
sub·lim·i·ty \sə-ˈbli-mə-tē\ *n, pl* **-ties** (15c) **1** : the quality or state of being sublime **2** : something sublime or exalted
sub·line \ˈsəb-ˌlīn\ *n* (1942) : an inbred or selectively cultured line (as of cells) within a strain
sub·lin·gual \ˌsəb-ˈliŋ-gwəl, -gyə-wəl\ *adj* [NL *sublingualis,* fr. L *sub-* + *lingua* tongue — more at TONGUE] (1661) : situated or administered under the tongue ⟨~ glands⟩ ⟨~ tablets⟩
sub·lit·er·ary \-ˈli-tə-ˌrer-ē\ *adj* (1936) : relating to or being subliterature
sub·lit·er·a·ture \-ˈli-tə-rə-ˌchu̇r, -ˈli-trə-ˌchu̇r, -ˈli-tə(r)-ˌchu̇r, -chər, -ˌtyu̇r, -ˌtu̇r\ *n* (1952) : popular writing (as mystery or adventure stories) considered inferior to standard literature
[1]**sub·lit·to·ral** \-ˈli-tə-rəl; ˌsəb-ˌli-tə-ˈral, -ˈräl\ *adj* (1846) **1** : situated, occurring, or formed on the aquatic side of a shoreline or littoral zone **2** : constituting the sublittoral
[2]**sublittoral** *n* (ca. 1935) : the deeper part of the littoral portion of a body of water; *esp* : the region in an ocean between the lowest point exposed by a low tide and the margin of the continental shelf
sub·lu·na·ry \ˌsəb-ˈlü-nə-rē, ˈsəb-lu̇-ˌner-ē\ *also* **sub·lu·nar** \ˌsəb-ˈlü-nər *also* -ˌnär\ *adj* [modif. of LL *sublunaris,* fr. L *sub-* + *luna* moon — more at LUNAR] (1592) : of, relating to, or characteristic of the terrestrial world ⟨dull ~ lovers —John Donne⟩
sub·lux·a·tion \ˌsə-ˌblək-ˈsā-shən\ *n* (1674) : partial dislocation (as of one of the bones in a joint)
sub·ma·chine gun \ˌsəb-mə-ˈshēn-ˌgən\ *n* (1920) : a portable automatic firearm that uses pistol-type ammunition and is fired from the shoulder or hip
[1]**sub·man·dib·u·lar** \ˌsəb-man-ˈdi-byə-lər\ *adj* (1875) **1** : of, relating to, situated in, or performed in the region below the lower jaw **2** : of, relating to, or associated with the salivary glands inside of and near the lower edge of the mandible on each side
[2]**submandibular** *n* (1974) : a submandibular part (as an artery or bone)
sub·mar·gin·al \ˌsəb-ˈmärj-nəl, -ˈmär-jə-nᵊl\ *adj* (1829) **1** : adjacent to a margin or a marginal part or structure ⟨~ spots on an insect wing⟩ **2** : falling below a necessary minimum ⟨~ economic conditions⟩

\ə\ **abut** \ᵊ\ kitten, F table \ər\ **further** \a\ **ash** \ā\ **ace** \ä\ **mop, mar**
\au̇\ **out** \ch\ **chin** \e\ **bet** \ē\ **easy** \g\ **go** \i\ **hit** \ī\ **ice** \j\ **job**
\ŋ\ **sing** \ō\ **go** \ȯ\ **law** \ȯi\ **boy** \th\ **thin** \t͟h\ **the** \ü\ **loot** \u̇\ **foot**
\y\ **yet** \zh\ **vision, beige** \k̲, ⁿ, œ, ue, ʸ\ *see* Guide to Pronunciation

[1]**sub·ma·rine** \ˈsəb-mə-ˌrēn, ˌsəb-mə-ˈ\ *adj* (1648) : UNDERWATER; *esp* : UNDERSEA ⟨~ plants⟩ ⟨~ minerals⟩

[2]**submarine** *n* (1703) **1** : something that functions or operates underwater; *specif* : a naval vessel designed to operate underwater **2** : a large sandwich on a long split roll with any of a variety of fillings (as meatballs or cold cuts, cheese, lettuce, and tomato) — called also *grinder, hero, hoagie, Italian sandwich, po'boy, sub, torpedo*

[3]**submarine** *vb* **-rined; -rin·ing** *vt* (1914) : to attack by or as if by a submarine : attack from beneath ~ *vi* : to dive or slide under something

sub·ma·ri·ner \ˌsəb-mə-ˈrē-nər, -ˈma-rə-nər\ *n* (1914) : a member of a submarine crew

sub·max·il·lary \ˌsəb-ˈmak-sə-ˌler-ē, ˈsəb-, *chiefly Brit* ˌsəb-mak-ˈsi-lə-rē\ *adj or n* (1787) : SUBMANDIBULAR

sub·me·di·ant \ˌsəb-ˈmē-dē-ənt\ *n* (1806) : the sixth tone of a major or minor scale

sub·merge \səb-ˈmərj\ *vb* **sub·merged; sub·merg·ing** [L *submergere*, fr. *sub-* + *mergere* to plunge — more at MERGE] *vt* (1606) **1** : to put under water **2** : to cover or overflow with water **3** : to make obscure or subordinate : SUPPRESS ⟨personal lives *submerged* by professional responsibilities⟩ ~ *vi* : to go under water — **sub·mer·gence** \-ˈmər-jən(t)s\ *n* — **sub·merg·ible** \-ˈmər-jə-bəl\ *adj*

submerged *adj* (1799) **1** : covered with water **2** : SUBMERSED b **3** : sunk in poverty and misery **4** : HIDDEN, SUPPRESSED ⟨~ emotions⟩

sub·merse \səb-ˈmərs\ *vt* **sub·mersed; sub·mers·ing** [L *submersus*, pp. of *submergere*] (1837) : SUBMERGE — **sub·mer·sion** \-ˈmər-zhən, -shən\ *n*

submersed *adj* (ca. 1727) : SUBMERGED: as **a** : covered with water **b** : growing or adapted to grow underwater ⟨~ weeds⟩

[1]**sub·mers·ible** \səb-ˈmər-sə-bəl\ *adj* (1866) : capable of being submerged

[2]**submersible** *n* (1900) : something that is submersible; *esp* : a usu. small underwater craft used esp. for deep-sea research

sub·meta·cen·tric \ˌsəb-ˌme-tə-ˈsen-trik\ *adj* (1962) : having the centromere situated so that one chromosome arm is somewhat shorter than the other — **submetacentric** *n*

sub·mi·cro·gram \ˌsəb-ˈmī-krə-ˌgram\ *adj* (1946) : relating to or having a mass of less than one microgram ⟨~ quantities of a chemical⟩

sub·mi·cron \-ˌkrän\ *adj* (1948) **1** : being less than a micron in a (specified) measurement and esp. in diameter ⟨a ~ particle⟩ **2** : having or consisting of submicron particles ⟨a ~ metal powder⟩

sub·mi·cro·scop·ic \ˌsəb-ˌmī-krə-ˈskä-pik\ *adj* [ISV] (1905) **1** : too small to be seen in an ordinary light microscope **2** : of, relating to, or dealing with the very minute ⟨the ~ world⟩ — **sub·mi·cro·scop·i·cal·ly** \-pi-k(ə-)lē\ *adv*

sub·mil·li·me·ter \ˌsəb-ˈmi-lə-ˌmē-tər\ *adj* (1955) : being less than a millimeter in diameter or wavelength ⟨a ~ particle⟩ ⟨a ~ radio wave⟩

sub·min·i·a·ture \ˌsəb-ˈmi-nē-ə-ˌchu̇r, -ˈmi-ni-ˌchu̇r, -ˈmin-yə-, -chər, -ˌtyu̇r, -ˌtu̇r\ *adj* [ISV] (1947) : very small — used esp. of a very compact assembly of electronic equipment

sub·miss \səb-ˈmis\ *adj* [L *submissus*, fr. pp. of *submittere*] (1570) *archaic* : SUBMISSIVE, HUMBLE

sub·mis·sion \səb-ˈmi-shən\ *n* [ME, fr. AF, fr. L *submission-, submissio* act of lowering, fr. *submittere*] (14c) **1 a** : a legal agreement to submit to the decision of arbitrators **b** : an act of submitting something (as for consideration or inspection); *also* : something submitted (as a manuscript) **2** : the condition of being submissive, humble, or compliant **3** : an act of submitting to the authority or control of another

sub·mis·sive \-ˈmi-siv\ *adj* (1575) : submitting to others ⟨~ employees⟩ — **sub·mis·sive·ly** *adv* — **sub·mis·sive·ness** *n*

sub·mit \səb-ˈmit\ *vb* **sub·mit·ted; sub·mit·ting** [ME *submitten*, fr. L *submittere* to lower, submit, fr. *sub-* + *mittere* to send] *vt* (14c) **1 a** : to yield to governance or authority **b** : to subject to a condition, treatment, or operation ⟨the metal was *submitted* to analysis⟩ **2** : to present or propose to another for review, consideration, or decision; *also* : to deliver formally ⟨*submitted* my resignation⟩ **3** : to put forward as an opinion or contention ⟨we ~ that the charge is not proved⟩ ~ *vi* **1 a** : to yield oneself to the authority or will of another : SURRENDER **b** : to permit oneself to be subjected to something ⟨had to ~ to surgery⟩ **2** : to defer to or consent to abide by the opinion or authority of another ***syn*** see YIELD — **sub·mit·tal** \-ˈmi-tᵊl\ *n*

sub·mi·to·chon·dri·al \ˌsəb-ˌmī-tə-ˈkän-drē-əl\ *adj* (1963) : relating to, composed of, or being parts and esp. fragments of mitochondria ⟨~ membranes⟩ ⟨~ particles⟩

sub·mu·co·sa \ˌsəb-myü-ˈkō-zə\ *n* [NL] (1885) : a supporting layer of loose connective tissue directly under a mucous membrane — **sub·mu·co·sal** \-zəl\ *adj*

sub·mul·ti·ple \-ˈməl-tə-pəl\ *n* (1758) : an exact divisor of a number ⟨8 is a ~ of 72⟩

sub·mu·ni·tion \(ˌ)səb-myü-ˈni-shən\ *n* (1975) : any of a group of smaller weapons carried as a warhead by a missile or projectile and expelled as the carrier approaches its target

sub·nor·mal \-ˈnȯr-məl\ *adj* [ISV] (ca. 1890) **1** : lower or smaller than normal **2** : having less of something and esp. of intelligence than is normal — **sub·nor·mal·i·ty** \ˌsəb-nȯr-ˈma-lə-tē\ *n* — **sub·nor·mal·ly** \ˌsəb-ˈnȯr-mə-lē\ *adv*

sub·note·book \ˈsəb-ˈnōt-ˌbu̇k\ *n* (1990) : a portable microcomputer similar to but smaller and lighter than a notebook computer

sub·nu·cle·ar \ˌsəb-ˈnü-klē-ər, -ˈnyü-, ÷-kyə-lər\ *adj* (1937) : of, relating to, or being a particle smaller than the atomic nucleus

sub·oce·an·ic \ˌsəb-ˌō-shē-ˈa-nik\ *adj* (1858) : situated, taking place, or formed beneath the ocean or its bottom ⟨~ oil resources⟩

sub·or·bit·al \ˌsəb-ˈȯr-bə-tᵊl\ *adj* (ca. 1827) **1** : situated beneath the eye or the orbit of the eye **2** : being or involving less than one orbit (as of the earth or moon); *also* : intended for suborbital flight

sub·or·der \ˈsəb-ˌȯr-dər\ *n* (1826) : a subdivision of an order ⟨a soil ~⟩; *esp* : a taxonomic category ranking between an order and a family

[1]**sub·or·di·nate** \sə-ˈbȯr-də-nət, -ˈbȯrd-nət\ *adj* [ME *subordinat*, fr. ML *subordinatus*, pp. of *subordinare* to subordinate, fr. L *sub-* + *ordinare* to order — more at ORDAIN] (15c) **1** : placed in or occupying a lower class, rank, or position : INFERIOR ⟨a ~ officer⟩ **2** : submissive to or controlled by authority **3 a** : of, relating to, or constituting a clause that functions as a noun, adjective, or adverb **b** : SUBORDINATING — **sub·or·di·nate·ly** *adv* — **sub·or·di·nate·ness** *n*

[2]**subordinate** *n* (1640) : one that is subordinate

[3]**sub·or·di·nate** \sə-ˈbȯr-də-ˌnāt\ *vt* **-nat·ed; -nat·ing** [ML *subordinatus*] (1597) **1** : to make subject or subservient **2** : to treat as of less value or importance — **sub·or·di·na·tion** \-ˌbȯr-də-ˈnā-shən\ *n* — **sub·or·di·na·tive** \-ˈbȯr-də-ˌnā-tiv\ *adj*

subordinating *adj* (1857) : introducing and linking a subordinate clause to a main clause ⟨~ conjunction⟩

sub·or·di·na·tor \-ˌnā-tər\ *n* (1959) : one that subordinates; *esp* : a subordinating conjunction

sub·orn \sə-ˈbȯrn\ *vt* [MF *suborner*, fr. L *subornare*, fr. *sub-* secretly + *ornare* to furnish, equip — more at ORNATE] (1534) **1** : to induce secretly to do an unlawful thing **2** : to induce to commit perjury; *also* : to obtain (perjured testimony) from a witness — **sub·or·na·tion** \ˌsə-ˌbȯr-ˈnā-shən\ *n* — **sub·orn·er** *n*

sub·phy·lum \ˈsəb-ˌfī-ləm\ *n* [NL] (1888) : a category in biological classification ranking below a phylum and above a class

sub·plot \ˈsəb-ˌplät\ *n* (1830) **1** : a subordinate plot in fiction or drama **2** : a subdivision of an experimental plot of land

[1]**sub·poe·na** \sə-ˈpē-nə, ÷-nē\ *n* [ME *suppena*, fr. L *sub poena* under penalty] (15c) : a writ commanding a person designated in it to appear in court under a penalty for failure

[2]**subpoena** *vt* **-naed; -na·ing** (1640) : to serve or summon with a writ of subpoena

subpoena ad tes·ti·fi·can·dum \-ˌad-ˌtes-tə-fi-ˈkan-dəm\ *n* [NL, under penalty to give testimony] (ca. 1769) : a writ commanding a person to appear in court to testify as a witness

subpoena du·ces te·cum \-ˌdü-səs ˈtē-kəm\ *n* [NL, under penalty you shall bring with you] (1768) : a writ commanding a person to produce in court certain designated documents or evidence

sub·po·lar \ˌsəb-ˈpō-lər\ *adj* (1826) **1** : SUBARCTIC **2** : SUBANTARCTIC

sub·pop·u·la·tion \ˈsəb-ˌpä-pyə-ˈlā-shən\ *n* (1944) : an identifiable fraction or subdivision of a population

sub·po·tent \ˌsəb-ˈpō-tᵊnt\ *adj* (ca. 1909) : less potent than normal ⟨~ drugs⟩ — **sub·po·ten·cy** \-ˈpō-tᵊn(t)-sē\ *n*

sub·prime \ˈsəb-ˌprīm\ *adj* (1995) **1** : having or being an interest rate that is higher than a prime rate and is extended esp. to low-income borrowers ⟨~ mortgages⟩ **2** : extending or obtaining a subprime loan ⟨~ lenders⟩ ⟨~ borrowers⟩

sub·prin·ci·pal \-ˈprin(t)-s(ə-)pəl, -sə-bəl\ *n* (1597) **1** : an assistant principal (as of a school) **2** : a secondary or bracing rafter

sub·prob·lem \ˈsəb-ˌprä-bləm\ *n* (1906) : a problem that is contingent on or forms a part of another more inclusive problem

sub·pro·fes·sion·al \ˌsəb-prə-ˈfesh-nəl, -ˈfe-shə-nᵊl\ *adj* (1941) : functioning or qualified to function below the professional level but distinctly above the clerical or labor level and usu. under the supervision of a professionally trained person — **subprofessional** *n*

sub·pro·gram \ˈsəb-ˌprō-ˌgram, -grəm\ *n* (1947) : a semi-independent portion of a program (as for a computer)

sub·re·gion \ˈsəb-ˌrē-jən\ *n* [ISV] (1864) **1** : a subdivision of a region **2** : one of the primary divisions of a biogeographic region — **sub·re·gion·al** \-ˌrēj-nəl, -ˌrē-jə-nᵊl\ *adj*

sub·rep·tion \(ˌ)səb-ˈrep-shən\ *n* [LL *subreption-, subreptio*, fr. L, act of stealing, fr. *subripere, surripere* to take away secretly — more at SURREPTITIOUS] (1600) : a deliberate misrepresentation; *also* : an inference drawn from it — **sub·rep·ti·tious** \ˌsəb-ˌrep-ˈti-shəs\ *adj* — **sub·rep·ti·tious·ly** *adv*

sub·ring \ˈsəb-ˌriŋ\ *n* (1937) : a subset of a mathematical ring which is itself a ring

sub·ro·gate \ˈsə-brō-ˌgāt\ *vt* **-gat·ed; -gat·ing** [ME, fr. L *subrogatus*, pp. of *subrogare, surrogare* — more at SURROGATE] (15c) : to put in the place of another; *esp* : to substitute (as a second creditor) for another with regard to a legal right or claim

sub·ro·ga·tion \ˌsə-brō-ˈgā-shən\ *n* (15c) : the act of subrogating; *specif* : the assumption by a third party (as a second creditor or an insurance company) of another's legal right to collect a debt or damages

sub–rosa *adj* (1904) : SECRETIVE, PRIVATE

sub ro·sa \ˌsəb-ˈrō-zə\ *adv* [NL, lit., under the rose; fr. the ancient association of the rose with secrecy] (1654) : in confidence : SECRETLY

sub·rou·tine \ˈsəb-(ˌ)rü-ˌtēn\ *n* [ISV] (1948) : a subordinate routine; *specif* : a sequence of computer instructions for performing a specified task that can be used repeatedly

sub–Sa·ha·ran \ˌsəb-sə-ˈher-ən, -ˈhär-\ *adj* (1955) : of, relating to, or being the part of Africa south of the Sahara

[1]**sub·sam·ple** \ˈsəb-ˌsam-pəl, ˌsəb-ˈsam-\ *vt* (ca. 1899) : to draw samples from (a previously selected group or population) : sample a sample of

[2]**subsample** *n* (ca. 1899) : a sample or specimen obtained by subsampling

sub·sat·el·lite \ˌsəb-ˈsa-tə-ˌlīt\ *n* (1894) : an object carried into orbit in and subsequently released from a satellite or spacecraft

sub·scribe \səb-ˈskrīb\ *vb* **sub·scribed; sub·scrib·ing** [ME, fr. L *subscribere*, lit., to write beneath, fr. *sub-* + *scribere* to write — more at SCRIBE] *vt* (15c) **1** : to write (one's name) underneath : SIGN **2 a** : to sign (as a document) with one's own hand in token of consent or obligation **b** : to attest by signing **c** : to pledge (a gift or contribution) by writing one's name with the amount **3** : to assent to : SUPPORT ~ *vi* **1** : to sign one's name to a document **2 a** : to give consent or approval to something written by signing ⟨unwilling to ~ to the agreement⟩ **b** : to set one's name to a paper in token of promise to give something (as a sum of money); *also* : to give something in accordance with such a promise **c** : to enter one's name for a publication or service; *also* : to receive a periodical or service regularly on order ⟨*subscribed* to many magazines⟩ **d** : to agree to purchase and pay for securities esp. of a new offering ⟨*subscribed* for 1000 shares⟩ **3** : to feel favorably disposed ⟨I ~ to your sentiments⟩ ***syn*** see ASSENT — **sub·scrib·er** *n*

sub·script \ˈsəb-ˌskript\ *n* [L *subscriptus*, pp. of *subscribere*] (1901) : a distinguishing symbol (as a letter or numeral) written immediately below or below and to the right or left of another character — **subscript** *adj*

sub·scrip·tion \səb-ˈskrip-shən\ *n* [ME *subscripcion* mark at the end of a document, concluding formula, fr. AF, fr. L *subscription-, subscriptio*, fr. *subscribere*] (15c) **1 a** : the act of signing one's name (as in attesting or witnessing a document) **b** : the acceptance (as of ecclesiastical articles of faith) attested by the signing of one's name **2** : something that is subscribed: as **a** : an autograph signature; *also* : a paper to which a signature is attached **b** : a sum subscribed or pledged **3** : an arrangement for providing, receiving, or making use of something of a continuing or periodic nature on a prepayment plan: as **a** : a purchase by prepayment for a certain number of issues (as of a periodical) **b** : application to purchase securities of a new issue **c** : a method of offering or presenting a series of public performances **d** *Brit* : membership dues

subscription TV *n* (1953) : pay-TV that broadcasts programs directly over the air to customers provided with a special receiver — called also *subscription television;* compare PAY-CABLE, PAY-TV

sub·sec·tion \ˈsəb-ˌsek-shən\ *n* (1621) **1** : a subdivision or a subordinate division of a section **2** : a subordinate part or branch

[1]**sub·se·quence** \ˈsəb-sə-ˌkwen(t)s, -si-kwən(t)s\ *n* (ca. 1500) : the quality or state of being subsequent; *also* : a subsequent event

[2]**sub·se·quence** \ˈsəb-ˌsē-kwən(t)s, -ˌkwen(t)s\ *n* (1908) : a mathematical sequence that is part of another sequence

sub·se·quent \ˈsəb-si-kwənt, -sə-ˌkwent\ *adj* [ME, fr. AF, fr. L *subsequent-, subsequens,* prp. of *subsequi* to follow close, fr. *sub-* near + *sequi* to follow — more at SUB-, SUE] (15c) : following in time, order, or place ⟨~ events⟩ ⟨a ~ clause in the treaty⟩ — **subsequent** *n* — **sub·se·quent·ly** \-ˌkwent-lē, -kwənt-\ *adv*

subsequent to *prep* (1621) : at a time later or more recent than : SINCE ⟨*subsequent to* our discussion⟩

sub·serve \(ˌ)səb-ˈsərv\ *vt* [L *subservire* to serve, be subservient, fr. *sub-* + *servire* to serve] (1661) **1** : to promote the welfare or purposes of **2** : to serve as an instrument or means in carrying out

sub·ser·vi·ence \səb-ˈsər-vē-ən(t)s\ *n* (ca. 1676) **1** : a subservient or subordinate place or function **2** : obsequious servility

sub·ser·vi·en·cy \-ən(t)-sē\ *n* (1651) : SUBSERVIENCE

sub·ser·vi·ent \-ənt\ *adj* [L *subservient-, subserviens,* prp. of *subservire*] (ca. 1626) **1** : useful in an inferior capacity : SUBORDINATE **2** : serving to promote some end **3** : obsequiously submissive : TRUCKLING — **sub·ser·vi·ent·ly** *adv*

syn SUBSERVIENT, SERVILE, SLAVISH, OBSEQUIOUS mean showing or characterized by extreme compliance or abject obedience. SUBSERVIENT implies the cringing manner of one very conscious of a subordinate position ⟨domestic help was expected to be properly *subservient*⟩. SERVILE suggests the mean or fawning behavior of a slave ⟨a political boss and his entourage of *servile* hangers-on⟩. SLAVISH suggests abject or debased servility ⟨the *slavish* status of migrant farm workers⟩. OBSEQUIOUS implies fawning or sycophantic compliance and exaggerated deference of manner ⟨waiters who are *obsequious* in the presence of celebrities⟩.

sub·set \ˈsəb-ˌset\ *n* (1902) **1** : a set each of whose elements is an element of an inclusive set **2** : DIVISION, PORTION ⟨a ~ of our community⟩

sub·shrub \-ˌshrəb, *esp Southern* -ˌsrəb\ *n* (1851) : a perennial plant having woody stems except for the terminal part of the new growth which is killed back annually; *also* : a low shrub

sub·side \səb-ˈsīd\ *vi* **sub·sid·ed; sub·sid·ing** [L *subsidere,* fr. *sub-* + *sidere* to sit down, sink; akin to L *sedēre* to sit — more at SIT] (1607) **1** : to sink or fall to the bottom : SETTLE **2** : to tend downward : DESCEND; *esp* : to flatten out so as to form a depression **3** : to let oneself settle down : SINK ⟨*subsided* into a chair⟩ **4** : to become quiet or less ⟨as the fever ~*s*⟩ ⟨my anger *subsided*⟩ ***syn*** see ABATE — **sub·si·dence** \səb-ˈsī-dᵊn(t)s, ˈsəb-sə-dən(t)s\ *n*

sub·sid·i·ar·i·ty \ˌsəb-si-dē-ˈer-ə-tē, səb-ˌsi-\ *n* (1936) **1** : the quality or state of being subsidiary **2** : a principle in social organization: functions which subordinate or local organizations perform effectively belong more properly to them than to a dominant central organization

[1]**sub·sid·i·ary** \səb-ˈsi-dē-ˌer-ē, -ˈsi-də-rē\ *adj* [L *subsidiarius,* fr. *subsidium* reserve troops] (1543) **1 a** : furnishing aid or support : AUXILIARY ⟨~ details⟩ **b** : of secondary importance ⟨a ~ stream⟩ **2** : of, relating to, or constituting a subsidy ⟨a ~ payment to an ally⟩ — **sub·sid·i·ari·ly** \-ˌsi-dē-ˈer-ə-lē\ *adv*

[2]**subsidiary** *n, pl* **-ar·ies** (1603) : one that is subsidiary; *esp* : a company wholly controlled by another

sub·si·dise *Brit var of* SUBSIDIZE

sub·si·dize \ˈsəb-sə-ˌdīz, -zə-\ *vt* **-dized; -diz·ing** (1769) : to furnish with a subsidy: as **a** : to purchase the assistance of by payment of a subsidy **b** : to aid or promote (as a private enterprise) with public money ⟨~ soybean farmers⟩ ⟨~ public transportation⟩ — **sub·si·di·za·tion** \ˌsəb-sə-də-ˈzā-shən, -zə-\ *n* — **sub·si·diz·er** *n*

sub·si·dy \ˈsəb-sə-dē, -zə-\ *n, pl* **-dies** [ME *subsidie,* fr. AF, fr. L *subsidium* reserve troops, support, assistance, fr. *sub-* near + *sedēre* to sit — more at SUB-, SIT] (14c) : a grant or gift of money: as **a** : a sum of money formerly granted by the British Parliament to the crown and raised by special taxation **b** : money granted by one state to another **c** : a grant by a government to a private person or company to assist an enterprise deemed advantageous to the public

sub·sist \səb-ˈsist\ *vb* [LL *subsistere* to exist, fr. L, to come to a halt, remain, fr. *sub-* + *sistere* to come to a stand; akin to L *stare* to stand — more at STAND] *vi* (1549) **1 a** : to have existence : BE **b** : PERSIST, CONTINUE **2** : to have or acquire the necessities of life (as food and clothing); *esp* : to nourish oneself ⟨~*ing* on roots, berries and grubs⟩ **3 a** : to hold true **b** : to be logically conceivable as the subject of true statements ~ *vt* : to support with provisions

sub·sis·tence \səb-ˈsis-tən(t)s\ *n* [ME, fr. LL *subsistentia,* fr. *subsistent-, subsistens,* prp. of *subsistere*] (15c) **1 a (1)** : real being : EXISTENCE **(2)** : the condition of remaining in existence : CONTINUATION, PERSISTENCE **b** : an essential characteristic quality of something that exists **c** : the character possessed by whatever is logically conceivable **2** : means of subsisting: as **a** : the minimum (as of food and shelter) necessary to support life **b** : a source or means of obtaining the necessities of life — **sub·sis·tent** \-tənt\ *adj*

subsistence farming *n* (1938) **1** : farming or a system of farming that provides all or almost all the goods required by the farm family usu. without any significant surplus for sale **2** : farming or a system of farming that produces a minimum and often inadequate return to the farmer — called also *subsistence agriculture* — **subsistence farmer** *n*

sub·so·cial \ˌsəb-ˈsō-shəl\ *adj* (ca. 1909) : incompletely social; *esp* : tending to associate gregariously but lacking fixed or complex social organization ⟨~ insects⟩

[1]**sub·soil** \ˈsəb-ˌsȯi(-ə)l\ *n* (1796) : the stratum of weathered material that underlies the surface soil

[2]**subsoil** *vt* (1840) : to turn, break, or stir the subsoil of — **sub·soil·er** *n*

sub·so·lar point \ˌsəb-ˈsō-lər-\ *n* (ca. 1908) : the point on the surface of the earth or a planet at which the sun is at the zenith

sub·son·ic \ˌsəb-ˈsä-nik\ *adj* [ISV] (1937) **1** : of, relating to, or being a speed less than that of sound in air **2** : moving, capable of moving, or utilizing air currents moving at a subsonic speed **3** : INFRASONIC 1 — **sub·son·i·cal·ly** \-ni-k(ə-)lē\ *adv*

sub·space \ˈsəb-ˌspās\ *n* (1926) : a subset of a space; *esp* : one that has the essential properties (as those of a vector space or topological space) of the including space

sub spe·cie ae·ter·ni·ta·tis \su̇b-ˈspe-kē-ˌā-ˌī-ˌter-nə-ˈtä-təs\ *adv* [NL, lit., under the aspect of eternity] (1895) : in its essential or universal form or nature

sub·spe·cies \ˈsəb-ˌspē-shēz, -sēz\ *n* [NL] (1699) : a subdivision of a species: as **a** : a category in biological classification that ranks immediately below a species and designates a population of a particular geographic region genetically distinguishable from other such populations of the same species and capable of interbreeding successfully with them where its range overlaps theirs **b** : a named subdivision (as a race or variety) of a taxonomic species **c** : SUBGROUP 1 ⟨a political ~⟩ — **sub·spe·cif·ic** \ˌsəb-spi-ˈsi-fik\ *adj*

sub·stage \ˈsəb-ˌstāj\ *n* (1888) : an attachment to a microscope by means of which accessories (as mirrors, diaphragms, or condensers) are held in place beneath the stage of the instrument

sub·stance \ˈsəb-stən(t)s\ *n* [ME, fr. AF, fr. L *substantia,* fr. *substant-, substans,* prp. of *substare* to stand under, fr. *sub-* + *stare* to stand — more at STAND] (14c) **1 a** : essential nature : ESSENCE **b** : a fundamental or characteristic part or quality **c** *Christian Science* : GOD 1b **2 a** : ultimate reality that underlies all outward manifestations and change **b** : practical importance : MEANING, USEFULNESS ⟨the . . . bill—which will be without ~ in the sense that it will authorize nothing more than a set of ideas —Richard Reeves⟩ **3 a** : physical material from which something is made or which has discrete existence **b** : matter of particular or definite chemical constitution **c** : something (as drugs or alcoholic beverages) deemed harmful and usu. subject to legal restriction ⟨possession of a controlled ~⟩ ⟨~ abuse⟩ **4** : material possessions : PROPERTY ⟨a family of ~⟩ — **sub·stance·less** \-ləs\ *adj* — **in substance** : in respect to essentials : FUNDAMENTALLY

substance P *n* (1934) : a neuropeptide that consists of 11 amino acid residues, that is present in the nervous system and gastrointestinal tract, that causes the contraction of smooth muscle and dilation of blood vessels, and that acts as a potent neurotransmitter esp. in the transmission of signals from pain receptors

sub·stan·dard \ˌsəb-ˈstan-dərd\ *adj* (1897) : deviating from or falling short of a standard or norm: as **a** : of a quality lower than that prescribed by law ⟨~ housing⟩ **b** : conforming to a pattern of linguistic usage existing within a speech community but not that of the prestige group in that community **c** : constituting a greater than normal risk to an insurer

sub·stan·tial \səb-ˈstan(t)-shəl\ *adj* (14c) **1 a** : consisting of or relating to substance **b** : not imaginary or illusory : REAL, TRUE **c** : IMPORTANT, ESSENTIAL **2** : ample to satisfy and nourish : FULL ⟨a ~ meal⟩ **3 a** : possessed of means : WELL-TO-DO **b** : considerable in quantity : significantly great ⟨earned a ~ wage⟩ **4** : firmly constructed : STURDY ⟨a ~ house⟩ **5** : being largely but not wholly that which is specified ⟨a ~ lie⟩ — **substantial** *n* — **sub·stan·ti·al·i·ty** \-ˌstan(t)-shē-ˈa-lə-tē\ *n* — **sub·stan·tial·ly** \-ˈstan(t)-sh(ə-)lē\ *adv* — **sub·stan·tial·ness** \-ˈstan(t)-shəl-nəs\ *n*

sub·stan·tia ni·gra \səb-ˌstan(t)-shē-ə-ˈnī-grə, -ˈni-\ *n, pl* **sub·stan·ti·ae ni·grae** \-chē-ˌē-ˈnī-(ˌ)grē, -ˈni-\ [NL, lit., black substance] (ca. 1882) : a layer of deeply pigmented gray matter situated in the midbrain and containing the cell bodies of a tract of dopamine-producing nerve cells whose secretion tends to be deficient in Parkinson's disease

sub·stan·ti·ate \səb-ˈstan(t)-shē-ˌāt\ *vt* **-at·ed; -at·ing** (1657) **1** : to give substance or form to : EMBODY **2** : to establish by proof or competent evidence : VERIFY ⟨~ a charge⟩ ***syn*** see CONFIRM — **sub·stan·ti·a·tion** \-ˌstan(t)-shē-ˈā-shən\ *n* — **sub·stan·ti·a·tive** \-ˈstan(t)-shē-ˌā-tiv\ *adj*

sub·stan·ti·val \ˌsəb-stən-ˈtī-vəl\ *adj* (ca. 1832) : of, relating to, or serving as a substantive — **sub·stan·ti·val·ly** \-və-lē\ *adv*

[1]**sub·stan·tive** \ˈsəb-stən-tiv\ *n* [ME *substantif,* fr. AF *sustentif,* fr. *sustentif,* adj., having or expressing substance, fr. LL *substantivus,* fr. L *substantia*] (14c) : NOUN; *broadly* : a word or word group functioning syntactically as a noun — **sub·stan·tiv·ize** \-ti-ˌvīz\ *vt*

[2]**sub·stan·tive** \ˈsəb-stən-tiv; *2c & 3 also* səb-ˈstan-tiv\ *adj* [ME, fr. AF *sustentif*] (14c) **1** : being a totally independent entity **2 a** : real rather than apparent : FIRM ⟨need ~ evidence to prove her guilt⟩; *also* : PERMANENT, ENDURING **b** : belonging to the substance of a thing : ESSENTIAL **c** : expressing existence ⟨the ~ verb is the verb *to be*⟩ **d** : requiring or involving no mordant ⟨a ~ dyeing process⟩ **3 a** : having the nature or function of a grammatical substantive ⟨a ~ phrase⟩ **b** : relating to or having the character of a noun or pronominal term in logic **4** : considerable in amount or numbers : SUBSTANTIAL ⟨made ~ progress⟩ **5** : creating and defining rights and duties ⟨~ law⟩ — compare PROCEDURAL **6** : having substance : involving matters of major or practical importance to all concerned ⟨~ discussions among world leaders⟩ — **sub·stan·tive·ly** *adv* — **sub·stan·tive·ness** *n*

substantive due process *n* (1954) : DUE PROCESS 2

substantive right *n* (1939) : a right (as of life, liberty, property, or reputation) held to exist for its own sake and to constitute part of the normal legal order of society

sub·sta·tion \ˈsəb-ˌstā-shən\ *n* (1881) : a subordinate or subsidiary station: as **a** : a branch post office **b** : a subsidiary station in which

\ə\ **abut** \ᵊ\ **kitten**, F **table** \ər\ **further** \a\ **ash** \ā\ **ace** \ä\ **mop, mar**
\au̇\ **out** \ch\ **chin** \e\ **bet** \ē\ **easy** \g\ **go** \i\ **hit** \ī\ **ice** \j\ **job**
\ŋ\ **sing** \ō\ **go** \ȯ\ **law** \ȯi\ **boy** \th\ **thin** \t͟h\ **the** \ü\ **loot** \u̇\ **foot**
\y\ **yet** \zh\ **vision, beige** \k̲, ⁿ, œ, ue, ʸ\ *see* Guide to Pronunciation

electric current is transformed **c :** a police station serving a particular area

sub·stit·u·ent \səb-ˈsti-chə-wənt, -ˈstich-wənt\ *n* [L *substituent-, substituens,* prp. of *substituere*] (ca. 1896) **:** an atom or group that replaces another atom or group in a molecule — **substituent** *adj*

sub·sti·tut·able \ˈsəb-stə-ˌtü-tə-bəl, -ˈtyü-\ *adj* (1805) **:** capable of being substituted — **sub·sti·tut·abil·i·ty** \ˌsəb-stə-ˌtü-tə-ˈbi-lə-tē, -ˌtyü-\ *n*

1**sub·sti·tute** \ˈsəb-stə-ˌtüt, -ˌtyüt\ *n* [ME, fr. AF *substitut,* fr. L *substitutus,* pp. of *substituere* to put in place of, fr. *sub-* + *statuere* to set up, place — more at STATUTE] (15c) **:** a person or thing that takes the place or function of another — **substitute** *adj*

2**substitute** *vb* **-tut·ed; -tut·ing** *vt* (ca. 1594) **1 a :** to put or use in the place of another **b :** to introduce (an atom or group) as a substituent; *also* **:** to alter (as a compound) by introduction of a substituent ⟨a *substituted* benzene ring⟩ **2 :** to take the place of **:** REPLACE ~ *vi* **:** to serve as a substitute

sub·sti·tu·tion \ˌsəb-stə-ˈtü-shən, -ˈtyü-\ *n* [ME *substitucion,* fr. MF, fr. LL *substitution-, substitutio,* fr. *substituere*] (14c) **1 a :** the act, process, or result of substituting one thing for another **b :** replacement of one mathematical entity by another of equal value **2 :** one that is substituted for another — **sub·sti·tu·tion·al** \-shnəl, -shə-nᵊl\ *adj* — **sub·sti·tu·tion·al·ly** *adv* — **sub·sti·tu·tion·ary** \-shə-ˌner-ē\ *adj*

substitution cipher *n* (1936) **:** a cipher in which the letters of the plaintext are systematically replaced by substitute letters — compare TRANSPOSITION CIPHER

sub·sti·tu·tive \ˈsəb-stə-ˌtü-tiv, -ˌtyü-\ *adj* (1668) **:** serving or suitable as a substitute — **sub·sti·tu·tive·ly** *adv*

sub·strate \ˈsəb-ˌstrāt\ *n* [ML *substratum*] (1807) **1 :** SUBSTRATUM **2 :** the base on which an organism lives ⟨the soil is the ~ of most seed plants⟩ **3 :** a substance acted upon (as by an enzyme)

sub·stra·tum \ˈsəb-ˌstrā-təm, -ˌstra-, ˌsəb-ˈ\ *n, pl* **-stra·ta** \-tə\ [ML, fr. L, neut. of *substratus,* pp. of *substernere* to spread under, fr. *sub-* + *sternere* to spread — more at STREW] (1631) **:** an underlying support **:** FOUNDATION: as **a :** substance that is a permanent subject of qualities or phenomena **b :** the material of which something is made and from which it derives its special qualities **c :** a layer beneath the surface soil; *specif* **:** SUBSOIL **d :** SUBSTRATE 2

sub·struc·ture \ˈsəb-ˌstrək-chər\ *n* (1726) **:** an underlying or supporting part of a structure — **sub·struc·tur·al** \-chə-rəl, -shrəl\ *adj*

sub·sume \səb-ˈsüm\ *vt* **sub·sumed; sub·sum·ing** [NL *subsumere,* fr. L *sub-* + *sumere* to take up — more at CONSUME] (1825) **:** to include or place within something larger or more comprehensive **:** encompass as a subordinate or component element ⟨red, green, and yellow are *subsumed* under the term "color"⟩ — **sub·sum·able** \-ˈsü-mə-bəl\ *adj*

sub·sump·tion \səb-ˈsəm(p)-shən\ *n* [NL *subsumption-, subsumptio,* fr. *subsumere*] (1652) **:** the act or process of subsuming

1**sub·sur·face** \ˈsəb-ˌsər-fəs\ *n* (1778) **:** earth material (as rock) near but not exposed at the surface of the ground

2**sub·sur·face** \ˌsəb-ˈsər-fəs\ *adj* (1875) **:** of, relating to, or being something located beneath a surface and esp. underground

sub·teen \ˈsəb-ˈtēn\ *n* (1951) **:** a preadolescent child

sub·tem·per·ate \ˌsəb-ˈtem-p(ə-)rət\ *adj* (1852) **:** of or occurring in the colder parts of the temperate zones

sub·ten·an·cy \-ˈte-nən(t)-sē\ *n* (ca. 1861) **:** the state of being a subtenant

sub·ten·ant \-ˈte-nənt\ *n* (15c) **:** one who rents from a tenant

sub·tend \səb-ˈtend\ *vt* [L *subtendere* to stretch beneath, fr. *sub-* + *tendere* to stretch — more at THIN] (1570) **1 a :** to be opposite to and extend from one side to the other of ⟨a hypotenuse ~*s* a right angle⟩ **b :** to fix the angular extent of with respect to a fixed point or object taken as the vertex ⟨a central angle ~*ed* by an arc⟩ ⟨the angle ~*ed* at the eye by an object of given width and a fixed distance away⟩ **c :** to determine the measure of by marking off the endpoints of ⟨a chord ~*s* an arc⟩ **2 a :** to underlie so as to include **b :** to occupy an adjacent and usu. lower position to and often so as to embrace or enclose ⟨a bract that ~*s* a flower⟩

sub·ter·fuge \ˈsəb-tər-ˌfyüj\ *n* [LL *subterfugium,* fr. L *subterfugere* to escape, evade, fr. *subter-* secretly (fr. *subter* underneath; akin to L *sub* under) + *fugere* to flee — more at UP, FUGITIVE] (1573) **1 :** deception by artifice or stratagem in order to conceal, escape, or evade **2 :** a deceptive device or stratagem ***syn*** see DECEPTION

sub·ter·mi·nal \ˌsəb-ˈtərm-nəl, -ˈtər-mə-nᵊl\ *adj* (1828) **:** situated or occurring near but not precisely at an end ⟨~ spots on tail feathers⟩

sub·ter·ra·nean \ˌsəb-tə-ˈrā-nē-ən, -nyən\ *also* **sub·ter·ra·neous** \-nē-əs, -nyəs\ *adj* [L *subterraneus,* fr. *sub-* + *terra* earth — more at THIRST] (1603) **1 :** being, lying, or operating under the surface of the earth **2 :** existing or working in secret **:** HIDDEN ⟨a ~ network of criminals⟩ — **sub·ter·ra·nean·ly** *also* **sub·ter·ra·neous·ly** *adv*

sub·text \ˈsəb-ˌtekst\ *n* (1950) **:** the implicit or metaphorical meaning (as of a literary text) — **sub·tex·tu·al** \ˌsəb-ˈteks-chə-wəl, -chəl\ *adj* — **sub·tex·tu·al·ly** *adv*

sub·thresh·old \ˌsəb-ˈthre-ˌshōld, -ˈthresh-ˌhōld\ *adj* (1942) **:** inadequate to produce a response ⟨~ dosage⟩ ⟨a ~ stimulus⟩

sub·tile \ˈsə-tᵊl, ˈsəb-tᵊl\ *adj* **sub·til·er** \ˈsət-lər, ˈsə-tᵊl-ər; ˈsəb-tə-lər\; **sub·til·est** \ˈsət-ləst, ˈsə-tᵊl-əst; ˈsəb-tə-ləst\ [ME *subtile, sotil* subtle] (14c) **1 :** SUBTLE, ELUSIVE ⟨a ~ aroma⟩ **2 a :** CUNNING, CRAFTY **b :** SAGACIOUS, DISCERNING — **sub·tile·ly** \ˈsət-lē, ˈsə-tᵊl-(l)ē; ˈsəb-tə-lē\ *adv* — **sub·tile·ness** \ˈsə-tᵊl-nəs, ˈsəb-tᵊl-\ *n*

sub·til·i·sin \ˌsəb-ˈti-lə-sən\ *n* [NL *subtilis,* specific epithet of *Bacillus subtilis,* species to which *Bacillus amyloliquefaciens* was once thought to belong] (1953) **:** a protease secreted by a soil bacillus (*Bacillus amyloliquefaciens*)

sub·til·ize \ˈsə-tᵊl-ˌīz, ˈsəb-tə-ˌlīz\ *vb* **-ized; -iz·ing** *vi* (1592) **:** to act or think subtly ~ *vt* **:** to make subtile — **sub·til·i·za·tion** \ˌsə-tᵊl-ə-ˈzā-shən, ˌsəb-tə-lə-\ *n*

sub·til·ty \ˈsə-tᵊl-tē, ˈsəb-tᵊl-\ *n, pl* **-ties** (14c) **:** SUBTLETY

1**sub·ti·tle** \ˈsəb-ˌtī-tᵊl\ *n* (1825) **1 :** a secondary or explanatory title **2 :** a printed statement or fragment of dialogue appearing on the screen between the scenes of a silent motion picture or appearing as a translation at the bottom of the screen during the scenes of a motion picture or television show in a foreign language

2**subtitle** *vt* (1891) **:** to give a subtitle to

sub·tle \ˈsə-tᵊl\ *adj* **sub·tler** \ˈsət-lər, ˈsə-tᵊl-ər\; **sub·tlest** \ˈsət-ləst, ˈsə-tᵊl-əst\ [ME *sotil, subtile,* fr. AF, fr. L *subtilis,* lit., finely textured, fr. *sub-* + *tela* cloth on a loom; akin to L *texere* to weave — more at TECHNICAL] (14c) **1 a :** DELICATE, ELUSIVE ⟨a ~ fragrance⟩ **b :** difficult to understand or perceive **:** OBSCURE ⟨~ differences in sound⟩ **2 a :** PERCEPTIVE, REFINED ⟨a writer's sharp and ~ moral sense⟩ **b :** having or marked by keen insight and ability to penetrate deeply and thoroughly ⟨a ~ scholar⟩ **3 a :** highly skillful **:** EXPERT ⟨a ~ craftsman⟩ **b :** cunningly made or contrived **:** INGENIOUS **4 :** ARTFUL, CRAFTY ⟨a ~ rogue⟩ **5 :** operating insidiously ⟨~ poisons⟩ — **sub·tle·ness** \ˈsə-tᵊl-nəs\ *n* — **sub·tly** \ˈsət-lē, ˈsə-tᵊl-(l)ē\ *adv*

sub·tle·ty \ˈsə-tᵊl-tē\ *n, pl* **-ties** [ME *sotilte, subtilte,* fr. AF *sotilté,* fr. L *subtilitat-, subtilitas,* fr. *subtilis*] (14c) **1 :** the quality or state of being subtle **2 :** something subtle

sub·ton·ic \ˌsəb-ˈtä-nik\ *n* [fr. its being a half tone below the upper tonic] (ca. 1854) **:** LEADING TONE

1**sub·to·tal** \ˈsəb-ˌtō-tᵊl\ *n* (1906) **:** the sum of part of a series of figures

2**sub·to·tal** \ˌsəb-ˈtō-tᵊl\ *adj* (1908) **:** somewhat less than complete **:** nearly total ⟨~ thyroidectomy⟩ — **sub·to·tal·ly** *adv*

sub·tract \səb-ˈtrakt\ *vb* [L *subtractus,* pp. of *subtrahere* to draw from beneath, withdraw, fr. *sub-* + *trahere* to draw] *vt* (1557) **:** to take away by or as if by deducting ⟨~ 5 from 9⟩ ⟨~ funds from the project⟩ ~ *vi* **:** to perform a subtraction — **sub·tract·er** *n*

sub·trac·tion \səb-ˈtrak-shən\ *n* [ME *subtraccion,* fr. AF *sustraction, subtraction,* fr. LL *subtraction-, subtractio,* fr. L *subtrahere*] (15c) **:** an act, operation, or instance of subtracting: as **a :** the withdrawing or withholding of a right to which an individual is entitled **b :** the operation of deducting one number from another

sub·trac·tive \-ˈtrak-tiv\ *adj* (1690) **1 :** tending to subtract **2 :** constituting or involving subtraction

sub·tra·hend \ˈsəb-trə-ˌhend\ *n* [L *subtrahendus,* gerundive of *subtrahere*] (1674) **:** a number that is to be subtracted from a minuend

sub·trop·i·cal \ˌsəb-ˈträ-pi-kəl\ *also* **sub·trop·ic** \-pik\ *adj* [ISV] (1842) **:** of, relating to, or being the regions bordering on the tropical zone ⟨~ environment⟩ ⟨~ grasses⟩

sub·trop·ics \-piks\ *n pl* (1886) **:** subtropical regions

su·bu·late \ˈsü-byə-lət, ˈsə-, -ˌlāt\ *adj* [NL *subulatus,* fr. L *subula* awl, fr. *suere* to sew — more at SEW] (1748) **:** linear and tapering to a fine point ⟨a ~ leaf⟩

sub·um·brel·la \ˌsəb-(ˌ)əm-ˈbre-lə\ *n* (1878) **:** the concave undersurface of a jellyfish

sub·urb \ˈsə-ˌbərb\ *n* [ME *suburbe,* fr. AF, fr. L *suburbium,* fr. *sub-* near + *urbs* city — more at SUB-] (14c) **1 a :** an outlying part of a city or town **b :** a smaller community adjacent to or within commuting distance of a city **c** *pl* **:** the residential area on the outskirts of a city or large town **2** *pl* **:** the near vicinity **:** ENVIRONS — **sub·ur·ban** \sə-ˈbər-bən\ *adj or n* — **sub·ur·ban·ite** \-bə-ˌnīt\ *n*

sub·ur·ban·ise *Brit var of* SUBURBANIZE

sub·ur·ban·ize \sə-ˈbər-bə-ˌnīz\ *vt* **-ized; -iz·ing** (1893) **:** to make suburban **:** give a suburban character to — **sub·ur·ban·i·za·tion** \-ˌbər-bə-nə-ˈzā-shən\ *n*

sub·ur·bia \sə-ˈbər-bē-ə\ *n* [NL, fr. E *suburb*] (1895) **1 :** the suburbs of a city **2 :** people who live in the suburbs **3 :** suburban life

sub·ven·tion \səb-ˈven(t)-shən\ *n* [ME *subvencion,* fr. MF & LL; MF *subvención,* fr. LL *subvention-, subventio* assistance, fr. L *subvenire* to come up, come to the rescue, fr. *sub-* up + *venire* to come — more at SUB-, COME] (15c) **:** the provision of assistance or financial support: as **a :** ENDOWMENT **b :** a subsidy from a government or foundation — **sub·ven·tion·ary** \-shə-ˌner-ē\ *adj*

sub·ver·sion \səb-ˈvər-zhən, -shən\ *n* [ME, fr. AF, fr. LL *subversion-, subversio,* fr. L *subvertere*] (14c) **1 :** the act of subverting **:** the state of being subverted; *esp* **:** a systematic attempt to overthrow or undermine a government or political system by persons working secretly from within **2** *obs* **:** a cause of overthrow or destruction — **sub·ver·sion·ary** \-zhə-ˌner-ē, -shə-\ *adj* — **sub·ver·sive** \-ˈvər-siv, -ziv\ *adj or n* — **sub·ver·sive·ly** *adv* — **sub·ver·sive·ness** *n*

sub·vert \səb-ˈvərt\ *vt* [ME, fr. AF *subvertir,* fr. L *subvertere,* lit., to turn from beneath, fr. *sub-* + *vertere* to turn — more at WORTH] (14c) **1 :** to overturn or overthrow from the foundation **:** RUIN **2 :** to pervert or corrupt by an undermining of morals, allegiance, or faith — **sub·vert·er** *n*

sub·vi·ral \ˌsəb-ˈvī-rəl\ *adj* (1963) **:** relating to, being, or caused by a piece or a structural part (as a protein) of a virus ⟨~ infection⟩

sub·vo·cal \-ˈvō-kəl\ *adj* (1924) **:** characterized by the occurrence in the mind of words in speech order with or without inaudible articulation of the speech organs — **sub·vo·cal·ly** \-kə-lē\ *adv*

sub·vo·cal·i·za·tion \ˌsəb-ˌvō-kə-lə-ˈzā-shən\ *n* (1947) **:** the act or process of inaudibly articulating speech with the speech organs — **sub·vo·cal·ize** \ˌsəb-ˈvō-kə-ˌlīz\ *vb*

sub·way \ˈsəb-ˌwā\ *n* (1825) **:** an underground way: as **a :** a passage under a street (as for pedestrians, power cables, or water or gas mains) **b :** a usu. electric underground railway **c :** UNDERPASS — **subway** *vi*

sub·woof·er \ˈsəb-ˈwu̇-fər\ *n* (1978) **:** a loudspeaker responsive only to the lowest acoustic frequencies

suc·ce·da·ne·um \ˌsək-sə-ˈdā-nē-əm\ *n, pl* **-ne·ums** *or* **-nea** \-nē-ə\ [NL, fr. L, neut. of *succedaneus* substituted, fr. *succedere* to follow after] (1641) **:** SUBSTITUTE — **suc·ce·da·ne·ous** \-nē-əs\ *adj*

suc·ce·dent \sək-ˈsē-dᵊnt\ *adj* [ME, fr. L *succedent-, succedens,* prp. of *succedere*] (15c) **:** coming next **:** SUCCEEDING, SUBSEQUENT

suc·ceed \sək-ˈsēd\ *vb* [ME *succeden,* fr. AF *succeeder,* fr. L *succedere* to go up, follow after, succeed, fr. *sub-* near + *cedere* to go — more at SUB-] *vi* (14c) **1 a :** to come next after another in office or position or in possession of an estate; *esp* **:** to inherit sovereignty, rank, or title **b :** to follow after another in order **2 a :** to turn out well **b :** to attain a desired object or end ⟨students who ~ in college⟩ **3** *obs* **:** to pass to a person by inheritance ~ *vt* **1 :** to follow in sequence and esp. immediately **2 :** to come after as heir or successor ***syn*** see FOLLOW — **suc·ceed·er** *n*

suc·cès de scan·dale \sək-ˌsā-də-skäⁿ-ˈdäl, (ˌ)sük-\ *n* [F, lit., success of scandal] (1896) **:** something (as a work of art) that wins popularity or notoriety because of its scandalous nature; *also* **:** the reception accorded such a piece

suc·cès d'es·time \-ˌdes-ˈtēm\ *n* [F, lit., success of esteem] (1859) **:** something (as a work of art) that wins critical respect but not popular success; *also* **:** the reception accorded such a piece

suc·cès fou \-ˈfü\ *n* [F, lit., mad success] (1878) **:** an extraordinary success

suc·cess \sək-ˈses\ *n* [L *successus,* fr. *succedere*] (1537) **1** *obs* **:** OUTCOME, RESULT **2 a :** degree or measure of succeeding **b :** favorable or desired outcome; *also* **:** the attainment of wealth, favor, or eminence **3 :** one that succeeds

suc·cess·ful \-fəl\ *adj* (1588) **1 :** resulting or terminating in success ⟨a ~ attempt⟩ **2 :** gaining or having gained success ⟨a ~ investor⟩ — **suc·cess·ful·ly** \-fə-lē\ *adv* — **suc·cess·ful·ness** *n*

suc·ces·sion \sək-ˈse-shən\ *n* [ME, fr. AF or L; AF, fr. L *succession-, successio,* fr. *succedere*] (14c) **1 a :** the order in which or the conditions under which one person after another succeeds to a property, dignity, title, or throne **b :** the right of a person or line to succeed **c :** the line having such a right **2 a :** the act or process of following in order **:** SEQUENCE **b** (1) **:** the act or process of one person's taking the place of another in the enjoyment of or liability for rights or duties or both (2) **:** the act or process of a person's becoming beneficially entitled to a property or property interest of a deceased person **c :** the continuance of corporate personality **d :** unidirectional change in the composition of an ecosystem as the available competing organisms and esp. the plants respond to and modify the environment **3 a :** a number of persons or things that follow each other in sequence **b :** a group, type, or series that succeeds or displaces another — **suc·ces·sion·al** \-ˈsesh-nəl, -ˈse-shə-nᵊl\ *adj* — **suc·ces·sion·al·ly** *adv*

succession duty *n* (1853) *chiefly Brit* **:** INHERITANCE TAX

suc·ces·sive \sək-ˈse-siv\ *adj* (15c) **1 :** following in order **:** following each other without interruption ⟨their fourth ~ victory⟩ **2 :** characterized by or produced in succession — **suc·ces·sive·ly** *adv* — **suc·ces·sive·ness** *n*

suc·ces·sor \sək-ˈse-sər\ *n* [ME *successour,* fr. AF, fr. L *successor,* fr. *succedere*] (14c) **:** one that follows; *esp* **:** one who succeeds to a throne, title, estate, or office

suc·ci·nate \ˈsək-sə-ˌnāt\ *n* (1790) **:** a salt or ester of succinic acid

succinate dehydrogenase *n* (1962) **:** an iron-containing flavoprotein enzyme that catalyzes often reversibly the dehydrogenation of succinic acid to fumaric acid in the Krebs cycle and that is widely distributed esp. in animal tissues, bacteria, and yeast — called also *succinic dehydrogenase*

suc·cinct \(ˌ)sək-ˈsiŋ(k)t, sə-ˈsiŋ(k)t\ *adj* [ME, fr. L *succinctus* having one's clothes gathered up by a belt, tightly wrapped, concise, fr. *sub-* + *cinctus,* pp. of *cingere* to gird — more at CINCTURE] (15c) **1** *archaic* **a :** being girded **b :** close-fitting **2 :** marked by compact precise expression without wasted words ⟨a ~ description⟩ ***syn*** see CONCISE — **suc·cinct·ly** \-ˈsiŋ(k)t-lē, -ˈsiŋ-klē\ *adv* — **suc·cinct·ness** \-ˈsiŋt-nəs, -ˈsiŋk-nəs\ *n*

suc·cin·ic acid \(ˌ)sək-ˈsi-nik-\ *n* [F *succinique,* fr. L *succinum* amber] (1790) **:** a crystalline dicarboxylic acid $C_4H_6O_4$ found widely in nature and active in energy-yielding metabolic reactions

suc·ci·nyl \ˈsək-sə-nᵊl, -ˌnil\ *n* [ISV] (ca. 1868) **:** either of two radicals derived from succinic acid by removal of one or both hydroxyl groups: **a :** a divalent radical $OCCH_2CH_2CO$ **b :** a monovalent radical $HOOCCH_2CH_2CO$

suc·ci·nyl·cho·line \ˌsək-sə-nᵊl-ˈkō-ˌlēn, -ˌnil-\ *n* (1950) **:** a basic compound that is used intravenously chiefly in the form of a hydrated chloride $C_{14}H_{30}Cl_2N_2O_4{\cdot}2H_2O$ as a muscle relaxant in surgery

1**suc·cor** \ˈsə-kər\ *n* [ME *socour, sucurs* (taken as pl.), fr. AF *sucur, sucors,* fr. ML *succursus,* fr. L *succurrere* to run to the rescue, bring aid, fr. *sub-* + *currere* to run — more at CAR] (13c) **1 :** RELIEF; *also* **:** AID, HELP **2 :** something that furnishes relief

2**succor** *vt* **suc·cored; suc·cor·ing** \ˈsə-k(ə-)riŋ\ (13c) **:** to go to the aid of **:** RELIEVE — **suc·cor·er** \ˈsə-kər-ər\ *n*

suc·co·ry \ˈsə-k(ə-)rē\ *n* [alter. of ME *cicoree*] (1533) **:** CHICORY

suc·co·tash \ˈsə-kə-ˌtash\ *n* [Narragansett *msickquatash* boiled corn kernels] (1751) **:** lima or shell beans and kernels of green corn cooked together

suc·cour \ˈsə-kər\ *chiefly Brit var of* SUCCOR

suc·cu·ba \ˈsə-kyə-bə\ *n, pl* **-bae** \-ˌbē, -ˌbī\ [L, paramour] (1559) **:** SUCCUBUS

suc·cu·bus \-bəs\ *n, pl* **-bi** \-ˌbī, -ˌbē\ [ME, fr. ML, alter. of L *succuba* paramour, fr. *succubare* to lie under, fr. *sub-* + *cubare* to lie, recline] (14c) **:** a demon assuming female form to have sexual intercourse with men in their sleep — compare INCUBUS

suc·cu·lence \ˈsə-kyə-lən(t)s\ *n* (1787) **1 :** the state of being succulent **2 :** succulent feed ⟨wild game subsisting on ~⟩

1**suc·cu·lent** \-lənt\ *adj* [L *suculentus,* fr. *sucus* juice, sap; perh. akin to L *sugere* to suck — more at SUCK] (1601) **1 a :** full of juice **:** JUICY **b :** moist and tasty **:** TOOTHSOME ⟨a ~ meal⟩ **c** *of a plant* **:** having fleshy tissues that conserve moisture **2 :** rich in interest — **suc·cu·lent·ly** *adv*

2**succulent** *n* (1825) **:** a succulent plant (as a cactus or an aloe)

suc·cumb \sə-ˈkəm\ *vi* [F & L; F *succomber,* fr. L *succumbere,* fr. *sub-* + *-cumbere* to lie down; akin to L *cubare* to lie] (1604) **1 :** to yield to superior strength or force or overpowering appeal or desire ⟨~ to temptation⟩ **2 :** to be brought to an end (as death) by the effect of destructive or disruptive forces ***syn*** see YIELD

1**such** \ˈsəch, ˈsich\ *adj* [ME, fr. OE *swilc;* akin to OHG *sulīh* such, OE *swā* so, *gelīk* like — more at SO, LIKE] (bef. 12c) **1 a :** of a kind or character to be indicated or suggested ⟨a bag ~ as a doctor carries⟩ **b :** having a quality to a degree to be indicated ⟨his excitement was ~ that he shouted⟩ **2 :** of the character, quality, or extent previously indicated or implied ⟨in the past few years many ~ women have shifted to full-time jobs⟩ **3 :** of so extreme a degree or quality ⟨never heard ~ a hubbub⟩ **4 :** of the same class, type, or sort ⟨other ~ clinics throughout the state⟩ **5 :** not specified

2**such** *pron* (bef. 12c) **1 :** such a person or thing **2 :** someone or something stated, implied, or exemplified ⟨~ was the result⟩ **3 :** someone or something similar **:** similar persons or things ⟨tin and glass and ~⟩ — **as such :** intrinsically considered **:** in itself ⟨*as such* the gift was worth little⟩

usage For reasons that are hard to understand, commentators on usage disapprove of *such* used as a pronoun. Dictionaries, however, recognize it as standard; all of the citations upon which our definitions of this word are based are clearly standard.

3**such** *adv* (bef. 12c) **1 a :** to such a degree **:** SO ⟨~ tall buildings⟩ ⟨~ a fine person⟩ **b :** VERY, ESPECIALLY ⟨hasn't been in ~ good spirits lately⟩ **2 :** in such a way ⟨related ~ that each excludes the other⟩

1**such and such** *adj* (13c) **:** not named or specified

2**such and such** *pron* (15c) **:** something not specified

1**such·like** \ˈsəch-ˌlīk\ *adj* (15c) **:** of like kind **:** SIMILAR

2**suchlike** *pron* (15c) **:** SUCH 3

1**suck** \ˈsək\ *vb* [ME *suken,* fr. OE *sūcan;* akin to OHG *sūgan* to suck, L *sugere*] *vt* (bef. 12c) **1 a :** to draw (as liquid) into the mouth through a suction force produced by movements of the lips and tongue ⟨~*ed* milk from his mother's breast⟩ **b :** to draw something from or consume by such movements ⟨~ an orange⟩ ⟨~ a lollipop⟩ **c :** to apply the mouth to in order to or as if to suck out a liquid ⟨~*ed* his burned finger⟩ **2 a :** to draw by or as if by suction ⟨when a receding wave ~*s* the sand from under your feet —Kenneth Brower⟩ ⟨inadvertently ~*ed* into the . . . intrigue —Martin Levin⟩ **b :** to take in and consume by or as if by suction ⟨a vacuum cleaner ~*ing* up dirt⟩ ⟨~ up a few beers⟩ ⟨opponents say that malls ~ the life out of downtown areas —Michael Knight⟩ ~ *vi* **1 :** to draw something in by or as if by exerting a suction force; *esp* **:** to draw milk from a breast or udder with the mouth **2 :** to make a sound or motion associated with or caused by suction ⟨his pipe ~*ed* wetly⟩ ⟨flanks ~*ed* in and out, the long nose resting on his paws —Virginia Woolf⟩ **3 :** to act in an obsequious manner ⟨when they want votes . . . the candidates come ~*ing* around —W. G. Hardy⟩ — usu. used with *up* ⟨~*ed* up to the boss⟩ **4** *slang* **:** to be objectionable or inadequate ⟨our lifestyle ~*s* —*Playboy*⟩ ⟨people who went said it ~*ed* —H. S. Thompson⟩ — **suck it up :** to make the effort required to do or deal with something difficult or unpleasant

2**suck** *n* (13c) **1 :** a sucking movement or force **2 :** the act of sucking

1**suck·er** \ˈsə-kər\ *n* (14c) **1 a :** one that sucks esp. a breast or udder **:** SUCKLING **b :** a device for creating or regulating suction (as a piston or valve in a pump) **c :** a pipe or tube through which something is drawn by suction **d** (1) **:** an organ in various animals for adhering or holding (2) **:** a mouth (as of a leech) adapted for sucking or adhering **2 :** a shoot from the roots or lower part of the stem of a plant **3 :** any of numerous chiefly No. American freshwater bony fishes (family Catostomidae) closely related to the carps but distinguished from them esp. by the structure of the mouth which usu. has thick soft lips — compare HOG SUCKER, WHITE SUCKER **4 :** LOLLIPOP 1 **5 a :** a person easily cheated or deceived **b :** a person irresistibly attracted by something specified ⟨a ~ for ghost stories⟩ **c** — used as a generalized term of reference ⟨see if you can get that ~ working again⟩

2**sucker** *vb* **suck·ered; suck·er·ing** \ˈsə-k(ə-)riŋ\ *vt* (1607) **1 :** to remove suckers from ⟨~ tobacco⟩ **2 :** HOODWINK 3 ~ *vi* **:** to send out suckers ⟨corn ~*s* abundantly⟩

sucker punch *vt* (1964) **:** to punch (a person) suddenly without warning and often without apparent provocation — **sucker punch** *n*

suck in *vt* (1840) **1 :** DUPE, HOODWINK **2 :** to contract, flatten, and tighten (the abdomen) esp. by inhaling deeply

suck·ing \ˈsə-kiŋ\ *adj* (bef. 12c) **:** not yet weaned; *broadly* **:** very young

sucking louse *n* (ca. 1907) **:** any of an order (Anoplura) of wingless insects comprising the true lice with mouthparts adapted to sucking body fluids

suck·le \ˈsə-kəl\ *vb* **suck·led; suck·ling** \-k(ə-)liŋ\ [ME *suklen,* prob. back-formation fr. *suklyng*] *vt* (14c) **1 a :** to give milk to from the breast or udder ⟨a mother *suckling* her child⟩ **b :** to nurture as if by giving milk from the breast ⟨was *suckled* on pulp magazines⟩ **2 :** to draw milk from the breast or udder of ⟨lambs *suckling* the ewes⟩ ~ *vi* **:** to draw milk from the breast or udder

suck·ling \ˈsə-kliŋ\ *n* [ME *suklyng,* fr. *suken* to suck] (13c) **:** a young unweaned animal

suck–up \ˈsək-ˌəp\ *n* (1976) **:** a person who is ingratiating or fawning ⟨a ~ to the teacher⟩

sucky \ˈsə-kē\ *adj* **suck·i·er; -est** (1984) *slang* **:** AWFUL 3

su·cra·lose \ˈsü-krə-ˌlōs\ *n* [prob. fr. *sucrose* + 3*-al* + 2*-ose*] (1985) **:** a white crystalline powder $C_{12}H_{19}Cl_3O_3$ that is derived from sucrose and is used as a low-calorie sweetener having a sweetness of much greater intensity than sucrose

su·crase \ˈsü-ˌkrās, -ˌkrāz\ *n* [ISV, fr. F *sucre* sugar, fr. MF — more at SUGAR] (ca. 1900) **:** INVERTASE

su·cre \ˈsü-(ˌ)krā\ *n* [Sp, fr. Antonio José de *Sucre*] (1886) **:** the basic monetary unit of Ecuador until 2000

su·crose \ˈsü-ˌkrōs, -ˌkrōz\ *n* [ISV, fr. F *sucre* sugar] (1857) **:** a sweet crystalline dextrorotatory disaccharide sugar $C_{12}H_{22}O_{11}$ that occurs naturally in most plants and is obtained commercially esp. from sugarcane or sugar beets

1**suc·tion** \ˈsək-shən\ *n* [LL *suction-, suctio,* fr. L *sugere* to suck — more at SUCK] (1626) **1 :** the act or process of sucking **2 a :** the act or process of exerting a force upon a solid, liquid, or gaseous body by reason of reduced air pressure over part of its surface **b :** force so exerted **3 :** a device (as a pipe or fitting) used in a machine that operates by suction — **suc·tion·al** \-shə-nᵊl, -shnəl\ *adj*

2**suction** *vt* (1954) **:** to remove (as from a body cavity or passage) by suction

suction cup *n* (1942) **:** a cup-shaped device in which a partial vacuum can be produced when applied to a surface

suction pump *n* (1825) **:** a common pump in which the liquid to be raised is pushed by atmospheric pressure into the partial vacuum under a retreating valved piston on the upstroke and reflux is prevented by a check valve in the pipe

suction stop *n* (1887) **:** a voice stop in the formation of which air behind the articulation is rarefied with consequent inrush of air when articulation is broken

suc·to·ri·al \ˌsək-ˈtȯr-ē-əl\ *adj* [NL *suctorius,* fr. L *sugere*] (1833) **:** adapted for sucking; *esp* **:** serving to draw up fluid or to adhere by suction ⟨~ mouths⟩

suc·to·ri·an \-ē-ən\ *n* [NL *Suctoria,* fr. neut. pl. of *suctorius* suctorial] (ca. 1842) **:** any of a class or subclass (Suctoria) of complex protozoans which are ciliated only early in development and in which the mature form is fixed to the substrate, lacks locomotor organelles or a mouth, and obtains food through specialized suctorial tentacles

Su·dan grass \sü-ˈdan-, -ˈdän-\ *n* [the *Sudan,* region in Africa] (1911) **:** a vigorous tall-growing annual sorghum grass (*Sorghum sudanense* syn. *S. vulgare sudanense*) widely grown for hay and fodder

su·da·to·ri·um \ˌsü-də-ˈtȯr-ē-əm\ *n* [L, fr. *sudare* to sweat — more at SWEAT] (ca. 1757) **:** a sweat room in a bath

su·da·to·ry \ˈsü-də-ˌtȯr-ē\ *n, pl* **-ries** (1615) **:** SUDATORIUM

sudd \ˈsəd\ *n* [Ar, lit., obstruction] (1874) **:** floating vegetable matter that forms obstructive masses esp. in the upper White Nile

[1]**sud·den** \ˈsə-dᵊn\ *adj* [ME *sodain,* fr. AF *sudain,* fr. L *subitaneus,* fr. *subitus* sudden, fr. pp. of *subire* to come up, fr. *sub-* up + *ire* to go — more at SUB-, ISSUE] (14c) **1 a :** happening or coming unexpectedly ⟨a ~ shower⟩ **b :** changing angle or character all at once ⟨a ~ drop in the ocean bottom⟩ **2 :** marked by or manifesting abruptness or haste ⟨a ~ departure⟩ **3 :** made or brought about in a short time **:** PROMPT ***syn*** see PRECIPITATE — **sud·den·ly** *adv* — **sud·den·ness** \ˈsə-dᵊn-(n)əs\ *n*

[2]**sudden** *n* (1558) *obs* **:** an unexpected occurrence **:** EMERGENCY — **all of a sudden** *also* **on a sudden :** sooner than was expected **:** at once

sudden death *n* (14c) **1 :** unexpected death that is instantaneous or occurs within minutes from any cause other than violence ⟨*sudden death* following coronary occlusion⟩ **2 :** extra play to break a tie in a sports contest in which the first to score or gain the lead wins

sudden infant death syndrome *n* (1970) **:** death of an apparently healthy infant usu. before one year of age that is of unknown cause and occurs esp. during sleep — abbr. *SIDS;* called also *crib death*

su·do·ku \sü-ˈdō-kü\ *n* [Jp *sūdoku,* short for *sūji wa dokushin ni kagiru* "the numerals must remain single" (i.e., the digits can occur only once)] (2004) **:** a puzzle in which several numbers are to be filled into a 9x9 grid of squares so that every row, every column, and every 3x3 box contains the numbers 1 through 9

su·do·rif·er·ous \ˌsü-də-ˈri-f(ə-)rəs\ *adj* [LL *sudorifer,* fr. L *sudor* sweat (fr. *sudare* to sweat) + *-ifer* -iferous — more at SWEAT] (1597) **:** producing or conveying sweat ⟨~ glands⟩ ⟨a ~ duct⟩

su·do·rif·ic \-ˈri-fik\ *adj* [NL *sudorificus,* fr. L *sudor*] (1626) **:** causing or inducing sweat **:** DIAPHORETIC ⟨~ herbs⟩ — **sudorific** *n*

Su·dra \ˈsü-drə, ˈshü-\ *n* [Skt *śūdra*] (1630) **:** a Hindu of a lower caste traditionally assigned to menial occupations — **Sudra** *adj*

[1]**suds** \ˈsədz\ *n pl but sing or pl in constr* [prob. fr. MD *sudse* marsh; akin to OE *sēothan* to seethe — more at SEETHE] (1581) **1 :** water impregnated with soap or a synthetic detergent compound and worked up into froth; *also* **:** the lather or froth on such water **2 a :** FOAM, FROTH **b :** BEER — **suds·less** \-ləs\ *adj*

[2]**suds** *vt* (1834) **:** to wash in suds ~ *vi* **:** to form suds

suds·er \ˈsəd-zər\ *n* (1967) **:** SOAP OPERA

sudsy \ˈsəd-zē\ *adj* **suds·i·er; -est** (1866) **1 :** full of suds **:** FROTHY, FOAMY **2 :** SOAPY 4

sue \ˈsü\ *vb* **sued; su·ing** [ME *sewen, siuen* to follow, strive for, petition, fr. AF *sivre, siure,* fr. VL **sequere,* fr. L *sequi* to follow; akin to Gk *hepesthai* to follow, Skt *sacate* he accompanies] *vt* (14c) **1** *obs* **:** to make petition to or for **2** *archaic* **:** to pay court or suit to **:** WOO **3 a :** to seek justice or right from (a person) by legal process; *specif* **:** to bring an action against **b :** to proceed with and follow up (a legal action) to proper termination ~ *vi* **1 :** to make a request or application **:** PLEAD — usu. used with *for* or *to* ⟨~ for peace⟩ **2 :** to pay court **:** WOO ⟨he loved . . . but *sued* in vain —William Wordsworth⟩ **3 :** to take legal proceedings in court — **su·er** *n*

[1]**suede** *also* **suède** \ˈswād\ *n* [F *gants de Suède* Swedish gloves] (1883) **1 :** leather with a napped surface **2 :** a fabric finished with a nap to simulate suede

[2]**suede** *vb* **sued·ed; sued·ing** *vt* (1921) **:** to give a suede finish or nap to (a fabric or leather) ~ *vi* **:** to give cloth or leather a suede finish

su·et \ˈsü-ət\ *n* [ME *sewet,* fr. AF *suet, siuet,* fr. *seu, su* hard animal fat, fr. L *sebum*] (14c) **:** the hard fat about the kidneys and loins in beef and mutton that yields tallow

suf·fer \ˈsə-fər\ *vb* **suf·fered; suf·fer·ing** \-f(ə-)riŋ\ [ME *suffren,* fr. AF *suffrir,* fr. VL **sufferire,* fr. L *sufferre,* fr. *sub-* up + *ferre* to bear — more at SUB-, BEAR] *vt* (13c) **1 a :** to submit to or be forced to endure ⟨~ martyrdom⟩ **b :** to feel keenly **:** labor under ⟨~ thirst⟩ **2 :** UNDERGO, EXPERIENCE **3 :** to put up with esp. as inevitable or unavoidable **4 :** to allow esp. by reason of indifference ⟨the eagle ~*s* little birds to sing —Shak.⟩ ~ *vi* **1 :** to endure death, pain, or distress **2 :** to sustain loss or damage **3 :** to be subject to disability or handicap ***syn*** see BEAR — **suf·fer·able** \ˈsə-f(ə-)rə-bəl\ *adj* — **suf·fer·able·ness** *n* — **suf·fer·ably** \-blē\ *adv* — **suf·fer·er** \ˈsə-fər-ər\ *n*

suf·fer·ance \ˈsə-f(ə-)rən(t)s\ *n* (14c) **1 :** patient endurance **2 :** PAIN, MISERY **3 :** consent or sanction implied by a lack of interference or failure to enforce a prohibition **4 :** ENDURANCE 2

suffering *n* (14c) **1 :** the state or experience of one that suffers **2 :** PAIN ***syn*** see DISTRESS

suf·fice \sə-ˈfīs *also* -ˈfīz\ *vb* **suf·ficed; suf·fic·ing** [ME, fr. AF *suffis-,* stem of *suffire,* fr. L *sufficere* to provide, be adequate, fr. *sub-* + *facere* to make, do — more at DO] *vi* (14c) **1 :** to meet or satisfy a need **:** be sufficient ⟨a brief note will ~⟩ — often used with an impersonal *it* ⟨~ it to say that they are dedicated, serious personalities —Cheryl Aldridge⟩ **2 :** to be competent or capable ~ *vt* **:** to be enough for ⟨a few more should ~ them⟩ — **suf·fic·er** *n*

suf·fi·cien·cy \sə-ˈfi-shən(t)-sē\ *n, pl* **-cies** (15c) **1 :** sufficient means to meet one's needs **:** COMPETENCY; *also* **:** a modest but adequate scale of living **2 :** the quality or state of being sufficient **:** ADEQUACY

suf·fi·cient \sə-ˈfi-shənt\ *adj* [ME, fr. L *sufficient-, sufficiens,* fr. prp. of *sufficere*] (14c) **1 a :** enough to meet the needs of a situation or a proposed end ⟨~ provisions for a month⟩ **b :** being a sufficient condition **2** *archaic* **:** QUALIFIED, COMPETENT — **suf·fi·cient·ly** *adv*

syn SUFFICIENT, ENOUGH, ADEQUATE, COMPETENT mean being what is necessary or desirable. SUFFICIENT suggests a close meeting of a need ⟨*sufficient* savings⟩. ENOUGH is less exact in suggestion than SUFFICIENT ⟨do you have *enough* food?⟩. ADEQUATE may imply barely meeting a requirement ⟨the service was *adequate*⟩. COMPETENT suggests measuring up to all requirements without question or being adequately adapted to an end ⟨had no *competent* notion of what was going on⟩.

sufficient condition *n* (1885) **1 :** a proposition whose truth assures the truth of another proposition **2 :** a state of affairs whose existence assures the existence of another state of affairs

[1]**suf·fix** \ˈsə-fiks\ *n* [NL *suffixum,* fr. L, neut. of *suffixus,* pp. of *suffigere* to fasten underneath, fr. *sub-* + *figere* to fasten — more at FIX] (1778) **:** an affix occurring at the end of a word, base, or phrase — compare PREFIX — **suf·fix·al** \ˈsə-fik-səl, (ˌ)sə-ˈfik-səl\ *adj*

[2]**suf·fix** \ˈsə-fiks, (ˌ)sə-ˈfiks\ *vt* (1778) **:** to attach as a suffix — **suf·fix·a·tion** \ˌsə-fik-ˈsā-shən\ *n*

suf·fo·cate \ˈsə-fə-ˌkāt\ *vb* **-cat·ed; -cat·ing** [ME, fr. L *suffocatus,* pp. of *suffocare* to choke, stifle, fr. *sub-* + *fauces* throat] *vt* (15c) **1 a** (1) **:** to stop the respiration of (as by strangling or asphyxiation) (2) **:** to deprive of oxygen **b :** to make uncomfortable by want of fresh air **2 :** to impede or stop the development of ~ *vi* **1 :** to become suffocated: **a** (1) **:** to die from being unable to breathe (2) **:** to die from lack of oxygen **b :** to be uncomfortable through lack of fresh air **2 :** to become checked in development — **suf·fo·ca·tion** \ˌsə-fə-ˈkā-shən\ *n* — **suf·fo·ca·tive** \ˈsə-fə-ˌkā-tiv\ *adj*

suffocating *adj* (1604) **:** tending or serving to suffocate or overpower **:** OVERWHELMING — **suf·fo·cat·ing·ly** *adv*

Suf·folk \ˈsə-fək, -ˌfōk\ *n* [*Suffolk,* England] (1831) **1 :** any of a breed of chestnut-colored draft horses of English origin — called also *Suffolk punch* **2 :** any of a breed of large hornless black-faced sheep of English origin raised chiefly for mutton

[1]**suf·fra·gan** \ˈsə-fri-gən, -jən\ *n* [ME, fr. AF, fr. ML *suffraganeus,* fr. *suffragium* support, prayer] (14c) **1 :** a diocesan bishop (as in the Roman Catholic Church and the Church of England) subordinate to a metropolitan **2 :** an Anglican or Episcopal bishop assisting a diocesan bishop and not having the right of succession

[2]**suffragan** *adj* (15c) **1 :** of or being a suffragan **2 :** subordinate to a metropolitan or archiepiscopal see

suf·frage \ˈsə-frij, *sometimes* -fə-rij\ *n* [in sense 1, fr. ME, fr. AF, fr. ML *suffragium,* fr. L, vote, political support, fr. *suffragari* to support with one's vote; in other senses, fr. L *suffragium*] (14c) **1 :** a short intercessory prayer usu. in a series **2 :** a vote given in deciding a controverted question or electing a person for an office or trust **3 :** the right of voting **:** FRANCHISE; *also* **:** the exercise of such right

suf·frag·ette \ˌsə-fri-ˈjet\ *n* (1906) **:** a woman who advocates suffrage for women

suf·frag·ist \ˈsəf-ri-jist\ *n* (1822) **:** one who advocates extension of suffrage esp. to women

suf·fuse \sə-ˈfyüz\ *vt* **suf·fused; suf·fus·ing** [L *suffusus,* pp. of *suffundere,* lit., to pour beneath, fr. *sub-* + *fundere* to pour — more at FOUND] (1590) **:** to spread over or through in the manner of fluid or light **:** FLUSH, FILL ⟨the northern horizon was *suffused* with a deep red glow —P. M. Leschak⟩ ***syn*** see INFUSE — **suf·fu·sion** \-ˈfyü-zhən\ *n* — **suf·fu·sive** \-ˈfyü-siv, -ziv\ *adj*

Su·fi \ˈsü-(ˌ)fē\ *n* [Ar *ṣūfī,* perh. fr. *ṣūf* wool] (1653) **:** a Muslim mystic — **Sufi** *adj* — **Su·fic** \-fik\ *adj* — **Su·fism** \-ˌfi-zəm\ *n*

[1]**sug·ar** \ˈshu̇-gər\ *n* [ME *sugre, sucre,* fr. AF *sucre,* fr. ML *zuccarum,* fr. OIt *zucchero,* fr. Ar *sukkar,* fr. Pers *shakar,* ultim. fr. Skt *śarkarā;* akin to Skt *śarkara* pebble — more at CROCODILE] (14c) **1 a :** a sweet crystallizable material that consists wholly or essentially of sucrose, is colorless or white when pure tending to brown when less refined, is obtained commercially from sugarcane or sugar beet and less extensively from sorghum, maples, and palms, and is important as a source of dietary carbohydrate and as a sweetener and preservative of other foods **b :** any of various water-soluble compounds that vary widely in sweetness, include the monosaccharides and oligosaccharides, and typically are optically active **2 :** a unit (as a spoonful, cube, or lump) of sugar **3 :** a sugar bowl — **sug·ar·less** \-ləs\ *adj*

[2]**sugar** *vb* **sug·ared; sug·ar·ing** \ˈshu̇-g(ə-)riŋ\ *vt* (15c) **1 :** to make palatable or attractive **:** SWEETEN ⟨a story ~*ed* with romance⟩ **2 :** to sprinkle or mix with sugar ~ *vi* **1 :** to form or be converted into sugar **2 :** to become granular **3 :** to make maple syrup or maple sugar

sugar apple *n* (1738) **:** a tropical American tree (*Annona squamosa*) of the custard-apple family; *also* **:** its edible sweet pulpy fruit with thick green scaly rind and shining black seeds

sugar beet *n* (1817) **:** a white-rooted beet grown for the sugar in its roots

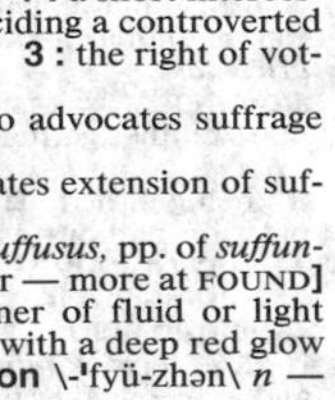

sugar beet

sug·ar·ber·ry \ˈshu̇-gər-ˌber-ē\ *n* (ca. 1818) **:** any of several hackberries (esp. *Celtis laevigata* and *C. occidentalis*) with sweet edible fruits

sugar bush *n* (1823) **:** a woods in which sugar maples predominate

sug·ar·cane \ˈshu̇-gər-ˌkān\ *n* (15c) **:** a stout tall perennial grass (*Saccharum officinarum*) native to tropical southeast Asia that has a large terminal panicle and is widely grown in warm regions as a source of sugar

sug·ar·coat \ˈshu̇-gər-ˌkōt\ *vt* [back-formation fr. *sugarcoated*] (1858) **1 :** to coat with sugar **2 :** to make superficially attractive or palatable

sugar daddy *n* (1926) **1 :** a well-to-do usu. older man who supports or spends lavishly on a mistress, girlfriend, or boyfriend **2 :** a generous benefactor of a cause or undertaking

sug·ar·house \ˈshu̇-gər-ˌhau̇s\ *n* (1600) **:** a building where sugar is made or refined; *specif* **:** one where maple sap is boiled and maple syrup and maple sugar are made

sugaring off *n* (1836) **1 :** the act or process of converting maple syrup into sugar **2 :** a party held at the time of sugaring off

sug·ar·loaf \ˈshu̇-gər-ˌlōf\ *n* (15c) **1 :** refined sugar molded into a cone **2 :** a hill or mountain shaped like a sugarloaf — **sugar–loaf** *adj*

sugar maple *n* (1731) **1 :** a maple (*Acer saccharum*) of eastern No. America with 3- to 5-lobed leaves, hard close-grained wood much used for cabinetwork, and sap that is the chief source of maple syrup and maple sugar — called also *rock maple, hard maple* **2 :** any of several maples (esp. *Acer nigrum* and *A. grandidentatum*) often considered subspecies of the sugar maple

sugar off *vi* (1836) **1 :** to complete the process of boiling down the syrup in making maple sugar until it is thick enough to crystallize **2 :** to approach or reach the state of granulation

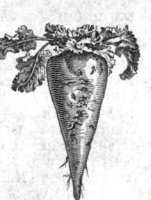

sugar orchard *n* (1833) *chiefly NewEng* : SUGAR BUSH
sugar pea *n* (1707) : SNOW PEA
sugar pill *n* (1852) : a pharmacologically inert pill : PLACEBO
sugar pine *n* (1846) : a very tall pine (*Pinus lambertiana*) found from Oregon to Baja California and having needles in clusters of five, cones up to 18 inches (46 cm) long, and soft reddish-brown wood; *also* : its wood
sug·ar·plum \ˈshu̇-gər-ˌpləm\ *n* (1627) : a small candy in the shape of a ball or disk : SWEETMEAT
sugar snap pea *n* (1979) : SNAP PEA
sug·ary \ˈshu̇-g(ə-)rē\ *adj* (1591) **1 a** : exaggeratedly sweet : HONEYED ⟨his ~ deprecating voice —D. H. Lawrence⟩ **b** : cloyingly sweet : SENTIMENTAL **2** : containing, resembling, or tasting of sugar
sug·gest \səg-ˈjest, sə-ˈjest\ *vt* [L *suggestus,* pp. of *suggerere* to pile up, furnish, suggest, fr. *sub-* + *gerere* to carry] (1526) **1 a** *obs* : to seek to influence : SEDUCE **b** : to call forth : EVOKE **c** : to mention or imply as a possibility ⟨~*ed* that he might bring his family⟩ **d** : to propose as desirable or fitting ⟨~ a stroll⟩ **e** : to offer for consideration or as a hypothesis ⟨~ a solution to a problem⟩ **2 a** : to call to mind by thought or association ⟨the explosion . . . ~*ed* sabotage —F. L. Paxson⟩ **b** : to serve as a motive or inspiration for ⟨a play ~*ed* by a historic incident⟩ — **sug·gest·er** *n*
syn SUGGEST, IMPLY, HINT, INTIMATE, INSINUATE mean to convey an idea indirectly. SUGGEST may stress putting into the mind by association of ideas, awakening of a desire, or initiating a train of thought ⟨a film title that *suggests* its subject matter⟩. IMPLY is close to SUGGEST but may indicate a more definite or logical relation of the unexpressed idea to the expressed ⟨measures *implying* that bankruptcy was imminent⟩. HINT implies the use of slight or remote suggestion with a minimum of overt statement ⟨*hinted* that she might get the job⟩. INTIMATE stresses delicacy of suggestion without connoting any lack of candor ⟨*intimates* that there is more to the situation than meets the eye⟩. INSINUATE applies to the conveying of a usually unpleasant idea in a sly underhanded manner ⟨*insinuated* that there were shady dealings⟩.
sug·gest·ible \səg-ˈjes-tə-bəl, sə-ˈjes-\ *adj* (1890) : easily influenced by suggestion — **sug·gest·ibil·i·ty** \-ˌjes-tə-ˈbi-lə-tē\ *n*
sug·ges·tion \səg-ˈjes-chən, sə-ˈjes-, -ˈjesh-\ *n* (14c) **1 a** : the act or process of suggesting **b** : something suggested **2 a** : the process by which a physical or mental state is influenced by a thought or idea ⟨the power of ~⟩ **b** : the process by which one thought leads to another esp. through association of ideas **3** : a slight indication : TRACE ⟨a ~ of a smile⟩
sug·ges·tive \səg-ˈjes-tiv, sə-ˈjes-\ *adj* (1631) **1 a** : giving a suggestion : INDICATIVE ⟨~ of a past era⟩ **b** : full of suggestions : stimulating thought ⟨provided a ~ . . . commentary on the era —Lloyd Morris⟩ **c** : stirring mental associations : EVOCATIVE **2** : suggesting or tending to suggest something improper or indecent : RISQUÉ — **sug·ges·tive·ly** *adv* — **sug·ges·tive·ness** *n*
sui·cid·al \ˌsü-ə-ˈsī-dᵊl\ *adj* (1777) **1 a** : dangerous esp. to life **b** : destructive to one's own interests **2** : relating to or of the nature of suicide **3** : marked by an impulse to commit suicide — **sui·cid·al·ly** *adv*
[1]**sui·cide** \ˈsü-ə-ˌsīd\ *n* [L *sui* (gen.) of oneself + E *-cide;* akin to OE & OHG *sīn* his, L *suus* one's own, *sed, se* without, Skt *sva* oneself, one's own] (1643) **1 a** : the act or an instance of taking one's own life voluntarily and intentionally esp. by a person of years of discretion and of sound mind **b** : ruin of one's own interests ⟨political ~⟩ **c** : APOPTOSIS ⟨cell ~⟩ **2** : one that commits or attempts suicide
[2]**suicide** *adj* (1773) : of or relating to suicide; *esp* : being or performing a deliberate act resulting in the voluntary death of the person who does it ⟨a ~ mission⟩ ⟨a ~ bomber⟩
[3]**suicide** *vb* **sui·cid·ed; sui·cid·ing** *vi* (1841) : to commit suicide ~ *vt* : to put (oneself) to death
suicide squeeze *n* (1955) : a squeeze play in which the runner runs all out at the pitch without knowing whether the batter will contact the ball
sui ge·ner·is \ˌsü-ˌī-ˈje-nə-rəs; ˌsü-ē-ˈje-, -ˈge-\ *adj* [L, of its own kind] (1754) : constituting a class alone : UNIQUE, PECULIAR
sui ju·ris \ˌsü-ˌī-ˈju̇r-əs, ˌsü-ē-ˈyu̇r-\ *adj* [L, of one's own right] (1675) : having full legal rights or capacity
su·int \ˈsü-ənt, ˈswint\ *n* [F, fr. MF, fr. *suer* to sweat, fr. L *sudare* — more at SWEAT] (1791) : dried perspiration of sheep deposited in the wool and rich in potassium salts
[1]**suit** \ˈsüt\ *n* [ME *sute, seute* pursuit, retinue, set, legal action, fr. AF *siute, suite,* fr. VL **sequita,* fr. fem. of **sequitus,* pp. of **sequere* to follow — more at SUE] (14c) **1** *archaic* : SUITE 1 **2 a** : recourse or appeal to a feudal superior for justice or redress **b** : an action or process in a court for the recovery of a right or claim **3** : an act or instance of suing or seeking by entreaty : APPEAL; *specif* : COURTSHIP **4** : a group of things forming a unit : SUITE — used chiefly of armor, sails, and counters in games **5** : a set of garments: as **a** : an ensemble of two or more usu. matching outer garments (as a jacket, vest, and trousers) ⟨businessmen wearing three-piece ~*s*⟩ **b** : a costume to be worn for a special purpose or under particular conditions ⟨gym ~*s*⟩ **6 a** : all the playing cards in a pack bearing the same symbol **b** : all the dominoes bearing the same number **c** : all the cards or counters in a particular suit held by one player ⟨a 5-card ~⟩ **d** : the suit led ⟨follow ~⟩ **7** *slang* : a business executive — usu. used in pl. — **suit·ed** \ˈsü-təd\ *adj*
[2]**suit** *vt* (14c) **1 a** : to be becoming to ⟨that dress ~*s* you⟩ **b** : to be proper for : BEFIT ⟨a mood that ~*s* the occasion⟩ **2** : to outfit with clothes : DRESS **3** : ACCOMMODATE, ADAPT ⟨~ the action to the word⟩ **4** : to meet the needs or desires of : PLEASE ⟨~*s* me fine⟩ ~ *vi* **1** : to be in accordance : AGREE ⟨the position ~*s* with your abilities⟩ **2** : to be appropriate or satisfactory ⟨these prices don't ~⟩ **3** : to put on specially required clothing (as a uniform or protective garb) — usu. used with *up* ⟨players ~*ing* up for the game⟩
suit·able \ˈsü-tə-bəl\ *adj* (1581) **1** *obs* : SIMILAR, MATCHING **2 a** : adapted to a use or purpose ⟨~ for kitchen use⟩ **b** : satisfying propriety : PROPER ⟨~ dress⟩ **c** : ABLE, QUALIFIED ⟨a ~ candidate for the job⟩ *syn* see FIT — **suit·abil·i·ty** \ˌsü-tə-ˈbi-lə-tē\ *n* — **suit·able·ness** *n* — **suit·ably** \-blē\ *adv*
suit·case \ˈsüt-ˌkās\ *n* (1897) : portable case designed to hold a traveler's clothing and personal articles
suite \ˈswēt, *2d is also* ˈsüt\ *n* [F, fr. OF *siute, suite* — more at SUIT] (1673) **1** : RETINUE; *esp* : the personal staff accompanying a ruler, diplomat, or dignitary on official business **2** : a group of things forming a unit or constituting a collection : SET: as **a** : a group of rooms occupied as a unit **b** (1) : a 17th and 18th century instrumental musical form consisting of a series of dances in the same or related keys (2) : a modern instrumental composition in several movements of different character (3) : a long orchestral concert arrangement in suite form of material drawn from a longer work (as a ballet) **c** : a collection of minerals or rocks having some characteristic in common (as type or origin) **d** : a set of matched furniture **e** : a set of computer programs designed to work together and usu. sold as a single unit
suit·er \ˈsü-tər\ *n* (1952) : a suitcase for holding a specified number of suits — usu. used in combination ⟨a two-*suiter*⟩
suit·ing \ˈsü-tiŋ\ *n* (1883) **1** : fabric for suits **2** : a suit of clothes
suit·or \ˈsü-tər\ *n* [ME *sutour, suytour,* follower, petitioner, fr. AF *siuter, suytour,* fr. L *secutor* follower, fr. *sequi* to follow — more at SUE] (15c) **1** : one that petitions or entreats **2** : a party to a suit at law **3** : one who courts a woman or seeks to marry her **4** : one who seeks to take over a business
su·ki·ya·ki \skē-ˈyä-kē; ˌsu̇-kē-ˈ, ˌsü-\ *n* [Jp, fr. *suki-* slice + *yaki* broil] (1919) : a dish consisting of thin slices of meat, tofu, and vegetables cooked in soy sauce and sugar
suk·kah \ˈsu̇-kə\ *n* [Heb *sukkāh*] (1875) : a booth or shelter with a roof of branches and leaves that is used esp. for meals during the Sukkoth
Suk·koth *or* **Suk·kot** \ˈsu̇-kəs, -ˌkōt, -ˌkōth, -ˌkōs\ *n* [Heb *sukkōth,* pl. of *sukkāh*] (ca. 1868) : a Jewish harvest festival beginning on the 15th of Tishri and commemorating the temporary shelters used by the Jews during their wandering in the wilderness
sul·cate \ˈsəl-ˌkāt\ *adj* [L *sulcatus,* pp. of *sulcare* to furrow, fr. *sulcus*] (1760) : scored with usu. longitudinal furrows ⟨a ~ seedpod⟩
sul·cus \ˈsəl-kəs\ *n, pl* **sul·ci** \-ˌkī, -ˌkē, -ˌsī\ [L; akin to OE *sulh* plow, Gk *holkos* furrow, *helkein* to pull] (1662) : FURROW, GROOVE; *esp* : a shallow furrow on the surface of the brain separating adjacent convolutions
sulf- *or* **sulfo-** *comb form* [F *sulf-, sulfo-,* fr. L *sulfur*] : sulfur : containing sulfur ⟨*sulf*ide⟩
sul·fa \ˈsəl-fə\ *adj* [short for *sulfanilamide*] (1940) **1** : related chemically to sulfanilamide **2** : of, relating to, or containing sulfa drugs
sul·fa·di·a·zine \ˌsəl-fə-ˈdī-ə-ˌzēn\ *n* [*sulfa* + *diazine* ($C_4H_4N_2$)] (1940) : a sulfa drug $C_{10}H_{10}N_4O_2S$ used esp. in the treatment of toxoplasmosis
sulfa drug *n* (1940) : any of various synthetic organic bacteria-inhibiting drugs that are sulfonamides derived esp. from sulfanilamide
sul·fa·meth·ox·a·zole \ˌsəl-fə-ˌme-ˈthäk-sə-ˌzōl\ *n* [*sulfa* + *meth*yl + *oxazole,* a compound C_3H_3NO (fr. ISV *ox-* + *azole*)] (1960) : an antibacterial sulfonamide $C_{10}H_{11}N_3O_3S$ used alone or in combination with trimethoprim (as in the treatment of urinary tract infections or acute otitis media)
sul·fa·nil·amide \ˌsəl-fə-ˈni-lə-ˌmīd, -məd\ *n* [*sulfanil*ic acid ($C_6H_7NO_3S$, fr. ISV *sulf-* + *anil*ine + *-ic*) + *amide*] (1937) : a crystalline sulfonamide $C_6H_8N_2O_2S$ that is the parent compound of most of the sulfa drugs
sul·fa·tase \ˈsəl-fə-ˌtās, -ˌtāz\ *n* [[1]*sulfate*] (1924) : any of various esterases that accelerate the hydrolysis of sulfuric esters and that are found in animal tissues and in microorganisms (as bacteria)
[1]**sul·fate** \ˈsəl-ˌfāt\ *n* [F, fr. L *sulfur*] (1788) **1** : a salt or ester of sulfuric acid **2** : a divalent group or anion SO_4 characteristic of sulfuric acid and the sulfates
[2]**sulfate** *vt* **sul·fat·ed; sul·fat·ing** (1888) : to treat or combine with sulfuric acid or a sulfate
sulf·hy·dryl \ˌsəlf-ˈ(h)ī-drəl\ *n* [ISV] (ca. 1901) : THIOL 2 — used chiefly in molecular biology
sul·fide \ˈsəl-ˌfīd\ *n* (1836) **1** : any of various organic compounds characterized by a sulfur atom attached to two carbon atoms **2** : a binary compound (as CuS) of sulfur usu. with a more electropositive element or group : a salt of hydrogen sulfide
sul·fin·py·ra·zone \ˌsəl-fən-ˈpī-rə-ˌzōn\ *n* [*sulfin*ic acid (RSO_2H) + *pyr-* + *azole* + *-one*] (1958) : a uricosuric drug $C_{23}H_{20}N_2O_3S$ used in long-term treatment of chronic gout
sul·fite \ˈsəl-ˌfīt\ *n* [F *sulfite,* alter. of *sulfate*] (1788) : a salt or ester of sulfurous acid — **sul·fit·ic** \ˌsəl-ˈfi-tik\ *adj*
sul·fon·amide \ˌsəl-ˈfä-nə-ˌmīd, -məd; -ˈfō-nə-ˌmīd\ *n* [*sulfon*ic + *amide*] (1881) : any of various amides (as sulfanilamide) of a sulfonic acid; *also* : SULFA DRUG
[1]**sul·fo·nate** \ˈsəl-fə-ˌnāt\ *n* (1876) : a salt or ester of a sulfonic acid
[2]**sulfonate** *vt* **-nat·ed; -nat·ing** (1882) : to introduce the SO_3H group into; *broadly* : to treat (an organic substance) with sulfuric acid — **sul·fo·na·tion** \ˌsəl-fə-ˈnā-shən\ *n*
sul·fone \ˈsəl-ˌfōn\ *n* (1872) : any of various compounds containing the sulfonyl group with its sulfur atom having two bonds with carbon
sul·fon·ic \ˌsəl-ˈfä-nik, -ˈfō-\ *adj* (1873) : of, relating to, being, or derived from the monovalent acid group SO_3H
sulfonic acid *n* (1873) : any of numerous acids that contain the SO_3H group and may be derived from sulfuric acid by replacement of a hydroxyl group by either an inorganic anion or a monovalent organic group
sul·fo·ni·um \ˌsəl-ˈfō-nē-əm\ *n* [NL, fr. *sulf-* + *-onium*] (1885) : a monovalent group or cation SR_3 or derivative SR_3
sul·fo·nyl \ˈsəl-fə-ˌnil\ *n* (1920) : the divalent group SO_2
sul·fo·nyl·urea \ˌsəl-fə-ˌnil-ˈyu̇r-ē-ə\ *n* [NL, fr. ISV *sulfonyl* + NL *urea*] (1956) : any of several hypoglycemic compounds related to the sulfonamides and used in the oral treatment of diabetes
sul·fo·raph·ane \ˌsəl-fō-ˈra-ˌfan, -ˈrā-\ *n* [*sulforaph*en, a chemically similar substance (fr. *sulfo-* + *-raphen,* perh. alter. of *raphanin,* an alternate name, fr. NL *Raphanus,* a cruciferous plant genus) + *-ane*] (1992) : an anticarcinogenic isothiocyanate $C_6H_{11}NOS_2$ found in cruciferous vegetables (as broccoli and cauliflower) that is thought to function by

\ə\ **abut** \ᵊ\ **kitten**, F table \ər\ **further** \a\ **ash** \ā\ **ace** \ä\ **mop**, **mar** \au̇\ **out** \ch\ **chin** \e\ **bet** \ē\ **easy** \g\ **go** \i\ **hit** \ī\ **ice** \j\ **job** \ŋ\ **sing** \ō\ **go** \ȯ\ **law** \ȯi\ **boy** \th\ **thin** \t͟h\ **the** \ü\ **loot** \u̇\ **foot** \y\ **yet** \zh\ **vision, beige** \k̟, ⁿ, œ, ue, ʸ\ *see* Guide to Pronunciation

stimulating the production of enzymes in the body that detoxify cancer-causing substances

sulf·ox·ide \ˌsəl-ˈfäk-ˌsīd\ *n* [ISV] (ca. 1894) **:** any of a class of organic compounds characterized by an SO group with its sulfur atom having two bonds with carbon

sul·fur *also* **sul·phur** \ˈsəl-fər\ *n* [ME *sulphur* brimstone, fr. L *sulpur, sulphur, sulfur*] (14c) **:** a nonmetallic element that occurs either free or combined esp. in sulfides and sulfates, is a constituent of proteins, exists in several allotropic forms including yellow orthorhombic crystals, resembles oxygen chemically but is less active and more acidic, and is used esp. in the chemical and paper industries, in rubber vulcanization, and in medicine for treating skin diseases — see ELEMENT table — **sul·fury** *or* **sul·phury** \-ē\ *adj*

usage The spelling *sulfur* predominates in U.S. technical usage, while both *sulfur* and *sulphur* are common in general usage. British usage tends to favor *sulphur* for all applications. The same pattern is seen in most of the words derived from *sulfur.*

sulfur bacterium *n* (1891) **:** any of various bacteria (esp. genus *Thiobacillus*) capable of metabolizing sulfur compounds

sulfur dioxide *n* (1869) **:** a heavy pungent toxic gas SO_2 that is easily condensed to a colorless liquid, is used esp. in making sulfuric acid, in bleaching, as a preservative, and as a refrigerant, and is a major air pollutant esp. in industrial areas

sul·fu·ric \ˌsəl-ˈfyu̇r-ik\ *adj* (1788) **:** of, relating to, or containing sulfur esp. with a higher valence than sulfurous compounds ⟨~ esters⟩

sulfuric acid *or* **sul·phu·ric acid** \ˌsəl-ˈfyu̇r-ik-\ *n* (1788) **:** a heavy corrosive oily dibasic strong acid H_2SO_4 that is colorless when pure and is a vigorous oxidizing and dehydrating agent ***usage*** see SULFUR

sul·fu·rize \ˈsəl-fə-ˌrīz, -fyə-\ *vt* **-rized; -riz·ing** (1794) **:** to treat with sulfur or a sulfur compound

sul·fu·rous *also* **sul·phu·rous** \ˈsəl-fə-rəs, -fyə- *also esp for 1a* ˌsəl-ˈfyu̇r-əs\ *adj* (15c) **1 a :** of, relating to, or containing sulfur esp. with a lower valence than sulfuric compounds ⟨~ esters⟩ **b :** resembling or emanating from sulfur and esp. burning sulfur **2 a :** of, relating to, or dealing with the fire of hell **:** INFERNAL **b :** SCATHING, VIRULENT ⟨~ denunciations⟩ **c :** PROFANE, BLASPHEMOUS ⟨~ language⟩ ***usage*** see SULFUR — **sul·fu·rous·ly** *adv* — **sul·fu·rous·ness** *n*

sulfurous acid *n* (1790) **:** a weak unstable dibasic acid H_2SO_3 known in solution and through its salts and used as a reducing and bleaching agent

sul·fu·ryl \ˈsəl-fə-ˌril, -fyə-\ *n* [ISV] (1867) **:** SULFONYL — used esp. in names of inorganic compounds

[1]**sulk** \ˈsəlk\ *vi* [back-formation fr. *sulky*] (1781) **:** to be moodily silent

[2]**sulk** *n* (1804) **1 :** the state of one sulking — often used in pl. ⟨had a case of the ~*s*⟩ **2 :** a sulky mood or spell ⟨in a ~⟩

[1]**sulky** \ˈsəl-kē\ *adj* **sulk·i·er; -est** [prob. alter. of obs. *sulke* sluggish] (1744) **1 a :** sulking or given to spells of sulking **b :** relating to or indicating a sulk ⟨a ~ expression⟩ **2** [[2]*sulky*] **:** having wheels and usu. a seat for the driver ⟨a ~ plow⟩ ***syn*** see SULLEN — **sulk·i·ly** \-kə-lē\ *adv* — **sulk·i·ness** \-kē-nəs\ *n*

[2]**sulky** *n, pl* **sulkies** [prob. fr. [1]*sulky;* fr. its having room for only one person] (1756) **:** a light 2-wheeled vehicle (as for harness racing) having a seat for the driver only and usu. no body

sul·lage \ˈsə-lij\ *n* [prob. fr. AF **sollage, *suillage,* fr. *suiller, soiller* to soil — more at SOIL] (1553) **:** REFUSE, SEWAGE

sul·len \ˈsə-lən\ *adj* [ME *solein* solitary, fr. AF *sulein, solain,* perh. fr. *sol, soul* single, sole + *-ain* after OF *soltain* solitary, private, fr. LL *solitaneus,* ultim. fr. L *solus* alone] (14c) **1 a :** gloomily or resentfully silent or repressed ⟨a ~ crowd⟩ **b :** suggesting a sullen state **:** LOWERING ⟨a ~ countenance⟩ **2 :** dull or somber in sound or color **3 :** DISMAL, GLOOMY ⟨a ~ morning⟩ **4 :** moving sluggishly ⟨a ~ river⟩ — **sul·len·ly** *adv* — **sul·len·ness** \ˈsə-lə(n)-nəs\ *n*

syn SULLEN, GLUM, MOROSE, SURLY, SULKY, CRABBED, SATURNINE, GLOOMY mean showing a forbidding or disagreeable mood. SULLEN implies a silent ill humor and a refusal to be sociable ⟨remained *sullen* amid the festivities⟩. GLUM suggests a silent dispiritedness ⟨a *glum* candidate left to ponder a stunning defeat⟩. MOROSE adds to GLUM an element of bitterness or misanthropy ⟨*morose* job seekers who are inured to rejection⟩. SURLY implies gruffness and sullenness of speech or manner ⟨a typical *surly* teenager⟩. SULKY suggests childish resentment expressed in peevish sullenness ⟨grew *sulky* after every spat⟩. CRABBED applies to a forbidding morose harshness of manner ⟨the school's notoriously *crabbed* headmaster⟩. SATURNINE describes a heavy forbidding aspect or suggests a bitter disposition ⟨a *saturnine* cynic always finding fault⟩. GLOOMY implies a depression in mood making for seeming sullenness or glumness ⟨a *gloomy* mood ushered in by bad news⟩.

[1]**sul·ly** \ˈsə-lē\ *vt* **sul·lied; sul·ly·ing** [ME **sullien,* prob. alter. (influenced by AF *suillier, soiller* to soil) of *sulen* to soil, fr. OE *sylian*] (15c) **:** to make soiled or tarnished **:** DEFILE

[2]**sully** *n, pl* **sullies** (1601) *archaic* **:** SOIL, STAIN

sulph- *or* **sulpho-** *chiefly Brit var of* SULF-

sul·phate, sul·phide *chiefly Brit var of* SULFATE, SULFIDE

sulphur butterfly *n* (1879) **:** any of numerous butterflies (esp. *Colias* and related genera of the family Pieridae) having the wings usu. yellow or orange with a black border — called also *sulphur*

sul·phu·re·ous \ˌsəl-ˈfyu̇r-ē-əs\ *adj* (ca. 1552) **:** SULFUROUS

sul·phu·rise *Brit var of* SULFURIZE

sulphur yellow *n* (1814) **:** a brilliant greenish yellow

Sul·pi·cian \ˌsəl-ˈpi-shən\ *n* [F *sulpicien,* fr. Compagnie de Saint-*Sulpice* Society of St. Sulpice] (1786) **:** a member of the Society of Priests of St. Sulpice founded by Jean Jacques Olier in Paris, France, in 1642 and dedicated to the teaching of seminarians

sul·tan \ˈsəl-tᵊn\ *n* [MF, fr. Ar *sulṭān*] (1555) **:** a king or sovereign esp. of a Muslim state — **sul·tan·ic** \ˌsəl-ˈta-nik\ *adj*

sul·ta·na \(ˌ)səl-ˈta-nə\ *n* [It, fem. of *sultano* sultan, fr. Ar *sulṭān*] (1585) **1 :** a woman who is a member of a sultan's family; *esp* **:** a sultan's wife **2 a :** a pale yellow seedless grape grown for raisins and wine **b :** the raisin of a sultana

sul·tan·ate \ˈsəl-tᵊn-ˌāt\ *n* (1822) **1 :** a state or country governed by a sultan **2 :** the office, dignity, or power of a sultan

sul·tan·ess \ˈsəl-tə-nəs\ *n* (1611) **:** SULTANA 1

sul·try \ˈsəl-trē\ *adj* **sul·tri·er; -est** [obs. E *sulter* to swelter, alter. of E *swelter*] (1594) **1 a :** very hot and humid **:** SWELTERING ⟨a ~ day⟩ **b :** burning hot **:** TORRID ⟨a ~ sun⟩ **2 a :** hot with passion or anger **b :** exciting or capable of exciting strong sexual desire ⟨~ glances⟩ — **sul·tri·ly** \-trə-lē\ *adv* — **sul·tri·ness** \-trē-nəs\ *n*

[1]**sum** \ˈsəm\ *n* [ME *summe,* fr. AF *sume, somme,* fr. L *summa,* fr. fem. of *summus* highest; akin to L *super* over — more at OVER] (14c) **1 :** an indefinite or specified amount of money **2 :** the whole amount **:** AGGREGATE **3 :** the utmost degree **:** SUMMIT ⟨reached the ~ of human happiness⟩ **4 a :** a summary of the chief points or thoughts **:** SUMMATION ⟨the ~ of this criticism follows —C. W. Hendel⟩ **b :** GIST ⟨the ~ and substance of an argument⟩ **5 a** (1) **:** the result of adding numbers ⟨the ~ of 5 and 7 is 12⟩ (2) **:** the limit of the sum of the first *n* terms of an infinite series as *n* increases indefinitely **b :** numbers to be added; *broadly* **:** a problem in arithmetic **c** (1) **:** DISJUNCTION 2 (2) **:** UNION 2d — **sum·ma·bil·i·ty** \ˌsə-mə-ˈbi-lə-tē\ *n* — **sum·ma·ble** \ˈsə-mə-bəl\ *adj* — **in sum :** in short **:** BRIEFLY

[2]**sum** *vb* **summed; sum·ming** *vt* (14c) **1 :** to calculate the sum of **:** TOTAL **2 :** SUMMARIZE ~ *vi* **:** to reach a sum **:** AMOUNT

[3]**sum** \ˈsəm\ *n, pl* **sums** [Uzbek *so'm* ruble] (1993) — see MONEY table

su·mac *also* **su·mach** \ˈshü-ˌmak, ˈsü-\ *n* [ME *sumac,* fr. AF, ultim. fr. Ar *summāq*] (14c) **1 :** a material used in tanning and dyeing that consists of dried powdered leaves and flowers of various sumacs **2 :** any of a genus (*Rhus*) of trees, shrubs, and woody vines of the cashew family that have leaves turning to brilliant colors in the autumn, small usu. dioecious flowers, and spikes or loose clusters of red or whitish berries — compare POISON IVY, POISON OAK, POISON SUMAC

su·ma·trip·tan \ˌsü-mə-ˈtrip-ˌtan, -tən\ *n* [perh. fr. *suma-* (by shortening & alter. fr. *sulfonamide*) + *-triptan* (by shortening & alter. fr. *tryptamine*)] (1989) **:** a triptan $C_{14}H_{21}N_3O_2S$ that is administered as a nasal spray or in the form of its succinate by mouth or by injection and is used in the treatment of migraine attacks

Su·me·ri·an \sü-ˈmer-ē-ən, -ˈmir-\ *n* (1878) **1 :** a native of Sumer **2 :** the language of the Sumerians that has no known linguistic affinities — **Sumerian** *adj*

Su·me·rol·o·gy \ˌsü-mə-ˈrä-lə-jē\ *n* (1897) **:** the study of Sumerian culture, language, and history — **Su·me·rol·o·gist** \-jist\ *n*

sum·ma \ˈsu̇-mə, ˈsü-, ˈsə-\ *n, pl* **sum·mae** \ˈsu̇-ˌmī, ˈsü-, -ˌmā; ˈsə-ˌmē, -ˌmī\ [ML, fr. L, sum] (1725) **1 :** a comprehensive treatise; *esp* **:** one by a scholastic philosopher **2 :** a synthesis or summary of any subject

sum·ma cum lau·de \ˌsu̇-mə-(ˌ)ku̇m-ˈlau̇-də, ˌsü-, -ˈlau̇-dē; ˌsə-mə-ˌkəm-ˈlȯ-dē\ *adv or adj* [L, with highest praise] (1882) **:** with highest distinction ⟨graduated *summa cum laude*⟩ — compare CUM LAUDE, MAGNA CUM LAUDE

sum·mand \ˈsə-ˌmand, ˌsə-ˈmand\ *n* [ML *summandus,* gerund of *summare* to sum, fr. *summa*] (1846) **:** a term in a summation **:** ADDEND

sum·ma·rise *Brit var of* SUMMARIZE

sum·ma·ri·za·tion \ˌsə-mə-rə-ˈzā-shən, ˌsəm-rə-\ *n* (1865) **1 :** the act of summarizing **2 :** SUMMARY

sum·ma·rize \ˈsə-mə-ˌrīz\ *vb* **-rized; -riz·ing** *vt* (1871) **:** to tell in or reduce to a summary ~ *vi* **:** to make a summary — **sum·ma·riz·able** \ˌsə-mə-ˈrī-zə-bəl\ *adj* — **sum·ma·riz·er** *n*

[1]**sum·ma·ry** \ˈsə-mə-rē *also* ˈsəm-rē *or* -ˌmer-ē\ *adj* [ME, fr. ML *summarius,* fr. L *summa* sum] (15c) **1 :** COMPREHENSIVE; *esp* **:** covering the main points succinctly **2 a :** done without delay or formality **:** quickly executed ⟨a ~ dismissal⟩ **b :** of, relating to, or using a summary proceeding ⟨a ~ trial⟩ ***syn*** see CONCISE — **sum·mar·i·ly** \(ˌ)sə-ˈmer-ə-lē\ *adv*

[2]**sum·ma·ry** \ˈsə-mə-rē *also* ˈsəm-rē\ *n, pl* **-ries** (1509) **:** an abstract, abridgment, or compendium esp. of a preceding discourse

summary judgment *n* (1798) **:** judgment that may be granted upon a party's motion when the pleadings, discovery, and any affidavits show that there is no issue of material fact and that the party is entitled to judgment in its favor as a matter of law

summary proceeding *n* (1643) **:** a civil or criminal proceeding conducted without formalities (as pleadings) for the speedy disposition of a matter

sum·mate \ˈsə-ˌmāt\ *vb* **sum·mat·ed; sum·mat·ing** [back-formation fr. *summation*] *vt* (1900) **:** to add together **:** SUM UP ~ *vi* **:** to form a sum or cumulative effect

sum·ma·tion \(ˌ)sə-ˈmā-shən\ *n* (1760) **1 :** the act or process of forming a sum **:** ADDITION **2 :** SUM, TOTAL **3 :** cumulative action or effect; *esp* **:** the process by which a sequence of stimuli that are individually inadequate to produce a response are cumulatively able to induce a nerve impulse **4 :** a final part of an argument reviewing points made and expressing conclusions — **sum·ma·tion·al** \-shnəl, -shə-nᵊl\ *adj*

sum·ma·tive \ˈsə-mə-tiv, -ˌmā-\ *adj* (1881) **:** ADDITIVE, CUMULATIVE

[1]**sum·mer** \ˈsə-mər\ *n* [ME *sumer,* fr. OE *sumor;* akin to OHG & ON *sumer* summer, Skt *samā* year, season] (bef. 12c) **1 :** the season between spring and autumn comprising in the northern hemisphere usu. the months of June, July, and August or as reckoned astronomically extending from the June solstice to the September equinox **2 :** the warmer half of the year **3 :** YEAR ⟨a girl of seventeen ~*s*⟩ **4 :** a period of maturing powers — **sum·mer·like** \-ˌlīk\ *adj*

[2]**summer** *adj* (14c) **1 :** of, relating to, or suitable for summer ⟨~ vacation⟩ ⟨a ~ home⟩ **2 :** sown in the spring and harvested in the same year as sown ⟨~ wheat⟩ — compare WINTER

[3]**summer** *vb* **sum·mered; sum·mer·ing** \ˈsə-mə-riŋ, ˈsəm-riŋ\ *vi* (15c) **:** to pass the summer ~ *vt* **:** to keep or carry through the summer; *esp* **:** to provide (as cattle or sheep) with pasture during the summer

summer cypress *n* (1767) **:** a densely branched Eurasian herb (*Kochia scoparia*) of the goosefoot family grown for its foliage which turns red in autumn

summer flounder *n* (1859) **:** a greenish-brown white-spotted flounder (*Paralichthys dentatus* of the family Bothidae) that occurs along the Atlantic coast of the U.S. from Maine to Florida and is used for food

sum·mer·house \ˈsə-mər-ˌhau̇s\ *n* (bef. 12c) **1 :** a country house for summer residence **2 :** a covered structure in a garden or park designed to provide a shady resting place in summer

summer kitchen *n* (1874) **:** a small building or shed that is usu. adjacent to a house and is used as a kitchen in warm weather

sum·mer·long \-ˌlȯŋ, -ˈlȯŋ\ *adj* (1960) **:** lasting through the summer

sum·mers \ˈsə-mərz\ *adv* (1907) **:** during the summers ⟨worked ~ as a waiter⟩

summersault *var of* SOMERSAULT

summer savory *n* (ca. 1573) **:** an aromatic annual European mint (*Satureja hortensis*) with leaves used for seasoning; *also* **:** its leaves — compare WINTER SAVORY
summer school *n* (1860) **:** a school or school session conducted in summer enabling students to accelerate progress toward a diploma or degree, to make up credits lost through absence or failure, or to round out professional education
summer squash *n* (1815) **:** any of various squashes that are cultivars of a variety (*Cucurbita pepo* var. *melopepo*) and are used as a vegetable while immature and before hardening of the seeds and rind
summer stock *n* (1927) **:** theatrical productions of stock companies presented during the summer
summer theater *n* (1801) **:** a theater that presents several different plays or musicals during the summer
sum·mer·time \ˈsə-mər-ˌtīm\ *n* (14c) **:** the summer season or a period like summer
summer time *n* (1916) *chiefly Brit* **:** DAYLIGHT SAVING TIME
sum·mer·wood \ˈsə-mər-ˌwu̇d\ *n* (1896) **:** the harder less porous portion of an annual ring of wood that develops late in the growing season — compare SPRINGWOOD
sum·mery \ˈsə-mə-rē, ˈsəm-rē\ *adj* (1824) **:** of, resembling, or fit for summer
sum·ming–up \ˌsə-miŋ-ˈəp\ *n, pl* **sum·mings–up** \-miŋz-\ (1658) **:** the act or statement of one who sums up
1**sum·mit** \ˈsə-mət\ *n* [ME *somete,* fr. AF *sumet,* dim. of *sum* top, fr. L *summum,* neut. of *summus* highest — more at SUM] (15c) **1 :** TOP, APEX; *esp* **:** the highest point **:** PEAK **2 :** the topmost level attainable ⟨the ~ of human fame⟩ **3 a :** the highest level of officials; *esp* **:** the diplomatic level of heads of government **b :** a conference of highest-level officials (as heads of government) ⟨an economic ~⟩
syn SUMMIT, PEAK, PINNACLE, CLIMAX, APEX, ACME, CULMINATION mean the highest point attained or attainable. SUMMIT implies the topmost level attainable ⟨at the *summit* of the Victorian social scene⟩. PEAK suggests the highest among other high points ⟨an artist working at the *peak* of her powers⟩. PINNACLE suggests a dizzying and often insecure height ⟨the *pinnacle* of worldly success⟩. CLIMAX implies the highest point in an ascending series ⟨the war was the *climax* to a series of hostile actions⟩. APEX implies the point where all ascending lines converge ⟨the *apex* of Dutch culture⟩. ACME implies a level of quality representing the perfection of a thing ⟨a statue that was once deemed the *acme* of beauty⟩. CULMINATION suggests the outcome of a growth or development representing an attained objective ⟨the *culmination* of years of effort⟩.
2**summit** *vi* (1972) **1 :** to participate in a summit conference **2 :** to climb to the summit ⟨~*ed* on May 29⟩
sum·mit·eer \ˌsə-mə-ˈtir\ *n* (1957) **:** one who takes part in a summit
sum·mit·ry \ˈsə-mə-trē\ *n* (1958) **:** the use of a summit conference for international negotiation
sum·mon \ˈsə-mən\ *vt* **sum·moned; sum·mon·ing** \ˈsə-mə-niŋ, ˈsəm-niŋ\ [ME *somnen, somonen,* fr. AF *somondre,* fr. VL **summonere,* alter. of L *summonēre* to remind secretly, fr. *sub-* secretly + *monēre* to warn — more at SUB-, MIND] (13c) **1 :** to issue a call to convene **:** CONVOKE **2 :** to command by service of a summons to appear in court **3 :** to call upon for specified action **4 :** to bid to come **:** send for ⟨~ a physician⟩ **5 :** to call forth **:** EVOKE — often used with *up* — **sum·mon·able** \ˈsə-mə-nə-bəl\ *adj* — **sum·mon·er** \ˈsə-mə-nər, ˈsəm-nər\ *n*
syn SUMMON, CALL, CITE, CONVOKE, CONVENE, MUSTER mean to demand the presence of. SUMMON implies the exercise of authority ⟨was *summoned* to answer charges⟩. CALL may be used less formally for SUMMON ⟨*called* the legislature into special session⟩. CITE implies a summoning to court usu. to answer a charge ⟨*cited* for drunken driving⟩. CONVOKE implies a summons to assemble for deliberative or legislative purposes ⟨*convoked* a Vatican council⟩. CONVENE is somewhat less formal than CONVOKE ⟨*convened* the students⟩. MUSTER suggests a calling up of a number of things that form a group in order that they may be exhibited, displayed, or utilized as a whole ⟨*mustered* the troops⟩.
1**sum·mons** \ˈsə-mənz\ *n, pl* **sum·mons·es** [ME *somouns,* fr. AF *somonse,* fr. pp. of *somondre*] (13c) **1 :** the act of summoning; *esp* **:** a call by authority to appear at a place named or to attend to a duty **2 :** a warning or citation to appear in court: as **a :** a written notification to be served on a person as a warning to appear in court at a day specified to answer to the plaintiff **b :** a subpoena to appear as a witness **3 :** something (as a call) that summons
2**summons** *vt* (1683) **:** SUMMON 2
sum·mum bo·num \ˌsu̇-məm-ˈbō-nəm, ˌsü-, ˌsə-\ *n* [L] (1563) **:** the supreme good from which all others are derived
su·mo \ˈsü-(ˌ)mō\ *n* [Jp *sumō*] (1880) **:** a Japanese form of wrestling in which a contestant loses if he is forced out of the ring or if any part of his body except the soles of his feet touches the ground
sump \ˈsəmp\ *n* [ME *sompe* swamp — more at SWAMP] (1653) **1 :** a pit or reservoir serving as a drain or receptacle for liquids: as **a :** CESSPOOL **b :** a pit at the lowest point in a circulating or drainage system (as the oil-circulating system of an internal combustion engine) **c** *chiefly Brit* **:** OIL PAN **2** *Brit* **:** CRANKCASE **3** [G *Sumpf,* lit., marsh, fr. MHG — more at SWAMP] **a :** the lowest part of a mine shaft into which water drains **b :** an excavation ahead of regular work in driving a mine tunnel or sinking a mine shaft **4 :** something resembling a sump **:** SINK 2
sump pump *n* (ca. 1899) **:** a pump (as in a basement) to remove accumulations of liquid (as water) from a sump pit
sump·ter \ˈsəm(p)-tər\ *n* [ME, short for *sompter hors,* fr. *sompter* driver of a packhorse, fr. AF *sumeter,* fr. VL **sagmatarius,* fr. LL *sagmat-, sagma* packsaddle, fr. Gk; akin to Gk *sattein* to pack, stuff] (15c) **:** a pack animal
sump·tu·ary \ˈsəm(p)-chə-ˌwer-ē\ *adj* [L *sumptuarius,* fr. *sumptus* expense, fr. *sumere* to take, spend — more at CONSUME] (1600) **1 :** relating to personal expenditures and esp. to prevent extravagance and luxury ⟨conservative ~ tastes —John Cheever⟩ **2 :** designed to regulate extravagant expenditures or habits esp. on moral or religious grounds ⟨~ laws⟩ ⟨~ tax⟩
sump·tu·ous \ˈsəm(p)(t)-shə-wəs, -shəs, -shwəs\ *adj* [ME, fr. L *sumptuosus,* fr. *sumptus*] (15c) **:** extremely costly, rich, luxurious, or magnificent ⟨~ banquets⟩ ⟨a ~ residence⟩; *also* **:** MAGNIFICENT 4 — **sump·tu·ous·ly** *adv* — **sump·tu·ous·ness** *n*
sum total *n* (14c) **1 :** a total arrived at through the counting of sums **2 :** total result **:** TOTALITY
sum–up \ˈsəm-ˌəp\ *n* (1894) **:** SUMMARY
sum up *vt* (15c) **1 :** to be the sum of **:** bring to a total ⟨10 victories *summed up* his record⟩ **2 a :** to present or show succinctly **:** SUMMARIZE ⟨*sum up* the evidence presented⟩ **b :** to assess and then describe briefly **:** size up ~ *vi* **:** to present a summary or recapitulation
1**sun** \ˈsən\ *n* [ME *sunne,* fr. OE; akin to OHG *sunna* sun, L *sol* — more at SOLAR] (bef. 12c) **1 a** *often cap* **:** the luminous celestial body around which the earth and other planets revolve, from which they receive heat and light, which is composed mainly of hydrogen and helium, and which has a mean distance from earth of about 93,000,000 miles (150,000,000 kilometers), a linear diameter of 864,000 miles (1,390,000 kilometers), and a mass 332,000 times greater than earth **b :** a celestial body like the sun **:** STAR **2 :** the heat or light radiated from the sun ⟨played in the ~ all day⟩ **3 :** one resembling the sun (as in warmth or brilliance) **4 :** the rising or setting of the sun ⟨from ~ to ~⟩ **5 :** GLORY, SPLENDOR — **in the sun :** in the public eye — **under the sun :** in the world **:** on earth
2**sun** *vb* **sunned; sun·ning** *vt* (15c) **:** to expose to or as if to the rays of the sun ~ *vi* **:** to sun oneself
Sun *abbr* Sunday
sun·baked \ˈsən-ˌbākt\ *adj* (1628) **1 :** heated, parched, or compacted esp. by excessive sunlight **2 :** baked by exposure to sunshine
sun·bath \ˈsən-ˌbath, -ˌbäth\ *n* (1866) **:** an exposure to sunlight or a sunlamp
sun·bathe \-ˌbāth\ *vi* [back-formation fr. *sunbather*] (1941) **:** to take a sunbath — **sun·bath·er** \-ˌbā-thər\ *n*
sun·beam \-ˌbēm\ *n* (bef. 12c) **:** a ray of sunlight
sun bear *n* (1842) **:** a small forest-dwelling bear (*Ursus malayanus* syn. *Helarctos malayanus*) of southeastern Asia that has short glossy black fur with a lighter muzzle and often an orange or white breast mark
sun·bird \-ˌbərd\ *n* (1826) **:** any of numerous small brilliantly colored oscine birds (family Nectariniidae) of the tropical Old World somewhat resembling hummingbirds
sun·block \-ˌbläk\ *n* (1972) **:** a preparation (as a lotion) applied to the skin to prevent sunburn (as by physically blocking out ultraviolet radiation); *also* **:** its active ingredient (as titanium dioxide) — compare SUNSCREEN
sun·bon·net \-ˌbä-nət\ *n* (1824) **:** a woman's bonnet with a wide brim framing the face and usu. having a ruffle at the back to protect the neck from the sun
sun·bow \-ˌbō\ *n* (1816) **:** an arch resembling a rainbow made by the sun shining through vapor or mist
1**sun·burn** \-ˌbərn\ *vb* **-burned** \-ˌbərnd\ *or* **-burnt** \-ˌbərnt\; **-burn·ing** [back-formation fr. *sunburned,* fr. *sun* + *burned*] *vt* (1530) **:** to burn or discolor by the sun ~ *vi* **:** to become sunburned
2**sunburn** *n* (1652) **:** inflammation of the skin caused by overexposure to ultraviolet radiation esp. from sunlight
sun·burst \ˈsən-ˌbərst\ *n, often attrib* (1816) **1 :** a flash of sunlight esp. through a break in clouds **2 a :** a jeweled brooch representing a sun surrounded by rays **b :** a design in the form of rays diverging from a central point
sun·choke \-ˌchōk\ *n* (1980) **:** JERUSALEM ARTICHOKE
sun·dae \ˈsən-(ˌ)dā, -dē\ *n* [prob. alter. of *Sunday*] (1897) **:** ice cream served with topping (as crushed fruit, syrup, nuts, or whipped cream)
sun dance *n, often cap S&D* (1849) **:** a solo or group solstice rite of American Indians
1**Sun·day** \ˈsən-(ˌ)dā, -dē\ *n* [ME, fr. OE *sunnandæg* (akin to OHG *sunnūntag*), fr. *sunne* sun + *dæg* day] (bef. 12c) **:** the first day of the week **:** the Christian analogue of the Jewish Sabbath — **Sun·days** \-(ˌ)dāz, -dēz\ *adv*
2**Sunday** *adj* (14c) **1 :** of, relating to, or associated with Sunday **2** [fr. the practice of wearing one's best clothes on Sunday to attend church] **:** BEST ⟨~ suit⟩ **3 :** AMATEUR ⟨~ painters⟩
Sun·day–go–to–meet·ing \ˈsən-dē-ˌgō-tə-ˈmē-tiŋ\ *adj* (1831) **:** appropriate for Sunday churchgoing
Sunday punch *n* (1929) **1 :** a powerful or devastating blow; *esp* **:** a knockout punch **2 :** something capable of delivering a powerful or devastating blow to the opposition ⟨saving his *Sunday punch* for the end of the campaign —*Newsweek*⟩
Sunday school *n* (1783) **:** a school held on Sunday for religious education; *also* **:** the teachers and pupils of such a school
sun·deck \ˈsən-ˌdek\ *n* (1897) **1 :** the usu. upper deck of a ship that is exposed to the most sun **2 :** a roof, deck, or terrace for sunning
sun·der \ˈsən-dər\ *vb* **sun·dered; sun·der·ing** \-d(ə-)riŋ\ [ME, fr. OE *gesundrian, syndrian;* akin to OHG *suntarōn* to sunder, OE *sundor* apart, L *sine* without, Skt *sanutar* away] *vt* (bef. 12c) **:** to break apart or in two **:** separate by or as if by violence or by intervening time or space ~ *vi* **:** to become parted, disunited, or severed ***syn*** see SEPARATE
sun·dew \ˈsən-(ˌ)dü, -(ˌ)dyü\ *n* (1578) **:** any of a genus (*Drosera* of the family Droseraceae, the sundew family) of bog-inhabiting insectivorous herbs having leaves covered with gland-tipped adhesive hairs
sun·di·al \-ˌdī(-ə)l\ *n* (1599) **:** an instrument to show the time of day by the shadow of a gnomon on a usu. horizontal plate or on a cylindrical surface
sun disk *n* (1877) **:** an ancient Near Eastern symbol consisting of a disk with conventionalized wings emblematic of the sun god (as Ra in Egypt)

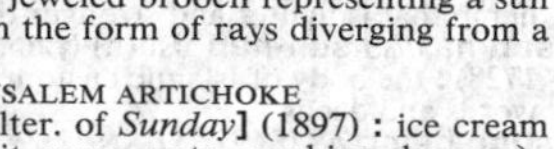
sun disk

sun dog *n* (1635) **1 :** PARHELION **2 :** a small nearly round halo on the parhelic circle most frequently just outside the halo of 22 degrees
sun·down \ˈsən-ˌdau̇n\ *n* (1620) **:** SUNSET 2

sun·down·er \-ˌdau̇-nər\ *n* (1868) **1** [fr. his habit of arriving at a place where he hopes to obtain food and lodging too late to do any work] *Austral* : HOBO, TRAMP **2** *chiefly Brit* : a drink taken at sundown
sun·dress \-ˌdres\ *n* (1942) : a dress with an abbreviated bodice usu. exposing the shoulders, arms, and back
sun·dries \ˈsən-drēz\ *n pl* [[1]*sundry*] (1755) : miscellaneous small articles, details, or items
sun·drops \ˈsən-ˌdräps\ *n pl but sing or pl in constr* (1784) : any of several day-flowering herbs (genera *Oenothera* and *Calylophus*) of the evening-primrose family
[1]**sun·dry** \ˈsən-drē\ *adj* [ME, different for each, fr. OE *syndrig,* fr. *sundor* apart — more at SUNDER] (13c) : MISCELLANEOUS, VARIOUS ⟨~ articles⟩
[2]**sundry** *pron, pl in constr* (15c) : an indeterminate number ⟨recommended for reading by all and ~ —Edward Huberman⟩
sun·fish \-ˌfish\ *n* (1629) **1** : OCEAN SUNFISH **2** : any of numerous No. American freshwater bony fishes (family Centrarchidae, esp. genus *Lepomis*) usu. with a deep compressed body and metallic luster
Sunfish *trademark* used for a small light sailboat that has one sail
sun·flow·er \-ˌflau̇(-ə)r\ *n* (1597) : any of a genus (*Helianthus,* esp. *H. annuus*) of New World composite plants with large yellow-rayed flower heads bearing edible seeds that yield an edible oil
sung *past and past part of* SING
Sung \ˈsu̇ŋ\ *n* [Chin (Beijing) *Sòng*] (1673) : a Chinese dynasty dated A.D. 960–1280 and marked by cultural refinement and achievements in philosophy, literature, and art — **Sung** *adj*
sun·glass \ˈsən-ˌglas\ *n* (1804) **1** : a convex lens for converging the sun's rays **2** *pl* : glasses to protect the eyes from the sun
sung mass *n* (1931) : HIGH MASS
sun god *n, often cap S&G* (1592) : a god that represents or personifies the sun in various religions
sun goddess *n, often cap S&G* (1861) : a goddess that represents or personifies the sun in various religions
sun–grebe \ˈsən-ˌgrēb\ *n* (1860) : any of a small family (Heliornithidae) of semiaquatic African, Asian, and American tropical birds that have lobed feet and are related to the rails
[1]**sunk** *past and past part of* SINK
[2]**sunk** *adj* (1719) **1** : depressed in spirits **2** : DONE FOR, RUINED
sunk·en \ˈsəŋ-kən\ *adj* [ME *sonkyn,* pp. of *sinken* to sink] (14c) **1** : SUBMERGED; *esp* : lying at the bottom of a body of water **2 a** : HOLLOW, RECESSED ⟨~ cheeks⟩ **b** : lying in a depression ⟨a ~ garden⟩ **c** : settled below the normal level **d** : constructed below the normal floor level ⟨a ~ living room⟩
sunk fence *n* (ca. 1771) : a ditch with a retaining wall used to divide lands without defacing a landscape — called also *ha-ha*
sun·lamp \ˈsən-ˌlamp\ *n* (1885) : an electric lamp designed to emit radiation of wavelengths from ultraviolet to infrared
sun·less \-ləs\ *adj* (1589) : lacking sunshine : DARK, CHEERLESS
sun·light \-ˌlīt\ *n* (13c) : the light of the sun : SUNSHINE
sun·lit \-ˌlit\ *adj* (1792) : lighted by or as if by the sun
sunn \ˈsən\ *n* [Hindi & Urdu *san,* fr. Skt *śaṇa*] (1774) : an annual Indian herb (*Crotalaria juncea*) of the legume family with slender branches, simple leaves, and yellow flowers; *also* : its valuable fiber resembling hemp that is lighter and stronger than jute
sun·na *also* **sun·nah** \ˈsu̇(n)-(ˌ)nə, ˈsə(n)-\ *n, often cap* [Ar *sunna*] (ca. 1728) : the body of Islamic custom and practice based on Muhammad's words and deeds
sunn hemp *n* (1849) : SUNN
Sun·ni \ˈsu̇(n)-(ˌ)nē\ *n* [Ar *sunnī,* fr. *sunna*] (1595) **1** : the Muslims of the branch of Islam that adheres to the orthodox tradition and acknowledges the first four caliphs as rightful successors of Muhammad — compare SHIA **2** : a Sunni Muslim — **Sunni** *adj*
Sun·nism \ˈsu̇(n)-ˌni-zəm\ *n* (1892) : the religious system or distinctive tenets of the Sunni
Sun·nite \-ˌnīt\ *n* (1718) : SUNNI 2 — **Sun·nite** \ˈsu̇(n)-ˌnīt\ *adj*
sun·ny \ˈsə-nē\ *adj* **sun·ni·er; -est** (14c) **1** : marked by brilliant sunlight : full of sunshine **2** : CHEERFUL, OPTIMISTIC ⟨a ~ disposition⟩ **3** : exposed to, brightened by, or warmed by the sun ⟨a ~ room⟩ — **sun·ni·ly** \ˈsə-nə-lē\ *adv* — **sun·ni·ness** \ˈsə-nē-nəs\ *n*
sun·ny–side up \ˌsə-nē-ˌsīd-ˈəp\ *adj* (ca. 1901) *of an egg* : fried on one side only
sun·porch \-ˌpȯrch\ *n* (1918) : a screened-in or glassed-in porch with a sunny exposure
sun protection factor *n* (1978) : a number assigned to a sunscreen that is the factor by which the time required for unprotected skin to become sunburned is increased when the sunscreen is used — abbr. SPF
sun·rise \ˈsən-ˌrīz\ *n* (15c) **1** : the apparent rising of the sun above the horizon; *also* : the accompanying atmospheric effects **2** : the time when the upper limb of the sun appears above the horizon as a result of the diurnal rotation of the earth
sun·roof \-ˌrüf, -ˌru̇f\ *n* (1952) : a panel in an automobile roof that can be opened
sun·room \-ˌrüm, -ˌru̇m\ *n* (ca. 1902) : a glass-enclosed porch or living room with a sunny exposure — called also *sun parlor*
sun·scald \-ˌskȯld\ *n* (1855) : an injury of woody plants (as fruit or forest trees) characterized by localized death of the tissues and sometimes by cankers and caused when it occurs in the summer by the combined action of both the heat and light of the sun and in the winter by the combined action of sun and low temperature to produce freezing of bark and underlying tissues
sun·screen \-ˌskrēn\ *n* (1738) **1** : a screen to protect against sun **2** : a preparation (as a lotion) applied to the skin to prevent sunburn (as by chemically absorbing ultraviolet radiation); *also* : its active ingredient (as benzophenone) — compare SUNBLOCK — **sun·screen·ing** *adj*
sun·seek·er \-ˌsē-kər\ *n* (1954) : a person who travels to an area of warmth and sun esp. in winter
[1]**sun·set** \-ˌset\ *n* (14c) **1** : the apparent descent of the sun below the horizon; *also* : the accompanying atmospheric effects **2** : the time when the upper limb of the sun disappears below the horizon as a result of the diurnal rotation of the earth **3** : a period of decline; *esp* : old age
[2]**sunset** *adj* (1976) : stipulating the periodic review of government agencies and programs in order to continue their existence ⟨~ laws⟩
sun·shade \ˈsən-ˌshād\ *n* (1842) : something used as a protection from the sun's rays: as **a** : PARASOL **b** : AWNING
[1]**sun·shine** \-ˌshīn\ *n* (13c) **1 a** : the sun's light or direct rays **b** : the warmth and light given by the sun's rays **c** : a spot or surface on which the sun's light shines **2** : something (as a person, condition, or influence) that radiates warmth, cheer, or happiness — **sun·shiny** \-ˌshī-nē\ *adj*
[2]**sunshine** *adj* (1972) : forbidding or restricting closed meetings of legislative or executive bodies and sometimes providing for public access to records ⟨~ laws⟩
sun·spot \-ˌspät\ *n* (1868) : any of the dark spots that appear at times on the sun's surface and are usu. visible only through a telescope
sun·stroke \-ˌstrōk\ *n* (1829) : heatstroke caused by direct exposure to the sun
sun·struck \-ˌstrək\ *adj* (1794) : affected or touched by the sun
sun·suit \-ˌsüt\ *n* (1929) : an outfit worn usu. for sunbathing and play
sun·tan \-ˌtan\ *n* (1867) **1** : a browning of the skin from exposure to the rays of the sun **2** *pl* : a tan-colored summer uniform — **sun·tanned** \-ˌtand\ *adj*
sun·tan·ning \ˈsən-ˌta-niŋ\ *n* (1959) : the process of tanning the skin by exposure to the sun or artificial light — **suntanning** *adj*
sun·up \-ˌəp\ *n* (1653) : SUNRISE
[1]**sun·ward** \ˈsən-wərd\ *or* **sun·wards** \-wərdz\ *adv* (1611) : toward the sun
[2]**sunward** *adj* (1769) : facing the sun
sun·wise \ˈsən-ˌwīz\ *adv* (ca. 1864) : CLOCKWISE
[1]**sup** \ˈsəp\ *vb* **supped; sup·ping** [ME *suppen,* fr. OE *sūpan, suppan;* akin to OHG *sūfan* to drink, sip, OE *sopp* sop] *vt* (bef. 12c) : to take or drink in swallows or gulps ~ *vi, chiefly dial* : to take food and esp. liquid food into the mouth a little at a time
[2]**sup** *n* (1551) : a mouthful esp. of liquor or broth : SIP; *also* : a small quantity of liquid ⟨pour me just a ~ of tea⟩
[3]**sup** *vi* **supped; sup·ping** [ME *soupen, suppen,* fr. AF *super,* fr. *supe* sop, soup — more at SOUP] (14c) **1** : to eat the evening meal **2** : to make one's supper — used with *on* or *off* ⟨~ on roast beef⟩
[4]**sup** *abbr* **1** superior **2** supra
[1]**su·per** \ˈsü-pər\ *adj* [*super-*] (1842) **1 a** : of high grade or quality **b** — used as a generalized term of approval ⟨a ~ cook⟩ **2** : very large or powerful ⟨a ~ atomic bomb⟩ **3** : exhibiting the characteristics of its type to an extreme or excessive degree ⟨~ secrecy⟩
[2]**super** *n* (1838) **1** [by shortening] **a** : SUPERNUMERARY; *esp* : a supernumerary actor **b** : SUPERINTENDENT, SUPERVISOR; *esp* : the superintendent of an apartment building **2** [short for obs. *superhive*] : a removable upper story of a beehive **3** [[1]*super*] : a superfine grade or extra large size **4** [origin unknown] : a thin loosely woven open-meshed starched cotton fabric used esp. for reinforcing books
[3]**super** *adv* [*super-*] (1946) **1** : VERY, EXTREMELY ⟨a ~ fast car⟩ **2** : to an excessive degree
super- *prefix* [L, over, above, in addition, fr. *super* over, above, on top of — more at OVER] **1 a (1)** : over and above : higher in quantity, quality, or degree than : more than ⟨*super*human⟩ **(2)** : in addition : extra ⟨*super*tax⟩ **b (1)** : exceeding or so as to exceed a norm ⟨*super*heat⟩ **(2)** : in or to an extreme or excessive degree or intensity ⟨*super*subtle⟩ **c** : surpassing all or most others of its kind ⟨*super*highway⟩ **2 a** : situated or placed above, on, or at the top of ⟨*super*lunary⟩; *specif* : situated on the dorsal side of **b** : next above or higher ⟨*super*tonic⟩ **3** : having the (specified) ingredient present in a large or unusually large proportion ⟨*super*phosphate⟩ **4** : constituting a more inclusive category than that specified ⟨*super*family⟩ **5** : superior in status, title, or position ⟨*super*power⟩

su·per·ab·sor·bent
su·per·ac·cu·rate
su·per·achiev·er
su·per·ac·tiv·i·ty
su·per·ad·di·tion
su·per·ad·min·is·tra·tor
su·per·agent
su·per·am·bi·tious
su·per·ath·lete
su·per·bad
su·per·bank
su·per·bil·lion·aire
su·per·bitch
su·per·board
su·per·bomb
su·per·bomb·er
su·per·bright
su·per·bu·reau·crat
su·per·cab·i·net
su·per·car·ri·er
su·per·cau·tious
su·per·cheap
su·per·chic
su·per·church
su·per·civ·i·li·za·tion
su·per·civ·i·lized
su·per·clean
su·per·club
su·per·co·los·sal
su·per·com·fort·able
su·per·com·pe·tent
su·per·com·pet·i·tive
su·per·con·fi·dent
su·per·con·glom·er·ate
su·per·con·ser·va·tive
su·per·con·ve·nient
su·per·cop
su·per·cor·po·ra·tion
su·per·crim·i·nal
su·per·cute
su·per·de·luxe
su·per·dip·lo·mat
su·per·ef·fec·tive
su·per·ef·fi·cien·cy
su·per·ef·fi·cient
su·per·ego·ist
su·per·elite
su·per·em·i·nence
su·per·em·i·nent
su·per·em·i·nent·ly
su·per·ex·pen·sive
su·per·ex·press
su·per·fan
su·per·farm
su·per·fast
su·per·firm
su·per·flack
su·per·good
su·per·gov·ern·ment
su·per·growth
su·per·hard·en
su·per·heavy
su·per·her·o·ine
su·per·hit
su·per·hot
su·per·hype
su·per·in·su·lat·ed
su·per·in·tel·lec·tu·al
su·per·in·tel·li·gence
su·per·in·tel·li·gent
su·per·in·ten·si·ty
su·per·jock
su·per·large
su·per·law·yer
su·per·light
su·per·lob·by·ist
su·per·long
su·per·loy·al·ist
su·per·lux·u·ri·ous
su·per·lux·u·ry
su·per·ma·cho
su·per·ma·jor·i·ty
su·per·male
su·per·mas·cu·line
su·per·mas·sive
su·per·mil·i·tant
su·per·mil·lion·aire
su·per·mind
su·per·min·is·ter
su·per·mod·ern
su·per·na·tion
su·per·na·tion·al
su·per·nu·tri·tion
su·per·or·gan·ic
su·per·or·gasm
su·per·pa·tri·ot
su·per·pa·tri·ot·ic
su·per·pa·tri·o·tism
su·per·per·son
su·per·per·son·al
su·per·phe·nom·e·non
su·per·pimp
su·per·plane
su·per·play·er
su·per·po·lite
su·per·port
su·per·pow·er·ful
su·per·pre·mi·um
su·per·pro
su·per·prof·it
su·per·qual·i·ty
su·per·race
su·per·real
su·per·re·al·ism
su·per·re·gion·al
su·per·rich
su·per·road
su·per·ro·man·tic
su·per·ro·man·ti·cism
su·per·safe
su·per·sale
su·per·sales·man
su·per·scale
su·per·school
su·per·scout
su·per·se·cre·cy
su·per·se·cret
su·per·sell

su·per·sell·er
su·per·sen·si·tive
su·per·sen·si·tiv·i·ty
su·per·sex·u·al·i·ty
su·per·sharp
su·per·show
su·per·sing·er
su·per·size
su·per·sized
su·per·sleuth
su·per·slick
su·per·smart
su·per·smooth
su·per·soft
su·per·so·phis·ti·cat·ed
su·per·spe·cial
su·per·spe·cial·ist
su·per·spe·cial·i·za·tion
su·per·spe·cial·ized
su·per·spec·ta·cle
su·per·spec·tac·u·lar
su·per·spec·u·la·tion
su·per·spy
su·per·state
su·per·sta·tion
su·per·stim·u·late
su·per·stock
su·per·stra·tum
su·per·strength
su·per·strike
su·per·strong
su·per·stud
su·per·sub·tle
su·per·sub·tle·ty
su·per·sur·geon
su·per·sweet
su·per·tank·er
su·per·ter·rif·ic
su·per·thick
su·per·thin
su·per·thril·ler
su·per·tight
su·per·vir·ile
su·per·vir·tu·o·so
su·per·wave
su·per·weap·on
su·per·wide
su·per·wife

su·per·a·ble \ˈsü-p(ə-)rə-bəl\ *adj* [L *superabilis,* fr. *superare* to surmount — more at INSUPERABLE] (1629) : capable of being overcome or conquered — **su·per·a·ble·ness** *n* — **su·per·a·bly** \-blē\ *adv*

su·per·abound \ˌsü-pər-ə-ˈbau̇nd\ *vi* [ME, fr. LL *superabundare,* fr. L *super-* + *abundare* to abound] (14c) : to abound or prevail in greater measure or to excess

su·per·abun·dant \-ˈbən-dənt\ *adj* [ME, fr. LL *superabundant-, superabundans,* fr. prp. of *superabundare*] (15c) : EXCESSIVE — **su·per·abun·dance** \-dən(t)s\ *n* — **su·per·abun·dant·ly** *adv*

su·per·add \ˌsü-pər-ˈad\ *vt* [ME, fr. L *superaddere,* fr. *super-* + *addere* to add] (15c) : to add esp. in a way that compounds an effect

su·per·agen·cy \ˈsü-pər-ˌā-jən(t)-sē\ *n* (1943) : a large complex governmental agency esp. when set up to supervise other agencies

su·per·al·loy \ˌsü-pər-ˈa-ˌlȯi, -ə-ˈlȯi\ *n* (1948) : any of various high-strength often complex alloys resistant to high temperature

su·per·al·tern \ˌsü-pər-ˈȯl-tərn\ *n* [*super-* + sub*altern*] (1921) : a universal proposition (as "every P is Q") that in traditional logic is held to be grounds for the immediate inference of the truth of a corresponding subaltern (as "some P is Q")

su·per·an·nu·ate \ˌsü-pər-ˈan-yə-ˌwāt\ *vb* **-at·ed; -at·ing** [back-formation fr. *superannuated*] *vt* (ca. 1633) **1 :** to make, declare, or prove obsolete or out-of-date **2 :** to retire and pension because of age or infirmity ~ *vi* **1 :** to become retired **2 :** to become antiquated — **su·per·an·nu·a·tion** \-ˌan-yə-ˈwā-shən\ *n*

superannuated *adj* [ML *superannuatus,* pp. of *superannuari* to be too old, fr. L *super-* + *annus* year — more at ANNUAL] (ca. 1633) **1 :** OUTMODED, OLD-FASHIONED ⟨~ slang⟩ ⟨~ planes⟩ **2 a :** incapacitated or disqualified for active duty by advanced age **b :** older than the typical member of a specified group ⟨a ~ graduate student⟩

su·perb \su̇-ˈpərb\ *adj* [L *superbus* excellent, proud, fr. *super* above + *-bus* (akin to OE *bēon* to be) — more at OVER, BE] (1549) : marked to the highest degree by grandeur, excellence, brilliance, or competence ***syn*** see SPLENDID — **su·perb·ly** *adv* — **su·perb·ness** *n*

Super Ball *trademark* — used for a toy rubber ball with a high bounce

su·per·block \-ˌbläk\ *n* (1928) : a very large commercial or residential block barred to through traffic, crossed by pedestrian walks and sometimes access roads, and often spotted with grassed malls

Super Bowl *service mark* — used for the annual championship game of the National Football League

su·per·bug \ˈsü-pər-ˌbəg\ *n* (1985) : a pathogenic microorganism and esp. a bacterium that has developed resistance to the medications normally used against it

[1]**su·per·cal·en·der** \ˈsü-pər-ˌka-lən-dər\ *vt* (1888) : to process (paper) in a supercalender

[2]**supercalender** *n* (1894) : a stack of highly polished calender rolls used to give an extra finish to paper

su·per·car·go \ˌsü-pər-ˈkär-(ˌ)gō, ˈsü-pər-ˌ\ *n* [Sp *sobrecargo,* fr. *sobre-* over (fr. L *super-*) + *cargo* cargo] (1697) : an officer on a merchant ship in charge of the commercial concerns of the voyage

su·per·cede *var of* SUPERSEDE

usage *Supercede* has occurred as a spelling variant of *supersede* since the 17th century, and it is common in current published writing. It continues, however, to be widely regarded as an error.

su·per·cell \ˈsü-pər-ˌsel\ *n* (1985) : an unusually large storm cell; *specif* : a severe storm generated by such a cell

su·per·cen·ter \ˈsü-pər-ˌsen-tər\ *n* (1977) : a very large discount department store that also sells a complete line of grocery merchandise

su·per·charge \ˈsü-pər-ˌchärj\ *vt* (1876) **1 :** to charge greatly or excessively (as with vigor or tension) **2 :** to supply a charge to the intake of (as an engine) at a pressure higher than that of the surrounding atmosphere **3 :** PRESSURIZE 1 — **supercharge** *n*

su·per·charg·er \-ˌchär-jər\ *n* (1919) : a device (as a blower or compressor) for pressurizing the cabin of an airplane or for increasing the volume air charge of an internal combustion engine over that which would normally be drawn in through the pumping action of the pistons

su·per·cil·i·ary \ˌsü-pər-ˈsi-lē-ˌer-ē\ *adj* [NL *superciliaris,* fr. L *supercilium*] (1732) : of, relating to, or adjoining the eyebrow : SUPRAORBITAL

su·per·cil·ious \-ˈsi-lē-əs, -ˈsil-yəs\ *adj* [L *superciliosus,* fr. *supercilium* eyebrow, haughtiness, fr. *super-* + *-cilium* eyelid (akin to *celare* to hide) — more at HELL] (1614) : coolly and patronizingly haughty ***syn*** see PROUD — **su·per·cil·ious·ly** *adv* — **su·per·cil·ious·ness** *n*

su·per·city \ˈsü-pər-ˌsi-tē\ *n* (1925) : MEGALOPOLIS

su·per·class \-ˌklas\ *n* (ca. 1891) : a category in biological classification ranking below a phylum or division and above a class

su·per·clu·ster \ˈsü-pər-ˌkləs-tər\ *n* (1926) : a group of gravitationally associated clusters of galaxies

su·per·coil \-ˌkȯi(-ə)l\ *n* (1965) : a double helix (as of DNA) that has undergone additional twisting in the same direction as or in the opposite direction from the turns in the original helix — **supercoil** *vb*

su·per·col·lid·er \-kə-ˌlī-dər\ *n* (1984) : a very large collider capable of accelerating particles to very high energies

su·per·com·put·er \-kəm-ˌpyü-tər\ *n* (1967) : a large very fast mainframe used esp. for scientific computations

su·per·con·duct \ˌsü-pər-kən-ˈdəkt\ *vi* (1952) : to exhibit superconductivity — **su·per·con·duc·tive** \-ˈdək-tiv\ *adj*

su·per·con·duc·tiv·i·ty \-ˌkän-ˌdək-ˈti-və-tē, -kən-\ *n* (1913) : a complete disappearance of electrical resistance in a substance esp. at very low temperatures — **su·per·con·duc·tor** \-kən-ˈdək-tər\ *n*

su·per·con·ti·nent \ˈsü-pər-ˌkän-tə-nənt, -ˌkänt-nənt\ *n* (1960) : a hypothetical former large continent from which other continents are held to have broken off and drifted away

[1]**su·per·cool** \ˌsü-pər-ˈkül\ *vt* (1906) : to cool below the freezing point without solidification or crystallization ~ *vi* : to become supercooled

[2]**supercool** *adj* (1970) : extremely cool: as **a :** showing extraordinary reserve and self-control **b :** being the latest style or fashion

su·per·crit·i·cal \-ˈkri-ti-kəl\ *adj* (1934) : being or having a temperature above a critical temperature ⟨~ fluid⟩

su·per·cross \ˈsü-pər-ˌkrȯs\ *n* [*super-* + motocross] (1983) : a motorcycle race held in a stadium on a dirt track having hairpin turns and high jumps

su·per·cur·rent \ˈsü-pər-ˌkər-ənt, -ˌkə-rənt\ *n* (1940) : a current of electricity flowing in a superconductor

su·per·del·e·gate \ˈsü-pər-ˌde-li-gət\ *n* (1983) : a political party leader or an elected official selected to vote at a presidential nominating convention who may or may not be pledged to support a particular candidate

su·per–du·per \ˈsü-pər-ˈdü-pər\ *adj* [redupl. of [1]*super*] (1940) : of the greatest excellence, size, effectiveness, or impressiveness

su·per·ego \ˌsü-pər-ˈē-(ˌ)gō *also* -ˈe-(ˌ)gō\ *n* [NL, trans. of G *Über-ich,* fr. *über* over + *ich* I] (1919) : the one of the three divisions of the psyche in psychoanalytic theory that is only partly conscious, represents internalization of parental conscience and the rules of society, and functions to reward and punish through a system of moral attitudes, conscience, and a sense of guilt — compare EGO, ID

su·per·el·e·vate \-ˈe-lə-ˌvāt\ *vt* (ca. 1945) : BANK 1c

su·per·el·e·va·tion \-ˌe-lə-ˈvā-shən\ *n* (1889) **1 :** the vertical distance between the heights of inner and outer edges of highway pavement or railroad rails **2 :** additional elevation

su·per·er·o·ga·tion \ˌsü-pər-ˌer-ə-ˈgā-shən\ *n* [ML *supererogation-, supererogatio,* fr. *supererogare* to perform beyond the call of duty, fr. LL, to expend in addition, fr. L *super-* + *erogare* to expend public funds after asking the consent of the people, fr. *e-* + *rogare* to ask — more at RIGHT] (1526) : the act of performing more than is required by duty, obligation, or need

su·per·erog·a·to·ry \ˌsü-pər-i-ˈrä-gə-ˌtȯr-ē\ *adj* (1593) **1 :** observed or performed to an extent not enjoined or required **2 :** SUPERFLUOUS

su·per·fam·i·ly \ˈsü-pər-ˌfam-lē, -ˈfa-mə-\ *n* (ca. 1890) **1 :** a category of biological classification ranking below an order and above a family **2 :** a large group of closely related molecules or chemical compounds usu. possessing a similar function

su·per·fat·ted \-ˌfa-təd\ *adj* (1891) : containing extra oil or fat

su·per·fe·cun·da·tion \ˌsü-pər-ˌfe-kən-ˈdā-shən, -ˌfē-\ *n* (ca. 1855) **1 :** successive fertilization of two or more ova from the same ovulation esp. by different sires **2 :** fertilization at one time of a number of ova excessive for the species

su·per·fe·ta·tion \-fē-ˈtā-shən\ *n* [ML *superfetation-, superfetatio,* fr. L *superfetare* to conceive while already pregnant, fr. *super-* + *fetare* to bear young, fr. *fetus* newly delivered — more at FETUS] (1642) : a progressive accumulation or accretion reaching an excessive degree

su·per·fi·cial \ˌsü-pər-ˈfi-shəl\ *adj* [ME, fr. LL *superficialis,* fr. L *superficies*] (15c) **1 a (1) :** of, relating to, or located near a surface **(2) :** lying on, not penetrating below, or affecting only the surface ⟨~ wounds⟩ **b** *Brit, of a unit of measure* : SQUARE ⟨~ foot⟩ **2 a :** concerned only with the obvious or apparent : SHALLOW **b :** seen on the surface : EXTERNAL **c :** presenting only an appearance without substance or significance — **su·per·fi·cial·ly** \-ˈfi-sh(ə-)lē\ *adv*

syn SUPERFICIAL, SHALLOW, CURSORY mean lacking in depth or solidity. SUPERFICIAL implies a concern only with surface aspects or obvious features ⟨a *superficial* analysis⟩. SHALLOW is more generally derogatory in implying lack of depth in knowledge, reasoning, emotions, or character ⟨a *shallow* review⟩. CURSORY suggests a lack of thoroughness or a neglect of details ⟨a *cursory* reading⟩.

superficial fascia *n* (1876) : the thin layer of loose fatty connective tissue underlying the skin and binding it to the parts beneath — called also *hypodermis*

su·per·fi·ci·al·i·ty \ˌsü-pər-ˌfi-shē-ˈa-lə-tē\ *n, pl* **-ties** (1530) **1 :** the quality or state of being superficial **2 :** something superficial

su·per·fi·cies \-ˈfi-(ˌ)shēz, -shē-ˌēz\ *n, pl* **superficies** [L, surface, fr. *super-* + *facies* face, aspect — more at FACE] (1530) **1 :** a surface of a body or a region of space **2 :** the external aspects or appearance of a thing

su·per·fine \ˌsü-pər-ˈfīn\ *adj* (1575) **1 :** overly refined or nice **2 :** of extremely fine size or texture ⟨~ toothbrush bristles⟩ ⟨~ sugar⟩ **3 :** of high quality or grade — used esp. of merchandise

su·per·fix \ˈsü-pər-ˌfiks\ *n* [*super-* + *-fix* (as in *prefix*)] (ca. 1948) : a morpheme consisting of a pattern of stress, intonation, or juncture features that are associated with the syllables of a word or phrase (as the distinctive stress patterns of the noun *subject* and the verb *subject*)

su·per·flu·id \ˌsü-pər-ˈflü-əd\ *n* (1938) : an unusual state of matter noted only in liquid helium cooled to near absolute zero and characterized by apparently frictionless flow (as through fine holes) — **superfluid** *adj* — **su·per·flu·id·i·ty** \-flü-ˈi-də-tē\ *n*

su·per·flu·i·ty \ˌsü-pər-ˈflü-ə-tē\ *n, pl* **-ties** [ME *superfluitee,* fr. AF *superfluité,* fr. LL *superfluitat-, superfluitas,* fr. L *superfluus*] (14c) **1 a :** EXCESS, OVERSUPPLY **b :** something unnecessary or superfluous **2 :** immoderate and esp. luxurious living, habits, or desires

su·per·flu·ous \su̇-ˈpər-flü-əs\ *adj* [ME, fr. L *superfluus,* lit., running over, fr. *superfluere* to overflow, fr. *super-* + *fluere* to flow — more at FLUID] (15c) **1 a :** exceeding what is sufficient or necessary : EXTRA **b :** not needed : UNNECESSARY **2** *obs* **:** marked by wastefulness : EXTRAVAGANT — **su·per·flu·ous·ly** *adv* — **su·per·flu·ous·ness** *n*

su·per·gene \ˈsü-pər-ˌjēn\ *n* (1949) : a group of linked genes acting as an allelic unit esp. when due to the suppression of crossing-over

\ə\ **abut** \ᵊ\ kitten, F table \ər\ **fur**ther \a\ **ash** \ā\ **ace** \ä\ **mop, mar**
\au̇\ **out** \ch\ **chin** \e\ **bet** \ē\ **easy** \g\ **go** \i\ **hit** \ī\ **ice** \j\ **job**
\ŋ\ **sing** \ō\ **go** \ȯ\ **law** \ȯi\ **boy** \th\ **thin** \t͟h\ **the** \ü\ **loot** \u̇\ **foot**
\y\ **yet** \zh\ **vision, beige** \k͟, ⁿ, œ, ue, ʸ\ *see* Guide to Pronunciation

su·per·gi·ant \-ˌjī-ənt\ *n* (1926) **:** something that is extremely large; *esp* **:** a star of very great intrinsic luminosity and enormous size — **super·giant** *adj*

su·per·glue \ˈsü-pər-ˌglü\ *n* (1946) **:** a very strong glue; *specif* **:** a glue whose chief ingredient is a cyanoacrylate that becomes adhesive through polymerization rather than evaporation of a solvent — **super·glue** *vt*

su·per·graph·ics \-ˌgra-fiks\ *n pl but sing or pl in constr* (1969) **:** billboard-sized graphic shapes usu. of bright color and simple design

su·per·grav·i·ty \ˌsü-pər-ˈgra-və-tē\ *n* (1976) **:** any of various theories in physics that are based on supersymmetry and attempt to unify general relativity and quantum theory and that state that the principal transmitter of gravity is the graviton

su·per·group \ˈsü-pər-ˌgrüp\ *n* (1968) **:** a rock group made up of prominent former members of other rock groups; *also* **:** an extremely successful rock group

[1]**su·per·heat** \ˌsü-pər-ˈhēt\ *vt* (1859) **1 :** to heat (a vapor not in contact with its own liquid) so as to cause to remain free from suspended liquid droplets ⟨~*ed* steam⟩ **2 :** to heat (a liquid) above the boiling point without converting into vapor — **su·per·heat·er** *n*

[2]**su·per·heat** \ˈsü-pər-ˌhēt, ˌsü-pər-ˈ\ *n* (1884) **:** the extra heat imparted to a vapor in superheating it from a dry and saturated condition; *also* **:** the corresponding rise of temperature

su·per·heat·ed \-ˌhē-təd, -ˈhē-\ *adj* (1857) **1 :** subjected to superheating **2 :** very hot; *also* **:** exceedingly emotional or intense ⟨~ debate⟩

su·per·hea·vy·weight \ˌsü-pər-ˈhe-vē-ˌwāt\ *n* (1971) **:** an athlete (as an Olympic weightlifter, boxer, or wrestler) who competes in the heaviest class or division

su·per·he·lix \ˈsü-pər-ˌhē-liks\ *n* (1964) **:** SUPERCOIL — **su·per·he·li·cal** \ˌsü-pər-ˈhe-li-kəl, -ˈhē-\ *adj*

su·per·hero \-ˌhir-(ˌ)ō, -ˌhē-(ˌ)rō\ *n* (1917) **:** a fictional hero having extraordinary or superhuman powers; *also* **:** an exceptionally skillful or successful person

su·per·het·ero·dyne \ˌsü-pər-ˈhe-tə-rə-ˌdīn, -ˈhe-trə-\ *adj* [*super*sonic + *heterodyne*] (1922) **:** used in or being a radio receiver in which an incoming signal is mixed with a locally generated frequency to produce an ultrasonic signal that is then rectified, amplified, and rectified again to reproduce the sound — **superheterodyne** *n*

su·per·high frequency \ˈsü-pər-ˌhī-\ *n* (1945) **:** a radio frequency in the next to the highest range of the radio spectrum — see RADIO FREQUENCY table

su·per·high·way \ˌsü-pər-ˈhī-ˌwā, ˈsü-pər-ˌ\ *n* (1925) **1 :** a multilane highway (as an expressway or turnpike) designed for high-speed traffic **2 :** INFORMATION SUPERHIGHWAY

su·per·hu·man \ˌsü-pər-ˈhyü-mən, -ˈyü-\ *adj* (1633) **1 :** being above the human **:** DIVINE ⟨~ beings⟩ **2 :** exceeding normal human power, size, or capability **:** HERCULEAN ⟨a ~ effort⟩ ⟨~ strength⟩; *also* **:** having such power, size, or capability — **su·per·hu·man·i·ty** \-hyü-ˈma-nə-tē, -yü-\ *n* — **su·per·hu·man·ly** \-ˈhyü-mən-lē, -ˈyü-\ *adv* — **su·per·hu·man·ness** \-mən-nəs\ *n*

su·per·im·pose \ˌsü-pər-im-ˈpōz\ *vt* (1794) **:** to place or lay over or above something ⟨*superimposed* images⟩ — **su·per·im·pos·able** \-ˈpō-zə-bəl\ *adj* — **su·per·im·po·si·tion** \-ˌim-pə-ˈzi-shən\ *n*

su·per·in·cum·bent \-in-ˈkəm-bənt\ *adj* [L *superincumbent-, superincumbens,* prp. of *superincumbere* to lie on top of, fr. *super-* + *incumbere* to lie down on — more at INCUMBENT] (1664) **:** lying or resting and usu. exerting pressure on something else — **su·per·in·cum·bent·ly** *adv*

su·per·in·di·vid·u·al \ˌsü-pər-ˌin-də-ˈvij-wəl, -ˈvi-jə-wəl, -ˈvi-jəl\ *adj* (1916) **:** of, relating to, or being an organism, entity, or complex of more than individual complexity or nature

su·per·in·duce \-in-ˈdüs, -ˈdyüs\ *vt* [L *superinducere,* fr. *super-* + *inducere* to lead in — more at INDUCE] (ca. 1555) **1 :** to introduce as an addition over or above something already existing **2 :** BRING ON, INDUCE — **su·per·in·duc·tion** \-ˈdək-shən\ *n*

su·per·in·fec·tion \-in-ˈfek-shən\ *n* (ca. 1922) **:** reinfection or a second infection with a microbial agent (as a bacterium, fungus, or virus) — **su·per·in·fect** \-ˈfekt\ *vt*

su·per·in·tend \ˌsü-p(ə-)rin-ˈtend, ˌsü-pərn-\ *vt* [LL *superintendere,* fr. L *super-* + *intendere* to stretch out, direct — more at INTEND] (ca. 1615) **:** to have or exercise the charge and oversight of **:** DIRECT

su·per·in·ten·dence \-ˈten-dən(t)s\ *n* (1603) **:** the act or function of superintending or directing **:** SUPERVISION

su·per·in·ten·den·cy \-dən(t)-sē\ *n, pl* **-cies** (1598) **:** the office, post, or jurisdiction of a superintendent; *also* **:** SUPERINTENDENCE

su·per·in·ten·dent \-dənt\ *n* [ML *superintendent-, superintendens,* fr. LL, prp. of *superintendere*] (1554) **:** one who has executive oversight and charge — **superintendent** *adj*

[1]**su·pe·ri·or** \sü-ˈpir-ē-ər\ *adj* [ME, fr. MF, fr. L, compar. of *superus* upper, fr. *super* over, above — more at OVER] (14c) **1 :** situated higher up **:** UPPER **2 :** of higher rank, quality, or importance **3 :** courageously or serenely indifferent (as to something painful or disheartening) **4 a :** greater in quantity or numbers ⟨escaped by ~ speed⟩ **b :** excellent of its kind **:** BETTER ⟨her ~ memory⟩ **5 :** being a superscript **6 a** *of an animal structure* **:** situated above or anterior or dorsal to another and esp. a corresponding part ⟨a ~ artery⟩ **b** *of a plant structure* **:** situated above or near the top of another part: as (1) *of a calyx* **:** attached to and apparently arising from the ovary (2) *of an ovary* **:** free from the calyx or other floral envelope **7 :** more comprehensive ⟨a genus is ~ to a species⟩ **8 :** affecting or assuming an air of superiority **:** SUPERCILIOUS — **su·pe·ri·or·ly** *adv*

[2]**superior** *n* (15c) **1 :** one who is above another in rank, station, or office; *esp* **:** the head of a religious house or order **2 :** one that surpasses another in quality or merit **3 :** SUPERSCRIPT

superior conjunction *n* (1833) **:** a conjunction of a planet with the sun in which the sun is aligned between the earth and the planet

superior court *n* (1686) **1 :** a court of general jurisdiction intermediate between the inferior courts (as a justice of the peace court) and the higher appellate courts **2 :** a court with juries having original jurisdiction

superior general *n, pl* **superiors general** (1774) **:** the superior of a religious order or congregation

su·pe·ri·or·i·ty \sü-ˌpir-ē-ˈȯr-ə-tē, ˌsü-, -ˈär-\ *n, pl* **-ties** (15c) **:** the quality or state of being superior; *also* **:** a superior characteristic

superiority complex *n* (ca. 1924) **:** an exaggerated opinion of oneself

superior planet *n* (1583) **:** a planet (as Jupiter) whose orbit lies outside that of Earth

superior vena cava *n* (1875) **:** the branch of the vena cava of a vertebrate that brings blood back from the head and anterior part of the body to the heart

su·per·ja·cent \ˌsü-pər-ˈjā-sᵊnt\ *adj* [L *superjacent-, superjacens,* prp. of *superjacēre* to lie over or upon, fr. *super-* + *jacēre* to lie; akin to L *jacere* to throw — more at JET] (1610) **:** lying above or upon **:** OVERLYING ⟨~ rocks⟩

su·per·jet \ˈsü-pər-ˌjet\ *n* (1958) **:** a very large jet airplane

su·per·jum·bo \ˈsü-pər-ˌjəm-bō\ *n* (1991) **:** an extremely large passenger jet airplane **:** SUPERJET

[1]**su·per·la·tive** \sü-ˈpər-lə-tiv\ *adj* [ME *superlatif,* fr. AF, fr. LL *superlativus,* fr. L *superlatus* (pp. of *superferre* to carry over, raise high), fr. *super-* + *latus,* pp. of *ferre* to carry — more at TOLERATE, BEAR] (14c) **1 :** of, relating to, or constituting the degree of grammatical comparison that denotes an extreme or unsurpassed level or extent **2 a :** surpassing all others **:** SUPREME **b :** of very high quality **:** EXCELLENT ⟨~ work⟩ **3 :** EXCESSIVE, EXAGGERATED — **su·per·la·tive·ly** *adv* — **su·per·la·tive·ness** *n*

[2]**superlative** *n* (15c) **1 a :** the superlative degree of comparison in a language **b :** a superlative form of an adjective or adverb **2 :** the superlative or utmost degree of something **:** ACME **3 :** a superlative person or thing **4 :** an admiring sometimes exaggerated expression esp. of praise

su·per·lin·er \ˈsü-pər-ˌlī-nər\ *n* (1919) **:** a fast luxurious passenger liner of great size

su·per·lu·na·ry \ˌsü-pər-ˈlü-nə-rē\ *or* **su·per·lu·nar** \-nər, -ˌnär\ *adj* [L *super-* + *luna* moon — more at LUNAR] (1614) *archaic* **:** being above the moon **:** CELESTIAL

su·per·ma·jor·i·ty \ˈsü-pər-mə-ˌjȯr-ə-tē, -ˌjär-\ *n* (1977) **:** a majority (as two-thirds or three-fifths) greater than a simple majority

su·per·man \ˈsü-pər-ˌman\ *n* [trans. of G *Übermensch,* fr. *über* over, super- + *Mensch* man] (1903) **1 :** a superior man that according to Nietzsche has learned to forgo fleeting pleasures and attain happiness and dominance through the exercise of creative power **2 :** a person of extraordinary or superhuman power or achievements

su·per·mar·ket \-ˌmär-kət\ *n, often attrib* (1933) **1 :** a self-service retail market selling esp. foods and household merchandise **2 :** something resembling a supermarket esp. in the variety or volume of its goods or services

su·per·mi·cro \-ˌmī-(ˌ)krō\ *n* (1982) **:** a very fast and powerful microcomputer

su·per·mini·com·put·er \-ˈmi-nē-kəm-ˌpyü-tər\ *n* (1980) **:** a very fast and powerful minicomputer — called also *supermini*

su·per·mod·el \ˈsü-pər-ˌmä-dᵊl\ *n* (1977) **:** a famous and successful fashion model

su·per·mom \ˈsü-pər-ˌmäm\ *n* (1974) **:** an exemplary mother; *also* **:** a woman who performs the traditional duties of housekeeping and child-rearing while also having a full-time job

su·per·nal \sü-ˈpər-nᵊl\ *adj* [ME, fr. MF *supernel,* fr. L *supernus,* fr. *super* over, above — more at OVER] (15c) **1 a :** being or coming from on high **b :** HEAVENLY, ETHEREAL ⟨~ melodies⟩ **c :** superlatively good ⟨~ trumpet playing⟩ **2 :** located in or belonging to the sky — **su·per·nal·ly** \-nᵊl-ē\ *adv*

su·per·na·tant \ˌsü-pər-ˈnā-tᵊnt\ *n* [L *supernatant-, supernatans,* prp. of *supernatare* to float, fr. *super-* + *natare* to swim — more at NATANT] (1922) **:** the usu. clear liquid overlying material deposited by settling, precipitation, or centrifugation — **supernatant** *adj*

su·per·nat·u·ral \ˌsü-pər-ˈna-chə-rəl, -ˈnach-rəl\ *adj* [ME, fr. ML *supernaturalis,* fr. L *super-* + *natura* nature] (15c) **1 :** of or relating to an order of existence beyond the visible observable universe; *esp* **:** of or relating to God or a god, demigod, spirit, or devil **2 a :** departing from what is usual or normal esp. so as to appear to transcend the laws of nature **b :** attributed to an invisible agent (as a ghost or spirit) — **supernatural** *n* — **su·per·nat·u·ral·ly** \-ˈna-chər-ə-lē, -ˈnach-rə-, -ˈna-chər-lē\ *adv* — **su·per·nat·u·ral·ness** *n*

su·per·nat·u·ral·ism \ˌsü-pər-ˈna-chə-rə-ˌli-zəm, -ˈnach-rə-\ *n* (1799) **1 :** the quality or state of being supernatural **2 :** belief in a supernatural power and order of existence — **su·per·nat·u·ral·ist** \-list\ *n or adj* — **su·per·nat·u·ral·is·tic** \-ˌna-chə-rə-ˈlis-tik, -ˌnach-rə-\ *adj*

su·per·na·ture \ˈsü-pər-ˌnā-chər\ *n* [back-formation fr. *supernatural*] (1844) **:** the realm of the supernatural

su·per·nor·mal \ˌsü-pər-ˈnȯr-məl\ *adj* (1868) **1 :** exceeding the normal or average **2 :** being beyond normal human powers **:** PARANORMAL — **su·per·nor·mal·i·ty** \-nȯr-ˈma-lə-tē\ *n* — **su·per·nor·mal·ly** \-ˈnȯr-mə-lē\ *adv*

su·per·no·va \ˌsü-pər-ˈnō-və\ *n* [NL] (1926) **1 :** the explosion of a star in which the star may reach a maximum intrinsic luminosity one billion times that of the sun **2 :** one that explodes into prominence or popularity; *also* **:** SUPERSTAR

[1]**su·per·nu·mer·ary** \ˌsü-pər-ˈnü-mə-ˌrer-ē, -ˈnyü-, -mə-rē; -ˈn(y)üm-rē\ *adj* [LL *supernumerarius,* fr. L *super-* + *numerus* number] (1605) **1 a :** exceeding the usual, stated, or prescribed number ⟨a ~ tooth⟩ **b :** not enumerated among the regular components of a group and esp. of a military organization **2 :** exceeding what is necessary, required, or desired **3 :** more numerous

[2]**supernumerary** *n, pl* **-ar·ies** (1639) **1 :** a supernumerary person or thing **2 :** an actor employed to play a walk-on

su·per·or·der \ˈsü-pər-ˌȯr-dər\ *n* (ca. 1890) **:** a category of biological classification ranking below a class and above an order

su·per·or·di·nate \ˌsü-pər-ˈȯrd-nət, -ˈȯr-də-nət, -ˈȯr-də-ˌnāt\ *adj* [*super-* + sub*ordinate*] (1620) **:** superior in rank, class, or status

su·per·or·gan·ism \-ˈȯr-gə-ˌni-zəm\ *n* (ca. 1899) **:** an organized society (as of a social insect) that functions as an organic whole

su·per·ovu·la·tion \-ˌäv-yə-ˈlā-shən, -ˌōv-\ *n* (1927) **:** production of exceptional numbers of ova at one time — **su·per·ovu·late** \-ˈäv-yə-ˌlāt, -ˈōv-\ *vb*

su·per·ox·ide \-ˈäk-ˌsīd\ *n* (ca. 1847) **:** the monovalent anion O_2^- or a compound containing it ⟨potassium ~ KO_2⟩

superoxide dis·mut·ase \-dis-ˈmyü-ˌtās, -ˌtāz\ *n* [*dismut*ation (simultaneous oxidation and reduction) + *-ase*] (1969) **:** a metal-containing antioxidant enzyme that reduces harmful free radicals of oxygen formed during normal metabolic cell processes to oxygen and hydrogen peroxide

su·per·par·a·sit·ism \ˌsü-pər-ˈpa-rə-ˌsī-ˌti-zəm, -sə-\ *n* (ca. 1899) **:** parasitization of a host by more than one parasitic individual usu. of one kind — used esp. of parasitic insects

su·per·phos·phate \ˌsü-pər-ˈfäs-ˌfāt\ *n* (1797) **1 :** an acid phosphate **2 :** a soluble mixture of phosphates used as fertilizer and made from insoluble mineral phosphates by treatment with sulfuric acid

su·per·phys·i·cal \-ˈfi-zi-kəl\ *adj* (ca. 1603) **:** being above or beyond the physical world or explanation on physical principles

su·per·plas·tic \-ˈplas-tik\ *adj* (1947) **1 :** capable of plastic deformation under low stress at an elevated temperature — used of metals and alloys **2 :** of or relating to superplastic materials ‹∼ molding› — **su·per·plas·tic·i·ty** \-pla-ˈsti-sə-tē\ *n*

su·per·pose \ˌsü-pər-ˈpōz\ *vt* **-posed; -pos·ing** [prob. fr. F *superposer,* back-formation fr. *superposition,* fr. LL *superposition-, superpositio,* fr. L *superponere* to superpose, fr. *super-* + *ponere* to place — more at POSITION] (1823) **1 :** to place or lay over or above whether in or not in contact **:** SUPERIMPOSE **2 :** to lay (as a geometric figure) upon another so as to make all like parts coincide — **su·per·pos·able** \-ˈpō-zə-bəl\ *adj* — **su·per·po·si·tion** \-pə-ˈzi-shən\ *n*

su·per·posed \-ˈpōzd\ *adj* (1823) **:** situated vertically over another layer or part

su·per·pow·er \ˈsü-pər-ˌpau̇(-ə)r\ *n* (1920) **1 :** excessive or superior power **2 a :** an extremely powerful nation; *specif* **:** one of a very few dominant states in an era when the world is divided politically into these states and their satellites **b :** an international governing body able to enforce its will upon the most powerful states — **su·per·pow·ered** \-ˌpau̇(-ə)rd\ *adj*

su·per·sat·u·rate \ˌsü-pər-ˈsa-chə-ˌrāt\ *vt* (1788) **:** to add to (a solution) beyond saturation

su·per·sat·u·rat·ed \-ˌrā-təd\ *adj* (1794) **:** containing an amount of a substance greater than that required for saturation as a result of having been cooled from a higher temperature to a temperature below that at which saturation occurs ‹a ∼ solution› ‹air ∼ with water vapor›

su·per·sat·u·ra·tion \-ˌsa-chə-ˈrā-shən\ *n* (1791) **:** the state of being supersaturated

su·per·scribe \ˈsü-pər-ˌskrīb, ˌsü-pər-ˈ\ *vt* **-scribed; -scrib·ing** [ME, fr. L *superscribere,* fr. *super-* + *scribere* to write — more at SCRIBE] (15c) **1 :** to write (as a name or address) on the outside or cover of **:** ADDRESS **2 :** to write or engrave on the top or outside

su·per·script \ˈsü-pər-ˌskript\ *n* [L *superscriptus,* pp. of *superscribere*] (1901) **:** a distinguishing symbol (as a numeral or letter) written immediately above or above and to the right or left of another character — **superscript** *adj*

su·per·scrip·tion \ˌsü-pər-ˈskrip-shən\ *n* [ME, fr. LL *superscription-, superscriptio,* fr. L *superscribere*] (14c) **1 :** something written or engraved on the surface of, outside, or above something else **:** INSCRIPTION; *also* **:** ADDRESS **2 :** the act of superscribing

su·per·sede \ˌsü-pər-ˈsēd\ *vt* **-sed·ed; -sed·ing** [ME (Sc) *superceden* to defer, fr. MF, fr. L *supersedēre* to sit on top, refrain from, fr. *super-* + *sedēre* to sit — more at SIT] (1654) **1 a :** to cause to be set aside **b :** to force out of use as inferior **2 :** to take the place or position of **3 :** to displace in favor of another ***syn*** see REPLACE — **su·per·sed·er** *n*

su·per·se·de·as \-ˈsē-dē-əs\ *n, pl* **supersedeas** [ME, fr. L, you shall refrain, fr. *supersedēre*] (14c) **1 :** a common-law writ commanding a stay of legal proceedings that is issued under various conditions and esp. to stay an officer from proceeding under another writ **2 :** an order staying proceedings of an inferior court

su·per·se·dure \-ˈsē-jər\ *n* (1788) **:** the act or process of superseding; *esp* **:** the replacement of an old or inferior queen bee by a young or superior queen

su·per·sen·si·ble \ˌsü-pər-ˈsen(t)-sə-bəl\ *adj* (1798) **:** being above or beyond that which is apparent to the senses **:** SPIRITUAL

su·per·sen·so·ry \-ˈsen(t)-sə-rē, -ˈsen(t)s-rē\ *adj* (1883) **:** SUPERSENSIBLE

su·per·ser·vice·able \-ˈsər-və-sə-bəl\ *adj* (ca. 1606) **:** offering unwanted services **:** OFFICIOUS

su·per·ses·sion \ˌsü-pər-ˈse-shən\ *n* [ML *supersession-, supersessio,* fr. L *supersedēre*] (1790) **:** the act of superseding **:** the state of being superseded

su·per·size \ˈsü-pər-ˌsīz\ *vt* **-ized; -iz·ing** (1994) **:** to increase considerably the size, amount, or extent of

1**su·per·son·ic** \ˌsü-pər-ˈsä-nik\ *adj* [L *super-* + *sonus* sound — more at SOUND] (1919) **1 :** ULTRASONIC **2 :** of, being, or relating to speeds from one to five times the speed of sound in air — compare SONIC **3 :** moving, capable of moving, or utilizing air currents moving at supersonic speed **4 :** relating to supersonic airplanes or missiles ‹the ∼ age› — **su·per·son·i·cal·ly** \-ni-k(ə-)lē\ *adv*

2**supersonic** *n* (ca. 1924) **1 :** a supersonic wave or frequency **2 :** a supersonic airplane

su·per·son·ics \ˌsü-pər-ˈsä-niks\ *n pl but sing in constr* (1925) **:** the science of supersonic phenomena

supersonic transport *n* (1961) **:** a supersonic transport airplane

su·per·star \ˈsü-pər-ˌstär\ *n* (1924) **1 :** a star (as in sports or the movies) who is considered extremely talented, has great public appeal, and can usu. command a high salary **2 :** one that is very prominent or is a prime attraction ‹a diplomatic ∼› — **su·per·star·dom** \-dəm\ *n*

su·per·sti·tion \ˌsü-pər-ˈsti-shən\ *n* [ME *superisticion,* fr. AF, fr. L *superstition-, superstitio,* fr. *superstit-, superstes* standing over (as witness or survivor), fr. *super-* + *stare* to stand — more at STAND] (13c) **1 a :** a belief or practice resulting from ignorance, fear of the unknown, trust in magic or chance, or a false conception of causation **b :** an irrational abject attitude of mind toward the supernatural, nature, or God resulting from superstition **2 :** a notion maintained despite evidence to the contrary

su·per·sti·tious \-ˈsti-shəs\ *adj* [ME *supersticious,* fr. AF *supersticius,* fr. L *superstitiosus,* fr. *superstitio*] (14c) **:** of, relating to, or swayed by superstition ‹a ∼ ritual› — **su·per·sti·tious·ly** *adv*

su·per·store \ˈsü-pər-ˌstȯr\ *n* (1943) **:** a very large store often offering a wide variety of merchandise for sale

su·per·string \-ˌstriŋ\ *n* (1982) **:** a hypothetical string obeying the rules of supersymmetry whose vibrations manifest themselves as particles existing in ten dimensions of which only four are evident

su·per·struc·ture \-ˌstrək-chər\ *n* (1638) **1 a :** an entity, concept, or complex based on a more fundamental one **b :** social institutions (as the law or politics) that are in Marxist theory erected upon the economic base **2 :** a structure built as a vertical extension of something else: as **a :** all of a building above the basement **b :** the structural part of a ship above the main deck — **su·per·struc·tur·al** \ˌsü-pər-ˈstrək-chə-rəl, -ˈstrək-shrəl\ *adj*

su·per·sub·stan·tial \ˌsü-pər-səb-ˈstan(t)-shəl\ *adj* [LL *supersubstantialis,* fr. L *super-* + *substantia* substance] (1534) **:** being above material substance **:** of a transcending substance

su·per·sym·me·try \-ˈsi-mə-trē\ *n* (1974) **:** the correspondence between fermions and bosons of identical mass that is postulated to have existed during the opening moments of the big bang and that relates gravity to the other forces of nature — **su·per·sym·met·ric** \-sə-ˈme-trik\ *adj*

su·per·sys·tem \ˈsü-pər-ˌsis-təm\ *n* (ca. 1928) **:** a system that is made up of systems

su·per·tax \-ˌtaks\ *n* (1906) **:** SURTAX

su·per·ti·tle \ˈsü-pər-ˌtī-tᵊl\ *n* (1984) **:** a translation of foreign-language dialogue displayed above a screen or performance ‹an opera with ∼*s*› — compare SUBTITLE

su·per·ton·ic \ˌsü-pər-ˈtä-nik\ *n* (1806) **:** the second tone of a major or minor scale

su·per·vene \ˌsü-pər-ˈvēn\ *vi* **-vened; -ven·ing** [L *supervenire,* fr. *super-* + *venire* to come — more at COME] (ca. 1648) **:** to follow or result as an additional, adventitious, or unlooked-for development ***syn*** see FOLLOW — **su·per·ven·tion** \-ˈven(t)-shən\ *n*

su·per·ve·nient \-ˈvē-nyənt\ *adj* [L *supervenient-, superveniens,* prp. of *supervenire*] (1594) **:** coming or occurring as something additional, extraneous, or unexpected

su·per·vise \ˈsü-pər-ˌvīz\ *vt* **-vised; -vis·ing** [ML *supervisus,* pp. of *supervidēre,* fr. L *super-* + *vidēre* to see — more at WIT] (ca. 1645) **:** SUPERINTEND, OVERSEE

su·per·vi·sion \ˌsü-pər-ˈvi-zhən\ *n* (1640) **:** the action, process, or occupation of supervising; *esp* **:** a critical watching and directing (as of activities or a course of action)

su·per·vi·sor \ˈsü-pər-ˌvī-zər\ *n* [ME, fr. ML, fr. *supervidēre*] (15c) **:** one that supervises; *esp* **:** an administrative officer in charge of a business, government, or school unit or operation — **su·per·vi·so·ry** \ˌsü-pər-ˈvī-zə-rē, -ˈvīz-rē\ *adj*

su·per·wom·an \ˈsü-pər-ˌwu̇-mən\ *n* (1906) **:** an exceptional woman; *esp* **:** a woman who succeeds in having a career and raising a family

su·pi·nate \ˈsü-pə-ˌnāt\ *vb* **-nat·ed; -nat·ing** [L *supinatus,* pp. of *supinare* to lay backward or on the back, fr. *supinus*] *vt* (1831) **:** to cause to undergo supination ∼ *vi* **:** to undergo supination

su·pi·na·tion \ˌsü-pə-ˈnā-shən\ *n* (1666) **1 :** rotation of the forearm and hand so that the palm faces forward or upward; *also* **:** a corresponding movement of the foot and leg in which the foot rolls outward with an elevated arch **2 :** the position resulting from supination

su·pi·na·tor \ˈsü-pə-ˌnā-tər\ *n* [NL, fr. L *supinare*] (1615) **:** a muscle that produces the motion of supination

1**su·pine** \ˈsü-ˌpīn\ *n* [ME *supyn,* fr. LL *supinum,* fr. L, neut. of *supinus,* adj.] (15c) **1 :** a Latin verbal noun having an accusative of purpose in *-um* and an ablative of specification in *-u* **2 :** an English infinitive with *to*

2**su·pine** \su̇-ˈpīn, *attrib also* ˈsü-ˌpīn\ *adj* [ME *suppyne,* fr. L *supinus;* akin to L *sub* under, up to — more at UP] (15c) **1 a :** lying on the back or with the face upward **b :** marked by supination **2 :** exhibiting indolent or apathetic inertia or passivity; *esp* **:** mentally or morally slack **3** *archaic* **:** leaning or sloping backward ***syn*** see PRONE, INACTIVE — **su·pine·ly** \su̇-ˈpīn-lē\ *adv* — **su·pine·ness** \-ˈpīn-nəs\ *n*

supp *abbr* supplement

sup·per \ˈsə-pər\ *n* [ME *soper,* fr. AF *super,* fr. *super* to sup — more at SUP] (13c) **1 a :** the evening meal esp. when dinner is taken at midday **b :** a social affair featuring a supper; *esp* **:** an evening social esp. for raising funds ‹a church ∼› **2 :** the food served as a supper ‹eat your ∼› **3 :** a light meal served late in the evening

supper club *n* (1925) **:** NIGHTCLUB

sup·plant \sə-ˈplant\ *vt* [ME, fr. AF *supplanter,* fr. L *supplantare* to trip up, cause to stumble, fr. *sub-* + *planta* sole of the foot — more at PLACE] (14c) **1 :** to supersede (another) esp. by force or treachery **2 a** (1) *obs* **:** UPROOT (2) **:** to eradicate and supply a substitute for ‹efforts to ∼ the vernacular› **b :** to take the place of and serve as a substitute for esp. by reason of superior excellence or power ***syn*** see REPLACE — **sup·plan·ta·tion** \(ˌ)sə-ˌplan-ˈtā-shən\ *n* — **sup·plant·er** \sə-ˈplan-tər\ *n*

1**sup·ple** \ˈsə-pəl *also* ˈsü-\ *adj* **sup·pler** \-p(ə-)lər\; **sup·plest** \-p(ə-)ləst\ [ME *souple,* fr. AF *suple,* fr. L *supplic-, supplex* entreating for mercy, supplicant, perh. fr. *sub-* + *-plic-* (akin to *plicare* to fold) — more at PLY] (14c) **1 a :** compliant often to the point of obsequiousness **b :** readily adaptable or responsive to new situations **2 a :** capable of being bent or folded without creases, cracks, or breaks **:** PLIANT ‹∼ leather› **b :** able to perform bending or twisting movements with ease **:** LIMBER ‹∼ legs of a dancer› **c :** easy and fluent without stiffness or awkwardness ‹sang with a lively, ∼ voice —Douglas Watt› ***syn*** see ELASTIC — **sup·ple·ly** \-pə(l)-lē\ *or* **sup·ply** \-p(ə-)lē\ *adv* — **sup·ple·ness** \-pəl-nəs\ *n*

2**supple** *vb* **sup·pled; sup·pling** \-p(ə-)liŋ\ *vt* (14c) **1 :** to make pacific or complaisant ‹∼ the tempers of your race —Laurence Sterne› **2 :** to alleviate with a salve **3 :** to make flexible or pliant ∼ *vi* **:** to become soft and pliant

sup·ple·jack \ˈsə-pəl-ˌjak *also* ˈsü-\ *n* (ca. 1725) **:** any of various woody climbers having tough pliant stems; *esp* **:** a southern U.S. vine (*Berchemia scandens*) of the buckthorn family

1**sup·ple·ment** \ˈsə-plə-mənt\ *n* [ME, fr. L *supplementum,* fr. *supplēre* to fill up, complete — more at SUPPLY] (14c) **1 a :** something that completes or makes an addition **b :** DIETARY SUPPLEMENT **2 :** a part added to or issued as a continuation of a book or periodical to correct errors or make additions **3 :** an angle or arc that when added to a given angle or arc equals 180°

2sup·ple·ment \ˈsə-plə-ˌment\ *vt* (1749) **:** to add or serve as a supplement to ⟨does odd jobs to ~ his income⟩ — **sup·ple·men·ta·tion** \ˌsə-plə-ˌmen-ˈtā-shən, -mən-\ *n* — **sup·ple·ment·er** \ˈsə-plə-ˌmen-tər\ *n*

sup·ple·men·tal \ˌsə-plə-ˈmen-tᵊl\ *adj* (1605) **1 :** serving to supplement **2 :** NONSCHEDULED ⟨a ~ airline⟩ — **supplemental** *n*

sup·ple·men·ta·ry \ˌsə-plə-ˈmen-tə-rē, -ˈmen-trē\ *adj* (1667) **1 :** added or serving as a supplement **:** ADDITIONAL ⟨~ reading⟩ **2 :** being or relating to a supplement or a supplementary angle

supplementary angle *n* (ca. 1924) **:** one of two angles or arcs whose sum is 180° — usu. used in pl.

sup·ple·tion \sə-ˈplē-shən\ *n* [ML *suppletion-, suppletio* act of supplementing, fr. L *supplēre*] (1914) **:** the occurrence of phonemically unrelated allomorphs of the same morpheme (as *went* as the past tense of *go* or *better* as the comparative form of *good*) — **sup·ple·tive** \sə-ˈplē-tiv, ˈsə-plə-\ *adj*

sup·ple·to·ry \sə-ˈplē-tə-rē; ˈsə-plə-ˌtȯr-ē\ *adj* [L *supplēre*] (1628) **:** supplying deficiencies **:** SUPPLEMENTARY ⟨rules ~ to the contract⟩

sup·pli·ance \ˈsə-plē-ən(t)s\ *n* (ca. 1611) **:** ENTREATY, SUPPLICATION

1sup·pli·ant \-ənt\ *n* [ME, fr. AF, fr. prp. of *supplier* to supplicate, fr. L *supplicare*] (15c) **:** SUPPLICANT

2suppliant *adj* [MF, prp.] (ca. 1567) **1 :** humbly imploring **:** ENTREATING ⟨a ~ sinner seeking forgiveness —O. J. Baab⟩ **2 :** expressing supplication ⟨upraised to the heavens . . . ~ arms —William Styron⟩ — **sup·pli·ant·ly** *adv*

1sup·pli·cant \ˈsə-pli-kənt\ *n* (1591) **:** one who supplicates

2supplicant *adj* (1597) **:** SUPPLIANT

sup·pli·cate \ˈsə-plə-ˌkāt\ *vb* **-cat·ed; -cat·ing** [ME, fr. L *supplicatus*, pp. of *supplicare*, fr. *supplic-, supplex* supplicant — more at SUPPLE] *vi* (15c) **:** to make a humble entreaty; *esp* **:** to pray to God ~ *vt* **1 :** to ask humbly and earnestly of **2 :** to ask for earnestly and humbly ***syn*** see BEG — **sup·pli·ca·tion** \ˌsə-plə-ˈkā-shən\ *n*

sup·pli·ca·to·ry \ˈsə-pli-kə-ˌtȯr-ē\ *adj* (15c) **:** expressing supplication **:** SUPPLIANT ⟨a ~ prayer⟩

1sup·ply \sə-ˈplī\ *vb* **sup·plied; sup·ply·ing** [ME *supplien* to complete, compensate for, fr. MF *soupplier*, fr. L *supplēre* to fill up, complete, raise (a military unit, crew) to its full complement, substitute, fr. *sub-* up + *plēre* to fill — more at SUB-, FULL] *vt* (14c) **1 :** to add as a supplement **2** [MF *souploier*, alter. of *soupplier*] **a :** to provide for **:** SATISFY ⟨laws by which the material wants of men are *supplied* —*Bull. of Bates Coll.*⟩ **b :** to make available for use **:** PROVIDE ⟨*supplied* the necessary funds⟩ **c :** to satisfy the needs or wishes of **d :** to furnish (organs, tissues, or cells) with a vital element (as blood or nerve fibers) **3 :** to substitute for another in; *specif* **:** to serve as a supply in (a church or pulpit) ~ *vi* **:** to serve as a supply or substitute — **sup·pli·er** \-ˈplī(-ə)r\ *n*

2supply *n, pl* **supplies** (15c) **1** *obs* **:** ASSISTANCE, SUCCOR **2 a** *obs* **:** REINFORCEMENTS — often used in pl. **b :** a member of the clergy filling a vacant pulpit temporarily **c :** the quantity or amount (as of a commodity) needed or available ⟨beer was in short ~ in that hot weather —Nevil Shute⟩ **d :** PROVISIONS, STORES — usu. used in pl. **3 :** the act or process of filling a want or need ⟨engaged in the ~ of raw materials to industry⟩ **4 :** the quantities of goods or services offered for sale at a particular time or at one price **5 :** something that maintains or constitutes a supply

sup·ply–side \sə-ˈplī-ˈsīd\ *adj* (1976) **:** of, relating to, or being an economic theory that reduction of tax rates encourages more earnings, savings, and investment and thereby expands economic activity and the total taxable national income — **sup·ply–sid·er** \-ˈsī-dər\ *n*

1sup·port \sə-ˈpȯrt\ *vt* [ME, fr. AF *supporter*, fr. LL *supportare*, fr. L, to transport, fr. *sub-* + *portare* to carry — more at FARE] (14c) **1 :** to endure bravely or quietly **:** BEAR **2 a** (1) **:** to promote the interests or cause of (2) **:** to uphold or defend as valid or right **:** ADVOCATE ⟨~s fair play⟩ (3) **:** to argue or vote for ⟨~ed the motion to lower taxes⟩ **b** (1) **:** ASSIST, HELP ⟨bombers ~ed the ground troops⟩ (2) **:** to act with (a star actor) (3) **:** to bid in bridge so as to show support for **c :** to provide with substantiation **:** CORROBORATE ⟨~ an alibi⟩ **3 a :** to pay the costs of **:** MAINTAIN ⟨~ a family⟩ **b :** to provide a basis for the existence or subsistence of ⟨the island could probably ~ three —A. B. C. Whipple⟩ ⟨~ a habit⟩ **4 a :** to hold up or serve as a foundation or prop for **b :** to maintain (a price) at a desired level by purchases or loans; *also* **:** to maintain the price of by purchases or loans **5 :** to keep from fainting, yielding, or losing courage **:** COMFORT **6 :** to keep (something) going — **sup·port·abil·i·ty** \sə-ˌpȯr-tə-ˈbi-lə-tē\ *n* — **sup·port·able** \-ˈpȯr-tə-bəl\ *adj* — **sup·port·ive** \-ˈpȯr-tiv\ *adj* — **sup·port·ive·ness** \-nəs\ *n*

syn SUPPORT, UPHOLD, ADVOCATE, BACK, CHAMPION mean to favor actively one that meets opposition. SUPPORT is least explicit about the nature of the assistance given ⟨*supports* waterfront development⟩. UPHOLD implies extended support given to something attacked ⟨*upheld* the legitimacy of the military action⟩. ADVOCATE stresses urging or pleading ⟨*advocated* prison reform⟩. BACK suggests supporting by lending assistance to one failing or falling ⟨refusing to *back* the call for sanctions⟩. CHAMPION suggests publicly defending one unjustly attacked or too weak to advocate his or her own cause ⟨*championed* the rights of children⟩.

2support *n* (14c) **1 a :** the act or process of supporting **:** the condition of being supported **b :** assistance provided by a company to users of its products ⟨customer ~⟩ **2 :** one that supports — often used attributively ⟨a ~ staff⟩ **3 :** sufficient strength in a suit bid by one's partner in bridge to justify raising the suit

sup·port·er \sə-ˈpȯr-tər\ *n* (15c) **:** one that supports or acts as a support: as **a :** ADHERENT, PARTISAN **b :** one of two figures (as of men or animals) placed one on each side of an escutcheon and exterior to it **c :** GARTER 1 **d :** ATHLETIC SUPPORTER

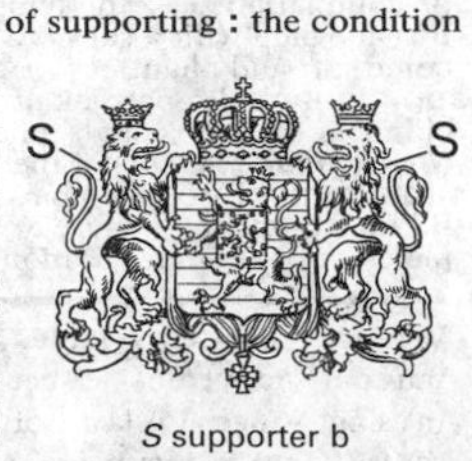

S supporter b

support group *n* (1969) **:** a group of people with common experiences and concerns who provide emotional and moral support for one another

support hose *n* (1963) **:** elastic stockings worn esp. to provide mild compression of the leg (as to prevent formation of varicose veins)

support level *n* (1953) **:** a price level on a declining market at which a security resists further decline due to increased attractiveness to traders and investors — called also *support area*

support system *n* (1980) **:** a network of people who provide an individual with practical or emotional support

sup·pos·able \sə-ˈpō-zə-bəl\ *adj* (1627) **:** capable of being supposed **:** CONCEIVABLE — **sup·pos·ably** \-blē\ *adv*

sup·pos·al \-ˈpō-zəl\ *n* (14c) **1 :** the act or process of supposing **2 :** something supposed **:** HYPOTHESIS, SUPPOSITION

sup·pose \sə-ˈpōz, *oftenest after "I"* ˈspōz\ *vb* **sup·posed; sup·pos·ing** [ME, fr. AF *supposer*, fr. ML *supponere* (perf. indic. *supposui*), fr. L, to put under, substitute, fr. *sub-* + *ponere* to put — more at POSITION] *vt* (14c) **1 a :** to lay down tentatively as a hypothesis, assumption, or proposal ⟨~ a fire broke out⟩ ⟨~ you bring the salad⟩ **b** (1) **:** to hold as an opinion **:** BELIEVE ⟨they *supposed* they were early⟩ (2) **:** to think probable or in keeping with the facts ⟨seems reasonable to ~ that he would profit⟩ **2 a :** CONCEIVE, IMAGINE **b :** to have a suspicion of **3 :** PRESUPPOSE ~ *vi* **:** CONJECTURE, OPINE

sup·posed \sə-ˈpōzd; *1b & 2a usu* -ˈpō-zəd, *3 & 4 often* -ˈpōst\ *adj* (1566) **1 a :** PRETENDED ⟨twelve hours are ~ to elapse between Acts I and II —W. S. Gilbert⟩ **b :** ALLEGED ⟨trusted my ~ friends⟩ **2 a :** held as an opinion **:** BELIEVED; *also* **:** mistakenly believed **:** IMAGINED ⟨the sight which makes ~ terror true —Shak.⟩ **b :** considered probable or certain **:** EXPECTED ⟨it was not ~ that everybody could master the technical aspects —J. C. Murray⟩ **c :** UNDERSTOOD ⟨you will be ~ to refer to my grandaunt —G. B. Shaw⟩ **3 :** made or fashioned by intent or design ⟨what's that button ~ to do⟩ **4 a :** required by or as if by authority ⟨soldiers are ~ to obey their commanding officers⟩ **b :** given permission **:** PERMITTED ⟨was not ~ to have visitors⟩ — **sup·pos·ed·ly** \-ˈpō-zəd-lē *also* -ˈpōzd-lē\ *adv*

supposing *conj* (1663) **:** if by way of hypothesis **:** on the assumption that ⟨~ I did agree with you⟩

sup·po·si·tion \ˌsə-pə-ˈzi-shən\ *n* [ME *supposicioun*, fr. AF *supposicion*, fr. LL *supposition-, suppositio*, fr. L, act of placing beneath, fr. *supponere*] (15c) **1 :** something that is supposed **:** HYPOTHESIS **2 :** the act of supposing — **sup·po·si·tion·al** \-ˈzish-nəl, -ˈzi-shə-nᵊl\ *adj*

sup·po·si·tious \-ˈzi-shəs\ *adj* [by contr.] (1624) **:** SUPPOSITITIOUS

sup·pos·i·ti·tious \sə-ˌpä-zə-ˈti-shəs\ *adj* [L *suppositicius*, fr. *suppositus*, pp. of *supponere* to substitute] (1610) **1 a :** fraudulently substituted **:** SPURIOUS **b** *of a child* (1) **:** falsely presented as a genuine heir (2) **:** ILLEGITIMATE **2** [influenced in meaning by *supposition*] **a :** IMAGINARY **b :** of the nature of or based on a supposition **:** HYPOTHETICAL — **sup·pos·i·ti·tious·ly** *adv*

sup·pos·i·to·ry \sə-ˈpä-zə-ˌtȯr-ē\ *n, pl* **-ries** [ME *suppositorie*, fr. AF, fr. ML *suppositorium*, fr. LL, neut. of *suppositorius* placed beneath, fr. L *supponere* to put under] (14c) **:** a solid but readily meltable cone or cylinder of usu. medicated material for insertion into a bodily passage or cavity (as the rectum)

sup·press \sə-ˈpres\ *vt* [ME, fr. L *suppressus*, pp. of *supprimere*, fr. *sub-* + *premere* to press — more at PRESS] (14c) **1 :** to put down by authority or force **:** SUBDUE ⟨~ a riot⟩ **2 :** to keep from public knowledge: as **a :** to keep secret **b :** to stop or prohibit the publication or revelation of ⟨~ the test results⟩ **3 a :** to exclude from consciousness **b :** to keep from giving vent to **:** CHECK ⟨~ed her anger⟩ **4** *obs* **:** to press down **5 a :** to restrain from a usual course or action ⟨~ a cough⟩ **b :** to inhibit the growth or development of **6 :** to inhibit the genetic expression of ⟨~ a mutation⟩ — **sup·press·ibil·i·ty** \-ˌpre-sə-ˈbi-lə-tē\ *n* — **sup·press·ible** \-ˈpre-sə-bəl\ *adj* — **sup·pres·sive** \-ˈpre-siv\ *adj* — **sup·pres·sive·ness** \-nəs\ *n*

sup·pres·sant \sə-ˈpre-sᵊnt\ *n* (1942) **:** an agent (as a drug) that tends to suppress or reduce in intensity rather than eliminate something

sup·pres·sion \sə-ˈpre-shən\ *n* (15c) **1 :** an act or instance of suppressing **:** the state of being suppressed **2 :** the conscious intentional exclusion from consciousness of a thought or feeling

sup·pres·sor \-ˈpre-sər\ *n* (1560) **:** one that suppresses; *esp* **:** a mutant gene that suppresses the expression of another nonallelic mutant gene when both are present

suppressor T cell *n* (1972) **:** a T cell that suppresses the immune response of B cells and other T cells to an antigen — called also *suppressor cell*

sup·pu·rate \ˈsə-pyə-ˌrāt\ *vi* **-rat·ed; -rat·ing** [L *suppuratus*, pp. of *suppurare*, fr. *sub-* + *pur-, pus* pus — more at FOUL] (1656) **:** to form or discharge pus — **sup·pu·ra·tion** \ˌsə-pyə-ˈrā-shən\ *n* — **sup·pu·ra·tive** \ˈsə-pyə-rə-tiv, -ˌrā-; ˈsə-prə-tiv\ *adj*

su·pra \ˈsü-prə, -ˌprä\ *adv* [L] (15c) **:** earlier in this writing **:** ABOVE

supra- *prefix* [L, fr. *supra* above, beyond, earlier; akin to L *super* over — more at OVER] **1 :** SUPER- 2a ⟨*supra*orbital⟩ **2 :** transcending ⟨*supra*national⟩

su·pra·chi·as·mat·ic nucleus \ˌsü-prə-ˌkī-əz-ˈma-tik-\ *n* (1938) **:** either of a pair of neuron clusters in the hypothalamus situated directly above the optic chiasma that receive photic input from the retina via the optic nerve and that regulate the body's circadian rhythms

su·pra·lim·i·nal \ˌsü-prə-ˈli-mə-nᵊl, -ˌprä-\ *adj* [*supra-* + L *limin-, limen* threshold] (1892) **1 :** existing above the threshold of consciousness **2 :** adequate to evoke a response or induce a sensation

su·pra·mo·lec·u·lar \-mə-ˈle-kyə-lər\ *adj* (ca. 1909) **:** more complex than a molecule; *also* **:** composed of many molecules

su·pra·na·tion·al \-ˈnash-nəl, -ˈna-shə-nᵊl\ *adj* (1908) **:** transcending national boundaries, authority, or interests ⟨a ~ authority, regulating ocean usage —N. H. Jacoby⟩ — **su·pra·na·tion·al·ism** \-ˈnash-nə-ˌli-zəm, -ˈna-shə-nə-ˌli-\ *n* — **su·pra·na·tion·al·ist** \-list\ *n* — **su·pra·na·tion·al·i·ty** \-ˌna-shə-ˈna-lə-tē\ *n*

su·pra·op·tic \-ˈäp-tik\ *adj* (1921) **:** situated above the optic chiasma; *also* **:** being a small nucleus of closely packed neurons overlying the optic chiasma and intimately connected with the neurohypophysis

su·pra·or·bit·al \-ˈȯr-bə-tᵊl\ *adj* [NL *supraorbitalis*, fr. L *supra-* + ML *orbita* orbit] (1828) **:** situated or occurring above the orbit of the eye

su·pra·ra·tio·nal \-ˈrash-nəl, -ˈra-shə-nᵊl\ *adj* (1894) **:** transcending the rational **:** based on or involving factors not to be comprehended by reason alone ⟨the stars inspire ~ dreams —R. J. Dubos⟩

[1]**su·pra·re·nal** \-ˈrē-nᵊl\ *adj* [NL *suprarenalis,* fr. L *supra-* + *renes* kidneys] (1828) **:** situated above or anterior to the kidneys

[2]**suprarenal** *n* (1841) **:** a suprarenal part; *esp* **:** ADRENAL GLAND

suprarenal gland *n* (1830) **:** ADRENAL GLAND

su·pra·seg·men·tal \ˌsü-prə-seg-ˈmen-tᵊl, -ˌprä-\ *adj* (1941) **:** of or relating to significant features (as stress, pitch, or juncture) that occur simultaneously with vowels and consonants in an utterance

sup·ra·ven·tric·u·lar \-ven-ˈtri-kyə-lər, -vən-\ *adj* (1951) **:** relating to or being a rhythmic abnormality of the heart caused by impulses originating above the ventricles ⟨~ tachycardia⟩

su·pra·vi·tal \-ˈvī-tᵊl\ *adj* [ISV] (1919) **:** having or utilizing the property of staining cells or tissues removed from a living body ⟨~ dyes⟩ — compare INTRAVITAL — **su·pra·vi·tal·ly** \-tᵊl-ē\ *adv*

su·prem·a·cist \sə-ˈpre-mə-sist, sü-\ *n* (1949) **1 :** an advocate or adherent of group supremacy **2 :** WHITE SUPREMACIST

su·prem·a·cy \sə-ˈpre-mə-sē, sü- *also* -ˈprē-\ *n, pl* **-cies** [*supreme* + *-acy* (as in *primacy*)] (1537) **:** the quality or state of being supreme; *also* **:** supreme authority or power

su·prem·a·tism \-mə-ˌti-zəm\ *n, often cap* [Russ *suprematizm,* fr. F *suprématie* supremacy + Russ *-izm* -ism] (1933) **:** an early 20th century art movement in Russia producing abstract works featuring flat geometric forms — **su·prem·a·tist** \-tist\ *adj or n, often cap*

su·preme \sə-ˈprēm, sü-\ *adj* [L *supremus,* superl. of *superus* upper — more at SUPERIOR] (1513) **1 :** highest in rank or authority ⟨the ~ commander⟩ **2 :** highest in degree or quality ⟨~ endurance in war and in labour —R. W. Emerson⟩ **3 :** ULTIMATE, FINAL ⟨the ~ sacrifice⟩ — **su·preme·ly** *adv* — **su·preme·ness** *n*

Supreme Being *n* (1668) **:** GOD 1

supreme court *n, often cap S&C* (1647) **1 :** the highest judicial tribunal in a political unit (as a nation or state) **2 :** a court of original jurisdiction in New York state subordinate to a final court of appeals

Supreme Soviet *n* (1936) **:** the highest legislative body of a nation (as the former Soviet Union or former Soviet republics)

su·pre·mo \sə-ˈprē-(ˌ)mō, sü-\ *n, pl* **-mos** [Sp & It, fr. *supremo,* adj., supreme, fr. L *supremus*] (1937) *chiefly Brit* **:** one who is highest in rank or authority

supt *abbr* superintendent

suq *var of* SOUK

sur- *prefix* [ME, fr. AF, fr. L *super-*] **1 :** over **:** SUPER- ⟨*sur*print⟩ ⟨*sur*tax⟩ **2 :** above **:** up ⟨*sur*base⟩

su·ra \ˈsu̇r-ə\ *n* [Ar *sūra,* lit., row] (1661) **:** a chapter of the Koran

su·rah \ˈsu̇r-ə\ *n* [prob. alter. of *surat,* a cotton produced in Surat, India] (1873) **:** a soft twilled fabric of silk or rayon

[1]**sur·cease** \(ˌ)sər-ˈsēs, ˈsər-ˌ\ *vb* **sur·ceased; sur·ceas·ing** [ME *sursesen, surcesen,* fr. AF *surcesser,* alter. of *surseer, surseoir,* fr. L *supersedēre* — more at SUPERSEDE] *vi* (15c) **:** to desist from action; *also* **:** to come to an end **:** CEASE ~ *vt* **:** to put an end to **:** DISCONTINUE

[2]**sur·cease** \ˈsər-ˌsēs, (ˌ)sər-ˈ\ *n* (1586) **:** CESSATION; *esp* **:** a temporary respite or end ⟨to borrow from my books ~ of sorrow —E. A. Poe⟩

[1]**sur·charge** \ˈsər-ˌchärj\ *vt* [ME, fr. AF *surcharger,* fr. *sur-* + *charger* to load, charge — more at CHARGE] (15c) **1 a :** OVERCHARGE **b :** to charge an extra fee **c :** to show an omission in (an account) for which credit ought to have been given **2** *Brit* **:** OVERSTOCK **3 :** to fill or load to excess ⟨the atmosphere . . . was *surcharged* with war hysteria —H. A. Chippendale⟩ **4 a :** to mark a surcharge on (a stamp) **b :** OVERPRINT ⟨~ a banknote⟩

[2]**surcharge** *n* (15c) **1 a :** an additional tax, cost, or impost **b :** an extra fare ⟨a sleeping car ~⟩ **c :** an instance of surcharging an account **2 :** an excessive load or burden **3 :** the action of surcharging **:** the state of being surcharged **4 a (1) :** an overprint on a stamp; *specif* **:** one that alters the denomination **(2) :** a stamp bearing such an overprint **b :** an overprint on a currency note

sur·cin·gle \ˈsər-ˌsiŋ-gəl\ *n* [ME *sursengle,* fr. AF *surcengle,* fr. *sur-* + *cengle* girdle, fr. L *cingulum* — more at CINGULUM] (14c) **1 :** a belt, band, or girth passing around the body of a horse to bind a saddle or pack fast to the horse's back **2** *archaic* **:** the cincture of a cassock

sur·coat \ˈsər-ˌkōt\ *n* [ME *surcote,* fr. AF, fr. *sur-* + *cote* coat] (13c) **:** an outer coat or cloak; *specif* **:** a tunic worn over armor

[1]**surd** \ˈsərd\ *adj* [L *surdus* deaf, silent, stupid] (1610) **1 :** lacking sense **:** IRRATIONAL ⟨~ conceits of scripture's sense —Thomas Jackson⟩ **2 :** VOICELESS — used of speech sounds

[2]**surd** *n* (1557) **1 a :** an irrational root (as $\sqrt{3}$) **b :** IRRATIONAL NUMBER **2 :** a surd speech sound

[1]**sure** \ˈshu̇r, *esp Southern* ˈshōr\ *adj* **sur·er; sur·est** [ME *seur, sure,* fr. AF *seur,* fr. L *securus* secure] (13c) **1** *obs* **:** safe from danger or harm **2 :** firmly established **:** STEADFAST ⟨a ~ hold⟩ **3 :** RELIABLE, TRUSTWORTHY ⟨a ~ friend⟩ **4 a :** marked by or given to feelings of confident certainty ⟨I'm ~ I'm right⟩ **b :** characterized by a lack of wavering or hesitation ⟨~ brush strokes⟩ ⟨a ~ hand⟩ **5 :** admitting of no doubt **:** INDISPUTABLE ⟨spoke from ~ knowledge⟩ **6 a :** bound to happen **:** INEVITABLE ⟨~ disaster⟩ **b :** BOUND, DESTINED ⟨is ~ to win⟩ **7 :** careful to remember, attend to, or find out something ⟨be ~ to lock the door⟩ — **sure·ness** *n* — **for sure :** without doubt or question **:** CERTAINLY — **to be sure :** it must be acknowledged **:** ADMITTEDLY

syn SURE, CERTAIN, POSITIVE, COCKSURE mean having no doubt or uncertainty. SURE usu. stresses the subjective or intuitive feeling of assurance ⟨felt *sure* that I had forgotten something⟩. CERTAIN may apply to a basing of a conclusion or conviction on definite grounds or indubitable evidence ⟨police are *certain* about the cause of the fire⟩. POSITIVE intensifies sureness or certainty and may imply opinionated conviction or forceful expression of it ⟨I'm *positive* that's the person I saw⟩. COCKSURE implies presumptuous or careless positiveness ⟨you're always so *cocksure* about everything⟩.

[2]**sure** *adv* (14c) **:** SURELY

usage Most commentators consider the adverb *sure* to be something less than completely standard; *surely* is usu. recommended as a substitute. Our current evidence shows, however, that *sure* and *surely* have become differentiated in use. *Sure* is used in much more informal contexts than *surely.* It is used as a simple intensive ⟨I can never know how much I bored her, but, be certain, she *sure* amused me —Norman Mailer⟩ and, because it connotes strong affirmation, it is used when the speaker or writer expects to be agreed with ⟨it's a moot point whether politicians are less venal than in Twain's day. But they're *sure* as the devil more intrusive —Alan Abelson⟩ ⟨he *sure* gets them to play —D. S. Looney⟩. *Surely,* like *sure,* is used as a simple intensive ⟨I *surely* don't want to leave the impression that I had an unhappy childhood —E. C. Welsh⟩ but it occurs in more formal contexts than *sure.* Unlike *sure* it may be used neutrally—the reader or hearer may or may not agree ⟨it would *surely* be possible, within a few years, to program a computer to construct a grammar —Noam Chomsky⟩ and it is often used when the writer is trying to persuade ⟨*surely* a book on the avant-garde cannot be so conventional —Karl Shapiro⟩.

sure–enough \ˈshu̇r-ə-ˈnəf\ *adj* (ca. 1846) **:** ACTUAL, GENUINE, REAL

sure enough *adv* (ca. 1545) **:** as one might expect **:** CERTAINLY

sure·fire \ˈshu̇r-ˈfī(-ə)r\ *adj* (ca. 1909) **:** certain to get successful or expected results ⟨a ~ recipe⟩

sure–foot·ed \-ˈfu̇-təd\ *adj* (1633) **:** not liable to stumble, fall, or err — **sure–foot·ed·ly** *adv* — **sure–foot·ed·ness** *n*

sure–hand·ed \-ˈhan-dəd\ *adj* (1930) **:** proficient and confident in performance esp. using the hands — **sure–hand·ed·ness** *n*

sure·ly \ˈshu̇r-lē, *esp Southern* ˈshōr-\ *adv* (14c) **1 :** in a sure manner: **a** *archaic* **:** without danger or risk of injury or loss **:** SAFELY **b (1) :** with assurance **:** CONFIDENTLY ⟨answered quickly and ~⟩ **(2) :** without doubt **:** CERTAINLY ⟨they will ~ be heard from in the future —R. J. Lifton⟩ **2 :** INDEED, REALLY — often used as an intensive ⟨you ~ don't believe that⟩ ***usage*** see [2]SURE

sure thing *n* (1767) **:** one that is certain to succeed **:** a sure bet

sure·ty \ˈshu̇r(-ə)-tē\ *n, pl* **-ties** [ME *seurte,* fr. AF *seurté,* fr. L *securitat-, securitas* security, fr. *securus*] (14c) **1 :** the state of being sure: as **a :** sure knowledge **:** CERTAINTY **b :** confidence in manner or behavior **:** ASSURANCE **2 a :** a formal engagement (as a pledge) given for the fulfillment of an undertaking **:** GUARANTEE **b :** a basis of confidence or security **3 :** one who has become legally liable for the debt, default, or failure in duty of another — **sure·ty·ship** \-ˌship\ *n*

surety bond *n* (1911) **:** a bond guaranteeing performance of a contract or obligation

[1]**surf** \ˈsərf\ *n* [origin unknown] (1685) **1 :** the swell of the sea that breaks upon the shore **2 :** the foam, splash, and sound of breaking waves

[2]**surf** *vi* (1917) **1 :** to ride the surf (as on a surfboard) **2 :** to scan a wide range of offerings for something of interest ~ *vt* **:** to scan the offerings of (as television or the Internet) for something of interest — **surf·er** *n*

[1]**sur·face** \ˈsər-fəs\ *n* [F, fr. MF, fr. *sur-* + *face* face, fr. OF — more at FACE] (ca. 1600) **1 :** the exterior or upper boundary of an object or body ⟨on the ~ of the water⟩ ⟨the earth's ~⟩ **2 :** a plane or curved two-dimensional locus of points (as the boundary of a three-dimensional region) ⟨plane ~⟩ ⟨~ of a sphere⟩ **3 a :** the external or superficial aspect of something ⟨trouble lurks below the ~⟩ **b :** an external part or layer ⟨sanded the rough ~*s*⟩ — **on the surface :** to all outward appearances

[2]**surface** *adj* (1642) **1 a :** of, located on, or designed for use at the surface of something **b :** situated, transported, or employed on the surface of the earth ⟨~ mail⟩ ⟨~ vehicles⟩ **2 :** appearing to be such on the surface only **:** SUPERFICIAL ⟨~ friendships⟩

[3]**surface** *vb* **sur·faced; sur·fac·ing** *vt* (1778) **1 :** to give a surface to: as **a :** to plane or make smooth **b :** to apply the surface layer to ⟨~ a highway⟩ **2 :** to bring to the surface ⟨~ a sunken ship⟩ ~ *vi* **1 :** to work on or at the surface **2 :** to come to the surface **3 :** to come into public view **:** SHOW UP ⟨letters that have recently *surfaced*⟩ — **sur·fac·er** *n*

surface–active *adj* (1920) **:** altering the properties and esp. lowering the tension at the surface of contact between phases ⟨soaps and wetting agents are typical ~ substances⟩

surface of revolution (1840) **:** a surface formed by the revolution of a plane curve about a line in its plane

sur·face–rip·ened \ˈsər-fəs-ˌrī-pənd, -ˌrī-pᵊmd\ *adj* (1945) *of cheese* **:** ripened by the action of microorganisms (as molds) on the surface

surface structure *n* (1964) **:** a formal representation of the phonetic form of a sentence; *also* **:** the structure which such a representation describes

surface tension *n* (1876) **:** the attractive force exerted upon the surface molecules of a liquid by the molecules beneath that tends to draw the surface molecules into the bulk of the liquid and makes the liquid assume the shape having the least surface area

surface–to–air *adj* (1949) **:** launched from the ground against a target in the air

surfacing *n* (1861) **:** material forming or used to form a surface

sur·fac·tant \(ˌ)sər-ˈfak-tənt, ˈsər-ˌ\ *n* [*surf*ace-*act*ive + *-ant*] (1950) **:** a surface-active substance (as a detergent) — **surfactant** *adj*

surf and turf *n* (ca. 1968) **:** seafood and steak served as a single course

surf·bird \ˈsərf-ˌbərd\ *n* (1839) **:** a shorebird (*Aphriza virgata*) of the sandpiper family that occurs along the Pacific coasts of America and has a black-tipped white tail

surf·board \-ˌbōrd\ *n* (ca. 1826) **:** a long narrow buoyant board (as of lightweight wood or fiberglass-covered foam) used in the sport of surfing — **surf·board·er** *n* — **surf·board·ing** \-ˌbōr-diŋ\ *n*

surf·boat \-ˌbōt\ *n* (1847) **:** a boat for use in heavy surf

surf casting *n* (1928) **:** a method of fishing in which artificial or natural bait is cast into the open ocean or in a bay where waves break on a beach — **surf caster** *n*

surf clam *n* (1884) **:** any of various typically rather large surf-dwelling edible clams (family Mactridae); *esp* **:** a common clam (*Spisula solidissima*) of the Atlantic coast chiefly from Nova Scotia to So. Carolina

[1]**sur·feit** \ˈsər-fət\ *n* [ME *surfet,* fr. AF, fr. *surfaire* to overdo, fr. *sur-* + *faire* to do, fr. L *facere* — more at DO] (14c) **1 :** an overabundant supply **:** EXCESS **2 :** an intemperate or immoderate indulgence in something (as food or drink) **3 :** disgust caused by excess

\ə\ **a**but \ᵊ\ kitten, F table \ər\ f**ur**ther \a\ **a**sh \ā\ **a**ce \ä\ m**o**p, m**a**r
\au̇\ **ou**t \ch\ **ch**in \e\ b**e**t \ē\ **ea**sy \g\ **g**o \i\ h**i**t \ī\ **i**ce \j\ **j**ob
\ŋ\ si**ng** \ō\ g**o** \ȯ\ l**aw** \ȯi\ b**oy** \th\ **th**in \t͟h\ **th**e \ü\ l**oo**t \u̇\ f**oo**t
\y\ **y**et \zh\ vi**s**ion, beige \k, ⁿ, œ, ue, ʸ\ *see* Guide to Pronunciation

[2]**surfeit** *vt* (14c) : to feed, supply, or give to surfeit ~ *vi, archaic* : to indulge to satiety in a gratification (as indulgence of the appetite or senses) ***syn*** see SATIATE — **sur·feit·er** *n*

sur·fi·cial \ˌsər-ˈfi-shəl\ *adj* [*surf*ace + *-icial* (as in *superficial*)] (1892) : of or relating to a surface ⟨~ geologic processes⟩

surf·ing \ˈsər-fiŋ\ *n* (1926) : the sport of riding the surf esp. on a surfboard

surf·man \ˈsərf-mən\ *n* (1879) : one who is skilled in handling a boat in surf

surf·perch \ˈsərf-ˌpərch\ *n* (1885) : any of a family (Embiotocidae) of small or medium-sized viviparous bony fishes chiefly of shallow water along the Pacific coast of No. America that resemble the perches

surg *abbr* surgeon; surgery; surgical

[1]**surge** \ˈsərj\ *vb* **surged; surg·ing** [earlier, to ride (at anchor) prob. in part fr. MF *sourgir* to cast anchor, land, fr. Catal *surgir* to heave, cast anchor, fr. L *surgere* to rise, spring up; fr. *sub-* up + *regere* to lead straight; in part fr. L *surgere* — more at SUB-, RIGHT] *vi* (1511) **1 :** to rise and fall actively : TOSS ⟨a ship *surging* in heavy seas⟩ **2 :** to rise and move in waves or billows : SWELL ⟨the sea was *surging*⟩ **3 :** to slip around a windlass, capstan, or bitts — used esp. of a rope **4 :** to rise suddenly to an excessive or abnormal value ⟨the stock market ~*ed* to a record high⟩ **5 :** to move with a surge or in surges ⟨felt the blood *surging* into his face —Harry Hervey⟩ ⟨she *surged* past the other runners⟩ ~ *vt* : to let go or slacken gradually (as a rope)

[2]**surge** *n* (1520) **1 :** a swelling, rolling, or sweeping forward like that of a wave or series of waves ⟨a ~ of interest⟩ **2 a :** a large wave or billow : SWELL **b** (1) **:** a series of such swells or billows (2) **:** the resulting elevation of water level **3 a :** a movement (as a slipping or slackening) of a rope or cable **b :** a sudden jerk or strain caused by such a movement **4 :** a transient sudden rise of current or voltage in an electrical circuit

sur·geon \ˈsər-jən\ *n* [ME *surgien,* fr. AF, alter. of *cirurgien,* fr. *cirurgerie* surgery] (14c) : a medical specialist who practices surgery

sur·geon·fish \-ˌfish\ *n* (1871) : any of a family (Acanthuridae) of tropical bony fishes that have a laterally compressed body and typically a movable spine on each side of the body near the base of the tail capable of inflicting a painful wound

surgeon general *n, pl* **surgeons general** (1706) : the chief medical officer of a branch of the armed services or of a public health service

surgeon's knot *n* (1733) : a reef knot in which the first knot has two turns — see KNOT illustration

sur·gery \ˈsərj-rē, ˈsər-jə-\ *n, pl* **-ger·ies** [ME *surgerie,* fr. AF *cirurgerie, surgerie,* fr. L *chirurgia,* fr. Gk *cheirourgia,* fr. *cheirourgos* surgeon, fr. *cheirourgos* doing by hand, fr. *cheir* hand + *ergon* work — more at CHIR-, WORK] (14c) **1 :** a branch of medicine concerned with diseases and conditions requiring or amenable to operative or manual procedures **2 :** alterations made as if by surgery ⟨literary ~⟩ **3 a** *Brit* **:** a physician's or dentist's office **b :** a room or area where surgery is performed **4 a :** the work done by a surgeon **b :** OPERATION

sur·gi·cal \ˈsər-ji-kəl\ *adj* [*surg*eon + *-ical*] (1770) **1 a :** of or relating to surgeons or surgery ⟨~ skills⟩ **b :** used in or in connection with surgery ⟨~ gauze⟩ **c :** following or resulting from surgery ⟨~ fevers⟩ **2 :** characteristic of or resembling surgery or a surgeon esp. in control or incisiveness ⟨~ precision⟩ — **sur·gi·cal·ly** \-k(ə-)lē\ *adv*

su·ri·mi \sü-ˈrē-mē\ *n* [Jp, chopped meat or fish] (1976) : a fish product made from inexpensive whitefish and often processed to resemble more expensive seafood (as crabmeat)

sur·jec·tion \(ˌ)sər-ˈjek-shən\ *n* [prob. fr. *sur-* + *-jection* (as in *projection*)] (1964) : a mathematical function that is an onto mapping — compare BIJECTION, INJECTION 3

sur·jec·tive \-ˈjek-tiv\ *adj* (1956) : ONTO ⟨a set of ~ functions⟩

sur·ly \ˈsər-lē\ *adj* **sur·li·er; -est** [alter. of ME *serreli* lordly, imperious, prob. fr. *sire, ser* sire] (1523) **1 :** menacing or threatening in appearance ⟨~ weather⟩ **2** *obs* **:** ARROGANT, IMPERIOUS **3 :** irritably sullen and churlish in mood or manner : CRABBED ***syn*** see SULLEN — **sur·li·ly** \-lə-lē\ *adv* — **sur·li·ness** \-lē-nəs\ *n* — **surly** *adv*

[1]**sur·mise** \sər-ˈmīz, ˈsər-ˌ\ *n* [ME, allegation, charge, fr. AF, fr. fem. of *surmis,* pp. of *surmettre* to place on, suppose, accuse, fr. ML *supermittere,* fr. LL, to place on, fr. L *super-* + *mittere* to let go, send] (1569) : a thought or idea based on scanty evidence : CONJECTURE

[2]**sur·mise** \sər-ˈmīz\ *vt* **sur·mised; sur·mis·ing** [ME, to allege, fr. *surmise,* n.] (1700) : to form a notion of from scanty evidence : IMAGINE, INFER

sur·mount \sər-ˈmau̇nt\ *vt* [ME, fr. AF *surmunter,* fr. *sur-* + *munter* to mount] (14c) **1** *obs* **:** to surpass in quality or attainment : EXCEL **2 :** to prevail over : OVERCOME ⟨~ an obstacle⟩ **3 :** to get to the top of : CLIMB **4 :** to stand or lie at the top of — **sur·mount·able** \-ˈmau̇n-tə-bəl\ *adj*

[1]**sur·name** \ˈsər-ˌnām\ *n* (14c) **1 :** an added name derived from occupation or other circumstance : NICKNAME 1 **2 :** the name borne in common by members of a family

[2]**surname** *vt* (15c) : to give a surname to

sur·pass \sər-ˈpas\ *vt* [MF *surpasser,* fr. *sur-* + *passer* to pass] (1555) **1 :** to become better, greater, or stronger than : EXCEED ⟨~*ed* her rivals⟩ ⟨~*ed* all expectations⟩ **2 :** to go beyond : OVERSTEP **3 :** to transcend the reach, capacity, or powers of ⟨a beauty that ~*es* description⟩ ***syn*** see EXCEED — **sur·pass·able** \-ˈpa-sə-bəl\ *adj*

sur·pass·ing \sər-ˈpa-siŋ\ *adj* (1566) : greatly exceeding others : of a very high degree — **sur·pass·ing·ly** *adv*

[1]**sur·plice** \ˈsər-pləs\ *n* [ME *surplis,* fr. AF, fr. ML *superpellicium,* fr. *super-* + *pellicium* coat of skins, fr. L, neut. of *pellicius* made of skins, fr. *pellis* skin — more at FELL] (13c) : a loose white outer ecclesiastical vestment usu. of knee length with large open sleeves

[2]**surplice** *adj* (ca. 1897) : having a diagonally overlapping neckline or closing ⟨a ~ collar⟩ ⟨~ sweaters⟩

sur·plus \ˈsər-(ˌ)pləs\ *n* [ME, fr. AF, fr. ML *superplus,* fr. L *super-* + *plus* more — more at PLUS] (14c) **1 a :** the amount that remains when use or need is satisfied **b :** an excess of receipts over disbursements **2 :** the excess of a corporation's net worth over the par or stated value of its stock — **surplus** *adj*

sur·plus·age \-(ˌ)plə-sij\ *n* (15c) **1 :** SURPLUS 1a **2 a :** excessive or nonessential matter **b :** matter introduced in legal pleading which is not necessary or relevant to the case

surplus value *n* (1887) : the difference in Marxist theory between the value of work done or of commodities produced by labor and the usu. subsistence wages paid by the employer

sur·print \ˈsər-ˌprint\ *vt* (1917) : OVERPRINT — **surprint** *n*

sur·pris·al \sə(r)-ˈprī-zəl\ *n* (1591) : the action of surprising : the state of being surprised

[1]**sur·prise** *also* **sur·prize** \sə(r)-ˈprīz\ *n* [ME *suppryse* exaction, seizure, fr. AF *sousprise, supprise,* fr. fem. of *supris, surpris, suspris,* pp. of *surprendre & susprendre* to capture, take by surprise, fr. *sur- & sus-, suz* under + *prendre* to take — more at PRIZE, SOUS] (15c) **1 a :** an attack made without warning **b :** a taking unawares **2 :** something that surprises **3 :** the state of being surprised : ASTONISHMENT

[2]**surprise** *also* **surprize** *vb* **sur·prised** *also* **sur·prized; sur·pris·ing** *also* **sur·priz·ing** *vt* (15c) **1 :** to attack unexpectedly; *also* **:** to capture by an unexpected attack **2 a :** to take unawares ⟨police *surprised* the burglars in the store⟩ **b :** to detect or elicit by a taking unawares ⟨sometimes *surprised* a tragic shadow in her eyes —Willa Cather⟩ **3 :** to strike with wonder or amazement esp. because unexpected ⟨his conduct *surprised* me⟩ ~ *vi* : to cause astonishment or surprise ⟨her success didn't ~⟩ — **sur·pris·er** *n*

syn SURPRISE, ASTONISH, ASTOUND, AMAZE, FLABBERGAST mean to impress forcibly through unexpectedness. SURPRISE stresses causing an effect through being unexpected but not necessarily unusual or novel ⟨*surprised* to find them at home⟩. ASTONISH implies surprising so greatly as to seem incredible ⟨a discovery that *astonished* the world⟩. ASTOUND stresses the shock of astonishment ⟨too *astounded* to respond⟩. AMAZE suggests an effect of bewilderment ⟨*amazed* by the immense size of the place⟩. FLABBERGAST may suggest thorough astonishment and bewilderment or dismay ⟨*flabbergasted* by his angry refusal⟩.

surprising *adj* (1614) : of a nature that excites surprise

sur·pris·ing·ly \sə(r)-ˈprī-ziŋ-lē\ *adv* (1661) **1 :** in a surprising manner : to a surprising degree ⟨a ~ fast runner⟩ **2 :** it is surprising that ⟨~, voter turnout was high⟩

sur·ra \ˈsu̇r-ə\ *n* [Marathi *sūra* wheezing sound] (1883) : a serious tropical or subtropical disease of domestic animals that is caused by a trypanosome (*Trypanosoma evansi*), is transmitted by biting flies, and is marked esp. by fever, anemia, edema, emaciation, and petechiae

sur·re·al \sə-ˈrē(-ə)l *also* -ˈrā-əl\ *adj* [back-formation fr. *surrealism*] (1937) **1 :** marked by the intense irrational reality of a dream; *also* **:** UNBELIEVABLE, FANTASTIC ⟨~ sums of money⟩ **2 :** SURREALISTIC — **sur·re·al·i·ty** \(ˌ)sə-rē-ˈa-lə-tē\ *n* — **sur·re·al·ly** *adv*

sur·re·al·ism \sə-ˈrē-ə-ˌli-zəm *also* -ˈrā-\ *n* [F *surréalisme,* fr. *sur-* + *réalisme* realism] (1925) : the principles, ideals, or practice of producing fantastic or incongruous imagery or effects in art, literature, film, or theater by means of unnatural or irrational juxtapositions and combinations — **sur·re·al·ist** \-list\ *n or adj*

sur·re·al·is·tic \-ˌrē-ə-ˈlis-tik *also* -ˌrā-\ *adj* (1925) **1 :** of or relating to surrealism **2 :** having a strange dreamlike atmosphere or quality like that of a surrealist painting — **sur·re·al·is·ti·cal·ly** \-ti-k(ə-)lē\ *adv*

sur·re·but·ter \ˌsər-(r)i-ˈbə-tər\ *n* (ca. 1601) : the reply in common law pleading of a plaintiff to a defendant's rebutter

sur·re·join·der \-(r)i-ˈjȯin-dər\ *n* (ca. 1543) : the reply in common law pleading of a plaintiff to a defendant's rejoinder

[1]**sur·ren·der** \sə-ˈren-dər\ *vb* **-dered; -der·ing** \-d(ə-)riŋ\ [ME *surrendren,* fr. *surrendre,* n.] *vt* (15c) **1 a :** to yield to the power, control, or possession of another upon compulsion or demand ⟨~*ed* the fort⟩ **b :** to give up completely or agree to forgo esp. in favor of another **2 a :** to give (oneself) up into the power of another esp. as a prisoner **b :** to give (oneself) over to something (as an influence) ~ *vi* : to give oneself up into the power of another : YIELD ***syn*** see RELINQUISH

[2]**surrender** *n* [ME *surrendre,* fr. AF, fr. *surrendre, susrendre* to relinquish, fr. *sur- & sus-, suz* under + *rendre* to give back — more at RENDER, SOUS] (15c) **1 a :** the action of yielding one's person or giving up the possession of something esp. into the power of another **b :** the relinquishment by a patentee of rights or claims under a patent **c :** the delivery of a principal into lawful custody by bail — called also *surrender by bail* **d :** the voluntary cancellation of the legal liability of an insurance company by the insured and beneficiary for a consideration **e :** the delivery of a fugitive from justice by one government to another **2 :** an instance of surrendering

sur·rep·ti·tious \ˌsər-əp-ˈti-shəs, ˌsə-rəp-, sə-ˌrep-\ *adj* [ME, fr. L *surrepticius,* fr. *surreptus,* pp. of *surripere* to snatch secretly, fr. *sub-* + *rapere* to seize — more at RAPID] (15c) **1 :** done, made, or acquired by stealth : CLANDESTINE **2 :** acting or doing something clandestinely : STEALTHY ⟨a ~ glance⟩ ***syn*** see SECRET — **sur·rep·ti·tious·ly** *adv*

sur·rey \ˈsər-ē, ˈsə-rē\ *n, pl* **surreys** [*Surrey,* England] (ca. 1891) : a four-wheel two-seated horse-drawn pleasure carriage

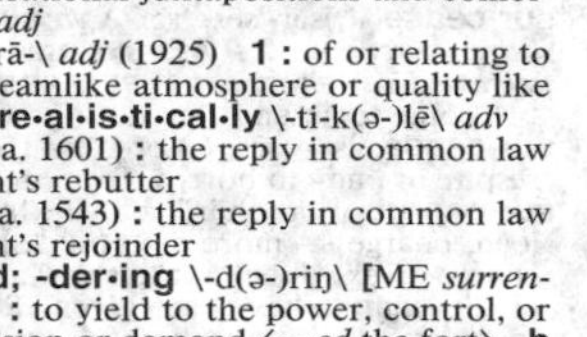
surrey

sur·ro·ga·cy \ˈsər-ə-gə-sē\ *n* (1982) : the practice of serving as a surrogate mother

[1]**sur·ro·gate** \ˈsər-ə-ˌgāt, ˈsə-rə-\ *vt* **-gat·ed; -gat·ing** [L *surrogatus,* pp. of *surrogare* to choose in place of another, substitute, fr. *sub-* + *rogare* to ask — more at RIGHT] (1533) : to put in the place of another: **a :** to appoint as successor, deputy, or substitute for oneself **b :** SUBSTITUTE

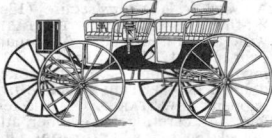

[2]**sur·ro·gate** \-ˌgāt, -gət\ *n, often attrib* (1603) **1 a :** one appointed to act in place of another : DEPUTY **b :** a local judicial officer in some states (as New York) who has jurisdiction over the probate of wills, the settlement of estates, and the appointment and supervision of guardians **2 :** one that serves as a substitute **3 :** SURROGATE MOTHER

surrogate mother *n* (1978) : a woman who becomes pregnant usu. by artificial insemination or surgical implantation of a fertilized egg for the purpose of carrying the fetus to term for another woman — **surrogate motherhood** *n*

[1]**sur·round** \sə-ˈrau̇nd\ *vt* [ME, to flood, inundate, fr. AF *surunder,* fr. LL *superundare,* to overflow, fr. L *super-* + *unda* wave; influenced in meaning by [5]*round* — more at WATER] (ca. 1616) **1 a** (1) **:** to enclose on all sides : ENVELOP ⟨the crowd ~*ed* her⟩ (2) **:** to enclose so as to cut off communication or retreat : INVEST **b :** to form or be a mem-

ber of the entourage of ⟨flatterers who ~ the king⟩ **c** : to constitute part of the environment of ⟨~*ed* by poverty⟩ **d** : to extend around the margin or edge of : ENCIRCLE ⟨a wall ~*s* the old city⟩ **2** : to cause to be surrounded by something ⟨~*ed* himself with friends⟩

²**surround** *n* (1893) : something (as a border or ambient environment) that surrounds ⟨from urban centre to rural ~ —Emrys Jones⟩

sur·round·ings \sə-ˈrau̇n-diŋz\ *n pl* (1841) : the circumstances, conditions, or objects by which one is surrounded : ENVIRONMENT

surround sound *n* (1969) : sound reproduction that often uses three or more transmission channels to enhance the illusion of a live hearing

sur·sum cor·da \ˌsu̇r-səm-ˈkȯr-də, -ˌdä\ *n* [LL, (lift) up (your) hearts; fr. the opening words] (1537) **1** *often cap S&C* : a versicle that in traditional eucharistic liturgies exhorts the faithful to enthusiastic worship **2** : something inspiriting

sur·tax \ˈsər-ˌtaks\ *n* (1881) **1** : an extra tax or charge **2** : a graduated income tax in addition to the normal income tax imposed on the amount by which one's net income exceeds a specified sum

sur·tout \(ˌ)sər-ˈtü, ˈsər-ˌ\ *n* [F, fr. *sur* over (fr. L *super*) + *tout* all, fr. L *totus* whole — more at OVER] (1686) : a man's long close-fitting overcoat

surv *abbr* survey

sur·veil \sər-ˈvāl\ *vt* **sur·veilled; sur·veil·ling** [back-formation fr. *surveillance*] (1914) : to subject to surveillance

sur·veil·lance \sər-ˈvā-lən(t)s *also* -ˈvāl-yən(t)s *or* -ˈvā-ən(t)s\ *n* [F, fr. *surveiller* to watch over, fr. *sur-* + *veiller* to watch, fr. OF *veillier*, fr. L *vigilare*, fr. *vigil* watchful — more at VIGIL] (1802) : close watch kept over someone or something (as by a detective); *also* : SUPERVISION

sur·veil·lant \-ˈvā-lənt *also* -ˈvāl-yənt *or* -ˈvā-ənt\ *n* (1819) : one that exercises surveillance

¹**sur·vey** \sər-ˈvā, ˈsər-ˌ\ *vb* **sur·veyed; sur·vey·ing** [ME, fr. AF *surveer*, to look over, fr. *sur-* + *veer* to see — more at VIEW] *vt* (15c) **1 a** : to examine as to condition, situation, or value : APPRAISE **b** : to query (someone) in order to collect data for the analysis of some aspect of a group or area **2** : to determine and delineate the form, extent, and position of (as a tract of land) by taking linear and angular measurements and by applying the principles of geometry and trigonometry **3** : to view or consider comprehensively **4** : INSPECT, SCRUTINIZE ⟨he ~*ed* us in a lordly way —Alan Harrington⟩ ~ *vi* : to make a survey

²**sur·vey** \ˈsər-ˌvā, sər-ˈ\ *n, pl* **surveys** (1548) **1** : the act or an instance of surveying: as **a** : a broad treatment of a subject **b** : POLL 5a **2** : something that is surveyed

survey course \ˈsər-ˌvā-\ *n* (1916) : a course treating briefly the chief topics of a broad field of knowledge

surveying *n* (1682) : a branch of applied mathematics that is concerned with determining the area of any portion of the earth's surface, the lengths and directions of the bounding lines, and the contour of the surface and with accurately delineating the whole on paper

sur·vey·or \sər-ˈvā-ər\ *n* (15c) : one that surveys; *esp* : one whose occupation is surveying land

sur·viv·able \sər-ˈvī-və-bəl\ *adj* (1955) : resulting in or permitting survival — **sur·viv·abil·i·ty** \-ˌvī-və-ˈbi-lə-tē\ *n*

sur·viv·al \sər-ˈvī-vəl\ *n, often attrib* (1598) **1 a** : the act or fact of living or continuing longer than another person or thing **b** : the continuation of life or existence ⟨problems of ~ in arctic conditions⟩ **2** : one that survives

sur·viv·al·ism \sər-ˈvī-və-ˌli-zəm\ *n* (1928) : an attitude, policy, or practice based on the primacy of survival as a value

sur·viv·al·ist \-və-list\ *n* (1970) : a person who advocates or practices survivalism; *esp* : one who has prepared to survive in the anarchy of an anticipated breakdown of society — **survivalist** *adj*

survival of the fittest (1864) : NATURAL SELECTION

sur·viv·ance \sər-ˈvī-vən(t)s\ *n* (ca. 1623) : SURVIVAL

sur·vive \sər-ˈvīv\ *vb* **sur·vived; sur·viv·ing** [ME, to outlive, fr. AF *survivre*, fr. L *supervivere*, fr. *super-* + *vivere* to live — more at QUICK] *vi* (15c) **1** : to remain alive or in existence : live on **2** : to continue to function or prosper ~ *vt* **1** : to remain alive after the death of ⟨he is *survived* by his wife⟩ **2** : to continue to exist or live after ⟨*survived* the earthquake⟩ **3** : to continue to function or prosper despite : WITHSTAND ⟨they *survived* many hardships⟩ — **sur·vi·vor** \-ˈvī-vər\ *n*

sur·viv·er \-ˈvī-vər\ *n* (1556) *archaic* : one that survives : SURVIVOR

sur·vi·vor·ship \-ˈvī-vər-ˌship\ *n* (ca. 1625) **1** : the legal right of the survivor of persons having joint interests in property to take the interest of the person who has died **2** : the state of being a survivor : SURVIVAL **3** : the probability of surviving to a particular age; *also* : the number or proportion of survivors (as of an age group or population)

Su·san B. An·tho·ny Day \ˈsü-zᵊn-ˌbē-ˈan(t)-thə-nē-\ *n* (ca. 1951) : February 15 observed to commemorate the birth of Susan B. Anthony

sus·cep·ti·bil·i·ty \sə-ˌsep-tə-ˈbi-lə-tē\ *n, pl* **-ties** (1644) **1** : the quality or state of being susceptible; *esp* : lack of ability to resist some extraneous agent (as a pathogen or drug) : SENSITIVITY **2 a** : a susceptible temperament or constitution **b** *pl* : FEELINGS, SENSIBILITIES **3 a** : the ratio of the magnetization in a substance to the corresponding magnetizing force **b** : the ratio of the electric polarization to the electric intensity in a polarized dielectric

sus·cep·ti·ble \sə-ˈsep-tə-bəl\ *adj* [LL *susceptibilis*, fr. L *susceptus*, pp. of *suscipere* to take up, admit, fr. *sub-*, *sus-* up + *capere* to take — more at SUB-, HEAVE] (1605) **1** : capable of submitting to an action, process, or operation ⟨a theory ~ to proof⟩ **2** : open, subject, or unresistant to some stimulus, influence, or agency ⟨~ to pneumonia⟩ **3** : IMPRESSIONABLE, RESPONSIVE ⟨a ~ mind⟩ ***syn*** see LIABLE — **sus·cep·ti·ble·ness** *n* — **sus·cep·ti·bly** \-blē\ *adv*

su·shi \ˈsü-shē *also* ˈsu̇-\ *n* [Jp] (1893) : cold rice dressed with vinegar, formed into any of various shapes, and garnished esp. with bits of raw seafood or vegetables

su·slik \ˈsü-slik\ *n* [Russ] (1774) **1** : any of several rather large short-tailed ground squirrels (genus *Spermophilus*) of eastern Europe or northern Asia **2** : the mottled grayish-black fur of a suslik

¹**sus·pect** \ˈsəs-ˌpekt, sə-ˈspekt\ *adj* [ME, fr. AF, fr. L *suspectus*, fr. pp. of *suspicere*] (14c) **1** : regarded or deserving to be regarded with suspicion : SUSPECTED ⟨investigates ~ employees⟩ **2** : DOUBTFUL, QUESTIONABLE ⟨whose skills are ~ —Peter Vecsey⟩

²**sus·pect** \ˈsəs-ˌpekt\ *n* (1591) : one that is suspected; *esp* : a person suspected of a crime

³**sus·pect** \sə-ˈspekt\ *vb* [ME, fr. L *suspectare*, freq. of *suspicere* to look up at, regard with awe, suspect, fr. *sub-*, *sus-* up, secretly + *specere* to look at — more at SUB-, SPY] *vt* (15c) **1** : to imagine (one) to be guilty or culpable on slight evidence or without proof ⟨~ him of giving false information⟩ **2** : to have doubts of : DISTRUST ⟨~*s* her motives⟩ **3** : to imagine to exist or be true, likely, or probable ⟨I ~ he's right⟩ ~ *vi* : to imagine something to be true or likely

sus·pend \sə-ˈspend\ *vb* [ME, fr. AF *suspendre*, fr. L *suspendere*, fr. *sub-*, *sus-* up + *pendere* to cause to hang, weigh] *vt* (14c) **1** : to debar temporarily esp. from a privilege, office, or function ⟨~ a student from school⟩ **2 a** : to cause to stop temporarily ⟨~ bus service⟩ **b** : to set aside or make temporarily inoperative ⟨~ the rules⟩ **3** : to defer to a later time on specified conditions ⟨~ sentence⟩ **4** : to hold in an undetermined or undecided state awaiting further information ⟨~ judgment⟩ ⟨~ disbelief⟩ **5 a** : HANG; *esp* : to hang so as to be free on all sides except at the point of support ⟨~ a ball by a thread⟩ **b** : to keep from falling or sinking by some invisible support (as buoyancy) ⟨dust ~*ed* in the air⟩ **c** : to put or hold in suspension ⟨~*ed* sediment⟩ **6 a** : to keep fixed or lost (as in wonder or contemplation) **b** : to keep waiting in suspense or indecision **7** : to hold (a musical note) over into the following chord ~ *vi* **1** : to cease operation temporarily **2** : to stop payment or fail to meet obligations **3** : HANG ***syn*** see DEFER

suspended animation *n* (1787) **1** : temporary suspension of the vital functions (as in persons nearly drowned) **2** : a condition (as inactivity) likened to suspended animation

sus·pend·er \sə-ˈspen-dər\ *n* (1524) **1** : one that suspends **2** : a device by which something may be suspended: as **a** : one of two supporting bands worn across the shoulders to support trousers, skirt, or belt — usu. used in pl. and often with *pair* **b** *Brit* : a fastener attached to a garment or garter to hold up a stocking or sock; *also* : a device consisting of garter and fastener — **sus·pend·ered** \-dərd\ *adj*

sus·pense \sə-ˈspen(t)s\ *n* [ME, fr. AF, fr. *suspendre*] (15c) **1** : the state of being suspended : SUSPENSION **2 a** : mental uncertainty : ANXIETY **b** : pleasant excitement as to a decision or outcome ⟨a novel of ~⟩ **3** : the state or character of being undecided or doubtful : INDECISIVENESS — **sus·pense·ful** \-fəl\ *adj* — **sus·pense·ful·ly** \-fə-lē\ *adv* — **sus·pense·ful·ness** \-fəl-nəs\ *n* — **sus·pense·less** \-ləs\ *adj*

suspense account *n* (1851) : an account for the temporary entry of charges or credits or esp. of doubtful accounts receivable pending determination of their ultimate disposition

sus·pens·er \sə-ˈspen(t)-sər\ *n* (ca. 1960) : a suspenseful film

sus·pen·sion \sə-ˈspen(t)-shən\ *n* [ME *suspensyon*, fr. AF *suspension*, fr. LL *suspension-*, *suspensio*, fr. L *suspendere*] (15c) **1** : the act of suspending : the state or period of being suspended: as **a** : temporary removal (as from office or privileges) **b** : temporary withholding (as of belief or decision) **c** : temporary abrogation of a law or rule **d** (1) : the holding over of one or more musical tones of a chord into the following chord producing a momentary discord and suspending the concord which the ear expects; *specif* : such a dissonance which resolves downward — compare ANTICIPATION, RETARDATION (2) : the tone thus held over **e** : stoppage of payment of business obligations : FAILURE — used esp. of a business or a bank **f** : a rhetorical device whereby the principal idea is deferred to the end of a sentence or longer unit **2 a** : the act of hanging : the state of being hung **b** (1) : the state of a substance when its particles are mixed with but undissolved in a fluid or solid (2) : a substance in this state (3) : a system consisting of a solid dispersed in a solid, liquid, or gas usu. in particles of larger than colloidal size — compare EMULSION **3** : something suspended **4** : the means by which something is suspended; *esp* : the system of devices (as springs) supporting the upper part of a vehicle on the axles

suspension bridge *n* (1821) : a bridge that has its roadway suspended from two or more cables usu. passing over towers and securely anchored at the ends — see BRIDGE illustration

suspension points *n pl* (1919) *chiefly Brit* : usu. three spaced periods used to show the omission of a word or word group from a written context

sus·pen·sive \sə-ˈspen(t)-siv\ *adj* (15c) **1** : stopping temporarily : SUSPENDING ⟨a ~ veto⟩ **2** : characterized by suspense, suspended judgment, or indecisiveness **3** : characterized by suspension — **sus·pen·sive·ly** *adv*

sus·pen·sor \sə-ˈspen(t)-sər\ *n* [NL, fr. L *suspendere*] (1832) : a suspending part or structure: as **a** : a group or chain of cells that is produced from the zygote of a seed plant and serves to push the developing embryo into the endosperm **b** : either of a pair of gametangia-bearing hyphal outgrowths in fungi (order Mucorales) that extend from two sexually compatible hyphae and support the resulting zygospore

¹**sus·pen·so·ry** \sə-ˈspen(t)-sə-rē, -ˈspen(t)s-rē\ *adj* (15c) **1** : held in suspension; *also* : fitted or serving to suspend **2** : temporarily leaving undetermined : SUSPENSIVE 1

²**suspensory** *n, pl* **-ries** (15c) : something that suspends or holds up; *esp* : a fabric supporter for the scrotum

suspensory ligament *n* (1831) : a ligament or fibrous membrane suspending an organ or part; *esp* : a ringlike fibrous membrane connecting the ciliary body and the lens of the eye and holding the lens in place — see EYE illustration

¹**sus·pi·cion** \sə-ˈspi-shən\ *n* [ME *suspecioun*, fr. AF, fr. L *suspicion-*, *suspicio*, fr. *suspicere* to suspect — more at SUSPECT] (14c) **1 a** : the act or an instance of suspecting something wrong without proof or on slight evidence : MISTRUST **b** : a state of mental uneasiness and uncertainty : DOUBT **2** : a barely detectable amount : TRACE ⟨just a ~ of garlic⟩ ***syn*** see UNCERTAINTY

²**suspicion** *vt* **sus·pi·cioned; sus·pi·cion·ing** \-ˈspi-sh(ə-)niŋ\ (ca. 1637) *chiefly dial* : SUSPECT

sus·pi·cious \sə-ˈspi-shəs\ *adj* (14c) **1 :** tending to arouse suspicion : QUESTIONABLE ⟨~ characters⟩ **2 :** disposed to suspect : DISTRUSTFUL ⟨~ of strangers⟩ **3 :** expressing or indicative of suspicion ⟨a ~ glance⟩ — **sus·pi·cious·ly** *adv* — **sus·pi·cious·ness** *n*

sus·pi·ra·tion \ˌsəs-pə-ˈrā-shən\ *n* (15c) : a long deep breath : SIGH

sus·pire \sə-ˈspī(-ə)r\ *vi* **sus·pired; sus·pir·ing** [ME, fr. L *suspirare,* fr. *sub-* + *spirare* to breathe] (15c) : to draw a long deep breath : SIGH

suss \ˈsəs\ *vt* [by shortening & alter. fr. *suspect*] (1966) **1** *chiefly Brit* : FIGURE OUT — usu. used with *out* **2** *chiefly Brit* : to inspect or investigate so as to gain more knowledge — usu. used with *out*

Sus·sex spaniel \ˈsə-siks-, -ˌseks-\ *n* [*Sussex,* England] (1856) : any of a breed of short-legged short-necked long-bodied spaniels of English origin with a flat or slightly wavy golden liver-colored coat

[1]**sus·tain** \sə-ˈstān\ *vt* [ME *sustenen,* fr. AF *sustein-,* stem of *sustenir,* fr. L *sustinēre* to hold up, sustain, fr. *sub-, sus-* up + *tenēre* to hold — more at SUB-, THIN] (13c) **1 :** to give support or relief to **2 :** to supply with sustenance : NOURISH **3 :** KEEP UP, PROLONG **4 :** to support the weight of : PROP; *also* : to carry or withstand (a weight or pressure) **5 :** to buoy up ⟨~*ed* by hope⟩ **6 a :** to bear up under **b :** SUFFER, UNDERGO ⟨~*ed* heavy losses⟩ **7 a :** to support as true, legal, or just **b :** to allow or admit as valid ⟨the court ~*ed* the motion⟩ **8 :** to support by adequate proof : CONFIRM ⟨testimony that ~*s* our contention⟩ — **sus·tained·ly** \-ˈstā-nəd-lē, -ˈstānd-lē\ *adv* — **sus·tain·er** *n*

[2]**sustain** *n* (1972) : a musical effect that prolongs a note's resonance ⟨utilizing heavy ~ on his guitar —Bill Dahl⟩

sus·tain·able \sə-ˈstā-nə-bəl\ *adj* (ca. 1727) **1 :** capable of being sustained **2 a :** of, relating to, or being a method of harvesting or using a resource so that the resource is not depleted or permanently damaged ⟨~ techniques⟩ ⟨~ agriculture⟩ **b :** of or relating to a lifestyle involving the use of sustainable methods ⟨~ society⟩ — **sus·tain·abil·i·ty** \-ˌstā-nə-ˈbi-lə-tē\ *n* — **sus·tain·ably** \-ˈstā-nə-blē\ *adv*

sus·tained–re·lease \sə-ˈstānd-ri-ˈlēs\ *adj* (1956) : designed to release a drug in the body slowly over an extended period of time

sustained yield *n* (ca. 1905) : production of a biological resource (as timber or fish) under management procedures which ensure replacement of the part harvested by regrowth or reproduction before another harvest occurs — **sustained–yield** *adj*

sus·tain·ing \sə-ˈstā-niŋ\ *adj* (1573) **1 :** serving to sustain **2 :** aiding in the support of an organization through a special fee ⟨a ~ member⟩

sus·te·nance \ˈsəs-tə-nən(t)s\ *n* [ME, fr. AF, fr. *sustenir*] (14c) **1 a :** means of support, maintenance, or subsistence : LIVING **b :** FOOD, PROVISIONS; *also* : NOURISHMENT **2 a :** the act of sustaining : the state of being sustained **b :** a supplying or being supplied with the necessaries of life **3 :** something that gives support, endurance, or strength

sus·ten·tac·u·lar cell \ˌsəs-tən-ˈta-kyə-lər-, -ˌten-\ *n* [NL *sustentaculum* supporting part, fr. L, prop, fr. *sustentare*] (1901) : a supporting epithelial cell (as a Sertoli cell or a cell of the olfactory epithelium) that lacks a specialized function (as nerve-impulse conduction)

sus·ten·ta·tion \-ˈtā-shən\ *n* [ME, fr. AF, fr. L *sustentation-, sustentatio* act of holding up, fr. *sustentare* to hold up, freq. of *sustinēre* to sustain] (14c) **1 :** the act of sustaining : the state of being sustained: as **a :** MAINTENANCE, UPKEEP **b :** PRESERVATION, CONSERVATION **c :** maintenance of life, growth, or morale **d :** provision with sustenance **2 :** something that sustains : SUPPORT — **sus·ten·ta·tive** \ˈsəs-tən-ˌtā-tiv, sə-ˈsten-tə-tiv\ *adj*

Su·su \ˈsü-(ˌ)sü\ *n, pl* **Susu** *or* **Susus** (1786) **1 :** a member of a West African people of Mali, Guinea, and the area along the northern border of Sierra Leone **2 :** the Mande language of the Susu people

su·sur·ra·tion \ˌsü-sə-ˈrā-shən\ *n* (14c) : a whispering sound : MURMUR

su·sur·rous \sü-ˈsər-əs, -ˈsə-rəs\ *adj* (1859) : full of whispering sounds

su·sur·rus \sü-ˈsər-əs, -ˈsə-rəs\ *n* [L, hum, whisper — more at SWARM] (1826) : a whispering or rustling sound — **su·sur·rant** \-ˈsər-ənt, -ˈsə-rənt\ *adj*

sut·ler \ˈsət-lər\ *n* [obs. D *soeteler,* fr. LG *suteler* sloppy worker, camp cook] (1599) : a civilian provisioner to an army post often with a shop on the post

su·tra \ˈsü-trə\ *n* [Skt *sūtra* precept, lit., thread; akin to L *suere* to sew — more at SEW] (1801) **1 :** a precept summarizing Vedic teaching; *also* : a collection of these precepts **2 :** one of the discourses of the Buddha that constitute the basic text of Buddhist scripture

sut·tee *also* **sa·ti** \(ˌ)sə-ˈtē, ˈsə-ˌtē\ *n* [Hindi *satī* wife who performs suttee, fr. Skt, devoted woman, fr. fem. of *sat* true, good; akin to OE *sōth* true — more at SOOTH] (1786) : the act or custom of a Hindu widow burning herself to death or being burned to death on the funeral pyre of her husband; *also* : a woman burned to death in this way

[1]**su·ture** \ˈsü-chər\ *n* [ME, fr. AF & L; AF, fr. L *sutura* seam, suture, fr. *sutus,* pp. of *suere* to sew — more at SEW] (15c) **1 a :** a strand or fiber used to sew parts of the living body; *also* : a stitch made with a suture **b :** the act or process of sewing with sutures **2 a :** a uniting of parts **b :** the seam or seamlike line along which two things or parts are sewed or united **3 a :** the line of union in an immovable articulation (as between the bones of the skull); *also* : such an articulation **b :** a furrow at the junction of adjacent bodily parts; *esp* : a line of dehiscence (as on a fruit) — **su·tur·al** \ˈsü-chə-rəl, ˈsüch-rəl\ *adj* — **su·tur·al·ly** \-rə-lē\ *adv*

[2]**suture** *vt* **su·tured; su·tur·ing** \ˈsü-chə-riŋ, ˈsüch-riŋ\ (1777) : to unite, close, or secure with sutures ⟨~ a wound⟩

SUV \ˌes-(ˌ)yü-ˈvē\ *n, pl* **SUVs** (1986) : SPORT-UTILITY VEHICLE

su·zer·ain \ˈsü-zə-rən, -ˌrān; ˈsüz-rən\ *n* [F, fr. MF *souserain,* fr. *sus* up (fr. L *sursum,* fr. *sub-* up + *versum* -ward, fr. neut. of *versus,* pp. of *vertere* to turn) + *-erain* (as in *soverain* sovereign) — more at SUB-, WORTH] (1807) **1 :** a superior feudal lord to whom fealty is due : OVERLORD **2 :** a dominant state controlling the foreign relations of a vassal state but allowing it sovereign authority in its internal affairs

su·zer·ain·ty \-tē\ *n* [F *suzeraineté,* fr. MF *suserenete,* fr. *suserain*] (1823) : the dominion of a suzerain : OVERLORDSHIP

sv *abbr* **1** saves **2** [L *sub verbo* or *sub voce*] under the word

svc *abbr* service

sved·berg \ˈsved-ˌbərg, ˈsfed-, -ˌber-ē\ *n* [The *Svedberg*] (1937) : a unit of time amounting to 10^{-13} second that is used to measure the sedimentation velocity of a colloidal solution (as of a protein) in an ultracentrifuge and to determine molecular weight by substitution in an equation — called also *svedberg unit*

svelte \ˈsvelt, ˈsfelt\ *adj* **svelt·er; svelt·est** [F, fr. It *svelto,* fr. pp. of *svellere* to pluck out, modif. of L *evellere,* fr. *e-* + *vellere* to pluck — more at VULNERABLE] (ca. 1817) **1 a :** SLENDER, LITHE **b :** having clean lines : SLEEK **2 :** URBANE, SUAVE — **svelte·ly** *adv* — **svelte·ness** *n*

Sven·ga·li \sven-ˈgä-lē, sfen-\ *n* [*Svengali,* villainous hypnotist in the novel *Trilby* (1894) by George du Maurier] (1919) : a person who manipulates or exerts excessive control over another

SVGA *abbr* super video graphics array

S–Vid·eo \ˈes-ˌvi-dē-ˌō\ *n* [*separate*] (1987) : an analog video data interface that transmits intensity and color value information in separate channels

sw *abbr* switch

SW *abbr* **1** shortwave **2** southwest

[1]**swab** \ˈswäb\ *n* [prob. fr. obs. D *swabbe;* akin to LG *swabber* mop] (1653) **1 a :** MOP; *esp* : a yarn mop **b** (1) **:** a wad of absorbent material usu. wound around one end of a small stick and used esp. for applying medication or for removing material from an area (2) **:** a specimen taken with a swab **c :** a sponge or cloth patch attached to a long handle and used to clean the bore of a firearm **2 a :** a useless or contemptible person **b :** SAILOR, GOB

[2]**swab** *vt* **swabbed; swab·bing** [back-formation fr. *swabber*] (1719) **1 :** to clean with or as if with a swab **2 :** to apply medication to with a swab ⟨*swabbed* the wound with iodine⟩

swab·ber \ˈswä-bər\ *n* [akin to LG *swabber* mop, ME *swabben* to sway] (1592) **1 :** one that swabs **2 :** SWAB 2a

swab·bie *also* **swab·by** \ˈswä-bē\ *n, pl* **swabbies** (1944) *slang* : SWAB 2b

swad·dle \ˈswä-dᵊl\ *vt* **swad·dled; swad·dling** \ˈswäd-liŋ, ˈswä-dᵊl-iŋ\ [ME *swadelen, swathelen,* prob. alter. of *swedelen, swethelen,* fr. *swethel* swaddling band, fr. OE; akin to OE *swathian* to swathe] (14c) **1 a :** to wrap (an infant) with swaddling clothes **b :** ENVELOP, SWATHE ⟨legs *swaddled* in bandages⟩ **2 :** RESTRAIN, RESTRICT ⟨marriage . . . *swaddled* him in a domesticity he came to loathe —Nina Auerbach⟩

swaddling clothes *n pl* (1526) **1 :** narrow strips of cloth wrapped around an infant to restrict movement **2 :** limitations or restrictions imposed on the immature or inexperienced

[1]**swag** \ˈswag\ *vb* **swagged; swag·ging** [perh. of Scand origin; akin to Norw *svagga* to sway, rock; akin to MLG *swacken* to rock] *vi* (1530) **1 :** SWAY, LURCH **2 :** SAG, DROOP ~ *vt* **1 :** to adorn with swags **2 :** to arrange (as drapery) in swags

[2]**swag** *n* (1660) **1 :** SWAY 1 **2 a :** something (as a decoration) hanging in a curve between two points : FESTOON **b :** a suspended cluster (as of evergreen branches) **3 a :** goods acquired by unlawful means : LOOT **b :** SPOILS, PROFITS **4 :** a depression in the earth **5** *chiefly Austral* : a pack of personal belongings

[1]**swage** \ˈswāj, ˈswej\ *n* [ME, ornamental border, fr. MF *souage*] (ca. 1812) : a tool used by metalworkers for shaping their work by holding it on the work or the work on it and striking with a hammer or sledge

[2]**swage** *vt* **swaged; swag·ing** (1831) : to shape by or as if by means of a swage

swage block *n* (1843) : a perforated cast-iron or steel block with grooved sides that is used in heading bolts and swaging bars by hand

[1]**swag·ger** \ˈswa-gər\ *vb* **swag·gered; swag·ger·ing** \-g(ə-)riŋ\ [prob. fr. [1]*swag* + *-er* (as in *chatter*)] *vi* (ca. 1596) **1 :** to conduct oneself in an arrogant or superciliously pompous manner; *esp* : to walk with an air of overbearing self-confidence **2 :** BOAST, BRAG ~ *vt* : to force by argument or threat : BULLY — **swag·ger·er** \-gər-ər\ *n* — **swag·ger·ing·ly** \-g(ə-)riŋ-lē\ *adv*

[2]**swagger** *n* (1725) **1 a :** an act or instance of swaggering **b :** arrogant or conceitedly self-assured behavior **c :** ostentatious display or bravado **2 :** a self-confident outlook : COCKINESS

[3]**swagger** *adj* (1879) : marked by elegance or showiness : POSH

swagger stick *n* (1887) : a short light stick usu. covered with leather and tipped with metal at each end and intended for carrying in the hand (as by military officers)

swag·gie \ˈswa-gē\ *n* [by shortening & alter.] (1891) *chiefly Austral* : SWAGMAN

swag·man \ˈswag-mən\ *n* (1851) *chiefly Austral* : DRIFTER; *esp* : one who carries a swag when traveling

Swa·hi·li \swä-ˈhē-lē\ *n, pl* **Swahili** *or* **Swahilis** [Ar *sawāḥil,* pl. of *sāḥil* coast] (1814) **1 :** a member of a Bantu-speaking people of Zanzibar and the adjacent coast **2 :** a Bantu language that is a trade and governmental language over much of East Africa and in the Congo region

swain \ˈswān\ *n* [ME *swein* boy, servant, fr. ON *sveinn;* akin to OE *swān* swain, L *suus* one's own — more at SUICIDE] (14c) **1 :** RUSTIC, PEASANT; *specif* : SHEPHERD **2 :** a male admirer or suitor — **swain·ish** \ˈswā-nish\ *adj* — **swain·ish·ness** *n*

Swain·son's hawk \ˈswān(t)-sənz-\ *n* [William *Swainson* †1855 Eng. naturalist] (1895) : a buteo (*Buteo swainsonii*) chiefly of western No. America and So. America having pointed wings and usu. a dark breast

SWAK *abbr* sealed with a kiss

swale \ˈswāl\ *n* [origin unknown] (1584) : a low-lying or depressed and often wet stretch of land; *also* : a shallow depression on a golf course

[1]**swal·low** \ˈswä-(ˌ)lō\ *n* [ME *swalowe,* fr. OE *swealwe;* akin to OHG *swalawa* swallow] (bef. 12c) **1 :** any of numerous small widely distributed oscine birds (family Hirundinidae, the swallow family) that have a short bill, long pointed wings, and often a deeply forked tail and that feed on insects caught on the wing **2 :** any of several birds that superficially resemble swallows

[2]**swallow** *vb* [ME *swalowen,* fr. OE *swelgan;* akin to OHG *swelgan* to swallow] *vt* (bef. 12c) **1 :** to take through the mouth and esophagus into the stomach **2 :** to envelop or take in as if by swallowing : ABSORB ⟨~ the financial loss⟩ ⟨watch night ~ the valley⟩ **3 :** to accept without question, protest, or resentment ⟨~ an insult⟩ ⟨a hard story to ~⟩ **4 :** TAKE BACK, RETRACT ⟨had to ~ my words⟩ **5 :** to keep from expressing or showing : REPRESS ⟨~*ed* my anger⟩ **6 :** to utter (as words) indistinctly ~ *vi* **1 :** to receive something into the body through the mouth and esophagus **2 :** to perform the action characteristic of swallowing something esp. under emotional stress — **swal·low·able** \ˈswä-lō-ə-bəl\ *adj* — **swal·low·er** \ˈswä-lə-wər\ *n*

[3]**swallow** *n* (14c) **1 :** the passage connecting the mouth to the stomach **2 :** a capacity for swallowing **3 a :** an act of swallowing **b :** an amount that can be swallowed at one time

swal·low·tail \ˈswä-lō-ˌtāl, -lə-\ *n* (1703) **1 :** a deeply forked and tapering tail (as of a swallow) **2 :** TAILCOAT **3 :** any of various usu. large brightly marked butterflies (family Papilionidae, esp. genus *Papilio*) with each hind wing typically having an elongated process — **swal·low–tailed** \-ˌtāld\ *adj*
swam *past of* SWIM
swa·mi \ˈswä-mē\ *n* [Hindi *svāmī,* fr. Skt *svāmin* owner, lord, fr. *sva* one's own — more at SUICIDE] (1895) **1 :** a Hindu ascetic or religious teacher; *specif* **:** a senior member of a religious order — used as a title **2 :** one that resembles or emulates a swami **:** PUNDIT, SEER
[1]**swamp** \ˈswämp, ˈswȯmp\ *n* [perh. alter. of ME *sompe,* fr. MD *somp* morass; akin to MHG *sumpf* marsh, Gk *somphos* spongy] (1624) **1 :** a wetland often partially or intermittently covered with water; *esp* **:** one dominated by woody vegetation **2 :** a tract of swamp **3 :** a difficult or troublesome situation or subject — **swamp** *adj*
[2]**swamp** *vt* (1784) **1 a :** to fill with or as if with water **:** INUNDATE, SUBMERGE **b :** to overwhelm numerically or by an excess of something **:** FLOOD ⟨~*ed* with work⟩ **2 :** to open by removing underbrush and debris ~ *vi* **:** to become submerged
swamp buggy *n* (1941) **:** a vehicle designed to travel over swampy terrain; *esp* **:** a four-wheel motor vehicle with oversize tires
swamp·er \ˈswäm-pər, ˈswȯm-\ *n* (1775) **1 a :** an inhabitant of swamps or lowlands **b :** one familiar with swampy terrain **2 :** a general assistant **:** HANDYMAN, HELPER
swamp·land \ˈswämp-ˌland, ˈswȯmp-\ *n* (1662) **:** SWAMP 1
swampy \ˈswäm-pē, ˈswȯm-\ *adj* **swamp·i·er; -est** (1649) **:** consisting of, suggestive of, or resembling swamp **:** MARSHY — **swamp·i·ness** *n*
[1]**swan** \ˈswän\ *n, pl* **swans** [ME, fr. OE; akin to MHG *swan* and perh. to L *sonus* sound — more at SOUND] (bef. 12c) **1** *pl also* **swan :** any of various large heavy-bodied long-necked mostly pure white aquatic birds (family Anatidae, esp. genus *Cygnus*) that have webbed feet and are related to but larger than the geese **2 :** one that resembles or is likened to a swan **3** *cap* **:** the constellation Cygnus

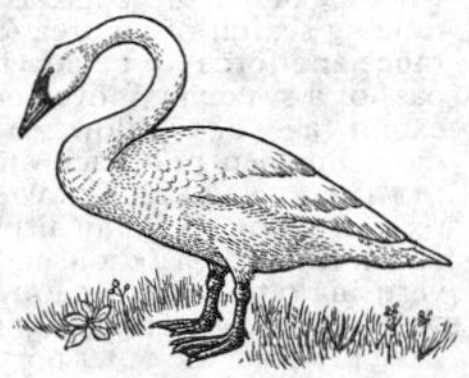
swan 1

[2]**swan** *vi* **swanned; swan·ning** (1942) **:** to wander aimlessly or idly **:** DALLY
[3]**swan** *vi* **swanned; swan·ning** [perh. euphemism for *swear*] (1784) *dial* **:** DECLARE, SWEAR
swan boat *n* (1953) **:** a small paddleboat usu. for children or sightseers that is a large model of a swan
swan dive *n* (1898) **:** a front dive executed with the head back, back arched, and arms spread sideways and then brought together above the head to form a straight line with the body as the diver enters the water
[1]**swank** *vi* [perh. akin to MHG *swanken* to sway; akin to MD *swanc* supple] (1708) **:** SHOW OFF, SWAGGER; *also* **:** BOAST 1
[2]**swank** \ˈswaŋk\ *adj* [MLG or MD *swanc* supple; akin to OHG *swingan* to swing] (1773) *Scot* **:** full of life or energy **:** ACTIVE
[3]**swank** *or* **swanky** \ˈswaŋ-kē\ *adj* **swank·er** *or* **swank·i·er; -est** (ca. 1842) **1 :** characterized by showy display **:** OSTENTATIOUS ⟨a ~ limousine⟩ **2 :** fashionably elegant **:** SMART ⟨a ~ restaurant⟩ — **swank·i·ly** \-kə-lē\ *adv* — **swank·i·ness** \-kē-nəs\ *n*
[4]**swank** *n* (ca. 1854) **1 :** arrogance or ostentation of dress or manner **:** PRETENTIOUSNESS, SWAGGER **2 :** ELEGANCE, FASHIONABLENESS
swan·nery \ˈswä-nə-rē, ˈswän-rē\ *n, pl* **-ner·ies** (1701) **:** a place where swans are bred or kept
swans·down \ˈswänz-ˌdau̇n\ *n* (1606) **1 :** the soft downy feathers of the swan often used as trimming on articles of dress **2 :** a heavy cotton flannel that has a thick nap on the face and is made with sateen weave
swan·skin \ˈswän-ˌskin\ *n* (1610) **1 :** the skin of a swan with the down or feathers on it **2 :** fabric resembling flannel and having a soft nap or surface
swan song *n* (1831) **1 :** a song of great sweetness said to be sung by a dying swan **2 :** a farewell appearance or final act or pronouncement
[1]**swap** \ˈswäp\ *vb* **swapped; swap·ping** [ME *swappen* to strike; fr. the practice of striking hands in closing a business deal] *vt* (14c) **1 a :** to give in trade **:** BARTER **b :** EXCHANGE 2 **2 :** to take turns in telling ⟨~ stories⟩ ~ *vi* **:** to make an exchange — **swap·per** *n*
[2]**swap** *n* (1625) **:** an act, instance, or process of exchanging one thing for another
swap meet *n* (1965) **:** a gathering for the sale or barter of usu. secondhand objects
swa·raj \swə-ˈräj\ *n* [Hindi *svarāj,* fr. Skt *sva* own + Hindi *rāj* rule — more at SUICIDE, RAJ] (1908) **:** national or local self-government in India — **swa·raj·ist** \-ˈrä-jist\ *n*
sward \ˈswȯrd\ *n* [ME, fr. OE *sweard, swearth* skin, rind; akin to MHG *swart* skin, hide] (15c) **1 :** a portion of ground covered with grass **2 :** the grassy surface of land — **sward·ed** \ˈswȯr-dəd\ *adj*
swarf \ˈswȯrf\ *n* [prob. fr. ME **swerf,* fr. OE *geswearf, gesweorf;* akin to OE *sweorfan* to file away — more at SWERVE] (1565) **:** material (as metallic particles and abrasive fragments) removed by a cutting or grinding tool
[1]**swarm** \ˈswȯrm\ *n* [ME, fr. OE *swearm;* akin to OHG *swaram* swarm and prob. to L *susurrus* hum] (bef. 12c) **1 a :** a great number of honeybees emigrating together from a hive in company with a queen to start a new colony elsewhere **b :** a colony of honeybees settled in a hive **2 a :** a large number of animate or inanimate things massed together and usu. in motion **:** THRONG ⟨~*s* of sightseers⟩ ⟨a ~ of locusts⟩ ⟨a ~ of meteors⟩ **b :** a number of similar geological features or phenomena close together in space or time ⟨a ~ of dikes⟩ ⟨an earthquake ~⟩
[2]**swarm** *vi* (14c) **1 :** to form and depart from a hive in a swarm **2 a :** to move or assemble in a crowd **:** THRONG **b :** to hover about in the manner of a bee in a swarm **3 :** to contain a swarm **:** TEEM ⟨~*ing* with bugs⟩ ~ *vt* **1 :** to fill with a swarm **2 :** to beset or surround in a swarm ⟨players ~*ing* the quarterback⟩ — **swarm·er** *n*
[3]**swarm** *vb* [origin unknown] *vi* (14c) **:** to climb with the hands and feet; *specif* **:** SHIN ⟨~ up a pole⟩ ~ *vt* **:** to climb up **:** MOUNT
swarm spore *n* (1859) **:** ZOOSPORE
swart \ˈswȯrt\ *adj* [ME, fr. OE *sweart;* akin to OHG *swarz* black, L *sordes* dirt] (bef. 12c) **1 a :** SWARTHY **b** *archaic* **:** producing a swarthy complexion **2 :** BANEFUL, MALIGNANT — **swart·ness** *n*
swar·thy \ˈswȯr-t͟hē, -thē\ *adj* **swar·thi·er; -est** [alter. of obs. *swarty,* fr. *swart*] (1587) **:** of a dark color, complexion, or cast — **swar·thi·ness** *n*
[1]**swash** \ˈswäsh, ˈswȯsh\ *vb* [prob. imit.] *vi* (1556) **1 :** BLUSTER, SWAGGER **2 :** to make violent noisy movements **3 :** to move with a splashing sound ~ *vt* **:** to cause to splash
[2]**swash** *n* (1593) **1 :** SWAGGER **2 :** a narrow channel of water lying within a sandbank or between a sandbank and the shore **3 :** a dashing of water against or on something; *esp* **:** the rush of water up a beach from a breaking wave
[3]**swash** *n* [obs. E *swash* slanting] (1683) **:** an extended flourish on a printed character
[4]**swash** *adj* (1683) **:** having one or more swashes ⟨~ capitals⟩
swash·buck·le \ˈswäsh-ˌbə-kəl, ˈswȯsh-\ *vi* **-led; -ling** \-ˌbə-k(ə-)liŋ\ [back-formation fr. *swashbuckler*] (1897) **:** to act the part of a swashbuckler
swash·buck·ler \-ˌbə-klər\ *n* [[1]*swash* + *buckler*] (1560) **1 :** a swaggering or daring soldier or adventurer **2 :** a novel or drama dealing with a swashbuckler
swash·buck·ling \-ˌbə-k(ə-)liŋ\ *adj* [*swashbuckler*] (ca. 1693) **1 :** acting in the manner of a swashbuckler **2 :** characteristic of, marked by, or done by swashbucklers
swash·er \ˈswä-shər, ˈswȯ-\ *n* (1580) **:** SWASHBUCKLER
swas·ti·ka \ˈswäs-ti-kə *also* swä-ˈstē-\ *n* [Skt *svastika,* fr. *svasti* well-being, fr. *su-* well + *as-* to be; akin to Skt *asti* he is, OE *is;* fr. its being regarded as a good luck symbol] (1871) **1 :** a symbol or ornament in the form of a Greek cross with the ends of the arms extended at right angles all in the same rotary direction **2 :** a swastika used as a symbol of anti-Semitism or of Nazism
[1]**swat** \ˈswät\ *vt* **swat·ted; swat·ting** [E dial., to squat, alter. of E *squat*] (ca. 1796) **:** to hit with a sharp slapping blow usu. with an instrument (as a bat or flyswatter) ⟨*swatted* the ball for a home run⟩
[2]**swat** *n* (ca. 1800) **1 :** a powerful or crushing blow **2 :** a long hit in baseball; *esp* **:** HOME RUN
SWAT \ˈswät\ *n, often attrib* [*s*pecial *w*eapons *a*nd *t*actics] (1968) **:** a police or military unit specially trained and equipped to handle unusually hazardous situations or missions
swatch \ˈswäch\ *n* [origin unknown] (1647) **1 a :** a sample piece (as of fabric) or a collection of samples **b :** a characteristic specimen **2 :** PATCH **3 :** a small collection **4 :** SWATH 2
swath \ˈswäth, ˈswȯth\ *or* **swathe** \ˈswät͟h, ˈswȯt͟h, ˈswāt͟h\ *n* [ME, fr. OE *swæth* footstep, trace; akin to MHG *swade* swath] (14c) **1 a :** a row of cut grain or grass left by a scythe or mowing machine **b :** the sweep of a scythe or a machine in mowing or the path cut in one course **2 :** a long broad strip or belt **3 :** a stroke of or as if of a scythe **4 :** a space devastated as if by a scythe
[1]**swathe** \ˈswät͟h, ˈswȯt͟h, ˈswāt͟h\ *or* **swath** \ˈswät͟h, ˈswäth, ˈswȯt͟h, ˈswȯth\ *n* [ME, fr. OE **swæth;* akin to OE *swathian* to swathe] (bef. 12c) **1 :** a band used in swathing **2 :** an enveloping medium
[2]**swathe** \ˈswät͟h, ˈswȯt͟h, ˈswāt͟h\ *vt* **swathed; swath·ing** [ME, fr. OE *swathian*] (12c) **1 :** to bind, wrap, or swaddle with or as if with a bandage **2 :** ENVELOP ⟨a mountain *swathed* by clouds⟩
swath·er \ˈswä-thər, -t͟hər\ *n* (ca. 1875) **:** a harvesting machine that cuts and windrows grain and seed crops; *also* **:** a mower attachment that windrows the swath
swathing clothes *n pl* [ME] (14c) *obs* **:** SWADDLING CLOTHES
swats \ˈswäts\ *n pl* [ME (Sc) **swats,* fr. OE *swātan,* pl., beer] (1508) *Scot* **:** DRINK; *esp* **:** new ale
swat·ter \ˈswä-tər\ *n* (1888) **:** one that swats; *esp* **:** FLYSWATTER
S wave *n* [*s*econdary] (1913) **:** a wave (as from an earthquake) in which the propagated disturbance is a shear in an elastic medium (as the earth) — compare PRESSURE WAVE
[1]**sway** \ˈswā\ *n* [ME *sweigh,* fr. *sweyen*] (14c) **1 :** the action or an instance of swaying or of being swayed **:** an oscillating, fluctuating, or sweeping motion **2 :** an inclination or deflection caused by or as if by swaying **3 a :** a controlling influence **b :** sovereign power **:** DOMINION **c :** the ability to exercise influence or authority **:** DOMINANCE ***syn*** see POWER
[2]**sway** *vb* [alter. of earlier *swey* to fall, swoon, fr. ME *sweyen,* prob. of Scand origin; akin to ON *sveigja* to sway; akin to Lith *svaigti* to become dizzy] *vi* (ca. 1500) **1 a :** to swing slowly and rhythmically back and forth from a base or pivot **b :** to move gently from an upright to a leaning position **2 :** to hold sway **:** act as ruler or governor **3 :** to fluctuate or veer between one point, position, or opinion and another ~ *vt* **1 a :** to cause to sway **:** set to swinging, rocking, or oscillating **b :** to cause to bend downward to one side **c :** to cause to turn aside **:** DEFLECT, DIVERT **2** *archaic* **a :** WIELD **b :** GOVERN, RULE **3 a :** to cause to vacillate **b :** to exert a guiding or controlling influence on **4 :** to hoist in place ⟨~ up a mast⟩ ***syn*** see SWING, AFFECT — **sway·er** *n*
sway·backed \ˈswā-ˌbakt\ *also* **sway·back** \-ˌbak\ *adj* (1680) **:** having an abnormally hollow or sagging back ⟨a ~ mare⟩ — **sway·back** *n*
sway bar *n* (1949) **:** a bar that torsionally couples the right and left front-wheel suspensions of an automobile to reduce roll and sway
Swa·zi \ˈswä-zē\ *n, pl* **Swazi** *or* **Swazis** [Zulu *iSwazi, iliSwazi*] (1878) **1 :** a member of a Bantu people of southeastern Africa **2 :** SISWATI
[1]**swear** \ˈswer\ *vb* **swore** \ˈswȯr\; **sworn** \ˈswȯrn\; **swear·ing** [ME *sweren,* fr. OE *swerian;* akin to OHG *swerien* to swear and perh. to OCS *svarŭ* quarrel] *vt* (bef. 12c) **1 :** to utter or take solemnly (an oath) **2 a :** to assert as true or promise under oath ⟨a *sworn* affidavit⟩ ⟨*swore* to uphold the Constitution⟩ **b :** to assert or promise emphatically or earnestly ⟨*swore* he'd study harder next time⟩ **3 a :** to put to an oath **:** administer an oath to **b :** to bind by an oath ⟨*swore* them to secrecy⟩ **4** *obs* **:** to invoke the name of (a sacred being) in an oath **5 :** to bring

into a specified state by swearing ⟨*swore* his life away⟩ ~ *vi* **1 :** to take an oath **2 :** to use profane or obscene language **:** CURSE — **swear·er** *n* — **swear by :** to place great confidence in ⟨*swears by* his mechanic⟩ — **swear for :** to give assurance for **:** GUARANTEE — **swear off :** to vow to abstain from **:** RENOUNCE ⟨*swear off* smoking⟩

[2]**swear** *n* (14c) **:** OATH, SWEARWORD

swear in *vt* (1536) **:** to induct into office by administration of an oath

swear out *vt* (1850) **:** to procure (a warrant for arrest) by making a sworn accusation

swear·word \ˈswer-ˌwərd\ *n* (1833) **:** a profane or obscene oath or word

[1]**sweat** \ˈswet\ *vb* **sweat** *or* **sweat·ed; sweat·ing** [ME *sweten,* fr. OE *swǣtan,* fr. *swāt* sweat; akin to OHG *sweiz* sweat, L *sudare* to sweat, Gk *hidrōs* sweat] *vi* (bef. 12c) **1 a :** to excrete moisture in visible quantities through the openings of the sweat glands **:** PERSPIRE **b :** to labor or exert oneself so as to cause perspiration **2 a :** to emit or exude moisture ⟨cheese ~*s* in ripening⟩ **b :** to gather surface moisture in beads as a result of condensation ⟨stones ~ at night⟩ **c** (1) **:** FERMENT (2) **:** PUTREFY **3 :** to undergo anxiety or mental or emotional distress ⟨~ through final exams⟩ **4 :** to become exuded through pores or a porous surface **:** OOZE ~ *vt* **1 :** to emit or seem to emit from pores **:** EXUDE **2 :** to manipulate or produce by hard work or drudgery **3 :** to get rid of or lose (weight) by or as if by sweating or being sweated **4 :** to make wet with perspiration **5 a :** to cause to excrete moisture from the skin **b :** to drive hard **:** OVERWORK **c :** to exact work from at low wages and under unfair or unhealthful conditions **d** *slang* **:** to give the third degree to **6 :** to cause to exude or lose moisture; *esp* **:** to subject (as tobacco leaves) to fermentation **7 a :** to extract something valuable from by unfair or dishonest means **:** FLEECE **b :** to remove particles of metal from (a coin) by abrasion **8 a :** to heat (as solder) so as to melt and cause to run esp. between surfaces to unite them; *also* **:** to unite by such means ⟨~ a pipe joint⟩ **b :** to heat so as to extract an easily fusible constituent ⟨~ bismuth ore⟩ **c :** to sauté in a covered vessel until natural juices are exuded **9** *slang* **:** to worry about ⟨doesn't ~ the small stuff —Barry McDermott⟩ — **sweat blood :** to work or worry intensely ⟨in preparing speeches each *sweats blood* in his own way —Stewart Cockburn⟩

[2]**sweat** *n* (13c) **1 :** hard work **:** DRUDGERY **2 :** the fluid excreted from the sweat glands of the skin **:** PERSPIRATION **3 :** moisture issuing from or gathering in drops on a surface **4 a :** the condition of one sweating or sweated **b :** a spell of sweating **5 :** a state of anxiety or impatience **6** *pl* **a :** SWEAT SUIT **b :** SWEATPANTS — **no sweat** *slang* **:** with little or no difficulty **:** EASILY; *also* **:** EASY — often used interjectionally

sweat·band \ˈswet-ˌband\ *n* (1862) **1 :** a usu. leather band lining the inner edge of a hat or cap to prevent sweat damage **2 :** a band of material worn around the head or wrist to absorb sweat

sweat bee *n* (1894) **:** any of various small black or brownish bees (family Halictidae) that are attracted to perspiration

sweat·box \-ˌbäks\ *n* (1864) **1 :** a place in which one is made to sweat; *esp* **:** a narrow box or cell in which a prisoner is placed for punishment **2 :** a device for sweating something (as hides in tanning or dried figs)

sweat·ed \ˈswe-təd\ *adj* (1882) **:** of, subjected to, or produced under sweatshop conditions ⟨~ labor⟩ ⟨~ goods⟩

sweat equity *n* (1966) **:** equity in a property resulting from labor invested in improvements that increase its value; *also* **:** the labor so invested

sweat·er \ˈswe-tər\ *n* (15c) **1 :** one that sweats or causes sweating **2 a :** a knitted or crocheted jacket or pullover **b :** a heavy jersey worn in ice hockey

sweat·er·dress \-ˌdres\ *n* (1952) **:** a knitted or crocheted dress

sweater girl *n* (1940) **:** a woman with a shapely bust

sweat·er–vest \ˈswe-tər-ˌvest\ *n* (1952) **:** a sleeveless pullover or buttoned sweater

sweat gland *n* (1845) **:** a simple tubular gland of the skin that excretes perspiration, is widely distributed in nearly all parts of the human skin, and consists typically of an epithelial tube extending spirally from a minute pore on the surface of the skin into the dermis or subcutaneous tissues where it ends in a convoluted tuft

sweat lodge *n* (1850) **:** a hut, lodge, or cavern heated by steam from water poured on hot stones and used esp. by American Indians for ritual or therapeutic sweating

sweat out *vt* (1589) **1 :** to work one's way painfully through or to **2 :** to endure or wait through the course of

sweat·pants \ˈswet-ˌpan(t)s\ *n pl* (1925) **:** pants having a drawstring or elastic waist and usu. elastic cuffs at the ankle that are worn esp. for exercise

sweat·shirt \-ˌshərt\ *n* (1925) **:** a loose collarless pullover or jacket usu. of heavy cotton jersey

sweat·shop \-ˌshäp\ *n* (1892) **:** a shop or factory in which employees work for long hours at low wages and under unhealthy conditions

sweat suit *n* (1930) **:** a suit worn usu. for exercise that consists of a sweatshirt and sweatpants

sweat test *n* (1978) **:** a test for cystic fibrosis that involves measuring the subject's sweat for abnormally high sodium chloride content

sweaty \ˈswe-tē\ *adj* **sweat·i·er; -est** (14c) **1 :** causing sweat ⟨a ~ day⟩ ⟨~ work⟩ **2 :** wet or stained with or smelling of sweat ⟨~ socks⟩ — **sweat·i·ly** \ˈswe-tə-lē\ *adv* — **sweat·i·ness** \ˈswe-tē-nəs\ *n*

swede \ˈswēd\ *n* [LG or obs. D] (1589) **1** *cap* **a :** a native or inhabitant of Sweden **b :** a person of Swedish descent **2** *chiefly Brit* **:** RUTABAGA

Swe·den·bor·gian \ˌswē-dᵊn-ˈbȯr-j(ē-)ən, -ˈbȯr-gē-ən\ *adj* (1807) **:** of or relating to the teachings of Emanuel Swedenborg or the Church of the New Jerusalem based on his teachings — **Swedenborgian** *n* — **Swe·den·bor·gian·ism** \-j(ē-)ə-ˌni-zəm, -gē-ə-\ *n*

Swed·ish \ˈswē-dish\ *n* (1605) **1 :** the North Germanic language spoken in Sweden and a part of Finland **2** *pl in constr* **:** the people of Sweden — **Swedish** *adj*

Swedish massage *n* (1911) **:** massage involving a system of active and passive exercise of muscles and joints

[1]**sweep** \ˈswēp\ *vb* **swept** \ˈswept\; **sweep·ing** [ME *swepen;* akin to OE *swāpan* to sweep, OHG *sweifen* to wander] *vt* (14c) **1 a :** to remove from a surface with or as if with a broom or brush ⟨*swept* the crumbs from the table⟩ **b :** to destroy completely **:** WIPE OUT — usu. used with *away* ⟨everything she cherished, might be *swept* away overnight —Louis Bromfield⟩ **c :** to remove or take with a single continuous forceful action ⟨*swept* the books off the desk⟩ **d :** to remove from sight or consideration ⟨the problem can't be *swept* under the rug⟩ **e :** to drive or carry along with irresistible force ⟨a wave of protest that *swept* the opposition into office⟩ **2 a :** to clean with or as if with a broom or brush **b :** to clear by repeated and forcible action **c :** to move across or along swiftly, violently, or overwhelmingly ⟨fire *swept* the business district —*Amer. Guide Series: Md.*⟩ **d :** to win an overwhelming victory in or on ⟨~ the elections⟩ **e :** to win all the games or contests of ⟨~ a double-header⟩ ⟨~ a series⟩ **3 :** to touch in passing with a swift continuous movement **4 :** to trace or describe the locus or extent of (as a line, circle, or angle) **5 :** to cover the entire range of ⟨his eyes *swept* the horizon⟩ ~ *vi* **1 a :** to clean a surface with or as if with a broom **b :** to move swiftly, forcefully, or devastatingly ⟨the wind *swept* through the treetops⟩ **2 :** to go with stately or sweeping movements ⟨proudly *swept* into the room⟩ **3 :** to move or extend in a wide curve or range — **sweep one off one's feet :** to gain immediate and unquestioning support, approval, or acceptance by a person — **sweep the board** *or* **sweep the table 1 :** to win all the bets on the table **2 :** to win everything **:** beat all competitors

[2]**sweep** *n* (1548) **1 :** something that sweeps or works with a sweeping motion: as **a :** a long pole or timber pivoted on a tall post and used to raise and lower a bucket in a well **b :** a triangular cultivator blade that cuts off weeds under the soil surface **c :** a windmill sail **2 a :** an instance of sweeping; *esp* **:** a clearing out or away with or as if with a broom **b :** the removal from the table in one play in casino of all the cards by pairing or combining **c :** an overwhelming victory **d :** a winning of all the contests or prizes in a competition **e :** a wide-ranging search of an area (as by police) **3 a :** a movement of great range and force **b :** a curving or circular course or line **c :** the compass of a sweeping movement **:** SCOPE **d :** a broad unbroken area or extent ⟨a ~ of wildflowers⟩ **e :** an end run in football in which one or more linemen pull back and run interference for the ballcarrier **4 :** CHIMNEY SWEEP **5 :** SWEEPSTAKES **6 :** obliquity with respect to a reference line ⟨~ of an airplane wing⟩; *esp* **:** SWEEPBACK **7** *pl* **:** a television ratings period during which surveys are taken to determine advertising rates ***syn*** see RANGE

sweep·back \ˈswēp-ˌbak\ *n* (1914) **:** the backward slant of an airplane wing in which the outer portion of the wing is downstream from the inner portion

sweep·er \ˈswē-pər\ *n* (15c) **1 :** one that sweeps **2 :** a lone back in soccer who plays between the line of the defenders and the goal

sweep hand *n* (1943) **:** SWEEP-SECOND HAND

[1]**sweeping** *n* (14c) **1 :** the act or action of one that sweeps ⟨gave the room a good ~⟩ **2** *pl* **:** things collected by sweeping **:** REFUSE

[2]**sweeping** *adj* (1573) **1 a :** moving or extending in a wide curve or over a wide area **b :** having a curving line or form **2 a :** EXTENSIVE ⟨~ reforms⟩ **b :** marked by wholesale and indiscriminate inclusion ⟨~ generalities⟩ — **sweep·ing·ly** *adv* — **sweep·ing·ness** *n*

sweep–sec·ond hand \ˈswēp-ˌse-kənd-, -kənt-\ *n* (1937) **:** a hand marking seconds on a timepiece mounted concentrically with the other hands and read from the same dial as the minute hand

sweep·stakes \-ˌstāks\ *n pl but sing or pl in constr, also* **sweep–stake** \-ˌstāk\ [ME *swepestake* one who wins all the stakes in a game, fr. *swepen* to sweep + *stake*] (1774) **1 a :** a race or contest in which the entire prize may be awarded to the winner; *specif* **:** STAKES RACE **b :** CONTEST, COMPETITION **2 :** any of various lotteries

sweepy \ˈswē-pē\ *adj* **sweep·i·er; -est** (1697) **:** sweeping in motion, line, or force

[1]**sweet** \ˈswēt\ *adj* [ME *swete,* fr. OE *swēte;* akin to OHG *suozi* sweet, L *suadēre* to urge, *suavis* sweet, Gk *hēdys*] (bef. 12c) **1 a** (1) **:** pleasing to the taste (2) **:** being or inducing the one of the four basic taste sensations that is typically induced by disaccharides and is mediated esp. by receptors in taste buds at the front of the tongue — compare BITTER, SALT, SOUR **b** (1) *of a beverage* **:** containing a sweetening ingredient **:** not dry (2) *of wine* **:** retaining a portion of natural sugar **2 a :** pleasing to the mind or feelings **:** AGREEABLE, GRATIFYING — often used as a generalized term of approval ⟨how ~ it is⟩ **b :** marked by gentle good humor or kindliness ⟨a ~ disposition⟩ **c :** FRAGRANT ⟨a ~ aroma⟩ **d** (1) **:** delicately pleasing to the ear or eye ⟨a ~ melody⟩ (2) **:** played in a straightforward melodic style ⟨~ jazz⟩ **e :** SACCHARINE, CLOYING **f :** very good or appealing ⟨a ~ job offer⟩ ⟨a ~ sports car⟩ **3 :** much loved **:** DEAR **4 a :** not sour, rancid, decaying, or stale **:** WHOLESOME ⟨~ milk⟩ **b :** not salt or salted **:** FRESH ⟨~ water⟩ ⟨~ butter⟩ **c :** free from excessive acidity — used esp. of soil **d :** free from noxious gases and odors **e :** free from excess of acid, sulfur, or corrosive salts ⟨~ crude oil⟩ **5 :** SKILLFUL, PROFICIENT ⟨a ~ golf swing⟩ **6 —** used as an intensive ⟨take your own ~ time⟩ — **sweet·ly** *adv* — **sweet·ness** *n* — **sweet on :** having a crush on

[2]**sweet** *adv* (13c) **:** in a sweet manner

[3]**sweet** *n* (14c) **1 :** something that is sweet to the taste: as **a :** a food (as a candy or preserve) having a high sugar content ⟨fill up on ~*s*⟩ **b** *Brit* **:** DESSERT **c** *Brit* **:** HARD CANDY **2 :** a sweet taste sensation **3 :** a pleasant or gratifying experience, possession, or state **4 :** DARLING, SWEETHEART **5 a** *archaic* **:** FRAGRANCE **b** *pl, archaic* **:** things having a sweet smell

sweet alyssum *n* (1822) **:** a widely cultivated European herb (*Lobularia maritima*) of the mustard family having narrow leaves and clusters of small fragrant usu. white or pink flowers

sweet–and–sour \ˌswē-tᵊn-ˈsau̇(-ə)r\ *adj* (1928) **:** seasoned with a sauce containing sugar and vinegar or lemon juice ⟨~ shrimp⟩

sweet basil *n* (ca. 1647) **:** a basil (*Ocimum basilicum*) with whitish or purple flowers that includes several cultivars (as bush basil); *also* **:** its dried or fresh leaves used esp. as a seasoning

sweet bay *n* (1716) **1 :** LAUREL 1 **2 :** a magnolia (*Magnolia virginiana*) of the eastern U.S. that has fragrant white flowers and leaves with glaucous undersides

sweet birch *n* (1785) **:** a common aromatic birch (*Betula lenta*) of eastern No. America that has shiny brown bark when young, hard dark-colored wood, and a volatile oil in its bark resembling wintergreen — called also *black birch*

sweet·bread \ˈswēt-ˌbred\ *n* (1565) **:** the thymus or pancreas of a young animal (as a calf) used for food

sweet·bri·ar *or* **sweet·bri·er** \-ˌbrī(-ə)r\ *n* (1538) **:** an Old World rose (esp. *Rosa eleganteria*) with stout recurved prickles and white to deep rosy-pink single flowers — called also *eglantine*
sweet cherry *n* (ca. 1901) **:** a white-flowered Eurasian cherry (*Prunus avium*) widely grown for its large sweet-flavored fruits; *also* **:** its fruit
sweet chocolate *n* (1846) **:** chocolate that contains added sugar
sweet cic·e·ly \-ˈsi-s(ə-)lē\ *n* [*cicely* fr. L *seselis,* fr. Gk] (1577) **:** any of a genus (*Osmorhiza*) of American and eastern Asian herbs of the carrot family that typically have thick fleshy roots and grow in moist woodlands
sweet clover *n* (1860) **:** any of a genus (*Melilotus*) of Old World legumes that have trifoliolate leaves and are widely grown for soil improvement or hay
sweet corn *n* (1646) **:** corn of a variety (*Zea mays rugosa* syn. *Z. m. saccharata*) with soft kernels containing a high percentage of sugar
sweet·en \ˈswē-tᵊn\ *vb* **sweet·ened; sweet·en·ing** \ˈswēt-niŋ, ˈswē-tᵊn-iŋ\ *vt* (ca. 1552) **1 :** to make sweet **2 :** to soften the mood or attitude of **3 :** to make less painful or trying **4 :** to free from a harmful or undesirable quality or substance; *esp* **:** to remove sulfur compounds from ⟨~ natural gas⟩ **5 :** to make more valuable or attractive ⟨~ the deal⟩: as **a :** to increase (a pot not won on the previous deal) by anteing prior to another deal **b :** to place additional securities as collateral for (a loan) ~ *vi* **:** to become sweet — **sweet·en·er** \ˈswēt-nər, ˈswē-tᵊn-ər\ *n*
sweetening *n* (1819) **:** something that sweetens
sweet fern *n* (1654) **:** a small No. American shrub (*Comptonia peregrina*) of the wax-myrtle family with aromatic leaves
sweet flag *n* (1765) **:** a perennial marsh herb (*Acorus calamus*) of the arum family with long narrow sword-shaped leaves and an aromatic rootstock — called also *calamus*
sweet·grass \ˈswēt-ˌgras\ *n* (1926) **:** a slender fragrant perennial grass (*Hierochloe odorata*) that typically grows in moist soils and is used esp. in basketry
sweet gum *n* (1700) **1 :** a No. American tree (*Liquidambar styraciflua*) of the witch-hazel family with palmately lobed glossy green leaves, corky twigs, a round spiny brown fruit cluster, and hard wood **2 :** the smooth reddish-brown wood of the sweet gum
[1]**sweet·heart** \ˈswēt-ˌhärt\ *n* (14c) **1 :** DARLING **2 :** one who is loved **3 :** a generally likable person **4 :** a remarkable one of its kind
[2]**sweetheart** *adj* (1942) **:** of or relating to an agreement between an employer and a labor union official arranged privately for their benefit usu. at the expense of the workers ⟨a ~ contract⟩; *broadly* **:** arranged in private for the benefit of a few at the expense of many ⟨a ~ deal⟩
sweetheart neckline *n* (1941) **:** a neckline for women's clothing that is high in back and low in front where it is scalloped to resemble the top of a heart
sweet·ie \ˈswē-tē\ *n* (1705) **1** *pl, Brit* **:** SWEET 1a **2 :** SWEETHEART
sweetie pie *n* (1928) **:** SWEETHEART
sweet·ing \ˈswē-tiŋ\ *n* (13c) **1** *archaic* **:** SWEETHEART **2 :** a sweet apple
sweet·ish \-tish\ *adj* (1580) **1 :** somewhat sweet **2 :** unpleasantly sweet — **sweet·ish·ly** *adv*
sweet marjoram *n* (1565) **:** a perennial marjoram (*Origanum majorana* syn. *Majorana hortensis*) with dense spikelike flower clusters
sweet·meat \ˈswēt-ˌmēt\ *n* (14c) **:** a food rich in sugar: as **a :** a candied or crystallized fruit **b :** CANDY, CONFECTION
sweetness and light *n* (1869) **1 :** a harmonious combination of beauty and enlightenment viewed as a hallmark of culture **2 a :** amiable reasonableness of disposition ⟨they were all *sweetness and light*⟩ **b :** an untroubled or harmonious state or condition ⟨but all was not *sweetness and light*⟩
sweet orange *n* (1538) **1 a :** an orange (*Citrus sinensis*) that is prob. native to southeastern Asia, has a fruit with a pithy central axis, and is the source of the widely cultivated oranges of commerce **b :** a cultivated orange derived from the sweet orange and usu. having fruit with a relatively thin rind and sweet juicy edible pulp **2 :** the fruit of a sweet orange
sweet pea *n* (1732) **1 :** a widely cultivated Italian legume (*Lathyrus odoratus*) having slender usu. climbing stems, ovate leaves, and large fragrant flowers **2 :** the flower of a sweet pea
sweet pepper *n* (1814) **:** any of various large mild thick-walled capsicum fruits; *also* **:** a pepper plant (*Capsicum annuum*) bearing sweet peppers — compare BELL PEPPER
sweet potato *n* (1750) **1 :** a tropical vine (*Ipomoea batatas*) of the morning-glory family with variously shaped leaves and purplish flowers; *also* **:** its large thick sweet and nutritious tuberous root that is cooked and eaten as a vegetable — compare YAM 2 **2 :** OCARINA
sweet·shop \ˈswēt-ˌshäp\ *n* (1878) *chiefly Brit* **:** a candy store
sweet·sop \-ˌsäp\ *n* (1696) **:** SUGAR APPLE
sweet sorghum *n* (1858) **:** SORGO
sweet spot *n* (ca. 1949) **:** the area around the center of mass of a bat, racket, or head of a club that is the most effective part with which to hit a ball
sweet–talk \ˈswēt-ˌtȯk\ *vt* (1928) **:** CAJOLE, COAX ~ *vi* **:** to use flattery
sweet talk *n* (1901) **:** FLATTERY
sweet tooth *n* (14c) **:** a craving or fondness for sweet food
sweet wil·liam \ˌswēt-ˈwil-yəm\ *n, often cap W* [fr. the name *William*] (1573) **:** a widely cultivated Old World pink (*Dianthus barbatus*) with small white to deep red or purple flowers often showily spotted, banded, or mottled and borne in flat-topped cymes
sweet woodruff *n* (1800) **:** a small Eurasian and No. African sweet-scented herb (*Galium odoratum* syn. *Asperula odorata*) of the madder family that has small white flowers and is used esp. in perfumery and for flavoring wine
[1]**swell** \ˈswel\ *vb* **swelled; swelled** *or* **swol·len** \ˈswō-lən\; **swell·ing** [ME, fr. OE *swellan;* akin to OHG *swellan* to swell] *vi* (bef. 12c) **1 a :** to expand (as in size, volume, or numbers) gradually beyond a normal or original limit ⟨the population ~*ed*⟩ **b :** to become distended or puffed up ⟨her ankle is badly *swollen*⟩ **c :** to form a bulge or rounded elevation **2 a :** to become filled with pride and arrogance **b :** to behave or speak in a pompous, blustering, or self-important manner **c :** to play the swell **3 :** to become distended with emotion ~ *vt* **1 :** to affect with a powerful or expansive emotion **2 :** to increase the size, number, or intensity of ⟨~ the applicant pool⟩ ***syn*** see EXPAND
[2]**swell** *n* (1606) **1 :** a long often massive and crestless wave or succession of waves often continuing beyond or after its cause (as a gale) **2 a :** the condition of being protuberant **b :** a rounded elevation **3 a :** the act or process of swelling **b** (1) **:** a gradual increase and decrease of the loudness of a musical sound; *also* **:** a sign indicating a swell (2) **:** a device used in an organ for governing loudness **4 a** *archaic* **:** an impressive, pompous, or fashionable air or display **b :** a person dressed in the height of fashion **c :** a person of high social position or outstanding competence
[3]**swell** *adj* (1785) **1 a :** STYLISH **b :** socially prominent **2 :** EXCELLENT — used as a generalized term of enthusiasm
swell box *n* (ca. 1801) **:** a chamber in an organ containing a set of pipes and having shutters that open or shut to regulate the volume of tone
swelled head *n* (1870) **:** an exaggerated opinion of oneself **:** SELF-CONCEIT — **swelled–head·ed** \ˈsweld-ˌhe-dəd\ *adj* — **swelled–head·ed·ness** *n*
swell·fish \ˈswel-ˌfish\ *n* (1807) **:** PUFFER FISH 1
swell–front \ˈswel-ˌfrənt\ *adj* (1914) **:** BOWFRONT 1
swell·head \-ˌhed\ *n* (1845) **:** one who has a swelled head **:** a conceited person — **swell·head·ed** \-ˌhe-dəd\ *adj* — **swell·head·ed·ness** *n*
swelling *n* (bef. 12c) **1 :** something that is swollen; *specif* **:** an abnormal bodily protuberance or localized enlargement **2 :** the condition of being swollen
[1]**swel·ter** \ˈswel-tər\ *vb* **swel·tered; swel·ter·ing** \-t(ə-)riŋ\ [ME *sweltren,* freq. of *swelten* to die, be overcome by heat, fr. OE *sweltan* to die; akin to Goth *swiltan* to die] *vi* (14c) **1 :** to suffer, sweat, or be faint from heat **2 :** to become exceedingly hot ⟨in summer, the place ~*s*⟩ ~ *vt* **1 :** to oppress with heat **2** *archaic* **:** EXUDE ⟨~*ed* venom —Shak.⟩
[2]**swelter** *n* (1851) **1 :** a state of oppressive heat **2 :** WELTER **3 :** an excited or overwrought state of mind **:** SWEAT ⟨in a ~⟩
sweltering *adj* (1566) **:** oppressively hot — **swel·ter·ing·ly** *adv*
swept *adj* [*swept,* pp. of *sweep*] (1903) **:** slanted backward
swept–back \ˈswep(t)-ˈbak\ *adj* (1914) **:** possessing sweepback
swerve \ˈswərv\ *vb* **swerved; swerv·ing** [ME, fr. OE *sweorfan* to wipe, file away; akin to OHG *swerban* to wipe off, W *chwerfu* to whirl] *vi* (14c) **:** to turn aside abruptly from a straight line or course **:** DEVIATE ~ *vt* **:** to cause to turn aside or deviate — **swerve** *n*
syn SWERVE, VEER, DEVIATE, DEPART, DIGRESS, DIVERGE mean to turn aside from a straight course. SWERVE may suggest a physical, mental, or moral turning away from a given course, often with abruptness ⟨*swerved* to avoid hitting the dog⟩. VEER implies a major change in direction ⟨at that point the path *veers* to the right⟩. DEVIATE implies a turning from a customary or prescribed course ⟨never *deviated* from her daily routine⟩. DEPART suggests a deviation from a traditional or conventional course or type ⟨occasionally *departs* from his own guidelines⟩. DIGRESS applies to a departing from the subject of one's discourse ⟨a professor prone to *digress*⟩. DIVERGE may equal DEPART but usu. suggests a branching of a main path into two or more leading in different directions ⟨after school their paths *diverged*⟩.
swev·en \ˈswe-vən\ *n* [ME, fr. OE *swefn* sleep, dream, vision — more at SOMNOLENT] (bef. 12c) *archaic* **:** DREAM, VISION
swid·den \ˈswi-dᵊn\ *n, often attrib* [E dial., burned clearing, prob. fr. ON *svithinn,* pp. of *svitha* to burn, singe] (ca. 1868) **:** a temporary agricultural plot formed by cutting back and burning off vegetative cover
[1]**swift** \ˈswift\ *adj* [ME, fr. OE; akin to OE *swīfan* to revolve — more at SWIVEL] (bef. 12c) **1 :** moving or capable of moving with great speed ⟨a ~ runner⟩ **2 :** occurring suddenly or within a very short time ⟨a ~ transition⟩ **3 :** quick to respond **:** READY ***syn*** see FAST
[2]**swift** *adv* (14c) **:** SWIFTLY ⟨*swift*-flowing⟩
[3]**swift** *n* (15c) **1 :** any of several lizards (esp. of the genus *Sceloporus*) that run swiftly **2 :** a reel for winding yarn or thread **3 :** any of numerous small plainly colored birds (family Apodidae) that are related to the hummingbirds but superficially much resemble swallows
swift fox *n* (1845) **:** a small fox (*Vulpes velox*) with large ears that occurs on the plains of western No. America
swift·let \ˈswif(t)-lət\ *n* (ca. 1890) **:** any of various cave-dwelling swifts (genus *Collocalia* syn. *Aerodramus*) of Asia including one (*C. fuciphaga*) that produces the nest used in bird's nest soup
swift·ly *adv* (bef. 12c) **:** in a swift manner **:** with speed **:** QUICKLY
swift·ness \ˈswif(t)-nəs\ *n* (bef. 12c) **1 :** the quality or state of being swift **:** CELERITY **2 :** the fact of being swift
[1]**swig** \ˈswig\ *n* [origin unknown] (ca. 1623) **:** a quantity drunk at one time
[2]**swig** *vb* **swigged; swig·ging** *vt* (ca. 1650) **:** to drink in long drafts ⟨~ cider⟩ ~ *vi* **:** to take a swig **:** DRINK — **swig·ger** *n*
[1]**swill** \ˈswil\ *vb* [ME *swilen,* fr. OE *swillan*] *vt* (bef. 12c) **1 :** WASH, DRENCH **2 :** to drink great drafts of **:** GUZZLE ⟨~ beer⟩ **3 :** to feed (as a pig) with swill ~ *vi* **1 :** to drink or eat freely, greedily, or to excess **2 :** SWASH — **swill·er** *n*
[2]**swill** *n* (1553) **1 :** something suggestive of slop or garbage **:** REFUSE **2 a :** a semiliquid food for animals (as swine) composed of edible refuse mixed with water or skimmed or sour milk **b :** GARBAGE
[1]**swim** \ˈswim\ *vb* **swam** \ˈswam\; **swum** \ˈswəm\; **swim·ming** [ME *swimmen,* fr. OE *swimman;* akin to OHG *swimman* to swim] *vi* (bef. 12c) **1 a :** to propel oneself in water by natural means (as movements of the limbs, fins, or tail) **b :** to play in the water (as at a beach or swimming pool) **2 :** to move with a motion like that of swimming **:** GLIDE ⟨a cloud *swam* slowly across the moon⟩ **3 a :** to float on a liquid **:** not sink **b :** to surmount difficulties **:** not go under ⟨sink or ~, live or die, survive or perish —Daniel Webster⟩ **4 :** to become immersed in or flooded with or as if with a liquid ⟨potatoes *swimming* in gravy⟩ **5 :** to have a floating or reeling appearance or sensation ~ *vt* **1 a :** to cross by propelling oneself through water ⟨~ a stream⟩ **b :** to execute in swimming **2 :** to cause to swim or float — **swim·mer** *n*

2swim *n* (1599) **1 :** a smooth gliding motion **2 :** an act or period of swimming **3 :** a temporary dizziness or unconsciousness **4 a :** an area frequented by fish **b :** the main current of activity ⟨in the ~⟩
3swim *adj* (1924) **:** of, relating to, or used in or for swimming
swim bladder *n* (1837) **:** the air bladder of a fish
swim fin *n* (1947) **:** FLIPPER 1b
swim·ma·ble \ˈswi-mə-bəl\ *adj* (1852) **:** that can be swum
swim·mer·et \ˌswi-mə-ˈret, ˈswi-mə-ˌ\ *n* (1840) **:** one of a series of small unspecialized appendages under the abdomen of many crustaceans that are best developed in some decapods (as a lobster) and usu. function in locomotion or reproduction
swimmer's ear *n* (1961) **:** inflammation of the canal in the outer ear that is characterized by itching, redness, swelling, pain, and discharge and that typically occurs when water trapped in the outer ear during swimming becomes infected usu. with a bacterium
swimmer's itch *n* (1928) **:** a severe urticarial reaction to the presence in the skin of larval schistosomes
1swimming *adj* (bef. 12c) **1** [prp. of *swim*] **:** that swims ⟨a ~ bird⟩ **2** [gerund of *swim*] **:** adapted to or used in or for swimming
2swimming *n* (14c) **:** the act, art, or sport of one that swims and dives
swim·ming·ly \ˈswi-miŋ-lē\ *adv* (1622) **:** very well **:** SPLENDIDLY ⟨the event went ~⟩
swimming pool *n* (1868) **:** a pool suitable for swimming; *esp* **:** a tank (as of concrete or plastic) made for swimming
swim·my \ˈswi-mē\ *adj* **swim·mi·er; -est** (1836) **1 :** verging on, causing, or affected by dizziness or giddiness **2** *of vision* **:** UNSTEADY, BLURRED — **swim·mi·ly** \ˈswi-mə-lē\ *adv*
swim·suit \ˈswim-ˌsüt\ *n* (1926) **:** a suit for swimming or bathing
swim·wear \-ˌwer\ *n* (1935) **:** clothing suitable for wear while swimming or bathing
1swin·dle \ˈswin-dᵊl\ *vb* **swin·dled; swin·dling** \ˈswin(d)-liŋ, ˈswin-dᵊl-iŋ\ [back-formation fr. *swindler,* fr. G *Schwindler* giddy person, fr. *schwindeln* to be dizzy, fr. OHG *swintilōn,* freq. of *swintan* to diminish, vanish; akin to OE *swindan* to vanish] *vi* (ca. 1782) **:** to obtain money or property by fraud or deceit ~ *vt* **:** to take money or property from by fraud or deceit ***syn*** see CHEAT — **swin·dler** \ˈswin(d)-lər, ˈswin-dᵊl-ər\ *n*
2swindle *n* (1821) **:** an act or instance of swindling **:** FRAUD
swine \ˈswīn\ *n, pl* **swine** [ME, fr. OE *swīn;* akin to OHG *swīn* swine, L *sus* — more at SOW] (bef. 12c) **1 :** any of various stout-bodied short-legged omnivorous artiodactyl mammals (family Suidae) with a thick bristly skin and a long flexible snout; *esp* **:** a domesticated one descended from the wild boar **2 :** a contemptible person
swine fever *n* (1886) **1 :** HOG CHOLERA **2 :** an acute highly contagious usu. fatal disease of swine that is caused by a double-stranded DNA virus (species *African swine fever virus* of the genus *Asfivirus,* family *Asfarviridae*), that resembles but is more severe than hog cholera, and that is indigenous to Africa — called also *African swine fever*
swine flu *n* (1921) **:** SWINE INFLUENZA; *also* **:** influenza A of humans that is caused by a different strain of an orthomyxovirus subtype (H1N1) from those found in swine and that is marked esp. by fever, sore throat, cough, chills, body aches, fatigue, and sometimes diarrhea and vomiting
swine·herd \-ˌhərd\ *n* (bef. 12c) **:** one who tends swine
swine influenza *n* (1919) **:** influenza A of swine that is caused by any of several subtypes (as H1N1 or H3N2) of the causative orthomyxovirus and in which sporadic transmission to humans has occurred — compare SWINE FLU
1swing \ˈswiŋ\ *vb* **swung** \ˈswəŋ\; **swing·ing** \ˈswiŋ-iŋ\ [ME, to beat, fling, hurl, rush, fr. OE *swingan* to beat, fling oneself, rush; akin to OHG *swingan* to fling, rush] *vt* (13c) **1 a :** to cause to move vigorously through a wide arc or circle ⟨~ an ax⟩ **b :** to cause to sway to and fro **c** (1) **:** to cause to turn on an axis (2) **:** to cause to face or move in another direction ⟨~ the car into a side road⟩ **2 :** to suspend so as to permit swaying or turning **3 :** to convey by suspension ⟨cranes ~*ing* cargo into the ship's hold⟩ **4 a** (1) **:** to influence decisively ⟨~ a lot of votes⟩ (2) **:** to bring around by influence **b :** to handle successfully **:** MANAGE ⟨wasn't able to ~ a new car on his income⟩ ⟨~ a deal⟩ **5 :** to play or sing (as a melody) in the style of swing music ~ *vi* **1 :** to move freely to and fro esp. in suspension from an overhead support **2 a :** to die by hanging **b :** to hang freely from a support **3 :** to move in or describe a circle or arc: **a :** to turn on a hinge or pivot **b :** to turn in place **c :** to convey oneself by grasping a fixed support ⟨~ aboard the train⟩ **4 a :** to have a steady pulsing rhythm **b :** to play or sing with a lively compelling rhythm; *specif* **:** to play swing music **5 :** to shift or fluctuate from one condition, form, position, or object of attention or favor to another ⟨~ constantly from optimism to pessimism and back —Sinclair Lewis⟩ **6 a :** to move along rhythmically **b :** to start up in a smooth vigorous manner ⟨ready to ~ into action⟩ **7 :** to hit or aim at something with a sweeping arm movement **8 a :** to be lively, exciting, and up-to-date **b :** to engage freely in sex

syn SWING, WAVE, FLOURISH, BRANDISH, THRASH mean to wield or cause to move to and fro or up and down. SWING implies regular or uniform movement ⟨*swing* the rope back and forth⟩. WAVE usu. implies smooth or continuous motion ⟨*waving* the flag⟩. FLOURISH suggests vigorous, ostentatious, graceful movement ⟨*flourished* the winning lottery ticket⟩. BRANDISH implies threatening or menacing motion ⟨*brandishing* a knife⟩. THRASH suggests vigorous, abrupt, violent movement ⟨an infant *thrashing* his arms about⟩.

syn SWING, SWAY, OSCILLATE, VIBRATE, FLUCTUATE, WAVER, UNDULATE mean to move from one direction to its opposite. SWING implies a movement of something attached at one end or one side ⟨the door suddenly *swung* open⟩. SWAY implies a slow swinging or teetering movement ⟨trees *swaying* in the breeze⟩. OSCILLATE stresses a usu. regular alternation of direction ⟨an *oscillating* fan⟩. VIBRATE suggests the rapid oscillation of an elastic body under stress or impact ⟨the *vibrating* strings of a piano⟩. FLUCTUATE suggests constant irregular changes of level, intensity, or value ⟨*fluctuating* interest rates⟩. WAVER stresses irregular motion suggestive of reeling or tottering ⟨the exhausted runner *wavered* before collapsing⟩. UNDULATE suggests a gentle wavelike motion ⟨an *undulating* sea of grass⟩.

2swing *n* (14c) **1 :** an act or instance of swinging **:** swinging movement: as **a** (1) **:** a stroke or blow delivered with a sweeping arm movement ⟨a batter with a powerful ~⟩ (2) **:** a sweeping or rhythmic movement of the body or a bodily part (3) **:** a dance figure in which two dancers revolve with joined arms or hands (4) **:** jazz dancing in moderate tempo with a lilting syncopation **b** (1) **:** the regular movement of a freely suspended object (as a pendulum) along an arc and back (2) **:** back and forth sweep ⟨the ~ of the tides⟩ **c** (1) **:** steady pulsing rhythm (as in poetry or music) (2) **:** a steady vigorous movement characterizing an activity or creative work **d** (1) **:** a trend toward a high or low point in a fluctuating cycle (as of business activity) (2) **:** an often periodic shift from one condition, form, position, or object of attention or favor to another **2 a :** liberty of action **b** (1) **:** the driving power of something swung or hurled (2) **:** steady vigorous advance **:** driving speed ⟨a train approaching at full ~⟩ **3 :** the progression of an activity, process, or phase of existence ⟨the work is in full ~⟩ **4 :** the arc or range through which something swings **5 :** something that swings freely from or on a support; *esp* **:** a seat suspended by a rope or chains for swinging to and fro on for pleasure **6 a :** a curving course or outline **b :** a course from and back to a point **:** a circular tour **7 :** jazz that is played (as by a big band) with a steady beat and that uses the harmonic structures of popular songs and the blues as a basis for improvisations and arrangements **8 :** a short pass in football thrown to a back running to the outside
3swing *adj* (1933) **1 :** of or relating to musical swing ⟨a ~ band⟩ ⟨~ music⟩ ⟨~ dancing⟩ **2 :** that may swing often decisively either way on an issue or in an election ⟨~ voters⟩ ⟨a ~ state⟩
1swinge \ˈswinj\ *vt* **swinged; swinge·ing** [ME *swengen* to shake, fr. OE *swengan;* akin to OE *swingan*] (12c) *chiefly dial* **:** BEAT, SCOURGE
2swinge *vt* **swinged; swinge·ing** [alter. of *singe*] (1590) *dial* **:** SINGE, SCORCH
1swinge·ing *also* **swing·ing** \ˈswin-jiŋ\ *adj* [fr. prp. of *1swinge*] (1575) *chiefly Brit* **:** very large, high, or severe ⟨~ fines⟩ ⟨~ taxes⟩
2swingeing *or* **swinging** *adv* (1690) *chiefly Brit* **:** VERY, SUPERLATIVELY
1swing·er \ˈswiŋ-ər\ *n* (1543) **:** one that swings: as **a :** a person who is lively, exciting, and up-to-date **b :** one who engages freely in sex
2swing·er \ˈswin-jər\ *n* [*1swinge*] (1583) **:** WHOPPER 1
swing·ing \ˈswiŋ-iŋ\ *adj* [prp. of *1swing*] (1956) **:** being lively, exciting, and up-to-date; *also* **:** abounding in swingers and swinging entertainment ⟨a ~ coffeehouse⟩
1swing·ing·ly \ˈswin-jiŋ-lē\ *adv* (1671) *chiefly Brit* **:** VERY, EXTREMELY
2swing·ing·ly \ˈswiŋ-iŋ-lē\ *adv* (1882) **:** in a swinging manner **:** with a swinging movement
swin·gle·tree \ˈswiŋ-gəl-(ˌ)trē\ *n* [ME *swyngyll tre,* fr. *swyngyll* rod for beating flax (fr. MD *swengel*) + *tre* tree] (15c) **:** WHIFFLETREE
swing·man \ˈswiŋ-ˌman, -mən\ *n* (1965) **:** a player capable of playing effectively in two different positions and esp. of playing both guard and forward on a basketball team
swing shift *n* (1940) **1 :** the work shift between the day and night shifts (as from 4 P.M. to midnight) **2 :** a group of workers in a factory operating seven days a week that work as needed to permit the regular shift workers to have one or more free days per week
swingy \ˈswiŋ-ē\ *adj* **swing·i·er; -est** (1915) **:** marked by swing
swin·ish \ˈswī-nish\ *adj* (13c) **:** of, suggesting, or characteristic of swine **:** BEASTLY — **swin·ish·ly** *adv* — **swin·ish·ness** *n*
1swink \ˈswiŋk\ *vi* [ME, fr. OE *swincan;* akin to OHG *swingan* to rush — more at SWING] (bef. 12c) *archaic* **:** TOIL, SLAVE
2swink *n* (12c) *archaic* **:** LABOR, DRUDGERY
1swipe \ˈswīp\ *n* [prob. alter. of *sweep*] (1739) **1 :** a strong sweeping blow ⟨a ~ of a paw⟩ **2 :** a sharp often critical remark ⟨took a parting ~ at management⟩
2swipe *vb* **swiped; swip·ing** *vi* (ca. 1825) **:** to strike or move with a sweeping motion ~ *vt* **1 :** to strike or wipe with a sweeping motion **2 :** STEAL, PILFER **3 :** to slide (a card with a magnetic strip or bar code) through a slot in a reading device so that information stored on the strip can be processed (as in making a purchase)
swipes \ˈswīps\ *n pl* [origin unknown] (1794) *Brit* **:** poor, thin, or spoiled beer; *also* **:** BEER
1swirl \ˈswər(-ə)l\ *vb* [ME] *vi* (14c) **1 a :** to move with an eddying or whirling motion ⟨~*ing* water⟩ **b :** to pass in whirling confusion **2 :** to have a twist or convolution ~ *vt* **:** to cause to swirl ⟨~*ed* her drink⟩ — **swirl·ing·ly** \ˈswər-liŋ-lē\ *adv*
2swirl *n* (15c) **1 a :** a whirling mass or motion **:** EDDY **b :** whirling confusion ⟨a ~ of events⟩ **2 :** a twisting shape, mark, or pattern **3 :** an act or instance of swirling
swirly \ˈswər-lē\ *adj* **swirl·i·er; -est** (1785) **1** *Scot* **:** KNOTTED, TWISTED **2 :** that swirls **:** SWIRLING ⟨the ~ water of the rapids⟩
1swish \ˈswish\ *vb* [imit.] *vi* (1756) **:** to move, pass, swing, or whirl with the sound of a swish ~ *vt* **1 :** to move, cut, or strike with a swish ⟨the horse ~*ed* its tail⟩ **2 :** to make (a basketball shot) so that the ball falls through the rim without touching it ⟨~*ed* a 3-point jumper⟩ — **swish·er** *n* — **swish·ing·ly** \ˈswi-shiŋ-lē\ *adv*
2swish *n* (1820) **1 a :** a prolonged hissing sound (as of a whip cutting the air) **b :** a light sweeping or brushing sound **2 :** a swishing movement **3** *usu disparaging* **:** an effeminate homosexual
3swish *adj* [origin unknown] (1766) **:** SMART, FASHIONABLE
swishy \ˈswi-shē\ *adj* **swish·i·er; -est** (1828) **1 :** producing a swishing sound **2** *usu disparaging* **:** characterized by effeminate behavior
1Swiss \ˈswis\ *n* [MF *Suisse,* fr. MHG *Swīzer,* fr. *Swīz* Switzerland] (1515) **1** *pl* **Swiss a :** a native or inhabitant of Switzerland **b :** one that is of Swiss descent **2** *often not cap* **:** any of various fine sheer fabrics of cotton orig. made in Switzerland; *esp* **:** DOTTED SWISS **3 :** SWISS CHEESE
2Swiss *adj* (1530) **:** of, relating to, or characteristic of Switzerland or the Swiss
Swiss chard *n* (1832) **:** a beet (*Beta vulgaris cicla*) having large leaves and succulent stalks often cooked as a vegetable — called also *chard*
Swiss cheese *n* (1783) **:** a hard cheese characterized by elastic texture, mild nutlike flavor, and large holes that form during ripening
Swiss steak *n* (ca. 1911) **:** a slice of steak pounded with flour and braised usu. with vegetables and seasonings
1switch \ˈswich\ *n* [perh. fr. MD *swijch* twig] (1592) **1 :** a slender flexible whip, rod, or twig ⟨a riding ~⟩ **2 :** an act of switching: as **a :** a blow with a switch **b :** a shift from one to another **c :** a change from the usual ⟨that outfit is a ~⟩ **3 :** a tuft of long hairs at the end of the tail of an animal (as a cow) — see COW illustration **4 :** a device made usu. of two movable rails and necessary connections and designed to

turn a locomotive or train from one track to another **5 :** a device for making, breaking, or changing the connections in an electrical circuit **6 :** a heavy strand of hair used in addition to a person's own hair for some coiffures

[2]**switch** *vt* (ca. 1611) **1 :** to strike or beat with or as if with a switch **2 :** WHISK, LASH ⟨a cat ~*ing* its tail⟩ **3 a** (1) **:** to turn from one railroad track to another **:** SHUNT (2) **:** to move (cars) to different positions on the same track within terminal areas **b :** to make a shift in or exchange of ⟨~ seats⟩ **4 a :** to shift to another electrical circuit by means of a switch **b** (1) **:** to operate an electrical switch so as to turn (as a device) on or off — usu. used with *on* or *off* (2) **:** to change to or from an active state — usu. used with *on* or *off* ⟨~*ed* on the gene⟩ ~ *vi* **1 :** to lash from side to side **2 :** to make a shift or exchange — **switch·able** \ˈswi-chə-bəl\ *adj* — **switch·er** *n*

[1]**switch·back** \ˈswich-ˌbak\ *n* (1863) **:** a zigzag road, trail, or section of railroad tracks for climbing a steep hill — **switchback** *adj*

[2]**switchback** *vi* (1903) **:** to follow a zigzag course esp. for ascent or descent ⟨a trail that ~*s*⟩

switch·blade \-ˌblād\ *n* (1932) **:** a pocketknife having the blade spring-operated so that pressure on a release catch causes it to fly open — called also *switchblade knife*

switch·board \-ˌbȯrd\ *n* (1873) **:** an apparatus (as in a telephone exchange) consisting of a panel on which are mounted electric switches so arranged that a number of circuits may be connected, combined, and controlled

switch engine *n* (1867) **:** a railroad engine used in switching cars

switch·er·oo \ˌswi-chə-ˈrü\ *n, pl* **-oos** [alter. of *switch*] (1933) **:** a surprising variation **:** REVERSAL

switch·grass \ˈswich-ˌgras\ *n* [alter. of *quitch (grass)*] (1840) **:** a tall No. American panic grass (*Panicum virgatum*) that is used for hay and forage

switch–hit \-ˈhit\ *vi* **-hit; -hit·ting** [back-formation fr. *switch-hitter*] (1938) **:** to bat right-handed against a left-handed pitcher and left-handed against a right-handed pitcher in baseball

switch–hit·ter \-ˈhi-tər\ *n* (1928) **1 :** a baseball player who switch-hits **2** *slang* **:** BISEXUAL **3 :** one that is flexible or adaptable; *esp* **:** a person who can work equally well in either of two jobs or capacities

switch knife *n* (1950) **:** SWITCHBLADE

switch·man \ˈswich-mən\ *n* (1843) **:** one who attends a switch (as in a railroad yard)

switch·yard \-ˌyärd\ *n* (1943) **:** a usu. enclosed area for the switching facilities of a power station

swith \ˈswith\ *adv* [ME, strongly, quickly, fr. OE *swīthe* strongly, fr. *swīth* strong; akin to Goth *swinths* strong, OE *gesund* sound — more at SOUND] (13c) *chiefly dial* **:** INSTANTLY, QUICKLY

swith·er \ˈswi-t͟hər\ *vi* [origin unknown] (1501) *dial chiefly Brit* **:** DOUBT, WAVER — **swither** *n, dial chiefly Brit*

Switz *abbr* Switzerland

Swit·zer \ˈswit-sər\ *n* [MHG *Swīzer*] (1549) **:** SWISS

[1]**swiv·el** \ˈswi-vəl\ *n, often attrib* [ME; akin to OE *swīfan* to revolve, OHG *swebōn* to roll, heave] (14c) **:** a device joining two parts so that one or both can pivot freely (as on a bolt or pin)

[2]**swivel** *vb* **-eled** *or* **-elled; -el·ing** *or* **-el·ling** \ˈswi-və-liŋ, ˈswiv-liŋ\ *vt* (1775) **:** to turn on or as if on a swivel ⟨~*ed* his eyes in various directions⟩ ~ *vi* **:** to swing or turn on or as if on a swivel

swivel chair *n* (1860) **:** a chair that swivels on its base

swiv·el–hipped \ˈswi-vəl-ˌhipt\ *adj* (1947) **:** moving with or characterized by movement with a twisting motion of the hips

swiv·et \ˈswi-vət\ *n* [origin unknown] (ca. 1892) **:** a state of extreme agitation ⟨in a ~⟩

[1]**swiz·zle** \ˈswi-zəl\ *n* [origin unknown] (1813) **:** an iced cocktail stirred with a swizzle stick

[2]**swizzle** *vb* **swiz·zled; swiz·zling** \ˈswi-zə-liŋ, ˈswiz-liŋ\ *vi* (1820) **:** to drink esp. to excess **:** GUZZLE ~ *vt* **:** to mix or stir with or as if with a swizzle stick — **swiz·zler** \ˈswi-zə-lər, ˈswiz-lər\ *n*

swizzle stick *n* (1879) **:** a stick used to stir mixed drinks

swob *archaic var of* SWAB

swollen *past part of* SWELL

[1]**swoon** \ˈswün\ *vi* [ME *swounen,* prob. back-formation fr. *swouning, swowening,* fr. *iswowen, aswoune,* fr. OE *geswōgen* in a swoon] (13c) **1 a :** FAINT **b :** to become enraptured ⟨~*ing* with joy⟩ **2 :** DROOP, FADE — **swoon·er** *n* — **swoon·ing·ly** \ˈswü-niŋ-lē\ *adv*

[2]**swoon** *n* (13c) **1 a :** a partial or total loss of consciousness **b :** a state of bewilderment or ecstasy **:** DAZE, RAPTURE **2 :** a state of suspended animation **:** TORPOR — **swoony** \ˈswü-nē\ *adj*

[1]**swoop** \ˈswüp\ *vb* [alter. of ME *swopen* to sweep, fr. OE *swāpan* — more at SWEEP] *vi* (1566) **:** to move with a sweep ~ *vt* **:** to gain or carry off in or as if in a swoop — usu. used with *up* — **swoop·er** *n*

[2]**swoop** *n* (1605) **1 :** an act or instance of swooping **2 :** a single concentrated and quickly effective effort ⟨was done in one ~⟩ — often used with *fell* ⟨solved everything at one fell ~⟩

swoop·stake \ˈswüp-ˌstāk\ *adv* [alter. of *sweepstake*] (1602) *obs* **:** in an indiscriminate manner

swoopy \ˈswü-pē\ *adj* (1978) **:** having sweeping lines or movement ⟨a ~ silhouette⟩

[1]**swoosh** \ˈswüsh, ˈswu̇sh\ *vb* [imit.] *vi* (1867) **1 :** to make or move with a rushing sound ⟨a car ~*ed* by⟩ **2 :** GUSH, SWIRL ~ *vt* **:** to discharge or transport with a rushing sound

[2]**swoosh** *n* (1885) **:** an act or instance of swooshing

swop *chiefly Brit var of* SWAP

sword \ˈsȯrd\ *n, often attrib* [ME, fr. OE *sweord;* akin to OHG *swert* sword] (bef. 12c) **1 :** a weapon (as a cutlass or rapier) with a long blade for cutting or thrusting that is often used as a symbol of honor or authority **2 a :** an agency or instrument of destruction or combat **b :** the use of force ⟨the pen is mightier than the ~ —E. G. Bulwer-Lytton⟩ **3 :** coercive power **4 :** something that resembles a sword — **sword·like** \-ˌlīk\ *adj* — **at swords' points :** mutually antagonistic **:** ready to fight

sword cane *n* (1823) **:** a cane in which a sword blade is concealed

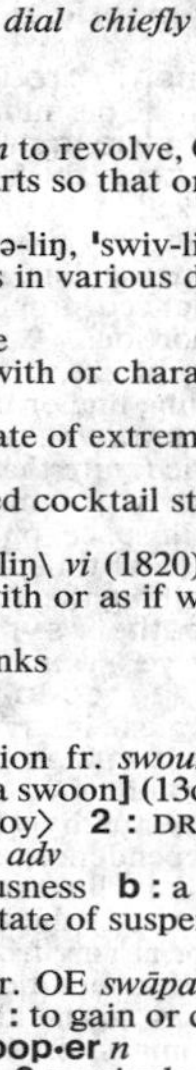

sword 1: *1* pommel, *2* hilt, *3* guard, *4* blade

sword dance *n* (1604) **1 :** a dance performed by men in a circle holding a sword in the right hand and grasping the tip of a neighbor's sword in the left hand **2 :** a dance performed over or around swords — **sword dancer** *n*

sword fern *n* (ca. 1829) **:** any of several ferns with long narrow more or less sword-shaped fronds: as **a :** a tropical fern (*Nephrolepis exaltata*) from which the Boston fern has been developed **b :** a fern (*Polystichum munitum*) of western No. America with a large fleshy rhizome

sword·fish \ˈsȯrd-ˌfish\ *n* (15c) **:** a very large scombroid fish (*Xiphias gladius* of the family Xiphiidae) that has a long swordlike beak formed by the bones of the upper jaw and is an important food and game fish

sword grass *n* (1598) **:** any of various grasses or sedges having leaves with a sharp or toothed edge

sword knot *n* (1676) **:** an ornamental cord or tassel tied to the hilt of a sword

sword of Dam·o·cles \-ˈda-mə-ˌklēz\ *often cap S* (1820) **:** an impending disaster

sword·play \ˈsȯrd-ˌplā\ *n* (1602) **1 :** the art or skill of wielding a sword esp. in fencing **2 :** an exhibition of swordplay — **sword·play·er** *n*

swords·man \ˈsȯrdz-mən\ *n* (1657) **1 :** one skilled in swordplay; *esp* **:** a saber fencer **2** *archaic* **:** a soldier armed with a sword

swords·man·ship \-ˌship\ *n* (1834) **:** SWORDPLAY

sword·tail \ˈsȯrd-ˌtāl\ *n* (1858) **:** a small brightly marked Central American live-bearer (*Xiphophorus helleri* of the family Poeciliidae) often kept in tropical aquariums and bred in many colors

swore *past of* SWEAR

sworn *past part of* SWEAR

[1]**swot** \ˈswät\ *n* [E dial., sweat, fr. ME *swot,* fr. OE *swāt* — more at SWEAT] (1850) *Brit* **:** GRIND 2b

[2]**swot** *vi* **swot·ted; swot·ting** (ca. 1860) *Brit* **:** GRIND 4

[1]**swound** \ˈswau̇nd, ˈswünd\ *n* [ME, alter. of *swoun* swoon, fr. *swounen* to swoon] (15c) *archaic* **:** SWOON 1a

[2]**swound** *vi* (1530) *archaic* **:** SWOON

swum *past part of* SWIM

swung *past and past part of* SWING

swung dash *n* (1951) **:** a character ~ used in printing to conserve space by representing part or all of a previously spelled-out word

syb·a·rite \ˈsi-bə-ˌrīt\ *n* (ca. 1555) **1** [fr. the notorious luxury of the Sybarites] **:** VOLUPTUARY, SENSUALIST **2** *cap* **:** a native or resident of the ancient city of Sybaris — **syb·a·rit·ic** \ˌsi-bə-ˈri-tik\ *adj* — **syb·a·rit·i·cal·ly** \-ti-k(ə-)lē\ *adv* — **syb·a·rit·ism** \ˈsi-bə-ˌrī-ˌti-zəm\ *n*

syc·a·mine \ˈsi-kə-ˌmīn, -mən\ *n* [L *sycaminus,* fr. Gk *sykaminos,* of Sem origin; akin to Heb *shiqmāh* mulberry tree, sycamore] (1526) **:** a tree of the Bible that is usu. considered a mulberry (*Morus nigra*)

syc·a·more \ˈsi-kə-ˌmȯr\ *n* [ME *sicamour,* fr. AF *sicamour,* fr. L *sycomorus,* fr. Gk *sykomoros,* prob. modif. of a Sem word akin to Heb *shiqmāh* sycamore] (14c) **1** *also* **syc·o·more** \ˈsi-kə-\ **:** a fig tree (*Ficus sycomorus*) of Africa and the Middle East that is the sycamore of Scripture and has edible fruit similar but inferior to the common fig **2 :** a Eurasian maple (*Acer pseudoplatanus*) with long racemes of showy yellowish-green flowers that is widely planted as a shade tree **3 :** [2]PLANE; *esp* **:** a very large spreading tree (*Platanus occidentalis*) chiefly of the eastern and central U.S. with 3- to 5-lobed broadly ovate leaves

syce \ˈsīs\ *n* [Hindi & Urdu *sāīs,* fr. Ar *sā'is*] (1653) **:** an attendant (as a groom) esp. in India

sy·cee \ˈsī-ˌsē\ *n* [Chin (Guangdong) *sai-sì,* lit., fine silk] (1711) **:** silver money made in the form of ingots and formerly used in China

sy·co·ni·um \sī-ˈkō-nē-əm\ *n, pl* **-nia** \-nē-ə\ [NL, fr. Gk *sykon* fig + NL *-ium*] (ca. 1856) **:** the multiple fleshy fruit of a fig in which the ovaries are borne within an enlarged succulent concave or hollow receptacle

sy·co·phan·cy \ˈsi-kə-fən(t)-sē *also* ˈsī- & -ˌfan(t)-sē\ *n* (1637) **:** obsequious flattery; *also* **:** the character or behavior of a sycophant

sy·co·phant \-fənt *also* -ˌfant\ *n* [L *sycophanta* slanderer, swindler, fr. Gk *sykophantēs* slanderer, fr. *sykon* fig + *phainein* to show — more at FANCY] (1575) **:** a servile self-seeking flatterer ***syn*** see PARASITE — **sycophant** *adj*

sy·co·phan·tic \ˌsi-kə-ˈfan-tik *also* ˌsī-\ *adj* (1676) **:** of, relating to, or characteristic of a sycophant **:** FAWNING, OBSEQUIOUS ⟨~ compliments⟩ — **sy·co·phan·ti·cal·ly** \-ˈfan-ti-k(ə-)lē\ *adv*

sy·co·phant·ish \ˌsi-kə-ˈfan-tish *also* ˌsī-\ *adj* (1794) **:** SYCOPHANTIC — **sy·co·phant·ish·ly** *adv*

sy·co·phant·ism \ˈsi-kə-fən-ˌti-zəm *also* ˈsī- & -ˌfan-\ *n* (1774) **:** SYCOPHANCY

sy·co·phant·ly \-lē\ *adv* (1672) **:** in a sycophantic manner

sy·co·sis \sī-ˈkō-səs\ *n* [NL, fr. Gk *sykōsis,* fr. *sykon* fig] (ca. 1827) **:** a chronic inflammatory disorder of the hair follicles esp. of the bearded part of the face

sy·e·nite \ˈsī-ə-ˌnīt\ *n* [L *Syenites* (*lapis*) stone of Syene, fr. *Syene,* ancient city in Egypt] (ca. 1796) **:** an igneous rock composed chiefly of feldspar — **sy·e·nit·ic** \ˌsī-ə-ˈni-tik\ *adj*

sy·li \ˈsē-lē\ *n, pl* **sylis** [Susu *sìlí,* lit., elephant] (1974) **:** the monetary unit of Guinea from 1972 to 1986

syl·la·bary \ˈsi-lə-ˌber-ē\ *n, pl* **-bar·ies** [NL *syllabarium,* fr. L *syllaba* syllable] (1586) **:** a table or listing of syllables; *specif* **:** a series or set of written characters each one of which is used to represent a syllable

[1]**syl·lab·ic** \sə-ˈla-bik\ *adj* [LL *syllabicus,* fr. Gk *syllabikos,* fr. *syllabē* syllable] (1728) **1 :** constituting a syllable or the nucleus of a syllable: **a :** not accompanied in the same syllable by a vowel ⟨a ~ consonant⟩ **b :** having vowel quality more prominent than that of another vowel in the syllable ⟨the first vowel of a falling diphthong, as \ȯ\ in \ȯi\, is ~⟩ **2 :** of, relating to, or denoting syllables ⟨~ accent⟩ **3 :** characterized by distinct enunciation or separation of syllables **4 :** of, relating to, or constituting a type of verse distinguished primarily by count of syllables rather than by rhythmical arrangement of accents or quantities — **syl·lab·i·cal·ly** \-bi-k(ə-)lē\ *adv*

[2]**syllabic** *n* (1880) **:** a syllabic character or sound

\ə\ **abut** \ᵊ\ **kitten,** F **table** \ər\ **further** \a\ **ash** \ā\ **ace** \ä\ **mop, mar**
\au̇\ **out** \ch\ **chin** \e\ **bet** \ē\ **easy** \g\ **go** \i\ **hit** \ī\ **ice** \j\ **job**
\ŋ\ **sing** \ō\ **go** \ȯ\ **law** \ȯi\ **boy** \th\ **thin** \t͟h\ **the** \ü\ **loot** \u̇\ **foot**
\y\ **yet** \zh\ **vision, beige** \k͟, ⁿ, œ, ue, ʸ\ *see* Guide to Pronunciation

syl·lab·i·cate \sə-ˈla-bə-ˌkāt\ *vt* **-cat·ed; -cat·ing** (ca. 1654) : SYLLABIFY

syl·lab·i·ca·tion \sə-ˌla-bə-ˈkā-shən\ *n* (15c) : the act, process, or method of forming or dividing words into syllables

syl·la·bic·i·ty \ˌsi-lə-ˈbi-sə-tē\ *n* (1933) : the state of being or the power of forming a syllable

syl·lab·i·fi·ca·tion \sə-ˌla-bə-fə-ˈkā-shən\ *n* (1838) : SYLLABICATION

syl·lab·i·fy \sə-ˈla-bə-ˌfī\ *vt* **-fied; -fy·ing** [L *syllaba* syllable] (ca. 1859) : to form or divide into syllables

1**syl·la·ble** \ˈsi-lə-bəl\ *n* [ME, fr. AF *sillabe, silable,* fr. L *syllaba,* fr. Gk *syllabē,* fr. *syllambanein* to gather together, fr. *syn-* + *lambanein* to take — more at LATCH] (14c) **1 :** a unit of spoken language that is next bigger than a speech sound and consists of one or more vowel sounds alone or of a syllabic consonant alone or of either with one or more consonant sounds preceding or following **2 :** one or more letters (as *syl, la,* and *ble*) in a word (as *syl·la·ble*) usu. set off from the rest of the word by a centered dot or a hyphen and roughly corresponding to the syllables of spoken language and treated as helps to pronunciation or as guides to placing hyphens at the end of a line **3 :** the smallest conceivable expression or unit of something : JOT **4 :** SOL-FA SYLLABLES

2**syllable** *vt* **syl·la·bled; syl·la·bling** \-b(ə-)liŋ\ (15c) **1 :** to give a number or arrangement of syllables to (a word or verse) **2 :** to express or utter in or as if in syllables

syl·la·bub *also* **sil·la·bub** \ˈsi-lə-ˌbəb\ *n* [origin unknown] (ca. 1537) **:** milk or cream that is curdled with an acid beverage (as wine or cider) and often sweetened and served as a drink or topping or thickened with gelatin and served as a dessert

syl·la·bus \-bəs\ *n, pl* **-bi** \-ˌbī, -ˌbē\ *or* **-bus·es** [LL, alter. of L *sillybus* label for a book, fr. Gk *sillybos*] (ca. 1656) **1 :** a summary outline of a discourse, treatise, or course of study or of examination requirements **2 :** HEADNOTE 2

syl·lep·sis \sə-ˈlep-səs\ *n, pl* **-lep·ses** \-ˌsēz\ [L, fr. Gk *syllēpsis,* fr. *syllambanein*] (ca. 1550) **1 :** the use of a word to modify or govern syntactically two or more words with only one of which it formally agrees in gender, number, or case **2 :** the use of a word in the same grammatical relation to two adjacent words in the context with one literal and the other metaphorical in sense — **syl·lep·tic** \-ˈlep-tik\ *adj*

syl·lo·gism \ˈsi-lə-ˌji-zəm\ *n* [ME *silogisme,* fr. AF *sillogisme,* fr. L *syllogismus,* fr. Gk *syllogismos,* fr. *syllogizesthai* to syllogize, fr. *syn-* + *logizesthai* to calculate, fr. *logos* reckoning, word — more at LEGEND] (14c) **1 :** a deductive scheme of a formal argument consisting of a major and a minor premise and a conclusion (as in "every virtue is laudable; kindness is a virtue; therefore kindness is laudable") **2 :** a subtle, specious, or crafty argument **3 :** deductive reasoning — **syl·lo·gis·tic** \ˌsi-lə-ˈjis-tik\ *adj* — **syl·lo·gis·ti·cal·ly** \-ti-k(ə-)lē\ *adv*

syl·lo·gist \ˈsi-lə-jist\ *n* (1799) : one who applies or is skilled in syllogistic reasoning

syl·lo·gize \ˈsi-lə-ˌjīz\ *vb* **-gized; -giz·ing** [ME *sylogysen,* fr. LL *syllogizare,* fr. Gk *syllogizesthai*] *vi* (15c) : to reason by means of syllogisms ~ *vt* : to deduce by syllogism ⟨~*s* moral laws⟩

sylph \ˈsilf\ *n* [NL *sylphus*] (1657) **1 :** an elemental being in the theory of Paracelsus that inhabits air **2 :** a slender graceful woman or girl — **sylph·like** \ˈsil-ˌflīk\ *adj*

sylph·id \ˈsil-fəd\ *n* (1680) : a young or diminutive sylph

1**syl·van** \ˈsil-vən\ *n* (1565) : one that frequents groves or woods

2**sylvan** *adj* [ML *silvanus, sylvanus,* fr. L *silva, sylva* wood] (ca. 1583) **1 a :** living or located in the woods or forest **b :** of, relating to, or characteristic of the woods or forest **2 a :** made, shaped, or formed of woods or trees **b :** abounding in woods, groves, or trees : WOODED

syl·vat·ic \sil-ˈva-tik\ *adj* [L *silvaticus* of the woods, wild — more at SAVAGE] (1661) **1 :** SYLVAN ⟨~ rodents⟩ **2 :** occurring in or affecting wild animals ⟨~ diseases⟩

syl·vite \ˈsil-ˌvīt\ *also* **syl·vine** \-ˌvēn\ *n* [alter. of *sylvine,* fr. F, fr. NL *sal digestivus Sylvii* digestive salt of Sylvius, fr. *Sylvius* latinized name of Jacques Dubois †1555 Fr. physician] (1868) : a mineral that is a natural potassium chloride and occurs in colorless cubes or crystalline masses

sym *abbr* symmetrical

sym- — see SYN-

sym·bi·ont \ˈsim-bē-ˌänt\ *n* [prob. fr. G, modif. of Gk *symbiount-, symbiōn,* prp. of *symbioun*] (1887) : an organism living in symbiosis; *esp* : the smaller member of a symbiotic pair

sym·bi·o·sis \ˌsim-bē-ˈō-səs, -ˌbī-\ *n, pl* **-bi·o·ses** \-ˌsēz\ [NL, fr. G *Symbiose,* fr. Gk *symbiōsis* state of living together, fr. *symbioun* to live together, fr. *symbios* living together, fr. *syn-* + *bios* life — more at QUICK] (1622) **1 :** the living together in more or less intimate association or close union of two dissimilar organisms (as in parasitism or commensalism); *esp* : MUTUALISM **2 :** a cooperative relationship (as between two persons or groups) ⟨the ~ . . . between the resident population and the immigrants —John Geipel⟩ — **sym·bi·ot·ic** \-ˈä-tik\ *adj* — **sym·bi·ot·i·cal·ly** \-ti-k(ə-)lē\ *adv*

sym·bi·ote \ˈsim-bē-ˌōt, -bī-\ *n* [F, fr. Gk *symbiōtēs* companion, fr. *symbioun* to live together] (ca. 1909) : SYMBIONT

1**sym·bol** \ˈsim-bəl\ *n* [in sense 1, fr. LL *symbolum,* fr. LGk *symbolon,* fr. Gk, token, sign; in other senses fr. L *symbolum* token, sign, symbol, fr. Gk *symbolon,* lit., token of identity verified by comparing its other half, fr. *symballein* to throw together, compare, fr. *syn-* + *ballein* to throw — more at DEVIL] (15c) **1 :** an authoritative summary of faith or doctrine : CREED **2 :** something that stands for or suggests something else by reason of relationship, association, convention, or accidental resemblance; *esp* : a visible sign of something invisible ⟨the lion is a ~ of courage⟩ **3 :** an arbitrary or conventional sign used in writing or printing relating to a particular field to represent operations, quantities, elements, relations, or qualities **4 :** an object or act representing something in the unconscious mind that has been repressed ⟨phallic ~*s*⟩ **5 :** an act, sound, or object having cultural significance and the capacity to excite or objectify a response

2**symbol** *vb* **-boled** *or* **-bolled; -bol·ing** *or* **-bol·ling** (1832) : SYMBOLIZE

sym·bol·ic \sim-ˈbä-lik\ *also* **sym·bol·i·cal** \-li-kəl\ *adj* (1610) **1 a :** using, employing, or exhibiting a symbol **b :** consisting of or proceeding by means of symbols **2 :** of, relating to, or constituting a symbol **3 :** characterized by or terminating in symbols ⟨~ thinking⟩ **4 :** characterized by symbolism ⟨a ~ dance⟩ — **sym·bol·i·cal·ly** \-li-k(ə-)lē\ *adv*

symbolic logic *n* (1856) : a science of developing and representing logical principles by means of a formalized system consisting of primitive symbols, combinations of these symbols, axioms, and rules of inference

sym·bol·ise *Brit var of* SYMBOLIZE

sym·bol·ism \ˈsim-bə-ˌli-zəm\ *n* (1654) **1 :** the art or practice of using symbols esp. by investing things with a symbolic meaning or by expressing the invisible or intangible by means of visible or sensuous representations: as **a :** artistic imitation or invention that is a method of revealing or suggesting immaterial, ideal, or otherwise intangible truth or states **b :** the use of conventional or traditional signs in the representation of divine beings and spirits **2 :** a system of symbols or representations

sym·bol·ist \ˈsim-bə-list\ *n* (1812) **1 :** one who employs symbols or symbolism **2 :** one skilled in the interpretation or explication of symbols **3** *often cap* : one of a group of writers and artists in France after 1880 reacting against realism, concerning themselves with general truths instead of actualities, exalting the metaphysical and the mysterious, and aiming to unify and blend the arts and the functions of the senses — **symbolist** *adj*

sym·bol·is·tic \ˌsim-bə-ˈlis-tik\ *adj* (ca. 1864) : SYMBOLIC

sym·bol·i·za·tion \ˌsim-bə-lə-ˈzā-shən\ *n* (1603) **1 :** an act or instance of symbolizing **2 :** the human capacity to develop a system of meaningful symbols

sym·bol·ize \ˈsim-bə-ˌlīz\ *vb* **-ized; -iz·ing** *vt* (1603) **1 :** to serve as a symbol of **2 :** to represent, express, or identify by a symbol ~ *vi* : to use symbols or symbolism — **sym·bol·iz·er** *n*

sym·bol·o·gy \sim-ˈbä-lə-jē\ *n, pl* **-gies** [*symbol* + *-logy*] (1840) **1 :** the art of expression by symbols **2 :** the study or interpretation of symbols **3 :** a system of symbols

sym·met·al·lism \(ˌ)si(m)-ˈme-tə-ˌli-zəm\ *n* [*syn-* + *-metallism* (as in *bimetallism*)] (ca. 1895) : a system of coinage in which the unit of currency consists of a particular weight of an alloy of two or more metals

sym·met·ri·cal \sə-ˈme-tri-kəl\ *or* **sym·met·ric** \-trik\ *adj* (1653) **1 :** having, involving, or exhibiting symmetry **2 :** having corresponding points whose connecting lines are bisected by a given point or perpendicularly bisected by a given line or plane ⟨~ curves⟩ **3** *symmetric* **:** being such that the terms or variables may be interchanged without altering the value, character, or truth ⟨*symmetric* equations⟩ ⟨R is a *symmetric* relation if *a*R*b* implies *b*R*a*⟩ **4 a :** capable of division by a longitudinal plane into similar halves ⟨~ plant parts⟩ **b :** having the same number of members in each whorl of floral leaves ⟨~ flowers⟩ **5 :** affecting corresponding parts simultaneously and similarly ⟨~ rash⟩ **6 :** exhibiting symmetry in a structural formula; *esp* : being a derivative with groups substituted symmetrically in the molecule — **sym·met·ri·cal·ly** \-tri-k(ə-)lē\ *adv* — **sym·met·ri·cal·ness** \-kəl-nəs\ *n*

symmetric group *n* (1897) : a permutation group that is composed of all of the permutations of *n* things

symmetric matrix *n* (ca. 1949) : a matrix that is its own transpose

sym·me·trize \ˈsi-mə-ˌtrīz\ *vt* **-trized; -triz·ing** (1796) : to make symmetrical — **sym·me·tri·za·tion** \ˌsi-mə-trə-ˈzā-shən\ *n*

sym·me·try \ˈsi-mə-trē\ *n, pl* **-tries** [L *symmetria,* fr. Gk, fr. *symmetros* symmetrical, fr. *syn-* + *metron* measure — more at MEASURE] (1563) **1 :** balanced proportions; *also* : beauty of form arising from balanced proportions **2 :** the property of being symmetrical; *esp* : correspondence in size, shape, and relative position of parts on opposite sides of a dividing line or median plane or about a center or axis — compare BILATERAL SYMMETRY, RADIAL SYMMETRY **3 :** a rigid motion of a geometric figure that determines a one-to-one mapping onto itself **4 :** the property of remaining invariant under certain changes (as of orientation in space, of the sign of the electric charge, of parity, or of the direction of time flow) — used of physical phenomena and of equations describing them

sympath- *or* **sympatho-** *comb form* [ISV, fr. *sympathetic*] : sympathetic nerve ⟨*sympatho*lytic⟩

sym·pa·thec·to·my \ˌsim-pə-ˈthek-tə-mē\ *n, pl* **-mies** [ISV] (1900) : surgical interruption of sympathetic nerve pathways — **sym·pa·thec·to·mized** \-ˌmīzd\ *adj*

1**sym·pa·thet·ic** \ˌsim-pə-ˈthe-tik\ *adj* [NL *sympatheticus,* fr. L *sympathia* sympathy] (1644) **1 :** existing or operating through an affinity, interdependence, or mutual association **2 a :** appropriate to one's mood, inclinations, or disposition **b :** marked by kindly or pleased appreciation ⟨the biographer's approach was ~⟩ **3 :** given to, marked by, or arising from sympathy, compassion, friendliness, and sensitivity to others' emotions ⟨a ~ gesture⟩ **4 :** favorably inclined : APPROVING ⟨not ~ to the idea⟩ **5 a :** showing empathy **b :** arousing sympathy or compassion ⟨a ~ role in the play⟩ **6 a :** of or relating to the sympathetic nervous system **b :** mediated by or acting on the sympathetic nerves **7 :** relating to musical tones produced by sympathetic vibration or to strings so tuned as to sound by sympathetic vibration — **sym·pa·thet·i·cal·ly** \-ti-k(ə-)lē\ *adv*

2**sympathetic** *n* (1808) : a sympathetic structure; *esp* : SYMPATHETIC NERVOUS SYSTEM

sympathetic magic *n* (1905) : magic based on the assumption that a person or thing can be supernaturally affected through its name or an object representing it

sympathetic nervous system *n* (1850) : the part of the autonomic nervous system that contains chiefly adrenergic fibers and tends to depress secretion, decrease the tone and contractility of smooth muscle, and increase heart rate — compare PARASYMPATHETIC NERVOUS SYSTEM

sympathetic strike *n* (1895) : SYMPATHY STRIKE

sympathetic vibration *n* (1898) : a vibration produced in one body by the vibrations of exactly the same period in a neighboring body

sym·pa·thise *chiefly Brit var of* SYMPATHIZE

sym·pa·thize \ˈsim-pə-ˌthīz\ *vi* **-thized; -thiz·ing** (1600) **1 :** to be in keeping, accord, or harmony **2 :** to react or respond in sympathy **3 :** to share in suffering or grief : COMMISERATE ⟨~ with a friend in trouble⟩; *also* : to express such sympathy **4 :** to be in sympathy intellectually ⟨~ with a proposal⟩ — **sym·pa·thiz·er** *n*

sym·pa·tho·lyt·ic \ˌsim-pə-thō-ˈli-tik\ *adj* [ISV] (1943) : tending to oppose the physiological results of sympathetic nervous activity or of sympathomimetic drugs ⟨a ~ agent⟩ — **sympatholytic** *n*

sym·pa·tho·mi·met·ic \-mə-ˈme-tik, -(ˌ)mī-\ *adj* [ISV] (1910) : simulating sympathetic nervous action in physiological effect ⟨~ drugs⟩ — **sympathomimetic** *n*

sym·pa·thy \ˈsim-pə-thē\ *n, pl* **-thies** [L *sympathia,* fr. Gk *sympatheia,* fr. *sympathēs* having common feelings, sympathetic, fr. *syn-* + *pathos* feelings, emotion, experience — more at PATHOS] (1579) **1 a** : an affinity, association, or relationship between persons or things wherein whatever affects one similarly affects the other **b** : mutual or parallel susceptibility or a condition brought about by it **c** : unity or harmony in action or effect ⟨every part is in complete ~ with the scheme as a whole —Edwin Benson⟩ **2 a** : inclination to think or feel alike : emotional or intellectual accord ⟨in ~ with their goals⟩ **b** : feeling of loyalty : tendency to favor or support ⟨republican *sympathies*⟩ **3 a** : the act or capacity of entering into or sharing the feelings or interests of another **b** : the feeling or mental state brought about by such sensitivity ⟨have ~ for the poor⟩ **4** : the correlation existing between bodies capable of communicating their vibrational energy to one another through some medium ***syn*** see ATTRACTION, PITY

sympathy strike *n* (1912) : a strike in which the strikers have no direct grievance against their own employer but attempt to support or aid usu. another group of workers on strike

sym·pat·ric \sim-ˈpa-trik\ *adj* [*syn-* + Gk *patra* fatherland, fr. *patēr* father — more at FATHER] (ca. 1904) **1** : occurring in the same area **2** : occupying the same geographical range without loss of identity from interbreeding ⟨~ species⟩; *also* : occurring between populations that are not geographically separated ⟨~ speciation⟩ — compare ALLOPATRIC — **sym·pat·ri·cal·ly** \-tri-k(ə-)lē\ *adv* — **sym·pat·ry** \ˈsim-ˌpa-trē\ *n*

sym·phon·ic \sim-ˈfä-nik\ *adj* (1856) **1** : HARMONIOUS, SYMPHONIOUS **2** : relating to or having the form or character of a symphony ⟨~ music⟩ **3** : suggestive of a symphony esp. in form, interweaving of themes, or harmonious arrangement ⟨a ~ drama⟩ — **sym·phon·i·cal·ly** \-ni-k(ə-)lē\ *adv*

symphonic poem *n* (1873) : an extended programmatic composition for symphony orchestra usu. freer in form than a symphony

sym·pho·ni·ous \sim-ˈfō-nē-əs\ *adj* (1652) : agreeing esp. in sound : HARMONIOUS — **sym·pho·ni·ous·ly** *adv*

sym·pho·nist \ˈsim(p)-fə-nist\ *n* (1767) **1** : a member of a symphony orchestra **2** : a composer of symphonies

sym·pho·ny \-nē\ *n, pl* **-nies** [ME *symphonie,* fr. MF, fr. L *symphonia,* fr. Gk *symphōnia,* fr. *symphōnos* concordant in sound, fr. *syn-* + *phōnē* voice, sound — more at BAN] (15c) **1** : consonance of sounds **2 a** : RITORNELLO 1 **b** : SINFONIA 1 **c** (1) : a usu. long and complex sonata for symphony orchestra (2) : a musical composition (as for organ) resembling such a symphony in complexity or variety **3** : consonance or harmony of color (as in a painting) **4 a** : SYMPHONY ORCHESTRA **b** : a symphony orchestra concert **5** : something that in its harmonious complexity or variety suggests a symphonic composition ⟨a ~ of flavors⟩

symphony orchestra *n* (ca. 1881) : a large orchestra of winds, strings, and percussion that plays symphonic works

sym·phy·se·al \ˌsim(p)-fə-ˈsē-əl\ *also* **sym·phys·i·al** \sim-ˈfi-zē-əl\ *adj* [Gk *symphyse-, symphysis* symphysis] (ca. 1836) : of, relating to, or constituting a symphysis

sym·phy·sis \ˈsim(p)-fə-səs\ *n, pl* **-phy·ses** \-ˌsēz\ [NL, fr. Gk, state of growing together, fr. *symphyesthai* to grow together, fr. *syn-* + *phyein* to make grow, bring forth — more at BE] (ca. 1578) **1** : an immovable or more or less movable articulation of various bones in the median plane of the body **2** : an articulation in which the bony surfaces are connected by pads of fibrous cartilage without a synovial membrane

sym·po·di·al \sim-ˈpō-dē-əl\ *adj* [NL *sympodium* apparent main axis formed from secondary axes, fr. Gk *syn-* + *podion* base — more at -PODIUM] (1875) : having or involving the formation of an apparent main axis from successive secondary axes ⟨~ branching of a cyme⟩

sym·po·si·ast \-zē-ˌast, -əst\ *n* [Gk *symposiazein* to take part in a symposium, fr. *symposion*] (1878) : a contributor to a symposium

sym·po·sium \sim-ˈpō-zē-əm *also* -zh(ē-)əm\ *n, pl* **-sia** \-zē-ə, -zh(ē-)ə\ *or* **-siums** [L, fr. Gk *symposion,* fr. *sympinein* to drink together, fr. *syn-* + *pinein* to drink — more at POTABLE] (1711) **1 a** : a convivial party (as after a banquet in ancient Greece) with music and conversation **b** : a social gathering at which there is free interchange of ideas **2 a** : a formal meeting at which several specialists deliver short addresses on a topic or on related topics — compare COLLOQUIUM **b** : a collection of opinions on a subject; *esp* : one published by a periodical **c** : DISCUSSION

symp·tom \ˈsim(p)-təm\ *n* [LL *symptomat-, symptoma,* fr. Gk *symptōmat-, symptōma* happening, attribute, symptom, fr. *sympiptein* to happen, fr. *syn-* + *piptein* to fall — more at FEATHER] (1541) **1 a** : subjective evidence of disease or physical disturbance; *broadly* : something that indicates the presence of bodily disorder **b** : an evident reaction by a plant to a pathogen **2 a** : something that indicates the existence of something else ⟨~*s* of an inner turmoil⟩ **b** : a slight indication : TRACE ***syn*** see SIGN — **symp·tom·less** \-ləs\ *adj*

symp·tom·at·ic \ˌsim(p)-tə-ˈma-tik\ *adj* (1698) **1 a** : being a symptom of a disease **b** : having the characteristics of a particular disease but arising from another cause ⟨~ epilepsy resulting from brain damage⟩ **2** : concerned with, affecting, or having symptoms ⟨~ treatment⟩ ⟨a ~ patient⟩ **3** : CHARACTERISTIC, INDICATIVE ⟨his behavior was ~ of his character⟩ — **symp·tom·at·i·cal·ly** \-ti-k(ə-)lē\ *adv*

symp·tom·atol·o·gy \ˌsim(p)-tə-mə-ˈtä-lə-jē\ *n* (1798) **1** : the symptom complex of a disease **2** : a branch of medical science concerned with symptoms of diseases — **symp·tom·at·o·log·i·cal** \-ˌma-tᵊl-ˈä-ji-kəl\ *or* **symp·tom·at·o·log·ic** \-ˈä-jik\ *adj* — **symp·tom·at·o·log·i·cal·ly** \-ji-k(ə-)lē\ *adv*

syn- *or* **sym-** *prefix* [NL, fr. Gk, fr. *syn* with, together with] **1** : with : along with : together ⟨*syn*clinal⟩ ⟨*sym*petalous⟩ **2** : at the same time ⟨*syn*esthesia⟩

syn·aes·the·sia *chiefly Brit var of* SYNESTHESIA

syn·a·gogue *also* **syn·a·gog** \ˈsi-nə-ˌgäg\ *n* [ME *synagoge,* fr. AF, fr. LL *synagoga,* fr. Gk *synagōgē* assembly, synagogue, fr. *synagein* to bring together, fr. *syn-* + *agein* to lead — more at AGENT] (13c) **1** : a Jewish congregation **2** : the house of worship and communal center of a Jewish congregation — **syn·a·gog·al** \ˌsi-nə-ˈgä-gəl\ *adj*

syn·ap·o·mor·phy \(ˌ)si-ˈna-pə-ˌmȯr-fē\ *n, pl* **-phies** [ISV *syn-* + *apomorphy* derived evolutionary trait or feature (fr. *apo-* + *-morphy*)] (1965) : a character or trait that is shared by two or more taxonomic groups and is derived through evolution from a common ancestral form

1**syn·apse** \ˈsi-ˌnaps, sə-ˈnaps\ *n* [NL *synapsis,* fr. Gk, juncture, fr. *synaptein* to fasten together, fr. *syn-* + *haptein* to fasten] (1899) : the point at which a nervous impulse passes from one neuron to another

2**synapse** *vi* **syn·apsed; syn·aps·ing** (1910) **1** : to form a synapse **2** : to come together in synapsis

syn·ap·sid \sə-ˈnap-səd\ *n* [NL *Synapsida,* fr. Gk *syn-* + *apsid-, apsis* arch, vault — more at APSIS] (1956) : any of a subclass (Synapsida) of extinct chiefly Permian and Triassic reptiles (as the pelycosaurs) that resembled mammals, had a single pair of lateral temporal skull openings, and are usu. held to be ancestral to mammals — **synapsid** *adj*

syn·ap·sis \sə-ˈnap-səs\ *n, pl* **-ap·ses** \-ˌsēz\ [NL] (1895) : the association of homologous chromosomes that is characteristic of the first meiotic prophase

syn·ap·tic \sə-ˈnap-tik\ *adj* [NL *synapsis*] (1895) **1** : of or relating to a synapsis **2** : of or relating to a synapse — **syn·ap·ti·cal·ly** \-ti-k(ə-)lē\ *adv*

syn·ap·to·ne·mal complex \sə-ˌnap-tə-ˈnē-məl-\ *n* [*synapt*ic + *-o-* or *-i-* + Gk *nēma* thread — more at NEMAT-] (1958) : a complex tripartite protein structure that spans the region between synapsed chromosomes in meiotic prophase — called also *syn·ap·ti·ne·mal complex* \sə-ˌnap-tə-ˈnē-məl-\

syn·ap·to·some \sə-ˈnap-tə-ˌsōm\ *n* [*synapt*ic + *-o-* + 3*-some*] (1964) : a nerve ending that is isolated from homogenized nerve tissue (as of the brain) — **syn·ap·to·som·al** \-ˌnap-tə-ˈsō-məl\ *adj*

syn·ar·thro·di·al \ˌsin-är-ˈthrō-dē-əl\ *adj* [NL *synarthrodia* synarthrosis] (1830) : of, relating to, or being a synarthrosis

syn·ar·thro·sis \-ˈthrō-səs\ *n, pl* **-thro·ses** \-ˌsēz\ [Gk *synarthrōsis,* fr. *syn-* + *arthrōsis* arthrosis] (1578) : an immovable articulation in which the bones are united by intervening fibrous connective tissues

1**sync** *also* **synch** \ˈsiŋk\ *vt* **synced** *also* **synched** \ˈsiŋ(k)t\; **sync·ing** *also* **synch·ing** \ˈsiŋ-kiŋ\ (1945) : SYNCHRONIZE

2**sync** *also* **synch** *n* (1929) : SYNCHRONIZATION, SYNCHRONISM ⟨moving in ~⟩ ⟨out of ~ with the world⟩ — **sync** *adj*

syn·car·pous \(ˌ)sin-ˈkär-pəs\ *adj* (ca. 1830) : having the carpels of the gynoecium united in a compound ovary — **syn·car·py** \ˈsin-ˌkär-pē\ *n*

syn·cat·e·gor·e·mat·ic \ˌsin-ˌka-tə-ˌgȯr-ə-ˈma-tik, -ˌgȯr-ē-\ *adj* [LL *syncategoremat-, syncategorema* syncategorematic term, fr. Gk *synkatēgorēma,* fr. *synkatēgorein* to predicate jointly, fr. *syn-* + *katēgorein* to predicate — more at CATEGORY] (1827) : forming a meaningful expression only in conjunction with a denotative expression (as a content word) ⟨logical operators and function words are ~⟩ — **syn·cat·e·gor·e·mat·i·cal·ly** \-ti-k(ə-)lē\ *adv*

1**syn·chro** \ˈsiŋ-(ˌ)krō, ˈsin-\ *adj* [*synchro-*] (1947) : adapted to synchronization

2**synchro** *n* (1968) : SYNCHRONIZED SWIMMING

synchro- *comb form* [*synchronized* & *synchronous*] : synchronized : synchronous ⟨*synchro*mesh⟩

syn·chro·cy·clo·tron \ˌsiŋ-(ˌ)krō-ˈsī-klə-ˌträn, ˌsin-\ *n* (1947) : a modified cyclotron that achieves greater energies for the charged particles by compensating for the variation in mass that the particles experience with increasing velocity

syn·chro·mesh \ˈsiŋ-krō-ˌmesh, ˈsin-\ *adj* (1928) : designed for effecting synchronized shifting of gears — **synchromesh** *n*

syn·chro·ne·ity \ˌsiŋ-krə-ˈnē-ə-tē, ˌsin-, -ˈnā-\ *n, pl* **-ities** [*synchronous* + *-eity* (as in *spontaneity*)] (ca. 1909) : the state of being synchronous

syn·chron·ic \sin-ˈkrä-nik, siŋ-\ *adj* (1833) **1** : SYNCHRONOUS **2 a** : DESCRIPTIVE 4 ⟨~ linguistics⟩ **b** : concerned with events existing in a limited time period and ignoring historical antecedents — **syn·chron·i·cal** \-ni-kəl\ *adj* — **syn·chron·i·cal·ly** \-ni-k(ə-)lē\ *adv*

syn·chro·nic·i·ty \ˌsiŋ-krə-ˈni-sə-tē, ˌsin-\ *n, pl* **-ties** (ca. 1889) **1** : the quality or fact of being synchronous **2** : the coincidental occurrence of events and esp. psychic events (as similar thoughts in widely separated persons or a mental image of an unexpected event before it happens) that seem related but are not explained by conventional mechanisms of causality — used esp. in the psychology of C. G. Jung

syn·chro·ni·sa·tion, syn·chro·nise *Brit var of* SYNCHRONIZATION, SYNCHRONIZE

syn·chro·nism \ˈsiŋ-krə-ˌni-zəm, ˈsin-\ *n* (1588) **1** : the quality or state of being synchronous : SIMULTANEOUSNESS **2** : chronological arrangement of historical events and personages so as to indicate coincidence or coexistence; *also* : a table showing such concurrences — **syn·chro·nis·tic** \ˌsiŋ-krə-ˈnis-tik, ˌsin-\ *adj*

syn·chro·ni·za·tion \ˌsiŋ-krə-nə-ˈzā-shən, ˌsin-\ *n* (1828) **1** : the act or result of synchronizing **2** : the state of being synchronous

syn·chro·nize \ˈsiŋ-krə-ˌnīz, ˈsin-\ *vb* **-nized; -niz·ing** *vi* (ca. 1624) : to happen at the same time ~ *vt* **1** : to represent or arrange (events) to indicate coincidence or coexistence **2** : to make synchronous in operation **3** : to make (motion-picture sound) exactly simultaneous with the action — **syn·chro·niz·er** *n*

synchronized swimming *n* (1950) : swimming in which the movements of one or more swimmers are synchronized with a musical accompaniment so as to form changing patterns — **synchronized swimmer** *n*

syn·chro·nous \ˈsiŋ-krə-nəs, ˈsin-\ *adj* [LL *synchronos,* fr. Gk, fr. *syn-* + *chronos* time] (1669) **1** : happening, existing, or arising at precisely the same time **2** : recurring or operating at exactly the same periods **3** : involving or indicating synchronism **4 a** : having the same period; *also* : having the same period and phase **b** : GEOSTATIONARY **5** : of, used in, or being digital communication (as between computers) in which a common timing signal is established that dictates when individual bits can be transmitted and which allows for very high rates of

\ə\ **abut** \ᵊ\ **kitten**, F **table** \ər\ **further** \a\ **ash** \ā\ **ace** \ä\ **mop**, **mar**
\au̇\ **out** \ch\ **chin** \e\ **bet** \ē\ **easy** \g\ **go** \i\ **hit** \ī\ **ice** \j\ **job**
\ŋ\ **sing** \ō\ **go** \ȯ\ **law** \ȯi\ **boy** \th\ **thin** \t͟h\ **the** \ü\ **loot** \u̇\ **foot**
\y\ **yet** \zh\ **vision**, **beige** \k̲, ⁿ, œ, ue, ʸ\ *see* Guide to Pronunciation

data transfer *syn* see CONTEMPORARY — **syn·chro·nous·ly** *adv* — **syn·chro·nous·ness** *n*
synchronous motor *n* (1897) **:** an electric motor having a speed strictly proportional to the frequency of the operating current
syn·chro·ny \ˈsiŋ-krə-nē, ˈsin-\ *n, pl* **-nies** (1848) **:** synchronistic occurrence, arrangement, or treatment
syn·chro·scope \-ˌskōp\ *n* (1907) **:** any of several devices for showing whether two associated machines or moving parts are operating in synchronism with each other
syn·chro·tron \ˈsiŋ-krə-ˌträn, ˈsin-\ *n* (1945) **1 :** an apparatus for imparting very high speeds to charged particles by means of a combination of a high-frequency electric field and a low-frequency magnetic field **2 :** SYNCHROTRON RADIATION
synchrotron radiation *n* [fr. its having been first observed in a synchrotron] (1956) **:** radiation emitted by high-energy charged relativistic particles (as electrons) when they are accelerated by a magnetic field (as in a nebula)
syn·cli·nal \(ˌ)sin-ˈklī-nᵊl\ *adj* [Gk *syn-* + *klinein* to lean — more at LEAN] (1833) **1 :** inclined down from opposite directions so as to meet **2 :** having or relating to a folded rock structure in which the sides dip toward a common line or plane
syn·cline \ˈsin-ˌklīn\ *n* [back-formation fr. *synclinal*] (1873) **:** a trough of stratified rock in which the beds dip toward each other from either side — compare ANTICLINE

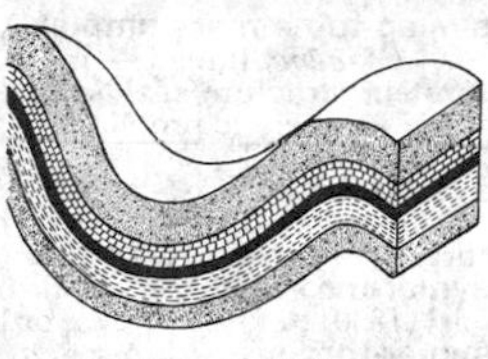

cross section of strata showing syncline

syn·co·pate \ˈsiŋ-kə-ˌpāt, ˈsin-\ *vt* **-pat·ed; -pat·ing** (1605) **1 a :** to shorten or produce by syncope ⟨~ *suppose* to *s'pose*⟩ **b :** to cut short **:** CLIP, ABBREVIATE **2 :** to modify or affect (musical rhythm) by syncopation — **syn·co·pa·tor** \-ˌpā-tər\ *n*
syncopated *adj* (1665) **1 :** cut short **:** ABBREVIATED **2 :** marked by or exhibiting syncopation ⟨~ rhythm⟩
syn·co·pa·tion \ˌsiŋ-kə-ˈpā-shən, ˌsin-\ *n* (1597) **1 :** a temporary displacement of the regular metrical accent in music caused typically by stressing the weak beat **2 :** a syncopated rhythm, passage, or dance step — **syn·co·pa·tive** \ˈsiŋ-kə-ˌpā-tiv, ˈsin-\ *adj*
syn·co·pe \ˈsiŋ-kə-(ˌ)pē, ˈsin-\ *n* [LL, fr. Gk *synkopē*, lit., cutting short, fr. *synkoptein* to cut short, fr. *syn-* + *koptein* to cut — more at CAPON] (ca. 1550) **1 :** loss of consciousness resulting from insufficient blood flow to the brain **:** FAINT **2 :** the loss of one or more sounds or letters in the interior of a word (as in *fo'c'sle* for *forecastle*) — **syn·co·pal** \-kə-pəl\ *adj*
syn·cret·ic \sin-ˈkre-tik, siŋ-\ *adj* (1840) **:** characterized or brought about by syncretism **:** SYNCRETISTIC ⟨a ~ religion⟩
syn·cre·tise *Brit var of* SYNCRETIZE
syn·cre·tism \ˈsiŋ-krə-ˌti-zəm, ˈsin-\ *n* [NL *syncretismus*, fr. Gk *synkrētismos* federation of Cretan cities, fr. *syn-* + *Krēt-*, *Krēs* Cretan] (1618) **1 :** the combination of different forms of belief or practice **2 :** the fusion of two or more orig. different inflectional forms — **syn·cre·tist** \-tist\ *n or adj* — **syn·cre·tis·tic** \ˌsiŋ-krə-ˈtis-tik, ˌsin-\ *adj*
syn·cre·tize \ˈsiŋ-krə-ˌtīz, ˈsin-\ *vt* **-tized; -tiz·ing** (1861) **:** to attempt to unite and harmonize esp. without critical examination or logical unity
syn·cy·tium \sin-ˈsi-sh(ē-)əm\ *n, pl* **-tia** \-sh(ē-)ə\ [NL, fr. *syn-* + *cyt-*] (1876) **1 :** a multinucleate mass of cytoplasm resulting from fusion of cells **2 :** COENOCYTE 1 — **syn·cy·tial** \-ˈsi-sh(ē-)əl\ *adj*
syn·dac·ty·lism \(ˌ)sin-ˈdak-tə-ˌli-zəm\ *n* (1889) **:** SYNDACTYLY
syn·dac·ty·ly \-lē\ *n* [NL *syndactylia*, fr. *syn-* + Gk *daktylos* finger] (1864) **:** a union of two or more digits that is normal in some animals (as various marsupials) and occurs as a human hereditary disorder marked by webbing of two or more fingers or toes
syn·des·mo·sis \ˌsin-ˌdez-ˈmō-səs, -ˌdes-\ *n, pl* **-mo·ses** \-ˌsēz\ [NL, fr. Gk *syndesmos* fastening, ligament, fr. *syndein*] (1726) **:** an articulation in which the contiguous surfaces of the bones are rough and are bound together by a ligament
syn·det·ic \sin-ˈde-tik\ *adj* [Gk *syndetikos*, fr. *syndein* to bind together — more at ASYNDETON] (1876) **:** CONNECTIVE, CONNECTING ⟨~ pronoun⟩; *also* **:** marked by a conjunctive ⟨~ relative clause⟩ — **syn·det·i·cal·ly** \-ti-k(ə-)lē\ *adv*
syn·dic \ˈsin-dik\ *n* [F, fr. LL *syndicus* representative of a corporation, fr. Gk *syndikos* assistant at law, advocate, representative of a state, fr. *syn-* + *dikē* judgment, case at law — more at DICTION] (1601) **1 :** a municipal magistrate in some countries **2 :** an agent of a university or corporation
syn·di·cal \-di-kəl\ *adj* (1855) **1 :** of or relating to a syndic or to a committee that assumes the powers of a syndic **2 :** of or relating to syndicalism
syn·di·cal·ism \ˈsin-di-kə-ˌli-zəm\ *n* [F *syndicalisme*, fr. *chambre syndicale* trade union] (1907) **1 :** a revolutionary doctrine by which workers seize control of the economy and the government by direct means (as a general strike) **2 :** a system of economic organization in which industries are owned and managed by the workers **3 :** a theory of government based on functional rather than territorial representation — **syn·di·cal·ist** \-list\ *adj or n*
[1]**syn·di·cate** \ˈsin-di-kət\ *n* [F *syndicat*, fr. *syndic*] (1624) **1 a :** a council or body of syndics **b :** the office or jurisdiction of a syndic **2 :** an association of persons officially authorized to undertake a duty or negotiate business **3 a :** a group of persons or concerns who combine to carry out a particular transaction or project **b :** CARTEL 2 **c :** a loose association of racketeers in control of organized crime **4 :** a business concern that sells materials for publication in a number of newspapers or periodicals simultaneously **5 :** a group of newspapers under one management
[2]**syn·di·cate** \ˈsin-də-ˌkāt\ *vb* **-cat·ed; -cat·ing** *vt* (1882) **1 :** to subject to or manage as a syndicate **2 a :** to sell (as a cartoon) to a syndicate or for publication in many newspapers or periodicals at once; *also* **:** to sell the work of (as a writer) in this way ⟨a *syndicated* columnist⟩ **b :** to sell (as a series of television programs) directly to local stations ~ *vi* **:** to unite to form a syndicate — **syn·di·ca·tion** \ˌsin-də-ˈkā-shən\ *n* — **syn·di·ca·tor** \ˈsin-də-ˌkā-tər\ *n*
syn·drome \ˈsin-ˌdrōm *also* -drəm\ *n* [NL, fr. Gk *syndromē* combination, syndrome, fr. *syn-* + *dramein* to run — more at DROMEDARY] (1541) **1 :** a group of signs and symptoms that occur together and characterize a particular abnormality or condition **2 :** a set of concurrent things (as emotions or actions) that usu. form an identifiable pattern
[1]**syne** \ˈsīn\ *adv* [ME (northern), prob. contr. of OE *siththan* since — more at SINCE] (14c) *chiefly Scot* **:** since then **:** AGO
[2]**syne** *conj or prep* (14c) *Scot* **:** SINCE
syn·ec·do·che \sə-ˈnek-də-(ˌ)kē\ *n* [L, fr. Gk *synekdochē*, fr. *syn-* + *ekdochē* sense, interpretation, fr. *ekdechesthai* to receive, understand, fr. *ex* from + *dechesthai* to receive; akin to Gk *dokein* to seem good — more at EX-, DECENT] (15c) **:** a figure of speech by which a part is put for the whole (as *fifty sail* for *fifty ships*), the whole for a part (as *society* for *high society*), the species for the genus (as *cutthroat* for *assassin*), the genus for the species (as *a creature* for *a man*), or the name of the material for the thing made (as *boards* for *stage*) — **syn·ec·doch·ic** \ˌsi-ˌnek-ˈdä-kik\ *adj* — **syn·ec·doch·i·cal** \-ˈdä-ki-kəl\ *adj* — **syn·ec·doch·i·cal·ly** \-ki-k(ə-)lē\ *adv*
syn·ecol·o·gy \ˌsi-ni-ˈkä-lə-jē, ˌsi-ne-\ *n* [G *Synökologie*, fr. *syn-* syn- + *Ökologie* ecology] (1910) **:** a branch of ecology that deals with the structure, development, and distribution of ecological communities — **syn·eco·log·i·cal** \ˌsi-ˌnē-kə-ˈlä-ji-kəl, ˌsi-ˌne-\ *adj*
syn·er·e·sis \sə-ˈner-ə-səs, -ˈnir-, *esp for 2* ˌsi-nə-ˈrē-\ *n* [LL *synaeresis*, fr. Gk *synairesis*, fr. *synairein* to contract, fr. *syn-* + *hairein* to take] (ca. 1577) **1 :** SYNIZESIS **2 :** the separation of liquid from a gel caused by contraction
syn·er·get·ic \ˌsi-nər-ˈje-tik\ *adj* [Gk *synergētikos*, fr. *synergein* to work with, cooperate, fr. *synergos* working together, fr. *syn-* + *ergon* work — more at WORK] (ca. 1836) **:** SYNERGIC
syn·er·gic \sə-ˈnər-jik\ *adj* (1850) **:** working together **:** COOPERATING ⟨~ muscles⟩ — **syn·er·gi·cal·ly** \-ji-k(ə-)lē\ *adv*
syn·er·gid \sə-ˈnər-jəd, ˈsi-nər-\ *n* [NL *synergida*, fr. Gk *synergos* working together] (1898) **:** one of two small cells lying near the micropyle of the embryo sac of an angiosperm
syn·er·gism \ˈsi-nər-ˌji-zəm\ *n* [NL *synergismus*, fr. Gk *synergos*] (1910) **:** interaction of discrete agencies (as industrial firms), agents (as drugs), or conditions such that the total effect is greater than the sum of the individual effects
syn·er·gist \-jist\ *n* (1876) **:** something (as a chemical or a muscle) that enhances the effectiveness of an active agent; *broadly* **:** either member of a synergistic pair
syn·er·gis·tic \ˌsi-nər-ˈjis-tik\ *adj* (ca. 1847) **1 :** having the capacity to act in synergism ⟨~ drugs⟩ **2 :** of, relating to, or resembling synergism ⟨a ~ reaction⟩ — **syn·er·gis·ti·cal·ly** \-ti-k(ə-)lē\ *adv*
syn·er·gy \ˈsi-nər-jē\ *n, pl* **-gies** [NL *synergia*, fr. Gk *synergos* working together] (1660) **1 :** SYNERGISM; *broadly* **:** combined action or operation **2 :** a mutually advantageous conjunction or compatibility of distinct business participants or elements (as resources or efforts)
syn·e·sis \ˈsi-nə-səs\ *n* [NL, fr. Gk, understanding, sense, fr. *synienai* to bring together, understand, fr. *syn-* + *hienai* to send — more at JET] (1856) **:** a grammatical construction in which agreement or reference is according to sense rather than strict syntax (as *anyone* and *them* in "if anyone calls, tell them I am out")
syn·es·the·sia \ˌsi-nəs-ˈthē-zh(ē-)ə\ *n* [NL, fr. *syn-* + *-esthesia* (as in *anesthesia*)] (ca. 1891) **1 :** a concomitant sensation; *esp* **:** a subjective sensation or image of a sense (as of color) other than the one (as of sound) being stimulated **2 :** the condition marked by the experience of such sensations — **syn·es·thet·ic** \-ˈthe-tik\ *adj*
syn·es·thete \ˈsi-nəs-ˌthēt\ *n* (1985) **:** a person affected with synesthesia
syn·fu·el \ˈsin-ˌfyü(-ə)l\ *n* [*syn*thetic + *fuel*] (1975) **:** a liquid or gaseous fuel derived esp. from a fossil fuel that is a solid (as coal) or part of a solid (as tar sand or oil shale)
syn·ga·my \ˈsiŋ-gə-mē\ *n* [ISV] (1904) **:** sexual reproduction by union of gametes **:** FERTILIZATION
syn·gas \ˈsin-ˌgas\ *n* (1975) **:** SYNTHESIS GAS
syn·ge·ne·ic \ˌsin-jə-ˈnē-ik\ *adj* [*syn-* + *-geneic* (as in *isogeneic*)] (1961) **:** involving, derived from, or being genetically identical or similar individuals of the same species esp. with respect to antigenic interaction ⟨~ tumor cells⟩ ⟨grafts between ~ mice⟩ — compare ALLOGENEIC
syn·i·ze·sis \ˌsi-nə-ˈzē-səs\ *n* [LL, fr. Gk *synizēsis*, fr. *synizein* to sit down together, collapse, blend, fr. *syn-* + *hizein* to sit down; akin to L *sidere* to sit down — more at SUBSIDE] (1846) **:** contraction of two syllables into one by uniting in pronunciation two adjacent vowels
syn·od \ˈsi-nəd *also* -ˌnäd\ *n* [ME *sinod*, fr. LL *synodus*, fr. LGk *synodos*, fr. Gk, meeting, assembly, fr. *syn-* + *hodos* way, journey] (14c) **1 :** an ecclesiastical governing or advisory council: as **a :** an assembly of bishops in the Roman Catholic Church **b :** the governing assembly of an Episcopal province **c :** a Presbyterian governing body ranking between the presbytery and the general assembly **d :** a regional or national organization of Lutheran congregations **2 :** the ecclesiastical district governed by a synod — **syn·od·al** \ˈsi-nə-dᵊl, -ˌnä-; sə-ˈnä-dᵊl\ *adj*
syn·od·ic \sə-ˈnä-dik\ *or* **syn·od·i·cal** \-di-kəl\ *adj* (1561) **1 :** of or relating to a synod **:** SYNODAL **2** *usu synodic* [Gk *synodikos*, fr. *synodos* meeting, conjunction] **:** relating to conjunction; *esp* **:** relating to the period between two successive conjunctions of the same celestial bodies (as the moon and the sun)
synodic month *n* (1654) **:** a lunar month
syn·o·nym \ˈsi-nə-ˌnim\ *n* [ME *sinonyme*, fr. L *synonymum*, fr. Gk *synōnymon*, fr. neut. of *synōnymos* synonymous, fr. *syn-* + *onyma* name — more at NAME] (15c) **1 :** one of two or more words or expressions of the same language that have the same or nearly the same meaning in some or all senses **2 a :** a word or phrase that by association is held to embody something (as a concept or quality) ⟨a tyrant whose name has become a ~ for oppression⟩ **b :** METONYM **3 :** one of two or more scientific names used to designate the same taxonomic group — compare HOMONYM — **syn·o·nym·ic** \ˌsi-nə-ˈni-mik\ *also* **syn·o·nym·i·cal** \-mi-kəl\ *adj* — **syn·o·nym·i·ty** \-ˈni-mə-tē\ *n*
syn·on·y·mist \sə-ˈnä-nə-mist\ *n* (ca. 1753) **:** one who lists, studies, or discriminates synonyms

syn·on·y·mize \-ˌmīz\ *vt* **-mized; -miz·ing** (ca. 1595) **1 a :** to give or analyze the synonyms of (a word) **b :** to provide (as a dictionary) with synonymies **2 :** to demonstrate (a taxonomic name) to be a synonym

syn·on·y·mous \-məs\ *adj* (1610) **1 :** having the character of a synonym; *also* **:** alike in meaning or significance **2 :** having the same connotations, implications, or reference ⟨to runners, Boston is ~ with marathon —*Runners World*⟩ — **syn·on·y·mous·ly** *adv*

syn·on·y·my \-mē\ *n, pl* **-mies** (1683) **1 a :** a list or collection of synonyms often defined and discriminated from each other **b :** the study or discrimination of synonyms **2 :** the scientific names that have been used to designate the same taxonomic group (as a species); *also* **:** a list of these **3 :** the quality or state of being synonymous

syn·op·sis \sə-ˈnäp-səs\ *n, pl* **-op·ses** \-ˌsēz\ [LL, fr. Gk, lit., comprehensive view, fr. *synopsesthai* to be going to see together, fr. *syn-* + *opsesthai* to be going to see — more at OPTIC] (1603) **1 :** a condensed statement or outline (as of a narrative or treatise) **:** ABSTRACT **2 :** the abbreviated conjugation of a verb in one person only

syn·op·size \-ˌsīz\ *vt* **-sized; -siz·ing** (1868) **1 :** EPITOMIZE **2 :** to make a synopsis of (as a novel)

syn·op·tic \sə-ˈnäp-tik\ *also* **syn·op·ti·cal** \-ti-kəl\ *adj* [Gk *synoptikos,* fr. *synopsesthai*] (1763) **1 :** affording a general view of a whole **2 :** manifesting or characterized by comprehensiveness or breadth of view **3 :** presenting or taking the same or common view; *specif, often cap* **:** of or relating to the first three Gospels of the New Testament **4 :** relating to or displaying conditions (as of the atmosphere or weather) as they exist simultaneously over a broad area — **syn·op·ti·cal·ly** \-ti-k(ə-)lē\ *adv*

syn·os·to·sis \ˌsi-ˌnäs-ˈtō-səs\ *n, pl* **-to·ses** \-ˌsēz\ [NL] (ca. 1848) **:** union of two or more separate bones to form a single bone

sy·no·via \sə-ˈnō-vē-ə, sī-\ *n* [NL, any of various bodily fluids or discharges] (1726) **:** SYNOVIAL FLUID

sy·no·vi·al \-vē-əl\ *adj* (1756) **:** of, relating to, or secreting synovial fluid ⟨~ membranes⟩; *also* **:** lined with synovial membrane

synovial fluid *n* (1846) **:** a transparent viscid lubricating fluid secreted by a membrane of an articulation, bursa, or tendon sheath

synovial joint *n* (1854) **:** DIARTHROSIS 2

sy·no·vi·tis \ˌsī-nə-ˈvī-təs\ *n* (ca. 1836) **:** inflammation of a synovial membrane

syn·tac·tic \sin-ˈtak-tik\ *or* **syn·tac·ti·cal** \-ti-kəl\ *adj* [NL *syntacticus,* fr. Gk *syntaktikos* arranging together, fr. *syntassein*] (1577) **:** of, relating to, or according to the rules of syntax or syntactics — **syn·tac·ti·cal·ly** \-ti-k(ə-)lē\ *adv*

syn·tac·ti·cian \ˌsin-ˌtak-ˈti-shən\ *n* (1900) **:** a specialist in syntax

syn·tac·tics \-tiks\ *n pl but sing or pl in constr* (1937) **:** a branch of semiotics that deals with the formal relations between signs or expressions in abstraction from their signification and their interpreters

syn·tagm \ˈsin-ˌtam\ *chiefly Brit var of* SYNTAGMA

syn·tag·ma \sin-ˈtag-mə\ *n, pl* **-mas** *or* **-ma·ta** \-mə-tə\ [Gk, fr. *syntassein*] (1937) **:** a syntactic element — **syn·tag·mat·ic** \ˌsin-ˌtag-ˈma-tik\ *adj*

syn·tax \ˈsin-ˌtaks\ *n* [MF or LL; MF *sintaxe,* fr. LL *syntaxis,* fr. Gk, fr. *syntassein* to arrange together, fr. *syn-* + *tassein* to arrange] (1574) **1 a :** the way in which linguistic elements (as words) are put together to form constituents (as phrases or clauses) **b :** the part of grammar dealing with this **2 :** a connected or orderly system **:** harmonious arrangement of parts or elements ⟨the ~ of classical architecture⟩ **3 :** syntactics esp. as dealing with the formal properties of languages or calculi

synth \ˈsin(t)th\ *n, often attrib* (1976) **:** SYNTHESIZER 2

syn·the·sis \ˈsin(t)-thə-səs\ *n, pl* **-the·ses** \-ˌsēz\ [Gk, fr. *syntithenai* to put together, fr. *syn-* + *tithenai* to put, place — more at DO] (1589) **1 a :** the composition or combination of parts or elements so as to form a whole **b :** the production of a substance by the union of chemical elements, groups, or simpler compounds or by the degradation of a complex compound **c :** the combining of often diverse conceptions into a coherent whole; *also* **:** the complex so formed **2 a :** deductive reasoning **b :** the dialectic combination of thesis and antithesis into a higher stage of truth **3 :** the frequent and systematic use of inflected forms as a characteristic device of a language — **syn·the·sist** \-sist\ *n*

synthesis gas *n* (ca. 1941) **:** a mixture of carbon monoxide and hydrogen used esp. in chemical synthesis

syn·the·size \-ˌsīz\ *vb* **-sized; -siz·ing** *vt* (1830) **1 :** to combine or produce by synthesis **2 :** to make a synthesis of **3 :** to produce (as music) by an electronic synthesizer ~ *vi* **:** to make a synthesis

syn·the·siz·er \-ˌsī-zər\ *n* (1869) **1 :** one that synthesizes ⟨an expert ~ of diverse views⟩ **2 :** a usu. computerized electronic apparatus for the production and control of sound (as for producing music)

syn·the·tase \ˈsin-thə-ˌtās, -ˌtāz\ *n* [*synthetic* + *-ase*] (1947) **:** an enzyme that catalyzes the linking together of two molecules usu. using the energy derived from the concurrent splitting off of a pyrophosphate group from a triphosphate (as ATP) — called also *ligase*

[1]**syn·thet·ic** \sin-ˈthe-tik\ *adj* [Gk *synthetikos* of composition, component, fr. *syntithenai* to put together] (1697) **1 :** relating to or involving synthesis **:** not analytic ⟨the ~ aspects of a philosophy⟩ **2 :** attributing to a subject something determined by observation rather than analysis of the nature of the subject and not resulting in self-contradiction if negated — compare ANALYTIC **3 :** characterized by frequent and systematic use of inflected forms to express grammatical relationships ⟨~ languages⟩ **4 a** (1) **:** of, relating to, or produced by chemical or biochemical synthesis; *esp* **:** produced artificially ⟨~ drugs⟩ ⟨~ silk⟩ (2) **:** of or relating to a synfuel **b :** devised, arranged, or fabricated for special situations to imitate or replace usual realities **c :** FACTITIOUS, BOGUS — **syn·thet·i·cal·ly** \-ti-k(ə-)lē\ *adv*

[2]**synthetic** *n* (1916) **:** something resulting from synthesis rather than occurring naturally; *esp* **:** a product (as a drug or plastic) of chemical synthesis

synthetic division *n* (1850) **:** a simplified method for dividing a polynomial by another polynomial of the first degree by writing down only the coefficients of the several powers of the variable and changing the sign of the constant term in the divisor so as to replace the usual subtractions by additions

synthetic geometry *n* (1856) **:** elementary euclidean geometry or projective geometry as distinguished from analytic geometry

synthetic resin *n* (1907) **:** RESIN 2

syph \ˈsif\ *n* (ca. 1914) *slang* **:** SYPHILIS

syph·i·lis \ˈsi-f(ə-)ləs\ *n* [NL, fr. *Syphilus,* hero of the poem *Syphilis sive Morbus Gallicus* (*Syphilis or the French disease*) (1530) by Girolamo Fracastoro †1553 Ital. poet and physician] (1718) **:** a chronic contagious usu. venereal and often congenital disease caused by a spirochete (*Treponema pallidum*) and if left untreated producing chancres, rashes, and systemic lesions in a clinical course with three stages continued over many years — compare PRIMARY SYPHILIS, SECONDARY SYPHILIS, TERTIARY SYPHILIS — **syph·i·lit·ic** \ˌsi-fə-ˈli-tik\ *adj or n*

syphon *var of* SIPHON

Sy·rah \sē-ˈrä\ *n* [F *syrah, syrac*] (1974) **1 :** a grape whose skin has a dark blue to bluish-black color that was orig. grown in the northern valley of the Rhone and is now widely grown elsewhere (as in California and Australia); *also* **:** a vine producing Syrah grapes **2 :** a red wine made from Syrah grapes

sy·rette \sə-ˈret\ *n* [fr. *Syrette,* a trademark] (1941) **:** a small collapsible tube fitted with a hypodermic needle for injecting a single dose of a medicinal agent (as morphine)

Syr·i·ac \ˈsir-ē-ˌak\ *n* [L *syriacus* Syrian, fr. Gk *syriakos,* fr. *Syria,* ancient country in Asia] (1598) **1 :** a literary language based on an eastern Aramaic dialect and used as the literary and liturgical language by several Eastern Christian churches **2 :** Aramaic spoken by Christian communities — **Syriac** *adj*

Syr·i·an hamster \ˈsir-ē-ən-\ *n* [*Syria,* Asia] (ca. 1949) **:** GOLDEN HAMSTER

sy·rin·ga \sə-ˈriŋ-gə\ *n* [NL, genus name, fr. Gk *syring-, syrinx* panpipe] (1664) **:** MOCK ORANGE 1

[1]**sy·ringe** \sə-ˈrinj *also* ˈsir-inj\ *n* [ME *syring,* fr. AF *siringe,* fr. ML *syringa,* fr. LL, injection, fr. Gk *syring-, syrinx* panpipe, tube] (14c) **:** a device used to inject fluids into or withdraw them from something (as the body or its cavities): as **a :** a device that consists of a nozzle of varying length and a compressible rubber bulb and is used for injection or irrigation **b :** an instrument (as for the injection of medicine or the withdrawal of bodily fluids) that consists of a hollow barrel fitted with a plunger and a hollow needle **c :** a gravity device consisting of a reservoir fitted with a long rubber tube ending with an exchangeable nozzle that is used for irrigation of the vagina or bowel

[2]**syringe** *vt* **sy·ringed; sy·ring·ing** (1610) **:** to irrigate or spray with or as if with a syringe

sy·rin·go·my·e·lia \sə-ˌriŋ-gō-mī-ˈē-lē-ə\ *n* [NL, fr. Gk *syring-, syrinx* tube, fistula + NL *myel-* + *-ia*] (1880) **:** a chronic progressive disease of the spinal cord associated with sensory disturbances, muscle atrophy, and spasticity — **sy·rin·go·my·el·ic** \-ˈe-lik\ *adj*

syr·inx \ˈsir-iŋ(k)s\ *n, pl* **sy·rin·ges** \sə-ˈriŋ-ˌgēz, -ˈrin-ˌjēz\ *or* **syr·inx·es** (1606) **1** [LL, fr. Gk] **:** PANPIPE **2** [NL, fr. Gk] **:** the vocal organ of birds that is a special modification of the lower part of the trachea or of the bronchi or of both

syr·phid fly \ˈsər-fəd-, ˈsir-\ *n* [NL *Syrphidae,* fr. *Syrphus,* genus of flies, fr. Gk *syrphos* gnat] (ca. 1891) **:** HOVERFLY

syr·up *also* **si·rup** \ˈsər-əp, ˈsir-əp, ˈsə-rəp\ *n* [ME *sirup,* fr. AF *sirop,* fr. ML *syrupus,* fr. Ar *sharāb*] (14c) **1 a :** a thick sticky solution of sugar and water often flavored or medicated **b :** the concentrated juice of a fruit or plant **2 :** cloying sweetness or sentimentality — **syr·upy** *adj*

sys·op \ˈsis-(ˌ)äp\ *n* [*sys*tem *op*erator] (1981) **:** the administrator of a computer bulletin board

syst *abbr* system

sys·tal·tic \sis-ˈtȯl-tik, -ˈtal-\ *adj* [LL *systalticus,* fr. Gk *systaltikos,* fr. *systellein* to contract — more at SYSTOLE] (1676) **:** marked by regular contraction and dilatation **:** PULSING

sys·tem \ˈsis-təm\ *n* [LL *systemat-, systema,* fr. Gk *systēmat-, systēma,* fr. *synistanai* to combine, fr. *syn-* + *histanai* to cause to stand — more at STAND] (1603) **1 :** a regularly interacting or interdependent group of items forming a unified whole ⟨a number ~⟩: as **a** (1) **:** a group of interacting bodies under the influence of related forces ⟨a gravitational ~⟩ (2) **:** an assemblage of substances that is in or tends to equilibrium ⟨a thermodynamic ~⟩ **b** (1) **:** a group of body organs that together perform one or more vital functions ⟨the digestive ~⟩ (2) **:** the body considered as a functional unit **c :** a group of related natural objects or forces ⟨a river ~⟩ **d :** a group of devices or artificial objects or an organization forming a network esp. for distributing something or serving a common purpose ⟨a telephone ~⟩ ⟨a heating ~⟩ ⟨a highway ~⟩ ⟨a computer ~⟩ **e :** a major division of rocks usu. larger than a series and including all formed during a period or era **f :** a form of social, economic, or political organization or practice ⟨the capitalist ~⟩ **2 :** an organized set of doctrines, ideas, or principles usu. intended to explain the arrangement or working of a systematic whole ⟨the Newtonian ~ of mechanics⟩ **3 a :** an organized or established procedure ⟨the touch ~ of typing⟩ **b :** a manner of classifying, symbolizing, or schematizing ⟨a taxonomic ~⟩ ⟨the decimal ~⟩ **4 :** harmonious arrangement or pattern **:** ORDER ⟨bring ~ out of confusion —Ellen Glasgow⟩ **5 :** an organized society or social situation regarded as stultifying or oppressive **:** ESTABLISHMENT 2 — usu. used with *the* **syn** see METHOD — **sys·tem·less** \-ləs\ *adj*

sys·tem·at·ic \ˌsis-tə-ˈma-tik\ *adj* [LL *systematicus,* fr. Gk *systēmatikos,* fr. *systēmat-, systēma*] (ca. 1680) **1 :** relating to or consisting of a system **2 :** presented or formulated as a coherent body of ideas or principles ⟨~ thought⟩ **3 a :** methodical in procedure or plan ⟨a ~ approach⟩ ⟨a ~ scholar⟩ **b :** marked by thoroughness and regularity ⟨~ efforts⟩ **4 :** of, relating to, or concerned with classification; *specif* **:** TAXONOMIC — **sys·tem·at·i·cal·ly** \-ti-k(ə-)lē\ *adv* — **sys·tem·at·ic·ness** \-tik-nəs\ *n*

systematic error *n* (1811) **:** an error that is not determined by chance but is introduced by an inaccuracy (as of observation or measurement) inherent in the system

sys·tem·at·ics \ˌsis-tə-ˈma-tiks\ *n pl but sing in constr* (1888) **1 :** the science of classification **2 a :** a system of classification **b :** the classi-

\ə\ **abut** \ᵊ\ **kitten**, F **table** \ər\ **further** \a\ **ash** \ā\ **ace** \ä\ **mop, mar**
\au̇\ **out** \ch\ **chin** \e\ **bet** \ē\ **easy** \g\ **go** \i\ **hit** \ī\ **ice** \j\ **job**
\ŋ\ **sing** \ō\ **go** \ȯ\ **law** \ȯi\ **boy** \th\ **thin** \th\ **the** \ü\ **loot** \u̇\ **foot**
\y\ **yet** \zh\ **vision, beige** \k, ⁿ, œ, ue, ʸ\ *see* Guide to Pronunciation

fication and study of organisms with regard to their natural relationships : TAXONOMY

sys·tem·at·ic the·ol·o·gy *n* (1830) : a branch of theology concerned with summarizing the doctrinal traditions of a religion (as Christianity) esp. with a view to relating the traditions convincingly to the religion's present-day setting

sys·tem·a·tise *Brit var of* SYSTEMATIZE

sys·tem·a·tism \'sis-tə-mə-ˌti-zəm, sis-'te-mə-\ *n* (1846) : the practice of forming intellectual systems

sys·tem·a·tist \'sis-tə-mə-tist, sis-'te-mə-\ *n* (1700) **1** : a maker or follower of a system **2** : a specialist in taxonomy : TAXONOMIST

sys·tem·a·tize \'sis-tə-mə-ˌtīz\ *vt* **-tized; -tiz·ing** (ca. 1767) : to arrange in accord with a definite plan or scheme : order systematically ⟨the need to ~ their work⟩ *syn* see ORDER — **sys·tem·a·ti·za·tion** \ˌsis-tə-mə-tə-'zā-shən, sis-ˌte-mə-\ *n* — **sys·tem·a·tiz·er** *n*

¹sys·tem·ic \sis-'te-mik\ *adj* (1803) : of, relating to, or common to a system: as **a** : affecting the body generally **b** : supplying those parts of the body that receive blood through the aorta rather than through the pulmonary artery **c** : of, relating to, or being a pesticide that as used is harmless to the plant or higher animal but when absorbed into its sap or bloodstream makes the entire organism toxic to pests (as an insect or fungus) — **sys·tem·i·cal·ly** \-mi-k(ə-)lē\ *adv*

²systemic *n* (1951) : a systemic pesticide

systemic risk *n* (1982) : the risk that the failure of one financial institution (as a bank) could cause other interconnected institutions to fail and harm the economy as a whole

systemic lupus er·y·the·ma·to·sus \-ˌer-ə-ˌthē-mə-'tō-səs\ *n* (1951) : an inflammatory connective tissue disease that is often held to be an autoimmune disease and that occurs chiefly in women, is characterized esp. by fever, skin rash, and arthritis, often by acute hemolytic anemia, by small hemorrhages in the skin and mucous membranes, by inflammation of the pericardium, and in serious cases by involvement of the kidneys and central nervous system

sys·tem·ize \'sis-tə-ˌmīz\ *vt* **-ized; -iz·ing** (1778) : SYSTEMATIZE — **sys·tem·i·za·tion** \ˌsis-tə-mə-'zā-shən\ *n*

systems analysis *n* (ca. 1950) : the act, process, or profession of studying an activity (as a procedure, a business, or a physiological function) typically by mathematical means in order to define its goals or purposes and to discover operations and procedures for accomplishing them most efficiently — **systems analyst** *n*

sys·to·le \'sis-tə-(ˌ)lē\ *n* [Gk *systolē*, fr. *systellein* to contract, fr. *syn-* + *stellein* to send] (1578) : a rhythmically recurrent contraction; *esp* : the contraction of the heart by which the blood is forced onward and the circulation kept up — **sys·tol·ic** \sis-'tä-lik\ *adj*

syz·y·gy \'si-zə-jē\ *n, pl* **-gies** [LL *syzygia* conjunction, fr. Gk, fr. *syzygos* yoked together, fr. *syn-* + *zygon* yoke — more at YOKE] (ca. 1847) : the nearly straight-line configuration of three celestial bodies (as the sun, moon, and earth during a solar or lunar eclipse) in a gravitational system

Szech·uan \'sech-ˌwän, 'sesh-\ *also* **Sich·uan** \'sēch-\ *or* **Szech·wan** \'sech-, 'sesh-\ *adj* [*Sichuan, Szechuan, Szechwan*, province in China] (1956) : of, relating to, or being a style of Chinese cooking that is spicy, oily, and esp. peppery

---

¹t \'tē\ *n, pl* **t's** *or* **ts** \'tēz\ *often cap, often attrib* (bef. 12c) **1 a** : the 20th letter of the English alphabet **b** : a graphic representation of this letter **c** : a speech counterpart of orthographic *t* **2** : a graphic device for reproducing the letter *t* **3** : one designated *t* esp. as the 20th in order or class **4** : something shaped like the letter T **5** : T FORMATION **6** : TECHNICAL FOUL — **to a T** [short for *to a tittle*] : to perfection

²t *abbr* **1** metric ton **2** tablespoon **3** teaspoon **4** technical **5** temperature **6** [L *tempore*] in the time of **7** tense **8** tertiary **9** time **10** ton **11** township **12** transitive **13** troy **14** true

T *abbr* **1** tera- **2** tesla **3** thymine **4** toddler **5** tritium **6** T-shirt

't \t\ *pron* (1598) : IT ⟨my country, 'tis of thee —S. F. Smith⟩

ta \'tä\ *n* [baby talk] (1772) *Brit* : THANKS

Ta *symbol* tantalum

TA *abbr* **1** teaching assistant **2** transactional analysis

¹tab \'tab\ *n, often attrib* [origin unknown] (1607) **1 a** : a short projecting device: as (1) : a small flap or loop by which something may be grasped or pulled (2) : a projection from a card used as an aid in filing **b** : a small insert, addition, or remnant **c** : APPENDAGE, EXTENSION; *esp* : one of a series of small pendants forming a decorative border or edge of a garment **d** : a small auxiliary airfoil hinged to a control surface (as a trailing edge) to help stabilize an airplane in flight — see AIRPLANE illustration **2** [partly short for *'table*; partly fr. sense 1] **a** : close surveillance : WATCH ⟨keep ~s on trends⟩ **b** : a creditor's statement : BILL, CHECK **c** : COST ⟨the ~ for the new program⟩ **3** [by shortening] **a** : TABLOID **b** : TABLET **4** [short for *tabulator*] : a key on a keyboard esp. for arranging data in columns

²tab *vt* **tabbed; tab·bing** (1872) **1** : to furnish or ornament with tabs **2** : to single out : DESIGNATE **3** : TABULATE

ta·ba·nid \'ta-'bā-nəd, -'ba-\ *n* [ultim. fr. L *tabanus* horsefly] (ca. 1891) : HORSEFLY

tab·ard \'ta-bərd *also* -ˌbärd\ *n* [ME, fr. AF] (14c) : a short loose-fitting sleeveless or short-sleeved coat or cape: as **a** : a tunic worn by a knight over his armor and emblazoned with his arms **b** : a herald's official cape or coat emblazoned with his lord's arms **c** : a woman's sleeveless outer garment often with side slits

Ta·bas·co \tə-'bas-(ˌ)kō\ *trademark* — used for a pungent condiment sauce made from hot peppers

tab·bou·leh *also* **ta·bou·leh** \tə-'bü-lə, -ˌlē\ *or* **ta·bou·li** \-ˌlē\ *n* [Ar *tabbūla*] (1939) : a salad of Lebanese origin consisting chiefly of cracked wheat, tomatoes, parsley, mint, onions, lemon juice, and olive oil

¹tab·by \'ta-bē\ *n, pl* **tabbies** [F *tabis*, fr. MF *atabis*, fr. ML *attabi*, fr. Ar *'attābī*, fr. Al-*'Attābīya*, quarter in Baghdad] (1638) **1 a** : *archaic* : a plain silk taffeta esp. with moiré finish **b** : a plain-woven fabric **2** [²*tabby*] **a** : a domestic cat with a striped and mottled coat **b** : a domestic cat; *esp* : a female cat

²tabby *adj* (1640) **1** : of, relating to, or made of tabby ⟨a ~ vest⟩ **2** : striped and mottled with darker color : BRINDLED ⟨a ~ cat⟩

³tabby *n* [Gullah *tabi*, ultim. fr. Sp *tapia* adobe wall] (1775) : a cement made of lime, sand or gravel, and oyster shells and used chiefly along the coast of Georgia and So. Carolina in the 17th and 18th centuries

¹tab·er·na·cle \'ta-bər-ˌna-kəl\ *n* [ME, fr. AF, fr. LL *tabernaculum*, fr. L, tent, fr. *taberna* hut] (13c) **1 a** *often cap* : a tent sanctuary used by the Israelites during the Exodus **b** *archaic* : a dwelling place **c** *archaic* : a temporary shelter : TENT **2** : a receptacle for the consecrated elements of the Eucharist; *esp* : an ornamental locked box used for reserving the Communion hosts **3** : a house of worship; *specif* : a large building or tent used for evangelistic services — **tab·er·nac·u·lar** \ˌta-bər-'na-kyə-lər\ *adj*

²tabernacle *vi* **tab·er·na·cled; tab·er·na·cling** \-ˌna-k(ə-)liŋ\ (1653) : to take up temporary residence; *esp* : to inhabit a physical body

ta·bes \'tā-(ˌ)bēz\ *n, pl* **tabes** [L, wasting disease, decay, fr. *tabēre* to decay — more at THAW] (1651) : wasting accompanying a chronic disease — **ta·bet·ic** \tə-'be-tik\ *adj or n*

tabes dor·sa·lis \-dòr-'sa-ləs, -'sä-, -'sä-\ *n* [NL, dorsal tabes] (ca. 1681) : a syphilitic disorder of the nervous system marked by wasting, pain, limb weakness, ataxia, and disorders of sensation and vision resulting from degeneration of the spinal cord — called also *locomotor ataxia*

ta·bla \'tä-blə\ *n* [Hindi & Urdu *tablā*, fr. Ar *ṭabla*] (1865) : a pair of small different-sized hand drums used esp. in music of India

tab·la·ture \'ta-blə-ˌchùr, -chər, -ˌtyùr, -ˌtùr\ *n* [MF, fr. ML *tabulatus* tablet, fr. L *tabula*] (1574) : an instrumental notation indicating the string, fret, key, or finger to be used instead of the tone to be sounded

¹ta·ble \'tā-bəl\ *n, often attrib* [ME, fr. OE *tabule* & AF *table*; both fr. L *tabula* board, tablet, list] (bef. 12c) **1** : TABLET 1a **2** *a pl* : BACKGAMMON **b** : one of the two leaves of a backgammon board or either half of a leaf **3 a** : a piece of furniture consisting of a smooth flat slab fixed on legs **b** (1) : a supply or source of food (2) : an act or instance of assembling to eat : MEAL ⟨sit down to ~⟩ **c** (1) : a group of people assembled at or as if at a table (2) : a legislative or negotiating session ⟨the bargaining ~⟩ **4** : STRINGCOURSE **5 a** : a systematic arrangement of data usu. in rows and columns for ready reference **b** : a condensed enumeration : LIST ⟨a ~ of contents⟩ **6** : something that resembles a table esp. in having a plane surface: as **a** : the upper flat surface of a cut precious stone — see BRILLIANT illustration **b** (1) : TABLELAND (2) : a horizontal stratum — **on the table** : up for consideration or negotiation ⟨the subject is not *on the table*⟩ — **under the table 1** : into a stupor ⟨can drink you *under the table*⟩ **2** : in a covert manner ⟨took money *under the table*⟩

²table *vt* **ta·bled; ta·bling** \-b(ə-)liŋ\ (15c) **1** : to enter in a table **2** *a Brit* : to place on the agenda **b** : to remove (as a parliamentary motion) from consideration indefinitely **c** : to put on a table

³table *adj* (1547) **1** : suitable for a table or for use at a table ⟨a ~ lamp⟩ **2** : suitable for serving at a table ⟨~ grapes⟩ **3** : proper for conduct at a table ⟨~ manners⟩

tab·leau \'ta-ˌblō, ta-'blō\ *n, pl* **tab·leaux** \-ˌblōz, -'blōz\ *also* **tableaus** [F, fr. MF *tablel*, dim. of *table*, fr. OF] (1660) **1** : a graphic description or representation : PICTURE ⟨winsome *tableaux* of old-fashioned literary days —J. D. Hart⟩ **2** : a striking or artistic grouping : ARRANGEMENT, SCENE **3** [short for *tableau vivant*] : a depiction of a scene usu. presented on a stage by silent and motionless costumed participants

tableau curtain *n* (1881) : a stage curtain that opens in the center and has its sections drawn upward as well as to the side

ta·ble·cloth \'tā-bəl-ˌklòth\ *n* (15c) : a covering spread over a dining table before the tableware is set

ta·ble d'hôte \ˌtä-bəl-'dōt, ˌta-\ *n* [F, lit., host's table] (ca. 1617) **1** : a meal served to all guests at a stated hour and fixed price **2** : a complete meal of several courses offered at a fixed price

ta·ble·ful \'tā-bəl-ˌfùl\ *n* (1535) : as much or as many as a table can hold or accommodate

ta·ble–hop \'tā-bəl-ˌhäp\ *vi* (1942) : to move from table to table (as in a restaurant) in order to chat with friends — **ta·ble–hop·per** *n*

ta·ble·land \-bə(l)-ˌland\ *n* (1697) : a broad level elevated area : PLATEAU

table linen *n* (15c) : linen (as tablecloths and napkins) for the table

ta·ble·mate \'tā-bəl-ˌmāt\ *n* (1624) : a dining companion

tabard b

table of organization (ca. 1918) **:** a table listing the number and duties of personnel and the major items of equipment authorized for a military unit
table salt *n* (1763) **:** salt suitable for use at the table and in cooking
table soccer *n* (1948) **:** FOOSBALL
ta·ble·spoon \ˈtā-bəl-ˌspün\ *n* (1761) **1 :** a large spoon used esp. for serving **2 :** a unit of measure used esp. in cookery equal to ½ fluid ounce (15 milliliters)
ta·ble·spoon·ful \ˌtā-bəl-ˈspün-ˌfu̇l, ˈtā-bəl-ˌ\ *n, pl* **tablespoonfuls** \-ˌfu̇lz\ *also* **ta·ble·spoons·ful** \-ˈspünz-ˌfu̇l, -ˌspünz-\ (1772) **1 :** enough to fill a tablespoon **2 :** TABLESPOON 2
table sugar *n* (1964) **:** SUGAR 1a; *esp* **:** granulated white sugar
tab·let \ˈta-blət\ *n* [ME *tablett,* fr. AF *tablet,* dim. of *table* table] (14c) **1 a :** a flat slab or plaque suited for or bearing an inscription **b :** a thin slab or one of a set of portable sheets used for writing **c :** PAD 4 **2 a :** a compressed or molded block of a solid material **b :** a small mass of medicated material ⟨an aspirin ~⟩ **3 :** GRAPHICS TABLET
table talk *n* (ca. 1569) **:** informal conversation at or as if at a dining table; *esp* **:** the social talk of a celebrity recorded for publication
table tennis *n* (1887) **:** a game resembling tennis that is played on a tabletop with wooden paddles and a small hollow plastic ball
ta·ble·top \ˈtā-bəl-ˌtäp\ *n* (1751) **1 :** the top of a table **2 :** a photograph of small objects or a miniature scene arranged on a table — **tabletop** *adj*
ta·ble·ware \-ˌwer\ *n* (1766) **:** utensils (as of china, glass, or silver) for table use
table wine *n* (1673) **:** an unfortified wine containing not more than 14 percent alcohol by volume and usu. suitable for serving with food
[1]**tab·loid** \ˈta-ˌblȯid\ *adj* [fr. *Tabloid,* a trademark] (1901) **1 :** compressed or condensed into small scope ⟨~ criticism⟩ **2 :** of, relating to, or resembling tabloids; *esp* **:** featuring stories of violence, crime, or scandal presented in a sensational manner ⟨~ television⟩ — **tab·loid·ism** \-ˌblȯi-ˌdi-zəm\ *n*
[2]**tabloid** *n* (1906) **1 :** DIGEST, SUMMARY **2 :** a newspaper that is about half the page size of an ordinary newspaper and that contains news in condensed form and much photographic matter
[1]**ta·boo** *also* **ta·bu** \tə-ˈbü, ta-\ *adj* [Tongan *tabu*] (1777) **1 :** forbidden to profane use or contact because of what are held to be dangerous supernatural powers **2 a :** banned on grounds of morality or taste ⟨the subject is ~⟩ **b :** banned as constituting a risk ⟨the area beyond is ~, still alive with explosives —Robert Leckie⟩
[2]**taboo** *also* **tabu** *n, pl* **taboos** *also* **tabus** (1777) **1 :** a prohibition against touching, saying, or doing something for fear of immediate harm from a supernatural force **2 :** a prohibition imposed by social custom or as a protective measure **3 :** belief in taboos
[3]**taboo** *also* **tabu** *vt* (1777) **1 :** to set apart as taboo esp. by marking with a ritualistic symbol **2 :** to avoid or ban as taboo
ta·bor *also* **ta·bour** \ˈtā-bər\ *n* [ME, fr. AF, ultim. fr. Pers *tabīr* drum] (14c) **:** a small drum with one head of soft calfskin used to accompany a pipe or fife played by the same person
ta·bor·er *also* **ta·bour·er** \-bər-ər\ *n* (15c) **:** one that plays on the tabor
tab·o·ret *or* **tab·ou·ret** \ˌta-bə-ˈret, -ˈrā\ *n* [F *tabouret,* lit., small drum, fr. MF, dim. of *tabor, tabour* drum, fr. OF] (1630) **1 :** a cylindrical seat or stool without arms or back **2 :** a small portable stand or cabinet
tabouleh *or* **tabouli** *var of* TABBOULEH
Ta·briz \tə-ˈbrēz\ *n, pl* **Tabriz** [*Tabriz,* Iran] (1900) **:** a Persian rug usu. having a cotton warp, firm wool pile, and a medallion design
tab·u·lar \ˈta-byə-lər\ *adj* [L *tabularis* of boards, fr. *tabula* board, tablet] (ca. 1656) **1 :** having a flat surface **:** LAMINAR ⟨a ~ crystal⟩ **2 a :** of, relating to, or arranged in a table; *specif* **:** set up in rows and columns **b :** computed by means of a table
ta·bu·la ra·sa \ˌta-byə-lə-ˈrä-zə, -sə\ *n, pl* **ta·bu·lae ra·sae** \-ˌlī-ˈrä-ˌzī, -ˌsī\ [L, smoothed or erased tablet] (1535) **1 :** the mind in its hypothetical primary blank or empty state before receiving outside impressions **2 :** something existing in its original pristine state
tab·u·late \ˈta-byə-ˌlāt\ *vt* **-lat·ed; -lat·ing** [L *tabula* tablet] (1734) **1 :** to put into tabular form **2 :** to count, record, or list systematically — **tab·u·la·tion** \ˌta-byə-ˈlā-shən\ *n* — **tab·u·la·tor** \ˈta-byə-ˌlā-tər\ *n*
ta·bun \ˈtä-ˌbu̇n\ *n* [G] (1948) **:** an extremely toxic chemical warfare agent $C_5H_{11}N_2O_2P$ similar to sarin in action
TAC *abbr* Tactical Air Command
tac·a·ma·hac \ˈta-kə-mə-ˌhak\ *n* [Sp *tacamahaca,* fr. Nahuatl *tecamac* medicinal resin] (1739) **:** BALSAM POPLAR
TACAN \ˈta-ˌkan\ *n, often attrib* [*ta*ctical *a*ir *n*avigation] (1955) **:** a system of navigation that uses ultrahigh frequency signals to determine the distance and bearing of an aircraft from a transmitting station
ta·cet \ˈtä-ˌket; ˈtā-sət, ˈta-sət\ [L, lit., (it) is silent, fr. *tacēre* to be silent — more at TACIT] (ca. 1724) — used as a direction in music to indicate that an instrument is not to play during a movement or long section
tach \ˈtak\ *n* (ca. 1930) **:** TACHOMETER
tach·i·nid \ˈta-kə-nəd, -ˌnid\ *n* [NL *Tachinidae,* fr. *Tachina,* genus of flies, fr. Gk *tachinos* fleet, fr. *tachys* swift] (1888) **:** any of a family (Tachinidae) of bristly usu. grayish or black dipteran flies whose parasitic larvae are often used in the biological control of insect pests — **tachinid** *adj*
tach·ism \ˈta-ˌshi-zəm\ *n, often cap* [F *tachisme,* fr. *tache* stain, spot, blob, fr. OF *teche, tache,* of Gmc origin; akin to OS *tēkan* sign, OHG *zeihhan* — more at TOKEN] (1955) **:** ACTION PAINTING — **tach·ist** \ˈta-shist\ *also* **ta·chiste** \ta-ˈshēst\ *adj or n, often cap*
ta·chis·to·scope \tə-ˈkis-tə-ˌskōp, ta-\ *n* [Gk *tachistos* (superl. of *tachys* swift) + ISV *-scope*] (ca. 1890) **:** an apparatus for the brief exposure of visual stimuli that is used in the study of learning, attention, and perception — **ta·chis·to·scop·ic** \-ˌkis-tə-ˈskä-pik\ *adj* — **ta·chis·to·scop·i·cal·ly** \-pi-k(ə-)lē\ *adv*
ta·chom·e·ter \ta-ˈkä-mə-tər, tə-\ *n* [Gk *tachos* speed + E *-meter*] (1810) **:** a device for indicating speed of rotation
tachy- *comb form* [Gk, fr. *tachys*] **:** rapid **:** accelerated ⟨*tachy*cardia⟩
tachy·ar·rhyth·mia \ˌta-kē-ā-ˈrith-mē-ə\ *n* [NL] (1926) **:** arrhythmia characterized by a rapid irregular heartbeat
tachy·car·dia \ˌta-ki-ˈkär-dē-ə\ *n* [NL] (1889) **:** relatively rapid heart action whether physiological (as after exercise) or pathological — compare BRADYCARDIA
tachy·on \ˈta-kē-ˌän\ *n* [*tachy-* + [2]*-on*] (1967) **:** a hypothetical particle held to travel only faster than light
tac·it \ˈta-sət\ *adj* [MF or L; MF *tacite,* fr. L *tacitus* silent, fr. pp. of *tacēre* to be silent; akin to OHG *dagēn* to be silent] (1576) **1 :** expressed or carried on without words or speech ⟨the blush was a ~ answer —Bram Stoker⟩ **2 :** implied or indicated (as by an act or by silence) but not actually expressed ⟨~ consent⟩ ⟨~ admission of guilt⟩ — **tac·it·ly** *adv* — **tac·it·ness** *n*
tac·i·turn \ˈta-sə-ˌtərn\ *adj* [F or L; F *taciturne,* fr. MF, fr. L *taciturnus,* fr. *tacitus*] (1734) **:** temperamentally disinclined to talk ***syn*** see SILENT — **tac·i·tur·ni·ty** \ˌta-sə-ˈtər-nə-tē\ *n*
[1]**tack** \ˈtak\ *vb* [ME *takken,* fr. *tak*] *vt* (14c) **1 :** ATTACH; *esp* **:** to fasten or affix with tacks **2 :** to join in a slight or hasty manner **3 a :** to add as a supplement **b :** to add (a rider) to a parliamentary bill **4 :** to change the direction of (a sailing ship) when sailing close-hauled by turning the bow to the wind and shifting the sails so as to fall off on the other side at about the same angle as before ~ *vi* **1 a :** to tack a sailing ship **b** *of a ship* **:** to change to an opposite tack by turning the bow to the wind **c :** to follow a course against the wind by a series of tacks **2 a :** to follow a zigzag course **b :** to modify one's policy or attitude abruptly — **tack·er** *n*
[2]**tack** *n* [ME *tak* fastener, rope tying down the windward corner of a sail, fr. MF (Norman dial.) *taque;* akin to MD *tac* sharp point] (1574) **1 :** a small short sharp-pointed nail usu. having a broad flat head **2 a :** the direction of a ship with respect to the trim of her sails ⟨starboard ~⟩ **b :** the run of a sailing ship on one tack **c :** a change when close-hauled from the starboard to the port tack or vice versa **d :** a zigzag movement on land **e :** a course or method of action; *esp* **:** one sharply divergent from that previously followed **3 :** any of various usu. temporary stitches **4 :** the lower forward corner of a fore-and-aft sail **5 :** a sticky or adhesive quality or condition
[3]**tack** *n* [origin unknown] (1841) **:** HARDTACK 1
[4]**tack** *n* [perh. short for *tackle*] (1924) **:** stable gear; *esp* **:** articles of harness (as saddle and bridle) for use on a saddle horse
tack·board \ˈtak-ˌbȯrd\ *n* (ca. 1927) **:** a board (as of cork) for tacking up notices and display materials
tack claw *n* (ca. 1876) **:** a small hand tool for removing tacks
tack·i·fy \ˈta-kə-ˌfī\ *vt* **-fied; -fy·ing** (1942) **:** to make (as a resin adhesive) tacky or more tacky — **tack·i·fi·er** \-ˌfī(-ə)r\ *n*
tack·i·ly \ˈta-kə-lē\ *adv* (1903) **:** in a tacky manner **:** so as to be tacky
tack·i·ness \ˈta-kē-nəs\ *n* (1883) **:** the quality or state of being tacky
[1]**tack·le** \ˈta-kəl, *naut often* ˈtā-\ *n* [ME *takel;* akin to MD *takel* ship's rigging] (13c) **1 :** a set of the equipment used in a particular activity **:** GEAR ⟨fishing ~⟩ **2 a :** a ship's rigging **b :** an assemblage of ropes and pulleys arranged to gain mechanical advantage for hoisting and pulling **3 a :** the act or an instance of tackling **b (1) :** either of two offensive football players positioned on each side of the center and between guard and end **(2) :** either of two football players positioned on the inside of a defensive line
[2]**tackle** *vb* **tack·led; tack·ling** \-k(ə-)liŋ\ *vt* (1600) **1 :** to attach or secure with or as if with tackle **2 a :** to seize, take hold of, or grapple with esp. with the intention of stopping or subduing **b :** to seize and throw down or stop (an opposing player with the ball) in football **3 :** to set about dealing with ⟨~ the problem⟩ ~ *vi* **:** to tackle an opposing player in football — **tack·ler** \-k(ə-)lər\ *n*
tack·ling \ˈta-kliŋ, *naut often* ˈtā-\ *n* (15c) **:** TACKLE, GEAR
[1]**tacky** \ˈta-kē\ *adj* **tack·i·er; -est** [[2]*tack*] (1788) **:** somewhat sticky to the touch ⟨~ varnish⟩; *also* **:** characterized by tack **:** ADHESIVE
[2]**tacky** *adj* **tacki·er; -est** [*tacky* a low-class person] (1862) **1 a :** characterized by lack of good breeding ⟨couldn't run around downtown . . . in a bikini, which was ~ —Cyra McFadden⟩ **b :** SHABBY, SEEDY ⟨a ~ town whose citrus groves were blighted by smoke —Bryce Nelson⟩ **2 :** not having or exhibiting good taste: as **a :** marked by lack of style **:** DOWDY **b :** marked by cheap showiness **:** GAUDY ⟨a ~ publicity stunt⟩ ⟨a ~ outfit⟩
ta·co \ˈtä-(ˌ)kō\ *n, pl* **tacos** \-(ˌ)kōz\ [MexSp] (1914) **:** a usu. fried tortilla that is folded or rolled and stuffed with a mixture (as of seasoned meat, cheese, and lettuce)
tac·o·nite \ˈta-kə-ˌnīt\ *n* [*Taconic* Range] (1892) **:** a flintlike rock high enough in iron content to constitute a low-grade iron ore
tac·rine \ˈta-ˌkrēn\ *n* [*t*etra- + *acridine*] (1965) **:** an anticholinesterase $C_{13}H_{14}N_2$ used in the form of its hydrochloride esp. for the palliative treatment of cognitive deficits associated with Alzheimer's disease
tact \ˈtakt\ *n* [F, sense of touch, fr. L *tactus,* fr. *tangere* to touch — more at TANGENT] (1797) **1 :** sensitive mental or aesthetic perception ⟨converted the novel into a play with remarkable skill and ~⟩ **2 :** a keen sense of what to do or say in order to maintain good relations with others or avoid offense

syn TACT, ADDRESS, POISE, SAVOIR FAIRE mean skill and grace in dealing with others. TACT implies delicate and considerate perception of what is appropriate ⟨questions showing a lack of *tact*⟩. ADDRESS stresses dexterity and grace in dealing with new and trying situations and may imply success in attaining one's ends ⟨brought it off with remarkable *address*⟩. POISE may imply both tact and address but stresses self-possession and ease in meeting difficult situations ⟨answered the accusations with unruffled *poise*⟩. SAVOIR FAIRE is likely to stress worldly experience and a sure awareness of what is proper or expedient ⟨the *savoir faire* of a seasoned traveler⟩.

tact·ful \ˈtakt-fəl\ *adj* (1864) **:** having or showing tact — **tact·ful·ly** \-fə-lē\ *adv* — **tact·ful·ness** *n*
[1]**tac·tic** \ˈtak-tik\ *n* [NL *tactica,* fr. Gk *taktikē,* fr. fem. of *taktikos*] (1640) **1 :** a device for accomplishing an end **2 :** a method of employing forces in combat
[2]**tactic** *adj* [NL *tacticus,* fr. Gk *taktikos*] (1871) **:** of or relating to arrangement or order
-tactic *adj comb form* [Gk *taktikos*] **1 :** of, relating to, or having (such) an arrangement or pattern ⟨para*tactic*⟩ **2 :** showing orientation or movement directed by a (specified) force or agent ⟨geo*tactic*⟩

tac·ti·cal \ˈtak-ti-kəl\ *adj* (1570) **1 :** of or relating to combat tactics: as **a** (1) **:** of or occurring at the battlefront ⟨a ~ defense⟩ ⟨a ~ first strike⟩ (2) **:** using or being weapons or forces employed at the battlefront ⟨~ missiles⟩ **b** *of an air force* **:** of, relating to, or designed for air attack in close support of friendly ground forces **2 a :** of or relating to tactics: as (1) **:** of or relating to small-scale actions serving a larger purpose (2) **:** made or carried out with only a limited or immediate end in view **b :** adroit in planning or maneuvering to accomplish a purpose — **tac·ti·cal·ly** \-k(ə-)lē\ *adv*

tac·ti·cian \tak-ˈti-shən\ *n* (1798) **:** one versed in tactics

tac·tics \ˈtak-tiks\ *n pl but sing or pl in constr* [NL *tactica,* pl., fr. Gk *taktika,* fr. neut. pl. of *taktikos* of order, of tactics, fit for arranging, fr. *tassein* to arrange, place in battle formation] (1626) **1 a :** the science and art of disposing and maneuvering forces in combat **b :** the art or skill of employing available means to accomplish an end **2 :** a system or mode of procedure **3 :** the study of the grammatical relations within a language including morphology and syntax

tac·tile \ˈtak-tᵊl, -ˌtī(-ə)l\ *adj* [F or L; F, fr. L *tactilis,* fr. *tangere* to touch — more at TANGENT] (1615) **1 :** perceptible by touch **2 :** of, relating to, or being the sense of touch — **tac·tile·ly** \-tə-lē, -ˌtīl-lē\ *adv*

tac·til·i·ty \tak-ˈti-lə-tē\ *n* (1659) **1 :** the capability of being felt or touched **2 :** responsiveness to stimulation of the sense of touch

tac·tion \ˈtak-shən\ *n* [L *taction-, tactio,* fr. *tangere*] (ca. 1623) **:** TOUCH

tact·less \ˈtakt-ləs\ *adj* (ca. 1847) **:** marked by lack of tact ⟨~ comments⟩ ⟨~ methods⟩ — **tact·less·ly** *adv* — **tact·less·ness** *n*

tac·tu·al \ˈtak-chə-wəl, -chəl\ *adj* [L *tactus* sense of touch — more at TACT] (1642) **:** TACTILE 2 — **tac·tu·al·ly** *adv*

tad \ˈtad\ *n* [prob. fr. E dial., toad, fr. ME *tode* — more at TOAD] (ca. 1877) **1 :** a small child; *esp* **:** BOY **2 :** a small or insignificant amount or degree **:** BIT ⟨might give him some water and a ~ to eat —C. T. Walker⟩ — **a tad :** SOMEWHAT, RATHER ⟨looked *a tad* bigger than me —Larry Hodgson⟩

ta–da *also* **ta–dah** \tä-ˈdä\ *interj* (1926) — used as mock fanfare to call attention to something remarkable

tad·pole \ˈtad-ˌpōl\ *n* [ME *taddepol,* fr. *tode* toad + *polle* head] (15c) **:** a larval amphibian; *specif* **:** a frog or toad larva that has a rounded body with a long tail bordered by fins and external gills soon replaced by internal gills and that undergoes a metamorphosis to the adult

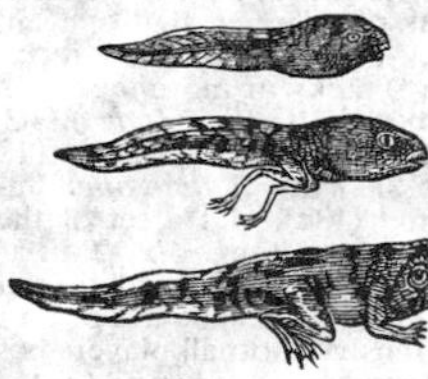
tadpole in stages

Tadzhik *var of* TAJIK

tae·di·um vi·tae \ˌtē-dē-əm-ˈvī-ˌtē, ˌtī-dē-əm-ˈwē-ˌtī\ *n* [L] (1759) **:** weariness or loathing of life

tae kwon do \ˈtī-ˈkwän-ˈdō\ *n, often cap T&K&D* [Korean *t'aekwŏndo,* fr. *t'ae-* to kick + *kwŏn* fist + *to* way] (1967) **:** a Korean art of unarmed self-defense characterized esp. by the extensive use of kicks

tael \ˈtāl\ *n* [Pg, fr. Malay *tahil*] (1588) **1 :** any of various Chinese units of value based on the value of a tael weight of silver **2 :** any of various units of weight of eastern Asia

tae·nia *also* **te·nia** \ˈtē-nē-ə\ *n, pl* **-ni·ae** \-nē-ˌī, -ˌē\ *or* **-nias** [L, ribbon, fillet, fr. Gk *tainia;* akin to Gk *teinein* to stretch — more at THIN] (1563) **1 :** a band on a Doric order separating the frieze from the architrave **2 :** TAPEWORM **3 :** an ancient Greek fillet

tae·ni·a·sis *also* **te·ni·a·sis** \tē-ˈnī-ə-səs\ *n* [NL, fr. L *taenia* tapeworm] (ca. 1890) **:** infestation with or disease caused by tapeworms

taf·fe·ta \ˈta-fə-tə\ *n* [ME *taffata,* fr. AF, fr. OIt *taffettà,* fr. Turk *tafta,* fr. Pers *tāftah* woven] (14c) **:** a crisp plain-woven lustrous fabric of various fibers used esp. for women's clothing

taf·fe·tized \ˈta-fə-ˌtīzd\ *adj* (1949) *of cloth* **:** having a crisp finish

taff·rail \ˈtaf-ˌrāl, -rəl\ *n* [modif. of D *tafereel,* fr. MD, panel, fr. OF *tablel* — more at TABLEAU] (ca. 1704) **1 :** the upper part of the stern of a wooden ship **2 :** a rail around the stern of a ship

taf·fy \ˈta-fē\ *n, pl* **taffies** [origin unknown] (ca. 1817) **1 :** a boiled candy usu. of molasses or brown sugar that is pulled until porous and light-colored **2 :** insincere flattery

[1]**tag** \ˈtag\ *n* [ME *tagge;* akin to MLG *tagge, tacke* twig, spike] (14c) **1 :** a loose hanging piece of cloth **:** TATTER **2 :** a metal or plastic binding on an end of a shoelace **3 :** a piece of hanging or attached material; *specif* **:** a loop, knot, or tassel on a garment **4 a :** a brief quotation used for rhetorical emphasis or sententious effect **b :** a recurrent or characteristic verbal expression **c :** TAGLINE 1 **5 a :** a cardboard, plastic, or metal marker used for identification or classification ⟨license ~*s*⟩ **b :** a descriptive or identifying epithet **c :** something used for identification or location **:** FLAG **d :** LABEL 3d **e :** PRICE TAG **f :** an element of code in a computer document used esp. to control format and layout or to establish a hyperlink **6 :** a detached fragmentary piece **:** BIT **7 :** a graffito in the form of an identifying name or symbol

[2]**tag** *vb* **tagged; tag·ging** *vt* (15c) **1 :** to provide or mark with or as if with a tag: as **a :** to supply with an identifying marker or price ⟨was *tagged* at $4.95⟩ **b :** to provide with a name or epithet **:** LABEL, BRAND ⟨*tagged* him a has-been⟩ **c :** to put a ticket on (a motor vehicle) for a traffic violation **d :** to deface with a graffito usu. in the form of the defacer's nickname **2 :** to attach as an addition **:** APPEND **3 :** to follow closely and persistently **4 :** to hold to account; *esp* **:** to charge with violating the law ⟨was *tagged* for . . . assault —Burt Woolis⟩ **5 :** LABEL 2 ~ *vi* **:** to keep close ⟨*tagging* at their heels —Corey Ford⟩

[3]**tag** *n* [origin unknown] (1738) **1 :** a game in which the player who is it chases others and tries to touch one of them who then becomes it **2 :** an act or instance of tagging a runner in baseball

[4]**tag** *vt* **tagged; tag·ging** (1878) **1 a :** to touch in or as if in a game of tag **b :** to put out (a runner) in baseball by a touch with the ball or the gloved hand containing the ball **2 :** to hit solidly **3 :** to choose usu. for a special purpose **:** SELECT **4 :** to make a hit or run off (a pitcher) in baseball ⟨the batter *tagged* him for a home run⟩

TAG *abbr* the adjutant general

Ta·ga·log \tə-ˈgä-ˌlȯg\ *n, pl* **Tagalog** *or* **Tagalogs** [Tag] (1808) **1 :** a member of a people of central Luzon **2 :** an Austronesian language of the Tagalog people — compare PILIPINO

tag·along \ˈta-gə-ˌlȯŋ\ *n* (1935) **:** one that persistently and often annoyingly follows the lead of another

tag along *vi* (1900) **:** to follow another's lead esp. in going from one place to another

tag·board \ˈtag-ˌbȯrd\ *n* (1904) **:** strong cardboard used esp. for making shipping tags

tag end *n* (1807) **1 :** the last part **2 :** a miscellaneous or random bit

tag·ger \ˈta-gər\ *n* (1648) **:** one that tags; *esp* **:** a person who marks surfaces with graffiti

ta·glia·tel·le \ˌtäl-yä-ˈte-(ˌ)lā\ *n* [It, fr. *tagliare* to cut, fr. LL *taliare* — more at TAILOR] (1899) **:** FETTUCCINE

tagline \ˈtag-ˌlīn\ *n* (1926) **1 :** a final line (as in a play or joke); *esp* **:** one that serves to clarify a point or create a dramatic effect **2 :** a reiterated phrase identified with an individual, group, or product **:** SLOGAN

tag question *n* (1933) **:** a question (as *isn't it* in "it's fine, isn't it?") added to a statement or command (as to gain the assent of or challenge the person addressed); *also* **:** a sentence ending in a tag question

tag, rag, and bobtail *or* **tagrag and bobtail** \ˌtag-ˌrag-ən-ˈbäb-ˌtāl, -ˌrag-ᵊŋ-\ *n* (1645) **:** RABBLE

tag sale *n* [fr. the price tag on each item] (1929) **:** GARAGE SALE

tag team *n* [[4]*tag*] (1952) **1 :** a team of two or more professional wrestlers who spell each other during a match **2 :** two or more people working in association toward the same goal — usu. hyphenated when used attributively

tag up *vi* (1942) **:** to touch a base before running in baseball after a fly ball is caught

ta·hi·ni \tə-ˈhē-nē, tä-\ *n* [Ar dial. *ṭaḥīna,* fr. *ṭaḥana* to grind] (1950) **:** a smooth paste of sesame seeds

Ta·hi·tian \tə-ˈhē-shən\ *n* (1825) **1 :** a native or inhabitant of Tahiti **2 :** the Polynesian language of the Tahitians — **Tahitian** *adj*

tahr \ˈtär\ *n* [Nepali *thār*] (1835) **:** any of a genus (*Hemitragus*) of wild Asian goats; *esp* **:** one (*H. jemlahicus*) of the Himalayas having a reddish-brown to dark brown coat and a long shaggy mane

tah·sil \tä-ˈsēl\ *n* [Hindi *tahsīl* & Urdu *taḥṣīl,* fr. Ar *taḥṣīl* collection of revenue] (1846) **:** a district administration or revenue subdivision in India

Tai \ˈtī\ *n, pl* **Tai** (1693) **1 :** a widespread group of peoples in southeast Asia associated ethnically with valley paddy-rice culture **2 :** a family of languages including Thai and Shan spoken in southeast Asia and China

tai chi *also* **t'ai chi** \ˈtī-ˈjē, ˈtī-ˈchē\ *n, often cap T&C* [Chin (Beijing) *tàijíquán,* fr. *tàijí* the Absolute in Chinese cosmology + *quán* fist, boxing] (1954) **:** an ancient Chinese discipline of meditative movements practiced as a system of exercises — called also *tai chi chuan, t'ai chi ch'uan* \-chü-ˈän\

tai·ga \ˈtī-gə\ *n* [Russ *taĭga*] (1888) **:** a moist subarctic forest dominated by conifers (as spruce and fir) that begins where the tundra ends

[1]**tail** \ˈtāl\ *n, often attrib* [ME, fr. OE *tægel;* akin to OHG *zagal* tail, MIr *dúal* lock of hair] (bef. 12c) **1 :** the rear end or a process or prolongation of the rear end of the body of an animal **2 :** something resembling an animal's tail in shape or position: as **a :** a luminous stream of particles, gases, or ions extending from a comet esp. in the antisolar direction **b :** the rear part of an airplane consisting usu. of horizontal and vertical stabilizing surfaces with attached control surfaces **3 :** RETINUE **4** *pl* **a :** TAILCOAT **b :** full evening dress for men **5 a :** BUTTOCKS, BUTT **b** *usu vulgar* **:** SEXUAL INTERCOURSE **6 :** the back, last, lower, or inferior part of something **7 :** TAILING 1 — usu. used in pl. **8 :** the reverse of a coin — usu. used in pl. ⟨~*s,* I win⟩ **9 :** one (as a detective) who follows or keeps watch on someone **10 :** the blank space at the bottom of a page **11 :** a location immediately or not far behind ⟨had a posse on his ~⟩ — **tailed** \ˈtāld\ *adj* — **tail·less** \ˈtāl-ləs\ *adj* — **tail·like** \-ˌlīk\ *adj*

[2]**tail** *vt* (1523) **1 :** to connect end to end **2 a :** to remove the tail of (an animal) **:** DOCK **b :** to remove the stem or bottom part of ⟨topping and ~*ing* gooseberries⟩ **3 a :** to make or furnish with a tail **b :** to follow or be drawn behind like a tail **4 :** to follow for purposes of surveillance ~ *vi* **1 :** to form or move in a straggling line **2 :** to grow progressively smaller, fainter, or more scattered **:** ABATE — usu. used with *off* ⟨productivity is ~*ing* off —Tom Nicholson⟩ **3 :** to swing or lie with the stern in a named direction — used of a ship at anchor **4 :** [2]TAG — **tail·er** *n*

[3]**tail** *n* [ME, fr. AF, fr. *tailler*] (14c) **:** ENTAIL 1a

[4]**tail** *adj* [ME *taille,* fr. AF *taylé,* pp. of *tailler* to cut, limit — more at TAILOR] (15c) **:** limited as to tenure **:** ENTAILED

tail·back \ˈtāl-ˌbak\ *n* (1930) **1 :** the offensive football back farthest from the line of scrimmage **2** *Brit* **:** a line of vehicles caused by a traffic slowdown or stoppage

tail·board \-ˌbȯrd\ *n* (1805) *chiefly Brit* **:** TAILGATE 1

tail·bone \-ˌbōn\ *n* (ca. 1577) **1 :** a caudal vertebra **2 :** COCCYX

tail·coat \-ˌkōt\ *n* (1847) **:** a coat with tails; *esp* **:** a man's full-dress coat with two long tapering skirts at the back — **tail·coat·ed** \-ˌkō-təd\ *adj*

tail covert *n* (1815) **:** one of the coverts of the tail quills

tail end *n* (14c) **1 :** BUTTOCKS, RUMP **2 :** the hindmost end **3 :** the concluding period ⟨the *tail end* of the session⟩

tail·end·er \ˈtāl-ˌen-dər\ *n* (1885) **:** one positioned at the end or in last place ⟨the ~*s* in a race⟩

tail fin *n* (1681) **1 :** the terminal fin of a fish or cetacean **2 :** FIN 2b

[1]**tail·gate** \ˈtāl-ˌgāt\ *n* (1854) **1 :** a board or gate at the rear of a vehicle that can be removed or let down (as for loading) **2** [fr. the custom of seating trombonists at the rear of trucks carrying jazz bands in parades] **:** a jazz trombone style marked by much use of slides to and from long sustained tones

[2]**tailgate** *vb* **tail·gat·ed; tail·gat·ing** *vi* (1949) **1 :** to drive dangerously close behind another vehicle **2 :** to hold a tailgate picnic ~ *vt* **:** to drive dangerously close behind — **tail·gat·er** *n*

[3]**tailgate** *adj* (1962) **:** relating to or being a picnic set up on the tailgate esp. of a station wagon

tail·ing \ˈtā-liŋ\ *n* (1764) **1 :** residue separated in the preparation of various products (as grain or ores) — usu. used in pl. **2 :** the part of a projecting stone or brick inserted in a wall

taille \ˈtä-yə, ˈtī-, ˈtāl\ *n* [MF, fr. OF, fr. *taillier* to cut, tax] (ca. 1533) **:** a tax formerly levied by a French king or seigneur on his subjects or on lands held of him

tail·light \ˈtāl-ˌlīt\ *n* (1844) **:** a usu. red warning light mounted at the rear of a vehicle — called also *taillamp*

[1]tai·lor \ˈtā-lər\ *n* [ME *taillour,* fr. AF *taillur,* fr. *tailler, taillier* to cut, fr. LL *taliare,* fr. L *talea* plant cutting, thin piece of wood] (13c) : a person whose occupation is making or altering outer garments

[2]tailor *vi* (1719) : to do the work of a tailor ∼ *vt* **1 a :** to make or fashion as the work of a tailor **b :** to make or adapt to suit a special need or purpose **2 :** to fit with clothes **3 :** to style with trim straight lines and finished handwork

tai·lor·bird \ˈta-lər-ˌbərd\ *n* (1769) : any of a genus (*Orthotomus* of the family Sylviidae) of chiefly Asian warblers that stitch leaves together to support and hide their nests

tai·lored \ˈtā-lərd\ *adj* (1862) **1 :** fashioned or fitted to resemble a tailor's work **2 :** CUSTOM-MADE **3 :** having the look of one fitted by a custom tailor

tai·lor·ing \ˈtā-lə-riŋ\ *n* (1662) **1 a :** the business or occupation of a tailor **b :** the work or workmanship of a tailor **2 :** the making or adapting of something to suit a particular purpose

[1]tai·lor–made \ˌtā-lər-ˈmād\ *adj* (1832) **1 :** made by a tailor or with a tailor's care and style **2 :** made or fitted esp. to a particular use or purpose **3 :** factory made rather than hand-rolled ⟨∼ cigarettes⟩

[2]tailor–made *n* (1892) : one that is tailor-made; *specif* : a woman's garment styled for a trim fit and with stiff straight lines

tail·piece \ˈtāl-ˌpēs\ *n* (1601) **1 :** a piece added at the end **2 :** a device from which the strings of a stringed instrument are stretched to the pegs — see VIOLIN illustration **3 :** an ornament placed below the text matter of a page

tail·pipe \-ˌpīp\ *n* (1922) : an outlet by which engine exhaust gases are expelled from a vehicle (as an automobile or jet aircraft)

tail·plane \-ˌplān\ *n* (1909) : the horizontal tail surfaces of an airplane including the stabilizer and the elevator

tail·race \ˈtāl-ˌrās\ *n* (1776) : a race for conveying water away from a point of industrial application (as a waterwheel or turbine) after use

tail·slide \-ˌslīd\ *n* (1916) : an aerobatic maneuver in which an aircraft that has been pulled into a steep climb stalls and then loses altitude by dropping backward

tail·spin \-ˌspin\ *n* (1917) **1 :** SPIN 2a **2 :** a mental or emotional letdown or collapse **3 :** a sustained and usu. severe decline or downturn ⟨stock prices in a ∼⟩

tail·wa·ter \-ˌwȯ-tər, -ˌwä-\ *n* (1759) **1 :** water below a dam or waterpower development **2 :** excess surface water draining esp. from a field under cultivation

tail·wind \-ˌwind\ *n* (1897) : a wind having the same general direction as a course of movement (as of an aircraft)

Tai·no \ˈtī-(ˌ)nō\ *n, pl* **Taino** *or* **Tainos** [Taino *nitaino, tayno* noble, lesser chief] (1836) **1 :** the language of the Taino people **2 :** a member of an aboriginal Arawakan people of the Greater Antilles and the Bahamas

[1]taint \ˈtānt\ *vb* [ME *teynten* to color & *taynten* to attaint; ME *teynten,* fr. AF *teinter,* fr. *teint,* pp. of *teindre,* fr. L *tingere;* ME *taynten,* short for *attaynten* — more at TINGE, ATTAIN] *vt* (1573) **1 :** to contaminate morally : CORRUPT ⟨scholarship ∼*ed* by envy⟩ **2 :** to affect with putrefaction : SPOIL **3 :** to touch or affect slightly with something bad ⟨persons ∼*ed* with prejudice⟩ ∼ *vi* **1** *obs* **:** to become weak **2 :** to become affected with putrefaction : SPOIL ***syn*** see CONTAMINATE

[2]taint *n* (1601) : a contaminating mark or influence ⟨the ∼ of scandal⟩ — **taint·less** \-ləs\ *adj*

'tain't \ˈtānt\ (1773) : it ain't

[1]tai·pan \ˈtī-ˌpan, ˈtī-ˈpän\ *n* [Chin (Guangdong) *daaih-bāan,* fr. *daaih* big + *bāan* class] (1834) : a powerful businessman and esp. formerly a foreigner living and operating in Hong Kong or China

[2]tai·pan \ˈtī-ˌpan\ *n* [Wik Munkan (Australian aboriginal language of northern Queensland) *dhayban*] (1933) : an exceedingly venomous elapid snake (*Oxyuranus scutellatus*) of northern Australia and New Guinea; *also* : a related snake (*O. microlepidotus*)

Ta·jik *or* **Ta·dzhik** \tä-ˈjik, tə-, -ˈjēk\ *n* (1815) **1 :** a member of a Persian-speaking ethnic group living in Tajikistan, Afghanistan, and adjacent areas of central Asia **2 :** the form of Persian spoken by the Tajiks

ta·ka \ˈtä-kə, -(ˌ)kä\ *n* [Bengali *ṭākā* rupee, taka, fr. Skt *ṭaṅka* stamped coin] (1972) — see MONEY table

ta·ka·he \tä-ˈkä-(ˌ)hā\ *n* [Maori] (1851) : a flightless bird (*Porphyrio mantelli* syn. *Notornis mantelli*) of the rail family that occurs in New Zealand

[1]take \ˈtāk\ *vb* **took** \ˈtu̇k\; **tak·en** \ˈtā-kən\; **tak·ing** [ME, fr. OE *tacan,* fr. ON *taka;* akin to MD *taken* to take] *vt* (bef. 12c) **1 :** to get into one's hands or into one's possession, power, or control: as **a :** to seize or capture physically ⟨*took* them as prisoners⟩ **b :** to get possession of (as fish or game) by killing or capturing **c** (1) **:** to move against (as an opponent's piece in chess) and remove from play (2) **:** to win in a card game ⟨able to ∼ 12 tricks⟩ **d :** to acquire by eminent domain **2 :** GRASP, GRIP ⟨∼ the ax by the handle⟩ **3 a :** to catch or attack through the effect of a sudden force or influence ⟨*taken* with a fit of laughing⟩ ⟨*taken* ill⟩ **b :** to catch or come upon in a particular situation or action ⟨was *taken* unawares⟩ **c :** to gain the approval or liking of : CAPTIVATE, DELIGHT ⟨was quite *taken* with her at their first meeting⟩ **4 a :** to receive into one's body (as by swallowing, drinking, or inhaling) ⟨∼ a pill⟩ **b :** to put oneself into (as sun, air, or water) for pleasure or physical benefit **c :** to partake of : EAT ⟨∼*s* dinner about seven⟩ **5 a :** to bring or receive into a relation or connection ⟨∼*s* just four students a year⟩ ⟨it's time he *took* a wife⟩ **b :** to copulate with **6 :** to transfer into one's own keeping: **a :** APPROPRIATE ⟨someone *took* my hat⟩ **b :** to obtain or secure for use (as by lease, subscription, or purchase) ⟨∼ a cottage for the summer⟩ ⟨I'll ∼ the red one⟩ ⟨*took* an ad in the paper⟩ **7 a :** ASSUME ⟨gods often *took* the likeness of a human being⟩ ⟨when the college *took* its present form⟩ **b** (1) **:** to enter into or undertake the duties of ⟨∼ a job⟩ ⟨∼ office⟩ (2) **:** to move onto or into : move into position on ⟨the home team *took* the field⟩ ⟨∼ the witness stand⟩ **c** (1) **:** to bind oneself by ⟨∼ the oath of office⟩ (2) **:** to make (a decision) esp. with finality or authority **d :** to impose upon oneself ⟨∼ the trouble to do good work⟩ ⟨∼ pains to make her feel welcome⟩ **e** (1) **:** to adopt as one's own ⟨∼ a stand on the issue⟩ ⟨∼ an interest⟩ (2) **:** to align or ally oneself with ⟨mother *took* his side⟩ **f :** to assume as if rightfully one's own or as if granted ⟨∼ the credit⟩ **g :** to accept the burden or consequences of ⟨*took* the blame⟩ **h :** to have or assume as a proper part of or accompaniment to itself ⟨transitive verbs ∼ an object⟩ **8 a :** to secure by winning in competition ⟨*took* first place⟩ **b :** DEFEAT **9 :** to pick out : CHOOSE, SELECT ⟨*took* the best apple⟩ **10 :** to adopt, choose, or avail oneself of for use: as **a :** to have recourse to as an instrument for doing something ⟨∼ a scythe to the weeds⟩ **b :** to use as a means of transportation or progression ⟨∼ the bus⟩ **c :** to have recourse to for safety or refuge ⟨∼ shelter⟩ **d :** to go along, into, or through ⟨*took* a different route⟩ **e** (1) **:** to proceed to occupy ⟨∼ a seat in the rear⟩ (2) **:** to use up (as space or time) ⟨∼*s* a long time to dry⟩ (3) **:** NEED, REQUIRE ⟨∼*s* a size nine shoe⟩ ⟨it ∼*s* two to start a fight⟩ **11 a :** to obtain by deriving from a source : DRAW ⟨∼*s* its title from the name of the hero⟩ **b** (1) **:** to obtain as the result of a special procedure : ASCERTAIN ⟨∼ the temperature⟩ ⟨∼ a census⟩ (2) **:** to get in or as if in writing ⟨∼ notes⟩ ⟨∼ an inventory⟩ (3) **:** to get by drawing or painting or by photography ⟨∼ a snapshot⟩ (4) **:** to get by transference from one surface to another ⟨∼ a proof⟩ ⟨∼ fingerprints⟩ **12 :** to receive or accept whether willingly or reluctantly ⟨∼ a bribe⟩ ⟨will you ∼ this call⟩ ⟨∼ a bet⟩: as **a** (1) **:** to submit to : ENDURE ⟨∼ a cut in pay⟩ (2) **:** WITHSTAND ⟨it will ∼ a lot of punishment⟩ (3) **:** SUFFER ⟨*took* a direct hit⟩ **b** (1) **:** to accept as true : BELIEVE ⟨I'll ∼ your word for it⟩ (2) **:** FOLLOW ⟨∼ my advice⟩ (3) **:** to accept or regard with the mind in a specified way ⟨*took* the news hard⟩ ⟨you ∼ yourself too seriously⟩ **c :** to indulge in and enjoy ⟨was *taking* his ease on the porch⟩ **d :** to receive or accept as a return (as in payment, compensation, or reparation) ⟨we don't ∼ credit cards⟩ **e :** to accept in a usu. professional relationship — often used with *on* ⟨agreed to ∼ him on as a client⟩ **f :** to refrain from hitting at (a pitched ball) ⟨∼ a strike⟩ **13 a** (1) **:** to let in : ADMIT ⟨the boat was *taking* water fast⟩ (2) **:** ACCOMMODATE ⟨the suitcase wouldn't ∼ another thing⟩ **b :** to be affected injuriously by (as a disease) : CONTRACT ⟨∼ cold⟩; *also* : to be seized by ⟨∼ a fit⟩ ⟨∼ fright⟩ **c :** to absorb or become impregnated with (as dye); *also* : to be effectively treated by ⟨a surface that ∼*s* a fine polish⟩ **14 a :** APPREHEND, UNDERSTAND ⟨how should I ∼ your remark⟩ **b :** CONSIDER, SUPPOSE ⟨I ∼ it you're not going⟩ **c :** RECKON, ACCEPT ⟨*taking* a stride at 30 inches⟩ **d :** FEEL, EXPERIENCE ⟨∼ pleasure⟩ ⟨∼ an instant dislike to someone⟩ ⟨∼ offense⟩ **15 a :** to lead, carry, or cause to go along to another place ⟨this bus will ∼ you into town⟩ ⟨*took* an umbrella with her⟩ **b :** to cause to move to a specified state, condition, or sphere of activity ⟨*took* the company public⟩ ⟨*took* his team to the finals⟩ **c :** to stop prescribing a specified regimen to — used with *off* ⟨*took* him off the medication⟩ **16 a :** REMOVE ⟨∼ eggs from a nest⟩ **b** (1) **:** to put an end to (life) (2) **:** to remove by death ⟨was *taken* in his prime⟩ **c :** SUBTRACT ⟨∼ two from four⟩ **d :** EXACT ⟨the weather *took* its toll⟩ **17 a :** to undertake and make, do, or perform ⟨∼ a walk⟩ ⟨∼ aim⟩ ⟨∼ legal action⟩ ⟨∼ a test⟩ ⟨∼ a look⟩ **b :** to participate in ⟨∼ a meeting⟩ **18 a :** to deal with ⟨∼ first things first⟩ **b :** to consider or view in a particular relation ⟨*taken* together, the details were significant⟩; *esp* : to consider as an example ⟨∼ style, for instance⟩ **c** (1) **:** to apply oneself to the study of ⟨∼ music lessons⟩ ⟨∼ French⟩ (2) **:** to study for esp. successfully ⟨*taking* a degree in engineering⟩ ⟨*took* holy orders⟩ **19 :** to obtain money from esp. fraudulently ⟨*took* me for all I had⟩ **20 :** to pass or attempt to pass through, along, or over ⟨*took* the curve too fast⟩ ⟨∼ the stairs two at a time⟩ ∼ *vi* **1 :** to obtain possession: as **a :** CAPTURE **b :** to receive property under law as one's own **2 :** to lay hold : CATCH, HOLD **3 :** to establish a take esp. by uniting or growing ⟨90 percent of the grafts ∼⟩ **4 a :** to betake oneself : set out : GO ⟨∼ after a purse snatcher⟩ **b** *chiefly dial* — used as an intensifier or redundantly with a following verb ⟨*took* and swung at the ball⟩ **5 a :** to take effect : ACT, OPERATE ⟨hoped the lesson he taught would ∼⟩ **b :** to show the natural or intended effect ⟨dry fuel ∼*s* readily⟩ **6 :** CHARM, CAPTIVATE ⟨a *taking* smile⟩ **7 :** DETRACT **8 :** to be seized or attacked in a specified way : BECOME ⟨*took* sick⟩ — **tak·er** *n* — **take a back seat :** to have or assume a secondary position or status — **take a bath :** to suffer a heavy financial loss — **take account of :** to take into account — **take advantage of 1 :** to use to advantage : profit by **2 :** to impose on : EXPLOIT; *also* : to exploit sexually — **take after :** to resemble in features, build, character, or disposition — **take a hike** *also* **take a walk :** to go away : LEAVE — **take aim at :** TARGET 1 ⟨new legislation that *takes aim at* crime⟩ — **take apart 1 :** to disconnect the pieces of : DISASSEMBLE **2 :** to treat roughly or harshly : tear into — **take a powder :** to leave hurriedly — **take care :** to be careful or watchful : exercise caution or prudence — **take care of :** to attend to or provide for the needs, operation, or treatment of — **take charge :** to assume care, custody, command, or control — **take effect 1 :** to become operative **2 :** to be effective — **take exception :** OBJECT ⟨*took exception* to the remark⟩ — **take five** *or* **take ten :** to take a break esp. from work — **take for :** to suppose to be; *esp* : to suppose mistakenly to be — **take for a ride :** TRICK, CHEAT — **take for granted 1 :** to assume as true, real, or expected **2 :** to value too lightly — **take heart :** to gain courage or confidence — **take hold 1 :** GRASP, GRIP, SEIZE **2 :** to become attached or established : take effect — **take into account :** to make allowance for — **take in vain :** to use (a name) profanely or without proper respect — **take issue :** DISAGREE — **take it on the chin :** to suffer from the results of a situation — **take kindly to :** to show an inclination to accept or approve — **take no prisoners :** to be merciless or relentless (as in exploiting an advantage) ⟨a politician who *takes no prisoners*⟩ — **take notice of :** to observe or treat with special attention — **take one's time :** to be leisurely about doing something — **take part :** JOIN, PARTICIPATE, SHARE — **take place :** HAPPEN, OCCUR — **take root 1 :** to become rooted **2 :** to become fixed or established — **take shape :** to assume a definite or distinctive form — **take ship :** set out on a voyage by ship — **take the cake :** to carry off the prize : rank first — **take the count 1** *of a boxer* **:** to be counted out **2 :** to go down in defeat — **take the floor :** to rise (as in a meeting or a legislative assembly) to make a formal address — **take the mickey** *Brit* **:** JOKE, KID — **take the mickey out of** *Brit* **:** to make fun of : TEASE — **take the plunge** : to do or undertake something decisively esp. after a period of hesitation or uncertainty — **take to** **1** : to go to or into ⟨*take to* the woods⟩ **2** : to apply or devote oneself to (as a practice, habit, or occupation) ⟨*take to* begging⟩ **3** : to adapt oneself to : respond to ⟨*takes to* water like a duck⟩ **4** : to conceive a liking for — **take to court** : to bring before a judicial body; *esp* : SUE 3 — **take to task** : to call to account for a shortcoming : CRITICIZE — **take to the cleaners** : to deprive of money or possessons : clean out — **take turns** : ALTERNATE

syn TAKE, SEIZE, GRASP, CLUTCH, SNATCH, GRAB mean to get hold of by or as if by catching up with the hand. TAKE is a general term applicable to any manner of getting something into one's possession or control ⟨*take* some salad from the bowl⟩. SEIZE implies a sudden and forcible movement in getting hold of something tangible or an apprehending of something fleeting or elusive when intangible ⟨*seized* the suspect⟩. GRASP stresses a laying hold so as to have firmly in possession ⟨*grasp* the handle and pull⟩. CLUTCH suggests avidity or anxiety in seizing or grasping and may imply less success in holding ⟨*clutching* her purse⟩. SNATCH suggests more suddenness or quickness but less force than SEIZE ⟨*snatched* a doughnut and ran⟩. GRAB implies more roughness or rudeness than SNATCH ⟨*grabbed* roughly by the arm⟩.

[2]**take** *n* (1654) **1** : something that is taken: **a** : the amount of money received : PROCEEDS, RECEIPTS, INCOME **b** : SHARE, CUT ⟨wanted a bigger ~⟩ **c** : the number or quantity (as of animals, fish, or pelts) taken at one time : CATCH, HAUL **d** : a section or installment done as a unit or at one time **e** (1) : a scene filmed or televised at one time without stopping the camera (2) : a sound recording made during a single recording period; *esp* : a trial recording **2** : an act or the action of taking: as **a** : the action of killing, capturing, or catching (as game or fish) **b** (1) : the uninterrupted photographing or televising of a scene (2) : the making of a sound recording **3 a** : a local or systemic reaction indicative of successful vaccination (as against smallpox) **b** : a successful union (as of a graft) **4** : a visible response or reaction (as to something unexpected) ⟨a delayed ~⟩ **5** : a distinct or personal point of view, outlook, or assessment ⟨was asked for her ~ on recent developments⟩; *also* : a distinct treatment or variation ⟨a new ~ on an old style⟩ — **on the take** : illegally paid for favors

take•away \ˈtāk-ə-ˌwā\ *n* (1961) **1** : the first movement of the backswing in golf **2** *chiefly Brit* : TAKEOUT **3** : an act or instance of taking possession of the ball or puck from an opposing team — **takeaway** *adj*

take back *vt* (1775) : to make a retraction of : WITHDRAW

take–charge \ˈtāk-ˈchärj\ *adj* (1954) : having the qualities of a forceful leader ⟨a ~ executive⟩

[1]**take•down** \ˈtāk-ˌdau̇n\ *n* (1893) **1** : the action or an act of taking down **2** : something (as a rifle) having takedown construction

[2]**take•down** \ˈtāk-ˈdau̇n\ *adj* (1907) : constructed so as to be readily taken apart ⟨a ~ rifle⟩

take down *vt* (15c) **1** : to lower without removing ⟨*took down* his pants⟩ **2 a** : to pull to pieces ⟨*take down* a building⟩ **b** : DISASSEMBLE ⟨*take* a rifle *down*⟩ **3** : to lower the spirit or vanity of **4 a** : to write down ⟨*took down* some notes⟩ **b** : to record by mechanical means ~ *vi* : to become seized or attacked esp. by illness

take–home pay \ˈtāk-ˌhōm-\ *n* (1943) : income remaining from salary or wages after deductions (as for income-tax withholding)

take–in \ˈtā-ˌkin\ *n* (1778) : an act of taking in esp. by deceiving

take in *vt* (ca. 1515) **1** : to draw into a smaller compass ⟨*take in* the slack of a line⟩: **a** : FURL **b** : to make (a garment) smaller by enlarging seams or tucks **2 a** : to receive as a guest or lodger **b** : to give shelter to **c** : to take to a police station as a prisoner **3** : to receive as payment or proceeds **4** : to receive (work) into one's house to be done for pay ⟨*take in* washing⟩ **5** : to encompass within its limits **6 a** : to include in an itinerary **b** : ATTEND ⟨*take in* a movie⟩ **7** : to receive into the mind : PERCEIVE ⟨*took in* the view⟩ **8** : DECEIVE, DUPE

taken *past part of* TAKE

take–no–prisoners *adj* (1978) : having a fierce, relentless, or merciless character ⟨~ politics⟩

take•off \ˈtāk-ˌȯf\ *n* (1846) **1** : an imitation esp. in the way of caricature **2 a** : a spot at which one takes off **b** : a starting point : point of departure **3 a** : a rise or leap from a surface in making a jump or flight or an ascent in an aircraft or in the launching of a rocket **b** : an action of starting out **c** : a rapid rise in activity, growth, or popularity ⟨an economic ~⟩ **4** : an action of removing something **5** : a mechanism for transmission of the power of an engine or vehicle to operate some other mechanism

take off *vt* (14c) **1** : REMOVE ⟨*take* your shoes *off*⟩ **2 a** : RELEASE ⟨*take* the brake *off*⟩ **b** : DISCONTINUE, WITHDRAW ⟨*took off* the morning train⟩ **c** : to take or allow as a discount : DEDUCT ⟨*took* 10 percent *off*⟩ **d** : to spend (a period of time) away from a usual occupation or activity ⟨*took* two weeks *off*⟩ **3** *slang* : ROB ~ *vi* **1** : to take away : DETRACT **2 a** : to start off or away often suddenly : SET OUT, DEPART ⟨*took off* for her trip⟩ **b** (1) : to branch off (as from a main stream or stem) (2) : to take a point of origin **c** : to begin a leap or spring **d** : to leave the surface : begin flight **e** : to embark on rapid activity, development, or growth **f** : to spring into wide use or popularity

take on *vt* (15c) **1 a** : to begin to perform or deal with : UNDERTAKE ⟨*took on* new responsibilities⟩ **b** : to contend with as an opponent ⟨*took on* the neighborhood bully⟩ **2** : ENGAGE, HIRE **3 a** : to assume or acquire as or as if one's own ⟨the city's plaza *takes on* a carnival air —W. T. LeViness⟩ **b** : to have as a mathematical domain or range ⟨what values does the function *take on*⟩ ~ *vi* : to show one's feelings esp. of grief or anger in a demonstrative way ⟨she cried, and *took on* like a distracted body —Daniel Defoe⟩

take•out \ˈtāk-ˌau̇t\ *n* (1917) **1** : the action or an act of taking out **2 a** : something taken out or prepared to be taken out **b** (1) : an article (as in a newspaper) printed on consecutive pages so as to be conveniently removed (2) : an intensive study or report **3 a** : prepared food packaged to be consumed away from its place of sale **b** : an establishment selling takeout

take–out \ˈtāk-ˌau̇t\ *adj* (1965) : of, relating to, selling, or being food not to be consumed on the premises ⟨~ counter⟩ ⟨a ~ supper⟩

take out *vt* (13c) **1 a** (1) : DEDUCT, SEPARATE (2) : EXCLUDE, OMIT (3) : WITHDRAW, WITHHOLD **b** : to find release for : VENT ⟨*take out* their resentments on one another —J. W. Aldridge⟩ **c** (1) : ELIMINATE (2) : KILL, DESTROY (3) : KNOCK OUT **2** : to take as an equivalent in another form ⟨*took* the debt *out* in trade⟩ **3 a** : to obtain from the proper authority ⟨*take out* a charter⟩ ⟨*take out* a second mortgage⟩ **b** : to arrange for (insurance) **4** : to overcall (a bridge partner) in a different suit ~ *vi* : to start on a course : SET OUT — **take it out on** : to expend anger, vexation, or frustration in harassment of

takeout double *n* (ca. 1944) : a double made in bridge to convey information to and request a bid from one's partner

take•over \ˈtāk-ˌō-vər\ *n* (ca. 1917) : the action or an act of taking over

take over *vt* (1884) : to assume control or possession of or responsibility for ⟨military leaders *took over* the government⟩ ~ *vi* **1** : to assume control or possession **2** : to become dominant

take–up \ˈtāk-ˌəp\ *n* (1838) : the action of taking up

take up *vt* (14c) **1** : PICK UP, LIFT ⟨*took up* the carpet⟩ **2 a** : to begin to occupy (land) **b** : to gather from a number of sources ⟨*took up* a collection⟩ **3 a** : to accept or adopt for the purpose of assisting **b** : to accept or adopt as one's own ⟨*took up* the life of a farmer⟩ **c** : to absorb or incorporate into itself ⟨plants *taking up* nutrients⟩ **4 a** : to enter upon (as a business, hobby, or subject of study) ⟨*take up* skiing⟩ ⟨*took up* the trumpet⟩ **b** : to proceed to consider or deal with ⟨*take up* one problem at a time⟩ **5** : to establish oneself in ⟨*took up* residence in town⟩ **6** : to occupy entirely or exclusively : fill up ⟨the meeting was *taken up* with old business⟩ **7** : to make tighter or shorter ⟨*take up* the slack⟩ **8** : to respond favorably to (as a person offering a bet, challenge, or proposal) ⟨*took* me *up* on it⟩ **9** : to begin again or take over from another ⟨we must *take* the good work *up* again⟩ ~ *vi* **1** : to make a beginning where another has left off **2** : to become shortened : draw together : SHRINK — **take up the cudgels** : to engage vigorously in a defense or dispute — **take up with** **1** : to become interested or absorbed in **2** : to begin to associate or consort with

ta•kin \ˈtä-ˌkēn\ *n* [Mishmi (Tibeto-Burman language of northeast India)] (1850) : a large heavily built bovid (*Budorcas taxicolor*) of Tibet and adjacent areas of Asia that is related to the goats and the musk ox and that has horns in both sexes arising near the midline of the head and sweeping abruptly outward and then backward and upward

tak•ings \ˈtā-kiŋz\ *n pl* (1606) *chiefly Brit* : receipts esp. of money

[1]**ta•la** \ˈtä-lə\ *n* [Skt *tāla,* lit., hand-clapping] (1891) : one of the ancient traditional rhythmic patterns of South Asian music — compare RAGA

[2]**ta•la** \ˈtä-lə, -(ˌ)lä\ *n, pl* **tala** [Samoan, fr. E *dollar*] (1967) — see MONEY table

Tal•bot \ˈtȯl-bət, ˈtal-\ *n* [prob. fr. *Talbot,* name of a Norman family in England] (1562) : a large heavy mostly white hound with pendulous ears and drooping flews held to be ancestral to the bloodhound

talc \ˈtalk\ *n* [F, fr. MF *talk,* fr. ML *talc, talcum,* fr. Ar *ṭalq*] (1610) **1** : a very soft mineral that is a basic silicate of magnesium, has a soapy feel, and is used esp. in making talcum powder **2** : TALCUM POWDER — **talc•ose** \ˈtal-ˌkōs\ *adj*

tal•cum powder \ˈtal-kəm-\ *n* [ML *talcum* talc] (ca. 1890) **1** : powdered talc **2** : a toilet powder composed of perfumed talc or talc and a mild antiseptic

tale \ˈtāl\ *n* [ME, fr. OE *talu;* akin to ON *tala* talk] (bef. 12c) **1** *obs* : DISCOURSE, TALK **2 a** : a series of events or facts told or presented : ACCOUNT **b** (1) : a report of a private or confidential matter ⟨dead men tell no ~*s*⟩ (2) : a libelous report or piece of gossip **3 a** : a usu. imaginative narrative of an event : STORY **b** : an intentionally untrue report : FALSEHOOD ⟨always preferred the ~ to the truth —Sir Winston Churchill⟩ **4 a** : COUNT, TALLY **b** : TOTAL

tale•bear•er \-ˌber-ər\ *n* (15c) : one that spreads gossip or rumors; *also* : TATTLETALE — **tale•bear•ing** \-iŋ\ *adj or n*

ta•leg•gio \tä-ˈle-j(ē-)ō\ *n, usu cap* [It, fr. *Taleggio* commune and valley in Italy] (1952) : a creamy cheese made from the whole milk of cows

tal•ent \ˈta-lənt\ *n* [ME, fr. OE *talente,* fr. L *talenta,* pl. of *talentum* unit of weight or money, fr. Gk *talanton* pan of a scale, weight; akin to Gk *tlēnai* to bear; in senses 2–5, fr. the parable of the talents in Mt 25:14–30 — more at TOLERATE] (bef. 12c) **1 a** : any of several ancient units of weight **b** : a unit of value equal to the value of a talent of gold or silver **2** *archaic* : a characteristic feature, aptitude, or disposition of a person or animal **3** : the natural endowments of a person **4 a** : a special often athletic, creative, or artistic aptitude **b** : general intelligence or mental power : ABILITY **5** : a person of talent or a group of persons of talent in a field or activity ***syn*** see GIFT — **tal•ent•ed** \-lən-təd\ *adj* — **tal•ent•less** \-lənt-ləs\ *adj*

talent scout *n* (1936) : a person engaged in discovering and recruiting people of talent for a specialized field or activity

talent show *n* (1953) : a show consisting of a series of individual performances (as singing) by amateurs who may be selected for special recognition as performing talent

ta•ler *also* **tha•ler** \ˈtä-lər\ *n* [G — more at DOLLAR] (ca. 1905) : any of numerous silver coins issued by various German states from the 15th to the 19th centuries

tales•man \ˈtālz-mən, ˈtā-lēz-\ *n* [ME *tales* talesmen, fr. ML *tales de circumstantibus* such (persons) of the bystanders; fr. the wording of the writ summoning them] (1679) **1** : a person added to a jury usu. from among bystanders to make up a deficiency in the available number of jurors **2** : a member of a large pool of persons called for jury duty from which jurors are selected

tale–tell•er \ˈtāl-ˌte-lər\ *n* (14c) **1** : one who tells tales or stories **2** : TALEBEARER — **tale–tell•ing** \-ˌte-liŋ\ *adj or n*

tali *pl of* TALUS

Tal•i•ban \ˈtä-li-bän, ˈta-li-ˌban\ *n pl* [Pashto & Pers *ṭālibān,* pl. of *ṭālib* student, seeker, fr. Ar] (1992) : a fundamentalist Islamic militia in Afghanistan

tali•pes \ˈta-lə-ˌpēz\ *n* [NL, fr. L *talus* ankle + *pes* foot — more at FOOT] (ca. 1841) : CLUBFOOT

tal•is•man \ˈta-ləs-mən, -ləz-\ *n, pl* **-mans** [F *talisman* or Sp *talismán* or It *talismano;* all fr. Ar *ṭilsam,* fr. MGk *telesma,* fr. Gk, consecration, fr. *telein* to initiate into the mysteries, complete, fr. *telos* end — more at TELOS] (1638) **1** : an object held to act as a charm to avert evil and bring good fortune **2** : something producing apparently magical or miraculous effects — **tal•is•man•ic** \ˌta-ləs-ˈma-nik, -ləz-\ *adj* — **tal•is•man•i•cal•ly** \-ni-k(ə-)lē\ *adv*

[1]**talk** \ˈtȯk\ *vb* [ME; akin to OE *talu* tale] *vt* (13c) **1** : to deliver or express in speech : UTTER **2** : to make the subject of conversation or discourse : DISCUSS ⟨~ business⟩ **3** : to influence, affect, or cause by

talking ⟨~*ed* them into going⟩ **4 :** to use (a language) for conversing or communicating : SPEAK ~ *vi* **1 a :** to express or exchange ideas by means of spoken words **b :** to convey information or communicate in any way (as with signs or sounds) ⟨can make a trumpet ~⟩ ⟨make the computer ~ to the printer⟩ **2 :** to use speech : SPEAK **3 a :** to speak idly : PRATE **b :** GOSSIP **c :** to reveal secret or confidential information **4 :** to give a talk : LECTURE — **talk·er** *n* — **talk back :** to answer impertinently — **talk sense :** to voice rational, logical, or sensible thoughts — **talk through one's hat :** to voice irrational, illogical, or erroneous ideas — **talk turkey :** to speak frankly or bluntly

[2]**talk** *n* (14c) **1 :** the act or an instance of talking : SPEECH **2 :** a way of speaking : LANGUAGE **3 :** pointless or fruitless discussion : VERBIAGE **4 :** a formal discussion, negotiation, or exchange of views — often used in pl. **5 a :** MENTION, REPORT **b :** RUMOR, GOSSIP **6 :** the topic of interested comment, conversation, or gossip ⟨it's the ~ of the town⟩ **7 a :** ADDRESS, LECTURE **b :** written analysis or discussion presented in an informal or conversational manner **8 :** communicative sounds or signs resembling or functioning as talk ⟨bird ~⟩

talk·a·thon \ˈtȯ-kə-ˌthän\ *n* (1934) **:** a long session of discussion or speech-making

talk·a·tive \ˈtȯ-kə-tiv\ *adj* (15c) **:** given to talking; *also* **:** full of talk — **talk·a·tive·ly** *adv* — **talk·a·tive·ness** *n*

syn TALKATIVE, LOQUACIOUS, GARRULOUS, VOLUBLE mean given to talk or talking. TALKATIVE may imply a readiness to engage in talk or a disposition to enjoy conversation ⟨a *talkative* neighbor⟩. LOQUACIOUS suggests the power of expressing oneself articulately, fluently, or glibly ⟨a *loquacious* spokesperson⟩. GARRULOUS implies prosy, rambling, or tedious loquacity ⟨*garrulous* traveling companions⟩. VOLUBLE suggests a free, easy, and unending loquacity ⟨a *voluble* raconteur⟩.

talk down *vi* (1844) **:** to speak in a condescending or oversimplified fashion ~ *vt* **:** to disparage or belittle by talking

talk·ie \ˈtȯ-kē\ *n* (1913) **:** a motion picture with a synchronized sound track

talking book *n* (1932) **:** AUDIOBOOK

talking head *n* (1968) **:** the televised head and shoulders shot of a person talking; *also* **:** a television personality who appears in such shots

talking machine *n* (1889) **:** an early phonograph

talking point *n* (ca. 1914) **:** something that lends support to an argument; *also* **:** a subject of discussion

talk·ing–to \ˈtȯ-kiŋ-ˌtü\ *n* (ca. 1875) **:** REPRIMAND, LECTURE

talk out *vt* (1954) **:** to clarify or settle by oral discussion

talk over *vt* (1734) **:** to review or consider in conversation : DISCUSS

talk radio *n* (1972) **:** radio programming consisting of call-in shows

talk show *n* (1965) **:** a radio or television program in which usu. well-known persons engage in discussions or are interviewed

talk therapy *n* (1979) **:** psychotherapy emphasizing conversation between therapist and patient

talk up *vt* (1722) **:** to discuss favorably : ADVOCATE, PROMOTE ⟨*talk up* the new product⟩ ~ *vi* **:** to speak up plainly or directly

talky \ˈtȯ-kē\ *adj* **talk·i·er; -est** (1815) **1 :** TALKATIVE **2 :** containing too much talk — **talk·i·ness** \-nəs\ *n*

tall \ˈtȯl\ *adj* [ME *tal,* prob. fr. OE *getæl* quick, ready; akin to OHG *gizal* quick] (15c) **1** *obs* **:** BRAVE, COURAGEOUS **2 a :** high in stature **b :** of a specified height ⟨five feet ~⟩ **3 a :** of considerable height ⟨~ trees⟩ **b :** long from bottom to top ⟨a ~ book⟩ **c :** of a higher growing variety or species of plant **4 a :** large or formidable in amount, extent, or degree ⟨a ~ order to fill⟩ **b :** POMPOUS, HIGH-FLOWN ⟨~ talk about the vast mysteries of life —W. A. White⟩ **c :** highly exaggerated : INCREDIBLE, IMPROBABLE ⟨a ~ story⟩ ***syn*** see HIGH — **tall** *adv* — **tall·ish** \ˈtȯ-lish\ *adj* — **tall·ness** \ˈtȯl-nəs\ *n*

tal·lage \ˈta-lij\ *n* [ME *taillage, tallage,* fr. AF, fr. *tailler* to cut, limit, tax — more at TAILOR] (14c) **:** an impost or due levied by a lord upon his tenants

tall·boy \ˈtȯl-ˌbȯi\ *n* (1769) **1 a :** HIGHBOY **b :** a double chest of drawers usu. with the upper section slightly smaller than the lower **2** *Brit* **:** CLOTHESPRESS

tall fescue *n* (ca. 1762) **:** a European fescue (*Festuca elatior* syn. *F. arundinacea*) with erect smooth stems three to four feet (about one meter) high that has been introduced into No. America — called also *tall fescue grass;* compare FESCUE FOOT

tall·grass prairie \ˈtȯl-ˌgras-\ *n* (1920) **:** PRAIRIE 2a

tal·lith \ˈtä-ləs, ˈta-, -lət, -ləth\ *or* **tal·lis** \-ləs\ *n* [Heb *ṭallīth* cover, cloak] (1613) **:** a shawl with fringed corners worn over the head or shoulders by Jewish men esp. during morning prayers

tall oil \ˈtäl-, ˈtȯl-\ *n* [part trans. of G *Tallöl,* part trans. of Sw *tallolja,* fr. *tall* pine + *olja* oil] (ca. 1926) **:** a resinous by-product from the manufacture of chemical wood pulp used esp. in making soaps, coatings, and oils

[1]**tal·low** \ˈta-(ˌ)lō\ *n* [ME *talgh, talow;* akin to MD *talch* tallow] (14c) **:** the white nearly tasteless solid rendered fat of cattle and sheep used chiefly in soap, candles, and lubricants — **tal·lowy** \ˈta-lə-wē\ *adj*

[2]**tallow** *vt* (15c) **:** to grease or smear with tallow

tall ship *n* (ca. 1548) **:** a sailing vessel with at least two masts; *esp* **:** SQUARE-RIGGER

[1]**tal·ly** \ˈta-lē\ *n, pl* **tallies** [ME *talye,* fr. AF *talie, taille,* in part fr. *tailler* to cut, measure, count; in part fr. ML *tallia,* alter. of L *talea* plant cutting, thin piece of wood] (15c) **1 :** a device (as a notched rod or mechanical counter) for visibly recording or accounting esp. business transactions **2 a :** a recorded reckoning or account (as of items or charges) ⟨keep a daily ~ of accidents⟩ **b :** a score or point made (as in a game) **3 a :** a part that corresponds to an opposite or companion member : COMPLEMENT **b :** a state of correspondence or agreement

[2]**tally** *vb* **tal·lied; tal·ly·ing** *vt* (15c) **1 a :** to record on or as if on a tally : TABULATE **b :** to list or check off (as a cargo) by items **c :** to register (as a score) in a contest **2 :** to make a count of : RECKON **3 :** to cause to correspond ~ *vi* **1 a :** to make a tally by or as if by tabulating **b :** to register a point in a contest : SCORE **2 :** CORRESPOND, MATCH

tal·ly·ho \ˌta-lē-ˈhō\ *n, pl* **-hos** [prob. fr. F *taïaut,* a cry used to excite hounds in deer hunting] (1772) **1 :** a call of a huntsman at sight of the fox **2** [*Tally-ho,* name of a coach formerly plying between London and Birmingham] **:** a four-in-hand coach

tal·ly·man \ˈta-lē-mən, -ˌman\ *n* (1654) **1** *Brit* **:** one who sells goods on the installment plan **2 :** one who tallies, checks, or keeps an account or record (as of receipt of goods)

Tal·mud \ˈtäl-ˌmu̇d, ˈtal-məd\ *n* [LHeb *talmūdh,* lit., instruction] (1532) **:** the authoritative body of Jewish tradition comprising the Mishnah and Gemara — **Tal·mu·dic** \tal-ˈmü-dik, -ˈmyü-, -ˈmə-; täl-ˈmu̇-\ *adj* — **tal·mud·ism** \ˈtäl-ˌmu̇-ˌdi-zəm, ˈtal-, -mə-\ *n, often cap*

Tal·mud·ist \ˈtäl-ˌmu̇-dist, ˈtal-, -mə-\ *n* (1569) **:** a specialist in Talmudic studies

tal·on \ˈta-lən\ *n* [ME *taloun* heel, hind claw of a bird of prey, fr. AF *talun,* fr. VL **talon-, *talo,* fr. L *talus* ankle, anklebone] (15c) **1 a :** the claw of an animal and esp. of a bird of prey **b :** a finger or hand of a human being **2 :** a part or object shaped like or suggestive of a heel or claw: as **a :** an ogee molding **b :** the shoulder of the bolt of a lock on which the key acts to shoot the bolt **3 a :** cards laid aside in a pile in solitaire **b :** STOCK 10c — **tal·oned** \-lənd\ *adj*

[1]**ta·lus** \ˈtā-ləs, ˈta-\ *n* [F, fr. MF, prob. fr. VL **talutum* side, slope; akin to L *talutium* slope indicating presence of gold under the soil] (1645) **1 :** a slope formed esp. by an accumulation of rock debris **2 :** rock debris at the base of a cliff

[2]**ta·lus** \ˈtā-ləs\ *n, pl* **ta·li** \ˈtā-ˌlī\ [NL, fr. L] (1578) **1 :** the human tarsal bone that bears the weight of the body and that together with the tibia and fibula forms the ankle joint **2 :** the entire ankle

tam \ˈtam\ *n* (1895) **:** TAM-O'-SHANTER

ta·ma·le \tə-ˈmä-lē\ *n* [MexSp *tamales,* pl. of *tamal* tamale, fr. Nahuatl *tamalli* steamed cornmeal dough] (1854) **:** cornmeal dough rolled with ground meat or beans seasoned usu. with chili, wrapped usu. in corn husks, and steamed

ta·man·dua \tə-ˈman-də-wə, -ˌman-də-ˈwä\ *n* [Pg *tamanduá,* fr. Tupi *tamanuá, tamanduá*] (1834) **:** either of two arboreal anteaters (*Tamandua mexicana* and *T. tetradactyla*) of Central and So. America having a nearly hairless tail

tam·a·rack \ˈta-mə-ˌrak, ˈtam-ˌrak\ *n* [origin unknown] (1805) **1 :** any of several American larches; *esp* **:** a larch (*Larix laricina*) of northern No. America that inhabits usu. moist or wet areas **2 :** the wood of a tamarack

ta·ma·ri \tə-ˈmär-ē\ *n* [Jp] (1965) **:** an aged soy sauce prepared with little or no added wheat

tam·a·ril·lo \ˌta-mə-ˈri-(ˌ)lō\ *n* [alter. of *tomatillo*] (1966) **:** the reddish edible fruit of an arborescent shrub (*Cyphomandra betacea*) of the nightshade family that is native to So. America but is grown commercially elsewhere; *also* **:** the shrub itself

tam·a·rin \ˈta-mə-rən, -ˌran\ *n* [F *tamary, tamarin,* perh. of Tupian origin] (1780) **:** any of numerous small chiefly So. American monkeys (genera *Saguinus* and *Leontopithecus*) that are related to the marmosets and have silky fur, a long tail, and lower canine teeth that are longer than the incisors

tam·a·rind \ˈta-mə-rənd, -ˌrind\ *n* [Sp & Pg *tamarindo,* fr. Ar *tamr hindī,* lit., Indian date] (15c) **:** a tropical Old World tree (*Tamarindus indica*) of the legume family with hard yellowish wood, pinnate leaves, and red-striped yellow flowers; *also* **:** its fruit which has an acid pulp often used for preserves or in a cooling laxative drink

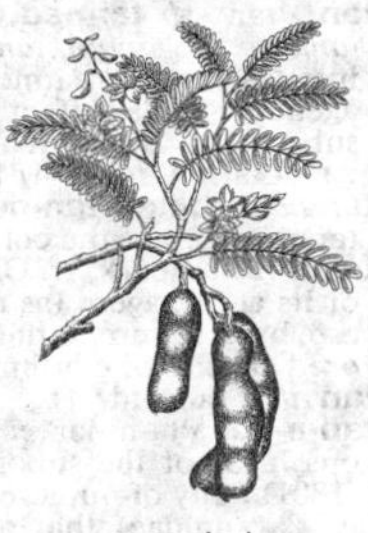

tamarind

tam·a·risk \ˈta-mə-ˌrisk\ *n* [ME *tamarisc,* fr. LL *tamariscus,* fr. L *tamaric-, tamarix*] (14c) **:** any of a genus (*Tamarix* of the family Tamaricaceae, the tamarisk family) of chiefly Old World desert shrubs and trees having tiny narrow leaves and masses of minute flowers with five stamens and a one-celled ovary — called also *salt cedar*

tam·ba·la \täm-ˈbä-lə\ *n, pl* **-la** *or* **-las** [Nyanja (Bantu language of Malawi), lit., cockerel] (1970) — see *kwacha* at MONEY table

[1]**tam·bour** \ˈtam-ˌbu̇r, tam-ˈ\ *n* [MF, drum, fr. Ar *ṭanbūr,* modif. of Pers *tabīr*] (15c) **1 :** [1]DRUM 1 **2 a :** an embroidery frame; *esp* **:** a set of two interlocking hoops between which cloth is stretched before stitching **b :** embroidery made on a tambour frame **3 :** a shallow metallic cup or drum with a thin elastic membrane supporting a writing lever used to transmit and register slight motions (as arterial pulsations) **4 :** a rolling top or front (as of a rolltop desk) of narrow strips of wood glued on canvas

[2]**tambour** *vt* (1774) **:** to embroider (cloth) with tambour ~ *vi* **:** to work at a tambour frame — **tam·bour·er** *n*

tam·bou·ra *or* **tam·bu·ra** \tam-ˈbu̇r-ə\ *n* [Pers *ṭambūra*] (1585) **:** an Asian musical instrument resembling a lute in construction but without frets and used to produce a drone accompaniment to singing

tam·bou·rine \ˌtam-bə-ˈrēn\ *n* [MF *tambourin,* dim. of *tambour*] (1579) **:** a small drum; *esp* **:** a shallow one-headed drum with loose metallic disks at the sides played esp. by shaking or striking with the hand

[1]**tame** \ˈtām\ *adj* **tam·er; tam·est** [ME, fr. OE *tam;* akin to OHG *zam* tame, L *domare* to tame, Gk *damnanai*] (bef. 12c) **1 :** reduced from a state of native wildness esp. so as to be tractable and useful to humans : DOMESTICATED ⟨~ animals⟩ **2 :** made docile and submissive : SUBDUED **3 :** lacking spirit, zest, interest, or the capacity to excite : INSIPID ⟨a ~ campaign⟩ — **tame·ly** *adv* — **tame·ness** *n*

[2]**tame** *vb* **tamed; tam·ing** *vt* (13c) **1 a :** to reduce from a wild to a domestic state **b :** to subject to cultivation **c :** to bring under control : HARNESS **2 :** to deprive of spirit : HUMBLE, SUBDUE ⟨the once revolutionary . . . party, long since *tamed* —*Times Lit. Supp.*⟩ **3 :** to tone down : SOFTEN ⟨*tamed* the language in the play⟩ ~ *vi* **:** to become tame — **tam·able** *or* **tame·able** \ˈtā-mə-bəl\ *adj* — **tam·er** *n*

tame·less \ˈtām-ləs\ *adj* (ca. 1598) **:** not tamed or not capable of being tamed

Tam·il \ˈta-məl, ˈtä-\ *n* [Tamil *Tamiẓ;* akin to Pali *Damiḷa,* a Dravidian-speaking people, Skt *Dravida*] (1734) **1 :** a Dravidian language of Tamil Nadu state, India, and of northern and eastern Sri Lanka **2 :** a Tamil-speaking person or a descendant of Tamil-speaking ancestors

Tam·ma·ny \ˈta-mə-nē\ *adj* [*Tammany Hall,* headquarters of the Tammany Society, political organization in New York City] (1872) **:** of, relating to, or constituting a group or organization exercising or seeking municipal political control by methods often associated with corruption and bossism — **Tam·ma·ny·ism** \-ˌi-zəm\ *n*

Tam·muz \ˈtä-ˌmu̇z\ *n* [Heb *Tammūz*] (1614) **:** the 10th month of the civil year or the 4th month of the ecclesiastical year in the Jewish calendar — see MONTH table

Tam o' Shan·ter *n* (1791) **1** \ˌta-mə-ˈshan-tər\ **:** the hero of Burns's poem *Tam o' Shanter* **2** *usu* **tam–o'–shanter** \ˈta-mə-ˌ\ **:** a woolen cap of Scottish origin with a tight headband, wide flat circular crown, and usu. a pompon in the center

ta·mox·i·fen \tə-ˈmäk-sə-ˌfen\ *n* [prob. by recombination & alter. of *trans-, oxy,* and *clomiphene*] (1972) **:** an estrogen antagonist $C_{26}H_{29}NO$ used in the form of its citrate esp. to treat postmenopausal breast cancer

[1]**tamp** \ˈtamp\ *vt* [prob. back-formation fr. obs. *tampion, tampin* plug, fr. ME, fr. MF *tapon, tampon,* of Gmc origin; akin to OHG *zapho* tap — more at TAP] (1834) **1 :** to drive in or down by a succession of light or medium blows ⟨~ wet concrete⟩ **2 :** to put a check on **:** REDUCE, LESSEN ⟨~ down rumors⟩ — **tamp·er** *n*

[2]**tamp** *n* (1920) **:** a tool for tamping

tam·per \ˈtam-pər\ *vi* **tam·pered; tam·per·ing** \-p(ə-)riŋ\ [prob. fr. MF *temprer* to temper, mix, meddle — more at TEMPER] (1567) **1 :** to carry on underhand or improper negotiations (as by bribery) **2 a :** to interfere so as to weaken or change for the worse — used with *with* ⟨did not want to ~ with tradition⟩ **b :** to try foolish or dangerous experiments — used with *with* **c :** to render something harmful or dangerous by altering its structure or composition ⟨was charged with ~*ing* with consumer products⟩ — **tam·per·er** \-pər-ər\ *n* — **tam·per-proof** \ˈtam-pər-ˌprüf\ *adj*

tam·pi·on \ˈtam-pē-ən, ˈtäm-\ *also* **tom·pi·on** \ˈtäm-pē-ən\ *n* [obs. *tampion, tampin* plug — more at TAMP] (ca. 1625) **:** a wooden plug or a metal or canvas cover for the muzzle of a gun

[1]**tam·pon** \ˈtam-ˌpän\ *n* [F, lit., plug, fr. MF — more at TAMP] (1848) **:** a wad of absorbent material (as of cotton) introduced into a body cavity or canal usu. to absorb secretions (as from menstruation) or to arrest hemorrhaging

[2]**tampon** *vt* (1860) **:** to place or insert a tampon into

tam–tam \ˈtam-ˌtam, ˈtäm-ˌtäm\ *n* [Hindi & Urdu *ṭamṭam*] (1782) **1 :** TOM-TOM **2 :** GONG; *esp* **:** one of a tuned set in a gamelan orchestra

Tam·worth \ˈtam-(ˌ)wərth\ *n* [*Tamworth,* borough in Staffordshire, England] (1860) **:** any of a breed of large long-bodied red swine developed in England esp. for the production of bacon

[1]**tan** \ˈtan\ *vb* **tanned; tan·ning** [ME *tannen,* fr. AF *tanner,* fr. ML *tannare,* fr. *tanum, tannum* tanbark] *vt* (13c) **1 a :** to convert (hide) into leather by treatment with an infusion of tannin-rich bark or other agent of similar effect **b :** to convert (protein) to leather or a similar substance **2 :** to make (skin) tan esp. by exposure to the sun **3 :** THRASH, WHIP ~ *vi* **:** to get or become tanned

[2]**tan** *adj* **tan·ner; tan·nest** (1586) **1 :** of, relating to, or used for tan or tanning **2 :** of the color tan

[3]**tan** *n* [F, tanbark, fr. OF, fr. ML *tanum*] (1674) **1 :** a tanning material or its active agent (as tannin) **2 :** a brown color imparted to the skin esp. by exposure to the sun **3 :** a light yellowish brown **4** *pl* **:** tan-colored articles of clothing

[4]**tan** *abbr* tangent

tan·a·ger \ˈta-ni-jər\ *n* [NL *tanagra,* modif. of Pg *tangará,* any of various birds of the suboscine family Pipridae, fr. Tupi *tagará, taŋgará*] (1801) **:** any of numerous chiefly tropical American oscine birds (family Thraupidae) that are often brightly colored and inhabit mostly woodlands — compare SCARLET TANAGER

tan·bark \ˈtan-ˌbärk\ *n* (1799) **1 :** a bark rich in tannin bruised or cut into small pieces and used in tanning **2 :** a surface (as a circus ring) covered with spent tanbark

T & A *n* [*t*its & *a*ss] (1979) **:** curvaceous and often scantily clothed women; *also* **:** entertainment featuring such women

[1]**tan·dem** \ˈtan-dəm\ *n* [L, at last, at length (taken to mean "lengthwise"), fr. *tam* so; akin to OE *thæt* that] (ca. 1785) **1 a** (1) **:** a 2-seated carriage drawn by horses harnessed one before the other (2) **:** a team so harnessed **b :** TANDEM BICYCLE **c :** a vehicle (as a motortruck) having close-coupled pairs of axles **2 :** a group of two or more arranged one behind the other or used or acting in conjunction — **in tandem 1 :** in a tandem arrangement **2 :** in partnership or conjunction

[2]**tandem** *adv* (ca. 1795) **:** one after or behind another ⟨ride ~⟩

[3]**tandem** *adj* (1815) **1 :** consisting of things or having parts arranged one behind the other **2 :** working or occurring in conjunction with each other

tandem bicycle *n* (ca. 1890) **:** a bicycle for usu. two persons sitting tandem

tandem repeat *n* (1973) **:** any of several identical DNA segments lying one after the other in a sequence

tan·door \tän-ˈdu̇r\ *n* [Hindi & Urdu *tandūr, tannūr,* fr. Pers *tanūr,* fr. Ar *tannūr*] (1840) **:** a cylindrical clay oven in which food is cooked over charcoal

tan·doori \tän-ˈdu̇r-ē\ *adj* [Hindi & Urdu *tandūrī,* fr. *tandūr*] (1958) **:** cooked in a tandoor ⟨~ chicken⟩ — **tandoori** *n*

[1]**tang** \ˈtaŋ\ *n* [ME, of Scand origin; akin to ON *tangi* point of land, tang] (15c) **1 :** a projecting shank, prong, fang, or tongue (as on a knife, file, or sword) to connect with the handle **2 a :** a sharp distinctive often lingering flavor **b :** a pungent odor **c :** something having the effect of a tang (as in stimulation of the senses) ⟨the ~ of the autumn air⟩ ⟨add ~ to your writing⟩ **3 a :** a faint suggestion **:** TRACE ⟨my comment held a ~ of sarcasm⟩ **b :** a distinguishing characteristic that sets apart or gives a special individuality **4 :** any of various surgeonfishes — compare BLUE TANG — **tanged** \ˈtaŋd\ *adj*

[2]**tang** *vt* (1566) **1 :** to furnish with a tang **2 :** to affect with a tang

[3]**tang** *vb* [imit.] (1556) **:** CLANG, RING

[4]**tang** *n* (1686) **:** a sharp twanging sound

Tang *or* **T'ang** \ˈtäŋ\ *n* [Chin (Beijing) *Táng*] (1669) **:** a Chinese dynasty dated A.D. 618–907 and marked by wide contacts with other cultures and by the development of printing and the flourishing of poetry and art

tan·ga \tən-ˈga\ *n, pl* **tanga** [Tajik, fr. Tajik & Pers, a silver coin, cash] (2000) **:** a former monetary unit equal to 1/100 Tajikistan ruble

tan·ge·lo \ˈtan-jə-ˌlō\ *n, pl* **-los** [*tangerine* + pom*elo*] (1903) **:** the fruit of a tree (*Citrus* × *tangelo*) that is a hybrid between a tangerine or mandarin orange and a grapefruit; *also* **:** the tree

tan·gen·cy \ˈtan-jən(t)-sē\ *n, pl* **-cies** (1819) **:** the quality or state of being tangent

[1]**tan·gent** \ˈtan-jənt\ *adj* [L *tangent-, tangens,* prp. of *tangere* to touch; perh. akin to OE *thaccian* to touch gently, stroke] (1594) **1 a :** meeting a curve or surface in a single point if a sufficiently small interval is considered ⟨straight line ~ to a curve⟩ **b** (1) **:** having a common tangent line at a point ⟨~ curves⟩ (2) **:** having a common tangent plane at a point ⟨~ surfaces⟩ **2 :** diverging from an original purpose or course **:** IRRELEVANT ⟨~ remarks⟩

[2]**tangent** *n* [NL *tangent-, tangens,* fr. *linea tangens* tangent line] (1594) **1 a :** the trigonometric function that for an acute angle is the ratio between the leg opposite to the angle when it is considered part of a right triangle and the leg adjacent **b :** a trigonometric function that is equal to the sine divided by the cosine for all real numbers θ for which the cosine is not equal to zero and is exactly equal to the tangent of an angle of measure θ in radians **2 :** a line that is tangent; *specif* **:** a straight line that is the limiting position of a secant of a curve through a fixed point and a variable point on the curve as the variable point approaches the fixed point **3 :** an abrupt change of course **:** DIGRESSION ⟨the speaker went off on a ~⟩ **4 :** a small upright flat-ended metal pin at the inner end of a clavichord key that strikes the string to produce the tone

tan·gen·tial \tan-ˈjen(t)-shəl\ *adj* (1630) **1 :** of, relating to, or of the nature of a tangent **2 :** acting along or lying in a tangent ⟨~ forces⟩ **3 a :** DIVERGENT, DIGRESSIVE **b :** touching lightly **:** INCIDENTAL, PERIPHERAL ⟨~ involvement⟩; *also* **:** of little relevance ⟨arguments ~ to the main point⟩ — **tan·gen·tial·ly** \-ˈjen(t)-sh(ə-)lē\ *adv*

tangent plane *n* (1856) **:** the plane through a point of a surface that contains the tangent lines to all the curves on the surface through the same point

tan·ger·ine \ˈtan-jə-ˌrēn, ˌtan-jə-ˈ\ *n* [*Tangerine (orange),* fr. F *Tanger* Tangier, Morocco + E [1]*-ine*] (1842) **1 a :** any of various mandarin oranges that have usu. deep orange skin and pulp; *broadly* **:** MANDARIN 3b **b :** a tree producing tangerines **2 :** a moderate to strong reddish orange

[1]**tan·gi·ble** \ˈtan-jə-bəl\ *adj* [LL *tangibilis,* fr. L *tangere* to touch] (1589) **1 a :** capable of being perceived esp. by the sense of touch **:** PALPABLE **b :** substantially real **:** MATERIAL **2 :** capable of being precisely identified or realized by the mind ⟨her grief was ~⟩ **3 :** capable of being appraised at an actual or approximate value ⟨~ assets⟩ ***syn*** see PERCEPTIBLE — **tan·gi·bil·i·ty** \ˌtan-jə-ˈbi-lə-tē\ *n* — **tan·gi·ble·ness** \ˈtan-jə-bəl-nəs\ *n* — **tan·gi·bly** \-blē\ *adv*

[2]**tangible** *n* (1890) **:** something tangible; *esp* **:** a tangible asset

[1]**tan·gle** \ˈtaŋ-gəl\ *vb* **tan·gled; tan·gling** \-g(ə-)liŋ\ [ME *tanglen, tagilen,* prob. short for *entanglen,* fr. AF *entagler, entangler* to prosecute (for), implicate] *vt* (14c) **1 :** to involve so as to hamper, obstruct, or embarrass **2 :** to seize and hold in or as if in a snare **:** ENTRAP **3 :** to unite or knit together in intricate confusion ~ *vi* **1 :** to interact in a contentious or conflicting way **2 :** to become entangled

[2]**tangle** *n* (1615) **1 :** a tangled twisted mass **:** SNARL **2 a :** a complicated or confused state or condition **b :** a state of perplexity or complete bewilderment **3 :** a serious altercation **:** DISPUTE **4 :** NEUROFIBRILLARY TANGLE

[3]**tangle** *n* [of Scand origin; akin to ON *thǫngull* tangle, *thang* seaweed] (1536) **:** a large seaweed

tangled *adj* (1596) **1 :** existing in or giving the appearance of a state of utter disorder **2 :** very involved **:** exceedingly complex

tan·gle·ment \-gəl-mənt\ *n* (1831) **:** ENTANGLEMENT

tan·gly \ˈtaŋ-g(ə-)lē\ *adj* (1813) **:** full of tangles or knots **:** INTRICATE

[1]**tan·go** \ˈtaŋ-(ˌ)gō\ *n, pl* **tangos** [AmerSp] (1913) **1 :** a ballroom dance of Latin-American origin in 2/4 time with a basic pattern of step-step-step-step-close and characterized by long pauses and stylized body positions; *also* **:** the music for this dance **2 :** interaction marked by a lack of straightforwardness ⟨the suspect's ~ with police⟩

[2]**tango** *vi* (1913) **:** to dance the tango

Tango (1952) — a communications code word for the letter *t*

tan·gram \ˈtaŋ-grəm, ˈtan-\ *n* [perh. fr. Chin (Beijing) *táng* Chinese + E *-gram*] (1861) **:** a Chinese puzzle made by cutting a square of thin material into five triangles, a square, and a rhomboid which are capable of being recombined in many different figures

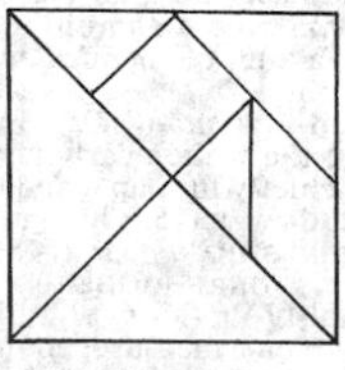

tangram

tangy \ˈtaŋ-ē\ *adj* **tang·i·er; -est** (1875) **:** having or suggestive of a tang

[1]**tank** \ˈtaŋk\ *n* [Pg *tanque,* alter. of *estanque,* fr. *estancar* to stanch, perh. fr. VL **stanticare* — more at STANCH] (1609) **1** *dial* **:** POND, POOL; *esp* **:** one built as a water supply **2 :** a usu. large receptacle for holding, transporting, or storing liquids (as water or fuel) **3 :** an enclosed heavily armed and armored combat vehicle that moves on tracks **4 :** a prison cell or enclosure used esp. for receiving prisoners **5 :** TANK TOP — **tank·ful** \-ˌfu̇l\ *n* — **tank·like** \-ˌlīk\ *adj* — **in the tank** *or* **into the tank :** in or into a decline or slump ⟨the sullen student's grades went *into the tank*⟩

[2]**tank** *vt* (1863) **1 :** to place, store, or treat in a tank **2 :** to make no effort to win **:** lose intentionally ⟨~*ed* the match⟩ ~ *vi* **1 :** to lose intentionally **:** give up in competition **2 :** to suffer rapid decline, failure, or collapse ⟨bought a stock that quickly ~*ed*⟩

tan·ka \ˈtäŋ-kə\ *n* [Jp] (ca. 1877) **:** an unrhymed Japanese verse form of five lines containing five, seven, five, seven, and seven syllables respectively; *also* **:** a poem in this form — compare HAIKU

tank·age \ˈtaŋ-kij\ *n* (1866) **1 a :** the aggregate of tanks required for a purpose **b :** the capacity or contents of a tank **2 :** dried animal residues usu. freed from the fat and gelatin and used as fertilizer and feedstuff **3** : the act or process of putting or storing in tanks

tan·kard \ˈtaŋ-kərd\ *n* [ME] (14c) : a tall one-handled drinking vessel; *esp* : a silver or pewter mug with a lid

tank car *n* (1862) : a railroad car for transporting liquids or gases in bulk

tank destroyer *n* (1941) : a highly mobile lightly armored vehicle usu. on a half-track or a tank chassis and mounting a cannon

tanked \ˈtaŋ(k)t\ *adj* (1893) *slang* : DRUNK 1a — often used with *up*

tank·er \ˈtaŋ-kər\ *n* (1900) **1 a** : a cargo ship fitted with tanks for carrying liquid in bulk **b** : a vehicle on which a tank is mounted to carry fluids; *also* : a cargo airplane for transporting fuel **2** : a member of a military tank crew

tank·i·ni \taŋ-ˈkē-nē\ *n* [blend of *tank* (*top*) and *bikini*] (1985) : a woman's two-piece swimsuit consisting of bikini briefs and a tank top

tank suit *n* (1940) : a one-piece bathing suit with usu. wide shoulder straps

tank top *n* (1950) : a sleeveless collarless shirt with usu. wide shoulder straps and no front opening

tank town *n* [fr. the fact that trains stopped at such towns only to take on water] (1906) : a small town

tan·nage \ˈta-nij\ *n* (1662) : the act, process, or result of tanning

tan·nate \ˈta-ˌnāt\ *n* [F, fr. *tannin*] (1802) : a compound of a tannin

[1]**tan·ner** \ˈta-nər\ *n* (bef. 12c) **1** : one that tans hides **2** : one who acquires or seeks to acquire a suntan

[2]**tanner** *n* [origin unknown] (ca. 1811) *Brit* : SIXPENCE

tanner crab *n* [prob. fr. NL *tanneri*, specific epithet of *Chionoecetes tanneri*, fr. Zera L. *Tanner* †1906 Am. naval officer] (1947) : any of several spider crabs (genus *Chionoecetes*); *esp* : SNOW CRAB

tan·nery \ˈta-nə-rē, ˈtan-rē\ *n, pl* **-ner·ies** (1694) : a place where tanning is carried on

tan·nic \ˈta-nik\ *adj* [F *tannique*, fr. *tannin*] (1836) **1** : of, resembling, or derived from tan or a tannin **2** *of wine* : containing an abundance of tannins : markedly astringent

tannic acid *n* (1836) : TANNIN 1

tan·nin \ˈta-nən\ *n* [F, fr. *tanner* to tan] (1802) **1** : any of various soluble astringent complex phenolic substances of plant origin used esp. in tanning leather and dyeing fabric, manufacturing ink, clarifying wine and beer, and in medicine **2** : a substance that has a tanning effect

tanning *n* (15c) **1** : the art or process by which a skin is tanned **2** : a browning of the skin esp. by exposure to sun **3** : a sound spanking **4** : a natural darkening and hardening of the cuticle of an insect immediately after molting

tan·nish \ˈta-nish\ *adj* (1935) : somewhat tan

tan oak *n* (ca. 1925) : a U.S. Pacific coast evergreen tree (*Lithocarpus densiflora*) of the beech family that has erect staminate catkins and furrowed brown bark rich in tannins

Ta·no·an \tə-ˈnō-ən, ˈtä-nə-wən\ *n* [*Tano*, a group of former pueblos in New Mexico] (1891) : a family of American Indian languages spoken in New Mexico and Arizona — **Tanoan** *adj*

tan·sy \ˈtan-zē\ *n, pl* **tansies** [ME *tansey*, fr. AF *tanesie*, fr. LL *tanacita*] (13c) : a common Old World composite herb (*Tanacetum vulgare*) that is naturalized in No. America and has bitter-tasting finely divided aromatic leaves and clustered yellow flower heads lacking ray flowers; *broadly* : a plant of the same genus

tansy ragwort *n* (ca. 1900) : an Old World yellow-flowered senecio (*Senecio jacobaea*) that is naturalized in No. America and is toxic to livestock

tan·ta·late \ˈtan-tə-ˌlāt\ *n* (1849) : a salt containing tantalum in combination with oxygen

tan·ta·lise, tan·ta·lis·ing *Brit var of* TANTALIZE, TANTALIZING

tan·ta·lite \ˈtan-tə-ˌlīt\ *n* (1805) : a mineral consisting of a heavy dark lustrous oxide of tantalum and usu. other metals (as iron or manganese)

tan·ta·lize \ˈtan-tə-ˌlīz\ *vb* **-lized; -liz·ing** [*Tantalus*] *vt* (1597) : to tease or torment by or as if by presenting something desirable to the view but continually keeping it out of reach ~ *vi* : to cause one to be tantalized — **tan·ta·liz·er** *n*

tantalizing *adj* (ca. 1683) : possessing a quality that arouses or stimulates desire or interest; *also* : mockingly or teasingly out of reach — **tan·ta·liz·ing·ly** *adv*

tan·ta·lum \ˈtan-tə-ləm\ *n* [NL, fr. L *Tantalus*; fr. its inability to absorb acid] (1809) : a gray-white ductile acid-resisting metallic element found combined in rare minerals (as tantalite and columbite) and used esp. in electronic components — see ELEMENT table

Tan·ta·lus \ˈtan-tə-ləs\ *n* [L, fr. Gk *Tantalos*] (14c) **1** : a legendary king of Lydia condemned to stand up to the chin in a pool of water in Hades and beneath fruit-laden boughs only to have the water or fruit recede at each attempt to drink or eat **2** *not cap* : a locked cellarette with contents visible but not obtainable without a key

tan·ta·mount \ˈtan-tə-ˌmau̇nt\ *adj* [obs. *tantamount*, n., equivalent, fr. AF *tant amunter* to amount to as much] (1641) : equivalent in value, significance, or effect ⟨a relationship ~ to marriage⟩

tan·ta·ra \tan-ˈta-rə, -ˈtär-ə\ *n* [L *taratantara*, of imit. origin] (1584) : the blare of a trumpet or horn

[1]**tan·tivy** \tan-ˈti-vē\ *adv* [origin unknown] (1641) : at a gallop

[2]**tantivy** *n, pl* **-tiv·ies** (ca. 1658) **1** : a rapid gallop or ride **2** : TANTARA

tan·tra \ˈtən-trə, ˈtän-, ˈtan-\ *n, often cap* [Skt, lit., warp, fr. *tanoti* he stretches, weaves; akin to Gk *teinein* to stretch — more at THIN] (1799) : one of the later Hindu or Buddhist scriptures dealing esp. with techniques and rituals including meditative and sexual practices; *also* : the rituals or practices outlined in the tantra — **tan·tric** \-trik\ *adj, often cap* — **Tan·trism** \-ˌtri-zəm\ *n* — **Tan·trist** \-trist\ *n*

tan·trum \ˈtan-trəm\ *n* [origin unknown] (1714) : a fit of bad temper

ta·nu·ki \tä-ˈnü-kē\ *n* [Jp, raccoon dog] (ca. 1929) : the fur of a raccoon dog; *also* : RACCOON DOG

tan·yard \ˈtan-ˌyärd\ *n* (1666) : the section or part of a tannery housing tanning vats

tan·za·nite \ˈtan-zə-ˌnīt\ *n* [*Tanzania*, Africa] (1968) : a mineral that is a deep blue variety of zoisite and is used as a gemstone

Tao \ˈdau̇, ˈtau̇\ *n* [Chin (Beijing) *dào*, lit., way] (1736) **1 a** : the unconditional and unknowable source and guiding principle of all reality as conceived by Taoists **b** : the process of nature by which all things change and which is to be followed for a life of harmony **2** *often not cap* : the path of virtuous conduct as conceived by Confucians **3** *often not cap* : the art or skill of doing something in harmony with the essential nature of the thing ⟨the ~ of archery⟩

Tao·ism \-ˌi-zəm\ *also* **Dao·ism** \ˈdau̇-\ *n* [*Tao*] (1838) **1** : a Chinese mystical philosophy traditionally founded by Lao-tzu in the sixth century B.C. that teaches conformity to the Tao by unassertive action and simplicity **2** : a religion developed from Taoist philosophy and folk and Buddhist religion and concerned with obtaining long life and good fortune often by magical means — **Tao·ist** \-ist\ *adj or n* — **Tao·is·tic** \dau̇-ˈis-tik, tau̇-\ *adj*

[1]**tap** \ˈtap\ *n* [ME *tappe*, fr. OE *tæppa*; akin to OHG *zapho* tap] (bef. 12c) **1 a** : a plug for a hole (as in a cask) : SPIGOT **b** : a device consisting of a spout and valve attached to the end of a pipe to control the flow of a fluid : FAUCET **2 a** : a liquor drawn through a tap **b** : the procedure of removing fluid (as from a body cavity) **3** : a tool for forming an internal screw thread **4** : an intermediate point in an electric circuit where a connection may be made **5** : WIRETAP — **on tap 1** : ready to be drawn from a large container (as a cask or keg) ⟨ale *on tap*⟩ **2** : broached or furnished with a tap **3** : on hand : AVAILABLE ⟨services instantly *on tap* —Hugh Dwan⟩ **4** : coming up ⟨other matches *on tap* —H. W. Wind⟩

[2]**tap** *vt* **tapped; tap·ping** (15c) **1** : to let out or cause to flow by piercing or by drawing a plug from the containing vessel ⟨~ wine from a cask⟩ **2 a** : to pierce so as to let out or draw off a fluid ⟨~ maple trees⟩ **b** : to draw out, from, or upon ⟨~ new sources of revenue⟩ ⟨the story ~*s* powerful emotions⟩ **3** : to cut in on (as a telephone or radio signal) to get information **4** : to form an internal screw thread in by means of a tap **5** : to get money from as a loan or gift **6** : to connect (a street gas or water main) with a local supply — **tap·per** *n* — **tap into** : to make a strong or advantageous connection with ⟨trying to *tap into* a new market⟩

[3]**tap** *vb* **tapped; tap·ping** [ME *tappen*, fr. OF *taper* to strike with the flat of the hand, of Gmc origin; akin to MHG *tāpe* paw, blow dealt with the paw] *vt* (13c) **1** : to strike lightly esp. with a slight sound **2** : to give a light blow with ⟨~ a pencil on the table⟩ **3** : to bring about by repeated light blows ⟨~ out a story on the typewriter⟩ **4** : to repair by putting a tap on **5** : SELECT, DESIGNATE ⟨was *tapped* for police commissioner⟩; *specif* : to elect to membership (as in a fraternity) ~ *vi* **1** : to strike a light audible blow : RAP **2** : to walk with light audible steps **3** : TAP-DANCE — **tap·per** *n*

[4]**tap** *n* (14c) **1 a** : a light usu. audible blow; *also* : its sound **b** : one of several usu. rapid drumbeats on a snare drum **2** : HALF SOLE **3** : a small metal plate for the sole or heel of a shoe **4** : TAP DANCE 1 **5** : FLAP 7

[1]**ta·pa** \ˈtä-pə, ˈta-\ *n* [Marquesan & Tahitian] (1817) : a coarse cloth made in the Pacific islands from the pounded bark esp. of the paper mulberry and usu. decorated with geometric patterns

[2]**tapa** *n* [Sp, lit., cover, lid, prob. of Gmc origin; akin to OE *tæppa* tap] (1939) : an hors d'oeuvre served with drinks esp. in Spanish bars — usu. used in pl.

tap dance *n* (1928) **1** : a step dance tapped out audibly by means of shoes with hard soles or soles and heels to which taps have been added **2** : something suggesting a tap dance; *esp* : an action or discourse intended to rationalize or distract ⟨does a clever *tap dance* to explain —Campbell Geeslin⟩ — **tap–dance** *vi* — **tap dancer** *n* — **tap dancing** *n*

[1]**tape** \ˈtāp\ *n* [ME, fr. OE *tæppe*] (bef. 12c) **1** : a narrow woven fabric **2** : a string or ribbon stretched breast-high above the finish line of a race **3** : a narrow flexible strip or band: as **a** : ADHESIVE TAPE **b** : MAGNETIC TAPE; *also* : CASSETTE 2b **4** : TAPE RECORDING

[2]**tape** *vb* **taped; tap·ing** *vt* (1609) **1** : to fasten, tie, bind, cover, or support with tape **2** : to record on tape and esp. magnetic tape ⟨~ an interview⟩ ~ *vi* : to record something on tape and esp. magnetic tape

[3]**tape** *adj* (1947) **1** : recorded on tape ⟨~ music⟩ **2** : intended for use with recording (as magnetic) tape ⟨a ~ cartridge⟩

tape deck *n* (1949) : a device used to play back and often to record on magnetic tape that usu. has to be connected to an audio system

tape grass *n* (ca. 1818) : any of several submerged aquatic monocotyledonous plants (genus *Vallisneria* of the family Hydrocharitaceae) with long ribbonlike leaves — called also *eelgrass, wild celery*

tape measure *n* (1845) : a narrow strip (as of a limp cloth or steel tape) marked off in units (as inches or centimeters) for measuring

ta·pe·nade \ˌtä-pə-ˈnäd\ *n* [F *tapénade*, fr. Occitan *tapenado*, fr. *tapeno* caper, ultim. fr. L *capparis* — more at CAPER] (1952) : a seasoned spread made chiefly with mashed black olives, capers, and anchovies

[1]**ta·per** \ˈtā-pər\ *n* [ME, fr. OE *tapor* candle, wick, perh. modif. of L *papyrus* papyrus] (bef. 12c) **1 a** : a slender candle **b** : a long waxed wick used esp. for lighting candles, lamps, pipes, or fires **c** : a feeble light **2 a** : a tapering form or figure **b** : gradual diminution of thickness, diameter, or width in an elongated object **c** : a gradual decrease

[2]**taper** *adj* (15c) **1** : progressively narrowed toward one end **2** : furnished with or adjusted to a scale : GRADUATED ⟨~ freight rates⟩

[3]**taper** *vb* **ta·pered; ta·per·ing** \ˈtā-p(ə-)riŋ\ *vi* (1610) **1** : to become progressively smaller toward one end **2** : to diminish gradually ~ *vt* : to cause to taper

[4]**tap·er** \ˈtā-pər\ *n* [[1]*tape*] (ca. 1920) : one that applies or dispenses tape

tape–re·cord \ˌtāp-ri-ˈkȯrd, ˈtāp-ri-ˌ\ *vt* [back-formation fr. *tape recording*] (1950) : to make a recording of on magnetic tape

tape recorder *n* (1932) : a device for recording on and playing back magnetic tape

tape recording *n* (1940) : magnetic recording on magnetic tape; *also* : a recording made by this process

ta·per·er \ˈtā-pər-ər\ *n* (15c) : one who bears a taper in a religious procession

taper off *vb* (1848) : TAPER ⟨housing starts *tapered off* in the fall⟩

ta·per·stick \ˈtā-pər-ˌstik\ *n* (1546) : a candlestick that holds tapers

tap·es·tried \ˈta-pə-strēd\ *adj* (1769) **1 :** covered or decorated with or as if with tapestry **2 :** woven or depicted in tapestry

tap·es·try \ˈta-pə-strē\ *n, pl* **-tries** [ME, modif. of AF *tapicerie,* fr. *tapit, tapis* carpet, hanging, fr. GK *tapētion,* dim. of *tapēt-, tapēs* carpet] (15c) **1 a :** a heavy handwoven reversible textile used for hangings, curtains, and upholstery and characterized by complicated pictorial designs **b :** a nonreversible imitation of tapestry used chiefly for upholstery **c :** embroidery on canvas resembling woven tapestry ⟨needlepoint ~⟩ **2 :** something resembling tapestry (as in complexity or richness of design) ⟨nature's rich ~⟩

tapestry carpet *n* (1852) **:** a carpet in which the designs are printed in colors on the threads before the fabric is woven

ta·pe·tum \tə-ˈpē-təm\ *n, pl* **ta·pe·ta** \-ˈpē-tə\ [NL, fr. L *tapete* carpet, tapestry, fr. Gk *tapēt-, tapēs* carpet] (1713) **1 :** any of various reflective membranous layers or areas esp. of the choroid and retina of the eye **2 :** a layer of nutritive cells that invests the sporogenous tissue in the sporangium of vascular plants

tape·worm \ˈtāp-ˌwərm\ *n* [fr. its shape] (1706) **:** any of a class (Cestoda) of bilaterally symmetrical flatworms parasitic esp. in the intestines of vertebrates — called also *cestode*

tap·hole \ˈtap-ˌhōl\ *n* (1594) **:** a hole for a tap; *specif* **:** a hole at or near the bottom of a furnace or ladle through which molten metal, matte, or slag can be tapped

ta·phon·o·my \tə-ˈfä-nə-mē, ta-\ *n* [Gk *taphē* burial + E *-nomy*] (1940) **:** the study of the processes (as burial, decay, and preservation) that affect animal and plant remains as they become fossilized; *also* **:** the processes themselves — **taph·o·nom·ic** \ˌta-fə-ˈnä-mik\ *adj* — **ta·phon·o·mist** \tə-ˈfä-nə-mist, ta-\ *n*

tap–in \ˈtap-ˌin\ *n* (1948) **1 :** TIP-IN **2 :** a very short easy putt in golf

tap·i·o·ca \ˌta-pē-ˈō-kə\ *n* [Pg, fr. Tupi *tipiˀóka*] (1707) **1 :** a usu. granular preparation of cassava starch used esp. in puddings and as a thickening in liquid food; *also* **:** a dish (as pudding) containing tapioca **2 :** CASSAVA

ta·pir \ˈtā-pər *also* ˈtā-ˌpir *or* tə-ˈpir\ *n, pl* **tapirs** *also* **tapir** [Pg *tapir, tapira,* fr. Tupi *tapiˀíra*] (1774) **:** any of a genus (*Tapirus*) of herbivorous chiefly nocturnal perissodactyl mammals of tropical America and southeastern Asia from Myanmar to Sumatra that have a heavy sparsely hairy body and the snout and upper lip prolonged into a short flexible proboscis

tap·is \ˈta-ˌpē, ta-ˈpē\ *n* [AF — more at TAPESTRY] (15c) *archaic* **:** a small tapestry used for hangings and floor and table coverings — **on the tapis :** under consideration

tap–off \ˈtap-ˌȯf\ *n* (ca. 1932) **:** 2TIP-OFF

tap out *vi* (1939) **:** to run out of money by betting

tap pants *n pl* (1977) **:** a loose-fitting woman's undergarment of a style similar to shorts formerly worn for tap dancing

tapped out *adj* (1950) **1 :** out of money **:** BROKE **2 :** SPENT, EXHAUSTED ⟨*tapped out* after months on the road⟩

tap·pet \ˈta-pət\ *n* [irreg. fr. 3*tap*] (1745) **:** a lever or projection moved by some other piece (as a cam) or intended to tap or touch something else to cause a particular motion

tapping *n* (15c) **:** the act, process, or means by which something is tapped

tap·pit hen \ˈta-pət-\ *n* [Sc *tappit,* alter. of E *topped*] (1721) *Scot* **:** a drinking vessel with a knob on the lid

tap·room \ˈtap-ˌrüm, -ˌru̇m\ *n* (1807) **:** BARROOM

tap·root \-ˌrüt, -ˌru̇t\ *n* [1*tap*] (1601) **1 :** a primary root that grows vertically downward and gives off small lateral roots **2 :** the central element or position in a line of growth or development

taps \ˈtaps\ *n pl but sing or pl in constr* [prob. alter. of earlier *taptoo* tattoo — more at TATTOO] (1824) **:** the last bugle call at night blown as a signal that lights are to be put out; *also* **:** a similar call blown at military funerals and memorial services

tap·sal–tee·rie \ˌtap-səl-ˈtē-rē\ *adv* [by alter.] (1784) *Scot* **:** TOPSY-TURVY

tap·ster \ˈtap-stər\ *n* (bef. 12c) **:** BARTENDER

tap water *n* (1881) **:** water as it comes from a tap (as in a home)

ta·que·ria *also* **ta·que·ría** \ˌtä-kə-ˈrē-ə\ *n* [MexSp, fr. *taco* taco] (1982) **:** a Mexican restaurant specializing esp. in tacos and burritos

1**tar** \ˈtär\ *n* [ME *terr, tarr,* fr. OE *teoru;* akin to OE *trēow* tree — more at TREE] (bef. 12c) **1 a :** a dark brown or black bituminous usu. odorous viscous liquid obtained by destructive distillation of organic material (as wood, coal, or peat) **b :** a substance in some respects resembling tar; *esp* **:** a condensable residue present in smoke from burning tobacco that contains combustion by-products (as resins, acids, phenols, and essential oils) **2** [short for *tarpaulin*] **:** SAILOR

2**tar** *vt* **tarred; tar·ring** (13c) **1 :** to cover with tar **2 :** to defile as if with tar ⟨least *tarred* by the scandal —*Newsweek*⟩ — **tar and feather :** to smear (a person) with tar and cover with feathers as a punishment or indignity — **tar with the same brush :** to mark or stain with the same fault or characteristic

3**tar** *or* **tarre** \ˈtär\ *vt* **tarred; tar·ring; tars** *or* **tarres** [ME *terren, tarren,* fr. OE *tyrwan*] (bef. 12c) **:** to urge to action — usu. used with *on*

tar·a·did·dle *or* **tar·ra·did·dle** \ˌtar-ə-ˈdi-dᵊl, ˈtar-ə-ˌ\ *n* [origin unknown] (ca. 1796) **1 :** FIB **2 :** pretentious nonsense

Tar·a·hu·ma·ra \ˌta-rə-hü-ˈmär-ə\ *n, pl* **Tarahumara** *or* **Tarahumaras** [Sp] (1874) **1 :** a member of an American Indian people living in the state of Chihuahua, Mexico **2 :** the Uto-Aztecan language of the Tarahumara people

tar·an·tel·la \ˌta-rən-ˈte-lə\ *n* [It, fr. *Taranto,* Italy] (1782) **:** a lively folk dance of southern Italy in 6/8 time

tar·an·tism \ˈta-rən-ˌti-zəm\ *n* [NL *tarantismus,* fr. *Taranto,* Italy] (ca. 1656) **:** a dancing mania or malady of late medieval Europe

ta·ran·tu·la \tə-ˈran-chə-lə, -tə-lə; -ˈranch-lə, -ˈrant-\ *n, pl* **ta·ran·tu·las** *also* **ta·ran·tu·lae** \-ˌlē\ [ML, fr. OIt *tarantola,* fr. *Taranto*] (1561) **1 :** a European wolf spider (*Lycosa tarentula*) popularly held to be the cause of tarantism **2 :** any of a family (Theraphosidae) of large hairy American spiders that are typically rather sluggish and capable of biting sharply though most forms are not significantly poisonous to humans

Ta·ras·can \tə-ˈras-kən, -ˈräs-\ *n* [Sp *tarasco*] (1922) **1 :** a member of an American Indian people of the state of Michoacán, Mexico **2 :** the language of the Tarascan people

tar baby *n* [fr. the tar baby that trapped Brer Rabbit in an Uncle Remus story by Joel Chandler Harris] (ca. 1910) **:** something from which it is nearly impossible to extricate oneself

tar·boosh *also* **tar·bush** \tär-ˈbüsh, ˈtär-ˌ\ *n* [Ar *ṭarbūsh*] (1702) **:** a red hat similar to the fez worn esp. by Muslim men

tar·di·grade \ˈtär-də-ˌgrād\ *n* [ultim. fr. L *tardigradus* slow-moving, fr. *tardus* slow + *gradi* to step, go — more at GRADE] (1860) **:** any of a phylum (Tardigrada) of microscopic invertebrates with four pairs of stout legs that live usu. in water or damp moss — called also *water bear*

tar·di·ly \ˈtär-də-lē\ *adv* (ca. 1598) **1 :** at a slow pace **2 :** LATE

tar·dive dyskinesia \ˈtär-div-\ *n* [*tardive* tending toward late development (fr. F, fem. of *tardif,* fr. MF) + *dyskinesia*] (1964) **:** a neurological disorder characterized by involuntary uncontrollable movements esp. of the mouth, tongue, trunk, and limbs and occurring esp. as a side effect of prolonged use of antipsychotic drugs (as phenothiazine)

tar·do \ˈtär-(ˌ)dō\ *adj* [It, fr. L *tardus*] (ca. 1843) **:** SLOW — used as a direction in music

1**tar·dy** \ˈtär-dē\ *adj* **tar·di·er; -est** [alter. of earlier *tardif,* fr. AF, fr. VL **tardivus,* fr. L *tardus*] (15c) **1 :** moving slowly **:** SLUGGISH ⟨the ~ pace at which she was obliged to walk —Charles Dickens⟩ **2 :** delayed beyond the expected or proper time **:** LATE ⟨a ~ arrival⟩ — **tar·di·ness** \ˈtär-dē-nəs\ *n*

2**tardy** *n, pl* **tardies** (1960) **:** an instance of being tardy (as to a class)

1**tare** \ˈter\ *n* [ME; prob. akin to MD *tarwe* wheat] (14c) **1 a :** the seed of a vetch **b :** any of several vetches (esp. *Vicia sativa* and *V. hirsuta*) **2 :** a weed of grain fields esp. of Biblical times that is usu. held to be the darnel **3** *pl* **:** an undesirable element

2**tare** *n* [ME, fr. AF, fr. OIt *tara,* fr. Ar *ṭarḥa,* lit., that which is removed] (15c) **1 :** a deduction from the gross weight of a substance and its container made in allowance for the weight of the container; *also* **:** the weight of the container **2 :** COUNTERWEIGHT

3**tare** *vt* **tared; tar·ing** (1812) **:** to ascertain or mark the tare of; *esp* **:** to weigh so as to determine the tare

targe \ˈtärj\ *n* [ME, fr. AF] (14c) **:** a light shield used esp. by the Scots

1**tar·get** \ˈtär-gət\ *n, often attrib* [ME, fr. MF *targette, targuete,* dim. of *targe* light shield, fr. OF, of Gmc origin; akin to ON *targa* shield] (14c) **1 :** a small round shield **2 a :** a mark to shoot at **b :** a target marked by shots fired at it **c :** something or someone fired at or marked for attack **d :** a goal to be achieved **3 a :** an object of ridicule or criticism **b :** something or someone to be affected by an action or development **4 a :** the metallic surface (as of platinum or tungsten) upon which the stream of electrons within an X-ray tube is focused and from which the X-rays are emitted **b :** a body, surface, or material bombarded with nuclear particles or electrons; *esp* **:** fluorescent material on which desired visual effects are produced in electronic devices (as in radar) — **off target :** not valid **:** INACCURATE — **on target :** precisely correct or valid esp. in interpreting or addressing a problem or vital issue

2**target** *vt* (1837) **1 :** to make a target of ⟨~*ed* her for promotion⟩; *esp* **:** to set as a goal **2 :** to direct or use toward a target

tar·get·able \ˈtär-gə-tə-bəl\ *adj* (1964) **:** capable of being aimed at a target ⟨missiles with ~ warheads⟩

target date *n* (1945) **:** the date set for an event or for the completion of a project, goal, or quota

target language *n* (1953) **1 :** a language into which another language is to be translated — compare SOURCE LANGUAGE **2 :** a language other than one's native language that is being learned

Tar·gum \ˈtär-ˌgüm, -ˌgüm\ *n* [LHeb *targūm,* fr. Aram, translation] (1587) **:** an Aramaic translation or paraphrase of a portion of the Old Testament

Tar Heel *n* (1864) **:** a native or resident of North Carolina — used as a nickname

1**tar·iff** \ˈter-əf, ˈta-rəf\ *n* [It *tariffa,* fr. Ar *taʿrīf* notification] (1592) **1 a :** a schedule of duties imposed by a government on imported or in some countries exported goods **b :** a duty or rate of duty imposed in such a schedule **2 :** a schedule of rates or charges of a business or a public utility **3 :** PRICE, CHARGE

2**tariff** *vt* (ca. 1828) **:** to subject to a tariff

tar·la·tan \ˈtär-lə-tən\ *n* [F *tarlatane*] (ca. 1741) **:** a sheer cotton fabric in open plain weave usu. heavily sized for stiffness

tar·mac \ˈtär-ˌmak\ *n* [fr. *Tarmac,* a trademark] (1919) **:** a tarmacadam road, apron, or runway

Tarmac *trademark* — used for a bituminous binder for roads

tar·mac·ad·am \ˌtär-mə-ˈka-dəm\ *n* (1882) **1 :** a pavement constructed by spraying or pouring a tar binder over layers of crushed stone and then rolling **2 :** a material of tar and aggregates mixed in a plant and shaped on the roadway

tarn \ˈtärn\ *n* [ME *terne, tarne,* of Scand origin; akin to ON *tjǫrn* small lake] (14c) **:** a small steep-banked mountain lake or pool

tar·na·tion \ˌtär-ˈnā-shən\ *n* [alter. of *darnation,* euphemism for *damnation*] (1790) **:** DAMNATION — often used as an interjection or intensive; often used with *in* ⟨~ strike me —James Joyce⟩ ⟨where in ~ you from? —Jessamyn West⟩

1**tar·nish** \ˈtär-nish\ *vb* [ME *ternysshen,* fr. MF *terniss-,* stem of *ternir,* prob. of Gmc origin; akin to OHG *tarnan* to hide] *vt* (15c) **1 :** to dull or destroy the luster of by or as if by air, dust, or dirt **:** SOIL, STAIN **2 a :** to detract from the good quality of **:** VITIATE ⟨his fine dreams now slightly ~*ed*⟩ **b :** to bring disgrace on **:** SULLY ⟨the scandal has ~*ed* his reputation⟩ ~ *vi* **:** to become tarnished — **tar·nish·able** \-ni-shə-bəl\ *adj*

2**tarnish** *n* (1684) **:** something that tarnishes; *esp* **:** a film of chemically altered material on the surface of a metal (as silver)

tarnished plant bug *n* (1902) **:** a common hemipterous brownish bug (*Lygus lineolaris*) of eastern No. America that causes injury to plants esp. by sucking sap from buds, leaves, and fruits

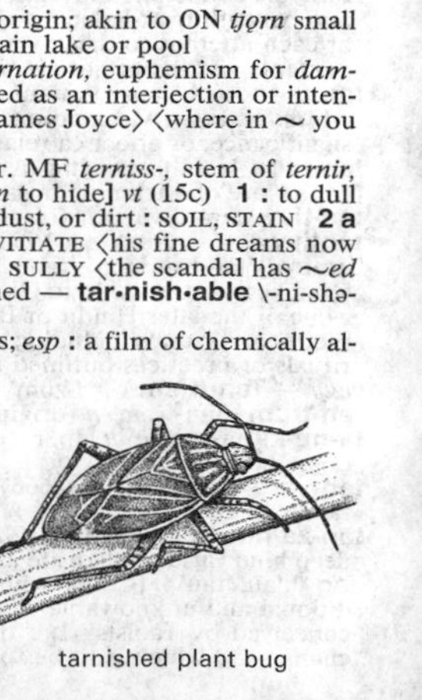
tarnished plant bug

ta·ro \ˈtär-(ˌ)ō, ˈter-\ *n, pl* **taros** [Tahitian & Maori] (1769) **:** a large-leaved tropical Asian plant (*Colocasia esculenta*) of the arum family grown throughout the tropics for its edible starchy corms and cormels and in temperate regions for ornament; *also* : its corms and cormels typically cooked as a vegetable or ground into flour

tar·ot \ˈter-(ˌ)ō, ˈta-(ˌ)rō\ *n* [MF, fr. It *tarocchi* (pl.)] (ca. 1623) : any of a set of usu. 78 playing cards including 22 pictorial cards used for fortune-telling

tarp \ˈtärp\ *n* (1906) : TARPAULIN

tar paper *n* (1886) : a heavy paper coated or impregnated with tar for use esp. in building

tar·pau·lin \tär-ˈpȯ-lən, ˈtär-pə-; ÷tär-ˈpōl-yən\ *n* [prob. fr. 1*tar* + *-palling, -pauling* (fr. *pall*)] (1605) **1** : a piece of material (as durable plastic) used for protecting exposed objects or areas **2** : SAILOR

tar pit *n* (1839) : an area in which natural bitumens collect and are exposed at the earth's surface and which tends to trap animals and preserve their hard parts (as bones or teeth)

tar·pon \ˈtär-pən\ *n, pl* **tarpon** *or* **tarpons** [origin unknown] (1685) : a large silvery elongate bony fish (*Megalops atlanticus* of the family Elopidae) that occurs esp. in the Gulf of Mexico, Caribbean, and warm coastal waters of the Atlantic, reaches a length of about six feet (two meters), and is often caught for sport

tar·ra·gon \ˈter-ə-ˌgän, ˈta-rə- *also* -gən\ *n* [MF *targon,* fr. ML *tarchon,* fr. MGk, fr. Ar *ṭarkhūn*] (1538) : a small widely cultivated perennial artemisia (*Artemisia dracunculus*) having aromatic narrow usu. entire leaves; *also* : its leaves used as a seasoning

tarre *var of* TAR

tar·ri·ance \ˈta-rē-ən(t)s\ *n* (15c) : the act or an instance of tarrying

1**tar·ry** \ˈter-ē, ˈta-rē\ *vi* **tar·ried; tar·ry·ing** [ME *tarien*] (14c) **1 a** : to delay or be tardy in acting or doing **b** : to linger in expectation : WAIT **2** : to abide or stay in or at a place

2**tarry** *n, pl* **tarries** (14c) : STAY, SOJOURN

3**tar·ry** \ˈtär-ē\ *adj* (1552) : of, resembling, or covered with tar

1**tar·sal** \ˈtär-səl\ *adj* (1817) **1** : of or relating to the tarsus **2** : being or relating to plates of dense connective tissue that serve to stiffen the eyelids

2**tarsal** *n* (1881) : a tarsal part (as a bone or cartilage)

tar sand *n* (1899) : a natural impregnation of sand or sandstone with petroleum from which the lighter portions have escaped

tar·si·er \ˈtär-sē-ər, -sē-ˌā\ *n* [F, fr. *tarse* tarsus, fr. NL *tarsus*] (ca. 1774) : any of a genus (*Tarsius* of the family Tarsiidae) of small chiefly nocturnal and arboreal carnivorous primates of the Malay Archipelago that have large round eyes, long legs, and a long nearly hairless tail

tar·so·meta·tar·sus \ˌtär-(ˌ)sō-ˌme-tə-ˈtär-səs\ *n* [NL, fr. *tarsus* + *-o-* + *metatarsus*] (1854) : the large compound bone of the tarsus of a bird; *also* : the segment of the limb it supports

tar·sus \ˈtär-səs\ *n, pl* **tar·si** \-ˌsī, -ˌsē\ [NL, fr. Gk *tarsos* wickerwork mat, flat of the foot, ankle, edge of the eyelid; akin to Gk *tersesthai* to become dry — more at THIRST] (ca. 1615) **1** : the part of the foot of a vertebrate between the metatarsus and the leg; *also* : the small bones that support this part of the limb **2** : the tarsal plate of the eyelid **3** : the distal part of the limb of an arthropod **4** : TARSOMETATARSUS

1**tart** \ˈtärt\ *adj* [ME, fr. OE *teart* sharp, severe; akin to MHG *traz* spite] (bef. 12c) **1** : agreeably sharp or acid to the taste ⟨a ~ apple⟩ **2** : marked by a biting, acrimonious, or cutting quality ⟨a ~ rejoinder⟩ — **tart·ish** \ˈtär-tish\ *adj* — **tart·ly** *adv* — **tart·ness** *n*

2**tart** *n* [ME *tarte,* fr. AF] (14c) **1** : a dish baked in a pastry shell : PIE: as **a** : a small pie or pastry shell without a top containing jelly, custard, or fruit **b** : a small pie made of pastry folded over a filling **2** [earlier slang, girlfriend, prob. short for *jam tart,* rhyming slang for *sweetheart*] : PROSTITUTE

tar·tan \ˈtär-tᵊn\ *n* [perh. fr. MF *tiretaine* linsey-woolsey] (ca. 1500) **1** : a plaid textile design of Scottish origin consisting of stripes of varying width and color usu. patterned to designate a distinctive clan **2 a** : a twilled woolen fabric with tartan design **b** : a fabric with tartan design **3** : a garment of tartan design

1**tar·tar** \ˈtär-tər\ *n* [ME, fr. AF, fr. ML *tartarum*] (14c) **1** : a substance consisting essentially of cream of tartar that is derived from the juice of grapes and deposited in wine casks together with yeast and other suspended matters as a pale or dark reddish crust or sediment; *esp* : a recrystallized product yielding cream of tartar on further purification **2** : an incrustation on the teeth consisting of plaque that has become hardened by the deposition of mineral salts (as calcium carbonate)

2**tartar** *n* [ME *Tartre,* fr. MF *Tartare,* prob. fr. ML *Tartarus,* modif. of Pers *Tātār* — more at TATAR] (14c) **1** *cap* : a native or inhabitant of Tartary **2** *cap* : TATAR 2 **3** *often cap* : a person of irritable or violent temper **4** : one that proves to be unexpectedly formidable — **Tartar** *adj* — **Tar·tar·i·an** \tär-ˈter-ē-ən\ *adj*

Tar·tar·e·an \tär-ˈter-ē-ən\ *adj* [L *tartareus,* fr. Gk *tartareios,* fr. *Tartaros* Tartarus] (1592) : of, relating to, or resembling Tartarus : INFERNAL ⟨were thrown headlong . . . into the ~ abyss —Edward Gibbon⟩

tartar emetic *n* (ca. 1704) : a poisonous efflorescent crystalline salt $C_8H_4K_2O_{12}Sb_2{\cdot}3H_2O$ of sweetish metallic taste that is used in dyeing as a mordant and esp. formerly in medicine as an emetic and expectorant

tar·tar·ic acid \(ˌ)tär-ˈta-rik-\ *n* (1810) : a strong dicarboxylic acid $C_4H_6O_6$ of plant origin that occurs in various isomeric forms, is usu. obtained from tartar, and is used esp. in food and medicines, in photography, in wine making, and in making salts and esters

tar·tar sauce *or* **tar·tare sauce** \ˈtär-tər-\ *n* [F *sauce tartare*] (1855) : a sauce made principally of mayonnaise and chopped pickles

Tar·ta·rus \ˈtär-tə-rəs\ *n* [L, fr. Gk *Tartaros*] (1513) : a section of Hades reserved for punishment of the wicked

tarte ta·tin \ˌtär(t)-tä-ˈtan, -ˈtaⁿ\ *n, pl* **tarte tatins** *also* **tartes tatin** *often cap 2d T* [F, Tatin tart, after the *Tatin* sisters of Lamotte-Beuvron, France] (1979) : a caramelized apple tart that is baked with pastry on top and then inverted for serving

tart·let \ˈtärt-lət\ *n* (14c) : a small tart

tar·trate \ˈtär-ˌtrāt\ *n* [ISV, fr. F *tartre* tartar, fr. MF, fr. ML *tartarum*] (1794) : a salt or ester of tartaric acid

Tar·tuffe \ˌtär-ˈtu̇f, -ˈtüf\ *n* [F *Tartufe*] (1686) : a religious hypocrite and protagonist in Molière's play *Tartuffe*

tart up *vt* (1938) : DRESS UP, FANCY UP ⟨*tarted up* the restaurant⟩

tarty \ˈtär-(ˌ)tē\ *adj* **tart·i·er; -est** [2*tart*] (1918) : resembling or suggestive of a prostitute (as in clothing or manner)

tase \ˈtāz\ *vt* **tased; tas·ing** *often cap* [back-formation fr. *Taser*] (1991) : to shoot with a Taser gun

Ta·ser \ˈtā-zər\ *trademark* — used for a gun that fires electrified darts to stun and immobilize a person

1**task** \ˈtask\ *n* [ME *taske,* fr. MF dial. (Picardy, Flanders) *tasque,* fr. ML *tasca* tax or service imposed by a feudal superior, alter. of **taxa,* fr. *taxare* to tax] (14c) **1 a** : a usu. assigned piece of work often to be finished within a certain time **b** : something hard or unpleasant that has to be done **c** : DUTY, FUNCTION **2** : subjection to adverse criticism : REPRIMAND — used in the expressions *to take, call,* or *bring to task*

syn TASK, DUTY, JOB, CHORE, STINT, ASSIGNMENT mean a piece of work to be done. TASK implies work imposed by a person in authority or an employer or by circumstance ⟨charged with a variety of *tasks*⟩. DUTY implies an obligation to perform or responsibility for performance ⟨the *duties* of a lifeguard⟩. JOB applies to a piece of work voluntarily performed; it may sometimes suggest difficulty or importance ⟨the *job* of turning the company around⟩. CHORE implies a minor routine activity necessary for maintaining a household or farm ⟨every child was assigned *chores*⟩. STINT implies a carefully allotted or measured quantity of assigned work or service ⟨a 2-month *stint* as a reporter⟩. ASSIGNMENT implies a definite limited task assigned by one in authority ⟨a reporter's *assignment*⟩.

2**task** *vt* (14c) **1** : to assign a task to ⟨employees ~*ed* with updating the files⟩ **2** *obs* : to impose a tax on **3** : to oppress with great labor ⟨~*s* his mind with petty details⟩

task force *n* (1941) : a temporary grouping under one leader for the purpose of accomplishing a definite objective

task·mas·ter \ˈtask-ˌmas-tər\ *n* (1530) : one that imposes a task or burdens another with labor

task·mis·tress \-ˌmis-trəs\ *n* (1603) : a woman who is a taskmaster

Tas·ma·nian devil \(ˌ)taz-ˈmā-nē-ən-, -nyən-\ *n* (ca. 1867) : a heavily built carnivorous nocturnal Tasmanian marsupial (*Sarcophilus harrisii*) that is about the size of a badger and has powerful jaws and teeth and a chiefly black coat marked with white on the chest

Tasmanian tiger *n* (ca. 1891) : a somewhat doglike carnivorous marsupial (*Thylacinus cynocephalus*) that formerly inhabited Tasmania but is now considered extinct — called also *Tasmanian wolf, thylacine*

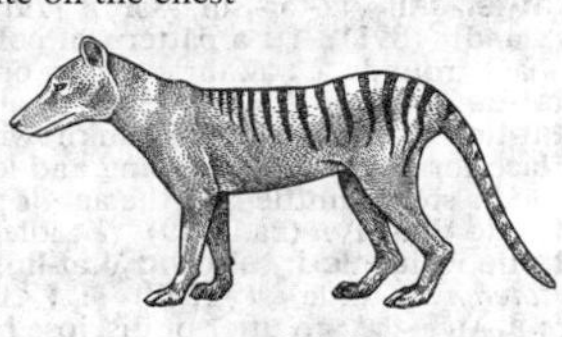

Tasmanian tiger

tasse \ˈtas\ *n* [ME, fr. MF dial. (Artois, Flanders) *taisse, tasse* purse, pouch] (15c) : one of a series of overlapping metal plates in a suit of armor that form a short skirt over the body below the waist — see ARMOR illustration

1**tas·sel** \ˈta-səl, *oftenest of corn* ˈtä-, ˈtȯ-\ *n* [ME, clasp, tassel, fr. AF, fr. VL **tassellus,* alter. of L *taxillus* small die; akin to L *talus* anklebone, die] (14c) **1** : a dangling ornament made by laying parallel a bunch of cords or threads of even length and fastening them at one end **2** : something resembling a tassel; *esp* : the terminal male inflorescence of some plants and esp. corn

2**tassel** *vb* **-seled** *or* **-selled; -sel·ing** *or* **-sel·ling** \-s(ə-)liŋ\ *vt* (14c) : to adorn with tassels ~ *vi* : to put forth tassel inflorescences

1**taste** \ˈtāst\ *vb* **tast·ed; tast·ing** [ME, to touch, test, taste, fr. AF *taster,* fr. VL **taxitare,* freq. of L *taxare* to touch, feel — more at TAX] *vt* (14c) **1** : to become acquainted with by experience ⟨has *tasted* the frustration of defeat⟩ **2** : to ascertain the flavor of by taking a little into the mouth **3** : to eat or drink esp. in small quantities **4** : to perceive or recognize as if by the sense of taste **5** *archaic* : APPRECIATE, ENJOY ~ *vi* **1** : to eat or drink a little **2** : to test the flavor of something by taking a small part into the mouth **3** : to have perception, experience, or enjoyment : PARTAKE — often used with *of* **4** : to have a specific flavor ⟨the apple ~*s* sour⟩

2**taste** *n* (14c) **1** *obs* : TEST **2 a** *obs* : the act of tasting **b** : a small amount tasted **c** : a small amount : BIT; *esp* : a sample of experience ⟨her first ~ of success⟩ **3** : the special sense that perceives and distinguishes the sweet, sour, bitter, or salty quality of a dissolved substance and is mediated by taste buds on the tongue **4** : the objective sweet, sour, bitter, or salty quality of a dissolved substance as perceived by the sense of taste **5 a** : a sensation obtained from a substance in the mouth that is typically produced by the stimulation of the sense of taste combined with those of touch and smell : FLAVOR **b** : the distinctive quality of an experience ⟨that gruesome scene left a bad ~ in my mouth⟩ **6** : individual preference : INCLINATION **7 a** : critical judgment, discernment, or appreciation **b** : manner or aesthetic quality indicative of such discernment or appreciation

taste bud *n* (1879) : an end organ mediating the sensation of taste and lying chiefly in the epithelium of the tongue

taste·ful \ˈtāst-fəl\ *adj* (1611) **1** : TASTY 1a **2** : having, exhibiting, or conforming to good taste ⟨a ~ display⟩ — **taste·ful·ly** \-fə-lē\ *adv* — **taste·ful·ness** *n*

taste·less \ˈtāst-ləs\ *adj* (1591) **1 a** : having no taste : INSIPID ⟨~ vegetables⟩ **b** : arousing no interest : DULL **2** : not having or exhibiting good taste ⟨a ~ joke⟩ — **taste·less·ly** *adv* — **taste·less·ness** *n*

taste·mak·er \-ˌmā-kər\ *n* (1954) : one who sets the standards of what is currently popular or fashionable

tast·er \ˈtā-stər\ *n* (14c) **1** : one that tastes: as **a** : one that tests (as tea) for quality by tasting **b** : a person who is able to taste the chemical phenylthiocarbamide **2** : a device for tasting or sampling

tast·ing \ˈtā-stiŋ\ *n* (1854) : an occasion for sampling a selection of foods or drinks in order to compare qualities ⟨a wine ~⟩

tasty \ˈtā-stē\ *adj* **tast·i·er; -est** (1603) **1 a** : having a marked and appetizing flavor ⟨a ~ meal⟩ **b** : strikingly attractive or interesting ⟨a ~ bit of gossip⟩ **2** : TASTEFUL ***syn*** see PALATABLE — **tast·i·ly** \-stə-lē\ *adv* — **tast·i·ness** \-stē-nəs\ *n*

1**tat** \ˈtat\ *vb* **tat·ted; tat·ting** [back-formation fr. *tatting*] *vi* (1858) : to work at tatting ~ *vt* : to make by tatting

---

\ə\ **abut** \ᵊ\ kitten, F table \ər\ **fur**ther \a\ **ash** \ā\ **ace** \ä\ **mop, mar**
\au̇\ **out** \ch\ **chin** \e\ **bet** \ē\ **easy** \g\ **go** \i\ **hit** \ī\ **ice** \j\ **job**
\ŋ\ **sing** \ō\ **go** \ȯ\ **law** \ȯi\ **boy** \th\ **thin** \t͟h\ **the** \ü\ **loot** \u̇\ **foot**
\y\ **yet** \zh\ **vision, beige** \k, ⁿ, œ, ue, ʸ\ *see* Guide to Pronunciation

[2]**tat** \ˈtat\ *n* [*t*rans-*a*ctivating *t*ranscriptional regulation] (1985) : a small protein produced by a lentivirus (as HIV) that greatly increases the rate of viral transcription and replication and enhances the susceptibility of T cells to infection; *also* : the viral gene that codes for the tat protein
[3]**tat** \ˈtat\ *n* [by shortening] (1987) : TATTOO — **tat** *vb*
TAT *abbr* thematic apperception test
ta–ta \tä-ˈtä\ *interj, chiefly Brit* [baby talk] (1823) — used to express farewell
ta·ta·mi \tä-ˈtä-mē, tə-\ *n, pl* **-mi** *or* **-mis** [Jp] (1614) : straw matting used as a floor covering in a Japanese home
Ta·tar \ˈtä-tər\ *n* [Pers *Tātār,* of Turkic origin; akin to Turk *Tatar* Tatar] (1842) **1** : a member of any of a group of Turkic peoples found mainly in the Tatar Republic of Russia and parts of Siberia and central Asia **2** : any of the Turkic languages spoken by the Tatar peoples
ta·ter \ˈtā-tər\ *n* [by shortening & alter.] (1759) **1** *dial* : POTATO **2** : HOME RUN 1
tat·soi \ˈtät-ˈsȯi\ *n* [Chin (Guangdong) *daat-choi,* fr. *daat-* sink, fall flat + *choi* vegetable (or fr. a cognate compound in another Chin dial.)] (1987) : an Asian mustard (*Brassica rapa rosularis*) having a rosette of edible dark green spoon-shaped glossy leaves; *also* : the leaves
[1]**tat·ter** \ˈta-tər\ *vt* (14c) : to make ragged ~ *vi* : to become ragged
[2]**tatter** *n* [ME, of Scand origin; akin to ON *tǫturr* tatter; akin to OE *tætteca* rag, OHG *zotta* matted hair, tuft] (15c) **1** : a part torn and left hanging : SHRED **2** *pl* : tattered clothing : RAGS
[1]**tat·ter·de·ma·lion** \ˌta-tər-di-ˈmāl-yən, -ˈmal-, -ˈma-lē-ən\ *n* [origin unknown] (1608) : a person dressed in ragged clothing : RAGAMUFFIN
[2]**tatterdemalion** *adj* (1614) **1** : ragged or disreputable in appearance **2** : being in a decayed state or condition : DILAPIDATED
tat·tered \ˈta-tərd\ *adj* (14c) **1** : wearing ragged clothes ⟨a ~ barefoot boy⟩ **2** : torn into shreds : RAGGED ⟨a ~ flag⟩ **3 a** : broken down : DILAPIDATED ⟨decaying houses along ~ paved streets —P. B. Martin⟩ **b** : being in a shattered condition ⟨led their ~ party to victory⟩
tat·ter·sall \ˈta-tər-ˌsȯl, -səl\ *n* [*Tattersall's* horse market, London, England] (1891) **1** : a pattern of colored lines forming squares of solid background **2** : a fabric woven or printed in a tattersall pattern
tat·tie \ˈta-tē\ *n* [by shortening & alter.] (1788) *Scot* : POTATO
tat·ting \ˈta-tiŋ\ *n* [origin unknown] (1842) **1** : a delicate handmade lace formed usu. by looping and knotting with a single cotton thread and a small shuttle **2** : the act or process of making tatting
[1]**tat·tle** \ˈta-tᵊl\ *n* (ca. 1529) **1** : idle talk : CHATTER **2** : GOSSIP
[2]**tattle** *vb* **tat·tled; tat·tling** \ˈtat-liŋ, ˈta-tᵊl-iŋ\ [MD *tatelen;* akin to ME *tateren* to tattle] *vi* (1547) **1** : CHATTER, PRATE **2** : to tell secrets : BLAB ~ *vt* : to utter or disclose in gossip or chatter
tat·tler \ˈtat-lər, ˈta-tᵊl-ər\ *n* (1550) **1** : TATTLETALE **2** : any of various slender long-legged shorebirds (as the willet, yellowlegs, and redshank) of the sandpiper family with a loud and frequent call
tat·tle·tale \ˈta-tᵊl-ˌtāl\ *n* (1888) : one that tattles : INFORMER
[1]**tat·too** \ta-ˈtü\ *n, pl* **tattoos** [alter. of earlier *taptoo,* fr. D *taptoe,* fr. the phrase *tap toe!* taps shut!] (ca. 1627) **1** : a rapid rhythmic rapping **2 a** : a call sounded shortly before taps as notice to go to quarters **b** : outdoor military exercise given by troops as evening entertainment
[2]**tattoo** *vt* (1780) : to beat or rap rhythmically on : drum on ~ *vi* : to give a series of rhythmic taps
[3]**tattoo** *vt* [Tahitian *tatau,* n., tattoo] (1769) **1** : to mark or color (the skin) with tattoos **2** : to mark the skin with (a tattoo) ⟨~*ed* a flag on his chest⟩ — **tat·too·er** *n* — **tat·too·ist** \-ˈtü-ist\ *n*
[4]**tattoo** *n, pl* **tattoos** (1777) **1** : the act of tattooing : the fact of being tattooed **2** : an indelible mark or figure fixed upon the body by insertion of pigment under the skin or by production of scars
tat·ty \ˈta-tē\ *adj* **tat·ti·er; -est** [perh. akin to OE *tætteca* rag — more at TATTER] (1513) : rather worn, frayed, or dilapidated : SHABBY ⟨a ~ shirt⟩ — **tat·ti·ness** \-nəs\ *n*
tau \ˈtau̇, ˈtȯ\ *n* [ME *taw,* fr. L *tau,* fr. Gk, of Sem origin; akin to Heb *tāw* taw] (14c) **1** : the 19th letter of the Greek alphabet — see ALPHABET table **2** : a short-lived elementary particle of the lepton family that exists in positive and negative charge states and has a mass about 3500 times greater than an electron — called also *tau particle* **3** : a protein that binds to and regulates the assembly and stability of neuronal microtubules and that is found in an abnormal form as the major component of neurofibrillary tangles
tau cross *n* (15c) : a T-shaped cross sometimes having expanded ends and foot — see CROSS illustration
taught *past and past part of* TEACH
[1]**taunt** \ˈtȯnt, ˈtänt\ *n* (ca. 1527) : a sarcastic challenge or insult
[2]**taunt** *vt* [perh. fr. MF *tenter* to try, tempt — more at TEMPT] (1539) : to reproach or challenge in a mocking or insulting manner : jeer at **syn** see RIDICULE — **taunt·er** *n* — **taunt·ing·ly** \ˈtȯn-tiŋ-lē, ˈtän-\ *adv*
taupe \ˈtōp\ *n* [F, lit., mole, fr. OF, fr. L *talpa*] (ca. 1909) : a brownish gray
Tau·re·an \ˈtȯr-ē-ən\ *n* (1911) : TAURUS 2b
[1]**tau·rine** \ˈtȯ-ˌrīn\ *adj* [L *taurinus,* fr. *taurus* bull; akin to Gk *tauros* bull, MIr *tarb*] (1613) : of or relating to a bull : BOVINE
[2]**tau·rine** \ˈtȯ-ˌrēn\ *n* [ISV, fr. L *taurus;* fr. its having been discovered in ox bile] (1845) : a crystalline acid $C_2H_7NO_3S$ that is synthesized in the body from cysteine and methionine, is similar to amino acids but is not a component of proteins, and is involved in various physiological functions (as bile acid conjugation and cell membrane stabilization)
tau·ro·cho·lic acid \ˌtȯr-ə-ˈkō-lik-, -ˈkä-\ *n* [L *taurus* + ISV *-o-* + *cholic (acid)*] (1857) : a bile acid $C_{26}H_{45}NO_7S$ derived from cholic acid and taurine and occurring as the sodium salt in the bile esp. of carnivores
Tau·rus \ˈtȯr-əs\ *n* [ME, fr. L (gen. *Tauri*), lit., bull] (14c) **1** : a zodiacal constellation that contains the Pleiades and Hyades and is represented pictorially by a bull's forequarters **2 a** : the second sign of the zodiac in astrology **b** : one born under the sign of Taurus — see ZODIAC table
[1]**taut** \ˈtȯt\ *adj* [ME *tought,* perh. fr. *tought, toughth* fierce, tough, alter. of *tough* tough] (14c) **1 a** : having no give or slack : tightly drawn ⟨a ~ rope⟩ **b** : HIGH-STRUNG, TENSE ⟨~ nerves⟩ **2 a** : kept in proper order or condition ⟨a ~ ship⟩ **b** (1) : not loose or flabby ⟨~ muscles⟩ (2) : marked by economy of structure and detail ⟨a ~ story⟩ — **taut·ly** *adv* — **taut·ness** *n*
[2]**taut** *vt* [origin unknown] (1721) *Scot* : MAT, TANGLE
taut- *or* **tauto-** *comb form* [LL, fr. Gk, fr. *tauto* the same, contr. of *to auto*] : same ⟨*tauto*merism⟩ ⟨*taut*onym⟩
taut·en \ˈtȯ-tᵊn\ *vb* **taut·ened; taut·en·ing** \ˈtȯt-niŋ, ˈtȯ-tᵊn-iŋ\ *vt* (ca. 1814) : to make taut ⟨~ the rope⟩ ~ *vi* : to become taut
tau·tog \ˈtȯ-ˌtȯg, -ˌtäg, tȯ-ˈ\ *n* [Narragansett *tautaûog,* pl.] (1643) : an edible fish (*Tautoga onitis*) of the wrasse family found along the Atlantic coast of the U.S. and adjacent Canada — called also *blackfish*
tau·to·log·i·cal \ˌtȯ-tə-ˈlä-ji-kəl\ *adj* (1620) : TAUTOLOGOUS — **tau·to·log·i·cal·ly** \-k(ə-)lē\ *adv*
tau·tol·o·gous \tȯ-ˈtä-lə-gəs\ *adj* [Gk *tautologos,* fr. *taut-* + *legein* to say — more at LEGEND] (1714) **1** : involving or containing rhetorical tautology : REDUNDANT **2** : true by virtue of its logical form alone — **tau·tol·o·gous·ly** *adv*
tau·tol·o·gy \tȯ-ˈtä-lə-jē\ *n, pl* **-gies** [LL *tautologia,* fr. Gk, fr. *tautologos*] (1574) **1 a** : needless repetition of an idea, statement, or word **b** : an instance of tautology **2** : a tautologous statement
tau·to·mer \ˈtȯ-tə-mər\ *n* [ISV, fr. *tautomeric*] (1903) : any of the forms of a tautomeric compound
tau·to·mer·ic \ˌtȯ-tə-ˈmer-ik\ *adj* [ISV] (ca. 1890) : of, relating to, or marked by tautomerism
tau·tom·er·ism \tȯ-ˈtä-mə-ˌri-zəm\ *n* (ca. 1890) : isomerism in which the isomers change into one another with great ease so that they ordinarily exist together in equilibrium
taut·o·nym \ˈtȯ-tə-ˌnim\ *n* (1899) : a taxonomic binomial in which the generic name and specific epithet are alike and which is common in zoology esp. to designate a typical form but is forbidden to botany under the International Code of Botanical Nomenclature — **tau·ton·y·my** \tȯ-ˈtä-nə-mē\ *n*
tav·ern \ˈta-vərn\ *n* [ME *taverne,* fr. AF, fr. L *taberna* hut, shop] (14c) **1** : an establishment where alcoholic beverages are sold to be drunk on the premises **2** : INN
ta·ver·na \tä-ˈver-nə\ *n* [ModGk *taberna,* prob. fr. LGk, drinking establishment, fr. L, hut, shop] (1914) : a café in Greece
tav·ern·er \ˈtav-ə(r)-nər\ *n* (14c) : one who keeps a tavern
[1]**taw** \ˈtȯ\ *vt* [ME, to prepare (soil), taw, fr. OE *tawian* to prepare, make; akin to OHG *zawjan* to hasten, Goth *taujan* to do, make] (bef. 12c) : to tan (skins) usu. by a dry process (as with alum or salt)
[2]**taw** \ˈtäf, ˈtȯf, ˈtäv, ˈtȯv\ *n* [Heb *tāw,* lit., mark, cross] (1701) : the 23d letter of the Hebrew alphabet — see ALPHABET table
[3]**taw** \ˈtȯ\ *n* [origin unknown] (1709) **1 a** : a marble used as a shooter **b** : RINGTAW **2** : the line from which players shoot at marbles **3** : a square-dance partner
[4]**taw** *vi* (1863) : to shoot a marble
[1]**taw·dry** \ˈtȯ-drē, ˈtä-\ *adj* **taw·dri·er; -est** [*tawdry lace* a tie of lace for the neck, fr. *St. Audrey* (St. Etheldreda) †679 queen of Northumbria] (1655) : cheap and gaudy in appearance or quality; *also* : IGNOBLE ⟨a ~ attempt to smear his opponent⟩ **syn** see GAUDY — **taw·dri·ly** \-drə-lē\ *adv* — **taw·dri·ness** \-drē-nəs\ *n*
[2]**tawdry** *n* (ca. 1680) : cheap showy finery
[1]**taw·ny** \ˈtȯ-nē, ˈtä-nē\ *adj* **taw·ni·er; -est** [ME, fr. AF *tané, tauné,* lit., tanned, fr. pp. of *tanner* to tan] (14c) **1** : of the color tawny **2** : of a warm sandy color ⟨the lion's ~ coat⟩ — **taw·ni·ness** *n*
[2]**tawny** *n, pl* **tawnies** (15c) : a brownish-orange to light brown color
taw·pie \ˈtȯ-pē\ *n* [of Scand origin; akin to Norw *tåpe* simpleton] (1728) *chiefly Scot* : a foolish or awkward young person
tawse *also* **taws** \ˈtȯz\ *n pl but sing or pl in constr* [prob. fr. pl. of obs. *taw* tawed leather] (ca. 1585) *Brit* : a leather strap slit into strips at the end and used esp. for disciplining children
[1]**tax** \ˈtaks\ *vt* [ME, to estimate, assess, tax, fr. AF *taxer,* fr. ML *taxare,* fr. L, to feel, estimate, censure, freq. of *tangere* to touch — more at TANGENT] (14c) **1** : to assess or determine judicially the amount of (costs in a court action) **2** : to levy a tax on **3** *obs* : to enter (a name) in a list ⟨there went out a decree . . . that all the world should be ~*ed* —Lk 2:1(AV)⟩ **4** : CHARGE, ACCUSE ⟨~*ed* him with neglect of duty⟩; *also* : CENSURE **5** : to make onerous and rigorous demands on ⟨the job ~*ed* her strength⟩ — **tax·able** \ˈtak-sə-bəl\ *adj* — **tax·er** *n*
[2]**tax** *n, often attrib* (14c) **1 a** : a charge usu. of money imposed by authority on persons or property for public purposes **b** : a sum levied on members of an organization to defray expenses **2** : a heavy demand
tax- *or* **taxo-** *also* **taxi-** *comb form* [Gk *taxi-,* fr. *taxis*] : arrangement ⟨*tax*eme⟩ ⟨*taxi*dermy⟩
taxa *pl of* TAXON
tax·a·tion \tak-ˈsā-shən\ *n* (14c) **1** : the action of taxing; *esp* : the imposition of taxes **2** : revenue obtained from taxes **3** : the amount assessed as a tax
tax base *n* (ca. 1943) : the wealth (as real estate or income) within a jurisdiction that is liable to taxation
tax–ex·empt \ˌtaks-ig-ˈzem(p)t\ *adj* (1923) **1** : exempted from a tax **2** : bearing interest that is free from federal or state income tax
[1]**taxi** \ˈtak-sē\ *n, pl* **tax·is** \-sēz\ *also* **tax·ies** (ca. 1907) : TAXICAB; *also* : a similarly operated boat or aircraft
[2]**taxi** *vb* **tax·ied; taxi·ing; tax·is** *or* **tax·ies** *vi* (1911) **1 a** *of an aircraft* : to go at low speed along the surface of the ground or water **b** : to operate an aircraft on the ground under its own power **2** : to ride in a taxicab ⟨~*ed* to the train station⟩ ~ *vt* **1** : to transport by or as if by taxi **2** : to cause (an aircraft) to taxi
taxi·cab \ˈtak-sē-ˌkab\ *n* [*taxi*meter *cab*] (1899) : an automobile that carries passengers for a fare usu. determined by the distance traveled
taxi dancer *n* (ca. 1927) : a woman employed by a dance hall, café, or cabaret to dance with patrons who pay an amount for each dance
taxi·der·my \ˈtak-sə-ˌdər-mē\ *n* [*tax-* + *derm-* + [2]*-y*] (1820) : the art of preparing, stuffing, and mounting the skins of animals and esp. vertebrates — **taxi·der·mic** \ˌtak-sə-ˈdər-mik\ *adj* — **taxi·der·mist** \ˈtak-sə-ˌdər-mist\ *n*
taxi·man \ˈtak-sē-mən\ *n* (1909) *chiefly Brit* : the operator of a taxi
taxi·me·ter \ˈtak-sē-ˌmē-tər\ *n* [F *taximètre,* modif. of G *Taxameter,* fr. ML *taxa* tax, charge (fr. *taxare* to tax) + G *-meter*] (1894) : an instrument for use in a hired vehicle (as a taxicab) for automatically showing the fare due
tax·ing \ˈtak-siŋ\ *adj* (1841) : ONEROUS, WEARING ⟨a ~ operatic role⟩ — **tax·ing·ly** \-siŋ-lē\ *adv*
tax·is \ˈtak-səs\ *n, pl* **tax·es** \-ˌsēz\ [Gk, lit., arrangement, order, fr. *tassein* to arrange] (1899) **1** : reflex translational or orientational movement by a freely motile and usu. simple organism in relation to a source of stimulation (as a light or a temperature or chemical gradient) **2** : a reflex reaction involving a taxis

-taxis *n comb form, pl* **-taxes** [NL, fr. Gk, fr. *taxis*] **1** : arrangement : ordering 〈thermo*taxis*〉 **2** : physiological taxis 〈chemo*taxis*〉

taxi stand *n* (1922) : a place where taxis may park while awaiting hire

taxi·way \'tak-sē-,wā\ *n* (ca. 1933) : a usu. paved strip for taxiing (as from the terminal to a runway) at an airport

Tax·ol \'tak-,sȯl\ *trademark* — used for a preparation of paclitaxel

tax·on \'tak-,sän\ *n, pl* **taxa** \-sə\ *also* **tax·ons** [NL, fr. ISV *taxonomy*] (1929) **1** : a taxonomic group or entity **2** : the name applied to a taxonomic group in a formal system of nomenclature

tax·on·o·my \tak-'sä-nə-mē\ *n* [F *taxonomie*, fr. *tax-* + *-nomie* *-nomy*] (ca. 1828) **1** : the study of the general principles of scientific classification : SYSTEMATICS **2** : CLASSIFICATION; *esp* : orderly classification of plants and animals according to their presumed natural relationships — **tax·o·nom·ic** \,tak-sə-'nä-mik\ *also* **tax·o·nom·i·cal** \-mi-kəl\ *adj* — **tax·o·nom·i·cal·ly** \-mi-k(ə-)lē\ *adv* — **tax·on·o·mist** \tak-'sä-nə-mist\ *n*

tax·pay·er \'taks-,pā-ər\ *n* (1797) : one that pays or is liable for a tax

tax·pay·ing \-,pā-iŋ\ *adj* (1832) : of, relating to, or subject to the paying of a tax

tax selling *n* (1963) : concerted selling of securities late in the year to establish gains and losses for income-tax purposes

tax shelter *n* (1952) : a strategy, investment, or tax code provision that reduces tax liability — **tax–shel·tered** \'taks-,shel-tərd\ *adj*

tax stamp *n* (ca. 1929) : a stamp marked on or affixed to a taxable item as evidence that the tax has been paid

tax·us \'tak-səs\ *n, pl* **tax·us** \-səs\ [NL, genus comprising the yews, fr. L, yew] (ca. 1945) : YEW 1a

-taxy *n comb form* [Gk *-taxia*, fr. *taktos*, verbal of *tassein* to arrange] : -TAXIS 〈epi*taxy*〉

Tay·lor·ism \'tā-lər-,i-zəm\ *n* [Frederick W. *Taylor* †1915 Am. engineer] (1928) : a factory management system developed in the late 19th century to increase efficiency by evaluating every step in a manufacturing process and breaking down production into specialized repetitive tasks

Tay·lor series \'tā-lər-\ *n* [Brook *Taylor* †1731 Eng. mathematician] (1842) : a power series that gives the expansion of a function $f(x)$ in the neighborhood of a point a provided that in the neighborhood of the function is continuous, all its derivatives exist, and the series converges to the function in which case it has the form

$$f(x) = f(a) + \frac{f^{[1]}(a)}{1!}(x-a) + \frac{f^{[2]}(a)}{2!}(x-a)^2 + \ldots + \frac{f^{[n]}(a)}{n!}(x-a)^n + \ldots$$

where $f^{[n]}(a)$ is the derivative of nth order of $f(x)$ evaluated at a — called also *Taylor's series*

Tay–Sachs disease \'tā-,saks-\ *n* [Warren *Tay* †1927 Brit. physician & Bernard P. *Sachs* †1944 Am. neurologist] (1907) : a hereditary disorder of lipid metabolism typically affecting individuals of eastern European Jewish ancestry that is characterized by the accumulation of lipids esp. in nervous tissue due to a deficiency of hexosaminidase, that is inherited as a recessive autosomal trait, and that causes death in early childhood — called also *Tay-Sachs*

taz·za \'tät-sə\ *n* [It, cup, tazza, fr. Ar *ṭassa*, *ṭass*, *ṭasht* basin, fr. Pers *tasht*] (1824) : a shallow cup or vase on a pedestal

tb *abbr* tablespoon; tablespoonful

Tb *symbol* terbium

¹TB \,tē-'bē\ *n* [*TB* (abbr. for *tubercle bacillus*)] (1912) : TUBERCULOSIS

²TB *abbr* **1** thoroughbred **2** tubercle bacillus

TBA *abbr* to be announced

T–ball \'tē-,bȯl\ *n* [²*tee*] (1976) : baseball modified for youngsters in which the ball is batted from a tee of adjustable height rather than being pitched

T–bar \'tē-,bär\ *n* (1948) : a ski lift having a series of T-shaped bars each of which pulls two skiers — called also *T-bar lift*

TBD *abbr* to be determined

T–bill \'tē-,bil\ *n* [*Treasury*] (1973) : a U.S. treasury note

¹T–bone \'tē-,bōn\ *n* (1934) : a small steak from the thin end of the short loin containing a T-shaped bone and a small piece of tenderloin; *also* : this bone — see BEEF illustration

²T–bone *vt* : BROADSIDE

tbs *or* **tbsp** *abbr* tablespoon; tablespoonful

Tc *symbol* technetium

TCDD \,tē-(,)sē-(,)dē-'dē\ *n* [*tetra-* + *chlor-* + *d*ibenzo- (containing two benzene rings) + *d*ioxin] (1971) : a carcinogenic dioxin $C_{12}H_4O_2Cl_4$ found esp. as a contaminant in 2,4,5-T

TCE *abbr* trichloroethylene

T cell *n* [*t*hymus-derived *cell*] (1970) : any of several lymphocytes (as a helper T cell) that differentiate in the thymus, possess highly specific cell-surface antigen receptors, and include some that control the initiation or suppression of cell-mediated and humoral immunity (as by the regulation of T and B cell maturation and proliferation) and others that lyse antigen-bearing cells — called also *T lymphocyte*; compare B CELL

tchotch·ke \'chäch-kə, 'tsäts-\ *n* [Yiddish *tshatshke* trinket, fr. obs. Pol *czaczko*] (1971) : KNICKKNACK, TRINKET

TCP/IP \,tē-(,)sē-'pē-,ī-'pē\ *n* [*t*ransmission-*c*ontrol *p*rotocol/*I*nternet *p*rotocol] (1980) : a set of communications protocols used for the exchange of information over networks and esp. over the Internet

TD *abbr* **1** tardive dyskinesia **2** touchdown

TDD *abbr* telecommunications device for the deaf

t distribution *n* (ca. 1957) : a probability density function that is used esp. in testing hypotheses concerning means of normal distributions whose standard deviations are unknown and that is the distribution of a random variable

$$t = \frac{u\sqrt{n}}{v}$$

where u and v are themselves independent random variables and u has a normal distribution with mean 0 and a standard deviation of 1 and v^2 has a chi-square distribution with n degrees of freedom — called also *student's t distribution*

TDN *abbr* total digestible nutrients

TDY *abbr* temporary duty

Te *symbol* tellurium

tea \'tē\ *n* [Chin (Xiamen) *dé*] (ca. 1655) **1 a** : a shrub (*Camellia sinensis* of the family Theaceae, the tea family) cultivated esp. in China, Japan, and the East Indies **b** : the leaves, leaf buds, and internodes of the tea plant prepared and cured for the market, classed according to method of manufacture into one set of types (as green tea, black tea, or oolong), and graded according to leaf size into another (as orange pekoe, pekoe, or souchong) **2** : an aromatic beverage prepared from tea leaves by infusion with boiling water **3 a** : any of various plants somewhat resembling tea in properties; *also* : an infusion of their leaves used medicinally or as a beverage **b** : TEA ROSE **4 a** : refreshments usu. including tea with sandwiches, crackers, or cookies served in late afternoon **b** : a reception, snack, or meal at which tea is served **5** *slang* : MARIJUANA — **tea·like** \-,līk\ *adj*

tea 1a

tea bag *n* (1935) : a bag usu. of filter paper holding enough tea for an individual serving

tea ball *n* (1886) : a perforated metal ball that holds tea leaves and is used in brewing tea in a pot or cup

tea·ber·ry \'tē-,ber-ē\ *n* [fr. the use of its leaves as a substitute for tea] (1818) : CHECKERBERRY

tea caddy *n* (1784) : CADDY

tea cake *n* (1805) **1** : a small flat cake usu. made with raisins **2** : COOKIE

tea cart *n* (1917) : TEA WAGON

teach \'tēch\ *vb* **taught** \'tȯt\; **teach·ing** [ME *techen* to show, instruct, fr. OE *tǣcan*; akin to OE *tācn* sign — more at TOKEN] *vt* (bef. 12c) **1 a** : to cause to know something 〈*taught* them a trade〉 **b** : to cause to know how 〈is ~*ing* me to drive〉 **c** : to accustom to some action or attitude 〈~ students to think for themselves〉 **d** : to cause to know the disagreeable consequences of some action 〈I'll ~ you to come home late〉 **2** : to guide the studies of **3** : to impart the knowledge of 〈~ algebra〉 **4 a** : to instruct by precept, example, or experience **b** : to make known and accepted 〈experience ~*es* us our limitations〉 **5** : to conduct instruction regularly in 〈~ school〉 ~ *vi* : to provide instruction : act as a teacher *usage* see LEARN

syn TEACH, INSTRUCT, EDUCATE, TRAIN, DISCIPLINE, SCHOOL mean to cause to acquire knowledge or skill. TEACH applies to any manner of imparting information or skill so that others may learn 〈*taught* us a lot about our planet〉. INSTRUCT suggests methodical or formal teaching 〈*instructs* raw recruits in military drill〉. EDUCATE implies development of the mind 〈more things than formal schooling serve to *educate* a person〉. TRAIN stresses instruction and drill with a specific end in view 〈*trained* foreign pilots to operate the new aircraft〉. DISCIPLINE implies training in habits of order and precision 〈a *disciplined* mind〉. SCHOOL implies training or disciplining esp. in what is hard to master 〈*schooled* the horse in five gaits〉.

teach·able \'tē-chə-bəl\ *adj* (15c) **1 a** : capable of being taught **b** : apt and willing to learn **2** : favorable to teaching — **teach·able·ness** *n* — **teach·ably** \-blē\ *adv*

teach·er \'tē-chər\ *n* (14c) **1** : one that teaches; *esp* : one whose occupation is to instruct **2** : a Mormon ranking above a deacon in the Aaronic priesthood

teach·er·ly \-lē\ *adj* (ca. 1683) : resembling, characteristic of, or befitting a teacher

teachers college *n* (ca. 1911) : a college for the training of teachers usu. offering a full 4-year course and granting a bachelor's degree

teacher's pet *n* (1914) **1** : a pupil who has won the teacher's special favor **2** : a person who is treated as a favorite by one in authority

teach–in \'tēch-,in\ *n* (1965) : an extended meeting usu. held on a college campus for lectures, debates, and discussions to raise awareness of or express a position on a social or political issue

¹teaching *n* (13c) **1** : the act, practice, or profession of a teacher **2** : something taught; *esp* : DOCTRINE 〈the ~*s* of Confucius〉

²teaching *adj* (1615) : of, relating to, used for, or engaged in teaching 〈a ~ aid〉 〈the ~ profession〉 〈a ~ assistant〉

teaching hospital *n* (1933) : a hospital that is affiliated with a medical school and provides means for medical education

tea·cup \'tē-,kəp\ *n* (1700) : a small cup usu. with a handle used with a saucer for hot beverages — **teacupful** *n*

tea dance *n* (1885) : a dance held in the late afternoon

tea garden *n* (1780) **1** : a public garden where tea and light refreshments are served **2** : a tea plantation

tea gown *n* (1878) : a semiformal gown of fine materials in graceful flowing lines worn esp. for afternoon entertaining at home

tea·house \'tē-,hau̇s\ *n* (1689) : a public house or restaurant where tea and light refreshments are sold

teak \'tēk\ *n* [Pg *teca*, fr. Malayalam *tēkka*] (1698) **1** : a tall tropical Asian timber tree (*Tectona grandis*) of the vervain family **2** : the hard yellowish-brown wood of teak used esp. for furniture and shipbuilding

tea·ket·tle \'tē-,ke-t³l\ *n* (1705) : a covered kettle with a handle and spout for boiling water

teak·wood \'tēk-,wu̇d\ *n* (1783) : TEAK 2

teal \'tēl\ *n, pl* **teal** *or* **teals** [ME *tele*; akin to MD *teling* teal] (14c) **1** : any of various widely distributed small short-necked dabblers (genus *Anas*) — compare BLUE-WINGED TEAL, GREEN-WINGED TEAL **2** : TEAL BLUE

teal blue *n* (1938) : a dark greenish blue

1team \ˈtēm\ *n* [ME *teme,* fr. OE *tēam* offspring, lineage, group of draft animals; akin to OHG *zoum* rein, OE *tēon* to draw, pull — more at TOW] (bef. 12c) **1 a :** two or more draft animals harnessed to the same vehicle or implement; *also* **:** these with their harness and attached vehicle **b :** a draft animal often with harness and vehicle **2** *obs* **:** LINEAGE, RACE **3 :** a group of animals: as **a :** a brood esp. of young pigs or ducks **b :** a matched group of animals for exhibition **4 :** a number of persons associated together in work or activity: as **a :** a group on one side (as in football or a debate) **b :** CREW, GANG

2team *adj* (14c) **:** of or performed by a team ⟨a ~ effort⟩; *also* **:** marked by devotion to teamwork rather than individual achievement ⟨a ~ player⟩

3team *vt* (1552) **1 :** to yoke or join in a team; *also* **:** to put together in a coordinated ensemble **2 :** to convey or haul with a team ~ *vi* **1 :** to drive a team or motortruck **2 :** to form a team or association

team foul *n* (1966) **:** one of a designated number of personal fouls the players on a basketball team may commit during a given period of play before the opposing team begins receiving bonus free throws

team handball *n* (1970) **:** a game developed from soccer which is played between two teams of seven players each and in which the ball is thrown, caught, and dribbled with the hands

team·mate \ˈtēm-ˌmāt\ *n* (1915) **:** a fellow member of a team

team·ster \ˈtēm(p)-stər\ *n* (1759) **:** one who drives a team or motortruck esp. as an occupation

team·work \ˈtēm-ˌwərk\ *n* (ca. 1828) **:** work done by several associates with each doing a part but all subordinating personal prominence to the efficiency of the whole

tea party *n* (1778) **1 :** an afternoon social gathering at which tea is served **2** [fr. the Boston Tea Party, name applied to the occasion in 1773 when a shipment of tea was thrown into Boston harbor in protest against the tax on imports] **:** an exciting disturbance or proceeding

tea·pot \ˈtē-ˌpät\ *n* (1685) **:** a vessel with a spout and a handle in which tea is brewed and from which it is served

tea·poy \ˈtē-ˌpȯi\ *n* [Hindi & Urdu *tipāī*] (1828) **1 :** a 3-legged ornamental stand **2** [influenced by *tea*] **:** a stand or table containing a tea chest or caddy and used for supporting a tea set; *also* **:** TEA CADDY

1tear \ˈtir\ *n* [ME, fr. OE *tæhher, tēar;* akin to OHG *zahar* tear, Gk *dakry*] (bef. 12c) **1 a :** a drop of clear saline fluid secreted by the lacrimal gland and diffused between the eye and eyelids to moisten the parts and facilitate their motion **b** *pl* **:** a secretion of profuse tears that overflow the eyelids and dampen the face **2 :** a transparent drop of fluid or hardened fluid matter (as resin) **3** *pl* **:** an act of weeping or grieving ⟨broke into ~*s*⟩ — **tear·less** *adj*

2tear *vi* (bef. 12c) **:** to fill with tears **:** shed tears ⟨eyes ~*ing* in the November wind —Saul Bellow⟩

3tear \ˈter\ *vb* **tore** \ˈtȯr\; **torn** \ˈtȯrn\; **tear·ing** [ME *teren,* fr. OE *teran;* akin to OHG *zeran* to destroy, Gk *derein* to skin, Skt *dṛṇāti* he bursts, tears] *vt* (bef. 12c) **1 a :** to separate parts of or pull apart by force **:** REND **b :** to wound by or as if by tearing **:** LACERATE ⟨~ the skin⟩ **2 :** to divide or disrupt by the pull of contrary forces ⟨a mind *torn* with doubts⟩ **3 a :** to remove by force **:** WRENCH — often used with *off* ⟨~ a cover off a box⟩ **b :** to remove as if by wrenching ⟨~ your thoughts away from the scene⟩ **4 :** to make or effect by or as if by tearing ⟨~ a hole in the wall⟩ ~ *vi* **1 :** to separate on being pulled **:** REND ⟨this cloth ~*s* easily⟩ **2 a :** to move or act with violence, haste, or force ⟨went ~*ing* down the street⟩ **b :** to smash or penetrate something with violent force ⟨the bullet *tore* through his leg⟩ — **tear·able** \ˈter-ə-bəl\ *adj* — **tear·er** *n* — **tear at :** to cause anguish to **:** DISTRESS ⟨her grief *tore at* his heart⟩ — **tear into :** to attack without restraint or caution — **tear it :** to cause frustration, defeat, or an end to plans or hopes ⟨that *tears it*⟩ — **tear one's hair :** to pull one's hair as an expression of grief, rage, frustration, desperation, or anxiety; *also* **:** to feel or display such an emotion

syn TEAR, RIP, REND, SPLIT, CLEAVE, RIVE mean to separate forcibly. TEAR implies pulling apart by force and leaving jagged edges ⟨*tear* up the letter⟩. RIP implies a pulling apart in one rapid uninterrupted motion often along a line or joint ⟨*ripped* the shirt on a nail⟩. REND implies very violent or ruthless severing or sundering ⟨an angry mob *rent* the prisoner's clothes⟩. SPLIT implies a cutting or breaking apart in a continuous, straight, and usu. lengthwise direction or in the direction of grain or layers ⟨*split* logs for firewood⟩. CLEAVE implies very forceful splitting or cutting with a blow ⟨a bolt of lightning *cleaved* the giant oak⟩. RIVE occurs most often in figurative use ⟨a political party *riven* by conflict⟩.

4tear \ˈter\ *n* (1611) **1 a :** damage from being torn; *esp* **:** a hole or flaw made by tearing **b :** the act of tearing **2 a :** a tearing pace **:** HURRY **b :** SPREE ⟨got paid and went on a ~⟩ **c :** a run of unusual success ⟨the team was on a ~⟩

tear·away \ˈter-ə-ˌwā\ *n* (1950) *Brit* **:** a rebellious and unruly or reckless young person

tear away *vt* (ca. 1699) **:** to remove (as oneself) reluctantly

tear·down \ˈter-ˌdau̇n\ *n* (1926) **:** the act or process of disassembling

tear down *vt* (14c) **1 a :** to cause to decompose or disintegrate **b :** VILIFY, DENIGRATE ⟨trying to *tear down* his reputation⟩ **2 :** to take apart **:** DISASSEMBLE ⟨*tear down* an engine⟩

tear·drop \ˈtir-ˌdräp\ *n* (1776) **1 :** 1TEAR 1a **2 :** something shaped like a dropping tear; *specif* **:** a pendent gem (as on an earring)

tear·ful \ˈtir-fəl\ *adj* (ca. 1586) **1 :** flowing with or accompanied by tears ⟨~ entreaties⟩ **2 :** causing tears **:** TEARY ⟨a ~ eulogy⟩ — **tear·ful·ly** \-fə-lē\ *adv* — **tear·ful·ness** *n*

tear·gas \-ˌgas\ *vt* (1946) **:** to use tear gas on

tear gas *n* (1917) **:** a solid, liquid, or gaseous substance that on dispersion in the atmosphere irritates mucous membranes resulting esp. in blinding of the eyes with tears and is used chiefly in dispelling mobs

tear·ing \ˈter-iŋ\ *adj* (1581) **1 :** causing continued or repeated pain or distress **2 :** HASTY, VIOLENT **3** *chiefly Brit* **:** SPLENDID

tear·jerk·er \ˈtir-ˌjər-kər\ *n* (1912) **:** a story, song, play, film, or broadcast that moves or is intended to move its audience to tears — **tear–jerk·ing** \-kiŋ\ *adj*

tea·room \ˈtē-ˌrüm, -ˌru̇m\ *n* (1778) **:** a small restaurant or café with service and decor designed primarily for a female clientele

tea rose *n* (1838) **:** a garden bush rose (*Rosa odorata*) of Chinese origin that includes several cultivars and is valued esp. for its abundant large usu. tea-scented blossoms — compare HYBRID TEA ROSE

tear sheet *n* (ca. 1924) **:** a sheet torn from a publication

tear·stain \ˈtir-ˌstān\ *n* (1922) **:** a spot or streak left by tears — **tear-stained** \-ˌstānd\ *adj*

tear up *vt* (1620) **1 :** to damage, remove, or effect an opening in ⟨*tore up* the street to lay a new water main⟩ **2 :** to perform or compete with great success on, in, or against ⟨couples *tearing up* the dance floor⟩ ⟨a batter who's *tearing up* the league⟩

teary \ˈtir-ē\ *adj* **tear·i·er; -est** (14c) **1 a :** wet or stained with tears **:** TEARFUL ⟨~ eyes⟩ **b :** consisting of tears or drops resembling tears **2 :** causing tears **:** PATHETIC ⟨a ~ story⟩

1tease \ˈtēz\ *vt* **teased; teas·ing** [ME *tesen,* fr. OE *tǣsan;* akin to OHG *zeisan* to tease] (bef. 12c) **1 a :** to disentangle and lay parallel by combing or carding ⟨~ wool⟩ **b :** TEASEL **2 :** to tear in pieces; *esp* **:** to shred (a tissue or specimen) for microscopic examination **3 a :** to disturb or annoy by persistent irritating or provoking esp. in a petty or mischievous way **b :** to annoy with petty persistent requests **:** PESTER; *also* **:** to obtain by repeated coaxing **c :** to persuade to acquiesce esp. by persistent small efforts **:** COAX **d :** to manipulate or influence as if by teasing **e :** to make fun of **:** KID **4 :** to comb (hair) by taking hold of a strand and pushing the short hairs toward the scalp with the comb **5 :** to tantalize esp. by arousing desire or curiosity often without intending to satisfy it ***syn*** see WORRY — **teas·ing·ly** \ˈtē-ziŋ-lē\ *adv*

2tease *n* (1680) **1 :** the act of teasing **:** the state of being teased **2 :** one that teases

1tea·sel \ˈtē-zəl\ *n* [ME *tesel,* fr. OE *tǣsel;* akin to OE *tǣsan* to tease] (bef. 12c) **1 a :** an Old World prickly herb (*Dipsacus fullonum* of the family Dipsacaceae, the teasel family) with flower heads that are covered with stiff hooked bracts and were used esp. formerly in the woolen industry — called also *fuller's teasel* **b :** a plant of the same genus as the teasel **2 a :** a flower head of the fuller's teasel used when dried to raise a nap on woolen cloth **b :** a wire substitute for the teasel

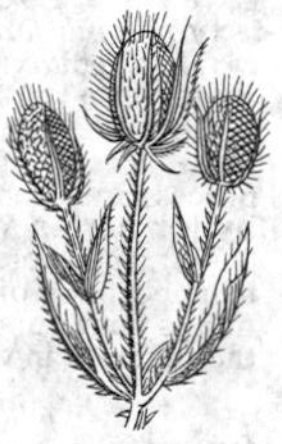

teasel 1a

2teasel *vt* **tea·seled** *or* **tea·selled; tea·sel·ing** *or* **tea·sel·ling** \ˈtēz-liŋ, ˈtē-zə-\ (1543) **:** to nap (cloth) with teasels

tease out *vt* (1828) **1 :** to obtain by or as if by disentangling and freeing with a pointed instrument **2 :** UNRAVEL 2

teas·er \ˈtē-zər\ *n* (14c) **1 :** one that teases **2 :** an advertising or promotional device intended to arouse interest or curiosity esp. in something to follow

tea service *n* (1809) **:** TEA SET

tea set *n* (1763) **:** a matching set of metalware or china (as a teapot, sugar bowl, creamer, and often plates, cups, and saucers) for serving tea and sometimes coffee at table

tea shop *n* (1851) *chiefly Brit* **:** a small restaurant or café **:** TEAROOM

tea·spoon \ˈtē-ˌspün, -ˈspün\ *n* (1686) **1 :** a small spoon that is used esp. for eating soft foods and stirring beverages and that holds about one third of a tablespoon **2 :** a unit of measure esp. in cookery equal to ⅙ fluid ounce or ⅓ tablespoon (5 milliliters)

tea·spoon·ful \-ˌfu̇l\ *n, pl* **teaspoonfuls** \-ˌfu̇lz\ *also* **tea·spoons·ful** \-ˌspünz-ˌfu̇l, -ˈspünz-\ (1731) **1 :** as much as a teaspoon can hold **2 :** TEASPOON 2

teat \ˈtit, ˈtēt\ *n* [ME *tete,* in part fr. OE *tit;* in part fr. AF, of Gmc origin; akin to OE *tit* teat, MHG *zitze*] (12c) **1 :** the protuberance through which milk is drawn from an udder or breast **:** NIPPLE **2 :** a small projection or a nib (as on a mechanical part) — **teat·ed** \ˈti-təd, ˈtē-\ *adj*

tea table *n* (1688) **:** a table used or spread for tea; *specif* **:** a small table for serving afternoon tea

tea·time \ˈtē-ˌtīm\ *n* (1727) **:** the customary time for tea **:** late afternoon or early evening

tea towel *n* (1863) **:** a cloth for drying dishes

tea tray *n* (1761) **:** a tray that accommodates a tea set

tea tree *n* [fr. the use of an infusion of their leaves as a beverage] (1790) **1 :** any of various Australasian shrubs or small trees (genus *Leptospermum*) of the myrtle family that form dense thickets and have aromatic evergreen foliage **2 :** any of various melaleucas (esp. *Melaleuca alternifolia*) with aromatic leaves that yield an essential oil used esp. as an antiseptic

tea wagon *n* (1921) **:** a small table on wheels used in serving tea

Te·bet \tā-ˈvāt, -ˈvāth, ˈtā-ˌves\ *n* [Heb *Ṭēbhēth*] (14c) **:** the 4th month of the civil year or the 10th month of the ecclesiastical year in the Jewish calendar — see MONTH table

1tech \ˈtek\ *n* (1942) **:** TECHNICIAN ⟨lab ~*s*⟩ ⟨a computer ~⟩

2tech *n, often attrib* (1972) **:** TECHNOLOGY ⟨the triumph of ~ . . . is far from complete —*Newsweek*⟩

3tech *abbr* **1** technical; technically **2** technological

teched *or* **tetched** \ˈtecht\ *adj* [alter. of *touched*] (1921) **:** mentally unbalanced

tech·ie \ˈte-kē\ *n* [by shortening & alter. fr. *technician*] (1970) **:** a person who is very knowledgeable or enthusiastic about technology and esp. high technology — **techie** *adj*

tech·ne·tium \tek-ˈnē-sh(ē-)əm\ *n* [NL, fr. Gk *technētos* artificial, fr. *technasthai* to devise by art, fr. *technē*] (ca. 1946) **:** a radioactive metallic element obtained esp. from nuclear fuel as a product of uranium fission and used as a diagnostic radiopharmaceutical — see ELEMENT table

tech·ne·tron·ic \ˌtek-nə-ˈträ-nik\ *adj* [*techno*logical + *electronic*] (1967) **:** shaped or influenced by the changes wrought by advances in technology and communications ⟨our modern ~ society⟩

tech·nic \ˈtek-nik, *for 1 also* tek-ˈnēk\ *n* (1855) **1 :** TECHNIQUE 1 **2** *pl but sing or pl in constr* **:** TECHNOLOGY 1a

tech·ni·cal \ˈtek-ni-kəl\ *adj* [Gk *technikos* of art, skillful, fr. *technē* art, craft, skill; akin to Gk *tektōn* builder, carpenter, L *texere* to weave, Skt *takṣati* he fashions] (1617) **1 a :** having special and usu. practical knowledge esp. of a mechanical or scientific subject ⟨a ~ consultant⟩ **b :** marked by or characteristic of specialization ⟨~ language⟩ **2 a :** of or relating to a particular subject **b :** of or relating to a practical subject organized on scientific principles ⟨a ~ school⟩ **c :** TECHNO-

LOGICAL 1 **3 a** : based on or marked by a strict or legal interpretation **b** : LEGAL 6 **4** : of or relating to technique **5** : of, relating to, or produced by ordinary commercial processes without being subjected to special purification ⟨~ sulfuric acid⟩ **6** : relating to or caused by the functioning of the market as a discrete mechanism not influenced by macroeconomic factors ⟨a ~ rally⟩ — **tech·ni·cal·ly** \-k(ə-)lē\ *adv*

technical foul *n* (ca. 1929) : a foul (as in basketball) that involves no physical contact with an opponent and that usu. is incurred by unsportsmanlike conduct — called also *technical*; compare PERSONAL FOUL

tech·ni·cal·i·ty \ˌtek-nə-ˈka-lə-tē\ *n, pl* **-ties** (1776) **1** : something technical; *esp* : a detail meaningful only to a specialist ⟨a legal ~⟩ **2** : the quality or state of being technical

tech·ni·cal·ize \ˈtek-ni-kə-ˌlīz\ *vt* **-ized; -iz·ing** (1852) : to give a technical slant to — **tech·ni·cal·i·za·tion** \ˌtek-ni-kə-lə-ˈzā-shən\ *n*

technical knockout *n* (1921) : the termination of a boxing match when a boxer is unable or is declared by the referee to be unable (as because of injuries) to continue the fight — called also *TKO*

technical sergeant *n* (ca. 1956) : a noncommissioned officer in the air force ranking above a staff sergeant and below a master sergeant

tech·ni·cian \tek-ˈni-shən\ *n* (1833) **1** : a specialist in the technical details of a subject or occupation ⟨a computer ~⟩ **2** : one who has acquired the technique of an art or other area of specialization ⟨a superb ~ and a musician of integrity —Irving Kolodin⟩

Tech·ni·col·or \ˈtek-ni-ˌkə-lər\ *trademark* — used for a process of color cinematography

tech·nique \tek-ˈnēk\ *n* [F, fr. *technique* technical, fr. Gk *technikos*] (1817) **1** : the manner in which technical details are treated (as by a writer) or basic physical movements are used (as by a dancer); *also* : ability to treat such details or use such movements ⟨good piano ~⟩ **2 a** : a body of technical methods (as in a craft or in scientific research) **b** : a method of accomplishing a desired aim

tech·no \ˈtek-nō\ *n, often attrib* [*techno-* (as in *techno-pop* or *techno-rock*, styles of popular music utilizing electronically created sounds)] (1987) : electronic dance music that features a fast beat and synthesized sounds usu. without vocals or a conventional song structure

techno- *comb form* [*technology*] : technical : technological ⟨*technocracy*⟩

tech·no·bab·ble \ˈtek-nə-ˌba-bəl\ *n* (1981) : technical jargon

tech·noc·ra·cy \tek-ˈnä-krə-sē\ *n, pl* **-cies** (1919) : government by technicians; *specif* : management of society by technical experts

tech·no·crat \ˈtek-nə-ˌkrat\ *n* (1932) **1** : an adherent of technocracy **2** : a technical expert; *esp* : one exercising managerial authority

tech·no·crat·ic \ˌtek-nə-ˈkra-tik\ *adj* (1932) : of, relating to, or suggestive of a technocrat or a technocracy

technol *abbr* technology

tech·no·log·i·cal \ˌtek-nə-ˈlä-ji-kəl\ *also* **tech·no·log·ic** \-ˈlä-jik\ *adj* (1800) **1** : of, relating to, or characterized by technology **2** : resulting from improvements in technical processes that increase productivity of machines and eliminate manual operations or operations done by older machines — **tech·no·log·i·cal·ly** \-ji-k(ə-)lē\ *adv*

tech·nol·o·gize \tek-ˈnä-lə-ˌjīz\ *vt* **-gized; -giz·ing** (1954) : to affect or alter by technology

tech·nol·o·gy \-jē\ *n, pl* **-gies** [Gk *technologia* systematic treatment of an art, fr. *technē* art, skill + *-o-* + *-logia* -logy] (1859) **1 a** : the practical application of knowledge esp. in a particular area : ENGINEERING 2 ⟨medical ~⟩ **b** : a capability given by the practical application of knowledge ⟨a car's fuel-saving ~⟩ **2** : a manner of accomplishing a task esp. using technical processes, methods, or knowledge ⟨new *technologies* for information storage⟩ **3** : the specialized aspects of a particular field of endeavor ⟨educational ~⟩ — **tech·nol·o·gist** \-jist\ *n*

tech·no·phile \ˈtek-nə-ˌfī(-ə)l\ *n* (1968) : an enthusiast of technology — **tech·no·phil·ia** \ˌtek-nō-ˈfi-lē-ə\ *n*

tech·no·pho·bia \ˌtek-nə-ˈfō-bē-ə\ *n* (1965) : fear or dislike of advanced technology or complex devices and esp. computers — **tech·no·phobe** \ˈtek-nə-ˌfōb\ *n* — **tech·no·pho·bic** \ˌtek-nə-ˈfō-bik\ *adj*

tech·no–pop \ˈtek-(ˌ)nō-ˌpäp\ *n* (1980) : popular music featuring extensive use of synthesizers

tech·no·pre·neur \ˌtek-nō-prə-ˈnər, -ˈn(y)u̇r\ *n* [*techno-* + entre*preneur*] (1987) : an entrepreneur involved with high technology

tech·no·struc·ture \ˈtek-nō-ˌstrək-chər\ *n* (1967) : the network of professionally skilled managers (as scientists, engineers, and administrators) that tends to control the economy both within and beyond individual corporate groups

tech·no–thrill·er \ˈtek-nō-ˌthri-lər, -nə-\ *n* (1986) : a thriller whose plot relies on modern technology

techy \ˈte-kē\ *adj* [*tech*nological + [1]*-y*] (1982) : characterized by technological sophistication : TECHNICAL ⟨~ innovations⟩

tec·ton·ic \tek-ˈtä-nik\ *adj* [LL *tectonicus*, fr. Gk *tektonikos* of a builder, fr. *tektōn* builder — more at TECHNICAL] (1894) **1** : of or relating to tectonics **2** : having a strong and widespread impact ⟨a ~ shift in voting patterns⟩ — **tec·ton·i·cal·ly** \-ni-k(ə-)lē\ *adv*

tec·ton·ics \tek-ˈtä-niks\ *n pl but sing or pl in constr* (1899) **1** : geological structural features as a whole **2 a** : a branch of geology concerned with the structure of the crust of a planet (as earth) or moon and esp. with the formation of folds and faults in it **b** : TECTONISM

tec·to·nism \ˈtek-tə-ˌni-zəm\ *n* [ISV] (1948) : the process of deformation that produces in the earth's crust its continents and ocean basins, plateaus and mountains, folds of strata, and faults — called also *diastrophism*

tec·tum \ˈtek-təm\ *n, pl* **tec·ta** \-tə\ [NL, fr. L, roof, dwelling, fr. neut. of *tectus*, pp. of *tegere* to cover — more at THATCH] (ca. 1905) : a bodily structure resembling or serving as a roof; *esp* : the dorsal part of the midbrain — **tec·tal** \ˈtek-tᵊl\ *adj*

ted \ˈted\ *vt* **ted·ded; ted·ding** [ME *tedden*, fr. OE **teddan*; akin to MD *tedden* to ted, ON *tethja* to manure, *tath* spread dung, OHG *zetten* to spread] (13c) : to spread or turn from the swath and scatter (as new-mown grass) for drying

ted·der \ˈte-dər\ *n* (15c) : one that teds; *specif* : a machine for stirring and spreading hay to hasten drying and curing

ted·dy \ˈte-dē\ *n, pl* **teddies** [origin unknown] (1924) : CHEMISE 1

ted·dy bear \ˈte-dē-ˌ\ *n* [*Teddy*, nickname of Theodore Roosevelt; fr. a cartoon depicting the president sparing the life of a bear cub while hunting] (1906) : a stuffed toy bear

teddy boy *n* [*Teddy*, nickname for Edward] (1954) : a young British thug esp. of the 1950s and 1960s characterized by Edwardian dress

Te De·um \ˌtā-ˈdā-əm, ˌtē-ˈdē-\ *n, pl* **Te Deums** [ME, fr. LL *te deum laudamus* thee, God, we praise; fr. the opening words of the hymn] (bef. 12c) : a liturgical Christian hymn of praise to God

te·dious \ˈtē-dē-əs, ˈtē-jəs\ *adj* [ME, fr. LL *taediosus*, fr. L *taedium*] (15c) : tiresome because of length or dullness : BORING ⟨a ~ public ceremony⟩ — **te·dious·ly** *adv* — **te·dious·ness** *n*

te·di·um \ˈtē-dē-əm\ *n* [L *taedium* disgust, irksomeness, fr. *taedēre* to disgust, weary] (1662) **1** : the quality or state of being tedious : TEDIOUSNESS; *also* : BOREDOM **2** : a tedious period of time

[1]**tee** \ˈtē\ *n* [ME] (15c) **1** : the letter *t* **2** : something shaped like a capital T **3** : a mark aimed at in various games (as curling) — **to a tee** : EXACTLY, PRECISELY ⟨the description fit her *to a tee*⟩

[2]**tee** *n* [origin unknown] (1673) **1 a** : a small mound or a peg on which a golf ball is placed before being struck at the beginning of play on a hole **b** : a device for holding a football in position for kicking **c** : an adjustable post on which a ball is placed for batting (as in T-ball) **2** : the area from which a golf ball is struck at the beginning of play on a hole

[3]**tee** *vt* **teed; tee·ing** (1673) : to place (a ball) on a tee — often used with *up*

teed off *adj* [prob. fr. *tee off* (on)] (1951) : ANGRY, ANNOYED

tee–hee \ˈtē-ˈhē\ *vi* [ME *tehee*, interj., of imit. origin] (13c) : GIGGLE, TITTER — **tee–hee** *n*

[1]**teem** \ˈtēm\ *vb* [ME *temen*, fr. OE *tīman, tǣman*; akin to OE *tēam* offspring — more at TEAM] *vt* (bef. 12c) *archaic* : BRING FORTH; give birth to : PRODUCE ~ *vi* **1** *obs* : to become pregnant : CONCEIVE **2 a** : to become filled to overflowing : ABOUND **b** : to be present in large quantity — **teem·ing·ly** \ˈtē-miŋ-lē\ *adv* — **teem·ing·ness** *n*

[2]**teem** *vt* [ME *temen*, fr. ON *tœma*; akin to OE *tōm* empty] (14c) : EMPTY, POUR ⟨~ molten metal into a mold⟩

[1]**teen** \ˈtēn\ *n* [ME *tene*, fr. OE *tēona* injury, grief; akin to ON *tjōn* loss, damage] (13c) *archaic* : MISERY, AFFLICTION

[2]**teen** *n* (1818) : a teenage person : TEENAGER — **teen** *adj*

teen·age \ˈtēn-ˌāj\ *or* **teen·aged** \-ˌājd\ *adj* (1921) : of, being, or relating to people in their teens — **teen·ag·er** \-ˌā-jər\ *n*

teen·er \ˈtē-nər\ *n* (1894) : TEEN, TEENAGER

teens \ˈtēnz\ *n pl* [*-teen* (as in *thirteen*)] (1604) : the numbers 13 to 19 inclusive; *specif* : the years 13 to 19 in a lifetime or century

teens·ploi·ta·tion \ˌtēn-(ˌ)splȯi-ˈtā-shən\ *n* [[2]*teen* + *-sploitation* (fr. *blaxploitation*)] (1982) : the exploitation of teenagers by producers of teen-oriented films

teen·sy \ˈtēn(t)-sē\ *adj* **teen·si·er; -est** [baby-talk alter. of *teeny*] (1899) : TINY

teen·sy–ween·sy \ˌtēn(t)-sē-ˈwēn(t)-sē\ *adj* [baby-talk alter. of *teeny-weeny*] (ca. 1906) : TINY

tee·ny \ˈtē-nē\ *adj* **tee·ni·er; -est** [by alter.] (1825) : TINY

teeny·bop \ˈtē-nē-ˌbäp\ *adj* [back-formation fr. *teenybopper*] (1967) : of, relating to, or being a teenybopper

teeny·bop·per \-ˌbä-pər\ *n* [*teeny* teenager + *-bopper*, perh. fr. [4]*bop*] (1965) **1** : a teenage girl **2** : a young teenager who is enthusiastically devoted to popular music and to current fads

tee·ny–wee·ny \ˌtē-nē-ˈwē-nē\ *adj* [*teeny* + *weeny*] (ca. 1879) : TINY

tee off *vi* (1895) **1** : to drive from a tee **2** : BEGIN, START **3** : to hit hard **4** : to make an angry denunciation — often used with *on*

teepee *var of* TEPEE

tee shirt *var of* T-SHIRT

[1]**tee·ter** \ˈtē-tər\ *vi* [ME *titeren* to totter, reel; akin to OHG *zittarōn* to shiver] (1844) **1 a** : to move unsteadily : WOBBLE **b** : WAVER, VACILLATE ⟨~*ed* on the brink of bankruptcy⟩ **2** : SEESAW

[2]**teeter** *n* (1860) : SEESAW 2b

tee·ter·board \-ˌbōrd\ *n* (1855) **1** : SEESAW 2b **2** : a board placed on a raised support so that a person standing on one end of the board is thrown into the air if another jumps on the opposite end

tee·ter–tot·ter \ˈtē-tər-ˌtä-tər\ *n* (ca. 1905) : SEESAW 2b

teeth *pl of* TOOTH

teethe \ˈtēth\ *vi* **teethed; teeth·ing** [back-formation fr. *teething*] (15c) : to experience the emergence of one's teeth through the gums

teeth·er \ˈtē-thər\ *n* (1946) : an object (as a teething ring) designed for a baby to bite on during teething

teething *n* [*teeth*] (1732) **1** : the first growth of teeth **2** : the phenomena accompanying growth of teeth through the gums

teething ring *n* (1872) : a usu. rubber or plastic ring for a teething infant to bite on

teeth·ridge \ˈtēth-ˌrij\ *n* (1928) : the inner surface of the gums of the upper front teeth

tee·to·tal \ˈtē-ˈtō-tᵊl, -ˌtō-\ *adj* [*total* + *total* (abstinence)] (1834) **1** : of, relating to, or practicing teetotalism **2** : TOTAL, COMPLETE — **tee·to·tal·ly** \-tᵊl-ē\ *adv*

tee·to·tal·er *or* **tee·to·tal·ler** \-ˈtō-tᵊl-ər\ *n* (1834) : one who practices or advocates teetotalism

tee·to·tal·ism \-tᵊl-ˌi-zəm\ *n* (1834) : the principle or practice of complete abstinence from alcoholic drinks — **tee·to·tal·ist** \-tᵊl-ist\ *n*

tee·to·tum \ˈtē-ˈtō-təm\ *n* [[1]*tee* + L *totum* all, fr. neut. of *totus* whole; fr. the letter *T* inscribed on one side as an abbr. of *totum* (take) all] (1720) : a small top usu. inscribed with letters and used in put-and-take

teff \ˈtef\ *n* [Amharic *ṭef*] (1790) : an economically important Ethiopian annual cereal grass (*Eragrostis tef* syn. *E. abyssinica*) grown for its small grain which yields a white flour and as a forage and hay crop

te·fil·lin \tē-ˈfi-lən *also* -ləm\ *n pl but sometimes sing in constr* [LHeb *tĕphillīn*, fr. Aram, attachments] (1613) : the phylacteries worn by Jews

TEFL *abbr* teaching English as a foreign language

Tef·lon \ˈte-ˌflän\ *trademark* — used for synthetic fluorine-containing resins used esp. for molding articles and for nonstick coatings

teg·men \ˈteg-mən\ *n, pl* **teg·mi·na** \-mə-nə\ [NL *tegmin-, tegmen*, fr. L, covering, fr. *tegere* to cover — more at THATCH] (1807) : a superficial layer or covering usu. of a plant or animal part

\ə\ **a**but \ᵊ\ kit**t**en, F ta**ble** \ər\ **fur**ther \a\ **a**sh \ā\ **a**ce \ä\ m**o**p, m**a**r \au̇\ **ou**t \ch\ **ch**in \e\ b**e**t \ē\ **ea**sy \g\ **g**o \i\ h**i**t \ī\ **i**ce \j\ **j**ob \ŋ\ si**ng** \ō\ g**o** \ȯ\ l**aw** \ȯi\ b**oy** \th\ **th**in \t͟h\ **th**e \ü\ l**oo**t \u̇\ f**oo**t \y\ **y**et \zh\ vi**si**on, bei**ge** \k, ⁿ, œ, ue, ʸ\ *see* Guide to Pronunciation

teg·men·tal \teg-ˈmen-tᵊl\ *adj* (ca. 1890) : of, relating to, or associated with an integument or a tegmentum

teg·men·tum \teg-ˈmen-təm\ *n, pl* **-men·ta** \-ˈmen-tə\ [NL, fr. L *tegumentum, tegmentum,* covering, fr. *tegere*] (1832) : an anatomical covering : TEGMEN; *esp* : the part of the ventral midbrain above the substantia nigra formed of longitudinal white fibers with arched transverse fibers and gray matter

teg·u·ment \ˈte-gyə-mənt\ *n* [ME, fr. L *tegumentum*] (15c) : INTEGUMENT

te·iid \ˈtē-əd, ˈtī-\ *n* [NL *Teiidae,* fr. *Teius,* genus of lizards, fr. Pg *teiú,* the lizard *Tupinambis teguixim,* fr. Tupi *tejú*] (1956) : any of a family (Teiidae) of mostly tropical American lizards (as the race runner) with an elongate forked tongue — **teiid** *adj*

Te·ja·no \tā-ˈhä-(ˌ)nō\ *n, pl* **-nos** *often attrib* [MexSp, fr. *Tejas* Texas] (1976) **1** : a Texan of Hispanic descent **2** [prob. short for *conjunto tejano,* lit., Texan ensemble] : Tex-Mex popular music combining elements of traditional, rock, and country music and often featuring an accordion

tek·tite \ˈtek-ˌtīt\ *n* [ISV, fr. Gk *tēktos* molten, fr. *tēkein* to melt — more at THAW] (1909) : a glassy body of probably meteoritic origin and of rounded but indefinite shape — **tek·tit·ic** \tek-ˈti-tik\ *adj*

tel *abbr* telephone

tel- *or* **telo-** *comb form* [ISV, fr. Gk *telos* — more at TELOS] : end ⟨*tel*angiectasia⟩

tel·a·mon \ˈte-lə-ˌmän\ *n, pl* **tel·a·mo·nes** \ˌte-lə-ˈmō-(ˌ)nēz\ [L, fr. Gk *telamōn* bearer, supporter; akin to Gk *tlēnai* to bear — more at TOLERATE] (ca. 1706) : ATLAS 5

tel·an·gi·ec·ta·sia \ˌte-ˌlan-jē-ˌek-ˈtā-zh(ē-)ə, ˌtē-, tə-\ *or* **tel·an·gi·ec·ta·sis** \-ˈek-tə-səs\ *n, pl* **-ta·sias** *or* **-ta·ses** \-tə-ˌsēz\ [NL, fr. *tel-* + *angi-* + *ectasia, ectasis* (as in *atelectasis*)] (1831) : an abnormal dilation of red, blue, or purple superficial capillaries, arterioles, or venules typically localized just below the skin's surface (as of the face) — compare SPIDER VEIN — **tel·an·gi·ec·tat·ic** \-ˌek-ˈta-tik\ *adj*

tel·co \ˈtel-(ˌ)kō\ *n* [*tel*ephone *co*mpany] (1975) : a telecommunications company

tele \ˈte-lē\ *n* (1936) *Brit* : TELEVISION

tele- *or* **tel-** *comb form* [NL, fr. Gk *tēle-, tēl-,* fr. *tēle* far off — more at PALE-] **1** : distant : at a distance : over a distance ⟨*tele*gram⟩ **2 a** : telegraph ⟨*tele*typewriter⟩ **b** : television ⟨*tele*cast⟩ **c** : telecommunication ⟨*tele*marketing⟩

tele·cast \ˈte-li-ˌkast\ *vb* **-cast** *also* **-cast·ed; -cast·ing** [*tele-* + *broadcast*] *vt* (1937) : to broadcast by television ~ *vi* : to broadcast a television program — **telecast** *n* — **tele·cast·er** *n*

tele·cine \ˈte-li-ˌsi-nē, ˌte-li-ˈsi-\ *n* [prob. short for *telecinema,* fr. F *télécinéma,* fr. *télé-* tele- + *cinéma* cinema] (1935) : the equipment used in the process of transferring a motion picture to videotape or converting it into television images; *also* : such a process

tel·e·com \ˈte-li-ˌkäm\ *n* (1948) **1** : TELECOMMUNICATION **2** : the telecommunications industry

tele·com·mu·ni·ca·tion \ˌte-li-kə-ˌmyü-nə-ˈkā-shən\ *n* [ISV] (1932) **1** : communication at a distance (as by telephone) **2** : technology that deals with telecommunication — usu. used in pl.

tele·com·mute \ˈte-li-kə-ˌmyüt\ *vi* (1974) : to work at home by the use of an electronic linkup with a central office — **tele·com·mut·er** *n*

tele·con·fer·enc·ing \ˈte-li-ˌkän-f(ə-)rən(t)-siŋ, -fərn(t)-\ *n* (1974) : the holding of a conference among people remote from one another by means of telecommunication devices (as telephones or computer terminals) — **tele·con·fer·ence** \-f(ə-)rən(t)s, -fərn(t)s\ *n*

Tele·copi·er \ˈte-lə-ˌkä-pē-ər\ *trademark* — used for transmitting and receiving equipment for producing facsimile copies of documents

tele·course \ˈte-li-ˌkȯrs\ *n* (1950) : a course of study conducted over television; *esp* : such a course taken at home for academic credit

tele·fac·sim·i·le \ˌte-li-fak-ˈsi-mə-(ˌ)lē\ *n* (1952) : FACSIMILE 2

tele·fax \ˈte-li-ˌfaks\ *n* (1943) : FACSIMILE 2

tele·film \ˈte-li-ˌfilm\ *n* (1939) : a motion picture made to be telecast

tele·ge·nic \ˌte-lə-ˈje-nik, -ˈjē-\ *adj* (1939) : having an appearance and manner that are markedly attractive to television viewers

[1]**tele·gram** \ˈte-lə-ˌgram, *Southern also* -grəm\ *n* (ca. 1852) : a telegraphic dispatch

[2]**tele·gram** \-ˌgram\ *vt* **-grammed; -gram·ming** (1864) : TELEGRAPH

[1]**tele·graph** \-ˌgraf\ *n* [F *télégraphe,* fr. *télé-* tele- (fr. Gk *tēle-*) + *-graphe* -graph] (1794) **1** : an apparatus for communication at a distance by coded signals; *esp* : an apparatus, system, or process for communication at a distance by electric transmission over wire **2** : TELEGRAM

[2]**telegraph** *vt* (1805) **1 a** : to send or communicate by or as if by telegraph **b** : to send a telegram to **c** : to send by means of a telegraphic order **2** : to make known by signs esp. unknowingly and in advance — **te·leg·ra·pher** \tə-ˈle-grə-fər\ *n* — **te·leg·ra·phist** \-fist\ *n*

tele·graph·ese \ˌte-lə-gra-ˈfēz, -ˈfēs\ *n* (1885) : language characterized by the terseness and ellipses that are common in telegrams

tele·graph·ic \ˌte-lə-ˈgra-fik\ *adj* (1794) **1** : of or relating to the telegraph **2** : CONCISE, TERSE — **tele·graph·i·cal·ly** \-fi-k(ə-)lē\ *adv*

te·leg·ra·phy \tə-ˈle-grə-fē\ *n* (1795) : the use or operation of a telegraph apparatus or system for communication

tele·ki·ne·sis \ˌte-li-kə-ˈnē-səs, -kī-\ *n* [NL] (1890) : the production of motion in objects (as by a spiritualistic medium) without contact or other physical means — **tele·ki·net·ic** \-ˈne-tik\ *adj* — **tele·ki·net·i·cal·ly** \-ti-k(ə-)lē\ *adv*

Te·lem·a·chus \tə-ˈle-mə-kəs\ *n* [L, fr. Gk *Tēlemachos*] (ca. 1556) : the son of Odysseus and Penelope who contrives with his father to slay his mother's suitors

tel·e·mark \ˈte-lə-ˌmärk\ *n, often cap* [Norw, fr. *Telemark,* region in Norway] (1904) : a turn in skiing in which the outside ski is advanced considerably ahead of the other ski and then turned inward at a steadily widening angle until the turn is completed

tele·mar·ket·ing \ˌte-lə-ˈmär-kə-tiŋ\ *n* (1980) : the marketing of goods or services by telephone — **tele·mar·ket·er** \-tər\ *n*

tel·e·mark·ing \ˈte-le-ˌmär-kiŋ\ *n* (1943) : the act or sport of performing telemarks — **tel·e·mark·er** \-kər\ *n*

tele·med·i·cine \ˌte-lə-ˈme-də-sən, -ˈmed-sən\ *n* (1970) : the practice of medicine when the doctor and patient are widely separated using two-way voice and visual communication (as by satellite or computer)

[1]**tele·me·ter** \ˈte-lə-ˌmē-tər\ *n* [ISV] (1860) **1** : an instrument for measuring the distance of an object from an observer **2** : an electrical apparatus for measuring a quantity (as pressure, speed, or temperature) and transmitting the result esp. by radio to a distant station

[2]**telemeter** *vt* (1925) : to transmit (as the measurement of a quantity) by telemeter ~ *vi* : to telemeter the measurement of a quantity

te·lem·e·try \tə-ˈle-mə-trē\ *n* (1885) **1** : the science or process of telemetering data **2** : data transmitted by telemetry **3** : BIOTELEMETRY — **tele·met·ric** \ˌte-lə-ˈme-trik\ *adj* — **tele·met·ri·cal·ly** \-tri-k(ə-)lē\ *adv*

tel·en·ceph·a·lon \ˌte-len-ˈse-fə-ˌlän, -lən\ *n* [NL, fr. *telo-* + *encephalon*] (1897) : the anterior subdivision of the embryonic forebrain or the corresponding part of the adult forebrain that includes the cerebral hemispheres and associated structures — **tel·en·ce·phal·ic** \-ˌlen(t)-sə-ˈfa-lik\ *adj*

tel·e·no·vela \ˌte-lə-nō-ˈve-lə\ *n* [Sp, fr. *tele-* tele- + *novela* novel, serial drama] (1976) : a soap opera produced in and televised in or from many Latin-American countries

tel·e·o·log·i·cal \ˌte-lē-ə-ˈlä-ji-kəl, ˌtē-\ *also* **tel·e·o·log·ic** \-ˈlä-jik\ *adj* (1798) : exhibiting or relating to design or purpose esp. in nature — **tel·e·o·log·i·cal·ly** \-ji-k(ə-)lē\ *adv*

tel·e·ol·o·gy \ˌte-lē-ˈä-lə-jē, ˌtē-\ *n* [NL *teleologia,* fr. Gk *tele-, telos* end, purpose + *-logia* -logy — more at WHEEL] (1740) **1 a** : the study of evidences of design in nature **b** : a doctrine (as in vitalism) that ends are immanent in nature **c** : a doctrine explaining phenomena by final causes **2** : the fact or character attributed to nature or natural processes of being directed toward an end or shaped by a purpose **3** : the use of design or purpose as an explanation of natural phenomena — **tel·e·ol·o·gist** \-jist\ *n*

tel·e·on·o·my \ˌte-lē-ˈä-nə-mē, ˌtē-\ *n* [*teleo-* (as in *teleology*) + *-nomy*] (1958) : the quality of apparent purposefulness of structure or function in living organisms due to evolutionary adaptation — **tel·e·o·nom·ic** \ˌte-lē-ə-ˈnä-mik, ˌtē-\ *adj*

tel·e·ost \ˈte-lē-ˌäst, ˈtē-\ *n* [ultim. fr. Gk *teleios* complete, perfect (fr. *telos* end) + *osteon* bone — more at OSSEOUS] (1862) : BONY FISH — **teleost** *adj* — **tel·e·os·te·an** \ˌte-lē-ˈäs-tē-ən, ˌtē-\ *adj*

tele·path \ˈte-lə-ˌpath\ *n* (1904) : one who is able to communicate by telepathy

te·lep·a·thy \tə-ˈle-pə-thē\ *n* (1882) : communication from one mind to another by extrasensory means — **tele·path·ic** \ˌte-lə-ˈpa-thik\ *adj* — **tele·path·i·cal·ly** \-thi-k(ə-)lē\ *adv*

[1]**tele·phone** \ˈte-lə-ˌfōn\ *n, often attrib* (1844) : an instrument for reproducing sounds at a distance; *specif* : one in which sound is converted into electrical impulses for transmission (as by wire or radio waves)

[2]**telephone** *vb* **-phoned; -phon·ing** *vt* (1877) **1** : to speak to or attempt to reach by telephone **2** : to send by telephone ~ *vi* : to communicate by telephone — **tele·phon·er** *n*

telephone book *n* (1915) : a book listing the names, addresses, and telephone numbers of telephone customers

telephone booth *n* (ca. 1895) : an enclosure within which one may stand or sit while making a telephone call

telephone box *n* (1904) *Brit* : a public telephone booth

telephone directory *n* (1907) : TELEPHONE BOOK

telephone number *n* (1885) : a number assigned to a telephone line for a specific location that is used to call that location

telephone tag *n* (1980) : telephoning back and forth by parties trying to reach each other without success

tele·phon·ic \ˌte-lə-ˈfä-nik\ *adj* (1840) : of, relating to, or conveyed by a telephone — **tele·phon·i·cal·ly** \-ni-k(ə-)lē\ *adv*

te·le·pho·nist \tə-ˈle-fə-nist, ˈte-lə-ˌfō-nist\ *n* (1880) *Brit* : a telephone switchboard operator

te·le·pho·ny \tə-ˈle-fə-nē *also* ˈte-lə-ˌfō-\ *n* (1835) : the use or operation of an apparatus (as a telephone) for transmission of sounds as electrical signals between widely removed points

[1]**tele·pho·to** \ˌte-lə-ˈfō-(ˌ)tō\ *adj* (ca. 1895) : being a camera lens system designed to give a large image of a distant object; *also* : relating to or being photography in which a telephoto lens is used

[2]**telephoto** *n, pl* **-tos** (1904) **1** : a telephoto lens **2** : a photograph taken with a camera having a telephoto lens

Telephoto *trademark* — used for an apparatus for transmitting photographs electrically or for a photograph so transmitted

tele·pho·tog·ra·phy \ˌte-lə-fə-ˈtä-grə-fē\ *n* [ISV] (1892) : the photography of distant objects (as by a camera provided with a telephoto lens)

tele·play \ˈte-li-ˌplā\ *n* (1952) : a story prepared for television production

tele·port \ˈte-lə-ˌpȯrt\ *vt* [back-formation fr. *teleportation*] (1947) : to transfer by teleportation

tele·por·ta·tion \ˌte-lə-ˌpȯr-ˈtā-shən, -pər-\ *n* [*tele-* + *transportation*] (1931) : the act or process of moving an object or person by psychokinesis

tele·print·er \ˈte-lə-ˌprin-tər\ *n* (1929) : a device capable of producing hard copy from signals received over a communications circuit; *esp* : TELETYPEWRITER

tele·pro·cess·ing \-ˈprä-ˌse-siŋ, -ˈprō-, -sə-siŋ\ *n* (1962) : computer processing via remote terminals

tele·prompt·er \ˈte-lə-ˌpräm(p)-tər\ *n* [fr. *TelePrompTer,* a trademark] (1951) : a device for displaying prepared text to a speaker or performer

[1]**tele·scope** \ˈte-lə-ˌskōp\ *n, often attrib* [NL *telescopium,* fr. Gk *tēleskopos* farseeing, fr. *tēle-* tele- + *skopos* watcher; akin to Gk *skopein* to look — more at SPY] (1648) **1** : a usu. tubular optical instrument for viewing distant objects by means of the refraction of light rays through a lens or the reflection of light rays by a concave mirror — compare REFLECTOR, REFRACTOR **2** : any of various tubular magnifying optical instruments **3** : RADIO TELESCOPE

[2]**telescope** *vb* **-scoped; -scop·ing** *vi* (1867) **1** : to become forced together lengthwise with one part entering another as the result of collision **2** : to slide or pass one within another like the cylindrical sections of a collapsible hand telescope **3** : to become compressed or condensed ~ *vt* **1** : to cause to telescope **2** : COMPRESS, CONDENSE

tele·scop·ic \ˌte-lə-ˈskä-pik\ *adj* (1705) **1 a** : of, relating to, or performed with a telescope **b** : suitable for seeing or magnifying distant objects **2** : seen or discoverable only by a telescope ⟨~ stars⟩ **3** : able to discern objects at a distance **4** : having parts that telescope — **tele·scop·i·cal·ly** \-pi-k(ə-)lē\ *adv*

tel·e·sis \ˈte-lə-səs\ *n, pl* **-e·ses** \-ˌsēz\ [NL, fr. Gk, fulfillment, fr. *telein* to complete, fr. *telos* end — more at TELOS] (1896) : progress that is intelligently planned and directed : the attainment of desired ends by the application of intelligent human effort to the means

Tel·es·tra·tor \ˈte-lə-ˌstrā-tər\ *trademark* — used for an electronic device that generates drawn video images over a background image

tele·text \ˈte-lə-ˌtekst\ *n* (1974) : a system for broadcasting text over an unused portion of a television signal and displaying it on a decoder-equipped television set — compare VIDEOTEX

tele·thon \ˈte-lə-ˌthän\ *n* [*tele-* + *-athon*] (1949) : a long television program usu. to solicit funds esp. for a charity

Tele·type \ˈte-lə-ˌtīp\ *trademark* — used for a teletypewriter

tele·type·writ·er \ˌte-lə-ˈtīp-ˌrī-tər\ *n* (1903) : a printing device resembling a typewriter that is used to send and receive telephonic signals

tel·evan·ge·list \ˌte-li-ˈvan-jə-list\ *n* (1973) : an evangelist who conducts regularly televised religious programs — **tel·evan·ge·lism** \-ˌli-zəm\ *n*

tele·view \ˈte-li-ˌvyü\ *vi* (1935) : to observe or watch by means of a television receiver — **tele·view·er** *n*

tele·vise \ˈte-lə-ˌvīz\ *vb* **-vised; -vis·ing** [back-formation fr. *television*] *vt* (1927) : to broadcast (as a baseball game) by television ~ *vi* : to broadcast by television

tele·vi·sion \ˈte-lə-ˌvi-zhən *esp Brit* ˌte-lə-ˈ\ *n, often attrib* [F *télévision,* fr. *télé-* tele- + *vision* vision] (1907) **1** : an electronic system of transmitting transient images of fixed or moving objects together with sound over a wire or through space by apparatus that converts light and sound into electrical waves and reconverts them into visible light rays and audible sound **2** : a television receiving set **3 a** : the television broadcasting industry **b** : television as a medium of communication

tele·vi·su·al \ˌte-lə-ˈvi-zhə-wəl, -zhəl; -ˈvizh-wəl\ *adj* (1926) *chiefly Brit* : of, relating to, or suitable for broadcast by television

¹**tel·ex** \ˈte-ˌleks\ *n* [*tel*eprinter + *ex*change] (1932) **1** : a communication service involving teletypewriters connected by wire through automatic exchanges; *also* : a teletypewriter used in telex **2** : a message sent by telex

²**telex** *vt* (1960) **1** : to send (as a message) by telex **2** : to communicate with by telex

te·lic \ˈte-lik, ˈtē-\ *adj* [Gk *telikos,* fr. *telos* end — more at TELOS] (1889) : tending toward an end or outcome — **te·li·cal·ly** \-li-k(ə-)lē\ *adv*

te·lio·spore \ˈtē-lē-ə-ˌspȯr\ *n* [Gk *teleios* complete (fr. *telos* end) + E *spore*] (1905) : a chlamydospore that is the final stage in the life cycle of a rust fungus and that gives rise to the basidium

te·li·um \ˈtē-lē-əm\ *n, pl* **te·lia** \-lē-ə\ [NL, fr. Gk *teleios* complete] (ca. 1905) : a teliospore-producing sorus or pustule on the host plant of a rust fungus — **te·li·al** \ˈtē-lē-əl\ *adj*

¹**tell** \ˈtel\ *vb* **told** \ˈtōld\; **tell·ing** [ME, fr. OE *tellan;* akin to OHG *zellen* to count, tell, OE *talu* tale] *vt* (bef. 12c) **1** : COUNT, ENUMERATE ⟨~ the stars, if thou be able to number them —Gen 15:5(AV)⟩ **2 a** : to relate in detail : NARRATE ⟨*told* the whole story to us⟩ **b** : to give utterance to : SAY ⟨could never ~ a lie⟩ **3 a** : to make known : DIVULGE, REVEAL ⟨don't ~ your password⟩ **b** : to express in words ⟨she never *told* her love —Shak.⟩ **4 a** : to give information to : INFORM ⟨~ us about your job⟩ **b** : to assure emphatically ⟨they did not do it, I ~ you⟩ **5** : ORDER, DIRECT ⟨*told* me to wait⟩ **6** : to find out by observing : RECOGNIZE ⟨you can ~ it's a masterpiece⟩ ~ *vi* **1** : to give an account ⟨an article *telling* of her experience⟩ **2** : to act as an informer — often used with *on* ⟨I'll get even with you if you ever ~ on me —*Inside Detective*⟩ **3** : to have a marked effect ⟨the pressure was beginning to ~ on him⟩ **4** : to serve as evidence or indication ***syn*** see REVEAL

²**tell** *n* [Ar *tall*] (1864) : HILL, MOUND; *specif* : an ancient mound in the Middle East composed of remains of successive settlements

tell–all \ˈtel-ˈȯl\ *n* (1954) : a written account (as a biography) that contains revealing and often scandalous information — **tell–all** *adj*

tell·er \ˈte-lər\ *n* (14c) **1** : one that relates or communicates ⟨a ~ of stories⟩ **2** : one that reckons or counts: as **a** : one appointed to count votes **b** : a member of a bank's staff concerned with the direct handling of money received or paid out

telling *adj* (1851) : carrying great weight and producing a marked effect : EFFECTIVE, EXPRESSIVE ⟨the most ~ evidence⟩ ***syn*** see VALID — **tell·ing·ly** \-liŋ-lē\ *adv*

tell off *vt* (1804) **1** : to number and set apart; *esp* : to assign to a special duty ⟨*told off* a detail and put them to opening a trench —J. F. Dobie⟩ **2** : REPRIMAND, EXCORIATE ⟨*told* him *off* for his arrogance⟩

tell·tale \ˈtel-ˌtāl\ *n* (ca. 1548) **1 a** : TALEBEARER, INFORMER **b** : an outward sign : INDICATION **2** : a device for indicating or recording something: as **a** : a wind-direction indicator often in the form of a ribbon **b** : a strip of metal on the front wall of a racquets or squash court above which the ball must be hit — **telltale** *adj*

tellur- *or* **telluro-** *comb form* [L *tellur-, tellus* — more at THILL] **1** : earth ⟨*tellur*ic⟩ **2** [NL *tellurium*] : tellurium ⟨*tellur*ide⟩

tel·lu·ric \tə-ˈlu̇r-ik, te-\ *adj* (1836) **1** : of or relating to the earth : TERRESTRIAL **2** : being or relating to a usu. natural electric current flowing near the earth's surface

tel·lu·ride \ˈtel-yə-ˌrīd\ *n* [ISV] (1849) : a binary compound of tellurium with a more electropositive element or group

tel·lu·ri·um \tə-ˈlu̇r-ē-əm, te-\ *n* [NL, fr. L *tellur-, tellus* earth] (1800) : a semimetallic element that occurs in a silvery-white brittle crystalline form of metallic luster, in a dark amorphous form, or combined with metals and that is used esp. in alloys and catalysts — see ELEMENT table

tel·lu·rom·e·ter \ˌtel-yə-ˈrä-mə-tər\ *n* (1957) : a device that measures distance by means of microwaves

tel·ly \ˈte-lē\ *n, pl* **tellys** *also* **tellies** [by shortening & alter.] (1939) *chiefly Brit* : TELEVISION

tel·net \ˈtel-ˌnet\ *n* [*tel*etype *net*work] (1969) : a telecommunications protocol providing specifications for emulating a remote computer terminal so that one can access a distant computer and function online using an interface that appears to be part of the user's local system — **telnet** *vi*

telo- — see TEL-

telo·cen·tric \ˌte-lə-ˈsen-trik, ˌtē-\ *adj* [ISV *tel-* + *centro*mere + *-ic*] (1939) : having the centromere terminally situated so that there is only one chromosomal arm ⟨a ~ chromosome⟩ — **telocentric** *n*

te·lome \ˈtē-ˌlōm\ *n* [ISV *tel-* + *-ome*] (1935) : a hypothetical plant structure in a theory of the evolution of leaves and sporophylls in vascular plants that consists of one of the vegetative or reproductive terminal branchlets of a dichotomously branched axis

tel·o·me·rase \te-ˈlō-mə-ˌrās, -ˌrāz\ *n* (1988) : a DNA polymerase that is a ribonucleoprotein catalyzing the elongation of chromosomal telomeres in eukaryotic cell division and is particularly active in cancer cells

telo·mere \ˈte-lə-ˌmir, ˈtē-\ *n* [ISV] (1940) : the natural end of a eukaryotic chromosome composed of a usu. repetitive DNA sequence and serving to stabilize the chromosome

telo·phase \ˈte-lə-ˌfāz, ˈtē-\ *n* [ISV] (1895) **1** : the final stage of mitosis and of the second division of meiosis in which the spindle disappears and the nuclear envelope reforms around each set of chromosomes **2** : the final stage in the first division of meiosis that may be missing in some organisms and is characterized by the gathering at opposite poles of the cell of half the original number of chromosomes including one from each homologous pair

te·los \ˈte-ˌläs, ˈtē-\ *n* [Gk; prob. akin to Gk *tellein* to accomplish, *tlēnai* to bear — more at TOLERATE] (1904) : an ultimate end

tel·son \ˈtel-sən\ *n* [NL, fr. Gk, end of a plowed field; perh. akin to Gk *telos* end] (1855) : the terminal segment of the body of an arthropod or segmented worm; *esp* : that of a crustacean forming the middle lobe of the tail

Tel·u·gu \ˈte-lə-ˌgü\ *n, pl* **Telugu** *or* **Telugus** [Telugu *telŭgu, tenŭngu*] (1789) **1** : a member of the largest group of people in Andhra Pradesh, India **2** : the Dravidian language of the Telugu people

TEM *abbr* transmission electron microscope; transmission electron microscopy

tem·blor \ˈtem-blər; ˈtem-ˌblȯr, tem-ˈ\ *n* [Sp, lit., trembling, fr. *temblar* to tremble, fr. ML *tremulare* — more at TREMBLE] (1876) : EARTHQUAKE

tem·er·ar·i·ous \ˌte-mə-ˈrer-ē-əs\ *adj* [L *temerarius,* fr. *temere*] (1532) : marked by temerity : rashly or presumptuously daring ⟨a ~ comment⟩ — **tem·er·ar·i·ous·ly** *adv* — **tem·er·ar·i·ous·ness** *n*

te·mer·i·ty \tə-ˈmer-ə-tē\ *n, pl* **-ties** [ME *temeryte,* fr. L *temeritas,* fr. *temere* blindly, recklessly; akin to OHG *demar* darkness, L *tenebrae,* Skt *tamas*] (15c) **1** : unreasonable or foolhardy contempt of danger or opposition : RASHNESS, RECKLESSNESS **2** : an act or instance of temerity

syn TEMERITY, AUDACITY, HARDIHOOD, EFFRONTERY, NERVE, CHEEK, GALL, CHUTZPAH mean conspicuous or flagrant boldness. TEMERITY suggests boldness arising from rashness and contempt of danger ⟨had the *temerity* to refuse⟩. AUDACITY implies a disregard of restraints commonly imposed by convention or prudence ⟨an entrepreneur with *audacity* and vision⟩. HARDIHOOD suggests firmness in daring and defiance ⟨admired for her *hardihood*⟩. EFFRONTERY implies shameless, insolent disregard of propriety or courtesy ⟨outraged at his *effrontery*⟩. NERVE, CHEEK, GALL, and CHUTZPAH are informal equivalents for EFFRONTERY ⟨the *nerve* of that guy⟩ ⟨has the *cheek* to call herself a singer⟩ ⟨had the *gall* to demand proof⟩ ⟨the *chutzpah* needed for a career in show business⟩.

¹**temp** \ˈtemp\ *n* (1850) **1** : TEMPERATURE 2a, c **2** : a temporary worker

²**temp** *vi* (1973) : to work as a temp

³**temp** *abbr* **1** temporary **2** [L *tempore*] in the time of

tem·peh \ˈtem-ˌpā\ *n* [Jav *témpé*] (1950) : an Asian food prepared by fermenting soybeans with a rhizopus

¹**tem·per** \ˈtem-pər\ *vt* **tem·pered; tem·per·ing** \-p(ə-)riŋ\ [ME, fr. OE & AF; OE *temprian* & AF *temprer,* fr. L *temperare* to moderate, mix, temper; prob. akin to L *tempor-, tempus* time] (bef. 12c) **1** : to dilute, qualify, or soften by the addition or influence of something else : MODERATE ⟨~ justice with mercy⟩ **2** *archaic* **a** : to exercise control over : GOVERN, RESTRAIN **b** : to cause to be well disposed : MOLLIFY ⟨~*ed* and reconciled them both —Richard Steele⟩ **3** : to bring to a suitable state by mixing in or adding a usu. liquid ingredient: as **a** : to mix (clay) with water or a modifier (as grog) and knead to a uniform texture **b** : to mix oil with (colors) in making paint ready for use **4 a** (1) : to soften (as hardened steel or cast iron) by reheating at a lower temperature (2) : to harden (as steel) by reheating and cooling in oil **b** : to anneal or toughen (glass) by a process of gradually heating and cooling **5** : to make stronger and more resilient through hardship : TOUGHEN ⟨troops ~*ed* in battle⟩ **6 a** : to put in tune with something : ATTUNE **b** : to adjust the pitch of (a note, chord, or instrument) to a temperament — **tem·per·able** \-p(ə-)rə-bəl\ *adj* — **tem·per·er** \-pər-ər\ *n*

²**temper** *n* (14c) **1 a** *archaic* : a suitable proportion or balance of qualities : a middle state between extremes : MEAN, MEDIUM ⟨virtue is . . . a just ~ between propensities —T. B. Macaulay⟩ **b** *archaic* : CHARACTER, QUALITY ⟨the ~ of the land you design to sow —John Mortimer⟩ **c** : characteristic tone : TREND ⟨the ~ of the times⟩ **d** : high quality of mind or spirit : COURAGE **2 a** : the state of a substance with respect to certain desired qualities (as hardness, elasticity, or workability); *esp* : the degree of hardness or resiliency given steel by tempering **b** : the feel and relative solidity of leather **3 a** : a characteristic cast of mind or state of feeling : DISPOSITION **b** : calmness of mind : COMPOSURE **c** : state of feeling or frame of mind at a particular time usu. dominated by a single strong emotion **d** : heat of mind or emotion : proneness to anger : PASSION ⟨she has a real ~⟩ **4** : a substance (as a metal) added to or mixed with something else (as another metal) to modify the properties of the latter ***syn*** see DISPOSITION

tem·pera \ˈtem-pə-rə\ *n* [It, lit., temper, fr. *temperare* to temper, fr. L] (1832) **1** : a process of painting in which an albuminous or colloidal medium (as egg yolk) is employed as a vehicle instead of oil; *also* : a painting done in tempera **2** : POSTER COLOR

tem·per·a·ment \ˈtem-p(ə-)rə-mənt, -pər-mənt\ *n* [ME, fr. L *temperamentum,* fr. *temperare* to mix, temper] (15c) **1** *obs* **a** : constitution of a substance, body, or organism with respect to the mixture or balance of its elements, qualities, or parts : MAKEUP **b** : COMPLEXION 1 **2** *obs* **a** : CLIMATE **b** : TEMPERATURE 2 **3 a** : the peculiar or distinguishing mental or physical character determined by the relative proportions of the humors according to medieval physiology **b** : characteristic or habitual inclination or mode of emotional response ⟨a nervous ~⟩ **c** : extremely high sensibility; *esp* : excessive sensitiveness or irritability **4 a** : the act or process of tempering or modifying : ADJUSTMENT, COMPROMISE **b** : middle course : MEAN **5** : the slight modification of acoustically pure intervals in tuning a musical instrument; *esp* : modification that produces a set of 12 equally spaced tones to the octave ***syn*** see DISPOSITION

tem·per·a·men·tal \ˌtem-p(ə-)rə-ˈmen-tᵊl, ˌtem-pər-ˈ\ *adj* (1646) **1** : of, relating to, or arising from temperament : CONSTITUTIONAL ⟨~ peculiarities⟩ **2 a** : marked by excessive sensitivity and impulsive mood changes ⟨a ~ child⟩ **b** : unpredictable in behavior or performance ⟨a ~ computer⟩ — **tem·per·a·men·tal·ly** \-tᵊl-ē\ *adv*

tem·per·ance \ˈtem-p(ə-)rən(t)s, -pərn(t)s\ *n* [ME, fr. AF, fr. L *temperantia,* fr. *temperant-, temperans,* prp. of *temperare* to moderate, be moderate] (14c) **1** : moderation in action, thought, or feeling : RESTRAINT **2 a** : habitual moderation in the indulgence of the appetites or passions **b** : moderation in or abstinence from the use of alcoholic beverages

tem·per·ate \ˈtem-p(ə-)rət\ *adj* [ME *temperat,* fr. L *temperatus,* fr. pp. of *temperare*] (14c) **1** : marked by moderation: as **a** : keeping or held within limits : not extreme or excessive : MILD **b** : moderate in indulgence of appetite or desire **c** : moderate in the use of alcoholic beverages **d** : marked by an absence or avoidance of extravagance, violence, or extreme partisanship **2 a** : having a moderate climate which esp. lacks extremes in temperature **b** : found in or associated with a moderate climate ⟨~ insects⟩ **3** : existing as a prophage in infected cells and rarely causing lysis ⟨~ bacteriophages⟩ — **tem·per·ate·ly** *adv* — **tem·per·ate·ness** *n*

temperate rain forest *n* (ca. 1930) : woodland of a usu. rather mild climatic area within the temperate zone that receives heavy rainfall, usu. includes numerous kinds of trees, and is distinguished from a tropical rain forest esp. by the presence of a dominant tree

temperate zone *n, often cap T&Z* (1551) : the area or region between the Tropic of Cancer and the arctic circle or between the Tropic of Capricorn and the antarctic circle

tem·per·a·ture \ˈtem-pə(r)-ˌchu̇r, -p(ə-)rə-, -chər, -ˌtyu̇r, -ˌtu̇r\ *n* [L *temperatura* mixture, moderation, fr. *temperatus,* pp. of *temperare*] (1533) **1** *archaic* **a** : COMPLEXION 1 **b** : TEMPERAMENT 3b **2 a** : degree of hotness or coldness measured on a definite scale **b** : the degree of heat that is natural to the body of a living being **c** : abnormally high body heat ⟨running a ~⟩ **3 a** : relative state of emotional warmth ⟨scandals raised the political ~⟩ **b** : MOOD ⟨testing the ~ of voters⟩

temperature inversion *n* (1921) : INVERSION 6

tem·pered \ˈtem-pərd\ *adj* (14c) **1 a** : having the elements mixed in satisfying proportions : TEMPERATE **b** : qualified, lessened, or diluted by the mixture or influence of an additional ingredient : MODERATED ⟨a pale gleam of ~ sunlight fell through the leaves —W. H. Hudson †1922⟩ **2** : treated by tempering; *esp, of glass* : treated so as to impart increased strength and the property of shattering into pellets when broken **3** : having a specified temper — used in combination ⟨short-tempered⟩ **4** : conforming to adjustment by temperament — used of a musical interval, intonation, semitone, or scale

[1]**tem·pest** \ˈtem-pəst\ *n* [ME *tempeste,* fr. AF, fr. VL **tempesta,* alter. of L *tempestas* season, weather, storm, fr. *tempus* time] (13c) **1** : a violent storm **2** : TUMULT, UPROAR

[2]**tempest** *vt* (14c) : to raise a tempest in or around

tempest in a teapot (1838) : a great commotion over an unimportant matter

tem·pes·tu·ous \tem-ˈpes-chə-wəs, -ˈpesh-\ *adj* [ME, fr. LL *tempestuosus,* fr. OL *tempestus* season, weather, storm, fr. *tempus*] (15c) : of, relating to, or resembling a tempest : TURBULENT, STORMY ⟨~ weather⟩ ⟨a ~ relationship⟩ — **tem·pes·tu·ous·ly** *adv* — **tem·pes·tu·ous·ness** *n*

Tem·plar \ˈtem-plər\ *n* [ME *templer,* fr. AF, fr. ML *templarius,* fr. L *templum* temple] (13c) **1** : a knight of a religious military order established in the early 12th century in Jerusalem for the protection of pilgrims and the Holy Sepulcher **2** : KNIGHT TEMPLAR 2

tem·plate \ˈtem-plət\ *n* [prob. fr. F *templet,* dim. of *temple,* part of a loom, prob. fr. L *templum*] (1677) **1** : a short piece or block placed horizontally in a wall under a beam to distribute its weight or pressure (as over a door) **2 a** (1) : a gauge, pattern, or mold (as a thin plate or board) used as a guide to the form of a piece being made (2) : a molecule (as of DNA) that serves as a pattern for the generation of another macromolecule (as messenger RNA) **b** : OVERLAY c **3** : something that establishes or serves as a pattern

[1]**tem·ple** \ˈtem-pəl\ *n* [ME, fr. OE & AF; OE *tempel* & AF *temple,* both fr. L *templum* space marked out for observation of auguries, temple, small timber; prob. akin to Gk *temenos* sacred precinct, *temnein* to cut — more at TOME] (bef. 12c) **1** : a building for religious practice: as **a** *often cap* : either of two successive national sanctuaries in ancient Jerusalem **b** : a building for Mormon sacred ordinances **c** : the house of worship of Reform and some Conservative Jewish congregations **2** : a local lodge of any of various fraternal orders; *also* : the building housing it **3** : a place devoted to a special purpose ⟨a ~ of cuisine⟩ — **tem·pled** \-pəld\ *adj*

[2]**temple** *n* [ME, fr. AF, fr. VL **tempula,* alter. of L *tempora* (pl.) temples] (14c) **1** : the flattened space on each side of the forehead of some mammals including humans **2** : one of the side supports of a pair of glasses jointed to the bows and passing on each side of the head

tem·po \ˈtem-(ˌ)pō\ *n, pl* **tem·pi** \-(ˌ)pē\ *or* **tempos** [It, lit., time, fr. L *tempus*] (ca. 1724) **1** : the rate of speed of a musical piece or passage indicated by one of a series of directions (as largo, presto, or allegro) and often by an exact metronome marking **2** : rate of motion or activity : PACE

[1]**tem·po·ral** \ˈtem-p(ə-)rəl\ *adj* [ME, fr. AF *temporel,* fr. L *temporalis,* fr. *tempor-, tempus* time] (14c) **1 a** : of or relating to time as opposed to eternity **b** : of or relating to earthly life **c** : lay or secular rather than clerical or sacred : CIVIL ⟨lords ~⟩ **2** : of or relating to grammatical tense or a distinction of time **3 a** : of or relating to time as distinguished from space **b** : of or relating to the sequence of time or to a particular time : CHRONOLOGICAL — **tem·po·ral·ly** *adv*

[2]**temporal** *n* [MF, fr. *temporal,* adj.] (1541) : a temporal part (as a bone or muscle)

[3]**temporal** *adj* [MF, fr. LL *temporalis,* fr. L *tempora* temples] (1597) : of or relating to the temples or the sides of the skull behind the orbits

temporal bone *n* (1771) : a compound bone of the side of the skull of some mammals including humans

tem·po·ral·i·ty \ˌtem-pə-ˈra-lə-tē\ *n, pl* **-ties** (14c) **1 a** : civil or political as distinguished from spiritual or ecclesiastical power or authority **b** : an ecclesiastical property or revenue — often used in pl. **2** : the quality or state of being temporal

tem·po·ral·ize \ˈtem-p(ə-)rə-ˌlīz\ *vt* **-ized; -iz·ing** (1828) **1** : SECULARIZE **2** : to place or define in time relations

temporal lobe *n* (1889) : a large lobe of each cerebral hemisphere that is situated in front of the occipital lobe and contains a sensory area associated with the organ of hearing

temporal summation *n* (1950) : sensory summation that involves the addition of single stimuli over a short period of time

tem·po·rar·i·ly \ˌtem-pə-ˈrer-ə-lē\ *adv* (1534) : during a limited time

[1]**tem·po·rary** \ˈtem-pə-ˌrer-ē\ *adj* [L *temporarius,* fr. *tempor-, tempus* time] (ca. 1564) : lasting for a limited time — **tem·po·rar·i·ness** *n*

[2]**temporary** *n, pl* **-rar·ies** (1848) : one serving for a limited time ⟨adding several *temporaries* as typists during the summer⟩

temporary duty *n* (1945) : temporary military service away from one's permanent duty station

tem·po·rise *Brit var of* TEMPORIZE

tem·po·rize \ˈtem-pə-ˌrīz\ *vi* **-rized; -riz·ing** [MF *temporiser,* fr. ML *temporizare* to pass the time, fr. L *tempor-, tempus*] (1579) **1** : to act to suit the time or occasion : yield to current or dominant opinion **2** : to draw out discussions or negotiations so as to gain time ⟨you'd have to ~ until you found out how she wanted to be advised —Mary Austin⟩ — **tem·po·ri·za·tion** \ˌtem-pə-rə-ˈzā-shən\ *n* — **tem·po·riz·er** *n*

tem·po·ro·man·dib·u·lar \ˈtem-pə-rō-man-ˈdi-byə-lər\ *adj* [[3]*temporal* + *-o-* + *mandibular*] (1889) : of, relating to, being, or affecting the joint between the temporal bone and the mandible that allows for the movement of the mandible ⟨~ dysfunction⟩

tempt \ˈtem(p)t\ *vt* [ME, fr. AF *tempter, tenter,* fr. L *temptare, tentare* to feel, try] (13c) **1** : to entice to do wrong by promise of pleasure or gain **2 a** *obs* : to make trial of : TEST **b** : to try presumptuously : PROVOKE ⟨~ fate⟩ **c** : to risk the dangers of **3 a** : to induce to do something **b** : to cause to be strongly inclined ⟨was ~*ed* to call it quits⟩ ***syn*** see LURE — **tempt·able** \ˈtem(p)-tə-bəl\ *adj*

temp·ta·tion \tem(p)-ˈtā-shən\ *n* (13c) **1** : the act of tempting or the state of being tempted esp. to evil : ENTICEMENT **2** : something tempting : a cause or occasion of enticement

tempt·er \ˈtem(p)-tər\ *n* (14c) : one that tempts or entices

tempt·ing \ˈtem(p)-tiŋ\ *adj* (1588) : having an appeal : ENTICING ⟨a ~ offer⟩ — **tempt·ing·ly** *adv*

tempt·ress \ˈtem(p)-trəs\ *n* (1594) : a woman who tempts or entices

tem·pu·ra \ˈtem-pə-rə, -ˌrä; tem-ˈpu̇r-ə\ *n* [Jp *tenpura*] (1920) : seafood or vegetables dipped in batter and fried in deep fat

ten \ˈten\ *n* [ME, fr. OE *tīene,* fr. *tīen,* adj., ten; akin to OHG *zehan* ten, L *decem,* Gk *deka*] (bef. 12c) **1** — see NUMBER table **2** : the 10th in a set or series ⟨wears a ~⟩ **3** : something having 10 units or members **4** : a 10-dollar bill **5** : one deserving the highest rating; *specif* : an exceptionally attractive person — **ten** *adj* — **ten** *pron, pl in constr*

ten·a·ble \ˈte-nə-bəl\ *adj* [MF, fr. OF, fr. *tenir* to hold, fr. L *tenēre* — more at THIN] (1579) : capable of being held, maintained, or defended : DEFENSIBLE, REASONABLE — **ten·a·bil·i·ty** \ˌte-nə-ˈbi-lə-tē\ *n* — **ten·a·ble·ness** *n* — **ten·a·bly** \ˈte-nə-blē\ *adv*

ten·ace \ˈte-ˌnās, te-ˈnās, ˈte-nəs\ *n* [modif. of Sp *tenaza,* lit., forceps, prob. fr. L *tenacia,* neut. pl. of *tenax*] (1655) : a combination of two high or relatively high cards (as ace and queen) of the same suit in one hand with one ranking two degrees below the other

te·na·cious \tə-ˈnā-shəs\ *adj* [L *tenac-, tenax* tending to hold fast, fr. *tenēre* to hold] (1607) **1 a** : not easily pulled apart : COHESIVE ⟨a ~ metal⟩ **b** : tending to adhere or cling esp. to another substance ⟨~ burs⟩ **2 a** : persistent in maintaining, adhering to, or seeking something valued or desired ⟨a ~ advocate of civil rights⟩ ⟨~ negotiators⟩ **b** : RETENTIVE ⟨a ~ memory⟩ ***syn*** see STRONG — **te·na·cious·ly** *adv* — **te·na·cious·ness** *n*

te·nac·i·ty \tə-ˈna-sə-tē\ *n* (15c) : the quality or state of being tenacious ***syn*** see COURAGE

te·nac·u·lum \tə-ˈna-kyə-ləm\ *n, pl* **-la** \-lə\ *or* **-lums** [NL, fr. LL, instrument for holding, fr. L *tenēre*] (ca. 1693) **1** : a slender sharp-pointed hook attached to a handle and used mainly in surgery for seizing and holding parts (as arteries) **2** : an adhesive animal structure

ten·an·cy \ˈte-nən(t)-sē\ *n, pl* **-cies** (1590) **1** : a holding of an estate or a mode of holding an estate; *specif* : the temporary possession or occupancy of something (as a house) that belongs to another **2** : the period of a tenant's occupancy or possession

[1]**ten·ant** \ˈte-nənt\ *n* [ME, fr. AF, fr. prp. of *tenir* to hold] (14c) **1 a** : one who holds or possesses real estate or sometimes personal property (as a security) by any kind of right **b** : one who has the occupation or temporary possession of lands or tenements of another; *specif* : one who rents or leases (as a house) from a landlord **2** : OCCUPANT, DWELLER — **ten·ant·less** \-ləs\ *adj*

[2]**tenant** *vt* (1634) : to hold or occupy as or as if as a tenant : INHABIT — **ten·ant·able** \-nən-tə-bəl\ *adj*

tenant farmer *n* (1748) : a farmer who works land owned by another and pays rent either in cash or in shares of produce

ten·ant·ry \ˈte-nən-trē\ *n, pl* **-ries** (14c) **1** : TENANCY **2** : a body of tenants

tench \ˈtench\ *n, pl* **tench** *or* **tench·es** [ME, fr. AF *tenche,* fr. LL *tinca*] (13c) : a cyprinid fish (*Tinca tinca*) native to Eurasia but introduced in the U.S. and noted for its ability to survive in poorly oxygenated waters

Ten Commandments *n pl* (13c) : the ethical commandments of God given according to biblical accounts to Moses by voice and by writing on stone tablets on Mount Sinai

[1]**tend** \ˈtend\ *vb* [ME, short for *attenden* to attend] *vi* (14c) **1** *archaic* : LISTEN **2** : to pay attention : apply oneself ⟨~ to your own affairs⟩ ⟨~ to our correspondence⟩ **3** : to act as an attendant : SERVE ⟨~*ed* to his wife⟩ **4** *obs* : AWAIT ~ *vt* **1** *archaic* : to attend as a servant **2**

a : to apply oneself to the care of : watch over ⟨~*ed* her sick father⟩ **b** : to have or take charge of as a caretaker or overseer ⟨~ the sheep⟩ **c** : CULTIVATE, FOSTER **d** : to manage the operations of : MIND ⟨~ the store⟩ ⟨~ the fire⟩ **3** : to stand by (as a rope) in readiness to prevent mischance (as fouling)

[2]**tend** *vi* [ME, to stretch, direct oneself, fr. AF *tendre* — more at TENDER] (14c) **1** : to move, direct, or develop one's course in a particular direction ⟨cannot tell where society is ~*ing*⟩ **2** : to exhibit an inclination or tendency : CONDUCE ⟨~*s* to be optimistic⟩

ten·dance \ˈten-dən(t)s\ *n* [short for *attendance*] (1573) **1** : watchful care **2** *archaic* : persons in attendance : RETINUE

ten·den·cious *chiefly Brit var of* TENDENTIOUS

ten·den·cy \ˈten-dən(t)-sē\ *n, pl* **-cies** [ML *tendentia,* fr. L *tendent-, tendens,* prp. of *tendere*] (1628) **1 a** : direction or approach toward a place, object, effect, or limit **b** : a proneness to a particular kind of thought or action **2 a** : the purposeful trend of something written or said : AIM **b** : deliberate but indirect advocacy

syn TENDENCY, TREND, DRIFT, TENOR, CURRENT mean movement in a particular direction. TENDENCY implies an inclination sometimes amounting to an impelling force ⟨a general *tendency* toward inflation⟩. TREND applies to the general direction maintained by a winding or irregular course ⟨the long-term *trend* of the stock market is upward⟩. DRIFT may apply to a tendency determined by external forces ⟨the *drift* of the population away from large cities⟩ or it may apply to an underlying or obscure trend of meaning or discourse ⟨got the *drift* of her argument⟩. TENOR stresses a clearly perceptible direction and a continuous, undeviating course ⟨the *tenor* of the times⟩. CURRENT implies a clearly defined but not necessarily unalterable course ⟨an encounter that changed the *current* of my life⟩.

ten·den·tious \ten-ˈden(t)-shəs\ *adj* (1900) : marked by a tendency in favor of a particular point of view : BIASED — **ten·den·tious·ly** *adv* — **ten·den·tious·ness** *n*

[1]**ten·der** \ˈten-dər\ *adj* [ME, fr. AF *tendre,* fr. L *tener;* perh. akin to L *tenuis* thin, slight — more at THIN] (13c) **1 a** : having a soft or yielding texture : easily broken, cut, or damaged : DELICATE, FRAGILE ⟨~ feet⟩ **b** : easily chewed : SUCCULENT **2 a** : physically weak : not able to endure hardship **b** : IMMATURE, YOUNG ⟨children of ~ age⟩ **c** : incapable of resisting cold : not hardy ⟨~ perennials⟩ **3** : marked by, responding to, or expressing the softer emotions : FOND, LOVING ⟨a ~ lover⟩ **4 a** : showing care : CONSIDERATE, SOLICITOUS ⟨~ regard⟩ **b** : highly susceptible to impressions or emotions : IMPRESSIONABLE ⟨a ~ conscience⟩ **5 a** : appropriate or conducive to a delicate or sensitive constitution or character : GENTLE, MILD ⟨~ breeding⟩ ⟨~ irony⟩ **b** : delicate or soft in quality or tone ⟨never before heard the piano sound so ~ —Elva S. Daniels⟩ **6** *obs* : DEAR, PRECIOUS **7 a** : sensitive to touch or palpation ⟨the bruise was still ~⟩ **b** : sensitive to injury or insult : TOUCHY ⟨~ pride⟩ **c** : demanding careful and sensitive handling : TICKLISH ⟨a ~ situation⟩ **d** *of a boat* : easily tipped by an external force — **ten·der·ly** *adv* — **ten·der·ness** *n*

[2]**tender** *n* [ˈ*tender*] (13c) *obs* : CONSIDERATION, REGARD

[3]**tender** *vb* **ten·dered; ten·der·ing** \-d(ə-)riŋ\ *vt* (14c) **1** : to make tender : SOFTEN, WEAKEN **2** *archaic* : to regard or treat with tenderness ~ *vi* : to become tender

[4]**tender** *vb* **ten·dered; ten·der·ing** \-d(ə-)riŋ\ [ME *tendren,* fr. AF *tendre* offer] *vt* (15c) **1** : to make a tender of **2** : to present for acceptance : OFFER ⟨~*ed* my resignation⟩ ~ *vi* : to make a bid or tender

[5]**tender** *n, often attrib* [ME *tendur* grant of a license, fr. AF *tendre* offer, tender, fr. *tendre,* v., to stretch, hold out, offer, direct, fr. L *tendere* to stretch, direct — more at THIN] (ca. 1543) **1** : an unconditional offer of money or service in satisfaction of a debt or obligation made to save a penalty or forfeiture for nonpayment or nonperformance **2** : an offer or proposal made for acceptance: as **a** : an offer of a bid for a contract **b** : TENDER OFFER **3** : something that may be offered in payment; *specif* : MONEY

[6]**tend·er** \ˈten-dər\ *n* (1675) : one that tends: as **a** (1) : a ship employed to attend other ships (as to supply provisions) (2) : a boat for communication or transportation between shore and a larger ship (3) : a warship that provides logistic support **b** : a car attached to a steam locomotive for carrying a supply of fuel and water

[7]**tender** *n* [prob. short for *tenderloin*] (1983) : an often breaded strip of usu. breast meat ⟨chicken ~*s*⟩; *also* : the tenderloin of a chicken

ten·der·foot \ˈten-dər-ˌfu̇t\ *n, pl* **ten·der·feet** \-ˌfēt\ *also* **ten·der·foots** \-ˌfu̇ts\ (1849) **1** : a newcomer in a comparatively rough or newly settled region; *esp* : one not hardened to frontier or outdoor life **2** : an inexperienced beginner : NOVICE ⟨a political ~⟩

ten·der·heart·ed \ˈten-dər-ˌhär-təd\ *adj* (15c) : easily moved to love, pity, or sorrow : COMPASSIONATE, IMPRESSIONABLE — **ten·der·heart·ed·ly** *adv* — **ten·der·heart·ed·ness** *n*

ten·der·ize \ˈten-də-ˌrīz\ *vt* **-ized; -iz·ing** (1930) : to make (meat or meat products) tender by applying a process or substance that breaks down connective tissue — **ten·der·i·za·tion** \ˌten-d(ə-)rə-ˈzā-shən\ *n* — **ten·der·iz·er** \ˈten-də-ˌrī-zər\ *n*

ten·der·loin \ˈten-dər-ˌlȯin\ *n* (ca. 1828) **1** : a strip of tender meat consisting of a large internal muscle of the loin on each side of the vertebral column **2** [fr. its making possible a luxurious diet for a corrupt police officer] : a district of a city largely devoted to vice

ten·der–mind·ed \ˈten-dər-ˌmīn-dəd\ *adj* (1593) : marked by idealism, optimism, and dogmatism

tender offer *n* (1967) : a public offer to buy not less than a specified number of shares of a stock at a fixed price from stockholders usu. in an attempt to gain control of the issuing company

ten·der·om·e·ter \ˌten-də-ˈrä-mə-tər\ *n* (1938) : a device for determining the maturity and tenderness of samples of fruits and vegetables

ten·di·ni·tis *or* **ten·don·itis** \ˌten-də-ˈnī-təs\ *n* [*tendinitis* fr. NL, fr. *tendin-, tendo* + *-itis; tendonitis* fr. *tendon* + *-itis*] (ca. 1900) : inflammation of a tendon

ten·di·nous \ˈten-də-nəs\ *adj* [NL *tendinosus,* fr. *tendin-, tendo* tendon, alter. of ML *tendon-, tendo*] (1578) **1** : consisting of tendons : SINEWY ⟨~ tissue⟩ **2** : of, relating to, or resembling a tendon

ten·don \ˈten-dən\ *n* [ML *tendon-, tendo,* fr. L *tendere* to stretch — more at THIN] (1541) : a tough cord or band of dense white fibrous connective tissue that unites a muscle with some other part (as a bone) and transmits the force which the muscle exerts

tendon of Achil·les \-ə-ˈki-lēz\ (ca. 1885) : ACHILLES TENDON

ten·dresse \tä^n-ˈdres\ *n* [ME, fr. AF, fr. *tendre* tender] (14c) : FONDNESS

ten·dril \ˈten-drəl\ *n* [prob. modif. of MF *tendron* bud, cartilage, alter. of OF *tenrum,* fr. VL **tenerumen,* fr. L *tener* tender — more at TENDER] (1538) **1** : a leaf, stipule, or stem modified into a slender spirally coiling sensitive organ serving to attach a climbing plant to its support **2** : something suggestive of a tendril ⟨creeping ~*s* of fog⟩ — **ten·driled** *or* **ten·drilled** \-drəld\ *adj* — **ten·dril·ous** \-drə-ləs\ *adj*

[1]**-tene** *adj comb form* [F *-tène,* fr. L *taenia* ribbon, band — more at TAENIA] : having (such or so many) chromosomal filaments ⟨poly*tene*⟩ ⟨pachy*tene*⟩

[2]**-tene** *n comb form* : stage of meiotic prophase characterized by (such) chromosomal filaments ⟨diplo*tene*⟩ ⟨pachy*tene*⟩

Ten·e·brae \ˈte-nə-ˌbrā, -ˌbrī, -ˌbrē\ *n pl but sing or pl in constr* [ML, fr. L, darkness — more at TEMERITY] (1651) : a church service observed during the final part of Holy Week commemorating the sufferings and death of Christ

ten·e·brif·ic \ˌte-nə-ˈbri-fik\ *adj* [L *tenebrae* darkness] (1785) **1** : GLOOMY **2** : causing gloom or darkness

te·ne·bri·o·nid \tə-ˈne-brē-ə-nəd, ˌte-nə-ˈbrī-ə-nəd\ *n* [NL *Tenebrionidae,* fr. *Tenebrion-, Tenebrio,* type genus, fr. L, one that shuns the light, fr. *tenebrae* darkness — more at TEMERITY] (1902) : DARKLING BEETLE — **tenebrionid** *adj*

te·neb·ri·ous \tə-ˈne-brē-əs\ *adj* [by alter.] (1594) : TENEBROUS

ten·e·brism \ˈte-nə-ˌbri-zəm\ *n, often cap* [L *tenebrae* darkness] (1954) : a style of painting esp. associated with the Italian painter Caravaggio and his followers in which most of the figures are engulfed in shadow but some are dramatically illuminated by a beam of light usu. from an identifiable source — **ten·e·brist** \-brist\ *n or adj, often cap*

ten·e·brous \ˈte-nə-brəs\ *adj* [ME, fr. AF *tenebreus,* fr. L *tenebrosus,* fr. *tenebrae*] (15c) **1** : shut off from the light : DARK, MURKY ⟨~ depths⟩ **2** : hard to understand : OBSCURE ⟨a ~ affair⟩ **3** : causing gloom

1080 *also* **ten–eighty** \(ˌ)ten-ˈā-tē\ *n* [fr. its laboratory serial number] (1945) : a poisonous preparation of sodium fluoroacetate used as a rodenticide and pesticide

ten·e·ment \ˈte-nə-mənt\ *n* [ME, fr. AF, fr. ML *tenementum,* fr. L *tenēre* to hold — more at THIN] (14c) **1** : any of various forms of corporeal property (as land) or incorporeal property that is held by one person from another **2** : DWELLING **3 a** : a house used as a dwelling : RESIDENCE **b** : APARTMENT, FLAT **c** : TENEMENT HOUSE

tenement house *n* (1858) : APARTMENT BUILDING; *esp* : one meeting minimum standards of sanitation, safety, and comfort and usu. located in a city

te·nes·mus \tə-ˈnez-məs\ *n* [L, fr. Gk *teinesmos,* fr. *teinein* to stretch, strain — more at THIN] (1527) : a distressing but ineffectual urge to evacuate the rectum or bladder

te·net \ˈte-nət *also* ˈtē-nət\ *n* [L, he holds, fr. *tenēre* to hold] (ca. 1600) : a principle, belief, or doctrine generally held to be true; *esp* : one held in common by members of an organization, movement, or profession

ten·fold \ˈten-ˌfōld, -ˈfōld\ *adj* (bef. 12c) **1** : having 10 units or members **2** : being 10 times as great or as many — **ten·fold** \-ˈfōld\ *adv*

ten–gallon hat *n* (1920) : COWBOY HAT

tenge \ˈteŋ-ˌgä\ *n, pl* **tenge** [Kazakh *teŋge* coin, ruble] (1992) — see MONEY table

tenia, teniasis *var of* TAENIA, TAENIASIS

Tenn *abbr* Tennessee

ten·ne \ˈteŋ-ä\ *n, pl* **ten·ne·si** \ˈteŋ-ə-sē\ [Turkmen (Turkic language of Turkmenistan) *teňňe* coin, ruble] (2001) — see *manat* at MONEY table

ten·ner \ˈte-nər\ *n* (1845) **1** : a 10-pound note **2** : a 10-dollar bill

Ten·nes·see walking horse \ˈte-nə-ˌsē-\ *n* [*Tennessee,* state of U.S.] (1938) : any of an American breed of large easy-gaited saddle horses largely of standardbred and Morgan ancestry — called also *Tennessee walker*

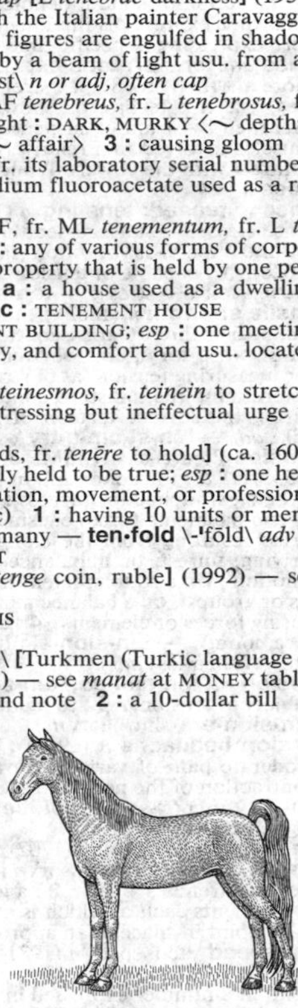

Tennessee walking horse

ten·nies \ˈte-nēz\ *n pl* [by shortening & alter.] (ca. 1951) : TENNIS SHOES, SNEAKERS

ten·nis \ˈte-nəs\ *n, often attrib* [ME *tenetz, tenys,* prob. fr. AF *tenez,* 2d pers. pl. imper. of *tenir* to hold — more at TENABLE] (15c) **1** : COURT TENNIS **2** : an indoor or outdoor game that is played with rackets and a light elastic ball by two players or pairs of players on a level court (as of clay or grass) divided by a low net

tennis elbow *n* (1883) : inflammation and pain over the outer side of the elbow usu. resulting from excessive strain on and twisting of the forearm

tennis shoe *n* (1886) : a lightweight usu. low-cut sneaker

ten·nist \ˈte-nist\ *n* [blend of *tennis* and *-ist*] (1932) : a tennis player

[1]**ten·on** \ˈte-nən\ *n* [ME, fr. AF, fr. *tenir* to hold — more at TENABLE] (14c) : a projecting member in a piece of wood or other material for insertion into a mortise to make a joint — see DOVETAIL illustration

[2]**tenon** *vt* (1596) **1** : to unite by a tenon **2** : to cut or fit for insertion in a mortise

[1]**ten·or** \ˈte-nər\ *n* [ME *tenour,* fr. AF, fr. L *tenor* uninterrupted course, fr. *tenēre* to hold — more at THIN] (14c) **1 a** : the drift of something spoken or written : PURPORT **b** : an exact copy of a writing : TRANSCRIPT **c** : the concept, object, or person meant in a metaphor **2 a** : the melodic line usu. forming the cantus firmus in medieval music **b** : the voice part next to the lowest in a 4-part chorus **c** : the highest natural adult male singing voice; *also* : a person having this voice **d** : a member of a family of instruments having a range next lower than that of the alto **3** : a continuance in a course, movement, or activity **4** : habitual condition : CHARACTER ***syn*** see TENDENCY

\ə\ **abut** \ᵊ\ kitten, F table \ər\ **further** \a\ **ash** \ā\ **ace** \ä\ mop, mar
\au̇\ **out** \ch\ **chin** \e\ **bet** \ē\ **easy** \g\ **go** \i\ **hit** \ī\ **ice** \j\ **job**
\ŋ\ **sing** \ō\ **go** \ȯ\ **law** \ȯi\ **boy** \th\ **thin** \t͟h\ **the** \ü\ **loot** \u̇\ **foot**
\y\ **yet** \zh\ **vision, beige** \ḵ, ^{n}, œ, ue, ^{y}\ *see* Guide to Pronunciation

^{2}**tenor** *adj* (1522) : relating to or having the range or part of a tenor

ten·or·ist \ˈte-nə-rist\ *n* (1865) : a person who sings tenor or plays a tenor instrument

te·no·syn·o·vi·tis \ˈte-nō-ˌsi-nə-ˈvī-təs, ˌtē-\ *n* [NL, fr. Gk *tenōn* tendon (akin to Gk *teinein* to stretch) + NL *synovitis* — more at THIN] (ca. 1860) : inflammation of a tendon sheath

ten·our \ˈte-nər\ *chiefly Brit var of* TENOR

ten·pen·ny \ˈten-ˈpe-nē, *Brit* -pə-nē\ *adj* (1592) : amounting to, worth, or costing 10 pennies

tenpenny nail *n* [fr. its original price per hundred] (15c) : a nail three inches (7.6 centimeters) long

ten·pin \ˈten-ˌpin\ *n* (1807) **1** : a bottle-shaped bowling pin 15 inches high **2** *pl but sing in constr* : a bowling game using 10 tenpins and a large ball 27 inches in circumference and allowing each player to bowl 2 balls in each of 10 frames

ten·pound·er \ˈten-ˈpau̇n-dər\ *n* (1699) : LADYFISH 2

ten·rec \ˈten-ˌrek\ *n* [F, fr. Malagasy *tàndraka*] (ca. 1785) : any of numerous small often spiny mammalian insectivores (family Tenrecidae) chiefly of Madagascar

TENS \ˈtenz\ *n* (1980) **1** [*t*ranscutaneous *e*lectrical *n*erve *s*timulation] : electrical stimulation of the skin to relieve pain by interfering with the neural transmission of signals from underlying pain receptors **2** [*t*ranscutaneous *e*lectrical *n*erve *s*timulator] : a device used for TENS

^{1}**tense** \ˈten(t)s\ *n* [ME *tens* time, tense, fr. AF, fr. L *tempus*] (14c) **1** : a distinction of form in a verb to express distinctions of time or duration of the action or state it denotes **2 a** : a set of inflectional forms of a verb that express distinctions of time **b** : an inflectional form of a verb expressing a specific time distinction

^{2}**tense** *adj* **tens·er; tens·est** [L *tensus,* fr. pp. of *tendere* to stretch — more at THIN] (1668) **1** : stretched tight : made taut : RIGID ⟨~ muscles⟩ **2 a** : feeling or showing nervous tension ⟨a ~ smile⟩ **b** : marked by strain or suspense ⟨a ~ thriller⟩ **3** : produced with the muscles involved in a relatively tense state ⟨the vowels \ē\ and \ü\ in contrast with the vowels \i\ and \u̇\ are ~⟩ — **tense·ly** *adv* — **tense·ness** *n*

^{3}**tense** *vb* **tensed; tens·ing** *vt* (1676) : to make tense ~ *vi* : to become tense ⟨*tensed* up and missed the putt⟩

ten·sile \ˈten(t)-səl *also* ˈten-ˌsī(-ə)l\ *adj* [NL *tensilis,* fr. L *tensus,* pp.] (1626) **1** : capable of tension : DUCTILE **2** : of, relating to, or involving tension ⟨~ stress⟩ — **ten·sil·i·ty** \ten-ˈsi-lə-tē\ *n*

tensile strength *n* (1862) : the greatest longitudinal stress a substance can bear without tearing apart

ten·si·om·e·ter \ˌten(t)-sē-ˈä-mə-tər\ *n* [*tension*] (1912) **1** : a device for measuring tension (as of structural material) **2** : an instrument for determining the moisture content of soil **3** : an instrument for measuring the surface tension of liquids — **ten·sio·met·ric** \-sē-ō-ˈme-trik\ *adj* — **ten·si·om·e·try** \-sē-ˈä-mə-trē\ *n*

^{1}**ten·sion** \ˈten(t)-shən\ *n* [MF or L; MF, fr. L *tension-, tensio,* fr. *tendere*] (1533) **1 a** : the act or action of stretching or the condition or degree of being stretched to stiffness : TAUTNESS **b** : STRESS 1b **2 a** : either of two balancing forces causing or tending to cause extension **b** : the stress resulting from the elongation of an elastic body **3 a** : inner striving, unrest, or imbalance often with physiological indication of emotion **b** : a state of latent hostility or opposition between individuals or groups **c** : a balance maintained in an artistic work between opposing forces or elements **4** : a device to produce a desired tension (as in a loom) — **ten·sion·al** \ˈten(t)-sh(ə-)nəl\ *adj* — **ten·sion·less** \ˈten(t)-shən-ləs\ *adj*

^{2}**tension** *vt* **ten·sioned; ten·sion·ing** \ˈten(t)-sh(ə-)niŋ\ (1891) : to subject to tension; *esp* : to tighten to a desired or appropriate degree — **ten·sion·er** \-sh(ə-)nər\ *n*

tension headache *n* (1953) : bilateral headache marked by mild to moderate pain of variable duration that typically is accompanied by contraction of the neck and scalp muscles

ten·si·ty \ˈten(t)-sə-tē\ *n, pl* **-ties** (ca. 1658) : the quality or state of being tense : TENSENESS

ten·sive \ˈten(t)-siv\ *adj* (1702) : of, relating to, or causing tension

ten·sor \ˈten(t)-sər, ˈten-ˌsȯr\ *n* [NL, fr. L *tendere*] (ca. 1704) **1** : a muscle that stretches a part **2** : a generalized vector with more than three components each of which is a function of the coordinates of an arbitrary point in space of an appropriate number of dimensions

ten–speed \ˈten-ˌspēd\ *n* (1971) : a bicycle with 10 gear combinations

tens place \ˈtenz-\ *n* (1937) : the place two to the left of the decimal point in a number expressed in the Arabic system of writing numbers

ten–strike \ˈten-ˌstrīk\ *n* (1840) **1** : a strike in tenpins **2** : a highly successful stroke or achievement

^{1}**tent** \ˈtent\ *n* [ME *tente,* fr. AF, fr. L *tenta,* fem. of *tentus,* pp. of *tendere* to stretch — more at THIN] (14c) **1** : a collapsible shelter of fabric (as nylon or canvas) stretched and sustained by poles and used for camping outdoors or as a temporary building **2** : DWELLING **3 a** : something that resembles a tent or that serves as a shelter; *esp* : a canopy or enclosure placed over the head and shoulders to retain vapors or oxygen being medically administered **b** : the web of a tent caterpillar — **tent·less** \ˈtent-ləs\ *adj* — **tent·like** \-ˌlīk\ *adj*

^{2}**tent** *vi* (ca. 1608) **1** : to reside for the time being : LODGE **2** : to live in a tent ~ *vt* **1** : to cover with or as if with a tent **2** : to lodge in tents

^{3}**tent** *vt* [ME, fr. *tent* attention, short for *attent,* fr. AF *atente,* fr. *atendre* to attend] (14c) *chiefly Scot* : to attend to

ten·ta·cle \ˈten-ti-kəl\ *n* [NL *tentaculum,* fr. L *tentare* to feel, touch — more at TEMPT] (ca. 1762) **1** : any of various elongate flexible usu. tactile or prehensile processes borne by animals and esp. invertebrates chiefly on the head or about the mouth **2 a** : something that resembles a tentacle esp. in or as if in grasping or feeling out ⟨corruption spreading its ~*s*⟩ **b** : a sensitive hair or emergence on a plant (as the sundew) — **ten·ta·cled** \-kəld\ *adj*

ten·tac·u·lar \ten-ˈta-kyə-lər\ *adj* [NL *tentaculum*] (1828) **1** : of, relating to, or resembling tentacles **2** : equipped with tentacles

tent·age \ˈten-tij\ *n* (1603) : a collection of tents : tent equipment

ten·ta·tive \ˈten-tə-tiv\ *adj* [ML *tentativus,* fr. L *tentatus,* pp. of *tentare, temptare* to feel, try] (1626) **1** : not fully worked out or developed ⟨~ plans⟩ **2** : HESITANT, UNCERTAIN ⟨a ~ smile⟩ — **tentative** *n* — **ten·ta·tive·ly** *adv* — **ten·ta·tive·ness** *n*

tent caterpillar *n* (1854) : any of several social caterpillars (genus *Malacosoma* and esp. *M. americanum* of the family Lasiocampidae) that form large silken webs on trees and may cause serious defoliation

tent·ed \ˈten-təd\ *adj* (1598) **1** : covered with a tent or tents ⟨~ camps⟩ **2** : shaped like a tent

^{1}**ten·ter** \ˈten-tər\ *n* [ME *teyntur,* prob. fr. ML *tentura,* fr. *tenta* tent frame, tent] (14c) **1** : a frame or endless track with hooks or clips along two sides that is used for drying and stretching cloth **2** *archaic* : TENTERHOOK

^{2}**tenter** *n* (1846) : one who lives in or occupies a tent

ten·ter·hook \ˈten-tər-ˌhu̇k\ *n* (15c) : a sharp hooked nail used esp. for fastening cloth on a tenter — **on tenterhooks** : in a state of uneasiness, strain, or suspense ⟨the waiting kept us *on tenterhooks*⟩

tenth \ˈten(t)th\ *n, pl* **tenths** \ˈten(t)s, ˈten(t)ths\ (13c) **1** — see NUMBER table **2 a** : a musical interval embracing an octave and a third **b** : the tone at this interval — **tenth** *adj or adv*

tenth–rate \ˈtenth-ˈrāt\ *adj* (1834) : of the lowest character or quality

tent·pole \ˈtent-ˌpōl\ *n* (1987) : a big-budget movie whose earnings are expected to compensate the studio for its less profitable movies

tent stitch *n* (1619) : a short stitch slanting to the right that is used in embroidery to form even lines of solid background

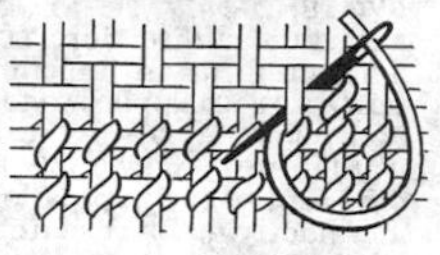

tent stitch

tenty *also* **tent·ie** \ˈten-tē\ *adj* [^{3}*tent*] (15c) *Scot* : ATTENTIVE, WATCHFUL

ten·u·is \ˈten-yə-wəs\ *n, pl* **-u·es** \-yə-ˌwēz, -ˌwās\ [ML, fr. L, thin, slight] (1650) : an unaspirated voiceless stop

te·nu·ity \te-ˈnü-ə-tē, tə-, -ˈnyü-\ *n* [ME *tenuite,* fr. L *tenuitas,* fr. *tenuis* thin, tenuous] (15c) **1** : lack of substance or strength **2** : lack of thickness : SLENDERNESS, THINNESS ⟨the ~ of poplars —Edith Wharton⟩ **3** : lack of density : rarefied quality or state

ten·u·ous \ˈten-yə-wəs, -yü-əs\ *adj* [L *tenuis* thin, slight, tenuous — more at THIN] (1597) **1** : not dense : RARE ⟨a ~ fluid⟩ **2** : not thick : SLENDER ⟨a ~ rope⟩ **3 a** : having little substance or strength : FLIMSY, WEAK ⟨~ influences⟩ **b** : SHAKY 2a ⟨~ reasons⟩ ***syn*** see THIN — **ten·u·ous·ly** *adv* — **ten·u·ous·ness** *n*

ten·ure \ˈten-yər *also* -ˌyu̇r\ *n* [ME, fr. AF *teneure, tenure,* fr. ML *tenitura,* fr. VL **tenitus,* pp. of L *tenēre* to hold — more at THIN] (15c) **1** : the act, right, manner, or term of holding something (as a landed property, a position, or an office); *esp* : a status granted after a trial period to a teacher that gives protection from summary dismissal **2** : GRASP, HOLD — **ten·ur·able** \-ə-bəl\ *adj* — **te·nur·ial** \te-ˈnyu̇r-ē-əl\ *adj* — **te·nur·ial·ly** \-ə-lē\ *adv*

ten·ured \ˈten-yərd\ *adj* (1965) : having tenure ⟨~ faculty members⟩

ten·ure–track \ˈten-yər-ˌtrak *also* -ˌyu̇r-\ *adj* (1976) : relating to or being a teaching position that may lead to a grant of tenure

te·nu·to \tā-ˈnü-(ˌ)tō\ *adj or adv* [It, fr. pp. of *tenere* to hold, fr. L *tenēre*] (1762) : held (as a tone or chord) to its full value — used as a direction in music

te·o·cal·li \ˌtē-ə-ˈka-lē, ˌtā-ə-ˈkä-\ *n* [Nahuatl *teōcalli,* fr. *teōtl* god + *calli* house] (ca. 1613) : an ancient temple of Mexico or Central America usu. built upon the summit of a truncated pyramidal mound; *also* : the mound itself

te·o·sin·te \ˌtā-ō-ˈsin-tē\ *n* [MexSp, fr. Nahuatl *teōcintli,* fr. *teōtl* god + *cintli* dried ears of maize] (ca. 1877) : any of several tall annual or perennial grasses (genus *Zea*) of Mexico and Central America that have small dark triangular seeds and include two species (*Z. mays parviglumis* and *Z. m. mexicana* syn. *Z. mexicana*) which are closely related to and often considered ancestral to corn

te·pa·ry bean \ˈte-pə-rē-\ *n* [MexSp *tépari,* fr. Ópata or Eudeve (Uto-Aztecan languages of Sonora, Mexico)] (1912) : an annual twining bean (*Phaseolus acutifolius* var. *latifolius*) that is native to the southwestern U.S. and Mexico and is cultivated for its roundish white, yellow, brown, or bluish-black edible seeds; *also* : the seed

te·pee *or* **tee·pee** *also* **ti·pi** \ˈtē-(ˌ)pē\ *n* [Dakota *tʰípi,* fr. *tʰi-* to dwell] (1743) : a conical tent usu. consisting of skins and used esp. by American Indians of the Great Plains

teph·ra \ˈte-frə\ *n* [NL, fr. Gk, ashes; akin to Skt *dahati* it burns — more at FOMENT] (ca. 1944) : solid material ejected into the air during a volcanic eruption; *esp* : ^{2}ASH 2b

tep·id \ˈte-pəd\ *adj* [ME *teped,* fr. L *tepidus,* fr. *tepēre* to be moderately warm; akin to Skt *tapati* it heats, OIr *tess* heat] (14c) **1** : moderately warm : LUKEWARM ⟨a ~ bath⟩ **2 a** : lacking in passion, force, or zest ⟨~ poetry⟩ **b** : marked by an absence of enthusiasm or conviction ⟨a ~ interest⟩ ⟨a ~ response⟩ — **te·pid·i·ty** \tə-ˈpi-də-tē, te-\ *n* — **tep·id·ly** \ˈte-pəd-lē\ *adv* — **tep·id·ness** *n*

TEPP \ˌtē-(ˌ)ē-(ˌ)pē-ˈpē\ *n* [*t*etra- + *e*thyl + *p*yro*p*hosphate] (1948) : a hygroscopic corrosive liquid organophosphate $C_8H_{20}O_7P_2$ that is a powerful anticholinesterase and is used esp. as an insecticide

tep·pan·ya·ki \ˌte-pän-ˈyä-kē\ *n* [Jp, fr. *teppan* griddle + *yaki* broiling] (ca. 1970) : a Japanese dish of meat, fish, or vegetables cooked on a large griddle usu. built into the diner's table; *also* : this style of cooking

te·qui·la \tə-ˈkē-lə, tā-\ *n* [Sp, fr. *Tequila,* town in Jalisco state, Mexico] (1849) : a Mexican liquor distilled from the fermented sap of an agave (*Agave tequilana*)

tequila sunrise *n* (1940) : a cocktail consisting of tequila, orange juice, and grenadine

ter *abbr* **1** terrace **2** territory

ter- *comb form* [L, fr. *ter;* akin to Gk & Skt *tris* three times, L *tres* three — more at THREE] : three times : threefold : three ⟨*ter*centenary⟩

tera- *comb form* [ISV, fr. Gk *terat-, teras* monster] : trillion (10^{12}) ⟨*tera*watt⟩

tera·byte \ˈter-ə-ˌbīt\ *n* (1984) : 1024 gigabytes or 1,099,511,627,776 bytes; *also* : one trillion bytes

te·rai \tə-ˈrī\ *n* [*Tarai,* lowland belt of India] (1888) : a wide-brimmed double felt sun hat worn esp. in subtropical regions

ter·aph \ˈter-əf\ *n, pl* **ter·a·phim** \ˈter-ə-ˌfim\ [Heb *tĕrāphīm* (pl. in form but sing. in meaning)] (14c) : an image of a Semitic household god

terat- *or* **terato-** *comb form* [Gk, fr. *terat-, teras* marvel, portent, monster] : developmental malformation ⟨*terato*genic⟩

te·rato·car·ci·no·ma \ˌter-ə-tō-ˌkär-sə-ˈnō-mə\ *n* (ca. 1946) : a malignant teratoma; *esp* : one involving germinal cells of the testis

te·rato·gen \tə-ˈra-tə-jən\ *n* (1959) : a teratogenic agent

ter·a·to·gen·e·sis \ˌter-ə-tə-ˈje-nə-səs\ *n* [NL] (1901) **:** production of developmental malformations

ter·a·to·gen·ic \-ˈje-nik\ *adj* (1879) **:** of, relating to, or causing developmental malformations ⟨∼ substances⟩ ⟨∼ effects⟩ — **ter·a·to·ge·nic·i·ty** \-jə-ˈni-sə-tē\ *n*

ter·a·to·log·i·cal \ˌter-ə-tə-ˈlä-ji-kəl\ *or* **ter·a·to·log·ic** \-jik\ *adj* (1857) **1 :** abnormal in growth or structure **2 :** of or relating to teratology

ter·a·tol·o·gy \ˌter-ə-ˈtä-lə-jē\ *n* (ca. 1842) **:** the study of malformations or serious deviations from the normal type in developing organisms — **ter·a·tol·o·gist** \-jist\ *n*

ter·a·to·ma \ˌter-ə-ˈtō-mə\ *n, pl* **-mas** *also* **-ma·ta** \-mə-tə\ [NL] (1879) **:** a tumor made up of a heterogeneous mixture of tissues

tera·watt \ˈter-ə-ˌwät\ *n* (1970) **:** a unit of power equal to one trillion watts

ter·bi·um \ˈtər-bē-əm\ *n* [NL, fr. *Ytterby,* Sweden] (1843) **:** a metallic element of the rare-earth group — see ELEMENT table

ter·bu·ta·line \tər-ˈbyü-tə-ˌlēn\ *n* [*tert-* tertiary + *-butaline,* perh. by shortening & alter. fr. *butyl* + *amino* + [2]*-ine*] (1973) **:** a bronchodilator $C_{12}H_{19}NO_3$ used esp. in the form of its sulfate

terce \ˈtərs\ *also* **tierce** \ˈtirs\ *n, often cap* [ME, third, terce — more at TIERCE] (14c) **:** the third of the canonical hours

tercel *var of* TIERCEL

ter·cen·te·na·ry \ˌtər-(ˌ)sen-ˈte-nə-rē, (ˌ)tər-ˈsen-tə-ˌner-ē\ *n, pl* **-ries** (1855) **:** a 300th anniversary or its celebration — **tercentenary** *adj*

ter·cen·ten·ni·al \ˌtər-(ˌ)sen-ˈte-nē-əl\ *adj or n* (1872) **:** TERCENTENARY

ter·cet \ˈtər-sət\ *n* [It *terzetto,* fr. dim. of *terzo* third, fr. L *tertius* — more at THIRD] (ca. 1598) **:** a unit or group of three lines of verse: **a :** one of the 3-line stanzas in terza rima **b :** one of the two groups of three lines forming the sestet in an Italian sonnet

ter·e·binth \ˈter-ə-ˌbin(t)th\ *n* [ME *terebynt,* fr. AF *terebinte,* fr. L *terebinthus* — more at TURPENTINE] (14c) **:** a small European tree (*Pistacia terebinthus*) of the cashew family yielding turpentine

te·re·do \tə-ˈrē-(ˌ)dō, -ˈrā-\ *n, pl* **-dos** [ME, fr. L *teredin-, teredo,* fr. Gk *terēdōn;* akin to Gk *tetrainein* to bore — more at THROW] (14c) **:** SHIPWORM

tere·phthal·ate \ˌter-ə(f)-ˈtha-ˌlāt\ *n* (1868) **:** a salt or ester of terephthalic acid; *esp* **:** a dimethyl-ester that is a major starting material for polyester fibers and coatings

tere·phthal·ic acid \ˌter-ə(f)-ˈtha-lik-\ *n* [ISV *terebene,* mixture of terpenes from distilled turpentine + *phthalic acid*] (1857) **:** a *p*-dicarboxylic acid $C_8H_6O_4$ that is obtained esp. by oxidation of xylene and is used chiefly in the synthesis of polyesters

te·rete \tə-ˈrēt, te-\ *adj* [L *teret-, teres* well turned, rounded; akin to L *terere* to rub — more at THROW] (ca. 1619) **:** approximately cylindrical but usu. tapering at both ends ⟨a ∼ seedpod⟩

Te·reus \ˈtir-ˌyüs, ˈtē-ˌrüs\ *n* [L, fr. Gk *Tēreus*] (14c) **:** the husband of Procne who rapes his sister-in-law Philomela

ter·gite \ˈtər-ˌgīt\ *n* [NL *tergum*] (1868) **:** the dorsal plate or dorsal portion of the covering of a metameric segment of an arthropod; *esp* **:** one on the abdomen

ter·gi·ver·sate \ˈtər-jə-vər-ˌsāt; ˌtər-ˈji-vər-ˌsāt, -ˈgi-; ˌtər-jə-ˈvər-\ *vi* **-sat·ed; -sat·ing** [L *tergiversatus,* pp. of *tergiversari* to show reluctance, fr. *tergum* back + *versare* to turn, freq. of *vertere* to turn — more at WORTH] (1590) **:** to engage in tergiversation — **ter·gi·ver·sa·tor** \-ˌsā-tər\ *n*

ter·gi·ver·sa·tion \ˌtər-ˌji-vər-ˈsā-shən, -ˌgi-; ˌtər-ji-(ˌ)vər-\ *n* (1570) **1 :** evasion of straightforward action or clear-cut statement **:** EQUIVOCATION **2 :** desertion of a cause, position, party, or faith

ter·gum \ˈtər-gəm\ *n, pl* **ter·ga** \-gə\ [NL, fr. L, back] (ca. 1826) **:** the dorsal part or plate of a segment of an arthropod — **ter·gal** \-gəl\ *adj*

ter·i·ya·ki \ˌter-ē-ˈyä-kē\ *n* [Jp, fr. *teri* glaze + *yaki* broiling] (1962) **:** a Japanese dish of meat or fish that is grilled or broiled after being soaked in a seasoned soy sauce marinade

[1]**term** \ˈtərm\ *n* [ME *terme,* fr. AF, fr. L *terminus* boundary marker, limit; akin to Gk *termōn* boundary, end, Skt *tarman* top of a post] (13c) **1 a :** END, TERMINATION; *also* **:** a point in time assigned to something (as a payment) **b :** the time at which a pregnancy of normal length terminates ⟨had her baby at full ∼⟩ **2 a :** a limited or definite extent of time; *esp* **:** the time for which something lasts **:** DURATION, TENURE ⟨∼ of office⟩ ⟨lost money in the short ∼⟩ **b :** the whole period for which an estate is granted; *also* **:** the estate or interest held by one for a term **c :** the time during which a court is in session **3** *pl* **:** provisions that determine the nature and scope of an agreement **:** CONDITIONS ⟨∼*s* of sale⟩ ⟨liberal credit ∼*s*⟩ **4 a :** a word or expression that has a precise meaning in some uses or is peculiar to a science, art, profession, or subject ⟨legal ∼*s*⟩ **b** *pl* **:** expression of a specified kind ⟨described in glowing ∼*s*⟩ **5 a :** a unitary or compound expression connected with another by a plus or minus sign **b :** an element of a fraction or proportion or of a series or sequence **6** *pl* **a :** mutual relationship **:** FOOTING ⟨on good ∼*s*⟩ **b :** AGREEMENT, CONCORD ⟨come to ∼*s* after extensive negotiations⟩ **c :** a state of acceptance or understanding ⟨came to ∼*s* with the failure of his marriage⟩ **7 :** any of the three substantive elements of a syllogism **8 :** a quadrangular pillar often tapering downward and adorned on the top with the figure of a head or the upper part of the body **9 :** division in a school year during which instruction is regularly given to students — **in terms of :** with respect to or in relation to ⟨thinks of everything *in terms of* money⟩ — **on one's own terms :** in accordance with one's wishes **:** in one's own way ⟨prefers to live *on his own terms*⟩

[2]**term** *vt* (ca. 1557) **:** to apply a term to **:** CALL, NAME

[1]**ter·ma·gant** \ˈtər-mə-gənt\ *n* [ME] (13c) **1** *cap* **:** a deity erroneously ascribed to Islam by medieval European Christians and represented in early English drama as a violent character **2 :** an overbearing or nagging woman **:** SHREW

[2]**termagant** *adj* (ca. 1598) **:** OVERBEARING, SHREWISH

term·er \ˈtər-mər\ *n* (1634) **:** a person serving for a specified term (as in a political office or in prison) ⟨a first ∼⟩

ter·mi·na·ble \ˈtər-mə-nə-bəl, ˈtərm-nə-\ *adj* [ME, fr. ML *terminabilis,* fr. L *terminare*] (15c) **:** capable of being terminated — **ter·mi·na·ble·ness** *n* — **ter·mi·na·bly** \-blē\ *adv*

[1]**ter·mi·nal** \ˈtərm-nəl, ˈtər-mə-nᵊl\ *adj* [L *terminalis,* fr. *terminus*] (1744) **1 a :** of or relating to an end, extremity, boundary, or terminus ⟨a ∼ pillar⟩ **b :** growing at the end of a branch or stem ⟨a ∼ bud⟩ **2 a :** of, relating to, or occurring in a term or each term ⟨∼ payments⟩ **b** (1) **:** leading ultimately to death **:** FATAL ⟨∼ cancer⟩ (2) **:** approaching or close to death **:** being in the final stages of a fatal disease ⟨a ∼ patient⟩ (3) **:** of or relating to patients with a terminal illness ⟨∼ care⟩ **c :** extremely or hopelessly severe ⟨∼ boredom⟩ **3 a :** occurring at or constituting the end of a period or series **:** CONCLUDING ⟨the ∼ moments of life⟩ **b :** not intended as preparation for further academic work ⟨a ∼ curriculum⟩ ***syn*** see LAST — **ter·mi·nal·ly** *adv*

[2]**terminal** *n* (1838) **1 :** a part that forms the end **:** EXTREMITY, TERMINATION **2 :** a terminating usu. ornamental detail **:** FINIAL **3 :** a device attached to the end of a wire or cable or to an electrical apparatus for convenience in making connections **4 a :** either end of a carrier line having facilities for the handling of freight and passengers **b :** a freight or passenger station that is central to a considerable area or serves as a junction at any point with other lines **c :** a town or city at the end of a carrier line **:** TERMINUS **5 :** a combination of a keyboard and output device (as a video display unit) by which data can be entered into or output from a computer or electronic communications system

terminal leave *n* (1944) **:** a final leave consisting of accumulated unused leave granted to a member of the armed forces just prior to separation or discharge from service

terminal side *n* (1927) **:** a straight line that has been rotated around a point on another line to form an angle measured in a clockwise or counterclockwise direction — compare INITIAL SIDE

[1]**ter·mi·nate** \ˈtər-mə-nət\ *adj* [ME, fr. L *terminatus,* pp. of *terminare,* fr. *terminus*] (15c) **:** coming to an end or capable of ending

[2]**ter·mi·nate** \ˈtər-mə-ˌnāt\ *vb* **-nat·ed; -nat·ing** *vi* (15c) **1 :** to extend only to a limit (as a point or line); *esp* **:** to reach a terminus **2 :** to form an ending **3 :** to come to an end in time ∼ *vt* **1 a :** to bring to an end **:** CLOSE ⟨∼ a marriage by divorce⟩ ⟨∼ a transmission line⟩ **b :** to form the conclusion of ⟨review questions ∼ each chapter⟩ **c :** to discontinue the employment of ⟨workers *terminated* because of slow business⟩ **2 :** to serve as an ending, limit, or boundary of **3 :** ASSASSINATE, KILL ***syn*** see CLOSE

terminating decimal *n* (ca. 1909) **:** a decimal which can be expressed in a finite number of figures or for which all figures to the right of some place are zero — compare REPEATING DECIMAL

ter·mi·na·tion \ˌtər-mə-ˈnā-shən\ *n* (ca. 1500) **1 :** end in time or existence **:** CONCLUSION ⟨the ∼ of life⟩ **2 :** the last part of a word; *esp* **:** an inflectional ending **3 :** the act of terminating **4 :** a limit in space or extent **:** BOUND **5 :** OUTCOME, RESULT — **ter·mi·na·tion·al** \-shnəl, -shə-nᵊl\ *adj*

ter·mi·na·tive \ˈtər-mə-ˌnā-tiv\ *adj* (15c) **:** tending or serving to terminate **:** ENDING — **ter·mi·na·tive·ly** *adv*

ter·mi·na·tor \ˈtər-mə-ˌnā-tər\ *n* (1770) **1 :** the dividing line between the illuminated and the unilluminated part of the moon's or a planet's disk **2 :** one that terminates

ter·mi·nol·o·gy \ˌtər-mə-ˈnä-lə-jē\ *n, pl* **-gies** [ML *terminus* term, expression (fr. L, limit) + E *-o-* + *-logy*] (1801) **1 :** the technical or special terms used in a business, art, science, or special subject **2 :** nomenclature as a field of study — **ter·mi·no·log·i·cal** \-mə-nə-ˈlä-ji-kəl\ *adj* — **ter·mi·no·log·i·cal·ly** \-ji-k(ə-)lē\ *adv*

term insurance *n* (1897) **:** insurance for a specified period that provides for no payment to the insured except on losses during the period and that becomes void upon its expiration

ter·mi·nus \ˈtər-mə-nəs\ *n, pl* **-ni** \-ˌnī, -ˌnē\ *or* **-nus·es** [L, boundary marker, limit — more at TERM] (ca. 1617) **1 :** a final goal **:** a finishing point **2 :** a post or stone marking a boundary **3 :** either end of a transportation line or travel route; *also* **:** the station, town, or city at such a place **:** TERMINAL **4 :** an extreme point or element **:** TIP ⟨the ∼ of a glacier⟩

terminus ad quem \-ˌäd-ˈkwem\ *n* [NL, lit., limit to which] (ca. 1555) **1 :** a goal, object, or course of action **:** DESTINATION, PURPOSE **2 :** a final limiting point in time

terminus a quo \-ˌä-ˈkwō\ *n* [NL, lit., limit from which] (ca. 1555) **1 :** a point of origin **2 :** a first limiting point in time

ter·mi·tar·i·um \ˌtər-mə-ˈter-ē-əm, -ˌmī-\ *n, pl* **-ia** \-ē-ə\ [NL] (1863) **:** a termites' nest

ter·mi·tary \ˈtər-mə-ˌter-ē, -ˌmī-ˌter-ē\ *n, pl* **-tar·ies** (1826) **:** TERMITARIUM

ter·mite \ˈtər-ˌmīt\ *n* [NL *Termit-, Termes,* genus of termites, fr. LL, a worm that eats wood, alter. of L *tarmit-, tarmes;* akin to Gk *tetrainein* to bore — more at THROW] (1781) **:** any of numerous pale-colored soft-bodied social insects (order Isoptera) that live in colonies consisting usu. of winged sexual forms, wingless sterile workers, and soldiers, feed on wood, and include some which are very destructive to wooden structures and trees — called also *white ant*

term·less \ˈtərm-ləs\ *adj* (ca. 1541) **1 :** having no term or end **:** BOUNDLESS, UNENDING **2 :** UNCONDITIONED, UNCONDITIONAL

term of art (1656) **:** a term that has a specialized meaning in a particular field or profession

term paper *n* (ca. 1926) **:** a major written assignment in a school or college course representative of a student's achievement during a term

tern \ˈtərn\ *n* [of Scand origin; akin to Dan *terne* tern] (1678) **:** any of various chiefly marine birds (subfamily Sterninae of the family Laridae and esp. genus *Sterna*) that differ from the related gulls in usu. smaller size, a more slender build, a sharply pointed bill, narrower wings, and an often forked tail

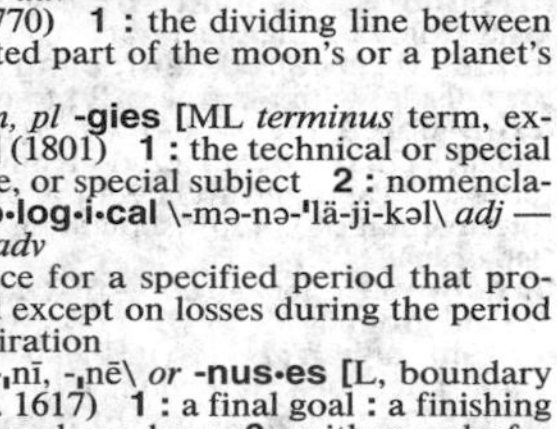

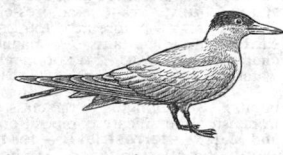

tern

ter·na·ry \ˈtər-nə-rē\ *adj* [ME, fr. L *ternarius,* fr. *terni* three each; akin to L *tres* three — more at THREE] (15c) **1 a :** of, relating to, or proceeding by threes **b :** having three elements, parts, or divisions **c**

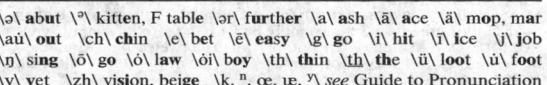

: arranged in threes ⟨~ petals⟩ **2** : using three as the base ⟨a ~ logarithm⟩ **3 a** : being or consisting of an alloy of three elements **b** : of, relating to, or containing three different elements, atoms, radicals, or groups ⟨sulfuric acid is a ~ acid⟩ **4** : third in order or rank

ter·nate \ˈtər-ˌnāt, -nət\ *adj* [NL *ternatus,* fr. ML, pp. of *ternare* to treble, fr. L *terni*] (1760) : arranged in threes or in subdivisions so arranged ⟨a ~ leaf⟩ — **ter·nate·ly** *adv*

terne \ˈtərn\ *n* [*terneplate*] (1891) **1** : an alloy of lead and tin typically in a ratio of four to one that is used as a coating in producing terneplate **2** : TERNEPLATE

terne·plate \-ˌplāt\ *n* [prob. fr. F *terne* dull (fr. MF, fr. *ternir* to tarnish) + E *plate*] (ca. 1858) : sheet iron or steel coated with an alloy of about four parts lead to one part tin

ter·pene \ˈtər-ˌpēn\ *n* [ISV *terp-* (fr. G *Terpentin* turpentine, fr. ML *terbentina*) + *-ene* — more at TURPENTINE] (ca. 1873) : any of various isomeric hydrocarbons $C_{10}H_{16}$ found present in essential oils (as from conifers) and used esp. as solvents and in organic synthesis; *broadly* : any of numerous hydrocarbons $(C_5H_8)_n$ found esp. in essential oils, resins, and balsams — **ter·pene·less** \-ləs\ *adj* — **ter·pe·noid** \ˈtər-pə-ˌnȯid, ˌtər-ˈpē-\ *adj or n*

ter·pin·e·ol \ˌtər-ˈpi-nē-ˌȯl, -ˌōl\ *n* [ISV, fr. *terpine* ($C_{10}H_{18}(OH)_2$)] (1848) : any of three fragrant isomeric alcohols $C_{10}H_{17}OH$ found in essential oils or made artificially and used esp. in perfume or as solvents

ter·poly·mer \ˌtər-ˈpä-lə-mər\ *n* (ca. 1947) : a polymer (as a complex resin) that results from copolymerization of three discrete monomers

Terp·sich·o·re \ˌtərp-ˈsi-kə-(ˌ)rē\ *n* [L, fr. Gk *Terpsichorē*] (1501) : the Greek Muse of dancing and choral song

terp·si·cho·re·an \ˌtərp-(ˌ)si-kə-ˈrē-ən; -sə-ˈkȯr-ē-, -ˈkȯr-\ *adj* (1825) : of or relating to dancing

terr *abbr* **1** terrace **2** territorial; territory

ter·ra \ˈter-ə\ *n, pl* **ter·rae** \-(ˌ)ē, -ˌī\ [NL, fr. L, land] (1946) : any of the relatively light-colored highland areas on the surface of the moon or a planet

1**ter·race** \ˈter-əs, ˈte-rəs\ *n* [MF, platform, terrace, fr. OF, fr. Old Occitan *terrassa,* fr. *terra* earth, fr. L, earth, land; akin to L *torrēre* to parch — more at THIRST] (1515) **1 a** : a colonnaded porch or promenade **b** : a flat roof or open platform **c** : a relatively level paved or planted area adjoining a building **2 a** : a raised embankment with the top leveled **b** : one of usu. a series of horizontal ridges made in a hillside to increase cultivatable land, conserve moisture, or minimize erosion **3** : a level ordinarily narrow plain usu. with steep front bordering a river, lake, or sea; *also* : a similar undersea feature **4 a** : a row of houses or apartments on raised ground or a sloping site **b** : a group of row houses **c** : a strip of park in the middle of a street often planted with trees or shrubs **d** : STREET **5** : a section of a British soccer stadium set aside for standing spectators

2**terrace** *vt* **ter·raced; ter·rac·ing** (1650) **1** : to provide (as a building or hillside) with a terrace **2** : to make into a terrace

ter·ra–cot·ta \ˌter-ə-ˈkä-tə\ *n, often attrib* [It *terra cotta,* lit., baked earth] (1722) **1** : a glazed or unglazed fired clay used esp. for statuettes and vases and architectural purposes (as roofing, facing, and relief ornamentation); *also* : something made of this material **2** : a brownish orange

terra fir·ma \-ˈfər-mə *also* -ˈfir-\ *n* [NL, lit., solid land] (1638) : dry land : solid ground

ter·rain \tə-ˈrān *also* te-\ *n* [F, land, ground, fr. OF *terrein,* fr. VL **terranum,* alter. of L *terrenum,* fr. neut. of *terrenus* of earth — more at TERRENE] (1766) **1 a** (1) : a geographic area (2) : a piece of land : GROUND **b** : the physical features of a tract of land **2** : TERRANE 1 **3 a** : a field of knowledge or interest **b** : ENVIRONMENT, MILIEU

ter·ra in·cog·ni·ta \ˈter-ə-ˌin-ˌkäg-ˈnē-tə, -in-ˈkäg-nə-tə\ *n, pl* **ter·rae in·cog·ni·tae** \ˈter-ˌī-ˌin-ˌkäg-ˈnē-ˌtī, -in-ˈkäg-nə-ˌtī\ [L] (1611) : unknown territory : an unexplored country or field of knowledge

Ter·ra·my·cin \ˌter-ə-ˈmī-sᵊn\ *trademark* — used for oxytetracycline

ter·rane \tə-ˈrān, te-\ *n* [alter. of *terrain*] (1864) **1** : the area or surface over which a particular rock or group of rocks is prevalent **2** : TERRAIN 1a

ter·ra·pin \ˈter-ə-pən\ *n* [alter. of earlier *torope,* fr. Virginia Algonquian **to·rəpe·w*] (1613) : any of various aquatic turtles (family Emydidae); *esp* : DIAMONDBACK TERRAPIN

terr·aque·ous \te-ˈrā-kwē-əs, tə-, -ˈra-\ *adj* [L *terra* land + E *aqueous*] (ca. 1658) : consisting of land and water

ter·rar·i·um \tə-ˈrer-ē-əm\ *n, pl* **-ia** \-ē-ə\ *or* **-i·ums** [NL, fr. L *terra* + *-arium* (as in *vivarium*)] (1890) : a usu. transparent enclosure for keeping or raising plants or usu. small animals (as turtles) indoors

ter·raz·zo \tə-ˈra-(ˌ)zō, -ˈrät-(ˌ)sō\ *n* [It, lit., terrace, perh. fr. Old Occitan *terrassa*] (1895) : a mosaic flooring consisting of small pieces of marble or granite set in mortar and given a high polish

1**ter·rene** \te-ˈrēn, tə-; ˈter-ˌēn\ *adj* [ME, fr. AF *terreine, terrin,* L *terrenus* of earth, fr. *terra* earth] (14c) : MUNDANE, EARTHLY

2**terrene** *n* (1667) : EARTH, TERRAIN

ter·re·plein \ˈter-ə-ˌplān\ *n* [MF, fr. OIt *terrapieno,* fr. ML *terraplenum,* fr. *terra plenus* filled with earth] (1591) : the level space behind a parapet of a rampart where guns are mounted

ter·res·tri·al \tə-ˈres-t(r)ē-əl; -ˈres-chəl, -ˈresh-\ *adj* [ME, fr. L *terrestris,* fr. *terra* earth — more at TERRACE] (15c) **1 a** : of or relating to the earth or its inhabitants ⟨~ magnetism⟩ **b** : mundane in scope or character : PROSAIC **2 a** : of or relating to land as distinct from air or water ⟨~ transportation⟩ **b** (1) : living on or in or growing from land ⟨~ plants⟩ ⟨~ birds⟩ (2) : of or relating to terrestrial organisms ⟨~ habits⟩ **3** : belonging to the class of planets that are like the earth (as in density and silicate composition) ⟨the ~ planets Mercury, Venus, and Mars⟩ — **terrestrial** *n* — **ter·res·tri·al·ly** *adv*

ter·ret \ˈter-ət\ *n* [alter. of ME *toret, turret* half-ring, eyelet, fr. AF *turette,* dim. of *tur* circuit, ring — more at TURN] (15c) : one of the rings on the top of a harness pad through which the reins pass

ter·ri·ble \ˈter-ə-bəl, ˈte-rə-\ *adj* [ME, fr. MF, fr. L *terribilis,* fr. *terrēre* to frighten — more at TERROR] (15c) **1 a** : exciting extreme alarm or intense fear : TERRIFYING **b** : formidable in nature : AWESOME ⟨a ~ responsibility⟩ **c** : DIFFICULT ⟨in a ~ bind⟩ **2** : EXTREME, GREAT ⟨a ~ disappointment⟩ **3** : extremely bad: as **a** : strongly repulsive : OBNOXIOUS ⟨a ~ smell⟩ **b** : notably unattractive or objectionable ⟨~ behavior⟩ **c** : of very poor quality ⟨a ~ movie⟩ — **ter·ri·ble·ness** *n* — **ter·ri·bly** \-blē\ *adv*

ter·ri·er \ˈter-ē-ər, ˈte-rē-\ *n* [ME *terryer, terrer,* fr. AF (*chen*) *terrer,* lit., earth dog, fr. *terre* earth, fr. L *terra*] (15c) : any of various usu. small energetic dogs orig. used by hunters to dig for small game and engage the quarry underground or drive it out

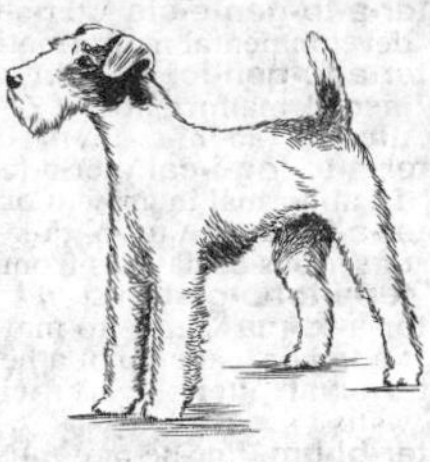

terrier

ter·rif·ic \tə-ˈri-fik\ *adj* [L *terrificus,* fr. *terrēre* to frighten] (1667) **1 a** : very bad : FRIGHTFUL **b** : exciting or fit to excite fear or awe ⟨a ~ thunderstorm⟩ **2** : EXTRAORDINARY ⟨~ speed⟩ **3** : unusually fine : MAGNIFICENT ⟨~ weather⟩ — **ter·rif·i·cal·ly** \-fi-k(ə-)lē\ *adv*

ter·ri·fy \ˈter-ə-ˌfī, ˈte-rə-\ *vt* **-fied; -fy·ing** [L *terrificare,* fr. *terrificus*] (15c) **1 a** : to drive or impel by menacing : SCARE **b** : DETER, INTIMIDATE **2** : to fill with terror

terrifying *adj* (ca. 1586) **1** : causing terror or apprehension **2** : of a formidable nature — **ter·ri·fy·ing·ly** *adv*

ter·rig·e·nous \te-ˈri-jə-nəs, tə-\ *adj* [L *terrigena* earthborn, fr. *terra* earth + *gignere* to beget — more at KIN] (1882) : being or relating to oceanic sediment derived directly from the destruction of rocks on the earth's surface

ter·rine \tə-ˈrēn, ter-ˈēn\ *n* [F — more at TUREEN] (ca. 1706) **1 a** : TUREEN 1 **b** : a usu. earthenware dish in which foods are cooked and served **2** : a mixture of chopped meat, fish, or vegetables cooked and served in a terrine

1**ter·ri·to·ri·al** \ˌter-ə-ˈtȯr-ē-əl\ *adj* (1625) **1 a** : NEARBY, LOCAL **b** : serving outlying areas : REGIONAL **2 a** : of or relating to a territory ⟨~ government⟩ **b** : of or relating to or organized chiefly for home defense **c** : of or relating to private property **3 a** : of or relating to an assigned or preempted area ⟨~ commanders⟩ **b** : exhibiting or involving territoriality ⟨~ birds⟩ — **ter·ri·to·ri·al·ly** \-ē-ə-lē\ *adv*

2**territorial** *n* (1907) : a member of a territorial military unit

territorial court *n* (1846) : a court in a U.S. territory that has jurisdiction over local and federal cases

ter·ri·to·ri·al·ism \ˌter-ə-ˈtȯr-ē-ə-ˌli-zəm\ *n* (1881) **1** : LANDLORDISM **2** : the principle established in 1555 requiring the inhabitants of a territory of the Holy Roman Empire to conform to the religion of their ruler or to emigrate — **ter·ri·to·ri·al·ist** \-list\ *n*

ter·ri·to·ri·al·i·ty \-ˌtȯr-ē-ˈa-lə-tē\ *n* (1864) **1** : territorial status **2 a** : persistent attachment to a specific territory **b** : the pattern of behavior associated with the defense of a territory

ter·ri·to·ri·al·ize \-ˈtȯr-ē-ə-ˌlīz\ *vt* **-ized; -iz·ing** (1818) : to organize on a territorial basis — **ter·ri·to·ri·al·i·za·tion** \-ˌtȯr-ē-ə-lə-ˈzā-shən\ *n*

territorial waters *n pl* (1841) : the waters under the sovereign jurisdiction of a nation or state including both marginal sea and inland waters

ter·ri·to·ry \ˈter-ə-ˌtȯr-ē\ *n, pl* **-ries** [ME, fr. L *territorium,* lit., land around a town, fr. *terra* land — more at TERRACE] (14c) **1 a** : a geographic area belonging to or under the jurisdiction of a governmental authority **b** : an administrative subdivision of a country **c** : a part of the U.S. not included within any state but organized with a separate legislature **d** : a geographic area (as a colonial possession) dependent on an external government but having some degree of autonomy **2 a** : an indeterminate geographic area **b** : a field of knowledge or interest **3 a** : an assigned area; *esp* : one in which a sales representative or distributor operates **b** : an area often including a nesting or denning site and a variable foraging range that is occupied and defended by an animal or group of animals — **go with the territory** *or* **come with the territory** : to be a natural or unavoidable aspect or accompaniment of a particular situation, position, or field ⟨criticism *goes with the territory* in this job⟩

ter·roir \ˌter-ˈwär\ *n* [F, land, country, stretch of land in reference to its agricultural features, fr. OF *tieroir,* fr. VL **terratorium,* alter. of L *territorium*] (1863) : the combination of factors including soil, climate, and sunlight that gives wine grapes their distinctive character

ter·ror \ˈter-ər, ˈte-rər\ *n* [ME, fr. AF *terrour,* fr. L *terror,* fr. *terrēre* to frighten; akin to Gk *trein* to be afraid, flee, *tremein* to tremble — more at TREMBLE] (14c) **1** : a state of intense fear **2 a** : one that inspires fear : SCOURGE **b** : a frightening aspect **c** : a cause of anxiety : WORRY **d** : an appalling person or thing; *esp* : BRAT **3** : REIGN OF TERROR **4** : violent or destructive acts (as bombing) committed by groups in order to intimidate a population or government into granting their demands ***syn*** see FEAR — **ter·ror·less** \-ləs\ *adj*

ter·ror·ise *chiefly Brit var of* TERRORIZE

ter·ror·ism \ˈter-ər-ˌi-zəm\ *n* (1795) : the systematic use of terror esp. as a means of coercion — **ter·ror·ist** \-ər-ist\ *adj or n* — **ter·ror·is·tic** \ˌter-ər-ˈis-tik\ *adj*

ter·ror·ize \ˈter-ər-ˌīz\ *vt* **-ized; -iz·ing** (1823) **1** : to fill with terror or anxiety : SCARE **2** : to coerce by threat or violence — **ter·ror·i·za·tion** \ˌter-ər-ə-ˈzā-shən\ *n*

ter·ry \ˈter-ē, ˈte-rē\ *n, pl* **terries** [perh. modif. of F *tiré,* pp. of *tirer* to draw] (1784) **1** : the loop forming the pile in uncut pile fabrics **2** : an absorbent fabric with such loops — called also *terry cloth*

terse \ˈtərs\ *adj* **ters·er; ters·est** [L *tersus* clean, neat, fr. pp. of *tergēre* to wipe off] (1601) **1** : smoothly elegant : POLISHED **2** : devoid of superfluity ⟨a ~ summary⟩; *also* : SHORT, BRUSQUE ⟨dismissed me with a ~ "no"⟩ ***syn*** see CONCISE — **terse·ly** *adv* — **terse·ness** *n*

1**ter·tian** \ˈtər-shən\ *adj* [ME *tercian,* fr. AF, fr. L *tertianus,* lit., of the third, fr. *tertius* third — more at THIRD] (14c) : recurring at approximately 48-hour intervals — used of malaria

2**tertian** *n* (14c) : a tertian fever (as vivax malaria)

1**ter·tia·ry** \ˈtər-shē-ˌer-ē, -shə-rē\ *n, pl* **-ries** (ca. 1550) **1** [ML *tertiarius,* fr. L, of a third] : a member of a monastic third order esp. of lay people **2** *cap* : the Tertiary period or system of rocks

2**tertiary** *adj* [L *tertiarius* of or containing a third, fr. *tertius* third] (ca. 1656) **1 a** : of third rank, importance, or value **b** *chiefly Brit* : of, relating to, or being higher education **c** : of, relating to, or constituting the third strongest of the three or four degrees of stress recognized by most linguists (as the stress of the third syllable of *basketball team*) **2** *cap* : of, relating to, or being the first period of the Cenozoic era or the corresponding system of rocks marked by the formation of high mountains (as the Alps, Caucasus, and Himalayas) and the dominance of mammals on land — see GEOLOGIC TIME table **3 a** : involving or resulting from the substitution of three atoms or groups ⟨a ∼ salt⟩ ⟨∼ amine⟩ **b** : being or containing a carbon atom having bonds to three other carbon atoms ⟨an acid containing a ∼ carbon⟩ ⟨∼ alcohols⟩ **c** : of, relating to, or being the normal folded structure of the coiled chain of a protein or of DNA or RNA **4** : occurring in or being a third stage: as **a** : being or relating to the recovery of oil and gas from old wells by means of the underground application of heat and chemicals **b** : being or relating to the purification of wastewater by removal of fine particles, nitrates, and phosphates

tertiary care *n* (1979) : highly specialized medical care usu. over an extended period of time that involves advanced and complex procedures and treatments performed by medical specialists in state-of-the-art facilities — compare PRIMARY CARE, SECONDARY CARE

tertiary color *n* (ca. 1864) **1** : a color produced by mixing two secondary colors **2** : a color produced by an equal mixture of a primary color with a secondary color adjacent to it on the color wheel

tertiary syphilis *n* (1875) : the third stage of syphilis that develops after disappearance of the symptoms of secondary syphilis and is marked by ulcers in and gummas under the skin and commonly by involvement of the skeletal, cardiovascular, and nervous systems

ter·ti·um quid \ˌtər-shē-əm-ˈkwid, ˌtər-tē-\ *n* [LL, lit., third something; fr. its failing to fit into a dichotomy] (ca. 1724) **1** : a middle course or an intermediate component ⟨where there are two systems of law and two orders of courts, there must . . . be some *tertium quid* to deal with conflicts of law and jurisdiction —Ernest Baker⟩ **2** : a third party of ambiguous status ⟨there was a man and his wife and a *tertium quid* —Rudyard Kipling⟩

ter·za ri·ma \ˌtert-sə-ˈrē-mə\ *n* [It, lit., third rhyme] (1819) : a verse form consisting of tercets usu. in iambic pentameter in English poetry with an interlaced rhyme scheme (as *aba, bcb, cdc*)

TESL *abbr* teaching English as a second language

tes·la \ˈtes-lə\ *n* [Nikola *Tesla*] (1958) : a unit of magnetic flux density in the meter-kilogram-second system equivalent to one weber per square meter

TESOL *abbr* Teachers of English to Speakers of Other Languages

tes·sel·late \ˈtes-ə-ˌlāt\ *vt* **-lat·ed; -lat·ing** [LL *tessellatus*, pp. of *tessellare* to pave with tesserae, fr. L *tessella*, dim. of *tessera*] (1789) : to form into or adorn with mosaic

tes·sel·lat·ed \-ˌlā-təd\ *adj* (1695) : having a checkered appearance

tes·sel·la·tion \ˌte-sə-ˈlā-shən\ *n* (1660) **1 a** : MOSAIC **b** : a covering of an infinite geometric plane without gaps or overlaps by congruent plane figures of one type or a few types **2** : an act of tessellating : the state of being tessellated

tes·sera \ˈte-sə-rə\ *n, pl* **-ser·ae** \-ˌrē, -ˌrī\ [L, prob. ultim. fr. Gk *tessares* four; fr. its having four corners — more at FOUR] (1538) **1** : a small tablet (as of wood, bone, or ivory) used by the ancient Romans as a ticket, tally, voucher, or means of identification **2** : a small piece (as of marble, glass, or tile) used in mosaic work

tes·ser·act \ˈte-sə-ˌrakt\ *n* [Gk *tessares* four + *aktis* ray — more at ACTIN-] (1888) : the four-dimensional analogue of a cube

tes·si·tu·ra \ˌte-sə-ˈtùr-ə\ *n* [It, lit., texture, fr. L *textura*] (1875) : the general range of a melody or voice part; *specif* : the part of the register in which most of the tones of a melody or voice part lie

¹**test** \ˈtest\ *n* [ME, vessel in which metals were assayed, potsherd, fr. AF *test, tees* pot, L *testum* earthen vessel; akin to L *testa* earthen pot, shell] (14c) **1 a** *chiefly Brit* : CUPEL **b** (1) : a critical examination, observation, or evaluation : TRIAL; *specif* : the procedure of submitting a statement to such conditions or operations as will lead to its proof or disproof or to its acceptance or rejection ⟨a ∼ of a statistical hypothesis⟩ (2) : a basis for evaluation : CRITERION **c** : an ordeal or oath required as proof of conformity with a set of beliefs **2 a** : a means of testing: as (1) : a procedure, reaction, or reagent used to identify or characterize a substance or constituent (2) : something (as a series of questions or exercises) for measuring the skill, knowledge, intelligence, capacities, or aptitudes of an individual or group **b** : a positive result in such a test **3** : a result or value determined by testing **4** : TEST MATCH

²**test** *adj* (1687) **1** : of, relating to, or constituting a test **2** : subjected to, used for, or revealed by testing ⟨a ∼ group⟩ ⟨∼ data⟩

³**test** *vt* (1748) **1** : to put to test or proof : TRY — often used with *out* **2** : to require a doctrinal oath of ∼ *vi* **1 a** : to undergo a test **b** : to be assigned a standing or evaluation on the basis of tests ⟨∼ed positive for cocaine⟩ ⟨the cake ∼ed done⟩ **2** : to apply a test as a means of analysis or diagnosis — used with *for* ⟨∼ for mechanical aptitude⟩ — **test·abil·i·ty** \ˌtes-tə-ˈbi-lə-tē\ *n* — **test·able** \ˈtes-tə-bəl\ *adj* — **test the waters** *also* **test the water** : to make a preliminary test or survey (as of reaction or interest) before embarking on a course of action

⁴**test** *n* [L *testa* shell] (ca. 1842) : an external hard or firm covering (as a shell) of many invertebrates (as a foraminifer or a mollusk)

Test *abbr* Testament

tes·ta \ˈtes-tə\ *n, pl* **tes·tae** \-ˌtē, -ˌtī\ [NL, fr. L, shell] (1796) : the hard external coating or integument of a seed

tes·ta·ceous \tes-ˈtā-shəs\ *adj* [L *testaceus*, fr. *testa* shell, earthen pot, brick] (1646) **1** : having a shell ⟨a ∼ protozoan⟩ **2** : of any of the several light colors of bricks

tes·ta·cy \ˈtes-tə-sē\ *n, pl* **-cies** (ca. 1864) : the state of being testate

tes·ta·ment \ˈtes-tə-mənt\ *n* [ME, fr. AF, fr. LL & L; LL *testamentum* covenant with God, holy scripture, fr. L, last will, fr. *testari* to be a witness, call to witness, make a will, fr. *testis* witness; akin to L *tres* three & to L *stare* to stand; fr. the witness's standing by as a third party in a litigation — more at THREE, STAND] (14c) **1 a** *archaic* : a covenant between God and the human race **b** *cap* : either of two main divisions of the Bible **2 a** : a tangible proof or tribute **b** : an expression of conviction : CREED **3 a** : an act by which a person determines the disposition of his or her property after death **b** : WILL — **tes·ta·men·ta·ry** \ˌtes-tə-ˈmen-tə-rē, -ˈmen-trē\ *adj*

tes·tate \ˈtes-ˌtāt, -tət\ *adj* [ME, fr. L *testatus*, pp. of *testari* to make a will] (15c) : having left a valid will ⟨she died ∼⟩

tes·ta·tor \ˈtes-ˌtā-tər, tes-ˈ\ *n* [ME, fr. AF, fr. LL *testator*, fr. L *testari*] (14c) : a person who dies leaving a will or testament in force

tes·ta·trix \ˈtes-ˌtā-triks, tes-ˈ\ *n* [LL, fem. of *testator*] (1564) : a woman who is a testator

test ban *n* (1958) : a self-imposed partial or complete ban on the testing of nuclear weapons that is mutually agreed to by countries possessing such weapons

test bed *n* (1914) : a vehicle (as an airplane) used for testing new equipment (as engines or weapons systems); *broadly* : any device, facility, or means for testing something in development

test case *n* (1850) **1** : a representative case whose outcome is likely to serve as a precedent **2** : a proceeding brought by agreement or on an understanding of the parties to obtain a decision as to the constitutionality of a statute

test·cross \ˈtes(t)-ˌkrȯs\ *n* (1934) : a genetic cross between a homozygous recessive individual and a corresponding suspected heterozygote to determine the genotype of the latter — **testcross** *vt*

test–drive \ˈtes(t)-ˌdrīv\ *vt* **-drove** \-ˌdrōv\; **-driv·en** \-ˌdri-vən\; **-driv·ing** \-ˌdrī-viŋ\ (1950) **1** : to drive (a motor vehicle) in order to evaluate performance **2** : to use or examine (as a computer program) in order to evaluate performance ⟨∼ the new game⟩ — **test–drive** *n*

test·ed \ˈtes-təd\ *adj* (1748) : subjected to or qualified through testing — often used in combination ⟨time-*tested* principles⟩

test·ee \tes-ˈtē\ *n* (1930) : one who takes an examination

¹**tes·ter** \ˈtēs-tər, ˈtes-\ *n* [ME, headboard of a bed, canopy, fr. AF, fr. *teste* head, fr. LL *testa* skull, fr. L, shell] (14c) : the canopy over a bed, pulpit, or altar

²**tes·ter** \ˈtes-tər\ *n* [modif. of MF *testart*, fr. *teston*] (1546) : TESTON a

³**test·er** \ˈtes-tər\ *n* (1661) : one that tests or is used for testing

testes *pl of* TESTIS

test–fly \ˈtest-ˌflī\ *vt* **-flew** \-ˌflü\; **-flown** \-ˌflōn\ **-fly·ing** (1936) : to subject to a flight test ⟨∼ an experimental plane⟩

tes·ti·cle \ˈtes-ti-kəl\ *n* [ME *testicule*, fr. L *testiculus*, dim. of *testis*] (15c) : TESTIS; *esp* : one of a higher mammal usu. with its enclosing structures — **tes·tic·u·lar** \tes-ˈti-kyə-lər\ *adj*

tes·ti·fy \ˈtes-tə-ˌfī\ *vb* **-fied; -fy·ing** [ME *testifien*, fr. AF *testifier*, fr. L *testificari*, fr. *testis* witness] *vi* (14c) **1 a** : to make a statement based on personal knowledge or belief : bear witness **b** : to serve as evidence or proof **2** : to express a personal conviction **3** : to make a solemn declaration under oath for the purpose of establishing a fact (as in a court) ∼ *vt* **1 a** : to bear witness to : ATTEST **b** : to serve as evidence of : PROVE **2** *archaic* : to make known (a personal conviction) **b** : to give evidence of : SHOW **3** : to declare under oath before a tribunal or officially constituted public body — **tes·ti·fi·er** \-ˌfī(-ə)r\ *n*

¹**tes·ti·mo·ni·al** \ˌtes-tə-ˈmō-nē-əl, -nyəl\ *adj* (15c) **1** : of, relating to, or constituting testimony **2** : expressive of appreciation or esteem ⟨a ∼ dinner⟩

²**testimonial** *n* (15c) **1** : EVIDENCE, TESTIMONY **2 a** : a statement testifying to benefits received **b** : a character reference : letter of recommendation **3** : an expression of appreciation : TRIBUTE

tes·ti·mo·ny \ˈtes-tə-ˌmō-nē\ *n, pl* **-nies** [ME *testimonie*, fr. AF, fr. LL & L; LL *testimonium* Decalogue, fr. L, evidence, witness, fr. *testis* witness — more at TESTAMENT] (14c) **1 a** (1) : the tablets inscribed with the Mosaic law (2) : the ark containing the tablets **b** : a divine decree attested in the Scriptures **2 a** : firsthand authentication of a fact : EVIDENCE **b** : an outward sign **c** : a solemn declaration usu. made orally by a witness under oath in response to interrogation by a lawyer or authorized public official **3 a** : an open acknowledgment **b** : a public profession of religious experience

test·ing \ˈtes-tiŋ\ *adj* (1858) : requiring maximum effort or ability ⟨a most difficult and ∼ problem —Ernest Bevin⟩

tes·tis \ˈtes-təs\ *n, pl* **tes·tes** \ˈtes-ˌtēz\ [L, witness, testis] (1650) : a typically paired male reproductive gland that produces sperm and secretes testosterone and that in most mammals is contained within the scrotum at sexual maturity

test–mar·ket \ˈtes(t)-ˌmär-kət\ *vt* (1953) : to subject (a product) to trial in a limited market

test match *n* (1862) **1** : any of a series of championship cricket matches played between teams representing Australia and England **2** : a championship game or series (as of cricket) played between teams representing different countries

tes·ton \ˈtes-ˌtän\ *or* **tes·toon** \tes-ˈtün\ *n* [MF, fr. OIt *testone*, aug. of *testa* head, fr. LL, skull — more at TESTER] (1536) : any of several old European coins: as **a** : a shilling of Henry VIII of England decreasing in value to ninepence and then to sixpence in Shakespeare's time **b** : a French silver coin of the 16th century worth between 10 and 14½ sous

tes·tos·ter·one \tes-ˈtäs-tə-ˌrōn\ *n* [*testis* + *-o-* + *-sterone*] (1935) **1** : a hormone that is a hydroxy steroid ketone $C_{19}H_{28}O_2$ produced esp. by the testes or made synthetically and that is responsible for inducing and maintaining male secondary sex characters **2** : qualities (as brawn and aggressiveness) usu. associated with males : MANLINESS

test pattern *n* (ca. 1946) : a fixed picture broadcast by a television station to assist viewers in adjusting their receivers

test pilot *n* (1917) : a pilot who specializes in putting new or experimental airplanes through maneuvers designed to test them (as for strength) by producing strains in excess of normal

test–tube \ˈtest-ˌtüb\ *adj* (1866) **1** : IN VITRO ⟨∼ experiments⟩ **2** : produced by in vitro fertilization ⟨∼ babies⟩

test tube *n* (1846) : a plain or lipped tube usu. of thin glass closed at one end and used esp. in chemistry and biology

tes·tu·do \tes-ˈtü-(ˌ)dō, -ˈtyü-\ *n, pl* **-dos** [L *testudin-, testudo*, lit., tortoise, tortoise shell; akin to L *testa* shell] (1609) : a cover of overlapping shields or a shed wheeled up to a wall used by the ancient Romans to protect an attacking force

tes·ty \ˈtes-tē\ *adj* **tes·ti·er; -est** [ME *testif*, fr. AF, headstrong, fr. *teste* head — more at TESTER] (1523) **1** : easily annoyed : IRRITABLE **2** : marked by impatience or ill humor ⟨∼ remarks⟩ — **tes·ti·ly** \-tə-lē\ *adv* — **tes·ti·ness** \-tē-nəs\ *n*

Tet \ˈtet\ *n* [Vietnamese *tết*] (1885) : the Vietnamese New Year observed during the first several days of the lunar calendar beginning at the second new moon after the winter solstice

---

\ə\ abut \ˈə, ˌə\ kitten, F table \ər\ further \a\ ash \ā\ ace \ä\ mop, mar \au̇\ out \ch\ chin \e\ bet \ē\ easy \g\ go \i\ hit \ī\ ice \j\ job \ŋ\ sing \ō\ go \ȯ\ law \ȯi\ boy \th\ thin \t͟h\ the \ü\ loot \u̇\ foot \y\ yet \zh\ vision, beige \k, ⁿ, œ, �, ᵊ\ *see* Guide to Pronunciation

tet·a·nal \ˈte-tə-nəl\ *adj* (1939) : of, relating to, or derived from tetanus
te·tan·ic \te-ˈta-nik\ *adj* (ca. 1727) : of, relating to, being, or tending to produce tetany or tetanus — **te·tan·i·cal·ly** \-ni-k(ə-)lē\ *adv*
tet·a·nize \ˈte-tə-ˌnīz\ *vt* **-nized; -niz·ing** (1849) : to induce tetanus in ⟨~ a muscle⟩ — **tet·a·ni·za·tion** \ˌte-tə-nə-ˈzā-shən, ˌtet-nə-\ *n*
tet·a·nus \ˈte-tə-nəs, ˈtet-nəs\ *n* [ME, fr. L, fr. Gk *tetanos,* fr. *tetanos* stretched, rigid; akin to Gk *teinein* to stretch — more at THIN] (14c) **1 a :** an acute infectious disease characterized by tonic spasm of voluntary muscles esp. of the jaw and caused by an exotoxin of a bacterium (*Clostridium tetani*) which is usu. introduced through a wound — compare LOCKJAW **b :** the bacterium that causes tetanus **2 :** prolonged contraction of a muscle resulting from rapidly repeated motor impulses
tet·a·ny \ˈte-tə-nē, ˈtet-nē\ *n* [ISV, fr. L *tetanus*] (ca. 1885) : a condition of physiological calcium imbalance marked by tonic spasm of muscles and often associated with deficient parathyroid secretion
te·tar·to·he·dral \te-ˌtär-tə-ˈhē-drəl\ *adj* [Gk *tetartos* fourth; akin to Gk *tettares* four — more at FOUR] (ca. 1858) *of a crystal* : having one fourth the number of planes required by complete symmetry — compare HEMIHEDRAL, HOLOHEDRAL
tetched *var of* TECHED
tetchy \ˈte-chē\ *adj* **tetch·i·er; -est** [perh. fr. obs. *tetch* habit] (1592) : irritably or peevishly sensitive : TOUCHY ⟨the ~ manner of two women living in the same house —Elizabeth Taylor †1975⟩ — **tetch·i·ly** \-chə-lē\ *adv* — **tetch·i·ness** \-chē-nəs\ *n*
[1]**tête–à–tête** \ˌtet-ə-ˈtet, ˌtāt-ə-ˈtāt, *2 is also* ˈtēt-ə-ˌtēt\ *n* [F, lit., head to head] (1696) **1 :** a private conversation between two persons **2 :** a short piece of furniture (as a sofa) intended to seat two persons esp. facing each other
[2]**tête–à–tête** \ˌtet-ə-ˈtet, ˌtāt-ə-ˈtāt\ *adv* (1700) : in private
[3]**tête–à–tête** \ˌtet-ə-ˌtet, ˌtāt-ə-ˌtāt\ *adj* (1728) : FACE-TO-FACE, PRIVATE
tête–bêche \ˈtet-ˈbesh\ *adj* [F, n., pair of inverted stamps, fr. *tête* head + *-bêche,* alter. of MF *bechevet* head against foot] (ca. 1913) : of or relating to a pair of stamps inverted in relation to one another either through a printing error or intentionally
teth \ˈtāt, ˈtāth, ˈtās\ *n* [Heb *ṭēth*] (ca. 1823) : the 9th letter of the Hebrew alphabet — see ALPHABET table
[1]**teth·er** \ˈte-t͟hər\ *n* [ME *tethir, teder,* prob. of Scand origin; akin to ON *tjōthr* tether; akin to OHG *zeotar* pole of a wagon] (14c) **1 :** something (as a rope or chain) by which an animal is fastened so that it can range only within a set radius **2 :** the limit of one's strength or resources ⟨at the end of my ~⟩
[2]**tether** *vt* **teth·ered; teth·er·ing** \-t͟h(ə-)riŋ\ (15c) : to fasten or restrain by or as if by a tether ⟨felt ~*ed* to her desk until the work was done⟩
teth·er·ball \ˈte-t͟hər-ˌbȯl\ *n* (1897) : a game played with a ball suspended by a string from an upright pole in which the object is to wrap the string around the pole by striking the ball in a direction opposite to that of one's opponent; *also* : the ball used in this game
Te·thys \ˈtē-thəs\ *n* [L, fr. Gk *Tēthys*] (1567) : a Titaness and wife of Oceanus
tet·ra \ˈte-trə\ *n* [by shortening fr. NL *Tetragonopterus,* former genus name, fr. LL *tetragonum* quadrangle + Gk *pteron* wing — more at TETRAGONAL, FEATHER] (1931) : any of numerous small often brightly colored So. American characin fishes often bred in tropical aquariums
tetra- *or* **tetr-** *comb form* [NL, fr. Gk; akin to Gk *tettares* four — more at FOUR] **1 :** four : having four : having four parts ⟨*tetra*valent⟩ **2 :** containing four atoms or groups (of a specified kind) ⟨*tetra*chloride⟩
tet·ra·caine \ˈte-trə-ˌkān\ *n* [*tetra-* + *-caine*] (ca. 1935) : a crystalline basic ester $C_{15}H_{24}N_2O_2$ that is closely related chemically to procaine and is used chiefly in the form of its hydrochloride as a local anesthetic
tet·ra·chlo·ride \ˌte-trə-ˈklȯr-ˌīd\ *n* (1866) : a chloride containing four atoms of chlorine
tet·ra·chord \ˈte-trə-ˌkȯrd\ *n* [Gk *tetrachordon,* fr. neut. of *tetrachordos* of four strings, fr. *tetra-* + *chordē* string — more at YARN] (1603) : a diatonic series of four tones with an interval of a perfect fourth between the first and last
tet·ra·cy·cline \ˌte-trə-ˈsī-ˌklēn\ *n* [ISV *tetracycl*ic having four fused hydrocarbon rings + [2]*-ine*] (1952) : a yellow crystalline broad-spectrum antibiotic $C_{22}H_{24}N_2O_8$ produced by streptomyces or synthetically; *also* : any of several chemically related antibiotics (as doxycycline)
tet·rad \ˈte-ˌtrad\ *n* [Gk *tetrad-, tetras,* fr. *tetra-*] (1653) : a group or arrangement of four: as **a :** a group of four cells produced by the successive divisions of a mother cell ⟨a ~ of spores⟩ **b :** a group of four synapsed chromatids that become visibly evident in the pachytene stage of meiotic prophase — **te·trad·ic** \te-ˈtra-dik\ *adj*
tet·ra·drachm \ˈte-trə-ˌdram\ *n* [Gk *tetradrachmon,* fr. *tetra-* + *drachmē* drachma] (ca. 1580) : an ancient Greek silver coin worth four drachmas
tet·ra·eth·yl lead \ˌte-trə-ˌe-thəl-ˈled\ *n* (1923) : a heavy oily poisonous liquid $Pb(C_2H_5)_4$ used esp. formerly as an antiknock agent
tet·ra·flu·o·ride \ˌte-trə-ˈflȯr-ˌīd, -ˈflu̇r-\ *n* (ca. 1909) : a fluoride containing four atoms of fluorine
te·trag·o·nal \te-ˈtra-gə-nᵊl\ *adj* [LL *tetragonalis* having four angles and four sides, fr. *tetragonum* quadrangle, fr. Gk *tetragōnon,* fr. neut. of *tetragōnos* tetragonal, fr. *tetra-* + *gōnia* angle — more at -GON] (1868) : of, relating to, or characteristic of the tetragonal system — **te·trag·o·nal·ly** \-nᵊl-ē\ *adv*
tetragonal system *n* (1879) : a crystal system characterized by three axes at right angles of which only the two lateral axes are equal
tet·ra·gram·ma·ton \ˌte-trə-ˈgra-mə-ˌtän\ *n* [ME, fr. LL, fr. Gk, fr. neut. of *tetragrammatos* having four letters, fr. *tetra-* + *grammat-, gramma* letter — more at GRAM] (15c) : the four Hebrew letters usu. transliterated YHWH or JHVH that form a biblical proper name of God — compare YAHWEH
tet·ra·he·dral \ˌte-trə-ˈhē-drəl\ *adj* (1794) **1 :** being a polyhedral angle with four faces **2 :** relating to, forming, or having the form of a tetrahedron — **tet·ra·he·dral·ly** \-drə-lē\ *adv*
tet·ra·he·dron \ˌte-trə-ˈhē-drən\ *n, pl* **-drons** *or* **-dra** \-drə\ [NL, fr. LGk *tetraedron,* neut. of *tetraedros* having four faces, fr. Gk *tetra-* + *hedra* seat, face — more at SIT] (1570) : a polyhedron that has four faces
tet·ra·hy·dro·can·nab·i·nol \-ˌhī-drə-kə-ˈna-bə-ˌnȯl, -ˌnōl\ *n* [*tetrahydro-* (combined with four atoms of hydrogen) + *cannabin* + [1]*-ol*] (1940) : THC
tet·ra·hy·dro·fu·ran \-ˈfyu̇r-ˌan, -fyu̇-ˈran\ *n* [*tetrahydro-* + *furan*] (ca. 1943) : a flammable liquid heterocyclic ether C_4H_8O that is derived from furan and used as a solvent and as an intermediate in organic synthesis
tet·ra·hy·me·na \ˌte-trə-ˈhī-mə-nə\ *n* [NL, fr. *tetra-* + Gk *hymēn* membrane] (1962) : any of a genus (*Tetrahymena*) of ciliate protozoans
te·tral·o·gy \te-ˈträ-lə-jē, -ˈtra-\ *n, pl* **-gies** [Gk *tetralogia,* fr. *tetra-* + *-logia* -logy] (1656) **1 :** a group of four dramatic pieces presented consecutively on the Attic stage at the Dionysiac festival **2 :** a series of four connected works (as operas or novels)
tet·ra·mer \ˈte-trə-mər\ *n* (1929) : a molecule (as an enzyme or a polymer) that consists of four structural subunits (as peptide chains or condensed monomers) — **tet·ra·mer·ic** \ˌte-trə-ˈmer-ik\ *adj*
te·tram·er·ous \te-ˈtra-mə-rəs\ *adj* [NL *tetramerus,* fr. Gk *tetramerēs,* fr. *tetra-* + *meros* part — more at MERIT] (1826) : having or characterized by the presence of four parts or of parts arranged in sets of four ⟨~ flowers⟩
te·tram·e·ter \te-ˈtra-mə-tər\ *n* [Gk *tetrametron,* fr. neut. of *tetrametros* having four measures, fr. *tetra-* + *metron* measure — more at MEASURE] (1612) : a line of verse consisting either of four dipodies (as in classical iambic, trochaic, and anapestic verse) or four metrical feet (as in modern English verse)
tet·ra·meth·yl·lead \ˌte-trə-ˌme-thəl-ˈled\ *n* (1964) : a volatile poisonous liquid $Pb(CH_3)_4$ used esp. formerly as an antiknock agent
[1]**tet·ra·ploid** \ˈte-trə-ˌplȯid\ *adj* [ISV] (1912) : having or being a chromosome number four times the monoploid number ⟨a ~ cell⟩ — **tet·ra·ploi·dy** \-ˌplȯi-dē\ *n*
[2]**tetraploid** *n* (1921) : a tetraploid individual
tet·ra·pod \ˈte-trə-ˌpäd\ *n* [NL *tetrapodus,* fr. Gk *tetrapod-, tetrapous* four-footed, fr. *tetra-* + *pod-, pous* foot — more at FOOT] (ca. 1891) : a vertebrate (as an amphibian, a bird, or a mammal) with two pairs of limbs
tet·ra·pyr·role \ˌte-trə-ˈpir-ˌōl\ *n* (ca. 1928) : a chemical group consisting of four pyrrole rings joined either in a straight chain or in a ring (as in chlorophyll)
te·trarch \ˈte-ˌträrk, ˈtē-\ *n* [ME, fr. L *tetrarcha,* fr. Gk *tetrarchēs,* fr. *tetra-* + *-archēs* -arch] (12c) **1 :** a governor of the fourth part of a province **2 :** a subordinate prince — **te·trar·chic** \te-ˈträr-kik, tē-\ *adj*
te·trar·chy \ˈte-ˌträr-kē, ˈtē-\ *n, pl* **-chies** (15c) : government by four persons ruling jointly
tet·ra·spore \ˈte-trə-ˌspȯr\ *n* [ISV] (1846) : one of the four haploid asexual spores developed meiotically in the red algae
tet·ra·va·lent \ˌte-trə-ˈvā-lənt\ *adj* [ISV] (1868) : having a valence of four
tet·ra·zo·li·um \ˌte-trə-ˈzō-lē-əm\ *n* [NL, fr. ISV *tetrazole* (CH_2N_4)] (1895) : a monovalent cation or group CH_3N_4 that is analogous to ammonium; *also* : any of several of its derivatives used esp. as electron acceptors to test for metabolic activity in living cells
tet·raz·zi·ni \ˌte-trə-ˈzē-nē\ *adj, often cap* [Luisa *Tetrazzini* †1940 Ital. opera singer] (1911) : prepared with pasta and a white sauce seasoned with sherry and served au gratin ⟨chicken ~⟩
tet·ri \ˈte-trē\ *n, pl* **tetri** [Georgian, lit., white, silver, a silver coin] (1994) — see *lari* at MONEY table
tet·rode \ˈte-ˌtrōd\ *n* (1886) : a vacuum tube with a cathode, an anode, a control grid, and an additional grid or other electrode
te·tro·do·tox·in \te-ˌtrō-də-ˈtäk-sən\ *n* [ISV *tetrodo-* (fr. NL *Tetrodon,* genus of tropical marine fishes) + *toxin*] (1911) : a neurotoxin $C_{11}H_{17}N_3O_8$ found esp. in puffer fish that blocks nerve conduction by suppressing permeability of the nerve fiber to sodium ions
te·trox·ide \te-ˈträk-ˌsīd\ *n* [ISV] (1863) : a compound of an element or group with four atoms of oxygen
tet·ryl \ˈte-trəl\ *n* [ISV] (1909) : a pale yellow crystalline explosive $C_7H_5N_5O_8$ used esp. as a detonator
tet·ter \ˈte-tər\ *n* [ME *teter,* fr. OE; akin to OHG *zittaroh* tetter, Skt *dadru* leprosy, *dṛṇāti* he tears — more at TEAR] (bef. 12c) : any of various vesicular skin diseases (as ringworm, eczema, and herpes)
Teu·ton \ˈtü-tᵊn, ˈtyü-, -ˌtän\ *n* [L *Teutoni,* pl.] (ca. 1580) **1 :** a member of an ancient prob. Germanic or Celtic people **2 :** a member of a people speaking a language of the Germanic branch of the Indo-European language family; *esp* : GERMAN
[1]**Teu·ton·ic** \tü-ˈtä-nik, tyü-\ *n* (1612) : GERMANIC
[2]**Teutonic** *adj* (1618) : of, relating to, or characteristic of the Teutons — **Teu·ton·i·cal·ly** \-ni-k(ə-)lē\ *adv*
Teu·ton·ism \ˈtü-tə-ˌni-zəm, ˈtyü-\ *n* (1854) : GERMANISM
Teu·ton·ist \-nist\ *n* (1882) : GERMANIST
teu·ton·ize \-ˌnīz\ *vt* **-ized; -iz·ing** *often cap* (1845) : GERMANIZE
TeV *abbr* tera-electron-volt; trillion electron-volts
Te·wa \ˈtā-wə, ˈtē-\ *n* [AmerSp *Tegua,* fr. Tewa *téwa,* a self-designation] (1844) **1 :** a member of a Pueblo Indian people of New Mexico and Arizona **2 :** the language of the Tewa people
Tex *abbr* Texas
tex·as \ˈtek-səs, -siz\ *n* [*Texas,* state of U.S.; fr. the naming of cabins on Mississippi steamboats after states, the officers' cabins being the largest] (1857) : a structure on the awning deck of a steamer that contains the officers' cabins and has the pilothouse in front or on top
Texas fever *n* (1866) : an infectious disease of cattle transmitted by the cattle tick and caused by a protozoan (*Babesia bigemina*) that multiplies in the blood and destroys the red blood cells
Texas Hold–'em \-ˈhōl-dəm\ *n* (1975) : poker in which each player is dealt two cards facedown and all players share five cards dealt faceup
Texas Independence Day *n* (ca. 1928) : March 2 observed as the anniversary of the declaration of independence of Texas from Mexico in 1836 and also as the birthday of Sam Houston
Texas leaguer *n* [*Texas League,* a baseball minor league] (1903) : a fly in baseball that falls too far out to be caught by an infielder and too close in to be caught by an outfielder
Texas longhorn *n* (1908) **1 :** LONGHORN 1a **2 :** any of a breed of relatively small cattle developed in the U.S. from descendants of the original longhorns and typically having a horn spread that averages 40 to 65 inches (100 to 165 centimeters) and a variable color pattern
Texas Ranger *n* (1846) : a member of a formerly mounted police force in Texas
Tex–Mex \ˈteks-ˈmeks\ *adj* [*Tex*as + *Mex*ico] (1949) : of, relating to, or being the Mexican-American culture or cuisine existing or originating in esp. southern Texas ⟨~ cooking⟩ ⟨~ music⟩ — **Tex–Mex** *n*

[1]text \ˈtekst\ *n* [ME, fr. AF *tiste, texte,* fr. ML *textus,* fr. L, texture, context, fr. *texere* to weave — more at TECHNICAL] (14c) **1 a (1) :** the original words and form of a written or printed work **(2) :** an edited or emended copy of an original work **b :** a work containing such text **2 a :** the main body of printed or written matter on a page **b :** the principal part of a book exclusive of front and back matter **c :** the printed score of a musical composition **3 a (1) :** a verse or passage of Scripture chosen esp. for the subject of a sermon or for authoritative support (as for a doctrine) **(2) :** a passage from an authoritative source providing an introduction or basis (as for a speech) **b :** a source of information or authority **4 :** THEME, TOPIC **5 a :** the words of something (as a poem) set to music **b :** matter chiefly in the form of words or symbols that is treated as data for processing by computerized equipment ⟨*text*-editing software⟩ **6 :** a type suitable for printing running text **7 :** TEXTBOOK **8 a :** something (as a story or movie) considered as an object to be examined, explicated, or deconstructed **b :** something likened to a text ⟨the surfaces of daily life are ~*s* to be explicated —Michiko Kakutani⟩ **9 :** FRAME OF REFERENCE 2 ⟨updated to fit the women's lib ~ for consciousness raising —Judith Crist⟩ **10 :** TEXT MESSAGE ⟨sent a ~ with the details⟩

[2]text *vt* (1998) **:** to send a text message from one cell phone to another ~ *vi* **:** to communicate by text messaging — **text·er** *n*

[1]text·book \ˈteks(t)-ˌbu̇k\ *n* (1779) **:** a book used in the study of a subject: as **a :** one containing a presentation of the principles of a subject **b :** a literary work relevant to the study of a subject

[2]textbook *adj* (1905) **:** of, suggesting, or suitable to a textbook; *esp* **:** CLASSIC ⟨a ~ example of bureaucratic waste⟩

text·book·ish \-ˌbu̇-kish\ *adj* (1914) **:** of, relating to, or having the characteristics of a textbook ⟨the style is heavy and ~ —*Nation*⟩

text edition *n* (1876) **:** an edition of a book prepared for use esp. in schools and colleges — compare TRADE EDITION

tex·tile \ˈtek-ˌstī(-ə)l, ˈteks-tᵊl\ *n* [L, fr. neut. of *textilis* woven, fr. *texere*] (1626) **1 :** CLOTH 1a; *esp* **:** a woven or knit cloth **2 :** a fiber, filament, or yarn used in making cloth

text message *n* (1978) **:** a short message sent electronically usu. from one cell phone to another

text messaging *n* (1982) **:** the sending of short text messages electronically esp. from one cell phone to another

tex·tu·al \ˈteks-chə-wəl, -chəl\ *adj* [ME *textuel,* fr. ML *textus* text] (15c) **:** of, relating to, or based on a text — **tex·tu·al·i·ty** \ˌteks-chə-ˈwa-lə-tē\ *n* — **tex·tu·al·ly** *adv*

textual critic *n* (1938) **:** a practitioner of textual criticism

textual criticism *n* (1859) **1 :** the study of a literary work that aims to establish the original text **2 :** a critical study of literature emphasizing a close reading and analysis of the text

tex·tu·al·ize \ˈteks-ch(ə-w)ə-ˌlīz\ *vt* **-ized; -iz·ing** (1981) **:** to put into text **:** set down as concrete and unchanging ⟨the novel ~*s* complex emotions⟩ — **tex·tu·al·i·za·tion** \ˌteks-ch(ə-w)ə-lə-ˈzā-shən\ *n*

[1]tex·tu·ary \ˈteks-chə-ˌwer-ē\ *n, pl* **-ar·ies** [ML *textus*] (1608) **:** one who is well informed in the Bible or in biblical scholarship

[2]textuary *adj* (1646) **:** TEXTUAL

[1]tex·ture \ˈteks-chər\ *n* [L *textura,* fr. *textus,* pp. of *texere* to weave — more at TECHNICAL] (1578) **1 a :** something composed of closely interwoven elements; *specif* **:** a woven cloth **b :** the structure formed by the threads of a fabric **2 a :** essential part **:** SUBSTANCE **b :** identifying quality **:** CHARACTER **3 a :** the disposition or manner of union of the particles of a body or substance **b :** the visual or tactile surface characteristics and appearance of something ⟨the ~ of an oil painting⟩ **4 a :** a composite of the elements of prose or poetry ⟨all these words . . . meet violently to form a ~ impressive and exciting —John Berryman⟩ **b :** a pattern of musical sound created by tones or lines played or sung together **5 a :** basic scheme or structure **b :** overall structure — **tex·tur·al** \-chə-rəl\ *adj* — **tex·tur·al·ly** \-rə-lē\ *adv* — **tex·tured** \-chərd\ *adj* — **tex·ture·less** \-chər-ləs\ *adj*

[2]texture *vt* **tex·tured; tex·tur·ing** (1694) **:** to give a particular texture to

textured vegetable protein *n* (1968) **:** protein from some vegetables and esp. soybeans used as a substitute for or added to meat

tex·tur·ize \ˈteks-chə-ˌrīz\ *vt* **-ized; -iz·ing** (ca. 1950) **:** TEXTURE

tex·tus re·cep·tus \ˌtek-stəs-ri-ˈsep-təs\ *n* [NL, lit., received text] (1851) **:** the generally accepted text of a literary work (as the Greek New Testament)

TF *abbr* task force

T formation *n* (1930) **:** an offensive football formation in which the fullback lines up behind the center and quarterback with one halfback stationed on each side of the fullback

T4 \ˈtē-ˈfȯr\ *n* [prob. fr. *t*hyronine, the amino acid of which thyroxine is a derivative + *4,* the number of iodine atoms it contains] (1974) **:** THYROXINE

T4 cell *n* [*T cell* + CD*4*] (1983) **:** any of the T cells (as a helper T cell) that display the CD4 molecule on their surface and become severely depleted in AIDS — called also *T4 lymphocyte*

TFT *abbr* thin-film transistor

TG *abbr* **1** transformational grammar **2** type genus

TGIF *abbr* thank God it's Friday

T–group \ˈtē-ˌgrüp\ *n* [*t*raining *group*] (1950) **:** a group of people under the leadership of a trainer who seek to develop self-awareness and sensitivity to others by verbalizing feelings uninhibitedly at group sessions — compare ENCOUNTER GROUP

TGV *abbr* [F *train à grande vitesse*] high-speed train

[1]Th *abbr* Thursday

[2]Th *symbol* thorium

[1]-th — see -ETH

[2]-th *or* **-eth** *adj suffix* [ME *-the, -te,* fr. OE *-tha, -ta;* akin to OHG *-do* -th, L *-tus,* Gk *-tos,* Skt *-tha*] — used in forming ordinal numbers ⟨hundred*th*⟩ ⟨forti*eth*⟩

[3]-th *n suffix* [ME, fr. OE; akin to OHG *-ida,* suffix forming abstract nouns, L *-ta,* Gk *-tē,* Skt *-tā*] **1 :** act or process ⟨spil*th*⟩ **2 :** state or condition ⟨dear*th*⟩

[4]-th *symbol* [[2]-th] — used with the figures 4, 5, 6, 7, 8, 9, and 0 and related Roman numerals to indicate an ordinal number ⟨25*th*⟩ ⟨50*th* wedding anniversary⟩ ⟨XXV*th* Olympiad⟩

[1]Thai \ˈtī\ *n, pl* **Thai** *or* **Thais** (1808) **1 :** TAI 2 **2 a :** a native or inhabitant of Thailand **b :** one who is descended from a Thai **3 :** the official language of Thailand

[2]Thai *adj* (1808) **:** of or relating to Thailand, its people, or their language or culture

thal·a·mus \ˈtha-lə-məs\ *n, pl* **-mi** \-ˌmī, -ˌmē\ [NL, fr. Gk *thalamos* chamber] (1859) **:** the largest subdivision of the diencephalon that consists chiefly of an ovoid mass of nuclei in each lateral wall of the third ventricle and serves chiefly to relay impulses and esp. sensory impulses to and from the cerebral cortex — see BRAIN illustration — **tha·lam·ic** \thə-ˈla-mik\ *adj*

thal·as·sae·mia *chiefly Brit var of* THALASSEMIA

thal·as·se·mia \ˌtha-lə-ˈsē-mē-ə\ *n* [NL, fr. Gk *thalassa* sea + NL *-emia*] (1932) **:** any of a group of inherited disorders of hemoglobin synthesis affecting the globin chain that are characterized usu. by mild to severe hemolytic anemia, are caused by a series of allelic genes, and tend to occur esp. in individuals of Mediterranean, black, or southeast Asian ancestry; *esp* **:** COOLEY'S ANEMIA — **thal·as·se·mic** \-mik\ *adj or n*

thalassemia major *n* [NL, greater thalassemia] (1944) **:** COOLEY'S ANEMIA

thalassemia minor *n* [NL, lesser thalassemia] (1944) **:** a mild form of thalassemia associated with the heterozygous condition for the gene involved

tha·las·sic \thə-ˈla-sik\ *adj* [F *thalassique,* fr. Gk *thalassa* sea] (1883) **:** of, relating to, or situated or developed about inland seas

thal·as·soc·ra·cy \ˌtha-lə-ˈsä-krə-sē\ *n* [Gk *thalassokratia,* fr. *thalassa* + *-kratia* -cracy] (1846) **:** maritime supremacy — **tha·las·so·crat** \thə-ˈla-sə-ˌkrat\ *n*

tha·las·so·ther·a·py \thə-ˌla-sō-ˈthe-rə-pē\ *n* [Gk *thalassa* + E *therapy*] (1899) **:** exposure to seawater (as in a hot tub) or application of sea products (as seaweed) to the body for health or beauty benefits

thaler *var of* TALER

Tha·lia \thə-ˈlī-ə\ *n* [L, fr. Gk *Thaleia*] (1523) **1 :** the Greek Muse of comedy **2 :** one of the three Graces

tha·lid·o·mide \thə-ˈli-də-ˌmīd, -məd\ *n* [ph*thal*ic acid + *-id-* (fr. *imide*) + *-o-* + *imide*] (1958) **:** a drug $C_{13}H_{10}N_2O_4$ that was formerly used as a sedative and is now used as an immunomodulatory agent esp. in the treatment of leprosy and that is known to cause malformations of infants born to mothers using it during pregnancy

thal·li·um \ˈtha-lē-əm\ *n* [NL, fr. Gk *thallos* green shoot; fr. the bright green line in its spectrum] (1861) **:** a soft poisonous metallic element that resembles lead in physical properties, occurs sparsely in a number of common ores, and is used chiefly in the form of compounds esp. in photosensitive devices and formerly as a pesticide — see ELEMENT table

thal·loid \ˈtha-ˌlȯid\ *adj* (1857) **:** of, relating to, resembling, or consisting of a thallus ⟨~ liverworts⟩

thal·lo·phyte \ˈtha-lə-ˌfīt\ *n* [ultim. fr. Gk *thallos* + *phyton* plant — more at PHYT-] (1854) **:** any of a group of plants or plantlike organisms (as algae and fungi) that lack differentiated stems, leaves, and roots and that were formerly classified as a primary division (Thallophyta) of the plant kingdom — **thal·lo·phyt·ic** \ˌtha-lə-ˈfi-tik\ *adj*

thal·lus \ˈtha-ləs\ *n, pl* **thal·li** \ˈtha-ˌlī, -ˌlē\ *or* **thal·lus·es** [NL, fr. Gk *thallos,* fr. *thallein* to sprout; akin to Arm *dalar* green, fresh, Alb *dal* I come forth] (1829) **:** a plant body that lacks differentiation into distinct parts (as stem, leaves, and roots), does not grow from an apical point, and is characteristic of organisms formerly classified as thallophytes

[1]than \t͟hən, ˈt͟han\ *conj* [ME *than, then* then, than — more at THEN] (bef. 12c) **1 a** — used as a function word to indicate the second member or the member taken as the point of departure in a comparison expressive of inequality; used with comparative adjectives and comparative adverbs ⟨older ~ I am⟩ ⟨easier said ~ done⟩ **b** — used as a function word to indicate difference of kind, manner, or identity; used esp. with some adjectives and adverbs that express diversity ⟨anywhere else ~ at home⟩ **2 :** rather than — usu. used only after *prefer, preferable,* and *preferably* **3 :** other than **4 :** WHEN 1b — used esp. after *scarcely* and *hardly*

[2]than *prep* (1560) **:** in comparison with ⟨you are older ~ me⟩

usage After 200 years of innocent if occasional use, the preposition *than* was called into question by 18th century grammarians. Some 200 years of elaborate reasoning have led to these present-day inconsistent conclusions: *than whom* is standard but clumsy ⟨T. S. Eliot, *than* whom nobody could have been more insularly English —Anthony Burgess⟩; *than me* may be acceptable in speech ⟨a man no mightier *than* thyself or me —Shak.⟩ ⟨why should a man be better *than* me because he's richer *than* me —William Faulkner, in a talk to students⟩; *than* followed by a third-person objective pronoun (*her, him, them*) is usu. frowned upon. Surveyed opinion tends to agree with these conclusions. Our evidence shows that *than* is used as a conjunction more commonly than as a preposition, that *than whom* is chiefly limited to writing, and that *me* is more common after the preposition than the third-person objective pronouns. In short, you can use *than* either as a conjunction or as a preposition.

than·a·tol·o·gy \ˌtha-nə-ˈtä-lə-jē\ *n* [Gk *thanatos* + E *-logy*] (ca. 1842) **:** the description or study of the phenomena of death and of psychological mechanisms for coping with them — **than·a·to·log·i·cal** \ˌtha-nə-tə-ˈlä-ji-kəl\ *adj* — **than·a·tol·o·gist** \-ə-ˈtä-lə-jist\ *n*

Than·a·tos \ˈtha-nə-ˌtäs\ *n* [Gk, death; akin to Skt *adhvanīt* it vanished] (1935) **:** DEATH INSTINCT

thane \ˈthān\ *n* [ME *theyn,* fr. OE *thegn;* akin to OHG *thegan* thane and perh. to Gk *tiktein* to bear, beget] (bef. 12c) **1 :** a free retainer of an Anglo-Saxon lord; *esp* **:** one resembling a feudal baron by holding lands of and performing military service for the king **2 :** a Scottish feudal lord — **thane·ship** \-ˌship\ *n*

thank \ˈthaŋk\ *vt* [ME, fr. OE *thancian;* akin to OE *thanc* gratitude — more at THANKS] (bef. 12c) **1 :** to express gratitude to ⟨~*ed* her for the present⟩ — used in the phrase *thank you* usu. without a subject to politely express gratitude ⟨~ you for your consideration⟩ or sometimes to emphasize a preceding statement esp. by implying that it is not subject to question ⟨likes her job just fine, *thank you*⟩; used in such phrases as *thank God, thank goodness* usu. without a subject to express gratitude or more often only the speaker's or writer's pleasure or satisfaction in something **2 :** to hold responsible ⟨had only himself to ~ for his loss⟩ — **thank·er** *n*

thank·ful \ˈthaŋk-fəl\ *adj* (bef. 12c) **1 :** conscious of benefit received ⟨for what we are about to receive make us truly ~⟩ **2 :** expressive of thanks ⟨~ service⟩ **3 :** well pleased : GLAD ⟨was ~ that it didn't rain⟩ — **thank·ful·ness** *n*

thank·ful·ly \-f(ə-)lē\ *adv* (bef. 12c) **1 :** in a thankful manner ⟨spoke ~⟩ **2 :** as makes one thankful ⟨graceless stadiums . . . ~ going out of fashion —R. G. Echevarriá⟩ ⟨~, those opinions are advanced with graceful prose —Ken Auletta⟩

thank·less \ˈthaŋk-ləs\ *adj* (15c) **1 :** not likely to obtain thanks : UNAPPRECIATED ⟨a ~ task⟩ **2 :** not expressing or feeling gratitude : UNGRATEFUL ⟨how sharper than a serpent's tooth it is to have a ~ child —Shak.⟩ — **thank·less·ly** *adv* — **thank·less·ness** *n*

thanks \ˈthaŋ(k)s\ *n pl* [pl. of ME *thank,* fr. OE *thanc* thought, gratitude; akin to OHG *dank* gratitude, L *tongēre* to know] (bef. 12c) **1 :** kindly or grateful thoughts : GRATITUDE **2 :** an expression of gratitude ⟨return ~ before the meal⟩ — often used in an utterance containing no verb and serving as a courteous and somewhat informal expression of gratitude ⟨many ~⟩

thanks·giv·ing \thaŋ(k)s-ˈgi-viŋ *also* ˈthaŋ(k)s-ˌ\ *n* (1533) **1 :** the act of giving thanks **2 :** a prayer expressing gratitude **3 a :** a public acknowledgment or celebration of divine goodness **b** *cap* **:** THANKSGIVING DAY

Thanksgiving Day *n* (1674) **:** a day appointed for giving thanks for divine goodness: as **a :** the fourth Thursday in November observed as a legal holiday in the U.S. **b :** the second Monday in October observed as a legal holiday in Canada

thanks to *prep* (1633) **:** with the help of : BECAUSE OF ⟨arrived early, *thanks to* good weather⟩ — **no thanks to :** not as a result of any benefit conferred by ⟨he feels better now, *no thanks to* you⟩

thank·wor·thy \ˈthaŋk-ˌwər-t͟hē\ *adj* (14c) **:** worthy of thanks or gratitude : MERITORIOUS

thank–you \ˈthaŋk-ˌyü\ *n* [fr. the phrase *thank you* used in expressing gratitude] (1792) **:** a polite expression of one's gratitude

thank–you–ma'am \ˈthaŋk-yü-ˌmam, -(y)ē-\ *n* [prob. fr. its causing a nodding of the head] (1849) **:** a bump or depression in a road; *esp* **:** a ridge or hollow made across a road on a hillside to cause water to run off

[1]**that** \ˈt͟hat, t͟hət\ *pron, pl* **those** \ˈt͟hōz\ [ME, fr. OE *thæt,* neut. demonstrative pron. & definite article; akin to OHG *daz,* neuter demonstrative pron. & definite article, Gk *to,* L *istud,* neut. demonstrative pron.] (bef. 12c) **1 a :** the person, thing, or idea indicated, mentioned, or understood from the situation ⟨~ is my father⟩ **b :** the time, action, or event specified ⟨after ~ I went to bed⟩ **c :** the kind or thing specified as follows ⟨the purest water is ~ produced by distillation⟩ **d :** one or a group of the indicated kind ⟨~'s a cat — quick and agile⟩ **2 a :** the one farther away or less immediately under observation or discussion ⟨*those* are maples and these are elms⟩ **b :** the former one **3 a** — used as a function word after *and* to indicate emphatic repetition of the idea expressed by a previous word or phrase ⟨he was helpful, and ~ to an unusual degree⟩ **b** — used as a function word immediately before or after a word group consisting of a verbal auxiliary or a form of the verb *be* preceded by *there* or a personal pronoun subject to indicate emphatic repetition of the idea expressed by a previous verb or predicate noun or predicate adjective ⟨is she capable? She is ~⟩ **4 a :** the one : the thing : the kind : SOMETHING, ANYTHING ⟨the truth of ~ which is true⟩ ⟨the senses are ~ whereby we experience the world⟩ ⟨what's ~ you say⟩ **b** *pl* **:** some persons ⟨*those* who think the time has come⟩ — **all that :** everything of the kind indicated ⟨tact, discretion, and *all that*⟩ — **at that 1 :** in spite of what has been said or implied **2 :** in addition : [2]BESIDES

[2]**that** \t͟hət, ˈt͟hat\ *conj* (bef. 12c) **1 a** (1) — used as a function word to introduce a noun clause that is usu. the subject or object of a verb or a predicate nominative ⟨said ~ he was afraid⟩ (2) — used as a function word to introduce a subordinate clause that is anticipated by the expletive *it* occurring as subject of the verb ⟨it is unlikely ~ he'll be in⟩ (3) — used as a function word to introduce a subordinate clause that is joined as complement to a noun or adjective ⟨we are certain ~ this is true⟩ ⟨the fact ~ you are here⟩ (4) — used as a function word to introduce a subordinate clause modifying an adverb or adverbial expression ⟨will go anywhere ~ he is invited⟩ **b** — used as a function word to introduce an exclamatory clause expressing a strong emotion esp. of surprise, sorrow, or indignation ⟨~ it should come to this!⟩ **2 a** (1) — used as a function word to introduce a subordinate clause expressing purpose or desired result ⟨cutting down expenses ~ her son might inherit an unencumbered estate —W. B. Yeats⟩ (2) — used as a function word to introduce a subordinate clause expressing a reason or cause ⟨rejoice ~ you are lightened of a load —Robert Browning⟩ (3) — used as a function word to introduce a subordinate clause expressing consequence, result, or effect ⟨are of sufficient importance ~ they cannot be neglected —Hannah Wormington⟩ **b** — used as a function word to introduce an exclamatory clause expressing a wish ⟨oh, ~ he would come⟩ **3** — used as a function word after a subordinating conjunction without modifying its meaning ⟨if ~ thy bent of love be honorable —Shak.⟩

[3]**that** *adj, pl* **those** (12c) **1 a :** being the person, thing, or idea specified, mentioned, or understood **b :** being the one specified — usu. used for emphasis ⟨~ rarity among leaders⟩ ⟨~ brother of yours⟩ **c :** so great a : SUCH **2 :** the farther away or less immediately under observation or discussion ⟨this chair or ~ one⟩

[4]**that** \t͟hət, ˈt͟hat\ *pron* [ME, fr. OE *thæt,* neut. rel. pron., fr. *thæt,* neut. demonstrative pron.] (bef. 12c) **1** — used as a function word to introduce a restrictive relative clause and to serve as a substitute within that clause for the substantive modified by the clause ⟨the house ~ Jack built⟩ ⟨I'll make a ghost of him ~ lets me —Shak.⟩ **2 a :** at which : in which : on which : by which : with which : to which ⟨each year ~ the lectures are given⟩ **b :** according to what : to the extent of what — used after a negative ⟨has never been here ~ I know of⟩ **3 a** *archaic* **:** that which **b** *obs* **:** the person who

usage *That, which, who:* In current usage *that* refers to persons or things, *which* chiefly to things and rarely to subhuman entities, *who* chiefly to persons and sometimes to animals. The notion that *that* should not be used to refer to persons is without foundation; such use is entirely standard. Because *that* has no genitive form or construction, *of which* or *whose* must be substituted for it in contexts that call for the genitive.

usage *That, which:* Although some handbooks say otherwise, *that* and *which* are both regularly used to introduce restrictive clauses in edited prose. *Which* is also used to introduce nonrestrictive clauses. *That* was formerly used to introduce nonrestrictive clauses; such use is virtually nonexistent in present-day edited prose, though it may occas. be found in poetry.

[5]**that** \ˈt͟hat\ *adv* (13c) **1 :** to such an extent ⟨a nail about ~ long⟩ **2 :** VERY, EXTREMELY — usu. used with the negative ⟨did not take the festival ~ seriously —Eric Goldman⟩

that·away \ˈt͟ha-də-ˌwā\ *adv* [alter. of *that way*] (1839) **:** in that direction

[1]**thatch** \ˈthach\ *vt* [ME *thecchen,* fr. OE *theccan* to cover; akin to OHG *decchen* to cover, L *tegere,* Gk *stegein* to cover, *stegos* roof, Skt *sthagati* he covers] (14c) **:** to cover with or as if with thatch — **thatch·er** *n*

[2]**thatch** *n* (14c) **1 a :** a plant material (as straw) used as a sheltering cover esp. of a house **b :** a sheltering cover (as a house roof) made of such material **c :** a mat of undecomposed plant material (as grass clippings) accumulated next to the soil in a grassy area (as a lawn) **2 :** something likened to the thatch of a house; *esp* **:** the hair of one's head

thau·ma·turge \ˈthȯ-mə-ˌtərj\ *n* [F, fr. NL *thaumaturgus,* fr. Gk *thaumatourgos* working miracles, fr. *thaumat-, thauma* miracle + *ergon* work — more at THEATER, WORK] (1715) **:** THAUMATURGIST

thau·ma·tur·gic \ˌthȯ-mə-ˈtər-jik\ *adj* (1680) **1 :** performing miracles **2 :** of, relating to, or dependent on thaumaturgy

thau·ma·tur·gist \ˈthȯ-mə-ˌtər-jist\ *n* (1829) **:** a performer of miracles; *esp* **:** MAGICIAN

thau·ma·tur·gy \ˈthȯ-mə-ˌtər-jē\ *n* (ca. 1727) **:** the performance of miracles; *specif* **:** MAGIC

[1]**thaw** \ˈthȯ\ *vb* [ME, fr. OE *thawian;* akin to OHG *douwen* to thaw, Gk *tēkein* to melt, L *tabēre* to waste away] *vt* (bef. 12c) **:** to cause to thaw ~ *vi* **1 a :** to go from a frozen to a liquid state : MELT **b :** to become free of the effect (as stiffness, numbness, or hardness) of cold as a result of exposure to warmth **2 :** to be warm enough to melt ice and snow — used with *it* in reference to the weather **3 :** to abandon aloofness, reserve, or hostility : UNBEND **4 :** to become mobile, active, or susceptible to change

[2]**thaw** *n* (15c) **1 :** the action, fact, or process of thawing **2 :** a period of weather warm enough to thaw ice ⟨the January ~⟩ **3 :** the action or process of becoming less aloof, less hostile, or more genial ⟨a ~ in international relations⟩

THC \ˌtē-(ˌ)āch-ˈsē\ *n* [*tetrahydrocannabinol*] (1967) **:** either of two physiologically active isomers $C_{21}H_{30}O_2$ from hemp plant resin; *esp* **:** one that is the chief intoxicant in marijuana

ThD *abbr* [NL *theologiae doctor*] doctor of theology

[1]**the** *before consonants usu* t͟hə, *before vowels usu* t͟hē, *sometime before vowels also* t͟hə; *for emphasis before titles and names or to suggest uniqueness often* ˈt͟hē\ *definite article* [ME, fr. OE *thē,* masc. demonstrative pron. & definite article, alter. (influenced by oblique cases — as *thæs,* gen. — & neut., *thæt*) of *sē;* akin to Gk *ho,* masc. demonstrative pron. & definite article — more at THAT] (bef. 12c) **1 a** — used as a function word to indicate that a following noun or noun equivalent is definite or has been previously specified by context or by circumstance ⟨put ~ cat out⟩ **b** — used as a function word to indicate that a following noun or noun equivalent is a unique or a particular member of its class ⟨~ President⟩ ⟨~ Lord⟩ **c** — used as a function word before nouns that designate natural phenomena or points of the compass ⟨~ night is cold⟩ **d** — used as a function word before a noun denoting time to indicate reference to what is present or immediate or is under consideration ⟨in ~ future⟩ **e** — used as a function word before names of some parts of the body or of the clothing as an equivalent of a possessive adjective ⟨how's ~ arm today⟩ **f** — used as a function word before the name of a branch of human endeavor or proficiency ⟨~ law⟩ **g** — used as a function word in prepositional phrases to indicate that the noun in the phrase serves as a basis for computation ⟨sold by ~ dozen⟩ **h** — used as a function word before a proper name (as of a ship or a well-known building) ⟨~ Mayflower⟩ **i** — used as a function word before a proper name to indicate the distinctive characteristics of a person or thing ⟨~ John Doe that we know wouldn't lie⟩ **j** — used as a function word before the plural form of a surname to indicate all the members of a family ⟨~ Johnsons⟩ **k** — used as a function word before the plural form of a numeral that is a multiple of ten to denote a particular decade of a century or of a person's life ⟨life in ~ twenties⟩ **l** — used as a function word before the name of a commodity or any familiar appurtenance of daily life to indicate reference to the individual thing, part, or supply thought of as at hand ⟨talked on ~ telephone⟩ **m** — used as a function word to designate one of a class as the best, most typical, best known, or most worth singling out ⟨this is ~ life⟩ ⟨~ pill⟩; sometimes used before a personal name to denote the most prominent bearer of that name **2 a** (1) — used as a function word with a noun modified by an adjective or by an attributive noun to limit the application of the modified noun to that specified by the adjective or by the attributive noun ⟨~ right answer⟩ ⟨Peter ~ Great⟩ (2) — used as a function word before an absolute adjective or an ordinal number ⟨nothing but ~ best⟩ ⟨due on ~ first⟩ **b** (1) — used as a function word before a noun to limit its application to that specified by a succeeding element in the sentence ⟨~ poet Wordsworth⟩ ⟨~ days of our youth⟩ ⟨didn't have ~ time to write⟩ (2) — used as a function word after a person's name to indicate a characteristic trait or notorious activity specified by the succeeding noun ⟨Jack ~ Ripper⟩ **3 a** — used as a function word before a singular noun to indicate that the noun is to be understood generically ⟨~ dog is a domestic animal⟩ **b** — used as a function word before a singular substantivized adjective to indicate an abstract idea ⟨an essay on ~ sublime⟩ **4** — used as a function word before a noun or a substantivized adjective to indicate reference to a group as a whole ⟨~ elite⟩

[2]**the** *adv* [ME, fr. OE *thȳ* by that, instrumental of *thæt* that] (bef. 12c) **1 :** than before : than otherwise — used before a comparative ⟨none ~ wiser for attending⟩ **2 a :** to what extent ⟨~ sooner the better⟩ **b**

: to that extent ⟨the sooner ~ better⟩ **3** : beyond all others ⟨likes this ~ best⟩
[3]the *prep* [ˈthē] (15c) : PER 2 ⟨a dollar ~ dozen⟩
the- *or* **theo-** *comb form* [ME *theo-*, fr. L, fr. Gk *the-, theo-,* fr. *theos*] : god : God ⟨*theism*⟩ ⟨*theocentric*⟩
[1]the·ater *or* **the·atre** \ˈthē-ə-tər, ˈthēə-, *oftenest in Southern* ˈthē-ˌā- *also* thē-ˈā-\ *n* [ME *theatre,* fr. MF, fr. L *theatrum,* fr. Gk *theatron,* fr. *theasthai* to view, fr. *thea* act of seeing; akin to Gk *thauma* miracle] (14c) **1 a** : an outdoor structure for dramatic performances or spectacles in ancient Greece and Rome **b** : a building or area for dramatic performances **c** : a building or area for showing motion pictures **2** : a place or sphere of enactment of usu. significant events or action ⟨the ~ of public life⟩ **3 a** : a place rising by steps or gradations ⟨a woody ~ of stateliest view —John Milton⟩ **b** : a room often with rising tiers of seats for assemblies (as for lectures or surgical demonstrations) **4 a** : dramatic literature : PLAYS **b** : dramatic representation as an art or profession : DRAMA **5 a** : dramatic or theatrical quality or effectiveness **b** : SPECTACLE 1a **c** : entertainment in the form of a dramatic or diverting situation or series of events ⟨their public feud made for good ~⟩ **6** : THEATER OF OPERATIONS
[2]theater *adj* (1977) : of, relating to, or appropriate for use in a theater of operations ⟨~ nuclear weapons⟩
the·ater·go·er \ˈthē-ə-tər-ˌgō-ər\ *n* (1870) : a person who frequently goes to the theater — **the·ater·go·ing** \-ˌgō-iŋ, -ˌgȯ(-)iŋ\ *n or adj*
theater–in–the–round *n, pl* **theaters–in–the–round** (1948) **1** : a theater in which the stage is located in the center of the auditorium — called also *arena theater* **2** : the style or method of staging plays in a theater-in-the-round
theater of operations (1868) : the part of a theater of war in which active combat operations are conducted
theater of the absurd (1961) : theater that seeks to represent the absurdity of human existence in a meaningless universe by bizarre or fantastic means
theater of war (ca. 1890) : the entire land, sea, and air area that is or may become involved directly in war operations
The·a·tine \ˈthē-ə-ˌtīn, -ˌtēn\ *n* [NL *Theatinus,* fr. L *Teatinus* inhabitant of Chieti, fr. *Teate* Chieti, Italy] (ca. 1598) : a priest of the Order of Clerks Regular founded in 1524 in Italy by St. Cajetan and Gian Pietro Caraffa to reform Catholic morality and combat Lutheranism — **Theatine** *adj*
[1]the·at·ri·cal \thē-ˈa-tri-kəl\ *also* **the·at·ric** \-trik\ *adj* (1558) **1** : of or relating to the theater or the presentation of plays ⟨a ~ costume⟩ **2** : marked by pretense or artificiality of emotion **3 a** : HISTRIONIC ⟨a ~ gesture⟩ **b** : marked by extravagant display or exhibitionism ***syn*** see DRAMATIC — **the·at·ri·cal·ism** \-kə-ˌli-zəm\ *n* — **the·at·ri·cal·i·ty** \-ˌa-trə-ˈka-lə-tē\ *n* — **the·at·ri·cal·ly** \-ˈa-tri-k(ə-)lē\ *adv*
[2]theatrical *n* (ca. 1683) **1** *pl* **a** : the performance of plays **b** : DRAMATICS **2** *Brit* : a professional actor **3** *pl* : showy or extravagant gestures
the·at·ri·cal·ize \thē-ˈa-tri-kə-ˌlīz\ *vt* **-ized; -iz·ing** (1778) **1** : to adapt to the theater : DRAMATIZE **2** : to display in showy fashion — **the·at·ri·cal·i·za·tion** \-ˌa-tri-kə-lə-ˈzā-shən\ *n*
the·at·rics \thē-ˈa-triks\ *n pl* (1807) **1** : THEATRICAL 1 **2** : staged or contrived effects
the·be \ˈthā-(ˌ)bā\ *n, pl* **thebe** [Tswana, lit., shield] (1967) — see *pula* at MONEY table
the·ca \ˈthē-kə\ *n, pl* **the·cae** \ˈthē-ˌsē, -ˌkē\ [NL, fr. Gk *thēkē* case — more at TICK] (ca. 1666) : an enveloping sheath or case of an animal or animal part — **the·cal** \ˈthē-kəl\ *adj*
-thecium *n comb form, pl* **-thecia** [NL, fr. Gk *thēkion,* dim. of *thēkē* case] : small containing structure ⟨endo*thecium*⟩
[1]the·co·dont \ˈthē-kə-ˌdänt\ *adj* [ISV *thec-* (fr. NL *theca*) + *-odont*] (1840) : having the teeth inserted in sockets
[2]thecodont *n* (1840) : any of an order (Thecodontia) of Triassic diapsid thecodont reptiles that were presumably on the common ancestral line of the dinosaurs, birds, and crocodiles
thé dan·sant \tā-dän-ˈsän\ *n, pl* **thés dansants** *same*\ [F] (1819) : TEA DANCE
thee \ˈthē\ *pron, archaic objective case of* THOU **1 a** — used esp. in ecclesiastical or literary language and by Friends esp. among themselves in contexts where the objective case form would be expected **b** — used by Friends esp. among themselves in contexts where the subjective case form would be expected **2** : THYSELF
thee·lin \ˈthē(-ə)-lən\ *n* [irreg. fr. Gk *thēlys* female; akin to Gk *thēlē* nipple — more at FEMININE] (1930) : ESTRONE
theft \ˈtheft\ *n* [ME *thiefthe,* fr. OE *thīefth;* akin to OE *thēof* thief] (bef. 12c) **1 a** : the act of stealing; *specif* : the felonious taking and removing of personal property with intent to deprive the rightful owner of it **b** : an unlawful taking (as by embezzlement or burglary) of property **2** *obs* : something stolen **3** : a stolen base in baseball
thegn \ˈthān\ *n* [OE — more at THANE] (1848) : THANE 1
thegn·ly \ˈthān-lē\ *adj* (1876) : of, relating to, or befitting a thegn
their \thər, ˈther\ *adj* [ME, fr. *their,* pron., fr. ON *theirra,* gen. pl. demonstrative & personal pron.; akin to OE *thæt* that] (13c) **1** : of or relating to them or themselves esp. as possessors, agents, or objects of an action ⟨~ furniture⟩ ⟨~ verses⟩ ⟨~ being seen⟩ **2** : his or her : HIS, HER, ITS — used with an indefinite third person singular antecedent ⟨anyone in ~ senses —W. H. Auden⟩ ***usage*** see THEY
theirs \ˈtherz\ *pron, sing or pl in constr* (14c) **1** : that which belongs to them — used without a following noun as a pronoun equivalent in meaning to the adjective *their* **2** : his or hers : HIS, HERS — used with an indefinite third person singular antecedent ⟨I will do my part if everybody else will do ~⟩
their·selves \thər-ˈselvz, (ˌ)ther-, *Southern also* -ˈsevz\ *pron pl* (14c) *chiefly dial* : THEMSELVES
the·ism \ˈthē-ˌi-zəm\ *n* (1678) : belief in the existence of a god or gods; *specif* : belief in the existence of one God viewed as the creative source of the human race and the world who transcends yet is immanent in the world — **the·ist** \-ist\ *n or adj* — **the·is·tic** \thē-ˈis-tik\ *also* **the·is·ti·cal** \-ti-kəl\ *adj* — **the·is·ti·cal·ly** \-ti-k(ə-)lē\ *adv*
T–help·er cell \ˈtē-ˈhel-pər-\ *n* (1980) : HELPER T CELL
[1]them \(th)əm, ˈthem, *after* p, b, v, f, *also* ᵊm\ *pron, objective case of* THEY (bef 12c) **1** : THEY 1 — used as object of a verb or preposition ⟨took ~ back⟩ ⟨gave it to ~⟩ **2** : THOSE — used esp. as antecedent to a relative pronoun ⟨the best of ~ that speak this speech —Shak.⟩; used as the subject of a verb chiefly in nonstandard speech and for humorous effect ⟨~ is fighting words⟩
[2]them \ˈthem\ *adj* (1594) *nonstand* : THOSE — used chiefly in nonstandard speech and for humorous effect
the·mat·ic \thi-ˈma-tik\ *adj* [Gk *thematikos,* fr. *themat-, thema* theme] (1697) **1** : of, relating to, or constituting a theme **2 a** : of or relating to the stem of a word **b** *of a vowel* : being the last part of a word stem before an inflectional ending — **the·mat·i·cal·ly** \-ti-k(ə-)lē\ *adv*
thematic apperception test *n* (1941) : a projective technique that is widely used in clinical psychology to make personality, psychodynamic, and diagnostic assessments based on the subject's verbal responses to a series of black-and-white pictures
theme \ˈthēm\ *n* [ME *teme, theme,* fr. AF & L; AF, fr. L *thema,* fr. Gk, lit., something laid down, fr. *tithenai* to place — more at DO] (14c) **1 a** : a subject or topic of discourse or of artistic representation ⟨guilt and punishment is the ~ of the story⟩ **b** : a specific and distinctive quality, characteristic, or concern ⟨the campaign has lacked a ~⟩ **2** : STEM 4 **3** : a written exercise : COMPOSITION ⟨a research ~⟩ **4** : a melodic subject of a musical composition or movement — **themed** \ˈthēmd\ *adj*
theme park *n* (1960) : an amusement park in which the structures and settings are based on a central theme
theme song *n* (1929) **1** : a melody recurring so often in a musical play that it characterizes the production or one of its characters **2** : a song used as a signature
them·selves \thəm-ˈselvz, them-\ *pron pl* (13c) **1 a** : those identical ones that are they — compare THEY 1a — used reflexively, for emphasis, or in absolute constructions ⟨nations that govern ~⟩ ⟨they ~ were present⟩ ⟨~ busy, they disliked idleness in others⟩ **b** : himself or herself : HIMSELF, HERSELF — used with an indefinite third person singular antecedent ⟨nobody can call ~ oppressed —Leonard Wibberley⟩ **2** : their normal, healthy, or sane condition ⟨were ~ again after a night's rest⟩ ***usage*** see THEY
[1]then \ˈthen\ *adv* [ME *than, then* then, than, fr. OE *thonne, thænne;* akin to OHG *denne* then, than, OE *thæt* that] (bef. 12c) **1** : at that time **2 a** : soon after that : next in order of time ⟨walked to the door, ~ turned⟩ **b** : following next after in order of position, narration, or enumeration : being next in a series ⟨first came the clowns, and ~ came the elephants⟩ **c** : in addition : BESIDES ⟨~ there is the interest to be paid⟩ **3 a** (1) : in that case ⟨take it, ~, if you want it so much⟩ (2) — used after *but* to qualify or offset a preceding statement ⟨she lost the race, but ~ she never really expected to win⟩ **b** : according to that : as may be inferred ⟨your mind is made up, ~⟩ **c** : as it appears : by way of summing up ⟨the cause of the accident, ~, is established⟩ **d** : as a necessary consequence ⟨if the angles are equal, ~ the complements are equal⟩ — **and then some** : with much more in addition ⟨would require all his strength *and then some*⟩
[2]then *n* (14c) : that time ⟨since ~, he's been more cautious⟩
[3]then *adj* (1584) : existing or acting at or belonging to the time mentioned ⟨the ~ secretary of state⟩
then and there *adv* (15c) : on the spot : IMMEDIATELY ⟨wanted the money right *then and there*⟩
the·nar \ˈthē-ˌnär, -nər\ *adj* [NL, palm of the hand, fr. Gk; akin to OHG *tenar* palm of the hand] (ca. 1857) : of, relating to, involving, or constituting the ball of the thumb or the intrinsic musculature of the thumb
thence \ˈthen(t)s *also* ˈthen(t)s\ *adv* [ME *thannes,* fr. *thanne* from that place, fr. OE *thanon;* akin to OHG *thanan* from that place, OE *thænne* then — more at THEN] (13c) **1** : from that place **2** *archaic* : from that time : THENCEFORTH **3** : from that fact or circumstance : THEREFROM — **from thence** : from that place
thence·forth \-ˌfōrth\ *adv* (14c) : from that time forward
thence·for·ward \then(t)s-ˈfȯr-wərd *also* then(t)s-\ *also* **thence·forwards** \-wərdz\ *adv* (15c) : onward from that place or time
theo- — see THE-
theo·bro·mine \ˌthē-ə-ˈbrō-ˌmēn, -mən\ *n* [NL *Theobroma,* genus that includes the cacao, fr. *the-* + Gk *brōma* food, fr. *bibrōskein* to devour — more at VORACIOUS] (1842) : a bitter alkaloid $C_7H_8N_4O_2$ closely related to caffeine that occurs esp. in cacao beans and has stimulant and diuretic properties
theo·cen·tric \ˌthē-ə-ˈsen-trik\ *adj* (1886) : having God as the central interest and ultimate concern ⟨a ~ culture⟩ — **theo·cen·tric·i·ty** \-ˌsen-ˈtri-sə-tē\ *n* — **theo·cen·trism** \-ˈsen-ˌtri-zəm\ *n*
the·oc·ra·cy \thē-ˈä-krə-sē\ *n, pl* **-cies** [Gk *theokratia,* fr. *the-* + *-kratia* -cracy] (1622) **1** : government of a state by immediate divine guidance or by officials who are regarded as divinely guided **2** : a state governed by a theocracy
theo·crat \ˈthē-ə-ˌkrat\ *n* (1827) **1** : one who rules in or lives under a theocratic form of government **2** : one who favors a theocratic form of government
theo·crat·ic \ˌthē-ə-ˈkra-tik\ *also* **theo·crat·i·cal** \-ti-kəl\ *adj* (1690) : of, relating to, or being a theocracy — **theo·crat·i·cal·ly** \-ti-k(ə-)lē\ *adv*
the·od·i·cy \thē-ˈä-də-sē\ *n, pl* **-cies** [modif. of F *théodicée,* fr. *théo-* the- (fr. L *theo-*) + Gk *dikē* judgment, right — more at DICTION] (1797) : defense of God's goodness and omnipotence in view of the existence of evil
the·od·o·lite \thē-ˈä-də-ˌlīt\ *n* [NL *theodelitus*] (1571) : a surveyor's instrument for measuring horizontal and usu. also vertical angles
the·og·o·ny \thē-ˈä-gə-nē\ *n, pl* **-nies** [Gk *theogonia,* fr. *the-* + *-gonia* -gony] (1612) : an account of the origin and descent of the gods — **theo·gon·ic** \ˌthē-ə-ˈgä-nik\ *adj*
theol *abbr* theological; theology
theo·lo·gian \ˌthē-ə-ˈlō-jən\ *n* (15c) : a specialist in theology
theo·log·i·cal \ˌthē-ə-ˈlä-ji-kəl\ *also* **theo·log·ic** \-jik\ *adj* (15c) **1** : of or relating to theology **2** : preparing for a religious vocation ⟨a ~ student⟩ — **theo·log·i·cal·ly** \-ji-k(ə-)lē\ *adv*

theological virtue *n* (1526) **:** one of the three spiritual graces faith, hope, and charity drawing the soul to God according to scholastic theology
the·ol·o·gise *Brit var of* THEOLOGIZE
the·ol·o·gize \thē-ˈä-lə-ˌjīz\ *vb* **-gized; -giz·ing** *vt* (1649) **:** to make theological **:** give a religious significance to ∼ *vi* **:** to theorize theologically — **the·ol·o·giz·er** *n*
theo·logue *also* **theo·log** \ˈthē-ə-ˌlȯg, -ˌläg\ *n* [L *theologus* theologian, fr. Gk *theologos,* fr. *the-* + *legein* to speak — more at LEGEND] (15c) **:** a theological student or specialist
the·ol·o·gy \thē-ˈä-lə-jē\ *n, pl* **-gies** [ME *theologie,* fr. AF, fr. L *theologia,* fr. Gk, fr. *the-* + *-logia* -logy] (14c) **1 :** the study of religious faith, practice, and experience; *esp* **:** the study of God and of God's relation to the world **2 a :** a theological theory or system ⟨Thomist ∼⟩ ⟨a ∼ of atonement⟩ **b :** a distinctive body of theological opinion ⟨Catholic ∼⟩ **3 :** a usu. 4-year course of specialized religious training in a Roman Catholic major seminary
the·on·o·mous \thē-ˈä-nə-məs\ *adj* [*the-* + *-nomous* (as in *autonomous*)] (1947) **:** governed by God **:** subject to God's authority
the·on·o·my \-mē\ *n* [G *Theonomie,* fr. *theo-* the- (fr. L) + *-nomie* -nomy] (1890) **:** the state of being theonomous **:** government by God
the·oph·a·ny \thē-ˈä-fə-nē\ *n, pl* **-nies** [ML *theophania,* fr. LGk *theophaneia,* fr. Gk *the-* + *-phaneia* (as in *epiphaneia* appearance) — more at EPIPHANY] (ca. 1633) **:** a visible manifestation of a deity — **theo·phan·ic** \ˌthē-ə-ˈfa-nik\ *adj*
the·oph·yl·line \thē-ˈä-fə-lən\ *n* [ISV *theo-* (fr. NL *thea* tea) + *phyll-* + [2]*-ine*] (ca. 1894) **:** a feebly basic bitter crystalline compound $C_7H_8N_4O_2$ present in tea leaves that is isomeric with theobromine and is used in medicine esp. as a bronchodilator
the·or·bo \thē-ˈȯr-(ˌ)bō\ *n, pl* **-bos** [modif. of It *tiorba, teorba*] (1605) **:** a stringed instrument of the 17th century resembling a large lute but having an extra set of long bass strings

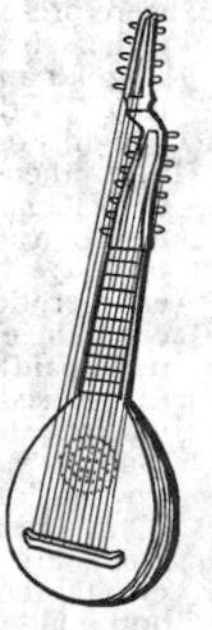
theorbo

the·o·rem \ˈthē-ə-rəm, ˈthir-əm\ *n* [LL *theorema,* fr. Gk *theōrēma,* fr. *theōrein* to look at, fr. *theōros* spectator, fr. *thea* act of seeing — more at THEATER] (1551) **1 :** a formula, proposition, or statement in mathematics or logic deduced or to be deduced from other formulas or propositions **2 :** an idea accepted or proposed as a demonstrable truth often as a part of a general theory **:** PROPOSITION ⟨the ∼ that the best defense is offense⟩ **3 :** STENCIL **4 :** a painting produced esp. on velvet by the use of stencils for each color — **the·o·rem·at·ic** \ˌthē-ə-rə-ˈmatik, ˌthir-ə-\ *adj*
the·o·ret·i·cal \ˌthē-ə-ˈre-ti-kəl, ˌthir-ˈe-\ *also* **the·o·ret·ic** \-tik\ *adj* [LL *theoreticus,* fr. Gk *theōrētikos,* fr. *theōrein* to look at] (1601) **1 a :** relating to or having the character of theory **:** ABSTRACT **b :** confined to theory or speculation often in contrast to practical applications **:** SPECULATIVE ⟨∼ physics⟩ **2 :** given to or skilled in theorizing ⟨a brilliant ∼ physicist⟩ **3 :** existing only in theory **:** HYPOTHETICAL ⟨gave as an example a ∼ situation⟩
the·o·ret·i·cal·ly \-ti-k(ə-)lē\ *adv* (1701) **1 :** in a theoretical way **2 :** according to an ideal or assumed set of facts or principles **:** in theory
the·o·re·ti·cian \ˌthē-ə-rə-ˈti-shən, -re-; ˌthir-ə-\ *n* (1886) **:** THEORIST
the·o·rise *Brit var of* THEORIZE
the·o·rist \ˈthē-ə-rist, ˈthir-ist\ *n* (1646) **:** a person who theorizes
the·o·rize \ˈthē-ə-ˌrīz, ˈthir-ˌīz\ *vb* **-rized; -riz·ing** *vi* (1638) **:** to form a theory **:** SPECULATE ∼ *vt* **1 :** to form a theory about **2 :** to propose as a theory — **the·o·ri·za·tion** \ˌthē-ə-rə-ˈzā-shən, ˌthir-ə-\ *n* — **the·o·riz·er** *n*
the·o·ry \ˈthē-ə-rē, ˈthir-ē\ *n, pl* **-ries** [LL *theoria,* fr. Gk *theōria,* fr. *theōrein*] (1592) **1 :** the analysis of a set of facts in their relation to one another **2 :** abstract thought **:** SPECULATION **3 :** the general or abstract principles of a body of fact, a science, or an art ⟨music ∼⟩ **4 a :** a belief, policy, or procedure proposed or followed as the basis of action ⟨her method is based on the ∼ that all children want to learn⟩ **b :** an ideal or hypothetical set of facts, principles, or circumstances — often used in the phrase *in theory* ⟨in ∼, we have always advocated freedom for all⟩ **5 :** a plausible or scientifically acceptable general principle or body of principles offered to explain phenomena ⟨the wave ∼ of light⟩ **6 a :** a hypothesis assumed for the sake of argument or investigation **b :** an unproved assumption **:** CONJECTURE **c :** a body of theorems presenting a concise systematic view of a subject ⟨∼ of equations⟩ ***syn*** see HYPOTHESIS
theory of games (1944) **:** GAME THEORY
theory of numbers (1811) **:** NUMBER THEORY
the·os·o·phist \thē-ˈä-sə-fist\ *n* (1656) **1 :** an adherent of theosophy **2** *cap* **:** a member of a theosophical society
the·os·o·phy \-fē\ *n* [ML *theosophia,* fr. LGk, fr. Gk *the-* + *sophia* wisdom — more at -SOPHY] (1650) **1 :** teaching about God and the world based on mystical insight **2** *often cap* **:** the teachings of a modern movement originating in the U.S. in 1875 and following chiefly Buddhist and Brahmanic theories esp. of pantheistic evolution and reincarnation — **theo·soph·i·cal** \ˌthē-ə-ˈsä-fi-kəl\ *adj* — **theo·soph·i·cal·ly** \-k(ə-)lē\ *adv*
Theo·to·kos \ˌthē-ə-ˈtō-(ˌ)kōs, ˌthā-, -kəs\ *n* [LGk, fr. Gk *the-* + *tokos* childbirth; akin to Gk *tiktein* to beget — more at THANE] (1868) **:** VIRGIN MARY
ther·a·peu·sis \ˌther-ə-ˈpyü-səs\ *n* [NL, fr. Gk, treatment, fr. *therapeuein*] (ca. 1857) **:** THERAPEUTICS
ther·a·peu·tic \ˌther-ə-ˈpyü-tik\ *adj* [Gk *therapeutikos,* fr. *therapeuein* to attend, treat, fr. *theraps* attendant] (1646) **1 :** of or relating to the treatment of disease or disorders by remedial agents or methods ⟨a ∼ rather than a diagnostic specialty⟩ **2 :** providing or assisting in a cure **:** CURATIVE, MEDICINAL ⟨∼ diets⟩ ⟨a ∼ investigation of government waste⟩ — **therapeutic** *n* — **ther·a·peu·ti·cal·ly** \-ti-k(ə-)lē\ *adv*
therapeutic index *n* (1926) **:** a measure of the relative desirability of a drug for the attaining of a particular medical end that is usu. expressed as the ratio of the largest dose producing no toxic symptoms to the smallest dose routinely producing cures
ther·a·peu·tics \ˌther-ə-ˈpyü-tiks\ *n pl but sing or pl in constr* (1671) **:** a branch of medical science dealing with the application of remedies to diseases
therapeutic touch *n* (1975) **:** a technique in alternative medicine that involves passing the hands over the body of the person being treated and that is held to induce relaxation, reduce pain, and promote healing
ther·a·pist \ˈther-ə-pist\ *n* (1886) **:** one specializing in therapy; *esp* **:** a person trained in methods of treatment and rehabilitation other than the use of drugs or surgery ⟨a speech ∼⟩
the·rap·sid \thə-ˈrap-səd\ *n* [NL *Therapsida,* fr. *ther-* mammal (fr. Gk *thēr* wild animal) + *apsid-, apsis* arch, vault — more at FIERCE, APSIS] (1912) **:** any of an order (Therapsida) of Permian and Triassic synapsid reptiles considered ancestors of the mammals — **therapsid** *adj*
ther·a·py \ˈther-ə-pē\ *n, pl* **-pies** [NL *therapia,* fr. Gk *therapeia,* fr. *therapeuein*] (ca. 1846) **:** therapeutic treatment esp. of bodily, mental, or behavioral disorder
Ther·a·va·da \ˌther-ə-ˈvä-də\ *n* [Pali *theravāda,* lit., doctrine of the elders] (1882) **:** a conservative branch of Buddhism comprising sects chiefly in Sri Lanka, Myanmar, Thailand, Laos, and Cambodia and adhering to the original Pali scriptures alone and to the nontheistic ideal of nirvana for a limited select number — compare MAHAYANA
[1]**there** \ˈt͟her\ *adv* [ME, fr. OE *thǣr;* akin to OHG *dār* there, OE *thæt* that] (bef. 12c) **1 :** in or at that place ⟨stand over ∼⟩ — often used interjectionally **2 :** to or into that place **:** THITHER ⟨went ∼ after church⟩ **3 :** at that point or stage ⟨stop right ∼ before you say something you'll regret⟩ **4 :** in that matter, respect, or relation ⟨∼ is where I disagree with you⟩ **5** — used interjectionally to express satisfaction, approval, encouragement or sympathy, or defiance ⟨∼, it's finished⟩
[2]**there** \ˈt͟her, *1 is also* t͟hər\ *pron* (bef. 12c) **1** — used as a function word to introduce a sentence or clause ⟨∼ shall come a time⟩ **2** — used as an indefinite substitute for a name ⟨hi ∼⟩
[3]**there** *same as* [1]\ *n* (1588) **1 :** that place or position ⟨there is no here and no ∼ . . . in pure space —James Ward⟩ **2 :** that point ⟨you take it from ∼⟩
[4]**there** *same as* [1]\ *adj* (1590) **1** — used for emphasis esp. after a demonstrative pronoun or a noun modified by a demonstrative adjective ⟨those men ∼ can tell you⟩ **2** *nonstand* — used for emphasis after a demonstrative adjective but before the noun modified ⟨I bet I cussed that ∼ blamed mule five hundred times —Elizabeth M. Roberts⟩ **3 :** capable of being relied on for support or aid ⟨she is always ∼ for him⟩ **4 :** fully conscious, rational, or aware ⟨not all ∼⟩
there·abouts \ˌt͟her-ə-ˈbau̇ts, ˈt͟her-ə-ˌ\ *also* **there·about** \-ˈbau̇t, -ˌbau̇t\ *adv* (bef. 12c) **1 :** near that place or time **2 :** near that number, degree, or quantity ⟨a boy of 18 or ∼⟩
there·af·ter \t͟her-ˈaf-tər\ *adv* (bef. 12c) **1 :** after that **2** *archaic* **:** according to that **:** ACCORDINGLY
there·at \-ˈat\ *adv* (bef. 12c) **1 :** at that place **2 :** at that occurrence
there·by \t͟her-ˈbī, ˈt͟her-ˌ\ *adv* (bef. 12c) **1 :** by that **:** by that means ⟨∼ lost her chance to win⟩ **2 :** connected with or with reference to that ⟨∼ hangs a tale —Shak.⟩
there'd \ˈt͟herd, ˈt͟her-əd\ (1691) **:** there had **:** there would
there·for \t͟her-ˈfȯr\ *adv* (12c) **:** for or in return for that ⟨ordered a change and gave his reasons ∼⟩
there·fore \ˈt͟her-ˌfȯr\ *adv* (14c) **1 a :** for that reason **:** CONSEQUENTLY **b :** because of that **c :** on that ground **2 :** to that end
there·from \t͟her-ˈfrəm, -ˈfräm\ *adv* (13c) **:** from that or it
there·in \t͟her-ˈin\ *adv* (bef. 12c) **1 :** in or into that place, time, or thing **2 :** in that particular or respect ⟨∼ lies the problem⟩
there·in·af·ter \ˌt͟her-in-ˈaf-tər\ *adv* (1818) **:** in the following part of that matter (as writing, document, or speech)
there·in·to \t͟her-ˈin-(ˌ)tü\ *adv* (14c) *archaic* **:** into that or it
there'll \ˈt͟her(-ə)l\ (1616) **:** there will **:** there shall
the·re·min \ˈther-ə-mən\ *n* [modif. of Russ *termen-voks* fr. Lev Sergeevich *Termen* (Léon Thérémin) †1993 Russ. engineer & inventor + L *vox* voice] (1927) **:** a purely melodic electronic musical instrument typically played by moving the hands in the electromagnetic fields surrounding two projecting antennae
there·of \t͟her-ˈəv, -ˈäv\ *adv* (bef. 12c) **1 :** of that or it **2 :** from that cause or particular **:** THEREFROM
there·on \-ˈȯn, -ˈän\ *adv* (bef. 12c) **1 :** on that ⟨a text with a commentary ∼⟩ **2** *archaic* **:** THEREUPON
there's \ˈt͟herz, t͟hərz\ (1580) **:** there is **:** there has
there·to \t͟her-ˈtü\ *adv* (bef. 12c) **:** to that ⟨a text and the notes ∼⟩
there·to·fore \ˈt͟her-tə-ˌfȯr; ˌt͟her-tə-ˈ\ *adv* (14c) **:** up to that time ⟨a ∼ unknown author⟩
there·un·der \t͟her-ˈən-dər\ *adv* (bef. 12c) **:** under that
there·un·to \-ˈən-(ˌ)tü; ˌt͟her-ən-ˈtü\ *adv* (14c) *archaic* **:** THERETO
there·up·on \ˈt͟her-ə-ˌpȯn, -ˌpän; ˌt͟her-ə-ˈ\ *adv* (13c) **1 :** on that matter **2 :** THEREFORE **3 :** immediately after that
there've \ˈt͟herv, t͟hərv\ (1846) **:** there have
there·with \t͟her-ˈwit͟h, -ˈwith\ *adv* (bef. 12c) **1 :** with that **2** *archaic* **:** THEREUPON, FORTHWITH
there·with·al \ˈt͟her-wi-ˌt͟hȯl, -thȯl\ *adv* (14c) **1** *archaic* **:** BESIDES **2 :** THEREWITH
the·ri·ac \ˈthir-ē-ˌak\ *n* [NL *theriaca*] (1568) **1 :** THERIACA **2 :** CURE-ALL
the·ri·a·ca \thi-ˈrī-ə-kə\ *n* [NL, fr. L, antidote against poison — more at TREACLE] (1562) **:** a mixture of many drugs and honey formerly held to be an antidote to poison — **the·ri·a·cal** \-kəl\ *adj*
the·ri·an \ˈthir-ē-ən\ *n* [NL *Theria,* fr. Gk *thēria,* pl. of *therion* wild animal — more at TREACLE] (1962) **:** any of a subclass (Theria) of mammals comprising the marsupials and the placental mammals — **therian** *adj*
the·rio·mor·phic \ˌthir-ē-ō-ˈmȯr-fik\ *adj* [Gk *thēriomorphos,* fr. *thērion* wild animal + *morphē* form — more at TREACLE] (1882) **:** having an animal form ⟨∼ gods⟩
therm \ˈthərm\ *n* [Gk *thermē* heat, fr. *thermos* hot; akin to L *formus* warm, Skt *gharma* heat] (1888) **:** a unit for quantity of heat that equals 100,000 British thermal units
therm- *or* **thermo-** *comb form* [Gk, fr. *thermē*] **1 :** heat ⟨*thermo*stat⟩ **2 :** thermoelectric ⟨*thermo*pile⟩
-therm *n comb form* [Gk *thermē* heat] **:** animal having a (specified) body temperature ⟨ecto*therm*⟩
[1]**ther·mal** \ˈthər-məl\ *adj* [Gk *thermē*] (1742) **1** [L *thermae* public baths, fr. Gk *thermai,* pl. of *thermē*] **:** of, relating to, or marked by the presence of hot springs ⟨∼ waters⟩ **2 a :** of, relating to, or caused by heat ⟨∼ stress⟩ ⟨∼ insulation⟩ **b :** being or involving a state of matter de-

pendent upon temperature ⟨~ conductivity⟩ ⟨~ agitation of molecular structure⟩ **c :** having low energies of the order of those due to thermal agitation ⟨~ neutrons⟩ **3 :** designed (as with insulating air spaces) to prevent the dissipation of body heat ⟨~ underwear⟩ — **ther·mal·ly** \-mə-lē\ *adv*

[2]**thermal** *n* (1933) **:** a rising body of warm air

ther·mal·ize \ˈthər-mə-ˌlīz\ *vt* **-ized; -iz·ing** (1948) **:** to change the effective speed of (a particle) to a thermal value ⟨~ a neutron⟩ — **ther·mal·i·za·tion** \ˌthər-mə-lə-ˈzā-shən\ *n*

thermal pollution *n* (1966) **:** the discharge of heated liquid (as wastewater from a factory) into natural waters at a temperature harmful to the environment

thermal printer *n* (1966) **:** a dot matrix printer (as for a computer) in which heat is applied to the pins of the matrix to form dots on usu. heat-sensitive paper

ther·mic \ˈthər-mik\ *adj* (1842) **:** THERMAL 2 ⟨~ energy⟩ — **ther·mi·cal·ly** \-mi-k(ə-)lē\ *adv*

therm·ion·ic \ˌthər-(ˌ)mī-ˈä-nik\ *adj* [*thermion* charged particle from an incandescent source, fr. *therm-* + *ion*] (1909) **:** relating to, using, or being the emission of charged particles (as electrons) by an incandescent material

therm·ion·ics \ˌthər-(ˌ)mī-ˈä-niks\ *n pl but sing in constr* (1909) **:** physics dealing with thermionic phenomena

therm·is·tor \ˈthər-ˌmis-tər\ *n* [*therm*al res*istor*] (1940) **:** an electrical resistor making use of a semiconductor whose resistance varies sharply in a known manner with the temperature

Ther·mit \ˈthər-mət, -ˌmīt\ *trademark* — used for thermite

ther·mite \ˈthər-ˌmīt\ *n* [*therm-* + [1]*-ite*] (1900) **:** a mixture of aluminum powder and a metal oxide (as iron oxide) that when ignited evolves a great deal of heat and is used in welding and in incendiary bombs

ther·mo·chem·is·try \ˌthər-mō-ˈke-mə-strē\ *n* (1844) **:** a branch of chemistry that deals with the interrelation of heat with chemical reaction or physical change of state — **ther·mo·chem·i·cal** \-ˈke-mi-kəl\ *adj* — **ther·mo·chem·ist** \-ˈke-mist\ *n*

ther·mo·cline \ˈthər-mə-ˌklīn\ *n* (1898) **:** the region in a thermally stratified body of water which separates warmer surface water from cold deep water and in which temperature decreases rapidly with depth

ther·mo·cou·ple \ˈthər-mə-ˌkə-pəl\ *n* (1890) **:** a device for measuring temperature in which a pair of wires of dissimilar metals (as copper and iron) are joined and the free ends of the wires are connected to an instrument (as a voltmeter) that measures the difference in potential created at the junction of the two metals

ther·mo·du·ric \ˌthər-mō-ˈdu̇r-ik, -ˈdyu̇r-\ *adj* [*therm-* + L *durare* to last — more at DURING] (1927) **:** able to survive high temperatures; *specif* **:** able to survive pasteurization — used of microorganisms

ther·mo·dy·nam·ic \ˌthər-mō-dī-ˈna-mik, -də-\ *also* **ther·mo·dy·nam·i·cal** \-mi-kəl\ *adj* (1849) **1 :** of or relating to thermodynamics **2 :** being or relating to a system of atoms, molecules, colloidal particles, or larger bodies considered as an isolated group in the study of thermodynamic processes — **ther·mo·dy·nam·i·cal·ly** \-mi-k(ə-)lē\ *adv*

ther·mo·dy·nam·ics \-miks\ *n pl but sing or pl in constr* (1854) **1 :** physics that deals with the mechanical action or relations of heat **2 :** thermodynamic processes and phenomena — **ther·mo·dy·nam·i·cist** \-ˈna-mə-sist\ *n*

ther·mo·elec·tric \ˌthər-mō-i-ˈlek-trik\ *adj* (1823) **:** of, relating to, or dependent on phenomena that involve relations between the temperature and the electrical condition in a metal or in contacting metals

ther·mo·elec·tric·i·ty \ˌthər-mō-i-ˌlek-ˈtri-sə-tē, -ˈtris-tē\ *n* (1823) **:** electricity produced by the direct action of heat (as by the unequal heating of a circuit composed of two dissimilar metals)

ther·mo·el·e·ment \-ˈe-lə-mənt\ *n* (ca. 1888) **:** a device for measuring small currents consisting of a wire heating element and a thermocouple in electrical contact with it

ther·mo·form \ˈthər-mə-ˌfȯrm\ *vt* (1956) **:** to give a final shape to (as a plastic) with the aid of heat and usu. pressure — **ther·mo·form·able** \-ˌfȯr-mə-bəl\ *adj*

ther·mo·gen·e·sis \ˌthər-mō-ˈje-nə-səs\ *n* [NL] (1891) **:** the production of heat esp. in the body (as by oxidation)

ther·mo·gen·ic \ˌthər-mə-ˈje-nik\ *adj* (1855) **:** relating to, caused by, or inducing the production of heat ⟨~ dietary supplements⟩ ⟨~ destruction of bacteria⟩; *also* **:** producing heat ⟨~ flowers⟩ ⟨~ organs⟩

ther·mo·gram \-ˌgram\ *n* (1883) **1 :** the record made by a thermograph **2 :** a photographic record made by thermography

ther·mo·graph \-ˌgraf\ *n* [ISV] (1843) **1 :** THERMOGRAM **2 :** a self-recording thermometer **3 :** the apparatus used in thermography

ther·mog·ra·phy \(ˌ)thər-ˈmä-grə-fē\ *n* (1840) **1 :** a process of writing or printing involving the use of heat; *esp* **:** a raised-printing process in which matter printed by letterpress is dusted with powder and heated to make the lettering rise **2 :** a technique for detecting and measuring variations in the heat emitted by various regions of the body and transforming them into visible signals that can be recorded photographically (as for diagnosing abnormal or diseased underlying conditions); *also* **:** a similar technique used elsewhere (as on buildings) — **ther·mog·ra·pher** \-grə-fər\ *n* — **ther·mo·graph·ic** \ˌthər-mə-ˈgra-fik\ *adj* — **ther·mo·graph·i·cal·ly** \-fi-k(ə-)lē\ *adv*

ther·mo·ha·line \ˌthər-mō-ˈhā-ˌlīn, -ˈha-\ *adj* [*therm-* + Gk *hal-, hals* salt — more at SALT] (1942) **:** involving or dependent upon the conjoint effect of temperature and salinity ⟨~ circulation in the Pacific⟩

ther·mo·junc·tion \-ˈjəŋ(k)-shən\ *n* (1889) **:** a junction of two dissimilar conductors used to produce a thermoelectric current

ther·mo·la·bile \-ˈlā-ˌbī(-ə)l, -bəl\ *adj* [ISV] (1904) **:** unstable when heated; *specif* **:** subject to loss of characteristic properties on being heated to or above 55°C (131°F) ⟨many immune bodies, enzymes, and vitamins are ~⟩ — **ther·mo·la·bil·i·ty** \-lā-ˈbi-lə-tē\ *n*

ther·mo·lu·mi·nes·cence \-ˌlü-mə-ˈne-sᵊn(t)s\ *n* [ISV] (1897) **1 :** phosphorescence developed in a previously excited substance upon gentle heating **2 :** the determination of the age of old material (as pottery) by the amount of thermoluminescence it produces — called also *thermoluminescence dating* — **ther·mo·lu·mi·nes·cent** \-sᵊnt\ *adj*

ther·mo·mag·net·ic \ˌthər-mō-mag-ˈne-tik\ *adj* (1823) **:** of or relating to the effects of heat upon the magnetic properties of substances or to the effects of a magnetic field upon thermal conduction

ther·mom·e·ter \thə(r)-ˈmä-mə-tər\ *n* [F *thermomètre,* fr. Gk *thermē* heat + F *-o-* + *-mètre* -meter — more at THERM] (1633) **:** an instrument for determining temperature; *esp* **:** one consisting of a glass bulb attached to a fine tube of glass with a numbered scale and containing a liquid (as mercury or colored alcohol) that is sealed in and rises and falls with changes of temperature — **ther·mo·met·ric** \ˌthər-mə-ˈme-trik\ *adj* — **ther·mo·met·ri·cal·ly** \-tri-k(ə-)lē\ *adv*

ther·mom·e·try \thə(r)-ˈmä-mə-trē\ *n* [ISV] (1848) **:** the measurement of temperature

ther·mo·nu·cle·ar \ˌthər-mō-ˈnü-klē-ər, -ˈnyü-, ÷-ˈn(y)ü-kyə-lər\ *adj* [ISV] (1938) **1 :** of, relating to, or employing transformations in the nuclei of atoms of low atomic weight (as hydrogen) that require a very high temperature for their inception (as in the hydrogen bomb or in the sun) ⟨~ reaction⟩ ⟨~ weapon⟩ **2 :** of, utilizing, or relating to a thermonuclear bomb ⟨~ war⟩ ⟨a ~ attack⟩

ther·mo·pe·ri·od·ism \ˌthər-mō-ˈpir-ē-ə-ˌdi-zəm\ *n* (ca. 1937) **:** the sum of the responses esp. of a plant to appropriately fluctuating temperatures

ther·mo·phil·ic \ˌthər-mə-ˈfi-lik\ *also* **ther·moph·i·lous** \(ˌ)thər-ˈmä-fə-ləs\ *or* **ther·mo·phile** \ˈthər-mə-ˌfī(-ə)l\ *adj* (ca. 1894) **:** of, relating to, or being an organism living at a high temperature ⟨~ fermentation⟩ ⟨~ bacteria⟩ — **thermophile** *n*

ther·mo·pile \ˈthər-mə-ˌpī(-ə)l\ *n* [[1]*pile*] (1849) **:** an apparatus consisting of thermocouples combined so as to multiply the effect and used for generating electric currents or determining intensities of radiation

ther·mo·plas·tic \ˌthər-mə-ˈplas-tik\ *adj* (1883) **:** capable of softening or fusing when heated and of hardening again when cooled ⟨~ synthetic resins⟩ — compare THERMOSETTING — **thermoplastic** *n* — **ther·mo·plas·tic·i·ty** \-ˌpla-ˈsti-sə-tē\ *n*

ther·mo·re·cep·tor \ˌthər-mō-ri-ˈsep-tər\ *n* (1937) **:** a sensory end organ that is stimulated by heat or cold

ther·mo·reg·u·la·tion \-ˌre-gyə-ˈlā-shən\ *n* [ISV] (1927) **:** the maintenance or regulation of temperature; *specif* **:** the maintenance of a particular temperature of the living body — **ther·mo·reg·u·late** \-ˈre-gyə-ˌlāt\ *vb*

ther·mo·reg·u·la·tor \-ˈre-gyə-ˌlā-tər\ *n* [ISV] (1875) **:** a device (as a thermostat) for the regulation of temperature

ther·mo·reg·u·la·to·ry \-ˈre-gyə-lə-ˌtȯr-ē\ *adj* (1941) **:** tending to maintain a body at a particular temperature whatever its environmental temperature ⟨~ mechanisms⟩

ther·mo·rem·a·nent \-ˈre-mə-nənt\ *adj* (1951) **:** being or relating to magnetic remanence (as in a rock cooled from a molten state or in a baked clay object containing magnetic minerals) that indicates the strength and direction of the earth's magnetic field at a former time — **ther·mo·rem·a·nence** \-nən(t)s\ *n*

ther·mos \ˈthər-məs\ *n* [fr. *Thermos,* a trademark] (1907) **:** a container (as a bottle or jar) with a vacuum between an inner and outer wall used to keep material and esp. liquids either hot or cold for considerable periods

ther·mo·set \ˈthər-mō-ˌset\ *n* (1947) **:** a thermosetting resin or plastic

ther·mo·set·ting \-ˌse-tiŋ\ *adj* (ca. 1931) **:** capable of becoming permanently rigid when heated or cured ⟨a ~ resin⟩ — compare THERMOPLASTIC

ther·mo·sphere \ˈthər-mə-ˌsfir\ *n* [ISV] (ca. 1950) **:** the part of the earth's atmosphere that begins at about 50 miles (80 kilometers) above the earth's surface, extends to outer space, and is characterized by steadily increasing temperature with height — **ther·mo·spher·ic** \ˌthər-mə-ˈsfir-ik, -ˈsfer-\ *adj*

ther·mo·sta·ble \ˌthər-mō-ˈstā-bəl\ *adj* (1904) **:** stable when heated; *specif* **:** retaining characteristic properties on being moderately heated ⟨a ~ bacterial enzyme⟩ — **ther·mo·sta·bil·i·ty** \-stə-ˈbi-lə-tē\ *n*

[1]**ther·mo·stat** \ˈthər-mə-ˌstat\ *n* (1831) **:** an automatic device for regulating temperature (as by controlling the supply of gas or electricity to a heating apparatus); *also* **:** a similar device for actuating fire alarms or for controlling automatic sprinklers — **ther·mo·stat·ic** \ˌthər-mə-ˈsta-tik\ *adj* — **ther·mo·stat·i·cal·ly** \-ti-k(ə-)lē\ *adv*

[2]**thermostat** *vt* **-stat·ed** \-ˌsta-təd\ *also* **-stat·ted; -stat·ing** *also* **-stat·ting** (1924) **:** to provide with or control the temperature of by a thermostat

ther·mo·tax·is \-ˈtak-səs\ *n* [NL] (ca. 1891) **1 :** the regulation of body temperature **2 :** a taxis in which temperature is the directive factor

ther·mo·trop·ic \-ˈträ-pik\ *adj* [ISV] (1885) **:** of, relating to, or exhibiting thermotropism

ther·mot·ro·pism \(ˌ)thər-ˈmä-trə-ˌpi-zəm\ *n* [ISV] (ca. 1890) **:** a tropism in which a temperature gradient determines the orientation

-thermy *n comb form* [NL *-thermia,* fr. Gk *thermē* heat — more at THERM] **1 :** state of heat ⟨endo*thermy*⟩ **2 :** generation of heat ⟨dia*thermy*⟩

the·ro·pod \ˈthir-ə-ˌpäd\ *n* [NL *Theropoda,* fr. Gk *thēr* wild animal + *pod-, pous* foot — more at FIERCE, FOOT] (ca. 1891) **:** any of a suborder (Theropoda) of carnivorous bipedal saurischian dinosaurs (as a tyrannosaur or velociraptor) usu. having small forelimbs

Ther·si·tes \(ˌ)thər-ˈsī-(ˌ)tēz\ *n* [L, fr. Gk *Thersitēs*] (ca. 1530) **:** a Greek warrior at Troy known as a carping critic and slain by Achilles for mocking him

the·sau·rus \thi-ˈsȯr-əs\ *n, pl* **-sau·ri** \-ˈsȯr-ˌī, -ˌē\ *or* **-sau·rus·es** \-ˈsȯr-ə-səz\ [NL, fr. L, treasure, collection, fr. Gk *thēsauros*] (ca. 1823) **1 :** TREASURY, STOREHOUSE **2 a :** a book of words or of information about a particular field or set of concepts; *esp* **:** a book of words and their synonyms **b :** a list of subject headings or descriptors usu. with a cross-reference system for use in the organization of a collection of documents for reference and retrieval — **the·sau·ral** \-ˈsȯr-əl\ *adj*

these *pl of* THIS

The·seus \ˈthē-ˌsüs, -sē-əs\ *n* [L, fr. Gk *Thēseus*] (14c) **:** a king of Athens in Greek mythology who kills Procrustes and the Minotaur before defeating the Amazons and marrying their queen

the·sis \ˈthē-səs, *Brit esp for 1* ˈthe-sis\ *n, pl* **the·ses** \ˈthē-ˌsēz\ [in sense 1, ME, lowering of the voice, fr. LL & Gk; LL, fr. Gk, downbeat, more important part of a foot, lit., act of laying down; in other senses, L, fr.

Gk, lit., act of laying down, fr. *tithenai* to put, lay down — more at DO] (14c) **1 a** (1) **:** the unstressed part of a poetic foot esp. in accentual verse (2) **:** the longer part of a poetic foot esp. in quantitative verse **b :** the accented part of a musical measure **:** DOWNBEAT — compare ARSIS **2 a :** a position or proposition that a person (as a candidate for scholastic honors) advances and offers to maintain by argument **b :** a proposition to be proved or one advanced without proof **:** HYPOTHESIS **3 :** the first and least adequate stage of dialectic — compare SYNTHESIS **4 :** a dissertation embodying results of original research and esp. substantiating a specific view; *esp* **:** one written by a candidate for an academic degree

thesp \ˈthesp\ *n* [short for *thespian*] (1962) **:** ACTOR

1**thes·pi·an** \ˈthes-pē-ən\ *adj* (1567) **1** *cap* **:** of or relating to Thespis **2** *often cap* [fr. the tradition that Thespis was the originator of the actor's role] **:** relating to the drama **:** DRAMATIC

2**thespian** *n* (1827) **:** ACTOR

Thess *abbr* Thessalonians

Thes·sa·lo·nians \ˌthe-sə-ˈlō-nyənz, -nē-ənz\ *n pl but sing in constr* [*Thessalonian* inhabitant of ancient Thessalonica, irreg. fr. *Thessalonica*] (1568) **:** either of two letters written by St. Paul to the Christians of Thessalonica and included as books in the New Testament — see BIBLE table

the·ta \ˈthā-tə, *chiefly Brit* ˈthē-tə\ *n* [ME, fr. L, fr. Gk *thēta,* of Sem origin; akin to Heb *ṭēth* teth] (15c) **1 :** the 8th letter of the Greek alphabet — see ALPHABET table **2 :** THETA RHYTHM

theta rhythm *n* (1944) **:** a relatively high amplitude brain wave pattern between approximately four and nine hertz that is characteristic esp. of the hippocampus — called also *theta wave*

thet·ic \ˈthe-tik, ˈthē-\ *adj* [Gk *thetikos* of a proposition, fr. *tithenai* to lay down — more at DO] (1815) **:** constituting or beginning with a poetic thesis ⟨a ~ syllable⟩ — **thet·i·cal·ly** \-ti-k(ə-)lē\ *adv*

The·tis \ˈthē-təs\ *n* [L, fr. Gk] (14c) **:** a sea goddess who marries Peleus and becomes the mother of Achilles

the·ur·gist \ˈthē-(ˌ)ər-jist\ *n* (1652) **:** WONDER-WORKER, MAGICIAN

the·ur·gy \ˈthē-(ˌ)ər-jē\ *n* [LL *theurgia,* fr. LGk *theourgia,* fr. *theourgos* miracle worker, fr. Gk *the-* + *ergon* work — more at WORK] (ca. 1569) **:** the art or technique of compelling or persuading a god or beneficent or supernatural power to do or refrain from doing something — **the·ur·gic** \thē-ˈər-jik\ *or* **the·ur·gi·cal** \-ji-kəl\ *adj*

thew \ˈthü, ˈthyü\ *n* [ME, personal quality, virtue, fr. OE *thēaw;* akin to OHG *thau* custom] (15c) **1 a :** muscular power or development **b :** STRENGTH, VITALITY **2 :** MUSCLE, SINEW — usu. used in pl.

they \ˈt͟hā\ *pron, pl in constr* [ME, fr. ON *their,* masc. pl. demonstrative & personal pron.; akin to OE *thæt* that] (13c) **1 a :** those ones — used as third person pronoun serving as the plural of *he, she,* or *it* or referring to a group of two or more individuals not all of the same sex ⟨~ dance well⟩ **b :** 1HE 2 — often used with an indefinite third person singular antecedent ⟨everyone knew where ~ stood —E. L. Doctorow⟩ ⟨nobody has to go to school if ~ don't want to —*N. Y. Times*⟩ **2 :** PEOPLE 2 — used in a generic sense ⟨as lazy as ~ come⟩

usage *They* used as an indefinite subject (sense 2) is sometimes objected to on the grounds that it does not have an antecedent. Not every pronoun requires an antecedent, however. The indefinite *they* is used in all varieties of contexts and is standard.

usage *They, their, them, themselves:* English lacks a common-gender third person singular pronoun that can be used to refer to indefinite pronouns (as *everyone, anyone, someone*). Writers and speakers have supplied this lack by using the plural pronouns ⟨and every one to rest *themselves* betake —Shak.⟩ ⟨I would have everybody marry if *they* can do it properly —Jane Austen⟩ ⟨it is too hideous for anyone in *their* senses to buy —W. H. Auden⟩. The plural pronouns have also been put to use as pronouns of indefinite number to refer to singular nouns that stand for many persons ⟨'tis meet that some more audience than a mother, since nature makes *them* partial, should o'erhear the speech —Shak.⟩ ⟨a person can't help *their* birth —W. M. Thackeray⟩ ⟨no man goes to battle to be killed. — But *they* do get killed —G. B. Shaw⟩. The use of *they, their, them,* and *themselves* as pronouns of indefinite gender and indefinite number is well established in speech and writing, even in literary and formal contexts. This gives you the option of using the plural pronouns where you think they sound best, and of using the singular pronouns (as *he, she, he or she,* and their inflected forms) where you think they sound best.

they'd \ˈt͟hād\ (1599) **:** they had **:** they would

they'll \ˈt͟hāl, ˈt͟hel\ (1567) **:** they will **:** they shall

they're \t͟hər, ˈt͟her\ (ca. 1595) **:** they are

they've \ˈt͟hāv\ (1611) **:** they have

thi- *or* **thio-** *comb form* [ISV, fr. Gk *thei-, theio-* sulfur, fr. *theion*] **:** containing sulfur ⟨*thiamine*⟩ ⟨*thiocyanate*⟩

thia·ben·da·zole \ˌthī-ə-ˈben-də-ˌzōl\ *n* [*thiazole* + *benz-* + imide + *azole*] (1961) **:** a drug $C_{10}H_7N_3S$ used in the control of parasitic nematode worms and fungus infections and as an agricultural fungicide

thi·ami·nase \thī-ˈa-mə-ˌnās, ˈthī-ə-mə-, -ˌnāz\ *n* [ISV] (1938) **:** an enzyme that catalyzes the breakdown of thiamine

thi·a·mine \ˈthī-ə-mən, -ˌmēn\ *also* **thi·a·min** \-mən\ *n* [*thiamine* alter. of *thiamin,* fr. *thi-* + *-amin* (as in *vitamin*)] (1937) **:** a vitamin $C_{12}H_{17}N_4OSCl$ of the vitamin B complex that is essential to normal metabolism and nerve function and is widespread in plants and animals — called also *vitamin* B_1

thi·a·zide \ˈthī-ə-ˌzīd, -zəd\ *n* [*thi-* + diazine + diox*ide*] (1959) **:** any of a group of drugs used as oral diuretics esp. in the control of high blood pressure

thi·a·zine \ˈthī-ə-ˌzēn\ *n* [ISV *thi-* + *azine*] (1900) **:** any of various compounds that are characterized by a ring composed of four carbon atoms, one sulfur atom, and one nitrogen atom and include some important as dyes and others as tranquilizers — compare PHENOTHIAZINE

thi·a·zole \ˈthī-ə-ˌzōl\ *n* [ISV *thi-* + *azole*] (1888) **1 :** a colorless basic liquid C_3H_3NS consisting of a 5-membered ring and having an odor like pyridine **2 :** any of various thiazole derivatives including some used in medicine and others important as chemical accelerators

1**thick** \ˈthik\ *adj* [ME *thikke,* fr. OE *thicce;* akin to OHG *dicki* thick, OIr *tiug*] (bef. 12c) **1 a :** having or being of relatively great depth or extent from one surface to its opposite ⟨a ~ plank⟩ **b :** heavily built **:** THICKSET **2 a :** close-packed with units or individuals ⟨the air was ~ with snow⟩ **b :** occurring in large numbers **:** NUMEROUS **c :** viscous in consistency ⟨~ syrup⟩ **d :** SULTRY, STUFFY **e :** marked by haze, fog, or mist ⟨~ weather⟩ **f :** impenetrable to the eye **:** PROFOUND ⟨~ darkness⟩ **g :** extremely intense ⟨~ silence⟩ **3 :** measuring in thickness ⟨12 inches ~⟩ **4 a :** imperfectly articulated **:** INDISTINCT ⟨~ speech⟩ **b :** plainly apparent **:** DECIDED ⟨a ~ French accent⟩ **c :** producing inarticulate speech ⟨a ~ tongue⟩ **5 :** OBTUSE, STUPID ⟨too ~ to understand⟩ **6 :** associated on close terms **:** INTIMATE ⟨was quite ~ with his pastor⟩ **7 :** exceeding bounds of propriety or fitness **:** EXCESSIVE ⟨called it a bit ~ to be fired without warning⟩ — **thick·ish** \ˈthi-kish\ *adj* — **thick·ly** *adv* — **thick on the ground :** PLENTIFUL, ABUNDANT

2**thick** *adv* (bef. 12c) **:** in a thick manner **:** THICKLY

3**thick** *n* (13c) **1 :** the most crowded or active part ⟨in the ~ of the battle⟩ **2 :** the part of greatest thickness ⟨the ~ of the thumb⟩

thick and thin *n* (14c) **:** every difficulty and obstacle — used esp. in the phrase *through thick and thin* ⟨was loyal through *thick and thin*⟩

thick·en \ˈthi-kən\ *vb* **thick·ened; thick·en·ing** \ˈthik-niŋ, ˈthi-kə-\ *vi* (14c) **1 a :** to become dense ⟨the mist ~*ed*⟩ **b :** to become concentrated in numbers, mass, or frequency **2 :** to grow blurred or obscure **3 :** to grow broader or bulkier **4 :** to grow complicated or keen ⟨the plot ~*s*⟩ ~ *vt* **1 a :** to make thick, dense, or viscous in consistency ⟨~ gravy with flour⟩ **b :** to make close or compact **2 :** to increase the depth or diameter of **3 :** to make inarticulate **:** BLUR ⟨alcohol ~*ed* his speech⟩ — **thick·en·er** \ˈthik-nər, ˈthi-kə-\ *n*

thickening *n* (15c) **1 :** a thickened part or place **2 :** the act of making or becoming thick **3 :** something used to thicken

thick·et \ˈthi-kət\ *n* [ME *thikket, fr. OE *thiccet,* fr. *thicce* thick] (bef. 12c) **1 :** a dense growth of shrubbery or small trees **:** COPPICE **2 :** something resembling a thicket in density or impenetrability **:** TANGLE ⟨a political ~⟩ ⟨a ~ of reporters⟩ — **thick·ety** \-kə-tē\ *adj*

thick·et·ed \ˈthi-kə-təd\ *adj* (ca. 1624) **:** dotted or covered with thickets

thick·head \ˈthik-ˌhed\ *n* (1797) **:** a stupid person **:** BLOCKHEAD

thick·head·ed \-ˌhe-dəd\ *adj* (1691) **1 :** sluggish and obtuse of mind **2 :** having a thick head

thick·ness \ˈthik-nəs\ *n* (bef. 12c) **1 :** the smallest of three dimensions ⟨length, width, and ~⟩ **2 :** the quality or state of being thick **3 a :** viscous consistency ⟨boiled to the ~ of honey⟩ **b :** the condition of being smoky, foul, or foggy **4 :** the thick part of something **5 :** CONCENTRATION, DENSITY **6 :** STUPIDITY, DULLNESS **7 :** LAYER, PLY, SHEET ⟨a single ~ of canvas⟩

thick·set \-ˌset\ *adj* (14c) **1 :** closely placed; *also* **:** growing thickly ⟨a ~ wood⟩ **2 :** having a thick body **:** BURLY

thick–skinned \-ˌskind\ *adj* (ca. 1545) **1 :** having a thick skin **:** PACHYDERMATOUS **2 a :** CALLOUS, INSENSITIVE **b :** impervious to criticism ⟨became ~ about his own work⟩

thick–wit·ted \-ˌwi-təd\ *adj* (1634) **:** dull or slow of mind **:** STUPID

thief \ˈthēf\ *n, pl* **thieves** \ˈthēvz\ [ME *theef,* fr. OE *thēof;* akin to OHG *diob* thief] (bef. 12c) **:** one that steals esp. stealthily or secretly; *also* **:** one who commits theft or larceny

thieve \ˈthēv\ *vb* **thieved; thiev·ing** (bef. 12c) **:** STEAL, ROB

thiev·ery \ˈthēv-rē, ˈthē-və-\ *n, pl* **-er·ies** (1568) **:** the act or practice or an instance of stealing **:** THEFT

thiev·ish \ˈthē-vish\ *adj* (14c) **1 :** of, relating to, or characteristic of a thief **2 :** given to stealing — **thiev·ish·ly** *adv* — **thiev·ish·ness** *n*

thigh \ˈthī\ *n* [ME, fr. OE *thēoh;* akin to OHG *dioh* thigh, Lith *taukai,* pl., fat] (bef. 12c) **1 a :** the proximal segment of the vertebrate hind or lower limb extending from the hip to the knee **b :** the segment of the leg immediately distal to the thigh in a bird or in a quadruped in which the true thigh is obscured **c :** the femur of an insect **2 :** something resembling or covering a thigh — **thighed** \ˈthīd\ *adj*

thigh·bone \ˈthī-ˌbōn\ *n* (15c) **:** FEMUR 1

thigh–slap·per \ˈthī-ˌsla-pər\ *n* (1965) **:** KNEE-SLAPPER

thig·mo·tax·is \ˌthig-mə-ˈtak-səs\ *n* [NL, fr. Gk *thigma* touch (fr. *thinganein* to touch) + NL *-taxis;* akin to L *fingere* to shape — more at DOUGH] (ca. 1900) **:** a taxis in which contact esp. with a solid body is the directive factor

thig·mot·ro·pism \thig-ˈmä-trə-ˌpi-zəm\ *n* [Gk *thigma* + ISV *-o-* + *-tropism*] (1899) **:** a tropism in which contact esp. with a solid or a rigid surface is the orienting factor

thill \ˈthil\ *n* [ME *thille,* perh. fr. OE, plank; akin to OE *thel* board, OHG *dili,* and prob. to L *tellus* earth] (14c) **:** a shaft of a vehicle

thim·ble \ˈthim-bəl\ *n* [ME *thymel, thymbyl,* fr. OE *thȳmel* covering for the thumb, fr. *thūma* thumb] (15c) **1 :** a pitted cap or cover worn on the finger to push the needle in sewing **2 a :** a grooved ring of thin metal used to fit in a spliced loop in a rope as protection from chafing **b :** a lining (as of metal) for an opening (as in a roof or wall) through which a stovepipe or chimney passes

thim·ble·ber·ry \-ˌber-ē\ *n* (1788) **:** any of several American raspberries or blackberries (esp. *Rubus occidentalis, R. parviflorus,* and *R. odoratus*) having thimble-shaped fruit

thim·ble·ful \-ˌfu̇l\ *n* (1604) **1 :** as much as a thimble will hold **2 :** a very small quantity ⟨not a ~ of common sense⟩

1**thim·ble·rig** \-ˌrig\ *n* (1826) **1 :** a swindling trick in which a small ball or pea is quickly shifted from under one to another of three small cups to fool the spectator guessing its location **2 :** one who manipulates the cup in thimblerig **:** THIMBLERIGGER

2**thimblerig** *vt* (1839) **1 :** to cheat by trickery **2 :** to swindle by thimblerig — **thim·ble·rig·ger** *n*

thim·ble·weed \ˈthim-bəl-ˌwēd\ *n* (1833) **:** any of various anemones (as *Anemone virginiana* and *A. cylindrica*) with cylindrical seed heads

thi·mer·o·sal \thī-ˈmer-ə-ˌsal\ *n* [prob. fr. *thi-* + *mer*cury + *-o-* + *sal*icylate] (1949) **:** a crystalline organic mercurial antiseptic $C_9H_9HgNaO_2S$ used esp. for its antifungal and bacteriostatic properties

1**thin** \ˈthin\ *adj* **thin·ner; thin·nest** [ME *thinne,* fr. OE *thynne;* akin to OHG *dunni* thin, L *tenuis* thin, *tenēre* to hold, *tendere* to stretch, Gk *teinein*] (bef. 12c) **1 a :** having little extent from one surface to its opposite ⟨~ paper⟩ **b :** measuring little in cross section or diameter ⟨~ rope⟩ **2 :** not dense in arrangement or distribution ⟨~ hair⟩ **3 :** not well fleshed **:** LEAN **4 a :** more fluid or rarefied than normal ⟨~ air⟩ **b :** having less than

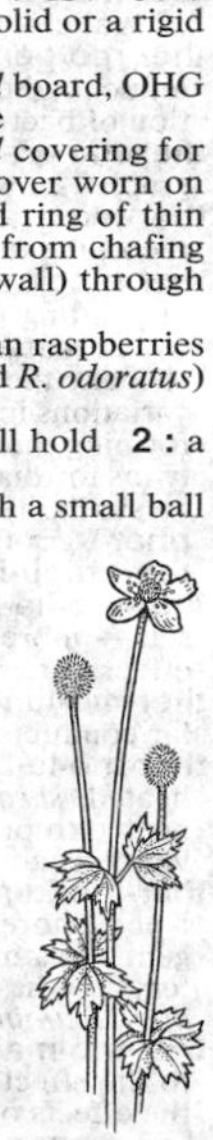

thimbleweed

the usual number : SCANTY ⟨~ attendance⟩ **c** : few in number : SCARCE **d** : scantily supplied **e** : characterized by a paucity of bids or offerings ⟨a ~ market⟩ **5 a** : lacking substance or strength ⟨~ broth⟩ ⟨a ~ plot⟩ **b** *of a soil* : INFERTILE, POOR **6 a** : FLIMSY, UNCONVINCING ⟨a ~ disguise⟩ **b** : disappointingly poor or hard ⟨had a ~ time of it⟩ **7** : somewhat feeble, shrill, and lacking in resonance ⟨a ~ voice⟩ **8** : lacking in intensity or brilliance ⟨~ light⟩ **9** : lacking sufficient photographic density or contrast — **thin·ly** *adv* — **thin·ness** \ˈthin-nəs\ *n* — **thin·nish** \ˈthi-nish\ *adj* — **thin on the ground** : SCARCE 1

syn THIN, SLENDER, SLIM, SLIGHT, TENUOUS mean not thick, broad, abundant, or dense. THIN implies comparatively little extension between surfaces or in diameter, or it may imply lack of substance, richness, or abundance ⟨*thin* wire⟩ ⟨a *thin* soup⟩. SLENDER implies leanness or spareness often with grace and good proportion ⟨the *slender* legs of a Sheraton chair⟩. SLIM applies to slenderness that suggests fragility or scantiness ⟨a *slim* volume of poetry⟩ ⟨a *slim* chance⟩. SLIGHT implies smallness as well as thinness ⟨a *slight* build⟩. TENUOUS implies extreme thinness, sheerness, or lack of substance and firmness ⟨a *tenuous* thread⟩.

[2]**thin** *vb* **thinned; thin·ning** *vt* (bef. 12c) : to make thin or thinner: **a** : to reduce in thickness or depth : ATTENUATE **b** : to make less dense or viscous **c** : DILUTE, WEAKEN **d** : to cause to lose flesh ⟨*thinned* by weeks of privation⟩ **e** : to reduce in number or bulk ~ *vi* **1** : to become thin or thinner **2** : to become weak

[3]**thin** *adv* **thin·ner; thin·nest** (13c) : in a thin manner : THINLY — used esp. in combination ⟨*thin*-clad⟩ ⟨*thin*-flowing⟩

[1]**thine** \ˈthīn\ *adj* [ME *thin,* fr. OE *thīn*] (bef. 12c) *archaic* : THY — used esp. before a word beginning with a vowel or *h*

[2]**thine** *pron, sing or pl in constr* [ME *thin,* fr. OE *thīn,* fr. *thīn* thy — more at THY] (bef. 12c) *archaic* : that which belongs to thee — used without a following noun as a pronoun equivalent in meaning to the adjective *thy*; used esp. in ecclesiastical or literary language and still surviving in the speech of Friends esp. among themselves

thin film *n* (1944) : a very thin layer of a substance on a supporting material; *esp* : a coating (as of a semiconductor) that is deposited in a layer one atom or one molecule thick

thing \ˈthiŋ\ *n* [ME, fr. OE, thing, assembly; akin to OHG *ding* thing, assembly, Goth *theihs* time] (bef. 12c) **1 a** : a matter of concern : AFFAIR ⟨many ~*s* to do⟩ **b** *pl* : state of affairs in general or within a specified or implied sphere ⟨~*s* are improving⟩ **c** : a particular state of affairs : SITUATION ⟨look at this ~ another way⟩ **d** : EVENT, CIRCUMSTANCE ⟨that shooting was a terrible ~⟩ **2 a** : DEED, ACT, ACCOMPLISHMENT ⟨do great ~*s*⟩ **b** : a product of work or activity ⟨likes to build ~*s*⟩ **c** : the aim of effort or activity ⟨the ~ is to get well⟩ **3 a** : a separate and distinct individual quality, fact, idea, or usu. entity **b** : the concrete entity as distinguished from its appearances **c** : a spatial entity **d** : an inanimate object distinguished from a living being **4 a** *pl* : POSSESSIONS, EFFECTS ⟨pack your ~*s*⟩ **b** : whatever may be possessed or owned or be the object of a right **c** : an article of clothing ⟨not a ~ to wear⟩ **d** *pl* : equipment or utensils esp. for a particular purpose ⟨bring the tea ~*s*⟩ **5** : an object or entity not precisely designated or capable of being designated ⟨use this ~⟩ **6 a** : DETAIL, POINT ⟨checks every little ~⟩ **b** : a material or substance of a specified kind ⟨avoid fatty ~*s*⟩ **7 a** : a spoken or written observation or point **b** : IDEA, NOTION ⟨says the first ~ he thinks of⟩ **c** : a piece of news or information ⟨couldn't get a ~ out of him⟩ **8** : INDIVIDUAL ⟨not a living ~ in sight⟩ **9** : the proper or fashionable way of behaving, talking, or dressing — used with *the* **10 a** : a mild obsession or phobia ⟨has a ~ about driving⟩; *also* : the object of such an obsession or phobia **b** : something (as an activity) that makes a strong appeal to the individual : FORTE, SPECIALTY ⟨letting students do their own ~ —*Newsweek*⟩ ⟨I think travelling is very much a novelist's ~ —Philip Larkin⟩

thing·am·a·bob \ˈthiŋ-ə-mə-ˌbäb\ *n* (1750) : THINGAMAJIG

thing·am·a·jig *or* **thing·um·a·jig** \ˈthiŋ-ə-mə-ˌjig\ *n* [alter. of earlier *thingum,* fr. *thing*] (1828) : something that is hard to classify or whose name is unknown or forgotten

thing–in–itself *n, pl* **things–in–themselves** [trans. of G *Ding an sich*] (1739) : NOUMENON

thing·ness \ˈthiŋ-nəs\ *n* (1896) : the quality or state of objective existence or reality

thing·um·my \ˈthiŋ-ə-mē\ *n, pl* **-mies** [alter. of earlier *thingum*] (1796) : THINGAMAJIG

[1]**think** \ˈthiŋk\ *vb* **thought** \ˈthȯt\; **think·ing** [ME *thenken,* fr. OE *thencan;* akin to OHG *denken* to think, L *tongēre* to know — more at THANKS] *vt* (bef. 12c) **1** : to form or have in the mind **2** : to have as an intention ⟨*thought* to return early⟩ **3 a** : to have as an opinion ⟨~ it's so⟩ **b** : to regard as : CONSIDER ⟨~ the rule unfair⟩ **4 a** : to reflect on : PONDER ⟨~ the matter over⟩ **b** : to determine by reflecting ⟨~ what to do next⟩ **5** : to call to mind : REMEMBER ⟨he never ~*s* to ask how we do⟩ **6** : to devise by thinking — usu. used with *up* ⟨*thought* up a plan to escape⟩ **7** : to have as an expectation : ANTICIPATE ⟨we didn't ~ we'd have any trouble⟩ **8 a** : to center one's thoughts on ⟨talks and ~*s* business⟩ **b** : to form a mental picture of **9** : to subject to the processes of logical thought ⟨~ things out⟩ ~ *vi* **1 a** : to exercise the powers of judgment, conception, or inference : REASON **b** : to have in the mind or call to mind a thought **2 a** : to have the mind engaged in reflection : MEDITATE **b** : to consider the suitability ⟨*thought* of her for president⟩ **3** : to have a view or opinion ⟨~*s* of himself as a poet⟩ **4** : to have concern — usu. used with *of* ⟨a man must ~ first of his family⟩ **5** : to consider something likely : SUSPECT ⟨may happen sooner than you ~⟩ — **think·er** *n* — **think better of** : to reconsider and make a wiser decision — **think much of** : to view with satisfaction : APPROVE — usu. used in negative constructions ⟨I didn't *think much of* the new car⟩

syn THINK, CONCEIVE, IMAGINE, FANCY, REALIZE, ENVISAGE, ENVISION mean to form an idea of. THINK implies the entrance of an idea into one's mind with or without deliberate consideration or reflection ⟨I just *thought* of a good joke⟩. CONCEIVE suggests the forming and bringing forth and usu. developing of an idea, plan, or design ⟨*conceived* of a new marketing approach⟩. IMAGINE stresses a visualization ⟨*imagine* you're at the beach⟩. FANCY suggests an imagining often unrestrained by reality but spurred by desires ⟨*fancied* himself a super athlete⟩. REALIZE stresses a grasping of the significance of what is conceived or imagined ⟨*realized* the enormity of the task ahead⟩. ENVISAGE and ENVISION imply a conceiving or imagining that is esp. clear or detailed ⟨*envisaged* a totally computerized operation⟩ ⟨*envisioned* a cure for the disease⟩.

syn THINK, COGITATE, REFLECT, REASON, SPECULATE, DELIBERATE mean to use one's powers of conception, judgment, or inference. THINK is general and may apply to any mental activity, but used alone often suggests attainment of clear ideas or conclusions ⟨teaches students how to *think*⟩. COGITATE implies deep or intent thinking ⟨*cogitated* on the mysteries of nature⟩. REFLECT suggests unhurried consideration of something recalled to the mind ⟨*reflecting* on fifty years of married life⟩. REASON stresses consecutive logical thinking ⟨able to *reason* brilliantly in debate⟩. SPECULATE implies reasoning about things theoretical or problematic ⟨*speculated* on the fate of the lost explorers⟩. DELIBERATE suggests slow or careful reasoning before forming an opinion or reaching a conclusion or decision ⟨the jury *deliberated* for five hours⟩.

[2]**think** *n* (1834) : an act of thinking ⟨has another ~ coming⟩

[3]**think** *adj* (1890) : relating to, requiring, or stimulating thinking

think·able \ˈthiŋ-kə-bəl\ *adj* (1805) **1** : conceivably possible ⟨a time when divorce was barely ~⟩ **2** : capable of being comprehended or reasoned about ⟨the ultimate nature of Deity is scarcely ~⟩ — **think·able·ness** *n* — **think·ably** \-blē\ *adv*

[1]**thinking** *n* (14c) **1** : the action of using one's mind to produce thoughts **2 a** : OPINION, JUDGMENT ⟨I'd like to know your ~ on this⟩ **b** : thought that is characteristic (as of a period, group, or person) ⟨the current student ~ on fraternities⟩

[2]**thinking** *adj* (1674) : marked by use of the intellect : RATIONAL ⟨~ citizens⟩ — **think·ing·ly** *adv* — **think·ing·ness** *n*

thinking cap *n* (1847) : a state or mood in which one thinks — usu. used in the phrase *put one's thinking cap on*

think piece *n* (1941) : a piece of writing meant to be thought-provoking and speculative that consists chiefly of background material and personal opinion and analysis

think tank *n* (1959) : an institute, corporation, or group organized for interdisciplinary research (as in technological and social problems) — called also *think factory*

thin–layer chromatography *n* (1957) : chromatography in which a liquid sample migrates by capillarity through a solid adsorbent medium (as alumina or silica gel) which is arranged as a thin layer on a rigid support (as a glass plate)

thin·ner \ˈthi-nər\ *n* (1832) : one that thins; *specif* : a volatile liquid (as turpentine) used esp. to thin paint

thin–skinned \ˈthin-ˌskind\ *adj* (1598) **1** : having a thin skin or rind ⟨~ oranges⟩ **2** : unduly susceptible to criticism or insult : TOUCHY

thio- — see THI-

thio acid \ˈthī-ō-\ *n* [ISV, fr. *thi-*] (1876) : an acid in which oxygen is partly or wholly replaced by sulfur

thio·cy·a·nate \ˌthī-ō-ˈsī-ə-ˌnāt, -nət\ *n* [ISV] (1877) : a compound that consists of the chemical group SCN bonded by the sulfur atom to a group or an atom other than a hydrogen atom

thi·ol \ˈthī-ˌȯl, -ˌōl\ *n* [ISV *thi-* + [1]*-ol*] (ca. 1890) **1** : any of various compounds having the general formula RSH which are analogous to alcohols but in which sulfur replaces the oxygen of the hydroxyl group and which have disagreeable odors **2** : the functional group –SH characteristic of thiols — **thi·o·lic** \thī-ˈō-lik\ *adj*

thion- *comb form* [ISV, fr. Gk *theion*] : sulfur ⟨*methionine*⟩

thio·pen·tal \ˌthī-ō-ˈpen-ˌtal, -ˌtȯl\ *n* [*thi-* + *pentobarbital*] (1947) : a barbiturate $C_{11}H_{18}N_2O_2S$ used in the form of its sodium salt esp. as an intravenous anesthetic — compare PENTOTHAL

thio·phene \ˈthī-ə-ˌfēn\ *n* [ISV *thi-* + *phene* benzene] (1883) : a heterocyclic liquid C_4H_4S from coal tar that resembles benzene

thi·o·rid·a·zine \ˌthī-ə-ˈri-də-ˌzēn, -zən\ *n* [*thi-* + piper*idine* + phenothi*azine*] (1959) : a phenothiazine tranquilizer $C_{21}H_{26}N_2S_2$ used in the form of its hydrochloride for relief of anxiety states and in the treatment of psychotic disorders and severe childhood behavioral problems

thio·sul·fate \-ˈsəl-ˌfāt\ *n* [ISV] (ca. 1872) : a salt containing the anion $S_2O_3^{2-}$

thio·te·pa \ˌthī-ə-ˈtē-pə\ *n* [*thi-* + *tepa,* the compound $C_6H_{12}N_3OP$, fr. *tri-* + *ethylene* + *phosphor-* + *amide*] (1953) : an alkylating agent $C_6H_{12}N_3PS$ that has been used as an antineoplastic agent and insect sterilant

thio·ura·cil \ˌthī-ō-ˈyu̇r-ə-ˌsil\ *n* [ISV] (1905) : a bitter crystalline compound $C_4H_4N_2OS$ that depresses the function of the thyroid gland

thio·urea \-yu̇-ˈrē-ə\ *n* [NL] (1884) : a colorless crystalline bitter compound $CS(NH_2)_2$ analogous to and resembling urea that is used esp. as a photographic and organic chemical reagent; *also* : a substituted derivative of this compound

thir \t͟hər, ˈthir, ˈthu̇r\ *pron or adj* [ME (northern), perh. irreg. fr. ME *this*] (14c) *dial Brit* : THESE

thi·ram \ˈthī-ˌram\ *n* [prob. by alter. fr. *thiuram* the chemical group NH_2CS] (1949) : a compound $C_6H_{12}N_2S_4$ used as a fungicide and seed disinfectant

[1]**third** \ˈthərd\ *adj* [ME *thridde, thirde,* fr. OE *thridda, thirdda;* akin to L *tertius* third, Gk *tritos, treis* three — more at THREE] (bef. 12c) **1 a** : being next after the second in place or time ⟨the ~ taxi in line⟩ **b** : ranking next after the second of a grade or degree in authority or precedence ⟨served as ~ mate⟩ **c** : being the forward speed or gear next higher than second esp. in a motor vehicle **2 a** : being one of three equal parts into which something is divisible ⟨a ~ share of the money⟩ **b** : being the last in each group of three in a series ⟨take out every ~ card⟩ — **third** *or* **third·ly** *adv*

[2]**third** *n* (14c) **1** : one of three equal parts of something ⟨a ~ of the pie⟩ **2 a** — see NUMBER table **b** : one that is next after second in rank, position, authority, or precedence ⟨the ~ in line⟩ **3 a** : the musical interval embracing three diatonic degrees **b** : a tone at this interval;

\ə\ **abut** \ᵊ\ kitten, F table \ər\ **further** \a\ **ash** \ā\ **ace** \ä\ **mop, mar** \au̇\ **out** \ch\ **chin** \e\ **bet** \ē\ **easy** \g\ **go** \i\ **hit** \ī\ **ice** \j\ **job** \ŋ\ **sing** \ō\ **go** \ȯ\ **law** \ȯi\ **boy** \th\ **thin** \t͟h\ **the** \ü\ **loot** \u̇\ **foot** \y\ **yet** \zh\ **vision, beige** \k̲, ⁿ, œ, ue, ʸ\ *see* Guide to Pronunciation

specif : MEDIANT **c** : the harmonic combination of two tones a third apart **4** *pl* : merchandise whose quality falls below the manufacturer's standard for seconds **5** : THIRD BASE **6** : the third forward gear or speed esp. of a motor vehicle

third base *n* (1845) **1** : the base that must be touched third by a base runner in baseball **2** : the player position for defending the area around third base — **third baseman** *n*

third–class *adj* (1839) : of or relating to a class, rank, or grade next below the second — **third–class** *adv*

third class *n* (1748) **1** : the third and usu. next below second class in a classification **2** : the least expensive class of accommodations (as on a passenger ship) **3** : a former class of U.S. mail comprising circulars, pamphlets, catalogs, and newsletters

third degree *n* (1900) : the subjection of a prisoner to mental or physical torture to extract a confession

third–degree burn *n* (1930) : a severe burn characterized by destruction of the skin through its deeper layers and possibly into underlying tissues, loss of fluid, and sometimes shock

third dimension *n* (1846) **1** : THICKNESS, DEPTH; *also* : a dimension that adds the effect of solidity to a two-dimensional system **2** : a quality that confers reality or lifelikeness ‹night sounds that stick in the mind and give a *third dimension* to the memory —Adie Suehsdorf› — **third–dimensional** *adj*

third estate *n, often cap T&E* (1604) : the third of the traditional political orders; *specif* : the commons

third force *n* (1936) : a grouping (as of political parties or international powers) intermediate between two opposing political forces

third–hand \ˈthərd-ˈhand\ *adj* (1598) **1** : received from or through two intermediaries ‹~ information› **2 a** : acquired after being used by two previous owners **b** : dealing in thirdhand merchandise

third house *n* (1841) : a legislative lobby

third market *n* (1964) : the over-the-counter market in listed securities

third order *n, often cap T&O* (1629) **1** : an organization composed of lay people living in secular society under a religious rule and directed by a religious order **2** : a congregation esp. of teaching or nursing sisters affiliated with a religious order

third–party *adj* (1901) **1** : of, relating to, or involving a third party ‹~ insurance› **2** : of, relating to, or being software that is created by a vendor to be compatible with the products of another vendor

third party *n* (1641) **1** : a person other than the principals ‹a *third party* to a divorce proceeding› ‹insurance against injury to *third parties*› **2 a** : a major political party operating over a limited period of time in addition to two other major parties in a nation or state normally characterized by a two-party system **b** : MINOR PARTY

third person *n* (ca. 1586) **1 a** : a set of linguistic forms (as verb forms, pronouns, and inflectional affixes) referring to one that is neither the speaker or writer of the utterance in which they occur nor the one to whom that utterance is addressed ‹"they" is a pronoun of the *third person*› **b** : a linguistic form belonging to such a set **c** : reference of a linguistic form to one that is neither the speaker or writer of the utterance in which it occurs nor the one to whom that utterance is addressed ‹referred to himself in the *third person*› **2** : a style of discourse marked by general use of verbs and pronouns of the third person ‹the story was written in the *third person*›

third rail *n* (1867) **1** : a metal rail through which electric current is led to the motors of an electric vehicle (as a subway car) **2** : a controversial issue usu. avoided by politicians

third–rate \ˈthərd-ˈrāt\ *adj* (1814) : extremely low in quality or value : worse than second-rate ‹~ hotels› ‹a ~ novelist› — **third–rat·er** \-ˈrā-tər\ *n*

third reading *n* (ca. 1571) : the final stage of the consideration of a legislative bill before a vote on its final disposition

third–stream *adj* (1962) : of, relating to, or being music that incorporates elements of classical music and jazz

third ventricle *n* (1615) : the median unpaired ventricle of the brain bounded by parts of the telencephalon and diencephalon

third world *n, often cap T&W* (1958) **1** : a group of nations esp. in Africa and Asia not aligned with either the Communist or the non-Communist blocs **2** : an aggregate of minority groups within a larger predominant culture **3** : the aggregate of the underdeveloped nations of the world — **third world·er** \-ˈwər(-ə)l-dər\ *n, often cap T&W*

[1]**thirl** \ˈthər(-ə)l\ *n* [ME, fr. OE *thyrel,* fr. *thurh* through — more at THROUGH] (bef. 12c) *dial* : HOLE, PERFORATION, OPENING

[2]**thirl** *vt* (bef. 12c) *dial Brit* : PIERCE, PERFORATE

[1]**thirst** \ˈthərst\ *n* [ME, fr. OE *thurst;* akin to OHG *durst* thirst, L *torrēre* to dry, parch, OIr *tart* dryness, thirst, Gk *tersesthai* to become dry] (bef. 12c) **1 a** : a sensation of dryness in the mouth and throat associated with a desire for liquids; *also* : the bodily condition (as of dehydration) that induces this sensation **b** : a desire or need to drink **2** : an ardent desire : CRAVING, LONGING ‹a ~ for success›

[2]**thirst** *vi* (bef. 12c) **1** : to feel thirsty : suffer thirst **2** : to crave vehemently and urgently ‹~*ed* for revenge› ‹~*ing* after justice› ***syn*** see LONG — **thirst·er** *n*

thirst·i·ly \ˈthər-stə-lē\ *adv* (1549) : with or on account of thirst

thirsty \ˈthər-stē\ *adj* **thirst·i·er; -est** (bef. 12c) **1 a** : feeling thirst **b** : deficient in moisture : PARCHED ‹~ land› **c** : highly absorbent ‹~ towels› **2** : having a strong desire : AVID ‹~ for knowledge› — **thirst·i·ness** \-stē-nəs\ *n*

thir·teen \ˌthər(t)-ˈtēn, ˈthər(t)-\ *n* [ME *thrittene,* fr. *thrittene,* adj., fr. OE *thrēotīne;* akin to OE *tīen* ten — more at TEN] (14c) — see NUMBER table — **thirteen** *adj* — **thirteen** *pron, pl in constr* — **thir·teenth** \-ˈtēn(t)th, -ˌtēn(t)th\ *adj or n*

thir·ty \ˈthər-tē\ *n, pl* **thirties** [ME *thritty,* fr. *thritty,* adj., fr. OE *thrītig,* fr. *thrītig* group of 30, fr. *thrīe* three + *-tig* group of ten; akin to OE *tīen* ten] (bef. 12c) **1** — see NUMBER table **2** *pl* : the numbers 30 to 39; *specif* : the years 30 to 39 in a lifetime or century **3** : a sign of completion : END — usu. written 30 ‹wrote ~ on the last page of the story› **4** : the second point scored by a side in a game of tennis — **thir·ti·eth** \-tē-əth\ *adj or n* — **thirty** *adj* — **thirty** *pron, pl in constr* — **thir·ty·ish** \-ish\ *adj*

thir·ty–eight \ˌthər-tē-ˈāt\ *n* (ca. 1541) **1** — see NUMBER table **2** : a handgun nominally of .38 caliber — usu. written .38 — **thirty–eight** *adj* — **thirty–eight** *pron, pl in constr*

thir·ty–sec·ond note \-ˈse-kən(d)-ˌnōt, -kən(t)-\ *n* (ca. 1890) : a musical note with the time value of $\frac{1}{32}$ of a whole note — see NOTE illustration

thirty–second rest *n* (ca. 1903) : a musical rest corresponding in time value to a thirty-second note

thir·ty·some·thing \ˈthər-tē-ˌsəm(p)-thiŋ\ *adj* (1987) : of, relating to, or being a person who is in his or her thirties ‹~ parents› — **thirty-something** *n*

thir·ty–thir·ty \ˌthər-tē-ˈthər-tē\ *n* (1929) : a rifle that fires a .30 caliber cartridge having a 30 grain powder charge — usu. written .30–30

thir·ty–three \ˌthər-tē-ˈthrē\ *n* (1590) **1** — see NUMBER table **2** : a microgroove phonograph record designed to be played at $33\frac{1}{3}$ revolutions per minute — usu. written 33 — **thirty–three** *adj* — **thirty–three** *pron, pl in constr*

thir·ty–two \-ˈtü\ *n* (15c) **1** — see NUMBER table **2** : a .32 caliber handgun — usu. written .32 — **thirty–two** *adj* — **thirty–two** *pron, pl in constr*

thir·ty–two·mo \-(ˌ)mō\ *n, pl* **-mos** (ca. 1841) : the size of a piece of paper cut 32 from a sheet; *also* : a book, a page, or paper of this size

[1]**this** \ˈt͟his, t͟həs\ *pron, pl* **these** \ˈt͟hēz\ [ME, pron. & adj., fr. OE *thes* (masc.), *this* (neut.); akin to OHG *dese* this, OE *thæt* that] (bef. 12c) **1 a** (1) : the person, thing, or idea that is present or near in place, time, or thought or that has just been mentioned ‹*these* are my hands› (2) : what is stated in the following phrase, clause, or discourse ‹I can only say ~: it wasn't here yesterday› **b** : this time or place ‹expected to return before ~› **2 a** : the one nearer or more immediately under observation or discussion ‹~ is iron and that is tin› **b** : the one more recently referred to

[2]**this** *adj, pl* **these** (bef. 12c) **1 a** : being the person, thing, or idea that is present or near in place, time, or thought or that has just been mentioned ‹~ book is mine› ‹early ~ morning› **b** : constituting the immediately following part of the present discourse **c** : constituting the immediate past or future ‹friends all *these* years› **d** : being one not previously mentioned — used esp. in narrative to give a sense of immediacy or vividness ‹then ~ guy runs in› ‹had ~ urge to go shopping› **2** : being the nearer at hand or more immediately under observation or discussion ‹~ car or that one›

[3]**this** \ˈt͟his\ *adv* (15c) : to the degree or extent indicated by something in the immediate context or situation ‹didn't expect to wait ~ long›

This·be \ˈthiz-bē\ *n* [L, fr. Gk *Thisbē*] (14c) : a legendary young woman of Babylon who dies for love of Pyramus

this·tle \ˈthi-səl\ *n* [ME *thistel,* fr. OE; akin to OHG *distill* thistle] (bef. 12c) : any of various prickly composite plants (esp. genera *Carduus, Cirsium,* and *Onopordum*) with often showy heads of mostly tubular flowers; *also* : any of various other prickly plants — **this·tly** \ˈthi-s(ə-)lē\ *adj*

this·tle·down \ˈthi-səl-ˌdau̇n\ *n* (1561) : the typically plumose pappus from the ripe flower head of a thistle

thistle tube *n* (ca. 1891) : a funnel tube usu. of glass with a bulging top and flaring mouth

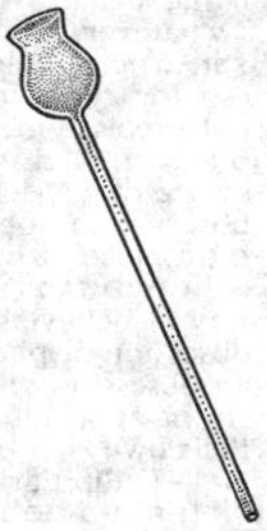

thistle tube

this–world·li·ness \ˈt͟his-ˈwərld-lē-nəs\ *n* (1887) : interest in, concern with, or devotion to things of this world esp. as opposed to a future stage of existence (as after death)

this–world·ly \-lē\ *adj* (1883) : characterized by or manifesting this-worldliness

[1]**thith·er** \ˈthi-t͟hər *also* ˈt͟hi-\ *adv* [ME, fr. OE *thider;* akin to ON *thathra* there, OE *thæt* that] (bef. 12c) : to that place : THERE

[2]**thither** *adj* (1830) : being on the other and farther side : more remote

thith·er·to \-ˌtü; ˌthi-t͟hər-ˈ, ˌt͟hi-\ *adv* (15c) : until that time

thith·er·ward \ˈthi-t͟hər-wərd, ˈt͟hi-\ *also* **thith·er·wards** \-wərdz\ *adv* (bef. 12c) : toward that place : THITHER

thix·ot·ro·py \thik-ˈsä-trə-pē\ *n* [ISV *thixo-* (fr. Gk *thixis* act of touching, fr. *thinganein* to touch) + *-tropy* — more at THIGMOTAXIS] (1927) : the property of various gels of becoming fluid when disturbed (as by shaking) — **thixo·tro·pic** \ˌthik-sə-ˈtrō-pik, -ˈträ-\ *adj*

ThM *abbr* [NL *theologiae magister*] master of theology

THM *abbr* trihalomethane

tho \ˈt͟hō\ *var of* THOUGH

usage While never extremely common, *tho* and *thru* have a long history of occasional use as spelling variants of *though* and *through.* Their greatest popularity occurred in the late 19th and early 20th centuries, when their adoption was advocated by spelling reformers. Their current use occurs chiefly in informal writing (as in personal letters) and in some technical journals.

[1]**thole** \ˈthōl\ *vb* **tholed; thol·ing** [ME, fr. OE *tholian* — more at TOLERATE] (bef. 12c) *chiefly dial* : ENDURE

[2]**thole** *n* [ME *tholle,* fr. OE *thol;* akin to ON *thollr* fir tree, peg, Gk *tylos* knob, callus] (bef. 12c) **1** : either of a pair of pins set in the gunwale of a boat to hold an oar in place **2** : PEG, PIN

tho·lei·ite \ˈtō-lə-ˌīt, ˈthō-\ *n* [G *Tholeiit,* fr. *Tholey,* village in Saarland, Germany + G *-it* -ite] (1866) : a basaltic rock that is rich in aluminum and low in potassium, is found typically in the ocean floor, and is prob. derived from the earth's mantle — **tho·lei·it·ic** \ˌtō-lə-ˈi-tik, ˌthō-\ *adj*

thole·pin \ˈthōl-ˌpin\ *n* (1598) : THOLE 1

Thom·as \ˈtä-məs\ *n* [Gk *Thōmas,* fr. Heb *t'ōm* twin] (bef. 12c) : an apostle who demanded proof of Jesus' resurrection

Tho·mism \ˈtō-ˌmi-zəm\ *n* [NL *Thomista* Thomist, fr. St. *Thomas* Aquinas] (ca. 1731) : the scholastic philosophical and theological system of St. Thomas Aquinas — **Tho·mist** \-mist\ *n or adj* — **Tho·mis·tic** \tō-ˈmis-tik\ *adj*

Thomp·son submachine gun \ˈtäm(p)-sən-\ *n* [John T. *Thompson* †1940 Am. army officer] (1920) : a .45 caliber submachine gun with a drum or stick magazine, a pistol grip, and a detachable buttstock

Thom·son's gazelle \ˈtäm(p)-sənz-\ *n* [Joseph *Thomson* †1895 Scot. explorer] (1897) : a small gazelle (*Gazella thomsonii*) of eastern Africa that is tan above and white below with a broad black stripe on each side

thong \ˈthȯŋ\ *n* [ME, fr. OE *thwong;* akin to ON *thvengr* thong] (bef. 12c) **1 :** a strip esp. of leather or hide **2 :** a sandal held on the foot by a thong fitting between the toes and connected to a strap across the top or around the sides of the foot **3 :** an article of swimwear or underwear consisting of a narrow strip of material that passes between the thighs and connects with a waistband — **thonged** \ˈthȯŋd\ *adj*
Thor \ˈthȯr\ *n* [ON *Thōrr*] (bef. 12c) **:** the Norse god of thunder, weather, and crops
tho·rac·ic \thə-ˈra-sik\ *adj* (ca. 1658) **:** of, relating to, located within, or involving the thorax — **tho·rac·i·cal·ly** \-si-k(ə-)lē\ *adv*
thoracic duct *n* (ca. 1741) **:** the main trunk of the system of lymphatic vessels that lies along the front of the spinal column and opens into the left subclavian vein
tho·ra·cot·o·my \ˌthȯr-ə-ˈkä-tə-mē\ *n, pl* **-mies** [L *thorac-, thorax* + ISV *-tomy*] (ca. 1857) **:** surgical incision of the chest wall
tho·rax \ˈthȯr-ˌaks\ *n, pl* **tho·rax·es** *or* **tho·ra·ces** \ˈthȯr-ə-ˌsēz\ [ME, fr. L *thorac-, thorax* breastplate, thorax, fr. Gk *thōrak-, thōrax*] (15c) **1 :** the part of the mammalian body between the neck and the abdomen; *also* **:** its cavity in which the heart and lungs lie **2 :** the middle of the three chief divisions of the body of an insect; *also* **:** the corresponding part of a crustacean or an arachnid
Tho·ra·zine \ˈthȯr-ə-ˌzēn\ *trademark* — used for chlorpromazine
tho·ria \ˈthȯr-ē-ə\ *n* [NL, fr. *thorium* + *-a*] (ca. 1841) **:** a powdery white oxide of thorium ThO_2 used esp. as a catalyst and in crucibles and refractories and optical glass
tho·ri·a·nite \-ē-ə-ˌnīt\ *n* [irreg. fr. *thoria*] (1904) **:** a strongly radioactive mineral that is an oxide of thorium and often contains rare earth elements
tho·rite \ˈthȯr-ˌīt\ *n* [Sw *thorit,* fr. NL *thorium*] (1832) **:** a rare mineral that is a brown to black or sometimes orange-yellow silicate of thorium resembling zircon
tho·ri·um \ˈthȯr-ē-əm\ *n* [NL, fr. ON *Thōrr* Thor] (1832) **:** a radioactive metallic element that is obtained esp. from monazite and is usu. associated with rare earths — see ELEMENT table
thorn \ˈthȯrn\ *n, often attrib* [ME, fr. OE; akin to OHG *dorn* thorn, Skt *tṛṇa* grass, blade of grass] (bef. 12c) **1 :** a woody plant bearing sharp impeding processes (as prickles or spines); *esp* **:** HAWTHORN **2 a :** a sharp rigid process on a plant; *specif* **:** a short, indurated, sharp-pointed, and leafless modified branch **b :** any of various sharp spinose structures on an animal **3 :** the runic letter þ used in Old English and Middle English to represent either of the fricatives \th\ or \th\ and in Icelandic to represent \th\ **4 :** something that causes distress or irritation — often used in the phrase *thorn in one's side* — **thorned** \ˈthȯrnd\ *adj* — **thorn·less** \ˈthȯrn-ləs\ *adj* — **thorn·like** \-ˌlīk\ *adj*
thorn apple *n* (1578) **1 :** JIMSONWEED; *also* **:** any plant of the same genus **2 :** the fruit of a hawthorn; *also* **:** HAWTHORN
thorn·back \ˈthȯrn-ˌbak\ *n* (14c) **:** any of various ray fishes having spines on the back
thorn·bush \-ˌbu̇sh\ *n* (15c) **1 :** any of various spiny or thorny shrubs or small trees **2 :** a low growth of thorny shrubs esp. of dry tropical regions
thorny \ˈthȯr-nē\ *adj* **thorn·i·er; -est** (bef. 12c) **1 :** full of thorns **2 :** full of difficulties or controversial points **:** TICKLISH ⟨a ~ problem⟩ — **thorn·i·ness** *n*
thoro *nonstand var of* THOROUGH
[1]**thor·ough** \ˈthər-(ˌ)ō, *sometimes* ˈthȯr-; ˈthə-(ˌ)rō\ *prep* [ME *thorow,* fr. OE *thurh, thuruh,* prep. & adv.] (bef. 12c) *archaic* **:** THROUGH
[2]**thorough** *adv* (bef. 12c) *archaic* **:** THROUGH
[3]**thorough** *adj* (15c) **1 :** carried through to completion **:** EXHAUSTIVE ⟨a ~ search⟩ **2 a :** marked by full detail ⟨a ~ description⟩ **b :** careful about detail **:** PAINSTAKING ⟨a ~ scholar⟩ **c :** complete in all respects ⟨~ pleasure⟩ **d :** having full mastery (as of an art) ⟨a ~ musician⟩ — **thor·ough·ly** *adv* — **thor·ough·ness** *n*
thor·ough·bass \ˈthər-ə-ˌbās, ˈthə-rə-\ *n* (1662) **:** CONTINUO
thor·ough·brace \-ˌbrās\ *n* (1837) **:** any of several leather straps supporting the body of a carriage and serving as springs
[1]**thor·ough·bred** \-ˌbred\ *adj* (1701) **1 :** thoroughly trained or skilled ⟨a ~ soldier⟩ **2 :** bred from the best blood through a long line **:** PUREBRED ⟨~ dogs⟩ **3 a** *cap* **:** of, relating to, or being a Thoroughbred horse **b :** having characteristics resembling those of a Thoroughbred
[2]**thoroughbred** *n* (1820) **1 :** a purebred or pedigreed animal **2 :** a thoroughly educated or skilled person **3** *cap* **:** any of an English breed of light speedy horses kept chiefly for racing that originated from crosses between English mares of uncertain ancestry and Arabian stallions
thor·ough·fare \-ˌfer\ *n* (14c) **1 :** a way or place for passage: as **a :** a street open at both ends **b :** a main road **2 a :** PASSAGE, TRANSIT **b :** the conditions necessary for passing through
thor·ough·go·ing \ˌthər-ə-ˈgō-iŋ, ˌthə-rə-, -ˈgȯ(-)iŋ\ *adj* (1800) **:** marked by thoroughness or zeal **:** THOROUGH, COMPLETE ⟨~ changes⟩ ⟨a ~ traditionalist⟩ — **thor·ough·go·ing·ly** *adv*
thor·ough–paced \-ˈpāst\ *adj* (1646) **1 :** THOROUGH, COMPLETE ⟨he has been a ~ little villain —Charles Dickens⟩ **2 :** thoroughly trained **:** ACCOMPLISHED
thor·ough·pin \ˈthər-ə-ˌpin, ˈthə-rə-\ *n* (1789) **:** a synovial swelling just above the hock of a horse on both sides of the leg and slightly anterior to the hamstring tendon that is sometimes associated with lameness
thor·ough·wort \-ˌwərt, -ˌwȯrt\ *n* (1814) **:** BONESET
thorp \ˈthȯrp\ *n* [ME, fr. OE *throp, thorp;* akin to OHG *dorf* village, L *trabs* beam, roof] (bef. 12c) *archaic* **:** VILLAGE, HAMLET
those [ME, fr. *those* these, fr. OE *thās,* pl. of *thes* this — more at THIS] *pl of* THAT
[1]**thou** \ˈthau̇\ *pron* [ME, fr. OE *thū;* akin to OHG *dū* thou, L *tu,* Gk *sy*] (bef. 12c) *archaic* **:** the one addressed ⟨~ shalt have no other gods before me —Exod 20:3(AV)⟩ — used esp. in ecclesiastical or literary language and by Friends as the universal form of address to one person; compare THEE, THINE, THY, YE, YOU
[2]**thou** *vt* (15c) **:** to address as *thou*
[3]**thou** \ˈthau̇\ *n, pl* **thou** [short for *thousand*] (1867) **:** a thousand of something (as dollars) ⟨paid 25 ~ for the car⟩
[1]**though** \ˈthō\ *conj* [ME, adv. & conj., of Scand origin; akin to ON *thō* nevertheless; akin to OE *thēah* nevertheless, OHG *doh*] (bef. 12c) **1 :** in spite of the fact that **:** WHILE ⟨~ they know the war is lost, they continue to fight —Bruce Bliven †1977⟩ **2 :** in spite of the possibility that **:** even if ⟨~ I may fail, I will try⟩
[2]**though** *adv* (13c) **:** HOWEVER, NEVERTHELESS ⟨It's hard work. I enjoy it ~⟩
[1]**thought** *past and past part of* THINK
[2]**thought** \ˈthȯt\ *n* [ME, fr. OE *thōht;* akin to OE *thencan* to think — more at THINK] (bef. 12c) **1 a :** the action or process of thinking **:** COGITATION **b :** serious consideration **:** REGARD **c** *archaic* **:** RECOLLECTION, REMEMBRANCE **2 a :** reasoning power **b :** the power to imagine **:** CONCEPTION **3 :** something that is thought: as **a :** an individual act or product of thinking **b :** a developed intention or plan ⟨had no ~ of leaving home⟩ **c :** something (as an opinion or belief) in the mind ⟨he spoke his ~*s* freely⟩ **d :** the intellectual product or the organized views and principles of a period, place, group, or individual ⟨contemporary Western ~⟩ *syn* see IDEA — **a thought :** a little **:** SOMEWHAT ⟨*a thought* too much vinegar in the dressing⟩
thought experiment *n* (1945) **:** GEDANKENEXPERIMENT
thought·ful \ˈthȯt-fəl\ *adj* (13c) **1 a :** absorbed in thought **:** MEDITATIVE **b :** characterized by careful reasoned thinking ⟨a ~ essay⟩ **2 a :** having thoughts **:** HEEDFUL ⟨became ~ about religion⟩ **b :** given to or chosen or made with heedful anticipation of the needs and wants of others ⟨a kind and ~ friend⟩ — **thought·ful·ly** \-fə-lē\ *adv* — **thought·ful·ness** *n*
thought·less \-ləs\ *adj* (1592) **1 a :** insufficiently alert **:** CARELESS **b :** RECKLESS, RASH ⟨~ actions⟩ **2 :** devoid of thought **:** INSENSATE **3 :** lacking concern for others **:** INCONSIDERATE ⟨rude and ~ behavior⟩ ⟨a ~ remark⟩ — **thought·less·ly** *adv* — **thought·less·ness** *n*
thought–out \-ˈau̇t\ *adj* (1865) **:** produced or arrived at through mental effort and esp. through careful and thorough consideration ⟨a ~ plan⟩
thought·way \-ˌwā\ *n* (ca. 1944) **:** a way of thinking that is characteristic of a particular group, time, or culture
thou·sand \ˈthau̇-zᵊn(d)\ *n, pl* **thousands** *or* **thousand** [ME, fr. OE *thūsend;* akin to OHG *dūsunt* thousand, Lith *tūkstantis,* and prob. to Skt *tavas* strong, L *tumēre* to swell — more at THUMB] (bef. 12c) **1 —** see NUMBER table **2 :** a very large number ⟨~*s* of ants⟩ — **thousand** *adj* — **thou·sand·fold** \-zᵊn(d)-ˌfōld\ *adj or adv* — **thou·sandth** \-zᵊn(t)th\ *adj or n*
Thousand Island dressing *n* [*Thousand Islands,* islands in the St. Lawrence River] (1924) **:** mayonnaise with chili sauce and seasonings (as chopped pimientos, green peppers, and onion)
thousand–leg·ger \ˌthau̇-zᵊn(d)-ˈle-gər, -ˈlā-\ *n* (1914) **:** MILLIPEDE
thousands place *n* (1937) **:** the place four to the left of the decimal point in a number expressed in the Arabic system of writing numbers
Thra·cian \ˈthrā-shən\ *n* (1565) **1 :** a native or inhabitant of Thrace **2 :** the Indo-European language of the ancient Thracians — see INDO-EUROPEAN LANGUAGES table — **Thracian** *adj*
[1]**thrall** \ˈthrȯl\ *n* [ME *thral,* fr. OE *thræl,* fr. ON *thræll*] (bef. 12c) **1 a :** a servant slave **:** BONDMAN; *also* **:** SERF **b :** a person in moral or mental servitude **2 a :** a state of servitude or submission ⟨in ~ to his emotions⟩ **b :** a state of complete absorption ⟨mountains could hold me in ~ with a subtle attraction of their own —Elyne Mitchell⟩ — **thrall** *adj* — **thrall·dom** *or* **thral·dom** \ˈthrȯl-dəm\ *n*
[2]**thrall** *vt* (13c) *archaic* **:** ENTHRALL, ENSLAVE
[1]**thrash** \ˈthrash\ *vb* [alter. of *thresh*] *vt* (1568) **1 :** to separate the seeds of from the husks and straw by beating **:** THRESH 1 **2 a :** to beat soundly with or as if with a stick or whip **:** FLOG **b :** to defeat decisively or severely ⟨~*ed* the visiting team⟩ **3 :** to swing, beat, or strike in the manner of a rapidly moving flail ⟨~*ing* his arms⟩ **4 a :** to go over again and again ⟨~ the matter over inconclusively⟩ **b :** to hammer out **:** FORGE ⟨~ out a plan⟩ ~ *vi* **1 :** THRESH 1 **2 :** to deal blows or strokes like one using a flail or whip **3 :** to move or stir about violently **:** toss about ⟨~ in bed with a fever⟩ *syn* see SWING
[2]**thrash** *n* (1840) **1 :** an act of thrashing **2 :** rock music (as heavy metal or punk rock) that is extremely fast and loud
[1]**thrash·er** \ˈthra-shər\ *n* (1632) **1 :** one that thrashes or threshes **2 :** an avid skateboarder
[2]**thrasher** *n* [perh. alter. of dial. *thresher* thrush] (ca. 1814) **:** any of various American oscine birds (family Mimidae, esp. genus *Toxostoma*) related to the mockingbird that resemble thrushes but have a usu. long curved bill and long tail

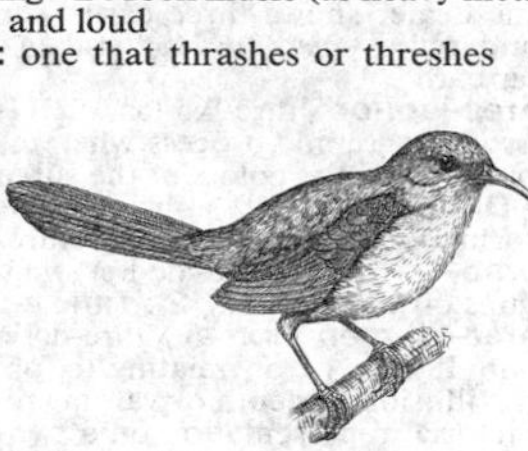
[2]thrasher

thra·son·i·cal \thrā-ˈsä-ni-kəl, thrə-\ *adj* [L *Thrason-, Thraso* Thraso, braggart soldier in the comedy *Eunuchus* by Terence] (1564) **:** of, relating to, resembling, or characteristic of Thraso **:** BRAGGING, BOASTFUL — **thra·son·i·cal·ly** \-k(ə-)lē\ *adv*
[1]**thraw** \ˈthrä\ *vb* [ME — more at THROW] *vt* (bef. 12c) **1** *chiefly Scot* **:** to cause to twist or turn **2** *chiefly Scot* **:** CROSS, THWART ~ *vi* **1** *chiefly Scot* **:** TWIST, TURN **2** *chiefly Scot* **:** to be in disagreement
[2]**thraw** *n* (1513) **1** *chiefly Scot* **:** TWIST, TURN **2** *chiefly Scot* **:** ill humor
thra·wart \ˈthrä-wərt\ *adj* [ME (Sc), alter. of ME *fraward, froward* froward] (15c) **1** *chiefly Scot* **:** STUBBORN **2** *Scot* **:** CROOKED
thrawn \ˈthrän\ *adj* [ME (Sc) *thrawin,* fr. pp. of ME *thrawen* to twist] (15c) *chiefly Scot* **:** lacking in pleasing or attractive qualities: as **a :** PERVERSE, RECALCITRANT **b :** CROOKED, MISSHAPEN — **thrawn·ly** *adv, chiefly Scot*
[1]**thread** \ˈthred\ *n* [ME *thred,* fr. OE *thrǣd;* akin to OHG *drāt* wire, OE *thrāwan* to cause to twist or turn — more at THROW] (bef. 12c) **1 a :** a filament, a group of filaments twisted together, or a filamentous length formed by spinning and twisting short textile fibers into a continuous strand **b :** a piece of thread **2 a :** any of various natural filaments

⟨the ∼s of a spiderweb⟩ **b** : a slender stream (as of water) **c** : a projecting helical rib (as in a fitting or on a pipe) by which parts can be screwed together : SCREW THREAD **3** : something continuous or drawn out: as **a** : a line of reasoning or train of thought that connects the parts in a sequence (as of ideas or events) ⟨lost the ∼ of the story⟩ **b** : a continuing element ⟨a ∼ of melancholy marked all his writing⟩ **c** : a series of newsgroup messages following a single topic **4** : a tenuous or feeble support ⟨hung on by a ∼⟩ **5** *pl* : CLOTHING — **thread·less** \-ləs\ *adj* — **thread·like** \-ˌlīk\ *adj*

²**thread** *vt* (14c) **1 a** : to pass a thread through the eye of (a needle) **b** : to arrange a thread, yarn, or lead-in piece in working position for use in (a machine) **2 a** (1) : to pass something through in the manner of a thread ⟨∼ a pipe with wire⟩ (2) : to pass (as a tape, line, or film) into or through something ⟨∼*ed* a fresh roll of film into the camera⟩ **b** : to make one's way through or between ⟨∼*ing* narrow alleys⟩; *also* : to make one's way usu. cautiously through a hazardous situation **3** : to put together on or as if on a thread : STRING ⟨∼ beads⟩ **4** : to interweave with or as if with threads : INTERSPERSE ⟨dark hair ∼*ed* with silver⟩ **5** : to form a screw thread on or in ∼ *vi* **1** : WEAVE 2 ⟨the car ∼*ed* through traffic⟩ **2** : to form a thread — **thread·er** *n*

thread·bare \ˈthred-ˌber\ *adj* (14c) **1 a** : having the nap worn off so that the thread shows : SHABBY ⟨∼ clothes⟩ **b** : wearing threadbare clothing : very poor ⟨took in ∼ relatives —Russell Baker⟩ **c** : barely adequate because of cheapness or shabbiness ⟨a ∼ production⟩ **2** : exhausted of interest or freshness ***syn*** see TRITE — **thread·bare·ness** *n*

thread·fin \-ˌfin\ *n* (ca. 1890) : any of various bony fishes (family Polynemidae, esp. genus *Polydactylus*) having elongated filamentous rays on the pectoral fin; *also* : a fish (as *Dorosoma pretense* of the herring family) having usu. one similar ray extending from a fin

thread·worm \-ˌwərm\ *n* (1802) : a long slender nematode worm (as a pinworm or strongyle)

thready \ˈthre-dē\ *adj* (1597) **1** : consisting of or bearing fibers or filaments ⟨a ∼ bark⟩ **2 a** : resembling a thread : FILAMENTOUS **b** : tending to form or draw out into strands : ROPY **3** : lacking in fullness, body, or vigor : THIN ⟨a ∼ voice⟩ — **thread·i·ness** *n*

threap \ˈthrēp\ *vt* [ME *threpen,* fr. OE *thrēapian*] (bef. 12c) **1** *chiefly Scot* : SCOLD, CHIDE **2** *chiefly Scot* : to maintain persistently

¹**threat** \ˈthret\ *n* [ME *thret* coercion, threat, fr. OE *thrēat* coercion; akin to MHG *drōz* annoyance, L *trudere* to push, thrust] (bef. 12c) **1** : an expression of intention to inflict evil, injury, or damage **2** : one that threatens **3** : an indication of something impending ⟨the sky held a ∼ of rain⟩

²**threat** *vb* (bef. 12c) *archaic* : THREATEN

threat·en \ˈthre-tᵊn\ *vb* **threat·ened; threat·en·ing** \ˈthret-niŋ, ˈthre-tᵊn-iŋ\ *vt* (13c) **1** : to utter threats against **2 a** : to give signs or warning of : PORTEND ⟨the clouds ∼*ed* rain⟩ **b** : to hang over dangerously : MENACE ⟨famine ∼*s* the city⟩ **3** : to announce as intended or possible ⟨the workers ∼*ed* a strike⟩ **4** : to cause to feel insecure or anxious ⟨felt ∼*ed* by his brother's success⟩ ∼ *vi* **1** : to utter threats **2** : to portend evil — **threat·en·er** \ˈthret-nər, ˈthre-tᵊn-ər\ *n* — **threat·en·ing·ly** \ˈthret-niŋ-lē, ˈthre-tᵊn-iŋ-\ *adv*

threatened *adj* (1960) : having an uncertain chance of continued survival ⟨a ∼ species⟩; *specif* : likely to become an endangered species

three \ˈthrē\ *n* [ME, fr. *three,* adj., fr. OE *thrīe* (masc.), *thrēo* (fem. & neut.); akin to OHG *drī* three, L *tres,* Gk *treis*] (bef. 12c) **1** — see NUMBER table **2** : the third in a set or series ⟨the ∼ of hearts⟩ **3 a** : something having three units or members **b** : THREE-POINTER — **three** *adj* — **three** *pron, pl in constr*

three–bag·ger \-ˈba-gər\ *n* (1881) : TRIPLE

three–ball \-ˌbȯl\ *adj* (1839) : relating to or being a golf match in which three players compete against one another with each playing a single ball

three–card monte \ˈthrē-ˈkärd-\ *n* (1854) : a gambling game in which the dealer shows three cards, shuffles them, places them face down, and invites spectators to bet they can identify the location of a particular card

three–col·or \ˈthrē-ˈkə-lər\ *adj* (1893) : being or relating to a printing or photographic process wherein three primary colors are used to reproduce all the colors of the subject

3–D \ˈthrē-ˈdē\ *n* [*D,* abbr. of *dimensional*] (1951) : a three-dimensional form; *also* : an image or a picture produced in it — **3–D** *adj*

three–deck·er \ˈthrē-ˈde-kər\ *n* (1795) **1** : a wooden warship carrying guns on three decks **2** : TRIPLE-DECKER

three–di·men·sion·al \ˈthrē-də-ˈmench-nəl, -ˈmen(t)-shə-nᵊl *also* -dī-\ *adj* (1872) **1** : of, relating to, or having three dimensions **2** : giving the illusion of depth or varying distances — used esp. of an image or a pictorial representation on a two-dimensional medium when this illusion is enhanced by stereoscopic means **3** : describing or being described in well-rounded completeness ⟨a ∼ analysis of multiple historical processes —L. L. Snyder⟩ **4** : true to life : LIFELIKE — **three–di·men·sion·al·i·ty** \-ˌmen(t)-shə-ˈna-lə-tē\ *n*

three·fold \ˈthrē-ˌfōld, -ˈfōld\ *adj* (bef. 12c) **1** : having three parts or members : TRIPLE ⟨a ∼ purpose⟩ **2** : being three times as great or as many ⟨a ∼ increase⟩ — **three·fold** \-ˈfōld\ *adv*

three–gait·ed \-ˈgā-təd\ *adj* (1948) *of a horse* : trained to use the walk, trot, and canter

three–hand·ed \-ˈhan-dəd\ *adj* (1680) : played by three players ⟨∼ bridge⟩

Three Hours *n* (ca. 1891) : a service of devotion between noon and three o'clock on Good Friday

three–legged \ˈthrē-ˈlegd, -ˈlāgd; -ˈle-gəd, -ˈlā-\ *adj* (1596) : having three legs ⟨a ∼ stool⟩

three–legged race *n* (1872) : a race between pairs of competitors with each pair having their adjacent legs bound together

three–mile limit *n* (1876) : the limit of the marginal sea of three miles included in the territorial waters of a state

three of a kind (ca. 1897) : three cards of the same rank in one hand — see POKER illustration

three–peat \ˈthrē-ˌpēt\ *n* [blend of *three* and *repeat*] (1988) : a third consecutive championship — **three–peat** *vi*

three·pence \ˈthre-pən(t)s, ˈthri-, ˈthrə-, *US also* ˈthrē-pen(t)s\ *n* (1589) **1** *pl* **threepence** *or* **three·penc·es** : a coin worth threepence **2** : the sum of three British pennies

three·pen·ny \ˈthre-p(ə-)nē, ˈthri-, ˈthrə-, *US also* ˈthrē-ˌpe-nē\ *adj* (15c) **1** : costing or worth threepence **2** : POOR

three–phase *adj* (1892) : of, relating to, or operating by means of a combination of three circuits energized by alternating electromotive forces that differ in phase by one third of a cycle

three–piece *adj* (1904) : consisting of or made in three pieces ⟨a ∼ suit⟩

three–pointer *n* (1977) : a basketball shot or field goal from beyond the three-point line

three–point landing *n* (1918) : an airplane landing in which the two main wheels of the landing gear and the tail wheel or skid or nose wheel touch the ground simultaneously

three–point line *n* (1977) : a line on a basketball court forming an arc at a set distance (as 22 feet) from the basket beyond which a field goal counts for three points

three–quarter *adj* (1606) : extending to three-quarters of the normal full length ⟨a ∼ sleeve⟩

three–quarter–bound *adj* (ca. 1951) *of a book* : bound like a half-bound book but having the material on the spine extended to cover about one third of the boards — **three–quarter binding** *n*

three–ring circus *n* (1902) **1** : a circus with simultaneous performances in three rings **2** : something wild, confusing, engrossing, or entertaining

three R's *n pl* [fr. the facetiously used phrase *reading, 'riting, and 'rithmetic*] (1828) **1** : the fundamentals taught in elementary school; *esp* : reading, writing, and arithmetic **2** : the fundamental skills in a field of endeavor

three·score \ˈthrē-ˈskȯr\ *adj* (14c) : being three times twenty : SIXTY

three·some \ˈthrē-səm\ *n* (14c) **1** : a group of three persons or things : TRIO **2** : a golf match in which one person plays his or her ball against the ball of two others playing each stroke alternately

three–spined stickleback \ˈthrē-ˈspīn(d)-\ *n* (1769) : a stickleback (*Gasterosteus aculeatus*) chiefly of fresh and brackish waters that typically has three dorsal spines — called also *three-spine stickleback*

three–toed sloth \ˈthrē-ˈtōd-\ *n* (1847) : any of a genus (*Bradypus*) of sloths having three clawed digits on each foot and eight or nine vertebrae in the neck — compare TWO-TOED SLOTH

three–wheel·er \-ˌhwē-lər, -ˌwē-\ *n* (1886) : any of various vehicles having three wheels

thre·node \ˈthrē-ˌnōd, ˈthre-\ *n* (1614) : THRENODY — **thre·nod·ic** \thri-ˈnä-dik\ *adj* — **thren·o·dist** \ˈthre-nə-dist\ *n*

thren·o·dy \ˈthre-nə-dē\ *n, pl* **-dies** [Gk *thrēnōidia,* fr. *thrēnos* dirge + *aeidein* to sing — more at DRONE, ODE] (1634) : a song of lamentation for the dead : ELEGY

thre·o·nine \ˈthrē-ə-ˌnēn\ *n* [prob. fr. *threonic acid* ($C_4H_8O_5$)] (1936) : a colorless crystalline essential amino acid $C_4H_9NO_3$

thresh \ˈthresh, ˈthrash\ *vb* [ME *thresshen,* fr. OE *threscan;* akin to OHG *dreskan* to thresh] *vt* (bef. 12c) **1** : to separate seed from (a harvested plant) mechanically; *also* : to separate (seed) in this way **2** : THRASH 4 **3** : to strike repeatedly ∼ *vi* **1** : to thresh grain **2 a** : THRASH 2 **b** : THRASH 3

thresh·er \ˈthre-shər, ˈthra-\ *n* (13c) **1** : one that threshes; *esp* : THRESHING MACHINE **2** : THRESHER SHARK

thresher shark *n* (1888) : a large nearly cosmopolitan shark (*Alopias vulpinus*) that has a greatly elongated curved upper lobe of the tail which is often used to thresh the water to round up the schooling fish on which it feeds — see SHARK illustration

thresh·ing machine \ˈthre-shiŋ-, ˈthra-\ *n* (1775) : a machine for separating grain crops into grain or seeds and straw

thresh·old \ˈthresh-ˌhōld, ˈthre-ˌshōld\ *n* [ME *thresshold,* fr. OE *threscwald;* akin to ON *threskjǫldr* threshold, OE *threscan* to thresh] (bef. 12c) **1** : the plank, stone, or piece of timber that lies under a door : SILL **2 a** : GATE, DOOR **b** (1) : END, BOUNDARY; *specif* : the end of a runway (2) : the place or point of entering or beginning : OUTSET ⟨on the ∼ of a new age⟩ **3 a** : the point at which a physiological or psychological effect begins to be produced ⟨has a high ∼ for pain⟩ **b** : a level, point, or value above which something is true or will take place and below which it is not or will not

threw *past of* THROW

thrice \ˈthrīs\ *adv* [ME *thrie, thries,* fr. OE *thriga;* akin to OFris *thria* three times, OE *thrīe* three] (13c) **1** : three times — often used in combination ⟨*thrice*-married⟩ **2 a** : in a threefold manner or degree **b** : to a high degree

thrift \ˈthrift\ *n* [ME, fr. ON, prosperity, fr. *thrīfask* to thrive] (13c) **1** : healthy and vigorous growth **2** : careful management esp. of money **3** *chiefly Scot* : gainful occupation **4** : any of a genus (*Armeria*) of low-growing perennial evergreen herbs of the plumbago family; *esp* : a tufted herb (*A. maritima*) with pink or white flower heads **5** : a savings bank or savings and loan association — called also *thrift institution*

thrift·less \ˈthrift-ləs\ *adj* (15c) **1** : lacking usefulness or worth **2** : careless, wasteful, or incompetent in handling money or resources : IMPROVIDENT — **thrift·less·ly** *adv* — **thrift·less·ness** *n*

thrift shop *n* (1944) : a shop that sells secondhand articles and esp. clothes and is often run for charitable purposes

thrifty \ˈthrif-tē\ *adj* **thrift·i·er; -est** (14c) **1** : thriving by industry and frugality : PROSPEROUS **2** : growing vigorously **3** : given to or marked by economy and good management ***syn*** see SPARING — **thrift·i·ly** \-tə-lē\ *adv* — **thrift·i·ness** \-tē-nəs\ *n*

thrill \ˈthril\ *vb* [ME *thirlen, thrillen* to pierce, fr. OE *thyrlian,* fr. *thyrel* hole, fr. *thurh* through — more at THROUGH] *vt* (1592) **1 a** : to cause to experience a sudden sharp feeling of excitement ⟨the news ∼*ed* him⟩ **b** : to cause to have a shivering or tingling sensation **2** : to cause to vibrate or tremble perceptibly ∼ *vi* **1** : to move or pass so as to cause a sudden wave of emotion **2** : to become thrilled: **a** : to experience a sudden sharp excitement **b** : TINGLE, THROB **3** : TREMBLE, VIBRATE — **thrill** *n* — **thrill·ing·ly** \ˈthri-liŋ-lē\ *adv*

thril·ler \ˈthri-lər\ *n* (1889) : one that thrills; *esp* : a work of fiction or drama designed to hold the interest by the use of a high degree of intrigue, adventure, or suspense

thrips \ˈthrips\ *n, pl* **thrips** [L, woodworm, fr. Gk] (1795) : any of an order (Thysanoptera) of small to minute sucking insects many of which feed often destructively on plant juices

thrive \ˈthrīv\ *vi* **thrived** *or* **throve** \ˈthrōv\; **thrived** *also* **thriv·en** \ˈthri-vən\; **thriv·ing** \ˈthrī-viŋ\ [ME, fr. ON *thrīfask,* prob. refl. of *thrīfa* to grasp] (13c) **1 :** to grow vigorously : FLOURISH **2 :** to gain in wealth or possessions : PROSPER **3 :** to progress toward or realize a goal despite or because of circumstances — often used with *on* ⟨~*s* on conflict⟩ — **thriv·er** \ˈthrī-vər\ *n*

thriving *adj* (1604) : characterized by success or prosperity ⟨a ~ business⟩ — **thriv·ing·ly** \ˈthrī-viŋ-lē\ *adv*

thro \ˈthrü\ *prep* (15c) *archaic* : THROUGH

[1]**throat** \ˈthrōt\ *n* [ME *throte,* fr. OE; akin to OHG *drozza* throat] (bef. 12c) **1 a** (1) : the part of the neck in front of the spinal column (2) : the passage through the neck to the stomach and lungs **b** (1) : VOICE (2) : the seat of the voice **2 :** something resembling the throat esp. in being an entrance, a passageway, a constriction, or a narrowed part: as **a :** the orifice of a tubular organ esp. of a plant **b :** the opening in the vamp of a shoe at the instep **c :** the part of a tennis racket that connects the head with the shaft **3 :** the curved part of an anchor's arm where it joins the shank — see ANCHOR illustration — **at each other's throats :** in open and aggressive conflict

[2]**throat** *vt* (ca. 1611) **1 :** to utter in the throat : MUTTER **2 :** to sing or enunciate in a throaty voice

throat·ed \ˈthrō-təd\ *adj* (ca. 1530) : having a throat esp. of a specified kind — usu. used in combination ⟨white-*throated*⟩

throat·latch \ˈthrōt-ˌlach\ *n* (1764) **1 :** a strap of a bridle or halter passing under a horse's throat **2 :** the part of a horse's throat around which the throatlatch passes — see HORSE illustration

throaty \ˈthrō-tē\ *adj* **throat·i·er; -est** (ca. 1645) **1 :** uttered or produced from low in the throat ⟨a ~ voice⟩ **2 :** heavy, thick, and deep as if from the throat ⟨~ notes of a horn⟩ — **throat·i·ly** \ˈthrō-tə-lē\ *adv* — **throat·i·ness** \ˈthrō-tē-nəs\ *n*

[1]**throb** \ˈthräb\ *vi* **throbbed; throb·bing** [ME *throbben*] (14c) **1 :** to pulsate or pound with abnormal force or rapidity **2 :** to beat or vibrate rhythmically — **throb·ber** *n*

[2]**throb** *n* (1579) : BEAT, PULSE

throe \ˈthrō\ *n* [ME *thrawe, throwe,* fr. OE *thrawu, thrēa* threat, pang; akin to OHG *drawa* threat] (13c) **1 :** PANG, SPASM ⟨death ~*s*⟩ ⟨~*s* of childbirth⟩ **2** *pl* : a hard or painful struggle ⟨the ~*s* of revolutionary social change —M. D. Geismar⟩

thromb- *or* **thrombo-** *comb form* [Gk *thrombos* clot] : blood clot : clotting of blood ⟨*thrombin*⟩ ⟨*thrombo*plastic⟩

throm·bin \ˈthräm-bən\ *n* [ISV] (1898) : a proteolytic enzyme that is formed from prothrombin and facilitates the clotting of blood by catalyzing conversion of fibrinogen to fibrin

throm·bo·cyte \-bə-ˌsīt\ *n* [ISV] (1893) : PLATELET; *also* : a cell with a similar clotting function — **throm·bo·cyt·ic** \ˌthräm-bə-ˈsi-tik\ *adj*

throm·bo·cy·to·pe·nia \ˌthräm-bə-ˌsī-tə-ˈpē-nē-ə, -nyə\ *n* [NL, fr. ISV *thrombocyte* + NL *-o-* + *-penia*] (1923) : persistent decrease in the number of platelets in the blood that is often associated with hemorrhagic conditions — **throm·bo·cy·to·pe·nic** \-nik\ *adj*

throm·bo·em·bo·lism \ˌthräm-bō-ˈem-bə-ˌli-zəm\ *n* (1907) : the blocking of a blood vessel by a particle that has broken away from a blood clot at its site of formation — **throm·bo·em·bol·ic** \-em-ˈbä-lik\ *adj*

throm·bo·ki·nase \ˌthräm-bō-ˈkī-ˌnās, -ˌnāz\ *n* [ISV] (1908) : THROMBOPLASTIN

[1]**throm·bo·lyt·ic** \ˌthräm-bə-ˈli-tik\ *adj* (1929) : destroying or breaking up a thrombus ⟨a ~ agent⟩ ⟨~ therapy⟩ — **throm·bol·y·sis** \-ˈbä-lə-səs\ *n*

[2]**thrombolytic** *n* (1965) : a thrombolytic drug : CLOT-BUSTER

throm·bo·phle·bi·tis \ˌthräm-bō-fli-ˈbī-təs\ *n* [NL] (ca. 1890) : inflammation of a vein with formation of a thrombus

throm·bo·plas·tic \-ˈplas-tik\ *adj* [ISV] (1911) : initiating or accelerating the clotting of blood

throm·bo·plas·tin \-ˈplas-tən\ *n* [ISV, fr. *thromboplastic*] (1911) : a complex enzyme found esp. in platelets that functions in the conversion of prothrombin into thrombin in the clotting of blood

throm·bo·sis \thräm-ˈbō-səs, thrəm-\ *n, pl* **-bo·ses** \-ˌsēz\ [NL, fr. Gk *thrombōsis* clotting, fr. *thrombousthai* to become clotted, fr. *thrombos* clot] (1866) : the formation or presence of a blood clot within a blood vessel — **throm·bot·ic** \-ˈbä-tik\ *adj*

throm·box·ane \thräm-ˈbäk-ˌsān\ *n* [*thromb-* + *ox-* + *-ane*] (1975) : any of several substances that are produced esp. by platelets, are formed from endoperoxides, cause constriction of vascular and bronchial smooth muscle, and promote blood clotting

throm·bus \ˈthräm-bəs\ *n, pl* **throm·bi** \-ˌbī, -ˌbē\ [NL, fr. Gk *thrombos* clot] (ca. 1693) : a clot of blood formed within a blood vessel and remaining attached to its place of origin — compare EMBOLUS

[1]**throne** \ˈthrōn\ *n* [ME *trone, throne,* fr. AF *trone,* fr. L *thronus,* fr. Gk *thronos* — more at FIRM] (13c) **1 a :** the chair of state of a sovereign or high dignitary (as a bishop) **b :** the seat of a deity **2 :** royal power and dignity : SOVEREIGNTY **3** *pl* : an order of angels — see CELESTIAL HIERARCHY

[2]**throne** *vb* **throned; thron·ing** *vt* (14c) **1 :** to seat on a throne **2 :** to invest with kingly rank or power ~ *vi* **1 :** to sit on a throne **2 :** to hold kingly power

throne room *n* (1845) : a formal audience room containing the throne of a sovereign

[1]**throng** \ˈthrȯŋ\ *n* [ME *thrang, throng,* fr. OE *thrang, gethrang;* akin to OE *thringan* to press, crowd, OHG *dringan,* Lith *trenkti* to jolt] (bef. 12c) **1 a :** a multitude of assembled persons **b :** a large number : HOST **2 a :** a crowding together of many persons **b :** a pressing increase of activity ⟨this ~ of business —S. R. Crockett⟩ ***syn*** see CROWD

[2]**throng** *vb* **thronged; throng·ing** \ˈthrȯŋ-iŋ\ *vt* (14c) **1 :** to crowd upon : PRESS ⟨a celebrity ~*ed* by fans⟩ **2 :** to crowd into : PACK ⟨shoppers ~*ing* the streets⟩ ~ *vi* : to crowd together in great numbers

thros·tle \ˈthrä-səl\ *n* [ME, fr. OE — more at THRUSH] (bef. 12c) : [1]THRUSH; *specif* : SONG THRUSH

[1]**throt·tle** \ˈthrä-tᵊl\ *vb* **throt·tled; throt·tling** \ˈthrät-liŋ, ˈthrä-tᵊl-iŋ\ [ME *throtelen,* fr. *throte* throat] *vt* (15c) **1 a** (1) : to compress the throat of : CHOKE (2) : to kill by such action **b :** to prevent or check expression or activity of : SUPPRESS ⟨policies that ~ creativity⟩ **2 a :** to decrease the flow of (as steam or fuel to an engine) by a valve **b :** to regulate and esp. to reduce the speed of (as an engine) by such means **c :** to vary the thrust of (a rocket engine) during flight ~ *vi* : to throttle something (as an engine) — usu. used with *back* or *down* ⟨the pilot *throttled* back⟩ — **throt·tler** \ˈthrät-lər, ˈthrä-tᵊl-ər\ *n*

[2]**throttle** *n* [perh. fr. ME **throtel,* dim. of *throte* throat] (ca. 1547) **1 a :** THROAT 1a **b :** TRACHEA 1 **2 a :** a valve for regulating the supply of a fluid (as steam) to an engine; *esp* : the valve controlling the volume of vaporized fuel charge delivered to the cylinders of an internal combustion engine **b :** the lever controlling this valve **c :** the condition of being throttled — **at full throttle :** at full speed ⟨the project is proceeding *at full throttle*⟩

throt·tle·able \ˈthrä-tᵊl-ə-bəl\ *adj* (1960) : capable of having the thrust varied — used of a rocket engine

throt·tle·hold \ˈthrä-tᵊl-ˌhōld\ *n* (1935) : a vicious, strangling, or stultifying control

[1]**through** \ˈthrü\ *prep* [ME *thurh, thruh, through,* fr. OE *thurh;* akin to OHG *durh* through, L *trans* across, beyond, Skt *tarati* he crosses over] (bef. 12c) **1 a** (1) — used as a function word to indicate movement into at one side or point and out at another and esp. the opposite side of ⟨drove a nail ~ the board⟩ (2) : by way of ⟨left ~ the door⟩ (3) — used as a function word to indicate passage from one end or boundary to another ⟨a highway ~ the forest⟩ ⟨a road ~ the desert⟩ (4) : without stopping for : PAST ⟨drove ~ a red light⟩ **b** — used as a function word to indicate passage into and out of a treatment, handling, or process ⟨the matter has already passed ~ her hands⟩ **2** — used as a function word to indicate means, agency, or intermediacy: as **a :** by means of : by the agency of **b :** because of ⟨failed ~ ignorance⟩ **c :** by common descent from or relationship with ⟨related ~ their grandfather⟩ **3 a :** over the whole surface or extent of : THROUGHOUT ⟨homes scattered ~ the valley⟩ **b** — used as a function word to indicate movement within a large expanse ⟨flew ~ the air⟩ **c** — used as a function word to indicate exposure to a specified set of conditions ⟨put him ~ hell⟩ **4** — used as a function word to indicate a period of time: as **a :** during the entire period of ⟨all ~ her life⟩ **b :** from the beginning to the end of ⟨the tower stood ~ the earthquake⟩ **c :** to and including ⟨Monday ~ Friday⟩ **5 a** — used as a function word to indicate completion or exhaustion ⟨got ~ the book⟩ ⟨went ~ the money in a year⟩ **b** — used as a function word to indicate acceptance or approval esp. by an official body ⟨got the bill ~ the legislature⟩

[2]**through** *adv* (bef. 12c) **1 :** from one end or side to the other **2 a :** from beginning to end **b :** to completion, conclusion, or accomplishment ⟨see it ~⟩ **3 :** to the core : COMPLETELY ⟨soaked ~⟩ **4 :** into the open : OUT ⟨break ~⟩

[3]**through** *adj* (15c) **1 a :** extending from one surface to another ⟨a ~ mortise⟩ **b :** admitting free or continuous passage : DIRECT ⟨a ~ road⟩ **2 a** (1) : going from point of origin to destination without change or reshipment ⟨a ~ train⟩ (2) : of or relating to such movement ⟨a ~ ticket⟩ **b :** initiated at and destined for points outside a local zone ⟨~ traffic⟩ **3 a :** arrived at completion or accomplishment ⟨is ~ with the job⟩ **b :** WASHED-UP, FINISHED

through and through *adv* (15c) : in every way : THOROUGHLY

through–com·posed \ˌthrü-kəm-ˈpōzd\ *adj* (1884) *of a song* : having new music provided for each stanza — compare STROPHIC

through·ith·er *or* **through·oth·er** \ˈthrü-(ə-)t͟hər\ *adv* [[1]*through* + *other*] (1596) *chiefly Scot* : in confusion : PROMISCUOUSLY

through·ly \ˈthrü-lē\ *adv* (15c) *archaic* : in a thorough manner

[1]**through·out** \thrü-ˈau̇t\ *adv* (13c) **1 :** in or to every part : EVERYWHERE ⟨of one color ~⟩ **2 :** during the whole time or action : from beginning to end ⟨remained loyal ~⟩

[2]**throughout** *prep* (13c) **1 :** all the way from one end to the other of : in or to every part of ⟨cities ~ the United States⟩ **2 :** during the whole course or period of ⟨troubled her ~ her life⟩

through·put \ˈthrü-ˌpu̇t\ *n* (ca. 1915) : OUTPUT, PRODUCTION ⟨the ~ of a computer⟩

through street *n* (1930) : a street on which the through movement of traffic is given preference

throve *past of* THRIVE

[1]**throw** \ˈthrō\ *vb* **threw** \ˈthrü\; **thrown** \ˈthrōn\; **throw·ing** [ME *thrawen, throwen* to cause to twist, throw, fr. OE *thrāwan* to cause to twist or turn; akin to OHG *drāen* to turn, L *terere* to rub, Gk *tribein* to rub, *tetrainein* to bore, pierce] *vt* (13c) **1 a :** to propel through the air by a forward motion of the hand and arm ⟨~ a baseball⟩ **b :** to propel through the air in any manner ⟨a rifle that can ~ a bullet a mile⟩ **c :** PITCH 6b ⟨*threw* a no-hitter⟩ **2 a :** to cause to fall ⟨*threw* his opponent⟩ **b :** to cause to fall off : UNSEAT ⟨the horse *threw* its rider⟩ **c :** to get the better of : OVERCOME ⟨the problem didn't ~ her⟩ **3 a :** to fling (oneself) precipitately ⟨*threw* herself down on the sofa⟩ **b :** to drive or impel violently : DASH ⟨the ship was *thrown* on a reef⟩ **4 a** (1) : to put in a particular position or condition ⟨*threw* her arms around him⟩ ⟨*thrown* into chaos⟩ ⟨*threw* him into prison⟩ (2) : to put on or off hastily or carelessly ⟨*threw* on a coat⟩ **b :** to bring to bear : EXERT ⟨*threw* all his efforts into the boy's defense⟩ ⟨~ their weight behind the proposal⟩ **c :** BUILD, CONSTRUCT ⟨*threw* a pontoon bridge over the river⟩ **5 :** to form or shape on a potter's wheel **6 :** to deliver (a blow) in or as if in boxing **7 :** to twist two or more filaments of into a thread or yarn **8 a :** to make a cast of (dice or a specified number on dice) **b :** ROLL 1a ⟨~ a bowling ball⟩ **9 :** to give up : ABANDON **10 :** to send forth : PROJECT ⟨the setting sun *threw* long shadows⟩; *also* : SHED 3c ⟨~ some light on the matter⟩ **11 :** to make (oneself) dependent : commit (oneself) for help, support, or protection ⟨*threw* himself on the mercy of the court⟩ **12 :** DEPOSIT 2b ⟨the wine ~*s* sediment⟩ **13 :** to perform (as a stunt) successfully ⟨~*ing* tricks on a skateboard⟩ **14 :** to indulge in : give way to ⟨*threw* a temper tantrum⟩ **15 a :** to bring forth ⟨~*s* a good crop⟩ **b :** to give birth to ⟨*threw* large litters⟩ **16 :** to lose intentionally ⟨~ a game⟩ **17 a :** to move (a lever) so as to connect or disconnect parts of a clutch or switch; *also* : to make or break (a connection) with a lever **b :** to put (an automobile) in a different gear esp. quickly or suddenly ⟨he *threw* the car into reverse⟩ **18 :** to give by way of entertainment ⟨~ a party⟩ ~ *vi* : CAST, HURL — **throw·er** \ˈthrō-ər\ *n* — **throw cold water on :** to discourage esp.

\ə\ **a**but \ᵊ\ kitten, F table \ər\ f**ur**ther \a\ **a**sh \ā\ **a**ce \ä\ m**o**p, m**a**r
\au̇\ **ou**t \ch\ **ch**in \e\ b**e**t \ē\ **ea**sy \g\ **g**o \i\ h**i**t \ī\ **i**ce \j\ **j**ob
\ŋ\ si**ng** \ō\ g**o** \ȯ\ l**aw** \ȯi\ b**oy** \th\ **th**in \t͟h\ **th**e \ü\ l**oo**t \u̇\ f**oo**t
\y\ **y**et \zh\ vi**si**on, bei**ge** \k̲, ⁿ, œ, ue, ʸ\ *see* Guide to Pronunciation

through pessimism or indifference — **throw money at** : to spend large sums of money on or for esp. recklessly or ineffectively ⟨trying to solve problems by *throwing money at* them⟩ — **throw one's weight around** *or* **throw one's weight about** : to exercise influence or authority esp. to an excessive degree or in an objectionable manner — **throw to the wolves** : to leave unprotected against fierce opposition or attack — **throw together** **1** : to put together in a hurried and usu. careless manner ⟨a bookshelf hastily *thrown together*⟩ **2** : to bring into casual association ⟨different kinds of people are *thrown together* —Richard Sennett⟩

syn THROW, CAST, TOSS, FLING, HURL, PITCH, SLING mean to cause to move swiftly through space by a propulsive movement or a propelling force. THROW is general and interchangeable with the other terms but may specif. imply a distinctive motion with bent arm ⟨can *throw* a fastball and a curve⟩. CAST usu. implies lightness in the thing thrown and sometimes a scattering ⟨*cast* it to the winds⟩. TOSS suggests a light or careless or aimless throwing and may imply an upward motion ⟨*tossed* the coat on the bed⟩. FLING stresses a violent throwing ⟨*flung* the ring back in his face⟩. HURL implies power as in throwing a massive weight ⟨*hurled* himself at the intruder⟩. PITCH suggests throwing carefully at a target ⟨*pitch* horseshoes⟩. SLING stresses either the use of whirling momentum in throwing or directness of aim ⟨*slung* the bag over his shoulder⟩.

[2]throw *n* (1530) **1 a** : an act of throwing, hurling, or flinging **b** (1) : an act of throwing dice (2) : the number thrown with a cast of dice **c** : a method of throwing an opponent in wrestling or judo **2** : the distance a missile may be thrown or light rays may be projected **3** : an undertaking involving chance or danger : RISK, VENTURE **4** : the amount of vertical displacement produced by a geological fault **5 a** : the extreme movement given to a pivoted or reciprocating piece by a cam, crank, or eccentric : STROKE **b** : the length of the radius of a crank or the virtual crank radius of an eccentric or cam **6 a** : a light coverlet (as for a bed) **b** : a woman's scarf or light wrap — **a throw** : for each one : APIECE ⟨copies are to be sold at $5 *a throw* —Harvey Breit⟩

[1]throw·away \ˈthrō-ə-ˌwā\ *n* (1903) **1** : one that is or is designed to be thrown away: as **a** : a free handbill or circular **b** : a line of dialogue (as in a play) de-emphasized by casual delivery; *esp* : a joke or witticism delivered casually **2** : something made or done without care or interest **3** : a child who has been forced to leave home or who has run away from indifferent or hostile parents

[2]throwaway *adj* (1928) **1** : designed to be thrown away : DISPOSABLE ⟨~ containers⟩ **2** : written or spoken (as in a play) in a low-key or unemphatic manner ⟨~ lines⟩ **3** : NONCHALANT, CASUAL **4** : marked by a tendency to discard things : overly wasteful ⟨a ~ society⟩

throw away *vt* (1530) **1 a** : to get rid of as worthless or unnecessary **b** : DISCARD 2b **2 a** : to use in a foolish or wasteful manner : SQUANDER **b** : to fail to take advantage of : WASTE ⟨*throw away* an opportunity⟩ **3** : to make (as a line in a play) unemphatic by casual delivery

throw·back \ˈthrō-ˌbak\ *n* (1888) **1 a** : reversion to an earlier type or phase : ATAVISM **b** : an instance or product of atavistic reversion **2** : one that is suggestive of or suited to an earlier time or style ⟨his manners were a ~ to a more polite era⟩

throw back *vt* (1840) **1** : to delay the progress or advance of : CHECK **2** : to cause to rely : make dependent ⟨they are *thrown back* upon . . . native intelligence —Michael Novak⟩ **3** : REFLECT ~ *vi* : to revert to an earlier type or phase

throw down *vt* (14c) **1** : to cause to fall : OVERTHROW **2** : PRECIPITATE **3** : to cast off : DISCARD **4** : to make (a slam dunk) with exceptional force

throw–in \ˈthrō-ˌin\ *n* (1881) **1** : an act or instance of throwing a ball in: as **a** : a throw made from the touchline in soccer to put the ball back in play after it has gone into touch **b** : a throw from an outfielder to the infield in baseball **c** : an inbounds pass in basketball **2** : something added as a bonus or supplement

throw in *vt* (1678) **1** : to add as a gratuity or supplement **2** : to introduce or interject in the course of something : CONTRIBUTE ⟨they *throw in* some . . . sound effects on several songs —Tom Phillips⟩ **3** : DISTRIBUTE 3b **4** : ENGAGE ⟨*throw in* the clutch⟩ ~ *vi* : to enter into association or partnership : JOIN ⟨agrees to *throw in* with a crooked excop —*Newsweek*⟩ — **throw in the towel** *also* **throw in the sponge** : to abandon a struggle or contest : acknowledge defeat : GIVE UP

throw off *vt* (1604) **1 a** : to free oneself from : get rid of ⟨*threw off* his inhibitions⟩ **b** : to cast off often in a hurried or vigorous manner : ABANDON ⟨*threw off* all restraint⟩ **c** : DISTRACT, DIVERT ⟨dogs *thrown off* by a false scent⟩ **2** : EMIT, GIVE OFF ⟨stacks *throwing off* plumes of smoke⟩ **3** : to produce in an offhand manner : execute with speed or facility ⟨some little . . . tune that the composer had *thrown off* —James Hilton⟩ **4 a** : to cause to depart from an expected or desired course ⟨mistakes *threw* his calculations *off* a bit⟩ **b** : to cause to make a mistake : MISLEAD **5** : EARN, GENERATE ⟨an investment that *throws off* a sizable income⟩ ~ *vi* **1** : to begin hunting **2** : to make derogatory comments

throw out *vt* (15c) **1 a** : to remove from a place, office, or employment usu. in a sudden or unexpected manner **b** : to get rid of as worthless or unnecessary **2** : to give expression to : UTTER ⟨*threw out* a remark . . . that utterly confounded him —Jean Stafford⟩ **3** : to dismiss from acceptance or consideration : REJECT ⟨the testimony was *thrown out*⟩ **4** : to make visible or manifest : DISPLAY ⟨the signal was *thrown out* for the . . . fleet to prepare for action —Archibald Duncan⟩ **5** : to leave behind : OUTDISTANCE **6** : to give forth from within : EMIT **7 a** : to send out **b** : to cause to project : EXTEND **8** : CONFUSE, DISCONCERT ⟨automobiles in line blocking the road . . . *threw* the whole schedule *out* —F. D. Roosevelt⟩ **9** : to cause to stand out : make prominent **10** : to make a throw that enables a teammate to put out (a base runner) — **throw out the baby with the bathwater** : to discard or lose something useful or beneficial in the process of discarding or rejecting something unwanted

throw over *vt* (1835) **1** : to forsake despite bonds of attachment or duty **2** : to refuse to accept : REJECT

throw pillow *n* (1956) : a small pillow used esp. as a decorative accessory

throw rug *n* (1928) : a rug of such a size that several can be used in a room

throw·ster \ˈthrō-stər\ *n* (15c) : one who throws textile filaments

throw up *vt* (15c) **1** : to raise quickly **2** : GIVE UP, QUIT ⟨the urge . . . to *throw up* all intellectual work —Norman Mailer⟩ **3** : to build hurriedly ⟨new houses *thrown up* almost overnight⟩ **4** : VOMIT **5** : to bring forth : PRODUCE **6** : to make distinct esp. by contrast : cause to stand out **7** : to mention repeatedly by way of reproach ~ *vi* : VOMIT — **throw up one's hands** : to admit defeat ⟨in the end *throws up his hands* in despair —Frank Conroy⟩

throw weight *n* (1969) : the maximum payload of an ICBM

thru *var of* THROUGH ***usage*** see THO

[1]thrum \ˈthrəm\ *n* [ME, fr. OE *-thrum* (in *tungethrum* ligament of the tongue); akin to OHG *drum* fragment] (14c) **1 a** (1) : a fringe of warp threads left on the loom after the cloth has been removed (2) : one of these warp threads **b** : a tuft or short piece of rope yarn used in thrumming canvas — usu. used in pl. **c** : BIT, PARTICLE **2** : a hair, fiber, or threadlike leaf on a plant; *also* : a tuft or fringe of such structures — **thrum** *adj*

[2]thrum *vt* **thrummed; thrum·ming** (15c) **1** : to furnish with thrums : FRINGE **2** : to insert short pieces of rope yarn or spun yarn in (a piece of canvas) to make a rough surface or a mat which can be wrapped about rigging to prevent chafing

[3]thrum *vb* **thrummed; thrum·ming** [imit.] *vi* (1592) **1** : to play or pluck a stringed instrument idly : STRUM **2** : to sound with a monotonous hum ~ *vt* **1** : to play (as a stringed instrument) in an idle or relaxed manner **2** : to recite tiresomely or monotonously

[4]thrum *n* (1798) : the monotonous sound of thrumming

[1]thrush \ˈthrəsh\ *n* [ME *thrusche,* fr. OE *thrysce;* akin to OE *throstle* thrush, OHG *droscala,* L *turdus*] (bef. 12c) : any of numerous small or medium-sized birds of an oscine family (Turdidae, the thrush family) or in some classifications a subfamily (Turdinae of the family Muscicapidae) which are mostly of a plain color often with spotted underparts and many of which are excellent singers

[2]thrush *n* [prob. of Scand origin; akin to Dan *trøske* thrush, Sw *torsk*] (1665) **1** : a disease that is caused by a fungus (*Candida albicans*), occurs esp. in infants and children, and is marked by white patches in the oral cavity; *broadly* : CANDIDIASIS ⟨vaginal ~⟩ **2** : a suppurative disorder of the feet in various animals (as a horse)

[1]thrust \ˈthrəst\ *vb* **thrust; thrust·ing** [ME *thrusten, thristen,* fr. ON *thrȳsta;* prob. akin to ON *thrjōta* to tire, OE *thrēat* coercion — more at THREAT] *vt* (13c) **1** : to push or drive with force : SHOVE **2** : to cause to enter or pierce something by or as if by pushing ⟨~ a dagger into his heart⟩ **3** : EXTEND, SPREAD **4** : STAB, PIERCE **5 a** : to put (as an unwilling person) forcibly into a course of action or position ⟨was *thrust* into the job⟩ **b** : to introduce often improperly into a position : INTERPOLATE **6** : to press, force, or impose the acceptance of upon someone ⟨~ new responsibilities upon her⟩ ~ *vi* **1 a** : to force an entrance or passage **b** : to push forward : press onward **c** : to push upward : PROJECT **2** : to make a thrust, stab, or lunge with or as if with a pointed weapon ⟨~ at them with a knife⟩

[2]thrust *n* (14c) **1 a** : a push or lunge with a pointed weapon **b** (1) : a verbal attack (2) : a military assault **2 a** : a strong continued pressure **b** : the sideways force or pressure of one part of a structure against another part (as of an arch against an abutment) **c** : the force produced by a propeller or by a jet or rocket engine that drives a vehicle (as an aircraft) forward **d** : a nearly horizontal geological fault **3 a** : a forward or upward push **b** : a movement (as by a group of people) in a specified direction **4 a** : salient or essential element or meaning ⟨the ~ of the argument⟩ **b** : principal concern or objective ⟨the plan's major ~ is testing —Ryan Lizza⟩

thrust·er *also* **thrust·or** \ˈthrəs-tər\ *n* (1597) : one that thrusts; *esp* : an engine (as a jet engine) that develops thrust by expelling a jet of fluid or a stream of particles

thrust·ful \ˈthrəst-fəl\ *adj* (1909) *Brit* : characterized by thrust : AGGRESSIVE ⟨~ young man on the make —*Current Literature*⟩

thrust stage *n* [*thrust,* pp. of [1]*thrust*] (1965) : a stage that projects beyond the proscenium so that the audience sits around the projection; *also* : a forestage that is extended into the auditorium to increase the stage area

thru·way \ˈthrü-ˌwā\ *n* (1930) : EXPRESSWAY

[1]thud \ˈthəd\ *n* [imit.] (1787) **1** : [5]BLOW **2 a** : a dull sound : THUMP

[2]thud *vi* **thud·ded; thud·ding** (1796) : to move or strike so as to make a thud

thug \ˈthəg\ *n* [Hindi & Urdu *ṭhag,* lit., thief] (1810) : a brutal ruffian or assassin : GANGSTER, TOUGH — **thug·gery** \ˈthə-g(ə-)rē\ *n* — **thug·gish** \ˈthə-gish\ *adj*

thu·ja \ˈthü-jə, ˈthyü-\ *n* [NL *Thuja,* fr. ML *thuia,* a cedar, fr. Gk *thyia,* fr. *thyein* to sacrifice — more at THYME] (ca. 1760) : any of a genus (*Thuja*) of evergreen shrubs and trees (as an arborvitae) of the cypress family having scalelike closely imbricated or compressed leaves

[1]Thu·le \ˈthü-lē, ˈthyü-\ *n* [ME *Tyle,* fr. OE, fr. L *Thule, Thyle,* fr. Gk *Thoulē, Thylē*] (bef. 12c) : the northernmost part of the habitable ancient world

[2]Thu·le \ˈtü-lē\ *adj* [*Thule,* Greenland] (1925) : of, relating to, or being the culture existing in the arctic lands from Alaska to Greenland from about A.D. 500 to A.D. 1400

thu·li·um \ˈthü-lē-əm, ˈthyü-\ *n* [NL, fr. L *Thule*] (1879) : a soft silvery metallic element of the rare-earth group — see ELEMENT table

[1]thumb \ˈthəm\ *n* [ME *thoume, thoumbe,* fr. OE *thūma;* akin to OHG *thūmo* thumb, L *tumēre* to swell] (bef. 12c) **1** : the short thick digit of the human hand that is analogous in position to the big toe and differs from the other fingers in having only two phalanges, allowing greater freedom of movement, and being opposable to each of them; *also* : a corresponding digit in lower animals **2** : the part of a glove or mitten that covers the thumb **3** : a convex molding : OVOLO — **all thumbs** : extremely awkward or clumsy — **under one's thumb** *or* **under the thumb** : under control : in a state of subservience ⟨her father did not have her that much *under his thumb* —Hamilton Basso⟩

[2]thumb *vt* (ca. 1647) **1 a** : to leaf through (pages) with the thumb : TURN **b** : to soil or wear by or as if by repeated thumbing ⟨a badly ~*ed* book⟩ **2** : to request or obtain (a ride) in a passing automobile by signaling with the thumb ~ *vi* **1** : to turn over pages ⟨~ through a book⟩ **2** : to travel by thumbing rides : HITCHHIKE ⟨~*ed* across the country⟩ — **thumb one's nose** **1** : to place the thumb at one's nose and extend the fingers as a gesture of scorn or defiance **2** : to express

disdain or defiance ⟨*thumb their nose* at opulence —*Sales Management*⟩
thumb drive *n* (2002) : a small usu. rectangular device used for storing and transferring computer data : FLASH DRIVE
thumb·hole \ˈthəm-ˌhōl\ *n* (1859) **1** : an opening in which to insert the thumb **2** : a hole in a wind musical instrument opened or closed by the thumb
thumb index *n* (1903) : a series of usu. labeled notches cut in the fore edge of a book (as a dictionary) to facilitate reference
[1]**thumb·nail** \ˈthəm-ˌnāl, -ˈnāl\ *n* (1604) **1** : the nail of the thumb **2** : a miniature computer graphic sometimes hyperlinked to a full-size version
[2]**thumbnail** *adj* (1852) : CONCISE, BRIEF ⟨a ~ sketch⟩
thumb piano *n* (1949) : MBIRA
thumb·print \ˈthəm-ˌprint\ *n* (1900) **1** : an impression made by the thumb; *esp* : a print made by the inside of the first joint **2** : something that identifies; *esp* : FINGERPRINT 2a
thumb·screw \-ˌskrü\ *n* (1788) **1** : an instrument of torture for compressing the thumb by a screw **2** : a screw having a flat-sided or knurled head so that it may be turned by the thumb and index finger
thumbs–down \ˈthəmz-ˈdau̇n\ *n* (1889) : an instance or gesture of rejection, disapproval, or condemnation
thumbs–up \-ˈəp\ *n* (1892) : an instance or gesture of approval or encouragement
[1]**thumb·tack** \ˈthəm-ˌtak\ *n* (1884) : a tack with a broad flat head for pressing into a surface with the thumb
[2]**thumbtack** *vt* (1914) : to fasten with a thumbtack
thumb·wheel \ˈthəm-ˌhwēl, -ˌwēl\ *n* (1903) : a control for various devices consisting of a partially exposed wheel that can be turned by moving the exposed edge with a finger
[1]**thump** \ˈthəmp\ *vb* [imit.] *vt* (1548) **1** : to strike or beat with or as if with something thick or heavy so as to cause a dull sound **2** : POUND, KNOCK **3** : WHIP, THRASH **4** : to produce (music) mechanically or in a mechanical manner — usu. used with *out* ⟨~*ed* out a tune on the piano⟩ ~ *vi* **1 a** : to inflict a thump **b** : to make or move with a thumping sound **2** : to make a vigorous endorsement ⟨got a couple of . . . senators to ~ for him —*N.Y. Herald Tribune*⟩ — **thump·er** *n*
[2]**thump** *n* (1552) : a blow or knock with or as if with something blunt or heavy; *also* : the sound made by such a blow
[1]**thump·ing** \ˈthəm-piŋ\ *adj* [*thumping,* prp. of [1]*thump*] (1576) : impressively large, great, or excellent ⟨a ~ majority⟩ — **thump·ing·ly** *adv*
[2]**thumping** *adv* (1835) : VERY, EXTREMELY ⟨a ~ good time⟩
[1]**thun·der** \ˈthən-dər\ *n* [ME *thoner, thunder,* fr. OE *thunor;* akin to OHG *thonar* thunder, L *tonare* to thunder] (bef. 12c) **1** : the sound that follows a flash of lightning and is caused by sudden expansion of the air in the path of the electrical discharge **2** : a loud utterance or threat **3** : BANG, RUMBLE ⟨the ~ of big guns⟩
[2]**thunder** *vb* **thun·dered; thun·der·ing** \-d(ə-)riŋ\ *vi* (bef. 12c) **1 a** : to produce thunder — usu. used impersonally ⟨it ~*ed*⟩ **b** : to give forth a sound that resembles thunder ⟨horses ~*ed* down the road⟩ **2** : ROAR, SHOUT ~ *vt* **1** : to utter loudly : ROAR **2** : to strike with a sound likened to thunder — **thun·der·er** \-dər-ər\ *n*
thun·der·bird \ˈthən-dər-ˌbərd\ *n* (1871) : a bird that causes lightning and thunder in American Indian myth
thun·der·bolt \-ˌbōlt\ *n* (15c) **1 a** : a single discharge of lightning with the accompanying thunder **b** : an imaginary elongated mass cast as a missile to earth in the lightning flash **2 a** : a person or thing that resembles lightning in suddenness, effectiveness, or destructive power **b** : a vehement threat or censure
thun·der·clap \-ˌklap\ *n* (14c) **1** : a clap of thunder **2** : something sharp, loud, or sudden like a clap of thunder
thun·der·cloud \-ˌklau̇d\ *n* (1697) : a cloud charged with electricity and producing lightning and thunder
thunder egg *n* (1941) : chalcedony in rounded concretionary nodules

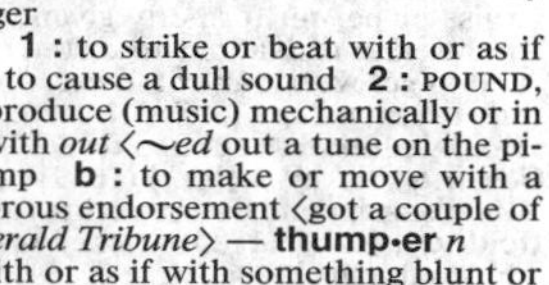

thunder egg: *1* nodule, *2* cutaway

thun·der·head \-ˌhed\ *n* (1843) : a rounded mass of cumulus or cumulonimbus cloud often appearing before a thunderstorm
thundering *adj* [*thundering,* prp. of [2]*thunder*] (1543) : awesomely great, intense, or unusual — **thun·der·ing·ly** *adv*
thunder lizard *n* [trans. of NL *Brontosaurus*] (1960) : BRONTOSAURUS
thun·der·ous \ˈthən-d(ə-)rəs\ *adj* (1582) **1 a** : producing thunder **b** : making or accompanied by a noise like thunder ⟨~ applause⟩ **2** : THUNDERING — **thun·der·ous·ly** *adv*
thun·der·show·er \-ˌshau̇(-ə)r\ *n* (1607) : a shower accompanied by lightning and thunder
thun·der·stone \-ˌstōn\ *n* (1598) **1** *archaic* : THUNDERBOLT 1b **2** : any of various stones (as a meteorite or an ancient artifact) regarded as having been cast to the earth as thunderbolts
thun·der·storm \-ˌstȯrm\ *n* (1652) : a storm accompanied by lightning and thunder
thun·der·strike \-ˌstrīk\ *vt* **-struck** \-ˌstrək\; **-struck** *also* **-strick·en** \-ˌstri-kən\; **-strik·ing** \-ˌstrī-kiŋ\ (ca. 1586) **1** : to strike dumb : ASTONISH ⟨was *thunderstruck* at the news⟩ **2** *archaic* : to strike by or as if by lightning
thun·der·stroke \-ˌstrōk\ *n* (14c) : a stroke of or as if of lightning with the attendant thunder
[1]**thunk** \ˈthəŋk\ *dial past and past part of* THINK
[2]**thunk** *n* [imit.] (1947) : a flat hollow sound
[3]**thunk** *vi* (1949) : to produce a flat hollow sound : make a thunk
thu·ri·ble \ˈthu̇r-ə-bəl, ˈthyu̇r-, ˈthər-\ *n* [ME *thurribul,* fr. L *thuribulum,* fr. *thur-, thus* incense, fr. Gk *thyos* incense, sacrifice, fr. *thyein* to sacrifice — more at THYME] (15c) : CENSER
thu·ri·fer \-ə-fər\ *n* [NL, fr. L *thurifer,* adj., incense-bearing, fr. *thur-, thus* + *-ifer* -iferous] (1849) : one who carries a censer in a liturgical service
Thu·rin·ger \ˈthu̇r-ən-jər, ˈthyu̇r-\ *n* [G *Thüringerwurst,* fr. *Thüringer* Thuringian + *Wurst* sausage] (ca. 1923) : a mildly seasoned fresh or smoked sausage
Thu·rin·gian \thu̇-ˈrin-j(ē-)ən, thyu̇r-\ *n* (1618) **1** : a member of an ancient Germanic people whose kingdom was overthrown by the Franks in the sixth century **2** : a native or inhabitant of Thuringia — **Thuringian** *adj*
thurl \ˈthər(-ə)l\ *n* [perh. fr. E dial., gaunt] (1920) : the hip joint in cattle — see COW illustration
Thurs *or* **Thur** *or* **Thu** *abbr* Thursday
Thurs·day \ˈthərz-(ˌ)dā, -dē\ *n* [ME, fr. OE *thursdæg,* fr. ON *thōrsdagr;* akin to OE *thunresdæg* Thursday, ON *Thōrr* Thor, OE *thunor* thunder — more at THUNDER] (bef. 12c) : the fifth day of the week — **Thursdays** \-dēz, -(ˌ)dāz\ *adv*
thus \ˈt͟həs\ *adv* [ME, fr. OE; akin to OS *thus* thus] (bef. 12c) **1** : in this or that manner or way ⟨described it ~⟩ **2** : to this degree or extent : so ⟨~ far⟩ **3** : because of this or that : HENCE, CONSEQUENTLY **4** : as an example
thus·ly \-lē\ *adv* (1865) : in this manner : THUS
[1]**thwack** \ˈthwak\ *vt* [imit.] (ca. 1530) : to strike with or as if with something flat or heavy : WHACK
[2]**thwack** *n* (1587) : a heavy blow : WHACK; *also* : the sound of or as if of such a blow
[1]**thwart** \ˈthwȯrt\ *vt* [ME *thwerten,* fr. *thwert,* adv.] (13c) **1 a** : to run counter to so as to effectively oppose or baffle : CONTRAVENE **b** : to oppose successfully : defeat the hopes or aspirations of **2** : to pass through or across ***syn*** see FRUSTRATE — **thwart·er** *n*
[2]**thwart** \ˈthwȯrt, *naut often* ˈthȯrt\ *adv* [ME *thwert,* fr. ON *thvert,* fr. neut. of *thverr* transverse, oblique; akin to OHG *dwerah* transverse, oblique] (14c) : ATHWART
[3]**thwart** *adj* (14c) : situated or placed across something else : TRANSVERSE — **thwart·ly** *adv*
[4]**thwart** *n* [alter. of obs. *thought, thoft,* fr. ME *thoft,* fr. OE *thofte;* akin to OHG *dofta* rower's seat] (ca. 1736) : a seat extending athwart a boat
thwart·wise \-ˌwīz\ *adv or adj* (1589) : CROSSWISE 1
thy \ˈt͟hī\ *adj* [ME *thin, thy,* fr. OE *thīn,* gen. of *thū* thou — more at THOU] (12c) *archaic* : of or relating to thee or thyself esp. as possessor or agent or as object of an action — used esp. in ecclesiastical or literary language and sometimes by Friends esp. among themselves
Thy·es·te·an \thī-ˈes-tē-ən\ *adj* [*Thyestes,* brother of Atreus who unwittingly ate the flesh of his children] (1667) : of or relating to the eating of human flesh : CANNIBAL
thy·la·cine \ˈthī-lə-ˌsīn\ *n* [NL *Thylacinus,* genus of marsupials, fr. Gk *thylakos* sack, pouch] (1838) : TASMANIAN TIGER
thy·la·koid \ˈthī-lə-ˌkȯid\ *n* [ISV *thylak-* (fr. Gk *thylakos* sack) + *-oid*] (1962) : any of the membranous disks of lamellae within plant chloroplasts that are composed of protein and lipid and are the sites of the photochemical reactions of photosynthesis
thym- *or* **thymo-** *comb form* [NL *thymus*] : thymus ⟨*thym*ic⟩ ⟨*thymo*cyte⟩
thyme \ˈtīm *also* ˈthīm\ *n* [ME, fr. AF *time, thime,* fr. L *thymum,* fr. Gk *thymon,* prob. fr. *thyein* to make a burnt offering, sacrifice; akin to L *fumus* smoke — more at FUME] (14c) **1** : any of a genus (*Thymus*) of Eurasian mints with small pungent aromatic leaves; *esp* : a Mediterranean garden herb (*T. vulgaris*) **2** : thyme leaves used as a seasoning
thy·mec·to·my \thī-ˈmek-tə-mē\ *n, pl* **-mies** (ca. 1905) : surgical removal of the thymus — **thy·mec·to·mize** \-ˌmīz\ *vt*
-thymia *n comb form* [NL, fr. Gk, fr. *thymos* mind] : condition of mind and will ⟨cyclo*thymia*⟩
thy·mic \ˈthī-mik\ *adj* (ca. 1656) : of or relating to the thymus
thy·mi·dine \ˈthī-mə-ˌdēn\ *n* [*thym*ine + *-idine*] (1912) : a nucleoside $C_{10}H_{14}N_2O_5$ that is composed of thymine and deoxyribose and occurs as a structural part of DNA
thy·mine \ˈthī-ˌmēn\ *n* [ISV, fr. NL *thymus*] (1894) : a pyrimidine base $C_5H_6N_2O_2$ that is one of the four bases coding genetic information in the polynucleotide chain of DNA — compare ADENINE, CYTOSINE, GUANINE, URACIL
thy·mo·cyte \ˈthī-mə-ˌsīt\ *n* [ISV] (ca. 1923) : a cell of the thymus; *esp* : a thymic lymphocyte
thy·mol \ˈthī-ˌmȯl, -ˌmōl\ *n* [ISV, fr. L *thymum* thyme] (1857) : a crystalline phenol $C_{10}H_{14}O$ of aromatic odor and antiseptic properties found esp. in thyme oil or made synthetically and used chiefly as a fungicide and preservative
thy·mo·sin \ˈthī-mə-sən\ *n* [Gk *thymos* thymus + E [1]*-in*] (1966) : a mixture of polypeptides isolated from the thymus; *also* : any of these
thy·mus \ˈthī-məs\ *n, pl* **thy·mus·es** *also* **thy·mi** \-ˌmī\ [NL, fr. Gk *thymos* warty excrescence, thymus] (1578) : a glandular structure of largely lymphoid tissue that functions esp. in the development of the body's immune system, is present in the young of most vertebrates typically in the upper anterior chest or at the base of the neck, and tends to atrophy in the adult
thymy *or* **thym·ey** \ˈtī-mē *also* ˈthī-\ *adj* (1727) : abounding in or fragrant with thyme
thyr- *or* **thyro-** *comb form* [*thyroid*] : thyroid ⟨*thyro*toxicosis⟩ ⟨*thyrox*ine⟩
thy·ra·tron \ˈthī-rə-ˌträn\ *n* [fr. *Thyratron,* a trademark] (1929) : a gas-filled hot-cathode electron tube in which the grid controls only the start of a continuous current thus giving the tube a trigger effect
thy·ris·tor \thī-ˈris-tər\ *n* [*thyr*atron + trans*istor*] (1958) : any of several semiconductor devices that act as switches, rectifiers, or voltage regulators
thy·ro·cal·ci·to·nin \ˌthī-rō-ˌkal-sə-ˈtō-nən\ *n* (1963) : CALCITONIN
thy·ro·glob·u·lin \-ˈglä-byə-lən\ *n* [ISV] (ca. 1905) : an iodine-containing protein of the thyroid gland that is the precursor of thyroxine and triiodothyronine
[1]**thy·roid** \ˈthī-ˌrȯid\ *also* **thy·roi·dal** \thī-ˈrȯi-dᵊl\ *adj* [NL *thyroides,* fr. Gk *thyreoeidēs* shield-shaped, thyroid, fr. *thyreos* shield shaped like a door, fr. *thyra* door — more at DOOR] (ca. 1741) **1 a** : of, relating to, or being the thyroid gland **b** : suggestive of a disordered thyroid ⟨a ~

personality⟩ **2 :** of, relating to, or being the chief cartilage of the larynx

[2]**thyroid** *n* (1787) **1 :** a large bilobed endocrine gland of vertebrates lying at the anterior base of the neck and producing esp. the hormones thyroxine and triiodothyronine **2 :** a preparation of the thyroid gland of various domestic animals used in treating thyroid disorders

thy·roid·ec·to·my \ˌthī-ˌrȯi-ˈdek-tə-mē, ˌthī-rə-\ *n, pl* **-mies** (1889) **:** surgical removal of thyroid gland tissue — **thy·roid·ec·to·mized** \-ˌmīzd\ *adj*

thy·roid·itis \ˌthī-ˌrȯi-ˈdī-təs, ˌthī-rə-\ *n* [NL] (ca. 1885) **:** inflammation of the thyroid gland

thyroid–stimulating hormone *n* (1941) **:** a hormone that is secreted by the anterior lobe of the pituitary gland and stimulates the thyroid gland — abbr. *TSH*; called also *thyrotropic hormone, thyrotropin*

thy·ro·tox·i·co·sis \ˌthī-rō-ˌtäk-sə-ˈkō-səs\ *n* [NL] (ca. 1911) **:** HYPERTHYROIDISM

thy·ro·tro·pic \ˌthī-rə-ˈtrō-pik, -ˈträ-\ *also* **thy·ro·tro·phic** \-ˈtrō-fik\ *adj* (ca. 1923) **:** exerting or characterized by a direct influence on the secretory activity of the thyroid gland ⟨~ functions⟩

thyrotropic hormone *n* (1940) **:** THYROID-STIMULATING HORMONE

thy·ro·tro·pin \ˌthī-rə-ˈtrō-pən\ *also* **thy·ro·tro·phin** \-fən\ *n* [*thyrotropic, thyrotrophic*] (1939) **:** THYROID-STIMULATING HORMONE

thyrotropin–releasing hormone *n* (1968) **:** a tripeptide hormone synthesized in the hypothalamus that stimulates secretion of thyroid-stimulating hormone — called also *thyrotropin-releasing factor*

thy·rox·ine *or* **thy·rox·in** \thī-ˈräk-ˌsēn, -sən\ *n* [*thyr-* + *oxy* + *indole*] (1918) **:** an iodine-containing hormone $C_{15}H_{11}I_4NO_4$ that is an amino acid produced by the thyroid gland as a product of the cleavage of thyroglobulin, increases metabolic rate, and is used to treat thyroid disorders

thyr·sus \ˈthər-səs\ *n, pl* **thyr·si** \-ˌsī, -ˌsē\ [L, fr. Gk *thyrsos*] (1591) **:** a staff surmounted by a pinecone or by a bunch of vine or ivy leaves with grapes or berries that is carried by Bacchus and by satyrs and others engaging in bacchic rites

thy·sa·nu·ran \ˌthī-sə-ˈnu̇r-ən, -ˈnyu̇r-\ *n* [ultim. fr. Gk *thysanos* tassel + *oura* tail — more at ASS] (1835) **:** BRISTLETAIL — **thysanuran** *adj*

thy·self \thī-ˈself\ *pron* (bef. 12c) *archaic* **:** YOURSELF — used esp. in ecclesiastical or literary language and sometimes by Friends esp. among themselves

[1]**ti** \ˈtē\ *n* [Tahitian, Marquesan, Samoan, & Maori] (1832) **:** any of several Asian and Pacific trees or shrubs (genus *Cordyline*) of the agave family with leaves in terminal tufts

[2]**ti** *n* [alter. of *si*] (1839) **:** the seventh tone of the diatonic scale in solmization

Ti *symbol* titanium

TIA *abbr* transient ischemic attack

ti·ara \tē-ˈer-ə, -ˈär-\ *n* [L, royal Persian headdress, fr. Gk] (1616) **1 :** a 3-tiered crown worn by the pope **2 :** a decorative jeweled or flowered headband or semicircle for formal wear by women

Ti·bet·an \tə-ˈbe-tᵊn\ *n* (1822) **1 :** a member of the predominant people of Tibet and adjacent areas of Asia; *also* **:** the Tibeto-Burman language of the Tibetan people **2 :** a native inhabitant of Tibet — **Tibetan** *adj*

Tibetan Buddhism *n* (1889) **:** a form of Mahayana Buddhism that evolved in Tibet and is dominated by the sect of the Dalai Lama

Tibetan terrier *n* (1905) **:** any of a breed of terriers resembling Old English sheepdogs but having a curled well-feathered tail

Ti·beto–Bur·man \tə-ˌbe-tō-ˈbər-mən\ *n* (1901) **1 :** a language family that includes Tibetan, Burmese, and related languages of southern and eastern Asia **2 :** a member of a people speaking a Tibeto-Burman language

tib·ia \ˈti-bē-ə\ *n, pl* **-i·ae** \-bē-ˌē, -bē-ˌī\ *also* **-i·as** [L] (ca. 1706) **1 :** the inner and usu. larger of the two bones of the vertebrate hind or lower limb between the knee and ankle **2 :** the fourth joint of the leg of an insect between the femur and tarsus — **tib·i·al** \-bē-əl\ *adj*

tib·io·fib·u·la \ˌti-bē-ō-ˈfi-byə-lə\ *n* [NL] (ca. 1909) **:** a bone esp. in frogs and toads that is formed by fusion of the tibia and fibula

tic \ˈtik\ *n* [F] (ca. 1834) **1 :** local and habitual spasmodic motion of particular muscles esp. of the face **:** TWITCHING **2 :** a frequent usu. unconscious quirk of behavior or speech ⟨"you know" is a verbal ~⟩

ti·cal \ti-ˈkäl, ˈti-kəl\ *n, pl* **ticals** *or* **tical** [Thai, fr. Pg, fr. Malay *tikal*, a monetary unit] (1662) **:** BAHT

tic dou·lou·reux \ˈtik-ˌdü-lə-ˈrü, -ˈrə(r)\ *n* [F, painful twitch] (1800) **:** TRIGEMINAL NEURALGIA

[1]**tick** \ˈtik\ *n* [ME *tyke, teke;* akin to MHG *zeche* tick, Arm *tiz*] (14c) **1 :** any of a superfamily (Ixodoidea) of bloodsucking acarid arachnids that are larger than the related mites, attach themselves to warm-blooded vertebrates to feed, and include important vectors of infectious diseases **2 :** any of various usu. wingless parasitic dipteran flies — compare SHEEP KED

[2]**tick** *n* [ME *tike,* prob. fr. MD (akin to OHG *ziahha* tick), fr. L *theca* cover, fr. Gk *thēkē* case; akin to Gk *tithenai* to place — more at DO] (15c) **1 :** the fabric case of a mattress, pillow, or bolster; *also* **:** a mattress consisting of a tick and its filling **2 :** [1]TICKING

[3]**tick** *n* [ME *tek* pat, light stroke; akin to MHG *zic* light push] (1680) **1 a :** a light rhythmic audible tap or beat; *also* **:** a series of such ticks **b :** the time taken by the tick of a clock **:** MOMENT **2 :** a small spot or mark; *esp* **:** one used to direct attention to something, to check an item on a list, or to represent a point on a scale

[4]**tick** *vi* (1721) **1 :** to make the sound of a tick or a series of ticks **2 :** to operate as a functioning mechanism **:** RUN ⟨tried to understand what made him ~⟩ ⟨the motor was *~ing* over quietly⟩ ~ *vt* **1 :** to mark with a written tick **:** CHECK — usu. used with *off* ⟨*~ed* off each item in the list⟩ **2 :** to mark, count, or announce by or as if by ticking beats ⟨a meter *~ing* off the cab fare⟩ **3 :** to touch with a momentary glancing blow ⟨*~ed* the ball⟩

[5]**tick** *n* [short for [1]*ticket*] (1642) *chiefly Brit* **:** CREDIT, TRUST; *also* **:** a credit account

tick–borne \ˈtik-ˌbȯrn\ *adj* (1921) **:** capable of being transmitted by the bites of ticks ⟨~ encephalitis⟩

[1]**ticked** \ˈtikt\ *adj* (ca. 1688) **1 :** marked with ticks **:** FLECKED **2 :** having or made of hair banded with two or more colors ⟨a ~ cat⟩ ⟨a ~ coat⟩

[2]**ticked** *adj* [*tick off*] (ca. 1959) **:** ANGRY, UPSET

tick·er \ˈti-kər\ *n* (1821) **:** something that ticks or produces a ticking sound: as **a :** WATCH **b** (1) **:** a telegraphic receiving instrument that automatically prints off information (as stock quotations or news) on a paper ribbon (2) **:** a graphic on which information is scrolled across the top or bottom of a television or computer screen **c** *slang* **:** HEART

ticker tape *n* (1895) **:** the paper ribbon on which a telegraphic ticker prints off its information

[1]**tick·et** \ˈti-kət\ *n* [MF *etiquet, estiquette* note attached to something indicating its contents, fr. MF dial. (Picard) *estiquier* to attach, fr. MD *steken* to stick; akin to OHG *sticken* to prick — more at STICK] (1529) **1 a :** a document that serves as a certificate, license, or permit; *esp* **:** a mariner's or airman's certificate **b :** TAG, LABEL **2 a :** a certificate or token showing that a fare or admission fee has been paid **b :** a means of access or passage ⟨education is the ~ to a good job⟩ **3 :** a list of candidates for nomination or election **:** SLATE **4 :** the correct or desirable thing ⟨cooperation, that's the ~ —K. E. Trombley⟩ **5 :** a slip or card recording a transaction or undertaking or giving instructions ⟨a savings deposit ~⟩ **6 :** a summons or warning issued to a traffic-law violator — **tick·et·less** \-ləs\ *adj*

[2]**ticket** *vt* (1611) **1 :** to attach a ticket to **:** LABEL; *also* **:** DESIGNATE **2 :** to furnish or serve with a ticket ⟨*~ed* for illegal parking⟩

ticket agency *n* (1923) **:** an agency selling transportation or theater and entertainment tickets

ticket agent *n* (1861) **:** one who sells transportation or theater and entertainment tickets

ticket office *n* (ca. 1667) **:** an office of a transportation company, theatrical or entertainment enterprise, or ticket agency where tickets are sold and reservations made

tick·et–of–leave \ˌti-kət-ə(v)-ˈlēv\ *n, pl* **tickets–of–leave** (1732) **:** a license or permit formerly given in the United Kingdom and the Commonwealth of Nations to a convict under imprisonment to go at large and to get work subject to certain specific conditions

tick fever *n* (ca. 1897) **1 :** TEXAS FEVER **2 :** a febrile disease (as Rocky Mountain spotted fever) transmitted by the bites of ticks

[1]**tick·ing** \ˈti-kiŋ\ *n* [[2]*tick*] (1649) **:** a strong linen or cotton fabric used in upholstering and as a covering for a mattress or pillow

[2]**ticking** *n* [[3]*tick*] (1885) **:** ticked marking on a bird or mammal or on individual hairs

[1]**tick·le** \ˈti-kəl\ *vb* **tick·led; tick·ling** \-k(ə-)liŋ\ [ME *tikelen;* akin to OE *tinclian* to tickle] *vt* (14c) **1 a :** to excite or stir up agreeably **:** PLEASE ⟨music . . . does more than ~ our sense of rhythm —Edward Sapir⟩ **b :** to provoke to laughter or merriment **:** AMUSE ⟨were *tickled* by the clown's antics⟩ **2 :** to touch (as a body part) lightly so as to excite the surface nerves and cause uneasiness, laughter, or spasmodic movements **3 :** to touch or stir gently ⟨a pianist *tickling* the ivories⟩ ~ *vi* **1 :** to have a tingling or prickling sensation ⟨my back *~s*⟩ **2 :** to excite the surface nerves to prickle

[2]**tickle** *n* (1801) **1 :** the act of tickling **2 :** a tickling sensation **3 :** something that tickles

tick·ler \ˈti-k(ə-)lər\ *n* (1680) **1 :** a person or device that tickles **2 :** a device for jogging the memory; *specif* **:** a file that serves as a reminder and is arranged to bring matters to timely attention

tick·lish \ˈti-k(ə-)lish\ *adj* (1581) **1 a :** TOUCHY, OVERSENSITIVE ⟨~ about his baldness⟩ **b :** easily overturned ⟨a canoe is a ~ craft⟩ **2 :** requiring delicate handling ⟨a ~ subject⟩ **3 :** sensitive to tickling — **tick·lish·ly** *adv* — **tick·lish·ness** *n*

tick off *vt* [[4]*tick*] (1915) **1 :** REPRIMAND, REBUKE ⟨his father *ticked* him *off* for his impudence⟩ **2 :** to make angry or indignant ⟨the cancellation really *ticked* me *off*⟩

tick·seed \ˈtik-ˌsēd\ *n* [[1]*tick*] (ca. 1760) **:** COREOPSIS

tick·tack *or* **tic·tac** \ˈtik-ˌtak\ *n* [redupl. of *tick*] (1549) **1 :** a ticking or tapping beat like that of a clock or watch **2 :** a contrivance used by children to tap on a window from a distance

tick·tock \ˈtik-ˈtäk, -ˌtäk\ *n* [imit.] (1848) **:** the ticking sound of a clock

tick trefoil *n* [[1]*tick*] (1853) **:** any of various leguminous plants (genus *Desmodium*) with trifoliolate leaves and rough sticky loments

[1]**ticky–tacky** \ˌti-kē-ˈta-kē\ *also* **ticky–tack** \-ˈtak\ *n, pl* **ticky–tackies** *also* **ticky–tacks** [redupl. of *tacky*] (1962) **:** sleazy or shoddy material used esp. in the construction of look-alike tract houses; *also* **:** something built of ticky-tacky

[2]**ticky–tacky** *also* **ticky–tack** *adj* (1964) **1 :** of an uninspired or monotonous sameness **2 :** TACKY **3 :** built of ticky-tacky

tic–tac–toe *or* **tick–tack–toe** \ˌtik-ˌtak-ˈtō\ *n* [*tic-tac-toe,* former game in which players with eyes shut brought a pencil down on a slate marked with numbers and scored the number hit] (ca. 1866) **:** a game in which two players alternately put Xs and Os in compartments of a figure formed by two vertical lines crossing two horizontal lines and each tries to get a row of three Xs or three Os before the opponent does

tid *abbr* [L *ter in die*] three times a day

tid·al \ˈtī-dᵊl\ *adj* (1807) **1 a :** of, relating to, caused by, or having tides ⟨~ cycles⟩ ⟨~ erosion⟩ **b :** periodically rising and falling or flowing and ebbing ⟨~ waters⟩ **2 :** dependent (as to the time of arrival or departure) upon the state of the tide ⟨a ~ steamer⟩ — **tid·al·ly** \-dᵊl-ē\ *adv*

tidal wave *n* (1851) **1 :** something overwhelming esp. in quantity or volume ⟨a *tidal wave* of tourists⟩ **2 a :** an unusually high sea wave that is triggered esp. by an earthquake **b :** an unusual rise of water alongshore due to strong winds

tid·bit \ˈtid-ˌbit\ *also* **tit·bit** \ˈtit-ˌbit\ *n* [perh. fr. *tit-* (as in *titmouse*) + *bit*] (ca. 1640) **1 :** a choice morsel of food **2 :** a choice or pleasing bit (as of information)

tid·dle·dy·winks \ˈti-dᵊl-dē-ˌwiŋ(k)s\ *or* **tid·dly·winks** \ˈti-dᵊl-ē-, ˈtid-lē-\ *n pl but sing in constr* [prob. fr. E dial. *tiddly* little, alter. of *little*] (1892) **:** a game whose object is to snap small disks from a flat surface into a small container

tid·dler \ˈti-dᵊl-ər, ˈtid-lər\ *n* [prob. fr. E dial. *tiddly* little] (1885) *Brit* **:** a small fish (as a stickleback or minnow)

tid·dly \ˈti-dᵊl-ē, ˈtid-lē\ *adj* [*tiddly* an alcoholic drink, prob. fr. E dial. *tiddly*] (1905) *chiefly Brit* **:** slightly drunk

[1]**tide** \ˈtīd\ *n* [ME, time, fr. OE *tīd;* akin to OHG *zīt* time and perh. to Gk *daiesthai* to divide] (bef. 12c) **1 a** *obs* **:** a space of time **:** PERIOD **b :** a fit or opportune time **:** OPPORTUNITY **c :** an ecclesiastical anniversary or festival; *also* **:** its season — usu. used in combination ⟨Eastertide⟩ **2 a** (1) **:** the alternate rising and falling of the surface of the ocean and

of water bodies (as gulfs and bays) connected with the ocean that occurs usu. twice a day and is the result of differing gravitational forces exerted at different parts of the earth by another body (as the moon or sun) (2) : a less marked rising and falling of an inland body of water (3) : a periodic movement in the earth's crust caused by the same forces that produce ocean tides (4) : a periodic distortion on one celestial body caused by the gravitational attraction of another (5) : one of the periodic movements of the atmosphere resembling those of the ocean and produced by gravitation or diurnal temperature changes **b** : FLOOD TIDE 1 **3 a** : something that fluctuates like the tides of the sea ⟨the ~ of public opinion⟩ **b** : a large and increasing quantity or volume ⟨a ~ of opportunists⟩ ⟨a swelling ~ of criticism⟩ **4 a** : a flowing stream : CURRENT **b** : the waters of the ocean **c** : the overflow of a flooding stream — **tide·less** \-ləs\ *adj*

[2]**tide** *vb* **tid·ed; tid·ing** *vi* (1593) : to flow as or in a tide : SURGE ~ *vt* : to cause to float with or as if with the tide

[3]**tide** *vi* **tid·ed; tid·ing** [ME, fr. OE *tīdan;* akin to MD *tiden* to go, come, OE *tīd* time] (bef. 12c) *archaic* : BETIDE, BEFALL

tide·land \ˈtīd-ˌland, -lənd\ *n* (1787) **1** : land overflowed during flood tide **2** : land underlying the ocean and lying beyond the low-water limit of the tide but being within the territorial waters of a nation — often used in pl.

tide·mark \-ˌmärk\ *n* (1799) **1 a** : a high-water or sometimes low-water mark left by tidal water or a flood **b** : a mark placed to indicate this point **2** : the point to which something has attained or below which it has receded ⟨the ~ of tolerance has risen —*New Republic*⟩

tide over *vt* [[2]*tide*] (1821) : to support or enable to survive temporarily ⟨money to *tide* us *over* until payday⟩

tide pool *n* (1853) : a pool of salt water left (as in a rock basin) by an ebbing tide — called also *tidal pool*

tide·wa·ter \-ˌwȯ-tər, -ˌwä-\ *n* (1772) **1** : water overflowing land at flood tide; *also* : water affected by the ebb and flow of the tide **2** : low-lying coastal land

tide·way \-ˌwā\ *n* (1798) : a channel in which the tide runs

tiding *n* [ME, fr. OE *tīdung,* fr. *tīdan* to betide] (12c) : a piece of news — usu. used in pl. ⟨good ~*s*⟩

[1]**ti·dy** \ˈtī-dē\ *adj* **ti·di·er; -est** [ME, timely, in good condition, fr. *tide* time] (13c) **1** : properly filled out : PLUMP **2** : adequately satisfactory : ACCEPTABLE, FAIR ⟨a ~ solution to their problem⟩ **3 a** : neat and orderly in appearance or habits : well ordered and cared for **b** : METHODICAL, PRECISE ⟨a ~ mind⟩ **4** : LARGE, SUBSTANTIAL ⟨a ~ profit⟩ — **ti·di·ly** \ˈtī-də-lē\ *adv* — **ti·di·ness** \ˈtī-dē-nəs\ *n*

[2]**tidy** *vb* **ti·died; ti·dy·ing** *vt* (1821) : to put in order ⟨~ up a room⟩ ~ *vi* : to make things tidy ⟨~*ing* up after supper⟩ — **ti·di·er** *n*

[3]**tidy** *n, pl* **tidies** (ca. 1828) **1** : a usu. compartmentalized receptacle for various small objects **2** : a piece of fancywork used to protect the back, arms, or headrest of a chair or sofa from wear or soil

ti·dy·tips \ˈtī-dē-ˌtips\ *n pl but sing or pl in constr* (1888) : an annual California composite herb (*Layia platyglossa*) having yellow-rayed flower heads often tipped with white

[1]**tie** \ˈtī\ *n* [ME *teg, tye,* fr. OE *tēag;* akin to ON *taug* rope, OE *tēon* to pull — more at TOW] (bef. 12c) **1 a** : a line, ribbon, or cord used for fastening, uniting, or drawing something closed; *esp* : SHOELACE **b** (1) : a structural element (as a rod or angle iron) holding two pieces together : a tension member in a construction (2) : any of the transverse supports to which railroad rails are fastened to keep them in line **2** : something that serves as a connecting link: as **a** : a moral or legal obligation to someone or something typically constituting a restraining power, influence, or duty **b** : a bond of kinship or affection **3** : a curved line that joins two musical notes of the same pitch to denote a single tone sustained through the time value of the two **4 a** : an equality in number (as of votes or scores) **b** : equality in a contest; *also* : a contest that ends in a draw **5** : a method or style of tying or knotting **6** : something that is knotted or is to be knotted when worn: as **a** : NECKTIE **b** : a low laced shoe : OXFORD — **tie·less** \-ləs\ *adj*

[2]**tie** *vb* **tied; ty·ing** \ˈtī-iŋ\ *or* **tie·ing** *vt* (bef. 12c) **1 a** : to fasten, attach, or close by means of a tie **b** : to form a knot or bow in ⟨~ your scarf⟩ **c** : to make by tying constituent elements ⟨*tied* a wreath⟩ ⟨~ a fishing fly⟩ **2 a** : to place or establish in relationship : CONNECT **b** : to unite in marriage **c** : to unite (musical notes) by a tie **d** : to join (power systems) electrically **3** : to restrain from independence or freedom of action or choice : constrain by or as if by authority, influence, agreement, or obligation **4 a** (1) : to make or have an equal score with in a contest (2) : to equalize (the score) in a game or contest (3) : to equalize the score of (a game) **b** : to provide or offer something equal to : EQUAL ~ *vi* : to make a tie: as **a** : to make a bond or connection **b** : to make an equal score **c** : to become attached **d** : to close by means of a tie — **tie into** : to attack with vigor — **tie one on** *slang* : to get drunk — **tie the knot** : to perform a marriage ceremony; *also* : to get married

tie–and–dye \ˈtī-ən-ˌdī\ *n* (1928) : TIE-DYEING

tie·back \ˈtī-ˌbak\ *n* (1926) **1** : a decorative strip or device of cloth, cord, or metal for draping a curtain to the side of a window **2** : a curtain with a tieback — usu. used in pl.

tie·break \ˈtī-ˌbrāk\ *n* (1970) : TIEBREAKER ⟨a tennis ~⟩

tie·break·er \ˈtī-ˌbrā-kər\ *n* (ca. 1932) : an additional contest or period of play used to select a winner when a competition ends in a tie

tied cottage *n* (1899) *Brit* : a cottage or house owned by an employer (as a farmer) and reserved for occupancy by an employee

tie–down \-ˌdau̇n\ *n* (ca. 1942) : a fitting or a system of lines and fittings used to secure something (as an aircraft or cargo)

tie–dye \ˈtī-ˌdī\ *n* (ca. 1939) **1** : TIE-DYEING **2** : a tie-dyed garment or fabric

tie–dyed *adj* (1904) : having patterns produced by tie-dyeing ⟨~ shirts⟩

tie–dye·ing \ˈtī-ˌdī-iŋ\ *n* (1904) : a hand method of producing patterns in textiles by tying portions of the fabric or yarn so that they will not absorb the dye

tie–in \ˈtī-ˌin\ *n* (1925) **1** : something that ties in, relates, or connects esp. in a promotional campaign **2** : a book that inspired or was inspired by a motion picture or television program

tie in *vt* (1793) : to bring into connection with something relevant: as **a** : to make the final connection of ⟨*tied in* the new branch pipeline⟩ **b** : to coordinate in such a manner as to produce balance and unity ⟨the illustrations were *tied in* with the text⟩ **c** : to use as a tie-in esp. in advertising ~ *vi* : to become tied in

tie–line \ˈtī-ˌlīn\ *n* (1923) : a telephone line that directly connects two or more private branch exchanges

tie·pin \ˈtī-ˌpin\ *n* (1780) : an ornamental straight pin that has usu. a sheath for the point and is used to hold the ends of a necktie in place

[1]**tier** \ˈtir\ *n* [MF *tire* rank, fr. OF — more at ATTIRE] (1569) **1 a** : a row, rank, or layer of articles; *esp* : one of two or more rows, levels, or ranks arranged one above another **b** : a group of political or geographic divisions that form a row across the map ⟨the southern ~ of states⟩ **2** : CLASS, CATEGORY

[2]**tier** *vt* (ca. 1889) : to place or arrange in tiers ~ *vi* : to rise in tiers

[3]**ti·er** *or* **ty·er** \ˈtī(-ə)r\ *n* (1633) : one that ties

[1]**tierce** *var of* TERCE

[2]**tierce** \ˈtirs\ *n* [ME *terce, tierce,* fr. AF, fr. fem. of *terz,* adj., third, fr. L *tertius* — more at THIRD] (15c) **1** *obs* : THIRD 2 **2** : a sequence of three playing cards of the same suit

tier·cel \ˈtir-səl\ *or* **ter·cel** \ˈtər-səl\ *n* [ME *tercel,* fr. AF, fr. VL **tertiolus,* fr. dim. of L *tertius* third; prob. fr. the fact that the male is about one third smaller than the female] (14c) : a male hawk

tiered \ˈtird\ *adj* (1807) : having or arranged in tiers, rows, or layers — often used in combination ⟨triple-*tiered*⟩

tie–rod \ˈtī-ˌräd\ *n* (1839) : a rod (as of steel) used as a connecting member or brace

tie silk *n* (ca. 1915) : a silk fabric of firm resilient pliable texture used for neckties and for blouses and accessories

tie tack *or* **tie tac** \-ˌtak\ *n* (1954) : an ornamented pin with a receiving button or clasp that is used to attach the two parts of a necktie together or to attach a necktie to a shirt

tie–up \ˈtī-ˌəp\ *n* (1851) **1 a** : a cow stable; *also* : a space for a single cow in a stable **b** : a mooring place for a boat **2** : a slowdown or stoppage of traffic, business, or operation (as by a mechanical breakdown) **3** : CONNECTION, ASSOCIATION ⟨helpful financial ~*s*⟩

tie up *vt* (1530) **1** : to attach, fasten, or bind securely; *also* : to wrap up and fasten **2 a** : to connect closely : JOIN ⟨*tie up* the loose ends⟩ **b** : to cause to be linked so as to depend on or relate to something **3 a** : to place or invest in such a manner as to make unavailable for other purposes ⟨their money was *tied up* in stocks⟩ **b** : to restrain from normal movement, operation, or progress ⟨traffic was *tied up* for miles⟩ **4 a** : to keep busy ⟨was *tied up* in conference all day⟩ **b** : to preempt the use of ⟨*tied up* the phone for an hour⟩ ~ *vi* **1** : DOCK ⟨the ferry *ties up* at the south slip⟩ **2** : to assume a definite relationship ⟨this *ties up* with what I told you before⟩

[1]**tiff** \ˈtif\ *vi* [origin unknown] (1700) : to have a petty quarrel

[2]**tiff** *n* (1754) : a petty quarrel

tif·fa·ny \ˈti-fə-nē\ *n, pl* **-nies** [perh. fr. obs. F *tiphanie* Epiphany, fr. LL *theophania,* fr. LGk, ultim. fr. Gk *theos* god + *phainein* to show] (1601) **1** : a sheer silk gauze formerly used for clothing and trimmings **2** : a plain-woven open-mesh cotton fabric (as cheesecloth)

Tif·fa·ny \ˈti-fə-nē\ *adj* (1936) : being glass or an article of glass made by or in the manner of Louis C. Tiffany; *esp* : made of pieces of stained glass ⟨a *Tiffany*-style lamp⟩ ⟨a ~ window⟩

tif·fin \ˈti-fən\ *n* [prob. alter. of *tiffing,* gerund of obs. E *tiff* to eat between meals] (1800) *chiefly Brit* : a light midday meal : LUNCHEON

ti·ger \ˈtī-gər\ *n, pl* **tigers** [ME *tigre,* fr. OE *tiger* & AF *tigre,* both fr. L *tigris,* fr. Gk, prob. of Iranian origin; akin to Av *tighra-* pointed; akin to Gk *stizein* to tattoo — more at STICK] (bef. 12c) **1** *pl also* **tiger a** : a large Asian carnivorous mammal (*Panthera tigris*) of the cat family having a usu. tawny coat transversely striped with black **b** : any of several large wildcats (as the jaguar or cougar) **c** : a domestic cat with striped pattern **d** *Austral* : TASMANIAN TIGER **2 a** : a fierce, daring, or aggressive person or quality ⟨aroused the ~ in him⟩ ⟨a ~ for work⟩ **b** : one (as a situation) that is formidable or impossible to control ⟨how the ~ of inflation can be tamed —J. A. Davenport⟩ — often used in the phrases *ride a tiger* and *have a tiger by the tail* **3** *Brit* : a groom in livery — **ti·ger·ish** \-g(ə-)rish\ *adj* — **ti·ger·ish·ly** *adv* — **ti·ger·ish·ness** *n* — **ti·ger·like** \-gər-ˌlīk\ *adj*

tiger beetle *n* (1826) : any of numerous active carnivorous beetles (family Cicindelidae) having larvae that tunnel in the soil

tiger cat *n* (1699) **1** : any of various wildcats (as the serval, ocelot, or margay) of moderate size and variegated coloration **2** : a striped or sometimes blotched tabby cat

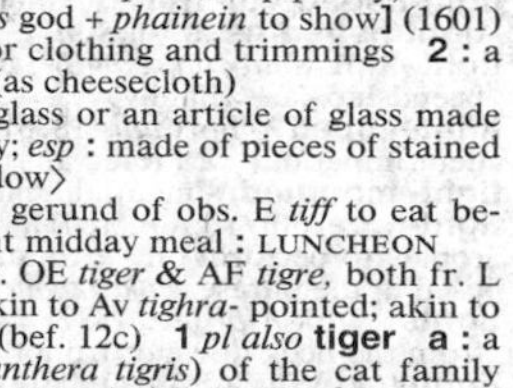

tiger cat 2

ti·ger·eye \ˈtī-gər-ˌī\ *or* **ti·ger's–eye** \-gərz-\ *n* (1888) : a usu. yellowish to brown chatoyant stone that consists of silicified crocidolite and is much used for ornament

tiger lily *n* (1824) : a common Asian garden lily (*Lilium lancifolium* syn. *L. tigrinum*) that has nodding orange-colored flowers densely spotted with black and alternate leaves with black bulblets in the leaf axils; *also* : any of various lilies with similar flowers

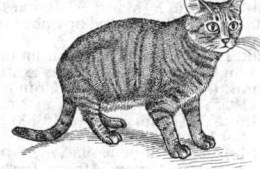

tiger maple *n* (1952) : maple lumber having a distinct irregularly striped pattern and much used for furniture

tiger mosquito *n* (1835) : ASIAN TIGER MOSQUITO

tiger moth *n* (1816) : any of a family (Arctiidae) of stout-bodied moths usu. with broad striped or spotted wings

tiger salamander *n* (1842) : a large widely distributed No. American salamander (*Ambystoma tigrinum* of the family Ambystomatidae) that is variably colored with contrasting blotches, spots, or bars

tiger shark *n* (ca. 1785) : a large gray or brown stocky-bodied requiem shark (*Galeocerdo cuvieri*) that is nearly cosmopolitan esp. in warm seas and can be dangerous to humans — see SHARK illustration

tiger shrimp *n* (1979) **:** a large shrimp (*Penaeus monodon* of the family Penaeidae) of the Indian and Pacific oceans that is often farmed and widely sold as food

tiger swallowtail *n* (1889) **:** a large widely distributed swallowtail (*Papilio glaucus*) of eastern No. America that in the male is largely yellow with black margins and black stripes on the wings and in the female is usu. similarly marked in the north but is very often all or mostly black in the south; *also* **:** any of several closely related black and yellow swallowtails (as *P. rutulus* of western No. America)

[1]**tight** \ˈtīt\ *adj* [ME *tiht, thyht* dense, solid, watertight, of Scand origin; akin to ON *thēttr* tight; akin to MHG *dīhte* thick, Skt *tanakti* it causes to coagulate] (14c) **1 a :** having elements close together ⟨a ~ formation⟩ ⟨a ~ line of type⟩ **b :** so close in structure as to prevent passage or escape (as of liquid, gas, or light) ⟨a ~ ship⟩ ⟨a ~ seal⟩ — compare LIGHTPROOF, WATERTIGHT **c :** fitting very close to the body ⟨~ jeans⟩; *also* **:** too snug ⟨~ shoes⟩ **d** (1) **:** closely packed **:** very full ⟨a ~ bale of hay⟩ (2) **:** barely allowing time for completion ⟨a ~ schedule⟩ ⟨~ deadlines⟩ **e :** allowing little or no room for free motion or movement ⟨a ~ connection⟩ ⟨a ~ crawl space⟩; *also* **:** having a small radius ⟨a ~ turn⟩ **2 a :** strongly fixed or held **:** SECURE ⟨a ~ jar lid⟩ ⟨a ~ grip on the ladder⟩ **b** (1) **:** not slack or loose **:** TAUT ⟨kept the reins ~⟩ ⟨a ~ knot⟩ ⟨a ~ drumhead⟩; *also* **:** marked by firmness and muscle tone ⟨a ~ stomach⟩ (2) **:** marked by unusual tension (as in the face or body) ⟨lips ~ with anger⟩ ⟨a family ~ with fear⟩ **3** *chiefly dial* **:** CAPABLE, COMPETENT **4 a :** difficult to cope with ⟨in a ~ spot financially⟩ **b :** relatively difficult to obtain ⟨money is ~ just now⟩; *also* **:** characterized by such difficulty ⟨a ~ job market⟩ **c :** not liberal in giving **:** STINGY ⟨~ with a penny⟩ **5 :** characterized by little difference in the relative positions of contestants with respect to final outcome **:** CLOSE ⟨a ~ race for mayor⟩ **6 :** somewhat drunk **7 a :** characterized by firmness or strictness in control or application or in attention to details ⟨~ security⟩ ⟨ran a ~ newsroom⟩ ⟨keeps a ~ hand on her investments⟩ **b :** marked by control or discipline in expression or style **:** having little or no extraneous matter ⟨~ writing⟩ **c :** characterized by a polished style and precise arrangements in music performance **8 :** having a close personal or working relationship **:** INTIMATE ⟨is ~ with the boss⟩ **9 :** being such that the subject fills the frame ⟨a ~ close-up⟩ — **tight·ly** *adv* — **tight·ness** *n*

[2]**tight** *adv* (1680) **1 :** FAST, TIGHTLY, FIRMLY ⟨the door was shut ~⟩ **2 :** in a sound manner **:** SOUNDLY ⟨sleep ~⟩

tight·en \ˈtī-tᵊn\ *vb* **tight·ened; tight·en·ing** \ˈtīt-niŋ, ˈtī-tᵊn-iŋ\ *vt* (ca. 1727) **:** to make tight or tighter ~ *vi* **:** to become tight or tighter — **tight·en·er** \ˈtīt-nər, ˈtī-tᵊn-ər\ *n* — **tighten one's belt :** to practice strict economy

tight end *n* (1962) **:** an offensive football end who lines up close to the tackle and can act as a lineman or receiver

tight·fist·ed \ˈtīt-ˈfis-təd\ *adj* (1844) **:** reluctant to part with money — **tight·fist·ed·ness** \-nəs\ *n*

tight–knit \-ˈnit\ *adj* (1946) **:** closely integrated and bound in love or friendship ⟨a ~ family⟩

tight–lipped \-ˈlipt\ *adj* (1876) **1 :** having the lips closed tight (as in determination) **2 :** reluctant to speak **:** TACITURN

tight–mouthed \-ˈmau̇thd, -ˈmau̇tht\ *adj* (1911) **:** CLOSEMOUTHED

tight·rope \ˈtīt-ˌrōp\ *n* (1801) **1 :** a rope or wire stretched taut for acrobats to perform on **2 :** a dangerously precarious situation — usu. used in the phrase *walk a tightrope*

tights \ˈtīts\ *n pl* (ca. 1837) **:** a skintight garment covering the body from the neck down or from the waist down; *also, Brit* **:** PANTY HOSE

tight·wad \ˈtīt-ˌwäd\ *n* (1906) **:** a close or miserly person

tight·wire \-ˌwī(-ə)r\ *n* (1928) **:** a tightrope made of wire

tighty–whit·ies *also* **tighty–whit·eys** \ˈtī-tē-ˈwī-tēz\ *n pl* (1990) *slang* **:** snug white underpants for men **:** white briefs

ti·glon \ˈtī-glən\ *n* [*tiger* + *lion*] (1942) **:** a hybrid between a male tiger and a female lion

ti·gon \ˈtī-gən\ *n* [*tiger* + *lion*] (1926) **:** TIGLON

Ti·gre \ˈti-(ˌ)grā, ˈtē-; tē-\ *n* (1878) **:** a Semitic language of northern Eritrea and adjacent parts of Sudan

ti·gress \ˈtī-grəs\ *n* (1611) **:** a female tiger; *also* **:** a tigerish woman

Ti·gri·nya \tə-ˈgrē-nyə\ *n* [Amharic *tigriñña*, fr. *Tigray* Tigre, Ethiopia] (1878) **:** a Semitic language of northern Ethiopia and Eritrea

tike *var of* TYKE

ti·ki \ˈtē-kē\ *n* [Maori & Marquesan, fr. *Tiki*, first man or creator of first man] (1777) **:** a wood or stone image of a Polynesian supernatural power

tiki bar *n* (1980) **:** a restaurant or bar decorated in a simulated Polynesian theme that usu. serves exotic cocktails

tik·ka \ˈti-kə\ *n* [Hindi & Urdu *tikkā* small piece of meat, fr. Pers *tikka*] (1955) **:** an Indian dish of marinated meat cooked on a skewer

til \ˈtil\ *n* [Hindi & Urdu, fr. Skt *tila*] (1840) **:** SESAME

'til *or* **til** *var of* [1]TILL 2, [2]TILL

ti·la·pia \tə-ˈlä-pē-ə, -ˈlā-\ *n, pl* **-pia** *also* **-pias** [NL, genus name] (1849) **:** any of numerous African freshwater cichlid fishes (genera *Oreochromis, Tilapia,* and *Sarotherodon*) often raised for food

til·bury \ˈtil-ˌber-ē, -b(ə-)rē\ *n, pl* **-bur·ies** [*Tilbury*, 19th cent. Eng. coach builder] (1814) **:** a light 2-wheeled carriage

til·de \ˈtil-də\ *n* [Sp, fr. ML *titulus* tittle] (ca. 1864) **1 :** a mark ˜ placed esp. over the letter *n* (as in Spanish *señor* sir) to denote the sound \nʸ\ or over vowels (as in Portuguese *irmã* sister) to indicate nasality **2 a :** the mark ~ used to indicate negation in logic and the geometric relation "is similar to" in mathematics **b :** the mark ~ used to indicate an approximate value

[1]**tile** \ˈtī(-ə)l\ *n, often attrib* [ME, fr. OE *tigele*, fr. L *tegula* tile; akin to L *tegere* to cover — more at THATCH] (bef. 12c) **1** *pl* **tiles** *or* **tile a :** a flat or curved piece of fired clay, stone, or concrete used esp. for roofs, floors, or walls and often for ornamental work **b :** a hollow or a semicircular and open earthenware or concrete piece used in constructing a drain **c :** a hollow building unit made of fired clay or of shale or gypsum **2 :** TILING **3 :** HAT; *esp* **:** a high silk hat **4 :** a thin piece of resilient material (as cork, linoleum, or rubber) used esp. for covering floors or walls **5 :** a thin piece resembling a ceramic tile that usu. bears a mark or letter and is used as a playing piece in a board game (as mah-jongg) — **on the tiles** *Brit* **:** engaged in late-night carousing

[2]**tile** *vt* **tiled; til·ing** (13c) **1 :** to cover with tiles **2 :** to install drainage tile in — **til·er** *n*

tile·fish \ˈtī(-ə)l-ˌfish\ *n* [*tile-* modif. of NL *Lopholatilus*] (1881) **:** any of various marine bony fishes (family Malacanthidae) used as food; *esp* **:** a large fish (*Lopholatilus chamaeleonticeps*) of deep waters of the Atlantic and Gulf of Mexico with a fleshy appendage on the head and yellow spots on the upper body and some of its fins

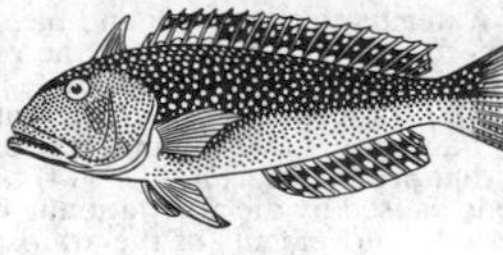

tilefish

til·ing *n* (15c) **1 :** the action or work of one who tiles **2 a :** TILES **b :** a surface of tiles **3 :** TESSELLATION 1b; *also* **:** a generalization of this to fill Euclidean space of three or higher dimensions using geometric objects of the same dimension as the space filled

[1]**till** \tᵊl, təl, ˈtil\ *prep* [ME, fr. OE *til;* akin to ON *til* to, till, OE *til* good] (bef. 12c) **1** *chiefly Scot* **:** TO **2** *or* **'til** *also* **til :** UNTIL

[2]**till** *or* **'til** *also* **til** *conj* (12c) **:** UNTIL

[3]**till** \ˈtil\ *vt* [ME *tilien, tillen*, fr. OE *tilian;* akin to OE *til* good, suitable, OHG *zil* goal] (12c) **:** to work by plowing, sowing, and raising crops **:** CULTIVATE — **till·able** \ˈti-lə-bəl\ *adj*

[4]**till** \ˈtil\ *n* [ME *tille* locker, chest] (15c) **1 a :** a box, drawer, or tray in a receptacle (as a cabinet or chest) used esp. for valuables **b :** a money drawer in a store or bank; *also* **:** CASH REGISTER **2 a :** the money contained in a till **b :** a supply of esp. ready money

[5]**till** \ˈtil\ *n* [origin unknown] (1842) **:** unstratified glacial drift consisting of clay, sand, gravel, and boulders intermingled

till·age \ˈti-lij\ *n* (15c) **1 :** the operation of tilling land **2 :** cultivated land

til·land·sia \tə-ˈlan(d)-zē-ə\ *n* [NL, fr. Elias *Tillands* †1693 Finn. botanist] (1759) **:** any of a large genus (*Tillandsia*) of chiefly epiphytic plants of the pineapple family native to tropical and subtropical America

[1]**til·ler** \ˈti-lər\ *n* [ME **tiller*, fr. OE *telgor, telgra* twig, shoot; akin to OHG *zelga* twig, OIr *dlongaid* he splits] (bef. 12c) **:** STALK, SPROUT; *esp* **:** one from the base of a plant or from the axils of its lower leaves

[2]**til·ler** *vi* **til·lered; til·ler·ing** \ˈti-lə-riŋ, ˈtil-riŋ\ (1677) *of a plant* **:** to put forth tillers

[3]**till·er** \ˈti-lər\ *n* (13c) **:** one that tills **:** CULTIVATOR

[4]**til·ler** \ˈti-lər\ *n* [ME *teler, tiller* stock of a crossbow, tiller, fr. AF *teiler* stock of a crossbow] (ca. 1625) **:** a lever used to turn the rudder of a boat from side to side; *broadly* **:** a device or system that plays a part in steering something

til·ler·man \ˈti-lər-mən\ *n* (ca. 1934) **:** one in charge of a tiller **:** STEERSMAN

Til·sit \ˈtil-sət\ *also* **Til·sit·er** \-sə-tər\ *n* [G *Tilsiter*, fr. *Tilsit* (now Sovetsk, Russia)] (ca. 1932) **:** a semisoft porous light yellow cheese with a flavor that ranges from mild to sharp

[1]**tilt** \ˈtilt\ *n* [ME *teld, telte* tent, canopy, fr. OE *teld;* akin to OHG *zelt* tent] (15c) **:** a canopy for a wagon, boat, or stall

[2]**tilt** *vt* (15c) **:** to cover or provide with a tilt

[3]**tilt** *n* [[4]*tilt*] (1507) **1 a :** a contest on horseback in which two combatants charging with lances or similar weapons try to unhorse each other **:** JOUST **b :** a tournament of tilts **2 a :** DISPUTE, CONTENTION **b :** SPEED — used in the phrase *full tilt* **3 a :** the act of tilting **:** the state or position of being tilted **b :** a sloping surface **c :** SLANT, BIAS ⟨a ~ toward military involvement⟩ **4 :** any of various contests resembling or suggesting tilting with lances — **tilt** *adj*

[4]**tilt** *vb* [ME *tulten, tilten* to fall over, cause to fall, fr. OE **tyltan, *tieltan*, akin to OE *tealt* unstable, *tealtian* to totter] *vt* (1594) **1 :** to cause to have an inclination **2 a :** to point or thrust in or as if in a tilt ⟨~ a lance⟩ **b :** to charge against ⟨~ an adversary⟩ ~ *vi* **1 a :** to move or shift so as to lean or incline **:** SLANT **b :** to incline, tend, or become drawn toward an opinion, course of action, or one side of a controversy **2 a :** to engage in a combat with lances **:** JOUST **b :** to make an impetuous attack ⟨~ at social evils⟩ — **tilt·able** \ˈtil-tə-bəl\ *adj* — **tilt·er** *n*

tilth \ˈtilth\ *n* [ME, fr. OE, fr. *tilian* to till] (bef. 12c) **1 :** cultivated land **:** TILLAGE **2 :** the state of aggregation of a soil esp. in relation to its suitability for crop growth

tilt·me·ter \ˈtilt-ˌmē-tər\ *n* (1932) **:** an instrument to measure the tilting of the earth's surface

tilt–ro·tor \-ˌrō-tər\ *n* (1961) **:** an aircraft that has rotors at the end of each wing which can be oriented vertically for vertical takeoffs and landings, horizontally for forward flight, or to any position in between

tilt·yard \ˈtilt-ˌyärd\ *n* (1528) **:** a yard or place for tilting contests

Tim *abbr* Timothy

tim·bale \ˈtim-bəl; tim-ˈbäl, tam-\ *n* [F, lit., kettledrum] (1824) **1 a :** a creamy mixture (as of meat or vegetables) baked in a mold; *also* **:** the mold in which it is baked **b :** a small pastry shell filled with a cooked timbale mixture **2** *also* **tim·bal** \ˈtim-bəl\ **:** one of a set of single-headed cylindrical drums played with sticks — usu. used in pl.

[1]**tim·ber** \ˈtim-bər\ *n* [ME, fr. OE, building, wood; akin to OHG *zimbar* wood, room, Gk *demein* to build, *domos* course of stones or bricks] (bef. 12c) **1 a :** growing trees or their wood **b** — used interjectionally to warn of a falling tree **2 :** wood suitable for building or for carpentry **3 :** MATERIAL, STUFF; *esp* **:** a person or type of person qualified for a particular position or status ⟨managerial ~⟩ **4 a :** a large squared or dressed piece of wood ready for use or forming part of a structure **b** *Brit* **:** LUMBER 2a **c :** a curving frame branching outward from the keel of a ship and bending upward in a vertical direction that is usu. composed of several pieces united **:** RIB — **timber** *adj*

[2]**timber** *vt* **tim·bered; tim·ber·ing** \-b(ə-)riŋ\ (bef. 12c) **:** to frame, cover, or support with timbers

tim·ber·doo·dle \ˌtim-bər-ˈdü-dᵊl\ *n* [[1]*timber* + *doodle* cock] (1856) **:** the No. American woodcock

tim·bered \ˈtim-bərd\ *adj* (15c) **1 :** having walls framed by exposed timbers **2 :** having a specified structure or constitution **3 :** covered with growing timber **:** WOODED

tim·ber·head \ˈtim-bər-ˌhed\ *n* (1794) **1 :** the top end of a ship's timber used above the gunwale (as for belaying ropes) **2 :** a bollard bolted to the deck where the end of a timber would come

timber hitch *n* (ca. 1815) **:** a knot used to secure a line to a log or spar — see KNOT illustration

tim•ber•ing \ˈtim-b(ə-)riŋ\ *n* (15c) : a set or arrangement of timbers

tim•ber•land \-bər-ˌland\ *n* (1654) : wooded land esp. with marketable timber

tim•ber•line \-ˌlīn\ *n* (1867) : the upper limit of arboreal growth in mountains or high latitudes — called also *tree line*

tim•ber•man \-mən\ *n* (1889) : LUMBERMAN

timber rattlesnake *n* (1895) : a widely distributed rattlesnake (*Crotalus horridus*) chiefly of the eastern U.S.

timber wolf *n* (1860) : GRAY WOLF

tim•ber•work \ˈtim-bər-ˌwərk\ *n* (14c) : timber construction

tim•bre *also* **tim•ber** \ˈtam-bər, ˈtim-; ˈtam(brᵊ)\ *n* [F, fr. MF, bell struck by a hammer, fr. OF, drum, fr. MGk *tymbanon* kettledrum, fr. Gk *tympanon* — more at TYMPANUM] (1845) : the quality given to a sound by its overtones: as **a** : the resonance by which the ear recognizes and identifies a voiced speech sound **b** : the quality of tone distinctive of a particular singing voice or musical instrument — **tim•bral** \ˈtam-brəl, ˈtim-\ *adj*

tim•brel \ˈtim-brəl\ *n* [dim. of obs. E *timbre* small drum, tambourine, fr. ME, fr. AF, drum] (ca. 1520) : a small hand drum or tambourine — **tim•brelled** \-brəld\ *adj*

[1]**time** \ˈtīm\ *n* [ME, fr. OE *tīma;* akin to ON *tīmi* time, OE *tīd* — more at TIDE] (bef. 12c) **1 a** : the measured or measurable period during which an action, process, or condition exists or continues : DURATION **b** : a nonspatial continuum that is measured in terms of events which succeed one another from past through present to future **c** : LEISURE ⟨∼ for reading⟩ **2** : the point or period when something occurs : OCCASION **3 a** : an appointed, fixed, or customary moment or hour for something to happen, begin, or end ⟨arrived ahead of ∼⟩ **b** : an opportune or suitable moment ⟨decided it was ∼ to retire⟩ — often used in the phrase *about time* ⟨about ∼ for a change⟩ **4 a** : a historical period : AGE **b** : a division of geologic chronology **c** : conditions at present or at some specified period — usu. used in pl. ⟨∼*s* are hard⟩ ⟨move with the ∼*s*⟩ **d** : the present time ⟨issues of the ∼⟩ **5 a** : LIFETIME **b** : a period of apprenticeship **c** : a term of military service **d** : a prison sentence **6** : SEASON ⟨very hot for this ∼ of year⟩ **7 a** : rate of speed : TEMPO **b** : the grouping of the beats of music : RHYTHM **8 a** : a moment, hour, day, or year as indicated by a clock or calendar ⟨what ∼ is it⟩ **b** : any of various systems (as sidereal or solar) of reckoning time **9 a** : one of a series of recurring instances or repeated actions ⟨you've been told many ∼*s*⟩ **b** *pl* (1) : added or accumulated quantities or instances ⟨five ∼*s* greater⟩ (2) : equal fractional parts of which an indicated number equal a comparatively greater quantity ⟨seven ∼*s* smaller⟩ ⟨three ∼*s* closer⟩ **c** : TURN ⟨three ∼*s* at bat⟩ **10** : finite as contrasted with infinite duration **11** : a person's experience during a specified period or on a particular occasion ⟨a good ∼⟩ ⟨a hard ∼⟩ **12 a** : the hours or days required to be occupied by one's work ⟨make up ∼⟩ ⟨on company ∼⟩ **b** : an hourly pay rate ⟨straight ∼⟩ **c** : wages paid at discharge or resignation ⟨pick up your ∼ and get out⟩ **13 a** : the playing time of a game **b** : TIME-OUT 1 **14** : a period during which something is used or available for use ⟨computer ∼⟩ — **at the same time** : NEVERTHELESS, YET ⟨slick and *at the same time* strangely unprofessional —Gerald Weaks⟩ — **at times** : at intervals : OCCASIONALLY — **for the time being** : for the present — **from time to time** : once in a while : OCCASIONALLY — **in no time** : very quickly or soon — **in time 1** : sufficiently early **2** : EVENTUALLY **3** : in correct tempo ⟨learn to play *in time*⟩ — **on time 1 a** : at the appointed time **b** : on schedule **2** : on the installment plan — **time and again** : FREQUENTLY, REPEATEDLY

[2]**time** *vb* **timed; tim•ing** *vt* (14c) **1 a** : to arrange or set the time of : SCHEDULE **b** : to regulate (a watch) to keep correct time **2** : to set the tempo, speed, or duration of ⟨*timed* his leap perfectly —Neil Amdur⟩ **3** : to cause to keep time with something **4** : to determine or record the time, duration, or rate of ⟨∼ a horse⟩ **5** : to dispose (as a mechanical part) so that an action occurs at a desired instant or in a desired way ∼ *vi* : to keep or beat time

[3]**time** *adj* (ca. 1711) **1 a** : of or relating to time **b** : recording time **2** : timed to ignite or explode at a specific moment ⟨a ∼ charge⟩ **3 a** : payable on a specified future day or a certain length of time after presentation for acceptance ⟨a ∼ draft⟩ ⟨∼ deposits⟩ **b** : based on installment payments ⟨a ∼ sale⟩

time and a half *n* (1888) : payment for work (as overtime or holiday work) at one and a half times the worker's regular wage rate

time bomb *n* (1893) **1** : a bomb so made as to explode at a predetermined time **2** : something with a potentially dangerous or detrimental delayed reaction

time capsule *n* (1938) **1** : a container holding historical records or objects representative of current culture that is deposited (as in a cornerstone) for preservation until discovery by some future age **2** : something resembling a time capsule ⟨sunken vessels are archaeological *time capsules* —Philip Trupp⟩

time card *n* (ca. 1891) : a card used with a time clock to record an employee's starting and quitting times each day or on each job

time chart *n* (ca. 1930) **1** : a chart showing the standard times in various parts of the world with reference to a specified time at a specified place **2** : TIME LINE 1

time clock *n* (1887) : a clock that stamps starting and quitting times on an employee's time card

time–con•sum•ing \ˈtīm-kən-ˈsü-miŋ\ *adj* (1600) **1** : using or taking up a great deal of time ⟨∼ chores⟩ **2** : wasteful of time ⟨∼ tactics⟩

timed *adj* (1631) **1** : done or taking place at a time of a specified sort ⟨an ill-*timed* arrival⟩ **2** : made to occur at or in a set time ⟨a ∼ explosion⟩

time dilation *n* (1934) : a slowing of time in accordance with the theory of relativity that occurs in a system in motion relative to an outside observer and that becomes apparent esp. as the speed of the system approaches that of light — called also *time dilatation*

timed–re•lease \ˈtīmd-ri-ˈlēs\ *or* **time–re•lease** \ˈtīm-\ *adj* (1966) : consisting of or containing a drug that is released in small amounts over time (as by dissolution of a coating) usu. in the gastrointestinal tract ⟨∼ capsules⟩

time exposure *n* (1893) : exposure of a photographic film for a definite time usu. of more than one half second; *also* : a photograph taken by such exposure

time frame *n* (1964) : a period of time esp. with respect to some action or project

time–hon•ored \ˈtīm-ˌä-nərd\ *adj* (ca. 1596) : honored because of age or long usage ⟨∼ traditions⟩

time immemorial *n* (1602) **1** : a time antedating a period legally fixed as the basis for a custom or right **2** : time so long past as to be indefinite in history or tradition — called also *time out of mind*

time•keep•er \ˈtīm-ˌkē-pər\ *n* (1686) **1** : TIMEPIECE **2** : a clerk who keeps records of the time worked by employees **3** : a person appointed to mark and announce the time in an athletic game or contest — **time•keep•ing** \-piŋ\ *n*

time killer *n* (1728) **1** : a person with free time **2** : something that passes the time : DIVERSION

time lag *n* (1892) : an interval of time between two related phenomena (as a cause and its effect)

time–lapse \ˈtīm-ˌlaps\ *adj* (1927) : of, relating to, or constituting a motion picture made so that when projected a slow action (as the opening of a flower bud) appears to be speeded up

time•less \ˈtīm-ləs\ *adj* (ca. 1560) **1** *archaic* : PREMATURE, UNTIMELY **2 a** : having no beginning or end : ETERNAL **b** : not restricted to a particular time or date ⟨the ∼ themes of love, solitude, joy, and nature —*Writer*⟩ **3** : not affected by time : AGELESS — **time•less•ly** *adv* — **time•less•ness** *n*

time line *n* (1951) **1** : a table listing important events for successive years within a particular historical period **2** *usu* **time•line** \ˈtīm-ˌlīn\ : a schedule of events and procedures : TIMETABLE 2

time lock *n* (ca. 1871) : a lock controlled by clockwork to prevent its being opened before a set time

[1]**time•ly** \ˈtīm-lē\ *adv* (bef. 12c) **1** *archaic* : EARLY, SOON **2** : in time : OPPORTUNELY ⟨the question was not . . . ∼ raised in the state court —W. O. Douglas⟩

[2]**timely** *adj* **time•li•er; -est** (13c) **1** : coming early or at the right time ⟨a ∼ decision⟩ ⟨∼ payment⟩ **2** : appropriate or adapted to the times or the occasion ⟨a ∼ book⟩ — **time•li•ness** *n*

time machine *n* (1895) : a hypothetical device that permits travel into the past and future

time–of–flight \ˈtīm-ə(v)-ˈflīt\ *adj* (1945) : of, relating to, being, or done with an instrument (as a mass spectrometer) that separates particles (as ions) according to the time required for them to traverse a tube of a certain length

time•ous \ˈtī-məs\ *adj* (ca. 1520) *chiefly Scot & SoAfr* : TIMELY — **time•ous•ly** *adv*

time–out \ˈtīm-ˈau̇t\ *n* (ca. 1896) **1** : a brief suspension of activity : BREAK; *esp* : a suspension of play in an athletic game **2** : a quiet period used esp. as a disciplinary measure for children

time out of mind (15c) : TIME IMMEMORIAL 2

time•piece \ˈtīm-ˌpēs\ *n* (1765) : a device (as a clock or watch) to measure or show progress of time; *esp* : one that does not chime

time•pleas•er \-ˌplē-zər\ *n* (1593) *obs* : TIMESERVER

tim•er \ˈtī-mər\ *n* (1841) : one that times: as **a** : TIMEPIECE; *esp* : a stopwatch for timing races **b** : TIMEKEEPER **c** : a device (as a clock) that indicates by a sound the end of an interval of time or that starts or stops a device at predetermined times

time reversal *n* (1955) : a formal operation in mathematical physics that reverses the order in which a sequence of events occurs

times \ˈtīmz\ *prep* (14c) : multiplied by ⟨two ∼ two is four⟩

time–sav•ing \ˈtīm-ˌsā-viŋ\ *adj* (1828) : intended or serving to expedite something ⟨∼ kitchen appliances⟩ — **time–sav•er** \-ˌsā-vər\ *n*

time•scale \-ˌskāl\ *n* (1890) : an arrangement of events used as a measure of the relative or absolute duration or antiquity of a period of history or geologic or cosmic time

time series *n* (1919) : a set of data collected sequentially usu. at fixed intervals of time

time•serv•er \-ˌsər-vər\ *n* (1584) : a person whose behavior is adjusted to the pattern of the times or to please superiors : TEMPORIZER

[1]**time•serv•ing** \-viŋ\ *n* (1621) : the behavior or practice of a timeserver

[2]**timeserving** *adj* (1621) : marked by or revealing a lack of independence or integrity ⟨a mean, ∼ little man, grovelling odiously before the wealthy people —Peter Forster⟩

time–shar•ing \ˈtīm-ˌsher-iŋ\ *n* (1953) **1** : simultaneous use of a central computer by many users at remote locations **2** *or* **time–share** \-ˌsher\ : joint ownership or rental of a vacation lodging (as a condominium) by several persons with each occupying the premises in turn for short periods — **time–share** *vt*

time sheet *n* (1904) **1** : a sheet for recording the time of arrival and departure of workers and for recording the amount of time spent on each job **2** : a sheet for summarizing hours worked by each worker during a pay period

time signature *n* (1875) : a sign used in music to indicate meter and usu. written as a fraction with the bottom number indicating the kind of note used as a unit of time and the top number indicating the number of units in each measure

times sign *n* (1948) : the symbol × used to indicate multiplication

time stamp *n* (1892) : a device for recording the date and time of day that letters or papers are received or sent out — **time–stamp** *vt*

time•ta•ble \ˈtīm-ˌtā-bəl\ *n* (1838) **1** : a table of departure and arrival times of trains, buses, or airplanes **2 a** : a schedule showing a planned order or sequence **b** : PROGRAM 3 — **time–table** *vt*

time–test•ed \-ˌtes-təd\ *adj* (1930) : having effectiveness that has been proved over a long period of time ⟨∼ methods⟩

time trial *n* (ca. 1949) : a competitive event (as in auto racing) in which individuals are successively timed over a set course or distance

time warp *n* (1954) : an anomaly, discontinuity, or suspension held to occur in the progress of time — **time–warp** *or* **time–warped** \ˈtīm-ˌwȯrpt\ *adj*

time•work \ˈtīm-ˌwərk\ *n* (1829) : work paid for at a standard rate for the hour or the day — **time•work•er** \-ˌwər-kər\ *n*

\ə\ **abut** \ᵊ\ kitten, F table \ər\ **fur**ther \a\ **ash** \ā\ **ace** \ä\ **mop, mar** \au̇\ **out** \ch\ **chin** \e\ **bet** \ē\ **easy** \g\ **go** \i\ **hit** \ī\ **ice** \j\ **job** \ŋ\ **sing** \ō\ **go** \ȯ\ **law** \ȯi\ **boy** \th\ **thin** \t͟h\ **the** \ü\ **loot** \u̇\ **foot** \y\ **yet** \zh\ **vision, beige** \k, ⁿ, œ, ue, ʸ\ *see* Guide to Pronunciation

time·worn \-ˌwōrn\ *adj* (1729) **1 :** worn or impaired by time ⟨~ mansions⟩ **2 a :** AGE-OLD, ANCIENT ⟨~ procedures⟩ **b :** HACKNEYED, STALE ⟨a ~ joke⟩
time zone *n* (1892) **:** a geographic region within which the same standard time is used

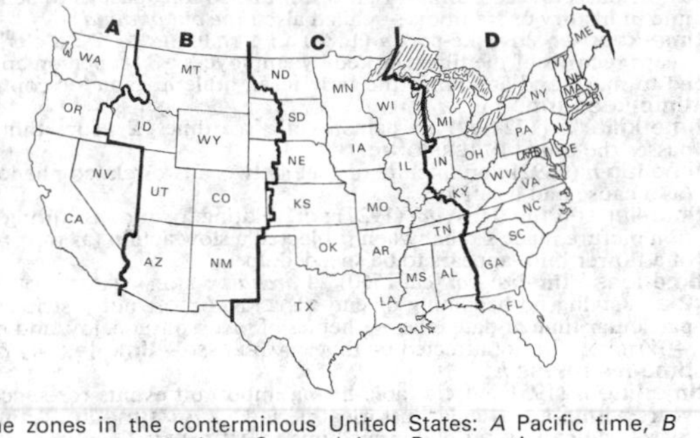

time zones in the conterminous United States: *A* Pacific time, *B* mountain time, *C* central time, *D* eastern time

tim·id \ˈti-məd\ *adj* [L *timidus,* fr. *timēre* to fear] (1549) **1 :** lacking in courage or self-confidence ⟨a ~ person⟩ **2 :** lacking in boldness or determination ⟨a ~ policy⟩ — **ti·mid·i·ty** \tə-ˈmi-də-tē\ *n* — **tim·id·ly** \ˈti-məd-lē\ *adv* — **tim·id·ness** *n*
timing *n* (ca. 1659) **1 a :** placement or occurrence in time ⟨the ~ of the sale couldn't have been better⟩ **b :** the ability to select the precise moment for doing something for optimum effect ⟨a boxer with impeccable ~⟩ **2 :** observation and recording (as by a stopwatch) of the elapsed time of an act, action, or process
ti·moc·ra·cy \tī-ˈmä-krə-sē\ *n* [ME *tymotracie,* fr. MF *tymocracie,* fr. ML *timocratia,* fr. Gk *timokratia,* fr. *timē* price, value, honor + *-kratia* -cracy; akin to Gk *tiein* to honor, Skt *cāyati* he respects] (15c) **1 :** government in which a certain amount of property is necessary for office **2 :** government in which love of honor is the ruling principle — **ti·mo·crat·ic** \ˌtī-mə-ˈkra-tik\ *or* **ti·mo·crat·i·cal** \-ti-kəl\ *adj*
ti·mo·lol \ˈtī-mə-ˌlōl, -ˌlȯl\ *n* [*tim-* (of unknown origin) + *-olol* (as in *propranolol*)] (1973) **:** a beta-blocker $C_{13}H_{24}N_4O_3S$ used in the form of its maleate salt to treat glaucoma and hypertension and to reduce the risk of second heart attacks
tim·o·rous \ˈti-mə-rəs, ˈtim-rəs\ *adj* [ME, fr. ML *timorosus,* fr. L *timor* fear, fr. *timēre* to fear] (15c) **1 :** of a timid disposition **:** FEARFUL ⟨reproached myself with being so ~ and cautious —Daniel Defoe⟩ **2 :** expressing or suggesting timidity ⟨proceed with doubtful and ~ steps —Edward Gibbon⟩ — **tim·o·rous·ly** *adv* — **tim·o·rous·ness** *n*
tim·o·thy \ˈti-mə-thē\ *n* [prob. after *Timothy* Hanson, 18th cent. Am. farmer said to have introduced it from New England to the southern states] (1747) **:** a European perennial grass (*Phleum pratense*) that has long cylindrical spikes and is widely grown for hay in the U.S.
Tim·o·thy \ˈti-mə-thē\ *n* [L *Timotheus,* fr. Gk *Timotheos*] (14c) **1 :** a disciple of the apostle Paul **2 :** either of two letters written with regard to pastoral care in the early church and included as books in the New Testament — see BIBLE table
tim·pa·ni *also* **tym·pa·ni** \ˈtim-pə-nē\ *n pl but sing or pl in constr* [It, pl. of *timpano* kettledrum, fr. L *tympanum* drum — more at TYMPANUM] (ca. 1854) **:** a set of two or more kettledrums played by one performer in an orchestra or band
tim·pa·nist *also* **tym·pa·nist** \-nist\ *n* (1906) **:** a person who plays the timpani
[1]**tin** \ˈtin\ *n* [ME, fr. OE; akin to OHG *zin* tin] (bef. 12c) **1 :** a soft faintly bluish-white lustrous low-melting crystalline metallic element that is malleable and ductile at ordinary temperatures and that is used esp. in containers, as a protective coating, in tinfoil, and in soft solders and alloys — see ELEMENT table **2 a :** a box, can, pan, vessel, or a sheet made of tinplate; *broadly* **:** such a container of any metal (as aluminum) **b :** a metal container and its contents ⟨a ~ of tomatoes⟩ — **tin** *adj* — **tin·ful** \-ˌfu̇l\ *n*
[2]**tin** *vt* **tinned; tin·ning** (14c) **1 :** to cover or plate with tin or a tin alloy **2 :** to put up or pack in tins **:** CAN ⟨*tinned* peaches⟩
TIN *abbr* taxpayer identification number
tin·a·mou \ˈti-nə-ˌmü\ *n* [F, fr. Carib *tinamu*] (ca. 1783) **:** any of a family (Tinamidae) of So. and Central American ground-dwelling birds that have a deeply keeled sternum and a rudimentary tail and that produce large glossy usu. colorful eggs
tin can *n* (1770) **1 :** a can made of tinplate; *broadly* **:** CAN 1c **2** *slang* **:** DESTROYER 2
[1]**tinct** \ˈtiŋ(k)t\ *adj* [L *tinctus,* pp.] (1579) **:** COLORED, TINGED
[2]**tinct** *n* (1602) **:** TINCTURE, TINGE
tinc·to·ri·al \tiŋ(k)-ˈtȯr-ē-əl\ *adj* [L *tinctorius,* fr. *tingere* to tinge] (1655) **:** of or relating to colors or to dyeing or staining; *also* **:** imparting color — **tinc·to·ri·al·ly** \-ē-ə-lē\ *adv*
[1]**tinc·ture** \ˈtiŋ(k)-chər\ *n* [ME, fr. L *tinctura* act of dyeing, fr. *tinctus,* pp. of *tingere* to tinge] (14c) **1 a** *archaic* **:** a substance that colors, dyes, or stains **b :** COLOR, TINT **2 a :** a characteristic quality **:** CAST **b :** a slight admixture **:** TRACE ⟨a ~ of doubt⟩ **3** *obs* **:** an active principle or extract **4 :** a heraldic metal, color, or fur **5 :** a solution of a medicinal substance in an alcoholic solvent
[2]**tincture** *vt* **tinc·tured; tinc·tur·ing** \ˈtiŋ(k)-chə-riŋ, -shriŋ\ (1616) **1 :** to tint or stain with a color **:** TINGE **2 a :** to infuse or instill with a property or entity **:** IMPREGNATE **b :** to imbue with a quality **:** AFFECT ⟨writing *tinctured* with wit and wisdom⟩
tin·der \ˈtin-dər\ *n* [ME, fr. OE *tynder;* akin to OHG *zuntra* tinder, OE *tendan* to kindle] (bef. 12c) **1 :** a very flammable substance adaptable for use as kindling **2 :** something that serves to incite or inflame ⟨that rhetoric was ready ~ for revolution —Margaret Peters⟩
tin·der·box \ˈtin-dər-ˌbäks\ *n* (1530) **1 a :** a metal box for holding tinder and usu. a flint and steel for striking a spark **b :** a highly inflammable object or place **2 :** a potentially explosive place or situation
[1]**tine** \ˈtīn\ *n* [ME *tind,* fr. OE; akin to OHG *zint* point, tine] (bef. 12c) **1 :** a slender pointed projecting part **:** PRONG **2 :** a pointed branch of an antler — **tined** \ˈtīnd\ *adj*
[2]**tine** *vb* **tined** \ˈtīnd\ *or* **tint** \ˈtint\; **tin·ing** \ˈtī-niŋ\ [ME, of Scand origin; akin to ON *tȳna* to lose, destroy, *tjōn* injury, loss — more at TEEN] *vt* (13c) *dial Brit* **:** LOSE ~ *vi, dial Brit* **:** to become lost
tin·ea \ˈti-nē-ə\ *n* [ME, fr. ML, fr. L, worm, moth] (14c) **:** any of several fungal infections of the skin; *esp* **:** RINGWORM — **tin·e·al** \-nē-əl\ *adj*
tinea cru·ris \-ˈkru̇r-əs\ *n* [NL, lit., tinea of the leg] (ca. 1923) **:** ringworm involving esp. the groin and perineum — called also *jock itch*
tinea pe·dis \-ˈpe-dəs\ *n* [NL, tinea of the foot] (1948) **:** ATHLETE'S FOOT
tin ear *n* (1935) **:** a deafened or insensitive ear
tin·foil \ˈtin-ˌfȯi(-ə)l\ *n* (14c) **:** a paper-thin metal sheeting usu. of aluminum or tin-lead alloy
ting \ˈtiŋ\ *n* [*ting,* vb., fr. ME *tingen,* of imit. origin] (1602) **:** a high-pitched sound like that made by a light stroke on a crystal goblet — **ting** *vi*
[1]**tinge** \ˈtinj\ *vt* **tinged; tinge·ing** *or* **ting·ing** \ˈtin-jiŋ\ [L *tingere* to dip, moisten, tinge; akin to Gk *tengein* to moisten and prob. to OHG *dunkōn* to dip] (1577) **1 a :** to color with a slight shade or stain **:** TINT **b :** to affect or modify with a slight odor or taste **2 :** to affect or modify in character
[2]**tinge** *n* (1752) **1 :** a slight staining or suffusing shade or color **2 :** an affective or modifying property or influence **:** TOUCH ⟨a ~ of guilt⟩
tin·gle \ˈtiŋ-gəl\ *vi* **tin·gled; tin·gling** \-g(ə-)liŋ\ [ME, alter. of *tinklen* to tinkle, tingle] (14c) **1 a :** to feel a ringing, stinging, prickling, or thrilling sensation **b :** to cause such a sensation **2 :** TINKLE 1 — **tingle** *n* — **tin·gling·ly** \-g(ə-)liŋ-lē\ *adv* — **tin·gly** \-g(ə-)lē\ *adj*
tin hat *n* (1903) **:** a metal helmet
tin·horn \ˈtin-ˌhȯrn\ *n* (1885) **:** one (as a gambler) who pretends to have money, ability, or influence
[1]**tin·ker** \ˈtiŋ-kər\ *n* [ME *tinkere*] (14c) **1 a :** a usu. itinerant mender of household utensils **b :** an unskillful mender **:** BUNGLER **2** *chiefly Irish* **:** GYPSY
[2]**tinker** *vb* **tin·kered; tin·ker·ing** \-k(ə-)riŋ\ *vi* (1592) **:** to work in the manner of a tinker; *esp* **:** to repair, adjust, or work with something in an unskilled or experimental manner **:** FIDDLE ⟨always ~*ing* with his car⟩ ~ *vt* **:** to repair, adjust, or experiment with — **tin·ker·er** \-kər-ər\ *n*
tinker's damn *also* **tinker's dam** \-ˈdam\ *n* [prob. fr. the tinkers' reputation for blasphemy] (1839) **:** a minimum amount or degree (as of care) ⟨didn't give a *tinker's damn* about poetry —James Blish⟩
Tin·ker·toy \ˈtiŋ-kər-ˌtȯi\ *trademark* — used for a construction toy of fitting parts
[1]**tin·kle** \ˈtiŋ-kəl\ *vb* **tin·kled; tin·kling** \-k(ə-)liŋ\ [ME, freq. of *tinken* to tinkle, of imit. origin] *vi* (15c) **1 :** to make or emit a tinkle or a sound suggestive of a tinkle **2 :** URINATE ~ *vt* **1 :** to sound or make known (the time) by a tinkle **2 a :** to cause to make a tinkle **b :** to produce by tinkling ⟨~ a tune⟩
[2]**tinkle** *n* (1725) **1 :** a jingling effect in verse or prose **2 :** a series of short high ringing or clinking sounds
tin·kly \ˈtiŋ-k(ə-)lē\ *adj* (1892) **:** that tinkles **:** TINKLING
tin liz·zie \-ˈli-zē\ *n* [fr. *Tin Lizzie,* nickname for the Model T Ford automobile] (1915) **:** a small inexpensive early automobile
tin·ner \ˈti-nər\ *n* (13c) **1 :** a tin miner **2 :** TINSMITH
tin·ni·tus \ˈti-nə-təs, tə-ˈnī-təs\ *n* [L, ringing, tinnitus, fr. *tinnire* to ring, of imit. origin] (1843) **:** a sensation of noise (as a ringing or roaring) that is caused by a bodily condition (as a disturbance of the auditory nerve or wax in the ear) and typically is of the subjective form which can only be heard by the one affected
tin·ny \ˈti-nē\ *adj* **tin·ni·er; -est** (1552) **1 :** of, abounding in, or yielding tin **2 a :** resembling tin **b :** LIGHT, CHEAP **c :** lacking depth or substance **:** EMPTY ⟨~ arguments⟩ **3 :** thin in tone ⟨a ~ voice⟩ — **tin·ni·ly** \ˈti-nᵊl-ē\ *adv* — **tin·ni·ness** \ˈti-nē-nəs\ *n*
Tin Pan Alley *n* (1908) **:** a district that is a center for composers and publishers of popular music; *also* **:** the body of such composers and publishers
tin·plate \ˈtin-ˈplāt\ *n* (1677) **:** thin sheet iron or steel coated with tin
tin–plate *vt* (1890) **:** to plate or coat (as a metal sheet) with tin
tin–pot \ˈtin-ˈpät\ *adj* (1838) **:** TWO-BIT 2 ⟨~ dictators⟩
[1]**tin·sel** \ˈtin(t)-səl *also* ˈtin-zəl\ *n* [ME *tyneseyle* cloth interwoven with metallic thread, prob. fr. AF *tencelé,* pp. of *tenceler, estenceler* to sparkle — more at STENCIL] (1538) **1 :** threads, strips, or sheets of metal, paper, or plastic used to produce a glittering and sparkling appearance in fabrics, yarns, or decorations **2 :** something superficially attractive or glamorous but of little real worth ⟨disfigured by no gaudy ~ of rhetoric or declamation —Thomas Jefferson⟩
[2]**tinsel** *adj* (1575) **1 :** made of or covered with tinsel **2 a :** cheaply gaudy **:** TAWDRY **b :** SPECIOUS, SUPERFICIAL ⟨~ promises⟩
[3]**tinsel** *vt* **tin·seled** *or* **tin·selled; tin·sel·ing** *or* **tin·sel·ling** \ˈtin(t)-s(ə-)liŋ *also* ˈtin-zə-liŋ\ (1594) **1 :** to interweave, overlay, or adorn with or as if with tinsel **2 :** to impart a specious brightness to
tin·sel·ly \ˈtin(t)-s(ə-)lē *also* ˈtin-zə-lē\ *adj* (1811) **:** TINSEL
Tin·sel·town \ˈtin(t)-səl-ˌtau̇n *also* ˈtin-zəl-\ *n* (1978) **:** HOLLYWOOD ⟨seduced by ~⟩ — **Tinseltown** *adj*
tin·smith \ˈtin-ˌsmith\ *n* (1812) **:** a worker who makes or repairs things of sheet metal (as tinplate) — **tin·smith·ing** \-ˌsmi-thiŋ\ *n*
tin·stone \ˈtin-ˌstōn\ *n* (1602) **:** CASSITERITE
[1]**tint** \ˈtint\ *n* [alter. of earlier *tinct,* fr. L *tinctus* act of dyeing, fr. *tingere* to tinge] (1717) **1 a :** a usu. slight or pale coloration **:** HUE **b :** any of various lighter or darker shades of a color **:** TINGE **2 :** a variation of a color produced by adding white to it and characterized by a low saturation with relatively high lightness **3 :** a usu. slight modifying quality or characteristic **:** TOUCH **4 :** a shaded effect in engraving produced by fine parallel lines close together **5 :** a panel of light color serving as background **6 :** dye for the hair
[2]**tint** *vt* (1791) **:** to impart or apply a tint to **:** COLOR — **tint·er** *n*
tint·ing \ˈtin-tiŋ\ *n* (ca. 1841) **1 :** the act or process of one that tints **2 :** the engraved or colored tint produced by tinting

tin·tin·nab·u·lary \ˌtin-tə-ˈna-byə-ˌler-ē\ *adj* [L *tintinnabulum* bell] (1787) **:** of, relating to, or characterized by bells or their sounds
tin·tin·nab·u·la·tion \ˌtin-tə-ˌna-byə-ˈlā-shən\ *n* [L *tintinnabulum* bell, fr. *tinnire* to ring, jingle, fr. *tinnire*] (1831) **1 :** the ringing or sounding of bells **2 :** a jingling or tinkling sound as if of bells
tint·less \ˈtint-ləs\ *adj* (1789) *archaic* **:** having no tints **:** lacking color
tin·type \-ˌtīp\ *n* (1864) **:** FERROTYPE 1
tin·ware \ˈtin-ˌwer\ *n* (1758) **:** articles and esp. utensils made of tinplate
tin·work \-ˌwərk\ *n* (ca. 1934) **:** work in tin
ti·ny \ˈtī-nē\ *adj* **ti·ni·er; -est** [alter. of ME *tine*] (1598) **:** very small or diminutive **:** MINUTE ***syn*** see SMALL — **ti·ni·ly** \ˈtī-nə-lē\ *adv* — **ti·ni·ness** \ˈtī-nē-nəs\ *n*
[1]**tip** \ˈtip\ *vb* **tipped; tip·ping** [ME] *vt* (14c) **1 :** OVERTURN, UPSET — usu. used with *over* **2 a :** CANT, TILT **b :** to raise and tilt forward in salute ⟨*tipped* his hat⟩ ~ *vi* **1 :** to become tipped **:** TOPPLE **2 :** LEAN, SLANT — **tip the scales 1 :** to register weight ⟨*tips the scales* at 285 pounds⟩ **2 :** to shift the balance of power or influence ⟨*tipped the scales* in favor of a declaration of war —S. F. Bemis⟩
[2]**tip** *n* (1673) **1 :** the act or an instance of tipping **:** TILT **2** *chiefly Brit* **:** a place for depositing something (as rubbish) by dumping
[3]**tip** *vt* **tipped; tip·ping** [ME *tipped* having a tip, fr. [4]*tip*] (14c) **1 a :** to furnish with a tip **b** (1) **:** to cover or adorn the tip of (2) **:** to blend (furs) for improved appearance by brushing the tips of the hair with dye **2 :** to affix (an insert) in a book — often used with *in* **3 :** to remove the ends of ⟨~ raspberries⟩
[4]**tip** *n* [ME; akin to MHG *zipf* tip, OE *tæppa* tap — more at TAP] (14c) **1 :** the usu. pointed end of something ⟨a pencil ~⟩ **2 :** a small piece or part serving as an end, cap, or point — **tipped** \ˈtipt\ *adj* — **on the tip of one's tongue 1 :** about to be uttered ⟨it was *on the tip of my tongue* to say exactly what I thought⟩ **2 :** just eluding recall
[5]**tip** *n* [ME *tippe;* akin to LG *tippen* to tap] (15c) **:** a light touch or blow
[6]**tip** *vb* **tipped; tip·ping** *vt* (1567) **1 :** to strike lightly **:** TAP **2 :** to give (as a baseball) a glancing blow ~ *vi* **:** TIPTOE
[7]**tip** *n* [origin unknown] (1567) **1 :** a piece of advice or expert or authoritative information **2 :** a piece of advance or confidential information given by one thought to have access to special or inside sources
[8]**tip** *vt* **tipped; tip·ping** (1883) **1 :** to impart a piece of information or advice about or to — often used with *off* **2** *chiefly Brit* **:** to mention as a likely candidate, prospective winner, or profitable investment **:** TOUT 4 — **tip one's hand** *also* **tip one's mitt :** to declare one's intentions or reveal one's opinions or resources ⟨the Justice Department wouldn't *tip its hand* by saying what its next move . . . would be —*Newsweek*⟩
[9]**tip** *vb* **tipped; tip·ping** [perh. fr. [6]*tip*] *vt* (ca. 1610) **1 :** GIVE, PRESENT ⟨this crew has *tipped* you the black spot —R. L. Stevenson⟩ **2 :** to give a gratuity to ~ *vi* **:** to bestow a gratuity
[10]**tip** *n* (1755) **:** a gift or a sum of money tendered for a service performed or anticipated **:** GRATUITY
tip·cart \ˈtip-ˌkärt\ *n* (ca. 1877) **:** a cart whose body can be tipped on the frame to empty its contents
tip·cat \-ˌkat\ *n* [[6]*tip*] (1676) **:** a game in which one player lightly bats a wooden peg and as it flies up strikes it again to drive it as far as possible while fielders try to recover it; *also* **:** the peg used in this game
tipi *var of* TEPEE
tip–in \ˈtip-ˌin\ *n* [[6]*tip*] (1948) **:** a goal (as in basketball or hockey) made by deflecting a shot into the basket or net from very close range
[1]**tip–off** \ˈtip-ˌóf\ *n* [[8]*tip*] (1901) **1 :** WARNING, TIP **2 :** a telltale sign
[2]**tip–off** *n* [[6]*tip*] (1922) **:** the act or an instance of putting the ball in play in basketball by a jump ball
tip of the iceberg [fr. an iceberg being mostly submerged] (1969) **:** the earliest, most obvious, or most superficial manifestation of some phenomenon
tip·per \ˈti-pər\ *n* (1819) **:** one that tips ⟨a generous ~⟩
tip·pet \ˈti-pət\ *n* [ME *tipet*] (14c) **1 :** a long hanging end of cloth attached to a sleeve, cap, or hood **2 :** a shoulder cape of fur or cloth often with hanging ends **3 :** a long black scarf worn over the robe by Anglican clergymen during morning and evening prayer
tipping point *n* (1959) **:** the critical point in a situation, process, or system beyond which a significant and often unstoppable effect or change takes place
[1]**tip·ple** \ˈti-pəl\ *vb* **tip·pled; tip·pling** \-p(ə-)liŋ\ [back-formation fr. obs. *tippler* alehouse keeper, fr. ME *tipler*] *vi* (1560) **:** to drink liquor esp. by habit or to excess ~ *vt* **:** to drink (liquor) esp. continuously in small amounts — **tip·pler** \-p(ə-)lər\ *n*
[2]**tipple** *n* (1581) **1 :** DRINK 1 **2 :** DRINK 2
[3]**tipple** *n* [E dial. *tipple* to tip over, freq. of E [1]*tip*] (1880) **1 :** a place where or an apparatus by which cars (as for coal) are loaded or emptied **2 :** a coal-screening plant
tip·py \ˈti-pē\ *adj* **tip·pi·er; -est** (1886) **:** liable to tip ⟨a ~ boat⟩
tip·staff \ˈtip-ˌstaf\ *n, pl* **tip·staves** \-ˌstavz, -ˌstāvz\ [obs. *tipstaff* staff tipped with metal] (1535) **:** a court officer whose duties include assisting the judge and acting as crier
tip·ster \ˈtip-stər\ *n* (1862) **:** one who gives or sells tips esp. for gambling or speculation
tip·sy \ˈtip-sē\ *adj* **tip·si·er; -est** [[1]*tip* + *-sy* (as in *tricksy*)] (1577) **1 :** unsteady, staggering, or foolish from the effects of liquor **:** FUDDLED **2 :** UNSTEADY, ASKEW ⟨a ~ angle⟩ — **tip·si·ly** \-sə-lē\ *adv* — **tip·si·ness** \-sē-nəs\ *n*
[1]**tip·toe** \ˈtip-ˌtō, -ˈtō\ *n* (14c) **:** the position of being balanced on the balls of the feet and toes with the heels raised — usu. used with *on; also* **:** the ends of the toes — **on tiptoe :** ALERT, AROUSED ⟨the contest of skill that puts one *on tiptoe* to win —*Deerfield (Wisc.) Independent*⟩
[2]**tiptoe** *adv* (1592) **:** on or as if on tiptoe
[3]**tiptoe** *adj* (1593) **1 :** standing or walking on or as if on tiptoe **2 :** CAUTIOUS, STEALTHY
[4]**tiptoe** *vi* **tip·toed; tip·toe·ing** (ca. 1661) **1 :** to stand or raise oneself on tiptoe **2 :** to walk or proceed quietly or cautiously on or as if on tiptoe ⟨~ around the issue⟩
[1]**tip–top** \ˈtip-ˈtäp, -ˌtäp\ *n* [[4]*tip* + *top*] (1702) **:** the highest point
[2]**tip–top** *adj* (1722) **:** EXCELLENT, FIRST-RATE ⟨~ working conditions⟩
[3]**tip–top** *adv* (1882) **:** very well
ti·rade \ˈtī-ˌrād *also* ti-ˈ\ *n* [F, shot, tirade, fr. MF, fr. OIt *tirata,* fr. *tirare* to draw, shoot] (1802) **:** a protracted speech usu. marked by intemperate, vituperative, or harshly censorious language
tir·a·mi·su \ˌtir-ə-ˈmē-(ˌ)sü, -ˈmi-; -mē-ˈsü\ *n* [It *tiramisù,* fr. *tirami su!,* lit., pull me up!] (1982) **:** a dessert made with ladyfingers, mascarpone, and espresso
[1]**tire** \ˈtī(-ə)r\ *vb* **tired; tir·ing** [ME *tyren,* fr. OE *tēorian, tȳrian*] *vi* (bef. 12c) **:** to become weary ~ *vt* **1 :** to exhaust or greatly decrease the physical strength of **:** FATIGUE **2 :** to wear out the patience of **:** BORE
syn TIRE, WEARY, FATIGUE, EXHAUST, JADE, FAG mean to make or become unable or unwilling to continue. TIRE implies a draining of one's strength or patience ⟨the long ride *tired* us out⟩. WEARY stresses tiring until one is unable to endure more of the same thing ⟨*wearied* of the constant arguing⟩. FATIGUE suggests great lassitude from excessive strain or undue effort ⟨*fatigued* by the day's chores⟩. EXHAUST implies complete draining of strength by hard exertion ⟨shoveling snow *exhausted* him⟩. JADE suggests the loss of all freshness and eagerness ⟨appetites *jaded* by overindulgence⟩. FAG implies a drooping with fatigue ⟨shoppers all *fagged* out by the Christmas rush⟩.
[2]**tire** *n* [ME, short for *attire*] (14c) **1** *obs* **:** ATTIRE **2** *archaic* **:** a woman's headband or hair ornament
[3]**tire** *vt* **tired; tir·ing** (14c) **1** *obs* **:** ATTIRE **2** *archaic* **:** to adorn (the hair) with an ornament
[4]**tire** *n, often attrib* [ME, prob. fr. [2]*tire*] (15c) **1 :** a metal hoop forming the tread of a wheel **2 :** a rubber cushion that fits around a wheel (as of an automobile) and usu. contains compressed air
tired *adj* (14c) **1 :** drained of strength and energy **:** fatigued often to the point of exhaustion **2 :** obviously worn by hard use **:** RUN-DOWN **3 :** TRITE, HACKNEYED — **tired·ly** *adv* — **tired·ness** *n*
tire·less \ˈtī(-ə)r-ləs\ *adj* (1591) **:** seemingly incapable of tiring **:** INDEFATIGABLE ⟨a ~ worker⟩ — **tire·less·ly** *adv* — **tire·less·ness** *n*
Ti·re·si·as \tī-ˈrē-sē-əs, -zē-\ *n* [L, fr. Gk *Teiresias*] (14c) **:** a blind seer of Thebes who in one Greek myth is changed into a woman for several years and then changed back to a man
tire·some \ˈtī(-ə)r-səm\ *adj* (ca. 1520) **:** WEARISOME, TEDIOUS ⟨a ~ lecture⟩ — **tire·some·ly** *adv* — **tire·some·ness** *n*
tir·ing–house \ˈtī-riŋ-ˌhau̇s\ *n* [[3]*tire*] (1590) **:** a section of a theater reserved for the actors and used esp. for dressing for stage entrances
tir·ing–room \-ˌrüm, -ˌru̇m\ *n* [[3]*tire*] (1623) **:** a dressing room esp. in a theater
tirl \ˈtərl\ *vb* [alter. of [1]*trill*] *vi* (ca. 1550) *chiefly Scot* **:** to make a rattling sound (as with a door latch) ~ *vt, chiefly Scot* **:** TWIRL
ti·ro *chiefly Brit var of* TYRO
'tis \ˈtiz, (ˌ)tiz, təz\ [contr.] (15c) **:** it is
ti·sane \ti-ˈzan, -ˈzän\ *n* [ME, fr. AF, fr. L *ptisana,* fr. Gk *ptisanē,* lit., crushed barley, fr. *ptissein* to crush — more at PESTLE] (14c) **:** an infusion (as of dried herbs) used as a beverage or for medicinal effects
Tish·ah–b'Ab \ˈti-shə-ˌbäv, -ˌbóv\ *n* [Heb *tishʿāh bĕ Ābh* ninth in Ab] (ca. 1902) **:** a Jewish holiday observed with fasting on the ninth of Ab in commemoration of the destruction of the temples at Jerusalem
Tish·ri \ˈtish-rē\ *n* [Heb *tishrī*] (ca. 1771) **:** the first month of the civil year or the seventh month of the ecclesiastical year in the Jewish calendar — see MONTH table
tis·sue \ˈti-(ˌ)shü, *chiefly Brit* ˈtis-(ˌ)yü\ *n* [ME *tysshewe, tyssew,* a rich fabric, fr. AF *tissue,* fr. pp. of *tistre* to weave, fr. L *texere* — more at TECHNICAL] (1563) **1 a :** a fine lightweight often sheer fabric **b :** MESH, NETWORK, WEB ⟨a ~ of lies⟩ **2 :** a piece of soft absorbent tissue paper used esp. as a handkerchief or for removing cosmetics **3 :** an aggregate of cells usu. of a particular kind together with their intercellular substance that form one of the structural materials of a plant or an animal — **tis·su·ey** \ˈti-shə-wē\ *adj*
tissue culture *n* (1912) **:** the process or technique of making body tissue grow in a culture medium outside the organism; *also* **:** a culture of tissue (as epithelium)
tissue fluid *n* (1900) **:** a fluid that permeates the spaces between individual cells, that is in osmotic contact with the blood and lymph, and that serves in interstitial transport of nutrients and waste
tissue paper *n* (1777) **:** a thin gauzy paper used esp. for protecting something (as by covering or wrapping)
tissue plasminogen activator *n* (1981) **:** a clot-dissolving enzyme with an affinity for fibrin that is produced naturally in blood vessel linings and is used in a genetically engineered form to prevent damage to heart muscle following a heart attack and reduce neurological damage following ischemic stroke — abbr. *TPA*
tis·su·lar \ˈti-shə-lər\ *adj* [*tissue* + *-lar* (as in *cellular*)] (ca. 1935) **:** of, relating to, or affecting organismic tissue ⟨~ grafts⟩ ⟨~ lesions⟩
[1]**tit** \ˈtit\ *n* [ME, fr. OE — more at TEAT] (bef. 12c) **1 :** TEAT **2** *usu vulgar* **:** BREAST — usu. used in pl.
[2]**tit** *n* (ca. 1706) **:** any of various small plump often long-tailed oscine birds (family Paridae) of Eurasia and Africa that are related to the chickadees and titmice
[3]**tit** *abbr* title
Tit *abbr* Titus
ti·tan \ˈtī-tᵊn\ *n* [Gk] (ca. 1741) **1** *cap* **:** any of a family of giants in Greek mythology born of Uranus and Gaea and ruling the earth until overthrown by the Olympian gods **2 :** one that is gigantic in size or power **:** one that stands out for greatness of achievement
titan- *or* **titani-** *comb form* [NL *titanium*] **:** titanium ⟨*titan*ate⟩
ti·ta·nate \ˈtī-tə-ˌnāt\ *n* (1839) **1 :** any of various multiple oxides of titanium dioxide with other metallic oxides **2 :** a titanium ester of the general formula $Ti(OR)_4$
ti·tan·ess \ˈtī-tᵊn-əs\ *n, often cap* (1596) **:** a female titan
ti·ta·nia \tī-ˈtā-nē-ə, tə-, -ˈtān-yə *also* -ˈta-nē-ə *or* -ˈtan-yə\ *n* [NL] (1922) **:** TITANIUM DIOXIDE
Ti·ta·nia \tə-ˈtān-yə, -ˈtän-; tī-ˈtān-\ *n* (1590) **:** the wife of Oberon and queen of the fairies in Shakespeare's *A Midsummer Night's Dream*
ti·tan·ic \tī-ˈta-nik *also* tə-\ *adj* [Gk *titanikos* of the Titans] (1709) **:** having great magnitude, force, or power **:** COLOSSAL ⟨a ~ struggle⟩ — **ti·tan·i·cal·ly** \-ni-k(ə-)lē\ *adv*
ti·ta·nif·er·ous \ˌtī-tə-ˈni-f(ə-)rəs\ *adj* (ca. 1828) **:** containing or yielding titanium ⟨~ minerals⟩

ti·tan·ism \ˈtī-tə-ˌni-zəm\ *n, often cap* [fr. the Titans' rebellion against their father Uranus] (1867) **:** defiance of and revolt against social or artistic conventions

ti·ta·ni·um \tī-ˈtā-nē-əm, tə- *also* -ˈta-nē-əm, -ˈtan-yəm\ *n* [NL, fr. Gk *Titan*] (1796) **:** a silvery-gray light strong metallic element obtained from ilmenite and rutile and used esp. in alloys and combined in refractory materials, pigments, and coatings — see ELEMENT table

titanium dioxide *n* (1877) **:** an oxide TiO_2 of titanium that occurs in rutile, anatase, and ilmenite and is used esp. as a pigment

titanium white *n* (1920) **:** TITANIUM DIOXIDE; *also* **:** a brilliant white lead-free pigment consisting of titanium dioxide often together with barium sulfate and zinc oxide

titbit *var of* TIDBIT

ti·ter \ˈtī-tər\ *n* [F *titre* title, proportion of gold or silver in a coin, fr. OF *title* inscription, title] (1868) **:** the strength of a solution or the concentration of a substance in solution as determined by titration

tit·fer \ˈtit-fər\ *n* [by shortening & alter. fr. *tit for tat,* rhyming slang for *hat*] (ca. 1930) *Brit* **:** HAT

tit for tat \ˌtit-fər-ˈtat\ [alter. of earlier *tip for tap,* fr. *tip* (blow) + *for* + *tap*] (1556) **:** an equivalent given in return (as for an injury) **:** retaliation in kind — **tit–for–tat** *adj*

tith·able \ˈtī-t͟hə-bəl\ *adj* (15c) **:** subject or liable to payment of tithes

[1]**tithe** \ˈtīt͟h\ *vb* **tithed; tith·ing** [ME, fr. OE *teogothian,* fr. *teogotha* tenth] *vt* (bef. 12c) **1 :** to pay or give a tenth part of esp. for the support of the church **2 :** to levy a tithe on ~ *vi* **:** to give a tenth of one's income as a tithe

[2]**tithe** *n* [ME, fr. OE *teogotha* tenth; akin to MLG *tegede* tenth, OE *tīen* ten — more at TEN] (bef. 12c) **1 :** a tenth part of something paid as a voluntary contribution or as a tax esp. for the support of a religious establishment **2 :** the obligation represented by individual tithes **3 :** TENTH; *broadly* **:** a small part **4 :** a small tax or levy

tith·er \ˈtī-t͟hər\ *n* (14c) **1 :** one that pays tithes **2 :** one that collects or advocates the payment of tithes

tith·ing \ˈtī-t͟hiŋ\ *n* [ME, fr. OE *tēothung,* fr. *teogothian, tēothian* to tithe, take one tenth] (bef. 12c) **:** a small administrative division preserved in parts of England apparently orig. made up of ten men with their families

ti·tho·nia \tə-ˈthō-nyə, tī-, -nē-ə\ *n* [NL, prob. fr. L *Tithonia,* poetic name of Aurora] (1940) **:** any of a genus (*Tithonia*) of tall composite herbs or shrubs of Mexico and Central America that have flower heads resembling sunflowers and that are sometimes grown as ornamentals

[1]**ti·ti** \ˈtī-ˌtī\ *n* [origin unknown] (1827) **1 :** a tree (*Cliftonia monophylla* of the family Cyrillaceae) of the southeastern U.S. with leathery leaves and racemes of fragrant white flowers **2 :** LEATHERWOOD 2

[2]**ti·ti** \ti-ˈtē\ *n* [AmerSp *tití*] (1832) **:** any of a genus (*Callicebus*) of small So. American monkeys having long thick variably colored fur and a tail that is not prehensile

ti·tian \ˈti-shən\ *adj, often cap* [*Titian* (Tiziano Vecellio)] (1892) **:** of a brownish-orange color

tit·il·late \ˈti-tə-ˌlāt\ *vb* **-lat·ed; -lat·ing** [L *titillatus,* pp. of *titillare*] *vt* (1620) **1 :** to excite pleasurably **:** arouse by stimulation **2 :** TICKLE 2 ~ *vi* **:** to act as a stimulant to pleasurable excitement — **tit·il·la·tion** \ˌti-tə-ˈlā-shən\ *n* — **tit·il·la·tive** \ˈti-tə-ˌlā-tiv\ *adj*

titillating *adj* (ca. 1714) **:** pleasantly stimulating or exciting ⟨~ reading⟩; *also* **:** EROTIC — **tit·il·lat·ing·ly** *adv*

tit·i·vate *or* **tit·ti·vate** \ˈti-tə-ˌvāt\ *vb* **-vat·ed; -vat·ing** [perh. fr. [1]*tidy* + ren*ovate*] *vt* (1824) **:** to make smart or spruce ~ *vi* **:** SMARTEN, SPRUCE — **tit·i·va·tion** \ˌti-tə-ˈvā-shən\ *n*

tit·lark \ˈtit-ˌlärk\ *n* [*tit-* (as in *titmouse*) + *lark*] (1668) **:** PIPIT

[1]**ti·tle** \ˈtī-tᵊl\ *n* [ME, fr. AF, fr. L *titulus* inscription, title] (14c) **1 a** *obs* **:** INSCRIPTION **b :** written material introduced into a motion picture or television program to give credits, explain an action, or represent dialogue — usu. used in pl. **2 a :** all the elements constituting legal ownership **b :** a legally just cause of exclusive possession **c :** the instrument (as a deed) that is evidence of a right **3 a :** something that justifies or substantiates a claim **b :** an alleged or recognized right **4 a :** a descriptive or general heading (as of a chapter in a book) **b :** the heading which names an act or statute **c :** the heading of a legal action or proceeding **5 a :** the distinguishing name of a written, printed, or filmed production **b :** a similar distinguishing name of a musical composition or a work of art **6 :** a descriptive name **:** APPELLATION **7 :** a division of an instrument, book, or bill; *esp* **:** one larger than a section or article **8 a :** an appellation of dignity, honor, distinction, or preeminence attached to a person or family by virtue of rank, office, precedent, privilege, attainment, or lands **b :** a person holding a title esp. of nobility **9 :** a usu. published work as distinguished from a particular copy ⟨published 25 new ~*s*⟩ **10 :** CHAMPIONSHIP 1

[2]**title** *vt* **ti·tled; ti·tling** \ˈtīt-liŋ, ˈtī-tᵊl-iŋ\ (14c) **1 :** to provide a title for **2 :** to designate or call by a title **:** TERM, STYLE

[3]**title** *adj* (1886) **:** of or relating to a title: as **a :** having the same name as the title of a production ⟨did the ~ role in *Hamlet*⟩ **b :** having the same title as or providing the title for the collection or production of which it forms a part ⟨the ~ song⟩ **c :** of, relating to, or involving a championship ⟨a ~ match⟩ **d :** of, relating to, or used with the titles that introduce a motion picture or television program ⟨~ music⟩

titled *adj* (1593) **:** having a title esp. of nobility

title deed *n* (ca. 1768) **:** the deed constituting the evidence of a person's legal ownership

ti·tle·hold·er \ˈtī-tᵊl-ˌhōl-dər\ *n* (1904) **:** one that holds a title; *specif* **:** CHAMPION

title insurance *n* (1886) **:** insurance against loss due to an unknown defect in a title or interest in real estate

title page *n* (1594) **:** a page of a book bearing the title and usu. the names of the author and publisher and the place and sometimes date of publication

ti·tlist \ˈtī-tᵊl-ist, ˈtīt-list\ *n* (1924) **:** TITLEHOLDER

tit·mouse \ˈtit-ˌmau̇s\ *n, pl* **tit·mice** \-ˌmīs\ [by folk etymology fr. ME *titmose,* fr. **tit* any small object or creature + *mose* titmouse, fr. OE *māse;* akin to OHG *meisa* titmouse] (14c) **:** any of several small No. American oscine birds (genus *Baeolophus* of the family Paridae) that are related to the chickadees, have small bills and usu. long tails, and have been sometimes placed esp. formerly in a related genus (*Parus*)

Ti·to·ism \ˈtē-(ˌ)tō-ˌi-zəm\ *n* (1949) **:** the political, economic, and social policies associated with Tito; *specif* **:** nationalistic policies and practices followed by a Communist state or group independently of and often in opposition to the U.S.S.R. — **Ti·to·ist** \-ˌō-ist\ *n or adj*

ti·trant \ˈtī-trənt\ *n* (1939) **:** a substance (as a reagent solution of precisely known concentration) that is added in titration

ti·trate \ˈtī-ˌtrāt\ *vb* **ti·trat·ed; ti·trat·ing** [*titer*] *vt* (ca. 1859) **:** to subject to titration ~ *vi* **:** to perform titration — **ti·trat·able** \-ˌtrā-tə-bəl\ *adj* — **ti·tra·tor** \-ˌtrā-tər\ *n*

ti·tra·tion \tī-ˈtrā-shən\ *n* (ca. 1859) **:** a method or process of determining the concentration of a dissolved substance in terms of the smallest amount of reagent of known concentration required to bring about a given effect in reaction with a known volume of the test solution

ti·tre \ˈtī-tər\ *chiefly Brit var of* TITER

ti·tri·met·ric \ˌtī-trə-ˈme-trik\ *adj* [*titration* + *-i-* + *-metric*] (1902) **:** employing or determined by titration

tit·ter \ˈti-tər\ *vi* [imit.] (ca. 1619) **:** to laugh in a nervous, affected, or partly suppressed manner **:** GIGGLE, SNICKER — **titter** *n*

tit·tie \ˈti-tē\ *n* [prob. baby talk alter. of *sister*] (ca. 1700) *chiefly Scot* **:** SISTER

tit·tle \ˈti-tᵊl\ *n* [ME *titel,* fr. ML *titulus,* fr. L, title] (14c) **1 :** a point or small sign used as a diacritical mark in writing or printing **2 :** a very small part

tit·tle–tat·tle \ˈti-tᵊl-ˌta-tᵊl\ *n* [redupl. of [1]*tattle*] (ca. 1529) **:** GOSSIP, PRATTLE — **tittle–tattle** *vi*

[1]**tit·tup** \ˈti-təp\ *n* [imit. of the sound of a horse's hooves] (1703) **:** lively, gay, or restless behavior

[2]**tittup** *vi* **-tupped** *or* **-tuped; -tup·ping** *or* **-tup·ing** (1785) **:** to move in a lively manner often with an exaggerated or affected action

[1]**tit·u·lar** \ˈti-chə-lər, ˈtich-lər\ *adj* [L *titulus* title] (1611) **1 a :** existing in title only; *esp* **:** bearing a title derived from a defunct ecclesiastical jurisdiction (as an episcopal see) **b :** having the title and usu. the honors belonging to an office or dignity without the duties, functions, or responsibilities **2 :** bearing a title **:** TITLED **3 :** of, relating to, or constituting a title ⟨the ~ hero of the play⟩ — **tit·u·lar·ly** *adv*

[2]**titular** *n* (1613) **:** a person holding a title

Ti·tus \ˈtī-təs\ *n* [LL, fr. Gk *Titos*] (bef. 12c) **1 :** an early Christian convert who assisted Paul in his missionary work **2 :** a letter written on the subject of pastoral care in the early church and included as a book in the New Testament — see BIBLE table

Tiu \ˈtē-(ˌ)ü\ *n* [OE *Tīw* — more at DEITY] (1872) **:** an ancient Germanic god of war identified with Tyr

Ti·Vo \ˈtē-(ˌ)vō\ *vt* [*TiVo,* proprietary name for a brand of DVR and associated software] (2000) **:** to record (as a television program) with a DVR

ti·yin \ˈtē-ēn\ *n, pl* **tiyin** [Uzbek, kopeck] (1993) — see *sum* at MONEY table

tiz·zy \ˈti-zē\ *n, pl* **tizzies** [origin unknown] (1935) **:** a highly excited and distracted state of mind

TKO \ˌtē-ˌkā-ˈō\ *n* [*t*echnical *k*nock*o*ut] (1941) **:** TECHNICAL KNOCKOUT

Tl *symbol* thallium

TLC *abbr* **1** tender loving care **2** thin-layer chromatography

Tlin·git \ˈtliŋ-kət, -gət *also* ˈkliŋ-\ *n, pl* **Tlingit** *or* **Tlingits** [Tlingit *łi·ngít* human being] (1865) **1 :** a member of a group of American Indian peoples of the islands and coast of southern Alaska **2 :** the language of the Tlingit peoples — **Tlingit** *adj*

T lymphocyte *n* [*t*hymus-derived] (1972) **:** T CELL

Tm *symbol* thulium

[1]**TM** \ˈtē-ˈem\ *service mark* — used for a Transcendental Meditation technique

[2]**TM** *abbr* trademark

T–man \ˈtē-ˌman\ *n* [*T*reasury *man*] (1937) **:** a special agent of the U.S. Treasury Department

tme·sis \(tə-)ˈmē-səs\ *n* [LL, fr. Gk *tmēsis* act of cutting, fr. *temnein* to cut — more at TOME] (1550) **:** separation of parts of a compound word by the intervention of one or more words (as *what place soever* for *whatsoever place*)

TMJ *abbr* temporomandibular joint

tn *abbr* **1** ton **2** town

TN *abbr* Tennessee

TNF *abbr* tumor necrosis factor

T–note \ˈtē-ˌnōt\ *n* (1968) **:** TREASURY NOTE

tnpk *abbr* turnpike

TNT \ˌtē-(ˌ)en-ˈtē\ *n* [*t*ri*n*itro*t*oluene] (1915) **:** a flammable toxic compound $C_7H_5N_3O_6$ used as a high explosive and in chemical synthesis

[1]**to** \tə, tu̇, ˈtü\ *prep* [ME, fr. OE *tō;* akin to OHG *zuo* to, L *do*nec as long as, until] (bef. 12c) **1 a** — used as a function word to indicate movement or an action or condition suggestive of movement toward a place, person, or thing reached ⟨drove ~ the city⟩ ⟨went back ~ the original idea⟩ ⟨went ~ lunch⟩ **b** — used as a function word to indicate direction ⟨a mile ~ the south⟩ ⟨turned his back ~ the door⟩ ⟨a tendency ~ silliness⟩ **c** — used as a function word to indicate contact or proximity ⟨applied polish ~ the table⟩ ⟨put her hand ~ her heart⟩ **d** (1) — used as a function word to indicate the place or point that is the far limit ⟨100 miles ~ the nearest town⟩ (2) — used as a function word to indicate the limit of extent ⟨stripped ~ the waist⟩ **e** — used as a function word to indicate relative position ⟨perpendicular ~ the floor⟩ **2 a** — used as a function word to indicate purpose, intention, tendency, result, or end ⟨came ~ our aid⟩ ⟨drink ~ his health⟩ **b** — used as a function word to indicate the result of an action or a process ⟨broken all ~ pieces⟩ ⟨go ~ seed⟩ ⟨~ their surprise, the train left on time⟩ **3** — used as a function word to indicate position or relation in time: as **a :** BEFORE ⟨five minutes ~ five⟩ **b :** TILL ⟨from eight ~ five⟩ ⟨up ~ now⟩ **4** — used as a function word to indicate addition, attachment, connection, belonging, possession, accompaniment, or response ⟨the key ~ the door⟩ ⟨danced ~ live music⟩ ⟨comes ~ her call⟩ **5** — used as a function word (1) to indicate the extent or degree (as of completeness or accuracy) ⟨loyal ~ a man⟩ ⟨generous ~ a fault⟩ or the extent and result (as of an action or a condition) ⟨beaten ~ death⟩ (2) to indicate the last or an intermediate point of a series ⟨moderate ~ cool temperatures⟩ **6 a** — used as a function word (1) to indicate a relation to one that serves as a standard ⟨inferior ~ her earlier works⟩ (2) to indicate similarity, correspondence, dissimilarity, or proportion ⟨compared him ~ a god⟩ **b** — used as a function word to indicate agreement or conformity ⟨add salt ~ taste⟩ ⟨~ my knowledge⟩ **c** — used as a function word to indicate a proportion in terms

of numbers or quantities ⟨400 ~ the box⟩ ⟨odds of ten ~ one⟩ **7 a** — used as a function word (1) to indicate the application of an adjective or a noun ⟨agreeable ~ everyone⟩ ⟨attitude ~ friends⟩ ⟨title ~ the property⟩ (2) to indicate the relation of a verb to its complement or to a complementary element ⟨refers ~ the traditions⟩ (3) to indicate the receiver of an action or the one for which something is done or exists ⟨gives a dollar ~ the man⟩ and often used with a reflexive pronoun to indicate exclusiveness (as of possession) or separateness ⟨had the house ~ themselves⟩ **b** — used as a function word to indicate agency ⟨falls ~ his opponent's blows⟩ **8** — used as a function word to indicate that the following verb is an infinitive ⟨wants ~ go⟩ and often used by itself at the end of a clause in place of an infinitive suggested by the preceding context ⟨knows more than she seems ~⟩

[2]**to** \'tü\ *adv* (bef. 12c) **1 a** — used as a function word to indicate direction toward ⟨run ~ and fro⟩ **b** : close to the wind ⟨the gale having gone over, we came ~ —R. H. Dana⟩ **2 a** : into contact esp. with the frame — used of a door or a window ⟨the door snapped ~⟩ **b** — used as a function word to indicate physical application or attachment ⟨he . . . hath set ~ his seal —Jn 3:33(AV)⟩ **3** — used as a function word to indicate application or attention ⟨will stand ~ —Shak.⟩ **4** : to a state of consciousness or awareness ⟨brings her ~ with smelling salts⟩ **5** : at hand : BY ⟨get to see 'em close ~ —Richard Llewellyn⟩

TO *abbr* **1** table of organization **2** traditional orthography **3** turnover

toad \'tōd\ *n* [ME *tode,* fr. OE *tāde, tādige*] (bef. 12c) **1** : any of numerous anuran amphibians (esp. family Bufonidae) that are distinguished from the related frogs by being more terrestrial in habit though returning to water to lay their eggs, by having a build that is squatter and shorter with weaker and shorter hind limbs, and by having skin that is rough, dry, and warty rather than smooth and moist **2** : a contemptible person or thing

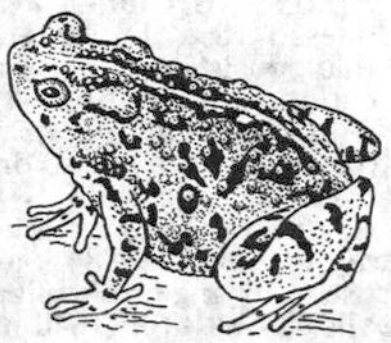

toad 1

toad·eat·er \-ˌē-tər\ *n* (ca. 1572) *archaic* : TOADY

toad·fish \-ˌfish\ *n* (1704) : any of a family (Batrachoididae) of chiefly marine bony fishes having a broad flat head, a wide mouth, and usu. scaleless slimy skin and producing sounds (as grunts) by means of a swim bladder

toad·flax \-ˌflaks\ *n* (1578) : BUTTER-AND-EGGS; *also* : any of several related plants (esp. genus *Linaria*) of the snapdragon family

toad·stone \-ˌstōn\ *n* (1558) : a stone or similar object held to have formed in the head or body of a toad and formerly often worn as a charm or antidote to poison

toad·stool \-ˌstül\ *n* (14c) : a fungus having an umbrella-shaped pileus : MUSHROOM; *esp* : a poisonous or inedible one as distinguished from an edible mushroom

[1]**toady** \'tō-dē\ *n, pl* **toad·ies** [by shortening & alter. fr. *toadeater*] (1826) : one who flatters in the hope of gaining favors : SYCOPHANT *syn* see PARASITE

[2]**toady** *vi* **toad·ied; toady·ing** (ca. 1859) : to behave as a toady : engage in sycophancy *syn* see FAWN — **toady·ism** \-ē-ˌi-zəm\ *n*

[1]**to–and–fro** \ˌtü-ən-'frō\ *n* (1553) : activity involving alternating movement in opposite directions ⟨the busy ~ of the holiday shoppers⟩

[2]**to–and–fro** *adj* (1749) : forward and backward

to and fro *adv* (14c) : from one place to another

[1]**toast** \'tōst\ *vb* [ME *tosten,* fr. AF *toster,* fr. LL *tostare* to roast, fr. L *tostus,* pp. of *torrēre* to dry, parch — more at THIRST] *vt* (14c) **1** : to warm thoroughly **2** : to make (as bread) crisp, hot, and brown by heat ~ *vi* : to become toasted; *esp* : to warm thoroughly

[2]**toast** *n* (15c) **1 a** : sliced bread browned on both sides by heat **b** : food prepared with toasted bread **2** [fr. the use of pieces of spiced toast to flavor drinks] **a** (1) : a person whose health is drunk (2) : something in honor of which persons usu. drink **b** : one that is highly admired ⟨she's the ~ of society⟩ **3** [[3]*toast*] : an act of proposing or of drinking in honor of a toast **4** : a rhyming narrative poem existing in oral tradition among black Americans **5** *slang* : one that is finished or done for ⟨soon their relationship was ~ —Rick Reilly⟩

[3]**toast** *vt* (1640) : to propose or drink to as a toast

toast·er \'tō-stər\ *n* (1582) : one that toasts; *esp* : an electrical appliance for toasting

toaster oven *n* (1961) : a usu. small electrical appliance that can function as an oven or a toaster

toast·mas·ter \'tōs(t)-ˌmas-tər\ *n* (1749) : one who presides at a banquet and introduces the after-dinner speakers

toast·mis·tress \-ˌmis-trəs\ *n* (1921) : a woman who acts as toastmaster

toasty \'tō-stē\ *adj* **toast·i·er; -est** (1953) **1** : pleasantly or comfortably warm ⟨felt snug and ~ by the fire⟩ **2** : suggestive of toast esp. in flavor

Tob *abbr* Tobit

to·bac·co \tə-'ba-(ˌ)kō\ *n, pl* **-cos** [Sp *tabaco,* prob. fr. Taino, roll of tobacco leaves] (ca. 1565) **1** : any of a genus (*Nicotiana*) of chiefly American plants of the nightshade family with viscid foliage and tubular flowers; *esp* : a tall erect annual tropical American herb (*N. tabacum*) cultivated for its leaves **2** : the leaves of cultivated tobacco prepared for use in smoking or chewing or as snuff **3** : manufactured products of tobacco (as cigars or cigarettes); *also* : smoking as a practice ⟨has sworn off ~⟩ **4** : a moderate brown

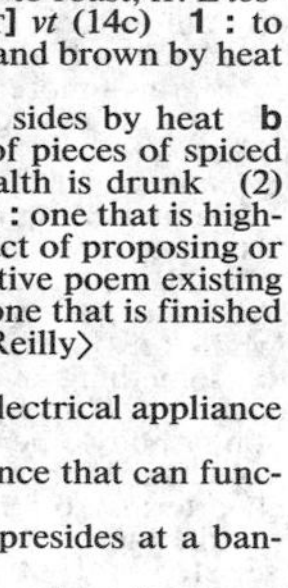

tobacco 1

tobacco budworm *n* (1918) : an American noctuid moth (*Heliothis virescens* syn. *Helicoverpa virescens*) whose striped and variably colored larva feeds on buds and young leaves esp. of tobacco and cotton

tobacco hornworm *n* (ca. 1909) : an American hawk moth (*Manduca sexta*) whose large usu. green larva is a hornworm that feeds on the leaves of plants of the nightshade family and esp. tobacco and tomato

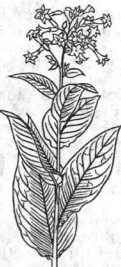

tobacco juice *n* (1833) : saliva colored brown by tobacco or snuff

tobacco mosaic virus *n* (1914) : a single-stranded RNA virus (species *Tobacco mosaic virus* of the genus *Tobamovirus*) that occurs worldwide and causes mosaic disease in plants (as tobacco and tomato) esp. of the nightshade family

to·bac·co·nist \tə-'ba-kə-nist\ *n* [irreg. fr. *tobacco* + *-ist*] (1657) : a dealer in tobacco esp. at retail

tobacco road *n, often cap T&R* [fr. *Tobacco Road,* novel (1932) by Erskine Caldwell and play (1933) by Jack Kirkland †1969 Am. playwright] (1937) : a squalid poverty-stricken rural area or community

to–be \tə-'bē\ *adj* (1594) : that is to be : FUTURE — usu. used postpositively and often in combination ⟨a bride-*to-be*⟩

To·bi·as \tə-'bī-əs\ *n* [Gk *Tobias*] (1535) **1** : a Jewish hero who with divine aid marries his kinswoman Sarah in spite of a jealous evil spirit and restores his father Tobit's sight **2** : TOBIT 2

To·bit \'tō-bət\ *n* [Gk *Tōbit*] (1587) **1** : the elderly father of Tobias **2** : a book of Scripture included in the Roman Catholic canon of the Old Testament and in the Protestant Apocrypha — see BIBLE table

[1]**to·bog·gan** \tə-'bä-gən\ *n* [CanF *tobogan,* of Algonquian origin; akin to Micmac *tobâgun* drag made of skin] (ca. 1820) **1** : a long flat-bottomed light sled made usu. of thin boards curved up at one end with usu. low handrails at the sides **2** : a downward course or a sharp decline **3** *chiefly Southern & Midland* : STOCKING CAP

[2]**toboggan** *vi* (1846) **1** : to coast on or as if on a toboggan **2** : to decline suddenly and sharply — **to·bog·gan·er** *n* — **to·bog·gan·ist** \-gə-nist\ *n*

to·bog·gan·ing \tə-'bä-gə-niŋ\ *n* (1849) : the act, art, or sport of riding a toboggan

to·by jug \'tō-bē-\ *n, often cap* [*Toby,* nickname fr. the name *Tobias*] (1840) : a small jug, pitcher, or mug shaped somewhat like a stout man with a cocked hat for the brim — called also *toby*

toc·ca·ta \tə-'kä-tə\ *n* [It, fr. *toccare* to touch, fr. VL — more at TOUCH] (ca. 1724) : a musical composition usu. for organ or harpsichord in a free style and characterized by full chords, rapid runs, and high harmonies

To·char·i·an *also* **To·khar·i·an** \tō-'ker-ē-ən,-'kär-\ *n* [Gk *Tocharoi*] (1926) **1 a** : a language of central Asia known from documents from the sixth to eighth centuries A.D. **b** : a branch of the Indo-European language family containing Tocharian — see INDO-EUROPEAN LANGUAGES table **2** : a member of a people of presumably Indo-European speech dwelling in central Asia during the first millennium of the Christian era

Tocharian A *n* (1926) : the eastern dialect of Tocharian — see INDO-EUROPEAN LANGUAGES table

Tocharian B *n* (1926) : the western dialect of Tocharian — see INDO-EUROPEAN LANGUAGES table

toch·er \'tä-k̲ər\ *n* [ME (Sc) *tochir,* fr. ScGael *tochar*] (15c) *chiefly Scot* **1** : DOWRY 2 **2** : DOWRY 3

to·coph·er·ol \tō-'kä-fə-ˌrȯl, -ˌrōl\ *n* [ISV, ultim. fr. Gk *tokos* childbirth, offspring (akin to Gk *tiktein* to beget) + *pherein* to carry, bear — more at THANE, BEAR] (ca. 1936) : any of several fat-soluble oily phenolic compounds with varying degrees of antioxidant vitamin E activity; *esp* : ALPHA-TOCOPHEROL

toc·sin \'täk-sən\ *n* [MF *toquassen,* fr. Old Occitan *tocasenh,* fr. *tocar* to touch, ring a bell (fr. VL **toccare*) + *senh* sign, bell, fr. ML & L *signum;* ML, bell, fr. LL, ringing of a bell, fr. L, mark, sign — more at TOUCH, SIGN] (1586) **1** : an alarm bell or the ringing of it **2** : a warning signal

[1]**tod** \'täd\ *n* [ME] (12c) *chiefly Scot* : FOX

[2]**tod** *n* [ME *todd, todde;* prob. akin to OHG *zotta* tuft of hair] (15c) **1** *archaic* : any of various units of weight for wool; *esp* : one equal to 28 pounds (13 kilograms) **2** *Brit* : a bushy clump (as of ivy)

[1]**to·day** \tə-'dā\ *adv* (bef. 12c) **1** : on or for this day **2** : at the present time

[2]**today** *n* (1535) : the present day, time, or age ⟨~'s youth⟩

[3]**today** *adj* (1966) : of or characteristic of today : NOW

tod·dle \'tä-dᵊl\ *vi* **tod·dled; tod·dling** \'täd-liŋ, 'tä-dᵊl-iŋ\ [origin unknown] (ca. 1600) **1** : to walk with short tottering steps in the manner of a young child **2** : to take a stroll : SAUNTER — **toddle** *n*

tod·dler \'täd-lər, 'tä-dᵊl-ər\ *n* (1793) : one that toddles; *esp* : a young child — **tod·dler·hood** \-ˌhu̇d\ *n*

tod·dy \'tä-dē\ *n, pl* **toddies** [Hindi & Urdu *tāṛī* juice of the palmyra palm, fr. *tāṛ* palmyra palm, fr. Skt *tāla*] (1609) **1** : the fresh or fermented sap of various chiefly Asian palms **2** : a usu. hot drink consisting of liquor (as rum), water, sugar, and spices

to–do \tə-'dü\ *n, pl* **to–dos** \-'düz\ (ca. 1576) : BUSTLE, STIR, FUSS

[1]**toe** \'tō\ *n* [ME *to,* fr. OE *tā;* akin to OHG *zēha* toe] (bef. 12c) **1 a** (1) : one of the terminal members of the vertebrate foot (2) : the fore end of a foot or hoof **b** : a terminal segment of a limb of an invertebrate **c** : the forepart of something worn on the foot ⟨the ~ of a boot⟩ **2** : a part that by its position or form is felt to resemble a toe ⟨the ~ of Italy⟩: as **a** : a lateral projection at one end or between the ends of a piece (as a rod or bolt) **b** : the lowest part (as of an embankment, dam, or cliff) **3** : TOE DANCE — **toe·less** \-ləs\ *adj* — **on one's toes** : ALERT 1 — **toe to toe** : facing one another

[2]**toe** *vb* **toed; toe·ing** *vt* (1660) **1** : to furnish with a toe ⟨~ a sock⟩ **2** : to touch, reach, or drive with the toe ⟨~ a football⟩ **3** : to drive (as a nail) obliquely; *also* : to clinch or fasten by or with nails or rods so driven ~ *vi* **1** : TIPTOE **2** : to stand, walk, or be placed so that the toes assume an indicated position or direction ⟨~ in⟩ — **toe the line** *or* **toe the mark** : to conform rigorously to a rule or standard

toea \'tȯi-ə\ *n, pl* **toea** [Hiri Motu (pidgin of Papua New Guinea based on Motu, an Austronesian language), a kind of shell] (1975) — see *kina* at MONEY table

toe cap *n* (1797) : a piece of material (as leather) covering the toe of a shoe and reinforcing or decorating it

toed \'tōd\ *adj* [[1]*toe*] (ca. 1611) **1** : having a toe or toes esp. of a specified kind or number — usu. used in combination ⟨five-*toed*⟩ ⟨round-

toed shoes⟩ **2** [fr. pp. of [2]*toe*] : driven obliquely ⟨a ~ nail⟩; *also* : secured by diagonal or oblique nailing

toe dance *n* (1898) : a dance executed on the tips of the toes by means of a ballet slipper with a reinforced toe — **toe–dance** *vi* — **toe dancer** *n* — **toe dancing** *n*

TOEFL \ˈtō-fəl\ *trademark* — used for a test to evaluate the English language skills of nonnative speakers

toe•hold \ˈtō-ˌhōld\ *n* (1880) **1 a** : a hold or place of support for the toes (as in climbing) **b** (1) : a means of progressing (as in surmounting barriers) (2) : a slight footing ⟨used his money to get a ~, then a foothold, then a near stranglehold on the political economy —R. W. Armstrong⟩ **2** : an illegal wrestling hold in which the aggressor bends or twists the other wrestler's foot

toe–in \ˈtō-ˌin\ *n* (1928) **1** : CAMBER 3 **2** : adjustment of the front wheels of an automotive vehicle so that they are closer together at the front than at the back

toe loop *n* (ca. 1964) : a backward jump in figure skating with a takeoff from the outside edge of one skate followed by a full turn in the air and a landing on the outside edge of the same skate

[1]**toe•nail** \ˈtō-ˌnāl, -ˈnāl\ *n* (1691) : a nail of a toe

[2]**toenail** *vt* (1900) : to fasten by toed nails : TOE

toe•piece \ˈtō-ˌpēs\ *n* (1860) : a piece designed to form a toe (as of a shoe) or cover the toes of the foot

toe•plate \-ˌplāt\ *n* (1894) : a tab attached to the toe of a shoe (as to prevent wear due to heavy use)

toe–to–toe *adj or adv* (ca. 1942) : slugging it out at or as if at close range ⟨a ~ confrontation over the new policy⟩

toff \ˈtäf\ *n* [prob. alter. of *tuft* titled college student] (1851) *chiefly Brit* : DANDY, SWELL

tof•fee *also* **tof•fy** \ˈtȯ-fē, ˈtä-\ *n, pl* **toffees** *also* **toffies** [alter. of *taffy*] (1825) : candy of brittle but tender texture made by boiling sugar and butter together

tof•fee–nosed \-ˈnōzd\ *adj* (ca. 1925) *chiefly Brit* : SNOBBISH

toft \ˈtȯft, ˈtäft\ *n* [ME, fr. OE, fr. ON *topt;* prob. akin to Gk *dapedon* floor, *demein* to build, *pedon* ground — more at TIMBER, PED] (bef. 12c) *Brit* : a site for a dwelling and its outbuildings; *also* : an entire holding comprising a homestead and additional land

to•fu \ˈtō-(ˌ)fü\ *n* [Jp *tōfu*] (1771) : a soft food product prepared by treating soybean milk with coagulants (as magnesium chloride or diluted acids) — called also *bean curd*

tog \ˈtäg, ˈtȯg\ *vt* **togged; tog•ging** [*togs*] (ca. 1785) : to dress esp. in fine clothing — usu. used with *up* or *out*

to•ga \ˈtō-gə\ *n* [L; akin to L *tegere* to cover — more at THATCH] (1600) : the loose outer garment worn in public by citizens of ancient Rome; *also* : a similar loose wrap or a professional, official, or academic gown — **to•gaed** \-gəd\ *adj*

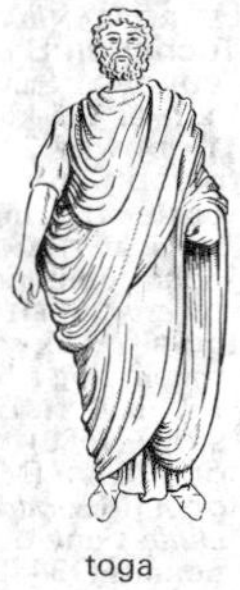

toga

to•ga vi•ri•lis \ˌtō-gə-və-ˈrē-ləs, -ˈri-\ *n, pl* **to•gae vi•ri•les** \ˈtō-ˌgī-və-ˈrē-ˌlās, -ˈri-\ [L, men's toga] (1600) : the white toga of manhood assumed by boys of ancient Rome at age 15

to•ga•vi•rus \ˈtō-gə-ˌvī-rəs\ *n* [NL, fr. L *toga* toga + NL *virus*] (1970) : any of a family (*Togaviridae*) of single-stranded RNA viruses that have a spherical virion and include the causative agents of German measles and the three forms of equine encephalitis

[1]**to•geth•er** \tə-ˈge-thər\ *adv* [ME *togedere,* fr. OE *togædere,* fr. *tō* to + *gædere* together; akin to MHG *gater* together, OE *gaderian* to gather] (bef. 12c) **1 a** : in or into one place, mass, collection, or group ⟨the men get ~ every Thursday for poker⟩ **b** : in a body : as a group ⟨students and faculty ~ presented the petition⟩ **2 a** : in or into contact (as connection, collision, or union) ⟨mix these ingredients ~⟩ **b** : in or into association or relationship ⟨colors that go well ~⟩ **3 a** : at one time : SIMULTANEOUSLY ⟨events that happened ~⟩ **b** : in succession ⟨was depressed for days ~⟩ **4 a** : by combined action : JOINTLY ⟨~ we forced the door⟩ **b** : in or into agreement or harmony ⟨the soloist and the orchestra weren't quite ~⟩ **c** : in or into a unified or coherent structure or an integrated whole ⟨can't even put a simple sentence ~⟩ **5 a** : with each other — used as an intensive after certain verbs ⟨join ~⟩ ⟨add ~⟩ **b** : as a unit : in the aggregate ⟨these arguments taken ~ make a convincing case⟩ **c** : considered as a whole : counted or summed up ⟨all ~, there were 21 entries⟩ — **to•geth•er•ness** *n*

[2]**together** *adj* (1963) **1** : appropriately prepared, organized, or balanced **2** : composed in mind or manner : SELF-POSSESSED

together with *prep* (15c) : in addition to : in association with

Tog•gen•burg \ˈtä-gən-ˌbərg\ *n* [*Toggenburg,* district in northeastern Switzerland] (1886) : any of a breed of brown hornless dairy goats of Swiss origin with white stripes on the face

tog•gery \ˈtä-g(ə-)rē, ˈtȯ-\ *n* [*togs*] (1810) : CLOTHING

[1]**tog•gle** \ˈtä-gəl\ *n* [origin unknown] (ca. 1775) **1** : a piece or device for holding or securing: as **a** : a pin inserted in a nautical knot to make it more secure or easier to slip **b** : a crosspiece attached to the end of or to a loop in something (as a chain, rope, line, strap, or belt) usu. to prevent slipping, to serve in twisting or tightening, or to hold something attached **2** : a device consisting of two bars jointed together end to end but not in line so that when a force is applied to the joint tending to straighten it pressure will be exerted on the parts adjacent or fixed to the outer ends of the bars; *also* : a device with a joint using a toggle

[2]**toggle** *vb* **tog•gled; tog•gling** \-g(ə-)liŋ\ *vt* (1836) **1** : to fasten with or as if with a toggle **2** : to furnish with a toggle ~ *vi* : to switch between two options esp. of an electronic device usu. by pressing a single button or a simple key combination

toggle bolt *n* (ca. 1794) : a bolt that has a nut with wings which close for passage through a small hole and spring open after passing through the hole to keep the bolt from slipping back through

toggle switch *n* (ca. 1924) : an electric switch operated by pushing a projecting lever through a small arc

togs \ˈtägz, ˈtȯgz\ *n pl* [pl. of E slang *tog* coat, short for obs. E argot *togeman, togman*] (1779) : CLOTHING; *esp* : a set of clothes and accessories for a specified use ⟨riding ~⟩

togue \ˈtōg\ *n* [CanF] (1839) : LAKE TROUT

To•ho•no O'odham \tō-ˈhō-nō-\ *n, pl* **Tohono O'odham** [O'odham *tóhono ʔóʔodham,* lit., desert people] (1986) : a member of an American Indian people of southwestern Arizona and northwestern Mexico

[1]**toil** \ˈtȯi(-ə)l\ *n* [ME *toile,* fr. AF *toyl,* fr. *toiller*] (14c) **1** *archaic* **a** : STRUGGLE, BATTLE **b** : laborious effort **2** : long strenuous fatiguing labor ***syn*** see WORK — **toil•ful** \-fəl\ *adj* — **toil•ful•ly** \-fə-lē\ *adv*

[2]**toil** *vb* [ME, to argue, struggle, fr. AF *toiller* to make dirty, fight, wrangle, fr. L *tudiculare* to crush, grind, fr. *tudicula* machine for crushing olives, dim. of *tudes* hammer; akin to L *tundere* to beat — more at CONTUSION] *vi* (14c) **1** : to work hard and long **2** : to proceed with laborious effort : PLOD ~ *vt* **1** *archaic* : OVERWORK **2** *archaic* : to get or accomplish with great effort — **toil•er** \ˈtȯi-lər\ *n*

[3]**toil** *n* [MF *toile* cloth, net, fr. OF *teile,* L *tela* cloth on a loom — more at SUBTLE] (ca. 1529) **1** : a net to trap game **2** : something by which one is held fast or inextricably involved : SNARE, TRAP — usu. used in pl. ⟨caught in the ~*s* of the law⟩

toile \ˈtwäl\ *n* [F, cloth, linen, fr. MF] (1794) **1** : any of many plain or simple twill weave fabrics; *esp* : LINEN **2** : a mock-up model of a garment

toile de Jouy \ˌtwäl-də-ˈzhwē\ *n* [F, lit., cloth of Jouy, fr. *Jouy-en-Josas, France*] (ca. 1920) : an 18th century French scenic pattern usu. printed on cotton, linen, or silk in one color on a light ground; *broadly* : a similar printed fabric

[1]**toi•let** \ˈtȯi-lət\ *n* [F *toilette* cloth on which items used for grooming are placed, fr. MF, piece of batiste, fr. dim. of *toile* cloth] (1667) **1** *archaic* : DRESSING TABLE **2** : the act or process of dressing and grooming oneself **3 a** (1) : BATHROOM, LAVATORY 2 (2) : PRIVY **b** : a fixture that consists usu. of a water-flushed bowl and seat and is used for defecation and urination **4** : cleansing in preparation for or in association with a medical or surgical procedure ⟨pulmonary ~⟩

[2]**toilet** *vi* (1840) **1** : to dress and groom oneself **2** : to use the toilet — usu. used of a child ~ *vt* **1** : DRESS, GARB **2** : to help (as a child or sick person) use the toilet

toilet paper *n* (1884) : a thin sanitary absorbent paper usu. in a roll for use in drying or cleaning oneself after defecation and urination

toilet powder *n* (1840) : a fine powder usu. with soothing or antiseptic ingredients for sprinkling or rubbing (as after bathing) over the skin

toi•let•ry \ˈtȯi-lə-trē\ *n, pl* **-ries** (1892) : an article or preparation (as toothpaste, shaving cream, or cologne) used in cleaning or grooming oneself — usu. used in pl.

toilet soap *n* (1839) : a mild soap that is often perfumed and colored and stabilized with preservatives

toi•lette \twä-ˈlet\ *n* [F, fr. MF] (1681) **1** : TOILET 2 **2 a** : formal or fashionable attire or style of dress **b** : a particular costume or outfit

toilet training *n* (1940) : the process of training a child to control bladder and bowel movements and to use the toilet — **toilet train** *vt*

toilet water *n* (1855) : EAU DE TOILETTE

toil•some \ˈtȯi(-ə)l-səm\ *adj* (1575) : marked by or full of toil or fatigue : LABORIOUS ⟨a ~ task⟩ — **toil•some•ly** *adv* — **toil•some•ness** *n*

toil•worn \ˈtȯi(-ə)l-ˌwȯrn\ *adj* (1751) : showing the effects of or worn out with toil ⟨~ hands⟩

to–ing and fro–ing \ˈtü-iŋ-ən(d)-ˈfrō-iŋ\ *n, pl* **to–ings and fro–ings** [*to and fro*] (1847) : a passing back and forth

to•ka•mak *also* **to•ko•mak** \ˈtō-kə-ˌmak, ˈtä-\ *n* [Russ, fr. *to*roidal'naya *kam*era s *a*ksial'nym magnitnym polem (toroidal chamber with an axial magnetic field)] (1965) : a toroidal device for producing controlled nuclear fusion that involves the confining and heating of a gaseous plasma by means of an electric current and magnetic field

To•kay \tō-ˈkā\ *n* (1696) **1** : a naturally sweet wine from the area around Tokaj, Hungary **2** : a blend of Angelica, port, and sherry made in California

toke \ˈtōk\ *n* [AmerSp *toque,* fr. Sp, touch, test, fr. *tocar* to touch, fr. VL **toccare* — more at TOUCH] (1968) *slang* : a puff on a marijuana cigarette or pipe — **toke** *vi, slang*

[1]**to•ken** \ˈtō-kən\ *n* [ME, fr. OE *tācen, tācn* sign, token; akin to OHG *zeihhan* sign, Gk *deiknynai* to show — more at DICTION] (bef. 12c) **1** : an outward sign or expression ⟨his tears were ~*s* of his grief⟩ **2 a** : SYMBOL, EMBLEM ⟨a white flag is a ~ of surrender⟩ **b** : an instance of a linguistic expression **3** : a distinguishing feature : CHARACTERISTIC **4 a** : SOUVENIR, KEEPSAKE **b** : a small part representing the whole : INDICATION ⟨this is only a ~ of what we hope to accomplish⟩ **c** : something given or shown as a guarantee (as of authority, right, or identity) **5 a** : a piece resembling a coin issued as money by some person or body other than a de jure government **b** : a piece resembling a coin issued for use (as for fare on a bus) by a particular group on specified terms **6** : a member of a group (as a minority) that is included within a larger group through tokenism; *esp* : a token employee ***syn*** see SIGN — **by the same token** : for the same reason

[2]**token** *adj* (1915) **1** : done or given as a token esp. in partial fulfillment of an obligation or engagement ⟨a ~ payment⟩ **2 a** : representing no more than a symbolic effort : MINIMAL, PERFUNCTORY ⟨~ resistance⟩ ⟨~ integration⟩ **b** : serving or intended to show absence of discrimination ⟨a ~ female employee⟩

to•ken•ism \ˈtō-kə-ˌni-zəm\ *n* (1961) : the policy or practice of making only a symbolic effort (as to desegregate)

token money *n* (1889) : money of regular government issue (as paper currency or coins) having a greater face value than intrinsic value

Tokharian *var of* TOCHARIAN

to•ko•no•ma \ˌtō-kə-ˈnō-mə\ *n* [Jp] (1871) : a niche or alcove in the wall of a Japanese house for the display of a decorative object

Tok Pis•in \ˈtȯk-ˈpi-zən, -sən\ *n* [Tok Pisin, lit., pidgin talk] (1974) : an English-based creole that is a national language of Papua New Guinea

tol- *or* **tolu-** *comb form* [ISV, fr. *toluene*] : toluene ⟨*tol*yl⟩

to•la \ˈtō-lə, tō-ˈlä\ *n* [Hindi & Urdu *tolā,* fr. Skt *tulā* weight; akin to L *tollere* to lift up] (1614) : a unit of weight of India equal to 180 grains troy or 0.375 ounce troy (11.7 grams)

to•lar \ˈtō-lär\ *n, pl* **to•lar•jev** \ˈtō-lär-ˌyev\ *or* **tolars** [Slovenian (nom. pl. *tolarji,* gen. pl. *tolarjev*), fr. G *Taler* taler] (1991) : the basic monetary unit of Slovenia from 1992 to 2007

tol•booth \ˈtō(l)-ˌbüth, ˈtäl-, ˈtȯl-\ *n* [ME *tolbothe, tollbothe* tollbooth, town hall, jail] (15c) **1** *Scot* : a town or market hall **2** *Scot* : JAIL, PRISON

tol•bu•ta•mide \täl-ˈbyü-tə-ˌmīd\ *n* [*tol-* + *butyric* + *amide*] (1956) : a sulfonylurea $C_{12}H_{18}N_2O_3S$ used in the treatment of diabetes

told *past and past part of* TELL

tole \ˈtōl\ *n, often attrib* [F *tôle,* fr. MF dial. *taule,* fr. L *tabula* board, tablet] (1927) **:** sheet metal and esp. tinplate for use in domestic and ornamental wares in which it is usu. japanned or painted and often elaborately decorated; *also* **:** objects made of tole

To·le·do \tə-ˈlē-(ˌ)dō\ *n, pl* **-dos** (1596) **:** a finely tempered sword of a kind made in Toledo, Spain

tol·er·a·ble \ˈtä-lə-rə-bəl, ˈtäl-rə-; ˈtä-lər-bəl\ *adj* (15c) **1 :** capable of being borne or endured ⟨~ pain⟩ **2 :** moderately good or agreeable **:** PASSABLE ⟨a ~ singing voice⟩ — **tol·er·a·bil·i·ty** \ˌtä-lə-rə-ˈbi-lə-tē, ˌtäl-rə-\ *n* — **tol·er·a·bly** \ˈtä-lə-rə-blē, ˈtäl-rə-; ˈtä-lər-blē\ *adv*

tol·er·ance \ˈtä-lə-rən(t)s, ˈtäl-rən(t)s\ *n* (15c) **1 :** capacity to endure pain or hardship **:** ENDURANCE, FORTITUDE, STAMINA **2 a :** sympathy or indulgence for beliefs or practices differing from or conflicting with one's own **b :** the act of allowing something **:** TOLERATION **3 :** the allowable deviation from a standard; *esp* **:** the range of variation permitted in maintaining a specified dimension in machining a piece **4 a** (1) **:** the capacity of the body to endure or become less responsive to a substance (as a drug) or a physiological insult esp. with repeated use or exposure ⟨developed a ~ to painkillers⟩; *also* **:** the immunological state marked by unresponsiveness to a specific antigen (2) **:** relative capacity of an organism to grow or thrive when subjected to an unfavorable environmental factor **b :** the maximum amount of a pesticide residue that may lawfully remain on or in food

tol·er·ant \ˈtä-lə-rənt, ˈtäl-rənt\ *adj* (1776) **1 :** inclined to tolerate; *esp* **:** marked by forbearance or endurance ⟨~ parents⟩ ⟨a culture ~ of religious differences⟩ **2 :** exhibiting tolerance (as for a drug or an environmental factor) — **tol·er·ant·ly** *adv*

tol·er·ate \ˈtä-lə-ˌrāt\ *vt* **-at·ed; -at·ing** [L *toleratus,* pp. of *tolerare* to endure, put up with; akin to OE *tholian* to bear, L *tollere* to lift up, *latus* carried (suppletive pp. of *ferre*), Gk *tlēnai* to bear] (1524) **1 :** to endure or resist the action of (as a drug or food) without serious side effects or discomfort **:** exhibit physiological tolerance for **2 a :** to allow to be or to be done without prohibition, hindrance, or contradiction **b :** to put up with ⟨learn to ~ one another⟩ ***syn*** see BEAR — **tol·er·a·tive** \-ˌrā-tiv\ *adj* — **tol·er·a·tor** \-ˌrā-tər\ *n*

tol·er·a·tion \ˌtä-lə-ˈrā-shən\ *n* (1531) **1 a :** the act or practice of tolerating something **b :** a government policy of permitting forms of religious belief and worship not officially established **2 :** TOLERANCE 4a(1)

tol·i·dine \ˈtä-lə-ˌdēn\ *n* [ISV *tol-* + *-idine*] (1879) **:** any of several isomeric aromatic diamines $C_{14}H_{16}N_2$ that are homologues of benzidine and used esp. as dye intermediates

¹toll \ˈtōl\ *n* [ME, fr. OE, fr. VL **tolonium,* alter. of LL *telonium* customhouse, fr. Gk *tolōnion,* fr. *telōnēs* collector of tolls, fr. *telos* tax, toll; perh. akin to Gk *tlēnai* to bear] (bef. 12c) **1 :** a tax or fee paid for some liberty or privilege (as of passing over a highway or bridge) **2 :** compensation for services rendered: as **a :** a charge for transportation **b :** a charge for a long-distance telephone call **3 :** a grievous or ruinous price ⟨inflation has taken its ~⟩; *esp* **:** cost in life or health ⟨the death ~ from the hurricane⟩

²toll *vi* (14c) **:** to take or levy toll ~ *vt* **1 a :** to exact part of as a toll **b :** to take as toll **2 :** to exact a toll from (someone)

³toll *or* **tole** \ˈtōl\ *vt* **tolled** *or* **toled; toll·ing** *or* **tol·ing** [ME *tollen, tolen;* akin to OE *fortyllan* to seduce] (13c) **1 :** ALLURE, ENTICE **2 a :** to entice (game) to approach **b :** to attract (fish) with scattered bait **c :** to lead or attract (domestic animals) to a desired point

⁴toll *vb* [ME, to pull, drag, toll (a bell), perh. alter. of *toilen* to struggle — more at TOIL] *vt* (15c) **1 :** to sound (a bell) by pulling the rope **2 a :** to give signal or announcement of ⟨the clock ~*ed* each hour⟩ **b :** to announce by tolling ⟨church bells ~*ed* the death of the bishop⟩ **c :** to call to or from a place or occasion ⟨bells ~*ed* the congregation to church⟩ ~ *vi* **:** to sound with slow measured strokes ⟨the bell ~*s* solemnly⟩

⁵toll *n* (15c) **:** the sound of a tolling bell

toll·booth \ˈtōl-ˌbüth\ *n* [ME *tolbothe, tollbothe* tollbooth, town hall, jail, fr. *tol, toll* toll + *bothe* booth] (14c) **:** a booth (as on a highway or bridge) where tolls are paid

toll call *n* (1912) **:** a long-distance telephone call at charges above a local rate

toll–free \ˈtōl-ˈfrē\ *adj or adv* (1970) **:** having or using a direct telephone line or number (as an 800 number) for a long-distance call that is not charged to the caller ⟨a ~ number⟩ ⟨called ~⟩

toll·gate \ˈtōl-ˌgāt\ *n* (1773) **:** a point where the driver of a vehicle must pay a toll

toll·house \-ˌhau̇s\ *n* (14c) **:** a house or booth where tolls are taken

Toll House *trademark* — used for cookies containing chocolate morsels

toll·way \-ˌwā\ *n* (1949) **:** TURNPIKE 2a(1)

Tol·tec \ˈtōl-ˌtek, ˈtäl-\ *n* [Sp *tolteca,* fr. Nahuatl *tōltēcah,* pl. of *tōltēcatl,* lit., person from *Tōllān* (now Tula de Allende, Mexico)] (1787) **:** a member of a people that dominated central and southern Mexico prior to the Aztecs — **Tol·tec·an** \-ən\ *adj*

tol·u·ene \ˈtäl-yə-ˌwēn\ *n* [F *toluène,* fr. *tolu* balsam from the tropical American tree *Myroxylon balsamum,* fr. Sp *tolú,* fr. Santiago de *Tolú,* Colombia] (1855) **:** a liquid aromatic hydrocarbon C_7H_8 that resembles benzene but is less volatile, flammable, and toxic and is used esp. as a solvent, in organic synthesis, and as an antiknock agent for gasoline

to·lu·i·dine \tə-ˈlü-ə-ˌdēn\ *n* [ISV] (1850) **:** any of three isomeric amino derivatives of toluene C_7H_9N that are analogous to aniline and are used as dye intermediates

toluidine blue *n* (1898) **:** a basic thiazine dye that is related to methylene blue and is used as a biological stain

tol·u·ol \ˈtäl-yə-ˌwȯl, -ˌwōl\ *n* (ca. 1848) **:** TOLUENE

tol·yl \ˈtä-ləl\ *n* [ISV] (ca. 1868) **:** any of three monovalent radicals $CH_3C_6H_4$ derived from toluene

tom \ˈtäm\ *n* [*Tom,* nickname for *Thomas*] (1762) **1 :** the male of various animals: as **a :** TOMCAT **b :** a male turkey **2** *cap* **:** UNCLE TOM 2

¹tom·a·hawk \ˈtä-mi-ˌhȯk\ *n* [Virginia Algonquian *tomahack*] (ca. 1612) **:** a light ax used as a missile and as a hand weapon esp. by No. American Indians

²tomahawk *vt* (ca. 1650) **:** to cut, strike, or kill with a tomahawk

to·mal·ley \tə-ˈma-lē, -ˈmä-; ˈtä-ˌma-lē, -mə-lē\ *n, pl* **-leys** [Carib *tumali* sauce of lobster livers] (ca. 1666) **:** the liver of the lobster

Tom and Jer·ry \ˌtäm-ən(d)-ˈjer-ē\ *n* [Corinthian *Tom & Jerry* Hawthorne, characters in *Life in London* (1821) by Pierce Egan †1849 Eng. sportswriter] (1845) **:** a hot drink that is a combination of a toddy and an eggnog

to·ma·til·lo \ˌtō-mə-ˈtē-(ˌ)yō, -ˈtēl-(ˌ)yō\ *n, pl* **-los** [Sp, dim. of *tomate*] (ca. 1913) **:** the small round yellow, purplish, and esp. pale green edible sticky fruit of a Mexican ground-cherry (*Physalis ixocarpa* syn. *P. philadelphica*); *also* **:** the plant that bears tomatillos

to·ma·to \tə-ˈmā-(ˌ)tō; *chiefly Brit, eNewEng, neVirginia, and sometimes elsewhere in cultivated speech* -ˈmä-; *chiefly Northern* -ˈma-\ *n, pl* **-toes** [alter. of earlier *tomate,* fr. Sp, fr. Nahuatl *tomatl*] (1604) **1 :** the usu. large rounded typically red or yellow pulpy berry of an herb (genus *Lycopersicon*) of the nightshade family native to So. America **2 :** a plant that produces tomatoes; *esp* **:** one (*Lycopersicon esculentum* syn. *L. lycopersicum*) that is a tender perennial widely cultivated as an annual for its edible fruit

to·ma·to·ey \-tə-wē\ *adj* (1972) **1 :** of, relating to, or characteristic of a tomato **2 :** richly flavored with tomatoes

tomato fruitworm *n* (ca. 1891) **:** CORN EARWORM

tomato hornworm *n* (1921) **:** a No. American hawk moth (*Manduca quinquemaculata*) whose green larva is a hornworm feeding on leaves of plants of the nightshade family and esp. tobacco and tomato

¹tomb \ˈtüm\ *n* [ME *tombe,* fr. AF *tumbe,* fr. LL *tumba* sepulchral mound, fr. Gk *tymbos;* perh. akin to L *tumēre* to be swollen — more at THUMB] (13c) **1 a :** an excavation in which a corpse is buried **:** GRAVE **b :** a place of interment **2 :** a house, chamber, or vault for the dead **3 :** a building or structure resembling a tomb (as in appearance) — **tomb·less** \-ləs\ *adj*

²tomb *vt* (14c) **:** BURY, ENTOMB

tom·bac \ˈtäm-ˌbak\ *n* [F, fr. D *tombak,* fr. Malay *tĕmbaga* copper] (1602) **:** an alloy essentially of copper and zinc and sometimes tin or arsenic that is used esp. for cheap jewelry and gilding

tom·bo·lo \ˈtōm-bə-ˌlō, ˈtäm-\ *n, pl* **-los** [It, fr. L *tumulus* mound, tumulus] (1899) **:** a sand or gravel bar connecting an island with the mainland or another island

tom·boy \ˈtäm-ˌbȯi\ *n* (1566) **:** a girl who behaves in a manner usu. considered boyish — **tom·boy·ish** \-ish\ *adj* — **tom·boy·ish·ness** *n*

tomb·stone \ˈtüm-ˌstōn\ *n* (1565) **:** GRAVESTONE

¹tom·cat \ˈtäm-ˌkat\ *n* (1789) **:** a male domestic cat

²tomcat *vi* (1927) **:** to seek sexual gratification promiscuously **:** CAT — often used with *around*

tom·cod \ˈtäm-ˌkäd\ *n* (1722) **:** either of two small fishes (*Microgadus tomcod* of the Atlantic and *M. proximus* of the Pacific) of the cod family

Tom Col·lins \ˈtäm-ˈkä-lənz\ *n* [fr. the name *Tom Collins*] (ca. 1909) **:** a collins with a base of gin

Tom, Dick, and Har·ry \ˌtäm-ˌdik-ən(d)-ˈha-rē\ *n, pl* **Toms, Dicks, and Harrys** (1805) **:** the common man **:** ANYONE — often used with *every* ⟨helps every *Tom, Dick, and Harry* in need⟩

tome \ˈtōm\ *n* [MF or L; MF, fr. L *tomus,* fr. Gk *tomos* section, roll of papyrus, tome, fr. *temnein* to cut; akin to MIr *tamnaid* he lops, Pol *ciąć* to cut, and perh. to L *tondēre* to shear] (1519) **1 :** a volume forming part of a larger work **2 :** BOOK; *esp* **:** a large or scholarly book

-tome *n comb form* [Gk *tomos*] **1 :** part **:** segment ⟨myo*tome*⟩ **2 :** cutting instrument ⟨micro*tome*⟩

to·men·tose \tō-ˈmen-ˌtōs, ˈtō-mən-\ *adj* [NL *tomentosus,* fr. *tomentum*] (1698) **:** covered with densely matted woolly hairs ⟨a ~ leaf⟩

to·men·tum \tō-ˈmen-təm\ *n, pl* **-ta** \-tə\ [NL, fr. L, cushion stuffing] (1699) **:** pubescence composed of densely matted woolly hairs

¹tom·fool \ˈtäm-ˈfül\ *n* (1640) **:** a great fool **:** BLOCKHEAD

²tomfool *adj* (1760) **:** extremely foolish, stupid, or doltish

tom·fool·ery \ˌtäm-ˈfül-rē, -ˈfü-lə-\ *n* (1812) **:** playful or foolish behavior

Tom·my \ˈtä-mē\ *n, pl* **Tommies** [*Thomas* Atkins, name used as model in official army forms] (1884) **:** a British soldier

Tommy At·kins \-ˈat-kənz\ *n* (1883) **:** TOMMY

tom·my–gun \ˈtä-mē-ˌgən\ *vt* (1942) **:** to shoot with a tommy gun

tommy gun *n* [by shortening & alter.] (1929) **:** THOMPSON SUBMACHINE GUN; *broadly* **:** SUBMACHINE GUN

tom·my·rot \ˈtä-mē-ˌrät\ *n* [E dial. *tommy* fool + E *rot*] (1884) **:** utter foolishness or nonsense

to·mo·gram \ˈtō-mə-ˌgram\ *n* (1936) **:** an image (as a radiograph) generated by tomography

to·mog·ra·phy \tō-ˈmä-grə-fē\ *n* [Gk *tomos* section + ISV *-graphy* — more at TOME] (1935) **:** a method of producing a three-dimensional image of the internal structures of a solid object (as the human body or the earth) by the observation and recording of the differences in the effects on the passage of waves of energy impinging on those structures — compare COMPUTED TOMOGRAPHY — **to·mo·graph·ic** \ˌtō-mə-ˈgra-fik\ *adj*

¹to·mor·row \tə-ˈmär-(ˌ)ō, -ˈmȯr-\ *adv* [ME *to morgen,* fr. OE *tō morgen,* fr. *tō* to + *morgen* morrow, morning — more at MORN] (13c) **:** on or for the day after today ⟨will do it ~⟩

²tomorrow *n* (14c) **1 :** the day after the present ⟨the court will recess until ~⟩ **2 :** FUTURE 1a ⟨the world of ~⟩

tompion *var of* TAMPION

Tom Thumb \ˈtäm-ˈthəm\ *n* (1579) **1 :** a legendary English dwarf **2 :** a dwarf type, race, or individual

tom·tit \ˈtäm-ˌtit, täm-ˈ\ *n* [prob. short for *tomtitmouse,* fr. the name *Tom* + *titmouse*] (1700) **:** any of various small active birds

tom–tom \ˈtäm-ˌtäm, ˈtəm-ˌtəm\ *n* [Hindi & Urdu *ṭamṭam*] (1693) **1 :** a usu. long and narrow small-headed drum commonly beaten with the hands **2 :** a monotonous beating, rhythm, or rhythmical sound

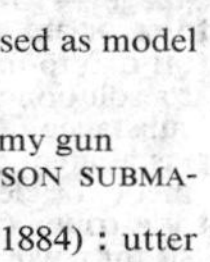

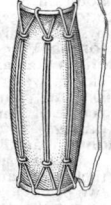

tom-tom 1

-tomy *n comb form* [NL *-tomia,* fr. Gk, fr. *-tomos* that cuts, fr. *temnein* to cut — more at TOME] : incision : section ⟨laparo*tomy*⟩

[1]**ton** \ˈtən\ *n, pl* **tons** *also* **ton** [ME *tunne* unit of weight or capacity — more at TUN] (14c) **1 a :** a unit of internal capacity for ships equal to 100 cubic feet — called also *register ton* **b :** a unit approximately equal to the volume of a long ton weight of seawater used in reckoning the displacement of ships and equal to 35 cubic feet **c :** a unit of volume for cargo freight usu. reckoned at 40 cubic feet — called also *measurement ton* **2 :** any of various units of weight: **a** — see WEIGHT table **b :** METRIC TON **3 :** a great quantity : LOT ⟨ate ~*s* of cookies⟩ ⟨has ~*s* of money⟩ ⟨a ~ of work to do⟩

[2]**ton** \ˈtō^{n}\ *n* [F, lit., tone, fr. OF, fr. L *tonus*] (1756) **1 :** the prevailing fashion : VOGUE **2 :** the quality or state of being smart or fashionable

ton·al \ˈtō-n^{ə}l\ *adj* (1776) **1 :** of or relating to tone, tonality, or tonicity **2 :** having tonality — **ton·al·ly** \-n^{ə}l-ē\ *adv*

to·nal·i·ty \tō-ˈna-lə-tē\ *n, pl* **-ties** (1838) **1 :** tonal quality **2 a :** KEY 7 **b :** the organization of all the tones and harmonies of a piece of music in relation to a tonic **3 :** the arrangement or interrelation of the tones of a work of visual art

ton·do \ˈtän-(ˌ)dō\ *n, pl* **ton·di** \-(ˌ)dē\ [It, fr. *tondo* round, short for *rotondo,* fr. L *rotundus* — more at ROTUND] (1890) **1 :** a circular painting **2 :** a sculptured medallion

[1]**tone** \ˈtōn\ *n* [ME, fr. AF *tun, ton,* fr. L *tonus* tension, tone, fr. Gk *tonos,* lit., act of stretching; akin to Gk *teinein* to stretch — more at THIN] (14c) **1 :** vocal or musical sound of a specific quality ⟨spoke in low ~*s*⟩ ⟨masculine ~*s*⟩; *esp* **:** musical sound with respect to timbre and manner of expression **2 a :** a sound of definite pitch and vibration **b :** WHOLE STEP **3 :** accent or inflection expressive of a mood or emotion **4 :** the pitch of a word often used to express differences of meaning **5 :** a particular pitch or change of pitch constituting an element in the intonation of a phrase or sentence ⟨high ~⟩ ⟨low ~⟩ ⟨mid ~⟩ ⟨low-rising ~⟩ ⟨falling ~⟩ **6 :** style or manner of expression in speaking or writing ⟨seemed wise to adopt a conciliatory ~⟩ **7 a** (1) **:** color quality or value (2) **:** a tint or shade of color **b :** the color that appreciably modifies a hue or white or black ⟨gray walls of greenish ~⟩ **8 :** the effect in painting of light and shade together with color **9 a :** the state of a living body or of any of its organs or parts in which the functions are healthy and performed with due vigor **b :** normal tension or responsiveness to stimuli; *specif* **:** muscular tonus **10 a :** healthy elasticity : RESILIENCY **b :** general character, quality, or trend ⟨a city's upbeat ~⟩ **c :** frame of mind : MOOD

[2]**tone** *vb* **toned; ton·ing** *vt* (1660) **1 :** INTONE **2 :** to give a particular intonation or inflection to **3 a :** to impart tone to : STRENGTHEN ⟨medicine to ~ up the system⟩ **b :** to soften or reduce in intensity, color, appearance, or sound : MELLOW — often used with *down* **c :** to change the normal silver image of (as a photographic print) into a colored image ~ *vi* **1 :** to assume a pleasing color quality or tint **2 :** to blend or harmonize in color

tone·arm \ˈtōn-ˌärm\ *n* (1907) **:** the movable part of a phonograph or record player that carries the pickup and permits the needle to follow the record groove

tone color *n* (1881) **:** TIMBRE

toned *adj* (15c) **1 :** having tone or a specified tone : characterized or distinguished by a tone **2** *of paper* **:** having a slight tint

tone–deaf \ˈtōn-ˌdef\ *adj* (1894) **:** relatively insensitive to differences in musical pitch — **tone deafness** *n*

tone language *n* (ca. 1909) **:** a language (as Chinese or Zulu) in which variations in tone distinguish words or phrases of different meaning that otherwise would sound alike

tone·less \ˈtōn-ləs\ *adj* (1773) **:** lacking in tone, modulation, or expression ⟨a ~ voice⟩ — **tone·less·ly** *adv* — **tone·less·ness** *n*

to·neme \ˈtō-ˌnēm\ *n* (1923) **:** an intonation phoneme in a tone language — **to·ne·mic** \tō-ˈnē-mik\ *adj*

tone poem *n* (1902) **:** SYMPHONIC POEM — **tone poet** *n*

ton·er \ˈtō-nər\ *n* (1888) **:** one that tones or is a source of tones: as **a :** a solution used to impart color to a silver photographic image **b :** a substance (as a thermoplastic powder) used esp. to develop an image (as a latent xerographic image) on a piece of paper **c :** a liquid cosmetic for cleansing the skin and contracting the pores

tone row *n* (1936) **:** the chosen sequence of tones that serves as the basis for a work of serial music; *specif* **:** TWELVE-TONE ROW

to·net·ic \tō-ˈne-tik\ *adj* (1922) **1 :** relating to linguistic tones or to tone languages **2 :** of or relating to intonation ⟨~ notation⟩ — **to·net·i·cal·ly** \-ti-k(ə-)lē\ *adv*

to·net·ics \-tiks\ *n pl but sing in constr* (1921) **:** the use or study of linguistic tones

to·nette \tō-ˈnet\ *n* [[1]*tone* + *-ette*] (1939) **:** a simple fipple flute with a range somewhat larger than an octave that is often used in elementary music education

toney *var of* TONY

[1]**tong** \ˈtäŋ, ˈtȯŋ\ *n* [Chin (Guangdong) *tòhng,* lit., hall] (1883) **:** a secret society or fraternal organization esp. of Chinese in the U.S. formerly notorious for gang warfare

[2]**tong** *vb* [*tongs*] *vt* (1868) **:** to take, gather, hold, or handle with tongs ⟨~ oysters⟩ ~ *vi* **:** to use tongs esp. in taking or gathering something — **tong·er** \ˈtäŋ-ər, ˈtȯŋ-\ *n*

ton·ga \ˈtäŋ-gə\ *n* [Hindi & Urdu *tāṅgā*] (1874) **:** a light 2-wheeled vehicle for two or four persons drawn by one horse and common in India

Ton·gan \ˈtäŋ-gən *also* -ən\ *n* (1853) **1 :** a member of a Polynesian people of Tonga **2 :** the Polynesian language of the Tongans — **Tongan** *adj*

tongs \ˈtäŋz, ˈtȯŋz\ *n pl but sing or pl in constr* [ME *tonges,* pl. of *tonge,* fr. OE *tang;* akin to OHG *zanga* tongs and perh. to Gk *daknein* to bite] (bef. 12c) **:** any of numerous grasping devices consisting commonly of two pieces joined at one end by a pivot or hinged like scissors

[1]**tongue** \ˈtəŋ\ *n* [ME *tunge,* fr. OE; akin to OHG *zunga* tongue, L *lingua*] (bef. 12c) **1 a :** a fleshy movable muscular process of the floor of the mouths of most vertebrates that bears sensory end organs and small glands and functions esp. in taking and swallowing food and in humans as a speech organ **b :** a part of various invertebrate animals that is analogous to the tongue **2 :** the flesh of a tongue (as of the ox or sheep) used as food **3 :** the power of communication through speech **4 a :** LANGUAGE; *esp* **:** a spoken language **b :** manner or quality of utterance with respect to tone or sound, the sense of what is expressed, or the intention of the speaker ⟨she has a clever ~⟩ ⟨a sharp ~⟩ **c :** ecstatic usu. unintelligible utterance usu. accompanying religious excitation — usu. used in pl. **d :** the cry of or as if of a hound pursuing or in sight of game — used esp. in the phrase *to give tongue* **5 :** a tapering flame ⟨~*s* of fire⟩ **6 :** a long narrow strip of land projecting into a body of water **7 :** something resembling an animal's tongue in being elongated and fastened at one end only: as **a :** a movable pin in a buckle **b :** a metal ball suspended inside a bell so as to strike against the sides as the bell is swung **c :** the pole of a vehicle **d :** the flap under the lacing or buckles of a shoe at the throat of the vamp **8 a :** the rib on one edge of a board that fits into a corresponding groove in an edge of another board to make a flush joint **b :** FEATHER 4 — **tongue·like** \-ˌlīk\ *adj*

[2]**tongue** *vb* **tongued; tongu·ing** \ˈtəŋ-iŋ\ *vt* (14c) **1** *archaic* **:** SCOLD **2 :** to touch or lick with or as if with the tongue **3 a :** to cut a tongue on ⟨~ a board⟩ **b :** to join (as boards) by means of a tongue and groove ⟨~ flooring together⟩ **4 :** to articulate (notes) by tonguing ~ *vi* **1 :** to project in a tongue **2 :** to articulate notes on a wind instrument by successively interrupting the stream of wind with the action of the tongue

tongue and groove *n* (1860) **:** a joint made by a tongue on one edge of a board fitting into a corresponding groove on the edge of another board — **tongue–and–groove** *adj*

tongued *adj* (14c) **:** having a tongue esp. of a specified kind — often used in combination ⟨sharp-*tongued*⟩

tongue–in–cheek *adj* (1933) **:** characterized by insincerity, irony, or whimsical exaggeration

tongue in cheek *adv* (ca. 1934) **:** with insincerity, irony, or whimsical exaggeration

tongue–lash \ˈtəŋ-ˌlash\ *vb* [back-formation fr. *tongue-lashing*] (1856) **:** CHIDE, SCOLD — **tongue–lash·ing** *n*

tongue·less \ˈtəŋ-ləs\ *adj* (14c) **1 :** having no tongue **2 :** lacking power of speech : MUTE

[1]**tongue–tie** \ˈtəŋ-ˌtī\ *vt* [back-formation fr. *tongue-tied*] (1555) **:** to deprive of speech or the power of distinct articulation

[2]**tongue–tie** *n* (ca. 1852) **:** limited mobility of the tongue due to a short frenulum connecting its underside to the floor of the mouth

tongue–tied \ˈtəŋ-ˌtīd\ *adj* (1529) **1 :** unable or disinclined to speak freely (as from shyness) **2 :** affected with tongue-tie

tongue twister *n* (1904) **:** a word, phrase, or sentence difficult to articulate because of a succession of similar consonantal sounds (as in "twin-screw steel cruiser")

-tonia *n comb form* [NL, fr. *tonus*] **:** condition or degree of tonus ⟨myo*tonia*⟩

[1]**ton·ic** \ˈtä-nik\ *adj* [Gk *tonikos,* fr. *tonos* tension, tone] (1649) **1 a :** characterized by tonus ⟨~ contraction of muscle⟩; *also* **:** marked by prolonged muscular contraction ⟨~ convulsions⟩ **b :** producing or adapted to produce healthy muscular condition and reaction of organs (as muscles) **2 a :** increasing or restoring physical or mental tone : REFRESHING **b :** yielding a tonic substance **3 :** relating to or based on the first tone of a scale ⟨~ harmony⟩ **4** *of a syllable* **:** bearing a principal stress or accent **5 :** of or relating to speech tones or to languages using them to distinguish words otherwise identical — **ton·i·cal·ly** \ˈtä-ni-k(ə-)lē\ *adv*

[2]**tonic** *n* (1797) **1 :** the first tone of a major or minor scale : KEYNOTE **2 a :** an agent (as a drug) that increases body tone **b :** one that invigorates, restores, refreshes, or stimulates ⟨a day in the country was a ~ for him⟩ **c :** a liquid preparation for the scalp or hair **d** *chiefly New-Eng* **:** a carbonated flavored beverage **e :** TONIC WATER **3 :** a voiced sound

tonic accent *n* (1867) **1 :** relative phonetic prominence (as from greater stress or higher pitch) of a spoken syllable or word **2 :** accent depending on pitch rather than stress

to·nic·i·ty \tō-ˈni-sə-tē\ *n* (1824) **1 :** the property of possessing tone; *esp* **:** healthy vigor of body or mind **2 :** muscular tonus

tonic sol–fa *n* (1852) **:** a system of solmization based on key relationships that replaces the normal notation with sol-fa syllables or their initials

tonic water *n* (1903) **:** a carbonated beverage flavored with a small amount of quinine, lemon, and lime

[1]**to·night** \tə-ˈnīt\ *adv* (bef. 12c) **:** on this present night or the night following this present day ⟨will do it ~⟩

[2]**tonight** *n* (14c) **:** the present night or the night following this present day

ton·ka bean \ˈtäŋ-kə-\ *n* [D *tonka(-boon)* & Pg *(fava-)tonca,* perh. of Cariban origin] (1796) **:** the coumarin-containing seed of any of several tropical American leguminous trees (genus *Dipteryx,* esp. *D. odorata*) that is used in perfumes and as an artificial vanilla flavoring; *also* **:** a tree bearing tonka beans

ton·nage \ˈtə-nij\ *n* [in sense 1, fr. ME, fr. AF, fr. *tonne* tun; in other senses, fr. [1]*ton* — more at TUNNEL] (15c) **1 :** a duty formerly levied on every tun of wine imported into England **2 a :** a duty or impost on vessels based on cargo capacity **b :** a duty on goods per ton transported **3 :** ships in terms of the total number of tons registered or carried or of their carrying capacity **4 a :** the cubical content of a merchant ship in units of 100 cubic feet **b :** the displacement of a warship **5 a :** total weight in tons shipped, carried, or produced **b :** impressively large amount or weight

tonne \ˈtən\ *n* [F, fr. *tonne* tun, fr. OF — more at TUNNEL] (1869) **:** METRIC TON

ton·neau \ˈtä-ˌnō, tə-ˈnō\ *n, pl* **tonneaus** [F, lit., tun, fr. OF *tonel* — more at TUNNEL] (1901) **1 :** the rear seating compartment of an automobile; *also* **:** the entire seating compartment **2 :** a shape of watch case or dial resembling a barrel in profile

ton·ner \ˈtə-nər\ *n* (1851) **:** an object (as a ship) having a specified tonnage — used in combination ⟨a thousand-*tonner*⟩

to·nom·e·ter \tō-ˈnä-mə-tər\ *n* [Gk *tonos* tone + E *-meter*] (1725) **1 :** an instrument or device for determining the exact pitch or the vibration rate of tones **2 :** an instrument for measuring tension or pressure and esp. intraocular pressure — **to·nom·e·try** \tō-ˈnä-mə-trē\ *n*

to·no·plast \ˈtō-nə-ˌplast\ *n* [ISV *tono-* (fr. Gk *tonos* tension) + *-plast* — more at TONE] (ca. 1888) **:** a semipermeable membrane surrounding a vacuole in a plant cell

ton·sil \ˈtän(t)-səl\ *n* [L *tonsillae, pl.*, tonsils] (1601) **1 :** either of a pair of prominent masses of lymphoid tissue that lie one on each side of the throat between two folds of soft tissue that bound the fauces **2 :** any of various masses of lymphoid tissue (as the adenoids) that are similar to tonsils — **ton·sil·lar** \ˈtän(t)-s(ə-)lər\ *adj*

tonsill- *comb form* [L *tonsillae*] **:** tonsil ⟨*tonsill*ectomy⟩

ton·sil·lec·to·my \ˌtän(t)-sə-ˈlek-tə-mē\ *n, pl* **-mies** (1899) **:** the surgical removal of the tonsils

ton·sil·li·tis \-ˈlī-təs\ *n* [NL] (1801) **:** inflammation of the tonsils

ton·so·ri·al \tän-ˈsȯr-ē-əl\ *adj* [L *tonsorius*, fr. *tondēre*] (1813) **:** of or relating to a barber or the work of a barber

[1]**ton·sure** \ˈtän(t)-shər\ *n* [ME, fr. AF, fr. ML *tonsura*, fr. L, act of shearing, fr. *tonsus*, pp. of *tondēre* to shear — more at TOME] (14c) **1 :** the Roman Catholic or Eastern rite of admission to the clerical state by the clipping or shaving of a portion of the head **2 :** the shaven crown or patch worn by monks and other clerics **3 :** a bald spot resembling a tonsure

[2]**tonsure** *vt* **ton·sured; ton·sur·ing** \ˈtän(t)-sh(ə-)riŋ\ (1706) **:** to shave the head of; *esp* **:** to confer the tonsure upon

ton·tine \ˈtän-ˌtēn, tän-ˈ\ *n* [F, fr. Lorenzo *Tonti* †1695 Ital. banker] (1765) **:** a joint financial arrangement whereby the participants usu. contribute equally to a prize that is awarded entirely to the participant who survives all the others

to·nus \ˈtō-nəs\ *n* [NL, fr. L, tension, tone] (1876) **:** TONE 9a; *esp* **:** a state of partial contraction characteristic of normal muscle

tony *also* **ton·ey** \ˈtō-nē\ *adj* **ton·i·er; -est** (1877) **:** marked by an aristocratic or high-toned manner or style ⟨~ private schools⟩

To·ny \ˈtō-nē\ *n, pl* **Tonys** [*Tony*, nickname of Antoinette Perry †1946 Am. actress & producer] (1947) **:** a medallion awarded annually by a professional organization for notable achievement in the theater

too \ˈtü\ *adv* [ME, fr. OE *tō* to, too — more at TO] (bef. 12c) **1 :** BESIDES, ALSO ⟨sell the house and furniture ~⟩ **2 a :** to an excessive degree **:** EXCESSIVELY ⟨~ large a house for us⟩ **b :** to such a degree as to be regrettable ⟨this time he has gone ~ far⟩ **c :** VERY ⟨didn't seem ~ interested⟩ **3 :** so 2d ⟨"I didn't do it." "You did ~."⟩

took *past of* TAKE

[1]**tool** \ˈtül\ *n* [ME, fr. OE *tōl;* akin to OE *tawian* to prepare for use — more at TAW] (bef. 12c) **1 a :** a handheld device that aids in accomplishing a task **b (1) :** the cutting or shaping part in a machine or machine tool **(2) :** a machine for shaping metal **:** MACHINE TOOL **2 a :** something (as an instrument or apparatus) used in performing an operation or necessary in the practice of a vocation or profession ⟨a scholar's books are his ~*s*⟩ **b :** an element of a computer program (as a graphics application) that activates and controls a particular function ⟨a drawing ~⟩ **c :** a means to an end ⟨a book's cover can be a marketing ~⟩ **d** *often vulgar* **:** PENIS **3 :** one that is used or manipulated by another **4** *pl* **:** natural ability ⟨has all the ~*s* to be a great pitcher⟩ ***syn*** see IMPLEMENT

[2]**tool** *vt* (1812) **1 a :** to cause (a vehicle) to go **:** DRIVE **b :** to convey in a vehicle **2 :** to shape, form, or finish with a tool; *esp* **:** to letter or ornament (as leather or gold) by means of hand tools **3 :** to equip (as a plant or industry) with tools, machines, and instruments for production ~ *vi* **1 :** DRIVE, RIDE **2 :** to equip a plant or industry with the means (as machines, machine tools, and instruments) of production — often used with *up*

[3]**tool** *n* (1881) **:** a design (as on the binding of a book) made by tooling

tool·bar \ˈtül-ˌbär\ *n* (1983) **:** a strip of icons on a computer display providing quick access to certain functions

tool·box \ˈtül-ˌbäks\ *n* (1832) **:** a chest for tools

tool·hold·er \-ˌhōl-dər\ *n* (1846) **:** a short steel bar having a shank at one end by which it is clamped to a machine and a clamp at the other end to hold small interchangeable cutting bits

tool·house \-ˌhau̇s\ *n* (1809) **:** TOOLSHED

tool·mak·er \ˈtül-ˌmā-kər\ *n* (1844) **:** one that makes tools; *esp* **:** a machinist who specializes in the construction, repair, maintenance, and calibration of the tools, jigs, fixtures, and instruments of a machine shop

tool·mak·ing \-kiŋ\ *n* (1848) **:** the action, process, or art of making tools; *also* **:** the trade of a toolmaker

tool·room \ˈtül-ˌrüm, -ˌru̇m\ *n* (1829) **:** a room where tools are kept; *esp* **:** a room in a machine shop in which tools are made, stored, and issued for use by workers

tool·shed \-ˌshed\ *n* (1840) **:** an outbuilding for storing tools

tools of ignorance [fr. the notion that a smart athlete would not play such a grueling position] (1939) **:** a baseball catcher's equipment

tool subject *n* (1925) **:** a subject studied to gain competence in a skill used in other subjects

toom \ˈtüm\ *adj* [ME, fr. OE *tōm* — more at TEEM] (bef. 12c) *chiefly Scot* **:** EMPTY

toon \ˈtün\ *n* [Hindi & Urdu *tūn*, fr. Skt *tunna*] (1810) **:** a southeast Asian and Australian tree (*Toona ciliata* syn. *Cedrela toona*) of the mahogany family with aromatic dark red to reddish-brown wood; *also* **:** its wood

[1]**toot** \ˈtüt\ *vb* [prob. imit.] *vi* (ca. 1510) **1 a :** to sound a short blast ⟨the horn ~*ed*⟩ **b :** to sound a note or call suggesting the short blast of a wind instrument **2 :** to blow or sound an instrument (as a horn) esp. so as to produce short blasts ~ *vt* **1 :** to cause to sound ⟨~ a whistle⟩ **2** *slang* **:** to take in (as cocaine) by inhalation **:** SNORT — **toot·er** *n*

[2]**toot** *n* (1641) **:** a short blast (as on a horn); *also* **:** a sound resembling such a blast

[3]**toot** *n* [Sc *toot* to drink heavily] (ca. 1790) **:** a drinking bout **:** SPREE

tooth \ˈtüth\ *n, pl* **teeth** \ˈtēth\ [ME, fr. OE *tōth;* akin to OHG *zand* tooth, L *dent-, dens*, Gk *odont-, odous*] (bef. 12c) **1 a :** one of the hard bony appendages that are borne on the jaws or in many of the lower vertebrates on other bones in the walls of the mouth or pharynx and serve esp. for the prehension and mastication of food and as weapons of offense and defense **b :** any of various usu. hard and sharp processes esp. about the mouth of an invertebrate **2 :** TASTE, LIKING **3 :** a projection resembling or suggesting the tooth of an animal in shape, arrangement, or action ⟨a saw ~⟩**:** as **a :** any of the regular projections on the circumference or sometimes the face of a wheel that engage with corresponding projections on another wheel esp. to transmit force **:** COG **b :** a small sharp-pointed marginal lobe or process on a plant **4 a :** something that injures, tortures, devours, or destroys ⟨jealousy with rankling ~ —Thomas Gray⟩ **b** *pl* **:** effective means of enforcement ⟨drug laws with *teeth*⟩ **5 :** a roughness of surface produced by mechanical or artificial means — **tooth·like** \ˈtüth-ˌlīk\ *adj* — **in the teeth of 1 :** in or into direct contact or collision with ⟨sailing *in the teeth of* a hurricane —*Current Biog.*⟩ **2 :** in direct opposition to ⟨rule had . . . been imposed by conquest *in the teeth of* obstinate resistance —A. J. Toynbee⟩ — **to the teeth :** FULLY, COMPLETELY ⟨armed *to the teeth*⟩

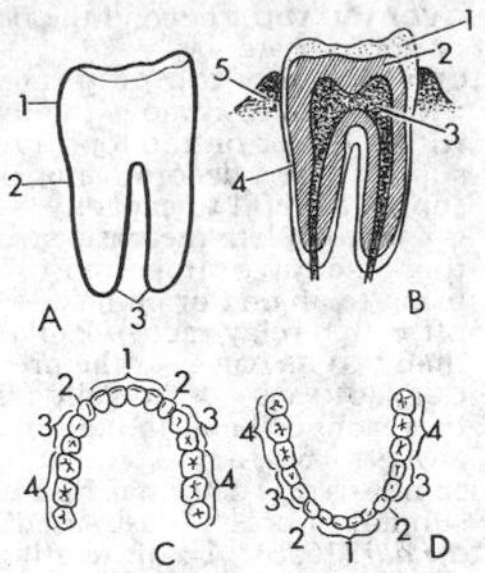

tooth 1a: *A* outside of a molar: *1* crown, *2* neck, *3* roots; *B* cross section of a molar: *1* enamel, *2* dentin, *3* pulp, *4* cementum, *5* gum; *C* dentition of adult human, upper; *D* dentition of adult human, lower: *1* incisors, *2* canines, *3* bicuspids, *4* molars

tooth·ache \ˈtüth-ˌāk\ *n* (14c) **:** pain in or about a tooth

tooth and nail *adv* (1550) **:** with every available means **:** ALL OUT ⟨fight *tooth and nail*⟩

tooth·brush \ˈtüth-ˌbrəsh\ *n* (1690) **:** a brush for cleaning the teeth

tooth·brush·ing *n* (1920) **:** the action of using a toothbrush to clean teeth

toothed \ˈtütht, *uncompounded also* ˈtü-thəd\ *adj* (14c) **:** having teeth esp. of a specified kind or number — often used in combination ⟨fine-*toothed*⟩

toothed whale \ˈtütht-, ˈtü-thəd-\ *n* (1843) **:** any of a suborder (Odontoceti) of cetaceans (as a dolphin, porpoise, or killer whale) bearing usu. numerous simple conical teeth — compare BALEEN WHALE

tooth fairy *n* (1962) **:** a fairy believed by children to leave money while they sleep in exchange for a tooth that has come out

tooth·less \ˈtüth-ləs\ *adj* (14c) **1 :** having no teeth **2 a :** lacking in sharpness or bite ⟨spoke in ~ generalities —Arthur Hepner⟩ **b :** lacking in means of enforcement or coercion **:** INEFFECTUAL

tooth·paste \-ˌpāst\ *n* (1832) **:** a paste for cleaning the teeth

tooth·pick \-ˌpik\ *n* (15c) **:** a pointed instrument (as a slender tapering piece of wood) for removing food particles lodged between the teeth

tooth powder *n* (1542) **:** a powder for cleaning the teeth

tooth shell *n* (ca. 1711) **:** any of a class (Scaphopoda) of burrowing marine mollusks with a tapering tubular shell; *also* **:** this shell

tooth·some \ˈtüth-səm\ *adj* (1551) **1 a :** AGREEABLE, ATTRACTIVE **b :** sexually attractive ⟨a ~ blonde⟩ **2 :** of palatable flavor and pleasing texture **:** DELICIOUS ⟨crisp ~ fried chicken⟩ ***syn*** see PALATABLE — **tooth·some·ly** *adv* — **tooth·some·ness** *n*

tooth·wort \-ˌwərt, -ˌwȯrt\ *n* (1597) **1 :** a European parasitic plant (*Lathraea squamaria*) of the broomrape family having pink-tinged white flowers and tooth-shaped scaly leaves **2 :** any of several cresses (genus *Dentaria*) that have usu. fleshy scaly rhizomes and are sometimes placed in the same genus as the bitter cresses

toothy \ˈtü-thē\ *adj* **tooth·i·er; -est** (1530) **1 :** having or showing prominent teeth ⟨~ grin⟩ **2 :** TOOTHSOME 2 — **tooth·i·ly** \-thə-lē\ *adv*

too·tle \ˈtü-tᵊl\ *vb* **too·tled; too·tling** \ˈtüt-liŋ, ˈtü-tᵊl-iŋ\ [freq. of [1]*toot*] *vi* (1820) **1 :** to toot gently, repeatedly, or continuously **2 :** to drive or move along in a leisurely manner ~ *vt* **:** to toot continuously on ⟨*tootled* his flute⟩ — **tootle** *n* — **too·tler** \ˈtüt-lər, ˈtü-tᵊl-ər\ *n*

too–too \ˈtü-ˈtü\ *adj* (1881) **1 :** going beyond the bounds of convention, good taste, or common sense **:** EXTREME **2 :** LA-DI-DA

toot·sie \ˈtu̇t-sē\ *n* [origin unknown] (1905) **1 :** DEAR, SWEETHEART **2 :** PROSTITUTE

toot·sy *also* **toot·sie** \ˈtu̇t-sē\ *n, pl* **tootsies** [baby-talk alter. of *foot*] (1854) **:** FOOT

[1]**top** \ˈtäp\ *n* [ME, fr. OE; akin to OHG *zopf* tip, tuft of hair] (bef. 12c) **1 a (1) :** the highest point, level, or part of something **:** SUMMIT, CROWN **(2) :** the head or top of the head — used esp. in the phrase *top to toe* **(3) :** the head of a plant; *esp* **:** the aboveground part of a plant having edible roots ⟨beet ~*s*⟩ **(4) :** a garment worn on the upper body **b (1) :** the highest or uppermost region or part **(2) :** the upper end, edge, or surface **2 :** a fitted, integral, or attached part or unit serving as an upper piece, lid, or covering **3 a :** a platform surrounding the head of a lower mast that serves to spread the topmast rigging, strengthen the mast, and furnish a standing place for men aloft **b :** a comparable part of the superstructure; *esp* **:** such a part on a warship used as a fire-control station or antiaircraft gun platform **4 a :** the highest degree or pitch conceivable or attained **:** ACME, PINNACLE **b :** the loudest or highest range of a sound **5 a :** the part that is nearest in space or time to the source or beginning **b :** the first half of an inning in baseball **6 a (1) :** the highest position (as in rank or achievement) **(2) :** a person or thing at the top **b** *pl* **:** aces and kings in a hand or the three highest honors in a suit **7 :** the choicest part **:** CREAM, PICK **8 :** a forward spin given to a ball (as in golf or billiards) by striking it on or near the top or above the center; *also* **:** the stroke so given **9 :** a fundamental quark that has an electric charge of + 2/3 and a measured energy of approximately 175 GeV; *also* **:** the flavor characterizing this particle — **topped** \ˈtäpt\ *adj* — **off the top of one's head :** in an impromptu manner ⟨sat down and wrote the . . . story *off the top of his head* —Jerome Beatty, Jr.⟩ — **on top of 1 a :** in control of ⟨acted like a man *on top of* his job —*Newsweek*⟩ **b :** informed about ⟨tried to keep *on top of* new developments⟩ **2 :** in sudden and unexpected proximity to ⟨the deadline was *on top of* them⟩ **3 :** in addition to — **on top of the world :** in a position of eminent success, happiness, or fame —

\ə\ **abut** \ᵊ\ kitten, F table \ər\ **further** \a\ ash \ā\ ace \ä\ mop, mar
\au̇\ **out** \ch\ **chin** \e\ bet \ē\ **easy** \g\ go \i\ **hit** \ī\ ice \j\ job
\ŋ\ sing \ō\ go \ȯ\ **law** \ȯi\ boy \th\ **thin** \t͟h\ **the** \ü\ **loot** \u̇\ **foot**
\y\ yet \zh\ vision, beige \k, ⁿ, œ, ue, ʸ\ *see* Guide to Pronunciation

over the top : beyond the bounds of what is expected, usual, normal, or appropriate
[2]**top** *vb* **topped; top·ping** *vt* (1509) **1** : to remove or cut the top of; *esp* : to shorten or remove the top of (a plant) : PINCH 1b **2 a** : to cover with a top or on the top : provide, form, or serve as a top for **b** : to supply with a decorative or protective finish or final touch **c** : to resupply or refill to capacity — usu. used with *off* ⟨*topped* off the tank⟩ **d** : to complete the basic structure of (as a high-rise building) by putting on a cap or uppermost section — usu. used with *out* or *off* **e** : to bring to an end or climax — usu. used with *off* ⟨the event was *topped* off with a relay race —Paula Rodenas⟩ **3 a** : to be or become higher than : OVERTOP ⟨~*s* the previous record⟩ **b** : to be superior to : EXCEL, SURPASS **c** : to gain ascendancy over : DOMINATE **4 a** : to rise to, reach, or be at the top of **b** : to go over the top of : CLEAR, SURMOUNT **5** : to strike (a ball) above the center thereby imparting topspin ~ *vi* **1** : to make an end, finish, or conclusion **2** : to reach a summit or crest — usu. used with *off* or *out*
[3]**top** *adj* (1556) **1** : of, relating to, or being at the top : UPPERMOST **2** : CHIEF, LEADING ⟨one of the world's ~ journalists⟩ **3** : of the highest quality, amount, or degree ⟨~ value⟩ ⟨~ form⟩
[4]**top** *n* [ME, fr. OE] (14c) : a commonly cylindrical or conoidal device that has a tapering point on which it is made to spin and that is used esp. as a toy
top- *or* **topo-** *comb form* [Gk, fr. *topos*] **1** : place : locality ⟨*top*ology⟩ ⟨*top*onymy⟩ **2** : topology ⟨*topo*isomerase⟩
to·paz \ˈtō-ˌpaz\ *n* [ME *topace*, fr. AF, fr. L *topazus*, fr. Gk *topazos*] (13c) **1 a** : a mineral that is essentially a silicate of aluminum and usu. occurs in orthorhombic translucent or transparent crystals or in white translucent masses **b** : a usu. yellow to brownish-yellow transparent mineral topaz used as a gem **c** : a yellow sapphire **d** : a yellow quartz **2** : either of two large brilliantly colored So. American hummingbirds (*Topaza pella* and *T. pyra*)
top banana *n* [fr. a burlesque routine involving three comedians in which the one that gets the punch line also gets a banana] (1952) : the leading comedian in a burlesque show; *broadly* : KINGPIN 2
top billing *n* (1945) **1** : prominent emphasis, featuring, or advertising **2** : the position at the top of a theatrical bill usu. featuring the star's name
top boot *n* (1768) : a high boot often with light-colored leather bands around the upper part
top·coat \ˈtäp-ˌkōt\ *n* (1804) **1** : a lightweight overcoat **2** : OVERCOAT 2
top·cross \-ˌkrȯs\ *n* (1890) : a cross between a superior or purebred male and inferior female stock to improve the average quality of the progeny; *also* : the product of such a cross
top dog *n* (1900) : a person, group, or thing in a position of authority esp. through victory in a hard-fought competition
top dollar *n* (1970) : the highest amount being paid for a commodity or service ⟨willing to pay *top dollar* to get them —Dean Failey⟩
top–down \ˈtäp-ˈdau̇n\ *adj* [fr. the phrase *from the top down*] (1941) **1** : controlled, directed, or instituted from the top level ⟨a ~ corporate structure⟩ **2** : proceeding by breaking large general aspects (as of a problem) into smaller more detailed constituents : working from the general to the specific ⟨~ programming⟩ ⟨~ design⟩
top drawer *n* (1905) : the highest level of society, authority, or excellence — **top–draw·er** \-ˈdrȯ(-ə)r\ *adj*
top–dress \ˈtäp-ˌdres\ *vt* (1733) : to apply material to (as land or a road) without working it in; *esp* : to scatter fertilizer over (land)
top·dress·ing \-ˌdre-siŋ\ *n* (1744) : a material used to top-dress soil
[1]**tope** \ˈtōp\ *vi* **toped; top·ing** [obs. E *tope*, interj. used to wish good health before drinking] (1664) : to drink liquor to excess
[2]**tope** *n* [origin unknown] (1686) : a small slender cosmopolitan shark (*Galeorhinus galeus*) valued for its flesh, fins, and oil-rich liver
[3]**tope** *n* [perh. fr. Punjabi *ṭop* hat] (1815) : STUPA
to·pee *or* **to·pi** \tō-ˈpē, ˈtō-(ˌ)pē\ *n* [Hindi & Urdu *ṭopī*] (1835) : a lightweight helmet-shaped hat made of pith or cork
top–end \ˈtäp-ˈend\ *adj* (1954) : TOPFLIGHT ⟨~ equipment⟩
top·er \ˈtō-pər\ *n* (1661) : one that topes; *esp* : DRUNKARD
top·flight \ˈtäp-ˈflīt\ *adj* (1931) : of, relating to, or being the highest level of achievement, excellence, or eminence — **top flight** *n*
[1]**Top 40** *n pl* (1965) : the forty best-selling audio recordings for a given period
[2]**Top 40** *adj* (1965) : constituting, playing, listing, or relating to the Top 40 ⟨*Top 40* hits⟩ ⟨*Top 40* stations⟩ ⟨*Top 40* charts⟩
top·ful *or* **top·full** \ˈtäp-ˈfu̇l\ *adj* (1553) : BRIMFUL
[1]**top·gal·lant** \(ˌ)täp-ˈga-lənt, tə-ˈga-\ *adj* [[1]*top* + [2]*gallant*] (1514) : of, relating to, or being a part next above the topmast and below the royal mast ⟨~ sails⟩ ⟨the ~ mast⟩
[2]**topgallant** *n* (1581) **1** *archaic* : the topmost point : SUMMIT ⟨the high ~ of my joy —Shak.⟩ **2** : a topgallant mast or sail
top gun *n* (1974) : one who is at the top (as in ability, rank, or prestige)
top–ham·per \ˈtäp-ˈham-pər\ *n* (1791) **1** : matter or weight (as spars or rigging) in the upper part of a ship **2** : unnecessary cumbersome matter
top hat *n* (1879) : a tall-crowned hat usu. of beaver or silk
top–heavy \ˈtäp-ˌhe-vē\ *adj* (ca. 1533) **1** : having the top part too heavy for the lower part **2** : having too high a proportion of administrators ⟨a ~ bureaucracy⟩ **3** : oversupplied with one element at the expense of others : lacking balance ⟨a novel ~ with description⟩
To·phet \ˈtō-fət\ *n* [ME, shrine south of ancient Jerusalem where human sacrifices were performed to Moloch in Jer 7:31, Gehenna, fr. LL *Topheth*, fr. Heb *tōpheth*] (14c) : HELL, GEHENNA
top–hole \ˈtäp-ˈhōl\ *adj* (1908) *chiefly Brit* : EXCELLENT, FIRST-CLASS
to·phus \ˈtō-fəs\ *n*, *pl* **to·phi** \ˈtō-ˌfī, -ˌfē\ [L, tufa] (1607) : a deposit of urates in tissues (as cartilage) that is characteristic of gout
to·pi \ˈtō-pē\ *n*, *pl* **topi** *or* **topis** [perh. fr. Swahili] (1894) : a sub-Saharan antelope (*Damaliscus lunatus* syn. *D. korrigum*) having a glossy usu. reddish-brown coat with purplish-black and yellowish markings
[1]**to·pi·ary** \ˈtō-pē-ˌer-ē\ *adj* [L *topiarius*, fr. *topia* ornamental gardening, irreg. fr. Gk *topos* place] (1592) : of, relating to, or being the practice or art of training, cutting, and trimming trees or shrubs into odd or ornamental shapes; *also* : characterized by such work
[2]**topiary** *n*, *pl* **-ar·ies** (1904) **1** : topiary art or gardening; *also* : a topiary garden **2 a** : a plant shaped by topiary art **b** : topiary plants
top·ic \ˈtä-pik\ *n* [L *Topica* Topics (work by Aristotle), fr. Gk *Topika*, fr. *topika*, neut. pl. of *topikos* of a place, of a topos, fr. *topos* place, topos] (ca. 1569) **1 a** : one of the general forms of argument employed in probable reasoning **b** : ARGUMENT, REASON **2 a** : a heading in an outlined argument or exposition **b** : the subject of a discourse or of a section of a discourse
top·i·cal \ˈtä-pi-kəl\ *adj* (ca. 1525) **1 a** : of, relating to, or arranged by topics ⟨set down in ~ form⟩ **b** : referring to the topics of the day or place : of local or temporary interest ⟨a ~ novel⟩ ⟨~ references⟩ **2** : designed for or involving local application and action (as on the body) ⟨a ~ anesthetic⟩ ⟨a ~ remedy⟩ — **top·i·cal·ly** \-k(ə-)lē\ *adv*
top·i·cal·i·ty \ˌtä-pə-ˈka-lə-tē\ *n*, *pl* **-ties** (1904) **1** : the quality or state of being topical **2** : an item of topical interest
topic sentence *n* (1885) : a sentence that states the main thought of a paragraph or of a larger unit of discourse and is usu. placed at or near the beginning
top·kick \ˈtäp-ˈkik\ *n* (1918) : FIRST SERGEANT 1
top·knot \-ˌnät\ *n* (ca. 1688) **1** : an ornament (as a knot of ribbons or a pompom) forming a headdress or worn as part of a coiffure **2** : a crest of feathers or tuft of hair on the top of the head
top·less \-ləs\ *adj* (1589) **1** *archaic* : so high as to reach up beyond sight ⟨and burnt the ~ towers of Ilium —Christopher Marlowe⟩ **2** : being without a top **3 a** : wearing no clothing on the upper body **b** : featuring topless waitresses or entertainers ⟨~ bars⟩ **c** : being a place where topless women are permitted ⟨a ~ beach⟩ — **top·less·ness** \-nəs\ *n*
top·line \-ˌlīn\ *n* (ca. 1909) : the outline of the top of the body of an animal (as a dog or horse)
top·lofty \ˈtäp-ˌlȯf-tē\ *also* **top·loft·i·cal** \täp-ˈlȯf-ti-kəl\ *adj* [prob. fr. the phrase *top loft*] (1823) : very superior in air or attitude — **top·loft·i·ly** \täp-ˈlȯf-tə-lē\ *adv* — **top·loft·i·ness** \ˈtäp-ˌlȯf-tē-nəs\ *n*
top·mast \ˈtäp-ˌmast, -məst\ *n* (15c) : the mast that is next above the lower mast and is topmost in a fore-and-aft rig
top milk *n* (1891) : the upper layer of milk in a container enriched by whatever cream has risen
top·min·now \ˈtäp-ˌmi-(ˌ)nō\ *n* (1884) : any of several live-bearers (family Poeciliidae) or killifish (family Cyprinodontidae)
top·most \ˈtäp-ˌmōst\ *adj* (1697) : highest of all : UPPERMOST
top–notch \-ˈnäch\ *adj* (1900) : of the highest quality : FIRST-RATE ⟨a ~ work⟩ — **top·notch·er** \-ˈnä-chər\ *n*
topo *abbr* topographic; topographical
to·po·cen·tric \ˌtä-pə-ˈsen-trik, ˌtō-\ *adj* (ca. 1942) : relating to, measured from, or as if observed from a particular point on the earth's surface : having or relating to such a point as origin ⟨~ coordinates⟩ — compare GEOCENTRIC
top–of–the–line *adj* (1963) : TOP-NOTCH; *esp* : being or belonging to the highest or most expensive class ⟨~ camera equipment⟩
to·pog·ra·pher \tə-ˈpä-grə-fər\ *n* (1603) : a specialist in topography
to·po·graph·ic \ˌtä-pə-ˈgra-fik, ˌtō-\ *adj* (1632) : of, relating to, or concerned with topography ⟨~ maps⟩
to·po·graph·i·cal \-fi-kəl\ *adj* (1571) **1** : TOPOGRAPHIC **2** : of, relating to, or concerned with the artistic representation of a particular locality ⟨a ~ poem⟩ ⟨~ painting⟩ — **to·po·graph·i·cal·ly** \-k(ə-)lē\ *adv*
to·pog·ra·phy \tə-ˈpä-grə-fē\ *n* [ME *topographie*, fr. LL *topographia*, fr. Gk, fr. *topographein* to describe a place, fr. *topos* place + *graphein* to write — more at CARVE] (15c) **1 a** : the art or practice of graphic delineation in detail usu. on maps or charts of natural and man-made features of a place or region esp. in a way to show their relative positions and elevations **b** : topographical surveying **2 a** : the configuration of a surface including its relief and the position of its natural and man-made features **b** : the physical or natural features of an object or entity and their structural relationships ⟨the ~ of human chromosomes⟩ ⟨the political ~ of our time⟩
topo·isom·er·ase \ˌtō-pō-ī-ˈsä-mə-ˌrās, -ˌrāz\ *n* [*top-* + *isomerase*] (1980) : any of a class of enzymes that reduce supercoiling in DNA by breaking and rejoining one or both strands of the DNA molecule
to·po·log·i·cal \ˌtä-pə-ˈlä-ji-kəl\ *adj* (1715) **1** : of or relating to topology **2** : being or involving properties unaltered under a homeomorphism ⟨continuity and connectedness are ~ properties⟩ — **to·po·log·i·cal·ly** \-k(ə-)lē\ *adv*
topological group *n* (1946) : a mathematical group which is also a topological space, whose multiplicative operation has the property that given any neighborhood of a product there exist neighborhoods of the elements composing the product such that any pair of elements representing each of these neighborhoods form a product belonging to the given neighborhood, and whose operation of taking inverses has the property that for any neighborhood of the inverse of an element there exists a neighborhood of the element itself in which every element has its inverse in the other neighborhood
topologically equivalent *adj* (1915) : related by a homeomorphism
topological space *n* (1926) : a set with a collection of subsets satisfying the conditions that both the empty set and the set itself belong to the collection, the union of any number of the subsets is also an element of the collection, and the intersection of any finite number of the subsets is an element of the collection
topological transformation *n* (1946) : HOMEOMORPHISM
to·pol·o·gy \tə-ˈpä-lə-jē, tä-\ *n*, *pl* **-gies** [ISV] (1850) **1** : topographic study of a particular place; *specif* : the history of a region as indicated by its topography **2 a (1)** : a branch of mathematics concerned with those properties of geometric configurations (as point sets) which are unaltered by elastic deformations (as a stretching or a twisting) that are homeomorphisms **(2)** : the set of all open subsets of a topological space **b** : CONFIGURATION ⟨~ of a molecule⟩ ⟨~ of a magnetic field⟩ — **to·pol·o·gist** \-jist\ *n*
top·o·nym \ˈtä-pə-ˌnim, ˈtō-\ *n* [ISV, back-formation fr. *toponymy*] (1899) : PLACE-NAME
top·o·nym·ic \ˌtä-pə-ˈni-mik, ˌtō-\ *adj* (1896) : of or relating to toponyms or toponymy — **top·o·nym·i·cal** \-mi-kəl\ *adj*
to·pon·y·my \tə-ˈpä-nə-mē, tō-\ *n* [ISV, fr. *top-* + Gk *onyma*, *onoma* name — more at NAME] (1876) : the place-names of a region or language or esp. the etymological study of them — **to·pon·y·mist** \-mist\ *n*

to·pos \ˈtō-ˌpäs, ˈtä-\ *n, pl* **to·poi** \-ˌpȯi\ [Gk, short for *koinos topos,* lit., common place] (1936) **:** a traditional or conventional literary or rhetorical theme or topic

top·per \ˈtä-pər\ *n* (1688) **1 :** one that puts on or takes off tops **2 :** one that is at or on the top **3 a :** SILK HAT **b :** OPERA HAT **4 :** something (as a joke) that caps everything preceding **5 :** a woman's usu. short and loose-fitting lightweight outer coat

[1]**topping** *n* (14c) **1 :** something that forms a top; *esp* **:** a garnish (as a sauce, bread crumbs, or whipped cream) placed on top of a food for flavor or decoration **2 :** the action of one that tops **3 :** something removed by topping

[2]**topping** *adj* (ca. 1685) **1 :** highest in rank or eminence **2** *NewEng* **:** PROUD, ARROGANT **3** *chiefly Brit* **:** EXCELLENT

top·ple \ˈtä-pəl\ *vb* **top·pled; top·pling** \-p(ə-)liŋ\ [freq. of [2]*top*] *vi* (1590) **:** to fall from or as if from being top-heavy ~ *vt* **1 :** to cause to topple **2 a :** OVERTHROW 2 ⟨~ a dictator⟩ **b :** DEFEAT 3

top round *n* (1903) **:** meat from the inner part of a round of beef

[1]**tops** \ˈtäps\ *adj* [pl. of [1]*top*] (1935) **:** topmost in quality, ability, popularity, or importance — used predicatively ⟨is ~ in his field⟩

[2]**tops** *adv* (1956) **:** at the very most ⟨will cost $50, ~⟩

top·sail \ˈtäp-ˌsāl, -səl\ *also* **top·s'l** \-səl\ *n* (14c) **1 :** the sail next above the lowermost sail on a mast in a square-rigged ship **2 :** the sail set above and sometimes on the gaff in a fore-and-aft rigged ship

top secret *adj* (1944) **1 :** protected by a high degree of secrecy ⟨a *top secret* weapon⟩ ⟨a *top secret* meeting⟩ **2 a :** containing or being information whose unauthorized disclosure could result in exceptionally grave danger to the nation ⟨*top secret* messages⟩ — compare CONFIDENTIAL, SECRET **b :** of or relating to top secret documents ⟨a *top secret* clearance⟩

top sergeant *n* (1898) **:** FIRST SERGEANT 1

top–shelf \ˈtäp-ˈshelf\ *adj* (ca. 1892) **:** of the best quality

[1]**top·side** \ˈtäp-ˈsīd\ *n* (1815) **1** *pl* **:** the top portion of the outer surface of a ship on each side above the waterline **2 :** the highest level of authority **3 :** the upper portion of the ionosphere

[2]**topside** *adv or adj* (1873) **1 :** to or on the top or surface **2 :** in a position of authority **3 :** on deck

Top–Sid·er \ˈtäp-ˌsī-dər\ *trademark* — used for a low casual shoe having a rubber sole

top·soil \ˈtäp-ˌsȯi(-ə)l\ *n* (1836) **:** surface soil usu. including the organic layer in which plants have most of their roots and which the farmer turns over in plowing

top·spin \-ˌspin\ *n* [[1]*top*] (1902) **:** a rotary motion imparted to a ball that causes it to rotate forward in the direction it is traveling

top·stitch \ˈtäp-ˌstich\ *vt* (1934) **:** to make a line of stitching on the outside of (a garment) close to a seam

top·sy–tur·vi·ness \ˌtäp-sē-ˈtər-vē-nəs\ *n* (1842) **:** the quality or state of being topsy-turvy

[1]**top·sy–tur·vy** \ˌtäp-sē-ˈtər-vē\ *adv* [prob. ultim. fr. *tops* (pl. of [1]*top*) + obs. E *terve* to turn upside down] (1528) **1 :** in utter confusion or disorder **2 :** with the top or head downward **:** UPSIDE DOWN

[2]**topsy–turvy** *adj* (1612) **:** turned topsy-turvy **:** totally disordered — **top·sy–tur·vi·ly** \-ˈtər-və-lē\ *adv* — **top·sy–tur·vy·dom** \-vē-dəm\ *n*

[3]**topsy–turvy** *n* (1655) **:** TOPSY-TURVINESS

top up *vt* (1937) *Brit* **:** to make up to the full quantity, capacity, or amount ~ *vi, Brit* **:** to replenish a supply — **top–up** \ˈtäp-ˌəp\ *n, Brit*

top·work \ˈtäp-ˌwərk\ *vt* (1882) **:** to graft scions of another variety on the main branches of (as fruit trees) usu. to obtain more desirable fruit

toque \ˈtōk\ *n* [MF, soft hat with a narrow brim worn esp. in the 16th cent., fr. OSp *toca* headdress] (1505) **1 :** a woman's small hat without a brim made in any of various soft close-fitting shapes **2 :** TUQUE **3 :** a tall brimless hat worn by a chef — called also *toque blanche*

tor \ˈtȯr\ *n* [ME, fr. OE *torr*] (bef. 12c) **:** a high craggy hill

To·rah \ˈtȯr-ə, ˈtȯi-rə\ *n* [Heb *tōrāh*] (1577) **1 :** the body of wisdom and law contained in Jewish Scripture and other sacred literature and oral tradition **2 :** the five books of Moses constituting the Pentateuch **3 :** a leather or parchment scroll of the Pentateuch used in a synagogue for liturgical purposes

[1]**torch** \ˈtȯrch\ *n, often attrib* [ME *torche,* fr. AF, fr. VL **torca,* alter. of L *torqua* something twisted, collar of twisted metal, alter. of *torques;* akin to L *torquēre* to twist — more at TORTURE] (13c) **1 :** a burning stick of resinous wood or twist of tow used to give light and usu. carried in the hand **:** FLAMBEAU **2 :** something (as tradition, wisdom, or knowledge) likened to a torch as giving light or guidance ⟨pass the ~ to the next generation⟩ **3 :** any of various portable devices for emitting an unusually hot flame — compare BLOWTORCH **4** *chiefly Brit* **:** FLASHLIGHT 2 **5 :** INCENDIARY 1a

[2]**torch** *vt* (1901) **:** to set fire to with or as if with a torch

torch·bear·er \-ˌber-ər\ *n* (15c) **1 :** one that carries a torch **2 :** someone in the forefront of a campaign, crusade, or movement

tor·chère \ˌtȯr-ˈsher\ *n* [F, fr. *torche* torch] (1904) **1 :** a tall ornamental stand for a candlestick or candelabra **2** *also* **tor·chiere** \-ˈsh(y)er\ **:** an electric floor lamp giving indirect light

torch·light \-ˌlīt\ *n* (15c) **1 :** light given by torches **2 :** TORCH

tor·chon \ˈtȯr-ˌshän\ *n* [F, dust cloth, fr. OF, handful of straw for wiping, fr. *torchier* to wipe, rub, fr. *torche* bundle of twisted straw, fr. VL **torca* — more at TORCH] (1865) **:** a coarse bobbin or machine-made lace made with fan-shaped designs forming a scalloped edge

torch singer *n* (ca. 1932) **:** a singer of torch songs

torch song *n* [fr. the phrase *to carry a torch for* (to be in love)] (1930) **:** a popular sentimental song of unrequited love

torch·wood \ˈtȯrch-ˌwu̇d\ *n* (1833) **1 :** any of a genus (*Amyris*) of tropical American trees and shrubs of the rue family with hard heavy fragrant resinous streaky yellowish-brown wood **2 :** the wood of a torchwood

torchy \ˈtȯr-chē\ *adj* **torch·i·er; -est** (1941) **:** of, relating to, characteristic of, or being a torch song or torch singer ⟨a ~ ballad⟩

tore *past of* TEAR

to·re·a·dor \ˈtȯr-ē-ə-ˌdȯr, ˈtär-\ *n* [Sp, fr. *torear* to fight bulls, fr. *toro* bull, fr. L *taurus* — more at TAURINE] (1618) **:** TORERO, BULLFIGHTER

to·re·ro \tə-ˈrer-(ˌ)ō\ *n, pl* **-ros** [Sp, fr. L *taurarius* bullfighter, fr. L *taurus* bull] (1728) **:** a matador or a member of the attending cuadrilla

to·reu·tics \tə-ˈrü-tiks\ *n pl but sing in constr* [*toreutic,* adj., fr. Gk *toreutikos,* fr. *toreuein* to bore through, chase, fr. *toreus* boring tool; akin to Gk *tetrainein* to bore — more at THROW] (1847) **:** the art or process of working in metal esp. by embossing or chasing — **to·reu·tic** \-ˈrü-tik\ *adj*

tori *pl of* TORUS

to·ric \ˈtȯr-ik\ *adj* (1890) **:** of, relating to, or shaped like a torus or segment of a torus ⟨a ~ lens⟩

to·rii \ˈtȯr-ē-ˌē\ *n, pl* **torii** [Jp] (1727) **:** a Japanese gateway of light construction commonly built at the approach to a Shinto shrine

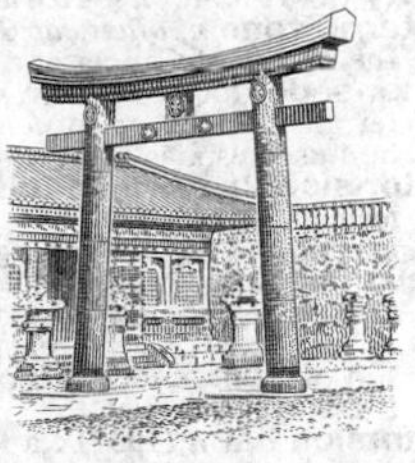

torii

[1]**tor·ment** \ˈtȯr-ˌment\ *n* [ME, fr. AF *turment, torment,* fr. L *tormentum* torture; akin to *torquēre* to twist — more at TORTURE] (14c) **1 :** the infliction of torture (as by rack or wheel) **2 :** extreme pain or anguish of body or mind **:** AGONY **3 :** a source of vexation or pain

[2]**tor·ment** \tȯr-ˈment, ˈtȯr-ˌ\ *vt* (14c) **1 :** to cause severe usu. persistent or recurrent distress of body or mind to ⟨cattle ~*ed* by flies⟩ **2 :** DISTORT, TWIST *syn* see AFFLICT

tor·men·til \ˈtȯr-mən-ˌtil\ *n* [ME *turmentille,* fr. AF, fr. ML *tormentilla,* fr. L *tormentum;* fr. its use in allaying pain] (14c) **:** a yellow-flowered Eurasian cinquefoil (*Potentilla erecta* syn. *P. tormentilla*) with a root sometimes used in tanning and dyeing

tor·men·tor *also* **tor·ment·er** \tȯr-ˈmen-tər, ˈtȯr-ˌ\ *n* (14c) **1 :** one that torments **2 :** a fixed curtain or flat on each side of a theater stage that prevents the audience from seeing into the wings

torn *past part of* TEAR

tor·na·dic \tȯr-ˈnā-dik, -ˈna-\ *adj* (1884) **:** relating to, characteristic of, or constituting a tornado ⟨~ winds⟩ ⟨a ~ storm⟩

tor·na·do \tȯr-ˈnā-(ˌ)dō\ *n, pl* **-does** *or* **-dos** [modif. of Sp *tronada* thunderstorm, fr. *tronar* to thunder, fr. L *tonare* — more at THUNDER] (1556) **1** *archaic* **:** a tropical thunderstorm **2 a :** a squall accompanying a thunderstorm in Africa **b :** a violent destructive whirling wind accompanied by a funnel-shaped cloud that progresses in a narrow path over the land **3 :** a violent windstorm **:** WHIRLWIND

tor·nil·lo \tȯr-ˈnē-(ˌ)yō, -ˈni-(ˌ)lō\ *n, pl* **-los** [Sp, lit., small lathe, screw, dim. of *torno* lathe, fr. L *tornus* — more at TURN] (ca. 1844) **:** SCREWBEAN 1

to·roid \ˈtȯr-ˌȯid\ *n* [NL *torus*] (1886) **1 :** a surface generated by a closed plane curve rotated about a line that lies in the same plane as the curve but does not intersect it **2 :** a body whose surface has the form of a toroid

to·roi·dal \tȯ-ˈrȯi-dᵊl\ *adj* (1881) **:** of, relating to, or shaped like a torus or toroid **:** doughnut-shaped ⟨a ~ resistance coil⟩ — **to·roi·dal·ly** \-dᵊl-ē\ *adv*

[1]**tor·pe·do** \tȯr-ˈpē-(ˌ)dō\ *n, pl* **-does** [L, lit., stiffness, numbness, fr. *torpēre* to be sluggish or numb — more at TORPID] (ca. 1520) **1 :** ELECTRIC RAY **2 :** a weapon for destroying ships by rupturing their hulls below the waterline: as **a :** a submarine mine **b :** a thin cylindrical self-propelled underwater projectile **3 :** a small firework that explodes when thrown against a hard object **4 :** a professional gunman or assassin **5 :** SUBMARINE 2

[2]**torpedo** *vt* **tor·pe·doed; tor·pe·do·ing** \-ˈpē-də-wiŋ\ (ca. 1879) **1 :** to hit or sink (a ship) with a naval torpedo **:** strike or destroy by torpedo **2 :** to destroy or nullify altogether **:** WRECK ⟨~ a plan⟩

torpedo boat *n* (1810) **:** a boat designed for launching torpedoes; *specif* **:** a small very fast boat with one or more torpedo tubes

torpedo bomber *n* (1930) **:** a military airplane designed to carry torpedoes — called also *torpedo plane*

torpedo tube *n* (ca. 1891) **:** a tube from which torpedoes are fired

tor·pid \ˈtȯr-pəd\ *adj* [ME, fr. L *torpidus,* fr. *torpēre* to be sluggish or numb; akin to Lith *tirpti* to become numb] (15c) **1 a :** having lost motion or the power of exertion or feeling **:** DORMANT, NUMB **b :** sluggish in functioning or acting ⟨a ~ frog⟩ ⟨a ~ mind⟩ **2 :** lacking in energy or vigor **:** APATHETIC, DULL — **tor·pid·i·ty** \tȯr-ˈpi-də-tē\ *n*

tor·por \ˈtȯr-pər\ *n* [ME, fr. L, fr. *torpēre*] (13c) **1 a :** a state of mental and motor inactivity with partial or total insensibility **b :** a state of lowered physiological activity typically characterized by reduced metabolism, heart rate, respiration, and body temperature that occurs in varying degrees esp. in hibernating and estivating animals **2 :** APATHY, DULLNESS *syn* see LETHARGY

[1]**torque** *or* **torc** \ˈtȯrk\ *n* [F, fr. L *torques,* fr. *torquēre* to twist — more at TORTURE] (1695) **:** a usu. metal collar or neck chain worn by the ancient Gauls, Germans, and Britons

[2]**torque** *n* [L *torquēre* to twist] (ca. 1884) **1 :** a force that produces or tends to produce rotation or torsion ⟨an automobile engine delivers ~ to the drive shaft⟩; *also* **:** a measure of the effectiveness of such a force that consists of the product of the force and the perpendicular distance from the line of action of the force to the axis of rotation **2 :** a turning or twisting force

[3]**torque** *vt* **torqued; torqu·ing** (1959) **:** to impart torque to **:** cause to twist (as about an axis) — **torqu·er** *n*

torque converter *n* (1927) **:** a device for transmitting and amplifying torque esp. by hydraulic means

torr \ˈtȯr\ *n, pl* **torr** [Evangelista *Torricelli*] (1949) **:** a unit of pressure equal to $\frac{1}{760}$ of an atmosphere (about 133.3 pascals)

[1]**tor·rent** \ˈtȯr-ənt, ˈtär-\ *n* [MF, fr. L *torrent-, torrens,* fr. *torrent-, torrens,* adj., burning, seething, rushing, fr. prp. of *torrēre* to parch, burn — more at THIRST] (1582) **1 :** a tumultuous outpouring **:** RUSH **2 :** a violent stream of a liquid (as water or lava) **3 :** a channel of a mountain stream

[2]**torrent** *adj* (1667) **:** TORRENTIAL

tor·ren·tial \tȯ-ˈren(t)-shəl, tə-\ *adj* (1849) **1 a :** relating to or having the character of a torrent ⟨~ rains⟩ **b :** caused by or resulting from action of rapid streams ⟨~ gravel⟩ **2 :** resembling a torrent in violence or rapidity of flow — **tor·ren·tial·ly** \-ˈren(t)-sh(ə-)lē\ *adv*

tor·rid \ˈtȯr-əd, ˈtär-\ *adj* [L *torridus,* fr. *torrēre*] (1545) **1 a :** parched with heat esp. of the sun : HOT ⟨~ sands⟩ **b :** giving off intense heat : SCORCHING **2 :** ARDENT, PASSIONATE ⟨~ love letters⟩ — **tor·rid·i·ty** \tȯ-ˈri-də-tē\ *n* — **tor·rid·ly** \ˈtȯr-əd-lē, ˈtär-\ *adv* — **tor·rid·ness** *n*

torrid zone *n, often cap T&Z* (1586) : the region of the earth between the Tropic of Cancer and the Tropic of Capricorn

tor·sade \tȯr-ˈsäd, -ˈsād\ *n* [F, fr. *tors* twisted, fr. OF, fr. VL **torsus,* alter. of L *tortus,* pp. of *torquēre* to twist] (1872) : a twisted cord or ribbon used esp. as a hat ornament

tor·sion \ˈtȯr-shən\ *n* [LL *torsion-, torsio* torment, alter. of L *tortio,* fr. *torquēre* to twist] (1543) **1 :** the twisting or wrenching of a body by the exertion of forces tending to turn one end or part about a longitudinal axis while the other is held fast or turned in the opposite direction; *also* **:** the state of being twisted **2 :** the twisting of a bodily organ or part on its own axis **3 :** the reactive torque that an elastic solid exerts by reason of being under torsion — **tor·sion·al** \ˈtȯr-shnəl, -shə-nᵊl\ *adj* — **tor·sion·al·ly** *adv*

torsion bar *n* (1937) : a long metal element in an automobile suspension that has one end held rigidly to the frame end and the other twisted and connected to the axle and that acts as a spring

tor·so \ˈtȯr-(ˌ)sō\ *n, pl* **torsos** *or* **tor·si** \ˈtȯr-ˌsē\ [It, lit., stalk, fr. L *thyrsus* stalk, thyrsus] (1722) **1 :** a sculptured representation of the trunk of a human body **2 :** something (as a piece of writing) that is mutilated or left unfinished **3 :** the human trunk

tort \ˈtȯrt\ *n* [ME, injury, fr. AF, fr. ML *tortum,* fr. L, neut. of *tortus* twisted, fr. pp. of *torquēre*] (1586) : a wrongful act other than a breach of contract for which relief may be obtained in the form of damages or an injunction

torte \ˈtȯrt-ə, ˈtȯrt\ *n, pl* **tor·ten** \ˈtȯr-tᵊn\ *or* **tortes** [G, prob. fr. It *torta* cake, fr. LL, round loaf of bread] (1748) : a cake made with many eggs and often grated nuts or dry bread crumbs and usu. covered with a rich frosting

tor·tel·li·ni \ˌtȯr-tə-ˈlē-nē\ *n, pl* **tortellini** *also* **tortellinis** [It, pl. of *tortellino* pasta round, dim. of *tortello,* fr. *torta* cake] (ca. 1911) : pasta in the form of little ring-shaped cases containing a filling (as of meat or cheese)

tor·ti·col·lis \ˌtȯr-tə-ˈkä-ləs\ *n* [NL, fr. L *tortus* twisted + *-i-* + *collum* neck — more at COLLAR] (ca. 1811) : a twisting of the neck to one side that results in abnormal carriage of the head and is usu. caused by muscle spasms — called also *wryneck*

tor·ti·lla \tȯr-ˈtē-yə\ *n* [AmerSp, fr. Sp, dim. of *torta* cake, fr. LL, round loaf of bread] (1648) : a thin round of unleavened cornmeal or wheat flour bread usu. eaten hot with a topping or filling (as of ground meat or cheese)

tor·tious \ˈtȯr-shəs\ *adj* (1544) : implying or involving tort ⟨~ acts⟩ — **tor·tious·ly** *adv*

tor·toise \ˈtȯr-təs\ *n* [ME *tortu, tortuse,* fr. AF *tortue* — more at TURTLE] (14c) **1 :** any of a family (Testudinidae) of terrestrial turtles; *broadly* **:** TURTLE **2 :** someone or something regarded as slow or laggard

tortoise beetle *n* (ca. 1711) : any of various chrysomelid beetles (subfamily Cassidinae) with leaf-eating larvae

[1]**tor·toise·shell** \ˈtȯr-tə-ˌshel, -əsh-ˌshel\ *n* (1632) **1 :** the mottled horny substance of the shell of the hawksbill turtle used esp. formerly in inlaying and in making various ornamental articles **2 :** any of several showy nymphalid butterflies (genera *Nymphalis* and *Aglais*)

[2]**tortoiseshell** *adj* (1651) **1 :** made of or resembling tortoiseshell esp. in mottled brown and yellow coloring ⟨~ glasses⟩ **2 :** of, relating to, or being a color pattern of the domestic cat consisting of patches of black, orange, and cream

tor·to·ni \tȯr-ˈtō-nē\ *n* [prob. fr. *Tortoni* 19th cent. Ital. restaurateur in Paris] (1911) : ice cream made of heavy cream often with minced almonds and chopped maraschino cherries and often flavored with rum

tor·tri·cid \ˈtȯr-trə-səd\ *n* [NL *Tortricidae,* fr. *Tortric-, Tortrix*] (ca. 1891) : any of a family (Tortricidae) of small stout-bodied moths many of whose larvae feed in fruits — **tortricid** *adj*

tor·trix \ˈtȯr-triks\ *n* [NL *Tortric-, Tortrix,* genus of moths, fr. L *tortus,* pp. of *torquēre* to twist; fr. the habit of twisting or rolling leaves to make a nest] (ca. 1797) : a tortricid moth

tor·tu·os·i·ty \ˌtȯr-chə-ˈwä-sə-tē\ *n, pl* **-ties** (15c) **1 :** the quality or state of being tortuous **2 :** something winding or twisted : BEND

tor·tu·ous \ˈtȯrch-wəs, ˈtȯr-chə-\ *adj* [ME, fr. MF *tortueux,* fr. L *tortuosus,* fr. *tortus* twist, fr. *torquēre* to twist] (15c) **1 :** marked by repeated twists, bends, or turns : WINDING ⟨a ~ path⟩ **2 a :** marked by devious or indirect tactics : CROOKED, TRICKY ⟨a ~ conspiracy⟩ **b :** CIRCUITOUS, INVOLVED ⟨the ~ jargon of legal forms⟩ — **tor·tu·ous·ly** *adv* — **tor·tu·ous·ness** *n*

[1]**tor·ture** \ˈtȯr-chər\ *n* [MF, fr. OF, fr. LL *tortura,* fr. L *tortus,* pp. of *torquēre* to twist; prob. akin to OHG *drāhsil* turner, Gk *atraktos* spindle] (1540) **1 a :** anguish of body or mind : AGONY **b :** something that causes agony or pain **2 :** the infliction of intense pain (as from burning, crushing, or wounding) to punish, coerce, or afford sadistic pleasure **3 :** distortion or overrefinement of a meaning or an argument : STRAINING

[2]**torture** *vt* **tor·tured; tor·tur·ing** \ˈtȯrch-riŋ, ˈtȯr-chə-\ (1588) **1 :** to cause intense suffering to : TORMENT **2 :** to punish or coerce by inflicting excruciating pain **3 :** to twist or wrench out of shape : DISTORT, WARP ***syn*** see AFFLICT — **tor·tur·er** \ˈtȯr-chər-ər\ *n*

tor·tur·ous \ˈtȯrch-rəs, ˈtȯr-chə-\ *adj* (15c) **1 a :** causing torture ⟨~ inquisitions⟩ **b :** very unpleasant or painful ⟨a ~ day⟩ ⟨~ self-doubts⟩ **2 :** painfully difficult or slow ⟨the ~ course of the negotiations⟩ — **tor·tur·ous·ly** *adv*

tor·u·la \ˈtȯr-yə-lə, ˈtär-, -ə-lə\ *n, pl* **-lae** \-ˌlē, -ˌlī\ *also* **-las** [NL, fr. L *torus* protuberance] (1862) : any of various fungi (genus *Torula*) and esp. yeasts that lack sexual spores, do not produce alcoholic fermentations, and are typically acid formers — called also *torula yeast*

to·rus \ˈtȯr-əs\ *n, pl* **to·ri** \ˈtȯr-ˌī, -ˌē\ [NL, fr. L, protuberance, bulge, torus molding] (1563) **1 :** a large molding of convex profile commonly occurring as the lowest molding in the base of a column **2 :** the thickening of a membrane closing a wood-cell pit (as of gymnosperm tracheids) having the secondary cell wall arched over the pit cavity **3 :** a doughnut-shaped surface generated by a circle rotated about an axis in its plane that does not intersect the circle; *broadly* **:** TOROID **4 :** a smooth rounded anatomical protuberance (as a bony ridge on the skull)

To·ry \ˈtȯr-ē\ *n, pl* **Tories** [Ir *tóraidhe* outlaw, robber, fr. MIr *tóir* pursuit] (1646) **1 :** a dispossessed Irishman subsisting as an outlaw chiefly in the 17th century **2** *obs* **:** BANDIT, OUTLAW **3 a :** a member or supporter of a major British political group of the 18th and early 19th centuries favoring at first the Stuarts and later royal authority and the established church and seeking to preserve the traditional political structure and defeat parliamentary reform — compare WHIG **b :** CONSERVATIVE 1b **4 :** an American upholding the cause of the British Crown against the supporters of colonial independence during the American Revolution : LOYALIST **5** *often not cap* **:** an extreme conservative esp. in political and economic principles — **Tory** *adj*

Tory Democracy *n* (1867) : a political philosophy advocating preservation of established institutions and traditional principles combined with political democracy and a social and economic program designed to benefit the common man

To·ry·ism \ˈtȯr-ē-ˌi-zəm\ *n* (1682) **1 :** the principles and practices of or associated with Tories **2 :** the British Tory party or its members

tosh \ˈtäsh\ *n* [origin unknown] (1528) : sheer nonsense : BOSH

[1]**toss** \ˈtȯs, ˈtäs\ *vb* [ME] *vt* (15c) **1 a :** to fling or heave continuously about, to and fro, or up and down ⟨a ship ~*ed* by waves⟩ **b :** BANDY 2 **c :** to mix lightly until well coated with a dressing or until the elements are thoroughly combined ⟨~ a salad⟩ **2 :** to make uneasy : stir up : DISTURB **3 a :** to throw with a quick, light, or careless motion or with a sudden jerk ⟨~ a ball around⟩ **b :** to throw up in the air ⟨~*ed* by a bull⟩ **c :** MATCH 5a **d :** to send as if by throwing ⟨~*ed* in jail⟩ ⟨~*ed* out of the game⟩ **e :** to get rid of : THROW AWAY **4 a :** to fling or lift with a sudden motion ⟨~*es* her head angrily⟩ **b :** to tilt suddenly so as to empty by drinking ⟨~*ed* his glass⟩; *also* **:** to consume by drinking ⟨~ down a drink⟩ **5 :** to accomplish, provide, or produce readily or easily ⟨~ off a few verses⟩ **6 :** THROW 18 ⟨~ a party⟩ **7 :** VOMIT 1 — often used in the phrase *toss one's cookies* ~ *vi* **1 a :** to move restlessly or turbulently; *esp* **:** to twist and turn repeatedly ⟨~*ed* sleeplessly all night⟩ **b :** to move with a quick or spirited gesture **2 :** to decide an issue by flipping a coin ***syn*** see THROW — **toss·er** *n*

[2]**toss** *n* (1634) **1 :** the state or fact of being tossed **2 :** an act or instance of tossing: as **a :** an abrupt tilting or upward fling **b :** a deciding by chance and esp. by flipping a coin **c :** THROW, PITCH

toss·pot \-ˌpät\ *n* (1568) : DRUNKARD, SOT

toss–up \-ˌəp\ *n* (1812) **1 :** TOSS 2b **2 :** an even chance **3 :** something that offers no clear basis for choice

tos·ta·da \tō-ˈstä-də\ *also* **tos·ta·do** \-(ˌ)dō\ *n* [MexSp *tostada,* fr. Sp, fem. of *tostado,* pp. of *tostar* to toast, roast, fr. LL *tostare* — more at TOAST] (1935) : a tortilla fried in deep fat

tos·to·ne \tō-ˈstō-nā\ *n* [AmerSp *tostón,* fr. Sp *tostar*] (1964) : a thick slice of green plantain that is fried, flattened, and then fried again

[1]**tot** \ˈtät\ *n* [origin unknown] (1725) **1 :** a small child : TODDLER **2 :** a small drink or allowance of liquor : SHOT

[2]**tot** *vb* **tot·ted; tot·ting** [*tot.,* abbr. of *total*] *vt* (ca. 1772) : to add together : TOTAL — usu. used with *up* ⟨~*s* up the score⟩ ~ *vi* : ADD

[1]**to·tal** \ˈtō-tᵊl\ *adj* [ME, fr. AF, fr. ML *totalis,* fr. L *totus* whole, entire] (14c) **1 :** comprising or constituting a whole : ENTIRE ⟨the ~ amount⟩ **2 :** ABSOLUTE, UTTER ⟨a ~ failure⟩ ⟨a ~ stranger⟩ **3 :** involving a complete and unified effort esp. to achieve a desired effect ⟨~ war⟩ ⟨~ theater⟩ ***syn*** see WHOLE

[2]**total** *n* (1557) **1 :** a product of addition : SUM **2 :** an entire quantity : AMOUNT

[3]**total** *adv* (1601) : TOTALLY

[4]**total** *vt* **to·taled** *or* **to·talled; to·tal·ing** *or* **to·tal·ling** (1716) **1 :** to add up : COMPUTE **2 :** to amount to : NUMBER **3 :** to make a total wreck of : DEMOLISH; *specif* **:** to damage so badly that the cost of repairs exceeds the market value of the vehicle ⟨~*ed* the car⟩

total depravity *n* (1794) : a state of corruption due to original sin held in Calvinism to infect every part of man's nature and to make the natural man unable to know or obey God

total eclipse *n* (1671) : an eclipse in which one celestial body is completely obscured by the shadow or body of another

to·tal·ism \ˈtō-tᵊl-ˌi-zəm\ *n* (1941) : TOTALITARIANISM — **to·tal·is·tic** \ˌtō-tᵊl-ˈis-tik\ *also* **to·tal·ist** \ˈtō-tᵊl-ist\ *adj*

[1]**to·tal·i·tar·i·an** \(ˌ)tō-ˌta-lə-ˈter-ē-ən\ *adj* [It *totalitario,* fr. *totalità* totality] (1926) **1 a :** of or relating to centralized control by an autocratic leader or hierarchy : AUTHORITARIAN, DICTATORIAL; *esp* **:** DESPOTIC **b :** of or relating to a political regime based on subordination of the individual to the state and strict control of all aspects of the life and productive capacity of the nation esp. by coercive measures (as censorship and terrorism) **2 a :** advocating or characteristic of totalitarianism **b :** completely regulated by the state esp. as an aid to national mobilization in an emergency **c :** exercising autocratic powers

[2]**totalitarian** *n* (ca. 1934) : an advocate or practitioner of totalitarianism

to·tal·i·tar·i·an·ism \(ˌ)tō-ˌta-lə-ˈter-ē-ə-ˌni-zəm\ *n* (1926) **1 :** centralized control by an autocratic authority **2 :** the political concept that the citizen should be totally subject to an absolute state authority

to·tal·i·ty \tō-ˈta-lə-tē\ *n, pl* **-ties** (1598) **1 :** an aggregate amount : SUM, WHOLE **2 a :** the quality or state of being total : WHOLENESS **b :** the phase of an eclipse during which it is total : state of total eclipse

to·tal·iza·tor *or* **to·tal·isa·tor** \ˈtō-tᵊl-ə-ˌzā-tər\ *n* (1879) : PARI-MUTUEL 2

to·tal·ize \ˈtō-tᵊl-ˌīz\ *vt* **-ized; -iz·ing** (1818) **1 :** to add up : TOTAL **2 :** to express as a whole

to·tal·iz·er \-ˌī-zər\ *n* (1887) : one that totalizes: as **a :** PARI-MUTUEL 2 **b :** a device (as a meter) that records a remaining total (as of fuel)

to·tal·ly \ˈtō-tᵊl-ē\ *adv* (1509) : in a total manner : to a total or complete degree : WHOLLY, ENTIRELY

total recall *n* (1926) : the faculty of remembering with complete clarity and in complete detail

[1]**tote** \ˈtōt\ *vt* **tot·ed; tot·ing** [prob. fr. an English-based creole; akin to Gullah & Krio *tot* to carry, of Bantu origin; akin to Kikongo *-tota* to pick up, Kimbundu *-tuta* to carry] (1677) **1 :** to carry by hand : bear on the person : LUG, PACK **2 :** HAUL, CONVEY — **tot·er** \ˈtō-tər\ *n*

[2]**tote** *n* (ca. 1772) **1 :** BURDEN, LOAD **2 :** TOTE BAG

[3]**tote** *vt* **tot·ed; tot·ing** [E dial. *tote,* n., total] (1888) : ADD, TOTAL — usu. used with *up* ⟨*toted* up his accomplishments —G. P. Morrill⟩

4**tote** *n* [short for *totalizator*] (1891) : PARI-MUTUEL 2
tote bag *n* (1900) : a large 2-handled open-topped bag (as of canvas)
tote board *n* [4*tote*] (ca. 1949) : an electrically operated board (as at a racetrack) on which pertinent information (as betting odds and race results) is posted
to·tem \ˈtō-təm\ *n* [Ojibwa *ototeːman* his totem] (ca. 1776) **1 a** : an object (as an animal or plant) serving as the emblem of a family or clan and often as a reminder of its ancestry; *also* : a usu. carved or painted representation of such an object **b** : a family or clan identified by a common totemic object **2** : one that serves as an emblem or revered symbol
to·tem·ic \tō-ˈte-mik\ *adj* (1846) **1** : of, relating to, suggestive of, or characteristic of a totem or totemism ⟨a ~ animal⟩ **2** : based on or practicing totemism ⟨~ clan structure⟩
to·tem·ism \ˈtō-tə-ˌmi-zəm\ *n* (1791) **1** : belief in kinship with or a mystical relationship between a group or an individual and a totem **2** : a system of social organization based on totemic affiliations
to·tem·is·tic \ˌtō-tə-ˈmis-tik\ *adj* (1873) : TOTEMIC
totem pole *n* (1880) **1** : a pole or pillar carved and painted with a series of totemic symbols representing family lineage and often mythical or historical incidents and erected by Indian tribes of the northwest coast of No. America **2** : an order of rank : HIERARCHY

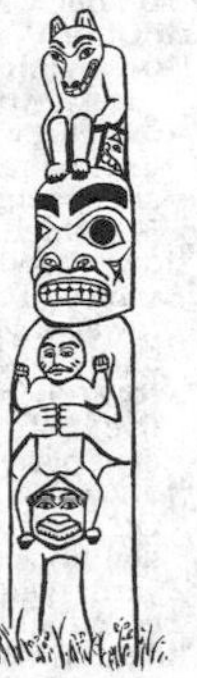
totem pole 1

toth·er *or* **t'oth·er** \ˈtə-t͟hər\ *pron or adj* [ME *tother,* alter. (resulting from misdivision of *thet other* the other, fr. *thet* the— fr. OE *thæt* — + *other*) of *other* — more at THAT] (13c) *chiefly dial* : the other
to·ti·po·tent \tō-ˈti-pə-tənt, ˌtō-tə-ˈpō-tᵊnt\ *adj* [L *totus* whole, entire + E *-i-* + *potent*] (ca. 1899) : capable of developing into a complete organism or differentiating into any of its cells or tissues ⟨~ stem cells⟩ — **to·ti·po·ten·cy** \tō-ˈti-pə-tən(t)-sē, ˌtō-tə-ˈpō-tᵊn-\ *n*
1**tot·ter** \ˈtä-tər\ *vi* [ME *toteren*] (15c) **1 a** : to tremble or rock as if about to fall : SWAY **b** : to become unstable : threaten to collapse **2** : to move unsteadily : STAGGER, WOBBLE
2**totter** *n* (1747) : an unsteady gait : WOBBLE
tot·ter·ing \ˈtä-tə-riŋ\ *adj* (1534) **1 a** : being in an unstable condition ⟨a ~ building⟩ **b** : walking unsteadily **2** : lacking firmness or stability : INSECURE ⟨a ~ regime⟩ — **tot·ter·ing·ly** *adv*
tot·tery \ˈtä-tə-rē\ *adj* (ca. 1755) : of an infirm or precarious nature
Touareg *var of* TUAREG
tou·can \ˈtü-ˌkan, -ˌkän, tü-ˈ\ *n* [F, fr. Pg *tucano,* fr. Tupi *tukána*] (1568) : any of a family (Ramphastidae) of chiefly fruit-eating birds of tropical America with brilliant coloring and a very large but light and thin-walled bill
1**touch** \ˈtəch\ *vb* [ME, fr. AF *tucher, tuchier,* fr. VL **toccare* to knock, strike a bell, touch, prob. of imit. origin] *vt* (14c) **1** : to bring a bodily part into contact with esp. so as to perceive through the tactile sense : handle or feel gently usu. with the intent to understand or appreciate ⟨loved to ~ the soft silk⟩ **2** : to strike or push lightly esp. with the hand or foot or an implement **3** : to lay hands upon (one afflicted with scrofula) with intent to heal **4** *archaic* **a** : to play on (a stringed instrument) **b** : to perform (a melody) by playing or singing **5 a** : to take into the hands or mouth ⟨never *~es* alcohol⟩ **b** : to put hands upon in any way or degree ⟨don't ~ anything before the police come⟩; *esp* : to commit violence upon ⟨swears he never *~ed* the child⟩ **6** : to deal with : become involved with ⟨a sticky situation and I wouldn't ~ it with a 10-foot pole⟩ **7** : to induce to give or lend ⟨*~ed* him for ten dollars⟩ **8** : to cause to be briefly in contact or conjunction with something ⟨*~ed* her spurs to the horse⟩ ⟨*~ed* his hand to his hat⟩ **9 a** (1) : to meet without overlapping or penetrating : ADJOIN (2) : to get to : REACH ⟨the speedometer needle *~ed* 80⟩ **b** : to be tangent to **c** : to rival in quality or value ⟨nothing can ~ that cloth for durability⟩ **10** : to speak or tell of esp. in passing ⟨barely *~ed* the incident in the speech⟩ **11 a** : to relate to : CONCERN **b** : to have an influence on : AFFECT **12 a** : to leave a mark or impression on ⟨few reagents will ~ gold⟩; *also* : TINGE **b** : to harm slightly by or as if by contact : TAINT, BLEMISH ⟨fruit *~ed* by frost⟩ **c** : to give a delicate tint, line, or expression to ⟨a smile *~ed* her lips⟩ **d** : to get a hit off or score a run against ⟨*~ed* him for three runs⟩ **13** : to draw or delineate with light strokes **14 a** : to hurt the feelings of : WOUND **b** : to move to sympathetic feeling ~ *vi* **1 a** : to feel something with a body part (as the hand or foot) **b** : to lay hand or finger on a person to cure disease (as scrofula) **2** : to be in contact **3** : to come close : VERGE ⟨your actions ~ on treason⟩ **4** : to have a bearing : RELATE — used with *on* or *upon* **5 a** : to make a brief or incidental stop on shore during a trip by water ⟨*~ed* at several ports⟩ **b** : to treat a topic in a brief or casual manner — used with *on* or *upon* ⟨*~ed* upon many points⟩ ***syn*** see AFFECT — **touch·able** \ˈtə-chə-bəl\ *adj* — **touch·er** *n* — **touch base** : to come in contact or communication ⟨coming in from the cold to *touch base* with civilization —Carla Hunt⟩
2**touch** *n* (14c) **1 a** : a light stroke, tap, or push **b** : a hit against an opponent in fencing **2** : the act or fact of touching; *also* : the act or an instance of handling or controlling a ball (as in basketball or soccer) **3** : the special sense by which pressure or traction exerted on the skin or mucous membrane is perceived **4** : mental or moral sensitiveness, responsiveness, or tact ⟨has a wonderful ~ with children⟩ **5** : a specified sensation that arises in response to stimulation of the tactile receptors : FEEL ⟨the velvety ~ of velour⟩ **6 a** *archaic* : the act of rubbing gold or silver on a touchstone to test its quality **b** : TEST, TRIAL — used chiefly in the phrase *put to the touch* **7 a** : a visible effect : MARK ⟨a ~ of the tropical sun⟩ **b** : WEAKNESS, DEFECT **8** : something slight of its kind: as **a** : a light attack ⟨a ~ of fever⟩ **b** : a small quantity or indication : HINT ⟨a ~ of spring in the air⟩ **c** : a transient emotion ⟨a momentary ~ of compunction⟩ **d** : a near approach : CLOSE CALL ⟨beaten in the championships by a mere ~⟩ **9 a** *archaic* : the playing of an instrument (as a lute or piano) with the fingers; *also* : musical notes or strains so produced **b** : particular action of a keyboard with reference to the resistance of its keys to pressure ⟨piano with a stiff ~⟩ **10** : control of the hands: as **a** : a manner or method of touching or striking esp. the keys of a keyboard instrument **b** : ability to precisely control the path and speed of a shot or pass ⟨a great shooting ~⟩ **11** : a set of changes in change ringing that is less than a peal **12 a** : an effective and subtle detail ⟨applies the finishing *~es* to the story⟩ **b** : distinctive and often effective manner or method ⟨the ~ of a master⟩ **c** : a characteristic or distinguishing trait or quality **13** *slang* : an act of soliciting or getting a gift or loan **14** : the state or fact of being in contact or communication or of having awareness ⟨lost ~ with her cousin⟩ ⟨let's keep in ~⟩ ⟨out of ~ with modern times⟩ **15** : the area outside of the touchlines in soccer or outside of and including the touchlines in rugby ⟨the ball went into ~⟩ — **a touch** : SOMEWHAT, RATHER ⟨aimed *a touch* too low and missed⟩
touch–and–go \ˌtəch-ən(d)-ˈgō\ *n* (1953) : an airplane landing followed immediately by application of power and a takeoff and usu. executed as one of a series for practice at landings
touch and go *adj* (1815) : unpredictable as to outcome : UNCERTAIN ⟨it was *touch and go* there for a while⟩
touch·back \ˈtəch-ˌbak\ *n* (ca. 1890) : a situation in football in which the ball is down behind the goal line after a kick or intercepted forward pass after which it is put in play by the team defending the goal on its own 20-yard line — compare SAFETY
touch·down \ˈtəch-ˌdau̇n\ *n* (1876) **1** : the act of touching a football to the ground behind an opponent's goal; *specif* : the act of scoring six points in American football by being lawfully in possession of the ball on, above, or behind an opponent's goal line when the ball is declared dead **2** : the act or moment of touching down (as with an airplane or spacecraft)
touch down *vt* (1864) : to place (the ball in rugby) by hand on the ground on or over an opponent's goal line in scoring a try or behind one's own goal line as a defensive measure ~ *vi* : to reach the ground : LAND
tou·ché \tü-ˈshā\ *interj* [F, fr. pp. of *toucher* to touch, fr. OF *tuchier*] (1904) — used to acknowledge a hit in fencing or the success or appropriateness of an argument, an accusation, or a witty point
touched \ˈtəcht\ *adj* (14c) **1** : emotionally stirred (as with gratitude) **2** : slightly unbalanced mentally
touch football *n* (1933) : football played informally and chiefly characterized by the substitution of touching for tackling
touch·hole \ˈtəch-ˌhōl\ *n* (1501) : the vent in muzzle-loading guns through which the charge is ignited
1**touch·ing** \ˈtə-chiŋ\ *prep* (14c) : in reference to : CONCERNING
2**touching** *adj* (1601) : capable of arousing emotions of tenderness or compassion ***syn*** see MOVING — **touch·ing·ly** *adv*
touch·line \ˈtəch-ˌlīn\ *n* (1868) : either of the lines that bound the long sides of the field of play in rugby and soccer
touch·mark \-ˌmärk\ *n* (1904) : an identifying maker's mark impressed on pewter
touch–me–not \ˈtəch-mē-ˌnät\ *n* [fr. the bursting of the ripe pods and scattering of their seeds when touched] (1659) : either of two No. American impatiens growing in moist areas: as **a** : one (*Impatiens capensis*) typically having orange flowers spotted with reddish brown **b** : one (*I. pallida*) having typically yellow flowers sometimes spotted with reddish brown
touch off *vt* (ca. 1765) **1** : to describe or characterize with precision **2 a** : to cause to explode by or as if by touching with fire **b** : to provoke or initiate with sudden intensity ⟨the verdict *touched off* local riots⟩
touch pad *n* (1979) : a keypad for an electronic device (as a microwave oven) that consists of a flat surface divided into several differently marked areas which are touched to choose options
touch screen *n* (1974) : a display screen on which the user selects options (as from a menu) by touching the screen
touch·stone \ˈtəch-ˌstōn\ *n* (1530) **1** : a black siliceous stone related to flint and formerly used to test the purity of gold and silver by the streak left on the stone when rubbed by the metal **2** : a test or criterion for determining the quality or genuineness of a thing **3** : a fundamental or quintessential part or feature : BASIS ⟨a ~ film of that decade⟩ ⟨now considered a ~ of the city's life —Michael Specter⟩ ***syn*** see STANDARD
touch system *n* (1918) : a method of typing that assigns a particular finger to each key and makes it possible to type without looking at the keyboard
touch–tone \ˈtəch-ˈtōn, -ˌtōn\ *adj* [fr. *Touch-Tone,* a trademark] (1962) : of, relating to, or being a telephone having push buttons that produce tones corresponding to numbers
touch–type \ˈtəch-ˌtīp\ *vi* (1943) : to type by the touch system — **touch typist** *n*
touch–up \ˈtəch-ˌəp\ *n* (1885) : an act or instance of touching up
touch up *vt* (1703) **1** : to improve or perfect by small additional strokes or alterations : fix the minor and usu. visible defects or damages of **2** : to stimulate by or as if by a flick of a whip
touch·wood \ˈtəch-ˌwu̇d\ *n* (1579) : 3PUNK
touchy \ˈtə-chē\ *adj* **touch·i·er; -est** (1605) **1** : marked by readiness to take offense on slight provocation ⟨he's a little ~ about his past⟩ **2 a** *of a body part* : acutely sensitive or irritable **b** *of a chemical* : highly explosive or inflammable **3** : calling for tact, care, or caution in treatment ⟨a ~ subject⟩ — **touch·i·ly** \ˈtə-chə-lē\ *adv* — **touch·i·ness** \ˈtə-chē-nəs\ *n*
touchy–feely \ˌtə-chē-ˈfē-lē\ *adj* (1968) : characterized by or encouraging interpersonal touching esp. in the free expression of emotions ⟨~ therapy⟩; *also* : openly or excessively emotional and personal ⟨gets all ~ with his adoring fans⟩
1**tough** \ˈtəf\ *adj* [ME, fr. OE *tōh;* akin to OHG *zāhi* tough] (bef. 12c) **1 a** : strong or firm in texture but flexible and not brittle **b** : not easily chewed ⟨~ meat⟩ **2** : GLUTINOUS, STICKY **3** : characterized by severity or uncompromising determination ⟨~ laws⟩ ⟨~ discipline⟩ **4** : capable of enduring strain, hardship, or severe labor ⟨~ soldiers⟩ **5** : very hard to influence : STUBBORN ⟨a ~ negotiator⟩ **6** : difficult to

---

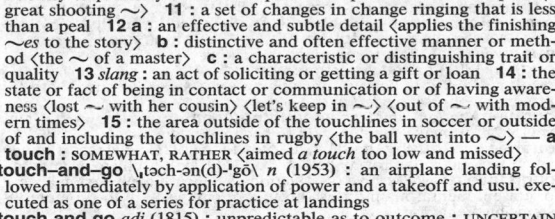

accomplish, resolve, endure, or deal with ⟨a ~ question⟩ ⟨~ luck⟩ **7** : stubbornly fought ⟨a ~ contest⟩ **8** : UNRULY, ROWDYISH ⟨a ~ gang⟩ **9** : marked by absence of softness or sentimentality ⟨a ~ critic⟩ ***syn*** see STRONG — **tough·ly** *adv* — **tough·ness** *n*

[2]**tough** *adv* (14c) : in a tough manner ⟨talking ~⟩

[3]**tough** *n* (1801) : a tough person : ROWDY

[4]**tough** *vt* (1830) : to bear unflinchingly : ENDURE — usu. used with *out* esp. in the phrase *tough it out*

tough·en \ˈtə-fən\ *vb* **tough·ened; tough·en·ing** \ˈtə-fə-niŋ, ˈtəf-niŋ\ *vt* (1582) : to make tough ~ *vi* : to become tough

tough·ie *also* **toughy** \ˈtə-fē\ *n, pl* **tough·ies** (1921) : one that is tough: as **a** : a loud rough rowdy person **b** : a difficult problem or question

tough love *n* (1968) : love or affectionate concern expressed in a stern or unsentimental manner (as through discipline) esp. to promote responsible behavior

tough–mind·ed \ˈtəf-ˌmīn-dəd\ *adj* (1907) : realistic or unsentimental in temper or outlook ⟨~ survivors⟩ — **tough–mind·ed·ness** *n*

tou·pee \tü-ˈpā\ *n* [F *toupet* forelock, fr. OF, dim. of *top, toup,* of Gmc origin; akin to OHG *zopf* tuft of hair — more at TOP] (1728) **1** : a curl or lock of hair made into a topknot on a periwig or natural coiffure; *also* : a periwig with such a topknot **2** : a wig or section of hair worn to cover a bald spot

[1]**tour** \ˈtu̇r, *1 is also* ˈtau̇(-ə)r\ *n* [ME, fr. AF *tur, tourn* turning, circuit, journey — more at TURN] (14c) **1 a** : one's turn in an orderly schedule : SHIFT **b** : a period during which an individual or unit is on a specific duty or at one place ⟨a ~ of duty⟩ **2 a** : a journey for business, pleasure, or education often involving a series of stops and ending at the starting point; *also* : something resembling such a tour ⟨a ~ of the history of philosophy⟩ **b** : a brief turn : ROUND **c** : a series of professional tournaments (as in golf or tennis)

[2]**tour** *vi* (1708) : to make a tour ~ *vt* **1** : to make a tour of **2** : to present (as a theatrical production) on a tour

touraco *var of* TURACO

tour·bil·lion \tu̇r-ˈbil-yən\ *or* **tour·bil·lon** \tür-bē-yōⁿ\ *n* [AF *turbeillun,* ultim. fr. L *turbin-, turbo* — more at TURBINE] (15c) **1** : WHIRLWIND **2** : a vortex esp. of a whirlwind or whirlpool

tour de force \ˌtu̇r-də-ˈfȯrs\ *n, pl* **tours de force** *same*\ [F] (1802) : a feat or display of strength, skill, or ingenuity ⟨the movie is a comic *tour de force*⟩

tour·er \ˈtu̇r-ər\ *n* (1924) **1** : TOURING CAR **2** : one that tours

Tou·rett·er \tu̇-ˈre-tər\ *n* (1985) : a person affected with Tourette's syndrome

Tou·rette's syndrome \tu̇-ˈrets-\ *n* [Georges Gille de la *Tourette* †1904 Fr. physician] (1970) : a familial neurological disorder of variable expression that is characterized by recurrent involuntary tics involving body movements (as eye blinks or grimaces) and vocalizations (as grunts or utterance of inappropriate words), often has one or more associated conditions (as obsessive-compulsive disorder), is more common in males than females, and usu. has an onset in childhood and often stabilizes or ameliorates in adulthood — called also *Tou·rette syndrome* \-ˈret-\

tour·ing \ˈtu̇r-iŋ\ *n* (1794) **1** : participation in a tour **2** : cross-country skiing for pleasure

touring car *n* (1903) : an automobile suitable for distance driving: as **a** : a vintage automobile with two cross seats, usu. four doors, and a folding top : PHAETON 2 **b** : a modern usu. 2-door sedan as distinguished from a sports car

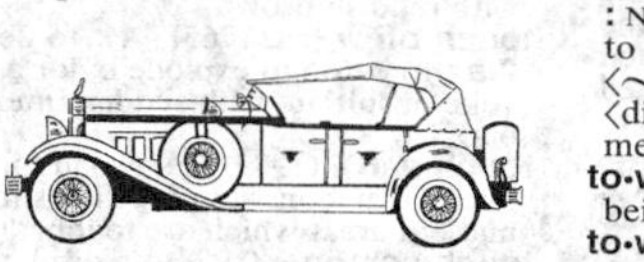

touring car a

tour·ism \ˈtu̇r-ˌi-zəm\ *n* (1811) **1** : the practice of traveling for recreation **2** : the guidance or management of tourists **3 a** : the promotion or encouragement of touring **b** : the accommodation of tourists

tour·ist \ˈtu̇r-ist\ *n* (1780) **1** : one that makes a tour for pleasure or culture **2** : TOURIST CLASS — **tourist** *adj or adv*

tourist card *n* (1948) : a citizenship identity card issued to a tourist usu. for a stated period of time in lieu of a passport or a visa

tourist class *n* (1935) : economy accommodations (as on a ship)

tourist court *n* (1937) : MOTEL

tour·ist·ed \ˈtu̇r-is-təd\ *adj* (1949) : frequented by tourists ⟨heavily ~ seaside towns⟩

tour·is·tic \tu̇r-ˈis-tik\ *adj* (1848) : of or relating to a tour, tourism, or tourists ⟨the ~ tradition of visiting Roman ruins by night —Naomi Rosenblum⟩ — **tour·is·ti·cal·ly** \-ti-k(ə-)lē\ *adv*

tourist trap *n* (1939) : a place that attracts and exploits tourists

tour·isty \ˈtu̇r-əs-tē\ *adj* (1906) **1** : characteristic of or relating to tourists ⟨~ behavior⟩ **2** : patronized by or appealing to tourists ⟨~ restaurants⟩

tour·ma·line \ˈtu̇r-mə-lən, -ˌlēn\ *n* [Sinhalese *toramalli* carnelian] (1759) : a mineral of variable color that consists of a complex borosilicate and is valued as a gem when transparent and cut

tour·na·ment \ˈtu̇r-nə-mənt *also* ˈtər- *or* ˈtȯr-\ *n* [ME *tornement,* fr. AF *turneiement,* fr. *turneier*] (13c) **1 a** : a knightly sport of the Middle Ages between mounted combatants armed with blunted lances or swords and divided into two parties contesting for a prize or favor bestowed by the lady of the tournament **b** : the whole series of knightly sports, jousts, and tilts occurring at one time and place **2** : a series of games or contests that make up a single unit of competition (as on a professional golf tour), the championship play-offs of a league or conference, or an invitational event

tour·ne·dos \ˌtu̇r-nə-ˈdō\ *n, pl* **tour·ne·dos** \-ˈdō(z)\ [F, fr. *tourner* to turn + *dos* back] (1877) : a small fillet of beef usu. cut from the tip of the tenderloin

[1]**tour·ney** \ˈtu̇r-nē, ˈtər- *also* ˈtȯr-\ *vi* **tour·neyed; tour·ney·ing** [ME, fr. AF *torneier,* to twist, whirl around, fight, tourney, fr. *tur, tourn* turning, circuit] (14c) : to perform in a tournament

[2]**tourney** *n, pl* **tourneys** (14c) : TOURNAMENT

tour·ni·quet \ˈtu̇r-ni-kət, ˈtər-\ *n* [F, turnstile, tourniquet, fr. *tourner* to turn, fr. OF — more at TURN] (1695) : a device (as a band of rubber) that checks bleeding or blood flow by compressing blood vessels

[1]**touse** \ˈtau̇z\ *vt* **toused; tous·ing** [ME *-tousen;* akin to OHG *zirzūsōn* to pull to pieces] (1598) : RUMPLE, TOUSLE

[2]**touse** *n* (1795) : a noisy disturbance

[1]**tou·sle** \ˈtau̇-zəl, -səl\ *vt* **tou·sled; tou·sling** \ˈtau̇z-liŋ, ˈtau̇s-; ˈtau̇-zə-, -sə-\ [ME *touselen,* freq. of *-tousen*] (15c) : DISHEVEL, RUMPLE ⟨*tousled* hair⟩

[2]**tou·sle** \ˈtau̇-zəl, *1 is also* ˈtü-\ *n* (1788) **1** *Scot* : rough dalliance : TUSSLE **2** : a tangled mass (as of hair)

[1]**tout** \ˈtau̇t, *in sense 4 also* ˈtüt\ *vb* [ME *tuten* to protrude, peer; prob. akin to OE *tōtian* to stick out, Norw *tyte*] *vt* (ca. 1700) **1** : to spy on : WATCH **2 a** *Brit* : to spy out information about (as a racing stable or horse) **b** : to give a tip or solicit bets on (a racehorse) **3** : to solicit, peddle, or persuade importunately ⟨not meant to ~ you off the movie —Russell Baker⟩ **4** : to make much of : PROMOTE, TALK UP ⟨~*ed* as the summer's blockbuster movie⟩ ⟨the college's much ~*ed* women's studies program⟩ ~ *vi* **1** : to solicit patronage **2 a** *chiefly Brit* : to spy on racehorses in training to gain information for betting **b** : to give a tip or solicit bets on a racehorse

[2]**tout** *n* (1853) : one who touts: as **a** : one who solicits patronage **b** *chiefly Brit* : one who spies out racing information for betting purposes **c** : one who gives tips or solicits bets on a racehorse

tout·er \ˈtau̇-tər\ *n* (ca. 1754) : one that touts

to·va·rich *or* **to·va·rish** \tə-ˈvär-ish, -ich\ *n* [Russ *tovarishch*] (ca. 1917) : COMRADE

[1]**tow** \ˈtō\ *vb* [ME, fr. OE *togian;* akin to OE *tēon* to draw, pull, OHG *ziohan* to draw, pull, L *ducere* to draw, lead] *vt* (bef. 12c) : to draw or pull along behind : HAUL ⟨~ a wagon⟩ ~ *vi* : to move in tow ⟨trailers that ~ behind the family auto —Bob Munger⟩

[2]**tow** *n* (1600) **1** : a rope or chain for towing **2 a** : the act or an instance of towing **b** : the fact or state of being towed **3 a** : something towed (as a boat or car) **b** : a group of barges lashed together and usu. pushed **4 a** : something (as a tugboat) that tows **b** : SKI TOW — **in tow 1** : under guidance or protection ⟨taken *in tow* by a friendly native⟩ **2** : accompanying or following usu. as an attending or dependent party ⟨not easy shopping with kids *in tow*⟩

[3]**tow** *n* [ME, fr. OE *tow-* spinning; akin to ON *tō* tuft of wool for spinning, OE *tawian* to prepare for use — more at TAW] (14c) **1** : short or broken fiber (as of flax, hemp, or synthetic material) that is used esp. for yarn, twine, or stuffing **2 a** : yarn or cloth made of tow **b** : a loose essentially untwisted strand of synthetic fibers

[4]**tow** *n* [ME (Sc), prob. fr. OE *toh-* (in *tohlīne* towline); akin to OE *togian* to tow] (14c) *chiefly Scot & dial Eng* : ROPE

tow·age \ˈtō-ij\ *n* (14c) **1** : the act of towing **2** : a charge for towing

[1]**to·ward** \ˈtō-ərd, ˈtȯ(-ə)rd\ *adj* [ME *toward,* fr. OE *tōweard* facing, imminent, fr. *tō,* prep., to + *-weard* -ward] (bef. 12c) **1** *also* **to·wards** \ˈtō-ərdz, ˈtȯ(-ə)rdz\ [ME *towardes,* fr. OE *tōweardes,* prep., toward, fr. *tōweard,* adj.] **a** : coming soon : IMMINENT **b** : happening at the moment : AFOOT **2 a** *obs* : quick to learn : APT **b** : PROPITIOUS, FAVORING ⟨a ~ breeze⟩

[2]**to·ward** *or* **to·wards** \ˈtō-ərd(z), ˈtȯ(-ə)rd(z), tə-ˈwȯrd(z), ˈtwȯrd(z), ˈtwōrd(z)\ *prep* (bef. 12c) **1** : in the direction of ⟨driving ~ town⟩ **2 a** : along a course leading to ⟨a long stride ~ disarmament⟩ **b** : in relation to ⟨an attitude ~ life⟩ **3 a** : at a point in the direction of : NEAR ⟨a cottage somewhere up ~ the lake⟩ **b** : in such a position as to be in the direction of ⟨your back was ~ me⟩ **4** : not long before ⟨~ the end of the afternoon⟩ **5 a** : in the way of help or assistance in ⟨did all he could ~ raising campaign funds⟩ **b** : for the partial payment of ⟨proceeds go ~ the establishment of a scholarship⟩

to·ward·li·ness \ˈtȯrd-lē-nəs\ *n* (1566) *archaic* : the quality or state of being toward or towardly

to·ward·ly \ˈtō-ərd-lē, ˈtȯ(-ə)rd-\ *adj* (15c) *archaic* **1** : PLEASANT, AFFABLE **2** : FAVORABLE, PROPITIOUS **3** : developing favorably : PROMISING — **towardly** *adv*

tow·boat \ˈtō-ˌbōt\ *n* (1815) **1** : TUGBOAT **2** : a compact shallow-draft boat with a squared bow designed and fitted for pushing tows of barges on inland waterways

[1]**tow·el** \ˈtau̇(-ə)l\ *n* [ME *towaille,* fr. AF *tuaille,* of Gmc origin; akin to OHG *dwahila* towel; akin to OHG *dwahan* to wash] (13c) : an absorbent cloth or paper for wiping or drying

[2]**towel** *vb* **-eled** *or* **-elled; -el·ing** *or* **-el·ling** *vt* (ca. 1839) : to rub or dry (as the body) with a towel ~ *vi* : to use a towel to dry oneself ⟨~*ed* down after swimming⟩

tow·el·ette \ˌtau̇-(ə-)ˈlet\ *n* (1902) : a small usu. premoistened piece of material used for personal cleansing (as of the hands)

tow·el·ing *or* **tow·el·ling** \ˈtau̇-(ə-)liŋ\ *n* (1583) : a cotton or linen fabric often used for making towels

[1]**tow·er** \ˈtau̇(-ə)r\ *n* [ME *tour, tor,* fr. OE *torr* & AF *tur, tour,* both fr. L *turris,* fr. Gk *tyrris, tyrsis*] (bef. 12c) **1** : a building or structure typically higher than its diameter and high relative to its surroundings that may stand apart (as a campanile) or be attached (as a church belfry) to a larger structure and that may be fully walled in or of skeleton framework (as an observation or transmission tower) **2** : a towering citadel : FORTRESS **3** : one that provides support or protection : BULWARK ⟨a ~ of strength⟩ **4** : a personal computer case that stands in an upright position — **tow·ered** \ˈtau̇(-ə)rd\ *adj* — **tow·er·like** \ˈtau̇(-ə)r-ˌlīk\ *adj*

[2]**tower** *vi* (15c) **1** : to reach or rise to a great height **2** : to exhibit superior qualities : SURPASS ⟨her intellect ~*ed* over the others'⟩

tower block *n* (1966) *chiefly Brit* : a tall building (as a high-rise apartment building)

tower house *n* (1687) : a medieval fortified castle (as in Scotland)

tow·er·ing \ˈtau̇(-ə)r-iŋ\ *adj* (1592) **1** : impressively high or great : IMPOSING ⟨~ pines⟩ **2** : reaching a high point of intensity : OVERWHELMING ⟨a ~ rage⟩ **3** : going beyond proper bounds : EXCESSIVE ⟨~ ambitions⟩ — **tow·er·ing·ly** *adv*

Tower of Babel (1718) : BABEL 2

tow·head \ˈtō-ˌhed\ *n* (1829) **1** : a low alluvial island or shoal in a river : SANDBAR **2** : a head of hair resembling tow esp. in being flaxen or tousled; *also* : a person having such a head of hair — **tow·head·ed** \-ˌhe-dəd\ *adj*

to·whee \ˈtō-ˌhē, ˈtō-(ˌ)ē, tō-ˈhē\ *n* [imit.] (ca. 1729) **1** : a common finch (*Pipilo erythrophthalmus* of the family Emberizidae) of eastern No. America with the male having reddish sides, white underparts, and black upperparts, head, and neck — called also *chewink* **2** : any of the No. American finches belonging to the same genus (*Pipilo*) as the towhee

to wit \tə-ˈwit\ *adv* [ME *to witen,* lit., to know — more at WIT] (14c) : that is to say : NAMELY

tow•line \ˈtō-ˌlīn\ *n* (1719) : TOWROPE

tow•mond \ˈtō-ˌmänd\ *n* [ME *towlmonyth,* fr. OE *twelf mōnath,* fr. *twelf* twelve + *mōnath* month] (15c) *Scot* : YEAR, TWELVEMONTH

town \ˈtau̇n\ *n* [ME, fr. OE *tūn* enclosure, village, town; akin to OHG *zūn* enclosure, OIr *dún* fortress] (bef. 12c) **1** *dial Eng* : a cluster or aggregation of houses recognized as a distinct place with a place-name : HAMLET **2 a** : a compactly settled area as distinguished from surrounding rural territory **b** : a compactly settled area usu. larger than a village but smaller than a city **c** : a large densely populated urban area : CITY **d** : an English village having a periodic fair or market **3** : a particular town or city under consideration ⟨the circus came to ~⟩ **4** : the city or urban life as contrasted with the country **5 a** : the inhabitants of a city or town ⟨practically the whole ~ turned out for the parade⟩ **b** : the townspeople of a college or university town as distinct from the academic community ⟨relations between ~ and gown⟩ **6** : a New England territorial and political unit usu. containing under a single town government both rural areas and urban areas not having their own charter of incorporation; *also* : a New England community governed by a town meeting **7** : a group of prairie dog burrows — **town** *adj* — **on the town** : in usu. carefree pursuit of entertainment or amusement (as city nightlife) esp. as a relief from routine

town car *n* (1907) : a 4-door automobile with a usu. open driver's compartment and a separate enclosed passenger compartment

town clerk *n* (14c) : a public officer charged with recording the official proceedings and vital statistics of a town

town crier *n* (1602) : a town officer who makes public proclamations

town•ee \tau̇-ˈnē\ *n* (1897) *chiefly Brit* : TOWNIE

town hall *n* (15c) : a public building used for town-government offices and meetings

town•home \ˈtau̇n-ˌhōm\ *n* (1975) : TOWN HOUSE 2

town house *n* (1586) **1** : a house in town; *specif* : the city residence of one having a countryseat or having a chief residence elsewhere ⟨stayed at their *town house* during the social season⟩ **2** : a usu. single-family house of two or sometimes three stories that is usu. connected to a similar house by a common sidewall; *also* : ROW HOUSE

town•ie *or* **towny** \ˈtau̇-nē\ *n, pl* **townies** (1852) : TOWNSMAN; *esp* : a permanent inhabitant of a town as distinguished from a member of another group (as the academic community)

town•let \ˈtau̇n-lət\ *n* (ca. 1552) : a very small town

town manager *n* (1922) : an official appointed to direct the administration of a town government

town meeting *n* (1636) : a meeting of inhabitants or taxpayers constituting the legislative authority of a town

town•scape \-ˌskāp\ *n* (1880) **1** : a representation of an urban scene **2** : a town or city viewed as a scene

towns•folk \ˈtau̇nz-ˌfōk\ *n pl* (1682) : TOWNSPEOPLE

town•ship \ˈtau̇n-ˌship\ *n* (12c) **1** : an ancient unit of administration in England identical in area with or a division of a parish **2 a** : TOWN 6 **b** : a unit of local government in some northeastern and north central states usu. having a chief administrative officer or board **c** : an unorganized subdivision of the county in Maine, New Hampshire, and Vermont **d** : an electoral and administrative district of the county in the southern U.S. **3** : a division of territory in surveys of U.S. public land containing 36 sections or 36 square miles **4** : an area in the Republic of South Africa that was segregated under apartheid for occupation by persons of non-European descent

towns•man \ˈtau̇nz-mən\ *n* (bef. 12c) **1 a** : a native or resident of a town or city **b** : an urban or urbane person **2** : a fellow citizen of a town

towns•peo•ple \-ˌpē-pəl\ *n pl* (1648) **1** : the inhabitants of a town or city : TOWNSMEN **2** : town-dwelling or town-bred persons

towns•wom•an \-ˌwu̇-mən\ *n* (1684) **1** : a woman who is a native or resident of a town or city **2** : a woman born or residing in the same town or city as another

tow•path \ˈtō-ˌpath, -ˌpäth\ *n* (1788) : a path (as along a canal) traveled esp. by draft animals towing boats — called also *towing path*

tow•plane \ˈtō-ˌplān\ *n* (1940) : an airplane that tows gliders

tow•rope \-ˌrōp\ *n* (1743) : a line used in towing something (as a boat)

tow sack \ˈtō-ˈsak\ *n* [[3]*tow*] (1926) *Midland & Southern* : GUNNYSACK

tow truck *n* (1944) : a truck with winches and hoist mechanisms for freeing stuck vehicles and towing wrecked or disabled vehicles

tox- *or* **toxi-** *or* **toxo-** *comb form* [LL, fr. L *toxicum* poison] : poisonous : poison ⟨*tox*emia⟩

tox•ae•mia *chiefly Brit var of* TOXEMIA

tox•a•phene \ˈtäk-sə-ˌfēn\ *n* [fr. *Toxaphene,* a trademark] (1947) : a persistent chlorinated insecticide mixture with the approximate empirical formula $C_{10}H_{10}Cl_8$ that is now banned in the U.S.

tox•e•mia \täk-ˈsē-mē-ə\ *n* [NL] (ca. 1860) **1** : an abnormal condition associated with the presence of toxic substances in the blood **2** : PREECLAMPSIA — **tox•e•mic** \-mik\ *adj*

[1]**tox•ic** \ˈtäk-sik\ *adj* [LL *toxicus,* fr. L *toxicum* poison, fr. Gk *toxikon* arrow poison, fr. neut. of *toxikos* of a bow, fr. *toxon* bow, arrow] (1664) **1** : containing or being poisonous material esp. when capable of causing death or serious debilitation ⟨~ waste⟩ ⟨a ~ radioactive gas⟩ ⟨an insecticide highly ~ to birds⟩ **2** : exhibiting symptoms of infection or toxicosis ⟨the patient became ~ two days later⟩ **3** : extremely harsh, malicious, or harmful ⟨~ sarcasm⟩ **4** : relating to or being an asset that has lost so much value that it cannot be sold on the market — **tox•ic•i•ty** \täk-ˈsi-sə-tē\ *n*

[2]**toxic** *n* (1890) : a toxic substance — usu. used in pl.

toxic- *or* **toxico-** *comb form* [NL, fr. L *toxicum*] : poison ⟨*toxico*logy⟩

tox•i•cant \ˈtäk-si-kənt\ *n* [ML *toxicant-, toxicans,* prp. of *toxicare* to poison, fr. L *toxicum*] (1879) : a toxic agent; *esp* : PESTICIDE

tox•i•co•log•i•cal \ˌtäk-si-kə-ˈlä-ji-kəl\ *also* **tox•i•co•log•ic** \-jik\ *adj* (1827) : of or relating to toxicology or toxins — **tox•i•co•log•i•cal•ly** \-ji-k(ə-)lē\ *adv*

tox•i•col•o•gy \-ˈkä-lə-jē\ *n* (ca. 1799) : a science that deals with poisons and their effect and with the problems involved (as clinical, industrial, or legal) — **tox•i•col•o•gist** \-jist\ *n*

tox•i•co•sis \ˌtäk-sə-ˈkō-səs\ *n, pl* **-co•ses** \-ˌsēz\ [NL] (ca. 1857) : a pathological condition caused by the action of a poison or toxin

toxic shock syndrome *n* (1978) : an acute disease that is characterized by fever, diarrhea, nausea, diffuse erythema, and shock, that is associated esp. with the presence of a bacterium (*Staphylococcus aureus*), and that occurs esp. in menstruating females using tampons — called also *toxic shock*

toxi•gen•ic \ˌtäk-sə-ˈje-nik\ *adj* (ca. 1923) : producing toxin ⟨~ bacteria and fungi⟩ — **toxi•ge•nic•i•ty** \ˌtäk-si-jə-ˈni-sə-tē\ *n*

tox•in \ˈtäk-sən\ *n* [ISV] (1886) : a poisonous substance that is a specific product of the metabolic activities of a living organism and is usu. very unstable, notably toxic when introduced into the tissues, and typically capable of inducing antibody formation

tox•oid \ˈtäk-ˌsȯid\ *n* [ISV] (ca. 1894) : a toxin of a pathogenic organism treated so as to destroy its toxicity but leave it capable of inducing the formation of antibodies on injection

tox•oph•i•lite \täk-ˈsä-fə-ˌlīt\ *n* [Gk *toxon* bow, arrow + *philos* dear, loving] (1794) : a person fond of or expert at archery — **toxophilite** *adj* — **tox•oph•i•ly** \-lē\ *n*

toxo•plas•ma \ˌtäk-sə-ˈplaz-mə\ *n* [NL] (1926) : any of a genus (*Toxoplasma*) of sporozoans that are typically serious pathogens of vertebrates — **toxo•plas•mic** \-mik\ *adj*

toxo•plas•mo•sis \-ˌplaz-ˈmō-səs\ *n, pl* **-mo•ses** \-ˌsēz\ [NL] (1926) : infection of humans, other mammals, or birds with disease caused by a toxoplasma (*Toxoplasma gondii*) that invades the tissues and may seriously damage the central nervous system esp. of infants

[1]**toy** \ˈtȯi\ *n* [ME *toye*] (15c) **1** *obs* **a** : flirtatious or seductive behavior **b** : PASTIME; *also* : a sportive or amusing act : ANTIC **2 a** : something (as a preoccupation) that is paltry or trifling **b** : a literary or musical trifle or diversion **c** : TRINKET, BAUBLE **3** : something for a child to play with **4** : something diminutive; *esp* : a diminutive animal (as of a small breed or variety) **5** : something that can be toyed with **6** *Scot* : a headdress of linen or woolen hanging down over the shoulders and formerly worn by old women of the lower classes — **toy•like** \-ˌlīk\ *adj*

[2]**toy** *vi* (ca. 1529) **1** : to act or deal with something lightly or without vigor or purpose ⟨~*ed* with the idea⟩ **2** : to engage in flirtation **3** : to amuse oneself as if with a toy : PLAY ⟨they're just ~*ing* with him⟩ ***syn*** see TRIFLE — **toy•er** \ˈtȯi-ər\ *n*

[3]**toy** *adj* (1801) **1** : of diminutive size compared to a standard form or breed ⟨a ~ dog⟩ **2** : designed or made for use as a toy ⟨a ~ stove⟩

toy Man•ches•ter terrier \-ˈman-ˌches-tər-, -chə-stər-\ *n* (1935) : any of a breed of toy dogs developed from the Manchester terrier that have erect ears of moderate size and weigh not more than 12 pounds (5.4 kilograms) — called also *toy Manchester*

toy•on \ˈtȯi-ˌän\ *n* [AmerSp *tollon*] (1848) : a chiefly Californian ornamental evergreen shrub (*Heteromeles arbutifolia*) of the rose family having white flowers succeeded by persistent usu. bright red berries

toy poodle *n* (1935) : a poodle developed from the standard poodle that is not more than 10 inches (25 centimeters) high at the withers and that is often considered to constitute a separate breed

tp *abbr* **1** title page **2** township

TP *abbr* triple play

TPA *abbr* tissue plasminogen activator

tpk *or* **tpke** *abbr* turnpike

TPN \ˌtē-ˌpē-ˈen\ *n* [*tri*phosphopyridine *n*ucleotide] (1938) : NADP

tr *abbr* **1** translated; translation; translator **2** transpose

tra•be•at•ed \ˈtrā-bē-ˌā-təd\ *also* **tra•be•ate** \-ˌāt\ *adj* [L *trabs, trabes* beam — more at THORP] (1843) : designed or constructed with horizontal beams or lintels — **tra•be•a•tion** \ˌtrā-bē-ˈā-shən\ *n*

tra•bec•u•la \trə-ˈbe-kyə-lə\ *n, pl* **-lae** \-ˌlē, -ˌlī\ *also* **-las** [NL, fr. L, little beam, dim. of *trabs, trabes* beam] (ca. 1866) **1** : a small bar, rod, bundle of fibers, or septal membrane in the framework of a body organ or part **2** : a fold, ridge, or bar projecting into or extending from a plant part; *esp* : a row of cells bridging an intercellular space — **tra•bec•u•lar** \-lər\ *adj* — **tra•bec•u•late** \-lət\ *adj*

[1]**trace** \ˈtrās\ *n* [ME, fr. AF, fr. *tracer* to trace] (14c) **1** *archaic* : a course or path that one follows **2 a** : a mark or line left by something that has passed; *also* : FOOTPRINT **b** : a path, trail, or road made by the passage of animals, people, or vehicles **3 a** : a sign or evidence of some past thing : VESTIGE **b** : ENGRAM **4** : something (as a line) traced or drawn: as **a** : the marking made by a recording instrument (as a seismograph or kymograph) **b** : the ground plan of a military installation or position either on a map or on the ground **5 a** : the intersection of a line or plane with a plane **b** : the usu. bright line or spot that moves across the screen of a cathode-ray tube; *also* : the path taken by such a line or spot **6 a** : a minute and often barely detectable amount or indication ⟨a ~ of a smile⟩ **b** : an amount of a chemical constituent not always quantitatively determinable because of minuteness — **trace•less** \-ləs\ *adj*

syn TRACE, VESTIGE, TRACK mean a perceptible sign made by something that has passed. TRACE may suggest any line, mark, or discernible effect ⟨the killer left no *traces*⟩. VESTIGE applies to a tangible reminder such as a fragment or remnant of what is past and gone ⟨boulders that are *vestiges* of the last ice age⟩. TRACK implies a continuous line that can be followed ⟨the fossilized *tracks* of dinosaurs⟩.

[2]**trace** *vb* **traced; trac•ing** [ME, fr. AF *tracer,* fr. VL **tractiare* to drag, fr. L *tractus,* pp. of *trahere* to pull] *vt* (14c) **1 a** : DELINEATE, SKETCH **b** : to form (as letters or figures) carefully or painstakingly **c** : to copy (as a drawing) by following the lines or letters as seen through a transparent superimposed sheet **d** : to impress or imprint (as a design or pattern) with a tracer **e** : to record a tracing of in the form of a curved, wavy, or broken line ⟨~ the heart action⟩ **f** : to adorn with linear ornamentation (as tracery or chasing) **2** *archaic* : to travel over : TRAVERSE **3 a** : to follow the footprints, track, or trail of **b** : to follow or study out in detail or step by step ⟨~ the history of the war⟩ **c** : to discover by going backward over the evidence step by step ⟨~ your ancestry⟩ **d** : to discover signs, evidence, or remains of **4** : to lay out the trace of (a military installation) ~ *vi* **1** : to make one's way; *esp* : to follow a track or trail **2** : to be traceable historically — **trace•abil•i•ty** \ˌtrā-sə-ˈbi-lə-tē\ *n* — **trace•able** \ˈtrā-sə-bəl\ *adj*

\ə\ **abut** \ᵊ\ kitten, F table \ər\ **further** \a\ **ash** \ā\ **ace** \ä\ **mop, mar**
\au̇\ **out** \ch\ **chin** \e\ **bet** \ē\ **easy** \g\ **go** \i\ **hit** \ī\ **ice** \j\ **job**
\ŋ\ **sing** \ō\ **go** \ȯ\ **law** \ȯi\ **boy** \th\ **thin** \t͟h\ **the** \ü\ **loot** \u̇\ **foot**
\y\ **yet** \zh\ **vision, beige** \ḵ, ⁿ, œ, ue, ʸ\ *see* Guide to Pronunciation

[3]**trace** *n* [ME *trais,* fr. AF *tres,* pl. of *trait* pull, draft, trace — more at TRAIT] (14c) **1 :** either of two straps, chains, or lines of a harness for attaching a draft animal to something (as a vehicle) to be drawn **2** : LEADER 1e(2) **3 :** one or more vascular bundles supplying a leaf or twig

trace element *n* (1932) **:** a chemical element present in minute quantities; *esp* **:** one used by organisms and held essential to their physiology

trace fossil *n* (1956) **:** a fossil (as of a dinosaur footprint) that shows the activity of an animal or plant but is not formed from the organism itself

trac·er \ˈtrā-sər\ *n* (14c) **1 :** one that traces, tracks down, or searches out: as **a :** a person who traces missing persons or property and esp. goods lost in transit **b :** an inquiry sent out in tracing a shipment lost in transit **2 :** one who traces designs, patterns, or markings **3 :** a device (as a stylus) used in tracing **4 a :** ammunition containing a chemical composition to mark the flight of projectiles by a trail of smoke or light **b :** a substance used to trace the course of a chemical or biological process; *esp* **:** LABEL 3d

trac·ery \ˈtrā-sə-rē, ˈtrās-rē\ *n, pl* **-er·ies** (1669) **1 :** architectural ornamental work with branching lines; *esp* **:** decorative openwork in the head of a Gothic window **2 :** a decorative interlacing of lines suggestive of Gothic tracery — **trac·er·ied** \-rēd\ *adj*

tracery 1

trache- *or* **tracheo-** *comb form* [NL, fr. ML *trachea*] **1 :** trachea ⟨*trache*itis⟩ ⟨*tracheo*tomy⟩ **2 :** tracheal and ⟨*tracheo*bronchial⟩

tra·chea \ˈtrā-kē-ə\ *n, pl* **-che·ae** \-kē-ˌē, -kē-ˌī\ *also* **-che·as** *or* **-chea** [ME, fr. ML, fr. LL *trachia,* fr. Gk *tracheia* (*artēria*) rough (artery), fr. fem. of *trachys* rough] (14c) **1 :** the main trunk of the system of tubes by which air passes to and from the lungs in vertebrates **2** [NL, fr. ML] **:** VESSEL 3b; *also* **:** one of its constituent cellular elements **3** [NL] **:** one of the air-conveying tubules forming the respiratory system of most insects and many other arthropods — **tra·che·al** \-kē-əl\ *adj*

tra·che·ary \ˈtrā-kē-ˌer-ē\ *adj* (1885) **:** of, relating to, or being plant tracheae ⟨~ elements⟩

tra·che·ate \-kē-ˌāt, -ət\ *or* **tra·che·at·ed** \-ˌā-təd\ *adj* (1877) **:** having tracheae as breathing organs

tra·cheid \ˈtrā-kē-əd, -ˌkēd\ *n* [ISV] (1875) **:** a long tubular pitted cell that is peculiar to xylem, functions in conduction and support, and has tapering closed ends and thickened lignified walls

tra·che·i·tis \ˌtrā-kē-ˈī-təs\ *n* [NL] (1859) **:** inflammation of the trachea

tra·cheo·bron·chi·al \ˌtrā-kē-ō-ˈbräŋ-kē-əl\ *adj* (1896) **:** of or relating to both trachea and bronchi ⟨~ lesions⟩

tra·che·ole \ˈtrā-kē-ˌōl\ *n* [NL *tracheola,* dim. of *trachea*] (1901) **:** one of the minute delicate endings of a branched trachea of an insect — **tra·che·o·lar** \trā-ˈkē-ə-lər\ *adj*

tra·cheo·phyte \ˈtrā-kē-ə-ˌfīt\ *n* [NL *Tracheophyta,* fr. *trache-* + Gk *phyton* plant; akin to Gk *phyein* to bring forth — more at BE] (1937) **:** any of a division (Tracheophyta) comprising green plants (as ferns and seed plants) with a vascular system that contains tracheids or tracheary elements

tra·che·os·to·my \ˌtrā-kē-ˈäs-tə-mē\ *n, pl* **-mies** (ca. 1923) **:** the surgical formation of an opening into the trachea through the neck esp. to allow the passage of air

tra·che·ot·o·my \ˌtrā-kē-ˈä-tə-mē\ *n, pl* **-mies** (ca. 1726) **:** the surgical operation of cutting into the trachea esp. through the skin

tra·cho·ma \trə-ˈkō-mə\ *n* [NL, fr. Gk *trachōma,* fr. *trachys* rough] (ca. 1693) **:** a chronic contagious bacterial conjunctivitis marked by inflammatory granulations on the conjunctival surfaces, caused by a chlamydia (*Chlamydia trachomatis*), and commonly resulting in blindness if left untreated

tra·chyte \ˈtra-ˌkīt, ˈtrā-\ *n* [F, fr. Gk *trachys* rough] (1821) **:** a usu. light-colored volcanic rock consisting chiefly of potash feldspar

tra·chyt·ic \trə-ˈki-tik\ *adj* (1827) **:** of or relating to a texture of igneous rocks in which lath-shaped feldspar crystals are in almost parallel lines

tracing *n* (14c) **1 :** something that is traced: as **a :** a copy made on a superimposed transparent sheet **b :** a graphic record made by an instrument (as a seismograph) that registers some movement **2 :** the act of one that traces

tracing paper *n* (1824) **:** a semitransparent paper for tracing drawings; *also* **:** a thin paper containing a clothing pattern to be transferred to fabric (as through carbon paper) by tracing

tracing wheel *n* (ca. 1891) **:** a usu. toothed wheel with a handle that is used on tracing paper to trace a pattern

[1]**track** \ˈtrak\ *n* [ME *trak,* fr. MF *trac*] (15c) **1 a :** detectable evidence (as the wake of a ship, a line of footprints, or a wheel rut) that something has passed **b :** a path made by or as if by repeated footfalls **:** TRAIL **c :** a course laid out esp. for racing **d :** the parallel rails of a railroad **e** (1) **:** one of a series of parallel or concentric paths along which material (as music or information) is recorded (as on a phonograph record or magnetic tape) (2) **:** a group of grooves on a phonograph record containing recorded sound (3) **:** material recorded esp. on or as if on a track ⟨a laugh ~⟩ ⟨instrumental *~s*⟩ ⟨a bonus commentary ~ on a DVD⟩ **f :** a usu. metal way (as a groove) serving as a guide (as for a movable lighting fixture) **2 :** a footprint whether recent or fossil ⟨the huge ~ of a dinosaur⟩ **3 a :** the course along which something moves or progresses **b :** a way of life, conduct, or action **c :** one of several curricula of study to which students are assigned according to their needs or levels of ability **d :** the projection on the earth's surface of the path along which something (as a missile or an airplane) has flown **4 a :** a sequence of events **:** a train of ideas **:** SUCCESSION **b :** an awareness of a fact, progression, or condition ⟨keep ~ of the costs⟩ ⟨lose ~ of the time⟩ **5 a :** the width of a wheeled vehicle from wheel to wheel and usu. from the outside of the rims **b :** the tread of an automobile tire **c :** either of two endless belts on which a tracklaying vehicle travels **6 :** track-and-field sports; *esp* **:** those performed on a running track ***syn*** see TRACE — **track·less** \ˈtrak-ləs\ *adj* — **in one's tracks :** where one stands or is at the moment **:** on the spot ⟨was stopped *in his tracks*⟩ — **on track :** achieving or doing what is necessary or expected

[2]**track** *vt* (1565) **1 a :** to follow the tracks or traces of **:** TRAIL **b :** to search for by following evidence until found ⟨~ down the source⟩ **2 a :** to follow by vestiges **:** TRACE **b :** to observe or plot the moving path of (as a spacecraft or missile) often instrumentally **3 :** to travel over **:** TRAVERSE ⟨~ a desert⟩ **4 a :** to make tracks upon **b :** to carry (as mud) on the feet and deposit **5 :** to keep track of (as a trend) **:** FOLLOW ~ *vi* **1 :** TRAVEL ⟨a comet *~ing* eastward⟩ **2 a** *of a phonograph needle* **:** to follow the groove undulations of a recording **b** *of a pair of wheels* (1) **:** to maintain a constant distance apart on the straightaway (2) **:** to fit a track or rails **c** *of a rear wheel of a vehicle* **:** to follow accurately the corresponding fore wheel on a straightaway **3 :** to leave tracks (as on a floor) — **track·er** *n*

track·age \ˈtra-kij\ *n* (1880) **1 :** lines of railway track **2 a :** a right to use the tracks of another railroad line **b :** the charge for such right

track–and–field \ˌtrak-ən(d)-ˈfēld\ *adj* (1905) **:** of, relating to, or being any of various competitive athletic events (as running, jumping, and weight throwing) performed on a running track and on the adjacent field

track·ball \ˈtrak-ˌbȯl\ *n* (1967) **:** a ball that is mounted usu. in a computer console so as to be only partially exposed and that is rotated to control the movement of a cursor on a display

tracked \ˈtrakt\ *adj* (1926) **1 :** traveling on endless metal belts instead of wheels **2 :** moving along a rail ⟨a ~ air-cushion vehicle⟩

track·ing \ˈtra-kiŋ\ *n* (ca. 1929) **:** the assigning of students to a curricular track

tracking shot *n* (ca. 1940) **:** a scene photographed from a moving dolly

tracking stock *n* (1989) **:** a stock the value of which is linked to the performance of a company division but which does not confer ownership in the company or the division

track·lay·er \ˈtrak-ˌlā-ər, -ˌler\ *n* (1853) **1 :** a worker engaged in tracklaying **2 :** a tracklaying vehicle

[1]**track·lay·ing** \-ˌlā-iŋ\ *n* (1852) **:** the laying of tracks on a railway line

[2]**tracklaying** *adj* (1884) **:** of, relating to, or being a vehicle that travels on two or more endless usu. metal belts

trackless trolley *n* (1921) **:** TROLLEYBUS

track lighting *n* (1972) **:** adjustable lamps mounted along an electrified metal track

track·man \ˈtrak-mən, -ˌman\ *n* (1922) **:** a runner on a track team

track record *n* [[1]*track* (track-and-field sports)] (1952) **:** a record of past performance often taken as an indicator of likely future performance

track·side \ˈtrak-ˌsīd\ *adj* (1886) **:** of, relating to, or situated in the area immediately adjacent to a track — **trackside** *n*

track·suit \ˈtrak-ˌsüt\ *n* (1922) **:** a suit of clothing consisting usu. of a jacket and pants that is often worn by athletes when working out

track·walk·er \-ˌwȯ-kər\ *n* (1872) **:** a worker employed to walk over and inspect a section of railroad tracks

track·way \-ˌwā\ *n* (1818) **1 :** a beaten or trodden path **2 :** a series of fossil footprints (as of a dinosaur)

[1]**tract** \ˈtrakt\ *n, often cap* [ME *tracte,* fr. ML *tractus,* fr. L, action of drawing, extension; perh. fr. its being sung without a break by one voice] (14c) **:** verses of Scripture (as from the Psalms) used between the gradual and the Gospel at some masses (as during penitential seasons)

[2]**tract** *n* [ME *tracte,* fr. L *tractus* action of drawing, extension, fr. *trahere* to pull, draw] (15c) **1 :** extent or lapse of time **2 :** an area either large or small: as **a :** an indefinite stretch of land **b :** a defined area of land **3 a :** a system of body parts or organs that act together to perform some function ⟨the digestive ~⟩ **b :** a bundle of nerve fibers having a common origin, termination, and function

[3]**tract** *n* [ME, treatise, fr. ML *tractus,* perh. alter. of L *tractatus* tractate] (1760) **:** a pamphlet or leaflet of political or religious propaganda; *also* **:** a piece of writing that is suggestive of such a tract

trac·ta·ble \ˈtrak-tə-bəl\ *adj* [L *tractabilis,* fr. *tractare* to handle, treat] (1502) **1 :** capable of being easily led, taught, or controlled **:** DOCILE ⟨a ~ horse⟩ **2 :** easily handled, managed, or wrought **:** MALLEABLE ***syn*** see OBEDIENT — **trac·ta·bil·i·ty** \ˌtrak-tə-ˈbi-lə-tē\ *n* — **trac·ta·ble·ness** \ˈtrak-tə-bəl-nəs\ *n* — **trac·ta·bly** \-blē\ *adv*

Trac·tar·i·an \trak-ˈter-ē-ən\ *n* [fr. *Tracts for the Times,* series of pamphlets expounding the Oxford movement] (ca. 1839) **:** a promoter or supporter of the Oxford movement

Trac·tar·i·an·ism \-ē-ə-ˌni-zəm\ *n* (1840) **:** a system of High Church principles set forth in a series of tracts at Oxford (1833–41)

trac·tate \ˈtrak-ˌtāt\ *n* [L *tractatus,* fr. *tractare* to draw out, handle, treat — more at TREAT] (15c) **:** TREATISE, DISSERTATION

tract house *n* (1956) **:** any of many similarly designed houses built on a tract of land

trac·tion \ˈtrak-shən\ *n* [ML *traction-, tractio,* fr. L *trahere*] (1608) **1 :** the act of drawing **:** the state of being drawn; *also* **:** the force exerted in drawing **2 :** the drawing of a vehicle by motive power; *also* **:** the motive power employed **3 a :** the adhesive friction of a body on a surface on which it moves ⟨the ~ of a wheel on a rail⟩ **b :** a pulling force exerted on a skeletal structure (as in a fracture) by means of a special device ⟨a ~ splint⟩; *also* **:** a state of tension created by such a pulling force ⟨a leg in ~⟩ — **trac·tion·al** \-shnəl, -shə-nᵊl\ *adj*

trac·tive \ˈtrak-tiv\ *adj* [L *tractus,* pp.] (1615) **1 :** serving to draw **2 :** of or relating to traction **:** TRACTIONAL

trac·tor \ˈtrak-tər\ *n* [NL, fr. L *trahere*] (1900) **1 a :** a 4-wheeled or tracklaying automotive vehicle used esp. for drawing farm equipment **b :** a smaller 2-wheeled apparatus controlled through handlebars by a walking operator **c :** [3]TRUCK 3f **2 :** an airplane having the propeller forward of the main supporting surfaces

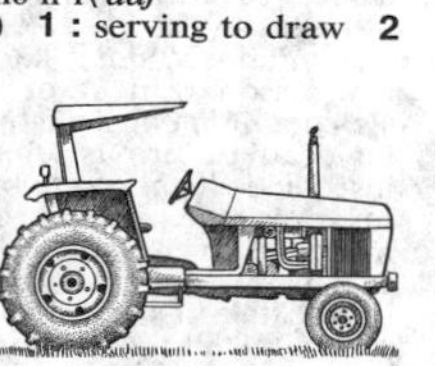
tractor 1a

trad \ˈtrad\ *adj* (1958) *chiefly Brit* **:** TRADITIONAL

[1]**trade** \ˈtrād\ *n* [ME, fr. MLG; akin to OHG *trata* track, course, OE *tredan* to tread] (14c) **1 a** *obs* **:** a path traversed **:** WAY **b** *archaic* **:** a track or trail left by a person or animal **:** TREAD 1 **2 :** a customary course of action **:** PRACTICE ⟨thy sin's not accidental, but a ~ —Shak.⟩ **3 a :** the business or work in which one engages regularly **:** OCCUPATION **b :** an occupation requiring manual or mechanical skill **:** CRAFT **c :** the persons engaged in an occupation, business, or industry **4 a** *obs* **:** dealings between persons or groups **b** (1) **:** the business of buying and selling or bartering commodities **:** COMMERCE (2) **:** BUSINESS, MARKET ⟨novelties for the tourist ~⟩ ⟨did a good ~ in small appliances⟩

5 a : an act or instance of trading : TRANSACTION; *also* : an exchange of property usu. without use of money **b** : a firm's customers : CLIENTELE **c** : the group of firms engaged in a business or industry **6** : TRADE WIND — usu. used in pl. **7** : a publication intended for persons in the entertainment business — usu. used in pl. ***syn*** see BUSINESS

[2]**trade** *vb* **trad·ed; trad·ing** *vi* (1553) **1** *obs* : to have dealings : NEGOTIATE **2 a** : to engage in the exchange, purchase, or sale of goods **b** : to make one's purchases : SHOP ⟨~*s* at his store⟩ **3** : to give one thing in exchange for another **4** : SELL 3 ~ *vt* **1** *archaic* : to do business with **2 a** : to give in exchange for another commodity : BARTER; *also* : to make an exchange of ⟨*traded* places⟩ **b** : to engage in frequent buying and selling of (as stocks or commodities) usu. in search of quick profits — **trad·able** *also* **trade·able** \ˈtrā-də-bəl\ *adj* — **trade on** : to take often unscrupulous advantage of : EXPLOIT ⟨*traded on* their influence . . . in securing special favors —T. C. Pease⟩

[3]**trade** *adj* (1633) **1** : of, relating to, or used in trade **2 a** : intended for or limited to persons in a business or industry ⟨a ~ publication⟩ ⟨~ sales⟩ **b** : serving others in the same business rather than the ultimate user or consumer ⟨a ~ printing house⟩ **3** *also* **trades** : of, composed of, or representing the trades or trade unions ⟨a ~ committee⟩ **4** : having a larger softcover format than that of a mass-market paperback and usu. sold only in bookstores ⟨~ paperbacks⟩; *also* : of or relating to the publishing of such books

trade acceptance *n* (1916) : a time draft or bill of exchange for the amount of a specific purchase drawn by the seller on the buyer, bearing the buyer's acceptance, and often noting the place of payment (as a bank)

trade agreement *n* (ca. 1921) **1** : an international agreement on conditions of trade in goods and services **2** : an agreement resulting from collective bargaining

trade book *n* (1928) **1** : a book intended for general readership **2** : TRADE EDITION

trade·craft \ˈtrād-ˌkraft\ *n* (1961) : the techniques and procedures of espionage

trade discount *n* (1898) : a deduction from the list price of goods allowed by a manufacturer or wholesaler to a retailer

trade dollar *n* (1873) : a U.S. silver dollar weighing 420 grains .900 fine issued 1873–85 for use in east Asian trade

trade down *vi* (1942) **1** : to trade something in (as an automobile) for something less expensive or valuable of its kind **2** : to stock or purchase lower-priced items : ECONOMIZE

trade edition *n* (1930) : an edition of a book intended for general distribution — compare TEXT EDITION

trade–in \ˈtrād-ˌin\ *n* (1917) : an item of merchandise (as an automobile or refrigerator) taken as payment or part payment for a purchase

trade in *vt* (1923) **1** : to turn in as payment or part payment for a purchase or bill ⟨*trade* the old car *in* on a new one⟩ **2** : EXCHANGE 2

trade language *n* (1662) : a restructured language (as a lingua franca or pidgin) used esp. in commercial communication

trade–last \ˈtrād-ˌlast\ *n* (1891) : a complimentary remark by a third person that a hearer offers to repeat to the person complimented if he or she will first report a compliment made about the hearer

[1]**trade·mark** \-ˌmärk\ *n* (1838) **1** : a device (as a word) pointing distinctly to the origin or ownership of merchandise to which it is applied and legally reserved to the exclusive use of the owner as maker or seller **2** : a distinguishing characteristic or feature firmly associated with a person or thing ⟨derringers . . . became almost a ~ of gamblers —Elmer Keith⟩ ⟨wearing his ~ bow tie and derby hat⟩

[2]**trademark** *vt* (1906) : to secure trademark rights for : register the trademark of

[1]**trade name** *n* (1860) **1 a** : the name used for an article among traders **b** : BRAND NAME **2** : the name or style under which a concern does business

[2]**trade name** *vt* (1945) : to designate with a trade name

trade–off \ˈtrād-ˌȯf\ *n* (1961) **1** : a balancing of factors all of which are not attainable at the same time ⟨the education versus experience ~ which governs personnel practices —H. S. White⟩ **2** : a giving up of one thing in return for another : EXCHANGE — **trade off** *vt*

trad·er \ˈtrā-dər\ *n* (1585) **1** : a person whose business is buying and selling or barter: as **a** : MERCHANT **b** : a person who buys and sells (as stocks or commodities futures) in search of short-term profits **2** : a ship engaged in the coastal or foreign trade

trade route *n* (1857) **1** : one of the sea-lanes ordinarily used by merchant ships **2** : a route followed by traders (as in caravans)

trad·es·can·tia \ˌtra-də-ˈskan(t)-sh(ē-)ə\ *n* [NL, genus name, fr. John *Tradescant* †1638 Eng. traveler & gardener] (1766) : SPIDERWORT

trade school *n* (1853) : a secondary school teaching the skilled trades

trade secret *n* (1862) : something (as a formula) which has economic value to a business because it is not generally known or easily discoverable by observation and for which efforts have been made to maintain secrecy

trade show *n* (1895) : a large exposition to promote awareness and sales of esp. new products within an industry ⟨a computer *trade show*⟩

trades·man \ˈtrādz-mən\ *n* (1596) **1** : a worker in a skilled trade : CRAFTSMAN **2** : one who runs a retail store : SHOPKEEPER

trades·peo·ple \-ˌpē-pəl\ *n pl* (1653) : people engaged in trade

trade union *n* (1835) : LABOR UNION — **trade unionism** *n* — **trade unionist** *n*

trade up *vi* (1926) **1** : to trade something in (as an automobile) for something more expensive or valuable of its kind **2** : to stock or purchase higher-priced items

trade wind *n* (1650) : a wind blowing almost constantly in one direction; *esp* : a wind blowing almost continually toward the equator from the northeast in the belt between the northern horse latitudes and the doldrums and from the southeast in the belt between the southern horse latitudes and the doldrums — usu. used in pl.

trading post *n* (1773) **1** : a station of a trader or trading company established in a sparsely settled region where trade in products of local origin (as furs) is carried on **2** : [6]POST 3b

trading stamp *n* (1897) : a printed stamp of value given as a premium to a retail customer to be redeemed in merchandise when accumulated in numbers

tra·di·tion \trə-ˈdi-shən\ *n* [ME *tradicioun,* fr. MF & L; MF *tradicion,* fr. L *tradition-, traditio* action of handing over, tradition — more at TREASON] (14c) **1 a** : an inherited, established, or customary pattern of thought, action, or behavior (as a religious practice or a social custom) **b** : a belief or story or a body of beliefs or stories relating to the past that are commonly accepted as historical though not verifiable **2** : the handing down of information, beliefs, and customs by word of mouth or by example from one generation to another without written instruction **3** : cultural continuity in social attitudes, customs, and institutions **4** : characteristic manner, method, or style ⟨in the best liberal ~⟩ — **tra·di·tion·al** \-ˈdish-nəl, -ˈdi-shə-nᵊl\ *adj* — **tra·di·tion·al·ly** *adv* — **tra·di·tion·less** \-ˈdi-shən-ləs\ *adj*

tra·di·tion·al·ism \trə-ˈdish-nə-ˌli-zəm, -ˈdi-shə-nᵊl-ˌi-\ *n* (1856) **1** : adherence to the doctrines or practices of a tradition **2** : the beliefs of those opposed to modernism, liberalism, or radicalism — **tra·di·tion·al·ist** \-list, -ist\ *n or adj* — **tra·di·tion·al·is·tic** \-ˌdish-nə-ˈlis-tik, -ˌdi-shə-nᵊl-ˈis-\ *adj*

tra·di·tion·al·ize \trə-ˈdish-nə-ˌlīz, -ˈdi-shə-nᵊl-ˌīz\ *vt* **-ized; -iz·ing** (1882) : to make traditional : imbue with traditions or traditionalism

tra·di·tion·ary \trə-ˈdi-shə-ˌner-ē\ *adj* (1661) : TRADITIONAL

tra·duce \trə-ˈdüs, -ˈdyüs\ *vt* **tra·duced; tra·duc·ing** [L *traducere* to lead across, transfer, degrade, fr. *tra-, trans-* trans- + *ducere* to lead — more at TOW] (1573) **1** : to expose to shame or blame by means of falsehood and misrepresentation **2** : VIOLATE, BETRAY ⟨~ a principle of law⟩ ***syn*** see MALIGN — **tra·duce·ment** \-mənt\ *n* — **tra·duc·er** *n*

[1]**traf·fic** \ˈtra-fik\ *n, often attrib* [MF *trafique,* fr. OIt *traffico,* fr. *trafficare* to trade in coastal waters] (1549) **1 a** : import and export trade **b** : the business of bartering or buying and selling **c** : illegal or disreputable usu. commercial activity ⟨the drug ~⟩ **2 a** : communication or dealings esp. between individuals or groups **b** : EXCHANGE ⟨a lively ~ in ideas —F. L. Allen⟩ **3** *archaic* : WARES, GOODS **4 a (1)** : the movement (as of vehicles or pedestrians) through an area or along a route **(2)** : the vehicles, pedestrians, ships, or planes moving along a route **(3)** : congestion of vehicles ⟨stuck in ~⟩ **b** : the information or signals transmitted over a communications system : MESSAGES **5 a** : the passengers or cargo carried by a transportation system **b** : the business of transporting passengers or freight **6** : the volume of customers visiting a business establishment ⟨restaurant ~⟩ **7** : a concentration of participants or players and esp. defensive players ⟨force difficult shots in ~⟩ ***syn*** see BUSINESS — **the traffic will bear** : existing conditions will allow or permit ⟨charge what *the traffic will bear*⟩

[2]**traffic** *vb* **traf·ficked; traf·fick·ing** *vi* (1540) **1** : to carry on traffic **2** : to concentrate one's effort or interest; *broadly* : ENGAGE, DEAL ⟨a writer who often ~*s* in hyperbole⟩ ~ *vt* **1 a** : to travel over ⟨heavily *trafficked* highways⟩ **b** : to visit as a customer ⟨a highly *trafficked* bookstore⟩ **2** : TRADE, BARTER — **traf·fick·er** *n*

traf·fic·abil·i·ty \ˌtra-fi-kə-ˈbi-lə-tē\ *n* (1899) : the quality of a terrain that permits passage (as of vehicles and troops) — **traf·fic·able** \ˈtra-fi-kə-bəl\ *adj*

traffic circle *n* (1942) : ROTARY 2

traffic cone *n* (1953) : a conical marker used on a road or highway (as for indicating an area under repair)

traffic court *n* (1919) : a minor court for disposition of petty prosecutions for violations of statutes, ordinances, and local regulations governing the use of highways and motor vehicles

traffic engineering *n* (1931) : engineering dealing with the design of streets and control of traffic — **traffic engineer** *n*

traffic island *n* (1931) : ISLAND 2a

traffic light *n* (1912) : a visual signal (as a system of colored lights) for controlling traffic

traffic signal *n* (1917) : a signal (as a traffic light) for controlling traffic

trag *abbr* tragedy; tragic

trag·a·canth \ˈtra-jə-ˌkan(t)th, ˈtra-gə-, -kən(t)th; *also* ˈtra-gə-ˌsan(t)th\ *n* [MF *tragacanthe,* fr. L *tragacantha,* fr. Gk *tragakantha,* fr. *tragos* goat + *akantha* thorn] (1573) : a gum obtained from various Asian or East European plants (genus *Astragalus* and esp. *A. gummifer*) of the legume family that swells in water and is used chiefly as an emulsifying, suspending, or thickening agent

tra·ge·di·an \trə-ˈjē-dē-ən\ *n* [ME *tragedien,* fr. MF, fr. *tragedie*] (14c) **1** : a writer of tragedies **2** : an actor specializing in tragic roles

tra·ge·di·enne \trə-ˌjē-dē-ˈen\ *n* [F *tragédienne,* fr. MF, fr. *tragedie*] (1850) : an actress who plays tragic roles

trag·e·dy \ˈtra-jə-dē\ *n, pl* **-dies** [ME *tragedie,* fr. MF, fr. L *tragoedia,* fr. Gk *tragōidia,* fr. *tragos* goat (akin to Gk *trōgein* to gnaw) + *aeidein* to sing — more at TROGLODYTE, ODE] (14c) **1 a** : a medieval narrative poem or tale typically describing the downfall of a great man **b** : a serious drama typically describing a conflict between the protagonist and a superior force (as destiny) and having a sorrowful or disastrous conclusion that elicits pity or terror **c** : the literary genre of tragic dramas **2 a** : a disastrous event : CALAMITY **b** : MISFORTUNE **3** : tragic quality or element

trag·ic \ˈtra-jik\ *also* **trag·i·cal** \-ji-kəl\ *adj* [ME, fr. L *tragicus,* fr. Gk *tragikos,* irreg. fr. *tragōidia* tragedy] (15c) **1** : of, marked by, or expressive of tragedy ⟨the ~ significance of the atomic bomb —H. S. Truman⟩ **2 a** : dealing with or treated in tragedy ⟨the ~ hero⟩ **b** : appropriate to or typical of tragedy **3 a** : regrettably serious or unpleasant : DEPLORABLE, LAMENTABLE ⟨a ~ mistake⟩ **b** : marked by a sense of tragedy — **trag·i·cal·ly** \-ji-k(ə-)lē\ *adv*

tragic flaw *n* (1913) : a flaw in character that brings about the downfall of the hero of a tragedy

tragic irony *n* (1833) : IRONY 3b

tragi·com·e·dy \ˌtra-ji-ˈkä-mə-dē\ *n* [MF *tragicomedie,* fr. OIt *tragicomedia,* fr. OSp, fr. L *tragicomoedia,* fr. *tragicus* + *comoedia* comedy] (ca. 1580) : a drama or a situation blending tragic and comic elements

tragi·com·ic \ˌtra-ji-ˈkä-mik\ *also* **tragi·com·i·cal** \-mi-kəl\ *adj* (1567) **1** : of, relating to, or resembling tragicomedy **2** : manifesting both tragic and comic aspects

\ə\ **abut** \ᵊ\ kitten, F table \ər\ **fur**ther \a\ **ash** \ā\ **ace** \ä\ mop, mar \au̇\ **out** \ch\ **chin** \e\ **bet** \ē\ **easy** \g\ **go** \i\ **hit** \ī\ **ice** \j\ **job** \ŋ\ **sing** \ō\ **go** \ȯ\ **law** \ȯi\ **boy** \th\ **thin** \th\ **the** \ü\ **loot** \u̇\ **foot** \y\ **yet** \zh\ vision, beige \k, n, œ, ue, y\ *see* Guide to Pronunciation

tra•gus \ˈtrā-gəs\ *n, pl* **tra•gi** \-ˌgī, -ˌjī\ [NL, fr. Gk *tragos,* a part of the ear, lit., goat] (ca. 1693) **:** the prominence in front of the external opening of the outer ear

[1]**trail** \ˈtrāl\ *vb* [ME, perh. fr. AF **trailer,* alter. of *trainer* to drag, trail on the ground — more at TRAIN] *vi* (13c) **1 a :** to hang down so as to drag along or sweep the ground **b :** to extend over a surface in a loose or straggling manner ⟨a vine that ~*s* over the ground⟩ **c :** to grow to such length as to droop over toward the ground ⟨~*ing* branches of a weeping birch⟩ **2 a :** to walk or proceed draggingly, heavily, or wearily **:** PLOD, TRUDGE **b :** to lag behind **:** do poorly in relation to others **3 :** to move, flow, or extend slowly in thin streams ⟨smoke ~*ing* from chimneys⟩ **4 a :** to extend in an erratic or uneven course or line **:** STRAGGLE **b :** DWINDLE ⟨her voice ~*ing* off⟩ **5 :** to follow a trail **:** track game ~ *vt* **1 a :** to draw or drag loosely along a surface **:** allow to sweep the ground **b :** HAUL, TOW **2 a :** to drag (as a limb or the body) heavily or wearily **b :** to carry or bring along as an addition, burden, or encumbrance **c :** to draw along in one's wake **3 a :** to follow upon the scent or trace of **:** TRACK **b :** to follow in the footsteps of **:** PURSUE **c :** to follow along behind **d :** to lag behind (as a competitor) ***syn*** see CHASE

[2]**trail** *n* (14c) **1 :** something that trails or is trailed: as **a :** a trailing plant **b :** the train of a gown **c :** a trailing arrangement (as of flowers) **:** SPRAY **d :** the part of a gun carriage that rests on the ground when the piece is unlimbered **2 a :** something that follows or moves along as if being drawn along **:** TRAIN ⟨a ~ of admirers⟩ **b (1) :** the streak produced by a meteor **(2) :** a continuous line produced photographically by permitting the image of a celestial body (as a star) to move over the plate **c :** a chain of consequences **:** AFTERMATH ⟨the . . . movement left a ~ of bitterness and prejudice behind it —Paul Blanshard⟩ **3 a :** a trace or mark left by something that has passed or been drawn along **:** SCENT, TRACK ⟨a ~ of blood⟩ **b (1) :** a track made by passage esp. through a wilderness **(2) :** a marked or established path or route esp. through a forest or mountainous region **c :** a course followed or to be followed ⟨hit the campaign ~⟩ — **trail•less** \ˈtrāl-ləs\ *adj*

trail bike *n* (1966) **:** a small motorcycle designed for off-road use

trail•blaz•er \ˈtrāl-ˌblā-zər\ *n* (1908) **1 :** one that blazes a trail to guide others **:** PATHFINDER **2 :** PIONEER 2 ⟨a ~ in astrophysics⟩

trail•blaz•ing \-ziŋ\ *adj* (1951) **:** making or pointing a new way ⟨~ legislation⟩

trail•break•er \-ˌbrā-kər\ *n* (1925) **:** TRAILBLAZER

[1]**trail•er** \ˈtrā-lər\ *n* (1590) **1 :** one that trails **2 :** a trailing plant **3 :** a nonautomotive vehicle designed to be hauled by road: as **a :** a vehicle for transporting something ⟨a boat ~⟩; *esp* **:** SEMITRAILER 1 **b :** a vehicle designed to serve wherever parked as a temporary dwelling or place of business **c :** MOBILE HOME **4 a :** PREVIEW 3 **b :** a short blank strip of film attached to the end of a reel

[2]**trailer** *vi* (1938) **1 :** to live or travel in or with a trailer **2 :** to be transportable by trailer ⟨a light boat that ~*s* easily⟩ ~ *vt* **:** to transport (as a boat) by means of a trailer — **trail•er•able** \-lə-rə-bəl\ *adj* — **trail•er•ing** *n*

trailer park *n* (1942) **:** an area equipped to accommodate mobile homes — called also *trailer camp, trailer court*

trail•head \ˈtrāl-ˌhed\ *n* (1948) **:** the point at which a trail begins

trailing arbutus *n* (1785) **:** ARBUTUS 2

trailing edge *n* (1909) **:** the rearmost edge of an object that moves and esp. of an airfoil

trail mix *n* (1977) **:** a mixture of seeds, nuts, and dried fruits eaten as a snack esp. by hikers

trail•side \ˈtrāl-ˌsīd\ *adj* (1923) **:** of, relating to, or situated in the area immediately adjacent to a trail

[1]**train** \ˈtrān\ *n* [ME *traine* treachery, fr. AF, fr. *trahir* to betray, fr. L *tradere* — more at TRAITOR] (14c) *obs* **:** SCHEME, TRICK

[2]**train** *n* [ME, fr. AF, fr. *trainer* to draw, drag] (14c) **1 :** a part of a gown that trails behind the wearer **2 a :** RETINUE, SUITE **b :** a moving file of persons, vehicles, or animals **3 :** the vehicles, personnel, and sometimes animals that furnish supply, maintenance, and evacuation services to a combat unit **4 a :** order of occurrence leading to some result — often used in the phrase *in train* ⟨this humiliating process had been in ~ for decades —Paul Fussell⟩ **b :** an orderly succession ⟨a ~ of thought⟩ **c :** accompanying or resultant circumstances **:** AFTERMATH ⟨consequences the discovery will bring in its ~⟩ **5 :** a line of combustible material laid to lead fire to a charge **6 :** a series of moving mechanical parts (as gears) that transmit and modify motion ⟨a gear ~⟩ **7 a :** a connected line of railroad cars with or without a locomotive **b :** an automotive tractor with one or more trailer units **8 :** a series of parts or elements that together constitute a system for producing a result and esp. for carrying on a process (as of manufacture) automatically — **train•ful** \ˈtrān-ˌfu̇l\ *n*

[3]**train** *vb* [ME, fr. AF *trainer,* fr. VL **traginare;* akin to L *trahere* to draw] *vt* (15c) **1 :** TRAIL, DRAG **2 :** to direct the growth of (a plant) usu. by bending, pruning, and tying **3 a :** to form by instruction, discipline, or drill **b :** to teach so as to make fit, qualified, or proficient **4 :** to make prepared (as by exercise) for a test of skill **5 :** to aim at an object or objective **:** DIRECT ⟨~*ed* his camera on the deer⟩ ⟨~*ing* every effort toward success⟩ ~ *vi* **1 :** to undergo instruction, discipline, or drill **2 :** to go by train ***syn*** see TEACH — **train•abil•i•ty** \ˌtrā-nə-ˈbi-lə-tē\ *n* — **train•able** \ˈtrā-nə-bəl\ *adj*

train•band \ˈtrān-ˌband\ *n* [alter. of *trained band*] (1630) **:** a 17th or 18th century militia company in England or America

train•bear•er \ˈtrān-ˌber-ər\ *n* (1708) **:** an attendant who holds up (as on a ceremonial occasion) the train of a robe or gown

train case *n* (1948) **:** a small boxlike piece of luggage used esp. for toilet articles

train dispatcher *n* (1857) **:** a railroad employee who directs the movement of trains within a division and coordinates their movement from one division to another

train•ee \trā-ˈnē\ *n* (1841) **:** one that is being trained esp. for a job — **train•ee•ship** \-ˈnē-ˌship\ *n*

train•er \ˈtrā-nər\ *n* (1598) **1 :** one that trains **2 :** one (as a machine or vehicle) used in training **3 :** a person who treats the ailments and minor injuries of the members of an athletic team **4** *chiefly Brit* **:** SNEAKER 2

train•ing \ˈtrā-niŋ\ *n* (1548) **1 a :** the act, process, or method of one that trains **b :** the skill, knowledge, or experience acquired by one that trains **2 :** the state of being trained

training college *n* (1850) *Brit* **:** TEACHERS COLLEGE

training school *n* (1829) **1 :** a school preparing students for a particular occupation **2 :** a correctional institution for the custody and reeducation of juvenile delinquents

training table *n* (1893) **:** a table where athletes under a training regimen eat meals planned to help in their conditioning

training wheels *n pl* (1964) **:** a pair of small wheels connected to the rear axle of a bicycle to help a beginning bicyclist maintain balance

train•load \ˈtrān-ˌlōd\ *n* (1854) **:** the full freight or passenger capacity of a railroad train; *also* **:** a load that fills a train

train•man \ˈtrān-mən, -ˌman\ *n* (1877) **:** a member of a train crew supervised by a conductor

train oil \ˈtrān-\ *n* [obs. *train* train oil, fr. ME *trane,* fr. MD *trane* or MLG *trān;* akin to OHG *trahan* tear] (ca. 1553) **:** oil from a marine animal (as a whale)

traipse \ˈtrāps\ *vb* **traipsed; traips•ing** [origin unknown] *vi* (1647) **:** to go on foot **:** WALK ⟨*traipsed* over to the restaurant⟩ ⟨children *traipsing* at her heels⟩; *also* **:** to walk or travel about without apparent plan but with or without a purpose ⟨a week *traipsing* through the Ozarks⟩ ⟨*traipsing* from office to office⟩ ~ *vt* **:** TRAMP, WALK ⟨~ the countryside⟩ ***syn*** see WANDER — **traipse** *n*

trait \ˈtrāt, *Brit usu* ˈtrā\ *n* [MF, lit., act of drawing, fr. L *tractus* — more at TRACT] (1589) **1 a :** a stroke of or as if of a pencil **b :** TOUCH, TRACE **2 a :** a distinguishing quality (as of personal character) ⟨curiosity is one of her notable ~*s*⟩ **b :** an inherited characteristic

trai•tor \ˈtrā-tər\ *n* [ME *traytour,* fr. AF *traitre,* fr. L *traditor,* fr. *tradere* to hand over, deliver, betray, fr. *trans-, tra-* trans- + *dare* to give — more at DATE] (13c) **1 :** one who betrays another's trust or is false to an obligation or duty **2 :** one who commits treason

trai•tor•ous \ˈtrā-tə-rəs, ˈtrā-trəs\ *adj* (14c) **1 :** guilty or capable of treason **2 :** constituting treason ⟨~ activities⟩ ***syn*** see FAITHLESS — **trai•tor•ous•ly** *adv*

trai•tress \ˈtrā-trəs\ *or* **trai•tor•ess** \ˈtrā-tə-rəs, ˈtrā-trəs\ *n* (14c) **:** a woman who is a traitor

tra•ject \trə-ˈjekt\ *vt* [L *trajectus,* pp. of *traicere*] (1657) **:** TRANSMIT — **tra•jec•tion** \-ˈjek-shən\ *n*

tra•jec•to•ry \trə-ˈjek-t(ə-)rē\ *n, pl* **-ries** [NL *trajectoria,* fr. fem. of *trajectorius* of passing, fr. L *traicere* to cause to cross, cross, fr. *trans-, tra-* trans- + *jacere* to throw — more at JET] (1696) **1 :** the curve that a body (as a planet or comet in its orbit or a rocket) describes in space **2 :** a path, progression, or line of development resembling a physical trajectory ⟨an upward career ~⟩

Tra•keh•ner \tra-ˈkā-nər\ *n* [G, fr. *Trakehnen,* site of the Prussian royal stud in East Prussia] (1926) **:** any of a breed of large powerful saddle horses of East Prussian origin that excel in dressage and jumping

[1]**tram** \ˈtram\ *n* [E dial., shaft of a wheelbarrow, prob. fr. LG *traam,* lit., beam] (ca. 1517) **1 :** any of various vehicles: as **a :** a boxlike wagon running on rails (as in a mine) **b** *chiefly Brit* **:** STREETCAR **c :** a carrier that travels on an overhead cable or rails **2** *pl, chiefly Brit* **:** a streetcar line

[2]**tram** *vt* **trammed; tram•ming** (1874) **:** to haul in a tram or over a tramway

tram•car \ˈtram-ˌkär\ *n* (1873) **1** *chiefly Brit* **:** STREETCAR **2 :** TRAM 1a

tram•line \-ˌlīn\ *n* (1886) *Brit* **:** a streetcar line

[1]**tram•mel** \ˈtra-məl\ *n* [ME *tramayle,* a kind of net, fr. OF *tramail,* fr. LL *tremaculum,* fr. L *tres* three + *macula* mesh, spot — more at THREE] (14c) **1 :** a net for catching birds or fish; *esp* **:** one having three layers with the middle one finer-meshed and slack so that fish passing through carry some of the center net through the coarser opposite net and are trapped **2 :** an adjustable pothook for a fireplace crane **3 :** a shackle used for making a horse amble **4 :** something impeding activity, progress, or freedom **:** RESTRAINT — usu. used in pl. **5 a :** an instrument for drawing ellipses **b :** a compass for drawing large circles that consists of a beam with two sliding parts — usu. used in pl. **c :** any of various gauges used for aligning or adjusting machine parts

[2]**trammel** *vt* **-meled** *or* **-melled; -mel•ing** *or* **-mel•ling** \ˈtra-mə-liŋ, ˈtram-liŋ\ (ca. 1606) **1 :** to catch or hold in or as if in a net **:** ENMESH **2 :** to prevent or impede the free play of **:** CONFINE ***syn*** see HAMPER

[1]**tra•mon•tane** \trə-ˈmän-ˌtān, ˌtra-mən-ˈ\ *n* (1593) **:** one dwelling in a tramontane region; *broadly* **:** FOREIGNER

[2]**tramontane** *adj* [It *tramontano,* fr. L *transmontanus,* fr. *trans-* + *mont-, mons* mountain — more at MOUNT] (1596) **1 :** TRANSALPINE **2 :** lying on or coming from the other side of a mountain range

[1]**tramp** \ˈtramp, *vi 1 & vt 1 are also* ˈträmp, ˈtrȯmp\ *vb* [ME; akin to MLG *trampen* to stamp] *vi* (14c) **1 :** to walk, tread, or step esp. heavily ⟨~*ed* loudly on the stairs⟩ **2 a :** to travel about on foot **:** HIKE **b :** to journey as a tramp ~ *vt* **1 :** to tread on forcibly and repeatedly **2 :** to travel or wander through or over on foot ⟨have ~*ed* all the woods on their property⟩ — **tramp•er** *n*

[2]**tramp** \ˈtramp, *3, 4 are also* ˈträmp, ˈtrȯmp\ *n* (1790) **1 a :** VAGRANT 1a **b :** a foot traveler **c :** a woman of loose morals; *specif* **:** PROSTITUTE **2 :** a walking trip **:** HIKE **3 :** the succession of sounds made by the beating of feet on a surface (as a road, pavement, or floor) **4 :** an iron plate to protect the sole of a shoe **5 :** a ship not making regular trips but taking cargo when and where it offers and to any port — called also *tramp steamer* — **trampy** \ˈtram-pē\ *adj*

[3]**tramp** \ˈtramp\ *adj* (1873) **:** having no fixed abode, connection, or destination ⟨a ~ dog⟩

tramp art *n* (1974) **:** a style of wood carving flourishing in the U.S. from about 1875 to 1930 that is characterized by ornate layered whittling of ten of cigar boxes or fruit crates; *also* **:** an object carved in this style

tram•ple \ˈtram-pəl\ *vb* **tram•pled; tram•pling** \-p(ə-)liŋ\ [ME, freq. of *trampen* to tramp] *vi* (14c) **1 :** TRAMP; *esp* **:** to tread heavily so as to bruise, crush, or injure **2 :** to inflict injury or destruction esp. contemptuously or ruthlessly — usu. used with *on, over,* or *upon* ⟨*trampling* on the rights of others⟩ ~ *vt* **:** to crush, injure, or destroy by or as if by treading ⟨*trampled* the flowers⟩ — **trample** *n* — **tram•pler** \-p(ə-)lər\ *n*

tram•po•line \ˌtram-pə-ˈlēn, ˈtram-pə-ˌ\ *n* [It *trampolino* springboard, fr. *trampoli* stilts, of Gmc origin; akin to MLG *trampen* to stamp]

(1798) : a resilient sheet or web (as of nylon) supported by springs in a metal frame and used as a springboard and landing area in tumbling — **tram·po·lin·er** \-ˈlē-nər, -ˌlē-\ *n* — **tram·po·lin·ist** \-nist\ *n*

tram·po·lin·ing \-ˈlē-niŋ, -ˌlē-\ *n* (1949) : the sport of jumping and tumbling on a trampoline

tram·way \-ˌwā\ *n* (1825) **1 a** : a railway for trams **b** *Brit* : a streetcar line **2** : an overhead cable for trams

[1]**trance** \ˈtran(t)s\ *n* [ME *traunce,* fr. AF *transe* death, coma, rapture, fr. *transir* to depart, die, fr. L *transire* to cross, pass by — more at TRANSIENT] (14c) **1** : STUPOR, DAZE **2** : a sleeplike state (as of deep hypnosis) usu. characterized by partly suspended animation with diminished or absent sensory and motor activity **3** : a state of profound abstraction or absorption — **trance·like** \-ˌlīk\ *adj*

[2]**trance** *vt* **tranced; tranc·ing** (ca. 1598) : ENTRANCE, ENRAPTURE

tranche \ˈträ^{n}sh\ *n* [F, lit., slice, fr. OF, fr. *trenchier, trancher* to cut — more at TRENCH] (1930) : a division or portion of a pool or whole; *specif* : an issue of bonds derived from a pooling of like obligations (as securitized mortgage debt) that is differentiated from other issues esp. by maturity or rate of return

tran·gam \ˈtraŋ-gəm\ *n* [origin unknown] (ca. 1658) *archaic* : TRINKET, GIMCRACK

tran·ny \ˈtra-nē\ *n, pl* **trannies** [by shortening & alter.] (1976) : TRANSMISSION 3

tran·quil \ˈtraŋ-kwəl, ˈtran-\ *adj* [ME *tranquill,* fr. L *tranquillus*] (15c) **1 a** : free from agitation of mind or spirit ⟨a ~ self-assurance⟩ **b** : free from disturbance or turmoil ⟨a ~ scene⟩ **2** : unvarying in aspect : STEADY, STABLE ***syn*** see CALM — **tran·quil·ly** \-kwə-lē\ *adv* — **tran·quil·ness** *n*

tran·quil·ize *also* **tran·quil·lize** \ˈtraŋ-kwə-ˌlīz, ˈtran-\ *vb* **-ized** *also* **-lized; -iz·ing** *also* **-liz·ing** *vt* (1623) : to make tranquil or calm : PACIFY; *esp* : to relieve of mental tension and anxiety by means of drugs ~ *vi* **1** : to become tranquil : RELAX 1 **2** : to make one tranquil

tran·quil·iz·er *also* **tran·quil·liz·er** \-ˌlī-zər\ *n* (1800) **1** : one that tranquilizes **2** : a drug used to reduce mental disturbance (as anxiety and tension) — compare ANTIPSYCHOTIC

tran·quil·li·ty *or* **tran·quil·i·ty** \tran-ˈkwi-lə-tē, traŋ-\ *n* (14c) : the quality or state of being tranquil ⟨the ~ of the quiet countryside⟩

[1]**trans** \ˈtran(t)s, ˈtranz\ *adj* (1892) : characterized by having certain groups of atoms on opposite sides of the longitudinal axis of a double bond or of the plane of a ring in a molecule

[2]**trans** *abbr* **1** transaction **2** transitive **3** translated; translation; translator **4** transmission **5** transportation **6** transverse

trans- *prefix* [L *trans-, tra-* across, beyond, through, so as to change, fr. *trans* across, beyond — more at THROUGH] **1** : on or to the other side of : across : beyond ⟨*trans*atlantic⟩ **2 a** : beyond (a specified chemical element) in the periodic table ⟨*trans*uranium⟩ **b** *usu ital* : trans ⟨*trans*-dichloro-ethylene⟩ — compare CIS- 2 **3** : through ⟨*trans*cutaneous⟩ **4** : so or such as to change or transfer ⟨*trans*literate⟩ ⟨*trans*location⟩ ⟨*trans*amination⟩ ⟨*trans*ship⟩

trans·act \tran-ˈzakt, tran(t)-ˈsakt\ *vb* [L *transactus,* pp. of *transigere* to drive through, complete, transact, fr. *trans-* + *agere* to drive, do — more at AGENT] *vi* (ca. 1585) : to carry on business ~ *vt* **1** : to carry to completion ⟨~ a sale⟩ **2** : to carry on the operation or management of : DO ⟨~ business⟩ — **trans·ac·tor** \-ˈzak-tər, -ˈsak-tər\ *n*

trans·ac·ti·nide \tran(t)-ˈsak-tə-ˌnīd, tran-ˈzak-\ *adj* (1969) : of, relating to, or being actual or hypothetical elements with atomic weights higher than those of the actinide series ⟨~ chemistry⟩

trans·ac·tion \tran-ˈzak-shən, tran(t)-ˈsak-\ *n* (1632) **1 a** : something transacted; *esp* : an exchange or transfer of goods, services, or funds ⟨electronic ~*s*⟩ **b** *pl* : the often published record of the meeting of a society or association **2 a** : an act, process, or instance of transacting **b** : a communicative action or activity involving two parties or things that reciprocally affect or influence each other — **trans·ac·tion·al** \-shnəl, -shə-n^{ə}l\ *adj*

transactional analysis *n* (1961) : a system of psychotherapy involving analysis of individual episodes of social interaction for insight that will aid communication

trans·al·pine \tran(t)s-ˈal-ˌpīn, tranz-\ *adj* [L *transalpinus,* fr. *trans-* + *Alpes* the Alps] (1590) : situated on the north side of the Alps ⟨*Transalpine* Gaul⟩ — compare CISALPINE

trans·am·i·nase \tran(t)s-ˈa-mə-ˌnās, tranz-, -ˌnāz\ *n* (1940) : an enzyme promoting transamination — called also *aminotransferase*

trans·am·i·na·tion \ˌtran(t)s-ˌa-mə-ˈnā-shən, ˌtranz-\ *n* [ISV *trans-* + *amine* + *-ation*] (1939) : a reversible oxidation-reduction reaction in which an amino group is transferred typically from an alpha-amino acid to the carbonyl carbon atom of an alpha-keto acid

trans·at·lan·tic \ˌtran(t)s-ət-ˈlan-tik, ˌtranz-\ *adj* (1779) **1 a** : crossing or extending across the Atlantic Ocean ⟨a ~ cable⟩ **b** : relating to or involving crossing the Atlantic Ocean ⟨~ airfares⟩ **2 a** : situated or originating from beyond the Atlantic Ocean **b** : of, relating to, or involving countries on both sides of the Atlantic Ocean and esp. the U.S. and Great Britain ⟨~ cooperation⟩

trans·ax·le \tran(t)s-ˈak-səl, tranz-\ *n* [*trans*mission + *axle*] (1958) : a unit that consists of a combination of a transmission and an axle's differential gear used esp. in front-wheel-drive automobiles

trans·bor·der \-ˈbȯr-dər\ *adj* (1897) : crossing or extending across a border

trans·ceiv·er \tran(t)-ˈsē-vər\ *n* [*trans*mitter + *receiver*] (1934) : a radio transmitter-receiver that uses many of the same components for both transmission and reception

tran·scend \tran(t)-ˈsend\ *vb* [ME, fr. L *transcendere* to climb across, transcend, fr. *trans-* + *scandere* to climb — more at SCAN] *vt* (14c) **1 a** : to rise above or go beyond the limits of **b** : to triumph over the negative or restrictive aspects of : OVERCOME **c** : to be prior to, beyond, and above (the universe or material existence) **2** : to outstrip or outdo in some attribute, quality, or power ~ *vi* : to rise above or extend notably beyond ordinary limits ***syn*** see EXCEED

tran·scen·dence \-ˈsen-dən(t)s\ *n* (1601) : the quality or state of being transcendent

tran·scen·den·cy \-dən(t)-sē\ *n* (1615) : TRANSCENDENCE

tran·scen·dent \-dənt\ *adj* [ME, fr. L *transcendent-, transcendens,* prp. of *transcendere*] (15c) **1 a** : exceeding usual limits : SURPASSING **b** : extending or lying beyond the limits of ordinary experience **c** *in Kantian philosophy* : being beyond the limits of all possible experience and knowledge **2** : being beyond comprehension **3** : transcending the universe or material existence — compare IMMANENT 2 **4** : universally applicable or significant ⟨the antislavery movement . . . recognized the ~ importance of liberty —L. H. Tribe⟩ — **tran·scen·dent·ly** *adv*

tran·scen·den·tal \ˌtran(t)-ˌsen-ˈden-t^{ə}l, -sən-\ *adj* (1624) **1 a** : TRANSCENDENT 1b **b** : SUPERNATURAL **c** : ABSTRUSE, ABSTRACT **d** : of or relating to transcendentalism **2 a** : incapable of being the root of an algebraic equation with rational coefficients ⟨π is a ~ number⟩ **b** : being, involving, or representing a function (as sin *x,* log *x,* e^x) that cannot be expressed by a finite number of algebraic operations ⟨~ curves⟩ **3** *in Kantian philosophy* **a** : of or relating to experience as determined by the mind's makeup **b** : transcending experience but not human knowledge **4** : TRANSCENDENT 1a — **tran·scen·den·tal·ly** \-t^{ə}l-ē\ *adv*

tran·scen·den·tal·ism \-tə-ˌli-zəm\ *n* (1803) **1** : a philosophy that emphasizes the a priori conditions of knowledge and experience or the unknowable character of ultimate reality or that emphasizes the transcendent as the fundamental reality **2** : a philosophy that asserts the primacy of the spiritual and transcendental over the material and empirical **3** : the quality or state of being transcendental; *esp* : visionary idealism — **tran·scen·den·tal·ist** \-tə-list\ *adj or n*

Transcendental Meditation *service mark* — used for a meditation technique

trans·con·ti·nen·tal \ˌtran(t)s-ˌkän-tə-ˈnen-t^{ə}l, ˌtranz-\ *adj* (1853) : extending or going across a continent ⟨a ~ railroad⟩

tran·scribe \tran(t)-ˈskrīb\ *vt* **tran·scribed; tran·scrib·ing** [L *transcribere,* fr. *trans-* + *scribere* to write — more at SCRIBE] (1552) **1 a** : to make a written copy of **b** : to make a copy of (dictated or recorded matter) in longhand or on a machine (as a typewriter) **c** : to paraphrase or summarize in writing **d** : WRITE DOWN, RECORD **2 a** : to represent (speech sounds) by means of phonetic symbols **b** : TRANSLATE 2a **c** : to transfer (data) from one recording form to another **d** : to record (as on magnetic tape) for later broadcast **3** : to make a musical transcription of **4** : to cause (as DNA) to undergo genetic transcription — **tran·scrib·er** *n*

tran·script \ˈtran(t)-ˌskript\ *n* [ME, fr. AF *transecrit,* fr. ML *transcriptum,* fr. L, neut. of *transcriptus,* pp. of *transcribere*] (14c) **1 a** : a written, printed, or typed copy; *esp* : a usu. typed copy of dictated or recorded material **b** : an official or legal and often published copy ⟨a court reporter's ~⟩; *esp* : an official copy of a student's educational record **2** : a representation (as of experience) in an art form **3** : a sequence of RNA produced by transcription from a DNA template

tran·scrip·tase \tran-ˈskrip-ˌtās, -ˌtāz\ *n* [*transcrip*tion + *-ase*] (1963) : RNA POLYMERASE; *also* : REVERSE TRANSCRIPTASE

tran·scrip·tion \tran(t)-ˈskrip-shən\ *n* (1598) **1** : an act, process, or instance of transcribing **2** : COPY, TRANSCRIPT: as **a** : an arrangement of a musical composition for some instrument or voice other than the original **b** : a recording (as on magnetic tape) made esp. for use in radio broadcasting **3** : the process of constructing a messenger RNA molecule using a DNA molecule as a template with resulting transfer of genetic information to the messenger RNA — compare TRANSLATION 2, REVERSE TRANSCRIPTION — **tran·scrip·tion·al** \-shnəl, -shə-n^{ə}l\ *adj* — **tran·scrip·tion·al·ly** *adv*

transcription factor *n* (1972) : any of various proteins that bind to DNA and play a role in the regulation of gene expression by promoting transcription

tran·scrip·tion·ist \-shə-nist\ *n* (1963) : one that transcribes; *esp* : a typist who transcribes dictated medical reports

trans·cul·tur·al \tran(t)s-ˈkəl-chə-rəl, tranz-, -ˈkəlch-rəl\ *adj* (1951) : involving, encompassing, or extending across two or more cultures

trans·cu·ta·ne·ous \ˌtran(t)s-kyu̇-ˈtā-nē-əs\ *adj* (ca. 1941) : passing, entering, or made by penetration through the skin ⟨~ infection⟩

trans·der·mal \tran(t)s-ˈdər-məl, tranz-\ *adj* (1944) : relating to, being, or supplying a medication in a form for absorption through the skin into the bloodstream ⟨~ drug delivery⟩ ⟨~ nitroglycerin⟩ ⟨~ nicotine patch⟩ — **trans·der·mal·ly** \-mə-lē\ *adv*

trans·dis·ci·plin·ary \-ˈdi-sə-plə-ˌner-ē\ *adj* (1948) : INTERDISCIPLINARY

trans·duce \tran(t)s-ˈdüs, tranz-, -ˈdyüs\ *vt* **trans·duced; trans·duc·ing** [L *transducere* to lead across, transfer, fr. *trans-* + *ducere* to lead — more at TOW] (1947) **1** : to convert (as energy or a message) into another form ⟨essentially sense organs ~ physical energy into a nervous signal⟩ **2** : to cause (genetic material) to undergo transduction

trans·duc·er \-ˈdü-sər, -ˈdyü-\ *n* (1924) : a device that is actuated by power from one system and supplies power usu. in another form to a second system ⟨a loudspeaker is a ~ that transforms electrical signals into sound energy⟩

trans·duc·tion \-ˈdək-shən\ *n* [L *transducere*] (1947) : the action or process of transducing; *esp* : the transfer of genetic material from one microorganism to another by a viral agent (as a bacteriophage) — **trans·duc·tant** \-tənt\ *n* — **trans·duc·tion·al** \-shnəl, -shə-n^{ə}l\ *adj*

[1]**tran·sect** \tran(t)-ˈsekt\ *vt* [*trans-* + *intersect*] (1634) : to cut transversely — **tran·sec·tion** \-ˈsek-shən\ *n*

[2]**tran·sect** \ˈtran(t)-ˌsekt\ *n* (1905) : a sample area (as of vegetation) usu. in the form of a long continuous strip

tran·sept \ˈtran(t)-ˌsept\ *n* [NL *transeptum,* fr. L *trans-* + *septum, saeptum* enclosure, wall] (ca. 1542) : the part of a cruciform church that crosses at right angles to the greatest length between the nave and the apse or choir; *also* : either of the projecting ends of a transept — **tran·sep·tal** \tran(t)-ˈsep-t^{ə}l\ *adj*

transexual *var of* TRANSSEXUAL

trans fat *n* (1978) : a fat containing trans-fatty acids

trans–fat·ty acid \ˈtran(t)s-ˈfa-tē-, ˈtranz-\ *n* (1953) : an unsaturated fatty acid characterized by a trans arrangement of alkyl chains that is formed esp. during the hydrogenation of vegetable oils and has been linked to an increase in blood cholesterol

trans·fec·tion \tran(t)s-ˈfek-shən, tranz-\ *n* [*trans-* + in*fection*] (1964) : infection of a cell with isolated viral nucleic acid followed by production of the complete virus in the cell; *also* : the incorporation of exogenous DNA into a cell — **trans·fect** \-ˈfekt\ *vt*

1**trans·fer** \tran(t)s-ˈfər, ˈtran(t)s-ˌ\ *vb* **trans·ferred; trans·fer·ring** [ME *transferren,* fr. AF *transferrer,* fr. L *transferre,* fr. *trans-* + *ferre* to carry — more at BEAR] *vt* (14c) **1 a** : to convey from one person, place, or situation to another : MOVE, SHIFT **b** : to cause to pass from one to another : TRANSMIT **c** : TRANSFORM, CHANGE **2** : to make over the possession or control of : CONVEY **3** : to print or otherwise copy from one surface to another by contact ~ *vi* **1** : to move to a different place, region, or situation; *esp* : to withdraw from one educational institution to enroll at another **2** : to change from one vehicle or transportation line to another — **trans·fer·abil·i·ty** \(ˌ)tran(t)s-ˌfər-ə-ˈbi-lə-tē\ *n* — **trans·fer·able** *also* **trans·fer·ra·ble** \tran(t)s-ˈfər-ə-bəl\ *adj* — **trans·fer·al** \-əl\ *n* — **trans·fer·rer** \-ər\ *n*

2**trans·fer** \ˈtran(t)s-ˌfər\ *n* (1674) **1 a** : conveyance of right, title, or interest in real or personal property from one person to another **b** : removal or acquisition of property by mere delivery with intent to transfer title **2 a** : an act, process, or instance of transferring : TRANSFERENCE 2 **b** : the carryover or generalization of learned responses from one type of situation to another **3** : one that transfers or is transferred; *esp* : a graphic image transferred by contact from one surface to another **4** : a place where a transfer is made (as of trains to ferries or as where one form of power is changed to another) **5** : a ticket entitling a passenger on a public conveyance to continue the trip on another route

trans·fer·ase \ˈtran(t)s-(ˌ)fər-ˌās, -ˌāz\ *n* (1948) : an enzyme that promotes transfer of a group from one molecule to another

trans·fer·ee \ˌtran(t)s-(ˌ)fər-ˈē\ *n* (ca. 1736) **1** : a person to whom a conveyance is made **2** : a person who is transferred

trans·fer·ence \tran(t)s-ˈfər-ən(t)s, ˈtran(t)s-(ˌ)\ *n* (1681) **1** : an act, process, or instance of transferring : CONVEYANCE, TRANSFER **2** : the redirection of feelings and desires and esp. of those unconsciously retained from childhood toward a new object (as a psychoanalyst conducting therapy) — **trans·fer·en·tial** \ˌtran(t)s-fə-ˈren(t)-shəl\ *adj*

transfer factor *n* (1956) : a substance that is produced and secreted by a lymphocyte functioning in cell-mediated immunity and that upon incorporation into a lymphocyte which has not been sensitized confers on it the same immunological specificity as the sensitized cell

trans·fer·or \ˌtran(t)s-(ˌ)fər-ˈȯr\ *n* (1875) : one that conveys a title, right, or property

transfer payment *n* (ca. 1945) **1** : a public expenditure made for a purpose (as unemployment compensation) other than procuring goods or services — usu. used in pl. **2** *pl* : money (as welfare payments) that is received by individuals and that is neither compensation for goods or services currently supplied nor income from investments

trans·fer·rin \tran(t)s-ˈfer-ən\ *n* [*trans-* + L *ferrum* iron] (1947) : a beta globulin in blood plasma capable of combining with ferric ions and transporting iron in the body

transfer RNA \ˈtran(t)s-ˌfər-\ *n* (1961) : a relatively small RNA that transfers a particular amino acid to a growing polypeptide chain at the ribosomal site of protein synthesis during translation — called also *tRNA*; compare MESSENGER RNA

transfer station *n* (1969) : a site where recyclables and refuse are collected and sorted in preparation for processing or landfill

trans·fig·u·ra·tion \(ˌ)tran(t)s-ˌfi-gyə-ˈrā-shən, -gə-\ *n* (14c) **1 a** : a change in form or appearance : METAMORPHOSIS **b** : an exalting, glorifying, or spiritual change **2** *cap* : a Christian feast that commemorates the transfiguration of Christ on a mountaintop in the presence of three disciples and that is observed on August 6 in the Roman Catholic and some Eastern churches and on the Sunday before Lent in most Protestant churches

trans·fig·ure \tran(t)s-ˈfi-gyər, *esp Brit* -ˈfi-gər\ *vt* **-ured; -ur·ing** [ME, fr. AF *transfigurer,* fr. L *transfigurare,* fr. *trans-* + *figurare* to shape, fashion, fr. *figura* figure] (14c) : to give a new and typically exalted or spiritual appearance to : transform outwardly and usu. for the better
syn see TRANSFORM

trans·fi·nite \(ˌ)tran(t)s-ˈfī-ˌnīt\ *adj* [G *transfinit,* fr. *trans-* (fr. L) + *finit* finite, fr. L *finitus*] (1902) **1** : going beyond or surpassing any finite number, group, or magnitude **2** : being or relating to the cardinal and ordinal numbers of infinite sets

trans·fix \tran(t)s-ˈfiks\ *vt* [L *transfixus,* pp. of *transfigere,* fr. *trans-* + *figere* to fasten, pierce — more at FIX] (1590) **1** : to pierce through with or as if with a pointed weapon : IMPALE **2** : to hold motionless by or as if by piercing ⟨he stood *~ed* by her gaze⟩ — **trans·fix·ion** \-ˈfik-shən\ *n*

1**trans·form** \tran(t)s-ˈfȯrm\ *vb* [ME, fr. MF *transformer,* fr. L *transformare,* fr. *trans-* + *formare* to form, fr. *forma* form] *vt* (14c) **1 a** : to change in composition or structure **b** : to change the outward form or appearance of **c** : to change in character or condition : CONVERT **2** : to subject to mathematical transformation **3** : to cause (a cell) to undergo genetic transformation ~ *vi* : to become transformed : CHANGE — **trans·form·able** \-ˈfȯr-mə-bəl\ *adj* — **trans·for·ma·tive** \-ˈfȯr-mə-tiv\ *adj*

syn TRANSFORM, METAMORPHOSE, TRANSMUTE, CONVERT, TRANSMOGRIFY, TRANSFIGURE mean to change a thing into a different thing. TRANSFORM implies a major change in form, nature, or function ⟨*transformed* a small company into a corporate giant⟩. METAMORPHOSE suggests an abrupt or startling change induced by or as if by magic or a supernatural power ⟨awkward girls *metamorphosed* into graceful ballerinas⟩. TRANSMUTE implies transforming into a higher element or thing ⟨attempted to *transmute* lead into gold⟩. CONVERT implies a change fitting something for a new or different use or function ⟨*converted* the study into a nursery⟩. TRANSMOGRIFY suggests a strange or preposterous metamorphosis ⟨a story in which a frog is *transmogrified* into a prince⟩. TRANSFIGURE implies a change that exalts or glorifies ⟨joy *transfigured* her face⟩.

2**trans·form** \ˈtran(t)s-ˌfȯrm\ *n* (1853) **1** : a mathematical element obtained from another by transformation **2** : TRANSFORMATION 3a(1), (2) **3** : a linguistic structure (as a sentence) produced by means of a transformation ⟨"the duckling is killed by the farmer" is a ~ of "the farmer kills the duckling"⟩

trans·for·ma·tion \ˌtran(t)s-fər-ˈmā-shən, -fȯr-\ *n* (15c) **1** : an act, process, or instance of transforming or being transformed **2** : false hair worn esp. by a woman to replace or supplement natural hair **3 a** (1) : the operation of changing (as by rotation or mapping) one configuration or expression into another in accordance with a mathematical rule; *esp* : a change of variables or coordinates in which a function of new variables or coordinates is substituted for each original variable or coordinate (2) : the formula that effects a transformation **b** : FUNCTION 5a **c** : an operation that converts (as by insertion, deletion, or permutation) one grammatical string (as a sentence) into another; *also* : a formal statement of such an operation **4** : genetic modification of a bacterium by incorporation of free DNA from another bacterial cell; *also* : genetic modification of a cell by the uptake and incorporation of exogenous DNA

trans·for·ma·tion·al \-shnəl, -shə-nᵊl\ *adj* (1894) : of, relating to, characterized by, or concerned with transformation and esp. linguistic transformation — **trans·for·ma·tion·al·ly** *adv*

transformational grammar *n* (1961) : a grammar that generates the deep structures of a language and converts these to the surface structures by means of transformations

trans·for·ma·tion·al·ist \ˌtran(t)s-fər-ˈmā-shnə-list, -shə-nə-list\ *n* (1964) : an exponent of transformational grammar

trans·form·er \tran(t)s-ˈfȯr-mər\ *n* (1596) : one that transforms; *specif* : a device employing the principle of mutual induction to convert variations of current in a primary circuit into variations of voltage and current in a secondary circuit

trans·form fault \ˈtran(t)s-ˌfȯrm-\ *n* (1965) : a strike-slip fault that occurs typically between segments of a mid-ocean ridge or other tectonic-plate boundary and that is characterized by shallow high-magnitude earthquakes

trans·fuse \tran(t)s-ˈfyüz\ *vt* **trans·fused; trans·fus·ing** [ME, fr. L *transfusus,* pp. of *transfundere,* fr. *trans-* + *fundere* to pour — more at FOUND] (15c) **1 a** : to cause to pass from one to another : TRANSMIT **b** : to diffuse into or through : PERMEATE ⟨sunlight *~s* the bay⟩ **2 a** : to transfer (as blood) into a vein or an artery of a person or animal **b** : to subject (a patient) to transfusion — **trans·fus·ible** *or* **trans·fus·able** \-ˈfyü-zə-bəl\ *adj*

trans·fu·sion \tran(t)s-ˈfyü-zhən\ *n* (1578) **1** : an act, process, or instance of transfusing; *esp* : the process of transfusing fluid (as blood) into a vein or artery **2** : something transfused — **trans·fu·sion·al** \-ˈfyüzh-nəl, -ˈfyü-zhə-nᵊl\ *adj*

trans·gen·der \-ˈjen-dər\ *or* **trans·gen·dered** \-dərd\ *adj* (1979) : of, relating to, or being a person (as a transsexual or transvestite) who identifies with or expresses a gender identity that differs from the one which corresponds to the person's sex at birth — **trans·gen·der·ism** \-ˌi-zəm\ *n*

trans·gene \ˈtran(t)s-ˌjēn, ˈtranz-\ *n* (1984) : a gene that is taken from the genome of one organism and introduced into the genome of another organism by artificial techniques

1**trans·gen·ic** \tran(t)s-ˈje-nik\ *adj* (1982) : being or used to produce an organism or cell of one species into which one or more genes of another species have been incorporated ⟨a ~ mouse⟩ ⟨~ crops⟩; *also* : produced by or consisting of transgenic plants or animals

2**transgenic** *n* (1986) **1** *pl but sing in constr* : a branch of biotechnology concerned with the production of transgenic plants, animals, and foods **2** : a transgenic plant or animal

trans·gress \tran(t)s-ˈgres, tranz-\ *vb* [ME, fr. MF *transgresser,* fr. L *transgressus,* pp. of *transgredi* to step beyond or across, fr. *trans-* + *gradi* to step — more at GRADE] *vi* (15c) **1** : to violate a command or law : SIN **2** : to go beyond a boundary or limit ~ *vt* **1** : to go beyond limits set or prescribed by : VIOLATE ⟨~ divine law⟩ **2** : to pass beyond or go over (a limit or boundary) — **trans·gres·sive** \-ˈgre-siv\ *adj* — **trans·gres·sor** \-ˈgre-sər\ *n*

trans·gres·sion \-ˈgre-shən\ *n* (14c) : an act, process, or instance of transgressing: as **a** : infringement or violation of a law, command, or duty **b** : the spread of the sea over land areas and the consequent unconformable deposit of sediments on older rocks

tranship *var of* TRANSSHIP

trans·his·tor·i·cal \ˌtran(t)s-(h)is-ˈtȯr-i-kəl, ˌtranz-, -ˈtär-\ *adj* (1909) : transcending historical bounds

trans·hu·mance \tran(t)s-ˈhyü-mən(t)s, tranz-, -ˈyü-\ *n* [F, fr. *transhumer* to practice transhumance, fr. Sp *trashumar,* fr. *tras-* trans- (fr. L *trans-*) + L *humus* earth — more at HUMBLE] (ca. 1901) : seasonal movement of livestock (as sheep) between mountain and lowland pastures either under the care of herders or in company with the owners — **trans·hu·mant** \-mənt\ *adj or n*

tran·sience \ˈtran(t)-sh(ē-)ən(t)s; ˈtran-zē-ən(t)s, ˈtran(t)-sē-; ˈtran-zhən(t)s, -jən(t)s\ *n* (1745) : the quality or state of being transient

tran·sien·cy \-sh(ē-)ən(t)-sē, -zē-ən(t)-, -sē-ən(t)-; -zhən(t)-sē, -jən(t)-\ *n* (1652) : TRANSIENCE

1**tran·sient** \-sh(ē-)ənt, -zē-ənt, -sē-; -zhənt, -jənt\ *adj* [L *transeunt-, transiens,* prp. of *transire* to cross, pass by, fr. *trans-* + *ire* to go — more at ISSUE] (1599) **1 a** : passing esp. quickly into and out of existence : TRANSITORY ⟨~ beauty⟩ **b** : passing through or by a place with only a brief stay or sojourn ⟨~ visitors⟩ **2** : affecting something or producing results beyond itself — **tran·sient·ly** *adv*

syn TRANSIENT, TRANSITORY, EPHEMERAL, MOMENTARY, FUGITIVE, FLEETING, EVANESCENT mean lasting or staying only a short time. TRANSIENT applies to what is actually short in its duration or stay ⟨a hotel catering primarily to *transient* guests⟩. TRANSITORY applies to what is by its nature or essence bound to change, pass, or come to an end ⟨fame in the movies is *transitory*⟩. EPHEMERAL implies striking brevity of life or duration ⟨many slang words are *ephemeral*⟩. MOMENTARY suggests coming and going quickly and therefore being merely a brief interruption of a more enduring state ⟨my feelings of guilt were only *momentary*⟩. FUGITIVE and FLEETING imply passing so quickly as to make apprehending difficult ⟨let a *fugitive* smile flit across his face⟩ ⟨*fleeting* moments of joy⟩. EVANESCENT suggests a quick vanishing and an airy or fragile quality ⟨the story has an *evanescent* touch of whimsy that is lost in translation⟩.

2**transient** *n* (1652) **1** : one that is transient: as **a** : a transient guest **b** : a person traveling about usu. in search of work **2 a** : a temporary oscillation that occurs in a circuit because of a sudden change of voltage or of load **b** : a transient current or voltage

transient ischemic attack *n* (1966) **:** a brief episode of cerebral ischemia that is usu. characterized by temporary blurring of vision, slurring of speech, numbness, paralysis, or syncope and is often predictive of a serious stroke — abbr. *TIA*; called also *ministroke*

trans·il·lu·mi·nate \ˌtran(t)s-ə-ˈlü-mə-ˌnāt, ˌtranz-\ *vt* (1900) **:** to cause light to pass through; *esp* **:** to pass light through (a body part) for medical examination — **trans·il·lu·mi·na·tion** \-ˌlü-mə-ˈnā-shən\ *n* — **trans·il·lu·mi·na·tor** \-ˈlü-mə-ˌnā-tər\ *n*

tran·sis·tor \tran-ˈzis-tər, tran(t)-ˈsis-\ *n* [ˈ*trans*fer + *resistor;* fr. its transferring an electrical signal across a resistor] (1948) **1 :** a solid-state electronic device that is used to control the flow of electricity in electronic equipment and usu. consists of a small block of a semiconductor (as germanium) with at least three electrodes **2 :** a transistorized radio

tran·sis·tor·ized \tran-ˈzis-tə-ˌrīzd, tran(t)-ˈsis-\ *adj* (1953) **:** equipped with transistors ⟨a ~ amplifier⟩

[1]**tran·sit** \ˈtran(t)-sət, ˈtran-zət\ *n* [ME *transite,* fr. L *transitus,* fr. *transire* to go across, pass] (15c) **1 a :** an act, process, or instance of passing through or over **b :** CHANGE, TRANSITION **c** (1) **:** conveyance of persons or things from one place to another (2) **:** usu. local transportation esp. of people by public conveyance; *also* **:** vehicles or a system engaged in such transportation **2 a :** passage of a celestial body over the meridian of a place or through the field of a telescope **b :** passage of a smaller body (as Venus) across the disk of a larger (as the sun) **3 :** a theodolite with the telescope mounted so that it can be transited

[2]**transit** *vi* (15c) **:** to make a transit ~ *vt* **1 a :** to pass over or through **b :** to cause to pass over or through **2 :** to pass across (a meridian, a celestial body, or the field of view of a telescope) **3 :** to turn (a telescope) over about the horizontal transverse axis in surveying

[1]**tran·si·tion** \tran(t)-ˈsi-shən, tran-ˈzi-, *chiefly Brit* tran(t)-ˈsi-zhən\ *n* [L *transition-, transitio,* fr. *transire*] (1551) **1 a :** passage from one state, stage, subject, or place to another **:** CHANGE **b :** a movement, development, or evolution from one form, stage, or style to another **2 a :** a musical modulation **b :** a musical passage leading from one section of a piece to another **3 :** an abrupt change in energy state or level (as of an atomic nucleus or a molecule) usu. accompanied by loss or gain of a single quantum of energy — **tran·si·tion·al** \-ˈsish-nəl, -ˈsizh-, -ˈzish-; -ˈsi-shə-nᵊl, -ˈzi-, -zhə-\ *adj* — **tran·si·tion·al·ly** *adv*

[2]**transition** *vi* (1946) **:** to make a transition ⟨~ into college⟩

transition metal *n* [fr. their being transitional between the more highly and the less highly electropositive elements] (1940) **:** any of various metallic elements (as chromium, iron, and nickel) that have valence electrons in two shells instead of only one — called also *transition element*

tran·si·tive \ˈtran(t)-sə-tiv, ˈtran-zə-; ˈtran(t)-stiv\ *adj* [LL *transitivus,* fr. L *transitus,* pp. of *transire*] (1590) **1 :** characterized by having or containing a direct object ⟨a ~ verb⟩ **2 :** being or relating to a relation with the property that if the relation holds between a first element and a second and between the second element and a third, it holds between the first and third elements ⟨equality is a ~ relation⟩ **3 :** of, relating to, or characterized by transition — **tran·si·tive·ly** *adv* — **tran·si·tive·ness** *n* — **tran·si·tiv·i·ty** \ˌtran(t)-sə-ˈti-və-tē, ˌtran-zə-\ *n*

tran·si·to·ry \ˈtran(t)-sə-ˌtȯr-ē, ˈtran-zə-\ *adj* [ME *transitorie,* fr. AF, fr. LL *transitorius,* fr. L, of or allowing passage, fr. *transire*] (14c) **1 :** tending to pass away **:** not persistent **2 :** of brief duration **:** TEMPORARY ⟨the ~ nature of earthly joy⟩ ***syn*** see TRANSIENT — **tran·si·to·ri·ly** \ˌtran(t)-sə-ˈtȯr-ə-lē, ˌtran-zə-\ *adv* — **tran·si·to·ri·ness** \ˈtran(t)-sə-ˌtȯr-ē-nəs, ˈtran-zə-\ *n*

transl *abbr* translated; translation; translator

trans·late \tran(t)s-ˈlāt, tranz-; ˈtran(t)s-ˌlāt, ˈtranz-\ *vb* **trans·lat·ed; trans·lat·ing** [ME, fr. AF *translater,* fr. L *translatus* (pp. of *transferre* to transfer, translate), fr. *trans-* + *latus,* pp. of *ferre* to carry — more at TOLERATE, BEAR] *vt* (14c) **1 a :** to bear, remove, or change from one place, state, form, or appearance to another **:** TRANSFER, TRANSFORM ⟨~ ideas into action⟩ **b :** to convey to heaven or to a nontemporal condition without death **c :** to transfer (a bishop) from one see to another **2 a :** to turn into one's own or another language **b :** to transfer or turn from one set of symbols into another **:** TRANSCRIBE **c** (1) **:** to express in different terms and esp. different words **:** PARAPHRASE (2) **:** to express in more comprehensible terms **:** EXPLAIN, INTERPRET **3 :** ENRAPTURE **4 :** to subject to mathematical translation **5 :** to subject (as genetic information) to translation in protein synthesis ~ *vi* **1 :** to practice translation or make a translation; *also* **:** to admit of or be adaptable to translation ⟨a word that doesn't ~ easily⟩ **2 :** to undergo a translation **3 :** LEAD, RESULT — usu. used with *into* ⟨believes that tax cuts will ~ into economic growth⟩ — **trans·lat·abil·i·ty** \(ˌ)tran(t)s-ˌlā-tə-ˈbi-lə-tē, (ˌ)tranz-\ *n* — **trans·lat·able** \tran(t)s-ˈlā-tə-bəl, tranz-\ *adj* — **trans·la·tor** \-ˈlā-tər\ *n*

trans·la·tion \tran(t)s-ˈlā-shən, tranz-\ *n* (14c) **1 :** an act, process, or instance of translating: as **a :** a rendering from one language into another; *also* **:** the product of such a rendering **b :** a change to a different substance, form, or appearance **:** CONVERSION **c** (1) **:** a transformation of coordinates in which the new axes are parallel to the old ones (2) **:** uniform motion of a body in a straight line **2 :** the process of forming a protein molecule at a ribosomal site of protein synthesis from information contained in messenger RNA — compare TRANSCRIPTION 3 — **trans·la·tion·al** \-shnəl, -shə-nᵊl\ *adj*

translational research *n* (1986) **:** medical research that is concerned with facilitating the practical application of scientific discoveries to the development and implementation of new ways to prevent, diagnose, and treat disease — called also *translational medicine*

trans·la·tive \-ˈlā-tiv\ *adj* (ca. 1682) **1 :** of, relating to, or involving removal or transference from one person or place to another **2 :** of, relating to, or serving in translation from one language or system into another

trans·la·to·ry \ˈtran(t)s-lə-ˌtȯr-ē, ˈtranz-; tran(t)s-ˈlā-tə-rē, tranz-\ *adj* (1849) **:** of, relating to, or involving uniform motion in one direction

trans·lit·er·ate \tran(t)s-ˈli-tə-ˌrāt, tranz-\ *vt* **-at·ed; -at·ing** [*trans-* + L *littera* letter] (1861) **:** to represent or spell in the characters of another alphabet — **trans·lit·er·a·tion** \(ˌ)tran(t)s-ˌli-tə-ˈrā-shən, (ˌ)tranz-\ *n*

trans·lo·ca·tion \ˌtran(t)s-lō-ˈkā-shən, ˌtranz-\ *n* (1624) **:** the act, process, or an instance of changing location or position: as **a :** the conduction of soluble material (as metabolic products) from one part of a plant to another **b :** transfer of part of a chromosome to a different position esp. on a nonhomologous chromosome; *esp* **:** the exchange of parts between nonhomologous chromosomes — **trans·lo·cate** \ˈtran(t)s-lō-ˌkāt, ˈtranz-, (ˌ)tran(t)s-ˈ, (ˌ)tranz-ˈ\ *vb*

trans·lu·cence \tran(t)s-ˈlü-sᵊn(t)s, tranz-\ *n* (1755) **:** the quality or state of being translucent

trans·lu·cen·cy \-sᵊn(t)-sē\ *n, pl* **-cies** (ca. 1610) **1 :** TRANSLUCENCE **2 :** something that is translucent

trans·lu·cent \-sᵊnt\ *adj* [L *translucent-, translucens,* prp. of *translucere* to shine through, fr. *trans-* + *lucēre* to shine — more at LIGHT] (1607) **1 :** permitting the passage of light: **a :** CLEAR, TRANSPARENT ⟨~ water⟩ **b :** transmitting and diffusing light so that objects beyond cannot be seen clearly **2 :** free from disguise or falseness ⟨his ~ patriotism —*Newsweek*⟩ ***syn*** see CLEAR — **trans·lu·cent·ly** *adv*

trans·ma·rine \ˌtran(t)s-mə-ˈrēn, ˌtranz-\ *adj* [L *transmarinus,* fr. *trans-* + *mare* sea — more at MARINE] (1583) **1 :** being or coming from beyond or across the sea **2 :** passing over or extending across the sea

trans·mem·brane \(ˌ)tran(t)s-ˈmem-ˌbrān, (ˌ)tranz-\ *adj* (1944) **:** taking place or existing across a membrane ⟨a ~ protein⟩

trans·mi·grate \(ˌ)tran(t)s-ˈmī-ˌgrāt, (ˌ)tranz-, ˈtran(t)s-ˌ, ˈtranz-ˌ\ *vb* [L *transmigratus,* pp. of *transmigrare* to migrate to another place, fr. *trans-* + *migrare* to migrate] *vt* (ca. 1559) **:** to cause to go from one state of existence or place to another ~ *vi* **1** *of the soul* **:** to pass at death from one body or being to another **2 :** MIGRATE — **trans·mi·gra·tion** \ˌtran(t)s-mī-ˈgrā-shən, ˌtranz-\ *n* — **trans·mi·gra·tor** \(ˌ)tran(t)s-ˈmī-ˌgrā-tər, (ˌ)tranz-, ˈtran(t)s-ˌ, ˈtranz-ˌ\ *n* — **trans·mi·gra·to·ry** \tran(t)s-ˈmī-grə-ˌtȯr-ē, tranz-\ *adj*

trans·mis·si·ble \tran(t)s-ˈmi-sə-bəl, tranz-\ *adj* (1644) **:** capable of being transmitted ⟨~ diseases⟩ — **trans·mis·si·bil·i·ty** \(ˌ)tran(t)s-ˌmi-sə-ˈbi-lə-tē, (ˌ)tranz-\ *n*

transmissible spongiform encephalopathy *n* (1990) **:** PRION DISEASE — abbr. *TSE*

trans·mis·sion \tran(t)s-ˈmi-shən, tranz-\ *n* [MF, fr. L *transmission-, transmissio,* fr. *transmittere* to transmit] (1611) **1 :** an act, process, or instance of transmitting ⟨~ of a nerve impulse across a synapse⟩ **2 :** the passage of radio waves in the space between transmitting and receiving stations; *also* **:** the act or process of transmitting by radio or television **3 :** an assembly of parts including the speed-changing gears and the propeller shaft by which the power is transmitted from an engine to a live axle; *also* **:** the speed-changing gears in such an assembly **4 :** something that is transmitted **:** MESSAGE — **trans·mis·sive** \-ˈmi-siv\ *adj* — **trans·mis·siv·i·ty** \ˌtran(t)s-(ˌ)mi-ˈsi-və-tē, ˌtranz-\ *n*

trans·mis·som·e·ter \ˌtran(t)s-(ˌ)mi-ˈsä-mə-tər, ˌtranz-\ *n* (ca. 1931) **:** an instrument for measuring the transmission of light through a fluid (as the atmosphere)

trans·mit \tran(t)s-ˈmit, tranz-\ *vb* **trans·mit·ted; trans·mit·ting** [ME *transmitten,* fr. L *transmittere,* fr. *trans-* + *mittere* to send] *vt* (15c) **1 a :** to send or convey from one person or place to another **:** FORWARD **b :** to cause or allow to spread: as (1) **:** to convey by or as if by inheritance or heredity **:** HAND DOWN (2) **:** to convey (infection) abroad or to another **2 a** (1) **:** to cause (as light or force) to pass or be conveyed through space or a medium (2) **:** to admit the passage of **:** CONDUCT ⟨glass ~s light⟩ **b :** to send out (a signal) either by radio waves or over a wire ~ *vi* **:** to send out a signal either by radio waves or over a wire — **trans·mit·ta·ble** \-ˈmi-tə-bəl\ *adj* — **trans·mit·tal** \-ˈmi-tᵊl\ *n*

trans·mit·tance \-ˈmi-tᵊn(t)s\ *n* (ca. 1855) **1 :** TRANSMISSION **2 :** the fraction of radiant energy that having entered a layer of absorbing matter reaches its farther boundary

trans·mit·ter \tran(t)s-ˈmi-tər, tranz-; ˈtran(t)s-ˌ, ˈtranz-\ *n* (1727) **:** one that transmits: as **a :** an apparatus for transmitting radio or television signals **b :** NEUROTRANSMITTER

trans·mog·ri·fy \tran(t)s-ˈmä-grə-ˌfī, tranz-\ *vb* **-fied; -fy·ing** [origin unknown] *vt* (1656) **:** to change or alter greatly and often with grotesque or humorous effect ~ *vi* **:** to become transmogrified ***syn*** see TRANSFORM — **trans·mog·ri·fi·ca·tion** \(ˌ)tran(t)s-ˌmä-grə-fə-ˈkā-shən, (ˌ)tranz-\ *n*

trans·mon·tane \(ˌ)tran(t)s-ˈmän-ˌtān, (ˌ)tranz-; ˌtran(t)s-(ˌ)män-ˈ, ˌtranz-\ *adj* [L *transmontanus*] (1727) **:** TRAMONTANE

trans·moun·tain \ˌtran(t)s-ˈmau̇n-tᵊn, ˌtranz-\ *adj* (1929) **:** crossing or extending over or through a mountain ⟨a ~ road⟩ ⟨a ~ tunnel⟩

trans·mu·ta·tion \ˌtran(t)s-myu̇-ˈtā-shən, ˌtranz-\ *n* [ME *transmutacioun,* fr. AF or L; AF *transmutacion,* fr. L *transmutation-, transmutatio,* fr. *transmutare*] (14c) **:** an act or instance of transmuting or being transmuted: as **a :** the conversion of base metals into gold or silver **b :** the conversion of one element or nuclide into another either naturally or artificially — **trans·mut·a·tive** \tran(t)s-ˈmyü-tə-tiv, tranz-\ *adj*

trans·mute \tran(t)s-ˈmyüt, tranz-\ *vb* **trans·mut·ed; trans·mut·ing** [ME, fr. L *transmutare,* fr. *trans-* + *mutare* to change — more at MUTABLE] *vt* (15c) **1 :** to change or alter in form, appearance, or nature and esp. to a higher form **2 :** to subject (as an element) to transmutation ~ *vi* **:** to undergo transmutation ***syn*** see TRANSFORM — **trans·mut·able** \-ˈmyü-tə-bəl\ *adj*

trans·na·tion·al \(ˌ)tran(t)s-ˈnash-nəl, (ˌ)tranz-, -ˈna-shə-nᵊl\ *adj* (1921) **:** extending or going beyond national boundaries ⟨~ corporations⟩ — **trans·na·tion·al·ism** \-ˈnash-nə-ˌli-zəm, -ˈna-shə-nə-\ *n*

trans·nat·u·ral \-ˈna-chə-rəl, -ˈnach-rəl\ *adj* (1569) **:** being above or beyond nature

trans·oce·an·ic \ˌtran(t)s-ˌō-shē-ˈa-nik, ˌtranz-\ *adj* (1827) **1 :** lying or dwelling beyond the ocean **2 :** crossing or extending across the ocean ⟨a ~ telephone cable⟩

tran·som \ˈtran(t)-səm\ *n* [ME *transyn, traunsom,* prob. alter. of *traversayn,* fr. MF *traversain* set crosswise, fr. VL **traversanus,* fr. L *transversus* transverse] (14c) **1 :** a transverse piece in a structure **:** CROSSPIECE: as **a :** LINTEL **b :** a horizontal crossbar in a window, over a door, or between a door and a window or fanlight above it **c :** the horizontal bar or member of a cross or gallows **d :** any of several transverse timbers or beams se-

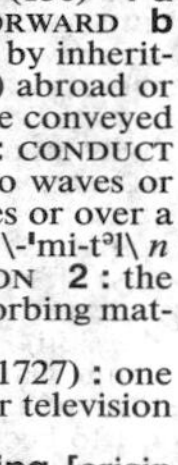

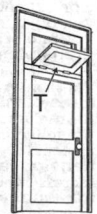

T transom 2

cured to the sternpost of a boat; *also* : the planking forming the stern of a square-ended boat **2 :** a window above a door or other window built on and commonly hinged to a transom — **over the transom** : without solicitation or prior arrangement ⟨the manuscript arrived *over the transom*⟩

tran·son·ic *also* **trans·son·ic** \tran(t)s-ˈsä-nik, tran-ˈsä-\ *adj* [*trans-* + super*sonic*] (1945) **1 :** being or relating to speeds near that of sound in air or about 741 miles (1185 kilometers) per hour at sea level and esp. to speeds slightly below the speed of sound at which the speed of airflow varies from subsonic to supersonic at different points along the surface of a body in motion relative to the surrounding air **2 :** moving, capable of moving, or utilizing air currents moving at a transonic speed

transp *abbr* transportation

trans·pa·cif·ic \ˌtran(t)s-pə-ˈsi-fik\ *adj* (1891) **1 a :** crossing or extending across the Pacific Ocean ⟨~ airlines⟩ **b :** relating to or involving crossing the Pacific Ocean ⟨~ airfares⟩ **2 a :** situated or occurring beyond the Pacific Ocean **b :** of, relating to, or involving countries on both sides of the Pacific Ocean ⟨the ~ economy⟩

trans·par·ence \tran(t)s-ˈper-ən(t)s\ *n* (1594) : TRANSPARENCY 2

trans·par·en·cy \tran(t)s-ˈper-ən(t)-sē\ *n, pl* **-cies** (1591) **1 :** something transparent; *esp* : a picture (as on film) viewed by light shining through it or by projection **2 :** the quality or state of being transparent

trans·par·ent \tran(t)s-ˈper-ənt\ *adj* [ME, fr. ML *transparent-, transparens,* prp. of *transparēre* to show through, fr. L *trans-* + *parēre* to show oneself] (15c) **1 a (1) :** having the property of transmitting light without appreciable scattering so that bodies lying beyond are seen clearly : PELLUCID **(2) :** allowing the passage of a specified form of radiation (as X-rays or ultraviolet light) **b :** fine or sheer enough to be seen through : DIAPHANOUS **2 a :** free from pretense or deceit : FRANK **b** : easily detected or seen through : OBVIOUS **c :** readily understood **d** : characterized by visibility or accessibility of information esp. concerning business practices ***syn*** see CLEAR — **trans·par·ent·ly** *adv* — **trans·par·ent·ness** *n*

trans·par·ent·ize \-ən-ˌtīz\ *vt* **-ized; -iz·ing** (1925) : to make transparent or more nearly transparent ⟨~ tracing paper⟩

trans·per·son·al \(ˌ)tran(t)s-ˈpərs-nəl, -ˈpər-sə-nᵊl\ *adj* (ca. 1906) **1** : extending or going beyond the personal or individual **2 :** of, relating to, or being psychology or psychotherapy concerned esp. with esoteric mental experience (as mysticism and altered states of consciousness) beyond the usual limits of ego and personality

tran·spic·u·ous \tran(t)s-ˈpi-kyə-wəs\ *adj* [NL *transpicuus,* fr. L *transpicere* to look through, fr. *trans-* + *specere* to look, see — more at SPY] (1638) : clearly seen through or understood

trans·pierce \tran(t)s-ˈpirs\ *vt* [MF *transpercer,* fr. OF, fr. *trans-* (fr. L) + *percer* to pierce] (1592) : to pierce through : PENETRATE

tran·spi·ra·tion \ˌtran(t)s-pə-ˈrā-shən\ *n* (15c) : the act or process or an instance of transpiring; *esp* : the passage of watery vapor from a living body (as of a plant) through a membrane or pores — **tran·spi·ra·tion·al** \-shnəl, -shə-nᵊl\ *adj*

tran·spire \tran(t)-ˈspī(-ə)r\ *vb* **tran·spired; tran·spir·ing** [MF *transpirer,* fr. ML *transpirare,* fr. L *trans-* + *spirare* to breathe] *vt* (1597) : to pass off or give passage to (a fluid) through pores or interstices; *esp* : to excrete (as water) in the form of a vapor through a living membrane (as the skin) ~ *vi* **1 :** to give off vaporous material; *specif* : to give off or exude watery vapor esp. from the surfaces of leaves **2 :** to pass in the form of a vapor from a living body **3 a :** to be revealed : come to light **b :** to become known or apparent : DEVELOP **4 :** to take place : GO ON, OCCUR

usage Sense 4 of *transpire* is the frequent whipping boy of those who suppose sense 3 to be the only meaning of the word. Sense 4 appears to have developed in the late 18th century; it was well enough known to have been used by Abigail Adams in a letter to her husband in 1775 ⟨there is nothing new *transpired* since I wrote you last —Abigail Adams⟩. Noah Webster recognized the new sense in his dictionary of 1828. *Transpire* was evidently a popular word with 19th century journalists; sense 4 turns up in such pretentiously worded statements as "The police drill will transpire under shelter to-day in consequence of the moist atmosphere prevailing." Around 1870 the sense began to be attacked as a misuse on the grounds of etymology, and modern critics echo the damnation of 1870. Sense 4 has been in existence for about two centuries; it is firmly established as standard; it occurs now primarily in serious prose, not the ostentatiously flamboyant prose typical of 19th century journalism.

trans·pla·cen·tal \ˌtran(t)s-plə-ˈsen-tᵊl\ *adj* [ISV] (1902) : passing through or occurring by way of the placenta ⟨~ immunization⟩ — **trans·pla·cen·tal·ly** \-tᵊl-ē\ *adv*

[1]**trans·plant** \ˌtran(t)s-ˈplant\ *vb* [ME *transplaunten,* fr. LL *transplantare,* fr. L *trans-* + *plantare* to plant] *vt* (15c) **1 :** to lift and reset (a plant) in another soil or situation **2 :** to remove from one place or context and settle or introduce elsewhere : RELOCATE **3 :** to transfer (an organ or tissue) from one part or individual to another ~ *vi* : to tolerate being transplanted ⟨does not ~ as well as other varieties⟩ — **trans·plant·abil·i·ty** \ˌtran(t)s-ˌplan-tə-ˈbi-lə-tē\ *n* — **trans·plant·able** \tran(t)s-ˈplan-tə-bəl\ *adj* — **trans·plan·ta·tion** \ˌtran(t)s-ˌplan-ˈtā-shən\ *n* — **trans·plant·er** \tran(t)s-ˈplan-tər\ *n*

[2]**trans·plant** \ˈtran(t)s-ˌplant\ *n* (1756) **1 a :** a person or thing that is transplanted **b :** a manufacturing plant set up locally by a foreign automobile company to save on shipping costs ⟨bumpers shipped to a Japanese ~ in the U.S.⟩ **2 :** the act or process of transplanting

trans·po·lar \(ˌ)tran(t)s-ˈpō-lər\ *adj* (1850) : crossing or extending across either of the polar regions

tran·spon·der \tran(t)-ˈspän-dər\ *n* [*trans*mitter + res*ponder*] (ca. 1944) : a radio or radar set that upon receiving a designated signal emits a radio signal of its own and that is used esp. for the detection, identification, and location of objects and in satellites for relaying communications signals

trans·pon·tine \tran(t)s-ˈpän-ˌtīn\ *adj* [*trans-* + L *pont-, pons* bridge — more at FIND] (1844) **1 :** situated on the farther side of a bridge **2** *Brit* : situated on the south side of the Thames

[1]**trans·port** \tran(t)s-ˈpȯrt, ˈtran(t)s-ˌ\ *vt* [ME, fr. AF or L; AF *transporter,* fr. L *transportare,* fr. *trans-* + *portare* to carry — more at FARE] (14c) **1 :** to transfer or convey from one place to another ⟨~*ing* ions across a living membrane⟩ **2 :** to carry away with strong and often intensely pleasant emotion **3 :** to send to a penal colony overseas ***syn*** see BANISH — **trans·port·abil·i·ty** \(ˌ)tran(t)s-ˌpȯr-tə-ˈbi-lə-tē\ *n* — **trans·port·able** \tran(t)s-ˈpȯr-tə-bəl\ *adj*

[2]**trans·port** \ˈtran(t)s-ˌpȯrt\ *n* (1611) **1 :** an act or process of transporting : TRANSPORTATION **2 :** strong or intensely pleasurable emotion ⟨~*s* of joy⟩ **3 a :** a ship for carrying soldiers or military equipment **b :** a vehicle (as a truck or airplane) used to transport persons or goods **c :** TRANSPORTATION 3 **4 :** a transported convict ***syn*** see ECSTASY

trans·por·ta·tion \ˌtran(t)s-pər-ˈtā-shən\ *n* (1540) **1 :** an act, process, or instance of transporting or being transported **2 :** banishment to a penal colony **3 a :** means of conveyance or travel from one place to another **b :** public conveyance of passengers or goods esp. as a commercial enterprise — **trans·por·ta·tion·al** \-shnəl, -shə-nᵊl\ *adj*

transport café \-ka-ˈfā, -ˈkaf\ *n* (1938) *Brit* : a roadside restaurant frequented chiefly by truck drivers

trans·port·er \tran(t)s-ˈpȯr-tər, ˈtran(t)s-ˌ\ *n* (1535) : one that transports; *esp* : a vehicle for transporting large or heavy loads

transposable element *n* (1979) : a segment of genetic material that is capable of changing its location in the genome or in some bacteria of undergoing transfer between an extrachromosomal plasmid and a chromosome

[1]**trans·pose** \tran(t)s-ˈpōz\ *vt* **trans·posed; trans·pos·ing** [ME, fr. AF *transposer,* fr. L *transponere* (perf. indic. *transposui*) to change the position of, fr. *trans-* + *ponere* to put, place — more at POSITION] (14c) **1 :** to change in form or nature : TRANSFORM **2 :** to render into another language, style, or manner of expression : TRANSLATE **3 :** to transfer from one place or period to another : SHIFT **4 :** to change the relative place or normal order of : alter the sequence of ⟨~ letters to change the spelling⟩ **5 :** to write or perform (a musical composition) in a different key **6 :** to bring (a term) from one side of an algebraic equation to the other with change of sign ***syn*** see REVERSE — **trans·pos·able** \-ˈpō-zə-bəl\ *adj*

[2]**trans·pose** \ˈtran(t)s-ˌpōz\ *n* (1937) : a matrix formed from another matrix by interchanging the rows and columns

trans·po·si·tion \ˌtran(t)s-pə-ˈzi-shən\ *n* [AF *transposicion,* fr. ML *transposition-, transpositio,* fr. L *transponere* to transpose] (1538) **1 a** : an act, process, or instance of transposing or being transposed **b** : the transfer of a segment of DNA from one site to another in the genome **2 a :** the transfer of any term of an equation from one side over to the other side with a corresponding change of the sign **b :** a mathematical permutation or interchange of two letters or symbols — **trans·po·si·tion·al** \-ˈzish-nəl, -ˈzi-shə-nᵊl\ *adj*

transposition cipher *n* (1939) : a cipher in which the letters of the plaintext are systematically rearranged into another sequence — compare SUBSTITUTION CIPHER

trans·po·son \tran(t)s-ˈpō-zän\ *n* [*transpose* + [2]*-on*] (1974) : a transposable element esp. when it contains genetic material controlling functions other than those related to its relocation

trans·ra·cial \(ˌ)tran(t)s-ˈrā-shəl, (ˌ)tranz-\ *adj* (1970) : involving, encompassing, or extending across two or more races ⟨~ adoption⟩

trans·sex·u·al *also* **tran·sex·u·al** \(ˌ)tran(t)s-ˈsek-sh(ə-)wəl, -shəl\ *n* (1957) : a person who strongly identifies with the opposite sex and may seek to live as a member of this sex esp. by undergoing surgery and hormone therapy to obtain the necessary physical appearance (as by changing the external sex organs) — **transsexual** *adj* — **trans·sex·u·al·ism** *also* **tran·sex·u·al·ism** \-sh(ə-)wə-ˌli-zəm, -shə-ˌli-\ *n* — **trans·sex·u·al·i·ty** *also* **tran·sex·u·al·i·ty** \-ˌsek-shə-ˈwa-lə-tē\ *n*

trans·shape \tran(sh)-ˈshāp, tran(t)s-\ *vt* (1575) *archaic* : to change into another shape : TRANSFORM

trans·ship *also* **tran·ship** \tran(sh)-ˈship, tran(t)s-\ *vt* (1792) : to transfer for further transportation from one ship or conveyance to another ~ *vi* : to change from one ship or conveyance to another — **trans·ship·ment** *also* **tran·ship·ment** \-mənt\ *n*

trans·tho·rac·ic \ˌtran(t)s-thə-ˈra-sik\ *adj* (1905) : done or made by way of the thoracic cavity — **trans·tho·rac·i·cal·ly** \-si-k(ə-)lē\ *adv*

tran·sub·stan·tial \ˌtran(t)-səb-ˈstan(t)-shəl\ *adj* (1567) : changed or capable of being changed from one substance to another

tran·sub·stan·ti·ate \ˌtran(t)-səb-ˈstan(t)-shē-ˌāt\ *vb* **-at·ed; -at·ing** [ME *transsubstanciaten,* fr. ML *transubstantiatus,* pp. of *transubstantiare,* fr. L *trans-* + *substantia* substance] *vt* (15c) **1 :** to effect transubstantiation in (sacramental bread and wine) **2 :** to change into another substance : TRANSMUTE ~ *vi* : to undergo transubstantiation

tran·sub·stan·ti·a·tion \-ˌstan(t)-shē-ˈā-shən\ *n* (14c) **1 :** an act or instance of transubstantiating or being transubstantiated **2 :** the miraculous change by which according to Roman Catholic and Eastern Orthodox dogma the eucharistic elements at their consecration become the body and blood of Christ while keeping only the appearances of bread and wine

tran·su·date \ˈtran(t)-sü-ˌdāt, -syü-; ˈtran-zü-, -zyü-\ *n* (1876) : a transuded substance

tran·su·da·tion \ˌtran(t)-sü-ˈdā-shən, -syü-; ˌtran-zü-, -zyü-\ *n* (1617) **1 :** the act or process of transuding or being transuded **2 :** TRANSUDATE

tran·sude \tran(t)-ˈsüd, -ˈsyüd; tran-ˈzüd, -ˈzyüd\ *vb* **tran·sud·ed; tran·sud·ing** [NL *transudare,* fr. L *trans-* + *sudare* to sweat — more at SWEAT] *vi* (1664) : to pass through a membrane or permeable substance : EXUDE ~ *vt* : to permit passage of

[1]**trans·ura·nic** \ˌtran(t)s-yü-ˈra-nik, -shə-, -ˈrā-; ˌtran-zyü-, -zhə-\ *or* **trans·ura·ni·um** \-ˈrā-nē-əm\ *adj* (1935) : of, relating to, or being an element with an atomic number greater than that of uranium

[2]**transuranic** *n* (1950) : a transuranic element

trans·ure·thral \ˌtran(t)s-yü-ˈrē-thrəl, ˌtranz-\ *adj* (1933) : passing through or performed by way of the urethra ⟨~ prostatectomy⟩

trans·val·u·ate \(ˌ)tran(t)s-ˈval-yə-ˌwāt, (ˌ)tranz-\ *vt* **-at·ed; -at·ing** [back-formation fr. *transvaluation*] (1912) : TRANSVALUE

trans·val·u·a·tion \ˌtran(t)s-ˌval-yə-ˈwā-shən, ˌtranz-\ *n* (1898) : the act or process of transvaluing

trans·val·ue \(ˌ)tran(t)s-ˈval-(ˌ)yü, (ˌ)tranz-\ *vt* **-val·ued; -valu·ing** (1899) : to reevaluate esp. on a basis that repudiates accepted standards

trans·ver·sal \tran(t)s-ˈvər-səl, tranz-\ *n* [*transversal,* adj., transverse, fr. ME, fr. ML *transversalis,* fr. L *transversus*] (ca. 1847) : a line that intersects a system of lines

[1]**trans·verse** \tran(t)s-ˈvərs, tranz-, ˈtran(t)s-ˌ, ˈtranz-ˌ\ *adj* [ME, fr. L *transversus,* fr. *trans-* + *-versus* (as in *adversus* adverse)] (15c) **1 :** acting, lying, or being across : set crosswise **2 :** made at right angles to the long axis of the body ⟨a ~ section⟩ — **trans·verse·ly** *adv*

[2]**trans·verse** \ˈtran(t)s-ˌvərs, ˈtranz-\ *n* (15c) : something (as a piece, section, or part) that is transverse

transverse colon *n* (ca. 1860) : the middle portion of the colon that extends across the abdominal cavity

transverse process *n* (1696) : a lateral process of a vertebra

transverse wave *n* (1912) : a wave in which the vibrating element moves in a direction perpendicular to the direction of advance of the wave

trans·ves·tite \tran(t)s-ˈves-ˌtīt, tranz-\ *n* [G *Transvestit,* fr. L *trans-* + *vestire* to clothe — more at VEST] (ca. 1922) : a person and esp. a male who adopts the dress and often the behavior typical of the opposite sex esp. for purposes of emotional or sexual gratification — **trans·ves·tism** \-ˈves-ˌti-zəm\ *also* **trans·ves·tit·ism** \-ˈves-ˌti-ˌti-zəm\ *n* — **transvestite** *adj*

[1]**trap** \ˈtrap\ *n* [ME, fr. OE *treppe* & AF *trape* (of Gmc origin); akin to MD *trappe* trap, stair, OE *treppan* to tread] (bef. 12c) **1 :** a device for taking game or other animals; *esp* : one that holds by springing shut suddenly **2 a :** something by which one is caught or stopped unawares; *also* : a position or situation from which it is difficult or impossible to escape **b :** a football play in which a defensive player is allowed to cross the line of scrimmage and then is blocked from the side while the ballcarrier advances through the spot vacated by the defensive player **c :** the act or an instance of trapping the ball in soccer **d :** a defensive maneuver in basketball in which two defenders converge quickly on the ball handler to steal the ball or force a bad pass **3 a :** a device for hurling clay pigeons into the air **b :** SAND TRAP **c :** a piece of leather or section of interwoven leather straps between the thumb and index finger of a baseball glove that forms an extension of the pocket **4** *slang* : MOUTH **5 :** a light usu. one-horse carriage with springs **6 :** any of various devices for preventing passage of something often while allowing other matter to proceed; *esp* : a device for drains or sewers consisting of a bend or partitioned chamber in which the liquid forms a seal to prevent the passage of sewer gas **7** *pl* : a group of percussion instruments (as a bass drum, snare drums, and cymbals) used esp. in a dance or jazz band **8 :** an arrangement of rock strata that favors the accumulation of oil and gas **9** *pl* [*speed trap*] : a measured stretch of a course over which electronic timing devices measure the speed of a vehicle (as a racing car or dragster)

[2]**trap** *vb* **trapped; trap·ping** *vt* (14c) **1 a :** to catch or take in or as if in a trap : ENTRAP **b :** to place in a restricted position : CONFINE ⟨*trapped* in the burning wreck⟩ **2 :** to provide or set (a place) with traps **3 a :** STOP, HOLD ⟨these mountains ~ rains and fogs generated over the ocean —*Amer. Guide Series: Calif.*⟩ **b :** to separate out (as water from steam) **4 a :** to catch (as a baseball) immediately after a bounce **b :** to block out (a defensive football player) by means of a trap **c :** to stop and gain control of (a soccer ball) with a part of the body other than the hands or arms ~ *vi* **1 :** to engage in trapping animals (as for furs) **2 :** to make a defensive trap in basketball ***syn*** see CATCH — **trap·per** *n*

[3]**trap** *vt* **trapped; trap·ping** [ME *trappen,* fr. *trappe* caparison, fr. AF *trape,* prob. fr. ML *trapus* cloth, by-form of LL *drappus*] (14c) : to adorn with or as if with trappings

[4]**trap** *n* [Sw *trapp,* fr. *trappa* stair, fr. MLG *trappe;* akin to MD *trappe* stair] (1794) : TRAPROCK

trap·door \ˈtrap-ˈdȯr\ *n* (14c) : a lifting or sliding door covering an opening (as in a roof, ceiling, or floor)

trap–door spider *n* (1826) : any of various often large burrowing spiders (esp. family Ctenizidae) that construct a tubular subterranean silk-lined nest topped with a hinged lid

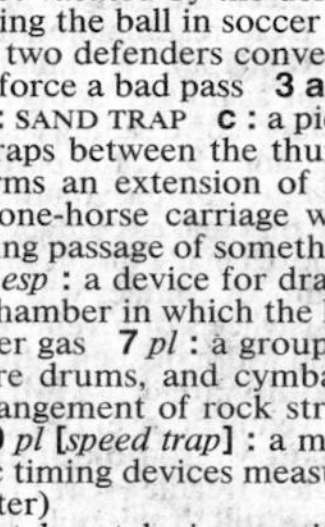

trap-door spider

tra·peze \tra-ˈpēz *also* trə-\ *n* [F *trapèze,* lit., trapezoid, fr. NL *trapezium*] (1861) : a gymnastic or acrobatic apparatus consisting of a short horizontal bar suspended by two parallel ropes

tra·pez·ist \-ˈpē-zist\ *n* (1875) : a performer on the trapeze — called also *trapeze artist*

tra·pe·zi·um \trə-ˈpē-zē-əm, tra-\ *n, pl* **-zi·ums** *or* **-zia** \-zē-ə\ [NL, fr. Gk *trapezion,* lit., small table, dim. of *trapeza* table, fr. *tra-* four (akin to *tettares* four) + *peza* foot; akin to Gk *pod-, pous* foot — more at FOUR, FOOT] (1570) **1 a :** a quadrilateral with no parallel sides **b** *Brit* : TRAPEZOID 1b **2 :** a bone in the wrist at the base of the metacarpal of the thumb

tra·pe·zi·us \-zē-əs\ *n, pl* **-zii** \-zē-ˌī\ *also* **-zi·us·es** [NL, fr. *trapezium;* fr. the pair on the back forming together the figure of a trapezium] (ca. 1704) : a large flat triangular superficial muscle of each side of the upper back

tra·pe·zo·he·dron \trə-ˌpē-zō-ˈhē-drən, ˌtra-pə-\ *n, pl* **-drons** *or* **-dra** \-drə\ [NL, fr. *trapezium* + *-o-* + *-hedron*] (ca. 1822) : a crystalline form whose faces are trapeziums

trap·e·zoid \ˈtra-pə-ˌzȯid\ *n* [NL *trapezoïdes,* fr. Gk *trapezoeidēs* trapezium-shaped, fr. *trapeza* table] (ca. 1706) **1 a** *Brit* : TRAPEZIUM 1a **b :** a quadrilateral having only two sides parallel **2 :** a bone in the wrist at the base of the metacarpal of the index finger — **trap·e·zoi·dal** \ˌtra-pə-ˈzȯi-dᵊl\ *adj*

trap·line \ˈtrap-ˌlīn\ *n* (1920) : a line or series of traps; *also* : the route along which such a line of traps is set

trapping *n* [ME, fr. gerund of *trappen* — more at TRAP] (14c) **1 :** CAPARISON 1 — usu. used in pl. **2** *pl* : outward decoration or dress : ornamental equipment **3** *pl* : outward signs ⟨conventional men with all the ~*s* . . . of banality —Robert Plank⟩

Trap·pist \ˈtra-pist\ *n* [F *trappiste,* fr. La *Trappe,* France] (1814) : a member of a reformed branch of the Roman Catholic Cistercian Order established by the Abbot de Rancé in 1664 at the monastery of La Trappe in Normandy — **Trappist** *adj*

trap·rock \ˈtrap-ˈräk\ *n* [[4]*trap*] (1813) : any of various dark-colored fine-grained igneous rocks (as basalt) used esp. in road making

traps \ˈtraps\ *n pl* [ME *trappe* caparison — more at TRAP] (1813) : personal belongings : LUGGAGE

trap·shoot·er \ˈtrap-ˌshü-tər\ *n* (1875) : a person who engages in trapshooting

trap·shoot·ing \-ˌshü-tiŋ\ *n* (1875) : shooting at clay pigeons sprung from a trap into the air away from the shooter

tra·pun·to \trə-ˈpün-(ˌ)tō, -ˈpu̇n-\ *n, pl* **-tos** [It, fr. pp. of *trapungere* to embroider, fr. *tra-* across (fr. L *trans-*) + *pungere* to prick, fr. L — more at TRANS-, PUNGENT] (ca. 1924) : a decorative quilted design in high relief worked through at least two layers of cloth by outlining the design in running stitch and padding it from the underside

[1]**trash** \ˈtrash\ *n* [ME *trasch* fallen leaves and twigs, perh. of Scand origin; akin to Norw dial. *trask* rubbish; ON *tros* fallen leaves and twigs, OE *trus*] (ca. 1518) **1 :** something worth little or nothing: as **a :** JUNK, RUBBISH **b** (1) **:** empty talk : NONSENSE (2) **:** inferior or worthless writing or artistic matter (as a television show); *esp* : such matter intended purely for sensational entertainment (3) **:** TRASH TALK **2 :** something in a crumbled or broken condition or mass; *esp* : debris from pruning or processing plant material **3 :** a worthless person; *also* : such persons as a group : RIFFRAFF

[2]**trash** *vt* (1902) **1 :** THROW AWAY 1 ⟨standards of reality and truth were ~*ed* —Edwin Diamond⟩ **2 :** VANDALIZE, DESTROY **3 :** ATTACK, ASSAULT **4 :** SPOIL, RUIN ⟨~*ing* the environment⟩ **5 :** to subject to criticism or invective; *esp* : to disparage strongly ⟨a film ~*ed* by the critics⟩ ~ *vi* : to trash something or someone

trash fish *n* (1944) **1 :** ROUGH FISH **2 :** a usu. marine fish having little or no market value as human food but used sometimes in the production of fish meal

trash·man \ˈtrash-ˌman, -mən\ *n* (1951) : a worker who collects and hauls away trash

trash talk *n* (1981) : disparaging, taunting, or boastful comments esp. between opponents trying to intimidate each other — **trash–talk** \ˈtrash-ˌtȯk\ *vb* — **trash–talk·er** \-ˌtȯ-kər\ *n*

trashy \ˈtra-shē\ *adj* **trash·i·er; -est** (ca. 1620) **1 :** being, resembling, or containing trash : of inferior quality **2 :** INDECENT — **trash·i·ly** \-shə-lē\ *adv* — **trash·i·ness** *n*

trat·to·ria \ˌträ-tə-ˈrē-ə\ *n, pl* **-ri·as** *or* **-rie** \-ˈrē-ˌā\ [It, fr. *trattore* restaurateur, fr. F *traiteur,* fr. *traiter* to treat, fr. OF *traitier* — more at TREAT] (1832) : RESTAURANT; *specif* : a usu. small Italian restaurant

trau·ma \ˈtrau̇-mə, ˈtrȯ-\ *n, pl* **traumas** *also* **trau·ma·ta** \-mə-tə\ [Gk *traumat-, trauma* wound, alter. of *trōma;* akin to Gk *titrōskein* to wound, *tetrainein* to pierce — more at THROW] (ca. 1693) **1 a :** an injury (as a wound) to living tissue caused by an extrinsic agent **b :** a disordered psychic or behavioral state resulting from severe mental or emotional stress or physical injury **c :** an emotional upset ⟨the personal ~ of an executive who is not living up to his own expectations —Karen W. Arenson⟩ **2 :** an agent, force, or mechanism that causes trauma — **trau·mat·ic** \trə-ˈma-tik, trȯ-, trau̇-\ *adj* — **trau·mat·i·cal·ly** \-ti-k(ə-)lē\ *adv*

trauma center *n* (1973) : a hospital unit specializing in the treatment of patients with acute and esp. life-threatening traumatic injuries

trau·ma·tise *Brit var of* TRAUMATIZE

trau·ma·tism \ˈtrau̇-mə-ˌti-zəm, ˈtrȯ-\ *n* (1857) : the development or occurrence of trauma; *also* : TRAUMA

trau·ma·tize \-ˌtīz\ *vt* **-tized; -tiz·ing** (1903) : to inflict a trauma upon — **trau·ma·ti·za·tion** \ˌtrau̇-mə-tə-ˈzā-shən, ˌtrȯ-\ *n*

trav *abbr* travel

[1]**tra·vail** \trə-ˈvāl, ˈtra-ˌvāl\ *n* [ME, fr. AF, fr. *travailler* to torment, labor, journey, fr. VL **trepaliare* to torture, fr. LL *trepalium* instrument of torture, fr. L *tripalis* having three stakes, fr. *tri-* + *palus* stake — more at POLE] (13c) **1 a :** work esp. of a painful or laborious nature : TOIL **b :** a physical or mental exertion or piece of work : TASK, EFFORT **c :** AGONY, TORMENT **2 :** LABOR, PARTURITION ***syn*** see WORK

[2]**travail** *same as* [1]; *in prayer-book communion service usu* ˈtra-ˌvāl\ *vi* (13c) **1 :** to labor hard : TOIL **2 :** LABOR 3

[1]**trav·el** \ˈtra-vəl\ *vb* **-eled** *or* **-elled; -el·ing** *or* **-el·ling** \ˈtra-və-liŋ, ˈtrav-liŋ\ [ME *travailen, travelen* to torment, labor, strive, journey, fr. AF *travailler*] *vi* (14c) **1 a :** to go on or as if on a trip or tour : JOURNEY **b** (1) **:** to go as if by traveling : PASS ⟨the news ~*ed* fast⟩ (2) **:** ASSOCIATE ⟨~*s* with a sophisticated crowd⟩ **c :** to go from place to place as a sales representative or business agent **2 a** (1) **:** to move or undergo transmission from one place to another ⟨goods ~*ing* by plane⟩ (2) **:** to withstand relocation successfully ⟨a dish that ~*s* well⟩ **b :** to move in a given direction or path or through a given distance ⟨the stylus ~*s* in a groove⟩ **c :** to move rapidly ⟨a car that can really ~⟩ **3 :** to take more steps while holding a basketball than the rules allow ~ *vt* **1 a :** to journey through or over **b :** to follow (a course or path) as if by traveling **2 :** to traverse (a specified distance) **3 :** to cover (an area) as a commercial traveler — **travel light :** to travel with a minimum of equipment or baggage

[2]**travel** *n* (14c) **1 a :** the act of traveling : PASSAGE **b :** a journey esp. to a distant or unfamiliar place : TOUR, TRIP — often used in pl. **2** *pl* : an account of one's travels **3 :** the number traveling : TRAFFIC **4 a :** MOVEMENT, PROGRESSION ⟨the ~ of satellites around the earth⟩ **b :** the motion of a piece of machinery; *esp* : reciprocating motion

travel agency *n* (1927) : an agency engaged in selling and arranging transportation, accommodations, tours, and trips for travelers — called also *travel bureau*

travel agent *n* (1925) : a person engaged in selling and arranging transportation, accommodations, tours, or trips for travelers

traveled *or* **travelled** *adj* (15c) **1 :** experienced in travel ⟨a widely ~ journalist⟩ **2 :** used by travelers ⟨a well-*traveled* road⟩

trav·el·er *or* **trav·el·ler** \ˈtra-və-lər, ˈtrav-lər\ *n* (14c) **1 :** one that travels: as **a :** one that goes on a trip or journey **b :** TRAVELING SALESMAN **2 a :** an iron ring sliding along a rope, bar, or rod of a ship **b :** a rod on the deck on which such a ring slides **3 :** any of various devices for handling something that is being transported laterally

traveler's check *n* (1891) **:** a draft purchased from a bank or express company and signed by the purchaser at the time of purchase and again at the time of cashing as a precaution against forgery

traveler's diarrhea *n* (1968) **:** intestinal sickness and diarrhea affecting a traveler that is typically caused by ingestion of pathogenic microorganisms (as some E. coli)

traveling *or* **travelling** *adj* (14c) **1 :** that travels ⟨a ~ opera company⟩ ⟨a ~ executive⟩ **2 :** carried, used by, or accompanying a traveler ⟨a ~ alarm clock⟩ ⟨a ~ companion⟩

traveling bag *n* (1826) **:** SUITCASE

traveling case *n* (1744) **:** a usu. rigid and box-shaped suitcase

traveling fellowship *n* (1789) **:** a fellowship whose terms permit or direct the holder to travel or go abroad for study or research

traveling salesman *n* (1885) **:** a traveling representative of a business concern who solicits orders usu. in an assigned territory

trav·el·ogue *or* **trav·el·og** \ˈtra-və-ˌlȯg, -ˌläg\ *n* [*travel* + *-logue*] (1903) **1 :** a talk or lecture on travel usu. accompanied by a film or slides **2 :** a narrated motion picture about travel **3 :** a piece of writing about travel

travel trailer *n* (1961) **:** a trailer drawn esp. by an automobile and equipped for use (as while traveling) as a dwelling

tra·vers·al \trə-ˈvər-səl *also* tra-ˈ *or* ˈtra-ˌ\ *n* (1897) **:** the act or an instance of traversing

[1]**tra·verse** \ˈtra-vərs *also* -ˌvərs, *esp for 6 & 8 also* trə-ˈ *or* tra-ˈ\ *n* [ME *travers,* fr. AF *travers* (as in *a travers, de travers* across), fr. L *transversum* (as in *in transversum* set crosswise), neut. of *transversus* lying across; senses 5–9 in part fr. [2]*traverse* — more at TRANSVERSE] (14c) **1 :** something that crosses or lies across **2 :** OBSTACLE, ADVERSITY **3 :** a formal denial of a matter of fact alleged by the opposing party in a legal pleading **4 a :** a compartment or recess formed by a partition, curtain, or screen **b :** a gallery or loft providing access from one side to another in a large building **5 :** a route or way across or over: as **a :** a zigzag course of a sailing ship with contrary winds **b :** a curving or zigzag way up a steep grade **c :** the course followed in traversing **6 :** the act or an instance of traversing **:** CROSSING **7 :** a protective projecting wall or bank of earth in a trench **8 a :** a lateral movement (as of the saddle of a lathe carriage); *also* **:** a device for imparting such movement **b :** the lateral movement of a gun about a pivot or on a carriage to change direction of fire **9 :** a line surveyed across a plot of ground

[2]**tra·verse** \trə-ˈvərs *also* tra-ˈ *or* ˈtra-(ˌ)\ *vb* **tra·versed; tra·vers·ing** [ME, fr. AF *traverser,* fr. LL *transversare,* fr. L *transversus*] *vt* (14c) **1 a :** to go against or act in opposition to **:** OPPOSE, THWART **b :** to deny (as an allegation of fact or an indictment) formally at law **2 a :** to go or travel across or over **b :** to move or pass along or through ⟨light rays *traversing* a crystal⟩ **3 :** to make a study of **:** EXAMINE **4 :** to lie or extend across **:** CROSS ⟨the bridge ~*s* a brook⟩ **5 a :** to move to and fro over or along **b :** to ascend, descend, or cross (a slope or gap) at an angle **c :** to move (a gun) to right or left on a pivot **6 :** to make or carry out a survey of by using traverses ~ *vi* **1 :** to move back and forth or from side to side **2 :** to move or turn laterally **:** SWIVEL **3 a :** to climb at an angle or in a zigzag course **b :** to ski across rather than straight down a hill **4 :** to make a survey by using traverses — **tra·vers·able** \-ˈvər-sə-bəl, -(ˌ)vər-\ *adj* — **tra·vers·er** *n*

[3]**tra·verse** \ˈtra-(ˌ)vərs, trə-ˈ, tra-ˈ\ *adj* (15c) **:** lying across **:** TRANSVERSE

tra·verse jury \ˈtra-vərs-\ *n* (1823) **:** PETIT JURY

traverse rod *n* (1948) **:** a metal rod or track with a pulley mechanism for drawing curtains

trav·er·tine \ˈtra-vər-ˌtēn, -tən\ *n* [F *travertin,* fr. It *travertino, trevertino,* fr. L *tiburtinus,* adj., of travertine, lit., of Tibur (Tivoli)] (1730) **:** a mineral consisting of a massive usu. layered calcium carbonate (as aragonite or calcite) formed by deposition from spring waters or esp. from hot springs

[1]**trav·es·ty** \ˈtra-və-stē\ *vt* **-tied; -ty·ing** (1673) **:** to make a travesty of **:** PARODY

[2]**travesty** *n, pl* **-ties** [obs. E *travesty* disguised, parodied, fr. F *travesti,* pp. of *travestir* to disguise, fr. It *travestire,* fr. *tra-* across (fr. L *trans-*) + *vestire* to dress, fr. L — more at VEST] (1674) **1 :** a burlesque translation or literary or artistic imitation usu. grotesquely incongruous in style, treatment, or subject matter **2 :** a debased, distorted, or grossly inferior imitation ⟨a ~ of justice⟩ ***syn*** see CARICATURE

tra·vois \trə-ˈvȯi, ˈtra-ˌvȯi\ *n, pl* **tra·vois** *also* **tra·voises** \-ˈvȯiz, -ˌvȯiz\ [AmerF *travail,* fr. CanF, shaft of a cart, fr. MF *traveil* catafalque, prop, fr. LL *trepalium* instrument of torture — more at TRAVAIL] (1847) **:** a simple vehicle used by Plains Indians consisting of two trailing poles serving as shafts and bearing a platform or net for the load

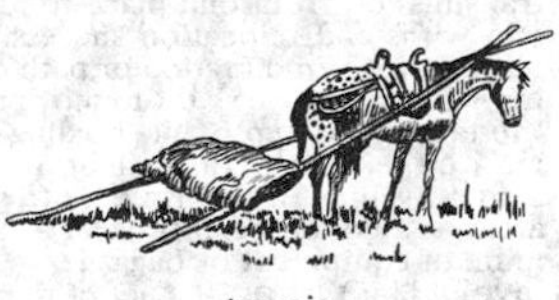
travois

[1]**trawl** \ˈtrȯl\ *vb* [prob. fr. obs. D *tragelen*] *vi* (1561) **1 a :** to fish with a trawl **b :** to make a search as if by trawling **2 :** TROLL 2a ~ *vt* **:** to catch (fish) with a trawl

[2]**trawl** *n* (1759) **1 :** a large conical net dragged along the sea bottom in gathering fish or other marine life **2 :** SETLINE

trawl·er \ˈtrȯ-lər\ *n* (1629) **1 :** a boat used in trawling **2 :** a person who fishes by trawling

trawl·er·man \-mən\ *n* (1633) **1 :** TRAWLER 2 **2 :** one who mans a trawler

tray \ˈtrā\ *n* [ME, fr. OE *trīg, trēg;* akin to OSw *trø* wooden grain measure and prob. to OE *trēow* tree — more at TREE] (bef. 12c) **:** an open receptacle with a flat bottom and a low rim for holding, carrying, or exhibiting articles — **tray·ful** \-ˌfu̇l\ *n*

traz·o·done \ˈtra-zə-ˌdōn\ *n* [perh. fr. ISV *triazo* azido + pyri*dine* + *-one*] (1971) **:** an antidepressant drug $C_{19}H_{22}ClN_5O$ administered in the form of its hydrochloride

treach·er·ous \ˈtre-chə-rəs, ˈtrech-rəs\ *adj* (14c) **1 :** characterized by or manifesting treachery **:** PERFIDIOUS **2 a :** likely to betray trust **:** UNRELIABLE ⟨a ~ memory⟩ **b :** providing insecure footing or support ⟨~ quicksand⟩ **c :** marked by hidden dangers, hazards, or perils ***syn*** see FAITHLESS — **treach·er·ous·ly** *adv* — **treach·er·ous·ness** *n*

treach·ery \-rē\ *n, pl* **-er·ies** [ME *trecherie,* fr. AF, fr. *trecher, tricher* to deceive, fr. VL **triccare* — more at TRICK] (13c) **1 :** violation of allegiance or of faith and confidence **:** TREASON **2 :** an act of perfidy or treason

trea·cle \ˈtrē-kəl\ *n* [ME *triacle,* fr. AF, fr. L *theriaca,* fr. Gk *thēriakē* antidote against a poisonous bite, fr. fem. of *thēriakos* of a wild animal, fr. *thērion* wild animal, dim. of *thēr* wild animal — more at FIERCE] (14c) **1 :** a medicinal compound formerly in wide use as a remedy against poison **2** *chiefly Brit* **a :** MOLASSES **b :** a blend of molasses, invert sugar, and corn syrup used as syrup — called also *golden syrup* **3 :** something (as a tone of voice) heavily sweet and cloying

trea·cly \-k(ə-)lē\ *adj* **trea·cli·er; -est** (1733) **:** resembling treacle (as in quality or appearance) ⟨~ sentimentality⟩

[1]**tread** \ˈtred\ *vb* **trod** \ˈträd\ *also* **tread·ed; trod·den** \ˈträ-dᵊn\ *or* **trod; tread·ing** [ME *treden,* fr. OE *tredan;* akin to OHG *tretan* to tread] *vt* (bef. 12c) **1 a :** to step or walk on or over **b :** to walk or proceed along **:** FOLLOW ⟨~*ing* a fine line between tradition and innovation⟩ **2 a :** to beat or press with the feet **:** TRAMPLE **b :** to subdue or repress as if by trampling **:** CRUSH **3 :** to copulate with — used of a male bird **4 a :** to form by treading **:** BEAT ⟨~ a path⟩ **b :** to execute by stepping or dancing ⟨~ a measure⟩ ~ *vi* **1 :** to move or proceed on or as if on foot ⟨must ~ lightly⟩ **2 a :** to set foot ⟨has gone where others fear to ~⟩ **b :** to put one's foot **:** STEP ⟨carelessly ~*ing* on the flowers⟩ **3 :** COPULATE — **tread·er** *n* — **tread on one's toes :** to give offense (as by encroaching on one's rights or feelings) — **tread water :** to keep the body nearly upright in the water and the head above water by a treading motion of the feet usu. aided by the hands

[2]**tread** *n* (13c) **1 :** a mark (as a footprint or the imprint of a tire) made by or as if by treading **2 a (1) :** the action of treading **(2) :** an act or instance of treading **:** STEP **b :** manner of stepping **c :** the sound of treading **3 a :** the part of a shoe or boot sole that touches the ground; *also* **:** the pattern on the bottom of a sole **b (1) :** the part of a wheel or tire that makes contact with a road or rail **(2) :** the pattern of ridges or grooves made or cut in the face of a tire **4 :** the distance between the points of contact with the ground of the two front wheels or the two rear wheels of a vehicle **5 a :** the upper horizontal part of a step **b :** the width of such a tread — **tread·less** \-ləs\ *adj*

[1]**trea·dle** \ˈtre-dᵊl\ *n* [ME *tredel* step of a stair, fr. OE, fr. *tredan*] (15c) **:** a swiveling or lever device pressed by the foot to drive a machine

[2]**treadle** *vb* **trea·dled; trea·dling** \ˈtred-liŋ, ˈtre-dᵊl-iŋ\ *vi* (1891) **:** to operate a treadle ~ *vt* **:** to operate (as a machine) by a treadle

tread·mill \ˈtred-ˌmil\ *n* (1822) **1 a :** a mill worked by persons treading on steps on the periphery of a wide wheel having a horizontal axis and used formerly in prison punishment **b :** a mill worked by an animal treading an endless belt **c :** a device having an endless belt on which an individual walks or runs in place for exercise or physiological testing **2 :** a wearisome or monotonous routine resembling continued activity on a treadmill ⟨the office ~⟩

treas *abbr* treasury

trea·son \ˈtrē-zᵊn\ *n* [ME *tresoun,* fr. AF *traisun,* fr. L *tradition-, traditio* act of handing over, fr. *tradere* to hand over, betray — more at TRAITOR] (13c) **1 :** the betrayal of a trust **:** TREACHERY **2 :** the offense of attempting by overt acts to overthrow the government of the state to which the offender owes allegiance or to kill or personally injure the sovereign or the sovereign's family

trea·son·able \ˈtrēz-nə-bəl, ˈtrē-zə-nə-bəl\ *adj* (14c) **:** relating to, consisting of, or involving treason ⟨~ words⟩ — **trea·son·ably** \-blē\ *adv*

trea·son·ous \ˈtrēz-nəs, ˈtrē-zə-nəs\ *adj* (1593) **:** TREASONABLE

trea·sur·able \ˈtre-zhə-rə-bəl, ˈtrā-; ˈtrezh-rə-, ˈtrāzh-rə-\ *adj* (1607) **:** worthy of being treasured **:** PRECIOUS

[1]**trea·sure** \ˈtre-zhər, ˈtrā-\ *n* [ME *tresor,* fr. AF, fr. L *thesaurus* — more at THESAURUS] (12c) **1 a (1) :** wealth (as money, jewels, or precious metals) stored up or hoarded ⟨buried ~⟩ **(2) :** wealth of any kind or in any form **:** RICHES **b :** a store of money in reserve **2 :** something of great worth or value; *also* **:** a person esteemed as rare or precious **3 :** a collection of precious things

[2]**treasure** *vt* **trea·sured; trea·sur·ing** \-zh(ə-)riŋ\ (14c) **1 :** to collect and store up (something of value) for future use **:** HOARD **2 :** to hold or keep as precious **:** CHERISH, PRIZE ⟨she *treasured* those memories⟩ ***syn*** see APPRECIATE

trea·sure–house \ˈtre-zhər-ˌhau̇s, ˈtrā-\ *n* (13c) **1 :** a building where treasure is kept **:** TREASURY **2 :** a place or source (as a collection) where many things of value can be found

trea·sur·er \ˈtre-zhə-rər, ˈtrā-; ˈtrezh-rər, ˈtrāzh-\ *n* (14c) **1 :** a guardian of a collection of treasures **:** CURATOR **2 :** an officer entrusted with the receipt, care, and disbursement of funds: as **a :** a governmental officer charged with receiving, keeping, and disbursing public revenues **b :** the executive financial officer of a club, society, or business corporation — **trea·sur·er·ship** \-ˌship\ *n*

treasure trove *n* [AF *tresor trové,* lit., found treasure] (1523) **1 :** treasure that anyone finds; *specif* **:** gold or silver in the form of money, plate, or bullion which is found hidden and whose ownership is not known **2 :** a valuable discovery, resource, or collection

trea·sury \ˈtre-zh(ə-)rē, ˈtrā-\ *n, pl* **-sur·ies** [ME *tresorie,* fr. AF, fr. *tresor* treasure] (14c) **1 a :** a place in which stores of wealth are kept **b :** the place of deposit and disbursement of collected funds; *esp* **:** one where public revenues are deposited, kept, and disbursed **c :** funds kept in such a depository **2** *obs* **:** TREASURE **3** *cap* **a :** a governmental department in charge of finances and esp. the collection, management, and expenditure of public revenues **b :** the building in which the business of such a governmental department is transacted **4** *cap* **:** a government security (as a note or bill) issued by the Treasury **5 :** a repository for treasures ⟨a ~ of poems⟩

treasury note *n* (1890) **1 :** a currency note issued by the U.S. Treasury in payment for silver bullion purchased under the Sherman Silver Purchase Act of 1890 **2 :** a U.S. government bond usu. with a maturity of not less than one year or more than seven years

treasury of merits (1636) **:** the superabundant satisfaction of Christ for human sins and the excess of merit of the saints which according to Roman Catholic theology is effective for salvation of others and is available for dispensation through indulgences

treasury stock *n* (1901) **:** issued stock reacquired by a corporation and held as an asset

[1]**treat** \ˈtrēt\ *vb* [ME *treten,* fr. AF *treter, traiter, traitier,* fr. L *tractare* to drag about, handle, deal with, freq. of *trahere* to drag, pull] *vi* (14c) **1** : to discuss terms of accommodation or settlement : NEGOTIATE **2** : to deal with a matter esp. in writing : DISCOURSE — usu. used with *of* ⟨a book ~*ing* of conservation⟩ **3** : to pay another's expenses (as for a meal or drink) esp. as a compliment or as an expression of regard or friendship ~ *vt* **1 a** : to deal with in speech or writing : EXPOUND **b** : to present or represent artistically **c** : to deal with : HANDLE ⟨food is plentiful and ~*ed* with imagination —Cecil Beaton⟩ **2 a** : to bear oneself toward : USE ⟨~ a horse cruelly⟩ **b** : to regard and deal with in a specified manner — usu. used with *as* ⟨~ the matter as confidential⟩ **3 a** : to provide with free food, drink, or entertainment ⟨they ~*ed* us to lunch⟩ **b** : to provide with enjoyment or gratification **4** : to care for or deal with medically or surgically ⟨~ a disease⟩ **5** : to act upon with some agent esp. to improve or alter ⟨~ a metal with acid⟩ — **treat·er** *n*

[2]**treat** *n* (1651) **1 a** : an entertainment given without expense to those invited **b** : the act of providing another with free food, drink, or entertainment ⟨dinner will be my ~⟩ **2** : an esp. unexpected source of joy, delight, or amusement ⟨seeing her again was a ~⟩

treat·able \ˈtrē-tə-bəl\ *adj* (14c) : capable of being treated : yielding or responsive to treatment ⟨a ~ disease⟩ — **treat·abil·i·ty** \ˌtrē-tə-ˈbi-lə-tē\ *n*

trea·tise \ˈtrē-təs *also* -təz\ *n* [ME *tretis,* fr. AF *tretiz,* alter. of *tretez, traitet,* fr. ML *tractatus,* fr. L *tractare* to treat, handle] (14c) **1** : a systematic exposition or argument in writing including a methodical discussion of the facts and principles involved and conclusions reached ⟨a ~ on higher education⟩ **2** *obs* : ACCOUNT, TALE

treat·ment \ˈtrēt-mənt\ *n* (ca. 1560) **1 a** : the act or manner or an instance of treating someone or something : HANDLING, USAGE ⟨the star requires careful ~⟩ **b** : the techniques or actions customarily applied in a specified situation **2 a** : a substance or technique used in treating **b** : an experimental condition

trea·ty \ˈtrē-tē\ *n, pl* **treaties** [ME *trete,* fr. AF *treté,* fr. pp. of *treter* to discuss, treat] (14c) **1** : the action of treating and esp. of negotiating **2 a** : an agreement or arrangement made by negotiation: (1) : PRIVATE TREATY (2) : a contract in writing between two or more political authorities (as states or sovereigns) formally signed by representatives duly authorized and usu. ratified by the lawmaking authority of the state **b** : a document in which such a contract is set down

treaty port *n* (1863) : any of numerous ports and inland cities in China, Japan, and Korea formerly open by treaty to foreign commerce

treb·bia·no \tre-ˈbyä-(ˌ)nō\ *n* [It] (1860) : a widely cultivated Italian white grape used esp. in making white wine and brandy

[1]**tre·ble** \ˈtre-bəl\ *n* [ME, the highest part in a three-part composition, fr. *treble,* adj.] (14c) **1 a** : the highest voice part in harmonic music : SOPRANO **b** : one that performs a treble part; *also* : a member of a family of instruments having the highest range **c** : a high-pitched or shrill voice, tone, or sound **d** : the upper half of the whole vocal or instrumental tonal range — compare BASS **e** : the higher portion of the audio frequency range in sound recording and broadcasting **2** : something treble in construction, uses, amount, number, or value

[2]**treble** *adj* [ME, fr. AF, fr. L *triplus* — more at TRIPLE] (14c) **1 a** : having three parts or uses : THREEFOLD **b** : triple in number or amount **2 a** : relating to or having the range or part of a treble **b** : HIGH-PITCHED, SHRILL **c** : of, relating to, or having the range of treble in sound recording and broadcasting ⟨~ frequencies⟩ — **tre·bly** \ˈtre-b(ə-)lē\ *adv*

[3]**treble** *vb* **tre·bled; tre·bling** \ˈtre-b(ə-)liŋ\ *vt* (14c) : to increase threefold ~ *vi* **1** : to sing treble **2** : to grow to three times the size, amount, or number

treble clef *n* [ˈ*treble;* fr. its use for the notation of treble parts] (1825) **1** : a clef that places G above middle C on the second line of the staff **2** : TREBLE STAFF

treble staff *n* (ca. 1854) : the musical staff carrying the treble clef

treb·u·chet \ˌtre-byə-ˈshet, -bə-, -ˈchet\ *or* **treb·uc·ket** \ˌtre-bə-ˈket\ *n* [ME *trebochet,* fr. AF *trebuchet*] (15c) : a medieval military engine for hurling heavy missiles (as rocks)

tre·cen·to \trā-ˈchen-(ˌ)tō\ *n* [It, lit., three hundred, fr. L *tres* three + *centum* hundred — more at THREE, HUNDRED] (1841) : the 14th century; *specif* : the 14th century in Italian literature and art

tre·de·cil·lion \ˌtrē-di-ˈsil-yən\ *n, often attrib* [L *tredecim* thirteen (fr. *tres* three + *decem* ten) + E *-illion* (as in *million*) — more at THREE, TEN] (1850) — see NUMBER table

[1]**tree** \ˈtrē\ *n* [ME, fr. OE *trēow;* akin to ON *trē* tree, Gk *drys,* Skt *dāru* wood] (bef. 12c) **1 a** : a woody perennial plant having a single usu. elongate main stem generally with few or no branches on its lower part **b** : a shrub or herb of arborescent form ⟨rose ~*s*⟩ ⟨a banana ~⟩ **2 a** (1) : a piece of wood (as a post or pole) usu. adapted to a particular use or forming part of a structure or implement (2) *archaic* : the cross on which Jesus was crucified **b** *archaic* : GALLOWS **3** : something in the form of or resembling a tree: as **a** : a diagram or graph that branches usu. from a simple stem or vertex without forming loops or polygons ⟨a genealogical ~⟩ ⟨phylogenetic ~*s*⟩ **b** : a much-branched system of channels esp. in an animal body ⟨the vascular ~⟩ **4** : SADDLETREE — **tree·less** \-ləs\ *adj* — **tree·like** \-ˌlīk\ *adj*

[2]**tree** *vt* **treed; tree·ing** (1575) **1 a** : to drive to or up a tree ⟨*treed* by a bull⟩ ⟨dogs ~*ing* game⟩ **b** : to put into a position of extreme disadvantage : CORNER; *esp* : to bring to bay **2** : to furnish or fit (as a shoe) with a tree

treed \ˈtrēd\ *adj* (1860) : planted or grown with trees : WOODED

tree ear *n* (1967) : WOOD EAR

tree farm *n* (1941) : an area of forest land managed to ensure continuous commercial production

tree fern *n* (1830) : any of various ferns (esp. families Cyatheaceae and Dicksoniaceae) of arborescent habit with a woody stem

tree frog *n* (1738) : any of numerous small anuran amphibians (esp. family Hylidae) of usu. arboreal habits that typically have adhesive disks on the toes

tree·hop·per \ˈtrē-ˌhä-pər\ *n* (ca. 1839) : any of a family (Membracidae) of small leaping homopterous insects that feed on the sap esp. of shrubs and trees

tree house *n* (1867) : a structure (as a playhouse) built among the branches of a tree

tree hugger *n* (1965) *sometimes disparaging* : ENVIRONMENTALIST 2; *esp* : an advocate for the preservation of woodlands

tree line *n* (1893) : TIMBERLINE

treen \ˈtrēn\ *n, sing or pl in constr* [*treen* wooden, fr. ME, fr. OE *trēowen,* fr. *trēow* tree, wood] (1927) : small woodenware — called also *treenware*

tree·nail *or* **trun·nel** *also* **tre·nail** \ˈtrə-nᵊl\ *n* (13c) : a wooden peg made usu. of dry compressed timber so as to swell in its hole when moistened

tree of heaven (1845) : a Chinese ailanthus (*Ailanthus altissima* syn. *A. glandulosa*) that has foliage similar to that of the sumacs, has ill-scented staminate flowers, and is grown as a shade and ornamental tree

tree of life (1880) : a conventionalized and often ornate representation of a tree used as a decorative motif

tree peony *n* (1811) : a shrubby Chinese peony (*Paeonia suffruticosa*) that has large showy flowers and is the source of many horticultural varieties

tree ring *n* (1919) : ANNUAL RING

tree shrew *n* (1893) : any of a family (Tupaiidae of the order Scandentia) of small southeast Asian mammals that resemble squirrels, are of semiarboreal or terrestrial habit, feed chiefly on insects and fruit, and are sometimes classified as true insectivores or primitive primates

tree sparrow *n* (ca. 1770) **1** : a Eurasian sparrow (*Passer montanus*) that has a black spot on the ear coverts **2** : a No. American sparrow (*Spizella arborea*) that has a single dark spot on the breast and breeds in Alaska and northern Canada and winters in the U.S.

tree surgery *n* (1902) : operative treatment of diseased trees esp. for control of decay; *broadly* : practices forming part of the professional care of specimen or shade trees — **tree surgeon** *n*

tree swallow *n* (1893) : an American swallow (*Tachycineta bicolor* syn. *Iridoprocne bicolor*) with iridescent greenish-blue upperparts and white underparts

tree toad *n* (1778) : TREE FROG

tree tomato *n* (ca. 1881) : TAMARILLO

tree·top \ˈtrē-ˌtäp\ *n* (1530) **1** : the topmost part of a tree **2** *pl* : the height or line marked by the tops of a group of trees

tre·foil \ˈtrē-ˌfȯi(-ə)l, ˈtre-\ *n* [ME, fr. AF, fr. L *trifolium,* fr. *tri-* + *folium* leaf — more at BLADE] (15c) **1 a** : CLOVER 1; *broadly* : any of several leguminous herbs (as bird's-foot trefoil) with leaves that have or appear to have three leaflets **b** : a trifoliolate leaf **2** : an ornament or symbol in the form of a stylized trifoliolate leaf

tre·ha·lose \tri-ˈhä-ˌlōs, -ˌlōz\ *n* [ISV *trehala,* a sweet substance constituting the pupal covering of a beetle + [2]*-ose*] (1862) : a crystalline disaccharide $C_{12}H_{22}O_{11}$ that is found in various organisms (as fungi and insects), is about half as sweet as sucrose, and is sometimes used as a sweetener in commercially prepared foods

treil·lage \tre-ˈyäzh\ *n* [F, fr. MF, fr. *treille* vine arbor — more at TRELLIS] (1698) : latticework for vines : TRELLIS 1

[1]**trek** \ˈtrek\ *vi* **trekked; trek·king** [Afrik, fr. D *trecken* to pull, haul, migrate; akin to OHG *trechan* to pull] (1835) **1** *chiefly SoAfr* **a** : to travel by ox wagon **b** : to migrate by ox wagon or in a train of such **2** : to make one's way arduously; *broadly* : JOURNEY — **trek·ker** *n*

[2]**trek** *n* [Afrik, fr. D *treck* pull, haul, fr. *trecken*] (1849) **1** *chiefly SoAfr* : a journey by ox wagon; *esp* : an organized migration by a group of settlers **2** : a trip or movement esp. when involving difficulties or complex organization : an arduous journey

[1]**trel·lis** \ˈtre-ləs\ *n* [ME *trelis,* fr. AF *treleis,* fr. OF *treille* arbor, fr. L *trichila* summerhouse] (14c) **1** : a frame of latticework used as a screen or as a support for climbing plants **2** : a construction (as a summerhouse) chiefly of latticework **3** : an arrangement that forms or gives the effect of a lattice ⟨a ~ of interlacing streams⟩ — **trel·lised** \ˈtre-ləst\ *adj*

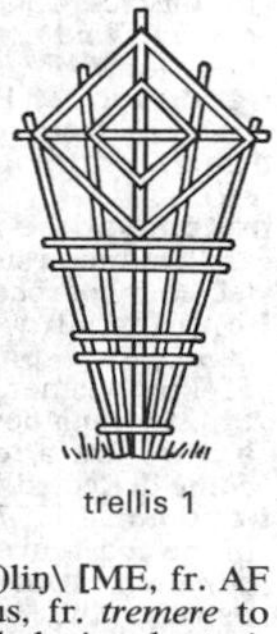

trellis 1

[2]**trellis** *vt* (15c) **1** : to provide with a trellis; *esp* : to train (as a vine) on a trellis **2** : to cross or interlace on or through : INTERWEAVE

trel·lis·work \ˈtre-ləs-ˌwərk\ *n* (1712) : LATTICEWORK

trem·a·tode \ˈtre-mə-ˌtōd\ *n* [ultim. fr. Gk *trēmatōdēs* pierced with holes, fr. *trēmat-, trēma* hole, fr. *tetrainein* to bore — more at THROW] (ca. 1859) : any of a class (Trematoda) of parasitic usu. hermaphroditic flatworms including the flukes — **trematode** *adj*

[1]**trem·ble** \ˈtrem-bəl\ *vi* **trem·bled; trem·bling** \-b(ə-)liŋ\ [ME, fr. AF *trembler,* fr. ML *tremulare,* fr. L *tremulus* tremulous, fr. *tremere* to tremble; akin to Gk *tremein* to tremble] (14c) **1** : to shake involuntarily (as with fear or cold) : SHIVER **2** : to move, sound, pass, or come to pass as if shaken or tremulous ⟨the building *trembled* from the blast⟩ **3** : to be affected with great fear or anxiety ⟨*trembled* for the safety of her child⟩ — **trem·bler** \-b(ə-)lər\ *n*

[2]**tremble** *n* (1609) **1** : an act or instance of trembling; *esp* : a fit or spell of involuntary shaking or quivering **2** *pl but sing in constr* : severe poisoning of livestock and esp. cattle by a toxic alcohol present in a snakeroot (*Eupatorium rugosum*) and rayless goldenrod that is characterized esp. by muscular tremors, weakness, and constipation

trem·bly \ˈtrem-b(ə-)lē\ *adj* (1848) : marked by trembling : TREMULOUS

tre·men·dous \tri-ˈmen-dəs\ *adj* [L *tremendus,* fr. gerundive of *tremere*] (1632) **1** : being such as may excite trembling or arouse dread, awe, or terror **2 a** : notable by reason of extreme size, power, greatness, or excellence ⟨~ problems⟩ ⟨a writer of ~ talent⟩ — often used as a generalized term of approval ⟨had a ~ time⟩ **b** : unusually large : HUGE ⟨a ~ number of people⟩ *syn* see MONSTROUS — **tre·men·dous·ly** *adv* — **tre·men·dous·ness** *n*

trem·o·lite \ˈtre-mə-ˌlīt\ *n* [F *trémolite,* fr. *Tremola,* valley in Switzerland] (1799) : a white or gray mineral of the amphibole group that is a silicate of calcium and magnesium — **trem·o·lit·ic** \ˌtre-mə-ˈli-tik\ *adj*

trem·o·lo \ˈtre-mə-ˌlō\ *n, pl* **-los** [It, fr. *tremolo* tremulous, fr. L *tremulus*] (ca. 1801) **1 a :** the rapid reiteration of a musical tone or of alternating tones to produce a tremulous effect **b :** vocal vibrato esp. when prominent or excessive **2 :** a mechanical device in an organ for causing a tremulous effect

trem·or \ˈtre-mər\ *n* [ME *tremour,* fr. AF *tremor,* fr. L, fr. *tremere*] (14c) **1 a :** a trembling or shaking usu. from physical weakness, emotional stress, or disease **b :** nervous excitement **2 :** a quivering or vibratory motion; *esp* **:** a discrete small movement following or preceding a major seismic event **3 a :** a feeling of uncertainty or insecurity ⟨a ~ of hesitation⟩ **b :** a cause of such a feeling

trem·u·lant \ˈtrem-yə-lənt\ *adj* [ML *tremulant-, tremulans,* prp. of *tremulare* — more at TREMBLE] (1837) **:** TREMULOUS, TREMBLING

trem·u·lous \-ləs\ *adj* [L *tremulus* — more at TREMBLE] (1611) **1 :** characterized by or affected with trembling or tremors **2 :** affected with timidity **:** TIMOROUS **3 :** such as is or might be caused by nervousness or shakiness ⟨a ~ smile⟩ **4 :** exceedingly sensitive **:** easily shaken or disordered — **trem·u·lous·ly** *adv* — **trem·u·lous·ness** *n*

[1]**trench** \ˈtrench\ *n* [ME *trenche* track cut through a wood, fr. AF, act of cutting, ditch, fr. *trencher, trenchier* to cut, prob. fr. VL **trinicare* to cut in three, fr. L *trini* three each — more at TRINE] (15c) **1 a :** a long cut in the ground **:** DITCH; *esp* **:** one used for military defense often with the excavated dirt thrown up in front **b** *pl* **:** a place, position, or level at which an activity is carried on in a manner likened to trench warfare — often used in the phrase *in the trenches* ⟨activists working in the ~*es*⟩ **2 :** a long, narrow, and usu. steep-sided depression in the ocean floor — compare TROUGH **3 :** TRENCH COAT

[2]**trench** *vt* (15c) **1 :** to make a cut in **:** CARVE **2 a :** to protect with or as if with a trench **b :** to cut a trench in **:** DITCH ~ *vi* **1 a :** ENTRENCH, ENCROACH ⟨~*ing* on other domains which were more vital —Sir Winston Churchill⟩ **b :** to come close **:** VERGE **2 :** to dig a trench

tren·chan·cy \ˈtren-chən(t)-sē\ *n* (1866) **:** the quality or state of being trenchant

tren·chant \-chənt\ *adj* [ME *trenchaunt,* fr. AF, prp. of *trencher*] (14c) **1 :** KEEN, SHARP **2 :** vigorously effective and articulate ⟨a ~ analysis⟩; *also* **:** CAUSTIC ⟨~ remarks⟩ **3 a :** sharply perceptive **:** PENETRATING ⟨a ~ view of current conditions⟩ **b :** CLEAR-CUT, DISTINCT ⟨the ~ divisions between right and wrong —Edith Wharton⟩ — **tren·chant·ly** *adv*

trench coat *n* (1916) **1 :** a waterproof overcoat with a removable lining designed for wear in trenches **2 :** a usu. double-breasted raincoat with deep pockets, wide belt, and often straps on the shoulders

trenched \ˈtrencht\ *adj* (1541) **1 :** furrowed or drained by trenches **2 :** provided with protective trenches

[1]**tren·cher** \ˈtren-chər\ *n* [ME *trenchour* knife, serving platter, fr. AF, fr. *trencher* to cut] (14c) **:** a wooden platter for serving food

[2]**trencher** *adj* (14c) **1 :** of or relating to a trencher or to meals **2** *archaic* **:** having the nature of a parasite **:** SYCOPHANTIC

[3]**trench·er** \ˈtren-chər\ *n* [[2]*trench*] (1851) **:** one that digs trenches; *specif* **:** a usu. self-propelled excavating machine typically employing a bucket conveyor and used to dig trenches esp. for pipelines and cables

tren·cher·man \ˈtren-chər-mən\ *n* (1590) **1 :** a hearty eater **2** *archaic* **:** HANGER-ON, SPONGER

trench fever *n* (1915) **:** a disease that is usu. marked by fever and pain in muscles, bones, and joints and that is caused by a bacterium (*Bartonella quintana* syn. *Rochalimaea quintana*) transmitted by the human body louse (*Pediculus humanus humanus*)

trench foot *n* (1915) **:** a painful foot disorder resembling frostbite and resulting from prolonged exposure to cold and wet

trench mouth *n* (1918) **1 :** VINCENT'S ANGINA **2 :** VINCENT'S INFECTION

trench warfare *n* (1915) **:** warfare in which the opposing forces attack and counterattack from a relatively permanent system of trenches protected by barbed-wire entanglements

[1]**trend** \ˈtrend\ *vi* [ME, to turn, revolve, fr. OE *trendan;* akin to MHG *trendel* disk, spinning top] (1598) **1 a :** to extend in a general direction **:** follow a general course ⟨mountain ranges ~*ing* north and south⟩ **b :** to veer in a new direction **:** BEND ⟨a coastline that ~*s* westward⟩ **2 a :** to show a tendency **:** INCLINE ⟨prices ~*ing* upward⟩ **b :** to become deflected **:** SHIFT ⟨opinions ~*ing* toward conservatism⟩

[2]**trend** *n* (ca. 1777) **1 :** a line of general direction or movement ⟨the ~ of the coast turned toward the west⟩ **2 a :** a prevailing tendency or inclination **:** DRIFT ⟨current ~*s* in education⟩ **b :** a general movement **:** SWING ⟨the ~ toward suburban living⟩ **c :** a current style or preference **:** VOGUE ⟨new fashion ~*s*⟩ **d :** a line of development **:** APPROACH ⟨new ~*s* in cancer research⟩ **3 :** the general movement over time of a statistically detectable change; *also* **:** a statistical curve reflecting such a change ***syn*** see TENDENCY

trend·oid \ˈtren-ˌdȯid\ *n* (1985) **:** a trendy person

trend·set·ter \ˈtren(d)-ˌse-tər\ *n* (1960) **:** one that sets a trend

trend·set·ting \-ˌse-tiŋ\ *adj* (1960) **:** that sets a trend ⟨a ~ design⟩

trendy \ˈtren-dē\ *adj* **trend·i·er; -est** (1962) **1 :** very fashionable **:** UP-TO-DATE ⟨he's a ~ dresser —*Sunday Mirror*⟩ **2 :** marked by ephemeral, superficial, or faddish appeal or taste ⟨~ ideas about success⟩ — **trend·i·ly** \-də-lē\ *adv* — **trend·i·ness** \-dē-nəs\ *n* — **trendy** \-dē\ *n*

[1]**tre·pan** \tri-ˈpan\ *vt* **tre·panned; tre·pan·ning** [ME, fr. *trepane* trephine] (15c) **1 :** to use a trephine on (the skull) **2 :** to remove a disk or cylindrical core (as from metal for testing) — **trep·a·na·tion** \ˌtre-pə-ˈnā-shən\ *n*

[2]**tre·pan** \ˈtrē-ˌpan, tri-ˈpan\ *n* [ME *trepane* trephine, AF *trepan,* fr. ML *trepanum,* fr. Gk *trypanon* auger, fr. *trypan* to bore] (ca. 1877) **:** a heavy tool used in boring mine shafts

[3]**tre·pan** \tri-ˈpan\ *n* [origin unknown] (1641) **1** *archaic* **:** TRICKSTER **2** *archaic* **:** a deceptive device **:** SNARE

[4]**tre·pan** \tri-ˈpan\ *vt* **tre·panned; tre·pan·ning** (ca. 1656) *archaic* **:** ENTRAP, LURE

tre·pang \tri-ˈpaŋ, ˈtrē-ˌ\ *n* [Malay *tĕripang*] (1783) **:** any of several large sea cucumbers (as of the genera *Actinopyga* and *Holothuria*) that are taken mostly in the southwestern Pacific and are boiled, dried, and used esp. in Asian cuisine — called also *bêche-de-mer*

treph·i·na·tion \ˌtre-fə-ˈnā-shən\ *n* (1874) **:** an act or instance of perforating the skull with a surgical instrument

tre·phine \ˈtrē-ˌfīn\ *n* [F *tréphine,* fr. obs. E *trefine, trafine,* fr. L *tres fines* three ends, fr. *tres* three + *fines,* pl. of *finis* end — more at THREE] (1628) **:** a surgical instrument for cutting out circular sections (as of bone or corneal tissue) — **trephine** *vt*

trep·id \ˈtre-pəd\ *adj* [L *trepidus*] (1650) **:** TIMOROUS, FEARFUL

trep·i·dant \ˈtre-pə-dənt\ *adj* [L *trepidant-, trepidans,* prp. of *trepidare*] (1892) **:** TIMID, TREMBLING

trep·i·da·tion \ˌtre-pə-ˈdā-shən\ *n* [L *trepidation-, trepidatio,* fr. *trepidare* to tremble, fr. *trepidus* agitated; prob. akin to OE *thrafian* to urge, push, Gk *trapein* to press grapes] (1605) **1** *archaic* **:** a tremulous motion **:** TREMOR **2 :** timorous uncertain agitation **:** APPREHENSION ⟨~ about starting a new job⟩ ***syn*** see FEAR

trep·i·da·tious *also* **trep·i·da·cious** \ˌtre-pə-ˈdā-shəs\ *adj* (1904) **:** feeling trepidation **:** APPREHENSIVE — **trep·i·da·tious·ly** *adv*

trep·o·ne·ma \ˌtre-pə-ˈnē-mə\ *n, pl* **-ma·ta** \-mə-tə\ *or* **-mas** [NL *Treponemat-, Treponema,* fr. Gk *trepein* to turn + *nēma* thread, fr. *nēn* to spin — more at NEEDLE] (1908) **:** any of a genus (*Treponema*) of spirochetes that are pathogenic in humans and other warm-blooded animals and include the causative agents of syphilis and yaws — **trep·o·ne·mal** \-məl\ *adj*

trep·o·ne·ma·to·sis \-ˌnē-mə-ˈtō-səs, -ˌne-\ *n, pl* **-to·ses** \-ˌsēz\ [NL] (1927) **:** infection with or disease caused by treponemata

trep·o·neme \ˈtre-pə-ˌnēm\ *n* (1919) **:** TREPONEMA

[1]**tres·pass** \ˈtres-pəs, -ˌpas\ *n* [ME *trespas,* fr. AF, passage, overstepping, misdeed, fr. *trespasser*] (13c) **1 a :** a violation of moral or social ethics **:** TRANSGRESSION; *esp* **:** SIN **b :** an unwarranted infringement **2 a :** an unlawful act committed on the person, property, or rights of another; *esp* **:** a wrongful entry on real property **b :** the legal action for injuries resulting from trespass

[2]**trespass** \-ˌpas *also* -pəs\ *vb* [ME, fr. AF *trespasser* to overtake, exceed, wrong, fr. *tres* to a high degree (fr. L *trans* beyond) + *passer* to pass — more at THROUGH, PASS] *vi* (14c) **1 a :** ERR, SIN **b :** to make an unwarranted or uninvited incursion **2 :** to commit a trespass; *esp* **:** to enter unlawfully upon the land of another ~ *vt* **:** VIOLATE ⟨~ the bounds of good taste⟩ — **tres·pass·er** *n*

syn TRESPASS, ENCROACH, INFRINGE, INVADE mean to make inroads upon the property, territory, or rights of another. TRESPASS implies an unwarranted or unlawful intrusion ⟨hunters *trespassing* on farmland⟩. ENCROACH suggests gradual or stealthy entrance upon another's territory or usurpation of another's rights or possessions ⟨the *encroaching* settlers displacing the native peoples⟩. INFRINGE implies an encroachment clearly violating a right or prerogative ⟨*infringing* a copyright⟩. INVADE implies a hostile and injurious entry into the territory or sphere of another ⟨accused of *invading* their privacy⟩.

tress \ˈtres\ *n* [ME *tresse,* fr. AF *tresce*] (14c) **1 :** a long lock of hair; *esp* **:** the long unbound hair of a woman — usu. used in pl. **2** *archaic* **:** a plait of hair **:** BRAID

tressed \ˈtrest\ *adj* (14c) **1** *obs* **:** being braided **:** PLAITED **2 :** having tresses — usu. used in combination ⟨golden-*tressed*⟩

tres·tle *also* **tres·sel** \ˈtre-səl *also* ˈtrə-\ *n* [ME *trestel,* fr. AF, fr. VL **trastellum,* fr. L *transtillum,* dim. of *transtrum* traverse beam, fr. *trans* across — more at THROUGH] (13c) **1 :** a braced frame serving as a support **2 :** HORSE 2b **3 :** a braced framework of timbers, piles, or steelwork for carrying a road or railroad over a depression

trestle table *n* (1883) **:** a table supported on trestles

tres·tle·work \-ˌwərk\ *n* (1848) **:** a system of connected trestles supporting a structure (as a railroad bridge)

tre·tin·o·in \tre-ˈti-nə-win\ *n* [perh. fr. trans- + *retino*ic acid] (1980) **:** the all-trans isomer of retinoic acid that is applied to the skin to treat severe acne and reduce facial wrinkles, roughness, and pigmented spots

tre·val·ly \trə-ˈva-lē\ *n, pl* **-lies** *also* **-lys** [origin unknown] (1871) **:** any of various carangid fishes (esp. genus *Caranx*)

trews \ˈtrüz\ *n pl* [ScGael *triubhas*] (ca. 1568) **1** *chiefly Brit* **:** [3]PANT 1; *esp* **:** tight-fitting trousers usu. of tartan **2 :** close-cut tartan shorts worn under the kilt in Highland dress

T. rex \ˈtē-ˈreks\ *n* [NL, short for *Tyrannosaurus rex*] (1982) **:** TYRANNOSAUR

trey \ˈtrā\ *n, pl* **treys** [ME *treye, treis,* fr. AF *trei, treis* three, fr. L *tres* — more at THREE] (14c) **1 :** the side of a die or domino that has three spots **2 :** a card numbered three or having three main pips **3 :** a shot in basketball that counts for three points

tri- *comb form* [L (fr. *tri-, tres*) & Gk, fr. *tri-, treis* — more at THREE] **1 :** three **:** having three elements or parts ⟨*tri*graph⟩ **2 :** into three ⟨*tri*sect⟩ **3 a :** thrice ⟨*tri*weekly⟩ **b :** every third ⟨*tri*monthly⟩

tri·able \ˈtrī-ə-bəl\ *adj* (15c) **:** liable or subject to judicial or quasi-judicial examination or trial

tri·ac·e·tate \(ˌ)trī-ˈa-sə-ˌtāt\ *n* [ISV] (1895) **1 :** an acetate containing three CH_3COO- groups **2 :** a textile fiber or fabric consisting of cellulose that is completely or almost completely acetylated

tri·ad \ˈtrī-ˌad *also* -əd\ *n* [L *triad-, trias,* fr. Gk, fr. *treis* three] (1546) **1 :** a union or group of three **:** TRINITY **2 :** a chord of three tones consisting of a root with its third and fifth and constituting the harmonic basis of tonal music — **tri·ad·ic** \trī-ˈa-dik\ *adj* — **tri·ad·i·cal·ly** \-di-k(ə-)lē\ *adv*

tri·age \trē-ˈäzh, ˈtrē-ˌ\ *n* [F, sorting, sifting, fr. *trier* to sort, fr. OF — more at TRY] (1918) **1 a :** the sorting of and allocation of treatment to patients and esp. battle and disaster victims according to a system of priorities designed to maximize the number of survivors **b :** the sorting of patients (as in an emergency room) according to the urgency of their need for care **2 :** the assigning of priority order to projects on the basis of where funds and other resources can be best used, are most needed, or are most likely to achieve success — **triage** *vt*

[1]**tri·al** \ˈtrī(-ə)l\ *n* [AF, fr. *trier* to try] (15c) **1 a :** the action or process of trying or putting to the proof **:** TEST **b :** a preliminary contest (as in a sport) **2 :** the formal examination before a competent tribunal of the matter in issue in a civil or criminal cause in order to determine such issue **3 :** a test of faith, patience, or stamina through subjection to suffering or temptation; *broadly* **:** a source of vexation or annoyance **4 a :** a tryout or experiment to test quality, value, or usefulness — compare CLINICAL TRIAL **b :** one of a number of repetitions of an experiment **5 :** ATTEMPT

[2]**trial** *adj* (1555) **1 :** of, relating to, or used in a trial **2 :** made or done as a test or experiment **3 :** used or tried out in a test or experiment
trial and error *n* (1806) **:** a finding out of the best way to reach a desired result or a correct solution by trying out one or more ways or means and by noting and eliminating errors or causes of failure; *also* **:** the trying of one thing or another until something succeeds
trial balance *n* (1838) **:** a list of the debit and credit balances of accounts in a double-entry ledger at a given date prepared primarily to test their equality
trial balloon *n* (1935) **:** a project or scheme tentatively announced in order to test public opinion
trial court *n* (1889) **:** the court before which issues of fact and law are first determined as distinguished from an appellate court
trial examiner *n* (1949) **:** a person appointed to hold hearings and to investigate and report facts sometimes with recommendations to an administrative or quasi-judicial agency or tribunal
trial horse *n* (1901) **:** one set up as an opponent for a champion in trial competitions or workouts
trial jury *n* (1884) **:** a jury impaneled to try a cause **:** PETIT JURY
trial lawyer *n* (ca. 1914) **:** a lawyer who engages chiefly in the trial of cases before courts of original jurisdiction
tri·a·logue \ˈtrī-ə-ˌlȯg, -ˌläg\ *n* [*tri-* + *-alogue* (as in *dialogue*)] (1532) **:** a scene, discourse, or colloquy in which three persons share
trial run *n* (1903) **:** a testing exercise **:** EXPERIMENT
tri·am·cin·o·lone \ˌtrī-ˌam-ˈsi-nə-ˌlōn\ *n* [*tri-* + *-amcin-* (alter. of *American Cyanimid* Company) + [1]*-ol* + *-one*] (1957) **:** a glucocorticoid drug $C_{21}H_{27}FO_6$ used chiefly in the form of its acetal or acetate derivatives esp. in treating skin disorders, asthma, and allergic rhinitis
tri·an·gle \ˈtrī-ˌaŋ-gəl\ *n* [ME, fr. AF, fr. L *triangulum*, fr. neut. of *triangulus* triangular, fr. *tri-* + *angulus* angle] (14c) **1 :** a polygon having three sides — compare SPHERICAL TRIANGLE **2 a :** a percussion instrument consisting of a rod of steel bent into the form of a triangle open at one angle and sounded by striking with a small metal rod **b :** a drafting instrument consisting of a thin flat right-angled triangle of wood or plastic with acute angles of 45 degrees or of 30 degrees and 60 degrees **3 :** a situation in which one member of a couple is involved in a love affair with a third person

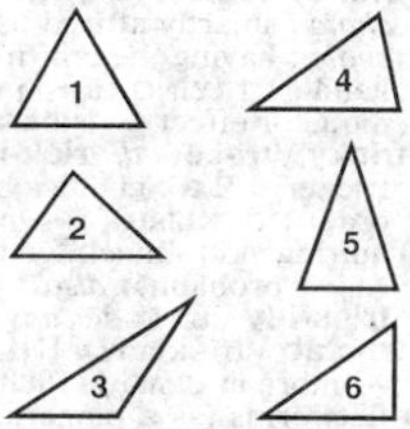

triangle 1: *1* equilateral, *2* acute, *3* obtuse, *4* scalene, *5* isosceles, *6* right triangle

triangle inequality *n* [fr. its application to the distances between three points in a coordinate system] (1941) **:** an inequality stating that the absolute value of a sum is less than or equal to the sum of the absolute values of the terms
tri·an·gu·lar \trī-ˈaŋ-gyə-lər\ *adj* [ME *trianguler*, fr. LL *triangularis*, fr. L *triangulum*] (14c) **1 a :** of, relating to, or having the form of a triangle ⟨a ~ plot of land⟩ **b :** having a triangular base or principal surface ⟨a ~ table⟩ ⟨a ~ pyramid⟩ **2 a** (1) **:** of, relating to, or involving three elements ⟨a ~ agreement⟩ (2) *of a military group* **:** based primarily on three units **b :** of or relating to a love triangle — **tri·an·gu·lar·i·ty** \(ˌ)trī-ˌaŋ-gyə-ˈla-rə-tē\ *n* — **tri·an·gu·lar·ly** \trī-ˈaŋ-gyə-lər-lē\ *adv*
triangular number *n* (1795) **:** a number (as 3, 6, 10, 15) representable by that many dots arranged in rows that form a triangle and that equals

$$\frac{n(n+1)}{2}$$

for some positive integer value of *n*
[1]**tri·an·gu·late** \trī-ˈaŋ-gyə-lət\ *adj* [ML *triangulatus*, pp. of *triangulare* to make triangles, fr. L *triangulum*] (1766) **:** consisting of or marked with triangles
[2]**tri·an·gu·late** \-ˌlāt\ *vt* **-lat·ed; -lat·ing** (1833) **1 :** to survey, map, or determine by triangulation **2 a :** to divide into triangles **b :** to give triangular form to
tri·an·gu·la·tion \(ˌ)trī-ˌaŋ-gyə-ˈlā-shən\ *n* (1818) **:** the measurement of the elements necessary to determine the network of triangles into which any part of the earth's surface is divided in surveying; *broadly* **:** any similar trigonometric operation for finding a position or location by means of bearings from two fixed points a known distance apart
tri·ar·chy \ˈtrī-ˌär-kē\ *n, pl* **-chies** [Gk *triarchia*, fr. *tri-* + *-archia* -archy] (ca. 1656) **1 :** government by three persons **:** TRIUMVIRATE **2 :** a country under three rulers
Tri·as·sic \trī-ˈa-sik\ *adj* [ISV, fr. L *trias* triad; fr. the three subdivisions of the European Triassic — more at TRIAD] (1841) **:** of, relating to, or being the earliest period of the Mesozoic era or the corresponding system of rocks marked by the first appearance of the dinosaurs — see GEOLOGIC TIME table — **Triassic** *n*
tri·ath·lete \trī-ˈath-ˌlēt, ÷-ˈa-thə-\ *n* (1982) **:** an athlete who competes in a triathlon
tri·ath·lon \trī-ˈath-lən, -ˌlän, ÷-ˈa-thə-\ *n* [*tri-* + *-athlon* (as in *decathlon*)] (1973) **:** an athletic contest that is a long-distance race consisting of three phases (as swimming, bicycling, and running)
tri·atom·ic \ˌtrī-ə-ˈtä-mik\ *adj* [ISV] (1862) **:** having three atoms in the molecule ⟨ozone is ~ oxygen⟩
tri·ax·i·al \(ˌ)trī-ˈak-sē-əl\ *adj* [ISV] (1886) **:** having or involving three axes — **tri·ax·i·al·i·ty** \-ˌak-sē-ˈa-lə-tē\ *n*
tri·azine \ˈtrī-ə-ˌzēn, trī-ˈa-ˌzēn\ *n* [ISV] (1894) **:** any of three compounds $C_3H_3N_3$ containing a ring composed of three carbon and three nitrogen atoms; *also* **:** any of various derivatives of these including several (as atrazine and simazine) used as herbicides
trib *abbr* tributary
[1]**trib·al** \ˈtrī-bəl\ *adj* (1632) **:** of, relating to, or characteristic of a tribe ⟨~ customs⟩ — **trib·al·ly** \-bə-lē\ *adv*
[2]**tribal** *n* (1953) **:** a member of an aboriginal people of India — usu. used in pl.
trib·al·ism \-bə-ˌli-zəm\ *n* (1861) **1 :** tribal consciousness and loyalty; *esp* **:** exaltation of the tribe above other groups **2 :** strong in-group loyalty
tri·ba·sic \(ˌ)trī-ˈbā-sik\ *adj* (1837) **:** having three replaceable hydrogen atoms — used of acids
tribe \ˈtrīb\ *n* [ME, fr. L *tribus*, a division of the Roman people, tribe] (13c) **1 a :** a social group comprising numerous families, clans, or generations together with slaves, dependents, or adopted strangers **b :** a political division of the Roman people orig. representing one of the three original tribes of ancient Rome **c :** PHYLE **2 :** a group of persons having a common character, occupation, or interest **3 :** a category of taxonomic classification ranking below a subfamily; *also* **:** a natural group irrespective of taxonomic rank ⟨the cat ~⟩ ⟨the rose ~⟩
tribes·man \ˈtrībz-mən\ *n* (1798) **:** a member of a tribe
tribes·peo·ple \-ˌpē-pəl\ *n pl* (1888) **:** members of a tribe
tribo- *comb form* [F, fr. Gk *tribein* to rub; prob. akin to L *terere* to rub — more at THROW] **:** friction ⟨*tribo*luminescence⟩
tri·bo·elec·tric·i·ty \ˌtrī-bō-i-ˌlek-ˈtri-sə-tē, ˌtri-, -ˈtris-tē\ *n* (ca. 1917) **:** a charge of electricity generated by friction (as by rubbing glass with silk) — **tri·bo·elec·tric** \-ˈlek-trik\ *adj*
tri·bol·o·gy \trī-ˈbä-lə-jē, tri-\ *n* (1966) **:** a study that deals with the design, friction, wear, and lubrication of interacting surfaces in relative motion (as in bearings or gears) — **tri·bo·log·i·cal** \ˌtrī-bə-ˈlä-ji-kəl, ˌtri-\ *adj* — **tri·bol·o·gist** \trī-ˈbä-lə-jist, tri-\ *n*
tri·bo·lu·mi·nes·cence \ˌtrī-bō-ˌlü-mə-ˈne-sᵊn(t)s, ˈtri-\ *n* [ISV] (1889) **:** luminescence due to friction — **tri·bo·lu·mi·nes·cent** \-sᵊnt\ *adj*
tri·brach \ˈtrī-ˌbrak\ *n* [L *tribrachys*, fr. Gk, having three short syllables, fr. *tri-* + *brachys* short — more at BRIEF] (1589) **:** a metrical foot of three short syllables of which two belong to the thesis and one to the arsis — **tri·brach·ic** \trī-ˈbra-kik\ *adj*
trib·u·late \ˈtri-byə-ˌlāt\ *vt* **-lat·ed; -lat·ing** [LL *tribulatus*, pp. of *tribulare*] (ca. 1637) **:** to cause to endure tribulation
trib·u·la·tion \ˌtri-byə-ˈlā-shən\ *n* [ME *tribulacion*, fr. AF, fr. L *tribulation-, tribulatio*, fr. *tribulare* to press, oppress, fr. *tribulum* drag used in threshing, fr. *terere* to rub — more at THROW] (13c) **:** distress or suffering resulting from oppression or persecution; *also* **:** a trying experience ⟨the trials and ~*s* of starting a new business⟩
tri·bu·nal \trī-ˈbyü-nᵊl, tri-\ *n* [ME, fr. L, platform for magistrates, fr. *tribunus* tribune] (15c) **1 :** [2]TRIBUNE **2 :** a court or forum of justice **3 :** something that decides or determines ⟨the ~ of public opinion⟩
tri·bu·nate \ˈtri-byə-ˌnāt, tri-ˈbyü-nət\ *n* (1546) **:** the office, function, or term of office of a tribune
[1]**tri·bune** \ˈtri-ˌbyün, tri-ˈ\ *n* [ME, fr. L *tribunus*, fr. *tribus* tribe] (14c) **1 :** a Roman official under the monarchy and the republic with the function of protecting the plebeian citizen from arbitrary action by the patrician magistrates **2 :** an unofficial defender of the rights of the individual — **tri·bune·ship** \-ˌship\ *n*
[2]**tribune** *n* [F, fr. It *tribuna*, fr. L *tribunal*] (ca. 1771) **:** a dais or platform from which an assembly is addressed
[1]**trib·u·tary** \ˈtri-byə-ˌter-ē\ *adj* (14c) **1 :** paying tribute to another to acknowledge submission, to obtain protection, or to purchase peace **:** SUBJECT **2 :** paid or owed as tribute ⟨~ gifts⟩ **3 :** channeling material or supplies into something more inclusive **:** CONTRIBUTORY
[2]**tributary** *n, pl* **-tar·ies** (14c) **1 :** a ruler or state that pays tribute to a conqueror **2 :** a stream feeding a larger stream or a lake
trib·ute \ˈtri-(ˌ)byüt, -byət\ *n* [ME *tribut*, fr. L *tributum*, fr. neut. of *tributus*, pp. of *tribuere* to allot, bestow, grant, pay, fr. *tribus* tribe] (14c) **1 a :** a payment by one ruler or nation to another in acknowledgment of submission or as the price of protection; *also* **:** the tax levied for such a payment **b** (1) **:** an excessive tax, rental, or tariff imposed by a government, sovereign, lord, or landlord (2) **:** an exorbitant charge levied by a person or group having the power of coercion **c :** the liability to pay tribute **2 a :** something given or contributed voluntarily as due or deserved; *esp* **:** a gift or service showing respect, gratitude, or affection ⟨a floral ~⟩ **b :** something (as material evidence or a formal attestation) that indicates the worth, virtue, or effectiveness of the one in question ⟨the design is a ~ to his ingenuity⟩ ***syn*** see ENCOMIUM
tri·bu·tyl·tin \trī-ˈbyü-tᵊl-tən\ *n* [*tri-* + *butyl* + [1]*tin*] (1962) **:** an organic compound of tin used as a biocide esp. in marine antifouling paints
tri·car·box·yl·ic \ˌtrī-ˌkär-ˌbäk-ˈsi-lik\ *adj* (1894) **:** containing three carboxyl groups in the molecule ⟨~ acid⟩
tricarboxylic acid cycle *n* (1945) **:** KREBS CYCLE
[1]**trice** \ˈtrīs\ *vt* **triced; tric·ing** [ME *trisen, tricen* to pull, trice, fr. MD *trisen* to hoist, fr. *trise* windlass] (15c) **:** to haul up or in and lash or secure (as a sail) with a small rope
[2]**trice** *n* [ME *trise*, lit., pull, fr. *trisen*] (15c) **:** a brief space of time **:** INSTANT — used chiefly in the phrase *in a trice*
tri·ceps \ˈtrī-ˌseps\ *n, pl* **triceps** [NL *tricipit-, triceps*, fr. L, three-headed, fr. *tri-* + *capit-, caput* head — more at HEAD] (1676) **:** a muscle that arises from three heads; *esp* **:** the large extensor muscle along the back of the upper arm
tri·cer·a·tops \(ˌ)trī-ˈser-ə-ˌtäps\ *n, pl* **-tops** *also* **-tops·es** \-ˌtäp-səz\ [NL, fr. *tri-* + Gk *kerat-, keras* horn + *ōps* face — more at HORN, EYE] (1892) **:** any of a genus (*Triceratops*) of large herbivorous quadrupedal ceratopsian dinosaurs of the Late Cretaceous with three horns, a bony hood or crest on the neck, and hoofed toes
-trices *pl of* -TRIX
trich- *or* **tricho-** *comb form* [NL, fr. Gk, fr. *trich-, thrix* hair] **:** hair **:** filament ⟨*tricho*gyne⟩
tri·chi·a·sis \tri-ˈkī-ə-səs\ *n* [LL, fr. Gk, fr. *trich-* + *-iasis*] (1661) **:** a turning inward of the eyelashes often causing irritation of the eyeball
tri·chi·na \tri-ˈkī-nə\ *n, pl* **-nae** \-(ˌ)nē\ *also* **-nas** [NL, fr. Gk *trichinos* made of hair, fr. *trich-, thrix* hair] (1835) **:** a small slender nematode worm (*Trichinella spiralis*) that is a parasite of flesh-eating mammals (as humans and swine) with larvae that migrate from the intestines to striated muscles where they become encysted — **tri·chi·nal** \-nᵊl\ *adj*
trich·i·nize \ˈtri-kə-ˌnīz\ *vt* **-nized; -niz·ing** (1864) **:** to infest with trichinae ⟨*trichinized* pork⟩

trich·i·no·sis \ˌtri-kə-ˈnō-səs\ *n* [NL] (1866) **:** infestation with or disease caused by trichinae and marked esp. by muscular pain, dyspnea, fever, weakness, and edema
tri·chi·nous \ˈtri-kə-nəs, tri-ˈkī-\ *adj* [ISV] (1857) **1 :** infested with trichinae ⟨~ meat⟩ **2 :** of, relating to, or involving trichinae or trichinosis ⟨~ infection⟩
tri·chlor·fon *also* **tri·chlor·phon** \(ˌ)trī-ˈklȯr-ˌfän\ *n* [*tri-* + *chlor-* + *-fon* (irreg. fr. *phosphonate,* a salt derived from phosphine)] (1960) **:** a crystalline compound $C_4H_8Cl_3O_4P$ used esp. as an insecticide
tri·chlo·ro·ace·tic acid \ˌtrī-ˌklȯr-ō-ə-ˈsē-tik-\ *also* **tri·chlor·ace·tic acid** \-ˌklȯr-ə-ˈsē-tik-\ *n* [ISV] (1885) **:** a strong vesicant pungent acid $C_2Cl_3HO_2$ used in weed control and in medicine as a caustic and astringent
tri·chlo·ro·eth·y·lene \-ˈe-thə-ˌlēn\ *n* (ca. 1919) **:** a nonflammable toxic liquid C_2HCl_3 used esp. as an industrial solvent
tricho·cyst \ˈtri-kə-ˌsist\ *n* (1859) **:** any of the minute lassoing or stinging organelles of protozoans and esp. of many ciliates
trich·o·gram·ma wasp \ˌtri-kə-ˈgra-mə-\ *n* [NL, fr. *trich-* + Gk *gramma* letter, small weight — more at GRAM] (1972) **:** any of a genus (*Trichogramma*) of minute chalcid wasps that are parasitic as larvae in the eggs of other insects and are used in the biological control of lepidopteran pests
tricho·gyne \-ˌjīn, -ˌgīn\ *n* [ISV] (ca. 1875) **:** a slender terminal prolongation of the ascogonium of a fungus that may serve as a fertilization tube; *also* **:** a similar reproductive structure in a red alga
tri·chol·o·gist \tri-ˈkä-lə-jist\ *n* (1887) **:** a person who specializes in hair and scalp care; *broadly* **:** HAIRDRESSER 1 — **tri·chol·o·gy** \-jē\ *n*
tri·chome \ˈtri-ˌkōm, ˈtrī-\ *n* [G *Trichom,* fr. Gk *trichōma* growth of hair, fr. *trichoun* to cover with hair, fr. *trich-, thrix* hair] (1875) **:** a filamentous outgrowth; *esp* **:** an epidermal hair structure on a plant
tricho·mo·nad \ˌtri-kə-ˈmō-ˌnad, -nəd\ *n* [NL *Trichomonad-, Trichomonas,* fr. *trich-* + LL *monad-, monas* monad] (1861) **:** any of a genus (*Trichomonas*) of flagellated protozoans parasitic in many animals — **trichomonad** *or* **tricho·mo·nal** \-ˈmō-nᵊl\ *adj*
trich·o·mo·nas \ˌtri-kə-ˈmō-nəs\ *n* [NL] (1917) **:** TRICHOMONAD
tricho·mo·ni·a·sis \ˌtri-kə-mə-ˈnī-ə-səs\ *n, pl* **-a·ses** \-ˌsēz\ [NL, fr. *Trichomonas* + *-iasis*] (1915) **:** infection with or disease caused by trichomonads: as **a :** a human sexually transmitted disease occurring esp. as vaginitis with a persistent discharge and caused by a trichomonad (*Trichomonas vaginalis*) that may also invade the male urethra and bladder **b :** a venereal disease of domestic cattle marked by abortion and sterility **c :** one or more diseases of various birds resembling blackhead
tri·chop·ter·an \tri-ˈkäp-tə-rən\ *n* [ultim. fr. Gk *trich-, thrix* hair + *pteron* wing — more at FEATHER] (ca. 1842) **:** CADDIS FLY — **trichopteran** *adj*
tricho·the·cene \ˌtri-kə-ˈthē-ˌsēn\ *n* [NL *Trichothecium* (fr. *trich-* + *-thecium*) + E *-ene*] (1971) **:** any of several mycotoxins that are produced by various fungi (as genera *Fusarium* and *Trichothecium*) and that include some contaminants of livestock feed and some held to be found in yellow rain
tricho·til·lo·ma·nia \ˌtri-kə-ˌti-lə-ˈmā-nē-ə\ *n* [NL, fr. *trich-* + Gk *tillein* to pull, pluck + NL *mania*] (ca. 1903) **:** an abnormal desire to pull out one's hair
tri·chot·o·mous \trī-ˈkä-tə-məs\ *adj* [LGk *trichotomein* to trisect, fr. Gk *tricha* in three (akin to *treis* three) + *-tomein* (akin to *temnein* to cut) — more at THREE, TOME] (1800) **:** divided or dividing into three parts or into threes ⟨~ branching⟩ — **tri·chot·o·mous·ly** *adv*
tri·chot·o·my \-mē\ *n, pl* **-mies** (1610) **:** division into three parts, elements, or classes
tri·chro·mat \ˈtrī-krō-ˌmat, (ˌ)trī-ˈ\ *n* [back-formation fr. *trichromatic*] (1929) **:** a person with trichromatism
tri·chro·mat·ic \ˌtrī-krō-ˈma-tik\ *adj* (ca. 1890) **1 :** of, relating to, or consisting of three colors ⟨~ light⟩ **2 a :** relating to or being the theory that human color vision involves three types of retinal sensory receptors **b :** characterized by trichromatism ⟨~ vision⟩
tri·chro·ma·tism \(ˌ)trī-ˈkrō-mə-ˌti-zəm\ *n* (ca. 1895) **:** color vision based on the perception of three primary colors and esp. red, green, and blue
¹**trick** \ˈtrik\ *n* [ME *trikke,* fr. AF **trik,* fr. *trikier* to deceive, cheat, fr. VL **triccare,* alter. of L *tricari* to behave evasively, shuffle, fr. *tricae* complications, trifles] (15c) **1 a :** a crafty procedure or practice meant to deceive or defraud **b :** a mischievous act **:** PRANK **c :** an indiscreet or childish action **d :** a deceptive, dexterous, or ingenious feat; *esp* **:** one designed to puzzle or amuse ⟨a juggler's ~*s*⟩ **2 a :** a habitual peculiarity of behavior or manner ⟨a horse with the ~ of shying⟩ **b :** a characteristic and identifying feature ⟨a ~ of speech⟩ **c :** a delusive appearance esp. when caused by art or legerdemain **:** an optical illusion ⟨a mere ~ of the light⟩ **3 a (1) :** a quick or artful way of getting a result **:** KNACK ⟨the ~ is to make it look natural⟩ **(2) :** an instance of getting a desired result ⟨one small adjustment will do the ~⟩ **b :** a technical device (as of an art or craft) ⟨the ~*s* of stage technique⟩ **4 :** the cards played in one round of a card game often used as a scoring unit **5 a :** a turn of duty at the helm usu. lasting for two hours **b :** SHIFT 4b(1) **c :** a trip taken as part of one's employment **d :** a sexual act performed by a prostitute ⟨turning ~*s*⟩; *also* **:** JOHN 2 **6 :** an attractive child or woman ⟨a cute little ~⟩
syn TRICK, RUSE, STRATAGEM, MANEUVER, ARTIFICE, WILE, FEINT mean an indirect means to gain an end. TRICK may imply deception, roguishness, illusion, and either an evil or harmless end ⟨the *tricks* of the trade⟩. RUSE stresses an attempt to mislead by a false impression ⟨the *ruses* of smugglers⟩. STRATAGEM implies a ruse used to entrap, outwit, circumvent, or surprise an opponent or enemy ⟨the *stratagem*-filled game⟩. MANEUVER suggests adroit and skillful avoidance of difficulty ⟨last-minute *maneuvers* to avert bankruptcy⟩. ARTIFICE implies ingenious contrivance or invention ⟨the clever *artifices* of the stage⟩. WILE suggests an attempt to entrap or deceive with false allurements ⟨used all of his *wiles* to ingratiate himself⟩. FEINT implies a diversion or distraction of attention away from one's real intent ⟨a *feint* toward the enemy's left flank⟩.
²**trick** *vt* (ca. 1500) **1 :** to dress or adorn fancifully or ornately **:** ORNAMENT ⟨~*ed* out in a gaudy uniform⟩ **2 :** to deceive by cunning or artifice **:** CHEAT
³**trick** *adj* (ca. 1530) **1 :** TRIG **2 a :** of or relating to or involving tricks or trickery ⟨~ photography⟩ ⟨~ dice⟩ **b :** skilled in or used for tricks ⟨a ~ horse⟩ **3 a :** somewhat defective and unreliable ⟨a ~ lock⟩ **b :** inclined to give way unexpectedly ⟨a ~ knee⟩
trick·er \ˈtri-kər\ *n* (1534) **:** one that tricks **:** TRICKSTER
trick·ery \ˈtri-k(ə-)rē\ *n* (1796) **:** the practice of crafty underhanded ingenuity to deceive or cheat ***syn*** see DECEPTION
trick·ish \ˈtri-kish\ *adj* (1703) **:** given to or characterized by tricks or trickery **:** TRICKY — **trick·ish·ly** *adv* — **trick·ish·ness** *n*
¹**trick·le** \ˈtri-kəl\ *vi* **trick·led; trick·ling** \-k(ə-)liŋ\ [ME *trikelen,* of imit. origin] (14c) **1 a :** to issue or fall in drops **b :** to flow in a thin gentle stream **2 a :** to move or go one by one or little by little ⟨customers began to ~ in⟩ **b :** to dissipate slowly ⟨his enthusiasm *trickled* away⟩
²**trickle** *n* (1580) **:** a thin, slow, or intermittent stream or movement
trickle–down *adj* (1944) **1 :** relating to or working on the principle of trickle-down theory ⟨~ economics⟩ **2 :** relating to or being an effect caused gradually by remote or indirect influences
trickle–down theory *n* (1954) **:** a theory that financial benefits given to big business will in turn pass down to smaller businesses and consumers
trick or treat *n* (ca. 1941) **:** a children's Halloween practice of asking for treats from door to door under threat of playing tricks on those who refuse — **trick–or–treat** *vi* — **trick–or–treater** *n*
trick·ster \ˈtrik-stər\ *n* (1711) **:** one who tricks: as **a :** a dishonest person who defrauds others by trickery **b :** a person (as a stage magician) skilled in the use of tricks and illusion **c :** a cunning or deceptive character appearing in various forms in the folklore of many cultures
tricksy \ˈtrik-sē\ *adj* **tricks·i·er; -est** [*tricks,* pl. of *trick*] (1552) **1** *archaic* **:** smartly attired **:** SPRUCE **2 :** full of tricks **:** PRANKISH **3 a** *archaic* **:** having the craftiness of a trickster **b :** difficult to cope with or handle **:** TRYING ⟨a ~ job⟩ **4** *chiefly Brit* **:** ornately contrived in technique or effect — **tricks·i·ness** *n*
tricky \ˈtri-kē\ *adj* **trick·i·er; -est** (1786) **1 :** inclined to or marked by trickery **2 a :** giving a deceptive impression of easiness, simplicity, or order **:** TICKLISH ⟨a ~ path through the swamp⟩ **b :** TRICK 3 **3 :** requiring skill, knack, or caution (as in doing or handling) **:** DIFFICULT ⟨a ~ problem⟩; *also* **:** INGENIOUS ⟨a ~ rhythm⟩ ***syn*** see SLY — **trick·i·ly** \ˈtri-kə-lē\ *adv* — **trick·i·ness** \ˈtri-kē-nəs\ *n*
tri·clad \ˈtrī-ˌklad\ *n* [NL *Tricladida,* ultim. fr. *tri-* + Gk *klados* branch — more at CLAD-] (1888) **:** any of an order (Tricladida) of turbellarian flatworms (as a planarian) having an intestine with one anterior and two posterior branches — **triclad** *adj*
tri·clin·ic \(ˌ)trī-ˈkli-nik\ *adj* [ISV] (1854) **:** of, relating to, or constituting a system of crystallization characterized by three unequal axes intersecting at oblique angles — used esp. of a crystal
tri·clin·i·um \trī-ˈkli-nē-əm\ *n, pl* **-ia** \-nē-ə\ [L, fr. Gk *triklinion,* fr. *tri-* + *klinein* to lean, recline — more at LEAN] (1646) **1 :** a couch extending around three sides of a table used by the ancient Romans for reclining at meals **2 :** a dining room furnished with a triclinium
tri·clo·san \trī-ˈklō-ˌsan\ *n* [*tri-* + *chlor-* + *-san* (of unknown origin)] (1973) **:** a whitish crystalline powder $C_{12}H_7Cl_3O_2$ that is a phenyl ether derivative used esp. as a broad-spectrum antibacterial agent (as in soaps, deodorants, and mouthwash)
tric·o·lette \ˌtri-kə-ˈlet\ *n* [*tricot* + *-lette* (as in *flannelette*)] (1919) **:** a usu. silk or rayon knitted fabric used esp. for women's clothing
¹**tri·col·or** \ˈtrī-ˌkə-lər *also* ˈtrē-, *esp Brit* ˈtri-kə-lər\ *adj* [F *tricolore* three-colored, fr. LL *tricolor,* fr. L *tri-* + *color* color] (1795) **1 a** *or* **tri·col·ored** \ˈtrī-ˈkə-lərd\ **:** having, using, or marked with three colors **b** *of a dog* **:** having a coat of black, tan, and white **2 :** of, relating to, or characteristic of a tricolor or a nation whose flag is a tricolor; *esp* **:** FRENCH
²**tricolor** *n* (1797) **1 :** a flag of three colors arranged in equal horizontal or vertical bands ⟨the French ~⟩ **2 :** a tricolor animal; *esp* **:** a tricolor dog
tri·corn \ˈtrī-ˌkȯrn\ *adj* [L *tricornis*] (1823) **:** having three horns or corners
tri·corne *or* **tri·corn** \ˈtrī-ˌkȯrn\ *n* [F *tricorne,* fr. *tricorne* three-cornered, fr. L *tricornis,* fr. *tri-* + *cornu* horn — more at HORN] (1857) **:** COCKED HAT 1
tri·cor·nered \ˈtrī-ˈkȯ(r)-nərd\ *adj* (1819) **:** having three corners
tri·cot \ˈtrē-(ˌ)kō, ˈtrī-kət\ *n* [F, fr. *tricoter* to move the legs rapidly, knit, fr. MF, to run, skip, ultim. fr. OF *estriquier* to stroke, of Gmc origin; akin to OE *strīcan* to stroke — more at STRIKE] (1859) **1 :** a plain warp-knitted fabric (as of nylon, wool, rayon, silk, or cotton) with a close inelastic knit and used esp. in clothing (as underwear) **2 :** a twilled clothing fabric of wool with fine warp ribs or of wool and cotton with fine weft ribs
tri·co·tine \ˌtri-kə-ˈtēn, ˌtrē-\ *n* [F, fr. *tricot*] (1886) **:** a sturdy suiting woven of tightly twisted yarns in a double twill
tric·trac \ˈtrik-ˌtrak\ *n* [F, of imit. origin] (1679) **:** an old form of backgammon played with pegs
¹**tri·cus·pid** \(ˌ)trī-ˈkəs-pəd\ *adj* [L *tricuspid-, tricuspis,* fr. *tri-* + *cuspid-, cuspis* point] (1834) **:** having three cusps ⟨a ~ molar⟩
²**tricuspid** *n* (1856) **:** a tricuspid anatomical structure; *esp* **:** a tooth having three cusps
tricuspid valve *n* (1670) **:** a valve of three flaps that prevents reflux of blood from the right ventricle to the right atrium
tri·cy·cle \ˈtrī-sə-kəl, -ˌsi-kəl\ *n* [F, fr. *tri-* + Gk *kyklos* wheel — more at WHEEL] (1868) **:** a 3-wheeled vehicle propelled by pedals or a motor
tri·cy·clic \(ˌ)trī-ˈsī-klik, -ˈsi-klik\ *adj* [*tri-* + *cyclic*] (1891) **:** being a chemical with three usu. fused rings in the molecular structure and esp. a tricyclic antidepressant
tricyclic antidepressant *n* (1966) **:** any of a group of antidepressant drugs (as imipramine and amitriptyline) that contain three fused benzene rings, potentiate the action of catecholamines (as norepinephrine and serotonin) by inhibiting their uptake by nerve endings, and do not inhibit the action of monoamine oxidase — called also *tricyclic*
¹**trident** *n* [L *trident-, tridens,* fr. *trident-, tridens* having three teeth, fr. *tri-* + *dent-, dens* tooth — more at TOOTH] (15c) **1 :** a 3-pronged spear serving in classical mythology as the attribute of a sea god (as Neptune) **2 :** a 3-pronged spear (as for fishing)
²**tri·dent** \ˈtrī-dᵊnt\ *adj* [L *trident-, tridens*] (1589) **:** having three teeth, processes, or points

Tri·den·tine \trī-ˈden-ˌtīn, -ˌtēn; ˈtrī-dᵊn-, ˈtri-\ *adj* [NL *Tridentinus,* fr. L *Tridentum* Trent, Italy] (1561) : of or relating to the Roman Catholic Church council held at Trent from 1545 to 1563 or its decrees

tri·di·men·sion·al \ˌtrī-də-ˈmench-nəl, -ˌdī-, -ˈmen(t)-shə-nᵊl\ *adj* [ISV] (1853) : of, relating to, or concerned with three dimensions ⟨~ space⟩ — **tri·di·men·sion·al·i·ty** \-ˌmen(t)-shə-ˈna-lə-tē\ *n*

trid·u·um \ˈtri-jə-wəm, ˈtri-dyə-\ *n* [L, space of three days, fr. *tri-* + *-duum* (akin to *dies* day) — more at DEITY] (1873) : a period of three days of prayer usu. preceding a Roman Catholic feast

tried \ˈtrīd\ *adj* [ME, fr. pp. of *trien* to try, test] (15c) **1 :** found good, faithful, or trustworthy through experience or testing ⟨a ~ recipe⟩ **2 :** subjected to trials or distress ⟨a kind but much-*tried* father⟩

tried–and–true *adj* (1792) : proved good, desirable, or feasible : shown or known to be worthy ⟨a ~ sales technique⟩

tri·ene \ˈtrī-ˌēn\ *n* (1917) : a chemical compound containing three double bonds

tri·en·ni·al \(ˌ)trī-ˈe-nē-əl\ *adj* (1562) **1 :** occurring or being done every three years ⟨the ~ convention⟩ **2 :** consisting of or lasting for three years ⟨a ~ contract⟩ — **triennial** *n* — **tri·en·ni·al·ly** \-nē-ə-lē\ *adv*

tri·en·ni·um \trī-ˈe-nē-əm\ *n, pl* **-ni·ums** *or* **-nia** \-nē-ə\ [L, fr. *tri-* + *annus* year — more at ANNUAL] (1847) : a period of three years

tri·er \ˈtrī(-ə)r\ *n* (14c) **1 :** someone or something that tries **2 :** an implement (as a tapered hollow tube) used in obtaining samples of bulk material for examination and testing

tri·er·arch \ˈtrī(-ə)-ˌrärk\ *n* [L *trierarchus,* fr. Gk *triērarchos,* fr. *triērēs* trireme (fr. *tri-* + *-ērēs* — akin to L *remus* oar) + *-archos* -arch — more at ROW] (ca. 1656) **1 :** the commander of a trireme **2 :** an Athenian citizen who had to fit out a trireme for the public service

tri·er·ar·chy \-ˌrär-kē\ *n* (ca. 1837) : the ancient Athenian plan whereby individual citizens furnished and maintained triremes as a civic duty

tri·fec·ta \trī-ˈfek-tə, ˈtrī-ˌ\ *n* [*tri-* + per*fecta*] (1974) **1 :** a variation of the perfecta in which a bettor wins by selecting the first three finishers of a race in the correct order of finish **2 :** TRIPLE 1b ⟨achieved a show-business ~ : a platinum record, hit TV series, and an Oscar⟩

tri·fid \ˈtrī-ˌfid, -fəd\ *adj* [L *trifidus* split into three, fr. *tri-* + *findere* to split — more at BITE] (ca. 1753) : being deeply and narrowly cleft into three teeth, processes, or points ⟨a spoon with a ~ top⟩

[1]**tri·fle** \ˈtrī-fəl\ *n* [ME *trufle, trifle,* fr. AF *trufle, triffle* fraud, trick, nonsense] (14c) **1 :** something of little value, substance, or importance **2 :** a dessert typically consisting of plain or sponge cake often soaked with wine or spirits (as brandy or rum) and topped with layers of preserves, custard, and cream — **a trifle :** to some small degree : SLIGHTLY ⟨*a trifle* annoyed⟩

[2]**trifle** *vb* **tri·fled; tri·fling** \-f(ə-)liŋ\ [ME *truflen, triflen,* fr. AF *trufler* to trick, talk nonsense] *vi* (14c) **1 a :** to talk in a jesting or mocking manner or with intent to delude or mislead **b :** to treat someone or something as unimportant **2 :** to handle something idly ~ *vt* : to spend or waste in trifling or on trifles — **tri·fler** \-f(ə-)lər\ *n*

syn TRIFLE, TOY, DALLY, FLIRT, COQUET mean to deal with or act toward without serious purpose. TRIFLE may imply playfulness, unconcern, indulgent contempt ⟨to *trifle* with a lover's feelings⟩. TOY implies acting without full attention or serious exertion of one's powers ⟨a political novice *toying* with great issues⟩. DALLY suggests indulging in thoughts or plans merely as an amusement ⟨*dallying* with the idea of building a boat someday⟩. FLIRT implies an interest or attention that soon passes to another object ⟨*flirted* with one fashionable ism after another⟩. COQUET implies attracting interest or admiration without serious intention ⟨companies that *coquet* with environmentalism solely for public relations⟩.

trifling *adj* (1535) : lacking in significance or solid worth: as **a :** FRIVOLOUS ⟨~ talk⟩ **b :** TRIVIAL ⟨a ~ gift⟩ **c** *chiefly dial* : LAZY, SHIFTLESS ⟨a ~ fellow⟩

tri·fluo·per·a·zine \ˌtrī-ˌflü-ō-ˈper-ə-ˌzēn, -zən\ *n* [*tri-* + *fluor-* + pi*perazine*] (ca. 1957) : a phenothiazine tranquilizer $C_{21}H_{24}F_3N_3S$ chiefly used to treat psychotic conditions and esp. schizophrenia

tri·flu·ra·lin \trī-ˈflu̇r-ə-lən\ *n* [*tri-* + *fluor-* + *aniline*] (ca. 1961) : an herbicide $C_{13}H_{16}F_3N_3O_4$ used in the control of weeds

[1]**tri·fo·cal** \(ˌ)trī-ˈfō-kəl\ *adj* (1826) : having three focal lengths

[2]**trifocal** *n* (1899) **1** *pl* : eyeglasses with trifocal lenses **2 :** a trifocal glass or lens

tri·fo·li·ate \(ˌ)trī-ˈfō-lē-ət\ *adj* [*tri-* + L *folium* leaf — more at BLADE] (ca. 1753) **1 :** having three leaves ⟨a ~ plant⟩ **2 :** TRIFOLIOLATE

trifoliate orange *n* (ca. 1900) : a thorny Chinese tree (*Poncirus trifoliata*) of the rue family related to the citruses that has trifoliolate leaves and a sour yellow fruit resembling a small orange and that is grown for ornament or hedges or used as a rootstock for citrus fruits

tri·fo·li·o·late \(ˌ)trī-ˈfō-lē-ə-ˌlāt\ *adj* [ISV *tri-* + LL *foliolum* leaflet, dim. of L *folium* leaf] (ca. 1828) : having three leaflets ⟨a ~ leaf⟩ — see LEAF illustration

tri·fo·li·um \trī-ˈfō-lē-əm\ *n* [NL, fr. L, trefoil — more at TREFOIL] (1541) : CLOVER 1

tri·fo·ri·um \trī-ˈfȯr-ē-əm\ *n, pl* **-ria** \-ē-ə\ [ML] (1703) : a gallery forming an upper story to the aisle of a church and typically an arcaded story between the nave arches and clerestory

tri·form \ˈtrī-ˌfȯrm\ *adj* [ME *triforme,* fr. L *triformis,* fr. *tri-* + *forma* form] (15c) : having a triple form or nature

tri·fur·cate \(ˌ)trī-ˈfər-kət, -ˌkāt; ˈtrī-(ˌ)fər-ˌkāt\ *adj* [L *trifurcus,* fr. *tri-* + *furca* fork] (ca. 1831) : having three branches or forks : TRICHOTOMOUS — **tri·fur·cate** \ˈtrī-(ˌ)fər-ˌkāt, trī-ˈfər-\ *vi* — **tri·fur·ca·tion** \ˌtrī-(ˌ)fər-ˈkā-shən\ *n*

[1]**trig** \ˈtrig\ *adj* [ME, trusty, nimble, of Scand origin; akin to ON *tryggr* faithful; akin to OE *trēowe* faithful — more at TRUE] (1513) **1 :** stylishly or jauntily trim ⟨everything was trim and ~ and bright —Mark Twain⟩ **2 :** extremely precise : PRIM **3** *dial chiefly Brit* : FIRM, VIGOROUS

[2]**trig** *n* [by shortening] (ca. 1878) : TRIGONOMETRY

tri·gem·i·nal \trī-ˈje-mə-nᵊl\ *adj* [NL *trigeminus* trigeminal nerve, fr. L, threefold, fr. *tri-* + *geminus* twin] (1830) : of or relating to the trigeminal nerve

trigeminal nerve *n* (1830) : either of a pair of large mixed nerves that are the fifth cranial nerves and supply motor and sensory fibers mostly to the face — called also *trigeminal*

trigeminal neuralgia *n* (1874) : an intense paroxysmal neuralgia involving one or more branches of the trigeminal nerve

[1]**trig·ger** \ˈtri-gər\ *n* [alter. of earlier *tricker,* fr. D *trekker,* fr. MD *trecker* one that pulls, fr. *trecken* to pull — more at TREK] (1621) **1 a :** a piece (as a lever) connected with a catch or detent as a means of releasing it; *esp* : the part of the action moved by the finger to fire a gun **b :** a similar movable part by which a mechanism is actuated ⟨~ of a spray gun⟩ **2 :** something that acts like a mechanical trigger in initiating a process or reaction — **trigger** *adj* — **trig·gered** \-gərd\ *adj*

[2]**trigger** *vb* **trig·gered; trig·ger·ing** \ˈtri-g(ə-)riŋ\ *vt* (1916) **1 a :** to release or activate by means of a trigger; *esp* : to fire by pulling a mechanical trigger ⟨~ a rifle⟩ **b :** to cause the explosion of ⟨~ a missile with a proximity fuse⟩ **2 :** to initiate, actuate, or set off by a trigger ⟨an indiscreet remark that ~*ed* a fight⟩ ⟨a stimulus that ~*ed* a reflex⟩ ~ *vi* : to release a mechanical trigger

trig·ger·fish \ˈtri-gər-ˌfish\ *n* (1849) : any of various deep-bodied bony fishes (family Balistidae, esp. genus *Balistes*) of warm seas having an anterior dorsal fin with two or three stout erectile spines

trig·ger–hap·py \-ˌha-pē\ *adj* (1943) **1 :** irresponsible in the use of firearms; *esp* : inclined to shoot before clearly identifying the target **2 a :** inclined to be irresponsible in matters that might precipitate war **b :** aggressively belligerent in attitude

trig·ger·man \-mən, -ˌman\ *n* (ca. 1930) : a gunman who shoots the victim (as in a gangland murder)

trigger point *n* (ca. 1891) : a localized usu. tender or painful area of the body and esp. of a muscle that when stimulated gives rise to pain elsewhere in the body

tri·glyc·er·ide \(ˌ)trī-ˈgli-sə-ˌrīd\ *n* [ISV] (1860) : any of a group of lipids that are esters formed from one molecule of glycerol and three molecules of one or more fatty acids, are widespread in adipose tissue, and commonly circulate in the blood in the form of lipoproteins

tri·glyph \ˈtrī-ˌglif\ *n* [L *triglyphus,* fr. Gk *triglyphos,* fr. *tri-* + *glyphein* to carve — more at CLEAVE] (1563) : a slightly projecting rectangular tablet in a Doric frieze with two vertical channels of V section and two corresponding chamfers or half channels on the vertical sides — **tri·glyph·ic** \trī-ˈgli-fik\ *or* **tri·glyph·i·cal** \-fi-kəl\ *adj*

tri·gon \ˈtrī-ˌgän\ *n* [L *trigonum,* fr. Gk *trigōnon,* fr. neut. of *trigōnos* triangular, fr. *tri-* + *gōnia* angle — more at -GON] (1563) : TRIPLICITY 1

tri·go·nal \trī-ˈgō-nᵊl\ *adj* (1878) : of, relating to, or being the division of the hexagonal crystal system or the forms belonging to it characterized by a vertical axis of threefold symmetry — **tri·go·nal·ly** \-nᵊl-ē\ *adv*

trig·o·no·met·ric \ˌtri-gə-nə-ˈme-trik\ *also* **trig·o·no·met·ri·cal** \-tri-kəl\ *adj* (1687) : of, relating to, or being in accordance with trigonometry — **trig·o·no·met·ri·cal·ly** \-tri-k(ə-)lē\ *adv*

trigonometric function *n* (1909) **1 :** a function (as the sine, cosine, tangent, cotangent, secant, or cosecant) of an arc or angle most simply expressed in terms of the ratios of pairs of sides of a right-angled triangle — called also *circular function* **2 :** the inverse (as the arcsine, arccosine, or arctangent) of a trigonometric function

trig·o·nom·e·try \ˌtri-gə-ˈnä-mə-trē\ *n* [NL *trigonometria,* fr. Gk *trigōnon* + *-metria* -metry] (1614) : the study of the properties of triangles and trigonometric functions and of their applications

tri·gram \ˈtrī-ˌgram\ *n* (1606) **1 :** TRIGRAPH 2 **2 :** any of the eight possible combinations of three whole or broken lines used esp. in Chinese divination

tri·graph \ˈtrī-ˌgraf\ *n* (ca. 1836) **1 :** three letters spelling a single consonant, vowel, or diphthong ⟨*eau* of *beau* is a ~⟩ **2 :** a cluster of three successive letters ⟨*the, ion,* and *ing* are high frequency ~*s*⟩ — **tri·graph·ic** \(ˌ)trī-ˈgra-fik\ *adj*

tri·halo·meth·ane \(ˌ)trī-ˌha-lə-ˈme-ˌthān, *Brit usu* -ˈmē-\ *n* (1968) : any of various derivatives CHX_3 of methane (as chloroform) that have three halogen atoms per molecule and are formed esp. during the chlorination of drinking water

tri·he·dral \-ˈhē-drəl\ *adj* (1789) **1 :** having three faces ⟨~ angle⟩ **2 :** of or relating to a trihedral angle — **trihedral** *n*

tri·hy·brid \-ˈhī-brəd\ *n* (1903) : an individual or strain that is heterozygous for three pairs of genes — **trihybrid** *adj*

tri·hy·droxy \ˌtrī-hī-ˈdräk-sē, -hə-\ *adj* [ISV] (1895) : containing three hydroxyl groups in the molecule

tri·io·do·thy·ro·nine \ˌtrī-ˌī-ə-dō-ˈthī-rə-ˌnēn\ *n* [*tri-* + *iod-* + *thyronine* an amino acid of which thyroxine is a derivative] (1952) : an iodine-containing hormone $C_{15}H_{12}I_3NO_4$ that is an amino acid derived from thyroxine

tri·jet \ˈtrī-ˌjet\ *n* (1967) : an aircraft powered with three jet engines

trike \ˈtrīk\ *n* [by shortening & alter.] (1883) : TRICYCLE

tri·lat·er·al \(ˌ)trī-ˈla-tə-rəl, -ˈla-trəl\ *adj* [L *trilaterus,* fr. *tri-* + *later-, latus* side] (1660) : having three sides or parties ⟨~ business ventures⟩ ⟨~ discussions⟩

tril·by \ˈtril-bē\ *n, pl* **trilbies** [fr. the fact that such a hat was worn in the London stage version of the novel *Trilby* (1894) by George du Maurier] (1897) *chiefly Brit* : a soft felt hat with indented crown

tri·lin·e·ar \(ˌ)trī-ˈli-nē-ər\ *adj* (1715) : of, relating to, or involving three lines ⟨~ coordinates⟩

tri·lin·gual \-ˈliŋ-gwəl *also* -ˈliŋ-gyə-wəl\ *adj* (1834) : consisting of, having, or expressed in three languages ⟨~ countries⟩ ⟨a ~ joke⟩; *also* : familiar with or able to use three languages ⟨a ~ teacher⟩ — **tri·lin·gual·ly** *adv*

[1]**tri·lit·er·al** \-ˈli-t(ə-)rəl\ *adj* [*tri-* + L *littera* letter] (1751) : consisting of three letters and esp. of three consonants ⟨~ roots in Semitic languages⟩ — **tri·lit·er·al·ism** \-t(ə-)rə-ˌli-zəm\ *n*

[2]**triliteral** *n* (ca. 1828) : a root or word that is triliteral

[1]**trill** \ˈtril\ *vb* [ME; akin to MD *trillen* to vibrate, Sw *trilla* to roll] *vi* (14c) **1 :** to flow in a small stream or in drops : TRICKLE **2 :** TWIRL, REVOLVE ~ *vt* : to cause to flow in a small stream

[2]**trill** *n* [It *trillo* prob. of imit. origin] (1649) **1 a :** the alternation of two musical tones a diatonic second apart — called also *shake* **b :** VIBRA-

\ə\ **abut** \ᵊ\ kitten, F table \ər\ **further** \a\ **ash** \ā\ **ace** \ä\ **mop, mar**
\au̇\ **out** \ch\ **chin** \e\ **bet** \ē\ **easy** \g\ **go** \i\ **hit** \ī\ **ice** \j\ **job**
\ŋ\ **sing** \ō\ **go** \ȯ\ **law** \ȯi\ **boy** \th\ **thin** \t͟h\ **the** \ü\ **loot** \u̇\ **foot**
\y\ **yet** \zh\ **vision, beige** \k̲, ⁿ, œ, ue, ʸ\ *see* Guide to Pronunciation

TO **c :** a rapid reiteration of the same tone esp. on a percussion instrument **2 :** a sound resembling a musical trill : WARBLE **3 a :** the rapid vibration of one speech organ against another (as of the tip of the tongue against the teethridge) **b :** a speech sound made by a trill

[3]**trill** *vi* (ca. 1667) **:** to play or sing with a trill : QUAVER ~ *vt* **:** to utter as or with or as if with a trill ‹~ the *r*› — **trill·er** *n*

tril·lion \ˈtri(l)-yən\ *n* [F, fr. *tri-* + *-illion* (as in *million*)] (1690) **1** — see NUMBER table **2 :** an indeterminately large number ‹a ~ mosquitoes out tonight› — **trillion** *adj* — **tril·lionth** \-yən(t)th\ *adj or n*

tril·li·um \ˈtri-lē-əm\ *n* [NL, fr. Sw *trilling* triplet; fr. its three leaves] (ca. 1760) **:** any of a genus (*Trillium*) of herbs of the lily family with an erect stem bearing a whorl of three leaves and a solitary typically spring-blooming flower

tri·lo·bate \(ˌ)trī-ˈlō-ˌbāt\ *adj* (1785) **:** TRILOBED

tri·lobed \ˈtrī-ˈlōbd\ *adj* (1826) **:** having three lobes ‹a ~ leaf›

tri·lo·bite \ˈtrī-lə-ˌbīt\ *n* [ultim. fr. Gk *trilobos* three-lobed, fr. *tri-* + *lobos* lobe] (1832) **:** any of numerous extinct Paleozoic marine arthropods (group Trilobita) having the segments of the body divided by furrows on the dorsal surface into three lobes

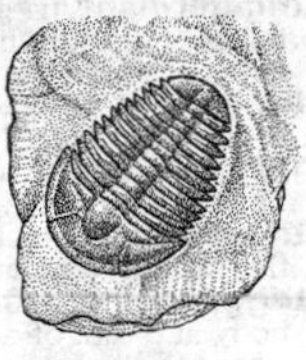

trilobite fossil

tril·o·gy \ˈtri-lə-jē\ *n, pl* **-gies** [Gk *trilogia,* fr. *tri-* + *-logia* -logy] (ca. 1661) **:** a series of three dramas or literary works or sometimes three musical compositions that are closely related and develop a single theme

[1]**trim** \ˈtrim\ *vb* **trimmed; trim·ming** [prob. fr. ME **trimmen* to prepare, put in order, fr. OE *trymian, trymman* to strengthen, arrange, fr. *trum* strong, firm; prob. akin to OE *trēo* tree, wood — more at TREE] *vt* (ca. 1521) **1 :** to embellish with or as if with ribbons, lace, or ornaments ‹~ the Christmas tree› ‹the coat was *trimmed* with fur› **2 a :** to administer a beating to : THRASH **b :** DEFEAT ‹*trimmed* me at chess› **3 a :** to make trim and neat esp. by cutting or clipping ‹~ the hedges› **b :** to free of excess or extraneous matter by or as if by cutting ‹~ a budget› ‹~ down the inventory› **c :** to remove by or as if by cutting ‹*trimmed* thousands from federal payrolls —*Grit*› **4 a** (1) **:** to cause (as a ship) to assume a desirable position in the water by arrangement of ballast, cargo, or passengers (2) **:** to adjust (as an airplane or submarine) for horizontal movement or for motion upward or downward **b :** to adjust (as cargo or a sail) to a desired position ~ *vi* **1 a :** to maintain neutrality between opposing parties or to favor each equally **b :** to change one's views for reasons of expediency **2 :** to assume or cause a boat to assume a desired position in the water ‹a boat that ~*s* badly› — **trim one's sails :** to adjust oneself or one's actions to prevailing conditions ‹compromise or *trim your sails* to suit the political winds —Philip Johnston›

[2]**trim** *adj* **trim·mer; trim·mest** (ca. 1521) **1** *obs* **:** EXCELLENT, FINE **2 :** ready for service or use; *also* **:** in good physical condition ‹keeps ~ by jogging› **3 :** exhibiting neatness, good order, or compactness of line or structure ‹~ houses› — **trim·ly** *adv* — **trim·ness** *n*

[3]**trim** *adv* (1529) **:** in a trim manner : TRIMLY — used chiefly in combination ‹the *trim*-cut forest vistas —W. M. Thackeray›

[4]**trim** *n* (ca. 1593) **1 :** suitable or excellent condition ‹tries to keep in ~› **2 a :** one's clothing or appearance **b :** material used for ornament or trimming **c :** the woodwork in the finish of a building esp. around openings **d :** the interior furnishings of an automobile **3 a :** the position of a ship or boat esp. with reference to the horizontal; *also* **:** the difference between the draft of a ship forward and that aft **b :** the relation between the plane of a sail and the direction of the ship **c :** the buoyancy status of a submarine **d :** the attitude of a lighter-than-air craft relative to a fore-and-aft horizontal plane **e :** the attitude with respect to wind axes at which an airplane will continue in level flight with free controls **4 :** something that is trimmed off or cut out **5 :** a haircut that neatens a previous haircut

tri·ma·ran \ˈtrī-mə-ˌran, ˌtrī-mə-ˈ\ *n* [*tri-* + cata*maran*] (1949) **:** a fast pleasure sailboat with three hulls side by side

tri·mer \ˈtrī-mər\ *n* [ISV] (ca. 1930) **:** a polymer formed from three molecules of a monomer — **tri·mer·ic** \trī-ˈmer-ik\ *adj*

trim·er·ous \ˈtri-mə-rəs\ *adj* [NL *trimerus,* fr. Gk *tri-* + *meros* part — more at MERIT] (1826) **:** having the parts in threes — used of a flower and often written *3-merous*

tri·mes·ter \(ˌ)trī-ˈmes-tər, ˈtrī-ˌ\ *n* [F *trimestre,* fr. L *trimestris* of three months, fr. *tri-* + *mensis* month — more at MOON] (1821) **1 :** a period of three or about three months; *esp* **:** any of three periods of approximately three months each into which a human pregnancy is divided **2 :** one of three terms into which the academic year is sometimes divided

trim·e·ter \ˈtri-mə-tər\ *n* [L *trimetrus,* fr. Gk *trimetros* having three measures, fr. *tri-* + *metron* measure — more at MEASURE] (1540) **:** a line of verse consisting of three dipodies or three metrical feet

tri·meth·o·prim \trī-ˈme-thə-ˌprim\ *n* [*tri-* + *meth-* + *-prim* (by shortening & alter. fr. *pyrimidine*)] (1964) **:** a synthetic antibacterial and antimalarial drug $C_{14}H_{18}N_4O_3$ used alone or in combination with sulfamethoxazole

trim·mer \ˈtri-mər\ *n* (1555) **1 a** (1) **:** one that trims articles (2) **:** one that stows coal or freight on a ship so as to distribute the weight properly **b :** an instrument or machine with which trimming is done **c :** a circuit element (as a capacitor) used to tune a circuit to a desired frequency **2 :** a beam that receives the end of a header in floor framing **3 :** a person who modifies a policy, position, or opinion esp. out of expediency

trimming *n* (ca. 1518) **1 :** DEFEAT, BEATING **2 :** the act of one who trims **3 a :** a decorative accessory or additional item ‹~*s* for a hat› **b :** an additional garnishing ‹turkey and all the ~*s*›

tri·month·ly \(ˌ)trī-ˈmən(t)th-lē\ *adj* (1856) **:** occurring every three months

tri·mor·phic \(ˌ)trī-ˈmȯr-fik\ *adj* [Gk *trimorphos* having three forms, fr. *tri-* + *-morphos* -morphous] (1866) **:** occurring in or having three distinct forms

tri·mo·tor \ˈtrī-ˌmō-tər, -ˈmō-\ *n* (1923) **:** an airplane powered by three engines

trim size *n* (ca. 1929) **:** the actual size (as of a book page) after excess material required in production has been cut off

Tri·mur·ti \tri-ˈmu̇r-tē\ *n* [Skt *-trimūrti,* fr. *trimūrti* having three forms, fr. *tri-* tri- + *mūrti* body, form] (1810) **:** the great triad of Hindu gods comprising Brahma, Vishnu, and Shiva

tri·nal \ˈtrī-nᵊl\ *adj* [ME, fr. LL *trinalis,* fr. L *trini* three each] (15c) **:** THREEFOLD

[1]**trine** \ˈtrīn\ *adj* [ME, fr. AF *trin,* fr. L *trinus,* fr. *trini* three each; akin to L *tres* three — more at THREE] (14c) **1 :** THREEFOLD, TRIPLE **2 :** of, relating to, or being the favorable astrological aspect of two celestial bodies 120 degrees apart

[2]**trine** *n* (1552) **1 :** a group of three : TRIAD **2 :** the trine astrological aspect of two celestial bodies

trine immersion *n* (1637) **:** the practice of immersing a candidate for baptism three times in the names of the members of the Trinity

trin·i·tar·i·an \ˌtri-nə-ˈter-ē-ən\ *adj* (1628) **1** *cap* **:** of or relating to the Trinity, the doctrine of the Trinity, or adherents to that doctrine **2 :** having three parts or aspects : THREEFOLD

Trinitarian *n* (1628) **1 :** a member of a religious teaching and nursing order for men founded in France in 1198 by John of Matha and Philip of Valois **2 :** one who subscribes to the doctrine of the Trinity — **Trin·i·tar·i·an·ism** \-ē-ə-ˌni-zəm\ *n*

tri·ni·tro·tol·u·ene \ˌtrī-ˌnī-trō-ˈtäl-yə-ˌwēn\ *n* [ISV] (ca. 1900) **:** TNT

Trin·i·ty \ˈtri-nə-tē\ *n* [ME *trinite,* fr. AF *trinité,* fr. LL *trinitat-, trinitas* state of being threefold, fr. L *trinus* threefold] (13c) **1 :** the unity of Father, Son, and Holy Spirit as three persons in one Godhead according to Christian dogma **2** *not cap* **:** a group of three closely related persons or things **3 :** the Sunday after Whitsunday observed as a feast in honor of the Trinity

Trin·i·ty·tide \-ˌtīd\ *n* (15c) **:** the season of the church year between Trinity Sunday and Advent

trin·ket \ˈtriŋ-kət\ *n* [origin unknown] (ca. 1527) **1 :** a small ornament (as a jewel or ring) **2 :** a small article of equipment **3 :** a thing of little value : TRIFLE

trin·ket·ry \-kə-trē\ *n* (1810) **:** small items of personal ornament

trin·oc·u·lar \(ˌ)trī-ˈnä-kyə-lər\ *adj* [*tri-* + bi*nocular*] (1960) **:** relating to or being a binocular microscope equipped with a lens for photographic recording during direct visual observation

[1]**tri·no·mi·al** \trī-ˈnō-mē-əl\ *n* [*tri-* + *-nomial* (as in *binomial*)] (1674) **1 :** a polynomial of three terms **2 :** a biological taxonomic name of three terms of which the first designates the genus, the second the species, and the third the subspecies or variety

[2]**trinomial** *adj* (ca. 1704) **1 :** consisting of three mathematical terms **2 :** of, relating to, or being a biological trinomial

tri·nu·cle·o·tide \(ˌ)trī-ˈnü-klē-ə-ˌtīd, -ˈnyü-\ *n* (1918) **:** a nucleotide consisting of three mononucleotides in combination : CODON

trio \ˈtrē-(ˌ)ō\ *n, pl* **tri·os** [F, fr. It, fr. *tri-* (fr. L)] (ca. 1724) **1 a :** a musical composition for three voice parts or three instruments **b :** the secondary or episodic division of a minuet or scherzo, a march, or of various dance forms **2 :** the performers of a musical or dance trio **3 :** a group or set of three

tri·ode \ˈtrī-ˌōd\ *n* (1919) **:** an electron tube with an anode, a cathode, and a controlling grid

tri·ol \ˈtrī-ˌȯl, -ˌōl\ *n* (1936) **:** a chemical compound (as glycerol) containing three hydroxyl groups

tri·o·let \ˈtrē-ə-lət, ˈtrī-\ *n* [F, fr. MF, lit., clover leaf, clover, ultim. fr. Gk *triphyllon,* fr. *tri-* tri- + *phyllon* leaf — more at BLADE] (1651) **:** a poem or stanza of eight lines in which the first line is repeated as the fourth and seventh and the second line as the eighth with a rhyme scheme of *ABaAabAB*

tri·ose \ˈtrī-ˌōs, -ˌōz\ *n* [ISV] (1894) **:** either of two monosaccharides $C_3H_6O_3$ containing three carbon atoms

tri·ox·ide \(ˌ)trī-ˈäk-ˌsīd\ *n* [ISV] (1863) **:** an oxide containing three atoms of oxygen

[1]**trip** \ˈtrip\ *vb* **tripped; trip·ping** [ME *trippen,* fr. AF *treper, triper,* of Gmc origin; akin to OE *treppan* to tread — more at TRAP] *vi* (14c) **1 a :** to dance, skip, or caper with light quick steps **b :** to walk with light quick steps **2 :** to catch the foot against something so as to stumble **3 :** to make a mistake or false step (as in morality or accuracy) **4 :** to stumble in articulation when speaking **5 :** to make a journey **6 a :** to actuate a mechanism **b :** to become operative **7 a :** to get high on a psychedelic drug (as LSD) : TURN ON — often used with *out* **b** *slang* **:** FREAK 3b ~ *vt* **1 a :** to cause to stumble — often used with *up* **b :** to cause to fail : OBSTRUCT — often used with *up* **2 :** to detect in a misstep, fault, or blunder; *also* **:** EXPOSE — usu. used with *up* **3** *archaic* **:** to perform (as a dance) lightly or nimbly **4 :** to raise (an anchor) from the bottom so as to hang free **5 a :** to pull (a yard) into a perpendicular position for lowering **b :** to hoist (a topmast) far enough to enable the fid to be withdrawn preparatory to housing or lowering **6 :** to release or operate (a mechanism) esp. by releasing a catch or detent ‹~ the fire alarm› — **trip the light fantastic :** DANCE

[2]**trip** *n* (14c) **1 :** a stroke or catch by which a wrestler is made to lose footing **2 a :** VOYAGE, JOURNEY **b :** a single round or tour on a business errand **3 :** ERROR, MISSTEP **4 :** a quick light step **5 :** a faltering step caused by stumbling **6 a :** the action of tripping mechanically **b :** a device for tripping a mechanism (as a catch or detent) **7 a :** an intense visionary experience undergone by a person who has taken a psychedelic drug (as LSD) **b :** an exciting or unusual experience ‹the party was a ~› **8 :** absorption in or obsession with an interest, attitude, or state of mind ‹a guilt ~› ‹on a nostalgia ~› **9 :** SCENE, LIFESTYLE

tri·pack \ˈtrī-ˌpak\ *n* (1911) **:** a combination of three superposed films or emulsions each sensitive to a different primary color for simultaneous exposure in one camera

tri·par·tite \(ˌ)trī-ˈpär-ˌtīt\ *adj* [ME, fr. AF, fr. L *tripartitus,* fr. *tri-* + *partitus* divided — more at PARTITE] (15c) **1 :** divided into or composed of three parts **2 :** having three corresponding parts or copies **3 :** made between or involving three parties ‹a ~ treaty›

tripe \ˈtrīp\ *n* [ME, fr. AF] (14c) **1 :** stomach tissue esp. of a ruminant (as an ox) used as food **2 :** something poor, worthless, or offensive

[1]**trip–ham·mer** \ˈtrip-ˌha-mər\ *n* (1781) **:** a massive power hammer having a head that is tripped and allowed to fall by cam or lever action

[2]**trip–hammer** *adj* (1846) **:** suggesting a trip-hammer in loud pounding or persistent action

tri·phe·nyl·meth·ane \ˌtrī-ˌfe-nᵊl-'me-ˌthän, -ˌfē-\ n [ISV] (ca. 1885) : a crystalline hydrocarbon $CH(C_6H_5)_3$ that is the parent compound of many dyes

trip–hop \'trip-ˌhäp\ n [prob. blend of ²trip (high from a psychedelic drug) + hip-hop] (1989) : electronic dance music usu. based on a slow hip-hop beat and incorporating hypnotic synthesized and prerecorded sounds

tri·phos·phate \(ˌ)trī-'fäs-ˌfāt\ n (ca. 1826) : a salt or acid that contains three phosphate groups — compare ATP, GTP

tri·phos·pho·pyr·i·dine nucleotide \ˌtrī-ˌfäs-fō-'pir-ə-ˌdēn-\ n (1937) : NADP

triph·thong \'trif-ˌthȯŋ, 'thȯŋ, 'trip-\ n [tri- + -phthong (as in diphthong)] (ca. 1599) 1 : a phonological unit consisting of three successive vocalic sounds in one syllable 2 : TRIGRAPH — **triph·thong·al** \trif-'thȯŋ-gəl, trip-, -ᵊl\ adj

tri·pin·nate \(ˌ)trī-'pi-ˌnāt\ adj (ca. 1760) : bipinnate with each division pinnate — **tri·pin·nate·ly** adv

tri·plane \'trī-ˌplān\ n (1909) : an airplane with three main supporting surfaces superposed

¹**tri·ple** \'tri-pəl\ vb **tri·pled; tri·pling** \-p(ə-)liŋ\ [ME (Sc), fr. LL triplare, fr. L triplus, adj.] vt (14c) 1 : to make three times as great or as many 2 a : to score (a base runner) by a triple b : to bring about the scoring of (a run) by a triple ~ vi 1 : to become three times as great or as numerous 〈their profits tripled last year〉 2 : to make a triple in baseball

²**triple** n [ME, fr. L triplus, adj.] (15c) 1 a : a triple sum, quantity, or number b : a combination, group, or series of three 2 : a base hit that allows the batter to reach third base safely 3 : TRIFECTA 1

³**triple** adj [ME, fr. L triplus, fr. tri- + -plus multiplied by — more at -FOLD] (15c) 1 : being three times as great or as many 2 : having or involving three units or members 〈~ bypass heart surgery〉 3 : having a threefold relation or character 〈worked as a double or even ~ agent —Time〉 4 a : three times repeated : TREBLE b : having three full revolutions 〈a ~ somersault〉 〈a ~ lutz〉 5 : marked by three beats per musical measure 〈~ meter〉 6 a : having units of three components 〈~ feet〉 b of rhyme : involving correspondence of three syllables (as in unfortunate-importunate)

triple bogey n (1963) : a golf score of three strokes over par on a hole — **triple–bogey** vt

triple bond n (1889) : a chemical bond in which three pairs of electrons are shared by two atoms in a molecule — compare DOUBLE BOND, SINGLE BOND

triple counterpoint n (ca. 1869) : three-part musical counterpoint so written that any part may be transposed above or below any other

Triple Crown n (ca. 1897) 1 : an unofficial title in horse racing representing the championship achieved by a horse that wins the three classic races for a designated category 2 : the unofficial title signifying the achievement of a baseball player who at the end of a season leads the league in batting average, home runs, and runs batted in 3 often not cap : a set of three noteworthy awards, wins, or achievements in a particular field

tri·ple–deck·er \ˌtri-pəl-'de-kər\ n, often attrib (1938) : something having three basic components or levels: as a : TRILOGY b : a sandwich consisting of three pieces of bread and two layers of filling c : a 3-story dwelling with an apartment on each floor

tri·ple–dou·ble \-'də-bəl\ n (1982) : an instance of a player accumulating 10 or more points, assists, and rebounds in one basketball game

tri·ple–head·er \-'he-dər\ n (ca. 1949) : a program consisting of three consecutive games, contests, or events

triple jump n (1964) : a jump for distance in track-and-field athletics usu. from a running start and combining a hop, a stride, and a jump in succession — **triple jumper** n

triple play n (1869) : a play in baseball by which three players are put out

triple point n (1872) : the condition of temperature and pressure under which the gaseous, liquid, and solid phases of a substance can exist in equilibrium

triple sec \-'sek\ n [fr. Triple Sec, a trademark] (1943) : a colorless orange-flavored liqueur

tri·ple–space \ˌtri-pəl-'spās\ vt (ca. 1939) : to type (text) leaving two blank lines between lines of copy ~ vi : to type on every third line

trip·let \'tri-plət\ n [²triple] (1656) 1 : a unit of three lines of verse 2 a : a combination, set, or group of three b : a group of three elementary particles (as positive, negative, and neutral pions) with different charge states but otherwise similar properties c : an atom or molecule with an even number of electrons that have a net magnetic moment d : CODON 3 : one of three children or offspring born at one birth 4 : a group of three musical notes or tones performed in the time of two of the same value

tri·ple–tail \'tri-pəl-ˌtāl\ n (ca. 1803) : a large marine bony fish (Lobotes surinamensis of the family Lobotidae) of warm and tropical waters that has long dorsal and anal fins which extend backward and together with the caudal fin appear like a 3-lobed tail

tri·ple–team \-ˌtēm\ vt (1973) : to block or guard (an opponent) with three players at one time — **triple–team** n

triple threat n (1924) 1 : a football player adept at running, kicking, and passing 2 : a person adept in three different fields of activity — **triple–threat** adj

tri·ple–tongue \ˌtri-pəl-'təŋ\ vi (1879) : to articulate the notes of triplets in fast tempo on a wind instrument by using the tongue positions esp. for t, k, t for the notes of each successive triplet

¹**tri·plex** \'tri-ˌpleks, 'trī-\ n (1571) : something (as an apartment) that is triplex

²**triplex** adj [L, fr. tri- + -plex -fold — more at -FOLD] (1655) 1 : THREEFOLD, TRIPLE 〈~ windows〉 2 : having three apartments, floors, or sections 〈~ buildings〉 〈a ~ theater〉

¹**trip·li·cate** \'tri-pli-kət\ adj [ME, fr. L triplicatus, pp. of triplicare to triple, fr. triplic-, triplex threefold] (15c) : consisting of or existing in three corresponding or identical parts or examples 〈~ invoices〉

²**trip·li·cate** \-plə-ˌkāt\ vt -cat·ed; -cat·ing (ca. 1623) 1 : to make triple or threefold 2 : to prepare in triplicate 〈~ the forms〉 — **trip·li·ca·tion** \ˌtri-plə-'kā-shən\ n

³**trip·li·cate** \-pli-kət\ n (1797) : three copies all alike — used with in 〈typed in ~〉

tri·plic·i·ty \tri-'pli-sə-tē, trī-\ n, pl -ties [ME triplicite, fr. LL triplicitas, condition of being threefold, fr. L triplic-, triplex] (14c) 1 : one of the groups of three signs each distant 120 degrees from the other two into which the signs of the zodiac are divided — called also trigon 2 : the quality or state of being triple or threefold

trip·lo·blas·tic \ˌtri-plō-'blas-tik\ adj [L triplus + E -o- + -blastic] (ca. 1888) : having three primary germ layers

trip·loid \'tri-ˌplȯid\ adj [ISV, fr. L triplus triple] (1911) : having or being a chromosome number three times the monoploid number — **trip·loi·dy** \'tri-ˌlȯi-dē\ n

tri·ply \'tri-p(ə-)lē\ adv (1641) : in a triple degree, amount, or manner

tri·pod \'trī-ˌpäd\ n [ME, fr. L tripod-, tripus, fr. Gk tripod-, tripous, fr. tripod-, tripous, adj., three-footed, fr. tri- + pod-, pous foot — more at FOOT] (15c) 1 : a vessel (as a cauldron) resting on three legs 2 : a stool, table, or altar with three legs 3 : a three-legged stand (as for a camera) — **tripod** or **tri·po·dal** \'trī-pə-dᵊl, 'trī-ˌpä-\ adj

trip·o·li \'tri-pə-lē\ n [F, fr. Tripoli, region of Africa] (ca. 1601) 1 : an earth consisting of very friable soft schistose deposits of silica and including diatomite and kieselguhr 2 : an earth consisting of friable dustlike silica not of diatomaceous origin

tri·pos \'trī-ˌpäs\ n [modif. of L tripus] (1589) 1 archaic : TRIPOD 2 [fr. the three-legged stool occupied by a participant in a disputation at the degree ceremonies] : a final honors examination at Cambridge university orig. in mathematics

trip·per \'tri-pər\ n (1813) 1 chiefly Brit : one that takes a trip : TOURIST 2 : a tripping device (as for operating a railroad signal)

trip·ping·ly \'tri-piŋ-lē\ adv (15c) : in a nimble or lively manner 〈the new name . . . may not roll ~ off the tongue —P. B. Carroll〉

trip·py \'tri-pē\ adj (1968) : of, relating to, or suggestive of a trip on psychedelic drugs or the culture associated with such drugs 〈~ music〉 〈a ~ experience〉

trip·tan \'trip-ˌtan, -tən\ n [-triptan (as in sumatriptan)] (1997) : any of a class of drugs (as sumatriptan) that bind to and are agonists of serotonin receptors and are used to treat migraine attacks

trip·tych \'trip-(ˌ)tik\ n [Gk triptychos having three folds, fr. tri- + ptychē fold] (1731) 1 : an ancient Roman writing tablet with three waxed leaves hinged together 2 a : a picture (as an altarpiece) or carving in three panels side by side b : something composed or presented in three parts or sections; esp : TRILOGY

trip wire n (1915) 1 : a low-placed concealed wire used esp. in warfare to trip an enemy or trespasser and usu. to trigger an alarm or explosive device when moved 2 : something (as a small military force) intended to function like a trip wire (as to set a larger military force in motion)

tri·ra·di·ate \(ˌ)trī-'rā-dē-ət, -dē-ˌāt\ adj (1846) : having three rays or radiating branches 〈a ~ sponge spicule〉

tri·reme \'trī-ˌrēm\ n [L triremis, fr. tri- + remus oar — more at ROW] (1600) : an ancient galley having three banks of oars

tri·sac·cha·ride \(ˌ)trī-'sa-kə-ˌrīd\ n [ISV] (ca. 1899) : a sugar that yields on complete hydrolysis three monosaccharide molecules

tri·sect \'trī-ˌsekt, trī-'\ vt [tri- + intersect] (1695) : to divide into three usu. equal parts — **tri·sec·tion** \trī-'sek-shən, trī-\ n — **tri·sec·tor** \'trī-ˌsek-tər, trī-'\ n

tri·shaw \'trī-ˌshȯ\ n [tri- + rickshaw] (1946) : PEDICAB

tris·kai·deka·pho·bia \ˌtris-ˌkī-ˌde-kə-'fō-bē-ə, ˌtris-kə-\ n [NL, fr. Gk treiskaideka thirteen (fr. treis three + kai and + deka ten) + NL phobia — more at THREE, TEN] (ca. 1911) : fear of the number 13

tris·kel·i·on \trī-'ske-lē-ən, trī-\ n [Gk tris thrice + E octahedron — more at TER-] (ca. 1847) : a solid (as a crystal) three-legged, fr. tri- + skelos leg; triskele fr. Gk triskelēs — more at ISOSCELES] (ca. 1857) : a figure composed of three usu. curved or bent branches radiating from a center

tris·mus \'triz-məs\ n [NL, fr. Gk trismos gnashing (of teeth), fr. trizein to squeak, gnash; akin to L stridēre to creak — more at STRIDENT] (ca. 1693) 1 : involuntary contraction of the muscles of mastication (as in tetanus or Parkinson's disease) 2 : LOCKJAW

triskelion

tris·oc·ta·he·dron \ˌtris-ˌsäk-tə-'hē-drən\ n [Gk tris thrice + E octahedron — more at TER-] (ca. 1847) : a solid (as a crystal) having 24 congruent faces meeting on the edges of a regular octahedron

tri·so·di·um phosphate \ˌtrī-'sō-dē-əm-\ n (1923) : a crystalline compound Na_3PO_4 that is used esp. in cleaning compositions

tri·so·my \'trī-ˌsō-mē\ n, pl -mies [tri- + ³-some + ²-y] (1930) : the condition (as in Down syndrome) of having one or a few chromosomes triploid in an otherwise diploid set — **tri·so·mic** \(ˌ)trī-'sō-mik\ adj or n

tri·so·my 21 \'trī-ˌsō-mē-ˌtwen-tē-'wən\ n [fr. the occurrence of trisomy in chromosome 21 of persons with Down syndrome] (1961) : DOWN SYNDROME

Tris·tan \'tris-tən, -ˌtän, -ˌtan\ n (1530) : TRISTRAM

tri·state \'trī-ˌstāt, -ˌstāt\ adj (1900) : of, relating to, or consisting of three adjoining states 〈the ~ area〉

triste \'trēst\ adj [F, fr. OF, fr. L tristis] (1756) : SAD, MOURNFUL; also : WISTFUL

tri·stea·rin \(ˌ)trī-'stē-ə-rən, -'stir-ən\ n [ISV] (ca. 1856) : a crystallizable triglyceride $C_{57}H_{110}O_6$ of stearic acid found esp. in hard fats

tris·te·za \tri-'stā-zə\ n [Pg, lit., sadness, fr. L tristitia, fr. tristis sad] (ca. 1902) : a highly infectious disease of citrus trees grafted on sour orange rootstocks that is caused by a single-stranded RNA virus (species Citrus tristeza virus of the genus Closterovirus, family Closteroviridae) transmitted by aphids and that eventually causes death of the trees

trist·ful \'trist-fəl\ adj [ME trist sad, fr. AF triste] (15c) : SAD, MELANCHOLY — **trist·ful·ly** \-fə-lē\ adv — **trist·ful·ness** n

tri·stim·u·lus \(ˌ)trī-'stim-yə-ləs\ adj (1933) : of or relating to values giving the amounts of the three colored lights red, green, and blue that

---

\ə\ abut \ᵊ\ kitten, F table \ər\ further \a\ ash \ā\ ace \ä\ mop, mar \aú\ out \ch\ chin \e\ bet \ē\ easy \g\ go \i\ hit \ī\ ice \j\ job \ŋ\ sing \ō\ go \ȯ\ law \ȯi\ boy \th\ thin \th\ the \ü\ loot \ú\ foot \y\ yet \zh\ vision, beige \k̟, ⁿ, œ, ᴜɛ, ᵞ\ see Guide to Pronunciation

when combined additively produce a match for the color being considered

Tris·tram \ˈtris-trəm\ *n* [ME *Tristrem,* fr. AF *Tristan*] (14c) **:** the lover of Isolde of Ireland and husband of Isolde of Brittany in medieval legend

tri·sub·sti·tut·ed \ˈtrī-ˈsəb-stə-ˌtü-təd, -ˌtyü-\ *adj* (ca. 1899) **:** having three substituent atoms or groups in the molecule

tri·sul·fide \-ˈsəl-ˌfīd\ *n* (1866) **:** a compound of an element or radical with three atoms of sulfur

tri·syl·lab·ic \ˌtrī-sə-ˈla-bik\ *adj* [L *trisyllabus,* fr. Gk *trisyllabos,* fr. *tri-* + *syllabē* syllable] (ca. 1637) **:** having three syllables ⟨a ~ word⟩

tri·syl·la·ble \ˈtrī-ˌsi-lə-bəl, (ˌ)trī-ˈ\ *n* (1589) **:** a word of three syllables

trite \ˈtrīt\ *adj* **trit·er; trit·est** [L *tritus,* fr. pp. of *terere* to rub, wear away — more at THROW] (1548) **:** hackneyed or boring from much use **:** not fresh or original — **trite·ly** *adv* — **trite·ness** *n*

syn TRITE, HACKNEYED, STEREOTYPED, THREADBARE mean lacking the freshness that evokes attention or interest. TRITE applies to a once effective phrase or idea spoiled from long familiarity ⟨"you win some, you lose some" is a *trite* expression⟩. HACKNEYED stresses being worn out by overuse so as to become dull and meaningless ⟨all of the metaphors and images in the poem are *hackneyed*⟩. STEREOTYPED implies falling invariably into the same pattern or form ⟨views of minorities that are *stereotyped* and out-of-date⟩. THREADBARE applies to what has been used until its possibilities of interest have been totally exhausted ⟨a mystery novel with a *threadbare* plot⟩.

tri·the·ism \ˈtrī-thē-ˌi-zəm\ *n* (1678) **:** the doctrine that the Father, Son, and Holy Spirit are three distinct Gods — **tri·the·ist** \-(ˌ)thē-ist\ *n or adj* — **tri·the·is·tic** \ˌtrī-thē-ˈis-tik\ *or* **tri·the·is·ti·cal** \-ˈis-ti-kəl\ *adj*

tri·thing \ˈtrī-thiŋ\ *n* [ME, alter. of OE **thrithing,* **thriding*] (12c) *archaic* **:** 3RIDING 1

tri·ti·at·ed \ˈtri-tē-ˌā-təd, ˈtri-shē-\ *adj* (1953) **:** containing and esp. labeled with tritium

trit·i·ca·le \ˌtri-tə-ˈkā-lē\ *n* [NL, blend of *Triticum,* genus of wheat, and *Secale,* genus of rye] (1952) **:** an amphidiploid hybrid between wheat and rye having protein-rich grain; *also* **:** its grain

tri·ti·um \ˈtri-tē-əm, ˈtri-shē-\ *n* [NL, fr. Gk *tritos* third — more at THIRD] (1933) **:** a radioactive isotope of hydrogen that has one proton and two neutrons in its nucleus and that has three times the mass of ordinary hydrogen — symbol *T*

trit·o·ma \ˈtri-tə-mə\ *n* [NL, genus name, fr. Gk *tritomos* thrice cut, fr. *tri-* + *temnein* to cut; fr. their trimerous flowers — more at TOME] (1804) **:** any of a genus (*Kniphofia*) of African herbs of the lily family that are often grown for their spikes of showy red or yellow flowers

1**tri·ton** \ˈtrī-tᵊn\ *n* [L, fr. Gk *Tritōn*] (1536) **1** *cap* **:** a son of Poseidon described as a demigod of the sea with the lower part of his body like that of a fish **2** [NL, genus name, fr. L *Triton*] **:** any of various large marine gastropod mollusks (family Ranellidae syn. Cymatiidae) with a heavy elongated conical shell; *also* **:** the shell

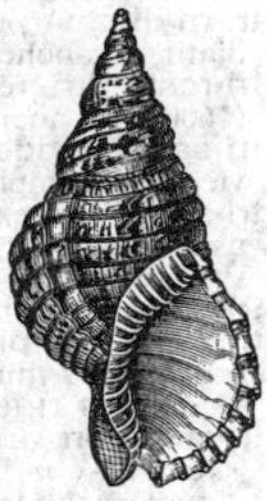

triton 2

2**tri·ton** \ˈtrī-ˌtän\ *n* [*trit*ium + 2*-on*] (1934) **:** the nucleus of tritium

tri·tone \ˈtrī-ˌtōn\ *n* [Gk *tritonon,* fr. *tri-* + *tonos* tone] (1609) **:** a musical interval of three whole steps

1**trit·u·rate** \ˈtri-chə-ˌrāt\ *vt* **-rat·ed; -rat·ing** [LL *trituratus,* pp. of *triturare* to thresh, fr. L *tritura* act of rubbing, threshing, fr. *tritus,* pp. — more at TRITE] (ca. 1755) **1 :** CRUSH, GRIND **2 :** to pulverize and comminute thoroughly by rubbing or grinding — **trit·u·ra·ble** \ˈtri-chə-rə-bəl\ *adj* — **trit·u·ra·tor** \-ˌrā-tər\ *n*

2**trit·u·rate** \-rət\ *n* (ca. 1891) **:** a triturated substance **:** TRITURATION 2

trit·u·ra·tion \ˌtri-chə-ˈrā-shən\ *n* (1646) **1 :** the act or process of triturating **:** the state of being triturated **:** COMMINUTION **2 :** a triturated medicinal powder made by triturating a substance with a diluent

1**tri·umph** \ˈtrī-əm(p)f\ *n, pl* **tri·umphs** \-əm(p)fs, -əm(p)s\ [ME *triumphe,* fr. OF, fr. L *triumphus*] (14c) **1 :** a ceremony attending the entering of Rome by a general who had won a decisive victory over a foreign enemy — compare OVATION 1 **2 :** the joy or exultation of victory or success **3 a :** a victory or conquest by or as if by military force **b :** a notable success ⟨the party was a ~⟩ — **tri·um·phal** \trī-ˈəm(p)-fəl\ *adj*

2**triumph** *vi* (1508) **1 :** to obtain victory **:** PREVAIL **2 a :** to receive the honor of a triumph **b :** to celebrate victory or success boastfully or exultingly

tri·um·phal·ism \trī-ˈəm(p)-fə-ˌli-zəm\ *n* (1964) **:** an attitude or feeling of victory or superiority: as **a :** the attitude that one religious creed is superior to all others **b :** smug or boastful pride in the success or dominance of one's nation or ideology over others — **tri·um·phal·ist** \-fə-list\ *n or adj*

tri·um·phant \trī-ˈəm(p)-fənt\ *adj* (15c) **1 :** VICTORIOUS, CONQUERING ⟨~ armies⟩ **2** *archaic* **:** of or relating to a triumph **3 :** rejoicing for or celebrating victory ⟨a ~ shout⟩ **4 :** notably successful ⟨a ~ performance⟩ — **tri·um·phant·ly** *adv*

tri·um·vir \trī-ˈəm-vər\ *n, pl* **-virs** *also* **-vi·ri** \-və-ˌrī, -ˌrē\ [ME, fr. L, back-formation fr. *triumviri,* pl., commission of three men, fr. *trium virum* of three men] (15c) **:** one of a commission or ruling body of three

tri·um·vi·rate \trī-ˈəm-və-rət\ *n* (1584) **1 :** a body of triumvirs **2 :** the office or government of triumvirs **3 :** a group or association of three

1**tri·une** \ˈtrī-ˌyün\ *n, often cap* [L *tri-* + *unus* one — more at ONE] (1605) **:** TRINITY 1

2**triune** *adj* (1632) **:** three in one: **a :** of or relating to the Trinity ⟨the ~ God⟩ **b :** consisting of three parts, members, or aspects

tri·va·lent \(ˌ)trī-ˈvā-lənt\ *adj* [ISV] (1865) **1 :** having a chemical valence of three **2 :** conferring immunity to three different pathogenic strains or species ⟨a ~ influenza vaccine⟩

triv·et \ˈtri-vət\ *n* [ME *trevet,* fr. OE *trefet,* prob. modif. of LL *triped-, tripes,* fr. L, three-footed, fr. *tri-* + *ped-, pes* foot — more at FOOT] (bef. 12c) **1 :** a three-legged stand **:** TRIPOD **2 :** a usu. metal stand with short feet for use under a hot dish

triv·ia \ˈtri-vē-ə\ *n pl but sing or pl in constr* [NL, back-formation fr. L *trivialis*] (1920) **:** unimportant matters **:** trivial facts or details; *also, sing in constr* **:** a quizzing game involving obscure facts

triv·i·al \ˈtri-vē-əl\ *adj* [L *trivialis* found everywhere, commonplace, fr. *trivium* crossroads, fr. *tri-* + *via* way — more at WAY] (1589) **1 :** COMMONPLACE, ORDINARY **2 a :** of little worth or importance ⟨a ~ objection⟩ ⟨~ problems⟩ **b :** relating to or being the mathematically simplest case; *specif* **:** characterized by having all variables equal to zero ⟨a ~ solution to a linear equation⟩ **3 :** SPECIFIC 4 — **triv·i·al·ist** \-ə-list\ *n* — **triv·i·al·ly** \-ə-lē\ *adv*

triv·i·al·ise *Brit var of* TRIVIALIZE

triv·i·al·i·ty \ˌtri-vē-ˈa-lə-tē\ *n, pl* **-ties** (1598) **1 :** the quality or state of being trivial **2 :** something trivial **:** TRIFLE

triv·i·al·ize \ˈtri-vē-ə-ˌlīz\ *vt* **-ized; -iz·ing** (1846) **:** to make trivial **:** reduce to triviality — **triv·i·al·i·za·tion** \ˌtri-vē-ə-lə-ˈzā-shən\ *n*

trivial name *n* (1759) **1 :** SPECIFIC EPITHET **2 :** a common or vernacular name of an organism or chemical

triv·i·um \ˈtri-vē-əm\ *n* [ML, fr. L, meeting of three ways, crossroads] (1647) **:** a group of studies consisting of grammar, rhetoric, and logic and forming the lower division of the seven liberal arts in medieval universities — compare QUADRIVIUM

1**tri·week·ly** \(ˌ)trī-ˈwē-klē\ *adj* (1832) **1 :** occurring or appearing three times a week **2 :** occurring or appearing every three weeks — **triweekly** *adv*

2**triweekly** *n, pl* **-lies** (1838) **:** a triweekly publication

-trix *n suffix, pl* **-trices** *or* **-trixes** [ME, fr. L, fem. of *-tor,* suffix denoting an agent] **1 :** female that does or is associated with a (specified) thing ⟨avia*trix*⟩ **2 :** geometric line, point, or surface ⟨genera*trix*⟩

tRNA \ˌtē-ˌär-ˌen-ˈā, ˈtē-ˌär-ˌen-ˌā\ *n* (1962) **:** TRANSFER RNA

tro·car *also* **tro·char** \ˈtrō-ˌkär\ *n* [F *trocart,* alter. of *trois-quart* fr. *trois* three + *carre* edge] (ca. 1706) **:** a sharp-pointed surgical instrument fitted with a cannula and used esp. to insert the cannula into a body cavity as a drainage outlet

tro·cha·ic \trō-ˈkā-ik\ *adj* [MF *trochaïque,* fr. L *trochaicus,* fr. Gk *trochaikos,* fr. *trochaios* trochee] (1589) **:** of, relating to, or consisting of trochees — **trochaic** *n*

tro·chan·ter \trō-ˈkan-tər\ *n* [Gk *trochantēr;* akin to Gk *trechein* to run] (1615) **1 :** a rough prominence at the upper part of the femur of many vertebrates serving usu. for the attachment of muscles **2 :** the second segment of an insect's leg adjacent to the coxa — **tro·chan·ter·al** \-tə-rəl\ *adj* — **tro·chan·ter·ic** \ˌtrō-kən-ˈter-ik, -ˌkan-\ *adj*

tro·che \ˈtrō-kē, *Brit usu* ˈtrōsh\ *n* [alter. of earlier *trochisk,* fr. LL *trochiscus,* fr. Gk *trochiskos,* fr. dim. of *trochos* wheel] (ca. 1597) **:** LOZENGE 3

tro·chee \ˈtrō-(ˌ)kē\ *n* [prob. fr. MF *trochée,* fr. L *trochaeus,* fr. Gk *trochaios,* fr. *trochaios* running, fr. *trochē* run, course, fr. *trechein* to run; akin to Gk *trochos* wheel, OIr *droch*] (1589) **:** a metrical foot consisting of one long syllable followed by one short syllable or of one stressed syllable followed by one unstressed syllable (as in *apple*)

troch·lea \ˈträ-klē-ə\ *n* [NL, fr. L, block of pulleys, fr. Gk *trochileia,* fr. *trochilos* sheave, fr. *trochos* wheel] (ca. 1693) **:** an anatomical structure that is held to resemble a pulley; *esp* **:** the articular surface on the medial condyle of the humerus that articulates with the ulna

troch·le·ar \-ər\ *adj* (ca. 1681) **1 :** of, relating to, or being a trochlea **2 :** of, relating to, or being a trochlear nerve

trochlear nerve *n* (ca. 1858) **:** either of the fourth pair of cranial nerves that supply some of the eye muscles with motor fibers — called also *trochlear*

tro·choid \ˈtrō-ˌkȯid, ˈträ-ˌkȯid\ *n* [Gk *trochoeidēs* like a wheel, fr. *trochos* wheel] (ca. 1704) **:** the curve generated by a point on the radius of a circle or the radius extended as the circle rolls on a fixed straight line — **tro·choi·dal** \trō-ˈkȯi-dᵊl, trä-\ *adj*

tro·cho·phore \ˈträ-kə-ˌfȯr\ *n* [ultim. fr. Gk *trochos* wheel + *pherein* to carry — more at BEAR] (1892) **:** a free-swimming ciliate larva occurring in several invertebrate groups (as the polychaete worms and mollusks)

trod *past and past part of* TREAD

trodden *past part of* TREAD

trof·fer \ˈträ-fər, ˈtrȯ-\ *n* [blend of *trough* and *coffer*] (1942) **:** an inverted trough serving as a support and reflector usu. for a fluorescent lighting unit

trog·lo·dyte \ˈträ-glə-ˌdīt\ *n* [L *troglodytae,* pl., fr. Gk *trōglodytai,* fr. *trōglē* hole, cave (akin to Gk *trōgein* to gnaw, Arm *aracem* I lead to pasture, graze) + *dyein* to enter] (1555) **1 :** a member of any of various peoples (as in antiquity) who lived or were reputed to live chiefly in caves **2 :** a person characterized by reclusive habits or outmoded or reactionary attitudes — **trog·lo·dyt·ic** \ˌträ-glə-ˈdi-tik\ *adj*

tro·gon \ˈtrō-ˌgän\ *n* [NL, genus name, fr. Gk *trōgōn,* prp. of *trōgein* to gnaw] (1792) **:** any of numerous nonpasserine tropical birds (family Trogonidae) with brilliant often iridescent plumage

troi·ka \ˈtrȯi-kə\ *n* [Russ *troĭka,* fr. *troe* three; akin to OE *thrīe* three] (1842) **1 :** a Russian vehicle drawn by three horses abreast; *also* **:** a team for such a vehicle **2 :** a group of three; *esp* **:** an administrative or ruling body of three

troi·lite \ˈtrō-ə-ˌlīt, ˈtrȯi-ˌlīt\ *n* [G *Troilit,* fr. Domenico *Troili,* 18th cent. Ital. scientist + G *-it* -ite] (ca. 1868) **:** a mineral that is a variety of pyrrhotite and that is widely but sparsely distributed (as on earth, in meteorites, and in lunar soil samples)

Troi·lus \ˈtrȯi-ləs, ˈtrō-ə-ləs\ *n* [ME, fr. L, fr. Gk *Trōilos*] (14c) **:** a son of Priam who in medieval legend loved Cressida and lost her to Diomedes

1**Tro·jan** \ˈtrō-jən\ *n* [ME, fr. L *trojanus* of Troy, fr. *Troia, Troja* Troy, fr. Gk *Trōia*] (14c) **1 :** a native or inhabitant of Troy **2 :** one who shows qualities (as pluck, endurance, or determined energy) attributed to the defenders of ancient Troy **3 :** a merry and often irresponsible or disreputable companion

2**Trojan** *adj* (14c) **1 :** of, relating to, or resembling ancient Troy or its inhabitants **2 :** of, relating to, or constituting a Trojan horse

Trojan horse *n* [fr. the large hollow wooden horse filled with Greek soldiers and introduced within the walls of Troy by a stratagem] (1837) **1 :** someone or something intended to defeat or subvert from within usu. by deceptive means **2 :** a seemingly useful computer program that contains concealed instructions which when activated perform an illicit or malicious action (as destroying data files); *also* **:** the concealed instructions of such a program — compare VIRUS

Trojan War *n* (1611) **:** a 10-year war between the Greeks and Trojans brought on by the abduction of Helen by Paris and ended with the destruction of Troy

[1]**troll** \ˈtrōl\ *vb* [ME, prob. fr. AF **troiller, *troller;* akin to AF *troil, trolle* winch] *vt* (15c) **1 :** to cause to move round and round : ROLL **2 a :** to sing the parts of (as a round or catch) in succession **b :** to sing loudly **c :** to celebrate in song **3 a :** to fish for by trolling **b :** to fish by trolling in ⟨∼ lakes⟩ **c :** to pull through the water in trolling ⟨∼ a lure⟩ **d :** to search in or at ⟨∼*s* flea markets for bargains⟩; *also* : PROWL ⟨∼ nightclubs⟩ ∼ *vi* **1 :** to move around : RAMBLE **2 a :** to fish by trailing a lure or baited hook from a moving boat **b :** SEARCH, LOOK ⟨∼*ing* for sponsors⟩; *also* : PROWL **3 :** to sing or play in a jovial manner **4 :** to speak rapidly — **troll·er** *n*

[2]**troll** *n* (1869) **:** a lure or a line with its lure and hook used in trolling

[3]**troll** *n* [Norw *troll* & Dan *trold,* fr. ON *troll* giant, demon; prob. akin to MHG *trolle* lout] (1616) **:** a dwarf or giant in Scandinavian folklore inhabiting caves or hills

[1]**trol·ley** *also* **trol·ly** \ˈträ-lē\ *n, pl* **trolleys** *also* **trollies** [prob. fr. [1]*troll*] (1823) **1** *dial Eng* **:** a cart of any of various kinds **2 a :** a device that carries electric current from an overhead wire to an electrically driven vehicle **b :** a streetcar powered electrically through a trolley — called also *trolley car* **3 :** a wheeled carriage running on an overhead rail or track **4** *chiefly Brit* **:** a cart or wheeled stand used for conveying something (as food or books)

[2]**trolley** *also* **trolly** *vb* **trol·leyed** *also* **trol·lied; trol·ley·ing** *also* **trol·ly·ing** *vt* (1882) **:** to convey by a trolley ∼ *vi* **:** to ride on a trolley

trol·ley·bus \ˈträ-lē-ˌbəs\ *n* (1921) **:** a bus that is powered electrically by two overhead wires

trol·lop \ˈträ-ləp\ *n* [perh. irreg. fr. *trull*] (1621) **:** a vulgar or disreputable woman; *esp* **:** one who engages in sex promiscuously or for money

Trombe wall \ˈtrōmb-, ˈträmb-, ˈtrōⁿb-\ *n* [Félix *Trombe* †1985 Fr. designer] (1978) **:** a masonry wall that is usu. separated from the outdoors by a glass wall and is designed to absorb solar heat and release it into the interior of a building

trom·bone \träm-ˈbōn, (ˌ)trəm-ˈ, ˈträm-ˌ\ *n* [It, aug. of *tromba* trumpet, of Gmc origin; akin to OHG *trumba, trumpa* trumpet] (ca. 1724) **:** a brass instrument consisting of a long cylindrical metal tube with two turns and having a movable slide or valves for varying the tone and a usual range one octave lower than that of the trumpet — **trom·bon·ist** \-ˈbō-nist, -ˌbō-\ *n*

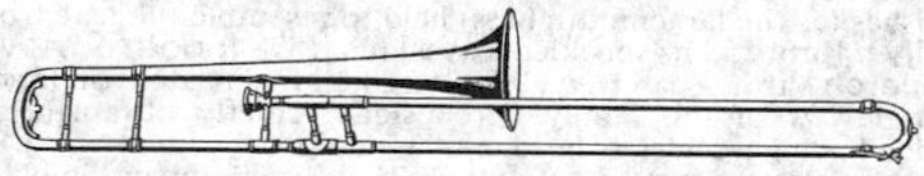

trombone

trom·mel \ˈträ-məl\ *n* [G, drum, fr. MHG *trummel,* dim. of *trumme* drum — more at DRUM] (ca. 1877) **:** a usu. cylindrical or conical revolving screen used esp. for screening or sizing rock, ore, or coal

tromp \ˈträmp, ˈtrȯmp\ *vb* [by alter.] *vi* (1846) **1 :** TRAMP 1 ⟨a lot of knocking on doors, ∼*ing* from room to room —Sara Davidson⟩ **2 :** to step hard : STAMP ⟨∼*ed* on the brake⟩ ∼ *vt* **1 :** TRAMP **2 :** STAMP ⟨∼*s* the accelerator to the floor —Jim Becker⟩ **3 a :** to give a physical beating to **b :** to defeat decisively

trompe l'oeil \(ˌ)trȯmp-ˈlə-ē, trōⁿp-ˈlœi\ *n, often attrib* [F *trompe-l'œil,* lit., deceives the eye] (1889) **1 :** a style of painting in which objects are depicted with photographically realistic detail; *also* **:** the use of similar technique in interior decorating **2 :** a trompe l'oeil painting or effect **3 :** something that misleads or deceives the senses : ILLUSION

-tron *n suffix* [Gk, suffix denoting an instrument; akin to OE *-thor,* suffix denoting an instrument, L *-trum*] **1 :** vacuum tube ⟨magne*tron*⟩ **2 :** device for the manipulation of subatomic particles ⟨cyclo*tron*⟩

tro·na \ˈtrō-nə\ *n* [Sw, prob. fr. Ar *natrūn* natron — more at NATRON] (1799) **:** a gray-white or yellowish-white monoclinic mineral consisting of a hydrous acid sodium carbonate

[1]**troop** \ˈtrüp\ *n* [MF *trope, troupe* company, herd, of Gmc origin; akin to OE *thorp, throp* village — more at THORP] (1545) **1 a :** a group of soldiers **b :** a cavalry unit corresponding to an infantry company **c** *pl* **:** ARMED FORCES, SOLDIERS **2 :** a collection of people or things : CREW 2 **3 :** a flock of mammals or birds **4 :** the basic organizational unit of Boy Scouts or Girl Scouts under an adult leader

[2]**troop** *vi* (1565) **1 :** to move or gather in crowds **2 :** to go one's way : WALK **3 :** to spend time together : ASSOCIATE **4 :** to move in large numbers

troop·er \ˈtrü-pər\ *n* (1640) **1 a (1) :** an enlisted cavalryman **(2) :** the horse of a cavalryman **b :** PARATROOPER **c :** SOLDIER **2 a :** a mounted police officer **b :** a state police officer **3 :** TROUPER 2

troop·ship \ˈtrüp-ˌship\ *n* (1800) **:** a ship or aircraft for carrying troops : TRANSPORT

trop *abbr* tropical

trop- *or* **tropo-** *comb form* [ISV, fr. Gk *tropos*] **1 :** turn : turning : change ⟨*tropo*sphere⟩ **2 :** tropism ⟨*trop*ic⟩

trope \ˈtrōp\ *n* [L *tropus,* fr. Gk *tropos* turn, way, manner, style, trope, fr. *trepein* to turn] (1533) **1 a :** a word or expression used in a figurative sense : FIGURE OF SPEECH **b :** a common or overused theme or device : CLICHÉ ⟨the usual horror movie ∼*s*⟩ **2 :** a phrase or verse added as an embellishment or interpolation to the sung parts of the Mass in the Middle Ages

troph- *or* **tropho-** *comb form* [F, fr. Gk, fr. *trophē* nourishment] **:** nutritive ⟨*tropho*blast⟩

troph·al·lax·is \ˌtrō-fə-ˈlak-səs\ *n* [NL, fr. *troph-* + Gk *allaxis* exchange, fr. *allassein* to change, exchange, fr. *allos* other — more at ELSE] (1918) **:** exchange of food (as from special glands) between social insects (as ants or termites)

tro·phic \ˈtrō-fik\ *adj* [F *trophique,* fr. Gk *trophikos,* fr. *trophē* nourishment, fr. *trephein* to nourish] (1873) **1 :** of or relating to nutrition : NUTRITIONAL ⟨∼ disorders⟩ **2 :** [3]TROPIC — **tro·phi·cal·ly** \-fi-k(ə-)lē\ *adv*

-trophic *adj comb form* [NL *-trophia* -trophy] **1 a :** of, relating to, or characterized by (such) nutrition ⟨ecto*trophic*⟩ **b :** requiring or utilizing (such) a kind of nutrition ⟨hetero*trophic*⟩ **2 :** -TROPIC 2 ⟨gonado*trophic*⟩

trophic level *n* (1942) **:** one of the hierarchical strata of a food web characterized by organisms which are the same number of steps removed from the primary producers

tro·pho·blast \ˈtrō-fə-ˌblast\ *n* [ISV] (1889) **:** the outer layer of the mammalian blastocyst that supplies nutrition to the embryo and facilitates implantation — **tro·pho·blas·tic** \ˌtrō-fə-ˈblas-tik\ *adj*

tro·pho·zo·ite \ˌtrō-fə-ˈzō-ˌīt\ *n* [*troph-* + *zo-* + [1]*-ite*] (ca. 1909) **:** a protozoan of a vegetative form as distinguished from one of a reproductive or resting form

tro·phy \ˈtrō-fē\ *n, pl* **trophies** [MF *trophee,* fr. ML tropheum, fr. L *tropaeum, trophaeum,* fr. Gk *tropaion,* fr. neut. of *tropaios* of a turning, of a rout, fr. *tropē* turn, rout, fr. *trepein* to turn] (15c) **1 :** something gained or given in victory or conquest esp. when preserved or mounted as a memorial **2 a :** a memorial of an ancient Greek or Roman victory raised on the field of battle or on the nearest land for a naval victory **b :** a representation of such a memorial (as on a medal); *also* **:** an architectural ornament representing a group of military weapons **3 :** a game animal or fish suitable for mounting as a trophy — usu. used attributively **4 :** one that is prized for qualities that enhance prestige or social status — usu. used attributively ⟨a ∼ wife⟩ ⟨a ∼ house⟩ — **trophy** *vt*

-trophy *n comb form* [NL *-trophia,* fr. Gk, fr. *-trophos* nourishing, fr. *trephein*] **:** nutrition : nurture : growth ⟨dys*trophy*⟩

[1]**trop·ic** \ˈträ-pik\ *n* [ME *tropik,* fr. L *tropicus* of the solstice, fr. Gk *tropikos,* fr. *tropē* turn] (1527) **1 :** either of the two parallels of terrestrial latitude at a distance of about 23½ degrees north or south of the equator where the sun is directly overhead when it reaches its most northerly or southerly point in the sky — compare TROPIC OF CANCER, TROPIC OF CAPRICORN **2** *pl, often cap* **:** the region lying between the tropics

[2]**tropic** *adj* (1551) **:** of, relating to, or occurring in the tropics

[3]**tro·pic** \ˈtrō-pik\ *adj* [*trop-*] (1903) **1 :** of, relating to, or characteristic of tropism or of a tropism **2** *of a hormone* **:** influencing the activity of a specified gland

-tropic *adj comb form* [F *-tropique,* fr. Gk *-tropos* -tropous] **1 :** turning, changing, or tending to turn or change in a (specified) manner or in response to a (specified) stimulus ⟨geo*tropic*⟩ **2 :** attracted to or acting upon (something specified) ⟨neuro*tropic*⟩

trop·i·cal *for 1* ˈträ-pi-kəl, *for 2* ˈtrō- *also* ˈträ-\ *adj* (1527) **1 a :** of, relating to, occurring in, or suitable for use in the tropics ⟨∼ forests⟩ ⟨a ∼ disease⟩ **b :** of, being, or characteristic of a region or climate that is frost-free with temperatures high enough to support year-round plant growth given sufficient moisture ⟨∼ Florida⟩ **2** [L *tropicus,* fr. Gk *tropikos,* fr. *tropos* trope] **:** FIGURATIVE 2 — **trop·i·cal·ly** \-pi-k(ə-)lē\ *adv*

tropical aquarium *n* (ca. 1948) **:** an aquarium kept at a uniform warmth and used esp. for tropical fish

tropical cyclone *n* (1920) **:** a cyclone originating in the tropics; *specif* : HURRICANE

tropical fish *n* (1931) **:** any of various small usu. showy fishes of tropical origin often kept in a tropical aquarium

trop·i·cal·ize \ˈträ-pi-kə-ˌlīz\ *vt* **-ized; -iz·ing** (1885) **1 :** to make tropical (as in character, conditions, or appearance) **2 :** to fit or adapt for use in a tropical climate esp. by measures designed to combat the effects of fungi and moisture

tropical oil *n* (1988) **:** any of several oils (as coconut oil and palm oil) that are high in saturated fatty acids and are used esp. in commercially prepared baked goods, snack products, and confections

tropical rain forest *n* (1909) **:** RAIN FOREST 1

tropical sprue *n* (ca. 1955) **:** [2]SPRUE 1

tropical storm *n* (1937) **:** a tropical cyclone with strong winds of over 39 miles (63 kilometers) per hour but less than hurricane intensity

tropic bird *n* (ca. 1671) **:** any of a genus (*Phaethon* of the family Phaethontidae) of web-footed birds that are related to the pelicans, are found chiefly in tropical seas often far from land, and have mostly white satiny plumage marked with a little black, a greatly elongated central pair of tail feathers, and a brightly colored bill

Tropic of Cancer [fr. the sign of the zodiac which its celestial projection intersects] (1545) **:** the parallel of latitude that is approximately 23½ degrees north of the equator and that is the northernmost latitude reached by the overhead sun

Tropic of Capricorn [fr. the sign of the zodiac which its celestial projection intersects] (1551) **:** the parallel of latitude that is approximately 23½ degrees south of the equator and that is the southernmost latitude reached by the overhead sun

-tropin *or* **-trophin** *n comb form* [*-tropin,* alter. of *-trophin,* fr. *-trophic* + [1]*-in*] **:** hormone ⟨gonado*tropin*⟩ ⟨somato*tropin*⟩

tro·pism \ˈtrō-ˌpi-zəm\ *n* [ISV *-tropism*] (1899) **1 a :** involuntary orientation by an organism or one of its parts that involves turning or curving by movement or by differential growth and is a positive or negative response to a source of stimulation **b :** a reflex reaction involving a tropism **2 :** an innate tendency to react in a definite manner to stimuli; *broadly* **:** a natural inclination : PROPENSITY ⟨encouraged his ∼ toward the theatrical —John Updike⟩ — **tro·pis·tic** \trō-ˈpis-tik\ *adj*

-tropism *n comb form* [ISV, fr. *trop-*] **:** tropism ⟨helio*tropism*⟩

tropo- — see TROP-

tro·po·col·la·gen \ˌträ-pə-ˈkä-lə-jən, ˌtrō-\ *n* (1954) **:** a subunit of collagen fibrils consisting of three polypeptide strands arranged in a helix

tro·po·log·i·cal \ˌtrō-pə-ˈlä-ji-kəl, ˌträ-\ *adj* (14c) **1 :** of, relating to, or involving biblical interpretation stressing moral metaphor; *also* : MORAL **2 :** characterized or varied by tropes : FIGURATIVE — **tro·po·log·i·cal·ly** \-ji-k(ə-)lē\ *adv*

tropo·my·o·sin \ˌträ-pə-ˈmī-ə-sən, ˌtrō-\ *n* (1946) **:** a protein of muscle that forms a complex with troponin regulating the interaction of actin and myosin in muscular contraction

tro·po·nin \ˈtrō-pə-nən, ˈträ-, -ˌnin\ *n* [by shortening & alter. fr. *tropomyosin*] (1966) **:** a protein of muscle that together with tropomyosin forms a regulatory protein complex controlling the interaction of actin and myosin and that when combined with calcium ions permits muscular contraction

tro·po·pause \ˈtrō-pə-ˌpȯz, ˈträ-\ *n* [ISV *tropo*sphere + *pause*] (1918) : the region at the top of the troposphere; *also* : a comparable layer of a celestial body

tro·po·sphere \ˈtrō-pə-ˌsfir, ˈträ-\ *n* [ISV] (1909) : the lowest densest part of the earth's atmosphere in which most weather changes occur and temperature generally decreases rapidly with altitude and which extends from the earth's surface to the bottom of the stratosphere — **tro·po·spher·ic** \ˌtrō-pə-ˈsfir-ik, ˌträ-, -ˈsfer-\ *adj*

tro·po·tax·is \ˌtrō-pə-ˈtak-səs, ˌträ-\ *n* [NL] (1934) : a taxis in which an organism orients itself by the simultaneous comparison of stimuli of different intensity acting on separate end organs

-tropous *adj comb form* [Gk *-tropos*, fr. *trepein* to turn] : turning or curving in (such) a way : exhibiting (such) a tropism ⟨ana*tropous*⟩

-tropy *n comb form* [F *-tropie*, fr. Gk *-tropia*, fr. *-tropos*] **1** : condition of exhibiting (such) a behavior ⟨allo*tropy*⟩ **2** : change in a (specified) way or in response to a (specified) stimulus ⟨thixo*tropy*⟩

[1]trot \ˈträt\ *n* [ME, fr. AF, fr. *troter* to trot, of Gmc origin; akin to OHG *trottōn* to tread, OE *tredan*] (14c) **1 a** (1) : a moderately fast gait of a quadruped (as a horse) in which the legs move in diagonal pairs (2) : a jogging gait of a human that falls between a walk and a run **b** : a ride on horseback **2** : an old woman **3** : a literal translation of a foreign text **4** *pl* : DIARRHEA — used with *the*

[2]trot *vb* **trot·ted; trot·ting** *vi* (14c) **1** : to ride, drive, or proceed at a trot ⟨the fox *trotted* over the knoll⟩ **2** : to proceed briskly : HURRY ~ *vt* **1** : to cause to go at a trot **2** : to traverse at a trot

[3]trot *n* (1883) : TROTLINE; *also* : one of the short lines with hooks that are attached to a trotline at intervals

Trot \ˈträt\ *n* (1962) : an adherent of Trotskyism : TROTSKYIST, TROTSKYITE

[1]troth \ˈträth, ˈtrȯth, ˈtrōth, *or with* th\ *n* [ME *trouth*, fr. OE *trēowth* — more at TRUTH] (12c) **1** : loyal or pledged faithfulness : FIDELITY ⟨pledged my ~⟩ **2** : one's pledged word ⟨I don't remember the details or, by my ~, even the gist —Stanley Elkin⟩; *also* : BETROTHAL

[2]troth *vt* (14c) : PLEDGE, BETROTH

[1]troth·plight \ˈträth-ˌplīt, ˈtrȯth-, ˈtrōth-\ *vt* (14c) *archaic* : BETROTH

[2]trothplight *n* (1513) *archaic* : BETROTHAL

trot·line \ˈträt-ˌlīn\ *n* [prob. fr. [3]*trot*] (1826) : SETLINE; *esp* : a comparatively short setline used near shore or along streams

trot out *vt* (1836) **1** : to lead out and show the paces of (as a horse) **2** : to bring forward for display or use ⟨*trotted out* a new excuse⟩

Trots·ky·ism \ˈträt-skē-ˌi-zəm, ˈtrȯt-\ *n* (1925) : the political, economic, and social principles advocated by Trotsky; *esp* : the theory and practice of communism developed by or associated with Trotsky and usu. including adherence to the concept of worldwide revolution as opposed to socialism in one country — **Trots·ky·ist** \-skē-ist\ *n or adj* — **Trots·ky·ite** \-skē-ˌīt\ *n or adj*

trot·ter \ˈträ-tər\ *n* (14c) **1** : one that trots; *specif* : a standardbred horse trained for harness racing **2** : a pig's foot used as food

trou·ba·dour \ˈtrü-bə-ˌdȯr, -ˌdu̇r\ *n* [F, fr. Old Occitan *trobador*, fr. *trobar* to compose, fr. VL **tropare*, fr. L *tropus* trope] (ca. 1741) **1** : one of a class of lyric poets and poet-musicians often of knightly rank who flourished from the 11th to the end of the 13th century chiefly in the south of France and the north of Italy and whose major theme was courtly love — compare TROUVÈRE **2** : a singer esp. of folk songs

[1]trou·ble \ˈtrə-bəl\ *vb* **trou·bled; trou·bling** \ˈtrə-b(ə-)liŋ\ [ME, fr. AF *trubler*, fr. VL **turbulare*, fr. **turbulus* agitated, alter. of L *turbulentus* — more at TURBULENT] *vt* (13c) **1 a** : to agitate mentally or spiritually : WORRY, DISTURB **b** (1) *archaic* : MISTREAT, OPPRESS (2) : to produce physical disorder in : AFFLICT ⟨*troubled* by a cold⟩ **c** : to put to exertion or inconvenience ⟨I'm sorry to ~ you⟩ **2** : to put into confused motion ⟨the wind *troubled* the sea⟩ ~ *vi* **1** : to become mentally agitated : WORRY ⟨refused to ~ over trifles⟩ **2** : to make an effort : be at pains ⟨did not ~ to come⟩ — **trou·bler** \-b(ə-)lər\ *n*

[2]trouble *n* (13c) **1** : the quality or state of being troubled esp. mentally **2** : public unrest or disturbance ⟨there's ~ brewing downtown⟩ **3** : an instance of trouble ⟨used to disguise her frustrations and despair by making light of her ~*s* —*Current Biog.*⟩ **4** : a state or condition of distress, annoyance, or difficulty ⟨in ~ with the law⟩ ⟨heading for ~⟩ ⟨got into financial ~⟩: as **a** : a condition of physical distress or ill health : AILMENT ⟨back ~⟩ ⟨heart ~⟩ **b** : a condition of mechanical malfunction ⟨engine ~⟩ **c** : a condition of doing something badly or only with great difficulty ⟨has ~ reading⟩ ⟨has ~ breathing⟩ **d** : pregnancy out of wedlock ⟨got a girl in ~⟩ **5** : an effort made : PAINS ⟨took the ~ to do it right⟩ **6 a** : a cause of distress, annoyance, or inconvenience ⟨don't mean to be any ~⟩ ⟨what's the ~?⟩ **b** : a negative feature : DRAWBACK ⟨the ~ with you is you're too honest⟩ ⟨the main ~ with electronic systems is the overreliance on them —John Perham⟩ **c** : the unhappy or sad fact ⟨the ~ is, I need the money⟩

troubled *adj* (14c) **1 a** : CONCERNED, WORRIED ⟨~ feelings about the decision⟩ **b** : exhibiting emotional or behavioral problems ⟨a program for ~ youth⟩ **2** : characterized by or indicative of trouble ⟨our ~ cities⟩ ⟨a gray and ~ sky⟩

trou·ble·mak·er \ˈtrə-bəl-ˌmā-kər\ *n* (ca. 1914) : a person who consciously or unconsciously causes trouble — **trou·ble·mak·ing** \-kiŋ\ *adj or n*

trou·ble·shoot \-ˌshüt\ *vb* **-shot** \-ˌshät\; **-shoot·ing** [back-formation fr. *troubleshooter*] *vi* (1918) : to operate or serve as a troubleshooter ⟨is ~*ing* for an electronics firm⟩ ~ *vt* : to investigate or deal with in the role of troubleshooter ⟨~*s* TV receivers⟩ ⟨~ a problem⟩

trou·ble·shoot·er \-ˌshü-tər\ *n* (1905) **1** : a skilled worker employed to locate trouble and make repairs in machinery and technical equipment **2** : an expert in resolving diplomatic or political disputes : a mediator of disputes that are at an impasse **3** : a person skilled at solving or anticipating problems or difficulties

trou·ble·some \-səm\ *adj* (1542) **1** : DIFFICULT, BURDENSOME **2** : giving trouble or anxiety : VEXATIOUS ⟨~ news⟩ — **trou·ble·some·ly** *adv* — **trou·ble·some·ness** *n*

trou·blous \ˈtrə-b(ə-)ləs\ *adj* (15c) **1** : full of trouble : STORMY ⟨these ~ times⟩ **2** : causing trouble : TROUBLESOME ⟨inflation is a ~ matter⟩ — **trou·blous·ly** *adv* — **trou·blous·ness** *n*

trough \ˈtrȯf, ˈtrȯth, *by bakers often* ˈtrō\ *n, pl* **troughs** \ˈtrȯfs, ˈtrȯvz; ˈtrȯths, ˈtrȯ(th)z; ˈtrōz\ [ME, fr. OE *trog*; akin to OHG *trog* trough, OE *trēow* tree, wood — more at TREE] (bef. 12c) **1 a** : a long shallow often V-shaped receptacle for the drinking water or feed of domestic animals **b** : any of various domestic or industrial containers **2 a** : a conduit, drain, or channel for water; *esp* : a gutter along the eaves of a building **b** : a long and narrow or shallow channel or depression (as between waves or hills); *esp* : a long but shallow depression in the bed of the sea — compare TRENCH **3** : the minimum point of a complete cycle of a periodic function: as **a** : an elongated area of low barometric pressure **b** : the low point in a business cycle

trounce \ˈtrau̇n(t)s\ *vt* **trounced; trounc·ing** [origin unknown] (1868) : to thrash or punish severely; *esp* : to defeat decisively

[1]troupe \ˈtrüp\ *n* [F, fr. MF — more at TROOP] (1776) : COMPANY, TROOP; *esp* : a group of theatrical performers

[2]troupe *vi* **trouped; troup·ing** (1851) : to travel in a troupe; *also* : to perform as a member of a theatrical troupe

troup·er \ˈtrü-pər\ *n* (1890) **1** : a member of a troupe; *esp* : ACTOR **2** : a person who deals with and persists through difficulty or hardship without complaint ⟨you're a real ~ to wait so long⟩

trou·pi·al \ˈtrü-pē-əl\ *n* [F *troupiale*, fr. *troupe*; fr. its living in flocks] (1825) : a large brightly colored oriole (*Icterus icterus*) of Central and So. America; *also* : any of various related birds (family Icteridae)

[1]trou·ser \ˈtrau̇-zər\ *n* [alter. of earlier *trouse*, fr. ScGael *triubhas*] (1681) : [3]PANT 1 — usu. used in pl.

[2]trouser *adj* (ca. 1771) **1** : of, relating to, or designed for trousers ⟨~ pockets⟩ **2** : of or relating to a male dramatic role played by a woman

trouser suit *n* (1939) *chiefly Brit* : PANTSUIT

trous·seau \ˈtrü-(ˌ)sō, trü-ˈ\ *n, pl* **trous·seaux** \-(ˌ)sōz, -ˈsōz\ *or* **trous·seaus** [F, fr. OF, dim. of *trousse* bundle, fr. *trousser* to truss] (1817) : the personal possessions of a bride usu. including clothes, accessories, and household linens and wares

trout \ˈtrau̇t\ *n, pl* **trout** *also* **trouts** [ME, fr. OE *trūht*, fr. LL *trocta, tructa*, a fish with sharp teeth, fr. Gk *trōktēs*, lit., gnawer, fr. *trōgein* to gnaw — more at TROGLODYTE] (bef. 12c) **1** : any of various salmonid food and sport fishes that are mostly smaller than the typical salmons and are anadromous or restricted to cool clear freshwater: **a** : any of various Old or New World fishes (genera *Salmo* and *Oncorhynchus*) — compare BROWN TROUT, RAINBOW TROUT **b** : [1]CHAR **2** : any of various fishes (as the largemouth bass) held to resemble the true trouts

trout lily *n* [prob. fr. its speckled leaves] (ca. 1898) : DOGTOOTH VIOLET

trout–perch \ˈtrau̇t-ˌpərch\ *n* (1883) : a small freshwater fish (*Percopsis omiscomaycus* of the family Percopsidae) chiefly of northern No. America having a scaleless head and large eyes

trouty \ˈtrau̇-tē\ *adj* **trout·i·er; -est** (1676) : containing or likely to contain abundant trout ⟨a ~ stream⟩

trou·vère \trü-ˈver\ *n* [F, fr. OF *troveor, troverre*, fr. *trover* to compose, find, fr. VL **tropare* — more at TROUBADOUR] (1795) : one of a school of poets who flourished from the 11th to the 14th centuries and who composed mostly narrative works (as chansons de geste and fabliaux) — compare TROUBADOUR

trove \ˈtrōv\ *n* [short for *treasure trove*] (1888) **1** : DISCOVERY, FIND **2** : a valuable collection : TREASURE; *also* : HAUL, COLLECTION

tro·ver \ˈtrō-vər\ *n* [AF, finding, trover, fr. *trover* to find] (1594) : a common law action to recover the value of goods wrongfully converted to another's own use

trow \ˈtrō\ *vb* [ME, fr. OE *trēowan*; akin to OE *trēowe* faithful, true — more at TRUE] (bef. 12c) **1** *obs* : BELIEVE **2** *archaic* : THINK

[1]trow·el \ˈtrau̇(-ə)l\ *n* [ME *truel*, fr. AF, fr. LL *truella*, fr. L *trulla* ladle] (13c) : any of various hand tools used to apply, spread, shape, or smooth loose or plastic material; *also* : a scoop-shaped or flat-bladed garden tool for taking up and setting small plants

[2]trowel *vt* **-eled** *or* **-elled; -el·ing** *or* **-el·ling** (ca. 1670) : to smooth, mix, or apply with or as if with a trowel — **trow·el·er** *n*

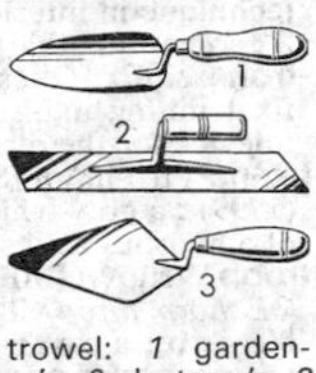

trowel: *1* gardener's, *2* plasterer's, *3* bricklayer's

troy \ˈtrȯi\ *adj* [ME *troye*, prob. fr. *Troyes*, France] (15c) : expressed in troy weight

troy weight *n* (15c) : a series of units of weight based on a pound of 12 ounces and an ounce of 480 grains — see WEIGHT table

tru·an·cy \ˈtrü-ən(t)-sē\ *n, pl* **-cies** (1784) : an act or instance of playing truant : the state of being truant

[1]tru·ant \ˈtrü-ənt\ *n* [ME, vagabond, idler, fr. AF, of Celt origin; akin to OIr *trógán* wretch, *trúag* wretched] (14c) : one who shirks duty; *esp* : one who stays out of school without permission

[2]truant *adj* (1561) **1** : shirking responsibility **2** : being, resembling, or characteristic of a truant

[3]truant *vi* (1580) : to idle away time esp. while playing truant

truant officer *n* (1868) : a person employed by a public-school system to investigate the continued absences of pupils — called also *attendance officer, truancy officer*

tru·ant·ry \ˈtrü-ən-trē\ *n, pl* **-ries** (15c) : TRUANCY

[1]truce \ˈtrüs\ *n* [ME *trewes*, pl. of *trewe* agreement, fr. OE *trēow* fidelity; akin to OE *trēowe* faithful — more at TRUE] (13c) **1** : a suspension of fighting esp. of considerable duration by agreement of opposing forces : ARMISTICE, CEASE-FIRE **2** : a respite esp. from a disagreeable or painful state or action

[2]truce *vb* **truced; truc·ing** *vi* (15c) : to make a truce ~ *vt* : to end with a truce

[1]truck \ˈtrək\ *vb* [ME *trukken*, fr. AF **truker, *troker*, fr. VL **troccare*, prob. of imit. origin] *vt* (13c) **1** : to give in exchange : SWAP **2** : to barter or dispose of by barter ~ *vi* **1** : to exchange commodities : BARTER **2** : to negotiate or traffic esp. in an underhanded way : have dealings

[2]truck *n* (1553) **1** : BARTER **2** : commodities appropriate for barter or for small trade **3** : close association or connection ⟨will have no ~ with crooks⟩ **4** : payment of wages in goods instead of cash **5** : vegetables grown for market **6** : heterogeneous small articles often of little value; *also* : RUBBISH

[3]truck *n* [prob. back-formation fr. *truckle* small wheel — more at TRUCKLE BED] (1611) **1** : a small wheel; *specif* : a small strong wheel for a gun carriage **2** : a small wooden cap at the top of a flagstaff or masthead usu. having holes for reeving flag or signal halyards **3 :** a wheeled vehicle for moving heavy articles: as **a :** a strong horse-drawn or automotive vehicle (as a pickup) for hauling **b :** a small barrow consisting of a rectangular frame having at one end a pair of handles and at the other end a pair of small heavy wheels and a projecting edge to slide under a load — called also *hand truck* **c :** a small heavy rectangular frame supported on four wheels for moving heavy objects **d :** a small flat-topped car pushed or pulled by hand **e :** a shelved stand mounted on casters **f :** an automotive vehicle with a short chassis equipped with a swivel for attaching a trailer and used esp. for the highway hauling of freight; *also* **:** a truck with attached trailer **4 a** *Brit* **:** an open railroad freight car **b :** a swiveling carriage consisting of a frame with one or more pairs of wheels and springs to carry and guide one end (as of a railroad car) in turning sharp curves — **truck·ful** \-ˌfu̇l\ *n*

[4]**truck** *vt* (1748) **:** to load or transport on a truck ~ *vi* **1 :** to transport goods by truck **2 :** to be employed in driving a truck **3 :** to roll along esp. in an easy untroubled way

[1]**truck·er** \ˈtrə-kər\ *n* [[1]*truck*] (1536) **1 :** one that barters **2** *Scot* **:** PEDDLER

[2]**trucker** *n* [[4]*truck*] (1878) **1 :** a person whose business is transporting goods by truck **2 :** a truck driver

truck farm *n* [[2]*truck*] (1866) **:** a farm devoted to the production of vegetables for the market — **truck farmer** *n*

truck·ing \ˈtrə-kiŋ\ *n* (1809) **:** the process or business of transporting goods on trucks

truck·le \ˈtrə-kəl\ *vi* **truck·led; truck·ling** \-k(ə-)liŋ\ [fr. the lower position of the truckle bed] (1647) **:** to act in a subservient manner **:** SUBMIT *syn* see FAWN — **truck·ler** \-k(ə-)lər\ *n*

truckle bed *n* [*truckle* small wheel, pulley, fr. ME *trokell,* fr. L *trochlea* block of pulleys — more at TROCHLEA] (15c) **:** TRUNDLE BED

truck·line \ˈtrək-ˌlīn\ *n* (1924) **:** a transportation line using trucks

truck·load \-ˈlōd, -ˌlōd\ *n* (1862) **1 :** a load or amount that fills or could fill a truck **2 :** the minimum weight required for shipping at truckload rates **3 :** a large amount ⟨~*s* of money⟩

truck·man \-mən\ *n* (1787) **1 :** [2]TRUCKER **2 :** a member of a fire department unit that operates a hook and ladder truck

truck·mas·ter \-ˌmas-tər\ *n* (1637) *archaic* **:** an officer in charge of trade with American Indians esp. among the early settlers

truck stop *n* (ca. 1951) **:** a facility esp. for truckers that is usu. by a highway and that includes a diner, fuel pumps, and a garage

truck system *n* (1830) **:** the system of paying wages in goods instead of cash

tru·cu·lence \ˈtrə-kyə-lən(t)s *also* ˈtrü-\ *n* (ca. 1727) **:** the quality or state of being truculent

tru·cu·len·cy \-lən(t)-sē\ *n* (1569) **:** TRUCULENCE

tru·cu·lent \-lənt\ *adj* [L *truculentus,* fr. *truc-, trux* savage; perh. akin to MIr *trú* doomed person] (ca. 1540) **1 :** feeling or displaying ferocity **:** CRUEL, SAVAGE **2 :** DEADLY, DESTRUCTIVE **3 :** scathingly harsh **:** VITRIOLIC ⟨~ criticism⟩ **4 :** aggressively self-assertive **:** BELLIGERENT — **tru·cu·lent·ly** *adv*

[1]**trudge** \ˈtrəj\ *vb* **trudged; trudg·ing** [origin unknown] *vi* (1547) **:** to walk or march steadily and usu. laboriously ⟨*trudged* through deep snow⟩ ~ *vt* **:** to trudge along or over — **trudg·er** *n*

[2]**trudge** *n* (1835) **:** a long tiring walk **:** TRAMP

trud·gen stroke \ˈtrə-jən-\ *n* [John *Trudgen* †1902 Eng. swimmer] (1893) **:** a swimming stroke consisting of alternating overarm strokes and a scissors kick

[1]**true** \ˈtrü\ *adj* **tru·er; tru·est** [ME *trewe,* fr. OE *trēowe* faithful; akin to OHG *gitriuwi* faithful, OIr *derb* sure, and prob. to Skt *dāruṇa* hard, *dāru* wood — more at TREE] (bef. 12c) **1 a :** STEADFAST, LOYAL **b :** HONEST, JUST **c** *archaic* **:** TRUTHFUL **2 a (1) :** being in accordance with the actual state of affairs ⟨~ description⟩ **(2) :** conformable to an essential reality **(3) :** fully realized or fulfilled ⟨dreams come ~⟩ **b :** IDEAL, ESSENTIAL **c :** being that which is the case rather than what is manifest or assumed ⟨the ~ dimension of the problem⟩ **d :** CONSISTENT ⟨~ to character⟩ **3 a :** properly so called ⟨~ love⟩ ⟨the ~ faith⟩ ⟨the ~ stomach of ruminant mammals⟩ **b (1) :** possessing the basic characters of and belonging to the same natural group as ⟨a whale is a ~ but not a typical mammal⟩ **(2) :** TYPICAL ⟨the ~ cats⟩ **4 :** LEGITIMATE, RIGHTFUL ⟨our ~ and lawful king⟩ **5 a :** that is fitted or formed or that functions accurately **b :** conformable to a standard or pattern **:** ACCURATE **6 :** determined with reference to the earth's axis rather than the magnetic poles ⟨~ north⟩ **7 :** logically necessary **8 :** NARROW, STRICT ⟨in the *truest* sense⟩ **9 :** corrected for error — **true·ness** *n*

[2]**true** *adv* (14c) **1 :** in accordance with fact or reality **2 a :** without deviation ⟨the bullet flew straight and ~⟩ **b :** without variation from type ⟨breed ~⟩

[3]**true** *n* (ca. 1536) **1 :** TRUTH, REALITY — usu. used with *the* **2 :** the quality or state of being accurate (as in alignment or adjustment) — used in the phrases *in true* and *out of true*

[4]**true** *vt* **trued; true·ing** *also* **tru·ing** (1841) **:** to make level, square, balanced, or concentric **:** bring or restore to a desired mechanical accuracy or form ⟨~ up a board⟩ ⟨~ up an engine cylinder⟩

true believer *n* (ca. 1820) **1 :** a person who professes absolute belief in something **2 :** a zealous supporter of a particular cause

true bill *n* (1766) **:** a bill of indictment endorsed by a grand jury as warranting prosecution of the accused

true–blue *adj* (1650) **1 :** marked by unswerving loyalty (as to a party) **2 :** GENUINE ⟨a ~ romantic⟩

true blue *n* [fr. the association of blue with constancy] (1762) **:** a person who is true-blue

true·born \ˈtrü-ˈbȯrn\ *adj* (1590) **:** genuinely such by birth ⟨a ~ Englishman —Shak.⟩

true bug *n* (1895) **:** BUG 1c

true–false test \ˈtrü-ˈfȯls-\ *n* (1924) **:** a test consisting of a series of statements to be marked as true or false

true·heart·ed \-ˈhär-təd\ *adj* (15c) **:** FAITHFUL, LOYAL ⟨a ~ soldier⟩ — **true·heart·ed·ness** *n*

true–life \ˈtrü-ˈlīf\ *adj* (1926) **:** true to life ⟨a ~ story⟩

true·love \ˈtrü-ˌləv\ *n* (14c) **:** one truly beloved or loving **:** SWEETHEART

true lover's knot *n* (1615) **:** a complicated ornamental knot not readily untied and symbolic of mutual love — called also *truelove knot;* see KNOT illustration

true·pen·ny \ˈtrü-ˌpe-nē\ *n* (1589) **:** an honest or trusty person

true porcelain *n* (1849) **:** PORCELAIN 1

true rib *n* (1741) **:** any of the ribs having costal cartilages connected directly with the sternum and in humans constituting the first seven pairs

true seal *n* (1923) **:** HAIR SEAL

truf·fle \ˈtrə-fəl, ˈtrü-\ *n* [modif. of MF *truffe,* fr. Old Occitan *trufa,* fr. VL **tufera;* akin to L *tuber* swelling, truffle — more at TUBER] (1591) **1 a :** the dark or light edible subterranean fruiting body of several European ascomycetous fungi (esp. genus *Tuber*); *also* **:** any of various similar fruiting bodies of related fungi **b :** a fungus that produces truffles **2 :** a candy made of chocolate, butter, sugar, and sometimes liqueur shaped into balls and often coated with cocoa

truf·fled \-fəld\ *adj* (1833) **:** cooked, stuffed, or garnished with truffles

trug \ˈtrəg\ *n* [origin unknown] (ca. 1864) *chiefly Brit* **:** a shallow rectangular gardening basket

tru·ism \ˈtrü-ˌi-zəm\ *n* (1708) **:** an undoubted or self-evident truth; *esp* **:** one too obvious for mention — **tru·is·tic** \trü-ˈis-tik\ *adj*

trull \ˈtrəl\ *n* [prob. fr. ME *trollen* (in *trollen forth* to travel about, wander), ultim. fr. OF *troller, treiller* to hunt for game without a scent or path] (1519) **:** PROSTITUTE, STRUMPET

tru·ly \ˈtrü-lē\ *adv* (13c) **1 a :** INDEED — often used as an intensive ⟨~, she is fair⟩ or interjectionally to express astonishment or doubt **b :** without feigning, falsity, or inaccuracy in truth or fact **2 :** in all sincerity **:** SINCERELY — often used with *yours* as a complimentary close **3 :** in agreement with fact **:** TRUTHFULLY **4 :** with exactness of construction or operation **5 :** in a proper or suitable manner

[1]**trump** \ˈtrəmp\ *n* [ME *trompe,* fr. AF *trumpe,* of Gmc origin; akin to OHG *trumba, trumpa* trumpet] (14c) **1 a :** TRUMPET **b** *chiefly Scot* **:** JEW'S HARP **2 :** a sound of or as if of trumpeting ⟨the ~ of doom⟩

[2]**trump** *n* [alter. of [1]*triumph*] (1529) **1 a :** a card of a suit any of whose cards will win over a card that is not of this suit — called also *trump card* **b :** the suit whose cards are trumps for a particular hand — often used in pl. **2 :** a decisive overriding factor or final resource — called also *trump card* **3 :** a dependable and exemplary person

[3]**trump** *vt* (1586) **1 :** to get the better of **:** OVERRIDE ⟨where ambition invariably ~*s* loyalty —Michael Kramer⟩ **2 :** to play a trump on (a card or trick) when another suit was led ~ *vi* **:** to play a trump when another suit was led

trumped–up \ˈtrəm(p)t-ˈəp\ *adj* (1728) **:** fraudulently concocted **:** SPURIOUS ⟨~ charges⟩

trum·pery \ˈtrəm-p(ə-)rē\ *n* [ME (Sc) *trompery* deceit, fr. MF, fr. *tromper* to deceive] (15c) **1 a :** worthless nonsense **b :** trivial or useless articles **:** JUNK ⟨a wagon loaded with household ~ —Washington Irving⟩ **2** *archaic* **:** tawdry finery — **trumpery** *adj*

[1]**trum·pet** \ˈtrəm-pət\ *n* [ME *trompette,* fr. AF, fr. *trumpe* trump] (14c) **1 a :** a wind instrument consisting of a conical or cylindrical usu. metal tube, a cup-shaped mouthpiece, and a flared bell; *specif* **:** a valved brass instrument having a cylindrical tube with two turns and a usual range from F sharp below middle C upward for 2½ octaves **b :** a musical instrument (as a cornet) resembling a trumpet **2 :** a trumpet player **3 :** something that resembles a trumpet or its tonal quality: as **a :** a funnel-shaped instrument (as a megaphone) for collecting, directing, or intensifying sound **b (1) :** a stentorian voice **(2) :** a penetrating cry (as of an elephant) — **trum·pet·like** *adj*

[2]**trumpet** *vi* (1530) **1 :** to blow a trumpet **2 :** to make a sound suggestive of that of a trumpet ~ *vt* **:** to sound or proclaim on or as if on a trumpet ⟨~ the news⟩

trumpet creeper *n* (ca. 1818) **:** TRUMPET VINE

trum·pet·er \ˈtrəm-pə-tər\ *n* (15c) **1 a :** a trumpet player; *specif* **:** one that gives signals with a trumpet **b :** one that praises or advocates **:** EULOGIST, SPOKESMAN **2 a :** any of a genus (*Psophia* of the family Psophiidae) of large gregarious long-legged So. American birds that are related to the cranes and have a long thin neck usu. held close to the body **b :** any of an Asian breed of pigeons with a rounded crest and heavily feathered feet

trumpeter swan *n* (1834) **:** a rare large pure white swan (*Cygnus buccinator*) of western No. America that is noted for its sonorous voice

trumpet flower *n* (ca. 1731) **1 :** any of various plants (as a trumpet vine or a datura) with trumpet-shaped flowers **2 :** the flower of a trumpet flower

trumpet honeysuckle *n* (ca. 1731) **:** a No. American honeysuckle (*Lonicera sempervirens*) with whorls of large coral-red or orange flowers having a narrow trumpet-shaped corolla

trumpet vine *n* (1709) **:** a No. American woody vine (*Campsis radicans*) of the bignonia family having pinnate leaves and large typically red trumpet-shaped flowers

trump up *vt* (1695) **1 :** to concoct esp. with intent to deceive **:** FABRICATE, INVENT **2** *archaic* **:** to cite as support for an action or claim

[1]**trun·cate** \ˈtrəŋ-ˌkāt, ˈtrən-\ *adj* [L *truncatus,* pp. of *truncare* to shorten, fr. *truncus* trunk] (1716) **:** having the end square or even ⟨~ leaves⟩

[2]**truncate** *vt* **trun·cat·ed; trun·cat·ing** (ca. 1727) **1 :** to shorten by or as if by cutting off **2 :** to replace (an edge or corner of a crystal) by a plane — **trun·ca·tion** \trəŋ-ˈkā-shən, trən-\ *n*

truncated *adj* (ca. 1704) **1 :** having the apex replaced by a plane section and esp. by one parallel to the base ⟨a ~ cone⟩ **2 a :** cut short **:** CURTAILED ⟨a ~ schedule⟩ **b :** lacking an expected or normal element (as a syllable) at the beginning or end **:** CATALECTIC

[1]**trun·cheon** \ˈtrən-chən\ *n* [ME *tronchoun,* fr. AF *trunchun,* fr. VL **truncion-,* **truncio,* fr. L *truncus* trunk] (14c) **1 :** a shattered spear or lance **2 a** *obs* **:** CLUB, BLUDGEON **b :** BATON **2 c :** a police officer's billy club

[2]**truncheon** *vt* (ca. 1598) *archaic* **:** to beat with a truncheon

[1]**trun·dle** \ˈtrən-d[ə]l\ *vb* **trun·dled; trun·dling** \ˈtrən(d)-liŋ, ˈtrən-d[ə]l-iŋ\ [[2]*trundle*] *vt* (ca. 1598) **1 a :** to propel by causing to rotate **:** ROLL

\ə\ **abut** \[ə]\ **kitten, F table** \ər\ **further** \a\ **ash** \ā\ **ace** \ä\ **mop, mar**
\au̇\ **out** \ch\ **chin** \e\ **bet** \ē\ **easy** \g\ **go** \i\ **hit** \ī\ **ice** \j\ **job**
\ŋ\ **sing** \ō\ **go** \ȯ\ **law** \ȯi\ **boy** \th\ **thin** \t͟h\ **the** \ü\ **loot** \u̇\ **foot**
\y\ **yet** \zh\ **vision, beige** \k̟, [n], œ, ue, [y]\ *see* Guide to Pronunciation

⟨a . . . child who was *trundling* a hoop —Charles Dickens⟩ **b** *archaic* **:** to cause to revolve **:** SPIN **2 :** to transport in or as if in a wheeled vehicle **:** HAUL, WHEEL ⟨*trundled* him off to school⟩ ~ *vi* **1 :** to progress by revolving **2 :** to move on or as if on wheels **:** ROLL ⟨buses *trundling* through the city⟩ — **trun·dler** \ˈtrən(d)-lər, ˈtrən-dᵊl-ər\ *n*

[2]trundle *n* [fr. *trundle* small wheel, alter. of earlier *trendle,* fr. ME, circle, ring, wheel, fr. OE *trendel;* akin to OE *trendan* to revolve — more at TREND] (ca. 1611) **1 :** the motion or sound of something rolling **2 :** TRUNDLE BED **3 :** a round or oval wooden tub

trundle bed *n* (1542) **:** a low bed usu. on casters that can be rolled or slid under a higher bed when not in use — called also *truckle bed*

trun·dle–tail \ˈtrən-dᵊl-ˌtāl\ *n* (15c) *archaic* **:** a curly-tailed dog

trunk \ˈtrəŋk\ *n* [ME *trunke* AF *trunc, trunke,* fr. L *truncus* trunk, torso] (15c) **1 a :** the main stem of a tree apart from limbs and roots — called also *bole* **b** (1) **:** the human or animal body apart from the head and appendages **:** TORSO (2) **:** the thorax of an insect **c :** the central part of anything; *specif* **:** the shaft of a column or pilaster **2 a** (1) **:** a large rigid piece of luggage used usu. for transporting clothing and personal effects (2) **:** the luggage compartment of an automobile **b** (1) **:** a superstructure over a ship's hatches usu. level with the poop deck (2) **:** the part of the cabin of a boat projecting above the deck (3) **:** the housing for a centerboard or rudder **3 :** PROBOSCIS; *esp* **:** the long muscular proboscis of the elephant **4** *pl* **:** men's shorts worn chiefly for sports ⟨swimming ~*s*⟩ **5 a :** a usu. major channel or passage (as a chute or shaft) **b :** a circuit between two telephone exchanges for making connections between subscribers; *broadly* **:** a usu. electronic path over which information is transmitted (as between computer systems) **6 a :** the principal channel or main body of a system or part that divides into branches ⟨a nerve ~⟩ ⟨the ~ of a river⟩ **b :** TRUNK LINE — **trunk·ful** \ˈtrəŋk-ˌfu̇l\ *n*

trunked \ˈtrəŋ(k)t\ *adj* (1640) **:** having a trunk esp. of a specified kind — usu. used in combination ⟨a gray-*trunked* tree⟩

trunk·fish \ˈtrəŋk-ˌfish\ *n* (ca. 1804) **:** any of numerous small often bright colored bony fishes (family Ostraciidae) of tropical seas with the body and head enclosed in a bony carapace

trunk hose \ˈtrəŋk-\ *n pl* [prob. fr. obs. E *trunk* to truncate] (1618) **:** short full breeches reaching about halfway down the thigh that were worn chiefly in the late 16th and early 17th centuries

trunk line *n* (1843) **1 :** a transportation system (as an airline, railroad, or highway) handling long-distance through traffic **2 a :** a main supply channel (as for gas or oil) **b :** TRUNK 5b

trunnel *var of* TREENAIL

trun·nion \ˈtrən-yən\ *n* [F *trognon* core, stump] (ca. 1625) **:** a pin or pivot on which something can be rotated or tilted; *esp* **:** either of two opposite gudgeons on which a cannon is swiveled

[1]truss \ˈtrəs\ *vt* [ME to pack, load, bind, fr. AF *trusser, trousser,* fr. VL **torsare,* fr. **torsus* twisted — more at TORSADE] (13c) **1 a :** to secure tightly **:** BIND **b :** to arrange for cooking by binding close the wings or legs of (a fowl) **2 :** to support, strengthen, or stiffen by or as if by a truss — **truss·er** *n*

[2]truss *n* (13c) **1 :** an iron band around a lower mast with an attachment by which a yard is secured to the mast **2 a :** BRACKET 1 **b :** an assemblage of members (as beams) forming a rigid framework **3 :** a device worn to reduce a hernia by pressure **4 :** a compact flower or fruit cluster

truss bridge *n* (1840) **:** a bridge supported mainly by trusses — see BRIDGE illustration

truss·ing \ˈtrə-siŋ\ *n* (1840) **1 :** the members forming a truss **2 :** the trusses and framework of a structure

[1]trust \ˈtrəst\ *n* [ME, prob. of Scand origin; akin to ON *traust* trust; akin to OE *trēowe* faithful — more at TRUE] (13c) **1 a :** assured reliance on the character, ability, strength, or truth of someone or something **b :** one in which confidence is placed **2 a :** dependence on something future or contingent **:** HOPE **b :** reliance on future payment for property (as merchandise) delivered **:** CREDIT ⟨bought furniture on ~⟩ **3 a :** a property interest held by one person for the benefit of another **b :** a combination of firms or corporations formed by a legal agreement; *esp* **:** one that reduces or threatens to reduce competition **4** *archaic* **:** TRUSTWORTHINESS **5 a** (1) **:** a charge or duty imposed in faith or confidence or as a condition of some relationship (2) **:** something committed or entrusted to one to be used or cared for in the interest of another **b :** responsible charge or office **c :** CARE, CUSTODY ⟨the child committed to her ~⟩ — **in trust :** in the care or possession of a trustee

[2]trust *vi* (13c) **1 a :** to place confidence **:** DEPEND ⟨~ in God⟩ ⟨~ to luck⟩ **b :** to be confident **:** HOPE **2 :** to sell or deliver on credit ~ *vt* **1 a :** to commit or place in one's care or keeping **:** ENTRUST **b :** to permit to stay or go or to do something without fear or misgiving **2 a :** to rely on the truthfulness or accuracy of **:** BELIEVE ⟨~ a rumor⟩ **b :** to place confidence in **:** rely on ⟨a friend you can ~⟩ **c :** to hope or expect confidently ⟨~*s* that the problem will be resolved soon⟩ **3 :** to extend credit to — **trust·abil·i·ty** \ˌtrəs-tə-ˈbi-lə-tē\ *n* — **trust·able** \ˈtrəs-tə-bəl\ *adj* — **trust·er** *n* — **trust·ing·ly** \ˈtrəs-tiŋ-lē\ *adv* — **trust·ing·ness** *n*

trust·bust·er \ˈtrəs(t)-ˌbəs-tər\ *n* (1903) **:** one who seeks to break up business trusts; *specif* **:** a federal official who prosecutes trusts under the antitrust laws — **trust–bust·ing** \-tiŋ\ *n*

trust company *n* (1834) **:** an incorporated trustee; *broadly* **:** a corporation that functions as a corporate and personal trustee and usu. also engages in the normal activities of a commercial bank

[1]trust·ee \ˌtrəs-ˈtē\ *n* (1647) **1 a :** one to whom something is entrusted **b :** a country charged with the supervision of a trust territory **2 a :** a natural or legal person to whom property is legally committed to be administered for the benefit of a beneficiary (as a person or a charitable organization) **b :** one (as a corporate director) occupying a position of trust and performing functions comparable to those of a trustee **3 :** TRUSTY

[2]trustee *vb* **trust·eed; trust·ee·ing** *vt* (1818) **:** to commit to the care of a trustee ~ *vi* **:** to serve as trustee

trust·ee·ship \ˌtrəs-ˈtē-ˌship\ *n* (ca. 1736) **1 :** the office or function of a trustee **2 :** supervisory control by one or more countries over a trust territory

trust·ful \ˈtrəst-fəl\ *adj* (1758) **:** full of trust **:** CONFIDING — **trust·ful·ly** \-fə-lē\ *adv* — **trust·ful·ness** *n*

trust fund *n* (1780) **:** property (as money or securities) settled or held in trust

trust·less \ˈtrəst-ləs\ *adj* (ca. 1530) **1 :** not deserving of trust **:** FAITHLESS **2 :** DISTRUSTFUL

trust territory *n* (1945) **:** a non-self-governing territory placed under an administrative authority by the Trusteeship Council of the United Nations

trust·wor·thy \ˈtrəst-ˌwər-t͟hē\ *adj* (1714) **:** worthy of confidence **:** DEPENDABLE ⟨a ~ guide⟩ ⟨~ information⟩ — **trust·wor·thi·ly** \-t͟hə-lē\ *adv* — **trust·wor·thi·ness** *n*

[1]trusty \ˈtrəs-tē\ *adj* **trust·i·er; -est** (14c) **:** TRUSTWORTHY, DEPENDABLE ⟨a ~ friend⟩ ⟨his ~ pocketknife⟩ — **trust·i·ness** *n*

[2]trusty \ˈtrəs-tē *also* ˌtrəs-ˈtē\ *n, pl* **trust·ies** (1573) **:** a trusty or trusted person; *specif* **:** a convict considered trustworthy and allowed special privileges

truth \ˈtrüth\ *n, pl* **truths** \ˈtrüt͟hz, ˈtrüths\ [ME *trewthe,* fr. OE *trēowth* fidelity; akin to OE *trēowe* faithful — more at TRUE] (bef. 12c) **1 a** *archaic* **:** FIDELITY, CONSTANCY **b :** sincerity in action, character, and utterance **2 a** (1) **:** the state of being the case **:** FACT (2) **:** the body of real things, events, and facts **:** ACTUALITY (3) *often cap* **:** a transcendent fundamental or spiritual reality **b :** a judgment, proposition, or idea that is true or accepted as true ⟨~*s* of thermodynamics⟩ **c :** the body of true statements and propositions **3 a :** the property (as of a statement) of being in accord with fact or reality **b** *chiefly Brit* **:** TRUE 2 **c :** fidelity to an original or to a standard **4** *cap, Christian Science* **:** GOD — **in truth :** in accordance with fact **:** ACTUALLY

truth·ful \ˈtrüth-fəl\ *adj* (ca. 1567) **:** telling or disposed to tell the truth ⟨a ~ witness⟩ — **truth·ful·ly** \-fə-lē\ *adv* — **truth·ful·ness** *n*

truth serum *n* (1924) **:** a hypnotic or anesthetic held to induce a subject under questioning to talk freely

truth set *n* (1940) **:** a mathematical or logical set containing all the elements that make a given statement of relationships true when substituted in it ⟨the equation $x + 7 = 10$ has as its *truth set* the single number 3⟩

truth table *n* (1921) **:** a table that shows the truth-value of a compound statement for every truth-value of its component statements; *also* **:** a similar table (as for a computer logic circuit) showing the value of the output for each value of each input

TRUTH TABLE

p a proposition	~*p* not *p* (negation)	*p* a proposition	*q* a proposition	*p* & *q* *p* and *q* (conjunction)	*p* or *q* *p* or *q*, inclusive (inclusive disjunction)	*p* or *q* *p* or *q*, exclusive (exclusive disjunction)	*p* → *q* if *p* then *q* (implication)	*p* ↔ *q* *p* if and only if *q* (biconditional)
T	F	T	T	T	T	F	T	T
F	T	T	F	F	T	T	F	F
T = true		F	T	F	T	T	T	F
F = false		F	F	F	F	F	T	T

truth–value *n* (1903) **:** the truth or falsity of a proposition or statement

[1]try \ˈtrī\ *vb* **tried; try·ing** [ME *trien,* fr. AF *trier* to select, sort, examine, determine, prob. fr. LL *tritare* to grind, freq. of L *terere* to rub — more at THROW] *vt* (14c) **1 a :** to examine or investigate judicially ⟨~ a case⟩ **b** (1) **:** to conduct the trial of (2) **:** to participate as counsel in the judicial examination of **2 a :** to put to test or trial ⟨~ one's luck⟩ — often used with *out* ⟨~ out a new method⟩ **b :** to subject to something (as undue strain or excessive hardship or provocation) that tests the powers of endurance **c :** DEMONSTRATE, PROVE **3 a** *obs* **:** PURIFY, REFINE **b :** to melt down and procure in a pure state **:** RENDER ⟨~ out whale oil from blubber⟩ **4 :** to fit or finish with accuracy **5 :** to make an attempt at — often used with an infinitive ⟨~ to fix the car⟩ ~ *vi* **:** to make an attempt ⟨you can do it if you ~⟩ ***syn*** see AFFLICT, ATTEMPT — **try one's hand :** to attempt something for the first time

[2]try *n, pl* **tries** (1832) **1 :** an experimental trial **:** ATTEMPT ⟨succeeded on the first ~⟩ **2 :** a play in rugby that is similar to a touchdown in football, scores usu. five points, and entitles the scoring side to attempt a placekick at the goal for additional points; *also* **:** the score made on a try

try for point (1929) **:** an attempt made after scoring a touchdown in football to score one or two additional points by kicking the ball over the crossbar or again carrying it into the opponents' end zone

trying *adj* (1718) **:** severely straining the powers of endurance ⟨a ~ experience⟩ — **try·ing·ly** *adv*

try on *vt* (1664) **1 :** to put on (a garment) in order to test the fit **2 :** to use or test experimentally — **try–on** \ˈtrī-ˌȯn, -ˌän\ *n*

try·out \ˈtrī-ˌau̇t\ *n* (1903) **:** an experimental performance or demonstration: as **a :** a test of the ability (as of an athlete or actor) to fill a part or meet standards **b :** a performance of a play prior to its official opening to determine response and discover weaknesses

try out *vi* (1909) **:** to compete for a position esp. on an athletic team or for a part in a play

try·pano·some \tri-ˈpa-nə-ˌsōm\ *n* [NL *Trypanosoma,* fr. Gk *trypanon* auger + NL *-soma* -some — more at TREPAN] (1903) **:** any of a genus (*Trypanosoma*) of parasitic flagellate protozoans that infest the blood of various vertebrates including humans, are usu. transmitted by the bite of an insect, and include some that cause serious diseases (as sleeping sickness and Chagas' disease)

try·pano·so·mi·a·sis \tri-ˌpa-nə-sə-ˈmī-ə-səs\ *n, pl* **-a·ses** \-ˌsēz\ [NL] (1902) **:** infection with or disease caused by trypanosomes
try–pot \ˈtrī-ˌpät\ *n* (1795) **:** a metallic pot used on a whaler or on shore to render whale oil from blubber
tryp·sin \ˈtrip-sən\ *n* [perh. fr. Gk *tryein* to wear down + E *pepsin;* akin to L *terere* to rub — more at THROW] (1876) **:** a proteolytic enzyme that is secreted in the pancreatic juice in the form of trypsinogen, is activated in the duodenum, and is most active in a slightly alkaline medium
tryp·sin·o·gen \trip-ˈsi-nə-jən\ *n* [ISV] (ca. 1890) **:** the inactive substance released by the pancreas into the duodenum to form trypsin
trypt·amine \ˈtrip-tə-ˌmēn\ *n* [*tryptophan* + *amine*] (1929) **:** a crystalline amine $C_{10}H_{12}N_2$ derived from tryptophan
tryp·tic \ˈtrip-tik\ *adj* [ISV, fr. *trypsin*] (1883) **:** of, relating to, or produced by trypsin or its action
tryp·to·phan \ˈtrip-tə-ˌfan\ *also* **tryp·to·phane** \-ˌfān\ *n* [ISV *tryptic* + *-o-* + *-phane*] (1890) **:** a crystalline essential amino acid $C_{11}H_{12}N_2O_2$ that is widely distributed in proteins
try·sail \ˈtrī-ˌsāl, -səl\ *n* [obs. *at try* lying to] (1769) **:** a fore-and-aft sail bent to a gaff and hoisted on a lower mast or a small mast close abaft
try square *n* (ca. 1877) **:** an instrument consisting of two straightedges fixed at right angles to each other and used for laying off right angles and testing whether work is square
[1]**tryst** \ˈtrist, *esp Brit* ˈtrīst\ *n* [ME *triste* appointed station for hunters, prob. fr. *trist, trust* confidence, trust] (14c) **1 :** an agreement (as between lovers) to meet **2 :** an appointed meeting or meeting place
[2]**tryst** *vi* (14c) **:** to make or keep a tryst — **tryst·er** \ˈtris-tər, ˈtrīs-\ *n*
try·works \ˈtrī-ˌwərks\ *n pl* (1792) **:** a brick furnace in which try-pots are placed; *also* **:** the furnace with the pots
TSA *abbr* Transportation Security Administration
tsade *var of* SADHE
tsar, tsarevitch, tsarina, tsarism *var of* CZAR, CZAREVITCH, CZARINA, CZARISM
TSE *abbr* transmissible spongiform encephalopathy
tset·se fly \ˈ(t)set-sē-, ˈtet-, ˈ(t)sēt-, ˈtēt-\ *n* [Afrik, fr. Tswana *tsètsê* fly] (1865) **:** any of several dipteran flies (genus *Glossina*) that occur in Africa south of the Sahara and include vectors of human and animal trypanosomes — called also *tsetse*; compare SLEEPING SICKNESS
TSgt *abbr* technical sergeant
TSH *abbr* thyroid-stimulating hormone
Tshi *var of* TWI
Tshi·lu·ba \chi-ˈlü-bə\ *n* (ca. 1961) **:** a Bantu language used as a lingua franca in the southeastern Democratic Republic of the Congo
T–shirt *also* **tee shirt** \ˈtē-ˌshərt\ *n* (1920) **:** a collarless short-sleeved or sleeveless usu. cotton undershirt; *also* **:** an outer shirt of similar design — **T–shirt·ed** *adj*
Tsim·shi·an \ˈchim-shē-ən, ˈ(t)si-\ *n, pl* **-an** *or* **-ans** [Tsimshian (Coast and Southern Tsimshian languages) *ćmsyan*, a self-designation, lit., inside the Skeena (River)] (1836) **1 :** a member of a group of American Indian peoples of west central British Columbia and southern Alaska **2 :** the family of closely related languages spoken by the Tsimshian peoples
tsk *a dental click; often read as* ˈtisk\ *interj* (1937) — used to express disapproval
tsk–tsk \ˈtisk-ˌtisk\ *vt* (1943) **:** to express disapproval of by or as if by uttering tsk ~ *vi* **:** to tsk-tsk someone or something
tsp *abbr* teaspoon; teaspoonful
TSP *abbr* trisodium phosphate
T square *n* (1785) **:** a ruler with a crosspiece or head at one end used in making parallel lines
TSS *abbr* toxic shock syndrome
tsu·na·mi \(t)sù-ˈnä-mē\ *n, pl* **tsunamis** *also* **tsunami** [Jp, fr. *tsu* harbor + *nami* wave] (1897) **:** a great sea wave produced esp. by submarine earth movement or volcanic eruption **:** TIDAL WAVE — **tsu·na·mic** \-mik\ *adj*
tsu·ris *also* **tsou·ris** \ˈtsü-ris, ˈtsùr-is\ *or* **tso·ris** \ˈtsȯr-is\ *n* [Yiddish *tsures, tsores,* pl. of *tsure, tsore* trouble, distress, fr. Heb *ṣārāh*] (1901) **:** TROUBLE, DISTRESS
tsu·tsu·ga·mu·shi disease \ˌ(t)süt-sə-gə-ˈmü-shē-, ˌtüt-\ *n* [Jp *tsutsugamushi* scrub typhus mite, fr. *tsutsuga* sickness + *mushi* insect] (1906) **:** SCRUB TYPHUS
Tswa·na \ˈ(t)swä-nə\ *n, pl* **Tswana** *or* **Tswanas** (1930) **1 :** a member of a Bantu-speaking people of Botswana and the Republic of South Africa **2 :** the language of the Tswana people
t–test \ˈtē-ˈtest\ *n* (1932) **:** a statistical test involving confidence limits for the random variable *t* of a t distribution and used esp. in testing hypotheses about means of normal distributions when the standard deviations are unknown
T_3 *also* **T–3** \ˈtē-ˈthrē\ *n* [*T,* abbr. for *thyronine + 3,* number of iodine atoms attached to the thyronine nucleus] (1956) **:** TRIIODOTHYRONINE
TTY *abbr* teletypewriter
Tu *abbr* Tuesday
Tua·reg *also* **Toua·reg** \ˈtwä-ˌreg\ *n, pl* **Tuareg** *or* **Tuaregs** *also* **Touareg** *or* **Touaregs** [Ar *Tawāriq*] (1821) **:** a member of a nomadic people of the central and western Sahara and along the middle Niger from Tombouctou to Nigeria
tu·a·ta·ra \ˌtü-ə-ˈtär-ə\ *n, pl* **-tara** *or* **-taras** [Maori *tuatàra*] (1890) **:** a large spiny quadrupedal reptile (*Sphenodon punctatum*) of islands off the coast of New Zealand that has a vestigial third eye in the middle of the forehead representing the pineal gland and that is the only surviving rhynchocephalian

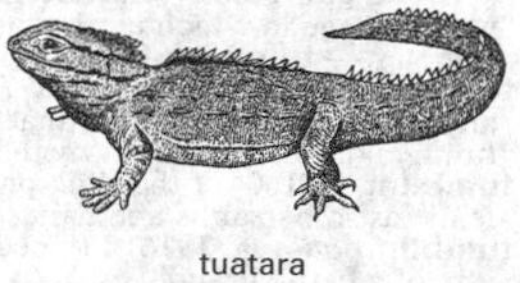

tuatara

[1]**tub** \ˈtəb\ *n* [ME *tubbe,* fr. MD; akin to MLG *tubbe* tub] (12c) **1 a :** a wide low vessel orig. formed with wooden staves, round bottom, and hoops **b :** a small round container in which a product is sold ⟨a ~ of butter⟩ **2 :** an old or slow boat **3 :** BATHTUB; *also* **:** BATH **4 :** the amount that a tub will hold — **tub·ful** \-ˌfu̇l\ *n* — **tub·like** \-ˌlīk\ *adj*
[2]**tub** *vb* **tubbed; tub·bing** *vt* (1610) **1 :** to wash or bathe in a tub **2 :** to put or store in a tub ~ *vi* **1 :** BATHE **2 :** to undergo washing — **tub·ba·ble** \ˈtə-bə-bəl\ *adj* — **tub·ber** *n*
tu·ba \ˈtü-bə, ˈtyü-\ *n* [It, fr. L, trumpet] (1852) **:** a large low-pitched brass instrument usu. oval in shape and having a conical tube, a cup-shaped mouthpiece, and a usual range an octave lower than that of the euphonium — **tu·ba·ist** \-bə(-i)st\ *or* **tub·ist** \-bist\ *n*
tub·al \ˈtü-bəl, ˈtyü-\ *adj* (ca. 1736) **:** of, relating to, or involving a tube and esp. a fallopian tube ⟨~ infection⟩
tubal ligation *n* (ca. 1948) **:** ligation of the fallopian tubes that by preventing passage of ova from the ovaries to the uterus serves as a method of female sterilization
tubal pregnancy *n* (ca. 1843) **:** ectopic pregnancy in a fallopian tube
tub·by \ˈtə-bē\ *adj* **tub·bi·er; -est** (ca. 1807) **1 :** sounding dull and without proper resonance or freedom of sound ⟨a ~ violin⟩ **2 :** PUDGY, FAT
tube \ˈtüb, ˈtyüb\ *n* [F, fr. L *tubus;* akin to L *tuba* trumpet] (1651) **1 :** any of various usu. cylindrical structures or devices: as **a :** a hollow elongated cylinder; *esp* **:** one to convey fluids **b :** a soft tubular container whose contents (as toothpaste) can be removed by squeezing **c** (1) **:** TUNNEL (2) *Brit* **:** SUBWAY b **d :** the basically cylindrical section between the mouthpiece and bell that is the fundamental part of a wind instrument **2 a :** a slender channel (as a fallopian tube or a pollen tube) within a plant or animal body **:** DUCT **b :** the narrow basal portion of a corolla with united petals or a calyx with united sepals **3 :** INNER TUBE **4 a :** ELECTRON TUBE; *esp* **:** VACUUM TUBE **b :** CATHODE-RAY TUBE; *esp* **:** a television picture tube **c :** TELEVISION **5 :** an article of clothing shaped like a tube ⟨a ~ top⟩ ⟨~ socks⟩ — **tubed** \ˈtübd, ˈtyübd\ *adj* — **tube·like** \ˈtüb-ˌlīk, ˈtyüb-\ *adj* — **down the tube** *or* **down the tubes :** into a state of collapse or deterioration
tube foot *n* (1888) **:** one of the small flexible tubular processes of most echinoderms that are extensions of the water-vascular system and are used esp. in locomotion and grasping
tube·less \ˈtüb-ləs, ˈtyüb-\ *adj* (1855) **:** lacking a tube; *specif* **:** being a pneumatic tire that does not depend on an inner tube for airtightness
tube nucleus *n* (1939) **:** the one of the two nuclei formed by mitotic division of a microspore during the formation of a pollen grain that is held to control subsequent growth of the pollen tube and that does not divide again — compare GENERATIVE NUCLEUS
tube pan *n* (1926) **:** a ring-shaped cake pan with a tubular center
tu·ber \ˈtü-bər, ˈtyü-\ *n* [L, swelling, truffle; perh. akin to L *tumēre* to swell — more at THUMB] (1668) **1 a :** a short fleshy usu. underground stem bearing minute scale leaves each of which bears a bud in its axil and is potentially able to produce a new plant — compare BULB, CORM **b :** a fleshy root or rhizome resembling a tuber **2 :** TUBEROSITY
tu·ber·cle \ˈtü-bər-kəl, ˈtyü-\ *n* [L *tuberculum,* dim. of *tuber*] (1578) **1 :** a small knobby prominence or excrescence esp. on a plant or animal **:** NODULE: as **a :** a protuberance near the head of a rib that articulates with the transverse process of a vertebra **b :** any of several prominences in the central nervous system **c :** NODULE b **2 :** a small abnormal discrete lump in the substance of an organ or in the skin; *esp* **:** the specific lesion of tuberculosis
tubercle bacillus *n* (ca. 1890) **:** a bacterium (*Mycobacterium tuberculosis*) that is a major cause of tuberculosis
tubercul- *comb form* [NL, fr. L *tuberculum*] **1 :** tubercle ⟨*tubercul*ar⟩ **2 :** tubercle bacillus ⟨*tubercul*in⟩ **3 :** tuberculosis ⟨*tubercul*oid⟩
[1]**tu·ber·cu·lar** \tu̇-ˈbər-kyə-lər, tyu̇-\ *adj* (1799) **1 a :** of, relating to, or affected with tuberculosis ⟨a ~ patient⟩ **b :** caused by the tubercle bacillus ⟨~ meningitis⟩ **2 :** characterized by lesions that are or resemble tubercles ⟨~ leprosy⟩ **3 :** relating to, resembling, or constituting a tubercle ⟨a ~ lump⟩
[2]**tubercular** *n* (1925) **:** a person with tuberculosis
tu·ber·cu·lat·ed \tu̇-ˈbər-kyə-ˌlā-təd, tyu̇-\ *also* **tu·ber·cu·late** \-lət\ *adj* (1771) **:** having tubercles **:** characterized by or beset with tubercles
tu·ber·cu·lin \tu̇-ˈbər-kyə-lən, tyu̇-\ *n* [ISV] (ca. 1890) **:** a sterile liquid containing the growth products of or specific substances extracted from the tubercle bacillus and used in the diagnosis of tuberculosis esp. in children and cattle
tuberculin test *n* (ca. 1900) **:** a test for hypersensitivity to tuberculin as an indication of past or present tubercular infection
tu·ber·cu·loid \tu̇-ˈbər-kyə-ˌlȯid, tyu̇-\ *adj* [ISV] (ca. 1923) **:** resembling tuberculosis esp. in the presence of tubercles ⟨~ leprosy⟩
tu·ber·cu·lo·sis \tu̇-ˌbər-kyə-ˈlō-səs, tyu̇-\ *n, pl* **-lo·ses** \-ˌsēz\ [NL] (1842) **:** a highly variable communicable disease of humans and some other vertebrates that is caused by the tubercle bacillus and rarely in the U.S. by a related mycobacterium (*Mycobacterium bovis*), that affects esp. the lungs but may spread to other areas (as the kidney or spinal column), and that is characterized by fever, cough, difficulty in breathing, formation of tubercles, caseation, pleural effusions, and fibrosis
tu·ber·cu·lous \tu̇-ˈbər-kyə-ləs, tyu̇-\ *adj* (1891) **1 :** constituting or affected with tuberculosis ⟨a ~ process⟩ **2 :** caused by or resulting from the presence or products of the tubercle bacillus ⟨~ peritonitis⟩
tube·rose \ˈtü-ˌbrōz, ˈtyü-, *also* -bə-ˌrōz, -bə-ˌrōs\ *n* [NL *tuberosa,* specific epithet, fr. L, fem. of *tuberosus* tuberous, fr. *tuber* tuber] (1664) **:** a Mexican bulbous herb (*Polianthes tuberosa*) of the agave family cultivated for its spike of fragrant white single or double flowers
tu·ber·os·i·ty \ˌtü-bə-ˈrä-sə-tē, ˌtyü-\ *n, pl* **-ties** (1611) **:** a rounded prominence; *esp* **:** a large prominence on a bone usu. serving for the attachment of muscles or ligaments
tu·ber·ous \ˈtü-b(ə-)rəs, ˈtyü-\ *adj* (1650) **1 :** consisting of, bearing, or resembling a tuber **2 :** of, relating to, or being a plant tuber or tuberous root of a plant
tuberous root *n* (ca. 1668) **:** a thick fleshy storage root (as of a dahlia) that is like a tuber but lacks buds or scale leaves — **tuberous–rooted** *adj*
tube worm *n* (ca. 1819) **:** a worm that lives in a tube: as **a :** any of various polychaetes or oligochaetes **b** (1) **:** POGONOPHORAN (2) **:** VESTIMENTIFERAN
tu·bi·fex worm \ˈtü-bə-ˌfeks-, ˈtyü-\ *n* [NL *Tubific-, Tubifex,* fr. L *tubus* tube + *facere* to make — more at DO] (1948) **:** any of a genus (*Tubifex*)

\ə\ **abut** \ᵊ\ **kitten,** F **table** \ər\ **further** \a\ **ash** \ā\ **ace** \ä\ **mop, mar**
\au̇\ **out** \ch\ **chin** \e\ **bet** \ē\ **easy** \g\ **go** \i\ **hit** \ī\ **ice** \j\ **job**
\ŋ\ **sing** \ō\ **go** \ȯ\ **law** \ȯi\ **boy** \th\ **thin** \t͟h\ **the** \ü\ **loot** \u̇\ **foot**
\y\ **yet** \zh\ **vision, beige** \k̲, ⁿ, œ, ue, ʸ\ *see* Guide to Pronunciation

of slender reddish tubificid worms that live in tubes in fresh or brackish water, are widely used as food for aquarium fish, and serve as a host for the protozoan causing whirling disease in fish — called also *tubifex*

tu·bi·fi·cid \tü-ˈbi-fə-səd, tyü-; ˌt(y)ü-bə-ˈfi-səd\ *n* [NL *Tubificidae,* fr. *Tubific-, Tubifex*] (1950) : any of a family (Tubificidae) of aquatic oligochaetes including the tubifex worms — **tubificid** *adj*

tub·ing \ˈtü-biŋ, ˈtyü-\ *n* (1845) **1** : material in the form of a tube; *also* : a length or piece of tube **2** : a series or system of tubes **3** : the sport or activity of riding an inner tube (as down a river or snowy slope)

tu·bo·cu·ra·rine \ˌtü-bō-kyu̇-ˈrär-ən, ˌtyü-, -ˌēn\ *n* [ISV *tubo-* (fr. L *tubus* tube) + *curare* + *-ine;* fr. its being shipped in sections of hollow bamboo] (1898) : a toxic alkaloid or its crystalline hydrochloride salt $C_{37}H_{42}Cl_2N_2O_6$ that is obtained chiefly from the bark and stems of a So. American vine (*Chondrodendron tomentosum* of the family Menispermaceae) and in its dextrorotatory form constitutes the chief active constituent of curare and is used esp. as a skeletal muscle relaxant

tub–thump·er \ˈtəb-ˌthəm-pər\ *n* (1662) : a vociferous supporter (as of a cause) — **tub–thump** \-ˌthəmp\ *vb*

tu·bu·lar \ˈtü-byə-lər, ˈtyü-\ *adj* (1673) **1 a** : having the form of or consisting of a tube ⟨a ~ calyx⟩ **b** : made or provided with tubes **2** : of, relating to, or sounding as if produced through tubes

tu·bule \ˈtü-(ˌ)byül, ˈtyü-\ *n* [L *tubulus,* dim. of *tubus*] (1677) : a small tube; *esp* : a slender elongated anatomical channel

tu·bu·lin \ˈtü-byə-lən, ˈtyü-\ *n* [*tubule* + [1]*-in*] (1968) : a globular protein that polymerizes to form microtubules

TUC *abbr* Trades Union Congress

tu·chun \ˈdü-ˈjün, -ˈju̇en\ *n* [Chin (Beijing) *dūjūn*] (1917) **1** : a Chinese military governor (as of a province) **2** : a Chinese warlord

[1]**tuck** \ˈtək\ *vb* [ME *tuken* to mistreat, finish (cloth) by stretching and beating, tuck, fr. OE *tūcian* to mistreat; akin to OHG *zuhhen* to jerk, OE *togian* to pull — more at TOW] *vt* (14c) **1 a** : to pull up into a fold **b** : to make a tuck in **2** : to put into a snug often concealing or isolating place ⟨a cottage *~ed* away in the hill⟩ **3 a** : to push in the loose end of so as to hold tightly ⟨~ in your shirt⟩ **b** : to cover by tucking in bedclothes — usu. used with *in* **4** : EAT — usu. used with *away* or *in* ⟨*~ed* away a big lunch⟩ **5** : to put into a tuck position ~ *vi* **1** : to draw together into tucks or folds **2** : to eat or drink heartily — usu. used with *into* ⟨*~ed* into their beer and pretzels⟩ **3** : to fit snugly

[2]**tuck** *n* (1532) **1** : a fold stitched into cloth to shorten, decorate, or control fullness **2** : the part of a vessel where the ends of the lower planks meet under the stern **3 a** : an act or instance of tucking **b** : something tucked or to be tucked in **4 a** : a body position (as in diving) in which the knees are bent, the thighs drawn tightly to the chest, and the hands clasped around the shins **b** : a skiing position in which the skier squats forward and holds the ski poles under the arms and parallel to the ground **5** : a cosmetic surgical operation for the removal of excess skin or fat from a body part ⟨a tummy ~⟩

[3]**tuck** *n* [ME (Sc) *tuicke* beat, stroke] (15c) : a sound of or as if of a drumbeat

[4]**tuck** *n* [MF *estoc,* fr. OF, sword point, fr. *estochier* to strike with the sword tip, thrust, of Gmc origin; akin to MD *stoken* to thrust, poke — more at STOKE] (1508) *archaic* : RAPIER

[5]**tuck** *n* [prob. fr. [2]*tuck*] (1878) : VIGOR, ENERGY ⟨seemed to kind of take the ~ all out of me —Mark Twain⟩

tuck·a·hoe \ˈtə-kə-ˌhō\ *n* [Virginia Algonquian *tockawhoughe*] (1612) **1** : either of two arums (*Peltandra virginica* and *Orontium aquaticum*) of the U.S. with rootstocks used as food by American Indians **2** : the large edible sclerotium of a subterranean fungus (*Poria cocos*)

[1]**tuck·er** \ˈtə-kər\ *n* (1688) **1** : a piece of lace or cloth in the neckline of a dress **2** : one that tucks **3** *chiefly Austral* : FOOD

[2]**tucker** *vt* **tuck·ered; tuck·er·ing** \ˈtə-k(ə-)riŋ\ [obs. E *tuck* to reproach + *-er* (as in [1]*batter*)] (1833) : EXHAUST — often used with *out* ⟨was all *~ed* out after a long day's work⟩

tuck·er–bag \ˈtə-kər-ˌbag\ *n* (1885) *chiefly Austral* : a bag used esp. by travelers in the bush to hold food

tuck·et \ˈtə-kət\ *n* [prob. fr. obs. E *tuk* to beat the drum, sound the trumpet] (1593) : a fanfare on a trumpet

tuck–point \ˈtək-ˌpȯint\ *vt* (1881) : to finish (the mortar joints between bricks or stones) with a narrow ridge of putty or fine lime mortar

tuckshop \-ˌshäp\ *n* [Brit *tuck* food, confectionery] (1857) *Brit* : a confectioner's shop : CONFECTIONERY

'tude \ˈtüd, ˈtyüd\ *n* [short for *attitude*] (1976) *slang* : a cocky or arrogant attitude

Tu·dor \ˈtü-dər, ˈtyü-\ *adj* [Henry *Tudor* (Henry VII of England)] (1779) **1** : of or relating to the English royal house that ruled from 1485 to 1603 **2** : of, relating to, or characteristic of the Tudor period — **Tudor** *n*

Tudor arch *n* (1815) : a low elliptical 3-, 4-, or 5-centered arch; *esp* : a 4-centered pointed arch — see ARCH illustration

Tues *or* **Tue** *abbr* Tuesday

Tues·day \ˈtüz-(ˌ)dā, ˈtyüz-, -dē\ *n* [ME *tiwesday,* fr. OE *tīwesdæg* (akin to OHG *zīostag* Tuesday), fr. OE *Tīw* Tiu + *dæg* day — more at DEITY] (bef. 12c) : the third day of the week — **Tues·days** \-dēz, -(ˌ)dāz\ *adv*

tu·fa \ˈtü-fə, ˈtyü-\ *n* [It *tufo,* fr. L *tofus*] (1770) **1** : TUFF **2** : a porous rock formed as a deposit from springs or streams; *specif* : TRAVERTINE — **tu·fa·ceous** \tü-ˈfā-shəs, tyü-\ *adj*

tuff \ˈtəf\ *n* [earlier *tuph, tuft* porous rock, fr. MF *tuf,* fr. OIt *tufo*] (1815) : a rock composed of the finer kinds of volcanic detritus usu. fused together by heat — **tuff·a·ceous** \ˌtə-ˈfā-shəs\ *adj*

tuf·fet \ˈtə-fət\ *n* [AF *tuffete,* fr. **tufe* tuft] (1553) **1** : TUFT 1a **2** : a low seat

[1]**tuft** \ˈtəft\ *n* [ME, modif. of MF *touffe,* prob. of Gmc origin; akin to OHG *zopf* tip — more at TOP] (14c) **1 a** : a small cluster of elongated flexible outgrowths attached or close together at the base and free at the opposite ends; *esp* : a growing bunch of grasses or close-set plants **b** : a bunch of soft fluffy threads cut off short and used as ornament **2** : CLUMP, CLUSTER **3** : MOUND **4** : any of the projections of yarns drawn through a fabric or making up a fabric so as to produce a surface of raised loops or cut pile — **tuft·ed** \ˈtəf-təd\ *adj* — **tufty** \ˈtəf-tē\ *adj*

[2]**tuft** *vt* (1535) **1 a** : to provide or adorn with a tuft **b** : to make (a fabric) of or with tufts **2** : to make (as a mattress) firm by stitching at intervals and sewing on tufts ~ *vi* : to form into or grow in tufts — **tuft·er** *n*

[1]**tug** \ˈtəg\ *vb* **tugged; tug·ging** [ME *tuggen;* akin to OE *togian* to pull — more at TOW] *vi* (14c) **1** : to pull hard **2** : to struggle in opposition : CONTEND **3** : to exert oneself laboriously : LABOR ~ *vt* **1** : to pull or strain hard at **2 a** : to move by pulling hard : HAUL **b** : to carry with difficulty : LUG **3** : to tow with a tugboat — **tug·ger** *n*

[2]**tug** *n* (15c) **1 a** : [3]TRACE 1 **b** : a short leather strap or loop **c** : a rope or chain used for pulling **2 a** : an act or instance of tugging : PULL **b** : a strong pulling force **3 a** : a straining effort **b** : a struggle between two people or opposite forces **4** : TUGBOAT

tug·boat \ˈtəg-ˌbōt\ *n* (1830) : a strongly built powerful boat used for towing and pushing — called also *towboat*

tug–of–war \ˌtəg-ə(v)-ˈwȯr\ *n, pl* **tugs–of–war** (1677) **1** : a struggle for supremacy or control usu. involving two antagonists **2** : a contest in which two teams pull against each other at opposite ends of a rope with the object of pulling the middle of the rope over a mark on the ground

tu·grik *or* **tu·ghrik** \ˈtü-grik\ *n* [Mongolian *tögrig,* lit., circle, wheel] (1927) — see MONEY table

tuille \ˈtwēl\ *n* [ME *toile,* fr. AF *toille,* prob. alter. of *tuille, tiule* tile, fr. L *tegula* — more at TILE] (15c) : one of the hinged plates before the thigh in plate armor — see ARMOR illustration

tu·ition \tə-ˈwi-shən, tyü-\ *n* [ME *tuicioun* protection, fr. AF, fr. L *tuition-, tuitio,* fr. *tueri* to look at, look after] (15c) **1** *archaic* : CUSTODY, GUARDIANSHIP **2** : the act or profession of teaching : INSTRUCTION ⟨pursued his studies under private ~⟩ **3** : the price of or payment for instruction — **tu·ition·al** \-ˈwish-nəl, -ˈwi-shə-nᵊl\ *adj*

tu·la·re·mia \ˌtü-lə-ˈrē-mē-ə, ˌtyü-\ *n* [NL, fr. *Tulare* County, Calif.] (1921) : an infectious zoonotic disease esp. of wild rabbits, rodents, humans, and some domestic animals that is caused by a bacterium (*Francisella tularensis*), is transmitted esp. by the bites of insects or ticks or by handling infected animals, and in humans is marked by variable symptoms — called also *rabbit fever* — **tu·la·re·mic** \-mik\ *adj*

tu·le \ˈtü-lē\ *n* [Sp, fr. Nahuatl *tōllin*] (1837) : either of two large New World bulrushes (*Scirpus californicus* and *S. acutus*)

tule elk *n* (1939) : a relatively small elk (*Cervus elaphus nannodes*) native to California

tu·lip \ˈtü-ləp, ˈtyü-\ *n* [NL *tulipa,* fr. Turk *tülbent* turban — more at TURBAN] (1578) : any of a genus (*Tulipa*) of Eurasian bulbous herbs of the lily family that have linear or broadly lanceolate leaves and are widely grown for their showy flowers; *also* : the flower or bulb of a tulip

tulip poplar *n* (1847) **1** : TULIP TREE 1 **2** : TULIPWOOD 1

tulip tree *n* (1705) **1** : a tall No. American timber tree (*Liriodendron tulipifera*) of the magnolia family having large greenish-yellow tulip-shaped flowers and soft white wood used esp. for cabinetwork and woodenware — called also *tulip poplar, yellow poplar* **2** : any of various trees other than the tulip tree with tulip-shaped flowers

tu·lip·wood \ˈtü-ləp-ˌwu̇d, ˈtyü-\ *n* (1843) **1** : wood of the No. American tulip tree **2 a** : any of several showily striped or variegated woods; *esp* : the rose-colored wood of a chiefly Brazilian tree (*Dalbergia frutescens*) of the legume family much used by cabinetmakers for inlaying **b** : a tree that yields tulipwood

tulle \ˈtül\ *n* [F, fr. *Tulle,* France] (ca. 1818) : a sheer often stiffened silk, rayon, or nylon net used chiefly for veils or ballet costumes

[1]**tum·ble** \ˈtəm-bəl\ *vb* **tum·bled; tum·bling** \-b(ə-)liŋ\ [ME, freq. of *tumben* to dance, fr. OE *tumbian;* akin to OHG *tūmōn* to reel] *vi* (14c) **1 a** : to fall suddenly and helplessly **b** : to suffer a sudden downfall, overthrow, or defeat **c** : to decline suddenly and sharply (as in price) : DROP ⟨the stock market *tumbled*⟩ **d** : to fall into ruin : COLLAPSE **2 a** : to perform gymnastic feats in tumbling **b** : to turn end over end in falling or flight **3** : to roll over and over, to and fro, or end over end : TOSS **4** : to issue forth hurriedly and confusedly **5** : to come by chance : STUMBLE **6** : to come to understand : CATCH ON ⟨didn't ~ to the seriousness of the problem⟩ ~ *vt* **1** : to cause to tumble (as by pushing or toppling) **2 a** : to throw together in a confused mass **b** : RUMPLE, DISORDER **3** : to whirl in a tumbling barrel

[2]**tumble** *n* (1634) **1 a** : a disordered mass of objects or material **b** : a disorderly state **2** : an act or instance of tumbling

tum·ble·bug \ˈtəm-bəl-ˌbəg\ *n* (1805) : any of various scarab beetles (esp. genera *Scarabaeus, Canthon, Copris,* or *Phanaeus*) that roll dung into small balls, bury them in the ground, and lay eggs in them

tum·ble·down \ˈtəm-bəl-ˈdau̇n\ *adj* (1818) : DILAPIDATED, RAMSHACKLE ⟨a ~ house at the edge of town —Sherwood Anderson⟩

tumble dry *vt* (1962) : to dry (as clothes) by tumbling in a dryer — **tumble dryer** *n* — **tumble drying** *n*

tum·bler \ˈtəm-blər\ *n* (14c) **1** : one that tumbles: as **a** : one who performs tumbling feats : ACROBAT **b** : any of various domestic pigeons that tumble or somersault backward in flight or on the ground **2** : a drinking glass without foot or stem and orig. with pointed or convex base **3 a** : a movable obstruction in a lock (as a lever, latch, wheel, slide, or pin) that must be adjusted to a particular position (as by a key) before the bolt can be thrown **b** : a piece on which the mainspring acts in a gun's lock **4** : a device or mechanism for tumbling (as a revolving cage in which clothes are dried) **5** : a worker who operates a tumbler — **tum·bler·ful** \-ˌfu̇l\ *n*

tum·ble·weed \ˈtəm-bəl-ˌwēd\ *n* (1887) : a plant (as Russian thistle or any of several amaranths) that breaks away from its roots in the autumn and is driven about by the wind as a light rolling mass

[1]**tumbling** *n* (1604) : the skill, practice, or sport of executing gymnastic feats (as somersaults and handsprings) without the use of apparatus

[2]**tumbling** *adj* (ca. 1916) : tipped or slanted out of the vertical — used esp. of a cattle brand

tumbling barrel *n* (ca. 1890) : a revolving cask in which objects or materials undergo a process (as drying or polishing) by being whirled about

tumbling verse *n* (1585) : an early modern English type of verse having four stresses but no prevailing type of foot and no regular number of syllables

tum·brel *or* **tum·bril** \ˈtəm-brəl\ *n* [ME *tomrel,* fr. OF (*tomberel,* fr. *tomber* to tumble, perh. of Gmc origin; akin to OHG *tūmōn* to reel — more at TUMBLE] (14c) **1** : a farm tipcart **2** : a vehicle carrying condemned persons (as political prisoners during the French Revolution) to a place of execution

tu·me·fac·tion \ˌtü-mə-ˈfak-shən, ˌtyü-\ *n* [ME *tumefaccioun,* fr. ML *tumefaccion-, tumefaccio,* fr. L *tumefacere* to cause to swell, fr. *tumēre* to swell + *facere* to make, do — more at THUMB, DO] (15c) **1 :** an action or process of swelling or becoming tumorous **2 :** SWELLING

tu·mes·cence \tü-ˈme-sᵊn(t)s, tyü-\ *n* (1859) **:** the quality or state of being tumescent; *esp* **:** readiness for sexual activity marked esp. by vascular congestion of the sex organs

tu·mes·cent \-sᵊnt\ *adj* [L *tumescent-, tumescens,* prp. of *tumescere* to swell up, incho. of *tumēre* to swell] (1882) **:** somewhat swollen ⟨~ tissue⟩

tu·mid \ˈtü-məd, ˈtyü-\ *adj* [L *tumidus,* fr. *tumēre*] (1541) **1 :** marked by swelling **:** SWOLLEN, ENLARGED ⟨a badly infected ~ leg⟩ **2 :** PROTUBERANT, BULGING ⟨sails ~ in the breeze⟩ **3 :** BOMBASTIC, TURGID

tumm·ler \ˈtùm-lər\ *n* [Yiddish *tumler,* lit., one who makes a racket] (1965) **:** a comic entertainer or social director at a Jewish resort

tum·my \ˈtə-mē\ *n, pl* **tummies** [baby-talk alter. of *stomach*] (1867) **:** STOMACH 1c

tu·mor \ˈtü-mər, ˈtyü-\ *n* [ME *tumour,* fr. L *tumor,* fr. *tumēre*] (15c) **1 :** a swollen or distended part **2 :** an abnormal benign or malignant new growth of tissue that possesses no physiological function and arises from uncontrolled usu. rapid cellular proliferation — called also *neoplasm* — **tu·mor·al** \-mə-rəl\ *adj* — **tu·mor·like** \-mər-ˌlīk\ *adj*

tu·mor·i·gen·ic \ˌtü-mə-rə-ˈje-nik, ˌtyü-\ *adj* (1941) **:** producing or tending to produce tumors; *also* **:** CARCINOGENIC — **tu·mor·i·gen·e·sis** \-ˈje-nə-səs\ *n* — **tu·mor·i·ge·nic·i·ty** \-jə-ˈni-sə-tē\ *n*

tumor necrosis factor *n* (1975) **:** a protein that is produced chiefly by monocytes and macrophages in response esp. to endotoxins and that mediates inflammation and induces the destruction of some tumor cells and the activation of white blood cells

tu·mor·ous \ˈtü-mə-rəs, ˈtyü-; ˈtüm-rəs, ˈtyüm-\ *adj* (1547) **:** of, relating to, or resembling a tumor ⟨~ cells⟩ ⟨a ~ growth⟩

tumor suppressor gene *n* (1985) **:** any of a class of genes (as p53) that act in normal cells to inhibit unrestrained cell division and that when inactivated (as by mutation) place the cell at increased risk for malignant proliferation

tu·mour \ˈtyü-mər\ *chiefly Brit var of* TUMOR

[1]**tump** \ˈtəmp\ *n* [origin unknown] (1589) **1** *dial chiefly Eng* **:** MOUND, HUMMOCK **2 :** a clump of vegetation

[2]**tump** *vb* [perh. akin to Brit. dial. *tumpoke* to fall head over heels] *vi* (1967) *chiefly Southern* **:** to tip or turn over esp. accidentally — usu. used with *over* ⟨sooner or later everybody ~s over. Nothing to worry about if you don't get caught under the canoe —Don Kennard⟩ ~ *vt, chiefly Southern* **:** to cause to tip over **:** OVERTURN, UPSET — usu. used with *over*

tump·line \ˈtəmp-ˌlīn\ *n* [*tump,* of Algonquian origin; akin to Eastern Abenaki *mádûmbi* pack strap] (1796) **:** a sling formed by a strap slung over the forehead or chest and used for carrying or helping to support a pack on the back or in hauling loads

tu·mult \ˈtü-ˌməlt, ˈtyü- *also* ˈtə-\ *n* [ME *tumulte,* fr. AF, fr. L *tumultus;* perh. akin to Skt *tumula* noisy] (15c) **1 a :** disorderly agitation or milling about of a crowd usu. with uproar and confusion of voices **:** COMMOTION **b :** a turbulent uprising **:** RIOT **2 :** HUBBUB, DIN **3 a :** violent agitation of mind or feelings **b :** a violent outburst

tu·mul·tu·ary \tù-ˈməl-chə-ˌwer-ē, tyù-, tə-\ *adj* (1590) **:** attended or marked by tumult, riot, lawlessness, confusion, or impetuosity

tu·mul·tu·ous \tù-ˈməl-chə-wəs, tyù-, tə-, -chəs; -ˈməlch-wəs\ *adj* (ca. 1548) **1 :** marked by tumult ⟨~ applause⟩ **2 :** tending or disposed to cause or incite a tumult ⟨the laws . . . were violated by a ~ faction —Edward Gibbon⟩ **3 :** marked by violent or overwhelming turbulence or upheaval ⟨~ passions⟩ — **tu·mul·tu·ous·ly** *adv* — **tu·mul·tu·ous·ness** *n*

tu·mu·lus \ˈtü-myə-ləs, ˈtyü-, ˈtə-\ *n, pl* **-li** \-ˌlī, -ˌlē\ [ME, fr. L; akin to L *tumēre* to swell — more at THUMB] (15c) **:** an artificial hillock or mound (as over a grave); *esp* **:** an ancient grave **:** BARROW

tun \ˈtən\ *n* [ME *tonne, tunne,* fr. OE & AF; OE, fr. ML *tunna;* AF *tone, tonne,* fr. ML] (bef. 12c) **1 :** a large cask esp. for wine **2 :** any of various units of liquid capacity; *esp* **:** one equal to 252 gallons

[1]**tu·na** \ˈtü-nə\ *n* [Sp, fr. Taino] (ca. 1555) **1 :** any of various flat-jointed prickly pears (genus *Opuntia*); *esp* **:** one (*O. tuna*) of tropical America **2 :** the edible fruit of a tuna

[2]**tu·na** \ˈtü-nə, ˈtyü-\ *n, pl* **tuna** *or* **tunas** [AmerSp, alter. of Sp *atún,* modif. of Ar *tūn,* fr. L *thunnus,* fr. Gk *thynnos*] (1881) **1 :** any of numerous large vigorous scombroid food and sport fishes (as an albacore or a bluefin tuna) **2 :** the flesh of a tuna esp. when canned for use as food — called also *tuna fish*

tun·able \ˈtü-nə-bəl, ˈtyü-\ *adj* (ca. 1500) **1** *archaic* **a :** TUNEFUL **b :** sounding in tune **:** CONCORDANT **2 :** capable of being tuned ⟨~ lasers⟩ — **tun·abil·i·ty** \ˌtü-nə-ˈbi-lə-tē, ˌtyü-\ *n* — **tun·able·ness** \ˈtü-nə-bəl-nəs, ˈtyü-\ *n* — **tun·ably** \-blē\ *adv*

tun·dish \ˈtən-ˌdish\ *n* [ME, funnel for filling a tun] (14c) **1 :** FUNNEL 1a **2 :** a reservoir in the top part of a mold into which molten metal is poured

tun·dra \ˈtən-drə *also* ˈtùn-\ *n* [Russ, fr. Russ dial. (northeast) *tundra, tundara,* fr. Kildin Sami (Sami language of the northern Kola Peninsula) *tūnter*] (ca. 1841) **:** a level or rolling treeless plain that is characteristic of arctic and subarctic regions, consists of black mucky soil with a permanently frozen subsoil, and has a dominant vegetation of mosses, lichens, herbs, and dwarf shrubs; *also* **:** a similar region confined to mountainous areas above timberline

tundra swan *n* (1984) **:** a native No. American swan (*Cygnus columbianus*) that has a soft high-pitched call, breeds in the Arctic tundra, and winters in shallow fresh or salt water esp. along the eastern and western coasts of the U.S. — called also *whistling swan*

[1]**tune** \ˈtün, ˈtyün\ *n* [ME, fr. AF *tun, tuen* tone] (14c) **1 a** *archaic* **:** quality of sound **:** TONE **b :** manner of utterance **:** INTONATION; *specif* **:** phonetic modulation **2 a :** a pleasing succession of musical tones **:** MELODY **b :** a dominant theme **3 :** correct musical pitch or consonance — used chiefly in the phrases *in tune* and *out of tune* **4 a** *archaic* **:** a frame of mind **:** MOOD **b :** AGREEMENT, HARMONY ⟨in ~ with the times⟩ **c :** general attitude **:** APPROACH ⟨changed his ~ when the going got rough⟩ **5 :** AMOUNT, EXTENT ⟨custom-made to the ~ of $40 to $50 apiece —*Amer. Fabrics*⟩

[2]**tune** *vb* **tuned; tun·ing** *vt* (15c) **1 :** to adjust in musical pitch or cause to be in tune ⟨*tuned* her guitar⟩ **2 a :** to bring into harmony **:** ATTUNE **b :** to adjust for precise functioning — often used with *up* ⟨~ up an engine⟩ **c :** to make more precise, intense, or effective **3 :** to adjust with respect to resonance at a particular frequency: as **a :** to adjust (a radio or television receiver) to respond to waves of a particular frequency — often used with *in* **b :** to establish radio contact with ⟨~ in a directional beacon⟩ **4 :** to adjust the frequency of the output of (a device) to a chosen frequency or range of frequencies; *also* **:** to alter the frequency of (radiation) ~ *vi* **1 :** to become attuned **2 :** to adjust a radio or television receiver to respond to waves of a particular frequency

tuned–in \ˈtünd-ˈin, ˈtyünd-\ *adj* (1958) **:** TURNED-ON

tune·ful \ˈtün-fəl, ˈtyün-\ *adj* (1591) **:** MELODIOUS, MUSICAL ⟨a ~ ballad⟩ — **tune·ful·ly** \-fə-lē\ *adv* — **tune·ful·ness** *n*

tune in *vt* (1913) **:** to listen to or view a broadcast of ⟨*tuned in* the weather report⟩ ~ *vi* **1 :** to listen to or view a broadcast ⟨*tune in* next week for the conclusion⟩ **2 :** to associate oneself with what is happening or one's surroundings

tune·less \ˈtün-ləs, ˈtyün-\ *adj* (1594) **1 :** not tuneful **2 :** not producing music — **tune·less·ly** *adv*

tune out *vt* (1908) **:** to become unresponsive to **:** IGNORE ~ *vi* **:** to dissociate oneself from what is happening or one's surroundings

tun·er \ˈtü-nər, ˈtyü-\ *n* (ca. 1801) **1 :** one that tunes ⟨a piano ~⟩ **2 :** something used for tuning; *specif* **:** the part of a receiving set that converts radio signals into audio or video signals

tune·smith \ˈtün-ˌsmith, ˈtyün-\ *n* (1926) **:** a composer esp. of popular songs

tune–up \-ˌəp\ *n* (1933) **1 :** a general adjustment to insure operation at peak efficiency ⟨an engine ~⟩ **2 :** a preliminary trial **:** WARM-UP

tung \ˈtəŋ\ *n* (1914) **:** TUNG TREE

tung oil *n* [part trans. of Chin (Beijing) *tóngyóu*] (1881) **:** a pale yellow pungent drying oil obtained from the seeds of tung trees and used chiefly in quick-drying varnishes and paints and as a waterproofing agent

tung·state \ˈtəŋ-ˌstāt\ *n* (1800) **:** a salt or ester of a tungstic acid and esp. of H_2WO_4

tung·sten \ˈtəŋ-stən\ *n* [Sw, fr. *tung* heavy + *sten* stone] (1796) **:** a gray-white heavy high-melting ductile hard polyvalent metallic element that resembles chromium and molybdenum in many of its properties and is used esp. in carbide materials and electrical components (as lamp filaments) and in hardening alloys (as steel) — see ELEMENT table

tung·stic acid \ˈtəŋ-stik-\ *n* [*tungsten*] (1796) **:** a yellow crystalline powder WO_3 that is the trioxide of tungsten; *also* **:** an acid (as H_2WO_4) derived from this trioxide

tung tree *n* [Chin (Beijing) *tóng*] (1889) **:** any of several trees (genus *Aleurites*) of the spurge family whose seeds yield tung oil; *esp* **:** an Asian tree (*A. fordii*) widely grown in warm regions

Tun·gus \tùŋ-ˈgüz, təŋ-\ *n, pl* **Tungus** *or* **Tun·gus·es** [Russ] (1674) **1 :** a member of an indigenous people of central and southeastern Siberia **2 :** the Tungusic language of the Tungus people

Tun·gu·sic \-ˈgü-zik\ *n* (1864) **:** a family of Altaic languages spoken in Manchuria and northward — **Tungusic** *adj*

tu·nic \ˈtü-nik, ˈtyü-\ *n* [OE *tunice,* fr. L *tunica,* of Sem origin; akin to Heb *kuttōneth* coat] (12c) **1 a :** a simple slip-on garment made with or without sleeves and usu. knee-length or longer, belted at the waist, and worn as an under or outer garment by men and women of ancient Greece and Rome **b :** SURCOAT **2 :** an enclosing or covering membrane or tissue ⟨the ~ of a seed⟩ **3 :** a long usu. plain close-fitting jacket with high collar worn esp. as part of a uniform **4 :** TUNICLE **5 a :** a short overskirt **b :** a hip-length or longer blouse or jacket

tu·ni·ca \ˈtü-ni-kə, ˈtyü-\ *n, pl* **tu·ni·cae** \-nə-ˌkē, -ˌkī, -ˌsē\ [L, tunic, membrane] (ca. 1698) **:** an enveloping membrane or layer of body tissue

[1]**tu·ni·cate** \ˈtü-ni-kət, ˈtyü-, -nə-ˌkāt\ *also* **tu·ni·cat·ed** \-nə-ˌkā-təd\ *adj* [L *tunicatus,* fr. *tunica*] (ca. 1623) **1 a :** having or covered with a tunic or tunica **b :** having, arranged in, or made up of concentric layers ⟨a ~ flower bulb⟩ **2 :** of or relating to the tunicates

[2]**tu·ni·cate** \-ni-kət, -nə-ˌkāt\ *n* [NL *Tunicata,* fr. neut. pl. of L *tunicatus*] (1889) **:** any of a subphylum (Urochordata syn. Tunicata) of marine chordate animals (as ascidians) that are filter feeders having a thick secreted covering layer, a greatly reduced nervous system, and only in the larval stage a notochord

tu·ni·cle \ˈtü-ni-kəl, ˈtyü-\ *n* [ME, fr. AF *tonicle,* L *tunicula,* dim. of *tunica*] (14c) **:** a short vestment worn by a subdeacon over the alb during mass and by a bishop under the dalmatic at pontifical ceremonies

tuning fork *n* (1799) **:** a 2-pronged metal implement that gives a fixed tone when struck and is useful for tuning musical instruments and ascertaining standard pitch

tuning pipe *n* (1897) **:** PITCH PIPE; *specif* **:** one of a set of pitch pipes used esp. for tuning stringed musical instruments

[1]**tun·nel** \ˈtə-nᵊl\ *n* [ME *tonel* cask, tun, fr. AF, fr. *tone* tun] (1508) **1 :** a hollow conduit or recess **:** TUBE, WELL **2 a :** a covered passageway; *specif* **:** a horizontal passageway through or under an obstruction **b :** a subterranean gallery (as in a mine) **c :** BURROW — **tun·nel·like** \-nᵊl-ˌ(l)īk\ *adj*

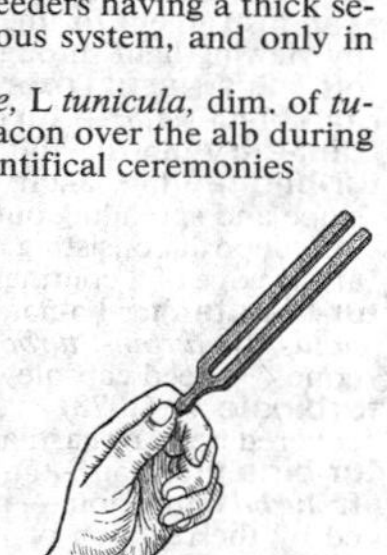

tuning fork

[2]**tunnel** *vb* **-neled** *or* **-nelled; -nel·ing** *or* **-nel·ling** \ˈtən-liŋ, ˈtə-nᵊl-iŋ\ *vi* (1795) **1 :** to make or use a tunnel **2** *physics* **:** to pass through a potential barrier ⟨electrons ~*ing* through an insulator between semiconductors⟩ ~ *vt* **:** to make a tunnel or similar opening through or under; *also* **:** to make (one's way) by or as if by making a tunnel — **tun·nel·er** \ˈtən-lər, ˈtə-nᵊl-ər\ *n*

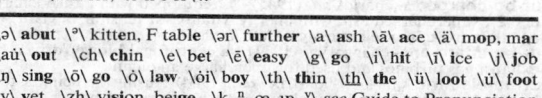

tunnel vision *n* (ca. 1942) **1 :** constriction of the visual field resulting in loss of peripheral vision **2 :** extreme narrowness of viewpoint : NARROW-MINDEDNESS; *also* : single-minded concentration on one objective — **tun·nel–vi·sioned** \-ˈvi-zhənd\ *adj*
tun·ny \ˈtə-nē\ *n, pl* **tunnies** *also* **tunny** [modif. of MF *thon* or OIt *tonno;* both fr. Old Occitan *ton,* fr. L *thunnus* — more at TUNA] (ca. 1530) : TUNA
[1]**tup** \ˈtəp\ *n* [ME *tupe*] (14c) **1** *chiefly Brit* : RAM 1a **2 :** a heavy metal body (as the weight of a pendulum)
[2]**tup** *vt* **tupped; tup·ping** (1604) *chiefly Brit* : to copulate with (a ewe)
tu·pe·lo \ˈtü-pə-ˌlō, ˈtyü-\ *n, pl* **-los** [perh. fr. Creek **topiló,* fr. *etó* tree + *piló:(fa), opiló:(fa)* swamp] (ca. 1730) **1 :** any of a genus (*Nyssa* of the family Nyssaceae) of No. American and Asian deciduous trees that have simple alternate leaves, small usu. greenish-white dioecious flowers, and a rounded drupe; *esp* : BLACK GUM **2 :** the pale soft wood of a tupelo
Tu·pi *also* **Tu·pí** \tü-ˈpē, ˈtü-(ˌ)\ *n, pl* **Tupi** *or* **Tupis** *also* **Tupí** *or* **Tupís** (1842) **1 :** TUPINAMBA **2 :** a language family of lowland South America that includes Tupi-Guarani and the speech of a number of other peoples living mainly in Brazil south of the Amazon River — **Tu·pi·an** \-ən\ *adj or n*
Tu·pi–Gua·ra·ni *also* **Tu·pí–Gua·ra·ní** \tü-ˌpē-ˌgwär-ə-ˈnē, ˈtü-(ˌ)pē-\ *n* (1850) **1 :** TUPI 2 **2 :** a branch of the Tupi language family that includes Tupinamba, Guarani, and a number of other languages spoken from French Guiana south to Paraguay and west to eastern Colombia — **Tupi–Gua·ra·ni·an** \-ˈnē-ən\ *adj or n*
Tu·pi·nam·ba *also* **Tu·pi·nam·bá** \tü-pə-ˈnam-bə, -ˌnam-ˈbä\ *n, pl* **-ba** *or* **-bas** *also* **-bá** *or* **-bás** (1810) **1 :** a member of a group of American Indian peoples who lived along a broad stretch of the Brazilian coast from the vicinity of Guanabara Bay to the mouth of the Amazon River **2 :** the extinct language of the Tupinamba
-tuple *n comb form* [quin*tuple,* sex*tuple*] : set of (so many) elements — usu. used of sets with ordered elements ⟨the ordered 2-*tuple* (*a, b*)⟩
tuppence *var of* TWOPENCE
tuque \ˈtük, ˈtyük\ *n* [CanF, fr. F *toque* — more at TOQUE] (1871) : a warm knitted usu. pointed stocking cap
tu quo·que \ˈtü-ˈkwō-kwē, ˈtyü-, -ˈkō-\ *n* [L, you too] (1614) : a retort charging an adversary with being or doing what he criticizes in others
tu·ra·co *or* **tou·ra·co** \ˈtu̇r-ə-(ˌ)kō\ *n, pl* **-cos** [origin unknown] (1743) : any of a family (Musophagidae) of typically crested African birds that are related to the cuckoos and have a long tail, a short stout often colored bill, and red wing feathers
Tu·ra·ni·an \tu̇-ˈrā-nē-ən, tyu̇-, -ˈrä-\ *n* [Pers *Tūrān* Turkestan, the region north of the Amu Darya] (ca. 1777) **1 :** a member of any of various peoples speaking Ural-Altaic languages **2 :** URAL-ALTAIC — **Turanian** *adj*
tur·ban \ˈtər-bən\ *n* [MF *turbant,* fr. It *turbante,* fr. Turk *tülbent,* fr. Pers *dulband*] (1588) **1 :** a headdress worn chiefly in countries of the eastern Mediterranean and southern Asia consisting of a long cloth that is wrapped around a cap (as by Muslims) or directly around the head (as by Sikhs and Hindus) **2 :** a headdress resembling a turban; *specif* : a woman's close-fitting hat without a brim **3 :** a rolled stuffed fillet of fish ⟨~ of sole⟩ — **turbaned** *or* **tur·banned** \-bənd\ *adj*

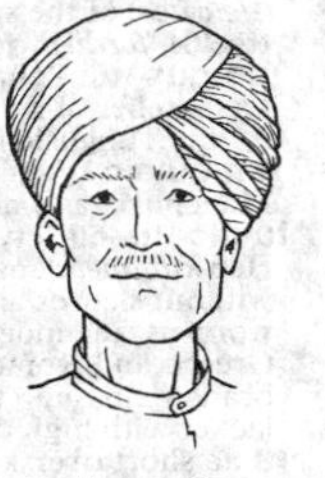
turban 1

tur·bel·lar·i·an \ˌtər-bə-ˈler-ē-ən\ *n* [ultim. fr. L *turbellae* (pl.) bustle, stir, dim. of *turba* confusion, crowd; fr. the tiny eddies created in water by the cilia] (1883) : any of a class (Turbellaria) of mostly aquatic and free-living flatworms (as a planarian) — **turbellarian** *adj*
tur·bid \ˈtər-bəd\ *adj* [L *turbidus* confused, turbid, fr. *turba* confusion, crowd, prob. fr. Gk *tyrbē* confusion] (1626) **1 a :** thick or opaque with or as if with roiled sediment ⟨a ~ stream⟩ **b :** heavy with smoke or mist **2 a :** deficient in clarity or purity : FOUL, MUDDY ⟨~ depths of degradation and misery —C. I. Glicksberg⟩ **b :** characterized by or producing obscurity (as of mind or emotions) ⟨an emotionally ~ response⟩ — **tur·bid·i·ty** \ˌtər-ˈbi-də-tē\ *n* — **tur·bid·ly** \ˈtər-bəd-lē\ *adv* — **tur·bid·ness** *n*
tur·bi·dim·e·ter \ˌtər-bə-ˈdi-mə-tər\ *n* [ISV *turbidity* + *-meter*] (1905) **1 :** an instrument for measuring and comparing the turbidity of liquids by viewing light through them and determining how much light is cut off **2 :** NEPHELOMETER — **tur·bi·di·met·ric** \ˌtər-bə-də-ˈme-trik, ˌtər-ˌbi-də-\ *adj* — **tur·bi·di·met·ri·cal·ly** \-tri-k(ə-)lē\ *adv* — **tur·bi·dim·e·try** \ˌtər-bə-ˈdi-mə-trē\ *n*
tur·bi·dite \ˈtər-bə-ˌdīt\ *n* [*turbidity* current (a current flowing down a slope and spreading out on the ocean floor) + [1]*-ite*] (1957) : a sedimentary deposit consisting of material that has moved down the steep slope at the edge of a continental shelf; *also* : a rock formed from this deposit
[1]**tur·bi·nate** \ˈtər-bə-nət, -ˌnāt\ *also* **tur·bi·nat·ed** \-ˌnā-təd\ *adj* [L *turbinatus,* fr. *turbin-, turbo*] (1661) **1 :** shaped like a top or an inverted cone ⟨~ seed capsule⟩ **2 :** relating to or being a turbinate
[2]**turbinate** *n* (1873) : one of usu. several thin plicated membrane-covered bony or cartilaginous plates on the walls of the nasal chambers
tur·bine \ˈtər-bən, -ˌbīn\ *n* [F, fr. L *turbin-, turbo* top, whirlwind, whirl, fr. *turba* confusion — more at TURBID] (1842) : a rotary engine actuated by the reaction or impulse or both of a current of fluid (as water, steam, or air) subject to pressure and usu. made with a series of curved vanes on a central rotating spindle
tur·bo \ˈtər-(ˌ)bō\ *n, pl* **turbos** [*turbo-*] (1904) **1 :** TURBINE **2** [by shortening] : TURBOCHARGER
turbo- *comb form* [*turbine*] **1 :** coupled directly to a driving turbine ⟨*turbo*fan⟩ **2 :** consisting of or incorporating a turbine ⟨*turbo*jet engine⟩
tur·bo·car \ˈtər-bō-ˌkär\ *n* (1950) : an automotive vehicle propelled by a gas turbine
tur·bo·charged \-ˌchärjd\ *adj* (1945) **1 :** equipped with a turbocharger **2 :** supercharged esp. with energy, vitality, or tension ⟨a giant, ~ ego that drove him relentlessly —Jeff Jarvis⟩
tur·bo·charg·er \-ˌchär-jər\ *n* (1934) : a centrifugal blower driven by exhaust gas turbines and used to supercharge an engine
tur·bo·elec·tric \ˌtər-bō-i-ˈlek-trik\ *adj* (1904) : using or being a turbine generator that produces electricity usu. for motive power
tur·bo·fan \ˈtər-bō-ˌfan\ *n* (1911) **1 :** a fan that is directly connected to and driven by a turbine and is used to supply air for cooling, ventilation, or combustion **2 :** a jet engine having a turbofan
tur·bo·gen·er·a·tor \ˌtər-bō-ˈje-nə-ˌrā-tər\ *n* (1898) : an electric generator driven by a turbine
tur·bo·jet \-ˌjet\ *n* (1945) **1 :** an airplane powered by turbojet engines **2 :** TURBOJET ENGINE
turbojet engine *n* (1944) : a jet engine in which a turbine drives a compressor that supplies air to a burner and hot gases from the burner drive the turbine before being discharged rearward
tur·bo·ma·chin·ery \ˌtər-bō-mə-ˈshē-nə-rē, -ˈshē-nə-\ *n* (1947) : machinery consisting of, incorporating, or constituting a turbine
tur·bo·prop \ˈtər-bō-ˌpräp\ *n* (1945) **1 :** TURBOPROP ENGINE **2 :** an airplane powered by turboprop engines
turboprop engine *n* (1947) : a jet engine designed to produce thrust principally by means of a propeller driven by a turbine with additional thrust usu. obtained by the rearward discharge of hot exhaust gases
tur·bo·shaft \ˈtər-bō-ˌshaft\ *n* (1958) : a gas turbine engine that is similar in operation to a turboprop engine but instead of being used to power a propeller is used through a transmission system for powering other devices (as helicopter rotors and pumps)
tur·bot \ˈtər-bət\ *n, pl* **turbot** *also* **turbots** [ME, fr. AF *turbut*] (14c) **1 :** a large European flatfish (*Psetta maxima*) that is a popular food fish and has a brownish upper surface marked with scattered tubercles and a white undersurface **2 :** any of various flatfishes (as *Scophthalmus maximus* or *Reinhardtius hippoglossoides*) resembling the turbot
tur·bu·lence \ˈtər-byə-lən(t)s\ *n* (1595) : the quality or state of being turbulent: as **a :** great commotion or agitation ⟨emotional ~⟩ **b :** irregular atmospheric motion esp. when characterized by up-and-down currents **c :** departure in a fluid from a smooth flow
tur·bu·len·cy \-lən(t)-sē\ *n, pl* **-cies** (1607) *archaic* : TURBULENCE
tur·bu·lent \-lənt\ *adj* [L *turbulentus,* fr. *turba* confusion, crowd — more at TURBID] (1538) **1 :** causing unrest, violence, or disturbance ⟨a set of mischievous, ~ rebels —Anne Brontë⟩ **2 a :** characterized by agitation or tumult : TEMPESTUOUS ⟨a ~ marriage⟩ **b :** exhibiting physical turbulence ⟨~ air⟩ — **tur·bu·lent·ly** *adv*
turbulent flow *n* (1895) : a fluid flow in which the velocity at a given point varies erratically in magnitude and direction — compare LAMINAR FLOW
Tur·co- *or* **Tur·ko-** \ˈtər-(ˌ)kō\ *comb form* [*Turco-* fr. ML *Turcus* Turk; *Turko-* fr. *Turk*] **1 :** Turkic : Turkish : Turk ⟨*Turco*phil⟩ **2 :** Turkish and ⟨*Turco*-Greek⟩
turd \ˈtərd\ *n* [ME *tord, turd,* fr. OE *tord;* akin to MD *tort* dung and prob. to OE *teran* to tear — more at TEAR] (bef. 12c) **1** *sometimes vulgar* : a piece of fecal matter **2** *usu vulgar* : a contemptible person
tur·duck·en \tər-ˈdə-kən\ *n* [*turkey* + [1]*duck* + [1]*chicken*] (1982) : a boneless chicken stuffed into a boneless duck stuffed into a boneless turkey
tu·reen \tə-ˈrēn, tyu̇-\ *n* [F *terrine,* fr. MF, fr. fem. of *terrin* of earth, fr. VL **terrinus,* fr. L *terra* earth — more at TERRACE] (ca. 1706) **1 :** a deep and usu. covered bowl from which foods (as soup) are served **2 :** CASSEROLE 1
[1]**turf** \ˈtərf\ *n, pl* **turfs** \ˈtərfs\ *also* **turves** \ˈtərvz\ [ME, fr. OE; akin to OHG *zurba* turf, Skt *darbha* tuft of grass] (bef. 12c) **1 a :** the upper stratum of soil bound by grass and plant roots into a thick mat; *also* : a piece of this **b :** an artificial substitute for this (as on a playing field) **c :** GRASS 3 **2 a :** PEAT 2 **b :** a piece of peat dried for fuel **3 a :** a track or course for horse racing **b :** the sport or business of horse racing **4 a :** territory considered by a teenage gang to be under its control **b :** TERRITORY 2 ⟨have to play two of the last three games on hostile ~ —Joe Klein⟩ ⟨in chapter two, the author is on unfamiliar ~⟩; *also* : a sphere of activity or influence ⟨people who could hurt him on his own foreign-policy ~ —*Wall Street Jour.*⟩ — **turfy** \ˈtər-fē\ *adj*
[2]**turf** *vt* (15c) **1 :** to cover with turf **2** *chiefly Brit* : to eject forcibly : KICK — usu. used with *out*
turf accountant *n* (1915) *Brit* : BOOKMAKER 2
turf·grass \ˈtərf-ˌgras\ *n* (1962) : any of various grasses (as Kentucky bluegrass or perennial ryegrass) grown to form turf
turf·man \ˈtərf-mən\ *n* (1818) : a devotee of horse racing; *esp* : a person who owns and races horses
turf·ski \-ˌskē\ *n* (1967) : a short ski with rollers on the bottom that can be used to ski down a grassy slope — **turf·ski·ing** *n*
turf toe *n* [fr. the occurrence of the injury among athletes who play on artificial turf] (1981) : a minor but painful usu. sports-related injury typically involving hyperextension of the big toe that results in spraining or tearing of the ligaments at the joint between the metatarsal and basal phalanx
tur·ges·cent \ˌtər-ˈje-sᵊnt\ *adj* [L *turgescent-, turgescens,* prp. of *turgescere* to swell, incho. of *turgēre* to be swollen] (ca. 1727) : becoming turgid, distended, or inflated — **tur·ges·cence** \-sᵊn(t)s\ *n*
tur·gid \ˈtər-jəd\ *adj* [L *turgidus,* fr. *turgēre* to be swollen] (1620) **1 :** being in a state of distension : SWOLLEN, TUMID ⟨~ limbs⟩; *esp* : exhibiting turgor **2 :** excessively embellished in style or language : BOMBASTIC, POMPOUS ⟨~ prose⟩ — **tur·gid·i·ty** \ˌtər-ˈji-də-tē\ *n* — **tur·gid·ly** \ˈtər-jəd-lē\ *adv* — **tur·gid·ness** *n*
tur·gor \ˈtər-gər, -ˌgȯr\ *n* [LL, turgidity, swelling, fr. L *turgēre*] (1876) : the normal state of turgidity and tension in living cells; *esp* : the distension of the protoplasmic layer and wall of a plant cell by the fluid contents
Tu·ring machine \ˈtu̇r-iŋ-, ˈtyu̇r-\ *n* [A. M. *Turing* †1954 Eng. mathematician] (1937) : a hypothetical computing machine that has an unlimited amount of information storage
tu·ris·ta \tü-ˈrē-stə\ *n* [Sp, tourist] (1962) : TRAVELER'S DIARRHEA
Turk \ˈtərk\ *n* [ME, fr. AF or Turk; AF *Turc,* fr. ML or Turk; ML *Turcus,* fr. Turk *Türk*] (14c) **1 :** a member of any of numerous Asian peoples speaking Turkic languages who live in a region extending from the Balkans to eastern Siberia and western China **2 :** a native or inhabitant of Turkey **3 :** MUSLIM; *specif* : a Muslim subject of the Turkish sultan **4 :** a Turkish horse; *specif* : a Turkish strain of Arab and crossbred horses **5** *often not cap* : a usu. young dynamic person eager for change; *esp* : YOUNG TURK
tur·key \ˈtər-kē\ *n, pl* **turkeys** [*Turkey,* country in western Asia and southeastern Europe; fr. confusion with the guinea fowl, supposed to be imported from Turkish territory] (1555) **1** *pl also* **turkey :** a large

No. American gallinaceous bird (*Meleagris gallopavo*) that is domesticated in most parts of the world **2 :** FAILURE, FLOP; *esp* **:** a theatrical production that has failed **3 :** three successive strikes in bowling **4 :** a stupid, foolish, or inept person

tur·key–cock \'tər-kē-ˌkäk\ *n* (1578) **1 :** [1]GOBBLER **2 :** a strutting pompous person

Turkey Day *n* (1870) **:** THANKSGIVING DAY

turkey oak *n* (1709) **:** a small oak (*Quercus laevis*) of the southeastern U.S.; *also* **:** a Eurasian oak (*Q. cerris*)

Tur·key red \'tər-kē-\ *n* [*Turkey*] (1734) **:** a brilliant durable red produced on cotton by means of alizarin in connection with an aluminum mordant and fatty matter

tur·key shoot \'tər-kē-\ *n* (1831) **:** a marksmanship contest using a moving target with a turkey offered as a prize

turkey trot *n* (1908) **:** a ragtime dance danced with the feet well apart and with a characteristic rise on the ball of the foot followed by a drop upon the heel

turkey vulture *n* (1823) **:** an American vulture (*Cathartes aura*) with a red head and whitish bill — called also *turkey buzzard*

Turk·ic \'tər-kik\ *adj* (1855) **1 a :** of, relating to, or constituting a family of Altaic languages including Turkish **b :** of or relating to the peoples speaking Turkic **2 :** TURKISH 1 — **Turkic** *n*

[1]Turk·ish \'tər-kish\ *adj* (14c) **1 :** of, relating to, or characteristic of Turkey, the Turks, or Turkish **2 :** TURKIC 1a

[2]Turkish *n* (1613) **:** the Turkic language of the Republic of Turkey

Turkish bath *n* (1644) **:** a bath in which the bather passes through a series of steam rooms of increasing temperature and then receives a rubdown, massage, and cold shower

Turkish coffee *n* (1854) **:** a sweetened decoction of pulverized coffee

Turkish delight *n* (1877) **:** a jellylike or gummy confection usu. cut in cubes and dusted with sugar — called also *Turkish paste*

Turkish towel *n* (1862) **:** a towel made of cotton terry cloth

Turk·ism \'tər-ˌki-zəm\ *n* (1877) **:** the customs, beliefs, institutions, and principles of the Turks

Tur·ko·man *or* **Tur·co·man** \'tər-kə-mən\ *n, pl* **Turkomans** *or* **Turcomans** [ML *Turcomannus,* fr. Pers *Turkmān,* fr. *turkmān* resembling a Turk, fr. *Turk*] (ca. 1520) **:** a member of a Turkic-speaking traditionally nomadic people living chiefly in Turkmenistan, Afghanistan, and Iran — **Turkoman** *or* **Turcoman** *adj*

Turk's head *n* (1833) **:** a turban-shaped knot worked on a rope with a piece of small line — see KNOT illustration

tur·mer·ic \'tər-mə-rik *also* 'tü-mə- *or* 'tyü-\ *n* [ME *turmeryte*] (15c) **1 :** an Indian perennial herb (*Curcuma longa* syn. *C. domestica*) of the ginger family with a large aromatic yellow rhizome **2 :** the boiled, dried, and usu. ground rhizome of the turmeric plant used as a coloring agent, a flavoring, or a stimulant **3 :** a yellow to reddish-brown dyestuff obtained from turmeric

tur·moil \'tər-ˌmȯi(-ə)l\ *n* [origin unknown] (1526) **:** a state or condition of extreme confusion, agitation, or commotion

[1]turn \'tərn\ *vb* [ME; partly fr. OE *tyrnan* & *turnian* to turn, fr. ML *tornare,* fr. L, to turn on a lathe, fr. *tornus* lathe, fr. Gk *tornos;* partly fr. AF *turner, tourner* to turn, fr. ML *tornare;* akin to L *terere* to rub — more at THROW] *vt* (bef. 12c) **1 a :** to cause to move around an axis or a center **:** make rotate or revolve ⟨~ a wheel⟩ ⟨~ a crank⟩ **b** (1) **:** to cause to move around so as to effect a desired end (as of locking, opening, or shutting) ⟨~*ed* the knob till the door opened⟩ (2) **:** to affect or alter the functioning of (as a mechanical device) or the level of (as sound) by such movement ⟨~ the oven to 400°⟩ ⟨~ the music to full volume⟩ **c :** to execute or perform by rotating or revolving ⟨~ handsprings⟩ **d :** to twist out of line or shape **:** WRENCH ⟨had ~*ed* his ankle⟩ **2 a** (1) **:** to cause to change position by moving through an arc of a circle ⟨~*ed* her chair to the fire⟩ (2) **:** to cause to move around a center so as to show another side of ⟨~ the page⟩ (3) **:** to cause (as a scale) to move so as to register weight **b :** to revolve mentally **:** think over **:** PONDER **3 a :** to reverse the sides or surfaces of **:** INVERT ⟨~ pancakes⟩ ⟨~ the shirt inside out⟩: as (1) **:** to dig or plow so as to bring the lower soil to the surface ⟨~ the compost weekly⟩ (2) **:** to make (as a garment) over by reversing the material and resewing ⟨~ a collar⟩ (3) **:** to invert feet up and face down (as a character, rule, or slug) in setting type **b :** to reverse or upset the order or disposition of ⟨everything was ~*ed* topsy-turvy⟩ **c :** to disturb or upset the mental balance of **:** DERANGE, UNSETTLE ⟨a mind ~*ed* by grief⟩ **d :** to set in another esp. contrary direction **4 a :** to bend or change the course of **:** DIVERT ⟨a battle that ~*ed* the tide of history⟩ **b :** to cause to retreat ⟨used fire hoses to ~ the mob⟩ **c :** to alter the drift, tendency, or expected result of **d :** to bend a course around or about **:** ROUND ⟨~*ed* the corner at full speed⟩ **5 a** (1) **:** to direct or point (as the face) in a specified way or direction (2) **:** to present by a change in direction or position ⟨~*ing* his back to his guests⟩ **b :** to bring to bear (as by aiming, pointing, or focusing) **:** TRAIN ⟨~*ed* the light into the dark doorway⟩ ⟨~*ed* a questioning eye toward her⟩ **c :** to direct (as the attention or mind) toward or away from something **d :** to direct the employment of **:** APPLY, DEVOTE ⟨~*ed* his skills to the service of humankind⟩ **e** (1) **:** to cause to rebound or recoil ⟨~*s* their argument against them⟩ (2) **:** to make antagonistic **:** PREJUDICE ⟨~ a child against its mother⟩ **f** (1) **:** to cause to go in a particular direction ⟨~*ed* our steps homeward⟩ (2) **:** DRIVE, SEND ⟨~ cows to pasture⟩ ⟨~*ing* hunters off his land⟩ (3) **:** to convey or direct out of an inverted receptacle ⟨~ the mixture into a baking dish⟩ **6 a** (1) **:** to make acid or sour (2) **:** to change the color of (as foliage) **b** (1) **:** CONVERT, TRANSFORM ⟨~ defeat into victory⟩ (2) **:** TRANSLATE, PARAPHRASE **c :** to cause to become of a specified nature or appearance ⟨~*ed* him into a frog⟩ ⟨embarrassment ~*ed* her face red⟩ **d :** to exchange for something else ⟨~ coins into paper money⟩ **e :** to cause to defect to another side **7 a :** to shape esp. in a rounded form by applying a cutting tool while revolving in a lathe **b :** to give a rounded form to by any means ⟨~ the heel of a sock⟩ **c :** to shape or mold artistically, gracefully, or neatly ⟨a well ~*ed* phrase⟩ **8 :** to make a fold, bend, or curve in: **a :** to form by bending ⟨~ a lead pipe⟩ **b :** to cause (the edge of a blade) to bend back or over **:** BLUNT, DULL **9 a :** to keep (as money or goods) moving; *specif* **:** to dispose of (a stock) to make room for another **b :** to gain in the course of business ⟨~*ing* a quick profit⟩ **c :** to make use of ⟨~*ed* her education to advantage⟩ **d :** to carry to completion **:** PULL OFF ⟨~*ed* a double play⟩ ⟨~ a deal⟩ **10 :** to engage in (an act of prostitution) ⟨~ tricks⟩ ~ *vi* **1 a :** to move around on an axis or through an arc of a circle **:** ROTATE **b :** to become giddy or dizzy **:** SPIN ⟨heights always made his head ~⟩ **c** (1) **:** to have as a decisive factor **:** HINGE ⟨the argument ~*s* on a point of logic⟩ ⟨the outcome of the game ~*ed* on an interception⟩ (2) **:** to have a center (as of interest) in something specified ⟨the discussion ~*ed* on the overall worth of the project⟩ (3) **:** to become focused on something specified ⟨the conversation ~*ed* to baseball⟩ **2 a :** to direct one's course **b** (1) **:** to reverse a course or direction ⟨the tide has ~*ed*⟩ (2) **:** to have a reactive usu. adverse effect **c :** to take a different course or direction ⟨~*ed* toward home⟩ ⟨the main road ~*s* sharply to the right⟩ **3 a :** to change position (as of one's head) so as to face another way ⟨everyone ~*ed* to stare⟩ **b :** to face toward or away from someone or something ⟨flowers ~ toward the light⟩ **c :** to change one's attitude or reverse one's course of action to one of opposition or hostility ⟨felt the world had ~*ed* against him⟩ **d :** to make a sudden violent assault esp. without evident cause ⟨dogs ~*ing* on their owners⟩ **4 a :** to direct one's attention to or away from someone or something **b** (1) **:** to change one's religion (2) **:** to go over to another side or party **:** DEFECT **c :** to have recourse **:** REFER, RESORT ⟨~*ed* to a friend for help⟩ ⟨~*ed* to his notes for the exact figures⟩ **d :** to direct one's efforts or activity **:** devote or apply oneself ⟨~*ed* to the study of the law⟩ ⟨~*ed* to a life of crime⟩ **5 a :** to become changed, altered, or transformed ⟨the weather ~*ed*⟩: as (1) *archaic* **:** to become different (2) **:** to change color ⟨the leaves have ~*ed*⟩ (3) **:** to become sour, rancid, or tainted ⟨the milk had ~*ed*⟩ (4) **:** to be variable or inconstant (5) **:** to become mentally unbalanced **:** become deranged **b** (1) **:** to pass from one state to another **:** CHANGE ⟨water had ~*ed* to ice⟩ (2) **:** BECOME, GROW ⟨his hair had ~*ed* gray⟩ ⟨the weather ~*ed* bad⟩ ⟨just ~*ed* twenty⟩ (3) **:** to become someone or something specified by change from another state **:** change into ⟨~ pro⟩ ⟨doctors ~*ed* authors⟩ (4) **:** to change by the passage of time ⟨days ~*ed* into weeks and months⟩ **6 :** to become curved or bent (as from pressure); *esp* **:** to become blunted by bending ⟨the edge of the knife had ~*ed*⟩ **7 :** to operate a lathe **8** *of merchandise* **:** to be stocked and disposed of **:** change hands — **turn·able** \'tər-nə-bəl\ *adj* — **turn a blind eye :** to refuse to see **:** be oblivious ⟨might *turn a blind eye* to the use of violence —Arthur Krock⟩ — **turn a deaf ear :** to refuse to listen — **turn a hair :** to give a sign of distress or disturbance ⟨did not *turn a hair* when told of the savage murder —*Times Lit. Supp.*⟩ — **turn color 1 :** to become of a different color **2 a :** BLUSH, FLUSH **b :** to grow pale — **turn heads :** to attract favorable attention ⟨the car's sleek design is bound to *turn heads*⟩ — **turn loose 1 a :** to set free ⟨*turned loose* the captured animal⟩ **b :** to free from all restraints ⟨*turned* them *loose* with a pile of theme paper to write whatever they liked —Elizabeth P. Schafer⟩ **2 :** to fire off **:** DISCHARGE **3 :** to open fire — **turn one's back on 1 :** REJECT, DENY ⟨would be *turning one's back on* history —Pius Walsh⟩ **2 :** FORSAKE ⟨*turned his back on* his obligations⟩ — **turn one's hand** *or* **turn a hand :** to set to work **:** apply oneself — **turn one's head :** to cause to become infatuated or conceited ⟨success had not *turned his head*⟩ — **turn one's stomach :** to disgust completely **:** NAUSEATE ⟨the foul smell *turned his stomach*⟩ — **turn tail :** to turn away so as to flee — **turn the other cheek :** to respond to injury or unkindness with patience **:** forgo retaliation — **turn the tables :** to bring about a reversal of the relative conditions or fortunes of two contending parties — **turn the trick :** to bring about the desired result or effect — **turn turtle :** CAPSIZE, OVERTURN

[2]turn *n* [ME; partly fr. AF *tur, tourn* turning, circuit (fr. *turner* to turn); partly fr. ME *turnen* to turn] (13c) **1 a :** the action or an act of turning about a center or axis **:** REVOLUTION, ROTATION **b :** any of various rotating or pivoting movements in dancing or gymnastics **2 a :** the action or an act of giving or taking a different direction **:** change of course or posture ⟨an illegal left ~⟩: as (1) **:** a drill maneuver in which troops in mass formation change direction without preserving alignment (2) **:** any of various shifts of direction in skiing (3) **:** an interruption of a curve in figure skating **b :** DEFLECTION, DEVIATION **c :** the action or an act of turning so as to face in the opposite direction **:** reversal of posture or course ⟨an about ~⟩ ⟨the ~ of the tide⟩ **d :** a change effected by turning over to another side ⟨a ~ of the cards⟩ **e :** a place at which something turns, turns off, or turns back **:** BEND, CURVE **3 :** a short trip out and back or round about ⟨took a ~ through the park⟩ **4 :** an act or deed affecting another esp. when incidental or unexpected ⟨one good ~ deserves another⟩ **5 a :** a period of action or activity **:** GO, SPELL ⟨took a ~ at the piano⟩ **b :** a place, time, or opportunity accorded an individual or unit of a series in simple succession or in a scheduled order ⟨waiting her ~ in line⟩ **c :** a period or tour of duty **:** SHIFT **d :** a short act or piece (as for a variety show); *also* **:** public appearance **:** PERFORMANCE ⟨makes frequent guest star ~*s*⟩ **e** (1) **:** an event in any gambling game after which bets are settled (2) **:** the order of the last three cards in faro — used in the phrase *call the turn* **6 :** something that revolves around a center: as **a** (1) **:** LATHE (2) **:** a catch or latch for a cupboard or cabinet door operated by turning a handle **b :** a musical ornament consisting of a group of four or more notes that wind about the principal note by including the notes next above and next below **7 :** a special purpose or requirement — used chiefly in the phrase *serve one's turn* **8 a :** an act of changing **:** ALTERATION, MODIFICATION ⟨a nasty ~ in the weather⟩ **b :** a change in tendency, trend, or drift ⟨hoped for a ~ in his luck⟩ ⟨a ~ for the better⟩ ⟨an unexpected ~ of events⟩ **c :** the beginning of a new period of time **:** the time when one period changes to the next ⟨the ~ of the century⟩ **9 a :** distinctive quality or character **b :** a fashioning of language or arrangement of words **:** manner of expression ⟨skillful ~*s* of phrase⟩ **c :** the shape or mold in which something is fashioned **:** CAST **10 a :** the state or manner of being coiled or twisted **b :** a single round (as of rope passed about an object or of wire wound on a core) **11 :** natural or special ability or aptitude **:** BENT, INCLINATION ⟨a ~ for logic⟩ ⟨an optimistic ~ of mind⟩ **12 :** a special twist,

\ə\ **a**but \ᵊ\ kitten, F table \ər\ **fur**ther \a\ **a**sh \ā\ **a**ce \ä\ m**o**p, m**a**r
\au̇\ **ou**t \ch\ **ch**in \e\ b**e**t \ē\ **ea**sy \g\ **g**o \i\ h**i**t \ī\ **i**ce \j\ **j**ob
\ŋ\ si**ng** \ō\ g**o** \ȯ\ l**aw** \ȯi\ b**oy** \th\ **th**in \t͟h\ **th**e \ü\ l**oo**t \u̇\ f**oo**t
\y\ **y**et \zh\ vi**si**on, bei**ge** \k, ⁿ, œ, ue, ʸ\ *see* Guide to Pronunciation

construction, or interpretation ‹gave the old yarn a new ~› **13 a :** a disordering spell or attack (as of illness, faintness, or dizziness) **b :** a nervous start or shock ‹snuck up on her and gave her quite a ~› **14 a :** a complete transaction involving a purchase and sale of securities; *also* **:** a profit from such a transaction **b :** TURNOVER 7b **15 :** something turned or to be turned: as **a :** a character or slug inverted in setting type **b :** a piece of type placed bottom up — **at every turn :** on every occasion **:** CONTINUALLY ‹they opposed her *at every turn*› — **by turns 1 :** one after another in regular succession **2 :** VARIOUSLY, ALTERNATELY ‹a book that is *by turns* pedantic, delightful, and infuriating› — **in turn :** in due order of succession — **on the turn :** at the point of turning ‹tide is *on the turn*› — **out of turn 1 :** not in due order of succession ‹play *out of turn*› **2 :** at a wrong time or place and usu. imprudently ‹talking *out of turn*› — **to a turn :** to perfection

turn·about \ˈtərn-ə-ˌbau̇t\ *n* (1789) **1 :** MERRY-GO-ROUND **2 a :** a change or reversal of direction, trend, policy, role, or character **b :** a changing from one allegiance to another **c :** TURNCOAT, RENEGADE **d :** an act or instance of retaliating ‹~ is fair play›

turn·around \-ˌrau̇nd\ *n* (1926) **1 a :** the process of readying a transport vehicle for departure after its arrival; *also* **:** the time spent in this process ‹a quick ~ between flights› **b :** the action of receiving, processing, and returning something ‹24-hour ~ time on most orders› **2 :** a space permitting the turning around of a vehicle **3 a :** TURNABOUT 2a ‹a corporate ~› **b :** TURNABOUT 2b **4 :** a jump shot by a player facing away from the basket who turns toward the basket while shooting — often used attributively ‹a ~ jumper›

turn around *vi* (1934) **1 :** to act in an abrupt, different, or surprising manner — used with *and* ‹after three years he just *turned around* and left school› **2 :** to become changed for the better ~ *vt* **:** to change for the better ‹*turned* her life *around*›

turn away *vt* (13c) **1 :** DEFLECT, AVERT **2 a :** to send away **:** REJECT, DISMISS **b :** REPEL **c :** to refuse admittance or acceptance to ~ *vi* **:** to start to go away **:** DEPART

turn back *vi* (15c) **1 a :** to go in the reverse direction **b :** to stop going forward **2 :** to refer to an earlier time or place ~ *vt* **1 :** to drive back or away **2 :** to stop the advance of **3 :** to fold back **4 :** GIVE BACK, RETURN — **turn back the clock :** to revert to or remind of a condition existing in the past

turn·buck·le \ˈtərn-ˌbə-kəl\ *n* (ca. 1877) **:** a device that usu. consists of a link with screw threads at both ends, that is turned to bring the ends closer together, and that is used for tightening a rod or stay

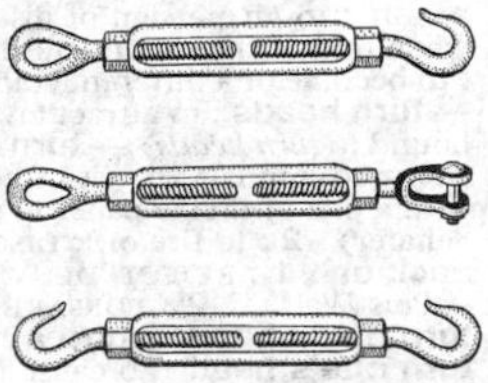

turnbuckles

turn·coat \-ˌkōt\ *n* (1557) **:** one who switches to an opposing side or party; *specif* **:** TRAITOR

¹turn·down \ˈtərn-ˈdau̇n\ *adj* (1763) **:** capable of being turned down; *esp* **:** worn turned down ‹a ~ collar›

²turn·down \ˈtərn-ˌdau̇n\ *n* (1849) **1 :** something turned down; *also* **:** an instance of turning something (as a bed sheet) down ‹hotel ~ service› **2 :** REJECTION **3 :** DOWNTURN

turn down *vt* (1601) **1 :** to fold or double down **2 :** to turn (a card) face downward **3 :** to reduce the height or intensity of by turning a control ‹*turn down* the radio› **4 :** to decline to accept **:** REJECT ‹*turned down* the offer› ~ *vi* **:** to be capable of being folded or doubled down ‹the collar *turns down*›

turned–on \ˈtərnd-ˈȯn, -ˈän\ *adj* (1966) **:** keenly aware of and responsive to what is new and fashionable **:** HIP

¹turn·er \ˈtər-nər\ *n* (13c) **:** one that turns or is used for turning ‹a pancake ~›; *esp* **:** a person who forms articles with a lathe

²tur·ner \ˈtər-nər, ˈtu̇r-\ *n* [G, fr. *turnen* to perform gymnastic exercises, fr. OHG *turnēn* to turn, fr. ML *tornare* — more at TURN] (1854) **:** a member of a turnverein **:** GYMNAST

Tur·ner's syndrome \ˈtər-nərz-\ *n* [Henry Hubert *Turner* †1970 Am. physician] (1942) **:** a genetically determined condition that is typically associated with the presence of only one complete X chromosome and no Y chromosome and is characterized esp. by a female phenotype with underdeveloped and usu. infertile ovaries and short stature

turn·ery \ˈtər-nə-rē\ *n, pl* **-er·ies** (1644) **:** the work, products, or shop of a turner

turn–in \ˈtərn-ˌin\ *n* (1873) **:** something that turns in or is turned in

turn in *vi* (1535) **1 :** to make an entrance by turning from a road or path **2 :** to go to bed ‹*turned in* early› ~ *vt* **1 :** to deliver up **:** HAND OVER ‹*turned in* his badge and quit› **2 a :** to inform on **:** BETRAY **b :** to deliver to an authority ‹urged the wanted man to *turn* himself *in*› **3 :** to acquit oneself of **:** PUT ON, PRODUCE ‹*turned in* a good performance›

turn·ing \ˈtər-niŋ\ *n* (14c) **1 :** the act or course of one that turns **2 :** a place of a change in direction **3 a :** a forming by use of a lathe; *broadly* **:** TURNERY **b** *pl* **:** waste produced in turning

turning point *n* (1817) **:** a point at which a significant change occurs

tur·nip \ˈtər-nəp\ *n* [ME *turnepe,* prob. fr. *turnen* to turn + *nepe* neep; fr. the well-rounded root] (1533) **1 a :** either of two biennial herbs of the mustard family with thick edible roots: (1) **:** one (*Brassica rapa rapifera*) with globular often flattened roots and leaves that are cooked as a vegetable (2) **:** RUTABAGA **b :** the root of a turnip **2 :** a large pocket watch

¹turn·key \ˈtərn-ˌkē\ *n, pl* **turnkeys** (1647) **:** one who has charge of a prison's keys

²turnkey *adj* (1927) **:** built, supplied, or installed complete and ready to operate ‹a ~ nuclear plant› ‹a ~ computer system›; *also* **:** of or relating to a turnkey building or installation ‹a ~ contract› ‹~ vendors›

turn·off \ˈtərn-ˌȯf\ *n* (ca. 1852) **1 :** a turning off **2 :** a place where one turns off; *esp* **:** EXIT 4 **3 :** one that causes loss of interest or enthusiasm ‹the music was a ~›

turn off *vt* (1564) **1 a :** DISMISS, DISCHARGE **b :** to dispose of **:** SELL **2 :** DEFLECT, EVADE **3 :** PRODUCE, ACCOMPLISH **4 :** to stop the flow of or shut off by or as if by turning a control ‹*turn* the water *off*› **5 :** HANG 1b **6 a :** to remove (material) by the process of turning **b :** to shape or produce by turning **7 :** to cause to lose interest **:** BORE ‹economics *turns* me *off*›; *also* **:** to evoke a negative feeling in ~ *vi* **1 :** to deviate from a straight course or from a main road ‹*turn off* into a side road› **2 a** *Brit* **:** to turn bad **:** SPOIL **b :** to change to a specified state **:** BECOME **3 :** to lose interest **:** WITHDRAW

turn on *vt* (1833) **1 :** to activate or cause to flow, operate, or function by or as if by turning a control ‹*turn* the water *on* full› ‹*turn on* the power› **2 a :** to cause to undergo an intense often visionary experience by taking a drug; *broadly* **:** to cause to get high **b :** to move pleasurably ‹rock music *turns* her *on*›; *also* **:** to excite sexually **c :** to cause to gain knowledge or appreciation of something specified ‹*turned* her *on* to ballet› ~ *vi* **:** to become turned on — **turn–on** \ˈtərn-ˌȯn, -ˌän\ *n*

turn·out \ˈtərn-ˌau̇t\ *n* (1688) **1 :** an act of turning out **2** *chiefly Brit* **a :** STRIKE 3a **b :** STRIKER 1d **3 :** the number of people who participate in or attend an event ‹a heavy voter ~› **4 a :** a place where something (as a road) turns out or branches off **b :** a space adjacent to a highway in which vehicles may park or pull into to enable others to pass **c :** a railroad siding **5 :** a clearing out and cleaning **6 a :** a coach or carriage together with the horses, harness, and attendants **b :** EQUIPMENT, RIG **c :** manner of dress **:** GETUP **7 :** net quantity of produce yielded

turn out *vt* (1546) **1 a :** EXPEL, EVICT **b :** to put (as a horse) to pasture **2 a :** to turn inside out ‹*turning out* his pockets› **b :** to empty the contents of esp. for cleaning or rearranging; *also* **:** CLEAN **3 :** to produce often rapidly or regularly by or as if by machine ‹a writer *turning out* stories› **4 :** to equip, dress, or finish in a careful or elaborate way **5 :** to put out by or as if by turning a switch ‹*turn out* the lights› **6 :** to call (as the guard or a company) out from rest or shelter and into formation ~ *vi* **1 a :** to come or go out from home in or as if in answer to a summons ‹voters *turned out* in droves› **b :** to get out of bed **2 a :** to prove to be in the result or end ‹the play *turned out* to be a flop› ‹it *turned out* that we were both wrong› **b :** to become in maturity ‹nobody thought he'd *turn out* like this› **c :** END ‹stories that *turn out* happily›

¹turn·over \ˈtərn-ˌō-vər\ *n* (14c) **1 :** an act or result of turning over **:** UPSET **2 :** a turning from one side, place, or direction to its opposite **:** SHIFT, REVERSAL **3 :** a reorganization with a view to a shift in personnel **:** SHAKE-UP **4 :** something that is turned over **5 :** a filled pastry made by folding half of the crust over the other half **6 :** the amount of business done; *esp* **:** the volume of shares traded on a stock exchange **7 a :** movement (as of goods or people) into, through, and out of a place **b** (1) **:** a cycle of purchase, sale, and replacement of a stock of goods (2) **:** the ratio of sales for a stated period to average inventory (3) **:** the amount received in sales for a stated period **c :** the number of persons hired within a period to replace those leaving or dropped from a workforce; *also* **:** the ratio of this number to the number in the average force maintained **8 :** the continuous process of loss and replacement of a constituent (as a cell or tissue) of a living system **9 :** the act or an instance of a team's losing possession of a ball through error or a minor violation of the rules (as in basketball or football)

²turnover *adj* (ca. 1849) **:** capable of being turned over

turn over *vt* (14c) **1 a :** to turn from an upright position **:** OVERTURN **b :** ROTATE ‹*turn over* a stiff valve with a wrench›; *also* **:** to cause (an internal combustion engine) to begin firing **2 :** to search (as clothes or papers) by lifting or moving one by one **3 :** to read or examine (as a book) slowly or idly **4 :** DELIVER, SURRENDER ‹I'm *turning* the job *over* to you›; *also* **:** to lose possession of ‹*turned* the ball *over* three times› **5 a :** to receive and dispose of (a stock of merchandise) **b :** to do business to the amount of ‹*turning over* $1000 a week› ~ *vi* **1 :** UPSET, CAPSIZE **2 a :** ROTATE **b** *of an engine* **:** to have crankshaft rotation esp. by external means (as by a starter) ‹the engine *turned over* but didn't start› **3 a** *of one's stomach* **:** to heave with nausea **b** *of one's heart* **:** to seem to leap or lurch convulsively with sudden fright — **turn over a new leaf :** to make a change for the better esp. in one's way of living

turn·pike \ˈtərn-ˌpīk\ *n* [ME *turnepike* revolving frame bearing spikes and serving as a barrier, fr. *turnen* to turn + *pike*] (1678) **1 :** TOLLGATE **2 a** (1) **:** a road (as an expressway) for the use of which tolls are collected (2) **:** a road formerly maintained as a turnpike **b :** a main road; *esp* **:** a paved highway with a rounded surface

turn·spit \-ˌspit\ *n* (1570) **1 a :** one that turns a spit; *specif* **:** a small dog formerly used in a treadmill to turn a spit **b :** a roasting jack **2 :** a rotatable spit

turn·stile \-ˌstī(-ə)l\ *n* (1643) **:** a post with arms pivoted on the top set in a passageway so that persons can pass through only on foot one by one

turn·stone \-ˌstōn\ *n* [fr. a habit of turning over stones to find food] (ca. 1674) **:** either of two shorebirds (genus *Arenaria*) of the sandpiper family: **a :** a bird (*A. interpres*) of worldwide distribution that has black and chestnut upperparts and a black breast **b :** a No. American bird (*A. melanocephala*) with black upperparts and breast

turn·ta·ble \-ˌtā-bəl\ *n* (1835) **:** a revolvable platform: as **a :** a platform with a track for turning wheeled vehicles (as locomotives) **b :** LAZY SUSAN **c :** a rotating platform that carries a phonograph record

turn to *vi* (1813) **:** to apply oneself to work **:** act vigorously ‹all hands *turn to* and build a church and a jail —Mark Twain›

¹turn·up \ˈtər-ˈnəp\ *adj* (1685) **1 :** turned up ‹a ~ nose› **2 :** made or fitted to be turned up ‹a ~ collar›

²turn·up \ˈtər-ˌnəp\ *n* (1688) **:** something that is turned up

turn up *vt* (1563) **1 :** FIND, DISCOVER **2 :** to raise or increase by or as if by turning a control ‹*turn up* the volume on the radio› **3** *Brit* **a :** to look up (as a word or fact) in a book **b :** to refer to or consult (a book) **4 :** to turn (a card) face upward ~ *vi* **1 :** to appear or come to light unexpectedly or after being lost ‹new evidence has *turned up*› **2 a** (1) **:** to turn out to be ‹he *turned up* missing at roll call› (2) **:** APPEAR 4 ‹her name is always *turning up* in the newspapers› **b :** to arrive or show up at an appointed or expected time or place ‹*turned up* half an hour late› **3 :** to happen or occur unexpectedly ‹something always *turned up* to prevent their meeting› **4** *of a ship* **:** TACK 1b — **turn up one's nose :** to show scorn or disdain

turn·ver·ein \ˈtərn-və-ˌrīn, ˈtu̇rn-\ *n* [G, fr. *turnen* to perform gymnastic exercises + *Verein* club] (1852) **:** an athletic club

tu·ro·phile \ˈtu̇r-ə-ˌfī(-ə)l, ˈtyu̇r-\ *n* [irreg. fr. Gk *tyros* cheese + E *-phile* — more at BUTTER] (1938) **:** a connoisseur of cheese **:** a cheese fancier

¹tur·pen·tine \ˈtər-pən-ˌtīn, ˈtər-pᵊm-\ *n* [ME *terbentyne, turpentyne,* fr. AF & ML; AF *terebentine,* fr. ML *terbentina,* fr. L *terebinthina,* fem. of *terebinthinus* of terebinth, fr. *terebinthus* terebinth, fr. Gk *terebinthos*] (14c) **1 a :** a yellow to brown semifluid oleoresin obtained as an exudate from the terebinth **b :** an oleoresin obtained from various conifers (as some pines and firs) **2 a :** an essential oil obtained from turpentines by distillation and used esp. as a solvent and thinner — called also *gum turpentine* **b :** a similar oil obtained by distillation or carbonization of pinewood — called also *wood turpentine*

[2]**turpentine** *vt* **-tined; -tin·ing** (1759) **1 :** to apply turpentine to **2 :** to extract turpentine from; *esp* **:** to tap (pine trees) in order to obtain turpentine

tur·pi·tude \ˈtər-pə-ˌtüd, -ˌtyüd\ *n* [MF, fr. L *turpitudo*, fr. *turpis* vile, base] (15c) **:** inherent baseness **:** DEPRAVITY ⟨moral ~⟩; *also* **:** a base act

turps \ˈtərps\ *n pl but sing in constr* [by shortening & alter.] (ca. 1823) **:** TURPENTINE

tur·quoise *also* **tur·quois** \ˈtər-ˌkȯiz, -ˌkwȯiz\ *n* [ME *turkeys*, fr. AF *turkeise*, fr. fem. of *turkeis* Turkish, fr. *Turc* Turk] (14c) **1 :** a mineral that is a blue, bluish-green, or greenish-gray hydrous basic phosphate of copper and aluminum, takes a high polish, and is valued as a gem when skyblue **2 :** a light greenish blue

turquoise blue *n* (1799) **:** a light greenish blue that is paler and slightly bluer than average turquoise

turquoise green *n* (1856) **:** a light bluish green

tur·ret \ˈtər-ət, ˈtə-rət, ˈtu̇r-ət\ *n* [ME *touret*, fr. AF *turette, tourette*, dim. of *tur, tour* tower — more at TOWER] (14c) **1 :** a little tower; *specif* **:** an ornamental structure at an angle of a larger structure **2 a :** a pivoted and revolvable holder in a machine tool **b :** a device (as on a microscope or a television camera) holding several lenses **3 a :** a tall building usu. moved on wheels and formerly used for carrying soldiers and equipment for breaching or scaling a wall **b** (1) **:** a gunner's fixed or movable enclosure in an airplane (2) **:** a revolving armored structure on a warship that protects one or more guns mounted within it (3) **:** a similar upper structure usu. for one gun on a tank

tur·ret·ed \ˈtər-ə-təd, ˈtə-rə-, ˈtu̇r-ə-\ *adj* (ca. 1550) **:** furnished with or as if with turrets ⟨a ~ fortress⟩

[1]**tur·tle** \ˈtər-tᵊl\ *n* [ME, fr. OE *turtla*, fr. L *turtur*] (bef. 12c) *archaic* **:** TURTLEDOVE

[2]**turtle** *n, pl* **turtles** *also* **turtle** *often attrib* [modif. of F *tortue*, fr. LL (*bestia*) *tartarucha*, fem. of *tartaruchus* of Tartarus, fr. Gk *tartarouchos*, fr. *Tartaros* Tartarus; fr. Mithraic and early Christian association of the turtle with infernal forces] (1612) **:** any of an order (Testudines syn. Chelonia) of terrestrial, freshwater, and marine reptiles that have a toothless horny beak and a shell of bony dermal plates usu. covered with horny shields enclosing the trunk and into which the head, limbs, and tail usu. may be withdrawn

[3]**turtle** *n* (1952) **:** TURTLENECK

tur·tle·back \ˈtər-tᵊl-ˌbak\ *n* (1872) **:** a raised convex surface — **turtle·back** *or* **tur·tle–backed** \-ˌbakt\ *adj*

turtle bean *n* (1923) **:** BLACK BEAN 1

tur·tle·dove \-ˌdəv\ *n* (14c) **:** any of several small wild pigeons (genus *Streptopelia* and esp. *S. turtur*) noted for plaintive cooing

turtle grass *n* (1735) **:** a submerged monocotyledonous marine plant (*Thalassia testudinum* of the family Hydrocharitaceae) of the coasts of Florida and the West Indies having long ribbonlike leaves

tur·tle·head \-ˌhed\ *n* (1857) **:** any of a genus (*Chelone*) of perennial No. American herbs of the snapdragon family with spikes of showy white or purple flowers

tur·tle·neck \-ˌnek\ *n* (1897) **1 :** a high close-fitting turnover collar used esp. for sweaters **2 :** a garment (as a sweater) with a turtleneck — **tur·tle·necked** \-ˌnekt\ *adj*

tur·tling \ˈtərt-liŋ, ˈtər-tᵊl-iŋ\ *n* (1669) **:** the action or process of catching turtles

turves *pl of* TURF

[1]**Tus·can** \ˈtəs-kən\ *n* [ME *Toscayne*, ultim. fr. ML *Tuscanus* Tuscan, Etruscan, fr. L *Tusci* Etruscans] (ca. 1509) **1 :** a native or inhabitant of Tuscany **2 a :** the Italian language as spoken in Tuscany **b :** the standard literary dialect of Italian

[2]**Tuscan** *adj* (1563) **1 :** of or relating to one of the five classical orders of architecture that is of Roman origin and plain in style **2 :** of, relating to, or characteristic of Tuscany, the Tuscans, or Tuscan

Tus·ca·ro·ra \ˌtəs-kə-ˈrȯr-ə\ *n, pl* **Tuscarora** *or* **Tuscaroras** [of Iroquoian origin; akin to Tuscarora *skarò·rǝʔ*, a self-designation] (1713) **1 :** a member of an American Indian people orig. of No. Carolina and later of New York and Ontario **2 :** the Iroquoian language of the Tuscarora people

tu·sche \ˈtüsh, ˈtü-shə\ *n* [G, fr. *tuschen* to lay on color, fr. F *toucher*, lit., to touch, fr. OF *tuchier* — more at TOUCH] (1885) **:** a black liquid used in lithography for drawing and painting and in etching and the silk-screen process as a resist

[1]**tush** \ˈtəsh\ *n* [ME *tusch*, fr. OE *tūsc*; akin to OFris *tusk* tooth, OE *tōth* tooth] (bef. 12c) **:** a long pointed tooth; *esp* **:** a horse's canine

[2]**tush** *interj* [ME *tussch*] (15c) — used to express disdain or reproach

[3]**tush** \ˈtu̇sh\ *n* [perh. modif. of Yiddish *tokhes*, fr. Heb *taḥath* under, beneath] (1970) *slang* **:** BUTTOCKS

[1]**tusk** \ˈtəsk\ *n* [ME, alter. of *tux*, fr. OE *tūx*; akin to OE *tūsc* tush] (bef. 12c) **1 :** an elongated greatly enlarged tooth (as of an elephant or walrus) that projects when the mouth is closed and serves esp. for digging food or as a weapon; *broadly* **:** a long protruding tooth **2 :** one of the small projections on a tusk tenon — **tusked** \ˈtəskt\ *adj* — **tusk·like** \ˈtəsk-ˌlīk\ *adj*

[2]**tusk** *vt* (1629) **:** to dig up with a tusk; *also* **:** to gash with a tusk

tusk·er \ˈtəs-kər\ *n* (1846) **:** an animal with tusks; *esp* **:** a male elephant with two normally developed tusks

tusk tenon *n* (ca. 1825) **:** a tenon strengthened by one or more smaller tenons underneath forming a steplike outline

tus·sah \ˈtə-sə, -ˌsȯ\ *or* **tus·sore** \-ˌsōr, -ˌsȯr\ *n* [Hindi & Urdu *tasar*] (1590) **:** silk or silk fabric from the brownish fiber produced by larvae of some saturniid moths (as *Antheraea paphia*)

tus·sive \ˈtə-siv\ *adj* [L *tussis* cough] (ca. 1857) **:** of, relating to, or involved in coughing

[1]**tus·sle** \ˈtə-səl\ *n* (1629) **1 :** a physical contest or struggle **:** SCUFFLE **2 :** an intense argument, controversy, or struggle

[2]**tussle** *vi* **tus·sled; tus·sling** \-s(ə-)liŋ\ [ME (Sc) *tussillen*, freq. of ME *-tusen, -tousen* to tousle — more at TOUSE] (1638) **:** to struggle roughly **:** SCUFFLE

tus·sock \ˈtə-sək\ *n* [origin unknown] (1607) **:** a compact tuft esp. of grass or sedge; *also* **:** an area of raised solid ground in a marsh or bog that is bound together by roots of low vegetation — **tus·socky** \-sə-kē\ *adj*

tussock grass *n* (1842) **:** a grass or sedge that typically grows in tussocks

tussock moth *n* (1826) **:** any of numerous dull-colored moths (family Lymantriidae) that usu. have wingless females and larvae with long tufts of hair

[1]**tut** *a dental or alveolar click; often read as* ˈtət\ *interj* (15c) — used to express disapproval or disbelief

[2]**tut** \ˈtət\ *vi* **tut·ted; tut·ting** (1849) **:** TUT-TUT

tu·tee \tü-ˈtē, tyü-\ *n* [*tut*or + *-ee*] (ca. 1927) **:** one who is being tutored

tu·te·lage \ˈtü-tə-lij, ˈtyü-\ *n* [L *tutela* protection, guardian (fr. *tutari* to protect, freq. of *tueri* to look at, guard) + E *-age*] (1605) **1 a :** an act or process of serving as guardian or protector **:** GUARDIANSHIP **b :** hegemony over a foreign territory **:** TRUSTEESHIP 2 **2 :** the state of being under a guardian or tutor **3 a :** instruction esp. of an individual **b :** a guiding influence ⟨a business under the ~ of a new director⟩

tu·te·lar \ˈtü-tə-lər, ˈtyü-, -ˌär\ *adj or n* (1600) **:** TUTELARY

[1]**tu·te·lary** \ˈtü-tə-ˌler-ē, ˈtyü-\ *adj* (1611) **1 :** having the guardianship of a person or a thing ⟨a ~ goddess⟩ **2 :** of or relating to a guardian

[2]**tutelary** *n, pl* **-lar·ies** (1652) **:** a tutelary power (as a deity)

[1]**tu·tor** \ˈtü-tər, ˈtyü-\ *n* [ME *tutour*, fr. AF & L; AF, fr. L *tutor*, fr. *tueri*] (14c) **:** a person charged with the instruction and guidance of another: as **a :** a private teacher **b :** a teacher in a British university who gives individual instruction to undergraduates

[2]**tutor** *vt* (1592) **1 :** to have the guardianship, tutelage, or care of **2 :** to teach or guide usu. individually in a special subject or for a particular purpose **:** COACH ~ *vi* **1 :** to do the work of a tutor **2 :** to receive instruction esp. privately

tu·tor·age \ˈtü-tə-rij, ˈtyü-\ *n* (1617) **:** the function or work of a tutor

tu·tor·ess \ˈtü-tə-rəs, ˈtyü-\ *n* (1614) **:** a woman or girl who is a tutor

[1]**tu·to·ri·al** \tü-ˈtȯr-ē-əl, tyü-\ *adj* (1822) **:** of, relating to, or involving a tutor or a tutorial

[2]**tutorial** *n* (1923) **1 :** a class conducted by a tutor for one student or a small number of students **2 :** a paper, book, film, or computer program that provides practical information about a specific subject

tu·tor·ship \ˈtü-tər-ˌship, ˈtyü-\ *n* (1581) **1 :** the office, function, or work of a tutor **2 :** TUTELAGE 3

tu·toy·er \tᵫ-twä-ˈyā\ *vt* [F, to address with the familiar pronoun *tu* thou, fr. MF, fr. *tu* thou (fr. L) + *toi* thee, fr. L *te* (acc. of *tu*) — more at THOU] (1697) **:** to address familiarly

Tut·si \ˈtü-sē, ˈtüt-\ *n, pl* **Tutsi** *or* **Tutsis** (1950) **:** a member of a people of Rwanda and Burundi prob. of Nilotic origin

[1]**tut·ti** \ˈtü-tē, ˈtu̇-; ˈtü-ˌtē, ˈtu̇-\ *adj or adv* [It, masc. pl. of *tutto* all, fr. VL **tottus*, alter. of L *totus*] (ca. 1724) **:** with all voices or instruments performing together — used as a direction in music

[2]**tutti** *n* (1816) **:** a passage or section performed by all the performers

tut·ti–frut·ti \ˌtü-ti-ˈfrü-tē, ˌtu̇-\ *n* [It *tutti frutti* all fruits] (ca. 1834) **:** a confection or ice cream containing chopped usu. candied fruits

[1]**tut–tut** *two alveolar or dental clicks; often read as* ˈtət-ˈtət\ *interj* (1566) **:** TUT

[2]**tut–tut** \ˈtət-ˈtət\ *vi* **tut–tut·ted; tut–tut·ting** (1873) **:** to express disapproval or disbelief by or as if by uttering tut ⟨editorialists *tut-tutted* over the recent congressional scandal⟩

tu·tu \ˈtü-(ˌ)tü\ *n* [F, fr. (baby talk) *tutu* backside] (1913) **:** a short projecting skirt worn by a ballerina

tu–whit tu–whoo \tə-ˌ(h)wit-tə-ˈ(h)wü\ *n* [imit.] (ca. 1595) **:** the cry of an owl

tux \ˈtəks\ *n* (1922) **:** TUXEDO

tux·e·do \ˌtək-ˈsē-(ˌ)dō\ *n, pl* **-dos** *or* **-does** [*Tuxedo* Park, N.Y.] (1889) **1 :** a men's single-breasted or double-breasted usu. black or blackish-blue jacket **2 :** a semiformal evening suit for men — **tux·e·doed** \-(ˌ)dōd\ *adj*

tu·yere \twē-ˈer\ *n* [F *tuyère*, fr. MF, fr. *tuyau* pipe] (1781) **:** a nozzle through which an air blast is delivered to a forge or blast furnace

[1]**TV** \ˈtē-ˈvē\ *n* [*television*] (1947) **:** TELEVISION

[2]**TV** *abbr* transvestite

TVA *abbr* Tennessee Valley Authority

TV dinner *n* [fr. its saving the television viewer from having to interrupt viewing to prepare and serve a meal] (1954) **:** a quick-frozen packaged dinner (as of meat, potatoes, and a vegetable) that requires only heating before it is served

TVP \ˌtē-(ˌ)vē-ˈpē\ *trademark* — used for textured vegetable protein

twa \ˈtwä\ *or* **twae** \ˈtwä, ˈtwē\ *Scot var of* TWO

[1]**twad·dle** \ˈtwä-dᵊl\ *n* [prob. alter. of E dial. *twattle* idle talk] (1782) **1 a :** silly idle talk **:** DRIVEL **b :** something insignificant or worthless **:** NONSENSE ⟨that idea is pure ~⟩ **2 :** one that twaddles **:** TWADDLER

[2]**twaddle** *vb* **twad·dled; twad·dling** \ˈtwäd-liŋ, ˈtwä-dᵊl-iŋ\ (1826) **:** PRATE, BABBLE — **twad·dler** \ˈtwäd-lər, ˈtwä-dᵊl-ər\ *n*

[1]**twain** \ˈtwān\ *adj* [ME, fr. OE *twēgen* — more at TWO] (bef. 12c) *archaic* **:** TWO

[2]**twain** *pron* (bef. 12c) **:** TWO; *esp* **:** two fathoms ⟨mark ~⟩

[3]**twain** *n* (12c) **1 :** TWO **2 :** COUPLE, PAIR

[1]**twang** \ˈtwaŋ\ *n* [imit.] (ca. 1553) **1 :** a harsh quick ringing sound like that of a plucked banjo string **2 a :** nasal speech or resonance **b :** the characteristic speech of a region, locality, or group of people **3 a :** an act of plucking **b :** PANG, TWINGE — **twangy** \ˈtwaŋ-ē\ *adj*

[2]**twang** *vb* **twanged; twang·ing** \ˈtwaŋ-iŋ\ *vi* (1570) **1 :** to sound with a twang ⟨the couch ~*ed* when he sat down⟩ **2 :** to speak or sound with a nasal intonation **3 :** to throb or twitch with pain or tension ~ *vt* **1 :** to cause to sound with a twang **2 :** to utter or pronounce with a nasal twang **3 :** to pluck the string of ⟨~ a guitar⟩ — **twang·er** *n*

\ə\ **abut** \ᵊ\ **kitten**, F **table** \ər\ **further** \a\ **ash** \ā\ **ace** \ä\ **mop**, **mar** \au̇\ **out** \ch\ **chin** \e\ **bet** \ē\ **easy** \g\ **go** \i\ **hit** \ī\ **ice** \j\ **job** \ŋ\ **sing** \ō\ **go** \ȯ\ **law** \ȯi\ **boy** \th\ **thin** \t͟h\ **the** \ü\ **loot** \u̇\ **foot** \y\ **yet** \zh\ **vision**, **beige** \k̟, ⁿ, œ, ᵫ, ʸ\ *see* Guide to Pronunciation

[3]**twang** *n* [alter. of *tang*] (ca. 1611) **1 :** a persisting flavor, taste, or odor **:** TANG **2 :** SUGGESTION, TRACE

'twas \ˈtwəz, ˈtwäz\ [by contr.] (1567) **:** it was

twat \ˈtwät\ *n* [origin unknown] (1656) *usu vulgar* **:** VULVA

tway·blade \ˈtwā-ˌblād\ *n* [E dial. *tway* two] (1578) **:** any of various orchids (genera *Listera* and *Liparis*) often having two leaves

tweak \ˈtwēk\ *vb* [prob. alter. of ME *twikken* to pull sharply, fr. OE *twiccian* to pluck — more at TWITCH] *vt* (1601) **1 :** to pinch and pull with a sudden jerk and twist **:** TWITCH ⟨∼*ed* a bud from the stem⟩ **2 :** to pinch (a person or a body part) lightly or playfully **3 :** to make usu. small adjustments in or to ⟨∼ the controls⟩; *esp* **:** FINE-TUNE **4 a :** ANNOY, BOTHER ⟨∼*ing* the establishment⟩ **b :** to criticize esp. in a sly or sharp manner **c :** to poke fun at **5 :** to injure slightly ∼ *vi* **1 :** PULL, PLUCK **2 :** to make small adjustments — **tweak** *n*

twee \ˈtwē\ *adj* [baby-talk alter. of *sweet*] (1905) *chiefly Brit* **:** affectedly or excessively dainty, delicate, cute, or quaint ⟨such a theme might sound ∼ or corny —*Times Lit. Supp.*⟩

tweed \ˈtwēd\ *n* [prob. short for Sc *tweedling, twidling* twilled cloth] (1841) **1 :** a rough woolen fabric made usu. in twill weaves and used esp. for suits and coats **2** *pl* **:** tweed clothing; *specif* **:** a tweed suit

Twee·dle·dum and Twee·dle·dee \ˌtwē-dᵊl-ˈdəm-ən(d)-ˌtwē-dᵊl-ˈdē\ *n* [E *tweedle* to chirp + *dum* (imit. of a low musical note) *&* *dee* (imit. of a high musical note)] (1725) **:** two individuals or groups that are practically indistinguishable

tweedy \ˈtwē-dē\ *adj* **tweed·i·er; -est** (1912) **1 :** of or resembling tweed ⟨a ∼ wool blend⟩ **2 a :** given to wearing tweeds **b :** informal or suggestive of the outdoors in taste or habits **c :** ACADEMIC, SCHOLARLY ⟨∼ authors⟩ — **tweed·i·ness** *n*

[1]**tween** \ˈtwēn\ *prep* [ME *twene,* short for *betwene*] (13c) **:** BETWEEN

[2]**tween** *n* [blend of be*tween* and [2]*teen*] (1967) **:** PRETEEN

tween·er \ˈtwē-nər\ *n* [*between* + [2]*-er*] (1978) **:** a player who has some but not all of the necessary characteristics for each of two or more positions (as in football or basketball)

tweep \ˈtwēp\ *n* [back-formation from *tweeps* an individual's followers on Twitter, blend of [1]*tweet* and *peeps*] (2008) **:** a person who uses the Twitter online message service to send and receive tweets

[1]**tweet** \ˈtwēt\ *n* [imit.] (1768) **1 :** a chirping note **2 :** a post made on the Twitter online message service

[2]**tweet** *vi* (1851) **1 :** to make a chirping sound ⟨birds ∼*ing* in the trees⟩ **2 :** to post a message to the Twitter online message service

tweet·er \ˈtwē-tər\ *n* (1934) **:** a small loudspeaker responsive only to the higher acoustic frequencies and reproducing sounds of high pitch — compare WOOFER

tweeze \ˈtwēz\ *vt* **tweezed; tweez·ing** [back-formation fr. *tweezers*] (1932) **:** to pluck, remove, or handle with tweezers

twee·zer \ˈtwē-zər\ *n* (1904) **:** TWEEZERS

twee·zers \ˈtwē-zərz\ *n pl but sing or pl in constr* [obs. E *tweeze,* n., etui, short for obs. E *etweese,* fr. pl. of obs. E *etwee,* fr. F *étui*] (1654) **:** any of various small metal instruments that are usu. held between the thumb and index finger, are used for plucking, holding, or manipulating, and consist of two legs joined at one end

Twelfth Day *n* [fr. its being the 12th day after Christmas] (bef. 12c) **:** EPIPHANY 1

Twelfth Night *n* (bef. 12c) **:** the evening or sometimes the eve of Epiphany

twelve \ˈtwelv\ *n* [ME, fr. OE *twelf;* akin to OHG *zwelif* twelve, OE *twā* two, *-leofan* (as in *endleofan* eleven) — more at TWO, ELEVEN] (bef. 12c) **1** — see NUMBER table **2** *cap* **a :** the twelve original disciples of Jesus **b :** the books of the Minor Prophets in the Jewish Scriptures **3 :** the 12th in a set or series **4 :** something having 12 units or members **5** *pl* **:** TWELVEMO — **twelfth** \ˈtwelf(t)th\ *adj or n* — **twelve** *adj* — **twelve** *pron, pl in constr*

twelve·mo \ˈtwelv-(ˌ)mō\ *n, pl* **-mos** (1816) **:** the size of a piece of paper cut 12 from a sheet; *also* **:** a book, a page, or paper of this size

twelve·month \-ˌmən(t)th\ *n* (12c) **:** YEAR

12–step \ˈtwelv-ˌstep\ *adj* (1983) **:** of, relating to, characteristic of, or being a program that is designed esp. to help an individual overcome an addiction, compulsion, serious shortcoming, or traumatic experience by adherence to 12 tenets emphasizing personal growth and dependence on a higher spiritual being

twelve–tone \-ˈtōn\ *adj* (1926) **:** of, relating to, or being serial music utilizing the 12 chromatic tones

twelve–tone row *n* (1941) **:** the 12 chromatic tones of the octave placed in a chosen fixed order and constituting with some permitted permutations and derivations the melodic and harmonic material of a serial musical piece

twen·ty \ˈtwen-tē, ˈtwən-\ *n, pl* **twenties** [ME, fr. *twenty,* adj., fr. OE *twēntig,* n., group of 20, fr. *twēn-* (akin to OE *twā* two) + *-tig* group of 10; akin to OE *tien* ten — more at TWO, TEN] (13c) **1** — see NUMBER table **2** *pl* **:** the numbers 20 to 29; *specif* **:** the years 20 to 29 in a lifetime or century **3 :** a 20-dollar bill — **twen·ti·eth** \-tē-əth\ *adj or n* — **twenty** *adj* — **twenty** *pron, pl in constr*

twen·ty–four·mo \ˌtwen-tē-ˈfȯr-(ˌ)mō, ˌtwən-\ *n, pl* **-mos** (ca. 1841) **:** the size of a piece of paper cut 24 from a sheet; *also* **:** a book, a page, or paper of this size

24–7 *or* **24/7** \ˈtwen-tē-ˈfȯr-ˈse-vən, ˈtwən-\ *adv or adj* (1985) **:** for twenty-four hours seven days a week ⟨can now shop ∼⟩

twen·ty–one \ˌtwen-tē-ˈwən, ˌtwən-\ *n* (ca. 1611) **1** — see NUMBER table **2** [trans. of F *vingt-et-un*] **:** BLACKJACK — **twenty–one** *adj* — **twenty–one** *pron, pl in constr*

twen·ty·some·thing \ˈtwen-tē-ˌsəm(p)-thiŋ, -ˈtwən-\ *adj* (1990) **:** of, relating to, or being a person who is in his or her twenties ⟨a ∼ professional⟩ — **twentysomething** *n*

twen·ty–twen·ty *or* **20/20** \-ˈtwen-tē, -ˈtwən-\ *adj* [fr. the testing of vision by reading letters at a distance of 20 feet] (1875) **1** *of the human eye* **:** meeting a standard of normal visual acuity ⟨∼ vision⟩ **2 :** marked by facilely accurate discernment, judgment, or assessment ⟨hindsight is ∼⟩

twen·ty–two \-ˈtü\ *n* (1526) **1** — see NUMBER table **2 :** a .22-caliber firearm; *esp* **:** one firing rimfire cartridges — usu. written .22 — **twenty–two** *adj* — **twenty–two** *pron, pl in constr*

'twere \ˈtwər\ [by contr.] (1578) **:** it were

twerp \ˈtwərp\ *n* [origin unknown] (ca. 1923) **:** a silly, insignificant, or contemptible person

Twi *also* **Tshi** \ˈchwē, chə-ˈwē, ˈtwē, ˈchē\ *n* [Akan *č*ʷ*ĩ*ĩ] (1874) **1 :** a dialect of Akan **2 :** a literary language based on the Twi dialect and used by the Akan-speaking peoples (as the Ashanti)

twi- \ˈtwī\ *prefix* [ME, fr. OE; akin to OHG *zwi-* twi-, L *bi-*, Gk *di-*, OE *twā* two] **:** two **:** double **:** doubly **:** twice ⟨*twi*-headed⟩

twice \ˈtwīs\ *adv* [ME *twiges, twies,* fr. OE *twiga;* akin to OE *twi-*] (12c) **1 :** on two occasions ⟨∼ absent⟩ **2 :** two times **:** in doubled quantity or degree ⟨∼ two is four⟩ ⟨∼ as much⟩

twice–born \-ˈbȯrn\ *adj* (13c) **1 :** born a second time **2 :** having undergone a definite experience of fundamental moral and spiritual renewal **3 :** of or forming one of the three upper Hindu caste groups in which boys undergo an initiation symbolizing spiritual birth

twice–laid \-ˈlād\ *adj* (ca. 1593) **:** made from the ends of rope and strands of used rope ⟨∼ rope⟩

twice–told \-ˈtōld\ *adj* (ca. 1597) **:** well known from repeated telling — used chiefly in the phrase *a twice-told tale*

[1]**twid·dle** \ˈtwi-dᵊl\ *vb* **twid·dled; twid·dling** \ˈtwid-liŋ, ˈtwi-dᵊl-iŋ\ [origin unknown] *vi* (ca. 1540) **1 :** to play negligently with something **:** FIDDLE **2 :** to turn or jounce lightly ⟨∼*s* round and round in the water —J. B. S. Haldane⟩ ∼ *vt* **:** to rotate lightly or idly ⟨*twiddled* his pen⟩ — **twiddle one's thumbs :** to spend time idly **:** do nothing

[2]**twiddle** *n* (1774) **:** TURN, TWIST

[1]**twig** \ˈtwig\ *n* [ME *twigge,* fr. OE; akin to OHG *zwīg* twig, OE *twā* two] (bef. 12c) **1 :** a small shoot or branch usu. without its leaves **2 :** a minute branch of a nerve or artery — **twigged** \ˈtwigd\ *adj* — **twiggy** \ˈtwi-gē\ *adj*

[2]**twig** *vb* **twigged; twig·ging** [perh. fr. Ir & ScGael *tuig-* understand] *vt* (1764) **1 :** NOTICE, OBSERVE **2 :** to understand the meaning of **:** COMPREHEND ∼ *vi* **:** to gain a grasp **:** UNDERSTAND ⟨*twigged* instinctively about things —H. E. Bates⟩

[3]**twig** *n* [origin unknown] (ca. 1811) *Brit* **:** FASHION, STYLE

twi·light \ˈtwī-ˌlīt\ *n, often attrib* (15c) **1 :** the light from the sky between full night and sunrise or between sunset and full night produced by diffusion of sunlight through the atmosphere and its dust; *also* **:** a time of twilight **2 a :** an intermediate state that is not clearly defined ⟨lived in the ∼ of neutrality —*Newsweek*⟩ **b :** a period of decline

twilight glow *n* (1819) **:** airglow seen at twilight

Twilight of the Gods (1768) **:** RAGNAROK

twilight zone *n* (1908) **1 a :** an area just beyond ordinary legal and ethical limits **b :** TWILIGHT 2a **2 :** a world of fantasy or illusion

twi·lit \ˈtwī-ˌlit\ *adj* [*twi*light + *lit*] (1869) **:** lighted by or as if by twilight

twill \ˈtwil\ *n* [ME *twyll, twylle,* fr. OE *twilic* having a double thread, part trans. of L *bilic-, bilix,* fr. *bi-* + *licium* thread] (14c) **1 :** a fabric with a twill weave **2 :** a textile weave in which the filling threads pass over one and under two or more warp threads to give an appearance of diagonal lines

twilled \ˈtwild\ *adj* (15c) **:** made with a twill weave

twill·ing \ˈtwi-liŋ\ *n* (1831) **:** twilled fabric; *also* **:** the process of making twilled fabric

[1]**twin** \ˈtwin\ *n* [ME, fr. *twin* twofold] (14c) **1 a :** either of two offspring produced at a birth **b** *pl, cap* **:** GEMINI **2 :** one of two persons or things closely related to or resembling each other **3 :** a compound crystal composed of two adjoining crystals or parts of crystals of the same kind that share a common plane of atoms — **twin·ship** \-ˌship\ *n*

[2]**twin** *vb* **twinned; twin·ning** *vt* (14c) **1 :** to bring together in close association **:** COUPLE **2 :** DUPLICATE, MATCH ∼ *vi* **1 :** to bring forth twins **2 :** to grow as a twin crystal

[3]**twin** *adj* [ME, twofold, double, fr. OE *twinn;* akin to ON *tvinnr* two by two, OE *twā* two] (1593) **1 :** born with one other or as a pair at one birth ⟨my ∼ brother⟩ ⟨∼ girls⟩ **2 a :** made up of two similar, related, or connected members or parts **:** DOUBLE **b :** paired in a close or necessary relationship **:** MATCHING **c :** having or consisting of two identical units **d :** being one of a pair

twin bed *n* (1919) **:** one of a pair of matching single beds; *also* **:** a twin-size bed

twin·ber·ry \ˈtwin-ˌber-ē\ *n* [fr. the occurrence of the berries in pairs] (1821) **1 :** a western No. American honeysuckle (*Lonicera involucrata*) with yellowish involucrate flowers **2 :** PARTRIDGEBERRY

twin bill *n* (ca. 1939) **:** DOUBLEHEADER

twin·born \ˈtwin-ˈbȯrn\ *adj* (1598) **:** born at the same birth

twin double *n* (1960) **:** a system of betting (as on horse races) in which the bettor must pick the winners of four stipulated races in order to win — compare DAILY DOUBLE

[1]**twine** \ˈtwīn\ *n* [ME *twin,* fr. OE *twīn;* akin to MD *twijn* twine, OE *twā* two] (bef. 12c) **1 :** a strong string of two or more strands twisted together **2** *archaic* **:** a twined or interlaced part or object **3** *archaic* **:** an act of twining, interlacing, or embracing — **twiny** \ˈtwī-nē\ *adj*

[2]**twine** *vb* **twined; twin·ing** *vt* (13c) **1 a :** to twist together **b :** to form by twisting **:** WEAVE **2 a :** INTERLACE ⟨the girl *twined* her hands —John Buchan⟩ **b :** to cause to encircle or enfold something **c :** to cause to be encircled ∼ *vi* **1 :** to coil about a support **2 :** to stretch or move in a sinuous manner **:** MEANDER ⟨the river ∼*s* through the valley⟩ — **twin·er** *n*

[3]**twine** *vb* **twined; twin·ing** [alter. of Sc *twin,* fr. ME *twinnen,* fr. *twin* double] *vt* (1722) *chiefly Scot* **:** to cause (one) to lose possession **:** DEPRIVE ⟨*twined* him of his nose —J. C. Ransom⟩ ∼ *vi, chiefly Scot* **:** PART ⟨you and me must ∼ —R. L. Stevenson⟩

twin·flow·er \ˈtwin-ˌflau̇(-ə)r\ *n* (ca. 1818) **:** a prostrate subshrub (*Linnaea borealis*) of the honeysuckle family that is found in cool regions of the northern hemisphere and has fragrant usu. pink flowers

[1]**twinge** \ˈtwinj\ *vb* **twinged; twing·ing** \ˈtwin-jiŋ\ *or* **twinge·ing** [ME *twengen,* fr. OE *twengan;* akin to OHG *zwengen* to pinch] *vt* (bef. 12c) **1** *dial* **:** PLUCK, TWEAK **2 :** to affect with a sharp pain or pang ∼ *vi* **:** to feel a sudden sharp local pain

[2]**twinge** *n* (1608) **1 :** a sudden sharp stab of pain **2 :** a moral or emotional pang ⟨a ∼ of conscience⟩ ⟨a ∼ of sympathy⟩

twi–night \ˈtwī-ˌnīt\ *adj* [*twi*light + *night*] (1946) **:** of, relating to, or being a baseball doubleheader in which the first game is played in the late afternoon and the second continues into the evening

[1]**twin·kle** \ˈtwiŋ-kəl\ *vb* **twin·kled; twin·kling** \-k(ə-)liŋ\ [ME, fr. OE *twinclian;* akin to MHG *zwinken* to blink] *vi* (bef. 12c) **1 :** to shine with a flickering or sparkling light **:** SCINTILLATE **2 a :** to flutter the eyelids **b :** to appear bright esp. with merriment ⟨his eyes *twinkled*⟩ **3 :** to flutter or flit rapidly ∼ *vt* **1 :** to cause to shine with fluctuating

light 2 : to flicker or flirt rapidly ⟨*twinkled* the straight, red-lacquered toes —Glenway Wescott⟩ — **twin·kler** \-k(ə-)lər\ *n*

[2]**twinkle** *n* (1548) 1 : a wink of the eyelids 2 : the instant's duration of a wink : TWINKLING 3 : an intermittent radiance : FLICKER, SPARKLE 4 : a rapid flashing motion : FLIT — **twin·kly** \-k(ə-)lē\ *adj*

twinkling *n* (14c) : the time required for a wink : INSTANT ⟨the kettle will boil in a ~ —*Punch*⟩

twin primes *n pl* (1930) : a pair of prime numbers (as 3 and 5 or 11 and 13) differing by two

twin·set \ˈtwin-ˈset\ *n* (1937) : a combination of a matching pullover and cardigan worn together

twin–size \ˈtwin-ˈsīz\ *adj* [*twin bed*] (1926) : having dimensions of 39 by 75 inches (about 1.0 by 1.9 meters) — used of a bed; compare FULL-SIZE, KING-SIZE, QUEEN-SIZE

[1]**twirl** \ˈtwər(-ə)l\ *vb* [perh. of Scand origin; akin to Norw dial. *tvirla* to twirl; akin to OHG *dweran* to stir] *vi* (1598) 1 : to revolve rapidly 2 : to pitch in a baseball game ~ *vt* 1 : to cause to rotate rapidly 2 : PITCH 2a — **twirl·er** \ˈtwər-lər\ *n*

[2]**twirl** *n* (1598) 1 : an act of twirling 2 : COIL, WHORL — **twirly** \ˈtwər-lē\ *adj*

twirp *var of* TWERP

[1]**twist** \ˈtwist\ *vb* [ME, prob. fr. MD *twisten,* fr. *twist* twine, discord, quarrel; akin to OE *-twist* (in *candeltwist* candlesnuffers, *mæsttwist* twin support for a mast), ME *twisten* to be forked, MHG *zwist* quarrel, OE *twi-* twi-] *vt* (15c) 1 a : to unite by winding ⟨~*ing* strands together⟩ b : to make by twisting strands together ⟨~ thread from yarn⟩ c : to mingle by interlacing 2 : TWINE, COIL 3 a : to wring or wrench so as to dislocate or distort; *esp* : SPRAIN ⟨~*ed* my ankle⟩ b : to alter the meaning of : DISTORT, PERVERT ⟨~*ed* the facts⟩ c : CONTORT ⟨~*ed* his face into a grin⟩ d : to pull off, turn, or break by torsion ⟨~ the nut off the bolt⟩ e : to cause to move with a turning motion ⟨~*ed* her chair to face the fire⟩ f : to form into a spiral shape g : to cause to take on moral, mental, or emotional deformity ⟨celebrity has ~*ed* their sense of decorum⟩ h : to make (one's way) in a winding or devious manner to a destination or objective ~ *vi* 1 : to follow a winding course : SNAKE 2 a : to turn or change shape under torsion b : to assume a spiral shape c : SQUIRM, WRITHE d : to dance the twist 3 *of a ball* : to rotate while taking a curving path or direction 4 : TURN 3a ⟨~*ed* around to see behind him⟩ — **twist in the wind** : to be left to face a difficult situation without support or help — **twist one's arm** : to bring strong pressure to bear on one

[2]**twist** *n* (1555) 1 : something formed by twisting or winding: as a : a thread, yarn, or cord formed by twisting two or more strands together b : a strong tightly twisted sewing silk c : a baked piece of twisted dough d : tobacco leaves twisted into a thick roll e : a strip of citrus peel used to flavor a drink 2 a : an act of twisting : the state of being twisted b : a dance performed with strenuous gyrations esp. of the hips c : the spin given the ball in any of various games d : a spiral turn or curve e (1) : torque or torsional stress applied to a body (as a rod or shaft) (2) : torsional strain (3) : the angle through which a thing is twisted 3 a : a turning off a straight course b : ECCENTRICITY, IDIOSYNCRASY c : a distortion of meaning or sense 4 a : an unexpected turn or development ⟨weird ~*s* of fate —W. L. Shirer⟩ b : a clever device : TRICK ⟨questions demanding special ~*s* of thinking —*New Yorker*⟩ c : a variant approach or method : GIMMICK ⟨a kind of ~ on the old triangle theme —Dave Fedo⟩ 5 : a front or back dive in which the diver twists sideways a half or full turn before entering the water — **twisty** \ˈtwis-tē\ *adj*

twist drill *n* (ca. 1875) : a drill having deep helical grooves extending from the point to the smooth portion of the shank

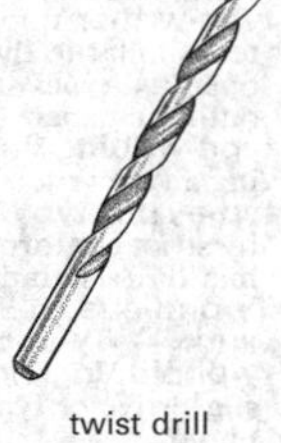

twist drill

twist·ed \ˈtwis-təd\ *adj* (ca. 1890) : mentally or emotionally unsound or disturbed : SICK

twist·er \ˈtwis-tər\ *n* (1579) 1 : one that twists; *esp* : a ball with a forward and spinning motion 2 : a tornado, waterspout, or dust devil in which the rotatory ascending movement of a column of air is esp. apparent

twist·ing \ˈtwis-tiŋ\ *n* (ca. 1905) : the use of misrepresentation or trickery to get someone to lapse a life insurance policy and buy another usu. in another company

twist tie *n* (1975) : a tie used for closing or securing (as a plastic bag) by twisting the ends together

[1]**twit** \ˈtwit\ *n* (1528) 1 : an act of twitting : TAUNT 2 : a silly annoying person : FOOL

[2]**twit** *vt* **twit·ted; twit·ting** [ME *atwiten* to reproach, fr. OE *ætwītan,* fr. *æt* at + *wītan* to reproach; akin to OHG *wīzan* to punish, OE *witan* to know] (1530) 1 : to subject to light ridicule or reproach : RALLY 2 : to make fun of as a fault

[1]**twitch** \ˈtwich\ *vb* [ME *twicchen;* akin to OE *twiccian* to pluck, OHG *gizwickan* to pinch] *vt* (14c) : to move or pull with a sudden motion : JERK ~ *vi* 1 : PULL, PLUCK ⟨~*ed* at my sleeve⟩ 2 : to move jerkily : QUIVER 3 : to undergo a brief spasmodic muscular contraction ⟨his hand ~*ed*⟩ — **twitch·er** *n*

[2]**twitch** *n* (1523) 1 : an act of twitching; *esp* : a short sudden pull or jerk 2 : a physical or mental pang ⟨a ~ of remorse⟩ 3 : a loop of rope or strap that is tightened over a horse's lip as a restraining device 4 a : a brief spasmodic contraction of the muscle fibers b : a slight jerk of a body part — **twitch·i·ly** \ˈtwi-chə-lē\ *adv* — **twitchy** \ˈtwi-chē\ *adj*

[3]**twitch** *n* [alter. of *quitch*] (1595) : QUACK GRASS

[1]**twit·ter** \ˈtwi-tər\ *vb* [ME *twiteren;* akin to OHG *zwizzirōn* to twitter] *vi* (14c) 1 : to utter successive chirping noises 2 a : to talk in a chattering fashion b : GIGGLE, TITTER 3 : to tremble with agitation : FLUTTER ~ *vt* 1 : to utter in chirps or twitters ⟨the robin ~*ed* its morning song⟩ 2 : to shake rapidly back and forth : FLUTTER

[2]**twitter** *n* (1678) 1 : a trembling agitation : QUIVER 2 : a small tremulous intermittent sound (as of birds) 3 a : a light chattering b : a light silly laugh : GIGGLE — **twit·tery** \ˈtwi-tə-rē\ *adj*

twixt \ˈtwikst\ *or* **'twixt** *prep* [ME *twix,* short for *betwix, betwixt*] (14c) : BETWEEN ⟨~ the two extremes⟩

[1]**two** \ˈtü\ *adj* [ME *twa, two,* fr. OE *twā* (fem. & neut.); akin to OE *twēgen* two (masc.), *tū* (neut.), OHG *zwēne,* L *duo,* Gk *dyo*] (bef. 12c) 1 : being one more than one in number 2 : being the second — used postpositively ⟨section ~ of the instructions⟩

[2]**two** *pron, pl in constr* (bef. 12c) 1 : two countable individuals not specified ⟨only ~ were found⟩ 2 : a small approximate number of indicated things ⟨only a shot or ~ were fired⟩

[3]**two** *n, pl* **twos** (13c) 1 — see NUMBER table 2 : the second in a set or series ⟨the ~ of spades⟩ 3 : a 2-dollar bill 4 : something having two units or members

two–bag·ger \-ˈba-gər\ *n* (1880) : DOUBLE 1b

two–bit \ˈtü-ˈbit\ *adj* (1802) 1 : of the value of two bits 2 : cheap or trivial of its kind : PETTY, SMALL-TIME ⟨a ~ chiseler⟩

two bits *n pl but sing or pl in constr* (1730) 1 : the value of a quarter of a dollar 2 : something of small worth or importance

[1]**two–by–four** \ˌtü-bī-ˈfȯr\ *n* (1884) : a piece of lumber approximately 2 by 4 inches as sawed and usu. 1 5/8 by 3 5/8 inches when dressed

[2]**two–by–four** *adj* (1897) 1 : small or petty of its kind ⟨this house and its ~ garden —Philip Barry⟩ 2 : measuring two units (as inches) by four

two cents *n* (ca. 1939) 1 *or* **two cents' worth** : an opinion offered on a topic under discussion ⟨send your *two cents' worth* to your senator⟩ 2 : a sum or object of very small value : practically nothing ⟨said angrily that for *two cents* he'd punch your nose⟩

two–cycle *adj* (1902) *of an internal combustion engine* : having a 2-stroke cycle

2–D \ˈtü-ˈdē\ *n* [*D,* abbr. of *dimensional*] (1963) : a two-dimensional form ⟨displayed in ~⟩ — **2–D** *adj*

two–dimensional *adj* (1883) 1 : of, relating to, or having two dimensions 2 : lacking the illusion of depth : not three-dimensional 3 : lacking depth of characterization ⟨~ characters⟩ — **two–dimensionality** *n*

two–edged sword \ˈtü-ˈejd-, -ˈe-jəd-\ *n* (1526) : DOUBLE-EDGED SWORD

two–faced \ˈtü-ˈfāst\ *adj* (1609) 1 : DOUBLE-DEALING, FALSE 2 : having two faces — **two–faced·ness** \-ˈfāst-nəs, -ˈfā-səd-nəs\ *n*

two·fer \ˈtü-fər\ *n* [alter. of *two for (one)*] (1885) 1 : a cheap item of merchandise; *esp* : a cigar selling at two for a nickel 2 : a free coupon entitling the bearer to purchase two tickets to a specified theatrical production for the price of one 3 : two articles available for the price of one or about the price of one 4 : something that satisfies two criteria or needs simultaneously

two–fist·ed \-ˈfis-təd\ *adj* (1774) : marked by vigorous often virile energy : HARD-HITTING ⟨~ journalism⟩

two·fold \ˈtü-ˌfōld, -ˈfōld\ *adj* (13c) 1 : having two parts or aspects 2 : being twice as great or as many — **twofold** \-ˈfōld\ *adv*

2,4–D \ˌtü-ˌfȯr-ˈdē\ *n* [*di-*] (ca. 1945) : a white crystalline irritant compound $C_8H_6Cl_2O_3$ used esp. as a weed killer

2,4,5–T \-ˌfīv-ˈtē\ *n* [*tri-*] (1946) : an irritant crystalline compound $C_8H_5Cl_3O_3$ used esp. formerly chiefly as an herbicide and defoliant

two–hand·ed \ˈtü-ˈhan-dəd\ *adj* (15c) 1 : used with both hands ⟨a ~ sword⟩ 2 : requiring two persons ⟨a ~ saw⟩ 3 *archaic* : STOUT, STRONG 4 a : having two hands b : efficient with either hand

two–party *adj* (1923) : characterized by two major political parties of comparable strength

two·pence \ˈtə-pən(t)s, *US also* ˈtü-ˌpen(t)s\ *or* **tup·pence** \ˈtə-pən(t)s\ *n* (15c) 1 : the sum of two British pennies 2 *pl* **twopence** *or* **two·pen·ces** : a coin worth twopence

two·pen·ny \ˈtəp-nē, ˈtə-pə-, *US also* ˈtü-ˌpe-nē\ *adj* (15c) : costing or worth twopence

two–phase *adj* (ca. 1896) : DIPHASIC

[1]**two–piece** \ˈtü-ˈpēs\ *adj* (ca. 1880) : forming a clothing ensemble with matching top and bottom parts

[2]**two–piece** \ˈtü-ˌpēs\ *n* (1942) : a garment (as a bathing suit) that is two-piece

two–piec·er \ˈtü-ˈpē-sər\ *n* (1943) : TWO-PIECE

two–ply \-ˈplī\ *adj* (1839) 1 : consisting of two thicknesses 2 a : woven with two sets of warp thread and two of filling ⟨a ~ carpet⟩ b : consisting of two strands ⟨~ yarn⟩

two's complement *n* (1958) : the negative of a binary number represented by switching all ones to zeros and all zeros to ones and then adding one to the result

two–sid·ed \-ˈsī-dəd\ *adj* (1856) : having two sides : BILATERAL

two·some \ˈtü-səm\ *n* (14c) 1 : a group of two persons or things : COUPLE 2 : a golf singles match

two–spot·ted spider mite \ˈtü-ˈspä-təd-\ *n* (1947) : a widely distributed spider mite (*Tetranychus urticae*) that feeds on soft plant parts and is a pest in greenhouses and gardens — called also *two-spotted mite*

two–step \ˈtü-ˌstep\ *n* (1895) 1 : a ballroom dance in 2/4 or 4/4 time having a basic pattern of step-close-step 2 : a piece of music for the two-step — **two–step** *vi*

two–suit·er \-ˈsü-tər\ *n* (1945) : a man's suitcase designed to hold two suits and accessories

two–tailed \ˈtü-ˈtāl(d)\ *also* **two–tail** \-ˈtāl\ *adj* (1945) : being a statistical test for which the critical region consists of all values of the test statistic greater than a given value plus the values less than another given value — compare ONE-TAILED

two–time \ˈtü-ˌtīm\ *vt* (1924) 1 : DOUBLE-CROSS 2 : to betray (a spouse or lover) by secret lovemaking with another — **two–tim·er** *n*

two–toed sloth \ˈtü-ˈtōd-\ *n* (1781) : any of a genus (*Choloepus* of the family Megalonychidae) of sloths having two clawed digits on each forefoot, three clawed digits on each hind foot, and usu. six or seven vertebrae in the neck — compare THREE-TOED SLOTH

two–tone \ˈtü-ˈtōn\ *adj* (1906) : colored in two colors or in two shades of one color ⟨~ shoes⟩

two–toned \ˈtü-ˈtōnd\ *adj* (1886) : TWO-TONE

two–way *adj* (1844) 1 : being a cock or valve that will connect a pipe or channel with either of two others 2 : moving or allowing movement in either direction ⟨a ~ bridge⟩ 3 a : involving or allowing an exchange between two individuals or groups ⟨there must be good ~ communication —Jerrold Orne⟩; *esp* : designed for both sending and receiving messages ⟨~ radio⟩ **b** : involving mutual responsibility or reciprocal relationships ⟨political alliance is a ~ thing —T. H. White †1986⟩ **4** : involving two participants ⟨a ~ race⟩ **5** : usable in either of two manners ⟨a ~ lamp⟩

two–way street *n* (1948) : a situation or relationship requiring give-and-take ⟨marriage is a *two-way street*⟩

2WD *abbr* two-wheel drive

two–wheel·er \-ˈhwē-lər, -ˈwē-\ *n* (1861) : a 2-wheeled vehicle (as a bicycle)

two–winged fly \ˈtü-ˈwiŋ(d)-\ *n* (1753) : [4]FLY 2a

twp *abbr* township

TWX *abbr* teletypewriter exchange

TX *abbr* Texas

-ty *n suffix* [var. of *-ity*] : quality : condition : degree ⟨apriori*ty*⟩

ty·coon \tī-ˈkün\ *n* [Jp *taikun*] (1857) **1** : SHOGUN **2 a** : a top leader (as in politics) **b** : a businessman of exceptional wealth and power : MAGNATE

tyer *var of* [3]TIER

tyin \ˈtēn\ *n, pl* **tyin** [Kazakh *tiïn, tiyin* kopeck, lit., squirrel, squirrel skin (formerly used as currency)] (1994) — see *tenge* at MONEY table

tying *pres part of* TIE

ty·iyn \tē-ˈyen\ *n, pl* **tyiyn** [Kyrgyz *tiyin* kopeck, lit., squirrel, squirrel skin (formerly used as currency)] (1993) — see *som* at MONEY table

tyke *also* **tike** \ˈtīk\ *n* [ME *tyke,* fr. ON *tīk* bitch; akin to MLG *tīke* bitch] (15c) **1** : DOG; *esp* : an inferior or mongrel dog **2 a** *chiefly Brit* : a clumsy, churlish, or eccentric person **b** : a small child

tym·bal \ˈtim-bəl\ *n* [alter. of *timbal*] (1929) : the vibrating membrane in the shrilling organ of a cicada

tym·pan \ˈtim-pən\ *n* [in sense 1, fr. ME, fr. OE *timpana,* fr. L *tympanum;* in other senses, fr. ML & L *tympanum*] (bef. 12c) **1** : [1]DRUM 1 **2** : a sheet (as of paper or cloth) placed between the impression surface of a press and the paper to be printed **3** : TYMPANUM 2

tympani, tympanist *var of* TIMPANI, TIMPANIST

tym·pan·ic \tim-ˈpa-nik\ *adj* [L & NL *tympanum*] (1808) : of, relating to, or being a tympanum

tympanic membrane *n* (1855) : a thin membrane that closes externally the cavity of the middle ear and functions in the mechanical reception of sound waves and in their transmission to the site of sensory reception — called also *eardrum;* see EAR illustration

tym·pa·ni·tes \ˌtim-pə-ˈnī-tēz\ *n* [ME, fr. LL, fr. Gk *tympanitēs,* fr. *tympanon*] (14c) : a distension of the abdomen caused by accumulation of gas in the intestinal tract or peritoneal cavity — **tym·pa·nit·ic** \-ˈni-tik\ *adj*

tym·pa·num \ˈtim-pə-nəm\ *n, pl* **-na** \-nə\ *also* **-nums** [ML & L; ML, eardrum, fr. L, drum, architectural panel, fr. Gk *tympanon* drum, kettledrum; perh. akin to Gk *typtein* to beat] (1619) **1 a (1)** : TYMPANIC MEMBRANE **(2)** : MIDDLE EAR **b** : a thin tense membrane covering an organ of hearing of an insect — see INSECT illustration **c** : a membranous resonator in a sound-producing organ **2 a** : the recessed usu. triangular face of a pediment within the frame made by the upper and lower cornices **b** : the space within an arch and above a lintel or a subordinate arch

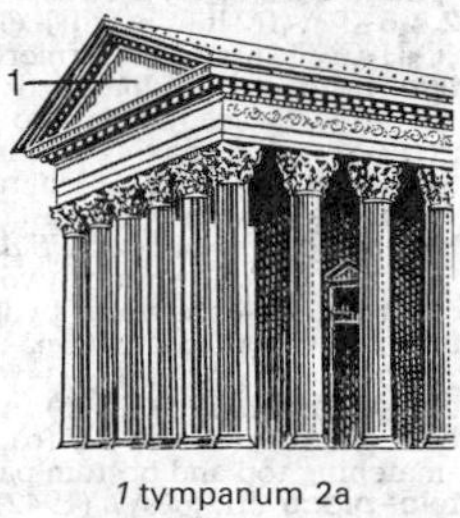

1 tympanum 2a

tym·pa·ny \-nē\ *n, pl* **-nies** [ML *tympanias,* fr. Gk, fr. *tympanon*] (1528) **1** : TYMPANITES **2** : BOMBAST, TURGIDITY

Tyn·dar·e·us \tin-ˈda-rē-əs\ *n* [L, fr. Gk] (1513) : a king of Sparta and husband of Leda in Greek mythology

typ·al \ˈtī-pəl\ *adj* (1853) **1** : serving as a type : TYPICAL **2** : of or relating to a type

[1]**type** \ˈtīp\ *n, often attrib* [ME, fr. LL *typus,* fr. L & Gk; L *typus* image, fr. Gk *typos* blow, impression, model, fr. *typtein* to strike, beat; akin to Skt *tupati* he injures and prob. to L *stupēre* to be benumbed] (15c) **1 a** : a person or thing (as in the Old Testament) believed to foreshadow another (as in the New Testament) **b** : one having qualities of a higher category : MODEL **c** : a lower taxonomic category selected as a standard of reference for a higher category; *also* : a specimen or series of specimens on which a taxonomic species or subspecies is actually based **2** : a distinctive mark or sign **3 a (1)** : a rectangular block usu. of metal bearing a relief character from which an inked print can be made **(2)** : a collection of such blocks ⟨a font of ~⟩ **(3)** : alphanumeric characters for printing ⟨the ~ for this book has been photoset⟩ **b** : TYPEFACE ⟨italic ~⟩ **c** : printed letters **d** : matter set in type **4 a** : qualities common to a number of individuals that distinguish them as an identifiable class: as **(1)** : the morphological, physiological, or ecological characters by which relationship between organisms may be recognized **(2)** : the form common to all instances of a linguistic element **b** : a typical and often superior specimen **c** : a member of an indicated class or variety of people ⟨the guests were mostly urban ~*s* —Lucy Cook⟩ **d** : a particular kind, class, or group ⟨oranges of the seedless ~⟩ ⟨leaders of the new ~ . . . did England yeoman's service —G. M. Trevelyan⟩ **e** : something distinguishable as a variety : SORT ⟨what ~ of food do you like?⟩

syn TYPE, KIND, SORT, NATURE, DESCRIPTION, CHARACTER mean a number of individuals thought of as a group because of a common quality or qualities. TYPE may suggest strong and clearly marked similarity throughout the items included so that each is typical of the group ⟨one of three basic body *types*⟩. KIND may suggest natural grouping ⟨a zoo seemingly having animals of every *kind*⟩. SORT often suggests some disparagement ⟨the *sort* of newspaper dealing in sensational stories⟩. NATURE may imply inherent, essential resemblance rather than obvious or superficial likenesses ⟨two problems of a similar *nature*⟩. DESCRIPTION implies a group marked by agreement in all details belonging to a type as described or defined ⟨not all acts of that *description* are actually illegal⟩. CHARACTER implies a group marked by distinctive likenesses peculiar to the type ⟨research on the subject so far has been of an elementary *character*⟩.

[2]**type** *vb* **typed; typ·ing** *vt* (1596) **1** : to represent beforehand as a type : PREFIGURE **2 a** : to produce a copy of **b** : to represent in terms of typical characteristics : TYPIFY **3** : to produce (as a character or document) using a keyboard (as on a typewriter or computer); *also* : KEYBOARD **4** : to identify as belonging to a type: as **a** : to determine the natural type of (as a blood sample) **b** : TYPECAST ~ *vi* : to write something on a typewriter or enter data into a computer by way of a keyboard — **type·able** \ˈtī-pə-bəl\ *adj*

type A *adj* (1970) : relating to, characteristic of, having, or being a personality that is marked by impatience, aggressiveness, and competitiveness and that is held to be associated with increased risk of cardiovascular disease ⟨*type A* behavior⟩

type B *adj* (1976) : relating to, characteristic of, having, or being a personality that is marked by a lack of aggressiveness and tension and that has been implicated by some studies as a factor decreasing the risk of cardiovascular disease ⟨*type B* behavior⟩

type·cast \ˈtīp-ˌkast\ *vt* **-cast; -cast·ing** (1927) **1** : to cast (an actor or actress) in a part calling for the same characteristics as those possessed by the performer **2** : to cast (an actor or actress) repeatedly in the same type of role **3** : STEREOTYPE 2

type·face \-ˌfās\ *n* (1887) **1** : the face of printing type **2** : all type of a single design

type·found·er \-ˌfau̇n-dər\ *n* (1797) : one engaged in the design and production of metal printing type for hand composition — **type·found·ing** \-diŋ\ *n*

type genus *n* (1840) : the genus of a taxonomic family or subfamily from which the name of the family or subfamily is formed

type 1 diabetes \ˈtīp-ˈwən-\ *n* (1982) : a form of diabetes mellitus that usu. develops during childhood or adolescence and is characterized by a severe deficiency in insulin secretion resulting from atrophy of the islets of Langerhans and causing hyperglycemia and a marked tendency toward ketoacidosis — called also *insulin-dependent diabetes, insulin-dependent diabetes mellitus, type 1 diabetes mellitus*

type I error *n* (1947) : rejection of the null hypothesis in statistical testing when it is true

type·script \ˈtīp-ˌskript\ *n* [*type* + manu*script*] (1893) : a typewritten manuscript; *esp* : one intended for use as printer's copy

type·set \-ˌset\ *vt* **-set; -set·ting** (1945) : to set in type : COMPOSE

type·set·ter \-ˌse-tər\ *n* (1833) : one that sets type or composes graphic matter for printing

type·set·ting \-ˌse-tiŋ\ *n* (1846) : the process of setting material in type or into a form to be used in printing; *also* : the process of producing graphic matter (as through a computer system)

type species *n* (1840) : the species of a genus with which the generic name is permanently associated

type specimen *n* (1852) : a specimen or individual designated as type of a species or lesser group and serving as the final criterion of the characteristics of that group

type·style \ˈtīp-ˌstī(-ə)l\ *n* (1954) : TYPEFACE

type 2 diabetes \-ˈtü-\ *n* (1982) : a common form of diabetes mellitus that develops esp. in adults and most often in obese individuals and that is characterized by hyperglycemia resulting from impaired insulin utilization coupled with the body's inability to compensate with increased insulin production — called also *non-insulin-dependent diabetes, non-insulin-dependent diabetes mellitus, type 2 diabetes mellitus*

type II error *n* (1947) : acceptance of the null hypothesis in statistical testing when it is false

type·write \ˈtīp-ˌrīt\ *vb* **-wrote** \-ˌrōt\; **-writ·ten** \-ˌri-tᵊn\ [back-formation fr. *typewriter*] *vt* (1887) : TYPE 3 ~ *vi* : TYPE

type·writ·er \ˈtīp-ˌrī-tər\ *n* (1868) **1** : a machine for writing in characters similar to those produced by printer's type by means of keyboard-operated types striking a ribbon to transfer ink or carbon impressions onto the paper **2** : TYPIST

type·writ·ing \ˈtīp-ˌrī-tiŋ\ *n* (1867) **1** : the act or study of or skill in using a typewriter **2** : writing produced with a typewriter

typ·ey *also* **typy** \ˈtī-pē\ *adj* **typ·i·er; -est** [[1]*type*] (1923) : characterized by strict conformance to type; *also* : exhibiting superior bodily conformation ⟨a sound ~ heifer⟩

Ty·pho·eus \tī-ˈfō-ˌyüs, -yəs\ *n* [L, fr. Gk *Typhōeus*] (ca. 1560) : TYPHON — **Ty·phoe·an** \-ˈfē-ən\ *adj*

[1]**ty·phoid** \ˈtī-ˌfȯid, (ˌ)tī-ˈ\ *adj* [NL *typhus*] (1800) **1** : of, relating to, or suggestive of typhus **2** [[2]*typhoid*] : of, relating to, or constituting typhoid

[2]**typhoid** *n* (1861) **1** : TYPHOID FEVER **2** : a disease of domestic animals resembling human typhus or typhoid

typhoid fever *n* (1829) : a communicable disease marked esp. by fever, diarrhea, prostration, headache, and intestinal inflammation and caused by a bacterium (*Salmonella typhi*)

Typhoid Mary *n, pl* **Typhoid Marys** [*Typhoid Mary,* nickname of Mary Mallon †1938 Irish cook in U.S. who was found to be a typhoid carrier] (1931) : one that is by force of circumstances a center from which something undesirable spreads ⟨the *Typhoid Marys* of the epidemics⟩

Ty·phon \ˈtī-ˌfän\ *n* [L, fr. Gk *Typhōn*] (14c) : a monster with a tremendous voice who according to classical mythology was father of Cerberus, the Chimera, and the Sphinx

ty·phoon \tī-ˈfün\ *n* [alter. (influenced by Chin — Guangdong — *daaih-fūng,* fr. *daaih* big + *fūng* wind) of earlier *touffon,* fr. Ar *ṭūfān* hurricane, fr. Gk *typhōn* violent storm] (1771) **1** : a hurricane occurring esp. in the region of the Philippines or the China sea **2** : WHIRLWIND 2a ⟨a ~ of activity⟩

ty·phus \ˈtī-fəs\ *n* [NL, fr. Gk *typhos* fever; akin to Gk *typhein* to smoke — more at DEAF] (1785) : any of various bacterial diseases caused by rickettsias: as **a** : a severe human febrile disease that is caused by one (*Rickettsia prowazekii*) transmitted esp. by body lice and is marked by high fever, stupor alternating with delirium, intense headache, and a dark red rash **b** : MURINE TYPHUS **c** : SCRUB TYPHUS

typ·ic \ˈti-pik\ *adj* (1596) : TYPICAL 1

typ·i·cal \ˈti-pi-kəl\ *adj* [LL *typicalis,* fr. *typicus,* fr. Gk *typikos,* fr. *typos* model — more at TYPE] (1609) **1** : constituting or having the nature of a type : SYMBOLIC **2 a** : combining or exhibiting the essential characteristics of a group ⟨~ suburban houses⟩ **b** : conforming to a type 〈a specimen ∼ of the species〉 *syn* see REGULAR — **typ·i·cal·i·ty** \ˌti-pə-ˈka-lə-tē\ *n* — **typ·i·cal·ness** \ˈti-pi-kəl-nəs\ *n*

typ·i·cal·ly \ˈti-pi-k(ə-)lē\ *adv* (1605) **1** : in a typical manner 〈∼ American〉 **2** : on a typical occasion : in typical circumstances 〈∼, members of our staff receive little . . . recognition —Brendan Gill〉

typ·i·fy \ˈti-pə-ˌfī\ *vt* **-fied; -fy·ing** (1622) **1** : to represent in typical fashion : to constitute a typical mark or instance of 〈realism . . . that *typified* his earlier work —*Current Biog.*〉 **2** : to embody the essential or salient characteristics of : be the type of — **typ·i·fi·ca·tion** \ˌti-pə-fə-ˈkā-shən\ *n*

typ·ist \ˈtī-pist\ *n* (1885) : a person who types esp. as a job

ty·po \ˈtī-(ˌ)pō\ *n, pl* **typos** [short for *typographical (error)*] (1878) : an error (as of spelling) in typed or typeset material

ty·po·graph \ˈtī-pə-ˌgraf\ *vt* (ca. 1933) : to produce (stamps) by letterpress

ty·pog·ra·pher \tī-ˈpä-grə-fər\ *n* (1643) : a person (as a compositor, printer, or designer) who specializes in the design, choice, and arrangement of type matter

ty·po·graph·ic \ˌtī-pə-ˈgra-fik\ *or* **ty·po·graph·i·cal** \-fi-kəl\ *adj* (1593) : of, relating to, or occurring or used in typography or typeset matter 〈a ∼ character〉 〈a *typographical* error〉 — **ty·po·graph·i·cal·ly** \-fi-k(ə-)lē\ *adv*

ty·pog·ra·phy \tī-ˈpä-grə-fē\ *n* [ML *typographia*, fr. Gk *typos* impression, cast + *-graphia* -graphy — more at TYPE] (1610) **1** : letterpress printing **2** : the style, arrangement, or appearance of typeset matter

ty·po·log·i·cal \ˌtī-pə-ˈlä-ji-kəl\ *adj* (1845) : of or relating to typology or types — **ty·po·log·i·cal·ly** \-ji-k(ə-)lē\ *adv*

ty·pol·o·gy \tī-ˈpä-lə-jē\ *n, pl* **-gies** (1845) **1** : a doctrine of theological types; *esp* : one holding that things in Christian belief are prefigured or symbolized by things in the Old Testament **2** : study of or analysis or classification based on types or categories — **ty·pol·o·gist** \-jist\ *n*

Tyr \ˈtir\ *n* [ON *Tȳr*; akin to OE *Tīw* Tiu — more at DEITY] (1793) : a god of war in Norse mythology

ty·ra·mine \ˈtī-rə-ˌmēn\ *n* [ISV *tyrosine* + *amine*] (1910) : a phenolic amine $C_8H_{11}NO$ found in various foods and beverages (as cheese and red wine) that has a sympathomimetic action and is derived from tyrosine

ty·ran·ni·cal \tə-ˈra-ni-kəl, tī-\ *also* **ty·ran·nic** \-nik\ *adj* [L *tyrannicus*, fr. Gk *tyrannikos*, fr. *tyrannos* tyrant] (15c) : being or characteristic of a tyrant or tyranny : DESPOTIC 〈a ∼ ruler〉 〈a ∼ ruler〉 — **ty·ran·ni·cal·ly** \-ni-k(ə-)lē\ *adv* — **ty·ran·ni·cal·ness** \-kəl-nəs\ *n*

ty·ran·ni·cide \tə-ˈra-nə-ˌsīd, tī-\ *n* [in sense 1, fr. F, fr. L *tyrannicidium*, fr. *tyrannus* + *-i-* + *-cidium* -cide (killing); in sense 2, fr. F, fr. L *tyrannicida*, fr. *tyrannus* + *-i-* + *-cida* -cide (killer)] (1650) **1** : the act of killing a tyrant **2** : the killer of a tyrant

tyr·an·nise *Brit var of* TYRANNIZE

tyr·an·nize \ˈtir-ə-ˌnīz\ *vb* **-nized; -niz·ing** *vi* (15c) : to exercise arbitrary oppressive power or severity 〈some ways the living ∼ over the dying —Thomas Powers〉 ∼ *vt* : to treat tyrannically : OPPRESS 〈a regime that ∼s its citizens〉 — **tyr·an·niz·er** *n*

ty·ran·no·saur \tə-ˈra-nə-ˌsȯr, tī-\ *n* [NL *Tyrannosaurus*, fr. Gk *tyrannos* tyrant + *sauros* lizard] (1924) **1** : a massive No. American tyrannosaurid (*Tyrannosaurus rex*) **2** : TYRANNOSAURID

ty·ran·no·sau·rid \-ˈsȯr-əd\ *n* [NL *Tyrannosauridae*, fr. *Tyrannosaurus*] (1966) : any of a family (*Tyrannosauridae*) of large bipedal carnivorous theropod dinosaurs of the Late Cretaceous in No. America and central and eastern Asia having forelegs reduced in size and including the tyrannosaur

ty·ran·no·sau·rus \tə-ˌra-nə-ˈsȯr-əs, (ˌ)tī-\ *n* [NL] (1905) : TYRANNOSAUR 1

tyr·an·nous \ˈtir-ə-nəs\ *adj* (15c) : marked by tyranny; *esp* : unjustly severe 〈∼ new laws〉 — **tyr·an·nous·ly** *adv*

tyr·an·ny \ˈtir-ə-nē\ *n, pl* **-nies** [ME *tyrannie*, fr. MF, fr. ML *tyrannia*, fr. L *tyrannus* tyrant] (14c) **1** : oppressive power 〈every form of ∼ over the mind of man —Thomas Jefferson〉; *esp* : oppressive power exerted by government 〈the ∼ of a police state〉 **2 a** : a government in which absolute power is vested in a single ruler; *esp* : one characteristic of an ancient Greek city-state **b** : the office, authority, and administration of a tyrant **3** : a rigorous condition imposed by some outside agency or force 〈living under the ∼ of the clock —Dixon Wecter〉 **4** : a tyrannical act 〈workers who had suffered *tyrannies*〉

ty·rant \ˈtī-rənt\ *n* [ME *tyraunt*, fr. AF *tyran, tyrant*, fr. L *tyrannus*, fr. Gk *tyrannos*] (14c) **1 a** : an absolute ruler unrestrained by law or constitution **b** : a usurper of sovereignty **2 a** : a ruler who exercises absolute power oppressively or brutally **b** : one resembling an oppressive ruler in the harsh use of authority or power

tyrant flycatcher *n* (ca. 1783) : any of a large family (Tyrannidae) of American flycatchers that are usu. strictly insectivorous and have a flattened bill often hooked at the tip and usu. bristly at the gape

tyre *chiefly Brit var of* TIRE

Tyr·i·an purple \ˈtir-ē-ən-\ *n* [*Tyre*, maritime city of ancient Phoenicia] (ca. 1586) : a crimson or purple dye that is related to indigo, was obtained by the ancient Greeks and Romans from gastropod mollusks, and is now made synthetically

ty·ro \ˈtī-(ˌ)rō\ *n, pl* **tyros** *often attrib* [ML, fr. L *tiro* young soldier, tyro] (1587) **1** : a beginner in learning : NOVICE *syn* see AMATEUR

ty·ro·ci·dine *also* **ty·ro·ci·din** \ˌtī-rə-ˈsī-dᵊn\ *n* [*tyrothricin* + *gramicidin*] (1940) : a basic polypeptide antibiotic produced by a soil bacillus (*Bacillus brevis*)

Ty·ro·le·an *also* **Ty·ro·li·an** \tə-ˈrō-lē-ən, tī-\ *adj* (1797) **1** : of or relating to the Tirol **2** *of a hat* : of a style originating in the Tirol and marked by soft often green felt, a narrow brim and pointed crown, and an ornamental feather

ty·ros·i·nase \tə-ˈrä-sə-ˌnās, tī-, -ˌnāz\ *n* (1896) : a copper-containing enzyme that promotes the oxidation of phenols (as tyrosine) and is widespread in plants and animals

ty·ro·sine \ˈtī-rə-ˌsēn\ *n* [ISV, irreg. fr. Gk *tyros* cheese — more at BUTTER] (1857) **1** : oppressive a phenolic amino acid $C_9H_{11}NO_3$ that is a precursor of several important substances (as epinephrine and melanin)

ty·ro·thri·cin \ˌtī-rə-ˈthrī-sᵊn\ *n* [NL *Tyrothoric-, Tyrothrix*, genus name formerly applied to various bacteria] (1940) : an antibiotic mixture consisting chiefly of tyrocidine and gramicidin and used topically esp. against gram-positive bacteria

tzaddik *var of* ZADDIK

tzar, tzarevitch, tzarina, tzarism *var of* CZAR, CZAREVITCH, CZARINA, CZARISM

tzi·gane \(t)sē-ˈgän\ *n* [F, fr. Hung *cigány*] (1763) **1** : GYPSY 1 **2** : ROMANY 2

tzim·mes \ˈtsi-məs\ *n* [Yiddish *tsimes*, fr. MHG *z, zuo* at, to + *imbīz* light meal] (1892) : a sweetened combination of vegetables (as carrots and potatoes) or of meat and vegetables often with dried fruits (as prunes) that is stewed or baked in a casserole

tzi·tzit *or* **tzi·tzis** *also* **zi·zith** \ˈtsit-səs, tsēt-ˈsēt\ *n pl* [Heb *ṣīṣīth*] (1675) : the fringes or tassels worn on traditional or ceremonial garments by Jewish males as reminders of the commandments of Deut 22:12 and Num 15:37–41

---

¹u \ˈyü\ *n, pl* **u's** *or* **us** \ˈyüz\ *often cap, often attrib* (bef. 12c) **1 a** : the 21st letter of the English alphabet **b** : a graphic representation of this letter **c** : a speech counterpart of orthographic *u* **2** : a graphic device for reproducing the letter *u* **3** : one designated *u* esp. as the 21st in order or class **4** [abbr. for *unsatisfactory*] **a** : a grade rating a student's work as unsatisfactory **b** : one graded or rated with a U **5** : something shaped like the letter U

²u *abbr* **1** unit **2** unsymmetrical **3** upper

¹U \ˈyü\ *adj* [upper class] (1954) : characteristic of the upper classes

²U *abbr* **1** unsatisfactory **2** uracil

³U *symbol* uranium

UAE *abbr* United Arab Emirates

ua·ka·ri \wä-ˈkä-rē\ *n, pl* **-ris** [fr. an unidentified language of western Brazilian Amazonia] (1863) : either of two short-tailed mostly naked-faced So. American monkeys (*Cacajao melanocephalus* and *C. calvus*)

UAR *abbr* United Arab Republic

UAV \ˌyü-ˌā-ˈvē\ *n* (1986) : RPV

UAW *abbr* United Automobile Workers

Uban·gi \yü-ˈbaŋ-gē, ü-, -ˈbaŋ-ē\ *n* [*Ubangi-Shari*, Africa] (1942) : a woman of the district of Kyabé village in Chad with lips pierced and distended to unusual dimensions with wooden disks — not used technically

über- *also* **uber-** \ˈü-bər, ˈue-bər\ *prefix* [G, fr. *über* over, beyond, fr. OHG *ubar* — more at OVER] **1** : being a superlative example of its kind or class : SUPER- 〈*über*nerd〉 **2** : to an extreme or excessive degree : SUPER- 〈*über*cool〉

ubi·qui·none \yü-ˈbi-kwə-ˌnōn, ˌyü-bə-kwi-ˈnōn\ *n* [blend of L *ubique* everywhere and E *quinone*; fr. its widespread occurrence in nature] (1958) : any of a group of lipid-soluble quinones that are found esp. in mitochondria, have an isoprenoid side chain, and function in oxidative phosphorylation as electron-carrying coenzymes in electron transport

ubiq·ui·tous \yü-ˈbi-kwə-təs\ *adj* (1830) : existing or being everywhere at the same time : constantly encountered : WIDESPREAD 〈a ∼ fashion〉 — **ubiq·ui·tous·ly** *adv* — **ubiq·ui·tous·ness** *n*

ubiq·ui·ty \yü-ˈbi-kwə-tē\ *n* [L *ubique* everywhere, fr. *ubi* where + *-que*, enclitic generalizing particle; akin to L *quis* who and to L *-que* and — more at WHO, SESQUI-] (1579) : presence everywhere or in many places esp. simultaneously : OMNIPRESENCE

U-boat \ˈyü-ˌbōt\ *n* [trans. of G *U-boot*, short for *Unterseeboot*, lit., undersea boat] (1916) : a German submarine

UC *abbr* uppercase

UDA *abbr* undocumented alien

ud·der \ˈə-dər\ *n* [ME, fr. OE *ūder*; akin to OHG *ūtar* udder, L *uber*, Gk *outhar*, Skt *ūdhar*] (bef. 12c) **1** : a large pendulous organ consisting of two or more mammary glands enclosed in a common envelope and each provided with a single nipple — see COW illustration **2** : MAMMARY GLAND

udon \ˈü-ˌdän\ *or* **udon noodle** *n* [Jp] (1902) : a thick Japanese noodle made from wheat flour and usu. served in a soup

UFO \ˌyü-(ˌ)ef-ˈō\ *n, pl* **UFO's** *or* **UFOs** \-ˈōz\ [*unidentified flying object*] (1953) : an unidentified flying object; *esp* : FLYING SAUCER

\ə\ abut \ᵊ\ kitten, F table \ər\ further \a\ ash \ā\ ace \ä\ mop, mar \aủ\ out \ch\ chin \e\ bet \ē\ easy \g\ go \i\ hit \ī\ ice \j\ job \ŋ\ sing \ō\ go \ȯ\ law \ȯi\ boy \th\ thin \t̲h̲\ the \ü\ loot \ủ\ foot \y\ yet \zh\ vision, beige \k̲, ⁿ, œ, ɶ, ʸ\ see Guide to Pronunciation

ufol·o·gy \yü-ˈfä-lə-jē\ *n, often cap U&F & 1st O* [*UFO* + *-logy*] (1959) : the study of unidentified flying objects — **ufo·log·i·cal** \ˌyü-fə-ˈlä-ji-kəl\ *adj, often cap U&F & 1st O* — **ufol·o·gist** \yü-ˈfä-lə-jist\ *n, often cap U&F & 1st O*

1**Uga·rit·ic** \ˌyü-gə-ˈri-tik, ˌü-gə-\ *n* (1936) : the Semitic language of ancient Ugarit closely related to Phoenician and Hebrew

2**Ugaritic** *adj* (1938) : of, relating to, or characteristic of the ancient city of Ugarit, its inhabitants, or Ugaritic

ugh *often read as* ˈəg *or* ˈə̲k̲ *or* ˈə\ *interj* (1678) — used to indicate the sound of a cough or grunt or to express disgust or horror

Ug·li \ˈə-glē\ *trademark* — used for a tangelo

ug·li·fy \ˈə-gli-ˌfī\ *vt* **-fied; -fy·ing** (1576) : to make ugly — **ug·li·fi·ca·tion** \ˌə-gli-fə-ˈkā-shən\ *n*

ug·li·ness \ˈə-glē-nəs\ *n* (14c) **1 :** the quality or state of being ugly **2 :** something that is ugly

1**ug·ly** \ˈə-glē\ *adj* **ug·li·er; -est** [ME, fr. ON *uggligr,* fr. *uggr* fear; akin to ON *ugga* to fear] (13c) **1 :** FRIGHTFUL, DIRE **2 a :** offensive to the sight : HIDEOUS **b :** offensive or unpleasant to any sense **3 :** morally offensive or objectionable ⟨corruption—the *ugliest* stain of all⟩ **4 a :** likely to cause inconvenience or discomfort ⟨the ~ truth⟩ **b :** SURLY, QUARRELSOME ⟨an ~ disposition⟩ — **ug·li·ly** \-glə-lē\ *adv*

2**ugly** *adv* (14c) : in an ugly manner ⟨was acting ~⟩

Ugly American *n* [*The Ugly American* (1958), collection of stories by Eugene Burdick and William J. Lederer Am. authors] (1965) : an American in a foreign country whose behavior is offensive to the people of that country

ugly duckling *n* [*The Ugly Duckling,* story by Hans Christian Andersen] (1869) : one that appears very unpromising but often has great potential

Ugri·an \ˈyü-grē-ən, ˈü-\ *n* [ORuss *Ugre* Hungarians] (1841) : a member of a division of the Finno-Ugric peoples that includes the Hungarians and two peoples of western Siberia — **Ugrian** *adj*

Ugric \ˈyü-grik, ˈü-\ *adj* (1854) : of, relating to, or characteristic of the languages of the Ugrians

ug·some \ˈəg-səm\ *adj* [ME, fr. *uggen* to fear, inspire fear, fr. ON *ugga* to fear] (15c) *archaic* : FRIGHTFUL, LOATHSOME

UHF *abbr* ultrahigh frequency

uh–huh *two* ᵊm*'s or two* ᵊn*'s separated by the voiceless sound* h; ˈən-(ˌ)hən, (ˌ)ən-ˈ\ *interj* (1889) — used to indicate affirmation, agreement, or gratification

uh·lan \ˈü-ˌlän, ü-ˈ; ˈyü-lən, ˈü-\ *n* [G, fr. Pol *ulan,* fr. Turk *oğlan* boy, servant] (1753) : any of a body of Prussian light cavalry orig. modeled on Tatar lancers

uh–oh \ˈə-ˌō, *usu with strong glottal stops before the vowels*\ *interj* (1971) — used to indicate dismay or concern

uh–uh *two* ᵊm*'s or two* ᵊn*'s preceded by glottal stops;* ˈən-ˌən\ *interj* (ca. 1924) — used to indicate negation

UI *abbr* unemployment insurance

Ui·ghur *also* **Ui·gur** \ˈwē-ˌgu̇r\ *n* [Uighur *Uighur*] (1747) **1 :** a member of a Turkic people powerful in Mongolia and eastern Turkestan between the 8th and 12th centuries A.D. who constitute a majority of the population of Chinese Turkestan **2 :** the Turkic language of the Uighurs — **Uighur** *also* **Uigur** *adj*

uil·leann pipes \ˈi-lən-\ *n pl, often cap* [*uilleann* fr. Ir, gen. sing. of *uillinn* elbow, fr. OIr *uilen;* akin to OE *eln* ell — more at ELL] (1906) : an Irish bagpipe with air supplied by a bellows held under and worked by the elbow

Uit·land·er \ˈāt-ˌlan-dər, ˈau̇t-, -ˌlän-\ *n* [Afrik, fr. MD *utelander* foreigner, fr. *utelant* foreign territory, fr. *ute* out + *lant* land] (1892) : FOREIGNER; *esp* : a British resident in the former republics of the Transvaal and Orange Free State

UK *abbr* United Kingdom

ukase \yü-ˈkās, -ˈkāz, ˈyü-ˌ; ü-ˈkäz\ *n* [F & Russ; F, fr. Russ *ukaz,* fr. *ukazat'* to show, order; akin to OCS *u-* away, L *au-,* Skt *ava-* and to OCS *kazati* to show] (1729) **1 :** a proclamation by a Russian emperor or government having the force of law **2 :** EDICT

uke \ˈyük\ *n* (1921) : UKULELE

uki·yo–e *also* **uki·yo–ye** \ü-ˌkē-ō-ˈyā, -ˈā\ *n* [Jp *ukiyo-e* genre picture, fr. *ukiyo* world, life + *e* picture] (1879) : a Japanese art movement that flourished from the 17th to the 19th century and produced paintings and prints depicting the everyday life and interests of the common people; *also* : the paintings and prints themselves

Ukrai·ni·an \yü-ˈkrā-nē-ən *also* -ˈkrī-\ *n* (1823) **1 :** a native or inhabitant of Ukraine **2 :** the Slavic language of the Ukrainian people — **Ukrainian** *adj*

uku·le·le *also* **uke·le·le** \ˌyü-kə-ˈlā-lē, ˌü-\ *n* [Hawaiian *ʻukulele,* fr. *ʻuku* flea + *lele* jumping] (1896) : a small guitar of Portuguese origin popularized in Hawaii in the 1880s and strung typically with four strings

-ular *adj suffix* [L *-ularis,* fr. *-ulus, -ula, -ulum* -ule + *-aris* -ar] : of, relating to, or resembling ⟨valv*ular*⟩

ul·cer \ˈəl-sər\ *n* [ME, fr. L *ulcer-, ulcus;* akin to Gk *helkos* wound] (14c) **1 :** a break in skin or mucous membrane with loss of surface tissue, disintegration and necrosis of epithelial tissue, and often pus **2 :** something that festers and corrupts like an open sore — **ulcer** *vb*

ul·cer·ate \ˈəl-sə-ˌrāt\ *vb* **-at·ed; -at·ing** *vi* (15c) : to become affected with or as if with an ulcer ~ *vt* : to affect with or as if with an ulcer

ul·cer·a·tion \ˌəl-sə-ˈrā-shən\ *n* (14c) **1 :** the process of becoming ulcerated : the state of being ulcerated **2 :** ULCER — **ul·cer·a·tive** \ˈəl-sə-ˌrā-tiv, ˈəls-rə-, ˈəl-sə-rə-\ *adj*

ulcerative colitis *n* (ca. 1928) : a nonspecific inflammatory disease of the colon of unknown cause characterized by diarrhea with discharge of mucus and blood, cramping abdominal pain, and inflammation and edema of the mucous membrane with patches of ulceration

ul·cero·gen·ic \ˌəl-sə-rō-ˈje-nik\ *adj* (1950) : tending to produce or develop into ulcers or ulceration

ul·cer·ous \ˈəls-rəs, ˈəl-sə-\ *adj* (1577) **1 :** characterized or caused by ulceration ⟨~ lesions⟩ **2 :** affected with or as if with an ulcer : ULCERATED

-ule *n suffix* [F & L; F, fr. L *-ulus,* masc. dim. suffix, *-ula,* fem. dim. suffix, *-ulum,* neut. dim. suffix] : little one ⟨duct*ule*⟩

ule·ma *or* **ula·ma** \ˌü-lə-ˈmä\ *n* [Ar, Turk, & Pers; Turk & Pers *ʻulemā,* fr. Ar *ʻulamā*] (1688) **1** *pl in constr* : the body of mullahs **2 :** MULLAH

-ulent *adj suffix* [L *-ulentus*] : that abounds in (a specified thing) ⟨floc*culent*⟩

ulex·ite \ˈyü-lək-ˌsīt\ *n* [George L. *Ulex* †1883 Ger. chemist] (1867) : a soft mineral consisting of a hydrous borate of sodium and calcium and usu. occurring in loose masses of white fibers

ul·lage \ˈə-lij\ *n* [ME *ulage,* fr. AF *ulliage,* fr. **ullier* to fill a partially empty cask, fr. OF (Picard dial.) *oel* bunghole, lit., eye, fr. L *oculus* eye — more at EYE] (15c) : the amount that a container (as a tank or cask) lacks of being full

ul·na \ˈəl-nə\ *n, pl* **ul·nae** \-nē\ *or* **ulnas** [NL, fr. L, elbow — more at ELL] (1541) : the bone on the little-finger side of the human forearm; *also* : a corresponding part of the forelimb of vertebrates above fishes — **ul·nar** \-nər, -ˌnär\ *adj*

ul·ster \ˈəl-stər\ *n* [*Ulster,* Ireland] (1876) : a long loose overcoat of Irish origin made of heavy material (as frieze)

ult *abbr* ultimo

ul·te·ri·or \ˌəl-ˈtir-ē-ər\ *adj* [L, farther, further, compar. of **ulter* situated beyond, fr. *uls* beyond; akin to L *ollus, ille,* that one, OIr *indoll* beyond] (1646) **1 a :** FURTHER, FUTURE **b :** more distant **c :** situated on the farther side **2 :** going beyond what is openly said or shown and esp. what is proper ⟨~ motives⟩ — **ul·te·ri·or·ly** *adv*

ul·ti·ma \ˈəl-tə-mə\ *n* [L, fem. of *ultimus* last] (ca. 1864) : the last syllable of a word

ul·ti·ma·cy \ˈəl-tə-mə-sē\ *n, pl* **-cies** (1842) **1 :** the quality or state of being ultimate **2 :** ULTIMATE 1

ul·ti·ma ra·tio \ˌu̇l-tə-mə-ˈrä-tē-ˌō\ *n* [NL] (1780) : the final argument; *also* : the last resort (as force)

1**ul·ti·mate** \ˈəl-tə-mət\ *adj* [ML *ultimatus* last, final, fr. LL, pp. of *ultimare* to come to an end, be last, fr. L *ultimus* farthest, last, final, superl. of L **ulter* situated beyond] (1640) **1 a :** most remote in space or time : FARTHEST **b :** last in a progression or series : FINAL ⟨their ~ destination was Paris⟩ **c :** EVENTUAL 2 ⟨they hoped for ~ success⟩ **d :** the best or most extreme of its kind : UTMOST ⟨the ~ sacrifice⟩ **2 :** arrived at as the last result ⟨the ~ question⟩ **3 a :** BASIC, FUNDAMENTAL ⟨the ~ nature of things —A. N. Whitehead⟩ **b :** ORIGINAL 1 ⟨the ~ source⟩ **c :** incapable of further analysis, division, or separation *syn* see LAST — **ul·ti·mate·ness** *n*

2**ultimate** *n* (1681) **1 :** something ultimate; *esp* : FUNDAMENTAL **2 :** ACME **3** *cap* : ULTIMATE FRISBEE

3**ul·ti·mate** \-mət, -ˌmāt\ *vb* **-mat·ed; -mat·ing** (ca. 1834) : END

Ultimate Frisbee *n, often not cap* (1972) : a game played on a rectangular field between two seven-player teams in which a plastic disc is advanced by being thrown from player to player and in which a team scores by catching a throw in the opponent's end zone — called also *Ultimate*

ul·ti·mate·ly \-mət-lē\ *adv* (1652) **1 :** in the end : FUNDAMENTALLY ⟨the word comes ~ from Latin⟩ **2 :** EVENTUALLY ⟨~, they agreed⟩

ul·ti·ma Thu·le \ˌəl-tə-mə-ˈthü-lē, -ˈthyü-\ *n* [L, farthest Thule] (1665) : THULE

ul·ti·ma·tum \ˌəl-tə-ˈmā-təm, -ˈmä-\ *n, pl* **-tums** *or* **-ta** \-tə\ [NL, fr. ML, neut. of *ultimatus* final] (1731) : a final proposition, condition, or demand; *esp* : one whose rejection will end negotiations and cause a resort to force or other direct action

ul·ti·mo \ˈəl-tə-ˌmō\ *adj* [L *ultimo mense* in the last month] (1616) : of or occurring in the month preceding the present

ul·ti·mo·gen·i·ture \ˌəl-tə-mō-ˈje-nə-ˌchu̇r, -ni-chər, -nə-ˌtyu̇r, -nə-ˌtu̇r\ *n* [L *ultimus* last + E *primogeniture*] (1882) : a system of inheritance by which the youngest child succeeds to the estate

1**ul·tra** \ˈəl-trə\ *adj* [*ultra-*] (1818) : going beyond others or beyond due limit : EXTREME

2**ultra** *n* [*ultra-*] (1819) : one that is ultra : EXTREMIST

ultra- *prefix* [L, fr. *ultra* beyond, adv. & prep., fr. **ulter* situated beyond — more at ULTERIOR] **1 :** beyond in space : on the other side : TRANS- ⟨*ultra*violet⟩ **2 :** beyond the range or limits of : transcending : SUPER- ⟨*ultra*microscopic⟩ **3 :** beyond what is ordinary, proper, or moderate : excessively : extremely ⟨*ultra*modern⟩

ul·tra·bright
ul·tra·care·ful
ul·tra·ca·su·al
ul·tra·cau·tious
ul·tra·cheap
ul·tra·chic
ul·tra·civ·i·lized
ul·tra·clean
ul·tra·cold
ul·tra·com·mer·cial
ul·tra·com·pact
ul·tra·com·pe·tent
ul·tra·com·pet·i·tive
ul·tra·con·ser·va·tism
ul·tra·con·ser·va·tive
ul·tra·con·tem·po·rary
ul·tra·con·ve·nient
ul·tra·cool
ul·tra·crit·i·cal
ul·tra·dem·o·crat·ic
ul·tra·dense
ul·tra·dis·tance
ul·tra·dis·tant
ul·tra·dry
ul·tra·ef·fi·cient
ul·tra·en·er·get·ic
ul·tra·ex·clu·sive
ul·tra·ex·pen·sive
ul·tra·fa·mil·iar
ul·tra·fast
ul·tra·fas·tid·i·ous
ul·tra·fem·i·nine
ul·tra·fine
ul·tra·glam·or·ous
ul·tra·haz·ard·ous
ul·tra·heat
ul·tra·heavy
ul·tra·high
ul·tra·hip
ul·tra·hot
ul·tra·hu·man
ul·tra·left
ul·tra·left·ism
ul·tra·left·ist
ul·tra·lib·er·al
ul·tra·lib·er·al·ism
ul·tra·light·weight
ul·tra·low
ul·tra·lu·mi·nous
ul·tra·mas·cu·line
ul·tra·mil·i·tant
ul·tra·min·i·a·tur·ized
ul·tra·mod·ern
ul·tra·mod·ern·ist
ul·tra·na·tion·al·ism
ul·tra·na·tion·al·ist
ul·tra·na·tion·al·is·tic
ul·tra·or·tho·dox
ul·tra·pa·tri·ot·ic
ul·tra·phys·i·cal
ul·tra·posh
ul·tra·pow·er·ful
ul·tra·prac·ti·cal
ul·tra·pre·cise
ul·tra·pre·ci·sion
ul·tra·pro·fes·sion·al
ul·tra·pro·gres·sive
ul·tra·pure
ul·tra·qui·et
ul·tra·rad·i·cal
ul·tra·rap·id
ul·tra·rare
ul·tra·ra·tio·nal
ul·tra·re·al·ism
ul·tra·re·al·ist
ul·tra·re·al·is·tic
ul·tra·re·fined
ul·tra·re·li·able
ul·tra·re·li·gious
ul·tra·re·spect·able
ul·tra·rev·o·lu·tion·ary
ul·tra·rich
ul·tra·right
ul·tra·right·ist
ul·tra·ro·man·tic
ul·tra·roy·al·ist
ul·tra·safe
ul·tra·se·cret
ul·tra·sen·si·tive
ul·tra·se·ri·ous
ul·tra·sharp
ul·tra·sim·ple
ul·tra·slick
ul·tra·slow
ul·tra·small
ul·tra·smart
ul·tra·smooth
ul·tra·soft
ul·tra·so·phis·ti·cat·ed
ul·tra·thin
ul·tra·ti·ny
ul·tra·tra·di·tion·al
ul·tra·vac·u·um
ul·tra·vi·o·lence
ul·tra·vi·o·lent
ul·tra·wide

ul·tra·ba·sic \ˌəl-trə-ˈbā-sik\ *adj* [ISV] (1881) : extremely basic ⟨an ~ system⟩; *specif* : very low in silica and rich in iron and magnesium minerals ⟨dunite and peridotite are ~ rocks⟩ — **ultrabasic** *n*

ul·tra·cen·trif·u·gal \-ˌsen-ˈtri-fyə-gəl, -fi-gəl\ *adj* (1930) **:** of, relating to, or obtained by means of an ultracentrifuge — **ul·tra·cen·trif·u·gal·ly** \-gə-lē\ *adv*

1**ul·tra·cen·tri·fuge** \-ˈsen-trə-ˌfyüj\ *n* (1924) **:** a high-speed centrifuge able to sediment colloidal and other small particles and used esp. in determining sizes of such particles and molecular weights of large molecules

2**ultracentrifuge** *vt* (1934) **:** to subject to an ultracentrifuge — **ul·tra·cen·tri·fu·ga·tion** \-ˌsen-trə-fyü-ˈgā-shən\ *n*

ul·tra·fiche \ˈəl-trə-ˌfēsh\ *n* (1969) **:** a microfiche whose microimages are of printed matter reduced 90 or more times

ul·tra·fil·tra·tion \ˌəl-trə-fil-ˈtrā-shən\ *n* (1908) **:** filtration through a medium (as a semipermeable capillary wall) which allows small molecules (as of water) to pass but holds back larger ones (as of protein) — **ul·tra·fil·trate** \-ˈfil-ˌtrāt\ *n*

ul·tra·high frequency \ˌəl-trə-ˈhī-\ *n* (1932) **:** a radio frequency between superhigh frequency and very high frequency — see RADIO FREQUENCY table

ul·tra·ism \ˈəl-trə-ˌi-zəm\ *n* (1821) **1 :** the principles of those who advocate extreme measures (as radicalism) **2 :** an instance or example of radicalism — **ul·tra·ist** \-trə-ist\ *adj or n* — **ul·tra·is·tic** \ˌəl-trə-ˈis-tik\ *adj*

1**ul·tra·light** \ˈəl-trə-ˌlīt\ *adj* (1974) **:** extremely light in mass or weight ⟨an ~ alloy⟩ ⟨an ~ pullover⟩

2**ultralight** *n* (1974) **:** a very light recreational aircraft typically for one person that is powered by a small gasoline engine

ul·tra·maf·ic \ˌəl-trə-ˈma-fik\ *adj* (1933) **:** ULTRABASIC

ul·tra·mar·a·thon \-ˈma-rə-ˌthän\ *n* (1977) **:** a footrace longer than a marathon — **ul·tra·mar·a·thon·er** \-ˌthä-nər\ *n*

1**ul·tra·ma·rine** \-mə-ˈrēn\ *n* [ML *ultramarinus* coming from beyond the sea, fr. L *ultra-* + *mare* sea — more at MARINE] (1598) **1 a** (1) **:** a blue pigment prepared by powdering lapis lazuli (2) **:** a similar pigment prepared from kaolin, soda ash, sulfur, and charcoal **b :** any of several related pigments **2 :** a vivid blue

2**ultramarine** *adj* (1652) **:** situated beyond the sea

ul·tra·mi·cro \ˌəl-trə-ˈmī-(ˌ)krō\ *adj* (1937) **:** being or dealing with something smaller than micro

ul·tra·mi·cro·scope \ˌəl-trə-ˈmī-krə-ˌskōp\ *n* [back-formation fr. *ultramicroscopic*] (1906) **:** an apparatus for making visible by scattered light particles too small to be perceived by an ordinary microscope

ul·tra·mi·cro·scop·ic \-ˌmī-krə-ˈskä-pik\ *also* **ul·tra·mi·cro·scop·i·cal** \-pi-kəl\ *adj* [ISV] (1870) **1 :** too small to be seen with an ordinary microscope **2 :** of or relating to an ultramicroscope — **ul·tra·mi·cro·scop·i·cal·ly** \-pi-k(ə-)lē\ *adv*

ul·tra·mi·cro·tome \-ˈmī-krə-ˌtōm\ *n* (1946) **:** a microtome for cutting extremely thin sections for electron microscopy — **ul·tra·mi·crot·o·my** \-mī-ˈkrä-tə-mē\ *n*

ul·tra·min·i·a·ture \-ˈmi-nē-ə-ˌchu̇r, -ˈmi-ni-ˌchu̇r, -ˈmin-yə-, -chər, -ˌtyu̇r, -ˌtu̇r\ *adj* (1942) **:** SUBMINIATURE

ul·tra·mon·tane \-ˈmän-ˌtān, -ˌmän-ˈ\ *adj* [ML *ultramontanus,* fr. L *ultra-* + *mont-, mons* mountain — more at MOUNT] (ca. 1618) **1 :** of or relating to countries or peoples beyond the mountains (as the Alps) **2 :** favoring greater or absolute supremacy of papal over national or diocesan authority in the Roman Catholic Church — **ultramontane** *n, often cap* — **ul·tra·mon·tan·ism** \-ˈmän-tə-ˌni-zəm\ *n*

ul·tra–pas·teur·ized \-ˈpas-chə-ˌrīzd, -ˈpas-tyə-, -tə-\ *adj* (1953) **:** subjected to pasteurization at higher than normal temperatures esp. to extend shelf life ⟨~ cream⟩

ul·tra·short \-ˈshȯrt\ *adj* (1926) **1 :** having a wavelength below 10 meters ⟨~ radiation⟩ **2 :** very short in duration ⟨an ~ pulse of light⟩

ul·tra·son·ic \-ˈsä-nik\ *adj* (1923) **1 :** having a frequency above the human ear's audibility limit of about 20,000 hertz — used of waves and vibrations **2 :** utilizing, produced by, or relating to ultrasonic waves or vibrations — **ul·tra·son·i·cal·ly** \-ni-k(ə-)lē\ *adv*

ul·tra·son·ics \ˌəl-trə-ˈsä-niks\ *n pl* (1924) **1 :** ultrasonic vibrations or compressional waves **2** *sing in constr* **:** the study of ultrasonic vibrations and their associated phenomena **3 :** ultrasonic devices

ul·tra·so·nog·ra·phy \-sə-ˈnä-grə-fē, -sō-\ *n* [*ultrasonic* + *-o-* + *-graphy*] (1951) **:** ULTRASOUND 2 — **ul·tra·so·nog·ra·pher** \-fər\ *n* — **ul·tra·so·no·graph·ic** \-ˌsō-nə-ˈgra-fik, -ˌsä-\ *adj*

ul·tra·sound \ˈəl-trə-ˌsau̇nd\ *n* (1923) **1 :** vibrations of the same physical nature as sound but with frequencies above the range of human hearing **2 :** the diagnostic or therapeutic use of ultrasound and esp. a noninvasive technique involving the formation of a two-dimensional image used for the examination and measurement of internal body structures and the detection of bodily abnormalities — called also *sonography* **3 :** a diagnostic examination using ultrasound

ul·tra·struc·ture \ˈəl-trə-ˌstrək-chər\ *n* (1939) **:** biological structure and esp. fine structure (as of a cell) not visible through an ordinary microscope — **ul·tra·struc·tur·al** \ˌəl-trə-ˈstrək-chə-rəl, -ˈstrək-shrəl\ *adj* — **ul·tra·struc·tur·al·ly** *adv*

ul·tra·vi·o·let \ˌəl-trə-ˈvī-(ə-)lət\ *adj* (1840) **1 :** situated beyond the visible spectrum at its violet end — used of radiation having a wavelength shorter than wavelengths of visible light and longer than those of X-rays **2 :** relating to, producing, or employing ultraviolet radiation — **ultraviolet** *n*

ul·tra vi·res \ˌəl-trə-ˈvī-(ˌ)rēz\ *adv or adj* [NL, lit., beyond power] (1793) **:** beyond the scope or in excess of legal power or authority

ul·u·lant \ˈəl-yə-lənt, ˈyül-\ *adj* (1855) **:** having a howling sound **:** WAILING ⟨dark wasteland . . . ~ with bitter wind —Rudi Blesh⟩

ul·u·late \ˈəl-yə-ˌlāt, ˈyül-\ *vi* **-lat·ed; -lat·ing** [L *ululatus,* pp. of *ululare,* of imit. origin] (ca. 1623) **:** HOWL, WAIL — **ul·u·la·tion** \ˌəl-yə-ˈlā-shən\ *n*

ul·va \ˈəl-və\ *n* [NL, genus name, fr. L, sedge] (ca. 1706) **:** SEA LETTUCE

Ulys·ses \yu̇-ˈli-(ˌ)sēz\ *n* [L *Ulysses, Ulixes,* fr. Gk *Oulixes, Olysseus, Odysseus*] (ca. 1530) **:** ODYSSEUS

um *a prolonged* m *sound,* əm\ *interj* (1672) — used to indicate hesitation ⟨well, ~, I don't know⟩

uma·mi \ü-ˈmä-mē\ *n* [Jp, savoriness, flavor] (1979) **:** a taste sensation that is meaty or savory and is produced by several amino acids and nucleotides (as glutamate and aspartate)

Umay·yad \ü-ˈmī-əd\ *n, often attrib* [Ar (*banū*) *umayya,* Meccan kin group to which the Umayyad caliphs belonged] (1758) **:** a member of a dynasty of caliphs based in Damascus that ruled from A.D. 661 to 750

um·bel \ˈəm-bəl\ *n* [NL *umbella,* fr. L, umbrella — more at UMBRELLA] (1597) **:** a racemose inflorescence typical of the carrot family in which the pedicels arise from about the same point to form a flat or rounded flower cluster — see INFLORESCENCE illustration

um·bel·late \ˈəm-bə-ˌlāt, ˌəm-ˈbe-lət\ *adj* (1760) **1 :** bearing, consisting of, or arranged in umbels **2 :** resembling an umbel in form

um·bel·li·fer \ˌəm-ˈbe-lə-fər\ *n* [NL *Umbelliferae,* group name, fem. pl. of *umbellifer* bearing umbels] (1718) **:** a plant of the carrot family

um·bel·lif·er·ous \ˌəm-bə-ˈli-f(ə-)rəs\ *adj* (1662) **:** of or relating to the carrot family ⟨~ flower heads⟩

1**um·ber** \ˈəm-bər\ *n* [prob. fr. obs. E, shade, color, fr. ME *ombre, umbre* shade, shadow, fr. AF, fr. L *umbra* — more at UMBRAGE] (1568) **1 :** a brown earth that is darker in color than ocher and sienna because of its content of manganese and iron oxides and is highly valued as a permanent pigment either in the raw or burnt state **2 a :** a moderate to dark yellowish brown **b :** a moderate brown

2**umber** *vt* **um·bered; um·ber·ing** \-b(ə-)riŋ\ (1610) **:** to darken with or as if with umber

3**umber** *adj* (1802) **:** of, relating to, or having the characteristics of umber; *specif* **:** of the color of umber

1**um·bil·i·cal** \ˌəm-ˈbi-li-kəl, *Brit also* ˌəm-bə-ˈlī-kəl\ *adj* (1541) **1 :** of, relating to, or used at the navel **2 :** of or relating to the central region of the abdomen **3 :** being a necessary or nurturing link or connection ⟨the town's ~ rail line⟩

2**umbilical** *n* (1774) **:** UMBILICAL CORD 2

umbilical cord *n* (1753) **1 a :** a cord arising from the navel that connects the fetus with the placenta and through which respiratory gases, nutrients, and wastes pass **b :** YOLK STALK **2 :** a tethering or supply line (as for an astronaut outside a spacecraft or a diver underwater) **3 :** a necessary, supportive, or nurturing link or connection

um·bil·i·cate \ˌəm-ˈbi-li-kət\ *or* **um·bil·i·cat·ed** \-lə-ˌkā-təd\ *adj* (1698) **1 :** depressed like a navel **2 :** having an umbilicus — **um·bil·i·ca·tion** \ˌəm-ˌbi-lə-ˈkā-shən\ *n*

um·bi·li·cus \ˌəm-ˈbi-li-kəs, ˌəm-bə-ˈlī-\ *n, pl* **um·bi·li·ci** \ˌəm-ˈbi-li-ˌkī, -ˌkē; ˌəm-bə-ˈlī-ˌkī, -ˌsī\ *or* **um·bi·li·cus·es** [L — more at NAVEL] (1799) **1 a :** NAVEL 1 **b :** any of several morphological depressions; *esp* **:** HILUM 1 **2 :** a central point **:** CORE, HEART

um·bles \ˈəm-bəlz\ *n pl* [ME, alter. of *noumbles,* fr. OF *nombles* loins, alter. of *lumbles,* fr. L *lumbuli,* dim. of *lumbi,* pl. of *lumbus* loin — more at LOIN] (15c) **:** the edible viscera of an animal (as a deer or hog)

um·bo \ˈəm-(ˌ)bō\ *n, pl* **um·bo·nes** \ˌəm-ˈbō-(ˌ)nēz\ *or* **umbos** [L; akin to L *umbilicus* — more at NAVEL] (1721) **1 :** the boss of a shield **2 :** a rounded elevation: as **a :** an inward projection of the tympanic membrane of the ear **b :** one of the lateral prominences just above the hinge of a bivalve shell — **um·bo·nal** \ˈəm-bə-nᵊl, ˌəm-ˈbō-\ *adj* — **um·bo·nate** \ˈəm-bə-ˌnāt, ˌəm-ˈbō-nət\ *adj*

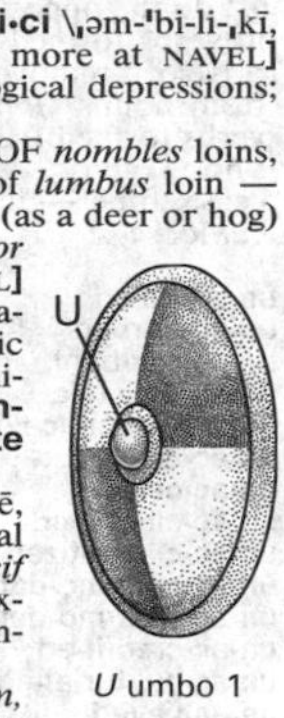

U umbo 1

um·bra \ˈəm-brə\ *n, pl* **umbras** *or* **um·brae** \-(ˌ)brē, -ˌbrī\ [L] (1638) **1 :** a shaded area **2 a :** a conical shadow excluding all light from a given source; *specif* **:** the conical part of the shadow of a celestial body excluding all light from the primary source **b :** the central dark part of a sunspot — **um·bral** \-brəl\ *adj*

um·brage \ˈəm-brij\ *n* [ME, fr. AF, fr. L *umbraticum,* neut. of *umbraticus* of shade, fr. *umbratus,* pp. of *umbrare* to shade, fr. *umbra* shade, shadow; akin to Lith *unksmė* shadow] (15c) **1 :** SHADE, SHADOW **2 :** shady branches **:** FOLIAGE **3 a :** an indistinct indication **:** vague suggestion **:** HINT **b :** a reason for doubt **:** SUSPICION **4 :** a feeling of pique or resentment at some often fancied slight or insult ⟨took ~ at the speaker's remarks⟩ ***syn*** see OFFENSE

um·bra·geous \ˌəm-ˈbrā-jəs\ *adj* (1587) **1 a :** affording shade **b :** spotted with shadows **2 :** inclined to take offense easily — **um·bra·geous·ly** *adv* — **um·bra·geous·ness** *n*

1**um·brel·la** \ˌəm-ˈbre-lə, *esp Southern* ˈəm-ˌ\ *n* [It *ombrella,* modif. of L *umbella,* dim. of *umbra*] (1611) **1 :** a collapsible shade for protection against weather consisting of fabric stretched over hinged ribs radiating from a central pole; *esp* **:** a small one for carrying in the hand **2 :** the bell-shaped or saucer-shaped largely gelatinous structure that forms the chief part of the body of most jellyfishes **3 :** something which provides protection: as **a :** defensive air cover (as over a battlefront) **b :** a heavy barrage **4 :** something which covers or embraces a broad range of elements or factors ⟨decided to expand . . . by building new colleges under a federation ~ —Diane Ravitch⟩

2**umbrella** *vt* **-laed; -la·ing** (1834) **:** to protect, cover, or provide with an umbrella

umbrella plant *n* (ca. 1909) **:** a perennial sedge (*Cyperus alternifolius*) of Madagascar that has large terminal whorls of slender leaves and is often grown as an ornamental

umbrella tree *n* (ca. 1790) **:** any of various trees or shrubs resembling an umbrella esp. in the arrangement of leaves or the shape of the crown; *esp* **:** a widely cultivated schefflera (*Schefflera actinophylla* syn. *Brassaia actinophylla*) of Australia and New Guinea having leaflets radiating from an elongate petiole

Um·bri·an \ˈəm-brē-ən\ *n* (1601) **1 :** a native or inhabitant of Umbria **2 :** the Italic language of ancient Umbria — see INDO-EUROPEAN LANGUAGES table — **Umbrian** *adj*

Um·bun·du \ˌəm-ˈbu̇n-(ˌ)dü\ *n* (ca. 1895) **:** a Bantu language of central Angola

umi·ak \ˈü-mē-ˌak\ *n* [Inuit *umiaq*] (1769) **:** an open Eskimo boat made of a wooden frame covered with hide

1**um·laut** \ˈüm-ˌlau̇t, ˈu̇m-\ *n* [G, fr. *um-* around, transforming + *Laut* sound] (ca. 1845) **1 a :** the change of a vowel (as \ü\ to \ē\ in *goose, geese*) that is caused by partial assimilation to a succeeding sound or that occurs as a reflex of the former presence of a succeeding sound which has been lost or altered **b :** a vowel resulting from such partial assimilation **2** : a diacritical mark ¨ placed over a vowel to indicate a more central or front articulation — compare DIAERESIS

²umlaut *vt* (1879) **1** : to produce by umlaut **2** : to write or print an umlaut over

¹ump \'əmp\ *n* (1912) : UMPIRE 2

²ump *vi* (1928) : to act as umpire

¹um·pire \'əm-ˌpī(-ə)r\ *n* [ME *oumpere*, alter. (fr. misdivision of *a noumpere*) of *noumpere*, fr. AF *nounpier*, *nompere*, fr. *nounpier*, adj., single, odd, fr. *non-* + *per* equal, fr. L *par*] (15c) **1** : one having authority to decide finally a controversy or question between parties: as **a** : one appointed to decide between arbitrators who have disagreed **b** : an impartial third party chosen to arbitrate disputes arising under the terms of a labor agreement **2** : an official in a sport who rules on plays **3** : a military officer who evaluates maneuvers

²umpire *vb* **um·pired; um·pir·ing** *vt* (1609) : to supervise or decide as umpire ~ *vi* : to act as umpire

ump·teen \ˌəm(p)-ˌtēn, ˌəm(p)-'\ *adj* [blend of *umpty* (such and such) and *-teen* (as in *thirteen*)] (1918) : very many : indefinitely numerous — **ump·teenth** \-ˌtēn(t)th, -'tēn(t)th\ *adj*

UMWA *abbr* United Mine Workers of America

UN *abbr* United Nations

¹un- \ˌən, *often* 'ən *before* '-*stressed syllable*\ *prefix* [ME, fr. OE; akin to OHG *un-* un-, L *in-*, Gk *a-*, *an-*, OE *ne* not — more at NO] **1** : not : IN-, NON- — in adjectives formed from adjectives ⟨*unambitious*⟩ ⟨*unskilled*⟩ or participles ⟨*undressed*⟩, in nouns formed from nouns ⟨*unavailability*⟩, and rarely in verbs formed from verbs ⟨*unbe*⟩; sometimes in words that have a meaning that merely negates that of the base word and are thereby distinguished from words that prefix *in-* or a variant of it (as *im-*) to the same base word and have a meaning positively opposite to that of the base word ⟨*unartistic*⟩ ⟨*unmoral*⟩ **2** : opposite of : contrary to — in adjectives formed from adjectives ⟨*unconstitutional*⟩ ⟨*ungraceful*⟩ ⟨*unmannered*⟩ or participles ⟨*unbelieving*⟩ and in nouns formed from nouns ⟨*unrest*⟩

²un- *prefix* [ME, fr. OE *un-*, *on-*, alter. of *and-* against — more at ANTE-] **1** : do the opposite of : reverse (a specified action) : DE- 1a, DIS- 1a — in verbs formed from verbs ⟨*unbend*⟩ ⟨*undress*⟩ ⟨*unfold*⟩ **2 a** : deprive of : remove (a specified thing) from : remove — in verbs formed from nouns ⟨*unfrock*⟩ ⟨*unsex*⟩ **b** : release from : free from — in verbs formed from nouns ⟨*unhand*⟩ **c** : remove from : extract from : bring out of — in verbs formed from nouns ⟨*unbosom*⟩ **d** : cause to cease to be — in verbs formed from nouns ⟨*unman*⟩ **3** : completely ⟨*unloose*⟩

un·abrad·ed
un·ab·sorbed
un·ab·sor·bent
un·ac·a·dem·ic
un·ac·a·dem·i·cal·ly
un·ac·cent·ed
un·ac·cept·ed
un·ac·cli·mat·ed
un·ac·cli·ma·tized
un·ac·com·mo·dat·ed
un·ac·com·mo·dat·ing
un·ac·cred·it·ed
un·ac·cul·tur·at·ed
un·achieved
un·ac·knowl·edged
un·ac·quaint·ed
un·act·able
un·act·ed
un·ac·tor·ish
un·adapt·able
un·adapt·ed
un·ad·dressed
un·ad·ju·di·cat·ed
un·ad·just·ed
un·ad·mired
un·ad·mit·ted
un·adopt·able
un·adult
un·ad·ven·tur·ous
un·ad·ver·tised
un·aes·thet·ic
un·af·fect·ing
un·af·fec·tion·ate
un·af·fec·tion·ate·ly
un·af·fil·i·at·ed
un·af·flu·ent
un·af·ford·able
un·afraid
un·ag·gres·sive
un·aid·ed
un·air–con·di·tioned
un·akin
un·alien·at·ed
un·alike
un·al·le·vi·at·ed
un·al·lo·cat·ed
un·al·lur·ing
un·al·tered
un·am·bi·tious
un·ame·na·ble
un·amend·ed
un·ami·a·ble
un·am·or·tized
un·am·pli·fied
un·amus·ing
un·an·a·lyz·able
un·an·a·lyzed
un·anes·the·tized
un·an·no·tat·ed
un·an·nounced
un·apol·o·giz·ing

un·ap·par·ent
un·ap·peased
un·ap·pre·ci·at·ed
un·ap·pre·cia·tive
un·ap·pro·pri·at·ed
un·ap·proved
un·ar·mored
un·ar·ro·gant
un·ar·tis·tic
un·as·pi·rat·ed
un·as·sailed
un·as·sem·bled
un·as·signed
un·as·sim·i·la·ble
un·as·sim·i·lat·ed
un·as·so·ci·at·ed
un·as·suaged
un·ath·let·ic
un·at·tain·able
un·at·tend·ed
un·at·ten·u·at·ed
un·at·test·ed
un·at·trib·ut·able
un·at·trib·ut·ed
un·at·tuned
un·au·dit·ed
un·au·then·tic
un·au·tho·rized
un·au·to·mat·ed
un·avail·abil·i·ty
un·avail·able
un·av·er·age
un·avowed
un·awak·ened
un·award·ed
un·awe·some
un·ban
un·bap·tized
un·barbed
un·bar·ri·cad·ed
un·be·hold·en
un·bel·lig·er·ent
un·be·loved
un·be·mused
un·billed
un·bit·ten
un·bit·ter
un·bleached
un·blem·ished
un·blend·ed
un·blink·ered
un·book·ish
un·bowd·ler·ized
un·brack·et·ed
un·brake
un·breach·able
un·break·able
un·bridge·able
un·bridged
un·briefed
un·bright

un·bril·liant
un·bruised
un·brushed
un·bud·get·ed
un·buf·fered
un·build·able
un·bulky
un·bu·reau·crat·ic
un·bur·ied
un·burn·able
un·burned
un·burnt
un·busi·ness·like
un·busy
un·but·tered
un·cal·ci·fied
un·cal·cined
un·cal·i·brat·ed
un·called
un·cal·loused
un·can·celed
un·can·did
un·can·did·ly
un·ca·non·i·cal
un·cap
un·cap·i·tal·ized
un·cap·tioned
un·cap·tur·able
un·cared–for
un·car·ing
un·car·pet·ed
un·case
un·cas·trat·ed
un·cat·a·loged
un·catch·able
un·catchy
un·cat·e·go·riz·able
un·caught
un·cen·sored
un·cen·so·ri·ous
un·cen·sured
un·cer·ti·fied
un·chal·lenge·able
un·chal·lenged
un·chal·leng·ing
un·changed
un·chan·neled
un·chap·er·oned
un·char·is·mat·ic
un·charm·ing
un·chart·ered
un·chau·vin·is·tic
un·check·able
un·checked
un·chew·able
un·chewed
un·chic
un·child·like
un·chlo·ri·nat·ed
un·cho·reo·graphed
un·chris·tened

un·chron·i·cled
un·chro·no·log·i·cal
un·church·ly
un·cil·i·at·ed
un·cin·e·mat·ic
un·clad
un·claimed
un·clar·i·fied
un·clas·si·fi·able
un·cleaned
un·clear
un·cli·chéd
un·clip
un·cloy·ing
un·co·alesce
un·coat·ed
un·cod·ed
un·cod·i·fied
un·co·erced
un·co·er·cive
un·co·er·cive·ly
un·col·lect·ed
un·col·lect·ible
un·co·lored
un·com·bat·ive
un·combed
un·com·bined
un·come·ly
un·com·ic
un·com·mer·cial·ized
un·com·pas·sion·ate
un·com·pel·ling
un·com·pen·sat·ed
un·com·pla·cent
un·com·plet·ed
un·com·pound·ed
un·com·pre·hend·ed
un·com·pressed
un·com·pu·ter·ized
un·con·cealed
un·con·fessed
un·con·fined
un·con·firmed
un·con·found·ed
un·con·fuse
un·con·ju·gat·ed
un·con·quered
un·con·se·crat·ed
un·con·strained
un·con·strict·ed
un·con·struc·tive
un·con·sumed
un·con·sum·mat·ed
un·con·tain·able
un·con·tam·i·nat·ed
un·con·tem·plat·ed
un·con·tem·po·rary
un·con·ten·tious
un·con·test·ed
un·con·tract·ed
un·con·tra·dict·ed
un·con·trived
un·con·trolled
un·con·tro·ver·sial
un·con·tro·ver·sial·ly
un·con·vert·ed
un·con·vinced
un·con·voyed
un·cooked
un·cooled
un·co·op·er·a·tive
un·co·or·di·nat·ed
un·copy·right·able
un·cor·rect·able
un·cor·rect·ed
un·cor·re·lat·ed
un·cor·rob·o·rat·ed
un·cor·rupt
un·count·able
un·cou·ra·geous
un·coy
un·cracked
un·crate
un·cra·zy
un·cre·a·tive
un·cre·den·tialed
un·cred·it·ed
un·crip·pled
un·cropped
un·cross·able
un·crowd·ed
un·crush·able
un·crys·tal·lized
un·cuff
un·cul·ti·va·ble
un·cul·ti·vat·ed
un·cul·tured
un·cured
un·cu·ri·ous
un·cur·rent
un·cur·tained
un·cus·tom·ar·i·ly
un·cus·tom·ary

un·cute
un·cyn·i·cal
un·cyn·i·cal·ly
un·dam·aged
un·damped
un·dance·able
un·dat·ed
un·dec·a·dent
un·de·cid·abil·i·ty
un·de·cid·able
un·de·cid·ed
un·de·ci·pher·able
un·de·ci·phered
un·de·clared
un·de·com·posed
un·dec·o·rat·ed
un·ded·i·cat·ed
un·de·feat·ed
un·de·fend·ed
un·de·filed
un·de·fin·able
un·de·fined
un·de·fo·li·at·ed
un·de·formed
un·del·e·gat·ed
un·de·liv·er·able
un·de·liv·ered
un·de·lud·ed
un·de·mand·ing
un·de·nom·i·na·tion·al
un·de·pend·able
un·de·scrib·able
un·de·served
un·de·serv·ing
un·des·ig·nat·ed
un·de·sired
un·de·tect·able
un·de·tect·ed
un·de·ter·min·able
un·de·ter·mined
un·de·terred
un·de·vel·oped
un·di·ag·nos·able
un·di·ag·nosed
un·di·a·lec·ti·cal
un·di·dac·tic
un·dif·fer·en·ti·at·ed
un·di·gest·ed
un·di·gest·ible
un·dig·ni·fied
un·di·lut·ed
un·di·min·ished
un·dimmed
un·dis·charged
un·dis·ci·plined
un·dis·closed
un·dis·cour·aged
un·dis·cov·er·able
un·dis·cov·ered
un·dis·crim·i·nat·ing
un·dis·cussed
un·dis·mayed
un·dis·pu·ta·ble
un·dis·put·ed
un·dis·solved
un·dis·tin·guished
un·dis·tort·ed
un·dis·tract·ed
un·dis·trib·ut·ed
un·dis·turbed
un·di·vid·ed
un·do·able
un·doc·ile
un·doc·tored
un·doc·tri·naire
un·do·mes·tic
un·do·mes·ti·cat·ed
un·dot·ted
un·doubt·able
un·doubt·ing
un·drained
un·dra·ma·tized
un·drilled
un·dubbed
un·dulled
un·du·pli·cat·ed
un·dyed
un·dy·nam·ic
un·ea·ger
un·ear·marked
un·eat·able
un·eat·en
un·ec·cen·tric
un·eco·log·i·cal
un·ed·i·fy·ing
un·ed·u·ca·ble
un·ed·u·cat·ed
un·elab·o·rate
un·elect·able
un·elect·ed
un·elec·tri·fied
un·em·bar·rassed
un·em·bel·lished
un·em·bit·tered

un·em·phat·ic
un·em·phat·i·cal·ly
un·em·pir·i·cal
un·en·chant·ed
un·en·closed
un·en·cour·ag·ing
un·en·dear·ing
un·en·dur·able
un·en·dur·able·ness
un·en·dur·ably
un·en·force·able
un·en·forced
un·en·larged
un·en·light·ened
un·en·light·en·ing
un·en·riched
un·en·ter·pris·ing
un·en·thu·si·as·tic
un·en·thu·si·as·ti·cal·ly
un·en·vi·able
un·en·vi·ous
un·erot·ic
un·es·cap·able
un·es·cort·ed
un·es·tab·lished
un·eth·i·cal
un·eval·u·at·ed
un·ex·am·ined
un·ex·celled
un·ex·cit·able
un·ex·cit·ed
un·ex·cit·ing
un·ex·cused
un·ex·ot·ic
un·ex·pend·ed
un·ex·pired
un·ex·plain·able
un·ex·plained
un·ex·plod·ed
un·ex·plored
un·ex·posed
un·ex·pressed
un·ex·pur·gat·ed
un·ex·traor·di·nary
un·faked
un·fa·mous
un·fan·cy
un·fas·tid·i·ous
un·fea·si·ble
un·felt
un·fem·i·nine
un·fenced
un·fer·ment·ed
un·fer·tile
un·fer·til·ized
un·filled
un·film·able
un·fired
un·flam·boy·ant
un·flashy
un·fly·able
un·fond
un·forced
un·fore·see·able
un·fore·seen
un·for·est·ed
un·for·giv·able
un·forked
un·for·mu·lat·ed
un·forth·com·ing
un·for·ti·fied
un·fos·sil·if·er·ous
un·framed
un·free
un·free·dom
un·friv·o·lous
un·ful·fill·able
un·ful·filled
un·fun·ny
un·fur·nished
un·fused
un·gal·lant
un·gal·lant·ly
un·gar·nished
un·ge·nial
un·gen·teel
un·gen·tle
un·gen·tle·man·ly
un·gen·tri·fied
un·ger·mi·nat·ed
un·gift·ed
un·gim·micky
un·glam·or·ized
un·glam·or·ous
un·glazed
un·grace·ful
un·grace·ful·ly
un·grad·ed
un·grasp·able
un·ground
un·grouped
un·guess·able
un·guid·ed
un·hack·neyed

un·ham·pered
un·harmed
un·har·ness
un·har·vest·ed
un·hatched
un·healed
un·health·ful
un·heat·ed
un·hedged
un·heed·ed
un·heed·ing
un·help·ful
un·help·ful·ly
un·her·ald·ed
un·he·ro·ic
un·hin·dered
un·hip
un·his·tor·i·cal
un·ho·mog·e·nized
un·hon·ored
un·hope·ful
un·housed
un·hu·mor·ous
un·hurt
un·hy·dro·lyzed
un·hy·gien·ic
un·hy·phen·at·ed
un·hys·ter·i·cal
un·hys·ter·i·cal·ly
un·iden·ti·fi·able
un·iden·ti·fied
un·ideo·log·i·cal
un·id·i·om·at·ic
un·ig·nor·able
un·il·lu·mi·nat·ing
un·imag·i·na·tive
un·imag·i·na·tive·ly
un·im·mu·nized
un·im·paired
un·im·pas·sioned
un·im·ped·ed
un·im·por·tant
un·im·pos·ing
un·im·pressed
un·im·pres·sive
un·in·cor·po·rat·ed
un·in·dexed
un·in·dict·ed
un·in·dus·tri·al·ized
un·in·fect·ed
un·in·flat·ed
un·in·flect·ed
un·in·flu·enced
un·in·for·ma·tive
un·in·for·ma·tive·ly
un·in·formed
un·in·gra·ti·at·ing
un·in·hab·it·able
un·in·hab·it·ed
un·ini·ti·at·ed
un·in·jured
un·in·oc·u·lat·ed
un·in·spect·ed
un·in·spired
un·in·spir·ing
un·in·struct·ed
un·in·struc·tive
un·in·su·lat·ed
un·in·sur·able
un·in·sured
un·in·te·grat·ed
un·in·tel·lec·tu·al
un·in·tel·li·gent
un·in·tel·li·gent·ly
un·in·tel·li·gi·bil·i·ty
un·in·tel·li·gi·ble
un·in·tel·li·gi·ble·ness
un·in·tel·li·gi·bly
un·in·tend·ed
un·in·ten·tion·al
un·in·ten·tion·al·ly
un·in·ter·est·ing
un·in·ter·pret·able
un·in·ter·rupt·ed
un·in·ter·rupt·ed·ly
un·in·tim·i·dat·ed
un·in·ven·tive
un·in·vit·ed
un·in·vit·ing
un·in·volved
un·iron·ic
un·iron·i·cal·ly
un·ir·ra·di·at·ed
un·ir·ri·gat·ed
un·is·sued
un·jad·ed
un·joined
un·joint·ed
un·jus·ti·fi·able
un·jus·ti·fi·ably
un·jus·ti·fied
un·kept
un·kill·able
un·knot

un·knowl·edge·able
un·ko·sher
un·la·beled
un·la·dy·like
un·la·ment·ed
un·laun·dered
un·learn·able
un·leav·ened
un·lib·er·at·ed
un·li·censed
un·lik·able
un·lined
un·lis·ten·able
un·lit
un·lit·er·ary
un·liv·able
un·lo·cal·ized
un·lov·able
un·loved
un·lov·ing
un·lyr·i·cal
un·ma·cho
un·mag·ni·fied
un·ma·li·cious
un·ma·li·cious·ly
un·man·age·able
un·man·age·ably
un·man·aged
un·ma·nip·u·lat·ed
un·mapped
un·marked
un·mar·ket·able
un·marred
un·mar·ried
un·mas·cu·line
un·match·able
un·matched
un·meant
un·mea·sur·able
un·mea·sured
un·mech·a·nized
un·med·i·cat·ed
un·me·lo·di·ous
un·me·lo·di·ous·ness
un·mem·o·ra·ble
un·mem·o·ra·bly
un·men·tioned
un·mer·it·ed
un·mer·ry
un·met
un·me·tab·o·lized
un·mil·i·tary
un·milled
un·mined
un·miss·able
un·mix
un·mix·able
un·mixed
un·mod·ern·ized
un·mod·i·fied
un·mod·ish
un·mod·u·lat·ed
un·mo·lest·ed
un·mon·i·tored
un·mo·ti·vat·ed
un·mount·ed
un·mov·able
un·moved
un·mu·si·cal
un·name·able
un·named
un·need·ed
un·ne·go·tia·ble
un·neu·rot·ic
un·news·wor·thy
un·no·tice·able
un·no·ticed
un·nour·ish·ing
un·nu·anced
un·ob·jec·tion·able
un·ob·serv·able
un·ob·served
un·ob·struct·ed
un·ob·tain·able
un·of·fi·cial
un·of·fi·cial·ly
un·open·able
un·opened
un·op·posed
un·or·dered
un·orig·i·nal
un·or·na·ment·ed
un·os·ten·ta·tious
un·os·ten·ta·tious·ly
un·owned
un·ox·y·gen·at·ed
un·paint·ed
un·par·a·sit·ized
un·par·don·able
un·pass·able
un·pas·teur·ized
un·pas·to·ral
un·pat·ent·able
un·pa·tri·ot·ic
un·paved

un·pe·dan·tic
un·peeled
un·per·ceived
un·per·cep·tive
un·per·form·able
un·per·formed
un·per·suad·ed
un·per·sua·sive
un·per·turbed
un·pic·tur·esque
un·place·able
un·planned
un·plau·si·ble
un·play·able
un·pleased
un·pleas·ing
un·plowed
un·po·et·ic
un·po·liced
un·pol·ished
un·pol·lut·ed
un·posed
un·prac·ti·cal
un·pre·dict·abil·i·ty
un·pre·dict·able
un·pre·dict·ably
un·prej·u·diced
un·pre·med·i·tat·ed
un·pre·pared
un·pre·pared·ness
un·pre·pos·sess·ing
un·pressed
un·pres·sured
un·pres·sur·ized
un·pret·ty
un·priv·i·leged
un·prob·lem·at·ic
un·pro·cessed
un·pro·duced
un·pro·duc·tive
un·pro·fes·sion·al
un·pro·gram·ma·ble
un·pro·grammed
un·pro·gres·sive
un·prompt·ed
un·pro·nounce·able
un·pro·pi·tious
un·pros·per·ous
un·prov·able
un·proved
un·prov·en
un·pro·voked
un·pruned
un·pub·li·cized
un·pub·lished
un·punc·tu·al
un·punc·tu·al·i·ty
un·punc·tu·at·ed
un·pun·ished
un·quan·ti·fi·able
un·quench·able
un·ques·tioned
un·raised
un·ranked
un·rat·ed
un·rav·ished
un·reach·able
un·reached
un·read·able
un·read·i·ness
un·ready
un·re·al·iz·able
un·re·al·ized
un·re·cep·tive
un·re·claim·able
un·re·claimed
un·rec·og·niz·able
un·rec·og·niz·ably
un·rec·og·nized
un·rec·on·cil·able
un·rec·on·ciled
un·re·cord·ed
un·re·cov·er·able
un·re·cov·ered
un·re·cy·cla·ble
un·re·deem·able
un·re·deemed
un·re·dressed
un·re·fined
un·re·flec·tive
un·re·formed
un·re·frig·er·at·ed
un·reg·is·tered
un·reg·u·lat·ed
un·re·hearsed
un·re·in·forced
un·re·lat·ed
un·re·laxed
un·re·li·abil·i·ty
un·re·li·able
un·re·lieved
un·re·liev·ed·ly
un·re·luc·tant
un·re·mark·able

un·re·mark·ably
un·re·mem·bered
un·rem·i·nis·cent
un·re·mov·able
un·re·peat·able
un·re·pen·tant
un·re·pen·tant·ly
un·re·port·ed
un·rep·re·sen·ta·tive
un·rep·re·sen·ta·tive-
   ness
un·rep·re·sent·ed
un·re·pressed
un·re·sis·tant
un·re·solv·able
un·re·solved
un·re·spect·able
un·re·spon·sive
un·re·spon·sive·ly
un·re·spon·sive·ness
un·rest·ful
un·re·stored
un·re·strict·ed
un·re·touched
un·re·turn·able
un·re·vealed
un·re·view·able
un·re·viewed
un·re·vised
un·rev·o·lu·tion·ary
un·re·ward·ed
un·re·ward·ing
un·rhe·tor·i·cal
un·rhymed
un·rhyth·mic
un·rid·able
un·ri·fled
un·rip·ened
un·ro·man·tic
un·ro·man·ti·cal·ly
un·ro·man·ti·cized
un·roofed
un·ruled
un·rushed
un·safe
un·sal·able
un·sal·a·ried
un·salt·ed
un·sal·vage·able
un·sanc·tioned
un·san·i·tary
un·sat·is·fied
un·scal·able
un·scarred
un·scent·ed
un·sched·uled
un·schol·ar·ly
un·screened
un·scrip·tur·al
un·sea·soned
un·sea·wor·thy
un·se·cured
un·seed·ed
un·seg·ment·ed
un·self–con·scious
un·self–con·scious·ly
un·self–con·scious-
   ness
un·sell·able
un·sen·sa·tion·al
un·sen·si·tized
un·sent
un·sen·ti·men·tal
un·sep·a·rat·ed
un·se·ri·ous
un·se·ri·ous·ness
un·served
un·ser·vice·able
un·sex·u·al
un·sexy
un·shad·ed
un·shak·able

un·shak·ably
un·shak·en
un·shape·ly
un·shared
un·sharp
un·shav·en
un·shelled
un·shock·able
un·shorn
un·showy
un·signed
un·sink·able
un·sized
un·slaked
un·slick
un·smart
un·smil·ing
un·smoothed
un·soiled
un·sol·dier·ly
un·so·lic·it·ed
un·solv·able
un·solved
un·sort·ed
un·sound·ed
un·sourced
un·sown
un·spe·cial·ized
un·spec·i·fi·able
un·spe·cif·ic
un·spec·i·fied
un·spec·tac·u·lar
un·spent
un·spir·i·tu·al
un·split
un·spoiled
un·spoilt
un·spo·ken
un·sprayed
un·stained
un·stan·dard·ized
un·star·tling
un·stat·ed
un·stayed
un·ster·ile
un·ster·il·ized
un·stint·ed
un·stitch
un·stop·per
un·strained
un·strat·i·fied
un·stuffy
un·styl·ish
un·sub·dued
un·sub·si·dized
un·sub·stan·ti·at·ed
un·sub·tle
un·sub·tly
un·suc·cess
un·suit·abil·i·ty
un·suit·able
un·suit·ably
un·suit·ed
un·sul·lied
un·su·per·vised
un·sup·port·able
un·sup·port·ed
un·sure
un·sur·pass·able
un·sur·passed
un·sur·prised
un·sus·cep·ti·ble
un·sus·pect·ed
un·sus·pect·ing
un·sus·pi·cious
un·sus·tain·able
un·sweet·ened
un·sym·pa·thet·ic
un·sym·pa·thet·i·cal·ly
un·syn·chro·nized
un·sys·tem·at·ic
un·sys·tem·at·i·cal·ly

un·sys·tem·a·tized
un·tact·ful
un·tagged
un·taint·ed
un·tal·ent·ed
un·tam·able
un·tamed
un·tanned
un·tar·nished
un·taxed
un·teach·able
un·tech·ni·cal
un·tem·pered
un·ten·ant·ed
un·tend·ed
un·ten·ured
un·test·able
un·test·ed
un·the·o·ret·i·cal
un·threat·en·ing
un·thrifty
un·till·able
un·tilled
un·to·geth·er
un·trace·able
un·tra·di·tion·al
un·tra·di·tion·al·ly
un·trained
un·tram·meled
un·trans·formed
un·trans·lat·abil·i·ty
un·trans·lat·able
un·trans·lat·ed
un·trav·eled
un·tra·versed
un·treat·ed
un·trendy
un·trimmed
un·trust·ing
un·trust·wor·thy
un·tucked
un·tuft·ed
un·typ·i·cal
un·typ·i·cal·ly
un·un·der·stand·able
un·us·able
un·uti·lized
un·vac·ci·nat·ed
un·var·ied
un·vary·ing
un·ven·ti·lat·ed
un·ver·bal·ized
un·ver·i·fi·able
un·versed
un·vi·a·ble
un·vis·it·ed
un·want·ed
un·war·like
un·war·rant·ed
un·wa·ver·ing
un·wa·ver·ing·ly
un·waxed
un·weaned
un·wear·able
un·weath·ered
un·wed
un·weight·ed
un·wel·come
un·white
un·willed
un·win·na·ble
un·wom·an·ly
un·won
un·work·abil·i·ty
un·work·able
un·worked
un·wor·ried
un·wound·ed
un·wo·ven
un·wrin·kled
un·young

un·abashed \ˌən-ə-ˈbasht\ *adj* [ME *unabaiste*, fr. *un-* + *abaiste*, pp. of *abaissen, abaishen* to abash] (15c) : not abashed : UNDISGUISED, UN-APOLOGETIC — **un·abash·ed·ly** \-ˈbash-əd-lē\ *adv*

un·abat·ed \ˌən-ə-ˈbā-təd\ *adj* (ca. 1611) : not abated : being at full strength or force — **un·abat·ed·ly** *adv*

un·able \ˌən-ˈā-bəl\ *adj* (14c) : not able : INCAPABLE: as **a** : UNQUALI-FIED, INCOMPETENT **b** : IMPOTENT, HELPLESS

un·abridged \ˌən-ə-ˈbrijd\ *adj* (1599) **1** : not abridged : COMPLETE ⟨an ~ reprint of a novel⟩ **2** : being the most complete of its class : not based on one larger ⟨an ~ dictionary⟩

un·ac·cept·able \ˌən-ik-ˈsep-tə-bəl, -ak-\ *adj* (15c) : not acceptable : not pleasing or welcome — **un·ac·cept·abil·i·ty** \-ˌsep-tə-ˈbi-lə-tē\ *n* — **un·ac·cept·ably** \-ˈsep-tə-blē\ *adv*

\ə\ abut \ˈə, ˌə\ kitten, F table \ər\ **fur**ther \a\ ash \ā\ ace \ä\ mop, mar
\au̇\ **out** \ch\ **chin** \e\ bet \ē\ **easy** \g\ go \i\ hit \ī\ **ice** \j\ job
\ŋ\ sing \ō\ go \ȯ\ law \ȯi\ **boy** \th\ **thin** \<u>th</u>\ the \ü\ loot \u̇\ foot
\y\ yet \zh\ vision, beige \k, ⁿ, œ, ɶ, ᵊ\ *see* Guide to Pronunciation

un·ac·com·pa·nied \ˌən-ə-ˈkəmp-nēd, -ˈkämp-; -ˈkəm-pə-, -ˈkäm-\ *adj* (1545) : not accompanied; *esp* : being without instrumental accompaniment
un·ac·count·able \ˌən-ə-ˈkau̇n-tə-bəl\ *adj* (1643) **1** : not to be accounted for : INEXPLICABLE, STRANGE **2** : not to be called to account : not responsible — **un·ac·count·abil·i·ty** \-ˌkau̇n-tə-ˈbi-lə-tē\ *n*
un·ac·count·ably \-ˈkau̇n-tə-blē\ *adv* (1687) **1** : in an unaccountable manner ⟨looking ~ upset⟩ ⟨heat was ~ disappearing⟩ **2** : for reasons that are hard to understand ⟨~, he stayed right there⟩
un·ac·count·ed \-ˈkau̇n-təd\ *adj* (1689) : not accounted : UNEXPLAINED — often used with *for*
un·ac·cus·tomed \ˌən-ə-ˈkəs-təmd\ *adj* (1526) **1** : not customary : not usual or common **2** : not habituated — usu. used with *to* — **un·ac·cus·tomed·ly** \-təmd-lē\ *adv*
una cor·da \ˌü-nə-ˈkȯr-də, -(ˌ)dä\ *adv or adj* [It, lit., one string] (ca. 1849) : with soft pedal depressed — used as a direction in piano music
un·adorned \ˌən-ə-ˈdȯrnd\ *adj* (1633) : not adorned : lacking embellishment or decoration : PLAIN, SIMPLE
un·adul·ter·at·ed \ˌən-ə-ˈdəl-tə-ˌrā-təd\ *adj* (ca. 1719) **1** : not adulterated : PURE ⟨~ food⟩ **2** : COMPLETE, UNQUALIFIED ⟨an ~ fool⟩ — **un·adul·ter·at·ed·ly** *adv*
un·ad·vised \ˌən-əd-ˈvīzd\ *adj* (15c) **1** : done without due consideration : RASH ⟨~ and dangerous dealings with the terrorists⟩ **2** : not prudent : ILL-ADVISED ⟨done with ~ haste⟩ — **un·ad·vis·ed·ly** \-ˈvī-zəd-lē\ *adv*
un·af·fect·ed \ˌən-ə-ˈfek-təd\ *adj* (ca. 1586) **1** : not influenced or changed mentally, physically, or chemically **2** : free from affectation : GENUINE — **un·af·fect·ed·ly** *adv* — **un·af·fect·ed·ness** *n*
un·ag·ing *or* **un·age·ing** \ˌən-ˈā-jiŋ\ *adj* (1860) : AGELESS
una·kite \ˈyü-nə-ˌkīt\ *n* [*Unaka* Mountains, Tenn. & N.C. + [1]*-ite*] (1874) : an altered igneous rock that is usu. opaque with green, black, pink, and white flecks and is usu. used as a gemstone
un·alien·able \ˌən-ˈāl-yə-nə-bəl, -ˈā-lē-ə-\ *adj* (ca. 1611) : INALIENABLE
un·aligned \ˌən-ə-ˈlīnd\ *adj* (ca. 1934) : NONALIGNED
un·al·loyed \ˌən-ə-ˈlȯid\ *adj* (1667) : not alloyed : UNMIXED, UNQUALIFIED, PURE ⟨~ metals⟩ ⟨~ happiness⟩
un·al·ter·able \ˌən-ˈȯl-t(ə-)rə-bəl\ *adj* (ca. 1605) : not capable of being altered or changed ⟨an ~ resolve⟩ ⟨~ hatred⟩ — **un·al·ter·abil·i·ty** \ˌən-ˌȯl-t(ə-)rə-ˈbi-lə-tē\ *n* — **un·al·ter·able·ness** \ˌən-ˈȯl-t(ə-)rə-bəl-nəs\ *n* — **un·al·ter·ably** \-blē\ *adv*
un·am·big·u·ous \ˌən-am-ˈbi-gyə-wəs\ *adj* (1743) : not ambiguous : CLEAR, PRECISE ⟨~ evidence⟩ — **un·am·big·u·ous·ly** *adv*
un·am·biv·a·lent \-ˈbi-və-lənt\ *adj* (1945) : not ambivalent : CLEAR-CUT, DEFINITE — **un·am·biv·a·lent·ly** *adv*
un–Amer·i·can \ˌən-ə-ˈmer-ə-kən\ *adj* (1818) : not American : not characteristic of or consistent with American customs, principles, or traditions
un·an·chored \ˌən-ˈaŋ-kərd\ *adj* (1651) **1** : not anchored : not at anchor **2** : not having a firm basis or foundation
un·aneled \ˌən-ə-ˈnēld\ *adj* [*un-* + *aneled*, pp. of *anele* to anoint, fr. ME, fr. *an* on + *elen* to anoint, fr. *ele* oil, fr. OE, fr. L *oleum* — more at OIL] (ca. 1601) *archaic* : not having received extreme unction
una·nim·i·ty \ˌyü-nə-ˈni-mə-tē\ *n* (15c) : the quality or state of being unanimous
unan·i·mous \yu̇-ˈna-nə-məs\ *adj* [L *unanimus*, fr. *unus* one + *animus* mind — more at ONE, ANIMATE] (1624) **1** : being of one mind : AGREEING **2** : formed with or indicating unanimity : having the agreement and consent of all — **unan·i·mous·ly** *adv*
un·an·swer·able \ˌən-ˈan(t)s-rə-bəl, -ˈan(t)-sə-\ *adj* (1613) : not capable of being answered; *also* : IRREFUTABLE — **un·an·swer·abil·i·ty** \ˌən-ˌan(t)s-rə-ˈbi-lə-tē, -ˌan(t)-sə-\ *n* — **un·an·swer·ably** \ˌən-ˈan(t)s-rə-blē, -ˈan(t)-sə-\ *adv*
un·an·swered \ˌən-ˈan(t)-sərd\ *adj* (14c) **1** : not answered ⟨~ letters⟩ **2** : scored in succession during a period in which an opponent fails to score ⟨scored 20 ~ points in the last quarter⟩
un·an·tic·i·pat·ed \ˌən-an-ˈti-sə-ˌpā-təd\ *adj* (ca. 1779) : not anticipated : UNEXPECTED, UNFORESEEN — **un·an·tic·i·pat·ed·ly** *adv*
un·apol·o·get·ic \ˌən-ə-ˌpä-lə-ˈje-tik\ *adj* (1834) : not apologetic : offered, put forward, or being such without apology or qualification ⟨an ~ liberal⟩ — **un·apol·o·get·i·cal·ly** \-ti-k(ə-)lē\ *adv*
un·ap·peal·able \ˌən-ə-ˈpē-lə-bəl\ *adj* (1635) : not appealable : not subject to appeal
un·ap·peal·ing \-ˈpē-liŋ\ *adj* (ca. 1846) : not appealing : UNATTRACTIVE — **un·ap·peal·ing·ly** \-liŋ-lē\ *adv*
un·ap·peas·able \-ˈpē-zə-bəl\ *adj* (1561) : not to be appeased : IMPLACABLE — **un·ap·peas·ably** \-blē\ *adv*
un·ap·pe·tiz·ing \ˌən-ˈa-pə-ˌtī-ziŋ\ *adj* (1884) : not appetizing : INSIPID, UNATTRACTIVE — **un·ap·pe·tiz·ing·ly** \-ziŋ-lē\ *adv*
un·ap·pre·ci·a·tion \ˌən-ə-ˌprē-shē-ˈā-shən\ *n* (1886) : failure to appreciate something
un·ap·proach·able \ˌən-ə-ˈprō-chə-bəl\ *adj* (1581) **1** : not approachable : physically inaccessible **2** : discouraging intimacies : RESERVED — **un·ap·proach·abil·i·ty** \-ˌprō-chə-ˈbi-lə-tē\ *n* — **un·ap·proach·ably** \-ˈprō-chə-blē\ *adv*
un·apt \ˌən-ˈapt\ *adj* (14c) **1** : INAPPROPRIATE, UNSUITABLE ⟨an ~ quote⟩ **2** : not accustomed and not likely ⟨a teacher ~ to tolerate carelessness⟩ **3** : DULL, BACKWARD ⟨~ scholars⟩ — **un·apt·ly** \-ˈap(t)-lē\ *adv* — **un·apt·ness** \-nəs\ *n*
un·ar·gu·able \ˌən-ˈär-gyə-wə-bəl\ *adj* (1881) : not arguable
un·ar·gu·ably \-blē\ *adv* (1929) : it cannot be argued : UNQUESTIONABLY
un·arm \ˌən-ˈärm\ *vt* (14c) : DISARM
un·armed \-ˈärmd\ *adj* (14c) **1** : not armed or armored ⟨~ civilians⟩; *also* : not using or involving a weapon ⟨~ robbery⟩ **2** : having no hard and sharp projections (as spines, spurs, or claws)
un·ar·tic·u·lat·ed \ˌən-är-ˈti-kyə-ˌlā-təd\ *adj* (ca. 1700) : not articulated; *esp* : not carefully reasoned or analyzed
una·ry \ˈyü-nə-rē\ *adj* [L *unus* one + E *-ary*] (1923) : having, consisting of, or acting on a single element, item, or component : MONADIC
un·ashamed \ˌən-ə-ˈshāmd\ *adj* (1600) : not ashamed : being without guilt, self-consciousness, or doubt — **un·asham·ed·ly** \-ˈshā-məd-lē\ *adv*
un·asked \ˌən-ˈas(k)t\ *adj* (13c) **1** : not being asked : UNINVITED **2** : not asked ⟨~ questions⟩ **3** : not asked for ⟨~ advice⟩
un·as·sail·able \ˌən-ə-ˈsā-lə-bəl\ *adj* (1596) : not assailable : not liable to doubt, attack, or question ⟨an ~ argument⟩ ⟨an ~ alibi⟩ — **un·as·sail·abil·i·ty** \-ˌsā-lə-ˈbi-lə-tē\ *n* — **un·as·sail·able·ness** \-ˈsā-lə-bəl-nəs\ *n* — **un·as·sail·ably** \-blē\ *adv*
un·as·ser·tive \ˌən-ə-ˈsər-tiv\ *adj* (1861) : not assertive : MODEST, SHY — **un·as·ser·tive·ly** *adv*
un·as·sist·ed \ˌən-ə-ˈsis-təd\ *adj* (1607) **1** : not assisted : lacking help **2** : made or performed without an assist ⟨an ~ double play⟩
un·as·suage·able \ˌən-ə-ˈswā-jə-bəl\ *adj* (ca. 1611) : not capable of being assuaged
un·as·sum·ing \ˌən-ə-ˈsü-miŋ\ *adj* (1722) : not assuming : MODEST ⟨an ~ librarian⟩ ⟨an ~ manner⟩ ⟨an ~ neighborhood⟩ — **un·as·sum·ing·ness** *n*
un·at·tached \ˌən-ə-ˈtacht\ *adj* (1796) **1 a** : not assigned or committed (as to a particular task, organization, or person); *esp* : not married or engaged **b** : not seized as security for a legal judgment **2** : not joined or united ⟨~ buildings⟩
un·at·trac·tive \-ˈtrak-tiv\ *adj* (1813) : not attractive : PLAIN, DULL — **un·at·trac·tive·ly** *adv* — **un·at·trac·tive·ness** *n*
un·avail·ing \-ˈvā-liŋ\ *adj* (1670) : not availing : FUTILE, USELESS — **un·avail·ing·ly** \-liŋ-lē\ *adv* — **un·avail·ing·ness** *n*
un·avoid·able \ˌən-ə-ˈvȯi-də-bəl\ *adj* (15c) : not avoidable : INEVITABLE ⟨the accident was ~⟩ — **un·avoid·ably** \-blē\ *adv*
[1]**un·aware** \-ə-ˈwer\ *adv* (1581) : UNAWARES
[2]**unaware** *adj* (1696) : not aware : IGNORANT ⟨~ of the problem⟩ — **un·aware·ly** *adv* — **un·aware·ness** *n*
un·awares \-ˈwerz\ *adv* [*un-* + *aware* + *-s*, adv. suffix, fr. ME, fr. *-s*, gen. sing. ending of nouns — more at -s] (1530) **1** : without design, attention, preparation, or premeditation **2** : without warning : SUDDENLY, UNEXPECTEDLY
un·backed \ˌən-ˈbakt\ *adj* (1609) : lacking support or aid
[1]**un·bal·ance** \-ˈba-lən(t)s\ *vt* (1854) : to put out of balance
[2]**unbalance** *n* (1855) : lack of balance : IMBALANCE
un·bal·anced \-lən(t)st\ *adj* (1650) : not balanced: as **a** : not in equilibrium **b** : mentally disordered or deranged **c** : not adjusted so as to make credits equal to debits ⟨an ~ account⟩
un·bal·last·ed \-ˈba-lə-stəd\ *adj* (1644) : not furnished with or steadied by ballast : UNSTEADY
un·ban·dage \-ˈban-dij\ *vt* (1835) : to remove a bandage from
un·bar \ˌən-ˈbär\ *vt* (14c) : to remove a bar from : UNBOLT, OPEN
un·bar·bered \-ˈbär-bərd\ *adj* (1845) : having long and esp. unkempt hair
un·barred \-ˈbärd\ *adj* (1603) **1** : not secured by a bar : UNLOCKED **2** : not marked with bars
un·bat·ed \-ˈbā-təd\ *adj* (ca. 1597) **1** : UNABATED **2** *archaic* : not blunted
un·be \-ˈbē\ *vi* (15c) *archaic* : to lack or cease to have being
un·bear·able \ˌən-ˈber-ə-bəl\ *adj* (15c) : not bearable : UNENDURABLE ⟨~ pain⟩ — **un·bear·ably** \-blē\ *adv*
un·beat·able \-ˈbē-tə-bəl\ *adj* (1855) **1** : not capable of being defeated **2** : possessing unsurpassable qualities — **un·beat·ably** \-blē\ *adv*
un·beat·en \-ˈbē-tᵊn\ *adj* (13c) **1** : not pounded or beaten : not whipped **2** : not traversed : UNTRODDEN **3** : not defeated
un·beau·ti·ful \-ˈbyü-ti-fəl\ *adj* (15c) : not beautiful : UNATTRACTIVE — **un·beau·ti·ful·ly** \-f(ə-)lē\ *adv*
un·be·com·ing \ˌən-bi-ˈkə-miŋ\ *adj* (1598) : not becoming ⟨an ~ dress⟩; *esp* : not according with the standards appropriate to one's position or condition of life ⟨~ conduct⟩ ***syn*** see INDECOROUS — **un·be·com·ing·ly** \-miŋ-lē\ *adv* — **un·be·com·ing·ness** *n*
un·be·knownst \ˌən-bi-ˈnōn(t)st\ *also* **un·be·known** \-ˈnōn\ *adj* [[1]*un-* + obs. E *beknown* known; *unbeknownst*, irreg. fr. *unbeknown*] (1636) **1** : happening or existing without the knowledge of someone specified — usu. used with *to* ⟨~ to us rumors were flying⟩ **2** : UNKNOWN
un·be·lief \ˌən-bə-ˈlēf\ *n* (12c) : incredulity or skepticism esp. in matters of religious faith
un·be·liev·able \-ˈlē-və-bəl\ *adj* (1548) : too improbable for belief ⟨the plot is unreal and ~⟩; *also* : of such a superlative degree as to be hard to believe ⟨the destruction was ~⟩ ⟨made an ~ catch in center field⟩ — **un·be·liev·ably** \-blē\ *adv*
un·be·liev·er \-ˈlē-vər\ *n* (1526) **1** : one that does not believe in a particular religious faith **2** : one that does not believe : an incredulous person : DOUBTER, SKEPTIC
un·be·liev·ing \-ˈlē-viŋ\ *adj* (14c) : marked by unbelief : INCREDULOUS, SKEPTICAL — **un·be·liev·ing·ly** \-viŋ-lē\ *adv*
un·belt·ed \ˌən-ˈbel-təd\ *adj* (1814) : not furnished with a belt
un·bend \-ˈbend\ *vb* **-bent** \-ˈbent\; **-bend·ing** *vt* (13c) **1** : to free from flexure : make or allow to become straight ⟨~ a bow⟩ **2** : to cause (as the mind) to relax **3 a** : to unfasten (as a sail) from a spar or stay **b** : to cast loose (as a rope) : UNTIE ~ *vi* **1** : to relax one's severity, stiffness, or austerity **2** : to cease to be bent : become straight
un·bend·able \-ˈben-də-bəl\ *adj* (1825) : SINGLE-MINDED, FIRM
un·bend·ing \-ˈben-diŋ\ *adj* [[1]*un-*] (ca. 1688) **1** : not bending : UNYIELDING, INFLEXIBLE ⟨an ~ will⟩ **2** : aloof or unsocial in manner : RESERVED
un·be·seem·ing \ˌən-bi-ˈsē-miŋ\ *adj* (1583) : not befitting : UNBECOMING
un·bi·ased \ˌən-ˈbī-əst\ *adj* (1607) **1** : free from bias; *esp* : free from all prejudice and favoritism : eminently fair ⟨an ~ opinion⟩ **2** : having an expected value equal to a population parameter being estimated ⟨an ~ estimate of the population mean⟩ ***syn*** see FAIR — **un·bi·ased·ness** \-əs(t)-nəs\ *n*
un·bib·li·cal \ˌən-ˈbi-bli-kəl\ *adj* (1828) : contrary to or unsanctioned by the Bible
un·bid·den \-ˈbi-dᵊn\ *also* **un·bid** \-ˈbid\ *adj* [ME *unbiden, unbeden*, fr. OE *unbeden*, fr. *un-* + *beden*, pp. of *biddan* to entreat — more at BID] (bef. 12c) : not bidden : UNASKED, UNINVITED ⟨barged in ~⟩
un·bind \-ˈbīnd\ *vt* **-bound** \-ˈbau̇nd\; **-bind·ing** (bef. 12c) **1** : to remove a band from : free from fastenings : UNTIE, UNFASTEN **2** : to set free : RELEASE
un·bit·ted \-ˈbi-təd\ *adj* [[2]*bit*] (ca. 1586) *archaic* : UNBRIDLED, UNCONTROLLED ⟨our ~ lusts —Shak.⟩
un·blenched \-ˈblencht\ *adj* (1634) : not disconcerted : UNDAUNTED
un·blessed *also* **un·blest** \ˌən-ˈblest\ *adj* (13c) **1** : EVIL, ACCURSED **2** : not blessed ⟨an ~ marriage⟩

un·blind·ed \-ˈblīn-dəd\ *adj* (ca. 1611) : not blinded; *esp* : free from illusion
un·blink·ing \-ˈbliŋ-kiŋ\ *adj* (1850) **1** : not blinking **2** : not showing signs of emotion, doubt, or confusion ⟨~ frankness⟩ — **un·blink·ing·ly** \-kiŋ-lē\ *adv*
un·block \-ˈbläk\ *vt* (ca. 1611) : to free from being blocked
un·blush·ing \-ˈblə-shiŋ\ *adj* (1567) **1** : not blushing **2** : SHAMELESS, UNABASHED ⟨~ greed⟩ — **un·blush·ing·ly** \-shiŋ-lē\ *adv*
un·bod·ied \-ˈbä-dēd\ *adj* (1513) **1** : having no body : INCORPOREAL; *also* : freed from the body ⟨~ souls⟩ **2** : FORMLESS
[1]**un·bolt** \ˌən-ˈbōlt\ *vt* (1581) : to open or unfasten by withdrawing a bolt
un·bolt·ed \-ˈbōl-təd\ *adj* [[2]*bolt*] (ca. 1580) : not fastened by bolts
[2]**unbolted** *adj* [[4]*bolt*] (ca. 1598) : not sifted ⟨~ flour⟩
un·bon·net·ed \ˌən-ˈbä-nə-təd\ *adj* (ca. 1605) : BAREHEADED
un·born \-ˈbȯrn\ *adj* (bef. 12c) **1** : not born : not brought into life **2** : still to appear : FUTURE **3** : existing without birth
un·bos·om \-ˈbu̇-zəm *also* -ˈbü-\ *vt* (ca. 1595) **1** : to give expression to : DISCLOSE, REVEAL **2** : to disclose the thoughts or feelings of (oneself) ~ *vi* : to unbosom oneself
un·bound \-ˈbau̇nd\ *adj* (bef. 12c) : not bound: as **a** (1) : not fastened (2) : not confined **b** : not having the leaves fastened together ⟨an ~ book⟩ **c** : not bound together with other issues ⟨~ periodicals⟩ **d** : not held in chemical or physical combination
un·bound·ed \-ˈbau̇n-dəd\ *adj* (1565) **1** : having no limit ⟨~ joy⟩ **2** : UNRESTRAINED, UNCONTROLLED — **un·bound·ed·ness** *n*
un·bowed \ˌən-ˈbau̇d\ *adj* (14c) **1** : not bowed down **2** : not subdued ⟨bloodied but ~⟩
un·box \-ˈbäks\ *vt* (ca. 1611) : to remove from a box
un·brace \-ˈbrās\ *vt* (15c) **1** : to free or detach by or as if by untying or removing a brace or bond **2** : ENFEEBLE, WEAKEN
un·braid \-ˈbrād\ *vt* (14c) : to separate the strands of : UNRAVEL
un·branched \-ˈbrancht\ *adj* (1665) **1** : having no branches ⟨a straight ~ trunk⟩ **2** : not divided into branches ⟨a leaf with ~ veins⟩
un·brand·ed \-ˈbran-dəd\ *adj* (1749) **1** : not marked with the owner's name or mark ⟨~ cattle⟩ **2** : not sold under a brand name
un·breath·able \-ˈbrē-t͟hə-bəl\ *adj* (1846) : not fit for being breathed
un·bred \-ˈbred\ *adj* (1622) **1** *obs* : ILL-BRED **2** : not taught : UNTRAINED **3** : not bred : never having been bred ⟨an ~ heifer⟩
un·bri·dle \ˌən-ˈbrī-dᵊl\ *vt* (15c) : to free or loose from a bridle; *broadly* : to set loose : free from restraint
un·bri·dled \-ˈbrī-dᵊld\ *adj* (14c) **1** : UNRESTRAINED ⟨~ enthusiasm⟩ **2** : not confined by a bridle
un·broke \-ˈbrōk\ *adj* (14c) : UNBROKEN
un·bro·ken \-ˈbrō-kən\ *adj* (14c) : not broken: as **a** : not violated **b** : WHOLE, INTACT **c** : not subdued : UNTAMED; *esp* : not trained for service or use ⟨~ colts⟩ **d** : CONTINUOUS ⟨miles of ~ forest⟩ **e** : not plowed **f** : not disorganized ⟨advanced in ~ ranks⟩
un·buck·le \-ˈbə-kəl\ *vt* (14c) : to loose the buckle of : UNFASTEN ~ *vi* **1** : to loosen buckles **2** : RELAX
un·budge·able \-ˈbə-jə-bəl\ *adj* (ca. 1929) : not able to be budged or changed : INFLEXIBLE ⟨an ~ optimist⟩ — **un·budge·ably** \-blē\ *adv*
un·budg·ing \-ˈbə-jiŋ\ *adj* (ca. 1934) : not budging : resisting movement or change — **un·budg·ing·ly** \-jiŋ-lē\ *adv*
un·build \ˌən-ˈbild\ *vb* **-built** \-ˈbilt\; **-build·ing** *vt* (ca. 1608) : to pull down : DEMOLISH, RAZE ~ *vi* : to destroy something
un·built \-ˈbilt\ *adj* (15c) **1** : not built : not yet constructed **2** : not built on ⟨an ~ plot⟩
un·bun·dle \-ˈbən-dᵊl\ *vi* (1969) : to give separate prices for equipment and supporting services ~ *vt* : to price separately
un·bur·den \-ˈbər-dᵊn\ *vt* (ca. 1538) **1** : to free or relieve from a burden **2** : to relieve oneself of (as cares, fears, or worries) : cast off
un·bur·dened \-ˈbər-dᵊnd\ *adj* (1548) : not burdened : having no weight or load ⟨~ by the expectations of others⟩
un·but·ton \-ˈbə-tᵊn\ *vt* (14c) **1** : to loose the buttons of **2** : to open by or as if by loosing buttons ~ *vi* : to undo buttons
un·but·toned \-tᵊnd\ *adj* (1583) **1 a** : not buttoned **b** : not provided with buttons **2** : not under constraint : free and unrestricted in action and expression ⟨the musicians' ~ energy⟩
Unc *abbr* uncirculated
un·cage \ˌən-ˈkāj\ *vt* (1620) : to release from or as if from a cage : free from restraint
un·cal·cu·lat·ed \-ˈkal-kyə-ˌlā-təd\ *adj* (1641) : not planned or thought out beforehand : SPONTANEOUS ⟨~ confrontations⟩
un·cal·cu·lat·ing \-ˌlā-tiŋ\ *adj* (1821) : not based on or marked by calculation ⟨~ love⟩ ⟨~ gallantry⟩
un·called–for \ˌən-ˈkȯl(d)-ˌfȯr\ *adj* (ca. 1656) **1** : not called for or needed : UNNECESSARY **2** : being or offered without provocation or justification ⟨an ~ display of temper⟩ ⟨~ insults⟩
un·can·ny \-ˈka-nē\ *adj* (1773) **1 a** : seeming to have a supernatural character or origin : EERIE, MYSTERIOUS **b** : being beyond what is normal or expected : suggesting superhuman or supernatural powers ⟨an ~ sense of direction⟩ **2** *chiefly Scot* : SEVERE, PUNISHING ***syn*** see WEIRD — **un·can·ni·ly** \-ˈka-nə-lē\ *adv* — **un·can·ni·ness** \-ˈka-nē-nəs\ *n*
un·caused \-ˈkȯzd\ *adj* (15c) : having no antecedent cause
un·ceas·ing \-ˈsē-siŋ\ *adj* (14c) : never ceasing : CONTINUOUS, INCESSANT ⟨~ efforts⟩ ⟨~ vigilance⟩ — **un·ceas·ing·ly** \-siŋ-lē\ *adv*
un·cel·e·brat·ed \-ˈse-lə-ˌbrā-təd\ *adj* (1660) **1** : not formally honored or commemorated **2** : not famous : OBSCURE ⟨solid but ~ players⟩
un·cer·e·mo·ni·ous \ˌən-ˌser-ə-ˈmō-nē-əs\ *adj* (1598) **1** : not ceremonious : INFORMAL **2** : ABRUPT, RUDE ⟨an ~ dismissal⟩ — **un·cer·e·mo·ni·ous·ly** *adv* — **un·cer·e·mo·ni·ous·ness** *n*
un·cer·tain \ˌən-ˈsər-tᵊn\ *adj* (14c) **1** : INDEFINITE, INDETERMINATE ⟨the time of departure is ~⟩ **2** : not certain to occur : PROBLEMATICAL ⟨his success was ~⟩ **3** : not reliable : UNTRUSTWORTHY ⟨an ~ ally⟩ **4 a** : not known beyond doubt : DUBIOUS ⟨an ~ claim⟩ **b** : not having certain knowledge : DOUBTFUL ⟨remains ~ about her plans⟩ **c** : not clearly identified or defined ⟨a fire of ~ origin⟩ **5** : not constant : VARIABLE, FITFUL ⟨an ~ breeze⟩ — **un·cer·tain·ly** *adv* — **un·cer·tain·ness** \-tᵊn-(n)əs\ *n*
un·cer·tain·ty \-tᵊn-tē\ *n* (14c) **1** : the quality or state of being uncertain : DOUBT **2** : something that is uncertain
syn UNCERTAINTY, DOUBT, DUBIETY, SKEPTICISM, SUSPICION, MISTRUST mean lack of sureness about someone or something. UNCERTAINTY may range from a falling short of certainty to an almost complete lack of conviction or knowledge esp. about an outcome or result ⟨assumed the role of manager without hesitation or *uncertainty*⟩. DOUBT suggests both uncertainty and inability to make a decision ⟨plagued by *doubts* as to what to do⟩. DUBIETY stresses a wavering between conclusions ⟨felt some *dubiety* about its practicality⟩. SKEPTICISM implies unwillingness to believe without conclusive evidence ⟨an economic forecast greeted with *skepticism*⟩. SUSPICION stresses lack of faith in the truth, reality, fairness, or reliability of something or someone ⟨regarded the stranger with *suspicion*⟩. MISTRUST implies a genuine doubt based upon suspicion ⟨had a great *mistrust* of doctors⟩.
uncertainty principle *n* (1929) : a principle in quantum mechanics: it is impossible to discern simultaneously and with high accuracy both the position and the momentum of a particle (as an electron) — called also *Heisenberg uncertainty principle*
UNCF *abbr* United Negro College Fund
un·chain \ˌən-ˈchān\ *vt* (1582) : to free by or as if by removing a chain : set loose ⟨~ workers from their desks⟩
un·chancy \-ˈchan(t)-sē\ *adj* (1533) **1** *chiefly Scot* : ILL-FATED **2** *chiefly Scot* : DANGEROUS
un·change·able \-ˈchān-jə-bəl\ *adj* (14c) : not changing or to be changed : IMMUTABLE ⟨~ documents⟩ ⟨~ facts⟩ — **un·change·abil·i·ty** \ˌən-ˌchān-jə-ˈbi-lə-tē\ *n* — **un·change·able·ness** \ˌən-ˈchān-jə-bəl-nəs\ *n* — **un·change·ably** \-blē\ *adv*
un·chang·ing \-ˈchān-jiŋ\ *adj* (1587) : CONSTANT, INVARIABLE ⟨~ beliefs⟩ — **un·chang·ing·ly** \-jiŋ-lē\ *adv* — **un·chang·ing·ness** *n*
un·char·ac·ter·is·tic \ˌən-ˌka-rik-tə-ˈris-tik\ *adj* (1748) : not characteristic : not typical or distinctive ⟨~ outbursts of temper⟩ — **un·char·ac·ter·is·ti·cal·ly** \-ti-k(ə-)lē\ *adv*
un·charge \ˌən-ˈchärj\ *vt* (14c) *obs* : ACQUIT
un·charged \-ˈchärjd\ *adj* (1815) : not charged; *specif* : having no electric charge
un·char·i·ta·ble \-ˈcha-rə-tə-bəl\ *adj* (15c) : lacking in charity : severe in judging : HARSH ⟨~ comments⟩ — **un·char·i·ta·ble·ness** *n* — **un·char·i·ta·bly** \-blē\ *adv*
un·chart·ed \-ˈchär-təd\ *adj* (1832) : not recorded or plotted on a map, chart, or plan ⟨an ~ island⟩; *broadly* : UNKNOWN ⟨a discussion moving into ~ territory⟩
un·chaste \-ˈchāst\ *adj* (14c) : not chaste : lacking in chastity — **un·chaste·ly** *adv* — **un·chaste·ness** \-ˈchās(t)-nəs\ *n*
un·chas·ti·ty \-ˈchas-tə-tē\ *n* (14c) : the quality or state of being unchaste
un·chiv·al·rous \-ˈshi-vəl-rəs\ *adj* (1830) : not chivalrous : lacking in chivalry ⟨an ~ rivalry⟩ — **un·chiv·al·rous·ly** *adv*
un·choke \-ˈchōk\ *vt* (1588) : to clear of obstruction
un·chris·tian \-ˈkris-chən, -ˈkrish-\ *adj* (1555) **1** : not of the Christian faith **2 a** : contrary to the Christian spirit or character **b** : UNCIVILIZED, BARBAROUS
un·church \-ˈchərch\ *vt* (ca. 1620) **1** : to expel from a church : EXCOMMUNICATE **2** : to deprive of a church or of status as a church
un·churched \-ˈchərcht\ *adj* (1657) : not belonging to or connected with a church
unci *pl of* UNCUS
[1]**un·cial** \ˈən(t)-shəl, -sē-əl\ *adj* [LL *unciales* (*litterae*) uncial (letters), fr. L, pl. of *uncialis* weighing an ounce, fr. *uncia* twelfth part, ounce — more at OUNCE] (1712) : written in the style or size of uncials — **un·cial·ly** *adv*
[2]**uncial** *n* (ca. 1775) **1** : a handwriting used esp. in Greek and Latin manuscripts of the fourth to the eighth centuries A.D. and made with somewhat rounded separated majuscules but having cursive forms for some letters **2** : an uncial letter **3** : a manuscript written in uncial

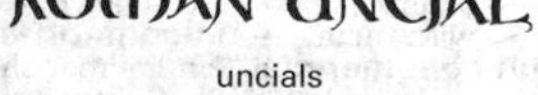

uncials

un·ci·form \ˈən(t)-sə-ˌfȯrm\ *adj* [NL *unciformis*, fr. L *uncus* hook + *-formis* -form — more at ANGLE] (ca. 1734) : hook-shaped : UNCINATE
un·ci·na·ri·a·sis \ˌən-ˌsi-nə-ˈrī-ə-səs\ *n* [NL, fr. *Uncinaria*, genus that includes hookworms, fr. L *uncinus* hook] (1902) : HOOKWORM 2
un·ci·nate \ˈən(t)-sə-ˌnāt\ *adj* [L *uncinatus*, fr. *uncinus* hook, fr. *uncus*] (ca. 1760) : bent at the tip like a hook : HOOKED ⟨an ~ achene⟩
un·cir·cu·lat·ed \ˌən-ˈsər-kyə-ˌlā-təd\ *adj* (1917) : issued for use as money but kept out of circulation (as for preservation in a collection)
un·cir·cum·cised \ˌən-ˈsər-kəm-ˌsīzd\ *adj* (14c) **1** : not circumcised **2** : spiritually impure : HEATHEN — **un·cir·cum·ci·sion** \ˌən-ˌsər-kəm-ˈsi-zhən\ *n*
un·civ·il \ˌən-ˈsi-vəl\ *adj* (1553) **1** : not civilized : BARBAROUS **2** : lacking in courtesy : ILL-MANNERED, IMPOLITE ⟨~ remarks⟩ **3** : not conducive to civic harmony and welfare — **un·civ·il·ly** \-və-lē\ *adv*
un·civ·i·lized \-ˈsi-və-ˌlīzd\ *adj* (1607) **1** : not civilized : BARBAROUS **2** : remote from settled areas : WILD
un·clamp \-ˈklamp\ *vt* (1809) : to loosen the clamp of : to free from a clamp
un·clar·i·ty \-ˈkla-rə-tē\ *n*, *pl* **-ties** (1923) : lack of clarity : AMBIGUITY, OBSCURITY
un·clasp \-ˈklasp\ *vt* (1530) **1** : to open the clasp of **2** : to open or cause to be opened (as a clenched hand) ~ *vi* : to loosen a hold
un·clas·si·cal \-ˈkla-si-kəl\ *adj* (1725) : not classical; *esp* : unconcerned with the classics
un·clas·si·fied \-ˈkla-sə-ˌfīd\ *adj* (1865) **1** : not placed or belonging in a class **2** : not subject to a security classification ⟨~ information⟩
un·cle \ˈəŋ-kəl\ *n* [ME, fr. AF, fr. L *avunculus* mother's brother; akin to OE *ēam* uncle, W *ewythr*, L *avus* grandfather] (14c) **1 a** : the brother of one's father or mother **b** : the husband of one's aunt **2** : one who helps, advises, or encourages **3** — used as a cry of surrender ⟨was forced to cry ~⟩ **4** *cap* : UNCLE SAM

\ə\ **abut** \ᵊ\ kitten, F table \ər\ **further** \a\ **ash** \ā\ **ace** \ä\ **mop, mar** \au̇\ **out** \ch\ **chin** \e\ **bet** \ē\ **easy** \g\ **go** \i\ **hit** \ī\ **ice** \j\ **job** \ŋ\ **sing** \ō\ **go** \ȯ\ **law** \ȯi\ **boy** \th\ **thin** \t͟h\ **the** \ü\ **loot** \u̇\ **foot** \y\ **yet** \zh\ **vision, beige** \k, ⁿ, œ, ue, ʸ\ *see* Guide to Pronunciation

un·clean \ˌən-ˈklēn\ *adj* (bef. 12c) **1 :** morally or spiritually impure **2 :** infected with a harmful supernatural contagion; *also* **:** prohibited by ritual law for use or contact **3 :** DIRTY, FILTHY **4 :** lacking in clarity and precision of conception or execution — **un·clean·ness** \-ˈklēn-nəs\ *n*

[1]**un·clean·ly** \-ˈklen-lē\ *adj* (bef. 12c) **:** morally or physically unclean — **un·clean·li·ness** *n*

[2]**un·clean·ly** \-ˈklēn-lē\ *adv* (bef. 12c) **:** in an unclean manner

un·clench \-ˈklench\ *vt* (1647) **1 :** to open from a clenched position **2 :** to release from a grip ~ *vi* **:** to become unclasped or relaxed

Un·cle Sam \ˌəŋ-kəl-ˈsam\ *n* [expansion of *U.S.*, abbr. of *United States*] (1813) **1 :** the U.S. government **2 :** the American nation or people

[1]**Uncle Tom** \-ˈtäm\ *n* [*Uncle Tom,* pious and faithful black slave in *Uncle Tom's Cabin* (1851–52) by Harriet Beecher Stowe] (1922) **1 :** a black who is overeager to win the approval of whites (as by obsequious behavior or uncritical acceptance of white values and goals) **2 :** a member of a low-status group who is overly subservient to or cooperative with authority ⟨the worst floor managers and supervisors by far are women . . . Some of them are regular *Uncle Toms* —Jane Fonda⟩ — **Uncle Tom·ism** \-ˈtä-ˌmi-zəm\ *n*

[2]**Uncle Tom** *vi* **Uncle Tommed; Uncle Tom·ming** (1947) **:** to behave like an Uncle Tom

un·climb·able \ˌən-ˈklī-mə-bəl\ *adj* (1553) **:** not able to be climbed — **un·climb·able·ness** *n*

un·clinch \ˌən-ˈklinch\ *vt* (1598) **:** UNCLENCH

un·cloak \-ˈklōk\ *vt* (ca. 1598) **1 :** to remove a cloak or cover from **2 :** REVEAL, UNMASK ⟨~ an impostor⟩ ~ *vi* **:** to take off a cloak

un·clog \-ˈkläg\ *vt* (ca. 1608) **:** to free from a difficulty or obstruction

un·close \-ˈklōz\ *vt* (14c) **1 :** OPEN **2 :** DISCLOSE, REVEAL ~ *vi* **:** to become opened

un·closed \-ˈklōzd\ *adj* (15c) **:** not closed or settled **:** not concluded

un·clothe \-ˈklōth\ *vt* (14c) **1 :** to strip of clothes **2 :** DIVEST, UNCOVER ⟨the hardest thing to ~ is still our fears —Joe Williams⟩

un·clothed \-ˈklōthd\ *adj* (15c) **:** not clothed

un·cloud·ed \-ˈklau̇-dəd\ *adj* (1594) **:** not covered by clouds **:** not darkened or obscured **:** CLEAR — **un·cloud·ed·ly** *adv*

un·club·ba·ble \ˌən-ˈklə-bə-bəl\ *adj* (ca. 1764) **:** UNSOCIABLE 1

un·clut·ter \-ˈklə-tər\ *vt* (1930) **:** to remove clutter from **:** make neat and orderly ⟨~ the garage⟩

un·clut·tered \-tərd\ *adj* (ca. 1925) **:** not cluttered ⟨an ~ desk⟩

[1]**un·co** \ˈəŋ-(ˌ)kō, -kə\ *adj* [ME (Sc) *unkow,* alter. of ME *uncouth*] (15c) **1** *chiefly Scot* **a :** STRANGE, UNKNOWN **b :** UNCANNY, WEIRD **2** *chiefly Scot* **:** EXTRAORDINARY

[2]**unco** *adv* (1721) **:** EXTREMELY, REMARKABLY, UNCOMMONLY ⟨you keep your room ~ hot —R. L. Stevenson⟩

[3]**unco** *n, pl* **uncos** (1785) **1** *pl, chiefly Scot* **:** NEWS, TIDINGS **2** *chiefly Scot* **:** STRANGER

un·cock \ˌən-ˈkäk\ *vt* (1693) **:** to remove the hammer of (a firearm) from a cocked position

un·cof·fin \-ˈkȯ-fən\ *vt* (1836) **:** to remove from or as if from a coffin

un·cof·fined \-fənd\ *adj* (1648) **:** not placed in a coffin

un·coil \ˌən-ˈkȯi(-ə)l\ *vt* (1713) **:** to release from a coiled state **:** UNWIND ~ *vi* **:** to become uncoiled

un·coiled \-ˈkȯi(-ə)ld\ *adj* (1713) **:** not coiled

un·coined \-ˈkȯind\ *adj* (15c) **1 :** not minted ⟨~ metal⟩ **2 :** not fabricated **:** NATURAL ⟨plain and ~ constancy —Shak.⟩

un·com·fort·able \ˌən-ˈkəm(p)(f)-tə(r)-bəl, -ˈkəm-fə(r)-bəl\ *adj* (1573) **1 :** causing discomfort or annoyance ⟨an ~ chair⟩ ⟨an ~ performance⟩ **2 :** feeling discomfort **:** UNEASY ⟨was ~ with them⟩ — **un·com·fort·ably** \-blē\ *adv*

un·com·mer·cial \ˌən-kə-ˈmər-shəl\ *adj* (1768) **1 :** not engaged in or related to commerce **2 :** not based on commercial principles **3 :** not likely to result in financial success ⟨an ~ book⟩

un·com·mit·ted \ˌən-kə-ˈmi-təd\ *adj* (15c) **:** not committed; *specif* **:** not pledged to a particular belief, allegiance, or program ⟨~ voters⟩

un·com·mon \ˌən-ˈkä-mən\ *adj* (ca. 1576) **1 :** not ordinarily encountered **:** UNUSUAL ⟨an ~ plant⟩ **2 :** REMARKABLE, EXCEPTIONAL ⟨a soldier of ~ courage⟩ ***syn*** see INFREQUENT — **un·com·mon·ly** *adv* — **un·com·mon·ness** \-mən-nəs\ *n*

un·com·mu·ni·ca·ble \ˌən-kə-ˈmyü-ni-kə-bəl\ *adj* (14c) **:** INCOMMUNICABLE ⟨~ grief⟩

un·com·mu·ni·ca·tive \-ˈmyü-nə-ˌkā-tiv, -ni-kə-tiv\ *adj* (1691) **:** not disposed to talk or impart information **:** RESERVED

un·com·pet·i·tive \-ˈpe-tə-tiv\ *adj* (1885) **:** not competitive **:** unable to compete — **un·com·pet·i·tive·ness** *n*

un·com·plain·ing \-ˈplā-niŋ\ *adj* (1738) **:** not complaining **:** PATIENT ⟨~ acceptance⟩ — **un·com·plain·ing·ly** \-niŋ-lē\ *adv*

un·com·pli·cat·ed \ˌən-ˈkäm-plə-ˌkā-təd\ *adj* (1704) **1 a :** not complicated by something outside itself **b :** not involving medical complications ⟨an ~ peptic ulcer⟩ **2 :** not complex **:** SIMPLE ⟨~ machinery⟩

un·com·pli·men·ta·ry \ˌən-ˌkäm-plə-ˈmen-tə-rē, -ˈmen-trē\ *adj* (1837) **:** not complimentary **:** DEROGATORY ⟨~ remarks⟩

un·com·pre·hend·ing \-pri-ˈhen-diŋ\ *adj* (1810) **:** not comprehending **:** lacking understanding — **un·com·pre·hend·ing·ly** \-diŋ-lē\ *adv*

un·com·pro·mis·able \ˌən-ˈkäm-prə-ˌmī-zə-bəl\ *adj* (1958) **:** not able to be compromised ⟨~ ideals⟩

un·com·pro·mis·ing \-ˌmī-ziŋ\ *adj* (1800) **:** not making or accepting a compromise **:** making no concessions **:** INFLEXIBLE, UNYIELDING — **un·com·pro·mis·ing·ly** \-ziŋ-lē\ *adv* — **un·com·pro·mis·ing·ness** \-nəs\ *n*

un·con·ceiv·able \ˌən-kən-ˈsē-və-bəl\ *adj* (ca. 1604) **:** INCONCEIVABLE

un·con·cern \ˌən-kən-ˈsərn\ *n* (1684) **1 :** lack of care or interest **:** INDIFFERENCE ⟨his ~ for personal gain⟩ **2 :** freedom from excessive concern or anxiety

un·con·cerned \-ˈsərnd\ *adj* (ca. 1635) **1 :** not involved **:** not having any part or interest **2 :** not anxious or upset **:** free of worry ***syn*** see INDIFFERENT — **un·con·cerned·ly** \-ˈsər-nəd-lē, -ˈsərnd-lē\ *adv* — **un·con·cerned·ness** \-ˈsər-nəd-nəs, -ˈsərn(d)-nəs\ *n*

un·con·di·tion·al \ˌən-kən-ˈdish-nəl, -ˈdi-shə-nᵊl\ *adj* (1666) **1 :** not conditional or limited **:** ABSOLUTE, UNQUALIFIED ⟨~ surrender⟩ ⟨~ love⟩ **2 :** UNCONDITIONED 2 — **un·con·di·tion·al·ly** *adv*

un·con·di·tioned \-ˈdi-shənd\ *adj* (ca. 1631) **1 :** not subject to conditions or limitations **2 a :** not dependent on or subjected to conditioning or learning **:** NATURAL ⟨~ responses⟩ **b :** producing an unconditioned response ⟨~ stimuli⟩

un·con·form·able \-ˈfȯr-mə-bəl\ *adj* (1594) **1 :** not conforming **2 :** exhibiting geological unconformity — **un·con·form·ably** \-blē\ *adv*

un·con·for·mi·ty \-ˈfȯr-mə-tē\ *n* (ca. 1600) **1** *archaic* **:** lack of conformity **2 a :** lack of continuity in deposition between rock strata in contact corresponding to a period of nondeposition, weathering, or erosion **b :** the surface of contact between unconformable strata

un·con·ge·nial \-ˈjē-nyəl, -nē-əl\ *adj* (1813) **1 :** not sympathetic or compatible ⟨~ roommates⟩ **2 a :** not fitted **:** UNSUITABLE ⟨a soil ~ to most crops⟩ **b :** not to one's taste **:** DISAGREEABLE ⟨an ~ task⟩ — **un·con·ge·nial·i·ty** \-ˌjē-nē-ˈa-lə-tē, -ˌjēn-ˈya-\ *n*

un·con·quer·able \ˌən-ˈkäŋ-k(ə-)rə-bəl\ *adj* (1582) **1 :** incapable of being conquered **:** INDOMITABLE ⟨an ~ will⟩ **2 :** incapable of being surmounted ⟨~ difficulties⟩ — **un·con·quer·ably** \-blē\ *adv*

un·con·scio·na·ble \-ˈkän(t)-sh(ə-)nə-bəl\ *adj* (1565) **1 :** not guided or controlled by conscience **:** UNSCRUPULOUS ⟨an ~ villain⟩ **2 a :** EXCESSIVE, UNREASONABLE ⟨found an ~ number of defects in the car⟩ **b :** shockingly unfair or unjust ⟨~ sales practices⟩ — **un·con·scio·na·bil·i·ty** \ˌən-ˌkän(t)-sh(ə-)nə-ˈbi-lə-tē\ *n* — **un·con·scio·na·ble·ness** \ˌən-ˈkän(t)-sh(ə-)nə-bəl-nəs\ *n* — **un·con·scio·na·bly** \-blē\ *adv*

[1]**un·con·scious** \ˌən-ˈkän(t)-shəs\ *adj* (1712) **1 a :** not knowing or perceiving **:** not aware **b :** free from self-awareness **2 a :** not possessing mind or consciousness ⟨~ matter⟩ **b** (1) **:** not marked by conscious thought, sensation, or feeling ⟨~ motivation⟩ (2) **:** of or relating to the unconscious **c :** having lost consciousness ⟨was ~ for three days⟩ **3 :** not consciously held or deliberately planned or carried out ⟨an ~ bias⟩ — **un·con·scious·ly** *adv* — **un·con·scious·ness** *n*

[2]**unconscious** *n* (ca. 1912) **:** the part of mental life that does not ordinarily enter the individual's awareness yet may influence behavior and perception or be revealed (as in slips of the tongue or in dreams)

un·con·sid·ered \ˌən-kən-ˈsi-dərd\ *adj* (1587) **1 :** not considered or worth consideration **2 :** not resulting from consideration ⟨~ remarks⟩

un·con·sol·i·dat·ed \-ˈsä-lə-ˌdā-təd\ *adj* (1802) **:** loosely arranged ⟨~ subsidiaries⟩; *esp* **:** not stratified ⟨~ soil⟩

un·con·sti·tu·tion·al \ˌən-ˌkän(t)-stə-ˈtü-shnəl, -ˈtyü-, -shə-nᵊl\ *adj* (1734) **:** not according or consistent with the constitution of a body politic (as a nation) ⟨an ~ infringement on rights⟩ — **un·con·sti·tu·tion·al·i·ty** \-ˌtü-shə-ˈna-lə-tē, -ˌtyü-\ *n* — **un·con·sti·tu·tion·al·ly** *adv*

un·con·straint \ˌən-kən-ˈstrānt\ *n* (1711) **:** freedom from constraint **:** EASE ⟨played the game with creative ~ —E. M. Swift⟩

un·con·struct·ed \-ˈstrək-təd\ *adj* (1970) *of clothing* **:** manufactured without added material for padding, stiffening, or shape retention

un·con·trol·la·ble \-ˈtrō-lə-bəl\ *adj* (1593) **1** *archaic* **:** free from control by a superior power **:** ABSOLUTE **2 :** incapable of being controlled **:** UNGOVERNABLE ⟨a rush of ~ emotions⟩ — **un·con·trol·la·bil·i·ty** \-ˌtrō-lə-ˈbi-lə-tē\ *n* — **un·con·trol·la·bly** \-ˈtrō-lə-blē\ *adv*

un·con·ven·tion·al \-ˈvench-nəl, -ˈven(t)-shə-nᵊl\ *adj* (1835) **:** not conventional **:** not bound by or in accordance with convention **:** being out of the ordinary ⟨an ~ outfit⟩ ⟨an ~ thinker⟩ — **un·con·ven·tion·al·i·ty** \-ˌven(t)-shə-ˈna-lə-tē\ *n* — **un·con·ven·tion·al·ly** *adv*

un·con·vinc·ing \-ˈvin(t)-siŋ\ *adj* (1653) **:** not convincing **:** IMPLAUSIBLE ⟨an ~ argument⟩ — **un·con·vinc·ing·ly** \-siŋ-lē\ *adv* — **un·con·vinc·ing·ness** *n*

un·cool \ˌən-ˈkül\ *adj* (1953) **1 :** lacking in assurance, sophistication, or self-control **2 :** failing to accord with the values or styles (as of dress or behavior) of a particular group **:** not accepted or admired as cool or proper ⟨driving an ~ car⟩ ⟨an ~ remark⟩

un·cork \ˌən-ˈkȯrk\ *vt* (1709) **1 :** to draw a cork from ⟨~ a bottle⟩ **2 a :** to release from a sealed or pent-up state ⟨~ a surprise⟩ **b :** to let go **:** RELEASE ⟨~ a wild pitch⟩

un·corked \-ˈkȯrkt\ *adj* (1777) **:** not provided with a cork

un·cor·set·ed \-ˈkȯr-sə-təd\ *adj* (1856) **1 :** not wearing a corset **2 :** not controlled or inhibited ⟨~ freedom⟩

un·count·ed \-ˈkau̇n-təd\ *adj* (15c) **1 :** not counted **2 :** INNUMERABLE

un·cou·ple \-ˈkə-pəl\ *vt* (14c) **1 :** to release (dogs) from a pair of joined collars **2 :** DETACH, DISCONNECT ⟨~ railroad cars⟩ — **un·cou·pler** \-p(ə-)lər\ *n*

un·couth \ən-ˈküth\ *adj* [ME, fr. OE *uncūth,* fr. *un-* + *cūth* familiar, known; akin to OHG *kund* known, OE *can* know — more at CAN] (bef. 12c) **1 a** *archaic* **:** not known or not familiar to one **:** seldom experienced **:** UNCOMMON, RARE **b** *obs* **:** MYSTERIOUS, UNCANNY **2 a :** strange or clumsy in shape or appearance **:** OUTLANDISH **b :** lacking in polish and grace **:** RUGGED ⟨~ verse⟩ **c :** awkward and uncultivated in appearance, manner, or behavior **:** RUDE — **un·couth·ly** *adv* — **un·couth·ness** *n*

un·cov·er \-ˈkə-vər\ *vt* (14c) **1 :** to make known **:** bring to light **:** DISCLOSE, REVEAL ⟨~ the truth⟩ **2 :** to expose to view by removing some covering **3 a :** to take the cover from **b :** to remove the hat from ⟨~*ed* his head⟩ **4 :** to deprive of protection ~ *vi* **1 :** to remove a cover or covering **2 :** to take off the hat as a token of respect

un·cov·ered \-vərd\ *adj* (14c) **:** not covered: as **a :** not supplied with a covering **b :** not covered by insurance or included in a social insurance or welfare program **c :** not covered by collateral ⟨an ~ note⟩

un·cre·at·ed \ˌən-krē-ˈā-təd\ *adj* (ca. 1549) **1 :** not existing by creation **:** ETERNAL, SELF-EXISTENT **2 :** not yet created

un·crit·i·cal \ˌən-ˈkri-ti-kəl\ *adj* (1659) **1 :** not critical **:** lacking in discrimination **2 :** showing lack or improper use of critical standards or procedures — **un·crit·i·cal·ly** \-k(ə-)lē\ *adv*

un·cross \-ˈkrȯs\ *vt* (1599) **:** to change from a crossed position

un·crown \-ˈkrau̇n\ *vt* (14c) **:** to take the crown from **:** DETHRONE

un·crum·ple \-ˈkrəm-pəl\ *vt* (1611) **:** to restore to an original smooth condition

unc·tion \ˈəŋ(k)-shən\ *n* [ME *unccioun,* fr. AF, fr. L *unction-, unctio,* fr. *unguere* to anoint — more at OINTMENT] (14c) **1 :** the act of anointing as a rite of consecration or healing **2 :** something used for anointing **:** OINTMENT, UNGUENT **3 a :** religious or spiritual fervor or the expression of such fervor **b :** exaggerated, assumed, or superficial earnestness of language or manner **:** UNCTUOUSNESS

unc·tu·ous \ˈəŋ(k)-chə-wəs, -chəs, -shwəs\ *adj* [ME, fr. MF or ML; MF *unctueus*, fr. ML *unctuosus*, fr. L *unctus* act of anointing, fr. *unguere* to anoint] (14c) **1 a :** FATTY, OILY **b :** smooth and greasy in texture or appearance **2 :** PLASTIC ⟨fine ~ clay⟩ **3 :** full of unction; *esp* **:** revealing or marked by a smug, ingratiating, and false earnestness or spirituality — **unc·tu·ous·ly** *adv* — **unc·tu·ous·ness** *n*

un·curl \ˌən-ˈkər(-ə)l\ *vi* (1588) **:** to become straightened out from a curled or coiled position ~ *vt* **:** to straighten the curls of **:** UNROLL

un·cus \ˈəŋ-kəs\ *n, pl* **un·ci** \ˈəŋ-ˌkī, -ˌkē; ˈən-ˌsī\ [NL, fr. L, hook — more at ANGLE] (ca. 1826) **:** a hooked anatomical part or process

un·cut \ˌən-ˈkət\ *adj* (14c) **1 :** not cut down or cut into **2 :** not shaped by cutting ⟨an ~ diamond⟩ **3** *of a book* **:** not having the folds of the leaves slit **4 :** not abridged, curtailed, or expurgated ⟨the film's ~ version⟩ **5 :** not diluted or adulterated ⟨~ gin⟩ ⟨~ heroin⟩

un·daunt·able \ˌən-ˈdȯn-tə-bəl, -ˈdän-\ *adj* (1587) **:** UNDAUNTED

un·daunt·ed \ˌən-ˈdȯn-təd, -ˈdän-\ *adj* (15c) **:** courageously resolute esp. in the face of danger or difficulty **:** not discouraged — **un·daunt·ed·ly** *adv*

un·dead \ˌən-ˈded\ *n, pl* **undead** (1897) **1 :** VAMPIRE 1 **2 :** ZOMBIE 1b

un·de·bat·able \ˌən-di-ˈbā-tə-bəl\ *adj* (1850) **:** not subject to debate **:** INDISPUTABLE — **un·de·bat·ably** \-blē\ *adv*

un·de·ceive \ˌən-di-ˈsēv\ *vt* (1598) **:** to free from deception, illusion, or error

un·de·cil·lion \ˌən-di-ˈsil-yən\ *n, often attrib* [L *undecim* eleven (fr. *unus* one + *decem* ten) + E *-illion* (as in *million*) — more at ONE, TEN] (1931) — see NUMBER table

un·dec·y·le·nic acid \ˌən-ˌde-sə-ˈle-nik-, -ˈlē-\ *n* [*undecylene* ($C_{11}H_{22}$)] (1879) **:** a fatty acid $C_{11}H_{20}O_2$ found in perspiration, obtained commercially from castor oil, and used esp. in the treatment of fungal infections (as ringworm) of the skin

un·dem·o·crat·ic \ˌən-ˌde-mə-ˈkra-tik\ *adj* (1839) **:** not democratic **:** not agreeing with democratic practice or ideals — **un·dem·o·crat·i·cal·ly** \-ti-k(ə-)lē\ *adv*

un·de·mon·stra·tive \ˌən-di-ˈmän(t)-strə-tiv\ *adj* (1836) **:** restrained in expression of feeling **:** RESERVED — **un·de·mon·stra·tive·ly** *adv* — **un·de·mon·stra·tive·ness** *n*

un·de·ni·able \ˌən-di-ˈnī-ə-bəl\ *adj* (1547) **1 :** plainly true **:** INCONTESTABLE ⟨an ~ fact⟩ **2 :** unquestionably excellent or genuine ⟨an applicant with ~ references⟩ — **un·de·ni·able·ness** *n* — **un·de·ni·ably** \-blē\ *adv*

[1]**un·der** \ˈən-dər\ *adv* [ME, adv. & prep., fr. OE; akin to OHG *untar* under, L *inferus* situated beneath, lower, *infra* below, Skt *adha*] (bef. 12c) **1 :** in or into a position below or beneath something **2 :** below or short of some quantity, level, or limit ⟨$10 or ~⟩ — often used in combination ⟨*under*staffed⟩ **3 :** in or into a condition of subjection, subordination, or unconsciousness ⟨put the patient ~ for surgery⟩ **4 :** down to defeat, ruin, or death ⟨weaker competitors will be forced ~⟩ **5 :** so as to be covered ⟨buried ~ by the avalanche⟩

[2]**under** *prep* (bef. 12c) **1 :** below or beneath so as to be overhung, surmounted, covered, protected, or concealed by ⟨~ sunny skies⟩ ⟨a soft heart ~ a stern exterior⟩ ⟨~ cover of darkness⟩ **2 a :** subject to the authority, control, guidance, or instruction of ⟨served ~ the general⟩ ⟨~ the terms of the contract⟩ ⟨a program that runs ~ any operating system⟩ **b :** receiving or undergoing the action or effect of ⟨~ pressure⟩ ⟨courage ~ fire⟩ ⟨~ the influence of alcohol⟩ ⟨the image of a point ~ a mapping⟩ ⟨~ oath⟩ **3 a :** within the group or designation of ⟨~ this heading⟩ **b :** having as name or title ⟨traveling ~ an alias⟩ **4 :** less or lower than (as in size, amount, or rank); *esp* **:** falling short of a standard or required degree ⟨~ the legal age⟩ ⟨~ par⟩

[3]**under** *adj* (13c) **1 a :** lying or placed below, beneath, or on the ventral side — often used in combination ⟨*under*lip⟩ **b :** facing or protruding downward **2 :** lower in rank or authority **:** SUBORDINATE **3 :** lower than usual, proper, or desired in amount, quality, or degree — often used in combination ⟨an *under*-dose of medicine⟩

un·der·achiev·er \ˌən-dər-ə-ˈchē-vər\ *n* (1952) **:** one (as a student) that fails to attain a predicted level of achievement or does not do as well as expected — **un·der·achieve** \-ə-ˈchēv\ *vi* — **un·der·achieve·ment** \-mənt\ *n*

un·der·act \ˌən-dər-ˈakt\ *vt* (ca. 1623) **:** to perform (a dramatic part) with restraint for effect **:** UNDERPLAY ~ *vi* **:** to perform feebly or with restraint

un·der·ac·tive \-ˈak-tiv\ *adj* (1959) **:** characterized by an abnormally low level of activity ⟨an ~ thyroid gland⟩ — **un·der·ac·tiv·i·ty** \-ˈti-və-tē\ *n*

un·der·age \ˌən-dər-ˈāj\ *adj* (1561) **1 :** of less than mature or legal age **2 :** done by or involving underage persons ⟨~ drinking⟩

un·der·ap·pre·ci·at·ed \ˌən-dər-ə-ˈprē-shē-ˌā-təd\ *adj* (1968) **:** not duly appreciated

[1]**un·der·arm** \ˈən-dər-ˈärm\ *adj* (1816) **1** *Brit* **:** UNDERHAND 3 **2 :** placed under or on the underside of the arm ⟨~ seams⟩

[2]**un·der·arm** \ˌən-dər-ˈärm\ *adv* (ca. 1909) **:** UNDERHAND

[3]**un·der·arm** \ˈən-dər-ˌärm\ *n* (1923) **1 :** ARMPIT 1 **2 :** the part of a garment that covers the underside of the arm

un·der·bel·ly \ˈən-dər-ˌbe-lē\ *n* (1942) **1 :** a vulnerable area; *also* **:** a corrupt or sordid part ⟨probing the ~ of the entertainment industry⟩ **2 :** the underside of a body or mass

un·der·bid \ˌən-dər-ˈbid\ *vb* **-bid; -bid·ding** *vt* (ca. 1677) **1 :** to bid less than (a competing bidder) **2 :** to bid (a hand of cards) at less than the strength of the hand warrants ~ *vi* **:** to bid too low — **un·der·bid·der** *n*

un·der·body \ˈən-dər-ˌbä-dē\ *n* (1870) **:** the lower part of something: as **a :** the lower part of an animal's body **:** UNDERPARTS **b :** the lower parts of the body of a vehicle

un·der·boss \ˈən-dər-ˌbȯs\ *n* (1942) **:** a boss ranking next below the head of a branch of a crime syndicate

un·der·bred \ˌən-dər-ˈbred\ *adj* (1650) **:** marked by lack of good breeding **:** ILL-BRED ⟨a degree of ~ pride —Emily Brontë⟩

un·der·brim \ˈən-dər-ˌbrim\ *n* (1856) **:** a facing on the underside of a hat brim

un·der·brush \ˈən-dər-ˌbrəsh\ *n* (1775) **1 :** shrubs, bushes, or small trees growing beneath large trees in a wood or forest **:** BRUSH **2 :** a tangled, obstructing, or impeding mass

un·der·bud·get·ed \ˌən-dər-ˈbə-jə-təd\ *adj* (1965) **:** provided with an inadequate budget

un·der·cap·i·tal·ized \-ˈka-pə-tə-ˌlīzd, -ˈkap-tə-\ *adj* (1962) **:** having too little capital for efficient operation ⟨an ~ business⟩

un·der·card \ˈən-dər-ˌkärd\ *n* (1948) **:** a program (as of boxing matches) supporting the featured match

un·der·car·riage \ˈən-dər-ˌka-rij\ *n* (ca. 1796) **1 :** a supporting framework or underside (as of an automobile) **2 :** the landing gear of an airplane

un·der·charge \ˌən-dər-ˈchärj\ *vt* (1633) **:** to charge (as a person) too little — **undercharge** \ˈən-dər-ˌ\ *n*

un·der·class \ˈən-dər-ˌklas\ *n* (1918) **:** the lowest social stratum usu. made up of disadvantaged minority groups

un·der·class·man \ˌən-dər-ˈklas-mən\ *n* (1871) **:** a member of the freshman or sophomore class in a school or college

un·der·clothes \ˈən-dər-ˌklō(th)z\ *n pl* (1835) **:** UNDERWEAR

un·der·cloth·ing \-ˌklō-thiŋ\ *n* (1804) **:** UNDERWEAR

un·der·coat \-ˌkōt\ *n* (1591) **1 :** a coat or jacket worn under another **2 :** a growth of short hair or fur partly concealed by the longer and usu. coarser guard hairs of a mammal **3 a :** a coat (as of paint) applied as a base for another coat **b :** UNDERCOATING **4** *dial* **:** PETTICOAT

un·der·coat·ing \-ˌkō-tiŋ\ *n* (1922) **:** a usu. asphalt-based waterproof coating applied to the underside of a vehicle

un·der·cool \ˌən-dər-ˈkül\ *vt* (1895) **:** SUPERCOOL

un·der·count \-ˈkau̇nt\ *vt* (1951) **:** to count fewer than the actual number of — **undercount** *n*

[1]**un·der·cov·er** \-ˈkə-vər\ *adj* (1920) **:** acting or executed in secret; *specif* **:** employed or engaged in spying or secret investigation ⟨an ~ agent⟩ — **undercover** *adv*

[2]**undercover** *n* (1962) **:** a person engaged in undercover activity **:** SPY

un·der·croft \ˈən-dər-ˌkrȯft\ *n* [ME, fr. *under* + *crofte* crypt, fr. MD, fr. ML *crupta*, fr. L *crypta* — more at CRYPT] (14c) **:** a subterranean room; *esp* **:** a vaulted chamber under a church

un·der·cur·rent \-ˌkər-ənt, -ˌkə-rənt\ *n* (1683) **1 :** a current below the upper currents or surface **2 :** a hidden opinion, feeling, or tendency often contrary to the one publicly shown — **undercurrent** *adj*

[1]**un·der·cut** \ˌən-dər-ˈkət\ *vb* **-cut; -cut·ting** *vt* (1598) **1 :** to cut away the underpart of ⟨~ a vein of ore⟩ **2 :** to cut away material from the underside of (an object) so as to leave an overhanging portion in relief **3 :** to offer to sell at lower prices than or to work for lower wages than (a competitor) **4 :** to cut obliquely into (a tree) below the main cut and on the side toward which the tree will fall **5 :** to strike (a ball) with a downward glancing blow so as to give a backspin or elevation to the shot **6 :** to undermine or destroy the force, value, or effectiveness of ⟨inflation ~*s* consumer buying power⟩ ~ *vi* **:** to perform the action of cutting away beneath

[2]**un·der·cut** \ˈən-dər-ˌkət\ *n* (1859) **1** *Brit* **:** TENDERLOIN 1 **2 :** the action or result of cutting away from the underside or lower part of something **3 :** a notch cut in the base of a tree before felling to determine the direction of falling and to prevent splitting

un·der·de·vel·oped \ˌən-dər-di-ˈve-ləpt\ *adj* (1892) **1 :** not normally or adequately developed ⟨~ muscles⟩ ⟨~ film⟩ **2 :** having a relatively low economic level of industrial production and standard of living (as from lack of capital) ⟨~ nations⟩ — **un·der·de·vel·op·ment** \-ləp-mənt\ *n*

un·der·di·ag·nose \ˌən-dər-ˈdī-ig-ˌnōs, -ˌnōz; -ˌdī-ig-ˈ, -əg-\ *vt* (1974) **:** to diagnose (a condition or disease) less often than it is actually present — **un·der·di·ag·no·sis** \-ˌdī-ig-ˈnō-səs, -əg-\ *n*

un·der·dog \ˈən-dər-ˌdȯg\ *n* (1859) **1 :** a loser or predicted loser in a struggle or contest **2 :** a victim of injustice or persecution

un·der·done \ˌən-dər-ˈdən\ *adj* (1683) **:** not thoroughly cooked **:** RARE

un·der·draw·ers \ˈən-dər-ˌdrȯ(-ə)rz\ *n pl* (1894) **:** an article of underwear for the lower body

un·der·draw·ing \ˈən-dər-ˌdrȯ-iŋ\ *n* (1968) **:** a preliminary sketch made on a surface (as a canvas or panel) prior to painting

un·der·dress \ˌən-dər-ˈdres\ *vi* (ca. 1784) **:** to dress in overly or inappropriately simple or informal clothing ~ *vt* **:** to dress (as oneself) more simply or informally than is appropriate

un·der·ed·u·cat·ed \ˌən-dər-ˈe-jə-ˌkā-təd\ *adj* (1848) **:** poorly educated

un·der·em·pha·sis \ˌən-dər-ˈem(p)-fə-səs\ *n* (1916) **:** less emphasis than is possible or desirable

un·der·em·pha·size \-ˌsīz\ *vt* (1955) **:** to fail to emphasize adequately

un·der·em·ployed \ˌən-dər-im-ˈplȯid\ *adj* (1908) **:** having less than full-time, regular, or adequate employment

un·der·em·ploy·ment \-ˈplȯi-mənt\ *n* (1909) **1 :** the condition in which people in a labor force are employed at less than full-time or regular jobs or at jobs inadequate with respect to their training or economic needs **2 :** the condition of being underemployed

un·der·es·ti·mate \ˌən-dər-ˈes-tə-ˌmāt\ *vt* (1792) **1 :** to estimate as being less than the actual size, quantity, or number **2 :** to place too low a value on **:** UNDERRATE — **un·der·es·ti·mate** \-mət\ *n* — **un·der·es·ti·ma·tion** \-ˌes-tə-ˈmā-shən\ *n*

un·der·ex·ploit·ed \ˌən-dər-ik-ˈsplȯi-təd\ *adj* (1952) **:** not fully or sufficiently utilized ⟨an ~ food source⟩

un·der·ex·pose \ˌən-dər-ik-ˈspōz\ *vt* (1861) **:** to expose insufficiently; *esp* **:** to expose (as film) to insufficient radiation (as light) — **un·der·ex·po·sure** \-ˈspō-zhər\ *n*

un·der·feed \ˌən-dər-ˈfēd\ *vt* **-fed** \-ˈfed\; **-feed·ing** (1659) **:** to feed with too little food

un·der·fi·nanced \-fə-ˈnan(t)st, -ˈfī-ˌ, -fī-ˈ\ *adj* (1922) **:** inadequately financed

un·der·foot \-ˈfu̇t\ *adv* (13c) **1 :** under the foot esp. against the ground ⟨trampled the flowers ~⟩ **2 :** below, at, or before one's feet ⟨warm sand ~⟩ **3 :** in the way ⟨children always getting ~⟩

un·der·fund \-ˈfənd\ *vt* (1963) **:** to provide insufficient funds for

un·der·fur \ˈən-dər-ˌfər\ *n* (1877) **:** an undercoat of fur esp. when thick and soft

un·der·gar·ment \-ˌgär-mənt\ *n* (1530) **:** a garment to be worn under another

\ə\ **abut** \ᵊ\ **kitten**, F **table** \ər\ **further** \a\ **ash** \ā\ **ace** \ä\ **mop, mar** \au̇\ **out** \ch\ **chin** \e\ **bet** \ē\ **easy** \g\ **go** \i\ **hit** \ī\ **ice** \j\ **job** \ŋ\ **sing** \ō\ **go** \ȯ\ **law** \ȯi\ **boy** \th\ **thin** \th\ **the** \ü\ **loot** \u̇\ **foot** \y\ **yet** \zh\ **vision, beige** \k, ⁿ, œ, ue, ʸ\ *see* Guide to Pronunciation

un·der·gird \ˌən-dər-ˈgərd\ *vt* (1526) **1** *archaic* : to make secure underneath ⟨took measures to ~ the ship —Acts 27:17(RSV)⟩ **2** : to form the basis or foundation of : STRENGTHEN, SUPPORT ⟨facts and statistics subtly ~ his commentary —Susan Q. Stranahan⟩

un·der·glaze \ˈən-dər-ˌglāz\ *adj* (1879) : applied or suitable for applying before the glaze is put on ⟨~ decorations⟩ ⟨~ colors⟩ — **underglaze** *n*

un·der·go \ˌən-dər-ˈgō\ *vt* **-went** \-ˈwent\; **-gone** \-ˈgȯn *also* -ˈgän\; **-go·ing** \-ˈgō-iŋ, -ˈgō(-)iŋ\ (14c) **1** : to submit to : ENDURE **2** : to go through : EXPERIENCE ⟨~ a transformation⟩ **3** *obs* : UNDERTAKE **4** *obs* : to partake of

un·der·grad \ˈən-dər-ˌgrad\ *n* (1827) : UNDERGRADUATE

un·der·grad·u·ate \ˌən-dər-ˈgra-jə-wət, -ˌwāt; -ˈgraj-wət\ *n* (1630) : a student at a college or university who has not received a first and esp. a bachelor's degree — **undergraduate** *adj*

[1]**un·der·ground** \ˌən-dər-ˈgrau̇nd\ *adv* (14c) **1** : beneath the surface of the earth **2** : in or into hiding or secret operation

[2]**underground** \ˈən-dər-ˌgrau̇nd\ *n* (1594) **1** : a subterranean space or channel **2** : an underground city railway system **3 a** : a movement or group organized in strict secrecy among citizens esp. in an occupied country for maintaining communications, popular solidarity, and concerted resistive action pending liberation **b** : a clandestine conspiratorial organization set up for revolutionary or other disruptive purposes esp. against a civil order **c** : an unofficial, unsanctioned, or illegal but informal movement or group; *esp* : a usu. avant-garde group or movement that functions outside the establishment

[3]**un·der·ground** \ˈən-dər-ˌgrau̇nd\ *adj* (1601) **1** : being, growing, operating, or situated below the surface of the ground **2** : conducted by secret means **3 a** : existing outside the establishment ⟨an ~ literary reputation⟩ **b** : existing outside the purview of tax collectors or statisticians ⟨the ~ economy⟩ **4 a** : produced or published outside the establishment esp. by the avant-garde ⟨~ movies⟩ ⟨~ newspapers⟩ **b** : of or relating to the avant-garde underground ⟨an ~ moviemaker⟩ ⟨an ~ theater⟩

un·der·ground·er \ˈən-dər-ˌgrau̇n-dər\ *n* (1882) : a member of the underground

Underground Railroad *n* (1842) : a system of cooperation among active antislavery people in the U.S. before 1863 by which fugitive slaves were secretly helped to reach the North or Canada — called also *Underground Railway*

un·der·growth \ˈən-dər-ˌgrōth\ *n* (1600) : low growth on the floor of a forest including seedlings and saplings, shrubs, and herbs

[1]**un·der·hand** \ˈən-dər-ˌhand\ *adv* (1538) **1 a** : in a clandestine manner **b** *archaic* : in a quiet or unobtrusive manner **2** : with an underhand motion ⟨bowl ~⟩ ⟨pitch ~⟩

[2]**underhand** *adj* (1592) **1** : UNDERHANDED **2** : done so as to evade notice **3** : made with the hand brought forward and up from below the shoulder level ⟨an ~ serve⟩

[1]**un·der·hand·ed** \ˌən-dər-ˈhan-dəd\ *adv* (ca. 1822) : UNDERHAND

[2]**underhanded** *adj* (1853) : marked by secrecy, chicanery, and deception : not honest and aboveboard : SLY ⟨an ~ attempt to gain power⟩ ***syn*** see SECRET — **un·der·hand·ed·ly** *adv* — **un·der·hand·ed·ness** *n*

un·der·in·flat·ed \ˌən-dər-in-ˈflā-təd\ *adj* (1928) : not sufficiently inflated ⟨~ tires⟩ — **un·der·in·fla·tion** \-ˈflā-shən\ *n*

un·der·in·sured \-ˈshu̇rd\ *adj* (1893) : not sufficiently insured

un·der·in·vest·ment \ˌən-dər-in-ˈves(t)-mənt\ *n* (1940) : an insufficient amount of investment

un·der·laid \ˌən-dər-ˈlād\ *adj* (bef. 12c) **1** : laid or placed underneath **2** : having something laid or lying underneath

[1]**un·der·lay** \-ˈlā\ *vt* **-laid** \-ˈlād\; **-lay·ing** (bef. 12c) **1** : to cover, line, or traverse the bottom of : give support to on the underside or below **2** : to raise or support by something laid under

[2]**un·der·lay** \ˈən-dər-ˌlā\ *n* (14c) : something that is or is designed to be laid under

un·der·lay·ment \ˌən-dər-ˈlā-mənt\ *n* (1949) : UNDERLAY

un·der·let \ˌən-dər-ˈlet\ *vt* **-let**; **-let·ting** (1677) **1** : to let below the real value **2** : SUBLET

un·der·lie \-ˈlī\ *vt* **-lay** \-ˈlā\; **-lain** \-ˈlān\; **-ly·ing** \-ˈlī-iŋ\ (bef. 12c) **1** *archaic* : to be subject or amenable to **2** : to lie or be situated under **3** : to be at the basis of : form the foundation of : SUPPORT ⟨ideas *underlying* the revolution⟩ **4** : to exist as a claim or security superior and prior to (another)

[1]**un·der·line** \ˈən-dər-ˌlīn, ˌən-dər-ˈ\ *vt* (1721) **1** : to mark (as a word) with a line underneath **2** : to put emphasis on : STRESS **3** : to show clearly or emphatically

[2]**un·der·line** \ˈən-dər-ˌlīn\ *n* (1886) **1** : the outline of a quadruped's underbody; *also* : the ventral surface of a quadruped's body **2** : a horizontal line placed underneath something

un·der·ling \ˈən-dər-liŋ\ *n* (12c) : one who is under the orders of another : SUBORDINATE, INFERIOR

un·der·lip \ˌən-dər-ˈlip\ *n* (1580) : the lower lip

un·der·ly·ing \ˌən-dər-ˈlī-iŋ\ *adj* (1611) **1 a** : lying beneath or below ⟨the ~ rock is shale⟩ **b** : BASIC, FUNDAMENTAL ⟨an investigation of the ~ issues⟩ **2** : evident only on close inspection : IMPLICIT **3** : anterior and prior in claim ⟨~ mortgage⟩ **4** : of or being present in deep structure ⟨~ word order⟩

un·der·ly·ing·ly \-ˈlī-iŋ-lē\ *adv* (1973) : in deep structure

un·der·manned \ˌən-dər-ˈmand\ *adj* (1848) : inadequately staffed

un·der·mine \ˌən-dər-ˈmīn\ *vt* (14c) **1** : to excavate the earth beneath : form a mine under : SAP **2** : to wash away supporting material from under **3** : to subvert or weaken insidiously or secretly ⟨trying to ~ his political rivals⟩ **4** : to weaken or ruin by degrees ***syn*** see WEAKEN

un·der·most \ˈən-dər-ˌmōst\ *adj* (1532) : lowest in relative position — **undermost** *adv*

[1]**un·der·neath** \ˌən-dər-ˈnēth\ *prep* [ME *undernethe,* prep. & adv., fr. OE *underneothan,* fr. *under* + *neothan* below — more at BENEATH] (bef. 12c) **1 a** : directly beneath ⟨write the date ~ the address⟩ **b** : close under esp. so as to be hidden ⟨treachery lying ~ a mask of friendliness⟩ ⟨wore a swimsuit ~ his slacks⟩ **2** : under subjection to

[2]**underneath** *adv* (bef. 12c) **1** : under or below an object or a surface : BENEATH **2** : on the lower side — **underneath** *adj*

un·der·nour·ished \ˌən-dər-ˈnər-isht, -ˈnə-risht\ *adj* (1910) **1** : supplied with less than the minimum amount of the foods essential for sound health and growth **2** : poorly supplied with vital elements or qualities ⟨~ independent libraries⟩ — **un·der·nour·ish·ment** \-ˈnər-ish-mənt, -ˈnə-rish-\ *n*

un·der·nu·tri·tion \-nu̇-ˈtri-shən, -nyu̇-\ *n* (1876) : deficient bodily nutrition due to inadequate food intake or faulty assimilation

un·der·paint·ing \ˈən-dər-ˌpān-tiŋ\ *n* (1866) : preliminary painting; *esp* : such painting done on a canvas or panel and covered completely or partially by the final layers of paint

un·der·pants \ˈən-dər-ˌpan(t)s\ *n pl* (1925) : a usu. short undergarment for the lower torso : DRAWERS

un·der·part \-ˌpärt\ *n* (1613) **1** : a part lying on the lower side (as of a bird or mammal) **2** : a subordinate or auxiliary part or role

un·der·pass \-ˌpas\ *n* (1903) : a crossing of a highway and another way (as a road or railroad) at different levels; *also* : the lower level of such a crossing

un·der·pay \ˌən-dər-ˈpā\ *vt* **-paid** \-ˈpād\; **-pay·ing** (1817) : to pay less than what is normal or required ⟨~ taxes⟩ — **un·der·pay·ment** *n*

un·der·per·form \ˌən-dər-pə(r)-ˈfȯrm\ *vt* (1971) : to do worse than ~ *vi* : to fail to do as well as expected — **un·der·per·for·mance** \-ˈfȯr-mən(t)s\ *n* — **un·der·per·form·er** \-ˈfȯr-mər\ *n*

un·der·pin \-ˈpin\ *vt* (1522) **1** : SUPPORT, SUBSTANTIATE ⟨~ a thesis with evidence⟩ **2** : to form part of, strengthen, or replace the foundation of ⟨~ a structure⟩ ⟨~ a sagging building⟩

un·der·pin·ning \ˈən-dər-ˌpi-niŋ\ *n* (15c) **1** : the material and construction (as a foundation) used for support of a structure **2** : something that serves as a foundation : BASIS, SUPPORT — often used in pl. ⟨the philosophical ~*s* of educational methods⟩ **3** : UNDERWEAR — usu. used in pl. **4** : a person's legs — usu. used in pl.

un·der·plant \ˌən-dər-ˈplant\ *vt* (1891) : to fill around, under, or among with lower-growing plants ⟨~ a tree with pansies⟩

un·der·play \ˌən-dər-ˈplā\ *vi* (1833) : to play a role with subdued force ~ *vt* **1** : to act or present (as a role or a scene) with restraint : PLAY DOWN **2** : to play a card lower than (a held high card)

un·der·plot \ˈən-dər-ˌplät\ *n* (1668) : SUBPLOT 1

un·der·pop·u·lat·ed \ˌən-dər-ˈpä-pyə-ˌlā-təd\ *adj* (1869) : having a lower density of population than is normal or desirable

un·der·pow·ered \-ˈpau̇(-ə)rd\ *adj* (1905) **1** : driven by an engine of insufficient power **2** : having or supplied with insufficient power

un·der·pre·pared \-prə-ˈperd\ *adj* (1964) : inadequately prepared

un·der·price \-ˈprīs\ *vt* (1756) **1** : to price below what is normal or below the real value **2** : to undercut (a competitor) in prices

un·der·priv·i·leged \-ˈpriv-lijd, -ˈpri-və-\ *adj* (1896) **1** : deprived through social or economic condition of some of the fundamental rights of all members of a civilized society **2** : of or relating to underprivileged people ⟨~ areas of the city⟩

un·der·pro·duc·tion \-prə-ˈdək-shən\ *n* (1887) : the production of less than enough to satisfy the demand or of less than the usual amount

un·der·pub·li·cized \-ˈpə-blə-ˌsīzd\ *adj* (1966) : insufficiently publicized

un·der·rate \ˌən-də(r)-ˈrāt\ *vt* (1632) : to rate too low : UNDERVALUE

un·der·re·act \-rē-ˈakt\ *vi* (1965) : to react with less than appropriate force or intensity

un·der·re·port \-ri-ˈpȯrt\ *vt* (1949) : to report to be less than is actually the case : UNDERSTATE ⟨~*s* his income⟩

un·der·rep·re·sent·ed \-ˌre-pri-ˈzen-təd\ *adj* (1853) : inadequately represented — **un·der·rep·re·sen·ta·tion** \-ˌzen-ˈtā-shən, -zən-\ *n*

[1]**un·der·run** \-ˈrən\ *vt* **-ran** \-ˈran\; **-run**; **-run·ning** (1547) **1** : to pass along under in order to examine (a cable) **2** : to pass or extend under

[2]**un·der·run** \ˈən-də(r)-ˌrən\ *n* (1926) : the amount by which something produced (as a cut of lumber) falls below an estimate

un·der·sat·u·rat·ed \ˌən-dər-ˈsa-chə-ˌrā-təd\ *adj* (ca. 1828) : less than normally or adequately saturated

[1]**un·der·score** \ˈən-dər-ˌskȯr\ *vt* (1771) **1** : to draw a line under : UNDERLINE **2** : to make evident : EMPHASIZE, STRESS ⟨arrived early to ~ the importance of the occasion⟩ **3** : to provide (action on film) with accompanying music

[2]**underscore** *n* (1901) **1** : a line drawn under a word or line esp. for emphasis or to indicate intent to italicize **2** : music accompanying the action and dialogue of a film

[1]**un·der·sea** \ˌən-dər-ˈsē\ *adj* (1613) **1** : being or carried on under the sea or under the surface of the sea ⟨~ oil deposits⟩ ⟨~ fighting⟩ **2** : designed for use under the surface of the sea ⟨an ~ fleet⟩

[2]**undersea** *or* **un·der·seas** \-ˈsēz\ *adv* (1645) : under the sea : beneath the surface of the sea ⟨photographs taken ~⟩

un·der·sec·re·tary \ˌən-dər-ˈse-krə-ˌter-ē, -ˈse-kə-\ *n* (1687) : a secretary immediately subordinate to a principal secretary ⟨~ of health⟩

un·der·sell \ˌən-dər-ˈsel\ *vt* **-sold** \-ˈsōld\; **-sell·ing** (1622) **1** : to sell articles cheaper than ⟨~ a competitor⟩ ⟨we will not be *undersold*⟩ **2** : to sell cheaper than ⟨imported cars that ~ domestic ones⟩

un·der·served \-ˈsərvd\ *adj* (1710) : provided with inadequate service

un·der·sexed \-ˈsekst\ *adj* (1931) : deficient in sexual desire

un·der·shirt \ˈən-dər-ˌshərt\ *n* (1648) : a collarless undergarment with or without sleeves — **un·der·shirt·ed** *adj*

un·der·shoot \ˌən-dər-ˈshüt\ *vt* **-shot** \-ˈshät\; **-shoot·ing** (ca. 1661) **1** : to shoot short of or below (a target) **2** : to fall short of (a runway) in landing an airplane

un·der·shorts \ˈən-dər-ˌshȯrts\ *n pl* (1944) : underpants for men or boys

un·der·shot \ˈən-dər-ˌshät\ *adj* (1610) **1** : moved by water passing beneath ⟨an ~ wheel⟩ **2** : having the lower incisor teeth or lower jaw projecting beyond the upper when the mouth is closed

un·der·shrub \ˈən-dər-ˌshrəb, *esp Southern* -ˌsrəb\ *n* (1598) : SUBSHRUB

un·der·side \ˈən-dər-ˌsīd, ˌən-dər-ˈ\ *n* (1660) **1** : the side or surface lying underneath **2** : a side usu. hidden from sight; *specif* : the more unpleasant or reprehensible side ⟨the ~ of politics⟩

un·der·signed \ˈən-dər-ˌsīnd\ *n, pl* **undersigned** (1643) : one whose name is signed at the end of a document ⟨the ~ all agree⟩

un·der·sized \ˌən-dər-ˈsīzd\ *also* **un·der·size** \-ˈsīz\ *adj* (1706) : of a size less than is common, proper, normal, or average ⟨~ trout⟩

un·der·skirt \ˈən-dər-ˌskərt\ *n* (1832) : a skirt worn under an outer skirt; *esp* : PETTICOAT

un·der·slung \ˌən-dər-ˈsləŋ\ *adj* (1903) **1** *of a vehicle frame* : suspended below the axles **2** : having a low center of gravity

un·der·spin \ˈən-dər-ˌspin\ *n* (1901) : BACKSPIN

un·der·staffed \ˌən-dər-ˈstaft\ *adj* (1891) : inadequately staffed — **un·der·staff·ing** \-ˈsta-fiŋ\ *n*

un·der·stand \ˌən-dər-ˈstand\ *vb* **-stood** \-ˈstu̇d\; **-stand·ing** [ME, fr. OE *understandan,* fr. *under* + *standan* to stand] *vt* (bef. 12c) **1 a :** to grasp the meaning of ⟨~ Russian⟩ **b :** to grasp the reasonableness of ⟨his behavior is hard to ~⟩ **c :** to have thorough or technical acquaintance with or expertness in the practice of ⟨~ finance⟩ **d :** to be thoroughly familiar with the character and propensities of ⟨~*s* children⟩ **2 :** to accept as a fact or truth or regard as plausible without utter certainty ⟨we ~ that he is returning from abroad⟩ **3 :** to interpret in one of a number of possible ways **4 :** to supply in thought as though expressed ⟨"to be married" is commonly *understood* after the word *engaged*⟩ ~ *vi* **1 :** to have understanding : have the power of comprehension **2 :** to achieve a grasp of the nature, significance, or explanation of something **3 :** to believe or infer something to be the case **4 :** to show a sympathetic or tolerant attitude toward something — **un·der·stand·abil·i·ty** \-ˌstan-də-ˈbi-lə-tē\ *n* — **un·der·stand·able** \-ˈstan-də-bəl\ *adj*

syn UNDERSTAND, COMPREHEND, APPRECIATE mean to have a clear or complete idea of. UNDERSTAND and COMPREHEND are very often interchangeable. UNDERSTAND may, however, stress the fact of having attained a firm mental grasp of something ⟨orders that were fully *understood* and promptly obeyed⟩. COMPREHEND may stress the process of coming to grips with something intellectually ⟨I have trouble *comprehending* your reasons for doing this⟩. APPRECIATE implies a just evaluation or judgment of a thing's value or nature ⟨failed to *appreciate* the risks involved⟩.

un·der·stand·ably \ˌən-dər-ˈstan-də-blē\ *adv* (ca. 1921) : as can be easily understood : for understandable reasons ⟨is ~ nervous⟩

1**un·der·stand·ing** \ˌən-dər-ˈstan-diŋ\ *n* (bef. 12c) **1 :** a mental grasp : COMPREHENSION **2 a :** the power of comprehending; *esp* : the capacity to apprehend general relations of particulars **b :** the power to make experience intelligible by applying concepts and categories **3 a :** friendly or harmonious relationship **b :** an agreement of opinion or feeling : adjustment of differences **c :** a mutual agreement not formally entered into but in some degree binding on each side **4 :** EXPLANATION, INTERPRETATION **5 :** SYMPATHY 3a

2**understanding** *adj* (13c) **1** *archaic* : KNOWING, INTELLIGENT **2 :** endowed with understanding : TOLERANT, SYMPATHETIC ⟨an ~ supervisor⟩ — **un·der·stand·ing·ly** \-ˈstan-diŋ-lē\ *adv*

un·der·state \ˌən-dər-ˈstāt\ *vt* (1824) **1 :** to represent as less than is the case ⟨~ taxable income⟩ **2 :** to state or present with restraint esp. for effect — **un·der·state·ment** \-mənt\ *n*

un·der·stat·ed \-ˈstā-təd\ *adj* (ca. 1909) : avoiding obvious emphasis or embellishment ⟨~ elegance⟩ — **un·der·stat·ed·ly** *adv*

un·der·steer \ˈən-dər-ˌstir\ *n* (1936) : the tendency of an automobile to turn less sharply than the driver intends — **un·der·steer** \ˌən-dər-ˈ\ *vi*

un·der·stood \ˌən-dər-ˈstu̇d\ *adj* (1605) **1 :** fully apprehended **2 :** agreed upon **3 :** IMPLICIT

un·der·sto·ry \ˈən-dər-ˌstȯr-ē\ *n* (1902) **1 :** an underlying layer of vegetation; *specif* : the vegetative layer and esp. the trees and shrubs between the forest canopy and the ground cover **2 :** the plants that form the understory

un·der·strap·per \-ˌstra-pər\ *n* [3*under* + *strapper* one who harnesses horses] (ca. 1704) : a petty agent or subordinate : UNDERLING

un·der·strength \ˌən-dər-ˈstreŋ(k)th\ *adj* (1925) : deficient in strength; *esp* : lacking sufficient or prescribed personnel

1**un·der·study** \ˈən-dər-ˌstə-dē, ˌən-dər-ˈ\ *vi* (1874) : to study another actor's part in order to substitute in an emergency ~ *vt* : to prepare (as a part) as understudy; *also* : to prepare as understudy to (as an actor)

2**un·der·study** \ˈən-dər-ˌstə-dē\ *n* (1882) : one who is prepared to act another's part or take over another's duties

un·der·sup·ply \ˌən-dər-sə-ˈplī\ *n* (1840) : an inadequate supply

1**un·der·sur·face** \ˈən-dər-ˌsər-fəs\ *n* (1733) : UNDERSIDE

2**un·der·sur·face** \ˌən-dər-ˈsər-fəs\ *adj* (ca. 1934) : existing or moving below the surface

un·der·take \ˌən-dər-ˈtāk\ *vb* **-took** \-ˈtu̇k\; **-tak·en** \-ˈtā-kən\; **-tak·ing** *vt* (14c) **1 :** to take upon oneself : set about : ATTEMPT ⟨~ a task⟩ ⟨~ to learn to swim⟩ **2 :** to put oneself under obligation to perform; *also* : to accept as a charge or responsibility ⟨the lawyer who *undertook* the case⟩ **3 :** GUARANTEE, PROMISE ⟨readily *undertook* that the letter should be securely conveyed —Sir Walter Scott⟩ ~ *vi, archaic* : to give surety or assume responsibility

un·der·tak·er \ˌən-dər-ˈtā-kər, *2 is* ˈən-dər-ˌ\ *n* (15c) **1 :** one that undertakes : one that takes the risk and management of business : ENTREPRENEUR **2 :** one whose business is to prepare the dead for burial and to arrange and manage funerals **3 :** an Englishman taking over forfeited lands in Ireland in the 16th and 17th centuries

un·der·tak·ing \ˈən-dər-ˌtā-kiŋ, ˌən-dər-ˈ; *1b is* ˈən-dər-ˌ *only*\ *n* (14c) **1 a :** the act of one who undertakes or engages in a project or business **b :** the business of an undertaker **2 :** something undertaken : ENTERPRISE **3 :** PLEDGE, GUARANTEE

un·der·ten·ant \ˈən-dər-ˌte-nənt\ *n* (1546) : one who holds lands or tenements by a sublease

under–the–counter *adj* [fr. the hiding of illicit wares under the counter of stores where they are sold] (1926) : surreptitious and usu. irregular or illicit ⟨~ liquor sales⟩

under–the–table *adj* (1948) : covert and usu. unlawful ⟨~ payoffs⟩

un·der·throw \ˈən-dər-ˌthrō\ *vt* (1963) : to throw (a ball or pass) short of the intended receiver in football; *also* : to throw a pass short of ⟨~ a receiver⟩

un·der·thrust \ˌən-dər-ˈthrəst\ *vt* **-thrust; -thrust·ing** (1893) : to insert (a faulted rock mass) into position under a passive rock mass

un·der·tone \ˈən-dər-ˌtōn\ *n* (1806) **1 :** a low or subdued utterance or accompanying sound **2 :** a quality (as of emotion) underlying the surface of an utterance or action **3 :** a subdued color; *specif* : a color seen through and modifying another color

un·der·tow \-ˌtō\ *n* (1817) **1 :** the current beneath the surface that sets seaward or along the beach when waves are breaking upon the shore **2 :** an underlying current, force, or tendency that is in opposition to what is apparent

un·der·treat \ˌən-dər-ˈtrēt\ *vt* (1908) : to treat inadequately ⟨~ a disease⟩

un·der·trick \-ˌtrik\ *n* (1903) : any of the tricks by which a declarer in bridge falls short of making the contract

un·der·used \ˌən-dər-ˈyüzd\ *adj* (1960) : not fully used : having more potential than is currently being realized or utilized ⟨~ land⟩ ⟨an ~ actress⟩

un·der·uti·lize \ˌən-dər-ˈyü-tə-ˌlīz\ *vt* (1951) : to utilize less than fully or below the potential use — **un·der·uti·li·za·tion** \ˈən-dər-ˌyü-tə-lə-ˈzā-shən\ *n*

un·der·val·u·a·tion \ˌən-dər-ˌval-yə-ˈwā-shən\ *n* (1629) **1 :** the act of undervaluing **2 :** a value below the real worth

un·der·val·ue \-ˈval-(ˌ)yü\ *vt* (1599) **1 :** to value, rate, or estimate below the real worth ⟨~ stock⟩ **2 :** to treat as having little value ⟨was *undervalued* as a poet⟩

un·der·wa·ter \ˌən-dər-ˈwȯ-tər, -ˈwä-\ *adj* (1627) **1 :** lying, growing, worn, performed, or operating below the surface of the water ⟨~ plants⟩ **2 :** being below the waterline of a ship **3 :** having, relating to, or being a mortgage loan for which more is owed than the property securing the loan is worth — **underwater** *adv*

un·der·way \ˌən-dər-ˈwā\ *adj* (1743) : occurring, performed, or used while traveling or in motion ⟨~ replenishment of fuel⟩

under way *adv* [prob. fr. D *onderweg,* fr. MD *onderwegen,* lit., under or among the ways] (1720) **1 :** in motion : not at anchor or aground **2 :** into motion from a standstill **3 :** in progress : AFOOT ⟨preparations were *under way*⟩ ⟨the season got *under way* with a bang⟩

un·der·wear \ˈən-dər-ˌwer\ *n* (1870) : clothing or an article of clothing worn next to the skin and under other clothing

under weigh *adv* [by folk etymology] (1749) : UNDER WAY

1**un·der·weight** \ˌən-dər-ˈwāt\ *n* (1596) : weight below normal, average, or requisite weight

2**underweight** *adj* (1675) : weighing less than the normal or requisite amount

un·der·whelm \-ˈhwelm, -ˈwelm\ *vt* [*under* + *overwhelm*] (1948) : to fail to impress or stimulate ⟨the movie ~*ed* most reviewers⟩

1**un·der·wing** \ˈən-dər-ˌwiŋ\ *n* (1535) **1 :** one of the posterior wings of an insect **2 :** any of various noctuid moths (esp. genus *Catocala*) that have the hind wings banded with contrasting colors (as red and black) — called also *underwing moth* **3 :** the underside of a bird's wing

2**underwing** *adj* (1896) : placed or growing underneath the wing ⟨~ rockets⟩

un·der·wire \ˈən-dər-ˌwī(-ə)r\ *n* (1973) : a wire running through the bottom edge of a brassiere to aid in support

un·der·wood \ˈən-dər-ˌwu̇d\ *n* (14c) : UNDERGROWTH, UNDERBRUSH

un·der·wool \-ˌwu̇l\ *n* (1939) : short woolly underfur

un·der·world \-ˌwərld\ *n* (1598) **1 :** the place of departed souls : HADES **2** *archaic* : EARTH **3 :** the side of the earth opposite to one : ANTIPODES **4 :** a social sphere below the level of ordinary life ⟨the town's seedy ~⟩; *esp* : the world of organized crime

un·der·write \ˈən-də(r)-ˌrīt, ˌən-də(r)-ˈ\ *vb* **-wrote** \-ˌrōt, -ˈrōt\; **-writ·ten** \-ˌri-tᵊn, -ˈri-tᵊn\; **-writ·ing** \-ˌrī-tiŋ, -ˈrī-\ *vt* (14c) **1 :** to write under or at the end of something else **2 :** to set one's name to (an insurance policy) for the purpose of thereby becoming answerable for a designated loss or damage on consideration of receiving a premium percent : insure on life or property; *also* : to assume liability for (a sum or risk) as an insurer **3 :** to subscribe to : agree to **4 a :** to agree to purchase (as security issue) usu. on a fixed date at a fixed price with a view to public distribution **b :** to guarantee financial support of ⟨~ a project⟩ ~ *vi* : to work as an underwriter

un·der·writ·er \ˈən-də(r)-ˌrī-tər\ *n* (1622) **1 :** one that underwrites : GUARANTOR **2 a :** one that underwrites a policy of insurance : INSURER **b :** one who selects risks to be solicited or rates the acceptability of risks solicited **3 :** one that underwrites a security issue

un·de·scend·ed \ˌən-di-ˈsen-dəd\ *adj* (1701) : retained within the inguinal region rather than descending into the scrotum ⟨an ~ testis⟩

un·de·sign·ing \ˌən-di-ˈzī-niŋ\ *adj* (1681) : having no ulterior or fraudulent purpose : SINCERE ⟨a child's ~ honesty⟩

1**un·de·sir·able** \-ˈzī-rə-bəl\ *adj* (1667) : not desirable : UNWANTED ⟨~ side effects⟩ — **un·de·sir·abil·i·ty** \-ˌzī-rə-ˈbi-lə-tē\ *n* — **un·de·sir·able·ness** \-ˈzī-rə-bəl-nəs\ *n* — **un·de·sir·ably** \-blē\ *adv*

2**undesirable** *n* (1883) : one that is undesirable

un·de·vi·at·ing \ˌən-ˈdē-vē-ˌā-tiŋ\ *adj* (1732) : keeping a true course : UNSWERVING ⟨served their country with ~ loyalty and devotion⟩ — **un·de·vi·at·ing·ly** \-tiŋ-lē\ *adv*

un·dies \ˈən-dēz\ *n pl* [by shortening & alter.] (1900) : UNDERWEAR; *esp* : women's underwear

un·dine \ˌən-ˈdēn, ˈən-ˌ\ *n* [NL *undina,* fr. L *unda* wave — more at WATER] (1819) : an elemental being in the theory of Paracelsus inhabiting water : WATER NYMPH

un·dip·lo·mat·ic \ˌən-ˌdi-plə-ˈma-tik\ *adj* (ca. 1828) : not diplomatic; *esp* : TACTLESS — **un·dip·lo·mat·i·cal·ly** \-ti-k(ə-)lē\ *adv*

un·di·rect·ed \ˌən-də-ˈrek-təd, -dī-\ *adj* (1596) : not directed : not planned or guided ⟨~ efforts⟩

un·dis·guised \ˌən-dis-ˈgīzd\ *adj* (15c) : not disguised or concealed ⟨~ impatience⟩ — **un·dis·guis·ed·ly** \-ˈgī-zəd-lē\ *adv*

un·dis·so·ci·at·ed \ˌən-di-ˈsō-shē-ˌā-təd, -sē-\ *adj* (1899) : not electrolytically dissociated

un·do \ˌən-ˈdü, ˈən-\ *vb* **-did** \-ˈdid\; **-done** \-ˈdən\; **-do·ing** \-ˈdü-iŋ\ *vt* (bef. 12c) **1 :** to open or loose by releasing a fastening **2 :** to make of no effect or as if not done : make null : REVERSE **3 a :** to ruin the worldly means, reputation, or hopes of ⟨a politician *undone* by scandal⟩ **b :** to disturb the composure of : UPSET ⟨she's come *undone*⟩ **c :** SEDUCE 3 ~ *vi* : to come open or apart — **un·do·er** \-ˈdü-ər\ *n*

un·dock \-ˈdäk\ *vi* (1750) : to move away from a dock (as at sailing time) ~ *vt* : UNCOUPLE ⟨~ the shuttle from the space station⟩

un·doc·u·ment·ed \ən-ˈdä-kyə-ˌmen-təd\ *adj* (1867) : not documented: as **a :** not supported by documentary evidence ⟨~ expenditures⟩ **b :** lacking documents required for legal immigration or residence ⟨~ workers⟩

\ə\ **abut** \ᵊ\ **kitten,** F **table** \ər\ **further** \a\ **ash** \ā\ **ace** \ä\ **mop, mar** \au̇\ **out** \ch\ **chin** \e\ **bet** \ē\ **easy** \g\ **go** \i\ **hit** \ī\ **ice** \j\ **job** \ŋ\ **sing** \ō\ **go** \ȯ\ **law** \ȯi\ **boy** \th\ **thin** \t͟h\ **the** \ü\ **loot** \u̇\ **foot** \y\ **yet** \zh\ **vision, beige** \k̲, ⁿ, œ, ue, ʸ\ *see* Guide to Pronunciation

un·dog·mat·ic \ˌən-dȯg-ˈma-tik, -däg-\ *adj* (1857) : not dogmatic : not committed to dogma — **un·dog·mat·i·cal·ly** \-ti-k(ə-)lē\ *adv*
un·do·ing \-ˈdü-iŋ\ *n* (14c) **1** : an act of loosening : UNFASTENING **2** : RUIN; *also* : a cause of ruin ⟨greed was to prove his ~⟩ **3** : ANNULMENT, REVERSAL
un·done \-ˈdən\ *adj* (14c) : not done : not performed or finished
un·dou·ble \ˌən-ˈdə-bəl\ *vb* (ca. 1611) : UNFOLD, UNCLENCH
un·dou·bled \-ˈdə-bəld\ *adj* (1598) : not doubled
un·doubt·ed \-ˈdau̇-təd\ *adj* (15c) : not doubted : GENUINE, UNDISPUTED ⟨the ~ truth⟩ ⟨an ~ friend⟩ — **un·doubt·ed·ly** *adv*
un·dra·mat·ic \ˌən-drə-ˈma-tik\ *adj* (1754) : lacking dramatic force or quality : UNSPECTACULAR — **un·dra·mat·i·cal·ly** \-ti-k(ə-)lē\ *adv*
un·drape \ˌən-ˈdrāp\ *vt* (1814) : to strip of drapery : UNVEIL
un·draw \-ˈdrȯ\ *vt* **-drew** \-ˈdrü\; **-drawn** \-ˈdrȯn\; **-draw·ing** (1671) : to draw aside (as a curtain) : OPEN
un·dreamed \-ˈdrem(p)t, -ˈdrēmd\ *also* **undreamt** \-ˈdrem(p)t\ *adj* (1611) : not dreamed : not thought of : UNIMAGINED ⟨technical advances ~ of a few years ago⟩
[1]**un·dress** \ən-ˈdres\ *vt* (1596) **1** : to remove the clothes or covering of : DIVEST, STRIP **2** : EXPOSE, REVEAL ~ *vi* : to take off one's clothes : DISROBE
[2]**undress** *n* (1677) **1** : informal dress: as **a** : a loose robe or dressing gown **b** : ordinary dress — compare FULL DRESS **2** : the state of being undressed
un·dressed \ˌən-ˈdrest\ *adj* (1535) : not dressed: as **a** : partially, improperly, or informally clothed **b** : not fully processed or finished ⟨~ hides⟩ **c** : not cared for or tended ⟨an ~ wound⟩ ⟨~ fields⟩
un·drink·able \ˌən-ˈdriŋ-kə-bəl\ *adj* (1611) : unsuitable or unpleasant to drink
un·drunk \-ˈdrəŋk\ *adj* (1637) : not swallowed
un·due \-ˈdü, -ˈdyü\ *adj* (14c) **1** : not due : not yet payable **2** : exceeding or violating propriety or fitness : EXCESSIVE ⟨~ force⟩
un·du·lant \ˈən-jə-lənt, ˈən-dyə-, ˈən-də-\ *adj* (1822) **1** : rising and falling in waves **2** : having a wavy form, outline, or surface ⟨played her approach shot onto the ~ green⟩
undulant fever *n* (1896) : a persistent human brucellosis marked esp. by remittent fever, weakness, headache, chills, and weight loss and contracted by contact with infected domestic animals or consumption of their products
[1]**un·du·late** \ˈən-jə-lət, ˈən-dyə-, ˈən-də-, -ˌlāt\ *or* **un·du·lat·ed** \-ˌlā-təd\ *adj* [L *undulatus*, fr. **undula*, dim. of *unda* wave — more at WATER] (1658) : having a wavy surface, edge, or markings ⟨the ~ margin of a leaf⟩
[2]**un·du·late** \-ˌlāt\ *vb* **-lat·ed; -lat·ing** [LL *undula* small wave, fr. L **undula*] *vi* (1664) **1** : to form or move in waves : FLUCTUATE **2** : to rise and fall in volume, pitch, or cadence **3** : to present a wavy appearance ~ *vt* : to cause to move in a wavy, sinuous, or flowing manner ***syn*** see SWING
un·du·la·tion \ˌən-jə-ˈlā-shən, ˌən-dyə-, ˌən-də-\ *n* (1646) **1 a** : a rising and falling in waves **b** : a wavelike motion to and fro in a fluid or elastic medium propagated continuously among its particles but with little or no permanent translation of the particles in the direction of the propagation : VIBRATION **2** : the pulsation caused by the vibrating together of two tones not quite in unison **3** : a wavy appearance, outline, or form : WAVINESS
un·du·la·to·ry \ˈən-jə-lə-ˌtōr-ē, ˈən-dyə-, ˈən-də-\ *adj* (1728) : of or relating to undulation : moving in or resembling waves : UNDULATING
undulatory theory *n* (ca. 1828) : WAVE THEORY
un·du·ly \ˌən-ˈdü-lē, -ˈdyü-\ *adv* (14c) : in an undue manner : EXCESSIVELY ⟨an ~ harsh punishment⟩ ⟨~ sensitive⟩
un·du·ti·ful \-ˈdü-ti-fəl, -ˈdyü-\ *adj* (1582) : not dutiful — **un·du·ti·ful·ly** \-fə-lē\ *adv* — **un·du·ti·ful·ness** *n*
un·dy·ing \-ˈdī-iŋ\ *adj* (14c) : not dying : IMMORTAL, PERPETUAL
un·earned \-ˈərnd\ *adj* (13c) **1** : not gained by labor, service, or skill ⟨~ income⟩ **2** : scored as a result of an error by the opposing team ⟨an ~ run⟩
unearned increment *n* (1871) : an increase in the value of property (as land) that is due to no labor or expenditure of the owner but to causes (as the increase of population) that create an increased demand for it
un·earth \ˌən-ˈərth\ *vt* (15c) **1** : to dig up out of or as if out of the earth : EXHUME ⟨~ treasure⟩ ⟨~ an old photo album⟩ **2** : to make known or public : bring to light ⟨~ a scandal⟩ ***syn*** see DISCOVER
un·earth·ly \-lē\ *adj* (1611) : not earthly: as **a** : not mundane : IDEAL ⟨~ love⟩ **b** : not terrestrial ⟨~ radio sources⟩ **c** : PRETERNATURAL, SUPERNATURAL ⟨an ~ light⟩ **d** : WEIRD, EERIE ⟨~ howls⟩ **e** : ABSURD, UNGODLY ⟨gets up at an ~ hour⟩ — **un·earth·li·ness** *n*
un·ease \ˌən-ˈēz\ *n* (14c) : mental or spiritual discomfort: as **a** : vague dissatisfaction : MISGIVING **b** : ANXIETY, DISQUIET **c** : lack of ease (as in social relations) : EMBARRASSMENT
un·eas·i·ly \-ˈē-zə-lē\ *adv* (14c) : in an uneasy manner
[1]**un·easy** \-ˈē-zē\ *adj* (14c) **1** : causing physical or mental discomfort ⟨~ news of captures and killings —Marjory S. Douglas⟩ **2** : not easy : DIFFICULT **3** : marked by lack of ease : AWKWARD, EMBARRASSED ⟨gave an ~ laugh⟩ **4** : APPREHENSIVE, WORRIED ⟨~ about the weather⟩ **5** : RESTLESS, UNQUIET ⟨an ~ night⟩ **6** : PRECARIOUS, UNSTABLE ⟨an ~ truce⟩ — **un·eas·i·ness** *n*
[2]**uneasy** *adv* (1596) : UNEASILY
un·eco·nom·ic \ˌən-ˌe-kə-ˈnä-mik, -ˌē-kə-\ *or* **un·eco·nom·i·cal** \-mi-kəl\ *adj* (1840) : not economically practicable ⟨~ transportation routes⟩; *also* : COSTLY, WASTEFUL ⟨an ~ nuclear technology⟩
un·ed·it·ed \ˌən-ˈe-də-təd\ *adj* (1829) : not edited: as **a** : left unrevised **b** : not yet edited ⟨~ books⟩ ⟨~ films⟩
un·emo·tion·al \ˌən-i-ˈmō-shnəl, -shə-nᵊl\ *adj* (1876) : not emotional: as **a** : not easily aroused or excited : COLD **b** : involving a minimum of emotion : INTELLECTUAL ⟨an ~ assessment⟩ — **un·emo·tion·al·ly** *adv*
un·em·ploy·able \ˌən-im-ˈplȯi-ə-bəl\ *adj* (1887) : not acceptable for employment — **un·em·ploy·abil·i·ty** \-ˌplȯi-ə-ˈbi-lə-tē\ *n* — **unemployable** *n*
un·em·ployed \-ˈplȯid\ *adj* (15c) : not employed: **a** : not being used **b** : not engaged in a gainful occupation **c** : not invested — **unemployed** *n*
un·em·ploy·ment \-ˈplȯi-mənt\ *n* (1888) **1** : the state of being unemployed : involuntary idleness of workers; *also* : the rate of such unemployment **2** : UNEMPLOYMENT COMPENSATION
unemployment compensation *n* (1944) : compensation paid at regular intervals (as by a government agency) to an unemployed worker and esp. one who has been laid off — called also *unemployment benefit*
unemployment insurance *n* (1923) : social insurance against involuntary unemployment that provides unemployment compensation for a limited period to unemployed workers; *also* : UNEMPLOYMENT COMPENSATION
un·en·cum·bered \ˌən-in-ˈkəm-bərd\ *adj* (1722) : free of encumbrance
un·end·ing \ˌən-ˈen-diŋ\ *adj* (1661) : never ending : ENDLESS — **un·end·ing·ly** \-diŋ-lē\ *adv*
un–En·glish \ˌən-ˈiŋ-glish *also* -ˈiŋ-lish\ *adj* (1633) **1** : not characteristically English **2** : not agreeing with standard or generally accepted usage of the English language
[1]**un·equal** \ˌən-ˈē-kwəl\ *adj* (1565) **1 a** : not of the same measurement, quantity, or number as another **b** : not like or not the same as another in degree, worth, or status **2** : not uniform : VARIABLE, UNEVEN **3 a** : badly balanced or matched ⟨an ~ contest⟩ **b** : contracted between unequals ⟨~ marriages⟩ **c** *archaic* : not equable **4** *archaic* : not equitable : UNJUST **5** : INADEQUATE, INSUFFICIENT ⟨~ to the task⟩ — **un·equal·ly** \-kwə-lē\ *adv*
[2]**unequal** *n* (1600) : one that is not equal to another
[3]**unequal** *adv* (1602) *archaic* : in an unequal manner ⟨~ match'd —Shak.⟩
un·equaled *or* **un·equalled** \-kwəld\ *adj* (1600) : not equaled : UNPARALLELED ⟨an artist of ~ talent⟩
un·equiv·o·ca·bly \ˌən-i-ˈkwi-və-kə-blē\ *adv* [by alter.] (1917) *nonstand* : UNEQUIVOCALLY
un·equiv·o·cal \ˌən-i-ˈkwi-və-kəl\ *adj* (1784) **1** : leaving no doubt : CLEAR, UNAMBIGUOUS **2** : UNQUESTIONABLE ⟨production of ~ masterpieces —Carole Cook⟩
un·equiv·o·cal·ly \-kə-lē, -klē\ *adv* (1794) : in an unequivocal manner
un·err·ing \ˌən-ˈer-iŋ, ˌən-ˈər-\ *adj* (1621) : committing no error : FAULTLESS, UNFAILING ⟨~ accuracy⟩ — **un·err·ing·ly** \-iŋ-lē\ *adv*
UNESCO *abbr* United Nations Educational, Scientific, and Cultural Organization
un·es·sen·tial \ˌən-ə-ˈsen(t)-shəl\ *adj* (ca. 1656) **1** : not essential : DISPENSABLE, UNIMPORTANT **2** *archaic* : void of essence : INSUBSTANTIAL
un–Eu·ro·pe·an \ˌən-ˌyu̇r-ə-ˈpē-ən\ *adj* (1846) : not characteristically European
un·even \ˌən-ˈē-vən\ *adj* (bef. 12c) **1 a** *archaic* : UNEQUAL 1a **b** : ODD 3a **2 a** : not even : not level or smooth : RUGGED, RAGGED ⟨large ~ teeth⟩ ⟨~ handwriting⟩ **b** : varying from the straight or parallel **c** : not uniform : IRREGULAR ⟨~ combustion⟩ **d** : varying in quality ⟨an ~ performance⟩ **3** : UNEQUAL 3a ⟨an ~ confrontation⟩ ***syn*** see ROUGH — **un·even·ly** *adv* — **un·even·ness** \-və(n)-nəs\ *n*
un·event·ful \ˌən-i-ˈvent-fəl\ *adj* (1800) : marked by no noteworthy or untoward incidents : PLACID ⟨an ~ weekend⟩ — **un·event·ful·ly** \-fə-lē\ *adv* — **un·event·ful·ness** \-fəl-nəs\ *n*
un·evolved \ˌən-i-ˈvälvd, -ˈvȯlvd\ *adj* (ca. 1775) : not evolved: as **a** : not fully developed ⟨an ~ wine⟩ **b** : lacking cultural refinement : UNENLIGHTENED
un·ex·am·pled \ˌən-ig-ˈzam-pəld\ *adj* (1610) : having no example or parallel : UNPRECEDENTED ⟨his ardent attachment and . . . ~ passion —Jane Austen⟩
un·ex·cep·tion·able \ˌən-ik-ˈsep-sh(ə-)nə-bəl\ *adj* [*un-* + obs. *exception* to take exception, object] (1664) : not open to objection or criticism : beyond reproach : UNIMPEACHABLE ⟨~ integrity⟩ — **un·ex·cep·tion·able·ness** *n* — **un·ex·cep·tion·ably** \-blē\ *adv*
un·ex·cep·tion·al \-shnəl, -shə-nᵊl\ *adj* (1806) : not out of the ordinary : COMMONPLACE
un·ex·er·cised \ˌən-ˈek-sər-ˌsīzd\ *adj* (14c) **1** : having terms that are not implemented ⟨~ options⟩ **2** : not subjected to exercise ⟨~ muscles⟩
un·ex·pect·ed \ˌən-ik-ˈspek-təd\ *adj* (ca. 1586) : not expected : UNFORESEEN — **un·ex·pect·ed·ly** *adv* — **un·ex·pect·ed·ness** *n*
un·ex·ploit·ed \ˌən-ik-ˈsplȯi-təd\ *adj* (1888) : not exploited or developed : not taken advantage of ⟨~ resources⟩
un·ex·pres·sive \ˌən-ik-ˈspre-siv\ *adj* (1600) **1** *obs* : INEFFABLE **2** : not expressive : failing to convey the feeling or meaning intended
un·fad·ing \ˌən-ˈfā-diŋ\ *adj* (1652) **1** : not losing color or freshness **2** : not losing value or effectiveness — **un·fad·ing·ly** \-diŋ-lē\ *adv*
un·fail·ing \ˌən-ˈfā-liŋ\ *adj* (14c) : not failing or liable to fail: **a** : CONSTANT, UNFLAGGING ⟨~ courtesy⟩ **b** : EVERLASTING, INEXHAUSTIBLE ⟨a subject of ~ interest⟩ **c** : INFALLIBLE, SURE ⟨an ~ test⟩ — **un·fail·ing·ly** \-liŋ-lē\ *adv*
un·fair \ˌən-ˈfer\ *adj* (1700) **1** : marked by injustice, partiality, or deception : UNJUST **2** : not equitable in business dealings — **un·fair·ness** *n*
un·fair·ly *adv* (1713) : in an unfair manner
un·faith \ˌən-ˈfāth, ˈən-ˌ\ *n* (15c) : absence of faith : DISBELIEF
un·faith·ful \ˌən-ˈfāth-fəl\ *adj* (15c) : not faithful: **a** : not adhering to vows, allegiance, or duty : DISLOYAL ⟨an ~ friend⟩ **b** : not faithful to marriage vows ⟨suspected her husband of being ~⟩ **c** : INACCURATE, UNTRUSTWORTHY ⟨an ~ copy of a document⟩ — **un·faith·ful·ly** \-fə-lē\ *adv* — **un·faith·ful·ness** *n*
un·fall·en \ˌən-ˈfȯ-lən\ *adj* (1653) : not morally fallen : INNOCENT 1a
un·fal·si·fi·able \ˌən-ˌfȯl-sə-ˈfī-ə-bəl\ *adj* (ca. 1934) : not capable of being proved false ⟨~ hypotheses⟩
un·fal·ter·ing \ˌən-ˈfȯl-t(ə-)riŋ\ *adj* (1727) : not wavering or weakening : FIRM ⟨~ loyalty⟩ — **un·fal·ter·ing·ly** \-t(ə-)riŋ-lē\ *adv*
un·fa·mil·iar \ˌən-fə-ˈmil-yər\ *adj* (1594) : not familiar: **a** : not well-known : STRANGE ⟨an ~ place⟩ **b** : not well acquainted ⟨~ with the subject⟩ — **un·fa·mil·iar·i·ty** \-ˌmil-ˈyar-ə-tē, -ˌmi-lē-ˈyar-\ *n* — **un·fa·mil·iar·ly** \-ˈmil-yər-lē\ *adv*
un·fash·ion·able \-ˈfa-sh(ə-)nə-bəl\ *adj* (1648) **1** : not in keeping with the current fashion ⟨~ clothes⟩ **2** : not favored socially ⟨~ neighborhoods⟩ — **un·fash·ion·able·ness** \-bəl-nəs\ *n* — **un·fash·ion·ably** \-blē\ *adv*

un·fas·ten \-ˈfa-sᵊn\ *vt* (14c) : to make loose: as **a** : UNPIN, UNBUCKLE **b** : UNDO ⟨~ a button⟩ **c** : DETACH ⟨~ a boat from its moorings⟩
un·fa·thered \-ˈfä-t͟hərd\ *adj* (1597) **1** : having no father : ILLEGITIMATE, BASTARD **2** : having no known origin ⟨~ slanders⟩
un·fath·om·able \-ˈfa-t͟hə-mə-bəl\ *adj* (1640) : not capable of being fathomed: **a** : IMMEASURABLE **b** : impossible to comprehend — **un·fath·om·ably** \-blē\ *adv*
un·fa·vor·able \ˌən-ˈfā-v(ə-)rə-bəl, -ˈfā-vər-bəl\ *adj* (1548) **1 a** : OPPOSED, CONTRARY **b** : expressing disapproval : NEGATIVE ⟨~ reviews⟩ **2** : not propitious : DISADVANTAGEOUS ⟨an ~ business climate⟩ **3** : not pleasing ⟨an ~ feature of the plan⟩ — **un·fa·vor·able·ness** *n* — **un·fa·vor·ably** \-blē\ *adv*
un·fa·vor·ite \-ˈfā-v(ə-)rət, -ˈfā-vərt\ *adj* (ca. 1934) : not being a favorite; *esp* : being regarded with special disfavor or dislike
un·fazed \ˌən-ˈfāzd\ *adj* (1945) : not fazed : UNDAUNTED
un·feel·ing \-ˈfē-liŋ\ *adj* (bef. 12c) **1** : devoid of feeling : INSENSATE ⟨an ~ corpse⟩ **2** : lacking kindness or sympathy : HARDHEARTED ⟨an ~ brute⟩ — **un·feel·ing·ly** \-liŋ-lē\ *adv* — **un·feel·ing·ness** *n*
un·feigned \-ˈfānd\ *adj* (14c) : not feigned or hypocritical : GENUINE *syn* see SINCERE — **un·feigned·ly** \-ˈfā-nəd-lē, -ˈfānd-lē\ *adv*
un·fet·ter \-ˈfe-tər\ *vt* (14c) **1** : to free from fetters ⟨~ a prisoner⟩ **2** : EMANCIPATE, LIBERATE ⟨~ the mind from prejudice⟩
un·fet·tered \-tərd\ *adj* (1601) : FREE, UNRESTRAINED ⟨~ access⟩
un·fil·ial \ˌən-ˈfi-lē-əl, -ˈfil-yəl\ *adj* (1611) : not observing the obligations of a child to a parent : UNDUTIFUL — **un·fil·ial·ly** *adv*
un·fil·tered \ˌən-ˈfil-tərd\ *adj* (ca. 1775) **1** : not filtered ⟨~ wine⟩; *also* : not modified, processed, or refined ⟨~ commercial publicity material —Paul Grimes⟩ **2** : lacking a filter ⟨an ~ cigarette⟩
un·find·able \ˌən-ˈfīn-də-bəl\ *adj* (1791) : not capable of being found
un·fin·ished \-ˈfi-nisht\ *adj* (1539) : not finished: **a** : not brought to an end or to the desired final state **b** : being in a rough state : UNPOLISHED **c** : subjected to no other processes (as bleaching or dyeing) after coming from the loom
[1]**un·fit** \-ˈfit\ *adj* (1545) : not fit: **a** : not adapted to a purpose : UNSUITABLE **b** : not qualified : INCAPABLE, INCOMPETENT **c** : physically or mentally unsound — **un·fit·ly** *adv* — **un·fit·ness** *n*
[2]**unfit** *vt* (1611) : to make unfit : DISABLE, DISQUALIFY
un·fit·ted \ˌən-ˈfi-təd\ *adj* (1592) : not adapted : UNQUALIFIED
un·fit·ting \-ˈfi-tiŋ\ *adj* (15c) : not fitting : UNSUITABLE
un·fix \-ˈfiks\ *vt* (1597) **1** : to loosen from a fastening : DETACH, DISENGAGE **2** : to make unstable : UNSETTLE
un·flag·ging \-ˈfla-giŋ\ *adj* (1715) **1** : not flagging : TIRELESS ⟨~ enthusiasm⟩ **2** : UNRELENTING 2 — **un·flag·ging·ly** \-giŋ-lē\ *adv*
un·flap·pa·ble \-ˈfla-pə-bəl\ *adj* [ˈ*un-* + ³*flap* (state of excitement) + *-able*] (1954) : marked by assurance and self-control — **un·flap·pa·bil·i·ty** \-ˌfla-pə-ˈbi-lə-tē\ *n* — **un·flap·pa·bly** \-ˈfla-pə-blē\ *adv*
un·flat·ter·ing \-ˈfla-tə-riŋ\ *adj* (1581) : not flattering ⟨an ~ portrait⟩; *esp* : UNFAVORABLE ⟨~ remarks⟩ — **un·flat·ter·ing·ly** \-riŋ-lē\ *adv*
un·fledged \ˌən-ˈflejd\ *adj* (1602) **1** : not feathered : not ready for flight **2** : not fully developed : IMMATURE ⟨an ~ writer⟩
un·flinch·ing \-ˈflin-chiŋ\ *adj* (1728) : not flinching or shrinking : STEADFAST, UNCOMPROMISING ⟨~ determination⟩ — **un·flinch·ing·ly** \-chiŋ-lē\ *adv*
un·fo·cused *also* **un·fo·cussed** \-ˈfō-kəst\ *adj* (1886) **1** : not adjusted to a focus **2** : not concentrated on one point or objective ⟨~ rage⟩
un·fold \-ˈfōld\ *vt* (bef. 12c) **1 a** : to open the folds of : spread or straighten out : EXPAND ⟨~*ed* the map⟩ **b** : to remove (as a package) from the folds : UNWRAP **2** : to open to the view : REVEAL; *esp* : to make clear by gradual disclosure and often by recital ~ *vi* **1 a** : to open from a folded state : open out : EXPAND **b** : BLOSSOM **2** : DEVELOP, EVOLVE ⟨as the story ~*s*⟩ **3** : to open out gradually to the view or understanding : become known ⟨a panorama ~*s* before their eyes⟩ — **un·fold·ment** \-ˈfōl(d)-mənt\ *n*
un·fold·ed \-ˈfōl-dəd\ *adj* (1683) : not folded
un·for·get·ta·ble \ˌən-fər-ˈge-tə-bəl\ *adj* (1806) : incapable of being forgotten : MEMORABLE — **un·for·get·ta·bly** \-ˈge-tə-blē\ *adv*
un·for·giv·ing \ˌən-fər-ˈgi-viŋ\ *adj* (1713) **1** : unwilling or unable to forgive **2** : having or making no allowance for error or weakness ⟨an ~ environment where false moves can prove fatal —Jaclyn Fierman⟩ — **un·for·giv·ing·ness** *n*
un·formed \-ˈfȯrmd\ *adj* (14c) : not arranged in regular shape, order, or relations; *esp* : IMMATURE, UNDEVELOPED
[1]**un·for·tu·nate** \-ˈfȯrch-nət, -ˈfȯr-chə-\ *adj* (15c) **1 a** : not favored by fortune : UNSUCCESSFUL, UNLUCKY ⟨an ~ young man⟩ **b** : marked or accompanied by or resulting in misfortune ⟨an ~ decision⟩ **2 a** : INFELICITOUS, UNSUITABLE ⟨an ~ choice of words⟩ **b** : DEPLORABLE, REGRETTABLE ⟨an ~ lack of taste⟩
[2]**unfortunate** *n* (1683) : an unfortunate person
un·for·tu·nate·ly \-lē\ *adv* (ca. 1548) **1** : in an unfortunate manner ⟨the marriage turned out ~⟩ **2** : it is unfortunate ⟨~ for him your letter has let the cat out of the bag —G. B. Shaw⟩
un·found·ed \ˌən-ˈfau̇n-dəd\ *adj* (1648) : lacking a sound basis : GROUNDLESS, UNWARRANTED ⟨an ~ accusation⟩
un·freeze \-ˈfrēz\ *vt* **-froze** \-ˈfrōz\; **-fro·zen** \-ˈfrō-zᵊn\; **-freez·ing** (1584) **1** : to cause to thaw **2** : to remove from a freeze ⟨~ wages⟩
un·fre·quent·ed \ˌən-frē-ˈkwen-təd; ˌən-ˈfrē-kwən-\ *adj* (1588) : not often visited or traveled over
un·friend \ˌən-ˈfrend\ *vt* (2003) : to remove (someone) from a list of designated friends on a person's social networking Web site
un·friend·ed \ˌən-ˈfren-dəd\ *adj* (1513) : having no friends : not befriended
un·friend·li·ness \-ˈfren(d)-lē-nəs\ *n* (ca. 1684) : the quality or state of being unfriendly : HOSTILITY
un·friend·ly \-ˈfren(d)-lē\ *adj* (15c) : not friendly: as **a** : HOSTILE, UNSYMPATHETIC ⟨an ~ nation⟩ **b** : INHOSPITABLE, UNFAVORABLE
un·frock \-ˈfräk\ *vt* (1644) : DEFROCK
un·fro·zen \-ˈfrō-zᵊn\ *adj* (1596) : not frozen ⟨~ ground⟩
un·fruit·ful \-ˈfrüt-fəl\ *adj* (14c) : not fruitful: as **a** : not producing offspring : BARREN **b** : yielding no valuable result : UNPROFITABLE ⟨an ~ conference⟩ — **un·fruit·ful·ly** \-fə-lē\ *adv* — **un·fruit·ful·ness** *n*
un·fund·ed \-ˈfən-dəd\ *adj* (ca. 1775) **1** : not funded : FLOATING ⟨an ~ debt⟩ **2** : not provided with funds ⟨~ schools⟩
un·furl \-ˈfər(-ə)l\ *vt* (1641) : to release from a furled state ~ *vi* : to open out from or as if from a furled state : UNFOLD
un·fussy \-ˈfə-sē\ *adj* (1823) : not fussy: as **a** : not particular : UNCONCERNED **b** : not cluttered with pretentious or nonessential matters : UNCOMPLICATED ⟨~ designs⟩ — **un·fuss·i·ly** \-ˈfə-sə-lē\ *adv*
un·gain·ly \-ˈgān-lē\ *adj* [obs. *gain* direct, fr. ME *gayn, geyn,* fr. OE *gēn,* fr. ON *gegn,* fr. *gegn,* prep., against; akin to OE *gēan-* against — more at AGAIN] (1611) **1 a** : lacking in smoothness or dexterity : CLUMSY ⟨~ movements⟩ **b** : hard to handle : UNWIELDY ⟨an ~ contraption⟩ **2** : having an awkward appearance ⟨a large ~ bird⟩ — **un·gain·li·ness** *n*
un·gen·er·os·i·ty \ˌən-ˌje-nə-ˈrä-sə-tē, -ˈräs-tē\ *n* (1757) : lack of generosity
un·gen·er·ous \ˌən-ˈjen-rəs, -ˈje-nə-\ *adj* (1641) : not generous: **a** : PETTY, MEAN ⟨~ criticisms⟩ **b** : deficient in liberality : STINGY ⟨an ~ offer⟩ — **un·gen·er·ous·ly** *adv*
un·gird \-ˈgərd\ *vt* (bef. 12c) : to divest of a restraining band or girdle : UNBIND
un·girt \-ˈgərt\ *adj* (14c) **1** : having the belt or girdle off or loose **2** : lacking in discipline or compactness : LOOSE, SLACK
un·glue \-ˈglü\ *vt* (ca. 1548) : to separate by or as if by dissolving an adhesive
un·glued \-ˈglüd\ *adj* (1922) : UPSET, DISORDERED — usu. used with *come* ⟨chief executives came ~ at the thought of a strike —H. E. Meyer⟩
un·god·li·ness \ˌən-ˈgäd-lē-nəs *also* -ˈgȯd-\ *n* (1526) : the quality or state of being ungodly
un·god·ly \-lē\ *adj* (14c) **1 a** : denying or disobeying God : IMPIOUS, IRRELIGIOUS **b** : contrary to moral law : SINFUL, WICKED **2** : OUTRAGEOUS ⟨gets up at an ~ hour⟩
un·got·ten \-ˈgä-tᵊn\ *or* **un·got** \-ˈgät\ *adj* (15c) **1** *obs* : not begotten **2** : not obtained
un·gov·ern·able \-ˈgə-vər-nə-bəl\ *adj* (1673) : not capable of being governed, guided, or restrained *syn* see UNRULY
un·gra·cious \-ˈgrā-shəs\ *adj* (13c) **1** *archaic* : WICKED **2** : not courteous : RUDE ⟨~ treatment⟩ **3** : not pleasing : DISAGREEABLE ⟨an ~ task⟩ — **un·gra·cious·ly** *adv* — **un·gra·cious·ness** *n*
un·gram·mat·i·cal \ˌən-grə-ˈma-ti-kəl\ *adj* (1654) : not following rules of grammar — **un·gram·mat·i·cal·i·ty** \-ˌma-tə-ˈka-lə-tē\ *n*
un·grate·ful \ˌən-ˈgrāt-fəl\ *adj* (1533) **1** : showing no gratitude : making a poor return ⟨an ~ child⟩ **2** : DISAGREEABLE; *also* : THANKLESS — **un·grate·ful·ly** \-fə-lē\ *adv* — **un·grate·ful·ness** *n*
un·grudg·ing \-ˈgrə-jiŋ\ *adj* (ca. 1774) : being without envy or reluctance ⟨~ efforts⟩ — **un·grudg·ing·ly** *adv*
un·gual \ˈəŋ-gwəl, ˈən-\ *adj* [L *unguis* nail, claw, hoof — more at NAIL] (1834) : of, relating to, or resembling a nail, claw, or hoof
un·guard \ˌən-ˈgärd\ *vt* [back-formation fr. *unguarded*] (1745) : to leave unprotected
un·guard·ed \-ˈgär-dəd\ *adj* (ca. 1593) **1** : vulnerable to attack : UNPROTECTED **2** : free from guile or wariness : DIRECT, INCAUTIOUS ⟨~ remarks⟩ — **un·guard·ed·ly** *adv* — **un·guard·ed·ness** *n*
un·guent \ˈəŋ-gwənt, ˈən-; ˈən-jənt\ *n* [ME, fr. AF, fr. L *unguentum* — more at OINTMENT] (15c) : a soothing or healing salve : OINTMENT
[1]**un·gu·late** \ˈəŋ-gyə-lət, ˈən-, -ˌlāt\ *adj* [LL *ungulatus,* fr. L *ungula* hoof, fr. *unguis* nail, hoof] (1839) **1** : having hooves **2** : of or relating to the ungulates
[2]**ungulate** *n* [NL *Ungulata,* fr. LL, neut. pl. of *ungulatus*] (ca. 1842) : a hoofed typically herbivorous quadruped mammal (as an artiodactyl or a perissodactyl) of a group formerly considered a major mammalian taxon (Ungulata)
un·hair \ˌən-ˈher\ *vt* (14c) *archaic* : to deprive of hair
un·hal·low \-ˈha-(ˌ)lō\ *vt* (1535) *archaic* : to make profane
un·hal·lowed \-(ˌ)lōd\ *adj* (bef. 12c) **1** : not blessed : UNCONSECRATED, UNHOLY ⟨~ ground⟩ **2 a** : unsanctioned by or showing lack of reverence for religion : IMPIOUS, PROFANE **b** : contrary to accepted standards : IMMORAL
un·hand \ˌən-ˈhand\ *vt* (1602) : to remove the hand from : let go
un·hand·some \-ˈhan(t)-səm\ *adj* (1530) : not handsome: as **a** : not beautiful : HOMELY **b** : UNBECOMING, UNSEEMLY **c** : lacking in courtesy or taste : RUDE — **un·hand·some·ly** *adv*
un·handy \-ˈhan-dē\ *adj* (1664) **1** : hard to handle : INCONVENIENT **2** : lacking in skill or dexterity : AWKWARD — **un·hand·i·ly** \-də-lē\ *adv* — **un·hand·i·ness** \-dē-nəs\ *n*
un·hap·pi·ly \ˌən-ˈha-pə-lē\ *adv* (14c) **1** : UNFORTUNATELY 2 ⟨~, medicine has not yet found a cure —Diana Trilling⟩ **2** : in an unhappy manner : without pleasure ⟨practiced law ~ for a few years⟩
un·hap·py \-ˈha-pē\ *adj* (14c) **1** : not fortunate : UNLUCKY ⟨an ~ coincidence⟩ **2** : not cheerful or glad : SAD, WRETCHED **3 a** : causing or subject to misfortune : INAUSPICIOUS **b** : INFELICITOUS, INAPPROPRIATE ⟨an ~ choice⟩ — **un·hap·pi·ness** *n*
un·har·ness \-ˈhär-nəs\ *vt* (1562) : to remove a harness from ⟨~ a horse⟩
un·healthy \-ˈhel-thē\ *adj* (1595) **1** : not conducive to health ⟨an ~ climate⟩ **2** : not in good health : SICKLY, DISEASED **3 a** : DANGEROUS, RISKY **b** : BAD, INJURIOUS **c** : morally contaminated : CORRUPT, UNWHOLESOME ⟨an ~ imagination⟩ — **un·health·i·ly** \-thə-lē\ *adv* — **un·health·i·ness** \-thē-nəs\ *n*
un·heard \-ˈhərd\ *adj* (14c) **1 a** : not perceived by the ear **b** : not given a hearing **2** *archaic* : UNHEARD-OF
un·heard–of \-ˌəv, -ˌäv\ *adj* (1592) : previously unknown; *esp* : UNPRECEDENTED ⟨moving at ~ speeds⟩
un·hes·i·tat·ing \-ˈhe-zə-ˌtā-tiŋ\ *adj* (1753) : not hesitating : not checked or qualified — **un·hes·i·tat·ing·ly** \-tiŋ-lē\ *adv*
un·hinge \-ˈhinj\ *vt* (1612) **1** : to make unstable : UNSETTLE, DISRUPT ⟨~ the balance of world peace⟩ ⟨pressure that would ~ a less experienced person⟩ **2** : to remove (as a door) from the hinges
un·hinged \-ˈhinjd\ *adj* (1652) : UPSET, UNGLUED; *esp* : mentally deranged ⟨attacked by an ~ extremist⟩
un·hitch \-ˈhich\ *vt* (1706) : to free from or as if from being hitched

\ə\ **abut** \ᵊ\ **kitten**, F **table** \ər\ **further** \a\ **ash** \ā\ **ace** \ä\ **mop, mar** \au̇\ **out** \ch\ **chin** \e\ **bet** \ē\ **easy** \g\ **go** \i\ **hit** \ī\ **ice** \j\ **job** \ŋ\ **sing** \ō\ **go** \ȯ\ **law** \ȯi\ **boy** \th\ **thin** \t͟h\ **the** \ü\ **loot** \u̇\ **foot** \y\ **yet** \zh\ **vision, beige** \k̲, ⁿ, œ, ue, ʸ\ *see* Guide to Pronunciation

un·ho·ly \ˌən-ˈhō-lē\ *adj* (bef. 12c) **1 :** showing disregard for what is holy : WICKED **2 :** deserving of censure ⟨an ~ alliance⟩ **3 :** very unpleasant : GOD-AWFUL ⟨an ~ mess⟩ — **un·ho·li·ness** *n*

un·hood \-ˈhu̇d\ *vt* (13c) : to remove a hood or covering from

un·hook \-ˈhu̇k\ *vt* (1611) **1 :** to remove from a hook **2 :** to unfasten by disengaging a hook **3 :** to free from a habit or dependency

un·hoped \-ˈhōpt\ *adj* (14c) *archaic* : not hoped for or expected

un·horse \-ˈhȯrs\ *vt* (14c) : to dislodge from or as if from a horse

un·hou·seled \-ˈhau̇-zəld\ *adj* (1532) *archaic* : not having received the Eucharist esp. shortly before death

un·hur·ried \-ˈhər-ēd, -ˈhə-rēd\ *adj* (ca. 1774) : not hurried : LEISURELY ⟨an ~ pace⟩ — **un·hur·ried·ly** *adv*

uni- *prefix* [L, fr. *unus* — more at ONE] : one : single ⟨*uni*cellular⟩

uni·al·gal \ˌyü-nē-ˈal-gəl\ *adj* (1914) : of, relating to, or derived from a single algal individual or cell ⟨a ~ culture⟩

Uni·ate *or* **Uni·at** \ˈyü-nē-ˌat, ˈü-\ *n* [Ukrainian *uniat, uniyat* one in favor of the union of the Greek and Roman Catholic churches, fr. *uniya* union, fr. Pol *unija*, fr. LL *unio* — more at UNION] (1833) : a Christian of a church adhering to an Eastern rite and discipline but submitting to papal authority — **Uniate** *adj*

uni·ax·i·al \ˌyü-nē-ˈak-sē-əl\ *adj* (ca. 1828) **1 :** having only one axis **2 :** of or relating to only one axis

uni·brow \ˈyü-nə-ˌbrau̇\ *n* (1988) : a single continuous brow resulting from the growing together of eyebrows

uni·cam·er·al \ˌyü-ni-ˈkam-rəl, -ˈka-mə-\ *adj* [*uni-* + LL *camera* room, chamber — more at CHAMBER] (1853) : having or consisting of a single legislative chamber — **uni·cam·er·al·ly** *adv*

UNICEF *abbr* [*United Nations International Children's Emergency Fund,* its former name] United Nations Children's Fund

uni·cel·lu·lar \ˌyü-ni-ˈsel-yə-lər\ *adj* (1858) : having or consisting of a single cell ⟨~ microorganisms⟩

uni·corn \ˈyü-nə-ˌkȯrn\ *n* [ME *unicorne,* fr. AF, fr. LL *unicornis,* fr. L, having one horn, fr. *uni-* + *cornu* horn — more at HORN] (13c) : a mythical animal generally depicted with the body and head of a horse, the hind legs of a stag, the tail of a lion, and a single horn in the middle of the forehead

unicorn plant *n* (1847) : DEVIL'S CLAW

uni·cy·cle \ˈyü-ni-ˌsī-kəl\ *n* [*uni-* + *-cycle* (as in *tricycle*)] (1869) : a vehicle that has a single wheel and is usu. propelled by pedals — **uni·cy·clist** \-ˌsī-k(ə-)list\ *n*

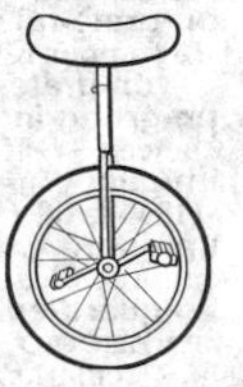
unicycle

uni·di·men·sion·al \ˌyü-ni-də-ˈmench-nəl, -ˈmen(t)-sh(ə-)nᵊl *also* -ˌdī-\ *adj* (1883) : ONE-DIMENSIONAL — **uni·di·men·sion·al·i·ty** \-ˌmen(t)-shə-ˈna-lə-tē\ *n*

uni·di·rec·tion·al \ˌyü-ni-də-ˈrek-shnəl, -dī-, -shə-nᵊl\ *adj* (1883) **1 :** involving, functioning, moving, or responsive in a single direction ⟨a ~ microphone⟩ **2 :** not subject to change or reversal of direction — **uni·di·rec·tion·al·ly** *adv*

unidirectional current *n* (1883) : DIRECT CURRENT

uni·fi·ca·tion \ˌyü-nə-fə-ˈkā-shən\ *n* (1851) : the act, process, or result of unifying : the state of being unified

uni·fo·li·ate \-ˈfō-lē-ət\ *adj* [*uni-* + L *folium* leaf — more at BLADE] (1849) **1 :** having only one leaf **2 :** UNIFOLIOLATE

uni·fo·li·o·late \-ˈfō-lē-ə-ˌlāt\ *adj* [*uni-* + LL *foliolum* leaflet, dim. of L *folium* leaf] (ca. 1859) *of a leaf* : compound but having only a single leaflet and distinguishable from a simple leaf by the basal joint

1**uni·form** \ˈyü-nə-ˌfȯrm\ *adj* [ME *uniforme,* fr. MF, fr. L *uniformis,* fr. *uni-* + *-formis* -form] (15c) **1 :** having always the same form, manner, or degree : not varying or variable ⟨~ procedures⟩ **2 :** consistent in conduct or opinion ⟨~ interpretation of laws⟩ **3 :** of the same form with others : conforming to one rule or mode : CONSONANT **4 :** presenting an unvaried appearance of surface, pattern, or color ⟨~ red brick houses⟩ **5 :** relating to or being convergence of a series whose terms are functions in such manner that the absolute value of the difference between the sum of the first *n* terms of the series and the sum of all terms can be made arbitrarily small for all values of the domain of the functions by choosing the *n*th term sufficiently far along in the series — **uni·form·ly** \ˈyü-nə-ˌfȯrm-lē, ˌyü-nə-ˈ\ *adv* — **uni·form·ness** \ˈyü-nə-ˌfȯrm-nəs\ *n*

2**uniform** *vt* (ca. 1681) **1 :** to bring into uniformity **2 :** to clothe with a uniform

3**uniform** *n* (1748) : dress of a distinctive design or fashion worn by members of a particular group and serving as a means of identification; *broadly* : distinctive or characteristic clothing

Uniform (1956) — a communications code word for the letter *u*

uni·for·mi·tar·i·an \ˌyü-nə-ˌfȯr-mə-ˈter-ē-ən\ *n* (1840) **1 :** an adherent of the doctrine of uniformitarianism **2 :** an advocate of uniformity — **uniformitarian** *adj*

uni·for·mi·tar·i·an·ism \-ē-ə-ˌni-zəm\ *n* (1865) : a geological doctrine that processes acting in the same manner as at present and over long spans of time are sufficient to account for all current geological features and all past geological changes — compare CATASTROPHISM

uni·for·mi·ty \ˌyü-nə-ˈfȯr-mə-tē\ *n, pl* **-ties** (15c) **1 :** the quality or state of being uniform **2 :** an instance of uniformity

uniform resource locator *n* (1993) : URL

uni·fy \ˈyü-nə-ˌfī\ *vt* **-fied; -fy·ing** [LL *unificare,* fr. L *uni-* + *-ficare* -fy] (1502) : to make into a unit or a coherent whole : UNITE — **uni·fi·able** \-ˌfī-ə-bəl\ *adj* — **uni·fi·er** \-ˌfī(-ə)r\ *n*

uni·lat·er·al \ˌyü-ni-ˈla-tə-rəl, -ˈla-trəl\ *adj* (1802) **1 a :** done or undertaken by one person or party **b :** of, relating to, or affecting one side of a subject : ONE-SIDED **c :** constituting or relating to a contract or engagement by which an express obligation to do or forbear is imposed on only one party **2 a :** having parts arranged on one side ⟨a ~ raceme⟩ **b :** occurring on, performed on, or affecting one side of the body or one of its parts ⟨~ exophthalmos⟩ **3 :** UNILINEAL **4 :** having only one side — **uni·lat·er·al·ly** *adv*

uni·lat·er·al·ism \ˌyü-ni-ˈla-t(ə-)rə-ˌli-zəm\ *n* (1926) : a policy of taking unilateral action (as in international affairs) regardless of outside support or reciprocity; *also* : advocacy of such a policy — **uni·lat·er·al·ist** \-list\ *n or adj*

uni·lin·e·al \-ˈli-nē-əl\ *adj* (1935) : tracing descent through either the maternal or paternal line only

uni·lin·e·ar \ˌyü-ni-ˈli-nē-ər\ *adj* (1910) : developing in or involving a series of stages usu. from the primitive to the more advanced

uni·lin·gual \ˌyü-ni-ˈliŋ-gwəl, -gyə-wəl\ *adj* [*uni-* + L *lingua* tongue, language — more at TONGUE] (1866) : composed in or using one language only

un·il·lu·sioned \ˌən-i-ˈlü-zhənd\ *adj* (1926) : free from illusion

uni·loc·u·lar \ˌyü-ni-ˈlä-kyə-lər\ *adj* (1753) : containing a single cavity

un·imag·in·able \ˌən-ə-ˈmaj-nə-bəl, -ˈma-jə-\ *adj* (1611) : not imaginable or comprehensible ⟨~ horror⟩ — **un·imag·in·ably** \-blē\ *adv*

un·im·peach·able \ˌən-im-ˈpē-chə-bəl\ *adj* (1784) : not impeachable: as **a :** reliable beyond a doubt ⟨~ evidence⟩ ⟨an ~ source⟩ **b :** not liable to accusation : IRREPROACHABLE ⟨an ~ reputation⟩ — **un·im·peach·ably** \-blē\ *adv*

1**un·im·proved** \-ˈprüvd\ *adj* (1602) *obs* : not reproved or admonished

2**unimproved** *adj* (1665) : not improved: as **a :** not tilled, built on, or otherwise improved for use ⟨~ land⟩ **b :** not used or employed advantageously ⟨~ opportunities⟩ **c :** not selectively bred for better quality or productiveness

un·in·hib·it·ed \ˌən-in-ˈhi-bə-təd\ *adj* (1880) : free from inhibition ⟨~ exuberance⟩; *also* : boisterously informal ⟨a festive ~ party⟩ — **un·in·hib·it·ed·ly** *adv* — **un·in·hib·it·ed·ness** *n*

un·ini·tiate \ˌən-ə-ˈni-sh(ē-)ət\ *adj* (1801) : not initiated : INEXPERIENCED — **uninitiate** *n*

un·in·stall \ˌən-in-ˈstȯl\ *vt* (1985) : to remove (software) from a computer system esp. by using a specially designed program

un·in·ter·est \ˌən-ˈin-trəst; -ˈin-tə-rəst, -tə-ˌrest, -tərst; -ˈin-ˌtrest\ *n* (1890) : lack of interest

uninterested *adj* (1661) : not interested : not having the mind or feelings engaged ***usage*** see DISINTERESTED

uni·nu·cle·ate \ˌyü-ni-ˈnü-klē-ət, -ˈnyü-\ *adj* (1885) : having a single nucleus ⟨a ~ yeast cell⟩

1**union** \ˈyün-yən\ *n* [ME, fr. AF, fr. LL *union-, unio* oneness, union, fr. L *unus* one — more at ONE] (15c) **1 a :** an act or instance of uniting or joining two or more things into one: as **(1) :** the formation of a single political unit from two or more separate and independent units **(2) :** a uniting in marriage; *also* : SEXUAL INTERCOURSE **(3) :** the growing together of severed parts **b :** a unified condition : COMBINATION, JUNCTION ⟨a gracious ~ of excellence and strength⟩ **2 :** something that is made one : something formed by a combining or coalition of parts or members: as **a :** a confederation of independent individuals (as nations or persons) for some common purpose **b (1) :** a political unit constituting an organic whole formed usu. from units which were previously governed separately (as England and Scotland in 1707) and which have surrendered or delegated their principal powers to the government of the whole or to a newly created government (as the U.S. in 1789) **(2)** *cap* : the federal union of states during the period of the American Civil War **c** *cap* : an organization on a college or university campus providing recreational, social, cultural, and sometimes dining facilities; *also* : the building housing such an organization **d :** the set of all elements belonging to one or more of a given collection of two or more sets — called also *join, sum* **e :** LABOR UNION **3 a :** a device emblematic of the union of two or more sovereignties borne on a national flag typically in the upper inner corner or constituting the whole design of the flag **b :** the upper inner corner of a flag **4 :** any of various devices for connecting parts (as of a machine); *esp* : a coupling for pipes or pipes and fittings

2**union** *adj* (1707) : of, relating to, dealing with, or constituting a union; *esp, cap* : of, relating to, or being the side favoring the Union in the American Civil War ⟨*Union* troops⟩

union card *n* (1874) **1 :** a card certifying personal membership in good standing in a labor union **2 :** something that resembles a union card esp. in being necessary for employment or in providing evidence of in-group status

union church *n* (1847) : a local church uniting members of diverse denominational backgrounds in an interdenominational congregation

un·ion·i·sa·tion, union·ise *Brit var of* UNIONIZATION, UNIONIZE

union·ism \ˈyün-yə-ˌni-zəm\ *n* (1845) : the principle or policy of forming or adhering to a union: as **a** *cap* : adherence to the policy of a firm federal union between the states of the United States esp. during the Civil War period **b :** the principles, theory, advocacy, or system of trade unions

union·ist \-nist\ *n* (1799) : an advocate or supporter of union or unionism

union·i·za·tion \ˌyün-yə-nə-ˈzā-shən\ *n* (1896) **1 :** the quality or state of being unionized **2 :** the action of unionizing

union·ize \ˈyün-yə-ˌnīz\ *vb* **-ized; -iz·ing** *vt* (1890) : to organize into a labor union ~ *vi* : to form or join a labor union

unionized *adj* (1900) : characterized by the presence of labor unions

union jack *n* (1674) **1 :** a jack consisting of the union of a national ensign **2** *cap U&J* : the state flag of the United Kingdom consisting of the union of the British national ensign

union shop *n* (1904) : an establishment in which the employer by agreement is free to hire nonmembers as well as members of the union but retains nonmembers on the payroll only on condition of their becoming members of the union within a specified time

union suit *n* (1892) : an undergarment with shirt and drawers in one piece

union territory *n* (1979) : a centrally administered subdivision of India

uni·pa·ren·tal \ˌyü-ni-pə-ˈren-tᵊl\ *adj* (1900) : having, involving, or derived from a single parent; *specif* : involving or being inheritance in which all or part of an offspring's genotype (as both members of a pair of homologous chromosomes) is derived from a single parent — **uni·pa·ren·tal·ly** \-tᵊl-ē\ *adv*

uni·po·lar \ˌyü-ni-ˈpō-lər\ *adj* (1965) : relating to, affected with, or being a manic-depressive disorder in which there is only a depressive phase ⟨~ depression⟩

unique \yu̇-ˈnēk\ *adj* [F, fr. L *unicus,* fr. *unus* one — more at ONE] (1602) **1 :** being the only one : SOLE ⟨his ~ concern was his own comfort⟩ ⟨I can't walk away with a ~ copy. Suppose I lost it? —Kingsley Amis⟩ ⟨the ~ factorization of a number into prime factors⟩ **2 a :** being without a like or equal : UNEQUALED ⟨could stare at the flames, each one new, violent, ~ —Robert Coover⟩ **b :** distinctively characteristic : PECULIAR 1

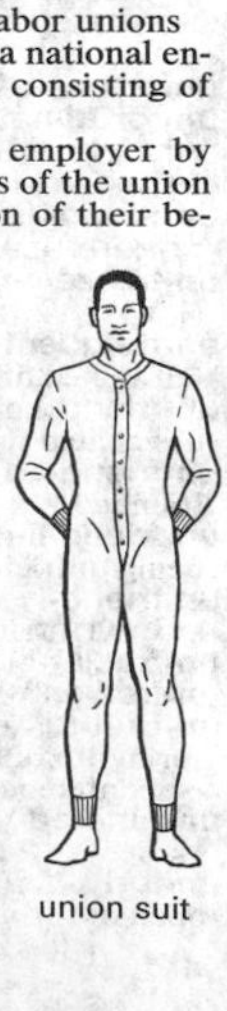
union suit

⟨this is not a condition ~ to California —Ronald Reagan⟩ **3 :** UNUSUAL ⟨a very ~ ball-point pen⟩ ⟨we were fairly ~, the sixty of us, in that there wasn't one good mixer in the bunch —J. D. Salinger⟩ ***syn*** see STRANGE — **unique·ly** *adv* — **unique·ness** *n*

usage Many commentators have objected to the comparison or modification (as by *somewhat* or *very*) of *unique,* often asserting that a thing is either unique or it is not. Objections are based chiefly on the assumption that *unique* has but a single absolute sense, an assumption contradicted by information readily available in a dictionary. *Unique* dates back to the 17th century but was little used until the end of the 18th when, according to the Oxford English Dictionary, it was reacquired from French. H. J. Todd entered it as a foreign word in his edition (1818) of Johnson's Dictionary, characterizing it as "affected and useless." Around the middle of the 19th century it ceased to be considered foreign and came into considerable popular use. With popular use came a broadening of application beyond the original two meanings (here numbered 1 and 2a). In modern use both comparison and modification are widespread and standard but are confined to the extended senses 2b and 3. When sense 1 or sense 2a is intended, *unique* is used without qualifying modifiers.

[1]**uni·sex** \ˈyü-nə-ˌseks\ *n* (1966) **:** the state or condition of not being distinguishable (as by hair or clothing) as to sex

[2]**unisex** *adj* (1968) **1 :** not distinguishable as male or female ⟨a ~ face⟩ **2 :** suitable or designed for both males and females ⟨~ clothes⟩

uni·sex·u·al \ˌyü-nə-ˈsek-sh(ə-)wəl, -shəl\ *adj* (ca. 1802) **1 :** of, relating to, or restricted to one sex: **a :** male or female but not hermaphroditic **b :** DICLINOUS ⟨a ~ flower⟩ **2 :** UNISEX — **uni·sex·u·al·i·ty** \-ˌsek-shə-ˈwa-lə-tē\ *n*

uni·son \ˈyü-nə-sən, -nə-zən\ *n* [ME *unisoun,* fr. MF *unisson,* fr. ML *unisonus* having the same sound, fr. L *uni-* + *sonus* sound — more at SOUND] (15c) **1 a :** identity in musical pitch; *specif* **:** the interval of a perfect prime **b :** the state of being so tuned or sounded **c :** the writing, playing, or singing of parts in a musical passage at the same pitch or in octaves **2 :** a harmonious agreement or union **:** CONCORD — **unison** *adj* — **in unison 1 :** in perfect agreement **:** so as to harmonize exactly ⟨a class reciting *in unison*⟩ **2 :** at the same time **:** SIMULTANEOUSLY

[1]**unit** \ˈyü-nət\ *n* [back-formation fr. *unity*] (1570) **1 a :** the first and least natural number **:** ONE **b :** a single quantity regarded as a whole in calculation **2 :** a determinate quantity (as of length, time, heat, or value) adopted as a standard of measurement: as **a :** an amount of work used in education in calculating student credits **b :** an amount of a biologically active agent (as a drug or antigen) required to produce a specific result — compare INTERNATIONAL UNIT **3 a :** a single thing, person, or group that is a constituent of a whole **b :** a part of a military establishment that has a prescribed organization (as of personnel and materiel) **c :** a piece or complex of apparatus serving to perform one particular function **d :** a part of a school course focusing on a central theme **e :** a local congregation of Jehovah's Witnesses **f :** a small molecule esp. when combined in a larger molecule ⟨repeating ~*s* of a polymer⟩ **g :** an area in a medical facility and esp. a hospital that is specially staffed and equipped to provide a particular type of care ⟨an intensive care ~⟩

[2]**unit** *adj* (1839) **:** being, relating to, or measuring one unit

unit·age \ˈyü-nə-tij\ *n* (1935) **1 :** specifications of the amount constituting a unit **2 :** amount in units

uni·tard \ˈyü-nə-ˌtärd\ *n* [*uni-* + leo*tard*] (1961) **:** a close-fitting one-piece garment for the torso and legs and often for the arms and feet

uni·tar·i·an \ˌyü-nə-ˈter-ē-ən\ *n* [NL *unitarius,* fr. L *unitas* unity] (1687) **1 a** *often cap* **:** one who believes that the deity exists only in one person **b** *cap* **:** a member of a denomination that stresses individual freedom of belief, the free use of reason in religion, a united world community, and liberal social action **2 :** an advocate of unity or a unitary system — **unitarian** *adj, often cap* — **uni·tar·i·an·ism** \-ē-ə-ˌni-zəm\ *n, often cap*

uni·tary \ˈyü-nə-ˌter-ē\ *adj* (1861) **1 a :** of or relating to a unit **b :** based on or characterized by unity or units **2 :** having the character of a unit **:** UNDIVIDED, WHOLE — **uni·tar·i·ly** \ˌyü-nə-ˈter-ə-lē\ *adv*

unit cell *n* (1915) **:** the simplest polyhedron that embodies all the structural characteristics of and by indefinite repetition makes up the lattice of a crystal

unit character *n* (1902) **:** a natural character inherited on an all-or-none basis; *esp* **:** one dependent on the presence or absence of a single gene

unit circle *n* (1955) **:** a circle having a radius of 1

[1]**unite** \yu̇-ˈnīt\ *vb* **unit·ed; unit·ing** [ME, fr. AF *uniter,* fr. L *unitus,* pp. of *unire,* fr. *unus* one — more at ONE] *vt* (15c) **1 a :** to put together to form a single unit **b :** to cause to adhere **c :** to link by a legal or moral bond **2 :** to possess (as qualities) in combination ~ *vi* **1 a :** to become one or as if one **b :** to become combined by or as if by adhesion or mixture **2 :** to act in concert ***syn*** see JOIN — **unit·er** *n*

[2]**unite** \ˈyü-ˌnīt\ *n* [obs. *unite* united, fr. ME *unit,* fr. L *unitus,* pp.] (1604) **:** an old British gold 20-shilling piece issued first by James I in 1604 for the newly united England and Scotland — called also *Jacobus*

united *adj* (ca. 1552) **1 :** made one **:** COMBINED **2 :** relating to or produced by joint action ⟨a ~ effort⟩ **3 :** being in agreement **:** HARMONIOUS ⟨a ~ family⟩ — **unit·ed·ly** *adv*

United Nations Day *n* (1947) **:** October 24 observed in commemoration of the founding of the United Nations

Unit·ed States \yu̇-ˈnī-təd-, *esp Southern* ˈyü-ˌ\ *n pl but sing or pl in constr* (1617) **:** a federation of states esp. when forming a nation in a usu. specified territory ⟨advocating a *United States* of Europe⟩

uni·tive \ˈyü-nə-tiv, yu̇-ˈnī-\ *adj* (15c) **:** characterized by or tending to produce union

unit·ize \ˈyü-nə-ˌtīz\ *vt* **-ized; -iz·ing** (ca. 1860) **1 :** to form or convert into a unit **2 :** to divide into units ⟨the added cost of *unitizing* bulk products⟩ — **unit·i·za·tion** \ˌyü-nə-tə-ˈzā-shən\ *n*

unit membrane *n* (1959) **:** the limiting membrane of cells and various organelles viewed formerly as a 3-layered structure with an inner lipid layer and two outer protein layers and currently as a fluid phospholipid bilayer with intercalating proteins

unit rule *n* (1884) **:** a rule under which a delegation to a national political convention casts its entire vote as a unit as determined by a majority vote

uni·trust \ˈyü-ni-ˌtrəst\ *n* (1970) **:** a trust from which the beneficiary receives annually a fixed percentage of the fair market value of its assets

units place *n* (1674) **:** the place just to the left of the decimal point in a number expressed in the Arabic system of writing numbers

unit train *n* (1964) **:** a railway train that transports a single commodity directly from producer to consumer

unit trust *n* (1936) **1** *Brit* **:** MUTUAL FUND **2 :** an investment company whose portfolio consists of long-term bonds that are held to maturity

uni·ty \ˈyü-nə-tē\ *n, pl* **-ties** [ME *unite,* fr. AF *unité,* fr. L *unitat-, unitas,* fr. *unus* one — more at ONE] (14c) **1 a :** the quality or state of not being multiple **:** ONENESS **b** (1) **:** a definite amount taken as one or for which 1 is made to stand in calculation ⟨in a table of natural sines the radius of the circle is regarded as ~⟩ (2) **:** IDENTITY ELEMENT **2 a :** a condition of harmony **:** ACCORD **b :** continuity without deviation or change (as in purpose or action) **3 a :** the quality or state of being made one **:** UNIFICATION **b :** a combination or ordering of parts in a literary or artistic production that constitutes a whole or promotes an undivided total effect; *also* **:** the resulting singleness of effect or symmetry and consistency of style and character **4 :** a totality of related parts **:** an entity that is a complex or systematic whole **5 :** any of three principles of dramatic structure derived by French classicists from Aristotle's *Poetics* and requiring a play to have a single action represented as occurring in one place and within one day **6** *cap* **:** a 20th century American religious movement that emphasizes spiritual sources of health and prosperity

univ *abbr* university

[1]**uni·va·lent** \ˌyü-ni-ˈvā-lənt\ *adj* (1868) **1 :** MONOVALENT 1 **2 :** being a chromosomal univalent

[2]**univalent** *n* (1912) **:** a chromosome that lacks a synaptic mate

uni·valve \ˈyü-ni-ˌvalv\ *n* (1668) **1 :** a mollusk with a shell consisting of one valve; *esp* **:** GASTROPOD **2 :** the shell of a univalve — **univalve** *adj*

uni·var·i·ate \ˌyü-ni-ˈver-ē-ət\ *adj* (1928) **:** characterized by or depending on only one random variable ⟨a ~ linear model⟩

[1]**uni·ver·sal** \ˌyü-nə-ˈvər-səl\ *adj* [ME, fr. AF, fr. L *universalis,* fr. *universum* universe] (14c) **1 :** including or covering all or a whole collectively or distributively without limit or exception; *esp* **:** available equitably to all members of a society ⟨~ health coverage⟩ **2 a :** present or occurring everywhere **b :** existent or operative everywhere or under all conditions ⟨~ cultural patterns⟩ **3 a :** embracing a major part or the greatest portion (as of humankind) ⟨a ~ state⟩ ⟨~ practices⟩ **b :** comprehensively broad and versatile ⟨a ~ genius⟩ **4 a :** affirming or denying something of all members of a class or of all values of a variable **b :** denoting every member of a class ⟨a ~ term⟩ **5 :** adapted or adjustable to meet varied requirements (as of use, shape, or size) ⟨a ~ gear cutter⟩ ⟨a ~ remote control⟩ — **uni·ver·sal·ly** \-s(ə-)lē\ *adv* — **uni·ver·sal·ness** \-səl-nəs\ *n*

[2]**universal** *n* (1553) **1 :** one that is universal: as **a :** a universal proposition in logic **b :** a predicable of traditional logic **c :** a general concept or term or something in reality to which it corresponds **:** ESSENCE **2 a :** a behavior pattern or institution (as the family) existing in all cultures **b :** a culture trait characteristic of all normal adult members of a particular society

universal donor *n* (1922) **:** a person with blood group O blood which can be donated to any recipient; *also* **:** the blood of such a person

universal grammar *n* (ca. 1750) **:** the study of general principles believed to underlie the grammatical phenomena of all languages; *also* **:** such principles viewed as part of an innate human capacity for learning a language

uni·ver·sal·ism \ˌyü-nə-ˈvər-sə-ˌli-zəm\ *n* (1805) **1** *often cap* **a :** a theological doctrine that all human beings will eventually be saved **b :** the principles and practices of a liberal Christian denomination founded in the 18th century orig. to uphold belief in universal salvation and now united with Unitarianism **2 :** something that is universal in scope **3 :** the state of being universal **:** UNIVERSALITY — **uni·ver·sal·ist** \-s(ə-)list\ *n or adj, often cap*

uni·ver·sal·is·tic \-ˌvər-sə-ˈlis-tik\ *adj* (1872) **:** of or relating to the whole **:** universal in scope or nature

uni·ver·sal·i·ty \-(ˌ)vər-ˈsa-lə-tē\ *n* (14c) **1 :** the quality or state of being universal **2 :** universal comprehensiveness in range

uni·ver·sal·ize \-ˈvər-sə-ˌlīz\ *vt* **-ized; -iz·ing** (1642) **:** to make universal **:** GENERALIZE — **uni·ver·sal·i·za·tion** \-ˌvər-sə-lə-ˈzā-shən\ *n*

universal joint *n* (1676) **:** a shaft coupling capable of transmitting rotation from one shaft to another not collinear with it — called also *universal coupling*

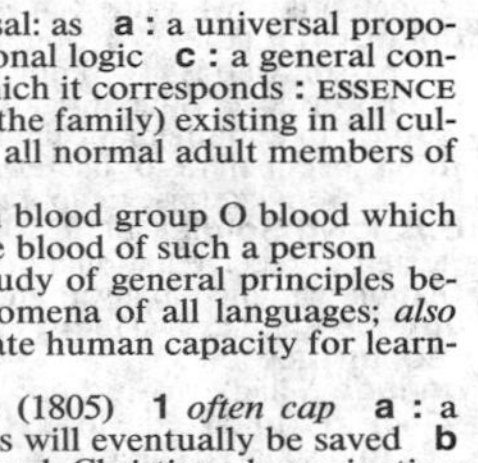
universal joint

universal motor *n* (1925) **:** an electric motor that can be used on either an alternating or a direct current supply

Universal Product Code *n* (1974) **:** a combination of a bar code and numbers by which a scanner can identify a product and usu. assign a price

universal recipient *n* (1922) **:** a person with blood group AB blood who can receive blood from any donor

universal resource locator *n* (1993) **:** URL

Universal Serial Bus *n* (1994) **:** USB

Universal time *n* (1882) **:** GREENWICH MEAN TIME

uni·verse \ˈyü-nə-ˌvərs\ *n* [ME, fr. L *universum,* fr. neut. of *universus* entire, whole, fr. *uni-* + *versus* turned toward, fr. pp. of *vertere* to turn — more at WORTH] (14c) **1 :** the whole body of things and phenomena observed or postulated **:** COSMOS: as **a :** a systematic whole held to arise by and persist through the direct intervention of divine power **b :** the world of human experience **c** (1) **:** the entire celestial cosmos (2) **:** MILKY WAY GALAXY (3) **:** an aggregate of stars comparable to the Milky Way galaxy **2 :** a distinct field or province of thought or reality

\ə\ **abut** \ᵊ\ kitten, F table \ər\ **further** \a\ **ash** \ā\ **ace** \ä\ **mop, mar** \au̇\ **out** \ch\ **chin** \e\ **bet** \ē\ **easy** \g\ **go** \i\ **hit** \ī\ **ice** \j\ **job** \ŋ\ **sing** \ō\ **go** \ȯ\ **law** \ȯi\ **boy** \th\ **thin** \t͟h\ **the** \ü\ **loot** \u̇\ **foot** \y\ **yet** \zh\ **vision, beige** \k, ⁿ, œ, ue, ʸ\ *see* Guide to Pronunciation

that forms a closed system or self-inclusive and independent organization **3 :** POPULATION 4 **4 :** a set that contains all elements relevant to a particular discussion or problem **5 :** a great number or quantity ⟨a large enough ~ of stocks . . . to choose from —G. B. Clairmont⟩

universe of discourse (1881) **:** an inclusive class of entities that is tacitly implied or explicitly delineated as the subject of a statement, discourse, or theory

uni·ver·si·ty \ˌyü-nə-ˈvər-sə-tē, -ˈvər-stē\ *n, pl* **-ties** [ME *universite,* fr. AF *université,* fr. ML *universitat-, universitas,* fr. L *universus*] (14c) **1 :** an institution of higher learning providing facilities for teaching and research and authorized to grant academic degrees; *specif* **:** one made up of an undergraduate division which confers bachelor's degrees and a graduate division which comprises a graduate school and professional schools each of which may confer master's degrees and doctorates **2 :** the physical plant of a university

univ·o·cal \yü-ˈni-və-kəl\ *adj* [LL *univocus,* fr. L *uni-* + *voc-, vox* voice — more at VOICE] (1599) **1 :** having one meaning only **2 :** UNAMBIGUOUS ⟨in search of a morally ~ answer⟩ — **univ·o·cal·ly** \-k(ə-)lē\ *adv*

un·just \ˌən-ˈjəst\ *adj* (14c) **1 :** characterized by injustice **:** UNFAIR **2** *archaic* **:** DISHONEST, FAITHLESS — **un·just·ly** *adv* — **un·just·ness** \-ˈjəs(t)-nəs\ *n*

un·kempt \-ˈkem(p)t\ *adj* [ME *unkemd, unkempt,* fr. *un-* + *kembed, kempt,* pp. of *kemben* to comb, fr. OE *cemban;* akin to OHG *chempen* to comb, OE *camb* comb — more at COMB] (14c) **1 :** not combed ⟨~ hair⟩ **2 :** deficient in order or neatness ⟨~ individuals⟩ ⟨~ hotel rooms⟩; *also* **:** ROUGH, UNPOLISHED ⟨~ prose⟩

un·kenned \-ˈkend\ *adj* (14c) *chiefly dial* **:** UNKNOWN, STRANGE

un·ken·nel \-ˈke-nᵊl\ *vt* (1575) **1 a :** to drive (as a fox) from a hiding place or den **b :** to free (dogs) from a kennel **2 :** to bring out into the open **:** UNCOVER

un·kind \-ˈkīnd\ *adj* (13c) **1 :** not pleasing or mild **:** INCLEMENT ⟨an ~ climate⟩ **2 :** lacking in kindness or sympathy **:** HARSH, CRUEL — **un·kind·ness** \-ˈkīn(d)-nəs\ *n*

1**un·kind·ly** \-ˈkīn(d)-lē\ *adj* (13c) **:** not kindly — **un·kind·li·ness** *n*

2**unkindly** *adv* (14c) **:** in an unkind manner ⟨dwells ~ long on his final decline —A. H. Johnston⟩

un·kink \ˌən-ˈkiŋk\ *vt* (1891) **:** to free from kinks **:** STRAIGHTEN ~ *vi* **:** to become lax or loose **:** RELAX

un·knit \-ˈnit\ *vb* **-knit** *or* **-knit·ted; -knit·ting** (bef. 12c) **:** UNDO, UNRAVEL

un·know·able \ˌən-ˈnō-ə-bəl\ *adj* (14c) **:** not knowable; *esp* **:** lying beyond the limits of human experience or understanding — **un·know·abil·i·ty** \-ˌnō-ə-ˈbi-lə-tē\ *n*

1**un·know·ing** \-ˈnō-iŋ\ *adj* (14c) **:** not knowing — **un·know·ing·ly** \-iŋ-lē\ *adv*

2**unknowing** *n* (14c) **:** IGNORANCE

1**un·known** \-ˈnōn\ *adj* (14c) **:** not known or not well-known; *also* **:** having an unknown value ⟨an ~ quantity⟩

2**unknown** *n* (1597) **1 :** one that is not known or not well-known; *esp* **:** a person who is little known (as to the public) **2 :** something that requires discovery, identification, or clarification: as **a :** a symbol (as *x, y,* or *z*) in a mathematical equation representing an unknown quantity **b :** a specimen (as of bacteria or mixed chemicals) required to be identified as an exercise in appropriate laboratory techniques

Unknown Soldier *n* (1923) **:** an unidentified soldier whose body is selected to receive national honors as a representative of all of the same nation who died in a war and esp. in one of the world wars

un·lace \ˌən-ˈlās\ *vt* (14c) **1 :** to loose by undoing a lacing **2** *obs* **:** UNDO, DISGRACE

un·lade \-ˈlād\ *vb* **-lad·ed; -laded** *or* **-lad·en** \-ˈlā-dᵊn\; **-lad·ing** *vt* (14c) **1 :** to take the load or cargo from **2 :** DISCHARGE, UNLOAD ~ *vi* **:** to discharge cargo

un·lash \-ˈlash\ *vt* (1739) **:** to untie the lashing of

un·latch \-ˈlach\ *vt* (1642) **:** to open or loose by lifting the latch ~ *vi* **:** to become loosed or opened

un·law·ful \ˌən-ˈlȯ-fəl\ *adj* (14c) **1 :** not lawful **:** ILLEGAL **2 :** not morally right or conventional — **un·law·ful·ly** \-f(ə-)lē\ *adv* — **un·law·ful·ness** \-fəl-nəs\ *n*

un·lay \-ˈlā\ *vb* **-laid** \-ˈlād\; **-lay·ing** *vt* (1726) **:** to untwist the strands of (as a rope) ~ *vi* **:** UNTWIST

un·lead·ed \-ˈle-dəd\ *adj* (ca. 1891) **1 :** not having leads between the lines in printing **2 :** not treated or mixed with lead or lead compounds ⟨~ fuels⟩

un·learn \-ˈlərn\ *vt* (15c) **1 :** to put out of one's knowledge or memory **2 :** to undo the effect of **:** discard the habit of

un·learned \-ˈlər-nəd *for 1, 2,* -ˈlərnd *for 3*\ *adj* (14c) **1 :** possessing inadequate learning or education; *esp* **:** deficient in scholarly attainments **2 :** characterized by or revealing ignorance **3 :** not gained by study or training ***syn*** see IGNORANT

un·leash \-ˈlēsh\ *vt* (ca. 1671) **1 :** to free from or as if from a leash **:** let loose ⟨~ the dogs⟩ ⟨~*ing* his anger⟩ **2 :** to throw, shoot, or set in motion forcefully ⟨~*ed* a superb shot . . . to earn his side a point —*N.Y. Times*⟩

1**un·less** \ən-ˈles, ˈən-ˌ\ *conj* [ME *unlesse,* alter. of *onlesse,* fr. *on* + *lesse* less] (14c) **1 :** except on the condition that **:** under any other circumstance than **2 :** without the accompanying circumstance or condition that **:** but that **:** BUT

2**unless** *prep* (ca. 1532) **:** except possibly **:** EXCEPT

un·let·tered \ˌən-ˈle-tərd\ *adj* (14c) **1 a :** lacking facility in reading and writing and ignorant of the knowledge to be gained from books **b :** ILLITERATE **2 :** not marked with letters ***syn*** see IGNORANT

un·licked \-ˈlikt\ *adj* (ca. 1592) **1 :** lacking proper form or shape **2** *archaic* **:** not licked dry

1**un·like** \-ˈlīk\ *adj* (13c) **:** not like: as **a :** marked by lack of resemblance **:** DIFFERENT ⟨the two books are quite ~⟩ **b :** marked by inequality **:** UNEQUAL ⟨contributed ~ amounts⟩ — **un·like·ness** *n*

2**unlike** *prep* (ca. 1592) **:** not like: as **a :** different from ⟨a landscape ~ any other⟩ **b :** not characteristic of ⟨it was ~ him to be late⟩ **c :** in a different manner from ⟨spoke clearly, ~ the others⟩

3**unlike** *conj* (1949) **:** in a manner that is different than **:** not as

usage The use of *unlike* as a conjunction is less common than conjunctive use of *like* and, while criticized, is not as frequently cited as an error. The conjunctive *unlike* almost always introduces a prepositional phrase ⟨~ in other areas, the judiciary cannot justify its attempt . . . as a necessary evil —Alexandra M. Walsh, *Stanford Law Rev.*⟩. In spite of criticism, this conjunctive use of *unlike* is well established in both American and British English.

un·like·li·hood \ˌən-ˈlī-klē-ˌhu̇d\ *n* (15c) **1 :** IMPROBABILITY **2 :** something unlikely

un·like·li·ness \-nəs\ *n* (1614) **:** IMPROBABILITY

un·like·ly \-ˈlī-klē\ *adj* (14c) **1 :** not likely **:** IMPROBABLE ⟨an ~ outcome⟩ **2 :** likely to fail **:** UNPROMISING

un·lim·ber \ˌən-ˈlim-bər\ *vt* (1802) **1 :** to detach the limber from and so make ready ⟨~ a gun for action⟩ **2 :** to prepare for operation or performance ⟨~*ed* his banjo and began to play⟩ ~ *vi* **:** to prepare something for action

un·lim·it·ed \-ˈli-mə-təd\ *adj* (15c) **1 :** lacking any controls **:** UNRESTRICTED ⟨~ access⟩ **2 :** BOUNDLESS, INFINITE ⟨~ possibilities⟩ **3 :** not bounded by exceptions **:** UNDEFINED ⟨the ~ and unconditional surrender of the enemy —Sir Winston Churchill⟩ — **un·lim·it·ed·ly** *adv*

un·link \-ˈliŋk\ *vt* (1600) **:** to unfasten the links of **:** SEPARATE, DISCONNECT ~ *vi* **:** to become detached

un·linked \-ˈliŋ(k)t\ *adj* (1966) **:** not belonging to the same genetic linkage group ⟨~ genes⟩

un·list·ed \-ˈlis-təd\ *adj* (1644) **1 :** not appearing on a list; *esp* **:** not appearing in a telephone book ⟨~ numbers⟩ **2 :** being or involving a security not listed formally on an organized exchange **:** OVER-THE-COUNTER

un·live \-ˈliv\ *vt* (1614) **:** ANNUL, REVERSE

un·load \ˌən-ˈlōd\ *vt* (1523) **1 a** (1) **:** to take off **:** DELIVER (2) **:** to take the cargo from ⟨~ the truck⟩ **b :** to give outlet to **:** pour forth ⟨~*ed* her bitter feelings⟩ **2 :** to relieve of something burdensome, unwanted, or oppressive ⟨~*ed* the pack animals⟩ ⟨~*ed* himself to his friend⟩ **3 :** to draw the charge from ⟨~*ed* the gun⟩ **4 :** to sell or dispose of esp. in large quantities **:** DUMP **5 :** to hit or propel with a great release of power ⟨~*ed* his ninth homer⟩ ~ *vi* **1 :** to perform the act of unloading **2 :** to release or deliver something esp. with power ⟨~*ed* on the ball⟩ **3 :** to give forth a usu. sudden angry outburst ⟨the coach ~*ed* on his players⟩ — **un·load·er** *n*

un·lock \-ˈläk\ *vt* (14c) **1 :** to unfasten the lock of **2 :** OPEN, UNDO **3 :** to free from restraints or restrictions ⟨the shock ~*ed* a flood of tears⟩ **4 :** to furnish a key to **:** DISCLOSE ~ *vi* **:** to become unfastened or freed from restraints

un·looked–for \-ˈlu̇kt-ˌfȯr\ *adj* (1535) **:** not foreseen **:** UNEXPECTED

un·loose \ˌən-ˈlüs\ *vt* (14c) **1 :** to relax the strain of ⟨~ a grip⟩ **2 :** to release from or as if from restraints **:** set free **3 :** to loosen the ties of ⟨~ traditional social bonds⟩

un·loos·en \-ˈlü-sᵊn\ *vt* (15c) **:** UNLOOSE

un·love·ly \-ˈləv-lē\ *adj* (14c) **:** not likable **:** DISAGREEABLE, UNPLEASANT — **un·love·li·ness** \-lē-nəs\ *n*

un·luck·i·ly \ˌən-ˈlə-kə-lē\ *adv* (1530) **:** UNFORTUNATELY ⟨~, it has a nasty way of turning to rain —Ambrose Bierce⟩ ⟨his ascent being ~ a little out of the perpendicular —T. L. Peacock⟩

un·lucky \-ˈlə-kē\ *adj* (1530) **1 :** marked by adversity or failure ⟨an ~ year⟩ **2 :** likely to bring misfortune **:** INAUSPICIOUS ⟨an ~ number⟩ **3 :** having or meeting with misfortune ⟨~ people⟩ **4 :** producing dissatisfaction **:** REGRETTABLE — **un·luck·i·ness** \-ˈlə-kē-nəs\ *n*

un·made \ˌən-ˈmād\ *adj* (13c) **:** not made ⟨an ~ bed⟩

un·make \-ˈmāk\ *vt* **-made** \-ˈmād\; **-mak·ing** (15c) **1 :** to cause to disappear **:** DESTROY **2 :** to deprive of rank or office **:** DEPOSE **3 :** to deprive of essential characteristics **:** change the nature of

un·man \ˌən-ˈman\ *vt* (ca. 1600) **1 :** to deprive of manly vigor, fortitude, or spirit **2 :** CASTRATE, EMASCULATE ***syn*** see UNNERVE

un·man·ly \-ˈman-lē\ *adj* (15c) **:** not manly: as **a :** being of weak character **:** COWARDLY **b :** EFFEMINATE — **un·man·li·ness** \-lē-nəs\ *n*

un·manned \-ˈmand\ *adj* (1544) **1 :** not manned ⟨an ~ spaceflight⟩ **2** *of a hawk* **:** not trained

un·man·nered \-ˈma-nərd\ *adj* (1594) **1 :** marked by a lack of good manners **:** RUDE **2 :** characterized by an absence of artificiality **:** UNAFFECTED — **un·man·nered·ly** *adv*

1**un·man·ner·ly** \-ˈma-nər-lē\ *adv* (14c) **:** in an unmannerly fashion

2**unmannerly** *adj* (14c) **:** not mannerly **:** DISCOURTEOUS — **un·man·ner·li·ness** \-lē-nəs\ *n*

un·mar·ried \-ˈma-rēd\ *adj* (14c) **:** not married: **a :** not now or previously married **b :** being divorced or widowed — **unmarried** *n*

un·mask \ˌən-ˈmask\ *vt* (ca. 1586) **1 :** to reveal the true nature of **:** EXPOSE **2 :** to remove a mask from ~ *vi* **:** to remove one's mask

un·mean·ing \-ˈmē-niŋ\ *adj* (1704) **1 :** lacking intelligence **:** VAPID **2 :** having no meaning **:** SENSELESS

un·me·di·at·ed \ˌən-ˈmē-dē-ˌā-təd\ *adj* (1648) **:** not mediated **:** not communicated or transformed by an intervening agency ⟨experience ~ by artifice⟩

un·meet \-ˈmēt\ *adj* (ca. 1529) **:** not meet **:** UNSUITABLE, IMPROPER

1**un·men·tion·able** \-ˈmen(t)-sh(ə-)nə-bəl\ *adj* (1837) **:** not fit or allowed to be mentioned or discussed **:** UNSPEAKABLE ⟨an ~ topic⟩

2**unmentionable** *n* (1823) **:** one that is not to be mentioned or discussed: as **a** *pl* **:** 3PANT 1 **b** *pl* **:** UNDERWEAR

un·mer·ci·ful \ˌən-ˈmər-si-fəl\ *adj* (14c) **1 :** not merciful **:** MERCILESS **2 :** EXCESSIVE, EXTREME ⟨chatted for an ~ length of time⟩ — **un·mer·ci·ful·ly** \-f(ə-)lē\ *adv*

un·mind·ful \-ˈmīn(d)-fəl\ *adj* (14c) **:** not consciously aware, attentive, or heedful **:** INATTENTIVE, CARELESS ⟨went shirtless, ~ of the sun's punishing rays⟩

un·mis·tak·able \ˌən-mə-ˈstā-kə-bəl\ *adj* (1666) **:** not capable of being mistaken or misunderstood **:** CLEAR — **un·mis·tak·ably** \-blē\ *adv*

un·mit·i·gat·ed \ˌən-ˈmi-tə-ˌgā-təd\ *adj* (1599) **1 :** not lessened **:** UNRELIEVED ⟨sufferings ~ by any hope of early relief⟩ **2 :** being so definitely what is stated as to offer little chance of change or relief ⟨an ~ disaster⟩ — **un·mit·i·gat·ed·ly** *adv* — **un·mit·i·gat·ed·ness** *n*

un·mold \ˌən-ˈmōld\ *vt* (ca. 1900) **:** to remove from a mold

un·moor \-ˈmu̇r\ *vt* (15c) **:** to loosen from or as if from moorings ~ *vi* **:** to cast off moorings

un·mor·al \-ˈmȯr-əl, -ˈmär-\ *adj* (1841) **1 :** having no moral perception or quality; *also* **:** not influenced or guided by moral considerations **2 :** lying outside the bounds of morals or ethics **:** AMORAL — **un·mo·ral·i·ty** \ˌən-mə-ˈra-lə-tē, -mȯ-\ *n*

un·muf·fle \ˌən-ˈmə-fəl\ *vt* (1611) : to free from something that muffles

un·muz·zle \-ˈmə-zəl\ *vt* (1600) : to free from or as if from a muzzle

un·my·elin·at·ed \-ˈmī-ə-lə-ˌnā-təd\ *adj* (1915) : lacking a myelin sheath ⟨~ axons⟩

un·nail \ˌən-ˈnāl\ *vt* (14c) : to unfasten by removing nails

un·nat·u·ral \ˌən-ˈna-chə-rəl, -ˈnach-rəl\ *adj* (14c) **1** : not being in accordance with nature or consistent with a normal course of events **2 a** : not being in accordance with normal human feelings or behavior : PERVERSE **b** : lacking ease and naturalness : CONTRIVED ⟨her manner was forced and ~⟩ **c** : inconsistent with what is reasonable or expected ⟨an ~ alliance⟩ ***syn*** see IRREGULAR — **un·nat·u·ral·ly** \-ˈna-chə-rə-lē, -ˈnach-rə-, -ˈna-chər-\ *adv* — **un·nat·u·ral·ness** \-ˈna-chə-rəl-nəs, -ˈnach-rəl-\ *n*

un·nec·es·sar·i·ly \ˌən-ˌne-sə-ˈser-ə-lē\ *adv* (1594) : not by necessity : to an unnecessary degree ⟨~ harsh criticism⟩

un·nec·es·sary \ˌən-ˈne-sə-ˌser-ē\ *adj* (15c) : not necessary

un·nerve \-ˈnərv\ *vt* (1601) **1** : to deprive of courage, strength, or steadiness **2** : to cause to become nervous : UPSET — **un·nerv·ing·ly** \-ˈnər-viŋ-lē\ *adv*

syn UNNERVE, ENERVATE, UNMAN, EMASCULATE mean to deprive of strength or vigor and the capacity for effective action. UNNERVE implies marked often temporary loss of courage, self-control, or power to act ⟨*unnerved* by the near collision⟩. ENERVATE suggests a gradual physical or moral weakening (as through luxury or indolence) until one is too feeble to make an effort ⟨a nation's youth *enervated* by affluence and leisure⟩. UNMAN implies a loss of manly vigor, fortitude, or spirit ⟨a soldier *unmanned* by the terrors of battle⟩. EMASCULATE stresses a depriving of characteristic force by removing something essential ⟨an amendment that *emasculates* existing safeguards⟩.

un·nil·hex·i·um \ˌyü-n^{ə}l-ˈhek-sē-əm\ *n* [NL, fr. *unnil-* (fr. L *unus* one + *nil* nothing, zero) + Gk *hex* six + NL *-ium* — more at ONE, NIL, SIX] (1981) : SEABORGIUM

un·nil·pen·ti·um \-ˈpen-tē-əm\ *n* [NL, fr. *unnil-* + Gk *pente* five + NL *-ium* — more at FIVE] (1981) : DUBNIUM

un·nil·qua·di·um \-ˈkwä-dē-əm\ *n* [NL, fr. *unnil-* + *quadri-* + *-ium*] (1979) : RUTHERFORDIUM

un·num·bered \ˌən-ˈnəm-bərd\ *adj* (14c) **1** : INNUMERABLE **2** : not having an identifying number ⟨~ pages⟩

un·ob·tru·sive \ˌən-əb-ˈtrü-siv, -ziv\ *adj* (1743) : not obtrusive : not blatant, arresting, or aggressive : INCONSPICUOUS — **un·ob·tru·sive·ly** *adv* — **un·ob·tru·sive·ness** *n*

un·oc·cu·pied \ˌən-ˈä-kyə-ˌpīd\ *adj* (14c) : not occupied: as **a** : not busy : UNEMPLOYED **b** : not lived in : EMPTY

un·or·ga·nized \-ˈȯr-gə-ˌnīzd\ *adj* (ca. 1828) **1** : not organized: as **a** : not brought into a coherent or well-ordered whole **b** : not belonging to a labor union **2** : not having the characteristics of a living organism

un·or·tho·dox \-ˈȯr-thə-ˌdäks\ *adj* (1657) : not orthodox — **un·or·tho·dox·ly** *adv*

un·or·tho·doxy \-ˌdäk-sē\ *n* (ca. 1704) **1** : the quality or state of being unorthodox **2** : something (as an opinion or doctrine) that is unorthodox

un·pack \ˌən-ˈpak\ *vt* (15c) **1 a** : to remove the contents of ⟨~ a suitcase⟩ **b** : UNBURDEN, REVEAL ⟨must . . . ~ my heart with words —Shak.⟩ **2** : to remove or undo from packing or a container ⟨~*ed* his gear⟩ **3** : to analyze the nature of by examining in detail : EXPLICATE ⟨~ a concept⟩ ~ *vi* : to engage in unpacking a container — **un·pack·er** *n*

un·paged \-ˈpājd\ *adj* (1874) : having no page numbers

un·paid \-ˈpād\ *adj* (14c) **1** : not paid ⟨an ~ volunteer⟩ **2** : not paying a salary ⟨an ~ position⟩

un·paired \-ˈperd\ *adj* (1648) : not paired: as **a** : not matched or mated **b** : being an electron that doesn't share its orbital with another electron

un·pal·at·able \-ˈpa-lə-tə-bəl\ *adj* (1682) **1** : not palatable : DISTASTEFUL ⟨~ wines⟩ **2** : UNPLEASANT, DISAGREEABLE ⟨raising income tax rates is politically ~ —Mary Rowland⟩ — **un·pal·at·abil·i·ty** \ˌən-ˌpa-lə-tə-ˈbi-lə-tē\ *n*

un·par·al·leled \ˌən-ˈpa-rə-ˌleld, -ləld\ *adj* (1594) : having no parallel; *esp* : having no equal or match : unique in kind or quality

un·par·lia·men·ta·ry \ˌən-ˌpär-lə-ˈmen-tə-rē, -ˌpärl-yə-, -ˈmen-trē\ *adj* (1626) : contrary to the practice of parliamentary bodies

un·peg \ˌən-ˈpeg\ *vt* (1602) **1** : to remove a peg from **2** : to unfasten by or as if by removing a peg

un·peo·ple \-ˈpē-pəl\ *vt* (ca. 1533) : DEPOPULATE

un·peo·pled \ˌən-ˈpē-pəld\ *adj* (ca. 1586) : not filled with or occupied by people ⟨an ~ wilderness⟩

un·per·fect \-ˈpər-fikt\ *adj* (14c) : IMPERFECT

un·per·son \ˈən-ˈpər-s^{ə}n, -ˌpər-\ *n* (1949) : an individual who usu. for political or ideological reasons is removed completely from recognition or consideration

un·pick \ˌən-ˈpik\ *vt* (ca. 1775) : to undo (as sewing) by taking out stitches

un·pile \-ˈpī(-ə)l\ *vt* (1611) : to take or disentangle from a pile

un·pin \-ˈpin\ *vt* (14c) **1** : to remove a pin from **2** : to loosen, free, or unfasten by or as if by removing a pin

un·placed \ˌən-ˈplāst\ *adj* (1512) **1** : not placed : not having a definite or assigned place ⟨taxonomically ~ organisms⟩ **2** : not finishing in one of the first three places in a horse race

un·pleas·ant \-ˈple-z^{ə}nt\ *adj* (15c) : not pleasant : not amiable or agreeable : DISPLEASING ⟨~ odors⟩ — **un·pleas·ant·ly** *adv*

un·pleas·ant·ness *n* (1548) **1** : the quality or state of being unpleasant **2** : an unpleasant situation, experience, or event

un·plug \ˌən-ˈpləg\ *vt* (ca. 1775) **1 a** : to take a plug out of **b** : to remove an obstruction from **2 a** : to remove (as an electric plug) from a socket or receptacle **b** : to disconnect from an electric circuit by removing a plug ⟨~ the refrigerator⟩

un·plugged \-ˈpləgd\ *adj* (1990) : ACOUSTIC 2 ⟨an ~ performance⟩

un·plumbed \-ˈpləmd\ *adj* (1623) **1** : not tested with a plumb line **2 a** : not measured with a plumb **b** : not thoroughly explored

un·po·lar·ized \-ˈpō-lə-ˌrīzd\ *adj* (ca. 1828) : not polarized; *specif* : having a random pattern of vibrations

un·po·lit·i·cal \ˌən-pə-ˈli-ti-kəl\ *adj* (1894) : APOLITICAL 1

un·pop·u·lar \ˌən-ˈpä-pyə-lər\ *adj* (1647) : not popular : viewed or received unfavorably by the public — **un·pop·u·lar·i·ty** \ˌən-ˌpä-pyə-ˈla-rə-tē\ *n* — **un·pop·u·lar·ly** *adv*

un·prec·e·dent·ed \ˌən-ˈpre-sə-ˌden-təd\ *adj* (1623) : having no precedent : NOVEL, UNEXAMPLED — **un·prec·e·dent·ed·ly** *adv*

un·preg·nant \ˌən-ˈpreg-nənt\ *adj* (1602) *obs* : INEPT 1

un·pre·tend·ing \ˌən-pri-ˈten-diŋ\ *adj* (1697) : UNPRETENTIOUS

un·pre·ten·tious \-ˈten(t)-shəs\ *adj* (1859) : free from ostentation, elegance, or affectation : MODEST ⟨~ homes⟩ ⟨an ~ celebrity⟩ — **un·pre·ten·tious·ly** *adv* — **un·pre·ten·tious·ness** *n*

un·prin·ci·pled \ˌən-ˈprin(t)-s(ə-)pəld, -sə-bəld\ *adj* (1644) : lacking moral principles : UNSCRUPULOUS — **un·prin·ci·pled·ness** *n*

un·print·able \-ˈprin-tə-bəl\ *adj* (1871) : unfit to be printed; *esp* : too obscene or offensive to be shown in print ⟨~ epithets⟩

un·pro·fessed \ˌən-prə-ˈfest\ *adj* (15c) : not professed ⟨an ~ aim⟩

un·prof·it·able \ˌən-ˈprä-fə-tə-bəl, -ˈpräf-tə-bəl\ *adj* (14c) : not profitable : producing no gain, good, or result ⟨an ~ venture⟩ — **un·prof·it·able·ness** *n* — **un·prof·it·ably** \-blē\ *adv*

un·prom·is·ing \-ˈprä-mə-siŋ\ *adj* (1663) : appearing unlikely to prove worthwhile or result favorably ⟨an ~ beginning⟩ — **un·prom·is·ing·ly** \-siŋ-lē\ *adv*

un·pro·nounced \ˌən-prə-ˈnau̇n(t)st\ *adj* (1611) : not pronounced; *esp* : MUTE

un·pro·tect·ed \-prə-ˈtek-təd\ *adj* (ca. 1593) **1** : lacking protection or defense ⟨~ troops⟩ ⟨skin ~ from the sun's rays⟩ **2** : performed without the use of birth control to prevent pregnancy; *also* : performed without the use of a condom to prevent spread of sexually transmitted disease ⟨~ sex⟩

un·pub·lish·able \-ˈpə-bli-shə-bəl\ *adj* (1815) : UNPRINTABLE

un·put·down·able \ˌən-ˌpu̇t-ˈdau̇n-ə-bəl\ *adj* (1947) : unable to be set aside : RIVETING ⟨an ~ book⟩

un·qual·i·fied \ˌən-ˈkwä-lə-ˌfīd\ *adj* (1556) **1** : not fit : not having requisite qualifications **2** : not modified or restricted by reservations : COMPLETE ⟨an ~ denial⟩ — **un·qual·i·fied·ly** \-ˌfī(-ə)d lē\ *adv*

un·ques·tion·able \-ˈkwes-chə-nə-bəl, -ˈkwesh-\ *adj* (1631) : not questionable : INDISPUTABLE ⟨~ evidence⟩ ⟨~ integrity⟩ — **un·ques·tion·ably** \-blē\ *adv*

un·ques·tion·ing \-ˈkwes-chə-niŋ, -ˈkwesh-\ *adj* (ca. 1828) : not questioning : not expressing or marked by doubt or hesitation ⟨~ obedience⟩ ⟨~ loyalty⟩ — **un·ques·tion·ing·ly** \-niŋ-lē\ *adv*

un·qui·et \-ˈkwī-ət\ *adj* (15c) **1** : not quiet : AGITATED, TURBULENT **2** : physically, emotionally, or mentally restless : UNEASY — **un·qui·et·ly** *adv* — **un·qui·et·ness** *n*

un·quote \ˈən-ˌkwōt *also* -ˌkōt\ *n* (1915) — used orally to indicate the end of a direct quotation

un·rav·el \ˌən-ˈra-vəl\ *vt* (1603) **1 a** : to disengage or separate the threads of : DISENTANGLE **b** : to cause to come apart by or as if by separating the threads of **2** : to resolve the intricacy, complexity, or obscurity of : clear up ⟨~ a mystery⟩ ~ *vi* : to become unraveled

un·read \-ˈred\ *adj* (15c) **1** : not read : left unexamined **2** : lacking the experience or the benefits of reading ⟨~ in political science⟩

un·re·al \-ˈrē(-ə)l\ *adj* (1605) : lacking in reality, substance, or genuineness : ARTIFICIAL, ILLUSORY; *also* : INCREDIBLE, FANTASTIC

un·re·al·is·tic \ˌən-ˌrē-ə-ˈlis-tik\ *adj* (1865) : not realistic : inappropriate to reality or fact — **un·re·al·is·ti·cal·ly** \-ti-k(ə-)lē\ *adv*

un·re·al·i·ty \ˌən-rē-ˈa-lə-tē\ *n* (1751) **1 a** : the quality or state of being unreal : lack of substance or validity **b** : something unreal, insubstantial, or visionary : FIGMENT **2** : ineptitude in dealing with reality

un·rea·son \ˌən-ˈrē-z^{ə}n, ˈən-ˌ\ *n* (1827) : the absence of reason or sanity : IRRATIONALITY, MADNESS

un·rea·son·able \-ˈrēz-nə-bəl, -ˈrē-z^{ə}n-ə-bəl\ *adj* (14c) **1 a** : not governed by or acting according to reason ⟨~ people⟩ **b** : not conformable to reason : ABSURD ⟨~ beliefs⟩ **2** : exceeding the bounds of reason or moderation ⟨working under ~ pressure⟩ — **un·rea·son·able·ness** \-nəs\ *n* — **un·rea·son·ably** \-blē\ *adv*

un·rea·soned \-ˈrē-z^{ə}nd\ *adj* (1790) : not founded on reason or reasoning ⟨~ fears⟩ ⟨an ~ decision⟩

un·rea·son·ing \-ˈrēz-niŋ, -ˈrē-z^{ə}n-iŋ\ *adj* (1751) : not reasoning; *esp* : not moderated or controlled by reason ⟨~ fear⟩ — **un·rea·son·ing·ly** \-ˈrēz-niŋ-lē, -ˈrē-z^{ə}n-iŋ-\ *adv*

un·re·con·struct·ed \ˌən-ˌrē-kən-ˈstrək-təd\ *adj* (1867) : not reconciled to some political, economic, or social change ⟨an ~ rebel⟩; *also* : holding stubbornly to a particular belief, view, place, or style ⟨an ~ hard-liner⟩

un·reel \ˌən-ˈrēl\ *vt* (1567) **1** : to unwind from a reel **2** : to perform successfully ⟨~*ed* a 66-yard pass play⟩ **3** : REEL OFF 2 ⟨~*ed* five birdies in a row⟩ ~ *vi* **1** : to become unwound **2** : to be presented ⟨the dress rehearsal ~*ed* flawlessly⟩

un·reeve \-ˈrēv\ *vt* **-rove** \-ˈrōv\ *or* **-reeved; -reev·ing** (1600) : to withdraw (a rope) from an opening (as a ship's block or thimble)

un·re·gen·er·ate \ˌən-ri-ˈje-nə-rət, -ˈjen-rət\ *adj* (1589) **1** : not regenerate ⟨the ~ condition of humanity⟩ ⟨~ pagans⟩ **2 a** : not reformed : UNRECONSTRUCTED ⟨~ liberals⟩ ⟨~ Confederates⟩ **b** : OBSTINATE, STUBBORN ⟨struggling against ~ impulses⟩ ⟨his ~ competitiveness⟩ — **un·re·gen·er·ate·ly** *adv*

un·re·lent·ing \-ˈlen-tiŋ\ *adj* (1588) **1** : not softening or yielding in determination : HARD, STERN ⟨an ~ leader⟩ **2** : not letting up or weakening in vigor or pace : CONSTANT ⟨the ~ struggle⟩ — **un·re·lent·ing·ly** \-tiŋ-lē\ *adv*

un·re·marked \-ˈmärkt\ *adj* (ca. 1775) : not remarked : UNNOTICED

un·re·mit·ting \-ˈmi-tiŋ\ *adj* (1728) : not remitting : CONSTANT, INCESSANT ⟨~ pain⟩ — **un·re·mit·ting·ly** \-tiŋ-lē\ *adv*

un·re·quit·ed \ˌən-ri-ˈkwī-təd\ *adj* (ca. 1542) : not requited : not reciprocated or returned in kind ⟨~ love⟩

un·re·serve \-ˈzərv\ *n* (1751) : absence of reserve : FRANKNESS

un·re·served \-ˈzərvd\ *adj* (1539) **1** : not limited or partial : ENTIRE, UNQUALIFIED ⟨~ enthusiasm⟩ **2** : not cautious or reticent : FRANK,

\ə\ **abut** \$^{ə}$\ **kitten**, F table \ər\ **further** \a\ **ash** \ā\ **ace** \ä\ **mop, mar** \au̇\ **out** \ch\ **chin** \e\ **bet** \ē\ **easy** \g\ **go** \i\ **hit** \ī\ **ice** \j\ **job** \ŋ\ **sing** \ō\ **go** \ȯ\ **law** \ȯi\ **boy** \th\ **thin** \th\ **the** \ü\ **loot** \u̇\ **foot** \y\ **yet** \zh\ **vision, beige** \k, ^{n}, œ, ue, ^{y}\ *see* Guide to Pronunciation

OPEN 3 : not set aside for special use — **un·re·serv·ed·ly** \-ˈzər-vəd-lē\ *adv* — **un·re·served·ness** \-ˈzər-vəd-nəs, -ˈzərv(d)-nəs\ *n*
un·rest \ˌən-ˈrest\ *n* (14c) : a disturbed or uneasy state : TURMOIL
un·re·strained \ˌən-ri-ˈstrānd\ *adj* (ca. 1586) **1** : not restrained : IMMODERATE, UNCONTROLLED ⟨~ proliferation of technology⟩ **2** : free of constraint : SPONTANEOUS ⟨felt happy and ~⟩ — **un·re·strain·ed·ly** \-ˈstrā-nəd-lē\ *adv* — **un·re·strained·ness** \-ˈstrā-nəd-nəs, -ˈstrān(d)-nəs\ *n*
un·re·straint \-ˈstrānt\ *n* (1804) : freedom from or lack of restraint
un·re·tire \ˌən-ri-ˈtī(-ə)r\ *vi* (1966) : to leave retirement : rejoin the workforce
un·rid·dle \ˌən-ˈri-dᵊl\ *vt* (ca. 1586) : to find the explanation of : FIGURE OUT, SOLVE ⟨~ a puzzle⟩ ⟨no trouble *unriddling* three-part syllogisms —*New Yorker*⟩; *also* : to make understandable : EXPLAIN ⟨just trying to ~ the man —Helen Dudar⟩
un·rig \-ˈrig\ *vt* (ca. 1580) : to strip of rigging ⟨~ a ship⟩
un·righ·teous \-ˈrī-chəs\ *adj* (bef. 12c) **1** : not righteous : SINFUL, WICKED **2** : UNJUST, UNMERITED ⟨intolerable and ~ interference in their lives —W. W. Wagar⟩ — **un·righ·teous·ly** *adv* — **un·righ·teous·ness** *n*
un·ripe \-ˈrīp\ *adj* (13c) **1** : not ripe : IMMATURE ⟨~ fruit⟩ **2** : not ready : UNPREPARED ⟨~ plans⟩ — **un·ripe·ness** *n*
un·ri·valed *or* **un·ri·valled** \ˌən-ˈrī-vəld\ *adj* (1591) : having no rival : INCOMPARABLE, SUPREME ⟨~ greatness⟩
un·roll \-ˈrōl\ *vt* (15c) **1** : to unwind a roll of : open out : UNCOIL **2** : to spread out like a scroll for reading or inspection : UNFOLD, REVEAL ~ *vi* : to be unrolled : UNWIND
un·roof \-ˈrüf, -ˈru̇f\ *vt* (1598) : to strip off the roof or covering of
[1]**un·round** \ˌən-ˈrau̇nd\ *vt* (1874) **1** : to pronounce (a sound) without lip rounding or with decreased lip rounding **2** : to spread (the lips) laterally ⟨necessary to ~ the lips in pronouncing \ē\⟩
[2]**unround** *adj* (1958) : pronounced with the lips not rounded
un·ruf·fled \ˌən-ˈrə-fəld\ *adj* (1659) **1** : poised and serene esp. in the face of setbacks or confusion **2** : not ruffled : SMOOTH ⟨~ water⟩ ***syn*** see COOL
un·ruly \-ˈrü-lē\ *adj* **un·rul·i·er; -est** [ME *unreuly,* fr. *un-* + *reuly* disciplined, fr. *reule* rule] (15c) : not readily ruled, disciplined, or managed ⟨an ~ crowd⟩ ⟨a mane of ~ hair⟩ — **un·rul·i·ness** *n*
syn UNRULY, UNGOVERNABLE, INTRACTABLE, REFRACTORY, RECALCITRANT, WILLFUL, HEADSTRONG mean not submissive to government or control. UNRULY implies lack of discipline or incapacity for discipline and often connotes waywardness or turbulence of behavior ⟨*unruly* children⟩. UNGOVERNABLE implies either an escape from control or guidance or a state of being unsubdued and incapable of controlling oneself or being controlled by others ⟨*ungovernable* rage⟩. INTRACTABLE suggests stubborn resistance to guidance or control ⟨*intractable* opponents of the hazardous-waste dump⟩. REFRACTORY stresses resistance to attempts to manage or to mold ⟨special schools for *refractory* children⟩. RECALCITRANT suggests determined resistance to or defiance of authority ⟨acts of sabotage by a *recalcitrant* populace⟩. WILLFUL implies an obstinate determination to have one's own way ⟨a *willful* disregard for the rights of others⟩. HEADSTRONG suggests self-will impatient of restraint, advice, or suggestion ⟨a *headstrong* young cavalry officer⟩.
UNRWA *abbr* United Nations Relief and Works Agency
un·sad·dle \ˌən-ˈsa-dᵊl\ *vt* (14c) **1** : to take the saddle from **2** : to throw from the saddle ~ *vi* : to remove the saddle from a horse
un·said \-ˈsed\ *adj* (bef. 12c) : not said; *esp* : not spoken aloud
un·sat·is·fac·to·ry \-ˌsa-təs-ˈfak-t(ə-)rē\ *adj* (ca. 1650) : not satisfactory — **un·sat·is·fac·to·ri·ly** \-t(ə-)rə-lē\ *adv* — **un·sat·is·fac·to·ri·ness** \-t(ə-)rē-nəs\ *n*
un·sat·u·rate \-ˈsa-chə-rət, -ˈsach-rət\ *n* (1934) : an unsaturated chemical compound
un·sat·u·rat·ed \-ˈsa-chə-ˌrā-təd\ *adj* (1758) : not saturated: as **a** : capable of absorbing or dissolving more of something ⟨an ~ solution⟩ **b** : able to form products by chemical addition; *esp* : containing double or triple bonds between carbon atoms ⟨~ fats⟩
un·saved \ˌən-ˈsāvd\ *adj* (13c) : not saved; *esp* : not absolved from eternal punishment : not regenerate
un·sa·vory \-ˈsā-və-rē, -ˈsāv-rē\ *adj* (13c) **1** : INSIPID, TASTELESS **2 a** : unpleasant to taste or smell **b** : DISAGREEABLE, DISTASTEFUL ⟨an ~ assignment⟩; *esp* : morally offensive ⟨~ business practices⟩
un·say \-ˈsā, *Southern also* -ˈse\ *vt* **-said** \-ˈsed\; **-say·ing** \-ˈsā-iŋ\ (15c) : to make as if not said : RECANT, RETRACT
un·say·able \-ˈsā-ə-bəl\ *adj* (1870) : not sayable : not easily expressed or related; *also* : not allowed to be said
un·scathed \-ˈskāt͟hd\ *adj* (14c) : wholly unharmed : not injured
un·schooled \-ˈsküld\ *adj* (1589) **1** : not schooled : UNTAUGHT, UNTRAINED ⟨an ~ woodsman⟩ **2** : not artificial : NATURAL ⟨~ talent⟩
un·sci·en·tif·ic \ˌən-ˌsī-ən-ˈti-fik\ *adj* (ca. 1775) : not scientific: as **a** : not used in scientific work **b** : not being in accord with the principles and methods of science ⟨~ management of woodlands⟩ ⟨an ~ survey⟩ **c** : not showing scientific knowledge or familiarity with scientific methods — **un·sci·en·tif·i·cal·ly** \-fi-k(ə-)lē\ *adv*
un·scram·ble \ˌən-ˈskram-bəl\ *vt* (ca. 1920) **1** : to separate (as a conglomeration or tangle) into original components : RESOLVE, CLARIFY **2** : to restore (scrambled communication) to intelligible form — **un·scram·bler** \-b(ə-)lər\ *n*
un·screw \-ˈskrü\ *vt* (1605) **1** : to draw the screws from **2** : to loosen or withdraw by turning ~ *vi* : to become or admit of being unscrewed
un·script·ed \-ˈskrip-təd\ *adj* (ca. 1950) : not following a prepared script
un·scru·pu·lous \-ˈskrü-pyə-ləs\ *adj* (1803) : not scrupulous : UNPRINCIPLED — **un·scru·pu·lous·ly** *adv* — **un·scru·pu·lous·ness** *n*
un·seal \-ˈsēl\ *vt* (12c) : to break or remove the seal of : OPEN
un·sealed \-ˈsēld\ *adj* (14c) : not sealed
un·seam \ˌən-ˈsēm\ *vt* (1592) : to open the seams of
un·search·able \-ˈsər-chə-bəl\ *adj* (14c) : not capable of being searched or explored : INSCRUTABLE — **un·search·ably** \-blē\ *adv*
un·sea·son·able \-ˈsēz-nə-bəl, -ˈsē-zᵊn-ə-\ *adj* (15c) **1** : occurring at other than the proper time : UNTIMELY **2** : not being in season **3 a** : not normal for the season of the year ⟨~ weather⟩ **b** : marked by unseasonable weather ⟨an ~ summer⟩ — **un·sea·son·able·ness** *n* — **un·sea·son·ably** \-blē\ *adv*
un·seat \-ˈsēt\ *vt* (1596) **1** : to dislodge from one's seat esp. on horseback **2** : to remove from a place or position; *esp* : to remove from political office
[1]**un·seem·ly** \-ˈsēm-lē\ *adj* (14c) : not seemly: as **a** : not according with established standards of good form or taste ⟨~ bickering⟩ **b** : not suitable for time or place : INAPPROPRIATE, UNSEASONABLE ***syn*** see INDECOROUS — **un·seem·li·ness** \-lē-nəs\ *n*
[2]**unseemly** *adv* (14c) : in an unseemly manner
un·seen \ˌən-ˈsēn\ *adj* (13c) **1** : not seen or perceived **2** : SIGHT 1 ⟨an ~ translation⟩
un·seg·re·gat·ed \-ˈse-gri-ˌgā-təd\ *adj* (1905) : not segregated; *esp* : free from racial segregation
un·se·lect·ed \ˌən-sə-ˈlek-təd\ *adj* (ca. 1891) : not selected ⟨will be held at a still ~ location⟩; *also* : chosen at random ⟨~ samples⟩
un·se·lec·tive \-ˈlek-tiv\ *adj* (ca. 1925) : not marked by selection : RANDOM, INDISCRIMINATE — **un·se·lec·tive·ly** \-lē\ *adv*
un·self·ish \ˌən-ˈsel-fish\ *adj* (1698) : not selfish : GENEROUS — **un·self·ish·ly** *adv* — **un·self·ish·ness** *n*
un·sell \-ˈsel\ *vt* **-sold** \-ˈsōld\; **-sel·ling** (ca. 1929) **1** : to dissuade from a belief in the truth, value, or desirability of something ⟨ads that ~ the public on energy consumption⟩ **2** : to discourage a belief in the truth, value, or desirability of ⟨I *unsold* the coat he wanted and sold him another⟩
un·set \-ˈset\ *adj* (14c) : not set: as **a** : not fixed in a setting : UNMOUNTED ⟨~ diamonds⟩ **b** : not firmed or solidified ⟨~ concrete⟩
un·set·tle \ˌən-ˈse-tᵊl\ *vt* (1598) **1** : to loosen or move from a settled state or condition : make unstable : DISORDER **2** : to perturb or agitate mentally or emotionally : DISCOMPOSE ~ *vi* : to become unsettled
un·set·tled \-ˈse-tᵊld\ *adj* (ca. 1586) : not settled: as **a** (1) : not calm or tranquil : DISTURBED ⟨~ political conditions⟩ (2) : likely to vary widely esp. in the near future : VARIABLE ⟨~ weather⟩ (3) : not settled down ⟨~ dust⟩ **b** (1) : not decided or determined : DOUBTFUL ⟨an ~ state of mind⟩ (2) : not resolved or worked out : UNDECIDED ⟨an ~ question⟩ **c** : characterized by irregularity ⟨an ~ life⟩ **d** : not inhabited or populated ⟨~ land⟩ **e** : mentally unbalanced **f** (1) : not disposed of according to law ⟨an ~ estate⟩ (2) : not paid or discharged ⟨~ debts⟩ — **un·set·tled·ness** \-tᵊl(d)-nəs\ *n*
un·set·tle·ment \-tᵊl-mənt\ *n* (1648) **1** : an act, process, or instance of unsettling **2** : the quality or state of being unsettled
un·set·tling \ˌən-ˈset-liŋ, -ˈse-tᵊl-iŋ\ *adj* (1665) : having the effect of upsetting, disturbing, or discomposing ⟨~ images of the war⟩ — **un·set·tling·ly** \-lē\ *adv*
un·sew \ˌən-ˈsō\ *vt* **-sewed; -sewn** \-ˈsōn\ *or* **-sewed; -sew·ing** (14c) : to undo the sewing of
un·sex \-ˈseks\ *vt* (1606) **1** : to deprive of sex or sexual power **2** : to deprive of the qualities typical of one's sex
un·shack·le \-ˈsha-kəl\ *vt* (1598) : to free from shackles
un·shaped \-ˈshāpt\ *adj* (1572) : not shaped: as **a** : not dressed or finished to final form ⟨an ~ timber⟩ **b** : imperfect in form or formulation ⟨~ ideas⟩
un·shap·en \-ˈshā-pən\ *adj* [ME, fr. [1]*un-* + *shapen,* pp. of *shapen* to shape] (12c) : UNSHAPED
un·sheathe \ˌən-ˈshēt͟h\ *vt* (14c) : to draw from or as if from a sheath or scabbard ⟨*unsheathed* his sword⟩
un·ship \-ˈship\ *vt* (15c) **1** : to take out of a ship : DISCHARGE, UNLOAD **2** : to remove (as an oar or tiller) from position : DETACH ~ *vi* : to become or admit of being detached or removed
un·shod \ˌən-ˈshäd\ *adj* (bef. 12c) : not wearing or provided with shoes
[1]**un·sight** \-ˈsīt\ *vt* (1615) : to prevent from seeing
[2]**unsight** *adj* (ca. 1622) : not sighted or examined
un·sight·ly \ˌən-ˈsīt-lē\ *adj* (15c) : not pleasing to the sight : not comely ⟨an ~ mess⟩ — **un·sight·li·ness** \-lē-nəs\ *n*
un·skilled \-ˈskild\ *adj* (1559) **1** : not skilled in a branch of work : lacking technical training ⟨an ~ worker⟩ **2** : not requiring skill ⟨~ jobs⟩ **3** : marked by lack of skill ⟨produced ~ poems⟩
un·skill·ful \-ˈskil-fəl\ *adj* (1565) : not skillful : lacking in skill or proficiency — **un·skill·ful·ly** \-fə-lē\ *adv* — **un·skill·ful·ness** *n*
un·slak·able \ˌən-ˈslā-kə-bəl\ *adj* (1820) : unable to be slaked : UNQUENCHABLE ⟨an ~ thirst⟩ ⟨an ~ desire for excellence⟩
un·sling \-ˈsliŋ\ *vt* **-slung** \-ˈsləŋ\; **-sling·ing** \-ˈsliŋ-iŋ\ (1630) : to remove from being slung ⟨*unslung* the carbine⟩
un·snap \-ˈsnap\ *vt* (1892) : to loosen or free by or as if by undoing a snap
un·snarl \-ˈsnär(-ə)l\ *vt* (1555) : to disentangle a snarl in
un·so·cia·ble \ˌən-ˈsō-shə-bəl\ *adj* (1600) **1** : having or showing a disinclination for social activity : SOLITARY, RESERVED **2** : not conducive to sociability — **un·so·cia·bil·i·ty** \ˌən-ˌsō-shə-ˈbi-lə-tē\ *n* — **un·so·cia·ble·ness** \ˌən-ˈsō-shə-bəl-nəs\ *n* — **un·so·cia·bly** \-blē\ *adv*
un·so·cial \-ˈsō-shəl\ *adj* (1731) : lacking a taste or desire for society or close association; *also* : marked by or arising from such a lack ⟨an ~ disposition⟩ — **un·so·cial·ly** \-ˈsō-sh(ə-)lē\ *adv*
un·sold \-ˈsōld\ *adj* (14c) : not sold
un·so·phis·ti·cat·ed \ˌən-sə-ˈfis-tə-ˌkā-təd\ *adj* (1630) : not sophisticated: as **a** : not changed or corrupted : GENUINE **b** (1) : not worldly-wise : lacking social or economic sophistication (2) : lacking complexity of structure : SIMPLE, STRAIGHTFORWARD ⟨an ~ analysis⟩ ⟨~ rhythms⟩ ***syn*** see NATURAL
un·so·phis·ti·ca·tion \-ˌfis-tə-ˈkā-shən\ *n* (1825) : lack of or freedom from sophistication
un·sought \ˌən-ˈsȯt\ *adj* (13c) : not searched for or sought out ⟨~ compliments⟩
un·sound \-ˈsau̇nd\ *adj* (14c) : not sound: as **a** : not healthy or whole ⟨an ~ horse⟩ **b** : not mentally normal : not wholly sane ⟨of ~ mind⟩ **c** : not firmly made, placed, or fixed ⟨structurally ~⟩ **d** : not valid or true : INVALID, SPECIOUS ⟨~ beliefs⟩ — **un·sound·ly** \-ˈsau̇n(d)-lē\ *adv*
un·sound·ness \-ˈsau̇n(d)-nəs\ *n* (1586) **1** : the quality or state of being unsound **2** : something (as a disease, injury, or defect) that causes one to be unsound
un·spar·ing \-ˈsper-iŋ\ *adj* (ca. 1586) **1** : not merciful or forbearing : HARD, RUTHLESS ⟨an ~ satire⟩ ⟨an ~ critic⟩ **2** : not frugal : LIBERAL, PROFUSE ⟨~ generosity⟩ — **un·spar·ing·ly** \-iŋ-lē\ *adv*
un·speak \-ˈspēk\ *vt* (1605) *obs* : UNSAY

un·speak·able \-ˈspē-kə-bəl\ *adj* (14c) **1 a** : incapable of being expressed in words : UNUTTERABLE **b** : inexpressibly bad : HORRENDOUS ⟨~ living conditions⟩ ⟨~ evil⟩ **2** : that may not or cannot be spoken ⟨the bawdy thoughts that come into one's head — the ~ words —L. P. Smith⟩ ⟨~ collections of consonants —Rosemary Jellis⟩ — **un·speak·ably** \-blē\ *adv*

un·spool \ˌən-ˈspül\ *vt* (1940) **1** : to unwind from a spool ⟨~ the cable⟩ **2** : to execute or present artfully or gracefully ⟨~*ed* a jump shot⟩ ⟨~*ing* an intricate tale⟩ ~ *vi* : to be presented or revealed on or as if on a motion-picture screen

un·sports·man·like \-ˈspȯrts-mən-ˌlīk\ *adj* (1754) : not characteristic of or exhibiting good sportsmanship : not sportsmanlike

un·spot·ted \-ˈspä-təd\ *adj* (14c) **1** : not spotted : free from spot or stain **2** : free from moral stain ⟨an ~ reputation⟩

un·sprung \-ˈsprəŋ\ *adj* (1600) : not sprung; *esp* : not equipped with springs

un·sta·ble \-ˈstā-bəl\ *adj* (13c) : not stable : not firm or fixed : not constant: as **a** : not steady in action or movement : IRREGULAR ⟨an ~ pulse⟩ **b** : wavering in purpose or intent : VACILLATING **c** : lacking steadiness : apt to move, sway, or fall ⟨an ~ tower⟩ **d (1)** : liable to change or alteration ⟨an ~ economy⟩ ⟨~ weather⟩ **(2)** : readily changing (as by decomposing) in chemical or physical composition or in biological activity **e** : characterized by lack of emotional control ***syn*** see INCONSTANT — **un·sta·ble·ness** *n* — **un·sta·bly** \-b(ə-)lē\ *adv*

unstable angina *n* (1972) : angina pectoris characterized by sudden changes (as an increase in the severity or length of anginal attacks or a decrease in the exertion required to precipitate an attack) esp. when symptoms were previously stable

1**un·steady** \ˌən-ˈste-dē\ *vt* (1532) : to make unsteady

2**unsteady** *adj* (1551) : not steady: as **a** : not firm or solid : not fixed in position : UNSTABLE **b** : marked by change or fluctuation : CHANGEABLE **c** : not uniform or even : IRREGULAR ⟨an ~ pulse⟩ — **un·stead·i·ly** \-ˈste-də-lē\ *adv* — **un·stead·i·ness** \-ˈste-dē-nəs\ *n*

un·step \ˌən-ˈstep\ *vt* (1853) : to remove (a mast) from a step

un·stick \-ˈstik\ *vt* **-stuck** \-ˈstək\; **-stick·ing** (1706) : to release from a state of adhesion

un·stint·ing \-ˈstin-tiŋ\ *adj* (1845) : not restricting or holding back : giving or being given freely or generously ⟨an ~ volunteer⟩ ⟨~ praise⟩ — **un·stint·ing·ly** *adv*

un·stop \-ˈstäp\ *vt* (14c) **1** : to free from an obstruction : OPEN ⟨~ a drain⟩ **2** : to remove a stopper from ⟨~ a flask⟩

un·stop·pa·ble \-ˈstä-pə-bəl\ *adj* (1836) : incapable of being stopped ⟨an ~ army⟩ ⟨an ~ rise to power⟩ — **un·stop·pa·bly** \-blē\ *adv*

un·strap \-ˈstrap\ *vt* (1779) : to remove or loose a strap from

un·stressed \ˌən-ˈstrest\ *adj* (1883) **1** : not bearing a stress or accent ⟨~ syllables⟩ **2** : not subjected to stress ⟨~ wires⟩

un·string \-ˈstriŋ\ *vt* **-strung** \-ˈstrəŋ\; **-string·ing** \-ˈstriŋ-iŋ\ (1611) **1** : to loosen or remove the strings of **2** : to remove from a string **3** : to make weak, disordered, or unstable ⟨was *unstrung* by the news⟩

un·struc·tured \-ˈstrək-chərd\ *adj* (1936) : lacking structure or organization: as **a** : not formally organized in a set or conventional pattern ⟨an ~ question⟩ ⟨feel insecure in an ~ situation⟩ **b** : not having a system or hierarchy typical of an organized society

un·stuck \ˌən-ˈstək\ *adj* (1911) : brought into a state of disarray, discomposure, or incoherence ⟨the deal came ~⟩

un·stud·ied \-ˈstə-dēd\ *adj* (14c) : not studied: as **a** : not acquired by study **b** : not forced : not done or planned for effect

un·sub·stan·tial \ˌən-səb-ˈstan(t)-shəl\ *adj* (15c) : not substantial : lacking substance, firmness, or strength ⟨~ shadows⟩ — **un·sub·stan·ti·al·i·ty** \-ˌstan(t)-shē-ˈa-lə-tē\ *n* — **un·sub·stan·tial·ly** \ˌən-səb-ˈstan(t)-sh(ə-)lē\ *adv*

un·suc·cess·ful \-fəl\ *adj* (1617) : not successful : not meeting with or producing success — **un·suc·cess·ful·ly** \-fə-lē\ *adv*

un·sul·fured \ˌən-ˈsəl-fərd\ *adj* (1853) : not treated or preserved with sulfur ⟨~ molasses⟩

un·sung \-ˈsəŋ\ *adj* (15c) **1** : not sung **2** : not celebrated or praised (as in song or verse) ⟨an ~ hero⟩

un·sur·pris·ing \ˌən-sə(r)-ˈprī-ziŋ\ *adj* (1671) : not surprising or unexpected

un·sur·pris·ing·ly \-ziŋ-lē\ *adv* (1950) **1** : as is not surprising ⟨matters complicate, ~ —Stanley Kauffmann⟩ **2** : in an unsurprising manner ⟨the story ended ~⟩

un·swathe \-ˈswāth, -ˈswȯth, -ˈswāth\ *vt* (14c) : to free from something that swathes

un·swear \-ˈswer\ *vb* **-swore** \-ˈswȯr\; **-sworn** \-ˈswȯrn\; **-swear·ing** *vi* (1596) *archaic* : to unsay or retract something sworn ~ *vt, archaic* : to recant or recall (as an oath) esp. by a second oath

un·swerv·ing \-ˈswər-viŋ\ *adj* (1694) **1** : not swerving or turning aside **2** : STEADY, UNFALTERING ⟨~ loyalty⟩

un·sym·met·ri·cal \ˌən-sə-ˈme-tri-kəl\ *adj* (1755) : ASYMMETRIC — **un·sym·met·ri·cal·ly** \-k(ə-)lē\ *adv*

un·tan·gle \ˌən-ˈtaŋ-gəl\ *vt* (1550) : to loose from tangles or entanglement : straighten out ⟨~ a knot⟩ ⟨~ a mystery⟩ ***syn*** see EXTRICATE

un·tapped \-ˈtapt\ *adj* (1779) **1** : not subjected to tapping ⟨an ~ keg⟩ **2** : not drawn upon or utilized ⟨as yet ~ markets⟩

un·taught \-ˈtȯt\ *adj* (14c) **1** : not instructed or trained : IGNORANT **2** : NATURAL, SPONTANEOUS ⟨~ kindness⟩

un·teach \-ˈtēch\ *vt* **-taught** \-ˈtȯt\; **-teach·ing** (1532) **1** : to cause to unlearn something **2** : to teach the contrary of ⟨~ bad habits⟩

un·ten·a·ble \-ˈte-nə-bəl\ *adj* (1647) **1** : not able to be defended ⟨an ~ position⟩ **2** : not able to be occupied ⟨~ apartments⟩ — **un·ten·a·bil·i·ty** \ˌən-ˌte-nə-ˈbi-lə-tē\ *n*

un·tent·ed \-ˈten-təd\ *adj* [¹*un-* + obs. E *tented,* pp. of *tent* to probe] (1606) *archaic* : not probed or dressed ⟨the ~ woundings of a father's curse —Shak.⟩

un·teth·er \-ˈte-thər\ *vt* (ca. 1775) : to free from or as if from a tether

un·think \-ˈthiŋk\ *vt* **-thought** \-ˈthȯt\; **-think·ing** (ca. 1600) : to put out of mind

un·think·able \-ˈthiŋ-kə-bəl\ *adj* (15c) **1** : not capable of being grasped by the mind **2** : being contrary to what is reasonable, desirable, or probable : being out of the question — **un·think·abil·i·ty** \ˌən-ˌthiŋ-kə-ˈbi-lə-tē\ *n* — **un·think·ably** \ˌən-ˈthiŋ-kə-blē\ *adv*

un·think·ing \ˌən-ˈthiŋ-kiŋ\ *adj* (1676) **1** : not taking thought : HEEDLESS, UNMINDFUL ⟨the ~ onlookers⟩ **2** : not indicating thought or reflection ⟨an ~ decision⟩ **3** : not having the power of thought — **un·think·ing·ly** \-kiŋ-lē\ *adv*

un·thought \-ˈthȯt\ *adj* (ca. 1548) : not anticipated : UNEXPECTED — often used with *of* ⟨an *unthought*-of development⟩

un·thread \ˌən-ˈthred\ *vt* (1597) **1** : to draw or take out a thread from ⟨~ a needle⟩ **2** : to loosen the threads or connections of **3** : to make one's way through ⟨~ a maze⟩

un·throne \-ˈthrōn\ *vt* (1611) : to remove from or as if from a throne

un·ti·dy \-ˈtī-dē\ *adj* (14c) **1 a** : not neat : SLOVENLY ⟨their ~ kitchen⟩ **b** : not neat or orderly in habits or procedure ⟨an ~ mind⟩ **2 a** : not neatly organized or carried out ⟨an ~ manuscript⟩ **b** : conducive to a lack of neatness ⟨~ tasks like bathing the baby —*New Yorker*⟩ — **un·ti·di·ly** \-ˈtī-də-lē\ *adv* — **un·ti·di·ness** \-ˈtī-dē-nəs\ *n*

un·tie \-ˈtī\ *vb* **-tied; -ty·ing** *or* **-tie·ing** *vt* (bef. 12c) **1** : to free from something that ties, fastens, or restrains : UNBIND ⟨*untied* our hands⟩ **2 a** : to disengage the knotted parts of ⟨~ a shoe⟩ **b** : DISENTANGLE, RESOLVE ⟨~ a traffic jam⟩ ~ *vi* : to become loosened or unbound

1**un·til** \ən-ˈtil, -ˈtel; ˈən-ˌ, -tᵊl\ *prep* [ME, fr. *un-* (prob. fr. ON **und* up to; akin to ON *unz* up to, until, OHG *unt,* OE *ende* end) + *til, till* till] (13c) **1** *chiefly Scot* : TO **2** — used as a function word to indicate continuance (as of an action or condition) to a specified time ⟨stayed ~ morning⟩ **3** : BEFORE 2 ⟨not available ~ tomorrow⟩ ⟨we don't open ~ ten⟩

2**until** *conj* (14c) : up to the time that : up to such time as ⟨play continued ~ it got dark⟩ ⟨never able to relax ~ he took up fishing⟩ ⟨ran ~ she was breathless⟩

1**un·time·ly** \ˌən-ˈtīm-lē\ *adv* (13c) **1** : at an inopportune time : UNSEASONABLY **2** : before the due, natural, or proper time : PREMATURELY ⟨went ~ to the grave⟩

2**untimely** *adj* (13c) **1** : INOPPORTUNE, UNSEASONABLE ⟨an ~ joke⟩ ⟨~ frost⟩ **2** : occurring or done before the due, natural, or proper time : too early : PREMATURE ⟨an ~ death⟩ — **un·time·li·ness** *n*

un·time·ous \-ˈtī-məs\ *adj* (15c) *chiefly Scot* : UNTIMELY

un·tir·ing \-ˈtī-riŋ\ *adj* (1822) : not becoming tired : INDEFATIGABLE ⟨an ~ worker⟩ — **un·tir·ing·ly** *adv*

un·ti·tled \-ˈtī-tᵊld\ *adj* (1590) **1** *obs* : having no title or right to rule **2** : not named ⟨an ~ novel⟩ **3** : not called by a title ⟨~ nobility⟩

un·to \ˈən-(ˌ)tü\ *prep* [ME, prob. fr. *un-* (as in *until*) + *to* to] (14c) **1** : TO **2** — used as a function word to indicate reference or concern ⟨they became a world ~ themselves —Anne T. Fleming⟩

un·told \ˌən-ˈtōld\ *adj* (14c) **1 a** : not told or related **b** : kept secret **2** : too great or numerous to count : INCALCULABLE, VAST

un·touch·abil·i·ty \ˌən-ˌtə-chə-ˈbi-lə-tē\ *n* (1919) : the quality or state of being untouchable; *esp* : the state of being an untouchable

1**un·touch·able** \ˌən-ˈtə-chə-bəl\ *adj* (1607) **1 a** : forbidden to the touch : not to be handled **b** : exempt from criticism or control **2** : lying beyond reach **3** : disagreeable or defiling to the touch

2**untouchable** *n* (1909) : one that is untouchable; *specif* : a member of a large formerly segregated hereditary group in India having in traditional Hindu belief the quality of defiling by contact a member of a higher caste

un·touched \ˌən-ˈtəcht\ *adj* (14c) **1** : not subjected to touching : not handled **2** : not described or dealt with **3 a** : not tasted **b** : being in the first or a primeval state or condition ⟨an ~ wilderness⟩ **4** : not influenced : UNAFFECTED

un·to·ward \ˌən-ˈtō-ərd, -ˈtȯ(-ə)rd; ˌən-tə-ˈwȯrd\ *adj* (15c) **1** : difficult to guide, manage, or work with : UNRULY, INTRACTABLE **2 a** : marked by trouble or unhappiness : UNLUCKY **b** : not favorable : ADVERSE, UNPROPITIOUS ⟨~ side effects⟩ **3** : IMPROPER, INDECOROUS — **un·to·ward·ly** *adv* — **un·to·ward·ness** *n*

un·track \ˌən-ˈtrak\ *vt* (1939) : to cause to escape from a slump ⟨couldn't get ~*ed* and played poorly throughout the game⟩

un·tread \ˌən-ˈtred\ *vt* (1593) *archaic* : to tread back : RETRACE

un·tried \-ˈtrīd\ *adj* (1526) **1** : not tested or proved by experience or trial ⟨a recruit ~ in combat⟩ **2** : not tried in court

un·trod·den \-ˈträ-dᵊn\ *also* **un·trod** \-ˈträd\ *adj* (14c) : not trod : UNTRAVERSED

un·trou·bled \-ˈtrə-bəld\ *adj* (15c) **1** : not given trouble : not made uneasy ⟨~ by the age difference⟩ **2** : CALM, TRANQUIL

un·true \-ˈtrü\ *adj* (bef. 12c) **1** : not faithful : DISLOYAL **2** : not according with a standard of correctness : not level or exact **3** : not according with the facts : FALSE — **un·tru·ly** \-ˈtrü-lē\ *adv*

un·truss \-ˈtrəs\ *vt* (15c) **1** *archaic* : UNTIE, UNFASTEN — used in the phrase *untruss one's points* **2** *archaic* : UNDRESS ~ *vi, archaic* : to unfasten or take off one's clothes and esp. one's breeches

un·truth \ˌən-ˈtrüth, ˈən-ˌ\ *n* (bef. 12c) **1** *archaic* : DISLOYALTY **2** : lack of truthfulness : FALSITY **3** : something that is untrue : FALSEHOOD

un·truth·ful \-ˈtrüth-fəl\ *adj* (ca. 1843) : not containing or telling the truth : FALSE, INACCURATE ⟨an ~ report⟩ ***syn*** see DISHONEST — **un·truth·ful·ly** \-fə-lē\ *adv* — **un·truth·ful·ness** *n*

un·tune \-ˈtün, -ˈtyün\ *vt* (1598) **1** : to put out of tune **2** : DISARRANGE, DISCOMPOSE

un·tu·tored \-ˈtü-tərd, -ˈtyü-\ *adj* (1593) **1 a** : having no formal learning or training **b** : NAIVE, UNSOPHISTICATED **2** : not produced or developed by instruction : NATIVE ⟨~ shrewdness⟩ ***syn*** see IGNORANT

un·twine \-ˈtwīn\ *vt* (15c) **1** : to unwind the twisted or tangled parts of : DISENTANGLE **2** : to remove by unwinding ~ *vi* : to become disentangled or unwound

un·twist \ˌən-ˈtwist\ *vt* (1538) : to separate the twisted parts of : UNTWINE ~ *vi* : to become untwined

un·twist·ed \-ˈtwis-təd\ *adj* (1575) : not twisted

un·used \-ˈyüzd, *in the phrase "unused to" usu* -ˈyüs(t)\ *adj* (14c) **1** : not habituated : UNACCUSTOMED ⟨~ to crowds⟩ **2** : not used: as **a**

: FRESH, NEW ⟨set an ~ canvas on the easel⟩ **b** : not put to use : IDLE ⟨~ land⟩ **c** : not consumed : ACCRUED ⟨~ sick leave⟩

un·usu·al \-ˈyü-zhə-wəl, -zhəl; -ˈyüzh-wəl\ *adj* (1579) : not usual : UNCOMMON, RARE — **un·usu·al·ly** *adv* — **un·usu·al·ness** *n*

un·ut·ter·able \ˌən-ˈə-tə-rə-bəl\ *adj* (ca. 1586) : being beyond the powers of description : INEXPRESSIBLE ⟨an ~ tragedy⟩ — **un·ut·ter·ably** \-blē\ *adv*

un·val·ued \-ˈval-(ˌ)yüd, -yəd\ *adj* (1586) **1** *obs* : INVALUABLE **2 a** : not important or prized : DISREGARDED **b** : not appraised

un·var·nished \-ˈvär-nisht\ *adj* (1605) **1 a** : not adorned or glossed : PLAIN, STRAIGHTFORWARD ⟨told the ~ truth⟩ **b** : ARTLESS, FRANK ⟨the ~ candor of old people and children —Janet Flanner⟩ **2** : not coated with or as if with varnish : CRUDE, UNFINISHED

un·veil \ˌən-ˈvāl\ *vt* (14c) **1** : to remove a veil or covering from **2** : to make public : DIVULGE, REVEAL ⟨a good time to ~ their plans⟩ ~ *vi* : to throw off a veil or protective cloak

un·veiled \-ˈvāld\ *adj* (14c) : not veiled : OPEN, REVEALED

un·vo·cal \ˌən-ˈvō-kəl\ *adj* (1773) **1** : not eloquent or outspoken : INARTICULATE **2** : not musical : DISCORDANT

un·voice \-ˈvȯis\ *vt* (1637) : DEVOICE

un·voiced \-ˈvȯist\ *adj* (1859) **1** : not verbally expressed ⟨~ fears⟩ **2** : VOICELESS 2 ⟨~ consonants⟩

un·war·rant·able \-ˈwȯr-ən-tə-bəl, -ˈwär-\ *adj* (1612) : not justifiable : INEXCUSABLE — **un·war·rant·ably** \-blē\ *adv*

un·wary \ˌən-ˈwer-ē\ *adj* (1579) : not alert : easily fooled or surprised : HEEDLESS, GULLIBLE ⟨cheats ~ tourists⟩ — **un·wari·ly** \-ˈwar-ə-lē, -ˈwer-\ *adv* — **un·wari·ness** \-ˈwer-ē-nəs\ *n*

[1]**un·washed** \-ˈwȯsht, -ˈwäsht\ *adj* (13c) **1** : not cleaned with or as if with soap and water **2** : IGNORANT, PLEBEIAN ⟨the ~ masses⟩ — **un·washed·ness** *n*

[2]**unwashed** *n* (1830) : an ignorant or underprivileged group : RABBLE — usu. used with *great* ⟨the great ~⟩

un·watch·able \ˌən-ˈwä-chə-bəl, -ˈwȯ-\ *adj* (1886) : not suitable or fit for watching : tending to discourage watching ⟨~ TV shows⟩

un·wea·ried \-ˈwir-ēd\ *adj* (13c) : not tired or jaded : FRESH ⟨~ travelers⟩ — **un·wea·ried·ly** *adv*

un·weave \-ˈwēv\ *vt* **-wove** \-ˈwōv\; **-wo·ven** \-ˈwō-vən\; **-weav·ing** (1542) : DISENTANGLE, UNRAVEL

un·weet·ing \-ˈwē-tiŋ\ *adj* (14c) *archaic* : UNWITTING — **un·weet·ing·ly** \-tiŋ-lē\ *adv, archaic*

un·weight \-ˈwāt\ *vt* (1930) : to reduce momentarily the force exerted by (as a ski) upon a surface by shifting the weight or position of one's body ~ *vi* : to unweight something by shifting the weight or position of one's body

un·well \ˌən-ˈwel\ *adj* (15c) **1** : being in poor health : AILING, SICK **2** : undergoing menstruation

un·whole·some \-ˈhōl-səm\ *adj* (13c) **1** : detrimental to physical, mental, or moral well-being : UNHEALTHY ⟨~ food⟩ ⟨~ pastimes⟩ **2 a** : CORRUPT, UNSOUND ⟨shady ~ dealings⟩ **b** : offensive to the senses : LOATHSOME ⟨the ~ stench⟩ — **un·whole·some·ly** *adv*

un·wieldy \-ˈwēl-dē\ *adj* (1530) : not easily managed, handled, or used (as because of bulk, weight, complexity, or awkwardness) : CUMBERSOME — **un·wield·i·ly** \-ˈwēl-də-lē\ *adv* — **un·wield·i·ness** \-dē-nəs\ *n*

un·will·ing \-ˈwi-liŋ\ *adj* (bef. 12c) : not willing: **a** : LOATH, RELUCTANT ⟨was ~ to learn⟩ **b** : done or given reluctantly ⟨~ approval⟩ **c** : offering opposition : OBSTINATE ⟨an ~ student⟩ — **un·will·ing·ly** \-liŋ-lē\ *adv* — **un·will·ing·ness** *n*

un·wind \-ˈwīnd\ *vb* **-wound** \-ˈwau̇nd\; **-wind·ing** *vt* (14c) **1 a** : to cause to uncoil : wind off : UNROLL **b** : to free from or as if from a binding or wrapping **c** : to release from tension : RELAX **2** *archaic* : to trace to the end ⟨~*ing* the labryinth and bringing the hero out —Laurence Sterne⟩ **3** : to undo (a financial arrangement or position) through the necessary legal or financial steps ⟨*unwound* most of its natural gas hedges —*N.Y. Times*⟩ ~ *vi* **1** : to become uncoiled or disentangled : UNFOLD **2** : to become released from tension ⟨take a bath to ~⟩

un·wis·dom \ˌən-ˈwiz-dəm\ *n* (bef. 12c) : lack of wisdom : FOOLISHNESS, FOLLY

un·wise \-ˈwīz\ *adj* (bef. 12c) : lacking wisdom or good sense : FOOLISH, IMPRUDENT — **un·wise·ly** *adv*

un·wish \-ˈwish\ *vt* (1594) *obs* : to wish away

un·wit·ting \-ˈwi-tiŋ\ *adj* (bef. 12c) **1** : not knowing : UNAWARE ⟨kept the truth from their ~ friends⟩ **2** : not intended : INADVERTENT ⟨an ~ mistake⟩ — **un·wit·ting·ly** \-tiŋ-lē\ *adv*

un·wont·ed \-ˈwȯn-təd, -ˈwōn- *also* -ˈwən- *or* -ˈwän-\ *adj* (1553) **1** : being out of the ordinary : RARE, UNUSUAL **2** : not accustomed by experience — **un·wont·ed·ly** *adv* — **un·wont·ed·ness** *n*

un·world·ly \-ˈwər(-ə)l-dlē, -ˈwərl-lē\ *adj* (1707) **1** : not of this world : UNEARTHLY; *specif* : SPIRITUAL **2 a** : not wise in the ways of the world : NAIVE **b** : not swayed by mundane considerations — **un·world·li·ness** \-ˈwərl(d)-lē-nəs\ *n*

un·worn \-ˈwȯrn\ *adj* (ca. 1586) **1 a** : not impaired by use : not worn away **b** : not worn : NEW **2** : not jaded : FRESH, ORIGINAL

un·wor·thy \ˌən-ˈwər-t͟hē\ *adj* (13c) **1 a** : lacking in excellence or value : POOR, WORTHLESS **b** : BASE, DISHONORABLE **2** : not meritorious : UNDESERVING ⟨~ of attention⟩ **3** : not deserved : UNMERITED ⟨~ treatment⟩ **4** : inappropriate to one's condition or station ⟨actions ~ of a gentleman⟩ — **un·wor·thi·ly** \-t͟hə-lē\ *adv* — **un·wor·thi·ness** \-t͟hē-nəs\ *n*

un·wrap \-ˈrap\ *vt* (14c) : to remove the wrapping from : DISCLOSE ⟨~ a package⟩ ⟨~ evidence in a criminal case⟩

un·wreathe \-ˈrēt͟h\ *vt* (1591) : UNCOIL, UNTWIST

un·writ·ten \-ˈri-tᵊn\ *adj* (14c) **1** : not expressed in writing : ORAL, TRADITIONAL ⟨an ~ rule⟩ **2** : containing no writing : BLANK

unwritten constitution *n* (1890) : a constitution not embodied in a single document but based chiefly on custom and precedent as expressed in statutes and judicial decisions

unwritten law *n* (1641) : law based chiefly on custom rather than legislative enactments

un·yield·ing \ˌən-ˈyēl-diŋ\ *adj* (1565) **1** : characterized by firmness or obduracy **2** : characterized by lack of softness or flexibility — **un·yield·ing·ly** \-diŋ-lē\ *adv*

un·yoke \-ˈyōk\ *vt* (bef. 12c) **1** : to free from a yoke or harness **2** : to take apart : DISJOIN ~ *vi* **1** *archaic* : to unharness a draft animal **2** *archaic* : to cease from work

un·zip \-ˈzip\ *vt* (1939) : to zip open ~ *vi* : to open by or as if by means of a zipper

[1]**up** \ˈəp\ *adv* [partly fr. ME *up* upward, fr. OE *ūp;* partly fr. ME *uppe* on high, fr. OE; both akin to OHG *ūf* up and prob. to L *sub* under, Gk *hypo* under, *hyper* over — more at OVER] (bef. 12c) **1 a** (1) : in or into a higher position or level; *esp* : away from the center of the earth (2) : from beneath the ground or water to the surface (3) : from below the horizon (4) : UPSTREAM 1 (5) : in or into an upright position ⟨sit ~⟩; *esp* : out of bed **b** : upward from the ground or surface ⟨pull ~ a daisy⟩ **c** : so as to expose a particular surface **2** : with greater intensity ⟨speak ~⟩ **3 a** : in or into a better or more advanced state **b** : at an end ⟨your time is ~⟩ **c** : in or into a state of greater intensity or excitement **d** : to or at a greater speed, rate, or amount ⟨prices went ~⟩ **e** : in a continual sequence : in continuance from a point or to a point ⟨from third grade ~⟩ ⟨at prices of $10 and ~⟩ ⟨~ until now⟩ **4 a** (1) : into existence, evidence, prominence, or prevalence (2) : into operation or practical form **b** : into consideration or attention ⟨bring ~ for discussion⟩ **5** : into possession or custody **6 a** : ENTIRELY, COMPLETELY ⟨button ~ your coat⟩ **b** — used as an intensifier ⟨clean ~ the house⟩ **7** : in or into storage : BY ⟨lay ~ supplies⟩ **8 a** : so as to arrive or approach **b** : in a direction conventionally the opposite of down: (1) : to windward (2) : NORTHWARD (3) : to or at the top (4) : to or at the rear of a theatrical stage **9** : in or into parts **10** : to a stop — usu. used with *draw, bring, fetch,* or *pull* **11** : for each side ⟨the score is 15 ~⟩

[2]**up** *adj* (bef. 12c) **1 a** : risen above the horizon ⟨the sun is ~⟩ **b** : STANDING **c** : being out of bed **d** : relatively high ⟨the river is ~⟩ ⟨was well ~ in her class⟩ **e** : being in a raised position : LIFTED ⟨windows are ~⟩ **f** : being in a state of completion : CONSTRUCTED, BUILT **g** : having the face upward **h** : mounted on a horse ⟨a new jockey ~⟩ **i** : grown above a surface ⟨the corn is ~⟩ **j** (1) : moving, inclining, or directed upward ⟨the ~ escalator⟩ (2) : bound in a direction regarded as up **2 a** (1) : marked by agitation, excitement, or activity (2) : positive or upbeat in mood or demeanor **b** : being above a former or normal level (as of quantity or intensity) ⟨attendance is ~⟩⟨the wind is ~⟩ **c** : exerting enough power (as for operation) ⟨sail when steam is ~⟩ **d** : READY; *specif* : highly prepared **e** : going on : taking place ⟨find out what is ~⟩ **3 a** : risen from a lower position ⟨men ~ from the ranks⟩ **b** : being at the same level or point ⟨did not feel ~ to par⟩ **c** (1) : well informed : ABREAST ⟨~ on the news⟩ (2) : being on schedule ⟨~ on his homework⟩ **d** : being ahead of one's opponent **4 a** : presented for or undergoing consideration ⟨contract ~ for negotiation⟩; *also* : charged before a court ⟨~ for robbery⟩ **b** : being the one whose turn it is ⟨you're ~ next⟩ — **up against** : confronted with : face-to-face with ⟨the problem we are *up against*⟩ — **up to** **1** : capable of performing or dealing with ⟨feels *up to* the task⟩ **2** : engaged in ⟨what is he *up to*⟩ **3** : being the responsibility of ⟨it's *up to* me⟩

[3]**up** *prep* (1509) **1 a** — used as a function word to indicate motion to or toward or situation at a higher point of ⟨went ~ the stairs⟩ **b** : up into or in the ⟨was hid away ~ garret —Mark Twain⟩ **2 a** : in a direction regarded as being toward or near the upper end or part of ⟨lives a few miles ~ the coast⟩ ⟨walked ~ the street⟩ **b** : toward or near a point closer to the source or beginning of ⟨sail ~ the river⟩ **3** : in the direction opposite to ⟨sailed ~ the wind⟩

[4]**up** *n* (1536) **1** : one in a high or advantageous position **2** : an upward slope **3** : a period or state of prosperity or success **4** : [3]UPPER **5** : a fundamental quark that has an electric charge of +2/3 and that is one of the constituents of a nucleon

[5]**up** *vb* **upped** \ˈəpt\ *or in vi 2* **up; upped; up·ping; ups** *or in vi 2* **up** *vi* (1643) **1 a** : to rise from a lying or sitting position **b** : to move upward : ASCEND **2** — used with *and* and another verb to indicate that the action of the following verb was either surprisingly or abruptly initiated ⟨he ~ and quit his job⟩ ~ *vt* **1** : RAISE, LIFT **2 a** : to advance to a higher level: (1) : INCREASE (2) : PROMOTE 1a **b** : RAISE 8d, e

UP *abbr* Upper Peninsula (of Michigan)

up–and–com·ing \ˌəp-ən(d)-ˈkə-miŋ, ˌəp-ᵊm-\ *adj* (1926) : gaining prominence and likely to advance or succeed ⟨an ~ young actor⟩ — **up–and–com·er** \-ˈkə-mər\ *n*

up–and–down \-ˈdau̇n\ *adj* (ca. 1755) **1** : marked by alternate upward and downward movement, action, or surface **2** : PERPENDICULAR

up and down *adv* (12c) **1** : TO AND FRO ⟨paced *up and down*⟩ **2** : alternately upward and downward ⟨jump *up and down*⟩ **3** *archaic* : here and there esp. throughout an area **4** : with regard to every particular : THOROUGHLY ⟨knew the territory *up and down*⟩ — **up and down** *prep*

up–and–up \ˈəp-ən-ˈəp\ *n* (1863) : an honest or respectable course — used in the phrase *on the up-and-up*

Upa·ni·shad \ü-ˈpä-ni-ˌshäd, yü-ˈpa-nə-ˌshad\ *n* [Skt *upaniṣad*] (1805) : one of a class of Vedic treatises dealing with broad philosophic problems — **Upa·ni·shad·ic** \(ˌ)ü-ˌpä-ni-ˈshä-dik, (ˌ)yü-ˌpa-nə-ˈsha-dik\ *adj*

upas \ˈyü-pəs\ *n* [Indonesian Malay *pohon upas* poison tree] (1814) **1** : a tall tropical Asian tree (*Antiaris toxicaria*) of the mulberry family with a latex that contains poisonous glycosides used as an arrow poison; *also* : a poisonous concentrate of the juice or latex of a upas **2** : a poisonous or harmful influence or institution

[1]**up·beat** \ˈəp-ˌbēt\ *n* (1869) **1** : an unaccented beat or portion of a beat in a musical measure; *specif* : the last beat of the measure **2** : an increase in activity or prosperity ⟨business that is on the ~⟩

[2]**upbeat** *adj* (1947) : CHEERFUL, OPTIMISTIC ⟨I'm feeling ~ today⟩

up–bow \ˈəp-ˌbō\ *n* (1876) : a stroke in playing a bowed instrument in which the bow is moved across the strings from the tip to the heel

up·braid \ˌəp-ˈbrād\ *vt* [ME *upbreyden,* fr. OE *ūpbregdan,* prob. fr. *ūp* up + *bregdan* to snatch, move suddenly — more at BRAID] (12c) **1** : to criticize severely : find fault with **2** : to reproach severely : scold vehemently ***syn*** see SCOLD — **up·braid·er** *n*

up·bring·ing \ˈəp-ˌbriŋ-iŋ\ *n* (1520) : early training; *esp* : a particular way of bringing up a child ⟨had a strict ~⟩

up·build \ˌəp-ˈbild\ *vt* **-built** \-ˈbilt\; **-build·ing** (1513) : BUILD UP

UPC *abbr* Universal Product Code

up·cast \ˈəp-ˌkast\ *n* (1883) : something cast up

up·chuck \ˈəp-ˌchək\ *vb* (1929) : VOMIT
up close *adv or adj* (1653) : at close range
up·coast \ˈəp-ˈkōst\ *adv* (1909) : up the coast
up·com·ing \ˈəp-ˌkə-miŋ\ *adj* (1943) : FORTHCOMING, APPROACHING
up–coun·try \ˈəp-ˌkən-trē\ *adj* (1910) : of, relating to, or characteristic of an inland, upland, or outlying region ⟨an ~ farm⟩ — **up–country** *n* — **up–country** \ˈəp-ˈ\ *adv*
[1]**up·date** \ˌəp-ˈdāt\ *vt* (1941) : to bring up to date
[2]**up·date** \ˈəp-ˌdāt\ *n* (1965) **1** : an act or instance of updating **2** : current information for updating something **3** : an up-to-date version, account, or report
up·do \ˈəp-(ˌ)dü\ *n, pl* **updos** [*up*swept hair*do*] (1938) : an upswept hairdo
up·draft \ˈəp-ˌdraft, -ˌdräft\ *n* (ca. 1887) : an upward movement of gas (as air)
up·end \ˌəp-ˈend\ *vt* (1823) **1** : to set or stand on end; *also* : OVERTURN 1 **2 a** : to affect to the point of being upset or flurried ⟨a . . . literary shocker, designed to ~ the credulous matrons —Wolcott Gibbs⟩ **b** : DEFEAT, BEAT ~ *vi* : to rise on an end
up·field \ˈəp-ˈfēld\ *adv or adj* (ca. 1934) : in or into the part of the field toward which the offensive team is headed
up–front \ˌəp-ˈfrənt, ˈəp-ˌ\ *adj* (1945) : being or coming in or at the front: as **a** (1) : being in a conspicuous or leading position (2) : FRANK, FORTHRIGHT **b** : playing in a front line (as in football) **c** : paid or payable in advance
up front *adv* (1937) **1** : in or at the front **2** : in advance **3** : in an up-front manner : FRANKLY, FORTHRIGHTLY
[1]**up·grade** \ˈəp-ˌgrād\ *n* (1873) **1** : an upward grade or slope **2** : INCREASE, RISE **3** : IMPROVEMENT 2b
[2]**up·grade** \ˈəp-ˌgrād, ˌəp-ˈ\ *vt* (1901) : to raise or improve the grade of: as **a** : to improve (livestock) by use of purebred sires **b** : to advance to a job requiring a higher level of skill esp. as part of a training program **c** : to raise the quality of **d** : to raise the classification and usu. the price of without improving the quality **e** : to extend the usefulness of (as a device) **f** : to assign a less serious status to ⟨*upgraded* the patient's condition to good⟩ ~ *vi* : to improve or replace esp. software or a device for increased usefulness — **up·grad·abil·i·ty** *or* **up·grade·abil·i·ty** \ˌəp-ˌgrā-də-ˈbi-lə-tē\ *n* — **up·grad·able** *or* **up·grade·able** \ˌəp-ˈgrā-də-bəl\ *adj*
up·growth \ˈəp-ˌgrōth\ *n* (1844) : the process of growing upward : DEVELOPMENT; *also* : a product or result of this
up·heav·al \ˌəp-ˈhē-vəl, (ˌ)ə-ˈpē-\ *n* (1838) **1** : the action or an instance of upheaving esp. of part of the earth's crust **2** : extreme agitation or disorder : radical change; *also* : an instance of this
up·heave \ˌəp-ˈhēv, (ˌ)ə-ˈpēv\ *vt* (13c) : to heave up : LIFT ~ *vi* : to move upward esp. with power — **up·heav·er** *n*
[1]**up·hill** \ˈəp-ˈhil\ *adv* (1535) **1** : upward on a hill or incline **2** : against difficulties ⟨seemed to be talking ~ —Willa Cather⟩
[2]**up·hill** \-ˌhil\ *n* (1548) : rising ground : ASCENT
[3]**up·hill** \-ˌhil\ *adj* (1613) **1** : situated on elevated ground **2 a** : going up : ASCENDING **b** : being the higher one or part esp. of a set; *specif* : being nearer the top of an incline **3** : DIFFICULT, LABORIOUS
up·hold \(ˌ)əp-ˈhōld\ *vt* **-held** \-ˈheld\; **-hold·ing** (13c) **1 a** : to give support to **b** : to support against an opponent **2 a** : to keep elevated **b** : to lift up ***syn*** see SUPPORT — **up·hold·er** *n*
up·hol·ster \(ˌ)əp-ˈhōl-stər, (ˌ)ə-ˈpōl-\ *vt* **-stered; -ster·ing** \-st(ə-)riŋ\ [back-formation fr. *upholstery*] (1849) : to furnish with or as if with upholstery — **up·hol·ster·er** \-stər-ər\ *n*
up·hol·stery \-st(ə-)rē\ *n, pl* **-ster·ies** [ME *upholdester* upholsterer, fr. *upholden* to uphold, fr. *up* + *holden* to hold] (1597) : materials (as fabric, padding, and springs) used to make a soft covering esp. for a seat
UPI *abbr* United Press International
up·keep \ˈəp-ˌkēp\ *n* (1884) **1** : the act of maintaining in good condition : the state of being maintained in good condition **2** : the cost of maintaining in good condition
up·land \ˈəp-lənd, -ˌland\ *n* (1566) **1** : high land esp. at some distance from the sea : PLATEAU **2** : ground elevated above the lowlands along rivers or between hills — **upland** *adj* — **up·land·er** \-lən-dər, -ˌlan-\ *n*
upland cotton *n* (1819) : a widely cultivated American cotton plant (*Gossypium hirsutum*) having short- to medium-staple fibers
upland sandpiper *n* (ca. 1890) : a large short-billed American sandpiper (*Bartramia longicauda*) that frequents fields and prairies — called also *upland plover*

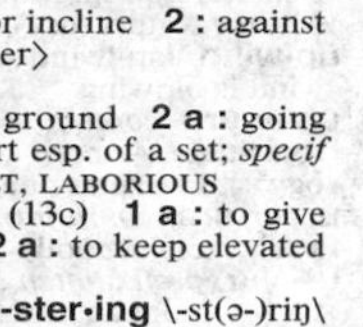
upland sandpiper

[1]**up·lift** \(ˌ)əp-ˈlift\ *vt* (14c) **1** : to lift up : ELEVATE; *esp* : to cause (a portion of the earth's surface) to rise above adjacent areas **2** : to improve the spiritual, social, or intellectual condition of ~ *vi* : RISE — **up·lift·er** *n*
[2]**up·lift** \ˈəp-ˌlift\ *n* (ca. 1845) **1** : an act, process, result, or cause of uplifting: as **a** (1) : the uplifting of a part of the earth's surface (2) : an uplifted mass of land **b** : a bettering of a condition esp. spiritually, socially, or intellectually **c** (1) : influences intended to uplift (2) : a social movement to improve esp. morally or culturally **2** : a brassiere designed to hold the breasts up
up·link \ˈəp-ˌliŋk\ *n* (1968) **1** : a communications channel for transmissions to a spacecraft or satellite; *also* : the transmissions themselves **2** : a facility on earth for transmitting to a spacecraft or satellite — **uplink** *vb*
up·load \(ˌ)əp-ˈlōd, ˈəp-ˌ\ *vt* (1977) : to transfer (as data or files) from a computer to the memory of another device (as a larger or remote computer)
up·man·ship \ˈəp-mən-ˌship\ *n* (1959) : ONE-UPMANSHIP
up·mar·ket \ˈəp-ˈmär-kət\ *adj* (1972) : UPSCALE — **upmarket** *adv*
up·most \ˈəp-ˌmōst\ *adj* (14c) : UPPERMOST
[1]**up·on** \ə-ˈpȯn, -ˈpän\ *prep* (12c) : ON
[2]**up·on** \ə-ˈpȯn, -ˈpän\ *adv* (13c) **1** *obs* : on the surface : on it **2** *obs* : THEREAFTER, THEREON
[1]**up·per** \ˈə-pər\ *adj* [ME, compar. of [2]*up*] (14c) **1 a** : higher in physical position, rank, or order ⟨the ~ lip⟩ ⟨~ management⟩ **b** : farther inland ⟨the ~ Mississippi⟩ **2** : constituting the branch of a bicameral legislature that is usu. smaller and more restricted in membership and possesses greater traditional prestige than the lower house **3 a** : constituting a stratum relatively near the earth's surface **b** *cap* : being a later epoch or series of the period or system named ⟨*Upper* Cretaceous⟩ ⟨*Upper* Paleolithic⟩ **4** : NORTHERN ⟨~ Manhattan⟩
[2]**upper** *n* (1789) : one that is upper: as **a** : the parts of a shoe or boot above the sole **b** : an upper tooth or denture **c** : an upper berth — **on one's uppers** : in straitened circumstances : DESTITUTE
[3]**upper** *n* [*up* + [2]*-er*] (ca. 1968) **1** : a stimulant drug; *esp* : AMPHETAMINE **2** : something that induces a state of good feeling or exhilaration
[1]**up·per·case** \ˌə-pər-ˈkās\ *adj* [fr. the compositor's practice of keeping capital letters in the upper of a pair of type cases] (1738) : CAPITAL 1
[2]**uppercase** *n* (ca. 1916) : capital letters
[3]**uppercase** *vt* **-cased; -cas·ing** (1949) : to print or set in capital letters
upper case *n* (1683) : a type case containing capitals and usu. small capitals, fractions, symbols, and accents
upper–class *adj* (1837) : of, relating to, or characteristic of the upper class
upper class *n* (1814) : a social class occupying a position above the middle class and having the highest status in a society
up·per·class·man \ˌə-pər-ˈklas-mən\ *n* (1871) : a member of the junior or senior class in a school or college
upper crust *n* (1836) : the highest social class or group; *esp* : the highest circle of the upper class — **upper–crust** *adj*
up·per·cut \ˈə-pər-ˌkət\ *n* (1842) : a swinging blow (as in boxing) directed upward with a bent arm — **uppercut** *vb*
upper hand *n* (15c) : MASTERY, ADVANTAGE, CONTROL ⟨was determined not to let the opposition get the *upper hand*⟩
up·per·most \ˈə-pər-ˌmōst\ *adj* (15c) : situated in the highest or most prominent position ⟨the ~ layer⟩ ⟨safety was ~ in their minds⟩ — **uppermost** *adv*
up·per·part \-ˌpärt\ *n* (1526) : a part lying on the upper side (as of a bird)
upper respiratory *adj* (1950) : of, affecting, or being the part of the respiratory system that includes the nose, nasal passages, and nasopharynx ⟨*upper respiratory* tract⟩ ⟨*upper respiratory* infection⟩
up·pish \ˈə-pish\ *adj* (1677) : UPPITY — **up·pish·ly** *adv* — **up·pish·ness** *n*
up·pi·ty \ˈə-pə-tē\ *adj* [prob. fr. *up* + *-ity* (as in *persnickity,* var. of *persnickety*)] (1880) : putting on or marked by airs of superiority : ARROGANT, PRESUMPTUOUS ⟨~ technicians⟩ ⟨a small ~ country⟩ — **up·pi·ti·ness** *also* **up·pi·ty·ness** *n*
up·raise \(ˌ)əp-ˈrāz\ *vt* (14c) : to raise or lift up : ELEVATE
up·rate \ˈəp-ˌrāt\ *vt* (1965) : UPGRADE; *specif* : to improve the power output of (as an engine)
up·rear \-ˈrir\ *vt* (14c) **1** : to lift up **2** : ERECT ~ *vi* : RISE
[1]**up·right** \ˈəp-ˌrīt\ *adj* (bef. 12c) **1 a** : PERPENDICULAR, VERTICAL **b** : erect in carriage or posture **c** : having the main axis or a main part perpendicular ⟨~ freezer⟩ **2** : marked by strong moral rectitude ⟨an ~ citizen⟩ — **up·right·ly** *adv* — **up·right·ness** *n*
syn UPRIGHT, HONEST, JUST, CONSCIENTIOUS, SCRUPULOUS, HONORABLE mean having or showing a strict regard for what is morally right. UPRIGHT implies a strict adherence to moral principles ⟨a stern and *upright* minister⟩. HONEST stresses adherence to such virtues as truthfulness, candor, fairness ⟨known for being *honest* in business dealings⟩. JUST stresses conscious choice and regular practice of what is right or equitable ⟨workers given *just* compensation⟩. CONSCIENTIOUS and SCRUPULOUS imply an active moral sense governing all one's actions and painstaking efforts to follow one's conscience ⟨*conscientious* in the completion of her assignments⟩ ⟨*scrupulous* in carrying out the terms of the will⟩. HONORABLE suggests a firm holding to codes of right behavior and the guidance of a high sense of honor and duty ⟨a difficult but *honorable* decision⟩.
[2]**upright** *adv* (12c) : vertically upward : in an upright position
[3]**upright** *n* (1683) **1** : the state of being upright : PERPENDICULAR ⟨a pillar out of ~⟩ **2** : something that stands upright; *esp* : a football goalpost — usu. used in pl. **3** : UPRIGHT PIANO
upright piano *n* (1857) : a piano with vertical frame and strings — compare GRAND PIANO
[1]**up·rise** \ˌəp-ˈrīz\ *vi* **up·rose** \-ˈrōz\; **up·ris·en** \-ˈri-zᵊn\; **up·ris·ing** \-ˈrī-ziŋ\ (14c) **1 a** : to rise to a higher position **b** (1) : STAND UP (2) : to get out of bed **c** : to come into view esp. from below the horizon **2** : to rise up in sound — **up·ris·er** \ˌəp-ˈrī-zər, ˈəp-ˌ\ *n*
[2]**up·rise** \ˈəp-ˌrīz\ *n* (14c) **1** : an act or instance of uprising **2** : an upward slope
up·ris·ing \ˈəp-ˌrī-ziŋ\ *n* (13c) : an act or instance of rising up; *esp* : a usu. localized act of popular violence in defiance usu. of an established government ***syn*** see REBELLION
up·riv·er \ˈəp-ˈri-vər\ *adv or adj* (1774) : toward or at a point nearer the source of a river
up·roar \ˈəp-ˌrȯr\ *n* [by folk etymology fr. D *oproer,* fr. MD, fr. *op* up (akin to OE *ūp*) + *roer* motion; akin to OE *hrēran* to stir] (1526) : a state of commotion, excitement, or violent disturbance
up·roar·i·ous \ˌəp-ˈrȯr-ē-əs\ *adj* (1800) **1** : marked by uproar **2** : very noisy and full **3** : extremely funny ⟨an ~ comedy⟩ — **up·roar·i·ous·ly** *adv* — **up·roar·i·ous·ness** *n*
up·root \(ˌ)əp-ˈrüt, -ˈru̇t\ *vt* (ca. 1620) **1** : to remove as if by pulling up **2** : to pull up by the roots **3** : to displace from a country or traditional habitat ***syn*** see EXTERMINATE — **up·root·ed·ness** *n* — **up·root·er** *n*
up·rush \ˈəp-ˌrəsh\ *n* (1871) **1** : an upward rush (as of gas or liquid) **2** : a sudden increase ⟨an ~ of energy⟩ ⟨an ~ of emotion⟩
UPS *abbr* uninterruptible power supply
ups and downs *n pl* (1659) : alternating rise and fall esp. in fortune
up·scale \ˈəp-ˈskāl\ *adj* (1966) : relating to, being, or appealing to affluent consumers; *also* : of a superior quality — **upscale** *adv or vt*
[1]**up·set** \(ˌ)əp-ˈset\ *vb* **-set; -set·ting** *vt* (1677) **1** : to thicken and shorten (as a heated bar of iron) by hammering on the end : SWAGE **2** : to

\ə\ **abut** \ᵊ\ **kitten, F table** \ər\ **further** \a\ **ash** \ā\ **ace** \ä\ **mop, mar** \au̇\ **out** \ch\ **chin** \e\ **bet** \ē\ **easy** \g\ **go** \i\ **hit** \ī\ **ice** \j\ **job** \ŋ\ **sing** \ō\ **go** \ȯ\ **law** \ȯi\ **boy** \th\ **thin** \t͟h\ **the** \ü\ **loot** \u̇\ **foot** \y\ **yet** \zh\ **vision, beige** \k̲, ⁿ, œ, ue, ʸ\ *see* Guide to Pronunciation

force out of the usual upright, level, or proper position : OVERTURN **3 a :** to trouble mentally or emotionally : disturb the poise of ⟨the news ~ me⟩ **b :** to throw into disorder **c :** INVALIDATE **d :** to defeat unexpectedly ⟨was ~ in the primary⟩ **4 :** to cause a physical disorder in; *specif* **:** to make somewhat ill ⟨spicy food ~*s* my stomach⟩ ~ *vi* **:** to become overturned ***syn*** see DISCOMPOSE — **up·set·ter** *n* — **upset the apple cart :** to disturb or overturn a natural or stable order

2**up·set** \ˈəp-ˌset\ *n* (1804) **1 :** an act of overturning : OVERTURN **2 a** (1) **:** an act of throwing into disorder : DERANGEMENT (2) **:** a state of disorder : CONFUSION **b :** an unexpected defeat **3 a :** a minor physical disorder ⟨a stomach ~⟩ **b :** an emotional disturbance ⟨went through a big ~ after his father's death⟩ **4 a :** a part of a rod (as the head on a bolt) that is upset **b :** the expansion of a bullet on striking

3**up·set** \(ˌ)əp-ˈset\ *adj* (1805) **:** emotionally disturbed or agitated ⟨was too ~ to speak to him⟩

up·set price \ˈəp-ˌset-\ *n* (1814) **:** the minimum price set for property offered at auction or public sale

up·shift \ˈəp-ˌshift\ *vi* (1952) **:** to shift an automotive vehicle into a higher gear — **upshift** *n*

up·shot \ˈəp-ˌshät\ *n* (1594) **:** the final result : OUTCOME

1**up·side** \ˈəp-ˌsīd\ *n* [2*up* + 1*side*] (1927) **1 :** an upward trend (as of prices) **2 a :** a positive aspect **b :** PROMISE, POTENTIAL ⟨a young star with lots of ~⟩

2**up·side** \ˈəp-ˈsīd\ *prep* [perh. fr. 1*up* + *-side* (as in *alongside*)] (1929) **:** up on or against the side of ⟨layin' in this death cell, writin' my time ~ the wall —Lonnie Johnson⟩ ⟨smacked him ~ the head⟩

up·side down \ˌəp-ˌsīd-ˈdau̇n\ *adv* [alter. of ME *up so doun,* fr. *up* + *so* + *doun* down] (15c) **1 :** in such a way that the upper and the lower parts are reversed in position **2 :** in or into great disorder ⟨turned their world *upside down*⟩ — **upside–down** *adj*

upside–down cake *n* (1925) **:** a cake baked with its batter covering an arrangement of fruit (as pineapple) and served with the fruit side up

up·si·lon \ˈüp-sə-ˌlän, ˈyüp-, ˈəp-, -lən, *Brit usu* yüp-ˈsī-lən\ *n* [MGk *y psilon,* lit., simple *y;* fr. the desire to distinguish it from *oi,* which was pronounced the same in later Greek] (1621) **1 :** the 20th letter of the Greek alphabet — see ALPHABET table **2 :** any of a group of unstable electrically neutral elementary particles of the meson family that have a mass about 10 times that of a proton

up·slope \ˈəp-ˈslōp\ *adj or adv* (1941) **:** being or moving to or toward the top of a slope : UPHILL ⟨~ winds⟩

up·spring \ˌəp-ˈspriŋ\ *vi* **-sprang** \-ˈspraŋ\ *or* **-sprung** \-ˈsprəŋ\; **-sprung; -spring·ing** \-ˈspriŋ-iŋ\ (bef. 12c) **1 :** to spring up **2 :** to come into being

1**up·stage** \ˈəp-ˈstāj\ *adv* (1870) **1 :** toward or at the rear of a theatrical stage **2 :** away from a motion-picture or television camera

2**upstage** *adj* (1918) **1** [3*upstage*] **:** HAUGHTY **2 :** of or relating to the rear of a stage

3**up·stage** \ˌəp-ˈstāj\ *vt* (1921) **1 :** to draw attention away from ⟨*upstaging* the competition⟩ **2 :** to force (an actor) to face away from the audience by staying upstage **3 :** to treat snobbishly

4**up·stage** \ˈəp-ˌstāj\ *n* (ca. 1931) **:** the part of a stage that is farthest from the audience or camera

1**up·stairs** \ˌəp-ˈsterz\ *adv* (1584) **1 :** up the stairs : on or to a higher floor **2 :** to or at a high altitude or higher position ⟨kicked ~ to company management⟩ **3 :** in the head : INTELLECTUALLY ⟨a little slow ~ —Tom Clancy⟩

2**up·stairs** \ˈəp-ˈsterz\ *adj* (1782) **:** situated above the stairs esp. on an upper floor ⟨an ~ bedroom⟩

3**up·stairs** \ˈəp-ˈsterz, ˈəp-ˌ\ *n pl but sing or pl in constr* (1842) **:** the part of a building above the ground floor

up·stand·ing \ˌəp-ˈstan-diŋ, ˈəp-ˌ\ *adj* (bef. 12c) **1 :** ERECT, UPRIGHT **2 :** marked by integrity ⟨an ~ businessman⟩ — **up·stand·ing·ness** *n*

1**up·start** \ˌəp-ˈstärt\ *vi* (14c) **:** to jump up (as to one's feet) suddenly

2**up·start** \ˈəp-ˌstärt\ *n* (1555) **1 :** one that has risen suddenly (as from a low position to wealth or power) : PARVENU; *esp* **:** one that claims more personal importance than is warranted **2 :** a start-up enterprise — **up·start** \ˈəp-ˈ\ *adj*

up·state \ˈəp-ˌstāt\ *n* (1901) **:** the chiefly northerly sections of a state; *also* **:** the chiefly rural part of a state when the major metropolitan area is in the south — **up·state** \-ˈstāt\ *adv or adj* — **up·stat·er** \-ˈstā-tər\ *n*

up·stream \ˈəp-ˈstrēm\ *adv or adj* (1681) **1 :** in the direction opposite to the flow of a stream **2 :** in or to a position within the production stream closer to manufacturing processes ⟨make most of its money ~, selling cheap crude . . . to refineries —John Quirt⟩

up·stroke \ˈəp-ˌstrōk\ *n* (1828) **:** a stroke (as of a pen) made in an upward direction

up·surge \ˈəp-ˌsərj\ *n* (1917) **:** a rapid or sudden rise ⟨an ~ in interest⟩

1**up·sweep** \ˈəp-ˌswēp\ *vi* **-swept** \-ˌswept\; **-sweep·ing** (1791) **:** to sweep upward

2**upsweep** *n* (ca. 1891) **1 :** an upward sweep **2 :** an upswept hairdo

up·swept \ˈəp-ˌswept\ *adj* (1938) **:** swept upward; *esp* **:** brushed up to the top of the head ⟨~ hair⟩

up·swing \ˈəp-ˌswiŋ\ *n* (1922) **1 :** an upward swing **2 :** a marked increase or improvement ⟨a dramatic ~ in profits⟩ — often used in the phrase *on the upswing* ⟨her career is on the ~⟩

up·take \ˈəp-ˌtāk\ *n* [Sc *uptake* to understand] (1816) **1 :** UNDERSTANDING, COMPREHENSION ⟨quick on the ~⟩ **2 :** a flue leading upward **3 :** an act or instance of absorbing and incorporating esp. into a living organism, tissue, or cell ⟨oxygen ~⟩

up–tem·po \ˈəp-ˌtem-(ˌ)pō\ *adj* (1948) **:** having a fast-moving tempo ⟨~ music⟩ ⟨an aggressive ~ style of basketball⟩

1**up·throw** \ˈəp-ˌthrō\ *vt* **-threw** \-ˌthrü\; **-thrown** \-ˌthrōn\; **-throw·ing** (14c) **:** to throw or thrust upward

2**upthrow** *n* (1807) **:** an upward displacement (as of a rock stratum) : UPHEAVAL, UPTHRUST

1**up·thrust** \ˈəp-ˌthrəst\ *vt* (1845) **:** to thrust up; *esp* **:** to elevate (a part of the earth's surface) in an upthrust ~ *vi* **:** to rise with an upward thrust

2**upthrust** *n* (1846) **:** an upward thrust; *specif* **:** an uplift of part of the earth's crust

up·tick \ˈəp-ˌtik\ *n* [2*up* + 3*tick*] (1955) **:** INCREASE, RISE ⟨an ~ in sales⟩ ⟨an ~ in hiring⟩

up·tight \ˈəp-ˈtīt, (ˌ)əp-ˈ\ *adj* (1934) **1 a :** being tense, nervous, or uneasy ⟨~ overachievers⟩ **b :** ANGRY, INDIGNANT **c :** rigidly conventional ⟨an ~ conservative⟩ **2 :** being in financial difficulties — **up·tight·ness** \(ˌ)əp-ˈtīt-nəs\ *n*

up·tilt \ˌəp-ˈtilt\ *vt* (1841) **:** to tilt upward

up·time \ˈəp-ˌtīm\ *n* (1958) **:** time during which a piece of equipment (as a computer) is functioning or able to function

up to *prep* (13c) **1 —** used as a function word to indicate extension as far as a specified place ⟨sank *up to* his knees in the mud⟩ **2 —** used as a function word to indicate a limit or boundary ⟨*up to* 50,000 copies a month⟩ ⟨worked *up to* the last minute⟩

up–to–date *adj* (1887) **1 :** extending up to the present time : including the latest information ⟨~ maps⟩ **2 :** abreast of the times : MODERN ⟨~ methods⟩ — **up–to–date·ly** *adv* — **up–to–date·ness** *n*

up–to–the–minute *adj* (1912) **1 :** extending up to the immediate present : including the very latest information ⟨~ scores⟩ **2 :** marked by complete up-to-dateness ⟨~ equipment⟩

1**up·town** \ˈəp-ˈtau̇n\ *adj* (1796) **1 :** of or relating to uptown **2 :** UPSCALE, FASHIONABLE ⟨an ~ dress⟩ — **uptown** *adv*

2**up·town** \ˈəp-ˌtau̇n\ *n* (1844) **:** the upper part of a town or city; *esp* **:** the residential district

up·trend \ˈəp-ˌtrend\ *n* (1926) **:** an upturn esp. in business or economic activity

1**up·turn** \ˈəp-ˌtərn, ˌəp-ˈ\ *vt* (1567) **1 :** to turn up or over **2 :** to direct upward ~ *vi* **:** to turn upward

2**up·turn** \ˈəp-ˌtərn\ *n* (1864) **:** an upward turn esp. toward better conditions or higher prices

1**up·ward** \ˈəp-wərd\ *or* **up·wards** \-wərdz\ *adv* (bef. 12c) **1 a :** in a direction from lower to higher ⟨the kite rose ~⟩ **b** (1) **:** toward the source (as of a river) (2) **:** toward the interior (as of a region) **c :** in a higher position ⟨held out his hand, palm ~⟩ **d :** in the upper parts : toward the head : ABOVE ⟨from the waist ~⟩ **2 :** toward a higher or better condition or level ⟨young lawyers moving ~⟩ **3 a :** to an indefinitely greater amount, figure, or rank ⟨from $5 ~⟩ **b :** toward a greater amount or higher number, degree, or rate ⟨attendance figures have risen ~⟩ **4 :** toward or into later years ⟨from youth ~⟩

2**upward** *adj* (15c) **1 :** directed toward or situated in a higher place or level : ASCENDING **2 :** rising to a higher pitch — **up·ward·ly** *adv* — **up·ward·ness** *n*

upward mobility *n* (1949) **:** the capacity or facility for rising to a higher social or economic position — **upwardly mobile** *adj*

upwards of *also* **upward of** *adv* (1683) **:** more than : in excess of ⟨they cost *upwards of* $25⟩

up·well \ˌəp-ˈwel\ *vi* (1885) **:** to well up; *specif* **:** to move or flow upward

up·well·ing \-ˈwe-liŋ\ *n* (1868) **:** the process or an instance of rising or appearing to rise to the surface and flowing outward; *esp* **:** the process of upward movement to the ocean surface of deeper cold usu. nutrient-rich waters esp. along some shores due to the offshore movement of surface waters (as from the action of winds and the Coriolis force)

up·wind \ˈəp-ˈwind\ *adv or adj* (1838) **:** in the direction from which the wind is blowing

1**ur-** *or* **uro-** *comb form* [NL, fr. Gk *our-, ouro-,* fr. *ouron* urine, fr. *ourein* to urinate — more at URINE] **1 :** urine ⟨*ur*ic⟩ **2 :** urinary tract ⟨*uro*logy⟩ **3 :** urinary and ⟨*uro*genital⟩ **4 :** urea ⟨*ur*acil⟩

2**ur-** *or* **uro-** *comb form* [NL, fr. Gk *our-, ouro-,* fr. *oura* tail — more at ASS] **:** tail ⟨*uro*pod⟩

3**ur-** \ˈu̇r\ *prefix, often cap* [G, fr. OHG *ir-, ur-* thoroughly (perfective prefix) — more at ABIDE] **1 :** original : primitive ⟨*ur*-form⟩ **2 :** original version of ⟨*ur*text⟩ **3 :** prototypical : ARCH- ⟨*ur*-anticommunist⟩

ura·cil \ˈyu̇r-ə-ˌsil, -səl\ *n* [ISV 1*ur-* + *acetic* + *-il* (substance relating to)] (1890) **:** a pyrimidine base $C_4H_4N_2O_2$ that is one of the four bases coding genetic information in the polynucleotide chain of RNA — compare ADENINE, CYTOSINE, GUANINE, THYMINE

urae·us \yu̇-ˈrē-əs\ *n, pl* **uraei** \-ˈrē-ˌī\ [NL, fr. LGk *ouraios,* a kind of snake] (1832) **:** a representation of the sacred asp (*Naja haje*) appearing in ancient Egyptian art and esp. on the headdress of rulers and serving as a symbol of sovereignty

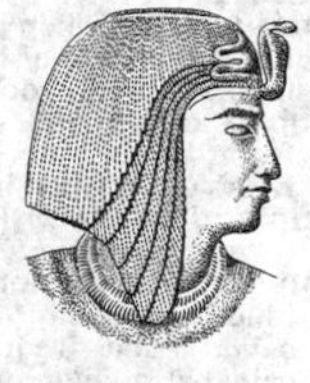

uraeus

Ural–Al·ta·ic \ˌyu̇r-əl-al-ˈtā-ik\ *n* (1853) **:** a postulated language family comprising the Uralic and Altaic languages — **Ural–Altaic** *adj*

Ura·li·an \yu̇-ˈrā-lē-ən, -ˈra-\ *adj* (1801) **1 :** of or relating to the Ural mountains **2 :** URALIC

1**Ural·ic** \yu̇-ˈra-lik\ *n* (1861) **:** a language family comprising the Finno-Ugric and Samoyed languages

2**Uralic** *adj* (1880) **:** of, relating to, or constituting the Finno-Ugric and Samoyed languages

Ura·nia \yu̇-ˈrā-nē-ə, -nyə\ *n* [L, fr. Gk *Ourania*] **:** the Greek Muse of astronomy

Ura·ni·an \yu̇-ˈrā-nē-ən, -nyən\ *adj* (1844) **:** of or relating to the planet Uranus

ura·ni·nite \yu̇-ˈrā-nə-ˌnīt\ *n* [G *Uranin* uraninite (fr. NL *uranium*) + E *-ite*] (1879) **:** a black octahedral mineral that consists of an oxide of uranium which usu. contains thorium, lead, and rare earth elements and is the chief ore of uranium

ura·ni·um \yu̇-ˈrā-nē-əm\ *n, often attrib* [NL, fr. *Uranus*] (ca. 1797) **:** a silvery heavy radioactive polyvalent metallic element that is found esp. in uraninite and exists naturally as a mixture of mostly nonfissionable isotopes — see ELEMENT table

uranium hexa·flu·o·ride \-ˌhek-sə-ˈflȯr-ˌīd, -ˈflu̇r-\ *n* (1899) **:** a volatile compound UF_6 of uranium and fluorine that is used in one major process of enriching uranium in uranium 235

uranium 238 *n* (1942) **:** an isotope of uranium of mass number 238 that is the most stable uranium isotope, that constitutes over 99 percent of natural uranium, that is not fissile but can be used to produce a fissile isotope of plutonium, and that has a half-life of 4.5 billion years

uranium 235 *n* (1940) **:** a light isotope of uranium of mass number 235 that constitutes less than one percent of natural uranium, that when bombarded with slow neutrons undergoes rapid fission into smaller atoms with the release of neutrons and energy, and that is used in nuclear reactors and atomic bombs

ura·nog·ra·phy \ˌyu̇r-ə-ˈnä-grə-fē\ *n* [Gk *ouranographia* description of the heavens, fr. *ouranos* sky + *-graphia* -graphy] (1675) **:** the construction of celestial representations (as maps)

Ura·nus \ˈyu̇r-ə-nəs, yu̇-ˈrā-\ *n* [LL, fr. Gk *Ouranos*] (1655) **1 :** the sky personified as a god and father of the Titans in Greek mythology **2** : the planet seventh in order from the sun — see PLANET table

ura·nyl \ˈyu̇r-ə-ˌnil, yu̇-ˈrā-nᵊl\ *n* [ISV, fr. NL *uran*ium + ISV *-yl*] (1850) : a divalent radical UO_2

urate \ˈyu̇r-ˌāt\ *n* [F, fr. *urique* uric, fr. E *uric*] (1800) : a salt of uric acid — **urat·ic** \yu̇-ˈra-tik\ *adj*

ur·ban \ˈər-bən\ *adj* [L *urbanus,* fr. *urbs* city] (1619) : of, relating to, characteristic of, or constituting a city

ur·bane \ˌər-ˈbān\ *adj* [L *urbanus* urban, urbane] (ca. 1623) : notably polite or polished in manner *syn* see SUAVE — **ur·bane·ly** *adv*

ur·ban·i·sa·tion, ur·ban·ise *Brit var of* URBANIZATION, URBANIZE

ur·ban·ism \ˈər-bə-ˌni-zəm\ *n* (1889) **1** : the characteristic way of life of city dwellers **2 a** : the study of the physical needs of urban societies **b** : CITY PLANNING **3** : URBANIZATION

ur·ban·ist \ˈər-bə-nist\ *n* (1930) : a specialist in city planning — **ur·ban·is·tic** \ˌər-bə-ˈnis-tik\ *adj* — **ur·ban·is·ti·cal·ly** \-ti-k(ə-)lē\ *adv*

ur·ban·ite \ˈər-bə-ˌnīt\ *n* (1897) : a person who lives in a city

ur·ban·i·ty \ˌər-ˈba-nə-tē\ *n, pl* **-ties** (15c) **1** : the quality or state of being urbane **2** *pl* : urbane acts or conduct

ur·ban·i·za·tion \ˌər-bə-nə-ˈzā-shən\ *n* (1888) : the quality or state of being urbanized or the process of becoming urbanized

ur·ban·ize \ˈər-bə-ˌnīz\ *vt* **-ized; -iz·ing** (1884) **1** : to cause to take on urban characteristics ⟨*urbanized* areas⟩ **2** : to impart an urban way of life to ⟨~ migrants from rural areas⟩

urban legend *n* (1968) : an often lurid story or anecdote that is based on hearsay and widely circulated as true ⟨the *urban legend* of alligators living in the sewers⟩ — called also *urban myth*

ur·ban·ol·o·gy \ˌər-bə-ˈnä-lə-jē\ *n* (1961) : a study dealing with specialized problems of cities (as planning, education, sociology, and politics) — **ur·ban·ol·o·gist** \-jist\ *n*

urban renewal *n* (1954) : a construction program to replace or restore substandard buildings in an urban area

urban sprawl *n* (1956) : the spreading of urban developments (as houses and shopping centers) on undeveloped land near a city

ur·ce·o·late \ˌər-ˈsē-ə-lət, ˈər-sē-ə-ˌlāt\ *adj* [NL *urceolatus,* fr. L *urceolus,* dim. of *urceus* pitcher] (1760) : shaped like an urn ⟨~ corollas⟩

ur·chin \ˈər-chən\ *n* [ME *yrchoun, urchoun,* fr. AF *heriçun, hirechoun,* fr. OF **eriz,* fr. L *ericius,* fr. *eris;* akin to Gk *chēr* hedgehog] (14c) **1** *archaic* : HEDGEHOG 1a **2** : a mischievous and often poor and raggedly clothed youngster ⟨street ~*s*⟩ **3** : SEA URCHIN

urd \ˈu̇rd, ˈərd\ *n* [Hindi & Urdu *urad, urad*] (ca. 1934) : an annual Asian legume (*Vigna mungo* syn. *Phaseolus mungo*) widely grown in warm regions for its edible blackish seed, for green manure, or for forage; *also* : the seed

Ur·du \ˈu̇r-(ˌ)dü, ˈər-\ *n* [Hindi & Urdu *urdū,* fr. Pers *zabān-e-urdū-e-muallā* language of the Exalted Camp (the imperial bazaar in Delhi)] (1796) : an Indo-Aryan language that has the same colloquial basis as standard Hindi, is an official language of Pakistan, and is widely used by Muslims in urban areas of India

-ure *n suffix* [ME, fr. AF, fr. L *-ura*] **1** : act : process ⟨*exposure*⟩ **2** : office : function; *also* : body performing (such) a function ⟨*legislature*⟩

urea \yu̇-ˈrē-ə\ *n* [NL, fr. F *urée,* fr. *urine*] (1806) : a soluble weakly basic nitrogenous compound $CO(NH_2)_2$ that is the chief solid component of mammalian urine and an end product of protein decomposition, is synthesized from carbon dioxide and ammonia, and is used esp. in synthesis (as of resins and plastics) and in fertilizers and animal rations

urea–formaldehyde *n* (1928) : a thermosetting synthetic resin made by condensing urea with formaldehyde

ure·ase \ˈyu̇r-ē-ˌās, -ˌāz\ *n* (1892) : an enzyme that catalyzes the hydrolysis of urea

ure·din·i·um \ˌyu̇r-ə-ˈdi-nē-əm\ *n, pl* **-ia** \-nē-ə\ [NL, fr. L *uredin-, uredo* burning, blight, fr. *urere* to burn — more at EMBER] (1905) : a usu. reddish or black mass of hyphae and spores of a rust fungus forming pustules that rupture the host's cuticle — **ure·din·i·al** \-nē-əl\ *adj*

ure·do·spore \yu̇-ˈrē-də-ˌspȯr\ *or* **ure·din·io·spore** \yu̇r-ə-ˈdi-nē-ə-\ *also* **ure·dio·spore** \yu̇-ˈrē-dē-ə-\ *n* [NL *ured*ium uredinium (fr. L *uredo*) + E *-o-* + *spore*] (1875) : one of the thin-walled spores that are produced by uredinial hyphae and spread the fungus vegetatively

ure·ide \ˈyu̇r-ē-ˌīd\ *n* (1857) : a cyclic or acyclic acyl derivative of urea

ure·mia \yu̇-ˈrē-mē-ə\ *n* [NL] (ca. 1857) **1** : accumulation in the blood of constituents normally eliminated in the urine that produces a severe toxic condition and usu. occurs in severe kidney disease **2** : the toxic bodily condition associated with uremia — **ure·mic** \-mik\ *adj*

ureo·tel·ic \yu̇-ˌrē-ə-ˈte-lik, ˌyu̇r-ē-ō-\ *adj* [*urea* + *-o-* + *tel-* + *-ic;* fr. the fact that urea is the end product] (1924) : excreting nitrogen mostly in the form of urea — **ureo·te·lism** \-ˈte-ˌli-zəm, ˌyu̇r-ē-ˈä-tə-ˌli-zəm\ *n*

ure·ter \ˈyu̇r-ə-tər, yu̇-ˈrē-tər\ *n* [NL, fr. Gk *ourētēr,* fr. *ourein* to urinate — more at URINE] (1543) : a duct that carries away the urine from a kidney to the bladder or cloaca — **ure·ter·al** \yu̇-ˈrē-tə-rəl\ *also* **ure·ter·ic** \ˌyu̇r-ə-ˈter-ik\ *adj*

ure·thane \ˈyu̇r-ə-ˌthān\ *also* **ure·than** \-ˌthan\ *n* [F *uréthane,* fr. *ur-* ¹ur- + *éth-* eth- + *-ane*] (1838) **1 a** : a crystalline compound $C_3H_7NO_2$ that is the ethyl ester of carbamic acid and is used esp. as a solvent and medicinally as an antineoplastic agent **b** : an ester of carbamic acid other than the ethyl ester **2** : POLYURETHANE

ure·thra \yu̇-ˈrē-thrə\ *n, pl* **-thras** *or* **-thrae** \-(ˌ)thrē\ [LL, fr. Gk *ourēthra,* fr. *ourein* to urinate] (1634) : the canal that in most mammals carries off the urine from the bladder and in the male serves also as a passageway for semen — **ure·thral** \-thrəl\ *adj*

ure·thri·tis \ˌyu̇r-i-ˈthrī-təs\ *n* [NL] (ca. 1823) : inflammation of the urethra

ure·thro·scope \yu̇-ˈrē-thrə-ˌskōp\ *n* [ISV] (1868) : an instrument for viewing the interior of the urethra

¹**urge** \ˈərj\ *vb* **urged; urg·ing** [L *urgēre* to press, push, entreat — more at WREAK] *vt* (ca. 1555) **1** : to present, advocate, or demand earnestly or pressingly ⟨his conviction was upheld on a theory never *urged* at his . . . trial —Leon Friedman⟩ **2** : to undertake the accomplishment of with energy, swiftness, or enthusiasm ⟨~ the attack⟩ **3 a** : SOLICIT, ENTREAT ⟨*urged* him to keep trying⟩ **b** : to serve as a motive or reason for ⟨*urged* by a sense of duty⟩ **4** : to force or impel in an indicated direction or into motion or greater speed ⟨the dog *urged* the sheep toward the gate⟩ **5** : STIMULATE, PROVOKE ⟨~ not my father's anger —Shak.⟩ ~ *vi* : to declare, advance, or press earnestly a statement, argument, charge, or claim ⟨~*ed* for the adoption of the proposal⟩ — **urg·er** *n*

²**urge** *n* (ca. 1618) **1** : the act or process of urging **2** : a force or impulse that urges; *esp* : a continuing impulse toward an activity or goal

urge incontinence *n* (1980) : involuntary leakage of urine from the bladder when a sudden strong need to urinate is felt — compare STRESS INCONTINENCE

ur·gen·cy \ˈər-jən(t)-sē\ *n, pl* **-cies** (1540) **1** : the quality or state of being urgent : INSISTENCE **2** : a force or impulse that impels or constrains : URGE

ur·gent \ˈər-jənt\ *adj* [ME, fr. MF, fr. L *urgent-, urgens,* prp. of *urgēre*] (15c) **1 a** : calling for immediate attention : PRESSING ⟨~ appeals⟩ ⟨an ~ need⟩ **b** : conveying a sense of urgency **2** : urging insistently : IMPORTUNATE — **ur·gent·ly** *adv*

-urgy *n comb form* [NL *-urgia,* fr. Gk *-ourgia,* fr. *-ourgos* working, fr. *-o-* + *ergon* work — more at WORK] : technique or art of dealing or working with (such) a product, matter, or tool ⟨metall*urgy*⟩

-uria *n comb form* [NL, fr. Gk *-ouria,* fr. *ouron* urine, fr. *ourein* to urinate — more at URINE] **1** : presence of (a specified substance) in urine ⟨albumin*uria*⟩ **2** : condition of having (such) urine ⟨poly*uria*⟩; *esp* : abnormal or diseased condition marked by the presence of (a specified substance) ⟨py*uria*⟩

uri·al \ˈu̇r-ē-əl, -ˌäl\ *n* [Punjabi *hureāl*] (1860) : an upland wild sheep (*Ovis vignei*) of southern and central Asia which is reddish brown and the males of which have a beard from the neck to the chest

uric \ˈyu̇r-ik\ *adj* (1797) : of, relating to, or found in urine

uric acid *n* (1800) : a white odorless and tasteless nearly insoluble acid $C_5H_4N_4O_3$ that is the chief nitrogenous waste present in the urine esp. of lower vertebrates (as birds and reptiles), is present in small quantity in human urine, and occurs pathologically in renal calculi and the tophi of gout

uri·co·su·ric \ˌyu̇r-i-kə-ˈshu̇r-ik, -ˈsu̇r-\ *adj* [irreg. fr. *uric*] (ca. 1947) : relating to or promoting the excretion of uric acid in the urine

uri·co·tel·ic \ˌyu̇r-i-kō-ˈte-lik\ *adj* [*uric* + *-o-* + *tel-* + *-ic;* fr. the fact that uric acid is the end product] (1924) : excreting nitrogen mostly in the form of uric acid ⟨birds are typical ~ animals⟩ — **uri·co·tel·ism** \-ˈte-ˌli-zəm, -ˈkä-tə-ˌli-zəm\ *n*

uri·dine \ˈyu̇r-ə-ˌdēn\ *n* [ISV ¹*ur-* + *-idine*] (1911) : a ribonucleoside $C_9H_{12}N_2O_6$ containing uracil that in the form of phosphate derivatives plays an important role in carbohydrate metabolism

Uri·el \ˈyu̇r-ē-əl\ *n* [Heb *Ūrī'ēl*] (1535) : one of the four archangels named in Hebrew tradition

Urim and Thum·mim \ˌyu̇r-ə-mən(d)-ˈthə-məm, ˌu̇r-; ˌu̇r-ēm-ən(d)-ˈtü-mēm\ *n pl* [part trans. of Heb *ūrīm wĕthummīm*] (1537) : sacred lots used in early times by the Hebrews

urin- *or* **urino-** *comb form* [NL, fr. L *urina* urine] : ¹UR- ⟨*urino*genital⟩ ⟨*urin*ary⟩

uri·nal \ˈyər-ə-nᵊl, ˈyu̇r-, *Brit also* yu̇-ˈrī-nᵊl\ *n* [ME, fr. AF, fr. LL, fr. L *urina*] (13c) **1** : a vessel for receiving urine **2 a** : a building or enclosure with facilities for urinating **b** : a fixture used for urinating

uri·nal·y·sis \ˌyər-ə-ˈna-lə-səs, ˌyu̇r-\ *n, pl* **-y·ses** [NL, irreg. fr. *urin-* + *analysis*] (1889) : chemical analysis of urine

uri·nary \ˈyər-ə-ˌner-ē, ˈyu̇r-\ *adj* (1578) **1** : relating to, occurring in, affecting, or constituting the organs concerned with the formation and discharge of urine ⟨the ~ system⟩ ⟨the ~ tract⟩ ⟨~ calculi⟩ **2** : of, relating to, or for urine **3** : excreted as or in urine ⟨~ sugar⟩

urinary bladder *n* (1728) : a membranous sac in many vertebrates that serves for the temporary retention of urine and discharges by the urethra

uri·nate \ˈyər-ə-ˌnāt, ˈyu̇r-\ *vi* **-nat·ed; -nat·ing** (1599) : to discharge urine : MICTURATE — **uri·na·tion** \ˌyər-ə-ˈnā-shən, ˈyu̇r-\ *n*

urine \ˈyər-ən, ˈyu̇r-\ *n* [ME, fr. AF, fr. L *urina,* fr. *urinari* to dive; akin to Skt *vār* water and perh. to Skt *varṣati* it rains, Gk *ourein* to urinate] (14c) : waste material that is secreted by the kidney in vertebrates, is rich in end products of protein metabolism together with salts and pigments, and forms a clear amber and usu. slightly acid fluid in mammals but is semisolid in birds and reptiles — **urin·ous** \ˈyər-ə-nəs, ˈyu̇r-\ *adj*

uri·no·gen·i·tal \ˌyu̇r-ə-nō-ˈje-nə-tᵊl\ *adj* (1836) : UROGENITAL

uri·nom·e·ter \ˌyu̇r-ə-ˈnä-mə-tər\ *n* [ISV] (1843) : a small hydrometer for determining the specific gravity of urine

URL \ˌyü-(ˌ)är-ˈel, ˈər(-ə)l\ *n* (1992) : the address of a resource (as a document or Web site) on the Internet that consists of a communications protocol followed by the name or address of a computer on the network and that often includes additional locating information (as directory and file names) ⟨our site's ~ is http://www.Merriam-Webster.com⟩ — called also *uniform resource locator, universal resource locator*

urn \ˈərn\ *n* [ME *urne,* fr. L *urna*] (14c) **1** : a vessel that is typically an ornamental vase on a pedestal and that is used for various purposes (as preserving the ashes of the dead after cremation) **2** : a closed vessel usu. with a spigot for serving a hot beverage ⟨a coffee ~⟩

uro- — see UR-

uro·ca·nic acid \ˌyu̇r-ə-ˈkā-nik-, -ˈka-\ *n* [¹*ur-* + *can*ine + *-ic;* fr. its being first obtained from the urine of a dog] (ca. 1903) : a crystalline acid $C_6H_6N_2O_2$ that is normally present in human skin

uro·chor·date \ˌyu̇r-ə-ˈkȯr-dət, -ˌdāt\ *n* [NL *Urochordata,* former group name, fr. ²*ur-* + *chordatus* having a notochord, fr. *chorda* notochord, fr. L, string, cord — more at CORD] (1948) : TUNICATE — **urochordate** *adj*

uro·chrome \ˈyu̇r-ə-ˌkrōm\ *n* (1864) : a yellow pigment to which the color of normal urine is principally due

uro·dele \ˈyu̇r-ə-ˌdēl\ *n* [F *urodèle,* ultim. fr. Gk *oura* tail + *dēlos* evident, showing — more at ASS] (1842) : any of an order (Caudata syn. Urodela) of amphibians

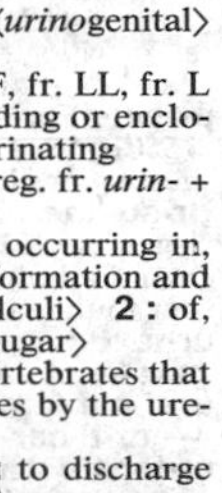

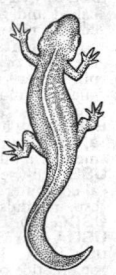

urodele

\ə\ **abut** \ᵊ\ **kitten, F table** \ər\ **further** \a\ **ash** \ā\ **ace** \ä\ **mop, mar** \au̇\ **out** \ch\ **chin** \e\ **bet** \ē\ **easy** \g\ **go** \i\ **hit** \ī\ **ice** \j\ **job** \ŋ\ **sing** \ō\ **go** \ȯ\ **law** \ȯi\ **boy** \th\ **thin** \t͟h\ **the** \ü\ **loot** \u̇\ **foot** \y\ **yet** \zh\ **vision, beige** \k͟, ⁿ, œ, ᵫ, ʸ\ *see* Guide to Pronunciation

(as newts and salamanders) that have a tail throughout life — **urodele** *adj*
uro·gen·i·tal \ˌyu̇r-ō-ˈje-nə-tᵊl\ *adj* [ISV] (1848) : of, relating to, or being the organs or functions of excretion and reproduction
uro·gy·ne·col·o·gy \ˌyu̇r-ō-ˌgī-nə-ˈkä-lə-jē, -ˌji-\ *n* (1989) : a branch of medicine concerned with urological problems affecting women — **uro·gy·ne·col·o·gist** \-jəst\ *n*
uro·ki·nase \ˌyu̇r-ō-ˈkī-ˌnās, -ˌnāz\ *n* (1952) : an enzyme that is produced by the kidney and found in urine, that activates plasminogen, and that is used therapeutically to dissolve blood clots (as in the heart)
uro·lith \ˈyu̇r-ə-ˌlith\ *n* [ISV] (ca. 1900) : a calculus in the urinary tract
uro·lith·ia·sis \ˌyu̇r-ə-li-ˈthī-ə-səs\ *n* [NL] (ca. 1860) : a condition that is marked by the formation or presence of calculi in the urinary tract
uro·logi·cal \ˌyu̇r-ə-ˈlä-ji-kəl\ *also* **uro·log·ic** \-jik\ *adj* (1855) : of or relating to the urinary tract or to urology
urol·o·gist \yu̇-ˈrä-lə-jist\ *n* (1879) : a physician who specializes in the urinary or urogenital tract — **urol·o·gy** \-jē\ *n*
-uronic *adj suffix* [Gk *ouron* urine] : connected with urine — in names of certain aldehyde-acids derived from sugars or compounds of such acids ⟨hyal*uronic*⟩
uron·ic acid \yu̇-ˈrä-nik-\ *n* (1925) : any of a class of acidic compounds of the general formula $HOOC(CHOH)_nCHO$ that contain both carboxylic and aldehydic groups, are oxidation products of sugars, and occur combined in many polysaccharides and in urine
uro·pod \ˈyu̇r-ə-ˌpäd\ *n* [ISV ²*ur-* + Gk *pod-, pous* foot — more at FOOT] (ca. 1890) : either of the flattened lateral appendages of the last abdominal segment of a crustacean; *broadly* : an abdominal appendage of a crustacean
uro·py·gi·al gland \ˌyu̇r-ə-ˈpī-jē-əl-\ *n* (1870) : a large gland that occurs in most birds, opens dorsally at the base of the tail feathers, and usu. secretes an oily fluid which the bird uses in preening its feathers — called also *oil gland*
uro·py·gi·um \ˌyu̇r-ə-ˈpī-jē-əm\ *n* [NL, fr. Gk *ouropygion,* fr. *ouro-* ²ur- + *pygē* rump] (1771) : the fleshy and bony prominence at the posterior extremity of a bird's body that supports the tail feathers
uro·style \ˈyu̇r-ə-ˌstī(-ə)l\ *n* [ISV ²*ur-* + Gk *stylos* pillar — more at STEER] (1875) : a long unsegmented bone that represents a number of fused vertebrae and forms the posterior part of the vertebral column of frogs and toads
Ur·sa Ma·jor \ˌər-sə-ˈmā-jər\ *n* [L (gen. *Ursae Majoris*), lit., greater bear] (ca. 1627) : a constellation that is the most conspicuous of the northern constellations, is situated near the north pole of the heavens, and contains the stars forming the Big Dipper two of which are in a line indicating the direction of the North Star — called also *Great Bear*
Ursa Mi·nor \-ˈmī-nər\ *n* [L (gen. *Ursae Minoris*), lit., lesser bear] (1638) : a constellation that includes the north pole of the heavens and the stars which form the Little Dipper with the North Star at the tip of the handle — called also *Little Bear*
ur·sine \ˈər-ˌsīn\ *adj* [L *ursinus,* fr. *ursus* bear — more at ARCTIC] (ca. 1550) **1** : of or relating to a bear or the bear family (Ursidae) **2** : suggesting or characteristic of a bear ⟨a lumbering ~ gait⟩
Ur·su·line \ˈər-sə-lən, -ˌlīn, -ˌlēn\ *n* [NL *Ursulina,* fr. *Ursula* St. Ursula, legendary Christian martyr] (1693) : a member of any of several Roman Catholic teaching orders of nuns; *esp* : a member of a teaching order founded by St. Angela Merici in Brescia, Italy, in 1535
ur·text \ˈu̇r-ˌtekst\ *n* [G, fr. *ur-* ³ur- + *Text* text] (ca. 1932) : the original text (as of a musical score)
ur·ti·car·ia \ˌər-tə-ˈker-ē-ə\ *n* [NL, fr. L *urtica* nettle] (ca. 1771) : HIVES — **ur·ti·car·i·al** \-ē-əl\ *adj*
ur·ti·cate \ˈər-tə-ˌkāt\ *vi* **-cat·ed; -cat·ing** [ML *urticatus,* pp. of *urticare* to sting, fr. L *urtica*] (1843) : to produce wheals or itching; *esp* : to induce hives — **ur·ti·ca·tion** \ˌər-tə-ˈkā-shən\ *n*
urus \ˈyu̇r-əs\ *n* [L, of Gmc origin; akin to OHG *ūro* aurochs — more at AUROCHS] (1601) : AUROCHS
uru·shi·ol \yu̇-ˈrü-shē-ˌȯl, u̇-ˈ, -ˌōl\ *n* [ISV, fr. Jp *urushi* lacquer + ISV ¹*-ol*] (1908) : a mixture of catechol derivatives with saturated or unsaturated side chains of 15 or 17 carbon atoms that is an oily toxic irritant principle present in poison ivy and some related plants (genus *Rhus*) and in lacquers derived from such plants
us \ˈəs\ *pron* [ME, fr. OE *ūs;* akin to OHG *uns* us, L *nos*] *objective case of* WE
US *abbr* United States
USA *abbr* **1** United States Army **2** United States of America
us·able *also* **use·able** \ˈyü-zə-bəl\ *adj* (14c) **1** : capable of being used **2** : convenient and practicable for use — **us·abil·i·ty** \ˌyü-zə-ˈbi-lə-tē\ *n* — **us·able·ness** \ˈyü-zə-bəl-nəs\ *n* — **us·ably** \-blē\ *adv*
USAF *abbr* United States Air Force
us·age \ˈyü-sij, -zij\ *n* [ME, fr. AF, fr. *us* use] (14c) **1 a** : firmly established and generally accepted practice or procedure **b** : a uniform certain reasonable lawful practice existing in a particular locality or occupation and binding persons entering into transactions chiefly on the basis of presumed familiarity **c** : the way in which words and phrases are actually used (as in a particular form or sense) in a language community **2 a** : the action, amount, or mode of using ⟨a decreased ~ of electricity⟩ **b** : manner of treating ***syn*** see HABIT
us·ance \ˈyü-zᵊn(t)s\ *n* (14c) **1** : USAGE 1a **2** : USE, EMPLOYMENT **3 a** *obs* : USURY **b** : INTEREST **4** : the time allowed by custom for payment of a bill of exchange in foreign commerce
USB \ˌyü-(ˌ)es-ˈbē\ *n* [*Universal Serial Bus*] (1995) : a standardized serial computer interface that allows simplified attachment of peripherals esp. in a daisy chain
USCG *abbr* United States Coast Guard
USDA *abbr* United States Department of Agriculture
¹**use** \ˈyüs\ *n* [ME *us,* fr. AF, fr. L *usus,* fr. *uti* to use] (13c) **1 a** : the act or practice of employing something : EMPLOYMENT, APPLICATION ⟨he made good ~ of his spare time⟩ **b** : the fact or state of being used ⟨a dish in daily ~⟩ **c** : a method or manner of employing or applying something ⟨gained practice in the ~ of the camera⟩ **2 a (1)** : habitual or customary usage **(2)** : an individual habit or group custom **b** : a liturgical form or observance; *esp* : a liturgy having modifications peculiar to a local church or religious order **3 a** : the privilege or benefit of using something ⟨gave him the ~ of her car⟩ **b** : the ability or power to use something (as a limb or faculty) **c** : the legal enjoyment of property that consists in its employment, occupation, exercise, or practice **4 a** : a particular service or end ⟨put learning to practical ~⟩ **b** : the quality of being suitable for employment ⟨saving things that might be of ~⟩ **c** : GOOD 2b ⟨it's no ~ arguing⟩ **d** : the occasion or need to employ ⟨took only what they had ~ for⟩ **5 a** : the benefit in law of one or more persons; *specif* : the benefit or profit of property established in one other than the legal possessor **b** : a legal arrangement by which such benefits and profits are so established **6** : a favorable attitude : LIKING ⟨had no ~ for modern art⟩
²**use** \ˈyüz\ *vb* **used** \ˈyüzd, *in the phrase "used to" usu* ˈyüs(t)\; **us·ing** \ˈyü-ziŋ\ *vt* (14c) **1** *archaic* : ACCUSTOM, HABITUATE **2** : to put into action or service : avail oneself of : EMPLOY **3** : to consume or take (as liquor or drugs) regularly **4** : to carry out a purpose or action by means of : UTILIZE; *also* : MANIPULATE 2b ⟨*used* him selfishly⟩ **5** : to expend or consume by putting to use — often used with *up* **6** : to behave toward : act with regard to : TREAT ⟨*used* the prisoners cruelly⟩ **7** : STAND 1d ⟨the house could ~ a coat of paint⟩ ~ *vi* **1** — used in the past with *to* to indicate a former fact or state ⟨we *used* to go more often⟩ ⟨didn't ~ to smoke⟩ **2** : to take illicit drugs regularly
syn USE, EMPLOY, UTILIZE mean to put into service esp. to attain an end. USE implies availing oneself of something as a means or instrument to an end ⟨*used* any means to achieve her ends⟩. EMPLOY suggests the use of a person or thing that is available but idle, inactive, or disengaged ⟨looking for better ways to *employ* their skills⟩. UTILIZE may suggest the discovery of a new, profitable, or practical use for something ⟨an old wooden bucket *utilized* as a planter⟩.
used \ˈyüzd, *in the phrase "used to" usu* ˈyüs(t)\ *adj* (14c) **1** : employed in accomplishing something **2** : that has endured use; *specif* : SECONDHAND ⟨a ~ car⟩ **3** : ACCUSTOMED, HABITUATED
use·ful \ˈyüs-fəl\ *adj* (1595) **1** : capable of being put to use; *esp* : serviceable for an end or purpose ⟨~ tools⟩ **2** : of a valuable or productive kind ⟨do something ~ with your life⟩ — **use·ful·ly** \-fə-lē\ *adv*
use·ful·ness *n* (1617) : the quality of having utility and esp. practical worth or applicability
use·less \ˈyüs-ləs\ *adj* (1592) : having or being of no use: **a** : INEFFECTUAL ⟨a ~ attempt⟩ **b** : not able to give service or aid : INEPT — **use·less·ly** *adv* — **use·less·ness** *n*
Use·net \ˈyüz-ˌnet\ *n* [prob. fr. *Use*nix, an association of computer programmers using the operating system Unix (fr. *users* of *U*nix) + ¹*net* (network)] (1980) : the aggregate of all newsgroups on the Internet
us·er \ˈyü-zər\ *n* (15c) : one that uses
user fee *n* (1967) : an excise tax often in the form of a license or supplemental charge levied to fund a public service — called also *user's fee*
us·er–friend·ly \ˌyü-zər-ˈfren(d)-lē\ *adj* (1977) : easy to learn, use, understand, or deal with ⟨~ software⟩; *also* : AGREEABLE, APPEALING ⟨a ~ atmosphere⟩ — **user–friendliness** *n*
us·er·name \ˈyü-zər-ˌnām\ *n* (1971) : a sequence of characters that identifies a user when logging onto a computer or Web site — called also *user ID*
USES *abbr* United States Employment Service
use up *vt* (1816) : to exhaust of strength or useful properties ⟨land that has been *used up*⟩
USG *abbr* United States government
USGA *abbr* United States Golf Association
USGS *abbr* United States Geological Survey
Ushak *var of* OUSHAK
¹**ush·er** \ˈə-shər\ *n* [ME *ussher,* fr. AF *ussier, usscher,* fr. VL **ustiarius* doorkeeper, fr. L *ostium, ustium* door, mouth of a river — more at OSTIUM] (13c) **1 a** : an officer or servant who has the care of the door of a court, hall, or chamber **b** : an officer who walks before a person of rank **c** : one who escorts persons to their seats (as in a theater) **2** *archaic* : an assistant teacher
²**usher** *vb* **ush·ered; ush·er·ing** \ˈə-sh(ə-)riŋ\ *vt* (1588) **1** : to conduct to a place **2** : to precede as an usher, forerunner, or harbinger **3** : to cause to enter : INTRODUCE ⟨a new theory ~*ed* into the world⟩ ~ *vi* : to serve as an usher ⟨~ at a wedding⟩
ush·er·ette \ˌə-shə-ˈret\ *n* (1921) : a girl or woman who is an usher
usher in *vt* (ca. 1600) **1** : to serve to bring into being ⟨a discovery that *ushered in* a period of change⟩ **2** : to mark or observe the beginning of ⟨*ushered in* the new year with merrymaking⟩ ***syn*** see BEGIN
USIA *abbr* United States Information Agency
USMC *abbr* United States Marine Corps
USN *abbr* United States Navy
us·nea \ˈəs-nē-ə, ˈəz-\ *n* [NL, fr. Ar *ushna* moss] (1597) : any of a genus (*Usnea* of the family Usneaceae) of widely distributed lichens (as old-man's beard) that have a grayish or yellow pendulous freely branched thallus
USNR *abbr* United States Naval Reserve
USNS *abbr* United States Naval Ship
USO *abbr* United Service Organizations
USP *abbr* United States Pharmacopeia
USPS *abbr* United States Postal Service
us·que·baugh \ˈəs-kwi-ˌbȯ, -ˌbä\ *n* [Ir *uisce beatha*] (1581) *Irish & Scot* : WHISKEY
USS *abbr* United States ship
USSR *abbr* Union of Soviet Socialist Republics
USTA *abbr* United States Tennis Association
usu *abbr* usual
¹**usu·al** \ˈyü-zhə-wəl, -zhəl; ˈyüzh-wəl\ *adj* [ME, fr. AF *usuel,* fr. LL *usualis,* fr. L *usus* use] (14c) **1** : accordant with usage, custom, or habit : NORMAL **2** : commonly or ordinarily used ⟨followed his ~ route⟩ **3** : found in ordinary practice or in the ordinary course of events : ORDINARY — **usu·al·ly** \ˈyü-zhə-wə-lē, -zhə-lē; ˈyüzh-wə-lē, ˈyüzh-lē\ *adv* — **usu·al·ness** \ˈyü-zhə-wəl-nəs, -zhəl-; ˈyüzh-wəl-\ *n* — **as usual** : in the accustomed or habitual way ⟨*as usual* they were late⟩
syn USUAL, CUSTOMARY, HABITUAL, WONTED, ACCUSTOMED mean familiar through frequent or regular repetition. USUAL stresses the absence of strangeness or unexpectedness ⟨my *usual* order for lunch⟩. CUSTOMARY applies to what accords with the practices, conventions, or usages of an individual or community ⟨the *customary* waiting period before the application is approved⟩. HABITUAL suggests a practice settled or established by much repetition ⟨a *habitual* morning routine⟩. WONTED stresses habituation but usu. applies to what is favored, sought, or purposefully cultivated ⟨his *wonted* determination⟩. ACCUSTOMED is less emphatic than WONTED or HABITUAL in suggest-

ing fixed habit or invariable custom ⟨accepted the compliment with her *accustomed* modesty⟩.

[2]**usual** *n* (1589) : something usual

usu·fruct \ˈyü-zə-ˌfrəkt, -sə-\ *n* [L *ususfructus,* fr. *usus et fructus* use and enjoyment] (ca. 1630) **1** : the legal right of using and enjoying the fruits or profits of something belonging to another **2** : the right to use or enjoy something

[1]**usu·fruc·tu·ary** \ˌyü-zə-ˈfrək-chə-ˌwer-ē, -sə-\ *n* (ca. 1618) **1** : one having the usufruct of property **2** : one having the use or enjoyment of something

[2]**usufructuary** *adj* (1710) : of, relating to, or having the character of a usufruct

usu·rer \ˈyü-zhər-ər, ˈyüzh-rər\ *n* (14c) : one that lends money esp. at an exorbitant rate

usu·ri·ous \yu̇-ˈzhu̇r-ē-əs, -ˈzu̇r-\ *adj* (1610) **1** : practicing usury **2** : involving usury : of the character of usury ⟨~ interest rates⟩ — **usu·ri·ous·ly** *adv* — **usu·ri·ous·ness** *n*

usurp \yu̇-ˈsərp *also* -ˈzərp\ *vb* [ME, fr. AF *usorper,* fr. L *usurpare* to take possession of without legal claim, fr. *usu* (abl. of *usus* use) + *rapere* to seize — more at RAPID] *vt* (14c) **1 a** : to seize and hold (as office, place, or powers) in possession by force or without right ⟨~ a throne⟩ **b** : to take or make use of without right ⟨~*ed* the rights to her life story⟩ **2** : to take the place of by or as if by force : SUPPLANT ⟨must not let stock responses based on inherited prejudice ~ careful judgment⟩ ~ *vi* : to seize or exercise authority or possession wrongfully — **usur·pa·tion** \ˌyü-sər-ˈpā-shən *also* ˌyü-zər-\ *n* — **usurp·er** \yu̇-ˈsər-pər *also* -ˈzər-\ *n*

usu·ry \ˈyü-zhə-rē, ˈyüzh-rē\ *n, pl* **-ries** [ME *usurie,* fr. AF, fr. ML *usuria,* alter. of L *usura,* fr. *usus,* pp. of *uti* to use] (14c) **1** *archaic* : INTEREST **2** : the lending of money with an interest charge for its use; *esp* : the lending of money at exorbitant interest rates **3** : an unconscionable or exorbitant rate or amount of interest; *specif* : interest in excess of a legal rate charged to a borrower for the use of money

USVI *abbr* United States Virgin Islands

ut \ˈət, ˈüt, ˈu̇t\ *n* [ME, first note in the diatonic scale, fr. ML, fr. the syllable sung to this note in a medieval hymn to St. John the Baptist] (14c) : a syllable used for the first note in the diatonic scale in an early solmization system and later replaced by *do*

UT *abbr* **1** Universal time **2** Utah

UTC *abbr* Coordinated Universal Time

ut dict *abbr* [L *ut dictum*] as directed

Ute \ˈyüt\ *n, pl* **Ute** *or* **Utes** [short for earlier *Utah, Utaw,* fr. AmerSp *Yuta*] (1776) **1** : a member of an American Indian people orig. ranging through Utah, Colorado, Arizona, and New Mexico **2** : the Uto-Aztecan language of the Ute people

uten·sil \yu̇-ˈten(t)-səl, ˈyü-ˌ\ *n* [ME, vessels for domestic use, fr. MF *utensile,* fr. L *utensilia,* fr. neut. pl. of *utensilis* useful, fr. *uti* to use] (14c) **1** : an implement, instrument, or vessel used in a household and esp. a kitchen **2** : a useful tool or implement ***syn*** see IMPLEMENT

uter·ine \ˈyü-tə-ˌrīn, -rən\ *adj* [ME, fr. LL *uterinus,* fr. L *uterus*] (15c) **1** : born of the same mother but by a different father ⟨~ brothers⟩ **2** : of, relating to, or affecting the uterus ⟨~ cancer⟩ ⟨the ~ lining⟩

uter·us \ˈyü-tə-rəs, ˈyü-trəs\ *n, pl* **uter·us·es** *or* **uteri** \ˈyü-tə-ˌrī\ [ME, fr. L, belly, womb; prob. akin to Gk *hoderos* belly, Skt *udara*] (14c) **1** : a muscular organ of the female mammal for containing and usu. for nourishing the young during development prior to birth — called also *womb* **2** : a structure in some lower animals analogous to the uterus in which eggs or young develop

Uther \ˈü-thər, ˈyü-\ *n* (13c) : a legendary British king and father of Arthur

UTI *abbr* urinary tract infection

util *abbr* utility

utile \ˈyü-tᵊl, ˈyü-ˌtī(-ə)l\ *adj* [MF, fr. L *utilis*] (15c) : USEFUL

uti·lise *Brit var of* UTILIZE

[1]**util·i·tar·i·an** \(ˌ)yü-ˌti-lə-ˈter-ē-ən\ *n* (ca. 1780) : an advocate or adherent of utilitarianism

[2]**utilitarian** *adj* (1802) **1** : of or relating to or advocating utilitarianism **2** : marked by utilitarian views or practices **3 a** : of, relating to, or aiming at utility **b** : exhibiting or preferring mere utility ⟨spare ~ furnishings⟩

util·i·tar·i·an·ism \-ē-ə-ˌni-zəm\ *n* (1827) **1** : a doctrine that the useful is the good and that the determining consideration of right conduct should be the usefulness of its consequences; *specif* : a theory that the aim of action should be the largest possible balance of pleasure over pain or the greatest happiness of the greatest number **2** : utilitarian character, spirit, or quality

[1]**util·i·ty** \yü-ˈti-lə-tē\ *n, pl* **-ties** [ME *utilite,* fr. AF *utilité,* fr. L *utilitat-, utilitas,* fr. *utilis* useful, fr. *uti* to use] (14c) **1** : fitness for some purpose or worth to some end **2** : something useful or designed for use **3 a** : PUBLIC UTILITY **b** (1) : a service (as light, power, or water) provided by a public utility (2) : equipment or a piece of equipment to provide such service or a comparable service **4** : a program or routine designed to perform or facilitate esp. routine operations (as copying files or editing text) on a computer

[2]**utility** *adj* (1851) **1** : capable of serving as a substitute in various roles or positions ⟨a ~ infielder⟩ **2 a** : kept to provide a useful product or service rather than for show or as a pet ⟨~ livestock⟩ ⟨a ~ dog⟩ **b** : being of a usable but inferior grade ⟨~ beef⟩ **3** : serving primarily for utility rather than beauty : UTILITARIAN **4** : designed or adapted for general use ⟨a ~ tool⟩ **5** : of or relating to a utility ⟨a ~ company⟩

utility knife *n* (1946) : a knife designed for general use ⟨a chef's *utility knife*⟩; *specif* : a cutting tool having a sharp replaceable blade that can be retracted into a usu. metal handle

utilization review *n* (1972) : a critical evaluation (as by a physician or nurse) of health-care services provided to patients that is made esp. for the purpose of controlling costs and monitoring quality of care

uti·lize \ˈyü-tə-ˌlīz\ *vt* **-lized; -liz·ing** [F *utiliser,* fr. *utile*] (1807) : to make use of : turn to practical use or account ⟨I'm a great person for *utilizing* waste power —Robert Frost⟩ ***syn*** see USE — **uti·liz·able** \-ˌlī-zə-bəl\ *adj* — **uti·li·za·tion** \ˌyü-tə-lə-ˈzā-shən\ *n* — **uti·liz·er** \ˈyü-tə-ˌlī-zər\ *n*

[1]**ut·most** \ˈət-ˌmōst, *esp Southern* -məst\ *adj* [ME, alter. of *utmest,* fr. OE *ūtmest,* superl. adj., fr. *ūt* out, adv. — more at OUT] (bef. 12c) **1** : situated at the farthest or most distant point : EXTREME ⟨the ~ point of the earth —John Hunt⟩ **2** : of the greatest or highest degree, quantity, number, or amount ⟨a matter of ~ concern⟩

[2]**utmost** *n* (bef. 12c) **1** : the most possible : the extreme limit : the highest attainable point or degree ⟨the ~ in reliability⟩ **2** : the highest, greatest, or best of one's abilities, powers, and resources ⟨will do our ~ to help⟩

Uto–Az·tec·an \ˌyü-tō-ˈaz-ˌte-kən\ *n* [*Ute* + *-o-* + *Aztec*] (1891) : a family of American Indian languages spoken by peoples from the U.S. Great Basin south to Central America — **Uto–Aztecan** *adj*

uto·pia \yu̇-ˈtō-pē-ə\ *n* [*Utopia,* imaginary and ideal country in *Utopia* (1516) by Sir Thomas More, fr. Gk *ou* not, no + *topos* place] (1597) **1** : an imaginary and indefinitely remote place **2** *often cap* : a place of ideal perfection esp. in laws, government, and social conditions **3** : an impractical scheme for social improvement

[1]**uto·pi·an** \-pē-ən\ *adj, often cap* (1551) **1** : of, relating to, or having the characteristics of a utopia; *esp* : having impossibly ideal conditions esp. of social organization **2** : proposing or advocating impractically ideal social and political schemes ⟨~ idealists⟩ **3** : impossibly ideal : VISIONARY ⟨recognised the ~ nature of his hopes —C. S. Kilby⟩ **4** : believing in, advocating, or having the characteristics of utopian socialism ⟨~ doctrines⟩ ⟨~ novels⟩

[2]**utopian** *n* (ca. 1873) **1** : one who believes in the perfectibility of human society **2** : one who proposes or advocates utopian schemes

uto·pi·an·ism \-pē-ə-ˌni-zəm\ *n* (ca. 1661) **1** : a utopian idea or theory **2** *often cap* : the body of ideas, views, or aims of a utopian

utopian socialism *n* (ca. 1923) : socialism based on a belief that social ownership of the means of production can be achieved by voluntary and peaceful surrender of their holdings by propertied groups — **utopian socialist** *n*

uto·pism \ˈyü-tə-ˌpi-zəm, yu̇-ˈtō-\ *n* (1888) : UTOPIANISM 2 — **utopist** \yu̇-ˈtō-pist\ *n* — **uto·pis·tic** \ˌyü-tə-ˈpis-tik, yu̇-ˌtō-\ *adj*

utri·cle \ˈyü-tri-kəl\ *n* [L *utriculus,* dim. of *uter* leather bag] (1731) : any of various small pouches or saccate parts of an animal or plant: as **a** : the part of the membranous labyrinth of the inner ear into which the semicircular canals open **b** : a small usu. indehiscent one-seeded fruit with thin membranous pericarp — **utric·u·lar** \yu̇-ˈtri-kyə-lər\ *adj*

utric·u·lus \yu̇-ˈtri-kyə-ləs\ *n* [L, small bag] (1847) : UTRICLE a

[1]**ut·ter** \ˈə-tər\ *adj* [ME, remote, fr. OE *ūtera* outer, compar. adj. fr. *ūt* out, adv. — more at OUT] (15c) : carried to the utmost point or highest degree : ABSOLUTE, TOTAL ⟨~ darkness⟩ ⟨~ strangers⟩ — **ut·ter·ly** *adv*

[2]**utter** *vb* [ME *uttren,* fr. *utter* outside, adv., fr. OE *ūtor,* compar. of *ūt* out] *vt* (15c) **1** *obs* : to offer for sale **2 a** : to send forth as a sound ⟨~ a sigh⟩ **b** : to give utterance to : PRONOUNCE, SPEAK ⟨refused to ~ his name⟩ **c** : to give public expression to : express in words ⟨~ an opinion⟩ **3** : to put (as currency) into circulation; *specif* : to circulate (as a counterfeit note) as if legal or genuine ⟨~ false tokens⟩ **4** : to put forth or out : DISCHARGE ~ *vi* : to make a statement or sound ***syn*** see EXPRESS — **ut·ter·able** \ˈə-tə-rə-bəl\ *adj* — **ut·ter·er** \ˈə-tər-ər\ *n*

[1]**ut·ter·ance** \ˈə-tə-rən(t)s, ˈə-trən(t)s\ *n* [ME *outraunce, uttraunce,* fr. MF *outrance,* fr. *outrer* to go beyond — more at OUTRÉ] (15c) *archaic* : the last extremity : BITTER END

[2]**ut·ter·ance** \ˈə-tə-rən(t)s *also* ˈə-trən(t)s\ *n* (15c) **1** : something uttered; *esp* : an oral or written statement : a stated or published expression **2** : vocal expression : SPEECH **3** : power, style, or manner of speaking

[1]**ut·ter·most** \ˈə-tər-ˌmōst\ *adj* [ME, alter. of *uttermest,* fr. [1]*utter* + *-mest* (as in *utmest* utmost)] (14c) **1** : OUTERMOST **2** : EXTREME, UTMOST

[2]**uttermost** *n* (14c) : UTMOST ⟨to the ~ of our capacity —H. S. Truman⟩

U–turn \ˈyü-ˌtərn\ *n* (1930) **1** : a turn resembling the letter U; *esp* : a 180-degree turn made by a vehicle in a road **2** : something (as a reversal of policy) resembling a U-turn

UV *abbr* ultraviolet

UVA \ˌyü-(ˌ)vē-ˈā\ *n* (1975) : radiation that is in the region of the ultraviolet spectrum which extends from about 320 to 400 nm in wavelength and that causes tanning and contributes to aging of the skin

U–val·ue \ˈyü-ˌval-(ˌ)yü\ *n* [*u*nit] (1949) : a measure of the heat transmission through a building part (as a wall or window) or a given thickness of a material (as insulation) with lower numbers indicating better insulating properties — compare R-VALUE

uva·rov·ite \yü-ˈvär-ə-ˌvīt, ü-\ *n* [G *Uwarowit,* fr. Count Sergei S. *Uvarov* †1855 Russ. statesman] (1837) : an emerald green calcium-chromium garnet

UVB \ˌyü-(ˌ)vē-ˈbē\ *n* (1975) : radiation that is in the region of the ultraviolet spectrum which extends from about 280 to 320 nm in wavelength and that is primarily responsible for sunburn, aging of the skin, and the development of skin cancer

UVC \ˌyü-(ˌ)vē-ˈsē\ *n* (1978) : radiation that is in the region of the ultraviolet spectrum which extends from about 200 to 280 nm in wavelength and that is more hazardous than UVB but is mostly absorbed by earth's upper atmosphere

uvea \ˈyü-vē-ə\ *n* [ML, fr. L *uva* grape] (1525) : the pigmented middle layer of the eye consisting of the iris and ciliary body together with the choroid — **uve·al** \-vē-əl\ *adj*

uve·itis \ˌyü-vē-ˈī-təs\ *n* [NL] (ca. 1848) : inflammation of the uvea

uvu·la \ˈyü-vyə-lə\ *n, pl* **-las** *or* **-lae** \-ˌlē, -ˌlī\ [ME, fr. ML, dim. of L *uva* cluster of grapes, uvula; prob. akin to Gk *oa* service tree, OE *īw* yew — more at YEW] (14c) : the pendent fleshy lobe in the middle of the posterior border of the soft palate

uvu·lar \-lər\ *adj* (1843) **1** : of or relating to the uvula ⟨~ glands⟩ **2** : produced with the aid of the uvula ⟨a ~ sound⟩

UW *abbr* underwriter

UXB *abbr* unexploded bomb

UXO *abbr* unexploded ordnance

\ə\ **abut** \ᵊ\ kitten, F table \ər\ **further** \a\ **ash** \ā\ **ace** \ä\ mop, mar
\au̇\ **out** \ch\ **chin** \e\ bet \ē\ **easy** \g\ **go** \i\ **hit** \ī\ **ice** \j\ **job**
\ŋ\ **sing** \ō\ **go** \ȯ\ **law** \ȯi\ **boy** \th\ **thin** \t͟h\ **the** \ü\ **loot** \u̇\ **foot**
\y\ yet \zh\ **vision, beige** \ḵ, ⁿ, œ, ue, ʸ\ *see* Guide to Pronunciation

ux·o·ri·al \ˌək-ˈsȯr-ē-əl, ˌəg-ˈzȯr-\ *adj* [L *uxorius*] (1800) : of, relating to, or characteristic of a wife
ux·or·i·cide \ˌək-ˈsȯr-ə-ˌsīd, -ˈsär-; ˌəg-ˈzȯr-, -ˈzär-\ *n* (1733) **1** [ML *uxoricidium,* fr. L *uxor* wife + *-i-* + *-cidium* -cide] : murder of a wife by her husband **2** [L *uxor* + E *-i-* + *-cide*] : a man who murders his wife

ux·o·ri·ous \ˌək-ˈsȯr-ē-əs, ˌəg-ˈzȯr-\ *adj* [L *uxorius* uxorious, uxorial, fr. *uxor* wife] (1598) : excessively fond of or submissive to a wife — **ux·o·ri·ous·ly** *adv* — **ux·o·ri·ous·ness** *n*
Uz·bek \ˈuz-ˌbek, ˈəz-, ˈuz-ˌ\ *or* **Uz·beg** \-ˌbeg, -ˈbeg\ *n* (1616) **1** : a member of a Turkic people of Uzbekistan and adjacent regions of central Asia **2** : the Turkic language of the Uzbek people

---

V

¹v \ˈvē\ *n, pl* **v's** *or* **vs** \ˈvēz\ *often cap, often attrib* (14c) **1 a** : the 22d letter of the English alphabet **b** : a graphic representation of this letter **c** : a speech counterpart of orthographic *v* **2** : FIVE — see NUMBER table **3** : a graphic device for reproducing the letter *v* **4** : one designated *v* esp. as the 22d in order or class **5** : something shaped like the letter V
²v *abbr* **1** vector **2** velocity **3** verse **4** verso **5** versus **6** very **7** vice **8** victory **9** vide **10** voice **11** voltage **12** volume **13** vowel
¹V *abbr* **1** violence; violent **2** volt
²V *symbol* vanadium
Va *abbr* Virginia
VA *abbr* **1** Veterans Administration **2** vice admiral **3** Virginia **4** visual aid **5** volt-ampere
vac *abbr* vacuum
va·can·cy \ˈvā-kən(t)-sē\ *n, pl* **-cies** (1598) **1** *archaic* : an interval of leisure **2** : physical or mental inactivity or relaxation : IDLENESS **3 a** : a vacating of an office, post, or piece of property **b** : the time such office or property is vacant **4** : a vacant office, post, or tenancy **5** : empty space : VOID; *specif* : an unoccupied site for an atom or ion in a crystal **6** : the state of being vacant : VACUITY
va·cant \ˈvā-kənt\ *adj* [ME, fr. AF, fr. L *vacant-, vacans,* prp. of *vacare* to be empty, be free] (14c) **1** : not occupied by an incumbent, possessor, or officer ⟨a ~ office⟩ ⟨~ thrones⟩ **2** : being without content or occupant ⟨a ~ seat on a bus⟩ ⟨a ~ room⟩ **3** : free from activity or work : DISENGAGED ⟨~ hours⟩ **4** : devoid of thought, reflection, or expression ⟨a ~ smile⟩ **5** : not lived in ⟨~ houses⟩ **6 a** : not put to use ⟨~ land⟩ **b** : having no heir or claimant : ABANDONED ⟨a ~ estate⟩ *syn* see EMPTY — **va·cant·ly** *adv* — **va·cant·ness** *n*
va·cate \ˈvā-ˌkāt, vā-ˈ\ *vb* **va·cat·ed; va·cat·ing** [L *vacatus,* pp. of *vacare*] *vt* (1643) **1** : to make legally void : ANNUL **2 a** : to deprive of an incumbent or occupant **b** : to give up the incumbency or occupancy of ~ *vi* : to vacate an office, post, or tenancy
¹va·ca·tion \vā-ˈkā-shən, və-\ *n, often attrib* [ME *vacacioun,* fr. AF *vacacion,* fr. L *vacation-, vacatio* freedom, exemption, fr. *vacare*] (14c) **1** : a respite or a time of respite from something : INTERMISSION **2 a** : a scheduled period during which activity (as of a court or school) is suspended **b** : a period of exemption from work granted to an employee **3** : a period spent away from home or business in travel or recreation ⟨had a restful ~ at the beach⟩ **4** : an act or an instance of vacating
²vacation *vi* **-tioned; -tion·ing** \-sh(ə-)niŋ\ (1883) : to take or spend a vacation ⟨~ed at the shore⟩ — **va·ca·tion·er** \-sh(ə-)nər\ *n*
va·ca·tion·ist \-sh(ə-)nist\ *n* (1885) : a person taking a vacation : VACATIONER
va·ca·tion·land \-shən-ˌland\ *n* (1927) : an area with recreational attractions and facilities for vacationers
vac·ci·nal \ˈvak-sə-n³l, vak-ˈsē-\ *adj* (ca. 1860) : of or relating to vaccine or vaccination ⟨a vaccine with ~ efficacy of 95 percent⟩
vac·ci·nate \ˈvak-sə-ˌnāt\ *vb* **-nat·ed; -nat·ing** *vt* (1803) : to administer a vaccine to usu. by injection ~ *vi* : to perform or practice vaccination — **vac·ci·na·tor** \-ˌnā-tər\ *n*
vac·ci·na·tion \ˌvak-sə-ˈnā-shən\ *n* (1800) **1** : the act of vaccinating **2** : the scar left by vaccinating
vac·cine \vak-ˈsēn, ˈvak-ˌ\ *n* [F *vaccin,* fr. *vaccine* cowpox, fr. NL *vaccina* (in *variolae vaccinae* cowpox), fr. L, fem. of *vaccinus,* adj., of or from cows, fr. *vacca* cow; akin to Skt *vaśā* cow] (1813) : a preparation of killed microorganisms, living attenuated organisms, or living fully virulent organisms that is administered to produce or artificially increase immunity to a particular disease — **vaccine** *adj*
vac·ci·nee \ˌvak-sə-ˈnē\ *n* (1889) : a vaccinated individual
vac·cin·ia \vak-ˈsi-nē-ə\ *n* [NL, fr. *vaccinus*] (1803) **1** : a poxvirus (species *Vaccinia virus* of the genus *Orthopoxvirus*) that differs from but is closely related to the viruses causing smallpox and cowpox and that includes a strain of uncertain natural origin used in making vaccines against smallpox — called also *vaccinia virus* **2** : a reaction to smallpox vaccine prepared from live vaccinia virus that may involve a rash, fever, headache, and body pain — **vac·cin·i·al** \-nē-əl\ *adj*
vac·il·late \ˈva-sə-ˌlāt\ *vi* **-lat·ed; -lat·ing** [L *vacillatus,* pp. of *vacillare* to sway, waver — more at WINK] (1597) **1 a** : to sway through lack of equilibrium **b** : FLUCTUATE, OSCILLATE **2** : to waver in mind, will, or feeling : hesitate in choice of opinions or courses *syn* see HESITATE — **vac·il·lat·ing·ly** \-ˌlā-tiŋ-lē\ *adv* — **vac·il·la·tor** \-ˌlā-tər\ *n*
vac·il·la·tion \ˌva-sə-ˈlā-shən\ *n* (15c) **1** : an act or instance of vacillating **2** : inability to take a stand : IRRESOLUTION, INDECISION
va·cu·i·ty \va-ˈkyü-ə-tē, və-\ *n, pl* **-ties** [ME *vacuite,* L *vacuitas,* fr. *vacuus* empty] (15c) **1** : an empty space **2** : the state, fact, or quality of being vacuous **3** : something (as an idea) that is vacuous or inane
vac·u·o·lat·ed \ˈva-kyə-(ˌ)wō-ˌlā-təd\ *or* **vac·u·o·late** \-ˌlāt\ *adj* (1859) : containing one or more vacuoles ⟨~ epithelial cells⟩

vac·u·o·la·tion \ˌva-kyə-(ˌ)wō-ˈlā-shən\ *n* (1858) : the development or formation of vacuoles
vac·u·ole \ˈva-kyə-ˌwōl\ *n* [F, lit., small vacuum, fr. L *vacuum*] (1853) **1** : a small cavity or space in the tissues of an organism containing air or fluid **2** : a cavity or vesicle in the cytoplasm of a cell usu. containing fluid — see CELL illustration — **vac·u·o·lar** \ˌva-kyə-ˈwō-lər, -ˌlär\ *adj*
vac·u·ous \ˈva-kyə-wəs\ *adj* [L *vacuus*] (ca. 1660) **1** : emptied of or lacking content **2** : marked by lack of ideas or intelligence : STUPID, INANE ⟨a ~ mind⟩ ⟨a ~ movie⟩ **3** : devoid of serious occupation : IDLE *syn* see EMPTY — **vac·u·ous·ly** *adv* — **vac·u·ous·ness** *n*
¹vac·u·um \ˈva-(ˌ)kyüm, -kyəm *also* -kyü-əm\ *n, pl* **vac·u·ums** *or* **vac·ua** \-kyə-wə\ [L, fr. neut. of *vacuus* empty, fr. *vacare* to be empty] (1550) **1** : emptiness of space **2 a** : a space absolutely devoid of matter **b** : a space partially exhausted (as to the highest degree possible) by artificial means (as an air pump) **c** : a degree of rarefaction below atmospheric pressure **3** : a state or condition resembling a vacuum : VOID ⟨the power ~ in Indochina after the departure of the French —Norman Cousins⟩ **b** : a state of isolation from outside influences ⟨people who live in a ~ . . . so that the world outside them is of no moment —W. S. Maugham⟩ **4** : a device creating or utilizing a partial vacuum; *esp* : VACUUM CLEANER
²vacuum *adj* (1825) **1** : of, containing, producing, or utilizing a partial vacuum ⟨separated by means of ~ distillation⟩ **2** : of or relating to a vacuum device or system
³vacuum *vt* (1922) **1** : to use a vacuum device (as a vacuum cleaner) on ⟨~ the living room⟩ **2** : to draw or take in by or as if by suction ~ *vi* : to operate a vacuum device
vacuum bottle *n* (1910) : THERMOS
vacuum cleaner *n* (1903) : a household appliance for cleaning (as floors, carpets, or upholstery) by suction — called also *vacuum sweeper*
vacuum flask *n* (1917) : THERMOS
vacuum gauge *n* (1851) : a gauge indicating degree of rarefaction below atmospheric pressure
vacuum–packed *adj* (ca. 1926) : having much of the air removed before being hermetically sealed
vacuum pan *n* (1833) : a tank with a vacuum pump for rapid evaporation and condensation (as of sugar syrup) by boiling at a low temperature
vacuum pump *n* (1844) : a pump for exhausting gas from an enclosed space
vacuum tube *n* (1859) : an electron tube evacuated to a high degree of vacuum
va·de me·cum \ˌvā-dē-ˈmē-kəm, ˌvä-dē-ˈmā-\ *n, pl* **vade mecums** [L, go with me] (1629) **1** : a book for ready reference : MANUAL **2** : something regularly carried about by a person
VADM *abbr* vice admiral
va·dose \ˈva-ˌdōs\ *adj* [L *vadosus* shallow, fr. *vadum,* n., shallow, ford; akin to L *vadere* to go — more at WADE] (1894) : of, relating to, or being water or solutions in the earth's crust above the permanent groundwater level
vag- *or* **vago-** *comb form* [ISV, fr. NL *vagus*] : vagus nerve ⟨*vagal*⟩ ⟨*vagotomy*⟩
¹vag·a·bond \ˈva-gə-ˌbänd\ *adj* [ME, fr. AF *vacabund,* fr. LL *vagabundus,* fr. L *vagari* to wander] (15c) **1** : moving from place to place without a fixed home : WANDERING **2** : of, relating to, or characteristic of a wanderer **b** : leading an unsettled, irresponsible, or disreputable life — **vag·a·bond·ish** \-ˌbän-dish\ *adj*
²vagabond *n* (15c) : one leading a vagabond life; *esp* : VAGRANT, TRAMP — **vag·a·bond·age** \-ˌbän-dij\ *n* — **vag·a·bond·ism** \-ˌbän-ˌdi-zəm\ *n*
³vagabond *vi* (ca. 1586) : to wander in the manner of a vagabond : roam about
va·gal \ˈvā-gəl\ *adj* [ISV] (1854) : of, relating to, mediated by, or being the vagus nerve — **va·gal·ly** \-gə-lē\ *adv*
va·gar·i·ous \vā-ˈger-ē-əs, və-, -ˈgar-\ *adj* (1798) : marked by vagaries : CAPRICIOUS, WHIMSICAL — **va·gar·i·ous·ly** *adv*
va·ga·ry \ˈvā-gə-rē; və-ˈger-ē, vā-\ *also* **va·ga·ry** \və-ˈger-ē\ *n, pl* **-ries** [prob. fr. L *vagari* to wander, fr. *vagus* wandering] (1579) : an erratic, unpredictable, or extravagant manifestation, action, or notion *syn* see CAPRICE
vag·ile \ˈva-jəl, -ˌjī(-ə)l\ *adj* [ISV, fr. L *vagus* wandering] (ca. 1890) : free to move about ⟨~ organisms⟩ — **va·gil·i·ty** \və-ˈji-lə-tē, va-\ *n*
va·gi·na \və-ˈjī-nə\ *n, pl* **-nae** \-(ˌ)nē\ *or* **-nas** [L, lit., sheath] (1682) **1** : a canal in a female mammal that leads from the uterus to the external orifice of the genital canal **2** : a canal that is similar in function or location to the vagina and occurs in various animals other than mammals
vag·i·nal \ˈva-jə-n³l\ *adj* (1726) **1** : of or relating to a theca **2** : of, relating to, or affecting the genital vagina — **vag·i·nal·ly** \-n³l-ē\ *adv*
vag·i·nis·mus \ˌva-jə-ˈniz-məs\ *n* [NL, fr. L *vagina*] (1866) : a painful spasmodic contraction of the vagina

vag·i·ni·tis \ˌva-jə-ˈnī-təs\ *n* [NL] (1846) : inflammation of the vagina or of a sheath (as a tendon sheath)

vag·i·no·sis \ˌva-jə-ˈnō-səs\ *n, pl* **-no·ses** \-ˌsēz\ [NL] (1984) : a disease or infection of the vagina; *specif* : BACTERIAL VAGINOSIS

va·got·o·my \vā-ˈgä-tə-mē\ *n, pl* **-mies** [ISV] (ca. 1903) : surgical division of the vagus nerve

va·go·to·nia \ˌvā-gə-ˈtō-nē-ə\ *n* [NL] (ca. 1915) : excessive excitability of the vagus nerve resulting typically in vasomotor instability, constipation, and sweating — **va·go·ton·ic** \-ˈtä-nik\ *adj*

va·gran·cy \ˈvā-grən(t)-sē\ *n, pl* **-cies** (1641) **1** : VAGARY **2** : the state or action of being vagrant **3** : the offense of being a vagrant

[1]**va·grant** \ˈvā-grənt\ *n* [ME *vagraunt,* fr. AF *vageraunt,* fr. prp. of *vagrer* to wander about, alter. (influenced by L *vagari* to wander) of *wacrer* to wander, of Gmc origin; akin to OE *wealcan* to roll — more at WALK] (15c) **1 a** : one who has no established residence and wanders idly from place to place without lawful or visible means of support **b** : one (as a prostitute or drunkard) whose conduct constitutes statutory vagrancy **2** : WANDERER, ROVER

[2]**vagrant** *adj* (15c) **1** : wandering about from place to place usu. with no means of support **2 a** : having a fleeting, wayward, or inconstant quality ⟨a ~ impulse⟩ **b** : having no fixed course : RANDOM ⟨a ~ breeze⟩ — **va·grant·ly** *adv*

va·grom \ˈvā-grəm\ *adj* [by alter.] (1599) : VAGRANT

vague \ˈvāg\ *adj* **vagu·er; vagu·est** [MF, fr. L *vagus,* lit., wandering] (1548) **1 a** : not clearly expressed : stated in indefinite terms ⟨~ accusations⟩ **b** : not having a precise meaning ⟨a ~ term of abuse⟩ **2 a** : not clearly defined, grasped, or understood : INDISTINCT ⟨only a ~ notion of what's needed⟩; *also* : SLIGHT ⟨a ~ hint of a thickening waistline⟩ ⟨hasn't the *vaguest* idea⟩ **b** : not clearly felt or sensed : somewhat subconscious ⟨a ~ longing⟩ **3** : not thinking or expressing one's thoughts clearly or precisely ⟨~ about dates and places⟩ **4** : lacking expression : VACANT ⟨~ eyes⟩ ⟨a ~ stare⟩ **5** : not sharply outlined : HAZY ⟨met by ~ figures with shaded torchlights —Earle Birney⟩ ***syn*** see OBSCURE — **vague·ly** *adv* — **vague·ness** *n*

va·gus nerve \ˈvā-gəs-\ *n* [NL *vagus nervus,* lit., wandering nerve] (1856) : either of the 10th pair of cranial nerves that arise from the medulla and supply chiefly the viscera esp. with autonomic sensory and motor fibers — called also *vagus*

vail \ˈvāl\ *vt* [ME *valen,* partly fr. AF *valer* (short for *avaler* to lower) & partly short for ME *avalen* to let fall, fr. AF *avaler,* fr. *aval* downward, fr. *a* to (fr. L *ad*) + *val* valley — more at AT, VALE] (14c) : to lower often as a sign of respect or submission

vain \ˈvān\ *adj* [ME, fr. AF, empty, futile, fr. L *vanus* — more at WANE] (14c) **1** : having no real value : IDLE, WORTHLESS ⟨~ pretensions⟩ **2** : marked by futility or ineffectualness : UNSUCCESSFUL, USELESS ⟨~ efforts to escape⟩ **3** *archaic* : FOOLISH, SILLY **4** : having or showing undue or excessive pride in one's appearance or achievements : CONCEITED ***syn*** see FUTILE — **vain·ly** *adv* — **vain·ness** \ˈvān-nəs\ *n* — **in vain** **1** : to no end : without success or result ⟨her efforts were *in vain*⟩ **2** : in an irreverent or blasphemous manner ⟨you shall not take the name of the Lord your God *in vain* —Deut 5:11 (RSV)⟩

syn VAIN, NUGATORY, OTIOSE, IDLE, EMPTY, HOLLOW mean being without worth or significance. VAIN implies either absolute or relative absence of value ⟨*vain* promises⟩. NUGATORY suggests triviality or insignificance ⟨a monarch with *nugatory* powers⟩. OTIOSE suggests that something serves no purpose and is either an encumbrance or a superfluity ⟨a film without a single *otiose* scene⟩. IDLE suggests being incapable of worthwhile use or effect ⟨*idle* speculations⟩. EMPTY and HOLLOW suggest a deceiving lack of real substance or soundness or genuineness ⟨an *empty* attempt at reconciliation⟩ ⟨a *hollow* victory⟩.

vain·glo·ri·ous \ˌvān-ˈglȯr-ē-əs\ *adj* (15c) : marked by vainglory : BOASTFUL — **vain·glo·ri·ous·ly** *adv* — **vain·glo·ri·ous·ness** *n*

vain·glo·ry \ˈvān-ˌglȯr-ē, ˌvān-ˈ\ *n* (13c) **1** : excessive or ostentatious pride esp. in one's achievements **2** : vain display or show : VANITY

vair \ˈver\ *n* [ME *veir,* fr. AF *vair,* fr. *vair,* adj., mottled, variegated, fr. L *varius* variegated, various] (13c) : the bluish-gray and white fur of a squirrel prized for ornamental use in medieval times

Vaish·na·va \ˈvīsh-nə-və\ *n* [Skt *vaiṣṇava* of Vishnu, fr. *Viṣṇu* Vishnu] (1808) : a member of a major Hindu sect devoted to the cult of Vishnu — **Vaishnava** *adj* — **Vaish·na·vism** \-ˌvi-zəm\ *n*

Vaish·ya *or* **Vais·ya** \ˈvīsh-yə, ˈvī-shə\ *n* [Skt *vaiśya,* fr. *viś* settlement; akin to Gk *oikos* house — more at VICINITY] (1665) : a Hindu of an upper caste traditionally assigned to commercial and agricultural occupations

val *abbr* value; valued

va·lance \ˈva-lən(t)s, ˈvā-\ *n* [ME *valaunce,* fr. AF *valence,* prob. fr. *valer* to lower — more at VAIL] (15c) **1** : a drapery hung along the edge of a bed, table, altar, canopy, or shelf **2** : a short drapery or wood or metal frame used as a decorative heading to conceal the top of curtains and fixtures — **va·lanced** \-lən(t)st\ *adj*

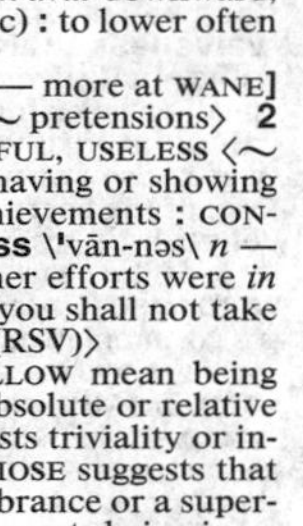

V valance 1

vale \ˈvāl\ *n* [ME, fr. AF *val,* fr. L *valles, vallis;* perh. akin to L *volvere* to roll — more at VOLUBLE] (14c) **1** : VALLEY, DALE **2** : WORLD ⟨this ~ of tears⟩

val·e·dic·tion \ˌva-lə-ˈdik-shən\ *n* [L *valedicere* to say farewell, fr. *vale* farewell + *dicere* to say — more at DICTION] (1613) **1** : an act of bidding farewell **2** : VALEDICTORY 1

val·e·dic·to·ri·an \-ˌdik-ˈtȯr-ē-ən\ *n* (1759) : the student usu. having the highest rank in a graduating class who delivers the valedictory address at the commencement exercises

[1]**val·e·dic·to·ry** \-ˈdik-t(ə-)rē\ *adj* [L *valedicere*] (1651) : of or relating to a valediction : expressing or containing a farewell

[2]**valedictory** *n, pl* **-ries** (1779) **1** : an address or statement of farewell or leave-taking **2** : VALEDICTION 1

va·lence \ˈvā-lən(t)s\ *n* [LL *valentia* power, capacity, fr. L *valent-, valens,* prp. of *valēre* to be strong — more at WIELD] (1884) **1** : the degree of combining power of an element as shown by the number of atomic weights of a monovalent element (as hydrogen) with which the atomic weight of the element will combine or for which it can be substituted or with which it can be compared **2 a** : relative capacity to unite, react, or interact (as with antigens or a biological substrate) **b** : the degree of attractiveness an individual, activity, or thing possesses as a behavioral goal ⟨the relative potency of the ~*s* of success and failure —Leon Festinger⟩

valence band *n* (1953) : the range of permissible energy values that are the highest energies an electron can have and still be associated with a particular atom of a solid material — compare CONDUCTION BAND

valence electron *n* (1922) : a single electron or one of two or more electrons in the outer shell of an atom that is responsible for the chemical properties of the atom

Va·len·cia orange \və-ˈlen-ch(ē-)ə, -len(t)-sē-ə\ *n* [*Valencia,* Spain] (1858) : a sweet orange of a juicy thin-skinned cultivar grown in the U.S. — called also *Valencia*

Va·len·ci·ennes \və-ˌlen(t)-sē-ˈen(z), ˌva-lən-sē-\ *n* [*Valenciennes,* France] (1717) : a fine bobbin lace

-valent *adj comb form* [ISV, fr. L *valent-, valens*] **1** : having a (specified) valence or valences ⟨bi*valent*⟩ ⟨multi*valent*⟩ **2** : having (so many) chromosomal strands or homologous chromosomes ⟨uni*valent*⟩

val·en·tine \ˈva-lən-ˌtīn\ *n* (15c) **1** : a sweetheart chosen or complimented on Valentine's Day **2 a** : a gift or greeting sent or given esp. to a sweetheart on Valentine's Day; *esp* : a greeting card sent on this day **b** : something (as a movie or piece of writing) expressing uncritical praise or affection : TRIBUTE

Valentine's Day *also* **Valentine Day** *n* (1668) : February 14 observed in honor of St. Valentine and as a time for sending valentines

val·er·ate \ˈva-lə-ˌrāt\ *n* (1852) : a salt or ester of valeric acid

va·le·ri·an \və-ˈlir-ē-ən\ *n* [ME, fr. AF or ML; AF *valeriane,* fr. ML *valeriana,* prob. fr. fem. of *valerianus* of Valeria, fr. *Valeria,* Roman province formerly part of Pannonia] (12c) **1** : any of a genus (*Valeriana* of the family Valerianaceae, the valerian family) of perennial herbs and shrubs many of which possess medicinal properties **2** : a preparation of the dried rhizome and roots of the garden heliotrope (*Valeriana officinalis*) used esp. formerly as a carminative and sedative

va·le·ric acid \və-ˈlir-ik-, -ˈler-\ *n* [*valerian;* fr. its occurrence in the root of valerian] (1857) : any of four isomeric fatty acids $C_5H_{10}O_2$ or a mixture of these; *esp* : a liquid acid of disagreeable odor obtained from valerian or made synthetically and used esp. in organic synthesis

[1]**va·let** \ˈva-lət, ˈva-(ˌ)lā, va-ˈlā\ *n* [ME *vadlet, valet,* fr. AF, young man of noble birth serving a lord, boy, servant, fr. ML **vassellittus,* dim. of *vassus* servant — more at VASSAL] (14c) **1 a** : a man's male servant who performs personal services (as taking care of clothing) **b** : an employee (as of a hotel or a public facility) who performs personal services for customers **2** : a device (as a rack or tray) for holding clothing or personal effects

[2]**valet** *vt* (1840) : to serve as a valet

va·let de cham·bre \(ˌ)va-ˌlā-də-ˈshä^{n}br^{ə}\ *n, pl* **va·lets de chambre** *same*\ [F, lit., chamber valet] (1646) : VALET 1a

valet parking *n* (1960) : a service that provides parking of motor vehicles by an attendant

[1]**val·e·tu·di·nar·i·an** \ˌva-lə-ˌtü-də-ˈner-ē-ən, -ˌtyü-\ *n* [L *valetudinarius* sickly, infirm, fr. *valetudin-, valetudo* state of health, sickness, fr. *valēre* to be strong, be well — more at WIELD] (1703) : a person of a weak or sickly constitution; *esp* : one whose chief concern is his or her ill health

[2]**valetudinarian** *adj* (1713) : of, relating to, or characteristic of a valetudinarian : SICKLY, WEAK

val·e·tu·di·nar·i·an·ism \-ē-ə-ˌni-zəm\ *n* (1839) : the condition or state of mind of a valetudinarian

[1]**val·e·tu·di·nary** \-ˈtü-də-ˈner-ē, -ˈtyü-\ *adj* [L *valetudinarius*] (1581) : VALETUDINARIAN

[2]**valetudinary** *n, pl* **-nar·ies** (1665) : VALETUDINARIAN

val·gus \ˈval-gəs\ *adj* [NL, fr. L, knock-kneed] (1884) **1** : of, relating to, or being a deformity in which an anatomical part is turned outward away from the midline of the body to an abnormal degree ⟨a ~ heel⟩ ⟨~ deformity of the big toe⟩ **2** : VARUS 1 — used of the knee — **valgus** *n*

Val·hal·la \val-ˈha-lə *also* väl-ˈhä-\ *n* [G & ON; G *Walhalla,* fr. ON *Valhǫll,* lit., hall of the slain, fr. *valr* the slain (akin to OE *wæl* slaughter, the slain) + *hǫll* hall; akin to OE *heall* hall] (1768) **1** : the great hall in Norse mythology where heroes slain in battle are received **2** : a place of honor, glory, or happiness : HEAVEN ⟨an academic's ~⟩

val·iance \ˈval-yən(t)s\ *n* (15c) : VALOR

val·ian·cy \-yən(t)-sē\ *n* (15c) : VALOR

[1]**val·iant** \ˈval-yənt\ *adj* [ME *vailant, valiant,* fr. AF *vaillant* worthy, strong, courageous, fr. prp. of *valer* to be of worth, fr. L *valēre* to be strong — more at WIELD] (14c) **1** : possessing or acting with bravery or boldness : COURAGEOUS ⟨~ soldiers⟩ **2** : marked by, exhibiting, or carried out with courage or determination : HEROIC ⟨~ feats⟩ — **val·iant·ly** *adv* — **val·iant·ness** *n*

[2]**valiant** *n* (1589) : a valiant person

val·id \ˈva-ləd\ *adj* [MF or ML; MF *valide,* fr. ML *validus,* fr. L, strong, potent, fr. *valēre*] (1571) **1** : having legal efficacy or force; *esp* : executed with the proper legal authority and formalities ⟨a ~ contract⟩ **2 a** : well-grounded or justifiable : being at once relevant and meaningful ⟨a ~ theory⟩ **b** : logically correct ⟨a ~ argument⟩ ⟨~ inference⟩ **3** : appropriate to the end in view : EFFECTIVE ⟨every craft has its own ~ methods⟩ **4** *of a taxon* : conforming to accepted principles of sound biological classification — **va·lid·i·ty** \və-ˈli-də-tē, va-\ *n* — **val·id·ly** \ˈva-ləd-lē\ *adv*

syn VALID, SOUND, COGENT, CONVINCING, TELLING mean having such force as to compel serious attention and usu. acceptance. VALID implies being supported by objective truth or generally accepted authority ⟨a *valid* reason for being absent⟩ ⟨a *valid* marriage⟩. SOUND implies a basis of flawless reasoning or of solid grounds ⟨a *sound* proposal for reviving the economy⟩. COGENT may stress either weight of sound argument and evidence or lucidity of presentation ⟨the prosecutor's *cogent* summation won over the jury⟩. CONVINCING suggests a power to overcome doubt, opposition, or reluctance to accept ⟨a *con-*

\ə\ **abut** \ᵊ\ kitten, F table \ər\ **further** \a\ **ash** \ā\ **ace** \ä\ **mop, mar**
\au̇\ **out** \ch\ **chin** \e\ **bet** \ē\ **easy** \g\ **go** \i\ **hit** \ī\ **ice** \j\ **job**
\ŋ\ **sing** \ō\ **go** \ȯ\ **law** \ȯi\ **boy** \th\ **thin** \t͟h\ **the** \ü\ **loot** \u̇\ **foot**
\y\ **yet** \zh\ **vision, beige** \k, ^{n}, œ, ue, ^{y}\ *see* Guide to Pronunciation

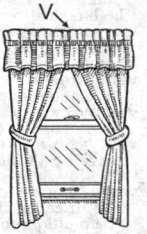

vincing argument for welfare reform〉. TELLING stresses an immediate and crucial effect striking at the heart of a matter 〈a *telling* example of bureaucratic waste〉.

val·i·date \ˈva-lə-ˌdāt\ *vt* **-dat·ed; -dat·ing** (1648) **1 a :** to make legally valid : RATIFY **b :** to grant official sanction to by marking 〈*validated* her passport〉 **c :** to confirm the validity of (an election); *also* : to declare (a person) elected **2 a :** to support or corroborate on a sound or authoritative basis 〈experiments designed to ~ the hypothesis〉 **b :** to recognize, establish, or illustrate the worthiness or legitimacy of 〈~ his concerns〉 ***syn*** see CONFIRM

val·i·da·tion \ˌva-lə-ˈdā-shən\ *n* (ca. 1656) : an act, process, or instance of validating; *esp* : the determination of the degree of validity of a measuring device

va·line \ˈva-ˌlēn, ˈvā-\ *n* [ISV, fr. *valeric (acid)*] (1907) : a crystalline essential amino acid $C_5H_{11}NO_2$ that is one of the building blocks of plant and animal proteins

va·lise \və-ˈlēs\ *n* [F, fr. It *valigia*] (1615) : SUITCASE

Val·ium \ˈva-lē-əm, ˈval-yəm\ *trademark* — used for a preparation of diazepam

Val·ky·rie \val-ˈkir-ē *also* val-ˈkī-rē, ˈval-kə-rē\ *n* [G & ON; G *Walküre*, fr. ON *valkyrja*, lit., chooser of the slain; akin to OE *wælcyrige* witch, ON *valr* the slain, OHG *kiosan* to choose — more at CHOOSE] (1770) : any of the maidens of Odin who choose the heroes to be slain in battle and conduct them to Valhalla

val·late \ˈva-ˌlāt\ *adj* [L *vallatus*, pp. of *vallare* to surround with a wall, fr. *vallum* wall, rampart — more at WALL] (1878) : having a raised edge surrounding a depression 〈~ papillae of the tongue〉

val·lec·u·la \va-ˈle-kyə-lə, və-\ *n, pl* **-u·lae** \-kyə-ˌlē, -ˌlī\ [NL, fr. LL, little valley, dim. of L *valles* valley — more at VALE] (1859) : an anatomical groove, channel, or depression; *esp* : one between the base of the tongue and the epiglottis — **val·lec·u·lar** \-lər\ *adj*

val·ley \ˈva-lē\ *n, pl* **valleys** [ME *valeye*, fr. AF *valee*, fr. *val* valley — more at VALE] (14c) **1 a :** an elongate depression of the earth's surface usu. between ranges of hills or mountains **b :** an area drained by a river and its tributaries **2 :** a low point or condition **3 a :** HOLLOW, DEPRESSION **b :** the place of meeting of two slopes of a roof that form on the plan a reentrant angle

valley fever *n* [fr. its prevalence in the San Joaquin valley of California] (1938) : COCCIDIOIDOMYCOSIS

Valley girl *n, often cap G* (1982) : an adolescent girl from the San Fernando Valley; *also* : one whose values, mannerisms, and esp. speech patterns resemble those of such a girl

Va·lois \ˈval-ˌwä, val-ˈ\ *adj* [Philippe de *Valois* (Philip VI of France)] (1883) : of or relating to the French royal house that ruled from 1328 to 1589

va·lo·nia \və-ˈlō-nē-ə, -nyə\ *n* [It *vallonia*, fr. MGk *balanidia*, pl. of *balanidion*, dim. of Gk *balanos* acorn — more at GLAND] (1722) : dried acorn cups esp. from a Eurasian evergreen oak (*Quercus macrolepis* syn. *Q. aegilops*) used in tanning or dressing leather

val·or \ˈva-lər\ *n* [ME *valour* worth, worthiness, bravery, fr. AF, fr. ML *valor*, fr. L *valēre* to be of worth, be strong — more at WIELD] (14c) : strength of mind or spirit that enables a person to encounter danger with firmness : personal bravery

val·o·rize \ˈva-lə-ˌrīz\ *vt* **-rized; -riz·ing** [Pg *valorizar*, fr. *valor* value, price, fr. ML] (ca. 1906) **1 :** to enhance or try to enhance the price, value, or status of by organized and usu. governmental action 〈using subsidies to ~ coffee〉 **2 :** to assign value or merit to : VALIDATE — **val·o·ri·za·tion** \ˌva-lə-rə-ˈzā-shən\ *n*

val·or·ous \ˈva-lə-rəs\ *adj* (15c) : VALIANT — **val·or·ous·ly** *adv*

val·our \ˈva-lər\ *chiefly Brit var of* VALOR

val·po·li·cel·la \ˌväl-ˌpō-lə-ˈche-lə, ˌval-\ *n, often cap* [*Valpolicella*, district in northern Italy] (1903) : a dry red Italian table wine

Val·sal·va maneuver \val-ˈsal-və-\ *n* [Antonio Maria *Valsalva* †1723 Ital. anatomist] (1886) : a forceful attempt at expiration when the airway is closed at some point; *esp* : a conscious attempt made while holding the nostrils closed and keeping the mouth shut (as for the purpose of adjusting middle ear pressure) — called also *Valsalva*

valse \ˈväls\ *n* [F, fr. G *Walzer* — more at WALTZ] (1796) : WALTZ; *specif* : a concert waltz

[1]**valu·able** \ˈval-yə-bəl, -yə-wə-bəl, -yü-ə-\ *adj* (ca. 1576) **1 a :** having monetary value **b :** worth a good price **2 a :** having desirable or esteemed characteristics or qualities 〈~ friendships〉 **b :** of great use or service 〈~ advice〉 — **valu·able·ness** *n* — **valu·ably** \-blē\ *adv*

[2]**valuable** *n* (ca. 1775) : a usu. personal possession (as jewelry) of relatively great monetary value — usu. used in pl.

valuable consideration *n* (1602) : an equivalent or compensation having value that is given for something acquired or promised (as money or marriage) and that may consist either in a benefit accruing to one party or a loss falling upon the other

val·u·ate \ˈval-yə-ˌwāt\ *vt* **-at·ed; -at·ing** (1873) : to place a value on : APPRAISE

val·u·a·tion \ˌval-yə-ˈwā-shən\ *n* [MF, fr. *valuer* to value, fr. *value*] (1529) **1 :** the act or process of valuing; *specif* : appraisal of property **2 :** the estimated or determined market value of a thing **3 :** judgment or appreciation of worth or character — **val·u·a·tion·al** \-shnəl, -shə-nᵊl\ *adj* — **val·u·a·tion·al·ly** *adv*

val·u·a·tor \ˈval-yə-ˌwā-tər\ *n* (1731) : one that valuates; *specif* : one that appraises

[1]**val·ue** \ˈval-(ˌ)yü\ *n* [ME, worth, high quality, fr. AF, fr. VL **valuta*, fr. fem. of **valutus*, pp. of L *valēre* to be of worth, be strong — more at WIELD] (14c) **1 :** a fair return or equivalent in goods, services, or money for something exchanged **2 :** the monetary worth of something : MARKET PRICE **3 :** relative worth, utility, or importance 〈a good ~ at the price〉 〈the ~ of base stealing in baseball〉 〈had nothing of ~ to say〉 **4 :** a numerical quantity that is assigned or is determined by calculation or measurement 〈let *x* take on positive ~*s*〉 〈a ~ for the age of the earth〉 **5 :** the relative duration of a musical note **6 a :** relative lightness or darkness of a color : LUMINOSITY **b :** the relation of one part in a picture to another with respect to lightness and darkness **7 :** something (as a principle or quality) intrinsically valuable or desirable 〈sought material ~*s* instead of human ~*s* —W. H. Jones〉 **8 :** DENOMINATION 2 — **val·ue·less** \-(ˌ)yü-ləs, -yə-\ *adj* — **val·ue·less·ness** *n*

[2]**value** *vt* **val·ued; val·u·ing** (15c) **1 a :** to estimate or assign the monetary worth of : APPRAISE 〈~ a necklace〉 **b :** to rate or scale in usefulness, importance, or general worth : EVALUATE **2 :** to consider or rate highly : PRIZE, ESTEEM 〈~*s* your opinion〉 ***syn*** see ESTIMATE, APPRECIATE — **val·u·er** \-yə-wər\ *n*

val·ue–add·ed \ˈval-(ˌ)yü-ˈa-dəd\ *adj* (1935) : of, relating to, or being a product whose value has been increased esp. by special manufacturing, marketing, or processing 〈~ goods〉

value–added tax *n* (1935) : an incremental excise that is levied on the value added at each stage of the processing of a raw material or the production and distribution of a commodity and that typically has the impact of a sales tax on the ultimate consumer

val·ued \ˈval-(ˌ)yüd, -yəd\ *adj* (1595) : having a value or values esp. of a specified kind or number — often used in combination 〈real-*valued*〉

val·ue–free \ˈval-(ˌ)yü-ˈfrē\ *adj* (1948) : making or having no value judgments 〈~ distinctions〉 〈~ instruction〉

value judgment *n* (1892) : a judgment assigning a value (as good or bad) to something

va·lu·ta \və-ˈlü-tə, -(ˌ)tä\ *n* [It, value, fr. VL **valuta*] (1920) **1 :** the agreed upon or exchange value of a currency **2 :** FOREIGN EXCHANGE 2

val·vate \ˈval-ˌvāt\ *adj* (1829) : having valves or parts resembling a valve; *esp* : meeting at the edges without overlapping 〈~ sepals〉

valve \ˈvalv\ *n* [L *valva*; akin to L *volvere* to roll — more at VOLUBLE] (14c) **1** *archaic* : a leaf of a folding or double door **2** [NL *valva*, fr. L] : a bodily structure (as the mitral valve) that closes temporarily a passage or orifice or permits movement of fluid in one direction only **3 a :** any of numerous mechanical devices by which the flow of liquid, gas, or loose material in bulk may be started, stopped, or regulated by a movable part that opens, shuts, or partially obstructs one or more ports or passageways; *also* : the movable part of such a device **b :** a device in a brass instrument for quickly channeling air flow through an added length of tube in order to change the fundamental tone by some definite interval **c** *chiefly Brit* : ELECTRON TUBE **4** [NL *valva*, fr. L] : one of the distinct usu. hinged and movable pieces of which the shell of some shell-bearing animals (as lamellibranch mollusks, brachiopods, and barnacles) consists **5** [NL *valva*, fr. L] **a :** one of the segments or pieces into which a dehiscing capsule or legume separates **b :** the portion of various anthers (as of the barberry) resembling a lid **c :** one of the two encasing membranes of a diatom — **valved** \ˈvalvd\ *adj* — **valve·less** \ˈvalv-ləs\ *adj*

val·vu·la \ˈval-vyə-lə\ *n, pl* **-lae** \-ˌlē, -ˌlī\ [NL, dim. of L *valva*] (1615) : a small valve or fold

val·vu·lar \ˈval-vyə-lər\ *adj* (1797) **1 :** resembling or functioning as a valve; *also* : opening by valves **2 :** of, relating to, or affecting a valve esp. of the heart 〈~ heart disease〉

val·vu·li·tis \ˌval-vyə-ˈlī-təs\ *n* [NL] (ca. 1891) : inflammation of a valve esp. of the heart

va·moose \və-ˈmüs, va-\ *vi* **va·moosed; va·moos·ing** [Sp *vamos* let us go, suppletive 1st pl. imper. (fr. L *vadere* to go) of *ir* to go, fr. L *ire* — more at WADE, ISSUE] (1859) : to depart quickly

[1]**vamp** *n* [ME *vampe* part of a hose leg or shoe covering the forefoot, vamp, fr. AF, alter. of *avanpié*, fr. *avant-* fore- + *pié* foot, fr. L *ped-, pes* — more at VANGUARD, FOOT] (14c) **1 :** the part of a shoe upper or boot upper covering esp. the forepart of the foot and sometimes also extending forward over the toe or backward to the back seam of the upper **2** [[2]*vamp*] : a short introductory musical passage often repeated several times (as in vaudeville) before a solo or between verses

[2]**vamp** \ˈvamp\ *vt* (1599) **1 a :** to provide (a shoe) with a new vamp **b :** to piece (something old) with a new part : PATCH 〈~ up old sermons〉 **2 :** INVENT, FABRICATE 〈~ up an excuse〉 ~ *vi* **1 :** to play a musical vamp **2 :** IMPROVISE, EXTEMPORIZE — **vamp·er** *n*

[3]**vamp** *n* [short for *vampire*] (ca. 1911) : a woman who uses her charm or wiles to seduce and exploit men — **vamp·ish** \ˈvam-pish\ *adj*

[4]**vamp** *vt* (ca. 1915) : to practice seductive wiles on ~ *vi* : to act like a vamp 〈~*ing* for the camera〉

vam·pire \ˈvam-ˌpī(-ə)r\ *n* [F, fr. G *Vampir*, fr. Serbian *vampir*] (1732) **1 :** the reanimated body of a dead person believed to come from the grave at night and suck the blood of persons asleep **2 a :** one who lives by preying on others **b :** a woman who exploits and ruins her lover **3 :** VAMPIRE BAT — **vam·pir·ic** \vam-ˈpir-ik\ *adj* — **vam·pir·ish** \ˈvam-ˌpī(-ə)r-ish\ *adj*

vampire bat *n* (1790) : any of several Central and So. American bats (*Desmodus rotundus*, *Diaemus youngi*, and *Diphylla ecaudata* of the subfamily Desmodontinae of the family Phyllostomidae) that feed on the blood of birds and mammals and esp. domestic animals and that are sometimes vectors of disease and esp. of rabies; *also* : any of several other bats (as of the families Megadermatidae and Phyllostomidae) that do not feed on blood but are sometimes reputed to do so

vam·pir·ism \-ˌpī(-ə)r-ˌi-zəm\ *n* (ca. 1796) **1 :** belief in vampires **2 :** the actions of a vampire

vampy \ˈvam-pē\ *adj* **vamp·i·er; -est** (1949) : of or relating to a vamp : VAMPISH; *also* : RISQUÉ 〈a ~ minidress〉

[1]**van** \ˈvan\ *n* [ME, fr. AF, fr. L *vannus* — more at WINNOW] (14c) **1** *dial Eng* : a winnowing device (as a fan) **2 :** WING 1a

[2]**van** *n* [by shortening] (1607) : VANGUARD

[3]**van** *n* [short for *caravan*] (1829) **1 a :** a usu. enclosed wagon or motortruck used for transportation of goods or animals; *also* : CARAVAN 2a **b :** a multipurpose enclosed motor vehicle having a boxlike shape, rear or side doors, and side panels often with windows **c :** a detachable passenger cabin transportable by aircraft or truck **2** *chiefly Brit* : an enclosed railroad freight or baggage car

[4]**van** *vt* **vanned; van·ning** (1840) : to transport by van

van·a·date \ˈva-nə-ˌdāt\ *n* [NL *vanadium* + E [1]*-ate*] (1835) : a salt derived from vanadium pentoxide and containing pentavalent vanadium

va·na·di·um \və-ˈnā-dē-əm\ *n* [NL, fr. ON *Vanadīs* Freya] (1833) : a silvery-grayish malleable ductile metallic element obtained from minerals and used esp. to form alloys and in catalysts — see ELEMENT table

vanadium pentoxide *n* (1869) : a yellowish-red crystalline compound V_2O_5 used esp. in glass manufacture and as a catalyst

Van Al·len belt \van-ˈa-lən-\ *n* [James A. *Van Allen*] (1958) : a belt of intense radiation in the magnetosphere composed of energetic charged particles trapped by the earth's magnetic field; *also* : a similar belt surrounding another planet

va·nas·pa·ti \və-ˈnəs-pə-tē, -ˈnäs-\ *n* [Hindi, short for *vanaspati ghī*, lit., ghee from vegetable matter] (ca. 1941) : a hydrogenated vegetable fat used as a butter substitute in India

van·co·my·cin \ˌvaŋ-kə-ˈmī-sᵊn\ *n* [*vanco-* (of unknown origin) + *-mycin*] (ca. 1956) : an antibiotic $C_{66}H_{75}Cl_2N_9O_{24}$ derived from an actinomycete (*Amycolatopsis orientalis* syn. *Streptomyces orientalis*) that is effective against gram-positive bacteria and is used chiefly in the form of its hydrochloride esp. against staphylococci resistant to methicillin

van·dal \ˈvan-dᵊl\ *n* [L *Vandalii* (pl.), of Gmc origin] (1530) **1** *cap* : a member of a Germanic people who lived in the area south of the Baltic Sea between the Vistula and the Oder rivers, overran Gaul, Spain, and northern Africa in the fourth and fifth centuries A.D., and in 455 sacked Rome **2** : one who willfully or ignorantly destroys, damages, or defaces property belonging to another or to the public — **vandal** *adj, often cap* — **Van·dal·ic** \van-ˈda-lik\ *adj*

van·dal·ise *Brit var of* VANDALIZE

van·dal·ism \ˈvan-də-ˌli-zəm\ *n* (1798) : willful or malicious destruction or defacement of public or private property

van·dal·is·tic \ˌvan-də-ˈlis-tik\ *adj* (1897) : of or relating to vandalism

van·dal·ize \ˈvan-də-ˌlīz\ *vt* **-ized; -iz·ing** (1832) : to subject to vandalism : DAMAGE — **van·dal·i·za·tion** \ˌvan-də-lə-ˈzā-shən\ *n*

van·da orchid \ˈvan-də-\ *n* [NL, fr. Skt *vandā* the orchid *Vanda tessellata*] (1943) : any of a large genus (*Vanda*) of eastern Asian epiphytic orchids often grown for their loose racemes of showy flowers — called also *vanda*

Van de Graaff generator \ˈvan-də-ˌgraf-\ *n* [Robert J. *Van de Graaff* †1967 Am. physicist] (1937) : an apparatus for the production of electrical discharges at high voltage commonly consisting of an insulated hollow conducting sphere that accumulates in its interior the charge continuously conveyed from a source of direct current by an endless belt of flexible nonconducting material

van der Waals forces \ˈvan-dər-ˌwȯlz-, ˈvän-dər-ˌvälz-\ *n pl* [Johannes D. *van der Waals* †1923 Du. physicist] (1939) : the relatively weak attractive forces that act on neutral atoms and molecules and that arise because of the electric polarization induced in each of the particles by the presence of other particles

Van·dyke \van-ˈdīk, vən-\ *n* [Sir Anthony *Vandyke*] (1754) **1 a** : a wide collar with a deeply indented edge **b** : one of several V-shaped points forming a decorative edging **c** : a border of such points **2** : a trim pointed beard — **van·dyked** \-ˈdīkt\ *adj*

Vandyke brown *n* [fr. its use by the painter Vandyke] (ca. 1850) : a natural brown-black pigment of organic matter obtained from bog earth or peat or lignite deposits; *also* : any of various synthetic brown pigments

vane \ˈvān\ *n* [ME (southern dial.), fr. OE *fana* banner; akin to OHG *fano* cloth, L *pannus* cloth, rag] (14c) **1 a** : a movable device attached to an elevated object (as a spire) for showing the direction of the wind **b** : one that is changeable or inconstant **2** : a thin flat or curved object that is rotated about an axis by a flow of fluid or that rotates to cause a fluid to flow or that redirects a flow of fluid ⟨the ~*s* of a windmill⟩ **3** : the web or flat expanded part of a feather — see FEATHER illustration **4** : a feather fastened to the shaft near the nock of an arrow — **vaned** \ˈvānd\ *adj*

van·guard \ˈvan-ˌgärd *also* ˈvaŋ-\ *n* [ME *vauntgard*, fr. AF *vantgarde, avantgarde*, fr. *avant-* fore- (fr. *avant* before, fr. LL *abante*) + *garde* guard — more at ADVANCE] (15c) **1** : the troops moving at the head of an army **2** : the forefront of an action or movement — **van·guard·ism** \-ˌgär-ˌdi-zəm\ *n* — **van·guard·ist** \-dist\ *n*

¹va·nil·la \və-ˈni-lə, -ˈne-\ *n* [NL, fr. Sp *vainilla* vanilla (plant and fruit), dim. of *vaina* sheath, fr. L *vagina* sheath, vagina] (1662) **1 a** : VANILLA BEAN **b** : a commercially important extract of the vanilla bean that is used esp. as a flavoring **2** : any of a genus (*Vanilla*) of tropical American climbing epiphytic orchids

²vanilla *adj* (1846) **1** : flavored with vanilla **2** : lacking distinction : PLAIN, ORDINARY, CONVENTIONAL

vanilla bean *n* (1874) : the long capsular fruit of a vanilla (esp. *Vanilla planifolia*) that is an important article of commerce

van·il·lin \ˈva-nə-lən\ *n* (ca. 1868) : a crystalline phenolic aldehyde $C_8H_8O_3$ that is extracted from vanilla beans or prepared synthetically and is used esp. in flavoring and in perfumery

Va·nir \ˈvä-ˌnir\ *n pl* [ON] (ca. 1875) : a race of Norse gods who warred against and later reconciled with the Aesir

van·ish \ˈva-nish\ *vb* [ME *vanisshen*, fr. AF *vaniss-*, stem of *vanir, envanir, esvanir*, fr. VL **exvanire*, alter. of L *evanescere* to dissipate like vapor, vanish, fr. *e-* + *vanescere* to vanish, fr. *vanus* empty] *vi* (14c) **1 a** : to pass quickly from sight : DISAPPEAR **b** : to pass completely from existence **2** : to assume the value zero ~ *vt* : to cause to disappear — **van·ish·er** *n*

vanishing cream \ˈva-ni-shiŋ-\ *n* (1916) : a cosmetic preparation that is used chiefly as a foundation for face powder

van·ish·ing·ly \ˈva-ni-shiŋ-lē\ *adv* (1870) : so as to be almost nonexistent or invisible ⟨the difference is ~ small⟩

vanishing point *n* (1797) **1** : a point at which receding parallel lines seem to meet when represented in linear perspective **2** : a point at which something disappears or ceases to exist

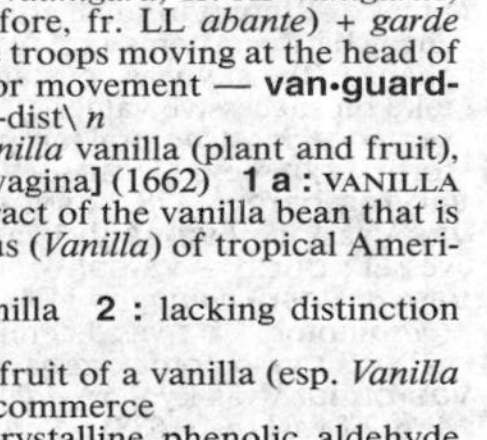

V vanishing point 1

¹van·i·ty \ˈva-nə-tē\ *n, pl* **-ties** [ME *vanite*, fr. AF *vanité*, fr. L *vanitat-, vanitas* quality of being empty or vain, fr. *vanus* empty, vain — more at WANE] (13c) **1** : something that is vain, empty, or valueless **2** : the quality or fact of being vain **3** : inflated pride in oneself or one's appearance : CONCEIT **4** : a fashionable trifle or knickknack **5 a** : ³COMPACT a **b** : a small case or handbag for toilet articles used by women **6 a** : DRESSING TABLE **b** : a bathroom cabinet containing a sink and usu. having a countertop

²vanity *adj* (ca. 1925) **1** : of, relating to, or being a work (as a book or recording) whose production cost is paid by the author or artist **2** : of, relating to, or being a showcase for a usu. famous performer or artist who is often also the project's creator or driving force ⟨write, direct, and star in a ~ film⟩

vanity fair *n, often cap V&F* [*Vanity-Fair*, a fair held in the frivolous town of Vanity in *Pilgrim's Progress* (1678) by John Bunyan] (1754) : a scene or place characterized by frivolity and ostentation

vanity plate *n* (1966) : a license plate bearing letters or numbers designated by the owner of the vehicle — called also *vanity license plate*

vanity press *n* (1950) : a publishing house that publishes books at the author's expense — called also *vanity publisher*

van·ner \ˈva-nər\ *n* (1927) : a person who owns a usu. customized van

van·pool \ˈvan-ˌpül\ *n* (1973) : an arrangement by which a group of people commute to work in a van — **van·pool·ing** *n*

van·quish \ˈvaŋ-kwish, ˈvan-\ *vt* [ME *venquishen*, fr. AF *venquis-*, preterit stem of *veintre* to conquer, fr. L *vincere* — more at VICTOR] (14c) **1** : to overcome in battle : subdue completely **2** : to defeat in a conflict or contest **3** : to gain mastery over (an emotion, passion, or temptation) ⟨~ your fear⟩ *syn* see CONQUER — **van·quish·able** \-kwi-shə-bəl\ *adj* — **van·quish·er** *n*

van·tage \ˈvan-tij\ *n* [ME, fr. AF *vantage, avantage* — more at ADVANTAGE] (14c) **1** *archaic* : BENEFIT, GAIN **2** : superiority in a contest **3** : a position giving a strategic advantage, commanding perspective, or comprehensive view **4** : ADVANTAGE 4 — **to the vantage** *obs* : in addition

vantage point *n* (1847) : a position or standpoint from which something is viewed or considered; *esp* : POINT OF VIEW

van·ward \ˈvan-wərd\ *adj* (1811) : located in the vanguard : ADVANCED — **vanward** *adv*

va·pid \ˈva-pəd, ˈvā-\ *adj* [L *vapidus* flat-tasting; akin to L *vappa* flat wine and perh. to L *vapor* steam] (ca. 1656) : lacking liveliness, tang, briskness, or force : FLAT, DULL ⟨a gossipy, ~ woman, obsessed by her own elegance —R. F. Delderfield⟩ ⟨London was not all ~ dissipation —V. S. Pritchett⟩ *syn* see INSIPID — **va·pid·ly** *adv* — **va·pid·ness** *n*

va·pid·i·ty \va-ˈpi-də-tē, vā-, və-\ *n, pl* **-ties** (ca. 1721) **1** : the quality or state of being vapid **2** : something vapid

¹va·por \ˈvā-pər\ *n* [ME *vapour*, fr. AF *vapor*, fr. L, steam, vapor] (14c) **1** : diffused matter (as smoke or fog) suspended floating in the air and impairing its transparency **2 a** : a substance in the gaseous state as distinguished from the liquid or solid state **b** : a substance (as gasoline, alcohol, mercury, or benzoin) vaporized for industrial, therapeutic, or military uses; *also* : a mixture (as the explosive mixture in an internal combustion engine) of such a vapor with air **3 a** : something unsubstantial or transitory : PHANTASM **b** : a foolish or fanciful idea **4** *pl* **a** *archaic* : exhalations of bodily organs (as the stomach) held to affect the physical or mental condition **b** : a depressed or hysterical nervous condition

²vapor *vi* **va·pored; va·por·ing** \-p(ə-)riŋ\ (15c) **1 a** : to rise or pass off in vapor **b** : to emit vapor **2** : to indulge in bragging, blustering, or idle talk — **va·por·er** \-pər-ər\ *n*

vapor barrier *n* (ca. 1941) : a layer of material (as roofing paper or polyethylene film) used to retard or prevent the absorption of moisture into a construction (as a wall or floor)

va·po·ret·to \ˌvä-pə-ˈre-(ˌ)tō\ *n, pl* **-ret·ti** \-ˈre-tē\ *also* **-ret·tos** [It, dim. of *vapore* steamboat, fr. F *vapeur*, fr. *bateau à vapeur* steamboat] (1926) : a motorboat serving as a canal bus in Venice, Italy

vaporing *n* (ca. 1630) : the act or speech of one that vapors; *specif* : an idle, extravagant, or high-flown expression or speech — usu. used in pl.

va·por·ise *Brit var of* VAPORIZE

va·por·ish \ˈvā-p(ə-)rish\ *adj* (ca. 1644) **1** : resembling or suggestive of vapor **2** : given to fits of the vapors — **va·por·ish·ness** *n*

va·por·ize \ˈvā-pə-ˌrīz\ *vb* **-ized; -iz·ing** *vt* (1803) **1** : to convert (as by the application of heat or by spraying) into vapor **2** : to cause to become dissipated **3** : to destroy by or as if by converting into vapor ⟨a tank *vaporized* by a shell⟩ ~ *vi* **1** : to become vaporized **2** : VAPOR 2 — **va·por·iz·able** \-ˌrī-zə-bəl\ *adj* — **va·por·i·za·tion** \ˌvā-pər-ə-ˈzā-shən\ *n*

va·por·iz·er \ˈvā-pə-ˌrī-zər\ *n* (ca. 1846) : one that vaporizes: as **a** : ATOMIZER **b** : a device for converting water or a medicated liquid into a vapor for inhalation

vapor lock *n* (1926) : partial or complete interruption of flow of a fluid (as fuel in an internal combustion engine) caused by the formation of bubbles of vapor in the feeding system

va·por·ous \ˈvā-p(ə-)rəs\ *adj* (1527) **1** : consisting or characteristic of vapor **2** : producing vapors : VOLATILE **3** : containing or obscured by vapors : MISTY **4 a** : ETHEREAL, UNSUBSTANTIAL **b** : consisting of or indulging in vaporings — **va·por·ous·ly** *adv* — **va·por·ous·ness** *n*

vapor pressure *n* (1865) : the pressure exerted by a vapor that is in equilibrium with its solid or liquid form — called also *vapor tension*

vapor trail *n* (1941) : CONTRAIL

va·por·ware \ˈvā-pər-ˌwer\ *n* (1984) : a computer-related product that has been widely advertised but has not and may never become available

va·pory \ˈvā-p(ə-)rē\ *adj* (1598) : VAPOROUS, MISTY

va·pour *chiefly Brit var of* VAPOR

va·que·ro \vä-ˈker-(ˌ)ō\ *n, pl* **-ros** [Sp — more at BUCKAROO] (1826) : HERDSMAN, COWBOY

var *abbr* **1** variable **2** variation **3** various

va·ra \ˈvär-ə\ *n* [AmerSp, fr. Sp, pole, fr. L, forked pole, fr. fem. of *varus* bent, bow-legged] (1831) : a Texas unit of length equal to 33.33 inches (84.66 centimeters)

vari- *or* **vario-** *comb form* [L *varius*] **1** : varied : diverse ⟨*vari*colored⟩ **2** : variation : variability ⟨*vario*meter⟩

var·ia \ˈver-ē-ə\ *n pl* [NL, fr. L, neut. pl. of *varius* various] (1926) : MISCELLANY; *esp* : a literary miscellany

¹var·i·able \ˈver-ē-ə-bəl\ *adj* [ME, fr. AF, fr. L *variabilis*, fr. *variare* to vary] (14c) **1 a** : able or apt to vary : subject to variation or changes ⟨~ winds⟩ ⟨~ costs⟩ **b** : FICKLE, INCONSTANT **2** : characterized by variations **3** : having the characteristics of a variable **4** : not true to type : ABERRANT — used of a biological group or character — **var·i-**

abil·i·ty \ˌver-ē-ə-ˈbi-lə-tē\ *n* — **var·i·able·ness** \ˈver-ē-ə-bəl-nəs\ *n* — **var·i·ably** \-blē\ *adv*

2**variable** *n* (1816) **1 a :** a quantity that may assume any one of a set of values **b :** a symbol representing a variable **2 :** something that is variable **3 :** VARIABLE STAR

variable rate mortgage *n* (1975) **:** ADJUSTABLE RATE MORTGAGE

variable star *n* (1788) **:** a star whose brightness changes usu. in more or less regular periods

var·i·ance \ˈver-ē-ən(t)s\ *n* (14c) **1 :** the fact, quality, or state of being variable or variant **:** DIFFERENCE, VARIATION ⟨yearly ~ in crops⟩ **2 :** the fact or state of being in disagreement **:** DISSENSION, DISPUTE **3 :** a disagreement between two parts of the same legal proceeding that must be consonant **4 :** a license to do some act contrary to the usual rule ⟨a zoning ~⟩ **5 :** the square of the standard deviation ***syn*** see DISCORD — **at variance :** not in harmony or agreement

1**var·i·ant** \ˈver-ē-ənt\ *adj* (14c) **1** *obs* **:** VARIABLE **2 :** manifesting variety, deviation, or disagreement **3 :** varying usu. slightly from the standard form ⟨~ readings⟩ ⟨~ spellings⟩

2**variant** *n* (ca. 1848) **:** one of two or more persons or things exhibiting usu. slight differences: as **a :** one that exhibits variation from a type or norm **b :** one of two or more different spellings (as *labor* and *labour*) or pronunciations (as of *economics* \ek-, ēk-\) of the same word **c :** one of two or more words (as *geographic* and *geographical*) or word elements (as *mon-* and *mono-*) of essentially the same meaning differing only in the presence or absence of an affix

variant Creutzfeldt–Jakob disease *n* (1996) **:** a fatal prion disease that is held to be a variant of Creutzfeldt-Jakob disease caused by the prion associated with bovine spongiform encephalopathy and contracted by consuming infected beef or beef products — abbr. *vCJD*; called also *variant CJD*

var·i·ate \ˈver-ē-ˌāt, -ət\ *n* (1909) **:** RANDOM VARIABLE

var·i·a·tion \ˌver-ē-ˈā-shən\ *n* (14c) **1 a :** the act or process of varying **:** the state or fact of being varied **b :** an instance of varying **c :** the extent to which or the range in which a thing varies **2 :** DECLINATION 6 **3 a :** a change of algebraic sign between successive terms of a sequence **b :** a measure of the change in data, a variable, or a function **4 :** the repetition of a musical theme with modifications in such elements as rhythm, melody, harmony, key, tempo, and accompaniment **5 a :** divergence in the structural or functional characteristics of an organism from the species or population norm or average **b :** something (as an individual or group) that exhibits variation **6 a :** a solo dance in classic ballet **b :** a repetition in modern ballet of a movement sequence with changes — **var·i·a·tion·al** \-shnəl, -shə-nᵊl\ *adj* — **var·i·a·tion·al·ly** *adv*

var·i·cel·la \ˌva-rə-ˈse-lə\ *n* [NL, irreg. dim. of *variola*] (1771) **:** CHICKEN POX

var·i·co·cele \ˈva-rə-kō-ˌsēl\ *n* [NL, fr. L *varic-*, *varix* + NL *-o-* + *-cele*] (1736) **:** a varicose enlargement of the veins of the spermatic cord

vari·col·ored \ˈver-i-ˌkə-lərd\ *adj* (1665) **:** having various colors **:** VARIEGATED ⟨a ~ butterfly⟩; *also* **:** of various colors

var·i·cose \ˈva-rə-ˌkōs\ *also* **var·i·cosed** \-ˌkōst\ *adj* [L *varicosus* full of dilated veins, fr. *varic-*, *varix* dilated vein] (ca. 1730) **1 :** abnormally swollen or dilated ⟨~ veins⟩ **2 :** affected with varicose veins ⟨~ legs⟩

var·i·cos·i·ty \ˌva-rə-ˈkä-sə-tē\ *n, pl* **-ties** (ca. 1842) **1 :** VARIX **2 :** the quality or state of being abnormally or markedly swollen or dilated

varied *adj* (1588) **1 :** VARIOUS, DIVERSE ⟨many and ~ comments⟩ **2 :** VARIEGATED 1 — **var·ied·ly** *adv*

var·ie·gate \ˈver-ē-ə-ˌgāt, ˈver-i-ˌgāt\ *vt* **-gat·ed; -gat·ing** [L *variegatus*, pp. of *variegare*, fr. *varius* various + *-egare* (akin to L *agere* to drive) — more at AGENT] (1653) **1 :** to diversify in external appearance esp. with different colors **:** DAPPLE **2 :** to enliven or give interest to by means of variety — **var·ie·ga·tor** \-ˌgā-tər\ *n*

variegated *adj* (1661) **1 :** having discrete markings of different colors ⟨~ leaves⟩ **2 :** VARIED 1

variegated cutworm *n* (1922) **:** a widespread noctuid moth (*Peridroma saucia*) whose larva is destructive to crops

var·ie·ga·tion \ˌver-ē-ə-ˈgā-shən, ˌver-i-ˈgā-\ *n* (1646) **:** the act of variegating **:** the state of being variegated; *esp* **:** diversity of colors

var·i·er \ˈver-ē-ər\ *n* (1860) **:** one that varies

1**va·ri·e·tal** \və-ˈrī-ə-tᵊl\ *adj* (1866) **1 :** of, relating to, or characterizing a variety ⟨~ names⟩; *also* **:** being a variety in distinction from an individual or species **2 :** of, relating to, or producing a varietal

2**varietal** *n* (1950) **:** a wine bearing the name of the principal grape from which it is made

va·ri·e·ty \və-ˈrī-ə-tē\ *n, pl* **-ties** [MF or L; MF *varieté*, fr. L *varietat-*, *varietas*, fr. *varius* various] (15c) **1 :** the quality or state of having different forms or types **:** MULTIFARIOUSNESS **2 :** a number or collection of different things esp. of a particular class **:** ASSORTMENT **3 a :** something differing from others of the same general kind **:** SORT **b :** any of various groups of plants or animals ranking below a species **:** SUBSPECIES **4 :** VARIETY SHOW

variety meat *n* (ca. 1946) **:** an edible part (as the liver or tongue) of a slaughter animal other than skeletal muscle

variety show *n* (1882) **:** a theatrical entertainment of successive separate performances (as of songs, dances, skits, and acrobatic feats)

variety store *n* (1768) **:** a retail store that carries a wide variety of merchandise esp. of low unit value

vario- — see VARI-

va·ri·o·la \və-ˈrī-ə-lə; ˌver-ē-ˈō-lə\ *n* [NL, fr. ML, pustule, pox, fr. LL, pustule, prob. fr. *varius* various] (1543) **:** SMALLPOX; *also* **:** its causative poxvirus (species *Variola virus* of the genus *Orthopoxvirus*)

var·i·om·e·ter \ˌver-ē-ˈä-mə-tər\ *n* (ca. 1889) **1 :** an instrument for measuring magnetic declination **2 :** an aeronautical instrument for indicating rate of climb

1**var·i·o·rum** \ˌver-ē-ˈȯr-əm\ *n* [L *variorum* of various persons (gen. pl. masc. of *varius*), in the phrase *cum notis variorum* with the notes of various persons] (1728) **1 :** an edition or text with notes by different persons **2 :** an edition containing variant readings of the text

2**variorum** *adj* (ca. 1763) **:** relating to or being a variorum ⟨a ~ edition⟩; *also* **:** VARIANT ⟨~ readings⟩

1**var·i·ous** \ˈver-ē-əs\ *adj* [ME, prob. fr. ML **variosus*, fr. L *varius*] (15c) **1** *archaic* **:** VARIABLE, INCONSTANT **2 :** VARICOLORED ⟨birds of ~ plumage⟩ **3 a :** of differing kinds **:** MULTIFARIOUS **b :** dissimilar in nature or form **:** UNLIKE **4 :** having a number of different aspects or characteristics ⟨a ~ place⟩ **5 :** of an indefinite number greater than one ⟨stop at ~ towns⟩ **6 :** INDIVIDUAL, SEPARATE ⟨rate increases granted in the ~ states⟩ ***syn*** see DIFFERENT — **var·i·ous·ness** *n*

2**various** *pron, pl in constr* (1877) **:** an indefinite number of separate individuals greater than one ⟨have read ~ of her essays⟩

var·i·ous·ly *adv* (1627) **1 :** in various ways **:** at various times ⟨was ~ occupied teaching, farming, and clerking⟩ **2 :** by various designations ⟨known ~ as principal, headmaster, and rector⟩

vari·sized \ˈver-i-ˌsīzd\ *adj* (1936) **:** of various sizes

va·ris·tor \va-ˈris-tər, ve-\ *n* [*vari-* + *resistor*] (1937) **:** an electrical resistor whose resistance depends on the applied voltage

var·ix \ˈva-riks\ *n, pl* **var·i·ces** \ˈva-rə-ˌsēz\ [ME, fr. L *varic-*, *varix*] (14c) **:** an abnormally dilated and lengthened vein, artery, or lymph vessel; *esp* **:** a varicose vein

var·let \ˈvär-lət\ *n* [ME *valet*, *vadlet*, *varlet* servant, boy — more at VALET] (15c) **1 a :** ATTENDANT, MENIAL **b :** a knight's page **2 :** a base unprincipled person **:** KNAVE

var·let·ry \-lə-trē\ *n* (1606) *archaic* **:** RABBLE

var·mint \ˈvär-mənt\ *n* [alter. of *vermin*] (ca. 1539) **1 :** an animal considered a pest; *specif* **:** one classed as vermin and unprotected by game law **2 :** a contemptible person **:** RASCAL; *broadly* **:** PERSON, FELLOW

1**var·nish** \ˈvär-nish\ *n* [ME *vernisch*, fr. AF *vernis*, fr. OIt or ML; OIt *vernice*, fr. ML *veronic-*, *veronix* sandarac] (14c) **1 a :** a liquid preparation that when applied to a surface dries to form a hard lustrous typically transparent coating **b :** the covering or glaze given by the application of varnish **c (1) :** something that suggests varnish by its gloss **(2) :** a coating (as of deposits in an internal combustion engine) comparable to varnish **2 :** outside show **:** 1GLOSS **3** *chiefly Brit* **:** a liquid nail polish — **var·nishy** \-ni-shē\ *adj*

2**varnish** *vt* (14c) **1 :** to apply varnish to **2 :** to cover or conceal (as something unpleasant) with something that gives an attractive appearance **:** 2GLOSS **3 :** ADORN, EMBELLISH — **var·nish·er** \ˈvär-ni-shər\ *n*

varnish tree *n* (1758) **:** any of various trees yielding a milky sap suitable for use as a varnish or lacquer; *esp* **:** an Asian tree (*Rhus verniciflua* syn. *Toxicodendron vernicifluum*) of the cashew family

var·roa mite \ˈva-rə-wə-\ *n* [NL *Varroa*, fr. Marcus Terentius *Varro*] (1983) **:** any of a genus (*Varroa*) of parasitic Asian mites that suck the hemolymph of honeybees and their larvae; *esp* **:** one (*V. destructor*) of worldwide distribution that is a serious pest of the European honeybee

var·si·ty \ˈvär-sə-tē, -stē\ *n, pl* **-ties** [by shortening & alter. fr. *university*] (1646) **1** *Brit* **:** UNIVERSITY **2 a :** the principal squad representing a university, college, school, or club esp. in a sport **b :** REGULAR 1d

Var·so·vi·an \ˌvär-ˈsō-vē-ən\ *n* [F *varsovien*, fr. *Varsovie* Warsaw] (1764) **:** a native or resident of Warsaw, Poland

Var·u·na \ˈva-rə-nə\ *n* [Skt *Varuṇa*] **:** a chief Vedic god responsible for natural and moral order in the cosmos

var·us \ˈver-əs\ *adj* [NL, fr. L, bent inward, bow-legged] (1945) **1 :** of, relating to, or being a deformity in which an anatomical part is turned inward toward the midline of the body to an abnormal degree ⟨a ~ heel⟩ **2 :** VALGUS 1 — used of the knee — **varus** *n*

varve \ˈvärv\ *n* [Sw *varv* turn, layer; akin to ON *hvarf* ring, OE *hweorfan* to turn — more at WHARF] (1912) **:** a pair of layers of alternately finer and coarser silt or clay believed to comprise an annual cycle of deposition in a body of still water — **varved** \ˈvärvd\ *adj*

vary \ˈver-ē\ *vb* **var·ied; vary·ing** [ME *varien*, fr. AF or L; AF *varier*, fr. L *variare*, fr. *varius* various] *vt* (14c) **1 :** to make a partial change in **:** make different in some attribute or characteristic **2 :** to make differences between items in **:** DIVERSIFY ~ *vi* **1 :** to exhibit or undergo change ⟨the sky was constantly ~*ing*⟩ **2 :** DEVIATE, DEPART **3 :** to take on successive values ⟨*y varies* inversely with *x*⟩ **4 :** to exhibit divergence in structural or physiological characters from the typical form ***syn*** see CHANGE — **vary·ing·ly** \-iŋ-lē\ *adv*

varying hare *n* (1781) **:** SNOWSHOE HARE

vas \ˈvas\ *n, pl* **va·sa** \ˈvā-zə\ [NL, fr. L, vessel] (1651) **:** an anatomical vessel **:** DUCT — **va·sal** \-zəl\ *adj*

vas- *or* **vaso-** *comb form* [NL, fr. L *vas*] **1 :** vessel: as **a :** blood vessel ⟨*vaso*motor⟩ **b :** vas deferens ⟨*vas*ectomy⟩ **2 :** vascular and ⟨*vaso*vagal⟩ **3 :** vasomotor ⟨*vaso*active⟩

vas·cu·lar \ˈvas-kyə-lər\ *adj* [NL *vascularis*, fr. L *vasculum* small vessel, dim. of *vas*] (ca. 1673) **1 :** of or relating to a channel for the conveyance of a body fluid (as blood of an animal or sap of a plant) or to a system of such channels; *also* **:** supplied with or made up of such channels and esp. blood vessels ⟨a ~ tumor⟩ ⟨a ~ system⟩ **2 :** marked by vigor and ardor **:** PASSIONATE — **vas·cu·lar·i·ty** \ˌvas-kyə-ˈla-rə-tē\ *n*

vascular bundle *n* (1842) **:** a strand of specialized vascular tissue of higher plants consisting mostly of xylem and phloem

vascular cylinder *n* (ca. 1889) **:** STELE

vas·cu·lar·i·za·tion \ˌvas-kyə-lə-rə-ˈzā-shən\ *n* (1818) **:** the process of becoming vascular; *also* **:** abnormal or excessive formation of blood vessels (as in the retina or on the cornea)

vascular plant *n* (1861) **:** a plant having a specialized conducting system that includes xylem and phloem **:** TRACHEOPHYTE

vascular ray *n* (ca. 1673) **:** a band of usu. parenchymatous cells extending from the cambium into both the xylem and phloem of a plant root or stem that conducts fluids radially and appears in a cross section like a spoke of a wheel

vascular tissue *n* (1842) **:** plant tissue concerned mainly with conduction; *esp* **:** the specialized tissue of higher plants consisting essentially of phloem and xylem

vas·cu·la·ture \ˈvas-kyə-lə-ˌchu̇r, -ˌtyu̇r, -ˌtu̇r\ *n* [L *vasculum* vessel + E *-ature* (as in *musculature*)] (ca. 1927) **:** the blood vessels or arrangement of blood vessels in an organ or part

vas·cu·li·tis \ˌvas-kyə-ˈlī-təs\ *n, pl* **-lit·i·des** \-ˈli-tə-ˌdēz\ [NL, fr. L *vasculum* vessel] (ca. 1900) **:** inflammation of a blood or lymph vessel

vas·cu·lum \ˈvas-kyə-ləm\ *n, pl* **-la** \-lə\ [NL, fr. L, small vessel] (1782) **:** a usu. metal and commonly cylindrical or flattened covered box used in collecting plants

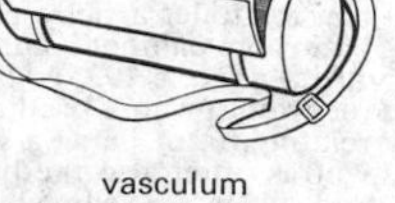

vasculum

vas def·er·ens \ˈvas-ˈde-fə-rənz, -ˌrenz\ *n, pl* **va·sa def·er·en·tia** \ˈvā-zə-ˌde-fə-ˈren(t)-sh(ē-)ə\ [NL, lit., deferent vessel] (1578) **:** a sperm-carrying duct esp. of a higher vertebrate that in the human male is a thick-walled tube about two feet (0.61

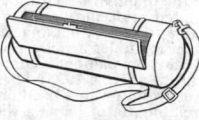

meters) long that begins at and is continuous with the tail of the epididymis and eventually joins the duct of the seminal vesicle to form the ejaculatory duct

vase \US *oftenest* ˈvās; *Canad usu & US also* ˈvāz; *Brit usu, Canad also, & US sometimes* ˈväz\ *n* [F, fr. L *vas* vessel] (1629) **:** a usu. round vessel of greater depth than width used chiefly as an ornament or for holding flowers — **vase·like** \-ˌlīk\ *adj*

va·sec·to·mize \və-ˈsek-tə-ˌmīz, vā-ˈzek-\ *vt* **-mized; -miz·ing** (1900) **:** to perform a vasectomy on

va·sec·to·my \-tə-mē\ *n, pl* **-mies** [ISV] (1899) **:** surgical division or resection of all or part of the vas deferens usu. to induce sterility

Vas·e·line \ˈva-sə-ˌlēn, ˌva-sə-ˈ\ *trademark* — used for petroleum jelly

va·so·ac·tive \ˌvā-zō-ˈak-tiv\ *adj* (ca. 1921) **:** affecting the blood vessels esp. in respect to the degree of their relaxation or contraction — **va·so·ac·tiv·i·ty** \-ak-ˈti-və-tē\ *n*

va·so·con·stric·tion \-kən-ˈstrik-shən\ *n* [ISV] (1899) **:** narrowing of the lumen of blood vessels

va·so·con·stric·tive \-ˈstrik-tiv\ *adj* (1890) **:** inducing vasoconstriction

va·so·con·stric·tor \-tər\ *n* (1877) **:** an agent (as a sympathetic nerve fiber or a drug) that induces or initiates vasoconstriction

va·so·di·la·tion \-dī-ˈlā-shən, -də-\ *or* **va·so·di·la·ta·tion** \-ˌdi-lə-ˈtā-shən, -ˌdī-lə-\ *n* [ISV] (1896) **:** widening of the lumen of blood vessels

va·so·di·la·tor \-dī-ˈlā-tər, -ˈdī-ˌlā-\ *n* (1881) **:** an agent (as a parasympathetic nerve fiber or a drug) that induces or initiates vasodilation

va·so·mo·tor \ˌvā-zə-ˈmō-tər\ *adj* [ISV] (1865) **:** of, relating to, or being nerves or centers controlling the size of blood vessels

va·so·pres·sin \ˌvā-zō-ˈpre-s^{ə}n\ *n* [fr. *Vasopressin,* a trademark] (1927) **:** a polypeptide hormone secreted by the posterior lobe of the pituitary gland or obtained synthetically that increases blood pressure and decreases urine flow — called also *antidiuretic hormone*

va·so·pres·sor \-ˈpre-sər\ *adj* (1928) **:** causing a rise in blood pressure by exerting a vasoconstrictor effect — **vasopressor** *n*

va·so·spasm \ˈvā-zō-ˌspa-zəm\ *n* [ISV] (1902) **:** sharp and often persistent contraction of a blood vessel reducing its lumen and blood flow — **va·so·spas·tic** \ˌvā-zō-ˈspas-tik\ *adj*

va·so·to·cin \ˌvā-zə-ˈtō-s^{ə}n\ *n* [*vaso-* + oxy*tocin*] (ca. 1963) **:** a polypeptide pituitary hormone of most vertebrates below mammals that has properties similar to oxytocin and vasopressin

va·so·va·gal \ˌvā-zō-ˈvā-gəl\ *adj* (1907) **:** relating to, involving, or caused by action of the vagus nerve on blood vessel dilation and heart rate ⟨∼ syncope⟩

vas·sal \ˈva-səl\ *n* [ME, fr. AF, fr. ML *vassallus,* fr. *vassus* servant, vassal, of Celt origin; akin to W *gwas* young man, servant] (14c) **1 :** a person under the protection of a feudal lord to whom he has vowed homage and fealty **:** a feudal tenant **2 :** one in a subservient or subordinate position — **vassal** *adj*

vas·sal·age \ˈva-sə-lij\ *n* (15c) **1 :** a position of subordination or submission (as to a political power) **2 :** the state of being a vassal **3 :** the homage, fealty, or services due from a vassal

[1]**vast** \ˈvast\ *adj* [L *vastus;* akin to OHG *wuosti* empty, desolate, OIr *fás*] (1585) **:** very great in size, amount, degree, intensity, or esp. in extent or range ⟨∼ knowledge⟩ ⟨a ∼ expanse⟩ ***syn*** see ENORMOUS — **vast·ly** *adv* — **vast·ness** \ˈvas(t)-nəs\ *n*

[2]**vast** *n* (1604) **:** a boundless space ⟨the ∼ of heaven —John Milton⟩

vas·ti·tude \ˈvas-tə-ˌtüd, -ˌtyüd\ *n* [L *vastitudo,* fr. *vastus*] (1623) **:** IMMENSITY, VASTNESS

vasty \ˈvas-tē\ *adj* (1596) **:** VAST ⟨call spirits from the ∼ deep —Shak.⟩

[1]**vat** \ˈvat\ *n* [ME *fat, vat,* fr. OE *fæt;* akin to OHG *vaz* vessel, Lith *puodas* pot] (12c) **1 :** a large vessel (as a cistern, tub, or barrel) esp. for holding liquors in an immature state or preparations for dyeing or tanning **2 :** a liquor containing a dye converted into a soluble reduced colorless or weakly colored form that on textile material steeped in the liquor and exposed to the air is converted by oxidation to the original insoluble dye and precipitated in the fiber

[2]**vat** *vt* **vat·ted; vat·ting** (1784) **:** to put into or treat in a vat

VAT *abbr* value-added tax

vat dye *n* (1903) **:** a water-insoluble generally fast dye used in the form of a vat liquor — called also *vat color*

vat–dyed \ˈvat-ˈdīd\ *adj* (1946) **:** dyed with one or more vat dyes

vat·ic \ˈva-tik\ *adj* [L *vates* seer, prophet; akin to OE *wōth* poetry, OHG *wuot* madness, OIr *fáith* seer, poet] (1603) **:** PROPHETIC, ORACULAR

Vat·i·can \ˈva-ti-kən\ *n* [L *Vaticanus* Vatican Hill (in Rome)] (1555) **1 :** the papal headquarters in Rome **2 :** the papal government — **Vatican** *adj*

va·tic·i·nal \və-ˈti-sə-nəl, va-\ *adj* [L *vaticinus,* fr. *vaticinari* to foretell, prophesy] (1586) **:** PROPHETIC

va·tic·i·nate \-sə-ˌnāt\ *vb* **-nat·ed; -nat·ing** [L *vaticinatus,* pp. of *vaticinari,* fr. *vates* + *-cinari* (akin to L *canere* to sing) — more at CHANT] (ca. 1623) **:** PROPHESY, PREDICT — **va·tic·i·na·tor** \-ˌnā-tər\ *n*

va·tic·i·na·tion \-ˌti-sə-ˈnā-shən\ *n* (1603) **1 :** PREDICTION **2 :** the act of prophesying

va·tu \ˈvä-ˌtü\ *n, pl* **vatu** [prob. alter. of *Vanuatu*] (1981) — see MONEY table

vaude·ville \ˈvȯd-vəl, ˈväd-, ˈvōd-, -ˌvil; ˈvȯ-də-, ˈvä-, ˈvō-\ *n* [F, fr. MF, popular satirical song, alter. of *vaudevire,* fr. *vau-de-Vire* valley of Vire, town in northwest France where such songs were composed] (1827) **1 :** a light often comic theatrical piece frequently combining pantomime, dialogue, dancing, and song **2 :** stage entertainment consisting of various acts (as performing animals, comedians, or singers) — **vaude·vil·lian** \ˌvȯd-ˈvil-yən, ˌväd-, ˌvōd-; ˌvȯ-də-, ˌvä-, ˌvō-\ *n or adj*

Vau·dois \vō-ˈdwä, ˈvō-ˌ\ *n pl* [MF, fr. ML *Valdenses*] (1560) **:** WALDENSES

[1]**vault** \ˈvȯlt\ *n* [ME *vaute, voute,* fr. AF *voute,* fr. VL **volvita* turn, vault, fr. fem. of **volvitus,* alter. of L *volutus,* pp. of *volvere* to roll — more at VOLUBLE] (14c) **1 a :** an arched structure of masonry usu. forming a ceiling or roof **b :** something (as the sky) resembling a vault **c :** an arched or dome-shaped anatomical structure ⟨the cranial ∼⟩ **2 a :** a space covered by an arched structure; *esp* **:** an underground passage or room **b :** an underground storage compartment **c :** a room or compartment for the safekeeping of valuables **3 a :** a burial chamber **b :** a prefabricated container usu. of metal or concrete into which a casket is placed at burial — **vaulty** \ˈvȯl-tē\ *adj*

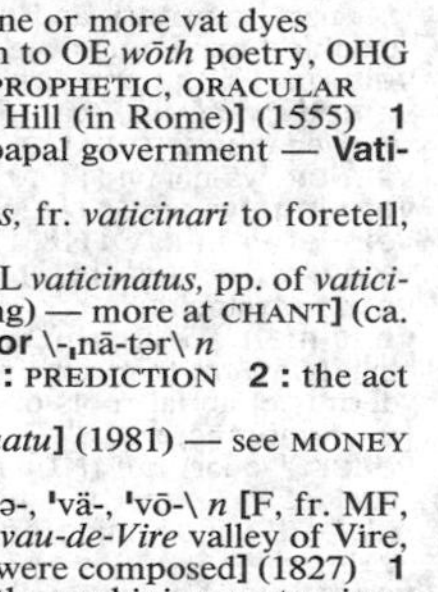

vault 1a

[2]**vault** *vt* (14c) **:** to form or cover with or as if with a vault **:** ARCH

[3]**vault** *vb* [MF *volter,* fr. OIt *voltare,* fr. VL **volvitare* to turn, leap, freq. of L *volvere*] *vi* (1538) **1 :** to leap vigorously; *esp* **:** to execute a leap using the hands or a pole **2 :** to do or achieve something as if by a leap ⟨∼*ed* to sudden prominence⟩ ∼ *vt* **:** to leap over; *esp* **:** to leap over by or as if by aid of the hands or a pole

[4]**vault** *n* (1576) **:** an act of vaulting **:** LEAP

vault·ed \ˈvȯl-təd\ *adj* (14c) **1 :** built in the form of a vault **:** ARCHED **2 :** covered with a vault

vault·er \-tər\ *n* (ca. 1552) **:** one that vaults; *esp* **:** an athlete who competes in the pole vault

[1]**vault·ing** \-tiŋ\ *n* (1512) **:** vaulted construction

[2]**vaulting** *adj* (1593) **1 :** reaching or stretching for the heights ⟨∼ ambition⟩ ⟨a ∼ imagination⟩ **2 :** designed for use in vaulting or in gymnastic exercises ⟨a ∼ block⟩ — **vault·ing·ly** \-tiŋ-lē\ *adv*

vaulting horse *n* (ca. 1875) **1 :** a gymnastics apparatus used in vaulting that consists of a padded rectangular or cylindrical form supported in a horizontal position above the floor **2 :** an event in which vaults are made over a vaulting horse

[1]**vaunt** \ˈvȯnt, ˈvänt\ *vb* [ME, fr. AF *vanter,* fr. LL *vanitare,* freq. of L **vanare,* fr. *vanus* vain] *vi* (15c) **:** to make a vain display of one's own worth or attainments **:** BRAG ∼ *vt* **:** to call attention to pridefully and often boastfully ⟨people who ∼ their ingenuity⟩ ***syn*** see BOAST — **vaunt·er** *n* — **vaunt·ing·ly** \ˈvȯn-tiŋ-lē, ˈvän-\ *adv*

[2]**vaunt** *n* (14c) **1 :** a vainglorious display of what one is or has or has done **2 :** a bragging assertive statement

vaunt–cou·ri·er \vȯnt-ˈku̇r-ē-ər, vänt-, -ˈkər-ē-, -ˈkə-rē-\ *n* [MF *avant-courrier,* lit., advance courier] (1560) *archaic* **:** FORERUNNER

vaunt·ed \ˈvȯn-təd, ˈvän-\ *adj* (1567) **:** highly or widely praised or boasted about ⟨his own much ∼ ferocity —Calvin Tomkins⟩

vaunt·ful \ˈvȯnt-fəl, ˈvänt-\ *adj* (1590) **:** VAINGLORIOUS, BOASTFUL

vaunty \ˈvȯn-tē, ˈvän-\ *adj* (1724) *Scot* **:** PROUD, BOASTFUL, VAIN

vav *var of* WAW

vav·a·sor *or* **vav·a·sour** \ˈva-və-ˌsȯr, -ˌsu̇r\ *n* [ME *vavasour,* fr. AF *vavassur,* prob. fr. ML *vassus vassorum* vassal of vassals] (14c) **:** a feudal tenant ranking directly below a baron

va·ward \ˈvau̇-ˌȯrd, -ˌwȯrd\ *n* [ME *vauntwarde, vanwarde, vaward,* fr. AF **vantwarde, vantgarde* vanguard] (14c) *archaic* **:** the foremost part **:** FOREFRONT ⟨the ∼ of our youth —Shak.⟩

VC *abbr* **1** venture capital; venture capitalist **2** Victoria Cross **3** Vietcong

V–chip \ˈvē-ˌchip\ *n* [*v*iolence] (1993) **:** a computer chip in a television set that can prevent the viewing of certain programs or channels esp. on the basis of content

vCJD *abbr* variant Creutzfeldt-Jakob disease

VCR \ˌvē-(ˌ)sē-ˈär\ *n* [*v*ideo*c*assette *r*ecorder] (1971) **:** a device that uses videocassettes for recording and playing back videotapes

VD *abbr* **1** various dates **2** venereal disease

V–day \ˈvē-ˌdā\ *n* [*v*ictory *day*] (1941) **:** a day of victory

VDT *abbr* video display terminal

VDU *abbr* visual display unit

've \v, əv\ *vb* [by contr.] (ca. 1576) **:** HAVE ⟨we*'ve* been there⟩

Ve·adar \ˈvā-ˌä-ˌdär, ˈvā-ə-\ *n* [Heb *wĕ-Adhār,* lit., and Adar (i.e., the second Adar)] (ca. 1648) **:** ADAR SHENI

[1]**veal** \ˈvēl\ *n* [ME *veel,* fr. AF, calf, veal, fr. L *vitellus* small calf, dim. of *vitulus* calf — more at WETHER] (14c) **1 :** the flesh of a young calf **2 :** CALF; *esp* **:** VEALER

[2]**veal** *vt* (ca. 1901) **:** to kill and dress (a calf) for veal

veal·er \ˈvē-lər\ *n* (ca. 1895) **:** a calf grown for or suitable for veal

vealy \ˈvē-lē\ *adj* (1769) **1 :** resembling or suggesting veal or a calf **2 :** IMMATURE

[1]**vec·tor** \ˈvek-tər\ *n* [NL, fr. L, carrier, fr. *vehere* to carry — more at WAY] (1846) **1 a :** a quantity that has magnitude and direction and that is commonly represented by a directed line segment whose length represents the magnitude and whose orientation in space represents the direction; *broadly* **:** an element of a vector space **b :** a course or compass direction esp. of an airplane **2 a :** an organism (as an insect) that transmits a pathogen **b :** POLLINATOR a **3 :** an agent (as a plasmid or virus) that contains or carries modified genetic material (as recombinant DNA) and can be used to introduce exogenous genes into the genome of an organism — **vector** *adj* — **vec·to·ri·al** \vek-ˈtȯr-ē-əl\ *adj* — **vec·to·ri·al·ly** \-ə-lē\ *adv*

[2]**vector** *vt* **vec·tored; vec·tor·ing** \-t(ə-)riŋ\ (1941) **1 :** to guide (as an airplane, its pilot, or a missile) in flight by means of a radioed vector **2 :** to change the direction of (the thrust of a jet engine) for steering

vector field *n* (ca. 1922) **:** a set of vectors that is defined in relation to a function such that each point of the function is associated with a vector from the set

vector product *n* (1878) **:** a vector *c* whose length is the product of the lengths of two vectors *a* and *b* and the sine of their included angle, whose direction is perpendicular to their plane, and whose direction is that in which a right-handed screw rotated from *a* toward *b* along axis *c* would move — called also *cross product*

vector space *n* (1937) **:** a set of vectors along with operations of addition and multiplication such that the set is a commutative group under addition, it includes a multiplicative inverse, and multiplication by scalars is both associative and distributive

vector sum *n* (ca. 1890) **:** the sum of a number of vectors that for the sum of two vectors is geometrically represented by the diagonal of a parallelogram whose sides represent the two vectors being added

Ve·da \ˈvā-də\ *n* [Skt, lit., knowledge; akin to Gk *eidenai* to know — more at WIT] (1734) **:** any of four canonical collections of hymns, prayers, and liturgical formulas that comprise the earliest Hindu sacred writings

\ə\ **a**but \$^{ə}$\ kitten, F table \ər\ **f**u**r**ther \a\ **a**sh \ā\ **a**ce \ä\ m**o**p, m**a**r \au̇\ **ou**t \ch\ **ch**in \e\ b**e**t \ē\ **ea**sy \g\ **g**o \i\ h**i**t \ī\ **i**ce \j\ **j**ob \ŋ\ si**ng** \ō\ g**o** \ȯ\ l**aw** \ȯi\ b**oy** \th\ **th**in \t͟h\ **th**e \ü\ l**oo**t \u̇\ f**oo**t \y\ **y**et \zh\ vi**si**on, beige \k͟, ^{n}, œ, ue, ^{y}\ *see* Guide to Pronunciation

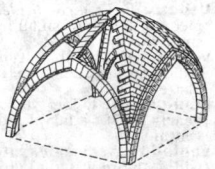

ve·da·lia \vi-ˈdāl-yə\ *n* [NL, genus name] (1889) **:** an Australian ladybug (*Rodolia cardinalis*) introduced to many countries to control scale insects — called also *vedalia beetle*
Ve·dan·ta \vā-ˈdän-tə, və-, -ˈdan-\ *n* [Skt *Vedānta,* lit., end of the Veda, fr. *Veda* + *anta* end; akin to OE *ende* end] (1788) **:** an orthodox system of Hindu philosophy developing esp. in a qualified monism the speculations of the Upanishads on ultimate reality and the liberation of the soul — **Ve·dan·tism** \-ˈdän-ˌti-zəm, -ˈdan-\ *n* — **Ve·dan·tist** \-ˈdän-tist, -ˈdan-\ *n*
Ve·dan·tic \-ˈdän-tik, -ˈdan-\ *adj* (1882) **1 :** of or relating to the Vedanta philosophy **2 :** VEDIC
Ved·da *or* **Ved·dah** \ˈve-də\ *n* [Sinhalese *vedda* hunter] (1681) **:** a member of an aboriginal people of Sri Lanka
Ved·doid \ˈve-ˌdȯid\ *n* (1928) **:** a member of a race of southern Asia traditionally classified by such physical features as wavy to curly hair, chocolate-brown skin color, and slender body build — **Veddoid** *adj*
ve·dette *or* **vi·dette** \vi-ˈdet\ *n* [F, fr. It *vedetta,* alter. of *veletta,* prob. fr. Sp *vela* watch, fr. *velar* to keep watch, fr. L *vigilare* to wake, watch, fr. *vigil* awake — more at VIGIL] (ca. 1611) **:** a mounted sentinel stationed in advance of pickets
Ve·dic \ˈvā-dik\ *adj* (1848) **:** of or relating to the Vedas, the language in which they are written, or Hindu history and culture between 1500 B.C. and 500 B.C.
vee \ˈvē\ *n* (ca. 1818) **1 :** the letter *v* **2 :** something shaped like the letter V
vee·jay \ˈvē-ˌjā\ *n* [*v*ideo *j*ockey] (ca. 1981) **:** an announcer of a program (as on television) that features music videos
veena *var of* VINA
veep \ˈvēp\ *n* [fr. *v. p.* (abbr. for *vice president*)] (1949) **:** VICE PRESIDENT
[1]**veer** \ˈvir\ *vt* [ME *veren,* of LG or D origin; akin to MD *vieren* to slacken, MLG *vīren*] (15c) **:** to let out (as a rope)
[2]**veer** *vb* [ME *veren,* fr. MF *virer,* fr. OF, to throw with a twisting motion, fr. VL **virare,* alter. of L *vibrare* to wave, propel suddenly — more at VIBRATE] *vi* (15c) **1 :** to change direction or course ⟨the economy ~*ed* sharply downward⟩ **2** *of the wind* **:** to shift in a clockwise direction — compare BACK **3** *of a ship* **:** to change course by turning the stern to the wind ~ *vt* **:** to direct to a different course; *specif* **:** WEAR 7 ***syn*** see SWERVE — **veer·ing·ly** \-iŋ-lē\ *adv*
[3]**veer** *n* (ca. 1611) **:** a change in course or direction ⟨a ~ to the right⟩
vee·ry \ˈvir-ē\ *n, pl* **veeries** [prob. imit.] (1838) **:** an American thrush (*Catharus fuscescens*) common in the eastern U.S.
veg \ˈvej\ *n, pl* **veg** (1918) *chiefly Brit* **:** VEGETABLE
Ve·ga \ˈvē-gə, ˈvā-\ *n* [NL, fr. Ar (*al-Nasr*) *al-Wāqiʿ,* lit., the falling (vulture)] (ca. 1638) **:** the brightest star in the constellation Lyra
veg·an \ˈvē-gən *also* ˈvā- *also* ˈve-jən *or* -ˌjan\ *n* [by contr. fr. *vegetarian*] (1944) **:** a strict vegetarian who consumes no animal food or dairy products; *also* **:** one who abstains from using animal products (as leather) — **vegan** *adj* — **veg·an·ism** \ˈvē-gə-ˌni-zəm, ˈvā-gə-, ˈve-jə-\ *n*
[1]**veg·e·ta·ble** \ˈvej-tə-bəl, ˈve-jə-\ *adj* [ME, fr. ML *vegetabilis* vegetative, fr. *vegetare* to grow, fr. L, to animate, fr. *vegetus* lively, fr. *vegēre* to enliven — more at WAKE] (15c) **1 a :** of, relating to, constituting, or growing like plants **b :** consisting of plants **:** VEGETATIONAL **2 :** made from, obtained from, or containing plants or plant products ⟨~ soup⟩ ⟨~ fat⟩ **3 :** resembling or suggesting a plant (as in inertness or passivity)
[2]**vegetable** *n* (15c) **1 :** PLANT 1b **2 :** a usu. herbaceous plant (as the cabbage, bean, or potato) grown for an edible part that is usu. eaten as part of a meal; *also* **:** such an edible part **3 :** a person whose mental and physical functioning is severely impaired and esp. one who requires supportive measures (as mechanical ventilation) to survive
vegetable ivory *n* (1842) **1 :** the hard white opaque endosperm of the ivory nut that takes a high polish and is used as a substitute for ivory **2 :** IVORY NUT
vegetable marrow *n* (ca. 1816) *chiefly Brit* **:** any of various smooth-skinned elongated summer squashes with creamy-white to deep green skins
vegetable oil *n* (1765) **:** an oil of plant origin; *esp* **:** a fatty oil from seeds or fruits
vegetable oyster *n* (ca. 1818) **:** SALSIFY
vegetable pear *n* (1887) **:** CHAYOTE
vegetable wax *n* (1815) **:** a wax of plant origin secreted commonly in thin flakes by the walls of epidermal cells
veg·e·ta·bly \ˈvej-tə-blē, ˈve-jə-\ *adv or adj* (1651) **:** in the manner of or like a vegetable
veg·e·tal \ˈve-jə-tᵊl\ *adj* [ML *vegetare* to grow] (15c) **1 :** VEGETABLE **2 :** VEGETATIVE **3 :** of or relating to the vegetal pole of an egg or to that part of an egg from which the endoderm normally develops ⟨~ blastomeres⟩
vegetal pole *n* (1896) **:** the point on the surface of an egg that is diametrically opposite to the animal pole and usu. marks the center of the protoplasm containing more yolk — see BLASTULA illustration
[1]**veg·e·tar·i·an** \ˌve-jə-ˈter-ē-ən\ *n* [[2]*vegetable* + *-arian*] (1839) **1 :** one who believes in or practices vegetarianism **2 :** HERBIVORE
[2]**vegetarian** *adj* (1847) **1 :** of or relating to vegetarians **2 :** consisting wholly of vegetables, fruits, grains, nuts, and sometimes eggs or dairy products ⟨a ~ diet⟩
veg·e·tar·i·an·ism \-ē-ə-ˌni-zəm\ *n* (ca. 1848) **:** the theory or practice of living on a vegetarian diet
veg·e·tate \ˈve-jə-ˌtāt\ *vb* **-tat·ed; -tat·ing** [ML *vegetatus,* pp. of *vegetare* to grow] *vi* (1605) **1 a :** to grow in the manner of a plant; *also* **:** to grow exuberantly or with proliferation of fleshy or warty outgrowths **b :** to produce vegetation **2 :** to lead a passive existence without exertion of body or mind ~ *vt* **:** to establish vegetation in or on
veg·e·ta·tion \ˌve-jə-ˈtā-shən\ *n* (1564) **1 :** the act or process of vegetating **2 :** inert existence **3 :** plant life or total plant cover (as of an area) **4 :** an abnormal growth upon a body part ⟨fibrin ~*s* on the mitral valve⟩ — **veg·e·ta·tion·al** \-shnəl, -shə-nᵊl\ *adj*
veg·e·ta·tive \ˈve-jə-ˌtā-tiv\ *adj* (14c) **1 a** (1) **:** growing or having the power of growing (2) **:** of, relating to, or engaged in nutritive and growth functions as contrasted with reproductive functions ⟨a ~ nucleus⟩ **b :** promoting plant growth ⟨the ~ properties of soil⟩ **c :** of, relating to, or involving propagation by nonsexual processes or methods **2 :** relating to, composed of, or suggesting vegetation **3 :** of or relating to the division of nature comprising the plant kingdom **4 a :** AUTONOMIC 1 **b :** characterized by, resulting from, or being a state in which there is total loss of cognitive functioning and in which only involuntary bodily functions (as breathing or blinking of the eyes) are sustained **5 :** VEGETABLE 3 — **veg·e·ta·tive·ly** *adv* — **veg·e·ta·tive·ness** *n*
ve·gete \və-ˈjēt\ *adj* [L *vegetus* — more at VEGETABLE] (1639) *archaic* **:** LIVELY, HEALTHY
veg·gie *also* **veg·ie** \ˈve-jē\ *n* [by shortening & alter.] (1955) **1 :** VEGETABLE **2** *slang* **:** VEGETARIAN
veggie burger *n* (1972) **:** a patty chiefly of vegetable-derived protein used as a meat substitute; *also* **:** a sandwich containing such a patty
veg out \ˈvej-\ *vi* **vegged out; veg·ging out** [short for *vegetate*] (1980) **:** to spend time idly or passively
ve·he·mence \ˈvē-ə-mən(t)s\ *n* (15c) **:** the quality or state of being vehement **:** INTENSITY
ve·he·ment \ˈvē-ə-mənt\ *adj* [ME, fr. MF, fr. L *vehement-, vehemens, vement-, vemens*] (15c) **:** marked by forceful energy **:** POWERFUL ⟨a ~ wind⟩: as **a :** intensely emotional **:** IMPASSIONED, FERVID ⟨~ patriotism⟩ **b** (1) **:** deeply felt ⟨a ~ suspicion⟩ (2) **:** forcibly expressed ⟨~ denunciations⟩ **c :** bitterly antagonistic ⟨a ~ debate⟩ — **ve·he·ment·ly** *adv*
ve·hi·cle \ˈvē-ə-kəl *also* ˈvē-ˌhi-kəl\ *n* [F *véhicule,* fr. L *vehiculum* carriage, conveyance, fr. *vehere* to carry — more at WAY] (1612) **1 a :** an inert medium (as a syrup) in which a medicinally active agent is administered **b :** any of various media acting usu. as solvents, carriers, or binders for active ingredients or pigments **2 :** an agent of transmission **:** CARRIER **3 :** a medium through which something is expressed, achieved, or displayed ⟨an investment ~⟩; *esp* **:** a work created esp. to display the talents of a particular performer **4 :** a means of carrying or transporting something ⟨planes, trains, and other ~*s*⟩: as **a :** MOTOR VEHICLE **b :** a piece of mechanized equipment
ve·hic·u·lar \vē-ˈhi-kyə-lər\ *adj* (1616) **1 a :** of, relating to, or designed for vehicles and esp. motor vehicles **b :** transported by vehicle **c :** caused by or resulting from the operation of a vehicle ⟨~ homicide⟩ **2 :** serving as a vehicle
V–8 \ˈvē-ˈāt\ *n* (1930) **:** an internal combustion engine having two banks of four cylinders each with the banks at an angle to each other; *also* **:** an automobile having such an engine
[1]**veil** \ˈvāl\ *n* [ME, fr. AF *veil, veille,* fr. L *vela,* pl. of *velum* sail, awning, curtain] (13c) **1 a :** a length of cloth worn by women as a covering for the head and shoulders and often esp. in Eastern countries for the face; *specif* **:** the outer covering of a nun's headdress **b :** a length of veiling or netting worn over the head or face or attached for protection or ornament to a hat or headdress ⟨a bridal ~⟩ **c :** any of various liturgical cloths; *esp* **:** a cloth used to cover the chalice **2 :** the life of a nun — often used in the phrase *take the veil* **3 :** a concealing curtain or cover of cloth **4 :** something that resembles a veil ⟨a ~ of stars⟩; *esp* **:** something that hides or obscures like a veil ⟨lift the ~ of secrecy⟩ **5 :** a covering body part or membrane: as **a :** VELUM **b :** CAUL
[2]**veil** *vt* (14c) **:** to cover, provide, obscure, or conceal with or as if with a veil ~ *vi* **:** to put on or wear a veil
veiled \ˈvāld\ *adj* (14c) **1 a :** having or wearing a veil or a concealing cover ⟨a ~ hat⟩ **b :** characterized by a softening tonal distortion **2 :** obscured as if by a veil **:** DISGUISED ⟨~ threats⟩
veil·ing \ˈvā-liŋ\ *n* (13c) **1 :** any of various light sheer fabrics **2 :** VEIL
[1]**vein** \ˈvān\ *n* [ME *veine,* fr. AF, fr. L *vena*] (14c) **1 a :** a narrow water channel in rock or earth or in ice **b** (1) **:** LODE 2 (2) **:** a bed of useful mineral matter **c :** LODE 3 **2 :** BLOOD VESSEL; *esp* **:** any of the tubular branching vessels that carry blood from the capillaries toward the heart **3 a :** any of the vascular bundles forming the framework of a leaf **b :** any of the thickened cuticular ribs that serve to stiffen the wings of an insect **4 :** something suggesting veins (as in reticulation); *specif* **:** a wavy variegation (as in marble) **5 a :** a distinctive mode of expression **:** STYLE ⟨stories in a romantic ~⟩ **b :** a distinctive element or quality **:** STRAIN ⟨introduced a welcome ~ of humor⟩ **c :** a line of thought or action **6 a :** a special aptitude ⟨inherited an artistic ~⟩ **b :** a usu. transitory and casually attained mood **c :** top form ⟨thou troublest me; I am not in the ~ —Shak.⟩ — **vein·al** \ˈvā-nᵊl\ *adj*
[2]**vein** *vt* (1502) **:** to pattern with or as if with veins
veined \ˈvānd\ *adj* (ca. 1529) **:** patterned with or as if with veins **:** having venation **:** STREAKED ⟨a ~ leaf⟩ ⟨~ marble⟩ ⟨~ cheese⟩
vein·er \ˈvā-nər\ *n* (1895) **:** a small V gouge used in wood carving
vein·ing \ˈvā-niŋ\ *n* (1826) **:** a pattern of veins **:** VENATION
vein·let \ˈvān-lət\ *n* (1831) **:** a small vein
veiny \ˈvā-nē\ *adj* (1611) **:** full of veins **:** noticeably veined ⟨~ hands⟩
vel *abbr* velocity
ve·la·men \və-ˈlā-mən\ *n, pl* **ve·lam·i·na** \-ˈla-mə-nə\ [NL, fr. L, covering, fr. *velare* to cover, fr. *velum* curtain] (1882) **:** the thick corky epidermis of aerial roots of an epiphytic orchid that absorbs water from the atmosphere
ve·lar \ˈvē-lər\ *adj* [NL *velaris,* fr. *velum*] (1876) **1 :** formed with the back of the tongue touching or near the soft palate ⟨the ~ \k\ of \ˈkül\ *cool*⟩ **2 :** of, forming, or relating to a velum and esp. the soft palate — **velar** *n*
ve·lar·i·um \vi-ˈler-ē-əm\ *n, pl* **-ia** \-ē-ə\ [L, fr. *velum* curtain] (1834) **:** an awning over an ancient Roman theater or amphitheater
ve·lar·i·za·tion \ˌvē-lə-rə-ˈzā-shən\ *n* (1915) **1 :** the quality or state of being velarized **2 :** an act or instance of velarizing
ve·lar·ize \ˈvē-lə-ˌrīz\ *vt* **-ized; -iz·ing** (1915) **:** to modify (as the \l\ of \ˈpül\ *pool*) by a simultaneous velar articulation
Vel·cro \ˈvel-(ˌ)krō\ *trademark* — used for a closure consisting of a piece of fabric of small hooks that sticks to a corresponding fabric of small loops
veld *or* **veldt** \ˈvelt, ˈfelt\ *n* [Afrik *veld,* fr. D, field; akin to OE *feld* field] (1835) **:** a grassland esp. of southern Africa usu. with scattered shrubs or trees
ve·li·ger \ˈvē-lə-jər, ˈve-\ *n* [NL, fr. *velum* + *-ger* bearing, fr. *gerere* to bear] (1877) **:** a larval mollusk in the stage when it has developed the velum
vel·le·i·ty \ve-ˈlē-ə-tē, və-\ *n, pl* **-ties** [NL *velleitas,* fr. L *velle* to wish, will — more at WILL] (1618) **1 :** the lowest degree of volition **2 :** a slight wish or tendency **:** INCLINATION

[1]**vel·lum** \ˈve-ləm\ *n* [ME *velym,* fr. AF *velim, veeslin,* fr. **veelin,* adj., of a calf, fr. *veel* calf — more at VEAL] (14c) **1 :** a fine-grained unsplit lambskin, kidskin, or calfskin prepared esp. for writing on or for binding books **2 :** a strong cream-colored paper

[2]**vellum** *adj* (15c) **1 :** of, resembling, or bound in vellum **2 :** slightly rough ⟨paper with a ~ finish⟩

ve·lo·ce \vā-ˈlō-(ˌ)chā\ *adv or adj* [It, fr. L *veloc-, velox*] (ca. 1823) : in a rapid manner — used as a direction in music

ve·lo·cim·e·ter \ˌvē-lō-ˈsi-mə-tər, ˌve-\ *n* [*velocity* + *-meter*] (1842) : a device for measuring speed (as of fluid flow or sound)

ve·loc·i·pede \və-ˈlä-sə-ˌpēd\ *n* [F *vélocipède,* fr. L *veloc-, velox* + *ped-, pes* foot — more at FOOT] (1818) : a lightweight wheeled vehicle propelled by the rider: as **a** *archaic* **:** BICYCLE **b :** TRICYCLE **c :** a 3-wheeled railroad handcar

ve·loc·i·rap·tor \və-ˈlä-sə-ˌrap-tər\ *n* [NL, fr. L *veloc-, velox* + *raptor* plunderer, predator — more at RAPTOR] (1990) : any of a genus (*Velociraptor*) of theropod dinosaurs of the Late Cretaceous having a long head with a flat snout and a large sickle-shaped claw on the second toe of each foot

ve·loc·i·ty \və-ˈlä-sə-tē, -ˈläs-tē\ *n, pl* **-ties** [MF *velocité,* fr. L *velocitat-, velocitas,* fr. *veloc-, velox* quick; prob. akin to L *vegēre* to enliven — more at WAKE] (15c) **1 a :** quickness of motion **:** SPEED ⟨the ~ of sound⟩ **b :** rapidity of movement ⟨[my horse's] strong suit is grace & personal comeliness, rather than ~ —Mark Twain⟩ **c :** speed imparted to something ⟨the power pitcher relies on ~ —Tony Scherman⟩ **2 :** the rate of change of position along a straight line with respect to time **:** the derivative of position with respect to time **3 a :** rate of occurrence or action **:** RAPIDITY ⟨the ~ of historical change —R. J. Lifton⟩ **b :** rate of turnover ⟨the ~ of money⟩

ve·lo·drome \ˈvē-lə-ˌdrōm, ˈve-, ˈvā-\ *n* [F *vélodrome,* fr. *vélo* cycle (short for *vélocipède*) + *-drome*] (1895) : a track designed for cycling

ve·lour *or* **ve·lours** \və-ˈlu̇r\ *n, pl* **velours** \-ˈlu̇rz\ *often attrib* [F *velours* velvet, velour, fr. MF *velours, velour,* fr. OF *velous,* fr. Old Occitan *velos,* fr. L *villosus* shaggy, fr. *villus* shaggy hair — more at VELVET] (1794) **1 :** any of various fabrics with a pile or napped surface resembling velvet used in heavy weights for upholstery and curtains and in lighter weights for clothing; *also* **:** the article of clothing itself **2 :** a fur felt (as of rabbit or nutria) finished with a long velvety nap and used esp. for hats

ve·lou·té \və-ˌlü-ˈtā\ *n* [F, lit., velvetiness, fr. MF *velluté,* fr. Old Occitan *velut* velvety, fr. VL **villutus*] (1830) : a soup or sauce made of chicken, veal, or fish stock and cream and thickened with butter and flour

ve·lum \ˈvē-ləm\ *n, pl* **ve·la** \-lə\ [NL, fr. L, curtain] (1753) **1 :** a membrane or membranous part resembling a veil or curtain: as **a :** SOFT PALATE **b :** an annular membrane projecting inward from the margin of the umbrella in some jellyfishes (as the hydromedusae) **2 :** a swimming organ that is esp. well developed in the later larval stages of many marine gastropods

ve·lure \ve-ˈlu̇r, vel-ˈyu̇r, ˈvel-yər\ *n* [modif. of MF *velour*] (1587) *obs* **:** VELVET; *also* **:** a fabric resembling velvet

[1]**vel·vet** \ˈvel-vət\ *n* [ME *veluet, velvet,* fr. AF, fr. *velu* shaggy, soft, velvety, fr. VL **villutus,* fr. L *villus* shaggy hair; akin to L *vellus* fleece — more at WOOL] (14c) **1 :** a clothing and upholstery fabric (as of silk, rayon, or wool) characterized by a short soft dense warp pile **2 a :** something suggesting velvet **b :** a characteristic (as softness or smoothness) of velvet **3 :** the soft vascular skin that envelops and nourishes the developing antlers of deer **4 a :** the winnings of a player in a gambling game **b :** a profit or gain beyond ordinary expectation — **vel·vet·like** \-ˌlīk\ *adj*

[2]**velvet** *adj* (14c) **1 :** made of or covered with velvet; *also* **:** clad in velvet **2 :** resembling or suggesting velvet **:** VELVETY ⟨a ~ voice⟩

velvet ant *n* (1748) : any of various solitary usu. brightly colored and hairy fossorial wasps (family Mutillidae) with the female wingless

velvet bean *n* (1898) : an annual legume (*Mucuna deeringiana* syn. *Stizolobium deeringianum*) grown esp. in the southern U.S. for green manure and grazing; *also* **:** its seed often used as stock feed

vel·ve·teen \ˌvel-və-ˈtēn\ *n* (1776) **1 :** a clothing fabric usu. of cotton in twill or plain weaves made with a short close weft pile in imitation of velvet **2** *pl* **:** clothes made of velveteen

vel·vety \ˈvel-və-tē\ *adj* (1752) **1 :** having the character of velvet as in being soft, smooth, thick, or richly hued ⟨~ hair⟩ ⟨a ~ green pasture⟩ **2 :** smooth to the taste **:** MILD ⟨a ~ wine⟩

Ven *abbr* venerable

ven- *or* **veni-** *or* **veno-** *comb form* [L *vena*] **:** vein ⟨*veni*puncture⟩ ⟨*veno*graphy⟩

ve·na \ˈvē-nə\ *n, pl* **ve·nae** \-(ˌ)nē\ [ME, fr. L] (14c) : VEIN

ve·na ca·va \ˌvē-nə-ˈkā-və\ *n, pl* **ve·nae ca·vae** \-(ˌ)nē-ˈkā-(ˌ)vē\ [NL, lit., hollow vein] (1598) : any of the large veins by which in air-breathing vertebrates the blood is returned to the right atrium of the heart — **vena ca·val** \-vəl\ *adj*

ve·nal \ˈvē-nᵊl\ *adj* [L *venalis,* fr. *venum* (acc.) sale; akin to Gk *ōneisthai* to buy, Skt *vasna* price] (1652) **1 :** capable of being bought or obtained for money or other valuable consideration **:** PURCHASABLE; *esp* **:** open to corrupt influence and esp. bribery **:** MERCENARY ⟨a ~ legislator⟩ **2 :** originating in, characterized by, or associated with corrupt bribery ⟨a ~ arrangement with the police⟩ — **ve·nal·i·ty** \vi-ˈna-lə-tē\ *n* — **ve·nal·ly** \ˈvē-nᵊl-ē\ *adv*

ve·na·tion \ve-ˈnā-shən, vē-\ *n* [L *vena* vein] (1646) : an arrangement or system of veins (as in the tissue of a leaf or the wing of an insect)

venation: *1* parallel-veined, *2* net-veined, *3* dichotomously veined

vend \ˈvend\ *vb* [L *vendere* to sell, v.t., contr. for *venum dare* to give for sale] *vt* (1651) **1 a :** to sell esp. as a hawker or peddler **b :** to sell by means of vending machines **2 :** to utter publicly ~ *vi* **:** to dispose of something by sale **:** SELL; *also* **:** to engage in selling

Ven·da \ˈven-də\ *n* (1908) **:** a Bantu language spoken by a people of Northern province, Republic of South Africa; *also* **:** a member of this people

vend·ee \ven-ˈdē\ *n* (1547) : one to whom a thing is sold **:** BUYER

ven·det·ta \ven-ˈde-tə\ *n* [It, lit., revenge, fr. L *vindicta* — more at VINDICTIVE] (1855) **1 :** BLOOD FEUD **2 :** an often prolonged series of retaliatory, vengeful, or hostile acts or exchange of such acts ⟨waged a personal ~ against those who opposed his nomination⟩

ven·deuse \väⁿ-ˈdə(r)z, vän-ˈdüz\ *n* [F, fem. of *vendeur* salesman, fr. MF] (1913) : a saleswoman esp. in the fashion industry

vend·ible *also* **vend·able** \ˈven-də-bəl\ *adj* (14c) : capable of being vended **:** SALABLE — **vend·ibil·i·ty** \ˌven-də-ˈbi-lə-tē\ *n*

vending machine *n* (ca. 1895) : a coin-operated machine for selling merchandise

ven·dor \ˈven-dər, *for 1 also* ven-ˈdȯr\ *also* **vend·er** \-dər\ *n* [AF *vendur,* fr. *vendre* to sell, fr. L *vendere*] (1594) **1 :** one that vends **:** SELLER **2 :** VENDING MACHINE

ven·due \ˈven-ˌdü, ˈvän-, ˈfen-, -ˌdyü; ven-ˈ, vän-ˈ\ *n* [obs. F, fr. MF, fr. *vendre*] (1668) : a public sale at auction

[1]**ve·neer** \və-ˈnir\ *n* [G *Furnier,* fr. *furnieren* to veneer, fr. F *fournir* to furnish, equip — more at FURNISH] (1702) **1 :** a thin sheet of a material: as **a :** a layer of wood of superior value or excellent grain to be glued to an inferior wood **b :** any of the thin layers bonded together to form plywood **c :** a plastic or porcelain coating bonded to the surface of a cosmetically imperfect tooth **2 :** a protective or ornamental facing (as of brick or stone) **3 :** a superficial or deceptively attractive appearance, display, or effect **:** FACADE, GLOSS ⟨a ~ of tolerance⟩

[2]**veneer** *vt* (1742) **1 :** to overlay or plate (as a common wood) with a thin layer of finer wood for outer finish or decoration; *broadly* **:** to face with a material giving a superior surface **2 :** to cover over with a veneer; *esp* **:** to conceal (as a defect of character) under a superficial and deceptive attractiveness — **ve·neer·er** *n*

ve·neer·ing \və-ˈnir-iŋ\ *n* (ca. 1706) **1 :** a veneered surface **2 :** material used as veneer

ven·er·a·ble \ˈve-nər(-ə)-bəl, ˈven-rə-bəl\ *adj* (15c) **1 :** deserving to be venerated — used as a title for an Anglican archdeacon or for a Roman Catholic who has been accorded the lowest of three degrees of recognition for sanctity **2 :** made sacred esp. by religious or historical association **3 a :** calling forth respect through age, character, and attainments ⟨a ~ jazz musician⟩; *broadly* **:** conveying an impression of aged goodness and benevolence ⟨encouraged by the ~ doctor's head-nodding⟩ **b :** impressive by reason of age ⟨under ~ pines⟩ ***syn*** see OLD — **ven·er·a·bil·i·ty** \ˌve-nə-rə-ˈbi-lə-tē, ˌven-rə-\ *n* — **ven·er·a·ble·ness** \ˈve-nər(-ə)-bəl-nəs, ˈven-rə-\ *n* — **ven·er·a·bly** \-blē\ *adv*

ven·er·ate \ˈve-nə-ˌrāt\ *vt* **-at·ed; -at·ing** [L *veneratus,* pp. of *venerari,* fr. *vener-, venus* love, charm — more at WIN] (ca. 1623) **1 :** to regard with reverential respect or with admiring deference **2 :** to honor (as an icon or a relic) with a ritual act of devotion ***syn*** see REVERE — **ven·er·a·tor** \-ˌrā-tər\ *n*

ven·er·a·tion \ˌve-nə-ˈrā-shən\ *n* (15c) **1 :** respect or awe inspired by the dignity, wisdom, dedication, or talent of a person **2 :** the act of venerating **3 :** the condition of one that is venerated

ve·ne·re·al \və-ˈnir-ē-əl\ *adj* [ME *venereall*e, fr. L *venereus,* fr. *vener-, venus* love, sexual desire] (15c) **1 :** of or relating to sexual pleasure or indulgence **2 a :** resulting from or contracted during sexual intercourse ⟨~ infections⟩ **b :** of, relating to, or affected with venereal disease ⟨a high ~ rate⟩ **c :** involving the genital organs ⟨~ sarcoma⟩ — **ve·ne·re·al·ly** *adv*

venereal disease *n* (1658) : a contagious disease (as gonorrhea or syphilis) that is typically acquired in sexual intercourse — compare STD

[1]**ven·ery** \ˈve-nə-rē\ *n* [ME *venerie,* fr. AF, fr. OF *vener* to hunt, fr. L *venari* — more at VENISON] (14c) **1 :** the art, act, or practice of hunting **2 :** animals that are hunted **:** GAME

[2]**venery** *n* [ME *venerie,* fr. ML *veneria,* fr. L *vener-, venus* sexual desire] (15c) **1 :** the pursuit of or indulgence in sexual pleasure **2 :** SEXUAL INTERCOURSE

ve·ne·sec·tion \ˈve-nə-ˌsek-shən, ˈvē-\ *n* [NL *venae section-, venae sectio,* lit., cutting of a vein] (1661) : PHLEBOTOMY

Ven·e·ti \ˈve-nə-ˌtī\ *n pl* [L *Veneti*] (1781) **1 :** an ancient people in Gaul conquered by Julius Caesar in 56 B.C. **2 :** an ancient people in northeastern Italy allied politically to the Romans

ve·ne·tian blind \və-ˈnē-shən-\ *n* [*Venetian* of Venice, Italy] (1770) : a blind (as for a window) having numerous horizontal slats that may be set simultaneously at any of several angles so as to vary the amount of light admitted

venetian glass *n, often cap V* (ca. 1845) : often colored glassware made at Murano near Venice of a soda-lime metal and typically elaborately decorated (as with gilt, enamel, or engraving)

Venetian red *n* (1753) : an earthy hematite used as a pigment; *also* **:** a synthetic iron oxide pigment

Ve·net·ic \və-ˈne-tik\ *n* [L *veneticus* of the Veneti, fr. *Veneti*] (1902) : the language of the ancient Veneti of Italy — see INDO-EUROPEAN LANGUAGES table — **Venetic** *adj*

venge \ˈvenj\ *vt* **venged; veng·ing** [ME, fr. AF *venger*] (14c) *archaic* **:** AVENGE

ven·geance \ˈven-jən(t)s\ *n* [ME, fr. AF, fr. *venger* to avenge, fr. L *vindicare* to lay claim to, avenge — more at VINDICATE] (14c) : punishment inflicted in retaliation for an injury or offense **:** RETRIBUTION — **with a vengeance 1 :** with great force or vehemence ⟨undertook reform *with a vengeance*⟩ **2 :** to an extreme or excessive degree ⟨the tourists are back—*with a vengeance*⟩

venge·ful \ˈvenj-fəl\ *adj* [obs. E *venge* revenge] (ca. 1586) : REVENGEFUL: as **a :** seeking to avenge **b :** serving to gain vengeance — **venge·ful·ly** \-fə-lē\ *adv* — **venge·ful·ness** *n*

V–en·gine \ˈvē-\ *n* (ca. 1922) : an internal combustion engine whose cylinders are arranged in two banks forming an acute or right angle

veni- *or* **veno-** — see VEN-

ve·nial \ˈvē-nē-əl, -nyəl\ *adj* [ME, fr. MF *veniel,* fr. LL *venialis,* fr. L *venia* favor, indulgence, pardon; akin to L *venus* love, charm — more at WIN] (14c) : of a kind that can be remitted **:** FORGIVABLE, PARDON-

ABLE; *also* : meriting no particular censure or notice : EXCUSABLE ⟨~ faults⟩ — **ve·nial·ly** *adv* — **ve·nial·ness** *n*
venial sin *n* (14c) **1** : a sin that is relatively slight or that is committed without full reflection or consent and so according to Thomist theology does not deprive the soul of sanctifying grace — compare MORTAL SIN **2** : a minor offense
ve·ni·punc·ture \ˈvē-nə-ˌpəŋ(k)-chər, ˈve-\ *n* (ca. 1903) : surgical puncture of a vein esp. for the withdrawal of blood or for intravenous medication
ve·ni·re \və-ˈnī-rē\ *n* [*venire facias*] (1807) : an entire panel from which a jury is drawn
ve·ni·re fa·ci·as \-ˌnī-rē-ˈfā-shē-əs\ *n* [ME, fr. ML, you should cause to come] (15c) : a judicial writ directing the sheriff to summon a specified number of qualified persons to serve as jurors
ve·ni·re·man \və-ˈnī-rē-mən, -ˈnir-ē-\ *n* (1776) : a member of a venire
ven·i·son \ˈve-nə-sən *also* -zən, *Brit usu* ˈven-zən\ *n, pl* **venisons** *also* **venison** [ME, fr. AF *veneisun* game, venison, fr. L *venation-, venatio* hunting, fr. *venari* to hunt, pursue; akin to Skt *vanoti* he strives for — more at WIN] (14c) : the edible flesh of a game animal and esp. a deer
Ve·ni·te \və-ˈnī-tē, -ˈnē-ˌtā\ *n* [ME, fr. L, O come, fr. *venire* to come; fr. the opening word of Ps 95:1 — more at COME] (13c) : a liturgical chant composed of parts of Psalms 95 and 96
Venn diagram \ˈven-\ *n* [John *Venn* †1923 Eng. logician] (1918) : a graph that employs closed curves and esp. circles to represent logical relations between and operations on sets and the terms of propositions by the inclusion, exclusion, or intersection of the curves

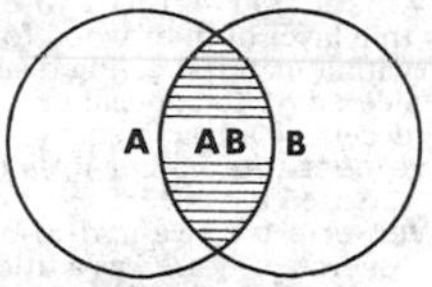

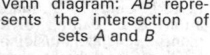

Venn diagram: *AB* represents the intersection of sets *A* and *B*

ve·nog·ra·phy \vi-ˈnä-grə-fē, vā-\ *n* [ISV] (1935) : radiography of a vein after injection of an opaque substance
1**ven·om** \ˈve-nəm\ *n* [ME *venim*, fr. AF, fr. VL **venimen*, alter. of L *venenum* magic charm, drug, poison; akin to L *venus* love, charm — more at WIN] (13c) **1** : poisonous matter normally secreted by some animals (as snakes, scorpions, or bees) and transmitted to prey or an enemy chiefly by biting or stinging; *broadly* : material that is poisonous **2** : ILL WILL, MALEVOLENCE
2**venom** *vt* (14c) : ENVENOM
ven·om·ous \ˈve-nə-məs\ *adj* (14c) **1** : full of venom: as **a** : POISONOUS, ENVENOMED **b** : NOXIOUS, PERNICIOUS ⟨expose a ~ dope ring —Don Porter⟩ **c** : SPITEFUL, MALEVOLENT ⟨~ criticism⟩ **2** : having a venom-producing gland and able to inflict a poisoned wound ⟨~ snakes⟩ — **ven·om·ous·ly** *adv* — **ven·om·ous·ness** *n*
ve·nous \ˈvē-nəs\ *adj* [L *venosus*, fr. *vena* vein] (1626) **1** : of, relating to, or full of veins ⟨a ~ thrombosis⟩ ⟨a ~ rock⟩ **2** *of blood* : having passed through the capillaries and given up oxygen for the tissues and become charged with carbon dioxide — **ve·nous·ly** *adv*
1**vent** \ˈvent\ *vb* [ME, in part fr. 2*vent*, in part short for *aventen* to release (air), fr. AF *aventer*, alter. of OF *esventer* to air, fr. *es-* ex- (fr. L *ex-*) + *vent* wind, fr. L *ventus* — more at WIND] *vt* (14c) **1** : to provide with a vent **2 a** : to serve as a vent for ⟨chimneys ~ smoke⟩ **b** : DISCHARGE, EXPEL **c** : to give often vigorous or emotional expression to ⟨~*ed* her frustration on her coworkers⟩ **3** : to relieve by means of a vent ⟨~*ed* himself in a fiery letter to the editor⟩ ~ *vi* : to relieve oneself by venting something (as anger) ⟨comes home from work and ~*s* to the kids⟩ ***syn*** see EXPRESS
2**vent** *n* [ME, anus, outlet, prob. fr. AF, wind, draft, outlet] (15c) **1** : an opening for the escape of a gas or liquid or for the relief of pressure: as **a** : the external opening of the rectum or cloaca : ANUS **b** (1) : PIPE 3c, FUMAROLE (2) : HYDROTHERMAL VENT **c** : an opening at the breech of a muzzle-loading gun through which fire is touched to the powder **d** *chiefly Scot* : CHIMNEY, FLUE **2** : an opportunity or means of escape, passage, or release : OUTLET ⟨finally gave ~ to his pent-up hostility⟩ — **vent·less** \-ləs\ *adj*
3**vent** *n* [ME *vente*, alter. of *fente*, fr. MF, slit, fissure, fr. *fendre* to split, fr. L *findere* — more at BITE] (15c) : a slit in a garment; *specif* : an opening in the lower part of a seam (as of a jacket or skirt) — **vent·less** *adj*
vent·age \ˈven-tij\ *n* (1602) : a small hole (as a flute stop)
ven·tail \ˈven-ˌtāl\ *n* [ME, fr. AF *ventaille*, fr. *venter* to blow, exhale, fr. *vent* wind] (14c) : the lower movable front of a medieval helmet
ven·ter \ˈven-tər\ *n* [AF *ventre* belly, womb, mother, fr. L, belly, womb; perh. akin to OHG *wanast* paunch, L *vesica* bladder, Skt *vasti*] (1544) **1** : a wife or mother that is a source of offspring **2** [NL, fr. L] : a protuberant and often hollow anatomical structure: as **a** : the undersurface of the abdomen of an arthropod **b** : the swollen basal portion of an archegonium in which an egg develops
ven·ti·fact \ˈven-tə-ˌfakt\ *n* [L *ven*tus + E arti*fact*] (1911) : a stone worn, polished, or faceted by windblown sand
ven·ti·late \ˈven-tə-ˌlāt\ *vt* **-lat·ed; -lat·ing** [ME, discussed, aired, fr. LL *ventilatus*, pp. of *ventilare*, fr. L, to fan, winnow, fr. *ventus* wind — more at WIND] (15c) **1 a** : to examine, discuss, or investigate freely and openly : EXPOSE ⟨*ventilating* family quarrels in public⟩ **b** : to make public : UTTER ⟨*ventilated* their objections at length⟩ **2** *archaic* : to free from chaff by winnowing **3 a** : to expose to air and esp. to a current of fresh air for purifying, curing, or refreshing ⟨~ stored grain⟩; *also* : OXYGENATE, AERATE ⟨~ blood in the lungs⟩ **b** : to subject the lungs to ventilation ⟨artificially ~ a patient in respiratory distress⟩ **4 a** *of a current of air* : to pass or circulate through so as to freshen **b** : to cause fresh air to circulate through (as a room or mine) **5** : to provide an opening in (a burning structure) to permit escape of smoke and heat
ven·ti·la·tion \ˌven-tə-ˈlā-shən\ *n* (1519) **1** : the act or process of ventilating **2 a** : circulation of air ⟨a room with good ~⟩ **b** : the circulation and exchange of gases in the lungs or gills that is basic to respiration **3** : a system or means of providing fresh air
ven·ti·la·tor \ˈven-tə-ˌlā-tər\ *n* (1743) : one that ventilates: as **a** : a contrivance for introducing fresh air or expelling foul or stagnant air **b** : RESPIRATOR 2
ven·ti·la·to·ry \ˈven-tə-lə-ˌtȯr-ē\ *adj* (1850) : of, relating to, or provided with ventilation ⟨~ capacity of the lung⟩
ventr- *or* **ventro-** *comb form* [L *ventr-, venter* belly] : ventral and ⟨*ventro*lateral⟩
1**ven·tral** \ˈven-trəl\ *adj* [F, fr. L *ventralis*, fr. *ventr-, venter*] (1739) **1 a** : of or relating to the belly : ABDOMINAL **b** : being or located near or on the anterior or lower surface of an animal opposite the back **2** : being or located on the lower surface of a dorsiventral plant structure — **ven·tral·ly** \-trə-lē\ *adv*
2**ventral** *n* (1834) : a ventral part (as a scale or fin)
ventral root *n* (ca. 1923) : the one of the two roots of a spinal nerve that passes ventrally from the spinal cord and consists of motor fibers — compare DORSAL ROOT
ven·tri·cle \ˈven-tri-kəl\ *n* [ME, fr. L *ventriculus*, fr. dim. of *ventr-, venter* belly] (14c) : a cavity of a bodily part or organ: as **a** : a chamber of the heart which receives blood from a corresponding atrium and from which blood is forced into the arteries — see HEART illustration **b** : any of a system of communicating cavities in the brain that are continuous with the central canal of the spinal cord — see BRAIN illustration
ven·tri·cose \-ˌkōs\ *adj* [NL *ventricosus*, fr. L *ventr-, venter* + *-icosus* (as in *varicosus* varicose)] (1756) : markedly swollen, distended, or inflated esp. on one side ⟨~ corollas⟩
ven·tric·u·lar \ven-ˈtri-kyə-lər, vən-\ *adj* (1838) : of, relating to, or being a ventricle ⟨~ fibrillation⟩ ⟨~ pressure⟩ ⟨~ myocardium⟩
ventricular assist device *n* (1970) : a device implanted in the chest or upper abdomen to assist a damaged or weakened heart in pumping blood
ven·tric·u·lus \ven-ˈtri-kyə-ləs, vən-\ *n, pl* **-li** \-ˌlī, -ˌlē\ [NL, fr. L, dim. of *venter*] (1693) : a digestive cavity (as a gizzard or stomach)
ven·tril·o·quism \ven-ˈtri-lə-ˌkwi-zəm\ *n* [LL *ventriloquus* ventriloquist, fr. L *ventr-, venter* + *loqui* to speak; fr. the belief that the voice is produced from the ventriloquist's stomach] (ca. 1797) **1** : the production of the voice in such a way that the sound seems to come from a source other than the vocal organs of the speaker **2** : the expression of one's views and attitudes through another; *esp* : such expression by a writer through a fictional character or literary persona — **ven·tri·lo·qui·al** \ˌven-trə-ˈlō-kwē-əl\ *adj* — **ven·tri·lo·qui·al·ly** \-ə-lē\ *adv*
ven·tril·o·quist \ven-ˈtri-lə-kwist\ *n* (ca. 1656) : one who uses or is skilled in ventriloquism; *esp* : one who provides entertainment by using ventriloquism to carry on an apparent conversation with a hand-manipulated dummy — **ven·tril·o·quis·tic** \(ˌ)ven-ˌtri-lə-ˈkwis-tik\ *adj*
ven·tril·o·quize \ven-ˈtri-lə-ˌkwīz\ *vb* **-quized; -quiz·ing** *vi* (1844) : to use ventriloquism ~ *vt* : to utter in the manner of a ventriloquist
ven·tril·o·quy \-kwē\ *n* (1584) : VENTRILOQUISM 1
ven·tro·lat·er·al \ˌven-ˌtrō-ˈla-tə-rəl, -ˈla-trəl\ *adj* (ca. 1836) : ventral and lateral
ven·tro·me·di·al \-ˈmē-dē-əl\ *adj* (1908) : ventral and medial
1**ven·ture** \ˈven(t)-shər\ *vb* **ven·tured; ven·tur·ing** \ˈven(t)-sh(ə-)riŋ\ [ME *venteren*, by shortening & alter. fr. *aventuren*, fr. *aventure* adventure] *vt* (15c) **1** : to expose to hazard : RISK, GAMBLE ⟨*ventured* a buck or two on the race⟩ **2** : to undertake the risks and dangers of : BRAVE ⟨*ventured* the stormy sea⟩ **3** : to offer at the risk of rebuff, rejection, or censure ⟨~ an opinion⟩ ~ *vi* : to proceed esp. in the face of danger — **ven·tur·er** \ˈven(t)-sh(ə-)rər\ *n*
2**venture** *n* (15c) **1** *obs* : DESTINY, FORTUNE, CHANCE **2 a** : an undertaking involving chance, risk, or danger; *esp* : a speculative business enterprise **b** : a venturesome act **3** : something (as money or property) at stake in a speculative venture — **at a venture** : at random ⟨a certain man drew a bow *at a venture*, and smote the king —1 Kings 22:34 (AV)⟩
venture capital *n* (1943) : capital (as retained corporate earnings or individual savings) invested or available for investment in the ownership element of new or fresh enterprise — called also *risk capital* — **venture capitalism** *n* — **venture capitalist** *n*
ven·ture·some \ˈven(t)-shər-səm\ *adj* (1661) **1** : involving risk : HAZARDOUS ⟨a ~ journey⟩ **2** : inclined to court or incur risk or danger : DARING ⟨a ~ investor⟩ ***syn*** see ADVENTUROUS — **ven·ture·some·ly** *adv* — **ven·ture·some·ness** *n*
ven·tu·ri \ven-ˈtu̇r-ē\ *n* [G. B. *Venturi* †1822 Ital. physicist] (1887) : a short tube with a tapering constriction in the middle that causes an increase in the velocity of flow of a fluid and a corresponding decrease in fluid pressure and that is used esp. in measuring fluid flow or for creating a suction (as for driving aircraft instruments or drawing fuel into the flow stream of a carburetor)
ven·tur·ous \ˈven(t)-sh(ə-)rəs\ *adj* (1565) : VENTURESOME — **ven·tur·ous·ly** *adv* — **ven·tur·ous·ness** *n*
ven·ue \ˈven-ˌyü\ *n* [AF, alter. (influenced by *venue* arrival, attendance) of *vinné, visné*, lit., neighborhood, neighbors, fr. VL **vicinatus*, alter. of L *vicinitas* vicinity] (1531) **1 a** : the place from which a jury is drawn and in which trial is held ⟨requested a change of ~⟩ **b** : the place or county in which take place the alleged events from which a legal action arises **c** : a statement showing that a case is brought to the proper court or authority **2 a** : LOCALE 1; *also* : a place where events of a specific type are held ⟨music ~*s*⟩ **b** : OUTLET 1c
ve·nule \ˈvēn-(ˌ)yül, ˈven-\ *n* [L *venula*, dim. of *vena* vein] (ca. 1850) : a small vein; *esp* : any of the minute veins connecting the capillaries with the larger systemic veins
Ve·nus \ˈvē-nəs\ *n* [ME, fr. L *Vener-, Venus*] (bef. 12c) **1** : the Roman goddess of love and beauty — compare APHRODITE **2** : the planet second in order from the sun — see PLANET table
Ve·nus·berg \-ˌbərg\ *n* : a mountain in central Germany containing a cavern where in medieval legend Venus held court
Venus fly·trap \-ˈflī-ˌtrap\ *n* (1930) : an insectivorous plant (*Dionaea muscipula*) of the sundew family of the Carolina coast with the leaf apex modified into an insect trap — called also *Venus's-flytrap*
Ve·nus–hair \-ˌher\ *n* (1548) : a delicate maidenhair fern (*Adiantum capillus-veneris*) that grows chiefly on wet calcareous rocks
Ve·nu·sian \vi-ˈnü-zhən, -ˈnyü-\ *adj* (1874) : of or relating to the planet Venus
Ve·nus's flow·er–bas·ket \ˈvē-nə-səz-, ˈvē-nəs-\ *n* (1872) : any of several glass sponges (genus *Euplectella*) of the western Pacific and Indian oceans — called also *Venus flower basket*
ve·ra·cious \və-ˈrā-shəs\ *adj* [L *verac-, verax* — more at VERY] (ca. 1677) **1** : TRUTHFUL, HONEST **2** : marked by truth : ACCURATE — **ve·ra·cious·ly** *adv* — **ve·ra·cious·ness** *n*

ve·rac·i·ty \və-ˈra-sə-tē\ *n, pl* **-ties** (ca. 1623) **1 :** devotion to the truth : TRUTHFULNESS **2 :** power of conveying or perceiving truth **3 :** conformity with truth or fact : ACCURACY **4 :** something true ⟨makes lies sound like *veracities*⟩

ve·ran·da *or* **ve·ran·dah** \və-ˈran-də\ *n* [Hindi & Urdu *varaṇḍā*] (1711) **:** a usu. roofed open gallery or portico attached to the exterior of a building

ve·ran·daed *also* **ve·ran·dahed** \-dəd\ *adj* (ca. 1818) **:** having a veranda

ve·rap·a·mil \və-ˈra-pə-ˌmil\ *n* [ISV *val*eric (acid) + *-apam-* (prob. alter. of *amino* + *propyl*) + nitr*ile*] (1967) **:** a calcium channel blocker $C_{27}H_{38}N_2O_4$ used esp. in the form of its hydrochloride

ve·rat·ri·dine \və-ˈra-trə-ˌdēn\ *n* [*veratr*ine + *-idine*] (1907) **:** a poisonous alkaloid $C_{36}H_{51}NO_{11}$ occurring esp. in sabadilla seed

ve·ra·trine \ˈver-ə-ˌtrēn, və-ˈra-trən\ *n* [NL *veratrina,* fr. *Veratrum,* genus of herbs] (1822) **:** a poisonous irritant mixture of alkaloids from sabadilla seed that has been used as a counterirritant and insecticide

ve·ra·trum \və-ˈrā-trəm\ *n* [NL, genus name, fr. L, hellebore] (1577) **:** HELLEBORE 2

verb \ˈvərb\ *n* [ME *verbe,* fr. AF, fr. L *verbum* word, verb — more at WORD] (14c) **:** a word that characteristically is the grammatical center of a predicate and expresses an act, occurrence, or mode of being, that in various languages is inflected for agreement with the subject, for tense, for voice, for mood, or for aspect, and that typically has rather full descriptive meaning and characterizing quality but is sometimes nearly devoid of these esp. when used as an auxiliary or linking verb — **verb·less** \ˈvər-bləs\ *adj*

[1]**ver·bal** \ˈvər-bəl\ *adj* [ME *verbale,* fr. LL *verbalis,* fr. L *verbum* word] (15c) **1 a :** of, relating to, or consisting of words ⟨~ instructions⟩ **b :** of, relating to, or involving words rather than meaning or substance ⟨a consistency that is merely ~ and scholastic —B. N. Cardozo⟩ **c :** consisting of or using words only and not involving action ⟨~ abuse⟩ **2 :** of, relating to, or formed from a verb ⟨a ~ adjective⟩ **3 :** spoken rather than written ⟨a ~ contract⟩ **4 :** VERBATIM, WORD-FOR-WORD ⟨a ~ translation⟩ **5 :** of or relating to facility in the use and comprehension of words ⟨~ aptitude⟩ — **ver·bal·ly** \-bə-lē\ *adv*

[2]**verbal** *n* (1530) **:** a word that combines characteristics of a verb with those of a noun or adjective — compare GERUND, INFINITIVE, PARTICIPLE

verbal auxiliary *n* (ca. 1958) **:** an auxiliary verb

ver·bal·ism \ˈvər-bə-ˌli-zəm\ *n* (1787) **1 a :** a verbal expression : TERM **b :** PHRASING, WORDING **2 :** words used as if they were more important than the realities they represent ⟨the emancipation of science from ~ —G. A. L. Sarton⟩ **3 a :** a wordy expression of little meaning **b :** VERBOSITY

ver·bal·ist \-list\ *n* (ca. 1609) **1 :** one who stresses words above substance or reality **2 :** a person who uses words skillfully — **ver·bal·is·tic** \ˌvər-bə-ˈlis-tik\ *adj*

ver·bal·ize \ˈvər-bə-ˌlīz\ *vb* **-ized; -iz·ing** *vi* (1609) **1 :** to speak or write verbosely **2 :** to express something in words ~ *vt* **1 :** to convert into a verb **2 :** to name or express in words — **ver·bal·i·za·tion** \ˌvər-bə-lə-ˈzā-shən\ *n* — **ver·bal·iz·er** \ˈvər-bə-ˌlī-zər\ *n*

verbal noun *n* (1652) **:** a noun derived directly from a verb or verb stem and in some uses having the sense and constructions of a verb

[1]**ver·ba·tim** \(ˌ)vər-ˈbā-təm\ *adv* [ME, fr. ML, fr. L *verbum* word] (15c) **:** in the exact words : word for word ⟨quoted the speech ~⟩

[2]**verbatim** *adj* (1613) **:** being in or following the exact words : WORD-FOR-WORD ⟨a ~ report of the meeting⟩

ver·be·na \(ˌ)vər-ˈbē-nə\ *n* [NL, genus of herbs or subshrubs, fr. L, leafy branch used ceremonially or medicinally — more at VERVAIN] (1562) **:** VERVAIN; *esp* **:** any of numerous garden vervains of hybrid origin widely grown for their showy spikes of white, pink, red, or blue flowers which are borne in profusion over a long season — compare LEMON VERBENA

ver·biage \ˈvər-bē-ij *also* -bij\ *n* [F, fr. MF *verbier* to chatter, alter. of OF *verboier, verbloier,* fr. OF (Picard dial.) *werbler* to trill — more at WARBLE] (ca. 1721) **1 :** a profusion of words usu. of little or obscure content ⟨such a tangled maze of evasive ~ as a typical party platform —Marcia Davenport⟩ **2 :** manner of expressing oneself in words : DICTION ⟨sportswriters guarded their ~ so jealously —R. A. Sokolov⟩

ver·bi·cide \ˈvər-bə-ˌsīd\ *n* [L *verbum* word + E *-cide*] (1858) **1 :** deliberate distortion of the sense of a word (as in punning) **2 :** one who distorts the sense of a word

ver·bid \ˈvər-bəd\ *n* (1914) **:** VERBAL

ver·big·er·a·tion \(ˌ)vər-ˌbi-jə-ˈrā-shən\ *n* [ISV, fr. L *verbigerare* to talk, chat, fr. *verbum* word + *gerere* to carry, wield — more at WORD] (1886) **:** continual repetition of stereotyped phrases (as in some forms of mental illness)

ver·bose \(ˌ)vər-ˈbōs\ *adj* [L *verbosus,* fr. *verbum*] (1672) **1 :** containing more words than necessary : WORDY ⟨a ~ reply⟩; *also* **:** impaired by wordiness ⟨a ~ style⟩ **2 :** given to wordiness ⟨a ~ orator⟩ ***syn*** see WORDY — **ver·bose·ly** *adv* — **ver·bose·ness** *n* — **ver·bos·i·ty** \-ˈbä-sə-tē\ *n*

ver·bo·ten \vər-ˈbō-tᵊn, fər-, ver-\ *adj* [G, fr. OHG *farboten,* pp. of *farbioten* to forbid (akin to OE *forbēodan* to forbid), fr. *far-, fur-* for- + *biotan* to offer — more at BID] (1916) **:** FORBIDDEN; *esp* **:** prohibited by dictate

verb sap \ˈvərb-ˈsap\ (1841) **:** VERBUM SAP

ver·bum sap \ˌvər-bəm-ˈsap\ [short for NL *verbum sapienti* (*sat est*) a word to the wise (is sufficient)] (1818) **:** enough said — used to indicate that something left unsaid may or should be inferred

ver·dant \ˈvər-dᵊnt\ *adj* [modif. of MF *verdoyant,* fr. prp. of *verdoyer* to be green, fr. OF *verdoier,* fr. *verd, vert* green, fr. L *viridis,* fr. *virēre* to be green] (1581) **1 a :** green in tint or color **b :** green with growing plants ⟨~ fields⟩ **2 :** unripe in experience or judgment : GREEN 9a, b — **ver·dan·cy** \-dᵊn(t)-sē\ *n* — **ver·dant·ly** \-dᵊnt-lē\ *adv*

verd an·tique *or* **verde an·tique** \ˌvərd-ˌan-ˈtēk\ *n* [It *verde antico,* lit., ancient green] (1745) **:** a green mottled or veined serpentine marble or calcareous serpentine much used for indoor decoration esp. by the ancient Romans

ver·der·er *also* **ver·der·or** \ˈvər-dər-ər\ *n* [AF *verder, verderer,* fr. *verd* green] (ca. 1538) **:** a onetime English judicial officer in charge of the king's forest

ver·dict \ˈvər-(ˌ)dikt\ *n* [ME *verdit, verdict,* fr. AF *veirdit,* fr. *veir* true (fr. L *verus*) + *dit* saying, dictum, fr. L *dictum* — more at VERY] (15c) **1 :** the finding or decision of a jury on the matter submitted to it in trial **2 :** OPINION, JUDGMENT

ver·di·gris \ˈvər-də-ˌgrēs, -ˌgris, -grəs *also* -ˌgrē\ *n* [ME *vertegrese,* fr. AF *verdegrece, vert de Grece,* lit., green of Greece] (14c) **1 a :** a green or greenish-blue poisonous pigment resulting from the action of acetic acid on copper and consisting of one or more basic copper acetates **b :** normal copper acetate $Cu(C_2H_3O_2)_2{\cdot}H_2O$ **2 :** a green or bluish deposit esp. of copper carbonates formed on copper, brass, or bronze surfaces

ver·din \ˈvər-dᵊn\ *n* [F, a green songbird of Indochina, alter. of *verdon, verdun* bunting, yellowhammer, fr. *vert* green, fr. OF *verd, vert*] (1881) **:** a very small yellow-headed bird (*Auriparus flaviceps*) of arid scrubland that is related to the chickadee and is found from Texas to California and southward to Mexico

ver·dure \ˈvər-jər *also* -dyər\ *n* [ME, fr. AF, fr. *verd* green] (14c) **1 :** the greenness of growing vegetation; *also* **:** such vegetation itself **2 :** a condition of health and vigor — **ver·dur·ous** \ˈverj-rəs; ˈver-jə-rəs, -dyə-\ *adj*

ver·dured \ˈvər-jərd *also* -dyərd\ *adj* (ca. 1718) **:** covered with verdure

[1]**verge** \ˈvərj\ *n* [ME, rod, measuring rod, margin, fr. AF, rod, area of jurisdiction, fr. L *virga* twig, rod, line] (15c) **1 a** (1) **:** a rod or staff carried as an emblem of authority or symbol of office (2) *obs* **:** a stick or wand held by a person being admitted to tenancy while he swears fealty **b :** the spindle of a watch balance; *esp* **:** a spindle with pallets in an old vertical escapement **c :** the male copulatory organ of any of various invertebrates **2 a :** something that borders, limits, or bounds: as (1) **:** an outer margin of an object or structural part (2) **:** the edge of roof covering (as tiling) projecting over the gable of a roof (3) *Brit* **:** a paved or planted strip of land at the edge of a road : SHOULDER **b :** BRINK, THRESHOLD ⟨a country on the ~ of destruction —Archibald MacLeish⟩

[2]**verge** *vi* **verged; verg·ing** (1787) **1 :** to be contiguous **2 :** to be on the verge or border ⟨the line where sentiment ~*s* on mawkishness —Thomas Hardy⟩

[3]**verge** *vi* **verged; verg·ing** [L *vergere* to bend, incline — more at WRENCH] (1610) **1 a** *of the sun* **:** to move or tend toward the horizon : SINK **b :** to move or extend in some direction or toward some condition ⟨*verging* to a hasty decline —Edward Gibbon⟩ **2 :** to be in transition or change

verg·er \ˈvər-jər\ *n* (15c) **1** *chiefly Brit* **:** an attendant that carries a verge (as before a bishop or justice) **2 :** a church official who keeps order during services or serves as an usher or a sacristan

ve·rid·i·cal \və-ˈri-di-kəl\ *adj* [L *veridicus,* fr. *verus* true + *dicere* to say — more at VERY, DICTION] (1653) **1 :** TRUTHFUL, VERACIOUS ⟨tried . . . to supply . . . a ~ background to the events and people portrayed —Laura Krey⟩ **2 :** not illusory : GENUINE ⟨it is assumed that . . . perception is ~ —George Lakoff⟩ — **ve·rid·i·cal·i·ty** \-ˌri-də-ˈka-lə-tē\ *n* — **ve·rid·i·cal·ly** \-ˈri-di-k(ə-)lē\ *adv*

ver·i·fi·able \ˌver-ə-ˈfī-ə-bəl\ *adj* (1593) **:** capable of being verified — **ver·i·fi·abil·i·ty** \ˌver-ə-ˌfī-ə-ˈbi-lə-tē\ *n* — **ver·i·fi·able·ness** *n*

ver·i·fi·ca·tion \ˌver-ə-fə-ˈkā-shən\ *n* (1523) **:** the act or process of verifying : the state of being verified

ver·i·fy \ˈver-ə-ˌfī\ *vt* **-fied; -fy·ing** [ME *verifien,* fr. AF *verifier,* fr. ML *verificare,* fr. L *verus* true] (14c) **1 :** to confirm or substantiate in law by oath **2 :** to establish the truth, accuracy, or reality of ⟨~ the claim⟩ ***syn*** see CONFIRM — **ver·i·fi·er** \-ˌfī(-ə)r\ *n*

ver·i·ly \ˈver-ə-lē\ *adv* [ME *verraily,* fr. *verray* very] (14c) **1 :** in truth : CERTAINLY **2 :** TRULY, CONFIDENTLY

veri·sim·i·lar \ˌver-ə-ˈsi-mə-lər, -ˈsim-lər\ *adj* [L *verisimilis*] (1681) **1 :** having the appearance of truth : PROBABLE **2 :** depicting realism (as in art or literature) — **veri·sim·i·lar·ly** *adv*

veri·si·mil·i·tude \-sə-ˈmi-lə-ˌtüd, -ˌtyüd\ *n* [L *verisimilitudo,* fr. *verisimilis* verisimilar, fr. *veri similis* like the truth] (ca. 1576) **1 :** the quality or state of being verisimilar **2 :** something verisimilar — **veri·si·mil·i·tu·di·nous** \-ˌmi-lə-ˈtüd-nəs, -ˈtyüd-; -ˈtü-də-nəs, -ˈtyü-\ *adj*

ve·rism \ˈvir-ˌi-zəm, ˈver-\ *n* [It *verismo,* fr. *vero* true, fr. L *verus*] (1892) **:** artistic use of contemporary everyday material in preference to the heroic or legendary esp. in grand opera — **ve·rist** \-ist\ *n or adj* — **ve·ris·tic** \vir-ˈis-tik, ver-\ *adj*

ve·ris·mo \vā-ˈrēz-(ˌ)mō\ *n* [It] (ca. 1908) **:** VERISM; *also* **:** REALISM 3

ver·i·ta·ble \ˈver-ə-tə-bəl\ *adj* [ME, fr. AF, fr. *verité*] (15c) **:** being in fact the thing named and not false, unreal, or imaginary — often used to stress the aptness of a metaphor ⟨a ~ mountain of references⟩ — **ver·i·ta·ble·ness** *n* — **ver·i·ta·bly** \-blē\ *adv*

vé·ri·té \ˌver-ə-ˈtā\ *n* [*cinema verité*] (1966) **:** the art or technique of filming (as a motion picture) so as to convey candid realism

ver·i·ty \ˈver-ə-tē\ *n, pl* **-ties** [ME *verite,* fr. AF *verité,* fr. L *veritat-, veritas,* fr. *verus* true] (14c) **1 :** the quality or state of being true or real **2 :** something (as a statement) that is true; *esp* **:** a fundamental and inevitably true value ⟨such eternal *verities* as honor, love, and patriotism⟩ **3 :** the quality or state of being truthful or honest ⟨the king-becoming graces, as justice, ~ —Shak.⟩

ver·juice \ˈvər-ˌjüs\ *n* [ME *vergeouse,* fr. AF *vertjous,* fr. *vert* green + *jous, jus* juice] (14c) **1 :** the sour juice of crab apples or of unripe fruit (as grapes or apples); *also* **:** an acid liquor made from verjuice **2 :** acidity of disposition or manner

ver·meil *n* [MF, fr. *vermeil,* adj. — more at VERMILION] (1530) **1** \ˈvər-məl, -ˌmāl\ **:** VERMILION **2** \ver-ˈmā\ **:** gilded silver — **vermeil** *adj*

vermi- *comb form* [NL, fr. LL, fr. L *vermis* — more at WORM] **:** worm ⟨*vermi*form⟩

ver·mi·cel·li \ˌvər-mə-ˈche-lē, -ˈse-\ *n* [It, fr. pl. of *vermicello,* dim. of *verme* worm, fr. L *vermis*] (1669) **:** pasta made in long solid strings smaller in diameter than spaghetti

ver·mi·cide \ˈvər-mə-ˌsīd\ *n* (1849) **:** an agent that destroys worms

ver·mic·u·lar \(ˌ)vər-ˈmi-kyə-lər\ *adj* [NL *vermicularis,* fr. L *vermiculus,* dim. of *vermis*] (1672) **1 a :** resembling a worm in form or motion **b :** VERMICULATE **2 :** of, relating to, or caused by worms
ver·mic·u·late \-lət\ *or* **ver·mic·u·lat·ed** \-ˌlā-təd\ *adj* [L *vermiculatus,* fr. *vermiculus*] (1605) **1 :** TORTUOUS, INVOLUTE **2 :** full of worms : WORM-EATEN **3 a :** VERMIFORM **b :** marked with irregular fine lines or with wavy impressed lines ⟨a ~ nut⟩ — **ver·mic·u·la·tion** \-ˌmi-kyə-ˈlā-shən\ *n*
ver·mic·u·lite \(ˌ)vər-ˈmi-kyə-ˌlīt\ *n* [L *vermiculus* little worm] (1824) : any of various micaceous minerals that are hydrous silicates resulting usu. from expansion of the granules of mica at high temperatures to give a lightweight highly water-absorbent material
ver·mi·cul·ture \ˈvər-mə-ˌkəl-chər\ *n* (1976) : the cultivation of annelid worms (as earthworms or bloodworms) esp. for use as bait or in composting
ver·mi·form \ˈvər-mə-ˌfȯrm\ *adj* [NL *vermiformis,* fr. *vermi-* + *-formis* -form] (ca. 1730) : resembling a worm in shape
vermiform appendix *n* (1778) : a narrow blind tube usu. about three to four inches (8 to 10 centimeters) long that extends from the cecum in the lower right-hand part of the abdomen
ver·mi·fuge \ˈvər-mə-ˌfyüj\ *n* (1718) : an agent that destroys or expels parasitic worms : ANTHELMINTIC
ver·mil·ion *also* **ver·mil·lion** \vər-ˈmil-yən\ *n* [ME *vermilioun,* fr. AF *vermeilloun,* fr. *vermeil,* adj., bright red, vermilion, fr. LL *vermiculus* kermes, fr. L, little worm] (13c) **1 :** a bright red pigment consisting of mercuric sulfide; *broadly* : any of various red pigments **2 :** a vivid reddish orange
ver·min \ˈvər-mən\ *n, pl* **vermin** [ME, fr. AF *vermin, vermine,* fr. *verm* worm, fr. L *vermis*] (14c) **1 a :** small common harmful or objectionable animals (as lice or fleas) that are difficult to control **b :** birds and mammals that prey on game **c :** animals that at a particular time and place compete (as for food) with humans or domestic animals **2 :** an offensive person
ver·min·ous \ˈvər-mə-nəs\ *adj* [L *verminosus* infested with maggots, fr. L **vermin-, vermen* worm; akin to L *vermis* worm — more at WORM] (ca. 1616) **1 :** consisting of or being vermin : NOXIOUS **2 :** forming a breeding place for or infested by vermin : FILTHY ⟨~ garbage⟩ **3 :** caused by vermin ⟨~ disease⟩
ver·mis \ˈvər-mis\ *n* [NL, fr. L, worm] (1876) : the constricted median lobe of the cerebellum that connects the two lateral lobes
ver·mouth \vər-ˈmüth\ *n* [F *vermout,* fr. G *Wermut* wormwood, fr. OHG *wermuota* — more at WORMWOOD] (1806) : a dry or sweet aperitif wine flavored with aromatic herbs and often used in mixed drinks
¹**ver·nac·u·lar** \və(r)-ˈna-kyə-lər\ *adj* [L *vernaculus* native, fr. *verna* slave born in the master's house, native] (1601) **1 a :** using a language or dialect native to a region or country rather than a literary, cultured, or foreign language **b :** of, relating to, or being a nonstandard language or dialect of a place, region, or country **c :** of, relating to, or being the normal spoken form of a language **2 :** applied to a plant or animal in the common native speech as distinguished from the Latin nomenclature of scientific classification ⟨the ~ name⟩ **3 :** of, relating to, or characteristic of a period, place, or group; *esp* : of, relating to, or being the common building style of a period or place ⟨~ architecture⟩ — **ver·nac·u·lar·ly** *adv*
²**vernacular** *n* (1661) **1 :** a vernacular language, expression, or mode of expression **2 :** the mode of expression of a group or class **3 :** a vernacular name of a plant or animal
ver·nac·u·lar·ism \və(r)-ˈna-kyə-lə-ˌri-zəm\ *n* (ca. 1841) : a vernacular word or idiom
ver·nal \ˈvər-nᵊl\ *adj* [L *vernalis,* alter. of *vernus,* fr. *ver* spring; akin to Gk *ear* spring, Skt *vasanta*] (1530) **1 :** of, relating to, or occurring in the spring ⟨~ equinox⟩ ⟨~ sunshine⟩ **2 :** fresh or new like the spring; *also* : YOUTHFUL — **ver·nal·ly** \-nᵊl-ē\ *adv*
ver·nal·i·za·tion \ˌvər-nə-lə-ˈzā-shən\ *n* (1933) : the act or process of hastening the flowering and fruiting of plants by treating seeds, bulbs, or seedlings so as to induce a shortening of the vegetative period — **ver·nal·ize** \ˈvər-nə-ˌlīz\ *vt*
ver·na·tion \(ˌ)vər-ˈnā-shən\ *n* [NL *vernation-, vernatio,* fr. L *vernare* to behave as in spring, fr. *vernus* vernal] (1793) : the arrangement of foliage leaves within the bud
Ver·ner's law \ˈver-nərz-\ *n* [Karl A. *Verner*] (1878) : a statement in historical linguistics: in medial or final position in voiced environments and when the immediately preceding vowel did not bear the principal accent in Proto-Indo-European, the Proto-Germanic voiceless fricatives *f,* þ, and *χ* derived from the Proto-Indo-European voiceless stops *p, t,* and *k* and the Proto-Germanic voiceless fricative *s* derived from Proto-Indo-European *s* became the voiced fricatives b, ð, g, and z represented in various recorded Germanic languages by *b, d, g,* and *r*
ver·ni·cle *or* **ver·na·cle** \ˈvər-ni-kəl\ *n* [ME *vernicle,* fr. AF, alter. of MF *veronique,* fr. ML *veronica*] (14c) : ²VERONICA
¹**ver·ni·er** \ˈvər-nē-ər\ *n* [Pierre *Vernier*] (1766) **1 :** a short scale made to slide along the divisions of a graduated instrument for indicating parts of divisions **2 a :** a small auxiliary device used with a main device to obtain fine adjustment **b :** any of two or more small supplementary rocket engines or gas nozzles on a missile or a rocket vehicle for making fine adjustments in the speed or course or controlling the attitude — called also *vernier engine*
²**vernier** *adj* (1788) : having or comprising a vernier
vernier caliper *n* (ca. 1876) : a measuring device that consists of a main scale with a fixed jaw and a sliding jaw with an attached vernier
ver·nis·sage \ˌver-ni-ˈsäzh\ *n* [F, day before an exhibition opens reserved for artists to varnish and put finishing touches to their paintings, lit., varnishing, fr. *vernis* varnish — more at VARNISH] (1912) : a private showing or preview of an art exhibition
¹**ve·ron·i·ca** \və-ˈrä-ni-kə\ *n* [NL, genus of herbs] (1527) : any of a genus (*Veronica*) of annual or perennial herbs of the snapdragon family that have small pink, white, blue or purple flowers with a 4- or 5-lobed calyx, a rotate corolla, two stamens, and the fruit a compressed capsule — compare SPEEDWELL
²**veronica** *n* [ME, fr. ML, fr. *Veronica,* legendary saint of the 1st cent. A.D.] (15c) : an image of Christ's face said to have been impressed on the cloth that St. Veronica gave him to wipe his face with on the way to his crucifixion; *also* : a cloth resembling the legendary one of St. Veronica
³**veronica** *n* [Sp *verónica,* fr. St. *Veronica*] (1926) : a pase in bullfighting in which the cape is swung slowly away from the charging bull while the matador keeps his feet in the same position
Vé·ro·nique *also* **Ve·ro·nique** \ˌvā-rō-ˈnēk\ *adj* [F *Véronique* Veronica] (1907) : prepared or garnished with usu. white seedless grapes ⟨sole ~⟩
ver·ru·ca \və-ˈrü-kə\ *n, pl* **-cae** \-(ˌ)kē, -ˌkī, -ˌsī\ [L, wart, hillock; akin to Lith *viršus* summit and prob. to OE *wearte* wart — more at WART] (1565) **1 :** a wart or warty skin lesion **2 :** a warty elevation on a plant or animal surface
ver·ru·cas *chiefly Brit pl of* VERRUCA
verruca vul·ga·ris \-ˌvəl-ˈger-əs\ *n* [NL, lit., common verruca] (1903) : WART 1a; *esp* : one occurring on the back of the fingers and hands
ver·ru·cose \və-ˈrü-ˌkōs\ *adj* (1686) : covered with warty elevations
ver·sal \ˈvər-səl, ˈvär-\ *adj* [short for *universal*] (1592) *archaic* : ENTIRE, WHOLE ⟨as pale as any clout in the ~ world —Shak.⟩
ver·sant \ˈvər-sᵊnt\ *adj* [L *versant-, versans,* prp. of *versare, versari* to turn, occupy oneself, meditate] (1645) **1** *archaic* : EXPERIENCED, PRACTICED **2 :** CONVERSANT
ver·sa·tile \ˈvər-sə-tᵊl, *esp Brit* -ˌtī(-ə)l\ *adj* [F or L; F, fr. L *versatilis* turning easily, fr. *versare* to turn, freq. of *vertere*] (1605) **1 :** changing or fluctuating readily : VARIABLE ⟨a ~ disposition⟩ **2 :** embracing a variety of subjects, fields, or skills; *also* : turning with ease from one thing to another **3 a (1) :** capable of turning forward or backward : REVERSIBLE ⟨a ~ toe of a bird⟩ **(2) :** capable of moving laterally and up and down ⟨~ antennae⟩ **b** *of an anther* : having the filaments attached at or near the middle so as to swing freely **4 :** having many uses or applications ⟨~ building material⟩ — **ver·sa·tile·ly** \-tᵊl-(l)ē, -ˌtī(-ə)l-lē\ *adv* — **ver·sa·tile·ness** \-tᵊl-nəs, -ˌtī(-ə)l-nəs\ *n*
ver·sa·til·i·ty \ˌvər-sə-ˈti-lə-tē\ *n* (1668) : the quality or state of being versatile ⟨a writer of great ~⟩
vers de so·ci·é·té \ˌver-də-ˌsō-sē-ə-ˈtā\ *n* [F, society verse] (1796) : witty and typically ironic light verse
¹**verse** \ˈvərs\ *n* [ME *vers, fers,* fr. AF *vers* & OE *fers,* both fr. L *versus,* lit., turning, fr. *vertere* to turn — more at WORTH] (bef. 12c) **1 :** a line of metrical writing **2 a (1) :** metrical language **(2) :** metrical writing distinguished from poetry esp. by its lower level of intensity **(3) :** POETRY 2 **b :** POEM **c :** a body of metrical writing (as of a period or country) **3 :** STANZA **4 :** one of the short divisions into which a chapter of the Bible is traditionally divided
²**verse** *vb* **versed; vers·ing** *vi* (bef. 12c) : to make verse : VERSIFY ~ *vt* **1 :** to tell or celebrate in verse **2 :** to turn into verse
³**verse** *vt* **versed; vers·ing** [back-formation fr. *versed,* fr. L *versatus,* pp. of *versari* to be active, be occupied (in), pass. of *versare* to turn] (1599) : to familiarize by close association, study, or experience ⟨well *versed* in the theater⟩
vers·et \ˈvər-sət, -ˌset; ˌvər-ˈset\ *n* [ME, fr. AF, dim. of *vers* verse] (13c) : a short verse esp. from a sacred book (as the Koran)
ver·si·cle \ˈvər-si-kəl\ *n* [ME, fr. L *versiculus,* dim. of *versus* verse] (14c) **1 :** a short verse or sentence (as from a psalm) said or sung by a leader in public worship and followed by a response from the people **2 :** a little verse
ver·sic·u·lar \ˌvər-ˈsi-kyə-lər\ *adj* [L *versiculus* little verse] (1812) : of or relating to verses or versicles
ver·si·fi·ca·tion \ˌvər-sə-fə-ˈkā-shən\ *n* (ca. 1576) **1 :** the making of verses **2 a :** metrical structure : PROSODY **b :** a particular metrical structure or style **3 :** a version in verse of something orig. in prose
ver·si·fi·er \ˈvər-sə-ˌfī(-ə)r\ *n* (14c) : one that versifies; *esp* : a writer of light or inferior verse
ver·si·fy \-ˌfī\ *vb* **-fied; -fy·ing** [ME *versifien,* fr. AF *versifier,* fr. L *versificare,* fr. *versus* verse, line] *vi* (14c) : to compose verses ~ *vt* **1 :** to relate or describe in verse **2 :** to turn into verse
ver·sion \ˈvər-zhən, -shən\ *n* [MF, fr. ML *version-, versio* act of turning, change, fr. L *vertere* to turn — more at WORTH] (1582) **1 :** a translation from another language; *esp* : a translation of the Bible or a part of it **2 a :** an account or description from a particular point of view esp. as contrasted with another account **b :** an adaptation of a literary work ⟨the movie ~ of the novel⟩ **c :** an arrangement of a musical composition **3 :** a form or variant of a type or original ⟨an experimental ~ of the airplane⟩ **4 a :** a condition in which an organ and esp. the uterus is turned from its normal position **b :** manual turning of a fetus in the uterus to aid delivery — **ver·sion·al** \ˈvərzh-nəl, ˈvərsh-; ˈvər-zhə-nᵊl, -shə-\ *adj*
vers li·bre \ver-ˈlēbrᵊ\ *n, pl* **vers li·bres** *same*\ [F] (1902) : FREE VERSE
vers–li·brist \-ˈlē-brist\ *n* [F *vers-libriste*] (1916) : a writer of free verse
ver·so \ˈvər-(ˌ)sō\ *n, pl* **versos** [NL *verso* (*folio*) the page being turned] (1839) **1 :** the side of a leaf (as of a manuscript) that is to be read second **2 :** a left-hand page — compare RECTO
verst \ˈvərst\ *n* [F *verste* & G *Werst;* both fr. Russ *versta;* akin to L *vertere* to turn] (1555) : a Russian unit of distance equal to 0.6629 mile (1.067 kilometers)
ver·sus \ˈvər-səs, -səz\ *prep* [ME, fr. ML, towards, against, fr. L, adv., so as to face, fr. pp. of *vertere* to turn] (15c) **1 :** AGAINST **2 :** in contrast to or as the alternative of ⟨free trade ~ protection⟩
¹**vert** \ˈvərt\ *n* [ME, fr. AF, fr. *vert* green — more at VERDANT] (15c) **1 a :** green forest vegetation esp. when forming cover or providing food for deer **b :** the right or privilege (as in England) of cutting living wood or sometimes of pasturing animals in a forest **2 :** the heraldic color green
²**vert** *abbr* vertical
ver·te·bra \ˈvər-tə-brə, -ˌbrā\ *n, pl* **-brae** \-ˌbrā, -(ˌ)brē, -brə\ *or* **-bras** [L, joint, vertebra, fr. *vertere* to turn] (1578) : one of the bony or cartilaginous segments composing the spinal column, consisting in some lower vertebrates of several distinct elements which never become united, and in higher vertebrates having a short more or less cylindrical body whose ends articulate by pads of elastic or cartilaginous tissue with those of adjacent vertebrae and a bony arch that encloses the spinal cord
ver·te·bral \(ˌ)vər-ˈtē-brəl, ˈvər-tə-\ *adj* (ca. 1681) : of, relating to, or being vertebrae or the vertebral column : SPINAL ⟨a ~ fracture⟩
vertebral canal *n* (1830) : a canal that contains the spinal cord and is delimited by the arches on the dorsal side of the vertebrae — called also *spinal canal*
vertebral column *n* (1822) : SPINAL COLUMN

[1]**ver·te·brate** \ˈvər-tə-brət, -ˌbrāt\ *adj* [NL *vertebratus,* fr. L, jointed, fr. *vertebra*] (1826) **1 a :** having a spinal column **b :** of or relating to the vertebrates **2 :** organized or constructed in orderly or developed form

[2]**vertebrate** *n* [NL *Vertebrata,* fr. neut. pl. of *vertebratus*] (1826) : any of a subphylum (Vertebrata) of chordates possessing a spinal column that includes the mammals, birds, reptiles, amphibians, and fishes

ver·tex \ˈvər-ˌteks\ *n, pl* **ver·ti·ces** \ˈvər-tə-ˌsēz\ *also* **ver·tex·es** [ME, top of the head, fr. L *vertic-, vertex, vortic-, vortex* whirl, whirlpool, top of the head, summit, fr. *vertere* to turn] (14c) **1 :** the top of the head **2 a :** the point opposite to and farthest from the base in a figure **b :** a point (as of an angle, polygon, polyhedron, graph, or network) that terminates a line or curve or comprises the intersection of two or more lines or curves **c :** a point where an axis of an ellipse, parabola, or hyperbola intersects the curve itself **3 :** a principal or highest point : SUMMIT ⟨the ~ of the hill⟩

ver·ti·cal \ˈvər-ti-kəl\ *adj* [MF or LL; MF, fr. LL *verticalis,* fr. L *vertic-, vertex*] (1559) **1 a :** situated at the highest point : directly overhead or in the zenith **b** *of an aerial photograph* **:** taken with the camera pointing straight down or nearly so **2 a :** perpendicular to the plane of the horizon or to a primary axis : UPRIGHT **b (1) :** located at right angles to the plane of a supporting surface **(2) :** lying in the direction of an axis : LENGTHWISE **3 a :** relating to, involving, or integrating economic activity from basic production to point of sale ⟨a ~ monopoly⟩ **b :** of, relating to, or comprising persons of different status ⟨the ~ arrangement of society⟩ — **vertical** *n* — **ver·ti·cal·i·ty** \ˌvər-tə-ˈka-lə-tē\ *n* — **ver·ti·cal·ly** \ˈvər-ti-k(ə-)lē\ *adv* — **ver·ti·cal·ness** \-kəl-nəs\ *n*

syn VERTICAL, PERPENDICULAR, PLUMB mean being at right angles to a base line. VERTICAL suggests a line or direction rising straight upward toward a zenith ⟨the side of the cliff is almost *vertical*⟩. PERPENDICULAR may stress the straightness of a line making a right angle with any other line, not necessarily a horizontal one ⟨the parallel bars are *perpendicular* to the support posts⟩. PLUMB stresses an exact verticality determined (as with a plumb line) by earth's gravity ⟨make sure that the wall is *plumb*⟩.

vertical angle *n* (1571) : either of two angles lying on opposite sides of two intersecting lines

vertical circle *n* (1559) : a great circle of the celestial sphere whose plane is perpendicular to that of the horizon — see AZIMUTH illustration

vertical file *n* (1906) : a collection of articles (as pamphlets and clippings) that is maintained (as in a library) to answer brief questions or to provide points of information not easily located

vertical union *n* (1933) : INDUSTRIAL UNION

ver·ti·cil \ˈvər-tə-ˌsil\ *n* [NL *verticillus,* dim. of L *vertex* whirl] (1793) : WHORL 2

ver·ti·cil·late \ˌvər-tə-ˈsi-lət\ *adj* (ca. 1793) : arranged in whorls

ver·ti·cil·li·um wilt \ˌvər-tə-ˈsi-lē-əm-\ *n* [NL *Verticillium,* fr. *verticillus*] (1916) : a wilt disease of various plants that is caused by a soil-borne imperfect fungus (genus *Verticillium*)

ver·tig·i·nous \(ˌ)vər-ˈti-jə-nəs\ *adj* [L *vertiginosus,* fr. *vertigin-, vertigo*] (1608) **1 a :** characterized by or suffering from vertigo or dizziness **b :** inclined to frequent and often pointless change : INCONSTANT **2 :** causing or tending to cause dizziness ⟨the ~ heights⟩ **3 :** marked by turning : ROTARY ⟨the ~ motion of the earth⟩ — **ver·tig·i·nous·ly** *adv*

ver·ti·go \ˈvər-ti-ˌgō\ *n, pl* **-goes** *or* **-gos** [ME, fr. L *vertigin-, vertigo,* fr. *vertere* to turn] (15c) **1 a :** a sensation of motion in which the individual or the individual's surroundings seem to whirl dizzily **b :** a dizzy confused state of mind **2 :** disordered vertiginous movement as a symptom of disease in lower animals; *also* : a disease (as gid) causing this

vertu *var of* VIRTU

ver·vain \ˈvər-ˌvān\ *n* [ME *verveine,* fr. AF, fr. L *verbena* leafy branch; akin to L *verber* rod, Lith *virbas,* and perh. to Gk *rhabdos* rod] (14c) : any of a genus (*Verbena* of the family Verbenaceae, the vervain family) of chiefly American plants having bracted spicate flowers, a corolla with a 5-lobed limb, and a fruit that separates into four nutlets

verve \ˈvərv\ *n* [F, fr. MF, caprice, fr. OF, word, gossip, fr. VL **verva,* fr. L *verba,* pl. of *verbum* word — more at WORD] (1697) **1** *archaic* **:** special ability or talent **2 a :** the spirit and enthusiasm animating artistic composition or performance : VIVACITY **b :** ENERGY, VITALITY

ver·vet \ˈvər-vət\ *n* [F *vervet*] (1893) : GREEN MONKEY

[1]**very** \ˈver-ē, ˈve-rē\ *adj* **veri·er; -est** [ME *verray, verry,* fr. AF *verai,* fr. VL **veracus,* alter. of L *verac-, verax* truthful, fr. *verus* true; akin to OE *wǣr* true, OHG *wāra* trust, care, Gk *ēra* (acc.) favor] (13c) **1 a :** properly entitled to the name or designation : TRUE ⟨the fierce hatred of a ~ woman —J. M. Barrie⟩ **b :** ACTUAL, REAL ⟨the ~ blood and bone of our grammar —H. L. Smith †1972⟩ **c :** SIMPLE, PLAIN ⟨in ~ truth⟩ **2 a :** EXACT, PRECISE ⟨the ~ heart of the city⟩ **b :** exactly suitable or necessary ⟨the ~ thing for the purpose⟩ **3 a :** ABSOLUTE, UTTER ⟨the *veriest* fool alive⟩ **b :** UNQUALIFIED, SHEER ⟨the ~ shame of it⟩ **4** — used as an intensive esp. to emphasize identity ⟨before my ~ eyes⟩ **5 :** MERE, BARE ⟨the ~ thought terrified him⟩ **6 :** being the same one : SELFSAME ⟨the ~ man I saw⟩ **7 :** SPECIAL, PARTICULAR ⟨the ~ essence of truth is plainness and brightness —John Milton⟩ ***syn*** see SAME

[2]**very** *adv* (14c) **1 :** in actual fact : TRULY ⟨the ~ best store in town⟩ ⟨told the ~ same story⟩ **2 :** to a high degree : EXCEEDINGLY ⟨~ hot⟩ ⟨didn't hurt ~ much⟩

very hard *adj* (ca. 1943) *of cheese* **:** suitable chiefly for grating

very high frequency *n* (1920) : a radio frequency between ultrahigh frequency and high frequency — see RADIO FREQUENCY table

Ve·ry light \ˈver-ē-, ˈvir-ē-\ *n* [Edward W. *Very* †1910 Am. naval officer] (1917) : a pyrotechnic signal in a system of signaling using white or colored balls of fire projected from a special pistol

very low–density lipoprotein *n* (1977) : VLDL

very low frequency *n* (1938) : a radio frequency between low frequency and voice frequency — see RADIO FREQUENCY table

Ve·ry pistol \ˈver-ē-, ˈvir-ē-\ *n* (1915) : a pistol for firing Very lights

Very Reverend \ˈver-ē-, ˈve-rē-\ (1748) — used as a title for various ecclesiastical officials (as cathedral deans and canons, rectors of Roman Catholic colleges and seminaries, and superiors of some religious houses)

ves·i·cal \ˈve-si-kəl\ *adj* [L *vesica* bladder — more at VENTER] (1797) : of or relating to the urinary bladder ⟨~ burning⟩

ves·i·cant \ˈve-si-kənt\ *n* [L *vesica* bladder, blister] (1661) : an agent (as a chemical weapon) that induces blistering — **vesicant** *adj*

ves·i·cle \ˈve-si-kəl\ *n* [MF *vesicule,* fr. L *vesicula* small bladder, blister, fr. dim. of *vesica*] (1578) **1 a :** a membranous and usu. fluid-filled pouch (as a cyst, vacuole, or cell) in a plant or animal **b :** a small abnormal elevation of the outer layer of skin enclosing a watery liquid : BLISTER **c :** a pocket of embryonic tissue that is the beginning of an organ **2 :** a small cavity in a mineral or rock

ve·sic·u·lar \və-ˈsi-kyə-lər, ve-\ *adj* [NL *vesicula* vesicle, fr. L, small bladder] (1715) **1 :** containing, composed of, or characterized by vesicles ⟨~ lava⟩ **2 :** having the form or structure of a vesicle **3 :** of or relating to vesicles — **ve·sic·u·lar·i·ty** \-ˌsi-kyə-ˈla-rə-tē\ *n*

vesicular stomatitis *n* (ca. 1903) : an acute viral disease esp. of various domesticated animals (as horses and cows) that resembles foot-and-mouth disease, is marked by erosive blisters in and about the mouth, and is caused by any of three rhabdoviruses (species *Vesicular stomatitis Alagoas virus, Vesicular stomatitis Indiana virus,* and *Vesicular stomatitis New Jersey virus* of the genus *Vesiculovirus*) which sometimes infect humans producing flu-like symptoms

ve·sic·u·late \və-ˈsi-kyə-ˌlāt, ve-\ *vb* **-lat·ed; -lat·ing** *vt* (1865) : to make vesicular ~ *vi* : to become vesicular — **ve·sic·u·la·tion** \-ˌsi-kyə-ˈlā-shən\ *n*

[1]**ves·per** \ˈves-pər\ *n* [ME, fr. L, evening, evening star — more at WEST] (14c) **1** *cap, archaic* **:** EVENING STAR **2 :** a vesper bell **3** *archaic* **:** EVENING, EVENTIDE

[2]**vesper** *adj* (1791) : of or relating to vespers or the evening

ves·per·al \ˈves-p(ə-)rəl\ *adj* (ca. 1623) : VESPER ⟨a ~ breeze⟩

ves·pers \ˈves-pərz\ *n pl but sing or pl in constr, often cap* [AF *vespres,* fr. ML *vesperae,* fr. L, pl. of *vespera* evening; akin to L *vesper* evening star] (1595) **1 :** the sixth of the canonical hours that is said or sung in the late afternoon **2 :** a service of evening worship

ves·per·til·ian \ˌves-pər-ˈti-lē-ən, -ˈtil-yən\ *adj* [L *vespertilio* bat, fr. *vesper*] (1874) : of, relating to, or resembling a bat ⟨flaunts ~ wing and cloven hoof —Robert Graves⟩

ves·per·tine \ˈves-pər-ˌtīn\ *adj* [L *vespertinus,* fr. *vesper*] (15c) **1 :** of, relating to, or occurring in the evening ⟨~ shadows⟩ **2 :** active, flowering, or flourishing in the evening : CREPUSCULAR

ves·pid \ˈves-pəd\ *n* [ultim. fr. L *vespa* wasp — more at WASP] (ca. 1900) : any of a cosmopolitan family (Vespidae) of chiefly social wasps that usu. live in colonies like bees — **vespid** *adj*

ves·pine \ˈves-ˌpīn\ *adj* [L *vespa* wasp] (1843) : of, relating to, or resembling wasps and esp. vespid wasps

ves·sel \ˈve-səl\ *n* [ME, fr. AF, fr. LL *vascellum,* dim. of L *vas* vase, vessel] (14c) **1 a :** a container (as a cask, bottle, kettle, cup, or bowl) for holding something **b :** a person into whom some quality (as grace) is infused ⟨a child of light, a true ~ of the Lord —H. J. Laski⟩ **2 :** a watercraft bigger than a rowboat; *esp* : SHIP 1 **3 a :** a tube or canal (as an artery) in which a body fluid is contained and conveyed or circulated **b :** a conducting tube in the xylem of a vascular plant formed by the fusion and loss of end walls of a series of cells

[1]**vest** \ˈvest\ *vb* [ME, fr. AF *vestir* to clothe, invest, vest, fr. L *vestire* to clothe, fr. *vestis* clothing, garment — more at WEAR] *vt* (15c) **1 a :** to place or give into the possession or discretion of some person or authority; *esp* : to give to a person a legally fixed immediate right of present or future enjoyment of (as an estate) **b :** to grant or endow with a particular authority, right, or property ⟨the plan ~*s* workers with pension benefits after 10 years of service⟩ **2 :** to clothe with or as if with a garment; *esp* : to robe in ecclesiastical vestments ~ *vi* **1 :** to become legally vested **2 :** to put on garments or vestments

[2]**vest** *n* [F *veste,* fr. It, fr. L *vestis* garment] (1613) **1** *archaic* **a :** a loose outer garment : ROBE **b :** CLOTHING, GARB **2 a :** a sleeveless garment for the upper body usu. worn over a shirt **b :** a protective usu. sleeveless garment (as a life preserver) that extends to the waist **c :** an insulated sleeveless waist-length garment often worn under or in place of a coat **3 a** *chiefly Brit* **:** a man's sleeveless undershirt **b :** a knitted undershirt for women **4 :** a plain or decorative piece used to fill in the front neckline of a woman's outer garment (as a blouse or dress) — **vest·like** \-ˌlīk\ *adj*

ves·ta \ˈves-tə\ *n* [L *Vesta*] (14c) **1** *cap* **:** the Roman goddess of the hearth — compare HESTIA **2 :** a short match with a shank of wax-coated threads; *also* : a short wooden match

[1]**ves·tal** \ˈves-tᵊl\ *adj* (15c) **1 :** of or relating to the Roman goddess Vesta **2 a :** of or relating to a vestal virgin **b :** CHASTE

[2]**vestal** *n* (15c) : VESTAL VIRGIN

vestal virgin *n* (ca. 1583) **1 :** a virgin consecrated to the Roman goddess Vesta and to the service of watching the sacred fire perpetually kept burning on her altar **2 :** a chaste woman

vest·ed \ˈves-təd\ *adj* (1766) **1 :** fully and unconditionally guaranteed as a legal right, benefit, or privilege ⟨the ~ benefits of the pension plan⟩ **2 :** having a vest ⟨a ~ suit⟩

vested interest *n* (1818) **1 :** an interest (as a title to an estate) carrying a legal right of present or future enjoyment; *specif* : a right vested in an employee under a pension plan **2 :** a special concern or stake in maintaining or influencing a condition, arrangement, or action esp. for selfish ends **3 :** one having a vested interest in something; *specif* : a group enjoying benefits from an existing economic or political privilege

vest·ee \ve-ˈstē\ *n* (1915) **1 :** DICKEY; *esp* : one made to resemble a vest **2 :** VEST 4

ves·ti·ary \ˈves-tē-ˌer-ē, ˈvesh-chē-\ *n* [ME *vestiarie,* fr. L *vestiarium* — more at VESTRY] (14c) **1 :** a room where clothing is kept **2 :** CLOTHING, RAIMENT

ves·tib·u·lar \ve-ˈsti-byə-lər\ *adj* (ca. 1839) **1 :** of, relating to, or functioning as a vestibule **2 :** of, relating to, or affecting the perception of body position and movement ⟨the ~ system of the inner ear⟩

ves·ti·bule \ˈves-tə-ˌbyül\ *n* [L *vestibulum* forecourt] (1726) **1 a :** a passage, hall, or room between the outer door and the interior of a building : LOBBY **b :** an enclosed entrance at the end of a railway passenger car **2 :** any of various bodily cavities esp. when serving as or resembling an entrance to some other cavity or space: as **a :** the central cavity of the bony labyrinth of the inner ear or the parts (as the saccule and utricle) of the membranous labyrinth that it contains **b :** the part of the left ventricle below the aortic orifice **c :** the space between the labia minora containing the orifice of the urethra **d :** the part of the mouth cavity outside the teeth and gums **3 :** a course that offers access (as to something new) — **ves·ti·buled** \-ˌbyüld\ *adj*

vestibule school *n* (1918) : a school organized in an industrial plant to train new workers in specific skills

ves·tib·u·lo·co·chle·ar nerve \ve-ˌsti-byə-lō-ˈkō-klē-ər-, -ˈkä-\ *n* (1962) : AUDITORY NERVE

ves·tige \ˈves-tij\ *n* [ME, fr. MF, fr. L *vestigium* footstep, footprint, track, vestige] (15c) **1 a (1) :** a trace, mark, or visible sign left by something (as an ancient city or a condition or practice) vanished or lost **(2) :** the smallest quantity or trace **b :** FOOTPRINT 1 **2 :** a bodily part or organ that is small and degenerate or imperfectly developed in comparison to one more fully developed in an earlier stage of the individual, in a past generation, or in closely related forms ***syn*** see TRACE — **ves·ti·gial** \ve-ˈsti-jē-əl, -jəl\ *adj* — **ves·ti·gial·ly** *adv*

ves·ti·men·tif·er·an \ˌves-tə-ˌmen-ˈti-f(ə-)rən\ *n* [NL *Vestimentifera,* fr. *vestimentum* muscular structure by which the worm emerges from its tube (fr. L, garment) + *-fera,* neut. pl. of *-fer* -fer] (1982) : any of a taxonomic group (Vestimentifera) of very large tube worms that may grow to 9 feet (3 meters) in length and more than an inch (3 centimeters) in diameter, are found esp. near deep-sea hydrothermal vents, and are considered pogonophorans or a separate phylum or polychaetes — **vestimentiferan** *adj*

vest·ing \ˈves-tiŋ\ *n* (1944) : the conveying to an employee of the inalienable right to share in a pension fund esp. in the event of termination of employment prior to the normal retirement age; *also* : the right so conveyed

vest·ment \ˈves(t)-mənt\ *n* [ME *vestement,* fr. AF, fr. L *vestimentum,* fr. *vestire* to clothe] (13c) **1 a :** an outer garment; *esp* : a robe of ceremony or office **b** *pl* : CLOTHING, GARB **2 :** a covering resembling a garment **3 :** one of the articles of the ceremonial attire and insignia worn by ecclesiastical officiants and assistants as indicative of their rank and appropriate to the rite being celebrated — **vest·men·tal** \ves(t)-ˈmen-tᵊl\ *adj*

vest–pocket *adj* (1848) **1 :** adapted to fit into the vest pocket ⟨a ~ edition of a book⟩ **2 :** of very small size or scope

vest–pocket park *n* (1966) : a very small urban park

ves·try \ˈves-trē\ *n, pl* **vestries** [ME *vestrie,* prob. fr. AF **vesterie,* alter. of MF *vestiarie,* fr. ML *vestiarium,* fr. L, cupboard for storing clothes, fr. *vestis* garment; fr. its use as a robing room for the clergy] (14c) **1 a :** SACRISTY **b :** a room used for church meetings and classes **2 a :** the business meeting of an English parish **b :** an elective body in an Episcopal parish composed of the rector and a group of elected parishioners administering the temporal affairs of the parish

ves·try·man \-trē-mən\ *n* (1614) : a member of a vestry

[1]**ves·ture** \ˈves-chər, ˈvesh-\ *n* [ME, fr. AF, fr. *vestir* to clothe — more at VEST] (14c) **1 a :** a covering garment (as a robe or vestment) **b :** CLOTHING, APPAREL **2 :** something that covers like a garment

[2]**vesture** *vt* **ves·tured; ves·tur·ing** (15c) : to cover with vesture : CLOTHE

ve·su·vi·an \və-ˈsü-vē-ən\ *n* [*Vesuvian*] (1853) : a match used esp. formerly for lighting cigars

Ve·su·vi·an \və-ˈsü-vē-ən\ *adj* (1661) **1 :** of, relating to, or resembling the volcano Vesuvius **2 :** marked by sudden outbursts ⟨has a ~ temper, but quickly controls himself —Sidney Shalett⟩

ve·su·vi·an·ite \-vē-ə-ˌnīt\ *n* (ca. 1888) : IDOCRASE

[1]**vet** \ˈvet\ *n* (1862) : VETERINARIAN, VETERINARY

[2]**vet** *vt* **vet·ted; vet·ting** (1891) **1 a :** to provide veterinary care for (an animal) or medical care for (a person) **b :** to subject (a person or animal) to a physical examination or checkup **2 a :** to subject to usu. expert appraisal or correction ⟨~ a manuscript⟩ **b :** to evaluate for possible approval or acceptance ⟨~ the candidates for a position⟩ — **vetter** *n*

[3]**vet** *adj or n* (1848) : VETERAN

vetch \ˈvech\ *n* [ME *fecche, veche,* fr. MF dial. (Norman & Picard) *veche,* fr. L *vicia;* perh. akin to L *vincire* to bind] (14c) : any of a genus (*Vicia*) of herbaceous twining leguminous plants including some grown for fodder and green manure — compare CROWN VETCH, HAIRY VETCH, MILK VETCH

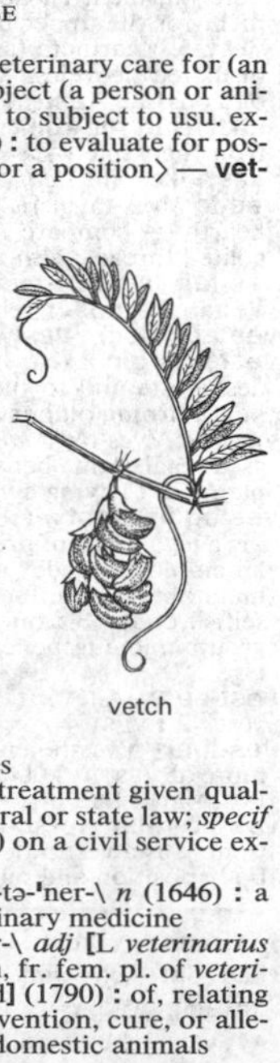

vetch

vetch·ling \ˈvech-liŋ\ *n* (1578) : any of various leguminous herbs (genus *Lathyrus* and esp. *L. pratensis*)

vet·er·an \ˈve-tə-rən, ˈve-trən\ *n* [L *veteranus,* fr. *veteranus,* adj., old, of long experience, fr. *veter-, vetus* old — more at WETHER] (1509) **1 a :** an old soldier of long service **b :** a former member of the armed forces **2 :** a person of long experience usu. in some occupation or skill (as politics or the arts) — **veteran** *adj*

Veterans Day *n* (1952) : November 11 set aside in commemoration of the end of hostilities in 1918 and 1945 and observed as a legal holiday in the U.S. to honor the veterans of the armed forces

veterans' preference *n* (ca. 1941) : preferential treatment given qualified veterans of the U.S. armed forces under federal or state law; *specif* : special consideration (as by allowance of points) on a civil service examination

vet·er·i·nar·i·an \ˌve-tə-rə-ˈner-ē-ən, ˌve-trə-, ˌve-tə-ˈner-\ *n* (1646) : a person qualified and authorized to practice veterinary medicine

[1]**vet·er·i·nary** \ˈve-tə-rə-ˌner-ē, ˈve-trə-, ˈve-tə-ˌner-\ *adj* [L *veterinarius* of beasts of burden, fr. *veterinae* beasts of burden, fr. fem. pl. of *veterinus* of beasts of burden; akin to L *veter-, vetus* old] (1790) : of, relating to, practicing, or being the science and art of prevention, cure, or alleviation of disease and injury in animals and esp. domestic animals

[2]**veterinary** *n, pl* **-nar·ies** (1861) : VETERINARIAN

veterinary surgeon *n* (ca. 1802) *Brit* : VETERINARIAN

vet·i·ver \ˈve-tə-vər\ *n* [F *vétiver,* fr. Tamil *veṭṭivēr*] (ca. 1858) : a tall perennial grass (*Vetiveria zizanioides*) of southeastern Asia cultivated in warm regions esp. for its fragrant roots which are used esp. in woven goods (as mats) and in perfumes; *also* : its root

[1]**ve·to** \ˈvē-(ˌ)tō\ *n, pl* **vetoes** [L, I forbid, fr. *vetare* to forbid] (1629) **1 :** an authoritative prohibition : INTERDICTION **2 a :** a power of one department or branch of a government to forbid or prohibit finally or provisionally the carrying out of projects attempted by another department; *esp* : a power vested in a chief executive to prevent permanently or temporarily the enactment of measures passed by a legislature **b (1) :** the exercise of such authority **(2) :** a message communicating the reasons of an executive and esp. the president of the U.S. for vetoing a proposed law

[2]**veto** *vt* **ve·toed; ve·to·ing** (1706) : to refuse to admit or approve : PROHIBIT; *also* : to refuse assent to (a legislative bill) so as to prevent enactment or cause reconsideration — **ve·to·er** \-ˌtō-ər\ *n*

ve·to–proof \-ˌprüf\ *adj* (1972) : having enough potential votes to be enacted over a veto or to override vetoes consistently ⟨a ~ bill⟩

vex \ˈveks\ *vt* **vexed** *also* **vext; vex·ing** [ME, fr. AF *vexer,* fr. L *vexare* to agitate, harry; prob. akin to L *vehere* to convey — more at WAY] (15c) **1 a :** to bring trouble, distress, or agitation to ⟨the restaurant is ~*ed* by slow service⟩ **b :** to bring physical distress to ⟨a headache ~*ed* him all morning⟩ **c :** to irritate or annoy by petty provocations : HARASS ⟨~*ed* by the children⟩ **d :** PUZZLE, BAFFLE ⟨a problem to ~ the keenest wit⟩ **2 :** to shake or toss about ***syn*** see ANNOY

vex·a·tion \vek-ˈsā-shən\ *n* (15c) **1 :** the act of harassing or vexing : TROUBLING **2 :** the quality or state of being vexed : IRRITATION **3 :** a cause of trouble : AFFLICTION

vex·a·tious \-shəs\ *adj* (1534) **1 a :** causing vexation : DISTRESSING ⟨~ delays⟩ **b :** intended to harass ⟨a ~ lawsuit⟩ **2 :** full of disorder or stress : TROUBLED ⟨a ~ period in her life⟩ — **vex·a·tious·ly** *adv* — **vex·a·tious·ness** *n*

vexed \ˈvekst\ *adj* (1657) : debated or discussed at length ⟨a ~ question⟩

vexed·ly \ˈvek-səd-lē, ˈvekst-lē\ *adv* (1748) : with vexation

vex·il·lol·o·gy \ˌvek-sə-ˈlä-lə-jē\ *n* [L *vexillum*] (1959) : the study of flags — **vex·il·lo·log·ic** \(ˌ)vek-ˌsi-lə-ˈlä-jik\ *or* **vex·il·lo·log·i·cal** \-ˈlä-ji-kəl\ *adj* — **vex·il·lol·o·gist** \ˌvek-sə-ˈlä-lə-jist\ *n*

vex·il·lum \vek-ˈsi-ləm\ *n, pl* **-la** \-lə\ [L; akin to L *velum* curtain, awning] (1726) **1 :** a square flag of the ancient Roman cavalry **2 :** the web or vane of a feather

vexing *adj* (1569) : causing or likely to cause vexation : VEXATIOUS ⟨a ~ problem⟩ — **vex·ing·ly** *adv*

VFR *abbr* visual flight rules

VFW *abbr* Veterans of Foreign Wars

VG *abbr* very good

VGA *abbr* video graphics array

VHF *abbr* very high frequency

VI *abbr* Virgin Islands

via \ˈvī-ə, ˈvē-ə\ *prep* [L, abl. of *via* way — more at WAY] (1779) **1 :** by way of **2 :** through the medium or agency of; *also* : by means of

vi·a·ble \ˈvī-ə-bəl\ *adj* [F, fr. MF, fr. *vie* life, fr. L *vita* — more at VITAL] (ca. 1832) **1 :** capable of living; *esp* : having attained such form and development as to be normally capable of surviving outside the mother's womb ⟨a ~ fetus⟩ **2 :** capable of growing or developing ⟨~ seeds⟩ ⟨~ eggs⟩ **3 a :** capable of working, functioning, or developing adequately ⟨~ alternatives⟩ **b :** capable of existence and development as an independent unit ⟨the colony is now a ~ state⟩ **c (1) :** having a reasonable chance of succeeding ⟨a ~ candidate⟩ **(2) :** financially sustainable ⟨a ~ enterprise⟩ — **vi·a·bil·i·ty** \ˌvī-ə-ˈbi-lə-tē\ *n* — **vi·a·bly** \ˈvī-ə-blē\ *adv*

via·duct \ˈvī-ə-ˌdəkt\ *n* [L *via* way, road + E aque*duct*] (1816) : a long elevated roadway usu. consisting of a series of short spans supported on arches, piers, or columns

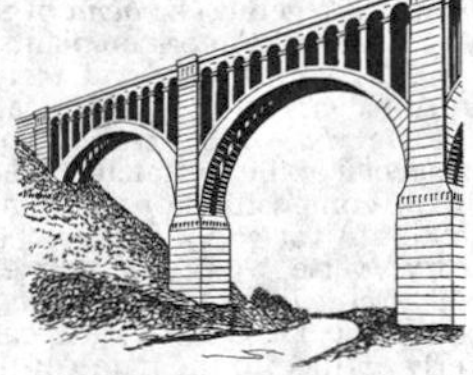

viaduct

Vi·ag·ra \vī-ˈa-grə\ *trademark* — used for a preparation of the citrate of sildenafil

vi·al \ˈvī(-ə)l\ *n* [ME *fiole, viole,* fr. AF, fr. LL *fiola,* alter. of L *phiala* — more at PHIAL] (14c) : a small closed or closable vessel esp. for liquids

via me·dia \ˌvī-ə-ˈmē-dē-ə; ˌvē-ə-ˈmā-dē-ə, -ˈme-\ *n* [L] (1834) : a middle way

vi·and \ˈvī-ənd\ *n* [ME, *viaunde,* fr. AF, fr. ML *vivanda* food, alter. of L *vivenda,* neut. pl. of *vivendus,* gerundive of *vivere* to live — more at QUICK] (15c) **1 :** an item of food; *esp* : a choice or tasty dish **2** *pl* : PROVISIONS, FOOD

vi·at·i·cal settlement \vī-ˈa-ti-kəl-\ *n* [prob. fr. *viaticum*] (1991) : an agreement by which the owner of a life insurance policy that covers a person (as the owner) who has a catastrophic or life-threatening illness receives compensation for less than the expected death benefit of the policy in return for a turning over (as by sale or bequest) of the death benefit or ownership of the policy to the other party (as a company specializing in such transfers) — called also *viatical*

vi·at·i·cum \vī-ˈa-ti-kəm, vē-\ *n, pl* **-cums** *or* **-ca** \-kə\ [L — more at VOYAGE] (1562) **1 :** the Christian Eucharist given to a person in danger of death **2 a :** an allowance (as of transportation or supplies and money) for traveling expenses **b :** provisions for a journey

vibe \ˈvīb\ *n* (1967) : VIBRATION 4 ⟨seems to be in on every conversation, every deal, every ~ that is winging through the room —Albert Goldman⟩ — usu. used in pl. ⟨got bad ~*s* from him⟩

vibes \ˈvībz\ *n pl* (1940) : VIBRAPHONE — **vib·ist** \ˈvī-bist\ *n*

vi·bra·harp \ˈvī-brə-ˌhärp\ *n* [fr. *Vibra-Harp,* a trademark] (1930) : VIBRAPHONE — **vi·bra·harp·ist** \-ˌhär-pist\ *n*

vi·brance \ˈvī-brən(t)s\ *n* (ca. 1900) : VIBRANCY

vi·bran·cy \ˈvī-brən(t)-sē\ *n* (ca. 1890) : the quality or state of being vibrant

vi·brant \-brənt\ *adj* (1616) **1 a (1) :** oscillating or pulsating rapidly **(2) :** pulsating with life, vigor, or activity ⟨a ~ personality⟩ **b (1)**

: readily set in vibration (2) : RESPONSIVE, SENSITIVE **2** : sounding as a result of vibration : RESONANT ⟨a ~ voice⟩ **3** : BRIGHT 4 ⟨a ~ orange⟩ — **vi·brant·ly** *adv*

vi·bra·phone \ˈvī-brə-ˌfōn\ *n* [L *vibrare* + ISV *-phone*] (1926) : a percussion instrument resembling the xylophone but having metal bars and motor-driven resonators for sustaining the tone and producing a vibrato — **vi·bra·phon·ist** \-ˌfō-nist\ *n*

vi·brate \ˈvī-ˌbrāt, *esp Brit* vī-ˈ\ *vb* **vi·brat·ed; vi·brat·ing** [L *vibratus,* pp. of *vibrare* to brandish, wave, rock — more at WIPE] *vt* (1616) **1** : to swing or move to and fro **2** : to emit with or as if with a vibratory motion **3** : to mark or measure by oscillation ⟨a pendulum *vibrating* seconds⟩ **4** : to set in vibration ~ *vi* **1 a** : to move to and fro or from side to side : OSCILLATE **b** : FLUCTUATE, VACILLATE ⟨~ between two choices⟩ **2** : to have an effect as or as if of vibration ⟨music, when soft voices die, ~*s* in the memory —P. B. Shelley⟩ **3** : to be in a state of vibration : QUIVER **4** : to respond sympathetically : THRILL ⟨~ to the opportunity⟩ ***syn*** see SWING

vi·bra·tile \ˈvī-brə-tᵊl, -ˌtī(-ə)l\ *adj* (ca. 1826) **1** : characterized by vibration **2** : adapted to, used in, or capable of vibratory motion ⟨~ cilia⟩

vi·bra·tion \vī-ˈbrā-shən\ *n* (1635) **1 a** : a periodic motion of the particles of an elastic body or medium in alternately opposite directions from the position of equilibrium when that equilibrium has been disturbed (as when a stretched cord produces musical tones or molecules in the air transmit sounds to the ear) **b** : the action of vibrating : the state of being vibrated or in vibratory motion: as (1) : OSCILLATION (2) : a quivering or trembling motion : QUIVER **2** : an instance of vibration **3** : vacillation in opinion or action : WAVERING **4 a** : a characteristic emanation, aura, or spirit that infuses or vitalizes someone or something and that can be instinctively sensed or experienced — often used in pl. **b** : a distinctive usu. emotional atmosphere capable of being sensed — usu. used in pl. — **vi·bra·tion·al** \-shnəl, -shə-nᵊl\ *adj* — **vi·bra·tion·less** \-shən-ləs\ *adj*

vi·bra·to \vi-ˈbrä-(ˌ)tō, vī-\ *n, pl* **-tos** [It, fr. pp. of *vibrare* to vibrate, fr. L] (ca. 1876) : a slightly tremulous effect imparted to vocal or instrumental tone for added warmth and expressiveness by slight and rapid variations in pitch — **vi·bra·to·less** \-ləs\ *adj*

vi·bra·tor \ˈvī-ˌbrā-tər\ *n* (1862) : one that vibrates or causes vibration: as **a** : a vibrating electrical apparatus used in massage or for sexual stimulation **b** : a vibrating device (as in an electric bell or buzzer)

vi·bra·to·ry \ˈvī-brə-ˌtȯr-ē\ *adj* (1728) **1** : consisting of, capable of, or causing vibration or oscillation **2** : characterized by vibration

vib·rio \ˈvi-brē-ˌō\ *n, pl* **-rios** [NL, *Vibrion-, Vibrio,* fr. L *vibrare* to wave] (ca. 1864) : any of a genus (*Vibrio*) of short rigid motile bacteria that are straight or curved rods and include pathogens esp. of gastrointestinal diseases (as cholera) — **vib·ri·on·ic** \ˌvi-brē-ˈä-nik\ *adj*

vib·ri·on \ˈvi-brē-ˌän\ *n* [NL *Vibrion-, Vibrio*] (1882) : VIBRIO; *also* : a motile bacterium

vib·ri·o·sis \ˌvi-brē-ˈō-səs\ *n, pl* **-o·ses** \-ˌsēz\ [NL, fr. *Vibrio*] (1950) : an infectious disease of sheep and cattle caused by a bacterium (*Campylobacter fetus* syn. *Vibrio fetus*) and marked by infertility and abortion; *also* : infection with or disease caused by a vibrio

vi·bris·sa \vī-ˈbri-sə, və-\ *n, pl* **vi·bris·sae** \vī-ˈbri-(ˌ)sē; və-ˈbri-(ˌ)sē, -ˌsī\ [ML, fr. L *vibrare*] (ca. 1693) **1** : one of the stiff hairs that are located esp. about the nostrils or on other parts of the face in many mammals and that often serve as tactile organs **2** : one of the bristly feathers near the mouth of many and esp. insectivorous birds that may help to prevent the escape of insects

vi·bur·num \vī-ˈbər-nəm\ *n* [NL, fr. L, a viburnum] (ca. 1731) : any of a genus (*Viburnum*) of widely distributed shrubs or small trees of the honeysuckle family with simple leaves and white or sometimes pink cymose flowers

vic *abbr* vicinity

Vic *abbr* Victoria

vic·ar \ˈvi-kər\ *n* [ME, fr. AF, fr. L *vicarius,* fr. *vicarius* vicarious] (14c) **1** : one serving as a substitute or agent; *specif* : an administrative deputy **2** : an ecclesiastical agent: as **a** : a Church of England incumbent receiving a stipend but not the tithes of a parish **b** : a member of the Episcopal clergy or laity who has charge of a mission or chapel **c** : a member of the clergy who exercises a broad pastoral responsibility as the representative of a prelate — **vic·ar·ship** \-ˌship\ *n*

vic·ar·age \ˈvi-k(ə-)rij\ *n* (15c) **1** : the benefice of a vicar **2** : the house of a vicar **3** : VICARIATE 1

vicar apostolic *n, pl* **vicars apostolic** (1766) : a Roman Catholic titular bishop who administers a territory not organized as a diocese

vic·ar·ate \ˈvi-kə-rət, -ˌrāt\ *n* (1883) : VICARIATE

vicar–general *n, pl* **vicars–general** (15c) : an administrative deputy of a Roman Catholic or Anglican bishop or of the head of a religious order

vi·car·i·al \vī-ˈker-ē-əl, və-\ *adj* [L *vicarius*] (1617) **1** : VICARIOUS 1 **2** : of or relating to a vicar

vi·car·i·ance \-ē-ən(t)s\ *n* (1957) : fragmentation of the environment (as by splitting of a tectonic plate) in contrast to dispersal as a factor in promoting biological evolution by division of large populations into isolated subpopulations — called also *vicariance biogeography*

vi·car·i·ant \-ē-ənt\ *adj* [trans. of G *vikarirend,* prp. of *vikarieren* to act as a substitute, fr. *Vikar* representative, proxy, fr. MHG *vicar,* fr. L *vicarius* substitute] (1952) : of, relating to, or being the process of vicariance or organisms that evolved through this process ⟨the possible ~ origin of the Antillean arthropod fauna⟩ — **vicariant** *n*

vi·car·i·ate \-ē-ət\ *n* [ML *vicariatus,* fr. L *vicarius* vicar] (1610) **1** : the office, jurisdiction, or tenure of a vicar **2** : the office or district of a governmental administrative deputy

vi·car·i·ous \vī-ˈker-ē-əs, və-\ *adj* [L *vicarius,* fr. *vicis* change, alternation, stead — more at WEEK] (1637) **1 a** : serving instead of someone or something else **b** : that has been delegated ⟨~ authority⟩ **2** : performed or suffered by one person as a substitute for another or to the benefit or advantage of another : SUBSTITUTIONARY ⟨a ~ sacrifice⟩ **3** : experienced or realized through imaginative or sympathetic participation in the experience of another **4** : occurring in an unexpected or abnormal part of the body instead of the usual one ⟨~ menstruation manifested by bleeding from the nose⟩ — **vi·car·i·ous·ly** *adv* — **vi·car·i·ous·ness** *n*

Vicar of Christ (15c) : POPE 1

[1]**vice** \ˈvīs\ *n* [ME, fr. AF, fr. L *vitium* fault, vice] (14c) **1 a** : moral depravity or corruption : WICKEDNESS **b** : a moral fault or failing **c** : a habitual and usu. trivial defect or shortcoming : FOIBLE ⟨suffered from the ~ of curiosity⟩ **2** : BLEMISH, DEFECT **3** : a physical imperfection, deformity, or taint **4 a** *often cap* : a character representing one of the vices in an English morality play **b** : BUFFOON, JESTER **5** : an abnormal behavior pattern in a domestic animal detrimental to its health or usefulness **6** : sexual immorality; *esp* : PROSTITUTION ***syn*** see FAULT, OFFENSE

[2]**vice** *chiefly Brit var of* VISE

[3]**vice** \ˈvīs *also* ˈvī-sē\ *prep* [L, abl. of *vicis* change, alternation, stead — more at WEEK] (1770) : in the place of ⟨I will preside, ~ the absent chairman⟩; *also* : rather than

vice- \ˈvīs, ˌvīs\ *prefix* [ME *vis-, vice-,* fr. AF, fr. LL *vice-,* fr. L *vice,* abl. of *vicis*] : one that takes the place of ⟨*vice*-chancellor⟩

vice admiral *n* [MF *visamiral,* fr. *vis-* vice- + *amiral* admiral] (15c) : a commissioned officer in the navy or coast guard who ranks above a rear admiral and whose insignia is three stars

vice–chan·cel·lor \ˈvīs-ˈchan(t)-s(ə-)lər, ˌvīs-\ *n* (15c) **1** : an officer ranking next below a chancellor and serving as deputy to the chancellor **2** : chief administrative officer in a British university **3** : a judge appointed to act for or to assist a chancellor

vice–con·sul \-ˈkän(t)-səl\ *n* (1559) : a consular officer subordinate to a consul general or to a consul

vice·ge·ren·cy \-ˈjir-ən(t)-sē\ *n, pl* **-cies** (1596) : the office or jurisdiction of a vicegerent

vice·ge·rent \-ˈjir-ənt\ *n* [ML *vicegerent-, vicegerens,* fr. LL *vice-* + L *gerent-, gerens,* prp. of *gerere* to carry, carry on] (1536) : an administrative deputy of a king or magistrate

vi·cen·ni·al \vī-ˈse-nē-əl\ *adj* [LL *vicennium* period of 20 years, fr. L *vicies* 20 times + *annus* year; akin to L *viginti* twenty — more at VIGESIMAL, ANNUAL] (ca. 1859) : occurring once every 20 years

vice presidency *n* (1804) : the office of vice president

vice president *n* (1540) **1** : an officer next in rank to a president and usu. empowered to serve as president in that officer's absence or disability **2** : any of several officers serving as a president's deputies in charge of particular locations or functions — **vice presidential** *adj*

vice·re·gal \ˈvīs-ˈrē-gəl, ˌvīs-\ *adj* (1806) : of or relating to a viceroy or viceroyalty — **vice·re·gal·ly** \-gə-lē\ *adv*

vice–re·gent \-ˈrē-jənt\ *n* (1556) : a regent's deputy

vice·reine \ˈvīs-ˌrān\ *n* [F, fr. *vice-* + *reine* queen, fr. OF, fr. L *regina,* fem. of *reg-, rex* king — more at ROYAL] (1823) **1** : the wife of a viceroy **2** : a woman who is a viceroy

vice·roy \ˈvīs-ˌrȯi\ *n* [MF *vice-roi,* fr. *vice-* + *roi* king, fr. OF *rei, roi,* fr. L *reg-, rex*] (1524) **1** : the governor of a country or province who rules as the representative of a king or sovereign **2** : a showy No. American nymphalid butterfly (*Limenitis archippus*) closely mimicking the monarch in coloration but smaller

vice·roy·al·ty \ˈvīs-ˌrȯi(-ə)l-tē, ˌvīs-ˈ\ *n* (1703) : the office, authority, or term of service of a viceroy; *also* : the territory or jurisdiction of a viceroy

vice·roy·ship \ˈvīs-ˌrȯi-ˌship\ *n* (1609) : VICEROYALTY

vice squad *n* (1905) : a police squad charged with enforcement of laws concerning gambling, pornography, prostitution, and the illegal use of liquor and narcotics

vice ver·sa \ˌvī-si-ˈvər-sə, ˈvīs-ˈvər-\ *adv* [L] (1601) : with the order changed : with the relations reversed : CONVERSELY

vi·chys·soise \ˌvi-shē-ˈswäz, ˌvē-\ *n* [F, fr. fem. of *vichyssois* of Vichy, fr. *Vichy,* France] (1939) : a soup typically made of pureed leeks or onions and potatoes, cream, and chicken stock and usu. served cold

Vi·chy water \ˈvi-shē-\ *n* (ca. 1858) : a natural sparkling mineral water from Vichy, France; *also* : an imitation of or substitute for this

vic·i·nage \ˈvi-sə-nij, ˈvis-nij\ *n* [ME *vesinage,* fr. AF *veisinage,* fr. neighboring, fr. VL **vecinus,* alter. of L *vicinus*] (14c) : a neighboring or surrounding district : VICINITY

vic·i·nal \ˈvi-sə-nəl, ˈvis-nəl\ *adj* [L *vicinalis,* fr. *vicinus* neighbor, fr. *vicinus,* adj., neighboring] (ca. 1623) **1** : of or relating to a limited district : LOCAL **2** : of, relating to, or substituted in adjacent sites in a molecule ⟨a ~ disulfide group⟩

vi·cin·i·ty \və-ˈsi-nə-tē\ *n, pl* **-ties** [MF *vicinité,* fr. L *vicinitat-, vicinitas,* fr. *vicinus* neighboring, fr. *vicus* row of houses, village; akin to Goth *weihs* village, OCS *vĭsĭ,* Gk *oikos, oikia* house] (1560) **1** : the quality or state of being near : PROXIMITY **2** : a surrounding area or district : NEIGHBORHOOD **3** : NEIGHBORHOOD 3b

vi·cious \ˈvi-shəs\ *adj* [ME, fr. AF *vicios,* fr. L *vitiosus* full of faults, corrupt, fr. *vitium* vice] (14c) **1** : having the nature or quality of vice or immorality : DEPRAVED **2** : DEFECTIVE, FAULTY; *also* : INVALID **3** : IMPURE, NOXIOUS **4 a** : dangerously aggressive : SAVAGE ⟨a ~ dog⟩ **b** : marked by violence or ferocity : FIERCE ⟨a ~ fight⟩ **5** : MALICIOUS, SPITEFUL ⟨~ gossip⟩ **6** : worsened by internal causes that reciprocally augment each other ⟨a ~ wage-price spiral⟩ — **vi·cious·ly** *adv* — **vi·cious·ness** *n*

syn VICIOUS, VILLAINOUS, INIQUITOUS, NEFARIOUS, CORRUPT, DEGENERATE mean highly reprehensible or offensive in character, nature, or conduct. VICIOUS may directly oppose *virtuous* in implying moral depravity, or may connote malignancy, cruelty, or destructive violence ⟨a *vicious* gangster⟩. VILLAINOUS applies to any evil, depraved, or vile conduct or characteristic ⟨a *villainous* assault⟩. INIQUITOUS implies absence of all signs of justice or fairness ⟨an *iniquitous* system of taxation⟩. NEFARIOUS suggests flagrant breaching of time-honored laws and traditions of conduct ⟨the *nefarious* rackets of organized crime⟩. CORRUPT stresses a loss of moral integrity or probity causing betrayal of principle or sworn obligations ⟨city hall was rife with *corrupt* politicians⟩. DEGENERATE suggests having sunk to an esp. vicious or enervated condition ⟨a *degenerate* regime propped up by foreign powers⟩.

vicious circle *n* (ca. 1792) **1 :** an argument or definition that begs the question **2 :** a chain of events in which the response to one difficulty creates a new problem that aggravates the original difficulty — called also *vicious cycle*

vi·cis·si·tude \və-ˈsi-sə-ˌtüd, vī-, -ˌtyüd\ *n* [MF, fr. L *vicissitudo,* fr. *vicissim* in turn, fr. *vicis* change, alternation — more at WEEK] (ca. 1576) **1 a :** the quality or state of being changeable **:** MUTABILITY **b :** natural change or mutation visible in nature or in human affairs **2 a :** a favorable or unfavorable event or situation that occurs by chance **:** a fluctuation of state or condition ⟨the ~*s* of daily life⟩ **b :** a difficulty or hardship attendant on a way of life, a career, or a course of action and usu. beyond one's control **c :** alternating change **:** SUCCESSION

vi·cis·si·tu·di·nous \və-ˌsi-sə-ˈtüd-nəs, (ˌ)vī-, -ˈtyüd-; -ˈtü-də-nəs, -ˈtyü-\ *adj* [L *vicissitudin-, vicissitudo*] (ca. 1846) **:** marked by or filled with vicissitudes

vic·tim \ˈvik-təm\ *n* [L *victima;* perh. akin to OHG *wīh* holy] (15c) **1 :** a living being sacrificed to a deity or in the performance of a religious rite **2 :** one that is acted on and usu. adversely affected by a force or agent ⟨the schools are ~*s* of the social system⟩: as **a** (1) **:** one that is injured, destroyed, or sacrificed under any of various conditions ⟨a ~ of cancer⟩ ⟨a ~ of the auto crash⟩ ⟨a murder ~⟩ (2) **:** one that is subjected to oppression, hardship, or mistreatment ⟨a frequent ~ of political attacks⟩ **b :** one that is tricked or duped ⟨a con man's ~⟩ — **vic·tim·hood** \-ˌhu̇d\ *n*

vic·tim·ise *Brit var of* VICTIMIZE

vic·tim·ize \ˈvik-tə-ˌmīz\ *vt* **-ized; -iz·ing** (1830) **1 :** to make a victim of **2 :** to subject to deception or fraud **:** CHEAT — **vic·tim·i·za·tion** \ˌvik-tə-mə-ˈzā-shən\ *n* — **vic·tim·iz·er** \ˈvik-tə-ˌmī-zər\ *n*

vic·tim·less \ˈvik-təm-ləs\ *adj* (1938) **:** having no victim **:** not of a nature that may produce a complainant ⟨a ~ crime⟩

vic·tim·ol·o·gy \ˌvik-tə-ˈmä-lə-jē\ *n* (1950) **1 :** the study of the ways in which the behavior of crime victims may have led to or contributed to their victimization **2 :** the claim that the problems of a person or group are the result of victimization — **vic·tim·ol·o·gist** \-jist\ *n*

vic·tor \ˈvik-tər\ *n* [ME, fr. AF, fr. L, fr. *vincere* to conquer, win; akin to OE *wīgan* to fight, Lith *veikti* to be active] (14c) **:** one that defeats an enemy or opponent **:** WINNER — **victor** *adj*

Victor (1942) — a communications code word for the letter *v*

vic·to·ria \vik-ˈtȯr-ē-ə\ *n* [Queen *Victoria*] (ca. 1864) **:** a low four-wheeled pleasure carriage for two with a folding top and a raised seat in front for the driver

Victoria Cross *n* (1856) **:** a bronze Maltese cross awarded to members of the British armed services for acts of remarkable valor

Victoria Day *n* [Queen *Victoria*] (1901) **1 :** formerly May 24 and now the Monday preceding May 25 observed in Canada as a legal holiday **2 :** COMMONWEALTH DAY

[1]**Vic·to·ri·an** \vik-ˈtȯr-ē-ən\ *adj* (1839) **1 :** of, relating to, or characteristic of the reign of Queen Victoria of England or the art, letters, or tastes of her time **2 :** typical of the moral standards, attitudes, or conduct of the age of Victoria esp. when considered stuffy, prudish, or hypocritical

[2]**Victorian** *n* (1876) **1 :** a person living during Queen Victoria's reign; *esp* **:** a representative figure of that time **2 :** a typically large and ornate house built during Queen Victoria's reign

Vic·to·ri·ana \(ˌ)vik-ˌtȯr-ē-ˈa-nə, -ˈä-, -ˈā-\ *n* [Queen *Victoria* + E *-ana*] (1940) **:** materials concerning or characteristic of the Victorian age; *also* **:** a collection of such materials

Vic·to·ri·an·ism \vik-ˈtȯr-ē-ə-ˌni-zəm\ *n* (1905) **1 :** a typical instance or product of Victorian expression, taste, or conduct **2 :** the quality or state of being Victorian esp. in taste or conduct

vic·to·ri·ous \vik-ˈtȯr-ē-əs\ *adj* (14c) **1 a :** having won a victory ⟨a ~ army⟩ **b :** of, relating to, or characteristic of victory ⟨~ exuberance⟩ **2 :** evincing moral harmony or a sense of fulfillment **:** FULFILLED — **vic·to·ri·ous·ly** *adv* — **vic·to·ri·ous·ness** *n*

vic·to·ry \ˈvik-t(ə-)rē\ *n, pl* **-ries** [ME *victorie,* fr. AF, fr. L *victoria,* fr. *victor*] (14c) **1 :** the overcoming of an enemy or antagonist **2 :** achievement of mastery or success in a struggle or endeavor against odds or difficulties

Vic·tro·la \vik-ˈtrō-lə\ *trademark* — used for a phonograph

[1]**vict·ual** \ˈvi-tᵊl\ *n* [ME *vitaille, victuayle,* fr. AF, fr. LL *victualia,* pl., provisions, victuals, fr. neut. pl. of *victualis* of nourishment, fr. L *victus* nourishment, way of living, fr. *vivere* to live — more at QUICK] (15c) **1 :** food usable by people **2** *pl* **:** supplies of food **:** PROVISIONS

[2]**victual** *vb* **-ualed** *or* **-ualled; -ual·ing** *or* **-ual·ling** *vt* (1558) **:** to supply with food ~ *vi* **1 :** EAT **2 :** to lay in provisions

vict·ual·ler *or* **vict·ual·er** \ˈvi-tᵊl-ər\ *n* (1514) **1 :** one that provisions an army, a navy, or a ship with food **2 :** the keeper of a restaurant or tavern **3 :** an army or navy provision ship

vi·cu·ña *or* **vi·cu·na** \vi-ˈkün-yə, vī-; vī-ˈkü-nə, və-, -ˈkyü-\ *n* [Sp *vicuña,* fr. Quechua *wik'uña*] (1604) **1 :** a wild ruminant (*Vicugna vicugna* syn. *Lama vicugna*) of the Andes from Peru to Argentina that is related to the llama and alpaca **2 a :** the wool from the vicuña's fine lustrous undercoat **b :** a fabric made of vicuña wool; *also* **:** a sheep's wool imitation of this

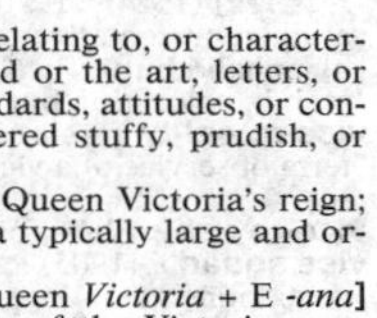
vicuña 1

vid \ˈvid\ *n* (1979) **:** VIDEO 2a, b

Vi·da·lia \və-ˈdāl-yə\ *certification mark* — used for certain mild sweet yellow onions grown in Georgia

vi·de \ˈvī-dē, ˈvē-ˌdā\ *vb imper* [L, fr. *vidēre* to see — more at WIT] (1552) **:** SEE — used to direct a reader to another item

vi·de·li·cet \və-ˈde-lə-ˌset, vī-; vi-ˈdā-li-ˌket\ *adv* [ME, fr. L, fr. *vidēre* to see + *licet* it is permitted, fr. *licēre* to be permitted] (15c) **:** that is to say **:** NAMELY

[1]**vid·eo** \ˈvi-dē-ˌō\ *n* [L *vidēre* to see + *-o* (as in *audio*)] (1937) **1 :** TELEVISION; *also* **:** the visual portion of television **2 :** VIDEOTAPE: as **a :** a recording of a motion picture or television program for playing through a television set **b :** a videotaped performance of a song often featuring an interpretation of the lyrics through visual images **3 :** a recording similar to a videotape but stored in digital form (as on an optical disk or a computer's hard drive)

[2]**video** *adj* (1935) **1 :** being, relating to, or used in the transmission or reception of the television image ⟨a ~ channel⟩ — compare AUDIO **2 :** being, relating to, or involving images on a television screen or computer display ⟨a ~ terminal⟩

video camera *n* (1949) **:** a camera that records video and usu. audio; *esp* **:** CAMCORDER

video card *n* (1982) **:** a circuit board in a computer system designed to generate output for the system's video display screen

vid·eo·cas·sette \ˌvi-dē-ō-kə-ˈset, -ka-\ *n* (1970) **1 :** a case containing videotape for use with a VCR **2 :** a recording on a videocassette

videocassette recorder *n* (1976) **:** VCR

vid·eo·con·fer·enc·ing \-ˈkän-f(ə-)rən(t)-siŋ, -fərn(t)-\ *n* (1977) **:** the holding of a conference among people at remote locations by means of transmitted audio and video signals — **vid·eo·con·fer·ence** \-ˈkän-f(ə-)rən(t)s, -fərn(t)s\ *n*

vid·eo·disc *or* **vid·eo·disk** \ˈvi-dē-ō-ˌdisk\ *n* (1967) **1 :** a disc similar in appearance and use to a phonograph record on which programs have been recorded for playback on a television set; *also* **:** OPTICAL DISK **2 :** a recording (as of a movie) on a videodisc

video game *n* (1973) **:** an electronic game played by means of images on a video screen and often emphasizing fast action

vid·e·o·gen·ic \ˌvi-dē-ō-ˈje-nik\ *adj* (1948) **:** TELEGENIC

vid·e·og·ra·phy \ˌvi-dē-ˈä-grə-fē\ *n* (1972) **:** the practice or art of recording images with a video camera — **vid·e·og·ra·pher** \-fər\ *n*

vid·eo·land \-ˌland\ *n* (1967) **:** television as a medium or industry

vid·eo·phile \ˈvi-dē-ə-ˌfī(-ə)l\ *n* (1966) **:** a person fond of video; *esp* **:** one interested in video equipment or in producing videos

vid·eo·phone \ˈvi-dē-ə-ˌfōn\ *n* (ca. 1950) **:** a telephone that can transmit video as well as audio signals so that users can see each other

[1]**vid·eo·tape** \ˈvi-dē-ō-ˌtāp\ *n* (1953) **:** a recording of visual images and sound (as of a television production) made on magnetic tape; *also* **:** the magnetic tape used for such a recording

[2]**videotape** *vt* (1958) **:** to make a videotape of ⟨~ a show⟩

videotape recorder *n* (1953) **:** a device for recording and playing back videotapes — called also *video recorder*

vid·eo·tex \-ˌteks\ *also* **vid·eo·text** \-ˌtekst\ *n* [[2]*video* + *-tex* (alter. of *text*)] (1978) **:** an electronic data retrieval system in which usu. textual information is transmitted via telephone or cable-television lines and displayed on a television set or video display terminal; *esp* **:** such a system that is interactive — compare TELETEXT

video vé·ri·té \-ˌver-ə-ˈtā\ *n* [*cinema verité*] (1969) **:** the filming or videotaping of a television program (as a documentary) so as to convey candid realism

vidette *var of* VEDETTE

vid·icon \ˈvi-di-ˌkän\ *n, often cap* [[2]*vid*eo + *icon*oscope] (1950) **:** a camera tube using the principle of photoconductivity

vie \ˈvī\ *vb* **vied; vy·ing** \ˈvī-iŋ\ [ME, short for *envien,* fr. AF *envier* to invite, call on, challenge, fr. L *invitare* to invite] *vt* (15c) *archaic* **:** WAGER, HAZARD; *also* **:** to exchange in rivalry **:** MATCH ~ *vi* **:** to strive for superiority **:** CONTEND, COMPETE — **vi·er** \ˈvī(-ə)r\ *n*

Vi·en·na sausage \vē-ˈe-nə-\ *n* [*Vienna,* Austria] (1873) **:** a short slender frankfurter

Viet·cong \vē-ˈet-ˈkäŋ, vyet-, ˌvē-ət-, vēt-, -ˈkȯŋ\ *n, pl* **Vietcong** [Vietnamese *Việt-cộng*] (1957) **:** a guerrilla member of the Vietnamese Communist movement

Viet·minh \-ˈmin\ *n, pl* **Vietminh** [Vietnamese *Việt-Minh,* short for *Việt-Nam Độc-Lập Đồng-Minh* League for the Independence of Vietnam] (1945) **:** an adherent of the Vietnamese Communist movement from 1941 to 1951

Viet·nam·ese \vē-ˌet-nə-ˈmēz, ˌvyet-, ˌvē-ət-, ˌvēt-, -na-, -nä-, -ˈmēs\ *n, pl* **Vietnamese** (1947) **1 :** a native or inhabitant of Vietnam **2 :** the language of the largest group in Vietnam and the official language of the country — **Vietnamese** *adj*

Vietnamese potbellied pig *n* (1985) **:** POTBELLIED PIG

[1]**view** \ˈvyü\ *n* [ME *vewe, vyewe,* fr. AF, fr. fem. of *veu, viewe,* pp. of *veer* to see, fr. L *vidēre* — more at WIT] (14c) **1 :** extent or range of vision **:** SIGHT ⟨tried to keep the ship in ~⟩ ⟨sat high in the bleachers to get a good ~⟩ **2 :** the act of seeing or examining **:** INSPECTION; *also* **:** SURVEY ⟨a ~ of English literature⟩ **3 a :** a mode or manner of looking at or regarding something **b :** an opinion or judgment colored by the feeling or bias of its holder ⟨in my ~ the plan will fail⟩ **4 :** SCENE, PROSPECT ⟨the lovely ~ from the balcony⟩ **5 :** the foreseeable future ⟨no hope in ~⟩ **6 :** a pictorial representation ***syn*** see OPINION — **in view of :** in regard to **:** in consideration of — **on view :** open to public inspection **:** on exhibition — **with a view to :** with the object of ⟨studied hard *with a view to* getting an A⟩

[2]**view** *vt* (1523) **1 :** to look at attentively **:** SCRUTINIZE, OBSERVE ⟨~ an exhibit⟩ **2 a :** SEE, WATCH **b :** to look on in a particular light **:** REGARD ⟨doesn't ~ himself as a rebel⟩ **3 :** to survey or examine mentally **:** CONSIDER ⟨~ all sides of a question⟩ — **view·able** \-ə-bəl\ *adj*

view·book \ˈvyü-ˌbu̇k\ *n* (1956) **:** a promotional booklet with pictures that is published by a college or university and used esp. for recruiting students; *also* **:** an online version of such a booklet

view·data \ˈvyü-ˌdā-tə *also* -ˌda-\ *n* (1975) **:** a videotex system usu. employing telephone lines

view·er \ˈvyü-ər\ *n* (15c) **:** one that views: as **a :** a person legally appointed to inspect and report on property **b :** an optical device used in viewing **c :** a person who watches television

view·er·ship \-ˌship\ *n* (1954) **:** a television audience esp. with respect to size or makeup

view·find·er \ˈvyü-ˌfīn-dər\ *n* (1889) **:** a device on a camera for showing the area of the subject to be included in the picture

view hal·loo \ˌvyü-hə-ˈlü\ *interj* (1761) — used in fox hunting on seeing a fox break cover

view·ing \ˈvyü-iŋ\ *n* (1535) **:** an act of seeing, watching, or taking a look; *esp* **:** an instance or the practice of watching television

view·less \ˈvyü-ləs\ *adj* (1605) **1 :** not perceivable **:** INVISIBLE **2 :** affording no view **3 :** expressing no views — **view·less·ly** *adv*

view·point \-ˌpȯint\ *n* (1855) **:** POINT OF VIEW, STANDPOINT

view·shed \ˈvyü-ˌshed\ *n* [*view* + *-shed* (as in *watershed*)] (1981) **:** the natural environment that is visible from one or more viewing points

viewy \ˈvyü-ē\ *adj* (1848) **1 :** possessing visionary, impractical, or fantastic views **2 :** spectacular or arresting in appearance **:** SHOWY

vig \ˈvig\ *n* (1968) **:** VIGORISH

vi·ga \'vē-gə\ *n* [Sp, beam, rafter] (1844) **:** one of the heavy rafters and esp. a log supporting the roof in American Indian and Spanish architecture of the Southwest

vi·ges·i·mal \vī-'je-sə-məl\ *adj* [L *vicesimus, vigesimus* twentieth; akin to L *viginti* twenty, Gk *eikosi*] (ca. 1656) **:** based on the number 20

vig·il \'vi-jəl\ *n* [ME *vigile,* fr. AF, fr. LL & L; LL *vigilia* watch on the eve of a feast, fr. L, wakefulness, watch, fr. *vigil* awake, watchful; akin to L *vigēre* to be vigorous, *vegēre* to enliven — more at WAKE] (13c) **1 a :** a watch formerly kept on the night before a religious feast with prayer or other devotions **b :** the day before a religious feast observed as a day of spiritual preparation **c :** evening or nocturnal devotions or prayers — usu. used in pl. **2 :** the act of keeping awake at times when sleep is customary; *also* **:** a period of wakefulness **3 :** an act or period of watching or surveillance **:** WATCH ⟨kept ~ at her bedside⟩

vig·i·lance \'vi-jə-lən(t)s\ *n* (1533) **:** the quality or state of being vigilant

vigilance committee *n* (1835) **:** a committee of vigilantes

vig·i·lant \'vi-jə-lənt\ *adj* [ME (Sc), fr. L *vigilant-, vigilans,* fr. prp. of *vigilare* to keep watch, stay awake, fr. *vigil* awake] (15c) **:** alertly watchful esp. to avoid danger ***syn*** see WATCHFUL — **vig·i·lant·ly** *adv*

vig·i·lan·te \ˌvi-jə-'lan-tē\ *n* [Sp, watchman, guard, fr. *vigilante* vigilant, fr. L *vigilant-, vigilans*] (1856) **:** a member of a volunteer committee organized to suppress and punish crime summarily (as when the processes of law are viewed as inadequate); *broadly* **:** a self-appointed doer of justice — **vig·i·lan·tism** \-'lan-ˌti-zəm\ *n*

vigil light *n* (ca. 1931) **:** a candle lighted devotionally (as in a Roman Catholic church) before a shrine or image — called also *vigil candle*

vi·gin·til·lion \ˌvī-ˌjin-'til-yən\ *n, often attrib* [L *viginti* twenty + E *-illion* (as in *million*) — more at VIGESIMAL] (1857) — see NUMBER table

vi·gne·ron \ˌvēn-yə-'rōn\ *n* [ME (Sc), fr. MF, fr. OF *vineron,* fr. *vine, vigne* vine, vineyard] (15c) **:** WINEGROWER

[1]**vi·gnette** \vin-'yet, vēn-\ *n* [F, fr. MF *vignete,* fr. dim. of *vigne* vine — more at VINE] (1611) **1 :** a running ornament (as of vine leaves, tendrils, and grapes) put on or just before a title page or at the beginning or end of a chapter; *also* **:** a small decorative design or picture so placed **2 a :** a picture (as an engraving or photograph) that shades off gradually into the surrounding paper **b :** the pictorial part of a postage stamp design as distinguished from the frame and lettering **3 a :** a short descriptive literary sketch **b :** a brief incident or scene (as in a play or movie) — **vi·gnett·ist** \-'ye-tist\ *n*

[2]**vignette** *vt* **vi·gnett·ed; vi·gnett·ing** (1853) **1 :** to finish (as a photograph) like a vignette **2 :** to describe briefly — **vi·gnett·er** *n*

vig·or \'vi-gər\ *n* [ME *vigour,* fr. AF, fr. L *vigor,* fr. *vigēre* to be vigorous] (14c) **1 :** active bodily or mental strength or force **2 :** active healthy well-balanced growth esp. of plants **3 :** intensity of action or effect **:** FORCE **4 :** effective legal status

vig·o·rish \'vi-gə-rish\ *n* [perh. fr. Ukrainian *vygrash* or Russ *vyigrysh* winnings, profit] (1912) **1 :** a charge taken (as by a bookie or a gambling house) on bets; *also* **:** the degree of such a charge ⟨a ~ of five percent⟩ **2 :** interest paid to a moneylender

vi·go·ro·so \ˌvi-gə-'rō-(ˌ)sō, ˌvē-, -(ˌ)zō\ *adj or adv* [It, lit., vigorous, fr. MF *vigorous*] (ca. 1724) **:** energetic in style — used as a direction in music

vig·or·ous \'vi-g(ə-)rəs\ *adj* [ME *vigorous, vigrous,* fr. AF, fr. *vigour*] (14c) **1 :** possessing vigor **:** full of physical or mental strength or active force **:** STRONG ⟨a ~ youth⟩ ⟨a ~ plant⟩ **2 :** done with vigor **:** carried out forcefully and energetically ⟨~ exercises⟩ — **vig·or·ous·ly** *adv* — **vig·or·ous·ness** *n*

syn VIGOROUS, ENERGETIC, STRENUOUS, LUSTY, NERVOUS mean having or showing great vitality and force. VIGOROUS further implies showing no signs of depletion or diminishing of freshness or robustness ⟨as *vigorous* as a youth half his age⟩. ENERGETIC suggests a capacity for intense activity ⟨an *energetic* campaigner⟩. STRENUOUS suggests a preference for coping with the arduous or the challenging ⟨the *strenuous* life on an oil rig⟩. LUSTY implies exuberant energy and capacity for enjoyment ⟨a *lusty* appetite for life⟩. NERVOUS suggests esp. the forcibleness and sustained effectiveness resulting from mental vigor ⟨full of *nervous* energy⟩.

vig·our \'vi-gər\ *chiefly Brit var of* VIGOR

Vi·king \'vī-kiŋ\ *n* [ON *vīkingr*] (1807) **1 a :** one of the pirate Norsemen plundering the coasts of Europe in the 8th to 10th centuries **b** *not cap* **:** SEA ROVER **2 :** SCANDINAVIAN

vile \'vī(-ə)l\ *adj* **vil·er** \'vī-lər\; **vil·est** \-ləst\ [ME, fr. AF *vil,* fr. L *vilis*] (14c) **1 a :** morally despicable or abhorrent ⟨nothing is so ~ as intellectual dishonesty⟩ **b :** physically repulsive **:** FOUL ⟨a ~ slum⟩ **2 :** of little worth or account **:** COMMON; *also* **:** MEAN **3 :** tending to degrade ⟨~ employments⟩ **4 :** disgustingly or utterly bad **:** OBNOXIOUS, CONTEMPTIBLE ⟨~ weather⟩ ⟨had a ~ temper⟩ ***syn*** see BASE — **vile·ly** \'vī(-ə)l-lē\ *adv* — **vile·ness** *n*

vil·i·fi·ca·tion \ˌvi-lə-fə-'kā-shən\ *n* (1630) **1 :** the act of vilifying **:** ABUSE **2 :** an instance of vilifying **:** a defamatory utterance

vil·i·fy \'vi-lə-ˌfī\ *vt* **-fied; -fy·ing** [ME *vilifien,* fr. LL *vilificare,* fr. L *vilis* cheap, vile] (15c) **1 :** to lower in estimation or importance **2 :** to utter slanderous and abusive statements against **:** DEFAME ***syn*** see MALIGN — **vil·i·fi·er** \-ˌfī(-ə)r\ *n*

vil·i·pend \'vi-lə-ˌpend\ *vt* [ME, fr. MF *vilipender,* fr. ML *vilipendere,* fr. L *vilis* + *pendere* to weigh, estimate] (15c) **1 :** to hold or treat as of little worth or account **:** CONTEMN **2 :** to express a low opinion of **:** DISPARAGE

vill \'vil\ *n* [AF *vil, ville* farmstead, township] (1596) **1 :** a division of a hundred **:** TOWNSHIP **2 :** VILLAGE

vil·la \'vi-lə\ *n* [It, fr. L; akin to L *vicus* village — more at VICINITY] (1611) **1 :** a country estate **2 :** the rural or suburban residence of a wealthy person **3** *Brit* **:** a detached or semidetached urban residence with yard and garden space

vil·la·dom \'vi-lə-dəm\ *n* (1880) *Brit* **:** the world constituted by villas and their occupants

vil·lage \'vi-lij\ *n, often attrib* [ME, fr. AF *vilage,* fr. *vil* manorial estate, farmstead, fr. L *villa*] (14c) **1 a :** a settlement usu. larger than a hamlet and smaller than a town **b :** an incorporated minor municipality **2 :** the residents of a village **3 :** something (as an aggregation of burrows or nests) suggesting a village **4 :** a territorial area having the status of a village esp. as a unit of local government

vil·lag·er \'vi-li-jər\ *n* (1570) **:** an inhabitant of a village

vil·lage·ry \'vi-lij-rē, -li-jə-\ *n* (1596) **:** VILLAGES

vil·lain \'vi-lən\ *n* [ME *vilain, vilein,* fr. AF, fr. ML *villanus,* fr. L *villa*] (14c) **1 :** VILLEIN **2 :** an uncouth person **:** BOOR **3 :** a deliberate scoundrel or criminal **4 :** a character in a story or play who opposes the hero **5 :** one blamed for a particular evil or difficulty ⟨automation as the ~ in job . . . displacement —M. H. Goldberg⟩

vil·lain·ess \-lə-nəs\ *n* (1586) **:** a woman who is a villain

vil·lain·ous \-lə-nəs\ *adj* (14c) **1 a :** befitting a villain (as in evil or depraved character) ⟨a ~ attack⟩ **b :** being or having the character of a villain **:** DEPRAVED ⟨the ~ foe⟩ **2 :** highly objectionable **:** WRETCHED ***syn*** see VICIOUS — **vil·lain·ous·ly** *adv* — **vil·lain·ous·ness** *n*

vil·lainy \-lə-nē\ *n, pl* **-lain·ies** (13c) **1 :** villainous conduct; *also* **:** a villainous act **2 :** the quality or state of being villainous **:** DEPRAVITY

vil·la·nel·la \ˌvi-lə-'ne-lə\ *n, pl* **-nel·le** \-'ne-lē\ [It, fr. *villano* villein, peasant, fr. ML *villanus*] (1596) **1 :** a 16th century Italian part-song in an intentionally unsophisticated style **2 :** an instrumental piece in the style of a rustic dance

vil·la·nelle \ˌvi-lə-'nel\ *n* [F, fr. It *villanella*] (1877) **:** a chiefly French verse form running on two rhymes and consisting typically of five tercets and a quatrain in which the first and third lines of the opening tercet recur alternately at the end of the other tercets and together as the last two lines of the quatrain

vil·lat·ic \vi-'la-tik\ *adj* [L *villaticus,* fr. *villa*] (1671) **:** RURAL

-ville \ˌvil, *esp Southern* vəl\ *n suffix* [*-ville,* suffix occurring in names of towns, fr. F, fr. OF, fr. *ville* village] **:** place, category, or quality of a specified nature ⟨dulls*ville*⟩

vil·lein \'vi-lən, 'vi-ˌlān, vi-'lān\ *n* [ME *vilain, vilein* — more at VILLAIN] (14c) **1 :** a free common villager or village peasant of any of the feudal classes lower in rank than the thane **2 :** a free peasant of a feudal class higher in rank than a cotter **3 :** an unfree peasant standing as the slave of a feudal lord but free in legal relations with respect to all others

vil·len·age \'vi-lə-nij\ *n* [ME, fr. AF, fr. *vilein, vilain*] (14c) **1 :** tenure at the will of a feudal lord by villein services **2 :** the status of a villein

vil·li·form \'vi-lə-ˌfȯrm\ *adj* [ISV] (1846) **:** having the form or appearance of villi

vil·lous \'vi-ləs\ *adj* [ME, fibrous, fr. L *villosus* hairy, shaggy, fr. *villus*] (14c) **1 :** covered or furnished with villi ⟨a ~ adenoma⟩ **2 :** having soft long hairs ⟨leaves ~ underneath⟩ — compare PUBESCENT

vil·lus \'vi-ləs\ *n, pl* **vil·li** \'vi-ˌlī, -(ˌ)lē\ [NL, fr. L, tuft of shaggy hair — more at VELVET] (1728) **:** a small slender often vascular process: as **a :** one of the minute finger-shaped processes of the mucous membrane of the small intestine that serve in the absorption of nutriment **b :** one of the branching processes of the surface of the chorion of the developing embryo of most mammals that help to form the placenta

vim \'vim\ *n* [L, accus. of *vis* strength; akin to Gk *is* strength, Skt *vaya* meal, strength] (1843) **:** robust energy and enthusiasm

VIN *abbr* vehicle identification number

vi·na \'vē-nə\ *n* [Hindi *vīṇā,* fr. Skt] (1788) **:** a stringed instrument of India having usu. four strings on a long bamboo fingerboard with movable frets and a gourd resonator at each end

vi·na·ceous \vī-'nā-shəs, vi-\ *adj* [L *vinaceus* of wine, fr. *vinum* wine — more at WINE] (1688) **:** of the color of red wine

vin·ai·grette \ˌvi-ni-'gret\ *n* [F, fr. *vinaigre* vinegar] (1811) **1 :** a small ornamental box or bottle with perforated top used for holding an aromatic preparation (as smelling salts) **2 :** a sauce made typically of oil, vinegar, and seasonings and used esp. on salads, cold meats, or fish — called also *vinaigrette dressing*

vi·nal \'vī-ˌnal\ *n* [polyvinyl *al*cohol] (ca. 1939) **:** a synthetic textile fiber that is a long-chain polymer consisting largely of vinyl alcohol units

vin·blas·tine \(ˌ)vin-'blas-ˌtēn\ *n* [contr. of *vincaleukoblastine,* fr. *vinca* + *leukoblast* developing leukocyte, fr. *leuk-* + *-blast*] (1962) **:** an alkaloid $C_{46}H_{58}N_4O_9$ from the rosy periwinkle used esp. in the form of its sulfate to treat human neoplastic diseases (as Hodgkin's disease)

vin·ca \'viŋ-kə\ *n* [NL, short for L *vincapervinca* periwinkle] (1868) **:** [1]PERIWINKLE

Vin·cen·tian \vin-'sen(t)-shən\ *n* (1854) **1 :** a member of the Roman Catholic Congregation of the Mission founded by St. Vincent de Paul in Paris, France, in 1625 and devoted to missions and seminaries **2 :** a native or inhabitant of the island of St. Vincent — **Vincentian** *adj*

Vin·cent's angina \'vin(t)-sən(t)s-, (ˌ)vaⁿ-'säⁿz-\ *n* [Jean Hyacinthe *Vincent* †1950 Fr. bacteriologist] (ca. 1903) **:** Vincent's infection in which the ulceration has spread to surrounding tissues (as of the pharynx and tonsils) — called also *trench mouth*

Vincent's infection *n* (ca. 1922) **:** a progressive painful disease of the mouth that is marked esp. by dirty gray ulceration of the mucous membranes, bleeding of the gums, and a foul odor to the breath and that is associated with the presence of large numbers of a rod-shaped bacterium (*Fusobacterium fusiforme* syn. *F. nucleatum*) and a spirochete (*Treponema vincentii* syn. *Borrelia vincentii*) in the lesions — called also *trench mouth*

vin·ci·ble \'vin(t)-sə-bəl\ *adj* [L *vincibilis,* fr. *vincere* to conquer — more at VICTOR] (1548) **:** capable of being overcome or subdued

vin·cris·tine \(ˌ)vin-'kris-ˌtēn\ *n* [*vinca* + L *crista* crest + E [2]*-ine* — more at CREST] (ca. 1962) **:** an alkaloid $C_{46}H_{56}N_4O_{10}$ from the rosy periwinkle used esp. in the form of its sulfate to treat some human neoplastic diseases (as acute leukemia)

vin·cu·lum \'viŋ-kyə-ləm\ *n, pl* **-lums** *or* **-la** \-lə\ [L, fr. *vincire* to bind] (1661) **1 :** a unifying bond **:** LINK, TIE **2 :** a straight horizontal mark placed over two or more members of a compound mathematical expression and equivalent to parentheses or brackets about them (as in $a-\overline{b-c}=a-[b-c]$)

vin·da·loo \'vin-də-ˌlü\ *n, pl* **-loos** [prob. fr. Konkani *vindalu,* fr. Indo-Portuguese (Pg creole of India) *vinh d'alho,* lit., wine of garlic, fr. Pg *vinho de alho*] (1888) **:** a curried dish of Indian origin made with meat or shellfish, garlic, and wine or vinegar

vin·di·ca·ble \'vin-di-kə-bəl\ *adj* (1647) **:** capable of being vindicated

vin·di·cate \ˈvin-də-ˌkāt\ *vt* **-cat·ed; -cat·ing** [L *vindicatus,* pp. of *vindicare* to lay claim to, avenge, fr. *vindic-, vindex* claimant, avenger] (ca. 1571) **1** *obs* **:** to set free **:** DELIVER **2 :** AVENGE **3 a :** to free from allegation or blame **b** (1) **:** CONFIRM, SUBSTANTIATE (2) **:** to provide justification or defense for **:** JUSTIFY **c :** to protect from attack or encroachment **:** DEFEND **4 :** to maintain a right to ***syn*** see EXCULPATE, MAINTAIN — **vin·di·ca·tor** \-ˌkā-tər\ *n*

vin·di·ca·tion \ˌvin-də-ˈkā-shən\ *n* (1613) **:** an act of vindicating **:** the state of being vindicated; *specif* **:** justification against denial or censure **:** DEFENSE

vin·dic·a·tive \vin-ˈdi-kə-tiv\ *adj* (1521) **1** *obs* **:** VINDICTIVE, VENGEFUL **2** *archaic* **:** PUNITIVE

vin·di·ca·to·ry *adj* (1647) **1** \ˈvin-di-kə-ˌtȯr-ē\ **:** providing vindication **:** JUSTIFICATORY **2** \vin-ˈdi-kə-\ **:** PUNITIVE, RETRIBUTIVE

vin·dic·tive \vin-ˈdik-tiv\ *adj* [L *vindicta* revenge, vindication, fr. *vindicare*] (15c) **1 a :** disposed to seek revenge **:** VENGEFUL **b :** intended for or involving revenge **2 :** intended to cause anguish or hurt **:** SPITEFUL — **vin·dic·tive·ly** *adv* — **vin·dic·tive·ness** *n*

[1]**vine** \ˈvīn\ *n* [ME, fr. AF *vigne,* fr. L *vinea* vine, vineyard, fr. fem. of *vineus* of wine, fr. *vinum* wine — more at WINE] (14c) **1 :** GRAPE 2 **2 a :** a plant whose stem requires support and which climbs by tendrils or twining or creeps along the ground; *also* **:** the stem of such a plant **b :** any of various sprawling herbaceous plants (as a tomato or potato) that lack specialized adaptations for climbing

[2]**vine** *vi* **vined; vin·ing** (1796) **:** to form or grow in the manner of a vine

vine·dress·er \ˈvīn-ˌdre-sər\ *n* (1560) **:** a person who cultivates and prunes grapevines

vin·e·gar \ˈvi-ni-gər\ *n* [ME *vinegre,* fr. AF *vin egre,* fr. *vin* wine (fr. L *vinum*) + *egre* keen, sour — more at EAGER] (13c) **1 :** a sour liquid obtained by fermentation of dilute alcoholic liquids and used as a condiment or preservative **2 :** ill humor **:** SOURNESS **3 :** VIM

vin·e·gared \-gərd\ *adj* (1845) **:** flavored or marinated with vinegar

vinegar eel *n* (ca. 1839) **:** a minute free-living nematode worm (*Turbatrix aceti*) often found in great numbers in acidic vegetable or vegetable-derived fermenting matter (as unpasteurized vinegar)

vinegar fly *n* [fr. its breeding in pickles] (1901) **:** DROSOPHILA

vin·e·gar·ish \ˈvi-ni-g(ə-)rish\ *adj* (1648) **:** VINEGARY 2

vin·e·gary \ˈvi-ni-g(ə-)rē\ *adj* (ca. 1730) **1 a :** resembling vinegar **:** SOUR **b :** flavored with vinegar **2 :** disagreeable, bitter, or irascible in character or manner ⟨two ~ fellows bickering⟩

vine maple *n* (1849) **:** a small maple (*Acer circinatum*) found from British Columbia to California that has spreading twisted branches that may form dense thickets

vin·ery \ˈvīn-rē, ˈvī-nə-\ *n, pl* **-er·ies** (15c) **:** an area or building in which vines are grown

vine·yard \ˈvin-yərd\ *n* (14c) **1 :** a planting of grapevines **2 :** a sphere of activity **:** field of endeavor ⟨toilers in the ~ of diplomacy —Daniel Schorr⟩

vine·yard·ist \-yər-dist\ *n* (1848) **:** a person who owns or cultivates a vineyard

vingt–et–un \ˌvan-ˌtā-ˈən\ *n* [F, lit., twenty-one] (1772) **:** BLACKJACK 5

vi·ni·cul·ture \ˈvi-nə-ˌkəl-chər, ˈvī-\ *n* [L *vinum* + ISV *-i-* + *culture*] (1871) **:** VITICULTURE

vi·nif·era \vī-ˈni-f(ə-)rə\ *n, pl* **-era** *or* **-eras** [NL, fr. L *vinifer* wine-producing, fr. *vinum* wine] (1888) **:** a common European grape (*Vitis vinifera*) that is the chief source of Old World wine and table grape varieties — **vinifera** *adj*

vi·ni·fi·ca·tion \ˌvi-nə-fə-ˈkā-shən, ˌvī-\ *n* [F, fr. *vin* wine + *-i-* + *-fication*] (1880) **:** the conversion of fruit juices (as grape juice) into wine by fermentation

vin·i·fy \ˈvi-nə-ˌfī, ˈvī-\ *vt* **-fied; -fy·ing** [prob. back-formation fr. *vinification*] (1969) **1 :** to make wine from (grapes often of a specified kind) **2 :** to make (wine) from grapes

vi·no \ˈvē-(ˌ)nō\ *n, pl* **vinos** [It & Sp, fr. L *vinum*] (ca. 1919) **:** WINE

vi·nos·i·ty \vī-ˈnä-sə-tē\ *n, pl* **-ties** (1658) **:** the characteristic body, flavor, and color of a wine

vi·nous \ˈvī-nəs\ *adj* [ME, fr. L *vinosus,* fr. *vinum* wine] (15c) **1 :** of, relating to, or made with wine ⟨~ medications⟩ **2 :** showing the effects of the use of wine **3 :** VINACEOUS — **vi·nous·ly** *adv*

[1]**vin·tage** \ˈvin-tij\ *n* [ME, prob. alter. of *vendage,* fr. AF *vendage, vendenge,* fr. L *vindemia* grape-gathering, vintage, fr. *vinum* wine, grapes + *demere* to take off, fr. *de-* + *emere* to take — more at WINE, REDEEM] (15c) **1 a** (1) **:** a season's yield of grapes or wine from a vineyard (2) **:** WINE; *esp* **:** a usu. superior wine all or most of which comes from a single year **b :** a collection of contemporaneous and similar persons or things **:** CROP **2 :** the act or time of harvesting grapes or making wine **3 a :** a period of origin or manufacture ⟨a piano of 1845 ~⟩ **b :** length of existence **:** AGE

[2]**vintage** *adj* (1601) **1** *of wine* **:** of, relating to, or produced in a particular vintage **2 :** of old, recognized, and enduring interest, importance, or quality **:** CLASSIC **3 a :** dating from the past **:** OLD **b :** OUTMODED, OLD-FASHIONED **4 :** of the best and most characteristic — used with a proper noun ⟨~ Shaw: a wise and winning comedy —*Time*⟩

vin·tag·er \ˈvin-ti-jər\ *n* (1589) **:** a person concerned with the production of grapes and wine

vintage year *n* (1878) **1 :** a year in which a vintage wine is produced **2 :** a year of outstanding distinction or success

vint·ner \ˈvint-nər\ *n* [ME, alter. of *vineter,* fr. AF, fr. ML *vinetarius,* fr. L *vinetum* vineyard, fr. *vinum* wine] (15c) **1 :** a wine merchant **2 :** a person who makes wine

viny \ˈvī-nē\ *adj* **vin·i·er; -est** (1570) **1 :** of, relating to, or resembling vines ⟨~ plants⟩ **2 :** covered with or abounding in vines

vi·nyl \ˈvī-nᵊl\ *n* [ISV, fr. L *vinum* wine] (1863) **1 :** a monovalent radical CH_2=CH derived from ethylene by removal of one hydrogen atom **2 :** a polymer of a vinyl compound or a product (as a resin or a textile fiber) made from such a polymer — **vi·nyl·ic** \vī-ˈni-lik\ *adj*

vinyl alcohol *n* (1873) **:** an unstable compound CH_2=CHOH isolated only in the form of its polymers or derivatives

vinyl chloride *n* (1872) **:** a flammable gaseous carcinogenic compound C_2H_3Cl that is used esp. to make vinyl resins

vi·nyl·i·dene \vī-ˈni-lə-ˌdēn\ *n* [ISV *vinyl* + *-ide* + *-ene*] (1898) **:** a divalent radical CH_2=C derived from ethylene by removal of two hydrogen atoms from one carbon atom

vinyl resin *n* (1933) **:** any of various thermoplastic resinous materials that are essentially polymers of vinyl compounds

vi·ol \ˈvī(-ə)l, ˈvī-(ˌ)ōl\ *n* [ME *vial,* fr. AF *viele, viole,* fr. Old Occitan *viola*] (15c) **:** a bowed stringed instrument chiefly of the 16th and 17th centuries made in treble, alto, tenor, and bass sizes and distinguished from members of the violin family esp. in having a deep body, a flat back, sloping shoulders, usu. six strings, a fretted fingerboard, and a low-arched bridge

[1]**vi·o·la** \vī-ˈō-lə, vē-; ˈvī-ə-\ *n* [ME, fr. L] (15c) **:** VIOLET 1a; *esp* **:** any of various garden hybrids with solitary white, yellow, or purple often variegated flowers resembling but smaller than typical pansies

[2]**vi·o·la** \vē-ˈō-lə\ *n* [It & Sp, viol, viola, fr. Old Occitan, viol] (ca. 1724) **:** a musical instrument of the violin family that is intermediate in size and compass between the violin and cello and is tuned a fifth below the violin — **vi·o·list** \-list\ *n*

vi·o·la·ble \ˈvī-ə-lə-bəl\ *adj* (1552) **:** capable of being or likely to be violated — **vi·o·la·bil·i·ty** \ˌvī-ə-lə-ˈbi-lə-tē\ *n* — **vi·o·la·ble·ness** \ˈvī-ə-lə-bəl-nəs\ *n* — **vi·o·la·bly** \-blē\ *adv*

vi·o·la·ceous \ˌvī-ə-ˈlā-shəs\ *adj* [L *violaceus,* fr. *viola* violet] (1657) **:** of the color violet

vi·o·la da gam·ba \vē-ˌō-lə-də-ˈgäm-bə, -ˈgam-\ *n, pl* **vi·o·las da gamba** \-ləz-də-\ *or* **vi·o·le da gamba** \-(ˌ)lā-\ [It, leg viol] (1597) **:** a bass member of the viol family having a range approximating the cello — **vi·o·list da gamba** \-lis(t)-də-\ *n*

viola d'a·mo·re \-də-ˈmȯr-ē, -(ˌ)ā\ *n, pl* **violas d'amore** *or* **viole d'amore** [It, viol of love] (ca. 1700) **:** a tenor viol having usu. seven gut and seven wire strings

[1]**vi·o·late** \ˈvī-ə-ˌlāt\ *vt* **-lat·ed; -lat·ing** [ME, fr. L *violatus,* pp. of *violare,* fr. *viol-* (as in *violentus* violent)] (15c) **1 :** BREAK, DISREGARD ⟨~ the law⟩ **2 :** to do harm to the person or esp. the chastity of; *specif* **:** RAPE 2 **3 :** to fail to show proper respect for **:** PROFANE ⟨~ a shrine⟩ **4 :** INTERRUPT, DISTURB ⟨~ the peace of a spring evening —Nancy Larter⟩ — **vi·o·la·tive** \-ˌlā-tiv\ *adj* — **vi·o·la·tor** \-ˌlā-tər\ *n*

[2]**vi·o·late** \ˈvī-ə-lət\ *adj* (15c) *archaic* **:** subjected to violation

vi·o·la·tion \ˌvī-ə-ˈlā-shən\ *n* (15c) **:** the act of violating **:** the state of being violated: as **a :** INFRINGEMENT, TRANSGRESSION; *specif* **:** an infringement of the rules in sports that is less serious than a foul and usu. involves technicalities of play **b :** an act of irreverence or desecration **:** PROFANATION **c :** DISTURBANCE, INTERRUPTION **d :** RAPE 2, RAVISHMENT

vi·o·lence \ˈvī-lən(t)s, ˈvī-ə-\ *n* (14c) **1 a :** exertion of physical force so as to injure or abuse (as in warfare effecting illegal entry into a house) **b :** an instance of violent treatment or procedure **2 :** injury by or as if by distortion, infringement, or profanation **:** OUTRAGE **3 a :** intense, turbulent, or furious and often destructive action or force ⟨the ~ of the storm⟩ **b :** vehement feeling or expression **:** FERVOR; *also* **:** an instance of such action or feeling **c :** a clashing or jarring quality **:** DISCORDANCE **4 :** undue alteration (as of wording or sense in editing a text)

vi·o·lent \-lənt\ *adj* [ME, fr. AF, fr. L *violentus;* akin to L *vis* strength — more at VIM] (14c) **1 :** marked by extreme force or sudden intense activity ⟨a ~ attack⟩ **2 a :** notably furious or vehement ⟨a ~ denunciation⟩ **b :** EXTREME, INTENSE ⟨~ pain⟩ ⟨~ colors⟩ **3 :** caused by force **:** not natural ⟨a ~ death⟩ **4 a :** emotionally agitated to the point of loss of self-control ⟨became ~ after an insult⟩ **b :** prone to commit acts of violence ⟨~ prison inmates⟩ — **vi·o·lent·ly** *adv*

violent storm *n* (ca. 1881) **:** STORM 1c(1) — see BEAUFORT SCALE table

vi·o·let \ˈvī-(ə-)lət\ *n* [ME, fr. AF *violete,* dim. of *viole* violet, fr. L *viola*] (14c) **1 a :** any of a genus (*Viola* of the family Violaceae, the violet family) of chiefly herbs with alternate stipulate leaves and showy flowers in spring and often cleistogamous flowers in summer; *esp* **:** one with smaller usu. solid-colored flowers as distinguished from the usu. larger-flowered violas and pansies **b :** any of several plants of genera other than that of the violet — compare DOGTOOTH VIOLET **2 :** any of a group of colors of reddish-blue hue, low lightness, and medium saturation

vi·o·lin \ˌvī-ə-ˈlin\ *n* [It *violino,* dim. of *viola*] (ca. 1576) **:** a bowed stringed instrument having four strings tuned at intervals of a fifth and a usual range from G below middle C upward for more than 4½ octaves and having a shallow body, shoulders at right angles to the neck, a fingerboard without frets, and a curved bridge — **vi·o·lin·ist** \-ist\ *n* — **vi·o·lin·is·tic** \-ə-lə-ˈnis-tik\ *adj*

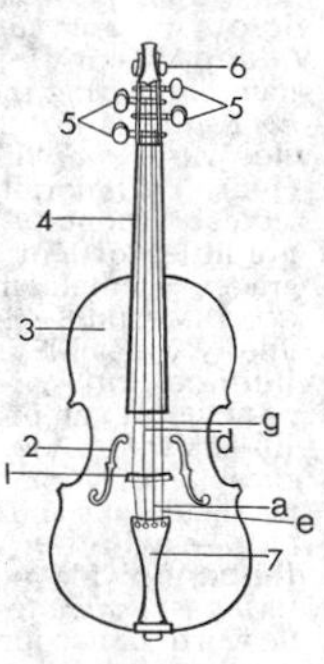

violin: *1* bridge, *2* sound hole, *3* soundboard, *4* fingerboard, *5* pegs, *6* scroll, *7* tailpiece, *g* G-string, *d* D-string, *a* A-string, *e* E-string

vi·o·lon·cel·lo \ˌvī-ə-lən-ˈche-(ˌ)lō, ˌvē-\ *n* [It, dim. of *violone,* aug. of *viola*] (ca. 1724) **:** CELLO — **vi·o·lon·cel·list** \-ˈche-list\ *n*

vio·my·cin \ˌvī-ə-ˈmī-sᵊn\ *n* [*vi*olet + *-mycin;* fr. the color of the soil organism] (1950) **:** a polypeptide antibiotic $C_{25}H_{43}N_{13}O_{10}$ that is produced by several soil actinomycetes (genus *Streptomyces*) and is administered in the form of its sulfate in the treatment of tuberculosis

VIP \ˌvē-ˌī-ˈpē\ *n, pl* **VIPs** \-ˈpēz\ [*v*ery *i*mportant *p*erson] (1933) **:** a person of great influence or prestige; *esp* **:** a high official with special privileges

vi·per \ˈvī-pər\ *n* [ME *vipere,* fr. L *vipera*] (15c) **1 a :** a common Eurasian venomous snake (*Vipera berus*) that attains a length of about two feet (0.6 meter), varies in color from red, brown, or gray with dark markings to black, and is usu. not fatal to humans; *broadly* **:** any of a family (Viperidae) of venomous snakes that includes Old World snakes (subfamily Viperinae) and the pit vipers **b :** a venomous or reputedly venomous snake **2 :** a vicious or treacherous person

vi·per·ine \-pə-ˌrīn\ *adj* (ca. 1550) **:** of, relating to, or resembling a viper **:** VENOMOUS

vi·per·ish \-p(ə-)rish\ *adj* (1755) **:** spitefully vituperative **:** VENOMOUS

vi·per·ous \-p(ə-)rəs\ *adj* (1535) **1 :** VIPERINE **2 :** having the qualities attributed to a viper **:** MALIGNANT, VENOMOUS ⟨the backstabbing of a ~ family⟩ — **vi·per·ous·ly** *adv*

viper's bugloss *n* (ca. 1597) : a coarse Old World herb (*Echium vulgare*) of the borage family that is naturalized in No. America and has showy blue tubular flowers with exserted stamens — called also *blueweed*

vi·ra·go \və-ˈrä-(ˌ)gō, -ˈrā-; ˈvir-ə-ˌgō\ *n, pl* **-goes** *or* **-gos** [ME, fr. L *viragin-, virago,* fr. *vir* man — more at VIRILE] (14c) **1** : a loud overbearing woman : TERMAGANT **2** : a woman of great stature, strength, and courage — **vi·rag·i·nous** \və-ˈra-jə-nəs\ *adj*

vi·ral \ˈvī-rəl\ *adj* (1937) **1** : of, relating to, or caused by a virus ⟨a ~ infection⟩ **2** : quickly and widely spread or popularized esp. by person-to-person electronic communication ⟨a ~ video⟩ — **vi·ral·ly** \-rə-lē\ *adv*

viral marketing *n* (1989) : marketing designed to disseminate information (as about a new product) very rapidly by making it likely to be passed from person to person esp. via electronic means

vir·e·lay \ˈvir-ə-ˌlā\ *n* [ME, fr. MF *virelai*] (14c) : a chiefly French verse form having stanzas of indeterminate length and number, alternating long and short lines, and interlaced rhyme (as *abab bcbc cdcd dada*)

vi·re·mia \vī-ˈrē-mē-ə\ *n* [NL, fr. *virus* + *-emia*] (1946) : the presence of viruses in the blood — **vi·re·mic** \-mik\ *adj*

vir·eo \ˈvir-ē-ˌō\ *n, pl* **-e·os** [L, a small bird, fr. *virēre* to be green] (1834) : any of various small insectivorous American oscine birds (family Vireonidae, esp. genus *Vireo*) that are chiefly olivaceous and grayish in color

vires *pl of* VIS

vi·res·cence \və-ˈre-sᵊn(t)s, vī-\ *n* (ca. 1888) : the state or condition of becoming green; *esp* : such a condition due to the development of chloroplasts in plant organs (as petals) normally white or colored

vi·res·cent \-sᵊnt\ *adj* [L *virescent-, virescens,* prp. of *virescere* to become green, incho. of *virēre* to be green] (1826) **1** : beginning to be green : GREENISH **2** : developing or displaying virescence

vir·ga \ˈvər-gə\ *n* [NL, fr. L, branch, rod, streak in the sky suggesting rain] (1938) : wisps of precipitation evaporating before reaching the ground

[1]**vir·gate** \ˈvər-ˌgāt\ *n* [ML *virgata,* fr. *virga,* a land measure, fr. L, rod] (1655) : a variable old English unit of land area equal to about one quarter of a hide or 30 acres

[2]**virgate** *adj* [NL *virgatus,* fr. L, made of twigs, fr. *virga*] (1821) : shaped like a rod or wand ⟨a ~ one-flowered branch⟩

[1]**vir·gin** \ˈvər-jən\ *n* [ME, fr. AF *virgine,* fr. L *virgin-, virgo* young woman, virgin] (13c) **1 a** : an unmarried woman devoted to religion **b** *cap* : VIRGO **2 a** : an absolutely chaste young woman **b** : an unmarried girl or woman **3** *cap* : VIRGIN MARY **4 a** : a person who has not had sexual intercourse **b** : a person who is inexperienced in a usu. specified sphere of activity **5** : a female animal that has never copulated

[2]**virgin** *adj* (14c) **1** : free of impurity or stain : UNSULLIED **2** : CHASTE **3** : characteristic of or befitting a virgin : MODEST **4** : FRESH, UNSPOILED; *specif* : not altered by human activity ⟨a ~ forest⟩ **5 a (1)** : being used or worked for the first time **(2)** *of a metal* : produced directly from ore by primary smelting **b** : INITIAL, FIRST **6** *of a vegetable oil* : obtained from the first light pressing and without heating **7** : containing no alcohol ⟨a ~ daiquiri⟩

[1]**vir·gin·al** \ˈvər-jə-nᵊl, ˈvərj-nəl\ *adj* (15c) **1** : of, relating to, or characteristic of a virgin or virginity; *esp* : PURE, CHASTE ⟨a ~ young girl⟩ **2** : PRISTINE, UNSULLIED ⟨a ~ snowfall⟩ — **vir·gin·al·ly** *adv*

[2]**virginal** *n* [prob. fr. L *virginalis* of a virgin, fr. *virgin-, virgo*] (1530) : a small rectangular spinet having no legs and only one wire to a note and popular in the 16th and 17th centuries — often used in pl.; called also *pair of virginals* — **vir·gin·al·ist** \ˈvər-jə-nᵊl-ist, ˈvərj-nə-list\ *n*

virgin birth *n* (1613) **1** : birth from a virgin **2** *often cap V&B* : the theological doctrine that Jesus was miraculously begotten of God and born of a virgin mother

Vir·gin·ia bluebells \vər-ˈji-nyə-, -ˈji-nē-ə-\ *n pl* [*Virginia,* state of the U.S.] (ca. 1922) : BLUEBELL 2b

Virginia creeper *n* (1704) : a common No. American tendril-climbing vine (*Parthenocissus quinquefolia*) of the grape family with palmately compound leaves and bluish-black berries — called also *woodbine*

Virginia fence *n* (1671) : WORM FENCE — called also *Virginia rail fence*

Virginia ham *n* (1795) : a dry-cured, smoked, and aged ham esp. from a peanut-fed hog

Virginia pine *n* (1862) : a pine (*Pinus virginiana*) of the eastern U.S. that has short needles occurring in pairs — called also *Jersey pine*

Virginia rail *n* (1813) : an American long-billed rail (*Rallus limicola*) that has gray cheeks

Virginia reel *n* (1817) : an American dance in which two lines of couples face each other and all couples in turn dance in a series of figures

Virginia snakeroot *n* (1694) : a birthwort (*Aristolochia serpentaria*) of the eastern U.S. with oblong leaves usu. cordate at the base and pointed at the tip and a solitary basal brownish-purple flower

vir·gin·i·ty \(ˌ)vər-ˈji-nə-tē\ *n, pl* **-ties** (14c) **1** : the quality or state of being virgin; *esp* : MAIDENHOOD **2** : the unmarried life : CELIBACY

Virgin Mary *n* (14c) : the mother of Jesus

virgin's bower *n* (ca. 1597) : any of several usu. small-flowered and climbing clematises (esp. *Clematis virginiana*)

virgin wool *n* (1915) : wool not used before in manufacture

Vir·go \ˈvər-(ˌ)gō, ˈvir-\ *n* [L (gen. *Virginis*), lit., virgin] (bef. 12c) **1** : a zodiacal constellation on the celestial equator that lies due south of the handle of the Big Dipper and is pictured as a woman holding a spike of grain **2 a** : the sixth sign of the zodiac in astrology — see ZODIAC table **b** : one born under the sign of Virgo — **Vir·go·an** *n*

vir·gule \ˈvər-(ˌ)gyül\ *n* [F, fr. L *virgula* small stripe, obelus, fr. dim. of *virga* rod] (1837) : SLASH 4

vi·ri·ci·dal \ˌvī-rə-ˈsī-dᵊl\ *adj* [NL *virus* + E *-i-* + *-cide*] (1924) : VIRUCIDAL — **vi·ri·cide** \ˈvī-rə-ˌsīd\ *n*

vir·id \ˈvir-əd\ *adj* [L *viridis* green] (1600) : vividly green : VERDANT

vir·i·des·cent \ˌvir-ə-ˈde-sᵊnt\ *adj* [L *viridis* green] (ca. 1847) : slightly green : GREENISH

vi·rid·i·an \və-ˈri-dē-ən\ *n* [L *viridis*] (1882) : a chrome green pigment that is a hydrated oxide of chromium

vi·rid·i·ty \və-ˈri-də-tē\ *n* [ME *viridite,* fr. L *viriditat-, viriditas,* fr. *viridis*] (15c) **1 a** : the quality or state of being green **b** : the color of grass or foliage **2** : naive innocence

vir·ile \ˈvir-əl, ˈvir-ˌī(-ə)l, *Brit also* ˈvī(-ə)r-ˌī(-ə)l\ *adj* [MF or L; MF *viril,* fr. L *virilis,* fr. *vir* man, male; akin to OE & OHG *wer* man, Skt *vīra*] (15c) **1** : having the nature, properties, or qualities of an adult male; *specif* : capable of functioning as a male in copulation **2** : ENERGETIC, VIGOROUS **3 a** : characteristic of or associated with men : MASCULINE **b** : having traditionally masculine traits esp. to a marked degree **4** : MASTERFUL, FORCEFUL — **vir·ile·ly** *adv*

vir·il·ism \ˈvir-ə-ˌli-zəm\ *n* (1922) : the appearance of secondary male characteristics (as facial hair) in the female

vi·ril·i·ty \və-ˈri-lə-tē, *Brit also* vī-\ *n* (1586) : the quality or state of being virile: as **a** : MANHOOD 3 **b** : manly vigor : MASCULINITY

vi·ri·on \ˈvī-rē-ˌän, ˈvir-ē-\ *n* [F, fr. *virien* viral (fr. *virus* virus) + *-on* [2]-on] (1959) : a complete virus particle that consists of an RNA or DNA core with a protein coat sometimes with external envelopes and that is the extracellular infective form of a virus

virl \ˈvər(-ə)l\ *n* [ME *virole* — more at FERRULE] (15c) *Scot* : FERRULE 1

vi·roid \ˈvī-ˌrȯid\ *n* [NL *virus* + E *-oid*] (1971) : any of two families (*Pospiviroidae* and *Avsunviroidae*) of subviral particles that consist of a small single-stranded RNA arranged in a closed loop without a protein shell and that replicate in their host plants where they may or may not be pathogenic

vi·rol·o·gy \vī-ˈrä-lə-jē\ *n* [NL *virus* + ISV *-logy*] (ca. 1935) : a branch of science that deals with viruses and viral diseases — **vi·ro·log·i·cal** \ˌvī-rə-ˈlä-ji-kəl\ *or* **vi·ro·log·ic** \-jik\ *adj* — **vi·ro·log·i·cal·ly** \-ji-k(ə-)lē\ *adv* — **vi·rol·o·gist** \vī-ˈrä-lə-jist\ *n*

vir·tu \ˌvər-ˈtü, ˌvir-\ *or* **ver·tu** \ˌvər-, ˌver-\ *n* [It *virtù,* lit., virtue, fr. L *virtut-, virtus*] (1722) **1** : a love of or taste for curios or objets d'art **2** : productions of art esp. of a curious or antique nature : OBJETS D'ART

vir·tu·al \ˈvər-chə-wəl, -chəl; ˈvərch-wəl\ *adj* [ME, efficacious, potential, fr. ML *virtualis,* fr. L *virtus* strength, virtue] (15c) **1** : being such in essence or effect though not formally recognized or admitted ⟨a ~ dictator⟩ **2** : of, relating to, or using virtual memory **3** : of, relating to, or being a hypothetical particle whose existence is inferred from indirect evidence ⟨~ photons⟩ — compare REAL 3 **4** : being on or simulated on a computer or computer network ⟨print or ~ books⟩ ⟨a ~ keyboard⟩: as **a** : occurring or existing primarily online ⟨~ shopping⟩ **b** : of, relating to, or existing within a virtual reality ⟨a ~ tour⟩

virtual colonoscopy *n* (1994) : COLONOGRAPHY — called also *virtual colonography*

virtual image *n* (1859) : an image (as seen in a plane mirror) formed of points from which divergent rays (as of light) seem to emanate without actually doing so

vir·tu·al·i·ty \ˌvər-chə-ˈwa-lə-tē\ *n, pl* **-ties** (1646) **1** : ESSENCE **2** : potential existence : POTENTIALITY

vir·tu·al·ly \ˈvər-chə-wə-lē, -chə-lē; ˈvərch-wə-lē\ *adv* (15c) **1** : almost entirely : NEARLY **2** : for all practical purposes ⟨~ unknown⟩

virtual memory *n* (1959) : a section of a hard drive that can be used as if it were an extension of a computer's random-access memory — called also *virtual storage*

virtual reality *n* (1987) : an artificial environment which is experienced through sensory stimuli (as sights and sounds) provided by a computer and in which one's actions partially determine what happens in the environment; *also* : the technology used to create or access a virtual reality

vir·tue \ˈvər-(ˌ)chü\ *n* [ME *vertu, virtu,* fr. AF, fr. L *virtut-, virtus* strength, manliness, virtue, fr. *vir* man — more at VIRILE] (13c) **1 a** : conformity to a standard of right : MORALITY **b** : a particular moral excellence **2** *pl* : an order of angels — see CELESTIAL HIERARCHY **3** : a beneficial quality or power of a thing **4** : manly strength or courage : VALOR **5** : a commendable quality or trait : MERIT **6** : a capacity to act : POTENCY **7** : chastity esp. in a woman — **vir·tue·less** \-(ˌ)chü-ləs\ *adj* — **by virtue of** *or* **in virtue of** : through the force of : by authority of

vir·tu·o·sa \ˌvər-chü-ˈō-sə, -zə\ *n* [It, fem. of *virtuoso*] (1668) : a girl or woman who is a virtuoso

vir·tu·os·i·ty \-ˈä-sə-tē\ *n, pl* **-ties** (1673) **1** : a taste for or interest in virtu **2** : great technical skill (as in the practice of a fine art)

vir·tu·o·so \-ˈō-(ˌ)sō, -(ˌ)zō\ *n, pl* **-sos** *or* **-si** \-(ˌ)sē, -(ˌ)zē\ [It, fr. *virtuoso,* adj., virtuous, skilled, fr. LL *virtuosus* virtuous, fr. L *virtus*] (1651) **1** : an experimenter or investigator esp. in the arts and sciences : SAVANT **2** : one skilled in or having a taste for the fine arts **3** : one who excels in the technique of an art; *esp* : a highly skilled musical performer (as on the violin) **4** : a person who has great skill at some endeavor ⟨a computer ~⟩ — **vir·tu·o·sic** \-ˈō-sik, -zik\ *adj* — **virtuoso** *adj*

vir·tu·ous \ˈvər-chə-wəs, ˈvərch-wəs\ *adj* (14c) **1** : POTENT, EFFICACIOUS **2 a** : having or exhibiting virtue **b** : morally excellent : RIGHTEOUS ⟨a ~ decision⟩ **3** : CHASTE ***syn*** see MORAL — **vir·tu·ous·ly** *adv* — **vir·tu·ous·ness** *n*

vi·ru·cid·al \ˌvī-rə-ˈsī-dᵊl\ *adj* [NL, *virus* + E *-cide*] (1925) : having the capacity to or tending to destroy or inactivate viruses ⟨~ agents⟩ ⟨~ activity⟩ — **vi·ru·cide** \ˈvī-rə-ˌsīd\ *n*

vir·u·lence \ˈvir-ə-lən(t)s, ˈvir-yə-\ *n* (1617) : the quality or state of being virulent: as **a** : extreme bitterness or malignity of temper : RANCOR **b** : MALIGNANCY, VENOMOUSNESS ⟨the ~ of a disease⟩ **c** : the relative capacity of a pathogen to overcome body defenses

vir·u·len·cy \-lən(t)-sē\ *n* (1616) : VIRULENCE

vir·u·lent \ˈvir-ə-lənt, ˈvir-yə-\ *adj* [ME, fr. L *virulentus,* fr. *virus* poison] (14c) **1 a** : marked by a rapid, severe, and destructive course ⟨a ~ infection⟩ **b** : able to overcome bodily defensive mechanisms : markedly pathogenic ⟨~ bacteria⟩ **2** : extremely poisonous or venomous **3** : full of malice : MALIGNANT ⟨~ racists⟩ **4** : objectionably harsh or strong ⟨~ criticism⟩ — **vir·u·lent·ly** *adv*

vir·u·lif·er·ous \ˌvir-ə-ˈli-f(ə-)rəs, ˌvir-yə-\ *adj* [*virul*ence + *-iferous*] (ca. 1899) : containing, producing, or conveying an agent of infection and esp. a virus ⟨~ insects⟩

vi·rus \ˈvī-rəs\ *n, pl* **vi·rus·es** [L, venom, poisonous emanation; akin to Gk *ios* poison, Skt *viṣa;* in senses 2 & 4, fr. NL, fr. L] (1599) **1** *archaic* : VENOM 1 **2 a** : the causative agent of an infectious disease **b** : any of a large group of submicroscopic infective agents that are regarded either as extremely simple microorganisms or as extremely complex molecules, that typically contain a protein coat surrounding an RNA or DNA core of genetic material but no semipermeable membrane, that are capable of growth and multiplication only in living cells, and that cause various important diseases in humans, lower animals, or plants; *also* : FILTERABLE VIRUS **c** : a disease or illness caused by a virus **3** : something that poisons the mind or soul ⟨the force of this ~ of prejudice —V. S. Waters⟩ **4** : a computer program that is usu. hidden within another seemingly innocuous program and that produces copies of itself and inserts them into other programs and usu. performs a malicious action (as destroying data)

[1]**vis** \ˈvis\ *n, pl* **vi·res** \ˈvī-ˌrēz\ [L — more at VIM] (ca. 1630) : FORCE, POWER

[2]**vis** *abbr* **1** visibility; visible **2** visual

[1]**vi·sa** \ˈvē-zə *also* -sə\ *n* [F, fr. L, neut. pl. of *visus,* pp.] (1831) **1** : an endorsement made on a passport by the proper authorities denoting that it has been examined and that the bearer may proceed **2** : a signature of formal approval by a superior upon a document

[2]**visa** *vt* **vi·saed** \-zəd, -səd\; **vi·sa·ing** \-zə-iŋ, -sə-\ (ca. 1847) : to give a visa to (a passport)

vis·age \ˈvi-zij\ *n* [ME, fr. AF, fr. *vis* face, fr. L *visus* sight, fr. *vidēre* to see — more at WIT] (14c) **1** : the face, countenance, or appearance of a person or sometimes an animal **2** : ASPECT, APPEARANCE ⟨the grimy ~ of a mining town⟩

vis·aged \ˈvi-zijd\ *adj* (1540) : having a visage of a specified kind — usu. used in combination ⟨grim-*visaged*⟩

[1]**vis–à–vis** \ˈvēz-ə-ˈvē, ˌvēs- *also* -ä-ˈvē\ *prep* [F, lit., face-to-face] (1755) **1** : face-to-face with **2** : in relation to **3** : as compared with

[2]**vis–à–vis** *n, pl* **vis–à–vis** \-ə-ˈvē(z), -ä-\ (ca. 1757) **1** : one that is face-to-face with another **2 a** : ESCORT, DATE **b** : COUNTERPART **3** : TÊTE-À-TÊTE 1

[3]**vis–à–vis** *adv* (1760) : in company : TOGETHER

Vi·sa·yan \və-ˈsī-ən\ *also* **Bi·sa·yan** \bə-ˈsī-ən\ *n* (1951) **1** : a member of any of several peoples in the Visayan Islands, Philippines **2** : the group of Austronesian languages of the Bisayans

vis·ca·cha *or* **viz·ca·cha** \vis-ˈkä-chə\ *n* [Sp *vizcacha,* fr. Quechua *wisk'acha*] (1604) : any of several So. American burrowing rodents (genera *Lagostomus* and *Lagidium*) closely related to the chinchilla

viscera *pl of* VISCUS

vis·cer·al \ˈvi-sə-rəl, ˈvis-rəl\ *adj* (1575) **1** : felt in or as if in the viscera : DEEP ⟨a ~ conviction⟩ **2** : not intellectual : INSTINCTIVE, UNREASONING ⟨~ drives⟩ **3** : dealing with crude or elemental emotions : EARTHY ⟨a ~ novel⟩ **4** : of, relating to, or located on or among the viscera : SPLANCHNIC ⟨~ organs⟩ — **vis·cer·al·ly** \-rə-lē\ *adv*

vis·cid \ˈvi-səd\ *adj* [LL *viscidus,* fr. L *viscum* birdlime — more at VISCOUS] (1635) **1 a** : having an adhesive quality : STICKY **b** : having a glutinous consistency : VISCOUS **2** : covered with a sticky layer — **vis·cid·i·ty** \vi-ˈsi-də-tē\ *n* — **vis·cid·ly** \ˈvi-səd-lē\ *adv*

vis·co·elas·tic \ˌvis-kō-ə-ˈlas-tik\ *adj* [*viscous* + *-o-* + *elastic*] (1935) : having appreciable and conjoint viscous and elastic properties ⟨such ~ materials as asphalt⟩; *also* : constituting or relating to the state of viscoelastic materials ⟨~ data⟩ ⟨~ properties⟩ — **vis·co·elas·tic·i·ty** \-ˌlas-ˈti-sə-tē, -ˈtis-tē\ *n*

vis·com·e·ter \vis-ˈkä-mə-tər\ *n* [*viscosity* + *-meter*] (ca. 1883) : an instrument with which to measure viscosity — **vis·co·met·ric** \ˌvis-kə-ˈme-trik\ *adj* — **vis·com·e·try** \-mə-trē\ *n*

[1]**vis·cose** \ˈvis-ˌkōs, -ˌkōz\ *n* [obs. *viscose,* adj., viscous] (1896) **1** : a viscous golden-brown solution made by treating cellulose with caustic alkali solution and carbon disulfide and used in making rayon and films of regenerated cellulose **2** : viscose rayon

[2]**viscose** *adj* (1900) : of, relating to, or made from viscose

vis·co·sim·e·ter \ˌvis-kə-ˈsi-mə-tər\ *n* [ISV *viscos*ity + *-meter*] (ca. 1868) : VISCOMETER — **vis·cosi·met·ric** \(ˌ)vis-ˌkä-sə-ˈme-trik\ *adj*

vis·cos·i·ty \vis-ˈkä-sə-tē\ *n, pl* **-ties** [ME *viscosite,* fr. AF *viscosité,* fr. ML *viscositat-, viscositas,* fr. LL *viscosus* viscous] (14c) **1** : the quality or state of being viscous **2** : the property of resistance to flow in a fluid or semifluid **3** : the ratio of the tangential frictional force per unit area to the velocity gradient perpendicular to the direction of flow of a liquid — called also *coefficient of viscosity*

viscosity index *n* (1929) : an arbitrary number assigned as a measure of the constancy of the viscosity of a lubricating oil with change of temperature with higher numbers indicating viscosities that change little with temperature

vis·count \ˈvī-ˌkau̇nt\ *n* [ME *viscounte* sheriff, viscount, fr. AF *visquens, visconte,* fr. ML *vicecomit-, vicecomes,* fr. LL *vice-* vice- + *comit-, comes* count — more at COUNT] (15c) : a member of the peerage in Great Britain ranking below an earl and above a baron — **vis·count·cy** \-ˌkau̇n(t)-sē\ *n* — **vis·county** \-ˌkau̇n-tē\ *n*

vis·count·ess \-ˌkau̇n-təs\ *n* (15c) **1** : the wife or widow of a viscount **2** : a woman who holds the rank of viscount in her own right

vis·cous \ˈvis-kəs\ *adj* [ME *viscouse,* fr. AF *viscos,* fr. LL *viscosus* full of birdlime, viscous, fr. L *viscum* mistletoe, birdlime; akin to OHG *wīhsila* cherry, Gk *ixos* mistletoe] (14c) **1** : VISCID **2** : having or characterized by viscosity ⟨~ lava⟩ — **vis·cous·ly** *adv* — **vis·cous·ness** *n*

vis·cus \ˈvis-kəs\ *n, pl* **vis·cera** \ˈvi-sə-rə\ [L (pl. *viscera*)] (1651) **1** : an internal organ of the body; *esp* : one (as the heart, liver, or intestine) located in the great cavity of the trunk proper **2** *pl* : HEART 4

[1]**vise** \ˈvīs\ *n* [ME *vys, vice* screw, fr. AF *vyz,* fr. L *vitis* vine — more at WITHY] (1500) **1** : any of various tools with two jaws for holding work that close usu. by a screw, lever, or cam **2** : something likened to a vise ⟨economic ~ of slow growth and rampant price increases —David Milne⟩ — **vise·like** \-ˌlīk\ *adj*

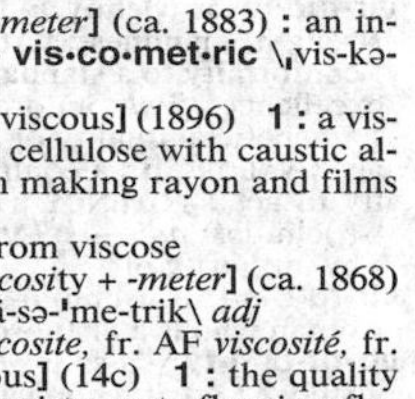

vise 1

[2]**vise** *vt* **vised; vis·ing** (1602) : to hold, force, or squeeze with or as if with a vise

[1]**vi·sé** \ˈvē-ˌzā, vē-ˈ\ *vt* **vi·séd** *or* **vi·séed; vi·sé·ing** [F, pp. of *viser* to visa, fr. *visa*] (1810) : VISA

[2]**visé** *n* (1842) : VISA

Vish·nu \ˈvish-(ˌ)nü\ *n* [Skt *Viṣṇu*] (1638) : the preserver god of the Hindu sacred triad — compare BRAHMA, SHIVA

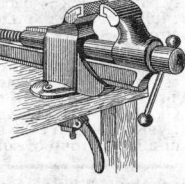

vis·i·bil·i·ty \ˌvi-zə-ˈbi-lə-tē\ *n, pl* **-ties** (15c) **1** : the quality or state of being visible **2 a** : the degree of clearness (as of the atmosphere or ocean); *specif* : the greatest distance through the atmosphere toward the horizon at which prominent objects can be identified with the naked eye **b** : capability of being readily noticed **c** : capability of affording an unobstructed view **d** : PUBLICITY 2d **3** : a measure of the ability of radiant energy to evoke visual sensation

vis·i·ble \ˈvi-zə-bəl\ *adj* [ME, fr. MF or L; MF, fr. L *visibilis,* fr. *visus,* pp. of *vidēre* to see] (14c) **1 a** : capable of being seen ⟨stars ~ to the naked eye⟩ **b** : situated in the region of the electromagnetic spectrum perceptible to human vision ⟨~ light⟩ — used of radiation having a wavelength between about 400 nanometers and 700 nanometers **2 a** : exposed to view ⟨the ~ horizon⟩ **b** (1) : CONSPICUOUS ⟨has played a highly ~ role in the negotiations⟩ (2) : WELL-KNOWN ⟨a highly ~ politician⟩ **3** : capable of being discovered or perceived : RECOGNIZABLE ⟨no ~ means of support⟩ **4** : ACCESSIBLE 4 ⟨~ resources⟩ **5** : devised to keep a particular part or item always in full view or readily seen or referred to ⟨a ~ index⟩ — **vis·i·ble·ness** *n* — **vis·i·bly** \-blē\ *adv*

visible speech *n* (1865) **1** : a set of phonetic symbols based on symbols for articulatory position **2** : speech reproduced spectrographically

Vis·i·goth \ˈvi-zə-ˌgäth\ *n* [LL *Visigothi,* pl.] (1597) : a member of the western division of the Goths — **Vis·i·goth·ic** \ˌvi-zə-ˈgä-thik\ *adj*

[1]**vi·sion** \ˈvi-zhən\ *n* [ME, fr. AF, fr. L *vision-, visio,* fr. *vidēre* to see — more at WIT] (14c) **1 a** : something seen in a dream, trance, or ecstasy; *esp* : a supernatural appearance that conveys a revelation **b** : a thought, concept, or object formed by the imagination **c** : a manifestation to the senses of something immaterial ⟨look, not at ~*s,* but at realities —Edith Wharton⟩ **2 a** : the act or power of imagination **b** (1) : mode of seeing or conceiving (2) : unusual discernment or foresight ⟨a person of ~⟩ **c** : direct mystical awareness of the supernatural usu. in visible form **3 a** : the act or power of seeing : SIGHT **b** : the special sense by which the qualities of an object (as color, luminosity, shape, and size) constituting its appearance are perceived through a process in which light rays entering the eye are transformed by the retina into electrical signals that are transmitted to the brain via the optic nerve **4 a** : something seen **b** : a lovely or charming sight — **vi·sion·al** \ˈvizh-nəl, ˈvi-zhə-nᵊl\ *adj* — **vi·sion·al·ly** *adv*

[2]**vision** *vt* **vi·sioned; vi·sion·ing** \ˈvi-zhə-niŋ, ˈvizh-niŋ\ (1743) : ENVISION

[1]**vi·sion·ary** \ˈvi-zhə-ˌner-ē\ *adj* (1648) **1 a** : of the nature of a vision : ILLUSORY **b** : incapable of being realized or achieved : UTOPIAN ⟨a ~ scheme⟩ **c** : existing only in imagination : UNREAL **2 a** : able or likely to see visions **b** : disposed to reverie or imagining : DREAMY **3** : of, relating to, or characterized by visions or the power of vision **4** : having or marked by foresight and imagination ⟨a ~ leader⟩ ⟨a ~ invention⟩ *syn* see IMAGINARY — **vi·sion·ar·i·ness** \-ē-nəs\ *n*

[2]**visionary** *n, pl* **-ar·ies** (1702) **1** : one whose ideas or projects are impractical : DREAMER **2** : one who sees visions : SEER **3** : one having unusual foresight and imagination ⟨a ~ in the computer industry⟩

vi·sioned \ˈvi-zhənd\ *adj* (1510) **1** : seen in a vision ⟨a ~ face⟩ **2** : produced by or experienced in a vision ⟨~ agony⟩ **3** : endowed with vision : INSPIRED

vi·sion·less \ˈvi-zhən-ləs\ *adj* (1820) **1** : SIGHTLESS, BLIND ⟨~ eyes⟩ **2** : lacking vision or inspiration ⟨a ~ leader⟩

vision quest *n* (1922) : a solitary vigil by an adolescent American Indian boy to seek spiritual power and learn through a vision the identity of his usu. animal or bird guardian spirit

[1]**vis·it** \ˈvi-zət\ *vb* **vis·it·ed** \ˈvi-zə-təd, ˈviz-təd\; **vis·it·ing** \ˈvi-zə-tiŋ, ˈviz-tiŋ\ [ME, fr. AF *visiter,* fr. L *visitare,* freq. of *visere* to go to see, freq. of *vidēre* to see] *vt* (13c) **1 a** *archaic* : COMFORT — used of the Deity ⟨~ us with Thy salvation —Charles Wesley⟩ **b** (1) : AFFLICT ⟨~*ed* his people with distempers —Tobias Smollett⟩ (2) : INFLICT, IMPOSE ⟨~*ed* his wrath upon them⟩ **c** : AVENGE ⟨~*ed* the sins of the fathers upon the children⟩ **d** : to present itself to or come over momentarily ⟨was ~*ed* by a strange notion⟩ **2** : to go to see in order to comfort or help **3 a** : to pay a call on as an act of friendship or courtesy **b** : to reside with temporarily as a guest **c** : to go to see or stay at (a place) for a particular purpose (as business or sightseeing) **d** : to go or come officially to inspect or oversee ⟨a bishop ~*ing* his parishes⟩ ~ *vi* **1** : to make a visit; *also* : to make frequent or regular visits **2** : CHAT, CONVERSE ⟨enjoys ~*ing* with the neighbors⟩

[2]**visit** *n* (1621) **1 a** : a short stay : CALL **b** : a brief residence as a guest **c** : an extended stay : SOJOURN **2** : a journey to and stay or short sojourn at a place **3** : an official or professional call or tour : VISITATION **4** : the act of a naval officer in boarding a merchant ship on the high seas in exercise of the right of search

vis·it·able \ˈvi-zə-tə-bəl, ˈviz-tə-\ *adj* (1605) **1** : subject to or allowing visitation or inspection **2** : socially eligible to receive visits

vis·i·tant \ˈvi-zə-tənt, ˈviz-tənt\ *n* (1599) **1** : VISITOR; *esp* : one thought to come from a spirit world **2** : a migratory bird that appears at intervals for a limited period — **visitant** *adj*

vis·i·ta·tion \ˌvi-zə-ˈtā-shən\ *n* (14c) **1** : an instance of visiting: as **a** : an official visit (as for inspection) **b** : [2]WAKE 3 **c** : temporary custody of a child granted to a noncustodial parent ⟨~ rights⟩ **2 a** : a special dispensation of divine favor or wrath **b** : a severe trial : AFFLICTION **3** *cap* : the visit of the Virgin Mary to Elizabeth recounted in Luke and celebrated July 2 by a Christian feast

vis·i·ta·to·ri·al \ˌvi-zə-tə-ˈtȯr-ē-əl, ˌviz-tə-\ *adj* (1688) : of or relating to visitation or to a judicial visitor or superintendent

visiting *adj* (1949) **1** : invited to join or attend an institution (as a university) for a limited time ⟨a ~ professor⟩ ⟨a ~ fellow⟩ **2** : playing on an opponent's grounds ⟨the ~ team⟩

visiting card *n* (1774) : a small card presented when visiting that bears the name and sometimes the address of the visitor

visiting fireman *n* (1926) : a usu. important or influential visitor whom it is desirable or expedient to entertain impressively

visiting nurse *n* (1918) : a nurse employed by a hospital or social-service agency to perform public health services and esp. to visit and provide care for sick persons in a community

vis·i·tor \ˈvi-zə-tər, ˈviz-tər\ *n* (14c) : one that visits; *esp* : one that makes formal visits of inspection

vi·sor *also* **vizor** \ˈvī-zər\ *n* [ME *viser,* fr. AF, fr. *vis* face — more at VISAGE] (14c) **1 :** the front piece of a helmet; *esp* **:** a movable upper piece **2 a :** a face mask **b :** DISGUISE **3 a :** a projecting front on a cap or headband for shading the eyes **b :** a usu. movable flat sunshade attached at the top of an automobile windshield — **vi·sored** \-zərd\ *adj* — **vi·sor·less** \-zər-ləs\ *adj*

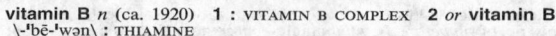

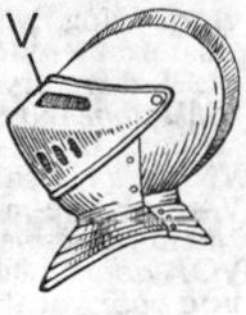
V visor 1

vis·ta \ˈvis-tə\ *n* [It, sight, fr. *visto,* pp. of *vedere* to see, fr. L *vidēre* — more at WIT] (1644) **1 :** a distant view through or along an avenue or opening **:** PROSPECT **2 :** an extensive mental view (as over a stretch of time or a series of events)
VISTA *abbr* Volunteers in Service to America
vis·taed \ˈvis-təd\ *adj* (1835) **1 :** affording or made to form a vista **2 :** seen in or as if in a vista
[1]**vi·su·al** \ˈvi-zhə-wəl, -zhəl; ˈvizh-wəl\ *adj* [ME, fr. LL *visualis,* fr. L *visus* sight, fr. *vidēre* to see] (15c) **1 :** of, relating to, or used in vision ⟨~ organs⟩ **2 :** attained or maintained by sight ⟨~ impressions⟩ **3 :** VISIBLE ⟨~ objects⟩ **4 :** producing mental images **:** VIVID **5 :** done or executed by sight only ⟨~ navigation⟩ **6 :** of, relating to, or employing visual aids — **vi·su·al·ly** \ˈvi-zhə-wə-lē, -zhə-lē; ˈvizh-wə-lē\ *adv*
[2]**visual** *n* (1938) **:** something (as a graphic) that appeals to the sight and is used for effect or illustration — usu. used in pl.
visual acuity *n* (1889) **:** the relative ability of the visual organ to resolve detail that is usu. expressed as the reciprocal of the minimum angular separation in minutes of two lines just resolvable as separate and that forms in the average human eye an angle of one minute
visual aid *n* (1911) **:** an instructional device (as a chart, map, or model) that appeals chiefly to vision; *esp* **:** an educational motion picture or filmstrip
visual cortex *n* (1954) **:** a sensory area of the occipital lobe of the cerebral cortex receiving afferent nerve fibers concerned with vision — called also *visual area*
visual field *n* (1875) **:** the entire expanse of space visible at a given instant without moving the eyes — called also *field of vision*
vi·su·al·i·sa·tion, vi·su·al·ise, vi·su·al·is·er *Brit var of* VISUALIZATION, VISUALIZE, VISUALIZER
vi·su·al·i·za·tion \ˌvi-zhə-wə-lə-ˈzā-shən, ˌvi-zhə-lə-, ˌvizh-wə-lə-\ *n* (1883) **1 :** formation of mental visual images **2 :** the act or process of interpreting in visual terms or of putting into visible form **3 :** the process of making an internal organ or part visible by the introduction (as by swallowing) of a radiopaque substance followed by radiography
vi·su·al·ize \ˈvi-zhə-wə-ˌlīz, ˈvi-zhə-ˌlīz, ˈvizh-wə-ˌlīz\ *vb* **-ized; -iz·ing** *vt* (1817) **:** to make visible: as **a :** to see or form a mental image of **:** ENVISAGE ⟨trying to ~ the problem⟩ **b :** to make (an internal organ or part) visible by radiographic visualization ~ *vi* **:** to form a mental visual image
vi·su·al·iz·er \-ˌlī-zər\ *n* (1886) **:** one that visualizes; *esp* **:** a person whose mental imagery is prevailingly visual
visual literacy *n* (1971) **:** the ability to recognize and understand ideas conveyed through visible actions or images (as pictures)
visual purple *n* (1878) **:** a photosensitive red or purple pigment in the retinal rods of various vertebrates; *esp* **:** RHODOPSIN
vi·suo·spa·tial \ˌvi-zhə-wō-ˈspā-shəl\ *adj* [*visu*al + *-o-* + *spatial*] (1960) **:** of, relating to, or being thought processes that involve visual and spatial awareness ⟨~ problem solving⟩
vi·ta \ˈvē-tə, ˈvī-tə\ *n, pl* **vi·tae** \ˈvē-ˌtī, -tē\ [L, lit., life] (1939) **1 :** a brief biographical sketch **2 :** CURRICULUM VITAE
vi·tal \ˈvī-tᵊl\ *adj* [ME, fr. L *vitalis* of life, fr. *vita* life; akin to L *vivere* to live — more at QUICK] (14c) **1 a :** existing as a manifestation of life **b :** concerned with or necessary to the maintenance of life ⟨~ organs⟩ ⟨blood and other ~ fluids⟩ **2 :** full of life and vigor **:** ANIMATED **3 :** characteristic of life or living beings **4 a :** fundamentally concerned with or affecting life or living beings: as (1) **:** tending to renew or refresh the living **:** INVIGORATING (2) **:** destructive to life **:** MORTAL **b :** of the utmost importance ⟨a ~ clue⟩ ⟨~ resources⟩ **5 :** recording data relating to lives **6 :** of, relating to, or constituting the staining of living tissues ***syn*** see ESSENTIAL — **vi·tal·ly** \-tᵊl-ē\ *adv*
vital capacity *n* (1852) **:** the breathing capacity of the lungs expressed as the number of cubic inches or cubic centimeters of air that can be forcibly exhaled after a full inspiration
vi·tal·ism \ˈvī-tə-ˌli-zəm\ *n* (1822) **1 :** a doctrine that the functions of a living organism are due to a vital principle distinct from physicochemical forces **2 :** a doctrine that the processes of life are not explicable by the laws of physics and chemistry alone and that life is in some part self-determining — **vi·tal·ist** \-list\ *n or adj* — **vi·tal·is·tic** \ˌvī-tə-ˈlis-tik\ *adj*
vi·tal·i·ty \vī-ˈta-lə-tē\ *n, pl* **-ties** (1592) **1 a :** the peculiarity distinguishing the living from the nonliving **b :** capacity to live and develop; *also* **:** physical or mental vigor esp. when highly developed **2 a :** power of enduring **b :** lively and animated character
vi·tal·ize \ˈvī-tə-ˌlīz\ *vt* **-ized; -iz·ing** (1678) **:** to endow with vitality **:** ANIMATE — **vi·tal·i·za·tion** \ˌvī-tə-lə-ˈzā-shən\ *n*
vi·tals \ˈvī-tᵊlz\ *n pl* (1607) **1 :** vital organs (as the heart, liver, lungs, and brain) **2 :** essential parts
vital signs *n pl* (1818) **:** signs of life; *specif* **:** the pulse rate, respiratory rate, body temperature, and often blood pressure of a person
vital statistics *n pl* (ca. 1837) **1 :** statistics relating to births, deaths, marriages, health, and disease **2 :** facts (as physical dimensions or quantities) considered to be interesting or important; *esp* **:** a woman's bust, waist, and hip measurements
vi·ta·min \ˈvī-tə-mən, *Brit usu* ˈvi-\ *n* [alter. of *vitamine,* fr. L *vita* life + E *amine*] (ca. 1912) **:** any of various organic substances that are essential in minute quantities to the nutrition of most animals and some plants, act esp. as coenzymes and precursors of coenzymes in the regulation of metabolic processes but do not provide energy or serve as building units, and are present in natural foodstuffs or sometimes produced within the body
vitamin A *n* (ca. 1920) **:** any of several fat-soluble vitamins (as retinol) found esp. in animal products (as egg yolk, milk, or fish-liver oils) or a mixture of them whose lack in the animal body causes epithelial tissues to become keratinous (as in the eye with resulting visual defects)
vitamin B *n* (ca. 1920) **1 :** VITAMIN B COMPLEX **2** *or* **vitamin B_1** \-ˈbē-ˈwən\ **:** THIAMINE
vitamin B complex *n* (1928) **:** a group of water-soluble vitamins that are found esp. in yeast, seed germs, eggs, liver and flesh, and vegetables and that have varied metabolic functions and include coenzymes and growth factors — called also *B complex;* compare BIOTIN, NIACIN, PANTOTHENIC ACID, RIBOFLAVIN
vitamin B_6 \-ˈbē-ˈsiks\ *n* (1934) **:** pyridoxine or a closely related compound found widely in combined form and considered essential to vertebrate nutrition
vitamin B_{12} \-ˈbē-ˈtwelv\ *n* (1948) **1 :** a complex cobalt-containing compound $C_{63}H_{88}CoN_{14}O_{14}P$ that occurs esp. in liver, is essential to normal blood formation, neural function, and growth, and is used esp. in treating pernicious and related anemias and in animal feed as a growth factor — called also *cyanocobalamin* **2 :** any of several compounds similar to vitamin B_{12} in action but having different chemistry
vitamin B_2 \-ˈbē-ˈtü\ *n* (1928) **:** RIBOFLAVIN
vitamin C *n* (ca. 1920) **:** a water-soluble vitamin $C_6H_8O_6$ found in plants and esp. in fruits and leafy vegetables or made synthetically and used in the prevention and treatment of scurvy and as an antioxidant for foods — called also *ascorbic acid*
vitamin D *n* (ca. 1921) **:** any or all of several fat-soluble vitamins chemically related to steroids, essential for normal bone and tooth structure, and found esp. in fish-liver oils, egg yolk, and milk or produced by activation (as by ultraviolet irradiation) of sterols: as **a** *or* **vitamin D_2** \-ˈdē-ˈtü\ **:** CALCIFEROL **b** *or* **vitamin D_3** \-ˈdē-ˈthrē\ **:** CHOLECALCIFEROL
vitamin E *n* (1925) **:** any of several fat-soluble vitamins that are chemically tocopherols, are essential in the nutrition of various vertebrates in which their absence is associated with infertility, degenerative changes in muscle, or vascular abnormalities, are found esp. in leaves and in seed germ oils, and are used chiefly in animal feeds and as antioxidants
vitamin H *n* [G *Haut* skin] (ca. 1935) **:** BIOTIN
vitamin K *n* [fr. the initial letter of Dan & Sw *koagulation* coagulation, Norw *koagulasjon* & G *Koagulation*] (ca. 1935) **1 :** either of two naturally occurring fat-soluble vitamins $C_{31}H_{46}O_2$ and $C_{41}H_{56}O_2$ essential for the clotting of blood because of their role in the production of prothrombin — called also respectively *vitamin K_1, vitamin K_2* **2 :** any of several synthetic compounds closely related chemically to natural vitamins K_1 and K_2 and of similar biological activity
vi·tel·line \vī-ˈte-lən, -ˌlēn, -ˌlīn\ *adj* [ME, fr. ML *vitellinus,* fr. L *vitellus* egg yolk] (15c) **1 :** resembling the yolk of an egg esp. in yellow color **2 :** of, relating to, or producing yolk
vitelline membrane *n* (1845) **:** a membrane enclosing an egg that comprises the zona pellucida in mammals and that upon fertilization splits off from the surface of the egg forming a fertilization membrane in many invertebrates and amphibians and in some fish
vi·tel·lo·gen·e·sis \vī-ˌte-lō-ˈje-nə-səs, və-\ *n* [NL, fr. L *vitellus* + NL *-o-* + *genesis*] (1947) **:** yolk formation
vi·tel·lo·gen·in \vī-ˌte-lō-ˈje-nən\ *n* [prob. fr. *vitellogen*esis + [1]*-in*] (1971) **:** a precursor protein of egg yolk normally in the blood or hemolymph only of females that is used as a biomarker in vertebrates of exposure to environmental estrogens which stimulate elevated levels in males as well as females
vi·ti·ate \ˈvi-shē-ˌāt\ *vt* **-at·ed; -at·ing** [L *vitiatus,* pp. of *vitiare,* fr. *vitium* fault, vice] (1534) **1 :** to make faulty or defective **:** IMPAIR ⟨the comic impact is *vitiated* by obvious haste —William Styron⟩ **2 :** to debase in moral or aesthetic status ⟨a mind *vitiated* by prejudice⟩ **3 :** to make ineffective ⟨fraud ~*s* a contract⟩ ***syn*** see DEBASE — **vi·ti·a·tion** \ˌvi-shē-ˈā-shən\ *n* — **vi·ti·a·tor** \ˈvi-shē-ˌā-tər\ *n*
vi·ti·cul·ture \ˈvi-tə-ˌkəl-chər, ˈvī-\ *n* [L *vitis* vine + E *culture* — more at WITHY] (1872) **:** the cultivation or culture of grapes esp. for wine making — **vi·ti·cul·tur·al** \ˌvi-tə-ˈkəl-chə-rəl, ˌvī-, -ˈkəlch-rəl\ *adj* — **vi·ti·cul·tur·al·ly** *adv* — **vi·ti·cul·tur·ist** \-rist\ *n*
vit·i·li·go \ˌvi-tə-ˈlī-(ˌ)gō, -ˈlē-\ *n* [NL, fr. L, skin eruption] (ca. 1842) **:** a skin disorder manifested by smooth white spots on various parts of the body
vit·rec·to·my \və-ˈtrek-tə-mē\ *n, pl* **-mies** [*vitr*eous humor + *-ectomy*] (1968) **:** surgical removal of all or part of the vitreous humor
[1]**vit·re·ous** \ˈvi-trē-əs\ *adj* [ME, fr. L, fr. *vitrum* glass] (14c) **1 a :** resembling glass (as in color, composition, brittleness, or luster) **:** GLASSY ⟨~ rocks⟩ **b :** characterized by low porosity and usu. translucence due to the presence of a glassy phase ⟨~ china⟩ **2 :** of, relating to, derived from, or consisting of glass **3 :** of, relating to, or constituting the vitreous humor ⟨~ surgery⟩
[2]**vitreous** *n* (1869) **:** VITREOUS HUMOR
vitreous humor *n* (14c) **:** the clear colorless transparent jelly that fills the eyeball posterior to the lens — see EYE illustration
vitreous silica *n* (1925) **:** a chemically stable and refractory glass made from silica alone — compare QUARTZ GLASS
vit·ri·fy \ˈvi-trə-ˌfī\ *vb* **-fied; -fy·ing** [MF *vitrifier,* fr. L *vitrum* glass] *vt* (1594) **:** to convert into glass or a glassy substance by heat and fusion ~ *vi* **:** to become vitrified — **vit·ri·fi·able** \ˌvi-trə-ˈfī-ə-bəl\ *adj* — **vit·ri·fi·ca·tion** \ˌvi-trə-fə-ˈkā-shən\ *n*
vi·trine \və-ˈtrēn\ *n* [F, fr. *vitre* pane of glass, fr. OF, fr. L *vitrum*] (1880) **:** a glass showcase or cabinet esp. for displaying fine wares or specimens
vit·ri·ol \ˈvi-trē-əl\ *n* [ME, fr. AF *vitriole,* fr. ML *vitriolum,* alter. of LL *vitreolum,* neut. of *vitreolus* glassy, fr. L *vitreus* vitreous] (14c) **1 a :** a sulfate of any of various metals (as copper, iron, or zinc); *esp* **:** a glassy hydrate of such a sulfate **b :** OIL OF VITRIOL **2 :** something felt to resemble vitriol esp. in caustic quality; *esp* **:** virulence of feeling or of speech — **vit·ri·ol·ic** \ˌvi-trē-ˈä-lik\ *adj*
vit·ta \ˈvi-tə\ *n, pl* **vit·tae** \ˈvi-tē, ˈvi-ˌtī\ [NL, fr. L, fillet; akin to L *viēre* to plait — more at WIRE] (1819) **1 :** STRIPE, STREAK **2 :** one of the oil tubes in the fruits of plants of the carrot family
vit·tles \ˈvi-tᵊlz\ *n pl* (14c) **:** VICTUALS

vi·tu·per·ate \vī-ˈtü-pə-ˌrāt, və-, -ˈtyü-\ *vb* **-at·ed; -at·ing** [L *vituperatus,* pp. of *vituperare,* fr. *vitium* fault + *parare* to make, prepare — more at PARE] *vt* (1542) **:** to abuse or censure severely or abusively **:** BERATE ~ *vi* **:** to use harsh condemnatory language ***syn*** see SCOLD — **vi·tu·per·a·tor** \-ˌrā-tər\ *n*

vi·tu·per·a·tion \(ˌ)vī-ˌtü-pə-ˈrā-shən, və-, -ˌtyü-\ *n* (15c) **1 :** sustained and bitter railing and condemnation **:** vituperative utterance **2 :** an act or instance of vituperating ***syn*** see ABUSE

vi·tu·per·a·tive \vī-ˈtü-p(ə-)rə-tiv, -pə-ˌrā-\ *adj* (1727) **:** uttering or given to censure **:** containing or characterized by verbal abuse — **vi·tu·per·a·tive·ly** *adv*

vi·tu·per·a·to·ry \-p(ə-)rə-ˌtȯr-ē\ *adj* (1586) **:** VITUPERATIVE

vi·va \ˈvē-və, -ˌvä\ *interj* [It & Sp, long live, fr. 3d pers. sing. pres. subj. of *vivere* to live, fr. L — more at QUICK] (1682) — used to express goodwill or approval

[1]**vi·va·ce** \vē-ˈvä-(ˌ)chā, -chē\ *n* (ca. 1683) **:** a musical composition or movement in vivace tempo

[2]**vivace** *adv or adj* [It, vivacious, fr. L *vivac-, vivax*] (ca. 1724) **:** in a brisk spirited manner — used as a direction in music

vi·va·cious \və-ˈvā-shəs *also* vī-\ *adj* [L *vivac-, vivax* long-lived, vigorous, high-spirited, fr. *vivere* to live] (ca. 1645) **:** lively in temper, conduct, or spirit **:** SPRIGHTLY ***syn*** see LIVELY — **vi·va·cious·ly** *adv* — **vi·va·cious·ness** *n*

vi·vac·i·ty \-ˈva-sə-tē\ *n* (15c) **:** the quality or state of being vivacious

vi·van·dière \ˌvē-ˌväⁿ-ˈdyer\ *n* [F, fem. of *vivandier* sutler, fr. OF, hospitable man, alter. of *viandier,* fr. *viande, viaunde* item of food — more at VIAND] (1844) **:** a woman who is a sutler

vi·var·i·um \vī-ˈver-ē-əm\ *n, pl* **-ia** \-ē-ə\ *or* **-i·ums** [L, park, preserve, fr. *vivus* alive — more at QUICK] (1853) **:** a terrarium used esp. for small animals

[1]**vi·va vo·ce** \ˌvī-və-ˈvō-(ˌ)sē *or* ˌvē-və-ˈvō-(ˌ)chā\ *adv* [ML, with the living voice] (1563) **:** by word of mouth **:** ORALLY

[2]**viva voce** *adj* (1654) **:** expressed or conducted by word of mouth

[3]**viva voce** *n* (1842) **:** an examination conducted viva voce — called also *viva*

vi·vax malaria \ˈvī-ˌvaks-\ *n* [NL *vivax,* specific epithet of *Plasmodium vivax,* fr. L] (1958) **:** malaria caused by a plasmodium (*Plasmodium vivax*) that induces paroxysms at 48-hour intervals

vi·ver·rid \vī-ˈver-əd\ *n* [NL *Viverridae,* fr. *Viverra,* type genus, fr. L *viverra* ferret; akin to OE *ācweorna* squirrel, Lith *voverė*] (1902) **:** any of a family (Viverridae) of carnivorous mammals that include the civets, genets, linsangs, and in some classifications the mongooses and that are rarely larger than a domestic cat but are long, slender, and like a weasel in build with short more or less retractile claws and rounded feet — **viverrid** *adj*

vi·vers \ˈvē-vərz, ˈvī-\ *n pl* [MF *vivres,* pl. of *vivre* food, fr. *vivre* to live, fr. L *vivere*] (1536) *chiefly Scot* **:** VICTUALS, FOOD

Viv·i·an *or* **Viv·i·en** \ˈvi-vē-ən\ *n* (1859) **:** the mistress of Merlin in Arthurian legend — called also *Lady of the Lake*

viv·id \ˈvi-vəd\ *adj* [L *vividus,* fr. *vivere* to live — more at QUICK] (1634) **1** *of a color* **:** very strong **:** very high in chroma **2 :** having the appearance of vigorous life or freshness **:** LIVELY ⟨a ~ sketch⟩ **3 :** producing a strong or clear impression on the senses **:** SHARP, INTENSE; *specif* **:** producing distinct mental images ⟨a ~ description⟩ **4 :** acting clearly and vigorously ⟨a ~ imagination⟩ ***syn*** see GRAPHIC — **viv·id·ly** *adv* — **viv·id·ness** *n*

vi·vif·ic \vī-ˈvi-fik\ *adj* [L *vivificus*] (1551) **:** imparting spirit or vivacity

viv·i·fy \ˈvi-və-ˌfī\ *vt* **-fied; -fy·ing** [ME *vivifien* to nourish, fr. AF *vivifier* to give life to, fr. LL *vivificare,* fr. L *vivificus* enlivening, fr. *vivus* alive — more at QUICK] (14c) **1 :** to endow with life or renewed life **:** ANIMATE ⟨rains that ~ the barren hills⟩ **2 :** to impart vitality or vividness to ⟨a long story *vivified* by specific details⟩ ***syn*** see QUICKEN — **viv·i·fi·ca·tion** \ˌvi-və-fə-ˈkā-shən\ *n* — **viv·i·fi·er** \ˈvi-və-ˌfī(-ə)r\ *n*

vi·vi·par·i·ty \ˌvī-və-ˈpa-rət-ē, ˌvi-\ *n* (1864) **:** the quality or state of being viviparous

vi·vip·a·rous \vī-ˈvi-p(ə-)rəs, və-\ *adj* [L *viviparus,* fr. *vivus* alive + *-parus* -parous] (1646) **1 :** producing living young instead of eggs from within the body in the manner of nearly all mammals, many reptiles, and a few fishes **2 :** germinating while still attached to the parent plant ⟨the ~ seed of the mangrove⟩ — **vi·vip·a·rous·ly** *adv*

viv·i·sect \ˈvi-və-ˌsekt\ *vb* [back-formation fr. *vivisection*] *vt* (1864) **:** to perform vivisection on **:** subject to vivisection ~ *vi* **:** to practice vivisection — **viv·i·sec·tor** \-ˌsek-tər\ *n*

viv·i·sec·tion \ˌvi-və-ˈsek-shən, ˈvi-və-ˌ\ *n* [L *vivus* + E *section*] (1707) **1 :** the cutting of or operation on a living animal usu. for physiological or pathological investigation; *broadly* **:** animal experimentation esp. if considered to cause distress to the subject **2 :** minute or pitiless examination or criticism — **viv·i·sec·tion·al** \ˌvi-və-ˈsek-shnəl, -shə-nᵊl\ *adj* — **viv·i·sec·tion·ist** \-ˈsek-sh(ə-)nist\ *n*

vix·en \ˈvik-sən\ *n* [ME (southern dial.) **vixen,* alter. of ME *fixen,* fr. OE *fyxe,* fem. of *fox*] (1590) **1 :** a shrewish ill-tempered woman **2 :** a female fox **3 :** a sexually attractive woman — **vix·en·ish** \-s(ə-)nish\ *adj*

viz *abbr* videlicet

viz·ard \ˈvi-zərd, -ˌzärd\ *n* [alter. of ME *viser* mask, visor] (ca. 1555) **1 :** a mask for disguise or protection **2 :** DISGUISE, GUISE

vizcacha *var of* VISCACHA

vi·zier \və-ˈzir\ *n* [Turk *vezir,* fr. Ar *wazīr*] (1599) **1 :** a high executive officer of various Muslim countries and esp. of the Ottoman Empire **2 :** a civil officer in ancient Egypt having viceregal powers — **vi·zier·ate** \-ˈzir-ət, -ˈzir-ˌāt\ *n* — **vi·zier·ial** \-ˈzir-ē-əl\ *adj* — **vi·zier·ship** \-ˈzir-ˌship\ *n*

vizor *var of* VISOR

vizs·la \ˈvēz-lə, ˈvēs-, ˈvizh-\ *n* [Hung] (1945) **:** any of a breed of hunting dogs of Hungarian origin that resemble the Weimaraner but have a rich deep red coat and brown eyes

VJ \ˈvē-ˌjā\ *n* (1982) **:** VEEJAY

VLDL \ˌvē-(ˌ)el-(ˌ)dē-ˈel\ *n* [*very low-density lipoprotein*] (1977) **:** a plasma lipoprotein that is produced primarily by the liver with lesser amounts contributed by the intestine, that contains relatively large amounts of triglycerides compared to protein, and that leaves a residue of cholesterol in the tissues during the process of conversion to LDL — compare HDL

VLF *abbr* very low frequency

vlog \ˈvlȯg, ˈvläg\ *n* [*video* + *blog*] (2002) **:** a blog that contains video material — **vlog** *vb* — **vlog·ger** *n*

VLSI *abbr* very large-scale integration

VMD *abbr* [NL *veterinariae medicinae doctor*] doctor of veterinary medicine

VNA *abbr* Visiting Nurse Association

V–neck \ˈvē-ˌnek\ *n* (1882) **:** a V-shaped neck of a garment; *also* **:** a garment (as a sweater) with a V-shaped neck — **V–necked** *adj*

VOA *abbr* Voice of America

voc *abbr* vocational

VOC *abbr* volatile organic compound

vo·cab \ˈvō-ˌkab\ *n* (1900) **:** VOCABULARY

vo·ca·ble \ˈvō-kə-bəl\ *n* [MF, fr. L *vocabulum,* fr. *vocare* to call, fr. *vox* voice — more at VOICE] (1530) **:** TERM; *specif* **:** a word composed of various sounds or letters without regard to its meaning

vo·cab·u·lar \vō-ˈka-byə-lər, və-\ *adj* [back-formation fr. *vocabulary*] (1608) **:** of or relating to words or phraseology **:** VERBAL

vo·cab·u·lary \vō-ˈka-byə-ˌler-ē, və-\ *n, pl* **-lar·ies** [MF *vocabulaire,* prob. fr. ML *vocabularium,* fr. neut. of *vocabularius* verbal, fr. L *vocabulum*] (1532) **1 :** a list or collection of words or of words and phrases usu. alphabetically arranged and explained or defined **:** LEXICON **2 a :** a sum or stock of words employed by a language, group, individual, or work or in a field of knowledge **b :** a list or collection of terms or codes available for use (as in an indexing system) **3 :** a supply of expressive techniques or devices (as of an art form)

vocabulary entry *n* (ca. 1934) **:** a word (as the noun *book*), hyphenated or open compound (as the verb *book-match* or the noun *book review*), word element (as the affix *pro-*), abbreviation (as *agt*), verbalized symbol (as *Na*), or term (as *man in the street*) entered alphabetically in a dictionary for the purpose of definition or identification or expressly included as an inflected form (as the noun *mice* or the verb *saw*) or as a derived form (as the noun *godlessness* or the adverb *globally*) or related phrase (as *one for the book*) run on at its base word and usu. set in a type (as boldface) readily distinguishable from that of the lightface running text which defines, explains, or identifies the entry

[1]**vo·cal** \ˈvō-kəl\ *adj* [ME, fr. L *vocalis,* fr. *voc-, vox* voice — more at VOICE] (14c) **1 a :** uttered by the voice **:** ORAL **b :** produced in the larynx **:** uttered with voice **2 :** relating to, composed or arranged for, or sung by the human voice ⟨~ music⟩ **3 :** VOCALIC **4 a :** having or exercising the power of producing voice, speech, or sound **b :** EXPRESSIVE **c :** full of voices **:** RESOUNDING **d :** given to expressing oneself freely or insistently **:** OUTSPOKEN ⟨a highly ~ critic⟩ **e :** expressed in words **5 :** of, relating to, or resembling the voice ⟨~ impairment⟩ — **vo·cal·i·ty** \vō-ˈka-lə-tē\ *n* — **vo·cal·ly** \ˈvō-kə-lē\ *adv*

[2]**vocal** *n* (1582) **1 :** a vocal sound **2 :** a usu. accompanied musical composition for the human voice **:** SONG; *also* **:** a performance of such a composition

vocal cords *n pl* (1852) **:** either of two pairs of folds of mucous membranes that project into the cavity of the larynx and have free edges extending dorsoventrally toward the middle line

vocal folds *n pl* (1924) **:** the lower pair of vocal cords each of which when drawn taut, approximated to the contralateral member of the pair, and subjected to a flow of breath produces the voice

[1]**vo·cal·ic** \vō-ˈka-lik, və-\ *adj* [L *vocalis* vowel, fr. *vocalis* vocal] (1814) **1 :** marked by or consisting of vowels **2 a :** being or functioning as a vowel **b :** of, relating to, or associated with a vowel — **vo·cal·i·cal·ly** \-li-k(ə-)lē\ *adv*

[2]**vocalic** *n* (1924) **:** a vowel sound or sequence in its function as the most sonorous part of a syllable

vo·cal·ise *Brit var of* VOCALIZE

vo·cal·ism \ˈvō-kə-ˌli-zəm\ *n* (1854) **1 a :** the vowel system of a language or dialect **b :** the pattern of vowels in a word or paradigm **2 :** VOCALIZATION **3 :** vocal art or technique **:** SINGING

vo·cal·ist \ˈvō-kə-list\ *n* (1826) **:** [1]SINGER

vo·cal·ize \ˈvō-kə-ˌlīz\ *vb* **-ized; -iz·ing** *vt* (1669) **1 :** to give voice to **:** UTTER; *specif* **:** SING **2 a :** to make voiced rather than voiceless **:** VOICE **b :** to convert to a vowel **3 :** to furnish (as a consonantal Hebrew or Arabic text) with vowels or vowel points ~ *vi* **1 :** to utter vocal sounds **2 :** SING; *specif* **:** to sing without words — **vo·cal·i·za·tion** \ˌvō-kə-lə-ˈzā-shən\ *n* — **vo·cal·iz·er** \ˈvō-kə-ˌlī-zər\ *n*

vo·ca·tion \vō-ˈkā-shən\ *n* [ME *vocacioun,* fr. AF *vocaciun,* fr. L *vocation-, vocatio* summons, fr. *vocare* to call, fr. *vox* voice — more at VOICE] (15c) **1 a :** a summons or strong inclination to a particular state or course of action; *esp* **:** a divine call to the religious life **b :** an entry into the priesthood or a religious order **2 a :** the work in which a person is employed **:** OCCUPATION **b :** the persons engaged in a particular occupation **3 :** the special function of an individual or group

vo·ca·tion·al \vō-ˈkā-shnəl, -shə-nᵊl\ *adj* (1652) **1 :** of, relating to, or concerned with a vocation **2 :** of, relating to, or undergoing training in a skill or trade to be pursued as a career ⟨a ~ school⟩ ⟨~ students⟩ — **vo·ca·tion·al·ly** *adv*

vo·ca·tion·al·ism \-shnə-ˌli-zəm, -shə-nᵊl-ˌi-zəm\ *n* (1924) **:** emphasis on vocational training in education — **vo·ca·tion·al·ist** \-list, -ist\ *n*

[1]**voc·a·tive** \ˈvä-kə-tiv\ *adj* [ME *vocatif,* fr. MF, fr. L *vocativus,* fr. *vocatus,* pp. of *vocare*] (15c) **1 :** of, relating to, or being a grammatical case marking the one addressed (as Latin *Domine* in *miserere, Domine* "have mercy, O Lord") **2** *of a word or word group* **:** marking the one addressed (as *mother* in "mother, come here") — **voc·a·tive·ly** *adv*

[2]**vocative** *n* (15c) **1 :** the vocative case of a language **2 :** a form in the vocative case

voc–ed \ˈvōk-ˌed\ *n* (1967) **:** vocational education

vo·cif·er·ant \vō-ˈsi-fə-rənt\ *adj* (1609) **:** CLAMOROUS, VOCIFEROUS

vo·cif·er·ate \-ˌrāt\ *vb* **-at·ed; -at·ing** [L *vociferatus,* pp. of *vociferari,* fr. *voc-, vox* voice + *ferre* to bear — more at VOICE, BEAR] *vt* (1599) **:** to utter loudly **:** SHOUT ~ *vi* **:** to cry out loudly **:** CLAMOR — **vo·cif·er·a·tion** \-ˌsi-fə-ˈrā-shən\ *n* — **vo·cif·er·a·tor** \-ˈsi-fə-ˌrā-tər\ *n*

vo·cif·er·ous \vō-ˈsi-f(ə-)rəs\ *adj* (ca. 1611) **:** marked by or given to vehement insistent outcry — **vo·cif·er·ous·ly** *adv* — **vo·cif·er·ous·ness** *n*

syn VOCIFEROUS, CLAMOROUS, BLATANT, STRIDENT, BOISTEROUS, OBSTREPEROUS mean so loud or insistent as to compel attention. VOCIFEROUS implies a vehement shouting or calling out ⟨*vociferous* cries of protest and outrage⟩. CLAMOROUS may imply insistency as well as vociferousness in demanding or protesting ⟨*clamorous* demands for prison reforms⟩. BLATANT implies an offensive bellowing or insensitive loudness ⟨*blatant* rock music⟩ ⟨a *blatant* clamor for impeachment⟩. STRIDENT suggests harsh and discordant noise ⟨heard the *strident* cry of the crow⟩. BOISTEROUS suggests a noisiness and turbulence due to high spirits ⟨a *boisterous* crowd of party goers⟩. OBSTREPEROUS suggests unruly and aggressive noisiness and resistance to restraint ⟨the *obstreperous* demonstrators were arrested⟩.

vo·cod·er \ˈvō-ˌkō-dər\ *n* [*voice coder*] (ca. 1939) **:** an electronic mechanism that reduces speech signals to slowly varying signals transmittable over communication systems of limited frequency bandwidth

vod·cast \ˈväd-ˌkast\ [[2]video + *podcast*] (2005) **:** a video podcast

vod·ka \ˈväd-kə\ *n* [Russ, fr. *voda* water; akin to OE *wæter* water] (ca. 1803) **:** a colorless liquor of neutral spirits distilled from a mash (as of rye or wheat)

vodka martini *n* (1948) **:** a martini made with vodka instead of gin

vodou *var of* VOODOO

vo·dun *also* **vo·doun** \vō-ˈdüⁿ\ *n* [Haitian Creole *vodoun, vodou*] (1920) **:** VOODOO 1

vog \ˈvȯg, ˈväg\ *n* [*vo*lcanic + sm*og*] (1987) **:** air pollution caused by volcanic emissions

vo·gie \ˈvō-gē\ *adj* [origin unknown] (1712) *Scot* **:** PROUD, VAIN

[1]vogue \ˈvōg\ *n* [MF, action of rowing, course, fashion, fr. *voguer* to sail, fr. OF, fr. OIt *vogare* to row] (1571) **1** *archaic* **:** the leading place in popularity or acceptance **2 a :** popular acceptation or favor **:** POPULARITY **b :** a period of popularity **3 :** one that is in fashion at a particular time ***syn*** see FASHION — **vogue** *adj*

[2]vogue *vi* **vogued; vogu·ing** *or* **vogue·ing** [fr. *Vogue,* a fashion magazine] (1989) **:** to strike poses in campy imitation of fashion models esp. as a kind of dance — **vogu·er** \ˈvō-gər\ *n*

vogu·ish \ˈvō-gish\ *adj* (1926) **1 :** FASHIONABLE, SMART **2 :** suddenly or temporarily popular ⟨a ~ term⟩ — **vogu·ish·ness** *n*

[1]voice \ˈvȯis\ *n* [ME, fr. OF *vois,* fr. L *voc-, vox;* akin to OHG *giwahanen* to mention, Gk *epos* word, speech, Skt *vāk* voice] (14c) **1 a :** sound produced by vertebrates by means of lungs, larynx, or syrinx; *esp* **:** sound so produced by human beings **b** (1) **:** musical sound produced by the vocal folds and resonated by the cavities of head and throat (2) **:** the power or ability to produce musical tones (3) **:** SINGER (4) **:** one of the melodic parts in a vocal or instrumental composition (5) **:** condition of the vocal organs with respect to production of musical tones (6) **:** the use of the voice (as in singing or acting) ⟨studying ~⟩ **c :** expiration of air with the vocal cords drawn close so as to vibrate audibly (as in uttering vowels and consonant sounds as \v\ or \z\) **d :** the faculty of utterance ⟨lost my ~⟩ **2 :** a sound resembling or suggesting vocal utterance **3 :** an instrument or medium of expression ⟨the party became the ~ of the workers⟩ **4 a :** wish, choice, or opinion openly or formally expressed ⟨the ~ of the people⟩ **b :** right of expression; *also* **:** influential power **5 :** distinction of form or a system of inflections of a verb to indicate the relation of the subject of the verb to the action which the verb expresses ⟨active and passive ~*s*⟩ — **with one voice :** without dissent **:** UNANIMOUSLY

[2]voice *vt* **voiced; voic·ing** (15c) **1 :** to express in words **:** UTTER ⟨~ a complaint⟩ **2 :** to adjust for producing the proper musical sounds **3 :** to pronounce (as a consonant) with voice ***syn*** see EXPRESS

voice box *n* (1912) **:** LARYNX

voiced *adj* (15c) **1 :** having or furnished with a voice esp. of a specified kind — often used in combination ⟨soft-*voiced*⟩ **2 :** uttered with vocal cord vibration ⟨a ~ consonant⟩

voice·ful \ˈvȯis-fəl\ *adj* (ca. 1611) **:** having a voice or vocal quality; *also* **:** having a loud voice or many voices — **voice·ful·ness** *n*

voice·less \-ləs\ *adj* (1535) **1 :** having no voice **:** MUTE **2 :** not voiced **:** SURD ⟨a ~ consonant⟩ — **voice·less·ly** *adv* — **voice·less·ness** *n*

voice mail *n* (1980) **:** an electronic communication system in which spoken messages are recorded or digitized for later playback to the intended recipient; *also* **:** such a message

voice–over \ˈvȯis-ˌō-vər\ *n* (ca. 1947) **1 a :** the voice of an unseen narrator speaking (as in a motion picture or television commercial) **b :** the voice of a visible character (as in a motion picture) expressing unspoken thoughts **2 :** a recording of a voice-over

voice part *n* (1776) **:** VOICE 1b(4)

voice·print \ˈvȯis-ˌprint\ *n* [*voice* + finger*print*] (1962) **:** an individually distinctive pattern of certain voice characteristics that is spectrographically produced

voic·er \ˈvȯi-sər\ *n* (1879) **:** one that voices; *specif* **:** one that voices organ pipes

voice vote *n* (1924) **:** a parliamentary vote taken by calling for ayes and noes and estimating which response is stronger

[1]void \ˈvȯid\ *adj* [ME *voyde,* fr. AF, fr. VL **vocitus,* alter. of L *vocivus, vacivus* empty, fr. *vacare* to be empty] (14c) **1 a :** not occupied **:** VACANT ⟨a ~ bishopric⟩ **b :** not inhabited **:** DESERTED **2 :** containing nothing ⟨~ space⟩ **3 :** IDLE, LEISURE **4 a :** being without something specified **:** DEVOID ⟨a nature ~ of all malice⟩ **b :** having no members or examples; *specif, of a suit* **:** having no cards represented in a particular hand **5 :** VAIN, USELESS **6 a :** of no legal force or effect **:** NULL ⟨a ~ contract⟩ **b :** VOIDABLE ***syn*** see EMPTY — **void·ness** *n*

[2]void *n* (1616) **1 a :** OPENING, GAP **b :** empty space **:** EMPTINESS, VACUUM **2 :** the quality or state of being without something **:** LACK, ABSENCE **3 :** a feeling of want or hollowness **4 :** absence of cards of a particular suit in a hand orig. dealt to a player

[3]void *vb* [ME, fr. AF *voider* (OF of Île-de-France *vuider*) VL **vocitare,* fr. **vocitus*] *vt* (14c) **1 a :** to make empty or vacant **:** CLEAR **b** *archaic* **:** VACATE, LEAVE **2 :** DISCHARGE, EMIT **3 :** NULLIFY, ANNUL ~ *vi* **:** to eliminate solid or liquid waste from the body — **void·er** *n*

void·able \ˈvȯi-də-bəl\ *adj* (15c) **:** capable of being voided; *specif* **:** capable of being adjudged void ⟨a ~ contract⟩ — **void·able·ness** *n*

void·ance \ˈvȯi-dᵊn(t)s\ *n* (14c) **1 :** the act of voiding **2** *of a benefice* **:** the state of being without an incumbent

void·ed \ˈvȯi-dəd\ *adj* (ca. 1539) **:** having the inner part cut away or left vacant with a narrow border left at the sides — used of a heraldic charge

voi·là *or* **voi·la** \vwä-ˈlä\ *interj* [F, lit., see there] (1739) — used to call attention, to express satisfaction or approval, or to suggest an appearance as if by magic

voile \ˈvȯi(-ə)l\ *n* [F, veil, fr. OF, fr. L *vela,* neut. pl. of *velum*] (1889) **:** a fine soft sheer fabric used esp. for women's summer clothing or curtains

voir dire \ˈvwär-ˈdir, ˈwär-\ *n* [AF, lit., to speak the truth] (1676) **:** a preliminary examination to determine the competency of a witness or juror

vol *abbr* **1** volcano **2** volume **3** volunteer

vo·lant \ˈvō-lənt\ *adj* [MF, fr. L *volant-, volans,* prp. of *volare* to fly] (1572) **1 :** having the wings extended as if in flight — used of a heraldic bird **2 :** flying or capable of flying **3 :** QUICK, NIMBLE

vo·lan·te \vō-ˈlän-(ˌ)tā\ *adj* [It, lit., flying, fr. L *volant-, volans,* prp.] (ca. 1854) **:** moving with light rapidity — used as a direction in music

Vo·la·pük \ˈvō-lə-ˌpu̇k, ˈvä-\ *n* [Volapük, lit., world's speech, fr. *vola* of the world (gen. of *vol* world, modif. of E *world*) + *pük* speech, modif. of E *speak*] (1885) **:** an artificial international language based largely on English but with some root words from German, French, and Latin

vo·lar \ˈvō-lər, -ˌlär\ *adj* [L *vola* hollow in the palm of the hand or sole of the foot] (1814) **:** relating to the palm of the hand or the sole of the foot; *specif* **:** located on the same side as the palm of the hand

[1]vol·a·tile \ˈvä-lə-tᵊl, *esp Brit* -ˌtīl(-ə)l\ *adj* [F, fr. L *volatilis,* fr. *volare* to fly] (1605) **1 :** readily vaporizable at a relatively low temperature **2 :** flying or having the power to fly **3 a :** LIGHTHEARTED, LIVELY **b :** easily aroused ⟨~ suspicions⟩ **c :** tending to erupt into violence **:** EXPLOSIVE ⟨a ~ temper⟩ **4 a :** unable to hold the attention fixed because of an inherent lightness or fickleness of disposition **b :** characterized by or subject to rapid or unexpected change ⟨a ~ market⟩ **5 :** difficult to capture or hold permanently **:** EVANESCENT, TRANSITORY — **vol·a·tile·ness** *n* — **vol·a·til·i·ty** \ˌvä-lə-ˈti-lə-tē\ *n*

[2]volatile *n* (1686) **:** a volatile substance

volatile oil *n* (1800) **:** an oil that vaporizes readily; *esp* **:** ESSENTIAL OIL

vol·a·til·ise *Brit var of* VOLATILIZE

vol·a·til·ize \ˈvä-lə-tə-ˌlīz, *Brit also* və-ˈla-\ *vb* **-ized; -iz·ing** *vt* (1657) **:** to make volatile; *esp* **:** to cause to pass off in vapor ~ *vi* **:** to pass off in vapor — **vol·a·til·iz·able** \-ˌlī-zə-bəl\ *adj* — **vol·a·til·i·za·tion** \ˌvä-lə-tə-lə-ˈzā-shən, *Brit also* və-ˌla-\ *n*

vol–au–vent \ˌvȯ-lō-ˈväⁿ\ *n* [F, lit., flight in the wind] (1828) **:** a baked patty shell filled with meat, fowl, game, or seafood in sauce

[1]vol·ca·nic \väl-ˈka-nik, vȯl- *also* -ˈkā-\ *adj* (1774) **1 a :** of, relating to, or produced by a volcano **b :** characterized by volcanoes ⟨a ~ range⟩ **c :** made of materials from volcanoes **2 :** explosively violent **:** VOLATILE ⟨~ emotions⟩ — **vol·ca·ni·cal·ly** \-ni-k(ə-)lē\ *adv*

[2]volcanic *n* (1894) **:** a volcanic rock

volcanic glass *n* (ca. 1840) **:** natural glass produced by the cooling of molten lava too rapidly to permit crystallization

vol·ca·nic·i·ty \ˌväl-kə-ˈni-sə-tē, ˌvȯl-\ *n* (1836) **:** VOLCANISM

vol·ca·nism \ˈväl-kə-ˌni-zəm, ˈvȯl-\ *n* (ca. 1864) **:** volcanic action or activity

vol·ca·no \väl-ˈkā-(ˌ)nō, vȯl-\ *n, pl* **-noes** *or* **-nos** [It or Sp; It *vulcano,* fr. Sp *volcán,* ultim. fr. L *Volcanus* Vulcan] (1613) **1 :** a vent in the crust of the earth or another planet or a moon from which usu. molten or hot rock and steam issue; *also* **:** a hill or mountain composed wholly or in part of the ejected material **2 :** something of explosively violent potential

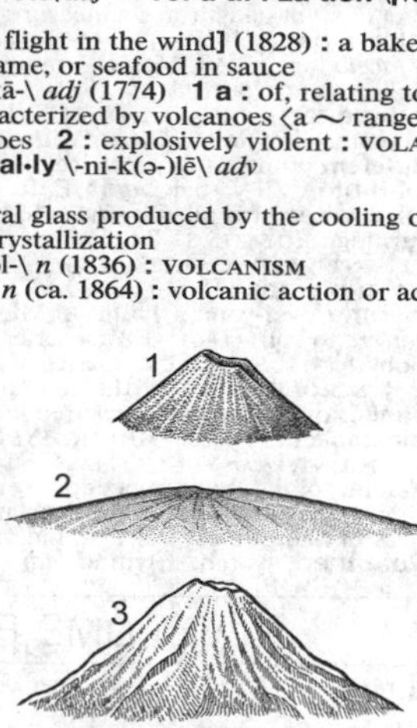

volcano 1: *1* cinder cone, *2* shield volcano, *3* stratovolcano

vol·ca·no·log·i·cal \ˌväl-kə-nə-ˈlä-ji-kəl, ˌvȯl-\ *also* **vol·ca·no·log·ic** \-jik\ *adj* (ca. 1891) **:** of, relating to, or involving volcanology or volcanic phenomena ⟨~ processes that shape the planets⟩

vol·ca·nol·o·gy \ˌväl-kə-ˈnä-lə-jē, ˌvȯl-\ *n* (1886) **:** a branch of science that deals with volcanic phenomena — **vol·ca·nol·o·gist** \-jist\ *n*

[1]vole \ˈvōl\ *n* [F, prob. fr. *voler* to fly — more at VOLLEY] (1679) **:** GRAND SLAM 1

[2]vole *n* [earlier *vole-mouse,* fr. *vole-* (of Scand origin; akin to ON *vǫllr* field) + *mouse;* akin to OE *weald* forest — more at WOLD] (1805) **:** any of various small rodents (*Microtus* and related genera) that typically have a stout body, rather blunt nose, and short ears, inhabit both moist meadows and dry uplands and do much damage to crops, and are closely related to muskrats and lemmings

vo·li·tion \vō-ˈli-shən, və-\ *n* [F, fr. ML *volition-, volitio,* fr. L *vol-* (stem of *velle* to will, wish) + *-ition-, -itio* (as in L *position-, positio* position) — more at WILL] (1615) **1 :** an act of making a choice or decision; *also* **:** a choice or decision made **2 :** the power of choosing or determining **:** WILL — **vo·li·tion·al** \-ˈlish-nəl, -ˈli-shə-nᵊl\ *adj*

vol·i·tive \ˈvä-lə-tiv\ *adj* (1660) **1 :** of or relating to the will **2 :** expressing a wish or permission

volks·lied \ˈfōks-ˌlēt, ˈfōlks-\ *n, pl* **volks·lie·der** \-ˌlē-dər\ [G, fr. *Volk* people + *Lied* song] (ca. 1854) **:** a folk song

[1]vol·ley \ˈvä-lē\ *n, pl* **volleys** [MF *volee* flight, fr. *voler* to fly, fr. OF, fr. L *volare*] (1573) **1 a :** a flight of missiles (as arrows) **b :** simultaneous discharge of a number of missile weapons **c :** one round per gun in a battery fired as soon as a gun is ready without regard to order **d** (1) **:** the flight of the ball (as in volleyball or tennis) or its course before striking the ground; *also* **:** a return of the ball before it touches the ground (2) **:** a kick of the ball in soccer before it rebounds (3) **:** the exchange of the shuttlecock in badminton following the serve **2 a :** a burst or emission of many things or a large amount at once ⟨received a ~ of angry letters⟩ **b :** a burst of simultaneous or immediately sequential nerve impulses passing to an end organ, synapse, or center

[2]volley *vb* **vol·leyed; vol·ley·ing** *vt* (1591) **1 :** to discharge in or as if in a volley **2 :** to propel (an object) while in the air and before touching the ground; *esp* : to hit (a tennis ball) on the volley ~ *vi* **1** : to become discharged in or as if in a volley **2** : to make a volley; *specif* : to volley an object of play (as in tennis) — **vol·ley·er** *n*

vol·ley·ball \ˈvä-lē-ˌbȯl\ *n* (1896) : a game played by volleying an inflated ball over a net; *also* : the ball used in this game

vol·plane \ˈväl-ˌplān, ˈvȯl-\ *vi* **vol·planed; vol·plan·ing** [F *vol plané* gliding flight] (1909) **1** : to glide in or as if in an airplane **2** : GLIDE 3

Vol·sci \ˈvȯl-ˌskē, ˈväl-ˌsī\ *n pl* [L] (ca. 1909) : a people of ancient Italy dwelling between the Latins and Samnites

Vol·scian \ˈväl-shən, ˈvȯl-skē-ən\ *n, pl* **Volscians** (1627) **1** : a member of the Volsci **2** : the Italic language of the Volsci — **Volscian** *adj*

[1]**volt** \ˈvōlt, ˈvȯlt\ *n* [F *volte,* fr. It *volta* turn, fr. *voltare* to turn, fr. VL **volvitare,* freq. of L *volvere* to roll — more at VOLUBLE] (1688) **1** : a leaping movement in fencing to avoid a thrust **2 a** : a tread or gait in which a horse going sideways makes a turn around a center **b** : a circle traced by a horse in this movement

[2]**volt** \ˈvōlt\ *n* [Alessandro *Volta*] (1873) : the practical meter-kilogram-second unit of electrical potential difference and electromotive force equal to the difference of potential between two points in a conducting wire carrying a constant current of one ampere when the power dissipated between these two points is equal to one watt and equivalent to the potential difference across a resistance of one ohm when one ampere is flowing through it

volt·age \ˈvōl-tij\ *n* (1890) **1** : electric potential or potential difference expressed in volts **2** : intensity of feeling

voltage divider *n* (1922) : a resistor or series of resistors provided with taps at certain points and used to provide various potential differences from a single power source

vol·ta·ic \väl-ˈtā-ik, vōl-, vȯl-\ *adj* [Alessandro *Volta*] (1812) : of, relating to, or producing direct electric current by chemical action (as in a battery) : GALVANIC ⟨~ cell⟩

volt–am·pere \ˈvōlt-ˈam-ˌpir *also* -ˌper\ *n* (1896) : a unit of electric measurement equal to the product of a volt and an ampere that for direct current constitutes a measure of power equivalent to a watt

volte–face \ˌvȯlt-ˈfäs, ˌvȯl-tə-\ *n* [F, fr. It *voltafaccia,* fr. *voltare* to turn + *faccia* face, fr. VL **facia* — more at VOLT, FACE] (1819) : a reversal in policy : ABOUT-FACE

volt·me·ter \ˈvōlt-ˌmē-tər\ *n* [ISV] (1869) : an instrument (as a galvanometer) for measuring in volts the differences in potential between different points of an electrical circuit

vol·u·ble \ˈväl-yə-bəl\ *adj* [ME, fr. L *volubilis,* fr. *volvere* to roll; akin to OE *wealwian* to roll, Gk *eilyein* to roll, wrap] (15c) **1** : easily rolling or turning : ROTATING **2** : characterized by ready or rapid speech : GLIB, FLUENT ***syn*** see TALKATIVE — **vol·u·bil·i·ty** \ˌväl-yə-ˈbi-lə-tē\ *n* — **vol·u·ble·ness** \ˈväl-yə-bəl-nəs\ *n* — **vol·u·bly** \-blē\ *adv*

[1]**vol·ume** \ˈväl-yəm, -(ˌ)yüm\ *n* [ME, fr. AF, fr. L *volumen* roll, scroll, fr. *volvere* to roll] (14c) **1 a** : a series of printed sheets bound typically in book form : BOOK **b** : a series of issues of a periodical **c** : ALBUM 1c **2** : SCROLL 1a **3** : the amount of space occupied by a three-dimensional object as measured in cubic units (as quarts or liters) : cubic capacity — see METRIC SYSTEM table, WEIGHT table **4 a** (1) : AMOUNT; *also* : BULK, MASS (2) : a considerable quantity **b** : the amount of a substance occupying a particular volume **c** : mass or the representation of mass in art or architecture **5** : the degree of loudness or the intensity of a sound; *also* : LOUDNESS ***syn*** see BULK — **vol·umed** \-yəmd, -(ˌ)yümd\ *adj*

VOLUME FORMULAS

FIGURE	FORMULA	MEANING OF LETTERS
cube	$V = a^3$	a = length of one edge
rectangular solid	$V = lwh$	l = length of base; w = width of base; h = height
pyramid	$V = \frac{Ah}{3}$	A = area of base; h = height
cylinder	$V = \pi r^2 h$	π = 3.1416; r = radius of the base; h = height
cone	$V = \frac{\pi r^2 h}{3}$	π = 3.1416; r = radius of the base; h = height
sphere	$V = \frac{4\pi r^3}{3}$	π = 3.1416; r = radius

[2]**volume** *vb* **vol·umed; vol·um·ing** *vt* (1815) : to send or give out in volume ~ *vi* : to roll or rise in volume

[3]**volume** *adj* (ca. 1945) : involving large quantities ⟨~ sales⟩

vol·u·me·ter \ˈväl-yü-ˌmē-tər\ *n* [ISV, blend of *volume* and *-meter*] (1829) : an instrument for measuring volumes (as of gases or liquids) directly or (as of solids) by displacement of a liquid

vol·u·met·ric \ˌväl-yü-ˈme-trik\ *adj* (1857) : of, relating to, or involving the measurement of volume — **vol·u·met·ri·cal·ly** \-tri-k(ə-)lē\ *adv*

vo·lu·mi·nos·i·ty \və-ˌlü-mə-ˈnä-sə-tē\ *n* (1782) : the quality or state of being voluminous

vo·lu·mi·nous \və-ˈlü-mə-nəs\ *adj* [LL *voluminosus,* fr. L *volumin-, volumen*] (1611) **1** : consisting of many folds, coils, or convolutions : WINDING **2 a** : having or marked by great volume or bulk : LARGE ⟨long ~ tresses⟩; *also* : FULL ⟨a ~ skirt⟩ **b** : NUMEROUS ⟨trying to keep track of ~ slips of paper⟩ **3 a** : filling or capable of filling a large volume or several volumes ⟨a ~ literature on the subject⟩ **b** : writing or speaking much or at great length ⟨a ~ correspondent⟩ — **vo·lu·mi·nous·ly** *adv* — **vo·lu·mi·nous·ness** *n*

vol·un·ta·rism \ˈvä-lən-tə-ˌri-zəm\ *n* (1838) **1** : the principle or system of doing something by or relying on voluntary action or volunteers **2** : a theory that conceives will to be the dominant factor in experience or in the world — **vol·un·ta·rist** \-rist\ *n* — **vol·un·ta·ris·tic** \ˌvä-lən-tə-ˈris-tik\ *adj*

[1]**vol·un·tary** \ˈvä-lən-ˌter-ē\ *adj* [ME, fr. AF *voluntarie,* fr. L *voluntarius,* fr. *voluntas* will, fr. *velle* to will, wish — more at WILL] (14c) **1** : proceeding from the will or from one's own choice or consent **2** : unconstrained by interference : SELF-DETERMINING **3** : done by design or intention : INTENTIONAL ⟨~ manslaughter⟩ **4** : of, relating to, subject to, or regulated by the will ⟨~ behavior⟩ **5** : having power of free choice **6** : provided or supported by voluntary action ⟨a ~ organization⟩ **7** : acting or done of one's own free will without valuable consideration or legal obligation — **vol·un·tar·i·ly** *adv* — **vol·un·tar·i·ness** *n*

syn VOLUNTARY, INTENTIONAL, DELIBERATE, WILLING mean done or brought about of one's own will. VOLUNTARY implies freedom and spontaneity of choice or action without external compulsion ⟨a *voluntary* confession⟩. INTENTIONAL stresses an awareness of an end to be achieved ⟨the *intentional* concealment of vital information⟩. DELIBERATE implies full consciousness of the nature of one's act and its consequences ⟨*deliberate* acts of sabotage⟩. WILLING implies a readiness and eagerness to accede to or anticipate the wishes of another ⟨*willing* obedience⟩.

[2]**voluntary** *n, pl* **-tar·ies** (1598) **1 a** : a prefatory often extemporized musical piece **b** : an improvisatory organ piece played before, during, or after a religious service **2** : one who participates voluntarily

vol·un·tary·ism \ˈvä-lən-ˌter-ē-ˌi-zəm\ *n* (1835) : VOLUNTARISM — **vol·un·tary·ist** \-ē-ist\ *n*

voluntary muscle *n* (1788) : muscle (as most striated muscle) under voluntary control

[1]**vol·un·teer** \ˌvä-lən-ˈtir\ *n* [obs. F *voluntaire* (now *volontaire*), fr. *voluntaire,* adj., voluntary, fr. OF, fr. L *voluntarius*] (ca. 1600) **1** : a person who voluntarily undertakes or expresses a willingness to undertake a service: as **a** : one who enters into military service voluntarily **b** (1) : one who renders a service or takes part in a transaction while having no legal concern or interest (2) : one who receives a conveyance or transfer of property without giving valuable consideration **2** : a volunteer plant **3** *cap* [*Volunteers of America*] : a member of a quasi-military religious and philanthropic organization founded in 1896 by Commander and Mrs. Ballington Booth

[2]**volunteer** *adj* (1649) **1** : being, consisting of, or engaged in by volunteers ⟨a ~ army⟩ ⟨busy with ~ activities⟩ **2** : growing spontaneously without direct human control or supervision esp. from seeds lost from a previous crop ⟨~ corn plants⟩

[3]**volunteer** *vi* (1709) : to offer oneself as a volunteer ⟨~*ed* to host the meeting⟩ ~ *vt* : to offer or bestow voluntarily ⟨~ one's services⟩

vol·un·teer·ism \ˌvä-lən-ˈtir-ˌi-zəm\ *n* (1844) **1** : VOLUNTARISM 1 **2** : the act or practice of doing volunteer work in community service

vol·un·tour·ism \ˌvä-lən-ˈtu̇r-ˌi-zəm\ *n* [blend of [2]*volunteer* and *tourism*] (2000) : the act or practice of doing volunteer work as needed in the community where one is vacationing — **vol·un·tour·ist** \-ist\ *n*

vo·lup·tu·ary \və-ˈləp(t)-shə-ˌwer-ē\ *n, pl* **-ar·ies** (ca. 1610) : a person whose chief interests are luxury and the gratification of sensual appetites — **voluptuary** *adj*

vo·lup·tu·ous \və-ˈləp(t)-shə-wəs, -shəs\ *adj* [ME, fr. L *voluptuosus,* irreg. fr. *voluptas* pleasure, fr. *volup* pleasurable; akin to Gk *elpesthai* to hope, L *velle* to wish — more at WILL] (14c) **1 a** : full of delight or pleasure to the senses : conducive to or arising from sensuous or sensual gratification : LUXURIOUS ⟨a ~ dance⟩ ⟨~ ornamentation⟩ ⟨a ~ wine⟩ **b** : suggesting sensual pleasure by fullness and beauty of form ⟨~ nudes⟩ **2** : given to or spent in enjoyment of luxury, pleasure, or sensual gratifications ⟨a long and ~ holiday —Edmund Wilson⟩ ***syn*** see SENSUOUS — **vo·lup·tu·ous·ly** *adv* — **vo·lup·tu·ous·ness** *n*

vo·lute \və-ˈlüt\ *n* [L *voluta,* fr. fem. of *volutus,* pp. of *volvere* to roll — more at VOLUBLE] (ca. 1696) **1** : a spiral or scroll-shaped form **2** : a spiral scroll-shaped ornament forming the chief feature of the Ionic capital **3 a** : any of various marine gastropod mollusks (family Volutidae) with a thick short-spired shell **b** : the shell of a volute — **volute** *or* **vo·lut·ed** \-ˈlü-təd\ *adj*

vo·lu·tin \ˈväl-yə-ˌtin, və-ˈlü-tᵊn\ *n* [G, fr. NL *volutans,* specific epithet of the bacterium *Spirillum volutans* in which it was first found] (1908) : a granular basophilic substance containing nucleic acids that is found esp. in cells of microorganisms

vol·va \ˈväl-və, ˈvȯl-\ *n* [NL, fr. L *volva, vulva* integument — more at VULVA] (ca. 1753) : a membranous sac or cup about the base of the stipe in many gilled fungi (as agarics)

vol·vox \-ˌväks\ *n* [NL, fr. L *volvere* to roll] (1798) : any of a genus (*Volvox*) of flagellated unicellular green algae that form spherical colonies

vol·vu·lus \ˈväl-vyə-ləs, ˈvȯl-\ *n* [NL, fr. L *volvere*] (1679) : a twisting of the intestine upon itself that causes obstruction

vo·mer \ˈvō-mər\ *n* [NL, fr. L, plowshare] (ca. 1704) : a bone of the skull of most vertebrates that is situated below the ethmoid region and in the human skull forms part of the nasal septum — **vo·mer·ine** \ˈvō-mə-ˌrīn\ *adj*

vom·ero·na·sal organ \ˌvä-mə-rō-ˈnā-zəl-, ˌvō-\ *n* (ca. 1926) : either of a pair of small blind pouches or tubes in many vertebrates that are situated one on either side of the nasal septum or in the buccal cavity and that are reduced to rudimentary pits in adult humans but are developed in reptiles, amphibians, and some mammals as chemoreceptors — called also *Jacobson's organ*

[1]**vom·it** \ˈvä-mət\ *n* [ME, fr. AF *vomite,* fr. L *vomitus,* fr. *vomere* to vomit; akin to ON *vāma* seasickness, Gk *emein* to vomit] (14c) **1** : an act or instance of disgorging the contents of the stomach through the mouth; *also* : the disgorged matter **2** : EMETIC

[2]**vomit** *vi* (15c) **1** : to disgorge the stomach contents **2** : to spew forth : BELCH, GUSH ~ *vt* **1** : to disgorge (the contents of the stomach) through the mouth **2** : to eject violently or abundantly : SPEW **3** : to cause to vomit — **vom·it·er** *n*

vom·i·to·ry \ˈvä-mə-ˌtȯr-ē\ *n, pl* **-ries** [LL *vomitorium,* fr. L *vomere;* fr. its disgorging the spectators] (1730) : an entrance piercing the banks of seats of a theater, amphitheater, or stadium

vom·i·tus \ˈvä-mə-təs\ *n* [L] (ca. 1899) : material ejected by vomiting

V–1 \ˈvē-ˈwən\ *n* [G, abbr. for *Vergeltungswaffe 1,* lit., reprisal weapon 1] (1944) : BUZZ BOMB

[1]**voo·doo** \ˈvü-(ˌ)dü\ *n, pl* **voodoos** [Louisiana Creole *voudou,* prob. fr. Ewe *vódũ* tutelary deity] (1850) **1** *also* **vo·dou** \vō-ˈdü\ : a religion that is derived from African polytheism and ancestor worship and is practiced chiefly in Haiti **2 a** : a person who deals in spells and necromancy **b** (1) : a sorcerer's spell : HEX (2) : a hexed object : CHARM

[2]**voodoo** *vt* (1880) : to bewitch by or as if by means of voodoo : HEX

[3]**voodoo** *adj* (1880) **1** : of, relating to, or practicing voodoo ⟨~ rituals⟩ **2** : based on highly improbable suppositions : extremely implausible or unrealistic ⟨~ economics⟩

voo·doo·ism \ˈvü-(ˌ)dü-ˌi-zəm\ *n* (1865) **1 :** VOODOO 1 **2 :** the practice of witchcraft — **voo·doo·ist** \-ist\ *n* — **voo·doo·is·tic** \ˌvü-(ˌ)dü-ˈis-tik\ *adj*

VOR *abbr* **1** very-high-frequency omnidirectional radio (range) **2** very-high-frequency omnidirectional radio (beacon)

vo·ra·cious \vȯ-ˈrā-shəs, və-\ *adj* [L *vorac-, vorax,* fr. *vorare* to devour; akin to OE *ācweorran* to guzzle, L *gurges* whirlpool, Gk *bibrōskein* to devour] (1635) **1 :** having a huge appetite : RAVENOUS **2 :** excessively eager : INSATIABLE ⟨a ~ reader⟩ — **vo·ra·cious·ly** *adv* — **vo·ra·cious·ness** *n*

syn VORACIOUS, GLUTTONOUS, RAVENOUS, RAPACIOUS mean excessively greedy. VORACIOUS applies esp. to habitual gorging with food or drink ⟨teenagers are often *voracious* eaters⟩. GLUTTONOUS applies to one who delights in eating or acquiring things esp. beyond the point of necessity or satiety ⟨an admiral who was *gluttonous* for glory⟩. RAVENOUS implies excessive hunger and suggests violent or grasping methods of dealing with food or with whatever satisfies an appetite ⟨a nation with a *ravenous* lust for territorial expansion⟩. RAPACIOUS often suggests excessive and utterly selfish acquisitiveness or avarice ⟨*rapacious* developers indifferent to environmental concerns⟩.

vo·rac·i·ty \vȯ-ˈra-sə-tē, və-\ *n* (1526) **:** the quality or state of being voracious

vor·la·ge \ˈfȯr-ˌlä-gə\ *n* [G, lit., forward position, fr. *vor* fore + *Lage* position] (1936) **:** the position of a skier leaning forward from the ankles usu. without lifting the heels from the skis

-vorous *adj comb form* [L *-vorus,* fr. *vorare* to devour] **:** eating : feeding on ⟨frugi*vorous*⟩

vor·tex \ˈvȯr-ˌteks\ *n, pl* **vor·ti·ces** \ˈvȯr-tə-ˌsēz\ *also* **vor·tex·es** \ˈvȯr-ˌtek-səz\ [NL *vortic-, vortex,* fr. L *vertex, vortex* whirlpool — more at VERTEX] (1652) **1 :** something that resembles a whirlpool ⟨the hellish ~ of battle —*Time*⟩ **2 a :** a mass of fluid (as a liquid) with a whirling or circular motion that tends to form a cavity or vacuum in the center of the circle and to draw toward this cavity or vacuum bodies subject to its action; *esp* **:** WHIRLPOOL, EDDY **b :** a region within a body of fluid in which the fluid elements have an angular velocity

vor·ti·cal \ˈvȯr-ti-kəl\ *adj* (1653) **:** of, relating to, or resembling a vortex : SWIRLING — **vor·ti·cal·ly** \-k(ə-)lē\ *adv*

vor·ti·cel·la \ˌvȯr-tə-ˈse-lə\ *n, pl* **-cel·lae** \-ˈse-(ˌ)lē\ *or* **-cellas** [NL, fr. L *vortic-, vortex*] (1787) **:** any of a genus (*Vorticella*) of stalked bell-shaped ciliates

vor·ti·cism \ˈvȯr-tə-ˌsi-zəm\ *n, often cap* [L *vortic-, vortex*] (1914) **:** an English abstract art movement from about 1912–15 embracing cubist and futurist concepts — **vor·ti·cist** \-sist\ *n or adj, often cap*

vor·tic·i·ty \vȯr-ˈti-sə-tē\ *n* (1888) **1 :** the state of a fluid in vortical motion; *broadly* **:** vortical motion **2 :** a measure of vortical motion; *esp* **:** a vector measure of local rotation in a fluid flow

vor·ti·cose \ˈvȯr-ti-ˌkōs\ *adj* (1783) *archaic* **:** VORTICAL

vo·ta·ress \ˈvō-tə-rəs\ *n* (1589) **:** a woman who is a votary

vo·ta·rist \-rist\ *n* (1603) **:** VOTARY

vo·ta·ry \ˈvō-tə-rē\ *n, pl* **-ries** [L *votum* vow] (1546) **1** *archaic* **:** a sworn adherent **2 a :** DEVOTEE **b :** a devoted admirer **3 a :** a devout or zealous worshipper **b :** a staunch believer or advocate

[1]**vote** \ˈvōt\ *n* [ME (Sc), fr. L *votum* vow, wish — more at VOW] (15c) **1 a :** a usu. formal expression of opinion or will in response to a proposed decision; *esp* **:** one given as an indication of approval or disapproval of a proposal, motion, or candidate for office **b :** the total number of such expressions of opinion made known at a single time (as at an election) **c :** an expression of opinion or preference that resembles a vote **d :** BALLOT 1 **2 :** the collective opinion or verdict of a body of persons expressed by voting **3 :** the right to cast a vote; *specif* **:** the right of suffrage : FRANCHISE **4 a :** the act or process of voting ⟨brought the question to a ~⟩ **b :** a method of voting **5 :** a formal expression of a wish, will, or choice voted by a meeting **6 a :** VOTER **b :** a group of voters with some common and identifying characteristics ⟨the labor ~⟩ **7** *chiefly Brit* **a :** a proposition to be voted on; *esp* **:** a legislative money item **b :** APPROPRIATION

[2]**vote** *vb* **vot·ed; vot·ing** *vi* (1552) **1 :** to express one's views in response to a poll; *esp* **:** to exercise a political franchise **2 :** to express an opinion ⟨consumers . . . ~ with their dollars —Lucia Mouat⟩ ~ *vt* **1 :** to choose, endorse, decide the disposition of, defeat, or authorize by vote ⟨he was *voted* out of office⟩ **2 a :** to adjudge by general agreement : DECLARE **b :** to offer as a suggestion : PROPOSE ⟨I ~ we all go home⟩ **3 a :** to cause to vote in a given way **b :** to cause to be cast for or against a proposal **4 :** to vote in accordance with or in the interest of ⟨~ your conscience⟩ ⟨*voted* their pocketbooks⟩ — **vote with one's feet :** to express one's disapproval or dissatisfaction by leaving

vo–tech \ˈvō-ˈtek\ *adj* [*vo*cational + *tech*nical] (1975) **:** relating to, providing, or receiving vocational and technical education and training

vote·less \ˈvōt-ləs\ *adj* (1672) **:** having no vote; *esp* **:** denied the political franchise

vot·er \ˈvō-tər\ *n* (ca. 1578) **:** one that votes or has the legal right to vote

voting machine *n* (1900) **:** a mechanical device for recording and counting votes cast in an election

vo·tive \ˈvō-tiv\ *adj* [L *votivus,* fr. *votum* vow] (1597) **1 :** consisting of or expressing a vow, wish, or desire ⟨a ~ prayer⟩ **2 :** offered or performed in fulfillment of a vow or in gratitude or devotion — **vo·tive·ly** *adv* — **vo·tive·ness** *n*

votive candle *n* (1824) **1 :** a candle lit in devotion or gratitude **2 :** a small squat candle — called also *votive*

votive mass *n* (1738) **:** a mass celebrated for a special intention (as for a wedding or funeral) in place of the mass of the day

vo·tress \ˈvō-trəs\ *n* [by alter.] (1590) *archaic* **:** VOTARESS

VO_2 max \ˌvē-ō-ˈtü-ˈmaks\ *n* [volume of O_2 *max*imum] (1970) **:** the maximum amount of oxygen the body can utilize during a specified period of usu. intense exercise

[1]**vouch** \ˈvau̇ch\ *vb* [ME *vochen, vouchen,* fr. AF *voucher* to call, vouch, fr. L *vocare* to call, summon, fr. *vox* voice — more at VOICE] *vt* (14c) **1 :** to summon into court to warrant or defend a title **2** *archaic* **:** ASSERT, AFFIRM **b :** ATTEST **3** *archaic* **:** to cite or refer to as authority or supporting evidence **4 a :** PROVE, SUBSTANTIATE **b :** to verify (a business transaction) by examining documentary evidence ~ *vi* **1 :** to give a guarantee : become surety **2 a :** to supply supporting evidence or testimony **b :** to give personal assurance ***syn*** see CERTIFY

[2]**vouch** *n* (1603) *obs* **:** ALLEGATION, DECLARATION

vouch·ee \vau̇-ˈchē\ *n* (15c) **:** a person for whom another vouches

[1]**vouch·er** \ˈvau̇-chər\ *n* [AF, summons to guarantee a title, fr. *voucher,* v.] (ca. 1523) **1 :** an act of vouching **2 a :** a piece of supporting evidence : PROOF **b :** a documentary record of a business transaction **c :** a written affidavit or authorization : CERTIFICATE **d :** a form or check indicating a credit against future purchases or expenditures **3 :** a coupon issued by government to a parent or guardian to be used to fund a child's education in either a public or private school

[2]**voucher** *vt* (1609) **1 :** to establish the authenticity of **2 :** to prepare a voucher for

[3]**voucher** *n* [[1]*vouch* + [2]*-er*] (1612) *archaic* **:** one that guarantees : SURETY

vouch·safe \vau̇ch-ˈsāf, ˈvau̇ch-ˌ\ *vt* **vouch·safed; vouch·saf·ing** [ME *vouchen sauf* to grant, consent, deign, fr. AF *voucher salf*] (14c) **1 a :** to grant or furnish often in a gracious or condescending manner **b :** to give by way of reply ⟨refused to ~ an explanation⟩ **2 :** to grant as a privilege or special favor ***syn*** see GRANT — **vouch·safe·ment** \vau̇ch-ˈsāf-mənt\ *n*

vous·soir \vü-ˈswär, ˈvü-ˌ\ *n* [F, fr. OF *vosoir,* fr. VL **volsorium,* fr. L *volvere* to roll — more at VOLUBLE] (1728) **:** one of the wedge-shaped pieces forming an arch or vault — see ARCH illustration

Vou·vray \vü-ˈvrā\ *n* [F, fr. *Vouvray,* village in France] (1885) **:** a semidry to semisweet white wine from the Loire Valley of France that is often produced as a sparkling wine

[1]**vow** \ˈvau̇\ *n* [ME *vowe,* fr. AF *vou,* fr. L *votum,* fr. neut. of *votus,* pp. of *vovēre* to vow; akin to Gk *euchesthai* to pray, vow, Skt *vāghat* sacrificer] (13c) **:** a solemn promise or assertion; *specif* **:** one by which a person is bound to an act, service, or condition

[2]**vow** *vt* (14c) **1 :** to promise solemnly : SWEAR **2 :** to bind or consecrate by a vow ~ *vi* **:** to make a vow — **vow·er** \ˈvau̇(-ə)r\ *n*

[3]**vow** *vt* [ME, short for *avowen*] (14c) **:** AVOW, DECLARE

vow·el \ˈvau̇(-ə)l\ *n* [ME, fr. AF *vowele,* fr. L *vocalis* — more at VOCALIC] (14c) **1 :** one of a class of speech sounds in the articulation of which the oral part of the breath channel is not blocked and is not constricted enough to cause audible friction; *broadly* **:** the one most prominent sound in a syllable **2 :** a letter or other symbol representing a vowel — usu. used in English of *a, e, i, o, u,* and sometimes *y*

vow·el·ize \ˈvau̇-(ə-)ˌlīz\ *vt* **-ized; -iz·ing** (1883) **:** to furnish with vowel points

vowel point *n* (1764) **:** a mark placed below or otherwise near a consonant in some languages (as Hebrew) and representing the vowel sound that precedes or follows the consonant sound

vowel rhyme *n* (1838) **:** ASSONANCE 2b

vox po·pu·li \ˈväks-ˈpä-pyü-ˌlī, -pyə-(ˌ)lē, -pə-(ˌ)lē\ *n* [L, voice of the people] (ca. 1550) **:** popular sentiment

[1]**voy·age** \ˈvȯi-ij, ˈvȯ(-)ij\ *n* [ME *viage, veyage,* fr. AF *veiage,* fr. LL *viaticum,* fr. L, traveling money, fr. neut. of *viaticus* of a journey, fr. *via* way — more at WAY] (14c) **1 :** an act or instance of traveling : JOURNEY **2 :** a course or period of traveling by other than land routes ⟨a long sea ~⟩ **3 :** an account of a journey esp. by sea

[2]**voyage** *vb* **voy·aged; voy·ag·ing** *vi* (15c) **:** to take a trip : TRAVEL ~ *vt* **:** SAIL, TRAVERSE — **voy·ag·er** *n*

voya·geur \ˌvȯi-ə-ˈzhər, ˌvwä-yä-\ *n* [CanF, fr. F, traveler, fr. *voyager* to travel, fr. *voyage* voyage, fr. OF *voiage, veiage*] (1793) **:** a man employed by a fur company to transport goods to and from remote stations esp. in the Canadian Northwest

voy·eur \vwä-ˈyər, vȯi-ˈər\ *n* [F, lit., one who sees, fr. MF, fr. *voir* to see, fr. L *vidēre* — more at WIT] (1900) **1 :** one obtaining sexual gratification from observing unsuspecting individuals who are partly undressed, naked, or engaged in sexual acts; *broadly* **:** one who habitually seeks sexual stimulation by visual means **2 :** a prying observer who is usu. seeking the sordid or the scandalous — **voy·eur·ism** \-ˌi-zəm\ *n* — **voy·eur·is·tic** \ˌvwä-(ˌ)yər-ˈis-tik, ˌvȯi-ər-\ *adj* — **voy·eur·is·ti·cal·ly** \-ti-k(ə-)lē\ *adv*

VP *abbr* **1** various places **2** verb phrase **3** vice president

VR *abbr* virtual reality

VRM *abbr* variable rate mortgage

vroom \ˈvrüm, və-ˈrüm\ *vi* [imit. of the noise of an engine] (1965) **:** to operate a motor vehicle at high speed or so as to create a great deal of engine noise

vs *abbr* **1** verse **2** versus — often punctuated

V sign *n* (1942) **:** a sign made by raising the index and middle fingers in a V and used as a victory salute or a gesture of approval

V–6 \ˈvē-ˈsiks\ *n* (1953) **:** an internal combustion engine having two banks of three cylinders each with the banks at an angle to each other; *also* **:** an automobile having such an engine — compare V-8

V/STOL *abbr* vertical or short takeoff and landing

Vt *abbr* Vermont

VT *abbr* **1** vacuum tube **2** Vermont

VTOL *abbr* vertical takeoff and landing

VTR *abbr* videotape recorder

V–2 \ˈvē-ˈtü\ *n* [G, abbr. for *Vergeltungswaffe 2,* lit., reprisal weapon 2] (1944) **:** a rocket-propelled bomb of German invention

vug \ˈvəg\ *n* [modif. of Late Corn *fugo* cave; akin to Old Corn *vooga* cave, Late Corn *ogo, googoo* sea cave, OW *guocof, guocob* cave] (1818) **:** a small unfilled cavity in a lode or in rock — **vug·gy** \ˈvə-gē\ *adj*

Vul·can \ˈvəl-kən\ *n* [L *Volcanus, Vulcanus*] (1513) **:** the Roman god of fire and metalworking — compare HEPHAESTUS

vul·ca·ni·an \ˌvəl-ˈkā-nē-ən\ *adj* (1602) **1** *cap* **:** of or relating to Vulcan or to working in metals (as iron) **2 :** of or relating to a volcanic eruption in which highly viscous or solid lava is blown into fragments and dust

vul·ca·nic·i·ty \ˌvəl-kə-ˈni-sə-tē\ *n* (1873) **:** VOLCANISM

vul·ca·ni·sate, vul·ca·ni·sa·tion, vul·ca·nise *Brit var of* VULCANIZATE, VULCANIZATION, VULCANIZE

vul·ca·nism \ˈvəl-kə-ˌni-zəm\ *n* (1877) **:** VOLCANISM

vul·ca·ni·zate \ˈvəl-kə-nə-ˌzāt, ˌvəl-kə-ˈnī-\ *n* [back-formation fr. *vulcanization*] (1926) **:** a vulcanized product

\ə\ **abut** \ᵊ\ **kitten**, F table \ər\ **further** \a\ **ash** \ā\ **ace** \ä\ **mop, mar**
\au̇\ **out** \ch\ **chin** \e\ **bet** \ē\ **easy** \g\ **go** \i\ **hit** \ī\ **ice** \j\ **job**
\ŋ\ **sing** \ō\ **go** \ȯ\ **law** \ȯi\ **boy** \th\ **thin** \t͟h\ **the** \ü\ **loot** \u̇\ **foot**
\y\ **yet** \zh\ **vision, beige** \k, ⁿ, œ, ue, ʸ\ *see* Guide to Pronunciation

vul·ca·ni·za·tion \ˌvəl-kə-nə-ˈzā-shən\ n (1846) : the process of treating crude or synthetic rubber or similar plastic material chemically to give it useful properties (as elasticity, strength, and stability)

vul·ca·nize \ˈvəl-kə-ˌnīz\ vb **-nized; -niz·ing** [ISV, fr. L *Vulcanus* Vulcan, fire] vt (1846) : to subject to vulcanization ~ vi : to undergo vulcanization — **vul·ca·niz·er** n

vulcanized fiber n [fr. *Vulcanized Fibre*, a trademark] (ca. 1884) : a tough substance made by treatment of cellulose and used for luggage and electrical insulation and in packaging

vul·ca·nol·o·gy \ˌvəl-kə-ˈnä-lə-jē\ n [ISV] (1858) : VOLCANOLOGY — **vul·ca·nol·o·gist** \-jist\ n

vul·gar \ˈvəl-gər\ adj [ME, fr. L *vulgaris* of the mob, vulgar, fr. *volgus, vulgus* mob, common people] (14c) **1 a** : generally used, applied, or accepted **b** : understood in or having the ordinary sense ⟨they reject the ~ conception of miracle —W. R. Inge⟩ **2** : VERNACULAR ⟨the ~ name of a plant⟩ **3 a** : of or relating to the common people : PLEBEIAN **b** : generally current : PUBLIC ⟨the ~ opinion of that time⟩ **c** : of the usual, typical, or ordinary kind **4 a** : lacking in cultivation, perception, or taste : COARSE **b** : morally crude, undeveloped, or unregenerate : GROSS **c** : ostentatious or excessive in expenditure or display : PRETENTIOUS **5 a** : offensive in language : EARTHY **b** : lewdly or profanely indecent **syn** see COMMON, COARSE — **vul·gar·ly** adv

vulgar era n (1716) : CHRISTIAN ERA

vul·gar·i·an \ˌvəlˈger-ē-ən\ n (1804) : a vulgar person

vul·gar·ise Brit var of VULGARIZE

vul·gar·ism \ˈvəl-gə-ˌri-zəm\ n (ca. 1676) **1** : VULGARITY **2 a** : a word or expression originated or used chiefly by illiterate persons **b** : a coarse word or phrase : OBSCENITY

vul·gar·i·ty \ˌvəl-ˈga-rə-tē\ n, pl **-ties** (1579) **1** : something vulgar **2** : the quality or state of being vulgar

vul·gar·ize \ˈvəl-gə-ˌrīz\ vt **-ized; -iz·ing** (1709) **1** : to diffuse generally : POPULARIZE **2** : to make vulgar : COARSEN — **vul·gar·i·za·tion** \ˌvəl-gə-rə-ˈzā-shən\ n — **vul·gar·iz·er** \ˈvəl-gə-ˌrī-zər\ n

Vulgar Latin n (1643) : the nonclassical Latin of ancient Rome including the speech of plebeians and the informal speech of the educated established by comparative evidence as the chief source of the Romance languages

vul·gate \ˈvəl-ˌgāt, -gət\ n [ML *vulgata*, fr. LL *vulgata editio* edition in general circulation] (1728) **1** cap : a Latin version of the Bible authorized and used by the Roman Catholic Church **2** : a commonly accepted text or reading **3** : the speech of the common people and esp. of uneducated people

vul·gus \ˈvəl-gəs\ n [prob. alter. of obs. *vulgars* English sentences to be translated into Latin] (1856) : a short composition in Latin verse formerly common as an exercise in some English public schools

vul·ner·a·ble \ˈvəl-n(ə-)rə-bəl, ˈvəl-nər-bəl\ adj [LL *vulnerabilis*, fr. L *vulnerare* to wound, fr. *vulner-, vulnus* wound; prob. akin to L *vellere* to pluck, Gk *oulē* wound] (1605) **1** : capable of being physically or emotionally wounded **2** : open to attack or damage : ASSAILABLE ⟨~ to criticism⟩ **3** : liable to increased penalties but entitled to increased bonuses after winning a game in contract bridge — **vul·ner·a·bil·i·ty** \ˌvəl-n(ə-)rə-ˈbi-lə-tē\ n — **vul·ner·a·ble·ness** \ˈvəl-n(ə-)rə-bəl-nəs, ˈvəl-nər-bəl-\ n — **vul·ner·a·bly** \-blē\ adv

¹vul·ner·ary \ˈvəl-nə-ˌrer-ē\ adj [L *vulnerarius*, fr. *vulner-, vulnus*] (1599) : used for or useful in healing wounds ⟨~ plants⟩

²vulnerary n, pl **-ar·ies** (1601) : a vulnerary remedy

vul·pine \ˈvəl-ˌpīn\ adj [ME, fr. L *vulpinus*, fr. *vulpes* fox; perh. akin to Gk *alōpēx* fox — more at ALOPECIA] (15c) **1** : of, relating to, or resembling a fox **2** : FOXY, CRAFTY ⟨a ~ smile⟩ ⟨~ charms⟩

vul·ture \ˈvəl-chər\ n [ME *vultur*, fr. AF, fr. L] (14c) **1** : any of various large birds (families Accipitridae and Cathartidae) that are related to the hawks, eagles, and falcons but have weaker claws and the head usu. naked and that subsist chiefly or entirely on carrion **2** : a rapacious or predatory person — **vul·tur·ish** \-chə-rish\ adj

vul·tur·ine \-chə-ˌrīn\ adj (1647) **1** : of, relating to, or characteristic of vultures **2** : RAPACIOUS, PREDATORY ⟨~ legislators⟩

vul·tur·ous \ˈvəl-chə-rəs, ˈvəlch-rəs\ adj (1623) : resembling a vulture esp. in rapacity or scavenging habits

vul·va \ˈvəl-və\ n, pl **vul·vae** \-ˌvē, -ˌvī\ [ME, fr. ML, fr. L *volva, vulva* womb, female genitals; akin to Skt *ulva* womb and perh. to L *volvere* to roll — more at VOLUBLE] (14c) : the external parts of the female genital organs — **vul·val** \ˈvəl-vəl\ or **vul·var** \-vər, -ˌvär\ adj

vul·vo·vag·i·ni·tis \ˌvəl-(ˌ)vō-ˌva-jə-ˈnī-təs\ n [NL] (1897) : coincident inflammation of the vulva and vagina

vv abbr verses

VX \ˈvē-ˈeks\ n [Am. or Brit. government code designation for the gas] (1965) : an extremely toxic chemical weapon $C_{11}H_{26}NO_2PS$ similar to sarin and tabun in action

vying pres part of VIE

W

¹w \ˈdə-bəl-(ˌ)yü, ˈdə-bə-; ˈdəb-(ˌ)yüz, -yə; ˈdəb-yē\ n, pl **w's** or **ws** \-(ˌ)yüz, -yəz, -yēz\ often cap, often attrib (15c) **1 a** : the 23d letter of the English alphabet **b** : a graphic representation of this letter **c** : a speech counterpart of orthographic w **2** : a graphic device for reproducing the letter w **3** : one designated w esp. as the 23d in order or class **4** : something shaped like the letter W

²w abbr **1** water **2** week **3** weight **4** white **5** wicket **6** wide; width **7** wife **8** with

¹W n (1960) : W PARTICLE

²W abbr watt

³W symbol [G *Wolfram*] tungsten

WA abbr Washington

wabble var of WOBBLE

Wac \ˈwak\ n [*Women's Army Corps*] (1943) : a member of a U.S. Army unit created for women during World War II and discontinued in the 1970s

wack \ˈwak\ adj [prob. alter. of *wacky*] (1984) slang : not up to the mark : LOUSY, LAME ⟨while there are skilled moments, there are ~ ones as well —Danyel Smith⟩

wacked-out var of WHACKED-OUT

¹wacko also **whacko** \ˈwa-(ˌ)kō\ adj [by alter.] (1975) : WACKY

²wacko also **whacko** n (1976) : a person who is wacky; also : PSYCHO

wacky also **whacky** \ˈwa-kē\ adj **wack·i·er; -est** [perh. fr. E dial. *whacky* fool] (ca. 1935) : absurdly or amusingly eccentric or irrational : CRAZY ⟨~ ideas⟩ ⟨a ~ comedian⟩ — **wack·i·ly** \ˈwa-kə-lē\ adv — **wack·i·ness** \ˈwa-kē-nəs\ n

¹wad \ˈwäd\ n [ME *wadde*, fr. ML *wadda*] (15c) **1** : a small mass, bundle, or tuft: as **a** : a soft mass esp. of a loose fibrous material variously used (as to stop an aperture, pad a garment, or hold grease around an axle) **b** (1) : a soft plug used to retain a powder charge or to avoid windage esp. in a muzzle-loading gun (2) : a felt or paper disk used to separate the components of a shotgun cartridge **c** : a small mass of a chewing substance ⟨a ~ of gum⟩ **2** : a considerable amount (as of money) **3 a** : a roll of paper money **b** : MONEY

²wad vt **wad·ded; wad·ding** (1579) **1 a** : to insert a wad into ⟨~ a gun⟩ **b** : to hold in by a wad ⟨~ a bullet in a gun⟩ **2** : to form into a wad or wadding; esp : to roll or crush into a tight wad **3** : to stuff or line with some soft substance — **wad·der** n

wadding n (1627) **1** : wads or material for making wads **2** : a soft mass or sheet of short loose fibers used for stuffing or padding

¹wad·dle \ˈwä-dᵊl\ vi **wad·dled; wad·dling** \ˈwäd-liŋ, ˈwä-dᵊl-iŋ\ [freq. of *wade*] (1592) **1** : to walk with short steps swinging the forepart of the body from side to side **2** : to move clumsily in a manner suggesting a waddle — **wad·dler** \ˈwäd-lər, ˈwä-dᵊl-ər\ n

²waddle n (1691) : an awkward clumsy swaying gait

¹wad·dy \ˈwä-dē\ n, pl **waddies** [Dharuk (Australian aboriginal language of the Port Jackson area) *wadi* stick, wooden weapon] (ca. 1790) *Austral* : CLUB 1a

²waddy vt **wad·died; wad·dy·ing** (1830) *Austral* : to attack or beat with a waddy

³wad·dy also **wad·die** \ˈwä-dē\ n, pl **waddies** [origin unknown] (1897) *West* : COWBOY

¹wade \ˈwād\ vb **wad·ed; wad·ing** [ME, fr. OE *wadan*; akin to OHG *watan* to go, wade, L *vadere* to go] vi (13c) **1** : to step in or through a medium (as water) offering more resistance than air **2** : to move or proceed with difficulty or labor ⟨~ through the crowd⟩ ⟨~ through all the evidence⟩ **3** : to set to work or attack with determination or vigor — used with in or into ⟨~ into a task⟩ ~ vt : to pass or cross by wading — **wad·able** or **wade·able** \ˈwā-də-bəl\ adj

²wade n (1665) : an act of wading ⟨a ~ in the brook⟩

Wade–Giles \ˈwād-ˈgī(-ə)lz, -ˈjī(-ə)lz\ n [Thomas F. *Wade* †1895 Brit. diplomat & Herbert A. *Giles* †1935 Brit. sinologist] (1943) : a system for romanizing Chinese ideograms in which tones are indicated by superscript numbers and consonantal aspiration is indicated by an apostrophe — compare PINYIN

wad·er \ˈwā-dər\ n (1673) **1** : one that wades **2** : SHOREBIRD; also : WADING BIRD **3** pl : high waterproof boots or a one-piece waterproof garment usu. consisting of pants with attached boots that are used for wading (as when fishing)

wa·di \ˈwä-dē\ n [Ar *wādī*] (1828) **1** : the bed or valley of a stream in regions of southwestern Asia and northern Africa that is usu. dry except during the rainy season and that often forms an oasis : GULLY, WASH **2** : a shallow usu. sharply defined depression in a desert region

wading bird n (1840) : any of an order (Ciconiiformes) of long-legged birds (as herons, bitterns, storks, and ibises) that wade in water in search of food

wading pool n (1921) : a shallow pool of portable or permanent construction used by children for wading

wad·mal or **wad·mol** or **wad·mel** \ˈwäd-məl\ n [ME *wadmale*, fr. ON *vathmál*, lit., standard cloth, fr. *vāth* cloth, clothing + *māl* measure; akin to L *metiri* to measure — more at WEED, MEASURE] (14c) : a coarse rough woolen fabric formerly used in the British Isles and Scandinavia for protective coverings and warm clothing

waders

wae·sucks \ˈwā-ˌsəks\ interj [Sc *wae* woe (fr. ME *wa*) + *sucks*, alter. of E *sakes* — more at WOE] (ca. 1774) *Scot* — used to express pity

Waf \ˈwaf\ *n* [*W*omen in the *A*ir *F*orce] (1948) **:** a member of the women's component of the U.S. Air Force formed after World War II and discontinued in the 1970s

[1]**wa·fer** \ˈwā-fər\ *n* [ME, fr. AF *wafer, walfre,* of Gmc origin; akin to MD *wafele* waffle] (14c) **1 a :** a thin crisp cake, candy, or cracker **b :** a round thin piece of unleavened bread used in the celebration of the Eucharist **2 :** an adhesive disk of dried paste with added coloring matter used as a seal **3 a :** a thin disk or ring resembling a wafer and variously used (as for a valve or diaphragm) **b :** a thin slice of semiconductor (as silicon) used as a base for an electronic component or circuit

[2]**wafer** *vt* **wa·fered; wa·fer·ing** \-f(ə-)riŋ\ (1748) **1 :** to seal, close, or fasten with a wafer **2 :** to divide (as a silicon rod) into wafers

waff \ˈwaf\ *n* [E dial. *waff* to wave] (1600) **1** *chiefly Scot* **:** a waving motion **2** *chiefly Scot* **:** PUFF, GUST

[1]**waf·fle** \ˈwä-fəl, ˈwȯ-\ *n* [D *wafel,* fr. MD *wafele;* akin to OHG *waba* honeycomb, OE *wefan* to weave] (1744) **:** a crisp cake of batter baked in a waffle iron

[2]**waffle** *vi* **waf·fled; waf·fling** \-f(ə-)liŋ\ [freq. of obs. *woff* to yelp, of imit. origin] (1868) **1 :** EQUIVOCATE, VACILLATE ⟨*waffled* on the important issues⟩; *also* **:** YO-YO, FLIP-FLOP **2 :** to talk or write foolishly **:** BLATHER ⟨can ~ . . . tiresomely off the point —*Times Lit. Supp.*⟩ — **waf·fler** \-f(ə-)lər\ *n*

[3]**waffle** *n* (ca. 1888) **:** empty or pretentious words **:** TRIPE

waffle iron *n* (1794) **:** a cooking utensil having two hinged metal parts that shut upon each other and impress surface projections on waffles that are being cooked

waf·fle·stomp·er \ˈwä-fəl-ˌstäm-pər, ˈwȯ-, -ˌstȯm-\ *n* [fr. the pattern left by the soles] (1972) **:** a hiking boot with a lug sole

[1]**waft** \ˈwäft, ˈwaft\ *vb* [ME, perh. fr. pp. of ME (northern dial.) *waffen,* by-form of ME *waven* to wave] *vi* (15c) **:** to move or go lightly on or as if on a buoyant medium ⟨heavenly aromas ~*ed* from the kitchen⟩ ~ *vt* **:** to cause to move or go lightly by or as if by the impulse of wind or waves — **waft·er** *n*

[2]**waft** *n* (1607) **1 :** something (as an odor) that is wafted **:** WHIFF **2 :** a slight breeze **:** PUFF **3 :** the act of waving **4 :** a pennant or flag used to signal or to show wind direction

waft·age \ˈwäf-tij, ˈwaf-\ *n* (1558) **:** the act of wafting or state of being wafted; *broadly* **:** CONVEYANCE

waf·ture \ˈwäf(t)-shər, ˈwaf(t)-\ *n* (1601) **:** the act of waving or a wavelike motion

[1]**wag** \ˈwag\ *vb* **wagged; wag·ging** [ME *waggen;* akin to MHG *wacken* to totter, OE *wegan* to move — more at WAY] *vi* (13c) **1 :** to be in motion **:** STIR **2 :** to move to and fro or up and down esp. with quick jerky motions **3 :** to move in chatter or gossip ⟨scandal caused tongues to ~⟩ **4** *archaic* **:** DEPART **5 :** WADDLE ~ *vt* **1 :** to swing to and fro or up and down esp. with quick jerky motions **:** SWITCH ⟨a dog *wagging* its tail⟩; *specif* **:** to nod (the head) or shake (a finger) at (as in assent or mild reproof) **2 :** to move (as the tongue) animatedly in conversation — **wag·ger** *n*

[2]**wag** *n* (1589) **:** an act of wagging **:** SHAKE

[3]**wag** *n* [prob. short for obs. E *waghalter* gallows bird, fr. E [1]*wag* + *halter*] (ca. 1553) **1 :** WIT, JOKER **2** *obs* **:** a young man **:** CHAP

[1]**wage** \ˈwāj\ *n* [ME, pledge, recompense, fr. AF *wage, gage,* of Gmc origin; akin to OHG *wetti* pledge — more at WED] (14c) **1 a :** a payment usu. of money for labor or services usu. according to contract and on an hourly, daily, or piecework basis — often used in pl. **b** *pl* **:** the share of the national product attributable to labor as a factor in production **2 :** RECOMPENSE, REWARD — usu. used in pl. but sing. or pl. in constr. ⟨the ~*s* of sin is death —Rom 6:23 (RSV)⟩ — **wage·less** \ˈwāj-ləs\ *adj*

[2]**wage** *vb* **waged; wag·ing** [ME, to offer surety, put up as a stake, hire, fr. AF **wager, gager,* fr. *wage*] *vt* (14c) **:** to engage in or carry on ⟨~ war⟩ ⟨~ a campaign⟩ ~ *vi* **:** to be in process of occurring ⟨the riot *waged* for several hours —*Amer. Guide Series: Md.*⟩

waged *adj* (15c) **:** compensated by wages ⟨~ workers⟩ ⟨~ labor⟩

wage earner *n* (1861) **:** a person who works for wages or salary

[1]**wa·ger** \ˈwā-jər\ *n* [ME *wageour* pledge, bet, fr. AF *wageure,* fr. **wager*] (14c) **1 a :** something (as a sum of money) risked on an uncertain event **:** STAKE **b :** something on which bets are laid **:** GAMBLE ⟨do a stunt as a ~⟩ **2** *archaic* **:** an act of giving a pledge to take and abide by the result of some action

[2]**wager** *vb* **wa·gered; wa·ger·ing** \ˈwāj-riŋ, ˈwā-jə-\ *vi* (1602) **:** to make a bet ~ *vt* **:** to risk or venture on a final outcome; *specif* **:** to lay as a gamble **:** BET ⟨~ $5 on a horse⟩ — **wa·ger·er** \ˈwā-jər-ər\ *n*

wage scale *n* (1900) **:** a schedule of wage rates for related tasks; *broadly* **:** the general level of wages in an industry or region

wage slave *n* (1882) **:** a person dependent on wages or a salary for a livelihood

wage·work·er \ˈwāj-ˌwər-kər\ *n* (1876) **:** WAGE EARNER

wag·gery \ˈwa-gə-rē\ *n, pl* **-ger·ies** (1594) **1 :** mischievous merriment **:** PLEASANTRY **2 :** JEST; *esp* **:** PRACTICAL JOKE

wag·gish \ˈwa-gish\ *adj* (1589) **1 :** resembling or characteristic of a wag ⟨a ~ friend⟩ ⟨a ~ prose style⟩ **2 :** done or made in waggery or for sport **:** HUMOROUS ⟨~ spoofs of popular songs⟩ — **wag·gish·ly** *adv* — **wag·gish·ness** *n*

[1]**wag·gle** \ˈwa-gəl\ *vb* **wag·gled; wag·gling** \-g(ə-)liŋ\ [freq. of [1]*wag*] *vi* (1588) **:** to reel, sway, or move from side to side **:** WAG ~ *vt* **:** to move frequently one way and the other **:** WAG — **wag·gly** \-g(ə-)lē\ *adj*

[2]**waggle** *n* (ca. 1866) **1 :** an instance of waggling **:** a jerky motion back and forth or up and down **2 :** a preliminary swinging of a golf club head back and forth over the ball before the swing

wag·gon *chiefly Brit var of* WAGON

[1]**Wag·ne·ri·an** \väg-ˈnir-ē-ən, -ˈner-\ *adj* [Richard *Wagner*] (1868) **:** of, relating to, characteristic, or suggestive of Wagner or his music, stage operas, or theories

[2]**Wagnerian** *n* (1874) **:** an admirer of the musical theories and style of Wagner

Wag·ner·ite \ˈväg-nə-ˌrīt\ *n* (1855) **:** WAGNERIAN

[1]**wag·on** \ˈwa-gən\ *n* [D *wagen,* fr. MD — more at WAIN] (15c) **1 a :** a usu. four-wheeled vehicle for transporting bulky commodities and drawn orig. by animals **b :** a lighter typically horse-drawn vehicle for transporting goods or passengers **c :** PADDY WAGON **2** *Brit* **:** a railway freight car **3 :** a low four-wheeled vehicle with an open rectangular body and a retroflex tongue made for the play or use of a child **4 :** a small wheeled table used for the service of a dining room ⟨the dessert ~⟩ **5 :** a delivery truck ⟨a milk ~⟩ **6 :** STATION WAGON — **off the wagon :** in or into a state of no longer abstaining from alcoholic beverages ⟨fell *off the wagon*⟩ — **on the wagon :** in or into a state of abstaining from alcoholic beverages

[2]**wagon** *vi* (1606) **:** to travel or transport goods by wagon ~ *vt* **:** to transport (goods) by wagon

wag·on·er \ˈwa-gə-nər\ *n* (1544) **1 :** a person who drives a wagon or transports goods by wagon **2** *cap, obs* **:** BOÖTES

wag·on·ette \ˌwa-gə-ˈnet\ *n* (ca. 1858) **:** a light wagon with two facing seats along the sides behind a transverse front seat

wa·gon–lit \vä-gōⁿ-ˈlē\ *n, pl* **wagons–lits** *or* **wagon–lits** \-gōⁿ-ˈlē(z)\ [F, fr. *wagon* railroad car + *lit* bed] (1884) **:** a railroad sleeping car

wa·gon·load \ˈwa-gən-ˌlōd\ *n* (1684) **1 :** a load that fills or could fill a wagon ⟨a ~ of apples⟩ **2 :** an indefinitely large quantity ⟨a ~ of options⟩

wagon master *n* (1645) **:** a person in charge of one or more wagons

wagon train *n* (1810) **:** a column of wagons (as of supplies for a group of settlers) traveling overland

wag·tail \ˈwag-ˌtāl\ *n* (1510) **:** any of various chiefly Old World oscine birds (family Motacillidae) related to the pipits and having a long tail that they habitually jerk up and down

Wah·habi *also* **Wa·habi** \wə-ˈhä-bē, wä-\ *n* [Ar *wahhābī,* fr. Muḥammad b. ʿAbd al-*Wahhāb* (Abdul-Wahhab) †1787 Arab religious reformer] (1807) **:** a member of a puritanical Muslim sect founded in Arabia in the 18th century by Muhammad ibn-Abdul Wahhab and revived by ibn-Saud in the 20th century — **Wah·hab·ism** *also* **Wa·hab·ism** \-ˈhä-ˌbi-zəm\ *n* — **Wah·hab·ite** *also* **Wa·hab·ite** \-ˌbīt\ *adj or n*

wa·hi·ne \wä-ˈhē-nē, -(ˌ)nā\ *n* [Maori & Hawaiian, woman] (1773) **1 :** a Polynesian woman **2 :** a female surfer

[1]**wa·hoo** \ˈwä-ˌhü, ˈwȯ-\ *n, pl* **wahoos** [origin unknown] (1770) **:** WINGED ELM

[2]**wahoo** *n, pl* **wahoos** [Dakota *wāhu,* fr. *wā-* arrow + *hu* wood] (1857) **:** a shrubby spindle tree (*Euonymus atropurpureus*) of chiefly eastern No. America that has purple capsules which in dehiscence expose scarlet-ariled seeds — called also *burning bush*

[3]**wahoo** *n, pl* **wahoos** [origin unknown] (ca. 1900) **:** a large vigorous mackerel (*Acanthocybium solandri*) that is common in warm seas and esteemed as a food and sport fish

[4]**wa·hoo** \ˈwä-ˈhü\ *interj* (ca. 1924) *chiefly West* — used to express exuberance and enthusiasm or to attract attention

wah–wah \ˈwä-ˌwä\ *n, often attrib* [imit.] (1925) **:** a fluctuating muted effect produced on a brass instrument by use of a mute or on an electric guitar by use of an electronic device connected to an amplifier and operated by a pedal

[1]**waif** \ˈwāf\ *n* [ME *weif, waif,* fr. AF, fr. *waif,* adj., stray, unclaimed, prob. of Scand origin; akin to ON *veif* something flapping, *veifa* to be in movement — more at WIPE] (14c) **1 a :** a piece of property found (as washed up by the sea) but unclaimed **b** *pl* **:** stolen goods thrown away by a thief in flight **2 a :** something found without an owner and esp. by chance **b :** a stray person or animal; *esp* **:** a homeless child — **waif·ish** \ˈwā-fish\ *adj* — **waif·like** \ˈwāf-ˌlīk\ *adj*

[2]**waif** *n* [perh. of Scand origin; akin to ON *veif* something flapping] (1530) **:** WAFT 4

[1]**wail** \ˈwāl\ *vb* [ME *weilen, waylen,* perh. modif. (influenced by ME *weilawei* wellaway) of ON *væla, vāla* to wail; akin to ON *vei* woe — more at WOE] *vi* (14c) **1 :** to express sorrow audibly **:** LAMENT **2 :** to make a sound suggestive of a mournful cry **3 :** to express dissatisfaction plaintively **:** COMPLAIN ~ *vt, archaic* **1 :** BEWAIL **2 :** to say or express plaintively ⟨~*ed* that her cake was ruined⟩ — **wail·er** \ˈwā-lər\ *n*

[2]**wail** *n* (15c) **1 :** the act or practice of wailing **:** loud lamentation **2 a :** a usu. prolonged cry or sound expressing grief or pain **b :** a sound suggestive of wailing ⟨the ~ of an air-raid siren⟩ **c :** a querulous expression of grievance **:** COMPLAINT

wail·ful \ˈwāl-fəl\ *adj* (1544) **1 :** uttering a sound suggestive of wailing **2 :** expressing grief or pain **:** SORROWFUL, MOURNFUL ⟨a ~ cry⟩ — **wail·ful·ly** \-fə-lē\ *adv*

wailing wall *n* (1890) **1** *cap* **:** a surviving section of the wall which in ancient times formed a part of the enclosure of Herod's temple near the Holy of Holies and at which Jews traditionally gather for prayer and religious lament **2 :** a source of comfort and consolation in misfortune

wain \ˈwān\ *n* [ME, wagon, chariot, fr. OE *wægn;* akin to MD *wagen* wagon, OE *wegan* to move — more at WAY] (bef. 12c) **1 :** a usu. large and heavy vehicle for farm use ⟨a hay ~⟩ **2** *cap* [short for *Charles's Wain*] **:** BIG DIPPER

[1]**wain·scot** \ˈwān-skət, -ˌskōt, -ˌskät\ *n* [ME, fr. MD *wagenschot,* prob. fr. *wagen* wagon + *schot* shot, crossbar] (14c) **1** *Brit* **:** a fine grade of oak imported for woodwork **2 a (1) :** a usu. paneled wooden lining of an interior wall **(2) :** a lining of an interior wall irrespective of material **b :** the lower three or four feet (about one meter) of an interior wall when finished differently from the remainder of the wall

[2]**wainscot** *vt* **-scot·ed** *or* **-scot·ted; -scot·ing** *or* **-scot·ting** (1570) **:** to line with or as if with boards or paneling

wain·scot·ing *or* **wain·scot·ting** \-ˌskō-tiŋ, -ˌskä-, -skə-\ *n* (1580) **1 :** WAINSCOT 2 **2 :** material used to wainscot a surface

wain·wright \ˈwān-ˌrīt\ *n* (bef. 12c) **:** a maker and repairer of wagons

waist \ˈwāst\ *n* [ME *wast;* prob. akin to OE *wæstm* growth, *weaxan* to grow — more at WAX] (14c) **1 a :** the typically narrowed part of the body between the thorax and hips **b :** the greatly constricted basal part of the abdomen of some insects (as wasps and flies) **2 :** the part of something corresponding to or resembling the human waist: as **a (1) :** the part of a ship's deck between the poop and forecastle **(2) :** the middle part of a sailing ship between foremast and mainmast **b :** the middle section of the fuselage of an airplane **3 :** a garment or the part of a garment covering the body from the neck to the waistline or just

\ə\ **abut** \ᵊ\ **kitten, F table** \ər\ **further** \a\ **ash** \ā\ **ace** \ä\ **mop, mar**
\au̇\ **out** \ch\ **chin** \e\ **bet** \ē\ **easy** \g\ **go** \i\ **hit** \ī\ **ice** \j\ **job**
\ŋ\ **sing** \ō\ **go** \ȯ\ **law** \ȯi\ **boy** \th\ **thin** \t͟h\ **the** \ü\ **loot** \u̇\ **foot**
\y\ **yet** \zh\ **vision, beige** \k̲, ⁿ, œ, ue, ʸ\ *see* **Guide to Pronunciation**

below: **a** : BODICE 1 **b** : BLOUSE **4** : WAISTLINE 1b — **waist·ed** \ˈwā-stəd\ *adj*

waist·band \ˈwās(t)-ˌband\ *n* (1584) : a band (as of trousers or a skirt) fitting around the waist

waist·coat \ˈwes-kət, ˈwās(t)-ˌkōt\ *n* (1519) **1** : an ornamental garment worn under a doublet **2** *chiefly Brit* : VEST 2a — **waist·coat·ed** \-ˌkō-təd\ *adj*

waist·line \ˈwāst-ˌlīn\ *n* (1857) **1 a** : an arbitrary line encircling the narrowest part of the waist **b** : the part of a garment that covers the waistline or may be above or below it as fashion dictates **2** : body circumference at the waist

[1]**wait** \ˈwāt\ *vb* [ME, fr. AF *waiter, guaiter* to watch over, await, of Gmc origin; akin to OHG *wahta* watch, OE *wæccan* to watch — more at WAKE] *vt* (14c) **1** : to stay in place in expectation of : AWAIT ⟨~*ed* the result of the advertisement —W. M. Thackeray⟩ ⟨~ your turn⟩ **2** : to delay serving (a meal) **3** : to serve as waiter for ⟨~ tables⟩ ~ *vi* **1 a** : to remain stationary in readiness or expectation ⟨~ for a train⟩ **b** : to pause for another to catch up — usu. used with *up* **2 a** : to look forward expectantly ⟨just ~*ing* to see his rival lose⟩ **b** : to hold back expectantly ⟨~*ing* for a chance to strike⟩ **3** : to serve at meals — usu. used in such phrases as *wait on tables* or *wait on table* **4 a** : to be ready and available ⟨slippers ~*ing* by the bed⟩ **b** : to remain temporarily neglected or unrealized ⟨the chores can ~⟩ — **wait on** *also* **wait upon 1 a** : to attend as a servant **b** : to supply the wants of : SERVE **2** : to make a formal call on **3** : to wait for — **wait up** : to delay going to bed : stay up

usage American dialectologists have evidence showing *wait on* (sense 3) to be more a Southern than a Northern form in speech. Handbook writers universally denigrate *wait on* and prescribe *wait for* in writing. Our evidence from printed sources does not show a regional preference; it does show that the handbooks' advice is not based on current usage ⟨settlement of the big problems still *waited on* Russia —*Time*⟩ ⟨I couldn't make out . . . whether Harper was *waiting on* me for approval —E. B. White⟩ ⟨the staggering bill that *waited on* them at the white commissary downtown —Maya Angelou⟩. One reason for the continuing use of *wait on* may lie in its being able to suggest protracted or irritating waits better than *wait for* ⟨for two days I've been *waiting on* weather —Charles A. Lindbergh⟩ ⟨the boredom of black Africans sitting there, *waiting on* the whims of a colonial bureaucracy —Vincent Canby⟩ ⟨doesn't care to sit around *waiting on* a House that's virtually paralyzed —Glenn A. Briere⟩. *Wait on* is less common than *wait for,* but if it seems natural, there is no reason to avoid it.

[2]**wait** *n* [ME *waite* watchman, observation, fr. AF, of Gmc origin; akin to OHG *wahta* watch] (14c) **1 a** : a hidden or concealed position — used chiefly in the expression *lie in wait* **b** : a state or attitude of watchfulness and expectancy ⟨anchored in ~ for early morning fishing —Fred Zimmer⟩ **2 a** : one of a band of public musicians in England employed to play for processions or public entertainments **b** (1) : one of a group who serenade for gratuities esp. at the Christmas season (2) : a piece of music by such a group **3** : an act or period of waiting ⟨a long ~ in line⟩

wait·er \ˈwā-tər\ *n* (15c) **1** : one that waits on another; *esp* : a person who waits tables (as in a restaurant) **2** : a tray on which something (as a tea service) is carried : SALVER

wait·ing game \ˈwā-tiŋ-\ *n* (1850) : a strategy in which one or more participants withhold action temporarily in the hope of having a favorable opportunity for more effective action later

waiting list *n* (1892) : a list or roster of those waiting (as for admission to an organization or institution)

waiting room *n* (1683) : a room (as in a doctor's office) for the use of persons (as patients) who are waiting

wait–list \ˈwāt-ˌlist\ *vt* (1960) : to put on a waiting list

wait out *vt* (1849) : to await an end to ⟨*wait* the storm *out*⟩

wait·per·son \ˈwāt-ˌpər-sᵊn\ *n* (ca. 1976) : a waiter or waitress

wait·ress \ˈwā-trəs\ *n* (1834) : a woman who waits tables (as in a restaurant) — **waitress** *vi*

wait·ron \ˈwā-ˌträn, -trən\ *n* [blend of *waiter* or *waitress* and *-tron* (suggesting the machinelike impersonality of such work), later (perh. influenced by *neutron*) taken as a gender-neutral term] (1980) : WAITPERSON

wait·staff \ˈwāt-ˌstaf\ *n* (1983) : the staff of servers at a restaurant

waive \ˈwāv\ *vt* **waived; waiv·ing** [ME *weiven* to decline, reject, give up, fr. AF *waiver, gaiver,* fr. *waif* lost, stray — more at WAIF] (14c) **1** *archaic* : GIVE UP, FORSAKE **2** : to throw away (stolen goods) **3** *archaic* : to shunt aside (as a danger or duty) : EVADE **4 a** : to relinquish voluntarily (as a legal right) ⟨~ a jury trial⟩ **b** : to refrain from pressing or enforcing (as a claim or rule) : FORGO ⟨~ the fee⟩ **5** : to put off from immediate consideration : POSTPONE **6** [influenced by [1]*wave*] : to dismiss with or as if with a wave of the hand ⟨*waived* the problem aside⟩ **7** : to place (a ball player) on waivers; *also* : to release after placing on waivers ***syn*** see RELINQUISH

waiv·er \ˈwā-vər\ *n* [AF *weyver,* fr. *waiver,* v.] (1628) **1** : the act of intentionally relinquishing or abandoning a known right, claim, or privilege; *also* : the legal instrument evidencing such an act **2** : the act of a club's waiving the right to claim a professional ball player who is being removed from another club's roster — often used in the phrase *on waivers* denoting the process by which a player to be removed from a roster is made available to other clubs

wa·ka·me \wä-ˈkä-me\ *n* [Jp] (1950) : an edible brown seaweed (*Undaria pinnatifida*) native to Asia

Wa·kash·an \wȯ-ˈka-shən, ˈwȯ-ˌ\ *n* [Nootka *wa·ka·š,* interj. used as a shout of approval] (ca. 1895) : a family of American Indian languages spoken in coastal areas of British Columbia and northwest Washington

[1]**wake** \ˈwāk\ *vb* **woke** \ˈwōk\ *also* **waked** \wākt\; **wo·ken** \ˈwō-kən\ *or* **waked** *also* **woke; wak·ing** [partly fr. ME *waken* (past *wook,* pp. *waken*), fr. OE *wacan* to awake (past *wōc,* pp. *wacen*); partly fr. ME *wakien, waken* (past & pp. *waked*), fr. OE *wacian* to be awake (past *wacode,* pp. *wacod*); akin to OE *wæccan* to watch, L *vegēre* to enliven] *vi* (bef. 12c) **1 a** : to be or remain awake **b** *archaic* : to remain awake on watch esp. over a corpse **c** *obs* : to stay up late in revelry **2** : AWAKE — often used with *up* ~ *vt* **1** : to stand watch over (as a dead body); *esp* : to hold a wake over **2 a** : to rouse from or as if from sleep : AWAKE — often used with *up* **b** : STIR, EXCITE ⟨*woke* up latent possibilities —Norman Douglas⟩ **c** : to arouse conscious interest in : ALERT — usu. used with *to* ⟨*woke* the public to the risks⟩ — **wak·er** *n*

[2]**wake** *n* (13c) **1** : the state of being awake **2 a** (1) : an annual English parish festival formerly held in commemoration of the church's patron saint (2) : VIGIL 1a **b** : the festivities orig. connected with the wake of an English parish church — usu. used in pl. but sing. or pl. in constr. **c** *Brit* : an annual holiday or vacation — usu. used in pl. but sing. or pl. in constr. **3** : a watch held over the body of a dead person prior to burial and sometimes accompanied by festivity

[3]**wake** *n* [akin to MLG *wake* wake, Norw dial. *vok,* ON *vǫk* hole in ice] (1627) **1** : the track left by a moving body (as a ship) in a fluid (as water); *broadly* : a track or path left **2** : AFTERMATH 3 — **in the wake of 1** : close behind and in the same path of travel ⟨missionaries arrived *in the wake of* conquistadors and soldiers —Sabine MacCormack⟩ **2** : as a result of : as a consequence of ⟨power vacuums left *in the wake of* the second world war —A. M. Schlesinger *b*1917⟩

wake·board \ˈwāk-ˌbȯrd\ *n* (1991) : a short board with foot bindings on which a rider is towed by a motorboat across its wake and esp. up off the crest for aerial maneuvers — **wake·board·er** *n* — **wake·board·ing** *n*

wake·ful \ˈwāk-fəl\ *adj* (15c) : not sleeping or able to sleep : SLEEPLESS — **wake·ful·ly** \-fə-lē\ *adv* — **wake·ful·ness** *n*

wake·less \ˈwā-kləs\ *adj* (1611) : SOUND, UNBROKEN ⟨~ sleep⟩

wak·en \ˈwā-kən\ *vb* **wak·ened; wak·en·ing** \ˈwāk-niŋ, ˈwā-kə-\ [ME *waknen,* fr. OE *wæcnian;* akin to ON *vakna* to awaken, OE *wæccan* to watch] *vi* (bef. 12c) : AWAKE — often used with *up* ~ *vt* : to rouse esp. out of sleep : WAKE

wak·en·er \ˈwāk-nər, ˈwā-kə-\ *n* (1597) *archaic* : one that causes to waken

wake·rife \ˈwāk-ˌrīf\ *adj* [ME (Sc) *walkryfe,* fr. *walk* awake (fr. *waken, walken* to wake) + *ryfe* rife] (15c) *Scot* : WAKEFUL, ALERT

wake–rob·in \ˈwāk-ˌrä-bən\ *n* (ca. 1530) **1** : TRILLIUM **2** : JACK-IN-THE-PULPIT

wake–up \ˈwāk-ˌəp\ *adj* (1946) : serving to wake up ⟨a ~ alarm⟩

wake–up call *n* (1976) **1** : something (as a telephone call from a hotel employee to a guest) that serves to wake a sleeper **2** : something that serves to alert a person to a problem, danger, or need ⟨a *wake-up call* to parents⟩

waking *adj* (1556) : passed in a conscious or alert state ⟨every ~ hour⟩

Wal·den·ses \wȯl-ˈden(t)-(ˌ)sēz, wäl-\ *n pl* [ME *Waldensis,* fr. ML *Waldenses, Valdenses,* fr. Peter *Waldo* (or *Valdo*)] (15c) : a Christian sect arising in southern France in the 12th century, adopting Calvinist doctrines in the 16th century, and later living chiefly in Piedmont — **Wal·den·sian** \-ˈden(t)-shən, -ˈden(t)-sē-ən\ *adj or n*

Wal·dorf salad \ˈwȯl-ˌdȯrf-\ *n* [*Waldorf*-Astoria Hotel, New York City] (1902) : a salad made typically of diced apples, celery, nuts, and mayonnaise

[1]**wale** \ˈwāl\ *n* [ME, fr. OE *walu;* akin to ON *vǫlr* staff and perh. to ON *valr* round, L *volvere* to roll — more at VOLUBLE] (bef. 12c) **1 a** : a streak or ridge made on the skin esp. by the stroke of a whip : WEAL **b** : a narrow raised surface : RIDGE **2** : any of a number of strakes usu. of extra thick and strong planks in the sides of a wooden ship — usu. used in pl. **3 a** : one of a series of even ribs in a fabric **b** : the texture esp. of a fabric **4** : a horizontal constructional member (as of timber or steel) used for bracing vertical members

[2]**wale** *vt* **waled; wal·ing** (15c) : to mark (as the skin) with welts

[3]**wale** *n* [ME (Sc & northern dial.) *wal,* fr. ON *val;* akin to OHG *wala* choice, OE *wyllan* to wish — more at WILL] (14c) **1** *dial Brit* : CHOICE **2** *dial Brit* : the best part : PICK

[4]**wale** *vb* (14c) *dial Brit* : CHOOSE

wal·er \ˈwā-lər\ *n, often cap* [New So. *Wales,* Australia] (ca. 1849) : a horse from New So. Wales; *esp* : a rather large rugged saddle horse of mixed ancestry formerly exported in quantity from Australia to British India for military use

Wal·hal·la \väl-ˈhä-lə\ *n* [G] (1851) : VALHALLA 1

[1]**walk** \ˈwȯk\ *vb* [partly fr. ME *walken* (past *welk,* pp. *walken*), fr. OE *wealcan* to roll, toss, journey about (past *weolc,* pp. *wealcen*) and partly fr. ME *walkien* (past *walked,* pp. *walked*), fr. OE *wealcian* to roll up, muffle up; akin to MD *walken* to knead, press, full] *vi* (bef. 12c) **1 a** *obs* : ROAM, WANDER **b** *of a spirit* : to move about in visible form : APPEAR **c** *of a ship* : to make headway **2 a** : to move along on foot : advance by steps **b** : to come or go easily or readily **c** : to go on foot for exercise or pleasure **d** : to go at a walk **3 a** : to pursue a course of action or way of life : conduct oneself : BEHAVE ⟨~ warily⟩ **b** : to be or act in association : continue in union ⟨the British and American peoples will . . . ~ together side by side . . . in peace —Sir Winston Churchill⟩ **c** : WALK OUT ⟨~*ed* over problems with management⟩ **4** : to go to first base as a result of a base on balls **5** *of an inanimate object* **a** : to move in a manner that is suggestive of walking **b** : to stand with an appearance suggestive of strides ⟨pylons ~*ing* across the valley⟩ **6** *of an astronaut* : to move about in space outside a spacecraft **7** : to avoid criminal prosecution or conviction ⟨~*ed* on a technicality⟩ ~ *vt* **1 a** : to pass on foot or as if on foot through, along, over, or upon : TRAVERSE, PERAMBULATE ⟨~ the streets⟩ ⟨~ a tightrope⟩ **b** : to perform or accomplish by going on foot ⟨~ guard⟩ **2 a** : to cause (an animal) to go at a walk : take for a walk ⟨~*ing* a dog⟩ **b** (1) : to cause to move by walking ⟨~*ed* her bicycle up the hill⟩ (2) : to haul (as an anchor) by walking round the capstan **3** : to follow on foot for the purpose of measuring, surveying, or inspecting ⟨~ a boundary⟩ **4 a** : to accompany on foot : walk with ⟨~*ed* her home⟩ **b** : to compel to walk (as by a command) **c** : to bring to a specified condition by walking ⟨~*ed* us off our feet⟩ **5** : to move (an object) in a manner suggestive of walking **6** : to perform (a dance) at a walking pace ⟨~ a quadrille⟩ **7** : to give a base on balls to — **walk away from 1** : to outrun or get the better of without difficulty **2** : to survive (an accident) with little or no injury **3** : to give up or leave behind willingly : ABANDON — **walk off with 1 a** : to steal and take away **b** : to take over unexpectedly from someone else : STEAL 1d ⟨*walked off with* the show⟩ **2** : to win or gain esp. by outdoing one's competitors without difficulty — **walk on** : to take advantage of : ABUSE — **walk on eggshells** *or* **walk on eggs** : to exercise extreme caution — **walk over** : to treat contemptuously — **walk the plank 1** : to walk under compulsion over the side of a ship into the sea **2** : to resign an office or position under compulsion — **walk through 1** : to go through (as a the-

atrical role or familiar activity) perfunctorily (as in an early stage of rehearsal) **2 :** to guide (as a novice) through an unfamiliar or complex procedure step-by-step **3 :** to deal with or carry out perfunctorily

[2]**walk** *n* (14c) **1 a :** an act or instance of going on foot esp. for exercise or pleasure ⟨go for a ~⟩ **b :** SPACE WALK **2 :** an accustomed place of walking : HAUNT **3 :** a place designed for walking: **a :** a railed platform above the roof of a dwelling house **b** (1) **:** a path specially arranged or paved for walking (2) **:** SIDEWALK **c :** a public avenue for promenading : PROMENADE **d :** ROPEWALK **4 :** a place or area of land in which animals feed and exercise with minimal restraint **5 :** distance to be walked ⟨a quarter mile ~ from here⟩ **6** *Brit* **:** a ceremonial procession **7 :** manner of living : CONDUCT, BEHAVIOR **8 a :** the gait of a biped in which the feet are lifted alternately with one foot not clear of the ground before the other touches **b :** the gait of a quadruped in which there are always at least two feet on the ground; *specif* **:** a 4-beat gait of a horse in which the feet strike the ground in the sequence near hind, near fore, off hind, off fore **c :** a low rate of speed ⟨the shortage of raw materials slowed production to a ~⟩ **9 :** a route regularly traversed by a person in the performance of a particular activity (as patrolling, begging, or vending) **10 :** characteristic manner of walking ⟨his ~ is just like his father's⟩ **11 a :** social or economic status ⟨all ~*s* of life⟩ **b** (1) **:** range or sphere of action : FIELD, PROVINCE (2) **:** VOCATION **12 :** BASE ON BALLS **13 :** an easy victory ⟨won in a ~⟩ — **walk in the park :** an easy or pleasurable experience

walk·able \ˈwȯ-kə-bəl\ *adj* (1736) **:** capable of or suitable for being walked ⟨a very ~ city⟩ ⟨a ~ distance⟩

walk·about \ˈwȯ-kə-ˌbau̇t\ *n* (1908) **1 :** a short period of wandering bush life engaged in by an Australian aborigine as an occasional interruption of regular work — often used in the phrase *go walkabout* ⟨the man who went ~ was making a ritual journey —Bruce Chatwin⟩ **2 :** something (as a journey) similar to a walkabout **3 :** a walking tour; *esp, Brit* **:** one in which a well-known person mingles with the public ⟨went ~ in the streets⟩

walk·a·thon \ˈwȯ-kə-ˌthän\ *n* [*walk* + *-athon*] (1932) **:** a walk covering a considerable distance organized esp. to raise money for a cause

walk·away \ˈwȯ-kə-ˌwā\ *n* (1888) **:** an easily won contest

walk·er \ˈwȯ-kər\ *n* (14c) **1 :** one that walks: as **a :** a competitor in a walking race **b :** a peddler going on foot **c :** a temporary male escort of socially prominent women attending usu. public events **2 :** something used in walking: as **a :** a framework designed to support a baby learning to walk or an infirm or disabled person **b :** a walking shoe

walk·ie–talk·ie \ˌwȯ-kē-ˈtȯ-kē, ˈwȯ-kē-ˌ\ *n* (ca. 1939) **:** a compact easily transportable battery-operated radio transmitting and receiving set

[1]**walk–in** \ˈwȯk-ˌin\ *adj* (1926) **1 :** large enough to be walked into ⟨a ~ closet⟩ **2 :** arranged so as to be entered directly rather than through a lobby ⟨a ~ apartment⟩ **3 a :** being a person who walks in without an appointment ⟨a ~ blood donor⟩ **b :** of, relating to, or intended for such persons ⟨a ~ clinic⟩

[2]**walk–in** *n* (1944) **1 :** a walk-in refrigerator or cold storage room **2 :** an easy election victory **3 :** a person who walks in without an appointment

[1]**walk·ing** \ˈwȯ-kiŋ\ *n* (14c) **1 :** the action of one that walks **2 :** the condition of a surface for one going on foot ⟨the ~ is slippery⟩

[2]**walking** *adj* (15c) **1 a :** able to walk : AMBULATORY ⟨the ~ wounded⟩ **b :** being the personification of a nonhuman quality or thing ⟨a ~ encyclopedia⟩ **2 a :** used for or in walking ⟨~ shoes⟩ **b :** characterized by or consisting of the action of walking ⟨a ~ tour⟩ **3 :** that moves or appears to move in a manner suggestive of walking; *esp* **:** that swings or rocks back and forth ⟨~ beam⟩ **4 :** guided or operated by a person on foot ⟨a ~ plow⟩

walking catfish *n* (1968) **:** an Asian freshwater catfish (*Clarias batrachus* of the family Clariidae) that is able to move about on land and has become established in Florida waters

walking delegate *n* (1886) **:** a labor union representative appointed to visit members and their places of employment, to secure enforcement of union rules and agreements, and at times to represent the union in dealing with employers

walking leaf *n* (1826) **:** any of a family (Phylliidae) of phasmid insects with wings and legs resembling leaves

walking papers *n pl* (1825) **:** DISMISSAL, DISCHARGE — called also *walking ticket*

walking pneumonia *n* (1964) **:** a usu. mild pneumonia caused by a mycoplasma (*Mycoplasma pneumoniae*) and characterized by malaise, cough, and often fever

walking stick *n* (1580) **1 :** a stick used in walking **2 :** STICK INSECT; *esp* **:** one (*Diapheromera femorata*) of the U.S. and Canada

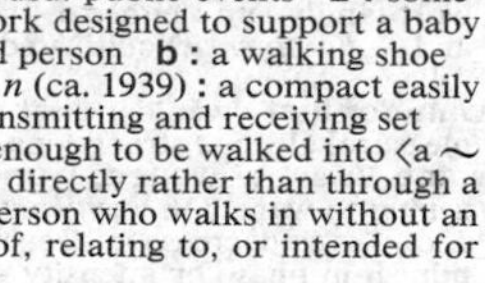

walking stick 2

Walk·man \ˈwȯk-mən, -ˌman\ *trademark* — used for a small portable audio player listened to by means of headphones or earphones

walk–off \ˈwȯk-ˌȯf\ *adj* (1990) **:** ending a baseball game immediately by causing the winning run to score for the home team in the bottom of the last inning ⟨a ~ homer⟩; *also* **:** won by the home team in the bottom of the last inning ⟨a ~ win⟩

walk–on \ˈwȯk-ˌȯn, -ˌän\ *n* (1902) **1 :** a minor part (as in a dramatic production); *also* **:** an actor having such a part **2 :** a college athlete who tries out for an athletic team without having been recruited or offered a scholarship

walk·out \ˈwȯk-ˌau̇t\ *n* (1888) **1 :** STRIKE 3a **2 :** the action of leaving a meeting or organization as an expression of disapproval

walk out *vi* (1840) **1 :** to leave suddenly often as an expression of disapproval **2 :** to go on strike — **walk out on :** to leave in the lurch : ABANDON, DESERT

walk·over \ˈwȯk-ˌō-vər\ *n* (1838) **1 :** a one-sided contest : an easy or uncontested victory **2 :** a horse race with only one starter

walk–through \ˈwȯk-ˌthrü\ *n* (1940) **1 :** a perfunctory performance of a play or acting part (as in an early stage of rehearsal) **2 :** a television rehearsal without cameras

[1]**walk–up** \ˈwȯk-ˌəp\ *adj* (ca. 1919) **1 :** located above the ground floor in a building with no elevator ⟨a ~ apartment⟩ **2 :** consisting of several stories and having no elevator ⟨a ~ tenement⟩ **3 :** designed to allow pedestrians to be served without entering a building ⟨the ~ window of a bank⟩

[2]**walk–up** *n* (1924) **:** an apartment or office building of several stories that has no elevator; *also* **:** an apartment or office in such a building

walk·way \ˈwȯk-ˌwā\ *n* (1792) **:** a passage for walking : WALK

Wal·ky·rie \väl-ˈkir-ē *also* väl-ˈkī-rē *or* ˈväl-kə-rē\ *n* [G *Walküre* & ON *valkyrja*] (bef. 12c) **:** VALKYRIE

[1]**wall** \ˈwȯl\ *n* [ME, fr. OE *weall;* akin to MHG *wall;* both fr. L *vallum* rampart, fr. *vallus* stake, palisade; perh. akin to ON *vǫlr* staff — more at WALE] (bef. 12c) **1 a :** a high thick masonry structure forming a long rampart or an enclosure chiefly for defense — often used in pl. **b :** a masonry fence around a garden, park, or estate **c :** a structure that serves to hold back pressure (as of water or sliding earth) **2 :** one of the sides of a room or building connecting floor and ceiling or foundation and roof **3 :** the side of a footpath next to buildings **4 :** an extreme or desperate position or a state of defeat, failure, or ruin ⟨the surrounded troops had their backs against the ~⟩ **5 :** a material layer enclosing space ⟨the ~ of a container⟩ ⟨heart ~*s*⟩ **6 :** something resembling a wall (as in appearance, function, or effect); *esp* **:** something that acts as a barrier or defense ⟨a ~ of reserve⟩ ⟨tariff ~⟩ — **wall–like** \ˈwȯl-ˌlīk\ *adj* — **off the wall** *slang* **:** CRAZY ⟨the plan was *off the wall*⟩ — **up the wall** *slang* **:** into a state of intense agitation, annoyance, or frustration ⟨the noise drove me *up the wall*⟩

[2]**wall** *vt* (13c) **1 a :** to provide, cover with, or surround with or as if with a wall ⟨~ in the garden⟩ **b :** to separate by or as if by a wall ⟨~*ed* off half the house⟩ **2 a :** IMMURE ⟨~*ed* the monster up within the tomb —E. A. Poe⟩ **b :** to close (an opening) with or as if with a wall

[3]**wall** *vb* [ME (Sc) *wawlen,* prob. fr. ME *wawil-* (in *wawil-eghed* walleyed)] *vi* (15c) *of the eyes* **:** to roll in a dramatic manner ~ *vt* **:** to roll (one's eyes) in a dramatic manner

wal·la·by \ˈwä-lə-bē\ *n, pl* **wallabies** *also* **wallaby** [Dharuk (Australian aboriginal language of the Port Jackson area) *walabi, waliba*] (ca. 1798) **:** any of various small or medium-sized kangaroos (esp. genus *Macropus*) — compare ROCK WALLABY

Wal·lace's line \ˈwä-lə-səz-\ *n* [Alfred Russel *Wallace*] (ca. 1868) **:** a hypothetical boundary that separates the highly distinctive faunas of the Asian and Australian biogeographic regions and passes between the islands of Bali and Lombok in Indonesia, between Borneo and Sulawesi, and between the Philippines and the Moluccas

wal·lah \ˈwä-lə, *in combination usu* ˌwä-lə\ *n* [Hindi & Urdu *-vālā* one in charge, fr. Skt *pāla* protector, fr. *pālayati, pārayati* he guards; akin to Skt *piparti* he brings over, saves, OE *faran* to go — more at FARE] (1782) **:** a person who is associated with a particular work or who performs a specific duty or service — usu. used in combination ⟨the book ~ was an itinerant peddler —George Orwell⟩

wal·la·roo \ˌwä-lə-ˈrü\ *n, pl* **-roos** [Dharuk (Australian aboriginal language of the Port Jackson area) *walaru*] (ca. 1826) **1 :** a large reddish-gray kangaroo (*Macropus robustus*) — called also *euro* **2 :** either of two kangaroos (*Macropus antelopinus* and *M. bernardus*) related to the wallaroo

wall·board \ˈwȯl-ˌbȯrd\ *n* (1906) **:** a structural boarding of any of various materials (as wood pulp, gypsum, or plastic) made in large rigid sheets and used esp. for sheathing interior walls and ceilings

wal·let \ˈwä-lət\ *n* [ME *walet*] (14c) **1 :** a bag for carrying miscellaneous articles while traveling **2 a :** a folding pocketbook with compartments for personal papers and usu. unfolded paper money; *also* **:** BILLFOLD **b :** a container that resembles a money wallet: as (1) **:** a usu. flexible folding case fitted for carrying specific items (as tools or fishing flies) (2) **:** FOLDER 3 **3 :** RESOURCES, FUNDS ⟨a shopping mall that seems to swallow your ~ —Karen Wright⟩

wall·eye \ˈwȯl-ˌī\ *n* [back-formation fr. *walleyed*] (1523) **1 a :** an eye with a whitish or bluish-white iris **b :** an eye with an opaque white cornea **2 a :** strabismus in which the eye turns outward away from the nose **b :** an eye affected with strabismus of this type **3 :** a large vigorous No. American freshwater food and sport fish (*Stizostedion vitreum*) that has large opaque eyes and is related to the perches but resembles the true pike — called also *walleyed pike*

wall·eyed \-ˈīd\ *adj* [by folk etymology fr. ME *wawil-eghed,* part trans. of ON *vagl-eygr* walleyed, fr. *vagl* beam (akin to Gk *ochleus* bar, OE *wegan* to move, carry) + *eygr* eyed — more at WAY] (15c) **1 :** having walleyes or affected with walleye **2 :** marked by a wild irrational staring of the eyes

walleye pollack *n* (1907) **:** POLLACK 2

wall·flow·er \ˈwȯl-ˌflau̇(-ə)r\ *n* (1577) **1 a :** any of several Old World perennial herbs (genus *Cheiranthus*) of the mustard family; *esp* **:** a hardy erect herb (*C. cheiri*) widely cultivated for its showy fragrant flowers **b :** any of a related genus (*Erysimum*) of herbs with showy flowers **2 a :** a person who from shyness or unpopularity remains on the sidelines of a social activity (as a dance) **b :** a shy or reserved person

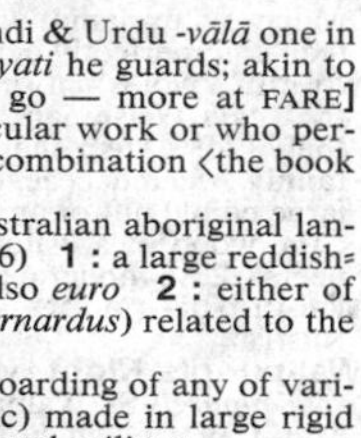

wallflower 1a

Wal·loon \wä-ˈlün\ *n* [MF *Wallon,* adj. & n., of Gmc origin; prob. akin to OHG *Walah* Celt, Roman, OE *Wealh* Celt, Welshman — more at WELSH] (1567) **1 :** a member of a people of southern and southeastern Belgium and adjacent parts of France **2 :** a French dialect of the Walloons — **Walloon** *adj*

[1]**wal·lop** \ˈwä-ləp\ *vb* [ME *walopen* to gallop, fr. OF (Picard dial.) *waloper*] *vi* (1579) **1 :** to boil noisily **2 a :** to move with reckless or disorganized haste **:** advance in a headlong rush **b :** WALLOW, FLOUNDER ~ *vt* **1 a :** to thrash soundly : LAMBASTE **b :** to beat by a wide margin : TROUNCE **2 :** to hit with force : SOCK — **wal·lop·er** *n*

[2]**wallop** *n* (ca. 1823) **1 a :** a powerful blow : PUNCH **b :** something resembling a wallop esp. in suddenness of force **c :** the ability (as of a boxer) to hit hard **2 a :** emotional, sensory, or psychological force or

\ə\ **abut** \ᵊ\ kitten, F table \ər\ **further** \a\ **ash** \ā\ **ace** \ä\ **mop, mar** \au̇\ **out** \ch\ **chin** \e\ **bet** \ē\ **easy** \g\ **go** \i\ **hit** \ī\ **ice** \j\ **job** \ŋ\ **sing** \ō\ **go** \ȯ\ **law** \ȯi\ **boy** \th\ **thin** \t͟h\ **the** \ü\ **loot** \u̇\ **foot** \y\ **yet** \zh\ **vision, beige** \k, ⁿ, œ, ue, ʸ\ *see* Guide to Pronunciation

influence : IMPACT ⟨a novel that packs a ~⟩ **b** : an exciting emotional response : THRILL **3** *Brit* : BEER

wal·lop·ing \ˈwä-lə-piŋ\ *adj* (1823) **1** : LARGE, WHOPPING **2** : exceptionally fine or impressive : SMASHING

[1]**wal·low** \ˈwä-(ˌ)lō\ *vi* [ME *walwen,* fr. OE *wealwian* to roll — more at VOLUBLE] (bef. 12c) **1** : to roll oneself about in a lazy, relaxed, or ungainly manner ⟨hogs ~*ing* in the mud⟩ **2** : to billow forth : SURGE **3** : to devote oneself entirely; *esp* : to take unrestrained pleasure : DELIGHT **4 a** : to become abundantly supplied : LUXURIATE ⟨a family that ~*s* in money⟩ **b** : to indulge oneself immoderately ⟨~*ing* in self-pity⟩ **5** : to become or remain helpless ⟨allowed them to ~ in their ignorance⟩ — **wal·low·er** \ˈwä-lə-wər\ *n*

[2]**wallow** *n* (15c) **1** : an act or instance of wallowing **2 a** : a muddy area or one filled with dust used by animals for wallowing **b** : a depression formed by or as if by the wallowing of animals **3** : a state of degradation or degeneracy

wall painting *n* (ca. 1688) : FRESCO

[1]**wall·pa·per** \ˈwȯl-ˌpā-pər\ *n* (1827) : decorative paper for the walls of a room

[2]**wallpaper** *vt* (1918) : to provide the walls of (a room) with wallpaper ~ *vi* : to put wallpaper on a wall

wall plate *n* (14c) : PLATE 5

wall plug *n* (1888) : an electric receptacle in a wall

wall rock *n* (1866) : a rock through which a fault or vein runs

wall rocket *n* (ca. 1611) : any of several Old World herbs (genus *Diplotaxis*) of the mustard family; *esp* : a yellow-flowered European herb (*D. tenuifolia*) naturalized in No. America

Wall Street \ˈwȯl-\ *n* [*Wall Street,* New York City, site of the New York Stock Exchange] (1831) : the influential financial interests of the U.S. economy

Wall Street·er \-ˌstrē-tər\ *n* (1885) : a person who is involved in Wall Street

wall system *n* (1968) : a set of shelves often with cabinets or bureaus that can be variously arranged along a wall

wall–to–wall *adj* (1946) **1** : covering the entire floor ⟨~ carpeting⟩ **2 a** : covering or filling one entire space or time ⟨a party crammed with ~ bodies⟩ **b** : occurring or found everywhere : UBIQUITOUS

wal·ly \ˈwā-lē\ *adj* [prob. fr. [3]*wale*] (ca. 1520) *Scot* : FINE, STURDY

wal·ly·drai·gle \ˈwā-lē-ˌdrā-gəl, ˈwä-lē-\ *n* [perh. fr. Sc *wally* (alter. of wallaway, exclamation of woe) + *dragle* draggle] (1508) *chiefly Scot* : a feeble, imperfectly developed, or slovenly creature

wal·nut \ˈwȯl-(ˌ)nət\ *n* [ME *walnot,* fr. OE *wealhhnutu,* lit., foreign nut, fr. *Wealh* Welshman, foreigner + *hnutu* nut — more at WELSH, NUT] (bef. 12c) **1 a** : the furrowed nut of any of a genus (*Juglans* of the family Juglandaceae, the walnut family) of deciduous trees; *esp* : the large edible nut of an English walnut **b** : a tree that bears walnuts **c** : the wood of a walnut that is often used for cabinetmaking and veneers **2** : a moderate reddish brown

Wal·pur·gis·nacht \väl-ˈpu̇r-gəs-ˌnäkt\ *n* [G] (1822) : WALPURGIS NIGHT

Wal·pur·gis Night \väl-ˈpu̇r-gəs-\ *n* [part trans. of G *Walpurgisnacht,* fr. *Walpurgis* St. Walburga †A.D. 779 Eng. saint whose feast day falls on May Day + G *Nacht* night] (1823) **1** : the eve of May Day on which witches are held to ride to an appointed rendezvous **2** : something (as an event or situation) having a nightmarish quality

wal·rus \ˈwȯl-rəs, ˈwäl-\ *n, pl* **walrus** *or* **wal·rus·es** [D, of Scand origin; akin to Dan & Norw *hvalros* walrus, ON *rosmhvalr*] (1728) : a large gregarious marine mammal (*Odobenus rosmarus* of the family Odobenidae) of arctic waters that is related to the seals and has long ivory tusks, a tough wrinkled hide, and stiff whiskers and that feeds mainly on bivalve mollusks

Wal·ter Mit·ty \ˌwȯl-tər-ˈmi-tē\ *n* [*Walter Mitty,* daydreaming hero of a story by James Thurber] (1949) : a commonplace unadventurous person who seeks escape from reality through daydreaming — **Walter Mit·ty·ish** \-ish\ *adj*

[1]**waltz** \ˈwȯl(t)s\ *n* [G *Walzer,* fr. *walzen* to roll, dance, fr. OHG *walzan* to turn, roll — more at WELTER] (1781) **1** : a ballroom dance in ¾ time with strong accent on the first beat and a basic pattern of step-step-close **2** : music for a waltz or a concert composition in ¾ time

[2]**waltz** *vi* (ca. 1794) **1** : to dance a waltz **2** : to move or advance in a lively or conspicuous manner : FLOUNCE **3 a** : to advance easily and successfully : BREEZE — often used with *through* **b** : to approach boldly — used with *up* ⟨can't just ~ up and introduce ourselves⟩ ~ *vt* **1** : to dance a waltz with **2** : to grab and lead (as a person) unceremoniously : MARCH — **waltz·er** *n*

[1]**wam·ble** \ˈwäm-bəl\ *vi* **wam·bled; wam·bling** \-b(ə-)liŋ\ [ME *wamlen;* akin to Dan *vamle* to become nauseated, L *vomere* to vomit — more at VOMIT] (14c) **1 a** : to feel nausea **b** *of a stomach* : RUMBLE 1 **2** : to move unsteadily or with a weaving or rolling motion

[2]**wamble** *n* (1552) **1** : a wambling esp. of the stomach **2** : a reeling or staggering gait or movement

wame \ˈwām\ *n* [ME, alter. of *wamb* — more at WOMB] (15c) *chiefly Scot* : BELLY

Wam·pa·no·ag \ˌwäm-pə-ˈnō-(ˌ)ag, ˌwȯm-\ *n, pl* **Wampanoag** *or* **Wampanoags** [Narragansett, lit., easterners] (1676) : a member of an American Indian people of Rhode Island east of Narragansett Bay and neighboring parts of Massachusetts

wam·pum \ˈwäm-pəm\ *n* [short for *wampumpeag*] (1636) **1** : beads of polished shells strung in strands, belts, or sashes and used by No. American Indians as money, ceremonial pledges, and ornaments **2** : MONEY

wam·pum·peag \-ˌpēg\ *n* [Massachusett *wampompeag,* fr. *wampan* white + *api* string + *-ag,* pl. suffix] (1627) : WAMPUM

[1]**wan** \ˈwän\ *adj* **wan·ner; wan·nest** [ME, fr. OE *wann* dark, livid] (14c) **1 a** : suggestive of poor health : SICKLY, PALLID **b** : lacking vitality : FEEBLE **2** : DIM, FAINT **3** : LANGUID ⟨a ~ smile⟩ — **wan·ly** *adv* — **wan·ness** \ˈwän-nəs\ *n*

[2]**wan** *vi* **wanned; wan·ning** (1578) : to grow or become pale or sickly

WAN \ˈwan\ *n* (1983) : WIDE AREA NETWORK

wand \ˈwänd\ *n* [ME, slender stick, fr. ON *vǫndr;* prob. akin to OE *windan* to wind, twist — more at WIND] (13c) **1** : a slender staff carried in a procession : VERGE **2** : a slender rod used by conjurers and magicians **3** : a slat six feet by two inches used as a target in archery; *also* : a narrow strip of paper pasted vertically on a target face **4** : any of various pipelike devices; *esp* : the rigid tube between the hose and the nozzle of a vacuum cleaner **5** : a handheld device used to enter information (as from a bar code) into a computer

wan·der \ˈwän-dər\ *vb* **wan·dered; wan·der·ing** \-d(ə-)riŋ\ [ME *wandren,* fr. OE *wandrian;* akin to MHG *wandern* to wander, OE *windan* to wind, twist] *vi* (bef. 12c) **1 a** : to move about without a fixed course, aim, or goal **b** : to go idly about : RAMBLE ⟨~*ing* around the house⟩ **2** : to follow a winding course : MEANDER **3 a** : to go astray (as from a course) : STRAY ⟨~*ed* away from the group⟩ **b** : to go astray morally : ERR **c** : to lose normal mental contact : stray in thought ⟨his mind ~*ed*⟩ ~ *vt* : to roam over ⟨~*ed* the halls⟩ — **wander** *n* — **wan·der·er** \-dər-ər\ *n*

syn WANDER, ROAM, RAMBLE, ROVE, TRAIPSE, MEANDER mean to go about from place to place usu. without a plan or definite purpose. WANDER implies an absence of or an indifference to a fixed course ⟨fond of *wandering* about the square just watching the people⟩. ROAM suggests wandering about freely and often far afield ⟨liked to *roam* through the woods⟩. RAMBLE stresses carelessness and indifference to one's course or objective ⟨the speaker *rambled* on without ever coming to the point⟩. ROVE suggests vigorous and sometimes purposeful roaming ⟨armed brigands *roved* over the countryside⟩. TRAIPSE implies a course that is erratic but may sometimes be purposeful ⟨*traipsed* all over town looking for the right dress⟩. MEANDER implies a winding or intricate course suggestive of aimless or listless wandering ⟨the river *meanders* for miles through rich farmland⟩.

[1]**wandering** *adj* (bef. 12c) : characterized by aimless, slow, or pointless movement: as **a** : that winds or meanders ⟨a ~ course⟩ **b** : not keeping a rational or sensible course : VAGRANT **c** : NOMADIC ⟨~ tribes⟩ **d** *of a plant* : having long runners or tendrils

[2]**wandering** *n* (14c) **1** : a going about from place to place — often used in pl. **2** : movement away from the proper, normal, or usual course or place — often used in pl.

wandering albatross *n* (1836) : a large white albatross (*Diomedea exulans*) of southern oceans that has black outer wing feathers and a wingspan of about 11 feet (3.4 meters)

Wandering Jew *n* (1628) **1** : a Jew of medieval legend condemned by Christ to wander the earth till Christ's second coming **2** *not cap W* : any of several plants (genera *Zebrina* and *Tradescantia*) of the spiderwort family; *esp* : either of two trailing or creeping plants (*Z. pendula* and *T. fluminensis*) cultivated for their showy and often white-striped foliage

wan·der·lust \ˈwän-dər-ˌləst\ *n* [G, fr. *wandern* to wander + *Lust* desire, pleasure] (1875) : strong longing for or impulse toward wandering

[1]**wane** \ˈwān\ *vi* **waned; wan·ing** [ME, fr. OE *wanian;* akin to OHG *wanōn* to wane, OE *wan* wanting, deficient, L *vanus* empty, vain] (bef. 12c) **1** : to decrease in size, extent, or degree : DWINDLE: as **a** : to diminish in phase or intensity — used chiefly of the moon, other satellites, and inferior planets **b** : to become less brilliant or powerful : DIM **c** : to flow out : EBB **2** : to fall gradually from power, prosperity, or influence ***syn*** see ABATE

[2]**wane** *n* (14c) **1 a** : the act or process of waning ⟨strength on the ~⟩ **b** : a period or time of waning; *specif* : the period from the full moon to the new moon **2** [ME, defect, fr. OE *wana;* akin to OE *wan* deficient] : a defect in lumber characterized by bark or a lack of wood at a corner or edge

wan·gle \ˈwaŋ-gəl\ *vb* **wan·gled; wan·gling** \-g(ə-)liŋ\ [perh. alter. of *waggle*] *vi* (1888) : to resort to trickery or devious methods ~ *vt* **1** : to adjust or manipulate for personal or fraudulent ends **2** : to make or get by devious means : FINAGLE ⟨~ an invitation⟩ — **wan·gler** \-g(ə-)lər\ *n*

wan·i·gan *or* **wan·ni·gan** \ˈwä-ni-gən\ *n* [Ojibwa *wa·nikka·n* pit] (ca. 1848) : a shelter (as for sleeping, eating, or storage) often mounted on wheels or tracks and towed by tractor or mounted on a raft or boat

wan·ion \ˈwän-yən\ *n* [fr. the obs. phrase *in the waniand* unluckily, lit., in the waning (moon), fr. ME, fr. *waniand,* northern prp. of *wanien, wanen* to wane] (1549) *archaic* : PLAGUE, VENGEANCE — used in the phrase *with a wanion*

wank \ˈwaŋk\ *vi* [origin unknown] (ca. 1950) *chiefly Brit, usu vulgar* : MASTURBATE

Wan·kel engine \ˈväŋ-kəl-, ˈwaŋ-\ *n* [Felix *Wankel* †1988 Ger. engineer] (1961) : an internal combustion rotary engine that has a rounded triangular rotor functioning as a piston and rotating in a space in the engine and that has only two major moving parts

wank·er \ˈwaŋ-kər\ *n* (ca. 1961) **1** *chiefly Brit, usu vulgar* : a person who masturbates **2** *chiefly Brit, usu vulgar* : JERK, DOLT

wan·na·be *also* **wan·na·bee** \ˈwä-nə-ˌbē\ *n* [fr. the phrase *want to be*] (1981) **1** : a person who wants or aspires to be someone or something else or who tries to look or act like someone else **2** : something (as a company, city, or product) intended to rival another of its kind that has been successful; *esp* : one for which hopes have failed or are likely to fail

[1]**want** \ˈwȯnt *also* ˈwänt & ˈwənt\ *vb* [ME, fr. ON *vanta;* akin to OE *wan* deficient] *vi* (13c) **1** : to be needy or destitute **2** : to have or feel need ⟨never ~*s* for friends⟩ **3** : to be necessary or needed **4** : to desire to come, go, or be ⟨the cat ~*s* in⟩ ⟨~*s* out of the deal⟩ ~ *vt* **1** : to fail to possess esp. in customary or required amount : LACK ⟨the answer ~*ed* courtesy⟩ **2 a** : to have a strong desire for ⟨~*ed* a chance to rest⟩ **b** : to have an inclination to : LIKE ⟨say what you ~, he is efficient⟩ **3 a** : to have need of : REQUIRE ⟨the motor ~*s* a tune-up⟩ **b** : to suffer from the lack of ⟨thousands still ~ food and shelter⟩ **4** : OUGHT — used with the infinitive ⟨you ~ to be very careful what you say —Claudia Cassidy⟩ **5** : to wish or demand the presence of **6** : to hunt or seek in order to apprehend ⟨~*ed* for murder⟩ ***syn*** see DESIRE

[2]**want** *n* (13c) **1 a** : DEFICIENCY, LACK ⟨suffers from a ~ of good sense⟩ **b** : grave and extreme poverty that deprives one of the necessities of life **2** : something wanted : NEED, DESIRE **3** : personal defect : FAULT ***syn*** see POVERTY

want ad *n* (1895) : a newspaper advertisement stating that something (as an employee, employment, or a specified item) is wanted

[1]**want·ing** \ˈwän-tiŋ\ *adj* (15c) **1** : not present or in evidence : ABSENT **2 a** : not being up to standards or expectations **b** : lacking in ability or capacity : DEFICIENT

[2]**wanting** *prep* (15c) **1 :** WITHOUT ⟨a book ~ a cover⟩ **2 :** LESS, MINUS ⟨a month ~ two days⟩

[1]**wan·ton** \ˈwȯn-tᵊn, ˈwän-\ *adj* [ME, fr. *wan-* deficient, wrong, mis- (fr. OE, fr. *wan* deficient) + *towen,* pp. of *teen* to draw, train, discipline, fr. OE *tēon* — more at TOW] (14c) **1 a** *archaic* **:** hard to control **:** UNDISCIPLINED, UNRULY **b :** playfully mean or cruel **:** MISCHIEVOUS **2 a :** LEWD, BAWDY **b :** causing sexual excitement **:** LUSTFUL, SENSUAL **3 a :** MERCILESS, INHUMANE ⟨~ cruelty⟩ **b :** having no just foundation or provocation **:** MALICIOUS ⟨a ~ attack⟩ **4 :** being without check or limitation: as **a :** luxuriantly rank ⟨~ vegetation⟩ **b :** unduly lavish **:** EXTRAVAGANT ⟨~ imagination⟩ — **wan·ton·ly** *adv* — **wan·ton·ness** \-tᵊn-nəs\ *n*

[2]**wanton** *n* (1509) **1 a :** one given to self-indulgent flirtation or trifling — used esp. in the phrase *play the wanton* **b :** a lewd or lascivious person **2 :** a pampered person or animal **:** PET; *esp* **:** a spoiled child **3 :** a frolicsome child or animal

[3]**wanton** *vi* (1582) **:** to be wanton or act wantonly ~ *vt* **:** to pass or waste wantonly or in wantonness — **wan·ton·er** *n*

wa·pen·take \ˈwa-pən-ˌtāk, ˈwä-\ *n* [ME, fr. OE *wǣpentæc,* fr. ON *vāpnatak* act of grasping weapons, fr. *vāpn* weapon + *tak* act of grasping, fr. *taka* to take; prob. fr. the brandishing of weapons as an expression of approval when the chief of the wapentake entered upon his office — more at WEAPON, TAKE] (bef. 12c) **:** a subdivision of some English shires corresponding to a hundred

wa·pi·ti \ˈwä-pə-tē\ *n, pl* **wapiti** *or* **wapitis** [Shawnee *wa·piti,* lit., white rump] (1806) **:** ELK 1b

wap·pen·schaw·ing \ˈwa-pən-ˌshȯ(-)iŋ, ˈwä-\ *n* [ME (northern dial.) *wapynschawing,* fr. *wapen* weapon (fr. ON *vāpn*) + *schawing,* gerund of *schawen* to show, fr. OE *scēawian* to look, look at — more at WEAPON, SHOW] (15c) **:** an inspection or muster of soldiers formerly held at various times in each district of Scotland

[1]**war** \ˈwȯr\ *n, often attrib* [ME *werre,* fr. AF *werre, guerre,* of Gmc origin; akin to OHG *werra* strife; akin to OHG *werran* to confuse] (12c) **1 a** (1) **:** a state of usu. open and declared armed hostile conflict between states or nations (2) **:** a period of such armed conflict (3) **:** STATE OF WAR **b :** the art or science of warfare **c** (1) *obs* **:** weapons and equipment for war (2) *archaic* **:** soldiers armed and equipped for war **2 a :** a state of hostility, conflict, or antagonism **b :** a struggle or competition between opposing forces or for a particular end ⟨a class ~⟩ ⟨a ~ against disease⟩ **c :** VARIANCE, ODDS 3 — **war·less** \-ləs\ *adj*

[2]**war** *vi* **warred; war·ring** (13c) **1 :** to be in active or vigorous conflict **2 :** to engage in warfare

[3]**war** \ˈwär\ *adv or adj* [ME *werre,* fr. ON *verri,* adj., *verr,* adv.; akin to OE *wiersa* worse — more at WORSE] (13c) *chiefly Scot* **:** WORSE

[4]**war** \ˈwär\ *vt* **warred; war·ring** (15c) *Scot* **:** WORST, OVERCOME

war baby *n* (1901) **:** a person born or conceived during a war

[1]**war·ble** \ˈwȯr-bəl\ *n* [ME *werble* tune, fr. OF (Picard dial.), fr. *werbler* to sing expressively, trill, of Gmc origin; akin to MD *wervelen* to turn, OHG *wirbil* whirlwind — more at WHIRL] (14c) **1 :** a melodious succession of low pleasing sounds **2 :** a musical trill **3 :** the action of warbling

[2]**warble** *vb* **war·bled; war·bling** \-b(ə-)liŋ\ *vi* (14c) **1 :** to sing in a trilling manner or with many turns and variations **2 :** to become sounded with trills, quavers, and rapid modulations in pitch **3 :** SING ~ *vt* **:** to render with turns, runs, or rapid modulations **:** TRILL

[3]**warble** *n* [perh. of Scand origin; akin to obs. Sw *varbulde* boil, fr. *var* pus + *bulde* swelling] (ca. 1585) **1 :** a swelling under the skin esp. of the back of cattle, horses, and wild mammals caused by infestation with maggots of a botfly or warble fly **2 :** the maggot of a warble fly — **war·bled** \-bəld\ *adj*

warble fly *n* (1877) **:** any of various dipteran flies (family Oestridae) whose larvae live under the skin of various mammals and cause warbles

war·bler \ˈwȯr-blər\ *n* (ca. 1611) **1 :** one that warbles **:** SINGER, SONGSTER **2 a :** any of numerous small chiefly Old World oscine birds (family Sylviidae) many of which are noted songsters and are closely related to the thrushes **b :** any of numerous small brightly colored American oscine birds (family Parulidae) with a usu. weak and unmusical song — called also *wood warbler*

warbler 2a

war·bon·net \ˈwȯr-ˌbä-nət\ *n* (1810) **:** an American Indian ceremonial headdress often with a feathered extension down the back

war bride *n* (1892) **1 :** a woman who marries a serviceman ordered into active service in time of war **2 :** a woman who marries a serviceman esp. of a foreign nation met during a time of war

war chest *n* (1871) **:** a fund accumulated to finance a war; *broadly* **:** a fund earmarked for a specific purpose, action, or campaign

war club *n* (1763) **:** a club-shaped implement used as a weapon esp. by American Indians

war crime *n* (1906) **:** a crime (as genocide or maltreatment of prisoners) committed during or in connection with war — usu. used in pl. — **war criminal** *n*

war cry *n* (1748) **1 :** a cry used by a body of fighters in war **2 :** a slogan used esp. to rally people to a cause

[1]**ward** \ˈwȯrd\ *n* [ME, fr. OE *weard* & AF *warde, garde,* of Gmc origin; akin to OHG *warta* act of watching, OE *warian* to beware of, guard, *wær* careful — more at GUARD, WARY] (bef. 12c) **1 a :** the action or process of guarding **b :** a body of guards **2 :** the state of being under guard; *esp* **:** CUSTODY **3 a :** the inner court of a castle or fortress **b :** a division (as a cell or block) of a prison **c :** a division in a hospital; *esp* **:** a large room in a hospital where a number of patients often requiring similar treatment are accommodated **4 a :** a division of a city for representative, electoral, or administrative purposes **b :** a division of some English and Scottish counties corresponding to a hundred **c :** the Mormon local congregation having auxiliary organizations (as Sunday schools and relief societies) and one or more quorums of each office of the Aaronic priesthood **5 :** a projecting ridge of metal in a lock casing or keyhole permitting only the insertion of a key with a corresponding notch; *also* **:** a corresponding notch in a bit of a key **6 :** a person or thing under guard, protection, or surveillance: as **a :** a minor subject to wardship **b :** a person who by reason of incapacity (as minority or mental illness) is under the protection of a court either directly or through a guardian appointed by the court — called also *ward of court* **c :** a person or body of persons under the protection or tutelage of a government **7 :** a means of defense **:** PROTECTION

[2]**ward** *vt* [ME, fr. OE *weardian* & AF *warder, garder,* of Gmc origin; akin to OHG *wartēn* to watch, ON *vartha* to guard, OE *weard* ward] (bef. 12c) **1 :** to keep watch over **:** GUARD **2 :** to turn aside (something threatening) **:** DEFLECT — usu. used with *off* ⟨~ off a blow⟩ ⟨trying to ~ off a cold⟩

[1]**-ward** *also* **-wards** *adj suffix* [*-ward* fr. ME, fr. OE *-weard;* akin to OHG *-wart, -wert* -ward, L *vertere* to turn; *-wards* fr. *-wards,* adv. suffix — more at WORTH] **1 :** that moves, tends, faces, or is directed toward ⟨river*ward*⟩ **2 :** that occurs or is situated in the direction of ⟨left*ward*⟩

[2]**-ward** *or* **-wards** *adv suffix* [*-ward* fr. ME, fr. OE *-weard,* fr. *-weard,* adj. suffix; *-wards* fr. ME, fr. OE *-weardes,* gen. sing. neut. of *-weard,* adj. suffix] **1 :** in a (specified) spatial or temporal direction ⟨up*ward*⟩ ⟨after*ward*⟩ **2 :** toward a (specified) point, position, or area ⟨earth*ward*⟩

war dance *n* (1711) **:** a dance performed (as by American Indians) in preparation for battle or in celebration of victory

ward·ed \ˈwȯr-dəd\ *adj* (14c) **:** provided with a ward ⟨a ~ lock⟩

war·den \ˈwȯr-dᵊn\ *n* [ME *wardein,* fr. AF *wardein, gardein,* fr. *warder* to guard] (13c) **1 :** one having care or charge of something **:** GUARDIAN, KEEPER **2 a :** REGENT 2 **b :** the governor of a town, district, or fortress **c :** a member of the governing body of a guild **3 a :** an official charged with special supervisory duties or with the enforcement of specified laws or regulations ⟨game ~⟩ ⟨air raid ~⟩ **b :** an official in charge of the operation of a prison **c :** any of various British officials having designated administrative functions ⟨~ of the mint⟩ **4 a :** one of two ranking lay officers of an Episcopal parish **b :** any of various British college officials whose duties range from the administration of academic matters to the supervision of student discipline

war·den·ship \-ˌship\ *n* (14c) **:** the office, jurisdiction, or powers of a warden

[1]**ward·er** \ˈwȯr-dər\ *n* [ME, fr. AF *wardere,* fr. *warde*] (15c) **1 :** WATCHMAN, PORTER **2** *Brit* **a :** WARDEN **b :** a prison guard

[2]**war·der** *n* [ME, staff, perh. fr. *warden* to ward] (ca. 1548) **:** a truncheon used by a king or commander in chief to signal orders

ward heeler *n* (1888) **:** a worker for a political boss in a ward or other local area

ward·ress \ˈwȯr-drəs\ *n* (1878) **:** a woman supervising female prisoners (as in a prison)

ward·robe \ˈwȯr-ˌdrōb\ *n* [ME *warderobe,* fr. AF **warderobe, garderobe,* fr. *warder, garder* to guard + *robe* robe] (14c) **1 a :** a room or closet where clothes are kept **b :** CLOTHESPRESS **c :** a large trunk in which clothes may be hung upright **2 a :** a collection of wearing apparel (as of one person or for one activity) ⟨a summer ~⟩ **b :** a collection of stage costumes and accessories **3 :** the department of a royal or noble household entrusted with the care of wearing apparel, jewels, and personal articles

ward·room \ˈwȯr-ˌdrüm, -ˌdru̇m\ *n* (1748) **:** the space in a warship allotted for living quarters to the commissioned officers excepting the captain; *specif* **:** the mess assigned to these officers

ward·ship \ˈwȯrd-ˌship\ *n* (15c) **1 a :** care and protection of a ward **b :** the right to the custody of an infant heir of a feudal tenant and of the heir's property **2 :** the state of being under a guardian

[1]**ware** \ˈwer\ *adj* [ME *war, ware* careful, aware, fr. OE *wær* — more at WARY] (bef. 12c) **1 :** AWARE, CONSCIOUS ⟨was ~ of black looks cast at me —Mary Webb⟩ **2** *archaic* **:** WARY, VIGILANT

[2]**ware** *vt* **wared; war·ing** [ME, fr. OE *warian;* akin to OHG bi*warōn* to protect, OE *wær* aware] (bef. 12c) **:** to beware of **:** AVOID — used chiefly as a command to hunting animals

[3]**ware** *n* [ME, fr. OE *waru;* akin to MHG *ware* ware and prob. to Skt *vasna* price — more at VENAL] (bef. 12c) **1 a :** manufactured articles, products of art or craft, or farm produce **:** GOODS — often used in combination ⟨tin*ware*⟩ **b :** an article of merchandise **2 :** articles (as pottery or dishes) of fired clay ⟨earthen*ware*⟩ **3 :** an intangible item (as a service or ability) that is a marketable commodity

[4]**ware** *vt* **wared; war·ing** [ME, prob. of Scand origin; akin to ON *verja* (pp. *varithr, varthr* to clothe, invest, spend — more at WEAR] (14c) *Scot* **:** SPEND, EXPEND

[1]**ware·house** \ˈwer-ˌhau̇s\ *n* (14c) **:** a structure or room for the storage of merchandise or commodities

[2]**ware·house** \-ˌhau̇z, -ˌhau̇s\ *vt* (1766) **1 :** to deposit, store, or stock in or as if in a warehouse **2 :** to confine or house (a person) in conditions suggestive of a warehouse

ware·house·man \-ˌhau̇s-mən\ *n* (1635) **:** a person who manages or works in a warehouse

ware·hous·er \-ˌhau̇-zər, -sər\ *n* (ca. 1927) **:** WAREHOUSEMAN

ware·room \ˈwer-ˌrüm, -ˌru̇m\ *n* (1811) **:** a room in which goods are exhibited for sale

war·fare \ˈwȯr-ˌfer\ *n* [ME, fr. *werre, warre* war + *fare* journey, passage — more at FARE] (15c) **1 :** military operations between enemies **:** HOSTILITIES, WAR; *also* **:** an activity undertaken by a political unit (as a nation) to weaken or destroy another ⟨economic ~⟩ **2 :** struggle between competing entities **:** CONFLICT

war·fa·rin \ˈwȯr-fə-rən\ *n* [*W*isconsin *A*lumni *R*esearch *F*oundation (its patentee) + cou*marin*] (1950) **:** a crystalline anticoagulant coumarin derivative $C_{19}H_{16}O_4$ used chiefly in the form of its sodium salt as a rodent poison and in medicine

war footing *n* (1800) **:** the condition of being prepared to undertake or maintain war

war–game *vt* (1942) **:** to plan or conduct in the manner of a war game ⟨*war-gamed* an invasion —*Newsweek*⟩ ~ *vi* **:** to conduct a war game

\ə\ **abut** \ᵊ\ kitten, F table \ər\ **further** \a\ **ash** \ā\ **ace** \ä\ **mop, mar** \au̇\ **out** \ch\ **chin** \e\ **bet** \ē\ **easy** \g\ **go** \i\ **hit** \ī\ **ice** \j\ **job** \ŋ\ **sing** \ō\ **go** \ȯ\ **law** \ȯi\ **boy** \th\ **thin** \t͟h\ **the** \ü\ **loot** \u̇\ **foot** \y\ **yet** \zh\ **vision, beige** \k͟, ⁿ, œ, ue, ʸ\ *see* Guide to Pronunciation

war game *n* (1828) **1** : a simulated battle or campaign to test military concepts and usu. conducted in conferences by officers acting as the opposing staffs **2** : a two-sided umpired training maneuver with actual elements of the armed forces participating

war hawk *n* (1798) : a person who clamors for war; *esp* : a jingoistic American favoring war with Britain around 1812

war·head \ˈwȯr-ˌhed\ *n* (1898) : the section of a missile containing the explosive, chemical, or incendiary charge

war·horse \-ˌhȯrs\ *n* (15c) **1** : a horse used in war : CHARGER **2** : a person with long experience in a field; *esp* : a veteran soldier or public person (as a politician) **3** : something (as a work of art or musical composition) that has become overly familiar or hackneyed due to much repetition in the standard repertoire

war·i·son \ˈwa-rə-sən\ *n* [prob. a misunderstanding by Sir Walter Scott of ME *waryson* reward, security, fr. AF **warison, garisun* healing, protection — more at GARRISON] (1805) : a bugle call to attack

Warks *abbr* Warwickshire

war·like \ˈwȯr-ˌlīk\ *adj* (15c) **1** *obs* : ready for war : equipped to fight **2** : fit for, disposed to, or fond of war : BELLICOSE ⟨a ~ people⟩ **3** : of, relating to, or useful in war ⟨~ preparations⟩ **4** : befitting or characteristic of war or a soldier ⟨~ cries⟩

war·lock \ˈwȯr-ˌläk\ *n* [ME *warloghe,* fr. OE *wǣrloga* one that breaks faith, the Devil, fr. *wǣr* faith, troth + *-loga* (fr. *lēogan* to lie); akin to OE *wǣr* true — more at VERY, LIE] (14c) **1** : a man practicing the black arts : SORCERER — compare WITCH **2** : CONJURER

war·lord \ˈwȯr-ˌlȯrd\ *n* (1856) **1** : a supreme military leader **2** : a military commander exercising civil power by force usu. in a limited area — **war·lord·ism** \-ˌlȯr-ˌdi-zəm\ *n*

[1]**warm** \ˈwȯrm\ *adj* [ME, fr. OE *wearm;* akin to OHG *warm* warm and prob. to Lith *virti* to cook, boil] (bef. 12c) **1 a** : having or giving out heat to a moderate or adequate degree ⟨~ weather⟩ ⟨a ~ fire⟩ **b** : serving to maintain or preserve heat esp. to a satisfactory degree ⟨a ~ sweater⟩ **c** : feeling or causing sensations of heat brought about by strenuous exertion **2** : comfortably established : SECURE **3 a** : marked by strong feeling : ARDENT **b** : marked by excitement, disagreement, or anger ⟨the argument grew ~⟩ **4** : marked by or readily showing affection, gratitude, cordiality, or sympathy ⟨a ~ welcome⟩ ⟨~ regards⟩ **5** : emphasizing or exploiting sexual imagery or incidents **6** : accompanied or marked by extreme danger or duress **7** : newly made : FRESH ⟨a ~ scent⟩ **8** : having the color or tone of something that imparts heat; *specif* : of a hue in the range yellow through orange to red **9** : near to a goal, object, or solution sought ⟨not there yet but getting ~⟩ — **warm·ish** \ˈwȯr-mish\ *adj* — **warm·ness** \ˈwȯrm-nəs\ *n*

[2]**warm** *vt* (bef. 12c) **1** : to make warm **2 a** : to infuse with a feeling of love, friendship, well-being, or pleasure **b** : to fill with anger, zeal, or passion **3** : to reheat (cooked food) for eating — often used with *over* **4** : to make ready for operation or performance by preliminary exercise or operation — often used with *up* ~ *vi* **1** : to become warm **2 a** : to become ardent, interested, or receptive — usu. used with *to* or *toward* ⟨~*ed* to the idea⟩ **b** : to become filled with affection or love — used with *to* or *toward* **3** : to experience feelings of pleasure : BASK **4** : to become ready for operation or performance by preliminary activity — often used with *up*

[3]**warm** *adv* (bef. 12c) : WARMLY — usu. used in combination ⟨*warm*-clad⟩

warm–blood·ed \ˈwȯrm-ˈblə-dəd\ *adj* (1793) **1** : having warm blood; *specif* : having a relatively high and constant internally regulated body temperature relatively independent of the surroundings **2** : fervent or ardent in spirit — **warm–blood·ed·ness** *n*

warmed–over \ˈwȯrmd-ˈō-vər\ *adj* (1887) **1** : not fresh or new : STALE ⟨~ ideas⟩ **2** : heated again ⟨~ beans⟩

warm·er \ˈwȯr-mər\ *n* (ca. 1595) : one that warms; *esp* : a device for keeping something warm ⟨a hand ~⟩

warm front *n* (1921) : an advancing edge of a warm air mass

warm fuzzies *n pl* (1981) : feelings of happiness, contentment, or sentimentality ⟨got *warm fuzzies* from the good news⟩

warm·heart·ed \ˈwȯrm-ˈhär-təd\ *adj* (ca. 1520) : marked by ready affection, cordiality, generosity, or sympathy — **warm·heart·ed·ness** *n*

warm·ing pan \ˈwȯr-miŋ-\ *n* (15c) : a long-handled covered pan filled with live coals that is used to warm a bed

warm·ly \ˈwȯrm-lē\ *adv* (1529) **1** : in a manner characterized or accompanied by warmth of emotion ⟨greeted us ~⟩ **2** : in a manner that causes or maintains warmth ⟨dressed ~⟩

war·mon·ger \ˈwȯr-ˌməŋ-gər, -ˌmäŋ-\ *n* (1817) : one who urges or attempts to stir up war — **war·mon·ger·ing** \-g(ə-)riŋ\ *n*

war·mouth \ˈwȯr-ˌmau̇th\ *n* [origin unknown] (ca. 1883) : a large-mouthed freshwater sunfish (*Lepomis gulosus*) chiefly of the eastern U.S. — called also *warmouth bass*

warm spot *n* (1886) : a lasting affection for a particular person or thing ⟨has a *warm spot* for her old classmates⟩

warmth \ˈwȯrm(p)th\ *n* (13c) **1** : the quality or state of being warm in temperature **2** : the quality or state of being warm in feeling ⟨a child needing human ~ and family life⟩ **3** : a glowing effect produced by the use of warm colors

warm–up \ˈwȯrm-ˌəp\ *n* (1915) **1** : the act or an instance of warming up; *also* : a preparatory activity or procedure **2** : a suit for exercise or casual wear consisting of a jacket or sweatshirt and pants — often used in pl.; called also *warm-up suit*

warm up *vi* (1846) : to engage in exercise or practice esp. before entering a game or contest; *broadly* : to get ready

warn \ˈwȯrn\ *vb* [ME, fr. OE *warnian;* akin to OHG *warnōn* to take heed, OE *wær* careful, aware — more at WARY] *vt* (bef. 12c) **1 a** : to give notice to beforehand esp. of danger or evil **b** : to give admonishing advice to : COUNSEL **c** : to call to one's attention : INFORM **2** : to order to go or stay away — often used with *off* ~ *vi* : to give a warning — **warn·er** *n*

[1]**warn·ing** \ˈwȯr-niŋ\ *n* (bef. 12c) **1** : the act of warning : the state of being warned ⟨he had ~ of his illness⟩ **2** : something that warns or serves to warn; *esp* : a notice or bulletin that alerts the public to an imminent hazard (as a tornado, thunderstorm, or flood)

[2]**warning** *adj* (1511) : serving as an alarm, signal, summons, or admonition ⟨a ~ bell⟩ ⟨a ~ shot⟩ — **warn·ing·ly** \ˈwȯr-niŋ-lē\ *adv*

warning coloration *n* (1928) : conspicuous coloration possessed by an animal (as an insect) otherwise effectively but not obviously defended that serves to warn off potential enemies

warning track *n* (1966) : a usu. dirt or cinder strip around the outside edge of a baseball outfield to warn a fielder when running to make a catch that the fence is near — called also *warning path*

war of nerves (1939) : a conflict characterized by psychological tactics (as bluff, threats, and intimidation) designed primarily to create confusion, indecision, or breakdown of morale

[1]**warp** \ˈwȯrp\ *n* [ME, fr. OE *wearp;* akin to OHG *warf* warp, OE *weorpan* to throw, ON *verpa*] (bef. 12c) **1 a** : a series of yarns extended lengthwise in a loom and crossed by the weft **b** : FOUNDATION, BASE ⟨the ~ of the economic structure is agriculture —*Amer. Guide Series: N.C.*⟩ **2** : a rope for warping or mooring a ship or boat **3** [[2]*warp*] **a** : a twist or curve that has developed in something orig. flat or straight ⟨a ~ in a door panel⟩ **b** : a mental aberration — **warp·age** \ˈwȯr-pij\ *n*

[2]**warp** *vt* (14c) **1** : to arrange (yarns) so as to form a warp **2 a** : to turn or twist out of or as if out of shape; *esp* : to twist or bend out of a plane **b** : to cause to judge, choose, or act wrongly or abnormally : PERVERT **c** : DISTORT ⟨intellect and learning . . . ~*ed* by prejudices —Irving Wallace⟩ ⟨~*s* space and time⟩ **d** : to deflect from a course **3** : to move (as a ship) by hauling on a line attached to a fixed object ~ *vi* **1** : to become warped **2** : to move a ship by warping ***syn*** see DEFORM — **warp·er** *n*

war paint *n* (1826) **1** : paint put on parts of the body (as the face) by American Indians as a sign of going to war **2** : MAKEUP 3a

warp and woof *n* (1842) : FOUNDATION, BASE ⟨the vigorous Anglo-Saxon base had become the *warp and woof* of English speech —H. R. Warfel⟩

war party *n* (1755) **1** : a group of American Indians on the warpath **2** : a usu. jingoistic political party advocating or upholding a war

war·path \ˈwȯr-ˌpath, -ˌpäth\ *n* (1755) **1** : the route taken by a party of American Indians going on a warlike expedition or to a war **2** : a hostile or combative course of action or frame of mind

warp beam *n* (ca. 1833) : a roll on which warp is wound for a loom

warp knit *n* (1853) : a knit fabric produced by machine with the yarns running in a lengthwise direction — compare WEFT KNIT — **warp–knit·ted** \-ˈni-təd\ *adj* — **warp knitting** *n*

war·plane \ˈwȯr-ˌplān\ *n* (ca. 1911) : a military airplane; *specif* : one armed for combat

war power *n* (1766) : the power to make war; *specif* : an extraordinary power exercised usu. by the executive branch of a government in the prosecution of a war

warp speed *n* [fr. the use in science fiction of space-time warps to allow faster-than-light travel] (1979) : the highest possible speed — **warp–speed** *adj*

[1]**war·rant** \ˈwȯr-ənt, ˈwär-\ *n* [ME *waraunt* protector, warrant, fr. AF *warant, garant,* of Gmc origin; akin to OHG *werēnto* guarantor, *werēn* to warrant; akin to OHG *wāra* trust, care — more at VERY] (14c) **1 a** (1) : SANCTION, AUTHORIZATION; *also* : evidence for or token of authorization (2) : GUARANTEE, SECURITY **b** (1) : GROUND, JUSTIFICATION (2) : CONFIRMATION, PROOF **2 a** : a commission or document giving authority to do something; *esp* : a writing that authorizes a person to pay or deliver to another and the other to receive money or other consideration **b** : a precept or writ issued by a competent magistrate authorizing an officer to make an arrest, a seizure, or a search or to do other acts incident to the administration of justice **c** : an official certificate of appointment issued to an officer of lower rank than a commissioned officer **d** (1) : a short-term obligation of a governmental body (as a municipality) issued in anticipation of revenue (2) : an instrument issued by a corporation giving to the holder the right to purchase the stock of the corporation at a stated price either prior to a stipulated date or at any future time — **war·rant·less** \-ləs\ *adj*

[2]**warrant** *vt* [ME, *waranten* to act as protector, guarantee, fr. AF *warentir, garantir,* fr. *warant*] (14c) **1 a** : to declare or maintain with certainty : be sure that ⟨I'll ~ he'll be here by noon⟩ **b** : to assure (a person) of the truth of what is said **2 a** : to guarantee to a person good title to and undisturbed possession of (as an estate) **b** : to provide a guarantee of the security of (as title to property sold) usu. by an express covenant in the deed of conveyance **c** : to guarantee to be as represented **d** : to guarantee (as goods sold) esp. in respect of the quality or quantity specified **3** : to guarantee security or immunity to : SECURE ⟨I'll ~ him from drowning —Shak.⟩ **4** : to give warrant or sanction to : AUTHORIZE ⟨the law ~*s* this procedure⟩ **5 a** : to give proof of the authenticity or truth of **b** : to give assurance of the nature of or for the undertaking of : GUARANTEE **6** : to serve as or give adequate ground or reason for ⟨promising enough to ~ further consideration⟩

war·rant·able \ˈwȯr-ən-tə-bəl, ˈwär-\ *adj* (1597) : capable of being warranted : JUSTIFIABLE ⟨take ~ action⟩ — **war·rant·able·ness** *n* — **war·rant·ably** \-blē\ *adv*

war·ran·tee \ˌwȯr-ən-ˈtē, ˌwär-\ *n* (1706) : the person to whom a warranty is made

warrant officer *n* (1693) **1** : an officer in the armed forces holding rank by virtue of a warrant and ranking above a noncommissioned officer and below a commissioned officer **2** : a commissioned officer ranking below an ensign in the navy or coast guard and below a second lieutenant in the marine corps

war·ran·tor \ˌwȯr-ən-ˈtȯr, ˌwär-; ˈwȯr-ən-tər, ˈwär-\ *also* **war·rant·er** \ˈwȯr-ən-tər, ˈwär-\ *n* (15c) : one that warrants or gives a warranty

war·ran·ty \ˈwȯr-ən-tē, ˈwär-\ *n, pl* **-ties** [ME *warantie,* fr. AF *warantie, garantie,* fr. *warentir* to warrant] (14c) **1 a** : a real covenant binding the grantor of an estate and the grantor's heirs to warrant and defend the title **b** : a collateral undertaking that a fact regarding the subject of a contract is or will be as it is expressly or by implication declared or promised to be **2** : something that authorizes, sanctions, supports, or justifies : WARRANT **3** : a usu. written guarantee of the integrity of a product and of the maker's responsibility for the repair or replacement of defective parts

warranty deed *n* (1751) : a deed warranting that the grantor has a good title free and clear of all liens and encumbrances and will defend the grantee against all claims

war·ren \ˈwȯr-ən, ˈwär-\ *n* [ME *wareine,* fr. AF *warenne, garenne*] (14c) **1** *chiefly Brit* **a** : a place legally authorized for keeping small game (as hare or pheasant) **b** : the privilege of hunting game in such a warren

2 a (1) **:** an area (as of uncultivated ground) where rabbits breed (2) **:** a structure where rabbits are kept or bred **b :** the rabbits of a warren **3 a :** a crowded tenement or district **b :** a maze of passageways or small rooms

war·ren·er \-ə-nər\ *n* (13c) **1 :** GAMEKEEPER **2 :** a person who maintains a rabbit warren

war·rior \ˈwȯr-yər, ˈwȯr-ē-ər, ˈwär-ē- *also* ˈwär-yər\ *n, often attrib* [ME *werreour,* fr. AF **werrier, guerreier,* fr. *warreier, guerreier* to wage war, fr. *werre* war — more at WAR] (14c) **:** a man engaged or experienced in warfare; *broadly* **:** a person engaged in some struggle or conflict ⟨poverty ~*s*⟩

war room *n* (1901) **1 :** a room at a military headquarters where maps showing the current status of troops in battle are maintained **2 :** a room (as at a business headquarters) used for conferences and planning that is often specially equipped (as with computers, or charts)

war·saw grouper \ˈwȯr-(ˌ)sȯ-\ *n* [*warsaw* modif. of AmerSp *guasa*] (1949) **:** any of several large groupers; *esp* **:** one (*Epinephelus nigritus*) of the western Atlantic and Gulf of Mexico — called also *warsaw*

war·ship \ˈwȯr-ˌship\ *n* (1533) **:** a naval vessel

war·sle *or* **wars·tle** \ˈwä(r)-səl\ *vb* [ME *werstelen, warstelen,* alter. of *wrestlen, wrastlen*] (14c) *Scot* **:** WRESTLE, STRUGGLE — **warsle** *n, Scot*

war story *n* (1839) **:** a story of a memorable personal experience typically involving an element of danger, hardship, or adventure ⟨politicians swapping *war stories* from past campaigns⟩

wart \ˈwȯrt\ *n* [ME, fr. OE *wearte;* akin to OHG *warza* wart, OCS *vrědŭ* injury] (bef. 12c) **1 a :** a horny projection on the skin usu. of the extremities produced by proliferation of the skin papillae and caused by any of numerous human papillomaviruses — called also *verruca vulgaris* **b :** any of numerous similar skin lesions not caused by viruses **2 :** an excrescence or protuberance resembling a true wart; *esp* **:** a glandular excrescence or hardened protuberance on a plant **3 a :** one that suggests a wart esp. in smallness, unpleasantness, or unattractiveness **b :** DEFECT, IMPERFECTION — often used in the phrase *warts and all* — **wart·ed** \ˈwȯr-təd\ *adj* — **wart·less** \ˈwȯrt-ləs\ *adj* — **warty** \ˈwȯr-tē\ *adj*

wart·hog \ˈwȯrt-ˌhȯg, -ˌhäg\ *n* (1840) **:** a wild African hog (*Phacochoerus aethiopicus*) that has large protruding tusks and in the male two pairs of rough warty excrescences on the face and that is sometimes placed in two separate species (*P. aethiopicus* and *P. africanus*)

warthog

war·time \ˈwȯr-ˌtīm\ *n, often attrib* (14c) **:** a period during which a war is in progress ⟨rationing during ~⟩

warts–and–all *adj* (1957) **:** showing defects or imperfections frankly **:** not idealized ⟨a ~ biography⟩

war whoop *n* (1739) **:** a war cry esp. of American Indians

wary \ˈwer-ē\ *adj* **war·i·er; -est** [[1]*ware,* fr. ME *war, ware,* fr. OE *wær* careful, aware, wary; akin to OHG gi*war* aware, attentive, L *vereri* to fear, Gk *horan* to see] (15c) **:** marked by keen caution, cunning, and watchfulness esp. in detecting and escaping danger ***syn*** see CAUTIOUS — **war·i·ly** \ˈwer-ə-lē\ *adv* — **war·i·ness** \ˈwer-ē-nəs\ *n*

war zone *n* (1914) **1 :** a zone in which belligerents are waging war; *broadly* **:** an area marked by extreme violence **2 :** a designated area esp. on the high seas within which rights of neutrals are not respected by a belligerent nation in time of war

was [ME, fr. OE, *wæs,* 1st & 3d sing. past indic. of *wesan* to be; akin to ON *vera* to be, *var* was, Skt *vasati* he lives, dwells] *past 1st & 3d sing of* BE

wa·sa·bi \ˈwä-sə-bē, wä-ˈsä-\ *n* [Jp] (1891) **1 :** a condiment that is prepared from the ground thick pungent greenish root of an Asian herb (*Wasabia japonica* syn. *Eutrema wasabi*) of the mustard family and is similar in flavor and use to horseradish; *also* **:** the root **2 :** the herb that yields wasabi

[1]**wash** \ˈwȯsh, ˈwäsh, *chiefly Midland also* ˈwȯrsh *or* ˈwärsh\ *vb* [ME, fr. OE *wascan;* akin to OHG *waskan* to wash and perh. to OE *wæter* water] *vt* (bef. 12c) **1 a :** to cleanse by or as if by the action of liquid (as water) **b :** to remove (as dirt) by rubbing or drenching with liquid **2 :** to cleanse (fur) by licking or by rubbing with a paw moistened with saliva **3 a :** to flush or moisten (a bodily part or injury) with a liquid **b** (1) **:** to wet thoroughly **:** DRENCH (2) **:** to overspread with light **:** SUFFUSE **c :** to pass a liquid (as water) over or through esp. so as to carry off material from the surface or interior **4 :** to flow along or dash or overflow against ⟨waves ~*ing* the shore⟩ **5 :** to move, carry, or deposit by or as if by the force of water in motion ⟨houses ~*ed* away by the flood⟩ **6 a :** to subject (as crushed ore) to the action of water to separate valuable material **b :** to separate (particles) from a substance (as ore) by agitation with or in water **c** (1) **:** to pass through a bath to carry off impurities or soluble components (2) **:** to pass (a gas or gaseous mixture) through or over a liquid to purify it esp. by removing soluble components **7 a :** to cover or daub lightly with or as if with an application of a thin liquid (as whitewash or varnish) **b :** to depict or paint by a broad sweep of thin color with a brush **8 :** to cause to swirl ⟨~*ing* coffee around in his cup⟩ **9 :** LAUNDER 3 ⟨how the mob ~*es* its money through corrupt bankers —Vincent Teresa⟩ ~ *vi* **1 :** to wash oneself or a part of one's body **2 :** to become worn away by the action of water **3 :** to clean something by rubbing or dipping in water **4 a :** to become carried along on water **:** DRIFT ⟨cakes of ice ~*ing* along⟩ **b :** to pour, sweep, or flow in a stream or current ⟨waves of pioneers ~*ing* westward —Green Peyton⟩ **5 :** to serve as a cleansing agent ⟨this soap ~*es* thoroughly⟩ **6 a :** to undergo laundering ⟨this dress doesn't ~ well⟩ **b** (1) **:** to undergo testing successfully **:** WORK 4 ⟨an interesting theory, but it just won't ~⟩ (2) **:** to gain acceptance **:** inspire belief ⟨the story didn't ~ with me⟩ — **wash one's hands of :** to disclaim interest in, responsibility for, or further connection with

[2]**wash** *n* (15c) **1 a :** a piece of ground washed by the sea or river **b :** BOG, MARSH **c** (1) **:** a shallow body of water (2) **:** a shallow creek **d** *West* **:** the dry bed of a stream — called also *dry wash* **2 a :** the act or process or an instance of washing or being washed **b :** articles to be washed, being washed, or having been washed **3 :** the surging action or sound of waves; *also* **:** something resembling this action or sound ⟨the warm ~ of applause that followed her . . . introduction —John Updike⟩ **4 a :** worthless esp. liquid waste **:** REFUSE **b :** an insipid beverage **c :** vapid writing or speech **5 a :** a sweep or splash esp. of color made by or as if by a long stroke of a brush ⟨in the gray ~ of early morning⟩ **b :** a thin coat of paint (as watercolor) **c :** a thin liquid used for coating a surface (as a wall) **6 :** LOTION **7 :** loose or eroded surface material of the earth (as rock debris) transported and deposited by running water **8 a :** BACKWASH 1 **b :** a disturbance in a fluid (as water or the air) produced by the passage of an airfoil or propeller **9 :** a situation in which losses and gains or advantages and disadvantages balance each other

[3]**wash** *adj* (1848) **1 :** involving essentially simultaneous purchase and sale of the same security ⟨spurious market activity resulting from ~ trading⟩ **2 :** WASHABLE ⟨~ fabric⟩

Wash *abbr* Washington

wash·able \ˈwȯ-shə-bəl, ˈwä-\ *adj* (1821) **:** capable of being washed without damage — **wash·abil·i·ty** \ˌwȯ-shə-ˈbi-lə-tē, ˌwä-\ *n*

wash–and–wear *adj* (1956) **:** of, relating to, or constituting a fabric or garment that needs little or no ironing after washing

wash·a·te·ria *also* **wash·e·te·ria** \ˌwä-shə-ˈtir-ē-ə, ˌwȯ-\ *n* [[2]*wash* + *-ateria* or *-eteria* (as in *cafeteria*)] (1937) *chiefly Southern* **:** a self-service laundry

wash·ba·sin \ˈwȯsh-ˌbā-sᵊn, ˈwäsh-\ *n* (1812) **:** WASHBOWL

wash·board \ˈwȯsh-ˌbȯrd, ˈwäsh-\ *n* (1742) **1 :** a broad thin plank along a gunwale or on the sill of a lower deck port to keep out the sea **2 :** BASEBOARD **3 a :** a corrugated rectangular surface that is used for scrubbing clothes or as a percussion instrument **b :** a road or pavement so worn by traffic as to be corrugated transversely **c :** an abdominal area characterized by prominent and well-defined musculature — usu. used attributively ⟨a bodybuilder with ~ abs⟩ ⟨a ~ stomach⟩

wash·bowl \-ˌbōl\ *n* (1647) **:** a large bowl for water that is used to wash one's hands and face

wash·cloth \-ˌklȯth\ *n* (1863) **:** a cloth that is used for washing one's face and body — called also *facecloth, washrag*

wash down *vt* (1600) **1 :** to move or carry downward by action of a liquid; *esp* **:** to facilitate the passage of (food) down the gullet with accompanying swallows of liquid ⟨pizza *washed down* with beer⟩ **2 :** to wash the whole length or extent of ⟨*washed down* and scrubbed the front porch⟩

wash drawing *n* (1887) **:** watercolor painting in or chiefly in washes esp. in black, white, and gray tones only

washed–out \ˈwȯsht-ˈau̇t, ˈwäsht-\ *adj* (1796) **1 :** faded in color **2 :** depleted in vigor or animation **:** EXHAUSTED

washed–up \ˈwȯsht-ˈəp, ˈwäsht-\ *adj* (1928) **:** no longer successful, skillful, popular, or needed ⟨~ athletes⟩ ⟨a ~ actor⟩

wash·er \ˈwȯ-shər, ˈwä-\ *n* (14c) **1 :** a flat thin ring or a perforated plate used in joints or assemblies to ensure tightness, prevent leakage, or relieve friction **2 :** one that washes; *esp* **:** WASHING MACHINE

wash·er·man \-mən\ *n* (1715) **:** LAUNDRYMAN; *also* **:** a man operating any of various industrial washing machines

wash·er·wom·an \-ˌwu̇-mən\ *n* (1632) **:** a woman whose occupation is washing clothes **:** LAUNDRESS

wash·house \ˈwȯsh-ˌhau̇s, ˈwäsh-\ *n* (1577) **:** a building used or equipped for washing; *esp* **:** one for washing clothes

wash·ing \ˈwȯ-shiŋ, ˈwä-\ *n* (13c) **1 :** the act or action of one that cleanses with water **2 :** material obtained by washing **3 :** articles washed or to be washed **:** WASH

washing machine *n* (ca. 1754) **:** a machine for washing; *esp* **:** one for washing clothes and household linen

washing soda *n* (1847) **:** a transparent crystalline hydrated sodium carbonate

Wash·ing·ton pie \ˈwȯ-shiŋ-tən-, ˈwä-, *chiefly Midland also* ˈwȯr-shiŋ- *or* ˈwär-shiŋ-\ *n* [George *Washington*] (1868) **:** cake layers put together with a jam or jelly filling

Washington's Birthday *n* [George *Washington*] (1829) **1 :** February 22 formerly observed as a legal holiday in most of the states of the U.S. **2 :** the third Monday in February observed as a legal holiday in most of the states of the U.S. — called also *Presidents' Day*

wash·out \ˈwȯsh-ˌau̇t, ˈwäsh-\ *n* (1873) **1 a :** the washing out or away of something and esp. of earth in a roadbed by a freshet **b :** a place where earth is washed away **2 :** one that fails to measure up **:** FAILURE: as **a :** one who fails in a course of training or study **b :** an unsuccessful enterprise or undertaking

wash out *vt* (1540) **1 :** to wash free of an extraneous substance (as dirt) **2 a :** to cause to fade by or as if by laundering **b :** to deplete the strength or vitality of **c :** to eliminate as useless or unsatisfactory **:** REJECT **3 a :** to destroy or make useless by the force or action of water ⟨the storm *washed out* the bridge⟩ **b :** RAIN OUT ⟨the game was *washed out*⟩ ~ *vi* **1 :** to become depleted of color or vitality **:** FADE **2 :** to fail to meet requirements or measure up to a standard

wash·rag \ˈwȯsh-ˌrag, ˈwäsh-\ *n* (1856) **:** WASHCLOTH

wash·room \-ˌrüm, -ˌru̇m\ *n* (1806) **:** a room that is equipped with washing and toilet facilities **:** LAVATORY

wash·stand \-ˌstand\ *n* (1789) **1 :** a stand holding articles needed for washing one's face and hands **2 :** a washbowl permanently set in place and attached to water and drainpipes

wash·tub \-ˌtəb\ *n* (1602) **:** a tub for washing or soaking clothes

wash·up \-ˌəp\ *n* (1884) **:** the act or process of washing clean

wash up *vi* (1664) **1 :** to be deposited by or as if by a swell of waves ⟨seaweed *washed up* on the shore⟩ **2 :** to wash one's face and hands **3** *Brit* **:** to wash the dishes after a meal ~ *vt* **1 :** to get rid of by washing ⟨*wash up* the spilled milk⟩ **2 :** EXHAUST, FINISH

wash·wom·an \ˈwȯsh-ˌwu̇-mən, ˈwäsh-\ *n* (1590) **:** WASHERWOMAN

washy \ˈwȯ-shē, ˈwä-\ *adj* **wash·i·er; -est** (1615) **1 a :** WEAK, WATERY ⟨~ tea⟩ **b :** deficient in color **c :** lacking in vigor, individuality, or definiteness **2 :** lacking in condition and in firmness of flesh

wasn't \ˈwə-zᵊnt, ˈwä-, *dial also* ˈwə-tᵊn(t)\ (ca. 1653) **:** was not

wasp \ˈwäsp, ˈwȯsp\ *n* [ME *waspe,* fr. OE *wæps, wæsp;* akin to OHG *wafsa* wasp, L *vespa* wasp] (bef. 12c) **1 :** any of numerous social or solitary winged hymenopterous insects (esp. families Sphecidae and Vespidae) that usu. have a slender smooth body with the abdomen attached by a narrow stalk, well-developed wings, biting mouthparts, and in the females and workers an often formidable sting, and that are largely carnivorous and often provision their nests with insects or spiders killed or paralyzed by stinging for their larvae to feed on — compare BEE **2 :** any of various hymenopterous insects (as a chalcid or ichneumon wasp) other than wasps with larvae that are parasitic on other arthropods — **wasp·like** \-ˌlīk\ *adj*

WASP *or* **Wasp** \ˈwäsp, ˈwȯsp\ *n, often attrib* [*w*hite *A*nglo-*S*axon *P*rotestant] (1957) *sometimes disparaging* **:** an American of Northern European and esp. British ancestry and of Protestant background; *esp* **:** a member of the dominant and the most privileged class of people in the U.S. — **Wasp·dom** \-dəm\ *n, sometimes disparaging* — **Wasp·ish** \ˈwäs-pish, ˈwȯs-\ *adj, sometimes disparaging* — **Wasp·ish·ness** *n, sometimes disparaging* — **Waspy** \-pē\ *adj, sometimes disparaging*

wasp·ish \ˈwäs-pish, ˈwȯs-\ *adj* (1566) **1 :** resembling a wasp in behavior; *esp* **:** SNAPPISH, PETULANT ⟨a ~ temper⟩ **2 :** resembling a wasp in form; *esp* **:** slightly built — **wasp·ish·ly** *adv* — **wasp·ish·ness** *n*

wasp waist *n* (1833) **:** a very slender waist — **wasp–waist·ed** \ˈwäsp-ˈwā-stəd, ˈwȯsp-\ *adj*

1**was·sail** \ˈwä-səl *also* wä-ˈsāl\ *n* [ME *wæs hæil, washayl,* fr. ON *ves heill* be well, fr. *ves* (imper. sing. of *vera* to be) + *heill* healthy — more at WAS, WHOLE] (12c) **1 :** an early English toast to someone's health **2 :** a hot drink that is made with wine, beer, or cider, spices, sugar, and usu. baked apples and is traditionally served in a large bowl esp. at Christmastime **3 :** riotous drinking **:** REVELRY

2**wassail** *vi* (14c) **1 :** to indulge in wassail **:** CAROUSE **2** *dial Eng* **:** to sing carols from house to house at Christmas ~ *vt* **:** to drink to the health or thriving of

was·sail bowl \ˈwä-səl-\ *n* (1606) **1 :** a bowl that is used for the serving of wassail **2 :** WASSAIL 2

was·sail·er \ˈwä-sə-lər *also* wä-ˈsā-lər\ *n* (1634) **1 :** one that carouses **:** REVELER **2** *archaic* **:** one who goes about singing carols

Was·ser·mann reaction \ˈwä-sər-mən-, ˈvä-\ *n* [August von *Wassermann*] (1911) **:** the complement-fixing reaction that occurs in a positive complement-fixation test for syphilis

Wassermann test *n* (1909) **:** a test for the detection of syphilis using the Wassermann reaction — called also *Wassermann*

wast \ˈwäst, ˈwəst\ *archaic past 2d sing of* BE

wast·age \ˈwā-stij\ *n* (1735) **:** loss, decrease, or destruction of something (as by use, decay, erosion, or leakage); *esp* **:** wasteful or avoidable loss of something valuable

1**waste** \ˈwāst\ *n* [ME *waste, wast;* in sense 1, fr. AF *wast,* fr. *wast, gast, guast,* adj., desolate, waste, fr. L *vastus;* in other senses, fr. ME *wasten* to waste — more at VAST] (13c) **1 a :** a sparsely settled or barren region **:** DESERT **b :** uncultivated land **c :** a broad and empty expanse (as of water) **2 :** the act or an instance of wasting **:** the state of being wasted **3 a :** loss through breaking down of bodily tissue **b :** gradual loss or decrease by use, wear, or decay **4 a :** damaged, defective, or superfluous material produced by a manufacturing process: as (1) **:** material rejected during a textile manufacturing process and used usu. for wiping away dirt and oil ⟨cotton ~⟩ (2) **:** SCRAP (3) **:** an unwanted by-product of a manufacturing process, chemical laboratory, or nuclear reactor ⟨toxic ~⟩ ⟨hazardous ~⟩ ⟨nuclear ~⟩ **b :** refuse from places of human or animal habitation: as (1) **:** GARBAGE, RUBBISH (2) **:** EXCREMENT — often used in pl. (3) **:** SEWAGE **c :** material derived by mechanical and chemical weathering of the land and moved down sloping surfaces or carried by streams to the sea

2**waste** *vb* **wast·ed; wast·ing** [ME, fr. AF *waster, gaster,* fr. L *vastare,* fr. *vastus* desolate, waste] *vt* (13c) **1 :** to lay waste; *esp* **:** to damage or destroy gradually and progressively ⟨reclaiming land *wasted* by strip-mining⟩ **2 :** to cause to shrink in physical bulk or strength **:** EMACIATE, ENFEEBLE ⟨a body *wasted* by disease⟩ **3 :** to wear away or diminish gradually **:** CONSUME **4 a :** to spend or use carelessly **:** SQUANDER ⟨~ valuable resources⟩ **b :** to allow to be used inefficiently or become dissipated ⟨a writer *wasting* her talent⟩ **5 :** KILL; *also* **:** to injure severely ~ *vi* **1 :** to lose weight, strength, or vitality — often used with *away* ⟨was *wasting* away from illness⟩ **2 a :** to become diminished in bulk or substance **b :** to become consumed **3 :** to spend money or consume property extravagantly or improvidently ***syn*** see RAVAGE — **waste one's breath :** to accomplish nothing by speaking

3**waste** *adj* [ME *waste, wast,* fr. AF *wast*] (14c) **1 a** (1) **:** being wild and uninhabited **:** DESOLATE (2) **:** ARID, EMPTY **b :** not cultivated **:** not productive **2 :** being in a ruined or devastated condition **3** [1*waste*] **a :** discarded as worthless, defective, or of no use **:** REFUSE ⟨~ material⟩ **b :** excreted from or stored in inert form in a living body as a byproduct of vital activity ⟨~ products⟩ **4** [1*waste*] **:** serving to conduct or hold refuse material ⟨a ~ barrel⟩; *specif* **:** carrying off superfluous water ⟨a ~ drain⟩ **5 :** WASTED 4

waste·bas·ket \ˈwās(t)-ˌbas-kət\ *n* (1850) **:** a receptacle for refuse and esp. for wastepaper — called also *wastepaper basket*

wasted *adj* (15c) **1 :** laid waste **:** RAVAGED **2 :** impaired in strength or health **:** EMACIATED **3** *archaic* **:** gone by **:** ELAPSED ⟨the chronicle of ~ time —Shak.⟩ **4 :** unprofitably used, made, or expended ⟨~ effort⟩ **5** *slang* **:** intoxicated from drugs or alcohol

waste·ful \ˈwāst-fəl\ *adj* (14c) **:** given to or marked by waste **:** LAVISH, PRODIGAL — **waste·ful·ly** \-fə-lē\ *adv* — **waste·ful·ness** *n*

waste·land \ˈwāst-ˌland *also* -lənd\ *n* (14c) **1 :** barren or uncultivated land ⟨a desert ~⟩ **2 :** an ugly often devastated or barely inhabitable place or area **3 :** something (as a way of life) that is spiritually and emotionally arid and unsatisfying

waste·pa·per \ˈwās(t)-ˈpā-pər\ *n* (1567) **:** paper discarded as used, superfluous, or not fit for use

waste pipe *n* (ca. 1512) **:** a pipe for carrying off waste fluid

wast·er \ˈwā-stər\ *n* (14c) **1 a** (1) **:** one that spends or consumes extravagantly and without thought for the future (2) **:** a dissolute person **b :** one that uses wastefully or causes or permits waste ⟨a procedure that is a ~ of time⟩ **c :** one that lays waste **:** DESTROYER **2 :** an imperfect or inferior manufactured article or object

waste·wa·ter \ˈwāst-ˌwȯ-tər, -ˌwä-\ *n* (15c) **:** water that has been used (as in a manufacturing process) **:** SEWAGE

wasting *adj* (13c) **1 :** laying waste **:** DEVASTATING **2 :** undergoing or causing decay or loss of strength ⟨~ diseases such as tuberculosis⟩

wast·rel \ˈwās-trəl *also* ˈwäs-\ *n* [irreg. fr. 2*waste*] (ca. 1841) **1 :** VAGABOND, WAIF **2 :** one who expends resources foolishly and self-indulgently **:** PROFLIGATE

1**watch** \ˈwäch, ˈwȯch\ *vb* [ME *wacchen,* fr. OE *wæccan* — more at WAKE] *vi* (bef. 12c) **1 a :** to keep vigil as a devotional exercise **b :** to be awake during the night **2 a :** to be attentive or vigilant **b :** to keep guard **3 a :** to keep someone or something under close observation **b :** to observe as a spectator ⟨the country ~*ed* as stocks fell sharply⟩ **4 :** to be expectant **:** WAIT ⟨~ for the signal⟩ ~ *vt* **1 :** to keep under guard **2 a :** to observe closely in order to check on action or change ⟨being ~*ed* by the police⟩ **b :** to look at **:** OBSERVE ⟨sat and ~*ed* the crowd⟩ **c :** to look on at ⟨~ television⟩ ⟨~ a ball game⟩ **3 a :** to take care of **:** TEND **b :** to be careful of ⟨~*es* his diet⟩ **4 :** to be on the alert for **:** BIDE ⟨~*ed* her opportunity⟩ — **watch it :** look out **:** be careful ⟨*watch it* when you handle the glassware⟩ — **watch one's step :** to proceed with extreme care **:** act or talk warily — **watch over :** to have charge of **:** SUPERINTEND

2**watch** *n* (bef. 12c) **1 a :** the act of keeping awake to guard, protect, or attend **b** *obs* **:** the state of being wakeful **c :** a wake over a dead body **d :** a state of alert and continuous attention **e :** close observation **:** SURVEILLANCE **f :** a notice or bulletin that alerts the public to the possibility of severe weather conditions occurring in the near future ⟨a winter storm ~⟩ **2 a :** any of the definite divisions of the night made by ancient peoples **b :** one of the indeterminate intervals marking the passage of night — usu. used in pl. ⟨the silent ~*es* of the night⟩ **3 a :** LOOKOUT, WATCHMAN **b** *archaic* **:** the office or function of a sentinel or guard **4 a :** a body of soldiers or sentinels making up a guard **b :** a watchman or body of watchmen formerly assigned to patrol the streets of a town at night, announce the hours, and act as police **5 a** (1) **:** a portion of time during which a part of a ship's company is on duty (2) **:** the part of a ship's company required to be on duty during a particular watch (3) **:** a sailor's assigned duty period **b :** a period of duty **:** SHIFT **c :** a term as holder esp. of an overseeing or managerial office ⟨the business grew on her ~⟩ **6 :** a portable timepiece designed to be worn (as on the wrist) or carried in the pocket — compare CLOCK

watch·able \ˈwä-chə-bəl, ˈwȯ-\ *adj* (1933) **:** worth watching ⟨a minor but highly ~ film⟩ — **watchable** *n*

watch and ward *n* (14c) **1 :** continuous unbroken vigilance and guard **2 :** service as a watchman or sentinel required from a feudal tenant

watch·band \ˈwäch-ˌband, ˈwȯch-\ *n* (1924) **:** the bracelet or strap of a wristwatch

watch cap *n* (1835) **:** a knitted close-fitting usu. navy-blue cap worn esp. by enlisted men in the U.S. navy in cold or stormy weather

watch·case \ˈwäch-ˌkās, ˈwȯch-\ *n* (1671) **:** the outside metal covering of a watch

1**watch·dog** \-ˌdȯg\ *n* (1612) **1 :** a dog kept to guard property **2 :** one that guards against loss, waste, theft, or undesirable practices

2**watchdog** *vt* (1902) **:** to act as a watchdog for

watch·er \ˈwä-chər, ˈwȯ-\ *n* (13c) **:** one that watches: as **a :** one that sits up or continues awake at night **b :** WATCHMAN **c** (1) **:** one that keeps watch beside a dead person (2) **:** one that attends a sick person at night **d :** a person who closely follows or observes someone or something ⟨a Supreme Court ~⟩ — often used in combination ⟨celebrity-*watchers*⟩ **e :** a representative of a party or candidate who is stationed at the polls on an election day to watch the conduct of officials and voters

watch fire *n* (1735) **:** a fire lighted as a signal or for the use of a guard

watch·ful \ˈwäch-fəl, ˈwȯch-\ *adj* (15c) **1** *archaic* **a :** not able or accustomed to sleep or rest **:** WAKEFUL **b :** causing sleeplessness **c :** spent in wakefulness **:** SLEEPLESS **2 :** carefully observant or attentive **:** being on the watch — **watch·ful·ly** \-fə-lē\ *adv* — **watch·ful·ness** *n*

syn WATCHFUL, VIGILANT, WIDE-AWAKE, ALERT mean being on the lookout esp. for danger or opportunity. WATCHFUL is the least explicit term ⟨the *watchful* eye of the department supervisor⟩. VIGILANT suggests intense, unremitting, wary watchfulness ⟨eternally *vigilant* in the safeguarding of democracy⟩. WIDE-AWAKE applies to watchfulness for opportunities and developments more often than dangers ⟨*wide-awake* companies latched onto the new technology⟩. ALERT stresses readiness or promptness in meeting danger or in seizing opportunity ⟨*alert* traders anticipated the stock market's slide⟩.

watch·mak·er \-ˌmā-kər\ *n* (1630) **:** one that makes or repairs watches or clocks — **watch·mak·ing** \-ˌmā-kiŋ\ *n*

watch·man \-mən\ *n* (15c) **:** a person who keeps watch **:** GUARD

watch night *n* (1742) **:** a devotional service lasting until after midnight esp. on New Year's Eve

watch out *vi* (1845) **:** to be vigilant or alert **:** be on the lookout ⟨you'd better *watch out*⟩ ⟨*watch out* for the tree!⟩

watch pocket *n* (1831) **:** a small pocket just below the front waistband of men's trousers

watch·tow·er \ˈwäch-ˌtau̇(-ə)r, ˈwȯch-\ *n* (1544) **:** a tower for a lookout

watch·word \-ˌwərd\ *n* (15c) **1 :** a word or phrase used as a sign of recognition among members of the same society, class, or group **2 a :** a word or motto that embodies a principle or guide to action of an individual or group **:** SLOGAN ⟨"safety" is our ~⟩ **b :** a guiding principle ⟨change is the ~ for both parties⟩

1**wa·ter** \ˈwȯ-tər, ˈwä-\ *n, often attrib* [ME, fr. OE *wæter;* akin to OHG *wazzar* water, Gk *hydōr,* L *unda* wave] (bef. 12c) **1 a :** the liquid that descends from the clouds as rain, forms streams, lakes, and seas, and is a major constituent of all living matter and that when pure is an odorless, tasteless, very slightly compressible liquid oxide of hydrogen H_2O which appears bluish in thick layers, freezes at 0° C and boils at 100° C, has a maximum density at 4° C and a high specific heat, is feebly ionized to hydrogen and hydroxyl ions, and is a poor conductor of electricity and a good solvent **b :** a natural mineral water — usu. used in pl. **2 :** a particular quantity or body of water: as **a** (1) *pl* **:** the water occupying or flowing in a particular bed (2) *chiefly Brit* **:** LAKE, POND

b : a quantity or depth of water adequate for some purpose (as navigation) **c** *pl* (1) **:** a band of seawater abutting on the land of a particular sovereignty and under the control of that sovereignty (2) **:** the sea of a particular part of the earth **d :** WATER SUPPLY ⟨threatened to turn off the ~⟩ **3 :** travel or transportation on water ⟨we went by ~⟩ **4 :** the level of water at a particular state of the tide **:** TIDE **5 :** liquid containing or resembling water: as **a** (1) **:** a pharmaceutical or cosmetic preparation made with water (2) **:** a watery solution of a gaseous or readily volatile substance — compare AMMONIA WATER **b** *archaic* **:** a distilled fluid (as an essence); *esp* **:** a distilled alcoholic liquor **c :** a watery fluid (as tears, urine, or sap) formed or circulating in a living body **d :** AMNIOTIC FLUID; *also* **:** BAG OF WATERS **6 a :** the degree of clarity and luster of a precious stone **b :** degree of excellence ⟨a scholar of the first ~⟩ **7 :** WATERCOLOR **8 a :** stock not representing assets of the issuing company and not backed by earning power **b :** fictitious or exaggerated asset entries that give a stock an unrealistic book value — **above water :** out of difficulty

[2]**water** *vt* (bef. 12c) **1 :** to moisten, sprinkle, or soak with water ⟨~ the lawn⟩ **2 :** to supply with water for drink ⟨~ cattle⟩ **3 :** to supply water to ⟨lands ~*ed* by the river⟩ **4 :** to treat with or as if with water; *specif* **:** to impart a lustrous appearance and wavy pattern to (cloth) by calendering **5 a :** to dilute by the addition of water — often used with *down* ⟨~ down the punch⟩ **b :** to add to the aggregate par value of (securities) without a corresponding addition to the assets represented by the securities ~ *vi* **1 :** to form or secrete water or watery matter (as tears or saliva) **2 :** to get or take water: as **a :** to take on a supply of water ⟨the boat docked to ~⟩ **b :** to drink water

water bag *n* (1638) **1 :** a bag for holding water; *esp* **:** one designed to keep water cool for drinking by evaporation through a slightly porous surface **2 :** BAG OF WATERS — used esp. of domestic animals

water balance *n* (1911) **:** the ratio between the water assimilated into the body and that lost from the body; *also* **:** the condition of the body when this ratio approximates equilibrium

water ballet *n* (1926) **:** a synchronized sequence of movements performed by a group of swimmers

water bear *n* (1852) **:** TARDIGRADE

Water Bearer *n* (1594) **1 :** AQUARIUS 1a **2 :** AQUARIUS 2

water bed *n* (1844) **:** a bed whose mattress is a watertight bag filled with water

water beetle *n* (ca. 1668) **:** any of numerous oval flattened aquatic beetles (as a diving beetle or whirligig beetle) that swim by means of their fringed hind legs which act together as oars

wa•ter•bird \ˈwȯ-tər-ˌbərd, ˈwä-\ *n* (15c) **:** a swimming or wading bird

water biscuit *n* (1786) **:** a cracker of flour and water and sometimes fat

water blister *n* (1836) **:** a blister with a clear watery content

water bloom *n* (1903) **:** BLOOM 1d

wa•ter•board•ing \ˈwȯ-tər-ˌbȯr-diŋ, ˈwä-\ *n* (2004) **:** an interrogation technique in which water is forced into a detainee's mouth and nose so as to induce the sensation of drowning

water boatman *n* (1815) **1 :** BACKSWIMMER **2 :** any of various oval flattened aquatic bugs (family Corixidae) of fresh or brackish water with fringed hind legs modified into paddles

wa•ter•borne \ˈwȯ-tər-ˌbȯrn, ˈwä-\ *adj* (ca. 1559) **:** supported, carried, or transmitted by water ⟨~ commerce⟩ ⟨~ diseases⟩

water boy *n* (1859) **:** one who keeps a group (as of football players) supplied with drinking water

wa•ter•buck \ˈwȯ-tər-ˌbək, ˈwä-\ *n, pl* **waterbuck** *or* **waterbucks** (1839) **:** a stocky antelope (*Kobus ellipsiprymnus*) of sub-Saharan Africa that commonly frequent streams or wet areas

water buffalo *n* (1847) **:** an often domesticated Asian buffalo (*Bubalus bubalis* syn. *B. arnee*)

water buffalo

water bug *n* (1750) **:** any of various small arthropods and esp. insects that frequent damp or wet places: as **a :** GERMAN COCKROACH **b :** WATER BOATMAN **c :** any of various large aquatic bugs (family Belostomatidae) with the hind legs flattened and used for swimming

water cannon *n* (1964) **:** a large truck-mounted nozzle for directing a high-pressure stream of water (as at a crowd of rioters or demonstrators)

water chestnut *n* (1847) **1 :** any of a genus (*Trapa*, esp. *T. natans* of the family Trapaceae, the water-chestnut family) of Old World aquatic herbs sometimes grown as ornamentals; *also* **:** its edible nutlike spiny fruit **2 :** a whitish crunchy vegetable used esp. in Chinese cooking that is the peeled and often sliced tuber of a sedge (*Eleocharis dulcis* syn. *E. tuberosa*) native to Asia but widely cultivated elsewhere; *also* **:** the tuber or the sedge itself

water clock *n* (1601) **:** an instrument designed to measure time by the fall or flow of a quantity of water — called also *clepsydra*

water closet *n* (1755) **1 :** a compartment or room with a toilet **2 :** a toilet bowl and its accessories

wa•ter•col•or \ˈwȯ-tər-ˌkə-lər, ˈwä-\ *n* (1596) **1 :** a paint of which the liquid is a water dispersion of the binding material (as glue, casein, or gum) **2 :** the art or method of painting with watercolors **3 :** a picture or design executed in watercolors — **watercolor** *adj* — **wa•ter•col•or•ist** \-ˌkə-lə-rist\ *n*

wa•ter•cool•er \ˈwȯ-tər-ˌkü-lər, ˈwä-\ *n* (1846) **:** a device for dispensing refrigerated drinking water

wa•ter•course \ˈwȯ-tər-ˌkȯrs\ *n* (1510) **1 :** a natural or artificial channel through which water flows **2 :** a stream of water (as a river, brook, or underground stream)

wa•ter•craft \-ˌkraft\ *n* (1566) **1 :** skill in aquatic activities (as managing boats) **2 a :** SHIP, BOAT **b :** craft for water transport

wa•ter•cress \-ˌkres\ *n* (14c) **1 :** any of several aquatic or semiaquatic cresses; *esp* **:** a perennial cress (*Nasturtium officinale*) native to Europe and southwestern Asia that is naturalized in the U.S. and has leaves used esp. in salads and as a potherb **2 :** the leaves of a watercress

water cycle *n* (1928) **:** HYDROLOGIC CYCLE

water dog *n* (1674) **1 :** a person (as a skilled sailor) who is quite at ease in or on water **2 :** any of several large American salamanders; *esp* **:** any of a genus (*Necturus* of the family Proteidae) with external gills

water down *vt* (1850) **:** to reduce or temper the force or effectiveness of ⟨*watered down* the plan⟩ — **wa•tered–down** *adj*

wa•ter•er \ˈwȯ-tər-ər, ˈwä-\ *n* (1549) **:** one that waters: as **a :** a person who obtains or supplies drinking water **b :** a device used for supplying water to livestock and poultry — called also *drinker*

wa•ter•fall \-ˌfȯl\ *n* (bef. 12c) **1 a :** a perpendicular or very steep descent of the water of a stream **b :** an artificial waterfall (as in a hotel lobby or a nightclub) **2 :** something resembling a waterfall

water flea *n* (ca. 1585) **:** any of various small active dark or brightly colored aquatic crustaceans (as a daphnia or cyclops)

[1]**wa•ter•flood** \-ˌfləd\ *n* (1928) **:** the process of waterflooding an oil well

[2]**waterflood** *vi* (1928) **:** to pump water into the ground around an oil well nearing depletion in order to loosen and force out additional oil

wa•ter•fowl \ˈwȯ-tər-ˌfau̇(-ə)l, ˈwä-\ *n, pl* **-fowl** *also* **-fowls** (14c) **:** a bird that frequents water; *esp* **:** a swimming game bird (as a duck or goose) as distinguished from an upland game bird or shorebird

wa•ter•fowl•er \-ˌfau̇-lər\ *n* (1968) **:** a hunter of waterfowl — **wa•ter•fowl•ing** \-liŋ\ *n*

wa•ter•front \-ˌfrənt\ *n* (1766) **:** land, land with buildings, or a section of a town fronting or abutting on a body of water

water gap *n* (1756) **:** a pass in a mountain ridge through which a stream runs — compare WIND GAP

water garden *n* (1852) **1 :** a garden in which aquatic plants predominate **2 :** a garden built about a stream or pool as a central feature

water gas *n* (1850) **:** a poisonous flammable gaseous mixture that consists chiefly of carbon monoxide and hydrogen with small amounts of methane, carbon dioxide, and nitrogen, is usu. made by blowing air and then steam over red-hot coke or coal, and is used as a fuel or after carbureting as an illuminant

Wa•ter•gate \-ˌgāt\ *n* [*Watergate*, apartment and office complex in Washington, D.C.; fr. the scandal following the break-in at the Democratic National Committee headquarters there in 1972] (1973) **:** a scandal usu. involving abuses of office, skulduggery, and a cover-up

water gate *n* (13c) **1 :** a gate (as of a building) giving access to a body of water **2 :** FLOODGATE

water gauge *n* (ca. 1706) **:** an instrument to measure or find the depth or quantity of water or to indicate the height of its surface esp. in a steam boiler

water glass *n* (1612) **1 :** a glass vessel (as a drinking glass) for holding water **2 :** an instrument consisting of an open box or tube with a glass bottom used for examining objects in or under water **3 :** a substance that consists usu. of the silicate of sodium, is found in commerce as a glassy mass, a stony powder, or dissolved in water as a viscous syrupy liquid, and is used esp. as a cement, a protective coating, and as a fireproofing agent

water gun *n* (1951) **:** WATER PISTOL

water hammer *n* (1850) **:** a concussion or sound of concussion of moving water against the sides of a containing pipe or vessel (as a steam pipe)

water haul *n* [fr. the figure of a fishing net that catches nothing but water] (1823) **:** a fruitless effort

water heater *n* (1853) **:** an apparatus for heating and usu. storing hot water (as for domestic use)

water hemlock *n* (ca. 1764) **:** a tall poisonous Eurasian perennial herb (*Cicuta virosa*) of the carrot family; *also* **:** any of several poisonous No. American plants (esp. *Cicuta maculata* and *C. douglasii*) of the same genus — compare POISON HEMLOCK

water hen *n* (ca. 1529) **:** any of various birds (as a coot or gallinule) of the rail family

water hole *n* (ca. 1653) **1 :** a natural hole or hollow containing water **2 :** a hole in a surface of ice

water hyacinth *n* (ca. 1890) **:** a showy floating aquatic herb (*Eichhornia crassipes*) of tropical So. America that has become naturalized in warm regions (as of the southern U.S.) often clogging waterways

water ice *n* (1818) **:** a frozen dessert of water, sugar, and flavoring

watering can *n* (1692) **:** a vessel usu. with a spout used to sprinkle or pour water esp. on plants — called also *watering pot*

watering hole *n* (1882) **1 :** WATER HOLE 1 **2 :** a place where people gather socially; *esp* **:** WATERING PLACE 3

watering place *n* (15c) **1 :** a place where water may be obtained; *esp* **:** one where animals and esp. livestock come to drink **2 :** a health or recreational resort featuring mineral springs or bathing **3 :** a place (as a nightclub, bar, or lounge) where drink is available

wa•ter•ish \ˈwȯ-tər-ish, ˈwä-\ *adj* (1542) **:** somewhat watery — **wa•ter•ish•ness** *n*

water jacket *n* (1853) **:** an outer casing which holds water or through which water circulates to cool the interior; *specif* **:** the enclosed space surrounding the cylinder block of an internal combustion engine and containing the cooling liquid

water jump *n* (1874) **:** an obstacle (as in a steeplechase) consisting of a pool, stream, or ditch of water

wa•ter•leaf \ˈwȯ-tər-ˌlēf, ˈwä-\ *n, pl* **-leafs** \-ˌlēfs\ (ca. 1760) **:** any of a genus (*Hydrophyllum* of the family Hydrophyllaceae, the waterleaf family) of perennial or biennial No. American woodland herbs with lobed or pinnate toothed leaves and cymes of bell-shaped flowers

wa•ter•less \-ləs\ *adj* (bef. 12c) **1 :** lacking or destitute of water **:** DRY **2 :** not requiring water (as for cooling) — **wa•ter•less•ness** *n*

water level *n* (1563) **1 :** an instrument to show the level by means of the surface of water in a trough or in a U-shaped tube **2 :** the surface of still water: as **a :** the level assumed by the surface of a particular body or column of water **b :** the waterline of a vessel

water lily *n* (14c) **:** any of various aquatic plants (esp. genera *Nymphaea* and *Nuphar* of the family Nymphaeaceae, the water-lily family) with floating leaves and usu. showy flowers; *broadly* **:** an aquatic plant (as a water hyacinth) with showy flowers

wa•ter•line \ˈwȯ-tər-ˌlīn, ˈwä-\ *n* (ca. 1625) **:** a line that marks the level of the surface of water on something: as **a** (1) **:** the point on the hull of a ship or boat to which the water rises (2) **:** a line marked on the outside of a ship that corresponds with the water's surface when the ship is afloat on an even keel under specified conditions of loading **b** **:** SHORELINE 1

wa•ter•log \-ˌlȯg, -ˌläg\ *vt* [back-formation fr. *waterlogged*] (1779) **:** to make waterlogged

wa•ter•logged \-ˌlȯgd, -ˌlägd\ *adj* [[1]*water* + *log* to accumulate in the hold] (ca. 1776) **1 :** so filled or soaked with water as to be heavy or hard to manage ⟨∼ boats⟩ **2 :** saturated with water ⟨∼ soil⟩

wa•ter•loo \ˌwȯ-tər-ˈlü, ˌwä-\ *n, pl* **-loos** *often cap* [*Waterloo*, Belgium, scene of Napoleon's defeat in 1815] (1816) **:** a decisive or final defeat or setback ⟨a political ∼⟩

water main *n* (1803) **:** a pipe or conduit for conveying water

wa•ter•man \ˈwȯ-tər-mən, ˈwä-\ *n* (12c) **:** one who works or lives on the water: as **a :** a man who makes his living from the water (as by fishing) **b :** a boatman who plies for hire usu. on inland waters or harbors

wa•ter•man•ship \-ˌship\ *n* (1882) **:** the business, skill, or art of a waterman: as **a :** technique or expertness in rowing **b :** technique or expertness in swimming

[1]**wa•ter•mark** \ˈwȯ-tər-ˌmärk, ˈwä-\ *n* (1640) **1 :** a mark indicating the height to which water has risen **2 :** a marking in paper resulting from differences in thickness usu. produced by pressure of a projecting design in the mold or on a processing roll and visible when the paper is held up to the light; *also* **:** the design of or the metal pattern producing the marking

[2]**watermark** *vt* (1866) **1 :** to mark (paper) with a watermark **2 :** to impress (a given design) as a watermark

wa•ter•mel•on \-ˌme-lən\ *n* (1615) **1 :** a large oblong or roundish fruit with a hard green or white rind often striped or variegated, a sweet watery pink, yellowish, or red pulp, and usu. many seeds **2 :** a widely cultivated African vine (*Citrullus lanatus* syn. *C. vulgaris*) of the gourd family that bears watermelons

water meter *n* (ca. 1858) **:** an instrument for recording the quantity of water passing through a particular outlet

water milfoil *n* (1578) **:** any of a genus (*Myriophyllum* of the family Haloragaceae) of aquatic herbs with finely pinnate submersed leaves

water mill *n* (15c) **:** a mill whose machinery is moved by water

water moccasin *n* (ca. 1821) **1 :** a venomous semiaquatic pit viper (*Agkistrodon piscivorus*) chiefly of the southeastern U.S. that is closely related to the copperhead — called also *cottonmouth, cottonmouth moccasin* **2 :** a harmless American colubrid water snake (genus *Nerodia*) resembling the true water moccasin

water mold *n* (1899) **:** any of various fungi of water or moist soils

water nymph *n* (14c) **:** a nymph (as a naiad, Nereid, or Oceanid) associated with a body of water

water oak *n* (1687) **:** any of several American oaks that thrive in wet soils; *esp* **:** one (*Quercus nigra*) of the eastern U.S.

water of crystallization (1791) **:** water of hydration present in many crystallized substances that is usu. essential for maintenance of a particular crystal structure

water of hydration (1864) **:** water that is chemically combined with a substance to form a hydrate and can be expelled (as by heating) without essentially altering the composition of the substance

water on the knee (ca. 1890) **:** an accumulation of synovial fluid in the knee joint (as from injury or disease) marked esp. by swelling

water ouzel *n* (1622) **:** DIPPER 2

water park *n* (1983) **:** an amusement park with facilities (as pools and wetted slides) for aquatic recreation

water parting *n* (1859) **:** DIVIDE 2a

water pepper *n* (ca. 1538) **:** an annual European smartweed (*Polygonum hydropiper*) of moist soils with extremely acrid peppery juice that is naturalized in No. America; *also* **:** a related American perennial (*P. hydropiperoides*) with mildly acrid juice

water pill *n* (ca. 1981) **:** a diuretic pill

water pimpernel *n* (ca. 1760) **:** either of two small white-flowered herbs (*Samolus valerandi* of Eurasia and *S. parviflorus* syn. *S. floribundus* of America) of the primrose family that grow in wet places

water pipe *n* (15c) **1 :** a pipe for conveying water **2 :** a smoking device that consists of a bowl mounted on a vessel of water which is provided with a long tube and arranged so that smoke is drawn through the water where it is cooled and up the tube to the mouth

water pistol *n* (1905) **:** a toy pistol designed to squirt a jet of liquid — called also *water gun, squirt gun*

water plantain *n* (ca. 1538) **:** any of a genus (*Alisma* of the family Alismataceae, the water-plantain family) of marsh or aquatic herbs with acrid sap and scapose 3-petaled flowers

water polo *n* (ca. 1884) **:** a goal game similar to soccer that is played in water by teams of swimmers using a ball resembling a soccer ball

wa•ter•pow•er \ˈwȯ-tər-ˌpau̇(-ə)r, ˈwä-\ *n* (1817) **1 :** the power of water employed to move machinery **2 :** a fall of water suitable for being used to move machinery

water privilege *n* (1804) **:** the right to use water esp. as a source of mechanical power

[1]**wa•ter•proof** \ˈwȯ-tər-ˌprüf, ˈwä-\ *adj* (1736) **:** impervious to water; *esp* **:** covered or treated with a material (as a solution of rubber) to prevent permeation by water — **wa•ter•proof•ness** *n*

[2]**waterproof** *n* (1799) **1 :** a waterproof fabric **2** *chiefly Brit* **:** RAINCOAT

[3]**waterproof** *vt* (1841) **:** to make waterproof — **wa•ter•proof•er** *n*

wa•ter•proof•ing \-ˌprü-fiŋ\ *n* (1845) **1 a :** the act or process of making something waterproof **b :** the condition of being made waterproof **2 :** something (as a coating) capable of imparting waterproofness

water rat *n* (ca. 1552) **1 :** a rodent that frequents water **2 :** a waterfront loafer or petty thief

wa•ter–re•pel•lent \ˌwȯ-tə(r)-ri-ˈpe-lənt, ˌwä-\ *adj* (1850) **:** treated with a finish that is resistant but not impervious to penetration by water

wa•ter–re•sis•tant \-ri-ˈzis-tənt\ *adj* (1889) **:** WATER-REPELLENT

water right *n* (1793) **:** a right to the use of water (as for irrigation); *esp* **:** RIPARIAN RIGHT

water sapphire *n* (ca. 1741) **:** a deep blue cordierite sometimes used as a gem

wa•ter•scape \ˈwȯ-tər-ˌskāp, ˈwä-\ *n* (1842) **:** a water or sea view **:** SEASCAPE 1

water scorpion *n* (1681) **:** any of numerous aquatic bugs (family Nepidae) with the end of the abdomen prolonged by a long breathing tube

wa•ter•shed \ˈwȯ-tər-ˌshed, ˈwä-\ *n* (1803) **1 a :** DIVIDE 2a **b :** a region or area bounded peripherally by a divide and draining ultimately to a particular watercourse or body of water **2 :** a crucial dividing point, line, or factor **:** TURNING POINT — **watershed** *adj*

water shield *n* (ca. 1818) **:** an aquatic herb (*Brasenia schreberi*) having floating oval leaves with a gelatinous coating and small dull purple flowers; *also* **:** any of a related genus (*Cabomba*)

[1]**wa•ter•side** \ˈwȯ-tər-ˌsīd, ˈwä-\ *n* (14c) **:** the margin of a body of water **:** WATERFRONT

[2]**waterside** *adj* (1663) **1 :** employed along the waterside ⟨∼ workers⟩; *also* **:** of or relating to the workers along the waterside ⟨a ∼ strike⟩ **2 :** of, relating to, or located on the waterside ⟨a ∼ café⟩

water ski *n* (1931) **:** a ski used in planing over water while being towed by a speedboat — **wa•ter–ski** *vi*

wa•ter–ski•er \ˈwȯ-tər-ˌskē-ər, ˈwä-\ *n* (1931) **:** one who water-skis

wa•ter•ski•ing \-ˌskē-iŋ\ *n* (1931) **:** the sport of planing and jumping on water skis

wa•ter•slide \ˈwȯ-tər-ˌslīd, ˈwä-\ *n* (1974) **:** a continuously wetted chute (as at an amusement park) down which people slide into a pool

water snake *n* (ca. 1601) **:** any of various snakes (esp. genus *Nerodia* formerly included in the genus *Natrix*) that frequent or inhabit freshwaters and feed largely on aquatic animals

wa•ter–soak \ˈwȯ-tər-ˌsōk, ˈwä-\ *vt* (1791) **:** to soak in water

water spaniel *n* (1566) **:** a spaniel of either of two breeds: **a :** AMERICAN WATER SPANIEL **b :** IRISH WATER SPANIEL

wa•ter•spout \ˈwȯ-tər-ˌspau̇t, ˈwä-\ *n* (14c) **1 :** a pipe, duct, or orifice from which water is spouted or through which it is carried **2 :** a funnel-shaped or tubular column of rotating cloud-filled wind usu. extending from the underside of a cumulus or cumulonimbus cloud down to a cloud of spray torn up by the whirling winds from the surface of an ocean or lake

water sprite *n* (1798) **:** a sprite believed to inhabit or haunt water **:** WATER NYMPH

water sprout *n* (ca. 1892) **:** a vigorous upright shoot from an adventitious or latent bud on the trunk or main branch of a tree

water strider *n* (1888) **:** any of various long-legged bugs (family Gerridae) that move about on the surface of the water

water supply *n* (1849) **:** a source, means, or process of supplying water (as for a community) usu. including reservoirs, tunnels, and pipelines

water table *n* (15c) **1 :** a stringcourse or similar member when projecting so as to throw off water **2 :** the upper limit of the portion of the ground wholly saturated with water

water taxi *n* (1928) **:** a boat functioning (as within a harbor) as a taxi

wa•ter•thrush \ˈwȯ-tər-ˌthrəsh, ˈwä-\ *n* (ca. 1813) **:** either of two No. American warblers (*Seiurus noveboracensis* and *S. motacilla* of the family Parulidae) found near freshwater (as a stream)

wa•ter•tight \ˌwȯ-tər-ˈtīt, ˌwä-\ *adj* (14c) **1 :** of such tight construction or fit as to be impermeable to water except when under sufficient pressure to produce structural discontinuity **2 :** leaving no possibility of misconstruction or evasion ⟨a ∼ lease⟩ — **wa•ter•tight•ness** *n*

water tower *n* (ca. 1883) **:** a tower or standpipe serving as a reservoir to deliver water at a required head

water turkey *n* (1836) **:** the New World anhinga (*Anhinga anhinga*)

water vapor *n* (1833) **:** water in a vaporous form esp. when below boiling temperature and diffused (as in the atmosphere)

water–vascular system *n* (1870) **:** a system of canals in echinoderms containing a circulating watery fluid that is used for the movement of the tentacles and tube feet

water wagon *n* (1902) **:** a wagon or motortruck equipped with a tank or barrels for hauling water or for sprinkling — **on the water wagon** **:** abstaining from alcoholic beverages **:** on the wagon

wa•ter•way \ˈwȯ-tər-ˌwā, ˈwä-\ *n* (15c) **1 :** a way or channel for water **2 :** a navigable body of water

wa•ter•weed \-ˌwēd\ *n* (1842) **:** any of various floating or submerged aquatic plants (as elodea) having usu. inconspicuous flowers

wa•ter•wheel \-ˌhwēl, -ˌwēl\ *n* (15c) **1 :** a wheel made to rotate by direct action of water **2 :** a wheel for raising water

waterwheel 1

water wings *n pl* (1907) **:** an air-filled device that fits around the arms of a person learning to swim so as to provide buoyancy

water witch *n* (1817) **:** one who dowses for water — **water witch•ing** \-ˌwi-chiŋ\ *n*

water witch•er \-ˌwi-chər\ *n* (1961) **:** WATER WITCH

wa•ter•works \ˈwȯ-tər-ˌwərks, ˈwä-\ *n pl* (1568) **1 :** the system of reservoirs, channels, mains, and pumping and purifying equipment by which a water supply is obtained and distributed (as to a city) **2 :** an ornamental fountain or cascade **3 :** the shedding of tears **:** TEARS

wa•ter•worn \-ˌwȯrn\ *adj* (1815) **:** worn, smoothed, or polished by the action of water

wa•tery \ˈwȯ-tə-rē, ˈwä-\ *adj* (bef. 12c) **1 a :** consisting of, filled with, or surrounded by water **b :** containing, sodden with, or yielding water or a thin liquid ⟨a ∼ solution⟩ ⟨∼ vesicles⟩ **2 a :** resembling water or watery matter esp. in thin fluidity, soggy texture, paleness, or lack of savor ⟨∼ sunlight⟩ ⟨a ∼ soup⟩ ⟨∼ diarrhea⟩ **b :** exhibiting weakness and vapidity **:** WISHY-WASHY ⟨a ∼ writing style⟩ — **wa•ter•i•ly** \-tə-rə-lē\ *adv* — **wa•ter•i•ness** \-tə-rē-nəs\ *n*

wa•ter•zooi \ˈvä-tər-ˌzȯi\ *n* [D dial., fr. *water* water + *zooi* quantity of cooked food] (1949) **:** a stew of fish or chicken and vegetables in a seasoned stock thickened with cream and egg yolks

WATS *abbr* Wide-Area Telecommunications Service

Wat•son–Crick \ˌwät-sən-ˈkrik\ *adj* (1964) **:** of or relating to the Watson-Crick model ⟨the ∼ helix⟩ ⟨the ∼ structure⟩ ⟨∼ base pairs⟩

Watson–Crick model *n* [J. D. *Watson* & F. H. C. *Crick*] (1958) **:** a model of DNA structure in which the molecule is a cross-linked double-stranded helix, each strand is composed of alternating links of phosphate and deoxyribose, and the strands are cross-linked by pairs of

watt • way **1415**

purine and pyrimidine bases projecting inward from the deoxyribose sugars and joined by hydrogen bonds with adenine paired with thymine and with cytosine paired with guanine — compare DOUBLE HELIX

watt \ˈwät\ *n* [James *Watt* †1819] (1882) **:** the absolute meter-kilogram-second unit of power equal to the work done at the rate of one joule per second or to the power produced by a current of one ampere across a potential difference of one volt **:** 1/746 horsepower

watt·age \ˈwä-tij\ *n* (1903) **1 :** amount of power expressed in watts **2 :** dynamic or mental energy or appeal ⟨the celebrity's high ~⟩

Wat·teau \(ˌ)wä-ˈtō\ *adj* [Antoine *Watteau*] (1861) **1** *of a hat* **:** shallow-crowned and having a wide brim turned up at the back to hold flower trimmings **2** *of women's dress* **:** having back pleats falling loosely from neckline to hem

watt–hour \ˈwät-ˈau̇(-ə)r\ *n* (1888) **:** a unit of work or energy equivalent to the power of one watt operating for one hour

[1]**wat·tle** \ˈwä-tᵊl\ *n* [ME *wattel,* fr. OE *watel;* akin to OHG *wadal* bandage] (bef. 12c) **1 a :** a fabrication of poles interwoven with slender branches, withes, or reeds and used esp. formerly in building **b :** material for such construction **c** *pl* **:** poles laid on a roof to support thatch **2** *Austral* **:** ACACIA 2 — **wat·tled** \-tᵊld\ *adj*

[2]**wattle** *vt* **wat·tled; wat·tling** \ˈwät-liŋ, ˈwä-tᵊl-iŋ\ (14c) **1 :** to form or build of or with wattle **2 a :** to form into wattle **:** interlace to form wattle **b :** to unite or make solid by interweaving light flexible material

[3]**wattle** *n* [origin unknown] (1513) **:** a fleshy pendulous process usu. about the head or neck (as of a bird)

wattle and daub *n* (ca. 1808) **:** a framework of woven rods and twigs covered and plastered with clay and used in building construction — **wattle–and–daub** *adj*

wat·tle·bird \ˈwä-tᵊl-ˌbərd\ *n* (1819) **:** any of several Australasian honeyeaters (genus *Anthochaera*) having ear wattles

watt·me·ter \ˈwät-ˌmē-tər\ *n* [ISV] (1887) **:** an instrument for measuring electric power in watts

Wa·tu·si \wä-ˈtü-sē\ *n, pl* **Watusi** *also* **Watusis** (1899) **:** TUTSI

[1]**wave** \ˈwāv\ *vb* **waved; wav·ing** [ME, fr. OE *wafian* to wave with the hands; akin to OE *wǣfan* to clothe and perh. to OE *wefan* to weave] *vi* (bef. 12c) **1 :** to motion with the hands or with something held in them in signal or salute **2 :** to float, play, or shake in an air current **:** move loosely to and fro **:** FLUTTER ⟨flags *waving* in the breeze⟩ **3** *of water* **:** to move in waves **:** HEAVE **4 :** to become moved or brandished to and fro ⟨signs *waved* in the crowd⟩ **5 :** to move before the wind with a wavelike motion ⟨field of *waving* grain⟩ **6 :** to follow a curving line or take a wavy form **:** UNDULATE ~ *vt* **1 :** to swing (something) back and forth or up and down **2 :** to impart a curving or undulating shape to ⟨*waved* her hair⟩ **3 a :** to motion to (someone) to go in an indicated direction or to stop **:** SIGNAL ⟨*waved* down a passing car⟩ **b :** to gesture with (the hand or an object) in greeting or farewell or in homage **c :** to dismiss or put out of mind **:** DISREGARD — usu. used with *aside* or *off* **d :** to convey by waving ⟨*waved* farewell⟩ **4 :** BRANDISH, FLOURISH ⟨*waved* a pistol menacingly⟩ ***syn*** see SWING

[2]**wave** *n* (1526) **1 a :** a moving ridge or swell on the surface of a liquid (as of the sea) **b :** open water **2 a :** a shape or outline having successive curves **b :** a waviness of the hair **c :** an undulating line or streak or a pattern formed by such lines **3 :** something that swells and dies away: as **a :** a surge of sensation or emotion ⟨a ~ of anger swept over her⟩ **b :** a movement sweeping large numbers in a common direction ⟨~*s* of protest⟩ **c :** a peak or climax of activity ⟨a ~ of buying⟩ **4 :** a sweep of hand or arm or of some object held in the hand used as a signal or greeting **5 :** a rolling or undulatory movement or one of a series of such movements passing along a surface or through the air **6 :** a movement like that of an ocean wave: as **a :** a surging movement of a group ⟨a big new ~ of women politicians⟩ **b :** one of a succession of influxes of people migrating into a region **c (1) :** a moving group of animals of one kind **(2) :** a sudden rapid increase in a population **d :** a line of attacking or advancing troops or airplanes **e :** a display of people in a large crowd (as at a sports event) successively rising, lifting their arms overhead, and quickly sitting so as to form a swell moving through the crowd **7 a :** a disturbance or variation that transfers energy progressively from point to point in a medium and that may take the form of an elastic deformation or of a variation of pressure, electric or magnetic intensity, electric potential, or temperature **b :** one complete cycle of such a disturbance **8 :** a marked change in temperature **:** a period of hot or cold weather **9 :** an undulating or jagged line constituting a graphic representation of an action — **wave·less** \ˈwāv-ləs\ *adj* — **wave·less·ly** *adv* — **wave·like** \-ˌlīk\ *adj*

Wave \ˈwāv\ *n* [*W*omen *A*ccepted for *V*olunteer *E*mergency Service] (1942) **:** a member of the women's component of the U.S. Navy formed during World War II and discontinued in the 1970s

wave band *n* (1923) **:** a band of radio-wave frequencies

waved *adj* (1599) **:** having a wavelike form or outline: as **a :** having wavy lines of color **:** WATERED ⟨~ cloth⟩ **b :** marked by undulations **:** CURVING ⟨the ~ cutting edge of a bread knife⟩

wave equation *n* (1926) **:** a partial differential equation of the second order whose solutions describe wave phenomena

wave·form \ˈwāv-ˌfȯrm\ *n* (1845) **:** a usu. graphic representation of the shape of a wave that indicates its characteristics (as frequency and amplitude) — called also *waveshape*

wave front *n* (ca. 1864) **:** a surface composed at any instant of all the points just reached by a vibrational disturbance in its propagation through a medium

wave·guide \ˈwāv-ˌgīd\ *n* (1932) **:** a device (as a duct, coaxial cable, or glass fiber) designed to confine and direct the propagation of electromagnetic waves (as light); *esp* **:** a metal tube for channeling ultrahigh-frequency waves

wave·length \-ˌleŋ(k)th\ *n* (1850) **1 :** the distance in the line of advance of a wave from any one point to the next point of corresponding phase **2 :** a particular course or line of thought esp. as related to mutual understanding ⟨two people on different ~*s*⟩

wave·let \-lət\ *n* (ca. 1810) **:** a little wave **:** RIPPLE

wave mechanics *n pl but sing or pl in constr* (1926) **1 :** the mathematical description of atomic and subatomic particles in terms of their wave characteristics **2 :** QUANTUM MECHANICS

wave number *n* (1873) **:** the number of waves per unit distance of radiant energy of a given wavelength **:** the reciprocal of the wavelength

wave of the future (1940) **:** an idea, product, or movement that is viewed as representing forces or a trend that will inevitably prevail

wave packet *n* (1928) **:** a pulse of radiant energy that is the resultant of a number of wave trains of differing wavelengths

wave pool *n* (1977) **:** a large swimming pool equipped with a machine for producing waves

[1]**wa·ver** \ˈwā-vər\ *vi* **wa·vered; wa·ver·ing** \ˈwāv-riŋ, ˈwā-və-riŋ\ [ME; akin to OE *wǣfre* restless, *wafian* to wave with the hands — more at WAVE] (14c) **1 :** to vacillate irresolutely between choices **:** fluctuate in opinion, allegiance, or direction **2 a :** to weave or sway unsteadily to and fro **:** REEL, TOTTER **b :** QUIVER, FLICKER ⟨~*ing* flames⟩ **c :** to hesitate as if about to give way **:** FALTER **3 :** to give an unsteady sound **:** QUAVER ***syn*** see SWING, HESITATE — **wa·ver·er** \ˈwā-və-rər\ *n* — **wa·ver·ing·ly** \ˈwāv-riŋ-lē, ˈwā-və-\ *adv*

[2]**waver** *n* (1519) **:** an act of wavering, quivering, or fluttering

[3]**wav·er** \ˈwā-vər\ *n* (1835) **:** one that waves

wa·very \ˈwāv-rē, ˈwā-və-rē\ *adj* (1820) **:** that waves **:** WAVERING

wave·shape \ˈwāv-ˌshāp\ *n* (1907) **:** WAVEFORM

wave theory *n* (1833) **:** a theory in physics: light is transmitted from luminous bodies to the eye and other objects by an undulatory movement — called also *undulatory theory*

wave train *n* (1897) **:** a succession of similar waves at equal intervals

wavy \ˈwā-vē\ *adj* **wav·i·er; -est** (ca. 1586) **1 :** rising or swelling in waves; *also* **:** abounding in waves ⟨~ hair⟩ **2 :** moving with an undulating motion **:** FLUCTUATING; *also* **:** marked by wavering ⟨~ lines⟩ **3 :** marked by undulation **:** ROLLING — **wav·i·ly** \ˈwā-və-lē\ *adv* — **wav·i·ness** \-vē-nəs\ *n*

waw *or* **vav** \ˈväv, ˈvȯv\ *n* [Heb *wāw*] (14c) **:** the 6th letter of the Hebrew alphabet — see ALPHABET table

[1]**wax** \ˈwaks\ *n* [ME, fr. OE *weax;* akin to OHG *wahs* wax, Lith *vaškas*] (bef. 12c) **1 :** a substance that is secreted by bees and is used by them for constructing the honeycomb, that is a dull yellow solid plastic when warm, and that is composed of a mixture of esters, cerotic acid, and hydrocarbons — called also *beeswax* **2 :** any of various substances resembling the wax of bees: as **a :** any of numerous substances of plant or animal origin that differ from fats in being less greasy, harder, and more brittle and in containing principally compounds of high molecular weight (as fatty acids, alcohols, and saturated hydrocarbons) **b :** a solid substance (as ozokerite or paraffin wax) of mineral origin consisting usu. of hydrocarbons of high molecular weight **c :** a pliable or liquid composition used esp. in uniting surfaces, excluding air, making patterns or impressions, or producing a polished surface **3 :** something likened to wax as soft, impressionable, or readily molded **4 :** a waxy secretion; *esp* **:** EARWAX **5 :** a phonograph recording — **wax·like** \ˈwaks-ˌlīk\ *adj*

[2]**wax** *vt* (14c) **1 a :** to treat or rub with wax usu. for polishing, stiffening, or reducing friction **b :** to apply wax to (as legs) as a depilatory **2 :** to record on phonograph records **3** *slang* **:** to defeat decisively (as in an athletic contest)

[3]**wax** *vi* [ME, fr. OE *weaxan;* akin to OHG *wahsan* to increase, Gk *auxanein,* L *augēre* — more at EKE] (bef. 12c) **1 a :** to increase in size, numbers, strength, prosperity, or intensity **b :** to grow in volume or duration **c :** to grow toward full development **2 :** to increase in phase or intensity — used chiefly of the moon, other satellites, and inferior planets **3 :** to assume a (specified) characteristic, quality, or state **:** BECOME ⟨~ indignant⟩ ⟨~ poetic⟩

[4]**wax** *n* (14c) **:** INCREASE, GROWTH — usu. used in the phrase *on the wax*

[5]**wax** *n* [perh. fr. [3]*wax*] (1854) **:** a fit of temper **:** RAGE

wax bean *n* (1897) **:** a kidney bean with pods that turn creamy yellow to bright yellow when mature enough for use as snap beans

wax·bill \ˈwaks-ˌbil\ *n* (1757) **:** any of numerous Old World oscine birds (family Estrildidae, esp. genus *Estrilda*) having white, pink, or reddish bills of a waxy appearance

waxed paper *n* (1853) **:** paper coated or treated with wax to make it resistant to water and grease and used esp. as a wrapping

wax·en \ˈwak-sən\ *adj* (bef. 12c) **1 :** made of or covered with wax **2 :** resembling wax: as **a :** easily molded **:** PLIABLE **b :** seeming to lack vitality or animation **:** PALLID **c :** lustrously smooth

wax·er \-sər\ *n* (ca. 1875) **1 :** a device for applying wax **2 :** one whose work is applying or polishing with wax

wax light *n* (1599) **:** a wax candle **:** TAPER

wax moth *n* (1766) **:** a dull brownish or ashen pyralid moth (*Galleria mellonella*) with a larva that feeds on the honeycomb wax of bees

wax museum *n* (1953) **:** a place where wax effigies (as of famous historical persons) are exhibited

wax myrtle *n* (1806) **:** any of a genus (*Myrica* of the family Myricaceae, the wax-myrtle family) of trees or shrubs with aromatic foliage; *esp* **:** a shrub or small tree (*M. cerifera*) of the eastern U.S. having small hard berries with a thick coating of bluish-white wax used for candles

wax palm *n* (ca. 1828) **:** any of several palms that yield wax: as **a :** an Andean pinnate-leaved palm (*Ceroxylon alpinum* syn. *C. andicola*) whose stem yields a resinous wax used in candles **b :** CARNAUBA

wax paper *n* (ca. 1844) **:** WAXED PAPER

wax·wing \ˈwaks-ˌwiŋ\ *n* (1817) **:** any of a genus (*Bombycilla*) of American and Eurasian chiefly brown to gray oscine birds (as a cedar waxwing) having a showy crest, red waxy material on the tips of the secondaries, and a yellow band on the tip of the tail

wax·work \-ˌwərk\ *n* (1663) **1 :** an effigy in wax usu. of a person **2** *pl but sing or pl in constr* **:** WAX MUSEUM

waxy \ˈwak-sē\ *adj* **wax·i·er; -est** (1552) **1 :** made of, abounding in, or covered with wax **:** WAXEN ⟨a ~ surface⟩ ⟨~ berries⟩ **2 :** resembling wax: as **a :** readily shaped or molded **b :** marked by smooth or lustrous whiteness ⟨a ~ complexion⟩ — **wax·i·ness** *n*

[1]**way** \ˈwā\ *n* [ME, fr. OE *weg;* akin to OHG *weg* way, OE *wegan* to move, L *vehere* to carry, *via* way] (bef. 12c) **1 a :** a thoroughfare for travel or transportation from place to place **b :** an opening for passage ⟨this door is the only ~ out of the room⟩ **2 :** the course traveled from one

place to another : ROUTE ⟨asked the ~ to the museum⟩ **3 a :** a course (as a series of actions or sequence of events) leading in a direction or toward an objective ⟨led the ~ to eventual open heart operations —*Current Biog.*⟩ **b** (1) **:** a course of action ⟨took the easy ~ out⟩ (2) **:** opportunity, capability, or fact of doing as one pleases ⟨always manages to get her own ~⟩ **c :** a possible decision, action, or outcome : POSSIBILITY ⟨they were rude—no two ~*s* about it⟩ **4 a :** manner or method of doing or happening ⟨admired her ~ of thinking⟩; *also* **:** method of accomplishing : MEANS ⟨that's the ~ to do it⟩ **b :** FEATURE, RESPECT ⟨in no ~ resembles her mother⟩ **c :** a usu. specified degree of participation in an activity or enterprise ⟨active in real estate in a small ~⟩ **5 a :** characteristic, regular, or habitual manner or mode of being, behaving, or happening ⟨knows nothing of the ~*s* of women⟩ **b :** ability to get along well or perform well ⟨she has a ~ with kids⟩ ⟨a ~ with words⟩ **6 :** the length of a course : DISTANCE ⟨has come a long ~ in her studies⟩ ⟨still have a ~ to go⟩ **7 :** movement or progress along a course ⟨worked her ~ up the corporate ladder⟩ **8 a :** DIRECTION ⟨is coming this ~⟩ **b :** PARTICIPANT — usu. used in combination ⟨three-*way* discussion⟩ **9 :** state of affairs : CONDITION, STATE ⟨that's the ~ things are⟩ **10 a** *pl but sometimes sing in constr* **:** an inclined structure upon which a ship is built or supported in launching **b** *pl* **:** the guiding surfaces on the bed of a machine along which a table or carriage moves **11 :** CATEGORY, KIND — usu. used in the phrase *in the way of* ⟨doesn't require much in the ~ of expensive equipment —*Forbes*⟩ **12 :** motion or speed of a ship or boat through the water ***syn*** see METHOD — **all the way :** to the full or entire extent : as far as possible ⟨ran *all the way* home⟩ ⟨seated *all the way* in the back⟩ — **by the way :** by way of interjection or digression : INCIDENTALLY — **by way of 1 :** for the purpose of **2 :** by the route through : VIA — **in a way 1 :** within limits : with reservations **2 :** from one point of view — **in one's way** *also* **in the way 1 :** in a position to be encountered by one : in or along one's course ⟨an opportunity had been put *in my way* —Ellen Glasgow⟩ **2 :** in a position to hinder or obstruct — **on the way** *or* **on one's way :** moving along in one's course : in progress — **out of the way 1 :** WRONG, IMPROPER ⟨didn't know I'd said anything *out of the way*⟩ **2 a :** in or to a secluded place **b :** UNUSUAL, REMARKABLE ⟨there's nothing *out of the way* about the plan⟩ **3 :** DONE, COMPLETED ⟨got his homework *out of the way*⟩ — **the way 1 :** in view of the manner in which ⟨you'd think she was rich, *the way* she spends money⟩ **2 :** LIKE, AS ⟨we have cats *the way* other people have mice —James Thurber⟩

[2]**way** *adj* (1799) **:** of, connected with, or constituting an intermediate point on a route

[3]**way** *adv* (1849) **1 a :** AWAY 7 ⟨is ~ ahead of the class⟩ **b :** by far : MUCH ⟨ate ~ too much⟩ **c :** VERY 2 ⟨~ cool⟩ ⟨~ excited⟩ **2 :** all the way ⟨pull the switch ~ back⟩ — **from way back :** of long standing ⟨friends *from way back*⟩

way·bill \ˈwā-ˌbil\ *n* (1821) **:** a document prepared by the carrier of a shipment of goods that contains details of the shipment, route, and charges

way·far·er \ˈwā-ˌfer-ər\ *n* [ME *weyfarere,* fr. *wey, way* way + *-farere* traveler, fr. *faren* to go — more at FARE] (15c) **:** a traveler esp. on foot — **way·far·ing** \-ˌfer-iŋ\ *adj*

wayfaring tree *n* (1597) **:** a Eurasian viburnum (*Viburnum lantana*) that has large ovate leaves and dense cymes of small white flowers and is common along waysides

way·go·ing \ˈwā-ˌgō-ən, -iŋ\ *n* (1633) *chiefly Scot* **:** the act of leaving : DEPARTURE

Way·land \ˈwā-lən(d)\ *n* [OE *Wēland*] (1849) **:** a heroic smith of Germanic legend

way·lay \ˈwā-ˌlā\ *vt* **-laid** \-ˌlād\; **-lay·ing** (1513) **:** to lie in wait for or attack from ambush

way·less \-ləs\ *adj* (12c) **:** having no road or path

Way of the Cross (1868) **:** STATIONS OF THE CROSS

way–out \ˈwā-ˈau̇t\ *adj* (1954) **:** FAR-OUT

way·point \ˈwā-ˌpȯint\ *n* (1880) **:** an intermediate point on a route or line of travel

ways \ˈwāz\ *n pl but sing in constr* [ME *wayes,* fr. gen. of [1]*way*] (1580) **:** WAY 6 ⟨a long ~ from home⟩

-ways *adv suffix* [ME, fr. *ways,* gen. of *way*] **:** in (such) a way, course, direction, or manner ⟨side*ways*⟩

ways and means *n pl* (15c) **1 :** methods and resources for accomplishing something and esp. for defraying expenses **2** *often cap W&M* **a :** methods and resources for raising the necessary revenues for the expenses of a nation or state **b :** a legislative committee concerned with this function

way·side \ˈwā-ˌsīd\ *n* (15c) **:** the side of or land adjacent to a road or path — **wayside** *adj* — **by the wayside :** out of consideration : into a condition of neglect or disuse — usu. used with *fall*

way station *n* (1850) **1 :** a station set between principal stations on a line of travel (as a railroad) **2 :** an intermediate stopping place

way·ward \ˈwā-wərd\ *adj* [ME, short for *awayward* turned away, fr. *away,* adv. + *-ward*] (14c) **1 :** following one's own capricious, wanton, or depraved inclinations : UNGOVERNABLE ⟨a ~ child⟩ **2 :** following no clear principle or law : UNPREDICTABLE **3 :** opposite to what is desired or expected : UNTOWARD ⟨~ fate⟩ ***syn*** see CONTRARY — **way·ward·ly** *adv* — **way·ward·ness** *n*

way·worn \-ˌwȯrn\ *adj* (1788) **:** wearied by traveling

wa·zoo \(ˌ)wä-ˈzü\ *n* [origin unknown] (1961) *slang* **:** ANUS — **up the wazoo** *also* **out the wazoo :** in excess ⟨we've got lawyers *up the wazoo* —Steven Bochco⟩

Wb *abbr* weber

WB *abbr* **1** waybill **2** westbound **3** wheelbase

WBC *abbr* white blood cell

WBF *abbr* wood-burning fireplace

WC *abbr* water closet

WCTU *abbr* Women's Christian Temperance Union

wd *abbr* **1** wood **2** word **3** would

we \ˈwē\ *pron, pl in constr* [ME, fr. OE *wē;* akin to OHG *wir* we, Skt *vayam*] (bef. 12c) **1 :** I and the rest of a group that includes me : you and I : you and I and another or others : I and another or others not including you — used as pronoun of the first person plural; compare I, OUR, OURS, US **2 :** [1]I — used by sovereigns; used by writers to keep an impersonal character

We *or* **Wed** *abbr* Wednesday

weak \ˈwēk\ *adj* [ME *weike,* fr. ON *veikr;* akin to OE *wīcan* to yield, Gk *eikein* to give way, Skt *vijate* he speeds, flees] (14c) **1 :** lacking strength: as **a :** deficient in physical vigor : FEEBLE, DEBILITATED **b :** not able to sustain or exert much weight, pressure, or strain **c :** not able to resist external force or withstand attack **d :** easily upset or nauseated ⟨a ~ stomach⟩ **2 a :** mentally or intellectually deficient **b :** not firmly decided : VACILLATING **c :** resulting from or indicating lack of judgment or discernment **d :** not able to withstand temptation or persuasion ⟨the spirit is willing but the flesh is ~⟩ **3 :** not factually grounded or logically presented ⟨a ~ argument⟩ **4 a :** not able to function properly ⟨~ eyes⟩ **b** (1) **:** lacking skill or proficiency ⟨tutoring for ~*er* students⟩ (2) **:** indicative of a lack of skill or aptitude ⟨history was my ~*est* subject⟩ **c :** wanting in vigor of expression or effect ⟨a ~ translation of the poem⟩ **5 a :** deficient in the usual or required ingredients : DILUTE ⟨~ coffee⟩ **b :** lacking normal intensity or potency ⟨a ~ radio signal⟩ ⟨a ~ strain of virus⟩ **6 a :** not having or exerting authority or political power ⟨~ government⟩ **b :** INEFFECTIVE, IMPOTENT **7 :** of, relating to, or constituting a verb or verb conjugation that in English forms the past tense and past participle by adding the suffix *-ed* or *-d* or *-t* **8 a :** bearing the minimal degree of stress occurring in the language ⟨a ~ syllable⟩ **b :** having little or no stress and obscured vowel sound ⟨*'d* in *he'd* is the ~ form of *would*⟩ **9 :** tending toward a lower price or value ⟨a ~ market⟩ ⟨a ~ dollar⟩ **10 :** ionizing only slightly in solution ⟨~ acids and bases⟩ — **weak·ly** *adv*

syn WEAK, FEEBLE, FRAIL, FRAGILE, INFIRM, DECREPIT mean not strong enough to endure strain, pressure, or strenuous effort. WEAK applies to deficiency or inferiority in strength or power of any sort ⟨felt *weak* after the surgery⟩. FEEBLE suggests extreme weakness inviting pity or contempt ⟨a *feeble* attempt to walk⟩. FRAIL implies delicacy and slightness of constitution or structure ⟨a *frail* teenager unable to enjoy sports⟩. FRAGILE suggests frailty and brittleness unable to resist rough usage ⟨a reclusive poet too *fragile* for the rigors of this world⟩. INFIRM suggests instability, unsoundness, and insecurity due to old age or crippling illness ⟨*infirm* residents requiring constant care⟩. DECREPIT implies being worn-out or broken-down from long use or old age ⟨the dowager's *decrepit* retainers⟩.

weak anthropic principle *n* (1985) **:** ANTHROPIC PRINCIPLE a

weak·en \ˈwē-kən\ *vb* **weak·ened; weak·en·ing** \ˈwēk-niŋ, ˈwē-kə-\ *vt* (1530) **1 :** to make weak : lessen the strength of **2 :** to reduce in intensity or effectiveness ~ *vi* **:** to become weak — **weak·en·er** \ˈwēk-nər, ˈwē-kə-\ *n*

syn WEAKEN, ENFEEBLE, DEBILITATE, UNDERMINE, SAP, CRIPPLE, DISABLE mean to lose or cause to lose strength or vigor. WEAKEN may imply loss of physical strength, health, soundness, or stability or of quality, intensity, or effective power ⟨a disease that *weakens* the body's defenses⟩. ENFEEBLE implies an obvious and pitiable condition of weakness and helplessness ⟨*enfeebled* by starvation⟩. DEBILITATE suggests a less marked or more temporary impairment of strength or vitality ⟨the *debilitating* effects of surgery⟩. UNDERMINE and SAP suggest a weakening by something working surreptitiously and insidiously ⟨a poor diet *undermines* your health⟩ ⟨drugs had *sapped* his ability to think⟩. CRIPPLE implies causing a serious loss of functioning power through damaging or removing an essential part or element ⟨*crippled* by arthritis⟩. DISABLE suggests a usu. sudden crippling or enfeebling ⟨*disabled* soldiers received an immediate discharge⟩.

weak·fish \ˈwēk-ˌfish\ *n* [obs. D *weekvis,* fr. D *week* soft + *vis* fish] (1791) **1 :** a common marine bony fish (*Cynoscion regalis* of the family Sciaenidae) of the eastern coast of the U.S. that is an important sport and food fish — called also *sea trout* **2 :** any of several fishes congeneric with the weakfish

weak force *n* (1968) **:** a fundamental physical force that governs interactions between hadrons and leptons (as in the emission and absorption of neutrinos) and is responsible for particle decay processes (as beta decay) in radioactivity, that is 10^{-5} times the strength of the strong force, and that acts over distances smaller than those between nucleons in an atomic nucleus — called also *weak interaction, weak nuclear force*; compare ELECTROMAGNETISM 2a, GRAVITY 3a(2), STRONG FORCE

weak·heart·ed \-ˈhär-təd\ *adj* (1549) **:** lacking courage : FAINTHEARTED

weak·ish \ˈwē-kish\ *adj* (1594) **:** somewhat weak ⟨~ tea⟩

weak–kneed \ˈwēk-ˈnēd\ *adj* (1863) **:** lacking willpower or resolution

weak·ling \ˈwē-kliŋ\ *n* (1548) **:** one that is weak in body, character, or mind — **weakling** *adj*

weak·ly \ˈwē-klē\ *adj* (1577) **:** FEEBLE, WEAK — **weak·li·ness** *n*

weak–mind·ed \ˈwēk-ˈmīn-dəd\ *adj* (1592) **:** having or indicating a weak mind: **a :** lacking in judgment or good sense : FOOLISH **b :** FEEBLEMINDED — **weak–mind·ed·ness** *n*

weak·ness \-nəs\ *n* (14c) **1 :** the quality or state of being weak; *also* **:** an instance or period of being weak ⟨backed down in a moment of ~⟩ **2 :** FAULT, DEFECT **3 a :** a special desire or fondness ⟨has a ~ for sweets⟩ **b :** an object of special desire or fondness ⟨pizza is my ~⟩

weak side *n* (1940) **1 :** the side of a football formation having the smaller number of players; *specif* **:** the side of a formation away from the tight end **2 :** the side of a court or field (as in basketball or soccer) away from the ball — **weak·side** \ˈwēk-ˌsīd\ *adj*

weak sister *n* (1857) **:** a member of a group who needs aid; *also* **:** something weak and ineffective as compared with others in a group

[1]**weal** \ˈwēl\ *n* [ME *wele,* fr. OE *wela;* akin to OE *wel* well] (bef. 12c) **1 :** a sound, healthy, or prosperous state : WELL-BEING **2** *obs* **:** BODY POLITIC, COMMONWEAL

[2]**weal** *n* [alter. of *wale*] (ca. 1798) **:** WELT

weald \ˈwēld\ *n* [the *Weald,* England, fr. ME *weeld,* fr. OE *weald* forest — more at WOLD] (bef. 12c) **1 :** a heavily wooded area : FOREST ⟨the *Weald* of Kent⟩ **2 :** a wild or uncultivated usu. upland region

wealth \ˈwelth *also* ˈweltth\ *n* [ME *welthe,* fr. *wele* weal] (13c) **1** *obs* **:** WEAL, WELFARE **2 :** abundance of valuable material possessions or resources **3 :** abundant supply : PROFUSION **4 a :** all property that has a money value or an exchangeable value **b :** all material objects that have economic utility; *esp* **:** the stock of useful goods having economic value in existence at any one time ⟨national ~⟩

wealthy \ˈwel-thē *also* ˈwelt-thē\ *adj* **wealth·i·er; -est** (15c) **1 :** having wealth : very affluent **2 :** characterized by abundance : AMPLE ***syn*** see RICH — **wealth·i·ly** \-thə-lē\ *adv* — **wealth·i·ness** \-thē-nəs\ *n*

wean \ˈwēn\ *vt* [ME *wenen,* fr. OE *wenian* to accustom, wean; akin to OE *wunian* to be used to — more at WONT] (bef. 12c) **1 :** to accustom (as a young child or animal) to take food otherwise than by nursing **2 :** to detach from a source of dependence ⟨being ~*ed* off the medication⟩ ⟨~ the bears from human food —*Sports Illus.*⟩; *also* **:** to free from a usu. unwholesome habit or interest ⟨~ him off his excessive drinking⟩ ⟨settling his soldiers on the land . . . , ~*ing* them from habits of violence —Geoffrey Carnall⟩ **3 :** to accustom to something from an early age — used in the passive esp. with *on* ⟨students ~*ed* on the Internet for research⟩ ⟨I was ~*ed* on greasepaint —Helen Hayes⟩ ⟨the principles upon which he had been ~*ed* —J. A. Michener⟩

wean·er \ˈwē-nər\ *n* (1579) **1 :** one that weans **2 :** a young animal recently weaned from its mother

wean·ling \ˈwēn-liŋ\ *n* (ca. 1533) **:** a child or animal newly weaned — **weanling** *adj*

[1]**weap·on** \ˈwe-pən\ *n* [ME *wepen,* fr. OE *wǣpen;* akin to OHG *wāffan* weapon, ON *vāpn*] (bef. 12c) **1 :** something (as a club, knife, or gun) used to injure, defeat, or destroy **2 :** a means of contending against another

[2]**weapon** *vt* (bef. 12c) **:** ARM

weap·on·ize \ˈwe-pə-ˌnīz\ *vt* **-ized; -iz·ing** (1957) **:** to adapt for use as a weapon of war — **weap·on·i·za·tion** \ˌwe-pə-nə-ˈzā-shən\ *n*

weap·on·less \-ləs\ *adj* (bef. 12c) **:** lacking weapons **:** UNARMED

weap·on·ry \-rē\ *n* (1844) **1 :** WEAPONS **2 :** the science of designing and making weapons

[1]**wear** \ˈwer\ *vb* **wore** \ˈwȯr\; **worn** \ˈwȯrn\; **wear·ing** [ME *weren,* fr. OE *werian;* akin to ON *verja* to clothe, invest, spend, L *vestis* clothing, garment, Gk *hennynai* to clothe] *vt* (bef. 12c) **1 :** to bear or have on the person ⟨*wore* a coat⟩ **2 a :** to use habitually for clothing, adornment, or assistance ⟨~*s* a size 10⟩ ⟨~ glasses⟩ **b :** to carry on the person ⟨~ a sword⟩ **3 a :** to hold the rank or dignity or position signified by (an ornament) ⟨~ the royal crown⟩ **b :** EXHIBIT, PRESENT ⟨*wore* a happy smile⟩ ⟨commend the book for ~*ing* its research so lightly —Brad Leithauser⟩ **c :** to show or fly (a flag or colors) on a ship **4 a :** to cause to deteriorate by use **b :** to impair or diminish by use or attrition **:** consume or waste gradually ⟨letters on the stone *worn* away by weathering⟩ **5 :** to produce gradually by friction or attrition ⟨~ a hole in the rug⟩ **6 :** to exhaust or lessen the strength of **:** WEARY, FATIGUE **7 :** to cause (a ship) to go about with the stern presented to the wind **8** *Brit* **:** to accept or tolerate without complaint **:** put up with — usu. used in negative constructions ⟨your mates wouldn't ~ it —Colin MacInnes⟩ **9 :** TAKE ON 3a ~ *vi* **1 a :** to endure use **:** last under use or the passage of time ⟨material that will ~ for years⟩ **b :** to retain quality or vitality ⟨the classics ~ well⟩ **2 a :** to diminish or decay through use ⟨the heels of his shoes began to ~⟩ **b :** to diminish or fail with the passage of time ⟨the effect of the drug *wore* off⟩ ⟨the day *wore* on⟩ **c :** to grow or become by attrition or use ⟨the blade *wore* dull⟩ **3** *of a ship* **:** to change to an opposite tack by turning the stern to the wind — compare TACK — **wear·er** *n* — **wear on :** IRRITATE, FRAY ⟨the constant beeping *wore* on my nerves⟩ — **wear the trousers** *or* **wear the pants :** to have the controlling authority in a household — **wear thin 1 :** to become weak or ready to give way ⟨my patience was *wearing thin*⟩ **2 :** to become trite, unconvincing, or out-of-date ⟨an argument that quickly *wore thin*⟩

[2]**wear** *n* (15c) **1 :** the act of wearing **:** the state of being worn **:** USE ⟨clothes for everyday ~⟩ **2 a :** clothing or an article of clothing usu. of a particular kind; *esp* **:** clothing worn for a special occasion or popular during a specific period **b :** FASHION, VOGUE **3 :** wearing quality **:** durability under use **4 :** the result of wearing or use **:** diminution or impairment due to use ⟨*wear*-resistant surface⟩

[1]**wear·able** \ˈwer-ə-bəl\ *adj* (1590) **:** capable of being worn **:** suitable to be worn — **wear·abil·i·ty** \ˌwer-ə-ˈbi-lə-tē\ *n*

[2]**wearable** *n* (1711) **:** GARMENT — usu. used in pl.

wear and tear *n* (1666) **:** the loss, injury, or stress to which something is subjected by or in the course of use; *esp* **:** normal depreciation

wear down *vt* (1774) **:** to weary and overcome by persistent resistance or pressure

wea·ri·ful \ˈwir-ē-fəl\ *adj* (15c) **1 :** causing weariness; *esp* **:** TEDIOUS **2 :** full of weariness **:** WEARIED — **wea·ri·ful·ly** \-fə-lē\ *adv* — **wea·ri·ful·ness** *n*

wea·ri·less \ˈwir-ē-ləs\ *adj* (15c) **:** TIRELESS — **wea·ri·less·ly** *adv*

[1]**wear·ing** \ˈwer-iŋ\ *adj* (15c) **:** intended for wear ⟨~ apparel⟩

[2]**wearing** *adj* (1811) **:** subjecting to or inflicting wear; *esp* **:** causing fatigue ⟨a ~ journey⟩ — **wear·ing·ly** \-iŋ-lē\ *adv*

wea·ri·some \ˈwir-ē-səm\ *adj* (15c) **:** causing weariness **:** TIRESOME — **wea·ri·some·ly** *adv* — **wea·ri·some·ness** *n*

wear out *vt* (14c) **1 :** TIRE, EXHAUST **2 :** to make useless esp. by long or hard usage **3 :** ERASE, EFFACE **4 :** to endure through **:** OUTLAST ⟨*wear out* a storm⟩ **5 :** to consume (as time) tediously ⟨*wear out* idle days⟩ ~ *vi* **:** to become useless from long or excessive wear or use

[1]**wea·ry** \ˈwir-ē\ *adj* **wea·ri·er; -est** [ME *wery,* fr. OE *wērig;* akin to OHG *wuorag* intoxicated and perh. to Gk *aōros* sleep] (bef. 12c) **1 :** exhausted in strength, endurance, vigor, or freshness **2 :** expressing or characteristic of weariness ⟨a ~ sign⟩ **3 :** having one's patience, tolerance, or pleasure exhausted — used with *of* **4 :** WEARISOME — **wea·ri·ly** \ˈwir-ə-lē\ *adv* — **wea·ri·ness** \ˈwir-ē-nəs\ *n*

[2]**weary** *vb* **wea·ried; wea·ry·ing** *vi* (bef. 12c) **:** to become weary ~ *vt* **:** to make weary ***syn*** see TIRE

wea·sand \ˈwē-zᵊnd, ˈwi-zᵊn(d)\ *n* [ME *wesand,* fr. OE **wǣsend* gullet; akin to OE *wāsend* gullet, OHG *weisunt* windpipe] (bef. 12c) **:** THROAT, GULLET; *also* **:** TRACHEA

[1]**wea·sel** \ˈwē-zəl\ *n, pl* **weasels** [ME *wesele,* fr. OE *weosule;* akin to OHG *wisula* weasel] (bef. 12c) **1** *or pl* **weasel :** any of various small slender active carnivorous mammals (genus *Mustela* of the family Mustelidae, the weasel family) that are able to prey on animals (as rabbits) larger than themselves, are mostly brown with white or yellowish underparts, and in northern forms turn white in winter — compare ERMINE 1a **2 :** a light self-propelled tracked vehicle built either for traveling over snow, ice, or sand or as an amphibious vehicle **3 :** a sneaky, untrustworthy, or insincere person

weasel 1

[2]**weasel** *vb* **wea·seled; wea·sel·ing** \ˈwēz-liŋ, ˈwē-zə-\ [*weasel word*] *vi* (1900) **1 :** to use weasel words **:** EQUIVOCATE **2 :** to escape from or evade a situation or obligation — often used with *out* ~ *vt* **:** to manipulate shiftily

wea·sel·ly *also* **wea·sely** \ˈwēz-lē, ˈwē-zə-\ *adj* (1838) **:** resembling or suggestive of a weasel

weasel word *n* [fr. the weasel's reputed habit of sucking the contents out of an egg while leaving the shell superficially intact] (1900) **:** a word used in order to evade or retreat from a direct or forthright statement or position

[1]**weath·er** \ˈwe-thər\ *n* [ME *weder,* fr. OE; akin to OHG *wetar* weather, OCS *vetrŭ* wind] (bef. 12c) **1 :** the state of the atmosphere with respect to heat or cold, wetness or dryness, calm or storm, clearness or cloudiness **2 :** state or vicissitude of life or fortune **3 :** disagreeable atmospheric conditions: as **a :** RAIN, STORM **b :** cold air with dampness **4 :** WEATHERING — **to weather :** in the direction from which the wind is blowing — **under the weather 1 :** ILL **2 :** DRUNK 1a

[2]**weather** *vb* **weath·ered; weath·er·ing** \ˈweth-riŋ, ˈwe-thə-\ *vt* (15c) **1 :** to expose to the open air **:** subject to the action of the elements **2 :** to bear up against and come safely through ⟨~ a storm⟩ ⟨~ a crisis⟩ ~ *vi* **:** to undergo or endure the action of the elements

[3]**weather** *adj* (1582) **:** of or relating to the side facing the wind — compare LEE

weath·er·abil·i·ty \ˌweth-rə-ˈbi-lə-tē, ˌwe-thə-\ *n* (1947) **:** capability of withstanding the weathering process ⟨~ of a plastic⟩

weath·er–beat·en \ˈwe-thər-ˌbē-tᵊn\ *adj* (1530) **1 :** toughened, tanned, or bronzed by the weather ⟨a ~ face⟩ **2 :** worn or damaged by exposure to weather

weath·er·board \-ˌbȯrd\ *n* (ca. 1540) **1 :** CLAPBOARD, SIDING **2 :** the weather side of a ship — **weath·er·board·ed** *adj*

weath·er·board·ing \-ˌbȯr-diŋ\ *n* (1632) **:** CLAPBOARDS, SIDING

weath·er–bound \-ˌbau̇nd\ *adj* (1590) **:** kept in port or at anchor or from travel or sport by bad weather

weather bureau *n* (1871) **:** a bureau engaged in the collection of weather reports as a basis for weather predictions, storm warnings, and the compiling of statistical records

weath·er·cast \-ˌkast\ *n* [[1]*weather* + [2]fore*cast*] (1866) **:** a weather forecast esp. on radio or television

weath·er·cast·er \-ˌkas-tər\ *n* (1607) **:** a weather forecaster esp. on radio or television

weath·er·cock \-ˌkäk\ *n* (13c) **1 :** a vane often in the figure of a cock mounted so as to turn freely with the wind and show its direction **2 :** a person or thing that changes readily or often

weather deck *n* (1850) **:** a deck having no overhead protection from the weather

weath·ered \ˈwe-thərd\ *adj* (1789) **1 :** seasoned by exposure to the weather **2 :** altered in color, texture, composition, or form by such exposure or by artificial means producing a similar effect ⟨~ oak⟩

weather eye *n* (1829) **1 :** an eye quick to observe coming changes in the weather **2 :** constant and shrewd watchfulness and alertness

weath·er·glass \ˈwe-thər-ˌglas\ *n* (1695) **:** a simple instrument for showing changes in atmospheric pressure by the changing level of liquid in a spout connected with a closed reservoir; *broadly* **:** BAROMETER

weathering *n* (1548) **:** the action of the weather conditions in altering the color, texture, composition, or form of exposed objects; *specif* **:** the physical disintegration and chemical decomposition of earth materials at or near the earth's surface

weath·er·ize \ˈwe-thə-ˌrīz\ *vt* **-ized; -iz·ing** (1943) **:** to make (as a house) better protected against winter weather (as by adding insulation) — **weath·er·i·za·tion** \ˌweth-rə-ˈzā-shən, ˌwe-thə-\ *n*

weath·er·ly \ˈwe-thər-lē\ *adj* (1729) **:** able to sail close to the wind with little leeway

weath·er·man \-ˌman\ *n* (1859) **:** one who reports and forecasts the weather **:** METEOROLOGIST

weather map *n* (1871) **:** a map or chart showing the principal meteorological elements at a given hour and over an extended region

weath·er·per·son \ˈwe-thər-ˌpər-sᵊn\ *n* (1974) **:** a person who reports and forecasts the weather **:** METEOROLOGIST

weath·er·proof \ˈwe-thər-ˌprüf\ *adj* (ca. 1620) **:** able to withstand exposure to weather without damage or loss of function — **weatherproof** *vt* — **weath·er·proof·ness** *n*

weather ship *n* (1946) **:** a ship that makes observations for use by meteorologists

weather station *n* (ca. 1895) **:** a station for taking, recording, and reporting meteorological observations

weather strip *n* (1847) **:** a strip of material to cover the joint of a door or window and the sill, casing, or threshold so as to exclude rain, snow, and cold air — called also *weather stripping* — **weath·er–strip** *vt*

weather vane *n* (ca. 1721) **:** VANE 1a

weath·er–wise \ˈwe-thər-ˌwīz\ *adj* (14c) **1 :** skillful in forecasting changes in the weather **2 :** skillful in forecasting changes in opinion or feeling ⟨a ~ politician⟩

weath·er·worn \-ˌwȯrn\ *adj* (1609) **:** worn by exposure to the weather

[1]**weave** \ˈwēv\ *vb* **wove** \ˈwōv\ *or* **weaved; wo·ven** \ˈwō-vən\ *or* **weaved; weav·ing** [ME *weven,* fr. OE *wefan;* akin to OHG *weban* to weave, Gk *hyphainein* to weave, *hyphos* web] *vt* (bef. 12c) **1 a :** to form (cloth) by interlacing strands (as of yarn); *specif* **:** to make (cloth) on a loom by interlacing warp and filling threads **b :** to interlace (as threads) into cloth **c :** to make (as a basket) by intertwining **2 :** SPIN 2 — used of spiders and insects **3 :** to interlace esp. to form a texture, fabric, or design **4 a :** to produce by elaborately combining elements **:** CONTRIVE **b :** to unite in a coherent whole **c :** to introduce as an appropriate element **:** work in — usu. used with *in* or *into* **5 :** to direct

(as the body) in a winding or zigzag course esp. to avoid obstacles ∼ *vi* **1 :** to work at weaving : make cloth **2 :** to move in a devious, winding, or zigzag course esp. to avoid obstacles

[2]**weave** *n* (1581) **1 :** something woven; *esp* **:** woven cloth **2 :** any of the patterns or methods for interlacing the threads of woven fabrics

[3]**weave** *vi* **weaved; weav·ing** [ME *weven* to move to and fro, wave; akin to ON *veifa* to be in movement — more at WIPE] (1596) **:** to move waveringly from side to side : SWAY

weav·er \ˈwē-vər\ *n* (14c) **1 :** one that weaves esp. as an occupation **2 :** any of numerous Old World passerine birds (family Ploceidae) that resemble finches and typically construct elaborate nests of interlaced vegetation

weaver ant *n* (1913) **:** any of various ants (esp. genus *Oecophylla*) that build nests from leaves bound together with silk secreted by larvae

weav·er·bird \-ˌbərd\ *n* (1826) **:** WEAVER 2

weaver's knot *n* (1532) **:** SHEET BEND — called also *weaver's hitch*

[1]**web** \ˈweb\ *n* [ME, fr. OE; akin to ON *vefr* web, OE *wefan* to weave] (bef. 12c) **1 :** a fabric on a loom or in process of being removed from a loom **2 a :** COBWEB, SPIDERWEB **b :** a network of silken thread spun esp. by the larvae of various insects (as a tent caterpillar) and usu. serving as a nest or shelter **3 :** a tissue or membrane of an animal or plant; *esp* **:** that uniting fingers or toes either at their bases (as in humans) or for a greater part of their length (as in many waterbirds) **4 a :** a thin metal sheet, plate, or strip **b :** the plate connecting the upper and lower flanges of a girder or rail **c :** the arm of a crank **5 :** something resembling a web: **a :** SNARE, ENTANGLEMENT ⟨a ∼ of intrigue⟩ ⟨ensnarled in a ∼ of folly —D. A. Stockman⟩ **b :** an intricate pattern or structure suggestive of something woven : NETWORK **6 :** the series of barbs on each side of the shaft of a feather : VANE **7 a :** a continuous sheet of paper manufactured or undergoing manufacture on a paper machine **b :** a roll of paper for use in a rotary printing press **8 :** the part of a ribbed vault between the ribs **9** *cap* **:** WORLD WIDE WEB — **webbed** \ˈwebd\ *adj* — **web·like** \ˈweb-ˌlīk\ *adj*

[2]**web** *vb* **webbed; web·bing** *vi* (1604) **:** to construct or form a web ∼ *vt* **1 :** to cover with a web or network **2 :** ENSNARE, ENTANGLE **3 :** to provide with a web

web belt *n* (1915) **:** a belt made of webbing and often worn as part of a uniform

webbing *n* (1796) **1 :** a strong narrow closely woven fabric designed for bearing weight and used esp. for straps or upholstery **2 :** TRAP 3c

web·by \ˈwe-bē\ *adj* (1661) **:** of, relating to, or consisting of a web

web·cam \ˈweb-ˌkam\ *n, often cap* (1995) **:** a camera used in transmitting live images over the World Wide Web

web·cast \-ˌkast\ *n, often cap* [World Wide *Web* + broad*cast*] (1995) **:** a transmission of sound and images (as of an event) via the World Wide Web — **webcast** *vb, often cap* — **web·cast·er** *n, often cap*

we·ber \ˈwe-bər, ˈvā-bər\ *n* [Wilhelm E. *Weber* †1891 Ger. physicist] (1891) **:** the practical meter-kilogram-second unit of magnetic flux equal to that flux which in linking a circuit of one turn produces in it an electromotive force of one volt as the flux is reduced to zero at a uniform rate in one second : 10^8 maxwells

We·be·ri·an \we-ˈbir-ē-ən, vā-, wē-\ *adj* (1943) **:** of or relating to the socioeconomic theories of Max Weber

web·fed \ˈweb-ˌfed\ *adj* (1947) **:** of, relating to, or printed by a web press

web·foot *n* (1765) **1** \ˈweb-ˈfu̇t\ **:** a foot having webbed toes **2** \-ˌfu̇t\ **:** an animal having web feet — **web–foot·ed** \-ˈfu̇-təd\ *adj*

web·i·nar \ˈwe-bə-ˌnär\ *n, often cap* [*web* + semi*nar*] (1998) **:** a live online educational presentation during which participating viewers can submit questions and comments

web·i·sode \ˈwe-bə-ˌsōd\ *n* [blend of *Web* and *episode*] (1996) **:** an episode esp. of a TV show that may or may not have been telecast but can be viewed at a Web site

Web·log \ˈweb-ˌlȯg, -ˌläg\ *n* (1997) **:** BLOG

web·mas·ter \ˈweb-ˌmas-tər\ *n, often cap* (1994) **:** a person responsible for the creation or maintenance of a Web site esp. for a company or organization

web member *n* (ca. 1890) **:** one of the several members joining the top and bottom chords of a truss or lattice girder

web–off·set \ˈweb-ˈȯf-ˌset\ *n, often attrib* (1959) **:** offset printing by web press

web press *n* (1875) **:** a press that prints a continuous roll of paper

Web site *or* **web·site** \ˈweb-ˌsīt\ *n* (1992) **:** a group of World Wide Web pages usu. containing hyperlinks to each other and made available online by an individual, company, educational institution, government, or organization

web spinner *n* (ca. 1907) **:** an insect that spins a web; *esp* **:** any of an order (Embioptera syn. Embiidina) of small slender gregarious insects with biting mouthparts that live in silken tunnels which they spin

web·ster \ˈweb-stər\ *n* [ME, fr. OE *webbestre* female weaver, fr. *webbian* to weave; akin to OE *wefan* to weave] (12c) *archaic* **:** WEAVER 1

web·work \ˈweb-ˌwərk\ *n* (1790) **:** WEB 5b ⟨a vast ∼ of land holdings⟩

web·worm \-ˌwərm\ *n* (1797) **:** any of various caterpillars that are more or less gregarious and spin large webs

wed \ˈwed\ *vb* **wed·ded** *also* **wed; wed·ding** [ME *wedden,* fr. OE *weddian;* akin to MHG *wetten* to pledge, OE *wedd* pledge, OHG *wetti,* Goth *wadi,* L *vad-, vas* bail, security] *vt* (bef. 12c) **1 :** to take for wife or husband by a formal ceremony : MARRY **2 :** to join in marriage **3 :** to unite as if by marriage: as **a :** to place in close or intimate association ⟨films that made me conscious of the power of *wedding* image to music —Gerald Early⟩ **b :** to link by commitment or custom ⟨was ∼ to the old ways⟩ ∼ *vi* **:** to enter into matrimony — **wed·der** *n*

we'd \ˈwēd\ (1603) **:** we had : we would : we should

Wed·dell seal \wi-ˈdel-, ˈwe-dᵊl-\ *n* [James *Weddell* †1834 Eng. navigator] (1914) **:** a vocal Antarctic hair seal (*Leptonychotes weddelli*) noted for its deep dives in search of food

wed·ding \ˈwe-diŋ\ *n, often attrib* (bef. 12c) **1 :** a marriage ceremony usu. with its accompanying festivities : NUPTIALS **2 :** an act, process, or instance of joining in close association **3 :** a wedding anniversary or its celebration — usu. used in combination ⟨a golden ∼⟩

wedding cake *n* (1648) **1 :** a usu. elaborately decorated and tiered cake made for the celebration of a wedding **2 :** something (as a large building) resembling a wedding cake esp. in elaborate ornamentation

wedding march *n* (1850) **:** a march of slow tempo and stately character that is composed or played to accompany the bridal procession

wedding ring *n* (14c) **:** a ring of metal (as gold) given by the groom to the bride during the wedding service; *also* **:** a similar ring given by the bride to the groom in a double-ring service

we·del \ˈvā-dᵊl\ *vi* [G *Wedeln*] (ca. 1963) **:** to ski by means of wedeln

we·deln \ˈvā-dᵊln\ *n* [G, fr. *wedeln,* lit., to fan, wag the tail, fr. *Wedel* fan, tail, fr. OHG *wadal;* akin to ON *vēli* bird's tail] (ca. 1957) **:** a style of skiing in which a skier rhythmically swings the rear of the skis from side to side while following the fall line

[1]**wedge** \ˈwej\ *n* [ME *wegge,* fr. OE *wecg;* akin to OHG *wecki* wedge, Lith *vagis*] (bef. 12c) **1 :** a piece of a substance (as wood or iron) that tapers to a thin edge and is used for splitting wood and rocks, raising heavy bodies, or for tightening by being driven into something **2 a :** something (as a policy) causing a breach or separation **b :** something used to initiate an action or development **3 :** something wedge-shaped: as **a :** an array of troops or tanks in the form of a wedge **b :** the wedge-shaped stroke in cuneiform characters **c :** a shoe having a heel extending from the back of the shoe to the front of the shank and a tread formed by an extension of the sole **d :** an iron golf club with a broad low-angled face for maximum loft **4 :** a golf shot made with a wedge — called also *wedge shot*

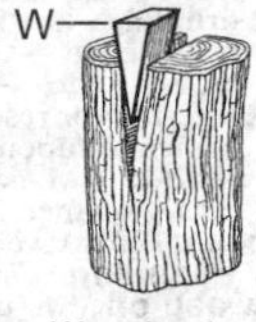

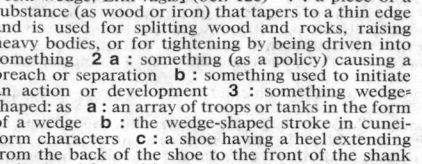

W wedge 1

[2]**wedge** *vb* **wedged; wedg·ing** *vt* (15c) **1 :** to fasten or tighten by driving in a wedge **2 a :** to force or press (something) into a narrow space : CRAM **b :** to force (one's way) into or through **3 :** to separate or force apart with or as if with a wedge ∼ *vi* **:** to become wedged

wedged \ˈwejd, ˈwe-jəd\ *adj* (1552) **:** shaped like a wedge

wedge issue *n* (1986) **:** a political issue that divides a candidate's supporters or the members of a party

wedg·ie \ˈwe-jē\ *n* (1939) **1 :** a shoe having a wedge-shaped piece serving as the heel and joining the half sole to form a continuous flat undersurface **2 :** the condition of having one's clothing wedged between the buttocks usu. from having one's pants or underpants yanked up from behind as a prank — often used with *get* or *give*

Wedg·wood \ˈwej-ˌwu̇d\ *trademark* — used for ceramic wares

wedgy \ˈwe-jē\ *adj* (1799) **:** resembling a wedge in shape

wed·lock \ˈwed-ˌläk\ *n* [ME *wedlok,* fr. OE *wedlāc* marriage bond, fr. *wedd* pledge + *-lāc,* suffix denoting activity] (13c) **:** the state of being married : MARRIAGE, MATRIMONY — **out of wedlock :** with the natural parents not legally married to each other

Wednes·day \ˈwenz-(ˌ)dā, -dē; *Brit also* ˈwe-dᵊnz-\ *n* [ME, fr. OE *wōdnesdæg* (akin to ON *ōthinsdagr* Wednesday); akin to OE *Wōden* Odin and *dæg* day] (bef. 12c) **:** the fourth day of the week — **Wednesdays** \-(ˌ)dāz, -dēz\ *adv*

wee \ˈwē\ *adj* [ME *we,* fr. *we,* n., little bit, fr. OE *wǣge* weight; akin to OE *wegan* to move, weigh — more at WAY] (15c) **1 :** very small : DIMINUTIVE **2 :** very early ⟨∼ hours of the morning⟩

[1]**weed** \ˈwēd\ *n* [ME, fr. OE *wēod* weed, herb; akin to OS *wiod* weed] (bef. 12c) **1 a (1) :** a plant that is not valued where it is growing and is usu. of vigorous growth; *esp* **:** one that tends to overgrow or choke out more desirable plants **(2) :** a weedy growth of plants **b :** an aquatic plant; *esp* **:** SEAWEED **c (1) :** tobacco products **(2) :** MARIJUANA **2 a :** an obnoxious growth, thing, or person **b :** something like a weed in detrimental quality; *esp* **:** an animal unfit to breed from

[2]**weed** *vi* (bef. 12c) **:** to remove weeds or something harmful ∼ *vt* **1 a :** to clear of weeds ⟨∼ a garden⟩ **b (1) :** to free from something hurtful or offensive **(2) :** to remove the less desirable portions of **2 :** to get rid of (something harmful or superfluous) — often used with *out*

[3]**weed** *n* [ME *wede,* fr. OE *wǣd, gewǣde;* akin to ON *vāth* cloth, clothing and perh. to Lith *austi* to weave] (bef. 12c) **1 :** GARMENT — often used in pl. **2 a :** dress worn as a sign of mourning (as by a widow) — usu. used in pl. **b :** a band of crape worn on a man's hat as a sign of mourning — usu. used in pl.

Weed eater *trademark* — used for a string trimmer

weed·er \ˈwē-dər\ *n* (15c) **:** one that weeds; *specif* **:** any of various devices for removing weeds from an area

Weed·wack·er \ˈwēd-ˌwa-kər\ *trademark* — used for a string trimmer

weedy \ˈwē-dē\ *adj* **weed·i·er; -est** (15c) **1 :** abounding with or consisting of weeds **2 :** resembling a weed esp. in vigorous growth or ready propagation **3 :** noticeably lean and scrawny : LANKY — **weed·i·ness** *n*

week \ˈwēk\ *n* [ME *weke,* fr. OE *wicu, wucu;* akin to OHG *wehha* week and perh. to L *vicis* change, alternation, OHG *wehsal* exchange] (bef. 12c) **1 a :** any of a series of 7-day cycles used in various calendars; *esp* **:** a 7-day cycle beginning on Sunday and ending on Saturday **b (1) :** a week beginning with a specified day or containing a specified holiday ⟨the ∼ of the 18th⟩ **(2) :** a week appointed for public recognition of some cause **2 a :** any seven consecutive days **b :** a series of regular working, business, or school days during each 7-day period **3** *Brit* **:** a time seven days before or after a specified day ⟨last Sunday ∼⟩

week·day \ˈwēk-ˌdā\ *n* (14c) **:** a day of the week except Sunday or sometimes except Saturday and Sunday

week·days \-ˌdāz\ *adv* (1694) **:** on weekdays repeatedly : on any weekday ⟨takes a bus ∼⟩

[1]**week·end** \ˈwēk-ˌend\ *n* (1638) **:** the end of the week; *specif* **:** the period between the close of one work or school week and the start of the next

[2]**weekend** *vi* (1901) **:** to spend the weekend ⟨∼*ing* in the country⟩

[3]**weekend** *adj* (1935) **:** active in a specified role only on weekends or part-time ⟨a ∼ father⟩ ⟨∼ athletes⟩

weekend bag *n* (1921) **:** a suitcase of a size to carry clothing and personal articles for a weekend trip — called also *weekend case*

week·end·er \ˈwēk-ˈen-dər\ *n* (1880) **1 :** one who vacations or visits for a weekend **2 :** WEEKEND BAG

week·ends \ˈwēk-ˌen(d)z\ *adv* (1946) **:** on weekends repeatedly : on any weekend ⟨travels ∼⟩

weekend warrior *n* (1981) **:** a person who participates in a usu. physically strenuous activity only on weekends or part-time

week·long \ˈwēk-ˈlȯŋ\ *adj* (1847) **:** lasting a week

[1]**week·ly** \ˈwē-klē\ *adv* (15c) **:** every week : once a week : by the week

[2]**weekly** *adj* (15c) **1 :** occurring, appearing, or done weekly ⟨∼ meetings⟩ **2 :** reckoned by the week ⟨∼ rental rates⟩

[3]**weekly** *n, pl* **weeklies** (1832) **:** a weekly newspaper or periodical

week·night \'wēk-ˌnīt\ *n* (1850) : a weekday night

week·nights \-ˌnīts\ *adv* (1965) : on weeknights repeatedly : on any weeknight

ween \'wēn\ *vt* [ME *wenen,* fr. OE *wēnan;* akin to ON *væna* to hope and prob. to L *venus* love, charm — more at WIN] (bef. 12c) *archaic* : BELIEVE 2

wee·nie \'wē-nē\ *n* [alter. of *wienie*] (ca. 1906) **1** : FRANKFURTER **2** *slang* : PENIS **3** : NERD ⟨computer ~*s*⟩

wee·ny \'wē-nē\ *also* **ween·sy** \'wēn(t)-sē\ *adj* [alter. of *wee*] (ca. 1781) : exceptionally small : TINY

weep \'wēp\ *vb* **wept** \'wept\; **weep·ing** [ME *wepen,* fr. OE *wēpan;* akin to OHG *wuoffan* to weep, Serbian & Croatian *vapiti* to cry out] *vt* (bef. 12c) **1** : to express deep sorrow for usu. by shedding tears : BEWAIL ⟨~*ing* the sins and errors of his youth —Edward Gibbon⟩ **2** : to pour forth (tears) from the eyes **3** : to exude (a fluid) slowly : OOZE ⟨a tree ~*ing* sap⟩ ~ *vi* **1** : to express passion (as grief) by shedding tears **2 a** : to give off or leak fluid slowly : OOZE **b** *of a fluid* : to flow sluggishly or in drops **3** : to droop over : BEND

weep·er \'wē-pər\ *n* (13c) **1 a** : one that weeps **b** : a professional mourner **2** : a small statue of a figure in mourning on a funeral monument **3** : a badge of mourning worn esp. in the 18th and 19th centuries **4** *pl* : long and flowing side-whiskers **5** : TEARJERKER

weep hole *n* (1851) : a hole (as in a wall or foundation) that is designed to drain off accumulated water

weep·ie \'wē-pē\ *n* (1928) : TEARJERKER

weeping *adj* (bef. 12c) **1** : TEARFUL **2** *archaic* : RAINY **3** : having slender pendent branches ⟨a ~ beech⟩

weeping fig *n* (1934) : an ornamental fig (*Ficus benjamina*) of southern Asia and Australia that is widely cultivated esp. as a houseplant for its glossy ovate leaves and drooping branches

weeping willow *n* (1621) : an Asian willow (*Salix babylonica*) introduced into No. America that has slender pendent branches

weepy \'wē-pē\ *adj* (15c) : inclined to weep : TEARFUL

weet \'wēt\ *vb* [ME *weten,* alter. of *witen* — more at WIT] (14c) *archaic* : KNOW

wee·vil \'wē-vəl\ *n* [ME *wevel,* fr. OE *wifel;* akin to OHG *wibil* beetle, OE *wefan* to weave] (bef. 12c) : any of a superfamily (Curculionoidea) of beetles which have the head prolonged into a more or less distinct snout and which include many that are destructive esp. as larvae to nuts, fruit, and grain or to living plants; *esp* : any of a family (Curculionidae) having a well-developed snout curved downward with the jaws at the tip and clubbed usu. elbowed antennae — **wee·vily** *or* **wee·vil·ly** \'wēv-lē, 'wē-və-lē\ *adj*

weft \'weft\ *n* [ME, fr. OE; akin to ON *veptr* weft, OE *wefan* to weave — more at WEAVE] (bef. 12c) **1 a** : a filling thread or yarn in weaving **b** : yarn used for the weft **2** : WEB, FABRIC; *also* : an article of woven fabric

weft knit *n* (1943) : a knit fabric produced in machine or hand knitting with the yarns running crosswise or in a circle — compare WARP KNIT — **weft–knit·ted** \-ˌni-təd\ *adj* — **weft knit·ting** *n*

wei·ge·la \wī-'jē-lə\ *n* [NL, fr. Christian E. *Weigel* †1831 Ger. physician] (1846) : any of a genus (*Weigela*) of showy eastern Asian shrubs of the honeysuckle family; *esp* : one (*W. florida*) widely grown for its usu. pink or red funnel-shaped flowers

¹weigh \'wā\ *vb* [ME *weyen,* fr. OE *wegan* to move, carry, weigh — more at WAY] *vt* (bef. 12c) **1** : to ascertain the heaviness of by or as if by a balance **2 a** : OUTWEIGH **b** : COUNTERBALANCE **c** : to make heavy : WEIGHT — often used with *down* **3** : to consider carefully esp. by balancing opposing factors or aspects in order to reach a choice or conclusion : EVALUATE ⟨~*ing* her options⟩ **4** : to heave up (an anchor) preparatory to sailing **5** : to measure or apportion (a definite quantity) on or as if on a scales ~ *vi* **1 a** : to have a certain heaviness : experience a specific force due to gravity **b** : to register a weight (as on a scales) — used with *in* or *out*; compare WEIGH IN **2** : to merit consideration as important : COUNT ⟨evidence will ~ heavily against him⟩ **3 a** : to press down with or as if with a heavy weight **b** : to have a saddening or disheartening effect ⟨guilt ~*ed* on my mind⟩ **4** : to weigh anchor **syn** see CONSIDER — **weigh·able** \'wā-ə-bəl\ *adj* — **weigh·er** *n*

²weigh *n* [alter. of *way*] (1777) : WAY — used in the phrase *under weigh*

weigh down *vt* (14c) **1** : to cause to bend down : OVERBURDEN **2** : OPPRESS, DEPRESS

weigh–in \'wā-ˌin\ *n* (1939) : an act or instance of weighing in as a contestant esp. in sport

weigh in *vi* (1868) **1** : to have oneself or one's possessions (as baggage) weighed; *esp* : to have oneself weighed in connection with an athletic contest **2** : to bring one's weight or influence to bear esp. as a participant, contributor, or mediator ⟨*weighed in* with an opinion⟩

¹weight \'wāt\ *n* [ME *wight, weght,* fr. OE *wiht;* akin to ON *vætt* weight, OE *wegan* to weigh] (bef. 12c) **1 a** : the amount that a thing weighs **b** (1) : the standard or established amount that a thing should weigh (2) : one of the classes into which contestants in a sports event are divided according to body weight (3) : poundage required to be carried by a horse in a handicap race **2 a** : a quantity or thing weighing a fixed and usu. specified amount **b** : a heavy object (as a metal ball) thrown, put, or lifted as an athletic exercise or contest **3 a** : a unit of weight or mass — see METRIC SYSTEM table **b** : a piece of material (as metal) of known specified weight for use in weighing articles **c** : a system of related units of weight **4 a** : something heavy : LOAD **b** : a heavy object to hold or press something down or to counterbalance **5 a** : BURDEN, PRESSURE ⟨the ~ of their responsibilities⟩ **b** : the quality or state of being ponderous **c** : CORPULENCE **6 a** : relative heaviness : MASS **b** : the force with which a body is attracted toward the earth or a celestial body by gravitation and which is equal to the product of the mass and the local gravitational acceleration **7 a** : the relative importance or authority accorded something ⟨the ~ of her opinions⟩ **b** : measurable influence esp. on others ⟨throwing his ~ behind the proposal⟩ **8** : overpowering force **9** : the quality (as lightness) that makes a fabric or garment suitable for a particular use or season — often used in combination ⟨summer-*weight*⟩ **10** : a numerical coefficient assigned to an item to express its relative importance in a frequency distribution **11** : the degree of thickness of the strokes of a type character **syn** see IMPORTANCE, INFLUENCE

☞ The Weights and Measures Table is on the following page.

²weight *vt* (1647) **1** : to oppress with a burden ⟨~*ed* down with cares⟩ **2 a** : to load or make heavy with or as if with a weight **b** : to increase in heaviness by adding an ingredient **3 a** : WEIGH 1 **b** : to feel the weight of : HEFT **4** : to assign a statistical weight to **5** : to cause to incline in a particular direction by manipulation ⟨the tax structure . . . which was ~*ed* so heavily in favor of the upper classes —A. S. Link⟩ **6** : to shift the burden of weight upon ⟨~ the inside ski⟩

weight·ed \'wā-təd\ *adj* (1597) **1** : made heavy : LOADED ⟨~ silk⟩ **2 a** : having a statistical weight attached ⟨a ~ test score⟩ **b** : compiled or calculated from weighted data ⟨a ~ mean⟩ **3** : INCLINED 1

weight·less \'wāt-ləs\ *adj* (ca. 1547) : having little weight : lacking apparent gravitational pull — **weight·less·ly** *adv* — **weight·less·ness** *n*

weight lifter *n* (1897) : one who lifts barbells in competition or as an exercise — **weight lifting** *n*

weight man *n* (ca. 1949) : an athlete who competes in any of the field events in which a weight is thrown or put

weight room *n* (1973) : a room containing equipment for weight training

weight training *n* (1955) : a system of conditioning involving lifting weights esp. for strength and endurance

weighty \'wā-tē\ *adj* **weight·i·er; -est** (15c) **1 a** : of much importance or consequence : MOMENTOUS ⟨a ~ problem⟩ **b** : SOLEMN **2 a** : weighing a considerable amount **b** : heavy in proportion to its bulk ⟨~ metal⟩ **3** : POWERFUL, TELLING ⟨~ arguments⟩ **syn** see HEAVY — **weight·i·ly** \'wā-tə-lē\ *adv* — **weight·i·ness** \'wā-tē-nəs\ *n*

Wei·ma·ra·ner \ˌvī-mə-'rä-nər, ˌwī-; 'vī-mə-ˌ, 'wī-\ *n* [G, fr. *Weimar,* Germany] (1943) : any of a breed of large light gray usu. short-haired pointers of German origin

weiner *var of* WIENER

weir \'wer, 'wir\ *n* [ME *were,* fr. OE *wer;* akin to ON *ver* fishing place, OHG *werien, werren* to defend] (bef. 12c) **1** : a fence or enclosure set in a waterway for taking fish **2** : a dam in a stream or river to raise the water level or divert its flow

¹weird \'wird\ *n* [ME *wird, werd,* fr. OE *wyrd;* akin to ON *urthr* fate, OE *weorthan* to become — more at WORTH] (bef. 12c) **1** : FATE, DESTINY; *esp* : ill fortune **2** : SOOTHSAYER

²weird *adj* (15c) **1** : of, relating to, or caused by witchcraft or the supernatural : MAGICAL **2** : of strange or extraordinary character : ODD, FANTASTIC — **weird·ly** *adv* — **weird·ness** *n* **syn** WEIRD, EERIE, UNCANNY mean mysteriously strange or fantastic. WEIRD may imply an unearthly or supernatural strangeness or it may stress queerness or oddness ⟨*weird* creatures from another world⟩. EERIE suggests an uneasy or fearful consciousness that mysterious and malign powers are at work ⟨an *eerie* calm preceded the bombing raid⟩. UNCANNY implies disquieting strangeness or mysteriousness ⟨an *uncanny* resemblance between total strangers⟩.

weird·ie \'wir-dē\ *or* **weirdy** *n, pl* **weird·ies** (1894) : WEIRDO

¹weirdo \'wir-(ˌ)dō\ *n, pl* **weird·os** (ca. 1955) : a person who is extraordinarily strange or eccentric

²weirdo *adj* (1962) : STRANGE, WEIRD

weird out *vt* (1973) : to make uneasy, bewildered, or disquieted by something considered very strange ⟨that movie *weirds* me *out*⟩

Weird Sisters *n pl* (15c) : FATES

weisenheimer *var of* WISENHEIMER

weka \'we-kə\ *n* [Maori] (1845) : a flightless New Zealand rail (*Gallirallus australis*)

welch *var of* WELSH

Welch *var of* WELSH

¹wel·come \'wel-kəm\ *vt* **wel·comed; wel·com·ing** [ME, fr. OE *welcumian, wylcumian,* fr. *wilcuma,* n.] (bef. 12c) **1** : to greet hospitably and with courtesy or cordiality **2** : to accept with pleasure the occurrence or presence of ⟨~*s* danger⟩ — **wel·com·er** *n*

²welcome *interj* [ME, alter. of *wilcume,* fr. OE, fr. *wilcuma* desirable guest (akin to OHG *willicomo* desirable guest); akin to OE *willa, will* desire, *cuman* to come — more at WILL, COME] (12c) — used to express a greeting to a guest or newcomer upon arrival

³welcome *adj* (12c) **1** : received gladly into one's presence or companionship ⟨was always ~ in their home⟩ **2** : giving pleasure : received with gladness or delight esp. in response to a need ⟨a ~ relief⟩ **3** : willingly permitted or admitted ⟨he was ~ to come and go —W. M. Thackeray⟩ **4** — used in the phrase "You're welcome" as a reply to an expression of thanks — **wel·come·ly** *adv* — **wel·come·ness** *n*

⁴welcome *n* (1525) **1** : a greeting or reception usu. upon arrival ⟨a warm ~⟩ **2** : the state of being welcome ⟨overstayed their ~⟩

welcome mat *n* (1946) : something likened to a mat placed before an entrance as a sign of welcome ⟨put out the *welcome mat* for foreign investors⟩

¹weld \'weld\ *vb* [alter. of obs. E *well* to weld, fr. ME *wellen* to boil, well, weld — more at WELL] *vi* (1599) : to become or be capable of being welded ~ *vt* **1 a** : to unite (metallic parts) by heating and allowing the metals to flow together or by hammering or compressing with or without previous heating **b** : to unite (plastics) in a similar manner by heating **c** : to repair (as an article) by this method **d** : to produce or create as if by such a process **2** : to unite or reunite closely or intimately ⟨architecture that ~*s* the past and the present⟩ — **weld·able** \'wel-də-bəl\ *adj*

²weld *n* (1831) **1** : a welded joint **2** : union by welding : the state or condition of being welded

weld·er \'wel-dər\ *n* (ca. 1828) : one that welds: as **a** *or* **wel·dor** : a person whose work is welding **b** : a machine used in welding

weld·ment \'wel(d)-mənt\ *n* (1941) : a unit formed by welding together an assembly of pieces

¹wel·fare \'wel-ˌfer\ *n* [ME, fr. the phrase *wel faren* to fare well] (14c) **1** : the state of doing well esp. in respect to good fortune, happiness, well-being, or prosperity ⟨must look out for your own ~⟩ **2 a** : aid in the

\ə\ abut \ᵊ\ kitten, F table \ər\ further \a\ ash \ā\ ace \ä\ mop, mar \au̇\ out \ch\ chin \e\ bet \ē\ easy \g\ go \i\ hit \ī\ ice \j\ job \ŋ\ sing \ō\ go \ȯ\ law \ȯi\ boy \th\ thin \t̲h̲\ the \ü\ loot \u̇\ foot \y\ yet \zh\ vision, beige \k̲, ⁿ, œ, ɶ, ᵫ\ see Guide to Pronunciation

WEIGHTS AND MEASURES[1]

UNIT	ABBREVIATION OR SYMBOL	EQUIVALENTS IN OTHER UNITS OF SAME SYSTEM	METRIC EQUIVALENT
WEIGHT			
Avoirdupois[2]			
ton			
short ton		2000 pounds, 20 short hundredweight	0.907 metric ton
long ton		2240 pounds, 20 long hundredweight	1.016 metric tons
hundredweight	cwt		
short hundredweight		100 pounds, 0.05 short ton	45.359 kilograms
long hundredweight		112 pounds, 0.05 long ton	50.802 kilograms
pound	lb *or* lb avdp *also* #	16 ounces, 7000 grains	0.454 kilogram
ounce	oz *or* oz avdp	16 drams, 437.5 grains, 0.0625 pound	28.350 grams
dram	dr *or* dr avdp	27.344 grains, 0.0625 ounce	1.772 grams
grain	gr	0.037 dram, 0.002286 ounce	0.0648 gram
Troy			
pound	lb t	12 ounces, 240 pennyweight, 5760 grains	0.373 kilogram
ounce	oz t	20 pennyweight, 480 grains, 0.083 pound	31.103 grams
pennyweight	dwt *also* pwt	24 grains, 0.05 ounce	1.555 grams
grain	gr	0.042 pennyweight, 0.002083 ounce	0.0648 gram
Apothecaries'			
pound	lb ap	12 ounces, 5760 grains	0.373 kilogram
ounce	oz ap *or* ℥	8 drams, 480 grains, 0.083 pound	31.103 grams
dram	dr ap *or* ʒ	3 scruples, 60 grains	3.888 grams
scruple	s ap *or* ℈	20 grains, 0.333 dram	1.296 grams
grain	gr	0.05 scruple, 0.002083 ounce, 0.0166 dram	0.0648 gram
CAPACITY			
U.S. liquid measure			
gallon	gal	4 quarts (231 cubic inches)	3.785 liters
quart	qt	2 pints (57.75 cubic inches)	0.946 liter
pint	pt	4 gills (28.875 cubic inches)	473.176 milliliters
gill	gi	4 fluid ounces (7.219 cubic inches)	118.294 milliliters
fluid ounce	fl oz *or* f℥	8 fluid drams (1.805 cubic inches)	29.573 milliliters
fluid dram	fl dr *or* fʒ	60 minims (0.226 cubic inch)	3.697 milliliters
minim	min *or* ℳ	1/60 fluid dram (0.003760 cubic inch)	0.061610 milliliter
U.S. dry measure			
bushel	bu	4 pecks (2150.42 cubic inches)	35.239 liters
peck	pk	8 quarts (537.605 cubic inches)	8.810 liters
quart	qt	2 pints (67.201 cubic inches)	1.101 liters
pint	pt	1/2 quart (33.600 cubic inches)	0.551 liter
British imperial liquid and dry measure			
bushel	bu	4 pecks (2219.36 cubic inches)	36.369 liters
peck	pk	2 gallons (554.84 cubic inches)	9.092 liters
gallon	gal	4 quarts (277.420 cubic inches)	4.546 liters
quart	qt	2 pints (69.355 cubic inches)	1.136 liters
pint	pt	4 gills (34.678 cubic inches)	568.26 milliliters
gill	gi	5 fluid ounces (8.669 cubic inches)	142.066 milliliters
fluid ounce	fl oz *or* f℥	8 fluid drams (1.7339 cubic inches)	28.412 milliliters
fluid dram	fl dr *or* fʒ	60 minims (0.216734 cubic inch)	3.5516 milliliters
minim	min *or* ℳ	1/60 fluid dram (0.003612 cubic inch)	0.059194 milliliter
LENGTH			
mile	mi	5280 feet, 1760 yards, 320 rods	1.609 kilometers
rod	rd	5.50 yards, 16.5 feet	5.029 meters
yard	yd	3 feet, 36 inches	0.9144 meter
foot	ft *or* '	12 inches, 0.333 yard	30.48 centimeters
inch	in *or* "	0.083 foot, 0.028 yard	2.54 centimeters
AREA			
square mile	sq mi *or* mi[2]	640 acres, 102,400 square rods	2.590 square kilometers
acre	ac	4840 square yards, 43,560 square feet	0.405 hectare, 4047 square meters
square rod	sq rd *or* rd[2]	30.25 square yards, 0.00625 acre	25.293 square meters
square yard	sq yd *or* yd[2]	9 square feet, 1296 square inches	0.836 square meter
square foot	sq ft *or* ft[2]	144 square inches, 0.111 square yard	0.093 square meter
square inch	sq in *or* in[2]	0.0069 square foot, 0.00077 square yard	6.452 square centimeters
VOLUME			
cubic yard	cu yd *or* yd[3]	27 cubic feet, 46,656 cubic inches	0.765 cubic meter
cubic foot	cu ft *or* ft[3]	1728 cubic inches, 0.0370 cubic yard	0.028 cubic meter
cubic inch	cu in *or* in[3]	0.00058 cubic foot, 0.000021 cubic yard	16.387 cubic centimeters

[1]For U.S. equivalents of the metric units see Metric System table.
[2]The U.S. uses the avoirdupois units as the common system of measuring weight.

form of money or necessities for those in need **b** : an agency or program through which such aid is distributed
²**welfare** *adj* (1903) **1** : of, relating to, or concerned with welfare and esp. with improvement of the welfare of disadvantaged social groups ⟨∼ legislation⟩ **2** : receiving public welfare benefits ⟨∼ families⟩
welfare state *n* (1894) **1** : a social system based on the assumption by a political state of primary responsibility for the individual and social welfare of its citizens **2** : a nation or state characterized by the operation of the welfare state system
wel·far·ism \'wel-ˌfer-ˌi-zəm\ *n* (1949) : the complex of policies, attitudes, and beliefs associated with the welfare state — **wel·far·ist** \-ist\ *n or adj*
wel·kin \'wel-kən\ *n* [ME, lit., cloud, fr. OE *wolcen;* akin to OHG *wolkan* cloud] (12c) **1 a** : the vault of the sky : FIRMAMENT ⟨the sun of heaven . . . made the western ∼ blush —Shak.⟩ **b** : the celestial abode of God or the gods : HEAVEN **2** : the upper atmosphere
¹**well** \'wel\ *n* [ME *welle,* fr. OE; akin to OE *weallan* to bubble, boil, OHG *wella* wave, Lith *vilnis*] (bef. 12c) **1 a** : an issue of water from the earth : a pool fed by a spring **b** : SOURCE, ORIGIN **2 a** : a pit or hole sunk into the earth to reach a supply of water **b** : a shaft or hole sunk

to obtain oil, brine, or gas **3 a** : an enclosure in the middle of a ship's hold to protect from damage and facilitate the inspection of the pumps **b** : a compartment in the hold of a fishing boat in which fish are kept alive **4** : an open space extending vertically through floors of a structure **5** : a space having a construction or shape suggesting a well for water **6 a** : something resembling a well in being damp, cool, deep, or dark **b** : a deep vertical hole **c** : a source from which something may be drawn as needed **7** : a pronounced minimum of a variable in physics ⟨a potential ∼⟩
²**well** *vb* [ME, fr. OE *wellan* to cause to well; akin to OE *weallan* to bubble, boil] *vi* (bef. 12c) **1** : to rise to the surface and usu. flow forth ⟨tears ∼ed from her eyes⟩ **2** : to rise like a flood of liquid ⟨longing ∼ed up in his breast⟩ ~ *vt* : to emit in a copious free flow
³**well** *adv* **bet·ter** \'be-tər\; **best** \'best\ [ME *wel,* fr. OE; akin to OHG *wela* well, OE *wyllan* to wish — more at WILL] (bef. 12c) **1 a** : in a good or proper manner : JUSTLY, RIGHTLY **b** : satisfactorily with respect to conduct or action ⟨did ∼ in math⟩ ⟨works ∼ under pressure⟩ **2** : in a kindly or friendly manner ⟨spoke ∼ of your idea⟩ ⟨wished them ∼⟩ **3 a** : with skill or aptitude : EXPERTLY, EXCELLENTLY ⟨paints ∼⟩ **b** : SATISFACTORILY ⟨the plan worked ∼⟩ **c** : with good

appearance or effect : ELEGANTLY ⟨carried himself ~⟩ **4 :** with careful or close attention : ATTENTIVELY ⟨watch ~ what I do⟩ **5 :** to a high degree ⟨~ deserved the honor⟩ ⟨a *well*-equipped kitchen⟩ — often used as an intensifier or qualifier ⟨there are . . . vacancies pretty ~ all the time —*Listener*⟩ **6 :** FULLY, QUITE ⟨~ worth the price⟩ **7 a :** in a way appropriate to the facts or circumstances : FITTINGLY, RIGHTLY ⟨~ said⟩ **b :** in a prudent manner : SENSIBLY — used with *do* ⟨you would do ~ to reread the material⟩ **8 :** in accordance with the occasion or circumstances : with propriety or good reason ⟨cannot ~ refuse⟩ ⟨the decision may ~ be questioned⟩ **9 a :** as one could wish : PLEASINGLY ⟨the idea didn't sit ~ with her⟩ **b :** with material success : ADVANTAGEOUSLY ⟨married ~⟩ **10 a :** EASILY, READILY ⟨could ~ afford a new car⟩ **b :** in all likelihood : INDEED ⟨it may ~ be true⟩ **11 :** in a prosperous or affluent manner ⟨he lives ~⟩ **12 :** to an extent approaching completeness : THOROUGHLY ⟨after being ~ dried with a towel⟩ **13 :** without doubt or question : CLEARLY ⟨~ knew the penalty⟩ **14 :** in a familiar manner ⟨knew her ~⟩ **15 :** to a large extent or degree : CONSIDERABLY, FAR ⟨~ over a million⟩ ***usage*** see GOOD — **as well 1 :** in addition : ALSO ⟨there were other features *as well*⟩ **2 :** to the same extent or degree : as much ⟨open *as well* to the poor as to the rich⟩ **3 :** with equivalent, comparable, or more favorable effect ⟨might just *as well* have stayed home⟩

4**well** *interj* (bef. 12c) **1** — used to indicate resumption of discourse or to introduce a remark ⟨they are, ~, not quite what you'd expect⟩ **2** — used to express surprise or expostulation ⟨~, what have we here?⟩

5**well** *adj* (bef. 12c) **1 a :** PROSPEROUS, WELL-OFF **b :** being in satisfactory condition or circumstances **2 :** being in good standing or favor **3 :** SATISFACTORY, PLEASING ⟨all's ~ that ends well⟩ **4 :** ADVISABLE, DESIRABLE ⟨it might be ~ for you to leave⟩ **5 a :** free or recovered from infirmity or disease : HEALTHY ⟨he's not a ~ man⟩ **b :** completely cured or healed ⟨the wound is nearly ~⟩ **6 :** pleasing or satisfactory in appearance ⟨our garden looks ~ —Conrad Aiken⟩ **7 :** being a cause for thankfulness : FORTUNATE ⟨it is ~ that this has happened⟩ ***syn*** see HEALTHY ***usage*** see GOOD

we'll \ˈwēl, ˈwil\ (1578) : we will : we shall

well–ad·just·ed \ˌwel-ə-ˈjəs-təd\ *adj* (1692) : WELL-BALANCED 2

well–ad·vised \ˈwel-əd-ˈvīzd\ *adj* (14c) **1 :** acting with wisdom, wise counsel, or proper deliberation : PRUDENT **2 :** resulting from, based on, or showing careful deliberation or wise counsel ⟨~ plans⟩

well–ap·point·ed \ˈwel-ə-ˈpȯin-təd\ *adj* (1530) : having good and complete equipment : properly fitted out ⟨a ~ house⟩

wel·la·way \ˌwe-lə-ˈwā, ˈwe-lə-ˌ\ *interj* [ME *welaway,* fr. OE *weilāwei,* lit., woe! lo! woe!, alter. of *wālāwā,* fr. *wā* woe + *lā* lo + *wā* woe — more at WOE] (bef. 12c) *archaic* — used to express sorrow or lamentation

well–ba·lanced \ˈwel-ˈba-lən(t)st\ *adj* (1629) **1 :** nicely or evenly balanced, arranged, or regulated ⟨a ~ diet⟩ ⟨a ~ attack in football⟩ **2 :** emotionally or psychologically untroubled

well–be·ing \ˈwel-ˈbē-iŋ\ *n* (1582) : the state of being happy, healthy, or prosperous : WELFARE

well–be·loved \ˌwel-bi-ˈləvd\ *adj* (14c) **1 :** sincerely and deeply loved ⟨my ~ wife⟩ **2 :** sincerely respected — used in various ceremonial forms of address

well·born \ˈwel-ˈbȯrn\ *adj* (bef. 12c) : born of noble or wealthy lineage

well–bred \-ˈbred\ *adj* (ca. 1589) **1 :** having or displaying good breeding : REFINED **2 :** having a good pedigree ⟨~ swine⟩

well–con·di·tioned \ˌwel-kən-ˈdi-shənd\ *adj* (15c) **1 :** characterized by proper disposition, morals, or behavior **2 :** having a good physical condition : SOUND

well deck *n* (1888) : a space on the weather deck of a ship lying at a lower level between a raised forecastle or poop and the bridge superstructure

well–de·fined \ˌwel-di-ˈfīnd\ *adj* (1704) **1 :** having clearly distinguishable limits, boundaries, or features ⟨a ~ scar⟩ **2 :** clearly stated or described ⟨~ policies⟩

well–dis·posed \-dis-ˈpōzd\ *adj* (14c) : having a good disposition; *esp* : disposed to be friendly, favorable, or sympathetic

well–done \ˈwel-ˈdən\ *adj* (14c) **1 :** rightly or properly performed **2 :** cooked thoroughly ⟨a ~ steak⟩

well–en·dowed \ˈwel-in-ˈdau̇d, -en-\ *adj* (1639) **1 :** well-supported financially : WELL-FIXED **2 :** having large breasts **3 :** having a large penis

Wel·ler·ism \ˈwe-lə-ˌri-zəm\ *n* [Sam *Weller,* witty servant of Mr. Pickwick in the story *Pickwick Papers* (1836–37) by Charles Dickens] (1839) : an expression of comparison comprising a usu. well-known quotation followed by a facetious sequel (as "'every one to his own taste,' said the old woman as she kissed the cow")

well–fa·vored \ˈwel-ˈfā-vərd\ *adj* (15c) : GOOD-LOOKING, HANDSOME ⟨a spacious, fair, ~ face —Henry James⟩ — **well–fa·vored·ness** *n*

well–fixed \-ˈfikst\ *adj* (1652) : having plenty of money or property

well–found \-ˈfau̇nd\ *adj* (1781) : fully furnished : properly equipped ⟨a ~ ship⟩

well–found·ed \-ˈfau̇n-dəd\ *adj* (14c) : based on excellent reasoning, information, judgment, or grounds

well–groomed \-ˈgrümd, -ˈgru̇md\ *adj* (1840) **1 :** well-dressed and scrupulously neat ⟨~ men⟩ **2 :** made neat, tidy, and attractive down to the smallest details ⟨a ~ lawn⟩

well–ground·ed \-ˈgrau̇n-dəd\ *adj* (14c) **1 :** having a firm foundation ⟨~ in Latin and Greek⟩ **2 :** WELL-FOUNDED

well–han·dled \-ˈhan-dᵊld\ *adj* (15c) **1 :** managed or administered efficiently **2 :** having been handled a great deal ⟨~ goods for sale⟩

well·head \ˈwel-ˌhed\ *n* (13c) **1 :** the source of a spring or a stream **2 :** principal source : FOUNTAINHEAD **3 :** the top of or a structure built over a well

wellhead price *n* (1953) : the price less transportation costs charged by the producer for petroleum or natural gas

well–heeled \-ˈhēld\ *adj* (1897) : having plenty of money : WELL-FIXED

wel·lie *or* **wel·ly** \ˈwe-lē\ *n, pl* **wellies** *often cap* [by shortening & alter.] (1961) *chiefly Brit* : WELLINGTON — usu. used in pl.

well–in·formed \-in-ˈfȯrmd\ *adj* (15c) **1 :** having extensive knowledge esp. of current topics and events **2 :** thoroughly knowledgeable in a particular subject

Wel·ling·ton \ˈwe-liŋ-tən\ *n* [Arthur Wellesley, 1st Duke of *Wellington*] (1817) : a boot having a loose top with the front usu. coming to or above the knee — usu. used in pl.

well–in·ten·tioned \ˌwel-in-ˈten(t)-shənd\ *adj* (1598) : WELL-MEANING

well–knit \ˈwel-ˈnit\ *adj* (15c) : firmly knit ⟨a ~ group⟩; *esp* : firmly and strongly constructed, compacted, or framed ⟨a ~ drama⟩

well–known \-ˈnōn\ *adj* (15c) : fully or widely known

well–mean·ing \-ˈmē-niŋ\ *adj* (15c) **1 :** having good intentions ⟨~ but misguided idealists⟩ **2 :** based on good intentions ⟨~ advice⟩

well–meant \-ˈment\ *adj* (15c) : WELL-MEANING 2

well·ness \ˈwel-nəs\ *n* (1653) : the quality or state of being in good health esp. as an actively sought goal ⟨lifestyles that promote ~⟩

well–nigh \-ˈnī\ *adv* (12c) : ALMOST, NEARLY ⟨~ impossible⟩

well–off \-ˈȯf\ *adj* (1722) **1 :** being in good condition or favorable circumstances ⟨doesn't know when he's ~⟩ **2 :** well provided : having no lack — usu. used with *for* **3 a :** being in easy or affluent circumstances : WELL-TO-DO **b :** suggesting prosperity ⟨the house had a sleek ~ look⟩

well–oiled \-ˈȯi(-ə)ld\ *adj* (1817) : smoothly functioning ⟨a ~ political machine⟩

well–or·dered \-ˈȯr-dərd\ *adj* (1589) **1 :** having an orderly procedure or arrangement ⟨a ~ household⟩ **2 :** partially ordered with every subset containing a first element and exactly one of the relationships "greater than", "less than", or "equal to" holding for any given pair of elements — **well–or·der·ing** \-ˈȯrd-riŋ, -ˈȯr-də-\ *n*

well–placed \-ˈplāst\ *adj* (1562) : well or advantageously directed or positioned ⟨~ informants⟩ ⟨~ trust⟩ ⟨a ~ blow⟩

well–read \-ˈred\ *adj* (1592) : well-informed or deeply versed through reading ⟨~ in history⟩

well–round·ed \-ˈrau̇n-dəd\ *adj* (1823) : fully or broadly developed: as **a :** having a broad educational background ⟨schools that turn out ~ graduates⟩ **b :** COMPREHENSIVE ⟨a ~ program of activities⟩

well–set \-ˈset\ *adj* (14c) **1 :** well or firmly established ⟨~ in his own values —William Johnson⟩ **2 :** strongly built ⟨a ~ athlete⟩

well–spo·ken \ˈwel-ˈspō-kən\ *adj* (15c) **1 :** speaking well, fitly, or courteously ⟨a ~ young woman⟩ **2 :** spoken with propriety ⟨~ words⟩

well·spring \-ˌspriŋ\ *n* (bef. 12c) : a source of continual supply ⟨a ~ of information⟩

well–tak·en \-ˈtā-kən\ *adj* (1761) : WELL-GROUNDED, JUSTIFIABLE ⟨your point is ~⟩

well–thought–of \wel-ˈthȯt-ˌəv, -ˌäv\ *adj* (1576) : being of good repute ⟨a ~ attorney⟩

well–timed \ˈwel-ˈtīmd\ *adj* (ca. 1656) : happening at an opportune moment : TIMELY ⟨a ~ announcement⟩

well–to–do \ˌwel-tə-ˈdü\ *adj* (1805) : having more than adequate financial resources : PROSPEROUS ⟨a ~ family⟩

well–turned \ˈwel-ˈtərnd\ *adj* (1616) **1 :** symmetrically shaped or rounded : SHAPELY **2 :** concisely and appropriately expressed ⟨a ~ phrase⟩ **3 :** expertly rounded or turned ⟨a ~ column⟩

well–wish·er \ˈwel-ˌwi-shər, -ˈwi-\ *n* (1590) : one who wishes well to another : an admiring supporter or fan — **well–wish·ing** \-shiŋ\ *adj or n*

well–worn \-ˈwȯrn\ *adj* (1621) **1 a :** made trite by overuse : HACKNEYED ⟨a ~ quotation⟩ **b :** having been much used or worn ⟨~ shoes⟩ **2** *archaic* : worn well or properly

welsh \ˈwelsh, ˈwelch\ *also* **welch** \ˈwelch\ *vi* [prob. fr. *Welsh,* adj.] (1905) **1** *sometimes offensive* : to avoid payment — used with *on* **2** *sometimes offensive* : to break one's word : RENEGE — **welsh·er** *n, sometimes offensive*

Welsh \ˈwelsh, ˈwelch\ *also* **Welch** \ˈwelch\ *n* [ME *Walsche, Welsse,* fr. *walisch, welisch,* adj., Welsh, fr. OE *wælisc, welisc* foreign, British, Welsh, fr. OE *Wealh* foreigner, Briton, Welshman, of Celt origin; akin to the source of L *Volcae,* a Celtic people of southeastern Gaul] (bef. 12c) **1 :** the Celtic language of the Welsh people **2** *pl in constr* : the natives or inhabitants of Wales **3 :** WELSH PONY — **Welsh** *also* **Welch** *adj*

Welsh black *n* (1919) : any of a breed of hardy medium-sized thick-haired horned black cattle of Welsh origin raised for meat and milk

Welsh cob *n* (1841) : any of a breed of medium-sized cobby horses developed by interbreeding Welsh mountain ponies with larger horses

Welsh corgi *n* (1926) : a short-legged long-backed dog with foxy head of either of two breeds of Welsh origin: **a :** CARDIGAN WELSH CORGI **b :** PEMBROKE WELSH CORGI

Welsh·man \-mən\ *n* (13c) : a native or inhabitant of Wales

Welsh mountain pony *n* (1947) : any of a breed of small sturdy ponies native to the mountains of Wales that do not exceed 12.2 hands (124 centimeters) in height

Welsh pony *n* (1771) : a pony of any of several breeds of Welsh origin; *esp* : any of a breed of riding and light draft ponies measuring 12.2 to 13.2 hands (124 to 134 centimeters) in height

Welsh rabbit *n* (1725) : melted often seasoned cheese poured over toast or crackers

Welsh rare·bit \-ˈrer-bət\ *n* [by alter.] (1785) : WELSH RABBIT

Welsh springer spaniel *n* (ca. 1929) : any of a breed of red and white relatively small-eared springer spaniels of Welsh origin

Welsh terrier *n* (1885) : any of a breed of wiry-coated terriers resembling Airedales but smaller and developed in Wales for hunting

Welsh·wom·an \ˈwelsh-ˌwu̇-mən, ˈwelch-\ *n* (15c) : a woman who is a native or inhabitant of Wales

1**welt** \ˈwelt\ *n* [ME *welte*] (15c) **1 :** a strip between a shoe sole and upper through which they are stitched or stapled together **2 :** a doubled edge, strip, insert, or seam (as on a garment) for ornament or reinforcement **3 a :** a ridge or lump raised on the body (as by a blow or allergic reaction) **b :** a heavy blow

2**welt** *vt* (15c) **1 :** to furnish with a welt **2 a :** to raise a welt on the body of **b :** to hit hard

welt·an·schau·ung \ˈvelt-ˌän-ˌshau̇-əŋ\ *n, pl* **weltanschauungs** \-əŋz\ *or* **welt·an·schau·ung·en** \-əŋ-ən\ *often cap* [G, fr. *Welt* world + *Anschauung* view] (1868) : a comprehensive conception or apprehension of the world esp. from a specific standpoint

---

\ə\ **abut** \ᵊ\ kitten, F table \ər\ **further** \a\ **ash** \ā\ **ace** \ä\ mop, mar
\au̇\ **out** \ch\ **chin** \e\ **bet** \ē\ **easy** \g\ **go** \i\ **hit** \ī\ **ice** \j\ **job**
\ŋ\ **sing** \ō\ **go** \ȯ\ **law** \ȯi\ **boy** \th\ **thin** \t͟h\ **the** \ü\ **loot** \u̇\ **foot**
\y\ **yet** \zh\ **vision, beige** \k̲, ⁿ, œ, ue, ʸ\ *see* Guide to Pronunciation

1wel·ter \ˈwel-tər\ *vi* **wel·tered; wel·ter·ing** \-t(ə-)riŋ\ [ME; akin to MD *welteren* to roll, OHG *walzan,* Lith *volioti,* L *volvere* — more at VOLUBLE] (14c) **1 a :** WRITHE, TOSS; *also* **:** WALLOW **b :** to rise and fall or toss about in or with waves **2 :** to become deeply sunk, soaked, or involved **3 :** to be in turmoil

2welter *n* (1596) **1 :** a state of wild disorder **:** TURMOIL **2 :** a chaotic mass or jumble ⟨a bewildering ~ of data⟩

3welter *n* (1900) **:** WELTERWEIGHT

wel·ter·weight \ˈwel-tər-ˌwāt\ *n* [*welter* (prob. fr. *1welt*) + *weight*] (ca. 1892) **:** a boxer in a weight division having a maximum limit of 147 pounds — compare LIGHTWEIGHT, MIDDLEWEIGHT

welt·schmerz \ˈvelt-ˌshmerts\ *n, often cap* [G, fr. *Welt* world + *Schmerz* pain] (1864) **1 :** mental depression or apathy caused by comparison of the actual state of the world with an ideal state **2 :** a mood of sentimental sadness

1wen \ˈwen\ *n* [ME *wenn,* fr. OE; akin to MLG *wene* wen] (bef. 12c) **:** an abnormal growth or a cyst protruding from a surface esp. of the skin

2wen *var of* WYNN

1wench \ˈwench\ *n* [ME *wenche,* short for *wenchel* child, fr. OE *wencel;* akin to OHG *wankōn* to totter, waver and prob. to OHG *winchan* to stagger — more at WINK] (14c) **1 a :** a young woman **:** GIRL **b :** a female servant **2 :** a lewd woman **:** PROSTITUTE

2wench *vi* (1590) **:** to consort with lewd women; *esp* **:** to practice fornication — **wench·er** *n*

wend \ˈwend\ *vb* [ME, fr. OE *wendan;* akin to OHG *wenten* to turn, OE *windan* to twist — more at WIND] *vi* (bef. 12c) **:** to direct one's course **:** TRAVEL ~ *vt* **:** to proceed on (one's way) **:** DIRECT

Wend \ˈwend\ *n* [G *Wende,* fr. OHG *Winida;* akin to OE *Winedas,* pl., Wends] (1786) **:** a member of a Slavic people of eastern Germany

1Wend·ish \ˈwen-dish\ *adj* (1614) **:** of or relating to the Wends or their language

2Wendish *n* (1617) **:** the West Slavic language of the Wends

Wens·ley·dale \ˈwenz-lē-ˌdāl\ *n* [fr. *Wensleydale,* valley in North Yorkshire] (1896) **:** a mild white friable cheese of English origin

went [ME, past & pp. of *wenden* to wend] *past of* GO

wen·tle·trap \ˈwen-tᵊl-ˌtrap\ *n* [D *wenteltrap* winding stair, fr. MD *wendeltrappe,* fr. *wendel* turning + *trappe* stairs] (1758) **:** any of a family (Epitoniidae) of marine snails with usu. white shells; *also* **:** one of the shells

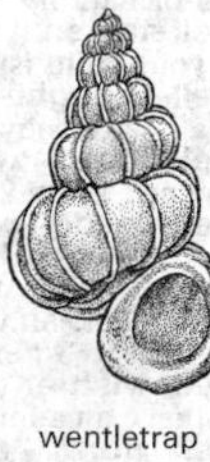

wentletrap

wept *past and past part of* WEEP

were [ME *were* (suppletive sing. past subj. & 2d sing. past indic. of *been* to be), *weren* (suppletive past pl. of *been*), fr. OE *wǣre* (sing. past subj. & 2d sing. past indic. of *wesan* to be), *wǣron* (past pl. indic. of *wesan*), *wǣren* (past pl. subj. of *wesan*) — more at WAS] *past 2d sing, past pl, or past subjunctive of* BE

we're \ˈwir, ˈwər, ˈwē-ər\ (ca. 1529) **:** we are

weren't \(ˈ)wərnt, ˈwər-ənt\ (1691) **:** were not

were·wolf \ˈwir-ˌwu̇lf, ˈwer-, ˈwər-\ *n, pl* **were·wolves** \-ˌwu̇lvz\ [ME, fr. OE *werwulf* (akin to OHG *werwolf* werewolf), fr. *wer* man + *wulf* wolf — more at VIRILE, WOLF] (bef. 12c) **:** a person transformed into a wolf or capable of assuming a wolf's form

wer·gild \ˈwər-ˌgild\ *or* **wer·geld** \-ˌgeld\ *n* [ME *wergeld,* fr. OE, fr. *wer* man + *-geld,* alter. of *gield, geld* payment, tribute — more at GELD] (13c) **:** the value set in Anglo-Saxon and Germanic law upon human life in accordance with rank and paid as compensation to the kindred or lord of a slain person

Wer·nick·e's area \ˈver-nə-kəz-, -kēz-\ *n* [Karl *Wernicke* †1905 Ger. neurologist] (1950) **:** an area of the brain that is located in the posterior left temporal lobe and is associated with comprehension of language

wert \ˈwərt\ *archaic past 2d sing of* BE

wes·kit \ˈwes-kət\ *n* [alter. of *waistcoat*] (1849) **:** VEST 2a

Wes·ley·an·ism \ˈwes-lē-ə-ˌni-zəm *also* ˈwez-\ *n* (1774) **:** METHODISM 1; *specif* **:** the system of Arminian Methodism taught by John Wesley — **Wes·ley·an** \-lē-ən\ *adj or n*

1west \ˈwest\ *adv* [ME, fr. OE; akin to OHG *westar* to the west and prob. to L *vesper* evening, Gk *hesperos*] (bef. 12c) **:** to, toward, or in the west

2west *adj* (bef. 12c) **1 :** situated toward or at the west ⟨the ~ exit⟩ **2 :** coming from the west ⟨a ~ wind⟩

3west *n* (12c) **1 a :** the general direction of sunset **:** the direction to the left of one facing north **b :** the compass point directly opposite to east **2** *cap* **a :** regions or countries lying to the west of a specified or implied point of orientation **b :** the noncommunist countries of Europe and America **3 :** the end of a church opposite the chancel **4** *often cap* **a :** the one of four positions at 90-degree intervals that lies to the west or at the left of a diagram **b :** a person (as a bridge player) occupying this position during a specified activity

west·bound \ˈwes(t)-ˌbau̇nd\ *adj* (1864) **:** traveling or heading west

west by north (1582) **:** a compass point that is one point north of due west **:** N78°45′W

west by south (1577) **:** a compass point that is one point south of due west **:** S78°45′W

west·er \ˈwes-tər\ *vi* **west·ered; west·er·ing** \-t(ə-)riŋ\ [ME *westren,* fr. *1west*] (14c) **:** to turn or move westward ⟨the half moon ~*s* low —A. E. Housman⟩

1west·er·ly \ˈwes-tər-lē\ *adj or adv* [obs. *wester* western] (15c) **1 :** situated toward or belonging to the west ⟨the ~ end of the farm⟩ **2 :** coming from the west ⟨a ~ breeze⟩

2westerly *n, pl* **-lies** (1876) **:** a wind from the west

1west·ern \ˈwes-tərn\ *adj* [ME *westerne,* fr. OE; akin to OHG *westrōni* western, OE *west*] (bef. 12c) **1 a :** coming from the west ⟨a ~ storm⟩ **b :** lying toward the west **2** *cap* **:** of, relating to, or characteristic of a region conventionally designated West: as **a :** steeped in or stemming from the Greco-Roman traditions ⟨*Western* culture⟩ **b :** of or relating to the noncommunist countries of Europe and America **c :** of or relating to the American West ⟨*Western* clothes⟩ **3** *cap* **:** of or relating to the Roman Catholic or Protestant segment of Christianity ⟨*Western* liturgies⟩ — **west·ern·most** \-ˌmōst\ *adj*

2western *n* (1612) **1 :** one that is produced in or characteristic of a western region and esp. the western U.S. **2** *often cap* **:** a novel, story, motion picture, or broadcast dealing with life in the western U.S. esp. during the latter half of the 19th century

Western blot *n* [after *Southern blot*] (1983) **:** a blot consisting of a sheet of nitrocellulose or nylon that contains spots of protein for identification by a suitable molecular probe and is used esp. for the detection of antibodies — **Western blotting** *n*

West·ern·er \ˈwes-tə(r)-nər\ *n* (1599) **1 :** a native or inhabitant of the West; *esp* **:** a native or resident of the western part of the U.S. **2 :** one advocating the adoption of western European culture esp. in 19th century Russia

western hemisphere *n, often cap W&H* (1624) **:** the half of the earth comprising No. and So. America and surrounding waters

west·ern·i·sa·tion, west·ern·ise *Brit var of* WESTERNIZATION, WESTERNIZE

west·ern·i·za·tion \ˌwes-tər-nə-ˈzā-shən\ *n, often cap* (1873) **:** conversion to or adoption of western traditions or techniques

west·ern·ize \ˈwes-tər-ˌnīz\ *vb* **-ized; -iz·ing** *often cap, vt* (1837) **:** to imbue with qualities native to or associated with a western region and esp. the noncommunist countries of Europe and America ~ *vi* **:** to become westernized — **west·ern·iz·er** *n, often cap*

western omelet *n* (1951) **:** an omelet made usu. with diced ham, green pepper, and onion — called also *Denver omelet*

western red cedar *n* (1886) **1 :** a large arborvitae (*Thuja plicata*) chiefly of the Pacific Northwest with reddish-brown bark and wood — called also *red cedar* **2 :** the wood of the western red cedar

western saddle *n, often cap W* (1897) **:** a deep-seated saddle used orig. by cattlemen that has broad skirts and fenders and a high pommel with a horn for holding the lariat — called also *stock saddle*

western sandwich *n* (1924) **:** a sandwich filled with a western omelet — called also *Denver sandwich*

western swing *n* (1968) **:** swing music played typically on country-music instruments (as guitar, fiddle, or steel guitar)

West Germanic *n* (1894) **:** a subdivision of the Germanic languages including English, Frisian, Dutch, and German — see INDO-EUROPEAN LANGUAGES table

West Highland white terrier *n* (ca. 1904) **:** any of a breed of small white long-coated terriers developed in Scotland

West·ie \ˈwes-tē\ *n* (1959) **:** WEST HIGHLAND WHITE TERRIER

west·ing \ˈwes-tiŋ\ *n* (1628) **:** westerly progress **:** a going westward

West Nile *n* (2003) **:** WEST NILE VIRUS

West Nile encephalitis *n* (1949) **:** a severe form of West Nile virus marked by encephalitis

West Nile fever *n* (1943) **:** WEST NILE VIRUS 2

West Nile virus *n* [fr. *West Nile* province of Uganda, where the virus was isolated in 1937] (1940) **1 :** a flavivirus (species *West Nile virus* of the genus *Flavivirus*) that causes an illness marked by fever, headache, muscle ache, skin rash, and sometimes encephalitis or meningitis and that is spread esp. from birds to humans by mosquitoes **2 :** the illness caused by West Nile virus

west–northwest *n* (15c) **:** a compass point that is two points north of due west **:** N67°30′W

West·pha·lian ham \wes(t)-ˈfāl-yən-, -ˈfā-lē-ən-\ *n* [*Westphalia,* Germany] (1722) **:** a ham of distinctive flavor produced by smoking with juniper brush

West Saxon *n* (14c) **1 :** a member or a descendant of the Saxons who occupied England largely south of the Thames, west of the Downs, and east of Dartmoor **2 :** a dialect of Old English used as the chief literary dialect in England before the Norman Conquest

west–southwest *n* (15c) **:** a compass point that is two points south of due west **:** S67°30′W

1west·ward \ˈwes-twərd\ *adv or adj* (bef. 12c) **:** toward the west — **west·wards** \-twərdz\ *adv*

2westward *n* (ca. 1596) **:** westward direction or part ⟨sail to the ~⟩

1wet \ˈwet\ *adj* **wet·ter; wet·test** [ME, partly fr. pp. of *weten* to wet & partly fr. OE *wǣt* wet; akin to ON *vātr* wet, OE *wæter* water] (bef. 12c) **1 a :** consisting of, containing, covered with, or soaked with liquid (as water) **b** *of natural gas* **:** containing appreciable quantities of readily condensable hydrocarbons **2 :** RAINY ⟨~ weather⟩ **3 :** still moist enough to smudge or smear ⟨~ paint⟩ **4 a :** DRUNK 1a ⟨a ~ driver⟩ **b :** having or advocating a policy permitting the manufacture and sale of alcoholic beverages ⟨a ~ county⟩ ⟨a ~ candidate⟩ **5 :** preserved in liquid **6 :** employing or done by means of or in the presence of water or other liquid ⟨~ extraction of copper⟩ **7 :** overly sentimental **8** *Brit* **a :** lacking strength of character **:** WEAK, SPINELESS **b :** belonging to the moderate or liberal wing of the Conservative party — **wet·ly** *adv* — **wet·ness** *n* — **all wet :** completely wrong **:** in error — **wet behind the ears :** IMMATURE, INEXPERIENCED

syn WET, DAMP, DANK, MOIST, HUMID mean covered or more or less soaked with liquid. WET usu. implies saturation but may suggest a covering of a surface with water or something (as paint) not yet dry ⟨slipped on the *wet* pavement⟩. DAMP implies a slight or moderate absorption and often connotes an unpleasant degree of moisture ⟨clothes will mildew if stored in a *damp* place⟩. DANK implies a more distinctly disagreeable or unwholesome dampness ⟨a prisoner in a cold, *dank* cell⟩. MOIST applies to what is slightly damp or not felt as dry ⟨treat the injury with *moist* heat⟩. HUMID applies to the presence of much water vapor in the air ⟨a hot, *humid* climate⟩.

2wet *n* (bef. 12c) **1 :** WATER; *also* **:** MOISTURE, WETNESS **2 :** rainy weather **:** RAIN **3 :** an advocate of a policy of permitting the sale of intoxicating liquors **4** *Brit* **:** one who is wet

3wet *vb* **wet** *or* **wet·ted; wet·ting** [ME *weten,* fr. OE *wǣtan,* fr. *wǣt,* adj.] *vt* (bef. 12c) **1 :** to make wet **2 :** to urinate in or on ⟨~ his pants⟩ ~ *vi* **1 :** to become wet **2 :** URINATE — **wet·ter** \ˈwe-tər\ *n* — **wet one's whistle :** to take a drink esp. of liquor

wet·back \ˈwet-ˌbak\ *n* [fr. the practice of wading or swimming the Rio Grande where it forms the U.S.-Mexico border] (1929) *usu offensive* **:** a Mexican who enters the U.S. illegally

wet bar *n* (1967) **:** a bar for mixing drinks (as in a home) that contains a sink with running water

wet blanket *n* (1844) **:** one that quenches or dampens enthusiasm or pleasure

wet down *vt* (1840) **:** to dampen by sprinkling with water

wet dream *n* (1851) **1 :** an erotic dream culminating in orgasm and in the male accompanied by ejaculation of semen **2 :** an exceedingly pleasurable or exciting experience, situation, or fantasy

weth·er \ˈwe-t͟hər\ *n* [ME, ram, fr. OE; akin to OHG *widar* ram, L *vitu-*

lus calf, *vetus* old, Gk *etos* year] (bef. 12c) **:** a male sheep castrated before sexual maturity; *also* **:** a castrated male goat

wet·land \ˈwet-ˌland, -lənd\ *n* (1669) **:** land or areas (as marshes or swamps) that are covered often intermittently with shallow water or have soil saturated with moisture — usu. used in pl.

wet–nurse *vt* (1784) **1 :** to act as wet nurse to **2 :** to give constant and often excessive care to

wet nurse *n* (1620) **:** a woman who cares for and suckles children not her own

wet suit *n* (1955) **:** a close-fitting suit made of material (as sponge rubber) that is worn (as by a skin diver) esp. in cold water to retain body heat and that traps a thin layer of water against the body

wet·ta·bil·i·ty \ˌwe-tə-ˈbi-lə-tē\ *n* (1913) **:** the quality or state of being wettable **:** the degree to which something can be wet

wet·ta·ble \ˈwe-tə-bəl\ *adj* (1885) **:** capable of being wetted

wetting agent *n* (1927) **:** a substance that by becoming adsorbed prevents a surface from being repellent to a wetting liquid and is used esp. in mixing solids with liquids or spreading liquids on surfaces

wet·tish \ˈwe-tish\ *adj* (1648) **:** somewhat wet **:** MOIST

wet·ware \ˈwet-ˌwer\ *n* [*wet* + soft*ware*] (1975) **:** the human brain or a human being considered esp. with respect to human logical and computational capabilities

wet wash *n* (1916) **:** laundry returned damp and not ironed

we've \ˈwēv\ (1604) **:** we have

wf *abbr* wrong font

WFTU *abbr* World Federation of Trade Unions

wh *abbr* white

WH *abbr* **1** watt-hour **2** withholding

[1]**whack** \ˈhwak, ˈwak\ *vb* [prob. imit. of the sound of a blow] *vt* (1719) **1 a :** to strike with a smart or resounding blow ⟨~ the ball⟩ **b :** to cut with or as if with a whack **:** CHOP **2** *chiefly Brit* **:** to get the better of **:** DEFEAT **3** *slang* **:** MURDER, KILL ~ *vi* **:** to strike a smart or resounding blow — **whack·er** *n*

[2]**whack** *n* (1736) **1 a :** a smart or resounding blow; *also* **:** the sound of or as if of such a blow **b :** a critical attack **2 :** PORTION, SHARE **3 :** CONDITION, STATE **4 a :** an opportunity or attempt to do something ⟨take a ~ at it⟩ **b :** a single action or occasion ⟨borrowed $50 all at one ~⟩ — **out of whack 1 :** out of proper order or shape ⟨threw his knee *out of whack*⟩ **2 :** not in accord ⟨feeling *out of whack* with her contemporaries —S. E. Rubin⟩

whacked–out *also* **wacked–out** \ˈ(h)wakt-ˌau̇t, ˌ(h)wakt-ˈ\ *adj* (1967) **1 :** WORN-OUT, EXHAUSTED **2 :** WACKY ⟨a ~ parody⟩ **3 :** STONED ⟨~ on drugs⟩

[1]**whack·ing** \ˈhwa-kiŋ, ˈwa-\ *adj* (1806) **:** very large **:** WHOPPING

[2]**whacking** *adv* (1853) **:** VERY ⟨a ~ good story⟩

whacko *var of* WACKO

whack off *vb* (1969) *usu vulgar* **:** MASTURBATE

whack up *vt* (ca. 1893) **:** to divide into shares

whacky *var of* WACKY

[1]**whale** \ˈhwāl, ˈwāl\ *n, pl* **whales** *often attrib* [ME, fr. OE *hwæl;* akin to OHG *hwal* whale and perh. to L *squalus* sea fish] (bef. 12c) **1** *or pl* **whale :** CETACEAN; *esp* **:** one (as a sperm whale or killer whale) of larger size **2 :** one that is impressive esp. in size ⟨a ~ of a difference⟩ ⟨a ~ of a good time⟩ — **whale·like** \-ˌlīk\ *adj*

[2]**whale** *vi* **whaled; whal·ing** (1700) **:** to engage in whale fishing

[3]**whale** *vt* **whaled; whal·ing** [origin unknown] (ca. 1790) **1 :** LASH, THRASH **2 :** to strike or hit vigorously **3 :** to defeat soundly

whale·back \ˈhwāl-ˌbak, ˈwāl-\ *n* (1886) **:** something shaped like the back of a whale

whale·boat \-ˌbōt\ *n* (1682) **1 :** a long narrow rowboat made with both ends sharp and raking, often steered with an oar, and formerly used by whalers for hunting whales **2 :** a long narrow rowboat or motorboat resembling the original whaleboats and often carried by warships and merchant ships

whale·bone \-ˌbōn\ *n* (15c) **1 :** BALEEN **2 :** an article made of whalebone

whalebone whale *n* (1725) **:** BALEEN WHALE

whal·er \ˈhwā-lər, ˈwā-\ *n* (1684) **1 :** a person or ship engaged in whale fishing **2 :** WHALEBOAT 2

whale shark *n* (ca. 1885) **:** a shark (*Rhincodon typus*) of warm waters that has small teeth, feeds chiefly on plankton strained by its gill rakers, may sometimes attain a length of up to 60 feet (18.3 meters), and is the largest known fish

whaling *n* (1688) **:** the occupation of catching and extracting commercial products from whales

[1]**wham** \ˈhwam, ˈwam\ *n* [imit.] (1739) **1 :** a solid blow **2 :** the loud sound of a hard impact

[2]**wham** *or* **wham·mo** \ˈhwa-(ˌ)mō, ˈwa-\ *adv* (1924) **:** with violent abruptness ⟨everything was going well; then ~ the deal fell through⟩

[3]**wham** *vb* **whammed; wham·ming** *vt* (1925) **:** to propel, strike, or beat so as to produce a loud impact ~ *vi* **:** to hit or explode with a loud impact

wham·my \ˈhwa-mē, ˈwa-\ *n, pl* **whammies** [prob. fr. [1]*wham*] (1940) **1 a :** a supernatural power bringing bad luck **b :** a magic curse or spell **:** JINX, HEX **2 :** a potent force or attack; *specif* **:** a paralyzing or lethal blow

[1]**whang** \ˈhwaŋ, ˈwaŋ\ *n* [alter. of ME *thong, thwang*] (1536) **1** *dial* **a :** THONG **b :** RAWHIDE **2** *Brit* **:** a large piece **:** CHUNK **3** *often vulgar* **:** PENIS

[2]**whang** *vt* (1684) **1** *dial* **:** BEAT, THRASH **2 :** to propel or strike with force ~ *vi* **:** to beat or work with force or violence

[3]**whang** *n* [imit.] (ca. 1824) **:** a loud sharp vibrant or resonant sound

[4]**whang** *vi* (1728) **:** to make a whang ~ *vt* **:** to strike with a whang

whan·gee \hwaŋ-ˈē, waŋ-, -ˈgē\ *n* [prob. modif. of Chin (Beijing) *huáng* bamboo] (1790) **1 :** the wood of any of several Asian bamboos (genus *Phyllostachys*) **2 :** a walking stick or riding crop of whangee

whap *var of* WHOP

wharf \ˈhwȯrf, ˈwȯrf\ *n, pl* **wharves** \ˈhwȯrvz, ˈwȯrvz\ *also* **wharfs** [ME, fr. OE *hwearf* embankment, wharf; akin to OE *hweorfan* to turn, OHG *hwerban,* Gk *karpos* wrist] (bef. 12c) **1 :** a structure built along or at an angle from the shore of navigable waters so that ships may lie alongside to receive and discharge cargo and passengers **2** *obs* **:** the bank of a river or the shore of the sea

wharf·age \ˈhwȯr-fij, ˈwȯr-\ *n* (14c) **1 a :** the provision or the use of a wharf **b :** the handling or stowing of goods on a wharf **2 :** the charge for the use of a wharf **3 :** the wharf accommodations of a place **:** WHARVES

wharf·in·ger \-fən-jər\ *n* [irreg. fr. *wharfage*] (1552) **:** the operator or manager of a commercial wharf

wharf·mas·ter \ˈhwȯrf-ˌmas-tər, ˈwȯrf-\ *n* (1618) **:** WHARFINGER

[1]**what** \ˈhwät, ˈhwət, ˈwät, ˈwət\ *pron* [ME, fr. OE *hwæt,* neut. of *hwā* who — more at WHO] (bef. 12c) **1 a** (1) — used as an interrogative expressing inquiry about the identity, nature, or value of an object or matter ⟨~ is this⟩ ⟨~ is wealth without friends⟩ ⟨~ does he earn⟩ ⟨~ hath God wrought⟩ (2) — often used to ask for repetition of an utterance or part of an utterance not properly heard or understood ⟨you said ~⟩ **b** (1) *archaic* **:** WHO 1 — used as an interrogative expressing inquiry about the identity of a person (2) — used as an interrogative expressing inquiry about the character, nature, occupation, position, or role of a person ⟨~ do you think I am, a fool⟩ ⟨~ is she, that all our swains commend her —Shak.⟩ **c** — used as an exclamation expressing surprise or excitement and frequently introducing a question ⟨~, no breakfast⟩ **d** — used in expressions directing attention to a statement that the speaker is about to make ⟨you know ~⟩ **e** (1) — used at the end of a question to express inquiry about additional possibilities ⟨is it raining, or snowing, or ~⟩ (2) — used with *or* at the end of a question usu. in expectation of agreement ⟨is this exciting, or ~⟩ **f** *chiefly Brit* — used at the end of an utterance as a form of tag question ⟨a clever play, ~⟩ **2** *chiefly dial* **:** [4]THAT 1, WHICH 3, WHO 3 **3 a :** that which **:** the one or ones that ⟨no income but ~ he gets from his writings⟩ — sometimes used in reference to a clause or phrase that is yet to come or is not yet complete ⟨gave also, ~ is more valuable, understanding⟩ **b :** the thing or things that ⟨~ you need is a vacation⟩ ⟨~ angered us was the tone of the article⟩ **4 a :** WHATEVER 1a ⟨say ~ you will⟩ **b** *obs* **:** WHOEVER — **what for 1 :** for what purpose or reason **:** WHY — usu. used with the other words of a question between *what* and *for* ⟨*what* did you do that *for*⟩ except when used alone **2 :** harsh treatment esp. by blows or by a sharp reprimand ⟨gave him *what for* in violent Spanish —*New Yorker*⟩ — **what have you :** WHATNOT ⟨novels, plays, short stories, travelogues, and *what have you* —Haldeen Braddy⟩ — **what if 1 :** what will or would be the result if **2 :** what does it matter if ⟨so *what if* he doesn't like it⟩ — **what of 1 :** what is the situation with respect to **2 :** what importance can be assigned to — **what's more :** in addition **:** FURTHERMORE — **what's what :** the true state of things ⟨knows *what's what* when it comes to fashion⟩ — **what though :** what does it matter if ⟨*what though* the rose have prickles, yet 'tis plucked —Shak.⟩

[2]**what** *adv* (bef. 12c) **1** *obs* **:** WHY **2 :** in what respect **:** HOW ⟨~ does he care⟩ **3** — used to introduce prepositional phrases in parallel construction or a prepositional phrase that expresses cause and usu. has more than one object; used principally before phrases beginning with *with* ⟨~ with unemployment increasing⟩ ⟨~ with the war, ~ with the sweat, ~ with the gallows, and ~ with poverty, I am custom-shrunk —Shak.⟩

[3]**what** *adj* (13c) **1 a** — used as an interrogative expressing inquiry about the identity, nature, or value of a person, object, or matter ⟨~ minerals do we export⟩ **b :** how remarkable or striking for good or bad qualities — used esp. in exclamatory utterances and dependent clauses ⟨~ mountains⟩ ⟨remember ~ fun we had⟩ ⟨~ a suggestion⟩ ⟨~ a charming girl⟩ **2 a** (1) **:** WHATEVER 1a (2) **:** ANY ⟨ornament of ~ description soever⟩ **b :** the . . . that **:** as much or as many . . . as ⟨rescued ~ survivors they found⟩

what all \ˈhwä-ˌdȯl, ˈwä-, ˈ(h)wə-\ *pron* (1702) **:** WHATNOT

what·cha·ma·call·it \ˈhwä-chə-mə-ˌkȯ-lət, ˈwä-, ˈ(h)wə-\ *n* [alter. of *what you may call it*] (1928) **:** THINGAMAJIG

[1]**what·ev·er** \hwät-ˈe-vər, wät-, (h)wət-\ *pron* (14c) **1 a :** anything or everything that ⟨take ~ you want⟩ **b :** no matter what ⟨~ he says, they won't believe him⟩ **c :** WHATNOT ⟨enjoys skiing, hiking, or ~⟩ **2 :** WHAT 1a(1) — used to express astonishment or perplexity ⟨~ do you mean by that⟩

[2]**whatever** *adj* (14c) **1 a :** any . . . that **:** all . . . that ⟨buy peace . . . on ~ terms could be obtained —C. S. Forester⟩ **b :** no matter what ⟨money, in ~ hands, will confer power —Samuel Johnson⟩ **2 :** of any kind at all — used after the substantive it modifies with *any* or with an expressed or implied negative ⟨in any order ~ —W. G. Moulton⟩ ⟨no food ~⟩

[3]**whatever** *adv* (1870) **:** in any case **:** whatever the case may be — sometimes used interjectionally to suggest the unimportance of an issue or decision between alternatives ⟨go see a movie, watch TV,— ~⟩

what–if \ˌhwät-ˈif, ˌwät-, ˌ(h)wət-\ *n* (1970) **:** a suppositional question — **what–if** *adj*

what·ness \ˈhwät-nəs, ˈwät-, ˈ(h)wət-\ *n* (1611) **:** QUIDDITY 1

[1]**what·not** \ˈhwät-ˌnät, ˈwät-, ˈ(h)wət-\ *pron* [*what not?*] (1540) **:** any of various other things that might also be mentioned ⟨paper clips, pins, and ~⟩

[2]**whatnot** *n* (1602) **1 :** a nondescript person or thing **2 :** a light open set of shelves for bric-a-brac

what·sit \ˈhwät-sət, ˈwät-, ˈ(h)wət-\ *also* **what·sis** \-səs\ *or* **what–is–it** \-iz-ət\ *n* [*whatsit* & *whatsis* contr. of *what-is-it*] (ca. 1882) **:** THINGAMAJIG

what·so·ev·er \ˌhwät-sə-ˈwe-vər, ˌwät-, ˌ(h)wət-\ *pron or adj* (13c) **:** WHATEVER

whaup \ˈhwȯp, ˈwȯp\ *n, pl* **whaup** *also* **whaups** [imit.] (ca. 1512) *chiefly Scot* **:** a European curlew (*Numenius arquata*)

wheal \ˈhwēl, ˈwēl\ *n* [alter. of [1]*wale*] (1808) **:** a suddenly formed elevation of the skin surface **:** WELT; *esp* **:** a flat burning or itching eminence on the skin

wheat \ˈhwēt, ˈwēt\ *n, often attrib* [ME *whete,* fr. OE *hwǣte;* akin to OHG *weizzi* wheat, *hwīz, wīz* white — more at WHITE] (bef. 12c) **1 :** a cereal grain that yields a fine white flour used chiefly in breads, baked goods (as cakes and crackers), and pastas (as macaroni or spaghetti), and is important in animal feeds **2 :** any of various Old World annual grasses (genus *Triticum,* esp. *T. aestivum* and *T. turgidum*) of wide climatic adaptability that are cultivated in most temperate areas for the wheat they yield **3 :** a light yellow

wheat berry *n* (1848) **:** an unprocessed whole kernel of wheat

wheat bread *n* (14c) **:** a bread made of a combination of white and whole wheat flours as distinguished from bread made entirely of white or whole wheat flour

wheat cake *n* (1703) **:** a pancake made of wheat flour

wheat·ear \ˈhwēt-ˌir, ˈwēt-\ *n* [back-formation fr. earlier *wheatears* wheatear, prob. by folk etymology or euphemism fr. *white* + *arse*] (1591) **:** any of various small thrushes (genus *Oenanthe*); *esp* **:** a white-rumped one (*O. oenanthe*) of northern No. America and the Old World

[1]**wheat·en** \ˈhwē-tᵊn, ˈwē-\ *adj* (bef. 12c) **:** of, relating to, or made of wheat

[2]**wheaten** *n* (ca. 1931) **:** a pale yellowish to ruddy-fawn color characteristic of the coat of some dogs

wheat germ *n* (1881) **:** the embryo of the wheat kernel separated in milling and used esp. as a source of vitamins and protein

wheat·grass \ˈhwēt-ˌgras, ˈwēt-\ *n* (1668) **:** any of a genus (*Agropyron*) of perennial grasses including some which are important pasture, hay, or turf grasses

wheat·land \ˈhwēt-ˌland, ˈwēt-\ *n* (bef. 12c) **:** land used or suitable for growing wheat

wheat rust *n* (1870) **:** a destructive disease of wheat caused by rust fungi; *also* **:** a fungus (as *Puccinia graminis*) causing a wheat rust

Wheat·stone bridge \ˈhwēt-ˌstōn-, ˈwēt-, *chiefly Brit* -stən-\ *n* [Sir Charles *Wheatstone*] (1872) **:** an electrical bridge consisting of two branches of a parallel circuit joined by a galvanometer and used for determining the value of an unknown resistance in one of the branches

whee \ˈhwē, ˈwē\ *interj* (1898) — used to express delight or exuberance

whee·dle \ˈhwē-dᵊl, ˈwē-\ *vb* **whee·dled; whee·dling** \ˈ(h)wēd-liŋ, ˈ(h)wē-dᵊl-iŋ\ [origin unknown] *vt* (ca. 1661) **1 :** to influence or entice by soft words or flattery **2 :** to gain or get by wheedling ⟨~ one's way into favor⟩ ~ *vi* **:** to use soft words or flattery ***syn*** see CAJOLE

[1]**wheel** \ˈhwēl, ˈwēl\ *n, often attrib* [ME, fr. OE *hweogol, hwēol;* akin to ON *hvēl* wheel, Gk *kyklos* circle, wheel, Skt *cakra,* L *colere* to cultivate, inhabit, Skt *carati* he moves, wanders] (bef. 12c) **1 :** a circular frame of hard material that may be solid, partly solid, or spoked and that is capable of turning on an axle **2 :** a contrivance or apparatus having as its principal part a wheel: as **a :** a chiefly medieval instrument of torture designed for mutilating a victim (as by stretching or disjointing) **b :** BICYCLE **c :** any of many revolving disks or drums used as gambling paraphernalia **d :** POTTER'S WHEEL **e :** STEERING WHEEL **3 a :** an imaginary turning wheel symbolizing the inconstancy of fortune **b :** a recurring course, development, or action **:** CYCLE **4 :** something (as a round flat cheese) resembling a wheel in shape **5 a :** a curving or circular movement **b :** a rotation or turn usu. about an axis or center; *specif* **:** a turning movement of troops or ships in line in which the units preserve alignment and relative positions as they change direction **6 a :** a moving or essential part of something compared to a machine ⟨the ~*s* of government⟩ **b :** a directing or controlling force **c :** a person of importance esp. in an organization ⟨a big ~⟩ **7 :** the refrain or burden of a song **8 a :** a circuit of theaters or places of entertainment **b :** a sports league **9** *pl, slang* **:** a wheeled vehicle; *esp* **:** AUTOMOBILE **10** *pl, slang* **:** LEGS — **wheel·less** \ˈhwēl-ləs, ˈwēl-\ *adj*

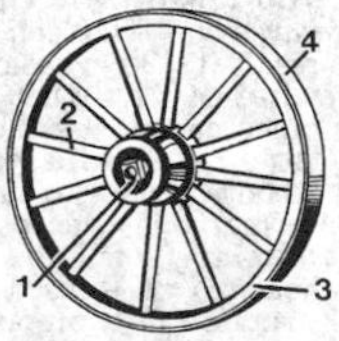

wheel 1: *1* hub, *2* spoke, *3* felly, *4* tire

[2]**wheel** *vi* (13c) **1 :** to turn on or as if on an axis **:** REVOLVE **2 :** to change direction as if revolving on a pivot ⟨the battalion would have ~*ed* to the flank —Walter Bernstein⟩ ⟨her mind will ~ around to the other extreme —Liam O'Flaherty⟩ ⟨~*ed* to face her opponent⟩ **3 :** to move or extend in a circle or curve ⟨birds in ~*ing* flight⟩ ⟨valleys where young cotton ~*ed* slowly in fanlike rows —William Faulkner⟩ **4 :** to travel on or as if on wheels or in a wheeled vehicle ~ *vt* **1 :** to cause to turn on or as if on an axis **:** ROTATE **2 :** to convey or move on or as if on wheels or in a wheeled vehicle ⟨~*ed* the patient back to his room⟩ ⟨~*ed* the car into the driveway⟩ ⟨~ in the experts⟩ **3 :** to cause to change direction as if revolving on a pivot **4 :** to make or perform in a circle or curve — **wheel and deal :** to make deals or do business esp. shrewdly or briskly

wheel and axle *n* (1759) **:** a mechanical device consisting of a grooved wheel turned by a cord or chain with a rigidly attached axle (as for winding up a weight) together with the supporting standards

wheel animal *n* (1788) **:** ROTIFER

[1]**wheel·bar·row** \ˈhwēl-ˌba-(ˌ)rō, ˈwēl-\ *n* (14c) **:** a small usu. single-wheeled vehicle that is used for carrying small loads and is fitted with handles at the rear by which it can be pushed and guided

[2]**wheelbarrow** *vt* (1721) **:** to convey in a wheelbarrow

wheel·base \ˈhwēl-ˌbās, ˈwēl-\ *n* (1863) **:** the distance in inches between the front and rear axles of an automotive vehicle

wheel bug *n* (1815) **:** a large No. American assassin bug (*Arilus cristatus*) that has a high serrated crest on its prothorax and preys on insects

wheel·chair \ˈhwēl-ˌcher, ˈwēl-\ *n* (ca. 1700) **:** a chair mounted on wheels esp. for the use of disabled persons

wheeled \ˈhwēld, ˈwēld\ *adj* (1572) **1 :** equipped with wheels ⟨~ vehicles⟩ **2 :** moving or functioning by means of wheels ⟨~ traffic⟩

wheel·er \ˈhwē-lər, ˈwē-\ *n* (1683) **1 :** one that wheels **2 :** a draft animal (as a horse) pulling in the position nearest the front wheels of a wagon **3 :** something (as a vehicle or ship) that has wheels — used esp. in combination ⟨a side-*wheeler*⟩ ⟨18-*wheelers*⟩

wheeler and dealer *n, pl* **wheelers and dealers** (1966) **:** WHEELER-DEALER

wheel·er–deal·er \ˌhwē-lər-ˈdē-lər, ˌwē-\ *n* (1954) **:** a shrewd operator esp. in business or politics

wheel·horse \ˈhwēl-ˌhȯrs, ˈwēl-\ *n* (1708) **1 :** a horse (as in a tandem) in a position nearest the wheels **2 :** a steady and effective worker esp. in a political body

wheel·house \-ˌhau̇s\ *n* (1835) **:** PILOTHOUSE

wheel·ie \ˈhwē-lē, ˈwē-\ *n* (ca. 1965) **:** a maneuver in which a wheeled vehicle (as a bicycle) is momentarily balanced on its rear wheel or wheels

wheel·ing \ˈhwē-liŋ, ˈwē-\ *n* (15c) **1 :** the act or process of one that wheels **2 :** the condition of a road relative to passage on wheels

wheel lock *n* (1670) **:** a gun's lock for a muzzle-loading firearm in which sparks are struck from a flint or a piece of pyrite by a revolving wheel

wheel·man \ˈhwēl-mən, ˈwēl-\ *n* (1865) **1 a :** HELMSMAN **b :** the driver of an automobile **2 :** CYCLIST

wheels·man \ˈhwēlz-mən, ˈwēlz-\ *n* (1866) **:** one who steers with a wheel; *esp* **:** HELMSMAN

wheel–thrown \ˈhwēl-ˌthrōn, ˈwēl-\ *adj* (1964) **:** made on a potter's wheel ⟨~ pottery⟩

wheel·work \ˈhwēl-ˌwərk, ˈwēl-\ *n* (1640) **:** wheels in gear and their connections in a machine or mechanism

wheel·wright \-ˌrīt\ *n* (13c) **:** a maker and repairer of wheels and wheeled vehicles

[1]**wheen** \ˈhwēn, ˈwēn\ *adj* [ME (Sc) *quheyne,* fr. OE *hwǣne, hwēne,* adv., somewhat, fr. instr. of *hwōn* little, few] (14c) *dial Brit* **:** FEW 2

[2]**wheen** *n* (1680) *dial Brit* **:** a considerable number or amount

[1]**wheeze** \ˈhwēz, ˈwēz\ *vi* **wheezed; wheez·ing** [ME *whesen,* prob. of Scand origin; akin to ON *hvæsa* to hiss; akin to OE *hwǣst* action of blowing, Skt *śvasiti* he blows, snorts] (15c) **1 :** to breathe with difficulty usu. with a whistling sound **2 :** to make a sound resembling that of wheezing ⟨the bellows *wheezed*⟩

[2]**wheeze** *n* (1800) **1 :** a sound of wheezing **2 a :** an often repeated and widely known joke used esp. by entertainers **b :** a trite saying or proverb

wheezy \ˈhwē-zē, ˈwē-\ *adj* **wheez·i·er; -est** (1818) **1 :** inclined to wheeze **2 :** having a wheezing sound ⟨a ~ cough⟩ ⟨the ~ call of a phoebe⟩ — **wheez·i·ly** \-zə-lē\ *adv* — **wheez·i·ness** \-zē-nəs\ *n*

[1]**whelk** \ˈhwelk, ˈwelk, ˈwilk\ *n* [ME *welke,* fr. OE *weoloc;* akin to MD *willoc* whelk and perh. to L *volvere* to turn — more at VOLUBLE] (bef. 12c) **:** any of numerous large marine snails (as of the genus *Buccinum*); *esp* **:** one (*B. undatum*) used as food in Europe

[2]**whelk** \ˈhwelk, ˈwelk\ *n* [ME *whelke,* fr. OE *hwylca,* fr. *hwelian* to suppurate] (bef. 12c) **:** PAPULE, PUSTULE

whelm \ˈhwelm, ˈwelm\ *vb* [ME] *vt* (14c) **1 :** to turn (as a dish or vessel) upside down usu. to cover something **:** cover or engulf completely with usu. disastrous effect **2 :** to overcome in thought or feeling **:** OVERWHELM ⟨~*ed* with a rush of joy —G. A. Wagner⟩ ~ *vi* **:** to pass or go over something so as to bury or submerge it

[1]**whelp** \ˈhwelp, ˈwelp\ *n* [ME, fr. OE *hwelp;* akin to OHG *hwelf* whelp] (bef. 12c) **1 :** any of the young of various carnivorous mammals and esp. of the dog **2 :** a young boy or girl

[2]**whelp** *vt* (13c) **:** to give birth to — used of various carnivores and esp. the dog ~ *vi* **:** to bring forth young

[1]**when** \ˈhwen, ˈwen, (h)wən\ *adv* [ME, fr. OE *hwanne, hwenne;* akin to OHG *hwanne* when, OE *hwā* who — more at WHO] (bef. 12c) **1 :** at what time ⟨~ will you return⟩ **2 a :** at or during which time **b :** and then **3 :** at a former and usu. less prosperous time ⟨brag fondly of having known him ~ —Vance Packard⟩

[2]**when** *conj* [ME, fr. OE *hwanne, hwenne,* fr. *hwanne, hwenne,* adv.] (bef. 12c) **1 a :** at or during the time that **:** WHILE ⟨went fishing ~ he was a boy⟩ **b :** just at the moment that ⟨stop writing ~ the bell rings⟩ **c :** at any or every time that ⟨~ he listens to music, he falls asleep⟩ **2 :** in the event that **:** IF ⟨a contestant is disqualified ~ he disobeys the rules⟩ **3 a :** considering that ⟨why use water at all ~ you can drown in it —Stuart Chase⟩ **b :** in spite of the fact that **:** ALTHOUGH ⟨quit politics ~ I might have had a great career in it⟩ **4 :** the time or occasion at or in which ⟨tomorrow is ~ we must decide⟩ ⟨humor is ~ you laugh —Earl Rovit⟩

[3]**when** \ˈhwen, ˈwen\ *pron* (14c) **:** what or which time ⟨life-long homes for those . . . who have lived here since ~ —Kim Waller⟩

[4]**when** *n* (1616) **:** the time in which something is done or comes about ⟨troubled his head very little about the hows and ~*s* of life —Laurence Sterne⟩

when·as \hwe-ˈnaz, we-, (h)wə-\ *conj* [ME (Sc) *when as,* fr. ME *when* + *as*] (15c) *archaic* **:** WHEN

[1]**whence** \ˈhwen(t)s, ˈwen(t)s\ *adv* [ME *whennes,* fr. *whenne* whence (fr. OE *hwanon*) + *-s,* adv. suffix, fr. *-s,* gen. sing. ending; akin to OHG *hwanān* whence, OE *hwā* who] (13c) **:** from what place, source, or cause ⟨then ~ comes this paradox —*Changing Times*⟩ — **from whence :** from what place, source, or cause ⟨no one could tell me *from whence* the gold had come —Graham Greene⟩

[2]**whence** *conj* (13c) **1 :** from what place, source, or cause ⟨inquired ~ the water came —Maria Edgeworth⟩ **2 a :** from or out of which place, source, or cause ⟨the lawless society ~ the ballads sprang —DeLancey Ferguson⟩ **b :** by reason of which fact **:** WHEREFORE ⟨nothing broke— ~ I infer that my bones are not yet chalky —O. W. Holmes †1935⟩

whence·so·ev·er \ˈhwen(t)(s)-sə-ˌwe-vər, ˈwen(t)(s)-\ *conj* (1511) **:** from whatever place or source

[1]**when·ev·er** \hwe-ˈne-vər, we-, (h)wə-\ *conj* (14c) **:** at any or every time that

[2]**whenever** *adv* (ca. 1576) **:** at whatever time

[1]**when·so·ev·er** \ˈhwen(t)-sə-ˌwe-vər, ˈwen(t)-\ *conj* (14c) **:** WHENEVER

[2]**whensoever** *adv* (1526) *obs* **:** at any time whatever

[1]**where** \ˈhwer, ˈwer, (ˌ)(h)wər\ *adv* [ME, fr. OE *hwǣr;* akin to OHG *hwār* where, OE *hwā* who — more at WHO] (bef. 12c) **1 a :** at, in, or to what place ⟨~ is the house⟩ ⟨~ are we going⟩ **b :** at, in, or to what situation, position, direction, circumstances, or respect ⟨~ does this plan lead⟩ ⟨~ am I wrong⟩ **2** *archaic* **:** HERE, THERE ⟨lo, ~ it comes again —Shak.⟩

[2]**where** *conj* (12c) **1 a :** at, in, or to what place ⟨knows ~ the house is⟩ **b :** at, in, or to what situation, position, direction, circumstances, or respect ⟨shows ~ the plan leads⟩ **c :** the place or point at, in, or to which ⟨couldn't see from ~ he was sitting⟩ ⟨kept that horse and gentled him to ~ I finally rode him —William Faulkner⟩ **2 :** WHEREVER ⟨goes ~ she likes⟩ **3 a :** at, in, or to which place ⟨the town ~ she lives⟩ **b :** at or in which ⟨has reached the size ~ traffic is a problem⟩ ⟨two fireplaces ~ you can bake bread in the ovens —Randall Jarrell⟩ **4 a :** at, in, or to the place at, in, or to which ⟨stay ~ you

are⟩ ⟨send him away ~ he'll forget⟩ **b :** in a case, situation, or respect in which ⟨outstanding ~ endurance is called for⟩ **5 :** THAT ⟨I've read ~ they do it that way in some Middle Eastern countries —Andy Rooney⟩

[3]where \ˈhwer, ˈwer\ *n* (15c) **1 :** PLACE, LOCATION ⟨the ~ and the how of the accident⟩ **2 :** what place, source, or cause ⟨I know ~ that comes from⟩ — **where it's at 1 a :** a place of central interest or activity **b :** something (as a topic or field of interest) of primary concern or importance ⟨education is *where it's at*⟩ **2 :** the true nature of things — **where one is at :** one's true position, state, or nature

[1]where·abouts \-ə-ˌbau̇ts\ *also* **where·about** \-ˌbau̇t\ *adv* [ME *wherabouts* (fr. *wher aboute* + *-s,* adv. suffix) & *wher aboute,* fr. *where, wher* where + *about, aboute* about — more at WHENCE] (14c) **:** about where **:** near what place ⟨~ is the house⟩

[2]whereabouts *also* **whereabout** *conj* (14c) **1** *obs* **:** on what business or errand **2 :** near what place **:** WHERE ⟨know ~ he lives⟩

[3]whereabouts *n pl but sing or pl in constr, also* **whereabout** (1605) **:** the place or general locality where a person or thing is ⟨their present ~ are a secret⟩

[1]where·as \hwer-ˈaz, wer-, (ˌ)(h)wər-\ *conj* [ME *where as,* fr. *where* + *as*] (14c) **1 a :** while on the contrary **b :** ALTHOUGH **2 :** in view of the fact that **:** SINCE — used esp. to introduce a preamble

[2]whereas *n* (1795) **1 :** an introductory statement of a formal document **:** PREAMBLE **2 :** a conditional or qualifying statement

where·at \-ˈat\ *conj* (14c) **1 :** at or toward which **2 :** in consequence of which **:** WHEREUPON

[1]where·by \-ˈbī\ *conj* (13c) **:** by, through, or in accordance with which

[2]whereby *adv* (14c) *obs* **:** by what **:** HOW

[1]where·fore \ˈhwer-ˌfȯr, ˈwer-\ *adv* [ME *wherfor, wherfore,* fr. *where, wher* + *for, fore* for] (13c) **1 :** for what reason or purpose **:** WHY **2 :** THEREFORE

[2]wherefore *n* (1590) **:** an answer or statement giving an explanation **:** REASON ⟨wants to know the whys and ~*s*⟩

where·from \-ˌfrəm, -ˌfräm\ *conj* (14c) **:** from which

[1]where·in \hwer-ˈin, wer-, (ˌ)(h)wər-\ *adv* (13c) **:** in what **:** in what particular or respect ⟨~ was I wrong⟩

[2]wherein *conj* (14c) **1 a :** in which **:** WHERE ⟨the city ~ he lives⟩ **b :** during which **2 :** in what way **:** HOW ⟨showed me ~ I was wrong⟩

where·in·to \-ˈin-(ˌ)tü\ *conj* (1539) **:** into which

[1]where·of \-ˈəv, -ˈäv\ *conj* (13c) **1** *archaic* **:** with or by which **2 :** of what ⟨knows ~ she speaks⟩ **3 a :** of which ⟨books ~ the best are lost⟩ **b :** of whom

[2]whereof *adv* (13c) *archaic* **:** of what ⟨~ are you made —Shak.⟩

[1]where·on \-ˈȯn, -ˈän\ *conj* (13c) **1** *archaic* **:** on what ⟨tell me ~ the likelihood depends —Shak.⟩ **2 :** on which ⟨the base ~ it rests⟩

[2]whereon *adv* (15c) *archaic* **:** on what ⟨~ do you look —Shak.⟩

where·so·ev·er \ˈhwer-sə-ˌwe-vər, ˈwer-\ *conj* (13c) **:** WHEREVER

where·through \ˈhwer-ˌthrü, ˈwer-\ *conj* (13c) **:** through which

[1]where·to \-ˌtü\ *adv* (13c) **:** to what place, purpose, or end ⟨~ tends all this —Shak.⟩

[2]whereto *conj* (14c) **:** to which

where·un·to \hwer-ˈən-(ˌ)tü, wer-, (ˌ)(h)wər-\ *adv or conj* (15c) **:** WHERETO

where·up·on \ˈhwer-ə-ˌpȯn, ˈwer-, -ˌpän\ *conj* (14c) **1 :** on which **2 :** closely following and in consequence of which

[1]wher·ev·er \hwer-ˈe-vər, wer-, (ˌ)(h)wər-\ *adv* (13c) **1 :** where in the world ⟨~ did you get that tie⟩ **2 :** anywhere at all ⟨explore northward or ~ —Bernard De Voto⟩

[2]wherever *conj* (14c) **1 :** at, in, or to any or all places that ⟨thrives ~ he goes⟩ **2 :** in any circumstance in which ⟨~ it is possible, we try to help⟩

[1]where·with \ˈhwer-ˌwith, ˈwer-, -ˌwith\ *pron* (13c) *archaic* **:** that with or by which — used with an infinitive ⟨so shall I have ~ to answer him —Ps 119:42 (AV)⟩

[2]wherewith *adv* (13c) *obs* **:** with what ⟨~ shall it be salted —Mt 5:13 (AV)⟩

[3]wherewith *conj* (14c) **:** with or by means of which ⟨metal tools ~ to break ground —Russell Lord⟩

[1]where·with·al \ˈhwer-wi-ˌthȯl, ˈwer-, -ˌthȯl\ *conj* [*where* + [2]*withal*] (1534) **:** WHEREWITH

[2]wherewithal *pron* (1583) **:** WHEREWITH

[3]wherewithal *n* (1809) **:** MEANS, RESOURCES; *specif* **:** MONEY ⟨didn't have the ~ for an expensive dinner⟩

wher·ry \ˈhwer-ē, ˈwer-\ *n, pl* **wherries** [ME *whery*] (15c) **1 :** any of various light boats: as **a :** a long light rowboat made sharp at both ends and used to transport passengers on rivers and about harbors **b :** a racing scull for one person **2 :** a large light barge, lighter, or fishing boat varying in type in different parts of Great Britain

[1]whet \ˈhwet, ˈwet\ *vt* **whet·ted; whet·ting** [ME *whetten,* fr. OE *hwettan;* akin to OHG *wezzen* to whet, *waz* sharp] (bef. 12c) **1 :** to sharpen by rubbing on or with something (as a stone) ⟨~ a knife⟩ **2 :** to make keen or more acute **:** EXCITE, STIMULATE ⟨~ the appetite⟩ ⟨*whetted* her curiosity⟩ — **whet·ter** *n*

[2]whet *n* (ca. 1628) **1** *dial* **a :** a spell of work done with a scythe between the time it is sharpened and the time it needs to be sharpened again **b :** TIME, WHILE **2 :** something that sharpens or makes keen: **a :** GOAD, INCITEMENT **b :** APPETIZER; *also* **:** a drink of liquor

[1]wheth·er \ˈhwe-thər, ˈwe-, (ˌ)(h)wə-\ *pron* [ME, fr. OE *hwæther, hwether;* akin to OHG *hwedar* which of two, L *uter,* Gk *poteros,* OE *hwā* who — more at WHO] (bef. 12c) **1** *archaic* **:** which one of the two **2** *archaic* **:** whichever one of the two

[2]whether *conj* (bef. 12c) — used as a function word usu. with correlative *or* or with *or whether* to indicate (1) until the early 19th century a direct question involving alternatives; (2) an indirect question involving stated or implied alternatives ⟨decide ~ he should agree or raise objections⟩ ⟨wondered ~ to stay⟩; (3) alternative conditions or possibilities ⟨see me no more, ~ he be dead or no —Shak.⟩ ⟨seated him next to her ~ by accident or design⟩ — **whether or no** *or* **whether or not :** in any case ⟨they've only been married a very few weeks, *whether or no* —Thomas Hardy⟩

whet·stone \ˈhwet-ˌstōn, ˈwet-\ *n* (bef. 12c) **:** a stone for whetting edge tools

whew *often read as* ˈhwü, ˈwü, ˈhyü; *the interj is a whistle concluded with a voiceless* ü\ *n* [imit.] (1513) **:** a whistling sound or a sound like a half-formed whistle uttered as an exclamation ⟨gave a long ~ when he realized the size of the job⟩ — used interjectionally chiefly to express amazement, discomfort, or relief

whey \ˈhwā, ˈwā\ *n* [ME, fr. OE *hwæg;* akin to MD *wey* whey] (bef. 12c) **:** the watery part of milk that is separated from the coagulable part or curd esp. in the process of making cheese and that is rich in lactose, minerals, and vitamins and contains lactalbumin and traces of fat — **whey·like** \-ˌlīk\ *adj*

whey–face \ˈhwā-ˌfās, ˈwā-\ *n* (1605) **:** a person having a pale face (as from fear) — **whey–faced** \-ˌfāst\ *adj*

[1]which \ˈhwich, ˈwich\ *adj* [ME, of what kind, which, fr. OE *hwilc;* akin to OHG *wilīh* of what kind, which, OE *hwā* who, *gelīk* like — more at WHO, LIKE] (bef. 12c) **1 :** being what one or ones out of a group — used as an interrogative ⟨~ tie should I wear⟩ ⟨kept a record of ~ employees took their vacations in July⟩ **2 :** WHICHEVER ⟨it will not fit, turn it ~ way you like⟩ **3** — used as a function word to introduce a nonrestrictive relative clause and to modify a noun in that clause and to refer together with that noun to a word or word group in a preceding clause or to an entire preceding clause or sentence or longer unit of discourse ⟨in German, ~ language might . . . have been the medium of transmission —Thomas Pyles⟩ ⟨that this city is a rebellious city . . . : for ~ cause was this city destroyed —Ezra 4:15 (AV)⟩

[2]which *pron* (bef. 12c) **1 :** what one or ones out of a group — used as an interrogative ⟨~ of those houses do you live in⟩ ⟨~ of you want tea and ~ want lemonade⟩ ⟨he is swimming or canoeing, I don't know ~⟩ **2 :** WHICHEVER ⟨take ~ you like⟩ **3** — used as a function word to introduce a relative clause; used in any grammatical relation except that of a possessive; used esp. in reference to animals, inanimate objects, groups, or ideas ⟨the bonds ~ represent the debt —G. B. Robinson⟩ ⟨the Samnite tribes, ~ settled south and southeast of Rome —Ernst Pulgram⟩; used freely in reference to persons as recently as the 17th century ⟨our Father ~ art in heaven —Mt 6:9(AV)⟩, and still occas. so used but usu. with some implication of emphasis on the function or role of the person rather than on the person as such ⟨chiefly they wanted husbands, ~ they got easily —Lynn White⟩; used by speakers on all educational levels and by many reputable writers, though disapproved by some grammarians, in reference to an idea expressed by a word or group of words that is not necessarily a noun or noun phrase ⟨he resigned that post, after ~ he engaged in ranching —*Current Biog.*⟩ ***usage*** see [4]THAT

[1]which·ev·er \hwich-ˈe-vər, wich-\ *adj* (14c) **:** being whatever one or ones out of a group **:** no matter which ⟨its soothing . . . effect will be the same ~ way you take it —*Punch*⟩

[2]whichever *pron* (14c) **:** whatever one or ones out of a group ⟨take two of the four elective subjects, ~ you prefer⟩

which·so·ev·er \ˌhwich-sə-ˈwe-vər, ˌwich-\ *pron or adj* (15c) *archaic* **:** WHICHEVER

whick·er \ˈhwi-kər, ˈwi-\ *vi* **whick·ered; whick·er·ing** \-k(ə-)riŋ\ [imit.] (1753) **:** NEIGH, WHINNY — **whicker** *n*

whid \ˈhwid, ˈwid\ *vi* **whid·ded; whid·ding** [Sc *whid* silent rapid motion] (1728) *Scot* **:** to move nimbly and silently

[1]whiff \ˈhwif, ˈwif\ *n* [imit.] (1591) **1 a :** a quick puff or slight gust esp. of air, odor, gas, smoke, or spray **b :** an inhalation of odor, gas, or smoke **c :** a slight puffing or whistling sound **2 :** a slight trace or indication ⟨a ~ of scandal⟩ **3 :** STRIKEOUT

[2]whiff *vi* (1591) **1 :** to move with or as if with a puff of air **2 :** to emit whiffs **:** PUFF **3 :** to inhale an odor **4 :** STRIKE OUT 3 ~ *vt* **1 a :** to carry or convey by or as if by a whiff **:** BLOW **b :** to expel or puff out in a whiff **:** EXHALE **c :** SMOKE 3 **2 :** FAN 8 ⟨~*ed* three batters⟩

whif·fet \ˈhwi-fət, ˈwi-\ *n* [prob. alter. of *whippet*] (1839) **:** a small, young, or unimportant person

whif·fle \ˈhwi-fəl, ˈwi-\ *vb* **whif·fled; whif·fling** \-f(ə-)liŋ\ [prob. freq. of *whiff*] *vi* (1568) **1 a** *of the wind* **:** to blow unsteadily or in gusts **b :** VACILLATE **2 :** to emit or produce a light whistling or puffing sound ~ *vt* **:** to blow, disperse, emit, or expel with or as if with a whiff

[1]whif·fler \ˈhwi-flər, ˈwi-\ *n* [alter. of earlier *wifler,* fr. obs. *wifle* battle-ax] (1539) *Brit* **:** one that clears the way for a procession

[2]whif·fler \ˈhwi-f(ə-)lər, ˈwi-\ *n* [*whiffle*] (1607) **1 :** a person who frequently changes opinions or course **2 :** a person who uses shifts and evasions in argument

whif·fle·tree \ˈhwi-fəl-(ˌ)trē, ˈwi-\ *n* [alter. of *whippletree*] (ca. 1806) **:** the pivoted swinging bar to which the traces of a harness are fastened and by which a vehicle or implement is drawn

Whig \ˈhwig, ˈwig\ *n* [short for *Whiggamore,* member of a Scottish group that marched to Edinburgh in 1648 to oppose the court party] (1702) **1 :** a member or supporter of a major British political group of the late 17th through early 19th centuries seeking to limit the royal authority and increase parliamentary power — compare TORY **2 :** an American favoring independence from Great Britain during the American Revolution **3 :** a member or supporter of an American political party formed about 1834 in opposition to the Jacksonian Democrats, associated chiefly with manufacturing, commercial, and financial interests, and succeeded about 1854 by the Republican party — **Whig** *adj* — **Whig·gism** \ˈhwi-ˌgi-zəm\ *n*

Whig·gery \ˈhwi-gə-rē, ˈwi-\ *n* (1714) **:** the principles or practices of Whigs

Whig·gish \ˈhwi-gish, ˈwi-\ *adj* (1684) **1 :** characteristic of Whigs or Whiggery **2 :** of, relating to, or characterized by a view which holds that history follows a path of inevitable progression and improvement and which judges the past in light of the present

whig·ma·lee·rie \ˌhwig-mə-ˈlir-ē, ˌwig-\ *n* [origin unknown] (1730) **1** *chiefly Scot* **:** WHIM **2** *chiefly Scot* **:** an odd or fanciful contrivance **:** GIMCRACK

[1]while \ˈhwī(-ə)l, ˈwī(-ə)l\ *n* [ME, fr. OE *hwīl;* akin to OHG *hwīla* time, L *quies* rest, quiet] (bef. 12c) **1 :** a period of time esp. when short and marked by the occurrence of an action or a condition **:** TIME ⟨stay here

---

\ə\ **abut** \ᵊ\ **kitten,** F **table** \ər\ **further** \a\ **ash** \ā\ **ace** \ä\ **mop, mar**
\au̇\ **out** \ch\ **chin** \e\ **bet** \ē\ **easy** \g\ **go** \i\ **hit** \ī\ **ice** \j\ **job**
\ŋ\ **sing** \ō\ **go** \ȯ\ **law** \ȯi\ **boy** \th\ **thin** \th\ **the** \ü\ **loot** \u̇\ **foot**
\y\ **yet** \zh\ **vision, beige** \k̲, ⁿ, œ, ue, ʸ\ *see* Guide to Pronunciation

for a ~⟩ **2 :** the time and effort used (as in the performance of an action) : TROUBLE ⟨worth your ~⟩
[2]**while** *conj* (12c) **1 a :** during the time that ⟨take a nap ~ I'm out⟩ **b :** as long as ⟨~ there's life there's hope⟩ **2 a :** when on the other hand : WHEREAS ⟨easy for an expert, ~ it is dangerous for a novice⟩ **b :** in spite of the fact that : ALTHOUGH ⟨~ respected, he is not liked⟩ **3 :** similarly and at the same time that ⟨~ the book will be welcomed by scholars, it will make an immediate appeal to the general reader —*Brit. Book News*⟩
[3]**while** *prep* (15c) *dial Brit* : UNTIL
[4]**while** *vt* **whiled; whil·ing** (1635) **:** to cause to pass esp. without boredom or in a pleasant manner — usu. used with *away* ⟨~ away the time⟩
[1]**whiles** \ˈhwī(-ə)lz, ˈwī(-ə)lz\ *conj* [ME, fr. *while* + *-s,* adv. suffix — more at WHENCE] (12c) *archaic* : WHILE
[2]**whiles** *adv* (15c) *chiefly Scot* : SOMETIMES
[1]**whi·lom** \ˈhwī-ləm, ˈwī-\ *adv* [ME, lit., at times, fr. OE *hwīlum,* dat. pl. of *hwīl* time, while] (12c) *archaic* : FORMERLY
[2]**whilom** *adj* (1837) : FORMER
whilst \ˈhwī(-ə)lst, ˈwī(-ə)lst\ *conj* [ME *whilest,* alter. of *whiles*] (14c) *chiefly Brit* : WHILE
whim \ˈhwim, ˈwim\ *n* [short for *whim-wham*] (1686) **1 :** a capricious or eccentric and often sudden idea or turn of the mind : FANCY ⟨quit his job on a ~⟩ **2 :** a large capstan that is made with one or more radiating arms to which a horse may be yoked and that is used in mines for raising ore or water ***syn*** see CAPRICE
whim·brel \ˈhwim-brəl, ˈwim-\ *n* [origin unknown] (ca. 1531) **:** a curlew (*Numenius phaeopus*) chiefly of the northern coastal regions of No. America and Eurasia
[1]**whim·per** \ˈhwim-pər, ˈwim-\ *vi* **whim·pered; whim·per·ing** \-p(ə-)riŋ\ [imit.] (1513) **1 :** to make a low whining plaintive or broken sound **2 :** to complain or protest with or as if with a whimper
[2]**whimper** *n* (ca. 1700) **1 :** a whimpering cry or sound **2 :** a petulant complaint or protest ⟨the bill passed without a ~⟩
whim·si·cal \ˈhwim-zi-kəl, ˈwim-\ *adj* [*whimsy*] (1653) **1 :** full of, actuated by, or exhibiting whims **2 a :** resulting from or characterized by whim or caprice; *esp* **:** lightly fanciful ⟨~ decorations⟩ **b :** subject to erratic behavior or unpredictable change — **whim·si·cal·i·ty** \ˌhwim-zə-ˈka-lə-tē, ˌwim-\ *n* — **whim·si·cal·ly** \ˈhwim-zi-k(ə-)lē, ˈwim-\ *adv* — **whim·si·cal·ness** \-kəl-nəs\ *n*
whim·sy *also* **whim·sey** \ˈhwim-zē, ˈwim-\ *n, pl* **whimsies** *also* **whimseys** [irreg. fr. *whim-wham*] (1605) **1 :** WHIM, CAPRICE **2 :** the quality or state of being whimsical or fanciful ⟨the designer's new line showed a touch of ~⟩ **3 :** a fanciful or fantastic device, object, or creation esp. in writing or art
whim–wham \ˈhwim-ˌhwam, ˈwim-ˌwam\ *n* [origin unknown] (1500) **1 :** a whimsical object or device esp. of ornament or dress **2 :** FANCY, WHIM **3** *pl* **:** JITTERS
whin \ˈhwin, ˈwin\ *n* [ME *whynne,* of Scand origin; akin to Norw *kvein* bent grass] (14c) : GORSE
whin·chat \ˈhwin-ˌchat, ˈwin-\ *n* [*whin*] (1678) **:** a small brown and buff European singing bird (*Saxicola rubetra*) of grassy meadows
[1]**whine** \ˈhwīn, ˈwīn\ *vb* **whined; whin·ing** [ME, fr. OE *hwīnan* to whiz; akin to ON *hvīna* to whiz] *vi* (13c) **1 a :** to utter a high-pitched plaintive or distressed cry **b :** to make a sound similar to such a cry ⟨the wind *whined* in the chimney⟩ **2 :** to complain with or as if with a whine ⟨always *whining* about the weather⟩ **3 :** to move or proceed with the sound of a whine ⟨the bullet *whined* . . . across the ice —Berton Roueché⟩ ~ *vt* **:** to utter or express with or as if with a whine — **whin·er** *n* — **whin·ing·ly** \ˈhwī-niŋ-lē, ˈwī-\ *adv*
[2]**whine** *n* (1633) **1 a :** a prolonged high-pitched cry usu. expressive of distress or pain **b :** a sound resembling such a cry **2 :** a complaint uttered with or as if with a whine — **whiny** *also* **whin·ey** \ˈhwī-nē, ˈwī-\ *adj*
whing–ding \ˈwiŋ-ˌdiŋ, ˈhwiŋ-\ *n* [by alter.] (ca. 1945) : WINGDING
whinge \ˈhwinj, ˈwinj\ *vi* **whinged; whing·ing** *or* **whinge·ing** [ME **whingen,* fr. OE *hwinsian;* akin to OHG *winsōn* to moan] (12c) *Brit* **:** to complain fretfully : WHINE — **whinge** *n, Brit*
[1]**whin·ny** \ˈhwi-nē, ˈwi-\ *vb* **whin·nied; whin·ny·ing** [prob. imit.] *vi* (1530) **:** to neigh esp. in a low or gentle way ~ *vt* **:** to utter with or as if with a whinny
[2]**whinny** *n, pl* **whinnies** (ca. 1823) **1 :** the neigh of a horse esp. when low or gentle **2 :** a sound resembling a neigh
whin·stone \ˈhwin-ˌstōn, ˈwin-\ *n* [*whin,* a hard rock] (1513) **:** basaltic rock : TRAP; *also* **:** any of various other dark resistant rocks (as chert)
[1]**whip** \ˈhwip, ˈwip\ *vb* **whipped; whip·ping** [ME *wippen, whippen;* akin to MD *wippen* to move up and down, sway, OE *wīpian* to wipe] *vt* (14c) **1 :** to take, pull, snatch, jerk, or otherwise move very quickly and forcefully ⟨*whipped* out his gun —Green Peyton⟩ **2 a (1) :** to strike with a slender lithe implement (as a lash or rod) esp. as a punishment **(2) :** SPANK **b :** to drive or urge on by or as if by using a whip **c :** to strike as a lash does ⟨rain *whipped* the pavement⟩ **3 a :** to bind or wrap (as a rope or fishing rod) with cord for protection and strength **b :** to wind or wrap around something **4 :** to belabor with stinging words : ABUSE **5 :** to seam or hem with shallow overcasting stitches **6 :** to overcome decisively : DEFEAT **7 :** to stir up : INCITE — usu. used with *up* ⟨trying to ~ up a new emotion —Ellen Glasgow⟩ **8 :** to produce in a hurry — usu. used with *up* ⟨a sketch . . . an artist might ~ up —*N.Y. Times*⟩ **9 :** to fish (water) with rod, line, and artificial lure **10 :** to beat (as eggs or cream) into a froth with a utensil (as a whisk or fork) **11 :** to gather together or hold together for united action in the manner of a party whip ~ *vi* **1 :** to proceed nimbly or quickly ⟨*whipping* through the supper dishes —C. B. Davis⟩ **2 :** to thrash about flexibly in the manner of a whiplash ⟨a flag . . . *whipping* out from its staff —H. A. Calahan⟩ — **whip·per** *n* — **whip into shape :** to bring forcefully to a desired state or condition
[2]**whip** *n* (14c) **1 :** an instrument consisting usu. of a handle and lash forming a flexible rod that is used for whipping **2 :** a stroke or cut with or as if with a whip **3 a :** a dessert made by whipping a portion of the ingredients ⟨prune ~⟩ **b :** a kitchen utensil made of braided or coiled wire or perforated metal with a handle and used in whipping **4 :** one that handles a whip: as **a :** a driver of horses : COACHMAN **b :** WHIPPER-IN 1 **5 a :** a member of a legislative body appointed by a political party to enforce party discipline and to secure the attendance of party members at important sessions **b** *often cap* **:** a notice of forthcoming business sent weekly to each member of a political party in the British House of Commons **6 :** a whipping or thrashing motion **7 :** the quality of resembling a whip esp. in being flexible **8 :** WHIP ANTENNA — **whip·like** \ˈhwip-ˌlīk, ˈwip-\ *adj*
whip antenna *n* (1942) **:** a flexible vertical rod radio antenna
whip·cord \ˈhwip-ˌkȯrd, ˈwip-\ *n* [fr. its use in making whips] (14c) **1 :** a thin tough cord made of braided or twisted hemp or catgut **2 :** a cloth that is made of hard-twisted yarns and has fine diagonal cords or ribs
whip hand *n* (1680) **1 :** positive control : ADVANTAGE **2 :** the hand holding the whip in driving
whip in *vt* (1742) **1 :** to collect or keep together (members of a political party) for legislative action **2 :** to keep (hounds in a pack) from scattering by use of a whip
whip·lash \ˈhwip-ˌlash, ˈwip-\ *n* (ca. 1580) **1 :** the lash of a whip **2 :** something resembling a blow from a whip ⟨the ~ of fear —R. S. Banay⟩ **3 :** injury resulting from a sudden sharp whipping movement of the neck and head (as of a person in a vehicle that is struck from the rear by another vehicle)
whip·per–in \ˌhwi-pər-ˈin, ˌwi-\ *n, pl* **whip·pers–in** \-pərz-\ (1739) **1 :** a huntsman's assistant who whips in the hounds **2 :** WHIP 5a
whip·per·snap·per \ˈhwi-pər-ˌsna-pər, ˈwi-\ *n* [alter. of *snippersnapper*] (1700) **:** a diminutive, insignificant, or presumptuous person
whip·pet \ˈhwi-pət, ˈwi-\ *n* [prob. fr. [1]*whip*] (1610) **:** any of a breed of small swift slender dogs used for coursing small game and racing
whipping *n* (1540) **1 :** the act of one that whips: as **a :** a severe beating or chastisement **b :** a stitching with small overcasting stitches **2 :** material used to whip or bind
whipping boy *n* (1647) **1 :** a boy formerly educated with a prince and punished in his stead **2 :** SCAPEGOAT 2
whipping cream *n* (1921) **:** a cream suitable for whipping that by law contains not less than 30 percent butterfat
whipping post *n* (1600) **:** a post to which offenders are tied to be legally whipped
whip·ple·tree \ˈhwi-pəl-(ˌ)trē, ˈwi-\ *n* [perh. irreg. fr. *whip* + *tree*] (1733) : WHIFFLETREE
whip–poor–will \ˈhwi-pər-ˌwil, ˌhwi-pər-ˈ, ˈwi-, ˌwi-\ *n* [imit.] (1709) **:** a nocturnal nightjar (*Caprimulgus vociferus*) of chiefly eastern No. America with a loud repeated call suggestive of its name

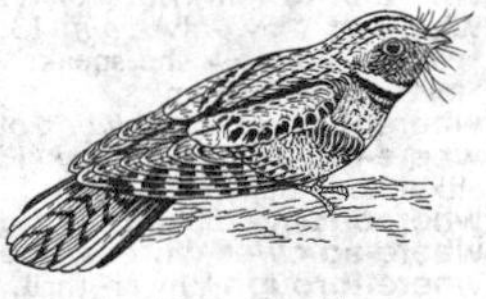
whip-poor-will

whip·py \ˈhwi-pē, ˈwi-\ *adj* **whip·pi·er; -est** (1867) **1 :** unusually resilient : SPRINGY ⟨a ~ fishing rod⟩ **2 :** of, relating to, or resembling a whip
whip–round \ˈhwip-ˌrau̇nd, ˈwip-\ *n* (1887) *chiefly Brit* **:** a collection of money made usu. for a benevolent purpose ⟨had a ~ to help the couple pay for a Paris honeymoon —*The People*⟩
[1]**whip·saw** \ˈhwip-ˌsȯ, ˈwip-\ *n* (15c) **:** a narrow pit saw averaging 5 to 7½ feet (1.5 to 2.3 meters) in length
[2]**whipsaw** *vt* (1842) **1 :** to saw with a whipsaw **2 :** to beset or victimize in two opposite ways at once, by a two-phase operation, or by the collusive action of two opponents ⟨wage earners were ~*ed* by inflation and high taxes⟩
whip·sawed \-ˌsȯd\ *adj* (1892) **:** subjected to a double market loss through trying inopportunely to recoup a loss by a subsequent short sale of the same security
whip scorpion *n* (ca. 1890) **:** any of an order (Uropygi) of chiefly tropical arachnids somewhat resembling true scorpions but having a long slender caudal process and no sting
whip stall *n* (1924) **:** a stall during a vertical climb in which the nose of the airplane whips violently forward and then downward
[1]**whip·stitch** \ˈhwip-ˌstich, ˈwip-\ *vt* (1592) : WHIP 5
[2]**whipstitch** *n* (1640) **:** a shallow overcasting stitch
whip·stock \-ˌstäk\ *n* (ca. 1530) **:** the handle of a whip
whip·tail \-ˌtāl\ *n* (1933) **:** any of various long slender American lizards (genus *Cnemidophorus*) having a whiplike tail and including some forms that are parthenogenetic
whip·worm \-ˌwərm\ *n* (1875) **:** a parasitic nematode worm (genus *Trichuris*) with a body that is thickened posteriorly and that is very long and slender anteriorly; *esp* **:** one (*T. trichiura*) of the human intestine
[1]**whir** *also* **whirr** \ˈhwər, ˈwər\ *vb* **whirred; whir·ring** [ME (Sc) *quirren,* prob. of Scand origin; akin to Dan *hvirre* to whirl, whir] *vi* (15c) **:** to fly, revolve, or move rapidly with a whir ⟨hummingbirds *whirring* past⟩ ~ *vt* **:** to move or carry rapidly with a whir
[2]**whir** *also* **whirr** *n* (1677) **:** a continuous fluttering or vibratory sound made by something in rapid motion ⟨the ~ of machinery⟩
[1]**whirl** \ˈhwər(-ə)l, ˈwər(-ə)l\ *vb* [ME, prob. of Scand origin; akin to ON *hvirfla* to whirl; akin to OHG *wirbil* whirlwind, OE *hweorfan* to turn — more at WHARF] *vi* (14c) **1 :** to move in a circle or similar curve esp. with force or speed **2 a :** to turn on or around an axis like a wheel : ROTATE **b :** to turn abruptly around or aside : WHEEL ⟨~*ed* around in surprise⟩ **3 :** to pass, move, or go quickly ⟨~*ed* down the hallway⟩ **4 :** to become giddy or dizzy : REEL ⟨my head is ~*ing*⟩ ~ *vt* **1 :** to drive, impel, or convey with or as if with a rotary motion **2 a :** to cause to turn usu. rapidly on or around an axis : ROTATE **b :** to cause to turn abruptly around or aside **3** *obs* **:** to throw or hurl violently with a revolving motion — **whirl·er** \ˈhwər-lər, ˈwər-\ *n*
[2]**whirl** *n* (15c) **1 a :** a rapid rotating or circling movement **b :** something undergoing such a movement **2 a :** a busy or fast-paced succession of events : BUSTLE ⟨a ~ of activity⟩ ⟨the social ~⟩ **b :** a confused or disturbed mental state : TURMOIL ⟨a ~ of febrile excitement —Emily Skeel⟩ **3 :** an experimental or brief attempt : TRY ⟨gave it a ~⟩
whirl·i·gig \ˈhwər-li-ˌgig, ˈwər-\ *n* [ME *whirlegigg,* fr. *whirlen* to whirl + *gigg* top — more at GIG] (15c) **1 :** a child's toy having a whirling motion **2 :** MERRY-GO-ROUND **3 a :** one that continuously whirls, moves, or changes **b :** a whirling or circling course (as of events)

whirligig beetle *n* (1855) **:** any of a family (Gyrinidae) of beetles with two pairs of eyes and clubbed antennae that live mostly on the surface of water where they swim swiftly about in circles

whirl·ing disease \ˈhwər-liŋ-, ˈwər-\ *n* (1946) **:** an infectious often fatal disease esp. of young salmonid fishes (as trout and salmon) that is caused by a protozoan (*Myxobolus cerebralis* syn. *Myxosoma cerebralis*) and is marked by skeletal deformities and a tendency to swim in circles

whirl·pool \ˈhwər(-ə)l-ˌpül, ˈwər(-ə)l-\ *n* (1529) **1 a :** a confused tumult and bustle **:** WHIRL **b :** a magnetic or impelling force by which something may be engulfed ⟨refusing to be drawn into this ~ of intrigue —A. D. White⟩ **2 a :** water moving rapidly in a circle so as to produce a depression in the center into which floating objects may be drawn **:** EDDY, VORTEX **b :** WHIRLPOOL BATH

whirlpool bath *n* (ca. 1916) **:** a therapeutic bath in which all or part of the body is exposed to forceful whirling currents of hot water

[1]**whirl·wind** \-ˌwind\ *n* (14c) **1 :** a small rotating windstorm of limited extent **2 a :** a confused rush **:** WHIRL ⟨a ~ of meetings⟩ **b :** a violent or destructive force or agency

[2]**whirlwind** *adj* (1614) **:** resembling a whirlwind esp. in speed or force ⟨a ~ campaign⟩ ⟨a ~ romance⟩

[1]**whirly** \ˈhwər-lē, ˈwər-\ *adj* (15c) **:** having a whirling motion

[2]**whirly** *n, pl* **whirl·ies** (1914) **:** a small whirlwind

whirly·bird \-ˌbərd\ *n* (1951) **:** HELICOPTER

whir·ry \ˈhwər-ē, ˈwər-, ˈ(h)wə-rē\ *vb* **whir·ried; whir·ry·ing** [perh. blend of *whir* and *hurry*] *vt* (1582) *Scot* **:** to convey quickly ~ *vi, Scot* **:** HURRY

[1]**whish** \ˈhwish, ˈwish\ *vb* [imit.] *vt* (1518) **:** to urge on or cause to move with a whish ~ *vi* **1 :** to make a sibilant sound **2 :** to move with a whish esp. at high speed ⟨an elevator . . . ~*es* down to the lower level —Natalie Cooper⟩

[2]**whish** *n* (ca. 1802) **:** a rushing sound **:** SWISH

whisht \ˈhwisht, ˈwisht\ *vi* [ME; imit.] (14c) *chiefly Irish* **:** HUSH — often used interjectionally to enjoin silence

[1]**whisk** \ˈhwisk, ˈwisk\ *n* [ME *wisk,* prob. of Scand origin; akin to ON *visk* wisp; akin to OE *wiscian* to plait] (14c) **1 :** a quick light brushing or whipping motion **2 a :** a usu. wire kitchen utensil used for beating food by hand **b :** a flexible bunch (as of twigs, feathers, or straw) attached to a handle for use as a brush

[2]**whisk** *vi* (15c) **:** to move nimbly and quickly ~ *vt* **1 :** to move or convey briskly ⟨~*ed* the children off to bed⟩ **2 :** to mix or fluff up by or as if by beating with a whisk ⟨~ egg whites⟩ **3 :** to brush or wipe off lightly

whisk broom *n* (1831) **:** a small broom with a short handle used esp. as a clothes brush or for light cleaning

whis·ker \ˈhwis-kər, ˈwis-\ *n* [sing. of *whiskers* mustache, fr. [2]*whisk*] (ca. 1600) **1 a :** a hair of the beard **b** *pl* (1) *archaic* **:** MUSTACHE (2) **:** the part of the beard growing on the sides of the face or on the chin **c :** HAIRBREADTH ⟨lost the race by a ~⟩ **2 :** one of the long projecting hairs or bristles growing near the mouth of an animal (as a cat or bird) **3 :** an outrigger extending on each side of the bowsprit to spread the jib and flying jib guys — usu. used in pl. **4 a :** a shred or filament resembling a whisker **b :** a thin hairlike crystal (as of sapphire or copper) of exceptional mechanical strength used esp. to reinforce composite structural material — **whis·kered** \-kərd\ *adj* — **whis·kery** \-k(ə-)rē\ *adj*

whis·key *or* **whis·ky** \ˈhwis-kē, ˈwis-\ *n, pl* **whiskeys** *or* **whiskies** [Ir *uisce beatha* & ScGael *uisge beatha,* lit., water of life] (1715) **1 :** a liquor distilled from fermented wort (as that obtained from rye, corn, or barley mash) **2 :** a drink of whiskey

Whiskey (1952) — a communications code word for the letter *w*

whiskey sour *n* (ca. 1889) **:** a cocktail usu. consisting of whiskey, sugar, and lemon juice shaken with ice

[1]**whis·per** \ˈhwis-pər, ˈwis-\ *vb* **whis·pered; whis·per·ing** \-p(ə-)riŋ\ [ME, fr. OE *hwisperian;* akin to OHG *hwispalōn* to whisper, ON *hvīsla* — more at WHISTLE] *vi* (bef. 12c) **1 :** to speak softly with little or no vibration of the vocal cords esp. to avoid being overheard **2 :** to make a sibilant sound that resembles whispering ~ *vt* **1 :** to address in a whisper **2 :** to utter or communicate in or as if in a whisper

[2]**whisper** *n* (1595) **1 :** something communicated by or as if by whispering; *esp* **:** RUMOR ⟨~*s* of scandal⟩ **2 a :** an act or instance of whispering; *esp* **:** speech without vibration of the vocal cords **b :** a sibilant sound that resembles whispered speech **3 :** HINT, TRACE

whis·per·er \-pər-ər\ *n* (1530) **1 :** one that whispers; *specif* **:** RUMORMONGER **2 :** a person who excels at calming or training hard-to-manage animals using noncoercive methods based esp. on an understanding of the animals' natural instincts

[1]**whispering** *n* (bef. 12c) **1 a :** whispered speech **b :** GOSSIP, RUMOR **2 :** a sibilant sound **:** WHISPER

[2]**whispering** *adj* (1547) **1 :** making a sibilant sound **2 :** spreading confidential and esp. derogatory reports ⟨~ tongues can poison truth —S. T. Coleridge⟩ — **whis·per·ing·ly** \-p(ə-)riŋ-lē\ *adv*

whispering campaign *n* (1920) **:** the systematic dissemination by word of mouth of derogatory rumors or charges esp. against a candidate for public office

whis·pery \ˈhwis-p(ə-)rē, ˈwis-\ *adj* (1834) **1 :** resembling a whisper **2 :** full of whispers

[1]**whist** \ˈhwist, ˈwist\ *vi* [ME; imit.] (14c) *dial Brit* **:** to be silent **:** HUSH — often used interjectionally to enjoin silence

[2]**whist** *adj* (15c) **:** QUIET, SILENT

[3]**whist** *n* [alter. of earlier *whisk,* prob. fr. [2]*whisk;* fr. whisking up the tricks] (1663) **:** a card game for four players in two partnerships that is played with a pack of 52 cards and that scores one point for each trick in excess of six

[1]**whis·tle** \ˈhwi-səl, ˈwi-\ *n, often attrib* [ME, fr. OE *hwistle;* akin to ON *hvīsla* to whisper] (bef. 12c) **1 a :** a small wind instrument in which sound is produced by the forcible passage of breath through a slit in a short tube ⟨a police ~⟩ **b :** a device through which air or steam is forced into a cavity or against a thin edge to produce a loud sound ⟨a factory ~⟩ **2 a :** a shrill clear sound produced by forcing breath out or air in through the puckered lips **b :** the sound produced by a whistle **c :** a signal given by or as if by whistling **3 :** a sound that resembles a whistle; *esp* **:** a shrill clear note of or as if of a bird

[2]**whistle** *vb* **whis·tled; whis·tling** \-s(ə-)liŋ\ *vi* (bef. 12c) **1 a :** to utter a shrill clear sound by blowing or drawing air through the puckered lips **b :** to utter a shrill note or call resembling a whistle **c :** to make a shrill clear sound esp. by rapid movement ⟨the wind *whistled*⟩ **d :** to blow or sound a whistle **2 a :** to give a signal or issue an order or summons by or as if by whistling **b :** to make a demand without result ⟨he did a sloppy job, so he can ~ for his money⟩ ~ *vt* **1 a :** to send, bring, signal, or call by or as if by whistling **b :** to charge (as a basketball or hockey player) with an infraction **2 :** to produce, utter, or express by whistling ⟨~ a tune⟩ — **whis·tle·able** \-sə-lə-bəl\ *adj* — **whistle in the dark :** to keep up one's courage by or as if by whistling

whis·tle–blow·er \-ˌblō-ər\ *n* (1970) **:** one who reveals something covert or who informs against another ⟨pledges to protect ~*s* who fear reprisals —*Wall Street Jour.*⟩ — **whis·tle–blow·ing** \-ˌblō-iŋ\ *n*

whis·tler \ˈhwi-s(ə-)lər, ˈwi-\ *n* (bef. 12c) **:** one that whistles: as **a :** any of various birds; *esp* **:** any of numerous oscine birds (esp. genus *Pachycephala*) found chiefly in Australia and South Pacific islands and having a whistling call **b :** a large marmot (*Marmota caligata*) of northwestern No. America having a shrill alarm call **c :** a broken-winded horse **d :** a very-low-frequency radio signal that is generated by lightning discharge, travels along the earth's magnetic-field lines, and produces a sound resembling a whistle of descending pitch in radio receivers

[1]**whis·tle–stop** \ˈhwi-səl-ˌstäp, ˈwi-\ *n, often attrib* (ca. 1925) **1 a :** a small station at which trains stop only on signal **:** FLAG STOP **b :** a small community **2 :** a brief personal appearance esp. by a political candidate usu. on the rear platform of a train during the course of a tour

[2]**whistle–stop** *vi* (1952) **:** to make a tour esp. in a political campaign with many brief personal appearances in small communities

whistling *n* (14c) **:** the act or sound of one that whistles **:** WHISTLE

whistling swan *n* (1785) **:** TUNDRA SWAN

whit \ˈhwit, ˈwit\ *n* [ME, prob. alter. of *wiht, wight* creature, thing — more at WIGHT] (15c) **:** the smallest part or particle imaginable **:** BIT ⟨what some people will do for a ~ of publicity —Patrick Quinn⟩

[1]**white** \ˈhwīt, ˈwīt\ *adj* **whit·er; whit·est** [ME, fr. OE *hwīt;* akin to OHG *hwīz* white and prob. to OCS *světŭ* light, Skt *śveta* white, bright] (bef. 12c) **1 a :** free from color **b :** of the color of new snow or milk; *specif* **:** of the color white **c :** light or pallid in color ⟨~ hair⟩ ⟨lips ~ with fear⟩ **d :** lustrous pale gray **:** SILVERY; *also* **:** made of silver **2 a :** being a member of a group or race characterized by light pigmentation of the skin **b :** of, relating to, characteristic of, or consisting of white people or their culture **c** [fr. the former stereotypical association of good character with northern European descent] **:** marked by upright fairness ⟨that's mighty ~ of you⟩ **3 :** free from spot or blemish: as **a** (1) **:** free from moral impurity **:** INNOCENT (2) **:** marked by the wearing of white by the woman as a symbol of purity ⟨a ~ wedding⟩ **b :** unmarked by writing or printing **c :** not intended to cause harm ⟨a ~ lie⟩ ⟨~ magic⟩ **d :** FAVORABLE, FORTUNATE ⟨one of the ~ days of his life —Sir Walter Scott⟩ **4 a :** wearing or habited in white **b :** marked by the presence of snow **:** SNOWY ⟨a ~ Christmas⟩ **5 a :** heated to the point of whiteness **b :** notably ardent **:** PASSIONATE ⟨~ fury⟩ **6 a :** conservative or reactionary in political outlook and action **b :** instigated or carried out by reactionary forces as a counterrevolutionary measure ⟨a ~ terror⟩ **7 :** of, relating to, or constituting a musical tone quality characterized by a controlled pure sound, a lack of warmth and color, and a lack of resonance **8 :** consisting of a wide range of frequencies — used of light, sound, and electromagnetic radiation — **whit·ish** \ˈhwī-tish, ˈwī-\ *adj*

[2]**white** *n* (bef. 12c) **1 :** the achromatic object color of greatest lightness characteristically perceived to belong to objects that reflect diffusely nearly all incident energy throughout the visible spectrum **2 a :** a white or light-colored part of something: as (1) **:** a mass of albuminous material surrounding the yolk of an egg (2) **:** the white part of the eyeball (3) **:** the light-colored pieces in a 2-player board game; *also* **:** the player by whom these are played (4) **:** the area of a page unmarked by writing, printing, or illustration **b** (1) *archaic* **:** a white target (2) **:** the fifth or outermost circle of an archery target; *also* **:** a shot that hits it **3 :** one that is or approaches white in color: as **a :** white clothing — often used in pl. **b :** WHITE WINE **c :** a white mammal (as a horse or a hog) **d** (1) **:** a white-colored product (as flour, pins, or sugar) — usu. used in pl. (2) **:** any of numerous butterflies (subfamily Pierinae of the family Pieridae) that usu. have the ground color of the wings white and are related to the sulphur butterflies **e** *pl* **:** TEETH — used in the phrase *pearly whites* **4** *pl* **:** LEUKORRHEA **5 :** a person belonging to a light-skinned race **6** *often cap* **:** a member of a conservative or reactionary political group

[3]**white** *vt* **whit·ed; whit·ing** [ME, fr. *white,* adj.] (bef. 12c) *archaic* **:** WHITEN

white amur \-ä-ˈmu̇r\ *n* [*amur* fr. *Amur* River] (1968) **:** GRASS CARP

white ant *n* (1684) **:** TERMITE

white ash *n* (1683) **:** a No. American ash (*Fraxinus americana*) having compound leaves with a pale green or silvery-white underside; *also* **:** its hard brownish wood

white·bait \ˈhwīt-ˌbāt, ˈwīt-\ *n* (1758) **1 :** the young of any of several European herrings and esp. of the common herring (*Clupea harengus*) or of the sprat (*Sprattus sprattus*) **2 :** any of various small fishes likened to the European whitebait and used as food

white bass *n* (1813) **:** a No. American freshwater bony fish (*Morone chrysops* of the family Percichthyidae) that is used for food

white bean *n* (1763) **:** a white kidney bean (as a cannellini bean)

white·beard \ˈhwīt-ˌbird, ˈwīt-\ *n* (15c) **:** an old man **:** GRAYBEARD

white birch *n* (1789) **1 :** PAPER BIRCH; *also* **:** GRAY BIRCH **2 :** either of two Eurasian birches (*Betula pubescens* and *B. pendula*) with white or ash-colored bark that are often planted as ornamentals in the U.S.

white blood cell *n* (1869) **:** any of the blood cells that are colorless, lack hemoglobin, contain a nucleus, and include the lymphocytes, monocytes, neutrophils, eosinophils, and basophils — called also *leukocyte, white blood corpuscle, white cell*

white·board \ˈhwīt-ˌbȯrd, ˈwīt-\ *n* (1951) : a hard smooth white surface used for writing or drawing on with markers

white book *n* (15c) : an official report of government affairs bound in white

white–bread \ˈhwīt-ˈbred, ˈwīt-\ *adj* (1977) : being, typical of, or having qualities (as blandness) associated with the white middle class

white·cap \ˈhwīt-ˌkap, ˈwīt-\ *n* (1773) : a wave crest breaking into white foam — usu. used in pl.

white cedar *n* (ca. 1671) **1** : an aromatic evergreen swamp tree (*Chamaecyparis thyoides*) of the cypress family that occurs along the eastern coast of the U.S. and has branchlets in fan-shaped sprays and small round cones; *also* : its wood **2** : NORTHERN WHITE CEDAR

white cell *n* (1852) : WHITE BLOOD CELL

white chip *n* (1897) **1** : a white-colored poker chip usu. of minimum value **2** : a thing or quantity of little worth

white chocolate *n* (1923) : a confection of cocoa butter, sugar, milk solids, lecithin, and flavorings

white clover *n* (bef. 12c) : a Eurasian clover (*Trifolium repens*) with round heads of white flowers that is widely used in lawn and pasture grass-seed mixtures and is an important source of nectar for bees — called also *white Dutch clover*

white–coat hypertension *n* [fr. the white laboratory coats worn by physicians] (1986) : a temporary elevation in a patient's blood pressure that occurs when measured in a medical setting (as a physician's office) and that is usu. due to anxiety on the part of the patient

white–col·lar \ˈhwīt-ˈkä-lər, ˈwīt-\ *adj* (1920) : of, relating to, or constituting the class of salaried employees whose duties do not call for the wearing of work clothes or protective clothing — compare BLUE-COLLAR

white crappie *n* (ca. 1926) : a silvery No. American sunfish (*Pomoxis annularis*) with five or six protruding spines on the dorsal fins that is used as a panfish and often for stocking small ponds

white–crowned sparrow \ˈhwīt-ˈkrau̇nd-, ˈwīt-\ *n* (1834) : a migratory sparrow (*Zonotrichia leucophrys*) that breeds in northern and western No. America and has a grayish breast, pink bill, and head striped with black and white

whited *adj* (13c) **1** : covered with white or whiting and esp. with whitewash **2** : made white : WHITENED

whited sepulcher *n* [fr. the simile in Mt 23:27] (1530) : a person inwardly corrupt or wicked but outwardly or professedly virtuous or holy : HYPOCRITE

white dwarf *n, pl* **white dwarfs** (1924) : a small hot whitish star of low intrinsic brightness usu. with a mass approximately equal to that of the sun but with a density many times larger

white elephant *n* (15c) **1** : an Indian elephant of a pale color that is sometimes venerated in India, Sri Lanka, Thailand, and Myanmar **2 a** : a property requiring much care and expense and yielding little profit **b** : an object no longer of value to its owner but of value to others **c** : something of little or no value

white·face \ˈhwīt-ˌfās, ˈwīt-\ *n* (1709) **1** : a white-faced animal; *specif* : HEREFORD **2** : dead-white facial makeup ⟨a clown in ~⟩

white–faced \-ˈfāst\ *adj* (1597) **1** : having the face white in whole or in part — used esp. of an animal otherwise dark in color **2** : having a wan pale face

white feather *n* [fr. the superstition that a white feather in the plumage of a gamecock is a mark of a poor fighter] (ca. 1785) : a mark or symbol of cowardice — used chiefly in the phrase *show the white feather*

white fir *n* (1849) : a large fir (*Abies concolor*) of western No. America with pale usu. bluish-green foliage, a narrow erect crown, and soft wood that is used for lumber

white·fish \ˈhwīt-ˌfish, ˈwīt-\ *n* (15c) **1 a** : any of various freshwater salmonid food fishes (esp. of genera *Coregonus* and *Prosopium*) found usu. in cold northern waters **b** : any of various fishes resembling the true whitefishes **c** *Brit* : any of various market fishes with white flesh that is not oily **2** : the flesh of a whitefish esp. as an article of food

white flag *n* (1555) **1** : a flag of plain white used as a flag of truce or as a token of surrender **2** : a token of weakness or yielding

white flight *n* (1967) : the departure of whites from places (as urban neighborhoods or schools) increasingly or predominantly populated by minorities

white·fly \ˈhwīt-ˌflī, ˈwīt-\ *n* (1813) : any of numerous small homopterous insects (family Aleyrodidae) that are injurious plant pests

white–foot·ed mouse \ˈhwīt-ˌfu̇-təd-, ˈwīt-\ *n* (1853) : any of various largely nocturnal mice (genus *Peromyscus*) of No. and Central America typically having whitish feet and underparts; *esp* : a common woodland mouse (*P. leucopus*) of No. America

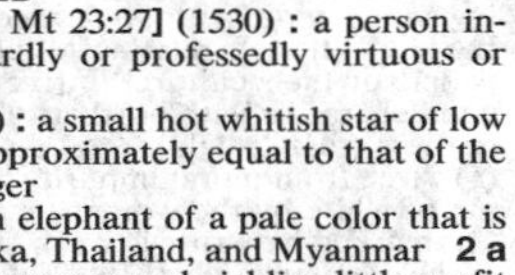

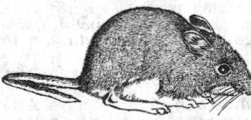

white-footed mouse

white friar *n, often cap W&F* [fr. his white habit] (15c) : CARMELITE

white gas *n* (1942) : unleaded gasoline used esp. to fuel portable stoves — called also *white gasoline*

white–glove \ˈhwīt-ˈgləv, ˈwīt-\ *adj* (1979) : marked by special care or attention : METICULOUS ⟨~ service⟩

white gold *n* (1666) : a pale alloy of gold esp. with nickel or palladium that resembles platinum in appearance

white goods *n pl* (ca. 1871) **1 a** : white fabrics esp. of cotton or linen **b** : articles (as sheets, towels, or curtains) orig. or typically made of white cloth **2** : major household appliances (as stoves and refrigerators) that are typically finished in white enamel

white grub *n* (1740) : a grub that is a destructive pest of grass roots and is the larva of various beetles and esp. june bugs

White·hall \ˈhwīt-ˌhȯl, ˈwīt-\ *n* [*Whitehall,* thoroughfare of London in which are located the chief offices of British government] (1827) : the British government

white hat *n* [fr. the white hats stereotypically worn by law-abiding characters in movie westerns] (1970) **1** : one who is admirable and honorable **2** : a mark or symbol of goodness ⟨could use a few more guys in *white hats* —Robert Christgau⟩

white·head \-ˌhed\ *n* (ca. 1931) : a small whitish lump in the skin due to retention of keratin in an oil gland duct — called also *milium*

white–head·ed \-ˈhe-dəd\ *adj* (1525) **1** : having the hair, fur, or plumage of the head white or very light **2** : specially favored : FORTUNATE — used esp. in the phrase *white-headed boy*

white heat *n* (ca. 1710) **1** : a temperature (as for copper and iron from 1500° to 1600° C) which is higher than red heat and at which a body becomes brightly incandescent **2** : a state of intense mental or physical strain, emotion, or activity

white hole *n* (1971) : a hypothetical extremely dense celestial object that radiates enormous amounts of energy and matter — compare BLACK HOLE 1

white hope *n* (1911) **1** : a white contender for a boxing championship held by a black; *also* : one who is felt to represent whites **2** : one from whom much is expected; *esp* : a person undertaking a difficult task

white–hot \ˈhwīt-ˈhät, ˈwīt-\ *adj* (1795) **1** : being at or radiating white heat **2 a** : extremely hot **b** : exhibiting or marked by extreme fervor or zeal ⟨~ enthusiasm⟩

White House \-ˌhau̇s\ *n* [the *White House,* mansion in Washington, D.C., assigned to the use of the president of the U.S.] (1811) **1** : a residence of the president of the U.S. **2** : the executive department of the U.S. government

white hunter *n* (1945) : a white man serving as guide and professional hunter to an African safari

white knight *n* (1951) **1** : one that comes to the rescue of another; *esp* : a corporation invited to buy out a second corporation in order to prevent an undesired takeover by a third **2** : one that champions a cause

white–knuck·le \ˈhwīt-ˈnə-kəl, ˈwīt-\ *also* **white–knuck·led** \-kəld\ *adj* (1974) : marked by, causing, or experiencing tense nervousness ⟨a ~ ride on a roller coaster⟩ ⟨a ~ passenger⟩

white lead *n* (15c) : any of several white lead-containing pigments; *esp* : a heavy poisonous basic carbonate of lead marketed as a powder or as a paste in linseed oil and used esp. formerly in paints

white lightning *n* (1915) : MOONSHINE 3

white line *n* (15c) : a band or edge of something white; *esp* : a stripe painted on a road and used to guide traffic

white list \-ˌlist\ *n* (1860) : a list of approved or favored items — compare BLACKLIST — **white–list·ed** \-ˌlis-təd\ *adj*

white–liv·ered \-ˈli-vərd\ *adj* [fr. the former belief that the choleric temperament depends on the body's producing large quantities of yellow bile] (1549) : PUSILLANIMOUS, LILY-LIVERED

white·ly \ˈhwīt-lē, ˈwīt-\ *adv* (14c) : with an effect of whiteness : so as to show or appear white

white man's burden *n* ["The White Man's Burden" (1899), poem by Rudyard Kipling] (1900) : the alleged duty of the white peoples to manage the affairs of the less developed nonwhite peoples

white marlin *n* (ca. 1950) : a marlin (*Tetrapturas albidus*) of the Atlantic Ocean that is blue above and silvery-white below

white matter *n* (1833) : neural tissue esp. of the brain and spinal cord that consists largely of myelinated nerve fibers bundled into tracts, has a whitish color, and typically underlies the cortical gray matter

white metal *n* (1613) **1** : any of several light-colored alloys used esp. as a base for plated silverware and ornaments and novelties **2** : any of several lead-base or tin-base alloys (as babbitt) used esp. for bearings, fusible plugs, and type metal

white mustard *n* (1548) : a Eurasian mustard (*Brassica hirta*) grown for its pale yellow seeds which yield mustard and mustard oil

whit·en \ˈhwī-tᵊn, ˈwī-\ *vb* **whit·ened; whit·en·ing** \ˈhwīt-niŋ, ˈwīt-, -ᵊn-iŋ\ *vt* (14c) : to make white or whiter ⟨snow ~*ed* the hills⟩ ~ *vi* : to become white or whiter

whit·en·er \ˈhwīt-nər, ˈwīt-; ˈhwī-tᵊn-ər, ˈwī-\ *n* (1611) : one that whitens; *specif* : an agent (as a bleach) used to impart whiteness to something

white·ness \ˈhwīt-nəs, ˈwīt-\ *n* (bef. 12c) **1** : the quality or state of being white: as **a** : white color **b** : PALLOR, PALENESS **c** : freedom from stain : CLEANNESS **2** : white substance

whitening *n* (1601) **1** : the act or process of making or becoming white **2** : something that is used to make white : WHITING

white noise *n* (1943) **1 a** : a heterogeneous mixture of sound waves extending over a wide frequency range — compare PINK NOISE **b** : a constant background noise; *esp* : one that drowns out other sounds **2** : meaningless or distracting commotion, hubbub, or chatter ⟨the *white noise* of policy and politics in America —Joseph Nocera⟩

white oak *n* (1634) : any of various oaks (esp. *Quercus alba* of eastern No. America) with acorns that mature in one year and leaf veins that never extend beyond the margin of the leaf; *also* : its hard strong durable wood

white oil *n* (1864) : any of various colorless odorless tasteless mineral oils used esp. in medicine and in pharmaceutical and cosmetic preparations

white·out \ˈhwīt-ˌau̇t, ˈwīt-\ *n* [*white* + black*out*] (1942) : a surface weather condition in a snow-covered area (as a polar region) in which no object casts a shadow, the horizon cannot be seen, and only dark objects are discernible; *also* : a blizzard that severely reduces visibility

white pages *n pl* (1952) : the section of a telephone directory that lists individuals and businesses alphabetically

white paper *n* (1899) **1** : a government report on any subject; *esp* : a British publication that is usu. less extensive than a blue book **2** : a detailed or authoritative report

white pepper *n* (14c) : a pungent condiment that consists of the fruit of a pepper plant (*Piper nigrum*) ground after the black husk has been removed

white perch *n* (1775) **1** : a silvery anadromous bass (*Morone americana*) chiefly of the coast and coastal streams of the eastern U.S. **2** : FRESHWATER DRUM **3** : WHITE CRAPPIE

white pine *n* (1682) **1 a** : a tall-growing pine (*Pinus strobus*) of eastern No. America with long needles in clusters of five — called also *eastern white pine* **b** : any of several pines that resemble the white pine esp. in having needles in bundles of five **2** : the wood of a white pine and esp. of the eastern white pine

white–pine blister rust *n* (1911) : a destructive disease of white pine caused by a rust fungus (*Cronartium ribicola*) that passes part of its complex life cycle on currant or gooseberry bushes; *also* : this fungus

white potato *n* (1847) : POTATO 2b

white rhinoceros *n* (1838) : a rhinoceros (*Ceratotherium simum*) of southern and central Africa that is distinguished from the black rhi-

noceros esp. by larger size and by a squared upper lip lacking a protrusion — called also *white rhino*
white rice *n* (1916) **:** rice from which the hull and bran have been removed by milling
white room *n* (1961) **:** CLEAN ROOM
White Russian *n* (1850) **1 :** BELARUSIAN **2 :** a cocktail made of vodka, coffee liqueur, and cream or milk
white rust *n* (ca. 1848) **:** any of various diseases of chiefly cruciferous plants caused by a fungus (genus *Albugo*) and marked by white spore-filled lesions; *also* **:** a fungus causing white rust
white sale *n* (1914) **:** a sale of white goods
white sauce *n* (1723) **:** a sauce consisting essentially of a roux with milk, cream, or stock and seasoning
white sea bass *n* (1884) **:** a large croaker (*Atractoscion nobilis*) of the Pacific coast of No. America that is an important sport and food fish
white shark *n* (1674) **:** GREAT WHITE SHARK
white–shoe \ˈhwīt-ˈshü, ˈwīt-\ *adj* (1957) **:** of, associated with, or characteristic of the privileged moneyed upper class **:** UPPER-CRUST ⟨a ~ law firm⟩
white slave *n* (1882) **:** a woman or girl held unwillingly for purposes of commercial prostitution
white slav·er \-ˈslā-vər\ *n* (1911) **:** one engaged in white-slave traffic
white slavery *n* (1857) **:** enforced prostitution
white·smith \ˈhwīt-ˌsmith, ˈwīt-\ *n* (14c) **1 :** TINSMITH **2 :** a worker in iron who finishes or polishes the work
white space *n* (1946) **:** the areas of a page without print or pictures
white spruce *n* (1741) **1 :** any of several spruces; *esp* **:** a widely distributed spruce (*Picea glauca*) of coniferous forests of Canada and the northern U.S. that has short stiff blue-green needles and slender cones — see CONE illustration **2 :** the wood of a white spruce; *esp* **:** the light pale tough straight-grained wood of the common white spruce (*Picea glauca*) used esp. for construction and as a source of paper pulp
white sucker *n* (1869) **:** a common and widespread edible sucker (*Catostomus commersoni*) of the U.S. and Canada
white supremacist *n* (1945) **:** a person who believes that the white race is inherently superior to other races and that white people should have control over people of other races — **white supremacy** *n*
white·tail \ˈhwīt-ˌtāl, ˈwīt-\ *n* (1872) **:** WHITE-TAILED DEER
white–tailed deer \-ˌtāld-\ *n* (1849) **:** a No. American deer (*Odocoileus virginianus*) with a rather long tail white on the undersurface and the males of which have forward-arching antlers — called also *whitetail deer*

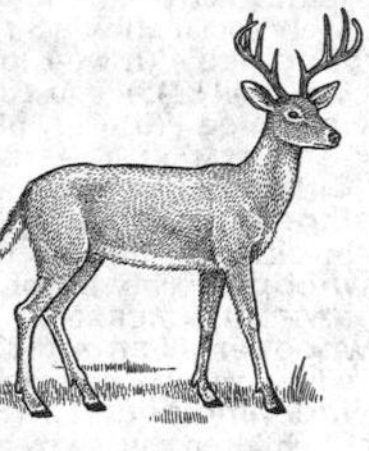

white-tailed deer

white tea *n* (1860) **:** tea that is light in color and made from buds and immature leaves that are covered with fine white hairs and undergo little to no oxidation before drying
white·throat \ˈhwīt-ˌthrōt, ˈwīt-\ *n* (1676) **:** any of several birds with white on the throat: as **a :** an Old World warbler (*Sylvia communis*) with rusty upper parts and largely pale buff underparts **b :** WHITE-THROATED SPARROW
white–throat·ed sparrow \-ˌthrō-təd-\ *n* (1811) **:** a common brown sparrow (*Zonotrichia albicollis*) chiefly of eastern No. America with a black-and-white striped crown and a white patch on the throat
white–tie *adj* (1930) **:** characterized by or requiring the wearing of formal evening clothes consisting of white tie and tailcoat for men and a formal gown for women ⟨a ~ dinner⟩ — compare BLACK-TIE
white trash *n sing but pl in constr* (1822) *usu disparaging* **:** a member of an inferior or underprivileged white social group
white·wall \ˈhwīt-ˌwȯl, ˈwīt-\ *n* (1953) **:** an automobile tire having a white band on the sidewall
white walnut *n* (1743) **1 :** BUTTERNUT 1 **2 :** the light-colored wood of a butternut
[1]**white·wash** \ˈhwīt-ˌwȯsh, ˈwīt-, -ˌwäsh\ *vt* (1591) **1 :** to whiten with whitewash **2 a :** to gloss over or cover up (as vices or crimes) ⟨refused to ~ the scandal⟩ **b :** to exonerate by means of a perfunctory investigation or through biased presentation of data **3 :** to hold (an opponent) scoreless in a game or contest — **white·wash·er** *n*
[2]**whitewash** *n* (1678) **1 :** a liquid composition for whitening a surface: as **a :** a preparation for whitening the skin **b :** a composition (as of lime and water or whiting, size, and water) for whitening structural surfaces **2 :** an act or instance of glossing over or of exonerating **3 :** a defeat in a contest in which the loser fails to score
white·wash·ing \-ˌwȯ-shiŋ, -ˌwä-\ *n* (1663) **:** an act or instance of applying whitewash; *also* **:** WHITEWASH 3
white water *n* (1586) **:** frothy water (as in breakers, rapids, or falls) — **white–water** *adj*
white way *n* [the *Great White Way,* nickname for the theatrical section of Broadway, New York City] (1920) **:** a brilliantly lighted street or avenue esp. in a city's business or theater district
white whale *n* (ca. 1834) **:** BELUGA 2
white wine *n* (14c) **:** a wine ranging in color from faintly yellow to amber that is produced from the juice alone of dark- or light-colored grapes
white·wing \ˈhwīt-ˌwiŋ, ˈwīt-\ *n* (1898) **:** a person and esp. a street sweeper wearing a white uniform
white·wood \-ˌwu̇d\ *n* (1631) **1 :** any of various trees with pale or white wood: as **a :** TULIP TREE 1 **b :** an Australian tree (*Atalaya hemiglauca*) of the soapberry family **2 :** the wood of a whitewood; *esp* **:** TULIPWOOD 1
whit·ey \ˈhwī-tē, ˈwī-\ *n, often cap* (1828) *usu disparaging* **:** the white man **:** white society
white zinfandel *n* (1976) **:** a blush wine made from zinfandel grapes
[1]**whith·er** \ˈhwi-t͟hər, ˈwi-\ *adv* [ME, fr. OE *hwider;* akin to L *quis* who and to OE hi*der* hither — more at WHO, HITHER] (bef. 12c) **1 :** to what place ⟨~ will they go⟩ **2 :** to what situation, position, degree, or end ⟨~ will this abuse drive him⟩
[2]**whither** *conj* (bef. 12c) **1 a :** to what place ⟨knew ~ to go —Daniel Defoe⟩ **b :** to what situation, position, degree, or end **2 a :** to the place at, in, or to which **b :** to which place **3 :** to whatever place

whith·er·so·ev·er \ˌhwi-t͟hər-sə-ˈwe-vər, ˌwi-\ *conj* (14c) **:** to whatever place ⟨will go ~ you lead⟩
whith·er·ward \ˈhwi-t͟hər-wərd, ˈwi-\ *adv* (13c) *archaic* **:** toward what or which place
[1]**whit·ing** \ˈhwī-tiŋ, ˈwī-\ *n, pl* **whiting** *also* **whit·ings** [ME, fr. MD *witinc,* fr. *wit* white; akin to OE *hwīt* white] (15c) **:** any of various marine food fishes: as **a :** a common European fish (*Merlangus merlangus*) of the cod family **b :** SILVER HAKE
[2]**whiting** *n* [ME, fr. gerund of *whiten* to white] (15c) **:** calcium carbonate ground into fine powder, washed, and used esp. as a pigment and extender, in putty, and in rubber compounding and paper coating
whit·low \ˈhwit-(ˌ)lō, ˈwit-\ *n* [ME *whitflawe, whitflowe, whitlowe*] (14c) **:** a deep usu. suppurative inflammation of the finger or toe esp. near the end or around the nail — called also *felon*
Whit·mon·day \ˈhwit-ˌmən-dē, ˈwit-, -ˈmən-\ *n* [*Whit*sunday + *Monday*] (1557) **:** the day after Whitsunday observed as a legal holiday in England, Wales, and Ireland
Whit·sun \ˈhwit-sən, ˈwit-\ *adj* [ME *Whitson,* fr. *Whitsonday*] (14c) **:** of, relating to, or observed on Whitsunday or at Whitsuntide
Whit·sun·day \-ˈsən-dē, -sən-ˌdā\ *n* [ME *Whitsonday,* fr. OE *hwīta sunnandæg,* lit., white Sunday; prob. fr. the custom of wearing white robes by those newly baptized at this season] (12c) **:** PENTECOST 2
Whit·sun·tide \-sən-ˌtīd\ *n* (13c) **:** the week beginning with Whitsunday and esp. the first three days of this week
[1]**whit·tle** \ˈhwi-tᵊl, ˈwi-\ *n* [ME *whittel,* alter. of *thwitel,* fr. *thwiten* to whittle, fr. OE *thwītan;* akin to ON *thveita* to hew] (15c) *archaic* **:** a large knife
[2]**whittle** *vb* **whit·tled; whit·tling** \ˈhwit-liŋ, ˈwit-; ˈhwi-tᵊl-iŋ, ˈwi-\ *vt* (1552) **1 a :** to pare or cut off chips from the surface of (wood) with a knife **b :** to shape or form by so paring or cutting **2 :** to reduce, remove, or destroy gradually as if by cutting off bits with a knife **:** PARE ⟨~ down expenses⟩ ~ *vi* **1 :** to cut or shape something (as wood) by or as if by paring it with a knife **2 :** to wear oneself or another out with fretting — **whit·tler** \ˈhwit-lər, ˈwit-; ˈhwi-tᵊl-ər, ˈwi-\ *n*
whit·tling *n* (1833) **1 :** the act or art of whittling **2 :** a piece cut away in whittling
whit·tret \ˈhwi-trət, ˈwi-\ *n* [ME *whitrat,* fr. *white, whit* white + *rat* rat] (15c) *chiefly Scot* **:** WEASEL
whity *or* **whit·ey** \ˈhwī-tē, ˈwī-\ *adj* (1593) **:** somewhat white **:** WHITISH — usu. used in combination
[1]**whiz** *or* **whizz** \ˈhwiz, ˈwiz\ *vb* **whizzed; whiz·zing** [imit.] *vi* (1582) **1 :** to hum, whir, or hiss like a speeding object (as an arrow or ball) passing through air **2 :** to fly or move swiftly esp. with a whiz ⟨cars *whizzing* by⟩ ~ *vt* **:** to cause to whiz; *esp* **:** to rotate very rapidly
[2]**whiz** *or* **whizz** *n, pl* **whiz·zes** (1620) **1 :** a hissing, buzzing, or whirring sound **2 :** a movement or passage of something accompanied by a whizzing sound **3** *sometimes vulgar* **:** an act of urinating — used esp. in the phrase *take a whiz*
[3]**whiz** *n, pl* **whiz·zes** [prob. by shortening & alter.] (1914) **:** WIZARD 3 ⟨a math ~⟩
whiz·bang *also* **whizz·bang** \ˈhwiz-ˌbaŋ, ˈwiz-, -ˈbaŋ\ *n* (1915) **:** one that is conspicuous for noise, speed, excellence, or startling effect — **whiz–bang** *adj*
whiz kid *also* **whizz kid** *n* [[3]*whiz*] (ca. 1942) **:** a person who is unusually intelligent, clever, or successful esp. at an early age
whiz·zer \ˈhwi-zər, ˈwi-\ *n* (1851) **:** one that whizzes; *esp* **:** a centrifugal machine for drying something (as grain, sugar, or nitrated cotton)
whiz·zy \ˈhwi-zē, ˈwi-\ *adj* **whiz·zi·er; -est** [[3]*whiz*] (1977) **:** WIZARDLY 2 ⟨~ technology⟩
who \ˈhü, ü\ *pron* [ME, fr. OE *hwā;* akin to OHG *hwer,* interrog. pron., who, L *quis,* Gk *tis,* L *qui,* rel. pron., who] (bef. 12c) **1 :** what or which person or persons — used as an interrogative ⟨~ was elected?⟩ ⟨find out ~ they are⟩; used by speakers on all educational levels and by many reputable writers, though disapproved by some grammarians, as the object of a verb or a following preposition ⟨~ did I see but a Spanish lady —Padraic Colum⟩ ⟨do not know ~ the message is from —G. K. Chesterton⟩ **2 :** the person or persons that **:** WHOEVER **3** — used as a function word to introduce a relative clause; used esp. in reference to persons ⟨my father, ~ was a lawyer⟩ but also in reference to groups ⟨a generation ~ had known nothing but war —R. B. West⟩ or to animals ⟨dogs ~ . . . fawn all over tramps —Nigel Balchin⟩ or to inanimate objects esp. with the implication that the reference is really to a person ⟨earlier sources ~ maintain a Davidic ancestry —F. M. Cross⟩; used by speakers on all educational levels and by many reputable writers, though disapproved by some grammarians, as the object of a verb or a following preposition ⟨a character ~ we are meant to pity —*Times Lit. Supp.*⟩ ***usage*** see WHOM, THAT — **as who** *archaic* **:** as one that **:** as if someone — **as who should say** *archaic* **:** so to speak — **who is who** *or* **who's who** *or* **who was who :** the identity of or the noteworthy facts about each of a number of persons
WHO *abbr* World Health Organization
whoa \ˈwō, ˈhō, ˈhwō\ *vb imper* [ME *whoo, who*] (15c) **1** — a command (as to a draft animal) to stand still **2 :** cease or slow a course of action or a line of thought **:** pause to consider or reconsider — often used to express a strong reaction (as alarm or astonishment)
who'd \ˈhüd\ (1640) **:** who had **:** who would
who·dun·it *also* **who·dun·nit** \hü-ˈdə-nət\ *n* [alter. of *who done it?*] (1929) **:** a detective story or mystery story
who·ev·er \hü-ˈe-vər\ *pron* (13c) **:** whatever person **:** no matter who — used in any grammatical relation except that of a possessive ⟨sells to ~ has the money to buy⟩
[1]**whole** \ˈhōl\ *adj* [ME *hool* healthy, unhurt, entire, fr. OE *hāl;* akin to OHG *heil* healthy, unhurt, ON *heill,* OCS *cělŭ*] (bef. 12c) **1 a (1) :** free of wound or injury **:** UNHURT **(2) :** recovered from a wound or injury **:** RESTORED **(3) :** being healed ⟨~ of an ancient evil, I sleep sound —A. E. Housman⟩ **b :** free of defect or impairment **:** INTACT **c :** physically sound and healthy **:** free of disease or deformity **d :** men-

\ə\ **abut** \ᵊ\ **kitten, F table** \ər\ **further** \a\ **ash** \ā\ **ace** \ä\ **mop, mar** \au̇\ **out** \ch\ **chin** \e\ **bet** \ē\ **easy** \g\ **go** \i\ **hit** \ī\ **ice** \j\ **job** \ŋ\ **sing** \ō\ **go** \ȯ\ **law** \ȯi\ **boy** \th\ **thin** \t͟h\ **the** \ü\ **loot** \u̇\ **foot** \y\ **yet** \zh\ **vision, beige** \k̲, ⁿ, œ, ue, ʸ\ *see* Guide to Pronunciation

tally or emotionally sound **2 :** having all its proper parts or components : COMPLETE, UNMODIFIED ⟨a ~ milk⟩ ⟨a ~ egg⟩ **3 a :** constituting the total sum or undiminished entirety : ENTIRE ⟨owns the ~ island⟩ **b :** each or all of the ⟨took part in the ~ series of athletic events⟩ **4 a :** constituting an undivided unit : UNBROKEN, UNCUT ⟨a ~ roast suckling pig⟩ **b :** directed to one end : CONCENTRATED ⟨your ~ attention⟩ **5 a :** seemingly complete or total ⟨the ~ idea is to help, not hinder⟩ **b :** very great in quantity, extent, or scope ⟨feels a ~ lot better now⟩ **6 :** constituting the entirety of a person's nature or development ⟨educate the ~ student⟩ **7 :** having the same father and mother ⟨~ brother⟩ ***syn*** see PERFECT — **whole•ness** *n*

syn WHOLE, ENTIRE, TOTAL, ALL mean including everything or everyone without exception. WHOLE implies that nothing has been omitted, ignored, abated, or taken away ⟨read the *whole* book⟩. ENTIRE may suggest a state of completeness or perfection to which nothing can be added ⟨the *entire* population was wiped out⟩. TOTAL implies that everything has been counted, weighed, measured, or considered ⟨the *total* number of people present⟩. ALL may equal WHOLE, ENTIRE, or TOTAL ⟨*all* proceeds go to charity⟩.

[2]**whole** *n* (14c) **1 :** a complete amount or sum : a number, aggregate, or totality lacking no part, member, or element **2 :** something constituting a complex unity : a coherent system or organization of parts fitting or working together as one — **in whole :** to the full or entire extent : WHOLLY — usu. used in the phrase *in whole or in part* — **on the whole 1 :** in view of all the circumstances or conditions : all things considered **2 :** in general : in most instances : TYPICALLY

[3]**whole** *adv* (14c) **1 :** WHOLLY, ENTIRELY ⟨a ~ new age group —Henry Chauncey⟩ **2 :** as a complete entity

whole cloth *n* (1840) : pure fabrication — usu. used in the phrase *out of whole cloth* ⟨the theory was created out of *whole cloth*⟩

whole food *n* (1970) : a natural food and esp. an unprocessed one (as a vegetable or fruit)

whole gale *n* (ca. 1805) : wind having a speed of 55 to 63 miles (88 to 102 kilometers) per hour — see BEAUFORT SCALE table

whole•heart•ed \ˈhōl-ˈhär-təd\ *adj* (1836) **1 :** completely and sincerely devoted, determined, or enthusiastic ⟨a ~ student of social problems⟩ **2 :** marked by complete earnest commitment : free from all reserve or hesitation ⟨gave the proposal ~ approval⟩ ***syn*** see SINCERE — **whole•heart•ed•ly** *adv*

whole–hog *adj* (1829) : committed without reservation : THOROUGHGOING ⟨a ~ patriot⟩

[1]**whole hog** *n* (1828) : the whole way or farthest limit — usu. used adverbially in the phrase *go the whole hog*

[2]**whole hog** *adv* (1844) : to the fullest extent : without reservation : COMPLETELY ⟨accepting *whole hog* the standards . . . of the majority —R. B. Kaplan⟩

whole language *n* (1984) : a method of teaching reading and writing that emphasizes learning whole words and phrases by encountering them in meaningful contexts rather than by phonics exercises

whole–life \ˈhōl-ˈlīf\ *adj* (1845) : of, relating to, or being life insurance with a fixed premium for the life of the policyholder and a cash value that can be redeemed on sale of the policy or can be the basis of low-interest loans

whole•meal \ˈhōl-ˌmēl\ *adj* (1828) *Brit* : WHOLE WHEAT

whole note *n* (1841) : a musical note equal in time value to four quarter notes or two half notes — see NOTE illustration

whole number *n* (1542) : any of the set of nonnegative integers; *also* : INTEGER

whole rest *n* (1851) : a musical rest corresponding in time value to a whole note

[1]**whole•sale** \ˈhōl-ˌsāl\ *n* (15c) : the sale of commodities in quantity usu. for resale (as by a retail merchant)

[2]**wholesale** *adj* (1642) **1 :** performed or existing on a large scale esp. without discrimination ⟨~ slaughter⟩ **2 :** of, relating to, or engaged in the sale of commodities in quantity for resale ⟨a ~ grocer⟩

[3]**wholesale** *adv* (1732) : in a wholesale manner

[4]**wholesale** *vb* **whole•saled; whole•sal•ing** *vt* (1800) : to sell (something) in quantity usu. for resale ~ *vi* : to sell in quantity usu. for resale

whole•sal•er \ˈhōl-ˌsā-lər\ *n* (1857) : a merchant middleman who sells chiefly to retailers, other merchants, or industrial, institutional, and commercial users mainly for resale or business use

whole•some \ˈhōl-səm\ *adj* (13c) **1 :** promoting health or well-being of mind or spirit **2 :** promoting health of body **3 a :** sound in body, mind, or morals **b :** having the simple health or vigor of normal domesticity **4 a :** based on well-grounded fear : PRUDENT ⟨a ~ respect for the law⟩ **b :** SAFE ⟨it wouldn't be ~ for you to go down there —Mark Twain⟩ ***syn*** see HEALTHFUL, HEALTHY — **whole•some•ly** *adv* — **whole•some•ness** *n*

whole–souled \ˈhōl-ˈsōld\ *adj* (1822) : moved by ardent enthusiasm or single-minded devotion : WHOLEHEARTED

whole step *n* (ca. 1899) : a musical interval (as C–D or C–B♭) comprising two half steps — called also *whole tone*

whole wheat *adj* (1848) : made of ground entire wheat kernels

whol•ly \ˈhō(l)-lē\ *adv* [ME *hoolly*, fr. *hool* whole] (14c) **1 :** to the full or entire extent : COMPLETELY ⟨a ~ owned subsidiary⟩ **2 :** to the exclusion of other things : SOLELY ⟨a book dealing ~ with herbs⟩

whom \ˈhüm, üm\ *pron, objective case of* WHO [ME, fr. OE *hwām*, dat. of *hwā* who] (bef. 12c) — used as an interrogative or relative; used as object of a verb or a preceding preposition ⟨to know for ~ the bell tolls —John Donne⟩ or less frequently as the object of a following preposition ⟨the man ~ you wrote to⟩ though now often considered stilted esp. as an interrogative and esp. in oral use; occas. used as predicate nominative with a copulative verb or as subject of a verb esp. in the vicinity of a preposition or a verb of which it might mistakenly be considered the object ⟨~ say ye that I am —Mt 16:15 (AV)⟩ ⟨people . . . ~ you never thought would sympathize —Shea Murphy⟩

usage Observers of the language have been predicting the demise of *whom* from about 1870 down to the present day ⟨one of the pronoun cases is visibly disappearing—the objective case *whom* —R. G. White (1870)⟩ ⟨*whom* is dying out in England, where "Whom did you see?" sounds affected —Anthony Burgess (1980)⟩. Our evidence shows that no one—English or not—should expect *whom* to disappear momentarily; it shows every indication of persisting quite a while yet. Actual usage of *who* and *whom*—accurately described at the entries in this dictionary—does not appear to be markedly different from the usage of Shakespeare's time. But the 18th century grammarians, propounding rules and analogies, rejecting other rules and analogies, and usu. justifying both with appeals to Latin or Greek, have intervened between us and Shakespeare. It seems clear that the grammarians' rules have had little effect on the traditional uses. One thing they have accomplished is to encourage hypercorrect uses of *whom* ⟨*whom* shall I say is calling?⟩. Another is that they have made some people unsure of themselves ⟨said he was asked to step down, although it is not known exactly *who* or *whom* asked him —*Redding (Conn.) Pilot*⟩.

whom•ev•er \hü-ˈme-vər\ *pron, objective case of* WHOEVER

[1]**whomp** \ˈhwämp, ˈhwȯmp, ˈwämp, ˈwȯmp\ *n* [imit.] (1926) : a loud slap, crash, or crunch

[2]**whomp** *vi* (1942) : to strike with a sharp noise or thump ~ *vt* **1 :** to hit or slap sharply **2 :** to defeat decisively : TROUNCE **3 :** to create or put together esp. hastily — usu. used with *up*

whomp up *vt* (1949) : to stir up : AROUSE

whom•so \ˈhüm-(ˌ)sō\ *pron, objective case of* WHOSO

whom•so•ev•er \ˌhüm-sə-ˈwe-vər\ *pron, objective case of* WHOSOEVER

whoo–hoo *var of* WOO-HOO

[1]**whoop** \ˈhüp, ˈhu̇p, ˈhwüp, ˈhwu̇p, ˈwüp, ˈwu̇p\ *vb* [ME *whopen, houpen*, fr. AF *huper*, of imit. origin] *vi* (14c) **1 :** to utter a whoop in expression of eagerness, enthusiasm, or enjoyment : SHOUT **2 :** to utter the cry of an owl : HOOT **3 :** to make the characteristic whoop of whooping cough **4 a :** to go or pass with a loud noise **b :** to be rushed through by acclamation or with noisy support ⟨the bill ~*ed* through both houses⟩ ~ *vt* **1 a :** to utter or express with a whoop **b :** to urge, drive, or cheer on with a whoop **2 :** to agitate in behalf of **3 :** RAISE, BOOST ⟨~ up the price⟩ — **whoop it up 1 :** to celebrate riotously : CAROUSE **2 :** to stir up enthusiasm

[2]**whoop** *n* (14c) **1 a :** a loud yell expressive of eagerness, exuberance, or jubilation — often used interjectionally **b :** a shout of hunters or of men in battle or pursuit **2 :** the cry of an owl : HOOT **3 :** the crowing intake of breath following a paroxysm in whooping cough **4 :** a minimum amount or degree : the least bit ⟨not worth a ~⟩

whoop–de–do *or* **whoop–de–doo** \ˌh(w)üp-dē-ˈdü, ˌh(w)u̇p-, -tē-\ *n* [prob. irreg. fr. [2]*whoop*] (1929) **1 :** noisy and exuberant or attention-getting activity (as at a social affair or in a political campaign) **2 :** a lively social affair **3 :** agitated public discussion or debate

[1]**whoop•ee** \ˈ(h)wu̇-(ˌ)pē, ˈ(h)wü-; (h)wu̇-ˈpē, (h)wü-\ *interj* [irreg. fr. [2]*whoop*] (1845) — used to express exuberance

[2]**whoop•ee** \ˈ(h)wu̇-(ˌ)pē, ˈ(h)wü-\ *n* (1924) **1 :** boisterous convivial fun : MERRYMAKING — usu. used with *make* **2 :** sexual play — usu. used with *make*

whoopee cushion *n* (1953) : a cushion that makes a sound like the breaking of wind when sat upon

whoop•er \ˈh(w)ü-pər, ˈh(w)u̇-\ *n* (1660) : one that whoops; *specif* : WHOOPING CRANE

whooper swan *n* (1879) : a chiefly Eurasian swan (*Cygnus cygnus*) with a yellow and black bill — compare TRUMPETER SWAN

whooping cough *n* (ca. 1670) : an infectious respiratory disease esp. of children caused by a bacterium (*Bordetella pertussis*) and marked by a convulsive spasmodic cough sometimes followed by a crowing intake of breath — called also *pertussis*

whooping crane *n* (ca. 1730) : a large white nearly extinct No. American crane (*Grus americana*) noted for its loud trumpeting call

whoop•la \ˈh(w)üp-ˌlä, ˈh(w)u̇p-\ *n* [alter. of *hoopla*] (1931) **1 :** HOOPLA **2 :** boisterous merrymaking

whoops *var of* OOPS

[1]**whoosh** \ˈhwüsh, ˈwüsh, ˈ(h)wu̇sh\ *n* [imit.] (1856) : a swift or explosive rush; *also* : the sound created by such a rush — often used interjectionally

[2]**whoosh** *vi* (1909) : to rush past or move explosively ⟨cars ~*ing* along the expressway⟩ ~ *vt* : to move (a person or thing) with or as if with a whoosh

[1]**whop** *or* **whap** \ˈhwäp, ˈwäp\ *vt* **whopped** *or* **whapped; whop•ping** *or* **whap•ping** [ME *whappen*, alter. of *wappen* to throw violently] (14c) **1 :** to pull or whip out **2 a :** BEAT, STRIKE **b :** to defeat totally

[2]**whop** *also* **whap** *n* (14c) : a heavy blow : THUMP

whop•per \ˈhwä-pər, ˈwä-\ *n* [[1]*whop*] (ca. 1712) **1 :** something unusually large or otherwise extreme of its kind **2 :** an extravagant or monstrous lie

whop•ping \ˈhwä-piŋ, ˈwä-\ *adj* (ca. 1625) : extremely large; *also* : EXTRAORDINARY, INCREDIBLE

[1]**whore** \ˈhȯr, ˈhu̇r\ *n* [ME *hore*, fr. OE *hōre*; akin to ON *hōra* whore, *hōrr* adulterer, L *carus* dear — more at CHARITY] (bef. 12c) **1 :** a woman who engages in sexual acts for money : PROSTITUTE; *also* : a promiscuous or immoral woman **2 :** a male who engages in sexual acts for money **3 :** a venal or unscrupulous person

[2]**whore** *vb* **whored; whor•ing** *vi* (1554) **1 :** to have unlawful sexual intercourse as or with a whore **2 :** to pursue a faithless, unworthy, or idolatrous desire ~ *vt, obs* : to corrupt by lewd intercourse : DEBAUCH

whore•dom \ˈhȯr-dəm, ˈhu̇r-\ *n* (12c) **1 :** the practice of whoring : PROSTITUTION **2 :** faithless, unworthy, or idolatrous practices or pursuits

whore•house \ˈhȯr-ˌhau̇s, ˈhu̇r-\ *n* (14c) : a building in which prostitutes are available : BORDELLO

whore•mas•ter \-ˌmas-tər\ *n* (14c) : a man consorting with whores or given to lechery

whore•mon•ger \-ˌməŋ-gər, -ˌmäŋ-\ *n* (1526) : WHOREMASTER

whore•son \ˈhȯr-sᵊn, ˈhu̇r-\ *n, often attrib* (14c) **1 :** BASTARD **2 :** a coarse fellow — used as a generalized term of abuse

Whorf•ian hypothesis \ˈwȯr-fē-ən-, ˈhwȯr-\ *n* [Benjamin Lee *Whorf* †1941 Am. anthropologist] (1954) : a theory in linguistics: one's language determines one's conception of the world

whor•ish \ˈhȯr-ish, ˈhu̇r-\ *adj* (1535) : of or befitting a whore

whorl \ˈhwȯr(-ə)l, ˈwȯr(-ə)l, ˈ(h)wər(-ə)l\ *n* [ME *wharle, whorle*, prob. alter. of *whirle*, fr. *whirlen* to whirl] (15c) **1 :** a drum-shaped section on the lower part of a spindle in spinning or weaving machinery serving as a pulley for the tape drive that rotates the spindle **2 :** an arrangement of similar anatomical parts (as leaves) in a circle around a point on an axis **3 :** something that whirls, coils, or spirals or whose form suggests such movement : SWIRL ⟨~*s* of snow⟩ **4 :** one of the turns of a univalve shell **5 :** a fingerprint in which the central papillary ridges turn through at least one complete circle

whorled \ˈhwȯr(-ə)ld, ˈwȯr(-ə)ld, ˈ(h)wər(-ə)ld\ *adj* (1567) **:** having or arranged in whorls ⟨leaves ~ at the nodes of the stem⟩

whor·tle·ber·ry \ˈhwər-tᵊl-ˌber-ē, ˈwər-\ *n* [alter. of earlier *hurtleberry,* fr. ME *hurtilberye,* irreg. fr. OE *horte* whortleberry + ME *berye* berry] (1578) **1 :** BILBERRY **2 :** BLUEBERRY

1whose \ˈhüz, üz\ *adj* [ME *whos,* gen. of *who, what*] (bef. 12c) **:** of or relating to whom or which esp. as possessor or possessors ⟨~ gorgeous vesture heaps the ground —Robert Browning⟩, agent or agents ⟨the law courts, ~ decisions were important —F. L. Mott⟩, or object or objects of an action ⟨the first poem ~ publication he ever sanctioned —J. W. Krutch⟩

2whose *pron, sing or pl in constr* (12c) **:** that which belongs to whom — used without a following noun as a pronoun equivalent in meaning to the adjective *whose* ⟨tell me ~ it was —Shak.⟩

whose·so·ev·er \ˌhüz-sə-ˈwe-vər\ *adj* (1611) **:** of or relating to whomsoever ⟨~ sins ye remit —Jn 20:23(AV)⟩

who·so \ˈhü-(ˌ)sō\ *pron* (12c) **:** WHOEVER

who·so·ev·er \ˌhü-sə-ˈwe-vər\ *pron* (13c) **:** WHOEVER

who's who \ˌhüz-ˈhü\ *n, often cap both Ws* (1917) **1 :** a compilation of brief biographical sketches of prominent persons in a particular field ⟨a *who's who* of sports figures⟩ **2 :** the leaders of a group **:** ELITE **3 :** a listing or grouping of notable persons or things

whump \ˈhwəmp, ˈwəmp\ *vi* [imit.] (1897) **:** BANG, THUMP — **whump** *n*

whup \ˈhwu̇p, ˈwu̇p\ *vt* **whupped; whup·ping** [alter. of *whip*] (1852) **1 :** to administer a beating to esp. as punishment **2 :** to defeat decisively

1why \ˈhwī, ˈwī\ *adv* [ME, fr. OE *hwȳ,* instr. case of *hwæt* what — more at WHAT] (bef. 12c) **:** for what cause, reason, or purpose ⟨~ did you do it?⟩

2why *conj* (bef. 12c) **1 :** the cause, reason, or purpose for which ⟨know ~ you did it⟩ ⟨that is ~ you did it⟩ **2 :** for which **:** on account of which ⟨know the reason ~ you did it⟩

3why *n, pl* **whys** (13c) **1 :** REASON, CAUSE ⟨wants to know the ~*s* and wherefores⟩ **2 :** a baffling problem **:** ENIGMA

4why *interj* (1519) — used to express mild surprise, hesitation, approval, disapproval, or impatience ⟨~, here's what I was looking for⟩

whyd·ah \ˈhwi-də, ˈwi-\ *n* [alter. of *widow (bird)*] (1783) **:** any of various mostly brownish African passerine birds (genera *Euplectes* and *Vidua*) often kept as cage birds and distinguished in the male by black-and-white plumage and by long tail feathers during the breeding season

wi *abbr* when issued

WI *abbr* Wisconsin

WIA *abbr* wounded in action

Wic·ca \ˈwi-kə\ *n* [prob. fr. OE *wicca* wizard — more at WITCH] (1959) **:** a religion influenced by pre-Christian beliefs and practices of western Europe that affirms the existence of supernatural power (as magic) and of both male and female deities who inhere in nature and that emphasizes ritual observance of seasonal and life cycles — **Wic·can** \ˈwi-kən\ *adj or n*

1wick \ˈwik\ *n* [ME *weke, wicke,* fr. OE *wēoce;* akin to OHG *wiohha* wick, MIr *figid* he weaves] (bef. 12c) **:** a bundle of fibers or a loosely twisted, braided, or woven cord, tape, or tube usu. of soft spun cotton threads that by capillary attraction draws up to be burned a steady supply of the oil in lamps or the melted tallow or wax in candles

2wick *vt* (1949) **:** to absorb or drain (as a fluid or moisture) like a wick ⟨a fabric that ~*s* away perspiration⟩

1wick·ed \ˈwi-kəd\ *adj* [ME, alter. of *wicke* wicked, perh. fr. OE *wicca*] (13c) **1 :** morally very bad **:** EVIL **2 a :** FIERCE, VICIOUS ⟨a ~ dog⟩ **b :** disposed to or marked by mischief **:** ROGUISH ⟨does ~ impersonations⟩ **3 a :** disgustingly unpleasant **:** VILE ⟨a ~ odor⟩ **b :** causing or likely to cause harm, distress, or trouble ⟨a ~ storm⟩ **4 :** going beyond reasonable or predictable limits **:** of exceptional quality or degree ⟨throws a ~ fastball⟩ — **wick·ed·ly** *adv*

2wicked *adv* (1980) **:** VERY, EXTREMELY ⟨~ fast⟩

wick·ed·ness *n* (14c) **1 :** the quality or state of being wicked **2 :** something wicked

wick·er \ˈwi-kər\ *n* [ME *wiker,* of Scand origin; akin to Sw dial. *vikker* willow, ON *veikr* weak — more at WEAK] (14c) **1 :** a small pliant twig or branch (as of osier) **:** WITHE **2 a :** WICKERWORK **b :** something made of wicker — **wicker** *adj*

wick·er·work \-ˌwərk\ *n* (1719) **:** work consisting of interlaced pliant twigs or branches ⟨a cage of ~⟩

wick·et \ˈwi-kət\ *n* [ME *wiket,* fr. AF, prob. of Gmc origin; akin to ON *vīk* inlet, corner] (13c) **1 :** a small gate or door; *esp* **:** one forming part of or placed near a larger gate or door **2 :** an opening like a window; *esp* **:** a grilled or grated window through which business is transacted **3 a :** either of the two sets of three stumps topped by two crosspieces and set 66 feet apart at which the ball is bowled in cricket **b :** an area 10 feet wide bounded by these wickets **c :** one innings of a batsman; *specif* **:** one that is not completed or never begun ⟨win by three ~*s*⟩ **4 :** an arch or hoop in croquet

wick·et·keep·er \ˈwi-kət-ˌkē-pər\ *n* (ca. 1750) **:** a fielder in cricket who stands behind the wicket at which the ball is being bowled

wick·ing \ˈwi-kiŋ\ *n* (1846) **:** material for wicks

wick·i·up \ˈwi-kē-ˌəp\ *n* [Fox (Algonquian language of the Fox, Sauk, and Kickapoo Indians) *wi·kiya·pi* house] (1843) **:** a hut used by the nomadic Indians of the arid regions of the western and southwestern U.S. with a usu. oval base and a rough frame covered with reed mats, grass, or brushwood; *also* **:** a rude temporary shelter or hut

wid·der·shins \ˈwi-dər-shənz\ *also* **with·er·shins** \ˈwi-t͟hər-shənz\ *adv* [MLG *weddersinnes,* fr. MHG *widersinnes,* fr. *widersinnen* to go against, fr. *wider* back against (fr. OHG *widar*) + *sinnen* to travel, go; akin to OHG *sendan* to send — more at WITH, SEND] (1545) **:** in a left-handed, wrong, or contrary direction **:** COUNTERCLOCKWISE — compare DEASIL

wid·dy \ˈwi-dē\ *n, pl* **widdies** [ME (Sc), fr. ME *withy*] (15c) **1** *Scot & dial Eng* **:** a rope of osiers **2** *Scot & dial Eng* **:** a hangman's noose

1wide \ˈwīd\ *adj* **wid·er; wid·est** [ME, fr. OE *wīd;* akin to OHG *wīt* wide] (bef. 12c) **1 a :** having great extent **:** VAST ⟨a ~ area⟩ **b :** extending over a vast area **:** EXTENSIVE ⟨a ~ reputation⟩ **c :** extending throughout a specified area or scope — usu. used in combination ⟨nation*wide*⟩ ⟨industry-*wide*⟩ **d :** COMPREHENSIVE, INCLUSIVE ⟨a ~ assortment⟩ **2 a :** having a specified extension from side to side ⟨3 feet ~⟩ **b :** having much extent between the sides **:** BROAD ⟨a ~ doorway⟩ **c :** fully opened ⟨*wide*-eyed⟩ **d :** LAX 4 **3 a :** extending or fluctuating considerably between limits ⟨a ~ variation⟩ **b :** straying or deviating from something specified — used with *of* ⟨the accusation was ~ of the truth⟩ **4** *of an animal ration* **:** relatively rich in carbohydrate as compared with protein ***syn*** see BROAD — **wide·ness** *n*

2wide *adv* **wid·er; wid·est** (bef. 12c) **1 a :** over a great distance or extent **:** WIDELY ⟨searched far and ~⟩ **b :** over a specified distance, area, or extent — usu. used in combination ⟨expanded the business country-*wide*⟩ **2 a :** so as to leave much space or distance between ⟨placed ~ apart⟩ **b :** so as to pass at or clear by a considerable distance ⟨ran ~ around left end⟩ **3 :** to the fullest extent **:** COMPLETELY, FULLY ⟨~ open⟩

wide–an·gle \ˈwīd-ˈaŋ-gəl\ *adj* (ca. 1878) **1 :** having or covering an angle of view wider than the ordinary — used esp. of lenses of shorter than normal focal length **2 :** having, involving the use of, or relating to a wide-angle lens ⟨a ~ shot⟩

wide area network *n* (1982) **:** a network of computers (as the Internet) in a large area (as a country or the globe) for sharing resources or exchanging data

wide·awake \ˌwīd-ə-ˈwāk\ *n* (1837) **1 :** a soft felt hat with a low crown and a wide brim **2 :** SOOTY TERN

wide–awake *adj* (1791) **1 :** fully awake **2 :** alertly watchful esp. for advantages or opportunities ***syn*** see WATCHFUL

wide·band \ˈwīd-ˌband\ *adj* (1935) **:** BROADBAND

wide–body \ˈwīd-ˌbä-dē\ *n* (1968) **:** a large jet aircraft characterized by a wide cabin

wide–eyed \ˈwīd-ˈīd\ *adj* (1838) **1 :** having or marked by unsophisticated or uncritical acceptance or admiration **:** NAIVE ⟨~ innocence⟩ **2 :** having the eyes wide open esp. with wonder or astonishment

wide·ly *adv* (1579) **1 :** over or through a wide area ⟨has traveled ~⟩ **2 :** to a great extent ⟨departed ~ from the previous edition⟩ **3 :** by or among a large well-dispersed group of people ⟨a ~ known political figure⟩ **4 :** over a broad range ⟨persons with ~ fluctuating incomes —*Current Biog.*⟩

wide·mouthed \ˈwīd-ˈmau̇t͟hd, -ˈmau̇tht\ *adj* (1593) **1 :** having one's mouth opened wide (as in awe) **2 :** having a wide mouth ⟨~ jars⟩

wid·en \ˈwī-dᵊn\ *vb* **wid·ened; wid·en·ing** \ˈwīd-niŋ, ˈwī-dᵊn-iŋ\ *vt* (1640) **:** to increase the width, scope, or extent of ⟨~ a road⟩ ⟨~ an investigation⟩ ~ *vi* **:** to become wide or wider ⟨a ~*ing gap*⟩ — **wid·en·er** \ˈwīd-nər, ˈwī-dᵊn-ər\ *n*

wide–open \ˈwīd-ˈō-pən, -ˌō-\ *adj* (1852) **:** having virtually no limits or restrictions ⟨a ~ town⟩

wide·out \ˈwīd-ˌau̇t\ *n* (1978) **:** WIDE RECEIVER

wide–rang·ing \ˈwīd-ˌrān-jiŋ\ *adj* (1816) **:** extensive in scope **:** COMPREHENSIVE ⟨~ interests⟩

wide receiver *n* (1968) **:** a football receiver who normally lines up several yards to the side of the offensive formation

wide–screen *adj* (1953) **:** of or relating to a projected picture whose aspect ratio is substantially greater than 1.33:1

wide·spread \ˈwīd-ˈspred\ *adj* (1582) **1 :** widely diffused or prevalent ⟨~ public interest⟩ **2 :** widely extended or spread out ⟨low, ~ hood and fenders —*Time*⟩ ⟨a ~ erosion surface —C. B. Hitchcock⟩

wide–spread·ing \-ˌspre-diŋ\ *adj* (1591) **:** stretching or extending over a wide space or area ⟨~ thatch roofs —*Nat'l Geographic*⟩

widgeon *var of* WIGEON

wid·get \ˈwi-jət\ *n* [alter. of *gadget*] (1926) **1 :** GADGET **2 :** an unnamed article considered for purposes of hypothetical example

wid·ish \ˈwī-dish\ *adj* (1823) **:** somewhat wide

1wid·ow \ˈwi-(ˌ)dō\ *n* [ME *widewe,* fr. OE *wuduwe;* akin to OHG *wituwa* widow, L *vidua,* Skt *vidhavā,* L *-videre* to separate] (bef. 12c) **1 a :** a woman who has lost her husband by death and usu. has not remarried **b :** GRASS WIDOW 2 **c :** a woman whose husband leaves her alone frequently or for long periods to engage in a usu. specified activity ⟨a golf ~⟩ **2 :** an extra hand or part of a hand of cards dealt face down and usu. placed at the disposal of the highest bidder **3 :** a single usu. short last line (as of a paragraph) separated from its related text and appearing at the top of a printed page or column

2widow *vt* (14c) **1 :** to cause to become a widow or widower **2** *obs* **:** to survive as the widow of **3 :** to deprive of something greatly valued or needed

wid·ow·bird \ˈwi-dō-ˌbərd\ *n* (1772) **:** any of several whydahs (genus *Euplectes*)

wid·ow·er \ˈwi-də-wər\ *n* [ME *widewer,* alter. of *wedow* widow, widower, fr. OE *wuduwa* widower; akin to OE *wuduwe* widow] (14c) **:** a man who has lost his wife by death and usu. has not remarried

wid·ow·er·hood \-ˌhu̇d\ *n* (ca. 1796) **1 :** the fact or state of being a widower **2 :** the period during which a man remains a widower

wid·ow·hood \ˈwi-dō-ˌhu̇d, -də-\ *n* (bef. 12c) **1 :** the fact or state of being a widow **2 :** the period during which a woman remains a widow **3 :** WIDOWERHOOD

widow's cruse *n* [fr. the widow's cruse of oil that miraculously supplies Elijah during a famine (I Kings 17:8–16)] (1729) **:** an inexhaustible supply

widow's peak *n* (ca. 1849) **:** a point formed by the hairline in front

widow's walk *n* (1937) **:** a railed observation platform atop a usu. coastal house

width \ˈwidth, ˈwitth\ *n* [1wide] (1627) **1 :** the horizontal measurement taken at right angles to the length **:** BREADTH **2 :** largeness of extent or scope **3 :** a measured and cut piece of material ⟨a ~ of calico⟩

wield \ˈwēld\ *vt* [ME *welden* to control, fr. OE *wieldan;* akin to OHG *waltan* to rule, L *valēre* to be strong, be worth] (bef. 12c) **1** *chiefly dial* **:** to deal successfully with **:** MANAGE **2 :** to handle (as a tool) esp. effectively ⟨~ a broom⟩ **3 a :** to exert one's authority by means of ⟨~ influence⟩ **b :** have at one's command or disposal ⟨did not ~ appropriate credentials —G. W. Bonham⟩ — **wield·er** *n*

\ə\ abut \ᵊ\ kitten, F table \ər\ further \a\ ash \ā\ ace \ä\ mop, mar
\au̇\ out \ch\ chin \e\ bet \ē\ easy \g\ go \i\ hit \ī\ ice \j\ job
\ŋ\ sing \ō\ go \ȯ\ law \ȯi\ boy \th\ thin \t͟h\ the \ü\ loot \u̇\ foot
\y\ yet \zh\ vision, beige \k̟, ⁿ, œ, ue, ʸ\ see Guide to Pronunciation

wieldy \ˈwēl-dē\ *adj* (14c) : capable of being wielded easily

wie·ner *also* **wei·ner** \ˈwē-nər, ˈwē-nē *also* ˈwi-nē\ *n* [short for *wienerwurst*] (1900) : FRANKFURTER

Wie·ner schnit·zel \ˈvē-nər-ˌshnit-səl, ˈwē-nər-ˌsnit-\ *n* [G, lit., Vienna cutlet] (1862) : a thin breaded veal cutlet

wie·ner·wurst \ˈwē-nə(r)-ˌwərst *also* -ˌwu̇rst *sometimes* -ˌwu̇sht *or* -ˌwu̇st; *also with* v *for* w\ *n* [G, fr. *Wiener* of Vienna + *Wurst* sausage] (1882) **1** : VIENNA SAUSAGE **2** : FRANKFURTER

wie·nie \ˈwē-nē *also* ˈwi-nē\ *n* [by shortening & alter. fr. *wienerwurst*] (1867) : FRANKFURTER

wife \ˈwīf\ *n, pl* **wives** \ˈwīvz\ [ME *wif,* fr. OE *wīf;* akin to OHG *wīb* wife and prob. to Toch B *kwīpe* female pudenda] (bef. 12c) **1 a** *dial* : WOMAN **b** : a woman acting in a specified capacity — used in combination ⟨fish*wife*⟩ **2** : a female partner in a marriage — **wife·hood** \ˈwīf-ˌhu̇d, ˈwī-ˌfu̇d\ *n* — **wife·less** \ˈwī-fləs\ *adj*

wife·beat·er \ˈwīf-ˌbē-tər\ *n* (1994) *slang* : a man's white tank top

[1]**wife·like** \ˈwīf-ˌlīk\ *adv* (1598) : in a wifely manner

[2]**wifelike** *adj* (1587) : WIFELY

wife·ly \ˈwī-flē\ *adj* (bef. 12c) : of, relating to, or befitting a wife — **wife·li·ness** \-flē-nəs\ *n*

wif·ey \ˈwī-fē\ *n* (1786) : WIFE

Wif·fle \ˈwi-fəl\ *trademark* — used for a hollow plastic ball with cutouts in one hemisphere

Wi–Fi \ˈwī-ˈfī\ *certification mark* — used to certify the interoperability of wireless computer networking devices

wif·ty \ˈwif-tē\ *adj* [origin unknown] (1979) : DITZY

[1]**wig** \ˈwig\ *n* [short for *periwig*] (1675) **1 a** : a manufactured covering of natural or synthetic hair for the head **b** : TOUPEE 2 **2** : an act of wigging : REBUKE

[2]**wig** *vb* **wigged; wig·ging** *vt* (1829) : to scold severely ~ *vi, slang* : to lose one's composure or reason : FREAK — usu. used with *out*

wig·an \ˈwi-gən\ *n* [*Wigan,* England] (1771) : a stiff plain-weave cotton fabric used for interlining

wi·geon *or* **wid·geon** \ˈwi-jən\ *n, pl* **wigeon** *or* **wigeons** *or* **widgeon** *or* **widgeons** [origin unknown] (1513) : any of several freshwater ducks (genus *Anas*): as **a** : an Old World duck (*Anas penelope*) having a large white patch on each wing with the male having a reddish-brown head and buff crown **b** : AMERICAN WIGEON

wigged *adj* (1777) : wearing a wig esp. of a specified kind

wigged–out \ˈwigd-ˈau̇t\ *adj* (1970) : mentally or emotionally discomposed : UPSET, CRAZY

[1]**wig·gle** \ˈwi-gəl\ *vb* **wig·gled; wig·gling** \-g(ə-)liŋ\ [ME *wiglen,* fr. or akin to MD or MLG *wiggelen* to totter; akin to OE *wegan* to move — more at WAY] *vi* (13c) **1** : to move to and fro with quick jerky or shaking motions : JIGGLE **2** : to proceed with or as if with twisting and turning movements : WRIGGLE ~ *vt* : to cause to wiggle

[2]**wiggle** *n* (1816) **1** : the act of wiggling **2** : shellfish or fish in cream sauce with peas — **wig·gly** \ˈwi-g(ə-)lē\ *adj*

wig·gler \ˈwi-g(ə-)lər\ *n* (1859) **1** : a larva or pupa of the mosquito — called also *wriggler* **2** : one that wiggles

wiggle room *n* (1965) : LEEWAY, LATITUDE ⟨a contract with *wiggle room* for further negotiations⟩

[1]**wight** \ˈwīt\ *n* [ME, creature, thing, fr. OE *wiht;* akin to OHG *wiht* creature, thing, OCS *veštĭ* thing] (bef. 12c) : a living being : CREATURE; *esp* : a human being

[2]**wight** *adj* [ME, of Scand origin; akin to ON *vīgr* skilled in fighting (neut. *vīgt*); akin to OE *wīgan* to fight — more at VICTOR] (13c) *archaic* : VALIANT, STALWART

wig·let \ˈwi-glət\ *n* (1831) : a small wig used esp. to enhance a hairstyle

[1]**wig·wag** \ˈwig-ˌwag\ *vb* [E dial. *wig* to move + E *wag*] *vt* (1892) **1** : to signal by wigwagging **2** : to cause to wigwag ~ *vi* **1** : to send a signal by or as if by a flag or light waved according to a code **2** : to make a signal (as by waving the hand or arm)

[2]**wigwag** *n* (1893) : the art or practice of wigwagging

wig·wam \ˈwig-ˌwäm\ *n* [Eastern Abenaki *wikəwαm* house] (1628) : a hut of the American Indians of the Great Lakes region and eastward having typically an arched framework of poles overlaid with bark, mats, or hides; *also* : a rough hut

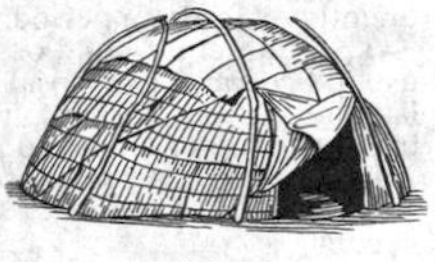

wigwam

wi·ki \ˈwi-kē, ˈwē-\ *n* [*WikiWikiWeb,* a Web site with such programming introduced in 1995] (1995) : a Web site that allows visitors to make changes, contributions, or corrections

wil·co \ˈwil-(ˌ)kō\ *interj* [*will* comply] (ca. 1938) — used esp. in radio and signaling to indicate that a message received will be complied with

[1]**wild** \ˈwī(-ə)ld\ *adj* [ME *wilde,* fr. OE; akin to OHG *wildi* wild, W *gwyllt*] (bef. 12c) **1 a** : living in a state of nature and not ordinarily tame or domesticated ⟨~ ducks⟩ **b** (1) : growing or produced without human aid or care ⟨~ honey⟩ (2) : related to or resembling a corresponding cultivated or domesticated organism **c** : of or relating to wild organisms ⟨the ~ state⟩ **2 a** : not inhabited or cultivated ⟨~ land⟩ **b** : not amenable to human habitation or cultivation; *also* : DESOLATE **3 a** (1) : not subject to restraint or regulation : UNCONTROLLED; *also* : UNRULY (2) : emotionally overcome ⟨~ with grief⟩; *also* : passionately eager or enthusiastic ⟨was ~ to own a toy train —J. C. Furnas⟩ **b** : marked by turbulent agitation : STORMY ⟨a ~ night⟩ **c** : going beyond normal or conventional bounds : FANTASTIC ⟨~ ideas⟩; *also* : SENSATIONAL **d** : indicative of strong passion, desire, or emotion ⟨a ~ gleam of delight in his eyes —*Irish Digest*⟩ **4** : UNCIVILIZED, BARBARIC **5** : characteristic of, appropriate to, or expressive of wilderness, wildlife, or a simple or uncivilized society **6 a** : deviating from the intended or expected course ⟨~ spelling —C. W. Cunnington⟩ ⟨the throw was ~⟩; *also* : tending to throw inaccurately ⟨a ~ pitcher⟩ **b** : having no basis in known or surmised fact ⟨a ~ guess⟩ **7** *of a playing card* : able to represent any card designated by the holder — **wildish** \ˈwī(-ə)l-dish\ *adj* — **wild·ness** \-nəs\ *n*

[2]**wild** *n* (13c) **1** : a sparsely inhabited or uncultivated region or tract : WILDERNESS **2** : a wild, free, or natural state or existence

[3]**wild** *adv* (ca. 1562) : in a wild manner: as **a** : without regulation or control ⟨plants that grow ~⟩ **b** : off an intended or expected course

wild bergamot *n* (1843) : a perennial aromatic No. American monarda (*Monarda fistulosa*) having a terminal cluster of pink or purple flowers

wild boar *n* (13c) : an Old World wild hog (*Sus scrofa*) from which most domestic swine have been derived

wild card *n* [*wild card,* playing card with arbitrarily determined value] (1971) **1** : an unknown or unpredictable factor **2** : one picked to fill a leftover playoff or tournament berth after regularly qualifying competitors have all been determined **3** *usu* **wild·card** : a symbol (as ? or *) used in a keyword database search to represent the presence of zero, one, or more than one unspecified characters

wild carrot *n* (ca. 1538) : QUEEN ANNE'S LACE

[1]**wild·cat** \ˈwī(-ə)l(d)-ˌkat\ *n, pl* **wildcats** (14c) **1 a** : an Old World cat (*Felis silvestris*) that resembles but is heavier in build than the domestic tabby cat and is usu. held to be among the ancestors of the domestic cat **b** *or pl* **wildcat** : any of various small or medium-sized cats (as the lynx or ocelot) **c** : a feral domestic cat **2** : a savage quick-tempered person **3 a** : wildcat money **b** : a wildcat oil or gas well **c** : a wildcat strike

[2]**wildcat** *adj* (1838) **1 a** (1) : issued by a financially irresponsible banking establishment ⟨~ currency⟩ (2) : financially irresponsible or unreliable ⟨~ banks⟩ **b** : operating, produced, or carried on outside the bounds of standard or legitimate business practices ⟨~ insurance schemes —H. H. Reichard⟩ **c** : of, relating to, or being an oil or gas well drilled in territory not known to be productive **d** : initiated by a group of workers without formal union approval or in violation of a contract ⟨a ~ strike⟩ ⟨~ work stoppages⟩ **2 a** *of a cartridge* : having a bullet of standard caliber but using an expanded case or a case designed for a bullet of greater caliber necked down for the smaller bullet **b** *of a firearm* : using wildcat cartridges

[3]**wildcat** *vi* **wild·cat·ted; wild·cat·ting** (ca. 1903) : to prospect and drill an experimental oil or gas well or sink a mine shaft in territory not known to be productive

wild·cat·ter \-ˌka-tər\ *n* (1883) **1** : one that drills wells in the hope of finding oil in territory not known to be an oil field **2** : one that promotes unsafe and unreliable enterprises; *esp* : one that sells stocks in such enterprises **3** : one that designs, builds, or fires wildcat cartridges and firearms **4** : a worker who goes out on a wildcat strike

wild celery *n* (1845) : TAPE GRASS

wild dog *n* (1786) : any of various undomesticated canids (as an African wild dog or a dingo) that resemble the domestic dog

wil·de·beest \ˈwil-də-ˌbēst\ *n, pl* **wildebeests** *also* **wildebeest** [Afrik *wildebees,* fr. *wilde* wild + *bees* ox] (ca. 1824) : either of two large African antelopes (*Connochaetes gnou* and *C. taurinus*) with a head like that of an ox, short mane, long tail, and horns in both sexes that curve downward and outward — called also *gnu*

wil·der \ˈwil-dər\ *vb* [prob. irreg. fr. *wilderness*] *vt* (1613) **1** *archaic* : to lead astray **2** *archaic* : BEWILDER, PERPLEX ~ *vi, archaic* : to move at random : WANDER — **wil·der·ment** \-dər-mənt\ *n, archaic*

wil·der·ness \ˈwil-dər-nəs\ *n* [ME, fr. *wildern* wild, fr. OE *wilddēoren* of wild beasts] (13c) **1 a** (1) : a tract or region uncultivated and uninhabited by human beings (2) : an area essentially undisturbed by human activity together with its naturally developed life community **b** : an empty or pathless area or region ⟨in remote ~*es* of space groups of nebulae are found —G. W. Gray †1960⟩ **c** : a part of a garden devoted to wild growth **2** *obs* : wild or uncultivated state **3 a** : a confusing multitude or mass : an indefinitely great number or quantity ⟨I would not have given it for a ~ of monkeys —Shak.⟩ **b** : a bewildering situation ⟨those moral ~*es* of civilized life —Norman Mailer⟩

wilderness area *n, often cap W&A* (1928) : an often large tract of public land maintained essentially in its natural state and protected against introduction of intrusive artifacts (as roads and buildings)

wild–eyed \ˈwī(-ə)ld-ˈīd\ *adj* (1791) **1** : having a wild expression in the eyes **2** : consisting of or favoring extreme or visionary ideas

wild·fire \-ˌfī(-ə)r\ *n* (12c) **1** : a sweeping and destructive conflagration esp. in a wilderness or a rural area **2** : GREEK FIRE **3** : a phosphorescent glow (as ignis fatuus or fox fire) **4** : a destructive leaf-spot disease of tobacco caused by several strains of a bacterium (*Pseudomonas syringae*) — **like wildfire** : very rapidly ⟨the news spread *like wildfire*⟩

wild·flow·er \-ˌflau̇(-ə)r\ *n* (1620) : the flower of a wild or uncultivated plant or the plant bearing it

wild·fowl \-ˌfau̇(-ə)l\ *n* (bef. 12c) : a game bird; *esp* : a game waterfowl (as a wild duck or goose) — **wild·fowl·er** \-ˌfau̇-lər\ *n* — **wild·fowl·ing** \-liŋ\ *n*

wild geranium *n* (1840) : a common geranium (*Geranium maculatum*) of eastern No. America with deeply parted leaves and flowers of rosy purple; *also* : any of several related geraniums

wild ginger *n* (1804) : any of a genus (*Asarum*) of perennial low-growing herbs of the birthwort family with an aromatic rhizome and usu. cordate leaves

wild–goose chase *n* (ca. 1595) : a complicated or lengthy and usu. fruitless pursuit or search

wild hyacinth *n* (ca. 1794) : any of several plants with flowers suggestive of hyacinths: as **a** : a camas (*Camassia scilloides*) of eastern No. America with white or bluish racemose flowers **b** : BLUEBELL 2a **c** : any of several western No. American herbs (genus *Brodiaea*) of the lily family with grasslike basal leaves and variously colored flowers

wild indigo *n* (1744) : BAPTISIA; *esp* : one (*Baptisia tinctoria*) of eastern No. America with bright yellow flowers and small trifoliolate leaves

[1]**wild·ing** \ˈwīl-diŋ\ *n* [[1]*wild* + [2]*-ing*] (ca. 1525) **1 a** : a plant growing uncultivated in the wild either as a native or an escape; *esp* : a wild apple or crab apple **b** : the fruit of a wilding **2** : a wild animal

[2]**wilding** *adj* (1697) : not domesticated or cultivated : WILD

wild·land \ˈwī(-ə)l(d)-ˌland\ *n* (1808) : land that is uncultivated or unfit for cultivation

wild·life \-ˌlīf\ *n, often attrib* (1879) : living things and esp. mammals, birds, and fishes that are neither human nor domesticated

wild·ling \-liŋ\ *n* (1840) : WILDING

wild·ly \ˈwī(-ə)l(d)-lē\ *adv* (14c) **1** : in a wild manner ⟨was talking ~⟩ **2** : EXTREMELY 2 ⟨~ popular⟩ ⟨~ enthusiastic⟩

wild marjoram *n* (ca. 1550) : OREGANO 1

wild mustard *n* (ca. 1611) : CHARLOCK

wild oat *n* (15c) **1** : any of several Old World wild grasses (genus *Avena*); *esp* : a Eurasian annual weed (*A. fatua*) common in meadows and pastures **2** *pl* : offenses and indiscretions ascribed to youthful exuberance — usu. used in the phrase *sow one's wild oats*

wild pansy *n* (1769) : JOHNNY-JUMP-UP

wild pink *n* (1814) : catchfly (*Silene caroliniana*) with pink or whitish flowers
wild pitch *n* (1867) : a baseball pitch not hit by the batter that cannot be caught or controlled by the catcher with ordinary effort and that enables a base runner to advance — compare PASSED BALL
wild rice *n* (1748) : a tall aquatic No. American perennial grass (*Zizania aquatica*) that yields an edible grain; *also* : the grain
wild rye *n* (ca. 1500) : any of several tall grasses (genus *Elymus*)
wild sarsaparilla *n* (1814) : a common No. American perennial herb (*Aralia nudicaulis*) of the ginseng family with long-stalked basal compound leaves, umbels of greenish flowers, and an aromatic root used as a substitute of true sarsaparilla
wild type *n* (1914) : a phenotype, genotype, or gene that predominates in a natural population of organisms or strain of organisms in contrast to that of natural or laboratory mutant forms; *also* : an organism or strain displaying the wild type — **wild–type** *adj*
Wild West *n* (1844) : the western U.S. in its frontier period characterized by roughness and lawlessness — **Wild West** *adj*
wild·wood \ˈwī(-ə)l(d)-ˌwu̇d\ *n* (12c) : a wood unaltered or unfrequented by humans
[1]**wile** \ˈwī(-ə)l\ *n* [ME *wil,* perh. of Scand origin; akin to ON *vēl* deceit, artifice] (12c) **1 :** a trick or stratagem intended to ensnare or deceive; *also* : a beguiling or playful trick **2 :** skill in outwitting : TRICKERY, GUILE ***syn*** see TRICK
[2]**wile** *vt* **wiled; wil·ing** (14c) **1 :** to lure by or as if by a magic spell : ENTICE **2** [by alter.] : WHILE
[1]**will** \wəl, (ə)l, ᵊl, ˈwil\ *vb, past* **would** \wəd, (ə)d, ˈwu̇d\ *pres sing & pl* **will** [ME (1st & 3d sing. pres. indic.), fr. OE *wille* (infin. *wyllan*); akin to OHG *wili* (3d sing. pres. indic.) wills, L *velle* to wish, will] *vt* (bef. 12c) : DESIRE, WISH ⟨call it what you ~⟩ ~ *verbal auxiliary* **1** — used to express desire, choice, willingness, consent, or in negative constructions refusal ⟨no one *would* take the job⟩ ⟨if we ~ all do our best⟩ ⟨~ you please stop that racket⟩ **2** — used to express frequent, customary, or habitual action or natural tendency or disposition ⟨~ get angry over nothing⟩ ⟨~ work one day and loaf the next⟩ **3** — used to express futurity ⟨tomorrow morning I ~ wake up in this first-class hotel suite —Tennessee Williams⟩ **4** — used to express capability or sufficiency ⟨the back seat ~ hold three passengers⟩ **5** — used to express probability and often equivalent to the simple verb ⟨that ~ be the babysitter⟩ **6 a** — used to express determination, insistence, persistence, or willfulness ⟨I have made up my mind to go and go I ~⟩ **b** — used to express inevitability ⟨accidents ~ happen⟩ **7** — used to express a command, exhortation, or injunction ⟨you ~ do as I say, at once⟩ ~ *vi* : to have a wish or desire ⟨whether we ~ or no⟩ ***usage*** see SHALL — **if you will :** if you wish to call it that ⟨a kind of preoccupation, or obsession *if you will* —Louis Auchincloss⟩
[2]**will** \ˈwil\ *n* [ME, fr. OE *willa* will, desire; akin to OE *wille*] (bef. 12c) **1 :** DESIRE, WISH: as **a :** DISPOSITION, INCLINATION ⟨where there's a ~ there's a way⟩ **b :** APPETITE, PASSION **c :** CHOICE, DETERMINATION **2 a :** something desired; *esp* : a choice or determination of one having authority or power **b** (1) *archaic* : REQUEST, COMMAND (2) [fr. the phrase *our will is* which introduces it] : the part of a summons expressing a royal command **3 :** the act, process, or experience of willing : VOLITION **4 a :** mental powers manifested as wishing, choosing, desiring, or intending **b :** a disposition to act according to principles or ends **c :** the collective desire of a group ⟨the ~ of the people⟩ **5 :** the power of control over one's own actions or emotions ⟨a man of iron ~⟩ **6 :** a legal declaration of a person's wishes regarding the disposal of his or her property or estate after death; *esp* : a written instrument legally executed by which a person makes disposition of his or her estate to take effect after death — **at will :** as one wishes : as or when it pleases or suits oneself
[3]**will** \ˈwil\ *vt* (bef. 12c) **1 a :** to order or direct by a will ⟨~*ed* that her property be divided among her children⟩ **b :** to dispose of by or as if by a will : BEQUEATH ⟨~*ed* his entire estate to this wife⟩ **2 a :** to determine by an act of choice **b :** DECREE, ORDAIN ⟨Providence ~*s* it⟩ **c :** INTEND, PURPOSE **d :** to cause or change by an act of will ⟨believed he could ~ himself to succeed⟩; *also* : to try to do so ~ *vi* **1 :** to exercise the will **2 :** CHOOSE ⟨do as you ~⟩
willed \ˈwild\ *adj* (14c) **1 :** having a will esp. of a specified kind — usu. used in combination ⟨strong-*willed*⟩ **2 :** DELIBERATE
wil·lem·ite \ˈwi-lə-ˌmīt\ *n* [G *Willemit,* fr. *Willem* (William) I †1843 king of the Netherlands] (ca. 1841) : a mineral of varying color consisting of a silicate of zinc and occurring esp. in massive or granular forms
wil·let \ˈwi-lət\ *n, pl* **willets** *also* **willet** [imit.] (1791) : a large American shorebird (*Catoptrophorus semipalmatus*) of the sandpiper family that resembles the greater yellowlegs but has a thicker bill and gray legs and that displays a black-and-white wing pattern when in flight
will·ful *or* **wil·ful** \ˈwil-fəl\ *adj* (13c) **1 :** obstinately and often perversely self-willed ⟨a stubborn and ~ child⟩ **2 :** done deliberately : INTENTIONAL ⟨~ disobedience⟩ ***syn*** see UNRULY — **will·ful·ly** \-fə-lē\ *adv* — **will·ful·ness** *n*
Wil·liams syndrome \ˈwil-yəmz-\ *n* [J. C. P. *Williams* b1922 New Zealand physician] (1981) : a rare genetic disorder marked esp. by hypercalcemia of infants, heart defects, characteristic facial abnormalities, and mild to moderate mental retardation but a high verbal aptitude
Wil·liam Tell \ˌwil-yəm-ˈtel\ *n* (1778) : a heroic archer in Swiss legend who complies with an order to shoot an apple off his son's head
wil·lies \ˈwi-lēz\ *n pl* [origin unknown] (ca. 1896) : a fit of nervousness : JITTERS — used with *the*
will·ing \ˈwi-liŋ\ *adj* (14c) **1 :** inclined or favorably disposed in mind : READY ⟨~ and eager to help⟩ **2 :** prompt to act or respond ⟨lending a ~ hand⟩ **3 :** done, borne, or accepted by choice or without reluctance ⟨a ~ sacrifice⟩ **4 :** of or relating to the will or power of choosing : VOLITIONAL ***syn*** see VOLUNTARY — **will·ing·ly** \-liŋ-lē\ *adv* — **will·ing·ness** *n*
wil·li·waw \ˈwi-li-ˌwȯ\ *n* [origin unknown] (ca. 1842) **1 a :** a sudden violent gust of cold land air common along mountainous coasts of high latitudes **b :** a sudden violent wind **2 :** a violent commotion
will–less \ˈwil-ləs\ *adj* (1747) **1 :** involving no exercise of the will : INVOLUNTARY ⟨~ obedience⟩ **2 :** not exercising the will ⟨life-benumbed, ~ characters —Norma Rosen⟩
will–o'–the–wisp \ˌwil-ə-t͟hə-ˈwisp\ *n* [*Will* (nickname for *William*) + *of* + *the* + *wisp*] (ca. 1661) **1 :** IGNIS FATUUS 1 **2 :** a delusive or elusive goal — **will–o'–the–wisp** *adj*
wil·low \ˈwi-(ˌ)lō\ *n* [ME *wilghe, wilowe,* fr. OE *welig;* akin to MHG *wilge* willow] (bef. 12c) **1 :** any of a genus (*Salix* of the family Salicaceae, the willow family) of trees and shrubs bearing catkins of apetalous flowers and including forms of value for wood, osiers, or tanbark and a few ornamentals **2 :** an object made of willow wood; *esp* : a cricket bat — **wil·low·like** \-lō-ˌlīk\ *adj*
willow herb *n* (1578) : any of a genus (*Epilobium*) of herbs of the evening-primrose family; *esp* : FIREWEED b
wil·low·ware \ˈwi-lə-ˌwer, ˈwi-lō-\ *n* (ca. 1885) : dinnerware that is usu. blue and white and that is decorated with a story-telling design featuring a large willow tree by a little bridge
wil·lowy \ˈwi-lə-wē\ *adj* (1766) **1 :** abounding with willows **2 :** resembling a willow: **a :** PLIANT **b :** gracefully tall and slender ⟨a ~ actress⟩
will·pow·er \ˈwil-ˌpau̇(-ə)r\ *n* (1858) : energetic determination
will to power (1907) **1 :** the drive of the superman in the philosophy of Nietzsche to perfect and transcend the self through the possession and exercise of creative power **2 :** a conscious or unconscious desire to exercise authority over others
wil·ly *also* **wil·lie** \ˈwi-lē\ *n* [fr. the name *Willy*] (ca. 1905) *slang* : PENIS
wil·ly–nil·ly \ˌwi-lē-ˈni-lē\ *adv or adj* [alter. of *will I nill I* or *will ye nill ye* or *will he nill he*] (1608) **1 :** by compulsion : without choice **2 :** in a haphazard or spontaneous manner
Wilms' tumor \ˈvilm-zəz-, ˈvilmz-\ *n* [Max *Wilms* †1918 Ger. surgeon] (ca. 1910) : a malignant tumor of the kidney that primarily affects children and is made up of embryonic elements
Wil·son's disease \ˈwil-sənz-\ *n* [Samuel A. K. *Wilson* †1937 Eng. neurologist] (ca. 1915) : a hereditary disease that is characterized by excessive accumulation of copper in the body (as in the liver or brain) due to abnormal copper metabolism, is determined by an autosomal recessive gene, and is marked esp. by liver dysfunction and neurologic disease
[1]**wilt** \wəlt, ˈwilt\ *archaic pres 2d sing of* WILL
[2]**wilt** \ˈwilt\ *vb* [alter. of earlier *welk,* fr. ME *welken,* prob. fr. MD; akin to OHG *erwelkēn* to wilt] *vi* (ca. 1691) **1 a :** to lose turgor from lack of water ⟨the plants ~*ed* in the heat⟩ **b :** to become limp **2 :** to grow weak or faint : LANGUISH ~ *vt* : to cause to wilt
[3]**wilt** \ˈwilt\ *n* (1855) **1 :** an act or instance of wilting : the state of being wilted **2 a :** a disorder (as a fungus disease) of plants marked by loss of turgidity in soft tissues with subsequent drooping and often shriveling — called also *wilt disease* **b :** polyhedrosis of caterpillars
Wil·ton \ˈwil-tᵊn\ *n* [*Wilton,* borough in England] (1774) : a carpet woven with loops like the Brussels carpet but having a velvet cut pile and being generally of better materials
wily \ˈwī-lē\ *adj* **wil·i·er; -est** (14c) : full of wiles : CRAFTY ⟨a ~ negotiator⟩ ***syn*** see SLY — **wil·i·ly** \-lə-lē\ *adv* — **wil·i·ness** \-lē-nəs\ *n*
[1]**wim·ble** \ˈwim-bəl\ *n* [ME, fr. AF, fr. MD *wimmel* auger; akin to MLG *wimmel* auger] (13c) : any of various instruments for boring holes
[2]**wimble** *vt* **wim·bled; wim·bling** \-b(ə-)liŋ\ (15c) *archaic* : to bore with or as if with a wimble
wimp \ˈwimp\ *n* [origin unknown] (1920) : a weak, cowardly, or ineffectual person — **wimp·i·ness** \ˈwim-pē-nəs\ *n* — **wimp·ish** \ˈwim-pish\ *adj* — **wimp·ish·ness** \-nəs\ *n* — **wimpy** \ˈwim-pē\ *adj*
[1]**wim·ple** \ˈwim-pəl\ *n* [ME *wimpel,* fr. OE; perh. akin to OE *wīpian* to wipe] (bef. 12c) **1 :** a cloth covering worn over the head and around the neck and chin esp. by women in the late medieval period and by some nuns **2** *Scot* **a :** a crafty turn : TWIST **b :** CURVE, BEND

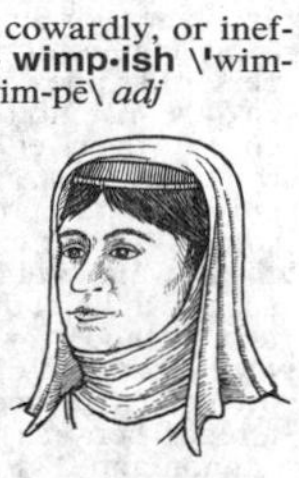
wimple 1

[2]**wimple** *vb* **wim·pled; wim·pling** \-p(ə-)liŋ\ *vt* (13c) **1 :** to cover with or as if with a wimple : VEIL **2 :** to cause to ripple ~ *vi* **1** *archaic* : to fall or lie in folds **2** *chiefly Scot* : to follow a winding course : MEANDER **3 :** RIPPLE
wimp out *vi* (1981) : to behave like a wimp : chicken out; *esp* : to choose the easiest course of action
[1]**win** \ˈwin\ *vb* **won** \ˈwən\; **win·ning** [ME *winnen,* fr. OE *winnan* to struggle; akin to OHG *winnan* to struggle and prob. to L *venus* sexual desire, charm, Skt *vanas* desire, *vanoti* he strives for] *vt* (bef. 12c) **1 a :** to get possession of by effort or fortune **b :** to obtain by work : EARN ⟨striving to ~ a living from the sterile soil⟩ **2 a :** to gain in or as if in battle or contest ⟨*won* the championship⟩ **b :** to be the victor in ⟨*won* the war⟩ **3 a :** to make friendly or favorable to oneself or to one's cause — often used with *over* ⟨*won* him over with persuasive arguments⟩ **b :** to induce to accept oneself in marriage ⟨was unable to ~ the woman he loved⟩ **4 a :** to obtain (as ore, coal, or clay) by mining **b :** to prepare (as a vein or bed) for regular mining **c :** to recover (as metal) from ore **5 :** to reach by expenditure of effort ~ *vi* **1 :** to gain the victory in a contest : SUCCEED **2 :** to succeed in arriving at a place or a state — **win·less** \ˈwin-ləs\ *adj* — **win·na·ble** \ˈwi-nə-bəl\ *adj*
[2]**win** *n* (1862) : VICTORY; *esp* : first place at the finish (as of a horse race)
wince \ˈwin(t)s\ *vi* **winced; winc·ing** [ME *wynsen* to kick out, start, fr. AF **wincer, *guincer* to shift direction, dodge, by-form of *guenchir,* prob. of Gmc origin; akin to OHG *wenken, wankōn* to totter — more at WENCH] (ca. 1748) : to shrink back involuntarily (as from pain) : FLINCH ***syn*** see RECOIL — **wince** *n*
[1]**winch** \ˈwinch\ *n* [ME *winche* roller, reel, fr. OE *wince;* akin to OE *wincian* to wink] (bef. 12c) **1 :** any of various machines or instruments for hauling or pulling; *esp* : a powerful machine with one or more drums on which to coil a rope, cable, or chain for hauling or hoisting : WINDLASS **2 :** a crank with a handle for giving motion to a machine (as a grindstone)
[2]**winch** *vt* (1529) : to hoist or haul with or as if with a winch — **winch·er** *n*

\ə\ abut \ᵊ\ kitten, F table \ər\ further \a\ ash \ā\ ace \ä\ mop, mar \au̇\ out \ch\ chin \e\ bet \ē\ easy \g\ go \i\ hit \ī\ ice \j\ job \ŋ\ sing \ō\ go \ȯ\ law \ȯi\ boy \th\ thin \t͟h\ the \ü\ loot \u̇\ foot \y\ yet \zh\ vision, beige \k, ⁿ, œ, ue, ʸ\ *see* Guide to Pronunciation

Win·ches·ter \ˈwin-ˌches-tər\ *adj* [fr. the code name used by the original developer] (1973) **:** relating to or being computer disk technology that permits high-density storage by sealing the rigid metal disks within the disk drive mechanism as protection against dust

[1]**wind** \ˈwind, *archaic or poetic* ˈwīnd\ *n, often attrib* [ME, fr. OE; akin to OHG *wint* wind, L *ventus,* Gk *aēnai* to blow, Skt *vāti* it blows] (bef. 12c) **1 a :** a natural movement of air of any velocity; *esp* **:** the earth's air or the gas surrounding a planet in natural motion horizontally **b :** an artificially produced movement of air **c :** SOLAR WIND, STELLAR WIND **2 a :** a destructive force or influence **b :** a force or agency that carries along or influences **:** TENDENCY, TREND ⟨withstood the ~*s* of popular opinion —Felix Frankfurter⟩ **3 a :** BREATH 4a **b :** BREATH 2a **c :** the pit of the stomach **:** SOLAR PLEXUS **4 :** gas generated in the stomach or the intestines ⟨pass ~⟩ **5 a :** compressed air or gas **b** *archaic* **:** AIR **6 :** something that is insubstantial: as **a :** mere talk **:** idle words **b :** NOTHING, NOTHINGNESS **c :** vain self-satisfaction **7 a :** air carrying a scent (as of a hunter or game) **b :** slight information esp. about something secret **:** INTIMATION ⟨got ~ of the plan⟩ **8 a :** musical wind instruments esp. as distinguished from strings and percussion **b** *pl* **:** players of wind instruments **9 a :** a direction from which the wind may blow **:** a point of the compass; *esp* **:** one of the cardinal points **b :** the direction from which the wind is blowing — **wind·less** \-ləs\ *adj* — **wind·less·ly** *adv* — **before the wind :** in the same direction as the main force of the wind — **close to the wind :** as nearly as possible against the main force of the wind — **have the wind of 1 :** to be to windward of **2 :** to be on the scent of **3 :** to have a superior position to — **in the wind :** about to happen **:** ASTIR, AFOOT ⟨change is *in the wind*⟩ — **near the wind 1 :** close to the wind **2 :** close to a point of danger **:** near the permissible limit — **off the wind :** away from the direction from which the wind is blowing — **on the wind :** toward the direction from which the wind is blowing — **to the wind** *or* **to the winds :** ASIDE, AWAY ⟨threw caution *to the wind*⟩ — **under the wind 1 :** to leeward **2 :** in a place protected from the wind **:** under the lee

[2]**wind** \ˈwind\ *vt* (15c) **1 :** to detect or follow by scent **2 :** to expose to the air or wind **:** dry by exposing to air **3 :** to make short of breath **4 :** to regulate the wind supply of (an organ pipe) **5 :** to rest (as a horse) in order to allow the breath to be recovered ~ *vi* **1 :** to scent game **2** *dial* **:** to pause for breath

[3]**wind** \ˈwīnd, ˈwind\ *vb* **wind·ed** \ˈwīn-dəd, ˈwin-\ *or* **wound** \ˈwau̇nd\; **wind·ing** [[1]*wind*] *vt* (1586) **1 :** to cause (as a horn) to sound by blowing **:** BLOW **2 :** to sound (as a call or note) on a horn ⟨*wound* a rousing call —R. L. Stevenson⟩ ~ *vi* **:** to produce a sound on a horn

[4]**wind** \ˈwīnd\ *vb* **wound** \ˈwau̇nd\ *also* **wind·ed; wind·ing** [ME, fr. OE *windan* to twist, move with speed or force, brandish; akin to OHG *wintan* to wind, Umbrian *ohavendu* let him turn aside] *vt* (bef. 12c) **1 a** *obs* **:** WEAVE **b :** ENTANGLE, INVOLVE **c :** to introduce sinuously or stealthily **:** INSINUATE **2 a :** to encircle or cover with something pliable **:** bind with loops or layers **b :** to turn completely or repeatedly about an object **:** COIL, TWINE **c** (1) **:** to hoist or haul by means of a rope or chain and a windlass (2) **:** to move (a ship) by hauling on a capstan **d** (1) **:** to tighten the spring of ⟨~ a clock⟩ (2) *obs* **:** to make tighter **:** TIGHTEN, TUNE (3) **:** CRANK **e :** to raise to a high level (as of excitement or tension) — usu. used with *up* **3 a :** to cause to move in a curving line or path **b** *archaic* **:** to turn the course of; *esp* **:** to lead (a person) as one wishes **c** (1) **:** to cause (as a ship) to change direction **:** TURN (2) **:** to turn (a ship) end for end **d :** to traverse on a curving course ⟨the river ~*s* the valley⟩ **e :** to effect by or as if by curving ~ *vi* **1 :** BEND, WARP **2 a :** to have a curving course or shape **:** extend in curves **b :** to proceed as if by winding **3 :** to move so as to encircle something **4 :** to turn when lying at anchor

[5]**wind** \ˈwīnd\ *n* (14c) **1 :** a mechanism (as a winch) for winding **2 :** an act of winding **:** the state of being wound **3 :** COIL, TURN **4 :** a particular method of winding

wind·age \ˈwin-dij\ *n* [[1]*wind*] (ca. 1710) **1 a :** the space between the projectile of a smoothbore gun and the surface of the bore **b :** the difference between the diameter of the bore of a muzzle-loading rifled cannon and that of the projectile cylinder **2 a :** the amount of sight deflection necessary to compensate for wind displacement in aiming a gun **b** (1) **:** the influence of the wind in deflecting the course of a projectile (2) **:** the amount of deflection due to the wind **3 :** the surface exposed (as by a ship) to the wind

wind·bag \ˈwin(d)-ˌbag\ *n* (1827) **:** an exhaustively talkative person

wind–bell \-ˌbel\ *n* (1897) **1 :** WIND CHIME — usu. used in pl. **2 :** a bell that is light enough to be moved and sounded by the wind

wind·blast \-ˌblast\ *n* (1582) **1 :** a gust of wind **2 :** the destructive effect of air friction on a pilot ejected from a high-speed airplane

wind·blown \-ˌblōn\ *adj* (1599) **:** blown by the wind; *esp* **:** having a permanent set or character of growth determined by the prevailing winds ⟨~ trees⟩

wind–borne \-ˌbȯrn\ *adj* (1823) **:** carried by the wind ⟨~ pollen⟩ ⟨~ soil deposits⟩

wind·break \-ˌbrāk\ *n* (1861) **:** a growth of trees or shrubs serving to break the force of wind; *broadly* **:** a shelter (as a fence) from the wind

Wind·break·er \-ˌbrā-kər\ *trademark* — used for a jacket made of wind-resistant material

wind–bro·ken \-ˌbrō-kən\ *adj* (1603) *of a horse* **:** affected with pulmonary emphysema or heaves

wind·burn \-ˌbərn\ *n* (1925) **:** irritation of the skin caused by wind — **wind·burned** \-ˌbərnd\ *adj*

wind·chill \ˈwin(d)-ˌchil\ *n* (1939) **:** a still-air temperature that would have the same cooling effect on exposed human skin as a given combination of temperature and wind speed — called also *chill factor, windchill factor, windchill index*

wind chime *n* (1927) **:** a cluster of small often sculptured pieces (as of metal or glass) suspended so as to chime when blown by the wind — usu. used in pl.

wind down *vi* (1952) **1 :** to draw gradually toward an end ⟨the party was *winding down*⟩ **2 :** RELAX, UNWIND ⟨*wind down* with a good book⟩ ~ *vt* **:** to cause a gradual lessening of usu. with the intention of bringing to an end

wind·er \ˈwīn-dər\ *n* (13c) **:** one that winds: as **a :** a worker or machine that winds thread and yarn **b :** a key for winding a mechanism (as a clock) **c :** a step that is wider at one end than at the other (as in a spiral staircase)

wind·fall \ˈwin(d)-ˌfȯl\ *n* (15c) **1 :** something (as a tree or fruit) blown down by the wind **2 :** an unexpected, unearned, or sudden gain or advantage

wind farm *n* (1980) **:** an area of land with a cluster of wind turbines for driving electrical generators

wind·flow·er \-ˌflau̇(-ə)r\ *n* (1551) **:** ANEMONE 1

wind·gall \-ˌgȯl\ *n* (ca. 1534) **:** a soft tumor or synovial swelling on a horse's leg in the region of the fetlock joint

wind gap *n* (1769) **:** a notch in the crest of a mountain ridge **:** a pass not occupied by a stream — compare WATER GAP

wind harp *n* (1813) **:** AEOLIAN HARP

wind·hov·er \ˈwind-ˌhə-vər, -ˌhä-\ *n* (1674) *Brit* **:** KESTREL

[1]**wind·ing** \ˈwīn-diŋ\ *n* (bef. 12c) **1 :** material (as wire) wound or coiled about an object (as an armature); *also* **:** a single turn of the wound material **2 a :** the act of one that winds **b :** the manner of winding something **3 :** a curved or sinuous course, line, or progress

[2]**winding** *adj* (1530) **:** marked by winding: as **a :** having a curved or spiral course or form ⟨a ~ stairway⟩ **b :** having a course that winds ⟨a ~ road⟩

wind·ing–sheet \ˈwīn-diŋ-ˌshēt\ *n* (15c) **:** a sheet in which a corpse is wrapped

wind·ing–up \ˌwīn-diŋ-ˈəp\ *n* (ca. 1858) *Brit* **:** the process of liquidating the assets of a partnership or corporation in order to pay creditors and make distributions to partners or shareholders upon dissolution

wind instrument *n* (1582) **:** a musical instrument (as a trumpet, clarinet, or organ) sounded by wind; *esp* **:** one sounded by the player's breath

wind·jam·mer \ˈwin(d)-ˌja-mər\ *n* (1880) **:** a sailing ship; *also* **:** one of its crew — **wind·jam·ming** \-miŋ\ *n*

[1]**wind·lass** \ˈwin(d)-ləs\ *n* [ME *wyneles, wyndlas,* alter. of *wyndase,* fr. OF *guindas, windas,* fr. ON *vindāss,* fr. *vinda* to wind (akin to OHG *wintan* to wind) + *āss* pole; akin to Goth *ans* beam] (13c) **:** any of various machines for hoisting or hauling: as **a :** a horizontal barrel supported on vertical posts and turned by a crank so that the hoisting rope is wound around the barrel **b :** a steam or electric winch with horizontal or vertical shaft and two drums used to raise a ship's anchor

[2]**windlass** *vt* (1834) **:** to hoist or haul with a windlass

win·dle·straw \ˈwin-dᵊl-ˌstrȯ, ˈwi-nᵊl-\ *n* [ME **windelstraw,* fr. OE *windelstrēaw,* fr. *windel-* (akin to ME *windel* caulking material) + *strēaw* straw] (bef. 12c) *Brit* **:** a dry thin stalk of grass

[1]**wind·mill** \ˈwin(d)-ˌmil\ *n* (14c) **1 a :** a mill or machine operated by the wind usu. acting on oblique vanes or sails that radiate from a horizontal shaft; *esp* **:** a wind-driven water pump or electric generator **b :** the wind-driven wheel of a windmill **2 :** something that resembles or suggests a windmill; *esp* **:** a calisthenic exercise that involves alternately lowering each outstretched hand to touch the toes of the opposite foot **3** [fr. the episode in *Don Quixote* by Cervantes in which the hero attacks windmills under the illusion that they are giants] **:** an imaginary wrong, evil, or opponent — usu. used in the phrase *to tilt at windmills*

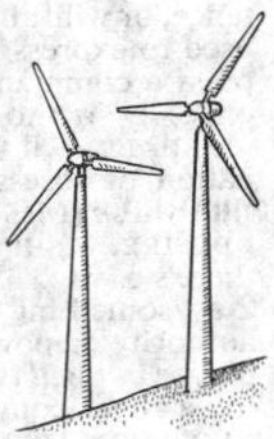

windmill 1a

[2]**windmill** *vt* (1914) **:** to cause to move like a windmill ~ *vi* **:** to move like a windmill; *esp* **:** to spin from the force of wind

win·dow \ˈwin-(ˌ)dō\ *n, often attrib* [ME *windowe,* fr. ON *vindauga,* fr. *vindr* wind (akin to OE *wind*) + *auga* eye; akin to OE *ēage* eye — more at EYE] (13c) **1 a :** an opening esp. in the wall of a building for admission of light and air that is usu. closed by casements or sashes containing transparent material (as glass) and capable of being opened and shut **b :** WINDOWPANE **c :** a space behind a window of a retail store containing displayed merchandise **d :** an opening in a partition or wall through which business is conducted ⟨a bank teller's ~⟩ **2 :** a means of entrance or access; *esp* **:** a means of obtaining information ⟨a ~ on history⟩ **3 :** an opening (as a shutter, slot, or valve) that resembles or suggests a window **4 :** the transparent panel or opening of a window envelope **5 :** the framework (as a shutter or sash with its fittings) that closes a window opening **6 :** CHAFF 4 **7 :** a range of wavelengths in the electromagnetic spectrum to which a planet's atmosphere is transparent **8 a :** an interval of time within which a rocket or spacecraft must be launched to accomplish a particular mission **b :** an interval of time during which certain conditions or an opportunity exists ⟨a ~ of vulnerability⟩ **9 :** an area at the limits of the earth's sensible atmosphere through which a spacecraft must pass for successful reentry **10 :** any of various rectangular boxes appearing on a computer screen that display files or program output, that can usu. be moved and resized, and that facilitate multitasking — **win·dow·less** \-dō-ləs, -də-\ *adj* — **out the window :** out of existence, use, or consideration

window box *n* (ca. 1885) **:** a box designed to hold soil for growing plants at a windowsill

window dressing *n* (1895) **1 :** the display of merchandise in a retail store window **2 a :** the act or an instance of making something appear deceptively attractive or favorable **b :** something used to create a deceptively favorable or attractive impression — **win·dow–dress** \ˈwin-dō-ˌdres\ *vt* — **window dresser** *n*

win·dowed \ˈwin-(ˌ)dōd, -dəd\ *adj* (15c) **:** having windows esp. of a specified kind — often used in combination

window envelope *n* (1914) **:** an envelope having an opening through which the address on the enclosure is visible

win·dow·pane \ˈwin-dō-ˌpān, -də-\ *n* (1819) **1 :** a pane in a window **2 :** TATTERSALL

window seat *n* (ca. 1745) **1 :** a seat built into a window recess **2 :** a seat next to a window (as in a bus or airplane)

window shade *n* (1810) **:** a shade or curtain for a window

win·dow–shop \ˈwin-dō-ˌshäp, -də-\ *vi* (1922) **:** to look at the displays in retail store windows without going inside the stores to make purchases — **win·dow–shop·per** *n*

win·dow·sill \-ˌsil\ *n* (1703) **:** the horizontal member at the bottom of a window opening

wind·pipe \ˈwin(d)-ˌpīp\ *n* (1530) **:** TRACHEA 1

wind–pol·li·nat·ed \-ˈpä-lə-ˌnā-təd\ *adj* (1884) **:** pollinated by wind-borne pollen

wind·proof \-ˈprüf\ *adj* (1616) : impervious to wind ⟨a ~ jacket⟩
wind rose \ˈwind-ˌrōz\ *n* [G *Windrose* compass card] (1846) : a diagram showing for a given place the relative frequency or frequency and strength of winds from different directions
[1]**wind·row** \ˈwin(d)-ˌrō\ *n* (ca. 1534) **1 a :** a row of hay raked up to dry before being baled or stored **b :** a similar row of cut vegetation (as grain) for drying **2 :** a row heaped up by or as if by the wind **3 a :** a long low ridge of road-making material scraped to the side of a road **b :** BANK, RIDGE, HEAP
[2]**windrow** *vt* (1729) : to form (as hay) into a windrow
wind·screen \ˈwin(d)-ˌskrēn\ *n* (1858) **1 :** a screen that protects against the wind **2** *chiefly Brit* : WINDSHIELD
wind shake *n* (1545) : a shake in timber attributed to high winds
wind shear *n* (1941) : a radical shift in wind speed and direction that occurs over a very short distance
wind·shield \ˈwin(d)-ˌshēld\ *n* (1902) : a transparent screen (as of glass) in front of the occupants of a vehicle
wind sock *n* (1928) : a truncated cloth cone open at both ends and mounted in an elevated position to indicate the direction of the wind
Wind·sor chair \ˈwin-zər-\ *n* [*Windsor*, England] (1740) : a wooden chair with spindle back, raking legs, and usu. a saddle seat — called also *Windsor*
Windsor knot *n* [prob. after Edward, Duke of *Windsor*] (1947) : a symmetrical necktie knot that is wider than the usual four-in-hand knot
Windsor tie *n* (1895) : a broad necktie usu. tied in a loose bow
wind sprint *n* (1948) : a sprint performed as a training exercise to develop breathing capacity esp. during exertion
wind·storm \ˈwin(d)-ˌstȯrm\ *n* (14c) : a storm marked by high wind with little or no precipitation
Wind·surf·er \-ˌsər-fər\ *trademark* — used for a sailboard
wind·surf·ing \-ˌsər-fiŋ\ *n* (1969) : the sport or activity of riding a sailboard — **wind·surf** \-ˌsərf\ *vi* — **wind·surf·er** *n*
wind·swept \ˈwin(d)-ˌswept\ *adj* (1812) : swept by or as if by wind
wind tee *n* (1932) : a large weather vane shaped like a horizontal letter T on or near a landing field
wind·throw \ˈwin(d)-ˌthrō\ *n* (1916) : the uprooting and overthrowing of trees by the wind
wind tunnel *n* (1911) : a tunnellike passage through which air is blown at a known velocity to investigate air flow around an object (as an airplane part or model) placed in the passage
wind turbine *n* (1909) : a wind-driven turbine for generating electricity
[1]**wind·up** \ˈwīnd-ˌəp\ *n* (1665) **1 a :** the act of bringing to an end **b :** a concluding act or part : FINISH **2 a :** a series of regular and distinctive motions (as swinging the arms) made by a pitcher preparatory to releasing a pitch **b :** an exaggerated backswing (as in tennis)
[2]**windup** *adj* (1784) : operated by a spring mechanism wound by hand
wind up *vt* (1583) **1 :** to bring to a conclusion : END **2 a :** to put in order for the purpose of bringing to an end ⟨*winds up* the meeting⟩ **b** *Brit* : to effectuate the winding up of ~ *vi* **1 a :** to come to a conclusion **b :** to arrive in a place, situation, or condition at the end or as a result of a course of action ⟨*wound up* as millionaires⟩ **2 :** to make a pitching windup
[1]**wind·ward** \ˈwin(d)-wərd\ *n* (1549) : the side or direction from which the wind is blowing — **to windward** : into or in an advantageous position
[2]**windward** *adj* (1627) : being in or facing the direction from which the wind is blowing — compare LEEWARD
wind·way \ˈwin(d)-ˌwā\ *n* (ca. 1875) : a passage for air (as in an organ pipe)
[1]**windy** \ˈwin-dē\ *adj* **wind·i·er; -est** (bef. 12c) **1 a (1) :** WINDSWEPT ⟨a ~ coast⟩ **(2) :** marked by strong wind or by more wind than usual ⟨a ~ day⟩ **b :** VIOLENT, STORMY **2 :** FLATULENT 1 ⟨a ~ bellyache⟩ **3 a :** VERBOSE, BOMBASTIC ⟨a ~ politician⟩ **b :** lacking substance : EMPTY ⟨~ promises⟩ — **wind·i·ly** \-də-lē\ *adv* — **wind·i·ness** \-dē-nəs\ *n*
[2]**windy** \ˈwīn-dē\ *adj* **wind·i·er; -est** (1871) : WINDING ⟨a ~ path⟩
[1]**wine** \ˈwīn\ *n, often attrib* [ME *win*, fr. OE *wīn;* akin to OHG *wīn* wine; both ultim. fr. L *vinum* wine, perh. of non-IE origin; akin to the source of Gk *oinos* wine] (bef. 12c) **1 a :** the alcoholic fermented juice of fresh grapes used as a beverage **b :** wine or a substitute used in Christian communion services **2 :** the alcoholic usu. fermented juice of a plant product (as a fruit) used as a beverage ⟨blackberry ~⟩ **3 :** something that invigorates or intoxicates **4 :** a dark red
[2]**wine** *vb* **wined; win·ing** *vi* (1829) : to drink wine ~ *vt* : to give wine to ⟨*wined* and dined his friends⟩
wine cellar *n* (14c) : a room for storing wines; *also* : a stock of wines
wine cooler *n* (1815) **1 :** a vessel or container in which wine is cooled **2 :** a usu. carbonated beverage that contains a mixture of wine and fruit juice
wine·glass \ˈwīn-ˌglas\ *n* (1709) : a stemware drinking glass for wine
wine·grow·er \-ˌgrō-ər\ *n* (1844) : a person who cultivates a vineyard and makes wine
wine·mak·er \ˈwīn-ˌmā-kər\ *n* (14c) : a person who makes wine; *specif* : one who supervises the wine-making process at a winery
wine·press \ˈwīn-ˌpres\ *n* (15c) : a vat in which juice is expressed from grapes by treading or by means of a plunger
win·ery \ˈwī-nə-rē, ˈwīn-rē\ *n, pl* **-er·ies** (1882) : a wine-making establishment
wine·sap \ˈwīn-ˌsap\ *n, often cap* (1826) : an apple with deep red skin and juicy somewhat tart flesh
wine·shop \ˈwīn-ˌshäp\ *n* (1848) : a tavern that specializes in serving wine
wine·skin \-ˌskin\ *n* (1821) : a bag that is made from the skin of an animal (as a goat) and that is used for holding wine
wine taster *n* (1632) **1 :** a person who tastes and evaluates wine esp. professionally **2 :** a small shallow vessel used to sample wine
win·ey *or* **winy** \ˈwī-nē\ *adj* **win·i·er; -est** (14c) **1 :** having the taste or qualities of wine ⟨a ~ sauce⟩ **2** *of the air* : crisply fresh : EXHILARATING
[1]**wing** \ˈwiŋ\ *n, often attrib* [ME *winge*, of Scand origin; akin to Dan & Sw *vinge* wing; akin to Skt *vāti* it blows — more at WIND] (13c) **1 a :** one of the movable feathered or membranous paired appendages by means of which a bird, bat, or insect is able to fly; *also* : such an appendage even though rudimentary if possessed by an animal belonging to a group characterized by the power of flight **b :** any of various anatomical structures (as of a flying fish or flying lemur) providing means of limited flight **2 :** an appendage or part resembling a wing in appearance, position, or function: as **a :** a device worn under the arms to aid a person in swimming or staying afloat **b :** ALA **c :** a turned-back or extended edge on an article of clothing **d :** a sidepiece at the top of an armchair **e (1) :** a foliaceous, membranous, or woody expansion of a plant esp. along a stem or on a samara or capsule **(2) :** either of the two lateral petals of a papilionaceous flower **f :** a vane of a windmill or arrow **g :** SAIL **h :** an airfoil that develops a major part of the lift which supports a heavier-than-air aircraft **i** *chiefly Brit* : FENDER d **3 :** a means of flight or rapid progress **4 :** the act or manner of flying : FLIGHT ⟨take ~⟩ **5 :** a side or outlying region or district **6 :** a part or feature of a building usu. projecting from and subordinate to the main or central part ⟨the servants' ~⟩ **7 a :** one of the pieces of scenery at the side of a stage **b** *pl* : the area at the side of the stage out of sight **8 a :** a left or right section of an army or fleet : FLANK **b :** one of the offensive positions or players on either side of a center position in certain team sports; *also* : FLANKER **9 a :** either of two opposing groups within an organization or society : FACTION **b :** a section of an organized body (as a legislative chamber) representing a group or faction holding distinct opinions or policies — compare LEFT WING, RIGHT WING **10 a :** a unit of the U.S. Air Force higher than a group and lower than a division **b :** two or more squadrons of naval airplanes **11 :** a dance step marked by a quick outward and inward rolling glide of one foot **12** *pl* : insignia consisting of an outspread pair of stylized bird's wings which are awarded on completion of prescribed training to a qualified pilot, aircrew member, or military balloon pilot — **wingy** \ˈwiŋ-ē\ *adj* — **in the wings 1 :** out of sight in the stage wings **2 :** close at hand in the background : readily available ⟨had a plan waiting *in the wings*⟩ — **on the wing 1 :** in flight : FLYING **2 :** in motion — **under one's wing** : under one's protection : in one's care ⟨took her *under his wing*⟩

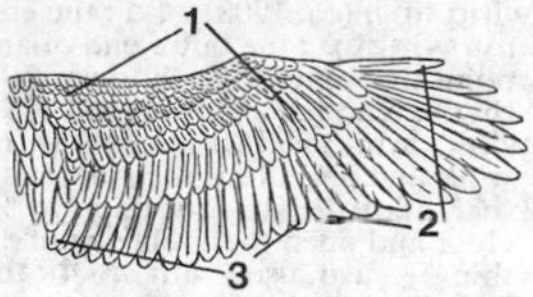

wing 1a: parts of a bird's wing *1* coverts, *2* primaries, *3* secondaries

[2]**wing** *vt* (1591) **1 a :** to fit with wings **b :** to enable to fly or move swiftly **2 a :** to traverse with or as if with wings **b :** to effect or achieve by flying **3 :** to let fly : DISPATCH ⟨would start to ~ punches —A. J. Liebling⟩ **4 a :** to wound in the wing : disable the wing of ⟨~*ed* the duck⟩ **b :** to wound (as with a bullet) without killing ⟨~*ed* by a sniper⟩ **5 :** to do or perform without preparation or guidelines : IMPROVISE ⟨~*ing it*⟩ ~ *vi* : to go with or as if with wings : FLY — often used with *it* ⟨~*ed* it to Europe⟩
wing and wing *adv* (1781) : with sails extended on both sides
wing·back \ˈwiŋ-ˌbak\ *n* (1933) : an offensive back in football who lines up outside the tight end; *also* : the position of such a player
wing bar *n* (1855) : a line of contrasting color across the middle of a bird's wing made by markings on the wing coverts
wing case *n* (1661) : ELYTRON
wing chair *n* (1904) : an upholstered armchair with high solid back and angled sides — called also *wingback chair*
wing commander *n* (1914) : a commissioned officer in the British air force who ranks with a lieutenant colonel in the army
wing covert *n* (1815) : one of the feathers covering the bases of the wing quills
wing·ding \ˈwiŋ-ˌdiŋ\ *n* [origin unknown] (1944) : a wild, lively, or lavish party
winged \ˈwiŋd *also except for 1a(2)* ˈwiŋ-əd\ *adj* (14c) **1 a (1) :** having wings ⟨~ seeds⟩ **(2) :** having wings of a specified kind — used in combination ⟨strong-*winged*⟩ **b :** using wings in flight **2 a :** soaring with or as if with wings : ELEVATED **b :** SWIFT, RAPID
winged bean \ˈwiŋd-\ *n* (1910) : an Asian twining legume (*Psophocarpus tetragonolobus*) cultivated in warm regions for its edible high-protein 4-winged pods; *also* : its pod
winged elm *n* (1820) : an elm (*Ulmus alata*) of the U.S. having twigs with prominent corky projections — called also *wahoo*
wing·er \ˈwiŋ-ər\ *n* (1896) : a player (as in soccer or ice hockey) in a wing position
wing–foot·ed \ˈwiŋ-ˈfu̇-təd\ *adj* (1591) **1 :** having winged feet **2 :** SWIFT
wing·less \ˈwiŋ-ləs\ *adj* (1582) : having no wings or very rudimentary wings — **wing·less·ness** *n*
wing·let \ˈwiŋ-lət\ *n* (1611) : a small wing; *also* : a nearly vertical airfoil at an airplane's wingtip that reduces drag by inhibiting turbulence
wing·like \-ˌlīk\ *adj* (ca. 1804) : resembling a wing in form or lateral position
wing·man \-mən\ *n* (1942) : a pilot who flies behind and outside the leader of a flying formation
wing nut *n* (ca. 1900) **1 :** a nut with wings that provide a grip for the thumb and finger **2** *slang* : a mentally deranged person **3** *slang* : one who advocates extreme measures or changes : RADICAL
wing·over \ˈwiŋ-ˌō-vər\ *n* (1927) : a flight maneuver in which a plane is put into a climbing turn until nearly stalled after which the nose is allowed to fall while the turn is continued until normal flight is attained in a direction opposite to that in which the maneuver was entered
wing shooting *n* (1881) : the act or practice of shooting at game birds in flight or at flying targets
wing·span \ˈwiŋ-ˌspan\ *n* (ca. 1917) : the distance from the tip of one of a pair of wings to that of the other; *also* : SPAN 2c
wing·spread \-ˌspred\ *n* (1897) : the spread of the wings : WINGSPAN; *specif* : the extreme measurement between the tips or outer margins of the wings (as of a bird or insect)

\ə\ **abut** \ᵊ\ **kitten**, F **table** \ər\ **further** \a\ **ash** \ā\ **ace** \ä\ **mop, mar**
\au̇\ **out** \ch\ **chin** \e\ **bet** \ē\ **easy** \g\ **go** \i\ **hit** \ī\ **ice** \j\ **job**
\ŋ\ **sing** \ō\ **go** \ȯ\ **law** \ȯi\ **boy** \th\ **thin** \t͟h\ **the** \ü\ **loot** \u̇\ **foot**
\y\ **yet** \zh\ **vision, beige** \k, ⁿ, œ, ue, ʸ\ *see* Guide to Pronunciation

wing tip *n* (ca. 1908) **1 a :** the edge or outer margin of a bird's wing **b** *usu* **wingtip :** the outer end of an airplane wing **2 :** a toe cap having a point that extends back toward the throat of the shoe and curving sides that extend toward the shank **3 :** a shoe having a wing tip

[1]**wink** \ˈwiŋk\ *vb* [ME, fr. OE *wincian;* akin to OHG *winchan* to stagger, wink and perh. to L *vacillare* to sway, Skt *vañcati* he goes crookedly] *vi* (bef. 12c) **1 :** to shut one eye briefly as a signal or in teasing **2 :** to close and open the eyelids quickly **3 :** to avoid seeing or noting something — usu. used with *at* **4 :** to gleam or flash intermittently : TWINKLE ⟨her glasses *~ing* in the sunlight —Harper Lee⟩ **5 a :** to come to an end — usu. used with *out* **b :** to stop shining — usu. used with *out* **6 :** to signal a message with a light **~** *vt* **1 :** to cause to open and shut **2 :** to affect or influence by or as if by blinking the eyes

[2]**wink** *n* (14c) **1 :** a brief period of sleep : NAP ⟨catching a **~**⟩ **2 a :** a hint or sign given by winking **b :** an act of winking **3 :** the time of a wink : INSTANT ⟨quick as a **~**⟩ **4 :** a flicker of the eyelids : BLINK

wink•er \ˈwiŋ-kər\ *n* (1549) **1 :** one that winks **2 :** a horse's blinder

[1]**win•kle** \ˈwiŋ-kəl\ *n* [by shortening] (1585) : [2]PERIWINKLE

[2]**winkle** *vi* **win•kled; win•kling** \-k(ə-)liŋ\ [freq. of *wink*] (1791) : TWINKLE

[3]**winkle** *vt* **win•kled; win•kling** \-k(ə-)liŋ\ [[1]*winkle;* fr. the process of extracting a winkle from its shell] (1918) **1** *chiefly Brit* **:** to displace, remove, or evict from a position — usu. used with *out* **2** *chiefly Brit* **:** to obtain or draw out by effort — usu. used with *out* ⟨no attempt to **~** out why they do it —Joan Bakewell⟩

win•ner \ˈwi-nər\ *n* (14c) **:** one that wins: as **a :** one that is successful esp. through praiseworthy ability and hard work **b :** a victor esp. in games and sports **c :** one that wins admiration **d :** a shot in a court game that is not returned and that scores for the player making it

winner's circle *n* (1951) **:** an enclosure near a racetrack where the winning horse and jockey are brought for photographs and awards

Win•nie \ˈwi-nē\ *n* [*winner* + *-ie*] (ca. 1944) **:** an award presented annually by a professional organization for notable achievement in fashion design

[1]**winning** *n* (14c) **1 :** the act of one that wins : VICTORY **2 :** something won: as **a :** a captured territory : CONQUEST **b :** money won by success in a game or competition — usu. used in pl.

[2]**winning** *adj* (15c) **1 a :** of or relating to winning **:** that wins ⟨the **~** ticket⟩ **b :** successful esp. in competition ⟨a **~** team⟩ **2 :** tending to please or delight ⟨a **~** personality⟩ — **win•ning•ly** \-niŋ-lē\ *adv*

win•ning•est *adj* (1972) **:** having achieved the most wins ⟨the **~** coach in football⟩

win•nock \ˈwi-nək\ *n* [ME (Sc) *windok, windowe*] (15c) *Scot* **:** WINDOW

[1]**win•now** \ˈwi-(ˌ)nō\ *vb* [ME *winewen,* fr. OE *windwian* to fan, winnow; akin to OHG *wintōn* to fan, L *vannus* winnowing fan, *ventus* wind — more at WIND] *vt* (bef. 12c) **1 a** (1) **:** to remove (as chaff) by a current of air (2) **:** to get rid of (something undesirable or unwanted) : REMOVE — often used with *out* ⟨**~** out certain inaccuracies —Stanley Walker⟩ **b** (1) **:** SEPARATE, SIFT ⟨an old hand at **~***ing* what is true and significant —Oscar Lewis⟩ (2) **:** SELECT **2 a :** to treat (as grain) by exposure to a current of air so that waste matter is eliminated **b :** to free of unwanted or inferior elements : PARE **c :** NARROW, REDUCE ⟨**~***ed* the field to four contenders⟩ **3 :** to blow on : FAN ⟨the wind **~***ing* his thin white hair —*Time*⟩ **~** *vi* **1 :** to separate chaff from grain by fanning **2 :** to separate desirable and undesirable elements — **win•now•er** \ˈwi-nə-wər\ *n*

[2]**winnow** *n* (1580) **1 :** a device for winnowing **2 a :** the action of winnowing **b :** a motion resembling that of winnowing

wino \ˈwī-(ˌ)nō\ *n, pl* **win•os** (ca. 1915) **:** a usu. indigent alcoholic who is addicted esp. to wine

win•some \ˈwin(t)-səm\ *adj* [ME *winsum,* fr. OE *wynsum,* fr. *wynn* joy; akin to OHG *wunna* joy, L *venus* desire — more at WIN] (bef. 12c) **1 :** generally pleasing and engaging often because of a childlike charm and innocence ⟨a **~** smile⟩ **2 :** CHEERFUL, LIGHTHEARTED — **win•some•ly** *adv* — **win•some•ness** *n*

[1]**win•ter** \ˈwin-tər\ *n* [ME, fr. OE; akin to OHG *wintar* winter and perh. to Lith *vanduo* water, OE *wæter* — more at WATER] (bef. 12c) **1 :** the season between autumn and spring comprising in the northern hemisphere usu. the months of December, January, and February or as reckoned astronomically extending from the December solstice to the March equinox **2 :** the colder half of the year **3 :** YEAR ⟨happened many **~***s* ago⟩ **4 :** a period of inactivity or decay

[2]**winter** *vb* **win•tered; win•ter•ing** \ˈwin-t(ə-)riŋ\ *vi* (14c) **1 :** to pass the winter ⟨**~***s* in the Caribbean⟩ **2 :** to feed or find food during the winter — used with *on* **~** *vt* **:** to keep, feed, or manage during the winter

[3]**winter** *adj* (14c) **1 :** of, relating to, or suitable for winter ⟨a **~** vacation⟩ ⟨**~** clothes⟩ **2 :** sown in the autumn and harvested in the following spring or summer ⟨**~** wheat⟩ ⟨**~** rye⟩ — compare SUMMER

winter aconite *n* (1794) **:** any of several low Eurasian perennial herbs (genus *Eranthis,* esp. *E. hyemalis*) of the buttercup family with solitary yellow or white flowers which often bloom through the snow

win•ter•ber•ry \ˈwin-tər-ˌber-ē\ *n* (1759) **1 :** an eastern No. American shrub (*Ilex verticillata*) of the holly family with axillary flowers, usu. bright red berries, and deciduous leaves that turn black in the fall — called also *black alder* **2 :** any of several congeneric shrubs or small trees (as *Ilex laevigata* of the eastern U.S.)

winter crookneck *n* (ca. 1909) **:** any of several crooknecks that are winter squashes (*Cucurbita moschata*) noted for their keeping qualities

win•ter•er \ˈwin-tər-ər\ *n* (1783) **:** one that winters; *specif* **:** a winter resident or visitor

winter flounder *n* (1814) **:** a rusty-brown flounder (*Pseudopleuronectes americanus* of the family Pleuronectidae) of the northwestern Atlantic important as a market fish esp. in winter

win•ter•green \ˈwin-tər-ˌgrēn\ *n* (1548) **1 :** any of a genus (*Pyrola* of the family Pyrolaceae, the wintergreen family) of evergreen perennial herbs (as the shinleafs) that have basal leaves and racemose flowers **2 a :** any of a genus (*Gaultheria*) of evergreen plants of the heath family; *esp* **:** a low creeping evergreen shrub (*G. procumbens*) of No. America with white flowers and spicy red berries — compare CHECKERBERRY **b** (1) **:** an essential oil from this plant (2) **:** the flavor of this oil ⟨**~** lozenges⟩

win•ter•ize \ˈwin-tə-ˌrīz\ *vt* **-ized; -iz•ing** (1934) **:** to make ready for winter or winter use and esp. resistant or proof against winter weather ⟨**~** a car⟩ — **win•ter•i•za•tion** \ˌwin-tə-rə-ˈzā-shən\ *n*

win•ter–kill \ˈwin-tər-ˌkil\ *vt* (ca. 1806) **:** to kill (as a plant) by exposure to winter conditions **~** *vi* **:** to die as a result of exposure to winter conditions — **winterkill** *n*

win•ter•ly \ˈwin-tər-lē\ *adj* (1559) **:** of, relating to, or occurring in winter : WINTRY

winter melon *n* (ca. 1900) **1 :** any of several muskmelons (as a casaba or honeydew melon) that are fruits of a cultivated vine (*Cucumis melo indorus*) **2 :** a large white-fleshed melon that is the fruit of an Asian vine (*Benincasa hispida*) and is used esp. in Chinese cooking

winter quarters *n pl but sing or pl in constr* (1641) **:** a winter residence or station (as of a military unit or a circus)

winter savory *n* (1597) **:** a perennial European mint (*Satureja montana*) with leaves used for seasoning — compare SUMMER SAVORY

winter squash *n* (1775) **:** any of various hard-shelled squashes that belong to cultivars derived from several species (esp. *Cucurbita maxima, C. moschata,* and *C. pepo*) and that can be stored for several months

win•ter•tide \ˈwin-tər-ˌtīd\ *n* (bef. 12c) **:** WINTERTIME

win•ter•time \-ˌtīm\ *n* (14c) **:** the season of winter

win through *vi* (1644) **:** to survive difficulties and reach a desired or satisfactory end ⟨*win through* to a better life beyond —B. F. Reilly⟩

win•tle \ˈwi-nᵊl, ˈwin-tᵊl\ *vi* **win•tled; win•tling** \ˈwin(t)-liŋ; ˈwi-nᵊl-iŋ, ˈwin-tᵊl-\ [perh. fr. D dial. *windtelen* to reel] (1786) **1** *Scot* **:** STAGGER, REEL **2** *Scot* **:** WRIGGLE

win•try \ˈwin-trē\ *also* **win•tery** \ˈwin-t(ə-)rē\ *adj* **win•tri•er; -est** (bef. 12c) **1 :** of, relating to, or characteristic of winter **2 a :** weathered by or as if by winter : AGED, HOARY **b :** CHEERLESS, CHILLING ⟨a **~** greeting⟩ — **win•tri•ness** \ˈwin-trē-nəs\ *n*

win–win \ˈwin-ˈwin, -ˌwin\ *adj* (1977) **:** advantageous or satisfactory to all parties involved ⟨a **~** situation⟩ ⟨a **~** deal⟩

winy *var of* WINEY

[1]**winze** \ˈwinz\ *n* [alter. of earlier *winds,* prob. fr. pl. of [5]*wind*] (1757) **:** a steeply inclined passageway in a mine

[2]**winze** *n* [prob. fr. D *wens* wish] (1785) *Scot* **:** CURSE

[1]**wipe** \ˈwīp\ *vb* **wiped; wip•ing** [ME *wipen,* fr. OE *wīpian;* akin to OHG *wīfan* to wind around, L *vibrare* to brandish, and prob. to ON *veipa* to be in movement, Skt *vepate* it trembles] *vt* (bef. 12c) **1 a :** to rub with or as if with something soft for cleaning **b :** to clean or dry by rubbing **c :** to draw, pass, or move for or as if for rubbing or cleaning ⟨*wiped* his hand across his brow⟩ **2 a :** to remove by or as if by rubbing ⟨**~** the spots off the glass⟩ **b :** to expunge completely ⟨**~** from memory the gruesome scenes —*Amer. Guide Series: Del.*⟩ **3 :** to spread by or as if by wiping **~** *vi* **:** to make a motion of or as if of wiping something — **wipe one's boots on :** to treat with indignity — **wipe the floor with** *or* **wipe the ground with :** to defeat decisively

[2]**wipe** *n* (1550) **1 a :** BLOW, STRIKE **b :** JEER, GIBE **2 a :** an act or instance of wiping **b :** a transition from one scene or picture to another (as in movies or television) made by a line moving across the screen **3 :** something (as a towel) used for wiping

wiped out *adj* (1965) **1** *slang* **:** INTOXICATED, HIGH **2 :** extremely tired : EXHAUSTED

wipe•out \ˈwīp-ˌau̇t\ *n* (1921) **1 :** the act or an instance of wiping out **:** complete or utter destruction **2 :** a fall or crash caused usu. by losing control **3 :** a total or decisive defeat : DRUBBING

wipe out *vt* (1535) **:** to destroy completely : ANNIHILATE **~** *vi* **:** to fall or crash usu. as a result of losing control

wip•er \ˈwī-pər\ *n* (1552) **1 :** a person who wipes **2 a :** something (as a towel or sponge) used for wiping **b :** a moving contact for making connections with the terminals of an electrical device (as a rheostat) **c :** a usu. motor-driven arm with a flexible blade for wiping a window (as the windshield of an automobile or airplane)

[1]**wire** \ˈwī(-ə)r\ *n, often attrib* [ME, fr. OE *wīr;* akin to OHG *wiara* fine gold work, L *viēre* to plait, and prob. to Gk *iris* rainbow] (bef. 12c) **1 a :** metal in the form of a usu. very flexible thread or slender rod **b :** a thread or rod of such material **2 a :** WIREWORK **b :** the meshwork of parallel or woven wire on which the wet web of paper forms **3 :** something (as a thin plant stem) that is wirelike **4** *pl* **a :** a system of wires used to operate the puppets in a puppet show **b :** hidden influences controlling the action of a person or organization **5 a :** a line of wire for conducting electric current — compare CORD 3b **b :** a telephone or telegraph wire or system; *esp* **:** WIRE SERVICE **c :** TELEGRAM, CABLEGRAM **6 :** fencing or a fence of usu. barbed wire **7 a :** the finish line of a race **b :** the final decisive moment (as of a contest) ⟨the negotiations came down to the **~**⟩ **8 :** WIREHAIR — **wire•like** \-ˌlīk\ *adj* — **under the wire 1 :** at the finish line **2 :** at the last moment — **wire to wire** *or* **from wire to wire :** from start to finish ⟨led the race *wire to wire*⟩

[2]**wire** *vb* **wired; wir•ing** *vt* (15c) **1 :** to provide with wire **:** use wire on for a specific purpose **2 :** to send or send word to by telegraph **3 :** to connect by or as if by a wire **4 :** to predispose, determine, or establish genetically or innately ⟨controversy over the extent to which human violence is *wired* biologically⟩ **~** *vi* **:** to send a telegraphic message — **wir•er** \ˈwī(-ə)r-ər\ *n*

wire cloth *n* (1798) **:** a fabric of woven metallic wire (as for strainers)

wired *adj* (15c) **1 :** reinforced by wire (as for strength) **2 a :** furnished with wires (as for electric connections) **b :** connected to a telecommunications network and esp. to the Internet **c :** characterized by a connection to the Internet ⟨the **~** world⟩ **3 :** bound with wire ⟨a **~** container⟩ **4 :** having a wirework netting or fence **5 :** feverishly excited

wire•draw \ˈwī(-ə)r-ˌdrȯ\ *vt* (1598) **1 :** to draw or stretch forcibly : ELONGATE **2 :** to draw or spin out to great length, tenuity, or overrefinement : ATTENUATE — **wire•draw•er** \-ˌdrȯ(-ə)r\ *n*

wire•drawn \-ˌdrȯn\ *adj* (1603) **:** excessively minute and subtle ⟨curious speculations, **~** comparisons, obsolete erudition —Virginia Woolf⟩

wire fox terrier *n* (1929) **:** any of a breed of fox terriers having a dense wiry chiefly white coat

wire fraud *n* (1976) **:** fraud committed using a means of electronic communication (as a telephone or computer)

wire gauge *n* (1833) **1 :** a gauge esp. for measuring the diameter of wire or the thickness of sheet metal **2 :** any of various systems consist-

ing of a series of standard sizes used in describing the diameter of wire or the thickness of sheet metal
wire gauze *n* (1816) : a gauzelike wire cloth
wire grass *n* (1751) : any of various grasses or rushes having wiry culms or leaves: as **a** : a Eurasian slender-stemmed meadow grass (*Poa compressa*) widely naturalized in the U.S. and Canada **b** : any of several coarse grasses (genus *Aristida*) with a 3-awned lemma that grow extensively in open dry, sandy, or sterile areas esp. of the southeastern and south-central U.S.
wire·hair \ˈwī(-ə)r-ˌher\ *n* (1884) : a wirehaired dog or cat
wire·haired \-ˈherd\ *adj* (1801) : having a stiff wiry outer coat of hair ⟨a ~ dog⟩ — compare ROUGH, SMOOTH
wirehaired pointing griffon *n* (1929) : any of a breed of dogs of Dutch origin that both hunt and retrieve and have a long head and a harsh wiry often chestnut or white and chestnut colored coat
wirehaired terrier *n* (ca. 1837) : WIRE FOX TERRIER
[1]**wire·less** \ˈwī(-ə)r-ləs\ *adj* (1894) **1** : having no wire or wires; *specif* : operating by means of transmitted electromagnetic waves ⟨a ~ remote⟩ **2 a** : of or relating to radiotelephony, radiotelegraphy, or radio ⟨a ~ phone⟩ **b** : of or relating to data communications using radio waves ⟨~ Internet access⟩ — **wire·less·ly** *adv*
[2]**wireless** *n* (1903) **1** : telecommunication (as radiotelegraphy or radiotelephony) involving signals transmitted by radio waves rather than over wires; *also* : the technology used in radio telecommunication **2** *chiefly Brit* : RADIO
wireless telegraphy *n* (1898) : telegraphy carried on by radio waves and without connecting wires — called also *wireless telegraph*
wireless telephone *n* (1894) : RADIOTELEPHONE
wire·man \ˈwī(-ə)r-mən\ *n* (ca. 1548) **1** : a maker of or worker with wire; *esp* : LINEMAN 1 **2** : WIRETAPPER
wire netting *n* (1801) : a wire cloth coarser than wire gauze
wire·pho·to \ˈwī(-ə)r-ˈfō-(ˌ)tō\ *n* [fr. *Wirephoto*, a trademark] (1935) : a photograph transmitted by electrical signals over telephone wires
wire–pull·er \-ˌpu̇-lər\ *n* (1825) : one who uses secret or underhanded means to influence the acts of a person or organization — **wire–pull·ing** \-ˌpu̇-liŋ\ *n*
wire recorder *n* (1943) : a magnetic recorder using a thin wire as the recording medium — **wire–re·cord·ing** *n*
wire rope *n* (1841) : a rope formed wholly or chiefly of wires
wire service *n* (1944) : a news agency that sends out syndicated news copy to subscribers by wire or by satellite transmission
[1]**wire·tap** \ˈwī(-ə)r-ˌtap\ *vi* (1904) : to tap a telephone or telegraph wire in order to get information ~ *vt* : to tap the telephone of
[2]**wiretap** *n* (1948) **1** : the act or an instance of wiretapping **2** : an electrical connection for wiretapping
wire·tap·per \-ˌta-pər\ *n* (1893) : one that taps telephone or telegraph wires
wire·work \-ˌwərk\ *n* (1587) **1** : a work of wires; *esp* : meshwork, netting, or grillwork of wire ⟨plan the ~ for new circuitry⟩ **2** : walking on wires esp. by acrobats
wire·worm \-ˌwərm\ *n* (ca. 1790) : any of the slender hard-coated larvae of various click beetles that include some destructive esp. to plant roots
wiring *n* (1809) **1** : the act of providing or using wire **2** : a system of wires; *esp* : an arrangement of wires used for electric distribution
wir·ra \ˈwir-ə\ *interj* [*oh wirra*, fr. Ir *a Mhuire*, lit., Mary!] (1829) *Irish* — usu. used to express lament, grief, or concern
wiry \ˈwī(-ə)r-ē\ *adj* **wir·i·er** \ˈwī-rē-ər\; **-est** (1588) **1 a** *archaic* : made of wire **b** : resembling wire esp. in form and flexibility ⟨the ~ coat of the Irish terrier⟩ ⟨~ stems⟩ **c** *of sound* : produced by or suggestive of the vibration of wire ⟨the violinist . . . often let his tone go nasal and ~ —D. J. Henahan⟩ **2** : being lean, supple, and vigorous : SINEWY ⟨the ~ figure of a long-distance runner —*Phoenix Flame*⟩ — **wir·i·ly** \ˈwī-rə-lē\ *adv* — **wir·i·ness** \-rē-nəs\ *n*
wis \ˈwis\ *vb* [by misdivision fr. *iwis* (understood as *I wis*, with *wis* taken to be an archaic pres. indic. of [1]*wit*)] (1508) *archaic* : KNOW
Wis *or* **Wisc** *abbr* Wisconsin
Wisd *abbr* Wisdom
wis·dom \ˈwiz-dəm\ *n* [ME, fr. OE *wīsdōm*, fr. *wīs* wise] (bef. 12c) **1 a** : accumulated philosophic or scientific learning : KNOWLEDGE **b** : ability to discern inner qualities and relationships : INSIGHT **c** : good sense : JUDGMENT **d** : generally accepted belief ⟨challenges what has become accepted ~ among many historians —Robert Darnton⟩ **2** : a wise attitude, belief, or course of action **3** : the teachings of the ancient wise men ***syn*** see SENSE
Wisdom *n* (ca. 1440) : a didactic book included in the Roman Catholic canon of the Old Testament and corresponding to the Wisdom of Solomon in the Protestant Apocrypha — see BIBLE table
Wisdom of Sol·o·mon \-ˈsä-lə-mən\ (1779) : a didactic book included in the Protestant Apocrypha — see BIBLE table
wisdom tooth *n* [fr. its being cut usu. in the late teens] (1824) : the third molar that is the last tooth to erupt on each side of the upper and lower jaws in humans
[1]**wise** \ˈwīz\ *n* [ME, fr. OE *wīse*; akin to OHG *wīsa* manner, Gk *eidos* form, *idein* to see — more at WIT] (bef. 12c) : MANNER, WAY ⟨in any ~⟩
[2]**wise** *adj* **wis·er; wis·est** [ME *wis*, fr. OE *wīs*; akin to OHG *wīs* wise, OE *witan* to know — more at WIT] (bef. 12c) **1 a** : characterized by wisdom : marked by deep understanding, keen discernment, and a capacity for sound judgment **b** : exercising or showing sound judgment : PRUDENT ⟨a ~ investor⟩ **2 a** : evidencing or hinting at the possession of inside information : KNOWING **b** : possessing inside information ⟨the police got ~ to his whereabouts⟩ **c** : CRAFTY, SHREWD **d** : aware of or informed about a particular matter — usu. used in the comparative in negative constructions with *the* ⟨was none the *wiser* about their plans⟩ **3** *archaic* : skilled in magic or divination **4** : INSOLENT, SMART-ALECKY, FRESH ⟨a tough kid with a ~ mouth⟩ — **wise·ly** *adv* — **wise·ness** *n*
syn WISE, SAGE, SAPIENT, JUDICIOUS, PRUDENT, SENSIBLE, SANE mean having or showing sound judgment. WISE suggests great understanding of people and of situations and unusual discernment and judgment in dealing with them ⟨*wise* beyond his tender years⟩. SAGE suggests wide experience, great learning, and wisdom ⟨the *sage* advice of my father⟩. SAPIENT suggests great sagacity and discernment ⟨the *sapient* musings of an old philosopher⟩. JUDICIOUS stresses a capacity for reaching wise decisions or just conclusions ⟨*judicious* parents using kindness and discipline in equal measure⟩. PRUDENT suggests exercise of the restraint of sound practical wisdom and discretion ⟨a *prudent* decision to wait out the storm⟩. SENSIBLE applies to action guided and restrained by good sense and rationality ⟨a *sensible* woman who was not fooled by flattery⟩. SANE stresses mental soundness, rationality, and levelheadedness ⟨remained *sane* even in times of crises⟩.
[3]**wise** *vb* **wised; wis·ing** *vt* (1905) : to give instruction or information to : TEACH — usu. used with *up* ⟨~ him up about procedures⟩ ~ *vi* : to become informed or knowledgeable : LEARN — used with *up*
[4]**wise** *vt* **wised; wis·ing** [ME, fr. OE *wīsian*; akin to ON *vīsa* to show the way, OE *wīs* wise] (bef. 12c) **1** *chiefly Scot* **a** : DIRECT, GUIDE **b** : ADVISE, PERSUADE **2** *chiefly Scot* : to divert or impel in a given direction : SEND
-wise *adv comb form* [ME, fr. OE *-wīsan*, fr. *wīse* manner] **1 a** : in the manner of ⟨crab*wise*⟩ ⟨fan*wise*⟩ **b** : in the position or direction of ⟨slant*wise*⟩ ⟨clock*wise*⟩ **2** : with regard to : in respect of ⟨dollar*wise*⟩
wise·acre \ˈwīz-ˌā-kər\ *n* [MD *wijssegger* soothsayer, modif. of OHG *wīzzago*; akin to OE *wītega* soothsayer, *witan* to know] (1595) : one who pretends to knowledge or cleverness; *esp* : SMART ALECK
wise·ass \ˈwīz-ˌas\ *n* (ca. 1971) : SMART ALECK — **wiseass** *adj*
[1]**wise·crack** \ˈwīz-ˌkrak\ *n* (1924) : a clever or sarcastic remark
[2]**wisecrack** *vi* (1924) : to make a wisecrack — **wise·crack·er** *n*
wised–up \ˈwīzd-ˈəp\ *adj* (1926) : KNOWING 1
wise guy \ˈwīz-ˌgī\ *n* (1896) **1** : SMART ALECK **2** *usu* **wiseguy** : MOBSTER
wise man *n* (bef. 12c) **1** : a man of unusual learning, judgment, or insight : SAGE **2** : a man versed in esoteric lore (as of magic or astrology); *esp* : MAGUS 1b
wi·sen·hei·mer *also* **wei·sen·hei·mer** \ˈwī-zᵊn-ˌhī-mər\ *n* [[2]*wise* + *-enheimer* (as in family names such as *Guggenheimer, Oppenheimer*)] (1904) : SMART ALECK
wi·sent \ˈvē-ˌzent\ *n* [G, fr. OHG *wisant* — more at BISON] (1866) : a European bison (*Bison bonasus*) sometimes considered conspecific with the No. American buffalo (*B. bison*) — called also *aurochs*
wise·wom·an \ˈwīz-ˌwu̇-mən\ *n* (14c) : a woman versed in charms, conjuring, or fortune-telling
[1]**wish** \ˈwish\ *vb* [ME *wisshen*, fr. OE *wȳscan*; akin to OHG *wunsken* to wish, Skt *vāñchati* he wishes, *vanoti* he strives for — more at WIN] *vt* (bef. 12c) **1** : to have a desire for (as something unattainable) ⟨~*ed* he could live his life over⟩ **2** : to give expression to as a wish : BID ⟨~ them good night⟩ **3 a** : to give form to (a wish) **b** : to express a wish for **c** : to request in the form of a wish : ORDER **d** : to desire (a person or thing) to be as specified ⟨cannot ~ our problems away⟩ **4** : to confer (something unwanted) on someone : FOIST ~ *vi* **1** : to have a desire : WANT ⟨~*ing* for more⟩ **2** : to make a wish ⟨~ on a falling star⟩ ***syn*** see DESIRE — **wish·er** *n*
[2]**wish** *n* (14c) **1 a** : an act or instance of wishing or desire : WANT ⟨a ~ to travel⟩ **b** : an object of desire : GOAL **2 a** : an expressed will or desire : MANDATE **b** : a request or command couched as a wish **3** : an invocation of good or evil fortune on someone
wisha \ˈwi-shə\ *interj* [Ir *mhuise, muise*, prob. alter. of *Muire* Mary (Jesus' mother)] (1826) *chiefly Irish* — used as an intensive or to express surprise
wish·bone \ˈwish-ˌbōn\ *n* [fr. the superstition that when two persons pull it apart the one getting the longer fragment will have a wish granted] (1847) **1** : a forked bone in front of the breastbone in a bird consisting chiefly of the two clavicles fused at their median or lower end **2** : a variation of the T formation in which the halfbacks line up farther from the line of scrimmage than the fullback does

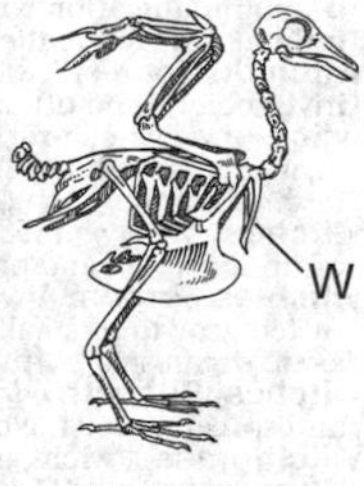

W wishbone 1

wish·ful \ˈwish-fəl\ *adj* (1593) **1 a** : expressive of a wish : HOPEFUL ⟨looked at the toys with ~ eyes⟩ **b** : having a wish : DESIROUS **2** : according with wishes rather than reality ⟨~ dreams⟩ — **wish·ful·ly** \-fə-lē\ *adv* — **wish·ful·ness** *n*
wish fulfillment *n* (1908) : the gratification of a desire esp. symbolically (as in dreams, daydreams, or neurotic symptoms)
wishful thinking *n* (1932) : the attribution of reality to what one wishes to be true or the tenuous justification of what one wants to believe
wish·ing \ˈwi-shiŋ\ *adj* (ca. 1530) **1** *archaic* : WISHFUL **2** : regarded as having the power to grant wishes ⟨threw a coin in the ~ well⟩
wish list *n* (1970) : a list of desired but often realistically unobtainable items ⟨a *wish list* of useful changes⟩
wish–wash \ˈwish-ˌwȯsh, -ˌwäsh\ *n* [redupl. of [2]*wash*] (1786) **1** : a weak drink **2** : insipid talk or writing
wishy–washy \ˈwi-shē-ˌwȯ-shē, -ˌwä-\ *adj* [redupl. of *washy*] (1703) **1** : lacking in character or determination : INEFFECTUAL ⟨~ leadership⟩ **2** : lacking in strength or flavor : WEAK ⟨~ wines⟩ — **wishy–wash·i·ness** *n*
[1]**wisp** \ˈwisp\ *n* [ME] (13c) **1** : a small handful (as of hay or straw) **2 a** : a thin strip or fragment **b** : a thready streak ⟨a ~ of smoke⟩ **c** : something frail, slight, or fleeting ⟨a ~ of a girl⟩ ⟨a ~ of a smile⟩ **3** *archaic* : WILL-O'-THE-WISP — **wisp·i·ly** \ˈwis-pə-lē\ *adv* — **wisp·i·ness** \ˈwis-pē-nəs\ *n* — **wispy** \ˈwis-pē\ *adj*
[2]**wisp** *vt* (1753) **1** : to roll into a wisp **2** : to make wisps of ⟨a cigarette ~*ing* smoke at the corner of his mouth —Raymond Chandler⟩ ~ *vi* : to emerge or drift in wisps ⟨her hair began to ~ into her eyes —Mary Manning⟩
wisp·ish \ˈwis-pish\ *adj* (1896) : resembling a wisp : INSUBSTANTIAL
wist \ˈwist\ *vt* [alter. of *wis*] (1508) *archaic* : KNOW

wis·te·ria \wis-ˈtir-ē-ə\ *also* **wis·tar·ia** \-ˈtir-ē-ə *also* -ˈter-\ *n* [NL *Wisteria,* fr. Caspar *Wistar* †1818 Am. physician] (1842) : any of a genus (*Wisteria*) of mostly woody leguminous vines of China, Japan, and the southeastern U.S. that have pinnately compound leaves and long racemes of showy blue, white, purple, or rose papilionaceous flowers and that include several (as *W. sinensis* and *W. floribunda*) grown as ornamentals

wist·ful \ˈwist-fəl\ *adj* [blend of *wishful* and obs. E *wistly* intently] (1714) **1** : full of yearning or desire tinged with melancholy; *also* : inspiring such yearning ⟨a ~ memoir⟩ **2** : musingly sad : PENSIVE ⟨a ~ glance⟩ — **wist·ful·ly** \-fə-lē\ *adv* — **wist·ful·ness** *n*

[1]**wit** \ˈwit\ *vb* **wist** \ˈwist\; **wit·ting** *pres 1st & 3d sing* **wot** \ˈwät\ [ME *witen* (1st & 3d sing. pres. *wot,* past *wiste*), fr. OE *witan* (1st & 3d sing. pres. *wāt,* past *wisse, wiste*); akin to OHG *wizzan* to know, L *vidēre* to see, Gk *eidenai* to know, *idein* to see] (bef. 12c) **1** *archaic* : KNOW **2** *archaic* : to come to know : LEARN

[2]**wit** *n* [ME, fr. OE; akin to OHG *wizzi* knowledge, OE *witan* to know] (bef. 12c) **1 a** : MIND, MEMORY **b** : reasoning power : INTELLIGENCE **2 a** : SENSE 2a — usu. used in pl. ⟨alone and warming his five ~*s,* the white owl in the belfry sits —Alfred Tennyson⟩ **b** (1) : mental soundness : SANITY — usu. used in pl. (2) : mental capability and resourcefulness : INGENUITY **3 a** : astuteness of perception or judgment : ACUMEN **b** : the ability to relate seemingly disparate things so as to illuminate or amuse **c** (1) : a talent for banter or persiflage (2) : a witty utterance or exchange **d** : clever or apt humor **4 a** : a person of superior intellect : THINKER **b** : an imaginatively perceptive and articulate individual esp. skilled in banter or persiflage — **at one's wit's end** *or* **at one's wits' end** : at a loss for a means of solving a problem

syn WIT, HUMOR, IRONY, SARCASM, SATIRE, REPARTEE mean a mode of expression intended to arouse amusement. WIT suggests the power to evoke laughter by remarks showing verbal felicity or ingenuity and swift perception esp. of the incongruous ⟨a playful *wit*⟩. HUMOR implies an ability to perceive the ludicrous, the comical, and the absurd in human life and to express these usu. without bitterness ⟨a sense of *humor*⟩. IRONY applies to a manner of expression in which the intended meaning is the opposite of what is seemingly expressed ⟨the *irony* of the title⟩. SARCASM applies to expression frequently in the form of irony that is intended to cut or wound ⟨given to heartless *sarcasm*⟩. SATIRE applies to writing that exposes or ridicules conduct, doctrines, or institutions either by direct criticism or more often through irony, parody, or caricature ⟨a *satire* on the Congress⟩. REPARTEE implies the power of answering quickly, pointedly, or wittily ⟨a dinner guest noted for *repartee*⟩.

wi·tan \ˈwi-ˌtän\ *n pl* [OE, pl. of *wita* sage, adviser; akin to OHG *wizzo* sage, OE *witan* to know] (1807) : members of the witenagemot

[1]**witch** \ˈwich\ *n* [ME *wicche,* fr. OE *wicca,* masc., wizard & *wicce,* fem., witch; akin to MHG *wicken* to bewitch, OE *wigle* divination, and perh. to OHG *wīh* holy — more at VICTIM] (bef. 12c) **1** : one that is credited with usu. malignant supernatural powers; *esp* : a woman practicing usu. black witchcraft often with the aid of a devil or familiar : SORCERESS — compare WARLOCK **2** : an ugly old woman : HAG **3** : a charming or alluring girl or woman **4** : a practitioner of Wicca **5** : WITCH OF AGNESI — **witch·like** \ˈwich-ˌlīk\ *adj* — **witchy** \ˈwi-chē\ *adj*

[2]**witch** *vt* (14c) **1** : to affect injuriously with witchcraft **2** *archaic* : to influence or beguile with allure or charm ~ *vi* : DOWSE

witch·craft \ˈwich-ˌkraft\ *n* (bef. 12c) **1 a** : the use of sorcery or magic **b** : communication with the devil or with a familiar **2** : an irresistible influence or fascination **3** : WICCA

witch doctor *n* (1718) : a professional worker of magic usu. in a primitive society who often works to cure sickness

witch·ery \ˈwi-chə-rē, ˈwich-rē\ *n, pl* **-er·ies** (1546) **1 a** : the practice of witchcraft : SORCERY **b** : an act of witchcraft **2** : an irresistible fascination

witches' brew *n* (1868) : a potent or fearsome mixture ⟨a *witches' brew* of untamed sex and brutality —Harrison Smith⟩

witch·es'–broom \ˈwi-chəz-ˌbrüm, -ˌbru̇m\ *n* (1881) : an abnormal tufted growth of small branches on a tree or shrub caused esp. by parasitic organisms (as fungi, viruses, or aphids)

witches' Sabbath *n* (ca. 1676) : a midnight assembly of witches, devils, and sorcerers for the celebration of rites and orgies

witch·grass \ˈwich-ˌgras\ *n* [prob. alter. of *quitch (grass)*] (1790) **1** : QUACK GRASS **2** [[1]*witch*] : a No. American grass (*Panicum capillare*) with slender brushy panicles that is often a weed on cultivated land

witch ha·zel \ˈwich-ˌhā-zəl\ *n* [*witch,* a tree with pliant branches, fr. ME *wyche,* fr. OE *wice;* prob. akin to OE *wīcan* to yield — more at WEAK] (ca. 1760) **1** : any of a genus (*Hamamelis* of the family Hamamelidaceae, the witch-hazel family) of shrubs or small trees with slender-petaled usu. yellow flowers borne in late fall or early spring; *esp* : one (*H. virginiana*) of eastern No. America that blooms in the fall **2** : an alcoholic solution of a distillate of the bark of a witch hazel (*H. virginiana*) used as a soothing and mildly astringent lotion

witch hunt *n* (1885) **1** : a searching out for persecution of persons accused of witchcraft **2** : the searching out and deliberate harassment of those (as political opponents) with unpopular views — **witch–hunt·er** *n* — **witch–hunt·ing** *n or adj*

[1]**witch·ing** \ˈwi-chiŋ\ *n* (bef. 12c) : the practice of witchcraft : SORCERY

[2]**witching** *adj* (14c) : of, relating to, or suitable for sorcery or supernatural occurrences ⟨the very ~ time of night —Shak.⟩

witch of Agne·si \-än-ˈyā-zē\ *n* [Maria Gaetana *Agnesi* †1799 Ital. mathematician; *witch,* trans. of It *versiera* cubic curve (influenced by It *versiera* female demon)] (1875) : a plane cubic curve that is symmetric about the y-axis and approaches the x-axis as an asymptote and that has the equation $x^2y = 4a^2(2a - y)$

witch·weed \ˈwich-ˌwēd\ *n* (1904) : any of a genus (*Striga*) of yellow-flowered Old World plants of the snapdragon family that are damaging root parasites of grasses (as sorghum and maize) and that include one (*S. asiatica*) which is an introduced pest in parts of the southeastern U.S.

[1]**wite** \ˈwīt\ *vt* **wit·ed; wit·ing** [ME, fr. OE *wītan;* akin to OHG *wīzan* to blame, OE *witan* to know] (bef. 12c) *chiefly Scot* : BLAME

[2]**wite** *n* (13c) *chiefly Scot* : BLAME, RESPONSIBILITY

wi·te·na·ge·mot *or* **wi·te·na·ge·mote** \ˈwi-tə-nə-gə-ˌmōt, -yə-ˌmōt\ *n* [OE *witena gemōt,* fr. *witena* (gen. pl. of *wita* sage, adviser) + *gemōt* gemot] (bef. 12c) : an Anglo-Saxon council made up of a varying number of nobles, prelates, and influential officials and convened from time to time to advise the king on administrative and judicial matters

with \ˈwit͟h, ˈwith, wət͟h, wəth\ *prep* [ME, against, from, with, fr. OE; akin to OE *wither* against, OHG *widar* against, back, Skt *vi* apart] (bef. 12c) **1 a** : in opposition to : AGAINST ⟨had a fight ~ his brother⟩ **b** : so as to be separated or detached from ⟨broke ~ her family⟩ **2 a** — used as a function word to indicate a participant in an action, transaction, or arrangement ⟨works ~ his father⟩ ⟨a talk ~ a friend⟩ ⟨got into an accident ~ the car⟩ **b** — used as a function word to indicate the object of attention, behavior, or feeling ⟨get tough ~ him⟩ ⟨angry ~ her⟩ **c** : in respect to : so far as concerns ⟨on friendly terms ~ all nations⟩ **d** — used to indicate the object of an adverbial expression of imperative force ⟨off ~ his head⟩ **e** : OVER, ON ⟨no longer has any influence ~ them⟩ **f** : in the performance, operation, or use of ⟨the trouble ~ this machine⟩ **3 a** — used as a function word to indicate the object of a statement of comparison or equality ⟨a dress identical ~ her hostess's⟩ **b** — used as a function word to express agreement or sympathy ⟨must conclude, ~ you, that the painting is a forgery⟩ **c** : on the side of : FOR ⟨if he's for lower taxes, I'm ~ him⟩ **d** : as well as ⟨can pitch ~ the best of them⟩ **4 a** — used as a function word to indicate combination, accompaniment, presence, or addition ⟨heat milk ~ honey⟩ ⟨went there ~ her⟩ ⟨his money, ~ his wife's, comes to a million⟩ **b** : inclusive of ⟨costs $5 ~ the tax⟩ **5 a** : in the judgment or estimation of ⟨stood well ~ her classmates⟩ **b** : in or according to the experience or practice of ⟨~ many of us, our ideas seem to fall by the wayside —W. J. Reilly⟩ **6 a** — used as a function word to indicate the means, cause, agent, or instrumentality ⟨hit him ~ a rock⟩ ⟨pale ~ anger⟩ ⟨threatened ~ tuberculosis⟩ ⟨he amused the crowd ~ his antics⟩ **b** *archaic* : by the direct act of **7 a** — used as a function word to indicate manner of action ⟨ran ~ effort⟩ ⟨acknowledge your contribution ~ thanks⟩ **b** — used as a function word to indicate an attendant fact or circumstance ⟨stood there ~ his hat on⟩ **c** — used as a function word to indicate a result attendant on a specified action ⟨got off ~ a light sentence⟩ **8 a** (1) : in possession of : HAVING ⟨came ~ good news⟩ (2) : in the possession or care of ⟨left the money ~ her mother⟩ **b** : characterized or distinguished by ⟨a person ~ a sharp nose⟩ **9 a** — used as a function word to indicate a close association in time ⟨~ the outbreak of war they went home⟩ ⟨mellows ~ time⟩ **b** : in proportion to ⟨the pressure varies ~ the depth⟩ **10 a** : in spite of : NOTWITHSTANDING ⟨a really tip-top man, ~ all his wrongheadedness —H. J. Laski⟩ **b** : except for ⟨finds that, ~ one group of omissions and one important addition, they reflect that curriculum —Gilbert Highet⟩ **11** : in the direction of ⟨~ the wind⟩ ⟨~ the grain⟩

[1]**with·al** \wi-ˈt͟hȯl, -ˈthȯl\ *adv* [ME, fr. *with* + *all, al* all] (13c) **1** : together with this : BESIDES ⟨a supporter of all constructive work and ~ an excellent businessman —A. W. Long⟩ **2** *archaic* : THEREWITH 1 **3** : on the other hand : NEVERTHELESS

[2]**withal** *prep* (14c) *archaic* : WITH — used postpositively with a relative or interrogative pronoun as object

with·draw \wit͟h-ˈdrȯ, with-\ *vb* **-drew** \-ˈdrü\; **-drawn** \-ˈdrȯn\; **-draw·ing** \-ˈdrȯ(-)iŋ\ [ME, fr. *with* from + *drawen* to draw] *vt* (13c) **1 a** : to take back or away : REMOVE ⟨pressure upon educational administrators to ~ academic credit —J. W. Scott⟩ **b** : to remove from use or cultivation **c** : to remove (money) from a place of deposit **d** : to turn away (as the eyes) from an object of attention ⟨*withdrew* her gaze⟩ **e** : to draw (as a curtain) back or aside **2 a** : to remove from consideration or set outside a group ⟨*withdrew* his name from the list of nominees⟩ ⟨*withdrew* their child from the school⟩ **b** (1) : TAKE BACK, RETRACT (2) : to recall or remove (a motion) under parliamentary procedure ~ *vi* **1 a** : to move back or away : RETIRE **b** : to draw back from a battlefield : RETREAT **2 a** : to remove oneself from participation **b** : to become socially or emotionally detached ⟨had *withdrawn* farther and farther into herself —Ethel Wilson⟩ **3** : to recall a motion under parliamentary procedure — **with·draw·able** \-ˈdrȯ-ə-bəl\ *adj*

with·draw·al \-ˈdrȯ(-ə)l\ *n* (1749) **1 a** : the act of taking back or away something that has been granted or possessed **b** : removal from a place of deposit or investment **c** (1) : the discontinuance of administration or use of a drug (2) : the syndrome of often painful physical and psychological symptoms that follows discontinuance of an addicting drug ⟨a heroin addict going through ~⟩ **2 a** : retreat or retirement esp. into a more secluded or less exposed place or position **b** : an operation by which a military force disengages from the enemy **c** (1) : social or emotional detachment (2) : a pathological retreat from objective reality (as in some schizophrenic states) **3** : RETRACTION, REVOCATION ⟨threatened us with ~ of consent⟩ **4 a** : the act of drawing someone or something back from or out of a place or position **b** : COITUS INTERRUPTUS

withdrawing room *n* (1591) : a room to retire to (as from a dining room); *esp* : DRAWING ROOM

with·drawn \wit͟h-ˈdrȯn, with-\ *adj* (1615) **1** : removed from immediate contact or easy approach : ISOLATED **2** : socially detached and unresponsive : exhibiting withdrawal : INTROVERTED ⟨a shy and ~ child⟩ — **with·drawn·ness** \-ˈdrȯn-nəs\ *n*

withe \ˈwith, ˈwit͟h, ˈwīt͟h\ *n* [ME, fr. OE *withthe;* akin to OE *wīthig* withy] (bef. 12c) : a slender flexible branch or twig; *esp* : one used as a band or line

[1]**with·er** \ˈwi-t͟hər\ *vb* **with·ered; with·er·ing** \ˈwit͟h-riŋ, ˈwi-t͟hə-\ [ME *widren;* prob. akin to ME *weder* weather] *vi* (14c) **1** : to become dry and sapless; *esp* : to shrivel from or as if from loss of bodily moisture **2** : to lose vitality, force, or freshness ⟨public support for the bill is ~*ing*⟩ ~ *vt* **1** : to cause to wither **2** : to make speechless or incapable of action : STUN ⟨~*ed* him with a look —Dorothy Sayers⟩

[2]**wither** *n* (1607) *chiefly Brit* : WITHERS

withering *adj* (1579) : acting or serving to cut down or destroy : DEVASTATING ⟨a ~ fire from the enemy⟩ ⟨a ~ rebuke⟩ — **with·er·ing·ly** \ˈwit͟h-riŋ-lē, ˈwi-t͟hə-\ *adv*

with·er·ite \ˈwi-t͟hə-ˌrīt\ *n* [G *Witherit,* irreg. fr. William *Withering* †1799 Eng. physician] (1794) : a translucent white or gray orthorhombic mineral consisting of a carbonate of barium

withe rod *n* (1846) : a viburnum (*Viburnum cassinoides*) of eastern No. America with tough slender shoots

with·ers \ˈwi-t͟hərz\ *n pl* [prob. fr. obs. E *wither-* against, fr. ME, fr. OE, fr. *wither* against; fr. the withers being the parts which resist the pull in drawing a load — more at WITH] (1580) **1 :** the ridge between the shoulder bones of a horse — see HORSE illustration **2 :** a part corresponding to the withers in a quadruped (as a dog) other than a horse
withershins *var of* WIDDERSHINS
with·hold \with-ˈhōld, wit͟h-\ *vb* **-held** \-ˈheld\; **-hold·ing** [ME, fr. *with* from + *holden* to hold — more at WITH] *vt* (13c) **1 :** to hold back from action **:** CHECK **2** *archaic* **:** to keep in custody **3 :** to refrain from granting, giving, or allowing ⟨~ permission⟩ **4 :** to deduct (withholding tax) from income ~ *vi* **:** FORBEAR, REFRAIN ⟨~ from commenting⟩ ***syn*** see KEEP — **with·hold·er** *n*
withholding tax *n* (1940) **:** a deduction (as from wages, fees, or dividends) levied at a source of income as advance payment on income tax
1**with·in** \wi-ˈt͟hin, -ˈthin\ *adv* [ME *withinne,* fr. OE *withinnan,* fr. *with* + *innan* inwardly, within, fr. *in*] (bef. 12c) **1 :** in or into the interior **:** INSIDE **2 :** in one's inner thought, disposition, or character **:** INWARDLY ⟨search ~ for a creative impulse —Kingman Brewster †1988⟩
2**within** *prep* (12c) **1** — used as a function word to indicate enclosure or containment **2** — used as a function word to indicate situation or circumstance in the limits or compass of: as **a :** before the end of ⟨gone ~ a week⟩ **b (1) :** not beyond the quantity, degree, or limitations of ⟨live ~ your income⟩ **(2) :** in or into the scope or sphere of ⟨~ the jurisdiction of the state⟩ **(3) :** in or into the range of ⟨~ reach⟩ ⟨~ sight⟩ **(4)** — used as a function word to indicate a specified difference or margin ⟨came ~ two points of a perfect mark⟩ ⟨~ a mile of the town⟩ **3 :** to the inside of **:** INTO ⟨sunk the sea ~ the earth —Shak.⟩
3**within** *n* (15c) **:** an inner place or area ⟨revolt from ~⟩
4**within** *adj* (1748) **:** being inside **:** ENCLOSED ⟨the ~ indictment⟩
with·in·doors \wi-ˌt͟hin-ˈdōrz, -ˌthin-, -ˈdȯrz\ *adv* (1581) **:** INDOORS
with–it \ˈwi-t͟hət, -thət\ *adj* (1959) **:** socially or culturally up-to-date ⟨the intelligent, disaffected, ~ young —Eliot Fremont-Smith⟩
1**with·out** \wi-ˈt͟hau̇t, -ˈthau̇t\ *prep* [ME *withoute,* fr. OE *withūtan,* fr. *with* + *ūtan* outside, fr. *ūt* out — more at OUT] (bef. 12c) **1 :** OUTSIDE **2** — used as a function word to indicate the absence or lack of something or someone ⟨fight ~ fear⟩ ⟨left ~ him⟩ ⟨looks ~ seeing⟩
2**without** *adv* (bef. 12c) **1 :** on the outside **:** EXTERNALLY **2 :** with something lacking or absent ⟨has learned to do ~⟩
3**without** *conj* (14c) *chiefly dial* **:** UNLESS ⟨you don't know about me ~ you have read a book —Mark Twain⟩
4**without** *n* (15c) **:** an outer place or area ⟨came from ~⟩
with·out·doors \wi-ˌt͟hau̇t-ˈdȯrz, -ˌthau̇t-\ *adv* (1617) **:** OUTDOORS
with·stand \with-ˈstand, wit͟h-\ *vt* **-stood** \-ˈstu̇d\; **-stand·ing** [ME, fr. OE *withstandan,* fr. *with* against + *standan* to stand] (bef. 12c) **1 a :** to stand up against **:** oppose with firm determination; *esp* **:** to resist successfully **b :** to be proof against **:** resist the effect of ⟨~ the impact of a landing —*Current Biog.*⟩ **2** *archaic* **:** to stop or obstruct the course of ***syn*** see OPPOSE
1**withy** \ˈwi-t͟hē\ *n, pl* **with·ies** [ME, fr. OE *wīthig;* akin to OHG *wīda* willow, L *vitis* vine, *viēre* to plait — more at WIRE] (bef. 12c) **1 :** WILLOW; *esp* **:** OSIER 1 **2 :** a flexible slender twig or branch (as of osier) **:** WITHE
2**withy** \ˈwi-thē, ˈwī-t͟hē\ *adj* [*withe*] (1598) **:** flexibly tough
wit·less \ˈwit-ləs\ *adj* (bef. 12c) **1 :** destitute of wit or understanding **:** FOOLISH **2 :** mentally deranged **:** CRAZY ⟨drive one ~ with anxiety —William Styron⟩ — **wit·less·ly** *adv* — **wit·less·ness** *n*
wit·ling \-liŋ\ *n* (1693) **1 :** a would-be wit **2 :** a person of little wit
wit·loof \ˈwit-ˌlōf, -ˌlüf\ *n* [D dial. *witloof* chicory, fr. D *wit* white + *loof* foliage] (1885) **:** CHICORY 1; *also* **:** BELGIAN ENDIVE
1**wit·ness** \ˈwit-nəs\ *n* [ME *witnesse,* fr. OE *witnes* knowledge, testimony, witness, fr. 2*wit*] (bef. 12c) **1 :** attestation of a fact or event **:** TESTIMONY **2 :** one that gives evidence; *specif* **:** one who testifies in a cause or before a judicial tribunal **3 :** one asked to be present at a transaction so as to be able to testify to its having taken place **4 :** one who has personal knowledge of something **5 a :** something serving as evidence or proof **:** SIGN **b :** public affirmation by word or example of usu. religious faith or conviction ⟨the heroic ~ to divine life —*Pilot*⟩ **6** *cap* **:** a member of the Jehovah's Witnesses
2**witness** *vt* (14c) **1 :** to testify to **:** ATTEST **2 :** to act as legal witness of **3 :** to furnish proof of **:** BETOKEN **4 a :** to have personal or direct cognizance of **:** see for oneself ⟨~*ed* the historic event⟩ **b :** to take note of ⟨our grammar— ~ our verb system—is a marvel of flexibility, variety, and exactitude —Charlton Laird⟩ **5 :** to constitute the scene or time of ⟨structures . . . which this striking Dorset hilltop once ~*ed* —*Times Lit. Supp.*⟩ ~ *vi* **1 :** to bear witness **:** TESTIFY **2 :** to bear witness to one's religious convictions ⟨opportunity to ~ for Christ —Billy Graham⟩ ***syn*** see CERTIFY
wit·ness–box \-ˌbäks\ *n* (1806) *chiefly Brit* **:** an enclosure in which a witness sits or stands while testifying in court
witness stand *n* (1853) **:** a stand or an enclosure from which a witness gives evidence in a court
wit·ted \ˈwi-təd\ *adj* (14c) **:** having wit or understanding — usu. used in combination ⟨dull-*witted*⟩ ⟨quick-*witted*⟩
wit·ti·cism \ˈwi-tə-ˌsi-zəm\ *n* [*witty* + *-cism* (as in *criticism*)] (1651) **:** a cleverly witty and often biting or ironic remark
1**wit·ting** \ˈwi-tᵊn, -tiŋ\ *n* (14c) **1** *chiefly dial* **:** knowledge or awareness of something **:** COGNIZANCE **2** *chiefly dial* **:** information obtained or communicated **:** NEWS
2**wit·ting** \-tiŋ\ *adj* (ca. 1520) **1 :** cognizant or aware of something **:** CONSCIOUS ⟨a ~ participant⟩ **2 :** done deliberately **:** INTENTIONAL ⟨a ~ violation⟩ — **wit·ting·ly** \-tiŋ-lē\ *adv*
wit·tol \ˈwi-tᵊl\ *n* [ME *wetewold,* fr. *weten, witen* to know + cokewold cuckold — more at WIT] (15c) **1** *archaic* **:** a man who knows of his wife's infidelity and puts up with it **2** *archaic* **:** a witless person
wit·ty \ˈwi-tē\ *adj* **wit·ti·er; -est** (bef. 12c) **1** *archaic* **:** having good intellectual capacity **:** INTELLIGENT **2 :** amusingly or ingeniously clever in conception or execution ⟨the costumes are sumptuous and ~ —Virgil Thomson⟩ ⟨the musical background is . . . often ~ —Wolcott Gibbs⟩ **3 :** marked by or full of wit **:** smartly facetious or jocular ⟨a ~ novel⟩ **4 :** quick or ready to see or express illuminating or amusing relationships or insights ⟨a ~ raconteur⟩ — **wit·ti·ly** \ˈwi-tə-lē\ *adv* — **wit·ti·ness** \ˈwi-tē-nəs\ *n*
syn WITTY, HUMOROUS, FACETIOUS, JOCULAR, JOCOSE mean provoking or intended to provoke laughter. WITTY suggests cleverness and quickness of mind ⟨a *witty* remark⟩. HUMOROUS applies broadly to anything that evokes usu. genial laughter and may contrast with *witty* in suggesting whimsicality or eccentricity ⟨*humorous* anecdotes⟩. FACETIOUS stresses a desire to produce laughter and may be derogatory in implying dubious or ill-timed attempts at wit or humor ⟨*facetious* comments⟩. JOCULAR implies a usu. habitual fondness for jesting and joking ⟨a *jocular* fellow⟩. JOCOSE is somewhat less derogatory than FACETIOUS in suggesting habitual waggishness or playfulness ⟨*jocose* proposals⟩.
wive \ˈwīv\ *vb* **wived; wiv·ing** [ME, fr. OE *wīfian,* fr. *wīf* woman, wife] *vi* (bef. 12c) **:** to marry a woman ~ *vt* **1 :** to marry to a woman **2 :** to take for a wife
wives *pl of* WIFE
wiz \ˈwiz\ *n* (1902) **:** WIZARD 3
1**wiz·ard** \ˈwi-zərd\ *n* [ME *wysard,* fr. *wis, wys* wise] (15c) **1** *archaic* **:** a wise man **:** SAGE **2 :** one skilled in magic **:** SORCERER **3 :** a very clever or skillful person ⟨computer ~*s*⟩
2**wizard** *adj* (1579) **1** *archaic* **:** having magical influence or power **2** *archaic* **:** of or relating to wizardry **:** ENCHANTED **3** *chiefly Brit* **:** worthy of the highest praise **:** EXCELLENT
wiz·ard·ly \ˈwi-zərd-lē\ *adj* (1588) **1 :** having characteristics of a wizard **2 :** marvelous in construction or operation ⟨uses ~ circuitry to distort images —*Time*⟩
wiz·ard·ry \ˈwi-zə(r)-drē\ *n, pl* **-ries** (1583) **1 :** the art or practices of a wizard **:** SORCERY **2 a :** a seemingly magical transforming power or influence ⟨electronic ~⟩ **b :** great skill or cleverness in an activity ⟨showed real ~ in legal maneuvering⟩
1**wiz·en** \ˈwi-zᵊn *also* ˈwē-\ *vb* **wiz·ened; wiz·en·ing** \ˈwiz-niŋ *also* ˈwēz-; ˈwi-zᵊn-iŋ *also* ˈwē-\ [ME *wisenen,* fr. OE *wisnian;* akin to OHG *wesanēn* to wither, Lith *vysti*] *vi* (bef. 12c) **:** to become dry, shrunken, and wrinkled often as a result of aging or of failing vitality ~ *vt* **:** to cause to wizen ⟨a face ~*ed* by age⟩
2**wizen** *adj* [alter. of *wizened*] (1786) **:** that is wizened
wk *abbr* **1** week **2** work
wkly *abbr* weekly
WL *abbr* waterline
WMD *abbr* weapons of mass destruction
WNBA *abbr* Women's National Basketball Association
WNW *abbr* west-northwest
w/o *abbr* without
WO *abbr* warrant officer
woad \ˈwōd\ *n* [ME *wod,* fr. OE *wād;* akin to OHG *weit* woad, L *vitrum*] (bef. 12c) **:** a European herb (*Isatis tinctoria*) of the mustard family formerly grown for the blue dyestuff yielded by its leaves; *also* **:** this dyestuff
1**wob·ble** *also* **wab·ble** \ˈwä-bəl\ *vb* **wob·bled** *also* **wab·bled; wob·bling** *also* **wab·bling** \-b(ə-)liŋ\ [prob. fr. LG *wabbeln;* akin to OE *wǣfre* restless — more at WAVER] *vi* (1657) **1 a :** to move or proceed with an irregular rocking or staggering motion or unsteadily and clumsily from side to side **b :** TREMBLE, QUAVER **2 :** WAVER, VACILLATE ~ *vt* **:** to cause to wobble — **wob·bler** *also* **wab·bler** \-b(ə-)lər\ *n* — **wob·bli·ness** *also* **wab·bli·ness** \ˈwä-blē-nəs\ *n* — **wob·bly** *also* **wab·bly** \ˈwä-b(ə-)lē\ *adj*
2**wobble** *also* **wabble** *n* (1699) **1 a :** a hobbling or rocking unequal motion (as of a wheel unevenly mounted) **b :** an uncertainly directed movement **2 :** an intermittent variation (as in volume of sound)
Wob·bly \ˈwä-blē\ *n, pl* **Wobblies** [origin unknown] (1914) **:** a member of the Industrial Workers of the World
WOC *abbr* without compensation
Wo·den \ˈwō-dᵊn\ *n* [OE *Wōden*] (13c) **:** ODIN
wodge \ˈwäj\ *n* [prob. alter. of *wedge*] (1860) *chiefly Brit* **:** a bulky mass or chunk **:** LUMP, WAD
1**woe** \ˈwō\ *interj* [ME *wa, wo,* fr. OE *wā;* akin to ON *vei,* interj., woe, L *vae*] (bef. 12c) — used to express grief, regret, or distress
2**woe** *n* (bef. 12c) **1 :** a condition of deep suffering from misfortune, affliction, or grief **2 :** ruinous trouble **:** CALAMITY, AFFLICTION ⟨economic ~*s*⟩ ***syn*** see SORROW
woe·be·gone \ˈwō-bi-ˌgȯn *also* -ˌgän\ *adj* [ME *wo begon,* fr. *wo,* n. + *begon,* pp. of *begon* to go about, beset, fr. OE *begān,* fr. *be-* + *gān* to go — more at GO] (14c) **1 :** strongly affected with woe **:** WOEFUL **2 a :** exhibiting great woe, sorrow, or misery ⟨a ~ expression⟩ **b :** being in a sorry state ⟨~ tattered clothes⟩ — **woe·be·gone·ness** *n*
woe·ful *also* **wo·ful** \ˈwō-fəl\ *adj* (14c) **1 :** full of woe **:** GRIEVOUS ⟨~ prophecies⟩ **2 :** involving or bringing woe **3 :** lamentably bad or serious **:** DEPLORABLE ⟨~ ignorance⟩ — **woe·ful·ly** \-f(ə-)lē\ *adv* — **woe·ful·ness** \-fəl-nəs\ *n*
wog \ˈwäg, ˈwȯg\ *n* [perh. short for *golliwog*] (ca. 1929) *chiefly Brit, usu disparaging* **:** a dark-skinned foreigner; *esp* **:** one from the Middle East or Far East
wok \ˈwäk\ *n* [Chin (Guangdong) *wohk*] (1952) **:** a large bowl-shaped cooking utensil used esp. in stir-frying
woke *past and past part of* WAKE
woken *past part of* WAKE
wold \ˈwōld\ *n* [ME *wald, wold,* fr. OE *weald, wald* forest; akin to OHG *wald* forest, ON *vǫllr* field] (bef. 12c) **1 :** a usu. upland area of open country **2** *cap* **:** a hilly or rolling region — used in names of various English geographic areas ⟨Yorkshire *Wolds*⟩
1**wolf** \ˈwu̇lf\ *n, pl* **wolves** \ˈwu̇lvz\ *often attrib* [ME, fr. OE *wulf;* akin to OHG *wolf* wolf, L *lupus,* Gk *lykos*] (bef. 12c) **1** *pl also* **wolf a :** any of several large predatory canids (genus *Canis*) that live and hunt in packs and resemble the related dogs; *esp* **:** GRAY WOLF — compare COYOTE, JACKAL **b :** the fur of a wolf **2 a (1) :** a fierce, rapacious, or destructive person **(2) :** a man forward, direct, and zealous in amatory attentions to women **b :** dire poverty **:** STARVATION ⟨keep the ~ from the door⟩ **c :** the maggot of a warble fly **3** [G; fr. the howling sound] **a (1) :** dissonance in some chords on organs, pianos, or other instruments with fixed tones tuned by unequal temperament **(2) :** an instance of such dissonance **b :** a harshness due to faulty vibration in various

\ə\ **abut** \ᵊ\ kitten, F table \ər\ **fur**ther \a\ **ash** \ā\ **ace** \ä\ m**o**p, m**ar** \au̇\ **out** \ch\ **chin** \e\ **bet** \ē\ **easy** \g\ **go** \i\ **hit** \ī\ **ice** \j\ **job** \ŋ\ **sing** \ō\ **go** \ȯ\ **law** \ȯi\ **boy** \th\ **thin** \t͟h\ **the** \ü\ **loot** \u̇\ **foot** \y\ **yet** \zh\ **vi**sion, beige \k̟, ⁿ, œ, ue, ʸ\ *see* Guide to Pronunciation

tones in a bowed instrument — **wolf·like** \'wu̇lf-ˌlīk\ *adj* — **wolf in sheep's clothing :** one who cloaks a hostile intention with a friendly manner

2**wolf** *vt* (1862) **:** to eat greedily **:** DEVOUR

wolf·ber·ry \'wu̇lf-ˌber-ē\ *n* (ca. 1834) **:** a white-berried No. American shrub (*Symphoricarpos occidentalis*) of the honeysuckle family

wolf dog *n* (1652) **1 :** any of various large dogs formerly kept for hunting wolves **2 :** the offspring of a wolf and a domestic dog

wolf·er \'wu̇l-fər\ *n* (1872) **:** a hunter of wolves

Wolff·ian duct \'wu̇l-fē-ən-\ *n* [Kaspar Friedrich *Wolff*] (1876) **:** the duct of the mesonephros that persists in the female chiefly as part of a vestigial organ and in the male as the duct system leaving the testis and including the epididymis, vas deferens, seminal vesicle, and ejaculatory duct

wolf·fish \'wu̇lf-ˌfish\ *n* (1569) **:** any of several large marine bony fishes (genus *Anarhichas* of the family Anarhichadidae) of cold northern waters having strong canine teeth in the front of the jaws and molar teeth on the sides and that feed chiefly on shellfish, starfish, and sea urchins

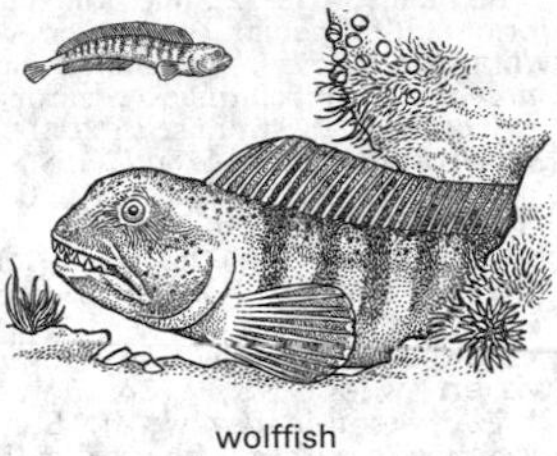
wolffish

wolf·hound \'wu̇lf-ˌhau̇nd\ *n* (1786) **:** any of several large dogs used esp. formerly in hunting large animals (as wolves) — compare BORZOI, IRISH WOLFHOUND

wolf·ish \'wu̇l-fish\ *adj* (15c) **1 a :** suggestive of a wolf ⟨~ mongrel dogs —Hoffman Birney⟩ ⟨a ~ and withdrawn youth —Marshall Frady⟩ **b :** befitting or characteristic of a wolf ⟨a ~ appetite⟩ **2 :** of or relating to wolves — **wolf·ish·ly** *adv* — **wolf·ish·ness** *n*

wolf pack *n* (1941) **:** a group of submarines that attack shipping

wol·fram \'wu̇l-frəm\ *n* [G] (1757) **1 :** WOLFRAMITE **2 :** TUNGSTEN

wol·fram·ite \'wu̇l-frə-ˌmīt\ *n* [G *Wolframit,* fr. *Wolfram*] (ca. 1868) **:** a brown to black mineral consisting of a tungstate of iron and manganese occurring esp. in monoclinic crystals and used as a source of tungsten

wolfs·bane \'wu̇lfs-ˌbān\ *n* (1548) **:** any of several monkshoods (esp. *Aconitum napellus* or *A. lycoctonum*)

wolf spider *n* (1608) **:** any of various active wandering ground spiders (family Lycosidae)

wolf tree *n* (1928) **:** a very large forest tree that has a wide-spreading crown and inhibits or prevents the growth of smaller trees around it

wolf whistle *n* (1946) **:** a distinctive 2-toned whistle sounded by a boy or man to express sexual admiration for a girl or woman in his vicinity

wol·las·ton·ite \'wu̇-lə-stə-ˌnīt, 'wä-\ *n* [William H. *Wollaston*] (1823) **:** a triclinic mineral consisting of a native calcium silicate occurring usu. in cleavable masses

Wo·lof \'wō-ˌlȯf\ *n* [Wolof, speaker of Wolof, the Wolof language] (1823) **:** a Niger-Congo language of Senegambia

wol·ver·ine \ˌwu̇l-və-'rēn\ *n, pl* **wolverines** [prob. irreg. fr. *wolv-* (as in *wolves*)] (1574) **1** *pl also* **wolverine a :** a carnivorous usu. solitary mammal (*Gulo gulo*) of the weasel family of northern forests and associated tundra that is dark brown with a light brown band on each side of the body and is noted for its strength **b :** the fur of the wolverine **2** *cap* **:** a native or resident of Michigan — used as a nickname

wom·an \'wu̇-mən, *esp Southern* 'wō- *or* 'wə-\ *n, pl* **wom·en** \'wi-mən\ [ME, fr. OE *wīfman,* fr. *wīf* woman, wife + *man* human being, man] (bef. 12c) **1 a :** an adult female person **b :** a woman belonging to a particular category (as by birth, residence, membership, or occupation) — usu. used in combination ⟨council*woman*⟩ **2 :** WOMANKIND **3 :** distinctively feminine nature **:** WOMANLINESS **4 :** a woman who is a servant or personal attendant **5 a** *chiefly dial* **:** WIFE **b :** MISTRESS **c :** GIRLFRIEND 2 — **woman** *adj* — **wom·an·less** \-ləs\ *adj*

wom·an·hood \-ˌhu̇d\ *n* (14c) **1 a :** the state of being a woman **b :** the distinguishing character or qualities of a woman or of womankind **2 :** WOMEN, WOMANKIND

wom·an·ise *Brit var of* WOMANIZE

wom·an·ish \'wu̇-mə-nish\ *adj* (14c) **1 :** associated with or characteristic of women rather than men **2 :** suggestive of a weak character **:** EFFEMINATE ⟨~ fears⟩ — **wom·an·ish·ly** *adv* — **wom·an·ish·ness** *n*

wom·an·ism \'wu̇-mə-ˌni-zəm\ *n* (1984) **:** a form of feminism focused esp. on the conditions and concerns of black women — **wom·an·ist** \-nist\ *n or adj*

wom·an·ize \'wu̇-mə-ˌnīz\ *vb* **-ized; -iz·ing** *vt* (1593) **:** to make effeminate ~ *vi* **:** to pursue casual sexual relationships with multiple women — **wom·an·iz·er** *n*

wom·an·kind \'wu̇-mən-ˌkīnd\ *n sing but sing or pl in constr* (13c) **:** female human beings **:** women esp. as distinguished from men

1**wom·an·like** \-ˌlīk\ *adj* (15c) **:** WOMANLY

2**womanlike** *adv* (15c) **:** in the manner of a woman

wom·an·ly \-lē\ *adj* (13c) **1 :** having qualities generally associated with a woman **2 :** appropriate in character to a woman — **wom·an·li·ness** *n*

woman of letters (1818) **1 :** a woman who is a scholar **2 :** a woman who is an author

woman of the street (1928) **:** PROSTITUTE

wom·an·pow·er \'wu̇-mən-ˌpau̇(-ə)r\ *n* (1938) **:** women available and prepared for work (as in industry or a particular line of endeavor)

woman's rights *n pl* (1833) **1 :** legal, political, and social rights for women equal to those of men **2 :** FEMINISM 2

woman suffrage *n* (1863) **:** possession and exercise of suffrage by women

womb \'wüm\ *n* [ME *wamb, womb,* fr. OE; akin to OHG *wamba* belly] (bef. 12c) **1 :** UTERUS **2 a :** a cavity or space that resembles a womb in containing and enveloping **b :** a place where something is generated — **wombed** \'wümd\ *adj*

wom·bat \'wäm-ˌbat\ *n* [Dharuk (Australian aboriginal language of the Port Jackson area) *wambad*] (1798) **:** any of several stocky burrowing Australian marsupials (genera *Vombatus* and *Lasiorhinus* of the family Vombatidae) resembling small bears

wom·en·folk \'wi-mən-ˌfōk\ *also* **wom·en·folks** \-ˌfōks\ *n pl* (1729) **:** WOMEN

wom·en·kind \-ˌkīnd\ *n* (13c) **:** WOMANKIND

women's rights *n pl* (1632) **:** WOMAN'S RIGHTS

women's room *n* (ca. 1937) **:** LADIES' ROOM

women's studies *n pl but sing or pl in constr* (1972) **:** the multidisciplinary study of the social status and societal contributions of women and the relationship between power and gender

wommera *var of* WOOMERA

1**won** \'wən, 'wōn\ *vi* **wonned; won·ning** [ME, fr. OE *wunian* — more at WONT] (bef. 12c) *archaic* **:** DWELL 2a, ABIDE 2

2**won** *past and past part of* WIN

3**won** \'wȯn\ *n, pl* **won** [Korean *wŏn*] (ca. 1917) — see MONEY table

1**won·der** \'wən-dər\ *n* [ME, fr. OE *wundor;* akin to OHG *wuntar* wonder] (bef. 12c) **1 a :** a cause of astonishment or admiration **:** MARVEL ⟨it's a ~ you weren't killed⟩ ⟨the pyramid is a ~ to behold⟩ **b :** MIRACLE **2 :** the quality of exciting amazed admiration **3 a :** rapt attention or astonishment at something awesomely mysterious or new to one's experience **b :** a feeling of doubt or uncertainty

2**wonder** *vb* **won·dered; won·der·ing** \-d(ə-)riŋ\ *vi* (bef. 12c) **1 a :** to be in a state of wonder **b :** to feel surprise **2 :** to feel curiosity or doubt ⟨~*ing* about the future⟩ ~ *vt* **:** to be curious or in doubt about ⟨~*s* why birds sing⟩ — **won·der·er** \-dər-ər\ *n*

3**wonder** *adj* (12c) **:** WONDROUS, WONDERFUL: as **a :** exciting amazement or admiration ⟨~ toys⟩ **b :** effective or efficient far beyond anything previously known or anticipated ⟨a ~ fabric⟩

wonder drug *n* (1939) **:** MIRACLE DRUG

won·der·ful \'wən-dər-fəl\ *adj* (bef. 12c) **1 :** exciting wonder **:** MARVELOUS, ASTONISHING ⟨a sight ~ to behold⟩ **2 :** unusually good **:** ADMIRABLE ⟨did a ~ job⟩ — **won·der·ful·ly** \-f(ə-)lē\ *adv* — **won·der·ful·ness** \-fəl-nəs\ *n*

won·der·land \'wən-dər-ˌland, -lənd\ *n* (1790) **1 :** an imaginary place of delicate beauty or magical charm **2 :** a place that excites admiration or wonder ⟨a scenic ~⟩

won·der·ment \-mənt\ *n* (15c) **1 :** a cause of or occasion for wonder **2 :** ASTONISHMENT, SURPRISE **3 :** curiosity about something

won·der·work \-də(r)-ˌwərk\ *n* (bef. 12c) **:** a marvelous act, work, or accomplishment

won·der–work·er \-ˌwər-kər\ *n* (1599) **:** one that performs wonders

won·der–work·ing \-kiŋ\ *adj* (1593) **:** producing wonders

won·drous \'wən-drəs\ *adj* [ME, alter. of *wonders,* fr. gen. of 1*wonder*] (15c) **:** that is to be marveled at **:** EXTRAORDINARY ⟨a ~ feat⟩ — **wondrous** *adv, archaic* — **won·drous·ly** *adv* — **won·drous·ness** *n*

wonk \'wäŋk, 'wȯŋk\ *n* [origin unknown] (1954) **:** a person preoccupied with arcane details or procedures in a specialized field; *broadly* **:** NERD ⟨a policy ~⟩ ⟨a computer ~⟩ — **wonk·ery** \'wäŋ-kə-rē\ *n* — **wonk·ish** \'wäŋ-kish\ *adj* — **wonk·ish·ness** *n*

won·ky \'wäŋ-kē\ *adj* **won·ki·er; -est** [prob. alter. of E dial. *wankle,* fr. ME *wankel,* fr. OE *wancol;* akin to OHG *wankōn* to totter — more at WENCH] (1918) **1** *Brit* **:** UNSTEADY, SHAKY **2** *chiefly Brit* **:** AWRY, WRONG

1**wont** \'wȯnt, 'wōnt *also* 'wənt, 'wänt\ *adj* [ME *woned, wont,* fr. pp. of *wonen* to dwell, be used to, fr. OE *wunian;* akin to OHG *wonēn* to dwell, be used to, Skt *vanoti* he strives for — more at WIN] (bef. 12c) **1 :** ACCUSTOMED, USED ⟨got up early as he is ~ to do⟩ **2 :** INCLINED, APT ⟨revealing as letters are ~ to be —Gladys M. Wrigley⟩

2**wont** *vb* **wont; wont** *or* **wont·ed; wont·ing** *vt* (15c) **:** ACCUSTOM, HABITUATE ~ *vi* **:** to have the habit of doing something

3**wont** *n* (1530) **:** habitual way of doing **:** USE ***syn*** see HABIT

won't \'wōnt; *NewEng, upstate NY, nPa* ˌwənt, 'wənt; *greater NYC* 'wünt; *eSC* 'wünt, 'wu̇nt\ (1562) **:** will not

wont·ed \'wȯn-təd, 'wōn- *also* 'wən- *or* 'wän-\ *adj* (15c) **:** usual or ordinary esp. by reason of established habit ⟨spoke with his ~ slowness⟩ ***syn*** see USUAL — **wont·ed·ly** *adv* — **wont·ed·ness** *n*

won·ton \'wän-ˌtän\ *n* [Chin (Guangdong) *wàhn-tān*] (1934) **:** filled pockets of noodle dough served boiled in soup or fried

woo \'wü\ *vb* [ME *wowen,* fr. OE *wōgian*] *vt* (bef. 12c) **1 :** to sue for the affection of and usu. marriage with **:** COURT **2 :** to solicit or entreat esp. with importunity ⟨~ new customers⟩ **3 :** to seek to gain or bring about ~ *vi* **:** to court a woman — **woo·er** *n*

1**wood** \'wüd, 'wōd, 'wu̇d\ *adj* [ME, fr. OE *wōd* insane; akin to OHG *wuot* madness — more at VATIC] (bef. 12c) *archaic* **:** violently mad

2**wood** \'wu̇d\ *n* [ME *wode,* fr. OE *widu, wudu;* akin to OHG *witu* wood, OIr *fid* tree] (bef. 12c) **1 a :** a dense growth of trees usu. greater in extent than a grove and smaller than a forest — often used in pl. but sing. or pl. in constr. **b :** WOODLAND **2 a :** the hard fibrous substance consisting basically of xylem that makes up the greater part of the stems, branches, and roots of trees or shrubs beneath the bark and is found to a limited extent in herbaceous plants **b :** wood suitable or prepared for some use (as burning or building) **3 a :** something made of wood **b :** a golf club having a thick wooden head; *also* **:** a golf club having a similar head made of metal — **out of the woods :** clear of danger or difficulty

3**wood** \'wu̇d\ *adj* (14c) **1 :** WOODEN **2 :** suitable for cutting or working with wood ⟨a ~ saw⟩ **3** *or* **woods** \'wu̇dz\ **:** living, growing, or existing in woods ⟨*woods* trails⟩

4**wood** \'wu̇d\ *vi* (1630) **:** to gather or take on wood ~ *vt* **:** to cover with a growth of trees or plant with trees

wood alcohol *n* (1854) **:** METHANOL

wood anemone *n* (1650) **:** any of several anemones; *esp* **:** one (*Anemone quinquefolia*) of No. America with solitary often pink-tinged flowers

wood bet·o·ny \-'be-tə-nē\ *n* [ME *betone,* fr. AF *betoine,* fr. L *vettonica, betonica,* fr. *Vettones,* an ancient people inhabiting the Iberian Peninsula] (1747) **:** a lousewort (*Pedicularis canadensis*) of eastern No. America with yellow or reddish flowers in bracted spikes

wood·bine \'wu̇d-ˌbīn\ *n* [ME *wodebinde,* fr. OE *wudubinde,* fr. *wudu* wood + *bindan* to tie, bind; fr. its winding around trees] (bef. 12c) **1 :** any of several honeysuckles; *esp*

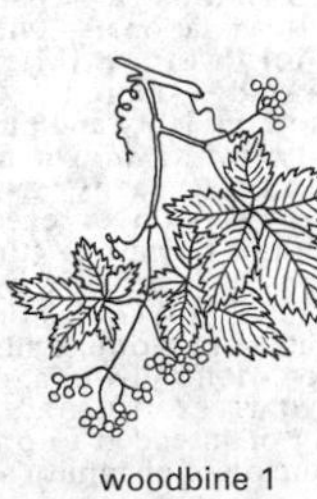
woodbine 1

: a Eurasian twining shrub (*Lonicera periclymenum*) **2 :** VIRGINIA CREEPER

wood·block \-ˌbläk\ *n* (1837) **:** WOODCUT — **wood–block** *adj*

wood–bor·ing \-ˌbȯr-iŋ\ *adj* (1815) **:** excavating galleries in wood in feeding or in constructing a nest — used chiefly of an insect

wood carving *n* (ca. 1710) **:** the art of fashioning or ornamenting objects of wood by cutting with a sharp handheld implement; *also* **:** an object of wood so fashioned or ornamented — **wood–carv·er** \-ˌkär-vər\ *n*

wood·chat shrike \ˈwu̇d-ˌchat-\ *n* (1781) **:** a black-and-white European shrike (*Lanius senator*) with a red crown and nape — called also *woodchat*

wood·chop·per \-ˌchä-pər\ *n* (1779) **:** one engaged in chopping wood and esp. in chopping down trees

wood·chuck \-ˌchək\ *n* [by folk etymology fr. a word of Algonquian origin; akin to Narragansett *ockqutchaun* woodchuck] (1674) **:** a grizzled thickset marmot (*Marmota monax*) chiefly of Alaska, Canada, and the northeastern U.S. — called also *groundhog*

wood·cock \ˈwu̇d-ˌkäk\ *n, pl* **woodcocks** (bef. 12c) **1** *or pl* **woodcock :** a widespread Old World woodland game bird (*Scolopax rusticola*) of the sandpiper family that has a long bill and large eyes; *also* **:** a smaller related woodland game bird (*S. minor* syn. *Philohela minor*) of eastern No. America **2** [fr. the ease with which the woodcock is snared] *archaic* **:** SIMPLETON

wood·craft \-ˌkraft\ *n* (14c) **1 :** skill and practice in anything relating to the woods and esp. in maintaining oneself and making one's way in the woods **2 :** skill in shaping or constructing articles from wood

wood·cut \-ˌkət\ *n* (1662) **1 :** a relief printing surface consisting of a wooden block with a usu. pictorial design cut with the grain **2 :** a print from a woodcut

wood·cut·ter \-ˌkə-tər\ *n* (1600) **:** one that cuts wood

wood·cut·ting \-ˌkə-tiŋ\ *n* (1683) **1 :** the action or occupation of cutting wood or timber **2 :** the producing of woodcuts

wood duck *n* (1777) **:** a showy American duck (*Aix sponsa*) which nests in tree cavities and the males of which have a large crest and iridescent plumage varied with green, purple, black, white, and chestnut

wood ear *n* (1917) **:** any of several ear- or cup-shaped basidiomycetous fungi (genus *Auricularia*) that grow on wood: as **a :** an edible brownish fungus (*A. auricula*) of No. America **b :** a cultivated usu. dark brown edible fungus (*A. polytricha*) used in Chinese cooking

wood·ed \ˈwu̇-dəd\ *adj* (1586) **:** covered with growing trees

wood·en \ˈwu̇-dᵊn\ *adj* (1538) **1 :** made or consisting of wood **2 :** lacking ease or flexibility **:** awkwardly stiff ⟨a ~ speech⟩ ⟨a ~ performer⟩ — **wood·en·ly** *adv* — **wood·en·ness** \-dᵊn-(n)əs\ *n*

wood engraving *n* (1816) **1 :** a relief printing surface consisting of a wooden block with a usu. pictorial design cut in the end grain **2 :** a print from a wood engraving

wood·en·head \ˈwu̇-dᵊn-ˌhed\ *n* (1831) **:** BLOCKHEAD

wood·en·head·ed \ˌwu̇-dᵊn-ˈhe-dəd\ *adj* (1773) **:** DENSE, STUPID

wooden Indian *n* (1855) **:** a wooden image of a standing American Indian brave used esp. formerly as a sign for a cigar store

wood·en·ware \ˈwu̇-dᵊn-ˌwer\ *n* (1639) **:** articles made of wood for domestic use

wood frog *n* (1839) **:** a common No. American frog (*Rana sylvatica*) that inhabits chiefly moist woodlands and is dark brown, yellowish-brown, or pink with a black stripe on each side of the head

[1]**wood·land** \ˈwu̇d-lənd, -ˌland\ *n* (bef. 12c) **:** land covered with woody vegetation **:** TIMBERLAND, FOREST — **wood·land·er** \-lən-dər, -ˌlan-\ *n*

[2]**woodland** *adj* (14c) **1 :** growing, living, or existing in woodland **2 :** of, relating to, or being woodland

wood·lore \ˈwu̇d-ˌlȯr\ *n* (1871) **:** knowledge of the woods

wood·lot \-ˌlät\ *n* (1643) **:** a restricted area of woodland usu. privately maintained as a source of fuel, posts, and lumber

wood louse *n* (1611) **:** a terrestrial isopod crustacean (suborder Oniscoidea) with a flattened elliptical body often capable of being rolled into a ball — called also *pill bug, sow bug*

wood·man \ˈwu̇d-mən\ *n* (15c) **1 :** WOODSMAN **2** *cap* [Modern *Woodmen* of America & *Woodmen* of the World] **:** a member of either of two independent benevolent and fraternal societies

wood·note \-ˌnōt\ *n* [fr. its likeness to the call of a bird in the woods] (1632) **:** verbal expression that is natural and artless

wood nymph *n* (1567) **:** a nymph living in woods — called also *dryad*

wood·peck·er \ˈwu̇d-ˌpe-kər\ *n* (ca. 1530) **:** any of numerous birds (family Picidae) with zygodactyl feet, stiff spiny tail feathers used in climbing or resting on tree trunks, a usu. extensible tongue, a very hard bill used to drill the bark or wood of trees for insect food or to excavate nesting cavities, and generally showy parti-colored plumage

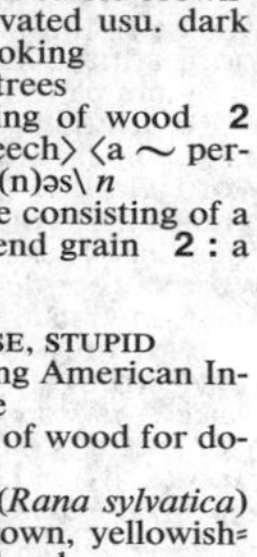

woodpecker

wood pigeon *n* (1714) **:** a large chiefly European pigeon (*Columba palumbus*) with a whitish patch on each side of the neck and wings edged with white — called also *ringdove*

wood·pile \-ˌpī(-ə)l\ *n* (ca. 1552) **:** a pile of wood (as firewood) — **in the woodpile :** doing or responsible for covert mischief

wood pulp *n* (1854) **:** pulp from wood used in making cellulose derivatives (as paper or rayon)

wood pussy *n* (ca. 1899) **:** SKUNK

wood rat *n* (1763) **:** any of numerous soft-furred cricetid rodents (esp. genus *Neotoma*) of No. and Central America that have well-furred tails, large ears, and a characteristic tendency to hoard food and debris on or near their dens — called also *pack rat*

wood ray *n* (1925) **:** XYLEM RAY

wood·ruff \ˈwu̇d-(ˌ)rəf\ *n* [ME *woderove,* fr. OE *wudurofe,* fr. *wudu* wood + *-rofe* (of unknown origin)] (bef. 12c) **1 :** any of a genus (*Asperula*) of Old World herbs of the madder family **2 :** SWEET WOODRUFF

[1]**wood·shed** \-ˌshed\ *n* (1777) **1 :** a shed for storing wood and esp. firewood **2 :** a place, means, or session for administering discipline

[2]**woodshed** *vi* **-shed·ded; -shed·ding** [prob. fr. the former use of woodsheds for private practicing] (1936) **:** PRACTICE; *esp* **:** to practice on a musical instrument

wood shot *n* (1927) **1 :** a golf shot played with a wood **2 :** a stroke in a racket game in which the ball or shuttlecock is hit with the frame of the racket rather than the strings

woods·man \ˈwu̇dz-mən\ *n* (1688) **:** a person who frequents or works in the woods; *esp* **:** one skilled in woodcraft

wood sorrel *n* (13c) **:** any of a genus (*Oxalis* of the family Oxalidaceae, the wood-sorrel family) of herbs with acid sap, compound leaves, and regular flowers having five usu. white, purple, or yellow petals; *esp* **:** either of two stemless herbs (*O. montana* of No. America and *O. acetosella* of Eurasia) with trifoliolate leaves

wood stork *n* (1884) **:** a white stork (*Mycteria americana*) with black wing flight feathers and tail that frequents wooded swamps from the southeastern U.S. to Argentina — called also *wood ibis*

wood·stove \ˈwu̇d-ˌstōv\ *n* (1847) **:** a stove that uses wood for fuel

wood sugar *n* (ca. 1900) **:** XYLOSE

woodsy \ˈwu̇d-zē\ *adj* **woods·i·er; -est** (1854) **:** characteristic or suggestive of woods ⟨the ~ flavor of mushrooms⟩

wood thrush *n* (1791) **:** a large woodland thrush (*Hylocichla mustelina*) of eastern No. America that is rusty brown on the head and back, has white underparts marked with large black spots, and is noted for its loud clear song

wood tick *n* (1668) **:** any of several ixodid ticks: as **a :** a widely distributed tick (*Dermacentor andersonii*) of western No. America that is a vector of Rocky Mountain spotted fever **b :** AMERICAN DOG TICK

wood turning *n* (1849) **:** the art or process of fashioning wooden pieces or blocks into various forms and shapes by means of a lathe

wood turpentine *n* (ca. 1909) **:** TURPENTINE 2b

wood warbler *n* (1817) **:** WARBLER 2b

wood·wind \ˈwu̇d-ˌwind\ *n* (1876) **1 :** any of a group of wind instruments (as a clarinet, flute, oboe, or saxophone) that are characterized by a cylindrical or conical tube of wood or metal usu. ending in a slightly flared bell, that produce tones by the vibration of one or two reeds in the mouthpiece or by the passing of air over a mouth hole, and that usu. have finger holes or keys by which the player may produce all the tones within an instrument's range **2** *pl* **:** the woodwind section of a band or orchestra

wood·work \-ˌwərk\ *n* (ca. 1609) **1 :** work made of wood; *esp* **:** interior fittings (as moldings or stairways) of wood **2 :** a place or state of concealment, seclusion, or anonymity ⟨witnesses came out of the ~ when a reward was offered⟩

[1]**wood·work·ing** \-ˌwər-kiŋ\ *adj* (1839) **:** used for woodworking

[2]**woodworking** *n* (1858) **:** the act, process, or occupation of working wood into a useful or desired form — **wood·work·er** \-kər\ *n*

wood·worm \ˈwu̇d-ˌwərm\ *n* (1725) **:** an insect larva (as of a furniture beetle) that bores esp. in dead wood; *also* **:** an infestation of woodworms

[1]**woody** \ˈwu̇-dē\ *adj* **wood·i·er; -est** (12c) **1 :** abounding or overgrown with woods **2 a :** of or containing wood or wood fibers **:** LIGNEOUS ⟨~ tissues⟩ **b :** having woody parts **:** rich in xylem and associated structures ⟨~ plants⟩ **3 :** characteristic of or suggestive of wood ⟨wine with a ~ flavor⟩ — **wood·i·ness** *n*

[2]**woody** *or* **wood·ie** \ˈwu̇-dē\ *n, pl* **woodies** [alter. of [3]*wood*] (1961) **:** a wood-paneled station wagon

[1]**woof** \ˈwu̇f, ˈwüf\ *n* [alter. of ME *oof,* fr. OE *ōwef,* fr. *ō-* (fr. *on*) + *wefan* to weave — more at WEAVE] (bef. 12c) **1 a :** WEFT 1a **b :** woven fabric; *also* **:** the texture of such a fabric **2 :** a basic or essential element or material

[2]**woof** \ˈwu̇f\ *vi* [imit.] (1804) **1 :** to make the low gruff sound typically produced by a dog **2 :** to express oneself in a usu. stylized boastful or aggressive manner

[3]**woof** *n* (1839) **1 :** a low gruff sound typically produced by a dog **2 :** a low note emitted by sound reproducing equipment

woof·er \ˈwu̇-fər\ *n* (1935) **:** a loudspeaker usu. larger than a tweeter, responsive only to the lower acoustic frequencies, and used for reproducing sounds of low pitch — compare TWEETER

woo–hoo *or* **whoo–hoo** \ˈwü-ˈhü, ˌwü-\ *interj* (1981) — used to express exuberant delight or approval

wool \ˈwu̇l\ *n, often attrib* [ME *wolle,* fr. OE *wull;* akin to OHG *wolla* wool, L *vellus* fleece, *lana* wool] (bef. 12c) **1 :** the soft wavy or curly usu. thick undercoat of various hairy mammals and esp. the sheep made up of a matrix of keratin fibers and covered with minute scales **2 :** a product of wool; *esp* **:** a woven fabric or garment of such fabric **3 a :** a dense felted pubescence esp. on a plant **:** TOMENTUM **b :** a filamentous mass — usu. used in combination; compare MINERAL WOOL, STEEL WOOL

wooled *also* **woolled** \ˈwu̇ld\ *adj* (15c) **:** having wool esp. of a specified kind — used in combination ⟨long-*wooled*⟩

[1]**wool·en** *or* **wool·len** \ˈwu̇-lən\ *adj* (bef. 12c) **1 :** made of wool **2 :** of or relating to the manufacture or sale of woolen products ⟨~ mills⟩

[2]**woolen** *or* **woollen** *n* (14c) **1 :** a fabric made of wool and esp. of woolen yarns having a fuzzy or napped face (as for use in clothing or blankets) — compare WORSTED **2 :** garments of woolen fabric — usu. used in pl.

wool fat *n* (1875) **:** wool grease esp. after refining **:** LANOLIN

wool·gath·er \ˈwu̇l-ˌga-t͟hər, -ˌge-t͟hər\ *vi* (1796) **:** to engage in woolgathering — **wool·gath·er·er** \-t͟hər-ər\ *n*

wool·gath·er·ing \-ˌga-t͟h(ə-)riŋ, -ˌge-t͟h(ə-)riŋ\ *n* (1553) **:** indulgence in idle daydreaming

wool grease *n* (1875) **:** a fatty slightly sticky wax coating the surface of the fibers of sheep's wool — compare WOOL FAT

[1]**wool·ly** *also* **wooly** \ˈwu̇-lē\ *adj* **wool·li·er; -est** (15c) **1 a :** resembling wool **b :** of, relating to, or bearing wool **2 a :** lacking in clearness or sharpness of outline ⟨a ~ TV picture⟩ **b :** marked by mental confusion ⟨~ thinking⟩ **3 :** marked by boisterous roughness or lack of order or restraint ⟨where the West is still ~ —Paul Schubert⟩ — used esp. in the phrase *wild and woolly* — **wool·li·ly** \-lə-lē\ *adv* — **wool·li·ness** *n*

[2]**wool·ly** *also* **wooly** *or* **wool·ie** \ˈwu̇-lē\ *n, pl* **wool·lies** *also* **wool·ies** (ca. 1865) **1 :** a garment made from wool; *esp* **:** underclothing of knitted wool — usu. used in pl. **2** *West & Austral* **:** SHEEP
woolly adel·gid \-ə-ˈdel-jəd\ *n* [*adelgid* ultim. fr. NL *Adelges,* prob. irreg. fr. Gk *adēlos* unseen] (1987) **:** either of two aphids (genus *Adelges*) with a white woolly coating that have been accidentally introduced into No. America: **a :** one (*A. piceae*) native to Europe that is a serious pest of fir trees **b :** one (*A. tsugae*) native to Asia that is a serious pest of hemlocks
woolly aphid *n* (1842) **:** any of several aphids (esp. genus *Eriosoma*) covered with a dense coat of white filaments — called also *woolly aphis*
woolly bear *n* (ca. 1841) **:** any of various rather large very hairy moth caterpillars; *esp* **:** one of a tiger moth
wool·ly–head·ed \ˌwu̇-lē-ˈhe-dəd\ *adj* (1650) **1 :** having hair suggesting wool **2 :** marked by vague or confused perception or thinking
woolly mammoth *n* (1874) **:** a heavy-coated mammoth (*Mammuthus primigenius*) formerly inhabiting the colder parts of the northern hemisphere
woolly monkey *n* (1877) **:** either of two large monkeys (*Lagothrix lagotricha* and *L. flavicauda*) chiefly of the Amazon basin that have short woolly hair, long limbs, and a long prehensile tail
woolly spider monkey *n* (1926) **:** a large monkey (*Brachyteles arachnoides*) of southeastern Brazil with woolly hair, long limbs, a long prehensile tail, and a thumb which is absent or rudimentary

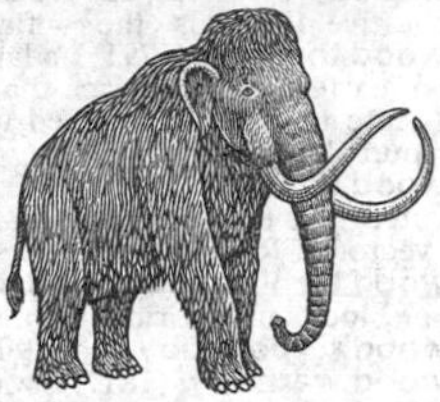
woolly mammoth

wool·pack \ˈwu̇l-ˌpak\ *n* (14c) **1 :** a wrapper of strong fabric into which fleeces are packed for shipment **2 :** the complete package of wool and wrapper
wool·sack \-ˌsak\ *n* (14c) **1** *archaic* **:** WOOLPACK 2 **2 :** a cushion that is the official seat of the Lord Chancellor or his deputy in presiding over the House of Lords
wool·shed \-ˌshed\ *n* (1844) **:** a building or group of buildings (as on an Australian ranch) in which sheep are sheared and wool is prepared for market
wool·skin \-ˌskin\ *n* (15c) **:** a sheepskin having the wool still on it
wool·sort·er's disease \ˈwu̇l-ˌsȯr-tərz-\ *n* (1880) **:** pulmonary anthrax resulting esp. from inhalation of bacterial spores from contaminated wool or hair
woom·era \ˈwu̇-mə-rə\ *also* **wom·mera** \ˈwä-\ *n* [Dharuk (Australian aboriginal language of the Port Jackson area) *wamara*] (1817) **:** a wooden rod with a hooked end used by Australian aborigines for throwing a spear
woops *var of* OOPS
woo·zy \ˈwü-zē, ˈwu̇-\ *adj* **woo·zi·er; -est** [origin unknown] (1897) **1 :** mentally unclear or hazy ⟨seems a little ~, not quite knowing what to say —J. A. Lukacs⟩ **2 :** affected with dizziness, mild nausea, or weakness **3 :** having a soft, indistinct, or unfocused quality **:** VAGUE, FUZZY ⟨~ . . . prose and vaguely beneficent statements —Roz Kaveney⟩ — **woo·zi·ly** *adv* — **woo·zi·ness** *n*
wop \ˈwäp\ *n, often cap* [It dial. *guappo* swaggerer, tough, fr. Sp *guapo,* prob. fr. MF dial. *vape, wape* weak, insipid, fr. L *vappa* wine gone flat] (1908) *usu offensive* **:** ITALIAN
Worces·ter \ˈwu̇s-tər\ *n* (1783) **:** low-fired porcelain containing a frit and steatite produced at Worcester, England, from about 1751 — called also *Worcester china, Worcester porcelain*
Worces·ter·shire sauce \ˈwu̇s-tə(r)-ˌshir-, -shər- *also* -ˌshī(-ə)r-\ *n* [*Worcestershire,* England, where it was orig. made] (1843) **:** a pungent sauce whose ingredients include soy, vinegar, and garlic — called also *Worcestershire*
[1]**word** \ˈwərd\ *n* [ME, fr. OE; akin to OHG *wort* word, L *verbum,* Gk *eirein* to say, speak, Hitt *weriya-* to call, name] (bef. 12c) **1 a :** something that is said **b** *pl* (1) **:** TALK, DISCOURSE ⟨putting one's feelings into ~*s*⟩ (2) **:** the text of a vocal musical composition **c :** a brief remark or conversation ⟨would like to have a ~ with you⟩ **2 a** (1) **:** a speech sound or series of speech sounds that symbolizes and communicates a meaning usu. without being divisible into smaller units capable of independent use (2) **:** the entire set of linguistic forms produced by combining a single base with various inflectional elements without change in the part of speech elements **b** (1) **:** a written or printed character or combination of characters representing a spoken word ⟨the number of ~*s* to a line⟩ — sometimes used with the first letter of a real or pretended taboo word prefixed as an often humorous euphemism ⟨the first man to utter the f ~ on British TV —*Time*⟩ ⟨we were not afraid to use the d ~ and talk about death —Erma Bombeck⟩ (2) **:** any segment of written or printed discourse ordinarily appearing between spaces or between a space and a punctuation mark **c :** a number of bytes processed as a unit and conveying a quantum of information in communication and computer work **3 :** ORDER, COMMAND ⟨don't move till I give the ~⟩ **4** *often cap* **a :** LOGOS **b :** GOSPEL 1a **c :** the expressed or manifested mind and will of God **5 a :** NEWS, INFORMATION ⟨sent ~ that he would be late⟩ **b :** RUMOR **6 :** the act of speaking or of making verbal communication **7 :** SAYING, PROVERB **8 :** PROMISE, DECLARATION ⟨kept her ~⟩ **9 :** a quarrelsome utterance or conversation — usu. used in pl. ⟨they had ~*s* and parted⟩ **10 :** a verbal signal **:** PASSWORD **11** *slang* — used interjectionally to express agreement — **good word 1 :** a favorable statement ⟨put in a *good word* for me⟩ **2 :** good news ⟨what's the *good word*⟩ — **in a word :** in short — **in so many words 1 :** in exactly those terms ⟨implied that such actions were criminal but did not say so *in so many words*⟩ **2 :** in plain forthright language ⟨*in so many words,* she wasn't fit to be seen —Jean Stafford⟩ — **of few words :** not inclined to say more than is necessary **:** LACONIC ⟨a man *of few words*⟩ — **of one's word :** that can be relied on to keep a promise — used only after *man* or *woman* ⟨a man *of his word*⟩ — **upon my word :** with my assurance **:** INDEED, ASSUREDLY ⟨*upon my word,* I've never heard of such a thing⟩
[2]**word** *vi* (13c) *archaic* **:** SPEAK ~ *vt* **:** to express in words **:** PHRASE ⟨a carefully ~*ed* reply⟩
word·age \ˈwər-dij\ *n* (1829) **1 a :** WORDS **b :** VERBIAGE 1 **2 :** the number or quantity of words **3 :** WORDING
word–association test *n* (1946) **:** a test of personality and mental function in which the subject is required to respond to each of a series of words with the first word that comes to mind or with a word of a specified class of words (as antonyms)
word·book \ˈwərd-ˌbu̇k\ *n* (1598) **:** VOCABULARY, DICTIONARY
word class *n* (1914) **:** a linguistic form class whose members are words; *esp* **:** PART OF SPEECH
word–for–word *adj* (ca. 1611) **:** being in or following the exact words **:** VERBATIM ⟨a ~ translation⟩
word for word *adv* (14c) **:** in the exact words **:** VERBATIM
word–hoard \ˈwərd-ˌhȯrd\ *n* [trans. of OE *wordhord*] (1850) **:** a supply of words **:** VOCABULARY
word·ing \ˈwər-diŋ\ *n* (1649) **:** the act or manner of expressing in words **:** PHRASEOLOGY
word·less \ˈwərd-ləs\ *adj* (15c) **1 :** not expressed in or accompanied by words ⟨a ~ picture book⟩ **2 :** SILENT, SPEECHLESS ⟨sat ~ throughout the meeting⟩ — **word·less·ly** *adv* — **word·less·ness** *n*
word·mon·ger \-ˌməŋ-gər, -ˌmäŋ-\ *n* (1590) **:** a writer who uses words for show or without particular regard for meaning
word–mon·ger·ing \-g(ə-)riŋ\ *n* (1851) **:** the use of empty or bombastic words
word–of–mouth \ˌwərd-ə(v)-ˈmau̇th\ *adj* (ca. 1812) **:** orally communicated; *also* **:** generated from or reliant on oral publicity ⟨~ customers⟩ ⟨a ~ business⟩
word of mouth (1553) **:** oral communication; *esp* **:** oral often inadvertent publicity
word order *n* (1882) **:** the order or arrangement of words in a phrase, clause, or sentence
word·play \ˈwərd-ˌplā\ *n* (1844) **:** playful use of words **:** verbal wit
word processing *n* (1970) **:** the production of typewritten documents (as business letters) with automated and usu. computerized typing and text-editing equipment — **word process** *vb*
word processor *n* (1970) **:** a keyboard-operated terminal usu. with a video display and a magnetic storage device for use in word processing; *also* **:** software (as for a computer system) to perform word processing
word·smith \ˈwərd-ˌsmith\ *n* (1873) **:** a person who works with words; *esp* **:** a skillful writer — **word·smith·ery** \-ˌsmi-thə-rē\ *n*
word square *n* (ca. 1879) **:** a series of words of equal length arranged in a square pattern to read the same horizontally and vertically
word stress *n* (1898) **:** the manner in which stresses are distributed on the syllables of a word — called also *word accent*
word wrap *n* (1977) **:** a word processing feature that automatically transfers a word for which there is insufficient space from the end of one line of text to the beginning of the next
wordy \ˈwər-dē\ *adj* **word·i·er; -est** (12c) **1 :** using or containing many and usu. too many words **2 :** of or relating to words **:** VERBAL — **word·i·ly** \ˈwər-də-lē\ *adv* — **word·i·ness** \ˈwər-dē-nəs\ *n*
syn WORDY, VERBOSE, PROLIX, DIFFUSE mean using more words than necessary to express thought. WORDY may also imply loquaciousness or garrulity ⟨a *wordy* speech⟩. VERBOSE suggests a resulting dullness, obscurity, or lack of incisiveness or precision ⟨the *verbose* position papers⟩. PROLIX suggests unreasonable and tedious dwelling on details ⟨habitually transformed brief anecdotes into *prolix* sagas⟩. DIFFUSE stresses lack of compactness and pointedness of style ⟨*diffuse* memoirs that are so many shaggy-dog stories⟩.
wore *past of* WEAR
[1]**work** \ˈwərk\ *n* [ME *werk, work,* fr. OE *werc, weorc;* akin to OHG *werc* work, Gk *ergon,* Av *varəzem* activity] (bef. 12c) **1 :** activity in which one exerts strength or faculties to do or perform something: **a :** sustained physical or mental effort to overcome obstacles and achieve an objective or result **b :** the labor, task, or duty that is one's accustomed means of livelihood **c :** a specific task, duty, function, or assignment often being a part or phase of some larger activity **2 a :** energy expended by natural phenomena **b :** the result of such energy ⟨sand dunes are the ~ of sea and wind⟩ **c :** the transference of energy that is produced by the motion of the point of application of a force and is measured by multiplying the force and the displacement of its point of application in the line of action **3 a :** something that results from a particular manner or method of working, operating, or devising ⟨careful police ~⟩ ⟨clever camera ~⟩ **b :** something that results from the use or fashioning of a particular material ⟨porcelain ~⟩ **4 a :** a fortified structure (as a fort, earthen barricade, or trench) **b** *pl* **:** structures in engineering (as docks, bridges, or embankments) or mining (as shafts or tunnels) **5** *pl but sing or pl in constr* **:** a place where industrial labor is carried on **:** PLANT, FACTORY **6** *pl* **:** the working or moving parts of a mechanism ⟨the ~*s* of a clock⟩ **7 a :** something produced or accomplished by effort, exertion, or exercise of skill ⟨this book is the ~ of many hands⟩ **b :** something produced by the exercise of creative talent or expenditure of creative effort **:** artistic production ⟨an early ~ by a major writer⟩ **8** *pl* **:** performance of moral or religious acts ⟨salvation by ~*s*⟩ **9 a :** effective operation **:** EFFECT, RESULT ⟨wait for time to do its healing ~⟩ **b :** manner of working **:** WORKMANSHIP, EXECUTION **10 :** the material or piece of material that is operated upon at any stage in the process of manufacture **11** *pl* **a :** everything possessed, available, or belonging ⟨the whole ~*s,* rod, reel, tackle box, went overboard⟩ ⟨ordered pizza with the ~*s*⟩ **b :** subjection to drastic treatment **:** all possible abuse — usu. used with *get* ⟨get the ~*s*⟩ or *give* ⟨gave them the ~*s*⟩ — **at work 1 :** engaged in working **:** BUSY; *esp* **:** engaged in one's regular occupation **2 :** having effect **:** OPERATING, FUNCTIONING — **in the works :** in process of preparation, development, or completion — **in work 1 :** in process of being done **2** *of a horse* **:** in training — **out of work :** without regular employment **:** JOBLESS
syn WORK, LABOR, TRAVAIL, TOIL, DRUDGERY, GRIND mean activity involving effort or exertion. WORK may imply activity of body, of mind, of a machine, or of a natural force ⟨too tired to do any *work*⟩. LABOR applies to physical or intellectual work involving great and often strenuous exertion ⟨farmers demanding fair compensation for their *labor*⟩. TRAVAIL is bookish for labor involving pain or suffering ⟨years of *travail* were lost when the house burned⟩. TOIL implies prolonged and fatiguing labor ⟨his lot would be years of back-breaking *toil*⟩. DRUDGERY suggests dull and irksome labor ⟨an editorial job

with a good deal of *drudgery*⟩. GRIND implies labor exhausting to mind or body ⟨the *grind* of the assembly line⟩.
syn WORK, EMPLOYMENT, OCCUPATION, CALLING, PURSUIT, MÉTIER, BUSINESS mean a specific sustained activity engaged in esp. in earning one's living. WORK may apply to any purposeful activity whether remunerative or not ⟨her *work* as a hospital volunteer⟩. EMPLOYMENT implies work for which one has been engaged and is being paid by an employer ⟨your *employment* with this firm is hereby terminated⟩. OCCUPATION implies work in which one engages regularly esp. as a result of training ⟨his *occupation* as a trained auto mechanic⟩. CALLING applies to an occupation viewed as a vocation or profession ⟨the ministry seemed my true *calling*⟩. PURSUIT suggests a trade, profession, or avocation followed with zeal or steady interest ⟨her family considered medicine the only proper *pursuit*⟩. MÉTIER implies a calling or pursuit for which one believes oneself to be esp. fitted ⟨acting was my one and only *métier*⟩. BUSINESS suggests activity in commerce or the management of money and affairs ⟨the *business* of managing a hotel⟩.

[2]**work** *adj* (14c) **1 :** used for work ⟨a ~ elephant⟩ **2 :** suitable or styled for wear while working ⟨~ clothes⟩ **3 :** involving or engaged in work ⟨a ~ gang⟩ ⟨~ hours⟩

[3]**work** *vb* **worked** \ˈwərkt\ *or* **wrought** \ˈrȯt\; **work·ing** [ME *werken, worken,* fr. OE *wyrcan;* akin to OE *weorc*] *vt* (bef. 12c) **1 :** to bring to pass **:** EFFECT ⟨~ miracles⟩ **2 a :** to fashion or create a useful or desired product by expending labor or exertion on **:** FORGE, SHAPE ⟨~ flint into tools⟩ **b :** to make or decorate with needlework; *esp* **:** EMBROIDER **3 a :** to prepare for use by stirring or kneading **b :** to bring into a desired form by a gradual process of cutting, hammering, scraping, pressing, or stretching ⟨~ cold steel⟩ **4 :** to set or keep in motion, operation, or activity **:** cause to operate or produce ⟨a pump *~ed* by hand⟩ ⟨~ farmland⟩ **5 :** to solve (a problem) by reasoning or calculation — often used with *out* **6 a :** to cause to toil or labor ⟨*~ed* their horses nearly to death⟩ **b :** to make use of **:** EXPLOIT **c :** to control or guide the operation of ⟨switches are *~ed* from a central tower⟩ **7 a :** to carry on an operation or perform a job through, at, in, or along ⟨the peddler *~ed* the corner⟩ ⟨a sportscaster hired to ~ the game⟩ **b :** to greet and talk with in a friendly way in order to ingratiate oneself or achieve a purpose ⟨politicians *~ing* the crowd⟩ ⟨*~ed* the room⟩ **8 :** to pay for or achieve with labor or service ⟨*~ed* my way through college⟩ ⟨*~ed* my way up in the company⟩ **9 a :** to get (oneself or an object) into or out of a condition or position by gradual stages **b :** CONTRIVE, ARRANGE ⟨we can ~ it so that you can take your vacation⟩ **10 a :** to practice trickery or cajolery on for some end ⟨*~ed* the management for a free ticket⟩ **b :** EXCITE, PROVOKE ⟨*~ed* myself into a rage⟩ ~ *vi* **1 a :** to exert oneself physically or mentally esp. in sustained effort for a purpose or under compulsion or necessity **b :** to perform or carry through a task requiring sustained effort or continuous repeated operations ⟨*~ed* all day over a hot stove⟩ **c :** to perform work or fulfill duties regularly for wages or salary ⟨*~s* in publishing⟩ **2 :** to function or operate according to plan or design ⟨hinges ~ better with oil⟩ **3 :** to exert an influence or tendency **4 :** to produce a desired effect or result **:** SUCCEED ⟨a plan that will ~⟩ **5 a :** to make way slowly and with difficulty **:** move or progress laboriously ⟨*~ed* up to the presidency⟩ **b :** to sail to windward **6 :** to permit of being worked **:** react in a specified way to being worked ⟨this wood *~s* easily⟩ **7 a :** to be in agitation or restless motion **b :** FERMENT 1 **c :** to move slightly in relation to another part **d :** to get into a specified condition by slow or imperceptible movements ⟨the knot *~ed* loose⟩ — **work on 1 :** AFFECT ⟨*worked on* my sympathies⟩ **2 :** to strive to influence or persuade — **work upon :** to have effect upon **:** operate on

work·able \ˈwər-kə-bəl\ *adj* (1545) **1 :** capable of being worked ⟨a ~ material⟩ **2 :** PRACTICABLE, FEASIBLE ⟨a ~ system⟩ — **work·abil·i·ty** \ˌwər-kə-ˈbi-lə-tē\ *n* — **work·able·ness** \ˈwər-kə-bəl-nəs\ *n*

work·a·day \ˈwər-kə-ˌdā\ *adj* [alter. of earlier *workyday,* fr. obs. *workyday,* n. workday] (1554) **1 :** of, relating to, or suited for working days ⟨~ clothes⟩ **2 :** ORDINARY, PROSAIC ⟨~ activities⟩ ⟨a ~ life⟩

work·a·hol·ic \ˌwər-kə-ˈhȯ-lik, -ˈhä-\ *n* [*work* + *-aholic*] (1968) **:** a compulsive worker — **workaholic** *adj* — **work·a·hol·ism** \ˈwər-kə-ˌhȯ-ˌli-zəm, -ˌhä-\ *n*

work–around \ˈwərk-ə-ˌrau̇nd\ *n* (1971) **:** a plan or method to circumvent a problem (as in computer software) without eliminating it

work·bag \ˈwərk-ˌbag\ *n* (1754) **:** a bag for implements or materials for work; *esp* **:** a bag for needlework

work·bas·ket \-ˌbas-kət\ *n* (1684) **:** a basket for needlework

work·bench \-ˌbench\ *n* (1677) **:** a bench on which work esp. of mechanics, machinists, and carpenters is performed

work·boat \-ˌbōt\ *n* (1937) **:** a boat used for work purposes (as commercial fishing and ferrying supplies) rather than for sport or for passenger or naval service

work·book \-ˌbu̇k\ *n* (1857) **1 :** a worker's manual **2 :** a booklet outlining a course of study **3 :** a record of work done **4 :** a student's book of problems to be solved directly on the pages

work·box \-ˌbäks\ *n* (1605) **:** a box for work instruments and materials

work camp *n* (1931) **:** a camp for workers: as **a :** PRISON CAMP 1 **b :** a short-term group project in which individuals from one or more religious organizations volunteer their labor

work·day \ˈwərk-ˌdā\ *n* (13c) **1 :** a day on which work is performed as distinguished from a day off **2 :** the period of time in a day during which work is performed — **workday** *adj*

worked \ˈwərkt\ *adj* (1740) **:** that has been subjected to some process of development, treatment, or manufacture ⟨a newly ~ field⟩

worked up *adj* (1874) **:** emotionally aroused **:** EXCITED

work·er \ˈwər-kər\ *n* (14c) **1 a :** one that works esp. at manual or industrial labor or with a particular material ⟨a factory ~⟩ — often used in combination **b :** a member of the working class **2 :** any of the sexually underdeveloped and usu. sterile members of a colony of social ants, bees, wasps, or termites that perform most of the labor and protective duties of the colony

worker–priest *n* (1949) **:** a French Roman Catholic priest who for missionary purposes spends part of each weekday as a worker in a secular job

workers' compensation *n* (1925) **:** a system of insurance that reimburses an employer for damages that must be paid to an employee for injury occurring in the course of employment — called also *workers' comp* \-ˈkämp\

work ethic *n* (1951) **:** a belief in work as a moral good

work·fare \ˈwərk-ˌfer\ *n* [*work* + wel*fare*] (1968) **:** a welfare program in which recipients are required to perform usu. public-service work

work farm *n* (1909) **:** a farm on which persons guilty of minor law violations are confined

work·folk \ˈwərk-ˌfōk\ *or* **work·folks** \-ˌfōks\ *n pl* (14c) **:** working people; *esp* **:** farm workers

work·force \ˈwərk-ˌfȯrs\ *n* (1931) **1 :** the workers engaged in a specific activity or enterprise ⟨the factory's ~⟩ **2 :** the number of workers potentially assignable for any purpose ⟨the nation's ~⟩

work·horse \ˈwərk-ˌhȯrs\ *n* (1543) **1 :** a horse used chiefly for labor as distinguished from driving, riding, or racing **2 a** (1) **:** a person who performs most of the work of a group task (2) **:** a hardworking person **b :** something that is markedly useful, durable, or dependable **c :** HORSE 7

work·house \-ˌhau̇s\ *n* (1630) **1** *Brit* **:** POORHOUSE **2 :** a house of correction for persons guilty of minor law violations

work in *vt* (1598) **1 :** to insert or cause to penetrate by repeated or continued effort **2 :** to interpose or insinuate gradually or unobtrusively ⟨*worked in* a few topical jokes⟩

[1]**work·ing** \ˈwər-kiŋ\ *n* (14c) **1 :** the manner of functioning or operating **:** OPERATION — usu. used in pl. ⟨the inner *~s* of the government⟩ **2 :** an excavation or group of excavations made in mining, quarrying, or tunneling — usu. used in pl.

[2]**working** *adj* (1532) **1 :** engaged in work esp. for wages or a salary ⟨a ~ journalist⟩ ⟨a ~ mother⟩ **2 :** adequate to permit work to be done ⟨a ~ majority⟩ **3 :** assumed or adopted to permit or facilitate further work or activity ⟨a ~ draft⟩ **4 :** spent at work ⟨~ life⟩ **5 :** being in use or operation ⟨a ~ farm⟩

working asset *n* (ca. 1914) **:** an asset other than a capital asset

working capital *n* (1889) **:** capital actively turned over in or available for use in the course of business activity: **a :** the excess of current assets over current liabilities **b :** all capital of a business except that invested in capital assets

working–class *adj* (1839) **:** of, relating to, deriving from, or suitable to the class of wage earners ⟨~ virtues⟩ ⟨a ~ family⟩

working class *n* (1789) **:** the class of people who work for wages usu. at manual labor

working day *n* (15c) **:** WORKDAY

working dog *n* (1885) **:** a dog suitable by size, breeding, or training for useful work (as draft or herding) esp. as distinguished from one suitable primarily for pet, show, or sporting use

working fluid *n* (1878) **:** a fluid working substance

work·ing·man \ˈwər-kiŋ-ˌman\ *n* (1638) **:** one who works for wages usu. at manual labor

working papers *n pl* (1928) **:** official documents legalizing the employment of a minor

working substance *n* (1855) **:** a usu. fluid substance that through changes of temperature, volume, and pressure is the means of carrying out thermodynamic processes or cycles (as in a heat engine)

work·ing·wom·an \ˈwər-kiŋ-ˌwu̇-mən\ *n* (ca. 1814) **:** WORKWOMAN

work·less \ˈwər-kləs\ *adj* (15c) **:** being without work **:** UNEMPLOYED — **work·less·ness** *n*

work·load \ˈwərk-ˌlōd\ *n* (1943) **1 :** the amount of work or of working time expected or assigned ⟨students with a heavy ~⟩ **2 :** the amount of work performed or capable of being performed (as by a mechanical device) usu. within a specific period

work·man \ˈwərk-mən\ *n* (bef. 12c) **1 :** WORKINGMAN **2 :** ARTISAN

work·man·like \-ˌlīk\ *adj* (1739) **:** characterized by the skill and efficiency typical of a good workman ⟨~ thoroughness⟩; *also* **:** competent and skillful but not outstanding or original ⟨an adequate . . . reporter who turned out ~ copy —Tom Clancy⟩

work·man·ly \-lē\ *adj* (1545) **:** WORKMANLIKE

work·man·ship \-ˌship\ *n* (1523) **1 :** something effected, made, or produced **:** WORK **2 :** the art or skill of a workman; *also* **:** the quality imparted to a thing in the process of making ⟨a vase of exquisite ~⟩

work·mate \ˈwərk-ˌmāt\ *n* (ca. 1837) *chiefly Brit* **:** a fellow worker

workmen's compensation insurance *n* (ca. 1917) **:** WORKERS' COMPENSATION

work of art (1629) **1 :** a product of one of the fine arts; *esp* **:** a painting or sculpture of high artistic quality **2 :** something giving high aesthetic satisfaction to the viewer or listener

work off *vt* (1662) **:** to dispose of or get rid of by work or activity

work·out \ˈwərk-ˌau̇t\ *n* (ca. 1894) **1 :** a practice or exercise to test or improve one's fitness for athletic competition, ability, or performance **2 :** a test of one's ability, capacity, stamina, or suitability **3 :** an undertaking or plan intended to resolve a problem of indebtedness esp. in lieu of bankruptcy or foreclosure proceedings

work out *vt* (1534) **1 a :** to bring about by labor and exertion ⟨*work out* your own salvation —Phil 2:12 (AV)⟩ **b :** to solve (as a problem) by a process of reasoning or calculation **c :** to devise, arrange, or achieve by resolving difficulties ⟨after many years of wrangling, *worked out* a definite agreement —A. A. Butkus⟩ **d :** DEVELOP ⟨the final situation is not *worked out* with psychological profundity —Leslie Rees⟩ **2 :** to discharge (as a debt) by labor **3 :** to exhaust (as a mine) by working ~ *vi* **1 a :** to prove effective, practicable, or suitable ⟨how this will actually *work out* I don't know —Milton Kotler⟩ **b :** to amount to a total or calculated figure — used with *at* or *to* **2 :** to engage in a workout ⟨*works out* regularly at the gym⟩

work over *vt* (1835) **1 :** to subject to thorough examination, study, or treatment ⟨shelf stock *worked over* by shoppers⟩ **2 :** to do over **:** REWORK ⟨saved the play by *working* the first act *over*⟩ **3 :** to beat up or manhandle with thoroughness ⟨the gang *worked* me *over*⟩

work·peo·ple \ˈwərk-ˌpē-pəl\ *n pl* (1708) *chiefly Brit* **:** WORKERS, EMPLOYEES

work·piece \-ˌpēs\ *n* (1919) **:** a piece of work in process of manufacture

\ə\ **abut** \ᵊ\ kitten, F table \ər\ **further** \a\ **ash** \ā\ **ace** \ä\ **mop, mar**
\au̇\ **out** \ch\ **chin** \e\ **bet** \ē\ **easy** \g\ **go** \i\ **hit** \ī\ **ice** \j\ **job**
\ŋ\ **sing** \ō\ **go** \ȯ\ **law** \ȯi\ **boy** \th\ **thin** \t͟h\ **the** \ü\ **loot** \u̇\ **foot**
\y\ yet \zh\ **vision, beige** \k̲, ⁿ, œ, ue, ʸ\ *see* Guide to Pronunciation

work·place \-ˌplās\ *n* (ca. 1828) **:** a place (as a shop or factory) where work is done
work print *n* (1937) **:** a completely edited motion-picture print used as a guide in cutting the original negative from which the final production prints will be made
work·room \ˈwərk-ˌrüm, -ˌru̇m\ *n* (1665) **:** a room used for work
work·shop \-ˌshäp\ *n* (1562) **1 :** a small establishment where manufacturing or handicrafts are carried on **2 :** WORKROOM **3 :** a usu. brief intensive educational program for a relatively small group of people that focuses esp. on techniques and skills in a particular field
work song *n* (1841) **:** a song sung in rhythm with work
work·sta·tion \-ˌstā-shən\ *n* (1931) **1 :** an area with equipment for the performance of a specialized task usu. by a single individual **2 a :** an intelligent terminal or personal computer usu. connected to a computer network **b :** a powerful microcomputer used esp. for scientific or engineering work
work stoppage *n* (1943) **:** concerted cessation of work by a group of employees usu. more spontaneous and less serious than a strike
work–study program *n* (1946) **:** a program planned to give high school or college students work experience
work·ta·ble \ˈwərk-ˌtā-bəl\ *n* (1788) **:** a table for holding working materials and implements; *esp* **:** a small table with drawers and other conveniences for needlework
work–to–rule *n* (1950) **:** the practice of working to the strictest interpretation of the rules as a job action
work·up \ˈwərk-ˌəp\ *n* (1939) **:** an intensive diagnostic study
work–up \ˈwərk-ˌəp\ *n* (1903) **:** an unintended mark on a printed sheet caused by the rising of spacing material
work up *vt* (15c) **1 :** to stir up **:** ROUSE **2 :** to produce by mental or physical work ⟨*worked up* a comedy act⟩ ⟨*worked up* a sweat in the gym⟩ **~** *vi* **:** to rise gradually in intensity or emotional tone
work·week \ˈwərk-ˌwēk\ *n* (1921) **:** the hours or days of work in a calendar week ⟨40-hour ~⟩ ⟨a 5-day ~⟩ ⟨a shortened ~⟩
work·wom·an \-ˌwu̇-mən\ *n* (14c) **:** a woman who works
[1]**world** \ˈwər(-ə)ld\ *n* [ME, fr. OE *woruld* human existence, this world, age (akin to OHG *weralt* age, world); akin to OE *wer* man, *eald* old — more at VIRILE, OLD] (bef. 12c) **1 a :** the earthly state of human existence **b :** life after death — used with a qualifier ⟨the next ~⟩ **2 :** the earth with its inhabitants and all things upon it **3 :** individual course of life **:** CAREER **4 :** the inhabitants of the earth **:** the human race **5 a :** the concerns of the earth and its affairs as distinguished from heaven and the life to come **b :** secular affairs **6 :** the system of created things **:** UNIVERSE **7 a :** a division or generation of the inhabitants of the earth distinguished by living together at the same place or at the same time ⟨the medieval ~⟩ **b :** a distinctive class of persons or their sphere of interest or activity ⟨the academic ~⟩ ⟨the digital ~⟩ **8 :** human society ⟨withdraw from the ~⟩ **9 :** a part or section of the earth that is a separate independent unit **10 :** the sphere or scene of one's life and action ⟨living in your own little ~⟩ **11 :** an indefinite multitude or a great quantity or distance ⟨makes a ~ of difference⟩ ⟨a ~ away⟩ **12 :** the whole body of living persons **:** PUBLIC ⟨announced their discovery to the ~⟩ **13 :** KINGDOM 5 ⟨the animal ~⟩ **14 :** a celestial body (as a planet) — **for all the world :** in every way **:** EXACTLY ⟨copies which look *for all the world* like the original⟩ — **in the world :** among innumerable possibilities **:** EVER — used as an intensive ⟨what *in the world* is it⟩ — **out of this world :** of extraordinary excellence **:** SUPERB
[2]**world** *adj* (12c) **1 :** of or relating to the world ⟨a ~ championship⟩ **2 a :** extending or found throughout the world **:** WORLDWIDE ⟨brought about ~ peace⟩ **b :** involving or applying to part of or the whole world ⟨a ~ tour⟩ ⟨a ~ state⟩ **c :** internationally recognized **:** RENOWNED, DISTINGUISHED ⟨a ~ authority on gemstones⟩
world beat *n* (1984) **:** WORLD MUSIC — usu. hyphenated when used attributively
world–beat·er \ˈwərl(d)-ˌbē-tər\ *n* (ca. 1888) **:** one that excels all others of its kind **:** CHAMPION
world–class *adj* (1950) **:** being of the highest caliber in the world ⟨a ~ athlete⟩
world federalism *n* (1950) **1 :** federalism on a worldwide basis **2** *cap W&F* **a :** the principles and policies of the World Federalists **b :** the body or movement composed of World Federalists
world federalist *n* (1951) **1 :** an adherent or advocate of world federalism **2** *cap W&F* **:** a member of a movement arising after World War II advocating the formation of a federal union of the nations of the world with limited but positive governmental powers
world·ling \ˈwər(-ə)ld-liŋ, ˈwərl-liŋ\ *n* (1549) **:** a person engrossed in the concerns of this present world
world·ly \ˈwər(-ə)ld-lē, ˈwərl-lē\ *adj* (bef. 12c) **1 :** of, relating to, or devoted to this world and its pursuits rather than to religion or spiritual affairs **2 :** WORLDLY-WISE ***syn*** see EARTHLY — **world·li·ness** *n*
world·ly–mind·ed \ˌwərl(d)-lē-ˈmīn-dəd\ *adj* (1579) **:** devoted to or engrossed in worldly interests — **world·ly–mind·ed·ness** *n*
world·ly–wise \ˈwərl(d)-lē-ˌwīz\ *adj* (15c) **:** possessing a practical and often shrewd understanding of human affairs ***syn*** see SOPHISTICATED
world music *n* (1982) **:** popular music originating from or influenced by non-Western musical traditions and often having a danceable rhythm — usu. hyphenated when used attributively
world power *n* (1860) **:** a political unit (as a nation or state) powerful enough to affect the entire world by its influence or actions
world premiere *n* (1925) **:** the first regular performance (as of a theatrical production) anywhere in the world
World Series *n* [fr. *World Series,* annual championship of Major League Baseball] (1951) **:** a contest or event that is the most important or prestigious of its kind ⟨the *World Series* of the equestrian world⟩
world's fair *n* (1850) **:** an international exposition featuring exhibits and participants from all over the world
world–shak·ing \ˈwərl(d)-ˌshā-kiŋ\ *adj* (1598) **:** EARTHSHAKING
world soul *n* (1844) **:** an animating spirit or creative principle related to the world as the soul is to the individual being
world·view \-ˌvyü\ *n* (1858) **:** WELTANSCHAUUNG
world war *n* (1909) **:** a war engaged in by all or most of the principal nations of the world; *esp, cap both Ws* **:** either of two such wars of the first half of the 20th century
world–wea·ry \ˈwərld-ˌwir-ē\ *adj* (1750) **:** feeling or showing fatigue from or boredom with the life of the world and esp. material pleasures — **world–wea·ri·ness** *n*
[1]**world·wide** \-ˈwīd\ *adj* (1632) **:** extended throughout or involving the entire world
[2]**worldwide** *adv* (1892) **:** throughout the world
World Wide Web *n* (1990) **:** a part of the Internet accessed through a graphical user interface and containing documents often connected by hyperlinks — called also *Web*
[1]**worm** \ˈwərm\ *n, often attrib* [ME, fr. OE *wyrm* serpent, worm; akin to OHG *wurm* serpent, worm, L *vermis* worm] (bef. 12c) **1 a :** EARTHWORM; *broadly* **:** an annelid worm **b :** any of numerous relatively small elongated usu. naked and soft-bodied animals (as a grub, pinworm, tapeworm, shipworm, or slowworm) **2 a :** a human being who is an object of contempt, loathing, or pity **:** WRETCH **b :** something that torments or devours from within **3** *archaic* **:** SNAKE, SERPENT **4 :** HELMINTHIASIS — usu. used in pl. **5 :** something (as a mechanical device) spiral or vermiculate in form or appearance: as **a :** the thread of a screw **b :** a short revolving screw whose threads gear with the teeth of a worm wheel or a rack **c :** ARCHIMEDES' SCREW; *also* **:** a conveyor working on the principle of such a screw **6 :** a usu. small self-contained and self-replicating computer program that invades computers on a network and usu. performs a destructive action — **worm·like** \-ˌlīk\ *adj*
[2]**worm** *vi* (1610) **:** to move or proceed sinuously or insidiously **~** *vt* **1 a :** to proceed or make (one's way) insidiously or deviously ⟨~ their way into positions of power —Bill Franzen⟩ **b :** to insinuate or introduce (oneself) by devious or subtle means **c :** to cause to move or proceed in or as if in the manner of a worm **2 :** to wind rope or yarn spirally round and between the strands of (a cable or rope) before serving **3 :** to obtain or extract by artful or insidious questioning or by pleading, asking, or persuading — usu. used with *out of* ⟨finally ~*ed* the truth out of him⟩ **4 :** to treat (an animal) with a drug to destroy or expel parasitic worms
worm–eat·en \ˈwərm-ˌē-tᵊn\ *adj* (14c) **1 a :** eaten or burrowed by worms ⟨~ timber⟩ **b :** PITTED **2 :** WORN-OUT, ANTIQUATED
worm·er \ˈwər-mər\ *n* (ca. 1934) **:** a drug used in veterinary medicine to worm an animal
worm fence *n* (1652) **:** a zigzag fence consisting of interlocking rails supported by crossed poles — called also *snake fence, Virginia fence*
worm gear *n* (1851) **1 :** WORM WHEEL **2 :** a gear of a worm and a worm wheel working together

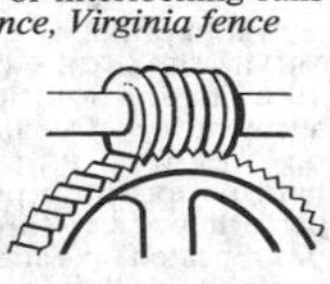
worm gear 2

worm·hole \ˈwərm-ˌhōl\ *n* (1593) **1 :** a hole or passage burrowed by a worm **2 :** a hypothetical structure of space-time envisioned as a long thin tunnel connecting points that are separated in space and time
worm·seed \-ˌsēd\ *n* (14c) **:** any of various plants whose seeds possess anthelmintic properties: as **a :** any of several artemisias **b :** a widely naturalized tropical American goosefoot (*Chenopodium ambrosioides*) — compare EPAZOTE
worm's–eye \ˈwərmz-ˌī\ *adj* (1908) **:** seen from ground level or from the lowest levels of a hierarchy ⟨the bird's-eye view of the executive and the ~ view of the employee —*Current Biog.*⟩
worm snake *n* (1885) **:** a small terrestrial colubrid snake (*Carphophis amoenus*) of the eastern U.S. that is dark above and pinkish red below
worm wheel *n* (1677) **:** a toothed wheel gearing with the thread of a worm
worm·wood \ˈwərm-ˌwu̇d\ *n* [ME *wormwode,* alter. of *wermode,* fr. OE *wermōd;* akin to OHG *wermuota* wormwood] (15c) **1 :** ARTEMISIA; *esp* **:** a European plant (*Artemisia absinthium*) that has silvery silky-haired leaves and drooping yellow flower heads and yields a bitter dark green oil used in absinthe **2 :** something bitter or grievous **:** BITTERNESS
wormy \ˈwər-mē\ *adj* **worm·i·er; -est** (15c) **1 :** containing, abounding in, or infested with or as if with worms ⟨~ flour⟩ ⟨a ~ dog⟩; *also* **:** damaged by worms **:** WORM-EATEN ⟨~ timbers⟩ **2 :** resembling or suggestive of a worm
worn *past part of* WEAR
worn–out \ˈwȯrn-ˈau̇t\ *adj* (15c) **:** exhausted or used up by or as if by wear
wor·ri·ment \ˈwər-ē-mənt, ˈwə-rē-\ *n* (1833) **:** an act or instance of worrying; *also* **:** TROUBLE, WORRY
wor·ri·some \-səm\ *adj* (1833) **1 :** causing distress or worry ⟨~ news⟩ **2 :** inclined to worry or fret ⟨investors feeling ~⟩ — **wor·ri·some·ly** *adv* — **wor·ri·some·ness** *n*
[1]**wor·ry** \ˈwər-ē, ˈwə-rē\ *vb* **wor·ried; wor·ry·ing** [ME *worien,* fr. OE *wyrgan;* akin to OHG *wurgen* to strangle, Lith *veržti* to constrict] *vt* (bef. 12c) **1** *dial Brit* **:** CHOKE, STRANGLE **2 a :** to harass by tearing, biting, or snapping esp. at the throat **b :** to shake or pull at with the teeth ⟨a terrier ~*ing* a rat⟩ **c :** to touch or disturb something repeatedly **d :** to change the position of or adjust by repeated pushing or hauling **3 a :** to assail with rough or aggressive attack or treatment **:** TORMENT **b :** to subject to persistent or nagging attention or effort **4 :** to afflict with mental distress or agitation **:** make anxious **~** *vi* **1** *dial Brit* **:** STRANGLE, CHOKE **2 :** to move, proceed, or progress by unceasing or difficult effort **:** STRUGGLE **3 :** to feel or experience concern or anxiety **:** FRET ⟨~*ing* about his health⟩ — **wor·ried·ly** \-(r)ēd-lē, -(r)əd-\ *adv* — **wor·ri·er** \-(r)ē-ər\ *n* — **wor·ry·ing·ly** *adv*
syn WORRY, ANNOY, HARASS, HARRY, PLAGUE, PESTER, TEASE mean to disturb or irritate by persistent acts. WORRY implies an incessant goading or attacking that drives one to desperation ⟨pursued a policy of *worrying* the enemy⟩. ANNOY implies disturbing one's composure or peace of mind by intrusion, interference, or petty attacks ⟨you're doing that just to *annoy* me⟩. HARASS implies petty persecutions or burdensome demands that exhaust one's nervous or mental power ⟨*harassed* on all sides by creditors⟩. HARRY may imply heavy oppression or maltreatment ⟨the strikers had been *harried* by thugs⟩. PLAGUE implies a painful and persistent affliction ⟨*plagued* all her life by poverty⟩. PESTER stresses the repetition of petty attacks ⟨constantly *pestered* with trivial complaints⟩. TEASE suggests an attempt to break down one's resistance or rouse to wrath ⟨children *teased* the dog⟩.

[2]**worry** *n, pl* **worries** (1804) **1 a :** mental distress or agitation resulting from concern usu. for something impending or anticipated **:** ANXIETY **b :** an instance or occurrence of such distress or agitation **2 :** a cause of worry **:** TROUBLE, DIFFICULTY ***syn*** see CARE

worry beads *n pl* (1956) **:** a string of beads that can be fingered to keep one's hands occupied

worry line *n* (1972) **:** a crease or wrinkle on the forehead or between the eyebrows

wor·ry·wart \ˈwər-ē-ˌwȯrt, ˈwə-rē-\ *n* (1936) **:** a person who is inclined to worry unduly

[1]**worse** \ˈwərs\ *adj, comparative of* BAD *or of* ILL [ME *werse, worse,* fr. OE *wiersa, wyrsa;* akin to OHG *wirsiro* worse] (bef. 12c) **1 :** of more inferior quality, value, or condition **2 a :** more unfavorable, difficult, unpleasant, or painful **b :** more faulty, unsuitable, or incorrect **c :** less skillful or efficient **3 :** bad, evil, or corrupt in a greater degree **:** more reprehensible **4 :** being in poorer health **:** SICKER

[2]**worse** *n* (bef. 12c) **:** one that is worse ⟨threatened expulsion and ~⟩

[3]**worse** *adv, comparative of* BAD *or of* ILL (bef. 12c) **1 :** in a worse manner **:** to a worse extent or degree **2 :** what is worse

wors·en \ˈwər-sᵊn\ *vb* **wors·ened; wors·en·ing** \ˈwərs-niŋ, ˈwər-sᵊn-iŋ\ *vt* (13c) **:** to make worse ~ *vi* **:** to become worse ⟨the weather began to ~⟩

wors·er \ˈwər-sər\ *adj or adv* (15c) *archaic* **:** WORSE ⟨I cannot hate thee ~ than I do —Shak.⟩

[1]**wor·ship** \ˈwər-shəp *also* ˈwȯr-\ *n* [ME *worshipe* worthiness, respect, reverence paid to a divine being, fr. OE *weorthscipe* worthiness, respect, fr. *weorth* worthy, worth + *-scipe* -ship] (bef. 12c) **1** *chiefly Brit* **:** a person of importance — used as a title for various officials (as magistrates and some mayors) **2 :** reverence offered a divine being or supernatural power; *also* **:** an act of expressing such reverence **3 :** a form of religious practice with its creed and ritual **4 :** extravagant respect or admiration for or devotion to an object of esteem ⟨~ of the dollar⟩

[2]**worship** *vb* **-shipped** *also* **-shiped; -ship·ping** *also* **-ship·ing** *vt* (13c) **1 :** to honor or reverence as a divine being or supernatural power **2 :** to regard with great or extravagant respect, honor, or devotion ⟨a celebrity *worshipped* by her fans⟩ ~ *vi* **:** to perform or take part in worship or an act of worship ***syn*** see REVERE — **wor·ship·per** *or* **wor·ship·er** *n*

wor·ship·ful \ˈwər-shəp-fəl *also* ˈwȯr-\ *adj* (14c) **1 a** *archaic* **:** NOTABLE, DISTINGUISHED **b** *chiefly Brit* — used as a title for various persons or groups of rank or distinction **2 :** giving or expressing worship or veneration — **wor·ship·ful·ly** \-fə-lē\ *adv* — **wor·ship·ful·ness** *n*

wor·ship·less \-shəp-ləs\ *adj* (1765) **:** lacking worship or worshippers

[1]**worst** \ˈwərst\ *adj, superlative of* BAD *or of* ILL [ME *werste, worste,* fr. OE *wierresta, wyrsta,* superl. of the root of OE *wiersa* worse] (bef. 12c) **1 :** most corrupt, bad, evil, or ill ⟨his ~ fault⟩ **2 a :** most unfavorable, difficult, unpleasant, or painful ⟨the ~ news⟩ ⟨your ~ enemy⟩ **b :** most unsuitable, faulty, unattractive, or ill-conceived ⟨has the ~ table manners⟩ **c :** least skillful or efficient ⟨the ~ person for the job⟩ **3 :** most wanting in quality, value, or condition ⟨the ~ results⟩ — **the worst way :** very much ⟨such men . . . need indoctrination *the worst way* —J. G. Cozzens⟩ — often used with *in* ⟨wanted a new bicycle in *the worst way*⟩

[2]**worst** *adv, superlative of* ILL *or* ILLY *or of* BAD *or* BADLY (bef. 12c) **1 :** to the extreme degree of badness or inferiority ⟨the ~ dressed person⟩ **2 :** to the greatest or highest degree ⟨groups who need the subsidies ~ lose out —T. W. Arnold⟩

[3]**worst** *n, pl* **worst** (13c) **:** one that is worst — **at worst :** under the worst circumstances

[4]**worst** *vt* (1636) **:** to get the better of **:** DEFEAT

worst–case *adj* (1964) **:** involving, projecting, or providing for the worst possible circumstances or outcome of a given situation ⟨a ~ scenario⟩

wor·sted \ˈwu̇s-təd, ˈwər-stəd\ *n* [ME, fr. *Worsted* (now *Worstead*), England] (13c) **:** a smooth compact yarn from long wool fibers used esp. for firm napless fabrics, carpeting, or knitting; *also* **:** a fabric made from worsted yarns — **worsted** *adj*

[1]**wort** \ˈwərt, ˈwȯrt\ *n* [ME, fr. OE *wyrt* root, herb, plant — more at ROOT] (bef. 12c) **:** PLANT; *esp* **:** an herbaceous plant — usu. used in combination ⟨louse*wort*⟩

[2]**wort** *n* [ME, fr. OE *wyrt;* akin to MHG *würze* brewer's wort, OE *wyrt* root, herb] (bef. 12c) **:** a sweet liquid drained from mash and fermented to make beer and whiskey

[1]**worth** \ˈwərth\ *vi* [ME, fr. OE *weorthan;* akin to OHG *werdan* to become, L *vertere* to turn, Lith *versti* to overturn, Skt *vartate* he turns] (bef. 12c) *archaic* **:** BECOME — usu. used in the phrase *woe worth*

[2]**worth** *adj* [ME, fr. OE *weorth* worthy, of (a specified) value; akin to OHG *werd* worthy, worth] (bef. 12c) **1** *archaic* **:** having monetary or material value **2** *archaic* **:** ESTIMABLE — **for all one is worth :** to the fullest extent of one's value or ability

[3]**worth** *n* (bef. 12c) **1 a :** monetary value ⟨farmhouse and lands of little ~⟩ **b :** the equivalent of a specified amount or figure ⟨a dollar's ~ of gas⟩ **2 :** the value of something measured by its qualities or by the esteem in which it is held ⟨a literary heritage of great ~⟩ **3 a :** moral or personal value ⟨trying to teach human ~⟩ **b :** MERIT, EXCELLENCE ⟨a field in which we have proved our ~⟩ **4 :** WEALTH, RICHES

[4]**worth** *prep* (13c) **1 a :** equal in value to **b :** having assets or income equal to **2 :** deserving of ⟨well ~ the effort⟩ — **worth one's salt :** of substantial or significant value or merit

worth·ful \ˈwərth-fəl\ *adj* (bef. 12c) **1 :** full of merit ⟨a good and ~ person⟩ **2 :** having value ⟨the ~ aspects of their culture⟩

worth·less \ˈwərth-ləs\ *adj* (ca. 1577) **1 a :** lacking worth **:** VALUELESS ⟨~ currency⟩ **b :** USELESS ⟨~ to continue searching⟩ **2 :** CONTEMPTIBLE, DESPICABLE ⟨a ~ criminal⟩ — **worth·less·ly** *adv* — **worth·less·ness** *n*

worth·while \-ˈhwī(-ə)l, -ˈwī(-ə)l\ *adj* (1662) **1 :** being worth the time or effort spent ⟨~ preparations⟩ **2 :** WORTHY 1 ⟨a ~ cause⟩ — **worth·while·ness** *n*

[1]**wor·thy** \ˈwər-t͟hē\ *adj* **wor·thi·er; -est** (13c) **1 a :** having worth or value **:** ESTIMABLE ⟨a ~ cause⟩ **b :** HONORABLE, MERITORIOUS ⟨~ candidates⟩ **2 :** having sufficient worth or importance ⟨~ to be remembered⟩ — **wor·thi·ly** \ˈwər-t͟hə-lē\ *adv* — **wor·thi·ness** \-t͟hē-nəs\ *n*

[2]**worthy** *n, pl* **worthies** (14c) **:** a worthy or prominent person

-worthy *adj comb form* **1 :** fit or safe for ⟨a sea*worthy* vessel⟩ **2 :** of sufficient worth for ⟨a news*worthy* event⟩

[1]**wot** *pres 1st & 3d sing of* WIT

[2]**wot** \ˈwät\ *vb* **wot·ted; wot·ting** [ME, alter. of *witen* — more at WIT] (14c) *chiefly Brit* **:** KNOW — often used with *of*

would \wəd, əd, d, ˈwu̇d\ *vb, past of* WILL [ME *wolde,* fr. OE; akin to OHG *wolta* wished, desired] (bef. 12c) **1 a** *archaic* **:** WISHED, DESIRED **b** *archaic* **:** wish for **:** WANT **c** (1) **:** strongly desire **:** WISH ⟨I ~ I were young again⟩ — often used without a subject and with *that* in a past or conditional construction ⟨~ that I had heeded your advice⟩ (2) — used in auxiliary function with *rather* or *sooner* to express preference ⟨he ~ sooner die than face them⟩ **2 a** — used in auxiliary function to express wish, desire, or intent ⟨those who ~ forbid gambling⟩ **b** — used in auxiliary function to express willingness or preference ⟨as ye ~ that men should do to you —Lk 6:31 (AV)⟩ **c** — used in auxiliary function to express plan or intention ⟨said we ~ come⟩ **3** — used in auxiliary function to express custom or habitual action ⟨we ~ meet often for lunch⟩ **4** — used in auxiliary function to express consent or choice ⟨~ put it off if he could⟩ **5 a** — used in auxiliary function in the conclusion of a conditional sentence to express a contingency or possibility ⟨if he were coming, he ~ be here now⟩ **b** — used in auxiliary function in a noun clause (as one completing a statement of desire, request, or advice) ⟨we wish that he ~ go⟩ **6** — used in auxiliary function to express probability or presumption in past or present time ⟨~ have won if I had not tripped⟩ **7 :** COULD ⟨the barrel ~ hold 20 gallons⟩ **8** — used in auxiliary function to express a request with which voluntary compliance is expected ⟨~ you please help us⟩ **9** — used in auxiliary function to express doubt or uncertainty ⟨the explanation . . . ~ seem satisfactory⟩ **10 :** SHOULD ⟨knew I ~ enjoy the trip⟩ ⟨~ be glad to know the answer⟩

would–be \ˈwu̇d-ˈbē\ *adj* (1647) **:** desiring, intending, professing, or having the potential to be ⟨a ~ actor⟩

would·est \ˈwu̇-dəst\ *archaic past 2d sing of* WILL

wouldn't \ˈwu̇-dᵊnt, -dᵊn, *dial also* ˈwu̇-tᵊn(t) *or* ˌwu̇nt\ (1675) **:** would not

wouldst \wu̇dst, ˈwu̇dst, wətst\ *archaic past 2d sing of* WILL

[1]**wound** \ˈwünd, *archaic or dial* ˈwau̇nd\ *n* [ME, fr. OE *wund;* akin to OHG *wunta* wound] (bef. 12c) **1 a :** an injury to the body (as from violence, accident, or surgery) that typically involves laceration or breaking of a membrane (as the skin) and usu. damage to underlying tissues **b :** a cut or breach in a plant usu. due to an external agent **2 :** a mental or emotional hurt or blow **3 :** something resembling a wound in appearance or effect; *esp* **:** a rift in or blow to a political body or social group

[2]**wound** *vt* (bef. 12c) **:** to cause a wound to or in ~ *vi* **:** to inflict a wound

[3]**wound** \ˈwau̇nd\ *past and past part of* WIND

[1]**wound·ed** \ˈwün-dəd\ *n pl* (bef. 12c) **:** wounded persons

[2]**wounded** *adj* (14c) **:** injured, hurt by, or suffering from a wound ⟨a ~ leg⟩ ⟨~ feelings⟩

wound·less \ˈwün(d)-ləs\ *adj* (1579) **1 :** free from wounds **:** UNWOUNDED **2** *obs* **:** INVULNERABLE ⟨the ~ air —Shak.⟩

wove *past of* WEAVE

[1]**woven** *past part of* WEAVE

[2]**wo·ven** \ˈwō-vən\ *n* (1930) **:** a woven fabric

wove paper \ˈwōv-\ *n* [*wove* (archaic pp. of *weave*)] (1795) **:** paper made with a revolving roller covered with wires so woven as to produce no fine lines running across the grain — compare LAID PAPER

[1]**wow** \ˈwau̇\ *interj* (1513) — used to express strong feeling (as pleasure or surprise)

[2]**wow** *n* (1920) **:** a striking success **:** HIT

[3]**wow** *vt* (1924) **:** to excite to enthusiastic admiration or approval ⟨a performance that ~*ed* the critics⟩

[4]**wow** *n* [imit.] (1932) **:** a distortion in reproduced sound consisting of a slow rise and fall of pitch caused by speed variation in the reproducing system

wow·ser \ˈwau̇-zər\ *n* [origin unknown] (1899) *chiefly Austral* **:** an obtrusively puritanical person

WP *abbr* **1** wettable powder **2** word processing; word processor

WPA *abbr* Works Progress Administration

W particle *n* [weak] (1963) **:** either of two particles about 80 times heavier than a proton that along with the Z particle are transmitters of the weak force and that can have a positive or negative charge

wpc *abbr* watts per channel

WPI *abbr* Wholesale Price Index

WPM *abbr* words per minute

WR *abbr* **1** warehouse receipt **2** world record

[1]**wrack** \ˈrak\ *n* [ME *wrak,* fr. MD or MLG; akin to OE *wræc* something driven by the sea] (14c) **1 a :** a wrecked ship **b :** WRECKAGE **c :** WRECK **d** *dial* **:** the violent destruction of a structure, machine, or vehicle **2 a :** marine vegetation; *esp* **:** KELP **b :** dried seaweeds

[2]**wrack** *n* [ME, fr. OE *wræc* misery, punishment, something driven by the sea; akin to OE *wrecan* to drive, punish — more at WREAK] (14c) **1 :** RUIN, DESTRUCTION **2 :** a remnant of something destroyed

[3]**wrack** *vt* (1562) **:** to utterly ruin **:** WRECK

[4]**wrack** *vb* [by alter.] (ca. 1555) **:** [4]RACK

[5]**wrack** *n* (1591) **:** [3]RACK 2

[6]**wrack** *n* (1794) **:** [1]RACK

wrack·ful \ˈrak-fəl\ *adj* (1558) **:** DESTRUCTIVE

wraith \ˈrāth\ *n, pl* **wraiths** \ˈrāths *also* ˈrāt͟hz\ [origin unknown] (1513) **1 :** the exact likeness of a living person seen usu. just before death as an apparition **b :** GHOST, SPECTER **2 :** an insubstantial form or semblance **:** SHADOW **3 :** a barely visible gaseous or vaporous column — **wraith·like** \-ˌlīk\ *adj*

[1]**wran·gle** \ˈraŋ-gəl\ *vb* **wran·gled; wran·gling** \-g(ə-)liŋ\ [ME; akin to OHG *ringan* to struggle — more at WRING] *vi* (14c) **1 :** to dispute angrily or peevishly **:** BICKER **2 :** to engage in argument or controversy

\ə\ **abut** \ᵊ\ kitten, F table \ər\ **further** \a\ **ash** \ā\ **ace** \ä\ mop, mar
\au̇\ **out** \ch\ **chin** \e\ **bet** \ē\ **easy** \g\ **go** \i\ **hit** \ī\ **ice** \j\ **job**
\ŋ\ **sing** \ō\ **go** \ȯ\ **law** \ȯi\ **boy** \th\ **thin** \t͟h\ **the** \ü\ **loot** \u̇\ **foot**
\y\ **yet** \zh\ **vision, beige** \k̲, ⁿ, œ, ue, ʸ\ *see* Guide to Pronunciation

~ *vt* **1 :** to obtain by persistent arguing or maneuvering : WANGLE **2** [back-formation fr. *wrangler*] **:** to herd and care for (livestock and esp. horses) on the range

[2]**wrangle** *n* (15c) **1 :** an angry, noisy, or prolonged dispute or quarrel **2 :** the action or process of wrangling ***syn*** see QUARREL

wran·gler \-g(ə-)lər\ *n* (ca. 1510) **1 :** a bickering disputant **2** [short for *horse-wrangler,* prob. part trans. of MexSp *caballerango* groom] **:** a ranch hand who takes care of the saddle horses; *broadly* : COWBOY

[1]**wrap** \'rap\ *vb* **wrapped; wrap·ping** [ME *wrappen*] *vt* (14c) **1 a :** to cover esp. by winding or folding **b :** to envelop and secure for transportation or storage : BUNDLE **c :** ENFOLD, EMBRACE **d :** to coil, fold, draw, or twine (as string or cloth) around something **2 a :** SURROUND, ENVELOP **b :** to suffuse or surround with an aura or state ⟨the affair was *wrapped* in scandal⟩ **c :** to involve completely : ENGROSS — usu. used with *up* **3 :** to conceal or obscure as if by enveloping **4 :** to enclose as if with a protective covering **5 :** to finish filming or recording ⟨~ a movie⟩ ~ *vi* **1 :** to wind, coil, or twine so as to encircle or cover something **2 :** to put on clothing : DRESS — usu. used with *up* **3 :** to be subject to covering, enclosing, or packaging — usu. used with *up* **4 :** to come to completion in filming or recording

[2]**wrap** *n* (15c) **1 a** (1) **:** WRAPPER, WRAPPING (2) **:** material used for wrapping ⟨plastic ~⟩ **b :** an article of clothing that may be wrapped around a person; *esp* **:** an outer garment (as a coat or shawl) **c :** BLANKET **d :** a treatment for the care of the skin in which material (as hot wet cloth or seaweed) is wrapped around the entire body; *also* **:** this material **2 :** a single turn or convolution of something wound around an object **3** *pl* **a :** RESTRAINT **b :** a shroud of secrecy ⟨a plan kept under ~*s*⟩ **4 :** the completion of a schedule or session for filming or recording **5 :** a thin flat piece of bread that is rolled around a filling (as of meat, fish, or vegetables)

[3]**wrap** *adj* (1923) **:** WRAPAROUND 1

[1]**wrap·around** \'rap-ə-ˌrau̇nd\ *adj* (1923) **1 :** made to be wrapped around something and esp. the body ⟨a ~ skirt⟩ **2 a :** shaped to follow a contour; *esp* **:** made to curve from the front around to the side ⟨~ sunglasses⟩ ⟨~ terraces⟩ **b :** extending laterally to the outermost limits of the field of vision ⟨a ~ movie screen⟩

[2]**wraparound** *n* (1924) **1 :** a garment (as a dress) made with a full-length opening and adjusted to the figure by wrapping around **2 :** an object that encircles or esp. curves and laps over another

wrap·per \'ra-pər\ *n* (15c) **1 :** that in which something is wrapped: as **a :** a tobacco leaf used for the outside covering esp. of cigars **b** (1) **:** JACKET 3c(1) (2) **:** the paper cover of a book not bound in boards **c :** a paper wrapped around a newspaper or magazine in the mail **2 :** one that wraps **3 :** an article of clothing worn wrapped around the body

wrapping *n* (14c) **:** something used to wrap an object : WRAPPER

wrap–up \'rap-ˌəp\ *n* (1951) **1 :** a summarizing report **2 :** a concluding part : FINALE

wrap up *vt* (ca. 1568) **1 :** SUMMARIZE, SUM UP **2 a :** to bring to a usu. successful conclusion **b :** CINCH, SEW UP ⟨has the nomination *wrapped up*⟩

wrasse \'ras\ *n, pl* **wrasses** *also* **wrasse** [Corn *gwragh, wragh* hag, wrasse] (ca. 1672) **:** any of a large family (Labridae) of elongate usu. brilliantly colored marine bony fishes that usu. bury themselves in sand at night and include important food fishes as well as a number of popular aquarium fishes

[1]**wrath** \'rath, *chiefly Brit* 'rȯth\ *n* [ME, fr. OE *wrǣththo,* fr. *wrāth* wroth — more at WROTH] (bef. 12c) **1 :** strong vengeful anger or indignation **2 :** retributory punishment for an offense or a crime : divine chastisement ***syn*** see ANGER

[2]**wrath** *adj* [alter. of *wroth*] (1535) *archaic* **:** WRATHFUL

wrath·ful \-fəl\ *adj* (13c) **1 :** filled with wrath : IRATE **2 :** arising from, marked by, or indicative of wrath — **wrath·ful·ly** \-fə-lē\ *adv* — **wrath·ful·ness** *n*

wrathy \'ra-thē, *chiefly Brit* 'rȯ-\ *adj* (1718) **:** WRATHFUL

wreak \'rēk *also* 'rek\ *vt* [ME *wreken,* fr. OE *wrecan* to drive, punish, avenge; akin to OHG *rehhan* to avenge and perh. to L *urgēre* to drive on, urge] (bef. 12c) **1 a** *archaic* **:** AVENGE **b :** to cause the infliction of (vengeance or punishment) **2 :** to give free play or course to (malevolent feeling) **3 :** BRING ABOUT, CAUSE ⟨~ havoc⟩

wreath \'rēth\ *n, pl* **wreaths** \'rēthz, 'rēths\ [ME *wrethe,* fr. OE *writha;* akin to OE *wrīthan* to twist — more at WRITHE] (bef. 12c) **1 :** something intertwined or arranged in a circular shape: as **a :** a band of intertwined flowers or leaves worn as a mark of honor or victory : GARLAND ⟨a laurel ~⟩ **b :** a decorative arrangement of foliage or flowers on a circular base ⟨a Christmas ~⟩ **2 :** something having a circular or coiling form ⟨a ~ of smoke⟩

wreathe \'rēth\ *vb* **wreathed; wreath·ing** [*wreath*] *vt* (1530) **1 a :** to shape into a wreath **b :** INTERWEAVE **c :** to cause to coil about something **2 :** to twist or contort so as to show folds or creases **3 :** to encircle or adorn with or as if with a wreath ~ *vi* **1 :** to twist in coils : WRITHE **2 a :** to take on the shape of a wreath **b :** to move or extend in circles or spirals

wreathy \'rē-thē, -thē\ *adj* (1644) **1 :** having the form of a wreath **2 :** constituting a wreath

[1]**wreck** \'rek\ *n* [ME *wrek,* fr. AF, of Scand origin; akin to ON *rek* wreck; akin to OE *wrecan* to drive] (12c) **1 :** something cast up on the land by the sea esp. after a shipwreck **2 a :** SHIPWRECK **b :** the action of wrecking or fact or state of being wrecked : DESTRUCTION **c :** a violent and destructive crash ⟨was injured in a car ~⟩ **3 a :** a hulk or the ruins of a wrecked ship **b :** the broken remains of something wrecked or otherwise ruined **c :** something disabled or in a state of ruin or dilapidation ⟨the house was a ~⟩; *also* **:** a person or animal of broken constitution, health, or spirits ⟨he's a nervous ~⟩

[2]**wreck** *vt* (14c) **1 :** to cast ashore **2 a :** to reduce to a ruinous state by or as if by violence ⟨a country ~*ed* by war⟩ ⟨ambition ~*ed* his marriage⟩ **b :** SHIPWRECK **c :** to ruin, damage, or imperil by a wreck ⟨~*ed* the car⟩ **3 :** BRING ABOUT, WREAK ⟨~ havoc⟩ ~ *vi* **1 :** to become wrecked **2 :** to rob, salvage, or repair wreckage or a wreck

wreck·age \'re-kij\ *n* (1837) **1 :** the act of wrecking : the state of being wrecked **2 a :** something that has been wrecked **b :** broken and disordered parts or material from something wrecked

wreck·er \'re-kər\ *n* (1693) **1 a :** one that searches for or works on the wrecks of ships (as for rescue or for plunder) **b :** TOW TRUCK **2 :** one that wrecks; *esp* **:** one whose work is the demolition of buildings

wrecking ball *n* (1947) **:** a heavy iron or steel ball swung or dropped by a derrick to demolish old buildings — called also *wrecker's ball*

wrecking bar *n* (1924) **:** a small crowbar with a claw for pulling nails at one end and a slight bend for prying at the other end

wren \'ren\ *n* [ME *wrenne,* fr. OE *wrenna;* akin to OHG *rentilo* wren] (bef. 12c) **1 :** any of a family (Troglodytidae) of small typically brownish oscine singing birds; *esp* **:** a very small widely distributed bird (*Troglodytes troglodytes*) that has a short erect tail and is noted for its song **2 :** any of various small singing birds resembling the true wrens in size and habits

[1]**wrench** \'rench\ *vb* [ME, fr. OE *wrencan;* akin to OHG *renken* to twist and perh. to L *vergere* to bend, incline] *vi* (bef. 12c) **1 :** to move with a violent twist; *also* **:** to undergo twisting **2 :** to pull or strain at something with violent twisting ~ *vt* **1 :** to twist violently **2 :** to injure or disable by a violent twisting or straining ⟨~*ed* her back⟩ **3 :** CHANGE; *esp* **:** DISTORT, PERVERT **4 a :** to pull or tighten by violent twisting or with violence **b :** to snatch forcibly : WREST **5 :** to cause to suffer mental anguish : RACK — **wrench·ing·ly** \'ren-chiŋ-lē\ *adv*

[2]**wrench** *n* (1530) **1 a :** a violent twisting or a pull with or as if with twisting **b :** a sharp twist or sudden jerk straining muscles or ligaments; *also* **:** the resultant injury (as of a joint) **c :** a distorting or perverting alteration **d :** acute emotional distress : sudden violent mental change **2 :** a hand or power tool for holding, twisting, or turning an object (as a bolt or nut) **3 :** MONKEY WRENCH 2

[1]**wrest** \'rest\ *vt* [ME *wrasten, wresten,* fr. OE *wrǣstan;* akin to ON *reista* to bend and prob. to OE *wrigian* to turn — more at WRY] (bef. 12c) **1 :** to pull, force, or move by violent wringing or twisting movements **2 :** to gain with difficulty by or as if by force, violence, or determined labor

[2]**wrest** *n* (14c) **1 :** the action of wresting : WRENCH **2** *archaic* **:** a key or wrench used for turning pins in a stringed instrument (as a piano)

[1]**wres·tle** \'re-səl, 'ra-\ *vb* **wres·tled; wres·tling** \'res-liŋ, 'ras-; 're-sᵊl-iŋ, 'ra-\ [ME *wrastlen, wrestlen,* fr. OE *wrǣstlian,* freq. of *wrǣstan*] *vi* (bef. 12c) **1 :** to contend by grappling with and striving to trip or throw an opponent down or off balance **2 :** to combat an opposing tendency or force ⟨*wrestling* with his conscience⟩ **3 :** to engage in deep thought, consideration, or debate **4 :** to engage in or as if in a violent or determined struggle ⟨*wrestling* with cumbersome luggage⟩ ~ *vt* **1 a :** to engage in (a match, bout, or fall) in wrestling **b :** to wrestle with ⟨~ an alligator⟩ **2 :** to move, maneuver, or force with difficulty — **wres·tler** \'res-lər, 'ras-; 're-sᵊl-ər, 'ra-\ *n*

[2]**wrestle** *n* (1593) **:** the action or an instance of wrestling : STRUGGLE; *esp* **:** a wrestling bout

wres·tling \'res-liŋ, 'ras-; 're-sᵊl-iŋ, 'ra-\ *n* (bef. 12c) **:** a sport or contest in which two unarmed individuals struggle hand to hand with each attempting to subdue or unbalance the other

wretch \'rech\ *n* [ME *wrecche,* fr. OE *wrecca* outcast, exile; akin to OHG *hrechjo* fugitive, OE *wrecan* to drive, drive out — more at WREAK] (bef. 12c) **1 :** a miserable person : one who is profoundly unhappy or in great misfortune **2 :** a base, despicable, or vile person

wretch·ed \'re-chəd\ *adj* [ME, irreg. fr. *wretch*] (12c) **1 :** deeply afflicted, dejected, or distressed in body or mind **2 :** extremely or deplorably bad or distressing ⟨was in ~ health⟩ ⟨a ~ accident⟩ **3 a :** being or appearing mean, miserable, or contemptible ⟨dressed in ~ old clothes⟩ **b :** very poor in quality or ability : INFERIOR ⟨~ workmanship⟩ — **wretch·ed·ly** *adv* — **wretch·ed·ness** *n*

[1]**wrig·gle** \'ri-gəl\ *vb* **wrig·gled; wrig·gling** \-g(ə-)liŋ\ [ME, fr. or akin to MLG *wriggeln* to wriggle; akin to OE *wrigian* to turn — more at WRY] *vi* (15c) **1 :** to move the body or a bodily part to and fro with short writhing motions like a worm : SQUIRM **2 :** to move or advance by twisting and turning **3 :** to extricate or insinuate oneself or reach a goal as if by wriggling ~ *vt* **1 :** to cause to move in short quick contortions **2 :** to introduce, insinuate, or bring into a state or place by or as if by wriggling — **wrig·gly** \-g(ə-)lē\ *adj*

[2]**wriggle** *n* (1709) **1 :** a short or quick writhing motion or contortion **2 :** a formation or marking of sinuous design

wrig·gler \'ri-g(ə-)lər\ *n* (1631) **:** one that wriggles; *esp* **:** WIGGLER 1

wright \'rīt\ *n* [ME, fr. OE *wyrhta, wryhta* worker, maker; akin to OE *weorc* work — more at WORK] (bef. 12c) **:** a worker skilled in the manufacture esp. of wooden objects — usu. used in combination ⟨ship*wright*⟩ ⟨wheel*wright*⟩

wring \'riŋ\ *vb* **wrung** \'rəŋ\; **wring·ing** \'riŋ-iŋ\ [ME, fr. OE *wringan;* akin to OHG *ringan* to struggle, Lith *rengtis* to bend down, OE *wyrgan* to strangle — more at WORRY] *vt* (bef. 12c) **1 :** to squeeze or twist esp. so as to make dry or to extract moisture or liquid ⟨~ a towel dry⟩ **2 :** to extract or obtain by or as if by twisting and compressing ⟨~ water from a towel⟩ ⟨~ a confession from the suspect⟩ **3 a :** to twist so as to strain or sprain into a distorted shape ⟨I could ~ your neck⟩ **b :** to twist together (clasped hands) as a sign of anguish **4 :** to affect painfully as if by wringing : TORMENT ⟨a tragedy that ~*s* the heart⟩ ~ *vi* **:** SQUIRM, WRITHE — **wring** *n*

wring·er \'riŋ-ər\ *n* (14c) **:** one that wrings: as **a :** a machine or device for pressing out liquid or moisture ⟨a clothes ~⟩ **b :** something that causes pain, hardship, or exertion ⟨his illness put them through the ~⟩

[1]**wrin·kle** \'riŋ-kəl\ *n* [ME, back-formation fr. *wrinkled* twisted, winding, prob. fr. OE *gewrinclod,* pp. of *gewrinclian* to wind, fr. *ge-,* perfective prefix + *-wrinclian* (akin to *wrencan* to wrench) — more at CO-] (14c) **1 :** a small ridge or furrow esp. when formed on a surface by the shrinking or contraction of a smooth substance : CREASE; *specif* **:** one in the skin esp. when due to age, worry, or fatigue **2 a :** METHOD, TECHNIQUE **b :** a change in a customary procedure or method **c :** something new or different : INNOVATION **3 :** IMPERFECTION, IRREGULARITY — **wrin·kly** \-k(ə-)lē\ *adj*

[2]**wrinkle** *vb* **wrin·kled; wrin·kling** \-k(ə-)liŋ\ *vi* (15c) **:** to become marked with or contracted into wrinkles ~ *vt* **:** to contract into wrinkles : PUCKER

wrist \'rist\ *n* [ME, fr. OE; akin to MHG *rist* wrist, ankle, OE *wrǣstan* to twist — more at WREST] (bef. 12c) **1 :** the joint or the region of the joint between the human hand and the arm or a corresponding part on a lower animal **2 :** the part of a garment or glove covering the wrist

wrist·band \'ris(t)-ˌband\ *n* (1571) **1 :** the part of a sleeve covering the wrist **2 :** a band encircling the wrist

wrist·let \ˈris(t)-lət\ *n* (1844) **:** a band encircling the wrist; *esp* **:** a close-fitting knitted band attached to the top of a glove or the end of a sleeve

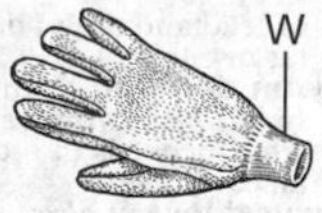

W wristlet

wrist·lock \ˈrist-ˌläk\ *n* (1921) **:** a wrestling hold in which one contestant is thrown or made helpless by a twisting grip on the wrist
wrist pin *n* (1853) **:** a stud or pin that forms a journal (as in a crosshead) for a connecting rod
wrist shot *n* (ca. 1899) **:** a quick usu. short-range shot in ice hockey made while the puck is against the blade of the stick by snapping the blade quickly forward
wrist·watch \ˈrist-ˌwäch\ *n* (1896) **:** a small watch that is attached to a bracelet or strap and is worn around the wrist
wrist wrestling *n* (1968) **:** a form of arm wrestling in which opponents interlock thumbs instead of gripping hands
wristy \ˈris-tē\ *adj* **wrist·i·er; -est** (1867) **:** involving or using a lot of wrist movement (as in stroking a ball)
writ \ˈrit\ *n* [ME, fr. OE; akin to OE *wrītan* to write] (bef. 12c) **1 :** something written **:** WRITING ⟨Sacred *Writ*⟩ **2 a :** a formal written document; *specif* **:** a legal instrument in epistolary form issued under seal in the name of the English monarch **b :** an order or mandatory process in writing issued in the name of the sovereign or of a court or judicial officer commanding the person to whom it is directed to perform or refrain from performing an act specified therein ⟨~ of detinue⟩ ⟨~ of entry⟩ ⟨~ of execution⟩ **c :** the power and authority of the issuer of such a written order — usu. used with *run* ⟨outside the United States where . . . our ~ does not run —Dean Acheson⟩
writ·able \ˈrī-tə-bəl\ *adj* (1782) **1 :** capable of being put in writing **2 :** being an electronic storage medium capable of having new data written on it ⟨a ~ DVD⟩
write \ˈrīt\ *vb* **wrote** \ˈrōt\; **writ·ten** \ˈri-tᵊn\ *also* **writ** \ˈrit\ *or dial* **wrote; writ·ing** \ˈrī-tiŋ\ [ME, fr. OE *wrītan* to scratch, draw, inscribe; akin to OHG *rīzan* to tear and perh. to Gk *rhinē* file, rasp] *vt* (bef. 12c) **1 a :** to form (as characters or symbols) on a surface with an instrument (as a pen) **b :** to form (as words) by inscribing the characters or symbols of on a surface **c :** to spell in writing ⟨words *written* alike but pronounced differently⟩ **d :** to cover, fill, or fill in by writing ⟨*wrote* ten pages⟩ ⟨~ a check⟩ **2 :** to set down in writing: as **a :** DRAW UP, DRAFT ⟨~ a will⟩ **b** (1) **:** to be the author of **:** COMPOSE ⟨~*s* poems and essays⟩ (2) **:** to compose in musical form ⟨~ a string quartet⟩ **c :** to express in literary form ⟨if I could ~ the beauty of your eyes —Shak.⟩ **d :** to communicate by letter ⟨~*s* that they are coming⟩ **e :** to use or exhibit (a specific script, language, or literary form or style) in writing ⟨~ Braille⟩ ⟨~*s* French with ease⟩ **f :** to write contracts or orders for; *esp* **:** UNDERWRITE ⟨~ life insurance⟩ **3 :** to make a permanent impression of **4 :** to communicate with in writing ⟨we'll ~ you when we get there⟩ **5 :** ORDAIN, FATE ⟨so be it, it is *written* —D. C. Peattie⟩ **6 :** to make evident or obvious ⟨guilt *written* on his face⟩ **7 :** to force, effect, introduce, or remove by writing ⟨~ oneself into fame and fortune —Charles Lee⟩ **8 :** to take part in or bring about (something worth recording) **9 a :** to introduce (information) into the storage device or medium of a computer **b :** to transfer (information) from the main memory of a computer to a storage or output device **10 :** SELL ⟨~ a stock option⟩ ~ *vi* **1 a :** to make significant characters or inscriptions; *also* **:** to permit or be adapted to writing **b :** to form or produce written letters, words, or sentences **2 :** to compose, communicate by, or send a letter **3 a :** to produce a written work **b :** to compose music — **write one's own ticket :** to select a course of action or position entirely according to one's wishes — **writ large :** on a larger scale or in a more prominent manner ⟨the problems of modern totalitarianism are only our own problems *writ large* —*Times Lit. Supp.*⟩ — **writ small :** on a smaller scale
write–down \ˈrīt-ˌdau̇n\ *n* (1932) **:** a deliberate reduction in the book value of an asset (as to reflect the effect of obsolescence)
write down *vt* (1588) **1 :** to record in written form **2 a :** to depreciate, disparage, or injure by writing **b :** to reduce in status, rank, or value; *esp* **:** to reduce the book value of ~ *vi* **:** to write so as to appeal to a lower level of taste, comprehension, or intelligence
write–in \ˈrīt-ˌin\ *n* (1932) **1 :** a vote cast by writing in the name of a candidate **2 :** a candidate whose name is written in
write in *vt* (14c) **1 :** to insert in a document or text **2 a :** to insert (a name not listed on a ballot or voting machine) in an appropriate space **b :** to cast (a vote) in this manner
write–off \ˈrīt-ˌȯf\ *n* (1905) **1 :** an elimination of an item from the books of account **2 a :** a reduction in book value of an item (as by way of depreciation) **b :** a tax deduction of an amount of depreciation, expense, or loss **3** *chiefly Brit* **:** something (as a damaged vehicle) or someone regarded or conceded as a loss
write off *vt* (1889) **1 :** to eliminate (an asset) from the books **:** enter as a loss or expense ⟨*write off* a bad loan⟩ **2 :** to regard or concede to be lost ⟨most were content to *write off* 1979 and look optimistically ahead —*Money*⟩; *also* **:** DISMISS ⟨was *written off* as an expatriate highbrow —Brendan Gill⟩
write out *vt* (15c) **:** to write esp. in a full and complete form
writ·er \ˈrī-tər\ *n* (bef. 12c) **:** one that writes: as **a :** AUTHOR **b :** one who writes stock options
writ·er·ly \ˈrī-tər-lē\ *adj* (1957) **:** of, relating to, or typical of a writer
writer's block *n* (1950) **:** a psychological inhibition preventing a writer from proceeding with a piece
writer's cramp *n* (1853) **:** a painful spasmodic contraction of muscles of the hand or fingers brought on by excessive writing
write–up \ˈrīt-ˌəp\ *n* (1885) **1 :** a written account; *esp* **:** a flattering article **2 :** a deliberate increase in the book value of an asset (as to reflect the effect of inflation)
write up *vt* (15c) **1 :** to make a write-up of **2 :** to report (a person) esp. for some violation of law or rules
writhe \ˈrīth\ *vb* **writhed; writh·ing** [ME, fr. OE *wrīthan;* akin to ON *rītha* to twist] *vt* (bef. 12c) **1 a :** to twist into coils or folds **b :** to twist so as to distort **:** WRENCH **c :** to twist (the body or a bodily part) in pain **2 :** INTERTWINE ~ *vi* **1 :** to move or proceed with twists and turns ⟨*writhed* to the music⟩ **2 :** to twist from or as if from pain or struggling **3 :** to suffer keenly — **writhe** *n*
writh·en \ˈri-thən\ *adj* [ME, fr. OE, fr. pp. of *wrīthan*] (bef. 12c) **:** being twisted or contorted ⟨~ trees⟩ ⟨a ~ smile⟩
writing *n* (13c) **1 :** the act or process of one who writes: as **a :** the act or art of forming visible letters or characters; *specif* **:** HANDWRITING 1 **b :** the act or practice of literary or musical composition **2 :** something written: as **a :** letters or characters that serve as visible signs of ideas, words, or symbols **b :** a letter, note, or notice used to communicate or record **c :** a written composition **d :** INSCRIPTION **3 :** a style or form of composition **4 :** the occupation of a writer; *esp* **:** the profession of authorship — **writing on the wall :** HANDWRITING ON THE WALL
writing desk *n* (1611) **:** a desk that often has a sloping top for writing on; *also* **:** a portable case that contains writing materials and has a surface for writing
writing paper *n* (1548) **:** paper that is usu. finished with a smooth surface and sized and that can be written on with ink
Writ·ings \ˈrī-tiŋz\ *n pl* [trans. of LHeb *kĕthūbhīm*] (14c) **:** the third part of the Jewish scriptures — see BIBLE table
writ of assistance (1706) **1 :** a writ issued to a law officer (as a sheriff or marshal) for the enforcement of a court order or decree; *esp* **:** one used to enforce an order for the possession of lands **2 :** a writ used esp. in colonial America authorizing a law officer to search in unspecified locations for unspecified illegal goods
writ of certiorari (ca. 1532) **:** CERTIORARI
writ of error (15c) **:** a common law writ directing an inferior court to remit the record of a legal action to the reviewing court in order that an error of law may be corrected if it exists
writ of extent (1590) **:** a writ formerly used to recover debts of record to the British crown and under which the lands, goods, and person of the debtor might all be seized to secure payment
writ of habeas corpus (1762) **:** HABEAS CORPUS
writ of mandamus (1820) **:** MANDAMUS
writ of prohibition (1802) **:** a writ issued by a superior court to prevent an inferior court from acting beyond its jurisdiction
writ of right (15c) **1 :** a common law writ for restoring to its owner property held by another **2 :** a writ granted as a matter of right
writ of summons (1660) **:** a writ issued on behalf of the British monarch summoning a lord spiritual or a lord temporal to attend parliament
wrnt *abbr* warrant
[1]**wrong** \ˈrȯŋ\ *n* [ME, fr. OE *wrang,* fr. **wrang,* adj., wrong] (bef. 12c) **1 a :** an injurious, unfair, or unjust act **:** action or conduct inflicting harm without due provocation or just cause **b :** a violation or invasion of the legal rights of another; *esp* **:** TORT **2 :** something wrong, immoral, or unethical; *esp* **:** principles, practices, or conduct contrary to justice, goodness, equity, or law **3 :** the state, position, or fact of being or doing wrong: as **a :** the state of being mistaken or incorrect **b :** the state of being guilty ***syn*** see INJUSTICE
[2]**wrong** *adj* **wrong·er** \ˈrȯŋ-ər\; **wrong·est** \ˈrȯŋ-əst\ [ME, fr. OE **wrang,* of Scand origin; akin to ON *rangr* awry, wrong, Dan *vrang* wrong side; akin to OE *wringan* to wring] (13c) **1 :** not according to the moral standard **:** SINFUL, IMMORAL ⟨thought that war was ~⟩ **2 :** not right or proper according to a code, standard, or convention **:** IMPROPER ⟨it was ~ not to thank your host⟩ **3 :** not according to truth or facts **:** INCORRECT ⟨gave a ~ date⟩ **4 :** not satisfactory (as in condition, results, health, or temper) **5 :** not in accordance with one's needs, intent, or expectations ⟨took the ~ bus⟩ **6 :** of, relating to, or constituting the side of something that is usu. held to be opposite to the principal one, that is the one naturally or by design turned down, inward, or away, or that is the least finished or polished — **wrong·ly** \ˈrȯŋ-lē\ *adv* — **wrong·ness** *n* — **wrong side of the tracks :** a run-down or unfashionable neighborhood
[3]**wrong** *adv* (13c) **1 :** without accuracy **:** INCORRECTLY ⟨guessed ~⟩ **2 :** without regard for what is proper or just ⟨was reprimanded for what he had done ~⟩ **3 :** in a wrong direction ⟨turned ~ at the junction⟩ **4 a :** in an unsuccessful or unfortunate way ⟨something went ~⟩ **b :** out of working order or condition **5 :** in a false light ⟨don't get me ~⟩
[4]**wrong** *vt* **wronged; wrong·ing** \ˈrȯŋ-iŋ\ (14c) **1 a :** to do wrong to **:** INJURE, HARM **b :** to treat disrespectfully or dishonorably **:** VIOLATE **2 :** DEFRAUD — usu. used with *of* ⟨~*ed* them of their land⟩ **3 :** DISCREDIT, MALIGN — **wrong·er** \ˈrȯŋ-ər\ *n*
syn WRONG, OPPRESS, PERSECUTE, AGGRIEVE mean to injure unjustly or outrageously. WRONG implies inflicting injury either unmerited or out of proportion to what one deserves ⟨a penal system that had *wronged* him⟩. OPPRESS suggests inhumane imposing of burdens one cannot endure or exacting more than one can perform ⟨a people *oppressed* by a warmongering tyrant⟩. PERSECUTE implies a relentless and unremitting subjection to annoyance or suffering ⟨a child *persecuted* by constant criticism⟩. AGGRIEVE implies suffering caused by an infringement or denial of rights ⟨a legal aid society representing *aggrieved* minority groups⟩.
wrong·do·er \ˈrȯŋ-ˌdü-ər\ *n* (15c) **:** one that does wrong; *esp* **:** one who transgresses moral laws
wrong·do·ing \-ˌdü-iŋ\ *n* (14c) **1 :** evil or improper behavior or action ⟨cleared of any ~⟩ **2 :** an instance of doing wrong
wronged *adj* (15c) **:** being injured unjustly **:** suffering a wrong
wrong–foot \ˈrȯŋ-ˌfu̇t\ *vt* (1928) *chiefly Brit* **:** to cause (as an opponent in soccer or tennis) to lean into or step with the wrong foot; *broadly* **:** to disrupt the equilibrium of ⟨a speed and flexibility that repeatedly ~*ed* his enemies —Anthony Lloyd⟩
wrong·ful \ˈrȯŋ-fəl\ *adj* (14c) **1 :** WRONG, UNJUST **2 a :** having no legal sanction **:** UNLAWFUL **b :** having no legal claim ⟨a ~ heir⟩ — **wrong·ful·ly** \-fə-lē\ *adv* — **wrong·ful·ness** *n*
wrongful birth *n* (1979) **:** a malpractice claim brought by the parents of a child born with a birth defect against a physician or health-care provider whose alleged negligence (as in diagnosis) effectively deprived the parents of the opportunity to make an informed decision whether

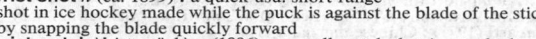

to avoid or terminate the pregnancy; *also* : the birth or injury at issue in such a claim

wrongful death *n* (1952) : a death caused by the negligent, willful, or wrongful act, neglect, omission, or default of another

wrong-head-ed \'rȯn-'he-dəd\ *adj* (1723) **1** : stubborn in adherence to wrong opinion or principles ⟨∼ in his opinions⟩ **2** : marked by perversity : contrary to sound judgment ⟨∼ advice⟩ — **wrong-head-ed-ly** *adv* — **wrong-head-ed-ness** *n*

wrote *past and dial past part of* WRITE

wroth \'rȯth *also* 'rȯth\ *adj* [ME, fr. OE *wrāth;* akin to OHG *reid* twisted, OE *wrīthan* to writhe] (bef. 12c) : intensely angry : highly incensed : WRATHFUL

¹wrought \'rȯt\ *past and past part of* WORK

²wrought *adj* [ME, fr. pp. of *worken* to work] (13c) **1** : worked into shape by artistry or effort ⟨carefully ∼ essays⟩ **2** : elaborately embellished : ORNAMENTED **3** : processed for use : MANUFACTURED ⟨∼ silk⟩ **4** : beaten into shape by tools : HAMMERED — used of metals **5** : deeply stirred : EXCITED — often used with *up* ⟨gets easily ∼ up over nothing⟩

wrought iron *n* (1678) : a commercial form of iron that is tough, malleable, and relatively soft, contains less than 0.3 percent and usu. less than 0.1 percent carbon, and carries 1 or 2 percent of slag mechanically mixed with it

wrung *past and past part of* WRING

¹wry \'rī\ *vb* **wried; wry-ing** [ME *wrien,* fr. OE *wrigian* to turn; akin to MHG *rigel* kerchief wound around the head, Gk *rhiknos* shriveled, Av *urvisyeiti* he turns] *vi* (14c) : TWIST, WRITHE ∼ *vt* : to pull out of or as if out of proper shape : make awry

²wry *adj* **wry-er** \'rī-(ə)r\; **wry-est** \'rī-əst\ (15c) **1** : having a bent or twisted shape or condition ⟨a ∼ smile⟩; *also* : turned abnormally to one side ⟨a ∼ neck⟩ **2** : WRONGHEADED **1 3** : cleverly and often ironically or grimly humorous — **wry-ly** \'rī-lē\ *adv* — **wry-ness** *n*

wry-neck \'rī-,nek\ *n* (1585) **1** : either of two Old World woodpeckers (*Jynx torquilla* or *J. ruficollis*) that differ from the typical woodpeckers in having soft tail feathers and a peculiar manner of writhing the neck **2** : TORTICOLLIS

WSW *abbr* west-southwest

wt *abbr* weight

WT *abbr* wireless telegraphy

wtd *abbr* wanted

WTO *abbr* World Trade Organization

Wu \'wü\ *n* [Chin (Beijing) *Wú,* historical kingdom coextensive with the dialect area] (1908) : a group of Chinese dialects spoken principally in Jiangsu and Zhejiang provinces

wud \'wüd\ *adj* [alter. of *wood*] (ca. 1699) *chiefly Scot* : INSANE, MAD

wul-fen-ite \'wu̇l-fə-,nīt\ *n* [G *Wulfenit,* fr. F. X. von *Wulfen* †1805 Austrian mineralogist] (1849) : a tetragonal mineral that is a complex oxide

of lead and molybdenum and occurs esp. in bright orange-yellow tabular crystals

wun-der-kind \'vu̇n-dər-,kint\ *n, pl* **wun-der-kin-der** \-,kin-dər\ [G, fr. *Wunder* wonder + *Kind* child] (1873) : a child prodigy; *also* : one who succeeds in a competitive or highly difficult field or profession at an early age

wurst \'wərst *also* 'wu̇rst *sometimes* 'wu̇sht *or* 'wu̇st; *also with* v *for* w\ *n* [G, fr. OHG] (1820) : SAUSAGE

wur-zel *n* [short for *mangel-wurzel*] (1869) : MANGEL

wu-shu \'wü-'shü\ *n* [Chin (Beijing) *wǔshù,* fr. *wǔ* martial, military + *shù* art] (1971) : Chinese martial arts

wuss \'wu̇s\ *also* **wus-sy** \'wu̇-sē\ *n, pl* **wuss-es** *also* **wus-sies** [origin unknown] (1976) : WIMP — **wussy** *adj*

wuth-er \'wə-thər\ *vi* [alter. of *whither* to rush, bluster, hurl] (1847) *dial Eng* : to blow with a dull roaring sound

WV *or* **W Va** *abbr* West Virginia

WVS *abbr* Women's Voluntary Services

w/w *abbr* wall-to-wall

WW *abbr* world war

www *abbr* World Wide Web

WY *or* **Wyo** *abbr* Wyoming

Wy-an-dot \'wī-ən-,dät *also* 'wīn-,dät\ *n* [of Iroquoian origin; akin to Huron (Iroquoian language of the Hurons) *ouendat,* a self-designation, Mohawk *skawę́·nat* one language] (1749) : a member of an American Indian group formed in the 17th century by Hurons and other Indians fleeing the Iroquois

wy-an-dotte \-,dät\ *n* [prob. fr. *Wyandotte* Wyandot] (1884) : any of a U.S. breed of medium-sized domestic chickens raised for meat and eggs

Wyc-liff-ite \'wi-klə-,fīt\ *n* [John *Wycliffe*] (1580) : LOLLARD — **Wycliffite** *adj*

wye \'wī\ *n* (1857) **1** : a Y-shaped part or object **2** : the letter *y*

wy-lie-coat \'wī-lē-,kōt, 'wi-\ *n* [ME (Sc) *wyle cot*] (15c) **1** *chiefly Scot* : a warm undergarment **2** *chiefly Scot* : PETTICOAT

wynd \'wīnd\ *n* [ME (Sc) *wynde,* prob. fr. *wynden* to wind, proceed, go, fr. OE *windan* to twist — more at WIND] (15c) *chiefly Scot* : a very narrow street

wynn *or* **wyn** \'win\ *also* **wen** \'wen\ *n* [OE *wynn,* lit., joy — more at WINSOME] (bef. 12c) : a runic letter used in Old English and Middle English to represent the consonant \w\

WYS-I-WYG \'wi-zē-,wig, -zə-\ *n, often attrib* [what you see is what you get] (1982) : a display generated by word-processing or desktop= publishing software that exactly reflects the appearance of the printed document

wy-vern \'wī-vərn\ *n* [alter. of ME *wyvere* viper, fr. AF *wivre, guivre,* fr. L *vipera*] (1610) : a mythical animal usu. represented as a 2-legged winged creature resembling a dragon

---

¹x \'eks\ *n, pl* **x's** *or* **xs** \'ek-səz\ *often cap, often attrib* (bef. 12c) **1 a** : the 24th letter of the English alphabet **b** : a graphic representation of this letter **c** : a speech counterpart of orthographic *x* **2** : TEN — see NUMBER table **3** : a graphic device for reproducing the letter *x* **4** : one designated *x* esp. as the 24th in order or class, or the first in an order or class that includes x, y, and sometimes z **5** : an unknown quantity **6** : something shaped like or marked with the letter X

²x *vt* **x–ed** *also* **x'd** *or* **xed** \'ekst\; **x–ing** *or* **x'ing** \'ek-siŋ\ (ca. 1849) **1** : to mark with an *x* **2** : to cancel or obliterate with a series of *x*'s — usu. used with *out* ⟨*x-ed* out the mistake⟩

³x *abbr* **1** cross **2** ex **3** experimental **4** extra

X \'eks\ *adj* (1970) *of a motion picture* : of such a nature that admission is denied to persons under a specified age (as 17) — used before the adoption of *NC-17*

Xan-a-du \'za-nə-,dü, -,dyü\ *n* [*Xanadu,* locality in *Kubla Khan* (1798), poem by Samuel T. Coleridge] (1919) : an idyllic, exotic, or luxurious place

xanth- *or* **xantho-** *comb form* [NL, fr. Gk, fr. *xanthos*] : yellow ⟨*xanthene*⟩

xan-than gum \'zan-thən-\ *n* [*xanth-* (fr. NL *Xanthomonas,* genus name) + ³-*an*] (1964) : a polysaccharide that is produced by fermentation of carbohydrates by a gram-negative bacterium (*Xanthomonas campestris*) and is a thickening and suspending agent used esp. in pharmaceuticals and prepared foods — called also *xanthan*

xan-thate \'zan-,thāt\ *n* (1831) : a salt or ester of any of various thio acids and esp. C₃H₆OS₂

xan-thene \'zan-,thēn\ *n* (1898) **1** : a white crystalline heterocyclic compound C₁₃H₁₀O; *also* : an isomer of this that is the parent of the colored forms of the xanthene dyes **2** : any of various derivatives of xanthene

xanthene dye *n* (1930) : any of various brilliant fluorescent yellow to pink to bluish-red dyes that are characterized by the presence of the xanthene nucleus

xan-thine \'zan-,thēn\ *n* [ISV] (1857) : a feebly basic compound C₅H₄N₄O₂ that occurs esp. in animal or plant tissue, is derived from

guanine and hypoxanthine, and yields uric acid on oxidation; *also* : any of various derivatives of xanthine (as methylxanthine)

Xan-thip-pe \zan-'thi-pē, -'ti-\ *or* **Xan-tip-pe** \-'ti-pē\ *n* [Gk *Xanthippē,* shrewish wife of Socrates] (1691) : an ill-tempered woman

xan-thone \'zan-,thōn\ *n* [ISV] (ca. 1894) : a ketone C₁₃H₈O₂ that is the parent of several natural yellow pigments

xan-tho-phyll \'zan(t)-thə-,fil\ *n* [F *xanthophylle,* fr. *xanth-* + *-phylle* -phyll] (1838) : any of several yellow to orange carotenoid pigments that are oxygen derivatives of carotenes; *esp* : LUTEIN

Xa-ve-ri-an Brother \zā-'vir-ē-ən-, za-\ *n* [*Xaverian* of St. Francis *Xavier*] (1882) : a member of a Roman Catholic congregation of lay brothers founded by Theodore J. Ryken in Brugge, Belgium, in 1839 and dedicated to education

x–ax-is \'eks-,ak-səs\ *n* (1886) **1** : the axis in a plane Cartesian coordinate system parallel to which abscissas are measured **2** : one of the three axes in a three-dimensional rectangular coordinate system

X band *n* (ca. 1946) : a segment of the superhigh-frequency radio spectrum that lies between 5.2 GHz and 10.9 GHz and is used esp. for radars and for spacecraft communication

X–C *abbr* cross-country

X chromosome *n* (1911) : a sex chromosome that usu. occurs paired in each female cell and single in each male cell in species in which the male typically has two unlike sex chromosomes — compare Y CHROMOSOME

x–co-or-di-nate \eks-kō-'ȯrd-nət; -'ȯr-də-nət, -də-,nāt\ *n* (1927) : a coordinate whose value is determined by measuring parallel to an x-axis; *specif* : ABSCISSA

Xe *symbol* xenon

xe-bec \'zē-,bek, zi-\ *n* [modif. of F *chebec,* fr. Ar *shabbāk*] (1756) : a usu. 3-masted Mediterranean sailing ship with long overhanging bow and stern

xen- *or* **xeno-** *comb form* [LL, fr. Gk, fr. *xenos* stranger, guest, host] **1 a** : guest : foreigner ⟨*xenophobia*⟩ **b** : that which is not the host ⟨*xenograft*⟩ **2 a** : strange : foreign ⟨*xenolith*⟩ **b** : not being the host ⟨*xenobiotic*⟩

xe-nia \'zē-nē-ə, -nyə\ *n* [NL, fr. Gk, hospitality, fr. *xenos* host] (1899) : the effect of

xebec

of genes introduced by pollen esp. on endosperm and embryo development

xe·no·bi·ot·ic \ˌze-nō-bī-ˈä-tik, ˌzē-, -bē-\ *n* (1965) : a chemical compound (as a drug, pesticide, or carcinogen) that is foreign to a living organism — **xenobiotic** *adj*

xe·no·di·ag·no·sis \-ˌdī-ig-ˈnō-səs\ *n* [NL] (ca. 1929) : the detection of a parasite (as of humans) by feeding a suitable intermediate host (as an insect) on supposedly infected material (as blood) and later examining the host for the parasite — **xe·no·di·ag·nos·tic** \-ˈnäs-tik\ *adj*

xe·no·ge·ne·ic \ˌze-jə-ˈnē-ik\ *adj* [*xen-* + *-geneic* (as in *isogeneic*)] (1961) : derived from, originating in, or being a member of another species

xe·no·graft \ˈze-nə-ˌgraft, ˈzē-\ *n* (1961) : a graft of tissue taken from a donor of one species and grafted into a recipient of another species — called also *heterograft*; compare HOMOGRAFT

xe·no·lith \ˈze-nə-ˌlith, ˈzē-\ *n* (1894) : a fragment of a rock included in another rock — **xe·no·lith·ic** \ˌze-nə-ˈli-thik, ˌzē-\ *adj*

xe·non \ˈzē-ˌnän, ˈze-\ *n* [Gk, neut. of *xenos* strange] (1898) : a heavy colorless and relatively inert gaseous element that occurs in air as about one part in 20 million and is used esp. in specialized electric lamps (as flashtubes) and in scientific research — see ELEMENT table

xe·no·phile \ˈze-nə-ˌfī(-ə)l, ˈzē-\ *n* [ISV] (1948) : one attracted to foreign things (as styles or people)

xe·no·phobe \ˈze-nə-ˌfōb, ˈzē-\ *n* [ISV] (1922) : one unduly fearful of what is foreign and esp. of people of foreign origin — **xe·no·pho·bic** \ˌze-nə-ˈfō-bik, ˌzē-\ *adj* — **xe·no·pho·bi·cal·ly** \-bi-k(ə-)lē\ *adv*

xe·no·pho·bia \ˌze-nə-ˈfō-bē-ə, ˌzē-\ *n* [NL] (1903) : fear and hatred of strangers or foreigners or of anything that is strange or foreign

xe·no·trans·plan·ta·tion \ˌze-nə-ˌtran(t)s-ˌplan-ˈtā-shən, ˌzē-\ *n* (1969) : transplantation of an organ, tissue, or cells between two different species — **xe·no·trans·plant** \-ˈtran(t)s-ˌplant\ *n*

xe·no·tro·pic \-ˈträ-pik, -trō-\ *adj* (1973) : replicating or reproducing only in cells other than those of the host species ⟨∼ viruses⟩

xer- *or* **xero-** *comb form* [LL, fr. Gk *xēr-, xēro-,* fr. *xēros*] : dry ⟨*xeric*⟩ ⟨*xerophyte*⟩

Xer \ˈek-sər\ *n* (1991) : a member of Generation X

xe·ric \ˈzir-ik, ˈzer-\ *adj* (1926) : characterized by, relating to, or requiring only a small amount of moisture ⟨a ∼ habitat⟩ ⟨a ∼ plant⟩ — compare HYDRIC, MESIC

xeri·scape \ˈzir-ə-ˌskāp, ˈzer-\ *n, often cap* (1985) : a landscaping method developed esp. for arid and semiarid climates that utilizes water-conserving techniques (as the use of drought-tolerant plants, mulch, and efficient irrigation)

xe·ro·der·ma pig·men·to·sum \ˌzir-ə-ˈdər-mə-ˌpig-mən-ˈtō-səm, -ˌmen-\ *n* [NL, lit., pigmented dryness of the skin] (1884) : a genetic disorder inherited as a recessive autosomal trait that is caused by a defect in mechanisms that repair DNA mutations (as those caused by ultraviolet light) and is characterized by the development of pigment abnormalities and multiple skin cancers in areas exposed to the sun

xe·rog·ra·phy \zə-ˈrä-grə-fē\ *n* [ISV] (1948) **1** : a process for copying graphic matter by the action of light on an electrically charged photoconductive insulating surface in which the latent image is developed with a resinous powder (as toner) **2** : XERORADIOGRAPHY — **xe·ro·graph·ic** \ˌzir-ə-ˈgra-fik\ *adj* — **xe·ro·graph·i·cal·ly** \-fi-k(ə-)lē\ *adv*

xe·roph·i·lous \zə-ˈrä-fə-ləs\ *or* **xe·ro·phile** \ˈzir-ə-ˌfī(-ə)l\ *adj* (1863) : thriving in or tolerant or characteristic of a xeric environment

xe·roph·thal·mia \ˌzir-ˌäf-ˈthal-mē-ə, -ˌäp-ˈthal-\ *n* [LL, fr. Gk *xērophthalmia,* fr. *xēr-* xer- + *ophthalmia* ophthalmia] (ca. 1656) : a dry thickened lusterless condition of the eyeball resulting esp. from a severe systemic deficiency of vitamin A — **xe·roph·thal·mic** \-mik\ *adj*

xe·ro·phyte \ˈzir-ə-ˌfīt\ *n* (1897) : a plant adapted for life and growth with a limited water supply — **xe·ro·phyt·ic** \ˌzir-ə-ˈfi-tik\ *adj*

xe·ro·ra·di·og·ra·phy \ˌzir-ō-ˌrā-dē-ˈä-grə-fē\ *n* (1949) : radiography used esp. in mammographic screening for breast cancer that produces an image using X-rays in a manner similar to the way an image is produced by light in xerography

xe·ro·ther·mic \ˌzir-ə-ˈthər-mik\ *adj* (1904) **1** : characterized by heat and dryness **2** : adapted to or thriving in a hot dry environment

xe·rox \ˈzir-ˌäks, ˈzē-ˌräks\ *vt* [fr. *Xerox*] (1965) **1** : to copy on a xerographic copier **2** : to make (a copy) on a xerographic copier

Xe·rox \ˈzir-ˌäks, ˈzē-ˌräks\ *trademark* — used for a xerographic copier

X factor *n* (1930) : a circumstance, quality, or person that has a strong but unpredictable influence

x–height \ˈeks-ˌhīt, -ˌhītth\ *n* (ca. 1945) : the height of a lowercase x used to represent the height of the main body of a lowercase letter

Xho·sa \ˈkō-sə, ˈhō-, ˈkȯ-\ *or with* ȯ *for* ō\ *n* [Xhosa *-xhosa* (as in *um-Xhosa* a Xhosa person)] (1801) **1** : a member of a Bantu-speaking people of Eastern Cape province **2** : a Bantu language of the Xhosas

xi \ˈzī, ˈksī\ *n, pl* **xis** [Gk *xei*] (15c) : the 14th letter of the Greek alphabet — see ALPHABET table

x–in·ter·cept \ˈeks-ˈin-tər-ˌsept\ *n* (ca. 1939) : the x-coordinate of a point where a line, curve, or surface intersects the x-axis

xi·phi·ster·num \ˌzī-fə-ˈstər-nəm, ˌzi-\ *n, pl* **-na** \-nə\ [NL, fr. Gk *xiphos* sword + NL *sternum*] (ca. 1860) : XIPHOID PROCESS

xi·phoid \ˈzī-ˌfȯid, ˈzi-\ *n* [NL *xiphoides,* fr. Gk *xiphoeidēs,* fr. *xiphos*] (ca. 1860) : XIPHOID PROCESS — **xiphoid** *adj*

xiphoid process *n* (1873) : the third and lowest segment of the human sternum

x–ir·ra·di·a·tion \ˌeks-i-ˌrā-dē-ˈā-shən\ *n, often cap* (1927) : X- RADIATION 1

XL *abbr* **1** extra large **2** extra long

X–linked \ˈeks-ˌliŋkt\ *adj* (1989) : located on an X chromosome ⟨an ∼ gene⟩; *also* : transmitted by an X-linked gene ⟨an ∼ disease⟩

Xmas \ˈkris-məs *also* ˈeks-məs\ *n* [*X* (symbol for *Christ,* fr. the Gk letter chi (X), initial of *Christos* Christ) + *-mas* (in *Christmas*)] (1551) : CHRISTMAS

XML \ˌeks-(ˌ)em-ˈel\ *n* [*X* (fr. *extensible*) + markup *language*] (1989) : a markup language with use and design similar to HTML but employing tags that indicate the logical structure in addition to the display specifications of the coded data

XO *abbr* executive office

x–ra·di·a·tion \ˌeks-ˌrā-dē-ˈā-shən\ *n, often cap* (1896) **1** : exposure to X-rays **2** : radiation composed of X-rays

X–rat·ed \ˈeks-ˈrā-təd\ *adj* (1970) **1** : having a rating of X; *broadly* : relating to or characterized by explicit sexual material or activity ⟨an ∼ book⟩ **2** : OBSCENE, VULGAR ⟨an ∼ gesture⟩

Xray \ˈeks-ˌrā\ (1943) — a communications code word for the letter x

x–ray \ˈeks-ˌrā\ *vt, often cap* (1899) : to examine, treat, or photograph with X-rays

X–ray \ˈeks-ˌrā\ *n* (1896) **1** : any of the electromagnetic radiations that have an extremely short wavelength of less than 100 angstroms and have the properties of penetrating various thicknesses of all solids, of producing secondary radiations by impinging on material bodies, and of acting on photographic films and plates as light does **2** : a photograph obtained by use of X-rays — **X–ray** *adj*

X–ray astronomy *n* (1963) : astronomy dealing with investigations of celestial bodies by means of the X-rays they emit

X–ray diffraction *n* (1924) : a scattering of X-rays by the atoms of a crystal that produces an interference effect so that the diffraction pattern gives information on the structure of the crystal or the identity of a crystalline substance

X–ray star *n* (1964) : a luminous celestial object emitting a major portion of its radiation in the form of X-rays — called also *X-ray source*

X–ray therapy *n* (1926) : medical treatment (as of cancer) by controlled application of X-rays

X–ray tube *n* (1896) : a vacuum tube in which a concentrated stream of electrons strikes a metal target and produces X-rays

XS *abbr* extra small

x–sec·tion \ˈkrȯs-ˈsek-shən, -ˌsek-\ *n* [*x,* rebus for *cross*] (1962) : CROSS SECTION — **x–sec·tion·al** \-shnəl, -shə-nᵊl\ *adj*

xu \ˈsü\ *n, pl* **xu** [Vietnamese, fr. F *sou* sou] (1948) **1** : a coin formerly minted by South Vietnam equivalent to the cent **2** — see *dong* at MONEY table

xyl- *or* **xylo-** *comb form* [L, fr. Gk, fr. *xylon*] **1** : wood ⟨*xylo*phone⟩ **2** : xylene ⟨*xyl*idine⟩

xy·lan \ˈzī-ˌlan\ *n* [ISV] (ca. 1894) : a yellow gummy pentosan that yields xylose on hydrolysis and is abundantly present in plant cell walls and woody tissue

xy·lem \ˈzī-ləm, -ˌlem\ *n* [G, fr. Gk *xylon*] (1873) : a complex tissue in the vascular system of higher plants that consists of vessels, tracheids, or both usu. together with wood fibers and parenchyma cells, functions chiefly in conduction of water and dissolved minerals but also in support and food storage, and typically constitutes the woody element (as of a plant stem) — compare PHLOEM

xylem ray *n* (1875) : a vascular ray or portion of a vascular ray located in xylem — called also *wood ray*; compare PHLOEM RAY

xy·lene \ˈzī-ˌlēn\ *n* [ISV] (1851) : any of three toxic flammable oily isomeric aromatic hydrocarbons C_8H_{10} that are di-methyl homologues of benzene and are usu. obtained from petroleum or natural gas distillates; *also* : a mixture of xylenes and ethyl benzene used chiefly as a solvent

xy·li·dine \ˈzī-lə-ˌdēn\ *n* [ISV] (1850) : any or a mixture of six toxic liquid or low-melting crystalline isomeric amino derivatives $C_8H_{11}N$ of the xylenes used chiefly as intermediates for azo dyes and in organic synthesis

xy·li·tol \ˈzī-lə-ˌtȯl, -ˌtōl\ *n* (1891) : a crystalline alcohol $C_5H_{12}O_5$ that is a derivative of xylose, is obtained esp. from birch bark, and is used as a sweetener

xy·log·ra·phy \zī-ˈlä-grə-fē\ *n* [F *xylographie,* fr. *xyl-* + *-graphie* -graphy] (1816) : the art of making engravings on wood esp. for printing — **xy·lo·graph** \ˈzī-lə-ˌgraf\ *n* — **xy·log·ra·pher** \zī-ˈlä-grə-fər\ *n* — **xy·lo·graph·ic** \ˌzī-lə-ˈgra-fik\ *also* **xy·lo·graph·i·cal** \-fi-kəl\ *adj*

xy·lol \ˈzī-ˌlȯl, -ˌlōl\ *n* [ISV] (1851) : XYLENE

xy·loph·a·gous \zī-ˈlä-fə-gəs\ *adj* [Gk *xylophagos,* fr. *xyl-* + *-phagos* -phagous] (1739) : feeding on or in wood ⟨∼ insects⟩

xy·lo·phone \ˈzī-lə-ˌfōn *also* ˈzi-\ *n* (1866) : a percussion instrument consisting of a series of wooden bars graduated in length to produce the musical scale, supported on belts of straw or felt, and sounded by striking with two small wooden hammers — **xy·lo·phon·ist** \-ˌfō-nist\ *n*

xy·lose \ˈzī-ˌlōs, -ˌlōz\ *n* [ISV] (ca. 1894) : a crystalline aldose sugar $C_5H_{10}O_5$ that is not fermentable with ordinary yeasts and occurs esp. as a constituent of xylans from which it is obtained by hydrolysis

---

\ə\ abut \ᵊ\ kitten, F table \ər\ further \a\ ash \ā\ ace \ä\ mop, mar
\au̇\ out \ch\ chin \e\ bet \ē\ easy \g\ go \i\ hit \ī\ ice \j\ job
\ŋ\ sing \ō\ go \ȯ\ law \ȯi\ boy \th\ thin \th̲\ the \ü\ loot \u̇\ foot
\y\ yet \zh\ vision, beige \k̲, ⁿ, œ, ɶ, ᵉ\ *see* Guide to Pronunciation

Y

[1]**y** \ˈwī\ *n, pl* **y's** *or* **ys** \ˈwīz\ *often cap, often attrib* (bef. 12c) **1 a :** the 25th letter of the English alphabet **b :** a graphic representation of this letter **c :** a speech counterpart of orthographic *y* **2 :** a graphic device for reproducing the letter *y* **3 :** one designated *y* esp. as the 25th in order or class or the second in order or class when x is made the first **4 :** something shaped like the letter Y

[2]**y** *abbr* **1** yard **2** year

[1]**Y** \ˈwī\ *n* (ca. 1915) **1 :** YMCA **2 :** YWCA

[2]**Y** *symbol* yttrium

[1]**-y** *also* **-ey** \ē; *in some dialects, esp Brit, Southern, & NewEng, often* i *but not shown at individual entries*\ *adj suffix* [ME, fr. OE *-ig;* akin to OHG *-īg* -y, L *-icus,* Gk *-ikos,* Skt *-ika*] **1 a :** characterized by : full of ⟨blossom*y*⟩ ⟨dirt*y*⟩ ⟨mudd*y*⟩ ⟨clay*ey*⟩ **b :** having the character of : composed of ⟨ic*y*⟩ ⟨wax*y*⟩ **c :** like : like that of ⟨hom*ey*⟩ ⟨wintr*y*⟩ — often with a disparaging connotation ⟨stag*y*⟩ **2 a :** tending or inclined to ⟨sleep*y*⟩ ⟨chatt*y*⟩ **b :** giving occasion for (specified) action ⟨tear*y*⟩ **c :** performing (specified) action ⟨curl*y*⟩

[2]**-y** *same*\ *n suffix, pl* **-ies** [ME *-ie,* fr. AF, fr. L *-ia,* fr. Gk *-ia, -eia*] **1 :** state : condition : quality ⟨beggar*y*⟩ **2 :** activity, place of business, or goods dealt with ⟨chandler*y*⟩ ⟨laundr*y*⟩ **3 :** whole body or group ⟨soldier*y*⟩

[3]**-y** *n suffix, pl* **-ies** [ME *-ie,* fr. AF, fr. L *-ium*] **:** instance of a (specified) action ⟨entreat*y*⟩ ⟨inquir*y*⟩

[4]**-y** — see -IE

YA *abbr* young adult

yab·ber \ˈya-bər\ *n* [perh. modif. of Wiradhuri (Australian aboriginal language of central New South Wales) *ya-* speak] (1855) *Austral* **:** TALK, JABBER ⟨all ~ and chatter ceased around the campfires —Francis Birtles⟩ — **yabber** *vi*

yab·by *or* **yab·bie** \ˈya-bē\ *n, pl* **yab·bies** [Wemba-Wemba (Australian aboriginal language of Victoria) *yabij*] (1894) **:** any of various burrowing Australian crayfishes (genus *Cherax,* esp. *C. destructor*) that are used for food

[1]**yacht** \ˈyät\ *n* [obs. D *jaght,* fr. MLG *jacht,* short for *jachtschip,* lit., hunting ship] (1557) **:** any of various recreational watercraft: as **a :** a sailboat used for racing **b :** a large usu. motor-driven craft used for pleasure cruising

[2]**yacht** *vi* (1836) **:** to race or cruise in a yacht

yacht club *n* (1834) **:** a club organized to promote and regulate yachting and boating

yacht·ing \ˈyä-tiŋ\ *n* (1836) **:** the action, fact, or pastime of racing or cruising in a yacht

yachts·man \ˈyäts-mən\ *n* (1862) **:** a person who owns or sails a yacht

ya·da ya·da *or* **yad·da yad·da** \ˈyä-də-ˈyä-də\ *or* **yada yada yada** *or* **yadda yadda yadda** \-ˈyä-də\ *n* [alter. of earlier *yatata* idle chatter, prob. ultim. fr. Brit. dial. and argot *yatter-yatter* to chatter, of imit. origin] (1980) **:** boring or empty talk ⟨listening to a lot of *yada yada* about the economy⟩ — often used interjectionally esp. in recounting words regarded as too dull or predictable to be worth repeating

YAG \ˈyag\ *n* [*y*ttrium *a*luminum *g*arnet] (1964) **:** a synthetic yttrium aluminum garnet of marked hardness and high refractive index that is used esp. as a gemstone and in laser technology

ya·gi \ˈyä-gē, ˈya-\ *n* [Hidetsugu *Yagi* †1976 Jp. engineer] (1943) **:** a highly directional and selective shortwave antenna consisting of a horizontal conductor of one or two dipoles connected with the receiver or transmitter and of a set of nearly equal insulated dipoles parallel to and on a level with the horizontal conductor

[1]**ya·hoo** \ˈyā-(ˌ)hü, ˈyä-\ *n, pl* **yahoos** (1726) **1** *cap* **:** a member of a race of brutes in Swift's *Gulliver's Travels* who have the form and all the vices of humans **2** [influenced by [2]*yahoo*] **:** a boorish, crass, or stupid person — **ya·hoo·ism** \-ˌi-zəm\ *n*

[2]**ya·hoo** \yä-ˈhü\ *interj* [perh. alter. of *yo-ho,* interj. used to attract attention, fr. *yo* + *ho*] (1870) **:** YIPPEE

Yah·weh \ˈyä-(ˌ)wā, -(ˌ)vā\ *also* **Jah·veh** *or* **Yah·veh** \-(ˌ)vā\ *n* [Heb *Yahweh*] (1869) **:** GOD 1a — used esp. by the ancient Hebrews; compare TETRAGRAMMATON

Yah·wism \-ˌwi-zəm, -ˌvi-\ *n* (1867) **:** the worship of Yahweh among the ancient Hebrews

Yah·wis·tic \yä-ˈwis-tik, -ˈvis-\ *adj* (1874) **1 :** characterized by the use of *Yahweh* as the name of God **2 :** of or relating to Yahwism

[1]**yak** \ˈyak\ *n, pl* **yaks** *also* **yak** [Tibetan (Lhasa dial.) *ya?* (spelled *gyag*)] (1795) **:** a large long-haired wild or domesticated ox (*Bos grunniens* syn. *B. mutus*) of Tibet and adjacent elevated parts of central Asia

[1]yak

[2]**yak** *var of* [1]YUK

[3]**yak** *also* **yack** *vi* **yakked** *also* **yacked; yak·king** *also* **yack·ing** [prob. imit.] (1949) **:** to talk persistently **:** CHATTER

[4]**yak** *also* **yack** \ˈyak\ *n* (1950) **:** persistent or voluble talk

Yak·a·ma *or* **Yak·i·ma** \ˈya-kə-ˌmȯ\ *n, pl* **Yakama** *or* **Yakamas** *or* **Yakima** *or* **Yakimas** [earlier *Eyakima,* the Yakima River, Yakamas, perh. fr. Sahaptin *iyakíma,* lit., pregnant ones] (1838) **1 :** a member of a group of Sahaptin peoples of the lower Yakima River valley, south central Washington **2 :** the language of the Yakama people

ya·ki·to·ri \ˌyä-ki-ˈtȯr-ē\ *n* [Jp, grilled chicken, fr. *yaki* broil, roast + *tori* bird] (1962) **:** bite-size marinated pieces of beef, seafood, or chicken on skewers

ya·ku·za \ˈyä-kü-ˌzä\ *n, pl* **yakuza** [Jp, ruffian, gangster] (1964) **1 :** a Japanese gangster **2 :** an organized crime syndicate in Japan

y'all *var of* YOU-ALL

yam \ˈyam\ *n* [earlier *iname,* fr. Pg *inhame* & Sp *ñame,* of African origin; akin to Fulani *nyami* to eat] (1657) **1 :** the edible starchy tuberous root of various plants (genus *Dioscorea* of the family Dioscoreaceae) used as a staple food in tropical areas; *also* **:** a plant producing yams **2 :** a moist usu. orange-fleshed sweet potato

ya·men \ˈyä-mən\ *n* [Chin (Beijing) *yámen*] (1747) **:** the headquarters or residence of a Chinese government official or department

yam·mer \ˈya-mər\ *vi* **yam·mered; yam·mer·ing** \ˈya-mə-riŋ, ˈyam-riŋ\ [ME *yameren,* alter. of *yomeren* to murmur, be sad, fr. OE *gēomrian;* akin to OHG *jāmaron* to be sad] (15c) **1 a :** to utter repeated cries of distress or sorrow **b :** WHIMPER **2 :** to utter persistent complaints **:** WHINE **3 :** to talk persistently or volubly and often loudly ⟨caused the purists to ~ for censorship —D. W. Maurer⟩ — **yammer** *n*

yang \ˈyäŋ, ˈyaŋ\ *n* [Chin (Beijing) *yáng*] (1671) **:** the masculine active principle in nature that in Chinese cosmology is exhibited in light, heat, or dryness and that combines with yin to produce all that comes to be

[1]**yank** \ˈyaŋk\ *vi* [origin unknown] (1822) **:** to pull on something with a quick vigorous movement ~ *vt* **1 :** to pull or extract with a quick vigorous movement **2 :** to remove in or as if in an abrupt manner ⟨~*ed* the story from the evening edition⟩

[2]**yank** *n* (ca. 1864) **:** a strong sudden pull **:** JERK

Yank \ˈyaŋk\ *n* (1778) **:** YANKEE

[1]**Yan·kee** \ˈyaŋ-kē\ *n* [origin unknown] (1758) **1 a :** a native or inhabitant of New England **b :** a native or inhabitant of the northern U.S. **2 :** a native or inhabitant of the U.S. — **Yan·kee·dom** \-kē-dəm\ *n* — **Yan·kee·ism** \-kē-ˌi-zəm\ *n*

[2]**Yankee** (1952) — a communications code word for the letter *y*

Yan·kee–Doo·dle \ˌyaŋ-kē-ˈdü-dᵊl\ *n* [*Yankee Doodle,* popular song during the American Revolution] (1767) **:** YANKEE

Ya·no·ma·mi \ˌyä-nō-ˈmä-mē\ *also* **Ya·no·ma·mo** \-mō\ *or* **Ya·no·ma·ma** \-mə\ *n, pl* **Yanomami** *also* **Yanomamis** *or* **Yanomamo** *or* **Yanomama** [Yanomami (language of the western Yanomami) *yanomami,* a self-designation] (1967) **1 :** an indigenous people inhabiting the rain forests of southern Venezuela and northern Brazil; *also* **:** a member of the Yanomami people **2 :** the family of four closely related languages spoken by the Yanomami

yan·qui \ˈyäŋ-kē\ *n, often cap* [Sp, fr. E [1]*Yankee*] (1928) **:** a citizen of the U.S. as distinguished from a Latin American

yan·tra \ˈyən-trə, ˈyan-, ˈyän-\ *n* [Skt] (1877) **:** a geometrical diagram used like an icon usu. in meditation

[1]**yap** \ˈyap\ *vi* **yapped; yap·ping** [imit.] (1596) **1 :** to talk in a shrill insistent way **:** CHATTER **2 :** to bark snappishly **:** YELP — **yap·per** *n*

[2]**yap** *n* (1822) **1 a :** a quick sharp bark **:** YELP **b :** shrill insistent talk **:** CHATTER **2 :** an unsophisticated, ignorant, or uncouth person **:** BUMPKIN **3** *slang* **:** MOUTH

Ya·qui \ˈyä-kē\ *n* [MexSp, alter. of earlier *hiaqui,* prob. fr. Yaqui *hiyaki,* the Yaqui River] (1861) **1 :** a member of an American Indian people of Sonora, Mexico **2 :** the Uto-Aztecan language of the Yaqui people

Yar·bor·ough \ˈyär-ˌbər-ə, -ˌbə-rə, -b(ə-)rə\ *n* [Charles Anderson Worsley, 2d Earl of *Yarborough* †1897 Eng. nobleman said to have bet a thousand to one against the dealing of such a hand] (1900) **:** a hand in bridge or whist containing no ace and no card higher than a nine

[1]**yard** \ˈyärd\ *n* [ME, fr. OE *geard* enclosure, yard; akin to OHG *gart* enclosure, L *hortus* garden] (bef. 12c) **1 a :** a small usu. walled and often paved area open to the sky and adjacent to a building **:** COURT **b :** the grounds of a building or group of buildings **2 :** the grounds immediately surrounding a house that are usu. covered with grass **3 a :** an enclosure for livestock (as poultry) **b** (1) **:** an area with its buildings and facilities set aside for a particular business or activity (2) **:** an assembly or storage area (as for dry-docked boats) **c :** a system of tracks for storage and maintenance of cars and making up trains **4 :** a locality in a forest where deer herd in winter

[2]**yard** *adj* (15c) **1 :** of, relating to, or employed in the yard surrounding a building ⟨~ light⟩ **2 :** of, relating to, or employed in a railroad yard ⟨a ~ engine⟩

[3]**yard** *vt* (1758) **1 :** to drive into or confine in a restricted area **:** HERD, PEN **2 :** to deliver to or store in a yard ~ *vi* **:** to congregate in or as if in a yard

[4]**yard** *n* [ME *yarde,* fr. OE *gierd* twig, measure, yard; akin to OHG *gart* stick, L *hasta* spear] (bef. 12c) **1 :** any of various units of measure: as **a :** a unit of length equal in the U.S. to 0.9144 meter — see WEIGHT table **b :** a unit of volume equal to a cubic yard **2 a :** a great length or quantity ⟨remembered ~*s* of facts and figures⟩ **b** *slang* **:** one hundred dollars **3 :** a long spar tapered toward the ends to support and spread the head of a square sail, lateen, or lugsail **4 :** a slender glass about three feet tall having a flared opening and a bulbous bottom; *also* **:** the amount it contains ⟨a ~ of ale⟩ — **the whole nine yards :** all of a related set of circumstances, conditions, or details ⟨who could learn the most about making records, about electronics and engineering, *the whole nine yards* —Stephen Stills⟩ — sometimes used adverbially with *go* to indicate an all-out effort

[1]**yard·age** \ˈyär-dij\ *n* [[1]*yard*] (1866) **1 :** the use of a livestock enclosure for animals in transit provided by a railroad at a station **2 :** a charge made by a railroad for the use of a livestock enclosure

[2]**yardage** *n* [[4]*yard*] (1900) **1 a :** an aggregate number of yards **b :** the length, extent, or volume of something as measured in yards **2 :** YARD GOODS

yard·arm \ˈyärd-ˌärm\ *n* (1553) **:** either end of the yard of a square-rigged ship

yard·bird \-ˌbərd\ *n* [[1]*yard*] (ca. 1941) **1 :** a soldier assigned to a menial task or restricted to a limited area as a disciplinary measure **2 :** an untrained or inept enlisted man

yard·er \ˈyär-dər\ *n* **:** one that is a specified number of yards in length — used in combination ⟨kicked a 42-*yarder*⟩

yard goods *n pl* (1895) **:** fabrics sold by the yard **:** PIECE GOODS

yard grass *n* [[1]*yard*] (1822) **:** a tall annual Old World grass (*Eleusine indica*) widely distributed as a weed — called also *goosegrass*

yard line *n* (1898) **:** any of a series of marked or imaginary lines one yard apart on a football field that are parallel to the goal lines and that indicate the distance to the nearest goal line

yard–long bean \ˈyärd-ˈlȯŋ-\ *n* (1926) **:** the edible 1- to 3-foot (0.3- to 0.9-meter) long thin stringless pod of a south Asian plant of a subspecies (*Vigna unguiculata sesquipedalis*) of the cowpea; *also* **:** the plant

yard·man \ˈyärd-mən, -ˌman\ *n* (ca. 1825) **1 :** a person employed to do outdoor work (as mowing lawns) **2 :** a person who works in the yard of a commercial establishment; *esp* **:** one who supervises the handling of building materials in a lumberyard **3 :** a railroad hand employed in yard service

yard·mas·ter \-ˌmas-tər\ *n* (1858) **:** the person in charge of operations in a railroad yard

yard sale *n* (1972) : GARAGE SALE
yard·stick \ˈyärd-ˌstik\ *n* (1610) **1 a :** a graduated measuring stick three feet (0.9144 meter) long **b :** a standard basis of calculation ⟨a ~ for measuring astronomical distances⟩ **2 :** a standard for making a critical judgment : CRITERION ⟨measured by the ~ of her first book⟩ ⟨was a great success by any ~⟩ ***syn*** see STANDARD
yare \ˈyer, ˈyär\ *adj* [ME, fr. OE *gearu;* akin to OHG *garo* ready] (bef. 12c) **1** *archaic* : set for action : READY **2** *or* **yar** \ˈyär\ **a :** characterized by speed and agility : NIMBLE, LIVELY **b :** HANDY 1c, MANEUVERABLE — **yare** *adv, archaic* — **yare·ly** *adv, archaic*
yar·mul·ke \ˈyä-mə-kə, ˈyär-mə(l)-kə\ *n* [Yiddish *yarmlke,* fr. Pol *jarmułka* & Ukrainian *yarmulka* skullcap, of Turkic origin; akin to Turk *yağmurluk* rainwear] (1903) : a skullcap worn esp. by Orthodox and Conservative Jewish males in the synagogue and the home
[1]**yarn** \ˈyärn\ *n* [ME, fr. OE *gearn;* akin to OHG *garn* yarn, Gk *chordē* string, L *hernia* rupture, Skt *hira* band] (bef. 12c) **1 a :** a continuous often plied strand composed of either natural or man-made fibers or filaments and used in weaving and knitting to form cloth **b :** a similar strand of another material (as metal, glass, or plastic) **2 :** a narrative of adventures; *esp* : a tall tale ⟨a roaring good ~⟩
[2]**yarn** *vi* (1812) : to tell a yarn — **yarn·er** *n*
yarn–dye \ˈyärn-ˌdī\ *vt* (1885) : to dye before weaving or knitting
yar·row \ˈya-(ˌ)rō\ *n* [ME *yarowe,* fr. OE *gearwe;* akin to OHG *garwa* yarrow] (bef. 12c) : a widely naturalized strong-scented Eurasian composite herb (*Achillea millefolium*) with finely dissected leaves and small usu. white corymbose flowers; *also* : any of several congeneric plants
yash·mak *also* **yas·mak** \ˈyash-ˌmak, ˈyas-\ *n* [Turk *yaşmak*] (1844) : a veil worn by Muslim women that is wrapped around the upper and lower parts of the face so that only the eyes remain exposed to public view
yat·a·ghan \ˈya-tə-ˌgan, ˈya-ti-gən\ *n* [Turk *yatağan*] (1815) : a long knife or short saber that lacks a guard for the hand at the juncture of blade and hilt and that usu. has a double curve to the edge and a nearly straight back
yauld \ˈyȯl(d)\ *adj* [origin unknown] (1786) *chiefly Scot* : VIGOROUS 1
yau·pon \ˈyü-ˌpän *also* ˈyō-, ˈyȯ-\ *n* [Catawba *yąpą,* fr. *yą-* tree + *pą* leaf] (1709) : a holly (*Ilex vomitoria*) of the southeastern U.S. that has smooth elliptical leaves with emetic and purgative properties
yau·tia \ˈyau̇-tē-ə\ *n* [AmerSp *yautía,* fr. Taino] (1899) : any of several aroid plants (genus *Xanthosoma,* esp. *X. sagittifolium*) chiefly of tropical America with starchy edible shaggy brown tubers that are cooked and eaten like yams or potatoes; *also* : one of these tubers
[1]**yaw** \ˈyȯ\ *n* [origin unknown] (1546) **1 :** the action of yawing; *esp* **:** a side to side movement **2 :** the extent of the movement in yawing
[2]**yaw** *vi* (1586) **1 a** *of a ship* **:** to deviate erratically from a course (as when struck by a heavy sea); *esp* **:** to move from side to side **b** *of an airplane, spacecraft, or projectile* **:** to turn by angular motion about the vertical axis **2 :** ALTERNATE ⟨restlessly ~*ing* between apparent extremes —Martin Kasindorf⟩
yawl \ˈyȯl\ *n* [LG *jolle*] (1670) **1 :** a ship's small boat : JOLLY BOAT **2 :** a fore-and-aft rigged sailboat carrying a mainsail and one or more jibs with a mizzenmast far aft

yawl 2

[1]**yawn** \ˈyȯn, ˈyän\ *vb* [ME *yenen, yanen,* fr. OE *ginian;* akin to OHG *ginēn* to yawn, L *hiare,* Gk *chainein*] *vi* (bef. 12c) **1 :** to open wide : GAPE **2 :** to open the mouth wide and take a deep breath usu. as an involuntary reaction to fatigue or boredom ~ *vt* **1 :** to utter with a yawn **2 :** to accomplish with or impel by yawns ⟨his grandchildren ~*ed* him to bed —L. L. King⟩
[2]**yawn** *n* (1602) **1 :** GAP, CAVITY **2 :** an opening of the mouth wide while taking a deep breath often as an involuntary reaction to fatigue or boredom; *also* **:** a reaction resembling a yawn ⟨a . . . success at the box office but drew only ~*s* from critics —*Current Biog.*⟩ **3 :** [5]BORE ⟨this book is kind of a ~ —Ilene L. Cooper⟩
yawn·er \ˈyȯ-nər\ *n* (1687) **1 :** one that yawns **2 :** something that causes boredom ⟨the show was a real ~⟩
yawn·ing \ˈyȯ-niŋ\ *adj* (bef. 12c) **1 :** wide open : CAVERNOUS ⟨a ~ hole⟩ ⟨~ gaps in the plot⟩ **2 :** showing fatigue or boredom by yawns ⟨a ~ audience⟩ — **yawn·ing·ly** \ˈyȯ-niŋ-lē\ *adv*
[1]**yawp** *or* **yaup** \ˈyȯp\ *vi* [ME *yolpen*] (14c) **1 :** to make a raucous noise : SQUAWK **2 :** CLAMOR, COMPLAIN — **yawp·er** *n*
[2]**yawp** *also* **yaup** *n* (1824) **1 :** a raucous noise : SQUAWK **2 :** something suggestive of a raucous noise; *specif* **:** rough vigorous language
yawp·ing \ˈyȯ-piŋ\ *n* (1876) : a strident utterance
yaws \ˈyȯz\ *n pl but sing or pl in constr* [prob. fr. an English-based creole of the Caribbean] (1679) : a contagious tropical disease caused by a spirochete (*Treponema pertenue*) closely resembling the causative agent of syphilis and marked by infectious ulcerative skin lesions with later bone involvement — called also *frambesia*
y–ax·is \ˈwī-ˌak-səs\ *n* (1875) **1 :** the axis of a plane Cartesian coordinate system parallel to which ordinates are measured **2 :** one of the three axes in a three-dimensional rectangular coordinate system
Yb *symbol* ytterbium
YBP *abbr* years before present
Y chromosome *n* (1911) : a sex chromosome that is characteristic of male cells in species in which the male typically has two unlike sex chromosomes — compare X CHROMOSOME
yclept *or* **ycleped** [ME, fr. OE *geclipod,* pp. of *clipian* to cry out, name] *past part of* CLEPE
y–co·or·di·nate \ˌwī-kō-ˈȯrd-nət, -ˈȯr-də-nət, -də-ˌnāt\ *n* (1927) : a coordinate whose value is determined by measuring parallel to a y-axis; *specif* : ORDINATE
yd *abbr* yard
[1]**ye** \ˈyē\ *pron* [ME, fr. OE *gē;* akin to OHG *ir* you — more at YOU] (bef. 12c) : YOU 1 — used orig. only as a plural pronoun of the second person in the subjective case and now used esp. in ecclesiastical or literary language and in various English dialects
[2]**ye** \yē, yə; *orig same as* [1]THE\ *definite article* [alter. of ME *þe* the, fr. OE *þē;* fr. the use of the letter *y* by printers and scribes of late ME to represent þ (*th*) of earlier manuscripts] (1551) *archaic* : THE ⟨*Ye* Olde Gifte Shoppe⟩
[1]**yea** \ˈyā\ *adv* [ME *ye, ya,* fr. OE *gēa;* akin to OHG *jā* yes] (bef. 12c) **1 :** YES — used in oral voting **2 :** more than this : not only so but — used to introduce a more explicit or emphatic phrase ⟨yet the impression, ~ the evidence, is inescapable —J. G. Harrison⟩
[2]**yea** *n* (13c) **1 :** AFFIRMATION, ASSENT **2 a :** an affirmative vote **b :** a person casting a yea vote
yeah \ˈyeə, ˈyaə\ *adv* [by alter.] (1902) : YES
yean \ˈyēn, ˈēn\ *vi* [ME *yenen,* fr. OE **geēanian,* fr. OE *ge-,* perfective prefix + *ēanian* to yean; akin to L *agnus* lamb, Gk *amnos*] (1548) : to bring forth young — used of a sheep or goat
yean·ling \-liŋ, -lən\ *n* (1637) : LAMB, KID 1a
year \ˈyir\ *n* [ME *yere,* fr. OE *gēar;* akin to OHG *jār* year, Gk *hōros* year, *hōra* season, hour] (bef. 12c) **1 a :** the period of about 365¼ solar days required for one revolution of the earth around the sun **b :** the time required for the apparent sun to return to an arbitrary fixed or moving reference point in the sky **c :** the time in which a planet completes a revolution about the sun ⟨two Mercury ~*s*⟩ **2 a :** a cycle in the Gregorian calendar of 365 or 366 days divided into 12 months beginning with January and ending with December **b :** a period of time equal to one year of the Gregorian calendar but beginning at a different time **3 :** a calendar year specified usu. by a number ⟨died in the ~ 1900⟩ **4** *pl* **:** a time or era having a special significance ⟨their glory ~*s*⟩ **5 a :** 12 months that constitute a measure of age or duration ⟨her 21st ~⟩ — often used in combination ⟨a *year*-old child⟩ **b** *pl* **:** AGE ⟨wise beyond her ~*s*⟩; *also* **:** the final stage of the normal life span **6 :** a period of time (as the usu. 9-month period in which a school is in session) other than a calendar year
year·book \-ˌbu̇k\ *n* (1677) **1 :** a book published yearly as a report or summary of statistics or facts : ANNUAL **2 :** a school publication that is compiled usu. by a graduating class and that serves as a record of the year's activities
[1]**year–end** \ˈyir-ˈend\ *n* (1872) : the end of usu. the fiscal year
[2]**year–end** *adj* (1899) : made, occurring, or existing at the year-end ⟨a ~ report⟩
year·ling \ˈyir-liŋ, ˈyər-lən\ *n* (15c) : one that is a year old: as **a :** an animal one year old or in the second year of its age **b :** a racehorse between January 1 of the year after the year in which it was foaled and the next January 1 — **yearling** *adj*
year·long \ˈyir-ˈlȯŋ\ *adj* (1813) : lasting through a year
[1]**year·ly** \ˈyir-lē\ *adj* (bef. 12c) **1 :** reckoned by the year **2 :** occurring, appearing, made, done, or acted upon every year or once a year : ANNUAL
[2]**yearly** *adv* (bef. 12c) : every year : ANNUALLY
Yearly Meeting *n* (1688) : an organization uniting several Quarterly Meetings of the Society of Friends
yearn \ˈyərn\ *vi* [ME *yernen,* fr. OE *giernan;* akin to OHG *gerōn* to desire, L *hortari* to urge, encourage, Gk *chairein* to rejoice] (bef. 12c) **1 :** to long persistently, wistfully, or sadly ⟨~*s* to make a difference⟩ **2 :** to feel tenderness or compassion ***syn*** see LONG — **yearn·er** *n* — **yearn·ing·ly** \ˈyər-niŋ-lē\ *adv*
yearn·ing \ˈyər-niŋ\ *n* (bef. 12c) : a tender or urgent longing ⟨a ~ for justice⟩
year of grace (14c) : a calendar year of the Christian era ⟨the *year of grace* 1993⟩
year–round \ˈyir-ˈrau̇nd\ *adj* (1924) : occurring, effective, employed, staying, or operating for the full year : not seasonal ⟨a ~ resort⟩ — **year–round** *adv* — **year–round·er** \-ˈrau̇n-dər\ *n*
yea–say·er \ˈyā-ˌsā-ər, -ˌser\ *n* (1920) **1 :** one whose attitude is that of confident affirmation **2 :** YES-MAN
[1]**yeast** \ˈyēst, *esp Southern & Midland* ˈēst\ *n* [ME *yest,* fr. OE *gist;* akin to OHG *jesen, gesen* to ferment, Gk *zein* to boil] (bef. 12c) **1 a :** a yellowish surface froth or sediment that occurs esp. in saccharine liquids (as fruit juices) in which it promotes alcoholic fermentation, consists largely of cells of a fungus (as the saccharomyces, *Saccharomyces cerevisiae*), and is used esp. in the making of alcoholic liquors and as a leaven in baking **b :** a commercial product containing yeast fungi in a moist or dry medium **c** (1) **:** a unicellular fungus that is present and functionally active in yeast, usu. has little or no mycelium, and reproduces by budding (2) **:** any of various similar fungi **2** *archaic* **:** the foam or spume of waves **3 :** something that causes ferment or activity ⟨were all seething with the ~ of revolt —J. F. Dobie⟩
[2]**yeast** *vi* (1819) : FERMENT, FROTH
yeast infection *n* (1966) : infection of the vagina with an overgrowth of a normally present candidal fungus (*Candida albicans*) that is characterized by a discharge and inflammation; *broadly* **:** an infection (as thrush) caused by a yeast fungus
yeasty \ˈyēs-tē, ˈēs-tē\ *adj* **yeast·i·er; -est** (1598) **1 :** of, relating to, or resembling yeast ⟨a ~ flavor⟩ **2 a :** IMMATURE, UNSETTLED **b :** marked by change ⟨a ~ period in history⟩ **c :** full of vitality **d :** FRIVOLOUS 1a **e :** FRIVOLOUS 2 — **yeast·i·ness** \-tē-nəs\ *n*
yech *or* **yecch** \ˈyək, ˈyək̲, ˈyek, ˈyek̲\ *interj* (1969) — used to express rejection or disgust
yegg \ˈyeg, ˈyāg\ *n* [origin unknown] (1903) : SAFECRACKER; *also* : ROBBER
[1]**yell** \ˈyel\ *vb* [ME, fr. OE *giellan;* akin to OHG *gellan* to yell, OE *galan* to sing] *vi* (bef. 12c) **1 :** to utter a loud cry, scream, or shout **2 :** to give a cheer usu. in unison ~ *vt* : to utter or declare with or as if with a yell : SHOUT — **yell·er** *n*
[2]**yell** *n* (14c) **1 :** SCREAM, SHOUT **2 :** a usu. rhythmic cheer used esp. in schools or colleges to encourage athletic teams

[1]**yel·low** \ˈye-(ˌ)lō, *dial* ˈye-lər *or* ˈya-\ *adj* [ME *yelwe, yelow,* fr. OE *geolu;* akin to OHG *gelo* yellow, L *helvus* light bay, Gk *chlōros* greenish yellow, Skt *hari* yellowish] (bef. 12c) **1 a :** of the color yellow **b :** become yellowish through age, disease, or discoloration **:** SALLOW **c** *sometimes offensive* **:** having a yellowish or light brown complexion or skin **2 a :** featuring sensational or scandalous items or ordinary news sensationally distorted ⟨~ journalism⟩ **b :** MEAN, COWARDLY — **yel·low·ish** \ˈye-lə-wish\ *adj*

[2]**yellow** *n* (bef. 12c) **1 :** something yellow or marked by a yellow color: as **a** *sometimes offensive* **:** a person having yellowish or light brown skin **b :** the yolk of an egg **2 a :** a color whose hue resembles that of ripe lemons or sunflowers or is that of the portion of the spectrum lying between green and orange **b :** a pigment or dye that colors yellow **3** *pl* **:** JAUNDICE **4** *pl but sing in constr* **:** any of several plant diseases caused esp. by phytoplasmas and marked by yellowing of the foliage and stunting

[3]**yellow** *vi* (15c) **:** to become or turn yellow ~ *vt* **:** to make yellow **:** give a yellow tinge or color to ⟨~*ed* by time⟩

yellow bile *n* (ca. 1823) **:** a humor believed in medieval physiology to be secreted by the liver and to cause irascibility

yellow birch *n* (1787) **:** a large birch (*Betula alleghaniensis* syn. *B. lutea*) of chiefly eastern No. America with thin lustrous gray or yellow bark forming plates with ragged edges in older trees; *also* **:** its strong hard dark brown to reddish-brown wood

yel·low·cake \ˈye-lō-ˌkāk, ˈye-lə-\ *n* (1950) **:** partially refined uranium ore that is often used as an intermediate step in the production of nuclear weapons

yel·low–dog \ˌye-lō-ˈdȯg, -lə-ˈdȯg\ *adj* (1880) **1 :** MEAN, CONTEMPTIBLE **2 :** of or relating to opposition to trade unionism or a labor union

yellow–dog contract *n* (1920) **:** an employment contract in which a worker disavows membership in and agrees not to join a labor union in order to get a job

yellow dwarf *n* (1928) **:** any of several plant diseases of cereal grasses (as oats and barley), onions, potatoes, tomatoes, or tobacco that are characterized by yellowing and stunting and are caused by viruses

yellow fever *n* (1738) **:** an acute infectious disease of warm regions (as sub-Saharan Africa and tropical So. America) marked by sudden onset, prostration, fever, and headache and sometimes albuminuria, jaundice, and hemorrhage and caused by a flavivirus (species *Yellow fever virus* of the genus *Flavivirus*) transmitted esp. by the yellow-fever mosquito

yellow–fever mosquito *n* (1905) **:** a small dark-colored mosquito (*Aedes aegypti*) that is the usual vector of yellow fever

yel·low·fin tuna \ˈye-lō-ˌfin-, ˈye-lə-\ *n* (1922) **:** a nearly cosmopolitan tuna (*Thunnus albacares*) with yellowish fins — called also *yellowfin*

yellow–green alga *n* (1930) **:** any of a class (Xanthophyceae of the division Chrysophyta) of algae with the chlorophyll masked by brown or yellow pigment

yel·low·ham·mer \ˈye-lō-ˌha-mər, ˈye-lə-\ *n* [alter. of earlier *yelambre,* fr. ME **yelwambre,* fr. *yelwe* yellow + **ambre* yellowhammer, fr. OE *amore;* akin to OHG *amaro* yellowhammer, *amari* emmer] (1587) **1 :** a common Palearctic finch (*Emberiza citrinella* of the family Emberizidae) having the male largely yellow and chestnut — called also *yellow bunting* **2 :** YELLOW-SHAFTED FLICKER

yellow jack *n* (ca. 1833) **1 :** YELLOW FEVER **2 :** a yellowish carangid marine food fish (*Caranx bartholomaei*) found from Massachusetts to Brazil

yellow jacket *n* (1796) **1 :** any of various small yellow-marked vespid wasps (esp. genus *Vespula*) that commonly nest in the ground and can sting repeatedly and painfully **2** *slang* **:** pentobarbital esp. in a yellow capsule

yellow jessamine *n* (1707) **:** a twining No. American evergreen shrub (*Gelsemium sempervirens* of the family Loganiaceae) with fragrant yellow flowers — called also *yellow jasmine*

yel·low·legs \ˈye-lō-ˌlegz, ˈye-lə-, -ˌlāgz\ *n pl but sing or pl in constr* (ca. 1772) **:** either of two American shorebirds of the sandpiper family with yellow legs: **a :** GREATER YELLOWLEGS **b :** LESSER YELLOWLEGS

yellow ocher *n* (15c) **1 :** a mixture of limonite usu. with clay and silica used as a pigment **2 :** a moderate orange yellow

yellow pages *n pl, often cap Y&P* (1927) **1 :** the section of a telephone book that lists business and professional firms alphabetically by category and that includes classified advertising; *also* **:** a listing of products or services that is independently published **2 :** a directory resembling yellow pages

yellow perch *n* (1796) **:** a common No. American freshwater fish (*Perca flavescens*) of the perch family that has yellowish sides with dark green vertical bands and is a popular food and sport fish

yellow peril *n, often cap Y&P* (1897) **1 :** a danger to Western civilization held to arise from expansion of the power and influence of eastern Asian peoples **2 :** a threat to Western living standards from the influx of eastern Asian laborers willing to work for very low wages

yellow pine *n* (1709) **1 :** any of several No. American pines (as a Ponderosa pine or longleaf pine) with yellowish wood **2 :** the wood of a yellow pine

yellow poplar *n* (1774) **1 :** TULIP TREE 1 **2 :** TULIPWOOD 1

yellow rain *n* (1979) **:** a yellow substance that has occurred in southeastern Asia as a mist or as spots on rocks and vegetation and has been held to be a biological warfare agent used in the Vietnam War but appears upon scientific examination to be identical to pollen-laden bee feces

yel·low–shaft·ed flicker \ˈye-lō-ˌshaf-təd-, ˈye-lə-\ *n* (1888) **:** a flicker of eastern No. America that is golden yellow on the underside of the tail and wings, has a red mark on the nape, and in the male has a black streak on each cheek

yellow spot *n* (1856) **:** MACULA LUTEA

yel·low·tail \ˈye-lō-ˌtāl, ˈye-lə-\ *n, pl* **yellowtail** *or* **yellowtails** (1709) **:** any of various fishes having a yellow or yellowish tail: as **a :** any of several carangid fishes (genus *Seriola*); *esp* **:** a food and sport fish (*S. lalandi*) of the Pacific and Indian oceans having a yellow stripe along each side of the body **b :** SILVER PERCH a **c :** a snapper (*Ocyurus chrysurus*) that is a sport and food fish found from Massachusetts to Brazil and is olive to bluish above with yellow spots and a broad yellow stripe along each side of the body — called also *yellowtail snapper*

yellowtail flounder *n* (1950) **:** a flounder (*Limanda ferruginea*) of the western Atlantic that is brownish above with rusty spots and yellow in front of the tail fin

yel·low·throat \-ˌthrōt\ *n* (1702) **:** any of several largely olive American warblers (genus *Geothlypis*); *esp* **:** one (*G. trichas*) with yellow breast and throat and in the male a black mask

yel·low·ware \-ˌwer\ *n* (1785) **:** pottery made from buff clay and covered with a yellowish transparent clay

yel·low·wood \-ˌwu̇d\ *n* (ca. 1666) **1 :** any of various trees having yellowish wood or yielding a yellow extract; *esp* **:** a leguminous tree (*Cladrastis lutea*) of the southern U.S. having showy white fragrant flowers and yielding a yellow dye **2 :** the wood of a yellowwood tree

yellowwood

[1]**yelp** \ˈyelp\ *n* [[2]*yelp*] (1501) **:** a sharp shrill bark or cry (as of a dog or turkey); *also* **:** SQUEAL

[2]**yelp** *vb* [ME, to boast, cry out, fr. OE *gielpan* to boast, exult; akin to OHG *gelph* outcry] *vi* (1553) **:** to utter a sharp quick shrill cry ⟨dogs ~⟩ ~ *vt* **:** to utter with a yelp

yelp·er \ˈyel-pər\ *n* (1673) **1 :** one that yelps; *esp* **:** a yelping dog **2 :** an instrument used by hunters to produce a call or whistle imitating the yelp of the wild turkey hen

[1]**yen** \ˈyen\ *n, pl* **yen** [Jp *en*] (1875) — see MONEY table

[2]**yen** *n* [obs. E argot *yen-yen* craving for opium, fr. Chin (Guangdong) *yīn-yáhn,* fr. *yīn* opium + *yáhn* craving] (1906) **:** a strong desire or propensity ⟨a ~ for the sea⟩; *also* **:** URGE, CRAVING ⟨a ~ for ice cream⟩

[3]**yen** *vi* **yenned; yen·ning** (ca. 1919) **:** to have an intense desire **:** LONG

yen–shee \ˈyen-ˈshē\ *n* [Chin (Guangdong) *yīn-sí,* fr. *yīn* opium + *sí* excrement, filth] (ca. 1882) **:** the residue formed in the bowl of an opium pipe by smoking

yen·ta \ˈyen-tə\ *n* [Yiddish *yente,* fr. the name *Yente*] (1923) **:** one that meddles; *also* **:** BLABBERMOUTH, GOSSIP

yeo·man \ˈyō-mən\ *n* [ME *yoman, yeman*] (14c) **1 a :** an attendant or officer in a royal or noble household **b :** a person attending or assisting another **:** RETAINER **c :** YEOMAN OF THE GUARD **d :** a naval petty officer who performs clerical duties **2 a :** a person who owns and cultivates a small farm; *specif* **:** one belonging to a class of English freeholders below the gentry **b :** a person of the social rank of yeoman **3 :** one that performs great and loyal service ⟨did a ~'s job in seeing the program through⟩

[1]**yeo·man·ly** \-lē\ *adv* (14c) *archaic* **:** in a manner befitting a yeoman **:** BRAVELY

[2]**yeomanly** *adj* (1576) **1 :** of, relating to, or having the rank of a yeoman **2 :** becoming or suitable to a yeoman **:** STURDY, LOYAL ⟨~ surveillance efforts⟩

yeoman of the guard (ca. 1520) **:** a member of a military corps attached to the British royal household that serves as ceremonial attendants of the sovereign

yeo·man·ry \ˈyō-mən-rē\ *n* (14c) **1 :** the body of yeomen; *specif* **:** the body of small landed proprietors of the middle class **2 :** a British volunteer cavalry force created from yeomen in 1761 as a home defense force and reorganized in 1907 as part of the territorial force

yeoman warder *n* (1573) **:** BEEFEATER 2

yep \ˈyep, *or with glottal stop instead of* p\ *or* **yup** \ˈyəp\ *adv* [by alter.] (1891) **:** YES

-yer — see -ER

yer·ba ma·té \ˌyer-bə-ˈmä-ˌtā, ˌyər-\ *n* [AmerSp *yerba mate,* fr. *yerba* herb + *mate* maté] (1839) **:** MATÉ

[1]**yerk** \ˈyərk\ *vt* [ME, to bind tightly] (ca. 1520) **1** *dial* **:** to beat vigorously **:** THRASH **2** *dial* **:** to attack or excite vigorously **:** GOAD

[2]**yerk** *n* (1581) **1** *Scot* **:** a lashing out **:** KICK **2** *dial* **:** JERK 1

[1]**yes** \ˈyes\ *adv* [ME, fr. OE *gēse*] (bef. 12c) **1** — used as a function word to express assent or agreement ⟨are you ready? *Yes,* I am⟩ **2** — used as a function word usu. to introduce correction or contradiction of a negative assertion or direction ⟨don't say that! *Yes,* I will⟩ **3** — used as a function word to introduce a more emphatic or explicit phrase **4** — used as a function word to indicate uncertainty or polite interest or attentiveness

[2]**yes** *n* (1712) **:** an affirmative reply **:** YEA

ye·shi·va *also* **ye·shi·vah** \yə-ˈshē-və\ *n, pl* **yeshivas** *or* **ye·shi·vot** \-ˌshē-ˈvōt, -ˈvōth\ [LHeb *yĕshībhāh*] (1760) **1 :** a school for talmudic study **2 :** an Orthodox Jewish rabbinical seminary **3 :** a Jewish day school providing secular and religious instruction

yes–man \ˈyes-ˌman\ *n* (1912) **:** a person who agrees with everything that is said; *esp* **:** one who endorses or supports without criticism every opinion or proposal of an associate or superior

yes·ter \ˈyes-tər\ *adj* (1520) *archaic* **:** of or relating to yesterday

[1]**yes·ter·day** \ˈyes-tər-(ˌ)dā, -dē\ *adv* [ME *yisterday,* fr. OE *giestran dæg,* fr. *giestran* yesterday + *dæg* day; akin to OHG *gestaron* yesterday, L *heri,* Gk *chthes*] (bef. 12c) **1 :** on the day last past **:** on the day preceding today **2 :** at a time not long past **:** only a short time ago ⟨I wasn't born ~⟩ — **yesterday** *adj*

[2]**yesterday** *n* (bef. 12c) **1 :** the day last past **:** the day next before the present **2 :** recent time **:** time not long past **3 :** past time — usu. used in pl.

[1]**yes·ter·night** \ˈyes-tər-ˌnīt\ *adv* [ME, fr. OE *gystran niht,* fr. *giestran* yesterday + *niht* night] (bef. 12c) *archaic* **:** on the night last past

[2]**yesternight** *n* (1513) **:** the night last past

yes·ter·year \ˈyes-tər-ˌyir\ *n* [*yesterday* + *year*] (1870) **1 :** last year **2 :** time gone by; *esp* **:** the recent past — **yesteryear** *adv*

yes·treen \ye-ˈstrēn\ *n* [ME (Sc) *yistrevin,* fr. *yister*day + *evin* evening, alter. of ME *even*] (1773) *chiefly Scot* **:** last evening or night — **yestreen** *adv*

[1]**yet** \ˈyet\ *adv* [ME, fr. OE *gīet;* akin to OFris *ieta* yet] (bef. 12c) **1 a :** in addition **:** BESIDES ⟨gives ~ another reason⟩ **b :** EVEN 2c ⟨a ~ higher speed⟩ **c :** on top of everything else **:** no less ⟨had wells going dry. Between two large lakes, ~ —J. H. Buzard⟩ **2 a** (1) **:** up to now **:** so far ⟨hasn't done much ~⟩ — often used to imply the negative of a following infinitive ⟨have ~ to win a game⟩ (2) **:** at this or that time **:** so soon as now ⟨not time to go ~⟩ **b :** continuously up to the present or a specified time **:** STILL ⟨is ~ a new country⟩ **c :** at a future time

: EVENTUALLY ⟨may ~ see the light⟩ **3 :** NEVERTHELESS, HOWEVER — **as yet :** up to the present or a specified time ⟨there are *as yet* few clues —Sharon Kingman⟩ — **yet again :** one more time ⟨arrived late *yet again*⟩

[2]**yet** *conj* (13c) : but nevertheless : BUT

ye·ti \ˈye-tē, ˈyā-\ *n* [Sherpa (Tibetan dial. of the Sherpas)] (ca. 1937) : ABOMINABLE SNOWMAN

yeuk \ˈyük\ *vi* [ME (northern) *yukyn,* fr. OE *giccan* — more at ITCH] (15c) *chiefly Scot* : ITCH

yew \ˈyü\ *n* [ME *ew,* fr. OE *īw;* akin to OHG *īwa* yew, MIr *eó*] (bef. 12c) **1 a :** any of a genus (*Taxus* of the family Taxaceae, the yew family) of evergreen gymnospermous trees and shrubs with stiff linear leaves and seeds surrounded by a fleshy red aril: as (1) : a long-lived Eurasian tree or shrub (*T. baccata*) — called also *English yew* (2) : a low straggling bush (*T. canadensis*) of the eastern U.S. and Canada (3) : PACIFIC YEW **b :** the wood of a yew; *esp* : the heavy fine-grained wood of the English yew **2** *archaic* : an archery bow made of yew

Ygerne \ē-ˈgern\ *n* (13c) : IGRAINE

Ygg·dra·sil \ˈig-drə-ˌsil\ *n* [ON] (1770) : a huge ash tree in Norse mythology that overspreads the world and binds earth, hell, and heaven together

YHWH *also* **JHVH** \ˈyä-(ˌ)wä, -(ˌ)vä\ *n* (1862) : YAHWEH — compare TETRAGRAMMATON

Yid \ˈyid\ *n* [Yiddish, fr. MHG *Jüde,* fr. OHG *Judeo,* fr. L *Judaeus* — more at JEW] (ca. 1874) *usu offensive* : JEW

Yid·dish \ˈyi-dish\ *n* [Yiddish *yidish,* short for *yidish daytsh,* lit., Jewish German, fr. MHG *jüdisch diutsch,* fr. *jüdisch* Jewish (fr. *Jude* Jew) + *diutsch* German] (1875) : a High German language written in Hebrew characters that is spoken by Jews and descendants of Jews of central and eastern European origin — **Yiddish** *adj*

Yid·dish·ism \ˈyi-di-ˌshi-zəm\ *n* (1904) **1 :** a usage, word, phrase, or idiom peculiar to Yiddish **2 :** a movement characterized by advocacy of the Yiddish language and culture — **Yid·dish·ist** \-shist\ *n or adj*

[1]**yield** \ˈyēld\ *vb* [ME, fr. OE *gieldan;* akin to OHG *geltan* to pay] *vt* (bef. 12c) **1** *archaic* : RECOMPENSE, REWARD **2 :** to give or render as fitting, rightfully owed, or required **3 :** to give up possession of on claim or demand: as **a :** to give up (as one's breath) and so die **b :** to surrender or relinquish to the physical control of another : hand over possession of **c :** to surrender or submit (oneself) to another **d :** to give (oneself) up to an inclination, temptation, or habit **e :** to relinquish one's possession of (as a position of advantage or point of superiority) ⟨~ precedence⟩ **4 a :** to bear or bring forth as a natural product esp. as a result of cultivation ⟨the tree always ~*s* good fruit⟩ **b :** to produce or furnish as return ⟨this soil should ~ good crops⟩ **c** (1) : to produce as return from an expenditure or investment : furnish as profit or interest ⟨a bond that ~*s* 12 percent⟩ (2) : to produce as revenue : BRING IN ⟨the tax is expected to ~ millions⟩ **5 :** to give up (as a hit or run) in baseball ⟨~*ed* two runs in the third inning⟩ ~ *vi* **1 :** to be fruitful or productive : BEAR, PRODUCE **2 :** to give up and cease resistance or contention : SUBMIT, SUCCUMB ⟨facing an enemy who would not ~⟩ ⟨~*ing* to temptation⟩ **3 :** to give way to pressure or influence : submit to urging, persuasion, or entreaty **4 :** to give way under physical force (as bending, stretching, or breaking) **5 a :** to give place or precedence : acknowledge the superiority of someone else **b :** to be inferior ⟨our dictionary ~*s* to none⟩ **c :** to give way to or become succeeded by someone or something else **6 :** to relinquish the floor of a legislative assembly

syn YIELD, SUBMIT, CAPITULATE, SUCCUMB, RELENT, DEFER mean to give way to someone or something that one can no longer resist. YIELD may apply to any sort or degree of giving way before force, argument, persuasion, or entreaty ⟨*yields* too easily in any argument⟩. SUBMIT suggests full surrendering after resistance or conflict to the will or control of another ⟨a repentant sinner vowing to *submit* to the will of God⟩. CAPITULATE stresses the fact of ending all resistance and may imply either a coming to terms (as with an adversary) or hopelessness in the face of an irresistible opposing force ⟨officials *capitulated* to the protesters' demands⟩. SUCCUMB implies weakness and helplessness to the one that gives way or an overwhelming power to the opposing force ⟨a stage actor *succumbing* to the lure of Hollywood⟩. RELENT implies a yielding through pity or mercy by one who holds the upper hand ⟨finally *relented* and let the children stay up late⟩. DEFER implies a voluntary yielding or submitting out of respect or reverence for or deference and affection toward another ⟨I *defer* to your expertise in these matters⟩. ***syn*** see in addition RELINQUISH

[2]**yield** *n* (15c) **1 :** something yielded : PRODUCT; *esp* : the amount or quantity produced or returned ⟨~ of wheat per acre⟩ **2 :** the capacity of yielding produce

yield·er \ˈyēl-dər\ *n* (1590) : one that yields: as **a :** a person who surrenders, concedes, or gives in **b :** something that yields produce or products

yield·ing \-diŋ\ *adj* (1533) **1 :** PRODUCTIVE ⟨a high-*yielding* wheat⟩ **2 :** lacking rigidity or stiffness : FLEXIBLE **3 :** disposed to submit or comply ⟨a docile and ~ temperament⟩

yikes \ˈyīks\ *interj* [prob. alter. of *yoicks*] (1957) — used to express fear or astonishment

yin \ˈyin\ *n* [Chin (Beijing) *yīn*] (1671) : the feminine passive principle in nature that in Chinese cosmology is exhibited in darkness, cold, or wetness and that combines with yang to produce all that comes to be

yin and yang *n* (1848) : opposite sides, elements, or extremes ⟨the daily *yin and yang* of the campaign —Steve Lopez⟩

Yin·glish \ˈyiŋ-glish, -lish\ *n* [blend of *Yiddish* and *English*] (1951) : English marked by numerous borrowings from Yiddish

y–in·ter·cept \ˈwī-ˈin-tər-ˌsept\ *n* (ca. 1939) : the y-coordinate of a point where a line, curve, or surface intersects the y-axis

yip \ˈyip\ *vi* **yipped; yip·ping** [imit.] (1907) **1 :** to bark sharply, quickly, and often continuously **2 :** to utter a short sharp cry — **yip** *n*

yip·pee \ˈyi-pē\ *interj* (1914) — used to express exuberant delight or triumph

yip·pie \ˈyi-pē\ *n* [*Y*outh *I*nternational *P*arty + *-ie* (as in *hippie*)] (1968) : a person belonging to or identified with a politically active group of hippies

yips \ˈyips\ *n pl* [origin unknown] (1962) : a state of nervous tension affecting an athlete (as a golfer) in the performance of a crucial action ⟨had a bad case of the ~ on short putts⟩

YK *abbr* Yukon Territory

-yl *n comb form* [Gk *hylē* matter, material, lit., wood] : chemical and usu. monovalent group or radical ⟨eth*yl*⟩ ⟨carbon*yl*⟩

ylang–ylang *also* **ilang–ilang** \ˌē-ˌläŋ-ˈē-ˌläŋ\ *n* [Tag] (1870) **1 :** a tree (*Cananga odorata*) of the custard-apple family that is native to the Malay Archipelago, the Philippines, and adjacent areas and has very fragrant greenish-yellow flowers **2 :** a perfume distilled from the flowers of the ylang-ylang tree

YMCA \ˌwī-ˌem-(ˌ)sē-ˈā\ *n* [*Y*oung *M*en's *C*hristian *A*ssociation] (1881) : an international organization that promotes the spiritual, intellectual, social, and physical welfare orig. of young men

YMHA \ˌwī-ˌem-ˌāch-ˈā\ *n* [*Y*oung *M*en's *H*ebrew *A*ssociation] (1918) : an organization that promotes the religious, intellectual, social, and physical welfare of Jewish young men

Ymir \ˈē-ˌmir\ *n* [ON] (1793) : a giant from whose body the gods create the world in Norse mythology

yo \ˈyō\ *interj* [ME *yo, io,* interj.] (15c) — used esp. to call attention, to indicate attentiveness, or to express affirmation

YO *abbr* year old; years old

yob \ˈyäb\ *n* [backward spelling for *boy*] (1908) *Brit* : YOBBO

YOB *abbr* year of birth

yob·bo \ˈyä-bō\ *n, pl* **yobbos** *or* **yobboes** [*yob* + [1]*-o*] (1922) **1** *Brit* : LOUT, YOKEL **2** *Brit* : HOODLUM

yock *var of* [1]YUK

yoc·to- *comb form* [ISV, alter. of *octo-*; fr. the fact that 10^{24} is the eighth power of 10^3] : one septillionth (10^{-24}) part of ⟨*yocto*second⟩

yoc·to·sec·ond \ˈyäk-tə-ˌse-kənd, -kənt\ *n* (1996) : one septillionth of a second

yod \ˈyȯd, ˈyu̇d\ *n* [Heb *yōdh*] (1735) : the 10th letter of the Hebrew alphabet — see ALPHABET table

[1]**yo·del** \ˈyō-dᵊl\ *vb* **-deled** *or* **-delled; -del·ing** *or* **-del·ling** \ˈyōd-liŋ, ˈyō-dᵊl-iŋ\ [G *jodeln*] *vi* (1827) : to sing by suddenly changing from a natural voice to a falsetto and back; *also* : to shout or call in a similar manner ~ *vt* : to sing (a tune) by yodeling — **yo·del·er** \ˈyōd-lər, ˈyō-dᵊl-ər\ *n*

[2]**yodel** *n* (1844) : a song or refrain sung by yodeling; *also* : a yodeled shout or cry

yo·ga \ˈyō-gə\ *n* [Skt, lit., yoking, fr. *yunakti* he yokes; akin to L *jungere* to join — more at YOKE] (1820) **1** *cap* : a Hindu theistic philosophy teaching the suppression of all activity of body, mind, and will in order that the self may realize its distinction from them and attain liberation **2 :** a system of exercises for attaining bodily or mental control and well-being — **yo·gic** \-gik\ *adj, often cap*

yogh \ˈyōk, ˈyōg, ˈyōk\ *n* [ME] (13c) : the letter ȝ used esp. in Middle English chiefly to represent voiced and voiceless velar and palatal fricatives

yo·gi \ˈyō-gē\ *also* **yo·gin** \-gən, -ˌgin\ *n* [Skt *yogin,* fr. *yoga*] (1619) **1 :** a person who practices yoga **2** *cap* : an adherent of Yoga philosophy **3 :** a markedly reflective or mystical person

yo·gurt *also* **yo·ghurt** \ˈyō-gərt\ *n* [Turk *yoğurt*] (1625) : a fermented slightly acid often flavored semisolid food made of milk and milk solids to which cultures of two bacteria (*Lactobacillus bulgaricus* and *Streptococcus thermophilus*) have been added

yo·him·be \yō-ˈhim-bā, yə-, -bē\ *n* [NL, prob. fr. a Bantu language of southern Cameroon] (1930) : a tropical African tree (*Pausinystalia yohimbe* syn. *Corynanthe yohimbe*) of the madder family whose bark yields yohimbine; *also* : a preparation of the bark that is used esp. as an aphrodisiac

yo·him·bine \yō-ˈhim-ˌbēn, -bən\ *n* [ISV, fr. *yohimbe*] (1898) : an alkaloid $C_{21}H_{26}N_2O_3$ obtained from the bark of the yohimbe that is a weak blocker of alpha-adrenergic receptors and has been used as an aphrodisiac

yoicks \ˈyȯiks\ *interj* (1774) — used as a cry of encouragement to foxhounds

[1]**yoke** \ˈyōk\ *n, pl* **yokes** [ME *yok,* fr. OE *geoc;* akin to OHG *joh* yoke, L *jugum,* Gk *zygon,* Skt *yuga,* L *jungere* to join] (bef. 12c) **1 a :** a wooden bar or frame by which two draft animals (as oxen) are joined at the heads or necks for working together **b :** an arched device formerly laid on the neck of a defeated person **c :** a frame fitted to a person's shoulders to carry a load in two equal portions **d :** a bar by which the end of the tongue of a wagon or carriage is suspended from the collars of the harness **e** (1) : a crosspiece on the head of a boat's rudder (2) : an airplane control operating the elevators and ailerons **f :** a frame from which a bell is hung **g :** a clamp or similar piece that embraces two parts to hold or unite them in position **2** *pl usu* **yoke** : two animals yoked or worked together **3 a** (1) : an oppressive agency (2) : SERVITUDE, BONDAGE **b :** TIE, LINK; *esp* : MARRIAGE **4 :** a fitted or shaped piece at the top of a skirt or at the shoulder of various garments

[2]**yoke** *vb* **yoked; yok·ing** *vt* (bef. 12c) **1 a** (1) : to put a yoke on (2) : to join in or with a yoke **b :** to attach a draft animal to; *also* : to attach (a draft animal) to something **2 :** to join as if by a yoke **3 :** to put to work ~ *vi* : to become joined or linked

yoke·fel·low \ˈyōk-ˌfe-(ˌ)lō\ *n* (1526) : a close companion : MATE

yo·kel \ˈyō-kəl\ *n* [perh. fr. E dial. *yokel* green woodpecker, of imit. origin] (ca. 1812) : a naive or gullible inhabitant of a rural area or small town

yolk \ˈyōk, ˈyelk (*in cultivated speech, esp Southern*), *also* ˈyōlk, ˈyȯlk, ˈyälk, ˈyəlk\ *also* **yoke** \ˈyōk\ *n* [ME *yolke,* fr. OE *geoloca,* fr. *geolu* yellow — more at YELLOW] (bef. 12c) **1 a :** the yellow spheroidal mass of stored food that forms the inner portion of the egg of a bird or reptile and is surrounded by the white — see EGG illustration **b** *archaic* : the whole contents of an animal ovum consisting of a protoplasmic formative portion and an inert nutritive portion **c :** material stored in an animal ovum that supplies food to the developing embryo and consists chiefly of proteins, lecithin, and cholesterol **2** [akin to MD *ieke* yolk (of wool), OE *ēowu* ewe] : oily material in unprocessed sheep wool consisting of wool fat, suint, and debris — **yolked** *adj* — **yolky** *adj*

\ə\ **abut** \ᵊ\ kitten, F table \ər\ **further** \a\ **ash** \ā\ **ace** \ä\ mop, mar
\au̇\ **out** \ch\ **chin** \e\ **bet** \ē\ **easy** \g\ **go** \i\ **hit** \ī\ **ice** \j\ **job**
\ŋ\ **sing** \ō\ **go** \ȯ\ **law** \ȯi\ **boy** \th\ **thin** \t͟h\ **the** \ü\ **loot** \u̇\ **foot**
\y\ **yet** \zh\ **vision, beige** \k, ⁿ, œ, ue, ʸ\ *see* Guide to Pronunciation

yolk sac *n* (1861) **:** a membranous sac of most vertebrates that encloses the yolk, is attached in most forms (as in humans) through the yolk stalk with the intestinal cavity of the embryo, and is supplied with blood vessels that transport nutritive yolk products to the developing embryo

yolk stalk *n* (1900) **:** the narrow tubular stalk connecting the yolk sac with the embryo

Yom Kip·pur \ˌyōm-ki-ˈpu̇r, ˌyȯm-, ˌyäm-; -ˈki-pər, -(ˌ)pu̇r\ *n* [Heb *yōm kippūr,* lit., day of atonement] (1854) **:** a Jewish holiday observed with fasting and prayer on the 10th day of Tishri in accordance with the rites described in Leviticus 16 — called also *Day of Atonement*

[1]**yon** \ˈyän\ *adj* [ME, fr. OE *geon;* akin to OHG *ienēr,* adj., that, Gk *enē* day after tomorrow] (bef. 12c) **:** YONDER

[2]**yon** *pron* (14c) *dial* **:** that or those yonder

[3]**yon** *adv* (14c) **1 :** YONDER **2 :** THITHER ⟨ran hither and ~⟩

[1]**yond** \ˈyänd\ *adv* [ME, fr. OE *geond;* akin to OE *geon*] (bef. 12c) *archaic* **:** YONDER

[2]**yond** *adj* (13c) *dial* **:** YONDER

[1]**yon·der** \ˈyän-dər\ *adv* [ME, fr. *yond* + *-er* (as in *hither*)] (14c) **:** at or in that indicated more or less distant place usu. within sight

[2]**yonder** *adj* (14c) **1 :** farther removed **:** more distant **2 :** being at a distance within view or at a place or in a direction known or indicated

[3]**yonder** *pron* (14c) **:** something that is or is in an indicated more or less distant place

yo·ni \ˈyō-nē\ *n* [Skt, vulva] (1799) **:** a stylized representation of the female genitalia that in Hinduism is a sign of generative power and that symbolizes the goddess Shakti — compare LINGAM — **yo·nic** \ˈyō-nik\ *adj*

yoo–hoo \ˈyü-(ˌ)hü\ *interj* [prob. alter. of *yo-ho,* interj. used to attract attention — more at YAHOO] (ca. 1924) — used to attract attention or as a call to persons

Yoop·er \ˈyu̇-pər\ *n* [*yoop-* (fr. the abbr. *UP*) + [2]*-er*] (1977) **:** a native or resident of the Upper Peninsula of Michigan — used as a nickname

yore \ˈyȯr\ *n* [ME, fr. *yore,* adv., long ago, fr. OE *gēara,* fr. *gēar* year — more at YEAR] (14c) **:** time past and esp. long past — usu. used in the phrase *of yore*

York·ie \ˈyȯr-kē\ *n* [by shortening & alter.] (1946) **:** YORKSHIRE TERRIER

York·ist \ˈyȯr-kist\ *adj* [Edward, Duke of *York* (Edward IV of England)] (1601) **:** of or relating to the English royal house that ruled from 1461 to 1485 — **Yorkist** *n*

York rite \ˈyȯrk-\ *n* [*York,* England] (ca. 1878) **1 :** a ceremonial observed by one of the Masonic systems **2 :** a system or organization that observes the York rite and confers in the U.S. 13 degrees of which the last three are in commanderies of Knights Templar — compare SCOTTISH RITE

York·shire \ˈyȯrk-ˌshir, -shər\ *n* (1869) **:** a white swine of any of several breeds or strains originated in Yorkshire, England

Yorkshire pudding *n* (1747) **:** a puffy bread dish made from a batter of eggs, flour, and milk that is baked in meat drippings

Yorkshire terrier *n* (1872) **:** any of a breed of compact toy terriers with long straight silky hair mostly bluish gray but tan on the head and chest

Yor·u·ba \ˈyȯr-ə-bə\ *n, pl* **Yoruba** *or* **Yorubas** [Yoruba *Yorùbá*] (1841) **:** a Niger-Congo language of southwestern Nigeria and parts of Benin and Togo; *also* **:** a member of any of the Yoruba-speaking peoples of this region — **Yo·ru·ban** \ˈyȯr-ə-bən\ *n or adj*

yot·ta- *comb form* [ISV, perh. alter. of It *otto* eight; fr. the fact that 10^{24} is the eighth power of 10^3] **:** septillion (10^{24}) ⟨*yotta*byte⟩

yot·ta·byte \ˈyä-tə-ˌbīt\ *n* (1993) **:** one septillion bytes

you \ˈyü, yə *also* yē\ *pron* [ME, fr. OE *ēow,* dat. & accus. of *gē* you; akin to OHG *iu,* dat. of *ir* you, Skt *yūyam* you] (bef. 12c) **1 :** the one or ones being addressed — used as the pronoun of the second person singular or plural in any grammatical relation except that of a possessive ⟨~ may sit in that chair⟩ ⟨~ are my friends⟩ ⟨can I pour ~ a cup of tea⟩; used formerly only as a plural pronoun of the second person in the dative or accusative case as direct or indirect object of a verb or as object of a preposition; compare THEE, THOU, YE, YOUR, YOURS **2 :** ONE 2a ⟨after a while, it grows on ~⟩

you–all \(ˌ)yü-ˈȯl, ˈyü-ˌ; ˈyȯl\ *or* **y'all** \ˈyȯl\ *pron* (1631) *chiefly Southern* **:** YOU — usu. used in addressing two or more persons

you'd \ˈyüd, ˈyu̇d, yəd\ (1599) **:** you had **:** you would

you'll \ˈyül, ˈyu̇l, yəl\ (1584) **:** you will **:** you shall

[1]**young** \ˈyəŋ\ *adj* **youn·ger** \ˈyəŋ-gər\; **youn·gest** \ˈyəŋ-gəst\ [ME *yong,* fr. OE *geong;* akin to OHG *jung* young, L *juvenis*] (bef. 12c) **1 a :** being in the first or an early stage of life, growth, or development **b :** JUNIOR 1a **c :** of an early, tender, or desirable age for use as food or drink ⟨fresh ~ lamb⟩ ⟨a ~ wine⟩ **2 :** having little experience **3 a :** recently come into being **:** NEW ⟨a ~ publishing company⟩ **b :** YOUTHFUL 5 **4 :** of, relating to, or having the characteristics of youth or a young person ⟨~ at heart⟩ **5** *cap* **:** representing a new or rejuvenated esp. political group or movement — **young·ish** \ˈyəŋ-ish\ *adj* — **young·ness** \ˈyəŋ-nəs\ *n*

[2]**young** *n, pl* **young** (bef. 12c) **1** *pl* **a :** young persons **:** YOUTH **b :** immature offspring — used esp. of animals **2 :** a single recently born or hatched animal — **with young** *of a female animal* **:** PREGNANT

young·ber·ry \ˈyəŋ-ˌber-ē\ *n* [B. M. *Young fl*1905 Am. fruit grower] (1927) **:** the large sweet reddish-black fruit of a cultivar of a bramble closely related to the boysenberry and loganberry and grown in the western and southern U.S.; *also* **:** a bramble bearing youngberries

young·blood \ˈyəŋ-ˌbləd\ *n* (1602) **1 :** a young inexperienced person; *esp* **:** one who is newly prominent in a field of endeavor ⟨jazz ~*s*⟩ **2 :** a young black American male

youn·ger \ˈyəŋ-gər\ *n* (bef. 12c) **:** an inferior in age **:** JUNIOR — usu. used with a possessive pronoun ⟨is several years his ~⟩

youn·gest \ˈyəŋ-gəst\ *n, pl* **youngest** (13c) **:** one that is the least old; *esp* **:** the youngest child or member of a family

young·ling \ˈyəŋ-liŋ\ *n* (bef. 12c) **:** one that is young; *esp* **:** a young person or animal — **youngling** *adj*

young·ster \ˈyəŋ(k)-stər\ *n* (1589) **1 a :** a young person **:** YOUTH **b :** CHILD **2 :** a young animal or plant esp. of a domesticated or cultivated breed or type

young Turk *n, often cap Y* [*Young Turks,* a 20th cent. revolutionary party in Turkey] (1908) **:** an insurgent or a member of an insurgent group esp. in a political party **:** RADICAL; *broadly* **:** one advocating changes within a usu. established group

youn·ker \ˈyəŋ-kər\ *n* [D *jonker* young nobleman] (1505) **1 :** a young man **2 :** CHILD, YOUNGSTER

your \yər, ˈyu̇r, ˈyȯr\ *adj* [ME, fr. OE *ēower;* akin to OE *ēow* you — more at YOU] (bef. 12c) **1 :** of or relating to you or yourself or yourselves esp. as possessor or possessors ⟨~ bodies⟩, agent or agents ⟨~ contributions⟩, or object or objects of an action ⟨~ discharge⟩ **2 :** of or relating to one or oneself ⟨when you face the north, east is at ~ right⟩ **3** — used with little or no meaning almost as an equivalent to the definite article *the* ⟨~ typical teenager⟩

you're \yər, ˈyu̇r, ˈyȯr, ˌyü-ər\ (ca. 1590) **:** you are

yours \ˈyu̇rz, ˈyȯrz\ *pron, sing or pl in constr* [ME, fr. *your* + *-s* -'s] (1526) **:** that which belongs to you — used without a following noun as a pronoun equivalent in meaning to the adjective *your* ⟨this book is ~⟩; often used esp. with an adverbial modifier in the complimentary close of a letter ⟨Yours truly⟩ ⟨Sincerely *yours*⟩ — **yours truly :** I, ME, MYSELF ⟨*yours truly* got stuck with the job⟩

your·self \yər-ˈself, *Southern also* -ˈsef\ *pron* (14c) **1 a :** that identical one that is you — used reflexively ⟨you might hurt ~⟩, for emphasis ⟨carry them ~⟩, or in absolute constructions **b :** your normal, healthy, or sane condition or self ⟨you haven't been ~ lately⟩ **2 :** ONESELF

your·selves \-ˈselvz, *Southern also* -ˈsevz\ *pron pl* (1523) **1 :** those identical ones that are you — used reflexively ⟨get ~ a treat⟩, for emphasis, or in absolute constructions **2 :** your normal, healthy, or sane condition or selves ⟨you will feel more like ~ after a good rest⟩

youth \ˈyüth\ *n, pl* **youths** \ˈyüt͟hz, ˈyüths\ *often attrib* [ME *youthe,* fr. OE *geoguth;* akin to OE *geong* young — more at YOUNG] (bef. 12c) **1 a :** the time of life when one is young; *esp* **:** the period between childhood and maturity **b :** the early period of existence, growth, or development **2 a :** a young person; *esp* **:** a young male between adolescence and maturity **b :** young persons or creatures — usu. pl. in constr. **3 :** the quality or state of being youthful **:** YOUTHFULNESS

youth·ful \ˈyüth-fəl\ *adj* (1557) **1 :** of, relating to, or characteristic of youth ⟨~ inexperience⟩ **2 :** being young and not yet mature **3 :** marked by or possessing youth ⟨~ dancers⟩ **4 :** having the vitality or freshness of youth **:** VIGOROUS ⟨my ~ grandparents⟩ **5 :** having accomplished or undergone little erosion ⟨~ mountains⟩ — **youth·ful·ly** \-fə-lē\ *adv* — **youth·ful·ness** *n*

youth hostel *n* (1929) **:** HOSTEL 2b

youth·quake \-ˌkwāk\ *n* [*youth* + earth*quake*] (1966) **:** a shift in cultural norms influenced by the values, tastes, and mores of young people

you've \ˈyüv, yəv\ (ca. 1600) **:** you have

[1]**yowl** \ˈyau̇(-ə)l\ *vb* [ME] *vi* (13c) **1 :** to utter a loud long cry of grief, pain, or distress **:** WAIL **2 :** to complain or protest with or as if with yowls ~ *vt* **:** to express with yowling

[2]**yowl** *n* (15c) **:** a loud long mournful wail or howl (as of a cat)

[1]**yo–yo** \ˈyō-(ˌ)yō\ *n, pl* **yo–yos** [prob. fr. Ilocano *yóyo,* or a cognate word in a language of the Philippines] (1915) **1 :** a thick grooved double disk with a string attached to its center axle that is made to fall and rise to the hand by unwinding and rewinding on the string **2 :** a condition or situation marked by regular fluctuations from one extreme to another **3 :** a stupid or foolish person

[2]**yo–yo** *adj* (1932) **:** shifting back and forth or up and down uncertainly or unexpectedly

[3]**yo–yo** *vi* **yo–yoed; yo–yo·ing** (1967) **:** to move from one position to another repeatedly **:** FLUCTUATE ⟨the stock price ~*ed*⟩

yr *abbr* **1** year **2** your

yrbk *abbr* yearbook

YT *abbr* Yukon Territory

yt·ter·bi·um \i-ˈtər-bē-əm\ *n* [NL, fr. *Ytterby,* town in southern Sweden] (1879) **:** a soft metallic element of the rare-earth group that occurs esp. with other rare earth elements in minerals and that has few commercial uses — see ELEMENT table

yt·tri·um \ˈi-trē-əm\ *n* [NL, fr. *yttria* yttrium oxide (Y_2O_3), irreg. fr. *Ytterby,* town in southern Sweden] (1814) **:** a metallic element usu. included in the rare-earth group that occurs usu. with other rare earth elements in minerals and is used esp. in phosphors, YAG lasers, and superalloys — see ELEMENT table

yu·an \ˈyü-ən, yü-ˈän\ *n, pl* **yuan** [Chin (Beijing) *yuán*] (1917) **1 —** see MONEY table **2 :** the dollar of the Republic of China (Taiwan)

yu·ca \ˈyü-kə\ *n* [NL *jucca,* fr. Taino *yuca*] (1555) **:** CASSAVA

Yu·ca·tec \ˈyü-kə-ˌtek\ *n* [Sp *yucateco*] (1843) **1 :** a member of an American Indian people of the Yucatán Peninsula, Mexico **2 :** the Mayan language of the Yucatecs — **Yu·ca·tec·an** \ˌyü-kə-ˈte-kən\ *adj or n*

yuc·ca \ˈyə-kə\ *n* [NL, fr. Sp *yuca,* of unknown origin] (1664) **1 :** any of a genus (*Yucca*) of sometimes arborescent plants of the agave family that occur in warm regions chiefly of western No. America and have long sword-shaped often stiff fibrous-margined leaves on a usu. woody base and bear a large panicle of white blossoms **2 :** CASSAVA

[1]**yuck** *var of* YUK

[2]**yuck** *also* **yuk** \ˈyək\ *interj* (1966) — used to express rejection or disgust ⟨looked at the meal I had prepared and said "~, I hate that"⟩

yucky *also* **yuk·ky** \ˈyə-kē\ *adj* **yuck·i·er** *also* **yuk·ki·er; -est** [*yuck*] (1970) **:** REPUGNANT, DISTASTEFUL; *also* **:** UNPLEASANT, DISAGREEABLE ⟨felt ~⟩ ⟨a ~ chore⟩

Yug *abbr* Yugoslavia

yu·ga \ˈyu̇-gə, ˈyü-\ *n* [Skt, yoke, age — more at YOKE] (1784) **:** one of the four ages of a Hindu world cycle

[1]**yuk** *or* **yuck** \ˈyək\ *also* **yak** \ˈyäk, ˈyak\ *or* **yock** \ˈyäk\ *n* (1946) **1** *slang* **:** LAUGH ⟨did it just for ~*s*⟩ **2** *slang* **:** JOKE, GAG

[2]**yuk** *or* **yuck** *vi* **yukked** *or* **yucked; yuk·king** *or* **yuck·ing** (1964) *slang* **:** LAUGH, JOKE — usu. used in the phrase *yuk it up*

Yu·kon Gold \ˈyü-ˌkän-\ *n* (1982) **:** a variety of potato developed in Canada that has light yellow flesh and smooth, yellowish-brown skin

yule \ˈyül\ *n, often cap* [ME *yol,* fr. OE *geōl;* akin to ON *jōl,* a pagan midwinter festival] (bef. 12c) **:** the feast of the nativity of Jesus Christ **:** CHRISTMAS

Yule log *n* (1725) **:** a large log formerly put on the hearth on Christmas Eve as the foundation of the fire

yule·tide \ˈyül-ˌtīd\ *n, often cap* (15c) **:** CHRISTMASTIDE

Yu·man \ˈyü-mən\ *n* [*Yuma* Quechan (member of a Yuman-speaking people of the lower Colorado River valley), fr. Sp, fr. O'odham *yuˈmĭ* (1891) : an American Indian language family of southwestern U.S. and northern Mexico — **Yuman** *adj*

yum·my \ˈyə-mē\ *adj* **yum·mi·er; -est** [*yum-yum*] (1899) : highly attractive or pleasing; *esp* : DELICIOUS, DELECTABLE

yum–yum \ˈyəm-ˈyəm\ *interj* (1878) — used to express pleasurable satisfaction esp. in the taste of food

¹yup *var of* YEP

²yup \ˈyəp\ *n* (1983) : YUPPIE

Yu·pik \ˈyü-pək\ *n, pl* **Yupiks** *or* **Yupik** [Central Alaskan Yupik *yúppik*, lit., authentic person] (1951) **1** : the language of the Eskimo people of southwestern Alaska **2** : a member of the Yupik-speaking people

yup·pie \ˈyə-pē\ *n, often cap* [prob. fr. *young* urban *professional* + *-ie*] (1980) : a young college-educated adult who is employed in a well-paying profession and who lives and works in or near a large city — **yup·pie·dom** \-dəm\ *n* — **yup·pie·ish** \-ish\ *adj*

yuppie flu *n* (1987) : CHRONIC FATIGUE SYNDROME

yup·pi·fy \ˈyə-pə-ˌfī\ *vt* **-fied; -fy·ing** (1984) : to make appealing to yuppies; *also* : to infuse with the qualities or values of yuppies — **yup-**

pi·fi·ca·tion \ˌyə-pə-fə-ˈkā-shən\ *n*

yurt \ˈyu̇rt\ *n* [Russ dial. *yurta*, of Turkic origin; akin to Turk *yurt* home] (1876) : a circular domed tent of skins or felt stretched over a collapsible lattice framework and used by pastoral peoples of inner Asia; *also* : a structure that resembles a yurt usu. in size and design

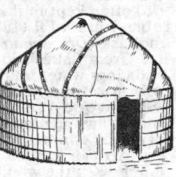

yurt

yu·zu \ˈyü-(ˌ)zü\ *n* (1977) : a green or yellow aromatic citrus fruit whose acidic rind and juice are often used in Japanese cuisine

YWCA \ˌwī-ˌdə-bəl-yü-(ˌ)sē-ˈā, ˌdə-bə-yü-\ *n* [Young Women's Christian Association] (1884) : an international organization that promotes the spiritual, intellectual, social, and physical welfare orig. of young women

YWHA \-ˌāch-ˈā\ *n* [Young Women's Hebrew Association] (1918) : an organization that promotes the religious, intellectual, social, and physical welfare of Jewish young women

---

¹z \ˈzē, *Canad, Brit, & Austral* ˈzed, *chiefly dial* ˈi-zərd\ *n, pl* **z's** *or* **zs** *often cap, often attrib* (bef. 12c) **1 a** : the 26th and last letter of the English alphabet **b** : a graphic representation of this letter **c** : a speech counterpart of orthographic *z* **2** : a graphic device for reproducing the letter *z* **3** : one designated *z* esp. as the 26th in order or class or the third in order or class when *x* is made the first **4** : something shaped like the letter Z **5** : WINK 1 — usu. used in pl. ⟨catch some *z's* before dinner⟩

²z *abbr* **1** zero **2** zone

¹Z *n* (1967) : Z PARTICLE

²Z *or* **ZD** *abbr* zenith distance

za *or* **'za** \ˈzä\ *n* [by alter.] (ca. 1970) *slang* : PIZZA

za·ba·glio·ne \ˌzä-bəl-ˈyō-nē\ *n* [It] (1899) : a whipped dessert or topping consisting of a mixture of egg yolks, sugar, and usu. Marsala wine

Zach *abbr* Zacharias

Zach·a·ri·as \ˌza-kə-ˈrī-əs\ *n* [LL, fr. Gk, fr. Heb *Zĕkharyāh*] (bef. 12c) : ZECHARIAH

zad·dik *or* **tzad·dik** \ˈtsä-dik\ *n, pl* **zad·dik·im** *or* **tzad·dik·im** \tsä-ˈdi-kəm\ [Yiddish *tsadek*, fr. Heb *ṣaddīq* just, righteous] (1873) **1** : a righteous and saintly person by Jewish religious standards **2** : the spiritual leader of a modern Hasidic community

zaf·tig \ˈzäf-tig, ˈzôf-\ *also* **zof·tig** \ˈzôf-\ *adj* [Yiddish *zaftik* juicy, succulent, fr. *zaft* juice, sap, fr. MHG *saf, saft*, fr. OHG *saf* — more at SAP] (ca. 1936) *of a woman* : having a full rounded figure : pleasingly plump

¹zag \ˈzag\ *n* [*zigzag*] (1793) **1 a** : one of the sharp turns, angles, or alterations in a zigzag course **b** : one of the short straight lines or sections of a zigzag course at an angle to a zag **2** : ZIG 2

²zag *vi* **zagged; zag·ging** (1900) : to execute a zag — usu. contrasted with *zig*

zai·bat·su \ˈzī-ˌbät-ˌsü\ *n* [Jp *zai* money, wealth + *batsu* clique, clan] (1947) : a powerful financial and industrial conglomerate of Japan

zaire \ˈzī-(ˌ)ər, zä-ˈir\ *n, pl* **zaires** *or* **zaire** [F *zaïre*, fr. *Zaïre*, former name (1971–97) of the Democratic Republic of the Congo] (1967) : the basic monetary unit of the Democratic Republic of the Congo (1967–71) and of Zaire (1971–96)

zal·cit·a·bine \zal-ˈsi-tə-ˌbēn, -ˌbīn\ *n* [origin unknown] (1991) : DDC

Zam·bo·ni \zam-ˈbō-nē\ *trademark* — used for an ice resurfacing machine

za·mia \ˈzä-mē-ə\ *n* [NL, fr. L *zamiae nuces*, false MS reading for *azaniae nuces* pine nuts] (1819) : any of a genus (*Zamia* of the family Zamiaceae) of American cycads with a short thick woody base, a crown of palmlike leaves, and oblong cones

za·min·dar *or* **ze·min·dar** \ˈzä-mən-ˌdär, ˈze-; zə-ˌmēn-ˈdär\ *n* [Hindi & Urdu *zamīndār*, fr. Pers, fr. *zamīn* land + *-dār* holder] (1683) **1** : a collector of the land revenue of a district for the government during the period of Mogul rule in India **2** : a feudal landlord in British India paying the government a fixed revenue

za·min·dari *or* **ze·min·dari** \ˈzä-mən-ˌdär-ē, ˌze-; zə-ˌmēn-\ *n, pl* **-dar·is** *or* **-dar·ies** [Hindi & Urdu *zamīndārī*, fr. Pers, fr. *zamīndār*] (1757) **1** : the system of landholding and revenue collection by zamindars **2** : the land held or administered by a zamindar

zan·der \ˈzan-dər, ˈtsän-\ *n, pl* **zander** *or* **zanders** [G] (1854) : a pike perch (*Stizostedion lucioperca*) of central Europe related to the walleye

¹za·ny \ˈzā-nē\ *n, pl* **zanies** [It *zanni*, a traditional masked clown, fr. It dial. *Zanni*, nickname for It *Giovanni* John] (1588) **1** : a subordinate clown or acrobat in old comedies who mimics ludicrously the tricks of the principal : MERRY-ANDREW **2** : a slavish follower : TOADY **3 a** : one who acts the buffoon to amuse others **b** : NUT, KOOK

²zany *adj* **za·ni·er; -est** (1609) **1** : being or having the characteristics of a zany **2** : fantastically or absurdly ludicrous ⟨a ~ movie⟩ — **za·ni·ly** \ˈzā-nə-lē\ *adv* — **za·ni·ness** \ˈzā-nē-nəs\ *n*

¹zap \ˈzap\ *interj* [imit.] (1929) **1** — used to express a sound made by or as if by a gun **2** — used to indicate a sudden or instantaneous occurrence

²zap *vb* **zapped; zap·ping** *vt* (1942) **1 a** : to get rid of, destroy, or kill esp. with or as if with sudden force **b** : to hit with or as if with a sudden concentrated application of force or energy ⟨~ to irradiate esp. with microwaves **2 a** : to propel suddenly or speedily **b** : to transport instantaneously **3** : to avoid watching (as a television commercial) by changing channels esp. with a remote control or by fast-forwarding a videotape ~ *vi* **1** : to move with speed or force **2** : to

change television channels using a remote control

³zap *n* (1963) : a pungent or zestful quality : ZIP; *also* : a sudden forceful blow

za·pa·te·ado \ˌzä-pə-tä-ˈä-(ˌ)dō, ˌsä-pə-tä-ˈaü\ *n, pl* **-a·dos** [Sp, fr. *zapatear* to strike or tap with the shoe, fr. *zapato* shoe] (1845) : a Latin American dance marked by rhythmic stamping or tapping of the feet

za·pa·teo \ˌzä-pə-ˈtä-(ˌ)ō, ˌsä-\ *n, pl* **-te·os** [Sp *zapatear*] (1922) : ZAPATEADO

Za·po·tec \ˈzä-pə-ˌtek, ˈsä-\ *n* [Sp *zapoteca*, fr. Nahuatl *tzapotēcah*, pl. of *tzapotēcatl*, lit., person of (the land of) sapodillas, fr. *tzapotl* sapodilla fruit + *-tēcatl* person (from)] (1843) : a member of an American Indian people of Oaxaca state, Mexico

zap·per \ˈza-pər\ *n* (1969) : one that zaps: as **a** : an electronic device designed to attract and kill insects **b** : a person who habitually changes channels (as to avoid commercials) **c** : a remote control device used for zapping

zap·py \ˈza-pē\ *adj* **zap·pi·er; -est** (1969) : ZIPPY

za·re·ba *or* **za·ri·ba** \zə-ˈrē-bə\ *n* [Ar *zarība* enclosure] (1849) : an improvised stockade constructed in parts of Africa esp. of thorny bushes

zar·zue·la \zär-zə-ˈwä-lə, ˌzär-ˈzwä-\ *n* [Sp, prob. fr. *La Zarzuela*, royal residence near Madrid where it was first performed] (1770) : a usu. comic Spanish operetta

z–ax·is \ˈzē-ˌak-səs; *Canad, Brit, & Austral* ˈzed-\ *n* (1929) : one of the axes in a three-dimensional rectangular coordinate system

za·yin \ˈzä-yən, ˈzī-(ə)n\ *n* [Heb] (1823) : the 7th letter of the Hebrew alphabet — *see* ALPHABET table

z–co·or·di·nate \ˈzē-kō-ˈórd-nət; -ˈôr-də-nət, -də-ˌnät; *Canad, Brit, & Austral* ˌzed-\ *n* (ca. 1956) : a coordinate whose value is determined by measuring parallel to a z-axis

z distribution *n* (1968) : a probability density function and esp. a normal distribution that has a mean equal to zero and a standard deviation equal to one and that is used esp. in testing hypotheses about means or proportions of samples drawn from populations whose population standard deviations are known — compare Z-TEST

zeal \ˈzēl\ *n* [ME *zele*, fr. LL *zelus*, fr. Gk *zēlos*] (14c) : eagerness and ardent interest in pursuit of something : FERVOR ⟨her ~ to succeed strained her relationships⟩ *syn* see PASSION

zeal·ot \ˈze-lət\ *n* [LL *zelotes*, fr. Gk *zēlōtēs*, fr. *zēlos*] (1537) **1** *cap* : a member of a fanatical sect arising in Judea during the first century A.D. and militantly opposing the Roman domination of Palestine **2** : a zealous person; *esp* : a fanatical partisan ⟨a religious ~⟩

zeal·ot·ry \ˈze-lə-trē\ *n, pl* **-ries** (1656) : excess of zeal : fanatical devotion

zeal·ous \ˈze-ləs\ *adj* (1526) : filled with or characterized by zeal : marked by fervent partisanship for a person, a cause, or an ideal ⟨~ missionaries⟩ — **zeal·ous·ly** *adv* — **zeal·ous·ness** *n*

ze·a·tin \ˈzē-ə-tən\ *n* [NL *Zea*, genus of grasses including corn + E *-tin* (as in kine*tin*) — more at ZEIN] (1963) : a cytokinin $C_{10}H_{13}N_5O$ first isolated from the endosperm of corn

ze·a·xan·thin \ˌzē-ə-ˈzan-thən\ *n* [ISV *zea-* (fr. NL *Zea*) + *xanthin* carotenoid pigment, fr. *xanth-* + *-in*] (1929) : an isomer of lutein occurring esp. in fruits and vegetables (as spinach and corn)

ze·bra \ˈzē-brə, *Canad & Brit also* ˈze-\ *n, pl* **zebras** [Pg *zebra, zebro* wild ass, perh. fr. L *equiferus*, kind of wild horse, fr. *equus* horse + *ferus* wild — more at EQUINE, FIERCE] (1600) **1** *pl also* **zebra** : any of several fleet African mammals (*Equus burchelli, E. grevyi*, and *E. zebra*) related to the horse but distinctively and conspicuously patterned in stripes of black or dark brown and white or buff **2** [fr. the shirts patterned in black-and-white stripes worn by football referees] : REFEREE 2 **3** : ZEBRA CROSSING — **ze·brine** \-ˌbrīn\ *adj or n*

ze·bra crossing *n* (1950) *Brit* : a crosswalk marked by a series of broad white stripes to indicate a crossing point at which pedestrians have the right of way

zebra finch *n* (1887) : a small Australian waxbill (*Taeniopygia guttata* syn. *Poephila guttata*) that is chiefly gray above and white below with a red or orange bill, a black-and-white barred tail, and in the male a black-barred throat and that is often kept as a cage bird

---

\ə\ abut \ᵊ\ kitten, F table \ər\ **further** \a\ ash \ā\ ace \ä\ mop, mar
\aü\ **out** \ch\ **chin** \e\ bet \ē\ **easy** \g\ go \i\ hit \ī\ ice \j\ **job**
\ŋ\ **sing** \ō\ go \ò\ law \òi\ **boy** \th\ **thin** \th\ **the** \ü\ **loot** \u̇\ **foot**
\y\ yet \zh\ vision, beige \k, ⁿ, œ, ᵫ, ᵓ\ *see* Guide to Pronunciation

zebra fish *n* (1771) **:** any of various barred fishes; *esp* **:** a very small blue-and-silver-striped Indian danio (*Danio rerio* syn. *Brachydanio rerio*) often kept in the tropical aquarium
zebra mussel *n* (1883) **:** a chiefly freshwater Eurasian lamellibranch mollusk (*Dreissena polymorpha*) that was accidentally introduced into the Great Lakes and has spread to other waterways where it colonizes and clogs water intake pipes and competes with native fish for food
ze•brano \zə-ˈbra-nō\ *n* [perh. irreg. fr. *zebra*] (1928) **:** ZEBRAWOOD
ze•bra•wood \ˈzē-brə-ˌwu̇d, ˈze-\ *n* (1783) **1 :** any of several trees or shrubs having mottled or striped wood: as **a :** a tall So. American timber tree (*Astronium fraxinifolium*) of the cashew family **b :** a tall western African timber tree (*Microberlinia brazzavillensis*) of the legume family **2 :** the wood of a zebrawood
ze•bu \ˈzē-(ˌ)bü, -(ˌ)byü\ *n* [F *zébu*] (1774) **:** any of various breeds of domestic oxen developed in India that are often considered conspecific with the common ox (*Bos taurus*) or sometimes as a separate species (*B. indicus*) and are characterized by a large fleshy hump over the shoulders, a dewlap, pendulous ears, and marked resistance to the injurious effects of heat and insect attack

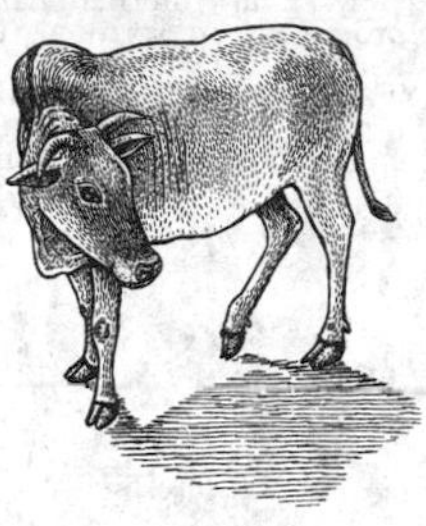
zebu

Zeb•u•lun \ˈze-byə-lən\ *n* [Heb *Zěbhūlūn*] (14c) **:** a son of Jacob and the traditional eponymous ancestor of one of the tribes of Israel
zec•chi•no \ze-ˈkē-(ˌ)nō, tse-\ *n, pl* **-ni** \-(ˌ)nē\ *or* **-nos** [It — more at SEQUIN] (1617) **:** SEQUIN 1
Zech *abbr* Zechariah
Zech•a•ri•ah \ˌze-kə-ˈrī-ə\ *n* [Heb *Zěkhar-yāh*] (14c) **1 :** a Hebrew prophet of the sixth century B.C. **2 :** a prophetic book of canonical Jewish and Christian Scripture — see BIBLE table
ze•chin \ˈze-kən, ze-ˈkēn\ *n* [It *zecchino*] (1575) **:** SEQUIN 1
zed \ˈzed\ *n* [ME, fr. MF *zede*, fr. LL *zeta* zeta, fr. Gk *zēta*] (13c) *chiefly Brit* **:** the letter *z*
zee \ˈzē\ *n* (1677) **:** the letter *z*
Zee•man effect \ˈzā-ˌmän-, -mən-\ *n* [Pieter *Zeeman*] (1899) **:** the splitting of a single spectral line into two or more lines of different frequencies observed when radiation (as light) originates in a magnetic field
ze•in \ˈzē-ən\ *n* [NL *Zea*, genus of grasses including corn, fr. Gk *zeai*, pl., wheat; akin to Skt *yava* barley] (1822) **:** a protein from corn that lacks lysine and tryptophan and is used esp. in making textile fibers, plastics, printing inks, coatings, and adhesives and sizes
zeit•ge•ber \ˈtsīt-ˌgā-bər, ˈzīt-\ *n* [G, fr. *Zeit* time + *Geber* giver] (1964) **:** an environmental agent or event (as the occurrence of light or dark) that provides the stimulus setting or resetting a biological clock of an organism
zeit•geist \ˈtsīt-ˌgīst, ˈzīt-\ *n, often cap* [G, fr. *Zeit* + *Geist* spirit] (1835) **:** the general intellectual, moral, and cultural climate of an era
zel•ko•va \ˈzel-kə-və, zel-ˈkō-və\ *n* [NL, fr. Russ *zel'kova, zel'kva*, fr. Georgian *dzelkva*] (ca. 1890) **:** a tall widely spreading Japanese tree (*Zelkova serrata*) of the elm family that is often used as an ornamental and shade tree in place of the American elm because of its resistance to Dutch elm disease
zemst•vo \ˈzem(p)st-(ˌ)vō, -və\ *n, pl* **zemstvos** [Russ; akin to Russ *zemlya* earth, land, L *humus* — more at HUMBLE] (1865) **:** one of the district and provincial assemblies established in Russia in 1864
Zen \ˈzen\ *n* [Jp, religious meditation] (1727) **:** a Japanese sect of Mahayana Buddhism that aims at enlightenment by direct intuition through meditation
ze•na•na \zə-ˈnä-nə\ *n* [Hindi & Urdu *zanāna*, fr. Pers, fr. *zan* woman] (1760) **:** HAREM 1a
Zend–Aves•ta \ˌzend-ə-ˈves-tə\ *n* [F, fr. MPers *Avastāk va Zand* Avesta and commentary] (1630) **:** AVESTA
ze•ner diode \ˈzē-nər-, ˈze-\ *n, often cap Z* [Clarence M. *Zener* †1993 Am. physicist] (1957) **:** a silicon semiconductor device used esp. as a voltage regulator
ze•nith \ˈzē-nəth, *Canad also & Brit usu* ˈze-nəth, -nith\ *n* [ME *cenyth, senyth*, fr. MF *cenit*, fr. ML, fr. OSp *zenit*, modif. of Ar *samt* (*al-ra's*) way (over one's head)] (14c) **1 :** the point of the celestial sphere that is directly opposite the nadir and vertically above the observer — see AZIMUTH illustration **2 :** the highest point reached in the heavens by a celestial body **3 :** culminating point **:** ACME ⟨at the ~ of his powers —John Buchan⟩
ze•nith•al \-nə-thəl\ *adj* (1860) **1 :** of, relating to, or located at or near the zenith **2 :** showing correct directions from the center ⟨a ~ map⟩
ze•o•lite \ˈzē-ə-ˌlīt\ *n* [Sw *zeolit*, fr. Gk *zein* to boil + *-o-* + Sw *-lit* -lite, fr. F *-lite* — more at YEAST] (ca. 1777) **:** any of various hydrous silicates that are analogous in composition to the feldspars, occur as secondary minerals in cavities of lavas, and can act as ion-exchangers; *also* **:** any of various natural or synthesized silicates of similar structure used esp. in water softening and as adsorbents and catalysts — **ze•o•lit•ic** \ˌzē-ə-ˈli-tik\ *adj*
Zeph *abbr* Zephaniah
Zeph•a•ni•ah \ˌze-fə-ˈnī-ə\ *n* [Heb *Ṣěphanyāh*] (14c) **1 :** a Hebrew prophet of the seventh century B.C. **2 :** an apocalyptic book of canonical Jewish and Christian Scripture — see BIBLE table
zeph•yr \ˈze-fər\ *n* [ME *Zephirus*, west wind (personified), fr. L *Zephyrus*, god of the west wind & *zephyrus* west wind, zephyr, fr. Gk *Zephyros & zephyros*] (1611) **1 a :** a breeze from the west **b :** a gentle breeze **2 :** any of various lightweight fabrics and articles of clothing
Zeph•y•rus \ˈze-fə-rəs\ *n* [L] (bef. 12c) **:** the Greek god of the west wind
zep•pe•lin \ˈze-p(ə-)lən\ *n* [Count Ferdinand von *Zeppelin*] (1900) **:** a rigid airship consisting of a cylindrical trussed and covered frame supported by internal gas cells; *broadly* **:** AIRSHIP
zep•to- *comb form* [ISV, prob. alter. of *hepta-*; fr. the fact that 10^{21} is the seventh power of 10^3] **:** one sextillionth (10^{-21}) part of ⟨*zepto*second⟩
zep•to•sec•ond \ˈzep-tə-ˌse-kənd, -kənt\ *n* (1994) **:** one sextillionth of a second
zerk \ˈzərk\ *n* [Oscar U. *Zerk* †1968 Am. (Austrian-born) inventor] (1926) **:** a grease fitting
[1]**ze•ro** \ˈzē-(ˌ)rō, ˈzir-(ˌ)ō\ *n, pl* **zeros** *also* **zeroes** [F or It; F *zéro*, fr. It *zero*, fr. ML *zephirum*, fr. Ar *ṣifr*] (1598) **1 a :** the arithmetical symbol 0 or Ø denoting the absence of all magnitude or quantity **b :** ADDITIVE IDENTITY; *specif* **:** the number between the set of all negative numbers and the set of all positive numbers **c :** a value of an independent variable that makes a function equal to zero ⟨+2 and –2 are ~*s* of $f(x)=x^2-4$⟩ **2** — see NUMBER table **3 a** (1) **:** the point of departure in reckoning; *specif* **:** the point from which the graduation of a scale (as of a thermometer) begins (2) **:** the temperature represented by the zero mark on a thermometer **b :** the setting or adjustment of the sights of a firearm that causes it to shoot to point of aim at a desired range **4 :** an insignificant person or thing **:** NONENTITY **5 a :** a state of total absence or neutrality **b :** the lowest point **:** NADIR **6 :** something arbitrarily or conveniently designated zero
[2]**zero** *adj* (1810) **1 a :** of, relating to, or being a zero **b :** having no magnitude or quantity **:** not any ⟨~ growth⟩ ⟨~ tolerance⟩ **c** (1) **:** having no phonetic manifestation ⟨the ~ modification in the past tense of *cut*⟩ (2) **:** having no modified inflectional form ⟨a ~ plural⟩ **2 a** *of a cloud ceiling* **:** limiting vision to 50 feet (15 meters) or less **b** *of horizontal visibility* **:** limited to 165 feet (50.3 meters) or less
[3]**zero** *vt* (1913) **1 :** to determine or adjust the zero of (as a rifle) **2 a :** to concentrate firepower on the exact range of — usu. used with *in* **b :** to bring to bear on the exact range of a target — usu. used with *in* ~ *vi* **1 :** to adjust fire on a specific target — usu. used with *in* **2 :** to close in on or focus attention on an objective — usu. used with *in* ⟨investigators are ~*ing* in on a suspect⟩
zero–based *or* **zero–base** *adj* (1970) **:** having each item justified on the basis of cost or need ⟨~ budgeting⟩
zero coupon *adj* (1979) **:** of, relating to, or being an investment security that is sold at a deep discount, is redeemable at face value on maturity, and that pays no periodic interest ⟨*zero coupon* municipal bonds⟩
zero gravity *n* (1951) **:** the state or condition of lacking apparent gravitational pull **:** WEIGHTLESSNESS
zero hour *n* [fr. its being marked by the count of zero in a countdown] (1915) **1 a :** the hour at which a planned military operation is scheduled to start **b :** the time at which a usu. significant or notable event is scheduled to take place **2 :** a time when a vital decision or decisive change must be made
zero–sum *adj* (1944) **:** of, relating to, or being a situation (as a game or relationship) in which a gain for one side entails a corresponding loss for the other side ⟨dividing up the budget is a ~ game⟩
ze•roth \ˈzē-(ˌ)rōth, ˈzir-(ˌ)ōth\ *adj* (1896) **:** being numbered zero in a series; *also* **:** ZERO 1 ⟨the ~ power of a number⟩
zero tillage *n* (1963) **:** NO-TILLAGE
zero vector *n* (ca. 1901) **:** a vector which is of zero length and all of whose components are zero
zero–zero *adj* (ca. 1939) **1 :** characterized by or being atmospheric conditions that reduce ceiling and visibility to zero **2 :** limited to zero by atmospheric conditions
zest \ˈzest\ *n* [obs. F (now *zeste*), orange or lemon peel (used as flavoring)] (ca. 1674) **1 :** a piece of the peel of a citrus fruit (as an orange or lemon) used as flavoring **2 :** an enjoyably exciting quality **:** PIQUANCY ⟨adds ~ to the performance⟩ **3 :** keen enjoyment **:** RELISH, GUSTO ⟨has a ~ for living⟩ — **zest•ful** \-fəl\ *adj* — **zest•ful•ly** \-fə-lē\ *adv* — **zest•ful•ness** *n* — **zest•less** \-ləs\ *adj*
zest•er \ˈzes-tər\ *n* (1967) **:** a small utensil for peeling zest (as of a lemon)
zesty \ˈzes-tē\ *adj* **zest•i•er; -est** (1868) **:** having or characterized by zest **:** appealingly piquant or lively ⟨a ~ sauce⟩ ⟨~ humor⟩ — **zest•i•ly** \-tə-lē\ *adv*
ze•ta \ˈzā-tə, ˈzē-\ *n* [Gk *zēta*] (1823) **:** the 6th letter of the Greek alphabet — see ALPHABET table
zet•ta- *comb form* [ISV, perh. alter. of It *sette* seven; fr. the fact that 10^{21} is the seventh power of 10^3] **:** sextillion (10^{21}) ⟨*zetta*byte⟩
zet•ta•byte \ˈze-tə-ˌbīt\ *n* (1993) **:** one sextillion bytes
zeug•ma \ˈzüg-mə\ *n* [ME *zeuma*, fr. ML, fr. L *zeugma*, fr. Gk, lit., joining, fr. *zeugnynai* to join; akin to L *jungere* to join — more at YOKE] (15c) **:** the use of a word to modify or govern two or more words usu. in such a manner that it applies to each in a different sense or makes sense with only one (as in "opened the door and her heart to the homeless boy")
Zeus \ˈzüs\ *n* [Gk] (1540) **:** the king of the gods and husband of Hera in Greek mythology — compare JUPITER
zib•e•line *or* **zib•el•line** \ˈzi-bə-ˌlēn, -ˌlīn\ *n* [*zibeline* (cloth), fr. earlier *zibeline*, n., sable, sable fur, fr. MF, fr. OIt *zibellino*, of Slav origin; akin to Russ *sobol'* sable] (1873) **:** a soft lustrous wool fabric with mohair, alpaca, or camel's hair
zi•do•vu•dine \zi-ˈdō-vyü-ˌdēn\ *n* [by shortening & alter. fr. *azidothymidine*] (1987) **:** AZT
ZIFT *abbr* zygote intrafallopian transfer
[1]**zig** \ˈzig\ *n* [*zigzag*] (1840) **1 a :** one of the sharp turns, angles, or alterations in a zigzag course **b :** one of the short straight lines or sections of a zigzag course at an angle to a zag **2 :** a sharp alteration or change of direction (as in a process or policy) ⟨the quick ~*s* and zags of his international maneuverings —*N.Y. Times*⟩
[2]**zig** *vi* **zigged; zig•ging** (1940) **:** to execute a zig — usu. contrasted with *zag* ⟨~*s* when others zag⟩
zig•gu•rat \ˈzi-gə-ˌrat\ *n* [Akkadian *ziqqurratu*] (1877) **:** an ancient Mesopotamian temple tower consisting of a lofty pyramidal structure built in successive stages with outside staircases and a shrine at the top; *also* **:** a structure or object of similar form

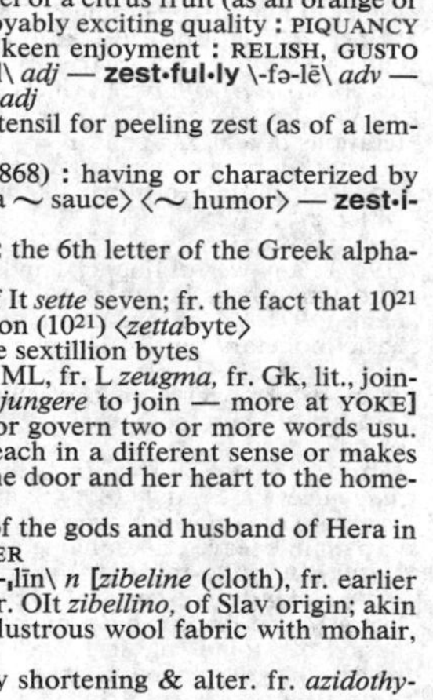
ziggurat

[1]**zig•zag** \ˈzig-ˌzag\ *n* [F] (1712) **:** one of a series of short sharp turns, angles, or alterations in a course; *also* **:** something having the form or character of such a series ⟨a blouse

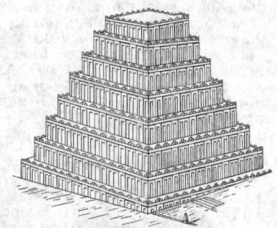

with green ~*s*⟩ ⟨endured the ~*s* of policy —Richard Bernstein⟩ — **zig·zag·gy** \-ˌza-gē\ *adj*
[2]**zigzag** *adv* (ca. 1730) **:** in or by a zigzag path or course
[3]**zigzag** *adj* (1750) **:** having short sharp turns or angles ⟨a ~ trail⟩
[4]**zigzag** *vb* **zig·zagged; zig·zag·ging** *vt* (1777) **:** to form into a zigzag or move along a zigzag course ~ *vi* **:** to lie in, proceed along, or consist of a zigzag course
zilch \ˈzilch\ *adj or n* [origin unknown] (1956) **:** ZERO, NOTHING
zil·lion \ˈzil-yən\ *n* [*z* + *-illion* (as in *million*)] (1934) **:** an indeterminately large number ⟨~*s* of mosquitoes⟩ — **zil·lionth** \-yən(t)th\ *adj*
zil·lion·aire \ˌzil-yə-ˈner\ *n* [*zillion* + *-aire* (as in *millionaire*)] (1946) **:** an immeasurably wealthy person
zin \ˈzin\ *n, often cap* (1980) **:** ZINFANDEL
[1]**zinc** \ˈziŋk\ *n, often attrib* [G *Zink*] (1651) **:** a bluish-white metallic element that is ductile when pure but in the commercial form is brittle at ordinary temperatures and becomes ductile on slight heating, occurs abundantly in minerals, is an essential micronutrient for both plants and animals, and is used esp. in alloys and as a protective coating in galvanizing iron and steel — see ELEMENT table
[2]**zinc** *vt* **zinced** *or* **zincked** \ˈziŋ(k)t\; **zinc·ing** *or* **zinck·ing** \ˈziŋ-kiŋ\ (1841) **:** to treat or coat with zinc **:** GALVANIZE
zinc blende *n* (1830) **:** SPHALERITE
zinc chloride *n* (1851) **:** a poisonous caustic deliquescent salt $ZnCl_2$ used esp. as a wood preservative, drying agent, and catalyst
zinc oxide *n* (1849) **:** an infusible white solid ZnO used esp. as a pigment, in compounding rubber, and in pharmaceutical and cosmetic preparations (as ointments and sunblocks)
zinc sulfate *n* (1851) **:** a crystalline salt $ZnSO_4$ used esp. in making a white paint pigment, in printing and dyeing, in sprays and fertilizers, and in medicine as an astringent, emetic, and weak antiseptic
zinc sulfide *n* (1851) **:** a fluorescent white to yellowish compound ZnS used esp. as a white pigment and a phosphor
zinc white *n* (1847) **:** a white pigment that consists of zinc oxide
zine \ˈzēn\ *n* [*-zine* (as in *fanzine*)] (1965) **:** MAGAZINE; *esp* **:** a noncommercial often homemade or online publication usu. devoted to specialized and often unconventional subject matter ⟨a feminist ~⟩
zin·eb \ˈzi-ˌneb\ *n* [*zinc* + ethylene + *bis*-] (1950) **:** an agricultural fungicide $C_4H_6N_2S_4Zn$ used esp. formerly on fruits and vegetables
zin·fan·del \ˈzin-fən-ˌdel\ *n, often cap* [prob. modif. of obs. Hung *tzinifándli, czirifandli,* a white wine grape (misapplied to a grape variety of Dalmatian origin), fr. G *Zierfandler*] (1858) **:** a dry red table wine made from a small black grape that is grown chiefly in California; *also* **:** the grape
[1]**zing** \ˈziŋ\ *n* [imit.] (1911) **1 :** a shrill humming noise **2 a :** an enjoyably exciting or stimulating quality **:** ZEST ⟨really put some ~ into this industry —Erwin Fine⟩ **b :** a sharply piquant flavor ⟨barbecue sauce with ~⟩
[2]**zing** *vi* (1920) **1 :** to make or move with a humming sound **2 :** ZIP, SPEED ~ *vt* **1 :** to hit suddenly **:** ZAP **2 :** to criticize in a pointed or witty manner
zing·er \ˈziŋ-ər\ *n* (1955) **1 :** something causing or meant to cause interest, surprise, or shock **2 :** a pointed witty remark or retort
zingy \ˈziŋ-ē\ *adj* **zing·i·er; -est** [ˈzing] (1945) **1 :** enjoyably exciting ⟨a ~ musical⟩ **2 :** strikingly attractive or appealing ⟨wore a ~ new outfit⟩ **3 :** sharply piquant ⟨a ~ salad⟩
zin·nia \ˈzi-nē-ə, ˈzē-; ˈzi-nyə, ˈzē-\ *n* [NL, fr. Johann G. *Zinn* †1759 Ger. botanist] (1767) **:** any of a genus (*Zinnia*) of tropical American composite herbs and low shrubs that have showy flower heads with long-lasting ray flowers
Zi·on \ˈzī-ən\ *also* **Si·on** \ˈsī-ən\ *n* [ME *Sion,* fr. OE, citadel in Palestine which was the nucleus of Jerusalem, fr. LL, fr. Gk *Seiōn,* fr. Heb *Ṣīyōn*] (14c) **1 a :** the Jewish people **:** ISRAEL **b :** the Jewish homeland that is symbolic of Judaism or of Jewish national aspiration **c :** the ideal nation or society envisaged by Judaism **2 :** HEAVEN **3 :** UTOPIA
Zi·on·ism \ˈzī-ə-ˌni-zəm\ *n* (1896) **:** an international movement orig. for the establishment of a Jewish national or religious community in Palestine and later for the support of modern Israel — **Zi·on·ist** \-nist\ *adj or n* — **Zi·on·is·tic** \ˌzī-ə-ˈnis-tik\ *adj*
[1]**zip** \ˈzip\ *vb* **zipped; zip·ping** [imit. of the sound of a speeding object] *vi* (1852) **1 :** to move, act, or function with speed and vigor **2 :** to travel with a sharp hissing or humming sound ~ *vt* **1 :** to impart speed or force to **2 :** to add zest, interest, or life to — often used with *up* **3 :** to transport or propel with speed
[2]**zip** *n* (1867) **1 :** a sudden sharp hissing or sibilant sound **2 :** ENERGY, VIM — **zip·less** \-ləs\ *adj*
[3]**zip** *n* [origin unknown] (ca. 1900) **:** NOTHING, ZERO ⟨the final score was 27 to ~⟩
[4]**zip** *n* (1920) *chiefly Brit* **:** ZIPPER
[5]**zip** *vb* **zipped; zip·ping** [back-formation fr. *zipper*] *vt* (1932) **1 a :** to close or open with or as if with a zipper **b :** to enclose or wrap by fastening a zipper **2 :** to cause (a zipper) to open or shut ~ *vi* **:** to become open, closed, or attached by means of a zipper
[6]**zip** *n, often all cap* (1969) **:** ZIP CODE 1
zip–code *vt* (1964) **:** to furnish with a zip code
zip code *n, often cap Z&I&P* [zone improvement plan] (1963) **1 :** a number that identifies a particular postal delivery area in the U.S. **2 :** the geographic area identified by a zip code
zip fastener *n* (1927) *chiefly Brit* **:** ZIPPER
zip gun *n* (1950) **:** a crude homemade single-shot pistol
zip line *n* (1970) **:** a cable suspended above an incline to which a pulley and harness are attached for a rider — **zip–line** *vi*
zip·lock \ˈzip-ˌläk\ *adj* [fr. *Ziploc,* trademark for a plastic bag with such a seal] (1980) **:** having an interlocking groove and ridge that form a tight seal when pressed together ⟨a ~ plastic bag⟩
[1]**zip·per** \ˈzi-pər\ *n* [fr. *Zipper,* a trademark] (1926) **:** a fastener consisting of two rows of metal or plastic teeth on strips of tape and a sliding piece that closes an opening by drawing the teeth together
[2]**zipper** *vt* (1930) **:** [5]ZIP
zip·pered \-pərd\ *adj* (1939) **:** equipped with a zipper
zip·py \ˈzi-pē\ *adj* **zip·pi·er; -est** (1904) **:** full of zip: as **a :** very quick or speedy ⟨a ~ sports car⟩ **b :** strikingly fresh, lively, or appealing in style ⟨~ clothes⟩
zip tie *n* (1992) **:** a plastic strip that can be threaded through its end and tightened so as to fasten something; *esp* **:** FLEX-CUFF — **zip–tie** *vb*

zi·ram \ˈzī-ˌram\ *n* [*z*inc + dithiocarb*amate*] (1949) **:** an organic zinc salt $C_6H_{12}N_2S_4Zn$ used esp. as an agricultural fungicide
zir·con \ˈzər-ˌkän, -kən\ *n* [G] (1794) **:** a tetragonal mineral consisting of a silicate of zirconium and occurring usu. in brown or grayish square prisms of adamantine luster or sometimes in transparent forms which are used as gems
zir·co·nia \ˌzər-ˈkō-nē-ə\ *n* [NL, fr. ISV *zircon*] (1797) **:** a white crystalline compound ZrO_2 used esp. in refractories, in thermal and electric insulation, in abrasives, and in enamels and glazes — called also *zirconium oxide*
zir·co·ni·um \ˌzər-ˈkō-nē-əm\ *n* [NL, fr. ISV *zircon*] (1808) **:** a steel-gray hard ductile metallic element with a high melting point that occurs widely in combined form (as in zircon), is highly resistant to corrosion, and is used esp. in alloys and in refractories and ceramics — see ELEMENT table
zit \ˈzit\ *n* [origin unknown] (ca. 1966) *slang* **:** PIMPLE 1
zith·er \ˈzi-thər, -thər\ *n* [G, fr. OHG *zitara, cithara,* fr. L *cithara* cithara — more at CITHER] (1850) **:** a stringed instrument having usu. 30 to 40 strings over a shallow horizontal soundboard and played with pick and fingers — **zith·er·ist** \-thə-rist, -thə-\ *n*
zi·ti \ˈzē-tē\ *n, pl* **ziti** [It, pl. of *zito,* alter. of *zita* piece of tubular pasta, prob. short for *maccheroni di zita,* lit., bride's macaroni] (ca. 1845) **:** medium-sized tubular pasta
zizith *var of* TZITZIT
Z line *n* (1916) **:** any of the dark thin bands across a striated muscle fiber that mark the junction of actin filaments in adjacent sarcomeres
zlo·ty \ˈzlȯ-tē\ *n, pl* **zlo·tys** \-tēz\ *or* **zlo·tych** \-tik\ [Pol *złoty* (gen. pl. złotych] (1915) — see MONEY table
[1]**Zn** *abbr* [azimuth + north] azimuth
[2]**Zn** *symbol* zinc
zo- *or* **zoo-** *comb form* [Gk *zōi-, zōio-,* fr. *zōion;* akin to Gk *zōē* life — more at QUICK] **1 :** animal **:** animal kingdom or kind ⟨*zooid*⟩ ⟨*zoology*⟩ **2** [Gk *zō-* alive, fr. *zōos;* akin to Gk *zōē*] **:** motile ⟨*zoospore*⟩
-zoa \ˈzō-ə\ *n pl comb form* [NL, fr. Gk *zōia,* pl. of *zōion*] **:** animals — in taxa ⟨Meta*zoa*⟩ ⟨Proto*zoa*⟩
zo·an·thar·i·an \ˌzō-ən-ˈther-ē-ən\ *n* [ultim. fr. *zo-* + Gk *anthos* flower — more at ANTHOLOGY] (1887) **:** any of a subclass (Hexacorallia syn. Zoantharia) of anthozoans having tentacles or septa or both that are typically six or a multiple of six in number and including most of the recent corals and sea anemones — **zoantharian** *adj*
zo·ca·lo \ˈzō-kə-ˌlō\ *n, pl* **-los** [MexSp, fr. *el Zócalo,* public square in Mexico City, fr. Sp *zócalo* socle, plinth, fr. It *zoccolo;* fr. the plinth of an unfinished monument in Mexico City's main square — more at SOCLE] (1882) **:** the public square of a Mexican city or town **:** PLAZA
zo·di·ac \ˈzō-dē-ˌak\ *n* [ME, fr. AF, fr. L *zodiacus,* fr. Gk *zōidiakos,* fr. *zōidiakos,* adj., of carved figures, of the zodiac, fr. *zōidion* carved figure, sign of the zodiac, fr. dim. of *zōion* living being, figure; akin to Gk *zōē* life] (14c) **1 a :** an imaginary band in the heavens centered on the ecliptic that encompasses the apparent paths of all the planets and is divided into 12 constellations or signs each taken for astrological purposes to extend 30 degrees of longitude **b :** a figure representing the signs of the zodiac and their symbols **2 :** a cyclic course ⟨a ~ of feasts and fasts —R. W. Emerson⟩ — **zo·di·a·cal** \zō-ˈdī-ə-kəl, zə-\ *adj*

SIGNS OF THE ZODIAC

NUMBER	NAME	SYMBOL	SUN ENTERS[1]
1	Aries the Ram	♈	March 21
2	Taurus the Bull	♉	April 20
3	Gemini the Twins	♊	May 21
4	Cancer the Crab	♋	June 22
5	Leo the Lion	♌	July 23
6	Virgo the Virgin	♍	August 23
7	Libra the Balance	♎	September 23
8	Scorpio the Scorpion	♏	October 24
9	Sagittarius the Archer	♐	November 22
10	Capricorn the Goat	♑	December 22
11	Aquarius the Water Bearer	♒	January 20
12	Pisces the Fishes	♓	February 19

[1] Though no longer astronomically accurate (because of precession of the equinoxes), these traditional dates continue to be used in astrology.

zodiacal light *n* (1734) **:** a diffuse glow seen in the west after twilight and in the east before dawn
zo·ea \zō-ˈē-ə\ *n, pl* **zo·eae** \-ˈē-ˌē\ *or* **zo·eas** \-ˈē-əz\ [NL, fr. Gk *zōē* life] (1877) **:** a free-swimming planktonic larval form of many decapod crustaceans and esp. crabs that has a relatively large cephalothorax, conspicuous eyes, and fringed antennae and mouthparts
zoftig *var of* ZAFTIG
[1]**-zoic** *adj comb form* [Gk *zōikos* of animals, fr. *zōion* animal — more at ZO-] **:** having a (specified) animal mode of existence ⟨holo*zoic*⟩
[2]**-zoic** *adj comb form* [Gk *zōē* life] **:** of, relating to, or being a (specified) geological era ⟨Protero*zoic*⟩ ⟨Meso*zoic*⟩
zois·ite \ˈzȯi-ˌsīt\ *n* [G *Zoisit,* fr. Sigismund *Zois* von Edelstein †1819 Slovene nobleman] (ca. 1805) **:** an orthorhombic mineral that consists of a basic silicate of calcium and aluminum and is related to epidote

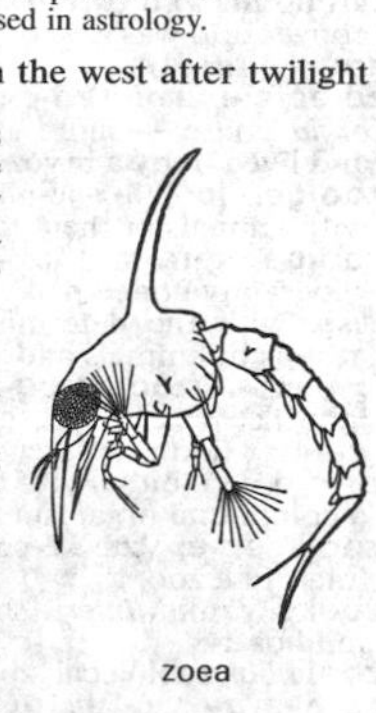
zoea

zom·bie *also* **zom·bi** \ˈzäm-bē\ *n* [Louisiana Creole or Haitian Creole *zonbi,* of Bantu origin; akin to Kimbundu *nzúmbe* ghost] (1760) **1** *usu* **zombi a :** the supernatural power

\ə\ abut \ᵊ\ kitten, F table \ər\ further \a\ ash \ā\ ace \ä\ mop, mar \au̇\ out \ch\ chin \e\ bet \ē\ easy \g\ go \i\ hit \ī\ ice \j\ job \ŋ\ sing \ō\ go \ȯ\ law \ȯi\ boy \th\ thin \th\ the \ü\ loot \u̇\ foot \y\ yet \zh\ vision, beige \k, ⁿ, œ, ue, ʸ\ see Guide to Pronunciation

that according to voodoo belief may enter into and reanimate a dead body **b** : a will-less and speechless human in the West Indies capable only of automatic movement who is held to have died and been supernaturally reanimated **2 a** : a person held to resemble the so-called walking dead; *esp* : AUTOMATON **b** : a person markedly strange in appearance or behavior **3** : a mixed drink made of several kinds of rum, liqueur, and fruit juice — **zom·bie·like** \-bē-ˌlīk\ *adj*

zom·bi·fy \ˈzäm-bə-ˌfī\ *vt* **-fied; -fy·ing** (1946) : to turn (an active alert person) into a zombie — **zom·bi·fi·ca·tion** \ˌzäm-bə-fə-ˈkā-shən\ *n*

zom·bi·ism \-bē-ˌi-zəm\ *n* (1932) : the beliefs and practices of the cult of the zombi

zon·al \ˈzō-nᵊl\ *adj* (1867) **1** : of, relating to, affecting, or having the form of a zone ⟨a ~ boundary⟩ **2** : of, relating to, or being a soil or a major soil group marked by well-developed characteristics that are determined primarily by the action of climate and organisms (as vegetation) — compare AZONAL, INTRAZONAL — **zon·al·ly** \-nᵊl-ē\ *adv*

zo·na pel·lu·ci·da \ˌzō-nə-pə-ˈlü-sə-də, -pel-ˈyü-\ *n, pl* **zo·nae pel·lu·ci·dae** \-(ˌ)nē . . . -(ˌ)dē, -ˌnī . . . -ˌdī\ [NL, transparent zone] (1841) : the transparent more or less elastic noncellular outer layer or envelope of a mammalian ovum that is composed of glycoproteins

zo·na·tion \zō-ˈnā-shən\ *n* (1898) **1** : structure or arrangement in zones **2** : distribution of kinds of organisms in biogeographic zones

¹**zone** \ˈzōn\ *n* [ME, fr. AF, fr. L *zona* belt, zone, fr. Gk *zōnē;* akin to Lith *juosti* to gird] (15c) **1 a** : any of five great divisions of the earth's surface with respect to latitude and temperature — compare FRIGID ZONE, TEMPERATE ZONE, TORRID ZONE **b** : a portion of the surface of a sphere included between two parallel planes **2** *archaic* : GIRDLE, BELT **3 a** : an encircling anatomical structure **b** (1) : a subdivision of a biogeographic region that supports a similar fauna and flora throughout its extent (2) : such a zone dominated by a particular life form **c** : a distinctive belt, layer, or series of layers of earth materials (as rock) **4** : a region or area set off as distinct from surrounding or adjoining parts **5** : one of the sections of an area or territory created for a particular purpose: as **a** : a zoned section of a city **b** (1) : any of the eight concentric bands of territory centered on a given postal shipment point designated as a distance bracket for U.S. parcel post to which mail is charged at a single rate (2) : a distance within which the same fare is charged by a common carrier **c** : an area on a field of play **d** : a stretch of roadway or a space in which certain traffic regulations are in force **6** : ZONE DEFENSE **7** : a temporary state of heightened concentration experienced by a performing athlete that enables peak performance ⟨players in the ~⟩

²**zone** *vt* **zoned; zon·ing** (1782) **1** : to surround with a zone : ENCIRCLE **2** : to arrange in or mark off into zones; *specif* : to partition (a city, borough, or township) by ordinance into sections reserved for different purposes (as residence or business) — **zon·er** *n*

³**zone** *adj* (1795) **1** : ZONAL 1 **2** : of, relating to, or occurring in a zone defense ⟨a ~ press⟩ ⟨a ~ blitz⟩

zone defense *n* (1927) : a system of defense (as in basketball or football) in which each player guards an assigned area rather than a specified opponent

zone out *vi* (1982) : to become oblivious to one's surroundings esp. in order to relax ⟨*zone out* in front of the TV⟩

zone refining *n* (1952) : a technique for the purification of a crystalline material and esp. a metal in which a molten region travels through the material to be refined, picks up impurities at its advancing edge, and then allows the purified part to recrystallize at its opposite edge — called also *zone melting* — **zone–refined** *adj*

Zon·ian \ˈzō-nē-ən, -nyən\ *n* (1910) : a U.S. citizen living in the Panama Canal Zone

zonk \ˈzäŋk, ˈzȯŋk\ *vb* [prob. imit.] *vt* (1950) : STUN, STUPEFY; *also* : STRIKE, ZAP — often used with *out* ~ *vi* : to pass out from or as if from alcohol or a drug — often used with *out*

zonked \ˈzäŋkt, ˈzȯŋ(k)t\ *adj* (ca. 1959) : stupefied by or as if by alcohol or a drug

zonked–out \-ˈau̇t\ *adj* (1967) : ZONKED

Zon·ti·an \ˈzän-tē-ən\ *n* [*Zonta International,* a service club] (1934) : a member of a service club made up of executive women each of whom is a sole representative of one business or profession in a community

zoo \ˈzü\ *n, pl* **zoos** [short for *zoological garden*] (ca. 1847) **1 a** : a garden or park where wild animals are kept for exhibition **b** : a collection of living animals usu. for public display **2** : a place, situation, or group marked by crowding, confusion, or unrestrained behavior ⟨the convention was a ~⟩

zoo- — see ZO-

zo·oe·ci·um *also* **zo·e·ci·um** \zō-ˈē-shē-əm\ *n, pl* **-cia** [NL, fr. *zo-* + Gk *oikia* house — more at VICINITY] (1880) : a sac or chamber secreted and lived in by a bryozoan zooid

zoo·gen·ic \ˌzō-ə-ˈje-nik\ *adj* [ISV] (ca. 1859) : caused by or associated with animals or their activities ⟨~ humus⟩

zoo·ge·og·ra·phy \ˌzō-ə-jē-ˈä-grə-fē\ *n* [ISV] (1868) : a branch of biogeography concerned with the geographic distribution of animals and esp. with the determination of the areas characterized by specific groups of animals and the study of the causes and significance of such groups — **zoo·ge·og·ra·pher** \-fər\ *n* — **zoo·geo·graph·ic** \-ˌjē-ə-ˈgra-fik\ *or* **zoo·geo·graph·i·cal** \-fi-kəl\ *adj* — **zoo·geo·graph·i·cal·ly** \-fi-k(ə-)lē\ *adv*

zo·oid \ˈzō-ˌȯid\ *n* (1851) : one of the asexually produced individuals of a compound organism (as a bryozoan, hydroid, or coral colony)

zoo·keep·er \ˈzü-ˌkē-pər\ *n* (1924) : one who maintains or cares for animals in a zoo

zooks \ˈzu̇ks\ *interj* [short for *gadzooks*] (1634) *archaic* — used as a mild oath

zool *abbr* zoological; zoology

zo·ol·a·try \zō-ˈä-lə-trē, zə-ˈwä-\ *n* [NL *zoolatria,* fr. *zo-* + LL *-latria* -latry] (1817) : animal worship

zoo·log·i·cal \ˌzō-ə-ˈlä-ji-kəl\ *also* **zoo·log·ic** \-jik\ *adj* (1807) **1** : of, relating to, or concerned with zoology **2** : of, relating to, or affecting lower animals often as distinguished from humans — **zoo·log·i·cal·ly** \-ji-k(ə-)lē\ *adv*

zoological garden *n* (1829) : ZOO 1a

zo·ol·o·gy \zō-ˈä-lə-jē, zə-ˈwä-\ *n* [NL *zoologia,* fr. *zo-* + *-logia* -logy] (1669) **1** : a branch of biology concerned with the classification and the properties and vital phenomena of animals **2 a** : animal life (as of a region) : FAUNA **b** : the properties and vital phenomena exhibited by an animal, animal type, or group — **zo·ol·o·gist** \-jist\ *n*

¹**zoom** \ˈzüm\ *vb* [imit.] *vi* (1903) **1 a** : to move with a loud low hum or buzz **b** : to go speedily : ZIP ⟨cars ~*ing* by on the highway⟩ **2** *of an airplane* : to climb for a short time at an angle greater than that which can be maintained in steady flight so that the machine is carried upward at the expense of stored kinetic energy **3 a** : to focus a camera or microscope on an object using a zoom lens so that the object's apparent distance from the observer changes — often used with *in* or *out* **b** : FOCUS, ZERO — used with *in* ⟨trying to ~ in on the cause of these problems⟩ **4** : to increase sharply ⟨retail sales ~*ed*⟩ ~ *vt* : to cause to zoom

²**zoom** *n* (1917) **1 a** : an act or process of zooming; *esp* : a sharp upward movement **b** : an image created by zooming **2** : a zooming sound **3** : a means of producing an enlarged image (as in a camera); *specif* : ZOOM LENS

zoom lens *n* (1936) : a lens (as of a camera or projector) in which the image size can be varied continuously while the image remains in focus

zoo·mor·phic \ˌzō-ə-ˈmȯr-fik\ *adj* [ISV] (1872) **1** : having the form of an animal **2** : of, relating to, or being a deity conceived of in animal form or with animal attributes — **zoo·morph** \ˈzō-ə-ˌmȯrf\ *n*

-zoon *n comb form, pl* **-zoa** [NL, fr. Gk *zōion*] : animal : zooid ⟨spermatozoon⟩

zoo·no·sis \zō-ˈä-nə-səs, ˌzō-ə-ˈnō-səs\ *n, pl* **-no·ses** \-ˌsēz\ [NL, fr. *zo-* + Gk *nosos* disease] (1876) : a disease communicable from animals to humans under natural conditions — **zoo·not·ic** \ˌzō-ə-ˈnä-tik\ *adj*

zoo·phil·ic \ˌzō-ə-ˈfi-lik\ *or* **zo·oph·i·lous** \zō-ˈä-fə-ləs, zə-ˈwä-\ *adj* (1886) : having an attraction to or preference for animals; *esp, of an insect* : preferring animals to humans as a source of food

zoo·phyte \ˈzō-ə-ˌfīt\ *n* [Gk *zōophyton,* fr. *zōi-, zō-* zo- + *phyton* plant — more at PHYT-] (1621) : an invertebrate animal (as a coral or sponge) more or less resembling a plant in appearance or mode of growth

zoo·plank·ter \ˈzō-ə-ˌplaŋ(k)-tər\ *n* [*zo-* + *plankter*] (1943) : a planktonic animal

zoo·plank·ton \ˌzō-ə-ˈplaŋ(k)-tən, -ˌtän\ *n* (1901) : plankton composed of animals — **zoo·plank·ton·ic** \-ˌplaŋ(k)-ˈtä-nik\ *adj*

zoo·spo·ran·gi·um \ˌzō-ə-spə-ˈran-jē-əm\ *n* [NL] (1874) : a spore case or sporangium bearing zoospores

zoo·spore \ˈzō-ə-ˌspȯr\ *n* [ISV] (1846) : an independently motile spore; *esp* : a motile usu. naked and flagellated asexual spore esp. of an alga or lower fungus — **zoo·spor·ic** \ˌzō-ə-ˈspȯr-ik\ *adj*

zoo·tech·ni·cal \ˌzō-ə-ˈtek-ni-kəl\ *adj* (1926) : of or relating to the technology of animal husbandry — **zoo·tech·nics** \-ˈtek-niks\ *n pl but sing or pl in constr*

zoot suit \ˈzüt-\ *n* [redupl. of ¹*suit*] (1942) : a suit of extreme cut typically consisting of a thigh-length jacket with wide padded shoulders and peg pants with narrow cuffs — **zoot–suit·er** \-ˌsü-tər\ *n*

zooty \ˈzü-tē\ *adj* (1946) : typical of a zoot-suiter : flashy in manner or style ⟨a ~ haircut⟩

zo·o·xan·thel·la \ˌzō-ə-zan-ˈthe-lə\ *n, pl* **-lae** \-(ˌ)lē\ [NL, fr. *zo-* + *xanth-* + *-ella* (dim. suffix)] (ca. 1891) : any of various symbiotic dinoflagellates that live within the cells of other organisms (as reef-building coral polyps)

zo·ri \ˈzȯr-ē\ *n, pl* **zori** *also* **zoris** [Jp *zōri*] (1823) : a flat thonged sandal usu. made of straw, cloth, leather, or rubber

Zorn's lemma \ˈzȯrnz-, ˈtsȯrnz-\ *n* [Max August *Zorn* †1993 Ger. mathematician] (ca. 1950) : a lemma in set theory: if a set S is partially ordered and if each subset for which every pair of elements is related by exactly one of the relationships "less than," "equal to," or "greater than" has an upper bound in S, then S contains at least one element for which there is no greater element in S — compare AXIOM OF CHOICE

Zo·ro·as·tri·an·ism \ˌzȯr-ə-ˈwas-trē-ə-ˌni-zəm\ *n* (1849) : a Persian religion founded in the sixth century B.C. by the prophet Zoroaster, promulgated in the Avesta, and characterized by worship of a supreme god Ahura Mazda who requires good deeds for help in his cosmic struggle against the evil spirit Ahriman — **Zo·ro·as·tri·an** \-trē-ən\ *adj or n*

zos·ter \ˈzäs-tər\ *n* [L, fr. Gk *zōstēr* girdle; akin to Gk *zōnē* zone] (ca. 1706) : SHINGLES

Zou·ave \zü-ˈäv\ *n* [F, fr. Ar dial. (Algeria) *Zwāwa,* Berber tribal confederation of Kabylia] (1844) **1** : a member of a French infantry unit orig. composed of Algerians wearing a brilliant uniform and conducting a quick spirited drill **2** : a member of a military unit adopting the dress and drill of the Zouaves

zouk \ˈzük\ *n* [Lesser Antillean F Creole, lit., dance party, dance, prob. alter. of *mazouk* Fr. Caribbean ballroom and club dance of the earlier 20th cent., alter. of F *mazurka* mazurka] (1986) : a form of French West Indian music blending African rhythms, reggae, calypso, and electronic dance music

zounds \ˈzau̇n(d)z, ˈzün(d)z, ˈzwau̇n(d)z, ˈzwün(d)z\ *interj* [euphemism for *God's wounds*] (1592) — used as a mild oath

zow·ie \ˈzau̇-ē\ *interj* [imit. of the sound of a speeding vehicle] (1902) — used to express astonishment or admiration esp. in response to something sudden or speedy

zoy·sia \ˈzȯi-shə, -zhə, -sē-ə, -zē-ə\ *n* [NL, alter. of *Zoisia,* fr. Karl von *Zois* †1799 Slovene botanist] (1924) : any of a genus (*Zoysia*) of creeping perennial grasses of southeastern Asia and New Zealand having fine wiry leaves and including some suitable for lawn grasses esp. in warm regions

Z particle *n* (1979) : a neutral elementary particle about 90 times heavier than a proton that along with the W particle is a transmitter of the weak force — called also Z^0 or Z^0 *particle*

ZPG *abbr* zero population growth

Zr *symbol* zirconium

z–score \ˈzē-ˌskȯr\ *n* (1966) : STANDARD SCORE

z–test \ˈzē-ˌtest\ *n* (1951) : any of several statistical tests that use a random variable having a z distribution to test hypotheses about the mean of a population based on a single sample or about the difference between the means of two populations based on a sample from each when the standard deviations of the populations are known or to test hypotheses about the proportion of successes in a single sample or the difference between the proportion of successes in two samples when the standard deviations are estimated from the sample data

zuc·chet·to \zu̇-ˈke-(ˌ)tō, tsü-\ *n, pl* **-tos** [It, dim. of *zucca* gourd, head]

(1853) : a small round skullcap worn by Roman Catholic ecclesiastics in colors that vary according to the rank of the wearer

zuc·chi·ni \zü-'kē-nē\ *n, pl* **-ni** *or* **-nis** [It, pl. of *zucchino,* dim. of *zucca* gourd] (1925) : a smooth cylindrical usu. dark green summer squash; *also* : a plant that bears zucchini

¹**Zu·lu** \'zü-(,)lü\ *n, pl* **Zulu** *or* **Zulus** [Zulu *-zula* (as in *isiZulu* the Zulu language] (1824) **1** : a member of a Bantu-speaking people of Natal **2** : the Bantu language of the Zulus — **Zulu** *adj*

²**Zulu** (1952) — a communications code word for the letter *z*

Zu·ni \'zü-nē\ *also* **Zu·ñi** \'zün-yē\ *n, pl* **Zuni** *or* **Zunis** *also* **Zuñi** *or* **Zuñis** [AmerSp *Zuñi*] (1834) **1** : a member of an American Indian people of western New Mexico **2** : the language of the Zuni people

zup·pa in·gle·se \,tsü-pə-iṇ-'glā-(,)zā, ,zü-, -in-, -(,)sā\ *n, often cap I* [It, lit., English soup] (1896) : a dessert consisting of sponge cake and custard or pudding that is flavored with rum, covered with cream, and garnished with fruit

zwie·back \'swē-,bak, 'swī-, 'zwē-, 'zwī-, -,bäk\ *n* [G, lit., twice baked, fr. *zwie-* twice (fr. OHG *zwi-*) + *backen* to bake, fr. OHG *bahhan* — more at TWI-, BAKE] (1863) : a usu. sweetened bread enriched with eggs that is baked and then sliced and toasted until dry and crisp

Zwing·li·an \'zwiṇ-glē-ən, 'swiṇ-, -lē-; 'tsfiṇ-lē-\ *adj* (1532) : of or relating to Ulrich Zwingli or his teachings and esp. his doctrine that Christ's presence in the Eucharist is not corporeal but symbolic — **Zwinglian** *n* — **Zwing·li·an·ism** \-ə-,ni-zəm\ *n*

zwit·ter·ion \'tsvi-tər-,ī-,än *also* 'zwi-\ *n* [G, fr. *Zwitter* hybrid (fr. OHG *zwitaran,* fr.,-wi-) + *Ion* ion — more at TWI-] (1906) : a dipolar ion — **zwit·ter·ion·ic** \,zwi-tər-ī-'ä-nik, ,swi-\ *adj*

zy·de·co \'zī-də-,kō\ *n, often attrib* [perh. modif. of F *les haricots* beans, fr. the Cajun dance tune *Les Haricots Sont Pas Salés*] (1960) : popular music of southern Louisiana that combines tunes of French origin with elements of Caribbean music and the blues and that features guitar, washboard, and accordion

zyg- *or* **zygo-** *comb form* [NL, fr. Gk, fr. *zygon* — more at YOKE] **1** : yoke ⟨zygomorphic⟩ **2** : pair ⟨zygodactyl⟩ **3** : union ⟨zygospore⟩

zyg·apoph·y·sis \,zī-gə-'pä-fə-səs\ *n, pl* **-y·ses** \-,sēz\ [NL] (1854) : any of the articular processes of the neural arch of a vertebra of which there are usu. two anterior and two posterior

zy·go·dac·tyl \,zī-gə-'dak-t°l\ *adj* [ISV *zyg-* + Gk *daktylos* toe] (1831) : having the toes arranged two in front and two behind — used of a bird

zy·go·dac·ty·lous \-tə-ləs\ *adj* (ca. 1828) : ZYGODACTYL

zy·go·ma \zī-'gō-mə\ *n, pl* **-ma·ta** \-mə-tə\ *also* **-mas** [NL *zygomat-, zygoma,* fr. Gk *zygōma,* fr. *zygoun* to join, fr. *zygon* yoke] (ca. 1684) **1 a** : ZYGOMATIC ARCH **b** : a slender bony process of the zygomatic arch **2** : ZYGOMATIC BONE

zy·go·mat·ic \,zī-gə-'ma-tik\ *adj* (1709) : of, relating to, constituting, or situated in the region of the zygomatic bone or zygomatic arch

zygomatic arch *n* (1825) : the arch of bone that extends along the front or side of the skull beneath the orbit

zygomatic bone *n* (1709) : a bone of the face below the eye that in mammals forms part of the zygomatic arch and part of the orbit — called also *cheekbone*

zygomatic process *n* (1741) : any of several bony processes that enter into or strengthen the zygomatic arch

zy·go·mor·phic \,zī-gə-'mȯr-fik\ *adj* (1875) *of a flower* : having floral parts unequal in size or form so that the flower is capable of division into essentially symmetrical halves by only one longitudinal plane passing through the axis — **zy·go·mor·phy** \'zī-gə-,mȯr-fē\ *n*

zy·gos·i·ty \zī-'gä-sə-tē\ *n* [prob. fr. *-zygous*] (1946) : the makeup or characteristics of a particular zygote; *also* : the genetic relationship between offspring of a single birth esp. in regard to being derived from the same or different zygotes

zy·go·spore \'zī-gə-,spȯr\ *n* [ISV] (1864) : a thick-walled spore of some algae and fungi that is formed by union of two similar sexual cells, usu. serves as a resting spore, and produces the sporophytic phase

zy·gote \'zī-,gōt\ *n* [Gk *zygōtos* yoked, fr. *zygoun* to join — more at ZYGOMA] (ca. 1887) : a cell formed by the union of two gametes; *broadly* : the developing individual produced from such a cell — **zy·got·ic** \zī-'gä-tik\ *adj*

zygote intrafallopian transfer *n* (1986) : a method of assisting reproduction in cases of infertility that is similar to gamete intrafallopian transfer but in which eggs are fertilized in vitro and some of the resulting fertilized eggs are inserted into a fallopian tube — abbr. ZIFT

zy·go·tene \'zī-gə-,tēn\ *n* [ISV] (1911) : the stage of meiotic prophase which immediately follows the leptotene and during which synapsis of homologous chromosomes occurs — **zygotene** *adj*

-zygous *adj comb form* [Gk *-zygos* yoked, fr. *zygon* yoke — more at YOKE] : having (such) a zygotic constitution ⟨hetero*zygous*⟩

zym- *or* **zymo-** *comb form* [ISV, fr. Gk, leaven, fr. *zymē* — more at JUICE] **1** : yeast ⟨*zymo*san⟩ **2** : enzyme ⟨*zymo*gen⟩

zy·mase \'zī-,mās, -,māz\ *n* [ISV] (ca. 1875) : an enzyme or enzyme complex of yeast that promotes fermentation of sugar

-zyme *n comb form* [Gk *zymē* leaven] : enzyme ⟨lyso*zyme*⟩

zy·mo·gen \'zī-mə-jən\ *n* [ISV] (1877) : an inactive protein precursor of an enzyme secreted by living cells and converted (as by a kinase or an acid) into an active form — called also *proenzyme*

zy·mo·gram \'zī-mə-,gram\ *n* (1957) : an electrophoretic strip (as of starch gel) or a representation of it exhibiting the pattern of separated enzymes and esp. isoenzymes after electrophoresis

zy·mo·san \'zī-mə-,san\ *n* [*zym-* + *-osan* (as in *hexosan*)] (1943) : an insoluble largely polysaccharide fraction of yeast cell walls

---

\ə\ **abut** \ᵊ\ **kitten,** F **table** \ər\ **further** \a\ **ash** \ā\ **ace** \ä\ **mop, mar**
\au̇\ **out** \ch\ **chin** \e\ **bet** \ē\ **easy** \g\ **go** \i\ **hit** \ī\ **ice** \j\ **job**
\ŋ\ **sing** \ō\ **go** \ȯ\ **law** \ȯi\ **boy** \th\ **thin** \t̲h\ **the** \ü\ **loot** \u̇\ **foot**
\y\ **yet** \zh\ **vision, beige** \k̲, ⁿ, œ, ᴜ, ᵞ\ *see* Guide to Pronunciation

Foreign Words & Phrases

ab·eunt stu·dia in mo·res \'ä-be-,ùnt-'stü-dē-,ä-,in-'mō-,räs\ [L] : practices zealously pursued pass into habits

à bien·tôt \ä-byaⁿ-tō\ [F] : so long

ab in·cu·na·bu·lis \,äb-,iṇ-kù-'nä-bù-,lēs\ [L] : from the cradle : from infancy

à bon chat, bon rat \ä-bōⁿ-'shä bōⁿ-'rä\ [F] : to a good cat, a good rat : retaliation in kind

à bouche ou·verte \ä-bü-shü-vert\ [F] : with open mouth : eagerly : uncritically

ab ovo us·que ad ma·la \äb-'ō-vō-,ùs-kwe-,äd-'mä-lä\ [L] : from egg to apples : from soup to nuts : from beginning to end

à bras ou·verts \ä-brä-zü-ver\ [F] : with open arms : cordially

ab·sit in·vi·dia \'äb-,sit-in-'wi-dē-,ä\ [L] : let there be no envy or ill will

ab uno dis·ce om·nes \äb-'ü-nō-,dis-ke-'ōm-,näs\ [L] : from one learn to know all

ab ur·be con·di·ta \äb-'ùr-be-'kōn-di-,tä\ [L] : from the founding of the city (Rome, founded 753 B.C.) — used by the Romans in reckoning dates

ab·usus non tol·lit usum \'ä-,bü-sùs-,nōn-,tò-lit-'ü-sùm\ [L] : abuse does not take away use, i.e., is not an argument against proper use

à compte \ä-'kōⁿt\ [F] : on account

à coup sûr \ä-kü-suer\ [F] : with sure stroke : surely

acte gra·tuit \äk-tə-grä-twⁱē\ [F] : gratuitous impulsive act

ad ar·bi·tri·um \,ad-är-'bi-trē-ùm\ [L] : at will : arbitrarily

ad as·tra per as·pe·ra \ad-'as-trə-,pər-'as-pə-ra\ [L] : to the stars by hard ways — motto of Kansas

ad ex·tre·mum \,äd-ek-'strä-,mùm, ,ad-ik-'strē-məm\ [L] : to the extreme : at last

ad ka·len·das Grae·cas \,äd-kä-'len-däs-'grī-,käs\ [L] : at the Greek calends : never (since the Greeks had no calends)

ad ma·jo·rem Dei glo·ri·am \äd-'mä-,yòr-,em-'de-,ē-'glòr-ē-,äm\ [L] : to the greater glory of God — motto of the Society of Jesus

ad pa·tres \äd-'pä-,träs\ [L] : (gathered) to his fathers : deceased

ad re·fe·ren·dum \,äd-,re-fe-'ren-dùm\ [L] : for reference : for further consideration by one having the authority to make a final decision

à droite \ä-drwät\ [F] : to or on the right hand

ad un·guem \äd-'ùṇ-,gwem\ [L] : to the fingernail : to a nicety : exactly (from the use of the fingernail to test the smoothness of marble)

ad utrum·que pa·ra·tus \,äd-ù-'trùm-kwe-pä-'rä-tùs\ [L] : prepared for either (event)

ad vi·vum \äd-'wē-,wùm\ [L] : to the life

ae·gri som·nia \,ī-grē-'sóm-nē-,ä\ [L] : a sick man's dreams

ae·quam ser·va·re men·tem \'ī-,kwäm-ser-,wä-rä-'men,tem\ [L] : to preserve a calm mind

ae·quo ani·mo \,ī-kwō-'ä-ni-,mō\ [L] : with even mind : calmly

ae·re per·en·ni·us \'ī-rä-pe-'re-nē-,ùs\ [L] : more lasting than bronze

à gauche \ä-gōsh\ [F] : to or on the left hand

age quod agis \'ä-ge-,kwòd-'ä-,gis\ [L] : do what you are doing : to the business at hand

à grands frais \ä-gräⁿ-fre\ [F] : at great expense

à huis clos \ä-wʸē-klō\ [F] : with closed doors : behind closed doors

aide-toi, le ciel t'ai·dera \ed-twä lə-'syel-te-drä\ [F] : help yourself (and) heaven will help you

aî·né \e-nā\ [F] : elder : senior (masc.)

aî·née \e-nā\ [F] : elder : senior (fem.)

à l'aban·don \ä-lä-bäⁿ-dōⁿ\ [F] : carelessly : in disorder

à la belle étoile \ä-lä-bel-ā-twäl\ [F] : under the beautiful star : in the open air at night

à la bonne heure \ä-lä-bò-nœr\ [F] : at a good time : well and good : all right

à la fran·çaise \ä-lä-fräⁿ-sez\ [F] : in the French manner

à l'amé·ri·caine \ä-lä-mä-rē-ken\ [F] : in the American manner : of the American kind

à l'an·glaise \ä-läⁿ-glez\ [F] : in the English manner

à la page \ä-lä-päzh\ [F] : at the page : up-to-the-minute

à la russe \ä-lä-rues\ [F] : in the Russian manner

alea jac·ta est \'ä-lē-,ä-,yäk-tä-'est\ [L] : the die is cast

à l'im·pro·viste \ä-laⁿ-prò-vēst\ [F] : unexpectedly

ali·quan·do bo·nus dor·mi·tat Ho·me·rus \,ä-li-,kwän-dō-'bò-nùs-dòr-'mē-,tät-hò-'mer-ùs\ [L] : sometimes (even) good Homer nods

alis vo·lat pro·pri·is \'ä-,lēs-'wò-,lät-'prō-prē-,ēs\ [L] : she flies with her own wings — motto of Oregon

al·ki \'äl-,kē\ [Chinook Jargon] : by and by — motto of Washington

alo·ha oe \ä-,lō-hä-'òi, -'ō-ē\ [Hawaiian] : love to you : greetings : farewell

al·ter Chris·tus \,äl-ter-'kris-tús\ [L] : another Christ

al·ter idem \,òl-ter-'ī-,dem, ,äl-ter-'ē-\ [L] : second self

a max·i·mis ad mi·ni·ma \ä-'mäk-si-,mēs-,äd-'mi-ni-,mä\ [L] : from the greatest to the least

à mer·veille \ä-mer-vā\ [F] : marvelously

ami·cus hu·ma·ni ge·ne·ris \ä-'me-kùs-hü-,mä-nē-'ge-ne-,ris\ [L] : friend of the human race

ami·cus us·que ad aras \-,ùs-kwe-,äd-'är-,äs\ [L] : a friend as far as to the altars, i.e., except in what is contrary to one's religion; *also* : a friend to the last extremity

ami de cour \ä-,mē-də-'kùr\ [F] : court friend : insincere friend

amor pa·tri·ae \'ä-,mòr-'pä-trē-,ī\ [L] : love of one's country

amor vin·cit om·nia \'ä-,mòr-,wiṇ-kit-'ōm-nē-,ä\ [L] : love conquers all things

an·cienne no·blesse \äⁿ-syen-nò-bles\ [F] : old-time nobility : the French nobility before the Revolution of 1789

an·guis in her·ba \,äṇ-gwis-in-'her-,bä\ [L] : snake in the grass

ani·mal bi·pes im·plu·me \'ä-ni-,mäl-,bi-,päs-im-'plü-me\ [L] : two-legged animal without feathers (i.e., the human race)

ani·mis opi·bus·que pa·ra·ti \'ä-ni-,mēs-,ó-pi-'bùs-kwe-pä-'rä-tē\ [L] : prepared in mind and resources — one of the mottoes of South Carolina

an·no ae·ta·tis su·ae \'ä-nō-ī-,tä-tis-'sü-,ī\ [L] : in the (specified) year of his (or her) age

an·no mun·di \,ä-nō-'mùn-dē\ [L] : in the year of the world — used in reckoning dates from the supposed period of the creation of the world, esp. as fixed by James Ussher at 4004 B.C. or by the Jews at 3761 B.C.

an·no ur·bis con·di·tae \,ä-nō-,ùr-bis-'kòn-di-,tī\ [L] : in the year of the founded city : in the year that the city was founded (Rome, founded 753 B.C.)

an·nu·it coep·tis \,ä-nü-,it-'kòip-,tēs\ [L] : He (God) has approved our beginnings — motto on the reverse of the Great Seal of the United States

à peu près \ä-pœ-pre\ [F] : nearly : approximately

à pied \ä-pyä\ [F] : on foot

à point \ä-pwaⁿ\ [F] : at the right time : at the peak of ripeness or perfect degree of doneness

ap·o·lo·gia pro vi·ta sua \,a-pə-'lō-j(ē-)ə-prō-'vē-tə-'sü-ə\ [L] : defense of one's life : a written justification for one's beliefs or course of conduct

après moi le dé·luge \ä-pre-mwä-lə-dā-luⱦh\ *or* **après nous le déluge** \ä-pre-nü-\ [F] : after me the deluge — attributed to Louis XV

à pro·pos de bottes \ä-prə-pō-də-bòt\ [F] : apropos of boots — used to change the subject

à pro·pos de rien \-ryaⁿ\ [F] : apropos of nothing

aqua et ig·ni in·ter·dic·tus \,ä-kwä-et-'ig-nē-,in-ter-'dik-tús\ [L] : forbidden to be furnished with water and fire : outlawed

Ar·ca·des am·bo \'är-kä-,des-'äm-bō\ [L] : both Arcadians : two persons of like occupations or tastes; *also* : two rascals

ar·gu·men·tum ad ba·cu·lum \,är-gù-'men-tùm-,äd-'bä-kù-lùm\ [L] : argument of the staff : appeal to force

ar·rec·tis au·ri·bus \ä-'rek-,tēs-'aù-ri-,bùs\ [L] : with ears pricked up : attentively

ar·ri·ve·der·ci \,är-ē-vä-'der-chē\ [It] : till we meet again : farewell

ars est ce·la·re ar·tem \,ärs-,est-kä-,lär-ä-'är-,tem\ [L] : it is (true) art to conceal art

ars lon·ga, vi·ta bre·vis \ärs-'lòṇ-,gä ,wē-,tä-'bre-wis\ [L] : art is long, life is short : human life span limits all that might be accomplished

as—sa·laam alai·kum \,əs-sə-'läm-ə-'lī-kúm\ [Ar *as-salāmu 'alaykum*] : peace to you — used as a traditional greeting among Muslims

a ter·go \ä-'ter-(,)gō\ [L] : from behind

à tort et à tra·vers \ä-tòr-ā-ä-trä-ver\ [F] : wrong and crosswise : at random : without rhyme or reason

au bout de son la·tin \ō-büd-sōⁿ-lä-taⁿ, -bü-də-\ [F] : at the end of one's Latin : at the end of one's mental resources

au con·traire \ō-kōⁿ-trer\ [F] : on the contrary

au·de·mus ju·ra nos·tra de·fen·de·re \aù-'dä-mùs,yùr-ä-'nò-strä-dā-'fen-de-rä\ [L] : we dare defend our rights — motto of Alabama

au·den·tes for·tu·na ju·vat \aù-'den-,täs-fòr-,tü-nä-'yü-,wät\ [L] : fortune favors the bold

au·di al·te·ram par·tem \'aù-,dē-,äl-te-,räm-'pär-,tem\ [L] : hear the other side

au fait \ō-fet, -fe\ [F] : to the point : fully competent : fully informed : socially correct

au fond \ō-fōⁿ\ [F] : at bottom : fundamentally

au grand sé·rieux \ō-gräⁿ-sā-ryœ\ [F] : in all seriousness

au mieux \ō-myœ\ [F] : on the best terms : on intimate terms

au pays des aveugles les borgnes sont rois \ō-pā-ē-dä-zä-vœglʸ-lä-bòrnʸ-ə-sōⁿ-rwä\ [F] : in the country of the blind the one-eyed men are kings

au·rea me·dio·cri·tas \'aù-rē-ä-,me-dē-'ò-kri-,täs\ [L] : the golden mean

au reste \ō-rest\ [F] : for the rest : besides

au sé·rieux \ō-sā-ry œ\ [F] : seriously

au·spi·ci·um me·li·o·ris ae·vi \aů-'spi-kē-,ům-,me-lē-,ŏr-is-'ī-,wē\ [L] : an omen of a better age — motto of the Order of St. Michael and St. George

aus·si·tôt dit, aus·si·tôt fait \ō-sē-tō-dē ō-sē-tō-fe\ [F] : no sooner said than done

aut Cae·sar aut ni·hil \aůt-'kī-sär-,aůt-'ni-,hil\ [L] : either a Caesar or nothing

aut Caesar aut nul·lus \-'nů-lůs\ [L] : either a Caesar or a nobody

au·tres temps, au·tres mœurs \ō-trə-täⁿ ō-trə-mœrs\ [F] : other times, other customs

aut vin·ce·re aut mo·ri \aůt-'wiŋ-ke-rä-,aůt-'mó-,rē\ [L] : either to conquer or to die

aux armes \ō-zärm\ [F] : to arms

avant la lettre \ä-väⁿ-lä-letrʳ\ [F] : before the letter : before a (specified) name or entity existed

avant—pro·pos \ä-väⁿ-prò-pō\ [F] : preface

ave at·que va·le \'ä-,wä-,ät-kwe-'wä-,lä\ [L] : hail and farewell

à vo·tre san·té \ä-vót-säⁿ-tā, -vó-trə-\ [F] : to your health — used as a toast

ax·is mun·di \'ak-səs-'můn-dē\ [L] : turning point of the world : line through the earth's center around which the universe revolves

beaux yeux \bō-zyœ\ [F] : beautiful eyes : beauty of face

bel·la fi·gu·ra \'bel-lə-fē-'gü-rä\ [It] : fine appearance or impression

belle laide \bel-led\ [F] : beautiful ugly woman : woman who is attractive though not conventionally beautiful

bel·lum om·ni·um con·tra om·nes \'be-lúm-'òm-nē-ùm-,kón-trä-'òm-,näs\ [L] : war of all against all

bien en·ten·du \byan-näⁿ-täⁿ-dœ\ [F] : well understood : of course

bien—pen·sant \byan-päⁿ-säⁿ\ [F] : right-minded : one who holds orthodox views

bien·sé·ance \byan-sā-äⁿs\ [F] : propriety

bien vu \byaⁿ-vœ\ [F] : well regarded

bis dat qui ci·to dat \'bis-,dät-kwē-'ki-tō-,dät\ [L] : he gives twice who gives promptly

bon ap·pé·tit \bò-nä-pā-tē\ [F] : good appetite : enjoy your meal

bon gré, mal gré \'bōⁿ-,grä 'mäl-,grä\ [F] : whether with good grace or bad : willy-nilly

bo·nis avi·bus \bò-,nēs-'ä-wi-,bůs\ [L] : under good auspices

bon·jour \bōⁿ-zhûr\ [F] : good day : good morning

bonne foi \bòn-fwä\ [F] : good faith

bon·soir \bōⁿ-swär\ [F] : good evening

bru·tum ful·men \,brü-tům-'fůl-men\ [L] : insensible thunderbolt : a futile threat or display of force

ca·dit quae·stio \kä-dit-'kwī-stē-,ō\ [L] : the question drops : the argument collapses

ca·pable de tout \kä-päblʳ-də-tü\ [F] : capable of anything : unpredictable

carte d'iden·ti·té \kärt-dē-däⁿ-tē-tā\ [F] : identity card

cau·sa si·ne qua non \'kaů-,sä-,si-nä-kwä-'nōn\ [L] : an indispensable cause or condition

ça va sans dire \sä-vä-säⁿ-dir\ [F] : it goes without saying

ca·ve·at lec·tor \'kä-wä-,ät-'lek,tór, 'ka-vē-, -,at-\ [L] : let the reader beware

ca·ve ca·nem \,kä-wā-'kä,nem\ [L] : beware the dog

ce·dant ar·ma to·gae \'kā-,dänt-,är-mə-'tō-,gī\ [L] : let arms yield to the toga : let military power give way to civil power — motto of Wyoming

ce n'est que le pre·mier pas qui coûte \snek-lə-prə-myä-pä-kē-küt\ [F] : it is only the first step that costs

c'est–à–dire \se-tä-'der\ [F] : that is to say : namely

c'est au·tre chose \se-tōt-shōz, -tō-trə-\ [F] : that's a different thing

c'est la guerre \se-lä-'ger\ [F] : that's war : it cannot be helped

c'est la vie \se-lä-vē\ [F] : that's life : that's how things happen

c'est plus qu'un crime, c'est une faute \se-plœ-kœⁿ-krēm se-tœn-fōt\ [F] : it is worse than a crime, it is a blunder

ce·te·ra de·sunt \,kā-te-rä-'dā-,sůnt\ [L] : the rest is missing

cha·cun à son goût \shä-kœⁿ-nä-sōⁿ-gü\ [F] : everyone to his taste

châ·teau en Es·pagne \shä-tō-äⁿ-nes-päⁿyʳ\ [F] : castle in Spain : a visionary project

cher·chez la femme \sher-shä-lä-fàm\ [F] : look for the woman

che sa·rà, sa·rà \kä-sä-'rä kä-'rä\ [It] : what will be, will be

che·val de ba·taille \shə-väl-də-bä-tāʳ\ [F] : warhorse : argument constantly relied on : favorite subject

ci—gît \sē-zhē\ [F] : here lies — used preceding a name on a tombstone

co·gi·to, er·go sum \'kō-gi-,tō ,er-gō-'sům\ [L] : I think, therefore I exist

co·mé·die hu·maine \kò-mā-dē-œ-men\ [F] : human comedy : the whole variety of human life

comédie lar·moy·ante \-lär-mwä-yäⁿt\ [F] : tearful comedy : sentimental comedy

comme ci, comme ça \kòm-sē kòm-sá\ [F] : so-so

com·pa·gnon de voy·age \kōⁿ-pä-nʸōⁿ-də-vwä-yäzh\ [F] : traveling companion

compte ren·du \kōⁿt-räⁿ-dœ\ [F] : report (as of proceedings in an investigation)

con·cor·dia dis·cors \kòn-'kòr-dē-ä-'dis-,kòrs\ [L] : discordant harmony

con·fes·sio fi·dei \kòn-'fe-sē-ō-'fi-dē-,ē\ [L] : confession of faith

con·temp·tus mun·di \kòn-'tem(p)-tůs-'můn-dē\ [L] : contempt for the world

cor·rup·tio op·ti·mi pes·si·ma \kò-'růp-tē-,ō-'äp-ti-,mē-'pe-si-,mä\ [L] : the corruption of the best is the worst of all

coup de maî·tre \küd-metrʳ, kü-də-\ [F] : masterstroke

coup d'es·sai \kü-dä-se\ [F] : experiment : trial

coûte que coûte \küt-kə-küt\ [F] : cost what it may

cre·do quia ab·sur·dum est \,krā-dō-'kwē-ä-äp,sůr-dům-'est\ [L] : I believe it because it is absurd

cre·do ut in·tel·li·gam \,krā-dō-,ůt-in-'te-lē-,gäm\ [L] : I believe so that I may understand

cres·cit eun·do \,kres-kit-'eůn-dō\ [L] : it grows as it goes — motto of New Mexico

crise de conscience \krēz-də-kōⁿ-syäⁿs\ [F] : crisis of conscience : agonizing period of moral uncertainty

crise de nerfs *or* **crise des nerfs** \krēz-də-ner\ [F] : crisis of nerves : nervous collapse : hysterical fit

crux cri·ti·co·rum \'krůks-,kri-ti-'kòr-ům\ [L] : crux of critics

cu·jus re·gio, ej·us re·li·gio \,kü-yůs-'re-gē-,ō ,e-yůs-re-'li-gē-,ō\ [L] : whose region, his or her religion : subjects are to accept the religion of their ruler

cum gra·no sa·lis \,kům-,grä-nō-'sä-lis\ [L] : with a grain of salt

cur·sus ho·no·rum \'kůr-sůs-hò-'nór-ům\ [L] : course of honors : succession of offices of increasing importance

cus·tos mo·rum \,kůs-tōs-'mòr-ům\ [L] : guardian of manners or morals : censor

d'ac·cord \dä-kòr\ [F] : in accord : agreed

dame d'hon·neur \däm-dò-nœr\ [F] : lady-in-waiting

dam·nant quod non in·tel·li·gunt \,däm-,nänt-,kwòd-,nōn-in-'te-li-,gůnt\ [L] : they condemn what they do not understand

de bonne grâce \də-bòn-gräs\ [F] : with good grace : willingly

de gus·ti·bus non est dis·pu·tan·dum \dā-'gůs-tə-,bůs-,nōn-,est-,dis-pů-'tän-,dům\ [L] : there is no disputing about tastes

Dei gra·tia \dā-,ē-'grä-tē-ä\ [L] : by the grace of God

de in·te·gro \dā-'in-te-,grō\ [L] : anew : afresh

de l'au·dace, en·core de l'au·dace, et tou·jours de l'au·dace \də-lō-'däs äⁿ-,kòr-də-lō-däs ā-tü-'zhür-də-lō-däs\ [F] : audacity, more audacity, and ever more audacity

de·len·da est Car·tha·go \dā-'len-dä-,est-kär-'tä-gō\ [L] : Carthage must be destroyed

de·li·ne·a·vit \dā-,lē-nä-'ä-wit\ [L] : he (or she) drew it

de mal en pis \də-mä-läⁿ-pē\ [F] : from bad to worse

de mi·ni·mis non cu·rat lex \dā-'mi-ni-,mēs-,nōn-,kü-,rät-'leks\ [L] : the law takes no account of trifles

de mor·tu·is nil ni·si bo·num \dā-'mòr-tů-,ēs-,nēl-,ni-sē-'bó-,nům\ [L] : of the dead (say) nothing but good

de nos jours \də-nō-zhür\ [F] : of our time : contemporary — used postpositively esp. after a proper name

Deo fa·ven·te \dā-ō-fä-'ven-tā\ [L] : with God's favor

Deo gra·ti·as \dā-ō-'grä-tē-,äs\ [L] : thanks (be) to God

de pro·fun·dis \dā-prō-'fůn-dēs, -'fən-\ [L] : out of the depths

der Geist der stets ver·neint \dər-'gīst-dər-,shtāts-fer-'nīnt\ [G] : the spirit that ever denies — applied originally to Mephistopheles

de·si·pe·re in lo·co \dā-'si-pe-rä-in-'lō-kō\ [L] : to indulge in trifling at the proper time

de te fa·bu·la nar·ra·tur \dā-,tā-'fä-bů-lä-nä-'rä-,tůr\ [L] : the story applies to you

De·us ab·scon·di·tus \dā-ůs-,äp-'skòn-di-,tůs\ [L] : hidden God : God unknowable by the human mind

De·us vult \,dā-ůs-'wůlt\ [L] : God wills it — rallying cry of the First Crusade

di·es fau·stus \,dē-,äs-'faů-stůs\ [L] : lucky day

dies in·fau·stus \-,in-'faů-stůs\ [L] : unlucky day

dies irae \-'ē-,rī, -,rä\ [L] : day of wrath — used of the Judgment Day

Dieu et mon droit \dyœ-ā-mōⁿ-drwä\ [F] : God and my right — motto on the British royal arms

Dieu vous garde \dyœ-vü-gärd\ [F] : God keep you

di·ri·go \'dē-ri-,gō\ [L] : I direct — motto of Maine

dis ali·ter vi·sum \,dēs-,ä-li-,ter-'wē-,sům\ [L] : the Gods decreed otherwise

dis·cor·dia con·cors \dis-'kòr-dē-ä-'kòn-,kòrs\ [L] : harmonious discord : harmony or unity gained by combining disparate or conflicting elements

di·tat De·us \,dē-,tät-'dā-ůs\ [L] : God enriches — motto of Arizona

di·vi·de et im·pe·ra \'dē-wi-,de-,et-'im-pe-,rä\ [L] : divide and rule

do·cen·do dis·ci·mus \dò-,ken-dō-'dis-ki-,můs\ [L] : we learn by teaching

dol·ce stil nuo·vo \'dòl-chä-stēl-'nwò-vō\ [It] : sweet new style

Do·mi·ne, di·ri·ge nos \'dò-mi-,ne 'dē-ri-,ge-'nòs\ [L] : Lord, direct us — motto of the City of London

Do·mi·nus vo·bis·cum \,dò-mi-,nůs-wō-'bēs-,kům\ [L] : the Lord be with you

dul·ce et de·co·rum est pro pa·tria mo·ri \,důl-,ke-et-de-'kòr-ům-,est-prō-,pä-trē-,ä-'mó-,rē\ [L] : it is sweet and seemly to die for one's country

dum spi·ro, spe·ro \dům-'spē-rō 'spä-rō\ [L] : while I breathe, I hope — one of the mottoes of South Carolina

dum vi·vi·mus vi·va·mus \dům-'wē-wē-,můs-wē-'wä-můs\ [L] : while we live, let us live

d'un cer·tain âge \dœⁿ-ser-te-näzh\ [F] : of a certain age : no longer young

dux fe·mi·na fac·ti \,důks-,fā-mi-nä-'fäk-,tē\ [L] : a woman was leader of the exploit

ec·ce sig·num \,e-ke-'sig-,nům\ [L] : behold the sign : look at the proof

e con·tra·rio \,ā-kòn-'trär-ē-,ō\ [L] : on the contrary

écra·sez l'in·fâme \ā-krä-,sez-laⁿ-fäm\ [F] : crush the infamous thing

eheu fu·ga·ces la·bun·tur an·ni \ā-,heů-fů-'gä-,käs-lä-'bůn-,tůr-'ä-,nē\ [L] : alas! the fleeting years glide on

ein' fes·te Burg ist un·ser Gott \īn-,fes-tə-'bůrk-ist-,ůn-zər-'gót\ [G] : a mighty fortress is our God

em·bar·ras de choix \äⁿ-bä-rä-də-shwä\ *or* **embarras du choix** \-dœ-shwä\ [F] : embarrassing variety of choice

em·bar·ras de ri·chesses \äⁿ-bä-räd-rē-shes, -rä-də-\ *or* **embarras de ri·chesse** [F] : embarrassing surplus of riches : confusing abundance

en ami \äⁿ-nä-mē\ [F] : as a friend

en ef·fet \äⁿ-nā-fe\ [F] : in fact : indeed

en fa·mille \äⁿ-fä-mē\ [F] : in or with one's family : at home : informally

en·fant ché·ri \äⁿ-fäⁿ-shā-rē\ [F] : loved or pampered child : one that is highly favored

---

\ə\ abut \ʳ\ kitten, F table \ər\ further \a\ ash \ā\ ace \ä\ mop, mar \aů\ out \ch\ chin \e\ bet \ē\ easy \g\ go \i\ hit \ī\ ice \j\ job \ŋ\ sing \ō\ go \ò\ law \òi\ boy \th\ thin \th̲\ the \ü\ loot \ů\ foot \y\ yet \zh\ vision, beige \ḵ, ⁿ, œ, œ, ʸ\ *see* Guide to Pronunciation

en·fant gâ·té \äⁿ-fäⁿ-gä-tā\ [F] : spoiled child

en·fants per·dus \äⁿ-fäⁿ-per-dœ\ [F] : lost children : soldiers sent to a dangerous post

en·fin \äⁿ-faⁿ\ [F] : in conclusion : in a word

en gar·çon \äⁿ-gär-sōⁿ\ [F] : as or like a bachelor

en garde \äⁿ-gärd\ [F] : on guard

en pan·tou·fles \äⁿ-pän-tüflᵉ\ [F] : in slippers : at ease : informally

en plein air \äⁿ-ple-ner\ [F] : in the open air

en plein jour \äⁿ-plaⁿ-zhür\ [F] : in broad day

en poste \äⁿ-pòst\ [F] : in a diplomatic post

en règle \äⁿ-reglᵉ\ [F] : in order : in due form

en re·tard \äⁿr-(ə-)tär\ [F] : behind time : late

en re·traite \äⁿr-(ə-)tret\ [F] : in retreat : in retirement

en re·vanche \äⁿr-(ə-)väⁿsh\ [F] : in return : in compensation

en se·condes noces \äⁿs-gōⁿd-nòs, äⁿ-sə-\ [F] : in a second marriage

en·se pe·tit pla·ci·dam sub li·ber·ta·te qui·e·tem \ᵉen-se-ᵖe-tit-'plä-ki-ᵈdäm-ᵊsub-ᵓlē-ber-ᵗtä-te-kwē-ᵉä-ᵗtem\ [L] : with the sword she seeks calm repose under liberty : by the sword we seek peace, but peace only under liberty — motto of Massachusetts

eo ip·so \ā-ō-'ip-(ᵓ)sō\ [L] : by that itself : by that fact alone

épa·ter le bour·geois \ā-pä-tā-lə-bür-zhwä\ or épater les bour·geois \-lā-bür-\ [F] : to shock the middle classes

e plu·ri·bus unum \ē-ᵓplür-ə-bəs-'(y)ü-nəm, ä-ᵓplür-i-bùs-'ü-nùm\ [L] : one out of many — used on the Great Seal of the U.S. and on several U.S. coins

ep·pur sl muo·ve \äp-ᵓpür-sē-'mwò-vä\ [It] : and yet it does move — attributed to Galileo after recanting his assertion of the earth's motion

Erin go bragh \er-ən-gə-'brò, -gō-'brä\ [Ir go brách or go bráth, lit., till doomsday] : Ireland forever

er·ra·re hu·ma·num est \e-'rär-ä-hü-ᵓmä-nùm-'est\ [L] : to err is human

es·prit de l'es·ca·lier \es-prēd-les-kä-lyä\ or es·prit d'es·ca·lier \-prē-des-\ [F] : wit of the staircase : repartee thought of only too late, on the way home

es·se quam vi·de·ri \'e-sä-ᵓkwäm-wi-'dä-rē\ [L] : to be rather than to seem — motto of North Carolina

est mo·dus in re·bus \est-'mò-ᵓdùs-in-'rā-ᵓbùs\ [L] : there is a proper measure in things, i.e., the golden mean should always be observed

es·to per·pe·tua \'es-ᵓtō-per-'pe-tù-ä\ [L] : may she endure forever — motto of Idaho

et hoc ge·nus om·ne \et-ᵓhòk-ᵓge-nùs-'òm-ne\ or et id genus omne \et-ᵓid-\ [L] : and everything of this kind

et in Ar·ca·dia ego \et-in-är-ᵓkä-dē-ä-'e-gō\ [L] : I too (lived) in Arcadia

et sic de si·mi·li·bus \et-ᵓsēk-dä-si-'mi-li-ᵓbùs\ [L] : and so of like things

et tu Bru·te \et-'tü-'brü-te\ [L] : thou too, Brutus — exclamation attributed to Julius Caesar on seeing his friend Brutus among his assassins

eu·re·ka \yù-'rē-kä\ [Gk] : I have found it — motto of California

Ewig–Weib·li·che \ā-vik-'vīp-li-kə\ [G] : eternal feminine

ex·al·té \eg-zäl-tā\ [F] : emotionally excited or elated : fanatic

ex ani·mo \eks-'ä-ni-ᵓmō\ [L] : from the heart : sincerely

ex·cel·si·or \ik-'sel-sē-ər, eks-'kel-sē-ᵓór\ [L] : still higher — motto of New York

ex·cep·tio pro·bat re·gu·lam de re·bus non ex·cep·tis \eks-'kep-tē-ᵓō-ᵓprò-bät-'rä-gù-ᵓläm-dä-'rä-ᵓbùs-ᵓnön-eks-'kep-ᵓtēs\ [L] : an exception establishes the rule as to things not excepted

ex·cep·tis ex·ci·pi·en·dis \eks-'kep-ᵓtēs-eks-ki-pē-'en-ᵓdēs\ [L] : with the proper or necessary exceptions

ex·i·tus ac·ta pro·bat \'ek-si-ᵓtùs-ᵓäk-tä-'prò-ᵓbät\ [L] : the outcome justifies the deed

ex me·ro mo·tu \eks-ᵓmer-ō-'mō-tü\ [L] : out of mere impulse : of one's own accord

ex ne·ces·si·ta·te rei \eks-ne-ᵓke-si-'tä-te-'rä(-ᵓē)\ [L] : from the necessity of the case

ex ni·hi·lo ni·hil fit \eks-'ni-hi-ᵓlō-ᵓni-ᵓhil-'fit\ [L] : from nothing nothing is produced

ex pe·de Her·cu·lem \eks-ᵓpe-de-'her-kù-ᵓlem\ [L] : from the foot (we may judge of the size of) Hercules : from a part we may judge of the whole

ex·per·to cre·de \eks-ᵓper-tō-'krā-de\ or experto cre·di·te \-'krā-di-ᵓte\ [L] : believe one who has had experience : trust me

ex un·gue le·o·nem \eks-'ùn-gwe-le-'ō-ᵓnem\ [L] : from the claw (we may judge of) the lion : from a part we may judge of the whole

ex vi ter·mi·ni \eks-ᵓwē-'ter-mə-ᵓnē\ [L] : from the force of the term

fa·ci·le prin·ceps \ᵓfä-ki-le-'prin-ᵓkeps\ [L] : easily first

fa·ci·lis de·scen·sus Aver·ni \'fä-ki-ᵓlis-dä-ᵓskän-ᵓsùs-ä-'wer-nō\ or facilis descensus Aver·ni \-(ᵓ)nē\ [L] : the descent to Avernus is easy : the road to evil is easy

fa·çon de par·ler \fä-sōⁿ-də-pär-lā\ [F] : manner of speaking : figurative or conventional expression

faire suivre \fer-swᵉēvrᵉ\ [F] : have forwarded : please forward

fas est et ab ho·ste do·ce·ri \fäs-'est-et-äb-'hò-ste-dò-'kä-(ᵓ)rē\ [L] : it is right to learn even from an enemy

Fa·ta vi·am in·ve·ni·ent \ᵓfä-tä-'wē-ᵓäm-in-'we-nē-ᵓent\ [L] : the Fates will find a way

fat·ti mas·chii, pa·ro·le fe·mi·ne \ᵓfät-tē-'mäs-ᵓkē pä-ᵓrò-lä-'fä-mē-ᵓnä\ [It] : deeds are males, words are females : deeds are more effective than words — motto of Maryland, where it is generally interpreted as meaning "manly deeds, womanly words"

faux bon·homme \fō-bò-nòm\ [F] : pretended good fellow

fe·lix cul·pa \'fä-liks-'kúl-pä\ [L] : fortunate fault — used esp. of original sin in relation to the consequent coming of Christ

femme de cham·bre \fäm-də-shäⁿbrᵉ\ [F] : chambermaid : lady's maid

fe·sti·na len·te \fe-ᵓstē-nä-'len-ᵓtä\ [L] : make haste slowly

feux d'ar·ti·fice \fœ-där-tē-fēs\ [F] : fireworks : display of wit

fi·at ex·pe·ri·men·tum in cor·po·re vi·li \'fē-ᵓät-ek-ᵓsper-ē-'men-ᵓtùm-in-ᵓkór-pò-re-'wē-ᵓlē\ [L] : let experiment be made on a worthless body

fi·at ju·sti·tia, ru·at cae·lum \ᵓfē-ᵓät-yùs-'ti-tē-ä ᵓrú-ᵓät-'kī-ᵓlúm\ [L] : let justice be done though the heavens fall

fi·at lux \ᵓfē-ᵓät-'lúks\ [L] : let there be light

Fi·dei De·fen·sor \ᵓfi-de-ᵓē-dä-'fän-ᵓsòr\ [L] : Defender of the Faith — a title of the sovereigns of England

fi·dus Acha·tes \fē-dùs-ä-'kä-ᵓtäs\ [L] : faithful Achates : trusty friend

fille de cham·bre \fē-də-shäⁿbrᵉ\ [F] : lady's maid

fille d'hon·neur \fē-dò-nœr\ [F] : maid of honor

fi·nem re·spi·ce \ᵓfē-ᵓnem-'rä-spi-ᵓke\ [L] : consider the end

fi·nis co·ro·nat opus \fē-nis-kó-ᵓrō-ᵓnät-'ō-ᵓpùs\ [L] : the end crowns the work

flo·re·at \'flò-re-ᵓät\ [L] : may (he, she, or it) flourish — usu. followed by a name

fluc·tu·at nec mer·gi·tur \'flúk-tù-ᵓät-ᵓnek-'mer-gi-ᵓtùr\ [L] : it is tossed by the waves but does not sink — motto of Paris

fo·lie de gran·deur or fo·lie des gran·deurs \fò-lē-də-grän-dœr\ [F] : delusion of greatness : megalomania

force de frappe \fòrs-də-fräp\ [F] : a force equipped to deal a quick offensive or retaliatory blow

fors·an et haec olim me·mi·nis·se ju·va·bit \ᵓfòr-ᵓsän-ᵓet-'hīk-ᵓō-lim-ᵓme-mi-'ni-se-yü-'wä-bit\ [L] : perhaps this too will be a pleasure to look back on one day

for·tes for·tu·na ju·vat \'fòr-ᵓtäs-fòr-'tü-nä-'yù-ᵓwät\ [L] : fortune favors the brave

fron·ti nul·la fi·des \'fròn-ᵓtē-ᵓnù-lä-'fi-ᵓdäs\ [L] : no reliance can be placed on appearance

fu·it Il·li·um \'fú-it-'i-lē-ùm\ [L] : Troy has been (i.e., is no more)

fu·ror lo·quen·di \'fúr-ᵓór-lò-'kwen-(ᵓ)dē\ [L] : rage for speaking

furor po·e·ti·cus \-ᵓpò-'ä-ti-ᵓkùs\ [L] : poetic frenzy

furor scri·ben·di \-skrē-'ben-(ᵓ)dē\ [L] : rage for writing

Gal·gen·hu·mor \ᵓgäl-gən-hü-ᵓmór\ [G] : gallows humor

Gal·li·ce \ᵓgä-li-ᵓke\ [L] : in French : after the French manner

gar·çon d'hon·neur \gär-sōⁿ-dò-nœr\ [F] : bridegroom's attendant

garde du corps \gärd-dœ-kór\ [F] : bodyguard

gar·dez la foi \gär-dā-lä-fwä\ [F] : keep faith

gau·de·a·mus igi·tur \ᵓgaù-dē-'ä-mùs-'i-gi-ᵓtúr\ [L] : let us then be merry

gens d'é·glise \zhäⁿ-dä-glēz\ [F] : church people : clergy

gens de guerre \zhäⁿ-də-ger\ [F] : military people : soldiery

gens du monde \zhäⁿ-dœ-mōⁿd\ [F] : people of the world : fashionable people

gno·thi se·au·ton \'gnō-thē-ᵓse-aù-'tòn\ [Gk] : know thyself

goût de ter·roir \gü-də-te-rwär\ [F] : taste of the earth

grande école \grä-dä-kól\ [F] : great school : French institution of higher education for postbaccalaureate professional or technological training

grand monde \gräⁿ-mōⁿd\ [F] : great world : high society

gros·so mo·do \'grós-(ᵓ)sō-ᵓmō-(ᵓ)dò\ [It] : roughly

guerre à ou·trance \ger-ä-ü-träⁿs\ [F] : war to the uttermost

gu·ten Tag \ᵓgü-tən-'täk\ [G] : good day

has·ta la vis·ta \ᵓäs-tə-lä-'vēs-tə\ [Sp] : good-bye

haute vul·ga·ri·sa·tion \ōt-vœl-gä-rē-zä-syōⁿ\ [F] : high popularization : effective presentation of a difficult subject to a general audience

haut goût \ō-gü\ [F] : high flavor : slight taint of decay

hic et nunc \ᵓhēk-et-'nùnk\ [L] : here and now

hic et ubi·que \ᵓhēk-et-ù-'bē-kwe\ [L] : here and everywhere

hic ja·cet \hik-'jä-sət, hēk-'yä-ket\ [L] : here lies — used preceding a name on a tombstone

hinc il·lae la·cri·mae \ᵓhink-ᵓi-lī-'lä-kri-ᵓmī\ [L] : hence those tears

hoc age \ᵓhòk-'ä-ge\ [L] : do this : apply yourself to what you are about

hoc opus, hic la·bor est \ᵓhòk-'ò-ᵓpùs ᵓhēk-'lä-ᵓbòr-'est\ [L] : this is the hard work, this is the toil

homme d'af·faires \òm-dä-fer\ [F] : man of business : business agent

homme de lettres \òm-də-letrᵉ\ [F] : man of letters

homme d'es·prit \òm-des-prē\ [F] : man of wit

homme moyen sen·suel \òm-mwä-yaⁿ-säⁿ-swᵉel\ [F] : the average nonintellectual man

ho·mo sum: hu·ma·ni nil a me ali·e·num pu·to \ᵓhò-mō-ᵓsùm hü-ᵓmä-nē-'nēl-ä-ᵓmä-ä-lē-'ä-nùm-'pú-tō\ [L] : I am a human being: I regard nothing of human concern as foreign to my interests

ho·ni soit qui mal y pense \ò-nē-swä-kē-mäl-ē-päⁿs\ [L] : shamed be he who thinks evil of it — motto of the Order of the Garter

hon·nête homme \ò-net-òm\ [F] : honest man : respectable and honorable citizen of the middle class

hors com·merce \òr-kò-mers\ [F] : outside the trade : not offered through regular commercial channels

hu·ma·num est er·ra·re \ᵓhü-ᵓmä-nùm-ᵓest-e-'rär-ä\ [L] : to err is human

ich dien \ik-'dēn\ [G] : I serve — motto of the Prince of Wales

ici on parle fran·çais \ē-se-ō̃ⁿ-pärl-fräⁿ-se, -pär-lə-\ [F] : French is spoken here

idées re·çues \ē-dār-(ə-)sœ\ [F] : received ideas : conventional opinions

id est \ᵓid-'est\ [L] : that is

ig·no·ran·tia ju·ris ne·mi·nem ex·cu·sat \ᵓig-nò-ᵓrän-tē-ä-'yùr-is-ᵓnä-mi-ᵓnem-eks-'kü-ᵓsät\ or ignorantia le·gis neminem excusat \-'lä-gis-\ [L] : ignorance of the law excuses no one

ig·no·tum per ig·no·ti·us \ig-'nò-tùm-ᵓper-ig-'nō-tē-ᵓùs\ [L] : (explaining) the unknown by means of the more unknown

il faut cul·ti·ver no·tre jar·din \ēl-fō-kœl-tē-vä-nòt-zhär-daⁿ, -nò-trə-zhär-\ [F] : we must cultivate our garden : we must tend to our own affairs

ils ne pas·se·ront pas \ēl-nə-päs-rōⁿ-pä, -pä-sə-rōⁿ-\ [F] : they shall not get past

in ae·ter·num \ᵓin-ī-'ter-ᵓnùm\ [L] : forever

in du·bio \in-'dù-bē-ᵓō\ [L] : in doubt : undetermined

in fu·tu·ro \in-fə-'tùr-ō\ [L] : in the future

in hoc sig·no vin·ces \in-ᵓhòk-'sig-nō-'win-ᵓkäs\ [L] : by this sign (the Cross) you will conquer

in li·mi·ne \in-'lē-mi-ᵓne\ [L] : on the threshold : at the beginning

In·nig·keit \'i-ni(k)-ᵓkīt\ [G] : poignant intimacy of feeling — used esp. of music

in om·nia pa·ra·tus \in-ᵓōm-nē-ä-pä-'rä-ᵓtùs\ [L] : ready for all things

in par·ti·bus in·fi·de·li·um \in-'pär-ti-ᵓbùs-ᵓin-fi-'dä-lē-ᵓùm\ [L] : in the regions of the infidels — used of a titular bishop having no diocesan jurisdiction, usu. in non-Christian countries

in prae·sen·ti \ᵓin-prī-'sen-ᵓtē\ [L] : at the present time

in sae·cu·la sae·cu·lo·rum \in-'sī-kù-,lä-,sī-kù-'lòr-ùm, -'sā-kù-lä-,sä-\ [L] : for ages of ages : forever and ever

in·shal·lah \,in-shä-'lä\ [Ar *in shāʾ Allāh*] : if Allah wills : God willing

in sta·tu quo an·te bel·lum \in-,stä-,tü-kwō-,än-te-'be-lùm\ [L] : in the same state as before the war

in·te·ger vi·tae sce·le·ris·que pu·rus \in-te-,ger-'wē-,tī-,ske-le-'ris-kwe-'pü-rùs\ [L] : upright of life and free from wickedness

in·ter ar·ma si·lent le·ges \,in-ter-'är-mä-,si-,lent 'lā-,gās\ [L] : in the midst of arms (i.e., in time of war) the laws are silent

in·ter nos \in-ter-'nōs\ [L] : between ourselves

in·tra mu·ros \in-trä-'mü-,rōs\ [L] : within the walls

in usum Del·phi·ni \in-'ü-sùm-del-'fē-nē\ [L] : for the use of the Dauphin : expurgated

in utrum·que pa·ra·tus \in-ü-'trùm-kwe-pä-'rä-,tùs\ [L] : prepared for either (event)

in·ve·nit \in-'wā-nit\ [L] : he or she devised it

in vi·no ve·ri·tas \in-wē-nō-'wā-ri-,täs\ [L] : there is truth in wine

in·vi·ta Mi·ner·va \in-'wē-,tä-mi-'ner-,wä\ [L] : Minerva being unwilling : without natural talent or inspiration

ira fu·ror bre·vis est \,ē-rä-'fùr-,òr-'bre-wis-,est\ [L] : anger is a brief madness

j'ac·cuse \zhä-kᵫz\ [F] : I accuse : bitter denunciation

jac·ta alea est \'yäk-,tä-,ä-lē-,ä-'est\ [L] : the die is cast

j'adoube \zhä-düb\ [F] : I adjust — used in chess when touching a piece without intending to move it

ja·nu·is clau·sis \,yä-nú-,ēs-'klaú-,sēs\ [L] : behind closed doors

je main·tien·drai \zhə-maⁿ-tyaⁿ-drā\ [F] : I will maintain — motto of the Netherlands

jeu de mots \zhœd-mō, zhœ-də-\ [F] : play on words : pun

Jo·an·nes est no·men eius \yō-'ä-näs-est-,nō-men-'ā-yùs\ [L] : John is his name — motto of Puerto Rico

jo·lie laide \zhò-lē-led\ [F] : good-looking ugly woman : woman who is attractive though not conventionally pretty

jouis·sance \zhwē-säⁿs\ [F] : pleasure : sexual pleasure : orgasm

jour·nal in·time \zhür-näl-aⁿ-tēm\ [F] : intimate journal : private diary

jus di·vi·num \yüs-di-'wē-,nùm\ [L] : divine law

jus·ti·tia om·ni·bus \yùs-,ti-tē-,ä-'òm-ni-,bùs\ [L] : justice for all — motto of the District of Columbia

j'y suis, j'y reste \zhē-swⁱē zhē-rest\ [F] : here I am, here I remain

Kin·der, Kir·che, Küche \'kin-dər 'kir-kə 'kᵫ-kə\ [G] : children, church, kitchen

kte·ma es aei \(kə-)'tä-,mä-,es-ä-'ā\ [Gk] : a possession for ever — applied to a work of art or literature of enduring significance

la belle dame sans mer·ci \lä-bel-däm-säⁿ-mer-sē\ [F] : the beautiful lady without mercy

la·bo·ra·re est ora·re \'lä-bō-,rär-ä-,est-'ō-,rär-ä\ [L] : to work is to pray

la·bor om·nia vin·cit \'lä-,bòr-,òm-nē-,ä-'wiŋ-kit\ [L] : labor conquers all things — motto of Oklahoma

la·cri·mae re·rum \,lä-kri-,mī-'rä-,rùm\ [L] : tears for things : pity for misfortune; *also* : tears in things : tragedy of life

lais·sez–al·ler *or* **lais·ser–al·ler** \le-sä-lä\ [F] : letting go : lack of restraint

lap·sus ca·la·mi \,läp-sùs-'kä-lä-,mē, ,lap-səs-'ka-lə-,mī\ [L] : slip of the pen

lap·sus lin·guae \,lap-səs-'liŋ-,gwī, ,läp-,sùs-\ [L] : slip of the tongue

la reine le veut \lä-ren-lə-vœ\ [F] : the queen wills it

la scia·te ogni spe·ran·za, voi ch'en·tra·te \läsh-'shä-tä-,ō-nʸē-spä-'rän-tsä ,vō-ē-kän-'trä-tä\ [It] : abandon all hope, ye who enter

lau·da·tor tem·po·ris ac·ti \laú-'dä-,tór-,tem-pó-ris-'äk-,tē\ [L] : one who praises past times

laus Deo \laús-'dā-ō\ [L] : praise (be) to God

Le·bens·welt \'lä-bəns-,velt\ [G] : life world : world of lived experience

le cœur a ses rai·sons que la rai·son ne con·naît point \lə-kœr-ä-sā-re-zōⁿ-kə-lä-re-zōⁿ-nə-kò-ne-pwäⁿ, -zōⁿ-nə-\ [F] : the heart has its reasons that reason knows nothing of

le roi est mort, vive le roi \lə-rwä-e-mòr vēv-lə-rwä\ [F] : the king is dead, long live the king

le roi le veut \lə-rwä-lə-vœ\ [F] : the king wills it

le roi s'avi·se·ra \lə-rwä-sä-ve-rä\ [F] : the king will consider

le style, c'est l'homme \lə-stēl se-lóm\ [F] : the style is the man

l'état, c'est moi \lā-tä se-mwä\ [F] : the state, it is I

l'étoile du nord \lā-twäl-dᵫ-nór\ [F] : the star of the north — motto of Minnesota

Lie·der·kranz \'lē-dər-,kränts\ [G] : wreath of songs : German singing society

lit·tera scrip·ta ma·net \,li-te-,rä-,skrip-tä-'mä-net\ [L] : the written letter abides

lo·cus in quo \,lò-kùs-in-'kwō\ [L] : place in which

l'union fait la force \lᵫ-nyōⁿ-fe-lä-fórs\ [F] : union makes strength — motto of Belgium

lu·sus na·tu·rae \,lü-sùs-nä-'tùr-,ē, -'tùr-,ī\ [L] : freak of nature

ma foi \mä-fwä\ [F] : my faith! : indeed

mag·na est ve·ri·tas et prae·va·le·bit \,mäg-nä-,est-'wā-ri-,täs-et-,prī-wä-'lä-bit\ [L] : truth is mighty and will prevail

mag·ni no·mi·nis um·bra \,mäg-nō-,mi-nis-'ùm-brä\ [L] : the shadow of a great name

ma·ha·lo \'mä-hä-lō [Hawaiian] : thank you

mai·son de san·té \mä-zōⁿd-säⁿ-tä, -zōⁿ-də-\ [F] : private hospital : asylum

ma·lade ima·gi·naire \mä-läd-ē-mä-zhē-ner\ [F] : imaginary invalid : hypochondriac

mal de siècle \mäl-də-syeklᵊ\ *or* **mal du siècle** \-dᵫ-\ [F] : illness from worldly concerns : world-weariness

ma·lis avi·bus \,mä-,lēs-'ä-wi-,bùs\ [L] : under evil auspices

mal vu \mäl-vᵫ\ [F] : badly regarded : disapproved of

man spricht Deutsch \män-shprikt-'dòich\ [G] : German spoken

ma·riage de con·ve·nance \mä-ryäzh-də-kōⁿv-näⁿs\ [F] : marriage of convenience

ma·ri com·plai·sant \mä-rē-kōⁿ-ple-zäⁿ\ [F] : complaisant husband : cuckold who accepts his wife's infidelity

mau·vaise honte \mò-vez-ōⁿt\ [F] : bad shame : bashfulness

mau·vais quart d'heure \mò-ve-kär-dœr\ [F] : bad quarter hour : an uncomfortable though brief experience

me·den agan \(,)mä-,den-'ä-,gän\ [Gk] : nothing in excess

me·dio tu·tis·si·mus ibis \'me-dē-,ō-tü-,ti-si-mùs-'ē-bis\ [L] : you will go most safely by the middle course

me ju·di·ce \mā-'yü-di-ke\ [L] : being judge : in my judgment

mens sa·na in cor·po·re sa·no \,mäns-'sä-nä-in-,kór-pó-re-'sä-nō\ [L] : a sound mind in a sound body

men·ta·li·té \mäⁿ-tä-lē-tā\ [F] : outlook : set of thought processes, values, and beliefs shared by members of a community

met·teur en scène \me-tœr-äⁿ-sen\ [F] : one who puts on the stage : director of a play or film

me·um et tu·um \,mē-əm-,et-'tü-əm, ,me-ùm-,et-'tü-ùm\ [L] : mine and thine : distinction of private property

mi·ra·bi·le vi·su \mi-,rä-bi-lä-'wē-sü\ [L] : wonderful to behold

mi·ra·bi·lia \,mir-ə-'bi-lē-,ä\ [L] : wonders : miracles

mise en abyme *or* **mise en abîme** \mē-zäⁿ-nä-bēm\ [F] : placement at the center of an escutcheon of a smaller copy of the same escutcheon : containment of an entity within another identical entity : image of an image

mise-en-page \mē-zäⁿ-päzh\ [F] : placement on a page : design of a printed or manuscript page

mœurs \mœr(s)\ [F] : mores : attitudes, customs, and manners of a society

mo·le ru·it sua \'mō-le-'rú-it-,sù-ä\ [L] : it collapses from its own bigness

monde \mōⁿd\ [F] : world : fashionable world : society

mon·ta·ni sem·per li·be·ri \,mòn-'tä-nē-,sem-per-'lē-be-,rē\ [L] : mountaineers are always free — motto of West Virginia

mo·nu·men·tum ae·re per·en·ni·us \,mò-nù-'men-tùm-,ī-re-pe-'re-nē-ùs\ [L] : a monument more lasting than bronze — used of an immortal work of art or literature

mo·re suo \,mòr-ā-'sü-ō\ [L] : in his (or her) own manner

mo·ri·tu·ri te sa·lu·ta·mus \,mòr-i-'tür-ē-,tä-,sä-lù-'tä-mùs\ *or* **mori·turi te sa·lu·tant** \-'sä-lù-,tänt\ [L] : we (or those) who are about to die salute thee

mul·tum in par·vo \,mùl-tùm-in-'pär-vō, -'pär-wō\ [L] : much in little

mu·sée ima·gi·naire \mᵫ-zä-ē-mä-zhē-ner\ [F] : imaginary museum

mu·ta·to no·mi·ne de te fa·bu·la nar·ra·tur \,mü-,tä-tō-'nō-mi-ne-,dä-,tä-'fä-bù-lä-nä-'rä-,tùr\ [L] : with the name changed the story applies to you

my·ster·i·um tre·men·dum \mi-'ster-ē-,ùm-tre-'men-dùm\ [L] : overwhelming mystery

na·tu·ram ex·pel·las fur·ca, ta·men us·que re·cur·ret \nä-'tü-,räm-ek-,spe-läs-'fùr-,kä ,tä-men-'ùs-kwe-re-'kùr-et\ [L] : you may drive nature out with a pitchfork, but she will keep coming back

na·tu·ra non fa·cit sal·tum \nä-'tü-rä-,nōn-,fä-kit-'säl-,tùm\ [L] : nature makes no leap

ne ce·de ma·lis \nā-,kä-de-'mä-,lēs\ [L] : yield not to misfortunes

ne·mo me im·pu·ne la·ces·sit \'nā-mō-'mä-im-,pü-nä-lä-'ke-sit\ [L] : no one attacks me with impunity — motto of Scotland and of the Order of the Thistle

ne quid ni·mis \,nā-,kwid-'ni-mis\ [L] : not anything in excess

n'est–ce pas? \nes-pä\ [F] : isn't it so?

nicht wahr? \nikt-'vär\ [G] : not true? : isn't it so?

nil ad·mi·ra·ri \,nēl-,äd-mi-'rär-ē\ [L] : to be excited by nothing : equanimity

nil de·spe·ran·dum \'nēl-dä-spä-'rän-dùm\ [L] : never despair

nil si·ne nu·mi·ne \'nēl-,si-nä-'nü-mi-ne\ [L] : nothing without the divine will — motto of Colorado

n'im·porte \naⁿ-pórt\ [F] : it's no matter

no·lens vo·lens \,nō-,lenz-'vō-,lenz\ [L] : unwilling (or) willing : willy-nilly

non om·nia pos·su·mus om·nes \nōn-'òm-nē-ä-,pó-sù-mùs-'òm-,nās\ [L] : we can't all (do) all things

non om·nis mo·ri·ar \nōn-'òm-nis-'mòr-ē-,är\ [L] : I shall not wholly die

non sans droict \nōⁿ-säⁿ-drwä\ [OF] : not without right — motto on Shakespeare's coat of arms

non sum qua·lis eram \,nōn-,sùm-,kwä-lis-'er-,äm\ [L] : I am not what I used to be

nos·ce te ip·sum \,nòs-ke-,tä-'ip-,sùm\ [L] : know thyself

nos·tal·gie de la boue \nòs-täl-zhēd-là-bü, -zhē-də-\ [F] : yearning for the mud : attraction to what is unworthy, crude, or degrading

nous avons chan·gé tout ce·la \nü-zä-vōⁿ-shäⁿ-zhä-tü-sä-lä\ [F] : we have changed all that

nous ver·rons ce que nous ver·rons \nü-ve-rōⁿs-kə-nü-ve-rōⁿ, -rōⁿ-sə-kə-\ [F] : we shall see what we shall see

no·vus ho·mo \,nò-wùs-'hò-mō\ [L] : new man : man newly ennobled : upstart

novus or·do se·clo·rum \-'òr-,dō-sä-'klòr-ùm\ [L] : a new cycle of the ages — motto on the reverse of the Great Seal of the United States

nu·gae \'nü-,gī\ [L] : trifles

nuit blanche \nwⁱē-bläⁿsh\ [F] : white night : a sleepless night

nyet \'nyet\ [Russ] : no

O al·ti·tu·do \'ō-,äl-ti-'tü-,dō\ [L] : O (the) height : feeling of spiritual exaltation

ob·iit \'ò-bē-,it\ [L] : he or she died

ob·scu·rum per ob·scu·ri·us \,òb-'skyùr-ùm-,per-òb-'skyùr-ē-ùs\ [L] : (explaining) the obscure by means of the more obscure

ode·rint dum me·tu·ant \'ō-de-,rint-,dùm-me-tù-,änt\ [L] : let them hate, so long as they fear

odi et amo \'ō-,dē-et-'ä-(,)mō\ [L] : I hate and I love

omer·tà \ò-'mer-tä\ [It] : conspiracy of silence

om·ne ig·no·tum pro mag·ni·fi·co \,òm-ne-ig-'nō-,tùm-prō-mäg-'ni-fi-,kō\ [L] : everything unknown (is taken) as grand : the unknown tends to be exaggerated in importance or difficulty

---

\ə\ abut \ᵊ\ kitten, F table \ər\ further \a\ ash \ā\ ace \ä\ mop, mar \aú\ out \ch\ chin \e\ bet \ē\ easy \g\ go \i\ hit \ī\ ice \j\ job \ŋ\ sing \ō\ go \ò\ law \òi\ boy \th\ thin \th\ the \ü\ loot \ù\ foot \y\ yet \zh\ vision, beige \k, ⁿ, œ, ᵫ, ʸ\ *see* Guide to Pronunciation

om·nia mu·tan·tur, nos et mu·ta·mur in il·lis \ˌóm-nē-ä-mü-ˈtän-ˌtu̇r ˌnōs-ˌet-mü-ˌtä-mu̇r-in-ˈi-ˌlēs\ [L] : all things are changing, and we are changing with them

om·nia vin·cit amor \ˈóm-nē-ä-ˈwiŋ-kit-ˈä-ˌmór\ [L] : love conquers all

onus pro·ban·di \ˌō-nu̇s-prō-ˈban-ˌdī, -dē\ [L] : burden of proof

ora pro no·bis \ˌō-rä-prō-ˈnō-ˌbēs\ [L] : pray for us

Ord·nung \ˈórd-nu̇ŋ\ [G] : order : orderliness : system of community norms

ore ro·tun·do \ˌōr-ē-rō-ˈtən-dō\ [L] : with round mouth : eloquently

oro y pla·ta \ˌōr-ō-ē-ˈplä-tə\ [Sp] : gold and silver — motto of Montana

o tem·po·ra! o mo·res! \ō-ˈtem-pò-rä ō-ˈmō-ˌrās\ [L] : oh the times! oh the manners!

oti·um cum dig·ni·ta·te \ˈō-tē-ˌu̇m-ku̇m-ˌdig-ni-ˈtä-te\ [L] : leisure with dignity

où sont les neiges d'an·tan? \ü-sōⁿ-lā-nezh-däⁿ-ˈtäⁿ\ [F] : where are the snows of yesteryear?

outre–mer \ütrᵊ-mer\ [F] : overseas : distant lands

pal·li·da Mors \ˌpa-li-dä-ˈmórz\ [L] : pale Death

pa·nem et cir·cen·ses \ˈpä-ˌnem-et-kir-ˈkān-ˌsās\ [L] : bread and circuses : provision of the means of life and recreation by government to appease discontent

pan·ta rhei \ˌpän-ˌtä-ˈrā, ˌpan-tə-ˈrā\ [Gk] : all things are in flux

par avance \pär-ä-väⁿs\ [F] : in advance : by anticipation

par avion \pär-ä-vyōⁿ\ [F] : by airplane — used on airmail

par ex·em·ple \pär-äg-zäⁿplᵊ\ [F] : for example

pars pro to·to \ˈpärs-(ˌ)prō-ˈtō-(ˌ)tō\ [L] : part (taken) for the whole

par·tu·ri·unt mon·tes, nas·ce·tur ri·di·cu·lus mus \pär-ˈtu̇r-ē-ˌu̇nt-ˈmòn-ˌtās näs-ˈkā-ˌtu̇r-ri-ˌdi-ku̇-lu̇s-ˈmüs\ [L] : the mountains are in labor, and a ridiculous mouse will be brought forth

pas·seg·gia·ta \päs-säd-ˈjä-tä\ [It] : stroll : evening stroll after work hours by the residents of a town

pa·ter pa·tri·ae \ˈpä-ˌter-ˈpä-trē-ˌī\ [L] : father of his country

pau·cis ver·bis \ˌpau̇-ˌkēs-ˈwer-ˌbēs\ [L] : in a few words

pax vo·bis·cum \ˌpäks-vō-ˈbēs-ˌku̇m\ [L] : peace (be) with you

peine forte et dure \pen-fȯr-tā-dᵫr\ [F] : strong and hard punishment : torture

per an·gus·ta ad au·gus·ta \per-ˈän-ˌgu̇s-tä-äd-ˈau̇-ˌgu̇s-tä, per-ˈäŋ-\ [L] : through difficulties to honors

per·eant qui an·te nos nos·tra dix·e·runt \ˈper-e-ˌänt-kwē-ˌän-te-ˈnōs-ˈnòs-trä-dēk-ˈsā-ˌru̇nt\ [L] : may they perish who have expressed our bright ideas before us

per·eunt et im·pu·tan·tur \ˈper-e-ˌu̇nt-et-ˌim-pu̇-ˈtän-ˌtu̇r\ [L] : they (the hours) pass away and are reckoned on (our) account

per·fide Al·bion \per-fēd-äl-byōⁿ\ [F] : perfidious Albion (England)

peu à peu \pœ-ä-pœ\ [F] : little by little

peu de chose \pœd-shōz, pœ-də-\ [F] : a trifle

pièce d'oc·ca·sion \pyes-dò-kä-zyōⁿ\ [F] : piece for a special occasion

pièce jus·ti·fi·ca·tive \pyes-zhᵫs-tē-fē-kä-tēv\ [F] : justificatory paper : document serving as evidence

pièce mon·tée \pyes-mōⁿ-tā\ [F] : set piece : food that has been decoratively shaped or arranged

pinx·it \ˈpiŋk-sit\ [L] : he or she painted it

place aux dames \pläs-ō-däm\ [F] : (make) room for the ladies

ple·no ju·re \ˌplā-nō-ˈyu̇r-e\ [L] : with full right

plus ça change, plus c'est la même chose \plᵫ-sä-shäⁿzh plᵫ-se-lä-mem-shōz\ [F] : the more that changes, the more it's the same thing — often shortened to *plus ça change*

plus roy·a·liste que le roi \plᵫ-rwä-yä-lēst-kəl-rwä\ [F] : more royalist than the king

po·cas pa·la·bras \ˌpō-käs-pä-ˈlä-vräs\ [Sp] : few words

po·eta nas·ci·tur, non fit \pò-ˌā-tä-ˈnäs-ki-ˌtu̇r nōn-ˈfit\ [L] : a poet is born, not made

po·ète mau·dit \pò-et-mō-dē\ [F] : accursed poet : a writer dogged by misfortune and lack of recognition

point de re·père \pwaⁿ-də-rä-per\ [F] : point of reference

pol·li·ce ver·so \ˌpò-li-ke-ˈwer-sō\ [L] : with thumb turned : with a gesture or expression of condemnation

post hoc, er·go prop·ter hoc \ˈpōst-ˌhōk ˌer-gō-ˈpròp-ter-ˌhōk\ [L] : after this, therefore on account of it (a fallacy of argument)

post ob·itum \pōst-ˈō-bi-ˌtu̇m\ [L] : after death

pour ac·quit \pür-ä-kē\ [F] : received payment

pour en·cou·ra·ger les autres \pür-äⁿ-kü-rä-zhā-lā-zōtrᵊ\ [F] : in order to encourage the others — said ironically of an action (as an execution) carried out in order to compel others to obey or submit

pour le mé·rite \pür-lə-mā-rēt\ [F] : for merit

pour rire \pür-rēr\ [F] : for laughing : not to be taken seriously

pri·mum non no·ce·re \ˌprē-mu̇m-ˌnōn-nò-ˈkā-rā\ [L] : the first thing (is) to do no harm

pro aris et fo·cis \prō-ˌä-ˌrēs-et-ˈfō-ˌkēs\ [L] : for altars and firesides

pro bo·no pu·bli·co \prō-ˌbò-nō-ˈpü-bli-ˌkō\ [L] : for the public good

pro hac vi·ce \prō-ˌhäk-ˈwi-ke\ [L] : for this occasion

pro pa·tria \prō-ˈpä-trē-ˌä\ [L] : for one's country

pro re·ge, le·ge, et gre·ge \prō-ˈrā-ˌge ˈlā-ˌge et-ˈgre-ˌge\ [L] : for the king, the law, and the people

pro re na·ta \ˌprō-ˌrā-ˈnä-tä\ [L] : for an occasion that has arisen : as needed — used in medical prescriptions

quand même \käⁿ-mem\ [F] : even so : all the same

quan·tum mu·ta·tus ab il·lo \ˌkwän-tu̇m-mü-ˈtä-tu̇s-äb-ˈi-lō\ [L] : how changed from what he once was

quan·tum suf·fi·cit \ˌkwän-təm-ˈsə-fə-ˌkit\ [L] : as much as suffices : a sufficient quantity — used chiefly in medical prescriptions

¿qué pa·sa? \kā-ˈpä-sä\ [Sp] : what's happening? — used as a greeting

¿quién sa·be? \kyān-ˈsä-vā\ [Sp] : who knows?

qui fa·cit per ali·um fa·cit per se \kwē-ˌfä-kit-ˌper-ˈä-lē-ˌu̇m-ˌfä-kit-ˌper-ˈsā\ [L] : he who does (something) through another does it through himself

quis cus·to·di·et ip·sos cus·to·des? \ˌkwis-ku̇s-ˈtō-dē-ˌet-ˌip-ˌsōs-ku̇s-ˈtō-ˌdās\ [L] : who will keep the keepers themselves?

qui s'ex·cuse s'ac·cuse \kē-ˈsek-ˌskᵫz-ˈsä-ˌkᵫz\ [F] : he who excuses himself accuses himself

quis se·pa·ra·bit? \ˌkwis-ˌsā-pə-ˈrä-bit\ [L] : who shall separate (us)? — motto of the Order of St. Patrick

qui trans·tu·lit sus·ti·net \kwē-ˈträns-tu̇-ˌlit-ˈsu̇s-ti-ˌnet\ [L] : He who transplanted sustains (us) — motto of Connecticut

qui va là? \kē-vä-lä\ [F] : who goes there?

quo·ad hoc \ˌkwò-ˌäd-ˈhōk\ [L] : as far as this : to this extent

quod erat de·mon·stran·dum \ˌkwòd-ˈer-ˌät-ˌde-mən-ˈstran-dəm, -ˌdā-ˌmòn-ˈsträn-ˌdu̇m\ [L] : which was to be proved

quod erat fa·ci·en·dum \-ˌfä-kē-ˈen-ˌdu̇m\ [L] : which was to be done

quod sem·per, quod ubi·que, quod ab om·ni·bus \kwòd-ˈsem-ˌper kwòd-ˈü-bi-ˌkwā ˌkwòd-äb-ˈòm-ni-ˌbu̇s, -ˌkwòd-u̇-ˈbē-(ˌ)kwā-\ [L] : what (has been held) always, everywhere, by everybody

quod vi·de \kwòd-ˈwi-ˌde\ [L] : which see

quo·rum pars mag·na fui \ˈkwór-u̇m-ˌpärs-ˌmäg-nä-ˈfu̇-ē\ [L] : in which I played a great part

quos de·us vult per·de·re pri·us de·men·tat \kwōs-ˈdā-u̇s-ˌwu̇lt-ˈper-de-ˌrā-ˌpri-u̇s-dā-ˈmen-ˌtät\ [L] : those whom a god wishes to destroy he first drives mad

quot ho·mi·nes, tot sen·ten·ti·ae \kwòt-ˈhò-mi-ˌnās ˌtòt-sen-ˈten-tē-ˌī\ [L] : there are as many opinions as there are men

quo va·dis? \kwō-ˈwä-dis, -ˈvä-dəs\ [L] : whither are you going?

raf·fi·né *or* **raf·fi·née** \rä-fē-nā\ [F] : refined : sophisticated

rai·son d'état \re-zōⁿ-dā-tä\ [F] : reason of state

re·cu·ler pour mieux sau·ter \rə-kᵫ-lā-pür-myœ-sō-tā\ [F] : to draw back in order to make a better jump

reg·nat po·pu·lus \ˌreg-ˌnät-ˈpò-pu̇-ˌlu̇s\ [L] : the people rule — motto of Arkansas

re in·fec·ta \ˌrā-in-ˈfek-ˌtä\ [L] : the business being unfinished : without accomplishing one's purpose

re·li·gio lo·ci \re-ˈli-ge-ˌo-ˈlò-ˌkē\ [L] : religious sanctity of a place

rem acu te·ti·gis·ti \rem-ˈä-ˌkü-ˌte-ti-ˈgis-tē\ [L] : you have touched the point with a needle : you have hit the nail on the head

ré·pon·dez s'il vous plaît \rā-pōⁿ-dā-sēl-vü-ple\ [F] : reply, if you please

re·qui·es·cat in pa·ce \ˌre-kwē-ˈes-ˌkät-in-ˈpä-ˌke, ˌrā-kwē-ˈes-ˌkät-in-ˈpä-ˌchā\ [L] : may he or she rest in peace — used on tombstones

re·spi·ce fi·nem \ˌrā-spi-ˌke-ˈfē-ˌnem\ [L] : look to the end : consider the outcome

re·sur·gam \re-ˈsu̇r-ˌgäm\ [L] : I shall rise again

re·te·nue \rət-nᵫ\ [F] : self-restraint : reserve

re·ve·nons à nos mou·tons \rəv-nōⁿ-ä-nō-mü-tōⁿ\ [F] : let us return to our sheep : let us get back to the subject

ruse de guerre \rᵫz-də-ger\ [F] : war stratagem

rus in ur·be \ˌrüs-in-ˈu̇r-ˌbe\ [L] : country in the city

sacre bleu \säkrᵊ-blœ\ [F] — used as a mild oath to express surprise or annoyance

sae·va in·dig·na·tio \ˌsī-wä-ˌin-dig-ˈnä-tē-ō\ [L] : fierce indignation

sa·laam alai·kum \sə-ˈläm-ə-ˈlī-ku̇m\ [Ar *as-salāmu ʿalaykum*] : peace to you — used as a traditional greeting among Muslims

sal At·ti·cum \sal-ˈa-ti-kəm\ [L] : Attic salt : wit

salle à man·ger \säl-ä-mäⁿ-zhā\ [F] : dining room

sa·lon des re·fu·sés \sä-lòⁿ-dār-(ə-)fᵫ-zā\ [F] : salon of the refused : exhibition of art that has been rejected by an official body

sal·to mor·ta·le \ˌsäl-tō-mòr-ˈtä-lā\ [It] : deadly jump : full somersault : dangerous or crucial undertaking

sa·lus po·pu·li su·pre·ma lex es·to \ˌsä-ˌlüs-ˈpò-pu̇-ˌlē-su̇-ˌprā-mä-ˌleks-ˈes-tō\ [L] : let the welfare of the people be the supreme law — motto of Missouri

sanc·ta sim·pli·ci·tas \ˌsäŋk-tä-sim-ˈpli-ki-ˌtäs\ [L] : holy simplicity — often used ironically in reference to another's naïveté

sans doute \säⁿ-düt\ [F] : without doubt

sans gêne \säⁿ-zhen\ [F] : without embarrassment or constraint

sans peur et sans re·proche \säⁿ-pœr-ā-säⁿ-rə-ˈpròsh\ [F] : without fear and without reproach

sans sou·ci \säⁿ-sü-sē\ [F] : without worry

sa·yo·na·ra \ˌsī-ə-ˈnär-ə, ˌsä-yə-\ [Jp] : good-bye

scène à faire \sen-ä-fer\ [F] : obligatory scene

sculp·sit \ˈskəlp-sət, ˈsku̇lp-sit\ [L] : he or she carved it

scu·to bo·nae vo·lun·ta·tis tu·ae co·ro·nas·ti nos \ˈskü-ˌtō-ˈbò-ˌnī-ˌvò-lu̇n-ˌtä-tis-ˈtü-ˌī-ˌkòr-ò-ˌnäs-tē-ˈnōs\ [L] : Thou hast crowned us with the shield of Thy good will — a motto on the Great Seal of Maryland

se·cun·dum ar·tem \se-ˌku̇n-du̇m-ˈär-ˌtem\ [L] : according to the art : according to the accepted practice of a profession or trade

secundum na·tu·ram \-nä-ˈtü-ˌräm\ [L] : according to nature : naturally

se de·fen·den·do \ˈsā-ˌdā-ˌfen-ˈden-dō\ [L] : in self-defense

se ha·bla es·pa·ñol \sā-ˌäv-lä-ˌäs-pä-ˈnʸōl\ [Sp] : Spanish spoken

sem·per ea·dem \ˌsem-ˌper-ˈe-ä-ˌdem\ [L] : always the same (fem.) — motto of Queen Elizabeth I

sem·per fi·de·lis \ˌsem-pər-fə-ˈdā-ləs\ [L] : always faithful — motto of the U.S. Marine Corps

sem·per idem \ˌsem-ˌper-ˈē-ˌdem\ [L] : always the same (masc.)

sem·per pa·ra·tus \ˌsem-pər-pə-ˈrä-təs\ [L] : always prepared — motto of the U.S. Coast Guard

se non è ve·ro, è ben tro·va·to \sā-ˌnōn-e-ˈvā-rō e-ˌben-trō-ˈvä-tō\ [It] : even if it is not true, it is well conceived

sha·lom alei·chem \ˌshò-ləm-ə-ˈlā-kəm, ˌshō-, -ˌkəm\ [Heb *shālōm ʿalēkhem*] : peace to you — used as a traditional Jewish greeting

sic itur ad as·tra \sēk-ˈi-ˌtu̇r-ˌäd-ˈäs-trə\ [L] : thus one goes to the stars : such is the way to immortality

sic sem·per ty·ran·nis \ˌsik-ˌsem-pər-tə-ˈra-nəs\ [L] : thus ever to tyrants — motto of Virginia

sic trans·it glo·ria mun·di \sēk-ˈträn-sit-ˌglòr-ē-ä-ˈmu̇n-dē\ [L] : so passes away the glory of the world

sic·ut pa·tri·bus sit De·us no·bis \ˌsē-ˌku̇t-ˈpä-tri-ˌbu̇s-sit-ˌdā-u̇s-ˈnō-ˌbēs\ [L] : as to our fathers may God be to us — motto of Boston

si jeu·nesse sa·vait, si vieil·lesse pou·vait! \sē-ˈzhœ-nes-ˈsä-ve sē-ˈvye-yes-ˈpü-ve\ [F] : if youth only knew, if age only could!

si·lent le·ges in·ter ar·ma \ˌsi-ˌlent-ˈlā-ˌgās-ˌin-ter-ˈär-mä\ [L] : the laws are silent in the midst of arms (i.e., in time of war)

s'il vous plaît \sēl-vü-ple\ [F] : if you please

si·mi·lia si·mi·li·bus cu·ran·tur \si-ˈmi-lē-ä-si-ˈmi-li-bu̇s-kü-ˈrän-ˌtu̇r\ [L] : like is cured by like

si·mi·lis si·mi·li gau·det \ˈsi-mi-lis-ˈsi-mi-lē-ˈgau̇-ˌdet\ [L] : like takes pleasure in like

si mo·nu·men·tum re·qui·ris, cir·cum·spi·ce \ˌsē-ˌmò-nu̇-ˌmen-tu̇m-re-ˈkwē-ris kir-ˈku̇m-spi-ke\ [L] : if you seek his monument, look around — epitaph of Sir Christopher Wren in St. Paul's, London, of which he was architect

sim·pliste \saⁿ-plēst\ [F] : simplistic : overly simple or naive

si quae·ris pen·in·su·lam amoe·nam, cir·cum·spi·ce \sē-'kwī-ris-pā-'nin-sə-,läm-ä-'mòi-,näm kir-'kùm-spi-ke\ [L] : if you seek a beautiful peninsula, look around — motto of Michigan

sis·te vi·a·tor \'sis-te-wē-'ä-,tòr\ [L] : stop, traveler — used on Roman roadside tombs

si vis pa·cem, pa·ra bel·lum \sē-'wēs-'pä-,kem 'pä-rä-'be-,lùm\ [L] : if you wish peace, prepare for war

sol·vi·tur am·bu·lan·do \'sòl-wi-,tùr-,äm-bù-'län-dō\ [L] : it is solved by walking : the problem is solved by a practical experiment

splen·di·de men·dax \,splen-di-,dā-'men-,däks\ [L] : nobly untruthful

spo·lia opi·ma \,spò-lē-ä-ō-'pē-mä\ [L] : rich spoils : the arms taken by the victorious from the vanquished general

sprez·za·tu·ra \sprät-tsä-'tü-rä\ [It] : studied nonchalance : perfect conduct or performance of something (as an artistic endeavor) without apparent effort

Sta·bat Ma·ter \,stä-bät-'mä-ter\ [L] : the mother was standing — title of a Latin hymn

sta·tus in quo \,stä-tùs-,in-'kwō\ [L] : state in which : the existing state

sta·tus quo an·te bel·lum \'stä-tùs-kwō-,än-te-'be-lùm\ [L] : the state existing before the war

Stim·mung \'shti-mùŋ\ [G] : tone : mood : atmosphere

sua·vi·ter in mo·do, for·ti·ter in re \'swä-wi-,ter-in-'mó-dō 'fòr-ti-,ter-in-'rä\ [L] : gently in manner, strongly in deed

sub ver·bo \sùb-'wer-bō, ,sab-'vər-bō\ or **sub vo·ce** \sùb-'wō-ke, ,sab-'vō-sē\ [L] : under the word — introducing a cross-reference in a dictionary or index

sunt la·cri·mae re·rum \sùnt-,lä-kri-,mī-'rä-rùm\ [L] : there are tears for things : tears attend trials

suo ju·re \,sù-ō-'yùr-e\ [L] : in his or her own right

suo lo·co \-'lō-kō\ [L] : in its proper place

suo Mar·te \-'mär-te\ [L] : by one's own exertions

sur place \sùr-'pläs\ [F] : in place : on the spot

su·um cui·que \,sù-ùm-'kwi-kwe\ [L] : to each his own

tant mieux \täⁿ-myœ\ [F] : so much the better

tant pis \-'pē\ [F] : so much the worse : too bad

tem·po·ra mu·tan·tur, nos et mu·ta·mur in il·lis \,tem-pò-rä-mü-'tän-,tùr ,nōs-,et-mü-,tä-mùr-in-'i-,lēs\ [L] : the times are changing, and we are changing with them

tem·pus edax re·rum \'tem-pùs-,e-,däks-'rä-rùm\ [L] : time, that devours all things

tem·pus fu·git \,tem-pəs-'fyü-jət, ,tem-pùs-'fü-git\ [L] : time flies

ti·meo Da·na·os et do·na fe·ren·tes \,ti-mē-,ō-'dä-nä-,ōs-,et-,dō-nä-fe-'ren-,tās\ [L] : I fear the Greeks even when they bring gifts

to·ti·dem ver·bis \,tò-ti-,dem-'wer-,bēs\ [L] : in so many words

to·tis vi·ri·bus \,tō-tis-'wē-ri-,bùs\ [L] : with all one's might

to·to cae·lo \,tō-tō-'kī-lō\ or **toto coe·lo** \-'kòi-lō\ [L] : by the whole extent of the heavens : diametrically

tou·jours per·drix \tü-zhür-per-drē\ [F] : always partridge : too much of a good thing

tour d'ho·ri·zon \tür-dò-rē-zōⁿ\ [F] : circuit of the horizon : general survey

tous frais faits \tü-fre-fe\ [F] : all expenses defrayed

tout à fait \tü-tä-fe\ [F] : altogether : quite

tout au con·traire \tü-tō-kōⁿ-'trer\ [F] : quite the contrary

tout à vous \tü-tä-vü\ [F] : wholly yours : at your service

tout bien ou rien \tü-'byaⁿ-nü-'ryaⁿ\ [F] : everything well (done) or nothing (attempted)

tout com·pren·dre c'est tout par·don·ner \'tü-kōⁿ-präⁿ-drə-se-'tü-pär,dò-nā\ [F] : to understand all is to forgive all

tout court \tü-kür\ [F] : quite short : and nothing else : simply : just; also : brusquely

tout de même \tüt-mem\ [F] : all the same : nevertheless

tout de suite \tüt-swēt\ [F] : immediately; also : all at once : consecutively

tout en·sem·ble \tü-täⁿ-säⁿblᵊ\ [F] : all together : general effect

tout est per·du fors l'hon·neur \tü-te-per-dœ-fòr-lò-nœr\ or **tout est perdu hors l'honneur** \-dœ-òr-\ [F] : all is lost save honor

tout le monde \tü-lə-mōⁿd\ [F] : all the world : everybody

tra·hi·son des clercs \trä-ē-zòⁿ-dä-klerk\ [F] : treason of the intellectuals

tranche de vie \träⁿsh-də-'vē\ [F] : slice of life

tria junc·ta in uno \,tri-ä-'yùŋk-tä-in-'ü-nō\ [L] : three joined in one — motto of the Order of the Bath

trist·esse \trē-stes\ [F] : melancholy

tru·di·tur di·es die \'trü-di-,tür-'di-,äs-'di-,ā\ [L] : day is pushed forth by day : one day hurries on another

tu·e·bor \tù-'ā-,bòr\ [L] : I will defend — a motto on the Great Seal of Michigan

ua mau ke ea o ka ai·na i ka po·no \,ù-ä-'mä-ù-kā-'ā-ä-ō-kä-'ä-ē-nä-,ē-kä-'pō-nō\ [Hawaiian] : the life of the land is perpetuated in righteousness — motto of Hawaii

über al·les \,ue-ber-'ä-les\ [G] : above everything else

Über·mensch \'ue-bər-,mench\ [G] : superman

ul·ti·ma ra·tio re·gum \'ùl-ti-mä-,rä-tē-ō-'rä-gùm\ [L] : the final argument of kings, i.e., war

und so wei·ter \ùnt-zō-'vī-tar\ [G] : and so on

uno ani·mo \,ü-nō-'ä-ni-,mō\ [L] : with one mind : unanimously

ur·bi et or·bi \,ùr-bē-,et-'òr-bē\ [L] : to the city (Rome) and the world : to everyone

uti·le dul·ci \,ü-ti-le-'dùl-,kē\ [L] : the useful with the agreeable

ut in·fra \ùt-'in-frä\ [L] : as below

ut su·pra \ùt-'sü-prä\ [L] : as above

va·de re·tro me, Sa·ta·na \wä-de-'rä-trō-,mä 'sä-tä-,nä\ [L] : get thee behind me, Satan

va et vient \vä-ā-vyäⁿ\ [F] : coming and going : active movement : traffic

vae vic·tis \wī-'wik-,tēs\ [L] : woe to the vanquished

va·ria lec·tio \,wär-ē-ä-'lek-tē-,ō\ pl **va·ri·ae lec·ti·o·nes** \'wär-ē-,ī-,lek-tē-'ō-,näs\ [L] : variant reading

va·ri·um et mu·ta·bi·le sem·per fe·mi·na \,wär-ē-ùm-,et-,mü-'tä-bi-le-,sem-,per-'fä-mi-nä\ [L] : woman is ever a fickle and changeable thing

ve·di Na·po·li e poi mo·ri \,vä-dē-'nä-pō-lē-ä-,pò-ē-'mó-rē\ [It] : see Naples and then die

ve·ni, vi·di, vi·ci \'wā-nē ,wē-dē 'wē-kē, ,vä-nē ,vē-dē 'vē-chē\ [L] : I came, I saw, I conquered

ven·tre à terre \väⁿ-trä-ter\ [F] : belly to the ground : at very great speed

ver·ba·tim ac lit·te·ra·tim \wer-'bä-tim-,äk-,li-te-'rä-tim\ [L] : word for word and letter for letter

ver·bum sat sa·pi·en·ti est \,wer-bùm-'sät-,sä-pē-'en-tē-,est\ [L] : a word to the wise is sufficient

Ver·frem·dung \'fer-frem-dùŋ\ [G] : distancing : alienation

via cru·cis \wē-ä-'krü-sis\ [L] : Way of the Cross : path of suffering

vieux jeu \vyœ-zhœ\ [F] : old game : old hat

vin·cit om·nia ve·ri·tas \,wiŋ-kit-'òm-nē-ä-'wä-ri-,täs\ [L] : truth conquers all things

vin·cu·lum ma·tri·mo·nii \,wiŋ-kù-lùm-,mä-tri-'mō-nē-,ē\ [L] : bond of marriage

vin du pays \vaⁿ-due-pä-ē\ or **vin de pays** \vaⁿ-də-\ [F] : wine of the locality

vir·gi·ni·bus pu·e·ris·que \wir-'gi-ni-bùs-,pù-e-'rēs-kwe\ [L] : for girls and boys

vir·go in·tac·ta \'vir-,gō-in-'täk-tä\ [L] : untouched virgin

vir·tu·te et ar·mis \wir-'tü-te-,et-'är-mēs\ [L] : by valor and arms — motto of Mississippi

vis me·di·ca·trix na·tu·rae \'wēs-,me-di-'kä-triks-nä-'tü-,rī\ [L] : the healing power of nature

vi·ta nuo·va \,vē-tä-'nwò-vä\ [It] : new life

vive la dif·fé·rence \vēv-lä-dē-fā-räⁿs, vē-və-\ [F] : long live the difference (between the sexes)

vive la reine \vēv-lä-ren\ [F] : long live the queen

vive le roi \vēv-lə-rwä\ [F] : long live the king

vix·e·re for·tes an·te Aga·mem·no·na \wik-,sä-re-'fòr-,täs-,än-te-,ä-gä-'mem-nò-,nä\ [L] : brave men lived before Agamemnon

vogue la ga·lère \vòg-lä-gä-ler\ [F] : let the galley be kept rowing : keep on, whatever may happen

voi·là tout \vwä-lä-tü\ [F] : that's all

vo·lup·té \vò-luep-tä\ [F] : pleasure : sensuality

vou·lu \vü-lue\ [F] : willed : contrived or forced

vox et prae·te·rea ni·hil \'wòks-et-prī-'ter-e-ä-'ni-,hil\ [L] : voice and nothing more

vox po·pu·li vox Dei \wòks-'pò-pù-,lē-,wòks-'dä-ē\ [L] : the voice of the people is the voice of God

Wan·der·jahr \'vän-dər-,yär\ [G] : year of wandering

Welt·bild \'velt-,bilt\ [G] : conception of the world

Wert·frei·heit \'vert-,frī-,hīt\ [G] : freedom from value judgments : ethical neutrality

wie geht's? \vē-'gāts\ [G] : how goes it? : how is it going? — used as a greeting

Wis·sen·schaft \'vi-sən-,shäft\ [G] : learning : science

wun·der·bar \'vùn-dər-,bär\ [G] : wonderful

Biographical Names

This section contains the names of many notable persons both living and dead. Persons are generally entered under the name or title by which they are most commonly known. Entries typically consist of last name, personal names, birth and death dates, nationality, and occupation or status. Also included, when appropriate, are pseudonyms, original names, epithets, alternate names, reign names, and titles. The pronunciation and end-of-line division of elements in boldface are usually shown. The pronunciation and end-of-line division of names or titles in italics or roman are given only occasionally. Transliterations of names from alphabets other than the Roman have been made as exact and consistent as possible. For most Chinese names, the traditional Wade-Giles system has been used. The Pinyin system has been used only for Chinese still living or recently deceased.

A number of names contain connectives like *d', de, di, van,* and *von.* With some exceptions, chiefly American or British, names are not alphabetized under these connectives but rather under the principal element of the surname. If the surname of a person is usually construed as containing this connective, the entry appears at the principal element and the connective appears immediately after, separated by a comma:

Gogh, van . . . Vincent

If the full name contains a connective which is not usually construed as an inseparable part of the surname, then the connective follows the personal name.

Bee·tho·ven . . . Ludwig van

Birth and death dates about which there is little or no doubt are entered without qualification. Doubtful dates are accompanied by a question mark, and approximate dates are preceded by *ca* (circa). In some instances only the years of principal activity are given, preceded by the abbreviation *fl* (flourished). The dates of a reign or other term of office are enclosed in parentheses.

At the end of many entries are derivative adjectives with such endings as *-ian, -ic,* or *-esque.* While it is possible to form these derivatives from any name, only the more common are shown:

Dan·te . . . — **Dan·te·an** . . . *or* **Dan·tes·can** . . . *or* **Dan·tesque** . . . *adj*

Of necessity many abbreviations have been used. For a key see the section Abbreviations in This Work in the front matter.

Aar·on \'er-ən\ Hank 1934–   *Henry Louis Aaron* Am. baseball player

Ab·bas \ä-'bäs\ Mahmoud 1935–   pres. of the Palestinian National Authority (2005–   )

Ab·bey \'a-bē\ Edwin Austin 1852–1911 Am. painter & illustrator

Ab·bott \'a-bət\ Berenice 1898–1991 Am. photographer

Abbott Sir John Joseph Caldwell 1821–1893 Canad. polit.; prime min. (1891–92)

Abbott Lyman 1835–1922 Am. clergyman & author

Ab·del·ka·der \,ab-,del-'kä-dər\ *or* **Abd al-Qā·dir** \,ab-dəl-\ 1808–1883 Arab leader in Algeria

Ab·dül·a·ziz \,ab-,dü-lə-'zēz\ 1830–1876 Ottoman sultan (1861–76)

Ab·dul·ha·mīd II \,ab-,dül-hä-'mēd\ 1842–1918 Ottoman sultan (1876–1909)

Ab·dul–Jab·bar \ab-'dül-jə-'bär\ Kareem 1947–   orig. *(Frederick) Lew(is) Alcindor, Jr.* Am. basketball player

Ab·dul·lah \,ab-də-'lä\ 1924–   *Abdullah bin Ab·dul·a·ziz Al Sa·ud* \bin-,ab-,dü-lə-'zēz-äl-sä-'üd\ king of Saudi Arabia (2005–   )

Abdullah I 1882–1951 *'Abd Allāh ibn al-Husayn* emir of Transjordan (1921–46); king of Jordan (1946–51)

Abdullah II 1962–   *great-grandson of prec.* king of Jordan (1999–   )

Ab·dül·me·cid I \,ab-,dül-mə-'jēd\ 1823–1861 Ottoman sultan (1839–61)

Abe \'ä-bā\ Shinzo 1954–   prime min. of Japan (2012–   )

Abel \'ä-bəl\ Sir Frederick Augustus 1827–1902 Eng. chem.

Ab·e·lard \'a-bə-,lärd\ Peter *F* Pierre Alé·lard *or* Abai·lard \,a-bā-'lär\ 1079–?1144 *husband of Héloïse* Fr. philos. & theol.

Ab·er·crom·bie *or* **Ab·er·crom·by** \'a-bər-,kräm-bē, -,krəm-\ James 1706–1781 Brit. gen. in America

Ab·er·nathy \'a-bər-,na-thē\ Ralph David 1926–1990 Am. clergyman & civil rights leader

Ab·ing·ton \'a-bin-tən\ Fanny 1737–1815 née *Frances Barton* Eng. actress

Abri·ko·sov \,ä-brē-'kó-,sóf\ Alexei (Alexeevich) 1928–   Russ. Am. physicist

Abū al–Qā·sim *or* **Abul Ka·sim** \ə-,bül-'kä-səm\ *L* **Al·bu·ca·sis** \,al-byü-'kä-səs\ *ca* 936–*ca* 1013 Span. Arab physician & medical writer

Abū Bakr \ə-,bü-'ba-kər\ *ca* 573–634 1st caliph of Mecca

Ache·be \ə-'che-bā\ Chinua 1930–2013 *Albert Chinualumogu Achebe* Nigerian writer

Ach·e·son \'a-chə-sən\ Dean Gooderham 1893–1971 Am. statesman

Ac·ton \'ak-tən\ 1st Baron 1834–1902 *John Emerich Edward Dal·berg=Acton* \,dal-,bərg-\ Eng. hist.

Ad·am \'a-dəm\ Robert 1728–1792 & his bro. James 1730–1794 Scot. architects & furniture designers

Ad·ams \'a-dəmz\ Ansel Easton 1902–1984 Am. photographer

Adams Charles Francis 1807–1886 *son of J.Q.* Am. author & diplomat

Adams Franklin Pierce 1881–1960 *known as F.P.A.* Am. journalist

Adams Henry Brooks 1838–1918 *son of C.F.* Am. hist.

Adams John 1735–1826 Am. diplomat; 2d pres. of the U.S. (1797–1801)

Adams John (Coolidge) 1947–   Am. composer

Adams John Quin·cy \'kwin-zē, 'kwin(t)-sē\ 1767–1848 *son of John* 6th pres. of the U.S. (1825–29)

Adams Maude 1872–1953 orig. *Maude Kiskadden* Am. actress

Adams Samuel 1722–1803 Am. Revolutionary patriot

Adams Samuel Hopkins 1871–1958 Am. author

Ad·dams \'a-dəmz\ Jane 1860–1935 Am. social worker

Ad·di·son \'a-də-sən\ Joseph 1672–1719 Eng. essayist & poet — **Ad·di·so·nian** \,a-də-'sō-nē-ən, -nyən\ *adj*

Ade \'ād\ George 1866–1944 Am. humorist & playwright

Ade·nau·er \'a-də-,naù(-ə)r, 'ä-\ Konrad 1876–1967 chancellor of West Germany (1949–63)

Ad·ler \'äd-lər, 'ad-\ Alfred 1870–1937 Austrian psychiatrist

Ad·ler \'ad-lər\ Cyrus 1863–1940 Am. educ. & scholar

Adler Felix 1851–1933 Am. educ. & reformer

Adler Mortimer Jerome 1902–2001 Am. philos.

Ador·no \ə-'dór-nō\ Theodor 1903–1969 orig. *Theodor Ludwig Wiesengrund* Ger. philos.

Adri·an \'ā-drē-ən\ name of 6 popes: esp. **IV** (*Nicholas Break·spear* \'brāk-,spir\) 1100?–1159 the only Eng. pope (1154–59)

Adrian Edgar Douglas 1889–1977 1st Baron of *Cambridge* Eng. physiol.

Æ — see George William RUSSELL

Æl·fric \'al-frik\ *ca* 955–*ca* 1010 Eng. abbot & writer

Aes·chi·nes \'es-kə-,nēz, 'ēs-\ 389–314 B.C. Athenian orator

Aes·chy·lus \'es-kə-ləs, 'ēs-\ 525–456 B.C. Greek dram. — **Aes·chy·le·an** \,es-kə-'lē-ən, ,ēs-\ *adj*

Ae·sop \'ē-,säp, -səp\ Greek fabulist; prob. legendary

Aeth·el·berht \'a-thəl-,berkt\ *or* **Eth·el·bert** \'e-thəl-,bert, -thəl-, -,bərt\ *or* **Aed·il·berct** \'a-d°l-,berkt\ *d* 616 king of Kent (560–616)

Aeth·el·red \'a-thəl-,red\ *or* **Eth·el·red II** \'é-thəl-\ 968?–1016 *the Unready* king of England (978–1016)

Afon·so \ə-'fōⁿ(n)-sü\ name of 6 kings of Portugal: esp. **I Hen·ri·ques** \äⁿ-'rē·kish\ 1109?–1185 (1st king of Portugal; reigned 1139–85); **V** 1432–1481 (reigned 1438–81)

Aga Khan III \ä·gə-'kän, ˌkä-\ 1877–1957 *Aga Sultan Sir Mohammed Shah* imam of a branch of Shiism (1885–1957)

Aga Khan IV 1936– *grandson of prec., Shah Karim* imam of a branch of Shiism (1957–)

Ag·as·siz \'a-gə-(ˌ)sē\ Alexander 1835–1910 *son of J.L.R.* Am. zool.

Agassiz (Jean) Louis (Rodolphe) 1807–1873 Am. (Swiss-born) naturalist

Agath·o·cles \ə-'ga-thə-ˌklēz\ 361–289 B.C. tyrant of Syracuse

Agee \'ä-(ˌ)jē\ James 1909–1955 Am. author

Ages·i·la·us II \ə-ˌje-sə-'lā-əs\ *ca* 444–360 B.C. king of Sparta (399–360)

Ag·nes \'ag-nəs\ Saint *d* A.D. 304 virgin martyr

Ag·new \'ag-ˌnü, -ˌnyü\ Spi·ro \'spir-(ˌ)ō\ Theodore 1918–1996 Am. polit.; vice pres. of the U.S. (1969–73)

Ag·non \'ag-ˌnän\ S(hmuel) Y(osef) 1888–1970 Israeli (Austrian-born) author

Ag·re \'ä-grä\ Peter 1949– Am. chemist

Agric·o·la \ə-'gri-kə-lə\ Gnaeus Julius A.D. 40–93 Rom. gen.

Agrip·pa \ə-'gri-pə\ Marcus Vipsanius 63?–12 B.C. Rom. statesman

Ag·rip·pi·na \ˌa-grə-'pī-nə, -'pē-\ the elder *ca* 14 B.C.–A.D. 33 *dau. of Agrippa, wife of Germanicus Caesar, mother of Caligula*

Agrippina the younger A.D. 15?–59 *dau. of prec. & mother of Emp. Nero*

Agui·nal·do \ä-gē-'näl-(ˌ)dō\ Emilio 1869–1964 Filipino leader

Ahern \ə-'hərn\ Bertie 1951– orig. *Bartholemew Ahern* prime min. of Ireland (1997–2008)

Ah·ma·di·ne·jad \ä-ˌmä-di-nē-'zhäd\ Mahmoud 1956– pres. of Iran (2005–13)

Ah·med III \ä-'met, -'med\ 1673–1736 Ottoman sultan (1703–30)

Ah·ti·saa·ri \'ä-tē-ˌsä-rē\ Martti 1937– pres. of Finland 1994–2000; U.N. mediator

Ai·ken \'ä-kən\ Conrad Potter 1889–1973 Am. writer

Ai·ley \'ä-lē\ Alvin 1931–1989 Am. dancer & choreographer

Ai·shah \'ä-ē-shə\ 611–678 *favorite wife of Muhammad*

Ak·bar \'ak-bər, -ˌbär\ 1542–1605 Mogul emp. of India (1556–1605)

Aken·side \'ä-kən-ˌsīd\ Mark 1721–1770 Eng. poet & physician

Ak·er·lof \'a-kər-ˌlȯf\ George Arthur 1940– Am. econ.

Akhe·na·ton \ˌäk-'nä-tᵊn, ä-kə-\ or **Ikh·na·ton** \ik-'nä-tᵊn\ *Amenhotep IV* king of Egypt (1379–1362 B.C.)

Aki·ba ben Jo·seph \ä-'ki-vä-ben-'jō-zəf\ A.D. 40–135 Jewish sage & martyr in Palestine

Aki·hi·to \ˌä-kē-'hē-(ˌ)tō\ 1933– emp. of Japan (1989–)

'Alam·gir \'ä-ləm-ˌgir\ Muhī-ud-Dīn Muhammad 1618–1707 *Au·rang·zeb* \aủ-rəŋ-ˌzeb, ȯ-, -'zeb\ Mogul emp. of India (1658–1707)

Alanbrooke Viscount — see Sir Alan Francis BROOKE

Alar·cón, de \ˌä-ˌlär-'kōn, -'kȯn\ Pedro Antonio 1833–1891 Span. writer & statesman

Al·a·ric \'a-lə-rik\ *ca* 370–410 Visigoth king; conqueror of Rome

Alaric II *d* 507 Visigoth king; issued legal code

Al·bee \'ȯl-(ˌ)bē, 'al-\ Edward Franklin 1928– Am. dram.

Al·bé·niz \äl-'bā-(ˌ)nēs, -(ˌ)nēth\ Isaac 1860–1909 Span. pianist & composer

Al·bers \'al-bərz, 'äl-bərs\ Josef 1888–1976 Am. (Ger.-born) painter

Al·bert \'al-bərt\ Carl Bert 1908–2000 Am. polit.

Albert I 1875–1934 king of Belgium (1909–34)

Albert II 1934– *son of Leopold III* king of Belgium (1993–2013)

Albert II 1958– *son of Rainier III & Grace Kelly* prince of Monaco (2005–)

Albert of Saxe–Coburg–Gotha 1819–1861 *prince consort of Queen Victoria of Great Britain* (1840–61)

Al·ber·tus Mag·nus \al-'bər-təs-'mag-nəs\ Saint *ca* 1200–1280 *Albert Count von Boll·städt* \'bȯl-ˌshtet\ Ger. philos. & theol.

Al·bi·no·ni \ˌäl-bē-'nō-nē\ Tomaso Giovanni 1671–1751 Ital. composer

Al·boin \'al-ˌbȯin, -bə-wən\ *d* 572 Lombard king (*ca* 565–572)

Al·bright \'ȯl-ˌbrīt\ Madeleine 1937– née *Korbel* U.S. secy. of state (1997–2001)

Al·bu·quer·que, de \'al-bə-ˌkər-kē, ˌal-bə-'\ Afonso 1453–1515 Port. viceroy & conqueror in India

Al·cae·us \al-'sē-əs\ *ca* 620–*ca* 580 B.C. Greek poet

Al·ci·bi·a·des \ˌal-sə-'bī-ə-ˌdēz\ *ca* 450–404 B.C. Athenian gen. & polit.

Al·cott \'ȯl-kət, 'al-, -ˌkät\ Amos Bronson 1799–1888 Am. teacher & philos.

Alcott Louisa May 1832–1888 *dau. of A.B.* Am. author

Al·cuin \'al-kwən\ *ca* 732–804 Anglo-Saxon theol. & scholar

Al·da \'äl-də, 'ȯl-, 'al-\ Frances 1883–1952 orig. *Frances Davies* N.Z.-born soprano

Al·den \'ȯl-dən\ John 1599?–1687 Am. colonist

Al·der \'al-dər\ Kurt 1902–1958 Ger. chem.

Al·drich \'ȯl-drich\ Thomas Bailey 1836–1907 Am. author

Al·drin \'ȯl-drən\ Buzz 1930– orig. *Edwin Eugene Aldrin, Jr.* Am. astronaut

Alei·chem Sho·lem \ˌshȯ-ləm-ə-'lä-kəm, ˌshō-\ 1859–1916 pseud. of *Sholem Ra·bin·o·vitz* \rə-'bi-nə-ˌvits\ Russ.-Am. writer in Yiddish

Aleix·an·dre \ˌä-lek-'sän-dre\ Vicente 1898–1984 Span. poet

Ale·mán \ˌä-lä-'män\ Mateo 1547–*ca* 1614 Span. nov.

Alemán Val·dés \väl-'des\ Miguel 1902–1983 Mex. lawyer; pres. of Mexico (1946–52)

Alem·bert, d' \ˌda-ləm-'ber\ Jean Le Rond 1717–1783 Fr. math. & philos.

Al·ex·an·der \ˌa-lig-'zan-dər, ˌe-\ name of 8 popes: esp. **VI** (*Rodrigo Borgia*) 1431–1503 (pope 1492–1503)

Alexander *Russ* Alek·sandr \ˌa-lik-'sän-dər\ name of 3 emps. of Russia: **I** 1777–1825 (reigned 1801–25); **II** 1818–1881 (reigned 1855–81); **III** 1845–1894 (reigned 1881–94)

Alexander *Serb* Alek·san·dar Obre·no·vić \ˌä-lik-'sän-dər-ō-'bre-nə-ˌvich\ 1876–1903 king of Serbia (1889–1903)

Alexander Harold Rupert Leofric George 1891–1969 1st Earl *Alexander of Tunis* Brit. field marshal; gov.-gen. of Canada (1946–52)

Alexander I 1888–1934 king of Yugoslavia (1929–34)

Alexander III of Macedon 356–323 B.C. *the Great* king (336–323) hero

Alexander Nev·sky \'nev-skē, 'nef-\ *ca* 1220–1263 Russ. saint & mil. hero

Alexander Se·ve·rus \sə-'vir-əs\ A.D. 208–235 Rom. emp. (222–235)

Alex·is I Mi·khay·lo·vich \ə-ˌlek-səs-mi-'kī-lə-ˌvich\ 1629–1676 *father of Peter the Great* czar of Russia (1645–76)

Alex·i·us I Com·ne·nus \ə-'lek-sē-əs-ˌkäm-'nē-nəs\ 1048–1118 Byzantine emp. (1081–1118)

Al·fer·ov \äl-'fyȯ-rȯf\ Zhores Ivanovich 1930– Russ. (Belarusian-born) physicist

Al·fie·ri \ˌäl-fē-'er-ē\ Conte Vittorio 1749–1803 Ital. tragic poet

Al·fon·so XIII \al-'fän(t)-(ˌ)sō, -'fän-(ˌ)zō\ 1886–1941 king of Spain (1886–1931)

Al·fred *or* **Æl·fred** \'al-frəd, -fərd\ 849–899 *the Great* king of Wessex (871–899)

Al·ger \'al-jər\ Horatio 1832–1899 Am. author

Al·gren \'ȯl-grən\ Nelson 1909–1981 Am. author

'Alī \ä-'lē, 'ä-lē\ *Ar* **'Alī ibn Abī Ṭā·lib** \-ˌi-bən-ˌä-bē-'tä-lib\ *ca* 600–661 *cousin & son-in-law of Muhammad* 4th orthodox caliph (656–661)

Ali \ä-'lē\ Muhammad 1942– orig. *Cassius Marcellus Clay* Am. boxer

Ali Pa·şa \'pä-shə, 'pa-; pə-'shä\ 1741–1822 *the Lion of Janina* Turk. pasha

Ali·to \ə-'lē-tō\ Samuel Anthony, Jr. 1950– Am. jurist

Al·lais \ä-'lä\ Maurice 1911–2010 Fr. econ.

Al·len \'a-lən\ Ethan 1738–1789 Am. Revolutionary soldier

Allen William 1532–1594 Eng. cardinal

Allen Woody 1935– orig. *Allen Stewart Konigsberg* Am. writer, actor, director

Al·len·by \'a-lən-bē\ Edmund Henry Hynman 1861–1936 1st Viscount *Allenby of Megiddo and Felixstowe* Brit. field marshal

Allen·de Gos·sens \ä-ˌyen-dā-'gȯ-ˌsen(t)s\ Salvador 1908–1973 Chilean Marxist; pres. of Chile (1970–73)

Al·leyne \'a-lən, -ˌlēn, -ˌlän\ Edward 1566–1626 Eng. actor

All·ston \'ȯl-stən\ Washington 1779–1843 Am. painter

Al·ma–Tad·e·ma \ˌal-mə-'ta-də-mə\ Sir Lawrence 1836–1912 Eng. (Du.-born) painter

Alt·man \'ȯlt-mən\ Robert (Bernard) 1925–2006 Am. film director

Altman Sidney 1939– Am. (Canad.-born) biophysicist

Al·va·ra·do, de \ˌäl-vä-'rä-thō\ Pedro *ca* 1485–1541 Span. conquistador

Al·va·rez \'al-və-ˌrez\ Luis Walter 1911–1988 Am. physicist

Al·va·rez de To·le·do \'äl-vä-ˌräth-thä-tō-'lä-thō\ Fernando 1507–1582 3d Duke of *Al·ba* \'al-bə\ *or Al·va* \'al-və\ Span. gen.

Alvarez Quin·te·ro \kēn-'tä-rō\ Serafín 1871–1938 & his bro. Joaquín 1873–1944 Span. dram.

Ama·ti \ä-'mä-tē, ə-\ family of Ital. violin makers of Cremona: esp. Nicolò 1596–1684

Am·brose \'am-ˌbrōz\ Saint 339–397 bishop of Milan — **Am·bro·sian** \am-'brō-zhən, -zē-ən\ *adj*

Amen·ho·tep \ˌä-mən-'hō-ˌtep, ˌa-\ *or* **Am·e·no·phis** \ˌa-mə-'nō-fəs\ name of 4 kings of Egypt: esp. **III** (1417–1379 B.C.); **IV** — see AKHENATON

Amerigo Vespucci — see VESPUCCI

Am·herst \'a-(ˌ)mərst\ Jeffery 1717–1797 Baron *Amherst* Brit. gen.; gov.-gen. of Brit. No. America (1760–63)

Amis \'ā-məs\ Sir Kingsley 1922–1995 Eng. author

Am·père \äⁿ-'per\ André-Marie 1775–1836 Fr. physicist

Amund·sen \'ä-mən-sən\ Roald 1872–1928 Norw. polar explorer

Anac·re·on \ə-'na-krē-ən\ *ca* 582–*ca* 485 B.C. Greek poet

An·ax·ag·o·ras \ˌa-ˌnak-'sa-gə-rəs\ *ca* 500–*ca* 428 B.C. Greek philos. — **An·ax·ag·o·re·an** \-ˌsa-gə-'rē-ən\ *adj*

Anax·i·man·der \ə-'nak-sə-ˌman-dər\ 610–*ca* 547 B.C. Greek philos. & astron. — **Anax·i·man·dri·an** \ə-ˌnak-sə-'man-drē-ən\ *adj*

An·ders \'än-dərs, -dərz\ Władysław 1892–1970 Pol. gen.

An·der·sen \'an-dər-sən\ Hans Christian 1805–1875 Dan. writer

An·der·son \'an-dər-sən\ Carl David 1905–1991 Am. physicist

Anderson John 1882–1958 1st Viscount *Wa·ver·ley* \'wā-vər-lē\ Brit. polit.

Anderson Dame Judith 1898–1992 orig. *Frances Margaret Anderson* Austral. actress

Anderson Marian 1897–1993 Am. contralto

Anderson Maxwell 1888–1959 Am. dram.

Anderson Sherwood 1876–1941 Am. writer

An·drás·sy \'ȯn-ˌdrä-shē\ Gyula, count; father 1823–1890 & son 1860–1929 Hung. statesmen

An·dré \'an-drē, 'än-(ˌ)drā\ John 1750–1780 Brit. spy

An·drea del Sar·to \än-'drā-ə-ˌdel-'sär-(ˌ)tō\ 1486–1530 *Andrea d'Agnolo* Florentine painter

An·dre·ot·ti \ˌän-drä-'ä-(ˌ)tē\ Giulio 1919–2013 prime min. of Italy (1972–73; 1976–79; 1989–92)

An·drews \'an-ˌdrüz\ Roy Chapman 1884–1960 Am. naturalist

An·dre·yev \än-'drä-yəf\ Leonid Nikolayevich 1871–1919 Russ. author

An·drić \'än-drēch\ Ivo 1892–1975 Serbo-Croatian author

An·dro·pov \an-'drō-ˌpȯv\ Yuri Vladimirovich 1914–1984 Russ. polit.; pres. U.S.S.R. (1982–84); 1st secy. of Communist party (1982–84)

An·dros \'an-ˌdräs, -drəs\ Sir Edmund 1637–1714 Brit. colonial gov. in America

An·ge·la Me·ri·ci \'an-jə-lə-mə-'rē-chē\ Saint 1474?–1540 Ital. religious & founder of Ursuline order

An·ge·li·co \an-'je-li-ˌkō\ Fra *ca* 1400–1455 orig. *Guido di Pietro* Florentine painter

An·gell \'än-jəl\ Sir Norman 1872–1967 orig. *Ralph Norman Angell Lane* Eng. author & lecturer

An·ge·lou \'an-jə-(ˌ)lō, commonly -ˌlü\ Maya 1928– orig. *Marguerite Annie Johnson* Am. writer

Ång·ström \'aŋ-strəm, 'ȯŋ-\ Anders Jonas 1814–1874 Swed. physicist

An·na Iva·nov·na \'a-nə-ē-'vä-nəv-nə\ 1693–1740 empress of Russia (1730–40)

An·nan \'a-ˌnan, 'ä-ˌnän\ Kofi (Atta) 1938– Ghanaian U.N. official; secy.-gen. (1997–2006)

\ə\ abut \ᵊ\ kitten, F table \ər\ further \a\ ash \ā\ ace \ä\ mop, mar \aủ\ out \ch\ chin \e\ bet \ē\ easy \g\ go \i\ hit \ī\ ice \j\ job \ŋ\ sing \ō\ go \ȯ\ law \ȯi\ boy \th\ thin \t͟h\ the \ü\ loot \ủ\ foot \y\ yet \zh\ vision, beige \ḵ, ⁿ, œ, ɶ, ᵀ\ *see* Guide to Pronunciation

Anne \'an\ 1665–1714 *dau. of James II* queen of Great Britain (1702–14)
Anne of Austria 1601–1666 *consort of Louis XIII of France* regent (1643–51) for her son Louis XIV
Anne of Cleves \'klēvz\ 1515–1557 *4th wife of Henry VIII of England*
Anouilh \a-'nü-ē\ Jean 1910–1987 Fr. dram.
An·selm \'an-ˌselm\ Saint 1033/34–1109 archbishop of Canterbury (1093–1109)
An·tho·ny \'an(t)-thə-nē, *chiefly Brit* 'an-tə-\ Saint *ca* 250–355 Egypt. monk
Anthony Mark — see Marcus ANTONIUS
Anthony Susan Brownell 1820–1906 Am. suffragist
Anthony *or* **An·to·ny** \'an-tə-nē\ **of Padua** Saint 1195–1231 Franciscan friar
An·tig·o·nus I \an-'ti-gə-nəs\ 382–301 B.C. *Antigonus Cyclops* gen. of Alexander the Great & king of Macedonia (306–301)
An·ti·o·chus \an-'tī-ə-kəs\ name of 13 Seleucid kings of Syria: esp. III *the Great* 242–187 B.C. (reigned 223–187), IV *Epiph·a·nes* \i-'pi-fə-ˌnēz\ *ca* 215–164 B.C. (reigned 175–164)
An·tip·a·ter \an-'ti-pə-tər\ *ca* 397–*ca* 319 B.C. Macedonian gen.
An·tis·the·nes \an-'tis-thə-ˌnēz\ *ca* 445–*ca* 365 B.C. Athenian philos.
An·to·ne·scu \ˌan-tə-'nes-(ˌ)kü\ Ion \'yòn\ 1882–1946 Romanian gen.; dictator (1940–44)
An·to·ni·nus \ˌan-tə-'nī-nəs\ Marcus Au·re·lius \ò-'rēl-yəs, -'rē-lē-əs\ A.D. 121–180 *nephew, son-in-law, and adopted son of Antoninus Pius* Rom. emp. (161–180) & Stoic philos.
Antoninus Pi·us \-'pī-əs\ A.D. 86–161 Rom. emp. (138–161)
An·to·ni·o·ni \an-ˌtō-nē-'ō-nē\ Michelangelo 1912–2007 Ital. film director
An·to·ni·us \an-'tō-nē-əs\ Marcus E Mark *or* Marc An·to·ny \'an-tə-nē\ *or* An·tho·ny \'an(t)-thə-nē, *chiefly Brit* 'an-tə-\ *ca* 82–30 B.C. Rom. orator, triumvir, & gen.
Apel·les \ə-'pe-lēz\ 4th cent. B.C. Greek painter
Apol·li·naire \ə-ˌpä-lə-'ner\ Guillaume 1880–1918 orig. *Wilhelm Apollinaris de Kos·tro·wit·zki* \ˌkòs-trə-'vēt-skē\ Fr. poet
Ap·ol·lo·ni·us \ˌa-pə-'lō-nē-əs\ **of Rhodes** 3d cent. B.C. Greek poet — **Ap·ol·lo·nian** \-nē-ən, -nyən\ *adj*
Appleseed Johnny — see John CHAPMAN
Ap·ple·ton \'a-pəl-tən\ Sir Edward 1892–1965 Eng. physicist
Ap·u·le·ius \ˌa-pə-'lā-əs\ Lucius *ca* A.D. 124–after 170? Rom. philos. & rhetorician
Aquinas Saint Thomas — see THOMAS AQUINAS
Aqui·no \ə-'kē-nō\ Benigno 1960–   in full *Benigno Simeon Cojuangco Aquino III, son of Corazon* pres. of Philippines (2010–   )
Aquino (Maria) Corazon 1933–2009 née *Co·juang·co* \kō-'hwäŋ-kō\ pres. of Philippines (1986–92)
ʿAr·a·fāt \är-ə-'fät, 'a-rə-ˌfat\ Yāsir 1929–2004 *Raḥmān ʿAbd Arra'üf Al= Qudwah* Palestinian polit. leader
Ar·am \'er-əm\ Eugene 1704–1759 Eng. philologist & murderer
Arblay, d' Madame — see Fanny BURNEY
Ar·bus \'är-bəs\ Diane 1923–71 née *Nemerov* Am. photographer
Ar·buth·not \är-'bəth-nət, är-bəth-ˌnät\ John 1667–1735 Scot. physician & author
Ar·cher \'är-chər\ William 1856–1924 Scot. critic & dram.
Ar·chi·me·des \ˌär-kə-'mē-dēz\ *ca* 287–212 B.C. Greek math. & inventor — **Ar·chi·me·de·an** \-'mē-dē-ən, -mi-'dē-\ *adj*
Ar·chi·pen·ko \ˌär-kə-'peŋ-(ˌ)kō\ Aleksandr Porfiryevich 1887–1964 Am. (Ukrainian-born) sculptor
Arendt \ə-'rent\ Hannah 1906–1975 Am. (Ger.-born) philos. & writer
Are·ti·no \ˌa-rə-'tē-(ˌ)nō\ Pietro 1492–1556 Ital. satirist
Ar·gall \'är-ˌgòl, -gəl\ Sir Samuel *ca* 1572–*ca* 1626 Eng. mariner
Ar·ge·rich \'är-gə-rich\ Martha 1941–   Argentine pianist
Ar·i·as Sánchez \ˌär-ē-'ò-(ˌ)stō\ Ludovico 1474–1533 Ital. poet
Ari·os·to \ˌär-ē-'ò-(ˌ)stō\ Ludovico 1474–1533 Ital. poet
Ar·is·tar·chus \ˌa-rə-'stär-kəs\ *ca* 217–145 B.C. Greek grammarian
Aristarchus of Samos *ca* 310–230 B.C. Greek astron.
Ar·is·tide \ˌa-ri-'stēd, ä-rē-'stēd\ Jean-Bertrand 1953–   pres. of Haiti (1991; 1994–96; 2001–04)
Ar·is·ti·des *or* **Ar·is·tei·des** \ˌa-rə-'stī-dēz\ *ca* 530–*ca* 468 B.C. *the Just* Athenian statesman
Ar·is·tip·pus \ˌa-rə-'sti-pəs\ *ca* 435–366 B.C. Greek philos.
Ar·is·toph·a·nes \ˌa-rə-'stä-fə-ˌnēz\ *ca* 450–*ca* 388 B.C. Athenian dram. — **Ar·is·to·phan·ic** \ˌa-rə-stə-'fa-nik\ *adj*
Aristophanes of Byzantium *ca* 257–180 B.C. Greek scholar
Ar·is·tot·le \'a-rə-ˌstä-t⁽ᵊ\l\ 384–322 B.C. Greek philos.
Ari·us \'er-ē-əs\ *ca* A.D. 250–336 Greek theol.
Ark·wright \'ärk-ˌrīt\ Sir Richard 1732–1792 Eng. inventor
Ar·len \'är-lən\ Harold 1905–1986 Am. composer
Ar·min·i·us \är-'mi-nē-əs\ *or* **Ar·min** \är-'mēn\ 18 B.C.?–A.D. 19 sometimes *Her·mann* \'her-ˌmän\ Ger. hero
Arminius Jacobus 1560–1609 *Jacob Har·men·sen* \'här-mən-sən\ *or Hermansz* \'her-ˌmän(t)s\ Du. theol.
Ar·mour \'är-mər\ Philip Danforth 1832–1901 Am. industrialist
Armstrong Louis 1901–1971 *Satch·mo* \'sach-ˌmō\ Am. jazz musician
Armstrong Neil Alden 1930–2012 Am. astronaut
Armstrong William George 1810–1900 Baron *Armstrong of Cragside* Eng. inventor & industrialist
Arne \'ärn\ Thomas Augustine 1710–1778 Eng. composer
Ar·nold \'är-n⁽ᵊ\ld\ Benedict 1741–1801 Am. Revolutionary gen. & traitor
Arnold Henry Harley 1886–1950 *Hap* Arnold Am. gen.
Arnold Matthew 1822–1888 *son of Thomas* Eng. poet & critic — **Ar·nold·ian** \är-'nòl-dē-ən\ *adj*
Arnold Thomas 1795–1842 Eng. educ.
Arou·et \ä-'rwe\ François-Marie — see VOLTAIRE
Arp \'ärp\ Jean (*or* Hans) 1887–1966 Fr. artist & poet
Ár·pád \'är-ˌpäd\ *d* 907 Hung. national hero
Ar·rau \ä-'raü\ Claudio 1903–1991 Am. (Chilean-born) pianist
Ar·rhe·ni·us \ä-'rē-nē-əs, -'rä-\ Svante August 1859–1927 Swed. physicist & chem.
Ar·son·val, d' \'där-s⁽ᵊ\n-ˌväl\ (Jacques) Arsène 1851–1940 Fr. biophysicist

Ar·ta·xer·xes \ˌär-tə(g)-'zərk-ˌsēz\ name of 3 Pers. kings: I *d* 425 B.C. (reigned 465–25); II *d* 359/58 B.C. (reigned 404–359/58); III *d* 338 B.C. (reigned 359/58–338)
Ar·te·vel·de, van \vän-'är-tə-ˌvel-də\ Jacob *ca* 1295–1345 & his son Philip 1340–1382 Flem. leaders
Ar·thur \'är-thər\ Chester Alan 1829–1886 21st pres. of the U.S. (1881–85)
As·bury \'az-ˌber-ē, -b(ə-)rē\ Francis 1745–1816 Am. (Eng.-born) Methodist bishop
Asch \'ash\ Sho·lem \'shò-ləm, 'shō-\ *or* Sha·lom \shə-'lōm\ *or* Sho·lom \'shò-ləm, 'shō-\ 1880–1957 Am. (Pol.-born) Yiddish writer
As·cham \'as-kəm\ Roger 1515–1568 Eng. scholar & author
Ash·croft \'ash-ˌkròft\ John (David) 1942–   U.S. atty. gen. (2001–05)
Ashcroft Dame Peggy 1907–1991 Brit. actress
Ashe \'ash\ Arthur Robert 1943–1993 Am. tennis player
Ashton Winifred — see Clemence DANE
Ashur·ba·ni·pal *also* **As·sur·ba·ni·pal** *or* **Asur·ba·ni·pal** \ˌä-sər-'bä-nə-ˌpäl, ä-shər-\ king of Assyria (668–627 B.C.)
As·i·mov \'a-zi-ˌmóf\ Isaac 1920–1992 Am. (Russ.-born) writer
Aśo·ka *or* **Aço·ka** \ə-'shō-kə, -'sō-\ *d* 238 *or* 232 B.C. king of India (*ca* 265–238 *or ca* 273–232 B.C.)
As·pa·sia \as-'pā-zh(ē-)ə\ 470?–410 B.C. *consort of Pericles*
As·quith \'as-ˌkwith, -kwəth\ Herbert Henry 1852–1928 1st Earl of *Oxford and Asquith* Brit. statesman
Assad, al- \'al-'ä-ˌsäd\ Bashar 1965–   pres. of Syria (2000–   )
Assad, al- Hafiz 1930–2000 *father of prec.* pres. of Syria (1971–2000)
Astaire \ə-'ster\ Fred 1899–1987 Am. dancer & actor
As·ton \'as-tən\ Francis William 1877–1945 Eng. physicist
As·tor \'as-tər\ John Jacob 1763–1848 Am. (Ger.-born) fur trader & capitalist
Astor Nancy Witcher 1879–1964 Viscountess *Astor* 1st woman member of Brit. Parliament (1919–45)
As·tu·ri·as \ə-'stùr-ē-əs, -'styùr-\ Miguel Ángel 1899–1974 Guatemalan author
Ata·huall·pa *or* **Ata·hual·pa** \ˌä-tə-'wäl-pə\ *ca* 1502–1533 last Incan king of Peru
Ata·türk \'a-tə-ˌtərk, ä-tä-'tùrk\ Kemal 1881–1938 orig. *Mustafa*; later surnamed *Kemal* Turk. gen. & statesman; pres. of Turkey (1923–38)
Ath·a·na·si·us \ˌa-thə-'nā-zh(ē-)əs, -sh(ē-)əs\ Saint *ca* 293–373 Greek (Egyptian-born) church father
Ath·el·stan \'a-thəl-ˌstan\ *d* 939 Anglo-Saxon ruler
Ath·er·ton \'a-thər-tən\ Gertrude Franklin 1857–1948 Am. nov.
ʿAt·tār \'a-tər, -ˌtär\ Farīd od-Dīn Mohammad ebn Ebrāhīm *ca* 1142–*ca* 1220 Pers. mystical poet
At·ti·la \'a-tə-lə, ə-'ti-lə\ 406?–453 *the Scourge of God* king of the Huns
Att·lee \'at-lē\ Clement Richard 1883–1967 1st Earl *Attlee* Eng. polit.
At·tucks \'a-təks\ Crispus 1723?–1770 Am. patriot
At·wood \'at-ˌwùd\ Margaret Eleanor 1939–   Canad. author
Au·ber \ō-'ber\ Daniel-François-Esprit 1782–1871 Fr. composer
Au·brey \'ò-brē\ John 1626–1697 Eng. antiquarian
Au·den \'ò-d⁽ᵊ\n\ W(ystan) H(ugh) 1907–1973 Am. (Eng.-born) poet — **Au·den·esque** \ˌò-də-'nesk\ *adj*
Au·du·bon \'ò-də-bən, -ˌbän\ John James 1785–1851 Am. (Haitian-born) artist & ornithologist
Au·gier \ō-'zhä, -'zhyä; ˌō-zhē-'ā\ Émile 1820–1889 Fr. poet & dram.
Au·gus·tine \'ò-gə-ˌstēn; ò-'gəs-tən, ə-\ Saint 354–430 church father; bishop of Hippo (396–430)
Augustine *also* **Aus·tin** \'òs-tən, 'äs-\ Saint *d* 604 *Apostle of the English* 1st archbishop of Canterbury (601–04)
Au·gus·tus \ò-'gəs-təs, ə-\ 63 B.C.–A.D. 14 orig. *Gaius Oc·ta·vi·us* \äk-'tā-vē-əs\ then *Gaius Julius Caesar* 1st Rom. emp. (27 B.C.–A.D. 14)
Au·mann \'aù-mən\ (Yisrael) Robert (John) 1930–   Israeli (Ger.=born) econ.
Aung San Suu Kyi \'òŋ-'sän-'sü-'chē\ 1945–   Burmese human rights activist
Aurangzeb — see ʿĀLAMGĪR
Au·re·lian \ò-'rēl-yən\ *ca* A.D. 215–275 *Lucius Domitius Aurelianus* Rom. emp. (270–275)
Au·riol \ˌòr-ē-'òl, -'òl\ Vincent 1884–1966 Fr. polit.; 1st pres. of 4th Republic (1947–54)
Au·ro·bin·do \ˌòr-ə-'bin-dō\ Sri 1872–1950 orig. *Sri Aurobindo Ghose* \'gōs\ Indian seer, poet, & nationalist
Aus·ten \'òs-tən, 'äs-\ Jane 1775–1817 Eng. nov.
Aus·tin \'òs-tən, 'äs-\ Alfred 1835–1913 Eng. poet; laureate (1896–1913)
Austin John 1790–1859 Eng. jurist
Austin John Langshaw 1911–1960 Eng. philos.
Austin Mary 1868–1934 née *Hunter* Am. nov.
Austin Stephen Fuller 1793–1836 Am. colonizer in Texas
Av·e·don \'a-və-ˌdän\ Richard 1923–2004 Am. photographer
Avenzoar — see IBN ZUHR
Aver·ro·ës *or* **Aver·rho·ës** \ə-'ver-ə-ˌwēz, ˌa-və-'rō-(ˌ)ēz\ 1126–1198 *also Ibn-Rushd* Span.-Arab philos. & physician
Avery \'ā-və-rē, 'āv-rē\ Milton Clark 1885–1965 Am. artist
Av·i·cen·na \ˌa-və-'se-nə\ 980–1037 *also Ibn Sīnā* Islamic (Pers.-born) philos. & scientist
Avi·la Ca·ma·cho \'ä-vē-lə-kə-'mä-(ˌ)chō\ Manuel 1897–1955 Mex. soldier & polit.; pres. of Mexico (1940–46)
Avo·ga·dro \ˌa-və-'gä-(ˌ)drō, ˌä-\ Amedeo 1776–1856 Conte *di Quaregna e Ceretto* Ital. chem. & physicist
Avon Earl of — see Anthony EDEN
Ax \'aks\ Emanuel 1949–   Am. (Ukrainian-born of Polish parents) pianist
Ax·el \'ak-səl\ Richard 1946–   Am. biochem.
Ayer \'er\ Sir Alfred Jules 1910–1989 Eng. philos.
Ayl·win Azó·car \'äl-win-ä-'sō-kär\ Patricio 1918–   pres. of Chile (1990–94)
Aza·ña y Di·az \ə-'thän-yə-ē-'thē-äth\ Manuel 1880–1940 Span. polit.; pres. of Spain (1936–39)
Az·nar (López) \'äs-när\ José María 1953–   prime min. of Spain (1996–2004)
Ba'al Shem Tov — see ISRAEL BEN ELIEZER
Bab·bage \'ba-bij\ Charles 1791–1871 Eng. math. & inventor

Bab·bitt \'ba-bət\ Irving 1865–1933 Am. scholar
Ba·beuf \bä-'bəf, bä-'bœf\ François-Noël 1760–1797 Fr. agitator
Bab·ing·ton \'ba-biŋ-tən\ Anthony 1561–1586 Eng. conspirator against Queen Elizabeth I
Bā·bur \'bä-bər\ 1483–1530 *Zahīr-ud-Dīn Muhammad* founder of Mogul dynasty of India; emp. (1526–30)
Bach \'bäk, 'bäk\ Carl Philipp Emanuel 1714–1788 *son of J.S.* Ger. composer
Bach Johann Christian 1735–1782 *son of J.S.* Ger. organist & composer
Bach Johann Sebastian 1685–1750 Ger. organist & composer
Bach Wilhelm Friedemann 1710–1784 *son of J.S.* Ger. composer
Ba·che·let \,bä-che-'lä\ (Jeria) \'he-rē-ä\, (Verónica) Michelle 1951– pres. of Chile (2006–10)
Ba·con \'bā-kən\ Francis 1561–1626 1st Baron *Ver·u·lam* \'ver-(y)ə-ləm\ Viscount *St. Al·bans* \sänt-'òl-bənz, sənt-\ Eng. philos.
Bacon Francis 1909–1992 Brit. (Irish-born) painter
Bacon Nathaniel 1647–1676 Am. colonial leader
Bacon Roger *ca* 1220–1292 Eng. philos. & scientist
Ba·den–Pow·ell \'bā-dᵊn-'pō-əl\ Robert Stephenson Smyth 1857–1941 1st Baron of *Gilwell* Brit. founder of Boy Scout movement
Ba·do·glio \bə-'dōl-(,)yō\ Pietro 1871–1956 Ital. gen.; prime min. (1943–44)
Bae·yer, von \'bā-ər\ Adolf 1835–1917 Ger. chem.
Baf·fin \'ba-fən\ William *ca* 1584–1622 Eng. navigator
Bage·hot \'ba-jət\ Walter 1826–1877 Eng. econ. & journalist
Ba·gra·tion \bä-grä-tē-'ón, -,grät-sē-; ,bä-grə-'tyòn\ Prince Pyotr Ivanovich 1765–1812 Russ. gen.
Ba·hā' Al·lāh *or* Ba·ha·ul·lah \bä-'hä-ù-'lä\ Mīrzā Ḥoseyn Alī Nūrī 1817–1892 Pers. founder of the Bahā'ī faith
Bai·ley \'bā-lē\ Liberty Hyde 1858–1954 Am. botanist
Bailey Nathan *or* Nathaniel *d* 1742 Eng. lexicographer
Bailey Pearl Mae 1918–1990 Am. singer
Bail·lie \'bā-lē\ Joanna 1762–1851 Scot. dram. & poet
Bain \'bān\ Alexander 1818–1903 Scot. psychol.
Baird \'berd\ John Logie 1888–1946 Scot. inventor
Bairns·fa·ther \'bernz-,fä-t͟hər\ Bruce 1888–1959 Eng. cartoonist
Ba·ker \'bā-kər\ James Addison 1930– U.S. secy. of treasury (1985–88); secy. of state (1989–92)
Baker Newton Diehl 1871–1937 Am. statesman
Baker Ray Stannard 1870–1946 pseud. *David Gray·son* \'grās-ᵊn\ Am. author
Bakst \'bäkst\ Léon 1866–1924 orig. *Lev Samoylovich Rosenberg* Russ. painter
Ba·ku·nin \bə-'kün-yən, bä-, -'kü-nən\ Mikhail Aleksandrovich 1814–1876 Russ. anarchist
Bal·an·chine \,ba-lən-'shēn, 'ba-lən-,\ George 1904–1983 *Georgy Melitonovich Balanchivadze* Am. (Russ.-born) choreographer
Bal·bo \'bäl-(,)bō\ Italo 1896–1940 Ital. aviator & polit.
Bal·boa \bal-'bō-ə\ Vasco Núñez de 1475–1519 Span. explorer & conquistador
Balch \'bólch\ Emily Greene 1867–1961 Am. econ. & sociol.
Bald·win \'bòl-dwən\ James 1924–1987 Am. writer
Baldwin James Mark 1861–1934 Am. psychol.
Baldwin Stanley 1867–1947 1st Earl *Baldwin of Bewd·ley* \'byüd-lē\ Eng. statesman; prime min. (1923–24; 1924–29; 1935–37)
Baldwin I 1058?–1118 *bro. of Godfrey of Bouillon* king of Jerusalem (1100–18)
Bal·four \'bal-fər, -,fòr\ Arthur James 1848–1930 1st Earl of Balfour; Brit. philos. & statesman; prime min. (1902–05)
Ba·liol *or* Bal·liol \'bāl-yəl\ John de 1249–1315 king of Scotland (1292–96)
Ball \'bòl\ John *d* 1381 Eng. priest & social agitator
Ball Lucille (Désirée) 1911–1989 Am. actress & comedienne
Bal·lan·tyne \'ba-lən-,tīn\ James 1772–1833 Scot. printer
Bal·lard \'ba-lərd\ Robert Duane 1942– Am. oceanographer
Bal·ti·more \'bòl-tə-,mór, -mər\ David 1938– Am. microbiologist
Baltimore Baron — see George CALVERT
Bal·zac \'bòl-,zak, 'bal-, F bäl-'zäk\ Honoré de 1799–1850 Fr. nov. — Bal·za·cian \bòl-'zā-shən, bal-, -'za-kē-ən\ *adj*
Ban·croft \'ban-,kròft, 'baŋ-\ George 1800–1891 Am. hist.
Bancroft Richard 1544–1610 archbishop of Canterbury (1604–10)
Ban·da·ra·nai·ke \,bän-də-rə-'nī-ə-kə\ Sirimavo Ratwatte Dias 1916–2000 prime min. of Sri Lanka (1960–65; 1970–77)
Ban·del·lo \bän-'de-(,)lō, bän-\ Matteo 1485–1561 Ital. writer
Ban Ki–moon \'bän-'kē-'mün\ 1944– So. Korean diplomat; secy.-gen. of U.N. (2007–)
Banks \'ban(k)s\ Sir Joseph 1743–1820 Eng. naturalist
Ban·nis·ter \'ba-nəs-tər\ Sir Roger (Gilbert) 1929– Brit. runner & neurologist
Ban·ting \'ban-tiŋ\ Sir Frederick Grant 1891–1941 Canad. physician
Ba·rak \bä-'räk\ Ehud 1942– Israeli soldier & polit.; prime min. of Israel (1999–2001)
Ba·ra·nov \bə-'rä-nəf\ Aleksandr Andreyevich 1747–1819 Russ. fur trader; 1st gov. of Russ. America
Bá·rány \'bär-,än-ə\ Robert 1876–1936 Austrian physician
Barbarossa — see FREDERICK I
Bar·ba·ros·sa \,bär-bə-'rä-sə, -'rò-\ *d* 1546 *Khayr ad-Dīn* Barbary pirate
Bar·ber \'bär-bər\ Samuel 1910–1981 Am. composer
Bar·bie \'bär-bē\ Klaus 1913–1991 Ger. Nazi leader
Bar·bour \'bär-bər\ Ian (Graeme) 1923– Am. (Chinese-born of Am.-Scot. parents) theol. & physicist
Bar·busse \bär-'bues; bär-'büs, -'byüs\ Henri 1873–1935 Fr. author
Bar·clay de Tol·ly \'bär-klē\ Robert 1648–1690 Scot. Quaker author
Bar·clay de Tol·ly \'bär-klē-də-'tò-lē, -'klä-\ Prince Mikhail Bogdanovich 1761–1818 Russ. field marshal
Bar·deen \bär-'dēn\ John 1908–1991 Am. physicist
Ba·rents \'bär-ən(t)s\ Willem *ca* 1550–1597 Du. navigator
Bar·ing \'ber-iŋ\ Alexander 1774–1848 1st Baron *Ash·bur·ton* \'ash-,bər-tᵊn\ Brit. financier & diplomat
Baring Evelyn 1841–1917 1st Earl of *Cro·mer* \'krō-mər\ Brit. diplomat
Bark·la \'bär-klə\ Charles Glover 1877–1944 Eng. physicist
Bark·ley \'bär-klē\ Al·ben \'al-bən\ William 1877–1956 Am. lawyer & polit.; vice pres. of U.S. (1949–53)

Bar·low \'bär-,lō\ Joel 1754–1812 Am. poet & diplomat
Bar·nard \'bär-nərd, -,närd\ Christiaan Neethling 1922–2001 So. African surgeon
Bar·nard \'bär-nərd\ George Grey 1863–1938 Am. sculptor
Bar·num \'bär-nəm\ Phineas Taylor 1810–1891 Am. showman — Bar·num·esque \,bär-nə-'mesk\ *adj*
Ba·ro·ja \bä-'rò-(,)hä\ Pío 1872–1956 Span. writer
Bar·rès \bä-'res\ Auguste-Maurice 1862–1923 Fr. nov. & polit.
Bar·ré–Si·nous·si \bä-'rä-sē-nü-'sē\ Françoise 1947– Fr. virologist
Bar·rie \'ba-rē\ Sir James Matthew 1860–1937 Scot. nov. & dram.
Bar·ros \'bär-üsh\ João de *ca* 1496–1570 Port. hist.
Bar·row \'ba-(,)rō\ Isaac 1630–1677 Eng. math. & theol.
Bar·ry \'ba-rē\ Jeanne Bécu 1743–1793 *Comtesse du Barry* mistress of Louis XV of France
Barry \'ba-rē\ Philip 1896–1949 Am. dram.
Bar·ry·more \'ba-ri-,mór\ family of Am. actors: Maurice 1847–1905 orig. *Herbert Blythe;* his wife Georgiana Emma 1854–1893 *dau. of John Drew;* their children Lionel 1878–1954, Ethel 1879–1959, & John Blythe 1882–1942
Bart \'bär\ *or* Barth \'bärt\ Jean 1650–1702 Fr. naval hero
Barth \'bärth\ John Simmons 1930– Am. author
Barth \'bärt, 'bärth\ Karl 1886–1968 Swiss theol. — Barth·ian \'bär-tē-ən, -thē-\ *adj*
Bar·thol·di \bär-'täl-dē, -'tòl-, -'thäl-, -'thòl-\ Frédéric-Auguste 1834–1904 Fr. sculptor
Bar·thol·o·mew I \bär-'thä-lə-,myü\ 1940– *Dimitrios Archontonis* archbishop of Constantinople & ecumenical patriarch (1991–)
Bart·lett \'bärt-lət\ John 1820–1905 Am. publisher & editor
Bar·tók \'bär-,täk, -,tòk\ Béla 1881–1945 Hung. composer
Bar·to·lom·meo \,bär-,tò-lə-'mā-(,)ō\ Fra 1472–1517 *Baccio della Porta* Florentine painter
Bar·ton \'bär-tᵊn\ Clara 1821–1912 in full *Clarissa Harlowe Barton* founder of Am. Red Cross Society
Bar·tram \'bär-trəm\ John 1699–1777 Am. botanist
Bartram William 1739–1823 *son of John* Am. naturalist
Ba·ruch \bə-'rük\ Bernard Man·nes \'ma-nəs\ 1870–1965 Am. businessman & statesman
Ba·rysh·ni·kov \bə-'rish-nə-,kòf\ Mikhail (Nikolaevitch) 1948– Am. (Latvian-born) ballet dancer
Bashō — see MATSUO
Ba·sie \'bā-sē\ William 1904–1984 *Count Basie* Am. bandleader & pianist
Bas·il \'bā-zəl, 'ba-, -səl\ *or* Ba·sil·i·us \bə-'si-lē-əs, -'zi-\ Saint *ca* 329–379 *the Great* church father; bishop of Caesarea
Bas·ker·ville \'bas-kər-,vil\ John 1706–1775 Eng. typographer
Bas·kin \'bas-kən\ Leonard 1922–2000 Am. sculptor & graphic artist
Bates \'bāts\ Katharine Lee 1859–1929 Am. poet & educ.
Ba·tis·ta (y Zal·dí·var) \bə-'tēs-tə-,ē-zäl-'dē-,vär\ Fulgencio 1901–1973 Cuban soldier; pres. of Cuba (1940–44; 1952–59)
Bat·tā·nī, al- \al-bə-'tä-nē\ *ca* 858–929 *Al·ba·te·gni* \,al-bə-'tän-yē\ *or Al·ba·te·ni·us* \-'tē-nē-əs\ Arab astron.
Bau·de·laire \bōd-'ler\ Charles-Pierre 1821–1867 Fr. poet — Bau·de·lair·ean *also* Bau·de·lair·ian \-ē-ən\ *adj*
Bau·douin \bō-'dwaⁿ\ 1930–1993 king of Belgium (1951–93)
Baum \'bäm\ L(yman) Frank 1856–1919 Am. journalist & writer
Baum \'baùm\ Vicki 1888–1960 orig. *Hedwig Baum* Am. (Austrian-born) nov.
Bau·mé \bō-'mā\ Antoine 1728–1804 Fr. chem.
Bax·ter \'bak-stər\ Richard 1615–1691 Eng. Puritan scholar & writer
Ba·yard \'bī-ərd, bā-' yär\ Pierre Terrail *ca* 1473–1524 *Seigneur de Bayard* Fr. mil. hero
Bayle \'bāl, 'bel\ Pierre 1647–1706 Fr. philos. & critic
Beard \'bird\ Charles Austin 1874–1948 & his wife Mary 1876–1958 née *Ritter* Am. historians
Beard Daniel Carter 1850–1941 Am. painter, illustrator, & organizer of Boy Scouts in U.S.
Beards·ley \'birdz-lē\ Aubrey Vincent 1872–1898 Eng. illustrator — Beards·ley·esque \,birdz-lē-'yesk\ *adj*
Be·a·trix \'bē-ə-,triks\ 1938– queen of the Netherlands (1980–2013)
Beat·tie \'bē-tē\ James 1735–1803 Scot. poet
Beau·fort \'bō-fərt\ Sir Francis 1774–1857 Brit. admiral
Beaufort Henry *ca* 1374–1447 Eng. cardinal & statesman
Beau·har·nais, de \,bō-är-'nā\ Fr. family including: Vicomte Alexandre 1760–1794 gen.; his wife Joséphine 1763–1814 later the *1st wife of Napoleon I;* their son Eugène 1781–1824 prince of Eich·stätt \'īk-,shtet\; their daughter Hor·tense \òr-'täⁿs\ 1783–1837 *wife of Louis Bonaparte & mother of Napoleon III*
Beau·mar·chais \,bō-,mär-'shä\ Pierre-Augustin Caron de 1732–1799 Fr. dram. & businessman
Beau·mont \'bō-,mänt, -mənt\ Francis 1584–1616 Eng. dram.
Beau·mont \-,mänt\ William 1785–1853 Am. surgeon
Beau·re·gard \'bòr-ə-,gärd\ Pierre Gustave Toutant 1818–1893 Am. Confed. gen.
Beau·voir, de \də-bō-'vwär\ Simone 1908–1986 Fr. author
Bea·ver·brook \'bē-vər-,brük\ 1st Baron 1879–1964 *William Maxwell Aitken* Brit. (Canad.-born) newspaper publisher
Be·bel \'bā-bəl\ August 1840–1913 Ger. Social Democrat leader & writer
Be·chet \bə-'shä\ Sidney 1897–1959 Am. jazz musician
Beck·er \'be-kər\ Gary Stanley 1930– Am. econ.
Beck·et \'be-kət\ Saint Thomas *ca* 1118–1170 *Thomas à Becket* archbishop of Canterbury (1162–70)
Beck·ett \'be-kət\ Samuel 1906–1989 Irish author in France — Beck·ett·ian \be-'ke-tē-ən\ *adj*
Beck·ford \'bek-fərd\ William 1760–1844 Eng. author

Beck·ham \'be-kəm\ David (Robert Joseph) 1975–   Brit. soccer player

Bec·que·rel \be-'krel, ˌbe-kə-'rel\ family of Fr. physicists including: Antoine-César 1788–1878; his son Alexandre-Edmond 1820–1891; the latter's son Antoine-Henri 1852–1908

Bede \'bēd\ or **Bae·da** or **Be·da** \'bē-də\ Saint ca 672–735 the Venerable Bede Anglo-Saxon scholar, hist., & theol.

Bed·norz \'bed-ˌnòrts\ Johannes Georg 1950–   Ger. physicist

Bee·be \'bē-bē\ Charles William 1877–1962 Am. naturalist & explorer

Bee·cham \'bē-chəm\ Sir Thomas 1879–1961 Eng. conductor

Bee·cher \'bē-chər\ Henry Ward 1813–1887 Am. clergyman

Beecher Lyman 1775–1863 father of prec. & of Harriet Beecher Stowe Am. Presbyterian clergyman

Beer·bohm \'bir-ˌbōm, -bəm\ Sir Max 1872–1956 Eng. critic & caricaturist

Bee·tho·ven \'bā-ˌtō-vən\ Ludwig van 1770–1827 Ger. composer — **Bee·tho·ve·nian** \ˌbā-ˌtō-'vē-nyən\ adj

Be·gin \'bā-gin\ Me·na·chem \mə-'nä-kəm\ 1913–1992 prime min. of Israel (1977–83)

Be·han \'bē-ən\ Brendan Francis 1923–1964 Irish dram.

Beh·ring \'ber-iŋ\ Emil von 1854–1917 Ger. bacteriol.

Behr·man \'ber-mən\ Samuel Nathaniel 1893–1973 Am. dram.

Bei·der·becke \'bī-dər-ˌbek\ (Leon) Bix 1903–1931 Am. jazz cornetist & composer

Be·las·co \bə-'las-(ˌ)kō\ David 1853–1931 Am. dram. & producer

Bel·i·sar·i·us \ˌbe-lə-'ser-ē-əs\ ca 505–565 Byzantine gen.

Bell \'bel\ Alexander Graham 1847–1922 Am. (Scot.-born) inventor

Bel·la·my \'be-lə-mē\ Edward 1850–1898 Am. author

Bel·lay, du \ˌdü-bə-'lā, ˌdyü-\ Joachim ca 1522–1560 Fr. poet

Bell Bur·nell \'bel-(ˌ)bər-'nel\ Dame (Susan) Jocelyn 1943–   née Bell Brit. astron.

Bel·li·ni \bə-'lē-nē\ family of Venetian painters including: Jacopo ca 1400–ca 1470 & his sons Gentile ca 1429–1507 & Giovanni ca 1430–1516

Bellini Vincenzo 1801–1835 Ital. composer

Bel·loc \'be-ˌläk, -lək\ (Joseph-Pierre) Hilaire 1870–1953 Eng. author

Bel·low \'be-(ˌ)lō\ Saul 1915–2005 Am. (Canad.-born) writer

Bel·lows \'be-(ˌ)lōz\ George Wesley 1882–1925 Am. painter

Be·lo \'be-(ˌ)lü\ Carlos Filipe Xi·men·es \shē-'me-nēsh\ 1948–   East Timorese bishop & peace activist

Be·na·ven·te y Mar·tí·nez \ˌbe-nə-'ven-tē-ē-mär-'tē-nəs\ Jacinto 1866–1954 Span. dram.

Bench \'bench\ Johnny (Lee) 1947–   Am. baseball player

Bench·ley \'bench-lē\ Robert Charles 1889–1945 Am. humorist

Ben·e·dict \'be-nə-ˌdikt\ name of 16 popes: esp. **XIV** (Prospero Lambertini) 1675–1758 (pope 1740–58); **XV** (Giacomo della Chiesa) 1854–1922 (pope 1914–22); **XVI** (Joseph Alois Ratz·ing·er \'rät-siŋ-ər\ ) 1927– (pope 2005–13)

Benedict Ruth 1887–1948 née Fulton Am. anthropol.

Benedict of Nur·sia \'nər-sh(ē-)ə\ Saint ca 480–ca 547 Ital. founder of Benedictine order

Be·neš \'be-ˌnesh\ Edvard 1884–1948 Czech pres. (1935–38; 1940–48)

Be·nét \bə-'nā\ Stephen Vincent 1898–1943 bro. of W.R. Am. poet

Benét William Rose 1886–1950 Am. poet, nov., & editor

Ben–Gu·rion \ˌben-gür-'yòn, ben-'gür-ē-ən\ David 1886–1973 Israeli (Pol.-born) statesman; prime min. of Israel (1949–53; 1955–63)

Ben·ja·min \'ben-jə-mən\ Judah Philip 1811–1884 Am. Confed. statesman & lawyer

Ben·nett \'be-nət\ (Enoch) Arnold 1867–1931 Eng. nov.

Bennett James Gordon 1795–1872 Am. (Scot.-born) journalist

Bennett Richard Bedford 1870–1947 Viscount Bennett Canad. prime min. (1930–35)

Be·noît de Sainte–Maure \ben-'wä-də-(ˌ)saⁿ(t)-'mòr\ 12th cent. Fr. trouvère

Ben·son \'ben(t)-sən\ Edward White 1829–1896 Brit. prelate; archbishop of Canterbury (1882–96)

Ben·tham \'ben(t)-thəm\ Jeremy 1748–1832 Eng. jurist & philos.

Ben·tinck \'ben-ti(ŋ)k\ Lord William Cavendish 1774–1839 son of W.H.C. 1st gov.-gen. of India (1833)

Bentinck William Henry Cavendish 1738–1809 3d Duke of Portland Brit. prime min. (1783; 1807–09)

Bent·ley \'bent-lē\ Richard 1662–1742 Eng. clergyman & scholar

Ben·ton \'ben-tⁿn\ Thomas Hart 1782–1858 Old Bullion Am. polit.

Benton Thomas Hart 1889–1975 grand-nephew of prec. Am. painter

Bé·ran·ger \bā-rä-'zhā\ Pierre-Jean de 1780–1857 Fr. poet

Ber·dya·yev \bərd-'yä-yəf, bər-'jä-\ Nikolay Aleksandrovich 1874–1948 Russ. philos.

Ber·en·son \'ber-ən-sən\ Bernard 1865–1959 Am. (Lith.-born) art critic

Berg \'berg\ Alban 1885–1935 Austrian composer

Bergerac, de Cyrano — see CYRANO DE BERGERAC

Ber·gi·us \'ber-gē-əs\ Friedrich 1884–1949 Ger. chem.

Berg·man \'bərg-mən, Sw 'ber-ē-män\ Ingmar 1918–2007 Swed. film & theater director

Bergman Ingrid 1915–1982 Swed. actress

Berg·son \'berg-sən, berk-'sōⁿ\ Henri-Louis 1859–1941 Fr. philos.

Be·ria or **Be·ri·ya** \'ber-ē-ə\ Lavrenty Pavlovich 1899–1953 Russ. polit.

Be·ring \'ber-iŋ, 'bir-\ Vitus Jonassen 1681–1741 Dan. navigator

Berke·ley \'bär-klē, 'bər-\ George 1685–1753 Irish bishop & philos.

Berke·ley \'bər-klē\ Sir William 1606–1677 colonial gov. of Virginia

Ber·lich·ing·en \'ber-li-ˌkiŋ-ən\ Götz von 1480–1562 Ger. knight

Ber·lin \(ˌ)bər-'lin\ Irving Israel Isidore Beilin 1888–1989 Am. (Russ.-born) composer

Ber·li·ner \'bər-lə-nər\ Emile 1851–1929 Am. (Ger.-born) inventor

Ber·li·oz \'ber-lē-ˌōz\ (Louis) Hector 1803–1869 Fr. composer — **Ber·li·oz·ian** \ˌber-lē-'ō-zē-ən\ adj

Ber·lu·sco·ni \ˌber-lü-'skō-nē\ Silvio 1936–   Ital. prime min. (1994; 2001–06; 2008–11)

Ber·na·dette of Lourdes \ˌbər-nə-'det\ Saint 1844–1879 Marie= Bernarde Sou·bi·rous \sü-bē-'rü\ Fr. religious

Ber·nan·ke \bər-'nan-kē\ Ben (Shalom) 1953–   Am. econ.

Ber·nard \bər-'när\ Claude 1813–1878 Fr. physiol.

Ber·nar·din de Saint–Pierre \ber-nər-'daⁿ-də-ˌsänt-pē-'er\ Jacques= Henri 1737–1814 Fr. author

Ber·nard of Clair·vaux \bər-'närd-əv-ˌkler-'vō, ber-'när-\ Saint 1090–1153 Fr. ecclesiastic — **Ber·nar·dine** \'bər-nə(r)-ˌdēn\ adj

Ber·ners–Lee \'bər-nərz-'lē\ Sir Tim(othy John) 1955–   Brit. inventor

Bern·hardt \'bərn-ˌhärt, ber-'när\ Sarah 1844–1923 orig. Henriette= Rosine Ber·nard \ber-'när\ Fr. actress

Ber·ni·ni \ber-'nē-nē\ Gian or Giovanni Lorenzo 1598–1680 Ital. sculptor, architect, & painter

Bern·stein \'bərn-ˌstīn also -ˌstēn\ Leonard 1918–1990 Am. conductor & composer

Bern·storff \'bern-ˌshtòrf\ Johann-Heinrich 1862–1939 Graf von Bernstorff Ger. diplomat

Ber·ra \'be-rə\ Yogi 1925–   Lawrence Peter Berra Am. baseball player & manager

Ber·ry·man \'ber-ē-mən\ John 1914–1972 Am. poet

Ber·thier \ber-'tyä\ Louis-Alexandre 1753–1815 Prince de Neuchâtel; Prince de Wagram Fr. soldier; marshal of France

Ber·til·lon \ber-tē-'yòⁿ\ Alphonse 1853–1914 Fr. criminologist

Ber·ton \'bər-tⁿn\ Pierre 1920–2004 Canad. writer

Ber·ze·li·us \(ˌ)bər-'zē-lē-əs, ber-'zā-\ Baron Jöns Jakob 1779–1848 Swed. chem.

Bes·ant \'be-sⁿnt, -zⁿnt\ Annie 1847–1933 née Wood Eng. theosophist

Bes·se·mer \'be-sə-mər\ Sir Henry 1813–1898 Eng. engineer

Best \'best\ Charles Herbert 1899–1978 Canad. (Am.-born) physiol.

Be·tan·court \ˌbe-ˌtän-'kùr(t), -tän-\ Rómulo 1908–1981 Venezuelan pres. (1959–64)

Be·the \'bā-tə\ Hans Albrecht 1906–2005 Am. (Ger.-born) physicist

Beth·mann–Holl·weg \'bet-mən-'hòl-ˌväg, -ˌmän-\ Theobald Theodor Friedrich Alfred von 1856–1921 Ger. statesman; chancellor (1909–17)

Be·thune \bə-'thün, -'thyün\ (Jennie) Louise 1856–1913 née Blanchard Am. architect

Bethune Mary 1875–1955 née McLeod Am. educ.

Bet·je·man \'be-chə-mən\ Sir John 1906–1984 Brit. author; poet laureate (1972–84)

Bet·tel·heim \'be-təl-ˌhīm\ Bruno 1903–1990 Am. (Austrian-born) psychol.

Bet·ter·ton \'be-tər-tən\ Thomas ca 1635–1710 Eng. actor

Beut·ler \'bòit-lər\ Bruce A(lan) 1957–   Am. immunologist

Beuys \'bòis\ Joseph 1921–1986 Ger. artist

Bev·er·idge \'be-və-rij, 'bev-rij\ Albert Jeremiah 1862–1927 Am. polit. & hist.

Beveridge William Henry 1879–1963 1st Baron Beveridge of Tug·gal \'tə-gəl\ Eng. econ.

Bev·in \'be-vən\ Ernest 1881–1951 Brit. labor leader & polit.

Be·zos \'bā-zōs\ Jeff(rey Preston) 1964–   Am. entrepreneur

Bhu·mi·bol Adul·ya·dej \'pü-mē-ˌpōn-ä-'dùn-lə-ˌdāt—sic\ 1927– king of Thailand (1946–)

Bhut·to \'bü-tō\ Benazir 1953–2007 prime min. of Pakistan (1988–90; 1993–96)

Bi·dault \bē-'dō\ Georges 1899–1983 Fr. statesman

Bid·dle \'bi-dⁿl\ John 1615–1662 founder of Eng. Unitarianism

Biddle Nicholas 1786–1844 Am. financier

Bi·den \'bī-dⁿn\ Joseph R(obinette) 1942–   Am. polit.; vice pres. of the U.S. (2009–)

Bien·ville \bē-'en-ˌvil, -vəl; byaⁿ-'vēl\ Jean-Baptiste Le Moyne, sieur de 1680–1768 Fr. colonial gov. of Louisiana

Bierce \'birs\ Ambrose Gwinnett 1842–?1914 Am. author

Bier·stadt \'bir-ˌstat\ Albert 1830–1902 Am. (Ger.-born) painter

Bing·ham \'biŋ-əm\ George Caleb 1811–1879 Am. painter

bin Lad·en \bin-'läd-ⁿn\ Osama 1957–2011 Saudi-born terrorist leader

Bin·nig \'bi-nik\ Gerd 1947–   Ger. physicist

Bird \'bərd\ Larry 1956–   Lawrence Joseph Bird Am. basketball player

Birk·beck \'bər(k)-ˌbek\ George 1776–1841 Eng. physician

Bir·ken·head \'bər-kən-ˌhed\ 1st Earl of 1872–1930 Frederick Edwin Smith Eng. jurist & statesman

Bish·op \'bi-shəp\ Elizabeth 1911–1979 Am. poet

Bishop John Michael 1936–   Am. microbiologist

Bis·marck \'biz-ˌmärk\ Prince Otto Eduard Leopold von 1815–1898 in full Bismarck-Schön·hau·sen \-shòen-'haù-zⁿn\ 1st chancellor of Ger. Empire (1871–90) — **Bis·marck·ian** \biz-'mär-kē-ən\ adj

Bi·zet \bē-'zā\ Alexandre-César-Léopold 1838–1875 called Georges Bizet Fr. composer

Bjørn·son \'byərn-sən\ Bjørnstjerne Martinius 1832–1910 Norw. poet, dram., & nov.

Black \'blak\ Hugo LaFayette 1886–1971 Am. jurist & polit.

Black Sir James Whyte 1924–2010 Brit. pharmacologist

Black·burn \'blak-(ˌ)bərn\ Elizabeth (Helen) 1948–   Austral.-Am. biol.

Black·ett \'bla-kət\ Patrick Maynard Stuart 1897–1974 Brit. physicist

Black Hawk \'blak-ˌhòk\ 1767–1838 Ma-ka-ta-i-me-she-kia-kiak Sauk Indian chief

Black·more \'blak-ˌmòr\ Richard Doddridge 1825–1900 Eng. nov.

Black·mun \'blak-mən\ Harry Andrew 1908–1999 Am. jurist

Black·stone \'blak-ˌstōn, chiefly Brit -stən\ Sir William 1723–1780 Eng. jurist

Black·well \'blak-ˌwel, -wəl\ Elizabeth 1821–1910 Am. physician

Black·wood \'blak-ˌwùd\ William 1776–1834 Scot. publisher

Blaine \'blān\ James Gillespie 1830–1893 Am. statesman

Blair \'bler\ Tony 1953–   Anthony Charles Lynton Blair Brit. prime min. (1997–2007)

Blake \'blāk\ Eugene Carson 1906–1985 Am. clergyman

Blake William 1757–1827 Eng. artist, poet, & mystic — **Blak·ean** \'blā-kē-ən\ adj

Blanc \'bläŋ\ Mel(vin Jerome) 1908–1989 Am. actor

Blas·co Ibá·ñez \'bläs-(ˌ)kō-ē-'bän-(ˌ)yäs\ Vicente 1867–1928 Span. nov.

Bla·vat·sky \blə-'vat-skē, -'vät-\ Helena Petrovna 1831–1891 née Hahn Russ. traveler & theosophist

Blé·riot \'bler-ē-(ˌ)ō\ Louis 1872–1936 Fr. engineer & pioneer aviator

Bligh \'blī\ William 1754–1817 Eng. naval officer

Blo·bel \'blō-bəl\ Günter 1936–   Am. (Ger.-born) biol.

Bloch \'bläk, 'blòk\ Ernest 1880–1959 Am. (Swiss-born) composer

Bloch \'bläk\ Felix 1905–1983 Am. (Swiss-born) physicist

Block \'bläk\ Herbert Lawrence 1909–2001 *Her·block* \'hər-ˌbläk\ Am. editorial cartoonist
Bloem·ber·gen \'blüm-ˌbər-gən\ Nicolaas 1920– Am. (Du.-born) physicist
Bloom \'blüm\ Harold 1930– Am. literary critic
Bloom·er \'blü-mər\ Amelia 1818–1894 née *Jenks* Am. reformer
Bloom·field \'blüm-ˌfēld\ Leonard 1887–1949 Am. linguist — **Bloom·field·ian** \ˌblüm-'fēl-dē-ən\ *adj*
Blü·cher \'blü-kər, 'blue-kər\ Gebhard Leberecht von 1742–1819 prince of *Wahlstatt* Pruss. field marshal
Blum \'blüm\ Léon 1872–1950 Fr. polit.; provisional pres. (1946–47)
Blunt·sch·li \'blünch-lē\ Johann Kaspar 1808–1881 Swiss legal scholar
Boabdil — see MUḤAMMAD XI
Boadicea — see BOUDICCA
Bo·as \'bō-ˌaz\ Franz 1858–1942 Am. (Ger.-born) anthropol. & ethnol.
Bo·ba·di·lla \ˌbō-bə-'dē-yə\ Francisco de *d* 1502 Span. viceroy of Indies
Boc·cac·cio \bō-'kä-ch(ē-ˌ)ō\ Giovanni 1313–1375 Ital. author
Boc·che·ri·ni \ˌbä-kə-'rē-nē\ Luigi 1743–1805 Ital. composer
Boc·cio·ni \bō-'chō-nē\ Umberto 1882–1916 Ital. artist
Bod·ley \'bäd-lē\ Sir Thomas 1545–1613 Eng. diplomat & founder of Bodleian Library
Bo·do·ni \bə-'dō-nē\ Giambattista 1740–1813 Ital. printer & type designer
Bo·e·thi·us \bō-'ē-thē-əs\ Anicius Manlius Severinus *ca* 480–524 Rom. philos.
Bo·gart \'bō-ˌgärt\ Humphrey (DeForest) 1899–1957 Am. actor
Böh·me \'bə(r)m-ə, 'bœ-mə\ Ja·kob \'yä-ˌkóp\ 1575–1624 Ger. mystic
Bohr \'bór\ Aage Niels 1922–2009 *son of Niels* Dan. physicist
Bohr Niels Henrik David 1885–1962 Dan. physicist
Bo·iar·do \bói-'är-(ˌ)dō, bō-'yär-\ Matteo Maria 1441?–1494 Ital. poet
Boi·leau-Des·pré·aux \ˌbwä-lō-ˌdā-prē-'ō\ Nicolas 1636–1711 Fr. critic & poet
Boj·er \'bói-ər\ Johan \yō-'hän\ 1872–1959 Norw. writer
Bok \'bäk\ Edward William 1863–1930 Am. (Du.-born) editor
Bo·leyn \bu̇-'lin, -'lēn; 'bu̇-lən\ Anne 1507?–1536 *2d wife of Henry VIII of England & mother of Queen Elizabeth I*
Bol·ger \'bäl-jər, 'bōl-\ James Brendan 1935– prime min. of New Zealand (1990–97)
Bo·lí·var Si·món \sē-ˌmōn-bə-'lē-ˌvär; ˌsī-mən-'bä-lə-ˌvär, -vər\ 1783–1830 So. Am. liberator
Böll \'bəl, 'bœl\ Heinrich Theodor 1917–1985 Ger. writer
Bo·na·parte \'bō-nə-ˌpärt\ *It* **Buo·na·par·te** \ˌbwó-nə-'pär-tē\ Corsican family including Na·po·léon I \nə-'pōl-yən, -'pō-lē-ən\ (*q.v.*) & his bros.: Joseph 1768–1844 king of Naples & Spain; Lucien 1775–1840 prince of Ca·ni·no \kə-'nē-(ˌ)nō\; Louis 1778–1846 *father of Napoléon III* king of Holland; Jérôme 1784–1860 king of Westphalia
Bon·a·ven·tu·ra \ˌbä-nə-ˌven-'tu̇r-ə, -'tyu̇r-\ *or* **Bon·a·ven·ture** \ˌbä-nə-'ven-chər, 'bä-nə-ˌ\ Saint *ca* 1217–1274 *the Seraphic Doctor* Ital. philos.
Bonds \'bän(d)z\ Barry (Lamar) 1964– Am. baseball player
Bone \'bōn\ Sir Muirhead 1876–1953 Scot. etcher & painter
Bon·heur \bä-'nər\ Rosa 1822–1899 *Marie-Rosalie* Fr. painter
Bon·i·face \'bä-nə-fəs, -ˌfäs\ Saint *ca* 675–754 *Wynfrid* or *Wynfrith* Eng. missionary in Germany
Boniface name of 9 popes: esp. **VIII** (*Benedict Caetani*) *ca* 1235(or 1240)–1303 (pope 1294–1303)
Bon·nard \bó-'när\ Pierre 1867–1947 Fr. painter
Bon·ner *or* **Bon·er** \'bä-nər\ Edmund *ca* 1500–1569 Eng. prelate
Bon·net \bó-'nā\ Georges-Étienne 1889–1973 Fr. polit. & diplomat
Bon·ney \'bä-nē\ William H., Jr. 1859–1881 *Billy the Kid* orig. *Henry McCarty?* Am. outlaw
Bon·temps \bän-'täm\ Arna Wendell 1902–1973 Am. writer
Boone \'bün\ Daniel 1734–1820 Am. pioneer
Booth \'büth, *chiefly Brit* 'bu̇th\ family of Am. actors: Junius Brutus 1796–1852 *b* in England & his sons Edwin Thomas 1833–1893 & John Wilkes 1838–1865 assassin of Lincoln
Booth William 1829–1912 Eng. founder of Salvation Army *father of:* William Bramwell 1856–1929 Salvation Army gen.; Ballington 1857–1940 founder of Volunteers of America; Evangeline Cory 1865–1950 Salvation Army gen.
Bo·rah \'bór-ə\ William Edgar 1865–1940 Am. polit.
Bor·den \'bór-dᵊn\ Sir Robert (Laird) 1854–1937 Canad. lawyer & statesman; prime min. (1911–20)
Bor·det \bór-'dā\ Jules 1870–1961 Belg. bacteriol.
Borg \'bórg\ Björn (Rune) 1956– Swed. tennis player
Bor·ges \'bór-ˌhäs\ Jorge Luis 1899–1986 Argentine author
Bor·gia \'bór-(ˌ)jä, -jə, -zhä\ Cesare 1475(or 1476)–1507 *son of Rodrigo* Ital. cardinal & mil. leader
Borgia Lucrezia 1480–1519 *dau. of Rodrigo* duchess of Ferrara
Borgia Rodrigo — see Pope ALEXANDER VI
Bor·glum \'bór-gləm\ (John) Gut·zon \'gət-sən\ (de la Mothe) 1867–1941 Am. sculptor
Bo·ris III \'bór-əs, 'bär-\ 1894–1943 czar of Bulgaria (1918–43)
Born \'bórn\ Max 1882–1970 Ger. physicist
Bo·ro·din \bór-ə-'dēn, ˌbär-\ Aleksandr 1833–1887 Russ. composer & chem.
Bor·row \'bär-(ˌ)ō\ George Henry 1803–1881 Eng. author
Bosch \'bäsh, 'bósh\ Carl 1874–1940 Ger. industrial chem.
Bosch \'bäsh, 'bósh, *D* 'bós\ Hieronymus *ca* 1450–*ca* 1516 Du. painter
Bo·sco \'bäs-kō\ Saint Giovanni Melchior 1815–1888 *Don Bosco* Ital. religious & founder of Society of St. Francis de Sales
Bose \'bōs, 'bós, 'bōsh\ Sir Ja·ga·dis \ˌjə-gə-'dēs\ Chan·dra \'chən-drə\ 1858–1937 Indian physicist & plant physiol.
Bos·suet \bó-'swä\ Jacques-Bénigne 1627–1704 Fr. bishop
Bos·well \'bäz-ˌwel, -wəl\ James 1740–1795 Scot. biographer & diarist
Bo·tha \'bü-tə, 'bü(ə)-\ Louis 1862–1919 Boer gen.; 1st prime min. of Transvaal (1907) & of Union of So. Africa (1910–19)
Botha Pieter Willem 1916–2006 *P.W. Botha* prime min. of Republic of So. Africa (1978–84); pres. (1984–89)
Bo·the \'bō-tə\ Walther Wilhelm Georg 1891–1957 Ger. physicist

Bot·ti·cel·li \ˌbä-tə-'che-lē\ Sandro 1445–1510 *Alessandro di Mariano Filipepi* Ital. painter
Bou·chard \bü-'shär(d)\ Lucien 1938– Canad. polit.
Bou·cher \bü-'shā\ François 1703–1770 Fr. painter
Bou·ci·cault \'bü-si-ˌkō\ *or* **Bour·ci·cault** \'bu̇r-\ Dion 1820(or 1822)–1890 *Dionysius Lardner Boursiquot* Am. (Irish-born) actor & dram.
Bou·dic·ca \bü-'di-kə\ *also* **Bo·a·di·cea** \ˌbō-ə-də-'sē-ə\ *d* A.D. 60 ancient Brit. queen
Bou·gain·ville \'bü-gən-ˌvil, bü-gaⁿ-'vēl\ Louis-Antoine de 1729–1811 Fr. navigator
Bou·lan·ger \bü-län-'zhā\ Georges-Ernest-Jean-Marie 1837–1891 Fr. gen.
Boulanger Nadia-Juliette 1887–1979 Fr. music teacher & conductor
Bou·lez \bü-'lez\ Pierre 1925– Fr. composer & conductor
Bour·bon \'bu̇r-bən, bu̇r-'bōⁿ\ Charles de 1490–1527 Duc *de Bourbon* Fr. gen.; constable of France
Bour·geois \bu̇rzh-'wä, 'bu̇rzh-ˌ\ Léon-Victor-Auguste 1851–1925 Fr. statesman
Bourgeois Louise 1911–2010 Am. (Fr.-born) sculptor
Bour·get \bu̇r-'zhā\ Paul-Charles-Joseph 1852–1935 Fr. author
Bour·gui·ba \bu̇r-'gē-bə\ Habib ibn Ali 1903–2000 Tunisian pres. (1957–87)
Bourke–White \ˌbərk-'(h)wīt\ Margaret 1906–1971 née *White* Am. photographer
Bou·tros–Gha·li \'bü-trōs-'gä-lē\ Boutros 1922– Egypt. U.N. official; secy.-gen. (1992–96)
Bow·ditch \'bau̇-dich\ Nathaniel 1773–1838 Am. math. & astron.
Bow·ell \'bō-əl\ Sir Mackenzie 1823–1917 Canad. polit.; prime min. of Canada (1894–96)
Bow·en \'bō-ən\ Elizabeth 1899–1973 Irish author
Bow·ie \'bü-ē, 'bō-ē\ James 1796–1836 hero of Texas revolution
Bowles \'bōlz\ Chester 1901–1986 Am. econ. & diplomat
Boy·den \'bói-dᵊn\ Seth 1788–1870 Am. inventor
Boy·er \'bói-ər\ Paul Delos 1918– Am. chem.
Boyle \'bói(-ə)l\ Kay 1902–1992 Am. author
Boyle Robert 1627–1691 Brit. physicist & chem.
Boyle Willard (Sterling) 1924–2011 Canad.-U.S. physicist
Brad·bury \'brad-ˌber-ē, -b(ə-)rē\ Ray Douglas 1920–2012 Am. writer
Brad·dock \'bra-dək\ Edward 1695–1755 Brit. gen. in America
Brad·ford \'brad-fərd\ Gamaliel 1863–1932 Am. biographer
Bradford William 1590–1657 Am. colonist; gov. of Plymouth colony
Bradford William 1663–1752 Am. printer
Brad·ley \'brad-lē\ Francis Herbert 1846–1924 Eng. philos. — **Brad·le·ian** *also* **Brad·ley·an** \'brad-lē-ən, brad-\ *adj*
Bradley Omar Nelson 1893–1981 Am. gen.
Brad·street \'brad-ˌstrēt\ Anne *ca* 1612–1672 née *Dudley; wife of Simon* Am. poet
Bradstreet Simon 1603–1697 colonial gov. of Massachusetts
Bra·dy \'brā-dē\ Mathew B. 1823?–1896 Am. photographer
Bragg \'brag\ Braxton 1817–1876 Am. Confed. gen.
Bragg Sir (William) Lawrence 1890–1971 *son of W.H.* Eng. physicist
Bragg Sir William Henry 1862–1942 Eng. physicist
Brahe \'brä; 'brä-hē, -hə\ Ty·cho \'tē-(ˌ)kō, 'tī-\ 1546–1601 Dan. astron.
Brahms \'brämz\ Johannes 1833–1897 Ger. composer & pianist — **Brahms·ian** \'bräm-zē-ən\ *adj*
Braille \'brāl, 'brī\ Louis 1809–1852 Fr. blind teacher of the blind
Bra·man·te \brə-'män-tē, -(ˌ)tā\ Donato 1444–1514 orig. *Donato d'Agnolo* or *d'Angelo* Ital. architect
Bran·cu·si \bran-'kü-sē\ Constantin 1876–1957 Fr. (Romanian-born) sculptor
Bran·deis \'bran-ˌdīs, -ˌdīz\ Louis Dembitz 1856–1941 Am. jurist
Bran·des \'brän-dəs\ Georg Morris 1842–1927 Dan. lit. critic
Bran·do \'bran-dō\ Marlon 1924–2004 Am. actor
Brandt \'bränt, 'brant\ Wil·ly \'vi-lē, 'wi-\ 1913–1992 orig. *Herbert Ernst Karl Frahm* W. Ger. polit.; chancellor of West Germany (1969–74)
Brant \'brant\ Joseph 1742–1807 *Thayendanegea* Mohawk Indian chief
Bran·ting \'bran-tin\ Karl Hjal·mar \'yäl-ˌmär\ 1860–1925 Swed. statesman & socialist leader
Braque \'brak, 'bräk\ Georges 1882–1963 Fr. painter
Brat·tain \'bra-tᵊn\ Walter Houser 1902–1987 Am. physicist
Brau·chitsch \'brau̇-kich, -ˌkich\ (Heinrich Alfred) Walther von 1881–1948 Ger. gen.
Braun \'brau̇n\ Karl Ferdinand 1850–1918 Ger. physicist
Braun Wernher von 1912–1977 Am. (Ger.-born) engineer
Breas·ted \'bres-təd\ James Henry 1865–1935 Am. orientalist
Brecht \'brekt, 'brekt\ Bertolt 1898–1956 Ger. dram. — **Brecht·ian** \'brek-tē-ən, 'brek-\ *adj*
Breck·in·ridge \'bre-kən-(ˌ)rij\ John Cabell 1821–1875 Am. polit.; vice pres. of the U.S. (1857–61)
Bren·nan \'bre-nən\ William Joseph, Jr. 1906–1997 Am. jurist
Bren·ner \'bre-nər\ Sydney 1927– Brit. (So. African-born) geneticist
Bre·ton \brə-'tōⁿ\ André 1896–1966 Fr. surrealist poet
Brew·ster \'brü-stər\ William 1567–1644 Am. colonist
Brey·er \'brī-ər\ Stephen Gerald 1938– Am. jurist
Brezh·nev \'brezh-ˌnef\ Leonid Ilyich 1906–1982 Russ. polit.; pres. of U.S.S.R. (1960–64; 1977–82); 1st secy. of Communist party (1964–82)
Bri·an \'brī-ən, 'brēn\ *also* **Brian Bo·ru** \bō-'rü\ 941–1014 king of Ireland (1002–14)
Bri·and \brē-'äⁿ\ Aristide 1862–1932 Fr. statesman
Brid·ger \'bri-jər\ James 1804–1881 Am. pioneer & scout
Brid·ges \'bri-jəz\ Robert Seymour 1844–1930 Eng. poet; poet laureate (1913–30)
Bright \'brīt\ John 1811–1889 Eng. orator & statesman
Brig·it \'bri-jət, 'brē-yit\ *also* **Brid·get** \'bri-jət\ *or* **Brig·id** \'bri-jəd, 'brē-yid\ *or* **Brighid** \'brēd\ Saint *d ca* 524–528 *Bride of Kildare* or **Bride of Ireland** a patron saint of Ireland

\ə\ abut \ᵊ\ kitten, F table \ər\ further \a\ ash \ā\ ace \ä\ mop, mar \au̇\ out \ch\ chin \e\ bet \ē\ easy \g\ go \i\ hit \ī\ ice \j\ job \n\ sing \ō\ go \ó\ law \ói\ boy \th\ thin \t͟h\ the \ü\ loot \u̇\ foot \y\ yet \zh\ vision, beige \k, ⁿ, œ, ᴜ, ᵞ\ *see* Guide to Pronunciation

Bril·lat–Sa·va·rin \brē-'yä-ˌsa-və-'raⁿ, -'sa-və-rən\ Anthelme 1755–1826 Fr. gastronome

Brit·ten \'bri-tⁿn\ (Edward) Benjamin 1913–1976 Baron *Britten of Aldeburgh* Eng. composer

Brock·house \'bräk-ˌhaůs\ Bertram Neville 1918–2003 Canad. physicist

Brod·sky \'bräd-skē\ Joseph 1940–1996 orig. *Iosip Aleksandrovich Brodsky* Am. (Russ.-born) poet & essayist

Broglie \'brŏi\ Louis-Victor-Pierre-Raymond de 1892–1987 Fr. physicist

Bron·të \'brän-tē, -(ˌ)tä\ family of Eng. writers: Charlotte 1816–1855 & her sisters Emily 1818–1848 & Anne 1820–1849

Brooke \'brůk\ Sir Alan Francis 1883–1963 1st Viscount *Al·an·brooke* \'a-lən-ˌbrůk\ Brit. field marshal

Brooke Edward William 1919–   Am. polit.

Brooke Rupert 1887–1915 Eng. poet

Brooks \'brůks\ Gwendolyn Elizabeth 1917–2000 Am. poet

Brooks Phillips 1835–1893 Am. bishop

Brooks Van Wyck \van-'wīk, vən-\ 1886–1963 Am. essayist & critic

Brow·der \'braů-dər\ Earl 1891–1973 Am. Communist polit.

Brown \'braůn\ Charles Brockden 1771–1810 Am. nov.

Brown Ford Mad·ox \'ma-dəks\ 1821–1893 Eng. painter

Brown George 1818–1880 Canad. (Scot.-born) journalist & polit.

Brown (James) Gordon 1951–   Brit. prime min. (2007–10)

Brown John 1800–1859 *Old Brown of Osa·wat·o·mie* \ˌō-sə-'wä-tə-mē\ Am. abolitionist

Brown Michael Stuart 1941–   Am. biochemist

Browne \'braůn\ Charles Farrar 1834–1867 pseud. *Ar·te·mus* \'är-tə-məs\ *Ward* Am. humorist

Browne Sir Thomas 1605–1682 Eng. physician & author

Brow·ning \'braů-niŋ\ Elizabeth Barrett 1806–1861 *wife of Robert* Eng. poet

Browning Robert 1812–1889 Eng. poet

Bruce \'brüs\ Sir David 1855–1931 Brit. physician & bacteriol.

Bruce Robert — see ROBERT I the Bruce

Bruce Stanley Melbourne 1883–1967 1st Viscount *Bruce of Melbourne* Austral. statesman; prime min. (1923–29)

Bruch \'brůk\ Max (Karl August) 1838–1920 Ger. composer

Bruck·ner \'brůk-nər\ Anton 1824–1896 Austrian composer — **Bruck·ner·ian** \ˌbrůk-'ner-ē-ən\ *adj*

Brue·ghel *or* **Breu·ghel** \'brü-gəl, 'brŏi-, *D* 'brœ-kəl\ family of Flem. painters including: Pieter *ca* 1525–1569 & his sons Pieter 1564–1638 & Jan 1568–1625

Brum·mell \'brə-məl\ George Bryan 1778–1840 *Beau Brummell* Eng. dandy

Brundt·land \'brůnt-ˌlän\ Gro Harlem 1939–   *née Harlem* prime min. of Norway (1981; 1986–89; 1990–96)

Bru·nel·le·schi \ˌbrů-nə-'les-kē\ *or* **Bru·nel·le·sco** \-(ˌ)kō\ Filippo 1377–1446 Ital. architect

Brü·ning \'brü-niŋ, 'brœ-\ Heinrich 1885–1970 chancellor of Germany (1930–32)

Bru·no \'brü-(ˌ)nō\ Giordano 1548–1600 Ital. philos.

Bru·tus \'brü-təs\ Marcus Junius 85–42 B.C. Rom. polit. & conspirator

Bry·an \'brī-ən\ William Jennings 1860–1925 Am. lawyer & polit.

Bry·ant \'brī-ənt\ William Cullen 1794–1878 Am. poet & editor

Bu·ber \'bü-bər\ Martin 1878–1965 Israeli (Austrian-born) philos.

Buch·an \'bə-kən, -ˌkən\ Sir John 1875–1940 1st Baron *Tweeds·muir* \'twēdz-ˌmyůr\ Scot. author; gov.-gen. of Canada (1935–40)

Bu·chan·an \byü-'ka-nən, bə-\ James 1791–1868 Am. polit. & diplomat; 15th pres. of the U.S. (1857–61)

Buchanan James McGill 1919–2013 Am. econ.

Buch·man \'bůk-mən, 'bək-\ Frank Nathan Daniel 1878–1961 Am. evangelist

Buck \'bək\ Linda B. 1947–   Am. biol.

Buck Pearl 1892–1973 née *Sy·den·strick·er* \'sī-dⁿn-ˌstri-kər\ Am. nov.

Buckingham 1st & 2d Dukes of — see VILLIERS

Buck·ley \'bək-lē\ William Frank 1925–2008 Am. editor & writer

Buck·ner \'bək-nər\ Simon Bolivar 1823–1914 Am. Confed. gen. & polit.

Buckner Simon Bolivar 1886–1945 *son of prec.* Am. gen.

Buddha — see SIDDHĀRTHA GAUTAMA

Bu·den·ny \bü-'dyó-nē, bü-'de-\ Semyon Mikhaylovich 1883–1973 Russ. gen.

Buffalo Bill — see William Frederick CODY

Buf·fett \'bə-fət\ Warren (Edward) 1930–   Am. investor & philanthropist

Buf·fon \ˌbə-'fōⁿ, byü-, bœ-\ Comte Georges-Louis Leclerc de 1707–1788 Fr. naturalist

Bu·kha·rin \bů-'kär-ən\ Nikolay Ivanovich 1888–1938 Russ. Communist leader & editor

Bul·finch \'bůl-ˌfinch\ Charles 1763–1844 Am. architect

Bul·ga·nin \bůl-'ga-nən\ Nikolay Aleksandrovich 1895–1975 Russ. polit. & marshal

Bull \'bůl\ Ole \'ō-lə\ Bornemann 1810–1880 Norw. violinist

Bü·low \'byü-(ˌ)lō, 'bœ-\ Bernhard Heinrich Martin Karl 1849–1929 Prince *von Bülow* Ger. diplomat & statesman; chancellor of Germany (1900–09)

Bult·mann \'bůlt-ˌmän\ Rudolf Karl 1884–1976 Ger. theol.

Bul·wer \'bůl-wər\ (William) Henry Lytton (Earle) 1801–1872 Baron *Dalling & Bulwer*; *bro. of 1st Baron Lytton* Brit. diplomat

Bulwer–Lytton — see LYTTON

Bunche \'bənch\ Ralph Johnson 1904–1971 Am. diplomat

Bu·nin \'bün-yən, -ˌyēn; 'bü-nən, -ˌnēn\ Ivan Alekseyevich 1870–1953 Russ. poet & nov.

Bun·ker \'bəŋ-kər\ Ellsworth 1894–1984 Am. diplomat

Bun·sen \'bůn-zən, 'bən(t)-sən\ Robert Wilhelm 1811–1899 Ger. chem.

Bu·ñu·el (Por·to·lés) \ˌbün-yü-'wel-pōr-tō-'läs\ Luis 1900–1983 Mex. (Span.-born) film director

Bun·yan \'bən-yən\ John 1628–1688 Eng. preacher & author

Bur·bage \'bər-bij\ Richard *ca* 1567–1619 Eng. actor

Bur·bank \'bər-ˌbaŋk\ Luther 1849–1926 Am. horticulturist

Burch·field \'bərch-ˌfēld\ Charles Ephraim 1893–1967 Am. painter

Bur·ger \'bər-gər\ Warren Earl 1907–1995 Am. jurist; chief justice U.S. Supreme Court (1969–86)

Bür·ger \'bůr-gər, 'bir-, 'bůer-\ Gottfried August 1747–1794 Ger. poet

Bur·gess \'bər-jəs\ Anthony 1917–1993 Brit. writer

Burgess (Frank) Gelett 1866–1951 Am. humorist & illustrator

Burgess Thornton Waldo 1874–1965 Am. writer

Burghley *or* **Burleigh** 1st Baron — see William CECIL

Bur·goyne \(ˌ)bər-'ˌgóin, 'bər-ˌ\ John 1722–1792 Brit. gen. in America

Burke \'bərk\ Edmund 1729–1797 Brit. statesman & orator — **Burk·ean** *or* **Burk·ian** \'bər-kē-ən\ *adj*

Bur·lin·game \'bər-lən-ˌgäm\ Anson 1820–1870 Am. diplomat

Burne–Jones \'bərn-'jōnz\ Sir Edward Co·ley \'kō-lē\ 1833–1898 orig. surname *Jones* Eng. painter & designer

Bur·nett \(ˌ)bər-'net, 'bər-nət\ Frances Eliza 1849–1924 née *Hodg·son* \'häj-sən\ Am. (Eng.-born) writer

Bur·ney \'bər-nē\ Fanny 1752–1840 orig. *Frances; Madame d'Ar·blay* \'där-ˌblä\ Eng. nov. & diarist

Burns \'bərnz\ Kenneth Lauren 1953–   Am. filmmaker

Burns Robert 1759–1796 Scot. poet — **Burns·ian** \'bərn-zē-ən\ *adj*

Burn·side \'bərn-ˌsīd\ Ambrose Everett 1824–1881 Am. gen.

Burr \'bər\ Aaron 1756–1836 3d vice pres. of the U.S. (1801–05)

Bur·roughs \'bər-(ˌ)ōz, 'bə-(ˌ)rōz\ Edgar Rice 1875–1950 Am. writer

Burroughs John 1837–1921 Am. naturalist

Burroughs William Seward 1914–1997 Am. writer

Bur·ton \'bər-tⁿn\ Harold Hitz 1888–1964 Am. jurist

Burton Richard 1925–1984 Brit. actor

Burton Sir Richard Francis 1821–1890 Brit. explorer & orientalist

Burton Robert 1577–1640 Eng. clergyman & author

Bush \'bůsh\ George (Herbert Walker) 1924–   Am. polit.; 41st pres. of the U.S. (1989–93)

Bush George W(alker) 1946–   *son of prec.* Am. polit.; 43d pres. of the U.S. (2001–09)

Bush Van·ne·var \və-'nē-vər\ 1890–1974 Am. electrical engineer

Bu·so·ni \byü-'zō-nē, bü-\ Ferruccio Benvenuto 1866–1924 Ital. composer & pianist

Bu·sta·man·te y Sir·vén \bü-stä-'män-(ˌ)tā-ē-sir-'ven\ Antonio Sánchez \'sän-(ˌ)chez\ 1865–1951 Cuban jurist

Bu·te·nandt \'bü-tə-ˌnänt\ Adolph 1903–1995 Ger. chem.

But·ler \'bət-lər\ Benjamin Franklin 1818–1893 Am. gen. & polit.

Butler Joseph 1692–1752 Eng. theol.

Butler Nicholas Murray 1862–1947 Am. educ.; pres. Columbia U. (1901–45)

Butler Samuel 1612–1680 Eng. satirical poet

Butler Samuel 1835–1902 Eng. nov. & satirist

Bux·te·hu·de \ˌbůk-stə-'hü-də\ Dietrich 1637–1707 Dan. organist & composer

By·att \'bī-ət\ Dame Antonia Susan 1936–   *A.S. Byatt* née *Drabble* Brit. writer

Byng \'biŋ\ Julian Hedworth George 1862–1935 1st Viscount *Byng of Vimy* Brit. gen.; gov.-gen. of Canada (1921–26)

Byrd \'bərd\ Richard Evelyn 1888–1957 Am. admiral & polar explorer

Byrd William 1543–1623 Eng. composer

Byrnes \'bərnz\ James Francis 1879–1972 Am. polit. & jurist

By·ron \'bī-rən\ Lord 1788–1824 in full *George Gordon Byron*, 6th Baron *Byron* Eng. poet — **By·ron·ic** \bī-'rä-nik\ *adj*

Ca·be·za de Va·ca \kə-'bā-zə-də-'vä-kə\ Álvar Núñez *ca* 1490–*ca* 1560 Span. explorer

Ca·ble \'kā-bəl\ George Washington 1844–1925 Am. nov.

Cab·ot \'kā-bət\ John *ca* 1450–*ca* 1499 It. *Giovanni Ca·bo·to* \kä-'bō-(ˌ)tō\ Venetian navigator & explorer for England

Cabot Sebastian 1476?–1557 *son of John* Eng. navigator & explorer

Ca·bral \kə-'bräl\ Pedro Álvares 1467(or 1468)–1520 Port. navigator

Ca·bril·ho \kə-'brē-(ˌ)yō, -'bri-(ˌ)lō\ João Rodrigues *d* 1543 Sp. *Juan Rodríguez Cabrillo* Span. (Port.-born) explorer in Mexico & California

Ca·bri·ni \kə-'brē-nē\ Saint Frances Xavier 1850–1917 *Mother Cabrini* 1st Am. citizen canonized (1946)

Cade \'kād\ John *d* 1450 *Jack Cade* Eng. rebel

Cad·il·lac \'kä-də-ˌlak, *F* kä-dē-'yäk\ Antoine de la Mothe, sieur de 1658–1730 Fr. founder of Detroit

Caed·mon \'kad-mən\ *fl* 658–680 Anglo-Saxon poet

Cae·sar \'sē-zər\ (Gaius) Julius 100–44 B.C. Rom. gen., statesman, & writer

Cage \'kāj\ John Milton 1912–1992 Am. composer

Ca·glio·stro \kal-'yó-(ˌ)strō, käl-\ Count Alessandro di 1743–1795 orig. *Giuseppe Bal·sa·mo* \'bäl-sə-ˌmō\ Ital. adventurer

Cain \'kān\ James Mallahan 1892–1977 Am. nov.

Caine \'kān\ Sir (Thomas Henry) Hall 1853–1931 Eng. nov.

Calamity Jane \jān\ 1852?–1903 *Martha Jane Burke* \'bərk\ née *Cannary* \'ka-nə-rē\ Am. frontier figure

Cal·der \'kól-dər\ Alexander 1898–1976 Am. sculptor

Cal·de·ra Rod·rí·guez \käl-'thä-rä-róth-'rē-gäs\ Rafael 1916–2009 pres. of Venezuela (1969–74; 1994–99)

Cal·de·rón (Hi·no·jo·sa) \ˌkäl-də-'rōn(-ˌē-nō-'hō-sä)\ Felipe (de Jesús) 1962–   pres. of Mexico (2006–12)

Cal·de·rón de la Bar·ca \ˌkäl-də-'rōn-dä-lə-'bär-kə\ Pedro 1600–1681 Span. dram. & poet

Cald·well \'kól-ˌdwel, -dwəl, 'käl-\ Erskine 1903–1987 Am. nov.

Caldwell (Janet) Taylor 1900–1985 Am. (Eng.-born) author

Cal·houn \kal-'hün\ John Caldwell 1782–1850 Am. polit.; vice pres. of the U.S. (1825–32)

Ca·lig·u·la \kə-'li-gyə-lə\ A.D. 12–41 *Gaius Caesar* Rom. emp. (37–41)

Cal·la·ghan \'ka-lə-ˌhan, -ˌhan\ (Leonard) James 1912–2005 Baron *Callaghan of Cardiff* Brit. prime min. (1976–79)

Callaghan Morley Edward 1903–1990 Canad. author

Cal·las \'ka-ləs, 'kä-\ Maria 1923–1977 orig. *Maria Anna Sofia Cecilia Kalogeropoulos* Am. soprano

Cal·les \'kä-ˌyäs\ Plutarco Elías 1877–1945 Mex. gen.; pres. of Mexico (1924–28)

Cal·lim·a·chus \kə-'li-mə-kəs\ 5th cent. B.C. Greek sculptor

Callimachus *ca* 305–*ca* 240 B.C. Greek scholar & Alexandrian librarian

Cal·lis·the·nes \kə-'lis-thə-ˌnēz\ *ca* 360–328 B.C. Greek philos. & hist.

Cal·lis·tra·tus \kə-'lis-trə-təs\ *d* 355 B.C. Athenian orator & gen.

Cal·vert \'kal-vərt\ George 1580?–1632 1st Baron *Baltimore* Eng. proprietor in America

Calvert Leonard 1606–1647 *son of George* gov. of Maryland province (1634–47)
Cal·vin \'kal-vən\ John 1509–1564 orig. *Jean Cau·vin* \kō-'va^n\ Fr. theol. & reformer
Calvin Melvin 1911–1997 Am. chem.
Camacho Manuel Ávila — see ÁVILA CAMACHO
Cam·ba·cé·rès \ˌkä^n-ˌba-sə-'res, -ˌbä-\ Jean-Jacques-Régis de 1753–1824 Duc de *Parme* Fr. jurist; counselor of Napoléon I
Cam·by·ses II \kam-'bī-(ˌ)sēz\ *d* 522 B.C. *son of Cyrus II the Great* king of Persia (529–22)
Cam·den \'kam-dən\ William 1551–1623 Eng. antiquarian & hist.
Cam·er·on \'ka-mə-rən, 'kam-rən\ David (William Donald) 1966– Brit. prime min. (2010–   )
Cameron James (Francis) 1954–   Am. (Canad.-born) filmmaker
Cameron of Loch·iel \lä-'kēl, -'kēl\ 1629–1719 Sir *Ewen Cameron* Scot. chieftain
Cameron of Lochiel 1695?–1748 *Donald Cameron; the gentle Lochiel* Scot. chieftain
Ca·mões \kə-'mói^nsh\ *E* **Ca·mo·ëns** \kə-'mō-ənz, 'ka-mə-wənz\ Luiz Vaz de 1524(or 1525)–1580 Port. poet
Camp \'kamp\ Walter Chauncey 1859–1925 Am. football coach
Camp·bell \'kam-bəl, 'ka-məl\ Alexander 1788–1866 Am. (Irish-born) founder of Disciples of Christ
Campbell Colin 1792–1863 orig. surname *Mac·li·ver* \mə-'klē-vər\; Baron *Clyde* Brit. field marshal
Campbell John 1705–1782 4th Earl of *Lou·doun* \'laú-d^n\ Brit. gen. in America
Campbell John Douglas Sutherland 1845–1914 9th Duke of *Argyll* gov.⹀gen. of Canada (1878–83)
Campbell Joseph 1904–1987 Am. mythologist & folklorist
Campbell Kim 1947–   orig. *Avril Phaedra Campbell* prime min. of Canada (1993)
Campbell Thomas 1777–1844 Brit. poet
Camp·bell–Ban·ner·man \-'ba-nər-mən\ Sir Henry 1836–1908 Brit. statesman; prime min. (1905–08)
Cam·pi \'käm-(ˌ)pē\ Ital. family of painters in Cremona including: Galeazzo 1477–1536 & his three sons Giulio 1502–1572, Antonio 1536–*ca* 1591, & Vincenzo 1536–1591
Cam·pi·on \'kam-pē-ən\ Thomas 1567–1620 Eng. poet & composer
Ca·mus \kä-'mᵫ\ Albert 1913–1960 Fr. nov., essayist, & dram.
Ca·na·let·to \ˌka-nə-'le-(ˌ)tō\ 1697–1768 orig. *Giovanni Antonio Canal* Ital. painter
Can·by \'kan-bē\ Henry Sei·del \'sī-d^l\ 1878–1961 Am. editor & author
Can·dolle \kä^n-'dól\ Augustin Pyrame de 1778–1841 Swiss botanist
Can·dra·gup·ta \ˌkən-drə-'gúp-tə\ *or* **Chan·dra·gup·ta** \'chən-\ *d ca* 297 B.C. Indian emp. (*ca* 321–*ca* 297 B.C.)
Can·dra Gup·ta II \'kən-drə-'gúp-tə\ *also* **Chan·dra Gup·ta II** \'chən-\ Indian ruler of Gupta dynasty (*ca* 380–*ca* 415)
Ca·net·ti \kə-'ne-tē\ Elias 1905–1994 Brit. (Bulg.-born) author writing in German
Can·ning \'ka-niŋ\ Charles John 1812–1862 Earl *Canning* Brit. gov.⹀gen. of India (1856–58); 1st viceroy of India (1858–62)
Canning George 1770–1827 *father of C.J.* Brit. statesman; prime min. (1827)
Canning Stratford 1786–1880 1st Viscount *Stratford de Red·cliffe* \'red-ˌklif\ Brit. diplomat
Can·non \'ka-nən\ Joseph Gurney 1836–1926 *Uncle Joe* Am. polit.
Ca·no·va \kə-'nō-və, -'nó-\ Antonio 1757–1822 Ital. sculptor
Ca·nute \kə-'nüt, -'nyüt\ *d* 1035 *the Great* king of England (1016–35); of Denmark (1018–35); of Norway (1028–35)
Ca·pec·chi \kə-'pe-kē\ Mario R(enato) 1937–   Am. (Ital.-born) geneticist
Ca·pek \'chä-ˌpek\ Ka·rel \'kär-əl\ 1890–1938 Czech nov. & dram.
Capet Hugh — see HUGH CAPET
Ca·pone \kə-'pōn\ Alphonse 1899–1947 *Scarface* Am. gangster
Ca·pote \kə-'pō-tē\ Truman 1924–1984 Am. writer
Cap·ra \'ka-prə\ Frank 1897–1991 Am. film director & producer — **Cap·ra·esque** \ˌka-prə-'esk\ *adj*
Car·a·cal·la \ˌka-rə-'ka-lə\ A.D. 188–217 *Marcus Aurelius Antoninus* orig. *Bas·si·a·nus* \ˌba-sē-'ä-nəs\ Rom. emp. (211–217)
Ca·rat·a·cus \kə-'ra-ti-kəs\ *also* **Ca·rac·ta·cus** \-'rak-ti-\ *W* **Ca·ra·doc** *or* **Ca·ra·dog** \kə-'rä-(ˌ)dóg\ 1st cent. A.D. Brit. chieftain
Ca·ra·vag·gio \ˌka-rə-'vä-j(ē-ˌ)ō, -'vä-zhō\ Michelangelo da 1571–1610 *Michelangelo Merisi* Ital. painter — **Ca·ra·vag·gesque** \ˌkär-ə-ˌvä-'jesk\ *adj*
Cár·de·nas \'kär-də-ˌnäs, 'kär-thä-ˌnäs\ Lázaro 1895–1970 Mex. gen. & polit.; pres. of Mexico (1934–40)
Car·do·so \kär-'dō-(ˌ)zü\ Fernando Henrique 1931–   pres. of Brazil (1995–2003)
Car·do·zo \kär-'dō-(ˌ)zō\ Benjamin Nathan 1870–1938 Am. jurist
Car·duc·ci \kär-'dü-(ˌ)chē\ Giosuè 1835–1907 Ital. poet
Ca·rew \kə-'rü, 'ker-ē\ Thomas 1595?–?1640 Eng. poet
Car·ey \'ker-ē\ George Leonard 1935–   Lord *Carey* archbishop of Canterbury (1991–2002)
Carl XVI Gus·taf \'kärl-'gəs-ˌtäv, -'gús-, -ˌtäf\ 1946–   king of Sweden (1973–   )
Carle·ton \'kär-(ə)l-tən\ Sir Guy 1724–1808 1st Baron *Dorchester* Brit. gen. & administrator in America
Car·los \'kär-ləs, -ˌlōs\ Don 1788–1855 infante & pretender to Span. throne
Carlos de Aus·tria \-'thä-ˌaú-strē-ə\ Don 1545–1568 *son of Philip II of Spain* prince of Asturias & heir to Span. throne
Car·lo·ta \kär-'lō-tə, -'lä-\ 1840–1927 *wife of Maximilian* empress of Mexico (1864–67)
Carls·son \'kär-(ə)l-sən\ Arvid 1923–   Swed. pharmacologist
Car·lyle \kär-'līl, 'kär-ˌ\ Thomas 1795–1881 Scot. essayist & hist. — **Car·lyl·ean** *or* **Car·lyl·ian** \kär-'lī-lē-ən\ *adj*
Car·mi·chael \kär-ˌmī-kəl\ Hoagy 1899–1981 *Hoagland Howard Carmichael* Am. songwriter
Car·mo·na \kär-'mō-nə\ António Óscar de Fragoso 1869–1951 Port. gen.; pres. of Portugal (1928–51)
Car·nap \'kär-ˌnap\ Rudolf 1891–1970 Am. (Ger.-born) philos.

Car·ne·gie \kär-'ne-gē, 'kär-nə-gē\ Andrew 1835–1919 Am. (Scot.-born) industrialist & philanthropist
Car·not \kär-'nō\ Lazare (-Nicolas-Marguerite) 1753–1823 Fr. statesman & gen.
Carnot (Marie-François-) Sadi 1837–1894 pres. of France (1887–94)
Car·ol II \'ka-rəl\ 1893–1953 king of Romania (1930–40)
Car·pac·cio \kär-'pä-ch(ē-ˌ)ō\ Vittore *ca* 1460–1525(or 1526) Ital. painter
Car·ran·za \kə-'rän-zə, -'rän-\ Venustiano 1859–1920 pres. of Mexico (1915–20)
Car·rel \kə-'rel, 'ka-rəl\ Alexis 1873–1944 Fr. surgeon & biol.
Car·rère \kə-'rer\ John Merven 1858–1911 Am. architect
Car·roll \'ka-rəl\ Charles 1737–1832 *Carroll of Carrollton* Am. patriot
Carroll Lewis — see Charles Lutwidge DODGSON — **Car·roll·ian** \kə-'rō-lē-ən\ *adj*
Car·son \'kär-s^n\ Christopher 1809–1868 *Kit* \'kit\ Carson Am. scout
Carson Rachel Louise 1907–1964 Am. biol. & writer
Carte, D'Oy·ly \ˌdói-lē-'kärt\ Richard 1844–1901 Eng. opera impresario
Car·ter \'kär-tər\ Elliott Cook 1908–2012 Am. composer
Carter Howard 1874–1939 Eng. archaeol.
Carter Jimmy 1924–   *James Earl Carter, Jr.* Am. polit.; 39th pres. of the U.S. (1977–81)
Car·ter·et \ˌkär-tə-'ret, 'kär-tə-ˌ\ John 1690–1763 Earl *Gran·ville* \'gran-ˌvil\ Eng. statesman
Car·tier \kär-'tyä, 'kär-tē-ˌä\ George Étienne 1814–1873 Canad. polit.
Cartier Jacques 1491–1557 Fr. navigator & explorer
Cart·wright \'kärt-ˌrīt\ Edmund 1743–1823 Eng. inventor
Ca·ru·so \kə-'rü-(ˌ)sō, -(ˌ)zō\ En·ri·co \en-'rē-(ˌ)kō\ 1873–1921 orig. *Errico* Ital. tenor
Car·ver \'kär-vər\ George Washington *ca* 1861–1943 Am. botanist
Carver John 1576–1621 Eng. *Mayflower* Pilgrim; 1st gov. of Plymouth colony
Cary \'ker-ē\ (Arthur) Joyce (Lunel) 1888–1957 Brit. nov.
Cary Henry Francis 1772–1844 Eng. clergyman & translator
Ca·sals \kə-'sälz, -'zälz\ Pablo 1876–1973 Catalan *Pau Casals* Span.-born cellist, conductor, & composer
Ca·sa·no·va \ˌka-zə-'nō-və, ˌka-sə-\ Giovanni Giacomo 1725–1798 orig. *Giacomo Girolamo Casanova*; alias *Jean-Jacques, Chevalier de Seingalt* Ital. adventurer & memoirist
Ca·sau·bon \kə-'sò-bən, ˌka-zō-'bō^n\ Isaac 1559–1614 Fr. scholar
Case·ment \'käs-mənt\ Sir Roger David 1864–1916 Irish rebel
Cas·lon \'kaz-lən\ William 1692–1766 Eng. typefounder
Cass \'kas\ Lewis 1782–1866 Am. statesman
Cas·satt \kə-'sat\ Mary Stevenson 1844–1926 Am. painter in France
Cas·sin \ka-'sa^n, kä-\ René-Samuel 1887–1976 Fr. statesman
Cas·si·o·do·rus \ˌka-sē-ə-'dór-əs\ Flavius Magnus Aurelius *ca* 490–*ca* 585 Rom. statesman & author
Cas·sius Lon·gi·nus \'ka-sh(ē-)əs-ˌlän-'jī-nəs, -s(ē-)əs-\ Gaius *d* 42 B.C. Rom. gen. & conspirator
Cas·te·lar y Ri·poll \ˌkas-tə-'lär-ē-rē-'pól\ Emilio 1832–1899 Span. statesman & writer
Ca·sti·glio·ne \ˌkäs-tēl-'yō-(ˌ)nä\ Baldassare 1478–1529 Ital. writer
Cas·ti·lho \kash-'tēl-(ˌ)yü, kas-\ Antônio Feliciano de 1800–1875 Port. poet
Castlereagh Viscount — see Robert STEWART
Cas·tro \'kas-(ˌ)trō, 'käs-\ Cipriano 1858–1924 Venezuelan gen.; pres. of Venezuela (1902–08)
Cas·tro \'käs-(ˌ)trō\ Inés \ē-'näs\ de 1320?–1355 Span. noblewoman
Cas·tro (Ruz) \'kas-(ˌ)trō-'rüs, 'käs-\ Fi·del \fē-'del\ 1926–   Cuban leader (1959–2008)
Castro (Ruz) Ra·úl \rä-'ül\ (Modesto) 1931–   *bro. of prec.* Cuban leader (2008–   )
Cates·by \'kāts-bē\ Mark 1679?–1749 Eng. naturalist
Catesby Robert 1573–1605 Eng. rebel
Cath·er \'ka-thər\ Willa Sibert 1873–1947 Am. nov.
Cath·er·ine \'ka-th(ə-)rən\ name of 1st, 5th, & 6th wives of Henry VIII of England: Catherine of Aragon 1485–1536; Catherine Howard 1520?–1542; Catherine Parr \'pär\ 1512–1548
Catherine I 1684–1727 *wife of Peter I* empress of Russia (1725–27)
Catherine II 1729–1796 *the Great* empress of Russia (1762–96)
Cath·er·ine de Mé·di·cis \-də-ˌmä-dē-'sēs, -'me-də-(ˌ)sēs\ *also* kä-'trēn-\ *It* **Ca·te·ri·na de' Me·di·ci** \ˌkä-tä-'rē-nä-dā-'me-dē-(ˌ)chē\ 1519–1589 *queen of Henry II of France*
Catherine of Bra·gan·za \brə-'gan-zə\ 1638–1705 *queen of Charles II of England*
Cat·i·line \'ka-tə-ˌlin\ *ca* 108–62 B.C. *Lucius Sergius Cat·i·li·na* \ˌka-tə-'lī-nə, -'lē-nə\ Rom. polit. & conspirator
Cat·lin \'kat-lən\ George 1796–1872 Am. artist
Ca·to \'kā-(ˌ)tō\ Marcus Porcius 234–149 B.C. *the Elder; the Censor* Rom. statesman
Cato Marcus Porcius 95–46 B.C. *the Younger; great-grandson of prec.* Rom. statesman
Catt \'kat\ Carrie Chapman 1859–1947 née *Lane* Am. suffragist
Cat·tell \kə-'tel\ James McKeen 1860–1944 Am. psychol. & editor
Cat·ton \'ka-t^n\ (Charles) Bruce 1899–1978 Am. journalist & hist.
Ca·tul·lus \kə-'tə-ləs\ Gaius Valerius *ca* 84–*ca* 54 B.C. Rom. poet
Cau·lain·court \ˌkō-ˌla^n-'kùr\ Marquis Armand-Augustin-Louis de 1773–1827 Fr. gen. & diplomat
Ca·va·co Sil·va \kə-ˌvä-kü-'sēl-və\ Aníbal (António) 1939–   Port. prime min. (1985–95); pres. (2006–   )
Ca·vell \'ka-vəl, kə-'vel\ Edith Louisa 1865–1915 Eng. nurse
Cav·en·dish \'ka-vən-(ˌ)dish\ Henry 1731–1810 Eng. scientist
Cavendish Spencer Compton 1833–1908 8th Duke of *Devonshire* Eng. statesman
Cavendish Sir William 1505?–1557 Eng. statesman
Cavendish William 1640–1707 1st Duke of *Devonshire* Eng. statesman

---

\ə\ abut \ᵊ\ kitten, F table \ər\ further \a\ ash \ā\ ace \ä\ mop, mar
\aú\ out \ch\ chin \e\ bet \ē\ easy \g\ go \i\ hit \ī\ ice \j\ job
\ŋ\ sing \ō\ go \ò\ law \òi\ boy \th\ thin \th\ the \ü\ loot \ù\ foot
\y\ yet \zh\ vision, beige \ḵ, ⁿ, œ, ᵫ, ᵛ\ *see* Guide to Pronunciation

Ca·vour \kə-'vûr, kä-\ **Con·te** \'kōn-(ˌ)tä\ Camillo Benso di 1810–1861 Ital. statesman

Ca·xi·as \kə-'shē-əs\ Du·que \'dü-kə\ de 1803–1880 *Luiz Alves de Lima e Silva* Braz. gen. & statesman

Cax·ton \'kak-stən\ William *ca* 1422–1491 1st Eng. printer

Ceau·şes·cu \chaù-'shes-(ˌ)kü\ Nicolae 1918–1989 pres. of Romania (1974–1989)

Cech \'chek\ Thomas Robert 1947–   Am. biochem.

Cec·il \'se-səl, 'si-\ (Edgar Algernon) Robert 1864–1958 1st Viscount *Cecil of Chel·wood* \'chel-ˌwùd\ Eng. statesman

Cecil Lord (Edward Christian) David 1902–1986 Eng. biographer

Cecil Robert 1563–1612 1st Earl of *Salisbury* & 1st Viscount *Cran·borne* \'kran-ˌbòrn\ Eng. statesman

Cecil Robert Arthur Talbot Gas·coyne– \'gas-ˌkòin\ 1830–1903 3d Marquis of *Salis·bury* \'sòlz-b(ə-)rē, 'sälz-\ Eng. statesman

Cecil William 1520–1598 1st Baron *Burgh·ley* or *Bur·leigh* \'bər-lē\ Eng. statesman

Ce·la \'sā-lə\ Camilo José 1916–2002 Span. writer

Cel·li·ni \chə-'lē-nē\ Ben·ve·nu·to \ˌben-və-'nü-(ˌ)tō\ 1500–1571 Ital. goldsmith & sculptor

Cel·sius \'sel-sē-əs, -shəs\ Anders 1701–1744 Swed. astron.

Cen·ci \'chen-(ˌ)chē\ Be·a·tri·ce \ˌbä-ä-'trē-(ˌ)chā\ 1577–1599 Ital. woman executed for parricide

Cer·van·tes \sər-'van-ˌtēz, -'vän-ˌtäs\ Miguel de 1547–1616 full surname *Cervantes Saa·ve·dra* \ˌsä-(ə-)'vä-drə\ Span. writer

Cé·zanne \sā-'zan\ Paul 1839–1906 Fr. painter — **Cé·zann·esque** \(ˌ)sā-ˌza-'nesk\ *adj*

Cha·bri·er \ˌshä-brē-'ā, ˌsha-\ (Alexis) Emmanuel 1841–1894 Fr. composer

Chad·wick \'chad-(ˌ)wik\ Sir James 1891–1974 Eng. physicist

Cha·gall \shə-'gäl, -'gal\ Marc 1887–1985 Russ. painter in France

Chag·a·tai \ˌcha-gə-'tī\ *d* 1241 *2d son of Genghis Khan* Mongol ruler

Chain \'chān\ Sir Ernst Boris 1906–1979 Brit. (Ger.-born) biochem.

Chal·fie \'chal-fē\ Martin 1947–   Am. biochem.

Cha·lia·pin \shəl-'yä-(ˌ)pēn, -pən\ Fyodor Ivanovich 1873–1938 Russ. basso

Chal·mers \'chal-mərz, 'chä-mərz\ Alexander 1759–1834 Scot. biographer & editor

Cham·ber·lain \'chām-bər-lən\ Joseph 1836–1914 & his sons Sir (Joseph) Austen 1863–1937 & (Arthur) Neville 1869–1940 Brit. statesmen

Chamberlain Wilton Norman 1936–1999 Am. basketball player

Cham·ber·lin \'chām-bər-lən\ Thomas Chrow·der \'kraù-dər\ 1843–1928 Am. geologist

Cham·bers \'chām-bərz\ Robert 1802–1871 Scot. publisher & editor

Cham·bord \shäⁿ-'bòr\ Comte de 1820–1883 *Henri-Charles-Ferdinand-Marie Dieudonné d'Artois* Duc de Bordeaux Bourbon claimant to Fr. throne

Cha·mor·ro \chä-'mór-rō\ Violeta Barrios de 1929–   pres. of Nicaragua (1990–97)

Cham·plain \sham-'plān, shäⁿ-'plaⁿ\ Samuel de *ca* 1567–1635 Fr. navigator, explorer, & founder of Quebec

Cham·pol·lion \shäⁿ-pól-'yōⁿ\ Jean-François 1790–1832 Fr. Egyptologist

Cham·pol·lion–Fi·geac \-fē-'zhäk\ Jacques-Joseph 1778–1867 *bro. of prec.* Fr. archaeol.

Chan·dler \'chan-(d)lər\ Raymond Thornton 1888–1959 Am. nov. & screenwriter

Chandragupta — see CANDRAGUPTA

Chandra Gupta II — see CANDRA GUPTA II

Chan·dra·se·khar \ˌchən-drə-'shä-kär\ Subrahmanyan 1910–1995 Am. (Indian-born) physicist

Cha·nel \shə-'nel, sha-\ Gabrielle 1883–1971 *Co·co* \'kō-(ˌ)kō\ *Chanel* Fr. fashion designer & perfumer

Chang Hsüeh–liang \'jäŋ-shù-'ä-lē-'äŋ\ 1898–2001 *son of Chang Tso-lin* Chin. gen.

Chang Tso–lin \-'(ˌ)tsō-'lin\ 1873–1928 Chin. gen.

Chan·ning \'cha-niŋ\ William Ellery 1780–1842 Am. clergyman

Chao K'uang–yin \'jaù-'kwäŋ-'yin\ 927–976 *T'ai Tsu* \'tīd-'zü\ Chin. emp. (960–976) & founder of Sung dynasty

Chap·lin \'cha-plən\ Sir Charles Spencer 1889–1977 *Charlie Chaplin* Brit. actor & director — **Chap·lin·esque** \ˌcha-plə-'nesk\ *adj*

Chap·man \'chap-mən\ Frank Mich·ler \'mi-klər\ 1864–1945 Am. ornithologist

Chapman George 1559?–1634 Eng. dram. & translator

Chapman John 1774–1845 *Johnny Ap·ple·seed* \'a-pəl-ˌsēd\ Am. pioneer

Char·cot \shär-'kō, 'shär-\ Jean-Mar·tin \'zhäⁿ-mär-'taⁿ\ 1825–1893 Fr. neurologist

Char·din \shär-'daⁿ\ Jean-Baptiste-Siméon 1699–1779 Fr. painter

Char·le·magne \'shär-lə-ˌmän\ 742–814 *Charles the Great* or *Charles I* Frankish king (768–814) & emp. of the West (800–814)

Charles \'chär(ˌ)lz\ 1948–   *son of Elizabeth II* prince of Wales

Charles 1771–1847 archduke of Austria

Charles Prince 1903–1983 *bro. of King Leopold* regent of Belgium (1944–50)

Charles I 1600–1649 *Charles Stuart* king of Great Britain (1625–49)

Charles I 1887–1922 *Charles Francis Joseph; nephew of Francis Ferdinand* emp. of Austria & (as *Charles IV*) king of Hungary (1916–18)

Charles I or II 823–877 *the Bald* king of France as *Charles I* (840–877); Holy Rom. emp. as *Charles II* (875–877)

Charles II 1630–1685 *son of Charles I* king of Great Britain (1660–85)

Charles IV 1294–1328 *the Fair* king of France (1322–28)

Charles V 1337–1380 *the Wise* king of France (1364–80)

Charles V 1500–1558 Holy Rom. emp. (1519–56); king of Spain as *Charles I* (1516–56)

Charles VI 1368–1422 *the Mad* or *the Beloved* king of France (1380–1422)

Charles VII 1403–1461 king of France (1422–61)

Charles IX 1550–1574 king of France (1560–74)

Charles X 1757–1836 king of France (1824–30)

Charles XII 1682–1718 king of Sweden (1697–1718)

Charles XIV John 1763–1844 orig. *Jean-Baptiste-Jules Ber·na·dotte* \ber-nà-dòt\ king of Sweden & Norway (1818–44)

Charles Edward 1720–1788 *the Young Pretender; (Bonnie) Prince Charlie* Brit. prince

Charles Mar·tel \-mär-'tel\ *ca* 688–741 *grandfather of Charlemagne* Frankish ruler (719–741)

Char·pak \shär-'päk\ Georges 1924–2010 Fr. (Pol.-born) physicist

Chase \'chäs\ Mary Ellen 1887–1973 Am. educ. & author

Chase Sal·mon \'sa-mən, 'sal-\ Portland 1808–1873 Am. statesman; chief justice U.S. Supreme Court (1864–73)

Cha·teau·bri·and \(ˌ)sha-ˌtō-brē-'äⁿ\ Vi·comte \vē-'kōⁿt\ François-Auguste-René de 1768–1848 Fr. author

Chatrian Alexandre — see ERCKMANN-CHATRIAN

Chat·ter·jee \'cha-tər-jē\ Ban·kim \'bòn-kim\ Chan·dra \'chən-(ˌ)drə\ 1838–1894 Indian nov.

Chat·ter·ton \'cha-tər-tən\ Thomas 1752–1770 Eng. poet

Chau·cer \'chò-sər\ Geoffrey *ca* 1342–1400 Eng. poet — **Chau·ce·ri·an** \chò-'sir-ē-ən\ *adj*

Chau·temps \shō-'täⁿ\ Camille 1885–1963 Fr. lawyer & polit.; premier (1930; 1933–34; 1937–38)

Chau·vin \shō-'vaⁿ\ Yves 1930–   Fr. chem.

Chavannes, de — see PUVIS DE CHAVANNES

Chá·vez \'chä-vəs, -ˌvez\ Carlos 1899–1978 Mex. composer

Chavez Cesar (Estrada) 1927–1993 Am. labor leader

Chá·vez (Frí·as) \'chä-ves-'frē-äs\ Hugo Rafael 1954–2013 pres. of Venezuela (1999–2013)

Chee·ver \'chē-vər\ John 1912–1982 Am. writer

Che·khov *also* **Che·kov** \'che-ˌkóf, -ˌkóv\ Anton Pavlovich 1860–1904 Russ. dram. & writer — **Che·kho·vi·an** \che-'kō-vē-ən\ *adj*

Che·ney \'chē-nē, *commonly* 'chā-\ Richard Bruce 1941–   Am. polit.; vice pres. of the U.S. (2001–09)

Ché·nier \shän-'yā\ André-Marie de 1762–1794 Fr. poet

Chen·nault \shə-'nòlt\ Claire Lee 1890–1958 Am. gen.

Cheops — see KHUFU

Che·ren·kov \chə-'reŋ-kəf\ Pavel Alekseyevich 1904–1990 Russ. physicist

Cher·nen·ko \cher-'nʸeŋ-kō\ Konstantin Ustinovich 1911–1985 Soviet polit.; pres. U.S.S.R. & 1st secy. of Communist party (1984–85)

Cher·ny·shev·sky \ˌcher-ni-'shef-skē, -'shev-\ Nikolay Gavrilovich 1829–1889 Russ. revolutionary & author

Cher·toff \'chər-ˌtóf\ Michael 1953–   U.S. secy. of homeland security (2005–09)

Che·ru·bi·ni \ˌker-ə-'bē-nē, ˌkä-rü-\ (Maria) Lu·i·gi \lü-'ē-(ˌ)jē\ Carlo Zenobio Salvatore 1760–1842 Ital. composer

Ches·ter·field \'ches-tər-ˌfēld\ 4th Earl of 1694–1773 *Philip Dormer Stan·hope* \'sta-nəp\ Eng. statesman & author

Ches·ter·ton \'ches-tər-tən\ Gilbert Keith 1874–1936 Eng. journalist & author — **Ches·ter·to·nian** \ˌches-tər-'tō-nē-ən, -nyən\ *adj*

Chiang Kai–shek \jē-'äŋ-'kī-'shek, ˌchaŋ-\ 1887–1975 Pinyin *Jiang Jieshī* \jē-'äŋ-jē-'ā-'shē\ Chin. gen. & polit.; pres. of China (1948–49; Taiwan, 1950–75)

Ch'ien–lung \chē-'en-'lùŋ\ 1711–1799 Chin. emp. (1736–96)

Chi·ka·ma·tsu \ˌchē-kə-'mät-(ˌ)sü\ Monzaemon 1653–1724 Jp. dram.

Child \'chī(-ə)ld\ Francis James 1825–1896 Am. ballad editor

Child Julia (Carolyn) 1912–2004 née *McWilliams* Am. chef

Childe \'chī(-ə)ld\ Vere Gordon 1892–1957 Brit. anthropol. & archaeol.

Chil·ders \'chil-dərz\ Erskine Hamilton 1905–1974 Irish (Eng.-born) polit.; pres. of Ireland (1973–74)

Chin·chi·lla (Mi·ran·da) \chēn-'chē-ä-mē-'rän-dä\ Laura 1959–   pres. of Costa Rica (2010–   )

Chip·pen·dale \'chi-pən-ˌdāl\ Thomas 1718–1779 Eng. cabinetmaker

Chi·rac \shē-'räk\ Jacques (René) 1932–   prime min. of France (1974–76; 1986–88); pres. (1995–2007)

Chi·ri·co, de \'kir-i-ˌkō, 'kē-ri-\ Gior·gio \'jòr-(ˌ)jō\ 1888–1978 Ital. painter

Choi·seul \shwä-'zəl, -'zər(-ə)l, -'zœl\ Étienne-François de 1719–1785 Duc de Choiseul Fr. statesman

Chom·sky \'chäm(p)-skē\ (Avram) Noam 1928–   Am. linguist — **Chom·sky·an** *also* **Chom·ski·an** \-skē-ən\ *adj*

Cho·pin \'shō-ˌpan, -ˌpaⁿ\ Frédéric François 1810–1849 orig. *Fryderyk Franciszek Chopin* Pol. pianist & composer

Cho·pin \'shō-ˌpan, shō-'\ Kate 1851–1904 orig. *Katherine O'Flaherty* Am. writer

Chou En–lai \'jō-'en-'lī\ 1898–1976 Pinyin *Zhou Enlai* Chin. Communist polit.; premier (1949–76)

Chré·tien \krā-'tyaⁿ\ (Joseph Jacques) Jean 1934–   prime min. of Canada (1993–2003)

Chré·tien de Troyes \krā-tyaⁿ-də-'trwä\ *fl* 1170 Fr. trouvère

Christ Jesus — see JESUS

Chris·tian X \'kris-chən, 'krish-\ 1870–1947 king of Denmark (1912–47)

Chris·tie \'kris-tē\ Dame Agatha 1890–1976 née *Miller* Eng. writer

Chris·ti·na \kris-'tē-nə\ 1626–1689 *dau. of Gustav II Adolphus* queen of Sweden (1632–54)

Chris·tine de Pi·san \krēs-tēn-də-pē-'zäⁿ\ 1364–*ca* 1430 Fr. poet

Chris·to \'kris-tō\ 1935–   *in full Christo Javacheff* Am. (Bulg.-born) artist

Chris·tophe \krē-'stóf\ Henri 1767–1820 king of Haiti (1811–20)

Chris·to·pher \'kris-tə-fər\ Warren Minor 1925–2011 U.S. secy. of state (1993–97)

Chris·ty \'kris-tē\ Howard Chandler 1873–1952 Am. artist

Chrys·ler \'krīs-lər\ Walter (Percy) 1875–1940 Am. auto manuf.

Chry·sos·tom \'kri-səs-təm, kri-'säs-təm\ Saint John *ca* 347–407 church father & patriarch of Constantinople

Chu \'chü\ Steven 1948–   Am. physicist; U.S. secy. of energy (2009–13)

Chu Hsi \'jü-'shē\ 1130–1200 Chin. philos.

Chun Doo–Hwan \'jùn-'dō-'hwän\ 1931–   pres. of So. Korea (1980–88)

Church \'chərch\ Frederic Edwin 1826–1900 Am. painter

Chur·chill \'chər-ˌchil, 'chərch-ˌhil\ John 1650–1722 1st Duke of *Marl·bor·ough* \'märl-ˌbər-ə, 'mòl-, -ˌbə-rə, -b(ə-)rə\ Eng. gen.

Churchill Randolph Henry Spencer 1849–1895 Lord *Randolph Churchill* Brit. statesman

Churchill Sir Winston Leonard Spencer 1874–1965 *son of Lord Randolph* Brit. statesman; prime min. (1940–45; 1951–55) — **Chur·chill·ian** \ˌchər-'chi-lē-ən, 'chərch-'hi-\ *adj*

Chu Teh \'jü-'də\ 1886–1976 Chin. gen.

Cia·no \'chä-(ˌ)nō\ Galeazzo 1903–1944 Conte *di Cortellazzo* Ital. statesman

Ciar·di \'chär-dē\ John 1916–1986 Am. poet

Cib·ber \'si-bər\ Col·ley \'kä-lē\ 1671–1757 Eng. dram. & actor; poet laureate (1730–57)

Cic·ero \'si-sə-ˌrō\ Marcus Tullius 106–43 B.C. Rom. statesman, orator, & author — **Cic·ero·nian** \ˌsi-sə-'rō-nyən, -nē-ən\ *adj*

Cid, El \'sid\ *ca* 1043–1099 *Rodrigo Dí·az de Vi·var* \'dē-ˌäs-də-vē-'vär, -ˌäz-\ Span. soldier & hero

Cie·cha·no·ver \chə-'kä-nə-vər\ Aaron 1947– Israeli biol.

Çil·ler \chi-'ler\ Tan·su \tän-'sü\ 1946– prime min. of Turkey (1993–96)

Ci·ma·bue \ˌchē-mə-'bü-(ˌ)ā\ Giovanni *ca* 1251–1302 orig. *Bencivieni di Pepo* Florentine painter

Ci·mon \'sī-mən, -ˌmän\ *ca* 570–*ca* 451 B.C. Athenian gen. & statesman

Cin·cin·na·tus \ˌsin(t)-sə-'na-təs, -'nä-\ Lucius Quinctius *b ca* 519 B.C. Rom. gen. & statesman

Clare \'kler\ John 1793–1864 Eng. poet

Clarendon Earl of — see Edward HYDE

Clare of Assisi Saint 1194–1253 Ital. religious

Clark \'klärk\ Champ \'champ\ 1850–1921 *James Beau·champ* \'bē-chəm\ *Clark* Am. polit.

Clark George Rogers 1752–1818 Am. soldier & frontiersman

Clark Helen (Elizabeth) 1950– prime min. of New Zealand (1999–2008)

Clark Joe 1939– *Charles Joseph Clark* Canad. polit.; prime min. (1979–80)

Clark Kenneth B(ancroft) 1914–2005 Am. psychol.

Clark Kenneth Mackenzie 1903–1983 Baron *Clark of Saltwood* Brit. art hist.

Clark Mark Wayne 1896–1984 Am. gen.

Clark Tom Campbell 1899–1977 Am. jurist

Clark William 1770–1838 *bro. of G.R.* Am. explorer

Clarke \'klärk\ Sir Arthur C(harles) 1917–2008 Brit. author

Clarke Charles Cow·den \'kaü-dᵊn\ 1787–1877 & his wife Mary Victoria Cowden-Clarke 1809–1898 Eng. Shakespearean scholars

Claude Lor·rain \klōd-lò-'raⁿ\ 1600–1682 pseud. of *Claude Gel·lée* \zhə-'lā\ Fr. painter

Clau·di·us \'klö-dē-əs\ Rom. gens including: **Ap·pi·us** \'a-pē-əs\ **Claudius Cras·sus** \'kra-səs\ consul (471 & 451 B.C.) & decemvir (451–450 B.C.); **Appius Claudius Cae·cus** \'sē-kəs\ censor (312–307 B.C.), consul (307 & 296 B.C.), & dictator

Claudius I 10 B.C.–A.D. 54 *Tiberius Claudius Drusus Ne·ro* \'nē-(ˌ)rō, 'nir-(ˌ)ō\ *Germanicus* Rom. emp. (41–54)

Claudius II A.D. 214–270 *Marcus Aurelius Claudius Gothicus* Rom. emp. (268–270)

Clau·se·witz \'klaü-zə-ˌvits\ Carl von 1780–1831 Pruss. gen. & military strategist — **Clau·se·witz·ian** \ˌklaü-zə-'vit-sē-ən\ *adj*

Clay \'klā\ Henry 1777–1852 Am. statesman & orator

Clay Lucius Du Bi·gnon \dü-'bin-yən\ 1897–1978 Am. gen.

Cle·an·thes \klē-'an-ˌthēz\ *ca* 331–*ca* 232 B.C. Greek Stoic philos.

Cle·ar·chus \klē-'är-kəs\ 5th cent. B.C. Greek soldier; gov. of Byzantium

Cleis·the·nes \'klīs-thə-ˌnēz\ *or* **Clis·the·nes** \'klis-\ *ca* 570–after 508 B.C. Athenian statesman

Cle·men·ceau \ˌkle-mən-'sō, klä-mäⁿ-'sō\ Georges 1841–1929 Fr. statesman; prime min. (1906–09, 1917–20)

Clem·ens \'kle-mənz\ Samuel Langhorne 1835–1910 pseud. *Mark Twain* \'twān\ Am. writer

Clem·ent \'kle-mənt\ name of 14 popes: esp. **VII** (*Giulio de'Me·di·ci* \'me-də-(ˌ)chē\) 1478–1534 (pope 1523–34)

Cle·men·te (Walker) \klə-'men-tā\ Roberto 1934–1972 Am. baseball player

Cle·men·ti \klə-'men-tē\ Muzio 1752–1832 Ital. pianist & composer in England

Clement of Alexandria Saint *ca* 150–between 211 & 215 *Titus Flavius Cle·mens* \'kle-ˌmenz\ Greek Christian theol. & church father

Cle·om·e·nes \klē-'ä-mə-ˌnēz\ name of 3 kings of Sparta: esp. **III** (reigned 235–222 B.C.)

Cle·o·pa·tra \ˌklē-ə-'pa-trə, -'pä-\ 69–30 B.C. queen of Egypt (51–30)

Cleve·land \'klēv-lənd\ (Stephen) Grover 1837–1908 22d & 24th pres. of the U.S. (1885–89; 1893–97)

Cli·burn \'klī-bərn\ Van 1934–2013 *Harvey Lavan Cliburn* Am. pianist

Clin·ton George 1739–1812 vice pres. of the U.S. (1805–12)

Clinton Sir Henry 1738–1795 Eng. gen. in America

Clinton Hillary Rodham 1947– *née Rodham, wife of W.J.* Am. polit.; U.S. secy. of state (2009–13)

Clinton William J(efferson) 1946– Am. polit.; 42d pres. of the U.S. (1993–2001)

Clive \'klīv\ Robert 1725–1774 Baron *Clive of Plassey* Brit. gen. & founder of the empire of Brit. India

Cloots \'klōts\ Baron de 1755–1794 *Jean-Baptiste du Val-de-Grâce;* known as *An·a·char·sis* \ˌa-nə-'kär-səs\ *Cloots* Pruss.-Fr. revolutionary

Close \'klōz, *commonly* 'klōs\ Chuck 1940– *Charles Thomas Close* Am. painter

Clough \'kləf\ Arthur Hugh 1819–1861 Eng. poet

Clo·vis I \'klō-vəs\ *G* **Chlod·wig** \'klöt-(ˌ)vik\ *ca* 466–511 king of the Salian Franks (481–511)

Coase \'kōz\ Ronald H(arry) 1910–2013 Am. (Brit.-born) econ.

Coates \'kōts\ Joseph Gordon 1878–1943 N.Z. statesman

Cobb \'käb\ Tyrus Raymond 1886–1961 *Ty* Am. baseball player

Cob·bett \'kä-bət\ William 1763–1835 pseud. *Peter Porcupine* Eng. polit. writer

Cob·den \'käb-dən\ Richard 1804–1865 Eng. statesman & econ.

Cobham Lord — see Sir John OLDCASTLE

Co·chise \kō-'chēs\ 1812?–1874 Chiricahua Apache Indian chief

Cock·croft \'kä(k)-ˌkröft\ Sir John Douglas 1897–1967 Brit. physicist

Coc·teau \kök-'tō\ Jean 1889–1963 Fr. author & artist

Co·dy \'kō-dē\ William Frederick 1846–1917 *Buffalo Bill* Am. scout & showman

Coen \'kün\ Jan Pieterszoon 1587–1629 Du. colonial gov. & founder of Du. East Indian empire

Coet·zee \kùt-'sē, -'siə\ J(ohn) M(axwell) 1940– So. African writer

Coeur de Lion — see RICHARD I of England

Cog·gan \'kä-gən\ Frederick Donald 1909–2000 archbishop of Canterbury (1974–80)

Co·han \'kō-ˌhan\ George Michael 1878–1942 Am. actor, dram., & producer

Co·hen \'kō-ən\ Stanley 1922– Am. biochem.

Co·hen–Tan·nou·dji \ˌkō-en-'tä-nü-jē\ Claude 1933– Fr. (Algerian-born) physicist

Cohn \'kōn\ Ferdinand Julius 1828–1898 Ger. botanist

Coke \'kùk, 'kōk\ Sir Edward 1552–1634 *Lord Coke* Eng. jurist

Col·bert \kòl-'ber, 'kòl-ˌ\ Jean-Baptiste 1619–1683 Fr. statesman & financier

Cole \'kōl\ Thomas 1801–1848 Am. (Eng.-born) painter

Cole·pep·er *or* **Cul·pep·er** \'kəl-ˌpe-pər\ Thomas 1635–1689 2d Baron *Colepeper* Eng. colonial administrator; gov. of Virginia

Cole·ridge \'kōl-rij, 'kō-lə-rij\ Samuel Taylor 1772–1834 Eng. poet — **Cole·ridge·an** *also* **Cole·ridg·ian** \ˌkōl-'ri-jē-ən, ˌkō-lə-\ *adj*

Col·et \'kä-lət\ John 1466(or 1467)–1519 Eng. theol. & scholar

Co·lette \kò-'let\ Sidonie-Gabrielle 1873–1954 Fr. author

Col·fax \'kōl-ˌfaks\ Schuy·ler \'skī-lər\ 1823–1885 vice pres. of the U.S. (1869–73)

Co·li·gny \ˌkò-lēn-'yē, kə-'lēn-yē\ Gaspard II de 1519–1572 *Seigneur de Châtillon* Fr. admiral & Huguenot leader

Col·lier \'käl-yər, 'kä-lē-ər\ Jeremy 1650–1726 Eng. clergyman

Collier John Payne 1789–1883 Eng. editor

Collier Peter Fen·e·lon \'fe-nə-lən\ 1849–1909 Am. publisher

Col·lins \'kä-lənz\ Billy 1941– *William Collins* Am. poet; poet laureate (2001–03)

Collins Francis S(ellers) 1950– Am. geneticist

Collins Michael 1890–1922 Irish revolutionary

Collins Michael 1930– Am. astronaut

Collins William 1721–1759 Eng. poet

Collins (William) Wilkie 1824–1889 Eng. nov.

Col·lor de Mel·lo \kō-'lòr-də-'me-lü\ Fernando Affonso 1949– pres. of Brazil (1990–92)

Col·man \'kōl-mən\ George 1732–1794 Eng. dram.

Col·trane \'kōl-trān\ John William 1926–1967 Am. jazz musician

Col·um \'kä-ləm\ Pad·raic \'pòth-rig\ 1881–1972 Am. (Irish-born) writer

Co·lum·ba \kə-'ləm-bə\ *Ir* **Col·um** \'kə-ləm\ *or* **Col·um·cille** \'kä-ləm-ˌkil\ Saint *ca* 521–597 Irish missionary in Scotland

Co·lum·bus \kə-'ləm-bəs\ Christopher *It* Christoforo **Co·lom·bo** \kə-'ləm-(ˌ)bō\ *Sp* Cristóbal **Co·lón** \kə-'lōn\ 1451–1506 Genoese navigator & explorer for Spain

Co·me·ni·us \kə-'mē-nē-əs\ John Amos *Czech* Jan Ámos **Ko·men·ský** \'kò-mən-skē\ 1592–1670 Czech theol. & educ.

Com·ma·ger \'kä-mi-jər\ Henry Steele 1902–1998 Am. hist.

Com·mo·dus \'kä-mə-dəs\ Lucius Aelius Aurelius A.D. 161–192 Rom. emp. (180–192)

Com·mo·ner \'kä-mə-nər\ Barry 1917–2012 Am. biol. & educ.

Com·mynes *or* **Co·mines** *or* **Com·mines** \kò-'mēn\ Philippe de *ca* 1447–1511 Fr. polit. & chronicler

Comp·ton \'käm(p)-tən\ Arthur Holly 1892–1962 Am. physicist

Compton Karl Taylor 1887–1954 *bro. of A.H.* Am. physicist

Com·stock \'käm-ˌstäk *also* 'kəm-\ Anthony 1844–1915 Am. reformer

Comte \'kōⁿt\ Auguste 1798–1857 in full *Isidore-Auguste-Marie-François-Xavier* Fr. sociologist & philos.

Conan Doyle — see DOYLE

Co·nant \'kō-nənt\ James Bryant 1893–1978 Am. chem. & educ.

Con·dé \kōⁿ-'dā\ Prince de 1621–1686 *Louis II de Bour·bon* \'bùr-bən, bùr-'bōⁿ\; Duc *d'En·ghien* \däⁿ-'gaⁿ\ Fr. gen.

Con·don \'kän-dən\ Edward Uhler 1902–1974 Am. physicist

Con·dor·cet \kōⁿ-dòr-'sā\ Marquis de 1743–1794 *Marie-Jean-Antoine-Nicholas de Ca·ri·tat* \ˌka-rə-'tä\ Fr. philos. & polit.

Con·fu·cius \kən-'fyü-shəs\ *Chin* **K'ung–Fu–tzu** \'kùŋ-'fü-'dzü\ *or* **K'ung–tzu** \kùŋ-'dzü\ 551–479 B.C. Chin. philos.

Con·greve \'kän-ˌgrēv, 'käŋ-\ William 1670–1729 Eng. dram.

Con·rad \'kän-ˌrad\ Joseph 1857–1924 orig. *Józef Teodor Konrad Korze·niow·ski* \ˌkò-zhən-'yòf-skē, -'yòv-\ Brit. (Ukrainian-born of Pol. parents) nov. — **Con·rad·ian** \ˌkän-'ra-dē-ən\ *adj*

Con·sta·ble \'kən(t)-stə-bəl, 'kän(t)-\ John 1776–1837 Eng. painter

Cons·tant de Re·becque \kōⁿ-'stäⁿ-də-rə-'bek\ Benjamin 1767–1830 Fr. writer & polit.

Con·stan·tine \'kän(t)-stən-ˌtēn, -ˌtīn\ name of 2 kings of Greece: **I** 1868–1923 (reigned 1913–17; 1920–22); **II** 1940– (reigned 1964–73; deposed)

Constantine I *d* 337 *the Great* Rom. emp. (306–337) — **Con·stan·tin·ian** \ˌkän(t)s-tən-'ti-nē-ən\ *adj*

Con·ta·ri·ni \ˌkän-tə-'rē-nē\ Venetian family including esp. Gasparo 1483–1542 cardinal & diplomat

Con·ti \'kōn-tē, 'kän-\ Niccolò de' *ca* 1395–1469 Venetian traveler

Cook \'kùk\ James 1728–1779 Eng. navigator & explorer

Cooke \'kùk\ Sir (Alfred) Al·is·tair \'a-lə-stər\ 1908–2004 Am. (Brit.-born) essayist & journalist

Cooke Terence James 1921–1983 Am. cardinal

Coo·lidge \'kü-lij\ (John) Calvin 1872–1933 30th pres. of the U.S. (1923–29)

Cooper Anthony Ashley — see SHAFTESBURY

Coo·per \'kü-pər, 'kù-\ James Fen·i·more \'fen-ə-ˌmòr\ 1789–1851 Am. nov.

Cooper Leon Neil 1930– Am. physicist

Cooper Peter 1791–1883 Am. manufacturer & philanthropist

Co·per·ni·cus \kō-'pər-ni-kəs\ Nicolaus *Pol* Mikołaj **Ko·per·nik** \kò-'per-nēk\ *or* Niklas **Ko·per·nigk** \'kä-pər-ˌnik\ 1473–1543 Pol. astron.

Cop·land \'kō-plənd\ Aaron 1900–1990 Am. composer

\ə\ abut \ᵊ\ kitten, F table \ər\ further \a\ ash \ā\ ace \ä\ mop, mar
\aù\ out \ch\ chin \e\ bet \ē\ easy \g\ go \i\ hit \ī\ ice \j\ job
\ŋ\ sing \ō\ go \ò\ law \òi\ boy \th\ thin \t̲h̲\ the \ü\ loot \ù\ foot
\y\ yet \zh\ vision, beige \k̲, ⁿ, œ, ɶ, ᵉ\ *see* Guide to Pronunciation

Cop·ley \'kä-plē\ John Sin·gle·ton \'siŋ-gəl-tən\ 1738–1815 Am. portrait painter

Co·que·lin \ˌkôk-'laⁿ, ˌkȯ-kə-\ Benoît-Constant 1841–1909 Fr. actor

Cor·bu·sier, Le \lə-ˌkȯr-büs-'yā\ 1887–1965 orig. *Charles-Édouard Jean·ne·ret* \zhän-'re\ Fr. (Swiss-born) architect, painter, & sculptor

Cor·day \kȯr-'dä, 'kȯr-\ Charlotte 1768–1793 *Marie-Anne-Charlotte Corday d'Ar·mont* \där-'mōⁿ\ Fr. patriot

Co·rel·li \kə-'re-lē\ Arcangelo 1653–1713 Ital. violinist & composer

Co·rey \'kȯr-ē\ Elias James 1928–   Am. chem.

Co·ri \'kȯr-ē\ Carl Ferdinand 1896–1984 & his wife Ger·ty \'ger-tē\ Theresa 1896–1957 née *Rad·nitz* \'räd-ˌnits\ Am. (Czech-born) biochemists

Cor·neille \kȯr-'nā\ Pierre 1606–1684 Fr. dram.

Cor·ne·lia \kȯr-'nēl-yə, -'nē-lē-ə\ 2d cent. B.C. *Mother of the Gracchi* Rom. matron

Cornelia d 67? B.C. *wife of Julius Caesar*

Cor·ne·lius \kȯr-'nāl-yəs, -'nā-lē-əs\ Pe·ter \'pā-tər\ von 1783–1867 Ger. painter

Cor·nell \kȯr-'nel\ Eric Allin 1961–   Am. physicist

Cornell Ezra 1807–1874 Am. financier & philanthropist

Cornell Joseph 1903–1972 Am. artist

Cornell Katharine 1893–1974 Am. actress

Corn·wal·lis \kȯrn-'wä-ləs\ 1st Marquis 1738–1805 *Charles Cornwallis* Brit. gen. & statesman

Co·ro·na·do \ˌkȯr-ə-'nä-(ˌ)dō, ˌkär-\ Francisco Vásquez de *ca* 1510–1554 Span. explorer & conquistador

Co·rot \kə-'rō, kȯ-\ (Jean-Baptiste-) Camille 1796–1875 Fr. painter

Cor·reg·gio \kə-'re-j(ē-ˌ)ō\ 1494–1534 *Antonio Allegri da Correggio* Ital. painter

Cor·tés \kȯr-'tez, 'kȯr-ˌ\ Hernán *or* Hernando 1485–1547 Span. conquistador

Cos·by \'käz-bē\ Bill 1937–   *William Henry Cosby, Jr.* Am. comedian

Cos·grave \'käz-ˌgräv\ Liam 1920–   prime min. of Ireland (1973–77)

Cosgrave William Thomas 1880–1965 *father of prec.* Irish statesman

Cos·ta Ca·bral \ˌkȯsh-tə-kə-'bräl, ˌkȯs-\ António Bernardo da 1803–1889 Conde *de Thomar* Port. statesman

Cos·tel·lo \käs-tə-ˌlō\ John Aloysius 1891–1976 prime min. of Ireland (1948–51; 1954–57)

Cot·ton \'kä-tⁿn\ Charles 1630–1687 Eng. author & translator

Cotton John 1585–1652 Am. (Eng.-born) Puritan clergyman

Co·ty \kȯ-'tē, kō-\ René (-Jules-Gustave) 1882–1962 Fr. lawyer; 2d pres. of Fourth Republic (1954–59)

Cou·lomb \kü-'lōⁿ; 'kü-ˌläm, -ˌlōm, kü-'\ Charles-Augustin de 1736–1806 Fr. physicist

Cou·pe·rin \ˌkü-'praⁿ, ˌkü-pə-'raⁿ\ François 1668–1733 Fr. composer

Cou·pe·rus \kü-'pā-rəs, -'per-əs\ Louis Marie Anne 1863–1923 Du. nov.

Cour·bet \kùr-'bā\ Gustave 1819–1877 Fr. painter

Cou·sin \kü-'zaⁿ\ Victor 1792–1867 Fr. philos.

Cous·ins \'kə-zⁿnz\ Norman 1912–1990 Am. editor & essayist

Cous·teau \kü-'stō\ Jacques-Yves 1910–1997 Fr. marine explorer

Co·var·ru·bias \ˌkō-və-'rü-bē-əs\ Miguel 1904–1957 Mex. artist

Cov·er·dale \'kə-vər-ˌdāl\ Miles 1488?–1569 Eng. Bible translator

Cow·ard \kaú(-ə)rd\ Sir Noël Peirce 1899–1973 Eng. actor & dram.

Cow·ell \kaú(-ə)l\ Henry Dixon 1887–1965 Am. composer

Cow·en \kaú-ən\ Brian 1960–   prime min. of Ireland (2008–11)

Cowl \'kaú(-ə)l\ Jane 1883–1950 orig. *Grace Bailey* Am. actress

Cow·ley \kaú-lē\ Abraham 1618–1667 Eng. poet

Cowley Malcolm 1898–1989 Am. lit. critic

Cow·per \'kü-pər, 'kü-, 'kaú\ William 1731–1800 Eng. poet

Cox·ey \'käk-sē\ Jacob Sechler 1854–1951 Am. polit. reformer

Coz·zens \'kə-zⁿnz\ James Gould 1903–1978 Am. author

Crabbe \'krab\ George 1754–1832 Eng. poet

Craig·av·on \krā-'ga-vən\ 1st Viscount 1871–1940 *James Craig* Brit. statesman; 1st prime min. of Northern Ireland (1921–40)

Crai·gie \'krā-gē\ Sir William Alexander 1867–1957 Brit. philologist & lexicographer

Cram \'kram\ Donald James 1919–2001 Am. chem.

Cram Ralph Adams 1863–1942 Am. architect & author

Cra·nach \'krä-ˌnäk\ Lucas 1472–1553 Ger. painter & engraver

Crane \'krān\ (Harold) Hart 1899–1932 Am. poet

Crane Stephen 1871–1900 Am. writer

Crane Walter 1845–1915 Eng. artist

Cran·mer \'kran-mər\ Thomas 1489–1556 Eng. reformer; archbishop of Canterbury (1533–56)

Cras·sus \'kra-səs\ Marcus Licinius 115?–53 B.C. *Di·ves* \'dī-(ˌ)vēz\ Rom. polit.

Cray \'krā\ Seymour R. 1925–1996 Am. computer scientist

Crazy Horse \'krā-zē-ˌhȯrs\ 1842–1877 *Ta-sunko-witko or Tashunca= Uitco* Sioux Indian chief

Cré·bil·lon \krā-bē-'yōⁿ\ 1674–1762 pseud. of *Prosper Jolyot* Fr. dram.

Cres·ton \'kres-tən\ Paul 1906–1985 orig. *Giuseppe Guttoveggio* Am. composer

Crève·coeur \krev-'kər, krēv-, -'kùr\ Michel-Guillaume-Jean de 1735–1813 pseud. *J. Hector St. John* Am. (Fr.-born) essayist

Crich·ton \'krī-tⁿn\ James 1560–1582 *the Admirable Crichton* Scot. man of letters

Crick \'krik\ Francis Harry Compton 1916–2004 Brit. biophysicist

Crile \'krī(-ə)l\ George Washington 1864–1943 Am. surgeon

Cripps \'krips\ Sir (Richard) Stafford 1889–1952 Brit. statesman

Cri·spi \'krēs-pē, 'krēs-\ Francesco 1819–1901 Ital. statesman; premier (1887–91; 1893–96)

Cris·ti·ani \ˌkris-tē-'ä-nē\ Alfredo 1947–   pres. of El Salvador (1989–94)

Cro·ce \'krō-(ˌ)chä\ Benedetto 1866–1952 Ital. philos. & statesman

Crock·ett \'krä-kət\ David 1786–1836 *Davy* Am. frontiersman & polit.

Croe·sus \'krē-səs\ *d ca* 546 B.C. king of Lydia (*ca* 560–546)

Cro·ker \'krō-kər\ John Wilson 1780–1857 Brit. essayist & editor

Cromp·ton \'kräm(p)-tən\ Samuel 1753–1827 Eng. inventor

Crom·well \'kräm-ˌwel, 'krȯm-, -wəl\ Oliver 1599–1658 Eng. gen. & statesman; lord protector of England (1653–58) — **Crom·well·ian** \kräm-'we-lē-ən, ˌkrȯm-\ *adj*

Cromwell Richard 1626–1712 *son of Oliver* lord protector (1658–59)

Cromwell Thomas 1485?–1540 Earl of *Essex* Eng. statesman

Cro·nin \'krō-nən\ Archibald Joseph 1896–1981 Eng. physician & nov.

Cron·jé \krȯn-'yä\ Piet Arnoldus *ca* 1835–1911 Boer leader & gen.

Cron·kite \'kräŋ-ˌkīt, 'krän-\ Walter 1916–2009 *Walter Leland Cronkite, Jr.* Am. journalist

Crookes \'krùks\ Sir William 1832–1919 Eng. physicist & chem.

Cros·by \'kräz-bē, 'krȯz-\ Bing 1904–1977 orig. *Harry Lillis Crosby* Am. singer & actor

Cross \'krȯs\ Wilbur Lucius 1862–1948 Am. educ. & polit.

Crouse \'kraùs\ Russel 1893–1966 Am. journalist & dram.

Cru·den \'krü-dⁿn\ Alexander 1701–1770 Scot. compiler of a biblical concordance

Cruik·shank \'krùk-ˌshaŋk\ George 1792–1878 Eng. caricaturist & illustrator

Crumb \'krəm\ George Henry 1929–   Am. composer

Crut·zen \'krət-sən, 'kruet-\ Paul J(osef) 1933–   Du. chem.

Cruz \'krüs\ Juana Inés de la 1651–1695 orig. *Juana Inés de Asbaje* Mex. religious & poet

Cud·worth \'kəd-(ˌ)wərth\ Ralph 1617–1688 Eng. philos.

Cu·kor \'kyü-kər\ George (Dewey) 1899–1983 Am. film director

Culpeper *var of* COLEPEPER

Cum·mings \'kə-miŋz\ Edward Estlin 1894–1962 known as *e. e. cummings* Am. poet

Cu·nha \'kün-yə\ Tris·tão da \ˌtris-tən-də-'kü-nə, trēsh-ˌtaúⁿ-də-'kün-yə, trēs-\ 1460–1540 Port. navigator & explorer

Cun·ning·ham \'kə-niŋ-ˌham, *chiefly Brit* -niŋ-əm\ Allan 1784–1842 Scot. author

Cunningham Merce 1919–2009 Am. choreographer

Cu·rie \kyù-'rē, 'kyùr-(ˌ)ē\ Eve 1904–2007 *dau. of Marie & Pierre* Am. (Fr.-born) author

Curie Marie 1867–1934 née *Maria Skło·dow·ska* \skłə-'dȯf-skə, -'dȯv-\ Fr. (Pol.-born) chem.

Curie Pierre 1859–1906 *husband of Marie* Fr. chem.

Curl \'kər(-ə)l\ Robert Floyd 1933–   Am. chem.

Cur·ley \'kər-lē\ James Michael 1874–1958 Am. polit.

Cur·ri·er \'kər-ē-ər, 'kə-rē-\ Nathaniel 1813–1888 Am. lithographer

Cur·ry \'kər-ē, 'kə-rē\ John Steuart 1897–1946 Am. painter

Cur·tin \'kər-tⁿn\ John 1885–1945 Austral. prime min. (1941–45)

Cur·tis \'kər-təs\ Charles 1860–1936 vice pres. of the U.S. (1929–33)

Curtis Cyrus (Hermann Kotzschmar) 1850–1933 Am. publisher

Curtis George William 1824–1892 Am. author & editor

Cur·tiss \'kər-təs\ Glenn Hammond 1878–1930 Am. aviator & inventor

Cur·ti·us \'kùrt-sē-əs\ Ernst 1814–1896 Ger. hist. & archaeol.

Cur·tiz \kər-'tēz\ Michael 1888–1962 orig. *Mi·haly Ker·tész* \'mē-hī-'ker-tes\ Am. (Hung.-born) film director

Cur·zon \'kər-zⁿn\ George Nathaniel 1859–1925 1st Baron & 1st Marquis *Curzon of Ked·le·ston* \'ke-dⁿl-stən\ Eng. statesman; viceroy of India (1899–1905)

Cush·ing \'kù-shiŋ\ Harvey 1869–1939 Am. surgeon

Cushing Richard James 1895–1970 Am. cardinal

Cush·man \'kùsh-mən\ Charlotte Saunders 1816–1876 Am. actress

Cus·ter \'kəs-tər\ George Armstrong 1839–1876 Am. gen.

Cuth·bert \'kəth-bərt\ Saint 635?–687 Eng. monk

Cu·vier \'kü-vē-ˌā, 'kyü-, kue-'vyā\ Baron Georges 1769–1832 orig. *Jean-Léopold-Nicolas-Frédéric Cuvier* Fr. naturalist

Cuyp *or* **Cuijp** \'kīp\ Aelbert Jacobsz 1620–1691 Du. painter

Cyn·e·wulf \'ki-nə-ˌwùlf\ *or* **Cyn·wulf** \'kin-ˌwùlf\ 9th cent. Anglo-Saxon poet

Cyp·ri·an \'si-prē-ən\ Saint *d* 258 *Thascius Caecilius Cyprianus* Christian martyr; bishop of Carthage (*ca* 248–258)

Cy·ran·kie·wicz \ˌ(t)sir-ən-'kyä-vich\ Józef 1911–1989 Pol. polit.; prime min. (1947–52; 1954–70)

Cy·ra·no de Ber·ge·rac \'sir-ə-ˌnō-də-'ber-zhə-ˌrak\ Savinien de 1619–1655 Fr. poet & soldier

Cyr·il \'sir-əl\ Saint *ca* 827–869 *Constantine* apostle to the Slavs

Cy·rus \'sī-rəs\ 424?–401 B.C. *the Younger* Persian prince & satrap

Cyrus II *ca* 585–*ca* 529 B.C. *the Great or the Elder* king of Persia (*ca* 550–529)

Czer·ny \'cher-nē, 'chər-\ Carl 1791–1857 Austrian pianist & composer

D' \d\ **De** \də, di; *in Dutch names* dē\ **Du** \dü, dyü, də\, etc. for many names beginning with these elements see the specific family names

Da·guerre \də-'ger\ Louis (-Jacques-Mandé) 1789–1851 Fr. painter & inventor

Dahl \'däl\ Roald 1916–1990 Brit. writer

Daim·ler \'dīm-lər\ Gottlieb Wilhelm 1834–1900 Ger. automotive manuf.

Da·kin \'dä-kən\ Henry Drysdale 1880–1952 Eng. chem.

Da·la·dier \ˌdä-lä-dē-ˌā, ˌdä-lə-'dyä\ Édouard 1884–1970 Fr. statesman

Da·lai La·ma \'dä-ˌlī-'lä-mə\ 1935–   *Tenzin Gyatso* Tibetan religious & political leader

D'Al·bert \'dal-bərt\ Eugen Francis Charles 1864–1932 Ger. (Scot.-born) pianist & composer

Dalcroze Émile Jaques — see Émile JAQUES-DALCROZE

Dale \'dāl\ Sir Henry Hallett 1875–1968 Eng. physiol.

Dale Sir Thomas *d* 1619 Eng. colonial administrator in Virginia

Da·lén \də-'län\ Nils Gustaf 1869–1937 Swed. inventor

Da·ley \'dä-lē\ Richard Joseph 1902–1976 & his son Richard Michael 1942–   Am. polits.

Dalhousie Earl & Marquis of — see RAMSAY

Da·li \'dä-lē, *by himself* dä-'lē\ Salvador 1904–1989 Span. surrealistic painter — **Da·li·esque** \ˌdä-lē-'esk\ *adj*

Dal·las \'da-ləs, -lis\ George Mifflin 1792–1864 vice pres. of the U.S. (1845–49)

Dal·rym·ple \dal-'rim-pəl, 'dal-ˌ\ Sir James 1619–1695 1st Viscount *Stair* \'ster\ Scot. jurist

Dal·ton \'dȯl-tⁿn\ John 1766–1844 Eng. chem. & physicist

Da·ly \'dä-lē\ (John) Augustin 1838–1899 Am. dram. & theater manager

Dam \'dam, 'däm\ (Carl Peter) Henrik 1895–1976 Dan. biochem.

Da·mien \'dä-mē-ən, ˌdä-mē-'aⁿ\ Father 1840–1889 orig. *Joseph de Veuster* Belg. R.C. missionary in Hawaiian Islands

Dam·pi·er \\'dam-pē-ər\ William 1652–1715 Eng. buccaneer & navigator
Dam·rosch \\'dam-ˌräsh\ Walter Johannes 1862–1950 Am. (Ger.-born) musician & conductor
Da·na \\'dā-nə\ Charles Anderson 1819–1897 Am. newspaper editor
Dana James Dwight 1813–1895 Am. geologist
Dana Richard Henry 1815–1882 Am. lawyer & author
Dane \\'dān\ Clemence 1888–1965 pseud. of *Winifred Ash·ton* \\'ash-tən\ Eng. nov.
Dan·iel \\'dan-yəl\ Samuel 1562?–1619 Eng. poet
Dan·iels \\'dan-yəlz\ Josephus 1862–1948 Am. journalist & statesman
Da·ni·lo·va \də-ˈnē-lə-və\ Aleksandra 1903?–1997 Am. (Russ.-born) choreographer & dancer
D'An·nun·zio \dä-ˈnün(t)-sē-ˌō\ Gabriele 1863–1938 Ital. author & soldier
Dan·te \\'dän-(ˌ)tā, 'dan-, -(ˌ)tē\ 1265–1321 *Dante* or *Durante Ali·ghie·ri* \ˌa-lə-ˈgyer-ē\ Ital. poet — **Dan·te·an** \\'dan-tē-ən, 'dän-\ *or* **Dan·tes·can** \dan-ˈtes-kən, dän-\ *or* **Dan·tesque** \-ˈtesk\ *adj*
Dan·ton \dä-ˈtōⁿ\ Georges-Jacques 1759–1794 Fr. revolutionary
Dare \\'der\ Virginia 1587–? 1st child born in America of Eng. parents
Da·río \dä-ˈrē-ō\ Rubén 1867–1916 orig. *Félix Rubén García Sarmiento* Nicaraguan poet
Da·ri·us \də-ˈrī-əs\ name of 3 kings of Persia: esp. **I** 550–486 B.C. (reigned 522–486) *Darius Hys·tas·pes* \his-ˈtas-pəs\; *the Great*
Dar·lan \där-ˈläⁿ\ Jean-Louis-Xavier-François 1881–1942 Fr. admiral
Darn·ley \\'därn-lē\ Lord 1545–1567 *Henry Stewart* or *Stuart; husband of Mary, Queen of Scots*
Dar·row \\'da-(ˌ)rō\ Clarence Seward 1857–1938 Am. lawyer & author
Dar·win \\'där-wən\ Charles Robert 1809–1882 Eng. naturalist
Darwin Erasmus 1731–1802 *grandfather of C.R.* Eng. physiol. & poet
Dau·bi·gny \ˌdō-bēn-ˈyē, dō-ˈbē-nyē\ Charles-François 1817–1878 Fr. painter
Dau·det \dō-ˈdā\ Alphonse 1840–1897 Fr. nov.
Daudet Léon 1867–1942 *son of Alphonse* Fr. journalist & writer
Dau·mier \dō-ˈmyā, 'dō-mē-ˌā\ Honoré 1808–1879 Fr. caricaturist & painter
Daus·set \dō-ˈse, -ˈsā\ Jean (-Baptiste-Gabriel-Joachim) 1916–2009 Fr. immunologist
Dav·e·nant *or* **D'Av·e·nant** \\'dav-nənt, 'da-və-\ Sir William 1606–1668 Eng. poet & dram.; poet laureate (1638–68)
Dav·en·port \\'da-vən-ˌpȯrt, 'da-vən-\ John 1597–1670 Am. (Eng.-born) clergyman & founder of New Haven colony
Da·vid \\'dä-vət\ Gerard *ca* 1460–1523 Du. painter
Da·vid \\'dä-vēt\ Jacques-Louis 1748–1825 Fr. painter
Da·vid I \\'dä-vəd\ *ca* 1082–1153 king of Scotland (1124–53)
David d'An·gers \däⁿ-ˈzhä\ Pierre-Jean 1788–1856 Fr. sculptor
Da·vid·son \\'dä-vəd-sən\ Jo 1883–1952 Am. sculptor
Da·vies \\'dā-vēz\ Arthur Bowen 1862–1928 Am. painter
Davies (William) Robertson 1913–1995 Canad. author
Dá·vi·la Pa·di·lla \\'dä-vi-lə-pä-ˈdē-yə\ Agustín 1562–1604 Mex. monk & hist.
Da·vis \\'dā-vəs\ Bet·te \\'be-tē\ 1908–1989 orig. *Ruth Elizabeth Davis* Am. actress
Davis Dwight Filley 1879–1945 Am. statesman
Davis Elmer Holmes 1890–1958 Am. radio broadcaster & news commentator
Davis Harold Le·noir \lə-ˈnȯr\ 1896–1960 Am. writer
Davis Jefferson 1808–1889 Am. statesman; pres. of Confed. states (1861–65)
Davis Miles 1926–1991 Am. jazz musician
Davis Raymond, Jr. 1914–2006 Am. astrophysicist
Da·vis·son \\'dā-və-sən\ Clinton Joseph 1881–1958 Am. physicist
Da·vout \da-ˈvü\ Louis-Nicolas 1770–1823 Duc *d'Au·er·städt* \\'daú(-ə)r-ˌstet\ & Prince *d'Eck·mühl* \\'dek-ˌmyül\ marshal of France
Da·vy \\'dā-vē\ Sir Humphry 1778–1829 Eng. chem.
Dawes \\'dȯz\ Charles Gates 1865–1951 Am. lawyer & financier; vice pres. of U.S. (1925–29)
Daw·son \\'dȯ-sᵊn\ Sir John William 1820–1899 Canad. geologist
Day \\'dā\ Clarence Shepard, Jr. 1874–1935 Am. author
Day Thomas 1748–1789 Eng. author
Day William Rufus 1849–1923 Am. statesman & jurist
Da·yan \dī-ˈän\ Moshe 1915–1981 Israeli soldier & polit.
Day–Le·wis \\'dā-ˈlü-əs\ Cecil 1904–1972 pseud. *Nicholas Blake* Brit. writer; poet laureate (1968–72)
De·ák \\'dā-ˌäk\ Fe·renc \\'fer-ˌen(t)s\ 1803–1876 Hung. statesman
Dean \\'dēn\ Sir Patrick 1909–1994 Brit. diplomat
Deane \\'dēn\ Silas 1737–1789 Am. lawyer & diplomat
De·bierne \də-ˈbyern\ André-Louis 1874–1949 Fr. chem.
Debs \\'debz\ Eugene Victor 1855–1926 Am. socialist
De·bus·sy \ˌde-byü-ˈsē, ˌdā-; də-ˈbyü-sē\ (Achille-) Claude 1862–1918 Fr. composer — **De·bus·sy·an** \ˌde-byü-ˈsē-ən, ˌdā-; də-ˈbyü-sē-ən\ *adj*
De·bye \də-ˈbī\ Peter Joseph William 1884–1966 Am. (Du.-born) physicist
De·ca·tur \di-ˈkā-tər\ Stephen 1779–1820 Am. naval officer
De·cazes \də-ˈkäz\ Duc Élie 1780–1860 Fr. statesman
De·cius \\'dē-sh(ē-)əs\ Gaius Messius Quintus Trajanus *ca* 201–251 Rom. emp. (249–51)
Dee·ping \\'dē-piŋ\ (George) Warwick 1877–1950 Eng. nov.
Deere \\'dir\ John 1804–1886 Am. inventor
Def·fand \də-ˈfäⁿ\ Marquise 1697–1780 née *Marie de Vichy-Chamrond* \də-vē-shē-shäⁿ-ˈrōⁿ\ Fr. woman of letters
De·foe \di-ˈfō\ Daniel 1660–1731 Eng. journalist & nov.
De For·est \di-ˈfȯr-əst, -ˈfär-\ Lee 1873–1961 Am. inventor
De·gas \də-ˈgä\ (Hilaire-Germain-) Edgar 1834–1917 Fr. artist
de Gaulle Charles — see GAULLE
De Gennes \də-ˈzhen\ Pierre-Gilles 1932–2007 Fr. physicist
Deh·melt \\'dā-məlt\ Hans Georg 1922– Am. (Ger.-born) physicist
Dei·sen·hof·er \\'dī-zən-ˌhō-fər\ Johann 1943– Ger. biochem.
Dek·ker \\'de-kər\ Thomas 1572?–?1632 Eng. dram.
de Klerk \də-ˈklərk, -ˈklerk\ F(rederik) W(illem) 1936– pres. of Republic of So. Africa (1989–94); vice pres. (1994–96)
de Koo·ning \də-ˈkō-niŋ\ Willem 1904–1997 Am. (Du.-born) painter
de Kruif \də-ˈkrīf\ Paul Henry 1890–1971 Am. bacteriol. & author

De·la·croix \ˌde-lə-ˈk(r)wä\ (Ferdinand-Victor-) Eugène 1798–1863 Fr. painter
de la Mare \ˌde-lə-ˈmer\ Walter John 1873–1956 Eng. poet & nov.
De·land \də-ˈland\ Margaret 1857–1945 née *Margaretta Wade Campbell* Am. nov.
De La Rey \ˌde-lə-ˈrī, -ˈrā\ Jacobus Hercules 1847–1914 Boer gen. & statesman
De·la·roche \ˌde-lə-ˈrȯsh, -ˈrȯsh\ (Hippolyte-) Paul 1797–1859 Fr. painter
De·la·vigne \ˌde-lə-ˈvēnʸ, -ˈvēn-yə\ Jean-François-Casimir 1793–1843 Fr. poet & dram.
De La Warr \\'de-lə-ˌwer\ Baron 1577–1618 *Thomas West; Lord Delaware* Eng. colonial administrator in America
De·Lay \di-ˈlā\ Thomas (Dale) 1947– Am. polit.
De·libes \də-ˈlēb\ (Clément-Philibert-) Léo 1836–1891 Fr. composer
De·Lil·lo \də-ˈli-lō\ Don(ald Richard) 1936– Am. writer
De·lius \\'dē-lē-əs, 'dēl-yəs\ Frederick 1862–1934 Eng. composer
Del·la Rob·bia \ˌde-lə-ˈrä-bē-ə, -ˈrō\ Luca 1399(or 1400)–1482 orig. *Luca di Simone di Marco* Florentine sculptor
De Long \də-ˈlȯŋ\ George Washington 1844–1881 Am. naval officer & explorer
De·lorme *or* **de l'Orme** \də-ˈlȯrm\ Philibert 1515?–1570 Fr. architect
de Mille \də-ˈmil\ Agnes George 1905–1993 Am. dancer & choreographer
De·Mille \də-ˈmil\ Cec·il \\'se-səl\ Blount \\'blənt\ 1881–1959 Am. film director & producer
De·moc·ri·tus \di-ˈmä-krə-təs\ *ca* 460–*ca* 370 B.C. *the Laughing Philosopher* Greek philos.
De Mor·gan \di-ˈmȯr-gən\ William Frend 1839–1917 Eng. artist & nov.
De·mos·the·nes \di-ˈmäs-thə-ˌnēz\ 384–322 B.C. Athenian orator & statesman — **De·mos·then·ic** \di-ˌmäs-ˈthe-nik, ˌdē-, -ˈthē-\ *adj*
Demp·sey \\'dem(p)-sē\ William Harrison 1895–1983 *Jack* Am. boxer
Deng Xiaoping — see TENG HSIAO-P'ING
De·ni·ker \dā-nē-ˈker\ Joseph 1852–1918 Fr. anthropol.
De·nis *or* **De·nys** \'de-nəs, də-nē\ Saint *d* 258? 1st bishop of Paris & patron saint of France
Dent \\'dent\ Joseph Mal·a·by \\'ma-lə-bē\ 1849–1926 Eng. publisher
De·pew \di-ˈpyü\ Chauncey Mitchell 1834–1928 Am. lawyer & polit.
De Quin·cey \di-ˈkwin(t)-sē, -ˈkwin-zē\ Thomas 1785–1859 Eng. author
De·rain \də-ˈräⁿ\ André 1880–1954 Fr. painter
Der·ri·da \ˌde-rē-ˈdä\ Jacques 1930–2004 Fr. philos. & critic — **Der·ri·de·an** *also* **Der·ri·di·an** \ˌde-ri-ˈdē-ən\ *adj*
Der·zha·vin \der-ˈzhä-vən\ Gavrila Romanovich 1743–1816 Russ. poet
De·sai \de-ˈsī\ Morarji Ranchhodji 1896–1995 prime min. of India (1977–79)
De·saix de Vey·goux \də-ˈsä-də-(ˌ)vā-ˈgü\ Louis-Charles-Antoine 1768–1800 Fr. gen.
De·sargues \dā-ˈzärg\ Gérard *or* Girard 1591–1661 Fr. math.
Des·cartes \dā-ˈkärt\ René 1596–1650 L. *Renatus Cartesius* Fr. math. & philos.
Des·cha·nel \ˌdā-shə-ˈnel\ Paul-Eugène-Louis 1855–1922 Fr. statesman; pres. of France (1920)
De Se·ver·sky \də-sə-ˈver-skē\ Alexander Procofieff 1894–1974 Am. (Russ.-born) aeronautical engineer
Des·mou·lins \dā-mü-ˈläⁿ\ Camille 1760–1794 *Lucie-Simplice-Camille-Benoît Desmoulins* Fr. revolutionary
de Soto Hernando — see SOTO
Des·sa·lines \ˌdā-sə-ˈlēn, -ˌdē-\ Jean-Jacques 1758?–1806 emp. as *Jacques I* \\'zhäk\ of Haiti (1804–06)
De·taille \də-ˈtī\ (Jean-Baptiste-) Édouard 1848–1912 Fr. painter
De·us Ra·mos \\'dā-əsh-ˈra-(ˌ)müsh\ João \\'zhwaúⁿ\ de 1830–1896 Port. poet
de Va·le·ra \ˌde-və-ˈler-ə, -ˈlir-ə\ Ea·mon \\'ā-mən\ 1882–1975 Irish polit.; prime min. of Ireland (1937–48; 1951–54; 1957–59); pres. of Ireland (1959–73)
De Vere \də-ˈvir\ Aubrey Thomas 1814–1902 Irish poet
Dev·er·eux \\'de-və-ˌrüks, -ˌrü\ Robert 1566–1601 2d Earl of *Essex* Eng. soldier & courtier
Devonshire dukes of — see CAVENDISH
De Vo·to \di-ˈvō-(ˌ)tō\ Bernard Augustine 1897–1955 Am. author
De Vries Hugo — see VRIES, DE
Dew·ar \\'dü-ər, 'dyü-\ Sir James 1842–1923 Scot. chem. & physicist
De Wet Christiaan Rudolph — see WET, DE
Dew·ey \\'dü-ē, 'dyü-\ George 1837–1917 Am. admiral
Dewey John 1859–1952 Am. philos. & educ. — **Dew·ey·an** \-ən\ *adj*
Dewey Melvil 1851–1931 Am. librarian
Dewey Thomas Edmund 1902–1971 Am. lawyer & polit.
De Witt Johan — see WITT, DE
De Witte Emanuel — see WITT, DE
Dia·ghi·lev \dē-ˈä-gə-ˌlef\ Sergey Pavlovich 1872–1929 Russ. ballet producer & art critic
Di·a·mond \\'dī-(ə-)mənd\ Peter A(rthur) 1940– Am. econ.
Di·as \\'dē-ˌäsh\ Bartholomeu *ca* 1450–1500 Port. navigator
Dí·az \\'dē-ˌäts\ Armando 1861–1928 Duca *della Vittoria* Ital. gen.; marshal of Italy
Dí·az \\'dē-ˌäs, -ˌäz\ (José de la Cruz) Porfirio 1830–1915 Mex. gen.; pres. of Mexico (1877–80; 1884–1911)
Dí·az Or·daz \\'dē-əs-ȯr-ˈdäz\ Gustavo 1911–1979 pres. of Mexico (1964–70)
Dick \\'dik\ George Frederick 1881–1967 & Gladys Henry 1881–1963 Am. physicians
Dick Philip K(indred) 1928–1982 Am. sci-fi writer
Dick·ens \\'di-kənz\ Charles John Huffam 1812–1870 pseud. *Boz* \\'bäz, 'bōz\ Eng. nov. — **Dick·en·si·an** \di-ˈken-zē-ən, -sē-\ *adj*
Dick·ey \\'di-kē\ James Lafayette 1923–1997 Am. poet, nov., & critic

---

\ə\ **abut** \ᵊ\ **kitten, F table** \ər\ **further** \a\ **ash** \ā\ **ace** \ä\ **mop, mar**
\aú\ **out** \ch\ **chin** \e\ **bet** \ē\ **easy** \g\ **go** \i\ **hit** \ī\ **ice** \j\ **job**
\ŋ\ **sing** \ō\ **go** \ȯ\ **law** \ȯi\ **boy** \th\ **thin** \th̷\ **the** \ü\ **loot** \ú\ **foot**
\y\ **yet** \zh\ **vision, beige** \k, ⁿ, œ, ᵫ, ʸ\ *see* Guide to Pronunciation

Dick·in·son \'di-kən-sən\ Emily Elizabeth 1830–1886 Am. poet

Dickinson John 1732–1808 Am. statesman

Di·de·rot \dē-'drō, 'dē-də-ˌrō\ Denis 1713–1784 Fr. encyclopedist

Die·fen·ba·ker \'dē-fən-ˌbä-kər\ John George 1895–1979 prime min. of Canada (1957–63)

Diels \'dēlz, 'dēls\ Otto Paul Hermann 1876–1954 Ger. chem.

Die·sel \'dē-zəl, -səl\ Rudolf 1858–1913 Ger. mechanical engineer

Die·trich \'dē-trik, -trik\ Marlene 1901?–1992 Am. (Ger.-born) actress & singer

Diez \'dēts\ Friedrich Christian 1794–1876 Ger. philologist

Dig·by \'dig-bē\ Sir Ken·elm \'ke-ˌnelm\ 1603–1665 Eng. naval commander, diplomat, & author

Dill \'dil\ Sir John Greer 1881–1944 Brit. gen.

Dil·lon \'di-lən\ John 1851–1927 Irish nationalist polit.

Di·Mag·gio \də-'mä-zhē-ˌō, -'ma-jē-(ˌ)ō, -'ma-jō\ Joseph Paul 1914–1999 *the Yankee Clipper* Am. baseball player

Di·mi·tri·os \thē-'mē-trē-ôs; də-'mē-trē-əs\ 1914–1991 *Dimitrios Papadopoulos* archbishop of Constantinople and ecumenical patriarch (1972–91)

Di·ne·sen \'dē-nə-sən, 'di-\ Isak \'ē-ˌsäk\ 1885–1962 pseud. of *Karen Christence Dinesen, Baroness Blixen-Finecke* Dan. author

Din·wid·die \din-'wi-dē\ Robert 1693–1770 Eng. colonial administrator in America

Di·o·cle·tian \ˌdī-ə-'klē-shən\ 245–316 *Gaius Aurelius Valerius Diocletianus* Rom. emp. (284–305)

Di·og·e·nes \dī-'ä-jə-ˌnēz\ *d ca* 320 B.C. Greek Cynic philos.

Di·o·ny·sius \ˌdī-ə-'ni-shē-əs, -sē-əs, -shəs; -'nī-sē-əs\ *ca* 430–367 B.C. *the Elder* Greek tyrant of Syracuse (405–367)

Dionysius *the Younger* tyrant of Syracuse (367–356; 346–343 B.C.)

Dionysius Ex·ig·u·us \eg-'zi-gyə-wəs\ *ca* 500–*ca* 560 Christian monk

Dionysius of Alexandria Saint *ca* 200–*ca* 265 theol. & bishop of Alexandria (247)

Dionysius of Hal·i·car·nas·sus \ˌha-lə-(ˌ)kär-'na-səs\ *fl ca* 20 B.C. Greek scholar

Dior \'dē-ˌôr, 'dē-ˌór; dyór\ Christian 1905–1957 Fr. fashion designer

Di·rac \di-'rak\ Paul Adrien Maurice 1902–1984 Eng. physicist

Dirk·sen \'dərk-sən\ Everett McKinley 1896–1969 Am. polit.

Dis·ney \'diz-nē\ Walter Elias 1901–1966 Am. film producer

Dis·rae·li \diz-'rā-lē\ Benjamin 1804–1881 1st Earl of *Bea·cons·field* \'bē-kənz-ˌfēld\ Brit. polit. & author; prime min. (1868; 1874–80)

Dit·mars \'dit-ˌmärz\ Raymond Lee 1876–1942 Am. naturalist

Dix \'diks\ Dorothea Lynde 1802–1887 Am. social reformer

Dix Dorothy — see Elizabeth Meriwether GILMER

Dix·on \'dik-sən\ Jeremiah *d* 1777 Eng. surveyor in America

Dö·be·rei·ner \'də(r)-bə-ˌrī-nər, 'dœ-\ Johann Wolfgang 1780–1849 Ger. chem.

Do·bie \'dō-bē\ J(ames) Frank 1888–1964 Am. folklorist

Do·brée \'dō-ˌbrä\ Bon·a·my \'bä-nə-mē\ 1891–1974 Eng. scholar

Dob·son \'däb-sən\ (Henry) Austin 1840–1921 Eng. poet & essayist

Dodge \'däj\ Mary Elizabeth 1831–1905 *née Mapes* \'māps\ Am. author

Dodg·son \'däd-sən, 'däj-\ Charles Lut·widge \'lət-wij\ 1832–1898 pseud. *Lewis Car·roll* \'ka-rəl\ Eng. math. & writer

Dods·ley \'dädz-lē\ Robert 1703–1764 Eng. author & bookseller

Do·her·ty \'dö-ər-tē, 'dō-, 'dä-\ Peter Charles 1940–   Am. (Austral.-born) immunologist

Doi·sy \'dói-zē\ Edward Adelbert 1893–1986 Am. biochem.

Dole \'dōl\ Bob 1923–   *Robert Joseph Dole* Am. polit.

Dole Sanford Ballard 1844–1926 Am. jurist; pres. (1894–1900) & gov. (1900–03) of Hawaii

Doll·fuss \'dól-ˌfüs\ Engelbert 1892–1934 Austrian statesman

Do·magk \'dō-ˌmäk\ Gerhard 1895–1964 Ger. bacteriol.

Do·me·ni·chi·no \(ˌ)dō-ˌmā-nə-'kē-(ˌ)nō\ 1581–1641 *Domenico Zampie·ri* \ˌtsäm-pē-'er-ē, ˌzäm-\ Ital. painter

Do·min·go \dō-'mēng-(ˌ)gō\ Plácido 1941–   Span. tenor

Do·min·ic \'dä-mə-(ˌ)nik\ Saint *ca* 1170–1221 *Domingo de Guz·mán* \güz-'män, güs-\ Span.-born founder of the Dominican order of friars

Do·mi·tian \də-'mi-shən\ A.D. 51–96 *Titus Flavius Domitianus* Rom. emp. (81–96)

Don·a·tel·lo \ˌdä-nə-'te-(ˌ)lō\ 1386?–1466 *Donato de Betto di Bardi* Florentine sculptor

Don·gen \'dón-ən\ Kees van 1877–1968 orig. *Cornelis Theodorus Maria Dongen* Fr. (Du.-born) painter

Dö·nitz \'də(r)-nəts, 'dœ-\ Karl 1891–1980 Ger. admiral

Don·i·zet·ti \ˌdä-nə(d)-'ze-tē, ˌdō-\ Gaetano 1797–1848 Ital. composer

Donne \'dən *also* 'dän\ John 1572–1631 Eng. poet & clergyman —
Donn·ean *or* **Donn·ian** \'dä-nē-ən\ *adj*

Don·o·van \'dä-nə-vən\ Shaun L. S. 1966–   U.S. secy. of housing & urban development (2009–   )

Don·o·van \'dä-nə-vən, 'dö-\ William Joseph 1883–1959 *Wild Bill* Am. lawyer & gen.

Doo·lit·tle \'dü-ˌli-t°l\ James Harold 1896–1993 Am. aviator & gen.

Dopp·ler \'dä-plər\ Christian Johann 1803–1853 Austrian physicist

Do·ré \dó-'rā, do-\ (Paul-) Gustave 1832–1883 Fr. illustrator & painter

Dor·ge·les \ˌdór-zhə-'les\ Roland 1886–1973 Fr. nov.

Dor·nier \'dórn-ˌyā\ Claudius 1884–1969 Ger. airplane builder

Dorr \'dór\ Thomas Wilson 1805–1854 Am. lawyer & polit.

Dor·sey \'dór-sē\ Tommy 1905–1956 *Thomas Francis Dorsey Jr.* Am. trombonist & bandleader

Dos Pas·sos \däs-'pa-səs\ John Roderigo 1896–1970 Am. writer

Dos·to·yev·sky \ˌdäs-tə-'yef-skē, -'yev-\ Fyodor Mikhaylovich 1821–1881 Russ. nov. — **Dos·to·yev·ski·an** *or* **Dos·to·ev·ski·an** \-skē-ən\ *adj*

Dou *or* **Douw** \'daù\ Gerrit *or* Gerard 1613–1675 Du. painter

Dou·ble·day \'də-bəl-ˌdā\ Abner 1819–1893 Am. soldier & reputed inventor of baseball

Doug·las \'də-gləs\ John Shol·to \'shól-(ˌ)tō\ 1844–1900 8th Marquess & Earl of *Queens·ber·ry* \'kwēnz-ˌber-ē, -b(ə-)rē\ Scot. boxing patron

Douglas Stephen Arnold 1813–1861 Am. polit.

Douglas William Orville 1898–1980 Am. jurist

Douglas–Home — see HOME

Douglas of Kir·tle·side \'kər-t°l-ˌsīd\ 1st Baron 1893–1969 *William Sholto Douglas* Brit. air marshal

Doug·lass \'də-gləs\ Frederick 1817–1895 orig. *Frederick Augustus Washington Bailey* Am. abolitionist

Dou·mer \dü-'mer\ Paul 1857–1932 pres. of France (1931–32)

Dou·mergue \dü-'merg\ Gaston 1863–1937 Fr. statesman; pres. of France (1924–31)

Dow·den \'daù-d°n\ Edward 1843–1913 Irish lit. critic

Dow·ie \'daù-ē\ John Alexander 1847–1907 Am. (Scot.-born) religious leader

Dow·son \'daù-s°n\ Ernest Christopher 1867–1900 Eng. lyric poet

Dox·ia·dis \ˌdók-sē-'ä-thēs\ Konstantinos Apostolos 1913–1975 Greek architect

Doyle \'dói-(ə)l\ Sir Arthur Co·nan \'kō-nən\ 1859–1930 Brit. physician, nov., & detective-story writer

D'Oyly Carte — see CARTE, D'OYLY

Dra·co \'drā-(ˌ)kō\ late 7th cent. B.C. Athenian lawgiver

Drake \'drāk\ Sir Francis 1540(or 1543)–1596 Eng. navigator & buccaneer

Dra·per \'drā-pər\ Henry 1837–1882 Am. astron.

Dray·ton \'drā-t°n\ Michael 1563–1631 Eng. poet

Drei·ser \'drī-sər, -zər\ Theodore 1871–1945 Am. editor & nov. —
Drei·ser·ian \ˌdrī-'ser-ē-ən, -'zər-\ *adj*

Drew \'drü\ John 1827–1862 Am. (Irish-born) actor

Drew John 1853–1927 *son of prec.* Am. actor

Drey·fus \'drī-fəs, 'drā-; dre-'füs\ Alfred 1859–1935 Fr. army officer

Driesch \'drēsh\ Hans Adolf Eduard 1867–1941 Ger. biol. & philos.

Drink·wa·ter \'drink-ˌwó-tər, -ˌwä-\ John 1882–1937 Eng. writer

Drou·et \drü-'e, -'ā\ Jean-Baptiste 1765–1844 Comte *d'Er·lon* \der-'lōⁿ\ Fr. gen.; marshal of France

Drum·mond \'drə-mənd\ Henry 1851–1897 Scot. clergyman & writer

Drummond William Henry 1854–1907 Canad. (Irish-born) poet

Drummond of Haw·thorn·den \'hó-ˌthórn-dən\ William 1585–1649 Scot. poet

Dru·sus \'drü-səs\ 38–9 B.C. *Ne·ro* \'nē-(ˌ)rō, 'nir-(ˌ)ō\ *Claudius Drusus Ger·man·i·cus* \(ˌ)jer-'ma-ni-kəs\ Rom. gen.

Dry·den \'drī-d°n\ John 1631–1700 Eng. poet & dram.; poet laureate (1668–88) — **Dry·de·ni·an** \drī-'dē-nē-ən, -'de-\ *adj*

Du Barry Comtesse — see Jeanne BARRY

Du·bois \dü-'bwä, dyü-; də-'bwä\ Paul 1829–1905 Fr. sculptor

DuBois \dü-'bóis, dyü-\ W(illiam) E(dward) B(urghardt) 1868–1963 Am. educ. & writer

Du·buf·fet \ˌdü-bə-'fä, ˌdyü-; də-bœ-'fe\ Jean 1901–1985 Fr. artist

Du Cange \dü-'käⁿzh, dyü-\ Sieur Charles Du Fresne 1610–1688 Fr. scholar & glossarist

Du Chail·lu \də-'shal-(ˌ)yü, -'shī-(ˌ)ü\ Paul Belloni 1831–1903 Am. (Fr.-born) explorer in Africa

Du·champ \dü-'shäⁿ, dyü-\ Marcel 1887–1968 Fr. painter — **Du·champ·ian** \-'shäm-pē-ən\ *adj*

Dudevant Aurore — see George SAND

Dud·ley \'dəd-lē\ Robert 1532(or 1533)–1588 1st Earl of *Leicester* Eng. courtier

Dudley Thomas 1576–1653 Eng. colonial administrator in America

Duf·fer·in and Ava \ˌdə-fə-rin-ən(d)-'ä-və\ 1st Marquis of 1826–1902 *Frederick Temple Hamilton-Temple-Blackwood* Brit. diplomat

Duff–Gor·don \ˌdəf-'gór-d°n\ Lady Lucie 1821–1869 Eng. author

Duf·fy \'də-fē\ Carol Ann 1955–   Brit. poet; poet laureate (2009–   )

Duffy Sir Charles Gavan 1816–1903 Irish nationalist & Austral. polit.

Du·fy \dü-'fē, dyü-\ Raoul 1877–1953 Fr. painter

Du Gard Roger Martin — see MARTIN DU GARD

Du·ha·mel \dü-ä-'mel, dyü-; dœ-ä'mel\ Georges 1884–1966 Fr. writer

Du·ka·kis \dü-'kä-kis\ Michael S(tanley) 1933–   Am. polit.

Duke \'dük, 'dyük\ Benjamin Newton 1855–1929 & his bro. James Buchanan 1856–1925 Am. tobacco industrialists

Dul·les \'də-ləs\ John Foster 1888–1959 Am. diplomat; secy. of state (1953–59)

Du·mas \dü-'mä, dyü-; 'd(y)ü-ˌ\ Alexandre 1802–1870 *Dumas père* \'per\ Fr. nov. & dram.

Dumas Alexandre 1824–1895 *Dumas fils* \'fēs\ Fr. nov. & dram.

du Mau·rier \dù-'mór-ē-ˌā, dyü-\ Dame Daphne 1907–1989 Brit. writer

du Maurier George Louis Palmella Busson 1834–1896 *grandfather of prec.* Brit. artist & nov.

Du·mou·riez \dü-'mùr-ē-ˌā, dyü-\ Charles-François du Périer 1739–1823 Fr. gen.

Du·nant \dü-'näⁿ, dyü-\ (Jean) Henri 1828–1910 Swiss philanthropist & founder of the Red Cross

Dun·bar \'dən-ˌbär\ Paul Laurence 1872–1906 Am. poet

Dunbar \'dən-ˌbär, ˌdən-\ William 1460?–?1530 Scot. poet

Dun·can \'dəŋ-kən\ Arne 1964–   U.S. secy. of education (2009–   )

Duncan Isadora 1877–1927 Am. dancer

Dun·das \ˌdən-'das\ Henry 1742–1811 1st Viscount *Melville* & Baron *Dun·ira* \ˌdə-'nir-ə\ Brit. statesman

Dun·lop \ˌdən-'läp, 'dən-\ John Boyd 1840–1921 Scot. inventor

Dunne \'dən\ Finley Peter 1867–1936 Am. humorist

Du·nois \dün-'wä, dyün-\ Comte de 1403–1468 *Jean d'Orléans; the Bastard of Orléans* Fr. gen.

Dun·sa·ny \ˌdən-'sä-nē\ 18th Baron 1878–1957 *Edward John Moreton Drax Plunkett* Irish poet & dram.

Duns Sco·tus \ˌdənz-'skō-təs\ John 1266?–1308 Scot. scholastic theol.

Dun·stan \'dən(t)-stən\ Saint 924–988 archbishop of Canterbury (959–988)

Du·pleix \dü-'pleks, dyü-\ Marquis Joseph-François 1697–1763 Fr. colonial administrator in India

Duplessis–Mornay — see Philippe de MORNAY

Du Pont \dü-'pänt, dyü-\ 'd(y)ü-ˌ\ Éleuthère Irénée 1771–1834 *son of P.S. Du Pont de Nemours* Fr.-born industrialist

Du Pont de Ne·mours \-də-nə-'mùr\ Pierre-Samuel 1739–1817 Fr. econ. & statesman

Du·quesne \dü-'kän, dyü-\ Marquis Abraham 1610–1688 Fr. naval officer

Du·rant \dù-'rant, dyù-\ Will(iam James) 1885–1981 & his wife Ariel 1898–1981 orig. *Ada Kaufman* Am. writers

Dü·rer \'dùr-ər, 'dyùr-, 'duer-\ Albrecht 1471–1528 Ger. painter & engraver — **Dü·rer·esque** \ˌdùr-ər-'esk, ˌdyür-, ˌduer-\ *adj*

D'Ur·fey \'dər-fē\ Thomas 1653–1723 Eng. songwriter & dram.
Durk·heim \dúr-'kem\ Émile 1858–1917 Fr. sociol. — **Durk·heim·ian** \-'ke-mē-ən\ *adj*
Du·roc \dü-'räk, dyü-\ Géraud-Christophe-Michel 1772–1813 Duc *de Fri·oul* \frē-'ül\ Fr. gen. under Napoleon
Dur·rell \'dər-əl, 'də-rəl\ Lawrence 1912–1990 Eng. nov. & poet
Dür·ren·matt \'dúer-ən-,mät, 'dúr-\ Friedrich 1921–1990 Swiss author
Du·ruy \dür-'wē, dŭe-'rw'e\ Victor 1811–1894 Fr. hist.
Du·se \'dü-(,)zā\ Eleonora 1858–1924 Ital. actress
Du·tra \'dü-trə\ Eurico Gaspar 1885–1974 Braz. gen.; pres. of Brazil (1946–51)
Du·va·lier \dù-'val-(,)yā, dyü-\ François 1907–1971 *Papa Doc* pres. of Haiti (1957–71)
Du Vi·gneaud \dü-'vēn-(,)yō, dyü-\ Vincent 1901–1978 Am. biochem.
Dvo·řák \(də-)'vör-,zhäk\ Antonín 1841–1904 Bohemian composer
Dwig·gins \'dwi-gənz\ William Addison 1880–1956 Am. type designer
Dwight \'dwīt\ Timothy 1752–1817 Am. clergyman; pres. Yale U. (1795–1817)
Dwight Timothy 1828–1916 *grandson of prec.* Am. clergyman; pres. Yale U. (1886–99)
Dyce \'dīs\ Alexander 1798–1869 Scot. editor
Dy·er \'dī(-ə)r\ John 1699–1757 Brit. poet
Dyer Mary *d* 1660 Am. Quaker martyr
Dy·lan \'di-lən\ Bob 1941– orig. *Robert Allen Zimmerman* Am. singer & songwriter
Eads \'ēdz\ James Buchanan 1820–1887 Am. engineer & inventor
Ea·kins \'ā-kənz\ Thomas 1844–1916 Am. artist
Ear·hart \'er-,härt, 'ir-\ Amelia 1897–1937 Am. aviator
Ear·ly \'ər-lē\ Ju·bal \'jü-bəl\ Anderson 1816–1894 Am. Confed. gen.
Earp \'ərp\ Wyatt 1848–1929 Am. lawman
East·man \'ēst-mən\ George 1854–1932 Am. inventor & industrialist
Eastman Max Forrester 1883–1969 Am. editor & writer
East·wood \'ēst-,wúd\ Clinton, Jr. 1930– *Clint Eastwood* Am. film actor & director
Ea·ton \'ē-t³n\ Theophilus 1590–1658 Eng. colonial administrator in America; gov. of New Haven colony (1638–58)
Eba·di \e-bò-dē\ Shirin 1947– Iranian human rights advocate
Ebert \'ā-bərt\ Friedrich 1871–1925 pres. of Germany (1919–25)
Ec·cles \'e-kəlz\ Marriner Stoddard 1890–1977 Am. banker & econ.
Eche·ver·ría **(Ál·va·rez)** \ā-chə-və-'rē-ə-'al-və-,rez, ,e-chə-\ Luis 1922– pres. of Mexico (1970–76)
Eck \'ek\ Johann 1486–1543 orig. *Johann Maier* Ger. R.C. theol.
Ecke·hart \'e-kə-,härt\ *or* **Eck·art** *or* **Eck·hart** \'ek-,härt, 'e-,kärt\ Johannes 1260?–?1327 *Meister Eckehart* Ger. mystic
Eck·er·mann \'e-kər-,män, -mən\ Johann Peter 1792–1854 Ger. writer
Ed·dy \'e-dē\ Mary (Morse) 1821–1910 née *Baker* Am. founder of the Christian Science Church
Eden \'ē-d³n\ (Robert) Anthony 1897–1977 Earl of *Avon* \'ā-vən\ Eng. statesman; prime min. (1955–57)
Ed·er·le \'e-dər-lē\ Gertrude (Caroline) 1905–2003 Am. swimmer
Edge·worth \'ej-(,)wərth\ Maria 1767–1849 Brit. nov.
Edinburgh Duke of — see PHILIP
Ed·i·son \'e-də-sən\ Thomas Alva 1847–1931 Am. inventor — **Ed·i·so·nian** \,e-də-'sō-nē-ən\ *adj*
Ed·mund *or* Ead·mund II \'ed-mənd\ *ca* 993–1016 *Ironside* king of the English (1016)
Ed·ward \'ed-wərd\ name of 8 post-Norman Eng. (Brit.) kings: I 1239–1307 (reigned 1272–1307); II 1284–1327 (reigned 1307–27); III 1312–1377 (reigned 1327–77); IV 1442–1483 (reigned 1461–70; 1471–83); V 1470–1483 (reigned 1483); VI 1537–1553 (reigned 1547–53) *son of Henry VIII & Jane Seymour;* VII 1841–1910 (reigned 1901–10) *Albert Edward, son of Victoria;* VIII 1894–1972 (reigned 1936; abdicated) Duke of *Windsor, son of George V*
Edward 1330–1376 *the Black Prince; son of Edward III* prince of Wales
Edward *or* Ead·ward \'ed-\ 1003?–1066 *the Confessor* king of the English (1042–66)
Ed·wards \'ed-wərdz\ Jonathan 1703–1758 Am. theol. — **Ed·ward·ean** \ed-'wär-dē-ən, -'wòr-\ *adj*
Edwards Sir Robert G(eoffrey) 1925–2013 Brit. physiologist
Ed·win *or* Ead·wine \'ed-wən\ 585?–633 king of Northumbria (616–633)
Egas Mo·niz \'ā-gäs-mō-'nēz\ António Caetano de Abreu Freire 1874–1955 Port. neurologist & polit.
Eg·bert \'eg-bərt\ *d* 839 king of the West Saxons (802–839) & 1st king of the English (828–839)
Eg·gle·ston \'e-gəl-stən\ Edward 1837–1902 Am. writer
Eggleston George Cary 1839–1911 *bro. of Edward* Am. writer
Eg·mond \'eg-,mänt\ *or* **Eg·mont** Lamoraal 1522–1568 Graaf *van Egmond* Flem. gen. & statesman
Eh·ren·burg \'er-ən-,bùrg, -,búrk\ Ilya Grigoryevich 1891–1967 Russ. writer
Ehr·lich \'er-lik\ Paul 1854–1915 Ger. bacteriol.
Ehr·lich \'ər-lik\ Paul Ralph 1932– Am. biol.
Eif·fel \'ī-fəl, e-fel\ Alexandre-Gustave 1832–1923 Fr. engineer
Eijk·man \'īk-,män, 'āk-\ Christiaan 1858–1930 Du. pathologist
Ein·stein \'īn-,stīn\ Albert 1879–1955 Am. (Ger.-born) physicist — **Ein·stein·ian** \īn-'stī-nē-ən\ *adj*
Eint·ho·ven \'īnt-,hō-vən, 'änt-\ Willem 1860–1927 Du. physiol.
Ei·sen·how·er \'ī-z³n-,haú(-ə)r\ Dwight David 1890–1969 Am. gen.; 34th pres. of the U.S. (1953–61)
Ei·sen·stein \'ī-z³n-,stīn\ Sergey Mikhaylovich 1898–1948 Soviet (Russ.-born) film director
El·a·gab·a·lus \,e-lə-'ga-bə-ləs\ *Gk* **He·li·o·gab·a·lus** \,hē-lē-ō-'ga-bə-ləs\ 204–222 Rom. emp. (218–222)
El·Ba·ra·dei \,el-'bä-rä-,dā\ Mohamed 1942– Egypt. diplomat
El·don \'el-dən\ John 1st Earl of 1751–1838 *John Scott* Eng. jurist
El·ea·nor \'e-lə-nər, -,nór\ **of Aquitaine** 1122?–1204 queen of Louis VII *of France (divorced 1152) & of Henry II of England*
Eleanor of Castile 1246–1290 queen of Edward I of England
Eleanor of Provence 1223–1291 *queen of Henry III of England*
El·gar \'el-,gär, -gər\ Sir Edward 1857–1934 Eng. composer
El·i·on \'e-lē-ən\ Gertrude Belle 1918–1999 Am. biochem.

El·iot \'e-lē-ət, 'el-yət\ Charles William 1834–1926 Am. educ.; pres. Harvard U. (1869–1909)
Eliot George 1819–1880 pseud. of *Mary Ann (or Marian) Evans* Eng. nov.
Eliot Sir John 1592–1632 Eng. statesman
Eliot John 1604–1690 *apostle to the Indians* Am. clergyman
Eliot T(homas) S(tearns) 1888–1965 Brit. (Am.-born) poet & critic — **Eli·ot·ian** \,e-lē-'ō-tē-ən, -'ōsh(ē-)ən\ *adj* — **Eli·ot·ic** \,e-lē-'ä-tik\ *adj*
Eliz·a·beth \i-'li-zə-bəth\ name of 2 Eng. (Brit.) queens: I 1533–1603 *dau. of Henry VIII & Anne Boleyn* (reigned 1558–1603); II 1926– *Elizabeth Alexandra Mary; dau. of George VI* (reigned 1952–   )
Elizabeth *also* Elizabeth Stu·art \-'stü-ərt, -'styü-; 'stúrt, 'styúrt\ 1596–1662 *queen of Frederick V of Bohemia*
Elizabeth 1900–2002 *Elizabeth Angela Marguerite Bowes-Ly·on* \'bōz-'lī-ən\; *queen of George VI of Great Britain*
Elizabeth 1843–1916 pseud. *Car·men Syl·va* \'kär-mən-'sil-və\ queen of Romania & writer
Elizabeth Pe·trov·na \pə-'tróv-nə\ 1709–1762 empress of Russia (1741–62)
Ellenborough 1st Baron — see LAW
El·ling·ton \'e-liŋ-tən\ Edward Kennedy 1899–1974 *Duke Ellington* Am. bandleader & composer
El·liott \'e-lē-ət, 'el-yət\ Maxine 1868–1940 orig. *Jessie Dermot* Am. actress
El·lis \'e-ləs\ Alexander John 1814–1890 orig. surname *Sharpe* Eng. philologist
Ellis (Henry) Have·lock \'hav-,läk, -lək\ 1859–1939 Eng. psychol. & writer
El·li·son \'e-lə-sən\ Ralph Waldo 1914–1994 Am. writer
Ells·worth \'elz-(,)wərth\ Lincoln 1880–1951 Am. explorer
Ellsworth Oliver 1745–1807 Am. jurist; chief justice U.S. Supreme Court (1796–1800)
El·man \'el-mən\ Mi·scha \'mē-shə\ 1891–1967 Am. (Russ.-born) violinist
El·phin·stone \'el-fən-,stōn, *chiefly Brit* -stən\ Mount·stu·art \maúnt-'st(y)ü-ərt\ 1779–1859 Brit. statesman in India
Elphinstone William 1431–1514 Scot. bishop & statesman
El·yot \'e-lē-ət, 'el-yət\ Sir Thomas 1490?–1546 Eng. scholar & diplomat
El·y·tis \e-'lē-(,)tēs\ Odysseus 1911–1996 Greek poet
El·ze·vir *or* El·ze·vier \'el-zə-,vir\ family of Du. printers including esp. Lodewijk *or* Louis 1546?–1617, his son Bonaventura 1583–1652, & his grandson Abraham 1592–1652
Em·er·son \'e-mər-sən\ Ralph Waldo 1803–1882 Am. essayist & poet — **Em·er·so·nian** \,e-mər-'sō-nē-ən, -nyən\ *adj*
Em·met \'e-mət\ Robert 1778–1803 Irish nationalist & rebel
Em·ped·o·cles \em-'pe-də-,klēz\ *ca* 490–430 B.C. Greek philos. & statesman
En·de·cott *or* En·di·cott \'en-di-kət, -də-,kät\ John 1588–1665 colonial gov. of Massachusetts
Enes·cu \-'nes-(,)kü\ Gheorghe *or* George *Fr* **Enes·co** \-(,)kō\ Georges 1881–1955 Romanian composer
En·gels \'en-gəlz, -əlz, *G* 'eŋ-əls\ Friedrich 1820–1895 Ger. socialist
En·gle \'eŋ-gəl\ Robert F. 1942– Am. econ.
En·glert \ä³-'glert\ François 1932– Belg. physicist
En·ver Pa·sa \'en-,ver-'pä-shə, -'pa-shə, -pə-'shä\ 1881–1922 Turk. soldier & polit.
Epam·i·non·das \i-,pa-mə-'nän-dəs\ *ca* 410–362 B.C. Theban gen. & statesman
Ep·ic·te·tus \,e-pik-'tē-təs\ *ca* A.D. 55–*ca* 135 Greek Stoic philos. in Rome — **Ep·ic·te·tian** \-'tē-shən\ *adj*
Ep·i·cu·rus \,e-pi-'kyúr-əs\ 341–270 B.C. Greek philos.
Ep·stein \'ep-,stīn\ Sir Jacob 1880–1959 Brit. (Am.-born) sculptor \-mē-ən\ *adj*
Eras·mus \i-'raz-məs\ Desiderius 1466?–1536 Du. scholar — **Eras·mi·an** \-mē-ən\ *adj*
Er·a·tos·the·nes \,er-ə-'täs-thə-,nēz\ *ca* 276–*ca* 194 B.C. Greek astron.
Erck·mann–Cha·tri·an \'erk-,mən-,shä-trē-ä³, -,sha-\ joint pseud. of *Émile Erckmann* 1822–1899 & *Alexandre Chatrian* 1826–1890 Fr. authors
Er·dos \'er-,dərsh\ Paul 1913–1996 Hung. math.
Er·hard \'er-härt\ Ludwig 1897–1977 chancellor of West Germany (1963–66)
Er·ics·son \'er-ik-sən\ John 1803–1889 Am. (Swed.-born) engineer & inventor
Erig·e·na \i-'ri-jə-nə\ John Sco·tus \'skō-təs\ *ca* 810–*ca* 877 Scot. (Irish-born) philos. & theol.
Er·ik \'er-ik\ *the Red* 10th cent. Norw. navigator & explorer
Eriksson Leif — see LEIF ERIKSSON
Er·lan·ger \'er-,län-dər\ Joseph 1874–1965 Am. physiol.
Er·len·mey·er \'ər-lən-,mī(-ə)r, 'er-\ Richard August Carl Emil 1825–1909 Ger. chem.
Ernst \'ern(t)st, 'ərn(t)st\ Max 1891–1976 Ger. painter
Ernst Richard Robert 1933– Swiss chem.
Er·skine \'ər-skən\ John 1879–1951 Am. educ. & writer
Er·tl \'er-t³l\ Gerhard 1936– Ger. chem.
Er·vine \'ər-vən\ St. John \sänt-'jän, sənt-; 'sin-jən\ Greer 1883–1971 Irish dram. & nov.
Erz·ber·ger \'erts-,ber-gər\ Matthias 1875–1921 Ger. statesman
Esch·er \'e-shər, 'es-kər\ M(aurits) C(ornelis) 1898–1972 Du. artist
Esh·kol \'esh-'kōl\ Levi 1895–1969 prime min. of Israel (1963–69)
Es·par·te·ro \,es-pər-'ter-(,)ō\ Baldomero 1793–1879 Conde *de Luchana* Span. gen. & statesman
Es·qui·vel \,ä-skē-'vel\ Adolfo Pérez 1931– Argentine sculptor & dissident
Es·sen \'e-s³n\ Count Hans Henrik von 1755–1824 Swed. field marshal & statesman

Essex 2d Earl of — see DEVEREUX
Es·taing, d' \des-'taⁿ\ Comte Jean-Baptiste-Charles-Henri-Hector 1729–1794 Fr. admiral
Este \'es-(‚)tā\ Ital. princely family beginning with *Alberto Az·zo II* \'äd-(‚)zō\ 996–1097 & ending with *Er·co·le III* \'er-kə-‚lā\ 1727–1803
Es·ter·ha·zy \'es-tər-‚hä-zē\ Marie-Charles-Ferdinand-Walsin 1847–1923 Fr. army officer
Es·tienne \ā-'tyen\ *or* **Étienne** Fr. family of printers & booksellers including esp.: Henri I *ca* 1470–1520; his son Robert 1503–1559; & Robert's son Henri II 1528–1598
Es·tra·da \ā-'strä-t̲h̲a\ Joseph 1937–   orig. surname *Ejercito* pres. of Philippines (1998–2001)
Estrada Pal·ma \'päl-mə\ Tomás 1835–1908 1st pres. of Cuba (1902–06)
Ethelbert — see AETHELBERHT
Ethelred — see AETHELRED
Eth·er·ege \'e-th(ə-)rij\ Sir George 1635?–1692 Eng. dram.
Eu·clid \'yü-kləd\ *fl ca* 300 B.C. Greek geometer
Eu·gene \yü-'jēn, 'yü-‚\ *F* œ-'zhen\ 1663–1736 *François-Eugène de Savoie-Carignan* prince of Savoy & Austrian gen.
Eu·gé·nie \'yü-jə-‚nē; yü-'jā-nē, -'jē-; *F* œ-zhā-'nē\ 1826–1920 *Eugénia Maria de Montijo de Guzmán; wife of Napoleon III* empress of the French (1853–71)
Eu·ler \'òi-lər\ Leonhard 1707–1783 Swiss math. & physicist
Eu·ler–Chel·pin \'òi-lər-'kel-pən\ Hans (Karl August Simon) von 1873–1964 Swed. (Ger.-born) chem.
Eu·rip·i·des \yù-'ri-pə-‚dēz\ *ca* 484–406 B.C. Greek dram. — **Eu·rip·i·de·an** \-‚ri-pə-'dē-ən\ *adj*
Eus·den \'yüz-dən\ Laurence 1688–1730 Eng. poet; poet laureate (1718–30)
Eu·se·bi·us of Caesarea \yü-'sē-bē-əs\ *ca* 260–*ca* 339 theol. & church hist.
Eu·sta·chio \eú-'stä-kē-‚ō\ Bartolomeo 1520–1574 L. *Eu·sta·chius* \yü-'stā-kē-əs, -'stä-sh(ē-)əs\ Ital. anatomist
Ev·ans \'e-vənz\ Sir Arthur John 1851–1941 Eng. archaeol.
Evans Herbert McLean 1882–1971 Am. anatomist & embryologist
Evans Sir Martin (John) 1941–   Brit. geneticist
Evans Maurice 1901–1989 Am. (Eng.-born) actor
Evans Rudulph 1878–1960 Am. sculptor
Evans Walker 1903–1975 Am. photographer
Ev·arts \'e-vərts\ William Maxwell 1818–1901 Am. lawyer & statesman
Ev·att \'e-vət\ Herbert Vere 1894–1965 Austral. jurist & statesman
Eve·lyn \'ēv-lən, 'ev-\ John 1620–1706 Eng. diarist
Ev·er·ett \'ev-rət, 'e-və-\ Edward 1794–1865 Am. clergyman, orator, & statesman
Ewald \'ī-‚väl\ Johannes 1743–1781 Dan. poet & dram.
Ew·ell \'yü-əl\ Richard Stoddert 1817–1872 Am. Confed. gen.
Eyck, van \van-'īk\ Hubert *or* Huybrecht *ca* 1370–1426 & his bro. Jan before 1395–1441 Flem. painters
Eze·kiel \i-'zēk-yəl\ Moses Jacob 1844–1917 Am. sculptor
Fa·bio·la \fä-bē-'ō-la, fə-'byō-\ 1928–   *Fabiola de Mo·ra y Ara·gón* \-‚t̲h̲ä-'mòr-ä-ē-ä-rä-'gōn\ *queen of Baudoin of Belgium*
Fa·bi·us \'fā-bē-əs\ *d* 203 B.C. *Quintus Fabius Maximus Verrucosus Cunc·ta·tor* \‚kəŋk-'tā-tər\ Rom. gen. against Hannibal
Fa·bre \'fäbrᵃ\ Jean-Henri 1823–1915 Fr. entomologist
Fad·den \'fa-dᵊn\ Sir Arthur William 1895–1973 Austral. statesman
Fad·i·man \'fa-də-mən\ Clifton 1904–1999 Am. writer & editor
Fahd \'fäd\ 1923–2005 *Fahd ibn 'Abd al-'Azīz as-Sa'ūd* king of Saudi Arabia (1982–2005)
Fah·ren·heit \'fa-rən-‚hīt, 'fär-ən-\ Daniel Gabriel 1686–1736 Ger. physicist
Fair·banks \'fer-‚baŋ(k)s\ Charles Warren 1852–1918 Am. lawyer & polit.; vice pres. of U.S. (1905–09)
Fairbanks Douglas Elton 1883–1939 Am. actor
Fair·child \'fer-‚chīld\ David Grandison 1869–1954 Am. botanist
Fair·fax \'fer-‚faks\ Baron Thomas 1612–1671 Eng. gen.
Fairfax Baron Thomas 1692–1782 proprietor in Virginia
Fai·sal *Ar* **Fay·ṣal** \'fī-səl, 'fā-\ *ca* 1906–1975 king of Saudi Arabia (1964–75)
Faisal I *Ar* **Fayṣal** 1885–1933 king of Syria (1920), of Iraq (1921–33)
Faisal II *Ar* **Fayṣal** 1935–1958 king of Iraq (1939–58)
Fa·lier \'yer\ *or* **Fa·lie·ro** \-(‚)ō\ Marino 1274–1355 doge of Venice (1354–55)
Fal·ken·hau·sen \'fäl-kən-‚haú-z°n, 'fal-\ Ludwig 1844–1936 Freiherr *von Falkenhausen* Ger. gen.
Fal·ken·hayn \'fäl-kən-‚hīn, 'fal-\ Erich von 1861–1922 Ger. gen.
Fal·la \'fä-yə, 'fäl-\ Manuel de 1876–1946 Span. composer
Fal·lières \fal-'yer\ (Clément-) Armand 1841–1931 Fr. statesman; pres. of France (1906–13)
Fama \'fä-mə\ Eugene F(rancis) 1939–   Am. econ.
Fan·euil \'fan-yəl, 'fa-nᵊl, 'fan-yə-wəl\ Peter 1700–1743 Am. merchant
Far·a·day \'fa-rə-‚dā, -dē\ Michael 1791–1867 Eng. chem. & physicist
Far·ley \'fär-lē\ James Aloysius 1888–1976 Am. polit.
Far·man \fär-'mäⁿ, 'fär-mən\ Henri 1874–1958 & his bro. Maurice 1877–1964 Fr. pioneer aviators & airplane manufacturers
Far·mer \'fär-mər\ Fannie Merritt 1857–1915 Am. cookery expert
Farmer James Leonard 1920–1999 Am. civil rights leader
Far·ne·se \fär-'nā-zē, -sē\ Alessandro 1545–1592 Duke of *Parma* Ital. gen. in Span. service
Farns·worth \'färnz-‚wərth\ Philo Taylor 1906–1971 Am. engineer
Fa·rouk I \fə-'rük\ *Ar* **Fā·rūq al–Aw·wal** \fär-'ük-al-'a-wal\ 1920–1965 king of Egypt (1936–52; abdicated)
Far·quhar \'fär-kər, -kwər\ George 1678–1707 Brit. dram.
Far·ra·gut \'fa-rə-gət\ David Glasgow 1801–1870 Am. admiral
Far·ra·khan \'fa-rə-‚kän, 'fer-\ Louis Abdul 1933–   orig. *Louis Eugene Walcott* Am. religious leader
Far·rar \fa-'rär\ Frederic William 1831–1903 Eng. clergyman & writer
Far·rar \fə-'rär\ Geraldine 1882–1967 Am. soprano
Far·rell \'fa-rəl\ James Thomas 1904–1979 Am. nov.
Farrell Suzanne 1945–   orig. *Roberta Sue Ficker* Am. dancer
Fass·bin·der \'fäs-‚bin-dər\ Rainer Werner (Maria) 1945–1982 Ger. film director
Fāṭ·i·mah \'fa-tə-mə\ *ca* 606–633 *az-Zahrā'* ('Shining One') dau. of Muḥammad

Faulk·ner \'fòk-nər\ William Cuthbert 1897–1962 orig. surname *Falkner* Am. nov. — **Faulk·ner·ian** \fòk-'nir-ē-ən, -'ner-\ *also* **Faulk·ner·esque** \‚fòk-nər-'esk\ *adj*
Faure \'fòr\ (François-) Félix 1841–1899 Fr. statesman; pres. of France (1895–99)
Fau·ré \fò-'rā\ Gabriel (-Urbain) 1845–1924 Fr. composer
Faus·ta \'fò-stə, 'faú-\ 289–326 *Flavia Maximiana Fausta; wife of Constantine the Great* Rom. empress
Fawkes \'fòks\ Guy 1570–1606 Eng. conspirator
Fech·ner \'fek-nər, 'fek-\ Gustav Theodor 1801–1887 Ger. physicist & psychol.
Fed·er·er \'fe-dər-ər\ Roger 1981–   Swiss tennis player
Feif·fer \'fī-fər\ Jules 1929–   Am. cartoonist & writer
Fei·ning·er \'fī-niŋ-ər\ Lyonel Charles Adrian 1871–1956 Am. painter
Fel·li·ni \fə-'lē-nē\ Federico 1920–1993 Ital. film director — **Fel·li·ni·esque** \fə-‚lē-nē-'esk\ *adj*
Fell·tham \'fel-thəm\ Owen 1602?–1668 Eng. writer
Fé·ne·lon \‚fā-nə-'lōⁿ, fen-'lòⁿ\ François de Salignac de La Mothe-1651–1715 Fr. prelate & writer
Feng Yü–hsiang \'fəŋ-'yü-shē-'äŋ\ 1882–1948 Chin. gen.
Fenn \'fen\ John B(ennett) 1917–2010 Am. chem.
Fer·ber \'fər-bər\ Edna 1887–1968 Am. writer
Fer·di·nand I \'fər-də-‚nand\ 1016(or 1018)–1065 *the Great* king of Castile (1035–65); of León (1037–65)
Ferdinand I 1503–1564 Holy Rom. emp. (1558–64)
Ferdinand I 1861–1948 king of Bulgaria (1908–18)
Ferdinand II 1578–1637 king of Bohemia (1617–19; 1620–27) & of Hungary (1618–25); Holy Rom. emp. (1619–37)
Ferdinand III 1608–1657 king of Hungary (1625–47); Holy Rom. emp. (1637–57)
Ferdinand II of Aragon *or* **V** of Castile 1452–1516 *the Catholic; husband of Isabella I* king of Castile (1474–1504); of Aragon (1479–1516); of Naples (1504–16); founder of the Span. monarchy
Ferdinand VII 1784–1833 king of Spain (1808; 1814–33)
Fer·mat \fer-'mä\ Pierre de 1601–1665 Fr. math.
Fer·mi \'fer-(‚)mē\ Enrico 1901–1954 Am. (Ital.-born) physicist
Fer·nán·dez \fər-'nan-‚dez\ Juan *ca* 1536–*ca* 1604 Span. navigator
Fernández de Cór·do·ba \-t̲h̲ä-'kòr-dò-ba, -ə-va\ Gon·za·lo \gòn-'zä-lō\ 1453–1515 *El Gran Capitán* Span. soldier & statesman
Fer·re·ro \fə-'rer-(‚)ō\ Guglielmo 1871–1943 Ital. hist. & author
Fert \'fer\ Albert 1938–   Fr. physicist
Fes·sen·den \'fe-s°n-dən\ William Pitt 1806–1869 Am. polit.; U.S. secy. of the treasury (1864–65)
Fes·tus \'fes-təs\ Porcius *d ca* A.D. 62 Rom. procurator of Judea (58 or 60–62)
Feucht·wang·er \'fòikt-‚väŋ-ər, 'fòikt-\ Li·on \'lē-‚òn\ 1884–1958 Ger. nov. & dram.
Feuil·let \fə-'yā\ Octave 1821–1890 Fr. nov. & dram.
Feyn·man \'fīn-mən\ Richard Phillips 1918–1988 Am. physicist
Fi·bi·ger \'fē-bē-gər\ Johannes Andreas Grib 1867–1928 Dan. pathologist
Fich·te \'fik-tə, 'fik-\ Johann Gottlieb 1762–1814 Ger. philos. — **Fich·te·an** \-tē-ən\ *adj*
Fied·ler \'fēd-lər\ Arthur 1894–1979 Am. conductor
Field \'fēld\ Cyrus West 1819–1892 Am. financier
Field Eugene 1850–1895 Am. poet & journalist
Field Marshall 1834–1906 Am. merchant
Fiel·ding \'fēl-diŋ\ Henry 1707–1754 Eng. nov.
Fields \'fēldz\ W.C. 1880–1946 orig. *Claude William Dukenfield* Am. actor
Fi·guei·re·do \‚fē-ge-'rā-(‚)dü\ João Baptista de Oliveira 1918–1999 pres. of Brazil (1979–85)
Fil·more \'fil-‚mór\ Millard 1800–1874 13th pres. of the U.S. (1850–53)
Fil·lon \fē-'yoⁿ\ François 1954–   prime min. of France (2007–12)
Fin·lay \fin-'lī\ Carlos Juan 1833–1915 Cuban physician & biol.
Finn·bo·ga·dót·tir \'fin-‚bō-gə-‚dō-tər\ Vigdís 1930–   pres. of Iceland (1980–96)
Fin·sen \'fin(t)-sən\ Niels Ryberg 1860–1904 Dan. physician
Fir·bank \'fər-‚baŋk\ (Arthur Annesley) Ronald 1886–1926 Eng. author
Fir·dow·sī *or* **Fer·dow·sī** \‚fər-'daú-sē, -'dò-\ *or* **Fir·du·si** \-'dü-sē\ *or* **Fer·du·si** \-'daú-, -'dò-\ *ca* 935–*ca* 1020(or 1026) orig. *Abū ol-Qāsem Manṣūr* Pers. poet
Fire \'fī(-ə)r\ Andrew Zachary 1959–   Am. geneticist
Fire·stone \'fī(-ə)r-‚stōn\ Harvey Samuel 1868–1938 Am. industrialist
Fi·scher \'fi-shər\ Edmond H(enri) 1920–   Am. (Chin.-born of Fr. parents) biochem.
Fischer Emil (Hermann) 1852–1919 Ger. chem.
Fi·scher–Dies·kau \'fi-shər-‚dēs-‚kaú\ Dietrich 1925–2012 Ger. baritone
Fish \'fish\ Hamilton 1808–1893 Am. statesman
Fish·bein \'fish-‚bīn\ Morris 1889–1976 Am. physician & editor
Fish·er \'fi-shər\ Dorothy 1879–1958 *Dorothea Frances* née *Can·field* \'kan-‚fēld\ Am. nov.
Fisher Irving 1867–1947 Am. econ.
Fisher John Arbuthnot 1841–1920 1st Baron *Fisher of Kil·ver·stone* \'kil-vər-stən\ Brit. admiral
Fisher Mary Frances Kennedy 1908–1992 Am. writer
Fiske \'fisk\ John 1842–1901 orig. *Edmund Fisk Green* Am. philos. & hist.
Fitch \'fich\ (William) Clyde 1865–1909 Am. dram.
Fitch John 1743–1798 Am. inventor
Fitz·ger·ald \fits-'jer-əld\ Ella 1917–1996 Am. singer
Fitzgerald F(rancis) Scott (Key) 1896–1940 Am. writer
FitzGerald Edward 1809–1883 Eng. poet & translator
FitzGerald Garret 1926–2011 prime min. of Ireland (1981–87)
Fitz·her·bert \fits-'hər-bərt\ Maria Anne 1756–1837 née *Smythe; secret wife of George IV of England as Prince of Wales* (1785–1808)
Flagg \'flag\ James Montgomery 1877–1960 Am. illustrator
Flag·ler \'flag-lər\ Henry M(orrison) 1830–1913 Am. financier
Flag·stad \'flag-‚stad, *Norw* 'fläg-‚stä\ Kir·sten \'kish-tən, 'kir-stən\ 1895–1962 Norw. soprano
Fla·min·i·us \flə-'mi-nē-əs\ Gaius *d* 217 B.C. Rom. gen. & statesman

Flam·ma·rion \flə-ˌma-rē-ˈōⁿ\ (Nicolas-) Camille 1842–1925 Fr. astron.
Flan·a·gan \ˈfla-ni-gən\ Edward Joseph 1886–1948 Am. (Irish-born) R.C. priest & founder of Boys Town
Flau·bert \flō-ˈber\ Gustave 1821–1880 Fr. nov. — **Flau·ber·tian** \-ˈbər-shən, -ˈber-tē-ən\ adj
Flax·man \ˈflaks-mən\ John 1755–1826 Eng. sculptor
Flem·ing \ˈfle-miŋ\ Sir Alexander 1881–1955 Brit. bacteriol.
Fleming Ian Lancaster 1908–1964 Brit. writer
Fleming Sir John Ambrose 1849–1945 Eng. electrical engineer
Fleming Renée 1959–   Am. soprano
Fletch·er \ˈfle-chər\ John 1579–1625 Eng. dram.
Fleu·ry \ˌflər-ˈē\ André-Hercule de 1653–1743 Fr. cardinal & statesman
Fleury Claude 1640–1723 Fr. ecclesiastical hist.
Flint \ˈflint\ Austin: father 1812–1886 & son 1836–1915 Am. physicians
Flo·res \ˈflȯr-ˌās\ Juan José 1800–1864 Ecuadorian soldier; pres. of Ecuador (1830–35; 1839–45)
Flo·rey \ˈflȯr-ē\ Sir Howard Walter 1898–1968 Brit. pathologist
Flo·rio \ˈflȯr-ē-ˌō\ John ca 1553–ca 1625 Eng. lexicographer & translator
Flynn \ˈflin\ Errol (Leslie) 1909–1959 Am. (Austral.-born) actor
Fo \ˈfō\ Dario 1926–   Ital. playwright
Foch \ˈfȯsh, ˈfäsh\ Ferdinand 1851–1929 Fr. gen.; marshal of France
Fo·gel \ˈfō-gəl\ Robert (William) 1926–2013 Am. econ.
Fo·kine \ˈfȯ-ˌkēn, fȯ-ˈ\ Michel 1880–1942 Am. (Russ.-born) choreographer
Fok·ker \ˈfä-kər, ˈfȯ-\ Anthony Herman Gerard 1890–1939 Am. (Du.-born) aircraft designer & builder
Fol·ger \ˈfōl-jər\ Henry Clay 1857–1930 Am. bibliophile
Fon·da \ˈfän-də\ Henry (Jaynes) 1905–1982 & his dau. Jane 1937– orig. Lady Jayne Seymour Fonda Am. actors
Fon·tanne \ˈfän-ˌtan, fän-ˈ\ Lynn 1887?–1983 wife of Alfred Lunt Am. (Eng.-born) actress
Fon·teyn \ˈfän-ˌtān, fän-ˈ\ Dame Margot 1919–1991 orig. Margot Hookham \ˈhu̇-kəm\ Eng. ballerina
Foote \ˈfu̇t\ Andrew Hull 1806–1863 Am. admiral
Foote Samuel 1720–1777 Eng. actor & playwright
Foote Shelby 1916–2005 Am. hist. & nov.
Forbes–Rob·ert·son \ˈfȯrbz-ˈrä-bərt-sən\ Sir Johnston 1853–1937 Eng. actor
Ford \ˈfȯrd\ Ford Mad·ox \ˈma-dəks\ 1873–1939 orig. Ford Hermann Huef·fer \ˈhü-fər; ˈhwe-fər, ˈwe-\ Eng. author
Ford Gerald R(udolph) 1913–2006 Am. polit.; 38th pres. of the U.S. (1974–77)
Ford Henry 1863–1947 Am. automobile manuf.
Ford John 1586–?1639 Eng. dram.
Ford John 1895–1973 orig. John Martin Feeney Am. film dir.
For·es·ter \ˈfȯr-əs-tər, ˈfär-\ C(ecil) S(cott) 1899–1966 Brit. writer
For·rest \ˈfȯr-əst, ˈfär-\ Edwin 1806–1872 Am. actor
Forrest Nathan Bedford 1821–1877 Am. Confed. gen.
For·res·tal \ˈfȯr-əs-tᵊl, ˈfär-, -ˌtȯl\ James Vincent 1892–1949 Am. banker; 1st secy. of defense (1947–49)
For·ster \ˈfȯr-stər\ E(dward) M(organ) 1879–1970 Brit. nov. — **For·ste·ri·an** \fȯr-ˈstir-ē-ən\ adj
For·syth \ˈfȯr-ˌsīth, fȯr-ˈ\ John 1780–1841 Am. statesman
For·tas \ˈfȯr-təs\ Abe 1910–1982 Am. jurist
Fos·dick \ˈfäz-ˌ(ˌ)dik\ Harry Emerson 1878–1969 Am. clergyman
Fos·sey \ˈfȯ-sē, ˈfä-\ Dian 1932–1985 Am. ethologist
Fos·ter \ˈfȯs-tər, ˈfäs-\ Stephen Collins 1826–1864 Am. songwriter
Foster William Z(ebulon) 1881–1961 Am. Communist
Fou·cault \fü-ˈkō\ Jean-Bernard-Léon 1819–1868 Fr. physicist
Foucault Michel 1926–1984 Fr. philos.
Fou·qué \fü-ˈkā\ Friedrich Heinrich Karl de la Motte \ˈmȯt\ 1777–1843 Freiherr Fouqué Ger. author
Fou·quet or **Fouc·quet** \fü-ˈkā\ Nicolas 1615–1680 Fr. govt. official
Four·dri·nier \ˈfȯr-drə-ˈnir; fu̇r-ˈdri-nē-ər, fȯr-\ Henry 1766–1854 & his bro. Sealy 1774–1847 Eng. papermakers & inventors
Fou·ri·er \ˈfu̇r-ē-ˌā\ (François-Marie-) Charles 1772–1837 Fr. sociol. & reformer
Fow·ler \ˈfau̇-lər\ Henry Watson 1858–1933 Eng. lexicographer
Fowler William Alfred 1911–1995 Am. physicist
Fowles \ˈfau̇(-ə)lz\ John (Robert) 1926–2005 Brit. writer
Fox \ˈfäks\ Charles James 1749–1806 Eng. statesman & orator
Fox George 1624–1691 Eng. preacher & founder of Society of Friends
Fox (Quesada) \ˈfȯks-ˌkā-ˈsä-ˌthä\ Vicente 1942–   pres. of Mexico (2000–06)
Foxe \ˈfäks\ John 1516–1587 Eng. martyrologist
Foxe or **Fox** Richard ca 1448–1528 Eng. prelate & statesman
Foxx \ˈfäks\ Anthony (Renard) 1971–   U.S. secy. of transportation (2013–)
Foyt \ˈfȯit\ A(nthony) J(oseph) Jr. 1935–   Am. auto racer
Fra·go·nard \ˌfra-gə-ˈnär\ Jean-Honoré 1732–1806 Fr. artist
France \ˈfran(t)s, fräⁿs\ Anatole 1844–1924 pseud. of Jacques-Anatole-François Thibault Fr. nov. & satirist
Francesca Piero della — see PIERO DELLA FRANCESCA
Francesca da Rimini — see POLENTA
Fran·cis \ˈfran(t)-səs\ 1936–   orig. Jorge Mario Bergoglio pope (2013–)
Francis I 1494–1547 king of France (1515–47)
Francis II 1768–1835 last Holy Rom. emp. (1792–1806); emp. of Austria (as Francis I) 1804–35
Francis Fer·di·nand \ˈfər-də-ˌnand, ˈfer-dē-ˌnänt\ 1863–1914 archduke of Austria
Francis Jo·seph I \ˈjō-səf, ˈyō-sef\ 1830–1916 emp. of Austria (1848–1916)
Francis of Assisi Saint 1181(or 1182)–1226 Francesco di Pietro di Bernardone Ital. friar; founder of Franciscan order
Francis of Sales \ˈsälz\ Saint 1567–1622 Fr. R.C. bishop of Geneva
Franck \ˈfräŋk\ César Auguste 1822–1890 Fr. (Belg.-born) organist & composer
Franck James 1882–1964 Am. (Ger.-born) physicist
Francke \ˈfräŋ-kə\ Kuno 1855–1930 Am. (Ger.-born) hist. & educ.
Fran·co \ˈfräŋ-(ˌ)kō, ˈfraŋ-\ Francisco 1892–1975 Francisco Paulino Hermenegildo Teódulo Franco Bahamonde Span. gen. & head of Span. state (1936–75)

Frank \ˈfraŋk, ˈfräŋk\ Anne 1929–1945 Ger.-born diarist during the Holocaust
Frank·en·thal·er \ˈfraŋ-kən-ˌtä-lər, -ˌthä-\ Helen 1928–2011 Am. artist
Frank·furt·er \ˈfraŋk-fə(r)-tər, -ˌfər-\ Felix 1882–1965 Am. (Austrian-born) jurist
Frank·lin \ˈfraŋ-klən\ Aretha (Louise) 1942–   Am. singer
Franklin Benjamin 1706–1790 Am. statesman & philos.
Franklin Sir John 1786–1847 Eng. arctic explorer
Franklin Rosalind Elsie 1920–1958 Eng. biophysicist
Fra·ser \ˈfrä-zər, -zhər\ James Earle 1876–1953 Am. sculptor
Fraser (John) Malcolm 1930–   prime min. of Australia (1975–83)
Fraser Peter 1884–1950 N.Z. statesman; prime min. (1940–49)
Fraser Simon 1776–1862 Canad. explorer & fur trader
Fraun·ho·fer \ˈfrau̇n-ˌhō-fər\ Joseph von 1787–1826 Ger. physicist
Fra·zer \ˈfrä-zər, -zhər\ Sir James George 1854–1941 Scot. anthropol.
Fré·chette \frā-ˈshet\ Louis-Honoré 1839–1908 Canad. poet
Fred·er·ick I \ˈfre-d(ə-)rik\ ca 1123–1190 Frederick Bar·ba·ros·sa \ˌbär-bə-ˈrä-sə, -ˈrȯ-\ Holy Rom. emp. (1152–90)
Frederick II 1194–1250 Holy Rom. emp. (1215–50); king of Sicily (1198–1250)
Frederick I 1657–1713 king of Prussia (1701–13)
Frederick II 1712–1786 the Great king of Prussia (1740–86)
Frederick IX 1899–1972 king of Denmark (1947–72)
Frederick William 1620–1688 the Great Elector elector of Brandenburg (1640–88)
Frederick William name of 4 kings of Prussia: **I** 1688–1740 (reigned 1713–40); **II** 1744–1797 (reigned 1786–97); **III** 1770–1840 (reigned 1797–1840); **IV** 1795–1861 (reigned 1840–61)
Free·man \ˈfrē-mən\ Douglas Sou·thall \ˈsau̇-ˌthȯl, -ˌthȯl\ 1886–1953 Am. editor & hist.
Freeman Mary Eleanor Wilkins 1852–1930 née Wilkins Am. writer
Fre·ge \ˈfrā-gə\ (Friedrich Ludwig) Gottlob 1848–1925 Ger. math. & philos.
Fre·ling·huy·sen \ˈfrē-liŋ-ˌhī-zᵊn\ Frederick Theodore 1817–1885 Am. statesman
Fré·mont \ˈfrē-ˌmänt\ John Charles 1813–1890 Am. gen. & explorer
French \ˈfrench\ Daniel Chester 1850–1931 Am. sculptor
Fre·neau \fri-ˈnō\ Philip Morin 1752–1832 Am. poet
Fres·co·bal·di \ˌfres-kə-ˈbäl-dē, -ˈbȯl-\ Girolamo 1583–1643 Ital. composer
Fres·nel \frā-ˈnel\ Augustin-Jean 1788–1827 Fr. physicist
Freud \ˈfrȯid\ Sigmund 1856–1939 Austrian neurologist
Frey·berg \ˈfrī-ˌbərg\ Bernard Cyril 1889–1963 Baron Freyberg N.Z. gen.
Frey·tag \ˈfrī-ˌtäk, -ˌtäg\ Gustav 1816–1895 Ger. author
Frick \ˈfrik\ Henry Clay 1849–1919 Am. industrialist
Frie·dan \frē-ˈdan\ Betty 1921–2006 née Bettye Naomi Goldstein Am. feminist
Fried·man \ˈfrēd-mən\ Jerome Isaac 1930–   Am. physicist
Friedman Milton 1912–2006 Am. econ.
Frie·drich \ˈfrē-driḵ\ Caspar David 1774–1840 Ger. painter
Frisch \ˈfrish\ Karl von 1886–1982 Austrian zool.
Fro·bi·sher \ˈfrō-bi-shər\ Sir Martin 1535?–1594 Eng. navigator
Froe·bel or **Frö·bel** \ˈfrā-bəl, ˈfrē-, ˈfrœ-\ Friedrich Wilhelm August 1782–1852 Ger. educ.
Frois·sart \ˈfrȯi-ˌsärt, frwä-ˈsär\ Jean 1333?–ca 1405 Fr. chronicler
Fromm \ˈfrōm, ˈfräm\ Erich 1900–1980 Am. (Ger.-born) psychoanalyst
Fron·di·zi \frän-ˈdē-zē, -sē\ Arturo 1908–1995 Argentine pres. (1958–62)
Fron·te·nac et Pal·lu·au \frōⁿ-tə-näk-ā-pä-ˈlwᵊyō\ Comte de 1622–1698 Louis de Buade \ˈbwᵊyäd\ Fr. gen. & colonial administrator in America
Frost \ˈfrȯst\ Robert Lee 1874–1963 Am. poet — **Frost·ian** \ˈfrȯs-tē-ən, -chən\ adj
Froude \ˈfrüd\ James Anthony 1818–1894 Eng. hist.
Fry \ˈfrī\ Christopher 1907–2005 Eng. dram.
Frye \ˈfrī\ (Herman) Northrop 1912–1991 Canad. lit. critic
Fu·ʾād I \fu̇-ˈäd\ 1868–1936 sultan (1917–22) & king (1922–36) of Egypt
Fu·en·tes \fü-ˈen-ˌtäs\ Carlos 1928–2012 Mex. author
Fuer·tes \ˈfyu̇r-(ˌ)tēz\ Louis Agassiz 1874–1927 Am. illustrator
Fu·gard \fü-ˈgärd\ Athol 1932–   So. African playwright
Fu·ji·mo·ri \ˌfü-jē-ˈmȯ-rē\ Alberto 1938–   pres. of Peru (1990–2000)
Ful·bright \ˈfu̇l-ˌbrīt\ (James) William 1905–1995 Am. polit.
Ful·ler \ˈfu̇-lər\ Melville Weston 1833–1910 Am. jurist; chief justice U.S. Supreme Court (1888–1910)
Fuller (Richard) Buckminster 1895–1983 Am. engineer
Fuller (Sarah) Margaret 1810–1850 Marchioness Os·so·li \ˈȯ-sə-(ˌ)lē\ Am. critic & reformer
Fuller Thomas 1608–1661 Eng. divine & author
Ful·ton \ˈfu̇l-tᵊn\ Robert 1765–1815 Am. engineer & inventor
Funk \ˈfu̇ŋk, ˈfəŋk\ Casimir 1884–1967 Am. (Pol.-born) biochem.
Funk \ˈfəŋk\ Isaac Kauffman 1839–1912 Am. editor & publisher
Furch·gott \ˈfərch-ˌgät\ Robert F(rancis) 1916–2009 Am. biochem.
Fur·ness \ˈfər-nəs, -ˌnes\ Horace Howard: father 1833–1912 & son 1865–1930 Am. Shakespearean scholars
Fur·ni·vall \ˈfər-nə-vəl\ Frederick James 1825–1910 Eng. philologist
Furt·wäng·ler \ˈfu̇rt-ˌveŋ-lər\ (Gustav Heinrich Ernst Martin) Wilhelm 1886–1954 Ger. conductor
Ga·ble \ˈgä-bəl\ (William) Clark 1901–1960 Am. actor
Ga·bo \ˈgä-(ˌ)bō\ Naum 1890–1977 orig. Naum Pevs·ner \ˈpevz-nər\ Am. (Russ.-born) sculptor
Ga·bor \ˈgä-(ˌ)bȯr, gə-ˈbȯr\ Dennis 1900–1979 Brit. (Hung.-born) physicist
Ga·bo·riau \ˌgä-bȯ-ˈryō, -ˈō\ Émile 1832?–1873 Fr. writer
Ga·bri·eli \ˌgä-brē-ˈe-lē\ Giovanni ca 1556–1612 Ital. composer

---

Gad·dha·fi \gə-'dä-fē, kə-, -'da-\ Mu'ammar Muḥammad al- 1942–2011 Libyan leader (1969–2011)

Gads·den \'gadz-dən\ James 1788–1858 Am. army officer & diplomat

Ga·ga·rin \gə-'gär-ən\ Yu·ry \'yùr-ē\ Alekseyevich 1934–1968 Russ. cosmonaut

Gage \'gāj\ Thomas 1721–1787 Brit. gen. & colonial gov. in America

Gail·lard \gil-'yärd\ David DuBose \dü-'bōz, dyü-\ 1859–1913 Am. army officer & engineer

Gaines \'gānz\ Edmund Pendleton 1777–1849 Am. gen.

Gains·bor·ough \'gānz-,bər-ə, -,bə-rə, -b(ə-)rə\ Thomas 1727–1788 Eng. painter

Gait·skell \'gāt-skəl\ Hugh Todd Naylor 1906–1963 Eng. polit.

Ga·ius \'gä-əs, 'gī-əs\ fl A.D. 130–180 Rom. jurist

Gal·ba \'gal-bə, 'gól-\ Servius Sulpicius 3 B.C.–A.D. 69 Rom. emp. (68–69)

Gal·braith \'gal-,brāth\ John Kenneth 1908–2006 Am. (Canad.-born) econ. — Gal·braith·ian \,gal-'brā-thē-ən, -'brāth-yən\ adj

Gale \'gāl\ Zona 1874–1938 Am. nov.

Ga·len \'gā-lən\ A.D. 129–ca 199 Greek physician & writer — Ga·len·ic \gə-'le-nik\ or Ga·len·i·cal \-ni-kəl\ adj

Ga·le·ri·us \gə-'lir-ē-əs\ d 311 Gaius Galerius Valerius Maximianus Rom. emp. (305–311)

Ga·li·leo \,ga-lə-'lē-(,)ō, -'lā-\ 1564–1642 in full Galileo Galilei Ital. astron. & physicist

Gal·land \ga-'län\ Antoine 1646–1715 Fr. orientalist & translator

Gal·lant \ga-'lant\ Mavis 1922–   orig. Mavis de Trafford Young Canad.-Fr. writer

Gal·la·tin \'ga-lə-tən\ (Abraham Alfonse) Albert 1761–1849 Am. (Swiss-born) financier & statesman

Gal·lau·det \,ga-lə-'det\ Thomas Hopkins 1787–1851 Am. teacher of the hearing- and speech-impaired

Ga·lle·gos Freí·re \gä-'yā-(,)gōs-'frā-(,)rä\ Rómulo 1884–1969 Venezuelan nov.; pres. of Venezuela (1948)

Gal·li–Cur·ci \,ga-li-'kúr-chē, gä-, -'kər-\ Amelita 1889–1963 née Galli Am. (Ital.-born) soprano

Gal·lie·ni \,gal-'yā-nē, gal-'yä-nē\ Joseph-Simon 1849–1916 Fr. gen. & colonial administrator

Gal·li·e·nus \,gal-ē-'ē-nəs, -'ā-nəs\ Publius Licinius Valerianus Egnatius d 268 Rom. emp. (253–268)

Gal·lup \'ga-ləp\ George Horace 1901–1984 Am. statistician

Ga·lois \gal-'wä\ Évariste 1811–1832 Fr. math.

Gals·wor·thy \'gólz-,wər-thē\ John 1867–1933 Eng. nov. & dram.

Galt \'gólt\ John 1779–1839 Scot. nov.

Gal·ton \'gól-tᵊn\ Sir Francis 1822–1911 Eng. scientist

Gal·va·ni \gal-'vä-nē, gäl-\ Luigi 1737–1798 Ital. physician & physicist

Gál·vez \'gäl-,ves\ José 1729–1787 Marqués de la Sonora Span. jurist & colonial administrator

Ga·ma, da \dä-'gä-mə, -'gä-\ Vas·co \'vas-kō, 'väs-\ ca 1460–1524 Port. navigator & explorer

Ga·mar·ra \gə-'mär-ə\ Augustín 1785–1841 Peruvian gen.; pres. of Peru (1829–33; 1839–41)

Gam·bet·ta \gam-'be-tə, ,gän-bə-'tä\ Léon (-Michel) 1838–1882 Fr. lawyer & statesman; premier (1881–82)

Ga·me·lin \,gam-'lᵃⁿ, ,ga-mə-\ Maurice-Gustave 1872–1958 Fr. gen.

Gan·dhi \'gän-dē, 'gan-\ Indira \in-'dir-ə, 'in-də-rə\ 1917–1984 dau. of Jawaharlal Nehru prime min. of India (1966–77; 1980–84)

Gandhi Mohandas Karamchand 1869–1948 Ma·hat·ma \mə-'hät-mə, -'hat-\ Indian nationalist leader — Gan·dhi·an \-ən\ adj

Gandhi Ra·jiv \rä-'jēv\ Ratna 1944–1991 son of Indira prime min. of India (1984–89)

Gao Xing·jian \gaù-'shiŋ-'jyen\ 1940–   Fr. (Chin.-born) nov., essayist, & dram.

Gar·a·mond \'ga-rə-,mänd, ,ga-rə-'mōⁿ\ or Gar·a·mont \-,mänt, -'mōⁿ\ Claude ca 1480–1561 Fr. typefounder

Ga·rand \gə-'rand, 'ga-rand\ John Cantius 1888–1974 Am. (Canad.-born) inventor

Gar·bo \'gär-(,)bō\ Greta 1905–1990 orig. Greta Lovisa Gustafsson Am. (Swed.-born) actress — Gar·bo·esque \,gär-bō-'wesk\ adj

Gar·cía (Pé·rez) \gär-'sē-ə(-'per-es)\ Alan (Gabriel Ludwig) 1949–   pres. of Peru (1985–90; 2006–11)

García Gu·tiér·rez \-gü-'tyer-əs\ Antonio 1813–1884 Span. dram.

García Lor·ca \-'lór-kə\ Federico 1898–1936 Span. poet & dram.

García Már·quez \-'mär-,käs\ Gabriel 1928–   Colombian author

García Mo·re·no \-,mo-'rā-(,)nō\ Gabriel 1821–1875 Ecuadoran journalist; pres. of Ecuador (1861–65; 1869–75)

Gar·ci·la·so de la Ve·ga \gär-si-'lä-sō-,dä-lə-'vä-gə\ 1539–1616 El Inca Peruvian hist.

Gar·di·ner \'gärd-nər, 'gär-dᵊn-ər\ Samuel Rawson 1829–1902 Eng. hist.

Gardiner Stephen ca 1482–1555 Eng. prelate & statesman

Gard·ner \'gärd-nər\ Erle Stanley 1889–1970 Am. writer

Gar·field \'gär-,fēld\ James Abram 1831–1881 20th pres. of the U.S. (1881)

Gar·i·bal·di \,gar-ə-'ból-dē\ Giuseppe 1807–1882 Ital. patriot

Gar·land \'gär-lənd\ (Hannibal) Hamlin 1860–1940 Am. nov.

Garland Judy 1922–1969 orig. Frances Gumm Am. actress & singer

Gar·ner \'gär-nər\ John Nance 1868–1967 Am. polit.; vice pres. of the U.S. (1933–41)

Gar·nett \'gär-nət\ Constance 1862–1946 née Black Eng. translator

Gar·rick \'ga-rik\ David 1717–1779 Eng. actor

Gar·ri·son \'ga-rə-sən\ William Lloyd 1805–1879 Am. abolitionist

Gar·shin \'gär-shən\ Vsevolod Mikhaylovich 1855–1888 Russ. writer

Gar·vey \'gär-vē\ Marcus Moziah 1887–1940 Jamaican black leader

Gary \'ger-ē\ Elbert Henry 1846–1927 Am. industrialist

Gas·coigne \'gas-,kòin\ George ca 1525–1577 Eng. poet

Gas·kell \'gas-kəl\ Elizabeth Cleghorn 1810–1865 née Stevenson Eng. nov.

Gas·ser \'ga-sər\ Herbert Spencer 1888–1963 Am. physiol.

Gates \'gāts\ Bill 1955–   William Henry Gates III Am. computer software manuf.

Gates Henry Louis, Jr. 1950–   Am. educator

Gates Horatio ca 1728–1806 Am. gen. in Revolution

Gates Robert Michael 1943–   U.S. secy. of defense (2006–11)

Gau·guin \gō-'gaⁿ\ (Eugène-Henri-) Paul 1848–1903 Fr. painter — Gau·guin·esque \(,)gō-,ga-'nesk\ adj

Gaulle, de \di-'gōl, -'gòl\ Charles (-André-Marie-Joseph) 1890–1970 Fr. gen. & polit.; pres. of Fifth Republic (1958–69)

Gauss \'gaùs\ Carl Friedrich 1777–1855 Ger. math. & astron.

Gau·tier \gō-'tyā\ Théophile 1811–1872 Fr. author

Gay \'gā\ John 1685–1732 Eng. poet & dram.

Gay–Lus·sac \gā-lə-'sak\ Joseph-Louis 1778–1850 Fr. chem. & physicist

Gbo·wee \'bō-ē\ Ley·mah \'lā-mə\ (Roberta) 1972–   Liberian peace activist

Ged·des \'ge-dēz\ Norman Bel 1893–1958 Am. designer

Geh·rig \'ger-ig\ Lou 1903–1941 Henry Louis Gehrig Am. baseball player

Gehry \'ger-ē\ Frank Owen 1929–   orig. Ephraim Owen Goldberg Am. (Canad.-born) architect

Geim \'gām, 'gīm\ Sir Andre (Konstantin) 1958–   Russ.-Dutch= Brit. physicist

Gei·sel \'gī-zəl\ Theodor Seuss 1904–1991 pseud. Dr. Seuss \'süs\ Am. writer & illustrator

Geith·ner \'gīt-nər\ Timothy (Franz) 1961–   U.S. secy. of treasury (2009–13)

Gell–Mann \'gel-'män\ Murray 1929–   Am. physicist

Ge·net \zhə-'nā\ Edmond-Charles-Édouard 1763–1834 Citizen Genet Fr. diplomat in U.S.

Genet Jean 1910–1986 Fr. dram. & nov.

Gen·ghis Khan \,jeŋ-gəs-'kän, ,gen-\ ca 1162–1227 Mongol conqueror

Gen·ser·ic \'gen(t)-sə-rik, 'jen(t)-\ or Gai·se·ric \'gī-zə-(,)rik, -sə-\ d 477 king of the Vandals (428–477)

Gen·ti·le da Fa·bri·a·no \jen-'tē-lē-də-,fä-brē-'ä-(,)nō\ ca 1370–1427 orig. Niccolo di Giovanni di Massio Ital. painter

Gen·ti·les·chi \,jen-tə-'les-kē\ Orazio Lomi 1562–ca 1639 & his dau. Artemisia 1593–after 1651 Ital. painters

Geof·frey of Monmouth \'jef-rē-əv-'män-məth\ ca 1100–1154 Brit. ecclesiastic & chronicler

George \'jórj\ Saint 3d cent. Christian martyr & patron saint of England

George name of 6 kings of Great Britain: I 1660–1727 (reigned 1714–27); II 1683–1760 (reigned 1727–60); III 1738–1820 (reigned 1760–1820); IV 1762–1830 (reigned 1820–30); V 1865–1936 (reigned 1910–36); VI 1895–1952 (reigned 1936–52)

George name of 2 kings of Greece: I 1845–1913 (reigned 1863–1913); II 1890–1947 (reigned 1922–23; 1935–47)

George David Lloyd — see David LLOYD GEORGE

George Henry 1839–1897 Am. econ.

Ge·rard \jə-'rärd, 'jer-,ärd\ Charles 1618?–1694 1st Baron Gerard of Bran·don \'bran-dən\; Viscount Brandon Eng. Royalist commander

Gé·rard \zhā-'rär\ Comte Étienne-Maurice 1773–1852 Fr. Napoleonic gen.; marshal of France

Ger·hard·sen \'ger-,härd-ha-sᵊn\ Einar Henry 1897–1987 Norw. polit.

Gé·ri·cault \,zhā-ri-'kō\ (Jean-Louis-André-) Théodore 1791–1824 Fr. painter

Ger·man·i·cus Cae·sar \jər-,ma-ni-kə(s)-'sē-zər\ 15 B.C.–A.D. 19 Rom. gen.

Gé·rôme \zhā-'rōm\ Jean-Léon 1824–1904 Fr. painter

Ge·ron·i·mo \jə-'rä-nə-,mō\ 1829–1909 Goyathlay Chiricahua Apache leader

Ger·ry \'ger-ē\ Elbridge 1744–1814 Am. polit.; vice pres. of the U.S. (1813–14)

Gersh·win \'gər-shwən\ George 1898–1937 orig. Jacob Gershvin Am. composer

Gersh·win Ira 1896–1983 Israel Gershvin; bro. of prec. Am. lyricist

Ge·sell \gə-'zel\ Arnold Lucius 1880–1961 Am. psychol. & pediatrician

Ges·ner \'ges-nər\ Conrad 1516–1565 Swiss naturalist

Get·ty \'ge-tē\ Jean Paul 1892–1976 Am. oil magnate

Gha·zā·lī, al- \,al-gə-'za-lē\ 1058–1111 Abu Ḥāmid Muḥammad ibn Muḥammad aṭ-Ṭūsī al-Ghazālī Islamic jurist, theol., & mystic

Ghi·ber·ti \gē-'ber-tē\ Lorenzo ca 1378–1455 Florentine goldsmith, painter, & sculptor

Ghir·lan·da·jo or Ghir·lan·da·io \,gir-lən-'dä-(,)yō\ Domenico 1449–1494 orig. Domenico di Tommaso Bigordi Florentine painter

Giac·co·ni \jə-'kō-nē\ Riccardo 1931–   Am. (Ital.-born) astrophysicist

Gia·co·met·ti \,jä-kə-'me-tē\ Alberto 1901–1966 Swiss artist

Gib·bon \'gi-bən\ Edward 1737–1794 Eng. hist. — Gib·bon·esque \,gi-bə-'nesk\ or Gib·bon·ian \gi-'bō-nē-ən\ adj

Gib·bons \'gi-bənz\ Orlando 1538–1625 Eng. organist & composer

Gibbs \'gibz\ James 1682–1754 Brit. architect

Gibbs J(osiah) Willard 1839–1903 Am. math. & physicist

Gib·ran or Jib·ran \jə-'brän\ Khalil 1883–1931 Jubrān Khalīl Jubrān Lebanese nov., poet, & artist in U.S.

Gib·son \'gib-sən\ Charles Dana 1867–1944 Am. illustrator

Gide \'zhēd\ André 1869–1951 Fr. nov., critic, & essayist

Giel·gud \'gil-,gùd, 'gēl-\ Sir (Arthur) John 1904–2000 Eng. actor

Gie·rek \'gyer-ek\ Edward 1913–2001 1st secy. of Polish Communist party (1970–80)

Gie·se·king \'gē-zə-kiŋ\ Walter Wilhelm 1895–1956 Ger. (Fr.-born) pianist

Gil·bert \'gil-bərt\ Cass 1859–1934 Am. architect

Gilbert Sir Humphrey ca 1539–1583 Eng. navigator

Gilbert William 1540–1603 Eng. physician & physicist

Gilbert Sir William Schwenck 1836–1911 Eng. librettist & poet — Gil·bert·ian \gil-'bər-tē-ən\ adj

Gil·lard \'gi-,lärd\ Julia (Eileen) 1961–   prime min. of Australia (2010–13)

Gil·les·pie \gə-'les-pē\ John Birks 1917–1993 Dizzy Am. jazz musician

Gil·lette \jə-'let\ King Camp 1855–1932 Am. inventor & manuf.

Gil·man \'gil-mən\ Alfred G(oodman) 1941–   Am. pharmacologist

Gilman Daniel Coit \'kòit\ 1831–1908 Am. educ.; pres. Johns Hopkins U. (1875–1901)

Gil·mer \'gil-mər\ Elizabeth 1870–1951 née Mer·i·weth·er \'mer-ə-,we-thər\ pseud. Dorothy Dix \'diks\ Am. journalist

Gil·pin \'gil-pən\ Charles Sidney 1878–1930 Am. actor

Gi·na·ste·ra \,hē-nə-'ster-ə\ Alberto Evaristo 1916–1983 Argentine composer

Gin·grich \'giŋ-(,)grich, -(,)rich\ Newton Leroy 1943–   Am. polit.

Gins·berg \'ginz-,bərg\ Allen 1926–1997 Am. poet

Gins·burg \'ginz-,bərg\ Ruth Bader 1933–   Am. jurist

Ginz·burg \'ginz-,bərg\ Vitaly Lazarevich 1916–2009 Russ. physicist

Gior·gio·ne \(,)jòr-'jō-nē\ ca 1477–1511 Giorgione da Castelfranco Venetlan painter

Giot·to \'jò(t)-(,)tō, jē-'ä-(,)tō\ 1266/67(or 1276)–1337 Giotto di Bondone Florentine painter, architect, & sculptor

Gi·rard \zhē-'rär\ Jean-Baptiste 1765–1850 Swiss Franciscan & educ.

Gi·rard \jə-'rärd\ Stephen 1750–1831 Am. (Fr.-born) financier

Gi·raud \zhē-'rō\ Henri-Honoré 1879–1949 Fr. gen.

Gi·rau·doux \'zhē-rō-'dü\ (Hyppolyte-) Jean 1882–1944 Fr. writer

Gir·tin \'gər-tᵊn\ Thomas 1775–1802 Eng. painter

Gis·card d'Es·taing \zhis-kär-des-'taⁿ, -,kär-des-'taŋ\ Valéry 1926–   pres. of France (1974–81)

Gish \'gish\ Lillian Diana 1893–1993 Am. actress

Gis·sing \'gi-siŋ\ George Robert 1857–1903 Eng. nov.

Giu·lio Ro·ma·no \'jül-yō-rə-'mä-(,)nō\ ca 1499–1546 Giulio di Pietro di Filippo de' Gianuzzi Ital. painter & architect

Glad·stone \'glad-,stōn, chiefly Brit -stən\ William Ewart 1809–1898 Brit. statesman; prime min. (1868–74; 1880–85; 1886; 1892–94) — Glad·ston·ian \,glad-'stō-nē-ən\ adj

Gla·ser \'glā-zər\ Donald A(rthur) 1926–2013 Am. physicist

Glas·gow \'glas-(,)kō, -(,)gō; 'glaz-(,)gō\ Ellen (Anderson Gholson) 1873–1945 Am. nov.

Glas·pell \'glas-,pel\ Susan 1882–1948 Am. nov. & dram.

Glass \'glas\ Carter 1858–1946 Am. statesman

Glass Philip 1937–   Am. composer

Glau·ber \'glaù-bər\ Roy J(ay) 1925–   Am. physicist

Gla·zu·nov \'gla-zə-,nóf, -,nóv, glä-zù-'\ Aleksandr Konstantinovich 1865–1936 Russ. composer

Glen·dow·er \glen-'daù(-ə)r\ Owen ca 1359–ca 1416 Welsh rebel

Glenn \'glen\ John 1921–   John Herschel Glenn, Jr. Am. astronaut & polit.

Glin·ka \'gliŋ-kə\ Mikhail Ivanovich 1804–1857 Russ. composer

Gloucester Duke of — see HUMPHREY

Glov·er \'glə-vər\ John 1732–1797 Am. gen. in Revolution

Gluck \'glük\ Alma 1884–1938 née (Reba) Fiersohn Am. (Romanian-born) soprano

Gluck Christoph Willibald 1714–1787 Ger. composer

Go·dard \gō-'där\ Jean-Luc 1930–   Fr. filmmaker

God·dard \'gä-dərd\ Robert Hutchings 1882–1945 Am. physicist

Gö·del \'gə(r)-dᵊl, 'gœ-\ Kurt 1906–1978 Am. (Austrian-born) mathematician

God·frey of Bouillon \,gäd-frē\ F Gode·froy de Bouillon \gòt-'frwä\ ca 1060–1100 Fr. crusader

Go·dol·phin \gə-'däl-fən\ Sidney 1645–1712 1st Earl of Godolphin Eng. statesman

Go·doy \gō-'dói\ Manuel de 1767–1851 Span. statesman

Go·du·nov \'gō-də-,nóf, 'gó-, 'gä-\ Boris Fyodorovich ca 1551–1605 czar of Russia (1598–1605)

God·win \'gäd-wən\ or God·wine \'gäd-(,)wi-nə\ d 1053 earl of Wessex

Godwin William 1756–1836 Eng. philos. & nov. — God·win·ian \gäd-'wi-nē-ən\ adj

Godwin–Aus·ten \-'òs-tən, -'äs-\ Henry Haversham 1834–1923 Eng. explorer & geologist

Goeb·bels \'gə(r)-bəlz, 'gœ-bəls\ (Paul) Joseph 1897–1945 Ger. Nazi propagandist

Goe·ring var of GÖRING

Goes \'güs\ Hugo van der ca 1440–1482 Du. painter

Goe·thals \'gō-thəlz\ George Washington 1858–1928 Am. gen. & engineer

Goe·the \'gə(r)-tə, 'gœ-tə\ Johann Wolfgang von 1749–1832 Ger. poet & dram. — Goe·the·an \-tē-ən\ adj

Gogh, van \van-'gō, -'gäk, -'kòk, Brit also -'gəf\ Vincent Willem 1853–1890 Du. painter

Go·gol \'gō-gəl, 'gò-,gòl\ Nikolay Vasilyevich 1809–1852 Russ. writer — Go·gol·ian \gò-'gòl-yən, gō-'gòl-\ adj

Gold·berg \'gōl(d)-,bərg\ Arthur Joseph 1908–1990 Am. lawyer & jurist; U.S. ambassador to U.N. (1965–68)

Gol·den·wei·ser \'gōl-dən-,wī-zər\ Alexander Alexandrovich 1880–1940 Am. (Russ.-born) anthropol. & sociol.

Gol·ding \'gōl-diŋ\ Sir William Gerald 1911–1993 Eng. author

Gol·do·ni \gäl-'dō-nē, gōl-\ Carlo 1707–1793 Ital. dram.

Gold·smith \'gōl(d)-,smith\ Oliver 1730–1774 Brit. author

Gold·stein \'gōl(d)-,stīn\ Joseph L(eonard) 1940–   Am. molecular geneticist

Gold·wa·ter \'gōld-,wò-tər, -,wä-\ Barry Morris 1909–1998 Am. polit.

Gold·wyn \'gōl-dwən\ Samuel 1879?–1974 orig. Schmuel Gelbfisz Am. (Pol.-born) motion-picture producer

Gol·gi \'gól-(,)jē\ Camillo \kä-'mēl-(,)lō\ 1843(or 1844)–1926 Ital. physician

Gol·lancz \gə-'lan(t)s\ Sir Hermann 1852–1930 Eng. Semitic scholar

Gó·mez \'gò-,mez\ Juan Vicente 1864–1935 Venezuelan gen. & polit.; dictator (1908–35)

Gom·pers \'gäm-pərz\ Samuel 1850–1924 Am. (Brit.-born) labor leader

Go·muł·ka \gō-'mül-kə, -'məl-\ Władysław 1905–1982 Pol. polit.

Gon·çal·ves Di·as \gən-'säl-vəs-'dē-əs\ Antônio 1823–1864 Braz. poet

Gon·cha·ro·va \gən-'chär-ə-və\ Nathalie 1883–1962 Russ. artist

Gon·court \gōⁿ-'kür\ Edmond (-Louis-Antoine Huot) de 1822–1896 & his bro. Jules (-Alfred Huot) de 1830–1870 Fr. nov. & collaborators

Gon·do·mar \,gän-də-'mär\ Conde de 1567–1626 Diego Sarmiento de Acuña Span. diplomat

Gon·za·ga \gən-'zä-gə, gän-, -'zä-\ Saint Aloysius 1568–1591 Ital. Jesuit

Gon·za·les \gən-'zä-ləs\ Alberto R. 1955–   U.S. atty. gen. (2005–2007)

Gon·zá·lez \gən-'zä-ləs\ Manuel 1833–1893 Mex. gen.; pres. of Mexico (1880–84)

Goo·dall \'gù-(,)dòl, -(,)däl\ Dame Jane 1934–   orig. Valerie Jane Morris-Goodall Brit. ethologist

Good·hue \'gùd-(,)hyü, -(,)yü\ Bertram Grosvenor 1869–1924 Am. architect

Good·man \'gùd-mən\ Benjamin David 1909–1986 Benny Goodman Am. musician & bandleader

Good·rich \'gùd-(,)rich\ Samuel Griswold 1793–1860 pseud. Peter Parley \'pär-lē\ Am. writer

Good·year \'gùd-,yir\ Charles 1800–1860 Am. inventor

Gor·ba·chev \,gòr-bə-'chóf, -'chef; 'gòr-bə-,\ Mikhail Sergeyevich 1931–   Soviet polit.; 1st secy. of Communist party (1985–91); pres. of U.S.S.R. (1990–91)

Gor·cha·kov \,gòr-chə-'kóf, -'kóv\ Prince Aleksandr Mikhaylovich 1798–1883 Russ. statesman & diplomat

Gor·di·mer \'gòr-də-mər\ Nadine 1923–   So. African writer

Gor·din \'gòr-dᵊn\ Jacob 1853–1909 Am. (Russ.-born) Yiddish dram.

Gor·don \'gòr-dᵊn\ Charles George 1833–1885 Chinese Gordon, Gordon Pasha Brit. soldier

Gordon Charles William 1860–1937 pseud. Ralph Connor Canad. clergyman & nov.

Gordon Lord George 1751–1793 Eng. polit. agitator

Gore \'gòr\ Albert, Jr. 1948–   Am. polit. & environmentalist; vice pres. of the U.S. (1993–2001)

Go·re·my·kin \,gòr-ə-'mē-kən\ Ivan Logginovich 1839–1917 Russ. statesman; prime min. (1906; 1914–16)

Gor·ey \'gòr-ē\ Edward St. John 1925–2000 Am. illustrator & writer

Gor·gas \'gòr-gəs\ William Crawford 1854–1920 Am. army surgeon & sanitation expert

Gö·ring \'gər-iŋ, 'ger-, 'gœr-\ Hermann 1893–1946 Ger. Nazi polit.

Gor·ky \'gòr-kē\ Arshile 1905–1948 Am. (Armenian-born) artist

Gorky Maksim 1868–1936 pseud. of Aleksey Maksimovich Pesh·kov \'pesh-,kóf, -,kóv\ Russ. writer

Gort Viscount — see VEREKER

Gosse \'gäs\ Sir Edmund William 1849–1928 Eng. poet & critic

Gott·schalk \'gä-,chòk, 'gät-,shòk\ Louis Moreau 1829–1869 Am. composer

Gou·dy \'gaù-dē\ Frederic William 1865–1947 Am. type designer

Gough \'gäf\ Hugh 1779–1869 1st Viscount Gough Eng. field marshal

Gould \'gùld\ Glenn (Herbert) 1932–1982 Canad. pianist

Gould Jay 1836–1892 orig. Jason Gould Am. financier

Gould Stephen Jay 1941–2002 Am. paleontologist

Gou·nod \gü-'nō; 'gü-,nō\ Charles-François 1818–1893 Fr. composer

Gour·mont \gùr-'mōⁿ\ Remy de 1858–1915 Fr. writer

Gove \'gōv\ Philip Babcock 1902–1972 Am. lexicographer

Gow·da \gō-(,)dä\ H(aradanahalli) D(oddegowda) Deve \'de-(,)vä, -ve\ 1933–   prime min. of India (1996–97)

Gow·er \'gaù(-ə)r, 'gò-ər\ John 1330?–1408 Eng. poet

Go·ya (y Lu·cien·tes) \'gói-ə-,ē-,lü-sē-'en-,tās\ Francisco José de 1746–1828 Span. painter — Go·ya·esque \,gói-ə-'esk\ or Go·yesque \,gói-'yesk\ adj

Goy·en or Goij·en, van \van-'gói-ən, -'kói-\ Jan Josephszoon 1596–1656 Du. painter

Grac·chus \'gra-kəs\ Gaius Sempronius 153–121 B.C. & his bro. Tiberius Sempronius 163–133 B.C. the Grac·chi \'gra-,kī\ Rom. statesmen

Gra·ham \'grā-əm, 'gra(-ə)m\ John 1648–1689 Graham of Claverhouse; Bonnie Dundee; 1st Viscount of Dundee Scot. Jacobite

Graham Martha 1893–1991 Am. choreographer & dancer

Graham Thomas 1805–1869 Scot. chem.

Graham William Franklin 1918–   Billy Graham Am. evangelist

Gra·hame \'grā-əm, 'gra(-ə)m\ Kenneth 1859–1932 Brit. writer

Gramme \'gram\ Zénobe Théophile 1826–1901 Belg. engineer

Gra·na·dos \grə-'nä-(,)dōs, -,thōs\ Enrique 1867–1916 Span. composer

Gran·di \'grän-(,)dē\ Dino 1895–1988 Conte di Mordano Ital. Fascist polit.

Gran·ger \'grän-jər\ Sir Clive W.J. 1934–2009 Brit. econ.

Grant \'grant\ Cary 1904–1986 orig. Archibald Alexander Leach Am. (Brit.-born) actor

Grant Ulysses S. 1822–1885 orig. Hiram Ulysses Grant Am. gen.; 18th pres. of the U.S. (1869–77)

Gran·ville–Bar·ker \'gran-,vil-'bär-kər\ Harley 1877–1946 Eng. actor, manager, & dram.

Grass \'gräs\ Günter Wilhelm 1927–   Ger. writer

Grasse \'gras, 'gräs\ François-Joseph-Paul 1722–1788 Comte de Grasse & Marquis de Grasse-Tilly \-tē-'yē\ Fr. naval officer

Gra·tian \'grā-sh(ē-)ən\ L Flavius Gratianus 359–383 Rom. emp. (367–383)

Grat·tan \'gra-tᵊn\ Henry 1746–1820 Irish orator & statesman

Grau San Mar·tín \'graù-,san-(,)mär-'tēn, -,sän-\ Ramón 1887–1969 Cuban physician & polit.; pres. of Cuba (1944–48)

Graves \'grävz\ Robert Ranke 1895–1985 Brit. author

Gray \'grä\ Asa 1810–1888 Am. botanist

Gray Thomas 1716–1771 Eng. poet

Gra·zia·ni \,grät-sē-'ä-nē\ Rodolfo 1882–1955 Marchese di Neghelli Ital. marshal & colonial administrator

Gre·co, El \el-'gre-(,)kō also -'grä-\ 1541–1614 Doménikos Theotokópoulos Span. (Cretan-born) painter

Gree·ley \'grē-lē\ Horace 1811–1872 Am. journalist & polit.

Gree·ly \'grē-lē\ Adolphus Washington 1844–1935 Am. gen. & arctic explorer

Green \'grēn\ Julien or Julian 1900–1998 Fr. nov.

Green William 1873–1952 Am. labor leader

Gree·na·way \'grē-nə-,wā\ Catherine 1846–1901 Kate Eng. artist

Greene \'grēn\ Graham 1904–1991 Brit. nov.

Greene Nathanael 1742–1786 Am. gen. in Revolution

Greene Robert 1558?–1592 Eng. poet & dram.

Green·gard \'grēn-,gärd\ Paul 1925–   Am. neuroscientist

Green·nough \'grē-,nō\ Horatio 1805–1852 Am. sculptor

Green·span \'grēn-,span\ Alan 1926–   Am. economist

Greg·o·ry \'greg-g(ə-)rē\ Saint 240–332 *the Illuminator* apostle & founder of the Armenian Church

Gregory name of 16 popes: esp. **I** Saint *ca* 540–604 *the Great* (pope 590–604); **VII** Saint orig. *Hil·de·brand* \'hil-də-,brand\ *ca* 1020–1085 (pope 1073–85); **XIII** orig. *Ugo Buon·com·pa·gni* \'ü-gō-bwòn-kōm-'pän-yē\ 1502–1585 (pope 1572–85)

Gregory (Isabella) Augusta 1852–1932 *Lady Gregory* née *Persse* Irish dram.

Gregory of Nys·sa \'nis-ə\ Saint *ca* 335–*ca* 394 Eastern church father

Gregory of Tours Saint 538–594 Frankish ecclesiastic & hist.

Grei·der \'grī-dər\ Carol (Widney) 1961–   Am. biol.

Gren·fell \'gren-,fel, -fəl\ Sir Wilfred Thomason 1865–1940 Eng. medical missionary

Gren·ville \'gren-,vil, -vəl\ *or* **Greyn·ville** \'grän-\ Sir Richard 1542–1591 Brit. naval commander

Gresh·am \'gre-shəm\ Sir Thomas 1519–1579 Eng. financier

Gretz·ky \'gret-(,)skē\ Wayne 1961–   Canad. ice hockey player

Greuze \'grə(r)z, 'grœz\ Jean-Baptiste 1725–1805 Fr. painter

Gré·vy \grā-'vē\ (François-Paul-) Jules 1807–1891 Fr. lawyer; 3d pres. of the Republic (1879–87)

Grey \'grā\ 2d Earl 1764–1845 *Charles Grey* Eng. statesman; prime min. (1830–34)

Grey Sir Edward 1862–1933 Viscount *Grey of Fal·lo·don* \'fa-lə-d⁺n\ Eng. polit.

Grey Lady Jane 1537–1554 titular queen of England for 9 days

Grey Zane 1875–1939 Am. nov.

Grieg \'grēg\ Edvard Hagerup 1843–1907 Norw. composer

Grif·fin \'gri-fən\ Walter Burley 1876–1937 Am. architect

Grif·fith \'gri-fəth\ Arthur 1872–1922 Irish journalist & nationalist

Griffith D(avid Lewelyn) W(ark) 1875–1948 Am. motion-picture producer & director

Grill·par·zer \'gril-,pärt-sər\ Franz 1791–1872 Austrian dram. & poet

Grimm \'grim\ Jacob 1785–1863 & his bro. Wilhelm 1786–1859 Ger. philologists & folklorists

Gris \'grēs\ Juan 1887–1927 *José Victoriano González* Span. painter in France

Gro·fé \'grō-,fā\ Fer·de \'fər-dē\ 1892–1972 Am. composer

Gro·lier de Ser·vières \,grōl-'yä-də-,ser-vē-'er, 'grōl-yər-\ Jean 1479–1565 Vicomte *d'Aguisy* Fr. bibliophile

Gro·my·ko \grə-'mē-(,)kō, grō-\ Andrey Andreyevich 1909–1989 Russ. econ. & diplomat; pres. of U.S.S.R. (1985–88)

Groo·te \'grō-tə\ Gerhard 1340–1384 *Ge·rar·dus Mag·nus* \jə-,rär-dəs-'mag-nəs\ Du. religious reformer

Gro·pi·us \'grō-pē-əs\ Walter 1883–1969 Am. (Ger.-born) architect

Gross \'grōs\ David J(onathan) 1941–   Am. physicist

Gros·ve·nor \'grōv-nər, 'grō-və-\ Gilbert Hovey 1875–1966 Am. geographer & editor

Grosz \'grōs\ George 1794–1871 Eng. hist.

Gro·tius \'grō-sh(ē-)əs\ Hugo 1583–1645 *Huigh de Groot* \də-'grōt\ Du. jurist & statesman

Grove \'grōv\ Sir George 1820–1900 Eng. musicologist

Groves \'grōvz\ Leslie Richard 1896–1970 Am. gen.

Grubbs \'grəbz\ Robert H(oward) 1942–   Am. chem.

Grün·berg \'grün-bərg, 'gruen-,berk\ Peter (Andreas) 1939–   Ger. physicist

Grü·ne·wald \'grü-nə-,wòld, 'grue-nə-,vält\ Matthias *ca* 1480–1528 Ger. painter

Gryph·i·us \'gri-fē-əs\ Andreas 1616–1664 *G Greif* \'grīf\ Ger. poet & dram.

Guar·ne·ri \gwär-'ner-ē\ *L* **Guar·ne·ri·us** \gwär-'nir-ē-əs, -'ner-\ family of Ital. violin makers: esp. Giuseppe Antonio 1687–1745

Gu·de·ri·an \gü-'der-ē-ən\ Heinz Wilhelm 1888–1954 Ger. gen.

Gue·rin \ger-ən\ Jules 1866–1946 Am. painter

Gues·clin \ges-'klaⁿ\ Bertrand du *ca* 1320–1380 Fr. soldier

Guesde \ged\ Jules 1845–1922 *Mathieu Basile* Fr. socialist

Guest \'gest\ Edgar Albert 1881–1959 Am. journalist & poet

Gue·va·ra \gə-'vär-ə\ gä-\ Ernesto 1928–1967 *Che* Latin-Am. (Argentine-born) revolutionary leader

Gui·do of Arezzo \'gwē-(,)dō\ *or* **Guido Are·ti·nus** \,ar-ə-'tē-nəs\ *ca* 991–1050 Benedictine monk & music reformer

Guil·laume \gē-'yōm\ Charles Édouard 1861–1938 Fr. physicist

Guille·min \gē(-ə)-'maⁿ\ Roger (Charles Louis) 1924–   Am. (Fr.-born) physiol.

Guin·ness \'gi-nis, -nəs\ Sir Alec 1914–2000 Brit. actor

Guiscard Robert — see ROBERT GUISCARD

Guise \'gēz *also* 'gwēz\ 2d Duc de 1519–1563 *François de Lorraine* Fr. soldier & polit.

Guise 3d Duc de 1550–1588 *Henri I de Lorraine* Fr. soldier & polit.

Gui·te·ras \gē-'ter-əs\ Juan 1852–1925 Cuban physician

Gui·zot \gē-'zō\ François (-Pierre-Guillaume) 1787–1874 Fr. hist. & statesman

Gull·strand \'gəl-,strand\ Allvar 1862–1930 Swed. ophthalmologist

Gun·nars·son \'gun-ər-sən\ Gunnar 1889–1975 Icelandic writer

Gun·ter \'gən-tər\ Edmund 1581–1626 Eng. math.

Gur·don \'gər-d⁺n\ Sir John B(ertrand) 1933–   Brit. biol.

Gus·mão \güzh-'maúⁿ\ Xanana 1946–   orig. *José Alexandre Gusmão* pres. of East Timor (2002–07); prime min. (2007–   )

Gus·tav \'güs-,täv\ *or* **Gus·ta·vus** \(,)gə-'stä-vəs, -'stä-\ name of 6 kings of Sweden, the first 4 of the Vasa dynasty: **I** (*Gustav Eriksson*) 1496?–1560 (reigned 1523–60); **II** (*Gustav Adolph*) 1594–1632 (reigned 1611–32); **III** 1746–1792 (reigned 1771–92); **IV** (*Gustav Adolph*) 1778–1837 (reigned 1792–1809); **V** 1858–1950 (reigned 1907–50); **VI** (*Gustav Adolph*) 1882–1973 (reigned 1950–73)

Gu·ten·berg \'gü-t⁺n-,bərg\ Johannes *ca* 1390–1468 Ger. inventor of printing from movable type

Guth·rie \'gə-thrē\ Woodrow Wilson 1912–1967 *Woody* Am. folksinger

Gutz·kow \'güts-(,)kō\ Karl Ferdinand 1811–1878 Ger. journalist, nov., & dram.

Guz·mán Blan·co \güs-,män-'blän-(,)kō\ Antonio 1829–1899 Venezuelan soldier & statesman; dictator of Venezuela (1870–89)

Gwin·nett \gwi-'net\ Button *ca* 1735–1777 Am. Revolutionary leader

Gwyn *or* **Gwynn** *or* **Gwynne** \'gwin\ Eleanor 1650–1687 *Nell* Eng. actress *mistress of Charles II*

Haa·kon VII \'hò-kən, -,kän\ 1872–1957 king of Norway (1905–57)

Haa·vel·mo \'hò-vəl-,mō\ Trygve 1911–1999 Norw. econ.

Ha·ber \'hä-bər\ Fritz 1868–1934 Ger. chem.

Ha·bi·bie \hə-'bē-bē, hä-\ B(acharuddin) J(usuf) 1936–   pres. of Indonesia (1998–99)

Há·cha \'hä-(,)kä\ Emil 1872–1945 Czech jurist & statesman

Had·field \'had-,fēld\ Sir Robert Abbott 1858–1940 Eng. metallurgist

Had·ley \'had-lē\ Henry Kimball 1871–1937 Am. composer

Had·ow \'ha-(,)dō\ Sir (William) Henry 1859–1937 Eng. educ. & musicologist

Hadrian A.D. 76–138 Rom. emp. (117–138)

Haeck·el \'he-kəl\ Ernst Heinrich 1834–1919 Ger. biol. & philos.

Hā·fez \hä-'fez\ 1325(or 1326)–1389(or 1390) *Mohammad Shams od-Dīn Hāfez* Pers. poet

Ha·gel \'hä-gəl\ Chuck 1946–   *Charles Timothy Hagel* Am. polit.; U.S. secy. of defense (2013–   )

Hag·gard \'ha-gərd\ Sir (Henry) Rider 1856–1925 Eng. nov.

Hahn \'hän\ Otto 1879–1968 Ger. physical chem.

Hah·ne·mann \'hä-nə-mən\ (Christian Friedrich) Samuel 1755–1843 Ger. physician

Haig \'hāg\ 1st Earl 1861–1928 *Douglas Haig* Brit. field marshal

Hai·le Se·las·sie \'hī-lē-sə-'la-sē, -'lä-\ 1892–1975 Ras *Tafari* emp. of Ethiopia (1930–36; 1941–74)

Hak·luyt \'hak-,lüt\ Richard *ca* 1552–1616 Eng. geographer & hist.

Hal·dane \'hòl-,dān, -dən\ J(ohn) B(urdon) S(anderson) 1892–1964 *son of J.S.* Brit. biol.

Haldane John Scott 1860–1936 Brit. physiol.

Haldane Richard Burdon 1856–1928 Viscount *Haldane of Cloan* \'klōn\; *bro. of J.S.* Brit. lawyer, philos., & statesman

Hal·der \'häl-dər\ Franz 1884–1972 Ger. gen.

Hale \'hāl\ Edward Everett 1822–1909 Am. Unitarian clergyman & writer

Hale George Ellery 1868–1938 Am. astron.

Hale Sir Matthew 1609–1676 Eng. jurist

Hale Nathan 1755–1776 Am. Revolutionary hero

Ha·lé·vy \,(h)a-lā-'vē, ,(h)ä-\ (Jacques-François-) Fromental (-Elíe) 1799–1862 orig. *Elias Lévy* \lä-'vē\ Fr. composer

Halévy Ludovic 1834–1908 *nephew of prec.* Fr. dram. & nov.

Hal·i·fax \'ha-lə-,faks\ Earl of 1881–1959 *Edward Frederick Lindley Wood* Eng. statesman & diplomat

Hall \'hòl\ Charles Francis 1821–1871 Am. arctic explorer

Hall Charles Martin 1863–1914 Am. chem. & manuf.

Hall G(ranville) Stanley 1844–1924 Am. psychol. & educ.

Hall James Norman 1887–1951 Am. nov.

Hall John L(ewis) 1934–   Am. physicist

Hal·lam \'ha-ləm\ Henry 1777–1859 Eng. hist.

Hal·leck \'ha-lək, -lik\ Fitz-Greene 1790–1867 Am. poet

Halleck Henry Wager 1815–1872 Am. gen.

Hal·ley \'ha-lē *also* 'hä-lē\ Edmond *or* Edmund 1656–1742 Eng. astron.

Hals \'hälz, 'häls\ Frans *ca* 1581–1666 Du. painter

Hal·sey \'hòl-sē, -zē\ William Frederick 1882–1959 Am. admiral

Hal·sted \'hòl-stəd, -,sted\ William Stewart 1852–1922 Am. surgeon

Ham·bro \'häm-,brō\ Carl Joachim 1885–1964 Norw. statesman

Ha·mil·car Bar·ca \hə-'mil-,kär-'bär-kə, ,ha-məl-\ *or* **Bar·cas** \'bär-kəs; 270?–229(or 228) B.C. *father of Hannibal* Carthaginian gen.

Ham·il·ton \'ha-məl-tən\ Alexander 1755–1804 Am. statesman

Hamilton Edith 1867–1963 Am. classicist

Hamilton Lady Emma 1765–1815 née *Amy Lyon* mistress of Lord Nelson

Ham·lin \'ham-lən\ Hannibal 1809–1891 Am. polit.; vice pres. of the U.S. (1861–65)

Ham·mar·skjöld \'ha-mər-,shəld, 'häm-, -,shùld, -,shēld\ Dag \'däg\ Hjalmar Agne Carl 1905–1961 Swed. U.N. official; secy.-gen. (1953–61)

Ham·mer·stein \'ha-mər-,stīn, -,stēn\ Oscar 1846–1919 Am. (Ger.-born) theater impresario

Hammerstein Oscar 1895–1960 *grandson of prec.* Am. lyricist & librettist

Ham·mett \'ha-met\ (Samuel) Dashiell 1894–1961 Am. writer

Ham·mond \'ha-mənd\ John Hays 1855–1936 Am. mining engineer

Hammond John Hays 1888–1965 *son of prec.* Am. electrical engineer & inventor

Hammond Laurens 1895–1973 Am. inventor

Ham·mu·ra·bi \,ha-mə-'rä-bē\ *or* **Ham·mu·ra·pi** \-'rä-pē\ *d* 1750 B.C. king of Babylon (1792–50)

Hamp·den \'ham(p)-dən\ John 1594–1643 Eng. statesman

Hamp·ton \'ham(p)-tən\ Wade 1751?–1835 Am. gen.

Hampton Wade 1818–1902 *grandson of prec.* Am. polit. & Confed. gen.

Ham·sun \'häm-sən\ Knut 1859–1952 pseud. of *Knut Pedersen* Norw. writer

Han·cock \'han-,käk\ John 1737–1793 Am. statesman in Revolution

Hancock Winfield Scott 1824–1886 Am. gen. & polit.

Hand \'hand\ (Billings) Learned 1872–1961 Am. jurist

Han·del \'han-d⁺l\ George Frideric 1685–1759 Brit. (Ger.-born) composer — **Han·de·li·an** \han-'dē-lē-ən\ *adj*

Han·dy \'han-dē\ W(illiam) C(hristopher) 1873–1958 Am. blues musician

Han·na \'ha-nə\ Marcus Alonzo 1837–1904 *Mark* Am. businessman & polit.

Han·ni·bal \'ha-nə-bəl\ 247–183 B.C. *son of Hamilcar Barca* Carthaginian gen.

Han·no \'ha-(,)nō\ 3d cent. B.C. *the Great* Carthaginian statesman

Ha·no·taux \,a-nə-'tō, ,ä-\ (Albert-Auguste-) Gabriel 1853–1944 Fr. hist. & statesman

Han·sard \'han-,särd, 'han(t)-sərd\ Luke 1752–1828 Eng. printer

Hänsch \'hensh\ Theodor W(olfgang) 1941–   Ger. physicist

Han·sen \'han(t)-sən\ Lars Peter 1952–   Am. econ.

Han·son \'han(t)-sən\ Howard 1896–1981 Am. composer

Hans·son \'han(t)-sən\ Per Albin 1885–1946 Swed. statesman

Han Wu Ti — see WU-TI

Han Yü \'hän-'yü\ 768–824 *Han Wen-kung* Chin. poet, essayist, & philos.

Har·ald V \'hä-,räl\ 1937–   *son of Olav V* king of Norway (1991–   )

Har·bach \'här-,bäk\ Otto Abels 1873–1963 Am. dram. & librettist

Har·de·ca·nute or Har·di·ca·nute \,här-di-kə-'nüt, -'nyüt\ ca 1019–1042 king of Denmark (1028–42) and of England (1040–42)
Har·den \'här-d°n\ Sir Arthur 1865–1940 Eng. chem.
Harden Maximilian 1861–1927 orig. Felix Ernst Witkowski Ger. writer
Har·den·berg \'här-d°n-,bərg, -,berk\ Prince Karl August von 1750–1822 Pruss. statesman
Har·ding \'här-diŋ\ Warren G(amaliel) 1865–1923 29th pres. of the U.S. (1921–23)
Har·dy \'här-dē\ Oliver 1892–1957 orig. Norvell Hardy Am. comic actor
Hardy Thomas 1840–1928 Eng. nov. & poet — Har·dy·esque \,här-dē-'esk\ adj
Har·greaves \'här-,grēvz\ James d 1778 Eng. inventor
Ha·ri·ri, al– \,al-hə-'rir-ē\ 1054–1122 Arab scholar & poet
Har·lan \'här-lən\ John Marshall 1833–1911 & his grandson 1899–1971 Am. jurists
Har·ley \'här-lē\ Robert 1661–1724 1st Earl of Oxford Eng. statesman
Harms·worth \'härmz-(,)wərth\ Alfred Charles William 1865–1922 Viscount North·cliffe \'nȯrth-,klif\ Eng. publisher & polit.
Harmsworth Harold Sidney 1868–1940 1st Viscount Roth·er·mere \'rä-thər-mir\ bro. of prec. Eng. publisher & polit.
Ha·roche \ä-'rȯsh\ Serge 1944– Fr. physicist
Har·old \'ha-rəld\ name of 2 kings of the English: I d 1040 Harold Harefoot \'her-,fût\ (reigned 1035–40); II ca 1022–1066 (reigned 1066)
Harold name of 3 kings of Norway: esp. III Hard·raa·de \'hȯr-,rȯ-də\ 1015–1066 (reigned 1045–66)
Har·per \'här-pər\ Stephen (Joseph) 1959– Canad. polit.; prime min. of Canada (2006–)
Har·ri·man \'ha-rə-mən\ W(illiam) Aver·ell \'āv-rəl, 'ā-və-\ 1891–1986 Am. businessman, diplomat, & polit.
Har·ris \'ha-rəs\ Barbara Clementine 1930– Am. bishop (1989–2002)
Harris Frank 1856–1931 Am. (Irish-born) writer
Harris Joel Chandler 1848–1908 Am. writer
Harris Roy 1898–1979 Am. composer
Harris William Torrey 1835–1909 Am. philos. & educ.
Har·ri·son \'ha-rə-sən\ Benjamin 1833–1901 grandson of W.H. Harrison 23d pres. of the U.S. (1889–93)
Harrison Sir Rex 1908–1990 orig. Reginald Carey Harrison Brit. actor
Harrison William Henry 1773–1841 9th pres. of the U.S. (1841)
Har·san·yi \här-'shä-nē\ John Charles 1920–2000 Am. (Hung.-born) econ.
Hart \'härt\ Albert Bushnell 1854–1943 Am. hist. & editor
Hart Lorenz 1895–1943 Am. lyricist
Hart Moss 1904–1961 Am. librettist & dram.
Hart Sir Robert 1835–1911 Brit. diplomat
Hart William S(urrey) 1872–1946 Am. actor
Harte \'härt\ Francis Brett 1836–1902 Bret Harte Am. writer
Har·tung \'här-,tûŋ\ Hans 1904–1989 Fr. (Ger.-born) painter
Hart·well \'härt-,wel\ Leland Harrison 1939– Am. geneticist
Hā·rūn ar–Ra·shīd \hə-'rün-ä-'shēd\ 763(or 766)–809 Hārūn ar-Rashīd ibn Muḥammad al-Mahdī ibn al-Manṣūr al-ʿAbbāsī caliph of Baghdad (786–809)
Har·vard \'här-vərd\ John 1607–1638 Am. clergyman & benefactor
Har·vey \'här-vē\ George Brinton McClellan 1864–1928 Am. journalist
Harvey Sir John Martin 1863–1944 Eng. actor & producer
Harvey William 1578–1657 Eng. physician & anatomist
Has·dru·bal \'haz-,drü-bəl, haz-\ d 207 B.C. bro. of Hannibal Carthaginian gen.
Has·sam \'ha-səm\ (Frederick) Childe 1859–1935 Am. artist
Hass·ler \'häs-lər\ Hans Leo 1564–1612 Ger. composer
Has·tert \'has-tərt\ (John) Dennis 1942– Am. polit.
Has·tings \'hās-tiŋz\ 1st Marquess of 1754–1826 Francis Raw·don-Hastings \'rȯ-d°n-\ Brit. gen. & colonial administrator
Hastings Warren 1732–1818 Eng. statesman & administrator in India
Ha·to·ya·ma \,hä-tō-'yä-mä\ Yukio 1947– prime min. of Japan (2009–10)
Haugh·ey \'hȯ-hē\ Charles James 1925–2006 prime min. of Ireland (1979–81; 1982; 1987–92)
Haupt·man \'haùpt-mən\ Herbert A(aron) 1917–2011 Am. biochem.
Haupt·mann \'haùpt-,män\ Gerhart 1862–1946 Ger. writer
Hau·sen \'haù-zən\ Harald zur 1936– Ger. virologist
Haus·ho·fer \'haùs-,hō-fər\ Karl Ernst 1869–1946 Ger. gen. & geographer
Hauss·mann \ōs-'män, 'haùs-mən\ Baron Georges-Eugène 1809–1891 Fr. administrator
Ha·vel \'hä-vel, -vəl\ Vá·clav \'vät-,släf\ 1936–2011 Czech writer & polit.; pres. of Czechoslovakia (1989–92); pres. of Czech Republic (1993–2003)
Have·lock \'hav-,läk, -lək\ Sir Henry 1795–1857 Brit. gen.
Hawke \'hȯk\ Bob 1929– Robert James Lee Hawke prime min. of Australia (1983–91)
Hawke 1st Baron 1705–1781 Edward Hawke Eng. admiral
Haw·king \'hȯ-kiŋ\ Stephen (William) 1942– Brit. physicist
Haw·kins \'hȯ-kənz\ Sir Anthony Hope 1863–1933 pseud. Anthony Hope Eng. nov. & dram.
Hawkins or Haw·kyns Sir John 1532–1595 Eng. admiral
Hawks \'hȯks\ Howard (Winchester) 1896–1977 Am. film director
Haw·orth \'haù-ərth\ Sir (Walter) Norman 1883–1950 Eng. chem.
Haw·thorne \'hȯ-,thȯrn\ Nathaniel 1804–1864 Am. author
Hay \'hā\ John Milton 1838–1905 Am. statesman
Haydn \'hī-d°n\ (Franz) Joseph 1732–1809 Austrian composer
Hay·ek \'hī-ek, 'hā-\ Friedrich (August) von 1899–1992 Brit. (Austrian-born) econ.
Hayes \'hāz\ Helen 1900–1993 Helen Hayes Brown Am. actress
Hayes Isaac Israel 1832–1881 Am. arctic explorer
Hayes Roland 1887–1977 Am. tenor
Hayes Rutherford B(irchard) 1822–1893 19th pres. of the U.S. (1877–81)
Haynes \'hānz\ Elwood 1857–1925 Am. inventor
Hays \'hāz\ Will Harrison 1879–1954 Am. lawyer & polit.
Haz·litt \'haz-lət, 'hāz-\ William 1778–1830 Eng. essayist
Hea·ly \'hē-lē\ Timothy Michael 1855–1931 Irish statesman
Hea·ney \'hē-nē\ Sea·mus \'shā-məs\ 1939–2013 Irish poet

Hearn \'hərn\ Laf·ca·dio \laf-'kä-dē-,ō\ 1850–1904 Jp. Yakumo Koizumi Am. (Greek-born) writer in Japan
Hearst \'hərst\ William Randolph 1863–1951 Am. newspaper publisher
Heath \'hēth\ Sir Edward (Richard George) 1916–2005 Brit. prime min. (1970–74)
Heav·i·side \'he-vē-,sīd\ Oliver 1850–1925 Eng. physicist
Heb·bel \'he-bəl\ (Christian) Friedrich 1813–1863 Ger. dram.
He·ber \'hē-bər\ Reginald 1783–1826 Eng. prelate & hymn writer
Hé·bert \ā-'ber\ Anne 1916–2000 Canad. nov., poet, & dram.
Hébert Jacques-René 1757–1794 Fr. radical journalist
Heck \'hek\ Richard F(red) 1931– Am. chem.
Heck·man \'hek-mən\ James (Joseph) 1944– Am. econ.
He·din \hä-'dēn\ Sven Anders 1865–1952 Swed. explorer
Hee·ger \'hē-gər\ Alan Jay 1936– Am. physicist
Heem \'hām\ Jan Davidsz de 1606–1683(or 1684) Du. painter
He·gel \'hā-gəl\ Georg Wilhelm Friedrich 1770–1831 Ger. philos.
Hei·deg·ger \'hī-,de-gər, 'hī-di-gər\ Martin 1889–1976 Ger. philos. — Hei·deg·ger·ian \,hī-di-'ger-ē-ən\ adj
Hei·fetz \'hī-fəts\ Ja·scha \'yä-shə\ 1901–1987 Am. (Russ.-born) violinist
Hei·ne \'hī-nə also -nē\ Heinrich 1797–1856 Ger. poet & critic
Hei·sen·berg \'hī-z°n-bərg, -,berk\ Werner Karl 1901–1976 Ger. physicist
Heliogabalus — see ELAGABALUS
Hel·ler \'he-lər\ Joseph 1923–1999 Am. nov.
Hell·man \'hel-mən\ Lillian 1905–1984 Am. dram.
Helm·holtz \'helm-,hōlts\ Hermann (Ludwig Ferdinand) von 1821–1894 Ger. physicist, anatomist, & physiol.
Hé·lo·ïse \'ā-lə-,wēz, 'e-lə-\ ca 1098–1164 wife of Abelard Fr. abbess
Hel·vé·tius \hel-'vä-sh(ē-)əs, -'vē-; ,(h)el-,väs-'yüs, -'yuιs\ Claude= Adrien 1715–1771 Fr. philos.
He·mans \'he-mənz, 'hē-\ Felicia Dorothea 1793–1835 née Browne Eng. poet
Hem·inge or Hem·minge \'he-miŋ\ John ca 1556–1630 Eng. actor
Hem·ing·way \'he-miŋ-,wā\ Ernest Miller 1899–1961 Am. writer & journalist — Hem·ing·way·esque \,he-miŋ-'wā-'esk\ adj
Hen·der·son \'hen-dər-sən\ Arthur 1863–1935 Brit. labor leader & statesman
Hen·dricks \'hen-driks\ Thomas Andrews 1819–1885 Am. polit.; vice pres. of the U.S. (1885)
Hen·gist or Hen·gest \'heŋ-gəst, -,gist\ & his bro. Hor·sa \'hȯr-sə\ 5th cent. Jute invaders of Britain
Hen·ley \'hen-lē\ William Ernest 1849–1903 Eng. editor & author
Hen·ne·pin \'he-nə-pən, ,e-nə-'paⁿ\ Louis 1626–after 1701 Belg. friar & explorer in America
Hen·ri \'hen-rē\ Robert 1865–1929 Am. painter
Hen·ry \'hen-rē\ name of 8 kings of England: I 1068–1135 (reigned 1100–35); II 1133–1189 (reigned 1154–89); III 1207–1272 (reigned 1216–72); IV 1366–1413 (reigned 1399–1413); V 1387–1422 (reigned 1413–22); VI 1421–1471 (reigned 1422–61 & 1470–71); VII 1457–1509 (reigned 1485–1509); VIII 1491–1547 (reigned 1509–47)
Henry name of 4 kings of France: I ca 1008–1060 (reigned 1031–60); II 1519–1559 (reigned 1547–59); III 1551–1589 (reigned 1574–89); IV (Henry III of Navarre) 1553–1610 (reigned 1589–1610)
Henry 1394–1460 the Navigator Port. prince
Henry Joseph 1797–1878 Am. physicist
Henry O. — see William Sydney PORTER
Henry Patrick 1736–1799 Am. statesman & orator
Hens·lowe \'henz-(,)lō\ Philip ca 1550–1616 Eng. theater manager
Hen·son \'hen(t)-sən\ James Maury 1936–1990 Am. puppeteer
Henson Matthew Alexander 1866–1955 Am. polar explorer
Hep·burn \'hep-(,)bərn\ Audrey 1929–1993 born Audrey Kathleen Ruston Brit. (Belg.-born) actress
Hepburn Katharine 1907–2003 Am. actress
Hep·ple·white \'he-pəl-,hwīt, -,wīt\ George d 1786 Eng. cabinetmaker & designer
Hep·worth \'hep-(,)wərth\ Dame Barbara 1903–1975 Brit. sculptor
Her·a·cli·tus \'her-,bärt\ Johann Friedrich 1776–1841 Ger. philos. & educ.
Her·a·clei·tus \,her-ə-'klī-təs\ ca 540–ca 480 B.C. Greek philos. — Her·a·cli·te·an \-'klī-tē-ən, -klī-'tē-\ adj
Her·a·cli·us \,her-ə-'klī-əs, hi-'ra-klē-\ ca 575–641 Byzantine emp. (610–641)
Her·bart \'her-,bärt\ Johann Friedrich 1776–1841 Ger. philos. & educ.
Her·bert \'hər-bərt\ George 1593–1633 Eng. divine & poet
Herbert Victor 1859–1924 Am. (Irish-born) composer & conductor
Herbert William 1580–1630 3d Earl of Pembroke Eng. statesman & patron
Herblock — see Herbert Lawrence BLOCK
Her·der \'her-dər\ Johann Gottfried von 1744–1803 Ger. philos.
He·re·dia \ā-rā-'dyä, (h)ä-'rä-dē-ə\ José María de 1842–1905 Fr. (Cuban-born) poet
He·ring \'her-iŋ, 'hā-riŋ\ Ewald 1834–1918 Ger. physiol. & psychol.
Her·ki·mer \'hər-kə-mər\ Nicholas 1728–1777 Am. gen.
Her·man \'hər-mən\ Woodrow Charles 1913–1987 Woody Herman Am. musician & bandleader
Hern·don \'hərn-dən\ William Henry 1818–1891 Am. lawyer
He·ro \'hē-(,)rō, 'hir-(,)ō\ or He·ron \'hē-,rän\ 1st cent. A.D. Greek scientist
Her·od \'her-əd\ 73–4 B.C. the Great Rom. king of Judea (37–4)
Herod An·ti·pas \'an-tə-pəs, -,pas\ 21 B.C.–A.D. 39 son of prec. Rom. tetrarch of Galilee (4 B.C.–A.D. 39)
He·rod·o·tus \hi-'räd-ə-təs\ ca 484–between 430 and 420 B.C. Greek hist. — He·rod·o·te·an \-,räd-ə-'tē-ən\ adj
Her·re·ra \(h)ə-'rer-ə\ Francisco de 1576–ca 1656 el Viejo Span. painter
Her·rick \'her-ik\ Robert 1591–1674 Eng. poet
Her·riot \,er-ē-'ō\ Édouard 1872–1957 Fr. statesman
Herr·mann \'hər-mən\ Bernard 1911–1975 Am. composer & conductor
Hersch·bach \'hərsh-,bäk\ Dudley R(obert) 1932– Am. chem.

Her·schel \'hər-shəl\ Sir John Frederick William 1792–1871 & his father Sir William 1738–1822 Eng. astronomers
Her·sey \'hər-sē\ John Richard 1914–1993 Am. nov. & journalist
Hersh·ko \'hersh-kō\ Avram 1937–   orig. *Hers·kó Ferenc* \'hersh-kō-'fer-ents\ Israeli (Hung.-born) biol.
Hertz \'herts, 'hərts\ Gustav Ludwig 1887–1975 Ger. physicist
Hertz Heinrich Rudolf 1857–1894 Ger. physicist
Hert·zog \'hert-ˌsȯk\ J(ames) B(arry) M(unnik) 1866–1942 So. African gen. & polit.; prime min. (1924–39)
Herz·berg \'hərts-ˌbərg\ Gerhard 1904–1999 Canad. (Ger.-born) physicist
Herzl \'hert-sᵊl\ Theodor 1860–1904 Austrian (Hung.-born) Zionist
Her·zog \'hert-ˌsȯg\ Werner 1942–   orig. *Werner Stipetic* Ger. film-maker
He·si·od \'hē-sē-əd, 'he-\ *fl ca* 800 B.C. Greek poet
Hess \'hes\ Dame Myra 1890–1965 Eng. pianist
Hess (Walther Richard) Rudolf 1894–1987 Ger. Nazi polit.
Hess Victor Franz 1883–1964 Austrian physicist
Hess Walter Rudolf 1881–1973 Swiss physiol.
Hes·se \'he-sə\ Hermann 1877–1962 Ger. author
Hew·ish \'hyü-ish\ Antony 1924–   Brit. astrophysicist
Hey·drich \'hī-drik, -drik\ Reinhard 1904–1942 *the Hangman* Ger. Nazi administrator
Hey·er·dahl \'hā-ər-ˌdäl\ Thor 1914–2002 Norw. explorer & writer
Hey·mans \ā-'män(t)s, -'man(t)s\ Corneille-Jean-François 1892–1968 Belg. physiol.
Hey·ward \'hā-wərd\ (Edwin) Du·Bose \dü-'bōz, dyü-\ 1885–1940 Am. author
Hey·wood \'hā-ˌwu̇d\ John 1497?–?1580 Eng. author
Heywood Thomas 1574?–1641 Eng. dram.
Hick·ok \'hi-ˌkäk\ James Butler 1837–1876 *Wild Bill Hickok* Am. scout & U.S. marshal
Hicks \'hiks\ Edward 1780–1849 Am. painter
Hi·dal·go (y Cos·ti·lla) \ē-'thäl-gō-ē-kȯ-'stē-yä\ Miguel 1753–1811 Mex. priest & revolutionary leader
Hi·ero I \'hī-ə-ˌrō\ *or* **Hi·er·on** \-ˌrän\ *d* 467(or 466) B.C. tyrant of Syracuse (478–467 or 466)
Hig·gin·son \'hi-gən-sən\ Thomas Wentworth Storrow 1823–1911 Am. clergyman & writer
Higgs \'higz\ Peter W(are) 1929–   Eng. physicist
Hil·bert \'hil-bərt\ David 1862–1943 Ger. math.
Hil·de·gard von Bin·gen \hil-də-ˌgärd-fȯn-'biŋ-ən, -ˌgärt-\ 1098–1179 Ger. mystic & composer
Hill \'hil\ Ambrose Powell 1825–1865 Am. Confed. gen.
Hill Archibald Vivian 1886–1977 Eng. physiol.
Hill James Jerome 1838–1916 Am. (Canad.-born) financier
Hill Sir Rowland 1795–1879 Eng. postal reformer
Hil·la·ry \'hi-lə-rē\ Sir Edmund Percival 1919–2008 N.Z. mountaineer & explorer
Hil·lel \'hi-ləl, -ˌlel\ 1st cent. B.C.–1st cent. A.D. Jewish teacher
Hil·liard \'hil-yərd\ Nicholas 1547–1619 Eng. painter
Hill·man \'hil-mən\ Sidney 1887–1946 Am. labor leader
Hil·ton \'hil-tᵊn\ Conrad Nicholson 1887–1979 Am. hotelier
Hilton James 1900–1954 Eng. nov.
Himm·ler \'him-lər\ Heinrich 1900–1945 Ger. Nazi polit.
Hin·de·mith \'hin-də-ˌmit, -ˌmith, -mət, -məth\ Paul 1895–1963 Am. (Ger.-born) violist & composer
Hin·den·burg \'hin-dən-ˌbȯrg, -ˌburg\ Paul von 1847–1934 *Paul Ludwig Hans Anton von Beneckendorff und von Hindenburg* Ger. field marshal; pres. of Germany (1925–34)
Hin·shel·wood \'hin(t)-shəl-ˌwu̇d\ Sir Cyril Norman 1897–1967 Brit. chem.
Hip·par·chus \hi-'pär-kəs\ *d* 514 B.C. tyrant of Athens (527–514)
Hipparchus \hi-'pär-kəs\ *fl* 146–127 B.C. Greek astron.
Hip·pi·as \'hi-pē-əs\ *d* 490 B.C. *bro. of Hipparchus* ruled Athens with his brother
Hip·poc·ra·tes \hi-'pä-krə-ˌtēz\ *ca* 460–*ca* 377 B.C. *father of medicine* Greek physician
Hi·ro·hi·to \ˌhir-ō-'hē-(ˌ)tō\ 1901–1989 emp. of Japan (1926–89)
Hi·ro·shi·ge \ˌhir-ə-'shē-gä\ Ando 1797–1858 Jp. painter
Hitch·cock \'hich-ˌkäk\ Sir Alfred Joseph 1899–1980 Brit. film director — **Hitch·cock·ian** \hich-'kä-kē-ən\ *adj*
Hitchcock Edward 1793–1864 Am. geologist
Hit·ler \'hit-lər\ Adolf 1889–1945 Ger. chancellor & führer (1933–45) — **Hit·ler·ian** \hit-'lir-ē-ən, -'ler-\ *adj*
Hit·ti \'hi-tē\ Philip Khuri 1886–1978 Am. (Lebanese-born) orientalist
Hit·torf \'hi-ˌtȯrf\ Johann Wilhelm 1824–1914 Ger. physicist
Hoare \'hȯr\ Sir Samuel John Gurney 1880–1959 Viscount *Templewood* Eng. statesman
Ho·bart \'hō-ˌbärt, -bərt\ Garret Augustus 1844–1899 Am. polit.; vice pres. of the U.S. (1897–99)
Hob·be·ma \'hä-bə-mə\ Mein·dert *or* Meyn·dert \'mīn-ˌdert\ 1638–1709 Du. painter
Hobbes \'häbz\ Thomas 1588–1679 Eng. philos.
Hoc·cleve \'häk-ˌlēv\ *or* **Oc·cleve** \'äk-\ Thomas 1368(or 1369)–*ca* 1450 Eng. poet
Ho Chi Minh \'hō-'chē-'min, -'shē-\ 1890–1969 orig. *Nguyen That Thanh* pres. of No. Vietnam (1945–69)
Hock·ing \'hä-kiŋ\ William Ernest 1873–1966 Am. philos.
Hock·ney \'häk-nē\ David 1937–   Brit. painter & photographer
Hodg·kin \'häj-kin\ Dorothy Mary Crowfoot 1910–1994 Brit. physicist
Hoe \'hō\ Richard March 1812–1886 *son of Robert* Am. inventor
Hoe Robert 1784–1833 Am. (Eng.-born) printing-press manuf.
Ho·fer \'hō-fər\ Andreas 1767–1810 Tyrolese patriot
Hof·fa \'hä-fə\ James Riddle 1913–?1975 Am. labor leader
Hoff·man \'häf-mən, 'hȯf-\ Mal·vi·na \mal-'vē-nə\ 1887–1966 Am. sculptor
Hoff·mann \'häf-mən, 'hȯf-, -ˌmän\ August Heinrich 1798–1874 Ger. poet, philologist, & hist.
Hoffmann Ernst Theodor Wilhelm 1776–1822 known as *Ernst Theodor Amadeus Hoffmann* Ger. composer, writer, & illustrator
Hoff·mann \ȯf-'män\ Jules A(lphonse) 1941–   Fr. immunologist
Hof·mann \'häf-mən, 'hȯf-, -ˌmän\ August Wilhelm von 1818–1892 Ger. chem.

Hofmann Hans 1880–1966 Am. (Ger.-born) painter
Hofmann Josef Casimir 1876–1957 Pol. pianist
Hof·manns·thal \'häf-mənz-ˌtäl, 'hȯf-\ Hugo von 1874–1929 Austrian poet & dram.
Ho·garth \'hō-ˌgärth\ William 1697–1764 Eng. painter & engraver — **Ho·garth·ian** \hō-'gär-thē-ən\ *adj*
Hog·ben \'hȯg-bən, 'häg-\ Lancelot Thomas 1895–1975 Eng. scientist
Hogg \'hȯg, 'häg\ James 1770–1835 *the Ettrick Shepherd* Scot. poet
Ho·hen·zol·lern \ˌhō-ənt-'sȯ-lərn\ Michael — see MICHAEL
Ho·ku·sai \'hō-ku̇-ˌsī, ˌhō-ku̇-\ Katsushika 1760–1849 Jp. artist
Hol·bein \'hȯl-ˌbīn, 'hōl-\ Hans 1465?–1524 *the Elder* & Hans 1497?–1543 *the Younger* Ger. painters
Hol·berg \'hōl-ˌberg\ Baron 1684–1754 *Ludwig Holberg* Dan. (Norw.-born) author
Hol·der \'hōl-dər\ Eric (Himpton, Jr.) 1951–   U.S. atty. gen. (2009–   )
Höl·der·lin \'hœl-dər-ˌlēn\ (Johann Christian) Friedrich 1770–1843 Ger. poet
Hol·i·day \'hä-lə-ˌdā\ Eleanora 1915–1959 *Billie* Am. jazz singer
Hol·in·shed \'hä-lən-ˌshed\ *or* **Hol·lings·head** \-liŋz-ˌhed\ Raphael *d ca* 1580 Eng. chronicler
Hol·land \'hä-lənd\ John Philip 1840–1914 Am. (Irish-born) inventor
Holland Sir Sidney George 1893–1961 prime min. of New Zealand (1945–57)
Hol·lande \ȯ-'länd\ François (Gérard Georges Nicolas) 1954–   pres. of France (2012–   )
Holmes \'hōmz, 'hōlmz\ Oliver Wendell 1809–1894 Am. physician & author
Holmes Oliver Wendell 1841–1935 *son of prec.* Am. jurist
Holst \'hōlst\ Gustav Theodore 1874–1934 Eng. composer
Holt \'hōlt\ Harold Edward 1908–1967 Austral. polit.; prime min. (1966–67)
Holt Luther Emmett 1855–1924 Am. pediatrician
Hol·yoake \'hōl-ˌyōk, 'hȯl-lē-ˌōk\ Sir Keith Jacka 1904–1983 prime min. of New Zealand (1960–72)
Home \'hyüm, 'hōm\ Sir Alec Douglas- 1903–1995 Brit. prime min. (1963–64)
Home William Douglas- 1912–1992 *bro. of prec.* Brit. dram.
Ho·mer \'hō-mər\ 9th–8th? cent. B.C. Greek epic poet
Homer Winslow 1836–1910 Am. artist
Ho·neck·er \'hō-nə-kər\ Erich 1912–1994 gen. secy. of East German Communist party (1971–89)
Ho·neg·ger \ȯ-nā-'ger, '(h)ä-ni-gər\ Arthur 1892–1955 Fr. composer
Ho·no·ri·us \hə-'nȯr-ē-əs\ Flavius 384–423 Rom. emp. of the West (395–423)
Hont·horst \'hȯnt-ˌhȯrst\ Gerrit van 1590–1656 Du. painter
Hooch *or* **Hoogh** \'hōk\ Pieter de 1629–after 1684 Du. painter
Hood \'hu̇d\ John Bell 1831–1879 Am. Confed. gen.
Hood Samuel 1724–1816 1st Viscount *Hood* Brit. admiral
Hood Thomas 1799–1845 Eng. poet
Hooke \'hu̇k\ Robert 1635–1703 Eng. scientist
Hook·er \'hu̇-kər\ Joseph 1814–1879 Am. gen.
Hooker Sir Joseph Dalton 1817–1911 Eng. botanist
Hooker Richard 1554–1600 Eng. theol.
Hooker Thomas 1586?–1647 Eng. Puritan clergyman & founder of Connecticut
Hoo·ver \'hü-vər\ Herbert Clark 1874–1964 31st pres. of the U.S. (1929–33)
Hoover J(ohn) Edgar 1895–1972 Am. F.B.I. director (1924–72)
Hope \'hōp\ Anthony — see Sir Anthony Hope HAWKINS
Hope Bob 1903–2003 orig. *Leslie Townes Hope* Am. (Brit.-born) comedian
Hope Victor Alexander John 1887–1951 2d Marquis of *Lin·lith·gow* \lin-'lith-(ˌ)gō\ Brit. soldier; viceroy of India (1936–43)
Hop·kins \'häp-kənz\ Sir Frederick Gow·land \'gau̇-lənd\ 1861–1947 Eng. biochem.
Hopkins Gerard Manley 1844–1889 Eng. poet
Hopkins Harry Lloyd 1890–1946 Am. polit. & administrator
Hopkins Johns \'jänz\ 1795–1873 Am. financier
Hop·kin·son \'häp-kən-sən\ Francis 1737–1791 Am. statesman & composer
Hop·pe \'hä-pē\ William Frederick 1887–1959 Am. billiard player
Hop·per \'hä-pər\ Edward 1882–1967 Am. artist
Hopper Grace 1906–1992 née *Grace Brewster Murray* Am. admiral, math., & computer scientist
Hopper (William) DeWolf 1858–1935 Am. actor
Hop·wood \'häp-ˌwu̇d\ (James) Avery 1882–1928 Am. dram.
Hor·ace \'hȯr-əs, 'här-\ 65–8 B.C. *Quintus Horatius Flaccus* Rom. poet & satirist — **Ho·ra·tian** \hə-'rā-shən\ *adj*
Hor·na·day \'hȯr-nə-ˌdā\ William Temple 1854–1937 Am. zool.
Hor·ney \'hȯr-ˌnī\ Karen 1885–1952 née *Danielsen* Am. (Ger.-born) psychoanalyst & author
Ho·ro·witz \'hȯr-ə-ˌwits, 'här-\ Vladimir 1903–1989 Am. (Russ.-born) pianist
Horsa — see HENGIST
Hortense de Beauharnais — see BEAUHARNAIS
Hor·thy de Nagy·bán·ya \'hȯr-tē-dä-'näj-ˌbán-yə\ Miklós 1868–1957 Hung. admiral; regent of Hungary (1920–44)
Hor·vitz \'hȯr-vits\ H(oward) Robert 1947–   Am. geneticist
Hou·di·ni \hü-'dē-nē\ Harry 1874–1926 orig. *Ehrich Weiss* Am. (Hung.-born) magician
Hou·don \'hü-ˌdän, ü-'dōⁿ\ Jean-Antoine 1741–1828 Fr. sculptor
House \'hau̇s\ Edward Mandell 1858–1938 *Colonel House* Am. diplomat
Hous·man \'hau̇s-mən\ A(lfred) E(dward) 1859–1936 Eng. classical scholar & poet
Housman Laurence 1865–1959 *bro. of prec.* Eng. writer & illustrator
Hous·say \ü-'sī\ Bernardo Alberto 1887–1971 Argentine physiol.
Hous·ton \'hyü-stən, 'yü-\ Samuel 1793–1863 Am. gen.; pres. of the Republic of Texas (1836–38; 1841–44)
Ho·vha·ness (Chakmajian) \hō-'vä-nəs\ Alan 1911–2000 Am. composer
How·ard \'hau̇(-ə)rd\ Catherine — see CATHERINE
Howard Henry 1517?–1547 Earl of *Surrey* Eng. soldier & poet

Howard John Winston 1939–   prime min. of Australia (1996–2007)
Howard Oliver Otis 1830–1909 Am. gen. & educ.
Howard Sidney Coe 1891–1939 Am. dram.
Howe \'haù\ Elias 1819–1867 Am. inventor
Howe Gordie 1928–   *Gordon Howe* Am. (Canad.-born) ice hockey player
Howe Julia 1819–1910 née *Ward* Am. suffragist & reformer
Howe Richard 1726–1799 *Earl Howe* Eng. admiral
Howe William 1729–1814 5th Viscount *Howe; bro. of prec.* Eng. gen. in America
How·ells \'haù-əlz\ William Dean 1837–1920 Am. author
Hoyle \'hòi(-ə)l\ Sir Fred 1915–2001 Brit. astrophysicist
Hr·dlič·ka \'hərd-lich-,kä\ Aleš \'ä-,lesh\ 1869–1943 Am. (Bohemianborn) anthropol.
Hsüan–t'ung \shü-'än-'tùŋ\ — see P'U-I
Hua Kuo–feng \'hwä-'gwō-'fəŋ\ 1920–2008 Pinyin *Hua Guofeng* Chin. premier (1976–80)
Huás·car \'wäs-,kär\ *d* 1532 Inca prince
Hub·bard \'hə-bərd\ Elbert Green 1856–1915 Am. writer & publisher
Hub·ble \'hə-bəl\ Edwin Powell 1889–1953 Am. astron.
Hu·ber \'hü-bər, 'hyü-\ Robert 1937–   Ger. biochem.
Hud·son \'həd-sən\ Henry *d* 1611 Eng. navigator & explorer
Hudson Manley Ottmer 1886–1960 Am. jurist
Hudson W(illiam) H(enry) 1841–1922 Eng. naturalist & writer
Huer·ta \'wer-tə, ü-'er-\ Victoriano 1854–1916 Mex. gen.; provisional pres. of Mexico (1913–14)
Hug·gins \'hə-gənz\ Sir William 1824–1910 Eng. astron.
Hugh Ca·pet \'hyü-'kä-pət, -'ka-, -ka-'pä\ *ca* 938–996 king of France (987–996)
Hughes \'hyüz *also* 'yüz\ Charles Evans 1862–1948 Am. jurist; chief justice U.S. Supreme Court (1930–41)
Hughes Howard Robard 1905–1976 Am. businessman
Hughes (James) Langston 1902–1967 Am. writer
Hughes Ted 1930–1998 Brit. poet; poet laureate (1984–98)
Hughes Thomas 1822–1896 Eng. jurist, reformer, & writer
Hughes William Morris 1864–1952 Austral. statesman
Hu·go \'hyü-(,)gō, 'yü-\ Victor (-Marie) 1802–1885 Fr. poet, nov., & dram. — Hu·go·esque \,hyü-(,)gō-'esk, ,yü-\ *adj*
Hui·zin·ga \'hī-ziŋ-gə\ Johan 1872–1945 Du. hist.
Hu Jin·tao \'hü-'jin-'taù\ 1942–   gen. secy. of Chin. Communist party (2002–12); pres. of China (2003–13)
Hü·le·gü \,hü-'lä-(,)gü\ *ca* 1217–*ca* 1265 *grandson of Genghis Khan* Mongol ruler
Hull \'həl\ Cordell 1871–1955 Am. statesman; secy. of state (1933–44)
Hull Isaac 1773–1843 Am. naval officer
Hull Bobby 1939–   *Robert Marvin Hull* Canad. ice hockey player
Hull William 1753–1825 Am. gen.
Hulse \'həls\ Russell Alan 1950–   Am. physicist
Hu·ma·la (Tas·so) \ü-'mä-lä('-tä-sō)\ Ollanta (Moisés) 1962–   Peruvian soldier; pres. of Peru (2011–)
Hu·mā·yūn \hü-'mä-,yün\ 1508–1556 Mogul emp. of India (1530–56)
Hum·boldt \'həm-,bōlt, 'hùm-\ (Friedrich Wilhelm Karl Heinrich) Alexander von 1769–1859 Ger. naturalist, traveler, & statesman
Humboldt (Karl) Wilhelm von 1767–1835 *bro. of prec.* Ger. philologist & diplomat
Hume \'hyüm *also* 'yüm\ David 1711–1776 Scot. philos. & hist. — Hum·ean *or* Hum·ian \'(h)yü-mē-ən\ *adj*
Hume John 1937–   Irish peace activist
Hum·per·dinck \'hùm-pər-,diŋk, 'həm-\ Engelbert 1854–1921 Ger. composer
Hum·phrey \'həm(p)-frē\ 1391–1447 *son of Henry IV Duke of Gloucester (the Good Duke) & Earl of Pembroke* Eng. statesman & bibliophile
Humphrey Hubert H(oratio) 1911–1978 Am. polit.; vice pres. of the U.S. (1965–69)
Hun·e·ker \'hə-ni-kər\ James Gibbons 1860–1921 Am. critic
Hung–wu \'hùŋ-'wü\ 1328–1398 *Chu Yüan-chang* \'jü-yü-'än-'jäŋ\ Chin. emp. (1368–98); founder of Ming dynasty
Hunt \'hənt\ (James Henry) Leigh 1784–1859 Eng. writer
Hunt Sir R(ichard) Timothy 1943–   Brit. molecular biol.
Hunt (William) Hol·man \'hōl-mən\ 1827–1910 Eng. painter
Hun·ter \'hən-tər\ John 1728–1793 Brit. anatomist & surgeon
Hun·ting·ton \'hən-tiŋ-tən\ Collis Potter 1821–1900 Am. railroad builder
Huntington Ellsworth 1876–1947 Am. geographer & explorer
Huntington Henry Edwards 1850–1927 Am. bibliophile
Huntington Samuel 1731–1796 Am. Revolutionary polit.
Hun·tzi·ger \,(h)ənt-sē-'zher\ Charles-Léon-Clément 1880–1941 Fr. gen.
Hu·nya·di \'hùn-,yä-dē, -,yò-\ Já·nos \'yä-(,)nōsh\ 1407?–1456 Hung. soldier & hero
Hur·ley \'hər-lē\ Patrick Jay 1883–1963 Am. lawyer & diplomat
Hurst \'hərst\ Sir Cecil James Barrington 1870–1963 Eng. jurist
Hurst Fannie 1889–1968 Am. writer
Hurs·ton \'hər-stən\ Zora Neale 1903–1960 Am. writer & folklorist
Hur·wicz \'hər-wich\ Leonid 1917–2008 Am. (Russ.-born of Polish parents) econ.
Hus \'həs, 'hùs\ Jan 1372(or 1373)–1415 Bohemian religious reformer
Hu·sák \'hü-(,)säk, 'hyü-\ Gustav 1913–1991 pres. of Czechoslovakia (1975–87)
Hu·sayn ibn ʿAlī \hü-'sän-,i-bən-ä-'lē\ *ca* 1854–1931 1st king of the Hejaz (1916–24)
Hu Shih \'hü-'shir\ 1891–1962 Chin. philos.
Hus·sein \hü-'sän\ Saddam al-Tikriti 1937–2006 pres. of Iraq (1979–2003)
Hussein I 1935–1999 king of Jordan (1952–99)
Hus·serl \'hú-sə-rəl\ Edmund 1859–1938 Ger. philos. — Hus·serl·ian \hú-'sər-lē-ən\ *adj*
Hus·ton \'hyü-stən, 'yü-\ John 1906–1987 Am. motion-picture director, writer, & actor
Hu·szár \'hü-,sär\ Károly 1882–1941 Hung. journalist & polit.
Hutch·ins \'hə-chənz\ Robert Maynard 1899–1977 Am. educ.
Hutch·in·son \'hə-chə(n)-sən\ Anne 1591–1643 née *Marbury* Am. (Eng.-born) religious dissident
Hutchinson Thomas 1711–1780 Am. colonial administrator

Hut·ten \'hù-tən\ Ulrich von 1488–1523 Ger. humanist & reformer
Hux·ley \'həks-lē\ Al·dous \'òl-dəs\ Leonard 1894–1963 *bro. of J.S.* Eng. nov. & critic — Hux·lei·an \,həks-'lē-ən, 'həks-lē-\ *or* Hux·ley·an \'həks-lē-ən\ *adj*
Huxley Sir Julian Sorell 1887–1975 *grandson of T.H.* Eng. biol.
Huxley T(homas) H(enry) 1825–1895 Eng. biol.
Huy·gens \'hī-gənz, 'hòi-\ Christian 1629–1695 Du. math., physicist, & astron.
Huys·mans \wē-'smä"s\ Camille 1871–1968 Belg. polit.
Huysmans Joris-Karl 1848–1907 orig. *Georges-Charles* Fr. nov.
Hy·att \'hī-ət\ Alpheus 1838–1902 Am. naturalist
Hyde \'hīd\ Douglas 1860–1949 pseud. *An Craoibhín Aoibhinn* Irish author; pres. of Republic of Ireland (1938–45)
Hyde Edward 1609–1674 1st Earl of *Clar·en·don* \'klar-ən-dən, 'kler-\ Eng. statesman & hist.
Hy·der Ali *or* Hai·dar Ali \'hī-dər-ä-'lē\ 1722–1782 Indian ruler & soldier
Hy·mans \'hī-,män(t)s, ē-'mä"s\ Paul 1865–1941 Belg. statesman
Hy·pse·lan·tes \,ēp-sə-'län-dēs\ *var of* YPSILANTIS
Ibáñez Vicente Blasco — see BLASCO IBÁÑEZ
Iber·ville \'ē-bər-,vil, -,vēl; 'ī-bər-,vil\ Sieur d' 1661–1706 *Pierre Le Moyne* \'mwän\ Fr.-Canad. explorer & founder of Louisiana
Ibn–Khal·dūn \,i-bən-,kal-'dün, -,kal-\ 1332–1406 Arab hist.
Ibn–Rushd \,i-bən-'rùsht\ — see AVERROËS
Ibn Sa·ʿūd \,i-bən-sä-'üd, -'saùd\ *ca* 1880–1953 king of Saudi Arabia (1932–53)
Ibn Zuhr \,i-bən-'zùr\ L Av·en·zo·ar \,a-vən-'zō-ər, -zō-'är\ *or* Abu·me·ron \,a-byü-'mer-,än\ *ca* 1090–1162 Muslim physician
Ibrā·hīm Pa·sha \,i-,brä-'him-'pä-shə, -'pa-shə, -pə-'shä\ 1789–1848 Egypt. gen. & viceroy
Ib·sen \'ib-sən, 'ip-\ Henrik 1828–1906 Norw. poet & dram. — Ib·se·ni·an \ib-'sē-nē-ən, ip-, -'se-nē-\ *or* Ib·sen·esque \,ib-sə-'nesk, ,ip-\ *adj*
Ick·es \'i-kəs\ Harold LeClair 1874–1952 Am. polit.
Ic·ti·nus \ik-'tī-nəs\ 5th cent. B.C. Greek architect
Ig·nar·ro \ig-'när-(,)ō\ Louis J(oseph) 1941–   Am. pharmacologist
Ig·na·tius \ig-'nä-sh(ē-)əs\ Saint *d ca* A.D. 110 *Theophorus* bishop of Antioch & church father
Ignatius of Loyola Saint 1491–1556 orig. *Iñigo de Oñaz y Loyola* Span. religious & founder of Society of Jesus — Ig·na·tian \-sh(ē-)ən\ *adj*
Ike·da \ē-'kä-də, -'ke-\ Hayato 1899–1965 Jp. polit.; prime min. (1960–64)
Ikhnaton — see AKHENATON
Il·ies·cu \i-lē-'es-(,)kü, il-'yes-\ Ion (Ilici) 1930–   pres. of Romania (1990–96, 2000–04)
Im·mel·mann \'i-məl-,män, -mən\ Max 1890–1916 Ger. aviator
In·dy, d' \'dan-dē; dan-'dē, da"-\ (Paul-Marie-Théodore-) Vincent 1851–1931 Fr. composer
Inés de Castro — see CASTRO
Inge \'inj\ William 1913–1973 Am. playwright
Inge \'iŋ\ William Ralph 1860–1954 Eng. prelate & author
In·ger·soll \'iŋ-gər-,sòl, -səl\ Robert Green 1833–1899 Am. orator
In·gres \'a"(n)grə\ Jean-Auguste-Dominique 1780–1867 Fr. painter
In·ness \'i-nəs\ George: father 1825–1894 & son 1854–1926 Am. painters
In·no·cent \'i-nə-sənt\ name of 13 popes: esp. II *d* 1143 (pope 1130–43); III 1160(or 1161)–1216 (pope 1198–1216); IV *d* 1254 (pope 1243–54); XI 1611–1689 (pope 1676–89)
Inö·nü \,i-nə-'nü, -'nyü\ İs·met \is-'met\ 1884–1973 Turk. statesman; pres. of Turkey (1938–50); premier (1961–65)
In·sull \'in(t)-səl\ Samuel 1859–1938 Am. (Eng.-born) financier
Io·nes·co \,ē-ə-'nes-(,)kō\ Eugène 1909–1994 Fr. (Rom.-born) dram.
Ipa·tieff \i-'pä-tē-,ef, -'pä-chəf\ Vladimir Nikolayevich 1867–1952 Am. (Russ.-born) chem.
Ire·dell \'ī(-ə)r-,del\ James 1751–1799 Am. jurist
Ire·ton \'ī(-ə)r-t°n\ Henry 1611–1651 Eng. soldier & polit.
Iri·go·yen \,ir-i-'gò-,yen\ Hi·pó·li·to \ē-'pò-lē-,tō\ 1852–1933 pres. of Argentina (1916–22; 1928–30)
Iron·side \'ī(-ə)rn-,sīd\ William Edmund 1880–1959 1st Baron *Ironside* Brit. field marshal
Ir·ving \'ər-viŋ\ Sir Henry 1838–1905 orig. *John Henry Brodribb* Eng. actor
Irving Washington 1783–1859 Am. essayist, nov., & hist.
Ir·win \'ər-wən\ William Henry 1873–1948 *Will Irwin* Am. journalist
Isaacs \'ī-ziks, -zəks\ Sir Isaac Alfred 1855–1948 Austral. jurist & statesman; gov.-gen. of Australia (1931–36)
Isaacs Rufus Daniel — see Marquis of READING
Is·a·bel·la I \,i-zə-'be-lə\ 1451–1504 *wife of Ferdinand V of Castile* queen of Castile (1474–1504) & of Aragon (1479–1504)
Ish·er·wood \'i-shər-,wùd\ Christopher William Bradshaw 1904–1986 Am. (Brit.-born) writer
Ishii \'ē-shē-,ē, 'i-\ Viscount Kikujiro 1866–1945 Jp. diplomat
Is·i·dore of Seville \'i-zə-,dòr\ Saint *ca* 560–636 L. *Isidorus Hispalensis* Span. prelate & scholar
Iskander Bey — see SKANDERBEG
Is·mā·ʿīl Pa·sha \is-'mä-,ēl-'pä-shə, -'pa-shə, -pə-'shä\ 1830–1895 viceroy of Egypt (1863–79)
Isoc·ra·tes \ī-'sä-krə-,tēz\ 436–338 B.C. Athenian orator
Is·ra·el ben Eli·ezer \'iz-rē-əl-,ben-,e-lē-'ä-zər\ *ca* 1700–1760 *Baʿal Shem Tov* \'bä(-ə)l-'shem-'tòv\ Pol.-Jewish religious leader
Ito \'ē-(,)tō\ Prince Hirobumi 1841–1909 Jp. statesman
Itur·bi \i-'tùr-bē\ José 1895–1980 Span.-born pianist & conductor
Itur·bi·de \,ē-,tùr-'bē-(,)thä\ Agustín de 1783–1824 Mex. soldier; emp. of Mexico (1822–23)
Ivan III \ē-'vän, 'ī-vən\ Va·si·lye·vich \və-'sil-yə-,vich\ 1440–1505 *the Great* grand prince of Russia (1462–1505)
Ivan IV Vasilyevich 1530–1584 *the Terrible* ruler of Russia (1533–84)

\ə\ abut \ə\ kitten, F table \ər\ further \a\ ash \ā\ ace \ä\ mop, mar
\aù\ out \ch\ chin \e\ bet \ē\ easy \g\ go \i\ hit \ī\ ice \j\ job
\ŋ\ sing \ō\ go \ò\ law \òi\ boy \th\ thin \th\ the \ü\ loot \ù\ foot
\y\ yet \zh\ vision, beige \k̲, ⁿ, œ, ʊ, ᵞ\ *see* Guide to Pronunciation

Ives \\'īvz\ Charles Edward 1874–1954 Am. composer — **Ives·ian** \\'īv-zē-ən\ *adj*

Ives James Merritt 1824–1895 Am. lithographer

Iyeyasu *or* **Ieyasu** — see TOKUGAWA

Jā·bir ibn Ḥay·yān \\'ja-ˌbir-ˌi-bən-hī-'yan\ Abū Mūsā *ca* 721–*ca* 851 L. *Ge·ber* \\'ja-ˌbir, 'ga-, 'ge-\ Arab alchemist & mystic

Jack·son \\'jak-sən\ Andrew 1767–1845 Am. gen.; 7th pres. of the U.S. (1829–37) — **Jack·son·ian** \jak-'sō-nē-ən\ *adj*

Jackson Helen (Maria) Hunt 1830–1885 née *Fiske* Am. nov.

Jackson Jesse (Louis) 1941–   Am. clergyman & polit. activist

Jackson Mahalia 1911–1972 Am. gospel singer

Jackson Michael (Joseph) 1958–2009 Am. pop singer, songwriter, & dancer

Jackson Robert H(ough·wout) \\'haů-ət\ 1892–1954 Am. jurist

Jackson Thomas Jonathan 1824–1863 *Stone·wall* \\'stōn-ˌwȯl\ *Jackson* Am. Confed. gen.

Ja·co·po del·la Quer·cia \yä-ˌkō-(ˌ)pō-ˌdä-lə-'kwer-chä\ *ca* 1374–1438 Ital. sculptor

Jac·quard \zha-'kär, 'ja-ˌkärd\ Joseph-Marie 1752–1834 Fr. inventor

Jacques I — see Jean-Jacques DESSALINES

Ja·hān·gīr \jə-'hän-ˌgir\ 1569–1627 emp. of India (1605–27)

Ja·lāl ad–Dīn ar–Rū·mī \jə-'lä-lə-'dē-när-'rü-mē\ *ca* 1207–1273 Pers. poet

James \\'jāmz\ name of 6 kings of Scotland & 2 kings of Great Britain: esp. **VI** 1566–1625 of Scotland (reigned 1567–1603) *or* **I** of Great Britain (reigned 1603–25); **II** 1633–1701 (reigned 1685–88)

James Henry 1811–1882 Am. philos.

James Henry 1843–1916 *son of prec.* Brit. (Am.-born) writer — **James·ian** \\'jäm-zē-ən\ *adj*

James Jesse Woodson 1847–1882 Am. outlaw

James P(hyllis) D(orothy) 1920–   Baroness *James of Holland Park* Brit. writer

James William 1842–1910 *bro. of Henry (writer)* Am. psychol. & philos. — **James·ian** \\'jäm-zē-ən\ *adj*

James Edward 1688–1766 *James Francis Edward Stuart; the Old Pretender; father of Charles Edward* Brit. prince

Jame·son \\'jäm-sən, 'je-mə-sən\ Sir Leander Starr 1853–1917 *Doctor Jameson* Scot. physician & administrator in So. Africa

Jā·mī \'jä-mē\ 1414–1492 Pers. poet & mystic

Ja·ná·ček \\'yä-nə-ˌchek\ Leoš 1854–1928 Czech composer

Jan·sen \\'jan(t)-sən, 'yän(t)-\ Cor·ne·lis \kȯr-'nā-ləs\ 1585–1638 L. *Cornelius Jansenius* Du. R.C. theol.

Jaques–Dal·croze \\'zhäk-ˌdal-'krōz, 'zhak-\ Émile 1865–1950 Swiss composer & creator of eurythmics

Ja·rīr \jə-'rir\ *ca* 650–*ca* 729 Arab poet

Jar·rell \jə-'rel, ja-\ Randall 1914–1965 Am. writer

Ja·ru·zel·ski \ˌyär-ü-'zel-skē\ Woj·ciech \'vȯi-ˌchek\ Witold 1923–   gen.; 1st secy. of the Communist party in Poland (1981–89)

Jas·pers \'jäs-pərs\ Karl Theodor 1883–1969 Ger. philos.

Jau·rès \zhō-'res\ (Auguste-Marie-Joseph-) Jean 1859–1914 Fr. socialist

Jay \'jā\ John 1745–1829 Am. jurist & statesman; 1st chief justice U.S. Supreme Court (1789–95)

Jeans \'jēnz\ Sir James Hopwood 1877–1946 Eng. physicist, astron., & author

Jef·fers \\'je-fərz\ (John) Robinson 1887–1962 Am. poet

Jef·fer·son \\'je-fər-sən\ Thomas 1743–1826 3d pres. of the U.S. (1801–09) — **Jef·fer·so·nian** \je-fər-'sō-nē-ən, -nyən\ *adj*

Jef·frey \\'je-frē\ Lord Francis 1773–1850 Scot. critic & jurist

Jef·freys \\'je-frēz\ George 1645–1689 1st Baron *Jeffreys of Wem* Eng. jurist

Jel·i·nek \\'yel-i-nek\ Elfriede 1946–   Austrian writer

Jel·li·coe \\'je-li-ˌkō\ 1st Earl 1859–1935 *John Rushworth Jellicoe* Brit. admiral

Jen·ner \\'je-nər\ Edward 1749–1823 Eng. physician — **Jen·ne·ri·an** \je-'nir-ē-ən\ *adj*

Jenner Sir William 1815–1898 Eng. physician

Jen·son \\'jen-sən, zhäⁿ-'sōⁿ\ Nicolas *ca* 1420–1480 Fr. printer & engraver in Venice

Je·rome \jə-'rōm *also* 'jer-əm\ Saint *ca* 347–419(or 420) L. *Eusebius Hieron·y·mus* \ˌhī-ə-'rä-nə-məs, hi-\ church father

Jer·vis \'jär-vəs, 'jär-\ John 1735–1823 Earl of *St. Vincent* Brit. admiral

Jes·per·sen \\'yes-pər-sən\ (Jens) Otto Harry 1860–1943 Dan. philologist

Je·sus \\'jē-zəs, -zəz\ *or* **Jesus Christ** \\'krīst\ *or* **Christ Jesus** *ca* 6 B.C.–*ca* A.D. 30 *Jesus of Nazareth; the Son of Mary* source of the Christian religion & Savior in the Christian faith

Jev·ons \\'je-vənz\ William Stanley 1835–1882 Eng. econ.

Jew·ell \\'jü(-ə)l\ Sally (Margaret) 1956–   née *Roffey* U.S. secy. of interior (2013–)

Jew·ett \\'jü-ət\ Sarah Orne 1849–1909 Am. writer

Ji·ang Ze·min \jē-'äŋ-zə-'min\ 1926–   gen. secy. of Chin. Communist party (1989–2002); pres. of China (1993–2003)

Ji·mé·nez \hē-'mā-nəs\ Juan Ramón 1881–1958 Span. poet

Jiménez de Cis·ne·ros \-ˌdä-sis-'ner-əs\ Francisco 1436–1517 Span. prelate & statesman

Jin·nah \\'ji-(ˌ)nä, 'ji-nə\ Mohammed Ali 1876–1948 Indian polit.; 1st gov.-gen. of dominion of Pakistan (1947–48)

Jo·achim \\'yō-'ä-kim, -ˌkim; 'yō-ə-ˌkim, -ˌkim\ Joseph 1831–1907 Hung. violinist

Joan of Arc \ˌjōn-əv-'ärk\ *F* **Jeanne d'Arc** \zhän-'därk\ Saint *ca* 1412–1431 *the Maid of Orleans* Fr. national heroine

Jobs \'jäbz\ Steven Paul 1955–2011 Am. computer entrepreneur

Jodl \'yō-dᵊl\ Alfred 1890–1946 Ger. gen.

Jof·fre \'zhȯfrᵊ\ Joseph-Jacques-Césaire 1852–1931 Fr. field marshal; marshal of France

John \'jän\ name of 21 popes: esp. **XXIII** (*Angelo Giuseppe Roncalli*) 1881–1963 (pope 1958–63)

John 1167–1216 *John Lack·land* \'lak-ˌland\ king of England (1199–1216)

John Augustus Edwin 1878–1961 Brit. painter & etcher

John I 1357–1433 *the Great* king of Portugal (1385–1433)

John III So·bies·ki \sō-'byes-kē, ˌsō-bē-'es-\ 1629–1696 king of Poland (1674–96)

John of Austria 1547–1578 Don *John* Span. gen.

John of Gaunt \'gȯnt, 'gänt\ 1340–1399 Duke of *Lancaster; son of Edward III of England*

John of Lancaster 1389–1435 Duke of *Bedford; son of Henry IV of England*

John of Salisbury 1115(or 1120)–1180 Eng. ecclesiastic

John of the Cross 1542–1591 *Juan de Yepes y Alvarez* Span. mystic & poet

John Paul \'pȯl\ name of 2 popes: esp. **II** (*Karol Wojtyla*) 1920–2005 (pope 1978–2005)

Johns \'jänz\ Jasper 1930–   Am. artist

John·son \'jän(t)-sən\ Andrew 1808–1875 17th pres. of the U.S. (1865–69) — **John·so·nian** \jän-'sō-nē-ən, -nyən\ *adj*

Johnson (Jonathan) Eastman 1824–1906 Am. painter

Johnson James Weldon 1871–1938 Am. author

Johnson Jeh (Charles) 1957–   U.S. secy. of homeland security (2013–)

Johnson Lyndon Baines 1908–1973 Am. polit.; 36th pres. of the U.S. (1963–69) — **John·so·nian** \jän-'sō-nē-ən, -nyən\ *adj*

Johnson Magic 1959–   *Earvin Johnson* Am. basketball player

Johnson Philip Cortelyou 1906–2005 Am. architect

Johnson Richard Mentor 1780–1850 vice pres. of the U.S. (1837–41)

Johnson Samuel 1709–1784 *Dr. Johnson* Eng. lexicographer & author

Johnson Sir William 1715–1774 Brit. administrator in America

Johnson Sir·leaf \'sər-ˌlēf\ Ellen née *Johnson* 1938–   Liberian activist; pres. of Liberia (2006–)

John·ston \'jän(t)-stən, -sən\ Albert Sidney 1803–1862 Am. Confed. gen.

Johnston Joseph Eggleston 1807–1891 Am. Confed. gen.

Join·ville \zhwaⁿ-'vēl\ Jean de *ca* 1224–1317 Fr. chronicler

Jo·liot–Cu·rie \ˌzhȯl-ˌyō-kyü-'rē, -'kyür-(ˌ)ē\ (Jean-) Frédéric 1900–1958 orig. surname *Joliot* Fr. physicist

Joliot–Curie Irène 1897–1956 formerly *Irène Curie-Joliot, dau. of Marie & Pierre Curie & wife of prec.* Fr. physicist

Jol·liet *or* **Jo·liet** \zhȯl-'yā, zhō-lē-ˌet; 'zhō-lē-ˌet\ Louis 1645–1700 Fr. explorer

Jol·son \'jōl-sən\ Al 1886–1950 born *Asa Yoelson* Am. (Lith.-born) singer

Jo·mi·ni \ˌzhō-mə-'nē\ Henri de 1779–1869 Swiss-born soldier & mil. strategist

Jon·a·than \'jä-nə-thən\ Goodluck (Ebele Azikiwe) 1957–   pres. of Nigeria (2010–)

Jones \'jōnz\ Anson 1798–1858 pres. of the Republic of Texas (1844–46)

Jones Howard Mumford 1892–1980 Am. educ. & critic

Jones In·i·go \'i-ni-ˌgō\ 1573–1652 Eng. architect

Jones John Paul 1747–1792 orig. in full *John Paul* Am. (Scot.-born) naval officer

Jones Quincy 1933–   Am. composer, bandleader, & producer

Jon·son \'jän(t)-sən\ Benjamin 1572–1637 *Ben Jonson* Eng. dram. — **Jon·so·nian** \jän-'sō-nē-ən, -nyən\ *adj*

Jop·lin \'jä-plən\ Scott 1868–1917 Am. pianist & composer

Jor·daens \'yȯr-dän(t)s\ Jacob 1593–1678 Flem. painter

Jor·dan \'yȯr-dän\ David Starr 1851–1931 Am. biol. & educ.

Jordan Michael (Jeffrey) 1963–   Am. basketball player

Jo·seph \'jō-zəf *also* -səf\ *ca* 1840–1904 *In-mut-too-yah-lat-lat* Nez Percé Indian chief

Joseph II 1741–1790 Holy Rom. emp. (1765–90)

Jo·se·phine \'jō-zə-ˌfēn\ Empress — see BEAUHARNAIS

Jo·seph·son \'jō-zəf-sən *also* -səf-\ Brian David 1940–   Brit. physicist

Jo·se·phus \jō-'sē-fəs\ Flavius *ca* A.D. 37–*ca* 100 Jewish hist.

Jos·quin des Prez \zhȯ-'skaⁿ-de-'prā\ *or* **Des·prez** \de-'prā\ *ca* 1440–1521 Fr. composer

Jou·bert \zhü-'ber\ Joseph 1754–1824 Fr. essayist & moralist

Joule \'jül\ James Prescott 1818–1889 Eng. physicist

Jour·dan \zhùr-'däⁿ\ Comte Jean-Baptiste 1762–1833 Fr. soldier; marshal of France

Jow·ett \'jaů-ət, 'jō-\ Benjamin 1817–1893 Eng. Greek scholar

Joyce \'jȯis\ James (Augustine Aloysius) 1882–1941 Irish writer — **Joyc·ean** \'jȯi-sē-ən\ *adj*

Juan Car·los \'(h)wän-'kär-ˌlōs\ 1938–   *grandson of Alfonso XIII* king of Spain (1975–)

Juá·rez \'hwär-əs, 'wär-\ Benito Pablo 1806–1872 Mex. lawyer; pres. of Mexico (1861–65; 1867–72)

Judas Maccabaeus — see MACCABEES

Ju·gur·tha \jù-'gər-thə\ *or* **Iu·gur·tha** \yù-\ *ca* 160–104 B.C. king of Numidia (118–105 B.C.)

Ju·lian \'jül-yən\ *ca* 331–363 *Flavius Claudius Julianus, the Apostate* Rom. emp. (361–363)

Ju·li·ana \ˌjü-lē-'a-nə\ 1909–2004 *dau. of Wilhelmina* queen of the Netherlands (1948–80)

Julius Caesar — see CAESAR

Jung \'yùŋ\ Carl Gustav 1875–1961 Swiss psychol.

Ju·nius \'jü-nyəs, -nē-əs\ Franciscus 1589–1677 Eng. (Ger.-born) philologist

Jun·kers \'yùŋ-kərz, -kərs\ Hugo 1859–1935 Ger. airplane designer & builder

Ju·not \zhǝ-'nō\ Andoche 1771–1813 Duc *d'Abran·tès* \ˌda-bräⁿ-'tes\ Fr. gen.

Jus·se·rand \zhǝs-'räⁿ, zhǝs-sə-\ Jean (Adrien-Antoine) Jules 1855–1932 Fr. scholar & diplomat

Jus·tin \'jəs-tən\ Saint *ca* 100–*ca* 165 *Justin (the) Martyr* church father

Jus·tin·i·an I \ˌjə-'sti-nē-ən\ 483–565 *the Great* Byzantine emp. (527–565)

Ju·ve·nal \'jü-və-nᵊl\ A.D. 55 to 60–*ca* 127 *Decimus Junius Juvenalis* Rom. poet & satirist — **Ju·ve·na·lian** \ˌjü-və-'näl-yən\ *adj*

Ka·bi·la \kä-'bē-lə\ Joseph 1971–   pres. of Democratic Republic of Congo (2001–)

Kabila Laurent (Désiré) 1938–2001 *father of prec.* pres. of Democratic Republic of Congo (1997–2001)

Ka·czyn·ski \kä-'chin-skē\ Lech (Aleksander) 1949–2010 pres. of Poland (2005–10)

Ká·dár \'kä-ˌdär\ János 1912–1989 1st secy. of Hung. Communist party (1956–88)

Kaf·ka \'käf-kə, 'kaf-\ Franz 1883–1924 Czech-born author writing in German

Ka·ga·me \kä-'gä-mā\ Paul 1957– pres. of Rwanda (2000–)

Ka·gan \'kä-gən\ Elena 1960– Am. jurist

Ka·ga·wa \kä-'gä-wə\ Toyohiko 1888–1960 Jp. social reformer

Kah·lo (de Ri·ve·ra) \'kä-lō-thä-ri-'ver-ə\ Frida 1907–1954 née *Magdalena Carmen Frida Kahlo y Calderón* Mex. painter

Kah·ne·man \'kä-nə-mən\ Daniel 1934– Am.-Israeli psychol.

Kai·ser \'kī-zər\ Henry John 1882–1967 Am. industrialist

Kalb \'kälp, 'kalb\ Johann 1721–1780 Baron *de Kalb* \di-'kalb\ Ger. gen. in Am. Revolution

Kā·li·dā·sa \ˌkä-li-'dä-sə\ 5th cent. A.D. Indian dram. & poet

Ka·li·nin \kə-'lē-nyən\ Mikhail Ivanovich 1875–1946 Russ. polit.; formal head of Soviet state (1919–46)

Ka·me·ha·me·ha I \kə-ˌmä-ə-'mä-(ˌ)hä\ 1758?–1819 *the Great* king of Hawaii (1795–1819)

Ka·me·nev \'käm-yə-ˌnef, 'kam-; 'kä-mə-, 'ka-\ Lev Borisovich 1883–1936 Russ. Communist leader

Ka·mer·lingh On·nes \ˌkä-mər-liŋ-'òn-əs\ Heike 1853–1926 Du. physicist

Kan·del \kan-'del\ Eric R(ichard) 1929– Am. (Austrian-born) neuroscientist

Kan·din·sky \kan-'din(t)-skē\ Wassily 1866–1944 Russ. painter

K'ang–hsi \'käŋ-'shē\ 1654–1722 Chin. emp. (1661–1722)

Kant \'kant, 'känt\ Immanuel 1724–1804 Ger. philos. — Kant·ian \'kan-tē-ən, 'kän-\ adj

Kao \'kaù\ Charles K(uen) 1933– Brit. (Chinese-born) physicist

Ka·pi·tsa \'kä-pyit-sə\ Pyotr Leonidovich 1894–1984 Russ. physicist

Kar·a·george \ˌka-rə-'jòrj\ 1762–1817 orig. *George Petrović Karageorge* Serbian leader & founder of Ka·ra·geor·ge·vić \-'jòr-jə-ˌvich\ dynasty

Ka·ra·jan \'kär-ə-ˌyän\ Herbert von 1908–1989 Austrian conductor

Ka·ra·man·lis \ˌkär-ə-ˌmän-'lēs, -'män-,\ Konstantinos 1907–1998 prime min. (1974–80) & pres. (1980–85; 1990–95) of Greece

Karamanlis Kostas 1956– *Konstantinos Karamanlis, nephew of prec.* prime min. of Greece (2004–09)

Kar·loff \'kär-(ˌ)lòf\ Boris 1887–1969 born *William Henry Pratt* Eng. actor

Kar·man \'kär-'män\ Ta·wak·kul \'tä-wä-ˌkül\ 1979– Yemeni activist

Ká·ro·lyi \'ka-rəl-yē, 'kär-əl-\ Count Mihály 1875–1955 Hung. polit.

Kar·plus \'kär-ˌpləs\ Martin 1930– Am. (Austrian-born) chem.

Kar·sa·vi·na \kär-'sä-və-nə, -'sa-\ Tamara 1885–1978 Russ. dancer

Kar·zai \'kär-ˌzī, ˌkär-'\ Hamid 1957– pres. of Afghanistan (2004–)

Kauf·man \'kòf-mən\ George S(imon) 1889–1961 Am. dram.

Ka·un·da \kä-'ün-də\ Kenneth David 1924– Zambian polit.; pres. (1964–91)

Kau·nitz \'kaù-nəts\ Wenzel Anton von 1711–1794 Prince *von Kaunitz-Rietberg* Austrian statesman

Kaut·sky \'kaùt-skē\ Karl Johann 1854–1938 Ger. socialist writer

Ka·wa·ba·ta \ˌkä-wə-'bä-tə, kə-'wä-bə-ˌtä\ Yasunari 1899–1972 Jp. writer

Ka·zan \kə-'zän\ Elia 1909–2003 orig. *Elias Kazanjoglous* Am. (Turk.-born) director

Ka·zan·tza·kis \ˌkä-z²n-'tsä-kēs, -'chä-\ Nikos 1885–1957 Greek poet, nov., & translator

Kean \'kēn\ Edmund 1789–1833 Eng. actor

Kear·ny \'kär-nē\ Philip 1814–1862 Am. gen.

Keat·ing \'kē-tiŋ\ Paul John 1944– prime min. of Australia (1991–96)

Kea·ton \'kē-t²n\ Buster 1895–1966 *Joseph Francis Keaton* Am. actor & director

Keats \'kēts\ John 1795–1821 Eng. poet — Keats·ian \'kēt-sē-ən\ adj

Ke·fau·ver \'kē-ˌfò-vər\ (Carey) Estes 1903–1963 Am. polit.

Kei·tel \'kī-t²l\ Wilhelm 1882–1946 Ger. field marshal

Kek·ko·nen \'ke-kə-nən, -ˌnen\ Urho Kaleva 1900–1986 pres. of Finland (1956–81)

Kel·ler \'ke-lər\ Helen Adams 1880–1968 Am. deaf & blind lecturer

Kel·logg \'ke-ˌlòg, -ˌläg\ Frank Billings 1856–1937 Am. statesman

Kel·ly \'ke-lē\ Ellsworth 1923– Am. artist

Kelly Gene 1912–1996 Am. dancer, actor, & director

Kelly Grace 1929–1982 *Princess Grace of Monaco* Am. actress

Kel·vin \'kel-vən\ 1st Baron 1824–1907 *William Thomson* Brit. math. & physicist

Kem·ble \'kem-bəl\ Frances Anne 1809–1893 *Fanny* Eng. actress

Kempis Thomas à — see THOMAS À KEMPIS

Ken·dall \'ken-d²l\ Henry Way 1926–1999 Am. physicist

Ken·nan \'ke-nən\ George F(rost) 1904–2005 Am. hist. & diplomat

Ken·ne·dy \'ke-nə-dē\ Anthony M(cLeod) 1936– Am. jurist

Kennedy John Fitzgerald 1917–1963 Am. polit.; 35th pres. of the U.S. (1961–63) — Ken·ne·dy·esque \ˌke-nə-dē-'esk\ adj

Kennedy Joseph Patrick 1888–1969 *father of J.F., R.F., & Ted* Am. businessman & diplomat

Kennedy Robert Francis 1925–1968 *bro. of J.F. & Ted* Am. polit.; atty. gen. (1961–64)

Kennedy Ted 1932–2009 *Edward Moore Kennedy, bro. of J.F. & R.F.* Am. polit.

Kennedy Onas·sis \ō-'na-səs\ Jacqueline 1929–1994 née *Bouvier; wife of J.F. Kennedy*

Ken·ny \'ke-nē\ Elizabeth 1880–1952 *Sister Kenny* Austral. nurse & physiotherapist

Kenny Enda 1951– prime min. of Ireland (2011–)

Kent \'kent\ Rockwell 1882–1971 Am. painter & illustrator

Ken·yat·ta \ken-'yä-tə\ Jomo 1894?–1978 pres. of Kenya (1964–78)

Kenyatta Uhuru (Muigai) 1961– *son of prec.* pres. of Kenya (2013–)

Ke·o·kuk \'kē-ə-ˌkək\ 1780?–1848 *Kiyo'kaga* Sauk & Fox tribal leader

Kep·ler \'ke-plər\ Johannes 1571–1630 Ger. astron. — Kep·ler·ian \ke-'plir-ē-ən, -'pler-\ adj

Ke·ren·sky \'ke-rən-skē, ke-'ren-\ Aleksandr Fyodorovich 1881–1970 Russ. revolutionary

Kern \'kərn\ Jerome David 1885–1945 Am. composer

Ker·ou·ac \'ker-ə-ˌwak\ Jack 1922–1969 *Jean-Louis* Am. writer

Ker·ry \'ker-ē\ John (Forbes) 1943– Am. polit.; U.S. secy. of state (2013–)

Ker·tész \'ker-tās\ Imre 1929– Hung. writer

Kes·sel·ring \'ke-səl-riŋ\ Albert 1885–1960 Ger. field marshal

Ket·ter·ing \'ke-tə-riŋ\ Charles Franklin 1876–1958 Am. electrical engineer & inventor

Ket·ter·le \'ke-tər-lə\ Wolfgang 1957– Ger. physicist

Key \'kē\ Francis Scott 1779–1843 Am. lawyer & author of "The Star-Spangled Banner"

Key John (Phillip) 1961– prime min. of New Zealand (2008–)

Keynes \'kānz\ John Maynard 1883–1946 1st Baron *Keynes of Tilton* Eng. econ.

Key·ser·ling \'kī-zər-liŋ\ Hermann Alexander 1880–1946 Graf *Keyserling* Ger. philos. & writer

Kha·cha·tu·ri·an \ˌkä-chə-'tùr-ē-ən, ˌka-\ Aram Ilich 1903–1978 Soviet (Armenian-born) composer

Kha·da·fy *var of* GADDHAFI

Khā·lid \'kä-lid, 'kä-\ in full *Khālid ibn 'Abd al-'Azīz ibn 'Abd ar-Raḥmān al-Saʻūd* 1913–1982 king of Saudi Arabia (1975–82)

Kha·me·nei \kə-'mä-nā\ Ayatollah Sayyid Ali 1939– supreme leader of Iran (1989–)

Kha·ta·mi \kä-'tä-mē\ Sayyid Mohammad 1943– pres. of Iran (1997–2005)

Khayyám Omar — see OMAR KHAYYÁM

Khe·ra·skov \kə-'räs-kəf\ Mikhail Matveyevich 1733–1807 Russ. poet

Kho·mei·ni \kō-'mä-nē, kō-, hō-\ Ayatollah Ruholla Mussaui 1900–1989 religious leader of Iran (1979–89)

Khru·shchev \krùsh-'chof, -'chòv; 'krùsh-,; *also with* e *for* ò\ Ni·ki·ta \nə-'kē-tə\ Sergeyevich 1894–1971 Soviet polit.; premier of Soviet Union (1958–64) — Khru·shchev·ian \krùsh-'chò-vē-ən, -'chō-\ adj — Khru·shchev·ite \krùsh-'chò-ˌvīt, -'che-ˌvīt; 'krùsh-,\ adj

Khu·fu \'kü-(ˌ)fü\ *Gk* Che·ops \'kē-ˌäps\ 26th cent. B.C. king of Egypt & pyramid builder

Khwā·riz·mī, al– \al-'kwär-əz-mē, -'kwär-\ *ca* 780–*ca* 850 *Muḥammad ibn Mūsā al-Khwārizmī* Islamic (Persian-born) math. & astron.

Ki·ba·ki \ki-'bä-kē\ (Emilio) Mwai 1931– pres. of Kenya (2002–13)

Kidd \'kid\ William *ca* 1645–1701 *Captain Kidd* Scot. pirate

Kier·ke·gaard \'kir-kə-ˌgär(d), -ˌgör\ Søren Aabye 1813–1855 Dan. philos. & theol. — Kier·ke·gaard·ian \ˌkir-kə-'gär-dē-ən, -'gör-\ adj

Kie·sing·er \'kē-ziŋ-ər\ Kurt Georg 1904–1988 chancellor of West Germany (1966–69)

Kil·by \'kil-bē\ Jack St. Clair 1923–2005 Am. electrical engineer

Kil·lian \'ki-lē-ən, 'kil-yən\ James Rhyne 1904–1988 Am. educ.

Kil·mer \'kil-mər\ (Alfred) Joyce 1886–1918 Am. poet

Kim Dae Jung \'kim-'dā-'jùn\ 1925–2009 pres. of So. Korea (1998–2003)

Kim Il Sung \'kim-'il-'səŋ, -'sùŋ\ 1912–1994 No. Korean Communist leader (1948–94) & pres. (1972–94)

Kim Jong Il \-'jòŋ-'il\ 1942–2011 *son of prec.* No. Korean Communist leader (1994–2011)

Kim Jong Un \-'jòŋ-'ən\ *ca* 1983– *son of prec.* No. Korean Communist leader (2011–)

Kim·mel \'ki-məl\ Husband Edward 1882–1968 Am. admiral

Kim Young Sam \'kim-'yəŋ-'säm, -'sam\ 1927– pres. of So. Korea (1993–98)

Kin·di, al– \al-'kin-dē\ *d ca* 870 Arab philos.

King \'kiŋ\ B. B. 1925– orig. *Riley B. King* Am. blues musician

King Billie Jean 1943– née *Moffitt* Am. tennis player

King Ernest Joseph 1878–1956 Am. admiral

King Martin Luther, Jr. 1929–1968 Am. clergyman & civil rights leader

King Rufus 1755–1827 Am. polit. & diplomat

King Stephen (Edwin) 1947– Am. writer

King William Lyon Mackenzie 1874–1950 Canad. statesman; prime min. (1921–26; 1926–30; 1935–48)

King William Rufus de Vane 1786–1853 Am. polit.; vice pres. of the U.S. (1853)

Kings·ley \'kiŋz-lē\ Charles 1819–1875 Eng. clergyman & nov.

Kin·kaid \kin-'kād\ Thomas Cassin 1888–1972 Am. admiral

Kin·sey \'kin-zē\ Alfred Charles 1894–1956 Am. sexologist

Kip·ling \'kip-liŋ\ (Joseph) Rud·yard \'rəd-yərd, 'rə-jərd\ 1865–1936 Eng. author — Kip·ling·esque \ˌkip-liŋ-'esk\ adj

Kirch·hoff \-ˌkòf\ Gustav Robert 1824–1887 Ger. physicist

Kirch·ner \'kirch-ner\ Cristina (Elisabet) Fernández de 1953– *wife of Néstor* pres. of Argentina (2007–)

Kirch·ner \'kirk-nər, 'kirk-\ Ernst Ludwig 1880–1938 Ger. painter

Kirch·ner \'kirch-ner\ Néstor (Carlos) 1950–2010 pres. of Argentina (2003–07)

Ki·rov \'kē-ˌròf, -ˌròv\ Sergey Mironovich 1886–1934 Soviet polit.

Kir·wan \'kir-wən\ Richard 1733–1812 Irish chem.

Kis·sin·ger \'ki-s²n-jər\ Henry (Alfred) 1923– Am. (Ger.-born) scholar & govt. official; U.S. secy. of state (1973–77)

Kitch·e·ner \'ki-chə-\ H(oratio) H(erbert) 1850–1916 1st Earl *Kitchener of Khartoum and of Broome* Brit. field marshal

Kit·tredge \'ki-trij\ George Lyman 1860–1941 Am. educ.

Klee \'klā\ Paul 1879–1940 Swiss painter

Kleist \'klīst\ (Bernd) Heinrich Wilhelm von 1777–1811 Ger. author

Kleist (Paul Ludwig) Ewald von 1881–1954 Ger. field marshal

Klem·per·er \'klem-pər-ər\ Otto 1885–1973 Ger. conductor

Klimt \'klimt\ Gustav 1862–1918 Austrian painter

Klitz·ing \'klit-siŋ\ Klaus von 1943– Ger. physicist

Klop·stock \'kläp-ˌstäk, 'klòp-ˌshtòk\ Friedrich Gottlieb 1724–1803 Ger. poet

Knel·ler \'ne-lər, 'kne-\ Sir Godfrey 1646 (or 1649)–1723 orig. *Gottfried Kniller* Ger. (Ger.-born) painter

Knowles \'nōlz\ William S(tandish) 1917–2012 Am. chem.

Knox \'näks\ Henry 1750–1806 Am. gen. in Revolution

Knox John *ca* 1514–1572 Scot. religious reformer

Knox Philander Chase 1853–1921 Am. statesman
Knut *var of* CANUTE
Ko·ba·ya·shi \ˌkō-bä-ˈyä-shē\ Makoto 1944–	Jp. physicist
Ko·bil·ka \kō-ˈbil-kə\ Brian K(ent) 1955–	Am. biol.
Koch \ˈkȯk, ˈkȯk, *or with* ō *or* ä *for* ȯ\ Robert 1843–1910 Ger. bacteriol.
Ko·cher \ˈkō-kər, -ˌkər\ Emil Theodor 1841–1917 Swiss surgeon
Ko·dály \ˈkō-ˌdī\ Zol·tán \ˈzōl-ˌtän\ 1882–1967 Hung. composer
Koest·ler \ˈkes(t)-lər\ Arthur 1905–1983 Brit. (Hung.-born) writer
Kohl \ˈkōl\ Helmut 1930–	chancellor of West Germany (1982–90) chancellor of Germany (1990–98)
Koh·ler \ˈkō-lər\ Foy David 1908–1990 Am. diplomat
Kohn \ˈkōn\ Walter 1923–	Am. (Austrian-born) physicist
Koi·so \ˈkȯi-(ˌ)sō, ˈkō-ē-(ˌ)sō\ Kuniaki 1880–1950 Jp. gen.
Koi·zu·mi \kȯi-ˈzü-mē\ Junichiro 1942–	prime min. of Japan (2001–06)
Kokh·ba \ˈkȯk-bä\ Bar *d* A.D. 135 orig. *Sim·e·on bar Ko·zi·ba* \ˈsi-mē-ən-bär-ˈkō-zē-ˌbä\ Jewish leader in Palestine
Ko·kosch·ka \kə-ˈkȯsh-kə\ Oskar 1886–1980 Brit. (Austrian-born) painter
Kol·chak \kȯl-ˈchäk\ Aleksandr Vasilyevich 1873–1920 Russ. admiral & counterrevolutionary
Kol·lon·tay \ˌkä-lən-ˈtī\ Aleksandra Mikhaylovna 1872–1952 Russ. diplomat
Koll·witz \ˈkȯl-ˌwits, ˈkȯl-ˌvits\ Käthe 1867–1945 née *Schmidt* Ger. artist
Kol·mo·go·rov \kəl-mə-ˈgȯ-rəf\ Andrey Nikolayevich 1903–1987 Soviet math.
Kol·tsov \kōlt-ˈsȯf, -ˈsȯv\ Aleksey Vasilyevich 1808–1842 Russ. poet
Ko·mo·row·ski \kȯ-mȯ-ˈrȯf-skē\ Bronislaw (Maria) 1952–	pres. of Poland (2010–	)
Ko·mu·ra \kō-ˈmùr-ä, ˈkō-mə-ˌrä\ Marquis Jutarō 1855–1911 Jp. diplomat
Kon·dí·lis \kȯn-ˈdē-ləs, -lēs\ Geórgios 1879–1936 Greek gen. & polit.
Ko·nev \ˈkȯn-ˌyef, -ˌyev, -yəf\ Ivan Stepanovich 1897–1973 Soviet gen.
Ko·noe \kə-ˈnȯ-(ˌ)ā\ Prince Fumimaro 1891–1945 Jp. statesman
Koo \ˈkü\ Vi Kyuin Wel·ling·ton \ˈwe-liŋ-tən\ 1888–1985 orig. *Ku Wei-chün* Chin. statesman & diplomat
Kool·haas \ˈkōl-ˌhäs\ Rem(ment Lucas) 1944–	Du. architect
Korn·berg \ˈkȯrn-bərg\ Roger David 1947–	Am. chem.
Korn·gold \ˈkȯrn-ˌgōld, -ˌgōlt\ Erich Wolfgang 1897–1957 Am. (Austrian-born) composer, conductor, & pianist
Kor·ni·lov \kȯr-ˈnē-ləf\ Lavr Georgiyevich 1870–1918 Russ. gen. & counterrevolutionary
Ko·ro·len·ko \ˌkȯr-ə-ˈlen-(ˌ)kō, ˌkär-\ Vladimir Galaktionovich 1853–1921 Russ. nov.
Kor·zyb·ski \kȯr-ˈzhip-skē, kȯr-ˈzib-\ Alfred Habdank Skarbek 1879–1950 Am. (Pol.-born) scientist & writer
Koś·ciusz·ko \kȯsh-ˈchùsh-(ˌ)kō, ˌkä-sē-ˈəs-ˌkō\ Tadeusz Andrzej Bonawentura 1746–1817 Pol. patriot & soldier in Am. Revolution
Ko·shi·ba \ˈkō-shē-bä\ Masatoshi 1926–	Jp. astrophysicist
Kos·sel \ˈkȯ-səl\ Albrecht 1853–1927 Ger. biochem.
Kos·suth \ˈkä-ˌsüth, kä-ˈ; ˈkȯ-ˌshüt\ La·jos \ˈlȯi-ˌōsh\ 1802–1894 Hung. patriot & statesman
Kos·tu·ni·ca \ˌkȯs-tü-ˈnēt-sä\ Vojislav 1944–	pres. of Yugoslavia (2000–03), prime min. of Serbia (2004–08)
Ko·sy·gin \kə-ˈsē-gən\ Aleksey Nikolayevich 1904–1980 Soviet polit.; premier of Soviet Union (1964–80)
Kot·ze·bue \ˈkät-sə-ˌbü, ˈkȯt-\ August (Friedrich Ferdinand) von 1761–1819 Ger. dram.
Kous·se·vitz·ky \ˌkü-sə-ˈvit-skē\ Serge \ˈsərj, ˈserzh\ 1874–1951 *Sergey Aleksandrovich Kusevitsky* Am. (Russ.-born) conductor
Krafft-Ebing \ˈkräft-ˈā-biŋ, ˈkraft-\ Richard 1840–1902 Freiherr *von Krafft-Ebing* Ger. neurologist
Kras·ner \ˈkraz-nər\ Lee 1908–1984 orig. *Lenore Krassner* Am. painter
Krebs \ˈkrebz\ Edwin Gerhard 1918–2009 Am. biochem.
Krebs Sir Hans Adolf 1900–1981 Brit. (Ger.-born) biochem.
Kreis·ky \ˈkrī-skē\ Bruno 1911–1990 chancellor of Austria (1970–83)
Kreis·ler \ˈkrīs-lər\ Fritz 1875–1962 Am. (Austrian-born) violinist
Kroe·mer \ˈkrō-mər\ Herbert 1928–	Am. (Ger.-born) electrical engineer
Kro·pot·kin \krə-ˈpät-kən\ Pyotr Alekseyevich 1842–1921 Russ. geographer & revolutionary
Kro·to \ˈkrō-(ˌ)tō\ Sir Harold Walter 1939–	orig. surname *Krotoschiner* Brit. chem.
Kru·ger \ˈkrü-gər\ Barbara 1945–	Am. artist
Kru·ger \ˈkrü-gər *Afrik* ˈkrʉ-ər\ Paul 1825–1904 *Stephanus Johannes Paulus* So. African statesman
Krug·man \ˈkrüg-mən\ Paul (Robin) 1953–	Am. econ.
Krupp \ˈkrüp, ˈkrəp\ family of Ger. munition makers: including Friedrich 1787–1826; his son Alfred 1812–1887; Alfred's son Friedrich Alfred 1854–1902; Friedrich Alfred's daughter Bertha 1886–1957; & Bertha's son Alfried 1907–1967
Krup·ska·ya \ˈkrüp-skə-yə\ Nadezhda Konstantinovna 1869–1939 *wife of Lenin* Russ. revolutionary
Krutch \ˈkrüch\ Joseph Wood 1893–1970 Am. author & critic
Ku·bi·tschek de Oli·vei·ra \ˈkü-bə-ˌchek-dā-ō-lē-ˈvā-rə\ Juscelino 1902–1976 pres. of Brazil (1956–61)
Ku·blai Khan \ˈkü-ˌblə-ˈkän, -ˌblī-\ 1215–1294 founder of Mongol dynasty in China
Ku·brick \ˈkü-brik, ˈkyü-\ Stanley 1928–1999 Am. film director, writer, & producer
Kuhn \ˈkün\ Richard 1900–1967 Austrian chem.
Kuhn Thomas Samuel 1922–1996 Am. philos. & scientist
Kun \ˈkün\ Bé·la \ˈbä-lə\ 1885–1937 Hung. Communist leader
Kun·de·ra \ˈkün-de-rä\ Milan 1929–	Czech-French writer
Kung \ˈgüŋ\ Prince 1833–1898 Manchu statesman
K'ung \ˈkùŋ\ H. H. 1881–1967 orig. *K'ung Hsiang-hsi* Chin. statesman
Ku·nitz \ˈkyü-nəts\ Stanley (Jasspon) 1905–2006 Am. poet & educ.
Ku·ro·pat·kin \ˌkùr-ə-ˈpat-kən, -ˈpät-\ Aleksey Nikolayevich 1848–1921 Russ. gen.
Ku·ro·sa·wa \ˌkùr-ə-ˈsaú-ə\ Akira 1910–1998 Jp. filmmaker
Kusch \ˈkùsh\ Polykarp 1911–1993 Am. (Ger.-born) physicist
Ku·tu·zov \kə-ˈtü-ˌzȯf, -ˌzȯv\ Mikhail Illarionovich 1745–1813 Prince of *Smolensk* Russ. field marshal

Kwas·niew·ski \kväsh-ˈnyef-skē\ Aleksander 1954–	pres. of Poland (1995–2005)
Kyd *or* **Kid** \ˈkid\ Thomas 1558–1594 Eng. dram.
Kyd·land \ˈshʉed-ˌländ—*sic*\ Finn E(rling) 1943–	Norwegian econ.
La Bru·yère \ˌlä-brü-ˈyer, -brē-ˈer\ Jean de 1645–1696 Fr. moralist
La·can \lä-ˈkäⁿ\ Jacques-Marie-Émile 1901–1981 Fr. psychoanalyst — **La·ca·ni·an** \lə-ˈkä-nē-ən\ *adj*
La·chaise \lə-ˈshäz\ Gaston 1882–1935 Am. (Fr.-born) sculptor
La Farge \lə-ˈfärzh, -ˈfärj\ John 1835–1910 Am. artist
La Farge Oliver Hazard Perry 1901–1963 Am. writer & anthropol.
La·fa·yette \ˌlä-fē-ˈet, ˌla-\ Marquis de 1757–1834 *Marie-Joseph-Paul-Yves-Roch-Gilbert du Motier* Fr. gen. & statesman
Laf·fite *or* **La·fitte** \lə-ˈfēt, la-\ Jean *ca* 1780–*ca* 1826 Fr. pirate in America
La Fol·lette \lə-ˈfä-lət\ Robert Marion 1855–1925 Am. polit.
La·Fon·taine \ˌlä-ˌfōⁿ-ˈten, lə-fän-ˈtän\ Sir Louis Hippolyte 1807–1864 Canad. polit.
La Fon·taine \ˌlä-ˌfōⁿ-ˈten\ Jean 1621–1695 Fr. poet
La·ger·kvist \ˈlä-gər-ˌkvist, -ˌkwist\ Pär Fabian 1891–1974 Swed. dram., poet, & nov.
La·ger·löf \ˈlä-gər-ˌlə(r)v\ Selma Ottiliana Lovisa 1858–1940 Swed. nov.
La·gos (Escobar) \ˈlä-gōs\ Ricardo (Froilán) 1938–	pres. of Chile (2000–06)
La·grange \lə-ˈgränj, -ˈgränzh\ Joseph-Louis 1736–1813 Comte *de Lagrange* Fr. math.
La Guar·dia \lə-ˈgwär-dē-ə\ Fi·o·rel·lo \ˌfē-ə-ˈre-(ˌ)lō\ Henry 1882–1947 Am. polit.
LaHood \lə-ˈhùd\ Raymond H. 1945–	U.S. secy. of transportation (2009–13)
Laing \ˈlaŋ\ R(onald) D(avid) 1927–1989 Brit. psychiatrist — **Laing·ian** \-ē-ən\ *adj*
La·marck \lə-ˈmärk\ Jean-Baptiste de Monet de 1744–1829 Chevalier *de Lamarck* Fr. naturalist
La·mar·tine \ˌlä-ˌmär-ˈtēn, ˌlä-mər\ Alphonse (-Marie-Louis de Prat) de 1790–1869 Fr. poet
Lamas Carlos Saavedra — see Carlos SAAVEDRA LAMAS
Lamb \ˈlam\ Charles 1775–1834 pseud. *Elia* \ˈe-lē-ə, *commonly* ˈē-\ Eng. essayist & critic
Lamb William 1779–1848 2d Viscount *Melbourne* Eng. statesman
Lamb Willis Eugene 1913–2008 Am. physicist
Lam·bert \ˈlam-bərt\ John 1619–1683 Eng. gen.
L'Amour \lä-ˈmòr, -ˈmùr\ Louis Dearborn 1908–1988 Am. writer
Land \ˈland\ Edwin Herbert 1909–1991 Am. inventor & industrialist
Lan·dau \län-ˈdaù\ Lev Davidovich 1908–1968 Russ. physicist
Lan·dis \ˈlan-dəs\ Ken·e·saw \ˈke-nə-ˌsò\ Mountain 1866–1944 Am. jurist & baseball commissioner
Lan·don \ˈlan-dən\ Alf(red Mossman) 1887–1987 Am. polit.
Lan·dor \ˈlan-ˌdȯr\ Walter Savage 1775–1864 Eng. author
Lan·dow·ska \lan-ˈdȯf-skə, -ˈdȯv-\ Wanda Louise 1879–1959 Pol. harpsichordist
Land·seer \ˈland-ˌsir\ Sir Edwin Henry 1802–1873 Eng. painter
Land·stei·ner \ˈland(-)ˌstī-nər, ˈländ-ˌshtī-\ Karl 1868–1943 Am. (Austrian-born) pathologist
Lane \ˈlän\ Edward William 1801–1876 Eng. orientalist
Lan·franc \ˈlan-ˌfraŋk\ 1005?–1089 Ital.-born prelate in England
Lang \ˈlaŋ\ Andrew 1844–1912 Scot. scholar & author
Lang Cosmo Gordon 1864–1945 Brit. prelate
Lang Fritz 1890–1976 *Friedrich Christian Anton Lang* Am. (Austrian-born) film director
Lange \ˈläŋ-ə\ Christian Louis 1869–1938 Norw. pacifist & hist.
Lange \ˈlaŋ\ Dorothea 1895–1965 Am. photographer
Lang·er \ˈlaŋ-ər\ Susanne Knauth 1895–1985 Am. philos. & educ.
Lang·land \ˈlaŋ-lənd\ William *ca* 1330–*ca* 1400 Eng. poet
Lang·ley \ˈlaŋ-lē\ Samuel Pierpont 1834–1906 Am. astron. & airplane pioneer
Lang·muir \ˈlaŋ-ˌmyùr\ Irving 1881–1957 Am. chem.
Lang·ton \ˈlaŋ(k)-tən\ Stephen *d* 1228 Eng. prelate
Lang·try \ˈlaŋ(k)-trē\ Lillie 1853–1929 née (*Emilie Charlotte*) *Le Breton; the Jersey Lily* Brit. actress
La·nier \lə-ˈnir\ Sidney 1842–1881 Am. poet
Lan·kes·ter \ˈlaŋ-kəs-tər; ˈlan-ˌkes-, ˈlaŋ-\ Sir Edwin Ray 1847–1929 Eng. zool.
Lannes \ˈlän, ˈlan\ Jean 1769–1809 Duc *de Montebello* Fr. soldier
Lan·sing \ˈlan(t)-siŋ\ Robert 1864–1928 Am. lawyer & statesman
Lao–tzu \ˈlaùd-ˈzə\ *orig.* Li Erh \ˈlē-ˈer\ 6th cent. B.C. Chin. philos.
La Pé·rouse \ˌlä-pā-ˈrüz, -pə-\ Comte de 1741–1788 *Jean-François de Galoup* Fr. navigator & explorer
La·pi·dus \ˈla-pə-dəs\ Morris 1902–2001 Am. (Russian-born) architect
La·place \lə-ˈpläs\ Pierre-Simon 1749–1827 Marquis *de Laplace* Fr. astron. & math.
Lard·ner \ˈlärd-nər\ Ring 1885–1933 in full *Ringgold Wilmer Lardner* Am. writer
La·re·do Brú \lə-ˈrä-dō-ˈbrü\ Federico 1875–1946 Cuban soldier; pres. of Cuba (1936–40)
Lar·kin \ˈlär-kən\ Philip (Arthur) 1922–1985 Brit. poet
La Roche·fou·cauld \lä-ˌrȯsh-fü-ˈkō, ˌrȯsh-\ François 1613–1680 Duc *de La Rochefoucauld* Fr. writer & moralist
La·rousse \lä-ˈrüs\ Pierre (-Athanase) 1817–1875 Fr. grammarian & lexicographer
Lar·tet \lär-ˈtā\ Édouard (Armand Isidore Hippolyte) 1801–1871 Fr. archaeol.
La Salle \lə-ˈsal\ Sieur de 1643–1687 *René-Robert Cavelier* Fr. explorer in America
Las Ca·sas \läs-ˈkä-səs\ Bartolomé de 1474–1566 Span. Dominican missionary & hist.
Las·ki \ˈlas-kē\ Harold Joseph 1893–1950 Eng. polit. scientist
Las·salle \lə-ˈsal, -ˈsäl\ Ferdinand 1825–1864 Ger. socialist
Lat·i·mer \ˈla-tə-mər\ Hugh *ca* 1485–1555 Eng. religious reformer
La Tour \lä-ˈtür\ Georges de 1593–1652 Fr. painter
La·trobe \lə-ˈtrōb\ Benjamin Henry 1764–1820 Am. (Eng.-born) architect & engineer
Lat·ti·more \ˈla-tə-ˌmȯr\ Owen 1900–1989 Am. orientalist
Lattimore Richmond 1906–1984 *bro. of prec.* Am. poet & translator

Lau·bach \'laù-ˌbäk\ Frank Charles 1884–1970 Am. educator & missionary

Laud \'lòd\ William 1573–1645 Eng. prelate; archbishop of Canterbury (1633–45) — **Laud·ian** \'lò-dē-ən\ adj

Lau·der \'lò-dər\ Sir Harry Maclennan 1870–1950 Scot. singer

Laue \'laù-\ Max von 1879–1960 Ger. physicist

Laugh·lin \'lòf-lən\ Robert B(etts) 1950–   Am. physicist

Laugh·ton \'lò-t°n\ Charles 1899–1962 Am. (Eng.-born) actor

Lau·rel \'lòr-əl, 'lär-\ Stan 1890–1965 born Arthur Stanley Jefferson Brit. comic actor in U.S.

Lau·rence \'lòr-ən(t)s, 'lär-\ (Jean) Margaret 1926–1987 née Wemyss Canad. author

Lau·ren·cin \lò-rän-'san\ Marie 1885–1956 Fr. painter

Lau·ri·er \'lòr-ē-ˌā, 'lär-\ Sir Wilfrid 1841–1919 Canad. statesman

Lau·ter·bur \'lò-tər-bər\ Paul C(hristian) 1929–2007 Am. biomed. scientist

La·val \lə-'val, -'väl\ Pierre 1883–1945 Fr. polit.

La Val·lière \lä-val-'yer\ Duchesse de 1644–1710 Françoise-Louise de La Baume Le Blanc mistress of Louis XIV of France

La·ver \'lā-vər\ Rod(ney George) 1938–   Austral. tennis player

La·ve·ran \ˌlä-və-'rä\ (Charles-Louis-) Alphonse 1845–1922 Fr. physiol. & bacteriol.

La Vé·ren·drye \lä-ˌver-ən-'drē, -'ver-ən-ˌdrī\ Sieur de 1685–1749 Pierre Gaultier de Varennes Canad. explorer in America

La·very \'lā-və-rē, 'la-; 'lāv-rē, 'lav-\ Sir John 1856–1941 Brit. painter

La·voi·sier \ləv-'wä-zē-ˌā\ Antoine-Laurent 1743–1794 Fr. chem.

Law \'lò\ (Andrew) Bon·ar \'bä-nər\ 1858–1923 Brit. (Canad.-born) statesman

Law Edward 1750–1818 1st Baron El·len·bor·ough \'e-lən-ˌbər-ə, -ˌbə-rə, -brə\ Eng. jurist

Law John 1671–1729 Scot. financier & speculator

Law William 1686–1761 Eng. writer

Lawes \'lòz\ Henry 1596–1662 Eng. composer

Lawes Lewis Edward 1883–1947 Am. penologist

Law·rence \'lòr-ən(t)s, 'lär-\ David 1888–1973 Am. journalist

Lawrence D(avid) H(erbert) 1885–1930 Eng. nov.

Lawrence Ernest Orlando 1901–1958 Am. physicist

Lawrence Gertrude 1898–1952 orig. Gertrud Alexandra Dagmar Lawrence Klasen Eng. actress

Lawrence James 1781–1813 Am. naval officer

Lawrence Sir Thomas 1769–1830 Eng. painter

Lawrence T(homas) E(dward) 1888–1935 Lawrence of Arabia later surname Shaw Brit. archaeol., soldier, & writer

Lax·ness \'läks-ˌnes\ Halldór Kiljan 1902–1998 Icelandic writer

Lay·a·mon \'lī-ə-mən, 'lä-\ fl 1200 Eng. poet

Lay·ard \'lā-ˌärd, -ərd\ Sir Austen Henry 1817–1894 Eng. archaeol. & diplomat

Lea·cock \'lē-ˌkäk\ Stephen Butler 1869–1944 Canad. humorist

Lea·hy \'lā-(ˌ)hē\ William Daniel 1875–1959 Am. admiral

Lea·key \'lē-kē\ Louis Seymour Bazett 1903–1972 & his wife Mary Douglas 1913–1996 née Nicol Brit. paleontologists

Lean \'lēn\ Sir David 1908–1991 Brit. film director

Lear \'lir\ Edward 1812–1888 Eng. painter & nonsense poet

Lea·vis \'lē-vəs\ F(rank) R(aymond) 1895–1978 Eng. critic — **Lea·vis·ian** \lē-'vi-zh(ē-)ən\ adj — **Lea·vis·ite** \'lē-və-ˌsīt\ adj

Le·brun \lə-'brœⁿ(n), -'brœⁿ\ Albert 1871–1950 Fr. statesman; pres. of France (1932–40)

Lebrun Mme. Vigée— see VIGÉE-LEBRUN

Le Brun or **Le·brun** \lə-'brœⁿ(n), -'brœⁿ\ Charles 1619–1690 Fr. painter

le Car·ré \lə-kä-'rā\ John 1931–   pseud. of David Corn·well \'kòrn-ˌwel\ Eng. nov.

Lecky \'le-kē\ William Edward Hartpole 1838–1903 Irish hist.

Le Clé·zio \lə-klāz-'yō\ J(ean-) M(arie) G(ustave) 1940–   Fr. author

Le·conte de Lisle \lə-ˌkōⁿ(n)t-də-'lēl\ Charles-Marie 1818–1894 orig. Leconte Fr. poet

Le Corbusier — see CORBUSIER

Led·bet·ter \'led-ˌbe-tər\ Huddie 1888–1949 Lead·bel·ly \'led-ˌbe-lē\ Am. blues singer

Le·der·berg \'lā-dər-ˌbərg\ Joshua 1925–2008 Am. geneticist

Led·er·man \'lā-dər-mən\ Leon Max 1922–   Am. physicist

Le Duc Tho \'lä-'dək-'tō\ 1911–1990 Vietnamese diplomat

Lee \'lē\ Ann 1736–1784 Am. (Eng.-born) Shaker

Lee Charles 1731–1782 Am. (Eng.-born) gen.

Lee David Morris 1931–   Am. physicist

Lee Fitzhugh 1835–1905 nephew of R.E. Am. gen.

Lee Francis Lightfoot 1734–1797 Am. statesman in Revolution

Lee (Nelle) Harper 1926–   Am. nov.

Lee Henry 1756–1818 Light-Horse Harry; father of R.E. Am. gen.

Lee Myung-bak 1941–   pres. of So. Korea (2008–13)

Lee Richard Henry 1732–1794 bro. of F.L. Am. statesman in Revolution

Lee Robert E(dward) 1807–1870 Am. Confed. gen.

Lee Sir Sidney 1859–1926 Eng. editor & scholar

Lee Yuan Tseh 1936–   Am. (Taiwanese-born) chem.

Leeu·wen·hoek \'lā-vən-ˌhùk\ Antoni van 1632–1723 Du. naturalist

Le·feb·vre \lə-'fevr°\ François-Joseph 1755–1820 Duc de Dantzig Fr. gen.; marshal of France

Lef·ko·witz \'lef-kə-ˌwits\ Robert J(oseph) 1943–   Am. biol.

Le Gal·lienne \lə-'gal-yən\ Eva 1899–1991 Am. (Eng.-born) actress

Le Gallienne Richard 1866–1947 Eng. writer

Le·gen·dre \lə-'zhäⁿdr°\ Adrien-Marie 1752–1833 Fr. math.

Lé·ger \lā-'zhā\ Alexis Saint-Léger 1887–1975 pseud. St. John Perse \sa°-ˌjòn-'pers\ Fr. diplomat & poet

Léger Fernand 1881–1955 Fr. painter

Leg·gett \'le-gət\ Sir Anthony (James) 1938–   Brit.-Am. physicist

Le·guía y Sal·ce·do \lā-'gē-ə-ē-säl-'sā-(ˌ)dō, -(ˌ)thō\ Augusto Bernardino 1863–1932 Peruvian banker; pres. of Peru (1908–12; 1919–30)

Le·hár \'lā-ˌhär\ Franz 1870–1948 Hung. composer

Leh·man \'lē-mən\ Herbert Henry 1878–1963 Am. banker & polit.

Leh·mann \'lā-ˌmän\ Lotte 1888–1976 Ger. soprano

Lehn \'lān\ Jean-Marie 1939–   Fr. chem.

Leib·niz \'līp-nəts\ Gottfried Wilhelm 1646–1716 Ger. philos. & math. — **Leib·niz·ian** \līb-'nit-sē-ən, līp-\ adj

Lei·bo·vitz \'lē-bō-ˌvits\ Annie 1949–   Am. photographer

Leicester 1st Earl of — see Robert DUDLEY; — see also de MONTFORT

Leif Er·iks·son \ˌlāv-'er-ik-sən, ˌlēf-\ or **Er·ics·son** \same\ fl 1000 son of Erik the Red Norw. explorer

Leigh·ton \'lā-t°n\ Frederick 1830–1896 Baron Leighton of Stretton Eng. painter

Leins·dorf \'līnz-ˌdòrf, 'līn(t)s-\ Erich 1912–1993 Am. (Austrian-born) conductor

Le·jeune \lə-'jün\ John Archer 1867–1942 Am. marine-corps gen.

Le·land \'lē-lənd\ John 1506?–1552 Eng. antiquarian

Le·ly \'lē-lē\ Sir Peter 1618–1680 orig. Pieter Van der Faes Brit. (Westphalian-born) painter

Le·maî·tre \lə-'metr°\ (Abbé) Georges Henri 1894–1966 Belg. astrophysicist

Le Moyne Pierre — see IBERVILLE

Len·clos \lä°-'klō\ Anne de 1620–1705 Ninon de Lenclos Fr. courtesan

L'En·fant \lä°-ˌfä°t, lä°-'fä°\ Pierre-Charles 1754–1825 Am. (Fr.-born) architect & engineer

Le·nin \'le-nən\ 1870–1924 orig. Vladimir Ilyich Ul·ya·nov \ül-'yä-nəf, -ˌnòf, -ˌnòv\ Russ. Communist leader

Len·non \'le-nən\ John (Winston) 1940–1980 Brit. singer & songwriter

Le Nô·tre \lə-'nō-tr°\ André 1613–1700 Fr. landscape architect

Leo \'lē-(ˌ)ō\ name of 13 popes: esp. I Saint d 461 (pope 440–61); III Saint d 816 (pope 795–816); XIII 1810–1903 (pope 878–1903)

Le·o·nar·do da Vin·ci \lē-ə-'när-(ˌ)dō-də-'vin-chē, ˌlā-, -'vēn-\ 1452–1519 It. painter, sculptor, architect, & engineer — **Le·o·nar·desque** \ˌlē-ə-när-'desk, ˌlā-\ adj

Le·on·ca·val·lo \ˌlā-ˌòn-kə-'vä-(ˌ)lō\ Ruggiero 1858–1919 Ital. composer & librettist

Le·on·i·das \lē-'ä-nə-dəs\ d 480 B.C. Greek hero; king of Sparta (490?–480)

Le·o·par·di \ˌlā-ə-'pär-dē\ Giacomo 1798–1837 Ital. poet

Le·o·pold I \'lē-ə-ˌpōld\ 1640–1705 king of Hungary (1655–1705) & Holy Rom. emp. (1658–1705)

Leopold I 1790–1865 king of Belgium (1831–65)

Leopold II 1747–1792 Holy Rom. emp. (1790–92)

Leopold II 1835–1909 king of Belgium (1865–1909)

Leopold III 1901–1983 king of Belgium (1934–51)

Lep·i·dus \'le-pə-dəs\ Marcus Aemilius d 13(or 12) B.C. Rom. triumvir

Ler·mon·tov \'ler-mən-ˌtóf, -ˌtòv\ Mikhail Yuryevich 1814–1841 Russ. poet & nov.

Ler·ner \'lər-nər\ Alan Jay 1918–1986 Am. dram. & librettist

Le·sage \lə-'säzh\ Alain-René 1668–1747 Fr. nov. & dram.

Le·sche·tiz·ky \ˌle-shə-'tit-skē\ Theodor 1830–1915 Pol. pianist

Les·seps \lā-'seps, 'le-səps\ Ferdinand-Marie de 1805–1894 Vicomte de Lesseps Fr. diplomat & promoter of Suez Canal

Les·sing \'le-sin\ Doris (May) 1919–   née Tayler Brit. writer

Lessing Gotthold Ephraim 1729–1781 Ger. critic & dram.

L'Es·trange \lə-'stränj\ Sir Roger 1616–1704 Eng. journalist

Let·ta \'le-tä\ Enrico 1966–   prime min. of Italy (2013–   )

Leu·tze \'lòit-sə\ Emanuel 1816–1868 Am. (Ger.-born) painter

Le·vi-Mon·tal·ci·ni \'lä-vē-ˌmòn-täl-'chē-nē\ Rita 1909–2012 Ital.-Am. neurologist

Le·vine \lə-'vīn\ James (Lawrence) 1943–   Am. conductor

Lé·vi-Strauss \'lā-vē-'straùs, 'le-vē-\ Claude 1908–2009 Fr. (Belg.-born) social anthropol. — **Lé·vi-Strauss·si·an** \-'straù-sē-ən\ adj

Lev·itt \'le-vət\ Michael 1947–   Eng.-Israeli-Am. (So. African-born) biophysicist

Lew \'lü\ Jacob (Joseph) 1955–   U.S. secy. of treasury (2013–   )

Lew·es \'lü-əs\ George Henry 1817–1878 Eng. philos. & critic

Lewis Cecil Day — see DAY-LEWIS

Lewis Edward B. 1918–2004 Am. biol.

Lewis C(live) S(taples) 1898–1963 Eng. nov. & essayist

Lewis John Llewellyn 1880–1969 Am. labor leader

Lewis Matthew Gregory 1775–1818 Monk Lewis Eng. author

Lewis Meriwether 1774–1809 Am. explorer

Lewis (Percy) Wyndham 1882–1957 Brit. painter & author

Lewis (Harry) Sinclair 1885–1951 Am. nov.

Lib·by \'li-bē\ Willard Frank 1908–1980 Am. chem.

Lich·ten·stein \'lik-tən-ˌstīn, -ˌshtīn\ Roy 1923–1997 Am. artist

Li·cin·i·us \lə-'si-nē-əs\ d 325 Valerius Licinianus Licinius Rom. emp. (308–324)

Lid·dell Hart \'li-d°l-'härt\ Sir Basil Henry 1895–1970 Eng. mil. hist.

Lie \'lē\ Jonas 1833–1908 Norw. nov. & dram.

Lie Trygve Halvdan 1896–1968 Norw. lawyer; secy.-gen. of U.N. (1946–52)

Lie·big \'lē-big\ Justus von 1803–1873 Freiherr von Liebig Ger. chem.

Lieb·knecht \'lēp-ˌknekt, -ˌnekt\ Karl 1871–1919 Ger. socialist leader

Li·far \'lē-ˌfär, lē-\ Serge 1905–1986 Fr. (Russ.-born) choreographer & dancer

Li Hung-chang \'lē-'hùn-'jän\ 1823–1901 Chin. statesman

Li Ke·qiang \'lē-'kə-'chyän\ 1955–   prime min. of China (2013–   )

Lil·ien·thal \'lil-yən-ˌtäl, -ˌthòl\ Otto 1848–1896 Ger. aeronautical engineer

Li·li·u·o·ka·la·ni \li-ˌlē-ə-(ˌ)wō-kə-'lä-nē\ 1838–1917 Lydia Paki Liliuokalani; Liliu Kamakaeha queen of the Hawaiian Islands (1891–93)

Li·món \li-'mòn\ José Arcadio 1908–1972 Am. (Mex.-born) dancer & choreographer

Lin \'lin\ Maya Ying 1959–   Am. architect & sculptor

Lin·a·cre \'li-ni-kər\ Thomas ca 1460–1524 Eng. humanist & physician

Lin·coln \'lin-kən\ Abraham 1809–1865 16th pres. of the U.S. (1861–65) — **Lin·coln·esque** \ˌlin-kə-'nesk\ or **Lin·coln·ian** \lin-'kō-nē-ən\ adj

Lincoln Benjamin 1733–1810 Am. gen. in Revolution

Lind \'lind\ Jenny 1820–1887 orig. Johanna Maria Lind; the Swedish Nightingale Swed. soprano

Lind·bergh \'lin(d)-ˌbərg\ Anne Spencer 1906–2001 née Morrow; wife of C.A. Am. author

---

\ə\ abut \°\ kitten, F table \ər\ further \a\ ash \ā\ ace \ä\ mop, mar
\aù\ out \ch\ chin \e\ bet \ē\ easy \g\ go \i\ hit \ī\ ice \j\ job
\ŋ\ sing \ō\ go \ò\ law \òi\ boy \th\ thin \tẖ\ the \ü\ loot \ù\ foot
\y\ yet \zh\ vision, beige \ḵ, ⁿ, œ, ʉ, ʏ\ see Guide to Pronunciation

Lindbergh Charles Augustus 1902–1974 Am. aviator
Lind·ley \'lin(d)-lē\ John 1799–1865 Eng. botanist — **Lind·ley·an** \-ən\ *adj*
Lind·say \'lin-zē\ Howard 1889–1968 Am. dram. & actor
Lindsay (Nicholas) Va·chel \'vā-chəl, 'va-\ 1879–1931 Am. poet
Link·la·ter \'liŋk-,lā-tər, -lə-tər\ Eric 1899–1974 Brit. writer
Linlithgow Marquis of — see HOPE
Lin·nae·us \lə-'nē-əs, -'nā-\ Carolus 1707–1778 Sw. *Carl von Lin·né* \lə-'nā\ Swed. botanist
Lin Yü–t'ang \'lin-'yü-'täŋ\ 1895–1976 Chin. author & philologist
Li·o·tard \,lē-ō-'tär\ Jean-Étienne 1702–1789 Swiss painter
Lip·chitz \'lip-shits\ Jacques 1891–1973 Am. (Latvian-born) sculptor
Li Peng \'lē-'pəŋ, -'peŋ\ 1928–   Chin. prime min. (1987–98)
Li Po \'lē-'bō, -'pō\ 701–762 Chin. poet
Lip·pi \'li-pē\ Fra Filippo *ca* 1406–1469 Florentine painter
Lippi Filippo *or* Filippino *fa* 1457–1504 *son of prec.* Florentine painter
Lipp·mann \lēp-'män, -'man\ Gabriel 1845–1921 Fr. physicist
Lipp·mann \'lip-mən\ Walter 1889–1974 Am. journalist & author
Lip·ton \'lip-tən\ Sir Thomas Johnstone 1850–1931 Eng. merchant & yachtsman
Lisle, de — see LECONTE DE LISLE, ROUGET DE LISLE
Lis·ter \'lis-tər\ Joseph 1827–1912 1st Baron *Lister of Lyme Regis* Eng. surgeon
Liszt \'list\ Franz 1811–1886 Hung. pianist & composer — **Liszt·ian** \'lis-tē-ən\ *adj*
Lit·tle·ton *or* **Lyt·tel·ton** \'li-t³l-tən\ *or* **Lut·tel·ton** \'lə-\ Sir Thomas 1422–1481 Eng. jurist
Lit·tré \li-'trā\ Maximilien-Paul-Émile 1801–1881 Fr. lexicographer
Lit·vi·nov \lit-'vē-,nȯf, -,nȯv, -nəf\ Maksim Maksimovich 1876–1951 Soviet diplomat
Liu Shao·bo \lē-'ü-'shaù-'bō\ 1955–   Chin. human-rights activist
Liu Shao–ch'i \lē-'ü-'shaù-'chē\ 1898–1974 Chin. Communist polit.
Liv·ing·ston \'li-viŋ-stən\ Robert R. 1746–1813 Am. statesman
Liv·ing·stone \'li-viŋ-stən\ David 1813–1873 Scot. missionary & explorer in Africa
Livy \'li-vē\ 59 B.C.–A.D. 17 *Titus Livius* Rom. hist.
Lloyd George \'lȯid-'jȯrj\ David 1863–1945 1st Earl of *Dwy·for* \'dü-ē-,vȯr\ Brit. statesman; prime min. (1916–22)
Llull \'lyül³\ Ramon *ca* 1235–1316 *Raymond Lul·ly* \'lù-lē\ Catalan mystic & poet
Lo·ba·chev·sky \,lō-bə-'chef-skē, ,lä-, -'chev-\ Nikolay Ivanovich 1792–1856 Russ. math.
Lo·ben·gu·la \,lō-bən-'gü-lə, -'gyü-\ *ca* 1836–1894 Zulu king of the Matabele
Locke \'läk\ Gary (Faye) 1950–   U.S. secy. of commerce (2009–11)
Locke John 1632–1704 Eng. philos. — **Lock·ean** *also* **Locke·ian** \'lä-kē-ən\ *adj*
Lock·hart \'lä-kərt, -,kärt; 'läk-,härt\ John Gibson 1794–1854 Scot. nov. & biographer
Lock·yer \'lä-kyər\ Sir Joseph Norman 1836–1920 Eng. astron.
Lodge \'läj\ Henry Cabot 1850–1924 Am. statesman & author
Lodge Henry Cabot 1902–1985 *grandson of prec.* Am. polit. & diplomat
Lodge Sir Oliver Joseph 1851–1940 Eng. physicist
Lodge Thomas 1558–1625 Eng. poet & dram.
Loeb \'lōb\ Jacques 1859–1924 Am. (Ger.-born) physiol.
Loewe \'lō\ Frederick 1901–1988 Am. (Austrian-born) composer
Loewi \'lō-ē\ Otto 1873–1961 Am. (Ger.-born) pharmacologist
Löff·ler \'le-flər\ Friedrich August Johannes 1852–1915 Ger. bacteriol.
Lo·max \'lō-,maks\ John Avery 1867–1948 & his son Alan 1915–2002 Am. folklorists
Lombard Peter — see PETER LOMBARD
Lom·bro·so \lȯm-'brō-(,)sō\ Ce·sa·re \'chā-zä-,rā\ 1836–1909 Ital. physician & psychiatrist
Lon·don \'lən-dən\ John Griffith 1876–1916 *Jack London* Am. writer
Long \'lȯŋ\ Crawford Williamson 1815–1878 Am. surgeon
Long Hu·ey \'hyü-ē\ Pierce 1893–1935 Am. polit.
Long Stephen Harriman 1784–1864 Am. army officer & explorer
Long·fel·low \'lȯŋ-,fe-(,)lō\ Henry Wads·worth \'wädz-(,)wərth\ 1807–1882 Am. poet
Lon·gi·nus \län-'jī-nəs\ 1st cent. A.D. Greek critic
Long·street \'lȯŋ-,strēt\ James 1821–1904 Am. Confed. gen.
Lönn·rot \'lœn-,rüt\ Elias 1802–1884 Finn. folklorist
Lons·dale \'länz-,dāl\ Frederick 1881–1954 Brit. dram.
Ló·pez \'lō-,pez\ Carlos Antonio 1790–1862 pres. of Paraguay (1844–62)
López Francisco Solano 1827–1870 *son of prec.* pres. of Paraguay (1862–70)
López Ma·te·os \-mə-'tā-əs, -(,)ōs\ Adolfo 1910–1969 pres. of Mexico (1958–64)
López Por·til·lo \-pȯr-'tē-yō\ José 1920–2004 pres. of Mexico (1976–82)
Lorca Federico García — see Federico GARCÍA LORCA
Lo·rentz \'lȯr-,en(t)s\ Hendrik Antoon 1853–1928 Du. physicist
Lo·renz \'lȯr-,en(t)s\ Konrad 1903–1989 Ger. (Austrian-born) ethologist
Lorrain Claude — see CLAUDE LORRAIN
Lo·thair I \lō-'ter, -'ther, lȯ-\ 795–855 Holy Rom. emp. (840–855)
Lothair II (*or* III) 1075–1137 king of Germany & Holy Rom. emp. (1125–37)
Lo·ti \lō-'tē, lȯ-\ Pierre 1850–1923 pseud. of *Louis-Marie-Julien Viaud* Fr. naval officer & nov.
Lott \'lät\ Trent 1941–   *Chester Trent Lott, Jr.* Am. polit.
Lou·bet \lü-'bā\ Émile-François 1838–1929 Fr. statesman; pres. of France (1899–1906)
Lou·is \'lü-ē, lü-ē\ name of 18 kings of France: esp. **I** 778–840 (reigned 814–840); **V** (*le Fainéant*) 967–987 (reigned—last Carolingian—986–987); **IX** (*Saint*) 1214–1270 (reigned 1226–70); **XI** 1423–1483 (reigned 1461–83); **XII** 1462–1515 (reigned 1498–1515); **XIII** 1601–1643 (reigned 1610–43); **XIV** 1638–1715 (reigned 1643–1715); **XV** 1710–1774 (reigned 1715–74); **XVI** 1754–1793 (reigned 1774–92; guillotined); **XVII** 1785–1795 (nominally reigned 1793–95); **XVIII** 1755–1824 (reigned 1814–15; 1815–24)
Louis \'lü-əs\ Joe 1914–1981 orig. *Joseph Louis Barrow* Am. boxer

Louis IV 1283?–1347 Duke of *Bavaria* king of Germany & Holy Rom. emp. (1314–47)
Louis–Napoléon — see NAPOLÉON III
Louis Phi·lippe \-fi-'lēp\ 1773–1850 *the Citizen King* king of the French (1830–48)
Louverture — see TOUSSAINT-LOUVERTURE
Louÿs \lü-'ēs\ Pierre 1870–1925 Fr. writer
Love·lace \'ləv-,lās\ Richard 1618–1657 Eng. poet
Lov·ell \'lə-vəl\ Sir (Alfred Charles) Bernard 1913–2012 Brit. astron.
Lov·er \'lə-vər\ Samuel 1797–1868 Irish nov.
Low \'lō\ Sir David Alexander Cecil 1891–1963 Brit. cartoonist
Low·ell \'lō-əl\ Amy 1874–1925 Am. poet & critic
Lowell James Russell 1819–1891 Am. poet, essayist, & dram.
Lowell Percival 1855–1916 *bro. of Amy* Am. astron.
Lowell Robert Traill Spence 1917–1977 Am. poet
Lowes \'lōz\ John Livingston 1867–1945 Am. educ.
Lowndes \'laùn(d)z\ William Thomas 1798–1843 Eng. bibliographer
Low·ry \'laù(-ə)r-ē\ (Clarence) Malcolm 1909–1957 Brit. writer
Loyola Saint Ignatius — see IGNATIUS OF LOYOLA
Lub·bock \'lə-bək\ Sir John 1834–1913 1st Baron *Ave·bury* \'āv-b(ə-)rē, 'ā-\ *son of Sir J.W.* Eng. financier & author
Lubbock Sir John William 1803–1865 Eng. astron. & math.
Luc·an \'lü-kən\ A.D. 39–65 *Marcus Annaeus Lucanus* Rom. poet
Lu·cas \'lü-kəs\ George Walton, Jr. 1944–   Am. filmmaker
Lucas Robert Emerson, Jr. 1937–   Am. econ.
Luce \'lüs\ Clare 1903–1987 *née Boothe* \'büth\ *wife of H.R.* Am. dram., polit., & diplomat
Luce Henry Robinson 1898–1967 Am. editor & publisher
Lu·cre·tius \lü-'krē-sh(ē-)əs\ *ca* 96–*ca* 55 B.C. *Titus Lucretius Carus* Rom. poet & philos. — **Lu·cre·tian** \-shən\ *adj*
Lu·cul·lus \lü-'kə-ləs\ Lucius Licinius *ca* 117–58(or 56) B.C. Rom. gen. & epicure
Lu·den·dorff \'lü-d³n-,dȯrf\ Erich Friedrich Wilhelm 1865–1937 Ger. gen.
Lu Hsün \'lü-'shün\ 1881–1936 pseud. of *Chou Shu-Jen* Chin. writer
Lu·i·gi Ame·deo \lə-'wē-jē-,ä-mə-'dā-(,)ō\ 1873–1933 Duca *D'Abruz·zi* \dä-'brüt-tsē\ & Prince of *Savoy-Aosta* Ital. explorer & naval officer
Lul·ly \lü-'lē\ Jean-Baptiste 1632–1687 Fr. (Ital.-born) composer
Lully Raymond — see Ramon LLULL
Lu·mum·ba \lə-'mùm-bə\ Patrice (Hemery) 1925–1961 Zaire polit.
Lunt \'lənt\ Alfred 1893–1977 *husband of Lynn Fontanne* Am. actor
Lu·ther \'lü-thər\ Martin 1483–1546 Ger. Reformation leader
Lu·thu·li \lù-'tü-lē, -'thü-\ Albert John 1898–1967 So. African reformer
Lux·em·burg \'lək-səm-,bərg, 'lùk-səm-,bùrk\ Rosa 1870–1919 Ger. socialist leader
Lyau·tey \lē-,ō-'tā\ Louis-Hubert-Gonzalve 1854–1934 Fr. soldier & colonial administrator
Ly·cur·gus \lī-'kər-gəs\ 9th cent. B.C. Spartan lawgiver
Lyd·gate \'lid-,gāt, -gət\ John *ca* 1370–*ca* 1450 Eng. poet
Ly·ell \'lī-əl\ Sir Charles 1797–1875 Brit. geologist
Lyly \'li-lē\ John 1554?–1606 Eng. author
Lynd \'lind\ Robert Staugh·ton \'stȯ-t³n\ 1892–1970 & his wife Helen née *Merrell* 1896–1982 Am. sociologists
Ly·on \'lī-ən\ Mary 1797–1849 Am. educ.
Ly·ons \'lī-ənz\ Joseph Aloysius 1879–1939 Austral. statesman; prime min. (1931–39)
Ly·san·der \lī-'san-dər\ *d* 395 B.C. Spartan commander
Ly·sen·ko \lə-'seŋ-(,)kō\ Trofim Denisovich 1898–1976 Soviet biol.
Lys·i·as \'li-sē-əs\ *ca* 445–after 380 B.C. Athenian orator
Ly·sim·a·chus \lī-'si-mə-kəs\ *ca* 355–*ca* 281 B.C. Macedonian gen. under Alexander the Great; king of Thrace (306)
Ly·sip·pus \lī-'si-pəs\ 4th cent. B.C. Greek sculptor
Lyt·ton \'li-t³n\ 1st Baron 1803–1873 *Edward George Earle Bul·wer= Lytton* \'bùl-wər-\; *bro. of Sir Henry Bulwer* Eng. author
Lytton 1st Earl of 1831–1891 (*Edward*) *Robert Bulwer-Lytton*; pseud. *Owen Meredith; son of prec.* Brit. statesman & poet
Ma \'mä\ Yo-Yo 1955–   Am. (Fr.-born of Chinese parents) cellist
Maa·thai \mä-'tī\ Wangari (Muta) 1940–2011 Kenyan environmentalist
Ma·ca·pa·gal–Ar·ro·yo \,mä-kə-pə-'gäl-ə-'rȯi-(,)ō\ Gloria 1947–   pres. of Philippines (2001–10)
Mac·Ar·thur \mə-'kär-thər\ Charles 1895–1956 Am. dram.
MacArthur Douglas 1880–1964 Am. gen.
Ma·cau·lay \mə-'kȯ-lē\ Dame Rose 1881–1958 Eng. nov.
Macaulay Thomas Babington 1800–1859 1st Baron *Macaulay* Eng. hist., author, & statesman
Mac·beth \mək-'beth\ *d* 1057 king of Scotland (1040–57)
Mac·Bride \mək-'brīd\ Seán 1904–1988 Irish statesman
Mac·ca·bees \'ma-kə-,bēz\ Judas *or* Judah *d* 161 B.C. surname *Mac·ca·ba·eus* \,ma-kə-'bē-əs\ Jewish patriot
Mac·Diar·mid \mək-'dər-məd, -mət\ Alan Graham 1927–2007 Am. (N.Z.-born) chem.
MacDiarmid Hugh 1892–1978 pseud. of *Christopher Murray Grieve* \'grēv\ Scot. poet
Mac·don·ald \mək-'dä-n³ld\ George 1824–1905 Scot. nov. & poet
Macdonald Sir John Alexander 1815–1891 Canad. statesman; 1st prime min. of Dominion of Canada (1867–73; 1878–91)
Mac·Don·ald \mək-'dä-n³ld\ (James) Ramsay 1866–1937 Brit. statesman; prime min. (1924; 1929–31; 1931–35)
Mac·don·ough \mək-'dä-nə, -'də-\ Thomas 1783–1825 Am. naval officer
Mac·Dow·ell \mək-'daù(-ə)l\ Edward Alexander 1860–1908 Am. composer
Mach \'mäk, 'mäk\ Ernst 1838–1916 Austrian physicist & philos.
Ma·cha·do y Mo·ra·les \mä-'chä-dō-,ē-mə-'rä-ləs\ Gerardo 1871–1939 pres. of Cuba (1925–33)
Ma·chi·a·vel·li \,ma-kē-ə-'ve-lē\ Niccolò 1469–1527 Ital. polit. philos.
Mac·Kaye \mə-'kī\ Percy 1875–1956 Am. poet & dram.
Mack·en·sen \'mä-kən-zən\ August von 1849–1945 Ger. field marshal
Mac·ken·zie \mə-'ken-zē\ Alexander 1822–1892 Canad. (Scot.-born) statesman; prime min. (1873–78)
Mackenzie Sir Compton 1883–1972 Eng. nov.
Mackenzie William Lyon 1795–1861 Canad. (Scot.-born) insurgent leader

Mac·kin·der \mə-'kin-dər\ Sir Halford John 1861–1947 Eng. geographer

Mac·Kin·non \mə-'ki-nən\ Roderick 1956–   Am. chemist

Maclaren Ian — see John WATSON

Mac·Leish \mə-'klēsh\ Archibald 1892–1982 Am. poet & administrator

Mac·Len·nan \mə-'kle-nən\ (John) Hugh 1907–1990 Canad. nov.

Mac·leod \mə-'klaud\ John James Rickard 1876–1935 Scot. physiol.

Mac–Ma·hon \'mäk-,mä-'ōⁿ; mä-'(-ə)n, -'mäⁿ\ Marie-Edme-Patrice-Maurice 1808–1893 Comte *de Mac-Mahon;* duc *de Magenta* marshal (1859) & pres. (1873–79) of France

Mac·mil·lan \mək-'mi-lən\ (Maurice) Harold 1894–1986 Brit. prime min. (1957–63)

Mac·Neice \mək-'nēs\ Louis 1907–1963 Irish poet

Mac·pher·son \mək-'far-sᵊn\ James 1736–1796 Scot. writer

Mac·rea·dy \mə-'krē-dē\ William Charles 1793–1873 Eng. actor

Ma·da·ria·ga y Ro·jo \,mä-də-rē-'ä-gə-(,)ē-'rō-(,)hō\ Salvador de 1886–1978 Span. writer & diplomat

Ma·de·ro \mə-'der-(,)ō\ Francisco Indalecio 1873–1913 pres. of Mexico (1911–13)

Mad·i·son \'ma-də-sən\ Dolley 1768–1849 *née (Dorothea) Payne; wife of James* Am. socialite

Madison James 1751–1836 4th pres. of the U.S. (1809–17) — **Mad·i·so·nian** \,ma-də-'sō-nē-ən, -nyən\ *adj*

Ma·du·ro (Mo·ros) \mə-'thü-rō(-'mō-rōs)\ Nicolás 1962–   pres. of Venezuela (2013–   )

Mae·ce·nas \mi-'sē-nəs\ Gaius *ca* 70–8 B.C. Rom. statesman & patron of literature

Maes \'mäs\ Nicolaes 1634–1693 *also called* Nicolas Maas Du. painter

Mae·ter·linck \'mä-tər-,liŋk *also* 'me-, 'ma-\ Maurice-Polydore-Marie-Bernard 1862–1949 Belg. poet, dram., & essayist

Ma·gel·lan \mə-'je-lən, *chiefly Brit* -'ge-\ Ferdinand *ca* 1480–1521 Pg. *Fernão de Magalhães* Port. navigator & explorer

Ma·gi·not \,ma-zhə-'nō, ,ma-jə-\ André 1877–1932 Fr. polit.

Ma·gritte \mə-'grēt\ René (-François-Ghislain) 1898–1967 Belg. painter

Mag·say·say \mäg-'sī-,sī, ,-sī-'sī\ Ramon 1907–1957 pres. of Philippines (1953–57)

Mah·fouz \'mäk-füz\ Naguib 1911–2006 Egypt. writer

Mah·ler \'mä-lər\ Gustav 1860–1911 Austrian composer — **Mah·ler·ian** \mä-'lir-ē-ən, -'ler-\ *adj*

Mah·mud II \mä-'müd\ 1785–1839 Ottoman sultan (1808–39)

Mai·ler \'mā-lər\ Norman 1923–2007 Am. author

Mail·lol \mä-'yól, -'yōl\ Aristide 1861–1944 Fr. sculptor

Mai·mon·i·des \mī-'mä-nə-,dēz\ Moses 1135–1204 Heb. *Moses ben Maimon* Jewish philos., jurist, & physician

Maine \'mān\ Sir Henry James Sumner 1822–1888 Eng. jurist

Main·te·non \,maⁿ(t)-tə-'nō⁺, ,maⁿ(t)t-'nō⁺\ Marquise de 1635–1719 *Françoise d'Aubigné; consort of Louis XIV*

Ma·jor \'mā-jər\ Sir John 1943–   Brit. prime min. (1990–97)

Mal·a·mud \'ma-lə-(,)məd\ Bernard 1914–1986 Am. writer

Ma·lan \mə-'län, -'län\ Daniel François 1874–1959 So. African editor; prime min. (1948–54)

Mal·colm X \'mal-kəm-'eks\ 1925–1965 orig. *Malcolm Little* Am. civil rights leader

Male·branche \,mal-'brä⁺sh, ,mäl-; ,ma-lə-, ,mä-\ Nicolas de 1638–1715 Fr. philos.

Ma·len·kov \mə-'len-,kóf, -,kóv, -'leŋ-kəf; ,ma-lən-'kóf, -'kóv\ Georgy Maksimilianovich 1902–1988 Soviet polit.

Mal·herbe \ma-'lerb, mä-\ François de 1555–1628 Fr. poet

Ma·li·ki \'mä-lə-kē\ Nuri (Ka·mal) al- \'nur-ē(-kä-'mäl)-äl\ 1950–   prime min. of Iraq (2006–   )

Ma·li·nov·sky \,ma-lə-'nóf-skē, ,mä-, -'nòv-\ Rodion Yakovlevich 1898–1967 Soviet gen.

Ma·li·now·ski \,ma-lə-'nóf-skē, ,mä-, -'nòv-\ Bronislaw Kasper 1884–1942 Am. (Pol.-born) anthropol.

Mal·lar·mé \,ma-,lär-'mā\ Stéphane 1842–1898 Fr. poet

Malle \'mäl\ Louis 1932–1995 Fr. film director

Mal·o·ry \'ma-lə-rē, 'mal-rē\ Sir Thomas *fl* 1470 Eng. author

Mal·pi·ghi \mal-'pē-gē, -'pi-\ Marcello 1628–1694 Ital. anatomist

Mal·raux \mal-'rō\ André 1901–1976 Fr. writer & art historian

Mal·thus \'mal-thəs\ Thomas Robert 1766–1834 Eng. econ.

Mam·et \'ma-mət\ David Alan 1947–   Am. dram. & director

Man·ci·ni \man-'sē-(,)nē\ Henry 1924–1994 orig. *Enrico Nicola Mancini* Am. composer & conductor

Man·del \'mäⁿ(n)-'del\ Georges 1885–1944 orig. *Louis-Georges Rothschild* Fr. polit.

Man·dela \man-'de-lə\ Nelson Rolihlahla 1918–2013 So. African black political leader; pres. of So. Africa (1994–99)

Man·del·brot \'man-dəl-,brōt\ Benoit B. 1924–2010 Am. (Pol.-born) math. & scientist

Man·de·ville \'man-də-,vil\ Bernard de 1670–1733 Brit. (Du.-born) satirist & philos.

Mandeville Sir John *fl* 1356 pseud. of an unidentified travel writer

Ma·net \ma-'nā, mä-\ Édouard 1832–1883 Fr. painter

Mann \'man\ Horace 1796–1859 Am. educ.

Mann \'män, 'man\ Thomas 1875–1955 Am. (Ger.-born) author

Man·ner·heim \'mä-nər-,häm, 'ma-, -,hīm\ Baron Carl Gustaf Emil von 1867–1951 Finn. gen. & statesman

Man·ning \'ma-niŋ\ Henry Edward 1808–1892 Eng. cardinal

Mans·field \'mans-,fēld, 'manz-\ Katherine 1888–1923 pseud. of *Kathleen Mansfield Beauchamp* \'bē-chəm\ Brit. (N.Z.-born) writer

Mansfield Sir Peter 1933–   Brit. physicist

Man·son \'man(t)-sən\ Sir Patrick 1844–1922 Brit. parasitologist

Man·stein \'män-shtīn\ Fritz Erich von 1887–1973 orig. surname *von Lewinski* Ger. field marshal

Man·ṣūr, al- \al-,man-'sür\ 709(to 714)–775 in full *Abū Ja'far al-Manṣūr* or *al-Manṣūr al-'Abbāsī* Arab caliph (754–775) & founder of Baghdad

Man·te·gna \män-'tän-yə\ Andrea 1431–1506 Ital. painter & engraver

Man·tle \'man-tᵊl\ Mickey (Charles) 1931–1995 Am. baseball player

Man·zo·ni \män(d)-'zō-nē\ Alessandro Francesco Tommaso Antonio 1785–1873 Ital. nov. & poet

Mao Tse-tung \'mau-(')(d)zə-'dùŋ, -(')tsə-\ 1893–1976 Pinyin *Mao Zedong* Chin. Communist; leader of People's Republic of China (1949–76)

Map \'map\ Walter *ca* 1140–*ca* 1209 Eng. writer

Ma·rat \mə-'rä\ Jean-Paul 1743–1793 Fr. (Swiss-born) revolutionary

Mar·cel·lus \mär-'se-ləs\ Marcus Claudius 268?–208 B.C. Rom. gen.

Mar·co·ni \mär-'kō-nē\ Guglielmo 1874–1937 Ital. physicist & inventor

Marco Polo — see POLO

Mar·cos \'mär-(,)kōs\ Ferdinand Edralin 1917–1989 pres. of the Philippines (1965–86)

Mar·cus \'mär-kəs\ Rudolph Arthur 1923–   Am. (Canad.-born) chem.

Marcus Aurelius — see Marcus Aurelius ANTONINUS

Mar·cu·se \mär-'kü-zə\ Herbert 1898–1979 Am. (Ger.-born) social & polit. philos.

Mar·ga·ret \'mär-g(ə-)rət\ **of Angoulême** 1492–1549 *queen of Henry of Navarre* & writer

Margaret of Anjou 1430–1482 *queen of Henry VI of England*

Margaret of Valois or **Margaret of France** 1553–1615 *queen consort of Henry of Navarre*

Mar·gre·the II \mär-'grā-tə\ 1940–   *dau. of Frederick IX* queen of Denmark (1972–   )

Ma·ria The·re·sa \mə-'rē-ə-tə-'rä-sə, -'rä-zə\ 1717–1780 *wife of Holy Rom. Emp. Francis I* archduchess of Austria & queen of Hungary & Bohemia

Ma·rie \mə-'rē\ 1875–1938 queen of Romania (1914–27); queen dowager (1927–38)

Marie An·toi·nette \,an-twə-'net, -tə-\ 1755–1793 *dau. of Maria Theresa & wife of Louis XVI of France*

Ma·rie de Mé·di·cis \mə-'rē-də-'me-də-(,)chē, -,mä-də-'sē(s)\ 1573–1642 *2d wife of Henry IV of France* regent for Louis XIII

Ma·rie–Lou·ise \mə-'rē-lə-'wēz, -'lwēz\ 1791–1847 *dau. of Francis II of Austria & 2d wife of Napoléon I*

Mar·in \'ma-rən\ John Cheri 1870–1953 Am. painter

Ma·ri·net·ti \,ma-rə-'ne-tē, ,mär-ə-\ (Emilio) Filippo Tommaso 1876–1944 Ital. poet

Ma·ri·ni \mə-'rē-nē\ or **Ma·ri·no** \-(,)nō\ Giambattista 1569–1625 Ital. poet

Ma·ri·on \'mer-ē-ən\ Francis 1732?–1795 *the Swamp Fox* Am. gen. in Revolution

Ma·ri·otte \mär-'yót\ Edme *ca* 1620–1684 Fr. physicist

Ma·ri·tain \,ma-rə-'taⁿ\ Jacques 1882–1973 Fr. philos. & diplomat

Mar·i·us \'mer-ē-əs\ Gaius *ca* 157–86 B.C. Rom. gen.

Ma·ri·vaux \,ma-rə-'vō\ Pierre (Carlet de Chamblain de) 1688–1763 Fr. dram. & nov.

Mark Antony or **Anthony** — see Marcus ANTONIUS

Mark·ham \'mär-kəm\ Beryl 1902–1986 Brit. aviator

Markham Edwin 1852–1940 orig. *Charles Edward Anson Markham* Am. poet

Mar·ko·va \mär-'kō-və\ Dame Ali·cia \ə-'lē-sē-ə\ 1910–2004 orig. *Lilian Alicia Marks* Eng. dancer

Mar·ko·witz \'mär-kə-,wits\ Harry M(ax) 1927–   Am. econ.

Marlborough 1st Duke of — see John CHURCHILL

Mar·lowe \'mär-,lō\ Christopher 1564–1593 Eng. dram.

Mar·mont \mär-'mō⁺\ Auguste-Frédéric-Louis Viesse de 1774–1852 Duc *de Raguse* Fr. gen.; marshal of France

Mar·mon·tel \,mär-(,)mō⁺-'tel\ Jean-François 1723–1799 Fr. author

Ma·rot \ma-'rō\ Clément 1496?–1544 Fr. poet

Mar·quand \mär-'kwänd\ John Phillips 1893–1960 Am. nov.

Mar·quette \mär-'ket\ Jacques 1637–1675 *Père* \,pir, ,per\ *Marquette* Fr.-born Jesuit missionary & explorer in America

Mar·quis \'mär-kwəs\ Donald Robert Perry 1878–1937 Am. humorist

Mar·ry·at \'ma-rē-ət\ Frederick 1792–1848 Eng. naval officer & nov.

Mar·sal·is \mär-'sa-lis\ Wynton (Learson) 1961–   Am. jazz musician

Marsh \'märsh\ Dame (Edith) Ngaio \'nī-(,)ō\ 1899–1982 N.Z. writer

Mar·shall \'mär-shəl\ Alfred 1842–1924 Eng. econ.

Marshall Barry J(ames) 1951–   Austral. microbiol.

Marshall George Catlett 1880–1959 Am. gen. & statesman

Marshall John 1755–1835 Am. jurist; chief justice U.S. Supreme Court (1801–35)

Marshall Thomas Riley 1854–1925 vice pres. of the U.S. (1913–21)

Marshall Thurgood 1908–1993 Am. jurist

Mar·sil·i·us \mär-'si-lē-əs\ **of Padua** *ca* 1280–*ca* 1343 Ital. scholar

Mar·ston \'mär-stən\ John 1576–1634 Eng. dram.

Mar·tel·ly \mär-tə-'lē\ Michel (Joseph) 1961–   pres. of Haiti (2011–   )

Mar·tens \'mär-tᵊnz\ Fyodor Fyodorovich 1845–1909 Russ. jurist

Mar·tí (y Pé·rez) \mär-'tē-ē-'pā-rās\ José (Julián) 1853–1895 Cuban writer & patriot

Mar·tial \'mär-shəl\ *ca* A.D. 40–*ca* 103 *Marcus Valerius Martialis* Rom. epigrammatist

Mar·tin \mär-tᵊn\ *Saint* ca 316–397 *Martin of Tours* patron saint of France

Mar·tin \mär-tᵊn\ Archer John Porter 1910–2002 Brit. chem.

Martin Glenn Luther 1886–1955 Am. airplane manuf.

Martin Joseph William 1884–1968 Am. publisher & polit.

Mar·tin \mär-tᵊn, -tᵊⁿ\ Paul (Edgar Philippe) 1938–   prime min. of Canada (2003–06)

Mar·tin du Gard \mär-taⁿ-due-'gär\ Roger 1881–1958 Fr. author

Mar·ti·neau \'mär-tᵊ-,nō\ Harriet 1802–1876 Eng. nov. & econ.

Martineau James 1805–1900 *bro. of Harriet* Eng. theol. & philos.

Mar·ti·ni \mär-'tē-nē\ Simone *ca* 1284–1344 Ital. painter

Mar·ti·nů \'mär-tyi-,nü\ Bohuslav Jan 1890–1959 Czech composer

Mar·vell \'mär-vəl\ Andrew 1621–1678 Eng. poet & satirist

Marx \'märks\ *family of* Am. comedians: *esp.* Groucho 1890–1977 *Julius Henry* & his bros. Chico 1887–1961 *Leonard* & Harpo 1888–1964 *Adolph*

Marx Karl Heinrich 1818–1883 Ger. polit. philos. & socialist

Mary I \'mer-ē, 'mä-rē\ 1516–1558 *Mary Tudor; Bloody Mary* queen of England (1553–58)

Mary II 1662–1694 joint Brit. sovereign with William III (1689–94)

Mary Stuart 1542–1587 *Mary, Queen of Scots* queen of Scotland (1542–67)

Ma·sac·cio \mə-'zä-ch(ē-,)ō\ 1401–1428 orig. *Tommaso di Giovanni di Simone Guidi* Ital. painter

Ma·sa·ryk \'mä-sə-,)rik, 'ma-\ Jan \'yän, 'yan\ Gar·rigue \gə-'rēg\ 1886–1948 *son of T.G.* Czech diplomat & polit.

Masaryk To·máš \'tȯ-,mäsh, 'tä-məs\ Garrigue 1850–1937 Czech philos. & statesman; 1st pres. of Czechoslovakia (1918–35)

Ma·sca·gni \mä-'skän-yē, ma-\ Pietro 1863–1945 Ital. composer

Mase·field \'mās-,fēld\ John 1878–1967 Eng. author; poet laureate (1930–67)

Mas·i·nis·sa \,ma-sə-'ni-sə\ *ca* 240–148 B.C. king of Numidia

Ma·ska·wa \mä-'skä-wä\ Toshihide 1940–   Jp. physicist

Mas·kin \'ma-skən\ Eric S(tark) 1950–   Am. econ.

Ma·son \'mä-s°n\ Charles 1728–1786 Eng. astron. & surveyor

Mason George 1725–1792 Am. statesman in Revolution

Mas·sa·soit \,ma-sä-'sȯit\ *d* 1661 Wampanoag Indian chief

Mas·sé·na \,ma-sā-'nä, mə-'sā-nə\ André 1758–1817 Duc *de Rivoli*; Prince *d'Ess·ling* \des-lēn\ Fr. gen.

Mas·se·net \,ma-sə-'nä, ma-'snā\ Jules (-Émile-Frédéric) 1842–1912 Fr. composer

Mas·sine \mä-'sēn\ Léonide 1896–1979 orig. *Leonid Fedorovich Miassin* Am. (Russ.-born) dancer & choreographer

Mas·sin·ger \'ma-s°n-jər\ Philip 1583–1640 Eng. dram.

Mas·sys \'ma-,sis\ *or* **Mat·sys** \'mät-sis\ *or* **Mes·sys** \'me-sis\ *or* **Met·sys** \'met-sis\ Quentin *ca* 1466–1530 Flem. painter

Mas·ters \'mas-tərz\ Edgar Lee 1869–1950 Am. author

Math·er \'ma-thər, -thər\ Cotton 1663–1728 Am. clergyman & author

Mather Increase 1639–1723 *father of Cotton* Am. clergyman & author; pres. Harvard College (1685–1701)

Mather John C(romwell) 1946–   Am. astrophysicist

Ma·tisse \ma-'tēs, mə-\ Henri (-Émile-Benoît) 1869–1954 Fr. painter

Ma·tsuo \mät-'sü-ō, 'mät-sü-ō\ Ba·shō \'bä-,shō\ 1644–1694 pseud. of *Matsuo Munefusa* Jp. haiku poet

Mat·te·ot·ti \,ma-tē-'ȯ-tē, ,mä-, -'ȯ-\ Giacomo 1885–1924 Ital. socialist

Mat·thews \'ma-(,)thyüz\ (James) Brander 1852–1929 Am. educ. & author

Maugham \'mȯm\ (William) Somerset 1874–1965 Eng. nov. & dram.

Mau·pas·sant \,mō-pə-'sän\ (Henri-René-Albert-) Guy de 1850–1893 Fr. writer

Mau·riac \mȯr-'yäk, ,mȯr-ē-'äk\ François 1885–1970 Fr. author

Mau·rice \'mȯr-əs, 'mär-; mȯ-'rēs\ *G* **Mo·ritz** \'mȯr-əts, 'mȯr-\ 1521–1553 elector of Saxony (1547–53) & gen.

Maurice of Nassau 1567–1625 Prince of *Orange* Du. gen. & statesman

Mau·rois \mȯr-'wä\ André 1885–1967 pseud. of *Émile-Salomon-Wilhelm Her·zog* \er-zȯg\ Fr. writer

Mau·ry \'mȯr-ē, 'mär-\ Matthew Fontaine 1806–1873 Am. naval officer & oceanographer

Mau·ser \'maú-zər\ Peter Paul 1838–1914 & his bro. Wilhelm 1834–1882 Ger. inventors

Maw·son \'mȯ-s°n\ Sir Douglas 1882–1958 Austral. polar explorer

Max·im \'mak-səm\ Sir Hiram Stevens 1840–1916 Brit. (Am.-born) inventor

Maxim Hudson 1853–1927 *bro. of prec.* Am. inventor

Max·i·mil·ian \,mak-sə-'mil-yən\ 1832–1867 *bro. of Francis Joseph I of Austria* emp. of Mexico (1864–67)

Maximilian I 1459–1519 Holy Rom. emp. (1493–1519)

Maximilian II 1527–1576 Holy Rom. emp. (1564–76)

Max·well \'maks-,wel, -wəl\ James Clerk \'klärk\ 1831–1879 Scot. physicist — **Max·wel·li·an** \maks-'we-lē-ən\ *adj*

Ma·ya·kov·ski \,mä-yə-'kȯf-skē, -'kȯv-\ Vladimir Vladimirovich 1893–1930 Russ. poet

May·er \'mā-ər, 'mer\ Louis B(urt) 1884–1957 orig. *Lazar Meir* Am. (Russ.-born) film producer & executive

Mayo \'mā-(,)ō\ Charles Horace 1865–1939 & his bro. William James 1861–1939 Am. surgeons

Mayr \'mī(-ə)r\ Ernst 1904–2005 Am. (Ger.-born) biol.

Mays \'māz\ Willie (Howard), Jr. 1931–   Am. baseball player

Ma·za·rin \,ma-zə-'ra°\ Jules 1602–1661 Fr. cardinal & statesman

Ma·zo·wie·cki \mä-zō-'vyet-skē\ Tadeusz 1927–2013 prime min. of Poland (1989–91)

Maz·zi·ni \mät-'sē-nē, mäd-'zē-\ Giuseppe 1805–1872 Ital. patriot

Mbe·ki \em-'be-kē, əm-\ Thabo (Mvuyelwa) 1942–   pres. of So. Africa (1999–2008)

Mc·Adoo \'ma-kə-,dü\ William Gibbs 1863–1941 Am. administrator

M'·Car·thy \mə-'kär-thē *also* -tē\ Justin 1830–1912 Irish writer & polit.

Mc·Cain \mə-'kān\ John 1936–   *John Sidney McCain III* Am. polit.

Mc·Car·thy \mə-'kär-thē\ Cormac 1933–   orig. *Charles McCarthy* Am. writer

McCarthy Eugene Joseph 1916–2005 Am. polit.

McCarthy Joseph Raymond 1908–1957 Am. polit.

McCarthy Mary Therese 1912–1989 Am. writer

Mc·Clel·lan \mə-'kle-lən\ George Brinton 1826–1885 Am. gen. & polit.

Mc·Clin·tock \mə-'klin-tək\ Barbara 1902–1992 Am. botanist

Mc·Clos·key \mə-'kläs-kē\ John 1810–1885 1st Am. cardinal

Mc·Cloy \mə-'klȯi\ John Jay 1895–1989 Am. banker & govt. official

Mc·Cor·mack \mə-'kȯr-mək, -mik\ John 1884–1945 Am. (Irish-born) tenor

McCormack John William 1891–1980 Am. polit.

Mc·Cor·mick \mə-'kȯr-mik\ Cyrus Hall 1809–1884 Am. inventor

McCormick Robert Rutherford 1880–1955 Am. newspaper publisher

Mc·Cul·lers \mə-'kə-lərz\ Carson 1917–1967 née *Smith* Am. writer

Mc·Dow·ell \mək-'daú(-ə)l\ Irvin 1818–1885 Am. gen.

Mc·Ew·an \mə-'kyü-ən\ Ian (Russell) 1948–   Brit. writer

Mc·Fad·den \mək-'fa-d°n\ Daniel L(ittle) 1937–   Am. econ.

Mc·Gill \mə-'gil\ James 1744–1813 Canad. (Scot.-born) businessman & philanthropist

Mc·Gov·ern \mə-'gə-vərn\ George Stanley 1922–2012 Am. polit.

Mc·Guf·fey \mə-'gə-fē\ William Holmes 1800–1873 Am. educ.

Mc·Ken·na \mə-'ke-nə\ Sio·bhan \shə-'vȯn\ 1923?–1986 Irish actress

Mc·Kim \mə-'kim\ Charles Follen 1847–1909 Am. architect

Mc·Kin·ley \mə-'kin-lē\ William 1843–1901 25th pres. of the U.S. (1897–1901)

Mc·Lu·han \mə-'klü-ən\ (Herbert) Marshall 1911–1980 Canad. educ.

Mc·Mil·lan \mək-'mi-lən\ Edwin Mattison 1907–1991 Am. chem.

Mc·Na·mara \,mak-nə-'ma-rə, 'mak-nə-,ma-rə\ Robert Strange 1916–2009 U.S. secy. of defense (1961–68)

Mc·Naugh·ton \mək-'nȯ-t°n\ Andrew George Latta 1887–1966 Canad. gen. & diplomat

Mead \'mēd\ Margaret 1901–1978 Am. anthropol.

Meade \'mēd\ George Gordon 1815–1872 Am. gen.

Mea·ny \'mē-nē\ George 1894–1980 Am. labor leader

Me·dei·ros \mə-'der-əs, -(,)ōs\ Humberto 1915–1983 Am. (Port.-born) cardinal

Me·di·ci, de' \'me-də-(,)chē\ Catherine — see CATHERINE DE MÉDICIS

Medici, de' Cosimo 1389–1464 *the Elder* Florentine financier & ruler

Medici, de' Cosimo I 1519–1574 *the Great;* Duke of *Florence;* Grand Duke of *Tuscany*

Medici, de' Lorenzo 1449–1492 *the Magnificent* Florentine statesman, ruler, & patron

Me·di·na-Si·do·nia \mə-'dē-nə-sə-'dōn-yə\ Duque de *d* 1619 *Alonso Pérez de Guzmán* Span. admiral

Med·ved·ev \mid-'vye-dif\ Dmitry (Anatolyevich) 1965–   pres. of Russia (2008–12); prime min. (2012–   )

Meigh·en \'mē-ən\ Arthur 1874–1960 Canad. statesman; prime min. (1920–21; 1926)

Mc·ir \mä 'ir\ Golda 1898–1978 orig. *Goldie Mabovitch,* later *Goldie Myerson* prime min. of Israel (1969–74)

Meis·so·nier \,mä-s°n-'yā\ Jean-Louis-Ernest 1815–1891 Fr. painter

Meit·ner \'mīt-nər\ Li·se \'lē-zə\ 1878–1968 Ger. physicist

Me·lanch·thon \mə-'laŋ(k)-thən, -tən\ Philipp 1497–1560 orig. surname *Schwartzerd* Ger. scholar & religious reformer

Mel·ba \'mel-bə\ Dame Nellie 1861–1931 orig. *Helen Porter Mitchell* Austral. soprano

Mel·chi·or \'mel-kē-,ȯr\ Lau·ritz \'laú-rəts\ Lebrecht Hommel 1890–1973 Am. (Dan.-born) tenor

Mel·lo \'me-lō\ Craig C(ameron) 1960–   Am. geneticist

Mel·lon \'me-lən\ Andrew William 1855–1937 Am. financier

Mel·ville \'mel-,vil\ Herman 1819–1891 Am. author — **Mel·vill·ean** \,mel-'vi-lē-ən\ *adj*

Mem·ling \'mem-liŋ\ *or* **Mem·linc** \-liŋk\ Hans *ca* 1430–1494 Flem. painter

Me·nan·der \mə-'nan-dər\ 342–292 B.C. Greek dram.

Men·chú (Tum) \'men-,chü\ Rigoberta 1959–   Guatemalan human rights activist

Mencius — see MENG-TZU

Menck·en \'meŋ-kən, 'men-\ H(enry) L(ouis) 1880–1956 Am. editor — **Menck·e·nian** \meŋ-kē-nē-ən, men-\ *adj*

Men·del \'men-d°l\ Gregor Johann 1822–1884 Austrian botanist — **Men·del·ian** \men-'dē-lē-ən, -'dēl-yən\ *adj*

Men·de·le·yev \,men-də-'lā-əf\ Dmitry Ivanovich 1834–1907 Russ. chem.

Men·dels·sohn \'men-d°l-sən\ Moses 1729–1786 Ger. philos.

Mendelssohn(–Bar·thol·dy) \-bär-'tȯl-dē, -'thȯl-\ (Jakob Ludwig) Felix 1809–1847 *grandson of prec.* Ger. composer, pianist, & conductor — **Men·dels·sohn·ian** \,men-d°l-'sō-nē-ən, -nyən\ *adj*

Mendès–France \ma°-des-'frä°s\ Pierre 1907–1982 Fr. statesman

Men·do·za \men-'dō-zə\ Antonio de *ca* 1490–1552 Span. colonial gov.

Men·e·lik II \'me-nə-(,)lik\ 1844–1913 emp. of Ethiopia (1889–1913)

Men·em \'me-,nem, -nəm\ Carlos Saúl 1930–   pres. of Argentina (1989–99)

Me·nén·dez de Av·i·lés \mə-'nen-dəs-dā-,ä-və-'läs\ Pedro 1519–1574 Span. navigator & explorer

Me·nes \'mē-,nēz\ *fl ca* 3100 B.C. king of Egypt

Mengs \'meŋ(k)s\ Anton Raphael 1728–1779 Ger. painter

Meng-tzu \'məŋ-'dzü\ *ca* 371–*ca* 289 B.C. orig. *Meng K'o* L. *Men·cius* \'men-ch(ē-)əs\ Chin. philos.

Men·ning·er \'me-niŋ-ər\ Karl Augustus 1893–1990 Am. psychiatrist

Men·no Si·mons \'me-nō-'sē-mōns, -'sī-\ 1469–1561 Du. religious reformer

Me·not·ti \mə-'nä-tē, -'nȯ-\ Gian Carlo 1911–2007 Am. (Ital.-born) composer

Me·nu·hin \'men-yə-wən\ Ye·hu·di \yə-'hü-dē\ 1916–1999 Am. violinist

Men·zies \'men-(,)zēz\ Sir Robert Gordon 1894–1978 Austral. statesman; prime min. (1939–41; 1949–66)

Mer·ca·tor \(,)mər-'kā-tər\ Gerardus 1512–1594 *Gerhard Kremer* Flem. cartographer

Mer·e·dith \'mer-ə-dəth\ George 1828–1909 Eng. nov. & poet

Mer·gen·tha·ler \'mər-gən-,thä-lər, 'mer-gən-,tä-\ Ottmar 1854–1899 Am. (Ger.-born) inventor

Mé·ri·mée \'mer-ə-,mā, ,mä-rə-\ Prosper 1803–1870 Fr. writer

Mer·kel \'mer-kəl\ Angela (Dorothea) 1954–   née *Kas·ner* \'käs-nər\ chancellor of Germany (2005–   )

Mer·rill \'mer-əl\ James Ingram 1926–1995 Am. poet

Mer·ton \'mər-t°n\ Robert C(ox) 1944–   Am. econ.

Merton Thomas 1915–1968 Am. religious & author

Mes·mer \'mez-mər, 'mes-\ Franz *or* Friedrich Anton 1734–1815 Ger. physician

Mes·sa·la (or Mes·sal·la) Cor·vi·nus \mə-'sä-lə-,kȯr-'vī-nəs\ Marcus Valerius *ca* 64 B.C.–A.D. 8 Rom. gen. & statesman

Mes·sa·li·na \,me-sə-'lī-nə, -'lē-\ Valeria *ca* A.D. 22–48 *3d wife of Emp. Claudius*

Mes·ser·schmitt \'me-sər-,shmit\ Willy 1898–1978 Ger. aircraft designer & manuf.

Mes·siaen \mes-'ya°\ Olivier 1908–1992 Fr. composer

Mes·sier \mäs-'yā, 'me-sē-,ā\ Charles 1730–1817 Fr. astron.

Meš·tro·vić \'mesh-trə-,vich, 'mes-\ Ivan 1883–1962 Am. (Yugoslavian-born) sculptor

Me·tax·as \me-'täk-'säs\ Ioannis 1871–1941 Greek gen. & dictator

Metch·ni·koff \'mech-nə-,kȯf\ Élie 1845–1916 orig. *Ilya Ilich Mech·ni·kov* \'myäch-nyi-,kȯf\ Fr. (Russ.-born) zool. & bacteriol.

Met·ter·nich \'me-tər-(,)nik, -(,)nik\ Klemens Wenzel Nepomuk Lothar 1773–1859 Fürst *von Metternich* Austrian statesman

Mey·er \'mī(-ə)r\ Annie 1867–1951 née *Nathan* Am. educ. & writer

Mey·er·beer \'mī-ər-ˌbir, -ˌber\ Giacomo 1791–1864 orig. *Jakob Liebmann Beer* Ger. composer

Mey·er·hof \'mī-ər-ˌhôf\ Otto 1884–1951 Ger. biochem.

Mi·chael \'mī-kəl\ *Romanian* Mi·hai \mē-'hī\ 1921– *Michael Hohenzollern* king of Romania (1927–30; 1940–47)

Mich·el \'mi-kəl\ Hartmut 1948– Ger. biochem.

Mi·chel·an·ge·lo \ˌmī-kə-'lan-jə-ˌlō, ˌmi-, ˌmē-kə-län-\ 1475–1564 *Michelangelo di Lodovico Buonarroti Simoni* Ital. sculptor, painter, architect, & poet — Mi·chel·an·ge·lesque \-ˌlan-jə-'lesk\ *adj*

Mi·che·let \ˌmēsh-'lā, ˌmē-shə-\ Jules 1798–1874 Fr. hist.

Mi·chel·son \'mī-kəl-sən\ Albert Abraham 1852–1931 Am. (Ger.-born) physicist

Mich·e·ner \'mich-nər, 'mi-chə-\ James Albert 1907–1997 Am. author

Mi·chu·rin \myi-'chür-yin\ Ivan Vladimirovich 1855–1935 Soviet horticulturist

Mic·kie·wicz \mits-'kyä-vich\ Adam 1798–1855 Pol. poet

Mid·dle·ton \'mi-dᵊl-tən\ Thomas 1570?–1627 Eng. dram.

Mies van der Ro·he \ˌmēs-van-der-'rō(-ə), ˌmēz-\ Ludwig 1886–1969 Am. (Ger.-born) architect — Mies·ian \'mē-sē-ən, 'mē-shən\ *adj*

Miff·lin \'mi-flən\ Thomas 1744–1800 Am. gen. in Revolution

Mi·haj·lo·vić \mi-'hī-lə-ˌvich\ Dragoljub 1893–1946 *Draža* \'drä-zhə\ Yugoslav gen.

Mi·ko·yan \ˌmē-kō-'yän\ Ana·stas \ˌä-nə-'stäs\ Ivanovich 1895–1978 Soviet polit.; head of Presidium (1964–65)

Mil·haud \mē-'ō\ Darius 1892–1974 Fr. composer

Mill \'mil\ James 1773–1836 Scot. philos., hist., & econ.

Mill John Stuart 1806–1873 *son of James* Eng. philos. & econ.

Mil·lais \'mi-ˌlā, mi-'lā\ Sir John Everett 1829–1896 Eng. painter

Mil·lay \'mi-ˌlā\ Edna St. Vincent 1892–1950 Am. poet

Mil·ler \'mi-lər\ Arthur 1915–2005 Am. dram. & nov.

Miller (Alton) Glenn 1904–1944 Am. bandleader

Miller Henry 1891–1980 Am. writer

Miller Joa·quin \wä-'kēn, wô-\ 1837–1913 pseud. of *Cincinnatus Hiner Miller* Am. poet

Miller Merton Howard 1923–2000 Am. econ.

Miller Perry Gilbert Eddy 1905–1963 Am. lit. critic & scholar

Miller William 1782–1849 Am. religious leader

Mil·le·rand \mēl-'rän, mē-lə-\ Alexandre 1859–1943 Fr. statesman; pres. of France (1920–24)

Mil·les \'mi-ləs\ Carl 1875–1955 Am. (Swed.-born) sculptor

Mil·let \mē-'yä, mi-'lā\ Jean-François 1814–1875 Fr. painter

Mil·li·kan \'mi-li-kən\ Robert Andrews 1868–1953 Am. physicist

Milne \'mil(n)\ A(lan) A(lexander) 1882–1956 Eng. poet & dram.

Mi·lo·še·vić \mə-'lō-sə-ˌvich, -shə-\ Slobodan 1941–2006 pres. of Serbia (1989–97); pres. of Yugoslavia (1997–2000)

Mi·losz \'mē-lôsh\ Czeslaw 1911–2004 Pol. writer

Mil·stein \'mil-ˌstīn, -ˌstēn\ César 1927–2002 Brit. (Argentine-born) immunologist

Mil·ti·a·des \mil-'tī-ə-ˌdēz\ *ca* 554–?489 B.C. *the Younger* Athenian gen.

Mil·ton \'mil-tən\ John 1608–1674 Eng. poet — Mil·to·nian \mil-'tō-nē-ən, -nyən\ *or* Mil·ton·ic \-'tä-nik\ *adj*

Mil·yu·kov \ˌmil-yə-'kóf, -'kóv\ Pavel Nikolayevich 1859–1943 Russ. polit. & hist.

Mi·not \'mī-nət\ George Richards 1885–1950 Am. physician

Min·u·it \'min-yə-wət\ *or* Min·ne·wit \'mi-nə-ˌwit\ Peter 1580–1638 Du. colonial administrator in America

Mi·ra·beau \'mir-ə-ˌbō\ Comte de 1749–1791 *Honoré-Gabriel Riqueti* Fr. orator & revolutionary

Mi·ró \mē-'rō\ Joan \zhü-'än\ 1893–1983 Span. painter

Mirr·lees \'mər-ˌlēz\ Sir James Alexander 1936– Brit. econ.

Mi·ses \'mē-zes\ Ludwig (Edler) von 1881–1973 Austrian econ.

Mi·shi·ma \'mi-shi-ˌmä, mə-'shē-mə\ Yukio 1925–1970 pseud. of *Hiracka Kimitake* Jp. writer

Mis·tral \'mi-strəl, -'stral\ Frédéric 1830–1914 Provençal poet

Mistral Gabriela 1889–1957 orig. *Lucila Godoy Alcayaga* Chilean poet & educ.

Mitch·ell \'mi-chəl\ Joni 1943– orig. *Roberta Joan Anderson* Canad. singer & songwriter

Mitchell Margaret Munnerlyn 1900–1949 Am. nov.

Mitchell Maria 1818–1889 Am. astron.

Mitchell Peter Dennis 1920–1992 Brit. chem.

Mitchell William 1879–1936 *Billy Mitchell* Am. gen.

Mith·ra·da·tes VI Eu·pa·tor \ˌmi-thrə-'dā-tēz-'yü-ˌpā-tər\ *d* 63 B.C. *the Great* king of Pontus (120–63)

Mi·tro·pou·los \mə-'trä-pə-ləs\ Di·mi·tri \də-'mē-trē\ 1896–1960 Am. (Greek-born) conductor

Mit·ter·rand \mē-ter-'äⁿ\ François (-Maurice) 1916–1996 pres. of France (1981–95)

Mo·bu·tu Se·se Se·ko \mə-'bü-(ˌ)tü-'sä-sä-'sä-(ˌ)kō\ 1930–1997 orig. *Joseph-Désiré Mobutu* pres. of Zaire (1965–97)

Mo·di·glia·ni \mó-dēl-'yä-nē, -dᵊl-\ Amedeo 1884–1920 Ital. painter

Modigliani Franco 1918–2003 Am. (Ital.-born) econ.

Mo·djes·ka \mō-'jes-kə\ Helena 1840–1909 Am. (Pol.-born) actress

Mo·ham·mad Re·za Pah·la·vi \mō-'ha-məd-ri-'zä-ˌpä-lə-(ˌ)vē, -'hä-\ 1919–1980 shah of Iran (1941–79)

Mo·ham·med *var of* MUHAMMAD

Moi \'mói\ Daniel arap 1924– pres. of Kenya (1978–2002)

Mois·san \mwä-'säⁿ\ Henri 1852–1907 Fr. chem.

Mo·ley \'mō-lē\ Raymond Charles 1886–1975 Am. journalist

Mo·lière \mō-'yer, 'mōl-ˌ\ 1622–1673 orig. *Jean-Baptiste Poquelin* Fr. actor & dram.

Mo·li·na \mō-'lē-nə\ Mario José 1943– Am. (Mex.-born) chem.

Molina Tirso de — see TIRSO DE MOLINA

Mol·nár \'mōl-ˌnär, 'mól-\ Fe·renc \'fer-ən(t)s\ 1878–1952 Hung. author

Mo·lo·tov \'mä-lə-ˌtóf, 'mó-, 'mō-, -ˌtóv\ Vyacheslav Mikhaylovich 1890–1986 orig. surname *Skryabin* Soviet statesman

Molt·ke \'mōlt-kə\ Helmuth Karl Bernhard 1800–1891 Graf *von Moltke* Pruss. field marshal

Momm·sen \'mäm-zən\ Theodor 1817–1903 Ger. scholar & hist.

Monck *or* Monk \'məŋk\ George 1608–1670 1st Duke of *Al·be·marle* \'al-bə-ˌmärl\ Eng. gen.

Mon·dale \'män-ˌdāl\ Walter Frederick 1928– Am. polit.; vice pres. of the U.S. (1977–81)

Mon·dri·an \'món-drē-ˌän\ Piet 1872–1944 *Pieter Cornelis Mondriaan* Du. painter

Mo·net \mō-'nä\ Claude 1840–1926 Fr. painter

Moniz Antonio Egas — see EGAS MONIZ

Mo·niz \mō-'nēz\ Ernest (Jeffrey) 1944– Am. nuclear physicist; U.S. secy. of energy (2013–)

Monk \'məŋk\ Thelonious Sphere 1920–1982 Am. jazz musician

Mon·mouth \'mən-məth, 'män-\ Duke of 1649–1685 *James Scott, son of Charles II of England* Eng. rebel & claimant to the throne

Mon·net \mō-'ne\ Jean (-Omer-Marie-Gabriel) 1888–1979 Fr. econ. & diplomat

Mon·roe \mən-'rō\ James 1758–1831 5th pres. of U.S. (1817–25)

Monroe Marilyn 1926–1962 orig. *Norma Jean Mor·ten·son* \'mór-tᵊn-sən\ Am. actress

Mon·ta·gna \mən-'tän-yə\ Bartolommeo *ca* 1450–1523 Ital. painter

Mon·ta·gnier \mōⁿ-tä-'nyä\ Luc Antoine 1932– Fr. virologist

Mon·ta·gu \'män-tə-ˌgyü, 'mən-\ Lady Mary Wortley 1689–1762 Eng. letter writer & poet

Mon·taigne \män-'tän, mōⁿ-'tenʸ\ Michel (Eyquem) de 1533–1592 Fr. essayist

Mon·ta·le \mōn-'tä-(ˌ)lä\ Eugenio 1896–1981 Ital. poet

Mont·calm de Saint–Vé·ran \mänt-'kälm-də-ˌsaⁿ-vä-'räⁿ, -'käm-\ Marquis de 1712–1759 *Louis-Joseph de Montcalm-Grozon* Fr. field marshal

Mon·tes·pan \mōⁿ-tes-'pä", 'män-tə-ˌspan\ Marquise de 1641–1707 née (*Françoise-Athénaïs*) *Rochechouart de Mortemart* mistress of Louis XIV

Mon·tes·quieu \ˌmän-təs-'kyü, -'kyœ(r), -ˌkyœ\ Baron *de La Brède et de* 1689–1755 *Charles-Louis de Secondat* Fr. lawyer & polit. philos.

Mon·tes·so·ri \ˌmän-tə-'sór-ē\ Maria 1870–1952 Ital. educ.

Mon·teux \mōⁿ-'tə(r), -'tœ\ Pierre 1875–1964 Am. (Fr.-born) conductor

Mon·te·ver·di \ˌmän-tə-'ver-dē, -'vər-\ Claudio 1567–1643 Ital. composer

Mon·te·zu·ma II \ˌmän-tə-'zü-mə\ *or* Moc·te·zu·ma \ˌmäk-tə-\ 1466–1520 last Aztec emp. of Mexico (1502–20)

Mont·fort \'mänt-fərt, mōⁿ-'fór\ Simon de 1165?–1218 *Simon IV de Montfort l'Amaury* Fr. soldier

Mont·fort \'mänt-fərt\ Simon de *ca* 1208–1265 Earl of *Leicester; son of prec.* Eng. soldier & statesman

Mont·gol·fier \mänt-'gäl-fē-ər, -fē-ˌä\ Joseph-Michel 1740–1810 & his bro. Jacques-Étienne 1745–1799 Fr. inventors & balloonists

Mont·gom·ery \(ˌ)mən(t)-'gəm-rē, män(t)-, -'gäm-; -'gə-mə-, -'gä-\ Bernard Law 1887–1976 1st Viscount *Montgomery of Alamein* Brit. field marshal

Montgomery Lucy Maud 1874–1942 Canad. nov.

Mon·ti \'mòn-tē\ Mario 1943– Ital. econ., prime min. of Italy (2011–13)

Mont·mo·ren·cy \ˌmänt-mə-'ren(t)-sē\ Anne 1493–1567 1st duc *de Montmorency* Fr. soldier; constable (1537)

Mon·trose \män-'tróz\ 1st Marquess of 1612–1650 *James Graham* Scot. Royalist

Moo·dy \'mü-dē\ Dwight Lyman 1837–1899 Am. evangelist

Moore \'mór, 'múr\ George 1852–1933 Irish author

Moore George Edward 1873–1958 Eng. philos.

Moore Henry 1898–1986 Brit. sculptor

Moore Marianne Craig 1887–1972 Am. poet

Moore Thomas 1779–1852 Irish poet

Mo·ra·les (Ay·ma) \mō-'rä-läs ('ī-mä)\ (Juan) Evo 1959– pres. of Bolivia (2006–)

Mo·ra·via \mō-'rä-vē-ə\ Alberto 1907–1990 pseud. of *Alberto Pincherle* Ital. writer

More \'mór\ Hannah 1745–1833 Eng. religious writer

More Henry 1614–1687 Eng. philos.

More Sir Thomas 1478–1535 *Saint Thomas More* Eng. statesman & author

Mo·reau \mò-'rō\ (Jean-) Victor-Marie 1763–1813 Fr. gen.

Mor·gan \'mór-gən\ Daniel 1736–1802 Am. gen. in Revolution

Morgan Sir Henry 1635–1688 Eng. buccaneer

Morgan John Hunt 1825–1864 Am. Confed. cavalry officer

Morgan J(ohn) P(ier·pont) \'pir-ˌpänt\ 1837–1913 Am. financier

Morgan J(ohn) P(ierpont) Jr. 1867–1943 *son of prec.* Am. financier

Morgan Thomas Hunt 1866–1945 Am. geneticist

Morgan William Wilson 1906–1994 Am. astron.

Mor·gen·thau \'mór-gən-ˌthó\ Henry 1891–1967 U.S. secy. of the treasury (1934–45)

Mor·i·son \'mór-ə-sən, 'mär-\ Samuel Eliot 1887–1976 Am. hist.

Morison Stanley 1889–1968 Eng. type designer

Mo·ri·sot \mò-rē-'zō\ Berthe 1841–1895 Fr. painter

Mor·ley \'mór-lē\ Christopher Darlington 1890–1957 Am. writer

Morley John 1838–1923 Viscount *Morley* Eng. statesman & writer

Mor·nay \mór-'nä\ Philippe de 1549–1623 Seigneur *du Plessis-Marly; usu. called Du·ples·sis-Mor·nay* \du-plä-sē-mór-'ne\ Fr. Huguenot

Mor·ris \'mór-əs, 'mär-\ Gou·ver·neur \ˌgə-və(r)-'nir\ 1752–1816 Am. statesman & diplomat

Morris Mark 1956– Am. choreographer

Morris Robert 1734–1806 Am. financier & statesman

Morris William 1834–1896 Eng. poet, artist, & socialist

Mor·ri·son \'mór-ə-sən, 'mär-\ Robert 1782–1834 Scot. missionary

Morrison Toni 1931– orig. *Chloe Anthony Wofford* Am. nov.

Morse \'mórs\ Samuel Finley Breese 1791–1872 Am. artist & inventor

Mor·ten·sen \'mór-tᵊn-sən\ Dale T(homas) 1939– Am. econ.

Mor·ti·mer \'mór-tə-mər\ Roger de 1287–1330 1st Earl of *March* & 8th Baron of *Wigmore* Welsh rebel

Mor·ton \'mór-tᵊn\ Jelly Roll 1890–1941 orig. *Ferdinand Joseph Lamothe* Am. jazz composer & musician

Morton Levi Parsons 1824–1920 Am. banker & polit.; vice pres. of the U.S. (1889–93)

Morton William Thomas Green 1819–1868 Am. dentist

Mos·by \'mōz-bē\ John Singleton 1833–1916 Am. Confed. officer
Moś·cic·ki \mòsh-'chēt-skē, -'chit-\ Ignacy 1867–1946 Pol. chem.; pres. of Poland (1926–39)
Mo·ses \'mō-zəz *also* -zəs\ Anna Mary 1860–1961 née *Robertson; Grandma Moses* Am. painter
Mos·ley \'mōz-lē\ Sir Oswald Er·nald \'ər-nᵊld\ 1896–1980 Eng. polit.
Möss·bau·er \'mœs‚baù(-ə)r, 'mes-\ Rudolf Ludwig 1929–2011 Ger. physicist
Moth·er·well \'mə-thər‚wel, -wəl\ Robert 1915–1991 Am. artist
Mo·tion \'mō-shən\ Sir Andrew 1952–   Brit. poet; poet laureate (1999–2009)
Mot·ley \'mät-lē\ John Lothrop 1814–1877 Am. hist.
Mo·ton \'mō-t°n\ Robert Russa 1867–1940 Am. educ.
Mott \'mät\ Lucretia 1793–1880 née *Coffin* Am. social reformer
Mot·tel·son \'mōd-t°l-sən, -(‚)sòn\ Ben Roy 1926–   Dan. (Am.-born) physicist
Mo–tzu \'mōd-'zə\ 470?–?391 B.C. orig. *Mo Ti* \'mō-'dē\ L. *Mi·cius* \'mē-sh(ē-)əs\ Chin. philos.
Moul·ton \'mōl-t°n\ Forest Ray 1872–1952 Am. astron.
Moul·trie \'mül-trē, 'mòl-\ William 1730–1805 Am. gen. in Revolution
Mount·bat·ten \maùnt-'ba-t°n\ Louis 1900–1979 1st Earl *Mountbatten of Burma* Brit. admiral; 1st gov.-gen. of India (1947–48); chief of U.K. defense staff (1959–65)
Mow·at \'mō-ət\ Farley McGill 1921–   Canad. writer
Mo Yan \'mō-'yen\ orig. *Guan Moye* 1955–   Chin. writer
Mo·zart \'mōt-‚särt\ Wolfgang Amadeus 1756–1791 Austrian composer — **Mo·zart·ean** *or* **Mo·zart·ian** \mōt-'sär-tē-ən\ *adj*
Mu·bar·ak \mù-'bär-ək\ (Muhammad) Hosni 1928–   pres. of Egypt (1981–2011)
Mu·ga·be \mù-'gä-bē\ Robert Gabriel 1924–   prime min. of Zimbabwe (1980–87); executive pres. (1987–   )
Mug·ge·ridge \'mə-gə-‚rij\ Malcolm Thomas 1903–1990 Brit. writer & social critic
Mu·ham·mad \mō-'ha-məd, -'hä- *also* mü-\ *ca* 570–632 *Abū al-Qāsim Muḥammad ibn ʿAbd Allāh ibn ʿAbd al-Muṭṭalib ibn Hāshim* Arab prophet & founder of Islam
Mu·ham·mad \mō-'ha-məd, mü-\ Elijah 1897–1975 orig. surname *Poole* Am. religious leader
Muḥammad XI \mō-'ha-məd, -'hä- *also* mü-\ *d* 1527 *Abū ʿAbd Allāh Muḥammad* Sp. *Bo·ab·dil* \bō-äv-'dēl\ last sultan of Granada
Müh·len·berg \'myü-lən-‚bərg\ Henry Melchior 1711–1787 Am. (Ger.-born) Lutheran clergyman
Muir \'myúr\ John 1838–1914 Am. (Scot.-born) naturalist
Mul·ler \'mə-lər\ Hermann Joseph 1890–1967 Am. geneticist
Mul·ler \'mue-lər\ Herta 1953–   Ger. (Romanian-born) writer
Mül·ler \'myü-lər, 'mi-, 'mə-\ (Friedrich) Max 1823–1900 Brit. (Ger.-born) philologist
Müller Johann 1436–1476 *Regiomontanus* Ger. astron.
Müller Karl Alexander 1927–   Swiss physicist
Müller Paul Hermann 1899–1965 Swiss chem.
Mul·li·ken \'mə-lə-kən\ Robert Sanderson 1896–1986 Am. chem. & physicist
Mul·lis \'mə-lis\ Kary Banks 1944–   Am. biochem.
Mul·ro·ney \məl-'rü-nē\ (Martin) Brian 1939–   Canad. polit.; prime min. (1984–93)
Mum·ford \'məm(p)-fərd\ Lewis 1895–1990 Am. writer
Munch \'mùnch, 'muench\ Charles 1891–1968 Alsatian-born conductor
Munch \'mùnk\ Edvard 1863–1944 Norw. painter
Münch·hau·sen \'muenk‚haù-z°n\ Karl Friedrich Hieronymus von 1720–1797 Baron *Mun·chau·sen* \'mən-‚chaú-z°n, 'mùn-\ Ger. hunter, soldier, & raconteur
Mun·dell \mən-'del\ Robert A(lexander) 1932–   Am. (Canad.-born) econ.
Mu·ñoz Ma·rín \(‚)mün-'yōs-mə-'rēn, -'yòz-\ Luis 1898–1980 Puerto Rican polit.
Mun·ro \(‚)mən-'rō\ Alice 1931–   née *Laidlaw* Canad. writer
Munro Hector Hugh 1870–1916 pseud. *Saki* Scot. writer
Mün·ster·berg \'mùn(t)-stər-‚bərg, 'myün(t)-, 'mən(t)-\ Hugo 1863–1916 Am. (Ger.-born) psychol.
Mu·rad \'myúr‚ad\ Ferid 1936–   Am. pharmacologist
Mu·ra·sa·ki \‚mùr-ə-'sä-kē, ‚myùr-\ Shikibu 978?–?1026 Jp. court lady & nov.
Mu·rat \myù-'rä, mue-\ Joachim 1767–1815 Fr. gen.; marshal of France; king of Naples (1808–15)
Mur·doch \'mər-dək, -‚däk\ Dame (Jean) Iris 1919–1999 Brit. (Irish-born) writer
Murdoch (Keith) Rupert 1931–   Am. (Austral.-born) newspaper publisher & media entrepreneur
Mu·ril·lo \myù-'ri-(‚)lō; mù-'rē-(‚)ō, myú-\ Bartolomé Esteban 1617–1682 Span. painter
Mur·phy \'mər-fē\ William Parry 1892–1987 Am. physician
Mur·ray \'mər-ē, 'mə-rē\ (George) Gilbert Aimé 1866–1957 Brit. classical scholar
Murray Sir James Augustus Henry 1837–1915 Brit. lexicographer
Murray Joseph Edward 1919–2012 Am. surgeon
Murray Philip 1886–1952 Am. labor leader
Mur·row \'mər-(‚)ō, 'mə-(‚)rō\ Edward Roscoe 1908–1965 Am. journalist
Mu·sev·e·ni \mü-'sev-ə-nē\ Yoweri (Kayibanda Kaguta) 1944–   pres. of Uganda (1986–   )
Mu·shar·raf \‚mù-'shär-əf\ Pervez 1943–   Pakistani gen.; pres. of Pakistan (2001–08)
Mus·set \myü-'sā\ (Louis-Charles-) Alfred de 1810–1857 Fr. poet
Mus·so·li·ni \‚mü-sə-'lē-nē, ‚mù-\ Be·ni·to \bə-'nē-(‚)tō\ 1883–1945 *Il Du·ce* \ēl-'dü-(‚)chā\ Ital. Fascist premier (1922–43)
Mus·sorg·sky \mù-'sòrg-skē, -'zòrg-\ Mo·dest \mō-'dest\ Petrovich 1839–1881 Russ. composer
Mu·tsu·hi·to \‚müt-sə-'hē-(‚)tō\ 1852–1912 *Mei·ji* \'mā-(‚)jē\ emp. of Japan (1867–1912)
My·er·son \'mī-ər-sən\ Roger Bruce 1951–   Am. econ.
Myr·dal \'muer-‚däl, 'mər-, 'mir-\ Alva 1902–1986 née *Reimer; wife of Gunnar* Swed. sociologist & diplomat
Myrdal (Karl) Gunnar 1898–1987 Swed. econ.
My·ron \'mī-rən\ *fl ca* 480–440 B.C. Greek sculptor

Na·bo·kov \nə-'bò-kəf\ Vladimir Vladimirovich 1899–1977 Am. (Russ.-born) nov. & poet — **Na·bo·ko·vi·an** \‚nä-bə-'kō-vē-ən\ *adj*
Na·der \'nä-dər\ Ralph 1934–   Am. consumer advocate
Nai·du \'nī-(‚)dü\ Sarojini 1879–1949 Indian poet & reformer
Nai·paul \'nī-‚pòl\ Sir V(idiadhar) S(urajprasad) 1932–   Brit. (Trinidadian-born of Indian parents) writer
Na·ka·so·ne \‚nä-kə-'sō-nē\ Yasuhiro 1918–   prime min. of Japan (1982–87)
Na·math \'nä-məth\ Joseph (William) 1943–   Am. football player
Nam·bu \'näm-bü\ Yoichiro 1921–   Am. (Jp.-born) physicist
Na·mier \'na-‚mir\ Sir Lewis Bernstein 1888–1960 Brit. hist.
Nā·nak \'nä-nək\ 1469–1539 founder of the Sikh faith in India
Nan·sen \'nän(t)-sən, 'nan(t)-\ Frid·tjof \'fri-‚chòf\ 1861–1930 Norw. arctic explorer, zool., & statesman
Na·pier \'nä-pē-ər, -‚pir; nə-'pir\ Sir Charles James 1782–1853 Brit. gen.
Napier *or* **Ne·per** \'nä-pər\ John 1550–1617 Laird of *Mer·chis·ton* \'mər-kə-stən\ Scot. math.
Napier Robert Cornelis 1810–1890 1st Baron *Napier of Mag·da·la* \'mag-də-lə\ Brit. field marshal
Na·po·léon I \nə-'pōl-yən, -'pō-lē-ən\ *or* **Napoléon Bo·na·parte** \'bō-nə-‚pärt\ 1769–1821 emp. of the French (1804–15) — **Na·po·le·on·ic** \nə-‚pō-lē-'ä-nik\ *adj*
Napoléon II 1811–1832 Duc *de Reichstadt; son of Napoléon I & Marie Louise*
Napoléon III 1808–1873 *Louis-Napoléon; son of Louis Bonaparte & nephew of Napoléon I* emp. of the French (1852–71)
Na·po·li·ta·no \nə-‚pä-lə-'ta-nō\ Janet (Ann) 1957–   U.S. secy. of homeland security (2009–13)
Nar·vá·ez \när-'vä-‚ās\ Pánfilo de *ca* 1480–1528 Span. soldier
Nash \'nash\ John Forbes, Jr. 1928–   Am. math.
Nash Ogden 1902–1971 Am. poet
Nash *or* **Nashe** \'nash\ Thomas 1567–1601 Eng. satirist & dram.
Na·smyth \'nā-‚smith, 'näz-məth\ Alexander 1758–1840 Scot. painter
Nas·ser \'nä-sər, 'na-\ Ga·mal \gə-'mäl\ Ab·del \'äb-d°l\ 1918–1970 Egypt. polit.; pres. of Egypt (1956–70)
Nast \'nast\ Thomas 1840–1902 Am. (Ger.-born) cartoonist
Na·than \'nä-thən\ George Jean 1882–1958 Am. editor & drama critic
Na·tion \'nä-shən\ Car·ry \'ka-rē\ Amelia 1846–1911 née *Moore* Am. temperance agitator
Nav·ra·ti·lo·va \‚na-vrə-ti-'lō-və\ Martina 1956–   born *Martina Subertova* Am. (Czech-born) tennis player
Neb·u·cha·drez·zar II \‚ne-byə-kə-'dre-zər, -bə-\ *or* **Neb·u·chad·nez·zar** \-kəd-'ne-\ *ca* 630–562 B.C. Chaldean king of Babylon (605–562)
Nec·ker \nä-'ker, 'ne-kər\ Jacques 1732–1804 *father of Mme. de Staël* Fr. (Swiss-born) financier & statesman
Ne·gi·shi \ne-'gē-shē\ Ei-ichi \'āch\ 1935–   Jp.-Am. chem.
Neh·er \'nä-ər\ Erwin 1944–   Ger. biochem.
Neh·ru \'ner-(‚)ü, 'nä-(‚)rü\ Ja·wa·har·lal \‚jə-'wä-hər-‚läl\ 1889–1964 *son of Motilal* Indian nationalist; prime min. (1947–64)
Nehru Pan·dit \'pən-dət\ Mo·ti·lal \'mō-tə-‚läl\ 1861–1931 Indian nationalist
Neil·son \'nēl-sən\ William Allan 1869–1946 Am. (Scot.-born) educ.; pres. Smith College (1917–39)
Nel·son \'nel-sən\ Horatio 1758–1805 Viscount *Nelson* Brit. admiral
Nem·e·rov \'ne-mə-‚ròf, -‚ròv\ Howard 1920–1991 Am. writer; poet laureate (1988–90)
Ne·pos \'nē-‚päs, 'ne-\ Cornelius *ca* 100–*ca* 25 B.C. Rom. hist.
Ne·ri \'ner-ē, 'nä-rē\ Saint Philip 1515–1595 It. *Filippo Neri* Ital. founder (1564) of "Fathers of the Oratory"
Nernst \'nern(t)st\ Walther Hermann 1864–1941 Ger. physicist & chem.
Ne·ro \'nē-(‚)rō, 'nir-(‚)ō\ A.D. 37–68 *Nero Claudius Caesar Drusus Germanicus* orig. *Lucius Domitius Ahenobarbus* Rom. emp. 54–68 — **Ne·ro·ni·an** \ni-'rō-nē-ən\ *or* **Ne·ron·ic** \-'rä-nik\ *adj*
Ne·ru·da \nä-'rü-də, -(‚)thä\ Pablo 1904–1973 *Neftalí Ricardo Reyes Basoalto* Chilean poet & diplomat
Ner·va \'nər-və\ Marcus Cocceius *ca* A.D. 30–98 Rom. emp. (96–98)
Ner·vi \'ner-vē\ Pier Luigi 1891–1979 Ital. engineer & architect
Nes·to·ri·us \ne-'stòr-ē-əs\ *d ca* 451 patriarch of Constantinople (428–431)
Net·an·ya·hu \‚ne-tän-'yä-(‚)hü, -net-°n-\ Benjamin 1949–   Israeli diplomat & polit.; prime min. of Israel (1996–99; 2009–   )
Neu·mann \'nòi-‚män\ John von 1903–1957 Am. math.
Neu·rath \'nòi-‚rät\ Konstantin 1873–1956 Freiherr *von Neurath* Ger. diplomat
Nev·el·son \'ne-vəl-sən\ Louise 1900–1988 Am. (Russ.-born) sculptor
Neville Richard — see Earl of WARWICK
Nev·ins \'ne-vəl-‚sän\ Allan 1890–1971 Am. hist.
New·comb \'nü-kəm, 'nyü-\ Simon 1835–1909 Am. (Canad.-born) astron.
New·co·men \'n(y)ü-kə-mən, n(y)ù-'kə-\ Thomas 1663–1729 Eng. inventor
New·man \'nü-mən, 'nyü-\ Barnett 1905–1970 orig. *Baruch Newman* Am. painter
Newman John Henry 1801–1890 Eng. cardinal & writer
Newman Paul (Leonard) 1925–2008 Am. actor
New·ton \'nü-t°n, 'nyü-\ Sir Isaac 1642–1727 Eng. math. & physicist
Ney \'nā\ Michel 1769–1815 Duc *d'Elchingen; Prince de la Moskova* Fr. soldier; marshal of France
Nich·o·las \'ni-k(ə-)ləs\ Saint 4th cent. Christian prelate
Nicholas name of 2 emps. of Russia: **I** 1796–1855 (reigned 1825–55); **II** 1868–1918 (reigned 1894–1917)
Nicholas Russ **Ni·ko·lay Ni·ko·lay·e·vich** \'nyē-kə-‚lī-‚nyē-kə-'lī(-ə)-‚vyich\ 1856–1929 Russ. grand duke & army officer
Nicholas of Cu·sa \-'kyü-sə, -zə\ 1401–1464 Ger. cardinal, math., & philos.
Nich·ol·son \'ni-kəl-sən\ Ben 1894–1982 Brit. painter
Nicholson Jack 1937–   *John Joseph Nicholson* Am. actor
Ni·ci·as \'ni-shē-əs, -sē-\ *d* 413 B.C. Athenian gen. & statesman
Nick·laus \'ni-kləs\ Jack (William) 1940–   Am. golfer
Ni·co·let \‚nē-kə-'lā, -'let\ Jean 1598–1642 Fr. explorer in No. America
Ni·colle \nē-'kòl\ Charles-Jean-Henri 1866–1936 Fr. bacteriol.
Nic·ol·son \'ni-kəl-sən\ Sir Harold George 1886–1968 Eng. biographer & diplomat

Nie·buhr \'nē-,bůr, -bər\ Reinhold \'rīn-,hōld\ 1892–1971 Am. theol. — Nie·buhr·ian \nē-'bůr-ē-ən\ adj
Niel·sen \'nēl-sən\ Carl August 1865–1931 Dan. composer
Niem·ce·wicz \nyemt-'sā-vich\ Julian Ursyn 1758–1841 Pol. patriot & writer
Nie·mey·er \'nē-,mī(-ə)r\ Oscar 1907–2012 in full Oscar Niemeyer Soares Filho Braz. architect
Nie·möl·ler \'nē-,mə(r)l-ər, -,mœl-\ (Friedrich Gustav Emil) Martin 1892–1984 Ger. Protestant theol.
Nietz·sche \'nē-chə, -chē\ Friedrich Wilhelm 1844–1900 Ger. philos. — Nietz·sche·an \-chē-ən\ adj
Night·in·gale \'nīt-ᵊn-,gāl, -tiŋ-\ Florence 1820–1910 Eng. nurse & philanthropist
Ni·jin·ska \nə-'zhin-skə, -'jin-\ Bro·ni·sła·wa \,brä-nə-'slä-və\ 1891–1972 sister of following Russ. (Pol.-born) dancer & choreographer
Ni·jin·sky \nə-'zhin-skē, -'jin-\ Vas·lav \'vät-släf\ Fomich 1890–1950 Russ. dancer
Nils·son \'nil-sən\ Birgit (Märta) 1918–2005 Swed. soprano
Nim·itz \'ni-məts\ Chester William 1885–1966 Am. admiral
Nin \'nēn\ Anaïs 1903–1977 Am. (Fr.-born) author
Nix·on \'nik-sən\ Richard Milhous 1913–1994 Am. polit.; 37th pres. of the U.S. (1969–74) — Nix·on·esque \,nik-sə-'nesk\ or Nix·o·ni·an \nik-'sō-nē-ən, -nyən\ adj
Nkru·mah \en-'krü-mə, eŋ-\ Kwa·me \'kwä-mē\ 1909–1972 prime min. (1952–60) & 1st pres. (1960–66) of Ghana
No·bel \nō-'bel\ Alfred Bernhard 1833–1896 Swed. manuf., inventor, & philanthropist
No·bi·le \'nō-bə-,lā\ Umberto 1885–1978 Ital. arctic explorer & aeronautical engineer
No·da \'nō-dä\ Yoshihiko 1957–   prime min. of Japan (2011–12)
No·el-Ba·ker \,nō-əl-'bā-kər\ Philip John 1889–1982 Brit. polit.
No·gu·chi \nō-'gü-chē\ Hideyo 1876–1928 Am. (Jp.-born) bacteriol.
Noguchi Isamu 1904–1988 Am. sculptor
Nor·dau \'nòr-,daü\ Max Simon 1849–1923 orig. surname Süd·feld \'zǔt-,felt\ Ger. (Hung.-born) physician, author, & Zionist
Nor·den·skiöld \'nůr-d'ᵊn-,shəld, -,shůld, -,shēld\ Baron (Nils) Adolf Erik 1832–1901 Swed. arctic explorer
Nor·man \'nòr-mən\ Jessye 1945–   Am. soprano
Nor·ris \'nòr-əs, 'när-\ Benjamin Franklin 1870–1902 Frank Norris Am. nov.
Norris George William 1861–1944 Am. statesman
North \'nòrth\ Douglass Cecil 1920–   Am. econ.
North Frederick 1732–1792 Lord North Eng. statesman; prime min. (1770–82)
North Sir Thomas 1535–?1603 Eng. translator
Northcliffe Viscount — see Alfred C. W. HARMSWORTH
Nor·throp \'nòr-thrəp\ John Howard 1891–1987 Am. biochem.
Nor·ton \'nòr-tᵊn\ Charles Eliot 1827–1908 Am. author & educ.
Norton Thomas 1532–1584 Eng. lawyer & poet
Nos·tra·da·mus \,näs-trə-'dä-məs, ,nōs-, -'dā-\ 1503–1566 Michel de Notredame or Nostredame Fr. physician & astrologer
No·vo·se·lov \,nō-və-'se-,lóf\ Sir Konstantin (Sergeevich) 1974–   Russ.-Brit. physicist
Noyes \'nóiz\ Alfred 1880–1958 Eng. poet
No·yo·ri \nō-'yór-ē\ Ryoji 1938–   Jp. chem.
Nu·re·yev \nü-'rā-yəf\ Rudolf Hametovich 1938–1993 Russ.-born ballet dancer
Nurse \'nərs\ Sir Paul Maxime 1949–   Brit. geneticist
Nüss·lein–Vol·hard \'nǔs-,līn-'fól,härt\ Christiane 1942–   Ger. biol.
Nut·ting \'nə-tiŋ\ Wallace 1861–1941 Am. antiquarian
Nye \'nī\ Edgar Wilson 1850–1896 Bill Nye Am. humorist
Nye·re·re \ni-'rer-ē\ Julius Kambarage 1922–1999 African polit.; pres. of Tanzania (1964–1985)
Oake·shott \'ōk-,shät\ Michael (Joseph) 1901–1990 Brit. philos.
Oates \'ōts\ Joyce Carol 1938–   Am. writer
Oates Titus 1649–1705 Brit. fabricator of the Popish Plot
Oba·ma \ō-'bä-mə\ Barack (Hussein) 1961–   Am. polit.; 44th pres. of the U.S. (2009–17)
Oba·san·jo \ō-'bä-sän-jō\ Olusegun 1937–   pres. of Nigeria (1999–2007)
O'·Boyle \ō-'bói(-ə)l\ Patrick Aloysius 1896–1987 Am. cardinal
O'·Bri·an \ō-'brī-ən\ Patrick 1914–2000 orig. Richard Patrick Russ Brit. nov.
Obu·chi \ō-'bü-chē\ Keizo 1937–2000 prime min. of Japan (1998–2000)
O'·Ca·sey \ō-'kā-sē\ Sean \'shòn\ 1880–1964 orig. John Casey Irish dram.
Occleve — see Thomas HOCCLEVE
Ochs \'äks\ Adolph Simon 1858–1935 Am. newspaper publisher
Ock·ham or Oc·cam \'ä-kəm\ William of ca 1285–?1349 Eng. philos. — Ock·ham·is·tic or Oc·cam·is·tic \,ä-kə-'mis-tik\ adj
O'·Con·nell \ō-'kä-nᵊl\ Daniel 1775–1847 Irish nationalist
O'Connell William Henry 1859–1944 Am. cardinal
O'·Con·nor \ō-'kä-nər\ (Mary) Flannery 1925–1964 Am. writer
O'Connor Frank 1903–1966 pseud. of Michael John O'Donovan Irish author
O'Connor Sandra Day 1930–   Am. jurist
O'Connor Thomas Power 1848–1929 Tay Pay \'tā-'pā\ Irish journalist
Octavius — see AUGUSTUS
Odets \'dets\ Clifford 1906–1963 Am. dram.
Odo·a·cer \'ō-də-,wā-sər, ,ō-\ also Odo·va·car or Odo·va·kar \-və-kər\ 433–493 1st barbarian ruler of Italy (476–493)
Oe \'ō-e\ Kenzaburo 1935–   Jp. writer
Oeh·len·schlä·ger \'ə(r)-lən-,shlä-gər, 'œl-\ Adam Gottlob 1779–1850 Dan. poet & dram.
O'·Fao·láin \ō-fə-'lón\ Seán \'shòn\ 1900–1991 Irish author
Of·fen·bach \'ò-fən-,bäk, -,bäk\ Jacques 1819–1880 orig. Jacob Eberst Fr. composer
O'·Fla·her·ty \ō-'fla-(h)ər-tē\ Li·am \'lē-əm\ 1896–1984 Irish nov.
Og·den \'óg-dən, 'äg-\ Charles Kay 1889–1957 Brit. psychol.
Ogle·thorpe \'ō-gəl-,thòrp\ James Edward 1696–1785 Eng. philanthropist, gen., & founder of Georgia
Ögö·dei \'ò-gə-,dä\ also Oga·dai \-,dī\ or Og·dai \'ò-,dī\ or Uge·dei \'ü-gə-,dä\ 1185–1241 Mongol Khan (1229–41)

O'·Hara \ō-'ha-rə\ John Henry 1905–1970 Am. author
O'·Hig·gins \ō-'hi-gənz, ō-'ē-gən(t)s\ Bernardo 1778–1842 Liberator of Chile Chilean soldier & statesman
Ohm \'ōm\ Georg Simon 1787–1854 Ger. physicist
Ois·trakh \'óis-trək\ David Fyodorovich 1908–1974 Russ. violinist
O'·Keeffe \ō-'kēf\ Georgia (Totto) 1887–1986 Am. painter
O'·Kel·ly \ō-'ke-lē\ Seán \'shòn\ Thomas 1883–1966 Irish journalist; pres. of Republic of Ireland (1945–59)
Olaf \'ō-ləf, -,läf, -laf; 'ü-läf\ name of 5 kings of Norway: esp. Olaf I Trygg·va·son \'trig-və-sən\ ca 964–1000 (reigned 995–1000); Olaf II Har·alds·son \'ha-rəl(d)-sən\ Saint Olaf 995?–1030 (reigned 1016–28); Olaf V 1903–1991 (reigned 1957–91)
Olah \'ō-lə\ George Andrew 1927–   Am. (Hung.-born) chem.
Old·cas·tle \'ōl(d)-,ka-səl\ Sir John 1377?–1417 Baron Cob·ham \-'kä-bəm\ Eng. Lollard leader
Ol·den·bar·ne·velt \,ōl-dən-'bär-nə-vəlt\ Johan van 1547–1619 Du. statesman
Ol·den·burg \'ōl-dən-,bərg\ Claes Thure 1929–   Am. (Swed.-born) sculptor
Oliv·i·er \ō-'li-vē-,ā\ Laurence Kerr 1907–1989 Baron Olivier of Brighton Eng. actor
Ol·mert \'ōl-mərt\ Ehud \e-'hüd\ 1945–   prime min. of Israel (2006–09)
Olm·sted \'ōm-,sted, 'äm-, -stəd\ Frederick Law 1822–1903 Am. landscape architect
Omar Khay·yám \,ō-,mär,-kī-'yäm, ,ō-mər-, -'yam\ 1048?–1122 Pers. poet & astron.
O'Neal \ō-'nēl\ Shaquille (Rashaun) 1972–   Am. basketball player
O'·Neill \ō-'nēl\ Eugene Gladstone 1888–1953 Am. dram.
On·ions \'ən-yənz\ Charles Talbut 1873–1965 Eng. lexicographer
On·sa·ger \'òn-,sä-gər\ Lars 1903–1976 Am. (Norw.-born) chem.
Op·pen·heim \'ä-pən-,hīm\ Edward Phillips 1866–1946 Eng. nov.
Op·pen·hei·mer \'ä-pən-,hī-mər\ (Julius) Robert 1904–1967 Am. physicist
Or·ca·gna \òr-'kän-yə\ Andrea ca 1308–ca 1368 Andrea di Cione Florentine painter, sculptor, & architect
Or·czy \'òrt-sē\ Baroness Em·mus·ka \'e-məsh-kə\ 1865–1947 Eng. (Hung.-born) nov. & dram.
Orff \'òrf\ Carl 1895–1982 Ger. composer & educator
Or·i·gen \'òr-ə-jən, 'är-\ 185?–?254 Oregenes Adamantius Greek (Egypt.-born) Christian writer, teacher, & mystic
Or·lan·do \òr-'lan-(,)dō, -'län-\ Vittorio Emanuele 1860–1952 Ital. statesman
Or·man·dy \'òr-mən-dē\ Eugene 1899–1985 orig. Jenö Ormandy Blau Am. (Hung.-born) conductor
Oroz·co \ō-'rò-(,)skō\ José Clemente 1883–1949 Mex. painter
Orr \'òr\ Bobby 1948–   Robert Gordon Orr Am. (Canad.-born) ice hockey player
Ør·sted \'ə(r)-stəd, 'œr-\ Hans Christian 1777–1851 Dan. physicist & chem.
Or·te·ga (Saa·ve·dra) \òr-'tā-gə-sä-'vä-drə\ (José) Daniel 1945–   pres. of Nicaragua (1985–90; 2007–   )
Or·te·ga y Gas·set \-'tā-gə-,ē-gä-'set\ José 1883–1955 Span. philos., writer, & statesman
Or·well \'òr-,wel, -wəl\ George 1903–1950 pseud. of Eric Arthur Blair Eng. author — Or·well·ian \òr-'we-lē-ən\ adj
Os·born \'äz-bərn, -,bòrn\ Henry Fairfield 1857–1935 Am. paleontologist
Os·borne \'äz-bərn, -,bòrn, -,bórn\ John James 1929–1994 Brit. dram.
Osborne Thomas Mott 1859–1926 Am. penologist
Os·car II \'äs-kər\ 1829–1907 king of Sweden (1872–1907) & of Norway (1872–905)
Osce·o·la \,ä-sē-'ō-lə, ,ō-\ ca 1800–1838 Seminole Indian chief
Osh·er·off \'ä-shər-,óf\ Douglas Dean 1945–   Am. physicist
Os·ler \'ōs-lər, 'óz-\ Sir William 1849–1919 Canad. physician
Os·man I \ōs-'män\ 1258–ca 1326 founder of the Ottoman Empire
Os·si·etz·ky \,ä-sē-'et-skē\ Carl von 1889–1938 Ger. writer & pacifist
Ostrom \'ō-strəm\ Elinor 1933–2012 née Awan Am. political scientist
Ost·wald \'òst-,wóld, -,vóld\ Friedrich Wilhelm 1853–1932 Ger. physical chem. & philos.
Otis \'ō-təs\ Harrison Gray 1837–1917 Am. gen. & journalist
Otis James 1725–1783 Am. statesman in Revolution
Ot·ter·bein \'ä-tər-,bīn\ Philip William 1726–1813 Am. (Ger.-born) clergyman
Ot·to I \'ä-(,)tō\ 912–973 the Great Holy Rom. emp. (936–973)
Ot·way \'ät-,wā\ Thomas 1652–1685 Eng. dram.
Ouida — see Marie Louise de la RAMÉE
Ov·id \'ä-vəd\ 43 B.C.–A.D. 17 Publius Ovidius Naso Rom. poet — Ovid·ian \ä-'vi-dē-ən\ adj
Ow·en \'ō-ən\ Robert 1771–1858 Welsh social reformer
Owen Wilfred 1893–1918 Brit. poet
Ow·ens \'ō-ənz\ Jesse 1913–1980 James Cleveland Owens Am. track-and-field athlete
Ox·en·stier·na \'úk-sen-,sher-nä\ Count Axel Gustafsson 1583–1654 Swed. statesman
Oz \'äz, 'òz\ Amos 1939–   born Amos Klausner Israeli writer
Paa·si·ki·vi \'pä-sə-,kē-vē\ Ju·ho \'yü-(,)hó\ Kusti 1870–1956 Finn. businessman; pres. of Finland (1946–56)
Pa·chel·bel \pä-'kel-,bel, 'pä-kəl-,bel\ Johann 1653–1706 Ger. composer & organist
Pa·de·rew·ski \,pa-də-'ref-skē, -'rev-\ Ignacy \ēn-'yäs\ Jan \'yän\ 1860–1941 Pol. pianist, composer, & statesman
Pa·ga·ni·ni \,pa-gə-'nē-nē, ,pä-\ Niccolò 1782–1840 Ital. violinist
Page \'pāj\ Walter Hines 1855–1918 Am. journalist & diplomat
Pag·et \'pa-jət\ Sir James 1814–1899 Eng. surgeon & pathologist
Pahlavi — see REZA SHAH PAHLAVI & MOHAMMAD REZA PAHLAVI

\ə\ abut \ᵊ\ kitten, F table \ər\ further \a\ ash \ā\ ace \ä\ mop, mar
\aú\ out \ch\ chin \e\ bet \ē\ easy \g\ go \i\ hit \ī\ ice \j\ job
\ŋ\ sing \ō\ go \ò\ law \òi\ boy \th\ thin \th̲\ the \ü\ loot \ů\ foot
\y\ yet \zh\ vision, beige \k̲, ⁿ, œ, ɶ, ᵜ\ see Guide to Pronunciation

Paige \'pāj\ Satchel 1906?–1982 *Leroy Robert Paige* Am. baseball player

Paine Thomas 1737–1809 Am. (Eng.-born) polit. philos. & author

Pain·le·vé \paⁿ-lə-'vā\ Paul 1863–1933 Fr. math. & statesman

Pa·le·stri·na \ˌpa-lə-'strē-nə\ Giovanni Pierluigi da *ca* 1525–1594 Ital. composer

Pa·ley \'pā-lē\ Grace 1922–2007 née *Goodside* Am. writer

Paley William 1743–1805 Eng. theol. & philos.

Pal·grave \'pal-ˌgrāv, 'pȯl-\ Francis Turner 1824–1897 Eng. writer

Pa·lin \'pā-lən\ Sarah (Louise) 1964–   née *Heath* Am. polit.

Pal·la·dio \pə-'lä-dē-ˌō\ Andrea 1508–1580 Ital. architect

Palm·er \'pä-mər, 'päl-mər\ Arnold (Daniel) 1929–   Am. golfer

Palmer Daniel David 1845–1913 Am. founder of chiropractic

Palm·er·ston \'pä-mər-stən, 'päl-\ 3d Viscount 1784–1865 *Henry John Temple* Eng. statesman; prime min. (1855–58; 1859–65) — **Palm·er·sto·nian** \ˌpä-mər-'stō-nē-ən, ˌpäl-, -nyən\ *adj*

Palm·gren \'päm-grən, 'pälm-\ Selim 1878–1951 Finn. composer

Pa·muk \pä-'mük\ (Ferit) Orhan 1952–   Turk. writer

Pa·net·ta \pə-'ne-tə\ Leon (Edward) 1938–   U.S. secy. of defense (2011–13)

Pank·hurst \'paŋk-ˌhərst\ Emmeline 1858–1928 née *Goulden* Eng. suffragist

Pan·ni·ni *or* **Pa·ni·ni** \pä-'nē-(ˌ)nē\ Giovanni Paolo 1691–1765 Ital. painter

Pa·nof·sky \pä-'nȯf-skē\ Erwin 1892–1968 Am. (Ger.-born) art hist.

Pa·o·li \'paȯ-lē, pä-ō-(ˌ)lē\ Pasquale 1725–1807 Corsican patriot

Pa·pan·dre·ou \ˌpä-pän-'drā-ü\ Andreas Georgios 1919–1996 prime min. of Greece (1981–89; 1993–96)

Papandreou George 1952–   *son of prec.* prime min. of Greece (2009–11)

Pa·pen \'pä-pən\ Franz von 1879–1969 Ger. diplomat

Pa·pi·neau \pä-pē-'nō\ Louis Joseph 1786–1871 Canad. polit.

Pap·pen·heim \'pä-pən-ˌhīm, 'pa-\ Gottfried Heinrich 1594–1632 Graf *zu Pappenheim* Ger. gen.

Par·a·cel·sus \ˌpa-rə-'sel-səs\ 1493–1541 pseud. of *Philippus Aureolus Theophrastus Bombastus von Hohenheim* Swiss-born alchemist & physician

Pa·re·to \pə-'rā-(ˌ)tō\ Vilfredo 1848–1923 Ital. econ. & sociol.

Park \'pärk\ Mungo 1771–1806 Scot. explorer

Park Chung Hee \'pärk-'chəŋ-'hē\ 1917–1979 So. Korean leader (1961–79) & pres. (1963–79)

Park Geun–hye \'pärk-'gün-'hye\ 1952–   *dau. of prec.* pres. of So. Korea (2012–   )

Par·ker \'pär-kər\ Charlie 1920–1955 *Charles Parker, Jr.; Bird or Yardbird* Am. jazz musician

Parker Dorothy 1893–1967 née *Rothschild* Am. writer

Parker Sir Gilbert 1862–1932 Canad. author

Parker Matthew 1504–1575 Eng. theol.

Parker Theodore 1810–1860 Am. Unitarian clergyman

Parkes \'pärks\ Sir Henry 1815–1896 Austral. statesman

Park·man \'pärk-mən\ Francis 1823–1893 Am. hist.

Parks \'pärks\ Rosa 1913–2005 née *McCauley* Am. civil rights activist

Parley Peter — see Samuel Griswold GOODRICH

Par·men·i·des \pär-'me-nə-ˌdēz\ *b ca* 515 B.C. Greek philos.

Par·mi·gia·ni·no \ˌpär-mi-jä-'nē-(ˌ)nō\ *or* **Par·mi·gia·no** \-mə-'jä-(ˌ)nō\ 1503–1540 *Girolamo Francesco Maria Mazzola* Ital. painter

Par·nell \pär-'nel\ Charles Stewart 1846–1891 Irish nationalist

Parr Catherine — see CATHERINE

Par·ra (Sandoval) \'pä-rä\ Nicanor 1914–   Chilean poet

Par·ring·ton \'pa-riŋ-tən\ Vernon Louis 1871–1929 Am. lit. hist.

Par·rish \'pa-rish\ Maxfield Frederick 1870–1966 Am. painter

Par·sons \'pär-sᵊnz\ Talcott 1902–1979 Am. sociol.

Parsons William 1800–1867 3d Earl of *Rosse* Irish astron.

Pas·cal \pa-'skal, päs-'käl\ Blaise 1623–1662 Fr. math. & philos. — **Pas·cal·ian** \pa-'skal-ē-ən\ *adj*

Pa·šić \'pä-(ˌ)shich\ Nicola \'nē-kō-lä\ 1845–1926 Serbian statesman

Pas·sy \pa-'sē, pä-\ Paul-Édouard 1859–1940 Fr. phonetician

Pas·ter·nak \'pas-tər-ˌnak\ Boris Leonidovich 1890–1960 Soviet (Russ.-born) poet, nov., & translator

Pas·teur \pas-'tər\ Louis 1822–1895 Fr. chem. & microbiologist

Pa·ter \'pā-tər\ Walter Horatio 1839–1894 Eng. essayist & critic

Pat·more \'pat-ˌmȯr\ Coventry (Kersey Dighton) 1823–1896 Eng. poet

Pa·ton \'pā-tᵊn\ Alan Stewart 1903–1988 So. African writer

Pat·rick \'pa-trik\ Saint *fl* 5th cent. A.D. apostle & patron saint of Ireland

Pat·ter·son \'pa-tər-sən\ Floyd 1935–2006 Am. boxer

Pat·ti \'pa-tē, 'pä-\ Adelina 1843–1919 Ital. (Span.-born) soprano

Pat·ton \'pa-tᵊn\ George Smith 1885–1945 Am. gen.

Paul \'pȯl\ name of 6 popes: esp. III *(Alessandro Farnese)* 1468–1549 (pope 1534–49); V 1552–1621 (pope 1605–21); VI *(Giovanni Battista Montini)* 1897–1978 (pope 1963–78)

Paul \'paȯ-(ə)l\ Wolfgang 1913–1993 Ger. physicist

Paul I \'pȯl\ 1754–1801 emp. of Russia (1796–1801)

Paul I 1901–1964 king of Greece (1947–64)

Paul·ding \'pȯl-diŋ\ James Kirke 1778–1860 Am. author

Pau·li \'paȯ-lē\ Wolfgang 1900–1958 Am. (Austrian-born) physicist

Pau·ling \'pȯ-liŋ\ Li·nus \'lī-nəs\ Carl 1901–1994 Am. chem.

Paul·son \'pȯl-sən\ Henry Merritt, Jr. 1946–   U.S. secy. of treasury (2006–09)

Pau·lus \'paȯ-ləs\ Friedrich 1890–1957 Ger. field marshal

Pau·sa·ni·as \pȯ-'sā-nē-əs\ *fl* A.D. 143–176 Greek hist. & geographer

Pa·va·rot·ti \ˌpa-və-'rä-tē, ˌpä-\ Luciano 1935–2007 Ital. tenor

Pav·lov \'pav-ˌlȯf, 'pav-, -ˌlȯv\ Ivan Petrovich 1849–1936 Russ. physiol. — **Pav·lov·ian** \pav-'lȯ-vē-ən, 'lȯ-; -'lȯ-fē-\ *adj*

Pav·lo·va \'pav-lə-və, pav-'lō-\ Anna 1882–1931 Russ. ballerina

Pay·ton \'pā-tᵊn\ Walter (Jerry) 1954–1999 Am. football player

Paz \'päs, 'päz\ Octavio 1914–1998 Mex. author

Pea·body \'pē-ˌbä-dē, -bə-dē\ Endicott 1857–1944 Am. educ.

Peabody George 1795–1869 Am. merchant & philanthropist

Pea·cock \'pē-ˌkäk\ Thomas Love 1785–1866 Eng. nov. & poet

Peale \'pēl\ Charles Willson 1741–1827 & his bro. James 1749–1831 & Charles's son Rembrandt 1778–1860 Am. painters

Pear·son \'pir-sᵊn\ Karl 1857–1936 Eng. math.

Pearson Lester Bowles 1897–1972 prime min. of Canada (1963–68)

Pea·ry \'pir-ē\ Robert Edwin 1856–1920 Am. polar explorer

Pe·dro \'pā-drō, -drü\ Dom; name of 2 emps. of Brazil: I 1798–1834 (reigned as emp. 1822–31; as king of Portugal 1826); II 1825–1891 (reigned 1831–89)

Peel \'pēl\ Sir Robert 1788–1850 Eng. statesman

Peele \'pēl\ George 1556–1596 Eng. dram. & poet

Pei \'pā\ I(eoh) M(ing) 1917–   Am. (Chin.-born) architect

Peirce \'pərs, 'pirs\ Charles Sanders 1839–1914 Am. physicist, math., & logician — **Peirc·ean** \'pər-sē-ən, 'pir'-\ *adj*

Pei·sis·tra·tus *or* **Pi·sis·tra·tus** \pi-'sis-trə-təs, pə-\ *d* 527 B.C. Athenian tyrant

Pe·la·gius \pə-'lā-j(ē-)əs\ *ca* 354–after 418 Brit. monk & theol.

Pe·lé \'pā-ˌlā\1940–   orig. *Edson Arantes do Nascimento* Braz. soccer player

Pe·lop·i·das \pə-'lä-pə-dəs\ *d* 364 B.C. Theban gen.

Pe·lo·si \pə-'lō-sē\ Nancy (Patricia) 1940–   née *D'Alesandro* Am. polit.

Pe·ña Nie·to \'pān-yä-'nyä-tō\ Enrique 1966–   pres. of Mexico (2012–   )

Pen·de·rec·ki \ˌpen-də-'ret-skē\ Krzysztof 1933–   Pol. composer

Penn \'pen\ Sir William 1621–1670 Eng. admiral

Penn William 1644–1718 *son of prec.* Eng. Quaker & founder of Pennsylvania

Pen·rose \'pen-ˌrōz, pen-'rōz\ Sir Roger 1931–   Brit. math. & physicist

Pen·zi·as \'pent-sē-əs\ Arno Allan 1933–   Am. (Ger.-born) physicist

Pép·in III \'pe-pən\ 714?–768 *the Short* king of the Franks (751–768) *adj*

Pepys \'pēps\ Samuel 1633–1703 Eng. diarist — **Pepys·ian** \'pēp-sē-ən\ *adj*

Per·cy \'pər-sē\ Sir Henry 1364–1403 *Hotspur* Eng. soldier

Percy Thomas 1729–1811 Eng. antiquarian & poet

Percy Walker 1916–1990 Am. writer

Per·el·man \'per-əl-mən *(his own pron.)*, 'pər(-ə)l-\ S(idney) J(oseph) 1904–1979 Am. writer

Per·es \'per-(ˌ)ez\ Shimon 1923–   born *Szymon Perski* Israeli (Pol.-born) prime min. (1984–86; 1995–96); pres. (2007–   )

Pe·rez \pə-'rez\ Thomas E(dward) 1961–   U.S. secy. of labor (2013–   )

Pé·rez de Cuél·lar \'per-es-thä-'kwä-yär\ Javier 1920–   Peruvian U.N. official; secy.-gen. (1982–91)

Pé·rez Gal·dós \'per-əs-(ˌ)gäl-'dȯs\ Benito 1843–1920 Span. writer

Per·go·le·si \ˌpər-gə-'lā-zē, ˌpər-gə-'lä-sē\ Giovanni Battista 1710–1736 Ital. composer

Per·i·cles \'per-ə-ˌklēz\ *ca* 495–429 B.C. Athenian statesman — **Per·i·cle·an** \ˌper-ə-'klē-ən\ *adj*

Per·kins \'pər-kənz\ Frances 1880–1965 Am. public official

Perl \'pərl\ Martin (Lewis) 1927–   Am. physicist

Perl·man \'per(-ə)l-mən, 'pər(-ə)l-\ Itzhak 1945–   Am. (Israeli-born) violinist

Perl·mut·ter \'pərl-ˌmə-tər\ Saul 1959–   Am. astrophysicist

Pe·rón \pā-'rōn, pə-\ Juan Domingo 1895–1974 Argentine polit.; pres. of Argentina (1946–55; 1973–74)

Per·rault \pə-'rō, pe-\ Charles 1628–1703 Fr. writer

Per·rin \pə-'raⁿ(n), pe-\ Jean-Baptiste 1870–1942 Fr. physicist

Per·ry \'per-ē\ Bliss 1860–1954 Am. educ. & critic

Perry Matthew Calbraith 1794–1858 Am. commodore

Perry Oliver Hazard 1785–1819 *bro. of prec.* Am. naval officer

Perse St. John — see Aléxis Saint-Léger LÉGER

Per·shing \'pər-shiŋ, -zhiŋ\ John Joseph 1860–1948 Am. gen.

Per·sius \'pər-shəs, 'pər-sē-əs\ A.D. 34–62 *Aulus Persius Flaccus* Rom. satirist

Pe·ru·gi·no \ˌper-ə-'jē-(ˌ)nō\ *ca* 1450–1523 *Pietro di Cristoforo Vannucci* Ital. painter

Pes·ta·loz·zi \ˌpes-tə-'lät-sē\ Johann Heinrich 1746–1827 Swiss educ.

Pé·tain \pā-'taⁿ\ (Henri-) Philippe 1856–1951 Fr. gen.; marshal of France; premier of Vichy France (1940–44)

Pe·ter \'pē-tər\ *ca* 1050–1115 *the Hermit* Fr. preacher of the 1st Crusade

Peter I 1672–1725 *the Great* czar of Russia (1682–1725)

Peter I 1844–1921 king of Serbia (1903–21)

Peter II 1923–1970 king of Yugoslavia (1934–45)

Peter Lom·bard \'läm-ˌbärd\ *ca* 1100–1160 L. *Petrus Lombardus* Ital. theol. in France

Pe·ters \'pā-tərz, -tᵊrs\ Carl 1856–1918 Ger. explorer

Pe·ter·son \'pē-tər-sən\ Roger Tory 1908–1996 Am. ornithologist

Pe·ti·pa \pä-tē-'pä\ Marius (Alphonse) 1818–1910 Russ. (Fr.-born) dancer & choreographer

Pe·tő·fi \'pe-tə-fē\ Sán·dor \'shän-ˌdȯr\ 1823–1849 Hung. poet

Pe·trarch \'pē-ˌträrk\ 1304–1374 It. *Francesco Petrarca* Ital. poet — **Pe·trarch·an** \pē-'trär-kən, pe-\ *adj*

Pe·trie \'pē-trē\ Sir (William Matthew) Flin·ders \'flin-dərz\ 1853–1942 Eng. Egyptologist

Pe·tro·ni·us \pə-'trō-nē-əs\ *d* A.D. 66 in full prob. *Titus Petronius Niger* Rom. satirist — **Pe·tro·ni·an** \-nē-ən\ *adj*

Pet·ty \'pe-tē\ Sir William 1623–1687 Eng. polit. econ.

Pevs·ner \'pevz-nər\ Sir Nikolaus 1902–1983 Brit. (Ger.-born) art hist.

Phae·drus \'fē-drəs\ *ca* 15 B.C.–*ca* A.D. 50 Rom. fabulist

Phelps \'felps\ Edmund Strother 1933–   Am. econ.

Phelps Michael (Fred) 1985–   Am. swimmer

Phid·i·as \'fi-dē-əs\ *or* **Phei·di·as** \'fī-\ *fl ca* 490–430 B.C. Greek sculptor

Phil·ip \'fi-ləp\ 1639?–1676 *Met·a·com·et* \ˌme-tə-'kä-mət\ Wampanoag Indian chief

Philip name of 6 kings of France: esp. II *or* Philip Augustus 1165–1223 (reigned 1179–1223); IV *(the Fair)* 1268–1314 (reigned 1285–1314); VI 1293–1350 (reigned 1328–50)

Philip name of 5 kings of Spain: esp. II 1527–1598 (reigned 1556–98); V 1683–1746 (reigned 1700–24; 1724–46)

Philip Prince 1921–   *consort of Queen Elizabeth II of Great Britain* 3d Duke of *Edinburgh*

Philip II 382–336 B.C. king of Macedon (359–336)

Philip III 1396–1467 *the Good* Duke of Burgundy (1419–67)

Phi·lippe \fē-'lēp\ 1960–   *son of Albert II* king of Belgium (2013–   )

Phil·lips \'fi-ləps\ Wendell 1811–1884 Am. orator & reformer

Phillips William D(aniel) 1948–   Am. physicist

Phi·lo Ju·dae·us \'fī-(,)lō-jü-'dē-əs, -'dä-\ *ca* 13 B.C.–A.D. 45 to 50 Jewish philos. of Alexandria

Pho·ci·on \'fō-sē-,än\ *ca* 402–318 B.C. Athenian gen. & statesman

Phyfe \'fīf\ Duncan 1768–1854 Am. (Scot.-born) cabinetmaker

Pi·af \pē-'af\ Edith \ā-'dēt\ 1915–1963 orig. *Edith Giovanna Gassion* Fr. singer

Pia·get \pyä-'zhā\ Jean 1896–1980 Swiss psychol. — **Pia·get·ian** \,pē-ə-'je-tē-ən, pyä-'zhā-ən\ *adj*

Pi·a·no \pē-'ä-(,)nō\ Renzo 1937–   Ital. architect

Pi·card \pē-'kär, pi-'kärd\ Jean 1620–1682 Fr. astron.

Pi·cas·so \pi-'kä-(,)sō, -'ka-\ Pablo 1881–1973 Span. painter & sculptor in France — **Pi·cas·so·esque** \-,kä-sō-'esk, -,ka-\ *adj*

Pic·card \pi-'kär, -'kärd\ Auguste 1884–1962 Swiss physicist

Piccard Jacques (-Ernest-Jean) 1922–2008 *son of prec.* Swiss (Belg.-born) oceanographer

Pick·er·ing \'pi-k(ə-)riŋ\ Edward Charles 1846–1919 & his bro. William Henry 1858–1938 Am. astronomers

Pick·ett \'pi-kət\ George Edward 1825–1875 Am. Confed. gen.

Pi·co del·la Mi·ran·do·la \'pē-(,)kō-,de-lə-mə-'ran-də-lə, -'rän-\ Conte Giovanni 1463–1494 Ital. humanist

Pierce \'pirs\ Franklin 1804–1869 14th pres. of the U.S. (1853–57)

Pie·ro del·la Fran·ces·ca \'pyer-ō-,de-lə-fran-'ches-kə, -frän-\ *or* de·Fran·ces·chi \-dä-fran-'ches-kē, -frän-\ *ca* 1420–1492 Ital. painter

Pike \'pīk\ Zebulon Montgomery 1779–1813 Am. gen. & explorer

Pi·late \'pī-lət\ Pon·tius \'pän-chəs, 'pän-chəs\ *d* after A.D. 36 Rom. procurator of Judea (26–*ca* 36)

Pił·sud·ski \pil-'süt-skē, -'züt-\ Józef Klemens 1867–1935 Pol. gen. & statesman

Pin·chot \'pin-,shō\ Gifford 1865–1946 Am. conservationist & polit.

Pinck·ney \'piŋk-nē\ Charles Cotesworth 1746–1825 Am. statesman

Pin·dar \'pin-dər, -,där\ *ca* 522–*ca* 438 B.C. Greek poet

Pi·ñe·ra (Eche·ni·que) \pēn-'yer-ä-ä-chā-'nē-kā\ (Miguel Juan) Sebastián 1949–   pres. of Chile (2010–)

Pi·ne·ro \pə-'nir-(,)ō, -'ner-\ Sir Arthur Wing 1855–1934 Eng. dram.

Pin·ker·ton \'piŋ-kər-tən\ Allan 1819–1884 Am. (Scot.-born) detective

Pi·no·chet (Ugar·te) \pē-nō-'chet-ü-'gär-tä\ Augusto 1915–2006 Chilean gen.; pres. of Chile (1974–90)

Pin·ter \'pin-tər\ Harold 1930–2008 Eng. dram. — **Pin·ter·esque** \,pin-tə-'resk\ *adj*

Pin·tu·ric·chio \,pin-tə-'rē-kē-,ō\ *ca* 1454–1513 *Bernardino di Betto di Biago* Ital. painter

Pin·zón \pin-'zōn\ Martín Alonso *ca* 1441–1493 & his bro. Vicente Yáñez *ca* 1460–*ca* 1523 Span. navigators & explorers

Pioz·zi \pē-'ot-sē\ Hester Lynch 1741–1821 *Mrs. Thrale* \'thrā(ə)l\ Eng. writer

Pi·ran·del·lo \,pir-ən-'de-(,)lō\ Luigi 1867–1936 Ital. author — **Pi·ran·del·li·an** \-'de-lē-ən\ *adj*

Pi·ra·ne·si \,pir-ə-'nä-zē\ Giambattista 1720–1778 Ital. architect, painter, & engraver

Pi·sa·no \pi-'sä-(,)nō, -'zä-\ Giovanni *ca* 1250–after 1314 & his father Nicola *ca* 1220–1278(or 1284) Ital. sculptors

Pisistratus — see PEISISTRATUS

Pis·sa·ri·des \,pi-sə-'rē-(,)dēz\ Christopher A(ntoniou) 1948–   Cypriot-Brit. econ.

Pis·sar·ro \pə-'sär-(,)ō\ Camille 1830–1903 Fr. painter

Pis·ton \'pis-tən\ Walter Hamor 1894–1976 Am. composer

Pitt \'pit\ William 1708–1778 Earl of *Chatham; the Elder Pitt* Brit. statesman

Pitt William 1759–1806 *the Younger Pitt; son of prec.* Brit. statesman; prime min. (1783–1801; 1804–06)

Pitt–Riv·ers \'pit-'ri-vərz\ Augustus Henry 1827–1900 Eng. archaeol.

Pi·us \'pī-əs\ name of 12 popes: esp. **II** (*Enea Silvio Piccolomini* or *Ae·ne·as Sil·vi·us* \i-'nē-əs-'sil-vē-əs\ or *Syl·vi·us* \'sil-vē-əs\) 1405–1464 (pope 1458–64); **VII** 1742–1823 (pope 1800–23); **IX** 1792–1878 (pope 1846–78); **X** 1835–1914 (pope 1903–14); **XI** (*Ambrogio Damiano Achille Ratti*) 1857–1939 (pope 1922–39); **XII** (*Eugenio Pacelli*) 1876–1958 (pope 1939–58)

Pi·zar·ro \pə-'zär-(,)ō\ Francisco *ca* 1475–1541 Span. conquistador

Planck \'plänk\ Max Karl Ernst Ludwig 1858–1947 Ger. physicist

Plan·tin \plä[n]-'ta[n]\ Christophe *ca* 1520–1589 Fr. printer

Plath \'plath\ Sylvia 1932–1963 Am. poet

Pla·to \'plā-(,)tō\ *ca* 428–348(or 347) B.C. Greek philos.

Plau·tus \'plȯ-təs\ Titus Maccius *ca* 254–184 B.C. Rom. dram. — **Plau·tine** \'plȯ-,tīn\ *adj*

Ple·kha·nov \plə-'kä-,nȯf, pli-'kä-\ Georgy Valentinovich 1857–1918 Russ. Marxist philos.

Pliny \'pli-nē\ A.D. 23–79 *Gaius Plinius Secundus; the Elder* Rom. scholar

Pliny A.D. 61(or 62)–*ca* 113 *Gaius Plinius Caecilius Secundus; the Younger; nephew of prec.* Rom. author

Plo·ti·nus \plō-'tī-nəs\ A.D. 205–270 Rom. (Egypt.-born) philos. — **Plo·tin·i·an** \-'ti-nē-ən\ *adj*

Plu·tarch \'plü-,tärk\ *ca* A.D. 46–after 119 Greek biographer & moralist — **Plu·tarch·an** \plü-'tär-kən\ *or* **Plu·tarch·ian** \-kē-ən\ *adj*

Po·ca·hon·tas \,pō-kə-'hän-təs\ *ca* 1595–1617 *dau. of Powhatan* Am. Indian

Poe \'pō\ Edgar Allan 1809–1849 Am. poet & short-story writer

Poin·ca·ré \,pwa[n]-,kä-'rā\ (Jules-) Henri 1854–1912 Fr. math.

Poincaré Raymond 1860–1934 *cousin of prec.* Fr. statesman; pres. of France (1913–20)

Poit·i·er \'pwȯi-tē-,ā, 'pwa-\ Sidney 1924–   Am. actor & director

Po·lan·yi \pō-'län-yē\ John Charles 1929–   Canad. (Ger.-born) chem.

Pole \'pōl, 'pül\ Reginald 1500–1558 Eng. cardinal; archbishop of Canterbury (1556–58)

Po·len·ta \pō-'len-tə\ Francesca da *d* 1283(or 1284) *Fran·ces·ca da Ri·mi·ni* \,fran-'ches-kə-dä-'ri-mə-(,)nē, ,frän-, -'rē-\ Ital. noblewoman famous for tragic adulterous love affair

Po·li·tian \pə-'li-shən\ 1454–1494 *Angelo Poliziano* or *Angelo Ambrogini* Ital. classical scholar & poet

Po·lit·zer \'pä-lət-sər\ H(ugh) David 1949–   Am. physicist

Polk \'pōk\ James Knox 1795–1849 11th pres. of the U.S. (1845–49)

Pol·lio \'pä-lē-,ō\ Gaius Asinius 76 B.C.–A.D. 4 Rom. soldier & polit.

Pol·lock \'pä-lək\ Sir Frederick 1845–1937 Eng. jurist

Pollock (Paul) Jackson 1912–1956 Am. painter

Po·lo \'pō-(,)lō\ Mar·co \'mär-(,)kō\ 1254–1324 Venetian traveler

Pol Pot \'päl-'pät\ 1925–1998 orig. *Saloth Sar* Cambodian leader

Po·lyb·i·us \pə-'li-bē-əs\ *ca* 200–*ca* 118 B.C. Greek hist.

Pol·y·carp \'pä-li-,kärp\ Saint 2d cent. Christian martyr & Apostolic Father; bishop of Smyrna

Pol·y·cli·tus *or* Pol·y·clei·tus \,pä-li-'klī-təs\ 5th cent. B.C. Greek sculptor & architect

Pol·yc·ra·tes \pə-'li-krə-,tēz\ *d ca* 522 B.C. tyrant of Samos

Pol·y·do·rus \,pä-li-'dȯr-əs\ 1st cent. B.C. Rhodian sculptor

Pol·yg·no·tus \,pä-lig-'nō-təs\ *ca* 500–*ca* 440 B.C. Greek painter

Pom·bal \'päm-,bäl\ Marquês de 1699–1782 orig. *Sebastião (José) de Carvalho (e Mello)* Port. reformer

Pom·pa·dour \'päm-pə-,dȯr, -,dür\ Madame de 1721–1764 *Jeanne=Antoinette Poisson; mistress of Louis XV*

Pom·pey \'päm-pē\ 106–48 B.C. *Gnaeus Pompeius Magnus; the Great* Rom. gen. & statesman

Pom·pi·dou \'päm-pi-,dü\ Georges (-Jean-Raymond) 1911–1974 Fr. polit.; prime min. (1962–68) & pres. (1969–74) of France

Ponce de Le·ón \,pän(t)-sə-,dā-lē-'ōn, ,pänts-dē-, -'lē-ən\ Juan 1460–1521 Span. explorer

Pon·chi·el·li \,pȯŋ-kē-'e-lē\ Amilcare 1834–1886 Ital. composer

Pons \'pänz, 'pō[n]s\ Lily 1904–1976 Am. (Fr.-born) soprano

Pon·selle \pän-'sel\ Rosa Melba 1897–1981 Am. soprano

Pon·ti·ac \'pän-tē-,ak\ *ca* 1720–1769 Ottawa Indian chief

Pon·tor·mo \pȯn-'tȯr-(,)mō\ Jacopo da 1494–1557 orig. *Jacopo Carrucci* Ital. painter

Pope \'pōp\ Alexander 1688–1744 Eng. poet — **Pop·ian** *also* **Pop·ean** \'pō-pē-ən\ *adj*

Pope John 1822–1892 Am. gen.

Po·ple \'pō-pəl\ Sir John Anthony 1925–2004 Brit. math. in U.S.

Por·tal \'pȯr-t[ə]l\ Charles Frederick Algernon 1893–1971 1st Viscount *Portal of Hungerford* Brit. air marshal

Por·ter \'pȯr-tər\ Cole Albert 1891–1964 Am. songwriter

Porter David 1780–1843 & his son David Dixon 1813–1891 Am. naval officers

Porter Gene 1868–1924 née *Stratton* Am. nov.

Porter Katherine Anne 1890–1980 Am. writer

Porter Noah 1811–1892 Am. philos. & lexicographer

Porter William Sydney 1862–1910 pseud. *O. Hen·ry* \(')ō-'hen-rē\ Am. short-story writer

Post \'pōst\ Emily 1872–1960 née *Price* Am. columnist & writer

Po·tem·kin \pə-'tyȯm(p)-kən, pō-'tem(p)-\ Grigory Aleksandrovich 1739–1791 Russ. field marshal & statesman

Pot·ter \'pä-tər\ Beatrix 1866–1943 Brit. writer & illustrator

Potter Paul *or* Paulus 1625–1654 Du. painter

Pou·lenc \'pü-,laŋk\ Fran·cis \frä[n]-'sēs\ 1899–1963 Fr. composer

Pound \'paund\ Ezra Loomis 1885–1972 Am. poet — **Pound·ian** \'paun-dē-ən\ *adj*

Pound Roscoe 1870–1964 Am. jurist

Pound·mak·er \'paund-,mā-kər\ 1826–1886 Canad. Cree chief

Pous·sin \pü-'sa[n]\ Nicolas 1594–1665 Fr. painter

Pow·ell \'paù(-ə)l\ Adam Clayton 1908–1972 Am. clergyman & polit.

Pow·ell \'pō-əl, 'paù(-ə)l\ Anthony 1905–2000 Eng. writer

Powell Cecil Frank 1903–1969 Brit. physicist

Pow·ell \'paù(-ə)l\ Colin (Luther) 1937–   Am. gen.; U.S. secy. of state (2001–05)

Powell John Wesley 1834–1902 Am. geologist & explorer

Powell Lewis Franklin 1907–1998 Am. jurist

Pow·ell \'pō-əl, 'paù(-ə)l\ Michael Latham 1905–1990 Brit. filmmaker

Pow·ers \'paù(-ə)rz\ Hiram 1805–1873 Am. sculptor

Pow·ha·tan \,paù-ə-'tan, paù-'ha-t[ə]n\ 1550?–1618 *Wa-hun-sen-a-cawh* or *Wahunsonacock; father of Pocahontas* Am. Indian chief

Pow·ys \'pō-əs\ John Cow·per \'kü-pər\ 1872–1963 & his bros. Theodore Francis 1875–1953 & Llewelyn 1884–1939 Eng. authors

Pra·do Ugar·te·che \'prä-(,)dō-,ü-gär-'tä-chē\ Manuel 1889–1967 Peruvian banker; pres. of Peru (1939–45; 1956–62)

Pra·ja·dhi·pok \prə-'chä-ti-,päk\ 1893–1941 king of Siam (1925–35)

Pratt \'prat\ Edwin John 1883–1964 Canad. poet

Prax·it·e·les \prak-'si-tə-,lēz\ *fl* 370–330 B.C. Athenian sculptor — **Prax·it·e·le·an** \(,)prak-,si-tə-'lē-ən\ *adj*

Pre·ble \'pre-bəl\ Edward 1761–1807 Am. naval officer

Pregl \'prā-gəl\ Fritz 1869–1930 Austrian chem.

Pres·cott \'pres-kət *also* -,kät\ Edward C(hristian) 1940–   Am. econ.

Prescott William Hickling 1796–1859 Am. hist.

Pres·ley \'prez-lē, 'pres-\ Elvis (Aaron) 1935–1977 Am. singer

Pre·to·ri·us \prē-'tȯr-ē-əs\ Andries Wilhelmus Jacobus 1798–1853 & his son Marthinus Wessels 1819–1901 So. African Du. colonizers & soldiers

Pré·val \prā-'väl\ René (Garcia) 1943–   pres. of Haiti (1996–2001, 2006–11)

Pré·vost d'Ex·iles \prā-'vō-,deg-'zēl\ Antoine-François 1697–1763 *Abbé Prévost* Fr. writer

Price \'prīs\ (Mary) Le·on·tyne \lē-'än-,tēn; 'lē-ən-,, 'lā-\ 1927–   Am. soprano

Pride \'prīd\ Thomas *d* 1658 Eng. Parliamentarian commander

Priest·ley \'prēst-lē\ John Boynton 1894–1984 Eng. author

Priestley Joseph 1733–1804 Eng. clergyman & chem.

Pri·mo de Ri·ve·ra y Or·ba·ne·ja \'prē-(,)mō-thä-ri-'ver-ə-,ē-,ȯr-bə-'nä-(,)hä\ Miguel 1870–1930 Marqués *de Estella* Span. gen. & polit.

Primrose Archibald Philip — see ROSEBERY

Prior \'prī(-ə)r\ Matthew 1664–1721 Eng. poet

Pris·cian \'pri-shən, 'pri-shē-ən\ *fl* A.D. 500 *Priscianus Caesariensis* Latin grammarian at Constantinople

Pro·clus \'prō-kləs, 'prä-\ 410?–485 Greek philos.
Pro·co·pi·us \prə-'kō-pē-əs\ 6th cent. Byzantine hist.
Pro·di \'prō-dē\ Romano 1939–   Ital. prime min. (1996–98; 2006–08)
Pro·kof·iev \prə-'kóf-yəf, -,yef, -,yev\ Sergey Sergeyevich 1891–1953 Russ. composer — Pro·kof·iev·ian \-,kóf-'ye-vē-ən\ adj
Pro·per·tius \prō-'pər-sh(ē-)əs\ Sextus ca 50–ca 15 B.C. Rom. poet
Pro·tag·o·ras \prō-'ta-gə-rəs\ ca 485–410 B.C. Greek philos. — Pro·tag·o·re·an \-,ta-gə-'rē-ən\ adj
Prou·dhon \prü-'dōⁿ\ Pierre-Joseph 1809–1865 Fr. journalist
Proulx \'prü\ (Edna) Annie 1935–   Am. writer
Proust \'prüst\ Marcel (Valentin Louis Georges Eugène) 1871–1922 Fr. nov. — Proust·ian \'prü-stē-ən\ adj
Pru·si·ner \'prü-sə-nər\ Stanley Ben 1942–   Am. neurologist
Prynne \'prin\ William 1600–1669 Eng. Puritan pamphleteer
Przhe·val·sky \,pər-zhə-'väl-skē, ,pshə-'väl-\ Nikolay Mikhaylovich 1839–1888 Russ. explorer
Ptol·e·my \'tä-lə-mē\ name of 15 kings of Egypt 323–30 B.C.
Ptolemy 2d cent. A.D. Claudius Ptolemaeus Alexandrian astron.
Puc·ci·ni \pü-'chē-nē\ Giacomo 1858–1924 Ital. composer — Puc·ci·ni·an \-nē-ən\ adj
P'u–i \'pü-'ē, -'yē\ Henry 1906–1967 Hsüan-T'ung Chin. emp. (1908–12); last of Manchu dynasty; puppet emp. of Manchukuo (1934–45)
Pu·las·ki \pə-'las-kē, pyü-\ Kazimierz 1747–1779 Pol. soldier in Am. Revolution
Pu·lit·zer \'pü-lət-sər (family's pron.), 'pyü-\ Joseph 1847–1911 Am. (Hung.-born) journalist
Pull·man \'pül-mən\ George Mortimer 1831–1897 Am. inventor
Pu·pin \pyü-'pēn, pü-\ Michael Idvorsky 1858–1935 Am. (Hung.-born) physicist & inventor
Pur·cell \(,)pər-'sel\ Edward Mills 1912–1997 Am. physicist
Pur·cell \'pər-səl, (,)pər-'sel\ Henry 1659–1695 Eng. composer
Pur·ky·ně or Pur·kin·je \'pür-kən-,yā\ Jan Evangelista 1787–1869 Bohemian physiol.
Pu·sey \'pyü-zē\ Edward Bouverie 1800–1882 Eng. theol.
Push·kin \'püsh-kən\ Aleksandr Sergeyevich 1799–1837 Russ. poet — Push·kin·ian \püsh-'ki-nē-ən\ adj
Pu·tin \'pü-tin\ Vladimir Vladimirovich 1952–   pres. of Russian Federation (2000–08); prime min. (2008–12); pres. (2012–   )
Put·nam \'pət-nəm\ Israel 1718–1790 Am. gen. in Revolution
Putnam Rufus 1738–1824 cousin of prec. Am. gen. in Revolution
Pu·vis de Cha·vannes \pü-vē-də-shä-'vän, -vēs-; pyü-,vē(s)-\ Pierre= Cécile 1824–1898 Fr. painter & muralist
Pu·zo \'pü-zō\ Mario 1920–1999 Am. writer
Pye \'pī\ Henry James 1745–1813 Eng. poet laureate (1790–1813)
Pyle \'pī(-ə)l\ Ernest Taylor 1900–1945 Ernie Pyle Am. journalist
Pym \'pim\ John 1584–1643 Eng. statesman
Pyn·chon \'pin-chən\ Thomas 1937–   Am. writer — Pyn·chon·esque \,pin-chə-'nesk\ adj
Pyr·rhus \'pir-əs\ 319–272 B.C. king of Epirus (306–302; 297–272 B.C.)
Py·thag·o·ras \pə-'tha-gə-rəs, pī-\ ca 580–ca 500 B.C. Greek philos. & math.

Qad·da·fi var of GADDHAFI
Quarles \'kwór(-ə)lz, 'kwär(-ə)lz\ Francis 1592–1644 Eng. poet
Qua·si·mo·do \kwä-'zē-mə-,dō\ Salvatore \,säl-vä-'tō-(,)rä\ 1901–1968 Ital. poet & critic
Quayle \'kwāl\ James Danforth 1947–   Dan Quayle Am. polit.; vice pres. of the U.S. (1989–93)
Queensberry Marquis of — see DOUGLAS
Quercia, della Jacopo — see JACOPO DELLA QUERCIA
Ques·nay \kā-'nā\ François 1694–1774 Fr. physician & econ.
Que·zon y Mo·li·na \'kā-,sòn-,ē-mə-'lē-nə\ Manuel Luis 1878–1944 pres. of the Philippine Commonwealth (1935–44)
Quil·ler–Couch \'kwi-lər-'küch\ Sir Arthur Thomas 1863–1944 pseud. Q Eng. author
Quin·cy \'kwin-zē, 'kwin(t)-sē\ Josiah 1744–1775 Am. lawyer
Quine \'kwīn\ Willard Van Orman 1908–2000 Am. philos.
Quintero Serafín & Joaquín — see ÁLVAREZ QUINTERO
Quin·til·ian \kwin-'til-yən\ ca A.D. 35–ca 100 Marcus Fabius Quintilianus Rom. rhetorician
Ra·be·lais \'ra-bə-,lā, ,ra-bə-'lā\ François ca 1483–1553 Fr. humorist & satirist
Ra·bi \'rä-bē\ Isidor Isaac 1898–1988 Am. (Austrian-born) physicist
Ra·bin \rä-'bēn\ Yitzhak 1922–1995 prime min. of Israel (1974–77; 1992–95)
Rach·ma·ni·noff \räk-'mä-nə-,nóf\ Sergey Vasilyevich 1873–1943 Russ. composer, pianist, & conductor
Ra·cine \ra-'sēn, rə-\ Jean 1639–1699 Fr. dram. — Ra·cin·ian \ra-'si-nē-ən, rə-\ adj
Rack·ham \'ra-kəm\ Arthur 1867–1939 Brit. illustrator
Rad·cliffe \'rad-,klif\ Ann 1764–1823 née Ward Eng. nov.
Ra·detz·ky \rə-'det-skē\ Joseph 1766–1858 Graf Radetzky von Radetz Austrian field marshal
Rae \'rä\ John 1813–1893 Scot. explorer
Rae·burn \'rä-(,)bərn\ Sir Henry 1756–1823 Scot. painter
Rae·der \'rä-dər\ Erich 1876–1960 Ger. admiral
Rae·mae·kers \'rä-,mä-kərz, -kərs\ Louis 1869–1956 Du. cartoonist
Raf·san·ja·ni \,räf-sän-'jä-nē\ (Ali Akbar) Hashemi 1934–   pres. of Iran (1989–97)
Rag·lan \'ra-glən\ 1st Baron 1788–1855 FitzRoy James Henry Somerset Brit. field marshal
Rai·mon·di \rī-'män-dē, -'mōn-\ Marcantonio ca 1480–ca 1534 Ital. engraver
Rai·nier III \rə-'nir, ra-, rä-\ 1923–2005 prince of Monaco (1949–2005)
Rain·wa·ter \'rān-,wò-tər, -,wä-\ L(eo) James 1917–1986 Am. physicist
Ra·ja·go·pa·la·cha·ri \,rä-jə-,gō-pə-lə-'chär-ē\ Chakravarti 1879–1972 Indian polit.; gov.-gen. of India (1948–50)
Ra·joy (Brey) \rä-'hói(-,)brä\ Mariano 1955–   prime min. of Spain (2011–   )
Ra·leigh or Ra·legh \'rò-lē, 'rä- also 'ra-\ Sir Walter 1554–1618 Eng. courtier, navigator, & hist.
Ra·ma·krish·na \,rä-mə-'krish-nə\ 1836–1886 Hindu religious
Ra·man \'rä-mən\ Sir Chan·dra·se·kha·ra \,chən-drə-'shä-kə-rə\ Venkata 1888–1970 Indian physicist

Ra·ma·krish·nan \,rä-mə-'krish-,nän\ Ven·ka·tra·man \'veŋ-kä-,trä-män\ 1952–   U.S. (Indian-born) biochem.
Ra·meau \ra-'mō\ Jean-Philippe 1683–1764 Fr. composer
Ra·mée \rə-'mä\ Marie Louise de la 1839–1908 pseud. Oui·da \'wē-də\ Eng. nov.
Ra·món y Ca·jal \rə-'mōn-(,)ē-kə-'häl\ Santiago 1852–1934 Span. histologist
Ra·mos \'rä-(,)mōs\ Fidel Valdez 1928–   pres. of the Philippines (1992–98)
Ra·mos–Hor·ta \'rä-(,)mōs-'hór-tə\ José (Manuel) 1949–   East Timorese peace activist; pres. of East Timor (2007–12)
Ram·pal \räm-'päl\ Jean-Pierre 1922–2000 Fr. flutist
Ram·say \ram-zē\ James Andrew Broun 1812–1860 10th Earl & 1st Marquis of Dal·hou·sie \dal-'haú-zē\ Brit. colonial administrator
Ramsay Sir William 1852–1916 Brit. chem.
Ram·ses \'ram-,sēz\ or Ram·e·ses \'ra-mə-,sēz\ name of 11 kings of Egypt: esp. II (reigned 1304–1237 B.C.); III (reigned 1198–1166 B.C.)
Ram·sey \'ram-zē\ (Arthur) Michael 1904–1988 archbishop of Canterbury (1961–74)
Ramsey Norman Foster 1915–2011 Am. physicist
Rand \'rand\ Ayn \'īn\ 1905–1982 Am. (Russ.-born) writer
Ran·dolph \'ran-,dälf\ A(sa) Philip 1889–1979 Am. labor leader
Randolph Edmund Jennings 1753–1813 Am. statesman
Randolph John 1773–1833 John Randolph of Roanoke Am. statesman
Ran·jit Singh \'rən-jət-'siŋ\ 1780–1839 Lion of the Punjab founder of Sikh kingdom
Ran·ke \'räŋ-kə\ Leopold von 1795–1886 Ger. hist.
Ran·som \'ran(t)-səm\ John Crowe 1888–1974 Am. educ. & poet
Rao \'raú, 'rä-ō\ Pamulaparti Venkata Narasimha 1921–2004 prime min. of India (1991–96)
Ra·pha·el \'ra-fē-əl, 'rä-, 'rä-\ 1483–1520 It. Raffaello Sanzio Ital. painter — Ra·pha·el·esque \,ra-fē-ə-'lesk, ,rä-, ,rä-\ adj
Rask \'rask, 'räsk\ Rasmus Kristian 1787–1832 Dan. philologist & orientalist
Ras·mus·sen \'ras-mə-sən, 'räs-,mü-sⁿ\ Knud Johan Victor 1879–1933 Dan. explorer & ethnologist
Ras·pu·tin \ra-'spyü-tⁿn, -'spyü-, -'spü-\ Grigory Yefimovich 1872–1916 Russ. mystic
Rausch·en·berg \'raú-shən-,berg\ Robert 1925–2008 Am. artist
Ra·vel \'ra-,vel, ra-\ (Joseph) Mau·rice \mó-'rēs\ 1875–1937 Fr. composer — Ra·vel·ian \rə-'ve-lyən, ra-, -'vēl-\ adj
Raw·lin·son \'rò-lən-sən\ Sir Henry Cres·wicke \'kre-zik\ 1810–1895 Eng. orientalist
Ray \'rä\ John 1627–1705 Eng. naturalist
Ray Nicholas 1911–1979 born Raymond Nicholas Kienzle Am. film director
Ray \'rī, 'rä\ Satyajit 1921–1992 Indian filmmaker
Ray·burn \'rä-(,)bərn\ Samuel Taliaferro 1882–1961 Am. polit.
Ray·leigh \'rä-lē\ Lord 1842–1919 John William Strutt Eng. math. & physicist
Read \'rēd\ George 1733–1798 Am. statesman in Revolution
Read Sir Herbert 1893–1968 Eng. writer
Reade \'rēd\ Charles 1814–1884 Eng. nov. & dram.
Rea·gan \'rā-gən\ Ronald Wilson 1911–2004 Am. actor & polit.; 40th pres. of the U.S. (1981–89) — Rea·gan·esque \-gə-'nesk\ adj
Ré·au·mur \,rā-ō-'myür, -'mуer\ René-Antoine Ferchault de 1683–1757 Fr. naturalist & physicist
Ré·ca·mi·er \rā-'ka-mē-,ā, rä-kä-'myā\ Jeanne-Françoise-Julie-Adélaïde 1777–1849 Madame de Récamier née Bernard Fr. society wit
Red Cloud \'red-,klaúd\ 1822–1909 Sioux Indian chief
Red·grave \'red-,grāv\ Vanessa 1937–   Brit. actress
Red·mond \'red-mənd\ John Edward 1856–1918 Irish polit.
Re·don \rə-'dōⁿ\ Odilon 1840–1916 Fr. artist
Reed \'rēd\ John 1887–1920 Am. journalist, poet, & Communist
Reed Stanley Forman 1884–1980 Am. jurist
Reed Thomas Brackett 1839–1902 Am. polit.
Reed Walter 1851–1902 Am. army surgeon
Reg·u·lus \'re-gyə-ləs\ Marcus Atilius d ca 250 B.C. Rom. gen.
Rehn·quist \'ren-,kwist, 'ren-kwəst\ William Hubbs 1924–2005 Am. jurist; chief justice U.S. Supreme Court (1986–2005)
Reich \'rīk\ Steve 1936–   Stephen Michael Reich Am. composer
Reich Wilhelm 1897–1957 Austrian psychol. — Reich·ian \'rī-kē-ən\ adj
Reich·stein \'rīk-,shtīn, -,stīn\ Tadeus 1897–1996 Swiss (Pol.-born) chem.
Reid \'rēd\ Thomas 1710–1796 Scot. philos.
Rei·ner \'rī-nər\ Fritz 1888–1963 Am. (Hung.-born) conductor
Reines \'rānz\ Frederick 1918–1998 Am. physicist
Rein·hardt \'rīn-,härt\ Max 1873–1943 orig. surname Goldmann Austrian theater director
Re·marque \rə-'märk\ Erich Maria 1898–1970 Am. (Ger.-born) nov.
Rem·brandt \'rem-,brant also -,bränt\ 1606–1669 in full Rembrandt Harmensz (or Harmenszoon) van Rijn (or Ryn) Du. painter — Rem·brandt·esque \,rem-,bran-'tesk, -,bränt-\ adj
Rem·ing·ton \'re-miŋ-tən\ Frederic 1861–1909 Am. artist
Rem·sen \'rem(p)-sən, 'rem-zən\ Ira 1846–1927 Am. chem.
Re·nan \rə-'nä(n)\ Joseph Ernest 1823–1892 Fr. philologist & hist.
Re·ni \'rä-nē\ Guido 1575–1642 Ital. painter
Ren·ner \'re-nər\ Karl 1870–1950 pres. of Austria (1945–50)
Re·no \'rē-(,)nō\ Janet 1938–   U.S. atty. gen. (1993–2001)
Re·noir \'ren-,wär, ren-'\ Jean 1894–1979 son of P.-A. Fr. film director & writer
Renoir (Pierre-) Auguste 1841–1919 Fr. painter
Ren·wick \'ren-(,)wik\ James 1818–1895 Am. architect
Rep·plier \'re-,plir, -plē-ər\ Agnes 1855–1950 Am. essayist
Re·spi·ghi \rə-'spē-gē, re-\ Ottorino 1879–1936 Ital. composer
Res·ton \'res-tən\ James Barrett 1909–1995 Am. journalist
Retz \'rets, F 're(s)\ Cardinal de 1613–1679 Jean-François-Paul de Gondi Fr. ecclesiastic & polit.
Reuch·lin \'ròi-klən; -,klēn, ròi-'\ Johannes 1455–1522 Cap·nio \'kap-nē-,ō\ Ger. humanist
Reu·ter \'ròi-tər\ Baron Paul Julius von 1816–1899 orig. Israel Beer Josaphat Brit. (Ger.-born) journalist
Reu·ther \'rü-thər\ Walter Philip 1907–1970 Am. labor leader

Re·vere \ri-'vir\ Paul 1735–1818 Am. patriot & silversmith

Rex·roth \'reks-,rȯth\ Kenneth 1905–1982 Am. writer

Rey·mont \'rā-,mȯnt\ *or* **Rej·ment** \'rā-,ment\ Władysław \vlä-'di-,släf\ Stanisław \stä-'nē-,släf\ 1867–1925 Pol. nov.

Rey·naud \rā-'nō\ Paul 1878–1966 premier of France (1940)

Reyn·olds \'re-nᵊl(d)z\ Sir Joshua 1723–1792 Eng. painter

Re·za Shah Pah·la·vi \ri-'zä-'shä-'pa-lə-(,)vē, -'shȯ-\ 1878–1944 *father of Mohammad Reza Pahlavi* shah of Iran (1925–41)

Rhee \'rē\ Syngman \'siŋ-mən, 'sig-\ 1875–1965 So. Korean polit.; pres. of So. Korea (1948–60)

Rhodes \'rōdz\ Cecil John 1853–1902 Brit. administrator & financier in So. Africa

Rhond·da \'rän-də, -thə\ 1st Viscount 1856–1918 *David Alfred Thomas* Brit. industrialist & administrator

Rib·ben·trop \'ri-bən-,träp, -,trȯp\ Joachim von 1893–1946 Ger. diplomat

Ri·be·ra \rē-'ber-ə\ José (*or* Jusepe) de 1591–1652 *Lo Spa·gno·let·to* \lō-,spän-yə-'let-tō\ Span. painter & etcher in Naples

Ri·car·do \ri-'kär-(,)dō\ David 1772–1823 Eng. econ.

Rice \'rīs\ Condoleezza 1954– U.S. secy. of state (2005–09)

Rice Elmer Leopold 1892–1967 orig. *Elmer Reizenstein* Am. dram.

Rich \'rich\ Adrienne Cecile 1929–2012 Am. poet

Rich·ard \'ri-chərd\ name of 3 kings of England: **I** (*Coeur de Lion* \,kər-də-'lī-ən, -'lē-; -lē-'ōⁿ\) 1157–1199 (reigned 1189–99); **II** 1367–1400 (reigned 1377–99); **III** 1452–1485 (reigned 1483–85)

Rich·ard·son \'ri-chərd-sən\ Henry Handel 1870–1946 pseud. of *Ethel Florence Lindesay Richardson* Austral. nov.

Richardson Henry Hobson 1838–1886 Am. architect

Richardson Sir Owen Willans 1879–1959 Eng. physicist

Richardson Sir Ralph David 1902–1983 Brit. actor

Richardson Robert Coleman 1937–2013 Am. physicist

Richardson Samuel 1689–1761 Eng. nov.

Ri·che·lieu \'ri-shə-,lü, -shəl-,yü; rē-shə-ˡlyœ\ Duc de 1585–1642 *Armand-Jean du Plessis* Fr. cardinal & statesman

Ri·chet \rē-'shā\ Charles Robert 1850–1935 Fr. physiol.

Rich·ler \'rich-lər\ Mordecai 1931–2001 Canad. nov.

Rich·ter \'rik-tər\ Charles Francis 1900–1985 Am. seismologist

Rich·ter \'rik-tər, 'rik-\ Gerhard 1932– Ger. artist

Rich·ter Jean Paul Friedrich 1763–1825 pseud. *Jean Paul* \'zhäⁿ-ˡpau̇(-ə)l\ Ger. writer

Ric·i·mer \'ri-sə-mər\ Flavius *d* 472 Rom. gen.

Rick·en·back·er \'ri-kən-,ba-kər\ Edward Vernon 1890–1973 Am. aviator

Rick·o·ver \'ri-,kō-vər\ Hyman George 1900–1986 Am. admiral

Ride \'rīd\ Sally Kristen 1951–2012 Am. astronaut

Rid·ley \'rid-lē\ Nicholas *ca* 1503–1555 Eng. reformer & martyr

Ri·el \rē-'el\ Louis 1844–1885 Canad. insurgent

Rie·mann \'rē-,män\ Georg Friedrich Bernhard 1826–1866 Ger. math. — **Rie·mann·ian** \rē-'mä-nē-ən\ *adj*

Rien·zo \'ryent-sō\ Cola di 1313–1354 orig. *Nicola di Lorenzo* Ital. leader

Ries·man \'rēs-mən\ David 1909–2002 Am. social scientist

Riess \'rēs\ Adam G(uy) 1969– Am. astrophysicist

Riis \'rēs\ Jacob August 1849–1914 Am. (Dan.-born) social reformer

Ri·ley \'rī-lē\ James Whitcomb \'hwit-kəm, 'wit-\ 1849–1916 Am. poet

Ril·ke \'ril-kə, -kē\ Rainer \'rī-nər\ Maria 1875–1926 Ger. poet

Rim·baud \raⁿ(m)-'bō, 'ram-,\ (Jean-Nicholas) Arthur 1854–1891 Fr. poet

Rimini Francesca da — see POLENTA

Rim·sky–Kor·sa·kov \,rim(p)-skē-'kȯr-sə-,kȯf, -,kȯv, -,kȯr-sə-\ Nikolay Andreyevich 1844–1908 Russ. composer

Rí·os \'rē-ōs\ Juan Antonio 1888–1946 pres. of Chile (1942–46)

Rip·ley \'ri-plē\ George 1802–1880 Am. lit. critic & socialist

Ri·ve·ra \ri-'ver-ə\ Diego 1886–1957 Mex. painter

Riv·ers \'ri-vərz\ Larry 1923–2002 orig. *Yitzroch Loiza Grossberg* Am. artist

Ri·zal \ri-'zäl, -'säl\ José Protasio 1861–1896 Filipino patriot

Riz·zio \'rit-sē-,ō\ *or* **Ric·cio** \'ri-chē-,ō\ David *ca* 1533–1566 Ital. musician & favorite of Mary, Queen of Scots

Robbe–Gril·let \,rȯ-bə-grē-'yā\ Alain 1922–2008 Fr. writer

Rob·bins \'rä-bənz\ Jerome 1918–1998 Am. dancer & choreographer

Rob·ert I \'rä-bərt\ *d* 1035 *the Devil* Duke of Normandy (1027–35) *father of William the Conqueror*

Robert I 1274–1329 *the Bruce* \'brüs\ king of Scotland (1306–1329)

Robert Guis·card \-gē-'skär\ *ca* 1015–1085 *Robert de Hauteville* Norman mil. leader

Rob·erts \'rä-bərts\ Sir Charles George Douglas 1860–1943 Canad. poet

Roberts Frederick Sleigh 1832–1914 1st Earl *Roberts* Brit. field marshal

Roberts John Glover, Jr. 1955– Am. jurist; chief justice U.S. Supreme Court (2005–)

Roberts Kenneth 1885–1957 Am. nov.

Roberts Owen Josephus 1875–1955 Am. jurist

Roberts Sir Richard John 1943– Brit. biol. in U.S.

Robe·son \'rōb-sən\ Paul Bustill 1898–1976 Am. actor & singer

Robes·pierre \'rōbz-,pir, -,pyer; ,rō-bəs-'pyer\ Maximilien (-François-Marie-Isidore) de 1758–1794 Fr. revolutionary

Rob·in·son \'rä-bən-sən\ Edwin Arlington 1869–1935 Am. poet

Robinson George Frederick Samuel 1827–1909 1st Marquis & 2d Earl of *Ripon* Brit. statesman

Robinson Jackie 1919–1972 *Jack Roosevelt Robinson* Am. baseball player

Robinson James Harvey 1863–1936 Am. hist.

Robinson Sir Robert 1886–1975 Eng. chemist

Robinson Sugar Ray 1921–1989 orig. *Walker Smith, Jr.* Am. boxer

Ro·cham·beau \,rō-,sham-'bō\ Comte de 1725–1807 *Jean-Baptiste-Donatien de Vimeur* Fr. field marshal

Rocke·fel·ler \'rä-ki,fe-lər\ John Davison 1839–1937 & his son John Davison, Jr. 1874–1960 Am. oil magnates & philanthropists

Rockefeller Nelson Aldrich 1908–1979 *grandson & son of prec.* Am. polit.; vice pres. of the U.S. (1974–77)

Rock·ing·ham \'rä-kiŋ-əm, *US also* -kiŋ-,ham\ 2d Marquis of 1730–1782 *Charles Watson-Wentworth* Eng. statesman

Rock·ne \'räk-nē\ Knute \'nüt\ Kenneth 1888–1931 Am. (Norw.-born) football coach

Rock·well \'räk-,wel, -wəl\ Norman 1894–1978 Am. illustrator — **Rock·well·ian** \,räk-'we-lē-ən\ *adj*

Rod·bell \'räd-(,)bel\ Martin 1925–1998 Am. biochem.

Rod·gers \'rä-jərz\ Richard 1902–1979 Am. composer

Ro·din \rō-'daⁿ(n)\ (François-) Auguste (-René) 1840–1917 Fr. sculptor — **Ro·din·esque** \,rō-,da-'nesk\ *adj*

Rod·ney \'räd-nē\ George Brydges \'bri-jəz\ 1718–1792 1st Baron *Rodney* Eng. admiral

Roeb·ling \'rō-bliŋ\ John Augustus 1806–1869 Am. (Ger.-born) civil engineer

Roentgen — see RÖNTGEN

Roeth·ke \'ret-kē, 'reth-\ Theodore 1908–1963 Am. poet

Rog·ers \'rä-jərz\ Carl Ranson 1902–1987 Am. psychol.

Rogers Robert 1731–1795 Am. frontiersman

Rogers William Penn Adair 1879–1935 *Will Rogers* Am. actor & humorist

Ro·get \rō-'zhā, 'rō-,\ Peter Mark 1779–1869 Eng. physician & scholar

Roh Moo Hyun \'rō-'mü-'hyən, 'nō-\ 1946–2009 pres. of So. Korea (2003–08)

Rohr·er \'rȯr-ər\ Heinrich 1933–2013 Swiss physicist

Roh Tae Woo \'rō-'tā-'ü, 'nō-, -'wü\ 1932– pres. of So. Korea (1988–93)

Ro·kos·sov·sky \,rä-kə-'sȯf-skē, -'sȯv-\ Konstantin Konstantinovich 1896–1968 marshal of Soviet Union

Rolfe \'rälf\ John 1585–1622 Eng. colonist

Rol·land \rō-ˡläⁿ, rȯ-\ Romain 1866–1944 Fr. author

Röl·vaag \'rōl-,väg\ Ole \'ō-lə\ Edvart \'ed-,värt\ 1876–1931 Am. (Norw.-born) educ. & nov.

Ro·mains \rō-'maⁿ\ Jules 1885–1972 pseud. of *Louis-Henri-Jean Farigoule* Fr. author

Romano Giulio — see GIULIO ROMANO

Ro·ma·nov *or* **Ro·ma·noff** \rō-'mä-nəf, 'rō-mə-,näf\ Michael 1596–1645 1st czar (1613–45) of Russ. Romanov dynasty (1613–1917)

Rom·berg \'räm-,bərg\ Sigmund 1887–1951 Am. (Hung.-born) composer

Rom·mel \'rä-məl\ Erwin Johannes Eugen 1891–1944 Ger. field marshal

Rom·ney \'räm-nē, 'rəm-\ George 1734–1802 Eng. painter

Rom·ney \'räm-nē\ (Willard) Mitt 1947– Am. businessman and polit.

Ron·sard \rōⁿ-'sär\ Pierre de 1524–1585 Fr. poet

Rönt·gen *or* **Roent·gen** \'rent-gən, 'rȯnt-, -jən; 'ren-chən, 'rən-\ Wilhelm Conrad 1845–1923 Ger. physicist

Roo·se·velt \'rō-zə-,velt (*Roosevelts' usual pron.*), -,velt *also* 'rü-\ (Anna) Eleanor 1884–1962 née *Roosevelt, wife of F.D.* Am. humanitarian & writer

Roosevelt Franklin Delano \'de-lə-,nō\ 1882–1945 32d pres. of the U.S. (1933–45) — **Roo·se·velt·ian** \,rō-zə-'vel-tē-ən, -sh(ē-)ən\ *adj*

Roosevelt Theodore 1858–1919 26th pres. of the U.S. (1901–09)

Root \'rüt, 'rut\ Elihu 1845–1937 Am. lawyer & statesman

Ro·sa \'rō-zə\ Salvator 1615–1673 Ital. painter & poet

Rose \'rōz\ Irwin A. 1926– Am. biol.

Rose·bery \'rōz-,ber-ē, -b(ə-)rē\ 5th Earl of 1847–1929 *Archibald Philip Prim·rose* \'prim-,rōz\ Eng. statesman

Rose·crans \'rō-zə-,kranz, 'rōz-,kran(t)s\ William Starke 1819–1898 Am. gen.

Ro·sen·berg \'rō-zᵊn-,bərg, -,berg\ Alfred 1893–1946 Ger. Nazi & writer

Ro·sen·wald \'rō-zᵊn-,wȯld\ Julius 1862–1932 Am. merchant & philanthropist

Ross \'rȯs\ Betsy 1752–1836 née *Griscom* reputed maker of 1st Am. flag

Ross Sir James Clark 1800–1862 Scot. explorer

Ross Sir John 1777–1856 *uncle of prec.* Scot. explorer

Ross Sir Ronald 1857–1932 Brit. physician

Rosse Earl of — see WILLIAM PARSONS

Ros·set·ti \rō-'ze-tē, -'se-\ Christina Georgina 1830–1894 *sister of D.G.* Eng. author

Rossetti Dante Gabriel 1828–1882 Eng. painter & poet

Ros·si \'rō-sē\ Bruno 1905–1993 Am. (Ital.-born) physicist

Ros·si·ni \rō-'sē-nē, rȯ-\ Gioacchino \,jō-ə-'kē-nō\ Antonio 1792–1868 Ital. composer — **Ros·si·ni·an** \-'sē-nē-ən\ *adj*

Ros·tand \rō-'stäⁿ, 'räs-,tand\ Edmond 1868–1918 Fr. poet & dram.

Ros·tro·po·vich \,rä-strə-'pō-,vich, ,rə-strə-'pó-\ Mstislav (Leopoldovich) 1927–2007 Russ. cellist

Ro·ta \'rō-(,)tä\ Nino 1911–1979 Ital. composer

Rot·blat \'rät-,blat, 'rȯt-\ Sir Joseph 1908–2005 Brit. (Pol.-born) physicist

Roth \'rȯth\ Alvin E(liot) 1951– Am. econ.

Roth Philip (Milton) 1933– Am. writer

Roth·ko \'räth-(,)kō\ Mark 1903–1970 Am. (Russ.-born) painter

Roth·man \'rȯth-mən\ James E(dward) 1950– Am. biochem.

Roth·schild \'rȯth(s)-,chī(-ə)ld, 'rȯs-, *G* 'rōt-,shilt\ Mayer Amschel 1744–1812 Ger. financier

Rothschild Nathan Mayer 1777–1836 *son of prec.* financier in London

Rou·ault \rü-'ō\ Georges 1871–1958 Fr. painter

Rou·get de Lisle \(,)rü-zhā-də-'lēl\ Claude-Joseph 1760–1836 Fr. army officer & composer

Rou·ha·ni \rō-'hä-nē\ Hassan 1948– pres. of Iran (2013–)

Rous·seau \rü-'sō, 'rü-,\ Henri (-Julien-Félix) 1844–1910 *le Douanier* Fr. painter

Rousseau Jean-Jacques 1712–1778 Fr. (Swiss-born) philos. & writer — **Rous·seau·esque** \,rü-sō-'esk, ,rü-\ *or* **Rous·seau·ian** \-'sō-ē-ən\ *adj*

Rousseau (Pierre-Étienne-) Théodore 1812–1867 Fr. painter

\ə\ abut \ᵊ\ kitten, F table \ər\ further \a\ ash \ā\ ace \ä\ mop, mar \au̇\ out \ch\ chin \e\ bet \ē\ easy \g\ go \i\ hit \ī\ ice \j\ job \ŋ\ sing \ō\ go \ȯ\ law \ȯi\ boy \th\ thin \th̷\ the \ü\ loot \u̇\ foot \y\ yet \zh\ vision, beige \k, ⁿ, œ, ᴜᴇ, ᵜ\ *see* Guide to Pronunciation

Rous·seff \rü-'sef\ Dilma (Vana) 1947–   pres. of Brazil (2011–)
Rowe \'rō\ Nicholas 1674–1718 Eng. poet & dram.; poet laureate (1715–18)
Row·land \'rō-lənd\ Frank Sherwood 1927–2012 Am. chem.
Row·land·son \'rō-lən(d)-sən\ Thomas 1756–1827 Eng. caricaturist
Row·ling \'rō-liŋ\ J(oanne) K(athleen) 1965–   Brit. writer
Ro·xas y Acu·ña \'rō-,häs-,ē-ə-'kün-yə\ Manuel 1892–1948 Philippine statesman; pres. of the Philippine Republic (1946–48)
Royce \'róis\ Josiah 1855–1916 Am. philos.
Rub·bia \'rü-bē-ə\ Carlo 1934–   Ital. physicist
Ru·bens \'rü-bənz\ Peter Paul 1577–1640 Flem. painter — **Ru·ben·si·an** \rü-ben-zē-ən\ adj
Ru·bin·stein \'rü-bən-,stīn\ An·ton \än-'tón\ 1829–1894 Russ. pianist & composer
Rubinstein Arthur 1887–1982 Am. (Pol.-born) pianist
Rudd \'rəd\ Kevin Michael 1957–   prime min. of Australia (2007–10; 2013)
Rud·olf \'rü-,dälf\ 1858–1889 archduke & crown prince of Austria
Rudolf I 1218–1291 Holy Rom. emp. (1273–91); 1st of the Hapsburgs
Ruis·dael or **Ruys·dael** \'rīz-,däl, 'rīs-\ Jacob van 1628(or 1629)–1682 & his uncle Salomon van ca 1602–1670 Du. painters
Rums·feld \'rəmz-,feld\ Donald Henry 1932–   U.S. secy. of defense (1975–77; 2001–06)
Run·cie \'rən(t)-sē\ Robert Alexander Kennedy 1921–2000 archbishop of Canterbury (1980–91)
Rund·stedt \'rün(t)-,shtet\ (Karl Rudolf) Gerd von 1875–1953 Ger. field marshal
Ru·ne·berg \'rü-nə-,bərg, -,ber-ē\ Johan Ludvig 1804–1877 Finn. poet
Run·yon \'rən-yən\ (Alfred) Da·mon \'dā-mən\ 1884–1946 Am. author — **Run·yon·esque** \,rən-yə-'nesk\ adj
Ru·pert \'rü-pərt\ Prince 1619–1682 Count Palatine of Rhine & Duke of Bavaria Eng. (Ger.-born) Royalist gen. & admiral
Rush \'rəsh\ Benjamin 1745–1813 Am. physician & patriot
Rush·die \'rəsh-(,)dē, 'rush-\ Sir (Ahmed) Salman 1947–   Brit. (Indian-born) writer
Rusk \'rəsk\ (David) Dean 1909–1994 U.S. secy. of state (1961–69)
Rus·ka \'rús-kə\ Ernst August Friedrich 1906–1988 Ger. physicist
Rus·kin \'rəs-kən\ John 1819–1900 Eng. essayist, critic, & reformer — **Rus·kin·ian** \,rəs-'ki-nē-ən\ adj
Rus·sell \'rə-səl\ Bertrand Arthur William 1872–1970 3d Earl Russell grandson of John Eng. math. & philos.
Russell Bill 1934–   William Felton Russell Am. basketball player
Russell Charles Taze 1852–1916 Am. religious leader
Russell George William 1867–1935 pseud. Æ \'ā-ē, 'ä\ Irish author
Russell John 1792–1878 1st Earl Russell of Kingston Russell Brit. statesman; prime min. (1846–52; 1865–66)
Russell Lillian 1861–1922 Helen Louise Leonard Am. singer & actress
Rus·tin \'rəs-tən\ Bayard 1910–1987 Am. civil rights leader
Ruth \'rüth\ George Herman 1895–1948 Babe Ruth or the Babe Am. baseball player — **Ruth·ian** \'rü-thē-ən\ adj
Ruth·er·ford \'rə-thə(r)-fərd, -thə(r)-\ Ernest 1871–1937 1st Baron Rutherford of Nelson Brit. physicist
Rutherford Joseph Franklin 1869–1942 Am. leader of Jehovah's Witnesses
Rut·ledge \'rət-lij\ John 1739–1800 Am. statesman & jurist; chief justice U.S. Supreme Court (1795)
Ru·žič·ka \'rü-,zhich-kə, -,zich-, -,zhits-\ Leopold 1887–1976 Swiss (Croatian-born) chem.
Ry·an \'rī-ən\ (Lynn) Nolan, Jr. 1947–   Am. baseball player
Ryan Paul (Davis) 1970–   Am. polit.
Ry·der \'rī-dər\ Albert Pinkham 1847–1917 Am. painter
Sa·a·kash·vi·li \,sä-ä-käsh-'vē-lē\ Mikheil (Nikolozis dze) 1967–   pres. of Georgia (2004–07; 2008–13)
Saa·ri·nen \'sär-ə-nən\ Ee·ro \'er-(,)ō\ 1910–1961 Am. architect
Saarinen (Gottlieb) Eliel 1873–1950 father of prec. Finn. architect
Sa·ba·ti·ni \,sa-bə-'tē-nē, ,sä-\ Rafael 1875–1950 Eng. (Ital.-born) author
Sa·bin \'sā-bin\ Albert Bruce 1906–1993 Am. physician
Sac·a·ga·wea also **Sac·a·ja·wea** \,sa-kə-jə-'wē-ə\ 1786?–1812 Am. Indian guide
Sac·co \'sa-(,)kō\ Nicola 1891–1927 & **Van·zet·ti** \van-'ze-tē\ Bartolomeo 1888–1927 Am. (Ital.-born) anarchists
Sachs \'zäks, 'saks\ Hans 1494–1576 Ger. poet & Meistersinger
Sachs \'saks, 'zäks\ Nelly 1891–1970 Swed. (Ger.-born) dram. & poet
Sack·ville \'sak-,vil\ Thomas 1536–1608 1st Earl of Dorset Eng. poet & diplomat
Sackville–West \-'west\ Victoria Mary 1892–1962 Vita Eng. writer
Sā·dāt \sə-'dat, -'dät\ Anwar el- 1918–1981 pres. of Egypt (1970–81)
Sade, de \də-'säd\ Comte Donatien-Alphonse-François 1740–1814 Marquis de Sade Fr. writer of erotica
Sa·gan \sā-gən\ Carl Edward 1934–1996 Am. astron.
Sa·gan \sä-'gäⁿ\ Françoise 1935–2004 pseud. of Françoise Quoi·rez \kwä-rä\ Fr. writer
Sage \'sāj\ Russell 1816–1906 Am. financier
St. Den·is \sānt-'de-nəs, sənt-\ Ruth 1878–1968 Am. dancer & choreographer
Sainte–Beuve \saⁿt-'bœv; sānt-'bə(r)v, sənt-\ Charles-Augustin 1804–1869 Fr. critic & author
Saint–Gau·dens \sānt-'gó-dⁿnz, sənt-\ Augustus 1848–1907 Am. (Irish-born) sculptor
Saint–Just \saⁿ-'zhœst; sānt-'jəst, sənt-\ Louis (-Antoine-Léon) de 1767–1794 Fr. revolutionary
St. Lau·rent \saⁿ-lȯ-'räⁿ\ Louis Stephen 1882–1973 Canad. polit.; prime min. (1948–57)
Saint–Saëns \saⁿ-'säⁿs\ (Charles-) Camille 1835–1921 Fr. composer
Saints·bury \'sānts-,ber-ē, -b(ə-)rē\ George Edward Bateman 1845–1933 Eng. critic
Saint–Si·mon \saⁿ-sē-'mōⁿ\ (Claude-) Henri de (Rouvroy) 1760–1825 Comte de Saint-Simon Fr. philos. & social scientist
Saint–Simon Louis de Rouvroy 1675–1755 Duc de Saint-Simon Fr. soldier, statesman, & writer
Sai·on·ji \sī-'än-jē, -'ón-\ Prince Kimmochi 1849–1940 Jp. statesman
Sa·kha·rov \'sä-kə-,róf, -,kə-, -,róv\ Andrey Dmitriyevich 1921–1989 Russ. physicist

Sa·ki \'sä-kē\ — see H. H. MUNRO
Sak·mann \'zäk-,män, 'säk-\ Bert 1942–   Ger. biochem.
Sal·a·din \'sa-lə-,dēn, -dən; ,sa-lə-'dēn\ 1137(or 1138)–1193 Salāḥ Ad-dīn Yūsuf Ibn Ayyūb Syrian commander & vizier in Egypt
Sa·la·zar \,sa-lə-'zär, ,sä-\ Antonio de Oliveira 1889–1970 Port. dictator (1932–68)
Sal·a·zar \,sa-lə-'zär, ,sä-\ Ken(neth Lee) 1955–   U.S. secy. of interior (2009–13)
Sa·lie·ri \säl-'yer-ē\ Antonio 1750–1825 Austrian (Ital.-born) composer
Sa·li·nas de Gor·ta·ri \sä-'lē-näs-thä-gór-'tä-rē\ Carlos 1948–   pres. of Mexico (1988–94)
Sal·in·ger \'sa-lən-jər\ J(erome) D(avid) 1919–2010 Am. nov.
Salisbury 1st Earl of & 3d Marquis of — see CECIL
Salk \'sò(l)k\ Jonas Edward 1914–1995 Am. physician
Sal·lust \'sa-ləst\ ca 86–35(or 34) B.C. Gaius Sallustius Crispus Rom. hist. & polit. — **Sal·lus·ti·an** \sə-'ləs-tē-ən, sa-\ adj
Sal·o·mon \'sa-lə-mən\ Haym 1740–1785 Am. (Pol.-born) merchant
Sa·ma·ras \'sä-mä-'räs\ Antonis 1951–   prime min. of Greece (2012–)
Sam·paio \säm-'pī-ü\ Jorge (Fernando Branco de) 1939–   pres. of Portugal (1996–2006)
Sam·pras \'sam-prəs\ Pete 1971–   Peter Am. tennis player
Sam·u·el·son \'sam-yə(-wə)l-sən\ Paul Anthony 1915–2009 Am. econ.
Sand \'sand, 'säⁿ(n)d, 'säⁿ\ George 1804–1876 pseud. of Amandine-Aurore-Lucie (or -Lucile) Du·de·vant \dùed-'väⁿ, dùe-də-\ née Dupin Fr. writer
Sand·burg \'san(d)-,bərg\ Carl (August) 1878–1967 Am. author
San·gal·lo \,sän-'gä-(,)lō, säŋ-\ Giuliano da 1445?–1516 Florentine architect & sculptor
Sang·er \'saŋ-ər\ Frederick 1918–   Brit. biochem.
Sanger Margaret 1883–1966 née Higgins Am. birth-control activist
San Mar·tín \,san-(,)mär-'tēn, ,sän-\ José de 1778–1850 So. Am. soldier & statesman
San·ta An·na \,san-tə-'a-nə, ,sän-tə-'ä-nə\ Antonio López de 1794–1876 Mex. gen., revolutionary, & pres.
San·tan·der \,sän-,tän-'der, ,san-,tan-\ Francisco de Paula 1792–1840 Colombian gen. & polit.
San·ta·ya·na \,san-tə-'yä-nə, ,san-tē-'ä-, ,sän-\ George 1863–1952 Am. (Span.-born) poet & philos.
San·tos \'sän-,tōs\ Juan Manuel 1951–   pres. of Colombia (2010–)
San·tos–Du·mont \,san-təs-dü-'mänt, -dyü-; säⁿ-tōs-dùe-'mōⁿ\ Alberto 1873–1932 Fr. (Braz.-born) aviation pioneer
Sa·pir \sə-'pir\ Edward 1884–1939 Am. (Pol.-born) anthropol. & linguist
Sap·pho \'sa-(,)fō\ fl ca 610–ca 570 B.C. Greek poet
Sa·ra·ma·go \,sä-rä-'mä-gü\ José (de Sousa) 1922–2010 Port. nov.
Sar·da·na·pa·lus or **Sar·da·na·pal·lus** \,sär-də-'na-p(ə-)ləs, -də-nə-'pä-ləs\ king of Assyria; sometimes identified with Ashurbanipal (reigned 668–627 B.C.)
Sar·dou \sär-'dü\ Victorien 1831–1908 Fr. dram.
Sar·gent \'sär-jənt\ John Sing·er \'siŋ-ər\ 1856–1925 Am. painter
Sargent Thomas J(ohn) 1943–   Am. econ.
Sar·gon II \'sär-,gän, -gən\ king of Assyria (722–705 B.C.)
Sar·ko·zy \,sär-kō-'zē\ Nicolas (Paul Stéphane) 1955–   orig. surname Sarközy de Nagy-Bocsa pres. of France (2007–12)
Sar·noff \'sär-nóf\ David 1891–1971 Am. (Russ.-born) communications executive
Sa·roy·an \sə-'rói-ən\ William 1908–1981 Am. writer
Sar·tre \'särtrᵊ\ Jean-Paul 1905–1980 Fr. philos., dram., & nov. — **Sar·tre·an** or **Sar·tri·an** \'sär-trē-ən\ adj
Sas·soon \sa-'sün, sə-\ Siegfried Lorraine 1886–1967 Eng. writer
Sa·tie \sa-'tē, sä-\ Erik (-Alfred-Leslie) 1866–1925 Fr. composer
Sa·ud \sä-'üd\ 1902–1969 king of Saudi Arabia (1953–64)
Saus·sure \sō-'sʏr\ Ferdinand de 1857–1913 Swiss linguist — **Saus·sur·ean** also **Saus·sur·ian** \sō-'sʏr-ē-ən, sò-\ adj
Sav·age \'sa-vij\ Michael Joseph 1872–1940 prime min. of New Zealand (1935–40)
Sa·vim·bi \sə-'vim-bē\ Jonas (Malheiro) 1934–2002 Angolan guerilla leader & polit.
Sa·vo·na·ro·la \,sa-və-nə-'rō-lə, sə-,vä-nə-'rō-\ Gi·ro·la·mo \ji-'rò-lə-,mō\ 1452–1498 Ital. reformer
Saxe \'saks\ (Hermann) Maurice 1696–1750 Comte de Saxe Fr. gen.
Saxo Gram·mat·i·cus \,sak-(,)sō-grə-'ma-ti-kəs\ ca 1150–after 1216 Dan. hist.
Say·ers \'sā-ərz, 'serz\ Dorothy Leigh 1893–1957 Eng. writer
Sca·lia \skə-'lē-ə\ Antonin (Gregory) 1936–   Am. jurist
Scal·i·ger \'ska-lə-jər\ Joseph Justus 1540–1609 Fr. scholar
Scaliger Julius Caesar 1484–1558 father of prec. Ital. physician
Scar·lat·ti \skär-'lä-tē\ (Pietro) Alessandro Gaspare 1660–1725 & his son (Giuseppe) Domenico 1685–1757 Ital. composers
Schacht \'shäkt, 'shäkt\ (Horace Greeley) Hjal·mar \'yäl-,mär\ 1877–1970 Ger. financier
Schal·ly \'sha-lē\ Andrew Victor 1926–   Am. (Pol.-born) physiol.
Scharn·horst \'shärn-,hórst\ Gerhard Johann David von 1755–1813 Pruss. gen.
Schei·de·mann \'shī-də-,män\ Philipp 1865–1939 Ger. polit.
Schek·man \'shek-mən\ Randy W(ayne) 1948–   Am. biochem.
Schel·ling \'she-liŋ\ Friedrich Wilhelm Joseph von 1775–1854 Ger. philos. — **Schel·ling·ian** \she-'liŋ-ē-ən\ adj
Schelling Thomas (Crombie) 1921–   Am. econ.
Schia·pa·rel·li \skē-,ä-pə-'re-lē\ Giovanni Virginio 1835–1910 Ital. astron.
Schick \'shik\ Bé·la \'bā-lə\ 1877–1967 Am. (Hung.-born) pediatrician
Schie·le \'shē-lə\ Egon 1890–1918 Austrian artist
Schil·ler \'shi-lər\ (Johann Christoph) Friedrich von 1759–1805 Ger. poet & dram.
Schin·dler \'shind-lər\ Oskar 1908–1974 Ger. humanitarian
Schi·rach \'shē-,räk, -,räk\ Baldur von 1907–1974 Ger. Nazi polit.
Schle·gel \'shlā-gəl\ August Wilhelm von 1767–1845 Ger. author
Schlegel Friedrich von 1772–1829 bro. of prec. Ger. philos. & writer
Schlei·cher \'shlī-kər, -,kər\ Kurt von 1882–1934 Ger. soldier & polit.
Schlei·er·ma·cher \'shlī-ər-,mä-kər, -,kər\ Friedrich Ernst Daniel 1768–1834 Ger. theol. & philos.

Schle·sing·er \'shlā-ziŋ-ər, 'shle-sin-jər\ Arthur M(eier) 1888–1965 & his son Arthur M(eier) Jr. 1917–2007 Am. historians

Schlie·mann \'shlē-ˌmän\ Heinrich 1822–1890 Ger. archaeol.

Schmidt \'shmit\ Brian P(aul) 1967–   Am.-Austral. astrophysicist

Schmidt Helmut 1918–   chancellor of West Germany (1974–82)

Schna·bel \'shnä-bəl\ Ar·tur \'är-ˌtür\ 1882–1951 Austrian pianist & composer

Schnabel Julian 1951–   Am. artist & filmmaker

Schnitz·ler \'shnits-lər\ Arthur 1862–1931 Austrian dram. & nov.

Schoen·berg \'sha(r)n-ˌbərg, 'shœn-ˌberk\ Arnold Franz Walter 1874–1951 Am. (Austrian-born) composer — Schoen·berg·ian \-ˌbər-gē-ən\ adj

Scho·field \'skō-ˌfēld\ John McAllister 1831–1906 Am. gen.

Scholes \'shōlz\ Myron Samuel 1941–   Am. (Canad.-born) econ.

Scho·pen·hau·er \'shō-pən-ˌhaú(-ə)r\ Arthur 1788–1860 Ger. philos. — Scho·pen·hau·er·ian \ˌshō-pən-ˌhaú-(ə-)rē-ən\ adj

Schrief·fer \'shrē-fər\ John Robert 1931–   Am. physicist

Schrock \'shräk\ Richard (Royce) 1945–   Am. chem.

Schrö·der \'shrœ-dər, 'shrä-\ Gerhard 1944–   chancellor of Germany (1998–2005)

Schrö·ding·er \'shrœ-diŋ-ər, shrä-\ Erwin 1887–1961 Austrian physicist

Schu·bert \'shü-bərt, -ˌbert\ Franz Peter 1797–1828 Austrian composer — Schu·bert·ian \shü-'bər-tē-ən, -'ber-\ adj

Schulz \'shúlts\ Charles Monroe 1922–2000 Am. cartoonist

Schu·man \'shü-ˌmän, -mən\ Robert 1886–1963 Fr. statesman

Schu·man \'shü-mən\ William Howard 1910–1992 Am. composer

Schu·mann \'shü-ˌmän, -mən\ Robert 1810–1856 Ger. composer

Schum·pe·ter \'shùm-ˌpā-tər\ Joseph Alois 1883–1950 Am. (Czech‑born) econ.

Schurz \'shùrts, 'shərts\ Carl 1829–1906 Am. (Ger.-born) lawyer, gen., & polit.

Schusch·nigg \'shùsh-(ˌ)nik, -(ˌ)nig\ Kurt von 1897–1977 Austrian statesman

Schuy·ler \'skī-lər\ Philip John 1733–1804 Am. gen. & statesman

Schwartz \'shwòrts\ Melvin 1932–2006 Am. physicist

Schwarz·kopf \'shwòrts-ˌkòf, 'swòrts-\ H. Norman 1934–2012 Am. gen.

Schwarz·kopf \'shvärts-ˌköpf\ Dame (Olga Maria) Elisabeth Friederike aunt of prec. 1915–2006 Ger. (Pol.-born) soprano

Schweit·zer \'shwīt-sər, 'shvīt-, 'swīt-\ Albert 1875–1965 Fr. theol., philos., missionary physician, & music scholar

Scip·io \'si-pē-ˌō, 'ski-\ Aemilianus Af·ri·ca·nus \-ˌa-frə-'ka-nəs, -'kä-, -'kā-\ & Numantinus Publius Cornelius 185(or 184)–129 B.C. Scipio the Younger Rom. gen.

Scipio Africanus Publius Cornelius 236–184(or 183) B.C. Scipio the Elder Rom. gen.

Scopes \'skōps\ John Thomas 1900–1970 Am. teacher

Scor·se·se \skòr-'sä-sē, -'se-, -zē\ Martin 1942–   Am. film director

Scott \'skät\ Dred \'dred\ 1795?–1858 Am. slave

Scott Sir George Gilbert 1811–1878 Eng. architect

Scott Robert Falcon 1868–1912 Eng. polar explorer

Scott Sir Walter 1771–1832 Scot. poet & nov.

Scott Winfield 1786–1866 Am. gen.

Scotus Duns — see DUNS SCOTUS

Scotus John — see ERIGENA

Scria·bin or Skrya·bin \skrē-'ä-bən\ Aleksandr Nikolayevich 1872–1915 Russ. composer

Scribe \skrēb\ (Augustin-) Eugène 1791–1861 Fr. dram.

Scu·dé·ry \ˌskü-də-'rē, skœ-dā-'rē\ Madeleine de 1607–1701 Sa·pho \sä-'fō\ Fr. poet, nov., & hostess of literary salon

Sea·borg \'sē-ˌbòrg\ Glenn Theodore 1912–1999 Am. chem.

Sears \'sirz\ Richard Warren 1863–1914 Am. merchant

Se·be·lius \sə-'bēl-yəs\ Kathleen 1948–   née Gilligan U.S. secy. of health & human services (2009–   )

See \'sē\ Thomas Jefferson Jackson 1866–1962 Am. astron. & math.

See·ger \'sē-gər\ Peter 1919–   Pete Seeger Am. folksinger

Se·fe·ri·a·des \ˌse-fə-rə-'ä-thēs\ Giorgos Stylianou 1900–1971 pseud. George Se·fer·is \se-'fer-ēs\ Greek diplomat & poet

Se·gal \'sē-gəl\ George 1924–2000 Am. sculptor

Se·go·via \sā-'gō-vyə, -vē-ə\ Andrés 1893–1987 Span. guitarist & composer

Sei·fert \'zī-fərt\ Jaroslav 1901–1986 Czech poet

Se·ja·nus \si-'jā-nəs\ Lucius Aelius d A.D. 31 Rom. conspirator

Se·leu·cus I Ni·ca·tor \sə-ˌlü-kəs-'ni-ˌkā-tər\ 358(to 354)–281 B.C. Macedonian gen. & founder of Seleucid dynasty

Sel·kirk \'sel-ˌkərk\ Alexander 1676–1721 Scot. marooned sailor

Sel·ten \'zel-tᵊn\ Reinhard 1930–   Ger. econ.

Selz·nick \'selz-nik\ David O(liver) 1902–1965 Am. film producer

Se·me·nov \sə-'myó-nəf\ Nikolay Nikolayevich 1896–1986 Soviet chem.

Semmes \'semz\ Raphael 1809–1877 Am. Confed. admiral

Sen \'sen\ Amartya Kumar 1933–   Brit. (Indian-born) econ.

Sen·dak \'sen-dak\ Maurice Bernard 1928–2012 Am. illustrator & writer

Sen·e·ca \'se-ni-kə\ Lucius Annaeus 4 B.C.?–A.D. 65 Rom. statesman, dram., & philos. — Sen·e·can \-kən\ adj

Sen·ghor \seŋ-'gòr, säⁿ-'gòr\ Léopold Sédar 1906–2001 Senegalese poet & statesman; pres. of Senegal (1960–80)

Sen·nach·er·ib \sə-'na-kə-rəb\ d 681 B.C. king of Assyria (704–681)

Se·quoya or Se·quoy·ah or Se·quoia \si-'kwòi-ə\ ca 1760–1843 George Guess Cherokee Indian scholar

Ser·kin \'sər-kən\ Rudolf 1903–1991 Am. (Bohemian-born) pianist

Ser·ra \'ser-ə\ Ju·ní·pe·ro \hü-'nē-pə-ˌrō\ 1713–1784 orig. Miguel José Serra Span. missionary in Mexico & California

Ser·to·ri·us \(ˌ)sər-'tòr-ē-əs\ Quintus ca 123–72 B.C. Rom. gen. & statesman

Ser·ve·tus \(ˌ)sər-'vē-təs\ Michael 1511?–1553 Span. Miguel Serveto Span. theol. & physician

Ser·vice \'sər-vəs\ Robert William 1874–1958 Canad. writer

Ses·sions \'se-shənz\ Roger Huntington 1896–1985 Am. composer

Se·ton \'sē-tᵊn\ Saint Elizabeth Ann 1774–1821 Mother Seton née Bayley Am. religious leader

Seton Ernest Thompson 1860–1946 orig. surname Thompson Am. (Eng.-born) writer & illustrator

Seu·rat \sə-'rä\ Georges 1859–1891 Fr. painter

Seuss — see Theodor Seuss GEISEL

Se·ve·rus \sə-'vir-əs\ Lucius Septimius A.D. 146–211 Rom. emp. (193–211)

Sé·vi·gné \ˌsā-(ˌ)vēn-'yā, sā-'vēn-(ˌ)yā\ Marquise de 1626–1696 née (Marie) de Rabutin-Chantal Fr. letter writer

Sew·ard \'sü-ərd, 'sürd\ William Henry 1801–1872 Am. statesman; secy. of state (1861–69)

Sew·ell \'sü-əl\ Anna 1820–1878 Brit. writer

Sey·mour \'sē-ˌmòr\ Jane 1509?–1537 3d wife of Henry VIII of England & mother of Edward VI

Seyss–In·quart \'zīs-'iŋk-ˌvärt\ Ar·tur \'är-ˌtür\ 1892–1946 Austrian Nazi polit.

Shack·le·ton \'sha-kəl-tən\ Sir Ernest Henry 1874–1922 Brit. polar explorer

Shad·well \'shad-ˌwel, -wəl\ Thomas 1642?–1692 Eng. dram.; poet laureate (1688–92)

Shaftes·bury \'shaf(t)s-ˌber-ē, -b(ə-)rē\ 1st Earl of 1621–1683 Anthony Ashley Coo·per \'kü-pər, 'kú-\ Eng. statesman

Shāh Jā·han \shä-jə-'hän\ 1592–1666 Mogul emp. of India (1628–57 or 58)

Shahn \'shän\ Ben 1898–1969 Am. (Lithuanian-born) painter

Shake·speare \'shāk-ˌspir\ William 1564–1616 Eng. dram. & poet

Sha·mir \shə-'mēr\ Yitzhak 1915–2012 orig. surname Yizernitzky prime min. of Israel (1983–84; 1986–92)

Shan·non \'sha-nən\ Claude Elwood 1916–2001 Am. math. & computer scientist

Sha·piro \shə-'pir-(ˌ)ō\ Karl Jay 1913–2000 Am. poet & critic

Shap·ley \shap-lē\ Lloyd S(towell) 1923–   Am. econ.

Sha·rif \shä-'rēf\ Nawaz 1949–   prime min. of Pakistan (1990–93; 1997–99; 2013–   )

Sha·ron \'shär-ˌrōn, shä-\ Ariel 1928–   Israeli soldier & polit.; prime min. of Israel (2001–06)

Sharp \'shärp\ Phillip Allen 1944–   Am. biol.

Sharpe \'shärp\ William Forsyth 1934–   Am. econ.

Sharp·less \'shärp-ləs\ K(arl) Barry 1941–   Am. chem.

Shaw \'shò\ George Bernard 1856–1950 Brit. (Irish-born) author

Shawn \'shòn\ Ted 1891–1972 Am. dancer & choreographer

Shays \'shāz\ Daniel 1747?–1825 Am. soldier & insurrectionist

Shecht·man \'shekt-ˌmän\ Dan(iel) 1941–   Israeli chem.

Shee·ler \'shē-lər\ Charles 1883–1965 Am. painter & photographer

Shel·ley \'she-lē\ Mary Woll·stone·craft \'wúl-stən-ˌkraft\ 1797–1851 née Godwin; wife of P.B. Eng. nov.

Shelley Percy Bysshe \'bish\ 1792–1822 Eng. poet — Shel·ley·an \'she-lē-ən\ or Shel·ley·esque \ˌshe-lē-'esk\ adj

Shen·stone \'shen-ˌstōn, 'shen(t)-stən\ William 1714–1763 Eng. poet

Shep·ard \'she-pərd\ Alan Bartlett 1923–1998 Am. astronaut

Shepard Sam 1943–   orig. Samuel Shepard Rogers Am. dram.

Sher·a·ton \'sher-ə-tən\ Thomas 1751–1806 Eng. furniture designer

Sher·i·dan \'sher-ə-dən\ Philip Henry 1831–1888 Am. gen.

Sheridan Richard Brins·ley \'brinz-lē\ 1751–1816 Irish dram. & orator

Sher·man \'shər-mən\ James Schoolcraft 1855–1912 vice pres. of the U.S. (1909–12)

Sherman John 1823–1900 bro. of W.T. Am. statesman

Sherman Roger 1721–1793 Am. jurist & statesman

Sherman William Tecumseh 1820–1891 Am. gen. — Sher·man·esque \ˌshər-mə-'nesk\ adj

Sher·riff \'sher-əf\ Robert Cedric 1896–1975 Eng. writer

Sher·ring·ton \'sher-iŋ-tən\ Sir Charles Scott 1857–1952 Eng. physiol.

Sher·wood \'shər-ˌwúd also 'sher-\ Robert Emmet 1896–1955 Am. dram.

Shev·ard·nad·ze \ˌshe-vər(d)-'näd-zə\ Eduard Amvrosiyevich 1928–   Soviet foreign min. (1985–90; 1991); pres. of Republic of Georgia (1995–2003)

Shev·chen·ko or Sev·čen·ko \shef-'cheŋ-(ˌ)kō\ Taras Hryhorovych 1814–1861 Ukrainian poet

Shi·de·ha·ra \shē-də-'här-ə\ Baron Kijūrō 1872–1951 Jp. statesman

Shi·ge·mi·tsu \shē-gə-'mit-(ˌ)sü, ˌshi-\ Mamoru 1887–1957 Jp. diplomat

Shil·ler \'shi-lər\ Robert J(ames) 1946–   Am. econ.

Shi·mo·mu·ra \shē-ˌmō-'mü-rə\ Osamu 1928–   Jp. chem. in U.S.

Shin·seki \shin-'se-kē\ Eric (Ken) 1942–   Am. gen.; U.S. secy. of veterans affairs (2009–   )

Ship·ley \'ship-lē\ Dame Jenny 1952–   née Jennifer Mary Robson prime min. of New Zealand (1997–99)

Shi·ra·ka·wa \shē-rä-'kä-wə\ Hideki 1936–   Jp. chem.

Shi·rer \'shī(-ə)r-ər\ William Lawrence 1904–1993 Am. author

Shir·ley \'shər-lē\ James 1596–1666 Eng. dram.

Shock·ley \'shä-klē\ William Bradford 1910–1989 Am. physicist

Shoe·mak·er \'shü-ˌmā-kər\ Eugene Merle 1928–1997 Am. planetary geologist

Sholem Aleichem — see ALEICHEM

Sho·lo·khov \'shò-lə-ˌkóf, -ˌkóv\ Mikhail Aleksandrovich 1905–1984 Soviet (Russ.-born) nov.

Sho·sta·ko·vich \ˌshäs-tə-'kō-vich, ˌshòs-, -'kò-\ Dmi·try \də-'mē-trē\ Dmitriyevich 1906–1975 Soviet (Russ.-born) composer

Shull \'shəl\ Clifford Glenwood 1915–2001 Am. physicist

Shultz \'shúlts\ George Pratt 1920–   U.S. secy. of labor (1969–70); secy. of the treasury (1972–74); secy. of state (1982–89)

Shute \'shüt\ Nev·il \'ne-vəl\ 1899–1960 pseud. of Nevil Shute Norway Eng. aeronautical engineer & writer in Australia

Shver·nik \'shver-nik\ Nikolay Mikhaylovich 1888–1970 Soviet polit.; chairman of the Presidium (1946–54)

Si·be·lius \sə-'bāl-yəs, -'bā-lē-əs\ Jean \'zhän, 'yän\ 1865–1957 Finn. composer

Sid·dhār·tha Gau·ta·ma \si-'där-tə-'gaú-tə-mə, -'gō-\ *ca* 563–*ca* 483 B.C. *The Bud·dha* \'bü-də, 'bù-\ Indian philos. & founder of Buddhism

Sid·dons \'si-d⁵nz\ Sarah 1755–1831 née *Kemble* Eng. actress

Sid·ney \'sid-nē\ Sir Philip 1554–1586 Eng. poet, statesman, & soldier

Sie·mens \'sē-mənz\ Sir William 1823–1883 Brit. (Ger.-born) inventor

Sien·kie·wicz \shen-'kyä-vich\ Henryk 1846–1916 pseud. *Litwas* Pol. nov.

Sie·yès \sē-,ā-'yes\ Emmanuel-Joseph 1748–1836 Fr. revolutionary

Sig·is·mund \'si-gəs-mənd\ 1368–1437 Holy Rom. emp. (1433–37)

Si·gurds·son \'si-gərd-sən, -gərth-\ Jón \'yōn\ 1811–1879 Icelandic statesman & author

Si·kor·ski \sə-'kor-skē\ Władysław 1881–1943 Pol. gen. & statesman

Si·kor·sky \sə-'kor-skē\ Igor Ivan 1889–1972 Am. (Russ.-born) aeronautical engineer

Si·lo·ne \si-'lō-nē\ Ignazio 1900–1978 pseud. of *Secondo Tranquilli* Ital. author

Sil·va, da \də-'sēl-və\ Luiz Inácio Lula 1945–   pres. of Brazil (2003–10)

Si·me·non \,sē-mə-'nō⁵\ Georges (-Joseph-Christian) 1903–1989 Fr. (Belg.-born) writer

Sim·e·on Sty·li·tes \'si-mē-ən-stə-'lī-tēz, -,stī-\ Saint *ca* 390–459 Syrian ascetic & pillar dweller

Si·mon \sē-'mō⁵\ Claude (-Eugène-Henri) 1913–2005 Fr. writer

Si·mon \'sī-mən\ 1st Viscount 1873–1954 *John Allsebrook Simon* Brit. jurist & statesman

Simon Herbert Alexander 1916–2001 Am. econ.

Simon (Marvin) Neil 1927–   Am. dram.

Simon Paul (Frederic) 1941–   Am. singer & songwriter

Si·mon·i·des \sī-'mä-nə-,dēz\ **of Ceos** *ca* 556–*ca* 468? B.C. Greek poet

Sims \'simz\ Christopher A(lbert) 1942–   Am. econ.

Sims William Sow·den \'saú-d⁵n\ 1858–1936 Am. admiral

Si·na·tra \sə-'nä-trə\ Frank 1915–1998 *Francis Albert Sinatra* Am. singer & actor

Sin·clair \sin-'kler, siŋ-\ Upton Beall \'bel\ 1878–1968 Am. writer & polit.

Sing·er \'siŋ-ər\ Isaac Ba·shev·is \bə-'she-vəs\ 1904–1991 Am. (Pol.-born) author

Singer Isaac Merrit 1811–1875 Am. inventor

Singh \'siŋ, 'si⁵-hə\ Manmohan 1932–   prime min. of India (2004–   )

Si·quei·ros \si-'kā-(,)rōs\ David Alfaro 1896–1974 Mex. painter

Si·rāj-ud–Daw·lah \sə-,räj-ə-'daú-lə\ *ca* 1732–1757 nabob of Bengal (1756–57)

Sirleaf Ellen Johnson — see Ellen JOHNSON SIRLEAF

Sis·ley \'siz-lē, sēs-'le\ Alfred 1839–1899 Fr. (Eng.-born) painter

Sis·mon·di \sis-'män-dē, sēs-mō⁵-'dē\ J(ean-) C(harles-) L(éonard) Simonde de 1773–1842 Swiss hist. & econ.

Sit·ter \'si-tər\ Willem de 1872–1934 Du. astron.

Sit·ting Bull \si-tiŋ-'búl\ 1831–1890 *Tatanka Iyotake* Sioux leader

Sit·well \'sit-,wel, -wəl\ Sir George Reres·by \'rirz-bē\ 1860–1943 & his 3 children: Dame Edith 1887–1964; Sir Osbert 1892–1969; & Sa·chev·er·ell \sə-'she-və-rəl\ 1897–1988 Eng. authors

Skan·der·beg or **Scan·der·beg** \'skan-dər-,beg\ 1405–1468 orig. *George Kas·tri·o·ti* \,käs-trē-'ō-(,)tē\ Turk. *Is·kan·der Bey* \i-skän-'der-'bä\ Albanian hero

Skeat \'skēt\ Walter William 1835–1912 Eng. philologist

Skel·ton \'skel-t⁵n\ John *ca* 1460–1529 Eng. poet — **Skel·ton·ic** \skel-'tä-nik\ *adj*

Skin·ner \'ski-nər\ B(urrhus) F(rederic) 1904–1990 Am. psychol. — **Skin·ner·ian** \ski-'nir-ē-ən, -'ner-\ *adj*

Skinner Cornelia Otis 1901–1979 *dau.* of Otis Am. actress & writer

Skinner Otis 1858–1942 Am. actor

Sko·da \'skō-də, 'shkō-(,)dä\ Emil von 1839–1900 Czech engineer & industrialist

Skou \'skō\ Jens C(hristian) 1918–   Dan. biophysicist

Sla·ter \'slā-tər\ Samuel 1768–1835 Am. (Eng.-born) industrialist

Sloan \'slōn\ Alfred P(ritchard), Jr. 1875–1966 Am. industrialist

Sloan John French 1871–1951 Am. painter

Small·ey \'smò-lē\ Richard Errett 1943–2005 Am. chem.

Sme·ta·na \'sme-tə-nə\ Be·dřich \'be-dər-,zhik\ 1824–1884 Czech composer

Smith \'smith\ Adam 1723–1790 Scot. econ.

Smith Alfred Emanuel 1873–1944 Am. polit.

Smith Bessie 1894–1937 Am. blues singer

Smith David 1906–1965 Am. sculptor

Smith George E(lwood) 1930–   Am. physicist

Smith John *ca* 1580–1631 Eng. explorer & colonist

Smith Joseph 1805–1844 Am. founder of Mormon Church

Smith Michael 1932–2000 Canad. (Brit.-born) biochem.

Smith Stevie 1902–1971 orig. *Florence Margaret Smith* Brit. poet

Smith Sydney 1771–1845 Eng. essayist

Smith Vernon Lomax 1927–   Am. econ.

Smith Walter Be·dell \bə-'del\ 1895–1961 Am. gen. & diplomat

Smith William 1769–1839 Eng. geologist

Smith·ies \'smi-thēz\ Oliver 1925–   Am. (Brit.-born) geneticist

Smith·son \'smith-sən\ James 1765–1829 Brit. chem. & mineralogist & benefactor of Smithsonian Inst.

Smol·lett \'smä-lət\ Tobias George 1721–1771 Brit. author

Smoot \'smüt\ George F(itzgerald) 1945–   Am. astrophysicist

Smuts \'smɔts, 'smœts\ Jan \'yän\ Christiaan 1870–1950 So. African field marshal; prime min. (1919–24; 1939–48)

Snead \'snēd\ Sam 1912–2002 *Samuel Jackson Snead* Am. golfer

Snor·ri Stur·lu·son \'snór-ē-'stər-lə-sən, ,snär-\ 1179–1241 Icelandic statesman & hist.

Snow \'snō\ C(harles) P(ercy) 1905–1980 Baron *Snow* Eng. nov. & physicist

Snow·den \'snō-d⁵n\ Philip 1864–1937 1st Viscount *Snowden of Ick·orn·shaw* \'i-,kórn-,shō\ Eng. polit.

Sny·ders \'snī-dərs\ Frans 1579–1657 Flem. painter

Soar·es \'swär-ish\ Mário (Alberto Nobre Lopes) 1924–   prime min. of Portugal (1976–78; 1983–85) & pres. (1986–96)

Sobieski John — see JOHN III SOBIESKI

So·ci·nus \sō-'sī-nəs\ Faustus 1539–1604 *Fausto Soz·zi·ni* or *So·ci·ni* or *So·zi·ni* \sōt-'sē-nē\ Ital. theol.

Soc·ra·tes \'sä-krə-,tēz\ *ca* 470–399 B.C. Greek philos.

Sod·dy \'sä-dē\ Frederick 1877–1956 Eng. chem.

So·do·ma \sō-'dō-mə\ Il 1477–1549 *Giovanni Antonio Bazzi* Ital. painter

So·lis \sō-'lēs\ Hilda (Lucia) 1957–   U.S. secy. of labor (2009–13)

So·lon \'sō-lən, -,län\ *ca* 630–*ca* 560 B.C. Athenian lawgiver

So·low \'sō-lō\ Robert M(erton) 1924–   Am. econ.

Sol·ti \'shōl-tē\ Sir Georg 1912–1997 orig. *György Stern* Brit. (Hung.-born) conductor & pianist

Sol·zhe·ni·tsyn \,sōl-zhə-'nēt-sən, ,sòl-\ Aleksandr Isayevich 1918–2008 Russ. nov.

Sond·heim \'sänd-(,)hīm\ Stephen Joshua 1930–   Am. composer

Son·tag \'sän-,tag\ Susan 1933–2004 née *Rosenblatt* Am. writer

Soong Ai–ling \'süŋ-'ī-'liŋ\ 1888–1973 *wife of H.H. K'ung*

Soong Ch'ing–ling \'chiŋ-'liŋ\ 1892–1981 *wife of Sun Yat-sen*

Soong Mei–ling \-'mā-'liŋ\ 1897–2003 *wife of Chiang Kai-shek*

Soong Tzu–wen or **Tse–ven** or **Tsŭ–wên** \-'tsü-'wən\ 1894–1971 *T. V. Soong; bro. of prec.* Chin. financier & statesman

Soph·o·cles \'sä-fə-,klēz\ *ca* 496–406 B.C. Greek dram. — **Soph·o·cle·an** \,sä-fə-'klē-ən\ *adj*

Sor·del·lo \sór-'de-(,)lō\ *ca* 1200–before 1269 Ital. troubadour

So·rol·la y Bas·ti·da \sə-'ról-yə-,ē-bä-'stē-də, -'rói-ə-, -'stē-thə\ Joaquín 1863–1923 Span. painter

So·ros \'sòr-(,)ōs\ George 1930–   born *György Schwartz* Am. (Hung.-born) financier

So·to, de \thä-'sōt-(,)ō, di-\ Hernando 1496(or 1499 or 1500)–1542 Span. explorer

So·to·may·or \,sō-tō-,mī-'ór, -,mä-\ Sonia (Maria) 1954–   Am. jurist

Soult \sült\ Nicolas-Jean de Dieu 1769–1851 Duc *de Dal·ma·tie* \däl-mä-'sē\ Fr. soldier; marshal of France

Sou·sa \'sü-zə, 'sü-sə\ John Philip 1854–1932 *the March King* Am. bandmaster & composer

Sou·ter \'sü-tər\ David 1939–   Am. jurist

South \'saúth\ Robert 1634–1716 Eng. clergyman

Sou·they \'saú-thē, 'sə-thē\ Robert 1774–1843 Eng. author; poet laureate (1813–43)

Sou·tine \sü-'tēn\ Chaim 1893–1943 Fr. (Lith.-born) painter

So·yin·ka \shō-'yiŋ-ka\ Wo·le \'wó-lā\ 1934–   in full *Akinwande Oluwole Soyinka* Nigerian dram. & poet

Spaak \'späk\ Paul-Henri Charles 1899–1972 Belg. lawyer & polit.; premier (1938–39; 1947–50); secy.-gen. of NATO (1957–61)

Spaatz \'späts\ Carl 1891–1974 Am. admiral

Spark \'spärk\ Dame Muriel (Sarah) 1918–2006 née *Camberg* Brit. writer

Sparks \'spärks\ Jar·ed \'jer-əd\ 1789–1866 Am. hist.

Spar·ta·cus \'spär-tə-kəs\ *d* 71 B.C. Rom. slave & insurrectionist

Spell·man \'spel-mən\ Francis Joseph 1889–1967 Am. cardinal

Spe·mann \'shpā-,män\ Hans 1869–1941 Ger. embryologist

Spence \'spen(t)s\ A(ndrew) Michael 1943–   Am. econ.

Spen·cer \'spen(t)-sər\ Herbert 1820–1903 Eng. philos.

Spen·der \'spen-dər\ Stephen Harold 1909–1995 Eng. poet & critic

Speng·ler \'shpeŋ-lər, 'speŋ-\ Oswald 1880–1936 Ger. philos.

Spen·ser \'spen(t)-sər\ Edmund 1552–1599 Eng. poet — **Spen·se·ri·an** \spen-'sir-ē-ən\ *adj*

Sper·ry \'sper-ē\ Elmer Ambrose 1860–1930 Am. inventor

Sperry Roger Wolcott 1913–1994 Am. psychobiologist

Spiel·berg \'spēl-,bərg\ Steven (Allan) 1946–   Am. film director, writer, & producer — **Spiel·berg·ian** \,spēl-'bər-gē-ən\ *adj*

Spil·lane \spi-'lān\ Mickey 1918–2006 *Frank Morrison Spillane* Am. nov.

Spi·no·za \spi-'nō-zə\ Benedict de 1632–1677 Hebrew prename *Baruch* Du. philos.

Spit·te·ler \'shpi-tə-lər, 'spi-; 'shpit-lər, 'spit-\ Carl 1845–1924 pseud. *Felix Tan·dem* \'tän-,dem\ Swiss writer

Spock \'späk\ Benjamin McLane 1903–1998 Am. physician

Spode \'spōd\ Josiah 1754–1827 Eng. potter

Spru·ance \'sprü-ən(t)s\ Raymond Ames 1886–1969 Am. admiral

Spy·ri \'shpir-ē, 'spir-\ Johanna 1827–1901 née *Heusser* Swiss author

Staël, de \də-'stäl\ Mme. Anne-Louise-Germaine 1766–1817 née *Necker* Baronne de Staël-Holstein Fr. writer & hostess of literary salon

Stáhl·berg \'stòl-,bərg, -,ber-ē\ Kaarlo Ju·ho \'yü-(,)hō\ 1865–1952 Finn. statesman

Sta·lin \'stä-lən, 'stä-, -,lēn\ Joseph 1879–1953 *Iosif Vissarionovich Dzhu·gash·vi·li* \,jü-gash-'vē-lē\ Soviet leader

Stan·dish \'stan-dish\ Myles or Miles 1584?–1656 Am. colonist

Stan·is·lav·sky \,sta-ni-'släf-skē\ Konstantin 1863–1938 pseud. of *Konstantin Sergeyevich Alekseyev* Russ. actor, director, & producer

Stan·is·law I \'sta-nə-,slóv, -,släv\ **Lesz·czyn·ski** \lesh-'chin-skē\ 1677–1766 king of Poland (1704–09; 1733–35)

Stan·ley \'stan-lē\ Edward George Geoffrey Smith 1799–1869 Earl of *Derby* Brit. statesman

Stanley Sir Henry Morton 1841–1904 orig. *John Rowlands* Brit. explorer

Stan·ton \'stan-t⁵n\ Edwin McMasters 1814–1869 Am. lawyer & secy. of war (1862–68)

Stanton Elizabeth 1815–1902 née *Cady* Am. suffragist

Star·hem·berg \'stär-əm-,bərg, 'shtär-əm-,berk\ Ernst Rüdiger 1899–1956 Fürst *von Starhemberg* Austrian polit.

Stark \'shtärk, 'stärk\ Johannes 1874–1957 Ger. physicist

Stark \'stärk\ John 1728–1822 Am. gen. in Revolution

Sta·tius \'stä-sh(ē-)əs\ Publius Papinius *ca* A.D. 45–96 Rom. poet

Stau·ding·er \'shtaú-diŋ-ər, 'staú-\ Hermann 1881–1965 Ger. chem.

Steele \'stēl\ Sir Richard 1672–1729 Brit. essayist & dram.

Steen \'stān\ Jan 1626–1679 Du. painter

Ste·fans·son \'ste-fən-sən\ Vil·hjal·mur \'vil-,yaúl-mər\ 1879–1962 Am. (Canad.-born) explorer

Stef·fens \'ste-fənz\ (Joseph) Lincoln 1866–1936 Am. journalist

Stei·chen \'stī-kən\ Edward Jean 1879–1973 Am. photographer

Stein \'stīn\ Gertrude 1874–1946 Am. writer

Stein \'shtīn, 'stīn\ (Heinrich Friedrich) Karl 1757–1831 Freiherr *vom und zum Stein* Pruss. statesman
Stein·beck \'stīn-,bek\ John Ernst 1902–1968 Am. nov.
Stein·berg·er \'stīn-,bər-gər\ Jack 1921– Am. (Ger.-born) physicist
Stei·nem \'stī-nəm\ Gloria 1934– Am. feminist writer & editor
Stein·man \'stīn-mən\ Ralph M(arvin) 1943–2011 Canad.-Am. immunologist
Stein·metz \'shtīn-,mets, 'stīn-\ Charles Proteus 1865–1923 Am. (Ger.-born) electrical engineer
Steitz \'stīts\ Thomas A(rthur) 1940– Am. biochem.
Stel·la \'ste-lə\ Frank Philip 1936– Am. artist
Sten·dhal \sten-'däl, stan-, *F* staⁿ-'däl\ 1783–1842 pseud. of *Marie-Henri Beyle* \'bel\ Fr. writer — **Sten·dhal·ian** \-'däl-ē-ən\ *adj*
Ste·phen \'stē-vən\ *ca* 1097–1154 king of England (1135–54)
Stephen Sir Leslie 1832–1904 Eng. philos., critic, & biographer
Ste·phens \'stē-vənz\ Alexander Hamilton 1812–1883 Am. polit.; vice pres. of the Confed. states
Stephens James 1882–1950 Irish poet & nov.
Ste·phen·son \'stē-vən-sən\ George 1781–1848 Eng. inventor & founder of railroads
Stephenson Robert 1803–1859 *son of prec.* Eng. engineer
Stern \'stərn\ Isaac 1920–2001 Am. (Russ.-born) violinist
Stern Otto 1888–1969 Am. (Ger.-born) physicist
Stern·berg \'stərn-,bərg\ George Miller 1838–1915 Am. physician & bacteriol.
Sterne \'stərn\ Laurence 1713–1768 Brit. nov.
Stet·tin·i·us \stə-'ti-nē-əs, ste-\ Edward Reilly 1900–1949 Am. financier & statesman
Steu·ben \'stü-bən, 'styü-, 'shtói-\ Baron Friedrich Wilhelm (Ludolf Gerhard Augustin) von 1730–1794 Pruss.-born gen. in Am. Revolution
Ste·vens \'stē-vənz\ John 1749–1838 Am. inventor
Stevens John Paul 1920– Am. jurist
Stevens Thaddeus 1792–1868 Am. polit.
Stevens Wallace 1879–1955 Am. poet
Ste·ven·son \'stē-vən-sən\ Ad·lai \'ad-lē, -(,)lā\ Ewing 1835–1914 Am. polit.; vice pres. of U.S. (1893–97)
Stevenson Adlai Ewing 1900–1965 *grandson of prec.* Am. polit.
Stevenson Robert Louis Balfour 1850–1894 Scot. author
Stew·art \'stü-ərt, 'styü-; 'st(y)ùrt\ Du·gald \'dü-gəld\ 1753–1828 Scot. philos.
Stewart James Maitland 1908–1997 Am. actor
Stewart Potter 1915–1985 Am. jurist
Stewart Robert 1769–1822 Viscount *Cas·tle·reagh* \'ka-səl-,rā\ Eng. statesman
Steyn \'stīn\ Marthinus Theunis 1857–1916 So. African statesman
Stieg·litz \'stē-gləts, -,glits\ Alfred 1864–1946 Am. photographer
Stig·litz \'sti-glits\ Joseph Eugene 1943– Am. econ.
Stil·i·cho \'sti-li-,kō\ Flavius *ca* 365–408 Rom. gen. & statesman
Still \'stil\ Andrew Taylor 1828–1917 Am. founder of osteopathy
Stil·well \'stil-,wel, -wəl\ Joseph Warren 1883–1946 Am. gen.
Stim·son \'stim(p)-sən\ Henry Lewis 1867–1950 Am. statesman
Stin·nes \'shti-nəs, 'stin-\ Hugo 1870–1924 Ger. industrialist
Stir·ling \'stər-liŋ\ Sir James Frazer 1926–1992 Brit. architect
Stock·hau·sen \'shtók-,haú-zən, 'stäk-\ Karlheinz 1928–2007 Ger. composer & theorist
Stock·mar \'stäk-,mär\ Christian Friedrich 1787–1863 Baron *von Stockmar* Anglo-Belg. statesman
Stock·ton \'stäk-tən\ Francis Richard 1834–1902 *Frank R. Stockton* Am. writer
Stod·dard \'stä-dərd\ Richard Henry 1825–1903 Am. poet & critic
Sto·ker \'stō-kər\ Bram 1847–1912 Irish writer
Stokes \'stōks\ Sir Frederick Wilfrid Scott 1860–1927 Eng. engineer & inventor
Sto·kow·ski \stə-'kóf-skē, -'kóv- *also* -'kaù-\ Leopold (Antoni Stanislaw Boleslawawicz) 1882–1977 Am. (Eng.-born) conductor
Stone \'stōn\ Harlan Fiske 1872–1946 Am. jurist; chief justice U.S. Supreme Court (1941–46)
Stone Irving 1903–1989 orig. surname *Tennenbaum* Am. writer
Stone Lucy 1818–1893 Am. suffragist
Stoph \'shtóf, 'stóf\ Willi 1914–1999 prime min. of East Germany (1976–89)
Stop·pard \'stäp-,ärd\ Sir Tom 1937– orig. *Tomas Straussler* Brit. (Czech-born) playwright & screenwriter
Stör·mer \'stór-mər\ Horst Ludwig 1949– Am. (Ger.-born) physicist
Sto·ry \'stór-ē\ Joseph 1779–1845 Am. jurist
Story William Wetmore 1819–1895 *son of prec.* Am. sculptor
Stow \'stō\ John 1525–1605 Eng. hist. & antiquarian
Stowe \'stō\ Harriet Elizabeth 1811–1896 née *Beecher* Am. author
Stra·bo \'strā-(,)bō\ 64(or 63) B.C.–after A.D. 23 Greek geographer
Stra·chey \'strā-chē\ (Evelyn) John St. Loe 1901–1963 Eng. socialist
Strachey (Giles) Lytton 1880–1932 Eng. biographer
Stra·di·va·ri \,stra-də-'vär-ē, -'ver-\ Antonio 1644–1737 L. *Antonius Strad·i·var·i·us* \,stra-də-'ver-ē-əs\ Ital. violin maker
Straf·ford \'stra-fərd\ 1st Earl of 1593–1641 *Thomas Wentworth* Eng. statesman
Strath·co·na \strath-'kō-nə\ **and Mount Royal** 1st Baron 1820–1914 *Donald Alexander Smith* Canad. (Scot.-born) railroad builder & polit.
Straus \'shtraús, 'straús\ Oscar 1870–1954 Fr. (Austrian-born) composer
Strauss \'shtraús, 'straús\ David Friedrich 1808–1874 Ger. theol. & philos.
Strauss Johann 1804–1849 & his sons Johann Baptist 1825–1899 & Josef 1827–1870 Austrian composers
Strauss Ri·chard \'ri-,kärt, -,kärt\ 1864–1949 Ger. composer — **Strauss·ian** \'strau-sē-ən, 'shtraú-\ *adj*
Stra·vin·sky \strə-'vin(t)-skē\ Igor \'ē-,gór\ Fyodorovich 1882–1971 Am. (Russ.-born) composer — **Stra·vin·sky·an** *or* **Stra·vin·ski·an** \-skē-ən\ *adj*
Streep \'strēp\ Meryl 1949– *Mary Louise Streep* Am. actress
Strei·cher \'shtrī-kər, 'strī-, -kər\ Julius 1885–1946 Ger. Nazi administrator
Stre·se·mann \'shtrā-zə-,män, 'strā-\ Gustav 1878–1929 Ger. polit.

Strind·berg \'strin(d)-,bərg, *Sw* 'strind-,ber-ē\ August 1849–1912 Swed. dram. & nov. — **Strind·berg·ian** \strin(d)-'bər-gē-ən\ *adj*
Stroess·ner \'stres-nər\ Alfredo 1912–2006 pres. of Paraguay (1954–89)
Stru·en·see \'shtrü-ən-,zā, 'strü-\ Johann Friedrich 1737–1772 Graf *Struensee* Dan. (Ger.-born) physician & polit.
Stu·art \'stü-ərt, 'styü-; 'st(y)ùrt\ — see CHARLES I & MARY STUART
Stuart Charles *the Young Pretender* — see CHARLES EDWARD
Stuart Gilbert Charles 1755–1828 Am. painter
Stuart James Ewell Brown 1833–1864 *Jeb Stuart* Am. Confed. gen.
Stuart James Francis Edward *the Old Pretender* — see JAMES EDWARD
Stubbs \'stəbz\ George 1724–1806 Eng. painter
Stubbs William 1825–1901 Eng. hist. & prelate
Stülp·na·gel \'shtùlp-,nä-gəl, 'stùlp-, 'shtùlp-\ Karl Heinrich von 1886–1944 Ger. gen.
Sturluson — see SNORRI STURLUSON
Stuy·ve·sant \'stī-və-sənt\ Peter *ca* 1610–1672 Du. colonial administrator in America
Sty·ron \'stī-rən\ William 1925–2006 Am. writer
Sua·rez Gon·zá·lez \'swär-əz-gən-'zä-ləs\ Adolfo 1932– prime min. of Spain (1976–81)
Su·choc·ka \sü-'ḵót-,skä\ Hanna 1946– prime min. of Poland (1992–93)
Suck·ling \'sə-kliŋ\ Sir John 1609–1642 Eng. Cavalier poet
Su·cre \'sü-(,)krā\ Antonio José de 1795–1830 So. Am. liberator
Süd·hof \'süd-,hóf, 'sùt-\ Thomas C(hristian) 1955– Ger.-Am. biochem.
Sue \'sü, 'sùe\ Eugène 1804–1857 orig. *Marie-Joseph Sue* Fr. nov.
Sue·to·ni·us \swē-'tō-nē-əs, ,sü-ə-'tō-\ *ca* A.D. 69–after 122 *Gaius Suetonius Tranquillus* Rom. biographer & hist.
Su·gi·ya·ma \,sü-gē-'yä-mə\ Hajime 1880–1945 Jp. field marshal
Su·har·to \sə-'här-(,)tō, sù-\ 1921–2008 pres. of Indonesia (1967–98)
Su·kar·no \sü-'kär-(,)nō\ 1901–1970 pres. of Indonesia (1945–67)
Su·kar·no·put·ri \sü-,kär-nō-'pü-trē\ Megawati 1947– pres. of Indonesia (2001–04)
Sü·ley·man *or* **So·li·man** *or* **Su·lei·man I** \'sü-lā-,män, -li-\ 1494(or 1495)–1566 *the Magnificent* Ottoman sultan (1520–66)
Sul·la \'sə-lə\ 138–78 B.C. *Lucius Cornelius Sulla Felix* Rom. gen. & polit.
Sul·li·van \'sə-lə-vən\ Sir Arthur Seymour 1842–1900 Eng. composer
Sullivan John 1740–1795 Am. gen. in Revolution
Sullivan John L(awrence) 1858–1918 Am. boxer
Sullivan Louis Henri 1856–1924 Am. architect
Sul·ly \'sə-lē, (,)sə-'lē, sùe-'lē\ Duc de 1560–1641 *Maximilien de Béthune* Baron *de Ros·ny* \də-rō-'nē\ Fr. statesman
Sul·ly \'sə-lē\ Thomas 1783–1872 Am. (Eng.-born) painter
Sul·ly Prud·homme \sùe-lē-prùe-'dəm\ 1839–1907 pseud. of *René-François-Armand Prudhomme* Fr. poet & critic
Sul·ston \'səl-stən\ Sir John Edward 1942– Brit. geneticist
Sum·mers \'sə-mərz\ Lawrence Henry 1954– Am. econ. & educ.; U.S. secy. of the treasury (1999–2001)
Sum·ner \'səm-nər\ Charles 1811–1874 Am. statesman & orator
Sumner James Batcheller 1887–1955 Am. biochem.
Sumner William Graham 1840–1910 Am. sociol. & educ.
Sun·day \'sən-dē\ William Ashley 1862–1935 *Billy Sunday* Am. evangelist
Sun Yat–sen \'sùn-'yät-'sen\ 1866–1925 orig. *Sun Wen* or *Sun Chung-shan* Chin. statesman
Surrey Earl of — see Henry HOWARD
Sur·tees \'sər-(,)tēz\ Robert Smith 1803–1864 Eng. nov. & editor
Suth·er·land \'sə-thər-lənd\ Dame Joan 1926–2010 Austral. soprano
Sut·ter \'sə-tər, 'sü-\ John Augustus 1803–1880 orig. *Johann August Suter* Am. (Ger.-born) pioneer
Sutt·ner \'zùt-nər, 'sùt-\ Bertha 1843–1914 née *Kinsky* Baroness *von Suttner* Austrian writer & pacifist
Su·vo·rov \sù-'vór-əf, -'vär-\ Aleksandr Vasilyevich 1729–1800 Russ. field marshal
Su·zu·ki \sü-'zü-kē\ Akira 1930– Jp. chem.
Sved·berg \'sved-,bərg, *Sw* -,ber-ē\ The *or* Theodor 1884–1971 Swed. chem.
Sver·drup \'sver-drəp\ Otto Neumann 1855–1930 Norw. explorer
Sver·rir \'sver-ər\ *ca* 1149–1202 *Sverrir Si·gurds·son* \'si-gərd-sən\ king of Norway (1184–1202)
Swe·den·borg \'swē-dⁿn-,bórg\ Emanuel 1688–1772 orig. *Svedberg* Swed. philos. & religious writer
Swee·linck \'swä-liŋk\ Jan Pieterszoon 1562–1621 Du. organist & composer
Sweet \'swēt\ Henry 1845–1912 Eng. phonetician
Swift \'swift\ Gustavus Franklin 1839–1903 Am. meatpacker
Swift Jonathan 1667–1745 Eng. (Irish-born) satirist — **Swift·ian** \'swif-tē-ən\ *adj*
Swin·burne \'swin-(,)bərn\ Algernon Charles 1837–1909 Eng. poet — **Swin·burn·ian** \swin-'bər-nē-ən\ *adj*
Sy·ming·ton \'sī-miŋ-tən\ (William) Stuart 1901–1988 Am. industrialist & polit.
Sy·monds \'si-mən(d)z, 'sī-\ John Addington 1840–1893 Eng. scholar
Sy·mons \'si-mənz, 'sī-\ Arthur William 1865–1945 Brit. poet & critic
Synge \'siŋ\ John Millington 1871–1909 Irish poet & dram.
Synge Richard Laurence Millington 1914–1994 Brit. biochem.
Szell \'sel, 'zel\ George 1897–1970 Am. (Hung.-born) conductor
Szent–Györ·gyi \sänt-'jórj, -'jór-jē\ Albert von Nagyrapolt 1893–1986 Am. (Hung.-born) chem.
Szi·lard \'zi-,lärd, zə-'lärd\ Leo 1898–1964 Am. (Hung.-born) physicist
Szold \'zōld\ Henrietta 1860–1945 Am. Zionist & founder of Hadassah
Szo·stak \'shō-,stak\ Jack W(illiam) 1952– Am. (Brit.-born) biol.
Szym·bor·ska \shim-'bór-skə\ Wis·la·wa \vēs-'wä-və\ 1923–2012 Pol. poet

---

Tac·i·tus \'ta-sə-təs\ Cornelius *ca* A.D. 56–*ca* 120 Rom. hist. — **Tac·i·te·an** \ˌta-sə-'tē-ən\ *adj*
Taft \'taft\ Lo·ra·do \lə-'rä-(ˌ)dō\ 1860–1936 Am. sculptor
Taft Robert Alphonso 1889–1953 *son of W.H.* Am. polit.
Taft William Howard 1857–1930 27th pres. of the U.S. (1909–13); chief justice U.S. Supreme Court (1921–30)
Ta·gore \tə-'gȯr\ Ra·bin·dra·nath \rə-'bin-drə-ˌnät\ 1861–1941 Indian poet
Taine \'tān, 'ten\ Hippolyte-Adolphe 1828–1893 Fr. philos. & critic
Tait \'tāt\ Archibald Campbell 1811–1882 archbishop of Canterbury (1869–82)
T'ai–tsu — see CHAO K'UANG-YIN
Ta·ke·shi·ta \tä-'kä-shə-ˌtä, tä-'kesh-tä\ Noboru 1924–2000 prime min. of Japan (1987–89)
Tall·chief \'tȯl-ˌchēf\ Maria 1925–2013 Am. dancer
Tal·ley·rand–Pé·ri·gord \'ta-lē-ˌran(d)-ˌper-ə-'gȯr, *F* tal-'rän-\ Charles-Maurice de 1754–1838 Prince *de Bénévent* Fr. statesman
Tal·lis *or* **Tal·lys** *or* **Tal·les** \'ta-ləs\ Thomas *ca* 1505–1585 Eng. composer & organist
Ta·ma·yo \tə-'mī-(ˌ)ō\ Rufino 1899–1991 Mex. painter
Tamerlane *or* **Tamburlaine** — see TIMUR
Ta·na·ka \tä-'nä-kə\ Koichi 1959–   Jp. biochemist
Tan·cred \'taŋ-krəd\ 1078?–1112 Norman leader in 1st Crusade
Tan·dy \'tan-dē\ Jessica 1909–1994 Am. (Brit.-born) actress
Ta·ney \'tȯ-nē\ Roger Brooke 1777–1864 Am. jurist; chief justice U.S. Supreme Court (1836–64)
Tan·ge \'tän-gā\ Kenzo 1913–2005 Jp. architect
T'ang T'ai Tsung \'täŋ-'tī-'dzuŋ\ 600–649 orig. *Li Shih-min* \'le-'shir-'min\ Chin. emp.
Tan·guy \'tän-ˌgē\ Yves 1900–1955 Am. (Fr.-born) artist
Tar·bell \'tär-bəl\ Ida Minerva 1857–1944 Am. author
Tar·dieu \tär-'dyə(r), -'dyœ\ André (-Pierre-Gabriel-Amédée) 1876–1945 Fr. statesman
Tar·king·ton \'tär-kiŋ-tən\ (Newton) Booth 1869–1946 Am. nov.
Tas·man \'taz-mən\ Abel Janszoon 1603?–?1659 Du. navigator & explorer
Tas·so \'ta-(ˌ)sō, 'tä-\ Tor·qua·to \tȯr-'kwä-(ˌ)tō\ 1544–1595 Ital. poet
Tate \'tāt\ (John Orley) Allen 1899–1979 Am. poet & critic
Tate Nahum 1652–1715 Brit. dram.; poet laureate (1692–1715)
Taube \'taúb\ Henry 1915–2005 Am. (Canad.-born) chem.
Taw·ney \'tȯ-nē\ Richard Henry 1880–1962 Eng. economic hist.
Tay·lor \'tā-lər\ (James) Bay·ard \'bī-ərd, 'bā-\ 1825–1878 Am. writer
Taylor (Joseph) Deems 1885–1966 Am. composer & music critic
Taylor Edward 1645?–1729 Am. clergyman & poet
Taylor Elizabeth (Rosemond) 1932–2011 Am. film actress
Taylor Jeremy 1613–1667 Eng. prelate & author
Taylor Joseph Hooton 1941–   Am. physicist
Taylor Maxwell Davenport 1901–1987 Am. gen.
Taylor Richard Edward 1929–   Canad. physicist
Taylor Tom 1817–1880 Eng. dram.
Taylor Zachary 1784–1850 12th pres. of the U.S. (1849–50)
Tchai·kov·sky \chī-'kȯf-skē, chə-, -'kóv-\ Pyotr Ilich 1840–1893 Russ. composer — **Tchai·kov·sky·an** *or* **Tchai·kov·ski·an** \-skē-ən\ *adj*
Teas·dale \'tēz-ˌdāl\ Sara 1884–1933 Am. poet
Te·cum·seh \tə-'kəm(p)-sə, -sē\ *or* **Te·cum·tha** \-'kəm(p)-thə\ *or* **Ti·kam·the** \-'kəm(p)-thə, -'käm(p)-\ 1768–1813 Shawnee Indian chief
Ted·der \'te-dər\ 1st Baron 1890–1967 *Arthur William Tedder* Brit. air marshal
Teil·hard de Char·din \tā-yär-də-shär-'daⁿ\ Pierre 1881–1955 Fr. philos. & paleontologist
Tek·a·kwitha \ˌte-kə-'kwi-thə\ *or* **Teg·a·kwitha** \ˌte-gə-\ *or* **Teg·a·kouita** \ˌte-gə-'kwi-tə\ Ka·teri \'kä-tə-rē\ 1656–1680 *Lily of the Mohawks* Am. Indian religious
Te·le·mann \'tā-lə-ˌmän, 'tē-\ Georg Philipp 1681–1767 Ger. composer
Tel·ler \'te-lər\ Edward 1908–2003 Am. (Hung.-born) physicist
Téllez Gabriel — see TIRSO DE MOLINA
Tem·in \'te-mən\ Howard Martin 1934–1994 Am. oncologist
Tem·ple \'tem-pəl\ Frederick 1821–1902 archbishop of Canterbury (1896–1902)
Temple Shirley 1928–   *Shirley Temple Black* Am. actress & diplomat
Temple Sir William 1628–1699 Brit. statesman
Temple William 1881–1944 *son of Frederick* archbishop of Canterbury (1942–44)
Teng Hsiao–p'ing *or* **Deng Xiao·ping** \'dəŋ-'shaú-'piŋ\ 1904–1997 Chin. Communist leader (1977–97)
Te·niers \tə-'nirs, tä-'nyä\ David *the Elder* 1582–1649 & *the Younger* 1610–1690 Flem. painters
Ten·niel \'ten-yəl\ Sir John 1820–1914 Eng. cartoonist & illustrator
Ten·ny·son \'te-nə-sən\ Alfred 1809–1892 1st Baron *Tennyson* known as *Alfred, Lord Tennyson* Eng. poet; poet laureate (1850–92) — **Ten·ny·so·nian** \ˌte-nə-'sō-nē-ən, -nyən\ *adj*
Ter·borch *or* **Ter Borch** \tər-'bȯrk, -'bȯrk\ Gerard 1617–1681 Du. painter
Ter·brug·ghen \tər-'brü-gən\ Hendrik 1588–1629 Du. painter
Ter·ence \'ter-ən(t)s\ 186(or 185)–?159 B.C. *Publius Terentius Afer* Rom. dram.
Te·re·sa \tə-'rā-zə, -'rē-sə\ Mother 1910–1997 *Agnes Gonxha Bojaxhiu* Albanian religious in India
Teresa of Avila Saint 1515–1582 Span. Carmelite & mystic
Te·resh·ko·va \ˌter-əsh-'kó-və, -'kō-\ Valentina Vladimirovna 1937–   Soviet (Russ.-born) cosmonaut
Ter·hune \(ˌ)tər-'hyün\ Albert Payson 1872–1942 Am. author
Ter·ry \'ter-ē\ (Alice) Ellen 1847–1928 Eng. actress
Ter·tul·lian \(ˌ)tər-'təl-yən\ *ca* A.D. 155(or 160)–after 220 *Quintus Septimius Florens Tertullianus* church father
Tes·la \'tes-lə\ Nikola 1856–1943 Am. (Croatian-born) electrical engineer & inventor
Tet·zel *or* **Te·zel** \'tet-səl\ Johann *ca* 1465–1519 Ger. Dominican friar
Thack·er·ay \'tha-k(ə-)rē\ William Makepeace 1811–1863 Eng. author — **Thack·er·ay·an** \-k(ə-)rē-ən\ *adj*
Tha·les \'thā-(ˌ)lēz\ of Miletus 625?–?547 B.C. Greek philos. — **Tha·le·sian** \thā-'lē-zhən\ *adj*

Thant \'thant, 'thänt\ U \'ü\ 1909–1974 Burmese U.N. official; secy.-gen. (1961–71)
Tharp \'thärp\ Twyla 1941–   Am. dancer, director, & choreographer
Thatch·er \'tha-chər\ Margaret Hilda 1925–2013 Baroness *Thatcher of Kesteven* née *Roberts* Brit. prime min. (1979–90)
Thayer \'ther, 'thā-ər\ Sylvanus 1785–1872 *father of West Point* Am. army officer & educ.
The·mis·to·cles \thə-'mis-tə-ˌklēz\ *ca* 524–*ca* 460 B.C. Athenian gen. & statesman
The·oc·ri·tus \thē-'ä-krə-təs\ *ca* 310–250 B.C. Greek poet
The·od·o·ric \thē-'ä-də-rik\ 454?–526 *the Great* king of the Ostrogoths (493–526)
The·o·do·sius I \ˌthē-ə-'dō-sh(ē-)əs\ 347–395 *the Great* Rom. gen. & emp. (379–395)
The·o·phras·tus \ˌthē-ə-'fras-təs\ *ca* 372–*ca* 287 B.C. Greek philos. & naturalist
Theresa Saint — see TERESA OF AVILA
Thes·pis \'thes-pəs\ 6th cent. B.C. Greek poet
Thiers \tē-'er\ (Louis-) Adolphe 1797–1877 Fr. statesman & hist.
Tho·mas \tó-'mä\ (Charles-Louis-) Ambroise 1811–1896 Fr. composer
Thom·as \'tä-məs\ Augustus 1857–1934 Am. dram.
Thomas Clarence 1948–   Am. jurist
Thomas Dyl·an \'di-lən\ Marlais 1914–1953 Welsh poet
Thomas E(dward) Donnall 1920–2012 Am. physician
Thomas Lowell (Jackson) 1892–1981 Am. traveler, journalist, & author
Thomas Norman Mat·toon \ma-'tün, mə-\ 1884–1968 Am. socialist polit.
Thomas Seth 1785–1859 Am. clock manuf.
Thomas (Christian Friedrich) Theodore 1835–1905 Am. (Ger.-born) conductor
Thomas à Becket — see BECKET
Thomas à Kem·pis \ə-'kem-pəs, (ˌ)ä-'kem-\ 1379(or 1380)–1471 orig. *Thomas Hemerken* Du. ecclesiastic & writer
Thomas Aqui·nas \ə-'kwī-nəs\ Saint 1224(or 1225)–1274 It. *Tommaso d'Aquino* Ital. religious & philos.
Thomas of Er·cel·doune \'ər-səl-ˌdün\ *fl* 1220–1297 *Thomas the Rhymer* and *Thomas Learmont* Scot. seer & poet
Thomp·son \'täm(p)-sən\ Benjamin 1753–1814 Count *Rum·ford* \'rəm(p)-fərd\ Brit. (Am.-born) physicist & statesman
Thompson Dorothy 1894–1961 Am. journalist
Thompson Francis 1859–1907 Eng. poet
Thompson Sir John Sparrow David 1844–1894 Canad. statesman; prime min. (1892–94)
Thompson Tommy (George) 1941–   U.S. secy. of health and human services (2001–05)
Thom·son \'täm(p)-sən\ Sir George Pag·et \'pa-jət\ 1892–1975 *son of Sir Joseph John* Eng. physicist
Thomson James 1700–1748 Scot. poet
Thomson James 1834–1882 *B. V.* or *Bysshe Vanolis* Scot. poet
Thomson John Arthur 1861–1933 Scot. biol.
Thomson Sir Joseph John 1856–1940 Eng. physicist
Thomson Virgil Garnett 1896–1989 Am. composer & critic
Thomson William — see Baron KELVIN
't Hooft \tə-'hōft\ Gerardus 1946–   Du. physicist
Tho·reau \thə-'rō, thȯ-; 'thȯr-(ˌ)ō, 'thər-(ˌ)ō\ Henry David 1817–1862 orig. *David Henry Thoreau* Am. writer — **Tho·reau·vi·an** \thə-'rō-vē-ən, thȯ-\ *adj*
Thorn·dike \'thȯrn-ˌdīk\ Edward Lee 1874–1949 Am. psychol.
Thorndike Dame (Agnes) Sybil 1882–1976 Brit. actress
Thorn·ton \'thȯrn-tᵊn\ William 1759–1828 Am. architect
Thorpe \'thȯrp\ James Francis 1888–1953 *Jim Thorpe* Am. athlete
Thor·vald·sen *or* **Thor·wald·sen** \'tȯr-ˌwȯl-sən, 'thȯr-; 'túr-ˌväl-sən\ Ber·tel \'ber-tᵊl\ 1768(or 1770)–1844 Dan. sculptor
Thras·y·bu·lus \ˌthra-sə-'byü-ləs\ *d* 388 B.C. Athenian gen.
Thu·cyd·i·des \thü-'si-də-ˌdēz, thyü-\ *d ca* 401 B.C. Greek hist. — **Thu·cyd·i·de·an** \(ˌ)thü-ˌsi-də-'dē-ən, (ˌ)thyü-\ *adj*
Thur·ber \'thər-bər\ James Grover 1894–1961 Am. writer — **Thur·ber·esque** \ˌthər-bə-'resk\ *adj*
Thut·mo·se \thüt-'mō-sə\ name of 4 kings of Egypt: esp. **III** *d* 1450 B.C. (reigned 1504–1450 B.C.)
Thys·sen \'ti-sᵊn\ Fritz 1873–1951 Ger. industrialist
Ti·be·ri·us \tī-'bir-ē-əs\ *id* 42 B.C.–A.D. 37 *Tiberius Claudius Nero Caesar Augustus* Rom. emp. (14–37)
Ti·bul·lus \tə-'bə-ləs\ Albius *ca* 55–*ca* 19 B.C. Rom. poet
Tieck \'tēk\ (Johann) Ludwig 1773–1853 Ger. author
Tie·po·lo \tē-'ä-pə-ˌlō, -'e-\ Giovanni Battista 1696–1770 Ital. painter
Tif·fa·ny \'ti-fə-nē\ Charles Lewis 1812–1902 Am. jeweler
Tiffany Louis Comfort 1848–1933 *son of C.L.* Am. painter & stained-glass artist
Tig·lath–pi·le·ser III \'ti-ˌglath-(ˌ)pī-'lē-zər, -pə-\ *d* 727 B.C. king of Assyria (745–727)
Til·den \'til-dən\ Samuel Jones 1814–1886 Am. polit.
Til·dy \'til-dē\ Zol·tán \'zȯl-ˌtän\ 1889–1961 Hung. polit.
Til·lich \'ti-lik, -lik\ Paul Johannes 1886–1965 Am. (Ger.-born) theol.
Til·lot·son \'ti-lət-sən\ John 1630–1694 Eng. prelate
Til·ly \'ti-lē\ Graf von 1559–1632 *Johann Tser·claes* \tsər-'kläs\ Bavarian gen.
Ti·mo·shen·ko \ˌti-mə-'shen-(ˌ)kō\ Sem·yon \səm-'yȯn\ Konstantinovich 1895–1970 Soviet marshal
Tim·ur \(ˌ)ti-ˌmùr\ *or* **Timur Lenk** \-ˌleŋk\ *E* **Tam·er·lane** \'ta-mər-ˌlän\ *or* **Tam·bur·laine** \'tam-bər-\ 1336–1405 Turkic conqueror
Tin·ber·gen \'tin-ˌber-kə(n)\ Nikolaas 1907–1988 Du. ethologist
Ting·ley \'tiŋ-lē\ Katherine Augusta 1847–1929 Am. theosophist
Tin·to·ret·to \ˌtin-tə-'re-(ˌ)tō\ *ca* 1518–1594 *Jacopo Robusti* Ital. painter
Ti·pu *or* **Tip·pu Sul·tan** \ˌti-(ˌ)pü-'sùl-ˌtän\ 1749(or 1753)–1799 sultan of Mysore (1782–99)
Tir·pitz \'tir-pəts, 'tər-\ Alfred von 1849–1930 Ger. admiral
Tir·so de Mo·li·na \ˌtir-sō-ˌdä-mə-'lē-nə\ *ca* 1584–1648 pseud. *of Gabriel Téllez* \'tä(l)-yäth\ Span. dram.
Ti·se·li·us \tə-'sä-lē-əs, -'zä-\ Arne Wilhelm Kaurin 1902–1971 Swed. biochem.

Ti·so \'tē-(,)sō\ Josef *or* Joseph 1887–1947 Slovak priest & polit.
Titch·e·ner \'ti-chə-nər\ Edward Bradford 1867–1927 Am. psychol.
Ti·tian \'ti-shən\ *ca* 1488–1576 *Tiziano Vecellio* Ital. painter — **Ti·tian·esque** \,ti-shə-'nesk\ *adj*
Ti·to \'tē-(,)tō\ 1892–1980 orig. *Josip Broz* \'brōz, 'brōz\ usu. called *Marshal Tito* leader of Yugoslavia (1943–80)
Ti·tus \'tī-təs\ A.D. 39–81 *Titus Flavius Vespasianus* Rom. emp. (79–81)
To·bin \'tō-bən\ James 1918–2002 Am. econ.
Tocque·ville \'tōk-,vil, 'tōk-, 'täk-, -,vēl, -vəl\ Alexis (-Charles-Henri= Maurice-Clérel) de 1805–1859 Fr. statesman & author
Todd \'täd\ Sir Alexander Robertus 1907–1997 Brit. chem.
Todt \'tōt\ Fritz 1891–1942 Ger. military engineer
To·gliat·ti \tōl-'yä-tē\ Pal·mi·ro \päl-'mē-(,)rō\ 1893–1964 Ital. polit.
Tō·gō \'tō-(,)gō\ Marquis Heihachirō 1848–1934 Jp. admiral
Tō·jō \'tō-(,)jō\ Hideki 1884–1948 Jp. gen. & polit.
To·ku·ga·wa \,tō-kù-'gä-wə\ Ieyasu 1543–1616 orig. *Matsudaira Takechiyo* Jp. shogun (1603–05); founder of last Jp. shogunate (1603–1867)
To·le·do \tō-'lā-thō\ Alejandro 1946– pres. of Peru (2001–06)
Tol·kien \'tól-,kēn\ J(ohn) R(onald) R(euel) 1892–1973 Eng. author — **Tol·kien·esque** \,tól-(,)kē-'nesk\ *adj*
Tol·ler \'tó-lər\ Ernst 1893–1939 Ger. dram. & polit.
Tol·stoy \tól-'stói, tōl-', tä̇l-', 'tól-, 'tōl-, 'täl-\ Count Lev Nikolayevich 1828–1910 Russ. nov., philos., & mystic — **Tol·stoy·an** *also* **Tol·stoi·an** \-ən\ *adj*
Tom·baugh \'täm-,bó\ Clyde William 1906–1997 Am. astron.
Tomp·kins \'täm(p)-kənz\ Daniel D. 1774–1825 Am. polit.; vice pres. of the U.S. (1817–25)
Tone \'tōn\ (Theobald) Wolfe 1763–1798 Irish revolutionary
To·ne·ga·wa \,tō-ne-'gä-wə\ Susumu 1939– Am. (Jp.-born) biol.
Tooke \'tůk\ (John) Horne 1736–1812 Eng. polit. radical & philologist
Toombs \'tümz\ Robert Augustus 1810–1885 Am. polit.
Tor·que·ma·da \,tór-kə-'mä-də, -thə\ Tomás de 1420–1498 Span. grand inquisitor
Tor·ri·cel·li \,tór-ə-'che-lē, ,tär-\ Evangelista 1608–1647 Ital. math. & physicist
Tos·ca·ni·ni \,täs-kə-'nē-nē, ,tós-\ Ar·tu·ro \är-'tùr-(,)ō\ 1867–1957 Ital. conductor
Tou·louse–Lau·trec (–Mon·fa) \tú-,lüz-lō-'trek-mōⁿ-'fä\ Henri (-Marie-Raymond) de 1864–1901 Fr. painter
Tour·neur \'tər-nər\ Cyril *ca* 1575–1626 Eng. dram.
Tous·saint–Lou·ver·ture \tü-,saⁿ-'lü-vər-,tür, -,tyùr\ *ca* 1743–1803 orig. *François-Dominique Toussaint* Haitian gen. & liberator
Toyn·bee \'tóin-bē\ Arnold Joseph 1889–1975 Eng. hist.
Tra·jan \'trä-jən\ A.D. 53–117 orig. *Marcus Ulpius Traiánus* usu. called *Germanicus* Rom. emp. (98–117)
Tran·strö·mer \'trän-,strœ-mər\ Tomas (Gösta) 1931– Swed. poet
Trau·bel \'traù-bəl\ Helen 1903–1972 Am. soprano
Tree \'trē\ Sir Herbert (Draper) Beerbohm 1853–1917 Eng. actor= manager
Treitsch·ke \'trīch-kə\ Heinrich von 1834–1896 Ger. hist.
Tre·vel·yan \tri-'vel-yən, -'vil-\ George Macaulay 1876–1962 Eng. hist.
Trevelyan Sir George Otto 1838–1928 *father of prec.* Eng. polit., biographer, & hist.
Tril·ling \'tri-liŋ\ Lionel 1905–1975 Am. literary critic
Trim·ble \'trim-bəl\ (William) David 1944– Lord *Trimble* Irish peace activist
Trol·lope \'trä-ləp\ Anthony 1815–1882 Eng. nov. — **Trol·lo·pi·an** \trä-'lō-pē-ən\ *adj*
Tromp \'trómp, 'trämp\ Maarten Harpertszoon 1598–1653 Du. admiral
Trots·ky \'trät-skē\ *also* \'trót-\ Leon 1879–1940 orig. *Lev Davidovich Bronstein* Russ. Communist leader
Tru·deau \'trü-(,)dō, trü-'\ Pierre Elliott 1919–2000 Canad. polit.; prime min. (1968–79; 1980–84)
Truf·faut \trü-'fō\ François (Roland) 1932–1984 Fr. filmmaker
Tru·ji·llo Mo·li·na \trü-'hē-(,)yō-mə-'lē-nə\ Rafael Leónidas 1891–1961 Dominican gen.; pres. of Dominican Republic (1930–38; 1942–52)
Tru·man \'trü-mən\ Harry S. 1884–1972 33d pres. of the U.S. (1945–53)
Trum·bull \'trəm-bəl\ John 1756–1843 Am. painter
Trumbull Jonathan 1710–1785 *father of prec.* Am. statesman
Truth \'trüth\ Sojourner *ca* 1797–1883 Am. evangelist & reformer
Ts'ao Chan \'tsaù-'jän\ 1715?–1763 *Ts'ao Hsüeh-ch'in* Chin. nov.
Tschaikovsky *var of* TCHAIKOVSKY
Tsien \'chen\ Roger Y(onchien) 1952– Am. biochem.
Tsui \'tsü-ē\ Daniel Chee 1939– Am. (Chin.-born) physicist
Tub·man \'təb-mən\ Harriet *ca* 1820–1913 Am. abolitionist
Tubman William W(acanarat) S(hadrach) 1895–1971 Liberian lawyer; pres. of Liberia (1944–71)
Tuch·man \'tək-mən\ Barbara 1912–1989 née *Wertheim* Am. hist.
Tu·dor \'tü-dər, 'tyü-\ Antony 1908(or 1909)–1987 orig. *William Cook* Am. (Brit.-born) ballet dancer & choreographer
Tu Fu \'dü-'fü\ 712–770 Chin. poet
Tul·si·dās \,tùl-sē-'däs\ 1543?–1623 Hindu poet
Tu·renne \tü-'ren\ Vicomte de 1611–1675 *Henri de La Tour d'Auvergne* marshal of France
Tur·ge·nev \tùr-'gän-yəf, -'gen-\ Ivan Sergeyevich 1818–1883 Russ. nov.
Tur·got \tùr-'gō\ Anne-Robert-Jacques 1727–1781 Baron *de l'Aulne* \'lōn\ Fr. statesman & econ.
Tu·ring \'tùr-iŋ\ Alan Mathison 1912–1954 Brit. math. & logician
Tur·ner \'tər-nər\ Frederick Jackson 1861–1932 Am. hist.
Turner J(oseph) M(allord) W(illiam) 1775–1851 Eng. painter
Turner Nat 1800–1831 Am. slave insurrectionist
Turner Ted 1938– *Robert Edward Turner III* Am. television executive
Tut·ankh·a·men \,tü-,taŋ-'kä-mən, -,täŋ-\ *or* **Tut·ankh·a·ten** \-'kä-tᵊn\ *ca* 1370–1352 B.C. king of Egypt (1361–1352 B.C.)
Tutu \'tü-,tü\ Desmond Mpilo 1931– So. African clergyman & polit. activist
Twacht·man \'twäkt-mən\ John Henry 1853–1902 Am. painter
Twain Mark — see CLEMENS
Tweed \'twēd\ William Marcy 1823–1878 *Boss Tweed* Am. polit.
Ty·ler \'tī-lər\ Anne 1941– Am. writer
Tyler John 1790–1862 10th pres. of the U.S. (1841–45)

Tyler Wat \'wät\ *or* Walter *d* 1381 Eng. leader of Peasants' Revolt (1381)
Tyn·dale *or* **Tin·dal** *or* **Tin·dale** \'tin-dᵊl\ William *ca* 1494–1536 Eng. reformer & translator
Tyn·dall \'tin-dᵊl\ John 1820–1893 Brit. physicist
Tz'u–hsi \'tsü-'shē\ 1835–1908 Chin. empress dowager
Uc·cel·lo \ü-'che-(,)lō\ Paolo 1397–1475 orig. *Paolo di Dono* Florentine painter
Udall \'yü-,dòl, 'yü-dᵊl\ Nicholas 1505–1556 Eng. schoolmaster & dram.
Ugar·te \ü-'gär-tē\ Manuel 1874–1951 Argentine writer
Uh·land \'ü-,länt\ Johann Ludwig 1787–1862 Ger. poet & hist.
Ul·bricht \'ùl-(,)brikt, -(,)brikt\ Walter 1893–1973 East German polit.
Ul·fi·las \'ùl-fə-ləs, 'əl-, -ləs, -,las\ *or* **Goth. Wul·fi·la** \'wùl-fə-lə\ *ca* 311–*ca* 382 Gothic missionary
Ul·pi·an \'əl-pē-ən\ *d* A.D. 228 *Domitius Ulpianus* Rom. jurist
Um·ber·to \,əm-'ber-(,)tō\ name of 2 kings of Italy: I 1844–1900 Duke of *Savoy* (reigned 1878–1900); II 1904–1983 Prince of *Piedmont*; Count of *Sarre* (reigned 1946)
Una·mu·no (y Ju·go) \,ü-nə-'mü-(,)nō-ē-'hü-(,)gō\ Miguel de 1864–1936 Span. philos. & writer
Un·cas \'əŋ-kəs\ 1588?–?1683 Pequot Indian chief
Und·set \'ùn-,set\ Si·grid \'si-grē, -grəd\ 1882–1949 Norw. nov.
Un·ter·mey·er \'ən-tər-,mī(-ə)r\ Louis 1885–1977 Am. poet
Up·dike \'əp-,dīk\ John (Hoyer) 1932–2009 Am. writer
Ur·ban \'ər-bən\ name of 8 popes: esp. II (*Odo* \'ō-(,)dō\ *of Lagery*) *ca* 1035–1099 (pope 1088–99)
Urey \'yùr-ē\ Harold Clayton 1893–1981 Am. chem.
Uri·be (Vélez) \ü-'rē-bā\ Álvaro 1952– pres. of Colombia (2002–10)
Ur·quhart \'ər-kərt, -,kärt\ *or* **Ur·chard** \'ər-chərd\ Sir Thomas 1611–1660 Scot. author & translator
Ussh·er \'ə-shər\ James 1581–1656 Irish prelate
Utril·lo \yü-'tri-(,)lō; ,yü-trē-'ō, ,ù-\ Maurice 1883–1955 Fr. painter
Vaj·pay·ee \'väj-,pī-ē\ Atal Be·ha·ri \'ä-täl-bi-'här-ē\ 1924– prime min. of India (1996; 1998–2004)
Val·de·mar \'väl-də-,mär, 'val-\ *or* **Wal·de·mar** \'wòl-\ name of 4 kings of Denmark: esp. I 1131–1182 (reigned 1157–82)
Valdes Peter — see WALDO
Val·di·via \väl-'dē-vē-ə\ Pedro de *ca* 1498–1553 Span. conquistador
Va·lens \'vä-lenz, -,lenz\ 328?–378 Rom. emp. of the East (364–378)
Val·en·tin·ian \,va-lən-'ti-nē-ən, -'tin-yən\ *L* **Val·en·tin·i·a·nus** \,va-lən-,ti-nē-'ä-nəs\ name of 3 Rom. emperors: I 321–375 (reigned 364–375); II 371–392 (reigned 375–392); III 419–455 (reigned 425–455)
Val·en·ti·no \,va-lən-'tē-(,)nō\ Rudolph 1895–1926 orig. *Rodolfo Guglielmi di Valentina d'An·ton·guol·la* \,dän-tən-'gwò-lä\ Am. (Ital.= born) actor
Valera Eamon de — see DE VALERA
Va·le·ra (y Al·ca·lá Ga·lia·no) \və-'ler-ə-,ē-,al-kə-'lä-,gä-lē-'ä-(,)nō, -,äl-kə-, -,gäl-\ Juan 1824–1905 Span. writer & statesman
Va·le·ri·an \və-'lir-ē-ən\ *d* A.D. 260 *Publius Licinius Valerianus* Rom. emp. (253–260)
Va·lé·ry \,va-lə-'rē, 'va-lə-rē\ (Ambroise-) Paul (-Toussaint-Jules) 1871–1945 Fr. poet & philos.
Val·le·jo \və-'lā-(,)ō, -'yä-(,)(h)ō\ Mariano Guadalupe 1808–1890 Am. soldier & pioneer
Van Al·len \van-'a-lən\ James Alfred 1914–2006 Am. physicist
Van·brugh \'van-brə, van-'brü\ Sir John 1664–1726 Eng. dram. & architect
Van Bu·ren \van-'byùr-ən, vən-\ Martin 1782–1862 8th pres. of the U.S. (1837–41)
Van·cou·ver \van-'kü-vər\ George 1757–1798 Eng. navigator
Van·de·grift \'van-də-,grift\ Alexander Archer 1887–1973 Am. gen.
Van·den·berg \'van-dən-,bərg\ Arthur Hendrick 1884–1951 Am. journalist & polit.
Van·der·bilt \'van-dər-,bilt\ Cornelius 1794–1877 Am. industrialist
van der Meer \,vän-dər-'mer\ Simon 1925–2011 Du. physicist
van Dongen Kees — see DONGEN
Van Do·ren \van-'dór-ən, vən-\ Carl Clinton 1885–1950 & his bro. Mark 1894–1972 Am. writers & editors
Van Dyck *or* **Van·dyke** \van-'dīk, vən-\ Sir Anthony 1599–1641 Flem. painter
Vane \'vān\ Sir Henry 1613–1662 *the Younger* Eng. statesman
Van Eyck — see EYCK, VAN
van Gogh Vincent Willem — see GOGH, VAN
Van·ier \,vän-'yā\ Georges-Philéas 1888–1967 Canad. polit.; gov.-gen. (1959–67)
Van Rens·se·laer \,van-,ren(t)-sə-'lir, -,ren-'slir, -,ren(t)-s(ə-)lər\ Stephen 1764–1839 Am. gen. & polit.
van't Hoff \vänt-'hóf, vant-\ Jacobus Hen·dri·cus \hen-'drē-kəs\ 1852–1911 Du. physical chem.
Vanzetti Bartolomeo — see Nicola SACCO
Va·rèse \və-'räz, -'rez\ Edgard 1883–1965 orig. *Edgar Victor Achille Charles Varèse* Am. (Fr.-born) composer
Var·gas \'vär-gəs\ Getúlio Dornelles 1883–1954 Braz. lawyer; pres. of Brazil (1930–45; 1951–54)
Var·gas Llo·sa \,bär-gäs-'lyō-sä\ (Jorge) Mario (Pedro) 1936– Peruvian writer
Var·mus \'vär-məs\ Harold Elliot 1939– Am. microbiologist
Var·ro \'va-(,)rō\ Marcus Terentius 116–27 B.C. Rom. scholar
Va·sa·ri \və-'zär-ē\ Giorgio 1511–1574 Ital. artist & art hist.
Vasco da Gama — see GAMA
Vau·ban \vō-'bäⁿ\ Sébastien Le Prestre de 1633–1707 Fr. mil. engineer; marshal of France
Vaughan \'vón, 'vän\ Henry 1621?–1695 Brit. poet
Vaughan Sarah Lois 1924–1990 Am. singer
Vaughan Wil·liams \'wil-yəmz\ Ralph 1872–1958 Eng. composer
Veb·len \'ve-blən\ Thorstein \'thór-,stīn\ Bunde 1857–1929 Am. sociol. & econ. — **Veb·le·ni·an** \ve-'blē-nē-ən\ *adj*

Ve·ga \'vä-gə\ Lo·pe \'lō-(,)pā\ de 1562–1635 *Lope Félix de Vega Carpio* Span. dram.

Ve·láz·quez \və-'läs-kəs, -'läs-, -kwiz, -(,)käs\ Diego Rodríguez de Silva 1599–1660 Span. painter

Velt·man \'velt-män\ Martinus J. G. 1931–   Du. physicist

Ven·dôme \väⁿ(n)-'dōm\ Duc de 1654–1712 *Louis-Joseph* Fr. soldier

Ve·ni·zé·los \,ve-nə-'zä-ləs, -'ze-ləs\ Eleuthérios 1864–1936 Greek statesman

Ven·ter \'ven-tər\ J(ohn) Craig 1946–   Am. geneticist

Ven·tu·ri \ven-'tür-ē\ Robert Charles 1925–   Am. architect

Ver·di \'ver-dē\ Giuseppe Fortunio Francesco 1813–1901 Ital. composer — **Ver·di·an** \-ən\ *adj*

Ve·re·ker \'ver-ə-kər\ John Standish Surtees Prendergast 1886–1946 6th Viscount *Gort* \'gört\ Brit. soldier

Ve·re·shcha·gin \,ver-əsh-'chä-gən, ,ver-ə-'shä-\ Vasily Vasilyevich 1842–1904 Russ. painter

Vergil — see VIRGIL

Ver·laine \ver-'län, -'len\ Paul(-Marie) 1844–1896 Fr. poet

Ver·meer \vər-'mer, -'mir\ Jan 1632–1675 also called *Jan van der Meer van Delft* \van-dər-'mer-van-'delft, -'mir-\ Du. painter

Verne \vərn, 'vern\ Jules \'jülz, 'zhuel\ (Gabriel) 1828–1905 Fr. writer

Ver·ner \'ver-nər\ Karl Adolph 1846–1896 Dan. philologist

Ver·nier \vern-'yā, 'vər-nē-ər\ Pierre *ca* 1580–1637 Fr. math.

Ver·non \'vər-nən\ Edward 1684–1757 Eng. admiral

Ve·ro·ne·se \,ver-ə-'nä-sē, -zē\ Paolo 1528–1588 orig. *Paolo Caliari* Ital. painter

Ver·ra·za·no or **Ver·raz·za·no** \,ver-ə-'zä-(,)nō, -ət-'sä-\ Giovanni da 1485–1528 Florentine navigator & explorer

Ver·roc·chio \və-'rō-kē-,ō\ Andrea del 1435–1488 orig. *Andrea di Michele Cione* Florentine sculptor & painter

Verulam — see Francis BACON

Ve·rus \'vir-əs\ Lucius Aurelius A.D. 130–169 orig. *Lucius Ceionius Commodus* Rom. emp. (161–169)

Ver·woerd \fər-'vürt, fer-\ Hendrik Frensch 1901–1966 So. African polit.; prime min. (1958–66)

Ve·sa·li·us \və-'sä-lē-əs, -'zä-\ Andreas 1514–1564 Belg. anatomist

Ve·sey \'vē-zē\ Denmark *ca* 1767–1822 Am. slave insurrectionist

Ves·pa·sian \ve-'spā-zh(ē-)ən\ A.D. 9–79 *Titus Flavius Sabinus Vespasianus* Rom. emp. (69–79)

Ves·puc·ci \ve-'spü-chē, -'spyü-\ Ame·ri·go \ə-'mer-i-,gō, *It* ,ä-mə-'rē-(,)gō\ 1454–1512 L. *Amer·i·cus Ves·pu·cius* \ə-'mer-ə-kəs,-,ves-'pyü-sh(ē-)əs\ Ital. navigator & explorer

Vick·rey \'vi-krē\ William Spencer 1914–1996 Am. (Canad.-born) econ.

Vi·co \'vē-kō\ Giambattista 1668–1744 Ital. philos.

Vic·tor Em·man·u·el I \'vik-tər-i-'man-yə-wəl\ 1759–1824 king of Sardinia (1802–21)

Victor Emmanuel II 1820–1878 king of Sardinia-Piedmont (1849–61) & 1st king of Italy (1861–78)

Victor Emmanuel III 1869–1947 king of Italy (1900–46)

Vic·to·ria \vik-'tòr-ē-ə\ 1819–1901 *Alexandrina Victoria* queen of the United Kingdom of Great Britain and Ireland (1837–1901)

Victoria Tomás Luis de *ca* 1548–1611 Span. composer

Vi·da \'vē-də\ Marco Girolamo *ca* 1490–1566 Ital. poet

Vi·gée–Le·brun \vē-'zhä-lə-'brəⁿ(n), -'brœⁿ\ (Marie-Louise-) Élisabeth 1755–1842 Fr. painter

Vi·gno·la \vēn-'yō-lə\ Giacomo da 1507–1573 *Giacomo Ba·roz·zi* \bä-'ròt-sē\ Ital. architect

Vi·gny \vēn-'yē\ Alfred-Victor 1797–1863 Comte *de Vigny* Fr. author

Vil·la \'vē-ə, 'vē-yä\ Francisco 1878–1923 *Pan·cho* \'pän-(,)chō, 'pan-\ *Villa* orig. *Doroteo Arango* Mex. bandit & revolutionary

Vil·la–Lo·bos \,vē-ə-'lō-(,)bōsh, -(,)bòs, -bəs\ Heitor \'ā-,tòr\ 1887–1959 Braz. composer

Vil·lars \vi-'lär\ Claude-Louis-Hector 1653–1734 Duc *de Villars* Fr. soldier; marshal of France

Ville·neuve \,vēl-'nə(r)v, -'nœv\ Pierre-Charles-Jean-Baptiste-Silvestre de 1763–1806 Fr. admiral

Ville·pin \vēl-'paⁿ\ Dominique (Marie François René Galouzeau) de 1953–   prime min. of France (2005–07)

Vil·liers \'vil-yərz, 'vi-lərz\ George 1592–1628 1st Duke of *Buck·ing·ham* \'bə-kiŋ-əm, *US also* -kiŋ-,ham\ Eng. courtier & polit.

Villiers George 1628–1687 2d Duke of *Buckingham; son of prec.* Eng. courtier & dram.

Vil·lon \vē-'yōⁿ *also* -'lōⁿ\ François 1431–after 1463 orig. *François de Montcorbier* or *Des Loges* Fr. poet

Vil·lon \vē-'lōⁿ, -'yōⁿ\ Jacques 1875–1963 orig. *Gaston Duchamp; bro. of Marcel Duchamp* Fr. painter

Vil·sack \'vil-,sak\ Thomas (James) 1950–   U.S. secy. of agriculture (2009–   )

Vin·cent de Paul \'vin(t)-sənt-də-'pòl\ Saint 1581–1660 Fr. religious

Vinci, da Leonardo — see LEONARDO DA VINCI

Vi·no·gra·doff \,vi-nə-'gra-,dóf\ Sir Paul Gavrilovitch 1854–1925 Brit. (Russ.-born) jurist & hist.

Vin·son \'vin(t)-sən\ Frederick Moore 1890–1953 Am. jurist; chief justice U.S. Supreme Court (1946–53)

Viol·let–le–Duc \,vyò-ə-'lä-lə-'dük, -'dyük; vyò-le-lə-'dœk\ Eugène-Emmanuel 1814–1879 Fr. architect

Vir·chow \'fir-(,)kō, 'vir-\ Rudolf 1821–1902 Ger. pathologist

Vir·gil *also* **Ver·gil** \'vər-jəl\ 70–19 B.C. *Publius Vergilius Maro* Rom. poet — **Vir·gil·ian** *also* **Ver·gil·ian** \vər-'jil-yən\ *adj*

Vir·ta·nen \'vir-tə-,nen\ Art·tu·ri \'är-tə-rē\ Ilmari 1895–1973 Finn. biochem.

Vi·tru·vi·us \və-'trü-vē-əs\ *fl* 1st cent. B.C. *Marcus Vitruvius Pollio* Rom. architect & engineer

Vi·val·di \vi-'väl-dē, -'vòl\ Antonio Lucio 1678–1741 Ital. composer

Vla·di·mir I \'vla-də-,mir, vlə-'dē-,mir\ Saint *ca* 956–1015 grand prince of Kiev (980–1015)

Vla·minck \vlə-'maŋk\ Maurice de 1876–1958 Fr. painter

Volck·er \'vòl-kər\ Paul Adolph 1927–   Am. economist

Vol·stead \'väl-,sted, 'vòl-, 'vòl-, -stəd\ Andrew John 1860–1947 Am. legislator

Vol·ta \'vōl-tə, 'väl-, 'vòl-\ Alessandro (Giuseppe Antonio Anastasio) Conte *Volta* 1745–1827 Ital. physicist

Vol·taire \vōl-'tar, väl-, vòl-, -'ter\ 1694–1778 orig. *François-Marie Arouet* Fr. writer — **Vol·tair·ean** or **Vol·tair·ian** \-'tar-ē-ən, -'ter-\ *adj*

Von Braun Wernher — see BRAUN

Von·ne·gut \'vä-ni-gət\ Kurt 1922–2007 Am. writer

Vo·ro·shi·lov \,vòr-ə-'shē-,lòf, ,vär-, -,lòv\ Kliment Yefremovich 1881–1969 Soviet marshal; chairman of the Presidium (1953–60)

Vor·ster \'fòr-stər\ John 1915–1983 orig. *Balthazar Johannes Vorster* prime min. of Republic of So. Africa (1966–78)

Voz·ne·sen·sky \,väz-nə-'sen(t)-skē\ Andrey 1933–2010 Russ. poet

Vries, de \də-'vrēs\ Hugo Marie 1848–1935 Du. botanist & geneticist

Vuil·lard \vwē-'yär\ (Jean-) Édouard 1868–1940 Fr. painter

Vy·shin·sky \və-'shin(t)-skē\ Andrey Yanuaryevich 1883–1954 Soviet lawyer, polit., & diplomat

Waals, van der \'van-dər-,wòlz\ Johannes Diderik 1837–1923 Du. physicist

Wace \'wäs, 'wäs\ *ca* 1100–after 1174 Anglo-Norman poet

Wag·ner \'väg-nər\ (Wilhelm) Ri·chard \'ri-,kärt, -,kärt\ 1813–1883 Ger. composer

Wagner von Jau·regg or **Wagner–Jau·regg** \-'yaù-,rek\ Julius 1857–1940 Austrian neurologist & psychiatrist

Wain·wright \'wän-,rīt\ Jonathan Mayhew 1883–1953 Am. gen.

Wainwright Richard 1817–1862 & his son Richard, Jr. 1849–1926 Am. naval officers

Waite \'wät\ Morrison Remick 1816–1888 Am. jurist; chief justice U.S. Supreme Court (1874–88)

Waks·man \'wäks-mən, 'waks-\ Sel·man \'sel-mən\ Abraham 1888–1973 Am. (Ukrainian-born) microbiologist

Wal·cott \'wäl-(,)kät\ Derek Alton 1930–   West Indian poet & playwright

Wald \'wòld\ George 1906–1997 Am. biol.

Wald Lillian D. 1867–1940 Am. social worker

Waldemar — see VALDEMAR

Wald·see \'väl-dər-,zā, 'wòl-\ Alfred von 1832–1904 Ger. soldier

Wald·heim \'vält-,hīm\ Kurt 1918–2007 Austrian U.N. official; secy. gen. (1972–82); pres. of Austria (1986–92)

Wal·do \'wòl-(,)dō, 'wäl-\ or **Val·des** \'val-(,)däs, 'väl-\ Peter *d* before 1218 Fr. religious leader

Wa·łe·sa \vä-'len(t)-sə, wä-; vä-'weⁿ-sə\ Lech \'lek, 'lek\ 1943–   Pol. polit.; pres. of Poland (1990–95)

Walk·er \'wò-kər\ Alice Malsenior 1944–   Am. writer

Walker John E(rnest) 1941–   Brit. biochem.

Walker William 1824–1860 Am. filibuster

Wal·lace \'wä-ləs\ Alfred Russel 1823–1913 Eng. naturalist

Wallace George Corley 1919–1998 Am. polit.

Wallace Henry Agard \'ä-,gärd\ 1888–1965 Am. agriculturist, editor, & polit.; vice pres. of the U.S. (1941–45)

Wallace Lewis 1827–1905 *Lew Wallace* Am. lawyer, gen., & nov.

Wallace Sir William *ca* 1270–1305 Scot. patriot

Wal·lach \'wä-lək, 'väl-\ Otto 1847–1931 Ger. chem.

Wal·len·berg \'wä-lən-,bərg, *Sw* -,ber-ē\ Raoul 1912–?1947 Swed. diplomat & hero of the Holocaust

Wal·len·stein \'vä-lən-,shtīn, 'wä-lən-,stīn\ Albrecht Wenzel Eusebius von 1583–1634 Duke of *Friedland and Mecklenburg;* Prince of *Sagan* Austrian gen.

Wal·ler \'wä-lər\ Edmund 1606–1687 Eng. poet

Waller Thomas Wright 1904–1943 *Fats Waller* Am. pianist & composer

Wal·pole \'wòl-,pōl, 'wäl-\ Horace 1717–1797 orig. *Horatio Walpole* 4th Earl of *Orford* \'òr-fərd\ Eng. author

Walpole Sir Hugh Seymour 1884–1941 Eng. nov.

Walpole Sir Robert 1676–1745 1st Earl of *Orford; father of Horace* Eng. statesman — **Wal·pol·ian** \wòl-'pō-lē-ən, wäl-\ *adj*

Wal·ter \'väl-tər, 'wòl-\ Bruno 1876–1962 orig. *Bruno Walter Schlesinger* \'shlä-ziŋ-ər\ Am. (Ger.-born) conductor

Wal·ther von der Vo·gel·wei·de \'väl-tər-,fòn-dər-'fō-gəl-,vī-də\ *ca* 1170–*ca* 1230 Ger. minnesinger & poet

Wal·ton \'wòl-t^ən\ Ernest Thomas Sinton 1903–1995 Irish physicist

Walton Izaak \'ī-zik, -zək\ 1593–1683 Eng. writer

Walton Samuel Moore 1918–1992 Am. merchant

Walton Sir William Turner 1902–1983 Eng. composer

Wan·a·mak·er \'wä-nə-,mā-kər\ John 1838–1922 Am. merchant

Wang Ching–wei \'wäŋ-'jiŋ-'wä\ 1883–1944 Chin. polit.

War·beck \'wòr-,bek\ Perkin 1474–1499 Flem. imposter & pretender to the English throne

War·burg \'wòr-,bərg, 'vär-,bùrk\ Otto Heinrich 1883–1970 Ger. biochem.

Ward \'wòrd\ (Aaron) Montgomery 1843–1913 Am. merchant

Ward Ar·te·mas \'är-tə-məs\ 1727–1800 Am. gen. in Revolution

Ward Artemus — see Charles Farrar BROWNE

Ward Barbara 1914–1981 Baroness *Jackson of Lodsworth* Eng. econ.

Ward Sir Joseph George 1856–1930 N.Z. statesman

Ward Mary Augusta 1851–1920 *Mrs. Humphry Ward* née *Arnold* Eng. nov.

War·hol \'wòr-,hól, -,hòl\ Andy 1928?–1987 orig. *Andrew Warhola* Am. artist & filmmaker — **War·hol·ian** \wòr-'hò-lē-ən, -'hō-\ *adj*

War·ner \'wòr-nər\ Charles Dudley 1829–1900 Am. editor & essayist

War·ren \'wòr-ən, 'wär-\ Earl 1891–1974 Am. jurist; chief justice U.S. Supreme Court (1953–69)

Warren Gou·ver·neur \,gə-və(r)-'nir\ Kemble 1830–1882 Am. gen.

Warren Joseph 1741–1775 Am. physician & gen. in Revolution

Warren J. Robin 1937–   Austral. pathologist

Warren Robert Penn 1905–1989 Am. author & educ.; poet laureate (1986–87)

War·shel \'wòr-shəl\ Arieh 1940–   Israeli-Am. biochem.

War·ton \'wòr-t^ən\ Thomas 1728–1790 Eng. lit. hist. & critic; poet laureate (1785–90)

War·wick \'wär-ik, *US also* 'wòr-ik, 'wòr-(,)wik\ Earl of 1428–1471 *Richard Nev·ille* \'ne-vəl\; *the Kingmaker* Eng. soldier & statesman

Wash·ing·ton \'wò-shiŋ-tən, 'wä-\ Book·er \'bu-kər\ Tal·ia·ferro \'tä-lə-vər—*sic*\ 1856–1915 Am. educ.

Washington George 1732–1799 Am. gen.; 1st pres. of the U.S. (1789–97) — **Wash·ing·to·nian** \,wò-shiŋ-'tō-nē-ən, ,wä-, -nyən\ *adj*

Was·mo·sy \wäs-'mō-sē\ Juan Carlos 1938–   pres. of Paraguay (1993–98)

Was·ser·mann \'wä-sər-mən, 'vä-\ August von 1866–1925 Ger. bacteriol.

Was·ser·stein \'wä-sər-ˌstīn\ Wendy 1950–2006 Am. dram.

Wa·ters \'wȯ-tərz, 'wä-\ Ethel 1896–1977 Am. actress & singer

Wat·son \'wät-sən\ James Dewey 1928– Am. geneticist

Watson John 1850–1907 pseud. *Ian Mac·lar·en* \mə-'klar-ən\ Scot. clergyman & author

Watson John Broadus 1878–1958 Am. psychol.

Watson Thomas (John) 1874–1956 & his son Thomas (John), Jr. 1914–1993 Am. industrialists

Watson Sir (John) William 1858–1935 Eng. poet

Watson–Watt \-'wät\ Sir Robert Alexander 1892–1973 Scot. physicist

Watt \'wät\ James 1736–1819 Scot. inventor

Wat·teau \wä-'tō, vä-\ (Jean-) Antoine 1684–1721 Fr. painter

Wat·ter·son \'wä-tər-sən, 'wȯ-\ Henry 1840–1921 Am. journalist

Watts \'wäts\ George Frederic 1817–1904 Eng. painter & sculptor

Watts Isaac 1674–1748 Eng. theol. & hymn writer

Watts–Dun·ton \-'dən-t°n\ Walter Theodore 1832–1914 Eng. critic & poet

Waugh \'wȯ\ Evelyn Arthur St. John 1903–1966 Eng. writer

Wa·vell \'wä-vəl\ 1st Earl 1883–1950 *Archibald Percival Wavell* Brit. field marshal; viceroy of India (1943–47)

Wayne \'wān\ Anthony 1745–1796 *Mad Anthony* Am. gen. in Revolution

Wayne John 1907–1979 born *Marion Michael Morrison* Am. film actor

Webb \'web\ Beatrice 1858–1943 née *Potter; wife of S.J.* Eng. socialist

Webb Sidney James 1859–1947 1st Baron *Passfield* Eng. socialist

We·ber \'web\ & Carl Maria von 1786–1826 Ger. composer & conductor

Weber Ernst Heinrich 1795–1878 Ger. physiol.

Weber Max 1864–1920 Ger. sociol. & econ. — We·be·ri·an \vä-'bir-ē-ən\ *adj*

Web·er \'we-bər\ Max 1881–1961 Am. (Russ.-born) painter

We·bern \'vä-bərn\ Anton von 1883–1945 Austrian composer

Web·ster \'web-stər\ Daniel 1782–1852 Am. statesman & orator

Webster John *ca* 1580–*ca* 1625 Eng. dram.

Webster Noah 1758–1843 Am. lexicographer & author

Wedg·wood \'wej-ˌwu̇d\ Josiah 1730–1795 Eng. potter

Weems \'wēmz\ Mason Locke 1759–1825 *Parson Weems* Am. clergyman & biographer

We·ge·ner \'vä-gə-nər\ Alfred Lothar 1880–1930 Ger. geophysicist & meteorologist

Weil \'vä\ André 1906–1998 Am. (Fr.-born) math.

Weill \'wī(-ə)l, 'vī(-ə)l\ Kurt \'ku̇rt\ 1900–1950 Am. (Ger.-born) composer

Weir \'wir\ Robert Walter 1803–1889 Am. painter

Weis·mann \'vīs-ˌmän, 'wīs-mən\ August Friedrich Leopold 1834–1914 Ger. biol.

Weiz·mann \'vīts-mən, 'wīts-\ Chaim \'k̲īm, 'hīm\ Azriel 1874–1952 Israeli (Russ.-born) chem.; 1st pres. of Israel (1949–52)

Welch \'welch, 'welsh\ William Henry 1850–1934 Am. pathologist

Welles \'welz\ (George) Or·son \'ȯr-s°n\ 1915–1985 Am. film & theater director, writer, producer, & actor

Welles Gideon 1802–1878 Am. polit. & writer

Welles Sumner 1892–1961 Am. diplomat

Welles·ley \'welz-lē\ 1st Marquis of 1760–1842 *Richard Colley Wellesley* Brit. statesman; gov.-gen. of India (1797–1805)

Wel·ling·ton \'we-liŋ-tən\ 1st Duke of 1769–1852 *Arthur Wellesley; the Iron Duke* Brit. gen. & statesman

Wells \'welz\ Herbert George 1866–1946 Eng. nov. & hist. — Wells·ian \'wel-zē-ən\ *adj*

Wel·ty \'wel-tē\ Eudora 1909–2001 Am. writer

Wen·ces·las \'wen(t)-sə-ˌsläs, -slȯs\ *G* Wen·zel \'ven(t)-səl\ 1361–1419 king of Germany & Holy Rom. emp. (1378–1400) & (as Wenceslas IV) king of Bohemia (1378–1419)

Wen Jia·bao \'wən-'jyä-'bau̇\ 1942– prime min. of China (2003–13)

Went·worth \'went-(ˌ)wərth\ William Charles 1793–1872 Austral. statesman

Wer·fel \'ver-fəl\ Franz 1890–1945 Ger. author

Wer·ner \'ver-nər\ Alfred 1866–1919 Swiss chem.

Wes·ley \'wes-lē, 'wez-\ Charles 1707–1788 *bro. of John* Eng. Methodist preacher & hymn writer

Wesley John 1703–1791 Eng. evangelist & founder of Methodism

West \'west\ Benjamin 1738–1820 Am. painter

West Nathanael 1903–1940 orig. *Nathan Wallenstein Weinstein* Am. nov.

West Dame Rebecca 1892–1983 pseud. of *Cicily Isabel Andrews* née *Fairfield* Eng. critic & nov.

West Thomas — see DE LA WARR

Wes·ter·marck \'wes-tər-ˌmärk\ Edward Alexander 1862–1939 Finn. philos. & anthropol.

Wes·ting·house \'wes-tiŋ-ˌhau̇s\ George 1846–1914 Am. inventor

Wet, de \də-'vet\ Christiaan Rudolf 1854–1922 Boer soldier & polit.

Wey·den \'vī-d°n, 'vä-\ Rogier van der 1399?–1464 Flem. painter

Wey·gand \vā-'gäⁿ\ Maxime 1867–1965 Fr. gen.

Whar·ton \'hwȯr-t°n, 'wȯr-\ Edith Newbold 1862–1937 née *Jones* Am. nov.

Whate·ly \'hwāt-lē, 'wāt-\ Richard 1787–1863 Eng. theol. & logician

Wheat·ley \'hwēt-lē, 'wēt-\ Phillis 1753?–1784 Am. (African-born) poet

Wheat·stone \'hwēt-ˌstōn, 'wēt-, *chiefly Brit* -stən\ Sir Charles 1802–1875 Eng. physicist & inventor

Whee·ler \'hwē-lər, 'wē-\ Joseph 1836–1906 Am. gen.

Wheeler William Almon 1819–1887 Am. polit.; vice pres. of the U.S. (1877–81)

Whee·lock \'hwē-ˌläk, 'wē-\ Eleazar 1711–1779 Am. clergyman & educ.

Whip·ple \'hwi-pəl, 'wi-\ George Hoyt 1878–1976 Am. pathologist

Whis·tler \'hwis-lər, 'wis-\ James (Abbott) McNeill 1834–1903 Am. painter & etcher — Whis·tler·ian \hwis-'lir-ē-ən, wis-\ *adj*

White \'hwīt, 'wīt\ Andrew Dickson 1832–1918 Am. educ. & diplomat

White Byron Raymond 1917–2002 Am. jurist

White Edward Douglass 1845–1921 Am. jurist; chief justice U.S. Supreme Court (1910–21)

White Elwyn Brooks 1899–1985 Am. journalist & writer

White Gilbert 1720–1793 Eng. clergyman & naturalist

White Patrick Victor Martindale 1912–1990 Austral. writer

White Stanford 1853–1906 Am. architect

White Theodore Harold 1915–1986 Am. journalist & writer

White William Allen 1868–1944 Am. journalist & writer

White·field \'hwit-ˌfēld, 'hwīt-, 'wit-, 'wīt-\ George 1714–1770 Eng. Methodist revivalist

White·head \'hwīt-ˌhed, 'wīt-\ Alfred North 1861–1947 Eng. math. & philos.

Whitehead William 1715–1785 Eng. dram.; poet laureate (1757–85)

Whit·man \'hwit-mən, 'wit-\ Marcus 1802–1847 & his wife Narcissa 1808–1847 née *Prentiss* Am. missionaries & pioneers

Whitman Walt \'wȯlt\ 1819–1892 orig. *Walter Whitman* Am. poet — Whit·man·esque \ˌhwit-mə-'nesk, ˌwit-\ *or* Whit·man·ian \hwit-'mä-nē-ən, wit-\ *adj*

Whit·ney \'hwit-nē, 'wit-\ Eli 1765–1825 Am. inventor

Whitney Josiah Dwight 1819–1896 Am. geologist

Whitney William Dwight 1827–1894 *bro. of prec.* Am. philologist

Whit·ta·ker \'hwi-ti-kər, 'wit-\ Charles Evans 1901–1973 Am. jurist

Whit·ti·er \'hwi-tē-ər, 'wit-\ John Greenleaf 1807–1892 Am. poet

Wi·dor \vē-'dȯr\ Charles-Marie 1844–1937 Fr. organist & composer

Wie·land \'vē-ˌlänt\ Christoph Martin 1733–1813 Ger. author

Wieland Heinrich 1877–1957 Ger. chem.

Wie·man \'wī-mən\ Carl E(dwin) 1951– Am. physicist

Wien \'vēn\ Wilhelm 1864–1928 Ger. physicist

Wie·ner \'wē-nər\ Norbert 1894–1964 Am. math.

Wie·schaus \'wē-ˌshau̇s\ Eric F. 1947– Am. biol.

Wie·sel \'vē-ˌzel, wē-\ El·ie \'e-lē\ 1928– Am. (Rom.-born) writer

Wie·sel \'vē-səl\ Torsten N(ils) 1924– Swed. neurobiologist

Wig·gin \'wi-gən\ Kate Douglas 1856–1923 Am. writer & educ.

Wig·ner \'wig-nər\ Eugene Paul 1902–1995 Am. (Hung.-born) physicist

Wil·ber·force \'wil-bər-ˌfȯrs\ William 1759–1833 Eng. philanthropist & abolitionist

Wil·bur \'wil-bər\ Richard Purdy 1921– Am. poet & translator; poet laureate (1987–88)

Wil·czek \'wil-ˌchek\ Frank 1951– Am. physicist

Wilde \'wī(-ə)ld\ Oscar Fingal O'Flahertie Wills 1854–1900 Irish writer — Wil·de·an \'wī(-ə)l-dē-ən\ *adj*

Wil·der \'wī(-ə)l-dər\ Billy 1906–2002 born *Samuel Wilder* Am. (Pol.-born) filmmaker

Wilder Thornton Niven 1897–1975 Am. author

Wi·ley \'wī-lē\ Harvey Washington 1844–1930 Am. chem. & reformer

Wil·hel·mi·na \ˌwil-(ˌ)hel-'mē-nə, ˌwi-lə-'mē-\ 1880–1962 queen of the Netherlands (1890–1948)

Wilkes \'wilks\ Charles 1798–1877 Am. naval officer & explorer

Wilkes John 1725–1797 Eng. polit.

Wil·kins \'wil-kənz\ Sir George Hubert 1888–1958 Austral. explorer

Wilkins Maurice (Hugh Frederick) 1916–2004 Brit. (New Zeal.-born) biophysicist

Wilkins Roy 1901–1981 Am. civil rights leader

Wil·kin·son \'wil-kən-sən\ Ellen Cicely 1891–1947 Eng. polit.

Wilkinson James 1757–1825 Am. gen. & adventurer

Wil·lard \'wi-lərd\ Emma 1787–1870 née *Hart* Am. educ.

Willard Frances Elizabeth Caroline 1839–1898 Am. educ. & reformer

Wil·lem–Al·ex·an·der \'wi-ləm-ˌä-lek-'sän-dər\ 1967– in full *Willem-Alexander Claus George Ferdinand, son of Beatrix* king of the Netherlands (2013–)

Wil·liam \'wil-yəm\ name of 4 kings of England: **I** (*the Conqueror*) *ca* 1028–1087 (reigned 1066–87); **II** (*Rufus* \'rü-fəs\) *ca* 1056–1100 (reigned 1087–1100); **III** 1650–1702 (reigned 1689–1702—see MARY II); **IV** 1765–1837 (reigned 1830–37)

William I 1533–1584 *the Silent* prince of Orange & founder of the Du. Republic

William I 1797–1888 *Wilhelm Friedrich Ludwig* king of Prussia (1861–88) Ger. emp. (1871–88)

William II 1859–1941 *Friedrich Wilhelm Viktor Albert* Ger. emp. & king of Prussia (1888–1918)

William of Malmes·bury \'mämz-ˌber-ē, 'mälmz-, -b(ə-)rē\ *ca* 1090–*ca* 1143 Eng. hist.

Wil·liams \'wil-yəmz\ Hank 1923–1953 *Hiram King Williams* Am. singer & guitarist

Williams Jody 1950– Am. peace activist

Williams John (Towner) 1932– Am. composer & conductor

Williams Ralph Vaughan — see VAUGHAN WILLIAMS

Williams Roger 1603?–1683 Am. (Eng.-born) clergyman & founder of Rhode Island colony

Williams Ted 1918–2002 *Theodore Samuel Williams* Am. baseball player

Williams Tennessee 1911–1983 orig. *Thomas Lanier Williams* Am. dram.

Williams William Carlos 1883–1963 Am. poet & physician

Wil·liam·son \'wil-yəm-sən\ Oliver E(aton) 1932– Am. econ.

Will·kie \'wil-kē\ Wendell Lewis 1892–1944 Am. polit.

Will·stät·ter \'vil-ˌshte-tər, 'wil-ˌste-\ Richard 1872–1942 Ger. chem.

Wil·son \'wil-sən\ August 1945–2005 orig. *Frederick August Kittel* Am. playwright

Wilson Charles Thomson Rees 1869–1959 Scot. physicist

Wilson Edmund 1895–1972 Am. writer

Wilson Edward Osborne 1929– Am. biol.

Wilson Sir (James) Harold 1916–1995 Brit. prime min. (1964–70; 1974–76)

Wilson Henry 1812–1875 orig. *Jeremiah Jones Colbath* Am. polit.; vice pres. of the U.S. (1873–75)

Wilson Robert Woodrow 1936– Am. physicist

Wilson (Thomas) Wood·row \'wu̇-ˌdrō\ 1856–1924 28th pres. of the U.S. (1913–21) — Wil·so·ni·an \wil-'sō-nē-ən\ *adj*

Winck·el·mann \'viŋ-kəl-ˌmän, 'wiŋ-kəl-mən\ Johann Joachim 1717–1768 Ger. archaeol. & art hist.

Win·daus \'vin-ˌdau̇s\ Adolf Otto Reinhold 1876–1959 Ger. chem.

\ə\ abut \ᵊ\ kitten, F table \ər\ further \a\ ash \ā\ ace \ä\ mop, mar \au̇\ out \ch\ chin \e\ bet \ē\ easy \g\ go \i\ hit \ī\ ice \j\ job \ŋ\ sing \ō\ go \ȯ\ law \ȯi\ boy \th\ thin \t̲h̲\ the \ü\ loot \u̇\ foot \y\ yet \zh\ vision, beige \k̲, ⁿ, œ, ᴜᴇ, ᵞ\ *see* Guide to Pronunciation

Win·disch·grätz \,vin-dish-'grets\ Alfred Candidus Ferdinand 1787–1862 Fürst *zu Windischgrätz* Austrian field marshal
Windsor Duke of — see EDWARD VIII
Wine·land \'wīn-lənd\ David J(effrey) 1944–   Am. physicist
Win·frey \'win-frē\ Oprah (Gail) 1954–   Am. television host & actress
Win·gate \'win-,gāt, -gət\ Orde \'ȯrd\ Charles 1903–1944 Brit. gen.
Wins·low \'winz-,lō\ Edward 1595–1655 gov. of Plymouth colony
Win·sor \'win-zər\ Justin 1831–1897 Am. librarian & hist.
Win·throp \'win(t)-thrəp\ John 1588–1649 1st gov. of Massachusetts Bay colony
Winthrop John 1606–1676 *the younger; son of prec.* gov. of Connecticut colony
Wise \'wīz\ Stephen Samuel 1874–1949 Am. (Hung.-born) rabbi
Wise Thomas James 1859–1937 Eng. bibliophile & forger
Wise·man \'wīz-mən\ Nicholas Patrick Stephen 1802–1865 Eng. cardinal & author
Wiss·ler \'wis-lər\ Clark 1870–1947 Am. anthropol.
Wis·ter \'wis-tər\ Owen 1860–1938 Am. nov.
With·er \'wi-thər\ George 1588–1667 Eng. poet & pamphleteer
Witt, de \də-'vit\ Johan 1625–1672 Du. statesman
Wit·te \'vi-tə\ Sergey Yulyevich 1849–1915 Russ. statesman
Wit·te, de \də-'vi-tə\ Emanuel 1617–1692 Du. painter
Wit·te·kind \'vi-tə-,kint\ *or* **Wi·du·kind** \'vē-də-\ *d ca* 807 Saxon warrior
Witt·gen·stein \'vit-gən-,shtīn, -,stīn\ Ludwig Josef Johan 1889–1951 Brit. (Austrian-born) philos. — **Witt·gen·stein·ian** \,vit-gən-'shtī-nē-ən, -'stī-\ *adj*
Wode·house \'wu̇d-,hau̇s\ Sir Pel·ham \'pe-ləm\ Grenville 1881–1975 Am. (Eng.-born) writer
Woese \'wōz\ Carl R(ichard) 1928–2012 Am. microbiologist
Wol·cott \'wu̇l-kət\ Oliver 1726–1797 Am. polit.
Wolcott Oliver 1760–1833 *son of prec.* Am. polit.
Wolf \'vȯlf\ Friedrich August 1759–1824 Ger. philologist
Wolf Hugo Philipp Jakob 1860–1903 Austrian composer
Wolfe \'wu̇lf\ Charles 1791–1823 Irish poet
Wolfe James 1727–1759 Brit. gen.
Wolfe Thomas Clayton 1900–1938 Am. nov.
Wolfe Tom 1931–   *Thomas Kennerly Wolfe, Jr.* Am. writer
Wolff \'vȯlf\ Caspar Friedrich 1734–1794 Ger. anatomist
Wolff *or* **Wolf** \'vȯlf\ Christian 1679–1754 Freiherr *von Wolff* Ger. philos. & math.
Wol·fram von Esch·en·bach \'wu̇l-frəm-vän-'e-shən-,bäk, 'vȯl-,främ-, -,bäk\ *ca* 1170–*ca* 1220 Ger. poet & minnesinger
Wol·las·ton \'wu̇-lə-stən\ William Hyde 1766–1828 Eng. chem. & physicist
Woll·stone·craft \'wu̇l-stən-,kraft\ Mary 1759–1797 *wife of William Godwin & mother of M.W. Shelley* Eng. feminist & writer
Wolse·ley \'wu̇lz-lē\ 1st Viscount 1833–1913 *Garnet Joseph Wolseley* Brit. field marshal
Wol·sey \'wu̇l-zē\ Thomas *ca* 1475–1530 Eng. cardinal & statesman
Won·der \'wən-dər\ Stevie 1950–   born *Stevland Hardaway Judkins* Am. singer, songwriter & instrumentalist
Wood \'wu̇d\ Grant (DeVolson) 1892–1942 Am. painter
Wood Leonard 1860–1927 Am. physician & gen.
Woods \'wu̇dz\ Tiger 1975–   *Eldrick Woods* Am. golfer
Wood·ward \'wu̇d-wərd\ Robert Burns 1917–1979 Am. chem.
Woolf \'wu̇lf\ (Adeline) Virginia 1882–1941 née *Stephen* Eng. author
Wooll·cott \'wu̇l-kət\ Alexander 1887–1943 Am. writer
Wool·worth \'wu̇l-(,)wərth\ Frank Winfield 1852–1919 Am. merchant
Worces·ter \'wu̇s-tər\ Joseph Emerson 1784–1865 Am. lexicographer
Worde \'wȯrd\ Wynkyn de *d* 1534? Eng. (Alsatian-born) printer
Words·worth \'wərdz-(,)wərth\ William 1770–1850 Eng. poet; poet laureate (1843–50) — **Words·worth·ian** \,wərdz-'wər-thē-ən, -,thē-\ *adj*
Wot·ton \'wu̇-tᵊn, 'wä-\ Sir Henry 1568–1639 Eng. diplomat & poet
Wran·gel \'raŋ-gəl\ Baron Pyotr Nikolayevich 1878–1928 Russ. gen.
Wren \'ren\ Sir Christopher 1632–1723 Eng. architect
Wright \'rīt\ Frank Lloyd 1867–1959 Am. architect
Wright Joseph 1734–1797 *Wright of Derby* Eng. painter
Wright Or·ville \'ȯr-vəl\ 1871–1948 & his bro. Wilbur 1867–1912 Am. pioneers in aviation
Wright Richard 1908–1960 Am. author
Wundt \'vu̇nt\ Wilhelm 1832–1920 Ger. physiol. & psychol.
Wüth·rich \'vue-trik\ Kurt 1938–   Swiss biophysicist
Wu–ti \'wü-'dē\ 156–87 B.C. orig. *Liu Ch'e* Chin. emp. (140–87)
Wy·att *or* **Wy·at** \'wī-ət\ Sir Thomas 1503–1543 Eng. poet & diplomat
Wych·er·ley \'wi-chər-lē\ William 1640–1716 Eng. dram.
Wyc·liffe \'wi-,klif, -kləf\ John *ca* 1330–1384 Eng. religious reformer & theol. — **Wyc·liff·ian** \wi-'kli-fē-ən\ *adj*
Wy·eth \'wī-əth\ Andrew Newell 1917–2009 Am. painter
Wyeth N(ewell) C(onvers) 1882–1945 *father of prec.* Am. painter
Wy·lie \'wī-lē\ Elinor Morton 1885–1928 née *Hoyt* Am. poet & nov.
Wylie Philip Gordon 1902–1971 Am. writer
Wynd·ham \'win-dəm\ George 1863–1913 Eng. polit. & writer
Xan·thip·pe \zan-'thi-pē, -'ti-\ 5th cent. B.C. *wife of Socrates*
Xa·vi·er \'zāv-yər, 'zā-vē-ər, ig-'zā-\ Saint Francis 1506–1552 Span. *Francisco Ja·vier* \hä-'vyer\ Span. Jesuit missionary
Xe·noc·ra·tes \zi-'nä-krə-,tēz\ 396–314 B.C. Greek philos.
Xe·noph·a·nes \zi-'nä-fə-,nēz\ *ca* 560–*ca* 478 B.C. Greek philos.
Xen·o·phon \'ze-nə-fən\ *ca* 431–*ca* 352 B.C. Greek hist.
Xer·xes I \'zərk-,sēz\ *ca* 519–465 B.C. *the Great* king of Persia (486–465)
Xi Jin·ping \'shē-'jin-'piŋ\ 1953–   gen. secy. of Chin. Communist Party (2012–   ); pres. of China (2013–   )
Yale \'yāl\ Elihu 1649–1721 Eng. (Am.-born) colonial administrator
Yal·ow \'ya-(,)lō\ Rosalyn 1921–2011 née *Sussman* Am. med. physicist
Ya·ma·ga·ta \,yä-mə-'gä-tə\ Prince Aritomo 1838–1922 Jp. gen. & statesman
Ya·ma·mo·to \,yä-mə-'mō-(,)tō\ Isoroku 1884–1943 Jp. admiral
Ya·ma·na·ka \,yä-mä-'nä-kä\ Shinya 1962–   Jp. biol.
Ya·ma·shi·ta \,yä-mä-'shē-tä\ Tomoyuki 1885–1946 Jp. gen.
Ya·nu·ko·vych \,yä-nü-'kō-vich\ Viktor (Fedorovych) 1950–   pres. of Ukraine (2010–   )

Yar·'A·dua \'yär-ə-'dü-ə\ Umaru Musa 1951–2010 pres. of Nigeria (2007–10)
Yeats \'yāts\ William Butler 1865–1939 Irish poet & dram. — **Yeats·ian** \'yāt-sē-ən\ *adj*
Yel·tsin \'yelt-sən, 'yel-sin\ Boris Nikolayevich 1931–2007 pres. of Russian Federation (1990–99)
Yer·kes \'yər-kēz\ Charles Ty·son \'tī-sᵊn\ 1837–1905 Am. financier
Yev·tu·shen·ko \,yef-tə-'sheŋ-(,)kō\ Yevgeny Aleksandrovich 1933–   Soviet (Russ.-born) writer
Yo·nath \'yō-,nät\ Ada E. 1939–   Israeli biochem.
York \'yȯrk\ Alvin Cullum 1887–1964 Am. soldier
Yo·shi·hi·to \,yō-shi-'hē-(,)tō\ 1879–1926 emp. of Japan (1912–26)
You·mans \'yü-mənz\ Vincent 1898–1946 Am. composer
Young \'yəŋ\ Andrew Jackson, Jr. 1932–   U.S. ambassador to U.N. (1977–79)
Young Brig·ham \'bri-gəm\ 1801–1877 Am. Mormon leader
Young Cy orig. *Denton True Young* 1867–1955 Am. baseball player
Young Owen D. 1874–1962 Am. lawyer
Young Whitney Moore 1921–1971 Am. civil rights leader
Young·hus·band \'yəŋ-,həz-bənd\ Sir Francis Edward 1863–1942 Brit. explorer & author
Your·ce·nar \,yür-sə-'när\ Marguerite 1903–1987 orig. surname *de Crayencour* Fr. author
Yp·si·lan·tis \,ip-sə-'lan-tē\ Alexandros 1792–1828 & his bro. Demetrios 1793–1832 Greek revolutionaries
Yüan Shlh–k'ai \yü-'än-'shir-'kī, -'shē\ 1859–1916 Chin. soldier & statesman; pres. of China (1913–16)
Yu·dho·yo·no \,yü-dō-'yō-nō\ Susilo Bambang 1949–   pres. of Indonesia (2004–   )
Yu·ka·wa \yü-'kä-wə\ Hideki 1907–1981 Jp. physicist
Yung–lo \'yu̇ŋ-'lō\ 1360–1424 orig. *Chu Ti; often called Ch'eng Tsu* Chin. emp. (1402–24)
Yu·nus \'yü-nəs\ Muhammad 1940–   Bangladeshi econ. & banker
Yush·chen·ko \'yüsh-'cheŋ-kō\ Viktor (Andriyovych) 1954–   pres. of Ukraine (2005–10)
Zagh·lūl \zag-'lül\ Saʻd \'säd\ 1857–1927 *Saʻd Zaghlūl Pasha ibn Ibrāhīm* Egypt. statesman
Za·har·ias \zə-'ha-rē-əs\ Babe 1914–1956 *Mildred Ella Zaharias* née *Di·drik·son* \'dē-drik-sən\ Am. athlete
Za·ha·roff \'zä-hər-əf, -,ȯf\ Sir Basil 1849–1936 orig. *Basileios Zacharias* Fr. (Russ.-born) banker & armament contractor
Zan·gwill \'zaŋ-,gwil, -,wil\ Israel 1864–1926 Eng. dram. & nov.
Za·pa·ta \sä-'pä-tä\ Emiliano 1879–1919 Mex. revolutionary
Za·pa·te·ro \,sä-pä-'tā-rō\ José Luis Rodríguez 1960–   prime min. of Spain (2004–11)
Zar·da·ri \zär-'där-ē\ Asif Ali 1955–   *husband of Benazir Bhutto* pres. of Pakistan (2008–13)
Ze·dil·lo (Pon·ce de Le·ón) \sä-'thē-(,)yō-'pȯn-sä-(,)thä-lā-'ȯn\ Ernesto 1951–   pres. of Mexico (1994–2000)
Zee·man \'zā-,män, -mən\ Pieter 1865–1943 Du. physicist
Ze·man \'ze-,män\ Milos 1944–   pres. of Czech Rep. (2013–   )
Zeng·er \'zeŋ-gər, -ər\ John Peter 1697–1746 Am. (Ger.-born) journalist & printer
Ze·no·bia \zə-'nō-bē-ə\ *d* after A.D. 274 queen of Palmyra (267?–272)
Ze·no of Ci·ti·um \'zē-(,)nō-əv-'si-sh(ē-)əm\ *ca* 335–*ca* 263 B.C. Greek philos. & founder of Stoic school
Zeno of Elea \'ē-lē-ə\ *ca* 495–*ca* 430 B.C. Greek philos.
Zep·pe·lin \,tse-pə-'lēn, 'ze-p(ə-)lən\ Ferdinand (Adolf August Heinrich) 1838–1917 Graf *von Zeppelin* Ger. gen. & aeronaut
Zeux·is \'zük-səs\ 5th cent. B.C. Greek painter
Ze·wail \zə-'wī(-ə)l\ Ahmed H(assan) 1946–   Am. (Egypt.-born) physicist & chem.
Zhao Zi·yang *or* **Chao Tzu–yang** \'jau̇-(d)zə-'yäŋ\ 1919–2005 Chin. Communist leader
Zhda·nov \zhə-'dä-nəf, 'shtä-\ Andrey Aleksandrovich 1896–1948 Soviet polit.
Zhu·kov \'zhü-,kȯf, -,kȯv\ Georgy Konstantinovich 1896–1974 Soviet marshal
Zhu Rong·ji \'jü-'rȯŋ-jē\ 1928–   prime min. of China (1998–2003)
Zieg·feld \'zig-,feld, 'zēg- *also* -,fēld, -fəld\ Florenz 1869–1932 Am. theatrical producer
Zim·mer·mann \'zi-mər-mən, 'tsi-mər-,män\ Arthur 1864–1940 Ger. statesman
Zin·ker·na·gel \'tsiŋ-kər-,näg-ᵊl\ Rolf Martin 1944–   Swiss immunologist
Zi·nov·yev *or* **Zi·nov·iev** \zyi-'nȯf-yəf\ Grigory Yevseyevich 1883–1936 orig. *Ovsel Gershon Aronov Radomylsky* Soviet revolutionary
Zins·ser \'zin(t)-sər\ Hans 1878–1940 Am. bacteriol.
Zin·zen·dorf \'zin-zən-,dȯrf, 'tsin-sən-\ Nikolaus Ludwig 1700–1760 Graf *von Zinzendorf* Ger. religious reformer
Žiž·ka \'zhish-kə\ Count Jan *ca* 1376–1424 Bohemian gen. & Hussite leader
Zog I \'zȯg\ 1895–1961 prename *Ahmed Bey Zogu* king of the Albanians (1928–39)
Zo·la \'zō-lə, 'zō-,lä, zō-'lä\ Émile 1840–1902 Fr. nov. — **Zo·la·esque** \,zō-lə-'esk, -lä-\ *adj*
Zorn \'sȯrn, 'zȯrn\ Anders Leonard 1860–1920 Swed. painter, etcher, & sculptor
Zo·ro·as·ter \'zȯr-ə-,was-tər, 'zȯr-\ *Old Iranian* Zar·a·thu·shtra \,zar-ə-'thüsh-trə, -'thəsh-, -'thüs-, -'thəs-\ *ca* 628–*ca* 551 B.C. founder of Zoroastrianism
Zor·ri·lla (y Mo·ral) \zə-'rē-yə-,ē-mə-'räl\ José 1817–1893 Span. poet & dram.
Zu·lo·a·ga \,zü-lə-'wä-gə\ Ignacio 1870–1945 Span. painter
Zu·ma \'zü-mə\ Jacob (Gedleyihlekisa) 1942–   pres. of South Africa (2009–   )
Zur·ba·rán \,zu̇r-bə-'rän\ Francisco de 1598–1664 Span. painter
Zweig \'zwīg, 'swīg, 'tsvīk\ Arnold 1887–1968 Ger. author
Zweig Stefan 1881–1942 Austrian writer
Zwing·li \'zwiŋ-glē, 'swiŋ-, -lē; 'tsfiŋ-lē\ Huldrych 1484–1531 Swiss Reformation leader
Zwor·y·kin \'zwȯr-i-kən, 'zvȯrʸ-kin\ Vladimir (Kosma) 1889–1982 Am. (Russ.-born) engineer & inventor

Geographical Names

This section gives basic information about the countries of the world and their most important regions, cities, and physical features. The information includes spelling, end-of-line division, and pronunciation of the name, nature of the feature, its location, and for the more important entries statistical data.

This section complements the A–Z vocabulary by entering many derivative forms:

Ab·ys·sin·ia . . . — **Ab·ys·sin·ian** . . . *adj or n*

Cos·ta Ri·ca . . . — **Cos·ta Ri·can** . . . *adj or n*

Mo·na·co . . . — **Mo·na·can** . . . *adj or n* — **Mon·e·gasque** . . . *adj or n*

The abbreviations used are listed in the section Abbreviations in This Work or in the A–Z vocabulary section. The letters N, E, S, and W when not followed by a period indicate direction and are not part of a place-name; thus N Vietnam indicates northern Vietnam and not North Vietnam. The symbol ✳ denotes a capital. Areas, altitudes, and lengths are given first in conventional units, with metric equivalents in parentheses.

The Pinyin transliteration of place-names for the People's Republic of China is the first spelling shown; the Wade-Giles transliteration is second. Where no variant is given, the two spellings are identical.

Aa·chen \'ä-kən, -kən\ *or F* **Aix–la–Cha·pelle** \ˌāks-ˌlä-shä-'pel, ˌeks-\ city W Germany near Belgian & Dutch borders *pop* 241,861

Aaiún, El — see LAAYOUNE

Aalborg — see ÅLBORG

Aalst \'älst\ *or* **Alost** \ä-'lóst\ commune *cen* Belgium WNW of Brussels *pop* 76,382

Aa·rau \'är-ˌaù\ commune N Switzerland ✳ of Aargau canton *pop* 15,300

Aa·re \'är-ə\ *or* **Aar** \'är\ river 183 *mi* (294 *km*) *cen* & N Switzerland flowing E & NE into the Rhine

Aar·gau \'är-ˌgaù\ *or F* **Ar·go·vie** \ˌär-gō-'vē\ canton N Switzerland ✳ Aarau *area* 542 *sq mi* (1409 *sq km*), *pop* 550,900

Aarhus — see ÅRHUS

Ab·a·co \'a-bə-ˌkō\ two islands of Bahamas (**Great Abaco** & **Little Abaco**) N of New Providence Is. *area* 776 *sq mi* (2018 *sq km*), *pop* 13,170

Aba·dan \ˌä-bə-'dän, ˌa-bə-'dan\ **1** island W Iran in delta of Shatt al Arab **2** town & port on Abadan Is.

Aba·kan \ˌä-bə-'kän\ town S Russia in Asia ✳ of Khakassia *pop* 158,000

Abay *or* **Ab·bai** \ä-'bī\ the upper course of the Blue Nile

Ab·be·ville \'ab-ˌvēl, 'a-bi-ˌvil\ commune N France on the Somme NW of Amiens *pop* 24,568 ·

Ab·bots·ford \'a-bəts-fərd\ city Canada in SW B.C. SE of Vancouver *pop* 133,497

Ab·er·dare \ˌa-bər-'der\ town S Wales NNW of Cardiff *pop* 36,621

Ab·er·deen \ˌa-bər-'dēn\ city NE S.Dak. *pop* 26,091 **2** \ˌa-bər-'dēn\ *or* **Ab·er·deen·shire** \-ˌshir, -shər\ administrative area NE Scotland *area* 2439 *sq mi* (6318 *sq km*) **3** city & port NE Scotland constituting an administrative area *area* 72 *sq mi* (186 *sq km*), *pop* 211,080 — **Ab·er·do·ni·an** \ˌa-bər-'dō-nē-ən\ *adj or n*

Ab·er·yst·wyth \ˌa-bə-'ris-ˌtwith, -'rəs-\ borough W Wales on Cardigan Bay *pop* 8666

Ab·i·djan \ˌa-bē-'jän, ˌa-bi-\ city & port, seat of government of Ivory Coast *pop* 1,934,342

Abila — see MUSA (Jebel)

Ab·i·lene \'a-bə-ˌlēn\ city NW *cen* Tex. *pop* 117,063

Ab·i·tibi \ˌa-bə-'ti-bē\ **1** lake Canada on Ont.-Que. border *area* 356 *sq mi* (926 *sq km*) **2** river 230 *mi* (368 *km*) Canada in E Ont. flowing N into Moose River

Ab·kha·zia \ab-'kä-zh(ē-)ə, -'kä-zē-ə\ autonomous republic NW Republic of Georgia on Black Sea ✳ Sukhumi *area* 3320 *sq mi* (8599 *sq km*), *pop* 180,000 — **Ab·khas** \-'käs\ *n* — **Ab·kha·zian** *or* **Ab·kha·sian** \-'kä-zh(ē-)ən, -'kä-zē-ən\ *adj or n*

Abo·mey \a-bō-'mā, ə-'bō-mē\ city S Benin *pop* 54,418

Abruz·zi \ä-'brüt-sē\ *or* **Abruz·zo** region *cen* Italy on the Adriatic including highest of the Apennines ✳ L'Aquila *pop* 1,281,283; with Molise (to S), formerly comprised **Abruzzi e Mo·li·se** \ˌä-'mò-li-ˌzä\ region

Ab·sa·ro·ka Range \ab-'sär-ə-kə, -'sór-kə, -'zór-\ mountain range S Mont. & NW Wyo. E of Yellowstone National Park — see FRANKS PEAK

Ab·se·con Inlet \ab-'sē-kən\ inlet SE N.J. bet. barrier islands N of Atlantic City

Ab·şe·ron *or* **Ab·she·ron** *or* **Ap·she·ron** \ˌap-shi-'rón\ peninsula E Azerbaijan projecting into the Caspian Sea

Abu Dha·bi \ˌä-bü-'dä-bē, -'thä-\ **1** sheikhdom, member of United Arab Emirates **2** town, its ✳ & ✳ of United Arab Emirates *pop* 347,000

Abu·ja \ä-'bü-jä\ city *cen* Nigeria, its ✳ since 1991

Abu Qir \ˌä-bü-'kir\ **1** bay N Egypt bet. Alexandria & Rosetta mouth of the Nile **2** village on this bay

Abu Sim·bel \ˌä-bü-'sim-bəl, ˌä-bü-sim-'bal\ locality S Egypt on left bank of the Nile SW of Aswân; site of two rock temples which were moved 1964–66 to higher ground when area was flooded after completion of Aswân High Dam

Aby·dos \ə-'bī-dəs\ **1** ancient town Asia Minor on the Hellespont **2** ancient town S Egypt on left bank of the Nile S of Thebes

Abyla — see MUSA (Jebel)

Ab·ys·sin·ia \ˌa-bə-'si-nē-ə, -nyə\ — see ETHIOPIA 2 — **Ab·ys·sin·ian** \-nē-ən, -nyən\ *adj or n*

Aca·dia \ə-'kā-dē-ə\ *or F* **Aca·die** \ä-kä-'dē\ NOVA SCOTIA — an early name

Acadia National Park section of coast of Maine including chiefly mountainous areas on Mount Desert Is. & Isle au Haut

Aca·pul·co \ˌä-kä-'pül-(ˌ)kō, ˌa-\ *or* **Acapulco de Juá·rez** \dā-'hwär-ˌes, thä-\ city & port S Mexico in Guerrero on the Pacific *pop* 687,292

Ac·ar·na·nia \ˌa-kər-'nā-nē-ə, -'nä-nyə\ region W Greece on Ionian Sea — **Ac·ar·na·nian** \-nē-ən, -nyən\ *adj or n*

Ac·cad \'a-ˌkad, 'ä-ˌkäd\ — see AKKAD — **Ac·ca·di·an** \ə-'kā-dē-ən, -'kä-\ *adj or n*

Ac·cra \'ä-krə, 'a-; ə-'krä\ city & port ✳ of Ghana on Gulf of Guinea *pop* 867,459

Ac·cring·ton \'a-kriŋ-tən\ town NW England in SE Lancashire N of Manchester

Achaea \ə-'kē-ə\ *or* **Acha·ia** \-'kī-ə, -'kā-\ region S Greece in N Peloponnese bordering on Gulfs of Corinth & Patras — **Achae·an** \ə-'kē-ən\ *or* **Acha·ian** \ə-'kī-ən, -'kä-\ *adj or n*

Ach·e·lo·us \ˌa-kə-'lō-əs\ *or ModGk* **Akhe·ló·os** \ˌä-ke-'lō-ōs\ river 137 *mi* (220 *km*) W Greece flowing S to Ionian Sea

Ach·ill \'a-kəl\ island 15 *mi* (24 *km*) long NW Ireland in County Mayo

Achray, Loch \-'krä\ lake *cen* Scotland SE of Loch Katrine

Acon·ca·gua \ˌä-kōn-'kä-gwä\ mountain 22,834 *ft* (6960 *m*) W Argentina WNW of Mendoza near Chilean border; highest in Andes & western hemisphere

Açores — see AZORES

A Co·ru·ña \ˌä-kō-'rü-nyä\ *or* **La Coruña** \lä-\ **1** province NW Spain in Galicia *area* 3041 *sq mi* (7876 *sq km*), *pop* 1,096,027 **2** *or* **Co·run·na** \kə-'rə-nə\ port, its ✳ *pop* 236,379

Acragas — see AGRIGENTO

Acre \'ä-krē, -(ˌ)krä\ state W Brazil bordering on Peru & Bolivia ✳ Rio Branco *area* 59,343 *sq mi* (153,698 *sq km*), *pop* 557,526

Acre \'ä-kər, 'ā-kər, 'ä-krə\ *or Heb* **'Ak·ko** *or Old Testament* **Ac·cho** \'ä-kō, 'ä-\ *or New Testament* **Ptol·e·ma·ïs** \ˌtä-lə-'mā-əs\ city & port NW Israel N of Mt. Carmel *pop* 37,400

Ac·te \'ak-tē\ *or Gk* **Ak·tí** \äk-'tē\ peninsula NE Greece, the most easterly of the three peninsulas of Chalcidice — see ATHOS (Mount)

Ac·ti·um \'ak-shē-əm, 'ak-tē-\ promontory & ancient town W Greece in NW Acarnania

Adak \'ä-ˌdak\ island SW Alaska in Andreanof group

Adalia — see ANTALYA

Ad·ams, Mount \'a-dəmz\ **1** mountain 5798 *ft* (1767 *m*) N N.H. in White Mountains N of Mt. Washington **2** mountain 12,307 *ft* (3751 *m*) SW Wash. in Cascade Range SSE of Mt. Rainier

Ad·am's Bridge \'a-dəmz\ chain of shoals 30 *mi* (48 *km*) long bet. Sri Lanka & SE India

Adam's Peak *or Sinhalese* **Sa·ma·na·la Kan·da** \'sə-mə-nə-lə-'kən-də\ mountain 7360 *ft* (2243 *m*) S *cen* Sri Lanka

Ada·na \ä-dä-'nä, ə-'dä-nə\ *or formerly* **Sey·han** \sä-'hän\ city S Turkey on Seyhan River *pop* 916,150

1512 Geographical Names

Ada·pa·za·rı \ˌä-də-ˌpä-zə-'rï\ city NW Turkey E of Istanbul *pop* 171,225

Ad Dam·mām \ˌäd-däm-'mäm\ *or* **Dam·mam** \də-'mam\ town & port Saudi Arabia on Persian Gulf

Ad·dis Aba·ba \ˌä-dis-'ä-bä-ˌbä, ˌa-dəs-'a-bə-bə\ city *cen* Ethiopia, its ✳ *pop* 2,970,000

Ad·di·son \'a-də-sən\ village NE Ill. W of Chicago *pop* 36,942

Ad·e·laide \'a-də-ˌlād\ city Australia ✳ of S. Australia *metropolitan area pop* 917,000

Aden \'ā-dᵊn, 'ä-\ **1** former Brit. protectorate S Arabia comprising the entire S coast of what is now Yemen; became part of People's Democratic Republic of Yemen 1967 *area* 112,000 *sq mi* (291,200 *sq km*) **2** former Brit. colony SW Arabia comprising Perim Is., the city of Aden, & the surrounding area; became part of People's Democratic Republic of Yemen 1967 *area* 75 *sq mi* (195 *sq km*) **3** city & port S Yemen; formerly ✳ of People's Democratic Republic of Yemen & before that ✳ of Aden colony & protectorate *pop* 240,370

Aden, Gulf of arm of Indian Ocean bet. Aden & Somalia

Adi·ge \'ä-dē-ˌjā\ river 255 *mi* (410 *km*) N Italy flowing SE into the Adriatic

Ad·i·ron·dack Mountains \ˌa-də-'rän-ˌdak\ mountains NE N.Y.

Ad·mi·ral·ty Inlet \'ad-m(ə-)rəl-tē\ branch of Puget Sound NW Washington

Admiralty Island island 90 *mi* (145 *km*) long SE Alaska in N Alexander Archipelago

Admiralty Islands islands W Pacific N of New Guinea in Bismarck Archipelago *area* 800 *sq mi* (2080 *sq km*), *pop* 30,160

Adour \ä-'du̇r\ river 208 *mi* (335 *km*) SW France flowing from the Pyrenees NW & W into Bay of Biscay

Adrianople — see EDIRNE

Adri·at·ic Sea \ˌā-drē-'a-tik, ˌa-\ arm of the Mediterranean bet. Italy & Balkan Peninsula

Ad·vent Bay \'ad-ˌvent, -vənt\ inlet of Arctic Ocean W Spitsbergen

Ad·wa \'äd-(ˌ)wä\ town N Ethiopia S of Asmara *pop* 17,476

Ady·ge·ya \ˌä-də-'gä-ə\ republic S Russia in Europe ✳ Maykop *area* 2934 *sq mi* (7599 *sq km*), *pop* 437,400

Adzharia — see AJARIA — **Adzhar** \'ä-jär, ə-'jär\ *n or adj*

Aegates Islands — see EGADI ISLANDS

Ae·ge·an Islands \i-'jē-ən\ islands Aegean Sea including the Cyclades & the Northern & Southern Sporades

Aegean Sea arm of the Mediterranean bet. Asia Minor & Greece

Ae·gi·na \i-'jī-nə\ *or Gk* **Aí·yi·na** \'e-yē-ˌnä\ island & ancient state SE Greece in Saronic Gulf — **Ae·gi·ne·tan** \ˌē-jə-'nē-tᵊn\ *adj or n*

Ae·gos·pot·a·mi \ˌē-gə-'spä-tə-ˌmī\ *or* **Ae·gos·pot·a·mos** \-məs\ river & town of ancient Thrace in the Chersonese

Aemilia — see EMILIA-ROMAGNA

Ae·o·lis \'ē-ə-ləs\ *or* **Ae·o·lia** \ē-'ō-lē-ə, -'ōl-yə\ ancient country of NW Asia Minor

Ae·to·lia \ē-'tō-lē-ə, -'tōl-yə\ region W *cen* Greece N of Gulf of Patras & E of Acarnania — **Ae·to·lian** \-lē-ən, -yən\ *adj or n*

Afars and the Issas, French Territory of the — see DJIBOUTI 1

Af·ghan·i·stan \af-'ga-nə-ˌstan, -'gä-nə-ˌstän\ country W Asia E of Iran ✳ Kabul *area* 250,775 *sq mi* (649,507 *sq km*), *pop* 22,576,000

Afog·nak \ə-'fōg-ˌnak, -'fäg-\ island S Alaska N of Kodiak Is.

Af·ri·ca \'a-fri-kə *also* 'ä-\ continent of the eastern hemisphere S of the Mediterranean & adjoining Asia on NE *area* 11,677,239 *sq mi* (30,244,049 *sq km*)

African Burial Ground National Monument site SE N.Y. in lower Manhattan, New York City

Afyon \ä-'fyȯn\ city W *cen* Turkey *pop* 98,618

Aga·dir \ˌä-gə-'dir, ˌa-\ city & port SW Morocco *area pop* 478,000

Agana — see HAGÁTÑA

Agar·ta·la \ˌə-gər-tə-'lä\ city E India ✳ of Tripura *pop* 189,327

Ag·ate Fossil Beds National Monument \'a-gət\ reservation W Nebr.

Ag·a·wam \'a-gə-ˌwäm\ city SW Mass. *pop* 28,438

Age·nais \ˌä-zhə-'nä\ *or* **Age·nois** \ˌä-zhe-'nwä\ ancient region SW France S of Périgord ✳ Agen

Aghrim — see AUGHRIM

Ag·in·court \'a-jin-ˌkȯrt, 'ä-zhən-ˌku̇r\ *or F* **Azin·court** \ˌä-zaⁿ-'ku̇r\ village N France WNW of Arras *pop* 276

Ag·no \'äg-(ˌ)nō\ river 128 *mi* (206 *km*) Philippines in NW Luzon

Agra \'ä-grə, 'ò-\ **1** region N India roughly equivalent to present Uttar Pradesh excluding Oudh region **2** city N India in W Uttar Pradesh SSE of Delhi *pop* 1,259,979

Agri Dagi — see ARARAT

Agri·gen·to \ˌä-grē-'jen-(ˌ)tō, ˌa-\ *or formerly* **Gir·gen·ti** \jər-'jen-tē\ *or anc* **Ag·ri·gen·tum** \ˌa-grə-'jen-təm\ *or* **Ac·ra·gas** \'ä-krä-ˌgäs\ commune Italy in SW Sicily near coast *pop* 55,446

Agua·dil·la \ˌä-gwä-'thä\ city NW Puerto Rico *pop* 41,959

Agua·di·lla \ˌä-gwä-'thē-yä\ city NW Puerto Rico *pop* 60,949

Aguas Bue·nas \ˌä-gwäs-'bwā-näs\ city E *cen* Puerto Rico *pop* 28,659

Aguas·ca·lien·tes \ˌä-gwäs-ˌkäl-'yen-ˌtäs\ **1** state *cen* Mexico *area* 2158 *sq mi* (5589 *sq km*), *pop* 719,659 **2** city, its ✳ *pop* 506,384

Agul·has, Cape \ə-'gəl-əs\ headland Republic of S. Africa in S Western Cape province; southernmost point of Africa, at 34°50'S, 20°E

Ahag·gar Mountains \ə-'hä-gər, ˌä-hə-'gär\ *or* **Hog·gar Mountains** \'hä-gər, hə-'gär\ mountains S Algeria in W *cen* Sahara; highest peak Tahat 9842 *ft* (3000 *m*)

Ah·mad·abad \'ä-mə-də-ˌbäd, -ˌbad\ city W India N of Bombay in Gujarat *pop* 3,515,361

Ah·vaz \ä-'väz\ *or* **Ah·waz** \ä-'wäz\ city SW Iran on the Karun *pop* 985,614

Ai·bo·ni·to \ˌī-bō-'nē-tō\ city *cen* Puerto Rico *pop* 25,900

Ai·ken \'ä-kən\ city W S.C. SW of Columbia *pop* 29,524

Ail·sa Craig \ˌāl-zə-'krāg\ small rocky island Scotland S of Arran at mouth of Firth of Clyde

Ain \'aⁿ\ river 120 *mi* (195 *km*) E France rising in Jura Mountains & flowing SSW into the Rhône

Aintab — see GAZIANTEP

Air·drie \'er-drē\ **1** burgh S *cen* Scotland E of Glasgow *pop* 45,643 **2** city Canada in S Alta. *pop* 42,564

Aire \'er\ river 70 *mi* (113 *km*) N England in W Yorkshire flowing to the Ouse; its valley is **Aire·dale** \-ˌdāl\

Aisne \'ān\ river *ab* 165 *mi* (265 *km*) N France flowing NW & W from Argonne Forest into the Oise near Compiègne

Aix–en–Pro·vence \ˌāks-ˌäⁿ-prō-'väⁿs, ˌeks-\ *or* **Aix** \'äks, 'eks\ city SE France N of Marseille *pop* 134,324

Aix–la–Chapelle — see AACHEN

Aix–les–Bains \ˌäks-lä-'baⁿ, ˌeks-\ commune E France N of Chambéry *pop* 25,721

Ai·zawl \i-'zau̇(-ə)l\ town E India ✳ of Mizoram *pop* 229,714

Ajac·cio \ä-'yä-(ˌ)chō, ä-zhäk-'syō\ city & port France in Corsica *pop* 52,851

Ajan·ta \ə-'jən-tə\ village W *cen* India in N *cen* Maharashtra in **Ajanta Range** (hills) NNE of Aurangabad; site of **Ajanta Caves** (temples excavated out of rock cliffs)

Ajar·ia *or* **Adzhar·ia** \ə-'jär-ē-ə\ autonomous republic SW Republic of Georgia on Black Sea ✳ Batumi *area* 1158 *sq mi* (2999 *sq km*), *pop* 381,500

Ajax \'ā-ˌjaks\ town Canada in SE Ont. *pop* 109,600

'Aj·man \äj-'män\ sheikhdom, member of United Arab Emirates

Aj·mer \ˌəj-'mir, -'mer\ city NW India in Rajasthan SW of Delhi *pop* 485,197

Akhelóos — see ACHELOUS

Ak·hi·sar \ˌäk-hi-'sär, ˌa-ki-\ *or anc* **Thy·a·ti·ra** \ˌthī-ə-'tī-rə\ city W Turkey in Asia NE of Izmir *pop* 151,957

Aki·ta \ä-'kē-tä, 'ä-kē-tä\ city & port Japan in N Honshu on Sea of Japan *pop* 317,625

Ak·kad *or* **Ac·cad** \'a-ˌkad, 'ä-ˌkäd\ **1** the N division of ancient Babylonia **2** *or* **Aga·de** \ə-'gä-də\ ancient city, its ✳

Akkerman — see BELGOROD-DNESTROVSKI

'Akko — see ACRE

Akmola — see ASTANA

Ak·ron \'a-krən\ city NE Ohio SE of Cleveland *pop* 199,110

Ak·sum *or* **Ax·um** \'äk-ˌsüm\ town N Ethiopia ✳ of an ancient kingdom (the Axumite Empire)

Aktí — see ACTE

Akyab — see SITTWE

Al·a·bama \ˌa-lə-'ba-mə\ **1** river 315 *mi* (507 *km*) S Ala. flowing SW into Tensaw & Mobile rivers — see TALLAPOOSA **2** state SE U.S. ✳ Montgomery *area* 51,705 *sq mi* (133,916 *sq km*), *pop* 4,779,736 — **Al·a·bam·i·an** \-'ba-mē-ən\ *or* **Al·a·bam·an** \-'ba-mən\ *adj or n*

Al·a·bas·ter \'a-lə-ˌbas-tər\ city *cen* Ala. S of Birmingham *pop* 30,352

Ala·go·as \ˌä-lə-'gō-əs\ state NE Brazil ✳ Maceió *area* 11,238 *sq mi* (29,184 *sq km*), *pop* 2,822,621

Alai \'ä-ˌlī\ mountain range SW Kyrgyzstan; highest peak 19,554 *ft* (5960 *m*)

Al ʿA·mā·rah \al-ha-'mär-ə\ city SE Iraq on the Tigris

Al·a·me·da \ˌa-lə-'mē-də\ city & port W Calif. on island in San Francisco Bay near Oakland *pop* 73,812

Alamein, El — see EL ALAMEIN

Al·a·mo·gor·do \ˌa-lə-mə-'gȯr-(ˌ)dō\ city S N.Mex. *pop* 30,403

Åland \'ō-ˌlän(d)\ *or* **Ahv·e·nan·maa** \'ä-ve-nän-ˌmä\ **1** archipelago SW Finland in Baltic Sea ✳ Mariehamn **2** island, chief of this group

Ala·nia \ə-'lä-nyə, -nē-ə\ *or* **North Os·se·tia** \ä-'sē-sh(ē-)ə\ autonomous republic SE Russia in Europe on the N slopes of Caucasus Mountains ✳ Vladikavkaz *area* 3089 *sq mi* (8001 *sq km*), *pop* 695,000

Al–ʿAqabah — see AQABA

Ala·şe·hir \ˌa-lə-shə-'hir, ˌä-\ *or anc* **Philadelphia** city W Turkey 75 *mi* (121 *km*) E of Izmir *pop* 36,535

Alas·ka \ə-'las-kə\ state (territory 1912–59) of the U.S. NW N. America ✳ Juneau *area* 591,004 *sq mi* (1,530,700 *sq km*), *pop* 710,231 — **Alas·kan** \-kən\ *adj or n*

Alaska, Gulf of inlet of the Pacific off S Alaska bet. Alaska Peninsula on W & Alexander Archipelago on E

Alaska Peninsula peninsula SW Alaska SW of Cook Inlet

Alaska Range mountain range S Alaska extending from Alaska Peninsula to Yukon boundary — see MCKINLEY (Mount)

Ala Tau \ˌä-lə-'tau̇\ several mountain ranges of the Tian Shan E Kazakhstan & Kyrgyzstan around & NE of Issyk Kul

Ala·va \'ä-lə-və\ province N Spain S of Vizcaya; in Basque Country ✳ Vitoria *area* 1176 *sq mi* (3046 *sq km*), *pop* 286,387

Al·a·va, Cape \'a-lə-və\ cape NW Wash. S of Cape Flattery; westernmost point of conterminous U.S., at 124°44'W

Al–ʿAyzarīyah — see BETHANY

Al·ba·ce·te \ˌäl-bä-'sä-tä\ **1** province SE Spain N of Murcia province *area* 5737 *sq mi* (14,859 *sq km*), *pop* 364,835 **2** commune, its ✳ *pop* 148,934

Al·ba Lon·ga \ˌal-bə-'lȯn-gə\ ancient city *cen* Italy SE of Rome

Al·ban Hills \'ȯl-bən, 'al-\ *or anc* **Al·ba·nus Mons** \ˌäl-'bä-nəs-'mȯn(t)s\ mountain group Italy SE of Rome

Al·ba·nia \al-'bā-nē-ə, -nyə *also* ȯl-\ **1** ancient country Europe in E Caucasus region on W side of Caspian Sea **2** country S Europe in Balkan Peninsula on the Adriatic; a republic ✳ Tiranë *area* 11,100 *sq mi* (28,749 *sq km*), *pop* 3,069,275

Al·ba·no, Lake \al-'bä-(ˌ)nō, äl-\ *or anc* **Al·ba·nus La·cus** \äl-'bä-nəs-'lä-kəs\ lake Italy SE of Rome

Al·ba·ny \'ȯl-bə-nē\ **1** city SW Ga. *pop* 77,434 **2** city ✳ of N.Y. on Hudson River *pop* 97,856 **3** city NW Oreg. S of Salem *pop* 50,158 **4** \'al-\ river 610 *mi* (982 *km*) Canada in N Ont. flowing E into James Bay — **Al·ba·ni·an** \ȯl-'bä-nē-ən\ *adj or n*

Al–Basrah — see BASRA

Al·be·marle Sound \'al-bə-ˌmärl\ inlet of the Atlantic NE N.C.

Al·bert, Lake \'al-bərt\ lake 100 *mi* (161 *km*) long E Africa bet. Uganda & Democratic Republic of the Congo in course of the Victoria Nile

Al·ber·ta \al-'bər-tə\ province W Canada ✳ Edmonton *area* 246,422 *sq mi* (638,232 *sq km*), *pop* 3,645,257 — **Al·ber·tan** \-'bər-tᵊn\ *adj or n*

Albert Nile — see NILE

Albertville — see KALEMIE

Al·bi \äl-'bē\ commune S France NE of Toulouse *pop* 46,299

Al Biqaʿ — see BEKAA

Ål·borg *or* **Aal·borg** \'ȯl-ˌbȯrg\ city & port Denmark in NE Jutland *pop* 162,521

Al·bu·quer·que \'al-bə-ˌkər-kē\ city *cen* N.Mex. *pop* 448,607 — **Al·bu·quer·que·an** \-kē-ən\ *n*

Al·ca·lá de He·na·res \ˌäl-kä-'lä-thä-ā-'när-äs\ commune *cen* Spain, ENE of Madrid *pop* 176,434

Al·ca·mo \'äl-kä-ˌmō\ commune Italy in NW Sicily *pop* 43,578

Al·ca·traz \'al-kə-ˌtraz\ island Calif. in San Francisco Bay

Al·cor·cón \ˌäl-kór-'kōn\ commune *cen* Spain, SW of Madrid *pop* 153,100

Al·da·bra \al-'dä-brə\ island (atoll) NW Indian Ocean N of Madagascar; chief of Aldabra group belonging to Seychelles

Al·dan \äl-'dän\ river 1393 *mi* (2241 *km*) E Russia in Asia in Sakha Republic flowing into the Lena

Al·der·ney \'ól-dər-nē\ island in English Channel; northernmost of the Channel Islands ✳ St. Anne *area* 3 *sq mi* (7.8 *sq km*), *pop* 2086

Al·der·shot \'ól-dər-ˌshät\ town S England in NE Hampshire *pop* 32,654

Aleksandrovsk — see ZAPORIZHZHYA

Aleksandrovsk–Grushevski — see SHAKHTY

Alen·çon \ˌa-lǟⁿ-'sóⁿ\ city NW France N of Le Mans *pop* 28,917

Alep·po \ə-'le-(ˌ)pō\ *or anc* **Be·roea** \bə-'rē-ə\ city N Syria *pop* 1,445,000 — **Alep·pine** \ə-'le-pən, -ˌpīn, -ˌpēn\ *adj or n*

Ales·san·dria \ˌä-le-'sän-drē-ä\ commune NW Italy *pop* 90,025

Aleu·tian Islands \ə-'lü-shən\ islands SW Alaska extending in an arc 1700 *mi* (2735 *km*) SW & W from Alaska Peninsula — see ANDREANOF ISLANDS, FOX ISLANDS, NEAR ISLANDS, RAT ISLANDS

Aleutian Range mountain range SW Alaska, the SW extension of Alaska Range running along NW shore of Cook Inlet to SW tip of Alaska Peninsula with mountains of the Aleutian Islands forming its SW extension — see SHISHALDIN

Al·ex·an·der Archipelago \ˌa-lig-'zan-dər, ˌe-\ archipelago of *ab* 1100 islands SE Alaska — see ADMIRALTY ISLAND, BARANOF, CHICHAGOF, KUPREANOF, PRINCE OF WALES ISLAND 1, REVILLAGIGEDO ISLAND

Alexander I Island island Antarctica W of base of Antarctic Peninsula

Alexandretta — see ISKENDERUN

Al·ex·an·dria \ˌa-lig-'zan-drē-ə, ˌe-\ **1** city *cen* La. *pop* 47,723 **2** city N Va. on the Potomac S of Washington, D.C. *pop* 139,966 **3** city & port N Egypt bet. Lake Mareotis & the Mediterranean *pop* 3,170,000 — **Al·ex·an·dri·an** \-drē-ən\ *adj or n*

Al Fal·lu·jah *or* **Fal·lu·jah** *or* **Al Fal·lu·ja** *or* **Falluja** \(ˌäl-)fə-'lü-jə\ town *cen* Iraq on the Euphrates

Al Fayyūm — see EL FAIYÛM

Al·föld \'ól-ˌfə(r)ld, -ˌfoeld\ the central plain of Hungary

Al Fu·jay·rah \ˌäl-fü-'jī-rə\ *or* **Fu·jai·rah** \-'jī-rə\ sheikhdom, member of United Arab Emirates *area* 450 *sq mi* (1166 *sq km*)

Al·gar·ve \äl-'gär-və, al-\ medieval Moorish kingdom now a province of Portugal on S coast

Al·ge·ci·ras \ˌal-jə-'sir-əs, ˌäl-hā-'thē-räs\ city & port SW Spain W of Gibraltar on Bay of Algeciras *pop* 101,468

Al·ge·ria \al-'jir-ē-ə\ country NW Africa bordering on the Mediterranean ✳ Algiers *area* 918,497 *sq mi* (2,390,315 *sq km*), *pop* 34,200,000 — **Al·ge·ri·an** \-ē-ən\ *adj or n*

Algiers \al-'jirz\ **1** former Barbary State N Africa now Algeria **2** city & port ✳ of Algeria on **Bay of Algiers** (inlet of Mediterranean) *pop* 1,365,400 — **Al·ge·rine** \ˌal-jə-'rēn\ *adj or n*

Algoa Bay \al-'gō-ə\ inlet of Indian Ocean S Republic of S. Africa on SE coast of Eastern Cape province

Al·gon·quin \al-'gän-kwən, -'gäŋ-\ village NE Ill. NW of Chicago *pop* 30,046

Al Hamad — see HAMAD (Al)

Al·ham·bra \al-'ham-brə, *for 2 also* ə-'lam-brə\ **1** city SW Calif. E of Los Angeles *pop* 83,089 **2** hill in Granada, Spain; site of remains of the palace of the Moorish kings

Al–Ha·sa \äl-'hä-sə\ *or* **Hasa** region NE Saudi Arabia in E Nejd bordering on Persian Gulf

Al Hijāz — see HEJAZ

Al Hu·day·dah \ˌäl-hó-'dä-də, -'dī-\ *or* **Ho·dei·da** \hō-'dä-də\ city & port W Yemen *pop* 155,110

Al Hu·fuf \ˌäl-hó-'füf\ *or* **Ho·fuf** \hō-'füf\ city NE Saudi Arabia in E Nejd

Al·i·ba·tes Flint Quarries National Monument \ˌa-lə-'bä-tēz\ archaeological site N Tex. NE of Amarillo

Ali·can·te \ˌa-lə-'kan-tē, ˌä-lē-'kän-tä\ **1** province E Spain on the Mediterranean S of Valencia province *area* 2264 *sq mi* (5864 *sq km*), *pop* 1,461,925 **2** city & port, its ✳ *pop* 284,580

Ali·garh \ˌə-lē-'gər, 'ä-lē-ˌgär\ city N India in NW Uttar Pradesh N of Agra *pop* (including old town of **Ko·il** \'kō-əl\) 667,732

Al Ittihad — see MADINAT ASH SHA'B

Al Jazirah — see GEZIRA

Al Jizah — see GIZA

Al Khums \äl-'kóms, al-'kümz\ town & port Libya ESE of Tripoli; nearby are ruins of ancient Leptis Magna

Alk·maar \'alk-ˌmär\ commune NW Netherlands *pop* 92,992

Al Ku·frah \äl-'kü-frə\ *or* **Ku·fra** \'kü-frə\ group of five oases SE Libya

Al Kut \al-'küt\ city SE *cen* Iraq on the Tigris SE of Baghdad

Al·lah·a·bad \'ä-lä-hä-ˌbäd, 'a-lə-hə-ˌbad\ city N India in S Uttar Pradesh on the Ganges W of Varanasi *pop* 990,298

Al·le·ghe·ny \ˌa-lə-'gä-nē *also* -'ge-\ river 325 *mi* (523 *km*) W Pa. & SW N.Y. uniting with the Monongahela at Pittsburgh to form the Ohio — **Al·le·ghe·ni·an** \-'gä-nē-ən, -'ge-\ *adj*

Allegheny Mountains mountains of Appalachian system E U.S. in Pa., Md., Va., & W.Va.

Al·len \'a-lən\ city N Tex. N of Dallas *pop* 84,246

Allen Park city SE Mich. WSW of Detroit *pop* 28,210

Allenstein — see OLSZTYN

Al·len·town \'a-lən-ˌtaún\ city E Pa. on the Lehigh *pop* 118,032

Al·li·ance \ə-'lī-ən(t)s\ city NE Ohio NE of Canton *pop* 22,322

Al·lier \äl-'yā\ river *ab* 250 *mi* (402 *km*) S *cen* France flowing to the Loire

Al·ma \'al-mə\ **1** river 50 *mi* (80 *km*) S W Crimea, Ukraine **2** city Canada in E Que. on the Saguenay *pop* 30,904

Al·ma·dén \ˌäl-mä-'dän, -'thän\ town S *cen* Spain in Sierra Morena *pop* 6830

Al Mansurah — see EL MANSÛRA

Al·maty \äl-'mä-tē\ *or* **Al·ma–Ata** \ˌal-mə-ə-'tä; ˌal-mə-'ä-tə, -ə-'tä\ *or formerly* **Ver·nyi** \'vern-yē\ city SE Kazakhstan; formerly its ✳ *pop* 1,156,200

Al·me·lo \'äl-mə-ˌlō\ commune E Netherlands *pop* 71,026

Al·me·re \'äl-mə-rə\ commune *cen* Netherlands *pop* 158,902

Al·me·ría \ˌäl-mä-'rē-ä\ **1** province S Spain SE of Granada province *area* 3388 *sq mi* (8775 *sq km*), *pop* 536,731 **2** city & port, its ✳ *pop* 166,328

Al Minya — see EL MINYA

Al Mu·kal·la \ˌäl-mù-'kä-ˌlä\ *or* **Mu·kal·la** \mù-'ka-lə\ town & port Yemen on Gulf of Aden; chief town of the Hadramawt

Al Mukha — see MOCHA

Alor \'a-ˌlór, 'ä-\ island Indonesia in Lesser Sunda Is. N of Timor; with **Pan·tar** \'pan-ˌtär\ forms **Alor Islands** group

Alor Se·tar \sə-'tär\ city Malaysia in NW Peninsular Malaysia ✳ of Kedah *pop* 66,179

Alost — see AALST

Al·pha·ret·ta \ˌal-fə-'re-tə\ city N Ga. NNE of Atlanta *pop* 57,551

Al·phe·us \al-'fē-əs\ *or ModGk* **Al·fiós** \äl-'fyòs\ river *ab* 75 *mi* (121 *km*) S Greece in W Peloponnese flowing NW into Ionian Sea

Alps \'alps\ mountain system *cen* Europe extending from Mediterranean coast at border bet. France & Italy to the W Balkan Peninsula — see MONT BLANC

Al·sace \al-'sas, -'säs; äl-'zäs\ *or* **El·sass** \'el-ˌzäs\ *or anc* **Al·sa·tia** \al-'sä-sh(ē-)ə\ region & former province NE France bet. Rhine River & Vosges Mountains — **Al·sa·tian** \al-'sä-shən\ *adj or n*

Alsace–Lor·raine \-lə-'rän, -lò-\ region NE France including Alsace & part of Lorraine

Al·sek \'al-ˌsek\ river 260 *mi* (418 *km*) NW Canada & SE Alaska flowing S into the Pacific

Al·ta California \'al-tə\ former Spanish & Mexican province (1772–1848) comprising the present state of Calif. — chiefly used to differentiate it from Baja California

Al·tai *or* **Al·tay** \al-'tī\ **1** mountain system *cen* Asia bet. Mongolia & China & bet. Kazakhstan & Russia **2** — see GORNO-ALTAY **3** territory SW Russia in Asia ✳ Barnaul *area* 101,042 *sq mi* (261,699 *sq km*), *pop* 2,666,000

Al·ta·ma·ha \'ól-tə-mə-ˌhò\ river 137 *mi* (220 *km*) SE Ga. formed by junction of the Ocmulgee & the Oconee & flowing SE into **Altamaha Sound** (estuary)

Al·ta·mi·ra \ˌäl-tä-'mē-rä\ caverns N Spain WSW of Santander

Al·ta·monte Springs \'al-tə-ˌmänt\ city *cen* Fla. *pop* 41,496

Alt·dorf \'alt-ˌdórf, 'ält-\ *or* **Al·torf** \-ˌtórf, 'äl-\ town *cen* Switzerland ✳ of Uri canton *pop* 8571

Al·ten·burg \'al-tⁿn-ˌbùrg\ city E *cen* Germany E of Weimar *pop* 48,926

Al·to Adi·ge \'äl-tō-'ä-dē-ˌjä\ *or* **Upper Adige** *or* **South Tirol** district N Italy in S Tirol in N Trentino-Alto Adige region

Al·ton \'ól-tⁿn\ city SW Ill. on the Mississippi *pop* 27,865

Al·too·na \al-'tü-nə\ city S *cen* Pa. *pop* 46,320

Alto Paraná — see PARANÁ

Al·trinc·ham \'ól-triŋ-əm\ town NW England in Greater Manchester SSW of Manchester *pop* 39,641

Al·tun *or* **Al·tyn** \äl-'tün\ mountain range W China in S Xinjiang Uygur; highest peak *ab* 25,000 *ft* (7620 *m*)

Ama·do·ra \ˌä-mə-'dòr-ə\ city W Portugal *pop* 175,872

Ama·ga·sa·ki \ˌä-mä-gä-'sä-kē\ city Japan in W *cen* Honshu on Osaka Bay *pop* 466,187

Amal·fi \ä-'mäl-fē\ commune & port S Italy in Campania on Gulf of Salerno *pop* 5527 — **Amal·fi·an** \-fē-ən\ *adj or n*

Ama·mi \ä-'mä-mē\ island group W Pacific in *cen* Ryukyus *area* 498 *sq mi* (1295 *sq km*)

Ama·pá \ˌä-mə-'pä\ state N Brazil NW of Amazon Delta ✳ Macapá *area* 54,965 *sq mi* (142,359 *sq km*), *pop* 477,032

Am·a·ril·lo \ˌa-mə-'ri-(ˌ)lō, -ə\ city NW Tex. *pop* 190,695 — **Am·a·ril·lo·an** \-'ri-lō-ən\ *n*

Am·a·zon \'a-mə-ˌzän, -zən\ river *ab* 3900 *mi* (6276 *km*) N S. America flowing from Peruvian Andes into the Atlantic in N Brazil — see UCAYALI, SOLIMÕES

Ama·zo·nas \ˌä-mə-'zō-nəs\ state NW Brazil ✳ Manaus *area* 604,032 *sq mi* (1,564,443 *sq km*), *pop* 2,812,557

Ama·zo·nia \ˌä-mə-'zō-nē-ə\ region N S. America; the basin of the Amazon

Am·ba·to \äm-'bä-(ˌ)tō\ city *cen* Ecuador S of Quito *pop* 124,166

Am·bon \äm-'bòn, ˌam-'bän\ *or* **Am·boi·na** \am-'bòi-nə\ **1** island E Indonesia in the Moluccas S of Ceram *area* 314 *sq mi* (816 *sq km*) **2** city & port on Ambon Is. *pop* 276,955 — **Am·bo·nese** \ˌam-bə-'nēz, -'nēs\ *also* **Am·boi·nese** \ˌam-ˌbòi-'nēz, -'nēs, am-'bòi-\ *adj or n*

Am·bra·cian Gulf \am-'brā-shən\ *or* **Gulf of Ar·ta** \'är-tə\ *or Gk* **Am·vra·ki·kós Kól·pos** \ˌäm-'vrä-kē-ˌkós-'kòl-ˌpòs\ inlet of Ionian Sea 25 *mi* (40 *km*) long W Greece in S Epirus

Am·brose \'am-ˌbrōz\ dredged channel SE N.Y. at entrance to N.Y. harbor N of Sandy Hook 40 *ft* (12 *m*) deep, 2000 *ft* (606 *m*) at widest point

Am·chit·ka \am-'chit-kə\ island SW Alaska in the Aleutians at E end of Rat Islands

Amer·i·ca \ə-'mer-ə-kə, -'me-rə-\ **1** either continent (N. America or S. America) of the western hemisphere **2** *or* **the Amer·i·cas** \-kəz\ the lands of the western hemisphere including N., Central, & S. America & the W. Indies **3** UNITED STATES OF AMERICA

American Samoa *or* **Eastern Samoa** island group of E Samoa SW *cen* Pacific ✳ Pago Pago (on Tutuila Is.) *area* 76 *sq mi* (198 *sq km*), *pop* 57,291

American Samoa, National Park of areas of cultural and ecological significance in three separate locations in American Samoa

Amers·foort \'ä-mərz-ˌfórt, -mərs-\ commune *cen* Netherlands NE of Utrecht *pop* 129,720

Ames \'āmz\ city *cen* Iowa N of Des Moines *pop* 58,965

Am·ga \əm-'gä\ river 800 *mi* (1280 *km*) E *cen* Russia in Asia flowing NE to the Aldan

Am·hara \am-'ha-rə, äm-'hä-rə\ former kingdom (now a province) NW Ethiopia ✳ Gondar

---

\ə\ abut \ᵊ\ kitten, F table \ər\ further \a\ ash \ā\ ace \ä\ mop, mar
\aú\ out \ch\ chin \e\ bet \ē\ easy \g\ go \i\ hit \ī\ ice \j\ job
\ŋ\ sing \ō\ go \ò\ law \òi\ boy \th\ thin \t͟h\ the \ü\ loot \ù\ foot
\y\ yet \zh\ vision, beige \ḵ, ⁿ, œ, ɶ, ᵞ\ see Guide to Pronunciation

Am·herst \'a-(,)mərst, *chiefly by outsiders* 'am-,hərst\ town W *cen* Mass. N of Springfield *pop* 37,819
Amiens \äm-'yaⁿ\ city N France on the Somme *pop* 135,449
Amin·di·vi Islands \,ə-mən-'dē-vē\ island group India in the N Laccadives
Am·i·rante Islands \'a-mə-,rant\ islands W Indian Ocean SW of Seychelles; a dependency of Seychelles
Am·man \ä-'män, a-, -'man\ *or anc* **Philadelphia** *or bib* **Rab·bah Am·mon** \'ra-bə-'a-mən\ *or* **Rab·bath Am·mon** \'ra-bəth\ city * of Jordan NE of Dead Sea *pop* 627,505
Am·mon \'a-mən\ ancient country NW Arabia E of Gilead * Rabbah
Ammonium — see SIWA
Amne Machin — see A'NYÊMAQÊN
Amo — see BLACK
Amor·gós \,ä-(,)mòr-'gòs\ island Greece in the Aegean in SE Cyclades SE of Naxos *area* 47 *sq mi* (122 *sq km*)
Amoy — see XIAMEN
Am·ra·va·ti \,əm-'rä-və-tē, äm-\ *or formerly* **Am·rao·ti** \-'raù-tē\ city *cen* India in NE Maharashtra; chief city of Berar region *pop* 549,370
Am·rit·sar \,əm-'rit-sər\ city N India in NW Punjab *pop* 975,695
Am·ster·dam \'am(p)-stər-,dam, 'äm(p)-stər-,däm\ city & port, official * of the Netherlands *pop* 735,526 — **Am·ster·dam·mer** \-,da-mər, -,dä-\ *n*
Amu Dar'·ya \,ä-mü-'där-yə\ *or anc* **Ox·us** \'äk-səs\ river over 1500 *mi* (2400 *km*), *cen* & W Asia flowing from Pamir plateau into Aral Sea
Amund·sen Gulf \'ä-mən-sən, 'a-\ arm of Beaufort Sea N Canada
Amundsen Sea arm of the S. Pacific W Antarctica off Marie Byrd Land
Amur \ä-'mùr\ *or Chin* **Hei·long** *or* **Hei–lung** \'hā-'lùŋ\ river *ab* 1780 *mi* (2865 *km*) E Asia formed by junction of the Shilka & the Argun, flowing into the Pacific at N end of Tatar Strait, & forming part of boundary bet. China & Russia
Ana·dyr \,ä-nə-'dir, ,a-\ river 694 *mi* (1117 *km*) E Russia in Asia flowing S & E to Gulf of Anadyr
Anadyr, Gulf of *or* **Gulf of Ana·dir** \,ä-nə-'dir, ,a-\ inlet of N Bering Sea E Russia in Asia S of Chukchi Peninsula
An·a·heim \'a-nə-,hīm\ city SW Calif. E of Long Beach *pop* 336,265
Anáhuac \ä-'nä-,wäk\ the central plateau of Mexico
Añas·co \ä-'nyäs-kō\ municipality W Puerto Rico N of Mayaguez *pop* 29,261
An·a·to·lia \,a-nə-'tō-lē-ə, -'tōl-yə\ the part of Turkey comprising the peninsula of Asia Minor
An–ch'ing — see ANQING
An·chor·age \'aŋ-k(ə-)rij\ municipality S *cen* Alaska at head of Cook Inlet *pop* 291,826
An·co·hu·ma \,än-kō-'ü-mä, -'hü-\ mountain peak 20,958 *ft* (6388 *m*) W Bolivia; highest in the Illampu Massif
An·co·na \aŋ-'kō-nə, an-\ city & port *cen* Italy * of Marche on the Adriatic *pop* 98,404
An·da·lu·sia \,an-də-'lü-zh(ē-)ə\ *or Sp* **An·da·lu·cía** \,än-dä-(,)lü-'sē-ä\ region S Spain including Sierra Nevada & valley of the Guadalquivir — **An·da·lu·sian** \,an-də-'lü-zhən\ *adj or n*
An·da·man and Nic·o·bar \'an-də-mən . . . 'ni-kə-,bär, -,man-\ union territory India comprising Andaman & Nicobar groups * Port Blair *area* 3202 *sq mi* (8293 *sq km*), *pop* 356,265
Andaman Islands islands India in Bay of Bengal S of Myanmar & N of Nicobar Islands *area* 2461 *sq mi* (6374 *sq km*) — **An·da·man·ese** \,an-də-mə-'nēz, -'nēs\ *adj or n*
Andaman Sea sea SE Asia, the E section of Bay of Bengal
An·der·lecht \'än-dər-,lekt\ commune *cen* Belgium *pop* 90,134
An·der·matt \'än-dər-,mät\ commune *cen* Switzerland S of Altdorf
An·der·son \'an-dər-sən\ **1** city *cen* Ind. *pop* 56,129 **2** city NW S.C. *pop* 26,686 **3** river 430 *mi* (692 *km*) NW Canada flowing W & N into Beaufort Sea
An·des \'an-(,)dēz\ mountain system of S. America extending along W coast from Panama to Tierra del Fuego — see ACONCAGUA — **An·de·an** \'an-(,)dē-ən, an-'\ *adj* — **An·dine** \'an-,dēn, -,dīn\ *adj*
An·dhra Pra·desh \,än-drə-prə-'däsh, -'desh\ state SE India N of Tamil Nadu state bordering on Bay of Bengal * Hyderabad *area* 106,272 *sq mi* (275,244 *sq km*), *pop* 75,727,541
An·di·jon \,an-di-'jōn\ *or* **An·di·zhan** \,an-di-'zhan, ,än-di-'zhän\ city Uzbekistan ESE of Tashkent *pop* 298,300
An·dor·ra \an-'dòr-ə, -'där-ə\ country SW Europe in E Pyrenees bet. France & Spain; a republic * **Andorra la Vel·la** \-lä-'vel-yä\ *area* 180 *sq mi* (482 *sq km*), *pop* 66,334 — **An·dor·ran** \-ən\ *adj or n*
An·do·ver \'an-,dō-vər, -də-\ **1** town NE Mass. *pop* 33,201 **2** city E Minn. N of Minneapolis *pop* 30,598
An·dre·a·nof Islands \,an-drē-'a-,nòf, ,än-drā-'ä-nəf\ islands SW Alaska in *cen* Aleutian chain — see ADAK, ATKA
An·dria \'än-drē-ə\ commune SE Italy in Puglia *pop* 95,073
Andropov — see RYBINSK
An·dros **1** \'an-drəs\ island, largest of Bahamas *area* 1600 *sq mi* (4160 *sq km*), *pop* 7686 **2** \'an-drəs, -,dräs; 'än-thròs\ island 25 *mi* (40 *km*) long Greece in N Cyclades
An·dros·cog·gin \,an-drə-'skä-gən\ river 157 *mi* (253 *km*) NE N.H. & SW Maine flowing into the Kennebec
Ane·to, Pi·co de \'pē-(,)kō-,dā-ä-'nā-(,)tō\ *or F* **Pic de Né·thou** \,pek-də-(,)nā-'tü\ mountain 11,168 *ft* (3404 *m*) NE Spain; highest in the Pyrenees
An·ga·ra \əŋ-gə-'rä, ,äŋ-gə-'rä\ river 1100 *mi* (1770 *km*) Russia flowing from Lake Baikal into the Yenisey — see TUNGUSKA
An·garsk \ən-'gärsk\ city S Russia in Asia on the Angara NW of Irkutsk *pop* 269,000
An·gel Falls \'ān-jəl\ waterfall 3212 *ft* (979 *m*) SE Venezuela on Auyán-tepuí Mountain in a headstream of the Caroní
An·gers \äⁿ-'zhā\ city W France ENE of Nantes *pop* 151,322
Ang·kor \'aŋ-,kòr\ ruins of ancient city NW Cambodia N of Tonle Sap; * of the Khmers
An·gle·sey *or* **An·gle·sea** \'aŋ-gəl-sē\ *or anc* **Mo·na** \'mō-nə\ island NW Wales
Anglia **1** — see ENGLAND **2** — see EAST ANGLIA — **An·gli·an** \'aŋ-glē-ən\ *adj or n*
Anglo–Egyptian Sudan — see SUDAN 2
An·go·la \aŋ-'gō-lə, an-\ *or formerly* **Portuguese West Africa** country SW Africa S of mouth of the Congo; until 1975 a dependency of Portugal * Luanda *area* 481,351 *sq mi* (1,251,513 *sq km*), *pop* 10,609,000 — **An·go·lan** \-lən\ *adj or n*
An·gou·lême \,äⁿ-gü-'lām, -'lem\ city W France *pop* 43,137
An·gou·mois \,äⁿ-gü-'mwä\ region & former duchy & province W France S of Poitou * Angoulême
An·guil·la \aŋ-'gwi-lə, an-\ island Brit. West Indies NW of St. Kitts *area* 35 *sq mi* (91 *sq km*) — **An·guil·lan** \-'gwi-lən\ *adj or n*
An·gus \'aŋ-gəs\ *or earlier* **For·far** \'fòr-fər\ *or* **For·far·shire** \-,shir, -shər\ administrative area E Scotland *area* 842 *sq mi* (2181 *sq km*)
An·halt \'än-,hält\ former state *cen* Germany * Dessau
An·hui *or* **An·hwei** \'än-'hwā, -'wā\ province E China W of Jiangsu * Hefei *area* 54,015 *sq mi* (140,439 *sq km*), *pop* 56,180,813
An·i·ak·chak Crater \,a-nē-'ak-,chak\ active volcano SW Alaska on Alaska Peninsula in **Aniakchak National Monument**
A–ni–ma–ch'ing — see A'NYÊMAQÊN
An·jou \'an-,jü, äⁿ-'zhü\ **1** region & former province NW France in Loire valley * Angers **2** former town Canada in S Que., now part of Montreal (city)
An·ka·ra \'aŋ-kə-rə, 'äŋ-\ *or formerly* **An·go·ra** \aŋ-'gòr-ə, an-\ *or anc* **An·cy·ra** \an-'sī-rə\ city * of Turkey in N *cen* Anatolia *pop* 2,559,471
An·ke·ny \'aŋ-kə-nē\ city S *cen* Iowa N of Des Moines *pop* 45,582
Ann, Cape \'an\ peninsula NE Mass.
An·na·ba \ä-'nä-bə\ *or formerly* **Bône** \'bōn\ commune & port NE Algeria NE of Constantine *pop* 305,526
An Na·fūd \,än-nä-'füd\ *or* **Na·fud** \na-'füd\ desert N Saudi Arabia in N Nejd
An Na·jaf \än-'nä-,jäf\ city S *cen* Iraq W of the Euphrates *pop* 242,603
An·nam \a-'nam, ə-; 'a-,nam\ region & former kingdom E Indochina in *cen* Vietnam * Hue *area ab* 57,000 *sq mi* (148,200 *sq km*)
An·nap·o·lis \ə-'na-pə-lis\ city & port * of Md. on Severn River *pop* 38,394
Annapolis Basin inlet of Bay of Fundy, Canada in W N.S.
An·na·pur·na \,a-nə-'pùr-nə, -'pər-\ massif N Nepal in the Himalayas; highest peak 26,504 *ft* (8078 *m*)
Ann Ar·bor \(,)an-'är-bər\ city SE Mich. W of Detroit *pop* 113,934
An·ne·cy \än-'sē\ city E France ENE of Lyon *pop* 50,324
An Nhon \'än-'nōn\ *or formerly* **Binh Dinh** \'bin-'din\ city *cen* Vietnam in S Annam
An·nis·ton \'a-nə-stən\ city NE Ala. *pop* 23,106
An·qing *or* **An–ch'ing** \'än-'chiŋ\ *or* **An·king** \'än-'kiŋ\ *or formerly* **Hwai·ning** \'hwī-'niŋ\ city E China in Anhui on the Chang *pop* 250,718
An·shan \'än-'shän\ city NE China in E *cen* Liaoning SSW of Shenyang *pop* 1,203,986
An·ta·kya \,än-tä-'kyä\ *or* **An·ta·ki·yah** \-'kē-yə\ *or anc* **An·ti·och** \'an-tē-,äk\ city S Turkey on the Orontes *pop* 123,871
An·tal·ya \,än-täl-'yä\ *or formerly* **Ada·lia** \ə-'dä-lē-ə\ city & port SW Turkey on Gulf of Antalya *pop* 378,208
An·ta·nan·a·ri·vo \,än-tä-,nä-nä-'rē-(,)vō\ *or Malagasy* **Ta·nan·a·ri·vo** \tä-,nä-nä-'rē-(,)vō\ *or formerly* **Ta·nan·a·rive** \tə-'na-nə-,rēv\ city * of Madagascar *urban area pop* 958,929
Ant·arc·tic \,ant-'ärk-tik, -'är-tik\ region including Antarctica, Antarctic Peninsula, and the surrounding ocean
Ant·arc·ti·ca \-'ärk-ti-kə, -'är-ti-\ body of land around the S. Pole; a plateau covered by a great ice cap & mountain peaks *area ab* 5,500,000 *sq mi* (14,300,000 *sq km*), divided into **West Antarctica** (including Antarctic Peninsula) & **East Antarctica** by Transantarctic Mountains
Antarctic Archipelago — see PALMER ARCHIPELAGO
Antarctic Ocean — see SOUTHERN OCEAN
Antarctic Peninsula *or formerly* **Palmer Peninsula** peninsula *ab* 700 *mi* (1126 *km*) long W Antarctica S of S end of S. America
An·tibes \äⁿ-'tēb\ city & port SE France SW of Nice *pop* 72,454
Antibes, Cap d' — see CAP D'ANTIBES
An·ti·cos·ti Island \,an-tə-'kò-stē\ island E Canada in E Que. at mouth of the St. Lawrence *area* 3043 *sq mi* (7912 *sq km*)
An·tie·tam Creek \an-'tē-təm\ creek S Pa. & N Md. flowing S into the Potomac N of Harpers Ferry, W.Va.
An·ti·gua \an-'tē-gə, -gwə\ **1** island Brit. West Indies in the Leewards *area* 108 *sq mi* (281 *sq km*); with Barbuda forms independent nation of **Antigua and Barbuda** (* St. John's, *pop* 75,741) since 1981 — see WEST INDIES ASSOCIATED STATES **2** *or* **Antigua Guatemala** city S *cen* Guatemala; former * of Guatemala *pop* 20,715 — **An·ti·guan** \-gən, -gwən\ *adj or n*
An·ti–Leb·a·non \,an-ti-'le-bə-nən, -,nän\ mountain range SW Asia E of Bekaa Valley on Syria-Lebanon border — see HERMON (Mount)
An·til·les \an-'ti-lēz\ the W. Indies excluding the Bahamas — see GREATER ANTILLES, LESSER ANTILLES — **An·til·le·an** \-lē-ən\ *adj*
An·ti·och \'an-tē-,äk\ **1** city W Calif. NE of Oakland *pop* 102,372 **2** — see ANTAKYA **3** ancient city Asia Minor in Pisidia, at certain periods within boundaries of Phrygia; ruins in W *cen* Turkey — **An·ti·o·chene** \an-'tī-ə-,kēn, ,an-tē-(,)ä-'kēn\ *adj or n* — **An·ti·och·i·an** \,an-tē-'ō-kē-ən, -'ä-\ *adj or n*
An·ti·sa·na \,än-tē-'sä-nä\ volcano 18,714 *ft* (5704 *m*) N *cen* Ecuador
An·to·fa·gas·ta \,än-tō-fä-'gäs-tä\ city & port N Chile *pop* 296,905
An·trim \'an-trəm\ **1** traditional county NE Northern Ireland **2** district E Northern Ireland, established 1974 *area* 217 *sq mi* (564 *sq km*), *pop* 44,322
An·tsi·ra·na·na \,än-tsē-'rä-nə-nə\ *or formerly* **Di·é·go–Sua·rez** \dē-'ā-gō-'swä-res\ city & port Madagascar near N tip of island *pop* 77,688
Antung — see DANDONG
Ant·werp \'ant-,wərp, 'an-,twərp\ *or F* **An·vers** \äⁿ-'ver(s)\ *or Flem* **Ant·wer·pen** \'änt-,ver-pə(n)\ **1** province N Belgium *area* 1104 *sq mi* (2870 *sq km*), *pop* 1,652,450 **2** city & port, its *, on the Schelde *pop* 448,709
Anu·ra·dha·pu·ra \ə-'nùr-ə-də-,pùr-ə\ town N *cen* Sri Lanka; an ancient * of Ceylon *pop* 37,000
An·yang \'än-'yäŋ\ **1** city E China in N Henan *pop* 480,668 **2** city NW S. Korea *pop* 361,577
A'·nyê·ma·qên \'ä-,nyä-,mä-'chen\ *or* **Am·ne Ma·chin** \'äm-nē-mä-'chin\ *or* **A–ni–ma–ch'ing** \'ä-nē-'mä-'chiŋ\ range of Kunlun Mountains W China in E *cen* Qinghai; highest peak 20,610 *ft* (6282 *m*)
An·zio \'änt-sē-,ō, 'an-zē-,ō\ city & port Italy SSE of Rome *pop* 33,523
Aomen — see MACAO

Ao·mo·ri \ä-'ō-mō-rē\ city & port N Japan in NE Honshu on Mutsu Bay *pop* 297,859

Aoraki *or* **Aorangi** — see COOK (Mount)

Aos·ta \ä-'ō-stä\ **1** commune NW Italy in Piedmont at junction of Great & Little Saint Bernard passes ✳ of Valle d'Aosta *pop* 34,644 **2** — see VALLE D'AOSTA

Apache Junction \ə-'pa-chē\ city S *cen* Ariz. SE of Phoenix *pop* 35,840

Ap·a·lach·i·co·la \ˌa-pə-ˌla-chi-'kō-lə\ river 90 *mi* (145 *km*) NW Fla. flowing from Lake Seminole S into **Apalachicola Bay** (inlet of Gulf of Mexico)

Apa·po·ris \ˌä-pä-'pòr-(ˌ)ēs\ river *ab* 550 *mi* (885 *km*) S Colombia flowing SE into the Japurá on Colombia-Brazil boundary

Apel·doorn \'ä-pəl-ˌdòrn\ commune E *cen* Netherlands N of Arnhem *pop* 154,859

Ap·en·nines \'a-pə-ˌnīnz\ mountain chain Italy extending the length of the peninsula — see CORNO (Monte) — **Ap·en·nine** \-ˌnīn\ *adj*

Apia \ä-'pē-ä\ town & port ✳ of independent Samoa on Upolu Is. *pop* 37,200

Apo, Mount \ä-(ˌ)pō\ volcano 9692 *ft* (2954 *m*) S Philippines in SE Mindanao; highest peak in the Philippines

Apop·ka \ə-'päp-kə\ city *cen* Fla. NW of Orlando *pop* 41,542

Ap·pa·la·chia \ˌa-pə-'lā-chə, -'la-chə, -'lā-shə\ region E U.S. comprising Appalachian Mountains from S *cen* N.Y. to *cen* Ala.

Ap·pa·la·chian Mountains \ˌa-pə-'lā-ch(ē-)ən, -sh(ē-)ən, -'la-ch(ē-)ən\ mountain system E N. America extending from Labrador & N.B. SW to N Ala.; highest peak Mt. Mitchell 6684 *ft* (2037 *m*)

Ap·pen·zell \'a-pən-ˌzel, -'tsel\ former canton NE Switzerland, now divided into **Appenzell Inner Rhodes** \'rōdz\ *or G* **Appenzell Inner Rho·den** \'i-nər(r)-'rō-dᵊn\ (✳ Appenzell *area* 67 *sq mi or* 174 *sq km, pop* 15,000) & **Appenzell Outer Rhodes** *or G* **Appenzell Aus·ser Rhoden** \'aú-sə(r)\ (✳ Herisau *area* 94 *sq mi or* 243 *sq km, pop* 53,200), which function as cantons

Ap·pi·an Way \'a-pē-ən\ ancient paved highway extending from Rome to the Adriatic

Ap·ple·ton \'a-pəl-tən\ city E Wis. *pop* 72,623

Apple Valley **1** town SE Calif. N of San Bernardino *pop* 69,135 **2** city SE Minn. *pop* 49,084

Apra Harbor \'ä-prä\ seaport Guam on W coast

Apsheron — see ABŞERON

Apu·lia — see PUGLIA — **Apu·lian** \ə-'pyül-yən, -'pyü-lē-ən\ *adj or n*

Apu·re \ä-'pü-rä\ river 509 *mi* (819 *km*) W Venezuela flowing E into the Orinoco

Apu·rí·mac \ˌä-pü-'rē-ˌmäk\ river 428 *mi* (689 *km*) S & *cen* Peru flowing N to unite with the Urubamba forming the Ucayali

Aqa·ba \'ä-kä-bə\ *or* **Al-'A·qa·bah** \ˌäl-\ *or anc* **Elath** \'ē-ˌlath\ town & port SW Jordan on border of Israel at head of NE arm (**Gulf of Aqaba**) of Red Sea *pop* 104,000

Aqmola — see ASTANA

Aquid·neck Island \ə-'kwid-ˌnek\ *or* **Rhode Island** island SE R.I. in Narragansett Bay; site of city of Newport

Aq·ui·taine \ˌa-kwə-'tān\ old region of SW France comprising area later known as Guienne ✳ Toulouse

Aq·ui·ta·nia \ˌa-kwə-'tā-nyə, -nē-ə\ a Roman division of SW Gaul under Caesar consisting of country bet. Pyrenees & Garonne River & under Augustus expanded to Loire & Allier rivers — **Aq·ui·ta·nian** \-nyən, -nē-ən\ *adj or n*

'Ara·bah, Wadi \'wä-dē-'är-ä-bə\ *or* **Wadi al-'Arabah** *or* **Wadi el-'Arabah** \ˌäl-, -ˌel-\ valley extending S from Dead Sea to Gulf of Aqaba

Ara·bia \ə-'rā-bē-ə\ *or* **Arabian Peninsula** peninsula SW Asia *ab* 1200 *mi* (1930 *km*) long & 1300 *mi* (2090 *km*) wide including Saudi Arabia, Yemen, & Persian Gulf States; in early times divided into **Arabia Petraea** \pə-'trē-ə\ "Rocky Arabia" (the NW part), **Arabia De·ser·ta** \di-'zər-tə\ "Desert Arabia" (the N part), & **Arabia Fe·lix** \fē-liks\ "Fertile Arabia" (the main part)

Arabian Desert — see EASTERN DESERT

Arabian Sea sea, NW section of the Indian Ocean bet. India & Arabia

Ar·a·by \'a-rə-bē\ ARABIA — an archaic, poetic, or informal name

Ara·ca·ju \ˌär-ə-kə-'zhü\ city & port NE Brazil ✳ of Sergipe *pop* 461,534

Arad \ä-'räd\ city W Romania on the Mures *pop* 172,824

Ara·fu·ra Sea \ˌär-ä-'fü-rä\ sea bet. N Australia & W New Guinea

Ar·a·gon \'a-rə-ˌgän, -gən; ä-rä-'gòn\ region NE Spain bordering on France; once an independent kingdom ✳ Saragossa — **Ar·a·go·nese** \ˌa-rə-gə-'nēz, -'nēs\ *adj or n*

Ara·gua·ia *or* **Ara·gua·ya** \ˌär-ä-'gwī-ə\ river *ab* 1365 *mi* (2195 *km*), *cen* Brazil flowing N into the Tocantins

Arāk \ä-'räk, ə-'rak\ city W Iran SW of Tehran *pop* 265,349

Ara·kan \ˌar-ə-'kän, -'kan\ coast region SW Myanmar on Bay of Bengal; chief town Sittwe

Ar·al Sea \'a-rəl\ *or formerly* **Lake Aral** brackish lake bet. Kazakhstan & Uzbekistan; now split into two parts *present area less than half its pre-1960 peak of 25,500 sq mi (66,000 sq km)*

Ar·am \'a-rəm, 'er-əm\ ancient Syria — its Hebrew name

Ar·an Islands \'a-rən\ islands W Ireland off coast of Galway; largest island Inishmore

Aran·sas Bay \ə-'ran(t)-səs\ inlet of Gulf of Mexico S Tex. NE of Corpus Christi Bay bet. mainland & San Jose Is.

Aransas Pass channel S Tex. bet. Mustang & San Jose islands leading to Corpus Christi & Aransas bays

Ar·a·rat \'a-rə-ˌrat\ *or* **Ağrı Da·gi** \ˌä-grē-dä-'gē\ mountain 16,946 *ft* (5165 *m*) E Turkey near border of Iran

Aras \ə-'räs\ *or* **Araks** \ə-'räks\ *or anc* **Arax·es** \ə-'rak-(ˌ)sēz\ river 635 *mi* (1022 *km*) W Asia rising in mountains of Turkish Armenia & flowing E to join the Kura in E Azerbaijan

Ara·val·li Range \ə-'rä-və-(ˌ)lē\ mountain range NW India E of Thar Desert; highest peak Mt. Abu 5650 *ft* (1722 *m*)

Ar·bil *or* **Ir·bil** \'är-ˌbēl\ *or* **Er·bil** \'är-ˌbēl\ city N Iraq E of Mosul *pop* 460,758

Ar·bon \'är-ˌbōⁿ\ commune NE Switzerland *pop* 11,333

Ar·buck·le Mountains \'är-ˌbək-\ hills S Okla.

Ar·ca·dia \är-'kā-dē-ə\ **1** city SW Calif. ENE of Los Angeles *pop* 56,364 **2** mountainous region S Greece in *cen* Peloponnese

Archangel, Gulf of — see DVINA BAY

Arch·es National Park \'är-chəz\ area of eroded natural arch formations E Utah

Ar·cos de la Fron·te·ra \är-kōs-ˌthä-lä-frōn-'tä-rä\ commune SW Spain NE of Cádiz *pop* 27,849

Ar·cot \är-'kät\ city SE India in N Tamil Nadu WSW of Madras; once ✳ of the nabobs of Carnatic *pop* 50,267

Arc·tic \'ärk-tik, 'är-tik\ the Arctic Ocean and lands in it and adjacent to it

Arctic Archipelago archipelago Canada in Nunavut & Northwest Territories in Arctic Ocean

Arctic Ocean ocean N of the Arctic Circle

Arctic Red river 310 *mi* (499 *km*) Canada in W Northwest Territories flowing N into the Mackenzie

Ar·cueil \är-'kœ-ē, -'kü-ē\ commune N France S of Paris *pop* 18,064

Ar·da·bil *or* **Ar·de·bil** \ˌär-də-'bēl\ city NW Iran in E Azerbaijan region *pop* 418,262

Ar·den \'är-dᵊn\ district *cen* England in SW Warwickshire W of Stratford-upon-Avon; site of former **Forest of Arden**

Ar·dennes \är-'den\ wooded plateau region in NE France, W Luxembourg, & SE Belgium E of the Meuse

Ard·more \'ärd-ˌmòr\ city S Okla. *pop* 24,283

Ards \'ärdz\ district E Northern Ireland, established 1974 *area* 143 *sq mi* (372 *sq km*), *pop* 64,026

Are·ci·bo \ˌä-rä-'sē-(ˌ)bō\ city & port N Puerto Rico *pop* 96,440

Are·na, Point \ə-'rē-nə\ promontory N Calif. on the Pacific *ab* midway bet. Cape Mendocino & San Francisco Bay

Are·qui·pa \ˌä-rā-'kē-pä\ city S Peru at foot of El Misti *pop* 710,000

Arez·zo \ä-'ret-(ˌ)sō\ commune *cen* Italy in Tuscany *pop* 92,297

Ar·gen·tan \ˌär-zhən-'täⁿ\ commune NW France in Normandy NNW of Alençon *pop* 16,596

Ar·gen·teuil \ˌär-zhən-'tœ-ē, -'tü-ē\ commune N France on the Seine NNW of Paris *pop* 93,932

Ar·gen·ti·na \ˌär-jən-'tē-nə\ country S S. America bet. the Andes & the Atlantic S of the Pilcomayo; a federal republic ✳ Buenos Aires *area* 1,072,156 *sq mi* (2,776,884 *sq km*), *pop* 36,260,130 — **Ar·gen·tine** \'är-jən-ˌtīn, -ˌtēn\ *adj or n* — **Ar·gen·tin·ean** *or* **Ar·gen·tin·i·an** \ˌär-jən-'ti-nē-ən\ *adj or n*

Ar·gi·nu·sae \ˌär-jə-'nü-(ˌ)sē, -'nyü-\ group of small islands in the Aegean SE of Lesbos

Ar·go·lis \'är-gə-ləs\ district & ancient country S Greece in E Peloponnese comprising a plain around Argos & area bet. Gulf of Argolis & Saronic Gulf — **Ar·gol·ic** \är-'gä-lik\ *adj*

Argolis, Gulf of inlet of the Aegean S Greece on E coast of Peloponnese

Ar·gonne \'är-ˌgòn, -ˌgän\ wooded plateau NE France S of the Ardennes near Belgian border bet. the Meuse & the Aisne

Ar·gos \'är-ˌgòs, -gəs\ town Greece in E Peloponnese on plain at head of Gulf of Argolis; once a Greek city-state

Argovie — see AARGAU

Ar·guel·lo, Point \är-'gwe-(ˌ)lō\ cape SW Calif. WNW of Santa Barbara

Ar·gun \är-'gün\ river 450 *mi* (724 *km*) NE Asia forming boundary bet. Inner Mongolia (China) & Russia & uniting with the Shilka to form the Amur

Ar·gyll \är-'gī(-ə)l, 'är-ˌgī(-ə)l\ *or* **Ar·gyll·shire** \-ˌshir, -shər\ former county W Scotland ✳ Lochgilphead

Argyll and Bute administrative area W Scotland *area* 2676 *sq mi* (6930 *sq km*)

Ar·hus *or* **Aar·hus** \'òr-ˌhüs\ city & port Denmark in E Jutland on the Kattegat *pop* 259,493

Aria \'a-rē-ə, ä-'rī-ə\ **1** an E province of ancient Persian Empire; district now in NW Afghanistan & E Iran **2** — see HERAT

Ari·ca \ə-'rē-kə\ city & port N Chile *pop* 185,268 — see TACNA

Ariha — see JERICHO 1

Ar·i·ma·thea \ˌa-rə-mə-'thē-ə\ town in ancient Palestine; location not certainly identified

Ariminum — see RIMINI

Ari·pua·nã \ˌär-ē-pwə-'näⁿ\ river 400 *mi* (644 *km*) W *cen* Brazil rising in Mato Grosso state & flowing N into the Madeira

Arius — see HARĪRŪD

Ar·i·zo·na \ˌa-rə-'zō-nə\ state SW U.S. ✳ Phoenix *area* 113,909 *sq mi* (296,163 *sq km*), *pop* 6,392,017 — **Ar·i·zo·nan** \-nən\ *or* **Ar·i·zo·nian** \-nē-ən, -nyən\ *adj or n*

Ar·kan·sas \'är-kən-ˌsò; 1 is also är-'kan-zəs\ **1** river 1450 *mi* (2334 *km*) SW *cen* U.S. rising in *cen* Colo. & flowing E & SE through S Kans., NE Okla., & Ark. into the Mississippi **2** state S *cen* U.S. ✳ Little Rock *area* 53,187 *sq mi* (137,754 *sq km*), *pop* 2,915,918 — **Ar·kan·san** \är-'kan-zən\ *adj or n*

Ar·khan·gel'sk \är-'kän-ˌgelsk, ər-'kän-gilsk\ *or* **Arch·an·gel** \'är-ˌkān-jəl\ city & port Russia in Europe on the Northern Dvina *pop* 414,000

Arl·berg \'är(-ə)l-ˌbərg, -ˌberk\ Alpine valley, pass, & tunnel W Austria in the Tirol

Arles \'är(-ə)l\ **1** medieval kingdom E & SE France; also called Kingdom of Burgundy **2** *or anc* **Ar·e·las** \'a-rə-ˌlas\ *or* **Ar·e·la·te** \ˌa-rə-'lā-tē\ city SE France on the Rhône *pop* 50,467 — **Ar·le·sian** \är-'lē-zhən\ *adj*

Ar·ling·ton \'är-liŋ-tən\ **1** town E Mass. NW of Boston *pop* 42,844 **2** city N Tex. E of Fort Worth *pop* 365,438 **3** unincorporated population center N Va. *pop* 207,627

Arlington Heights village N Ill. NW of Chicago *pop* 75,101

Ar·lon \är-'lōⁿ\ commune SE Belgium ✳ of Luxembourg province *pop* 25,261

Ar·magh \är-'mä, 'är-ˌ\ **1** traditional county SE Northern Ireland **2** district S Northern Ireland, established 1974 *area* 260 *sq mi* (676 *sq km*), *pop* 51,331 **3** town *cen* Armagh district, Northern Ireland *pop* 14,265

Ar·ma·gnac \är-män-ˈyäk\ district SW France in old province of Gascony; chief town Auch

Ar·me·nia \är-ˈmē-nē-ə, -nyə\ **1** *or bib* **Min·ni** \ˈmi-ˌnī\ former kingdom W Asia in mountainous region SE of Black Sea & SW of Caspian Sea; area now divided bet. Armenia, Turkey, & Iran **2** independent country W Asia; a constituent republic (**Armenian Republic**) of the U.S.S.R. 1936–91 * Yerevan *area* 11,506 *sq mi* (29,800 *sq km*), *pop* 3,802,400 — see LESSER ARMENIA

Ar·men·tières \ˌär-mä^{n}-ˈtyer, ˌär-mən-ˈtirz\ commune N France W of Lille *pop* 25,249

Ar·mor·i·ca \är-ˈmȯr-ə-kə, -ˈmär-\ **1** *or* **Ar·e·mor·i·ca** \ˌa-rə-\ ancient region NW France bet. the Seine & the Loire **2** BRITTANY

Arn·hem \ˈärn-ˌhem, ˈär-nəm\ commune E Netherlands * of Gelderland *pop* 140,736

Arn·hem Land \ˈär-nəm\ region N Australia on N coast of Northern Territory

Ar·no \ˈär-(ˌ)nō\ *or anc* **Ar·nus** \-nəs\ river 150 *mi* (241 *km*) *cen* Italy flowing W from the Apennines through Florence into Ligurian Sea

Aroos·took \ə-ˈrüs-tək, -ˈrùs-\ river 140 *mi* (225 *km*) N Maine flowing NE across N.B. border & into St. John River

Ar·ran \ˈa-rən\ island SW Scotland in Firth of Clyde *area* 165 *sq mi* (429 *sq km*)

Ar·ras \ä-ˈräs, ˈa-rəs\ city N France SSW of Lille *pop* 40,535

Arsanias — see MURAT

Arta, Gulf of — see AMBRACIAN GULF

Ar·tois \är-ˈtwä\ former province N France bet. Flanders & Picardy * Arras

Aru·ba \ə-ˈrü-bə\ internally self-governing Dutch island off NW Venezuela; chief town Oranjestad *area* 69 *sq mi* (179 *sq km*), *pop* 69,000 — **Aru·ban** \-bən\ *adj or n*

Aru Islands \ˈär-(ˌ)ü\ islands E Indonesia S of W New Guinea *area* 3305 *sq mi* (8593 *sq km*), *pop* 29,604

Aru·na·chal Pra·desh \ˈär-ə-ˌnä-chəl-prə-ˈdäsh, -ˈdesh\ *or formerly* **North East Frontier Agency** state NE India N of Assam * Itanagar *area* 32,269 *sq mi* (83,577 *sq km*), *pop* 1,091,117

Aru·wi·mi \ˌä-rü-ˈwē-mē\ river 620 *mi* (998 *km*) N Democratic Republic of the Congo flowing SW & W into Congo River

Ar·vada \är-ˈva-də\ city N *cen* Colo. NW of Denver *pop* 106,433

Ar·wad \är-ˈwad, -ˈwäd\ *or bib* **Ar·vad** \ˈär-ˌvad\ island Syria off coast of S Latakia

Asa·hi·ka·wa \ˌä-sə-hē-ˈkä-wə, ä-ˌsä-ˈhē-kä-\ *or* **Asa·hi·ga·wa** \-ˈgä-wə, -gä-wə\ city Japan in *cen* Hokkaido *pop* 359,536

Asa·ma \ä-ˈsä-mä\ *or* **Asa·ma·ya·ma** \ä-ˌsä-mä-ˈyä-mä\ volcano 8300 *ft* (2530 *m*) Japan in *cen* Honshu

Asan·sol \ˌə-sən-ˈsōl\ city NE India in W. Bengal *pop* 486,304

As·cen·sion \ə-ˈsen(t)-shən\ island in S. Atlantic belonging to Brit. colony of St. Helena *area* 34 *sq mi* (88 *sq km*), *pop* 1400

As·co·li Pi·ce·no \ˈäs-kō-(ˌ)lē-pē-ˈchā-(ˌ)nō\ *or anc* **As·cu·lum Pi·ce·num** \ˈas-kyə-ləm-(ˌ)pī-ˈsē-nəm\ commune *cen* Italy in Marche NE of Rome *pop* 51,814

Ascoli Sa·tria·no \ˌsä-trē-ˈä-(ˌ)nō\ *or anc* **As·cu·lum Ap·u·lum** \ˈas-kyə-ləm-ˈa-pyə-ləm\ *or* **Aus·cu·lum Apulum** \ˈȯs-\ commune SE Italy in Puglia S of Foggia *pop* 6528

As·cot \ˈas-kət\ village S England in Berkshire SW of London

As·cut·ney, Mount \ə-ˈskət-nē\ mountain 3320 *ft* (1012 *m*) SE Vt.

Ashan·ti \ə-ˈshan-tē, -ˈshän-\ former Brit. protectorate W Africa; now part of Ghana

Ash·bur·ton \ˈash-ˌbər-t^{ə}n\ river *ab* 400 *mi* (644 *km*) Australia in NW Western Australia flowing NW into Indian Ocean

Ash·dod \ˈash-ˌdäd\ city & port Israel W of Jerusalem *pop* 76,600

Ashe·ville \ˈash-ˌvil, -vəl\ city W N.C. *pop* 83,393

Ash·ga·bat \ˈäsh-gə-ˌbät\ *or* **Ashkh·a·bad** \ˈash-kə-ˌbad, -ˌbäd\ *or formerly* **Pol·to·ratsk** \ˌpäl-tə-ˈrätsk\ city * of Turkmenistan *pop* 412,200

Ash·ley \ˈash-lē\ river 40 *mi* (64 *km*) S S.C. flowing SE into Charleston harbor

Ash·qe·lon \ˈash-kə-ˌlän\ archaeological site Israel WSW of Jerusalem, an ancient city-state

Ash Sha·ri·qah \ˌäsh-ˈshä-rē-kə\ *or* **Shar·jah** \ˈshär-jə\ sheikhdom, member of United Arab Emirates

Asia \ˈā-zhə, -shə\ continent of the eastern hemisphere N of equator forming a single landmass with Europe (the conventional dividing line bet. Asia & Europe being the Ural Mountains & main range of the Caucasus Mountains); has numerous large offshore islands including Cyprus, Sri Lanka, Malay Archipelago, Taiwan, the Japanese chain, & Sakhalin *area* 17,139,445 *sq mi* (44,391,162 *sq km*)

Asia Minor peninsula forming W extremity of Asia bet. Black Sea on N, Mediterranean Sea on S, & Aegean Sea on W — see ANATOLIA

Asir \a-ˈsir\ province S Saudi Arabia on Red Sea SE of Hejaz * As Sabya *area* 40,130 *sq mi* (103,937 *sq km*)

As·ma·ra \az-ˈmä-rə, -ˈma-rə\ city * of Eritrea *pop* 342,706

As·nières \än-ˈyer\ commune N France NW of Paris

Aso, Mount \ˈä-(ˌ)sō\ *or* **Aso·san** \ˈä-sō-ˌsän\ volcanic mountain Japan in *cen* Kyushu; has five volcanic cones grouped around crater 15 *mi* (24 *km*) long with walls 2000 *ft* (610 *m*) high

Aso·lo \ˈä-zō-ˌlō\ commune NE Italy NW of Treviso *pop* 7636

Asphaltites, Lacus — see DEAD SEA

As·sam \ə-ˈsam, a-; ˈa-ˌsam\ state NE India on edge of Himalayas * Dispur *area* 30,318 *sq mi* (78,827 *sq km*), *pop* 26,638,407

As·sen \ˈä-s^{ə}n\ commune NE Netherlands * of Drenthe *pop* 60,230

As·sin·i·boine \ə-ˈsi-nə-ˌbȯin\ river 665 *mi* (1070 *km*) Canada rising in SE Sask. & flowing S & E across S Man. into Red River

Assiniboine, Mount mountain 11,870 *ft* (3618 *m*) Canada in SW Alta. on B.C. border

As·si·si \ə-ˈsi-sē, -ˈsē-, -zē\ commune *cen* Italy ESE of Perugia *pop* 25,637

Association of Southeast Asian Nations political organization consisting of Brunei, Cambodia, Indonesia, Laos, Malaysia, Myanmar, Philippines, Singapore, Thailand, & Vietnam; formed 1967

As·syr·ia \ə-ˈsir-ē-ə\ *or bib* **As·sur** \ä-ˈsùr, ˈä-ˌ\ *or* **Ashur** \ˈä-ˌshùr\ ancient empire W Asia extending along middle Tigris & over foothills to the E; early * Calah, later * Nineveh

Astacus — see IZMIT

As·ta·na \ä-stä-ˈnä\ *or formerly* **Aq·mo·la** *or* **Ak·mo·la** \ak-ˈmō-lə\ town N *cen* Kazakhstan, its * since 1997

Asti \ˈäs-tē\ commune NW Italy W of Alessandria *pop* 73,176

As·tra·khan \ˈas-trə-ˌkan, -kən\ city Russia in Europe on the Volga at head of its delta *pop* 512,000

As·tu·ri·as \ə-ˈstùr-ē-əs, a-, -ˈstyùr-\ **1** region & old kingdom NW Spain on Bay of Biscay **2** province NW Spain *area* 4079 *sq mi* (10,565 *sq km*), *pop* 1,062,998 — **As·tu·ri·an** \-ē-ən\ *adj or n*

Asun·ción \ä-sün-ˈsyōn\ city * of Paraguay on Paraguay River at confluence with the Pilcomayo *pop* 502,426

As·wân \a-ˈswän, ä-\ *or anc* **Sy·e·ne** \sī-ˈē-nē\ city S Egypt on right bank of the Nile near site of dam built 1898–1902 & of **Aswân High Dam** (completed 1970 to form **Lake Nas·ser** \ˈnä-sər, ˈna-\) *pop* 191,461

As·yût \äs'yüt\ city *cen* Egypt on left bank of the Nile *pop* 273,191

Atacama — see PUNA DE ATACAMA

Ata·ca·ma Desert \ˌä-tä-ˈkä-mä\ desert N Chile bet. Copiapó & Peru border

Atas·ca·de·ro \ə-ˌtas-kə-ˈder-(ˌ)ō\ city W Calif. *pop* 28,310

At·ba·ra \ˈat-bə-rə, ˈät-\ river *ab* 500 *mi* (805 *km*) NE Africa rising in N Ethiopia & flowing through E Sudan into the Nile

Atchaf·a·laya \(ə-)ˌcha-fə-ˈlī-ə\ river 225 *mi* (362 *km*) S La. flowing S into **Atchafalaya Bay** (inlet of Gulf of Mexico)

Ath·a·bas·ca *or* **Ath·a·bas·ka** \ˌa-thə-ˈbas-kə, ˌä-\ river 765 *mi* (1231 *km*) Canada in Alta. flowing NE & N into Lake Athabasca

Athabasca, Lake lake Canada on Alta.-Sask. boundary *area* 3058 *sq mi* (7951 *sq km*)

Ath·ens \ˈa-thənz\ **1** city NE Ga. coextensive with Clarke county *pop* 115,452 **2** *or Gk* **Athí·nai** \ä-ˈthē-(ˌ)ne\ *or anc* **Athe·nae** \ə-ˈthē-(ˌ)nē\ city * of Greece near Saronic Gulf *pop* 748,110 — **Athe·nian** \ə-ˈthē-nē-ən, -nyən\ *adj or n*

Athos, Mount \ˈa-ˌthōs, ˈä-\ mountain NE Greece at E end of Acte Peninsula; site of a number of monasteries

Ati·tlán \ˌä-tē-ˈtlän\ lake 12 *mi* (19 *km*) long SW Guatemala at 4700 *ft* (1432 *m*) altitude occupying a crater 1000 *ft* (305 *m*) deep N of **Atitlán Volcano**

At·ka \ˈat-kə, ˈät-\ island SW Alaska in Andreanof group

At·lan·ta \ət-ˈlan-tə, at-\ city NW *cen* Ga., its * *pop* 420,003 — **At·lan·tan** \-ˈlan-t^{ə}n\ *adj or n*

At·lan·tic City \ət-ˈlan-tik, at-\ city SE N.J. on Atlantic coast *pop* 39,558

Atlantic Ocean ocean separating N. & S. America from Europe & Africa *area* 31,814,640 *sq mi* (82,399,918 *sq km*), often divided into **North Atlantic Ocean & South Atlantic Ocean**

Atlantic Provinces the four Canadian provinces of Nfld.&Lab., N.B., N.S., & P.E.I. — see MARITIME PROVINCES

At·las Mountains \ˈat-ləs\ mountains NW Africa extending from SW Morocco to NE Tunisia; its highest peaks are in the **Grand,** or **High, Atlas** in SW *cen* Morocco — see TOUBKAL (Jebel)

Atrek \ä-ˈtrek\ *or* **Atrak** \-ˈtrak\ river 300 *mi* (483 *km*) NE Iran flowing into the Caspian Sea on Turkmenistan border

Atropatene — see AZERBAIJAN 1

At·ta·wa·pis·kat \ˌa-tə-wə-ˈpis-kət\ river 465 *mi* (748 *km*) Canada in N Ont. flowing E into James Bay

At·ti·ca \ˈa-ti-kə\ region E Greece; chief city Athens; a state of ancient Greece

At·tle·boro \ˈa-t^{ə}l-ˌbər-ō\ city SE Mass. *pop* 43,593

At·tu \ˈa-(ˌ)tü\ island SW Alaska in Near Islands; most westerly of the Aleutians — see WRANGELL (Cape)

At·wa·ter \ˈat-ˌwȯ-tər, -ˌwä-\ city *cen* Calif. *pop* 28,168

Aube \ˈōb\ river 154 *mi* (248 *km*) N *cen* France flowing into the Seine

Au·ber·vil·liers \ˌō-bər-ˌvēl-ˈyā\ commune N France *pop* 63,130

Au·burn \ˈȯ-bərn\ **1** city E Ala. *pop* 53,380 **2** city SW Maine *pop* 23,055 **3** city *cen* N.Y. *pop* 27,687 **4** city W Wash. *pop* 70,180

Auck·land \ˈȯ-klənd\ city & port N New Zealand on North Is. *pop* 367,737 — **Auck·land·er** \-klən-dər\ *n*

Audenarde — see OUDENAARDE

Au·ghrim *or* **Aghrim** \ˈȯ-grəm\ town W Ireland in E Galway

Au·gra·bies Falls \ȯ-ˈgrä-bēz\ waterfall 480 *ft* (146 *m*) Republic of S. Africa in Orange River in Northern Cape province

Augs·burg \ˈȯgz-ˌbərg, ˈaùgz-ˌbùrk\ city S Germany in Bavaria on the Lech *pop* 256,877

Au·gus·ta \ȯ-ˈgəs-tə, ə-\ **1** city E Ga. on Savannah River coextensive with Richmond county *pop* 195,844 **2** city * of Maine on the Kennebec *pop* 19,136

Au·la·vik National Park \ˈaù-lə-ˌvik\ Arctic landscape NW Canada on N Banks Is.

Au·lis \ˈȯ-ləs\ harbor E Greece in Boeotia on Evripos Strait

Au·nis \ō-ˈnēs\ former province W France on Gironde Estuary & Bay of Biscay * La Rochelle

Au·rang·a·bad \aù-ˈrəŋ-gə-ˌbäd, -ˈrəŋ-ə-, -ˌbad\ city W India in *cen* Maharashtra ENE of Bombay *pop* 872,667

Au·rès \ȯ-ˈres\ massif *ab* 7600 *ft* (2316 *m*) NE Algeria in Saharan Atlas

Au·ri·gnac \ˌȯ-rēn-ˈyäk\ village SW France SW of Toulouse *pop* 980

Au·ril·lac \ˌȯ-rē-ˈyak\ city S *cen* France *pop* 30,554

Au·ro·ra \ə-ˈrȯr-ə, ȯ-\ **1** city N *cen* Colo. E of Denver *pop* 325,078 **2** city NE Ill. *pop* 197,899 **3** town Canada in SE Ont. *pop* 53,203

Au·sa·ble \ȯ-ˈsā-bəl\ river 20 *mi* (32 *km*) NE N.Y. flowing E into Lake Champlain through **Ausable Chasm**

Auschwitz — see OŚWIĘCIM

Austerlitz — see SLAVKOV

Aus·tin \ˈȯs-tən, ˈäs-\ **1** city S Minn. *pop* 24,718 **2** city * of Tex. on the Colorado *pop* 790,390 — **Aus·tin·ite** \-tə-ˌnīt\ *n*

Aus·tral·asia \ˌȯs-trə-ˈlā-zhə, ˌäs-, -ˈlā-shə\ Australia, New Zealand, & Melanesia — **Aus·tral·asian** \-zhən, -shən\ *adj or n*

Aus·tra·lia \ȯ-ˈstrāl-yə, ä-, ə-\ **1** continent of the eastern hemisphere SE of Asia & S of the equator *area* 2,948,366 *sq mi* (7,665,751 *sq km*) **2** *or* **Commonwealth of Australia** dominion of the Commonwealth of Nations including the continent of Australia & island of Tasmania * Canberra *area* 2,967,909 *sq mi* (7,716,563 *sq km*), *pop* 17,562,000

Australian Alps mountain range SE Australia in E Victoria & SE New South Wales forming S end of Great Dividing Range

Australian Capital Territory *or formerly* **Federal Capital Territory** district SE Australia including two areas, one around Canberra & the other on Jervis Bay, surrounded by New South Wales *area* 939 *sq mi* (2441 *sq km*), *pop* 229,000

Aus·tral Islands \\'ós-trəl, 'äs-\\ islands S. Pacific S of Tahiti belonging to France *pop* 6509

Aus·tra·sia *or* **Os·tra·sia** \\ó-'strā-zhə, ä-, -shə\\ the E dominions of the Merovingian Franks extending from the Meuse to the Bohemian Forest — **Aus·tra·sian** \\-zhən, -shən\\ *adj or n*

Aus·tria \\'òs-trē-ə, 'ás-\\ *or* **G Os·ter·reich** \\'œ-stə(r)-rīk\\ country *cen* Europe in & N of E Alps with the Danube crossing it in N; a republic ✳ Vienna *area* 32,375 *sq mi* (84,175 *sq km*), *pop* 8,050,000 — **Aus·tri·an** \\-ən\\ *adj or n*

Austria–Hun·ga·ry \\'hən-gə-rē\\ dual monarchy 1867–1918 *cen* Europe including Bohemia, Moravia, Bukovina, Transylvania, Galicia, and what is now Austria, Hungary, Slovenia, Croatia, & NE Italy — **Aus·tro–Hun·gar·i·an** \\-'gä-rē-ən\\ *also* \\-'ás-\\ *adj or n*

Aus·tro·ne·sia \\ós-trə-'nē-zhə, 'ás-, -'nē-shə\\ **1** the islands of the S. Pacific **2** area extending from Madagascar through the Malay Peninsula & Archipelago to Hawaii & Easter Is.

Au·teuil \\ō-'tœ-ē, -'ta(r)\\ district in W Paris, France

Au·vergne \\ō-'vernʸ, -'vərn\\ region & former province S *cen* France ✳ Clermont (now Clermont-Ferrand)

Auvergne Mountains mountains S *cen* France; highest in the Massif Central — see SANCY (Puy de)

Aux Cayes — see CAYES

Aux Sources, Mont \\'mōⁿ-,tō-'sùrs\\ mountain 10,822 *ft* (3298 *m*) N Lesotho in Drakensberg Mountains on South Africa border

Au·yán–te·puí \\aú-,yän-tä-'pwē\\ *or* **Devil Mountain** plateau *ab* 20 *mi* (32 *km*) long SE Venezuela E of the Caroni — see ANGEL FALLS

Au·yuit·tuq National Park \\aú-'yü-ə-tək\\ mountainous landscape with abundant wildlife NE Canada in E Baffin Is.

Av·a·lon \\'a-və-,län\\ peninsula Canada in SE Newfoundland

Avalon, Isle of — see ISLE OF AVALON

Ava·rua \\ä-vä-'rü-ä\\ village ✳ of the Cook Islands on Rarotonga

Ave·bury \\'āv-b(ə-)rē, *US also* -,ber-ē\\ village S England in Wiltshire E of Bristol; has megalithic remains

Avel·la·ne·da \\ä-vā-zhä-'nä-thä\\ city E Argentina, E suburb of Buenos Aires, on Río de la Plata *pop* 346,620

Avenches \\ä-'väⁿsh\\ *or anc* **Aven·ti·cum** \\ə-'ven-ti-kəm\\ town W Switzerland in Vaud canton ✳ of ancient Helvetia

Av·en·tine \\'a-vən-,tīn, -,tēn\\ hill in Rome, Italy, one of seven (including also the Caelian, Capitoline, Esquiline, Palatine, Quirinal, & Viminal) on which the ancient city was built

Av·en·tu·ra \\,a-vən-'túr-ə\\ city SE Fla. NNE of Miami *pop* 35,762

Aver·nus, Lake \\ə-'vər-nəs\\ *or It* **Lago d'Aver·no** \\'lä-gō-dä-'ver-(,)nō\\ lake S Italy in crater of extinct volcano W of Naples

Avi·gnon \\a-(,)vēn-'yōⁿ\\ city SE France *pop* 85,937

Ávi·la \\'ä-vi-lə, -vē-,lä\\ **1** province *cen* Spain *area* 3107 *sq mi* (8047 *sq km*), *pop* 163,442 **2** city, its ✳, WNW of Madrid *pop* 49,712

Avlona — see VLORË

Avon \\'ā-vən, *US also* 'ā-,vän\\ **1** river 96 *mi* (154 *km*) *cen* England rising in Northamptonshire & flowing WSW past Stratford-upon-Avon into Severn River at Tewkesbury **2** river 65 *mi* (105 *km*) S England rising in Wiltshire & flowing S into English Channel **3** river 75 *mi* (121 *km*) SW England rising in Gloucestershire & flowing S & W through Bristol into Bristol Channel at Avonmouth **4** \\'a-vən\\ — see SWAN

Av·on·dale \\'a-vən-,dāl\\ city S *cen* Ariz. W of Tempe *pop* 76,238

Avranches \\äv-'rä°sh\\ town NW France in SW Normandy *pop* 8509

Awa·ji \\ä-'wä-jē\\ island Japan S of Honshu & NE of Shikoku

Awash \\'ä-,wäsh\\ river 500 *mi* (805 *km*) E Ethiopia flowing NE

Ax·el Hei·berg \\'ak-səl-'hī-,bərg\\ island N Canada in the Sverdrup Islands W of Ellesmere Is. *area* 15,779 *sq mi* (41,025 *sq km*)

Axum — see AKSUM — **Ax·um·ite** \\'ak-sə-,mīt\\ *adj or n*

Aya·cu·cho \\,ä-yä-'kü-(,)chō\\ town S Peru SE of Lima *pop* 101,600

Ay·din \\ī-'din\\ city SW Turkey SE of Izmir *pop* 107,011

Ayers Rock — see ULURU

Ayles·bury \\'ālz-b(ə-)rē, *US also* -,ber-ē\\ town SE *cen* England ✳ of Buckinghamshire *pop* 41,288

Ayl·mer \\'āl-mər\\ former town Canada in SW Que.; now part of Gatineau

Ayr \\'er\\ **1** *or* **Ayr·shire** \\-,shir, -shər\\ former county SW Scotland **2** burgh & port SW Scotland *pop* 49,481

Ayut·tha·ya \\,ä-yü-'tī-ə\\ *or in full* **Phra Na·khon Si Ayutthaya** \\,prä-nä-'kòn-sē-\\ city S Thailand N of Bangkok *pop* 60,561

Azer·bai·jan \\,a-zər-,bī-'jän, ,ä-\\ **1** *or anc* **At·ro·pa·te·ne** \\,a-trō-pə-'tē-nē\\ *or* **Me·dia Atropatene** \\'mē-dē-ə\\ region NW Iran; chief city Tabriz **2** independent country W Asia & SE Europe bordering on Caspian Sea; a constituent republic of the U.S.S.R. 1936–91 ✳ Baku *area* 33,200 *sq mi* (86,320 *sq km*), *pop* 8,200,000

Azincourt — see AGINCOURT

Azores \\'ā-,zòrz, ə-'\\ *or P* **Açores** \\ə-'sòr-ēsh\\ islands N. Atlantic belonging to Portugal & lying *ab* 800 *mi* (1287 *km*) off coast of Portugal; chief town Ponta Delgada *area* 905 *sq mi* (2344 *sq km*), *pop* 241,763 — **Azor·e·an** \\ā-'zòr-ē-ən, ə-\\ *adj or n*

Azov, Sea of \\'a-,zóf, 'ä-\\ *or R* \\-zòf\\ gulf of the Black Sea E of Crimea connected with the Black Sea by the Kerch Strait *area* 14,517 *sq mi* (37,599 *sq km*)

Az·tec Ruins National Monument \\'az-,tek\\ site of a prehistoric pueblo NW N.Mex. NE of Farmington

Azu·sa \\ə-'zü-sə\\ city SW Calif. ENE of Los Angeles *pop* 46,361

Az–Zaqāzīq — see ZAGAZIG

Baal·bek \\'bä-əl-,bek, 'bäl-,bek\\ town E Lebanon N of Damascus on site of ancient city of **He·li·op·o·lis** \\,hē-lē-'ä-pə-lis\\

Ba·bar Islands \\'bä-,bär\\ islands Indonesia ENE of Timor

Bab el Man·deb \\,bäb-el-'män-dəb\\ strait bet. SW Arabia & Africa connecting Red Sea & Gulf of Aden

Ba·bel·thu·ap \\,bäb-əl-'tü-,äp\\ island W Pacific, chief island in Palau *area* 143 *sq mi* (372 *sq km*)

Babruysk — see BOBRUYSK

Ba·bu·yan \\,bä-bü-'yän\\ chief island of the Babuyan group

Babuyan Islands *or* **Ba·bu·ya·nes** \\,bä-bü-'yä-näs\\ islands of N Philippines N of Luzon *area* 225 *sq mi* (585 *sq km*)

Bab·y·lon \\'ba-bə-lən, -,län\\ ancient city ✳ of Babylonia; its site *ab* 55 *mi* (89 *km*) S of Baghdad near the Euphrates

Bab·y·lo·nia \\,ba-bə-'lō-nyə, -nē-ə\\ ancient country in valley of the lower Euphrates & the Tigris ✳ Babylon

Ba·cau \\bə-'kaú\\ city E *cen* Romania *pop* 175,921

Back \\'bak\\ river 605 *mi* (974 *km*) Canada in Nunavut rising along border with Northwest Territories & flowing ENE into Arctic Ocean

Ba·co·lod \\bä-'kō-,lòd\\ city Philippines on Negros Is. *pop* 364,000

Bactra — see BALKH 2

Bac·tria \\'bak-trē-ə\\ ancient country SW Asia bet. Hindu Kush & Oxus River ✳ Bactra — see BALKH — **Bac·tri·an** \\'bak-trē-ən\\ *adj or n*

Ba·da·joz \\,bä-thä-'hōs, ,bä-də-'hōz\\ **1** province SW Spain in valley of the Guadiana *area* 8362 *sq mi* (21,658 *sq km*), *pop* 654,882 **2** city, its ✳ *pop* 133,519

Ba·da·lo·na \\,bä-thä-'lō-nä, ,bä-də-'lō-nə\\ city & port NE Spain on the Mediterranean NE of Barcelona *pop* 205,836

Bad Ems — see EMS

Ba·den \\'bä-dᵊn\\ **1** region SW Germany bordering on Switzerland & France; formerly a grand duchy (1805–1918), a state of the Weimar Republic (1918–33), an administrative division of the Third Reich (1933–49), & a state of the Bonn Republic (1949–51) ✳ Karlsruhe — see BADEN-WÜRTTEMBERG **2** BADEN-BADEN

Ba·den–Ba·den \\,bä-dᵊn-'bä-dᵊn\\ *or* **Baden** city & spa SW Germany in Baden-Württemberg SSW of Karlsruhe *pop* 52,524

Ba·den–Würt·tem·berg \\,bä-dᵊn-'wər-təm-,bərg, -'wùr-; -'vùr-təm-,berk\\ state SW Germany W of Bavaria; formed 1951 from former Baden, Württemberg-Baden, & Württemberg-Hohenzollern states ✳ Stuttgart *area* 13,803 *sq mi* (35,750 *sq km*), *pop* 9,822,000

Bad Godesberg — see GODESBERG

Bad Hom·burg \\,bät-'hòm-,bùrk, -'häm-,bərg\\ city SW *cen* Germany N of Frankfurt am Main *pop* 51,663

Badlands National Park area of badlands topography SW S. Dak. E of Black Hills

Bad Mergentheim — see MERGENTHEIM

Baer·um \\'ba-rəm\\ city SE Norway, a suburb of Oslo *pop* 100,013

Baf·fin Bay \\'ba-fən\\ inlet of the Atlantic bet. W Greenland & E Baffin Is.

Baffin Island island NE Canada in Nunavut N of Hudson Strait; largest in Arctic Archipelago *area* 183,810 *sq mi* (477,906 *sq km*)

Ba·fing \\bə-'faŋ, bä-'fēⁿ\\ river 350 *mi* (560 *km*) W Africa in W Mali & Guinea; the upper course of the Senegal

Bagh·dad \\'bag-,dad, ,bäg-'däd\\ city ✳ of Iraq on the middle Tigris *pop* 3,841,268 — **Bagh·dadi** \\bag-'da-dē\\ *n*

Ba·guio \\bä-gē-'ō\\ city Philippines in NW *cen* Luzon; formerly the nation's summer ✳ *pop* 183,000

Ba·ha·mas \\bə-'hä-məz, *by outsiders also* -'hä-\\ *or* **The Bahamas** islands in the Atlantic SE of Fla.; an independent member of the Commonwealth of Nations since 1973 ✳ Nassau *area* 4404 *sq mi* (11,450 *sq km*), *pop* 303,611 — see TURKS AND CAICOS — **Ba·ha·mi·an** \\bə-'hä-mē-ən, -'hā-\\ *adj or n*

Ba·ha·wal·pur \\bə-'hä-wəl-,pùr\\ region Pakistan in SW Punjab; until 1947 a princely state of India

Ba·hia \\bə-'hē-ə\\ **1** *or formerly* **Ba·ía** \\bä-'ē-ə\\ state E Brazil ✳ Salvador *area* 216,612 *sq mi* (561,025 *sq km*), *pop* 13,070,250 **2** — see SALVADOR — **Ba·hi·an** \\-ən\\ *adj or n*

Ba·hía Blan·ca \\bə-,hē-ə-'blaŋ-kə, bä-,ē-ə-'blän-kä\\ city & port E Argentina S of Buenos Aires *pop* 271,467

Bahnasa, El — see OXYRHYNCHUS

Bah·rain *also* **Bah·rein** \\bä-'rān\\ **1** islands in Persian Gulf off coast of Arabia **2** an independent kingdom ✳ Manama (on Bahrain Is.) *area* 255 *sq mi* (661 *sq km*), *pop* 650,604 **3** island, largest of the group, 27 *mi* (43 *km*) long — **Bah·raini** *also* **Bah·reini** \\-'rä-nē\\ *adj or n*

Bahr al–Gha·zal \\,bär-äl-gä-'zäl\\ river 445 *mi* (716 *km*) SW Sudan flowing E to unite with the Bahr el Jebel forming the White Nile

Ba·ia–Ma·re \\,bä-yä-'mä-rä\\ city NW Romania *pop* 137,976

Bai·kal, Lake *or* **Lake Bay·kal** \\bī-'käl, -'kal\\ lake Russia in Asia; 5315 *ft* (1620 *m*) deep, *ab* 395 *mi* (636 *km*) long

Baile Atha Cliath **1** — see DUBLIN 3 **2** — see DUBLIN 4

Ba·ja California \\'bä-(,)hä\\ peninsula 760 *mi* (1216 *km*) long NW Mexico bet. the Pacific & Gulf of California; divided into the states of **Baja California** (to the N ✳ Mexicali *area* 27,071 *sq mi* or 70,114 *sq km*, *pop* 1,660,855) & **Baja California Sur** \\-'sùr\\ (to the S ✳ La Paz *area* 28,447 *sq mi* or 73,678 *sq km*, *pop* 317,764)

Bakan — see SHIMONOSEKI

Baker, Mount mountain 10,778 *ft* (3266 *m*) NW Wash. in Cascade Range

Ba·ker Island \\'bā-kər\\ atoll *cen* Pacific near the equator at 176°31′W; belongs to U.S.

Baker Lake — see DUBAWNT

Ba·kers·field \\'bā-kərz-,fēld\\ city S *cen* Calif. on the Kern *pop* 347,483

Bākh·ta·rān \\,bäk-tə-'rän\\ *or formerly* **Ker·man·shah** \\,ker-,män-'shä\\ city W Iran *pop* 560,514

Ba·ku \\bä-'kü\\ city ✳ of Azerbaijan *pop* 1,150,000

Bakwanga — see MBUJI-MAYI

Ba·la·kla·va \\,bä-lə-'klä-və, -'kla-; ,bä-lə-'klä-və\\ village Ukraine in Crimea SE of Sevastopol

Ba·la·ton, Lake \\'ba-lə-,tän, 'bò-lò-,tōn\\ *or G* **Plat·ten·see** \\'plä-tᵊn-,zä\\ lake W Hungary; largest in *cen* Europe *area* 232 *sq mi* (601 *sq km*)

Bal·boa Heights \\,bal-'bō-ə\\ town Panama at Pacific entrance to Panama Canal adjacent to Panama (city); former administrative center of Canal Zone

Bald·win Park \\'bòl-dwən\\ city SW Calif. E of Los Angeles *pop* 75,390

Bâle — see BASEL

Bal·e·ar·es \\,bä-lē-'a-rēz, ,bä-lä-'är-äs\\ **1** BALEARIC ISLANDS **2** province E Spain comprising the Balearic Islands ✳ Palma *area* 1936 *sq mi* (5034 *sq km*), *pop* 841,669

Bal·e·ar·ic Islands \\,ba-lē-'a-rik\\ islands E Spain in the W Mediterranean — see BALEARES, IBIZA, MAJORCA, MINORCA

Ba·li \\'bä-lē, 'ba-\\ island Indonesia off E Java 2147 *sq mi* (5582 *sq km*), *pop* 2,777,811

\\ə\\ abut \\ᵊ\\ kitten, F table \\ər\\ further \\a\\ ash \\ā\\ ace \\ä\\ mop, mar
\\aú\\ out \\ch\\ chin \\e\\ bet \\ē\\ easy \\g\\ go \\i\\ hit \\ī\\ ice \\j\\ job
\\ŋ\\ sing \\ō\\ go \\ò\\ law \\òi\\ boy \\th\\ thin \\t͟h\\ the \\ü\\ loot \\ù\\ foot
\\y\\ yet \\zh\\ vision, beige \\k̲, ⁿ, œ, �, ʸ\\ *see* Guide to Pronunciation

Ba·lı·ke·sir \ˌbä-li-ke-ˈsir\ city NW Turkey in Asia *pop* 170,589
Ba·lik·pa·pan \ˌbä-lik-ˈpä-ˌpän\ city & port Indonesia on SE Borneo on inlet of Makassar Strait *pop* 309,492
Bal·kan Mountains \ˈbȯl-kən\ mountain range *cen* Bulgaria extending from border with Serbia to Black Sea; highest point Botev Peak 7793 *ft* (2375 *m*)
Balkan Peninsula peninsula SE Europe bet. Adriatic & Ionian seas on W & Aegean & Black seas on E — **Balkan** *adj* — **Bal·kan·ic** \bȯl-ˈka-nik\ *adj*
Bal·kans \ˈbȯl-kənz\ *also* **Balkan States** the countries occupying the Balkan Peninsula: Slovenia, Croatia, Bosnia and Herzegovina, Macedonia, Serbia, Montenegro, Kosovo, Romania, Bulgaria, Albania, Greece, & Turkey in Europe
Bal·kar·ia \bȯl-ˈker-ē-ə, bal-\ mountain region S Russia in Europe, in S Kabardino-Balkaria Republic
Balkh \ˈbälk\ **1** district N Afghanistan corresponding closely to ancient Bactria **2** *or anc* **Bac·tra** \ˈbak-trə\ town N Afghanistan ✻ of ancient Bactria
Bal·khash, Lake \bal-ˈkash, bäl-ˈkäsh\ lake 376 *mi* (605 *km*) long SE Kazakhstan *area ab* 7100 *sq mi* (18,390 *sq km*)
Bal·la·rat \ˈba-lə-ˌrat\ city SE Australia in *cen* Victoria *pop* 34,501
Ball·win \ˈbȯl-wən\ city E Mo. W of St. Louis *pop* 30,404
Bal·ly·me·na \ˌba-lē-ˈmē-nə\ district NE Northern Ireland, established 1974 *area* 246 *sq mi* (640 *sq km*), *pop* 56,032
Bal·ly·mon·ey \ˌba-lē-ˈmə-nē\ district N Northern Ireland, established 1974 *area* 162 *sq mi* (421 *sq km*), *pop* 23,984
Bal·sas \ˈbȯl-səs, ˈbäl-säs\ river 426 *mi* (682 *km*) *cen* Mexico flowing from Tlaxcala to the Pacific on border bet. Michoacán & Guerrero
Bal·tic Sea \ˈbȯl-tik\ arm of the Atlantic N Europe enclosed by Denmark, Sweden, Finland, Estonia, Latvia, Lithuania, Poland, & Germany *area ab* 160,000 *sq mi* (256,000 *sq km*)
Bal·ti·more \ˈbȯl-tə-ˌmȯr, -mər; ˈbȯlt-mər; *by residents usu* ˈbȯl-tē-ˌmȯr *or* ˈbȯl-mər\ city & port N *cen* Md. on estuary of the Patapsco River *pop* 620,961 — **Bal·ti·mor·e·an** \ˌbȯl-tə-ˈmȯr-ē-ən\ *n*
Bal·ti·stan \ˌbȯl-tə-ˈstan, ˌbəl-, -ˈstän\ region Ladakh district N Kashmir; under Pakistani control
Ba·lu·chi·stan \bə-ˌlü-chə-ˈstan, -ˈstän; bə-ˈlü-chə-ˌ\ **1** arid region S Asia bordering on Arabian Sea in SW Pakistan & SE Iran S & SW of Afghanistan **2** *or* **Ba·lo·chi·stan** \bə-ˌlō-chə-ˈ, bə-ˈlō-chə-ˌ\ province SW Pakistan ✻ Quetta *pop* 4,305,000
Ba·ma·ko \ˈbä-mä-ˌkō\ city ✻ of Mali on Niger River *pop* 1,016,167
Bam·ba·ri \ˈbäm-bä-rē\ town S *cen* Central African Republic *pop* 52,100
Bam·berg \ˈbam-ˌbərg, ˈbäm-ˌberk\ city S *cen* Germany in N Bavaria NNW of Nuremberg *pop* 70,689
Ba·na·ba \bä-ˈnä-bä\ *or* **Ocean Island** island W Pacific ESE of Nauru; belongs to Kiribati *area over* 2 *sq mi* (5 *sq km*), *pop* 284
Ba·na·hao, Mount \bä-ˈnä-ˌhau̇\ extinct volcano 7141 *ft* (2142 *m*) Philippines on S Luzon SE of Manila
Ba·nana River \bə-ˈna-nə\ lagoon E Fla. bet. Canaveral Peninsula & Merritt Is.
Banaras — see VARANASI
Ba·nat \bə-ˈnät, ˈbä-ˌnät\ region SE *cen* Europe in Danube basin bet. the Tisza & the Mures & the Transylvanian Alps; once entirely in Hungary, divided 1919 bet. Serbia & Romania
Ban·bridge \ban-ˈbrij\ district SE Northern Ireland, established 1974 *area* 171 *sq mi* (445 *sq km*), *pop* 33,102
Ban·da Islands \ˈban-də, ˈbän-\ islands Indonesia in Moluccas S of Ceram *area* 16 *sq mi* (42 *sq km*)
Banda Oriental — see URUGUAY 2
Banda Sea sea E Malay Archipelago SE of Sulawesi, S of the Moluccas, W of Aru Islands, & NE of Timor
Bandar — see MACHILIPATNAM
Bandar ʿAbbas *or* **Bandar–e–Abbas** \ˌbən-dər(-ē)-ə-ˈbäs\ city S Iran on Strait of Hormuz *pop* 379,301
Bandar–e Khomeyni *or* **Bandar Khomeyni** \ˌbən-dər(-ē)-ˌkō-mā-ˈnē, -kō-ˈmā-nē\ town & port SW Iran at head of Persian Gulf ENE of Abadan *pop* 67,000
Bandar Lampung — see TANJUNGKARANG
Ban·dar Se·ri Be·ga·wan \ˌbən-dər-ˌser-ē-bə-ˈgä-wän\ *or formerly* **Brunei** town ✻ of Brunei *pop* 27,285
Ban·de·lier National Monument \ˌban-də-ˈlir\ reservation N *cen* N.Mex. W of Santa Fe containing cliff-dweller ruins
Ban·dung *or D* **Ban·doeng** \ˈbän-ˌdu̇ŋ\ city Indonesia in W Java SE of Jakarta *pop* 2,057,442
Banff \ˈbam(p)f\ *or* **Banff·shire** \-ˌshir, -shər\ former county NE Scotland ✻ Banff
Banff National Park reservation W Canada in SW Alta. on E slope of Rocky Mountains
Ban·ga·lore \ˈbaŋ-gə-ˌlȯr\ *or* **Ben·ga·lu·ru** \ˈbeŋ-gə-ˌlü-rü\ city S India W of Madras ✻ of Karnataka *pop* 4,292,223
Banghazi — see BENGHAZI
Bang·ka *or* **Ban·ka** \ˈbaŋ-kə\ island Indonesia off SE Sumatra; chief town Pangkalpinang *area* 4609 *sq mi* (11,983 *sq km*), *pop* 251,639
Bang·kok \ˈbaŋ-ˌkäk, baŋ-ˈ\ *or Thai* **Krung Thep** \ˈkru̇ŋ-ˈtep\ city & port ✻ of Thailand on the Chao Phraya *ab* 25 *mi* (40 *km*) above its mouth *pop* 6,320,200
Ban·gla·desh \ˌbäŋ-glə-ˈdesh, ˌbaŋ-, ˌbəŋ-, -ˈdāsh\ country S Asia E of India on Bay of Bengal; a republic in the Commonwealth of Nations since 1971 ✻ Dhaka *area* 55,126 *sq mi* (143,328 *sq km*), *pop* 129,247,233 — see EAST PAKISTAN — **Ban·gla·deshi** \-ˈde-shē, -ˈdā-\ *adj or n*
Ban·gor \ˈbaŋ-ˌgȯr, ˈban-ˌgȯr (*these usual for 1*), ˈbaŋ-gər\ **1** city E *cen* Maine on the Penobscot *pop* 33,039 **2** town SE Northern Ireland in North Down (district) *pop* 46,585 **3** city NW Wales in Gwynedd *pop* 12,174
Ban·gui \bäŋ-ˈgē\ city ✻ of Central African Republic on the Ubangi *pop* 532,000
Bang·we·u·lu, Lake \ˌbäŋ-gwā-ˈü-(ˌ)lü\ lake *ab* 50 *mi* (80 *km*) long N Zambia in swamp region; its area fluctuates seasonally; drains into the Luapula, a headstream of Congo River
Ban·jar·ma·sin \ˈbän-jär-ˌmä-sin\ city Indonesia in S Borneo *pop* 481,371
Ban·jul \ˈbän-ˌjül\ *or formerly* **Bath·urst** \ˈba-(ˌ)thərst\ city & port ✻ of Gambia on island of St. Mary in Gambia River *pop* 35,000
Banks Island \ˈbaŋks\ island N Canada in Northwest Territories at W end of Arctic Archipelago *area ab* 27,000 *sq mi* (69,900 *sq km*)
Banks Islands islands SW Pacific; administered by Vanuatu *pop* 5521
Ban·ning \ˈba-niŋ\ city S Calif. ESE of Riverside *pop* 29,603
Ban·nock·burn \ˈba-nək-ˌbərn, ˌba-nək-ˈ\ town *cen* Scotland SSE of Stirling
Ban·tam \ˈban-təm\ former town Indonesia in NW corner of Java; once ✻ of Sultanate of Bantam
Ban·try Bay \ˈban-trē\ bay SW Ireland in SW County Cork
Bao·ding *or* **Pao–ting** \ˈbau̇-ˈdiŋ\ *or formerly* **Tsing·yuan** \ˈchiŋ-yü-ˈen\ city NE China SW of Beijing *pop* 483,155
Bao·ji *or* **Pao–chi** \ˈbau̇-ˈjē\ city N *cen* China in SW Shaanxi on the Wei W of Xi'an *pop* 337,765
Bao·tou *or* **Pao–t'ou** \ˈbau̇-ˈtō\ city N China in SW Inner Mongolia on the Huang *pop* 983,508
Ba·paume \bä-ˈpōm, ba-\ town N France S of Arras *pop* 4329
Ba·ra·coa \ˌbä-rä-ˈkō-ä\ city & port E Cuba on N coast near E tip of island *pop* 76,873
Ba·ra·nof \ˈba-rə-ˌnȯf, bə-ˈrä-nəf\ island SE Alaska in Alexander Archipelago S of Chichagof Is. *area ab* 1600 *sq mi* (4160 *sq km*)
Bar·a·tar·ia Bay \ˌba-rə-ˈter-ē-ə\ lagoon SE La. on coast NW of delta of Mississippi River
Bar·ba·dos \bär-ˈbā-(ˌ)dōs, -dəs, -(ˌ)dōz\ island Brit. West Indies in Lesser Antilles E of the Windward group; a dominion of the Commonwealth of Nations since 1966 ✻ Bridgetown *area* 166 *sq mi* (432 *sq km*), *pop* 270,800 — **Bar·ba·di·an** \-ˈbā-dē-ən\ *adj or n*
Bar·ba·ry Coast \ˈbär-b(ə-)rē\ **1** region N Africa extending from Egypt to the Atlantic & including the former **Barbary States** (Morocco, Algiers, Tunis, & Tripoli) — a chiefly former name **2** section of San Francisco formerly noted as a center of gambling, prostitution, and riotous nightlife — an informal name
Bar·bers Point \ˈbär-bərz\ *or* **Ka·la·e·loa Point** \kä-ˌlä-(ˌ)ā-ˈlō-ä\ cape Hawaii at SW corner of Oahu W of Pearl Harbor
Bar·ber·ton \ˈbär-bər-tən\ city NE Ohio SW of Akron *pop* 26,550
Bar·bi·zon \ˌbär-bē-ˈzōⁿ, ˈbär-bə-ˌzän\ village N France SSE of Paris *pop* 1493
Bar·bu·da \bär-ˈbü-də\ island Brit. West Indies in the Leewards *area* 62 *sq mi* (161 *sq km*), *pop* 1325 — see ANTIGUA 1
Bar·ce·lo·na \ˌbär-sə-ˈlō-nə\ **1** province NE Spain in Catalonia on the Mediterranean *area* 2986 *sq mi* (7734 *sq km*), *pop* 4,805,927 **2** city & port, its ✻ *pop* 1,503,884 **3** city NE Venezuela near coast *pop* 109,061 — **Bar·ce·lo·nan** \-ˈlō-nən\ *n* — **Bar·ce·lo·nese** \-lō-ˈnēz, -ˈnēs, -ˈlō-ˌ\ *adj or n*
Bar·di·yah *or* **Bar·dia** \ˈbär-dē-ə, bär-ˈdē-ə\ town & port Libya in NE Cyrenaica
Ba·reil·ly *or* **Ba·re·li** \bə-ˈrā-lē\ **1** city N India in NW *cen* Uttar Pradesh ESE of Delhi *pop* 699,839 **2** — see ROHILKHAND
Ba·rents Sea \ˈba-rən(t)s, ˈbär-ən(t)s\ sea comprising the part of the Arctic Ocean bet. Spitsbergen & Novaya Zemlya
Ba·ri \ˈbär-ē\ *or anc* **Bar·i·um** \ˈber-ē-əm\ commune & port SE Italy ✻ of Puglia on the Adriatic *pop* 332,143
Ba·ri·lo·che \ˌbä-rē-ˈlō-chā\ *or* **San Car·los de Bariloche** \sän-ˈkär-lōs-thā-\ town SW Argentina on Lake Nahuel Huapí *pop* 89,092
Ba·ri·nas \bä-ˈrē-näs\ town W *cen* Venezuela *pop* 152,853
Bar·i·sāl \ˈba-rə-ˌsäl\ city S Bangladesh in Ganges Delta *pop* 192,810
Bar·ka \ˈbär-kə\ town Libya in NW Cyrenaica
Bar·king and Dag·en·ham \ˈbär-kiŋ-ən(d)-ˈda-gə-nəm\ borough of E Greater London, England *pop* 139,900
Bar·let·ta \bär-ˈle-tə\ commune & port SE Italy in Puglia on the Adriatic *pop* 92,305
Bar·na·ul \ˌbär-nə-ˈül\ city Russia in Asia on the Ob' ✻ of Altai territory *pop* 606,000
Bar·ne·gat Bay \ˈbär-ni-ˌgat, -gət\ inlet of the Atlantic E N.J.
Barnes \ˈbärnz\ former municipal borough SE England, now part of Richmond
Bar·net \ˈbär-nət\ borough of N Greater London, England *pop* 283,000
Barns·ley \ˈbärnz-lē\ town N England in S. Yorkshire *pop* 217,300
Barn·sta·ble \ˈbärn-stə-bəl\ city SE Mass. on Cape Cod *pop* 45,193
Ba·ro·da \bə-ˈrō-də\ **1** former state W India near head of Gulf of Khambhat ✻ Baroda *area* 8176 *sq mi* (21,258 *sq km*) **2** — see VADODARA
Ba·rot·se·land \bä-ˈrȯt-sā-ˌland\ region W Zambia; formerly a protectorate
Bar·qui·si·me·to \ˌbär-kē-sə-ˈmā-(ˌ)tō\ city NW Venezuela *pop* 863,000
Bar·ran·quil·la \ˌbär-än-ˈkē-yä\ city & port N Colombia on the Magdalena *pop* 1,142,312
Bar·ran·qui·tas \ˌbär-rän-ˈkē-täs\ city *cen* Puerto Rico *pop* 30,318
Barren Grounds treeless plains N Canada W of Hudson Bay
Bar·rie \ˈba-rē\ city Canada in SE Ont. *pop* 135,711
Bar·row, Point \ˈba-(ˌ)rō\ most northerly point of Alaska & of the U.S., at *ab* 71°23′30″N, 156°28′30″W
Bar·row–in–Fur·ness \ˌba-rō-in-ˈfər-nəs\ port NW England in S Cumbria *pop* 71,900
Bar·tles·ville \ˈbär-tᵊlz-ˌvil\ city NE Okla. *pop* 35,750
Bart·lett \ˈbärt-lət\ **1** village NE Ill. W of Chicago *pop* 41,208 **2** city SW Tenn. *pop* 54,613
Ba·rú \bä-ˈrü\ *or formerly* **Chi·ri·quí** \ˌchē-rē-ˈkē\ volcano 11,400 *ft* (3475 *m*) Panama near Costa Rican border
Ba·sel \ˈbä-zəl\ *or F* **Bâle** *or older* **Basle** \ˈbäl\ **1** former canton NW Switzerland, now divided into two half cantons: **Ba·sel–Land** \ˈbä-zəl-ˌlänt\ (✻ Liestal *area* 165 *sq mi or* 429 *sq km, pop* 261,400) & **Ba·sel–Stadt** \-ˌshtät\ (✻ Basel *area* 14 *sq mi or* 36 *sq km, pop* 186,700) **2** city NW Switzerland ✻ of Basel-Stadt *pop* 164,850
Ba·shan \ˈbā-shən\ region in ancient Palestine E & NE of Sea of Galilee
Ba·shi Channel \ˈbä-shē\ strait bet. Philippines & Taiwan
Bash·kor·to·stan \bäsh-ˈkȯr-tə-ˌstän, -ˌstan\ *or* **Bash·kir Republic** \ˌbash-ˈkir, ˌbäsh-\ autonomous republic E Russia in Europe in S Ural Mountains ✻ Ufa *area* 55,443 *sq mi* (143,597 *sq km*), *pop* 4,008,000
Ba·si·lan \bä-ˈsē-ˌlän\ **1** island Philippines SW of Mindanao *area* 495 *sq mi* (1287 *sq km*) **2** city comprising Basilan Is. and several small nearby islands
Bas·il·don \ˈba-zəl-dən\ town SE England in Essex *pop* 157,500
Ba·si·li·ca·ta \ˌbä-ˌzē-lē-ˈkä-tä\ *or formerly* **Lu·ca·nia** \lü-ˈkā-nyə, -ˈkä-\ region S Italy on Gulf of Taranto ✻ Potenza *pop* 604,807

Basin Ranges — see GREAT BASIN

Basque Country \'bask, 'bäsk\ autonomous region N Spain on Bay of Biscay consisting of provinces of Álava, Guipúzcoa, & Vizcaya

Bas·ra \'bäs-rə, 'bȯs-, 'bas-, 'baz-, 'baz-\ or **Al–Bas·rah** \äl-'\ city & port S Iraq on Shatt al Arab pop 1,250,000

Bas·sein \bä-'sān\ city S Myanmar W of Yangon pop 216,000

Basse·terre \bas-'ter, bäs-\ town & port Brit. West Indies ✽ of St. Kitts Is. & of St. Kitts and Nevis state pop 13,220

Basse–Terre \bas-'ter, bäs-\ **1** island French West Indies constituting the W part of Guadeloupe area 364 sq mi (946 sq km), pop 173,000 **2** town & port ✽ of Guadeloupe pop 12,377

Bass Strait \'bas\ strait separating Tasmania & continent of Australia

Bas·tia \'bas-tē-ə, 'bäs-\ city & port France on NE coast of Corsica pop 37,880

Bas·togne \ba-'stȯn, -'stȯ-nyə\ town SE Belgium in the Ardennes pop 13,739

Basutoland — see LESOTHO

Ba·ta \'bä-tä\ city ✽ of Mbini, Equatorial Guinea pop 50,000

Ba·taan \bə-'tan, -'tän\ peninsula Philippines in W Luzon on W side of Manila Bay

Ba·ta·via \bə-'tā-vē-ə\ **1** city NE Ill. N of Aurora pop 26,045 **2** — see JAKARTA — **Ba·ta·vi·an** \-vē-ən\ adj or n

Batavian Republic the Netherlands under the French (1795–1806)

Bath \'bath, 'bäth\ city SW England in Somerset pop 79,900

Bathurst — see BANJUL

Bath·urst Island \'ba-(,)thərst\ island N Canada in Parry group

Bat·on Rouge \,ba-tᵊn-'rüzh\ city ✽ of La. on Mississippi River pop 229,493

Bat·ter·sea \'ba-tər-sē\ former metropolitan borough SW London, England, on S bank of the Thames, now part of Wandsworth

Bat·tle Creek \,ba-tᵊl-'krēk\ city S Mich. pop 52,347

Ba·tu·mi \bä-'tü-mē\ city & port SW Republic of Georgia on Black Sea ✽ of Ajaria pop 121,806

Baut·zen \'baut-sən\ city E Germany on the Spree ENE of Dresden pop 47,131

Ba·var·ia \bə-'ver-ē-ə\ or G **Bay·ern** \'bī-ərn\ state SE Germany bordering on Austria & the Czech Republic ✽ Munich area 27,239 sq mi (70,549 sq km), pop 11,448,800

Ba·ya·món \,bī-ä-'mōn\ city NE cen Puerto Rico pop 208,116

Bay City city E Mich. near head of Saginaw Bay pop 34,932

Ba·yeux \bä-'yü, bā-; bä-'yə(r); bä-'yœ\ town NW France WNW of Caen pop 14,961

Baykal, Lake — see BAIKAL

Bay·onne \bā-'ōn\ city & port NE N.J. pop 63,024

Ba·yonne \bā-'ōn, bā-'yȯn\ city SW France on the Adour near Bay of Biscay pop 40,113

Bay·reuth \bī-'rȯit, 'bī-,\ city Germany in Bavaria NE of Nuremberg pop 72,777

Baytin — see BETHEL

Bayt Lahm — see BETHLEHEM 2

Bay·town \'bā-,taun\ city SE Tex. on Galveston Bay pop 71,802

Beachy Head \'bē-chē\ headland SE England on coast of E. Sussex

Bear \'ber\ river 350 mi (563 km) N Utah, SW Wyo., & SE Idaho flowing to Great Salt Lake

Beard·more \'bird-,mȯr\ glacier Antarctica descending to Ross Ice Shelf at ab 170°E

Bear Mountain mountain 1305 ft (398 m) SE N.Y. on the Hudson

Bé·arn \bā-'ärn\ region & former province SW France in Pyrenees SW of Gascony ✽ Pau

Be·as \'bē-,äs\ river ab 300 mi (483 km) N India in the Punjab

Beau·fort Sea \'bō-fərt\ sea comprising the part of the Arctic Ocean NE of Alaska & NW of Canada

Beau·mar·is \bō-'ma-rəs\ town NW Wales in Gwynedd on E Anglesey Is. on **Beaumaris Bay** pop 2088

Beau·mont \'bō-,mänt, bō-'\ city & port SE Tex. on the Neches pop 118,296

Beaune \'bōn\ commune E France SSW of Dijon pop 21,917

Beau·port \bō-'pȯr, 'bō-(,)pȯrt\ former city Canada in S Que.; now part of Quebec (city)

Beau·so·leil \,bō-sə-'lā\ commune SE France N of Monaco pop 12,774

Beau·vais \bō-'vā\ commune N France NNW of Paris pop 55,371

Bea·ver \'bē-vər\ **1** river 280 mi (451 km) NW Okla. forming upper course of the N. Canadian **2** river 305 mi (491 km) Canada in Alta. & Sask. flowing E into the Churchill

Bea·ver·creek \'bē-vər-,krēk\ city SW Ohio E of Dayton pop 45,193

Bea·ver·head Mountains \'bē-vər-,hed\ mountains on Idaho-Mont. boundary; SE part of Bitterroot Range of the Rockies — see GARFIELD MOUNTAIN

Bea·ver·ton \'bē-vər-tən\ city NW Oreg. W of Portland pop 89,803

Bé·char \bā-'shär\ or formerly **Co·lomb–Béchar** \kə-,lōⁿ-\ commune NW Algeria SSE of Oran pop 134,000

Bech·u·a·na·land \,bech-'wä-nə-,land, ,be-chə-\ **1** region S Africa N of Orange River & including Kalahari Desert & Okavango Swamps **2** — see BOTSWANA **3** or **British Bechuanaland** former Brit. colony in the region S of the Molopo; became part of Union of South Africa 1895 — **Bech·u·a·na** \,bech-'wä-nə, ,be-chə-\ adj or n

Beck·en·ham \'be-kə-nəm, 'bek-nəm\ former urban district SE England in Kent, now part of Bromley

Bed·ford \'bed-fərd\ **1** city N Tex. pop 46,979 **2** town SE cen England ✽ of Bedfordshire pop 74,245

Bed·ford·shire \'bed-fərd-,shir, -shər\ or **Bedford** \'bed-fərd\ county SE cen England area 494 sq mi (1279 sq km), pop 514,200

Bedloe's Island — see LIBERTY ISLAND

Bę·dzin \'ben-,jēn\ commune S Poland in Silesia pop 75,800

Beer·she·ba \bir-'shē-bə, ber-, bər-\ town S Israel in N Negev; dating back to biblical times pop 128,400

Behistun — see BISITUN

Bei·jing \'bā-'jiŋ, ÷-'zhiŋ\ or **Pe·king** \'pē-'kiŋ, 'pā-\ or formerly **Pei·ping** \'pā-'piŋ, 'bā-\ municipality NE China, its ✽ pop 10,819,407 — **Bei·jing·er** \-'jiŋ-ər\ n

Bei·ra \'bā-rə\ town & port SE Mozambique; chief port for cen Mozambique & landlocked Zimbabwe & Malawi pop 436,240

Bei·rut \bā-'rüt\ or anc **Be·ry·tus** \bə-'rī-təs\ city & port ✽ of Lebanon — **Bei·ruti** \bā-'rü-tē\ n

Be·jaïa \bā-'zhī-ə\ or formerly **Bou·gie** \bü-'zhē\ city & port NE Algeria pop 173,000

Be·kaa \bi-'kä\ or **Al Bi·qa'** \,äl-be-'kä\ or anc **Coe·le–Syr·ia** \,sē-lē-'sir-ē-ə\ valley Lebanon bet. Lebanon & Anti-Lebanon ranges

Be·la·rus \,bē-lə-'rüs, ,byel-ə-\ country N cen Europe; a constituent republic (**Belorussia** or **Byelorussia**) of the U.S.S.R. 1919–91 ✽ Minsk area 80,154 sq mi (207,599 sq km), pop 9,500,000 — **Be·la·ru·san** \-'rü-sən\ adj or n — **Be·la·ru·si·an** \-'rü-sē-ən, -'rə-shən\ or **Be·la·rus·sian** \-'rə-shən\ adj or n

Belau — see PALAU

Be·la·wan \bā-'lä-,wän\ town & port Indonesia in NE Sumatra

Be·la·ya \'bye-lə-yə\ river Russia in Europe rising in the S Urals & flowing S, W, & NW to the Kama

Be·lém \be-'lem\ or **Pa·rá** \pä-'rä\ city N Brazil ✽ of Pará state on Pará River pop 1,280,614

Bel·fast \'bel-,fast, bel-'\ **1** district E Northern Ireland, established 1974 area 54 sq mi (140 sq km), pop 283,746 **2** city & port ✽ of Northern Ireland at head of **Belfast Lough** (inlet) pop 295,100

Bel·fort \bel-'fȯr, bā-'fȯr\ commune E France commanding **Belfort Gap** (wide pass bet. Vosges & Jura mountains) pop 50,406

Belgian Congo — see CONGO 2

Belgian East Africa — see RUANDA-URUNDI

Bel·gium \'bel-jəm\ or F **Bel·gique** \bel-'zhēk\ or Flem **Bel·gië** \'bel-kē-ə\ country W Europe bordering on North Sea; a constitutional monarchy ✽ Brussels area 11,781 sq mi (30,513 sq km), pop 10,309,725

Bel·go·rod–Dnes·trov·ski or **Belgorod–Dnestrov·skiy** \'bel-gə-,räd-(,)ne-'strȯf-skē, -'strȯv-, 'byel-gə-rət-dne-'\ or formerly **Turk** & **Russ Ak·ker·man** \'ä-kər-,män\ city SW Ukraine on the Dniester estuary pop 29,000

Bel·grade \'bel-,grād, -,gräd, -,grad, bel-'\ or **Beo·grad** \bā-'ȯ-,gräd\ city ✽ of Serbia pop 1,120,092

Bel·gra·via \bel-'grā-vē-ə\ district of W cen London, England, in Kensington and Chelsea borough S of Hyde Park

Be·li·tung \bā-'lē-təŋ\ or **Bil·li·ton** \bi-'lē-,tän\ island Indonesia bet. Sumatra & Borneo area 1866 sq mi (4852 sq km), pop 102,375

Be·lize \bə-'lēz\ or formerly **British Honduras** country Central America bordering on the Caribbean; an independent member of the Commonwealth of Nations ✽ Belmopan area 8867 sq mi (22,966 sq km), pop 345,000 — **Be·liz·ean** \-'lē-zē-ən\ adj or n

Belize City seaport Belize; formerly ✽ of British Honduras pop 49,050

Bell \'bel\ city SW Calif. SE of Los Angeles pop 35,477

Bel·la Coo·la \,be-lə-'kü-lə\ river ab 60 mi (96 km) Canada in B.C. flowing W to Burke Channel E of Queen Charlotte Sound

Bel·leau \be-'lō, 'be-,\ village N France NW of Château-Thierry & N of **Belleau Wood** (F Bois de Bel·leau \,bwä-də-be-'lō\)

Belle Fourche \,bel-'füsh\ river NE Wyo. & W S.Dak. flowing NE & E into Cheyenne River

Belle Isle, Strait of \bel-'ī(-ə)l\ channel bet. N tip of Newfoundland & SE Labrador

Belle·ville \'bel-,vil\ **1** city SW Ill. pop 44,478 **2** city Canada in SE Ont. pop 49,454

Belle·vue \'bel-,vyü\ **1** city E Nebr. S of Omaha pop 50,137 **2** city W Wash. E of Seattle pop 122,363

Bell·flow·er \'bel-,flaù(-ə)r\ city SW Calif. E of Los Angeles pop 76,616

Bell Gardens city SW Calif. E of Los Angeles pop 42,072

Bel·ling·ham \'be-liŋ-,ham\ city & port NW Wash. on **Bellingham Bay** (inlet at N end of Puget Sound) pop 80,885

Bel·lings·hau·sen Sea \'be-liŋz-,haù-zᵊn\ sea comprising a large bay of the S. Pacific W of base of Antarctic Peninsula

Bel·lin·zo·na \,be-lən-'zō-nə\ commune S Switzerland E of Locarno ✽ of Ticino pop 17,142

Bel·mont \'bel-,mänt\ **1** city W Calif. SE of San Francisco pop 25,835 **2** town E Mass. W of Boston pop 24,729

Bel·mo·pan \,bel-mō-'pän\ city ✽ of Belize pop 16,000

Be·lo Ho·ri·zon·te \'bā-lō-,ȯr-ē-'zȯn-tē\ city E Brazil ✽ of Minas Gerais pop 2,238,526

Be·loit \bə-'lȯit\ city S Wis. on Ill. border pop 36,966

Be·lo·rus·sia \,be-lō-'rə-shə, ,bye-lō-\ or **By·elo·rus·sia** \bē-,e-lō-, ,bye-lō-\ constituent republic of the U.S.S.R. bordering on Poland, Lithuania, & Latvia; became independent 1991 — see BELARUS

Beloye More — see WHITE SEA

Bel·sen \'bel-zən, -sən\ or **Ber·gen–Belsen** \,ber-gən-, ,bər-\ locality N Germany on Lüneburg Heath NW of Celle; site of Nazi concentration camp during World War II

Be·lu·kha \bə-'lü-kə\ mountain 15,157 ft (4620 m) Russia in Asia; highest in Altai Mountains

Benares — see VARANASI

Bend \'bend\ city cen Oreg. on the Deschutes pop 76,639

Ben·di·go \'ben-di-,gō\ city SE Australia in cen Victoria pop 30,133

Be·ne·lux \'be-nə-,ləks\ economic union comprising Belgium, the Netherlands, & Luxembourg; formed 1947

Be·ne·ven·to \,bā-nā-'ven-(,)tō\ commune S Italy in Campania NE of Naples pop 63,230

Ben·gal \ben-'gȯl, beŋ-, -'gäl\ region E India (subcontinent) including delta of the Ganges & the Brahmaputra; a province of Brit. India 1937–47; divided 1947 bet. Pakistan & India (republic) — see EAST BENGAL, EAST PAKISTAN, WEST BENGAL — **Ben·gal·ese** \,beŋ-gə-'lēz, ,ben-, -'lēs\ adj or n

Bengal, Bay of arm of the Indian Ocean bet. India & Sri Lanka on the W & Myanmar & Malay Peninsula on the E

Bengaluru — see BANGALORE

Beng·bu or **Pang–pu** or **Peng–pu** \all 'bəŋ-'bü\ city E China in N Anhui pop 449,245

Ben·gha·zi or **Ban·gha·zi** \ben-'gä-zē, beŋ-, -'ga-\ or anc **Ber·e·ni·ce** \,ber-ə-'nī-sē\ city & port NE Libya; former ✽ of Libya pop 685,000

Ben·guela \ben-'gwä-lä\ city & port W Angola pop 40,996

Be·ni \'bā-nē\ river *ab* 1000 *mi* (1609 *km*) *cen* & N Bolivia flowing N to unite with Mamoré River forming Madeira River

Be·ni·cia \bə-'nē-shə\ city *cen* Calif. NNE of Oakland *pop* 26,997

Be·nin \bə-'nēn, -'nin; 'bə-nən\ **1** river *ab* 100 *mi* (161 *km*) S Nigeria W of the Niger flowing into Bight of Benin **2** former kingdom W Africa on lower Niger River; incorporated in Nigeria after 1897 **3** *or formerly* **Da·ho·mey** \də-'hō-mē\ country W Africa on Gulf of Guinea; a republic, formerly a territory of French West Africa official ✳ Porto-Novo, seat of government Cotonou *area* 43,483 *sq mi* (112,621 *sq km*), *pop* 8,078,000 **4** *or* **Benin City** city SW Nigeria in W delta of Niger River *pop* 202,800 — **Be·ni·nese** \bə-,ni-'nēz, -,nē-, -'nēs; ,be-ni-'nēz, -'nēs\ *adj or n*

Benin, Bight of the S section of Gulf of Guinea W Africa SW of Nigeria

Be·ni Su·ef \,be-nē-sü-'āf\ city N *cen* Egypt on the Nile *pop* 174,000

Ben Lomond — see LOMOND (Ben)

Ben Nev·is \ben-'ne-vəs\ mountain 4406 *ft* (1343 *m*) W Scotland in Grampian Hills; highest in Great Britain

Be·no·ni \be-'nō-nē\ city NE Republic of South Africa in Gauteng on the Witwatersrand E of Johannesburg *pop* 151,294

Be·nue \'bān-(,)wā\ river 870 *mi* (1400 *km*) W Africa flowing W into Niger River

Ben Ve·nue \,ben-və-'nü, -'nyü\ mountain 2393 *ft* (729 *m*) *cen* Scotland S of Loch Katrine

Ben·xi \'bən-'shē\ *or* **Pen·hsi** \'bən-'shē\ *or* **Pen·ch'i** \-'chē\ city NE China in E *cen* Liaoning *pop* 834,000

Be·rar \bā-'rär, bə-\ region W *cen* India; in Central Provinces & Berar 1903–47, in Madhya Pradesh 1947–56, in Bombay 1956–60, in Maharashtra since 1960; chief city Amravati

Ber·be·ra \bər-b(ə-)rə\ town & port N Somalia *pop* 12,219

Berea — see VÉROIA

Be·re·zi·na \bə-'rā-zə-nə, -'re-\ river 365 *mi* (587 *km*) Belarus flowing SE into the Dnieper

Bergama — see PERGAMUM 2

Ber·ga·mo \'ber-gä-,mō, 'bər-gə-\ commune N Italy in Lombardy NE of Milan *pop* 117,415

Ber·gen **1** \'bər-gən, 'ber-\ city & port SW Norway *pop* 209,375 **2** — see MONS

Ber·gen·field \'bər-gən-,fēld\ borough NE N.J. *pop* 26,764

Be·ring Sea \'bir-iŋ, 'ber-\ arm of the N. Pacific bet. Alaska & NE Siberia & bet. the Aleutians & Bering Strait *area* 885,000 *sq mi* (2,292,150 *sq km*)

Bering Strait strait at narrowest point 53 *mi* (85 *km*) wide separating Asia (Russia) from N. America (Alaska)

Berke·ley \'bər-klē\ city W Calif. on San Francisco Bay N of Oakland *pop* 112,580

Berk·shire \'bärk-shər\ former county S England in Thames River basin ✳ Reading

Berk·shire Hills \'bərk-,shir, -shər\ hills W Mass. extending into Connecticut W of Connecticut River — see GREYLOCK (Mount)

Ber·lin \(,)bər-'lin, G ber-'lēn\ city comprising a state of Germany ✳ of (reunified) Germany on Spree River *pop* 3,388,434; before 1945 ✳ of Germany & of Prussia; divided under postwar occupation bet. E. & W. Germany, E. Berlin being made ✳ of E. Germany (1949) & W. Berlin a state (not formally incorporated) of W. Germany — **Ber·lin·er** \(,)bər-'li-nər\ *n*

Ber·me·jo \ber-'mā-(,)hō\ river 650 *mi* (1046 *km*) N Argentina rising on Bolivian border & flowing SE into Paraguay River

Ber·mond·sey \'bər-mən(d)-zē\ former metropolitan borough E *cen* London, England, now part of Southwark

Ber·mu·da \(,)bər-'myü-də\ islands W Atlantic ESE of Cape Hatteras; a self-governing Brit. colony ✳ Hamilton *area* 20 *sq mi* (52 *sq km*), *pop* 62,059 — **Ber·mu·dan** \-dᵊn\ *or* **Ber·mu·di·an** \-dē-ən\ *adj or n*

Bermuda Triangle triangular area N. Atlantic bet. Bermuda, Fla., & Puerto Rico; site of numerous reported disappearances of planes & ships

Bern \'bərn, 'bern\ **1** canton NW & W *cen* Switzerland *area* 2327 *sq mi* (6027 *sq km*), *pop* 947,100 **2** city, its ✳ & ✳ of Switzerland on the Aare *pop* 122,469 — **Ber·nese** \(,)bər-'nēz, -'nēs\ *adj or n*

Bern·burg \'bərn-,bərg, 'bern-,bürk\ city *cen* Germany W of Dessau *pop* 39,006

Ber·ner Al·pen \,ber-nər-'äl-pən\ *or* **Ber·nese Ober·land** \(,)bər-'nēz-'ō-bər-,länt, -'nēs-\ *or* **Bernese Alps** *or* **Oberland** section of the Alps S Switzerland in Bern & Valais cantons N of the Lake of Thun & Brienz on the N & the valley of the upper Rhône on the S — see FINSTERAARHORN

Ber·ni·cia \(,)bər-'ni-sh(ē-)ə\ Anglian kingdom of 6th century A.D. located bet. Tyne & Forth rivers ✳ Bamborough

Ber·ni·na \(,)bər-'nē-nə\ the S extension of Rhaetian Alps on border bet. Italy & Switzerland; highest peak **Piz Bernina** \,pēts-\ (highest in the Rhaetian Alps) 13,200 *ft* (4023 *m*)

Beroea **1** — see ALEPPO **2** — see VÉROIA

Ber·ry \be-'rē\ former province *cen* France ✳ Bourges

Ber·thoud Pass \'bər-thəd\ mountain pass 11,315 *ft* (3449 *m*) N Colo. in Front Range WNW of Denver

Ber·wick \'ber-ik\ *or* **Ber·wick·shire** \-,shir, -shər\ former county SE Scotland ✳ Duns

Ber·wyn \'bər-wən\ city NE Ill. W of Chicago *pop* 56,657

Berytus — see BEIRUT

Be·san·çon \bə-'zan(t)-sən, bə-zäⁿ-'sōⁿ\ city E France E of Dijon *pop* 117,691

Bes·kids \'bes-,kidz, be-'skēdz\ mountain ranges *cen* Europe in W Carpathians including **West Beskids** (in Poland, Slovakia, & the Czech Republic) & **East Beskids** (in Poland & NE Slovakia)

Bes·sa·ra·bia \,be-sə-'rā-bē-ə\ region SE Europe bet. the Dniester & Prut rivers; now mostly in Moldova — **Bes·sa·ra·bi·an** \-bē-ən\ *adj or n*

Bes·se·mer \'be-sə-mər\ city N *cen* Ala. *pop* 27,456

Beth·a·ny \'be-thə-nē\ biblical village of ancient Palestine E of Jerusalem on Mount of Olives; the present-day West Bank town is called **Al-'Ay·zar·ī·yah** \,äl-,ī-zä-'rē-yə\ *pop* 3560

Beth·el \'be-thəl, be-'thel\ city of ancient Palestine N of Jerusalem; the present-day West Bank town is called **Bay·tīn** \,bā-'tēn\

Beth·el Park \'be-thəl\ municipality SW Pa. *pop* 32,313

Be·thes·da \bə-'thez-də\ unincorporated population center Md., a N suburb of Washington, D.C. *pop* 60,858

Beth·le·hem \'beth-li-,hem, -lē-həm, -lē-əm\ **1** city E Pa. on the Lehigh *pop* 74,982 **2** city of ancient Palestine in Judea SW of Jerusalem; the present-day West Bank town is called **Bayt Lahm** \'bīt-'läm\ *pop* 34,180

Beth·nal Green \'beth-nəl\ former metropolitan borough E London, England, now part of Tower Hamlets

Be·thu·lia \bə-'thü-lē-ə\ locale thought to have been in *cen* ancient Palestine

Be·tio \'bā-chē-,ō, -shē-; 'bāt-sē-\ islet & village W Pacific in N Kiribati at S end of Tarawa

Bet·ten·dorf \'be-tᵊn-,dórf\ city E Iowa E of Davenport *pop* 33,217

Beuthen — see BYTOM

Bev·er·ley \'be-vər-lē\ town N England NNW of Hull *pop* 109,500

Bev·er·ly \'be-vər-lē\ city NE Mass. *pop* 39,502

Beverly Hills city SW Calif. within city of Los Angeles *pop* 34,109

Bex·ley \'bek-slē\ borough of E Greater London, England *pop* 211,200

Bey·o·glu \,bā-ō-'glü\ *or formerly* **Pera** \'per-ə\ section of Istanbul, Turkey comprising area N of the Golden Horn

Bé·ziers \bāz-'yā\ city S France SW of Montpellier *pop* 69,359

Bezwada — see VIJAYAWADA

Bha·gal·pur \'bä-gəl-,pur\ city E India on the Ganges in E Bihar *pop* 340,349

Bhak·ra Dam \bə-krə, 'bä-\ hydroelectric & irrigation dam 740 *ft* (226 *m*) N India in Punjab in gorge of the Sutlej

Bha·mo \bä-'mō\ city N Myanmar on the Irrawaddy *pop* 13,767

Bhat·pa·ra \bät-'pär-ə\ city E India in W. Bengal *pop* 441,956

Bhav·na·gar *or* **Bhau·na·gar** \baů-'nə-gər\ city & port W India in S Gujarat on Gulf of Khambhat *pop* 510,958

Bho·pal \bō-'päl\ **1** former state N *cen* India in & N of Vindhya Mountains ✳ Bhopal; now part of Madhya Pradesh **2** city N *cen* India NW of Nagpur ✳ of Madhya Pradesh *pop* 1,433,875

Bhu·ba·nes·war *or* **Bhu·ba·nesh·war** \,bù-və-'nāsh-wər\ city E India S of Cuttack ✳ of Orissa *pop* 647,302

Bhu·tan \bü-'tän, -'tan\ country Asia in Himalayas on NE border of India; ✳ Thimphu *area* 18,000 *sq mi* (46,800 *sq km*), *pop* 672,425 — **Bhu·ta·nese** \,bü-tə-'nēz, -'nēs\ *adj or n*

Bi·a·fra \bē-'ä-frə, bī-, -'a-\ former secessionist state (1967–70) in SE Nigeria — **Bi·a·fran** \-frən\ *adj or n*

Biafra, Bight of *or* **Bight of Bon·ny** \'bä-nē\ the E section of Gulf of Guinea W Africa

Bi·ak \bē-'yäk\ island off W New Guinea; largest of the Schoutens

Bia·ly·stok \bē-'ä-li-,stók, byä-'wi-stók\ city NE Poland *pop* 268,085

Biar·ritz \byä-'rēts\ commune SW France on Bay of Biscay *pop* 30,046

Bias — see BEAS

Biel \'bēl\ *or F* **Bienne** \bē-'en\ commune NW Switzerland in Bern canton *pop* 49,157

Bie·le·feld \'bē-lə-,felt\ city W *cen* Germany E of Münster *pop* 322,132

Biel·sko-Bia·la \bē-,el-skó-bē-'ä-lə, ,byel-skó-'byä-wä\ city S Poland *pop* 179,879

Big Bend **1** area W Tex. in large bend of the Rio Grande; partly included in **Big Bend National Park** **2** section of Columbia River E *cen* Wash.

Big Black river 330 *mi* (531 *km*) W *cen* Miss. flowing to Mississippi River

Big Diomede — see DIOMEDE ISLANDS

Big·horn \'big-,hórn\ river 336 *mi* (541 *km*) N Wyo. & SE Mont. flowing N into Yellowstone River — see WIND

Bighorn Mountains mountains N Wyo. extending S from Mont. border E of Bighorn River — see CLOUD PEAK

Big Sandy river 22 *mi* (35 *km*) bet. W.Va. & Ky. flowing N into Ohio River

Big Sioux \'sü\ river 420 *mi* (676 *km*) S.Dak. & Iowa flowing S to Missouri River & forming Iowa-S.Dak. boundary

Big Spring city W Tex. NE of Odessa *pop* 27,282

Big Stone lake *ab* 30 *mi* (48 *km*) long bet. W Minn. & NE S.Dak. — see MINNESOTA 1

Big Sur \'sər\ region W Calif. centering on Big Sur River & extending *ab* 80 *mi* (129 *km*) along coast SE of Point Sur

Big Thicket wilderness area E Tex. NE of Houston *area ab* 450 *sq mi* (1170 *sq km*)

Bi·har \bi-'här\ **1** state NE India ✳ Patna *area* 38,352 *sq mi* (99,332 *sq km*), *pop* 82,878,796 **2** city *cen* Bihar state SE of Patna *pop* 231,972

Bi·ka·ner \,bi-kə-'nir, 'be-kə-,ner\ city NW India in N Rajasthan in Thar Desert *pop* 529,007

Bi·ki·ni \bi-'kē-nē\ island (atoll) W Pacific in Marshall Islands — **Bi·ki·ni·an** \-nē-ən\ *n*

Bil·bao \bil-'bä-,ō, -'baů, -'bä-(,)ō\ city N Spain ✳ of Vizcaya *pop* 349,972

Bil·ler·i·ca \,bil-'ri-kə\ town NE Mass. *pop* 40,243

Bil·lings \'bi-liŋz\ city S *cen* Mont. *pop* 104,170

Billiton — see BELITUNG

Bi·loxi \bə-'lək-sē, -'läk-\ city & port SE Miss. *pop* 44,054

Bim·i·ni \'bi-mə-nē\ two islands of Bahamas NW of Andros *pop* 1717

Bing·en \'biŋ-ən\ city W Germany *pop* 24,272

Bing·ham·ton \'biŋ-əm-tən\ city S *cen* N.Y. *pop* 47,376

Binh Dinh — see AN NHON

Bío–Bío \,bē-ō-'bē-(,)ō\ river 238 *mi* (383 *km*) S *cen* Chile flowing into the Pacific at Concepción

Bi·o·ko \bē-'ō-(,)kō\ *or formerly* **Fer·nan·do Póo** \fer-'nän-(,)dō-'pō\ *or 1973–79* **Ma·cí·as Ngue·ma Bi·yo·go** \mä-'sē-äs-əŋ-'gwä-mə-bē-'yō-(,)gō\ island Equatorial Guinea in Bight of Biafra *area* 779 *sq mi* (2018 *sq km*)

Bir·ken·head \'bər-kən-,hed, ,bər-kən-'\ borough NW England in Merseyside on the Mersey estuary opposite Liverpool *pop* 123,907

Bir·ming·ham \'bər-miŋ-,ham, *Brit usu* -miŋ-əm\ **1** city N *cen* Ala. *pop* 212,237 **2** city *cen* England ✳ of West Midlands *pop* 934,900

Bi·ro·bi·dzhan \,bir-ō-bi-'jän, -'jan\ city Russia in Asia ✳ of Jewish Autonomous Oblast *pop* 86,300

Biscay *or* **Biscaya** — see VIZCAYA — **Bis·cay·an** \bis-'kī-ən, -'kā-\ *adj or n*

Bis·cay, Bay of \'bis-,kā, -kē\ inlet of the Atlantic bet. W coast of France & N coast of Spain

Bis·cayne Bay \bis-'kān, 'bis-\ inlet of the Atlantic SE Fla.; S part forms **Biscayne National Park**

Bish·kek \bish-'kek\ *or 1926–91* **Frun·ze** \'frün-zi\ city on Chu River ✻ of Kyrgyzstan *pop* 794,000

Bi·sho \'bē-(‚)shō\ town S Republic of South Africa; formerly ✻ of Ciskei

Bi·si·tun \‚bē-sə-'tün\ *or* **Be·his·tun** \‚bā-his-\ *or* **Bi·su·tun** \‚bē-sə-\ ruined town W Iran E of Kermanshah

Bis·kra \'bis-krə, -‚(‚)krä\ city NE Algeria at an oasis S edge of Atlas Mountains *pop* 128,747

Bis·marck \'biz-‚märk\ city ✻ of N.Dak. on Missouri River *pop* 61,272

Bismarck Archipelago archipelago W Pacific N of E end of New Guinea *area* 19,173 *sq mi* (49,658 *sq km*)

Bismarck Range mountain range Papua New Guinea NW of Owen Stanley Range; highest peak Mt. Wilhelm

Bismarck Sea sea comprising the part of the W Pacific enclosed by the islands of the Bismarck Archipelago

Bis·sau \bi-'saủ\ city & port ✻ of Guinea-Bissau *pop* 386,500

Bi·thyn·ia \bə-'thi-nē-ə\ ancient country NW Asia Minor bordering on the Sea of Marmara & Black Sea — **Bi·thyn·i·an** \-nē-ən\ *adj or n*

Bi·to·la \'bē-tō-lä\ *or* **Bi·tolj** \'bē-‚tōl(-yə), -‚toi\ *or* **Mon·a·stir** \‚mä-nə-'stir\ city S Macedonia *pop* 122,173

Bitter Lakes two lakes (Great Bitter Lake & Little Bitter Lake) in NE Egypt N of Suez connected & traversed by the Suez Canal

Bit·ter·root Range \'bi-tə(r)-‚rüt, -‚rủt\ range of the Rocky Mountains on Idaho-Mont. boundary — see BEAVERHEAD MOUNTAINS, GARFIELD MOUNTAIN

Bi·wa \'bē-(‚)wä\ lake 40 *mi* (64 *km*) long Japan on W *cen* Honshu

Biysk \'bēsk\ city Russia in Asia, in E Altai territory *pop* 235,000

Bi·zerte \bə-'zert\ *or* **Bi·zer·ta** \bə-'zər-tə\ city & port N Tunisia on **Lake Bizerte** (a deep lagoon) *pop* 62,856

Black 1 river 101 *mi* (162 *km*) E *cen* Louisiana flowing S into Red River 2 *or in China* **Amo** \'ä-'mō\ *or in Vietnam* **Da** \'dä\ river 500 *mi* (805 *km*) SE Asia rising in *cen* Yunnan, China & flowing SE to Red River in N Vietnam

Black·burn \'blak-(‚)bərn\ town NW England in Lancashire *pop* 132,800

Blackburn, Mount mountain 16,390 *ft* (4996 *m*) S Alaska; highest in the Wrangell Mountains

Black Canyon 1 canyon of Colorado River bet. Ariz. & Nev. S of Hoover Dam 2 canyon of the Gunnison SW *cen* Colo. partly in **Black Canyon of the Gunnison National Park**

Black Forest *or G* **Schwarz·wald** \'shvärts-‚vält\ forested mountain region SW Germany along the upper Rhine bet. the Neckar River & Swiss border

Black Hills mountains W S.Dak. & NE Wyo. — see HARNEY PEAK

Black Mountains mountains W N.C., a range of the Blue Ridge Mountains — see MITCHELL (Mount)

Black·pool \'blak-‚pül\ town NW England in Lancashire on Irish Sea *pop* 144,500

Blacks·burg \'blaks-‚bərg\ town W Va. W of Roanoke *pop* 42,620

Black Sea *or anc* **Pon·tus Eux·i·nus** \'pän-təs-‚yük-'sī-nəs\ *or* **Pontus** sea bet. Europe & Asia connected with Aegean Sea through the Bosporus, Sea of Marmara, & Dardanelles *area more than* 160,000 *sq mi* (414,400 *sq km*)

Black Volta — see VOLTA

Black Warrior river 178 *mi* (286 *km*) *cen* Ala. flowing into the Tombigbee

Blae·nau Gwent \'blī-‚nī-'gwent\ administrative area of SE Wales *area* 42 *sq mi* (109 *sq km*)

Bla·go·vesh·chensk \‚blä-gə-'vyäsh-chən(t)sk\ city Russia in Asia on the Amur *pop* 214,000

Blaine \'blān\ city E Minn. N of St. Paul *pop* 57,186

Blain·ville \'blän-‚vil, blen-'vēl\ town Canada in S Que. *pop* 53,510

Blanc, Cape \'blaŋk, 'bläⁿ\ 1 cape N Tunisia; northernmost point of Africa, at 37°14′N 2 promontory NW Africa on the Atlantic in Mauritania at SW tip of Río de Oro

Blanc, Mont — see MONT BLANC

Blan·ca Peak \'blaŋ-kə, 'bläŋ-\ mountain 14,345 *ft* (4372 *m*) S Colo.; highest in Sangre de Cristo Mountains

Blan·co, Cape \'blaŋ-(‚)kō\ cape SW Oreg.

Blan·tyre \'blan-‚tī(-ə)r\ city S Malawi *pop* 661,444

Blar·ney \'blär-nē\ town SW Ireland in *cen* County Cork *pop* 1952

Blen·heim \'ble-nəm\ *or* **Blind·heim** \'blint-‚hīm\ village S Germany in Bavaria NNW of Augsburg *pop* 1619

Bli·da \'blē-də\ city N Algeria SW of Algiers *pop* 170,182

Block Island \'bläk\ island R.I. in the Atlantic at E entrance to Long Island Sound

Bloem·fon·tein \'blüm-fən-‚tān, -‚fän-\ city *cen* Republic of South Africa, judicial ✻ of the Republic in the municipality of Mangaung 149,836

Blois \'blwä\ city N *cen* France SW of Orléans *pop* 49,062

Bloom·ing·ton \'blü-miŋ-tən\ 1 city *cen* Ill. *pop* 76,610 2 city SW *cen* Ind. *pop* 80,405 3 city SE Minn. *pop* 82,893

Blooms·bury \'blümz-b(ə-)rē, *US also* -‚ber-ē\ district of N *cen* London, England, in borough of Camden

Blue Grotto sea cave Italy on N shore of Capri

Blue Mountain city NE Ill. S of Chicago *pop* 23,706

Blue Mountains 1 mountains NE Oreg. & SE Wash.; highest Rock Creek Butte 9105 *ft* (2775 *m*) 2 mountains SE Australia in Great Dividing Range in E New South Wales; highest 4460 *ft* (1359 *m*) 3 mountains E Jamaica; highest Blue Mountain Peak 7402 *ft* (2256 *m*)

Blue Nile river 850 *mi* (1368 *km*) Ethiopia & Sudan flowing from Lake Tana NNW into the Nile at Khartoum — see ABAY

Blue Ridge the E range of the Appalachians E U.S. extending from South Mountain, S Pa. into N Ga. — see MITCHELL (Mount)

Blue Springs city W Mo. SE of Independence *pop* 52,575

Bluff \'bləf\ town S New Zealand; port for Invercargill *pop* 2720

Boa Vis·ta \‚bō-ə-'vēsh-tə\ city N Brazil ✻ of Roraima *pop* 200,568

Bo·bo–Diou·las·so \‚bō-(‚)bō-dyü-'lä-(‚)sō\ town W Burkina Faso *pop* 489,967

Bo·bruysk *or* **Ba·bruysk** \bə-'brü-isk\ city *cen* Belarus on the Berezina *pop* 223,000

Bo·ca Ra·ton \‚bō-kə-rə-'tōn\ city SE Fla. *pop* 84,392

Bo·chum \'bō-kəm\ city W Germany in Ruhr valley *pop* 398,578

Bodensee — see CONSTANCE (Lake)

Bodh Ga·ya \'bōd-'gī-ä\ *or* **Bud·dha Gaya** \'bủ-də\ *or* **Buddh Gaya** \'bủd\ village NE India in *cen* Bihar *pop* 30,883

Bod·min \'bäd-min\ town SW England in county of Cornwall and Isles of Scilly *pop* 12,148

Boe·o·tia \bē-'ō-sh(ē-)ə\ *or ModGk* **Voi·o·tía** \‚vē-ō-'tē-ä\ district E *cen* Greece NW of Attica — **Boe·o·tian** \bē-'ō-shən\ *adj or n*

Boetoeng — see BUTON

Bo·go·tá \‚bō-gō-'tä, -'tó, 'bō-gə-\ city ✻ of Colombia on plateau in the Andes *pop* 6,850,500

Bo Hai *or* **Po Hai** \'bō-'hī\ *or* **Gulf of Chih·li** \'chē-'lē, 'jir-\ arm of Yellow Sea NE China bounded on NE by Liaodong Peninsula & on SE by Shandong Peninsula

Bo·he·mia \bō-'hē-mē-ə\ *or* **Če·chy** \'che-kē, -‚kē\ region W Czech Republic; once a kingdom, later a province ✻ Prague

Bohemian Forest *or G* **Böh·mer Wald** \'bœ-mər-‚vält\ forested mountain region Czech Republic & Germany along boundary bet. E Bavaria & SW Bohemia

Bo·hol \bō-'hól\ island S *cen* Philippines, one of the Visayan Islands, N of Mindanao *area* 1492 *sq mi* (3879 *sq km*)

Bohol Sea *or* **Mindanao Sea** sea S Philippines N of Mindanao Island

Bois·bri·and \‚bwä-brē-'äⁿ\ town Canada in S Que. *pop* 26,816

Bois de Belleau — see BELLEAU

Bois de Bou·logne \‚bwä-də-bü-'lón, -'lō-nyə, -'lóin\ park France W of Paris

Boi·se \'bói-sē, -zē\ 1 river 60 *mi* (96 *km*) SW *cen* Idaho flowing W into Snake River 2 city ✻ of Idaho on Boise River *pop* 205,671

Bo·ja·dor, Cape \'bä-jə-‚dór\ headland NW Africa in the Atlantic on W coast of Western Sahara

Bokhara — see BUKHARA

Boks·burg \'bäks-‚bərg\ city NE Republic of South Africa in Gauteng E of Johannesburg *pop* 110,832

Bo·lan Pass \bō-'län\ mountain pass 5900 *ft* (1798 *m*) Pakistan in N Baluchistan

Bolbitine — see ROSETTA

Bo·ling·brook \'bō-liŋ-‚brủk\ village NE Ill. SW of Chicago *pop* 73,366

Bo·lí·var, Cer·ro \'ser-(‚)ō-bō-'lē-‚vär\ *or formerly* **La Pa·ri·da** \lä-pə-'rē-dä\ iron mountain 2018 *ft* (615 *m*) E Venezuela S of Ciudad Bolívar

Bo·lí·var, Pi·co \‚pē-(‚)kō-bō-'lē-‚vär\ mountain 16,427 *ft* (5007 *m*) W Venezuela in Cordillera de Mérida; highest in Venezuela

Bo·liv·ia \bə-'li-vē-ə\ country W *cen* S. America; a republic; administrative ✻ La Paz, constitutional ✻ Sucre *area ab* 424,200 *sq mi* (1,102,920 *sq km*), *pop* 9,947,000 — **Bo·liv·i·an** \-vē-ən\ *adj or n*

Bo·lo·gna \bə-'lō-nyä\ *or anc* **Bo·no·nia** \bə-'nō-nē-ə\ commune N Italy ✻ of Emilia-Romagna at foot of the Apennines *pop* 379,964 — **Bo·lo·gnan** \bə-'lō-nyən\ *or* **Bo·lo·gnese** \‚bō-lə-'nēz, -'nēs, -'nyēz, -'nyēs\ *adj or n*

Bol·se·na, Lake \bōl-'sä-nə\ lake *cen* Italy in W Lazio

Bol·ton \'bōl-t⁰n\ town NW England in NW Greater Manchester *pop* 253,300

Bol·za·no \bōlt-'sä-(‚)nō, bōl-'zä-\ 1 former province N Italy in S Tirol, now part of Trentino-Alto Adige region 2 commune in Trentino-Alto Adige region *pop* 97,300

Bo·ma \'bō-mə\ city & port W Republic of the Congo on Congo River *pop* 246,207

Bom·bay \bäm-'bā\ 1 former state W India ✻ Bombay; divided 1960 into Gujarat & Maharashtra states; a province of Brit. India 1937–47 2 *or* **Mum·bai** \'məm-‚bī\ city & port W India on **Bombay Island** (in Arabian Sea *area* 24 *sq mi* or 62 *sq km*) ✻ of Maharashtra & of former Bombay state *metropolitan area pop* 11,914,398

Bo·mu \'bō-(‚)mü\ *or* **Mbo·mou** \əm-'bō-(‚)mü\ river 500 *mi* (805 *km*) W *cen* Africa forming boundary bet. Democratic Republic of the Congo & Central African Republic & uniting with the Uele to form the Ubangi

Bon, Cape \'bōⁿ\ *or Ar* **Ra's at Tib** \‚räs-ät-'tēb\ headland NE Tunisia on **Cape Bon Peninsula**

Bo·na, Mount \'bō-nə\ mountain *ab* 16,500 *ft* (5030 *m*) S Alaska at W end of Wrangell Mountains

Bon·aire \bä-'ner\ internally self-governing Dutch island E of Curaçao *area* 111 *sq mi* (287 *sq km*), *pop* 10,791

Bon·di \'bän-‚dī\ town SE Australia S of entrance to Port Jackson on **Bondi Beach**; SE suburb of Sydney

Bône — see ANNABA

Bo·nin Islands \'bō-nən\ *or* **Oga·sa·wa·ra Islands** \(‚)ō-‚gä-sä-'wär-ä\ islands W Pacific *ab* 600 *mi* (966 *km*) SSE of Tokyo; belong to Japan; administered by U.S. 1945–68 *area* 40 *sq mi* (104 *sq km*), *pop* 1507

Bo·ni·ta Springs \bə-'nē-tə\ city SW Fla. *pop* 43,914

Bonn \'bän, 'bòn\ city W Germany on the Rhine SSE of Cologne; ✻ of Federal Republic of Germany (sometimes called **Bonn Republic**) before reunification; seat of reunified German parliament 1990–99 *pop* 296,244

Bon·ne·ville Salt Flats \'bä-nə-‚vil\ broad level area of Great Salt Lake Desert E of Wendover, Utah

Bonny, Bight of — see BIAFRA (Bight of)

Booker T. Washington National Monument historic site W *cen* Va. SE of Roanoke

Boo·thia, Gulf of \'bü-thē-ə\ gulf N Canada bet. Baffin Is. & Melville Peninsula on E & Boothia Peninsula on W

Boothia Peninsula peninsula N Canada W of Baffin Is.; its N tip (at *ab* 72°N, 94°W) is the northernmost point on N. American mainland

Boo·tle \'bü-t⁰l\ town NW England in W Merseyside *pop* 62,463

Bo·phu·tha·tswa·na \‚bō-(‚)pü-tät-'swä-nä\ former group of noncontiguous black enclaves in the Republic of South Africa ✻ Mmabatho; granted independence 1977; abolished 1994

Bo·ra–Bo·ra \‚bòr-ə-'bòr-ə\ island S. Pacific in Leeward group of the Society Islands NW of Tahiti *area ab* 15 *sq mi* (38 *sq km*)

Bo·rah Peak \'bȯr-ə\ mountain 12,662 *ft* (3859 *m*) E *cen* Idaho in Lost River Range; highest point in state

Bo·rås \bü-'rȯs\ city SW Sweden E of Göteborg *pop* 98,150

Bor·deaux \bȯr-'dō\ city & port SW France on the Garonne *pop* 215,374 — **Bor·de·lais** \ˌbȯr-də-'lā\ *n*

Borders — see SCOTTISH BORDERS

Bor·di·ghe·ra \ˌbȯr-di-'ger-ə\ commune & port NW Italy in Liguria *pop* 10,735

Borg·holm \'bȯrg-ˌhōm, 'bȯrʸ-ˌhȯlm\ seaport SE Sweden on W coast of Öland Island

Borgne, Lake \'bȯrn\ inlet of the Mississippi Sound E of New Orleans, La.

Bor·neo \'bȯr-nē-ˌō\ *or* Indonesian **Ka·li·man·tan** \ˌka-lə-'man-ˌtan, ˌkä-lē-'män-ˌtän\ island Malay Archipelago SW of Philippines *area* 290,320 *sq mi* (751,929 *sq km*) — see BRUNEI, KALIMANTAN, SABAH, SARAWAK — **Bor·ne·an** \-nē-ən\ *adj or n*

Born·holm \'bȯrn-ˌhōlm, -ˌhōm\ island Denmark in Baltic Sea ✳ Rønne *area* 227 *sq mi* (588 *sq km*), *pop* 43,956

Bos·nia \'bäz-nē-ə, 'bȯz-\ region S Europe in the Balkans; with Herzegovina forms independent state of **Bosnia and Her·ze·go·vi·na** \ˌhert-sə-gō-'vē-nə, ˌhərt-, -'gō-və-nə\; a federated republic of Yugoslavia 1946–92 ✳ Sarajevo *area* 19,904 *sq mi* (51,750 *sq km*), *pop* 4,422,000 — **Bos·ni·an** \-nē-ən\ *adj or n*

Bos·po·rus \'bäs-p(ə-)rəs\ *or* **Bos·pho·rus** \-f(ə-)rəs\ strait *ab* 18 *mi* (29 *km*) long bet. Turkey in Europe & Turkey in Asia connecting Sea of Marmara & Black Sea — **Bos·po·ran** \-pə-rən\ *adj*

Bos·sier City \'bō-zhər\ city NW La. *pop* 61,315

Bos·ton \'bȯs-tən\ 1 city & port ✳ of Mass. on Massachusetts Bay *pop* 617,594   2 port E England in SE Lincolnshire in Parts of Holland *pop* 52,600 — **Bos·to·nian** \bȯ-'stō-nē-ən, -nyən\ *adj or n*

Boston Mountains mountains NW Ark. & E Okla. in Ozark Plateau

Bo·ta·fo·go Bay \ˌbō-tä-'fō-(ˌ)gō\ inlet of Guanabara Bay in Rio de Janeiro, Brazil

Bot·a·ny Bay \ˌbä-tə-nē\ inlet of the S. Pacific SE Australia in New South Wales on S border of city of Sydney

Both·ell \'bä-thəl\ city W Wash. NNE of Seattle *pop* 33,505

Both·nia, Gulf of \'bäth-nē-ə\ arm of Baltic Sea bet. Sweden & Finland

Bo·tswa·na \bät-'swä-nə\ country S Africa N of the Molopo; an independent republic since 1966, formerly Brit. protectorate of Bechuanaland ✳ Gaborone *area ab* 220,000 *sq mi* (569,800 *sq km*), *pop* 1,611,021

Bot·trop \'bä-ˌträp\ city W Germany NNW of Essen *pop* 118,758

Bou·cher·ville \'bü-shər-ˌvil, ˌbü-shä-'vēl\ town Canada in S Que. NE of Montreal *pop* 40,753

Bou·gain·ville \'bü-gən-ˌvil, 'bō-, 'bü-\ island S. Pacific; largest of the Solomons; chief town Kieta *area* 3880 *sq mi* (10,088 *sq km*)

Bougie — see BEJAÏA

Bouil·lon \bü-'yōⁿ\ town SE Belgium in the Ardennes *pop* 5393

Boul·der \'bōl-dər\ city N cen Colo. *pop* 97,385

Boulder Dam — see HOOVER DAM

Bou·logne \bü-'lōn, -'lȯ-nyə, -'lȯin\ *or* **Bou·logne–sur–Mer** \-ˌsür-'mer\ city & port N France on English Channel *pop* 44,865

Boulogne–Bil·lan·court \-ˌbē-ˌyäⁿ-'kür\ commune N France SW of Paris on the Seine *pop* 106,316

Boundary Peak mountain 13,140 *ft* (4005 *m*) SW Nev. in White Mountains; highest in state

Bountiful city N Utah N of Salt Lake City *pop* 42,552

Bour·bon·nais \ˌbür-bȯ-'nā\ former province *cen* France W of Burgundy

Bourges \'bürzh\ commune *cen* France SSE of Orléans *pop* 72,434

Bourgogne — see BURGUNDY

Bourne·mouth \'bȯrn-məth, 'bürn-\ town S England in Dorset on English Channel *pop* 154,400

Bou·vet \bü-(ˌ)vā\ island S. Atlantic SSW of Cape of Good Hope at *ab* 54°S, 5°E; belongs to Norway

Bow \'bō\ river 315 *mi* (507 *km*) Canada in SW Alta. rising in Banff National Park

Bow·ie \'bü-ē\ city Md. NE of Washington, D.C. *pop* 54,727

Bowling Green 1 city S Ky. *pop* 58,067   2 city NW Ohio S of Toledo *pop* 30,028

Boyne \'bȯin\ river 70 *mi* (113 *km*) E Ireland in Leinster flowing to Irish Sea S of Drogheda

Boyn·ton Beach \'bȯin-t²n\ city SE Fla. *pop* 68,217

Bo·yo·ma Falls \bȯi-'ō-mä\ *or formerly* **Stanley Falls** series of seven cataracts NE Democratic Republic of the Congo in the Lualaba near head of Congo River with total fall of *ab* 200 *ft* (61 *m*) in 60 *mi* (96 *km*)

Boz·caa·da \ˌbȯz-jä-'dä\ *or anc* **Ten·e·dos** \'te-nə-ˌdäs\ island Turkey in NE Aegean Sea S of the Dardanelles

Boze·man \'bōz-mən\ city SW Mont. *pop* 37,280

Bra·bant \brä-'bänt; brə-'bant, -'bänt\ 1 old duchy of W Europe including region now forming N. Brabant province of Netherlands & Brabant & Antwerp provinces of Belgium   2 province *cen* Belgium ✳ Brussels *pop* 1,022,821

Bra·den·ton \'brä-d²n-tən\ city & port W Fla. N of Sarasota *pop* 49,546

Brad·ford \'brad-fərd\ city N England in W. Yorkshire *pop* 280,691

Bradford West Gwil·lim·bury \-'gwi-ləm-ˌber-ē\ town Canada in S Ont. *pop* 28,077

Bra·ga \'brä-gə\ commune NW Portugal NNE of Porto *pop* 164,192

Bra·gan·ça \brə-'gän-sə\ commune NE Portugal near Spanish border *pop* 34,750

Brah·ma·pu·tra \ˌbrä-mə-'pü-trə\ river *ab* 1800 *mi* (2900 *km*) S Asia flowing from the Himalayas in Tibet to the Ganges Delta in E India (subcontinent) — see JAMUNA, TSANGPO

Bra·i·la \brə-'ē-lə\ city E Romania on the Danube *pop* 216,929

Brain·tree \'brän-(ˌ)trē\ town E Mass. S of Boston *pop* 35,744

Brak·pan \'brak-ˌpan\ city NE Republic of South Africa in Gauteng on the Witwatersrand S of Johannesburg *pop* 85,044

Bramp·ton \'bramp-tən\ city Canada in SE Ont. W of Toronto *pop* 523,911

Bran·co, Rio \ˌrē-ō-'bräŋ-kü\ river 350 *mi* (563 *km*) N Brazil flowing S into Negro River

Bran·den·burg \'bran-dən-ˌbərg, 'brän-dən-ˌbůrk\ 1 region & former province NE *cen* Germany   2 state of E Germany ✳ Potsdam *area*

11,219 *sq mi* (29,057 *sq km*), *pop* 2,578,300   3 city E Germany *pop* 88,760

Bran·don \'bran-dən\ city Canada in SW Man. *pop* 46,061

Bran·dy·wine \'bran-dē-ˌwīn\ creek *ab* 20 *mi* (32 *km*) SE Pa. & N Del. flowing SE to Wilmington, Del.

Bran·ford \'bran-fərd\ town S Conn. E of New Haven *pop* 28,026

Brant \'brant\ city Canada in S Ont. *pop* 35,638

Brant·ford \'brant-fərd\ city Canada in SE Ont. *pop* 93,650

Bras d'Or Lake \brä-'dȯr\ tidal lake *ab* 50 *mi* (80 *km*) long Canada in N.S. on Cape Breton Is.

Bra·sí·lia \brə-'zil-yə\ city ✳ of Brazil in Federal District *metropolitan area pop* 2,051,146

Bra·sov \brä-'shȯv\ *or formerly* **Sta·lin** \'stä-lən, 'sta-, -ˌlēn\ city *cen* Romania in foothills of Transylvanian Alps *pop* 283,901

Bra·ti·sla·va \ˌbrä-tə-'slä-və, ˌbra-\ *or* G **Press·burg** \'pres-ˌbərg, -ˌbůrk\ *or* Hung **Po·zsony** \'pō-ˌzhō-nyə\ city SW Slovakia, its ✳, on the Danube *pop* 428,672

Bratsk \'brätsk\ city Russia in Asia, NNE of Irkutsk near site of **Bratsk Dam** (in the Angara) *pop* 259,000

Braunschweig 1 — see BRUNSWICK 2   2 — see BRUNSWICK 3

Bravo, Río — see RIO GRANDE 1

Bray \'brā\ town & port E Ireland *pop* 25,101

Bra·zil *or Pg* **Bra·sil** \brə-'zil\ country E S. America; a federal republic ✳ Brasília *area ab* 3,280,000 *sq mi* (8,495,200 *sq km*), *pop* 169,799,170 — **Bra·zil·ian** \brə-'zil-yən\ *adj or n*

Braz·os \'bra-zəs\ river *ab* 840 *mi* (1350 *km*) *cen* Tex. flowing SE into Gulf of Mexico

Braz·za·ville \'bra-zə-ˌvil, 'brä-zə-ˌvēl\ city & port ✳ of Republic of the Congo on W bank of Pool Malebo in Congo River *pop* 937,579

Brea \'brā-ə\ city SW Calif. SE of Los Angeles *pop* 39,282

Brec·on \'bre-kən\ *or* **Breck·nock** \'brek-ˌnäk, -ˌnək\ 1 *or* **Brec·on·shire** *or* **Breck·nock·shire** \-ˌshir, -shər\ former county SE Wales ✳ Brecon   2 town SE Wales in Powys *pop* 7422

Brecon Beacons two mountain peaks SE Wales in S Powys

Bre·da \brā-'dä\ commune S Netherlands in N. Brabant province *pop* 163,427

Bre·genz \'brā-ˌgents\ commune W Austria on Lake Constance ✳ of Vorarlberg *pop* 27,236

Bre·men \'bre-mən, 'brā-\ 1 former duchy N Germany bet. the lower Weser & the lower Elbe   2 state NW Germany *area* 156 *sq mi* (404 *sq km*), *pop* 681,700   3 city & port, its ✳, on the Weser *pop* 552,746

Bre·mer·ha·ven \'bre-mər-ˌhä-v²n, ˌbrä-mər-'hä-f²n\ city & port NW Germany in Bremen state at mouth of the Weser; includes former city of Wesermünde *pop* 130,938

Brem·er·ton \'bre-mər-tən\ city & port W Wash. on Puget Sound *pop* 37,729

Bren·ner Pass \'bre-nər\ mountain pass *ab* 4495 *ft* (1370 *m*) in the Alps bet. Austria & Italy

Brent \'brent\ *or formerly* **Brent·ford and Chis·wick** \'brent-fərd-²n-'chi-zik\ borough of W Greater London, England *pop* 226,100

Bren·ta \'bren-tä\ river 100 *mi* (161 *km*) N Italy flowing SE into the Adriatic S of Chioggia

Brent·wood \'brent-ˌwůd\ 1 city W *cen* Calif. E of Oakland *pop* 51,481   2 city W *cen* Tenn. S of Nashville *pop* 37,060

Bre·scia \'bre-shä, 'brä-\ *or anc* **Brix·ia** \'brik-sē-ə\ commune N Italy in E Lombardy ENE of Milan *pop* 194,697

Breslau — see WROCŁAW

Brest \'brest\ 1 *or formerly* **Brest Li·tovsk** \li-'tȯfsk\ city SW Belarus on Bug River *pop* 277,000   2 commune & port NW France in Brittany *pop* 149,649

Bre·ton, Cape \kap-'bre-t²n, kə-'bre-, -'bri-\ headland Canada; easternmost point of Cape Breton Is. & of N.S., at 59°48′W

Bridg·end \ˌbrij-'end\ administrative area of S Wales *area* 95 *sq mi* (246 *sq km*)

Bridge·port \'brij-ˌpȯrt\ city SW Conn. on Long Island Sound *pop* 144,229

Bridge·ton \'brij-tən\ city SW N.J. *pop* 25,349

Bridge·town \'brij-ˌtaůn\ city & port Brit. West Indies ✳ of Barbados *pop* 5996

Bridge·wa·ter \'brij-ˌwȯ-tər, -ˌwä-\ city SE Mass. *pop* 26,563

Brie \'brē\ district & medieval county NE France E of Paris; chief town Meaux

Bri·enne \brē-'en\ 1 former county NE France in Champagne NNE of Troyes   2 town, its ✳ *pop* 3332

Bri·enz \brē-'ents\ town Switzerland in SE Bern canton at NE end of **Lake of Brienz** (9 *mi* or 14 *km* long, in course of the Aare)

Brigh·ton \'brī-t²n\ town S England in E. Sussex on English Channel *pop* 133,400

Brin·di·si \'brin-də-(ˌ)zē, 'brēn-\ *or anc* **Brun·di·si·um** \ˌbrən-'di-zē-əm, -zhē-\ city & port SE Italy in Puglia *pop* 93,013

Bris·bane \'briz-bən, -ˌbān\ city & port E Australia ✳ of Queensland on Brisbane River (215 *mi* or 344 *km*) near its mouth *pop* 751,115

Bris·tol \'bris-t²l\ 1 city W *cen* Conn. WSW of Hartford *pop* 60,477   2 city NE Tenn. *pop* 26,702   3 city & port SW England on Avon River near Severn estuary *pop* 370,300 — **Bris·to·li·an** \bri-'stō-lē-ən, -'stōl-yən\ *n*

Bristol Bay arm of Bering Sea SW Alaska W of Alaska Peninsula

Bristol Channel channel bet. S Wales & SW England

Brit·ain \'bri-t²n\ 1 *or L* **Bri·tan·nia** \brə-'ta-nyə, -nē-ə\ the island of Great Britain   2 UNITED KINGDOM   3 COMMONWEALTH OF NATIONS

British America 1 *or* **British North America** CANADA   2 all Brit. possessions in & adjacent to N. & S. America

British Antarctic Territory islands & territories in the S. Atlantic & in Antarctica administered by the British including S. Orkney & S. Shetland islands, Antarctic Peninsula, & Palmer Archipelago

British Bechuanaland — see BECHUANALAND 3

British Columbia province W Canada on Pacific coast ✳ Victoria *area* 344,663 *sq mi* (892,677 *sq km*), *pop* 4,400,057 — **British Co·lum·bi·an** \kə-'ləm-bē-ən\ *n or adj*

British Commonwealth — see COMMONWEALTH OF NATIONS

British East Africa 1 — see KENYA   2 the former Brit. dependencies in E Africa: Kenya, Uganda, Zanzibar, & Tanganyika

British Empire a former empire consisting of Great Britain & the Brit. dominions & dependencies — see COMMONWEALTH OF NATIONS

British Guiana — see GUYANA
British Honduras — see BELIZE
British India the part of India formerly under direct Brit. administration — see INDIAN STATES
British Indian Ocean Territory Brit. colony in Indian Ocean comprising Chagos Archipelago & formerly Aldabra, Farquhar, & Desroches islands (returned to Seychelles 1976) *area* 23 *sq mi* (60 *sq km*)
British Isles island group W Europe comprising Great Britain, Ireland, & adjacent islands
British Malaya former dependencies of Great Britain on Malay Peninsula & in Malay Archipelago including Malaya (federation), Singapore, N. Borneo, Sarawak, & Brunei
British Solomon Islands former Brit. protectorate comprising the Solomons (except Bougainville, Buka, & adjacent small islands) & the Santa Cruz Islands ✻ Honiara (on Guadalcanal)
British Somaliland former Brit. protectorate E Africa bordering on Gulf of Aden ✻ Hargeisa; since 1960 part of Somalia
British Virgin Islands the E islands of the Virgin Islands group; a Brit. possession ✻ Road Town (on Tortola Is.) *area* 59 *sq mi* (153 *sq km*), *pop* 14,786
British West Indies islands of the West Indies including Jamaica, Bahamas, Caymans, Brit. Virgin Islands, Brit. Leeward & Windward islands, Trinidad, & Tobago
Brit·ta·ny \'bri-tə-nē\ *or F* **Bre·tagne** \brə-'tänʸ\ region & former province NW France SW of Normandy
Br·no \'bər-(,)nō\ *or G* **Brünn** \'bruen, 'brún\ city E Czech Republic, chief city of Moravia *pop* 376,172
Broad \'bröd\ **1** river 220 *mi* (354 *km*) N.C. & S.C. — see SALUDA **2** river 70 *mi* (113 *km*) S S.C. flowing into the Atlantic
Broads \'brödz\ low-lying district E England in Norfolk (the **Norfolk Broads**) & Suffolk (the **Suffolk Broads**)
Brock·en \'brä-kən\ mountain 3747 *ft* (1142 *m*) *cen* Germany near former E. Germany–W. Germany border; highest in Harz Mountains
Brock·ton \'bräk-tən\ city SE Mass. *pop* 93,810
Bro·ken Ar·row \'brō-kən-'a-rō\ city NE Okla. SE of Tulsa *pop* 98,850
Broken Hill **1** city SE Australia in W New South Wales *pop* 23,739 **2** — see KABWE
Bromberg — see BYDGOSZCZ
Brom·ley \'bräm-lē\ borough of SE Greater London, England *pop* 281,700
Bronx \'bränks\ *or* **the Bronx** borough of New York City on the mainland NE of Manhattan Is. *pop* 1,385,108
Brook·field \'bruk-,fēld\ city SE Wis. W of Milwaukee *pop* 37,920
Brook·line \'bruk-,līn\ town E Mass. W of Boston *pop* 58,732
Brook·lyn \'bru-klən\ borough of New York City at SW end of Long Is. *pop* 2,504,700 — **Brook·lyn·ite** \-klə-,nīt\ *n*
Brooklyn Center city SE Minn. NW of Minneapolis *pop* 30,104
Brooklyn Park city SE Minn. NW of Minneapolis *pop* 75,781
Brooks Range \'bruks\ mountain range N Alaska extending from Kotzebue Sound to Canadian border; highest peak over 9000 *ft* (2740 *m*)
Broom·field \'brüm-,fēld, 'brüm-\ city N *cen* Colo. *pop* 55,889
Bros·sard \brō-'sär(d)\ town Canada in S Que. *pop* 79,273
Browns·ville \'braúnz-,vil, -vəl\ city & port S Tex. *pop* 175,023
Bruce \'brüs\ peninsula SE Ont., Canada, projecting bet. Lake Huron & Georgian Bay; site of **Bruce Peninsula National Park** (area of varied landscapes)
Brug·ge \'brü-gə, 'brue-kə\ *or F* **Bruges** \'brüzh, 'bruezh\ commune NW Belgium ✻ of W. Flanders *pop* 116,836
Bru·nei \brú-'nī, 'brü-,nī\ **1** independent sultanate & former Brit. protectorate NW Borneo ✻ Bandar Seri Begawan *area* 2226 *sq mi* (5788 *sq km*), *pop* 332,844 **2** — see BANDAR SERI BEGAWAN — **Bru·nei·an** \brü-'nī-ən\ *adj or n*
Bruns·wick \'brənz-(,)wik\ **1** city NE Ohio SSW of Cleveland *pop* 34,255 **2** *or G* **Braun·schweig** \'braún-,shvīk\ former state *cen* Germany ✻ Brunswick **3** *or G* **Braunschweig** city N *cen* Germany W of Berlin *pop* 259,127
Brus·sels \'brə-səlz\ *or F* **Brux·elles** \brue(k)-'sel\ *or Flem* **Brus·sel** \'brue-səl\ city ✻ of Belgium & of Brabant 136,730 — **Bru·xel·lois** \,brue-səl-'wä also bruek-\ *adj or n*
Bruttium — see CALABRIA 2
Bry·an \'brī-ən\ city E *cen* Tex. *pop* 76,201
Bry·ansk \brē-'änsk\ city Russia in Europe SW of Moscow *pop* 461,000
Bryce Canyon National Park \'brīs\ canyon S Utah containing curiously eroded pinnacles
Bu·bas·tis \byü-'bas-təs\ ancient city N Egypt near modern Zagazig *pop* 349,400
Bu·ca·ra·man·ga \,bü-kä-rä-'mäŋ-gä\ city N Colombia NNE of Bogotá *pop* 349,400
Bu·cha·rest \'bü-kə-,rest, 'byü-\ *or Romanian* **Bu·cu·reş·ti** \,bü-kə-'resht\ *, -'resh-tē\ city ✻ of Romania *pop* 1,921,751
Bu·chen·wald \'bü-kən-,wöld, -kən-, -,vält\ village *cen* Germany NW of Weimar; site of Nazi concentration camp during World War II
Bucheon — see PUCHON
Buck·ing·ham·shire \'bə-kiŋ-əm-,shir, -shər, *US also* -kiŋ-,ham-\ *or* **Buckingham** *or* **Bucks** \'bəks\ county SE *cen* England ✻ Aylesbury *area* 753 *sq mi* (1950 *sq km*), *pop* 651,700
Buck Island Reef National Monument \'bək\ area of marine gardens on St. Croix in Virgin Islands of the U.S.
Bu·da·pest \'bü-də-,pest *also* 'bü-, 'byü-, -,pesht\ city ✻ of Hungary on the Danube *pop* 2,008,546
Buddha Gaya, Buddh Gaya — see BODH GAYA
Budweis — see CESKE BUDEJOVICE
Bue·na Park \'bwā-nə\ city Calif. W of Anaheim *pop* 80,530
Bue·na·ven·tu·ra \,bwä-nä-ven-'tü-rä\ city & port W Colombia on the Pacific *pop* 115,770
Bue·nos Ai·res \,bwā-nəs-'ī-rās, 'bō-\ city & port ✻ of Argentina on Río de la Plata *pop* 2,960,976
Buenos Aires, Lake 80 *mi* (129 *km*) long S Argentina & S Chile
Buf·fa·lo \'bə-fə-,lō\ city & port N.Y. on Lake Erie & Niagara River *pop* 261,310 — **Buf·fa·lo·ni·an** \,bə-fə-'lō-nē-ən\ *n*
Buffalo Grove village NE Ill. *pop* 41,496
Bug \'büg\ **1** river over 450 *mi* (720 *km*) *cen* Europe rising in W Ukraine, forming part of Ukraine-Poland and Poland-Belarus borders, & flowing into the Vistula in Poland **2** river over 500 *mi* (805 *km*) SW Ukraine flowing SE to the Dnieper estuary

Bu·gan·da \bü-'gän-dä, byü-\ region & former kingdom E Africa in SE Uganda ✻ Kampala
Bu·jum·bu·ra \,bü-jəm-'bur-ə\ *or formerly* **Usum·bu·ra** \,ü-səm-\ city ✻ of Burundi on Lake Tanganyika *pop* 236,334
Bu·ka \'bü-kä\ island W Pacific in the Solomons *pop* 33,770
Bu·ka·vu \bü-'kä-(,)vü\ *or formerly* **Cos·ter·mans·ville** \'käs-tər-mənz-,vil\ city E Democratic Republic of the Congo at S end of Lake Kivu *pop* 209,566
Bu·kha·ra \bü-'kär-ə, -'ka-rə, -'kär-ə\ *or chiefly formerly* **Bo·kha·ra** \bō-\ **1** former emirate W Asia around city of Bukhara **2** *or* **Bu·xo·ro** \bü-'kòr-ō\ city W Uzbekistan E of the Amu Dar'ya *pop* 249,600 — **Bu·kha·ran** \-(r)ən\ *adj or n*
Bu·ko·vi·na *or* **Bu·co·vi·na** \,bü-kō-'vē-nə\ region E *cen* Europe in foothills of E Carpathians; now in NE Romania & W Ukraine
Bu·la·wa·yo \,bü-lä-'wä-yō\ city SW Zimbabwe, chief town of Matabeleland *pop* 495,317
Bul·gar·ia \,bəl-'ger-ē-ə, bùl-\ country SE Europe on Black Sea; a republic ✻ Sofia *area* 42,823 *sq mi* (110,912 *sq km*), *pop* 7,932,984
Bull·head City \'bùl-,hed\ city W Ariz. across Colorado River from Nev. *pop* 39,540
Bull Run \'bùl-'rən\ stream 20 *mi* (32 *km*) N Va. W of Washington, D.C., flowing into Occoquan Creek (small tributary of the Potomac)
Bun·del·khand \'bùn-dᵊl-,kənd\ region N cen India containing headwaters of the Yamuna; now chiefly in N Madhya Pradesh
Bundesrepublik Deutschland — see GERMANY
Bun·ker Hill \'bəŋ-kər\ height in Charlestown section of Boston, Mass.
Bur·bank \'bər-,baŋk\ **1** city SW Calif. *pop* 103,340 **2** city NE Ill. *pop* 28,925
Bur·gas \bùr-'gäs\ city & port SE Bulgaria on an inlet of Black Sea *pop* 204,915
Bur·gen·land \'bər-gən-,land, 'bùr-gən-,länt\ province E Austria SE of Vienna on Hungarian border ✻ Eisenstadt
Bur·gos \'bùr-,gōs\ **1** province N Spain *area* 5509 *sq mi* (14,268 *sq km*), *pop* 348,934 **2** city, its ✻ & once ✻ of Old Castile *pop* 166,187
Bur·gun·dy \'bər-gən-dē\ *or F* **Bour·gogne** \bür-'gòn'\ **1** region ✻ with varying limits former kingdom, duchy, & province F France S of Champagne **2** former county France E of Burgundy province; later called **Franche–Com·té** \,fränʸh-kōⁿ-'tā\ — **Bur·gun·di·an** \(,)bər-'gən-dē-ən\ *adj or n*
Bu·ri·en \'byùr-ē-ən\ city W Wash. S of Seattle *pop* 33,313
Bur·ki·na Fa·so \bùr-'kē-nə-'fä-sō, bər-\ *or formerly* **Upper Vol·ta** \'vōl-tə, 'vòl-, 'väl-\ republic W Africa; until 1958 a French territory ✻ Ouagadougou *area* 105,869 *sq mi* (274,201 *sq km*), *pop* 13,730,258 — **Bur·ki·na·be** \bür-'kē-nə-,bä, bər-\ *adj or n*
Bur·lin·game \'bər-liŋ-,gām\ city W Calif. *pop* 28,806
Bur·ling·ton \'bər-liŋ-tən\ **1** city SE Iowa *pop* 25,663 **2** town NE Mass. *pop* 24,498 **3** city N *cen* N.C. *pop* 49,963 **4** city NW Vt. *pop* 42,417 **5** city Canada in SE Ont. N of Hamilton *pop* 175,779
Burma — see MYANMAR
Bur·na·by \'bər-nə-bē\ city Canada in SW B.C. *pop* 223,218
Burn·ley \'bərn-lē\ town NW England in SE Lancashire *pop* 89,000
Burns·ville \'bərnz-,vil\ village SE Minn. S of Minneapolis *pop* 60,306
Bur·rard Inlet \bə-'rärd\ inlet of Strait of Georgia W Canada in B.C. on which city of Vancouver is situated
Bur·sa \bùr-'sä, 'bər-sə\ *or formerly* **Bru·sa** \brü-'sä, 'brü-sə\ city NW Turkey in Asia near Sea of Marmara *pop* 834,576
Bur·ton \'bər-tᵊn\ city SE *cen* Mich. SE of Flint *pop* 29,999
Bu·run·di \bù-'rün-dē, -'rün-\ *or formerly* **Urun·di** \ù-'rün-\ country E *cen* Africa; a republic ✻ Bujumbura *area ab* 10,700 *sq mi* (27,700 *sq km*), *pop* 8,300,000 — see RUANDA-URUNDI — **Bu·run·di·an** \-dē-ən\ *adj or n*
Bury \'ber-ē\ town NW England in Greater Manchester *pop* 172,200
Bur·yat·ia *or* **Bur·yat·i·ya** \bùr-'yä-tē-ə\ *or* **Bur·yat Republic** \bùr-'yät, ,bùr-ē-'ät\ autonomous republic S Russia in Asia adjacent to Mongolia & E of Lake Baikal ✻ Ulan-Ude *area* 135,637 *sq mi* (351,300 *sq km*), *pop* 1,059,000 — **Buryat** ◊
Bury Saint Ed·munds \,ber-ē-sänt-'ed-mən(d)z, -sənt-\ town SE England in Suffolk *pop* 28,914
Busan — see PUSAN
Bu·shehr \bü-'sher\ city & port SW Iran *pop* 120,787
Bu·ta·ri·ta·ri \bü-,tä-rē-'tä-rē\ atoll W Pacific at N end of Kiribati *area* 4 *sq mi* (10 *sq km*)
Bute \'byüt\ **1** island SW Scotland W of Firth of Clyde **2** *or* **Bute·shire** \-,shir, -shər\ former county SW Scotland comprising several islands in the Firth of Clyde ✻ Rothesay (on Bute)
Bu·ton \'bü-,tón\ *or* **Bu·tung** *or D* **Boe·toeng** \'bü-,tùŋ\ island Indonesia off SE Sulawesi *area ab* 2000 *sq mi* (5200 *sq km*), *pop* 253,262
Butte \'byüt\ city SW Mont. in plateau of Rockies *pop* 32,996
Buxoro — see BUKHARA 2
Bu·zau \bü-'zō, -'zaú\ city E Romania *pop* 133,116
Buz·zards Bay \'bə-zərdz\ inlet of the Atlantic SE Mass. W of Cape Cod
Byd·goszcz \'bid-,gòsh(ch)\ *or G* **Brom·berg** \'bräm-,bərg, 'bròm-,berk\ city NW *cen* Poland NE of Poznan *pop* 380,385
Byelorussia — see BELORUSSIA — **Bye·lo·rus·sian** \bē-,e-lō-'rə-shən, ,bye-lō-\ *adj or n*
By·tom \'bē-,tòm, 'bi-\ *or G* **Beu·then** \'bòi-tᵊn\ city SW Poland in Silesia *pop* 229,851
Byzantium — see ISTANBUL
Ca·ba·na·tuan \,kä-bä-nä-'twän\ city Philippines in S *cen* Luzon *pop* 173,000
Ca·bi·mas \kä-'bē-mäs\ city NW Venezuela on NE coast of Lake Maracaibo *pop* 165,755
Ca·bin·da \kä-'bin-də\ territory W equatorial Africa on the Atlantic bet. Republic of the Congo & Democratic Republic of the Congo; belongs to Angola ✻ Cabinda *area* 3000 *sq mi* (7800 *sq km*), *pop* 260,000
Ca·bo Ro·jo \'kä-bō-'rō-hō\ city SW Puerto Rico *pop* 50,917

\ə\ abut \ᵊ\ kitten, F table \ər\ further \a\ ash \ā\ ace \ä\ mop, mar
\aú\ out \ch\ chin \e\ bet \ē\ easy \g\ go \i\ hit \ī\ ice \j\ job
\ŋ\ sing \ō\ go \ò\ law \òi\ boy \th\ thin \t̷h\ the \ü\ loot \ù\ foot
\y\ yet \zh\ vision, beige \k, ⁿ, œ, ɶ, ʸ\ *see* Guide to Pronunciation

Ca·bo San Lu·cas \ˌkä-bō-san-ˈlü-kəs\ resort W Mexico on **Cape San Lucas** (headland at S extremity of Baja California)

Cab·ot Strait \ˈka-bət\ strait *ab* 70 *mi* (113 *km*) wide E Canada bet. SW Newfoundland & Cape Breton Is. connecting Gulf of Saint Lawrence with the Atlantic

Ca·bril·lo National Monument \kə-ˈbrē-(ˌ)yō\ historic site SW Calif. on San Diego Bay

Ca·ca·hua·mil·pa \ˌkä-kä-wä-ˈmēl-pä\ caverns S Mexico in Guerrero NNE of Taxco

Cá·ce·res \ˈkä-sə-ˌrās\ **1** province W Spain in N Extremadura *area* 7701 *sq mi* (19,946 *sq km*), *pop* 403,621 **2** city, its ✱ *pop* 82,716

Cache la Pou·dre \ˌkash-lə-ˈpü-dər\ river 125 *mi* (201 *km*) N Colo. flowing into the S. Platte

Cad·do Lake \ˈka-(ˌ)dō\ lake 20 *mi* (32 *km*) long NW La. & NE Tex. draining to Red River

Cá·diz \kə-ˈdiz; ˈkā-dəz, ˈkä-, ˈka-; *Sp* ˈkä-(ˌ)thēs\ **1** province SW Spain in Andalusia *area* 2851 *sq mi* (7384 *sq km*), *pop* 1,116,491 **2** *or anc* **Ga·dir** \ˈgā-dər\ *or* **Ga·des** \ˈgā-(ˌ)dēz\ city & port, its ✱, on Bay of Cádiz NW of Gibraltar *pop* 133,363

Cádiz, Gulf of arm of the Atlantic SW Spain

Cae·li·an \ˈsē-lē-ən\ hill in Rome, Italy, one of seven on which the ancient city was built — see AVENTINE

Caen \ˈkä^{n}\ city NW France in Normandy *pop* 114,007

Caerdydd — see CARDIFF 2

Caer·nar·von *or* **Caer·nar·fon** \kär-ˈnär-vən, kə(r)-\ **1** *or* **Caer·nar·von·shire** \-ˌshir, -shər\ former county NW Wales **2** town and seaport NW Wales *pop* 9506

Caer·phil·ly \kər-ˈfi-lē\ administrative area SE Wales *area* 107 *sq mi* (277 *sq km*)

Cae·sa·rea \ˌsē-zə-ˈrē-ə; ˌse-sə-, ˌse-zə-\ **1** seaport of ancient Palestine; site S of modern Haifa, Israel **2** *or* **Caesarea Mazaca** — see KAYSERI

Caesarea Phi·lip·pi \ˈfi-lə-ˌpī, fə-ˈli-ˌpī\ city of ancient Palestine SW of Mt. Hermon; site at modern village of Baniyas \ˌba-nē-ˈyas\ in SW Syria

Caesena — see CESENA

Ca·ga·yan \ˌkä-gä-ˈyän\ *or* **Rio Gran·de de Cagayan** \ˌrē-ō-ˈgrän-dā-dā-\ river 220 *mi* (354 *km*) Philippines in NE Luzon flowing N

Ca·glia·ri \ˈkäl-yə-(ˌ)rē\ commune & port Italy ✱ of Sardinia *pop* 162,993

Ca·guas \ˈkä-ˌgwäs\ town E *cen* Puerto Rico *pop* 142,893

Ca·ho·kia Mounds \kə-ˈhō-kē-ə\ group of prehistoric Indian mounds Ill. ENE of E. St. Louis

Ca·hors \kä-ˈȯr\ city SW France N of Toulouse *pop* 20,022

Caicos — see TURKS AND CAICOS

Cairn·gorm Mountains \ˈkern-ˌgȯrm\ range of the Grampians NE *cen* Scotland; highest point Ben Macdhui 4296 *ft* (1309 *m*)

Cairns \ˈkernz\ city & port NE Australia in NE Queensland *pop* 54,862

Cai·ro \ˈkī-(ˌ)rō\ city N Egypt, its ✱ *pop* 7,786,640 — **Cai·rene** \kī-ˈrēn\ *adj or n*

Caith·ness \ˈkāth-nis, ˌkāth-ˈnes\ *or* **Caith·ness–shire** \-nish-ˌshir, -shər; -ˈnesh-\ former county N Scotland ✱ Wick

Ca·ja·mar·ca \ˌkä-hə-ˈmär-kä\ city NW Peru *pop* 92,600

Ca·jon Pass \kə-ˈhōn\ pass 4301 *ft* (1303 *m*) S Calif. NW of San Bernardino bet. San Bernardino Mountains & San Gabriel Mountains

Cal·a·bar \ˈka-lə-ˌbär\ city & port SE Nigeria *pop* 153,900

Ca·la·bria \kə-ˈlā-brē-ə, -ˈlä-\ **1** district of ancient Italy comprising area forming heel of the Italian Peninsula; now the S part of Puglia **2** *or It* **Le Ca·la·brie** \ˌlā-kä-ˈlä-brē-ˌā\ *or anc* **Brut·ti·um** \ˈbrü-tē-əm, ˈbrə-\ region S Italy occupying toe of the Italian Peninsula ✱ Catanzaro *area* 5822 *sq mi* (15,079 *sq km*), *pop* 2,043,288 — **Ca·la·bri·an** \kə-ˈlā-brē-ən, -ˈlä-\ *adj or n*

Ca·lah \ˈkā-lə\ ancient city ✱ of Assyria on the Tigris 20 *mi* (32 *km*) SE of modern Mosul, Iraq; site now called **Nim·rud** \nim-ˈrüd\

Ca·lais \ka-ˈlā\ city & port N France on Strait of Dover *pop* 77,317

Calais, Pas de — see DOVER (Strait of)

Ca·la·mian \ˌkä-lä-mē-ˈän\ islands W Philippines NE of Palawan Is.

Cal·ca·sieu \ˈkal-kə-ˌshü\ river 200 *mi* (322 *km*) SW La. flowing through **Calcasieu Lake** (*ab* 15 *mi or* 24 *km* long) & **Calcasieu Pass** (channel 5 *mi or* 8 *km* long) into Gulf of Mexico

Cal·cut·ta \kal-ˈkə-tə\ *or* **Kol·ka·ta** \kōl-ˈkä-tä\ city & port E India on the Hugli ✱ of W. Bengal *pop* 4,580,544 — **Cal·cut·tan** \-ˈkə-tᵊn\ *n*

Cald·well \ˈkȯl-ˌdwel, -dwəl, ˈkäl-\ city SW Idaho W of Boise *pop* 46,237

Cal·e·don \ˈka-lə-dən\ town Canada in SE Ont. *pop* 59,460

Cal·e·do·nia \ˌka-lə-ˈdō-nyə, -nē-ə\ **1** village SE Wisconsin *pop* 24,705 **2** — see SCOTLAND — **Cal·e·do·nian** \-nyən, -nē-ən\ *adj or n*

Caledonian Canal ship canal N Scotland connecting Loch Linnhe & Moray Firth & uniting Lochs Ness, Oich, Lochy, & Eil

Ca·lex·i·co \kə-ˈlek-si-ˌkō, ka-\ city SE Calif. near Mexican border *pop* 38,572

Cal·ga·ry \ˈkal-gə-rē\ city Canada in S Alta. *pop* 1,096,833 — **Cal·gar·i·an** \kal-ˈger-ē-ən\ *n*

Ca·li \ˈkä-lē\ city W Colombia on the Cauca *pop* 1,624,400

Cal·i·cut \ˈka-li-(ˌ)kət\ *or* **Ko·zhi·kode** \ˈkō-zhə-ˌkōd\ city & port SW India on Malabar Coast in Kerala *pop* 436,527

Cal·i·for·nia \ˌka-lə-ˈfȯr-nyə\ state SW U.S. ✱ Sacramento *area* 158,706 *sq mi* (411,048 *sq km*), *pop* 37,253,956 — **Cal·i·for·nian** \-nyən\ *adj or n* — **Cal·i·for·nio** \-nyō\ *n*

California, Gulf of arm of the Pacific NW Mexico bet. Baja California & states of Sonora & Sinaloa

Cal·lao \kä-ˈyä-(ˌ)ō, -ˈyau̇\ city & port W Peru on Callao Bay W of Lima *pop* 588,600

Ca·loo·sa·hatch·ee \kə-ˌlü-sə-ˈha-chē\ river 75 *mi* (121 *km*) S Fla. flowing W into Gulf of Mexico

Calpe — see GIBRALTAR (Rock of)

Cal·ta·nis·set·ta \ˌkäl-tä-nē-ˈse-tä\ commune Italy in *cen* Sicily *pop* 60,162

Cal·u·met \ˈkal-yə-ˌmet, -mət\ industrial region NW Ind. & NE Ill. SE of & adjacent to Chicago including cities of E. Chicago, Gary, & Hammond, Ind., & Calumet City & Lansing, Ill.

Calumet City city NE Ill. S of Chicago *pop* 37,042

Cal·va·dos Reef \ˌkal-və-ˈdōs\ *or F* **Ro·chers du Calvados** \rō-ˌshā-dᵫ-\ long reef of rocks NW France in English Channel at mouth of the Orne

Cal·va·ry \ˈkal-v(ə-)rē\ *or Heb* **Gol·go·tha** \ˈgäl-gə-thə, gäl-ˈgä-thə\ place outside ancient Jerusalem where Jesus was crucified

Cal·y·don \ˈka-lə-ˌdän, -dən\ ancient city *cen* Greece in S Aetolia near Gulf of Patras — **Cal·y·do·nian** \ˌka-lə-ˈdō-nyən, -nē-ən\ *adj*

Cam \ˈkam\ river 40 *mi* (64 *km*) E *cen* England in Cambridgeshire flowing into the Ouse

Ca·ma·güey \ˌkä-mä-ˈgwā\ city E *cen* Cuba *pop* 283,008

Ca·margue \kä-ˈmärg\ *or* **La Camargue** \ˌlä-\ marshy island S France in delta of the Rhône

Cam·a·ril·lo \ˌka-mə-ˈrē-(ˌ)ō\ city SW Calif. W of Los Angeles *pop* 65,201

Cambay — see KHAMBHAT

Cambay, Gulf of — see KHAMBHAT (Gulf of)

Cam·ber·well \ˈkam-bər-ˌwel, -wəl\ **1** city SE Australia in S Victoria E of Melbourne *pop* 83,799 **2** former metropolitan borough S London, England, now part of Southwark

Cam·bo·dia \kam-ˈbō-dē-ə\ *or* **Khmer Kam·pu·chea** \kə-ˈmer-ˌkam-pü-ˈchē-ə\ *or 1970–75* **Khmer Republic** country SE Asia bordering on Gulf of Thailand ✱ Phnom Penh *area* 69,898 *sq mi* (181,036 *sq km*), *pop* 14,400,000

Cam·brai *or formerly* **Cam·bray** \kam-ˈbrā, kä^{n}-ˈbre\ city N France on the Schelde *pop* 33,716

Cambria — see WALES

Cam·bri·an Mountains \ˈkam-brē-ən\ range *cen* Wales

Cam·bridge \ˈkām-brij\ **1** city E Mass. W of Boston *pop* 105,162 **2** city Canada in SE Ont. *pop* 126,748; includes former cities of Galt & Preston **3** *or ML* **Can·ta·brig·ia** \ˌkan-tə-ˈbri-j(ē-)ə\ city E England ✱ of Cambridgeshire *pop* 92,772

Cam·bridge·shire \ˈkām-brij-ˌshir, -shər\ *or* **Cambridge** *or formerly* **Cambridgeshire and Isle of Ely** \ˈē-lē\ county E England ✱ Cambridge *area* 1364 *sq mi* (3533 *sq km*), *pop* 640,700

Cam·den \ˈkam-dən\ **1** city & port SW N.J. on Delaware River opposite Philadelphia, Pa. *pop* 77,344 **2** borough of N Greater London, England *pop* 170,500

Cam·er·oon \ˌka-mə-ˈrün\ **1** massif *ab* 13,350 *ft* (4069 *m*) W Cameroon (republic) **2** *or* **Cam·er·oun** \-ˈrün\ country W equatorial Africa in Cameroons region; a republic, formerly a trust territory under France ✱ Yaoundé *area ab* 183,590 *sq mi* (475,500 *sq km*), *pop* 19,600,000

Cam·er·oons \ˌka-mə-ˈrünz\ region W Africa bordering on NE Gulf of Guinea formerly comprising Brit. & French Cameroons but now divided bet. Nigeria & Cameroon

Ca·mi·guin \ˌkä-mē-ˈgēn\ **1** island N Philippines N of Luzon; site of **Camiguin Volcano** 2602 *ft* (793 *m*) **2** island S Philippines off N coast of Mindanao

Ca·mo·tes Sea \kä-ˈmō-ˌtās\ sea S *cen* Philippines W of Leyte

Cam·pa·gna di Ro·ma \käm-ˈpä-nyä-dē-ˈrō-mä\ *or* **Roman Campagna** region *cen* Italy around Rome

Cam·pa·nia \käm-ˈpä-nyä, kam-ˈpā-nyə\ region S Italy bordering on Tyrrhenian Sea ✱ Naples *area* 5250 *sq mi* (13,598 *sq km*), *pop* 5,782,244 — **Cam·pa·nian** \-nyən, -nē-ən\ *adj or n*

Camp·bell \ˈkam-bel, ˈka-məl\ city W Calif. SW of San José *pop* 39,349

Campbell River city Canada in SW B.C. on Vancouver Is. *pop* 31,186

Cam·pe·che \kam-ˈpē-chē, käm-ˈpā-chā\ **1** state SE Mexico in W Yucatán Peninsula *area* 21,666 *sq mi* (56,115 *sq km*), *pop* 535,185 **2** city & port, its ✱, on Bay of Campeche *pop* 204,533

Campeche, Bay of the SW section of Gulf of Mexico

Cam·pi·nas \käm-ˈpē-nəs\ city SE Brazil in E São Paulo state *pop* 969,396

Cam·po·bel·lo \ˌkam-pə-ˈbe-(ˌ)lō\ island Canada in SW N.B. *area* 15 *sq mi* (40 *sq km*), *pop* 1056

Cam·po·for·mi·do \ˌkäm-(ˌ)pō-ˈfȯr-mə-ˌdō\ *or formerly* **Cam·po For·mio** \-mē-ˌō\ village NE Italy SW of Udine *pop* 7213

Cam·po Gran·de \ˌkäm-(ˌ)pü-ˈgrän-dē\ city SW Brazil ✱ of Mato Grosso do Sul *pop* 663,621

Cam·pos \ˈkäm-pəs\ city SE Brazil in Rio de Janeiro state on the Paraíba *pop* 406,989

Cam Ranh Bay \ˈkäm-ˈrän\ inlet of S. China Sea SE Vietnam *ab* 180 *mi* (290 *km*) NE of Ho Chi Minh City

Ca·muy \kä-ˈmwē\ city NW Puerto Rico *pop* 35,159

Ca·na \ˈkā-nə\ village in Galilee NE of Nazareth; now in Israel

Ca·naan \ˈkā-nən\ part of ancient Palestine bet. Jordan River & the Mediterranean — sometimes used to refer to all of ancient Palestine

Can·a·da \ˈka-nə-də\ country N N. America including Newfoundland & Arctic islands N of mainland; an independent state within the Commonwealth of Nations ✱ Ottawa *area* 3,851,809 *sq mi* (10,014,703 *sq km*), *pop* 33,476,688

Ca·na·di·an \kə-ˈnā-dē-ən\ *or, above its junction with the N. Canadian,* **South Canadian** river 906 *mi* (1458 *km*) S *cen* U.S. flowing E from NE N.Mex. to Arkansas River in E Okla.

Canadian Shield *or* **Lau·ren·tian Plateau** \lȯ-ˈren(t)-shən\ plateau region E Canada & NE U.S. extending from Mackenzie River basin E to Davis Strait & S to S Que., NE Minn., N Wis., NW Mich., & NE N.Y. including the Adirondacks

Canal Zone *or* **Panama Canal Zone** strip of territory Panama; ceased to exist as a formal political entity Oct. 1, 1979, but remained under U.S. control through 1999 for administration of the Panama Canal

Can·an·dai·gua \ˌka-nən-ˈdā-gwə\ lake 15 *mi* (24 *km*) long W *cen* N.Y.; one of the Finger Lakes

Ca·nary Islands \kə-ˈner-ē\ islands in the Atlantic off NW Africa belonging to Spain *area* 2796 *sq mi* (7242 *sq km*), *pop* 2,100,000 — see LAS PALMAS 1, SANTA CRUZ DE TENERIFE — **Ca·nar·i·an** \-ē-ən\ *adj or n*

Ca·nav·er·al, Cape \kə-ˈnav-rəl, -ˈna-və-\ *or 1963–73 officially* **Cape Ken·ne·dy** \ˈke-nə-dē\ cape on E shore of Canaveral Peninsula; site of Air Force satellite launch station & John F. Kennedy Space Center

Canaveral Peninsula peninsula E Fla. enclosing Indian River (lagoon)

Can·ber·ra \ˈkan-b(ə-)rə, -ˌber-ə\ city ✱ of Australia in Australian Capital Territory SW of Sydney — **Can·ber·ran** \-b(ə-)rən, -ˌber-ən\ *n*

Can·cún \ˌkan-ˈkün, kän-\ resort SE Mexico on island off NE coast of Yucatán Peninsula *pop* 397,191

Can·dia \ˈkan-dē-ə, kän-\ **1** — see CRETE **2** — see IRÁKLION

Candia, Sea of — see CRETE (Sea of)

Ca·nea \kə-ˈnē-ə\ *or anc* **Cy·do·nia** \sī-ˈdō-nē-ə, -nyə\ city & port Greece on N coast of W Crete *pop* 50,077

Can·i·a·pis·kau \ˌka-nē-ə-ˈpis-(ˌ)kō\ river 575 *mi* (925 *km*) Canada in N Que. flowing N to unite with the Larch forming the Koksoak

Can·nae \ˈka-(ˌ)nē\ ancient town SE Italy in Puglia WSW of modern Barletta

Can·na·nore \ˈka-nə-ˌnȯr\ 1 *or* Ka·na·nur \ˌka-nə-ˈnu̇r\ city SW India in Kerala NNW of Calicut *pop* 63,795 2 — *see* LACCADIVE ISLANDS

Cannes \ˈkan, ˈkän\ commune & port SE France SW of Nice *pop* 67,406

Ca·no·pus \kə-ˈnō-pəs\ ancient city N Egypt E of Alexandria at modern Abu Qir — Ca·no·pic \kə-ˈnō-pik, -ˈnä-\ *adj*

Ca·no·va·nas \kä-nō-bä-näs\ city Puerto Rico *pop* 47,648

Can·so, Cape \ˈkan(t)-(ˌ)sō\ cape Canada on NE N.S. mainland

Canso, Strait of narrow channel Canada separating Cape Breton Is. from N.S. mainland

Can·ta·bria \kan-ˈtä-brē-ä *or formerly* San·tan·der \ˌsän-ˈtän-der\ province N Spain in N Old Castile bordering on Bay of Biscay ✳ Santander *area* 2042 *sq mi* (5289 *sq km*), *pop* 535,131

Can·ta·bri·an Mountains \kan-ˈtä-brē-ən\ mountains N & NW Spain running E–W near coast of Bay of Biscay — *see* CERREDO

Cantabrigia — *see* CAMBRIDGE 3

Can·ter·bury \ˈkan-tə(r)-ˌber-ē, -b(ə-)rē\ 1 city SE Australia in E New South Wales, SW suburb of Sydney *pop* 129,232 2 city SE England in Kent *pop* 34,404 — Can·ter·bu·ri·an \ˌkan-tə(r)-ˈbyu̇r-ē-ən\ *adj*

Can·ti·gny \käⁿ-tē-ˈnyē\ village N France S of Amiens *pop* 125

Can·ton \ˈkan-tᵊn\ 1 city NE Ohio SSE of Akron *pop* 73,007 2 — *see* GUANGZHOU

Canyon de Chelly National Monument \də-ˈshā\ reservation NE Ariz. containing cliff-dweller ruins

Can·yon·lands National Park \ˈkan-yən-ˌlan(d)z\ reservation SE Utah surrounding junction of Colorado & Green rivers

Cap d'An·tibes \ˌkäp-däⁿ-ˈtēb\ cape SE France SW of Antibes

Cap de la Hague \ˌkäp-də-lä-ˈäg\ cape NW France at tip of Cotentin Peninsula

Cap·de·la·Ma·de·leine \ˌkäp-də-lä-ˌmäd-ˈlen\ former city Canada in S Que. on St. Lawrence River; now part of Trois-Rivières

Cape Bret·on \ˌkäp-ˈbre-tᵊn, kə-ˈbre-, -ˈbri-\ 1 regional municipality Canada in NE N.S. on Cape Breton Is. *pop* 97,398 2 — *see* BRETON (Cape)

Cape Breton Highlands National Park reservation Canada in NE N.S. near N end of Cape Breton Is.

Cape Breton Island island Canada in NE N.S. *area* 3970 *sq mi* (10,322 *sq km*)

Cape Cod — *see* COD (Cape)

Cape Cod Bay the S end of Massachusetts Bay W of Cape Cod

Cape Cor·al \ˈkȯr-əl, ˈkär-\ city SW Fla. *pop* 154,305

Cape Fear \ˈfir\ 1 river 202 *mi* (325 *km*) *cen* & SE N.C. flowing SE into the Atlantic 2 — *see* FEAR (Cape)

Cape Gi·rar·deau \jə-ˈrär-(ˌ)dō, jə-ˈrä-də\ city SE Mo. on Mississippi River *pop* 37,941

Cape Kru·sen·stern National Monument \ˈkrü-zən-ˌstərn\ reservation NW Alaska on Chukchi Sea

Cape of Good Hope 1 — *see* GOOD HOPE (Cape of) 2 *or* Cape Province *or* Kaap·land \ˈkäp-ˌlänt\ *or earlier* Cape Colony former province S Republic of South Africa ✳ Cape Town *area* 278,465 *sq mi* (724,009 *sq km*)

Ca·per·na·um \kə-ˈpər-nā-əm, -nē-\ city of ancient Palestine on NW shore of Sea of Galilee

Cape Sable — *see* SABLE (Cape)

Cape Sa·ble Island \ˈsā-bəl\ island 7 *mi* (11 *km*) long Canada off S coast of N.S.

Cape Town \ˈkäp-ˌtau̇n\ city & port, legislative ✳ of Republic of South Africa on Table Bay; formerly ✳ of Cape of Good Hope *pop* 776,617 — Cape·to·ni·an \ˌkäp-tō-nē-ən\ *n*

Cape Verde — *see* VERDE (Cape)

Cape Verde \ˈvərd\ country E Atlantic comprising the Cape Verde Islands; until 1975 belonged to Portugal ✳ Praia *area* 1557 *sq mi* (4048 *sq km*), *pop* 434,812 — Cape Verd·ean \ˈvər-dē-ən\ *adj or n*

Cape Verde Islands islands in the Atlantic off W Africa

Cape York Peninsula \ˈyȯrk\ peninsula NE Australia in N Queensland having at its N tip Cape York (on Torres Strait)

Cap Hai·tien \kap-ˈhä-shən\ *or F* Cap–Ha·ï·tien \kä-pä-ē-ˈsyaⁿ, -ē-ˈtyaⁿ\ city & port N Haiti *pop* 92,122

Cap·is·tra·no \ˌka-pə-ˈsträ-(ˌ)nō\ *or in full* San Juan Capistrano city SW Calif. SE of Los Angeles *pop* 34,593

Cap·i·to·line \ˈka-pə-tə-ˌlīn, Brit often kə-ˈpi-tə-\ hill in Rome, Italy, one of seven on which the ancient city was built — *see* AVENTINE

Capitol Reef National Park reservation S *cen* Utah containing archaeological remains, petrified forests, & unusual erosion forms

Capodistria — *see* KOPER

Caporetto — *see* KOBARID

Cap·pa·do·cia \ˌka-pə-ˈdō-sh(ē-)ə\ ancient district E Asia Minor chiefly in valley of the upper Kızıl Irmak in modern Turkey ✳ Caesarea Mazaca — Cap·pa·do·cian \-sh(ē-)ən\ *adj or n*

Ca·pri \kä-ˈprē, ˈkä-(ˌ)prē, ˈka-\ *or anc* Ca·pre·ae \ˈka-prē-ˌē\ island Italy S Bay of Naples *area* 4 *sq mi* (10 *sq km*), *pop* 7270 — Ca·pri·ote \ˈka-prē-ˌōt, ˈkä-, -prē-ət\ *n*

Ca·pri·vi Strip \kä-ˈprē-vē\ strip of land S Africa, a NE extension of Namibia running 300 *mi* (485 *km*) bet. Angola & Zambia on N and Botswana on S

Capsa — *see* GAFSA

Cap·ua \ˈka-pyu̇-wə, ˈkä-pü-ä\ commune S Italy on the Volturno N of Naples NW of site of ancient city of Capua *pop* 19,457

Cap·u·lin, Mount \ˈka-pyu̇-lən, -pü-\ cinder cone 8368 *ft* (2550 *m*) NE N.Mex.; main feature of Capulin Volcano National Monument

Cap Vert — *see* VERDE (Cape)

Ca·ra·cas \kə-ˈrä-käs\ city ✳ of Venezuela near Caribbean coast *pop* 1,836,000

Car·cas·sonne \ˌkär-kä-ˈsȯn, -ˈsȯn\ city S France *pop* 43,937

Car·che·mish \ˈkär-kə-ˌmish, kär-ˈkē-mish\ ruined city S Turkey on the Euphrates at Syrian border N of modern Jarabulus, Syria

Car·diff \ˈkär-dif\ *or W* Caer·dydd \kī-(-ə)r-ˈdēth\ 1 administrative area of S Wales *area* 54 *sq mi* (140 *sq km*) 2 city & port ✳ of Wales *pop* 272,600

Car·di·gan \ˈkär-di-gən\ *or* Car·di·gan·shire \-ˌshir, -shər\ former county W Wales ✳ Aberystwyth

Cardigan Bay inlet of St. George's Channel on W coast of Wales

Ca·ren·tan \ˌkä-rän-ˈtäⁿ\ town NW France at base of Cotentin Peninsula *pop* 6371

Car·ia \ˈker-ē-ə\ ancient region SW Asia Minor bordering on Aegean Sea ✳ Halicarnassus — Car·i·an \-ē-ən\ *adj or n*

Ca·rib·be·an Sea \ˌka-rə-ˈbē-ən, kə-ˈri-bē-\ arm of the Atlantic bounded on N & E by West Indies, on S by S. America, & on W by Central America

Car·ib·bees \ˈka-rə-ˌbēz\ LESSER ANTILLES

Car·i·boo Mountains \ˈka-rə-ˌbü\ range W Canada in E *cen* B.C. W of the Rocky Mountains; highest point *ab* 11,750 *ft* (3581 *m*)

Ca·rin·thia \kə-ˈrin(t)-thē-ə\ region *cen* Europe in E Alps; once a duchy; Austrian crown land 1849–1918; after 1918 most became part of Austria with parts going to Italy & the Kingdom of the Serbs, Croats, and Slovenes — Ca·rin·thi·an \-thē-ən\ *adj or n*

Car·lisle \kär-ˈlī(-ə)l, kər-, ˈkär-\ city NW England ✳ of Cumbria *pop* 99,800

Car·low \ˈkär-ˌlō\ 1 county SE Ireland in Leinster *area* 346 *sq mi* (900 *sq km*), *pop* 46,014 2 town, its ✳ *pop* 11,275

Carls·bad \ˈkär(-z)lz-ˌbad\ 1 caverns SE N.Mex. in Carlsbad Caverns National Park 2 city SW Calif. NNW of San Diego *pop* 105,328 3 city SE N.Mex. on the Pecos *pop* 26,138

Carmana, Carmania — *see* KERMAN

Car·mar·then \kär-ˈmär-thən, kə(r)-\ 1 *or* Car·mar·then·shire \-ˌshir, -shər\ administrative area of S Wales *area* 920 *sq mi* (2383 *sq km*) 2 port S Wales NW of Swansea *pop* 54,800

Car·mel 1 \ˈkär-ˈmel\ *or in full* Carmel–by–the–Sea city W Calif. S of Monterey Bay *pop* 3722 2 \ˈkär-məl\ city *cen* Ind. N of Indianapolis *pop* 79,191

Car·mel, Mount \ˈkär-məl\ mountain ridge NW Israel; highest point 1791 *ft* (546 *m*)

Car·men de Pa·ta·go·nes \ˈkär-men-thä-ˌpä-tä-ˈgō-näs\ town Argentina on the Negro River opposite Viedma *pop* 13,981

Car·nat·ic \kär-ˈna-tik\ region SE India bet. Eastern Ghats & Coromandel coast now in Andhra Pradesh & Karnataka

Car·nic Alps \ˈkär-nik\ mountain range E Alps bet. Austria & Italy

Car·nio·la \ˌkär-nē-ˈō-lə, kär-ˈnyō-\ region S & W Slovenia NE of Istrian Peninsula — Car·nio·lan \-lən\ *adj*

Car·o·li·na \ˌka-rə-ˈlī-nə\ English colony 1663–1729 on E coast of N. America, divided 1729 into N.C. & S.C. (the Car·o·li·nas \-nəz\) — Car·o·lin·ian \ˌka-rə-ˈli-nē-ən, -nyən\ *n*

Car·o·li·na \ˌka-rō-ˈlē-nä\ city NE *cen* Puerto Rico *pop* 176,762

Car·o·line Islands \ˈka-rə-ˌlīn, -lən\ islands W Pacific Ocean comprising Palau & the Federated States of Micronesia; formerly part of Trust Territory of the Pacific Islands

Car·ol Stream \ˈka-rəl\ village NE Ill. W of Chicago *pop* 39,711

Ca·ro·ni \kə-ˈrō-nē\ river E Venezuela flowing N into the Orinoco

Car·pa·thi·an Mountains \kär-ˈpä-thē-ən\ mountain system E *cen* Europe along boundary bet. Slovakia & Poland & extending through Ukraine & E Romania — *see* GERLACHOVSKY, TATRY, TRANSYLVANIAN ALPS

Carpathian Ruthenia — *see* ZAKARPATS'KA

Car·pen·tar·ia, Gulf of \ˌkär-pən-ˈter-ē-ə\ inlet of Arafura Sea on N coast of Australia

Car·pen·ters·ville \ˈkär-pən-tərz-ˌvil\ village NE Ill. *pop* 37,691

Car·qui·nez Strait \kär-ˈkē-nəs\ strait 8 *mi* (13 *km*) long Calif. joining San Pablo & Suisun bays

Car·ran·tuo·hill \ˌka-rən-ˈtü-əl\ mountain 3414 *ft* (1041 *m*) SW Ireland in County Kerry; highest in Macgillicuddy's Reeks & in Ireland

Car·ra·ra \kä-ˈrär-ä\ commune N Italy ESE of La Spezia *pop* 65,302

Car·rhae \ˈka-(ˌ)rē\ ancient city N Mesopotamia SSE of modern Şanlıurfa

Car·rick·fer·gus \ˌka-rik-ˈfər-gəs\ district E Northern Ireland, established 1974 *area* 34 *sq mi* (88 *sq km*), *pop* 32,439

Car·rick on Shan·non \ˌka-rik-ȯn-ˈsha-nən, -än-\ town N *cen* Ireland ✳ of County Leitrim *pop* 1621

Car·roll·ton \ˈka-rəl-tən\ city N Tex. *pop* 119,097

Car·shal·ton \kär-ˈshȯl-tᵊn, kər-\ former urban district S England in Surrey, now part of Sutton

Carso — *see* KARST

Car·son \ˈkär-sᵊn\ 1 river W Nev. flowing NE into Carson Lake 2 city SW Calif. SE of Los Angeles *pop* 91,714

Carson City city ✳ of Nev. E of Lake Tahoe *pop* 55,274

Carson Sink intermittent lake W Nev. S of Humboldt Lake

Carstensz, Mount — *see* PUNCAK JAYA

Car·ta·ge·na \ˌkär-tä-ˈgä-nä, -ˈhä-\ 1 city & port NW Colombia *pop* 688,300 2 city & port SE Spain on the Mediterranean *pop* 184,686

Car·ta·go \kär-ˈtä-(ˌ)gō\ city *cen* Costa Rica *pop* 21,753

Car·thage \ˈkär-thij\ *or anc* Car·tha·go \kär-ˈtä-(ˌ)gō, -ˈthä-\ ancient city & state N Africa on coast NE of modern Tunis — Car·tha·gin·ian \ˌkär-thə-ˈji-nyən, -nē-ən\ *adj or n*

Cary \ˈker-ē, ˈker-ē\ town E *cen* N.C. *pop* 135,234

Ca·sa·blan·ca \ˌka-sə-ˈblaŋ-kə, ˌkä-sə-ˈbläŋ-, -zə-\ *or Ar* Dar el Bei·da \ˌdär-ˌel-bā-ˈdä\ city & port W Morocco on the Atlantic *pop* 3,102,000

Casa Gran·de \ˌka-sə-ˈgran-dē\ city S *cen* Ariz. *pop* 48,571

Casa Grande Ruins National Monument reservation S Ariz. SE of Phoenix; site of prehistoric ruins

Cas·cade Range \(ˌ)kas-ˈkād\ mountain range W U.S., N continuation of the Sierra Nevada extending N from Lassen Peak across Oreg. & Wash. — *see* COAST MOUNTAINS, COAST RANGES, RAINIER (Mount)

Cas·co Bay \ˈkas-(ˌ)kō\ inlet of the Atlantic S Maine

Ca·ser·ta \kä-ˈzer-tä, -ˈzər-\ commune S Italy *pop* 74,801

\ə\ abut \ᵊ\ kitten, F table \ər\ further \a\ ash \ā\ ace \ä\ mop, mar

\au̇\ out \ch\ chin \e\ bet \ē\ easy \g\ go \i\ hit \ī\ ice \j\ job

\ŋ\ sing \ō\ go \ȯ\ law \ȯi\ boy \th\ thin \th\ the \ü\ loot \u̇\ foot

\y\ yet \zh\ vision, beige \ḵ, ⁿ, œ, ᵫ, ᵂ\ *see* Guide to Pronunciation

Cash·el \'ka-shəl\ town S Ireland in cen Tipperary South at base of Rock of Cashel (hill with ruins of cathedral & castle) pop 2473

Cashmere — see KASHMIR

Ca·si·quia·re or **Cas·si·quia·re** \,kä-sē-'kyä-rē\ river S Venezuela connecting the upper course of Negro River with Orinoco River

Cas·per \'kas-pər\ city cen Wyo. on N. Platte River pop 55,316

Cas·pi·an Gates \'kas-pē-ən\ pass on W shore of Caspian Sea near Derbent

Caspian Sea sea (salt lake) bet. Europe & Asia; ab 90 ft (27 m) below sea level area 143,550 sq mi (371,795 sq km)

Cas·sel·ber·ry \'kä-səl,-ber-ē\ city cen Fla. N of Orlando pop 26,241

Cas·si·no \kä-'sē-(,)nō\ commune cen Italy bet. Rome & Naples; site of Monte Cassino monastery pop 35,084

Cas·tel Gan·dol·fo \(,)kä-,stel-gän-'dōl-(,)fō\ commune cen Italy on Lake Albano SE of Rome pop 8436

Cas·tel·lón \,käs-tel-'yōn\ province E Spain area 2579 sq mi (6680 sq km), pop 484,566

Castellón de la Pla·na \-,thä-lä-'plä-nä\ city & port, ❋ of Castellón province, Spain, on the Mediterranean NE of Valencia pop 147,667

Castellorizo or **Castelrosso** — see KASTELLÓRIZON

Cas·tile \ka-'stēl\ or Sp **Cas·til·la** \kä-'stēl-yä, -'stē-yä\ region & ancient kingdom cen & N Spain divided by the Sierra de Guadarrama into regions & old provinces of **Old Castile** or Sp **Castilla la Vie·ja** \lä-'vyä-hä\ (to the N, ❋ Burgos) & **New Castile** or Sp **Castilla la Nue·va** \lä-'nwä-vä\ (to the S, ❋ Toledo)

Cas·til·lo de San Mar·cos National Monument \ka-'stē yō də san-'mär-(,)kōs\ historic site N Fla. containing a Spanish fort

Cas·tle·bar \,ka-səl-'bär\ town NW Ireland ❋ of Mayo pop 6071

Castle Clin·ton National Monument \'klin-tᵊn\ historic site Manhattan Is., SE N.Y. containing a fort

Cas·tle·reagh \'ka-səl-,(,)rā\ district E Northern Ireland, established 1974 area 33 sq mi (85 sq km), pop 60,649

Castres \'kästrᵃ\ city S France E of Toulouse pop 43,451

Cas·tries \'kas-,trēz, -,trēs\ city & port ❋ of St. Lucia pop 11,900

Ca·strop–Raux·el \,käs-,trōp-'rauk-səl\ city W Germany SSW of Münster pop 79,065

Ça·tal·ca \chä-tᵊl-'jä\ city Turkey in Europe W of Istanbul

Cat·a·li·na \,ka-tə-'lē-nə\ or **San·ta Catalina** \'san-tə\ island SW Calif. in Channel Islands area 70 sq mi (182 sq km)

Cat·a·lo·nia \,ka-tə-'lō-nyə, -nē-ə\ or Catal **Ca·ta·lu·nya** or Sp **Ca·ta·lu·ña** \,kä-tä-'lü-nyä\ autonomous region NE Spain bordering on France & the Mediterranean; chief city Barcelona area 12,328 sq mi (31,930 sq km), pop 6,059,494 — **Cat·a·lo·nian** \-'lō-nyən, -nē-ən\ adj or n

Ca·ta·mar·ca \,kä-tä-'mär-kä\ city NW Argentina pop 110,489

Ca·ta·nia \kə-'tä-nyə, -'tä-\ or anc **Cat·a·na** \'ka-tə-nə\ commune Italy in E Sicily on E coast on Gulf of Catania pop 336,222

Ca·ta·ño \kä-'tä-nyō\ city NE Puerto Rico S of San Juan pop 28,140

Ca·tan·za·ro \,kä-,tänd-'zär-(,)ō, -,tänt-'sär-\ city S Italy ❋ of Calabria pop 97,252

Ca·taw·ba \kə-'tȯ-bə\ river 250 mi (402 km) flowing S from W N.C. into S.C. — see WATEREE

Ca·thay \ka-'thā\ CHINA — an old name

Cathedral City city cen S Calif. pop 51,200

Catherine, Mount — see KATHERINA (Gebel)

Ca·toc·tin Mountain \kə-'täk-tən\ mountain ridge NW Md. & N Va. in Blue Ridge Mountains

Cats·kill Mountains \'kat-,skil\ mountains SE N.Y. in the Appalachian system W of Hudson River — see SLIDE MOUNTAIN

Cattaro — see KOTOR

Cau·ca \'kau̇-kä\ river 838 mi (1348 km) W Colombia flowing N into the Magdalena

Cau·ca·sus \'kȯ-kə-səs\ or **Cau·ca·sia** \kȯ-'kā-zhə, -shə\ region SE Europe bet. the Black & Caspian seas, divided by Caucasus Mountains into **Cis·cau·ca·sia** \,sis-\ (to the N) & **Trans·cau·ca·sia** \,tran(t)s-\ (to the S)

Caucasus Indicus — see HINDU KUSH

Caucasus Mountains mountain system SE Europe in Russia, Georgia, Azerbaijan, and Armenia — see EL'BRUS

Cau·dine Forks \'kȯ-,dīn, -,den\ two mountain passes S Italy in the Apennines bet. Benevento & Capua

Caul·field \'kȯl-,fēld\ city SE Australia in S Victoria; a SE suburb of Melbourne pop 67,776

Causses \'kōs\ limestone region S cen France on S border of Massif Central

Cau·ve·ry \'kȯ-və-rē\ or **Kā·ve·ri** \'kä-və-rē\ river 475 mi (764 km) S India flowing E & entering Bay of Bengal in a wide delta

Cauvery Falls or **Kā·ve·ri Falls** \'kä-və-rē\ waterfall India in the Cauvery on Karnataka-Tamil Nadu boundary

Cav·an \'ka-vən\ **1** county NE Ireland (republic) in Ulster area 730 sq mi (1898 sq km), pop 56,546 **2** town, its ❋ pop 3332

Ca·vi·te \kä-'vē-tē\ city Philippines in Luzon on **Cavite Peninsula** in Manila Bay SW of Manila pop 92,000

Caxias — see DUQUE DE CAXIAS

Cay·enne \kī-'en, kā-\ city & port ❋ of French Guiana on island in Cayenne River near the coast pop 37,097

Cayes \'kī\ or **Aux Cayes** \ō-'kī\ city & port SW Haiti pop 105,383

Ca·yey \kä-'yā\ city SE cen Puerto Rico pop 48,119

Cay·man Islands \(,)kā-'man, attributively 'kā-mən\ islands W. Indies NW of Jamaica; a Brit. colony ❋ George Town (on **Grand Cayman**, chief island) area 100 sq mi (259 sq km), pop 23,881 — **Cay·man·i·an** \kā-'ma-nē-ən\ adj or n

Ca·yu·ga \kā-'yü-gə, kī-, kē-, kə-\ lake 40 mi (64 km) long W cen N.Y.; one of the Finger Lakes

Ce·a·rá \,sā-ə-'rä\ state NE Brazil bordering on the Atlantic ❋ Fortaleza area 57,147 sq mi (148,011 sq km), pop 7,430,661

Ce·bu \sā-'bü\ **1** island E cen Philippines, one of the Visayan Islands area 1707 sq mi (4438 sq km) **2** city on E Cebu Is. pop 610,000

Čechy — see BOHEMIA

Ce·dar \'sē-dər\ river 329 mi (529 km) SE Minn. & E Iowa flowing SE into the Iowa River

Cedar Breaks National Monument reservation SW Utah NE of Zion National Park containing a vast natural amphitheater

Cedar Falls city NE Iowa NW of Waterloo pop 39,260

Cedar Hill town NE Tex. SW of Dallas pop 45,028

Cedar Park city cen Tex. NW of Austin pop 48,937

Cedar Rapids city E Iowa on the Cedar River pop 126,326

Celebes — see SULAWESI

Ce·le·bes Sea \'se-lə-,bēz, sə-'lē-bēz\ arm of W Pacific enclosed on N by Mindanao & the Sulu Archipelago, on S by Sulawesi, & on W by Borneo — **Ce·le·be·sian** \,se-lə-'bē-zhən\ adj

Celestial Empire the former Chinese Empire

Cel·le \'(t)se-lə\ city N cen Germany NE of Hannover pop 72,609

Celt·ic Sea \'kel-tik, 'sel-\ inlet of the Atlantic in British Isles SE of Ireland, SW of Wales, & W of England

Ce·nis, Mont \,mō⁸-sə-'nē\ **1** mountain pass 6831 ft (2082 m) bet. France & Italy over Mont Cenis Massif in Graian Alps **2** or **Fré·jus** \frä-'zhüs, -'zhues\ railroad tunnel 8.5 mi (13.6 km) long piercing the Fréjus Massif SW of Mont Cenis

Cen·ter·ville \'sen-tər,vil, -vəl\ city SW Ohio pop 23,999

Central African Republic or 1976–79 **Central African Empire** or earlier Ubangi–Shari republic N cen Africa ❋ Bangui area 240,376 sq mi (624,978 sq km), pop 3,895,139

Central America **1** the narrow S portion of N. America connecting with S. America & extending from the Isthmus of Tehuantepec to the Isthmus of Panama **2** the republics of Guatemala, El Salvador, Honduras, Nicaragua, Costa Rica, Panama, & Belize

Central Europe the countries of cen Europe — usu. considered to include the countries extending from Baltic Sea on the N to Alps on the S and from Russia, Lithuania, Belarus, & Ukraine on the E to North Sea & France on the W — **Central European** adj or n

Central India former group of 89 Indian states N cen India ❋ Indore; area now chiefly in W & N Madhya Pradesh

Central Karoo — see KAROO

Central Provinces and Be·rar \bā-'rär, bə-\ former province of India reorganized 1950 & renamed Madhya Pradesh

Central Valley valley cen Calif. comprising the valleys of the Sacramento & San Joaquin rivers

Ceos — see KEA

Ceph·a·lo·nia \,se-fə-'lō-nyə, -nē-ə\ or ModGk **Ke·fal·li·nía** \,ke-fä-lē-'nē-ä\ island W Greece in the Ionians area 288 sq mi (746 sq km)

Ce·ram or **Se·ram** \'sā-,räm\ island E Indonesia in cen Moluccas area 6621 sq mi (17,215 sq km), pop 96,797

Ce·re·di·gion \,ke-rə-'di-gē-,än\ administrative area of SW Wales area 693 sq mi (1795 sq km)

Ce·res \'sir-,(,)ēz\ city cen Calif. SE of Modesto pop 45,417

Cernauti — see CHERNIVTSI

Cer·re·do \se-'rā-(,)thō\ or **Tor·re de Cerredo** \'tȯr-ā-thä-\ mountain 8787 ft (2678 m) N Spain SW of Santander; highest in the Cantabrians

Cer·ri·tos \sə-'rē-təs\ city SW Calif. NE of Long Beach pop 49,041

Cerro Bolívar — see BOLÍVAR (Cerro)

Cer·ro de Pas·co \'ser-ō-thä-'päs-(,)kō\ **1** mountain 15,100 ft (4602 m) cen Peru NE of Lima **2** city near the mountain pop 170,500

Cerro de Pun·ta \thä-'pün-tä\ mountain ab 4390 ft (1338 m) cen Puerto Rico in Cordillera Central; highest on the island

Cerro Gor·do \'gȯr-(,)dō\ mountain pass E Mexico bet. Veracruz & Jalapa

Cervin, Mont — see MATTERHORN

Ce·se·na \chā-'zā-nä\ or anc **Cae·se·na** \sə-'zē-nə\ commune N Italy in Emilia-Romagna SE of Forlì pop 90,321

Ces·ke Bu·de·jo·vi·ce \'ches-ke-'bü-de-,yò-vĕt-se\ or G **Bud·weis** \'bút-,vīs\ city Czech Republic in S Bohemia pop 97,339

Ce·ti·nje \'(t)se-tē,nyə\ town S Montenegro SE of Kotor near coast; formerly ❋ of Montenegro pop 20,258

Cette — see SÈTE

Ceu·ta \'thā-ü-,tä, 'syü-tä\ city & port N Morocco opposite Gibraltar; a Spanish presidio pop 71,505

Cé·vennes \sā-'ven\ mountain range S France W of the Rhône at E edge of Massif Central — see MÉZENC

Cey·lon \si-'län, sā-\ **1** or Ar **Ser·en·dib** \'ser-ən-,dib, -,dip\ or L & Gk **Ta·prob·a·ne** \tə-'prä-bə-(,)nē\ island 270 mi (434 km) long & 140 mi (225 km) wide in Indian Ocean off S India **2** — see SRI LANKA — **Cey·lon·ese** \,sā-lə-'nēz, sē-, ,se-, -'nēs\ adj or n

Chaco — see GRAN CHACO

Chad or T **Tchad** \'chad\ country N cen Africa ❋ N'Djamena; a republic; until 1959 a territory of French Equatorial Africa area 495,752 sq mi (1,288,955 sq km), pop 11,594,000 — **Chad·ian** \'cha-dē-ən\ adj or n

Chad, Lake shallow lake N cen Africa at junction of boundaries of Chad, Niger, & Nigeria

Chae·ro·nea \,ke-ə-'nē-ə, ,kir-\ ancient city E cen Greece in W Boeotia SE of Mt. Parnassus

Cha·gos Archipelago \'chä-gəs\ archipelago cen Indian Ocean S of Maldives; comprises Brit. Indian Ocean Territory — see DIEGO GARCIA

Cha·gres \'chä-grəs, 'chä-\ river Panama flowing through Gatun Lake to the Caribbean

Cha·gua·ra·mas \,chä-gwä-'rä-mäs\ district NW Trinidad W of Port of Spain on **Chaguaramas Bay** (inlet of Gulf of Paria)

Cha·har \'chä-'här\ former province NE China in E Inner Mongolia ❋ Kalgan (Zhangjiakou)

Chalcedon — see KADIKOY

Chal·cid·i·ce \kal-'si-də-(,)sē\ or Gk **Khal·ki·di·kí** \,käl-kē-thē-'kē\ peninsula NE Greece in E Macedonia projecting SE into N Aegean Sea & terminating in three peninsulas: Kassandra (ancient Pallene), Sithonia, & Acte — see ACTE

Chalcis — see KHALKÍS — **Chal·cid·i·an** \kal-'si-dē-ən\ adj or n

Chal·dea \kal-'dē-ə\ ancient region SW Asia on Euphrates River & Persian Gulf

Cha·leur Bay \shə-'lu̇r, -'lər\ inlet of Gulf of St. Lawrence SE Canada bet. N N.B. & Gaspé Peninsula, Que.

Cha·lon \shä-'lō⁸\ or **Chalon–sur–Saône** \-,su̇r-'sōn\ city E cen France N of Mâcon pop 50,110

Châ·lons \shä-'lō⁸\ or **Châlons–en–Cham·pagne** \-ä⁸-shä⁸-'pän⁸\ commune NE France on the Marne pop 47,338

Cham·bal \'chəm-bəl\ river 650 mi (1046 km) cen India flowing from Vindhya Mountains E into the Yamuna

Cham·bé·ry \shä⁸-bā-'rē\ city E France E of Lyon pop 55,762

Cham·bord \shä⁸-'bȯr\ village N cen France NE of Blois pop 185

Cha·mi·zal \‚sha-mə-'zäl, ‚chä-mi-'säl\ tract of land 437 *acres* (177 *hectares*) on N bank of the Rio Grande formerly in El Paso, Tex.; ceded to Mexico 1963 — see CORDOVA ISLAND

Cha·mo·nix \‚sha-mō-'nē\ 1 valley SE France NW of Mont Blanc 2 *or* **Chamonix–Mont–Blanc** \-(‚)mōⁿ-'bläⁿ\ town SE France in Chamonix valley *pop* 9829

Cham·pagne \sham-'pān\ region & former province NE France W of Lorraine & N of Burgundy ✻ Troyes

Cham·paign \sham-'pān\ city E *cen* Ill. *pop* 81,055

Cham·pi·gny–sur–Marne \shäⁿ-(‚)pē-‚nyē-‚sᵫr-'märn\ commune N France, SSE suburb of Paris *pop* 74,232

Champlain, Lake \sham-'plān\ lake 125 *mi* (201 *km*) long bet. N.Y. & Vt. extending N into Que. *area* 430 *sq mi* (1114 *sq km*)

Chan·der·na·gore \‚chən-dər-nə-'gōr\ *or* **Chan·dan·na·gar** \‚chən-də-'nə-gər\ city E India in W. Bengal N of Calcutta; before 1950 part of French India *pop* 162,166

Chan·di·garh \'chən-dē-gər\ city N India N of Delhi; a union territory administered by the national government; ✻ of Punjabi Suba & of Haryana *pop* 808,796

Chan·dler \'chan(d)-lər\ city SW *cen* Ariz. *pop* 236,123

Chan·dra·pur \'chən-drə-'pür\ *or formerly* **Chan·da** \'chən-də\ town *cen* India in E Maharashtra *pop* 297,612; ✻ of Gond dynasty 12th–18th centuries

Chang \'chäŋ\ *or* **Yang·tze** \'yaŋ-'sē, 'yan(k)t-'sē; 'yäŋ-'tsə\ river *over* 3900 *mi* (6275 *km*) *cen* China flowing from Kunlun Mountains in SW Qinghai E into E. China Sea

Changan — see XI'AN

Chang–chia–k'ou — see ZHANGJIAKOU

Chang–chou — see ZHANGZHOU

Chang·chun \'chäŋ-'chün\ city NE China ✻ of Jilin *pop* 1,679,270

Chang·de *or* **Ch'ang·te** \'chäŋ-'də\ city SE *cen* China in N Hunan on the Yuan *pop* 301,276

Chang·sha \'chäŋ-'shä\ city SE *cen* China ✻ of Hunan on the Xiang *pop* 1,113,212

Chang·zhou *or* **Ch'ang·chou** \'chäŋ-'jō\ *or formerly* **Wu·tsin** \'wüd-'zin\ city E China in S Jiangsu *pop* 531,470

Channel Islands 1 *or* **Santa Barbara Islands** chain of islands Calif. in the Pacific off SW coast — see CATALINA, SAN CLEMENTE ISLAND, SANTA CRUZ 1, SANTA ROSA ISLAND 2 islands in English Channel; a possession of Brit. Crown *area* 75 *sq mi* (195 *sq km*), *pop* 149,900 — see ALDERNEY, GUERNSEY, JERSEY, SARK

Channel Islands National Park area of island landscapes SW Calif. including five of the Channel Islands

Chan·til·ly \‚shäⁿ-tē-'yē, shan-'ti-lē\ town N France NNE of Paris *pop* 10,916

Chao·an \'chaù-'än\ *or* **Chao·zhou** *or* **Ch'ao·chou** *or* **Chao·chow** \'chaù-'jō\ city E China in NE Guangdong on Han River *pop* 101,000

Chao Phra·ya \chaù-'prī-ə, -prä-'yä\ *or* **Me Nam** \mā-'näm\ river 227 *mi* (365 *km*) W *cen* Thailand formed by confluence of Nan & Ping rivers & flowing S into Gulf of Thailand

Cha·pa·la, Lake \chä-'pä-lä\ lake 50 *mi* (80 *km*) long W *cen* Mexico in Jalisco & Michoacán SE of Guadalajara

Chapel Hill town N N.C. SW of Durham *pop* 57,233

Cha·rente \shä-'räⁿt\ river *ab* 225 *mi* (362 *km*) W France flowing W into Bay of Biscay

Cha·ri *or* **Sha·ri** \'shär-ē\ river *ab* 590 *mi* (949 *km*) N *cen* Africa in Chad flowing NW into Lake Chad

Char·i·ton \'sha-rə-tən\ river 280 *mi* (451 *km*) S Iowa & N Mo. flowing S into the Missouri

Charle·roi \'shär-lə-‚rȯi, -lər-‚wä\ city SW Belgium in Hainaut *pop* 200,578

Charles \'chär(-ə)lz\ river 47 *mi* (76 *km*) Mass. flowing into Boston harbor

Charles, Cape cape E Va. N of entrance to Chesapeake Bay

Charles·bourg \shärl-'bür, 'chär(-ə)lz-‚bᵊrg\ former city Canada in SE Que.; now part of Quebec (city)

Charles·ton \'chär(-ə)l-stən\ 1 city & port SE S.C. *pop* 120,083 2 city ✻ of W.Va. on the Kanawha *pop* 51,400 — **Charles·to·nian** \‚chär(-ə)l-'stō-nē-ən, -nyən\ *n*

Charleston Peak mountain 11,919 *ft* (3633 *m*) SE Nev. WNW of Las Vegas; highest in Spring Mountains

Charles·town \'chär(-ə)lz-‚taùn\ section of Boston, Mass., on Charleston harbor bet. mouths of Charles & Mystic rivers

Char·lotte \'shär-lət\ city S N.C. near S.C. border *pop* 731,424

Charlotte Ama·lie \ə-'mäl-yə, 'a-mə-lē\ *or formerly* **Saint Thomas** city & port ✻ of Virgin Islands of the U.S. on St. Thomas Is. *pop* 11,004

Charlotte Harbor inlet of Gulf of Mexico SW Fla.

Char·lottes·ville \'shär-ləts-‚vil, -vəl\ city *cen* Va. *pop* 43,475

Char·lotte·town \'shär-lət-‚taùn\ city & port Canada ✻ of P.E.I. on Northumberland Strait *pop* 34,562

Chartres \'shärt, 'shärtrᵊ\ city N France SW of Paris *pop* 40,402

Châ·teau·guay \'sha-tə-‚gä\ town Canada in S Que. SW of Montreal *pop* 45,904

Châ·teau·roux \‚shä-tō-'rü\ commune *cen* France S of Orléans *pop* 34,192

Châ·teau–Thier·ry \‚shä-tō-‚tye-'rē\ town N France on the Marne SW of Reims *pop* 14,966

Chat·ham \'cha-təm\ 1 — see SAN CRISTÓBAL 1 2 town SE England in Kent *pop* 43,557

Chatham Islands islands S. Pacific belonging to New Zealand & comprising two islands (Chatham & Pitt) *area* 372 *sq mi* (967 *sq km*)

Chatham–Kent \-'kent\ municipality Canada in SE Ont. E of Lake Saint Clair *pop* 103,671

Chatham Strait strait SE Alaska bet. Admiralty Is. & Kuiu Is. on E & Baranof Is. & Chicagof Is. on W

Chat·ta·hoo·chee \‚cha-tə-'hü-chē\ river 436 *mi* (702 *km*) SE U.S. rising in N Ga. flowing SW & S along Ala.-Ga. boundary into Lake Seminole

Chat·ta·noo·ga \‚cha-tə-'nü-gə\ city SE Tenn. on Tennessee River *pop* 167,674

Chau·tau·qua \shə-'tȯ-kwə\ lake 18 *mi* (29 *km*) long SW N.Y.

Che·bok·sa·ry \‚che-‚bäk-'sär-ē\ city Russia in Europe ✻ of Chuvashia WNW of Kazan' *pop* 442,000

Che·cheno–In·gush Republic \chə-‚che-nō-in-'güsh\ former autonomous republic U.S.S.R. on N slopes of Caucasus Mountains; split into republics of Chechnya and Ingushetia within Russia 1992

Chech·nya *or* **Chech·e·nya** *or* **Chech·e·nia** \chech-'nyä, chech-nyə\ *or* **Che·chen Republic** \chi-'chen\ republic SE Russia in Europe on N slopes of Caucasus Mountains ✻ Grozny *area* 4750 *sq mi* (12,302 *sq km*), *pop* 1,103,686 — **Chechen** *adj or n*

Che·du·ba \chə-'dü-bə\ island W Myanmar *area* 202 *sq mi* (523 *sq km*), *pop* 2635

Chefoo — see YANTAI

Che·ju *or* **Je·ju** \'jä-jü\ *or formerly* **Quel·part** \'kwel-‚pärt\ island S. Korea in N E. China Sea *area* 706 *sq mi* (1829 *sq km*)

Chekiang — see ZHEJIANG

Che·lan, Lake \shə-'lan\ lake *ab* 55 *mi* (88 *km*) long N *cen* Wash.

Chelms·ford 1 \'chemz-fərd *also* 'chelmz-\ town NE Mass. *pop* 33,802 2 \'chelmz-, 'chemz-\ town SE England ✻ of Essex *pop* 150,000

Chel·sea \'chel-sē\ 1 city E Mass. NE of Boston *pop* 35,177 2 former metropolitan borough SW London, England, on N bank of Thames River, now part of Kensington and Chelsea

Chel·ten·ham \'chelt-nəm, 'chel-tə-nəm, *US also* -tᵊn-‚ham\ borough SW *cen* England in Gloucestershire *pop* 85,900

Che·lya·binsk \chel-'yä-bən(t)sk\ city W Russia in Asia *pop* 1,143,000

Che·lyu·skin, Cape \chel-'yü-skən\ headland Russia in Asia on Taymyr Peninsula; northernmost point of Asian mainland, at 77°35'N, 105°E

Chem·nitz \'kem-‚nits, -nəts\ *or* 1953–90 **Karl–Marx–Stadt** \(‚)kärl-'märk-‚shtät, -‚stät\ city E Germany SE of Leipzig *pop* 287,511

Chemulpo — see INCHON

Che·nab \chə-'näb\ river *ab* 600 *mi* (965 *km*) S Asia rising in Himachal Pradesh, India & flowing SW to unite with the Sutlej forming the Panjnad in Pakistan

Chen–chiang — see ZHENJIANG

Cheng·chou — see ZHENGZHOU

Cheng·de *or* **Ch'eng·te** \'chəŋ-'də\ *or* **Je·hol** \jə-'hōl, ‚rō-'hō\ city NE China in NE Hebei NE of Beijing *pop* 246,799

Cheng·du *or* **Ch'eng·tu** \'chəŋ-'dü\ city SW *cen* China ✻ of Sichuan on Min River *pop* 1,713,255

Chennai — see MADRAS 2

Chenstokhov — see CZESTOCHOWA

Cheongju — see CH'ONGJU

Cher \'sher\ river 217 *mi* (349 *km*) *cen* France flowing into the Loire

Cher·bourg \'sher-‚bür(g), sher-'bür\ city & port NW France on Cotentin Peninsula on English Channel *pop* 25,337

Che·rem·kho·vo \chə-'rem-kə-vō, ‚cher-əm-'kȯ-və\ city Russia in Asia NW of Irkutsk *pop* 73,600

Cher·kessk \chir-'kyesk\ city S Russia in Europe in N Caucasus region SE of Stavropol' ✻ of Karachay-Cherkessia *pop* 119,000

Cher·ni·hiv \‚cher-'nē-hē-ü\ *or* **Cher·ni·gov** \chir-'nē-gəf\ city N Ukraine *pop* 306,000

Cher·niv·tsi \chir-nift-sē\ *or* **Cher·nov·tsy** \chir-'nȯft-sē\ *or Romanian* **Cer·na·u·ti** \‚cher-nə-'üts, -'üt-sē\ city W Ukraine on the Prut near Romania border *pop* 259,000

Cher·no·byl \chər-'nō-bəl, (‚)cher-\ *or* **Chor·no·byl'** \chȯr-'nō-bəl\ site N Ukraine of town abandoned after 1986 nuclear accident

Cher·o·kee Outlet \'cher-ə-(‚)kē\ strip of land N Okla. along S border of Kans. E of 100°W; opened to settlement 1893; 50 *mi* (80 *km*) wide, *ab* 220 *mi* (354 *km*) long

Cher·so·nese \'kər-sə-‚nēz, -‚nēs\ *or anc* **Cher·so·ne·sus** \‚kər-sə-'nē-səs\ any of several peninsulas: as (1) Jutland (the **Cim·bri·an Chersonese** \'sim-brē-ən\ *or* **Cim·bric Chersonese** \-brik\); (2) the Malay Peninsula (the **Golden Chersonese**); (3) Crimea (the **Tau·ric Chersonese** \'tȯr-ik\); (4) Gallipoli (the **Thra·cian Chersonese** \'thrā-shən\)

Cher·well \'chär-wəl\ river 30 *mi* (48 *km*) *cen* England in Northamptonshire & Oxfordshire flowing S into the Thames at Oxford

Ches·a·peake \'che-sə-‚pēk, 'ches-‚pēk\ city SE Va. S of Norfolk *pop* 222,209

Chesapeake Bay inlet of the Atlantic 193 *mi* (311 *km*) long in Va. & Md.

Chesh·ire \'che-shər, -‚shir\ 1 town S Conn. SW of Meriden *pop* 29,261 2 *or* **Ches·ter** \'ches-tər\ county NW England ✻ Chester *area* 929 *sq mi* (2406 *sq km*), *pop* 937,300

Ches·ter \'ches-tər\ 1 city SE Pa. *pop* 33,972 2 city NW England ✻ of Cheshire on Dee River *pop* 58,436

Ches·ter·field \'ches-tər-‚fēld\ 1 city E Mo. W of St. Louis *pop* 47,484 2 town N *cen* England in Derbyshire S of Sheffield *pop* 99,700

Chesterfield Inlet inlet on NW coast of Hudson Bay, Canada in E mainland portion of Nunavut

Che·tu·mal \‚chā-tü-'mäl\ city SE Mexico ✻ of Quintana Roo

Chev·i·ot Hills \'chē-vē-ət, 'che-\ hills extending NE to SW along English-Scottish border; highest peak Cheviot 2676 *ft* (816 *m*)

Chey·enne \shī-'an, -'en\ 1 river 527 *mi* (850 *km*) S.Dak. flowing NE into Missouri River 2 city SE Wyo., its ✻ *pop* 59,466

Chhat·tis·garh \chə-'tēz-gər\ state *cen* India ✻ Raipur *area* 56,510 *sq mi* (146,361 *sq km*), *pop* 20,795,956

Chia–i \'jyä-'ē\ city W *cen* Taiwan *pop* 258,664

Chia–mu–ssu — see JIAMUSI

Chiang Mai \'jyäŋ-'mī\ city NW Thailand on the Ping *pop* 161,541

Chi·a·pas \chē-'ä-päs\ state SE Mexico bordering on the Pacific ✻ Tuxtla Gutiérrez *area* 28,528 *sq mi* (73,888 *sq km*), *pop* 3,210,496

Chi·ba \chē-bä\ city E Japan in Honshu on Tokyo Bay *pop* 887,164

Chi·ca·go \shə-'kä-(‚)gō, -'kȯ-, -gə\ 1 river Chicago, Ill., having a N branch & a S branch & *orig.* flowing E into Lake Michigan but now flowing S through S branch & Chicago Sanitary & Ship Canal into Des Plaines River 2 city & port NE Ill. on Lake Michigan *pop* 2,695,598 — **Chi·ca·go·an** \-'kä-gō-ən, -'kȯ-\ *n*

Chicago Heights city NE Ill. S of Chicago *pop* 30,276

Chich·a·gof \'chi-chə-ˌgóf, -ˌgäf\ island SE Alaska in Alexander Archipelago N of Baranof Is. *area* 2100 *sq mi* (5460 *sq km*)

Chi·chén It·zá \chē-ˌchen-ēt-'sä, -'ēt-sə\ village SE Mexico in Yucatán ESE of Mérida; site of ruins of important Mayan city

Chich·es·ter \'chi-chəs-tər\ town S England ENE of Portsmouth ✳ of W. Sussex *pop* 24,189

Ch'i–ch'i–ha–erh — see QIQIHAR

Chick·a·hom·i·ny \ˌchi-kə-'hä-mə-nē\ river 90 *mi* (145 *km*) E Va. flowing SE into James River

Chi·cla·yo \chē-'klī-(ˌ)ō\ city NW Peru near coast *pop* 419,600

Chi·co \'chē-(ˌ)kō\ city W Calif. N of Sacramento *pop* 86,187

Chic·o·pee \'chi-kə-(ˌ)pē\ city SW Mass. *pop* 55,298

Chi·cou·ti·mi \shə-'kü-tə-mē\ **1** river 100 *mi* (161 *km*) Canada in S Que. flowing N into the Saguenay **2** former city Canada in S cen Que. on the Saguenay; now part of the city of Saguenay

Chihli — see HEBEI

Chihli, Gulf of — see BO HAI

Chi·hua·hua \chē-'wä-(ˌ)wä, chə-, -wə\ **1** state N Mexico bordering on the U.S. *area* 95,400 *sq mi* (247,086 *sq km*), *pop* 2,441,873 **2** city, its ✳ *metropolitan area pop* 530,487

Chi·le \'chi-lē, 'chē-(ˌ)lā\ country S S. America bet. the Andes & the Pacific; a republic ✳ Santiago *area* 292,257 *sq mi* (756,946 *sq km*), *pop* 15,116,435 — **Chil·ean** \'chi-lē-ən, chə-'lā-ən\ *adj or n*

Chil·koot \'chil-ˌküt\ pass 3502 *ft* (1067 *m*) bet. SE Alaska & SW Yukon Territory, Canada, in N Coast Mountains

Chil·li·wack \'chi-lə-ˌwak\ city Canada in S B.C. *pop* 77,936

Chi·loé \ˌchē-lō-'ā\ island S cen Chile *area* 3241 *sq mi* (8394 *sq km*), *pop* 65,161

Chil·pan·cin·go \ˌchēl-pän-'sēŋ-(ˌ)gō\ city S Mexico ✳ of Guerrero *pop* 170,368

Chil·tern Hills \'chil-tərn\ hills S cen England in Oxfordshire, Buckinghamshire, Hertfordshire, & Bedfordshire

Chi–lung — see JILONG

Chim·bo·ra·zo \ˌchēm-bō-'rä-(ˌ)zō\ mountain 20,561 *ft* (6267 *m*) W cen Ecuador

Chimkent — see SHYMKENT

Chi·na, People's Republic of \'chī-nə\ country E Asia; a republic ✳ Beijing *area* 3,691,502 *sq mi* (9,597,905 *sq km*), *pop* 1,335,000,000

China, Republic of — see TAIWAN

Chinan — see JINAN

China Sea the E. & S. China seas

Chin–chou, Chinchow — see JINZHOU

Chin·co·teague Bay \ˌshiŋ-kə-'tēg\ bay Md. & Va. on Atlantic coast

Chin·dwin \'chin-'dwin\ river NW Myanmar flowing S into the Irrawaddy

Chinese Turkestan region W China in W & cen Xinjiang Uygur

Ch'ing–hai — see QINGHAI 1

Chin Hills \'chin\ hills W Myanmar; highest 10,016 *ft* (3053 *m*)

Ch'in–huang–tao, Chin·wang·tao — see QINHUANGDAO

Chinnampo — see NAMPO

Chinnereth, Sea of — see GALILEE (Sea of)

Chi·no \'chē-(ˌ)nō\ city SW Calif. E of Los Angeles *pop* 77,983

Chino Hills city S Calif. S of Pomona *pop* 74,799

Chiog·gia \kē-'ō-jä\ commune & port NE Italy on island in Lagoon of Venice *pop* 51,898

Chi·os \'kī-ˌäs\ *or ModGk* **Khí·os** \'kē-ˌós\ **1** island E Greece in the Aegean off W coast of Turkey *area* 325 *sq mi* (842 *sq km*), *pop* 52,691 **2** city & port Greece on E coast of Chios Is. — **Chi·an** \'kī-ən\ *adj or n*

Chip·pe·wa \'chi-pə-ˌwò, -ˌwä, -ˌwä, -wə\ river 183 *mi* (294 *km*) NW Wis. flowing S into Mississippi River

Chir·i·ca·hua National Monument \ˌchir-ə-'kä-wə, locally also 'chir-ə-ˌkaú\ area of curious rock formations SE Arizona

Chiriquí — see BARÚ

Chis·holm Trail \'chi-zəm\ pioneer cattle trail bet. San Antonio (Tex.) & Abilene (in E cen Kans.) used esp. 1866–85

Chi·și·nău \ˌkē-shē-'naú\ *or* **Ki·shi·nev** \ˌki-shi-'nyóf, 'ki-shə-ˌnef, -ˌnev\ city cen Moldova, its ✳ *pop* 665,000

Chis·le·hurst and Sid·cup \'chi-zəl-ˌhərst-ən(d)-'sid-kəp\ former urban district SE England in Kent, now partly in Bexley & partly in Bromley

Chi·ta \chi-'tä, 'chē-\ city Russia in Asia E of Lake Baikal *pop* 377,000

Chi·tral \chi-'träl\ river 300 *mi* (483 *km*) N Pakistan & Afghanistan flowing SW into Kabul River

Chit·ta·gong \'chi-tə-ˌgäŋ, -ˌgòŋ\ city & port SE Bangladesh on Bay of Bengal *pop* 1,566,070

Chi·tun·gwi·za \ˌchē-tüŋ-'gwē-zä\ city NE cen Zimbabwe, SSE of Harare *pop* 274,035

Chiu·si \'kyü-sē\ *or anc* **Clu·si·um** \'klü-zhē-əm, -zē-\ town cen Italy in Tuscany SE of Siena *pop* 8594

Chkalov — see ORENBURG

Choaspes — see KARKHEH

Choi·seul \shwä-'zə(r)l, -'zœl\ island W Pacific in the Solomons SE of Bougainville Is. nearly surrounded by barrier reef

Choi·sy \shwä-'zē\ *or* **Choi·sy–le–Roi** \shwä-ˌzē-lər-'wä\ commune N France on the Seine SSE of Paris *pop* 34,324

Cho·lon \shə-'lòn, chə-'lən\ former city S Vietnam, now part of Ho Chi Minh City

Cho·lu·la \chō-'lü-lä\ town SE cen Mexico in Puebla state

Cho·mo Lha·ri \ˌchō-mō-'lär-ē\ mountain 23,997 *ft* (7314 *m*) in the Himalayas bet. Tibet & NW Bhutan; sacred to Buddhists

Chomolungma — see EVEREST (Mount)

Ch'ong·ju *or* **Cheong·ju** \'chəŋ-ˌjü\ city W cen S. Korea N of Taejon *pop* 350,256

Chong·qing *or* **Ch'ung–ch'ing** \'chún-'chiŋ\ *or* **Chung·king** \'chúŋ-'kiŋ\ city SE Sichuan on the Chang; ✳ of China 1937–43 *pop* 2,266,772

Chon·ju *or* **Jeon·ju** \'jən-ˌjü\ city W cen S. Korea SW of Taejon *pop* 426,473

Cho Oyu \'chō-ō-'yü\ mountain 26,906 *ft* (8201 *m*) Nepal & Tibet in the Himalayas; 6th highest in the world

Cho·ras·mia \kə-'raz-mē-ə\ province of ancient Persia on Oxus River extending W to Caspian Sea; equivalent to Khwarazm — see KHIVA

Chornobyl' — see CHERNOBYL

Cho·rzow \'kò-ˌzhúf, 'kò-, -ˌzhúv\ city SW Poland in Silesia *pop* 132,674

Chosen — see KOREA

Cho·ta Nag·pur \ˌchō-tə-'näg-ˌpúr\ plateau region E India N of Mahanadi basin in N Orissa & S Bihar

Chou–shan — see ZHOUSHAN

Cho·wan \chə-'wän\ river 50 *mi* (80 *km*) NE N.C. flowing into Albemarle Sound

Christ·church \'krīs(t)-ˌchərch\ city New Zealand on E coast of South Is. *urban area pop* 334,107 — see LYTTELTON

Christiania — see OSLO

Chris·tian·sted \'kris-chən-ˌsted, 'krish-\ town Virgin Islands of the U.S. on E coast of St. Croix Is. *pop* 2555

Christ·mas Island \'kris-məs\ **1** island E Indian Ocean 225 *mi* (360 *km*) S of W end of Java; administered by Australia *area* 52 *sq mi* (135 *sq km*), *pop* 1000 **2** — see KIRITIMATI

Chu \'chü\ **1** — see ZHU **2** river *over* 1000 *mi* (1609 *km*) SE Kazakhstan flowing E into Issyk Kul

Ch'üan–chou, Chuanchow — see QUANZHOU

Chubb Crater — see NEW QUEBEC CRATER

Chu·but \chü-'büt, -'vüt\ river 500 *mi* (805 *km*) S Argentina flowing E across Patagonia into the Atlantic

Chu–chou, Chuchow — see ZHUZHOU

Chudskoe — see PEIPUS

Chu·gach Mountains \'chü-ˌgach also -ˌgash\ mountains S Alaska extending along coast from Cook Inlet to St. Elias Range; highest 13,176 *ft* (4016 *m*)

Chuk·chi Peninsula \'chək-chē, 'chúk-\ peninsula NE Russia in Asia bet. Bering & Chukchi seas

Chukchi Sea sea of the Arctic Ocean N of Bering Strait

Chu·la Vis·ta \ˌchü-lə-'vis-tə\ city SW Calif. S of San Diego *pop* 243,916

Chu·lym *or* **Chu·lim** \chə-'lim\ river Russia in Asia flowing W into the Ob'

Ch'ung–ch'ing, Chungking — see CHONGQING

Chun–ko–erh P'en–ti — see JUNGGAR PENDI

Chur \'kúr\ *or F* **Coire** \'kwär\ commune E Switzerland ✳ of Graubünden canton *pop* 31,078

Chur·chill \'chər-ˌchil\ **1** river ab 1000 *mi* (1609 *km*) Canada flowing E across N Sask. & N Man. into Hudson Bay **2** *or formerly* **Hamilton** river 208 *mi* (335 *km*) Canada in Nfld.&Lab. in S cen Labrador flowing E to Lake Melville

Churchill Falls *or formerly* **Grand Falls** waterfall 245 *ft* (75 *m*) high Canada in W Labrador in Churchill River

Chuuk \'chúk\ *or* **Truk** \'trək, 'trúk\ islands cen Carolines, part of Federated States of Micronesia *pop* 53,595

Chu·vash·ia *or* **Chu·va·shi·ya** \chü-'vä-shē-ə\ autonomous republic E cen Russia in Europe S of the Volga ✳ Cheboksary *area* 7066 *sq mi* (18,301 *sq km*), *pop* 1,393,000

Chu·zen·ji \chü-'zen-jē\ lake Japan in cen Honshu

Cí·bo·la \'sē-bə-lə, 'si-\ historical region in present N N.Mex. including seven pueblos (the **Seven Cities of Cíbola**) believed by early Spanish explorers to contain vast treasures

Cic·ero \'si-sə-ˌrō\ town NE Ill. W of Chicago *pop* 83,891

Ci·dra \'sē-drä\ city E cen Puerto Rico *pop* 43,480

Cien·fue·gos \syen-'fwä-(ˌ)gōs\ city & port W cen Cuba on S coast on **Cienfuegos Bay** *pop* 123,600

Cie·szyn \'che-shin\ *or G* **Te·schen** \'te-shən\ region cen Europe in Silesia; once an Austrian duchy; divided 1920 bet. Poland & Czechoslovakia (now the Czech Republic)

Ci·la·cap *or* **Tji·la·tjap** \chē-'lä-chäp\ city & port Indonesia in S Java ESE of Bandung

Ci·li·cia \sə-'li-sh(ē-)ə\ ancient country SE Asia Minor extending along Mediterranean coast S of Taurus Mountains — see LITTLE ARMENIA — **Ci·li·cian** \-'li-shən\ *adj or n*

Cilician Gates mountain pass S Turkey in Taurus Mountains

Cim·ar·ron \'si-mə-ˌrän, -ˌrōn, -rən\ river flowing E from NE N.Mex. through SW Kans. into Arkansas River in NE Okla.

Cimbrian Chersonese, Cimbric Chersonese — see CHERSONESE

Cimmerian Bosporus — see KERCH STRAIT

Cin·cin·nati \ˌsin(t)-sə-'na-tē, -'na-tə\ city SW Ohio on Ohio River *pop* 296,943 — **Cin·cin·nat·i·an** \-'na-tē-ən\ *n*

Cinque Ports \'siŋk\ group of seaports SE England in Kent & Sussex — Dover, Sandwich, Romney, Hastings, & Hythe to which were later added Winchelsea, Rye, & other minor places, granted privileges (until 19th century) in return for services in coast defense

Cintra — see SINTRA

Circars — see NORTHERN CIRCARS

Cir·cas·sia \(ˌ)sər-'ka-sh(ē-)ə\ region S Russia in Europe on Black Sea N of W end of Caucasus Mountains

Ci·re·bon \ˌchē-re-'bòn\ city Indonesia in W Java on N coast E of Jakarta *pop* 245,307

Cirenaica — see CYRENAICA

Cis·al·pine Gaul \(ˌ)sis-'al-ˌpīn\ the part of Gaul lying S & E of the Alps

Ciscaucasia — see CAUCASUS

Cis·kei \'sis-ˌkī\ former black enclave in the Republic of South Africa ✳ Bisho; granted independence 1981; abolished 1994 — **Cis·kei·an** \(ˌ)sis-'kī-ən\ *adj or n*

Ci·thae·ron \sə-'thē-ˌrän\ *or ModGk* **Ki·thai·rón** \ˌkē-the-'rón\ *or formerly* **El·a·tea** \ˌe-lə-'tē-ə\ mountain 4623 *ft* (1409 *m*) Greece on NW border of ancient Attica

Ci·tlal·té·petl \sēt-ˌläl-'tä-pe-tᵊl\ *or* **Ori·za·ba** \ˌór-ə-'zä-bə, ˌō-rē-'sä-vä\ inactive volcano 18,700 *ft* (5700 *m*) SE Mexico on Puebla-Veracruz boundary; highest mountain in Mexico & 3d highest in N. America

Citrus Heights city N cen Calif. NE of Sacramento *pop* 83,301

Città del Vaticano — see VATICAN CITY

Ciu·dad Bo·lí·var \syü-ˌthäth-bō-'lē-ˌvär, ˌsē-ù-'dad-\ city & port E cen Venezuela on the Orinoco *pop* 225,846

Ciudad Gua·ya·na \ˌgwä-'yä-nä\ city E Venezuela near junction of the Caroní & the Orinoco *pop* 536,506

Ciudad Juá·rez *or* **Juárez** \'hwär-es, 'wär-\ city Mexico in Chihuahua on Rio Grande opposite El Paso, Tex. *pop* 789,522

Ciudad Re·al \rā-'äl\ **1** province S cen Spain *area* 7625 *sq mi* (17,749 *sq km*), *pop* 478,957 **2** commune, its ✳, S of Toledo *pop* 63,251

Ciudad Trujillo — see SANTO DOMINGO 1

Ciudad Vic·to·ria \vik-'tòr-ē-ə\ city E cen Mexico ✳ of Tamaulipas pop 94,304

Ci·vi·ta·vec·chia \,chē-vē-tä-'ve-(,)kyä\ commune & port cen Italy in Lazio on Tyrrhenian Sea WNW of Rome pop 50,902

Clack·man·nan \klak-'ma-nən\ or **Clack·man·nan·shire** \-,shir, -shər\ administrative area cen Scotland bordering on the Forth area 61 sq mi (157 sq km)

Clac·ton \'klak-tən\ or **Clacton—on—Sea** town SE England in Essex on North Sea pop 43,571

Clare \'kler\ county W Ireland in Munster ✳ Ennis area 1231 sq mi (3201 sq km), pop 103,277

Clare·mont \-,mänt\ city SW Calif. E of Los Angeles pop 34,926

Clar·ing·ton \'kler-iŋ-tən\ municipality Canada in SE Ont. ENE of Toronto pop 84,548

Clark Fork \'klärk\ river 300 mi (483 km) W Mont. & N Idaho flowing NW into Pend Oreille Lake

Clarks·ville \'klärks-,vil, -vəl\ city N Tenn. NW of Nashville pop 132,929

Clear·field \'klir-,fēld\ city N Utah S of Ogden pop 30,112

Clear·wa·ter \'klir-,wò-tər, -,wä-\ city W Fla. NW of St. Petersburg on Gulf of Mexico pop 107,685

Clearwater Mountains mountains N cen Idaho; highest ab 8000 ft (2438 m)

Cle·burne \'klē-bərn\ city NE cen Tex. pop 29,337

Clee Hills \'klē\ hills W England in S Shropshire

Cler·mont—Fer·rand \,kler-,mòⁿ-fe-'räⁿ\ city S cen France in Allier valley on edge of Auvergne Mountains pop 137,154

Cleve·land \'klēv-lənd\ **1** city & port NE Ohio on Lake Erie pop 396,815 **2** city SE Tenn. ENE of Chattanooga pop 41,285 — **Cleve·land·er** \-lən-dər\ n

Cleveland, Mount mountain 10,455 ft (3185 m) N Mont.; highest in Glacier National Park

Cleveland Heights city NE Ohio E of Cleveland pop 46,121

Cli·chy \klē-'shē\ commune N France NW of Paris pop 50,237

Cliff·side Park \klif-(,)sīd\ borough NE N.J. pop 23,594

Clif·ton \'klif-tən\ city NE N.J. N of Newark pop 84,136

Clinch \'klinch\ river ab 300 mi (480 km) SW Va. & E Tenn. flowing SW into Tennessee River

Cling·mans Dome \'kliŋ-mənz\ mountain 6643 ft (2025 m) on N.C.- Tenn. boundary; highest in Great Smoky Mountains

Clin·ton \'klin-t³n\ **1** city E Iowa on Mississippi River pop 26,885 **2** town SW cen Miss. pop 25,216

Clon·mel \klän-'mel\ town S Ireland ✳ of County Tipperary South pop 11,759

Cloud Peak mountain 13,165 ft (4013 m) N Wyo.; highest in Bighorn Mountains

Clo·vis \'klō-vəs\ **1** city cen Calif. NE of Fresno pop 95,631 **2** city E N.Mex. pop 37,775

Cluj—Na·po·ca \'klüzh-'nä-pō-kə\ city NW cen Romania in Transylvania pop 318,027

Clu·ny \'klü-nē, klü-'\ town E cen France NNW of Lyon pop 4371

Clusium — see CHIUSI

Clu·tha \'klü-thə\ river 210 mi (338 km) New Zealand in SE South Is. flowing SE into the Pacific

Clyde \'klīd\ river 106 mi (171 km) SW Scotland flowing NW into **Firth of Clyde** (estuary)

Clyde·bank \'klīd-,baŋk\ burgh W cen Scotland on Clyde River pop 46,920

Clydes·dale \'klīdz-,dāl\ valley of the upper Clyde River in Scotland

Cni·dus \'nī-dəs\ ancient town SW Asia Minor in Caria

Cnossus — see KNOSSOS

Coa·chel·la \kō-'che-lə\ city S Calif. pop 40,704

Coachella Valley valley SE Calif. bet. Salton Sea & San Bernardino Mountains

Coa·hui·la \,kō-ä-'wē-lä, kwä-'wē-\ state N Mexico bordering on the U.S. ✳ Saltillo area 58,522 sq mi (151,572 sq km), pop 1,972,340

Co·a·mo \kō-'ä-mō\ city SE cen Puerto Rico pop 40,512

Coast Mountains mountains Canada in W B.C.; N continuation of Cascade Range

Coast Ranges mountain ranges W N. America extending along Pacific coast W of Sierra Nevada & Cascade Range & N through Vancouver Is., B.C., to Kenai Peninsula & Kodiak Is., Alaska — see LOGAN (Mount)

Coat·bridge \'kōt-(,)brij\ burgh S cen Scotland E of Glasgow pop 50,866

Coats Land \'kōts\ section of Antarctica SE of Weddell Sea

Cobh \'kōv\ or formerly **Queens·town** \'kwēnz-,taùn\ town & port SW Ireland on island in Cork harbor pop 6369

Coblenz — see KOBLENZ

Co·burg **1** \'kō-,bərg\ city SE Australia in S Victoria, N suburb of Melbourne pop 50,625 **2** \-,bərg, -,bùrk\ city cen Germany in N Bavaria NW of Bayreuth pop 44,693

Co·cha·bam·ba \,kō-chä-'bäm-bä\ city W cen Bolivia pop 404,102

Co·chin \'kō-,chin\ region SW India in Kerala on Malabar Coast — see TRAVANCORE

Co·chin China \'kō-,chin\ region S Vietnam bordering on S. China Sea & Gulf of Thailand area 29,974 sq mi (77,932 sq km)

Cochinos, Bahía de — see PIGS (Bay)

Co·co \'kō-(,)kō\ or formerly **Se·go·via** \sā-'gō-vyä, sə-, -vē-ə\ river over 450 mi (724 km) N Nicaragua flowing NE into the Caribbean & forming part of Honduras-Nicaragua boundary

Co·co·ni·no Plateau \,kō-kə-'nē-(,)nō, -'nē-nə\ plateau NW Ariz. S of Grand Canyon

Coconut Creek city SE Fla. NNW of Fort Lauderdale pop 52,909

Co·cos Islands \'kō-kəs\ or **Kee·ling Islands** \'kē-liŋ\ islands E Indian Ocean belonging to Australia area 5.5 sq mi (14 sq km), pop 600

Cod, Cape \'käd\ peninsula 65 mi (105 km) long SE Mass. — **Cape Cod·der** \'kä-dər\ n

Coele—Syria — see BEKAA

Coeur d'Alene \,kòr-də-'län, ,kər-\ city N Idaho pop 44,137

Coeur d'Alene Lake lake ab 37 mi (59 km) long N Idaho E of Spokane, Wash., drained by Spokane River

Co·glians, Mon·te \,mōn-tā-kōl-'yän(t)s\ mountain 9217 ft (2809 m) on Austria-Italy border; highest in the Carnic Alps

Coim·ba·tore \,kòim-bə-'tòr\ city S India in W Tamil Nadu on S slope of Nilgiri Hills pop 923,085

Co·im·bra \kō-'im-brə, kù-\ city W cen Portugal pop 148,443

Coire — see CHUR

Col·ches·ter \'kōl-,ches-tər, -chəs-\ town SE England in Essex pop 141,100

Col·chis \'käl-kəs\ ancient country bordering on Black Sea S of Caucasus Mountains; area now constitutes W part of Republic of Georgia — **Col·chi·an** \'käl-kē-ən\ adj or n

Cole·raine \kōl-'rān, 'kōl-,\ district N Northern Ireland, established 1974 area 187 sq mi (484 sq km), pop 51,062

Co·li·ma \kō-'lē-mä\ **1** volcano SW Mexico in S Jalisco **2** state SW Mexico bordering on the Pacific area 2106 sq mi (5454 sq km), pop 428,510 **3** city, its ✳, SSW of Guadalajara pop 106,967

College Park city SW Md. NE of Washington, D.C. pop 30,413

College Station city E cen Tex. SE of Bryan pop 93,857

Col·lier·ville \'käl-yər-,vil\ town SW Tenn. E of Memphis pop 43,965

Col·lins·ville \'kä-lənz-,vil\ city SW Ill. NE of E. St. Louis pop 25,579

Col·mar or G **Kol·mar** \'kōl-,mär, kōl-'\ commune NE France at E edge of Vosges Mountains pop 65,118

Co·logne \kə-'lōn\ or G **Köln** \'kœln\ city W Germany in N. Rhine= Westphalia on the Rhine pop 956,690

Colomb—Béchar — see BÉCHAR

Co·lombes \kə-'lōⁿb, -'lōm\ commune N France, NW suburb of Paris pop 76,690

Co·lom·bia \kə-'ləm-bē-ə also -'lōm-\ country NW S. America bordering on Caribbean Sea & Pacific Ocean ✳ Bogotá area 439,735 sq mi (1,138,914 sq km), pop 43,000,000 — **Co·lom·bi·an** \-ə-n\ adj or n

Co·lom·bo \kə-'ləm-(,)bō\ city & port ✳ of Sri Lanka pop 615,000

Co·lón \kō-'lōn\ city & port N Panama on the Caribbean at entrance to Panama Canal pop 54,469

Colón, Archipiélago de — see GALÁPAGOS ISLANDS

Col·o·phon \'kä-lə-,fän\ ancient city W Asia Minor in Lydia

Col·o·ra·do \,kä-lə-'ra-(,)dō, chiefly by outsiders -'rä-\ **1** river 1450 mi (2334 km) SW U.S. & NW Mexico rising in N Colo. & flowing SW into Gulf of California **2** river 600 mi (950 km) S Tex. flowing SE into Gulf of Mexico **3** state W U.S. ✳ Denver area 104,247 sq mi (271,042 sq km), pop 5,029,196 **4** river 530 mi (853 km) cen Argentina flowing SE to the Atlantic — **Col·o·ra·dan** \-'ra-d³n, -'rä-\ adj or n — **Col·o·ra·do·an** \-'ra-dō-ən, -'rä-\ adj or n

Colorado Desert desert SE Calif. W of Colorado River

Colorado National Monument reservation W Colo. W of Grand Junction containing many unusual erosion formations

Colorado Plateau plateau SW U.S. W of Rocky Mountains in Colorado River basin in N Ariz., S & E Utah, W Colo., & NW N.Mex.

Colorado Springs city cen Colo. E of Pikes Peak pop 416,427

Co·los·sae \kə-'lä-(,)sē\ ancient city SW cen Asia Minor in SW Phrygia — **Co·los·sian** \kə-'lä-shən\ adj or n

Col·ton \'kōl-t³n\ city SW Calif. S of San Bernardino pop 47,662

Co·lum·bia \kə-'ləm-bē-ə\ **1** river 1214 mi (1953 km) SW Canada & NW U.S. rising in SE B.C. & flowing S & W into the Pacific **2** city cen Mo. pop 108,500 **3** city cen S.C., its ✳ pop 129,272 **4** city cen Tenn. pop 34,681 — **Co·lum·bi·an** \-bē-ən\ adj or n

Columbia, Cape cape N Canada on Ellesmere Is.; northernmost point of Canada, at 83°07′N

Columbia, District of — see DISTRICT OF COLUMBIA

Columbia Plateau plateau E Wash., E Oreg., & SW Idaho in Columbia River basin

Co·lum·bus \kə-'ləm-bəs\ **1** city W Ga. on the Chattahoochee pop 189,885 **2** city S cen Ind. pop 44,061 **3** city E Miss. pop 23,640 **4** city cen Ohio, its ✳ pop 787,033

Col·ville \'kōl-,vil, 'käl-\ river 375 mi (603 km) N Alaska flowing NE into Beaufort Sea

Col·wyn Bay \'käl-wən\ town N Wales on Irish Sea pop 26,278

Co·mil·la or **Ku·mil·la** \kù-'mi-lə\ city E Bangladesh SE of Dhaka pop 164,509

Commander Islands — see KOMANDORSKI ISLANDS

Common Market — see EUROPEAN ECONOMIC COMMUNITY

Commonwealth of Independent States association formed in 1991 by the former constituent republics of the U.S.S.R. except for Lithuania, Latvia, and Estonia; Turkmenistan changed to associate member status in 2005; Georgia withdrew in 2009

Commonwealth of Nations or the **Commonwealth** or formerly **British Commonwealth** association of sovereign states consisting of the United Kingdom and a number of its former dependencies; formerly constituted, with several other British-controlled territories, the British Empire

Communism Peak — see QULLAI ISMAIL SOMONI

Co·mo \'kō-(,)mō\ commune N Italy in Lombardy at SW end of **Lake Como** (37 mi or 59 km long) pop 82,893

Co·mo·do·ro Ri·va·da·via \,kō-mō-'thòr-(,)ō-,rē-vä-'thä-vē-ä\ city & port S Argentina pop 135,632

Com·o·rin, Cape \'kä-mə-rən; kə-'mòr-ən, -'mär-\ cape S India in Tamil Nadu; southernmost point of India, at 8°5′N

Com·o·ros \'kä-mə-,rōz\ group of islands forming a country off SE Africa bet. Mozambique & Madagascar; formerly a French possession; a republic (except for Mayotte Is., which remains French) since 1975 ✳ Moroni area 719 sq mi (1862 sq km), pop 575,660 — **Com·o·ran** \'kä-mə-rən\ adj or n — **Co·mor·i·an** \kə-'mòr-ē-ən\ adj or n

Com·piègne \kòⁿ-'pyenⁿ\ town N France on the Oise pop 41,228

Compostela — see SANTIAGO 3

Comp·ton \'käm(p)-tən\ city SW Calif. SSE of Los Angeles pop 96,455

Com·stock Lode \'käm-,stäk\ gold & silver lode at Virginia City, Nev.

Con·a·kry \'kä-nə-krē\ city & port ✳ of Guinea on the Atlantic pop 581,000

Co·nan·i·cut Island \kə-'na-ni-kət\ island R.I. in Narragansett Bay

Con·cep·ción \kōn-sep-'syōn\ city S cen Chile pop 216,061

Con·chos \ˈkän-(ˌ)chōs\ river 300 *mi* (483 *km*) N Mexico flowing NE into Rio Grande
Con·cord 1 \ˈkän-ˌkȯrd, ˈkäŋ-\ city W Calif. NE of Oakland *pop* 122,067 2 \ˈkäŋ-kərd\ town E Mass. NW of Boston *pop* 17,668 3 \ˈkäŋ-kərd\ city * of N.H. on the Merrimack *pop* 42,695 4 \ˈkän-ˌkȯrd, ˈkäŋ-\ city S *cen* N.C. *pop* 79,066
Co·ney Island \ˈkō-nē\ resort section of New York City in S Brooklyn
Con·ga·ree \ˈkäŋ-gə-(ˌ)rē\ river 60 *mi* (96 *km*) *cen* S.C. flowing SE to unite with the Wateree forming the Santee
Congaree National Park reservation *cen* S.C. S of Columbia
Con·go \ˈkäŋ-(ˌ)gō\ 1 *or* **Zaire** river more than 2700 *mi* (4344 *km*) *cen* Africa flowing N, W, & SW into the Atlantic — see LUALABA 2 *or* **Democratic Republic of the Congo** *or 1971–97* **Zaire** *or 1908–60* **Belgian Congo** *or 1885–1908* **Congo Free State** country *cen* Africa comprising most of Congo River basin E of lower Congo River * Kinshasa *area* 905,356 *sq mi* (2,344,872 *sq km*), *pop* 67,800,000 3 *or* **Republic of the Congo** *or formerly* **Middle Congo** country W *cen* Africa W of the lower Congo * Brazzaville *area* 132,047 *sq mi* (342,002 *sq km*), *pop* 3,900,000 — see FRENCH EQUATORIAL AFRICA — **Con·go·lese** \ˌkäŋ-gə-ˈlēz, -ˈlēs\ *adj or n*
Con·nacht *or formerly* **Con·naught** \ˈkä-ˌnȯt\ province W Ireland *area* 6611 *sq mi* (17,189 *sq km*), *pop* 464,296
Con·nect·i·cut \kə-ˈne-ti-kət\ 1 river 407 *mi* (655 *km*) NE U.S. rising in N N.H. & flowing S into Long Island Sound from Connecticut 2 state NE U.S. * Hartford *area* 5018 *sq mi* (12,997 *sq km*), *pop* 3,574,097
Con·ne·ma·ra \ˌkä-nə-ˈmär-ə\ district Ireland in W Galway
Con·roe \ˈkän-(ˌ)rō\ city E Tex. N of Houston *pop* 56,207
Con·stance \ˈkän(t)-stən(t)s\ *or G* **Kon·stanz** \ˈkȯn-ˌshtänts\ commune S Germany on Lake Constance *pop* 76,162
Constance, Lake *or G* **Bo·den·see** \ˈbō-dᵊn-ˌzā\ lake 46 *mi* (74 *km*) long W Europe on border bet. Germany, Austria, & Switzerland
Con·stan·ța \kən-ˈstän(t)-sə\ city & port SE Romania on Black Sea *pop* 310,526
Con·stan·tine \ˈkän(t)-stən-ˌtēn\ city NE Algeria *pop* 440,842
Constantinople — see ISTANBUL — **Con·stan·ti·no·pol·i·tan** \ˌkän-ˌstan-tə-nō-ˈpä-lə-tən\ *adj*
Continental Divide *or* **Great Divide** the watershed of N. America comprising the line of highest points of land separating the waters flowing W from those flowing N or E, coinciding with various ranges of the Rockies, & extending SSE from NW Canada to NW S. America
Con·way \ˈkän-ˌwā\ city *cen* Ark. N of Little Rock *pop* 58,908
Con·wy \ˈkän-wē\ administrative area of N Wales *area* 436 *sq mi* (1130 *sq km*)
Cooch Be·har \ˌküch-bə-ˈhär\ former state NE India W of Assam; since 1947 attached to West Bengal
Cook, Mount \ˈku̇k\ *or Maori* **Ao·ra·ki** \au̇-ˈrä-kē\ *or formerly* **Aorangi** \au̇-ˈräŋ-ē\ mountain 12,316 *ft* (3754 *m*) New Zealand in W *cen* South Is.; highest peak in Southern Alps & New Zealand
Cooke·ville \ˈku̇k-ˌvil, -vəl\ city N *cen* Tenn. *pop* 30,435
Cook Inlet inlet of the Pacific S Alaska W of Kenai Peninsula
Cook Islands islands S. Pacific SW of Society Islands; self-governing territory of New Zealand * Avarua (on Rarotonga Is.) *area* 92 *sq mi* (238 *sq km*), *pop* 19,569
Cooks·town \ˈku̇ks-ˌtau̇n\ district *cen* Northern Ireland, established 1974 *area* 241 *sq mi* (627 *sq km*), *pop* 30,808
Cook Strait strait New Zealand bet. North Is. & South Is.
Coon Rapids \ˈkün\ city E Minn. N of St. Paul *pop* 61,476
Coo·per City \ˈkü-pər\ city SE Fla. WNW of Hollywood *pop* 28,547
Coorg *or* **Kurg** \ˈku̇rg\ former state S India * Mercara; merged with Mysore state (now Karnataka) 1956
Coo·sa \ˈkü-sə\ river 286 *mi* (460 *km*) NW Ga. & N Ala. flowing SW to join Tallapoosa River forming Alabama River
Coos Bay \ˈküs\ inlet of the Pacific SW Oreg.
Co·pán \kō-ˈpän\ ruins of Mayan city W Honduras
Co·pen·ha·gen \ˌkō-pən-ˈhā-gən, -ˈhä-; ˈkō-pən-ˌ\ *or Dan* **Kø·ben·havn** \ˌkœ-bən-ˈhau̇n\ city & port * of Denmark; located chiefly on E Sjælland Is. *pop* 501,285 — **Co·pen·ha·gen·er** \ˌkō-pən-ˈhā-gə-nər, -ˈhä-; ˈkō-pən-ˌ\ *n*
Co·pia·pó \ˌkō-pyä-ˈpō\ city N *cen* Chile *pop* 129,091
Cop·pell \ˈkä-pəl\ city Tex. NW of Dallas *pop* 38,659
Cop·per·as Cove \ˈkä-p(ə-)rəs\ city *cen* Tex. SW of Waco *pop* 32,032
Cop·per·mine \ˈkä-pər-ˌmīn\ river 525 *mi* (845 *km*) N Canada in Nunavut flowing NW into Arctic Ocean
Coquilhatville — see MBANDAKA
Co·quit·lam \kō-ˈkwit-ləm\ city Canada in S B.C. E of Vancouver *pop* 126,456
Coral Gables city SE Fla. SW of Miami *pop* 46,780
Coral Sea arm of the SW Pacific bounded on W by Queensland, Australia, on N by the Solomons, & on E by Vanuatu & New Caledonia
Coral Springs city SE Fla. NW of Fort Lauderdale *pop* 121,096
Cor·co·va·do \ˌkȯr-kō-ˈvä-(ˌ)dü\ mountain 2310 *ft* (704 *m*) SE Brazil on S side of city of Rio de Janeiro
Cor·dil·le·ra Cen·tral \ˌkȯr-dᵊl-ˈyer-ə-ˌsen-ˈträl, ˌkȯr-də-ˈler-, ˌkȯr-dē-ˈyer-\ 1 range of the Andes in Colombia 2 range of the Andes in Peru E of the Marañón 3 chief range of the Dominican Republic 4 range Philippines in N Luzon — see PULOG (Mount) 5 range S *cen* Puerto Rico — see CERRO DE PUNTA
Cordillera de Mé·ri·da \thā-ˈmā-rē-ˌthä\ *or* **Sier·ra Ne·va·da de Mérida** \ˈsyer-ä-ne-ˈvä-thä-ˌthā-\ mountain range W Venezuela — see BOLÍVAR (Pico)
Cór·do·ba \ˈkȯr-də-bə, ˈkȯr-thō-ˌvä\ 1 province S Spain *area* 5297 *sq mi* (13,179 *sq km*), *pop* 761,657 2 *or* **Cor·do·va** \ˈkȯr-də-və, ˈkȯr-thō-ˌvä\ city, its *, on the Guadalquivir *pop* 308,072 3 city N *cen* Argentina *pop* 1,179,067 — **Cor·do·ban** \-bən\ *adj or n*
Cor·do·va Island \ˈkȯr-də-və, ˈkȯr-thō-ˌvä\ tract on the Rio Grande 385 *acres* (156 *hectares*) adjoining Chamizal; formerly belonged entirely to Mexico; 193 *acres* (78 *hectares*) ceded to U.S. in 1963
Cor·fu \kȯr-ˈfü; ˈkȯr-(ˌ)fü, -(ˌ)fyü\ *or ModGk* **Kér·ky·ra** \ˈker-kē-ˌrä\ *or anc* **Cor·cy·ra** \kȯr-ˈsī-rə\ 1 island NW Greece, one of the Ionian Islands *area* 229 *sq mi* (593 *sq km*), *pop* 105,043 2 city & port on E Corfu *pop* 36,875 — **Cor·fi·ote** \ˈkȯr-fē-ˌōt, -ət\ *n*
Cor·inth \ˈkȯr-ən(t)th, ˈkär-\ *or ModGk* **Kó·rin·thos** \ˈkȯr-ēn-ˌthȯs\ *or Lat* **Co·rin·thia** \kə-ˈrin(t)-thē-ə\ region of ancient Greece occupying most of Isthmus of Corinth & part of NE Peloponnese
Corinth, Gulf of inlet of Ionian Sea *cen* Greece W of **Isthmus of Corinth** (neck of land 20 *mi or* 32 *km* long connecting Peloponnese with rest of Greece)
Cork \ˈkȯrk\ 1 county SW Ireland in Munster *area* 2880 *sq mi* (7459 *sq km*), *pop* 447,829 2 city & port, its *, at head of Cork harbor *pop* 123,062
Corneto — see TARQUINIA
Corn Islands \ˈkȯrn\ two small islands Nicaragua in the Caribbean
Cor·no, Mon·te \ˈmȯn-tā-ˈkȯr-(ˌ)nō\ mountain 9560 *ft* (2897 *m*) *cen* Italy NE of Rome; highest in the Apennines
Corn·wall \ˈkȯrn-ˌwȯl, -wəl\ 1 city Canada in SE Ont. *pop* 46,340 2 *or since 1974* **Cornwall and Isles of Scil·ly** \ˈsi-lē\ county SW England * Truro *area* 1418 *sq mi* (3673 *sq km*), *pop* 469,300
Co·ro \ˈkȯr-(ˌ)ō\ city NW Venezuela near coast *pop* 124,616
Cor·o·man·del \ˌkȯr-ə-ˈman-dᵊl, ˌkär-\ coast region SE India on Bay of Bengal S of mouths of the Krishna
Co·ro·na \kə-ˈrō-nə\ city S Calif. E of Los Angeles *pop* 152,374
Cor·o·na·do \ˌkȯr-ə-ˈnä-(ˌ)dō, ˌkär-\ city SW Calif. on San Diego Bay opposite San Diego *pop* 18,912
Co·ro·zal \ˌkȯ-rō-ˈsäl\ city N *cen* Puerto Rico *pop* 37,142
Cor·pus Chris·ti \ˌkȯr-pəs-ˈkris-tē\ city & port S Tex. on **Corpus Christi Bay** (inlet of Gulf of Mexico) at mouth of the Nueces *pop* 305,215
Cor·reg·i·dor \kə-ˈre-gə-ˌdȯr\ island N Philippines at entrance to Manila Bay *area ab* 2 *sq mi* (5 *sq km*)
Cor·rien·tes \ˌkȯr-ē-ˈen-ˌtās\ city NE Argentina *pop* 267,742
Cor·si·ca \ˈkȯr-si-kə\ *or F* **Corse** \ˈkȯrs\ island France in the Mediterranean N of Sardinia *area* 3360 *sq mi* (8702 *sq km*), *pop* 260,149 — **Cor·si·can** \ˈkȯr-si-kən\ *adj or n*
Cor·si·cana \ˌkȯr-sə-ˈka-nə\ city NE *cen* Tex. S of Dallas *pop* 23,770
Cor·ti·na *or* **Cortina d'Am·pez·zo** \kȯr-ˈtē-nä-ˌdäm-ˈpet-(ˌ)sō\ resort village N Italy in the Dolomites *pop* 6427
Cor·to·na \kȯr-ˈtō-nä\ commune *cen* Italy NW of Perugia *pop* 22,491
Coruña, La; Corunna — see A CORUÑA
Cor·val·lis \kȯr-ˈva-ləs\ city W Oreg. SW of Salem *pop* 54,462
Cos — see KOS
Co·sen·za \kō-ˈzen(t)-sä\ commune S Italy in Calabria *pop* 73,341
Cos·ta Bra·va \ˌkȯs-tä-ˈbrä-vä, ˌkōs-\ coast region NE Spain in Catalonia on the Mediterranean extending NE from Barcelona
Costa del Sol \-del-ˈsōl, -thel-, -ˈsȯl\ coast region S Spain on the Mediterranean extending E from Gibraltar
Cos·ta Me·sa \ˈkōs-tə-ˈmā-sə\ city SW Calif. SE of Long Beach on Pacific coast *pop* 108,724
Costa Ri·ca \ˈrē-kə\ country Central America bet. Nicaragua & Panama; a republic * San José *area* 19,652 *sq mi* (50,899 *sq km*), *pop* 4,346,500 — **Cos·ta Ri·can** \-kən\ *adj or n*
Costermansville — see BUKAVU
Côte d'A·zur \ˌkōt-də-ˈzu̇r, -dä-ˈzuer\ coast region SE France on the Mediterranean; part of the Riviera
Côte d'Ivoire — see IVORY COAST
Côte d'Or \kōt-ˈdȯr\ range of hills E France SW of Dijon
Co·ten·tin Peninsula \kō-ˌtäⁿ-ˈtaⁿ\ peninsula NW France projecting into English Channel W of mouth of the Seine
Côte–Saint–Luc \ˌkōt-saⁿ-ˈlük, -sānt-, -sənt-\ city Canada in S Que. W of Montreal *pop* 32,321
Co·to·nou \ˌkō-tō-ˈnü\ city & port, seat of government of Benin; former * of Dahomey *pop* 662,000
Co·to·paxi \ˌkō-tō-ˈpäk-sē\ volcano 19,347 *ft* (5897 *m*) N *cen* Ecuador
Cots·wold Hills \ˈkät-ˌswōld, -swəld\ range of hills SW *cen* England in Gloucestershire; highest point Cleeve Cloud 1031 *ft* (314 *m*)
Cottage Grove city E Minn. SE of St. Paul *pop* 34,589
Cott·bus *or* **Kott·bus** \ˈkät-bəs, -ˌbu̇s\ city E Germany on Spree River SE of Berlin *pop* 123,321
Cot·ti·an Alps \ˈkä-tē-ən\ range of W Alps France & Italy — see VISO
Coun·cil Bluffs \ˈkau̇n(t)-səl-ˈbləfs\ city SW Iowa on Missouri River *pop* 62,230
Cou·ran·tyne \ˈkȯr-ən-ˌtīn\ *or D* **Co·ran·tijn** \-ˌtīn\ river *ab* 475 *mi* (764 *km*) N S. America flowing N into the Atlantic & forming boundary bet. Guyana & Suriname
Cour·be·voie \ˌku̇r-bə-ˈvwä\ commune N France on the Seine NW of Paris *pop* 69,665
Cour·land \ˈku̇r-lənd, ˈkür-ˌlänt\ region W Latvia bordering on the Baltic & Gulf of Riga
Courland Lagoon *or Ger* **Kur·isch·es Haff** \ˈku̇r-i-shəs-ˈhäf\ *or Russ* **Kur·skiy Za·liv** \ˈku̇r-skē-ˈzä-lif\ inlet of the Baltic on border bet. Lithuania & Russia *area* 625 *sq mi* (1625 *sq km*)
Cour·ma·yeur \ˌku̇r-mə-ˈyər\ resort village NW Italy in Valle d'Aosta SE of Mont Blanc
Courtrai — see KORTRIJK
Cov·en·try 1 \ˈkə-vən-trē\ town W R.I. *pop* 35,014 2 \ˈkä-, ˈkə-\ city *cen* England in W. Midlands *pop* 292,500
Co·vi·na \kō-ˈvē-nə\ city SW Calif. E of Los Angeles *pop* 47,796
Cov·ing·ton \ˈkə-viŋ-tən\ city N Ky. *pop* 40,640
Cowes \ˈkau̇z\ town S England on Isle of Wight *pop* 19,663
Cow·litz \ˈkau̇-ləts\ river 130 *mi* (209 *km*) SW Wash. flowing into Columbia River
Co·zu·mel \ˌkō-sü-ˈmel, ˌkä-zə-\ island SE Mexico off Quintana Roo
Cracow — see KRAKÓW
Craig·av·on \krā-ˈga-vən\ district *cen* Northern Ireland, established 1974 *area* 147 *sq mi* (381 *sq km*), *pop* 74,494
Cra·io·va \krä-ˈyō-vä\ city S Romania *pop* 302,622
Cran·ston \ˈkran(t)-stən\ city E R.I. S of Providence *pop* 80,387
Cra·ter Lake \ˈkrā-tər\ lake 1932 *ft* (589 *m*) deep SW Oreg. in Cascade Range at altitude of 6164 *ft* (1879 *m*); main feature of **Crater Lake National Park**
Craters of the Moon National Monument area of lava flows & other volcanic formations SE *cen* Idaho
Cré·cy \krā-ˈsē, ˈkre-sē\ *or* **Cré·cy–en–Pon·thieu** \krā-ˈsē-ˌäⁿ-pōⁿ-ˈtyə(r), -ˈtyœ\ commune N France NW of Amiens
Cre·mo·na \krā-ˈmō-nä\ commune N Italy in Lombardy on the Po ESE of Milan *pop* 71,421 — **Crem·o·nese** \ˌkre-mə-ˈnēz, -ˈnēs\ *adj*
Crete \ˈkrēt\ *or Gk* **Krí·ti** \ˈkrē-tē\ *or It* **Can·dia** \ˈkan-dē-ə, ˈkän-\ island Greece in the E Mediterranean * Iráklion *area* 3189 *sq mi* (8260 *sq km*), *pop* 536,980 — **Cre·tan** \ˈkrē-tᵊn\ *adj or n*

Crete, Sea of *or formerly* **Sea of Can·dia** \ˈkan-dē-ə\ the S section of Aegean Sea bet. Crete & the Cyclades
Crewe \ˈkrü\ town NW England in Cheshire *pop* 47,759
Cri·mea \krī-ˈmē-ə, krə-\ *or* **Cri·me·an Peninsula** \krī-ˈmē-ən, krə-\ peninsula S Ukraine, extending into Black Sea SW of Sea of Azov — **Crimean** *adj*
Cris·to·bal \kri-ˈstō-bəl\ *or Sp* **Cris·tó·bal** \krē-ˈstō-väl\ town N Panama adjoining Colón at Caribbean entrance to Panama Canal
Cro·a·tia \krō-ˈā-sh(ē-)ə\ independent country SE Europe including Slavonia, most of Istria, & the Dalmatian coast; a constituent republic of Yugoslavia 1946–91 ✻ Zagreb *area* 21,829 *sq mi* (56,537 *sq km*), *pop* 4,437,460
Crocodile — see LIMPOPO
Cros·by \ˈkrȯz-bē\ *or* **Great Crosby** town NW England in Merseyside on Irish Sea NNW of Liverpool *pop* 53,660
Cross \ˈkrȯs\ river 300 *mi* (483 *km*) W Africa in W Cameroon & SE Nigeria flowing W & S into Gulf of Guinea
Cro·ton \ˈkrō-tᵊn\ river 60 *mi* (95 *km*) SE N.Y. flowing into the Hudson
Cro·to·ne \krō-ˈtō-nā\ *or anc* **Cro·to·na** \-nə\ *or* **Cro·ton** \ˈkrō-ˌtän, ˈkrō-tᵊn\ commune S Italy in Calabria on Gulf of Taranto *pop* 59,757
Croy·don \ˈkrȯi-dᵊn\ borough of S Greater London, England *pop* 299,600
Cro·zet Islands \krō-ˈzā\ islands S Indian Ocean WNW of Kerguelen; a French dependency
Crys·tal \ˈkris-tᵊl\ city SE Minn. N of Minneapolis *pop* 22,151
Crystal Lake city N Ill. *pop* 40,743
Cte·si·phon \ˈte-sə-ˌfän, ˈtē-\ ancient city *cen* Iraq on the Tigris opposite Seleucia ✻ of Parthia & of later Sassanid empire
Cuan·za *or* **Kwan·za** \ˈkwän-zä\ river 600 *mi* (965 *km*) SW Africa in *cen* Angola flowing NW into the Atlantic
Cu·ba \ˈkyü-bə, ˈkü-vä\ **1** island in the W. Indies N of Caribbean Sea *area* 41,620 *sq mi* (107,800 *sq km*) **2** country largely coextensive with island; a republic ✻ Havana *area* 42,804 *sq mi* (110,862 *sq km*), *pop* 11,177,743 — **Cu·ban** \ˈkyü-bən\ *adj or n*
Cubango — see OKAVANGO
Cú·cu·ta \ˈkü-kü-tä\ city N Colombia near Venezuela border *pop* 568,000
Cud·a·hy \ˈkə-də-ˌhē *by residents usu* -ˌhā\ city SW Calif. NW of Downey *pop* 23,805
Cuen·ca \ˈkweŋ-kä\ **1** city S Ecuador *pop* 194,981 **2** province E *cen* Spain *area* 6587 *sq mi* (17,060 *sq km*), *pop* 200,346 **3** commune, its ✻, ESE of Madrid *pop* 46,341
Cuer·na·va·ca \ˌkwer-nä-ˈvä-kä\ city S *cen* Mexico S of Mexico City ✻ of Morelos *pop* 281,752
Cu·ia·bá \ˌkü-yə-ˈbä\ city SW Brazil ✻ of Mato Grosso *pop* 483,346
Cu·lia·cán \ˌkül-yä-ˈkän\ **1** river 175 *mi* (282 *km*) NW Mexico flowing SW into the Pacific at mouth of Gulf of California **2** city NW Mexico on the Culiacán ✻ of Sinaloa *pop* 696,262
Cul·lo·den Moor \kə-ˈlä-dᵊn, -ˈlō-\ moorland N Scotland in N Highland region E of Inverness
Cul·ver City \ˈkəl-vər\ city SW Calif. *pop* 38,883
Cu·mae \ˈkyü-(ˌ)mē\ ancient town S Italy on Tyrrhenian coast W of modern Naples — **Cu·mae·an** \kyü-ˈmē-ən\ *adj*
Cu·ma·ná \ˌkü-mä-ˈnä\ city & port NE Venezuela on the Caribbean NE of Barcelona *pop* 212,492
Cum·ber·land \ˈkəm-bər-lənd\ **1** river 687 *mi* (1106 *km*) S Ky. & N Tenn. flowing W into Ohio River **2** town NE R.I. *pop* 33,506 **3** former county NW England ✻ Carlisle — see CUMBRIA
Cumberland Caverns caverns *cen* Tenn. SE of McMinnville
Cumberland Falls falls SE Ky. in upper course of Cumberland River
Cumberland Gap mountain pass 1640 *ft* (500 *m*) NE Tenn. through a ridge of the Cumberland Plateau SE of Middlesboro, Ky.
Cumberland Plateau tableland E U.S., part of the S Appalachian Mountains W of Tennessee River extending from S W.Va. to NE Ala.
Cumbre, La — see USPALLATA PASS
Cum·bria \ˈkəm-brē-ə\ county NW England including former counties of Cumberland & Westmorland ✻ Carlisle *area* 2724 *sq mi* (7055 *sq km*), *pop* 486,900 — **Cum·bri·an** \ˈkəm-brē-ən\ *adj or n*
Cumbrian Mountains mountains NW England chiefly in Cumbria & Lancashire — see SCAFELL PIKE
Cu·naxa \kyü-ˈnak-sə\ town in ancient Babylonia NW of Babylon
Cu·ne·ne *or* **Ku·ne·ne** \kü-ˈnā-nə\ river 700 *mi* (1126 *km*) SW Africa in SW Angola flowing S & W into the Atlantic
Cu·par \ˈkü-pər\ burgh E Scotland S of Dundee *pop* 6642
Cu·per·ti·no \ˌkü-pər-ˈtē-(ˌ)nō\ city W Calif. W of San José *pop* 58,302
Cu·ra·çao \ˌku̇r-ə-ˈsau̇, ˌkyu̇r-, -ˈsō, -ˈsä-ˌō\ internally self-governing Dutch island in the S Caribbean; chief town Willemstad *area* 182 *sq mi* (471 *sq km*), *pop* 143,816
Cu·ri·ti·ba \ˌku̇r-ə-ˈtē-bə\ city S Brazil ✻ of Paraná *pop* 1,587,315
Cush *or* **Kush** \ˈkəsh, ˈku̇sh\ ancient country NE Africa in Nile valley S of Egypt — **Cush·ite** \ˈkə-ˌshīt, ˈku̇-\ *adj or n* — **Cush·it·ic** \ˌkə-ˈshi-tik, ku̇-\ *adj*
Cut·tack \ˈkə-tək\ city E India in Orissa *pop* 535,139
Cux·ha·ven \ˈku̇ks-ˌhä-fᵊn\ city & port NW Germany on North Sea at mouth of the Elbe *pop* 56,328
Cuy·a·hoga \ˌkī-(ə-)ˈhō-gə, kə-ˈhō-, -ˈhä-, -ˈhȯ-\ river 100 *mi* (161 *km*) NE Ohio flowing into Lake Erie at Cleveland; part of its valley forms **Cuyahoga Valley National Park**
Cuyahoga Falls city NE Ohio N of Akron *pop* 49,652
Cu·yu·ni \kü-ˈyü-nē\ river 350 *mi* (563 *km*) N S. America rising in E Venezuela & flowing E into the Essequibo in N Guyana
Cuz·co *or* **Cus·co** \ˈküs-(ˌ)kō\ city S Peru *pop* 316,804
Cyc·la·des \ˈsi-klə-ˌdēz\ *or ModGk* **Ki·klá·dhes** \kē-ˈklä-(ˌ)t͟hes\ islands Greece in the S Aegean *area* 993 *sq mi* (2572 *sq km*), *pop* 95,083 — **Cy·clad·ic** \si-ˈkla-dik, sī-\ *adj*
Cydonia — see CANEA — **Cy·do·nian** \sī-ˈdō-nē-ən, -nyən\ *adj or n*
Cymru — see WALES
Cy·press \ˈsī-prəs\ city SW Calif. SE of Los Angeles *pop* 47,802
Cy·prus \ˈsī-prəs\ **1** island E Mediterranean S of Turkey **2** country coextensive with the island; a republic of the Commonwealth of Nations ✻ Nicosia *area* 3572 *sq mi* (9287 *sq km*), *pop* 1,100,000 — **Cyp·ri·ot** \ˈsi-prē-ət, -ˌät\ *or* **Cyp·ri·ote** \-ˌōt, -ət\ *adj or n*
Cy·re·na·ica \ˌsir-ə-ˈnā-ə-kə, ˌsī-rə-\ *or It* **Ci·re·na·ica** *same or* ˌchē-rä-ˈnä-ē-(ˌ)kä\ **1** *or* **Cy·re·ne** \sī-ˈrē-(ˌ)nē\ ancient coastal region N Africa dominated by city of Cyrene **2** region E Libya; formerly a province — **Cy·re·na·ic** \ˌsir-ə-ˈnā-ik, ˌsī-rə-\ *adj or n* — **Cy·re·na·ican** \-ˈnā-ə-kən\ *adj or n*
Cy·re·ne \sī-ˈrē-(ˌ)nē\ ancient city N Africa on the Mediterranean in NE Libya — **Cy·re·ni·an** \-nē-ən\ *adj or n*
Cyz·i·cus \ˈsi-zi-kəs\ **1** — see KAPIDAGI **2** ancient city in Mysia on isthmus leading to Kapidagi Peninsula
Czech·o·slo·va·kia \ˌche-kə-slō-ˈvä-kē-ə, -slə-, -ˈva-\ country 1918–92 *cen* Europe; a republic ✻ Prague *area* 49,371 *sq mi* (127,871 *sq km*); divided Jan. 1, 1993 into separate countries of Czech Republic & Slovakia — **Czech·o·slo·vak** \-ˈslō-ˌväk, -ˌvak\ *adj or n* — **Czech·o·slo·va·ki·an** \-slō-ˈvä-kē-ən, -slə-, -ˈva-\ *adj or n*
Czech Republic *or informally* **Czech·ia**\ˈche-kē-ə\country *cen* Europe; a constituent republic of Czechoslovakia 1918–92 ✻ Prague *area* 30,450 *sq mi* (78,866 *sq km*), *pop* 10,332,000
Cze·sto·cho·wa \ˌchen(t)-stə-ˈkō-və\ *or Russ* **Chen·sto·khov** \ˌchen(t)-stə-ˈkȯf, -ˈkȯv\ city S Poland on the Warta *pop* 258,700
Da — see BLACK
Da·bro·wa Gor·ni·cza \dȯⁿ-ˈbrȯ-vä-gu̇r-ˈnē-chä\ city S Poland *pop* 139,200
Dacca — see DHAKA
Da·chau \ˈdä-ˌkau̇, -ˌkau̇\ city S Germany in S Bavaria *pop* 35,892; site of Nazi concentration camp during World War II
Da·cia \ˈdā-sh(ē-)ə\ ancient country & Roman province SE Europe roughly equivalent to Romania & Bessarabia — **Da·cian** \-shən\ *adj or n*
Da·dra and Na·gar Ha·ve·li \də-ˈdrä . . . ˌnə-gər-ə-ˈve-lē\ union territory India bordering on Gujarat and Maharashtra ✻ Silvassa *area* 189 *sq mi* (491 *sq km*), *pop* 220,451
Daegu — see TAEGU
Daejeon — see TAEJON
Dag·en·ham \ˈda-gə-nəm, ˈdag-nəm\ former municipal borough SE England in Essex, now part of Barking and Dagenham
Da·ge·stan *or* **Da·ghe·stan** \ˌda-gə-ˈstan, ˌdä-gə-ˈstän\ autonomous republic SE Russia in Europe on W shore of the Caspian ✻ Makhachkala *area* 19,421 *sq mi* (50,300 *sq km*), *pop* 1,890,000
Dahomey — see BENIN — **Da·ho·man** \də-ˈhō-mən\ *adj or n* — **Da·ho·me·an** \-mē-ən\ *or* **Da·ho·mey·an** \-mē-ən\ *adj or n*
Da·kar \ˈda-ˌkär, dä-ˈkär\ city & port ✻ of Senegal *pop* 2,200,000
Dakh·la \ˈdä-klə\ *or formerly* **Vil·la Cis·ne·ros** \ˌvē-yə-sis-ˈner-ōs\ town & port NW Africa in Western Sahara ✻ of Río de Oro
Da·ko·ta \də-ˈkō-tə\ **1** — see JAMES 1 **2** territory (1861–89) NW U.S. divided 1889 into states of N.D. & S.D. (the **Da·ko·tas** \-təz\) — **Da·ko·tan** \-ˈkō-tᵊn\ *adj or n*
Dal·e·car·lia \ˌdä-lə-ˈkär-lē-ə\ region W *cen* Sweden — **Dal·e·car·li·an** \-lē-ən\ *adj*
Da·lian *or* **Ta–lien** \ˈdä-ˈlyen\ *or* **Lu·da** *or* **Lu–ta** \ˈlü-ˈdä\ *or* **Dai·ren** \ˈdī-ˈren\ city NE China in S Liaoning on Liaodong Peninsula *pop* 1,723,302
Dal·las \ˈda-ləs, -lis\ city NE Tex. on Trinity River *pop* 1,197,816 — **Dal·las·ite** \ˈda-lə-ˌsīt\ *n*
Dal·ma·tia \dal-ˈmā-sh(ē-)ə\ region W Balkan Peninsula on the Adriatic in Croatia extending into Bosnia and Herzegovina & Montenegro — **Dal·ma·tian** \-shən\ *adj or n*
Dal·ton \ˈdȯl-tᵊn\ city NW Ga. *pop* 33,128
Da·ly City \ˈdā-lē\ city W Calif. S of San Francisco *pop* 101,123
Da·man \də-ˈmän, -ˈman\ *or* **Da·mão** \də-ˈmau̇ⁿ\ district W India on Gulf of Khambhat; a constituent part of the union territory of **Daman and Diu** (*area* 36 *sq mi or* 93 *sq km*, *pop* 158,059) — see GOA, PORTUGUESE INDIA
Da·man·hûr \ˌda-mən-ˈhu̇r\ city N Egypt E of Alexandria *pop* 244,043
Da·mas·cus \də-ˈmas-kəs\ city SW Syria, its ✻ *pop* 1,451,000
Dam·a·vand \ˈda-mə-ˌvand\ *or* **Dem·a·vend** \ˈde-mə-ˌvend\ mountain 18,606 *ft* (5671 *m*) N Iran; highest in Elburz Mountains
Dam·i·et·ta \ˌda-mē-ˈe-tə\ city & port N Egypt *pop* 206,664
Dammam — see AD DAMMĀM
Da·mo·dar \ˈdä-mə-ˌdär\ river 368 *mi* (592 *km*) NE India in *cen* Bihar & W. Bengal flowing ESE into the Hugli
Dan \ˈdan\ **1** river 180 *mi* (290 *km*) S Va. & N N.C. flowing E into Roanoke River **2** village at N extremity of ancient Palestine
Da Nang \(ˌ)dä-ˈnäŋ, -ˈnaŋ\ *or formerly* **Tou·rane** \tü-ˈrän\ city & port *cen* Vietnam in Annam *pop* 724,000
Da·na Point \ˈdā-nə\ coastal city S Calif. S of Los Angeles *pop* 33,351
Dan·bury \ˈdan-ˌber-ē, -b(ə-)rē\ city SW Conn. *pop* 80,893
Dan·dong \ˈdän-ˈdu̇ŋ\ *or* **An·tung** \ˈän-ˈdu̇ŋ\ *or* **Tan–tung** \ˈdän-ˈdu̇ŋ\ city & port NE China in SE Liaoning at mouth of the Yalu *pop* 523,699
Danger Islands — see PUKAPUKA
Danish West Indies the W Virgin Islands that were until 1917 a Danish possession & now constitute the Virgin Islands of the U.S.
Danmark — see DENMARK
Dan·ube \ˈdan-(ˌ)yüb\ *or G* **Do·nau** \ˈdō-ˌnau̇\ *or anc* **Da·nu·bi·us** \də-ˈnü-bē-əs, da-, -ˈnyü-\ *or* **Is·ter** \ˈis-tər\ river 1771 *mi* (2850 *km*) *cen* & SE Europe flowing SE from SW Germany into Black Sea — **Da·nu·bi·an** \da-ˈnyü-bē-ən\ *adj*
Dan·vers \ˈdan-vərz\ town NE Mass. N of Lynn *pop* 26,493
Dan·ville \ˈdan-ˌvil\ **1** city W Calif. E of Oakland *pop* 42,039 **2** city E Ill. *pop* 33,027 **3** city S Va. on Dan River *pop* 43,055
Dan·zig \ˈdan(t)-sig, ˈdän(t)-\ **1** — see GDAŃSK **2** territory surrounding & including Gdańsk that (1920–39) constituted a free city under the League of Nations
Danzig, Gulf of — see GDAŃSK (Gulf of)
Dar·da·nelles \ˌdär-də-ˈnelz\ *or* **Hel·les·pont** \ˈhe-lə-ˌspänt\ *or anc* **Hel·les·pon·tus** \ˌhe-lə-ˈspän-təs\ strait NW Turkey connecting Sea of Marmara with the Aegean
Dar el Beida — see CASABLANCA
Dar es Sa·laam \ˌdär-ˌe(s)-sə-ˈläm\ city & port; historic ✻ of Tanzania on Indian Ocean *pop* 2,300,000

Dar·fur \där-'fúr\ region W Sudan; chief city El Fasher

Dar·i·én \‚där-ē-'en, ‚där-\ Spanish colonial settlement Central America W of Gulf of Darien

Darien, Gulf of inlet of the Caribbean bet. E Panama & NW Colombia

Darien, Isthmus of — see PANAMA (Isthmus of)

Dar·jee·ling or **Dar·ji·ling** \där-'jē-liŋ\ city NE India in W. Bengal on Sikkim border pop 107,530

Dar·ling \'där-liŋ\ river ab 1700 mi (2735 km) SE Australia in Queensland & New South Wales flowing SW into Murray River

Darling Range mountains SW Western Australia extending ab 250 mi (400 km) N–S along coast; highest point Mt. Cooke 1910 ft (582 m)

Dar·ling·ton \'där-liŋ-tən\ town N England in Durham pop 96,700

Darm·stadt \'därm-‚stat, -‚shtät, -‚stät\ city cen Germany in Hesse SSW of Frankfurt am Main pop 140,040

Dar·nah \'där-nə\ or **Der·na** \'der-\ city & port NE Libya

Dart·moor \'därt-‚múr, -‚mòr\ tableland SW England in S Devon area 365 sq mi (945 sq km)

Dart·mouth \'därt-məth\ 1 town SE Mass. W of New Bedford pop 34,032 2 town & port SW England in S Devon on Dart River pop 6298

Dar·win \'där-wən\ city & port N Australia ✲ of Northern Territory on **Port Darwin** (inlet of Timor Sea) pop 70,071

Da·tong \'dä-'túŋ\ or **Ta·tung** \'dä-'túŋ\ city NE China in N Shanxi pop 798,319

Dau·gav·pils \'daú-gəf-‚pilz\ or Russ **Dvinsk** \də-'vin(t)sk\ city E Latvia on Western Dvina River pop 113,409

Dau·phin \'dò-fin\ island SW Alabama at entrance to Mobile Bay

Dau·phi·né \‚dò-fē-'nā\ region & former province SE France N of Provence ✲ Grenoble

Da·vao \'dä-‚vaú, dä-'vaú\ city Philippines on Davao Gulf pop 850,000

Davao Gulf gulf of the Pacific Philippines in SE Mindanao

Dav·en·port \'da-vən-‚pòrt\ city E Iowa on Mississippi River pop 99,685

Da·vid \dä-'vēth\ town W Panama pop 77,057

Da·vie \'dä-vē\ city SE Fla. pop 91,992

Da·vis \'dä-vəs\ city W Calif. W of Sacramento pop 65,622

Davis Mountains mountains W Tex. N of the Big Bend of the Rio Grande

Davis Strait strait connecting Baffin Bay with the Atlantic

Daw·son \'dò-s°n\ town N Canada in Yukon pop 1319

Dax \'däks\ commune SW France in the Landes on the Adour NE of Biarritz pop 19,557

Day·ton \'dä-t°n\ city SW Ohio on Miami River pop 141,527

Day·to·na Beach \dä-'tō-nə, də-\ city NE Fla. pop 61,005

Da Yunhe — see GRAND CANAL

Dead Sea or bib **Salt Sea** or L **La·cus As·phal·ti·tes** \'lā-kəs-‚as-‚fòl-'tī-tēz\ salt lake ab 50 mi (80 km) long on boundary bet. Israel & Jordan area 350 sq mi (962 sq km), surface 1312 ft (400 m) below sea level

Dean, Forest of \'dēn\ forested district SW England in W Gloucestershire bet. Severn & Wye rivers; an ancient royal forest

Dear·born \'dir-‚bòrn, -bərn\ city SE Mich. pop 98,153

Dearborn Heights city SE Mich. W of Detroit pop 57,774

Death Valley arid valley E Calif. & S Nev. containing lowest point in the U.S. at 282 ft (86 m) below sea level; most of area included in **Death Valley National Park**

Deau·ville \'dò-‚vil, dō-'vēl\ town NW France on Bay of the Seine SSW of Le Havre pop 4371

De·bre·cen \'de-bret-‚sen\ city E Hungary pop 222,300

De·cap·o·lis \di-'ka-pə-lis\ confederation of 10 ancient cities N Palestine in region chiefly SE of Sea of Galilee

De·ca·tur \di-'kā-tər\ 1 city N Ala. pop 55,683 2 city cen Ill. pop 76,122

Dec·can \'de-kən, -‚kan\ plateau region S cen India lying bet. Eastern Ghats & Western Ghats

Ded·ham \'de-dəm\ town E Mass. SW of Boston pop 24,729

Dee \'dē\ 1 river 87 mi (140 km) NE Scotland flowing E into North Sea 2 river 50 mi (80 km) S Scotland flowing S into Solway Firth 3 river 70 mi (113 km) N Wales & W England flowing E & N into Irish Sea

Deep South region SE U.S. — usu. considered to include Ala., Ga., La., Miss., N.C., S.C., and all or part of the adjacent states of Fla., Va., Tenn., Ark., & Tex.

Deer·field Beach \'dir-‚fēld\ city SE Fla. N of Fort Lauderdale pop 75,018

Deer Park city SE Tex. pop 32,010

De·hi·wa·la–Mount La·vin·ia \dä-hē-'wä-lə . . . lə-'vi-nē-ə\ town W Sri Lanka on coast S of Colombo pop 193,000

Deh·ra Dun \‚der-ə-'dün\ city N India ✲ of Uttarakhand pop 447,808

De Kalb \di-'kalb\ city N Ill. pop 43,862

Del·a·goa Bay \‚de-lə-'gō-ə\ inlet of Indian Ocean S Mozambique

De·la·no \də-'lā-(‚)nō\ city S Calif. NNW of Bakersfield pop 53,041

Del·a·ware \'de-lə-‚wer, -wər\ 1 river 296 mi (476 km) E U.S. flowing S from S N.Y. into Delaware Bay 2 state E U.S. ✲ Dover area 2057 sq mi (5348 sq km), pop 897,934 3 city cen Ohio NNW of Columbus pop 34,753 — **Del·a·war·ean** \‚de-lə-'wer-ē-ən\ n

Delaware Bay inlet of the Atlantic bet. SW N.J. & E Del.

De·lé·mont \də-lā-'mō⁼⁼\ commune NW Switzerland ✲ of Jura canton pop 11,467

Delft \'delft\ commune SW Netherlands pop 96,936

Del·ga·do, Cape \del-'gä-(‚)dō\ cape NE Mozambique

Del·hi \'de-lē\ 1 union territory N India W of Uttar Pradesh ✲ Delhi area 573 sq mi (1484 sq km), pop 13,782,976 2 city, its ✲ pop 12,791,458 — see NEW DELHI

Del·mar·va Peninsula \del-'mär-və\ peninsula E U.S. bet. Chesapeake & Delaware bays comprising Del. & parts of Md. & Va. — see EASTERN SHORE

Del·men·horst \'del-mən-‚hòrst\ city NW Germany in Lower Saxony WSW of Bremen pop 75,067

De·los \'dē-‚läs\ or Gk **Dhí·los** \'thē-‚lòs\ island Greece in cen Cyclades area 2 sq mi (5.2 sq km) — **De·lian** \'dē-lē-ən, 'dēl-yən\ adj or n

Del·phi \'del-‚fī\ ancient town cen Greece in Phocis on S slope of Mt. Parnassus near present village of **Dhel·foí** \‚thel-'fē\

Del·ray Beach \del-'rā\ city SE Fla. S of W. Palm Beach pop 60,522

Del Rio \del-'rē-(‚)ō\ city S Tex. on Rio Grande pop 35,591

Del·ta \'del-tə\ municipality Canada in SW B.C. pop 99,863

Delta, The region NW Miss. bet. Mississippi & Yazoo rivers — **Delta** adj

Del·to·na \del-'tō-nə\ city Fla. N of Orlando pop 85,182

Demavend — see DAMAVEND

Dem·e·ra·ra \‚de-mə-'rär-ə, -'ra-rə\ river 200 mi (322 km) Guyana flowing N into the Atlantic

Denali, Denali National Park — see MCKINLEY (Mount)

Den·bigh \'den-bē\ or **Den·bigh·shire** \-‚shir, -shər\ administrative area of N Wales area 326 sq mi (844 sq km)

Den·der·mon·de \‚den-dər-'män-də\ or F **Ter·monde** \ter-'mō⁼⁼d\ commune NW cen Belgium pop 43,168

Den Hel·der \dən-'hel-dər\ commune W Netherlands in N. Holland on an outlet from Waddenzee to North Sea pop 60,083

Den·i·son \'de-nə-sən\ city NE Tex. on Red River pop 22,682

De·niz·li \de-naz-'lē\ city SW Turkey SE of Izmir pop 204,118

Den·mark \'den-‚märk\ or Dan **Dan·mark** \'dän-‚märk\ country N Europe occupying most of Jutland Peninsula & adjacent islands in Baltic & North seas; a kingdom ✲ Copenhagen area 16,629 sq mi (43,069 sq km), pop 5,500,000

Denmark Strait strait 130 mi (209 km) wide bet. SE Greenland & Iceland connecting Arctic Ocean with the Atlantic

Dent Blanche \dän-'blän̄sh\ mountain 14,295 ft (4357 m) S Switzerland in Pennine Alps

Dent du Mi·di \‚dän-dư-mē-'dē\ mountain 10,686 ft (3257 m) SW Switzerland in W Alps

Den·ton \'den-t°n\ city N Tex. NW of Dallas pop 113,383

D'En·tre·cas·teaux Islands \‚dän-trə-'kas-(‚)tō\ islands SW Pacific N of E tip of New Guinea belonging to Papua New Guinea area 1200 sq mi (3120 sq km), pop 38,894

Den·ver \'den-vər\ city NE cen Colo., its ✲ pop 600,158 — **Den·ver·ite** \-və-‚rīt\ n

Dept·ford \'det-fərd\ former metropolitan borough SE London, England, now part of Lewisham

Der·be \'dər-(‚)bē\ ancient town S Asia Minor in S Lycaonia on border of Cilicia; exact site unknown

Der·bent or **Der·bend** \dər-'bent\ city S Russia in Europe in Dagestan on Caspian Sea pop 81,500

Der·by \'där-bē, chiefly U.S. 'dər-\ city N cen England in Derbyshire pop 214,000

Der·by·shire \'där-bē-‚shir, -shər; US also 'dər-\ or **Derby** county N cen England ✲ Matlock area 1052 sq mi (2725 sq km), pop 914,600

Derna — see DARNAH

Der·ry \'der-ē\ 1 city SE N.H. SE of Manchester pop 33,109 2 or **Lon·don·der·ry** \‚lən-dən-'der-ē; 'lən-dən-‚der-ē, -d(ə-)rē\ district NW Northern Ireland, established 1974 area 148 sq mi (383 sq km), pop 94,918 3 or **Londonderry** port NW Derry district pop 62,697

Der·went \'dər-wənt\ river more than 105 mi (170 km) Australia in Tasmania flowing SE into Tasman Sea

Derwent Water lake NW England in Lake District in Cumbria

Desaguadero — see SALADO

Des·chutes \dā-'shüt\ river 250 mi (402 km) cen & N Oreg. E of Cascade Range flowing N into Columbia River

Des·er·et \‚de-zə-'ret\ provisional state of the U.S. S of 42d parallel & W of the Rockies organized 1849 by Mormons

Des Moines \di-'mòin\ 1 river 327 mi (526 km) Iowa flowing SE into Mississippi River 2 city ✲ of Iowa on Des Moines River pop 203,433 3 \also -'mòinz\ city W Wash. S of Seattle pop 29,673

Des·na \dyi-'snä\ river 550 mi (885 km) SW Russia in Europe & N Ukraine flowing S into the Dnieper

DeSo·to \di-'sō-(‚)tō\ city NE Tex. S of Dallas pop 49,047

Des Plaines \des-'plānz\ 1 river 150 mi (241 km) NE Ill. flowing S to unite with Kankakee River forming Illinois River 2 city NE Ill. NW of Chicago pop 58,364

Des·roches \dā-'ròsh\ island NW Indian Ocean NNE of Madagascar belonging to Seychelles

Des·sau \'de-‚saú\ city cen Germany NE of Halle pop 95,097

De·troit \di-'tròit, locally also 'dē-\ 1 river 31 mi (50 km) Ont. & SE Mich. connecting Lake Erie & Lake Saint Clair 2 city SE Mich. on Detroit River pop 713,777 — **De·troit·er** \di-'tròi-tər\ n

Detskoe Selo — see PUSHKIN

Deutsche Demokratische Republik — see GERMANY

Deutschland — see GERMANY

De·ven·ter \'dä-vən-tər\ commune E Netherlands pop 86,072

Devil Mountain — see AUYÁN-TEPUÍ

Devil's Island or F **Ile du Dia·ble** \‚ēl-dư-'dyäbl'\ island French Guiana in the Safety Islands group; former penal colony

Devils Post·pile \'pōst-‚pī(-ə)l\ lava formation E cen Calif. SE of Yosemite National Park in **Devils Postpile National Monument**

Devils Tower or **Ma·to Tepee** \'mä-tō\ columnar rock formation NE Wyo. rising 867 ft (264 m) in **Devils Tower National Monument**

Dev·on \'de-vən\ or **Dev·on·shire** \'de-vən-‚shir, -shər\ county SW England ✲ Exeter area 2686 sq mi (6957 sq km), pop 998,200

Devon Island island Nunavut, Canada, in E Parry Islands N of Baffin Is. area 20,861 sq mi (54,023 sq km)

Dews·bury \'dūz-‚ber-ē, 'dyüz-, -b(ə-)rē\ town N England in W. Yorkshire S of Leeds pop 48,339

Dez \'dez\ river 250 mi (402 km) W Iran flowing S to the Karun

Dezh·nev, Cape \'dezh-nyif\ or Russ **Mys Dezh·ne·va** \'mis-‚dezh-'nyò-və, -‚desh-\ cape NE Russia in Asia at E end of Chukchi Peninsula

Dhah·ran \dä-'rän, ‚thäh-'ran\ town SE Saudi Arabia on Persian Gulf near Bahrain Islands pop 12,500

Dha·ka \'dä-kə\ or **Dac·ca** \'da-kə, 'dä-\ city ✲ of Bangladesh pop 6,482,877

Dhau·la·gi·ri, Mount \‚daú-lə-'gir-ē\ mountain 26,810 ft (8172 m) W cen Nepal in the Himalayas

Di·a·blo, Mount \dē-'ä-(‚)blō, dē-'a-\ mountain 3849 ft (1173 m) cen Calif. at N end of **Diablo Range**

Di·a·man·ti·na \‚dī-ə-‚man-'tē-nə\ intermittent river maximum length 560 mi (901 km) E cen Australia in SW Queensland flowing SW into Warburton Creek 2 \dē-ə-‚män-\ city E Brazil in cen Minas Gerais pop 26,075

Di·a·mond \'dī-(ə-)mənd\ or **Kum·gang** \'kùm-‚gäŋ\ mountains SE N. Korea; highest 5374 ft (1638 m)

Diamond Bar city S Calif. E of Los Angeles pop 55,544

Diamond Head promontory Hawaii on Oahu Is. in SE Honolulu

Die·go Gar·cia \dē-ˌā-gō-gär-'sē-ə\ island in Indian Ocean, chief island of Chagos Archipelago

Diégo–Suarez — see ANTSIRANANA

Dien Bien Phu \dyen-ˌbyen-'fü\ village NW Vietnam

Dieppe \'dyep\ city & port N France N of Rouen *pop* 34,644

Di·jon \dē-'zhōⁿ\ city E France *pop* 150,138

Diks·mui·de or **Dix·mui·de** \dik-'smī-də\ or **Dix·mude** \dēk-'smued\ town W Belgium in W. Flanders N of Ieper *pop* 15,480

Di·li or **Dil·li** \'di-lē\ city & port N Timor ✳ of East Timor

Di·mi·trov·grad \də-'mē-trəf-ˌgrad, -ˌgrät\ city S Bulgaria on the Maritsa ESE of Plovdiv *pop* 56,882

Di·nar·ic Alps \də-'na-rik\ range of E Alps W Slovenia, W Croatia, Bosnia and Herzegovina, & Montenegro; highest point 8274 *ft* (2522 *m*)

Din·gle Bay \'diŋ-gəl\ inlet of the Atlantic SW Ireland

Ding·wall \'diŋ-ˌwȯl\ burgh N Scotland NW of Inverness *pop* 4815

Dinosaur National Monument area containing rich fossil deposits NW Colo. & NE Utah at junction of Green & Yampa rivers

Di·o·mede Islands \'dī-ə-ˌmēd\ islands in Bering Strait comprising **Big Diomede** (Russia) & **Little Diomede** (U.S.)

Diospolis — see THEBES 1

Di·re Da·wa \ˌdē-rä-'daü-ä\ city E Ethiopia *pop* 237,012

Disko — see QEQERTARSUAQ

Dismal Swamp or **Great Dismal Swamp** swamp SE Va. & NE N.C. bet. Chesapeake Bay & Albemarle Sound *ab* 37 *mi* (60 *km*) long, 10 *mi* (16 *km*) wide

Dis·pur \dis-'pür\ city E India ✳ of Assam

District of Co·lum·bia \kə-'ləm-bē-ə\ federal district E U.S. coextensive with city of Washington *area* 69 *sq mi* (179 *sq km*), *pop* 601,723

Dis·tri·to Fe·de·ral \dē-ˌstrē-tō-ˌfā-thä-'räl\ **1** district E Argentina largely comprising ✳ city of Buenos Aires *area* 77 *sq mi* (199 *sq km*), *pop* 2,960,976 **2** — see FEDERAL DISTRICT 1 **3** or **Federal District** district *cen* Mexico including ✳ city of Mexico City *area* 579 *sq mi* (1500 *sq km*), *pop* 8,235,744 **4** or **Federal District** district N Venezuela including ✳ city of Caracas *area* 745 *sq mi* (1937 *sq km*), *pop* 2,103,661

Diu \'dē-(ˌ)ü\ district W India at S end of Kathiawar Peninsula; a constituent part of the union territory of Daman and Diu — see GOA, PORTUGUESE INDIA

Dix·ie \'dik-sē\ the states of the SE U.S. & esp. those which constituted the Confederacy

Di·yar·ba·kir \di-ˌyär-bä-'kir\ or **Di·ar·bekr** \-'be-kər\ city SE Turkey on the Tigris *pop* 381,144

Djakarta — see JAKARTA

Djawa — see JAVA

Djerba — see JERBA

Dji·bou·ti \jə-'bü-tē\ **1** or formerly **French Territory of the Afars and the Is·sas** \ä-ˌfär(z) . . . ē-'sä(z)\ or earlier **French Somaliland** country E Africa on Gulf of Aden; a republic *area* 8880 *sq mi* (23,088 *sq km*), *pop* 510,000 **2** city, its ✳ *pop* 300,000 — **Dji·bou·ti·an** \jə-'bü-tē-ən\ adj or n

Dnie·per \'nē-pər\ river 1420 *mi* (2285 *km*) Ukraine, E Belarus, & W Russia in Europe rising in S Valdai Hills & flowing S into Black Sea

Dnies·ter \'nēs-tər\ river 877 *mi* (1411 *km*) W Ukraine & E Moldova rising on N slope of Carpathian Mountains near Polish border & flowing SE into Black Sea

Dni·pro·dzer·zhyns'k or **Dne·pro·dzer·zhinsk** \də-ˌnye-prə-dzir-'zhēnsk\ city E Ukraine on the Dnieper *pop* 284,000

Dni·pro·pe·trovs'k or **Dne·pro·pe·trovsk** \də-ˌnye-prə-pə-'trȯfsk\ or formerly **Eka·te·ri·no·slav** \i-ˌkä-ti-'rē-nə-ˌsläf, -ˌsläv\ city E Ukraine *pop* 1,189,000

Do·be·rai \'dō-bə-ˌrī\ or formerly **Vo·gel·kop** \'vō-gəl-ˌkäp\ peninsula Indonesia in NW West Papua

Do·bru·ja or **Do·bru·dja** \'dȯ-brü-jä, -jə\ region S Europe in Romania & Bulgaria on Black Sea S of the Danube

Do·de·ca·nese \dō-'de-kə-ˌnēz, -ˌnēs; ˌdō-di-kə-'\ islands Greece in the SE Aegean comprising the Southern Sporades S of Ikaria & Samos; belonged to Italy 1923–47 *area* 486 *sq mi* (1264 *sq km*), *pop* 162,439 — see RHODES — **Do·de·ca·ne·sian** \(ˌ)dō-ˌde-kə-'nē-zhən, ˌdō-di-kə-, -shən\ adj or n

Dodge City \'däj\ city S Kans. on Arkansas River *pop* 27,340

Do·do·ma \dō-'dō-(ˌ)mä\ town NE *cen* Tanzania, the nation's legislative ✳

Dog·ger Bank \'dȯ-gər, 'dä-\ submerged sandbank *ab* 150 *mi* (241 *km*) long in North Sea E of N England

Do·ha \'dō-(ˌ)hä\ city & port ✳ of Qatar on Persian Gulf *pop* 217,294

Dol·gel·lau \dȯl-'ge-(h)lī, -'geth-,lī\ town N Wales; formerly ✳ of Merionethshire

Dol·lard–des–Or·meaux \dȯ-'lär-ˌdā-ˌzȯr-'mō\ town Canada in S Que. NW of Montreal *pop* 49,637

Do·lo·mites \'dō-lə-ˌmīts, 'dä-\ range of E Alps NE Italy bet. Adige & Piave rivers — see MARMOLADA

Dol·ton \'dōl-tᵊn\ village NE Ill. S of Chicago *pop* 23,153

Dôme, Puy de \ˌpwē-də-'dōm\ mountain 4806 *ft* (1465 *m*) S *cen* France in Auvergne Mountains

Dom·i·ni·ca \ˌdä-mə-'nē-kə, ÷də-'mi-ni-kə\ island Brit. West Indies in the Lesser Antilles; a republic of the Commonwealth of Nations since 1978 ✳ Roseau *area* 289 *sq mi* (749 *sq km*), *pop* 69,625

Do·min·i·can Republic \də-'mi-ni-kən\ or formerly **San·to Do·min·go** \ˌsan-tə-də-'miŋ-(ˌ)gō, ˌsän-tō-thō-\ or **San Domingo** \ˌsan-də-, ˌsän-dō-\ country W. Indies on E Hispaniola; a republic ✳ Santo Domingo *area* 18,657 *sq mi* (48,322 *sq km*), *pop* 8,562,541 — **Dominican** adj or n

Don \'dän\ river 1224 *mi* (1969 *km*) Russia in Europe flowing SE & then SW into Sea of Azov

Donau — see DANUBE

Don·cas·ter \'däŋ-kəs-tər\ town N England in S. Yorkshire *pop* 81,610

Don·e·gal \ˌdä-ni-'gȯl, ˌdə-\ county NW Ireland (republic) in Ulster ✳ Lifford *area* 1865 *sq mi* (4849 *sq km*), *pop* 137,575

Donegal Bay inlet of the Atlantic NW Ireland

Do·nets \də-'nets, -'nyets\ river over 630 *mi* (1014 *km*) SE Ukraine & SW Russia in Europe flowing SE into Don River

Donets Basin or **Don·bass** or **Don·bas** \dən-'bas\ region E Ukraine SW of the Donets

Do·netsk \də-'nyetsk\ or formerly **Sta·li·no** \'stä-lyi-ˌnō, 'stä-\ or **Sta·lin** \'stä-lyin, 'stä-, -ˌlēn\ city E Ukraine in Donets Basin *pop* 1,121,000

Don·ner Pass \'dä-nər\ mountain pass *ab* 7090 *ft* (2160 *m*) E Calif. in Sierra Nevada

Don·ny·brook \'dä-nē-ˌbrúk\ city E Ireland in Leinster, SE suburb of Dublin

Do·nos·tia–San Se·bas·tián \ˌdō-nō-'stē-ə-ˌsän-ˌsä-bäs-'tyän\ seaport N Spain ✳ of Guipúzcoa province *pop* 178,377

Doornik — see TOURNAI

Door Peninsula \'dȯr\ peninsula E Wis. bet. Green Bay & Lake Michigan

Do·ra·do \dō-'rä-thō\ city N Puerto Rico *pop* 38,165

Dor·ches·ter \'dȯr-chəs-tər, -ˌches-\ town S England ✳ of Dorset *pop* 14,049

Dor·dogne \dȯr-'dōn, -'dȯ-nyə\ river 293 *mi* (471 *km*) SW France flowing SW & W to unite with the Garonne forming the Gironde Estuary

Dor·drecht \'dȯr-ˌdrekt, -ˌdrekt\ commune SW Netherlands in S. Holland on the Meuse *pop* 120,222

Dore, Monts \mōⁿ-'dȯr\ mountain group S *cen* France in Auvergne Mountains — see SANCY (Puy de)

Do·ris \'dȯr-əs, 'där-\ **1** ancient country *cen* Greece bet. Oeta Mountains & Mt. Parnassus **2** ancient district SW Asia Minor on coast of Caria

Dor·noch \'dȯr-nək, -nək\ royal burgh N Scotland N of Inverness

Dorpat — see TARTU

Dor·set \'dȯr-sət\ or **Dor·set·shire** \-ˌshir, -shər\ county S England ✳ Dorchester *area* 1062 *sq mi* (2750 *sq km*), *pop* 645,200

Dort·mund \'dȯrt-ˌmunt, -mənd\ city W Germany in the Ruhr *pop* 601,007

Do·than \'dō-thən\ city SE Ala. *pop* 65,496

Dou·ai \dü-'ä\ city N France S of Lille *pop* 42,812

Dou·a·la \dü-'ä-lä\ city & port SW Cameroon on Bight of Biafra *pop* 810,000

Doug·las \'də-gləs\ town United Kingdom ✳ of Isle of Man *pop* 22,214

Dou·ro \'dȯr-(ˌ)ü\ or **Sp Due·ro** \'dwä-rō\ river 556 *mi* (895 *km*) N Spain & N Portugal flowing W into the Atlantic

Do·ver \'dō-vər\ **1** city *cen* Del., its ✳ *pop* 36,047 **2** city SE N.H. *pop* 29,987 **3** port SE England in Kent on Strait of Dover *pop* 32,843

Dover, Strait of or **F Pas de Ca·lais** \ˌpäd-kä-'lā\ channel bet. SE England & N France, easternmost section of English Channel; 20 *mi* (32 *km*) wide at narrowest point

Down \'daún\ **1** district SE Northern Ireland, established 1974 *area* 250 *sq mi* (650 *sq km*), *pop* 57,511 **2** traditional county SE Northern Ireland

Dow·ners Grove \'daú-nərz\ village NE Ill. *pop* 47,833

Dow·ney \'daú-nē\ city SW Calif. SE of Los Angeles *pop* 111,772

Down·pat·rick \daún-'pa-trik\ town SE Northern Ireland in Down district *pop* 8245

Downs \'daúnz\ **1** two ranges of hills SE England — see NORTH DOWNS, SOUTH DOWNS **2** roadstead in English Channel along E coast of Kent protected by the Goodwin Sands

Down Under Australia or New Zealand

Dra·chen·fels \'drä-kən-ˌfels\ hill 1053 *ft* (321 *m*) W Germany in the Siebengebirge on the Rhine S of Bonn

Dra·cut \'drä-kət\ town NE Mass. N of Lowell *pop* 29,457

Dra·kens·berg \'drä-kənz-ˌbərg\ or **Kwath·lam·ba** \kwät-'läm-bə\ mountains Lesotho & E Republic of S. Africa; highest Thabana Ntlenyana 11,425 *ft* (3482 *m*)

Drake Passage \'drāk\ strait S of S. America bet. Cape Horn & S. Shetlands

Dram·men \'drä-mən\ city & port SE Norway *pop* 53,825

Dran·cy \dräⁿ-'sē\ commune N France, NE of Paris *pop* 62,271

Dra·per \'drä-pər\ city N *cen* Utah S of Salt Lake City *pop* 42,274

Dra·va or **Dra·ve** \'drä-və\ river 447 *mi* (719 *km*) S Austria, NE Slovenia, & N tip of Croatia flowing SE into the Danube

Dren·the \'dren-tə\ province NE Netherlands ✳ Assen *area* 1037 *sq mi* (2686 *sq km*), *pop* 478,799

Dres·den \'drez-dən\ city E Germany ✳ of Saxony *pop* 485,132

Dri·na \'drē-nə\ river 285 *mi* (459 *km*) flowing N along the border bet. Bosnia & Serbia into the Sava

Dro·ghe·da \'drȯi-ə-də, 'drȯi-i-də\ town & port E Ireland in County Louth on the Boyne *pop* 23,845

Drum·mond·ville \'drə-mən(d)-ˌvil\ town Canada in S Que. NE of Montreal *pop* 71,852

Dry Tor·tu·gas \tȯr-'tü-gəz\ island group S Fla. W of Key West; site of **Dry Tortugas National Park**

Du·bawnt \dü-'bȯnt\ river 580 *mi* (933 *km*) N Canada flowing NE through Dubawnt Lake to **Ba·ker Lake** \'bā-kər\ (W expansion of Chesterfield Inlet)

Dubawnt Lake lake N Canada in Nunavut E of Great Slave Lake

Du·bayy or **Du·bai** \(ˌ)dü-'bī\ **1** sheikhdom, member of United Arab Emirates 1500 *sq mi* (3885 *sq km*) **2** city, its ✳ *pop* 265,702

Dub·lin \'də-blən\ or for 3 and 4 *IrGael* **Bai·le Atha Cli·ath** \blä-'klē-ə\ **1** city W Calif. ESE of Oakland *pop* 46,036 **2** city *cen* Ohio, a suburb of Columbus *pop* 41,751 **3** county E Ireland in Leinster *area* 356 *sq mi* (926 *sq km*), *pop* 1,122,821 **4** city & port ✳ of Ireland (republic) & of County Dublin at mouth of the Liffey on **Dublin Bay** (inlet of Irish Sea) *pop* 495,781 — **Dub·lin·er** \'də-blə-nər\ n

Du·brov·nik \'dü-ˌbrȯv-nik, dú-'brȯv-nik\ city & port S Croatia *pop* 55,638

Du·buque \də-'byük\ city E Iowa on Mississippi River *pop* 57,637

Dud·ley \'dəd-lē\ town W *cen* England in W. Midlands WNW of Birmingham *pop* 300,400

Duis·burg \'düs-ˌbərg, 'düz-ˌ, 'dyüz-ˌ, *G* 'dues-ˌbúrk\ or formerly **Duis·burg–Ham·born** \-ˌhäm-'bȯrn\ city W Germany at junction of Rhine & Ruhr rivers *pop* 537,441

\ə\ abut \ᵊ\ kitten, F table \ər\ further \a\ ash \ā\ ace \ä\ mop, mar
\aú\ out \ch\ chin \e\ bet \ē\ easy \g\ go \i\ hit \ī\ ice \j\ job
\ŋ\ sing \ō\ go \ȯ\ law \ȯi\ boy \th\ thin \th\ the \ü\ loot \ú\ foot
\y\ yet \zh\ vision, beige \k̸, ⁿ, œ, ɶ, ᵇ\ *see* Guide to Pronunciation

Du·luth \də-'lüth\ city & port NE Minn. at W end of Lake Superior *pop* 86,265 — **Du·luth·ian** \-'lü-thē-ən\ *adj or n*

Dul·wich \'də-lij, -lich\ a SE district of London, England, in Southwark

Dum·bar·ton \,dəm-'bär-t°n\ **1** burgh W *cen* Scotland WNW of Glasgow *pop* 79,750   **2** *or* **Dum·bar·ton·shire** \-,shir, -shər\ DUNBARTON

Dum·fries \,dəm-'frēs, -'frēz\ **1** *or* **Dum·fries·shire** \-'frēsh-,shir, -shər\ former county S Scotland ✻ Dumfries   **2** burgh S Scotland *pop* 32,084

Dumfries and Gal·lo·way \'ga-lə-,wā\ administrative area S Scotland *area* 2481 *sq mi* (6425 *sq km*)

Dun·bar·ton \,dən-'bär-t°n\ *or* **Dun·bar·ton·shire** \-,shir, -shər\ former county W *cen* Scotland ✻ Dumbarton

Dun·can \'dən-kən\ city S Okla. *pop* 23,431

Dun·can·ville \'dən-kən-,vil, -vəl\ city NE Tex. *pop* 38,524

Dun·dalk \,dən-'dôl)k\ town & port NE Ireland (republic) on Dundalk Bay (inlet of Irish Sea) ✻ of County Louth *pop* 26,669

Dun·dee \,dən-'dē\ city & port E Scotland constituting an administrative area on Firth of Tay *area* 25 *sq mi* (65 *sq km*), *pop* 172,860

Dun·e·din \,dən-'nē-d°n\ **1** city W Fla. N of Clearwater *pop* 35,321   **2** — see EDINBURGH 1   **3** city New Zealand on SE coast of South Is. at head of Otago Harbour *urban area pop* 107,088

Dun·ferm·line \,dən-'fərm-lən\ royal burgh E Scotland NW of Edinburgh *pop* 129,910

Dun·gan·non \,dən-'ga-nən\ district S Northern Ireland, established 1974 *area* 301 *sq mi* (783 *sq km*), *pop* 45,322

Dun·kerque *or* **Dun·kirk** \'dən-,kərk, ,dən-'\ city & port N France on Strait of Dover *pop* 70,834

Dun Laoghai·re \,dən-'ler-ə\ *or formerly* **Kings·town** \'kiŋz-,taùn\ borough & port E Ireland in Leinster on Dublin Bay *pop* 54,715

Dun·net Head \'də-nət\ headland N Scotland on N coast W of John o' Groat's; northernmost point of mainland, at 58°50′N

Duns \'dənz\ burgh SE Scotland *pop* 2249

Du·que de Ca·xi·as \,dü-kē-dē-kə-'shē-əs\ *or* **Caxias** city SE Brazil in Rio de Janeiro state N of city of Rio de Janeiro *pop* 775,456

Du·ran·go \dù-'raŋ-(,)gō, dyù-; dü-'räŋ-gō\ **1** state NW *cen* Mexico *area* 46,196 *sq mi* (119,648 *sq km*), *pop* 1,349,378   **2** city, its ✻ *pop* 464,566

Dur·ban \'dər-bən\ city & port in the municipality of eThekwini E Republic of South Africa in E KwaZulu-Natal on inlet of Indian Ocean *municipality pop* 2,117,700

Dur·ham \'dər-əm, 'də-rəm, 'dùr-əm\ **1** city NE *cen* N.C. NW of Raleigh *pop* 228,330   **2** county N England bordering on North Sea *area* 974 *sq mi* (2523 *sq km*), *pop* 589,800   **3** city, its ✻ *pop* 26,422

Dur·res \'dùr-əs\ *or* **I** **Du·raz·zo** \dü-'rät-(,)sō\ *or anc* **Ep·i·dam·nus** \,e-pə-'dam-nəs\ *or* **Dyr·ra·chi·um** \də-'rā-kē-əm\ city & port Albania on Adriatic Sea W of Tiranë *pop* 181,662

Du·shan·be \dü-'sham-bə, dyü-, -'shäm-, 'dyü-,; dyü-shäm-'bä\ *or formerly* **Sta·lin·a·bad** \,stä-lyi-nə-'bäd, ,sta-li-nə-'bad\ city ✻ of Tajikistan *pop* 575,900

Düs·sel·dorf \'dü-səl-,dôrf, 'dyü-, 'dùe-\ city W Germany on the Rhine N of Cologne ✻ of N. Rhine-Westphalia *pop* 577,561

Dutch Borneo — see KALIMANTAN 2

Dutch Guiana — see SURINAME 1

Dvi·na, Northern \dvē-'nä, 'dvē-nə\ river 466 *mi* (750 *km*) N Russia in Europe flowing NW into White Sea

Dvina, Western river 634 *mi* (1020 *km*) Latvia, W Belarus, & W Russia in Europe rising in Valdai Hills & flowing W into Gulf of Riga

Dvina Bay *or formerly* **Gulf of Arch·an·gel** \'är-,kān-jəl\ arm of White Sea N Russia in Europe

Dvinsk — see DAUGAVPILS

Dzaudzhikau — see VLADIKAVKAZ

Dzer·zhinsk \dzər-'zhēn(t)sk\ city *cen* Russia in Europe on Oka River W of Nizhniy Novgorod *pop* 287,000

Dzungarian Basin — see JUNGGAR PENDI

Ea·gan \'ē-gən\ city SE Minn. *pop* 64,206

Ea·gle Lake \'ē-gəl\ lake 13 *mi* (21 *km*) long N Calif. ENE of Lassen Peak

Ea·ling \'ē-liŋ\ borough of W Greater London, England *pop* 263,600

East Africa region E Africa — usu. considered to include Tanzania, Kenya, Uganda, Rwanda, Burundi, & Somalia

East An·glia \'aŋ-glē-ə\ region E England including Norfolk & Suffolk; one of kingdoms in Anglo-Saxon heptarchy *pop* 1,366,300 — **East An·gli·an** \-ən\ *adj or n*

East Antarctica — see ANTARCTICA

East Ayrshire administrative area of W Scotland *area* 483 *sq mi* (1252 *sq km*)

East Bengal the part of Bengal now in Bangladesh

East Beskids — see BESKIDS

East·bourne \'ēs(t)-,bôrn\ town S England in E. Sussex on English Channel *pop* 83,200

East Chicago city NW Ind. SE of Chicago, Ill. *pop* 29,698

East China Sea sea W Pacific bet. China (on W), S. Korea (on N), Japan & Ryukyu Islands (on E), & Taiwan (on S)

East Cleveland city NE Ohio NE of Cleveland *pop* 17,843

East Dunbartonshire administrative area of W Scotland *area* 66 *sq mi* (172 *sq km*)

Eas·ter Island \'ē-stər\ *or* **Ra·pa Nui** \,rä-pə-'nü-ē\ *or Sp* **Is·la de Pas·cua** \,ēs-lä-thä-'päs-kwä\ island Chile in SE Pacific 2000 *mi* (3200 *km*) W of coast *area* 46 *sq mi* (119 *sq km*) — **Easter Islander** *n*

Eastern Cape *or* **Oos Kaap** \,ōs-'käp\ province SE Republic of South Africa *area* 65,483 *sq mi* (169,600 *sq km*), *pop* 6,504,000

Eastern Desert *or* **Arabian Desert** desert E Egypt bet. the Nile & the Red Sea

Eastern Ghats \'gäts, 'gòts, 'gəts\ chain of mountains SE India extending SW & S from near delta of the Mahanadi in Orissa to W Tamil Nadu; highest point Mt. Dodabetta (in Nilgiri Hills) 8640 *ft* (2633 *m*) — see WESTERN GHATS

Eastern Rumelia region S Bulgaria including Rhodope Mountains & the Maritsa valley

Eastern Samoa — see AMERICAN SAMOA

Eastern Shore region E Md. & E Va. E of Chesapeake Bay — sometimes considered to include Del. — see DELMARVA PENINSULA

Eastern Thrace — see THRACE

Eastern Transvaal — see MPUMALANGA

East Flanders province NW *cen* Belgium ✻ Ghent *area* 1151 *sq mi* (2981 *sq km*), *pop* 1,366,652

East Frisian Islands — see FRISIAN ISLANDS

East Germany the German Democratic Republic — see GERMANY

East Ham \'ēst-'ham\ former county borough SE England in Essex, now part of Newham

East Hartford town *cen* Conn. *pop* 51,252

East Ha·ven \'ēst-,hā-vən\ town S Conn. SE of New Haven *pop* 29,257

East Indies **1** *or* **East India** southeastern Asia including India, Indochina, & the Malay Archipelago — a chiefly former name   **2** the Malay Archipelago — **East Indian** *adj or n*

East Lansing city S Mich. *pop* 48,579

East London city & port S Republic of South Africa in SE Eastern Cape on Indian Ocean *pop* 119,727

East Lo·thi·an \'lō-thē-ən\ *or* **Had·ding·ton** \'ha-diŋ-tən\ *or* **Hadding·ton·shire** \-,shir, -shər\ administrative area of SE Scotland *area* 262 *sq mi* (678 *sq km*) — see LOTHIAN

East·main \'ēst-,mān\ river *ab* 500 *mi* (804 *km*) Canada in W Que.

East Malaysia the parts of Malaysia on Borneo

East Moline city NW Ill. on Mississippi River *pop* 21,302

Eas·ton \'ēs-tən\ city E Pa. NE of Allentown *pop* 26,800

East Orange city NE N.J. NW of Newark *pop* 64,270

East Pakistan the former E division of Pakistan comprising the E portion of Bengal — see BANGLADESH

East Palo Alto city SW Calif. *pop* 28,155

East Peoria city N *cen* Ill. *pop* 23,402

East Point city NW *cen* Ga. SW of Atlanta *pop* 33,712

East·pointe \'ēst-,pòint\ *or formerly* **East Detroit** city SE Mich. *pop* 32,442

East Providence city E R.I. *pop* 47,037

East Prussia region N Europe bordering on the Baltic E of Pomerania; formerly a province of Prussia; for a time (1919–39) separated from rest of Prussia by Polish Corridor; divided 1945 bet. Poland & U.S.S.R. (Russia & Lithuania)

East Punjab — see PUNJAB

East Renfrewshire administrative area of W Scotland *area* 67 *sq mi* (173 *sq km*)

East Riding — see YORK 3

East River strait SE N.Y. connecting Upper New York Bay with Long Island Sound & separating Manhattan Is. from Long Is.

East Saint Louis city SW Ill. *pop* 27,006

East Sea — see JAPAN (Sea of)

East Siberian Sea sea, arm of Arctic Ocean N of E Russia in Asia extending from New Siberian Islands to Wrangel Is.

East Suffolk — see SUFFOLK 2

East Sus·sex \'sə-siks, *US also* -,seks\ county SE England ✻ Lewes *area* 718 *sq mi* (1860 *sq km*), *pop* 670,600

East Timor *or* **Ti·mor–Leste** \tē-mòr-'lesh-,tā, tē-'mòr-\ country SE Asia on E Timor ✻ Dili *area* 5763 *sq mi* (14,926 *sq km*), *pop* 1,066,000

East York former borough Canada in SE Ont., now part of Toronto

Eau Claire \ō-'kler\ city W Wis. *pop* 65,883

Eb·bw Vale \'e-bü-'väl\ town SE Wales N of Cardiff *pop* 24,422

Eboracum — see YORK

Ebro \'ā-(,)brō\ river 565 *mi* (909 *km*) NE Spain flowing from Cantabrian Mountains ESE into the Mediterranean

Eca·te·pec de Mo·re·los \ā-,kä-tā-'pek-thā-mō-'rā-lōs\ city Mexico NE of Mexico City *pop* 1,621,100

Ecbatana — see HAMADAN

Ec·ua·dor \'e-kwə-,dòr, ,e-kwä-'thòr\ country W S. America bordering on the Pacific; a republic ✻ Quito *area* 109,483 *sq mi* (283,561 *sq km*), *pop* 14,219,000 — **Ec·ua·dor·an** \,e-kwə-'dòr-ən\ *adj or n* — **Ec·ua·dor·ean** *or* **Ec·ua·dor·ian** \-ē-ən\ *adj or n*

Edam \'ē-dəm, -,dam, *D* ā-'däm\ commune NW Netherlands on the IJsselmeer NNE of Amsterdam

Ede **1** \'ā-də\ commune E Netherlands NW of Arnhem *pop* 103,708   **2** \'ā-,dā\ city SW Nigeria NE of Ibadan *pop* 271,000

Eden Prairie \'ē-d°n\ city SE *cen* Minn., a suburb of Minneapolis *pop* 60,797

Edessa — see ŞANLIURFA

Edi·na \i-'dī-nə\ city SE Minn. SW of Minneapolis *pop* 47,941

Ed·in·burg \'e-d°n-,bərg\ city S Tex. NW of Brownsville *pop* 77,100

Ed·in·burgh \'e-d°n-,bər-ə, -,bə-rə, -b(ə-)rə\ **1** *or SCgael* **Dun·e·din** \,də-'nē-d°n\ city ✻ of Scotland constituting an administrative area on Firth of Forth *area* 101 *sq mi* (262 *sq km*), *pop* 434,520   **2** *or* **Ed·in·burgh·shire** \-,shir, -shər\ — see MIDLOTHIAN

Edir·ne \ā-'dir-nə\ *or formerly* **Adri·a·no·ple** \,ā-drē-ə-'nō-pəl\ city Turkey in Europe on the Maritsa *pop* 102,345

Ed·is·to \'e-də-,stō\ river 150 *mi* (241 *km*) S S.C. flowing SE into the Atlantic

Edith Ca·vell, Mount \'ē-dəth-'ka-vəl, -kə-'vel\ mountain 11,033 *ft* (3363 *m*) Canada in SW Alta. in Jasper National Park

Ed·mond \'ed-mənd\ city *cen* Okla. N of Oklahoma City *pop* 81,405

Ed·monds \'ed-mən(d)z\ city W Wash. N of Seattle *pop* 39,709

Ed·mon·ton \'ed-mən-tən\ **1** city Canada ✻ of Alta. on the N. Saskatchewan *pop* 812,201   **2** former municipal borough SE England in Middlesex, now part of Enfield — **Ed·mon·to·ni·an** \,ed-mən-'tō-nē-ən, -nyən\ *n*

Edo — see TOKYO

Edom \'ē-dəm\ *or* **Id·u·maea** *or* **Id·u·mea** \,i-dyù-'mē-ə\ ancient country SW Asia S of Judea & the Dead Sea

Ed·ward, Lake \'ed-wərd\ lake E Africa bet. NE Democratic Republic of the Congo & SW Uganda *area* 830 *sq mi* (2158 *sq km*)

Ed·wards Plateau \'ed-wərdz\ highland 2000–5000 *ft* (610–1524 *m*) SW Tex.

Eesti — see ESTONIA

Efa·te \ā-'fä-,tā\ *or F* **Va·té** \vä-'tā\ island SW Pacific in *cen* Vanuatu; chief town Port-Vila (✻ of Vanuatu) *area* 353 *sq mi* (914 *sq km*), *pop* 30,422

Effigy Mounds National Monument site NE Iowa on Mississippi River NW of Dubuque including prehistoric mounds

Ega·di Islands \'e-gə-dē\ *or anc* **Ae·ga·tes Islands** \ē-'gā-tēz\ islands Italy off W coast of Sicily *area* 15 *sq mi* (39 *sq km*), *pop* 4335

Eger \'ā-gər\ *or Czech* **Ohře** \'òr-zhə\ river 193 *mi* (311 *km*) E Germany & NW Czech Republic flowing NE into the Elbe

Eg·mont, Mount \\'eg-ˌmänt\ *or* **Ta·ra·na·ki** \ˌtä-rä-'nä-kē\ mountain 8260 *ft* (2518 *m*) New Zealand in W *cen* North Is.

Egypt \\'ē-jipt\ *or Ar* **Miṣr** \'misr\ country NE Africa bordering on Mediterranean & Red seas ✳ Cairo *area* 386,900 *sq mi* (1,002,071 *sq km*), *pop* 72,798,031 — see UNITED ARAB REPUBLIC

Ei·fel \\'ī-fəl\ plateau region W Germany NW of the Moselle & NE of Luxembourg

Ei·ger \\'ī-gər\ mountain 13,025 *ft* (3970 *m*) W *cen* Switzerland NE of the Jungfrau

Eilean Siar — see WESTERN ISLES 1

Eind·ho·ven \\'īnt-ˌhō-və(n), ˌänt-\ commune S Netherlands in N. Brabant *pop* 204,776

Eire — see IRELAND

Ei·se·nach \\'ī-zə-ˌnäk, -ˌnäk\ city *cen* Germany in Thuringia W of Erfurt *pop* 44,266

Ekaterinodar — see KRASNODAR

Ekaterinoslav — see DNIPROPETROVS'K

El Aaiún — see LAAYOUNE

El Al·a·mein \ˌel-ˌa-lə-'mān\ village NW Egypt on the Mediterranean N of NE corner of Qattara Depression

Elam \\'ē-ləm\ *or* **Su·si·ana** \ˌsü-zē-'a-nə, -'ä-, -'ā-\ ancient kingdom SW Asia at head of Persian Gulf E of Babylonia ✳ Susa — **Elam·ite** \'ē-lə-ˌmīt\ *adj or n*

Elat \\'ē-ˌlat, ā-'lät\ *or* **Ei·lat** \ā-'lät\ town & port S Israel at head of Gulf of Aqaba *pop* 29,900

Elatea — see CITHAERON

Elath — see AQABA

Ela·zig \\'e-lə-ˌzə, -'zē(g)\ city E *cen* Turkey in valley of the upper Murat *pop* 204,603

El·ba \\'el-bə\ island Italy in the Mediterranean bet. Corsica & mainland; chief town Portoferraio *area* 86 *sq mi* (224 *sq km*)

El Bahnasa — see OXYRHYNCHUS

El·be \\'el-bə, 'elb\ *or Czech* **La·be** \'lä-be\ river 720 *mi* (1159 *km*) N Czech Republic & NE Germany flowing NW into North Sea

El·bert, Mount \\'el-bərt\ mountain 14,433 *ft* (4399 *m*) *cen* Colo. in Sawatch Range; highest in Colo. & Rocky Mountains

El·blag \\'el-ˌblönk\ *or G* **El·bing** \'el-biŋ\ city & port N Poland near Vislinski Zaliv *pop* 125,154

El'·brus *or* **El·brus** \el-'brüz, -'brüs\ mountain 18,510 *ft* (5642 *m*) S Russia in Europe; highest in the Caucasus & in Europe

El·burz Mountains \el-'bu̇rz\ mountains N Iran parallel with S shore of Caspian Sea — see DAMAVAND

El Ca·jon \ˌel-kə-'hōn\ city SW Calif. E of San Diego *pop* 99,478

El Cen·tro \el-'sen-(ˌ)trō\ city S Calif. in Imperial Valley *pop* 42,598

El Cer·ri·to \el-kə-'rē-(ˌ)tō\ city W Calif. on San Francisco Bay N of Berkeley *pop* 23,549

El·che \\'el-(ˌ)chä\ *or* **Elx** \'älsh\ city SE Spain SW of Alicante *pop* 194,767

Electric Peak mountain 10,992 *ft* (3350 *m*) S Mont. in Yellowstone National Park; highest in Gallatin Range

El·e·phan·ta \ˌe-lə-'fan-tə\ *or* **Gha·ra·pu·ri** \ˌgär-ə-'pu̇r-ē\ island W India in Bombay harbor

El·e·phan·ti·ne \ˌe-lə-ˌfan-'tī-nē, -fən-, -'tē-\ island S Egypt in the Nile opposite Aswân *pop* 1814

Eleu·sis \i-'lü-səs\ ancient city W Attica NW of Athens; ruins at modern town of **Elev·sís** \ˌe-lef-'sēs\ in E Greece — **El·eu·sin·i·an** \ˌel-yù-'si-nē-ən\ *adj or n*

Eleu·thera \i-'lü-thə-rə\ island Bahamas E of New Providence Is. *area* 164 *sq mi* (425 *sq km*), *pop* 7999

El Fai·yūm \ˌel-fā-'yüm, -(ˌ)fī-\ *or* **Al Fay·yūm** \ˌal-\ city N Egypt SSW of Cairo *pop* 166,910

El Fa·sher \el-'fa-shər\ city W Sudan in Darfur

El Fer·rol \ˌel-fe-'rōl\ *or* **El Ferrol del Cau·dil·lo** \ˌthel-kau̇-'thē-(ˌ)yō, -'thēl-(ˌ)yō\ city & port N Spain on the Atlantic *pop* 77,950

El Gezira — see GEZIRA

El·gin 1 \\'el-jən\ city NE Ill. *pop* 108,188 2 \'el-gən\ *or* **El·gin·shire** \-ˌshir, -shər\ — see MORAY 2 3 \'el-gən\ royal burgh NE Scotland NE of Inverness *pop* 18,905

El Giza — see GIZA

El·gon, Mount \\'el-ˌgän\ extinct volcano 14,178 *ft* (4321 *m*) E Africa on boundary bet. Uganda & Kenya NE of Lake Victoria

Elikón — see HELICON

Elis \\'ē-ləs\ *or ModGk* **Ilía** \ē-'lē-ä\ region S Greece in NW Peloponnese S of Achaea bordering on Ionian Sea

Elisabethville — see LUBUMBASHI

Elisavetgrad — see KIROVOGRAD

Elisavetpol — see GANCA

Elis·ta \'lyē-stə, ē-'lis-tə\ town S Russia in Europe ✳ of Kalmykia *pop* 95,200

Eliz·a·beth 1 \i-'li-zə-bəth\ 1 short river SE Va. flowing bet. cities of Norfolk & Portsmouth into Hampton Roads 2 city & port NE N.J. SW of Newark on Newark Bay *pop* 124,969

Elizabeth Islands islands SE Mass. extending SW from SW point of Cape Cod

Eliz·a·beth·town \i-'li-zə-bəth-ˌtau̇n\ city Ky. SSW of Louisville *pop* 28,531

Elk Grove Village village NE Ill. NW of Chicago *pop* 33,127

Elk·hart \\'el-ˌkärt\ city N Ind. E of S. Bend *pop* 50,949

Elk Island National Park wildlife refuge & resort Canada in E *cen* Alta.

Ellás — see GREECE

Elles·mere Island \\'elz-ˌmir\ island Canada in Nunavut W of NW Greenland — see COLUMBIA (Cape)

Ellice Islands — see TUVALU

El·lis Island \\'e-ləs\ island SE N.Y. in Upper New York Bay; served as immigration station 1892–1954

El·lo·ra \e-'lōr-ə\ village W India in *cen* Maharashtra NW of Aurangabad; site of **Ellora Caves** (temples excavated out of rock cliffs)

Ells·worth Land \'elz-(ˌ)wəṙth\ region W Antarctica on Bellingshausen Sea

Ellsworth Mountains range Antarctica S of Ellsworth Land

El Ma·hal·la El Ku·bra \ˌel-mə-'ha-lə-ˌel-'kü-brə\ city N Egypt in Nile Delta NE of Tanta *pop* 400,000

El Mal·pa·is National Monument \ˌel-ˌmäl-pä-'ēs\ site W New Mexico including volcanic features

El Man·sû·ra \el-man-'sûr-ə\ *or* **Al Man·su·rah** \ˌal-\ city N Egypt in Nile Delta

Elm·hurst \\'elm-ˌhərst\ city NE Ill. W of Chicago *pop* 44,121

El Min·ya \el-'min-yə\ *or* **Al Minya** \ˌal-\ city *cen* Egypt on the Nile

El·mi·ra \el-'mī-rə\ city S N.Y. *pop* 29,200

El Misti — see MISTI (El)

El Mon·te \el-'män-tē\ city SW Calif. E of Los Angeles *pop* 113,475

El Mor·ro National Monument \el-'mär-(ˌ)ō, -'mȯr-\ site W N.Mex. SE of Gallup containing rock carvings & ruins of anc. pueblos

Elm·wood Park \\'elm-ˌwu̇d\ village NE Ill. *pop* 24,883

El Obeid \el-ō-'bād\ city *cen* Sudan in Kordofan *pop* 66,270

El Paso \el-'pa-(ˌ)sō\ city Tex. at W tip on Rio Grande *pop* 649,121 — **El Paso·an** \-ˌpa-sō-ən\ *n*

El Paso de Robles — see PASO ROBLES

El Sal·va·dor \el-'sal-və-ˌdȯr, -ˌsal-və-'; ˌel-ˌsäl-vä-'thȯr\ country Central America bordering on the Pacific; a republic ✳ San Salvador *area* 8124 *sq mi* (21,041 *sq km*), *pop* 5,517,000

Elsass — see ALSACE

Elsene — see IXELLES

Elu·ru \e-'luṙ-(ˌ)ü\ *or formerly* **El·lore** \e-'lōr\ city SE India in E Andhra Pradesh *pop* 189,772

Ely \\'ē-lē\ town E England in N *cen* Cambridgeshire

Ely, Isle of district & former administrative county (✳ Ely) E England in Cambridgeshire — see CAMBRIDGESHIRE

Elyr·ia \i-'lir-ē-ə\ city NE Ohio SW of Cleveland *pop* 54,533

Em·bar·ras \'am-ˌbrȯ—*sic*\ river 185 *mi* (298 *km*) E Ill. flowing SE into the Wabash

Em·den \\'em-dən\ city & port NW Germany at mouth of Ems River *pop* 51,103

Emesa — see HOMS

Emi·lia \ā-'mēl-yä\ 1 district N Italy comprising the W part of Emilia-Romagna region 2 — see EMILIA-ROMAGNA

Emilia–Ro·ma·gna \-rō-'mä-nyä\ *or formerly* **Emilia** *or anc* **Ae·mil·ia** \ē-'mil-yə\ region N Italy bounded by the Po, the Adriatic, & the Apennines ✳ Bologna *area* 8543 *sq mi* (22,126 *sq km*), *pop* 4,008,663

Em·me \\'e-mə\ river *ab* 50 *mi* (80 *km*) *cen* Switzerland in E Bern canton

Em·men \\'e-mən\ commune NE Netherlands *pop* 108,367

Em·po·ria \em-'pȯr-ē-ə\ city E *cen* Kans. *pop* 24,916

Empty Quarter RUB' AL-KHALI

Ems \'emz, 'em(p)s\ 1 river 231 *mi* (372 *km*) NW Germany flowing N into North Sea 2 *or* **Bad Ems** \ˌbät-\ town W Germany SE of Koblenz *pop* 10,358

Enchanted Mesa sandstone butte W N.Mex. NE of Acoma

En·ci·ni·tas \ˌen(t)-sə-'nē-təs\ city S Calif. on coast N of San Diego *pop* 59,518

En·der·bury \\'en-dər-ˌber-ē\ island (atoll) *cen* Pacific in the Phoenix Islands chain of Kiribati

En·di·cott Mountains \\'en-di-kət, -də-ˌkät\ mountains N Alaska, the *cen* part of the Brooks Range

En·field \\'en-ˌfēld\ 1 town N Conn. *pop* 44,654 2 borough of N Greater London, England *pop* 248,900

En·ga·dine \\'eŋ-gə-ˌdēn, ˌeŋ-gə-'\ valley of upper Inn River 60 *mi* (96 *km*) long E Switzerland in Graubünden

En·gland \\'iŋ-glənd, 'iŋ-lənd\ 1 *or LL* **An·glia** \'aŋ-glē-ə\ country S Great Britain; a division of the United Kingdom of Great Britain and Northern Ireland ✳ London *area* 50,333 *sq mi* (130,362 *sq km*), *pop* 49,138,831 2 *chiefly formerly* England & Wales 3 *chiefly formerly* UNITED KINGDOM

En·gle·wood \\'eŋ-gəl-ˌwu̇d\ 1 city N Colo. S of Denver *pop* 30,255 2 city NE N.J. on the Hudson *pop* 27,147

English Channel *or F* **La Manche** \lä-'mäⁿsh\ strait bet. S England & N France connecting North Sea & Atlantic Ocean

Enid \\'ē-nəd\ city N Okla. *pop* 49,379

Eni·we·tok \ˌe-ni-'wē-ˌtäk\ island (atoll) W Pacific in the NW Marshalls

En·na \\'e-nä\ commune Italy in *cen* Sicily *pop* 28,296

En·nis \\'e-nəs\ town W Ireland ✳ of County Clare *pop* 13,746

En·nis·kil·len \ˌe-nə-'ski-lən\ *or* **In·nis·kil·ling** \ˌi-nə-'ski-liŋ\ town SW Northern Ireland in *cen* Fermanagh district

Enns \'enz, 'en(t)s\ river 160 *mi* (257 *km*) *cen* Austria flowing E & N from Styria into the Danube

En·sche·de \\'en(t)-shə-ˌdä, -skə-\ commune E Netherlands in Overijssel near German border; *pop* 151,346

En·se·na·da \ˌen(t)-sə-'nä-də, ˌen-sä-'nä-thä\ city & port NW Mexico in Baja California in the NW part of Tijuana *pop* 315,289

En·teb·be \en-'te-bə, -bē\ town S Uganda on N shore of Lake Victoria; former ✳ of Uganda *pop* 41,638

Eph·e·sus \\'e-fə-səs\ ancient city W Asia Minor in Ionia near Aegean coast; site SSE of Izmir — **Ephe·sian** \i-'fē-zhən\ *adj or n*

Ephra·im \\'ē-frē-əm\ 1 *or* **Mount Ephraim** hilly region of ancient Palestine; now in West Bank 2 — see ISRAEL 2

Epidamnus — see DURRES

Ep·i·dau·rus \ˌe-pə-'dȯr-əs\ ancient town S Greece in Argolis on Saronic Gulf

Épi·nal \ˌā-pi-'näl\ commune NE France on the Moselle *pop* 35,782

Epi·rus \i-'pī-rəs\ *or Gk* **Epei·ros** \'ē-pē-ˌrós\ region NW Greece bordering on Ionian Sea — **Epi·rote** \i-'pī-ˌrōt, -rət\ *n*

Ep·ping Forest \\'e-piŋ\ forested region SE England in Essex NE of London & S of town of Epping

Equatorial Guinea country W Africa on Bight of Biafra comprising former Spanish Guinea; an independent republic since 1968 ✳ Malabo *area* 10,825 *sq mi* (28,037 *sq km*), *pop* 1,014,999 — see SPANISH GUINEA

Erbîl — see ARBIL

Er·ci·yas \er-jē-'yäs\ mountain 12,848 *ft* (3916 *m*) *cen* Turkey; highest in Asia Minor

---

\ə\ abut \ᵊ\ kitten, F table \ər\ further \a\ ash \ā\ ace \ä\ mop, mar \au̇\ out \ch\ chin \e\ bet \ē\ easy \g\ go \i\ hit \ī\ ice \j\ job \ŋ\ sing \ō\ go \ȯ\ law \ȯi\ boy \th\ thin \t͟h\ the \ü\ loot \u̇\ foot \y\ yet \zh\ vision, beige \k, ⁿ, œ, ɶ, ᵛ\ see Guide to Pronunciation

Er·e·bus, Mount \ˈer-ə-bəs\ volcano 12,448 *ft* (3794 *m*) E Antarctica on Ross Is. in SW Ross Sea

Ere·gli \ˌer-ā-ˈlē, -ˈglē\ **1** city S Turkey SSE of Ankara *pop* 74,332 **2** town & port NW Turkey in Asia on Black Sea *pop* 63,776

Er·furt \ˈer-fərt, -ˌfu̇rt\ city *cen* Germany ✻ of Thuringia *pop* 204,912

Erie \ˈir-ē\ city & port NW Pa. on Lake Erie *pop* 101,786

Erie, Lake lake E *cen* N. America on boundary bet. the U.S. & Canada; one of the Great Lakes *area* 9910 *sq mi* (25,667 *sq km*)

Erie Canal canal 363 *mi* (584 *km*) long N N.Y. from Hudson River at Albany to Lake Erie at Buffalo; built 1817–25; superseded by **New York State Barge Canal** (*ab* 525 *mi or* 840 *km* long)

Er·in \ˈer-ən\ IRELAND — a poetic name

Er·i·trea \ˌer-ə-ˈtrē-ə, -ˈtrā-\ country NE Africa bordering on Red Sea ✻ Asmara; became part of Ethiopia 1962, independent 1993; *area* 45,405 *sq mi* (117,599 *sq km*), *pop* 4,252,000 — **Er·i·tre·an** \-ən\ *adj or n*

Er·lang·en \ˈer-ˌläŋ-ən\ city S Germany in Bavaria NNW of Nuremberg *pop* 102,433

Er·mou·po·lis *or* **Her·mou·po·lis** \er-ˈmü-pə-lis, -pō-ˌlēs\ *or* **Sy·ros** \ˈsē-ˌrȯs\ port Greece on Syros; chief town of the Cyclades *pop* 12,987

Er Rif \er-ˈrif\ *or* **Rif** coastal mountain region N Morocco on the Mediterranean

Ertix — see IRTYSH

Erz·ge·bir·ge \ˈerts-gə-ˌbir-gə\ mountain range Germany & NW Czech Republic on boundary bet. Saxony & Bohemia; highest Klínovec (in Czech Republic) 4080 *ft* (1244 *m*)

Er·zin·can \ˌer-zin-ˈjän\ city E *cen* Turkey on the Euphrates *pop* 90,799

Er·zu·rum \ˌer-zu̇-ˈrüm\ city NE Turkey in mountainous area *pop* 242,391

Es·bjerg \ˈes-ˌbyer(g)\ city & port SW Denmark in SW Jutland Peninsula on North Sea *pop* 81,843

Escaut — see SCHELDE

Es·con·di·do \ˌes-kən-ˈdē-(ˌ)dō\ city SW Calif. N of San Diego *pop* 143,911

Es·dra·e·lon, Plain of \ˌez-drə-ˈē-lən\ plain N Israel NE of Mt. Carmel in valley of the upper Qishon

Es·fa·hān \ˌes-fə-ˈhän, -ˈhan\ *or* **Is·fa·han** \ˌis-\ *or formerly* **Is·pa·han** \ˌis-pə-\ city W *cen* Iran; former ✻ of Persia *pop* 986,753

Esher \ˈē-shər\ town S England in N Surrey *pop* 61,446

Es·kils·tu·na \ˈes-kəl-ˌstü-nə\ city SE Sweden *pop* 90,089

Es·ki·se·hir \ˌes-ki-shə-ˈhir\ *or* **Es·ki·shehr** \-ˈsher\ city W *cen* Turkey on tributary of the Sakarya *pop* 413,082

España — see SPAIN

Española — see HISPANIOLA

Es·pí·ri·to San·to \ə-ˈspir-ə-ˌtü-ˈsän-(ˌ)tü\ state E Brazil bordering on the Atlantic ✻ Vitória *area* 17,658 *sq mi* (45,734 *sq km*), *pop* 3,097,232

Es·pi·ri·tu San·to \ə-ˈspir-ə-ˌtü-ˈsan-(ˌ)tü\ island SW Pacific in NW Vanuatu; largest in the group *area* 1420 *sq mi* (3678 *sq km*), *pop* 22,663

Es·poo \ˈes-(ˌ)pō\ town S Finland W of Helsinki *pop* 216,836

Es·qui·line \ˈes-kwə-ˌlīn, -lən\ hill in Rome, Italy, one of seven on which the ancient city was built — see AVENTINE

Es·sa·oui·ra \ˌe-sə-ˈwir-ə\ *or formerly* **Mog·a·dor** \ˈmä-gə-ˌdȯr\ city & port W Morocco on the Atlantic W of Marrakech *pop* 83,000

Es·sen \ˈe-sᵊn\ city W Germany in the Ruhr *pop* 626,989

Es·se·qui·bo \ˌe-sə-ˈkē-(ˌ)bō\ river 630 *mi* (1014 *km*) Guyana flowing N into the Atlantic through a wide estuary

Es·sex \ˈe-siks\ county SE England bordering on North Sea & N shore of Thames River; one of kingdoms in Anglo-Saxon heptarchy ✻ Chelmsford *area* 1470 *sq mi* (3807 *sq km*), *pop* 1,495,600

Ess·ling·en \ˈes-liŋ-ən\ city SW Germany on the Neckar *pop* 91,829

Es·té·rel \ˌes-tā-ˈrel\ forested mountain region SE France on coast SW of Cannes; highest point 2020 *ft* (616 *m*)

Es·tes Park \ˈe-stəs\ valley N Colo. in Front Range of the Rocky Mountains at E border of Rocky Mountain National Park

Es·to·nia \e-ˈstō-nē-ə, -nyə\ *or Estonian* **Ees·ti** \ˈā-stē\ country N Europe bordering on Baltic Sea; one of the Baltic Provinces of Russia 1721–1917, an independent republic 1918–40, a constituent republic **(Estonian Republic)** of the U.S.S.R. 1940–91 ✻ Tallinn *area* 17,413 *sq mi* (45,100 *sq km*), *pop* 1,370,052

Es·to·ril \ˌesh-tə-ˈril\ resort town Portugal on coast W of Lisbon

Es·tre·ma·du·ra \ˌes-trə-mə-ˈdu̇r-ə\ region & old province W *cen* Portugal ✻ Lisbon

eThe·kwi·ni \ˈe-te-ˌkwē-nē\ municipality E Republic of South Africa including the city of Durban

Ethi·o·pia \ˌē-thē-ˈō-pē-ə\ **1** ancient country NE Africa bordering on Red Sea and extending from S Egypt to N (present-day) Ethiopia **2** *or historically* **Ab·ys·sin·ia** \ˌa-bə-ˈsi-nē-ə, -nyə\ country E Africa; formerly an empire; since 1975 a republic ✻ Addis Ababa *area* 426,370 *sq mi* (1,104,298 *sq km*), *pop* 73,053,000

Et·na, Mount \ˈet-nə\ volcano 10,902 *ft* (3323 *m*) Italy in NE Sicily

Eto·bi·coke \e-ˈtō-bi-ˌkō—*sic*\ former city Canada in SE Ont., now part of Toronto

Eton \ˈē-tᵊn\ town SE *cen* England in Berkshire

Etru·ria \i-ˈtru̇r-ē-ə\ ancient country *cen* Italy coextensive with modern Tuscany & part of Umbria; home of the Etruscans

Et·trick Forest \ˈe-trik\ region in SE Scotland; formerly a forest & hunting ground

Eu·boea \yu̇-ˈbē-ə\ *or* **Ev·voia** \ˈe-vē-ä\ island 90 *mi* (145 *km*) long E Greece in the Aegean NE of Attica & Boeotia *area* 1411 *sq mi* (3654 *sq km*) — **Eu·boe·an** \yu̇-ˈbē-ən\ *adj or n*

Eu·clid \ˈyü-kləd\ city NE Ohio NE of Cleveland *pop* 48,920

Eu·ga·ne·an Hills \yü-ˈgā-nē-ən, ˌyü-gə-ˈnē-\ hills NE Italy in SW Veneto bet. Padua & the Adige

Eu·gene \yü-ˈjēn\ city W Oreg. on the Willamette *pop* 156,185

Eu·less \ˈyü-ləs\ city NE Tex. NE of Fort Worth *pop* 51,277

Eu·pen \ˈȯi-pən; ˌə(r)-ˈpen, œ-ˈ\ commune E Belgium; formerly in Germany; transferred (with Malmédy) to Belgium 1919 *pop* 17,606

Eu·phra·tes \yu̇-ˈfrā-(ˌ)tēz\ river 1700 *mi* (2736 *km*) SW Asia flowing from E Turkey SE through Syria & Iraq to unite with the Tigris forming the Shatt al Arab — see KARA SU — **Eu·phra·te·an** \-ˈfrā-tē-ən\ *adj*

Eur·asia \yu̇-ˈrā-zhə, -shə\ landmass of Asia & Europe — chiefly used to refer to the two continents as one continent

Eure \ˈər, ˈœr\ river 140 *mi* (225 *km*) NW France flowing N into the Seine

Eu·re·ka \yu̇-ˈrē-kə\ city & port NW Calif. *pop* 27,191

Eu·rope \ˈyu̇r-əp\ **1** continent of the eastern hemisphere bet. Asia & the Atlantic *area* 3,997,929 *sq mi* (10,354,636 *sq km*) **2** the European continent exclusive of the British Isles

European Economic Community *or* **Common Market** economic organization subsumed within the European Union

European Union *or formerly* **European Communities** *or* **European Community** economic, scientific, and political organization consisting of Belgium, France, Italy, Luxembourg, Netherlands, Germany, Denmark, Greece, Ireland, United Kingdom, Spain, Portugal, Austria, Finland, Sweden, Cyprus, Czech Republic, Estonia, Hungary, Latvia, Lithuania, Malta, Poland, Slovakia, Slovenia, Bulgaria, Romania, & Croatia

Ev·ans, Mount \ˈe-vənz\ mountain 14,264 *ft* (4348 *m*) N *cen* Colo. in Front Range WSW of Denver

Ev·ans·ton \ˈe-vən(t)-stən\ city NE Ill. N of Chicago *pop* 74,486

Ev·ans·ville \ˈe-vənz-ˌvil\ city SW Ind. on Ohio River *pop* 117,429

Ev·er·est, Mount \ˈev-rəst, ˈe-və-\ *or Tibetan* **Cho·mo·lung·ma** \ˌchō-mō-ˈlu̇ŋ-mə\ mountain 29,035 *ft* (8850 *m*) S Asia on border bet. Nepal & Tibet in the Himalayas; highest in the world

Ev·er·ett \ˈev-rət, ˈe-və-\ **1** city E Mass. N of Boston *pop* 41,667 **2** city NW *cen* Wash. on Puget Sound N of Seattle *pop* 103,019

Ev·er·glades \ˈe-vər-ˌglādz\ swamp region S Fla. S of Lake Okeechobee; partly drained; SW part forms **Everglades National Park**

Eve·sham \ˈēv-shəm\ town W *cen* England in Worcester S of Birmingham in **Vale of Evesham** *pop* 15,271

Évian *or* **Évian–les–Bains** \ˌā-vyäⁿ-le-ˈbaⁿ\ commune E France on Lake Geneva; health resort *pop* 7278

Évo·ra \ˈe-vu̇-rə\ city S *cen* Portugal *pop* 56,519

Évreux \āv-ˈrœ, -ˈrə(r)\ commune N France WNW of Paris *pop* 51,159

Ev·ri·pos \ˈev-ri-ˌpȯs\ narrow strait E Greece bet. Euboea & mainland

Évros — see MARITSA

Ex·e·ter \ˈek-sə-tər\ city SW England ✻ of Devon *pop* 101,100

Ex·moor \ˈeks-ˌmu̇r, -ˌmȯr\ moorland SW England in Somerset & Devon *area* 32 *sq mi* (83 *sq km*)

Ex·tre·ma·du·ra \ˌek-strə-mə-ˈdu̇r-ə, ˌes-trā-mä-ˈthü-rä\ region & old province W Spain bordering on Portugal; area included in present Cáceres & Badajoz provinces

Ex·u·ma \ik-ˈsü-mə, ig-ˈzü-\ islands in *cen* Bahamas S of **Exuma Sound** (SE of New Providence Is.); chief island **Great Exuma**

Eyre, Lake \ˈer\ intermittent lake *cen* Australia in NE S. Australia

Eyre Peninsula peninsula Australia in S S. Australia W of Spencer Gulf

Eyzies, Les — see LES EYZIES

Fa·en·za \fä ˈen zä, ˈen(t)-sä\ commune N Italy *pop* 53,549

Faer·oe Islands *or* **Far·oe Islands** \ˈfer-(ˌ)ō\ islands Denmark in the NE Atlantic NW of the Shetlands ✻ Tórshavn *area* 540 *sq mi* (1404 *sq km*), *pop* 48,400

Fa·ial \fə-ˈyäl, fī-ˈäl\ island *cen* Azores *area* 66 *sq mi* (171 *sq km*)

Fair·banks \ˈfer-ˌbaŋks\ city E *cen* Alaska *pop* 31,535

Fair·born \ˈfer-ˌbȯrn\ city SW *cen* Ohio NE of Dayton *pop* 32,352

Fair·field \ˈfer-ˌfēld\ **1** city W Calif. NE of Berkeley *pop* 105,321 **2** city SW Conn. *pop* 59,404 **3** city SW Ohio *pop* 42,510

Fair Lawn borough NE N.J. NE of Paterson *pop* 32,457

Fair·weath·er, Mount *or esp in Canada* **Fairweather Mountain** \ˈfer-ˌwe-t͟hər\ mountain 15,300 *ft* (4663 *m*) on boundary bet. Alaska & B.C.

Fai·sa·la·bad \ˌfī-ˌsä-lə-ˈbäd, -ˌsa-lə-ˈbad\ *or formerly* **Lyall·pur** \lē-ˌäl-ˈpu̇r\ city NE Pakistan W of Lahore *pop* 2,008,861

Faiyûm, El — see EL FAIYÛM

Faiz·a·bad \ˈfī-zə-ˌbad, -ˌbäd\ **1** *or* **Fey·za·bad** \ˈfā-zä-ˌbäd\ city NE Afghanistan *pop* 70,871 **2** city N India in Uttar Pradesh *pop* 144,924

Fa·jar·do \fə-ˈhär-dō\ city NE Puerto Rico *pop* 40,712

Fa·ka·ra·va \ˌfä-kä-ˈrä-vä\ island (atoll) S. Pacific; principal island of the Tuamotu Archipelago *pop* 651

Fa·laise \fä-ˈlāz\ town NW France SSE of Caen *pop* 8434

Fal·kirk \ˈfȯl-(ˌ)kərk\ **1** administrative area *cen* Scotland *area* 115 *sq mi* (299 *sq km*) **2** burgh *cen* Scotland ENE of Glasgow *pop* 36,875

Falk·land Islands \ˈfȯ-klənd, ˈfȯl-\ *or Sp* **Is·las Mal·vi·nas** \ˌēs-läs-mäl-ˈvē-näs\ islands SW Atlantic E of S end of Argentina; a Brit. crown colony ✻ Stanley *area* 4700 *sq mi* (12,173 *sq km*), *pop* 2478

Fall River \ˈfȯl\ city & port SE Mass. *pop* 88,857

Falluja *or* **Fallujah** — see AL FALLŪJAH

Fal·mouth \ˈfal-məth\ town SE Mass. on Cape Cod *pop* 31,531

False Bay \ˈfȯls\ inlet Republic of South Africa in SW Western Cape province E of Cape of Good Hope

Fal·ster \ˈfäl-stər, ˈfȯl-\ island Denmark in Baltic Sea *pop* 43,537

Fa·ma·gus·ta \ˌfä-mä-ˈgüs-tä\ city & port E Cyprus on **Famagusta Bay** (inlet of the Mediterranean) *pop* 42,500

Fanning — see TABUAERAN

Far·al·lon Islands \ˈfa-rə-ˌlän\ islands in the Pacific W *cen* Calif. W of San Francisco

Far East the countries of E Asia & the Malay Archipelago — usu. considered to comprise the Asian countries bordering on the Pacific but sometimes also to include India, Sri Lanka, Bangladesh, Tibet, & Myanmar — **Far Eastern** *adj*

Fare·well, Cape \ˈfer-ˌwel\ cape Greenland at S tip

Far·go \ˈfär-(ˌ)gō\ city E N.Dak. on Red River *pop* 105,549

Fa·ri·da·bad \fä-ˈrē-dä-ˌbäd\ town N India in Haryana *pop* 1,054,981

Farm·ers Branch \ˈfär-mərz\ city NE Tex. NNE of Dallas *pop* 28,616

Far·ming·ton \ˈfär-miŋ-tən\ **1** town N Conn. W of Hartford *pop* 25,340 **2** city NW N.Mex. *pop* 45,877

Farmington Hills city SE Mich. NW of Detroit *pop* 79,740

Far·quhar Islands \ˈfär-kwər, -kər\ island group NW Indian Ocean NE of Madagascar belonging to Seychelles

Far·rukh·a·bad \fə-ˈrü-kə-ˌbad, -ˌbäd\ city N India in Uttar Pradesh on the Ganges WNW of Lucknow *pop* 227,876

Fársala — see PHARSALUS

Fashoda — see KODOK

Fá·ti·ma \ˈfa-tə-mə, ˈfä-tē-\ village *cen* Portugal NNE of Lisbon

Fatshan — see FOSHAN

Fay·ette·ville \ˈfā-ət-ˌvil, -vəl; *2 is also* ˈfed-vəl\ **1** city NW Ark. *pop* 73,580 **2** city SE *cen* N.C. on Cape Fear River *pop* 200,564

Fear, Cape \ˈfir\ cape SE N.C. at mouth of Cape Fear River

Feath·er \'fe-thər\ river 100 *mi* (161 *km*) N *cen* Calif. flowing S into Sacramento River
Federal Capital Territory — see AUSTRALIAN CAPITAL TERRITORY
Federal District 1 *or Pg* **Dis·tri·to Fe·de·ral** \dish-'trē-tü,-fe-ə-'räl\ district E *cen* Brazil including ✴ city of Brasília *area* 2245 *sq mi* (5814 *sq km*), *pop* 2,051,146 2 — see DISTRITO FEDERAL 3 3 — see DISTRITO FEDERAL 4
Federal Way city W Wash. NE of Tacoma *pop* 89,306
Federated Malay States former Brit. protectorate (1895–1945) comprising the Malay states of Negeri Sembilan, Pahang, Perak, & Selangor ✴ Kuala Lumpur
Fen \'fən, 'fen\ river 300 *mi* (483 *km*) N China in *cen* Shanxi flowing SSE into the Huang
Fengtien 1 — see LIAONING 2 — see SHENYANG
Fer·ga·na \fər-'gä-nə\ valley W *cen* Asia in the Tian Shan in Kyrgyzstan, Tajikistan, & Uzbekistan SE of Tashkent
Fer·man·agh \fər-'ma-nə\ 1 district SW Northern Ireland, established 1974 *area* 724 *sq mi* (1875 *sq km*), *pop* 54,062 2 traditional county W Northern Ireland
Fer·nan·do de No·ro·nha \fer-'nän-(,)dü-dē-nò-'rō-nyə\ island Brazil in the Atlantic NE of city of Natal *area* 10 *sq mi* (26 *sq km*)
Fernando Póo — see BIOKO
Fer·ra·ra \fe-'rär-ä\ commune N Italy in Emilia-Romagna NE of Bologna near the Po *pop* 131,713
Ferro — see HIERRO
Ferrol, El — see EL FERROL
Ferryville — see MENZEL-BOURGUIBA
Fertile Crescent semicircle of fertile land stretching from SE coast of Mediterranean around Syrian Desert N of Arabia to Persian Gulf
Fez \'fez\ *or* **Fès** \'fes\ city N *cen* Morocco *pop* 946,815
Fez·zan \fe-'zan\ region SW Libya, chiefly desert
Fich·tel·ge·bir·ge \'fiḵ-t°l-gə-,bir-gə\ mountains Germany in NE Bavaria; highest Schneeberg 3453 *ft* (1052 *m*)
Fie·so·le \'fyä-zō-,lä\ *or anc* **Fae·su·lae** \'fē-zə-,lē\ commune *cen* Italy in Tuscany NE of Florence *pop* 14,808
Fife \'fīf\ *or* **Fife·shire** \-,shir, -shər\ administrative area E Scotland bet. Firths of Tay & Forth *area* 509 *sq mi* (1319 *sq km*)
Fi·ji \'fē-(,)jē\ islands SW Pacific E of Vanuatu constituting (with Rotuma Is.) an independent dominion of the Commonwealth of Nations ✴ Suva (on Viti Levu) *area* 7055 *sq mi* (18,272 *sq km*), *pop* 821,000 — **Fi·ji·an** \'fē-(,)jē-ən, fi-\ *adj or n*
Filch·ner Ice Shelf \'filk-nər\ area of shelf ice Antarctica in Weddell Sea
Filipinas, República de — see PHILIPPINES
Finch·ley \'finch-lē\ former municipal borough SE England in Middlesex, now part of Barnet
Find·lay \'fin(d)-lē\ city NW Ohio *pop* 41,202
Fin·gal's Cave \'fiŋ-gəlz\ sea cave W Scotland on Staffa Is.
Fin·ger Lakes \'fiŋ-gər\ group of long narrow lakes W *cen* N.Y. comprising Cayuga, Seneca, Keuka, Canandaigua, Skaneateles, Owasco, & several smaller lakes
Fin·is·terre, Cape \,fi-nə-'ster, -'ster-ē\ cape NW Spain on coast of La Coruña; westernmost point of Spanish mainland, at 9°18′W
Fin·land \'fin-lənd\ *or* **Finn Suo·mi** \'swò-mē\ country N Europe bordering on Gulf of Bothnia & Gulf of Finland; a republic ✴ Helsinki *area* 130,128 *sq mi* (337,032 *sq km*), *pop* 5,181,100 — **Fin·land·er** *n*
Finland, Gulf of arm of Baltic Sea bet. Finland & Estonia
Fin·lay \'fin-lē\ river 250 *mi* (402 *km*) Canada in N cen B.C. flowing SE to unite with **Pars·nip** \'pär-snip\ River (145 *mi or* 232 *km*) forming Peace River
Fins·bury \'finz-,ber-ē, -b(ə-)rē\ former metropolitan borough E *cen* London, England, now part of Islington
Fin·ster·aar·horn \,fin(t)-stər-'är-,hórn\ mountain 14,019 *ft* (4273 *m*) S Switzerland; highest of the Berner Alpen
Fiord·land \'fē-órd-,land, 'fē-; 'fyórd-\ mountain region S New Zealand in SW South Is.
Fish·ers \'fi-shərz\ town *cen* Ind. N of Indianapolis *pop* 76,794
Fitch·burg \'fich-,bərg\ city N *cen* Mass. *pop* 40,318
Fiume — see RIJEKA
Fiu·mi·ci·no \,fyü-mē-'chē-(,)nō\ town *cen* Italy on Tyrrhenian Sea SW of Rome & WNW of Ostia *pop* 51,958
Flag·staff \'flag-,staf\ city N *cen* Ariz. *pop* 65,870
Flam·bor·ough Head \'flam-,bər-ə, -,bə-rə, -b(ə-)rə\ promontory NE England on North Sea coast
Flan·ders \'flan-dərz\ *or F* **Flan·dre** \'flän-dr°\ *or Flem* **Vlaan·de·ren** \'vlän-də-rə(n)\ 1 medieval county along coast of what is now Belgium and adjacent parts of France & Netherlands 2 semiautonomous region W Belgium *pop* 5,972,781 — see EAST FLANDERS, WEST FLANDERS
Flat·head \'flat-,hed\ river 245 *mi* (394 *km*) SE B.C. & NW Mont. flowing S through Flathead Lake (reservoir in Mont.) into Clark Fork
Flat·tery, Cape \'fla-tə-rē\ cape NW Wash. at entrance to Strait of Juan de Fuca
Flens·burg \'flenz-,bərg, 'flen(t)s-,bùrk\ city & port N Germany on inlet of the Baltic near Danish border *pop* 87,241
Fletsch·horn \'flech-,hòrn\ mountain 13,107 *ft* (3995 *m*) S Switzerland in Pennine Alps S of Simplon Pass
Flevo·land \'fle-vō-,land\ *province cen* Netherlands ✴ Lelystad *area* 549 *sq mi* (1422 *sq km*), *pop* 341,721
Flin·ders \'flin-dərz\ river 520 *mi* (837 *km*) Australia in *cen* Queensland flowing NW into Gulf of Carpentaria
Flinders Ranges mountain ranges Australia in E S. Australia E of Lake Torrens
Flint \'flint\ 1 river 265 *mi* (426 *km*) W Ga. flowing S & SW into Lake Seminole 2 city SE *cen* Mich. NNW of Detroit *pop* 102,434 3 *or* **Flint·shire** \-,shir, -shər\ administrative area of NE Wales *area* 169 *sq mi* (438 *sq km*)
Flod·den \'flä-d°n\ hill N England in N Northumberland near Scottish border
Flor·ence \'flór-ən(t)s, 'flär-\ 1 city NW Ala. on Tennessee River *pop* 39,319 2 city N Ky. SSW of Cincinnati, Ohio *pop* 29,951 3 city E S.C. *pop* 37,056 4 *or It* **Fi·ren·ze** \fē-'rent-sä\ commune *cen* Italy on the Arno ✴ of Tuscany *pop* 402,316 — **Flor·en·tine** \'flór-ən-,tēn, 'flär-, -,tīn\ *n*

Flo·res \'flór-əs\ 1 island NW Azores *area* 58 *sq mi* (150 *sq km*) 2 island Indonesia in Lesser Sunda Islands
Flo·ri·a·nó·po·lis \,flór-ē-ə-'nò-pú-lis\ city S Brazil ✴ of Santa Catarina state on island off coast *pop* 342,315
Flor·i·da \'flór-ə-də, 'flär-\ state SE U.S. ✴ Tallahassee *area* 58,664 *sq mi* (151,940 *sq km*), *pop* 18,801,310 — **Flo·rid·i·an** \flə-'ri-dē-ən\ *adj or n* — **Flor·i·dan** \'flór-ə-dən, 'flär-\ *adj or n*
Florida, Straits of channel bet. Florida Keys (on NW) & Cuba & Bahamas (on S & E) connecting Gulf of Mexico with the Atlantic
Flor·i·da Island \'flór-ə-də, 'flär-; flə-'rē-də\ island W Pacific in SE Solomons N of Guadalcanal
Florida Keys chain of islands S Florida extending SW from S tip of the peninsula
Flo·ris·sant \'flór-ə-sənt\ city E Mo. NNW of St. Louis *pop* 52,158
Florissant Fossil Beds National Monument reservation *cen* Colo.
Flower Mound town N Texas N of Arlington *pop* 64,669
Flush·ing \'flə-shiŋ\ 1 section of New York City on Long Is. in Queens 2 — see VLISSINGEN
Fly \'flī\ river 650 *mi* (1046 *km*) S New Guinea flowing SE into Gulf of Papua
Fog·gia \'fò-(,)jä\ commune SE Italy in Puglia *pop* 154,760
Foggy Bottom section of Washington, D.C., near the Potomac where the State Department building is located
Foix \'fwä\ region & former province S France in the Pyrenees SE of Gascony
Folke·stone \'fōk-stən, *US also* -,stōn\ seaport & summer resort SE England in Kent on Strait of Dover *pop* 43,742
Fol·som \'fōl-səm\ city N Calif. NE of Sacramento *pop* 72,203
Fond du Lac \'fän-də-,lak, 'fän-jə-\ city E Wis. on Lake Winnebago *pop* 43,021
Fon·se·ca, Gulf of \fón-'sä-kä\ *or* **Fonseca Bay** inlet of the Pacific in Central America in El Salvador, Honduras, & Nicaragua
Fon·taine·bleau \'fän-t°n-,blō, ,fön-,ten-'blō\ commune N France *pop* 15,949
Fon·tana \fän-'ta-nə\ city SW Calif. E of Los Angeles *pop* 196,069
Foochow — see FUZHOU
For·a·ker, Mount \'fòr-i-kər, 'fär-\ mountain 17,400 *ft* (5304 *m*) S Alaska in Alaska Range SW of Mt. McKinley
For·far \'fòr-fər\ 1 *or* **For·far·shire** \-,shir, -shər\ — see ANGUS 2 royal burgh E Scotland NNE of Dundee *pop* 12,742
Fo·ril·lon National Park \,fòr-ē(l)-'yōⁿ\ scenic & recreational reservation E Canada in Gaspé Peninsula
For·lì \fòr-'lē\ commune N Italy in Emilia-Romagna SE of Bologna *pop* 107,827
Formosa — see TAIWAN — **For·mo·san** \fòr-'mō-sᵊn, fər-, -'zᵊn\ *adj or n*
Formosa Strait — see TAIWAN STRAIT
For·ta·le·za \,fòr-tə-'lä-zə\ city & port NE Brazil on the Atlantic ✴ of Ceará *pop* 2,141,402
Fort Col·lins \'kä-lənz\ city N Colo. *pop* 143,986
Fort–de–France \,fòr-də-'fräⁿs\ city French West Indies ✴ of Martinique on W coast *pop* 94,152
Fort Dodge \'däj\ city NW *cen* Iowa *pop* 25,206
Fort Erie \'ir-ē\ town Canada in SE Ont. on Niagara River *pop* 29,960
Fort Fred·e·ri·ca National Monument \,fre-də-'rē-kə, fre-'drē-\ site SE Ga. on W shore of St. Simons Is. containing site of fort built by Oglethorpe 1736
Fort George \'jórj\ river 480 *mi* (772 *km*) Canada in *cen* Que. flowing W into James Bay
Forth \'fòrth\ river 116 *mi* (187 *km*) S *cen* Scotland flowing E into **Firth of Forth** (estuary 48 *mi or* 77 *km* long, inlet of North Sea)
Fort Knox \'näks\ military reservation N *cen* Ky. SSW of Louisville; location of U.S. Gold Bullion Depository
Fort–Lamy — see N'DJAMENA
Fort Lau·der·dale \'lò-dər-,dāl\ city SE Fla. on the Atlantic *pop* 165,521
Fort Lee \'lē\ borough NE N.J. on the Hudson *pop* 35,345
Fort Ma·tan·zas National Monument \mə-'tan-zəs\ site SSE of St. Augustine, Fla., containing fort built *ab* 1736 by the Spanish
Fort Mc·Hen·ry National Monument \mə-'ken-rē\ site in Baltimore, Md., of a fort bombarded 1814 by the British
Fort My·ers \'mī(-ə)rz\ city SW Fla. *pop* 62,298
Fort Nel·son \'nel-sən\ river 260 *mi* (418 *km*) Canada in NE B.C. flowing NW into the Liard
Fort Peck Lake \'pek\ reservoir *ab* 130 *mi* (209 *km*) long NE Mont. formed in Missouri River by **Fort Peck Dam**
Fort Pierce \'pirs\ city E Fla. on the Atlantic *pop* 41,590
Fort Pu·las·ki National Monument \pə-'las-kē, pyü-\ reservation E Ga. comprising island in mouth of Savannah River; site of a fort built 1829–47 to replace Revolutionary Fort Greene
Fort Smith \'smith\ city NW Ark. on Arkansas River *pop* 86,209
Fort Stan·wix National Monument \'stan-(,)wiks\ historic site E *cen* N.Y. in Rome
Fort Sum·ter National Monument \'səm(p)-tər\ reservation S.C. at entrance to Charleston harbor containing site of Fort Sumter
Fort Union National Monument NE N.Mex. ENE of Santa Fe containing site of military post 1851–91
Fort Wayne \'wān\ city NE Ind. *pop* 253,691
Fort William — see THUNDER BAY
Fort Worth \'wərth\ city N Tex. W of Dallas *pop* 741,206
Fo·shan \'fō-'shän\ *or formerly* **Fat·shan** \'fät-'shän\ city SE China in *cen* Guangdong SW of Guangzhou *pop* 303,160
Fossil Butte National Monument site SW Wyo. containing aquatic fossils
Fos·ter City \'fòs-tər, 'fäs-\ city W Calif. SSE of San Francisco *pop* 30,567
Fountain Valley city SW Calif. SE of Los Angeles *pop* 55,313

\ə\ abut \ᵊ\ kitten, F table \ər\ further \a\ ash \ā\ ace \ä\ mop, mar \aù\ out \ch\ chin \e\ bet \ē\ easy \g\ go \i\ hit \ī\ ice \j\ job \ŋ\ sing \ō\ go \ò\ law \òi\ boy \th\ thin \t̲h̲\ the \ü\ loot \ù\ foot \y\ yet \zh\ vision, beige \k̲, ⁿ, œ, ⱖ, ᵛ\ *see* Guide to Pronunciation

Four Forest Cantons the cantons of Uri, Schwyz, Unterwalden, & Lucerne in *cen* Switzerland surrounding Lake of Lucerne
Fou·ta Djal·lon \ˌfü-tə-jə-ˈlōn\ mountain region W Guinea; highest point *ab* 4970 *ft* (1515 *m*)
Fox \ˈfäks\ **1** river 220 *mi* (354 *km*) SE Wis. & NE Ill. flowing S into Illinois River **2** river 175 *mi* (282 *km*) E Wis. flowing NE & N through Lake Winnebago into Green Bay
Foxe Basin \ˈfäks\ inlet of the Atlantic N Canada in Nunavut W of Baffin Is., connected with Hudson Bay by **Foxe Channel**
Fox Islands islands SW Alaska in E Aleutians — see UMNAK, UNALASKA, UNIMAK
Foyle \ˈfȯi(-ə)l\ river *ab* 20 *mi* (32 *km*) N Ireland flowing NE past city of Derry to **Lough Foyle** (inlet of the Atlantic 18 *mi or* 29 *km* long)
Fra·ming·ham \ˈfrā-miŋ-ˌham\ town E Mass. WSW of Boston *pop* 68,318
France \ˈfran(t)s, ˈfrä^{n}s\ country W Europe bet. English Channel & the Mediterranean; a republic ✻ Paris *area* 210,025 *sq mi* (543,965 *sq km*), *pop* 62,962,000
Franche–Com·té \ˌfrä^{n}sh-kō^{n}-ˈtā\ region & former county & province E France E of the Saône ✻ Besançon — see BURGUNDY
Fran·cis Case, Lake \ˈfran(t)-səs-ˈkās\ reservoir *ab* 100 *mi* (161 *km*) long S S.Dak. formed in Missouri River by **Fort Ran·dall Dam** \ˈran-d^{ə}l\
Fran·co·nia \fraŋ-ˈkō-nē-ə, -nyə\ former duchy in Austrasia, now included chiefly in Baden-Württemberg, Bavaria, & Hesse states, Germany — **Fran·co·ni·an** \-nē-ən, -nyən\ *adj or n*
Frank·fort \ˈfraŋk-fərt\ city ✻ of Ky. on Kentucky River E of Louisville *pop* 25,527
Frank·furt \ˈfraŋk-fərt, ˈfräŋk-ˌfu̇rt\ **1** *or in full* **Frankfurt am Main** \(ˌ)äm-ˈmīn\ city W Germany on Main River *pop* 654,679 **2** *or in full* **Frankfurt an der Oder** \ˌän-dər-ˈō-dər\ city E Germany on Oder River *pop* 85,357
Frank·lin \ˈfraŋ-klən\ **1** city E *cen* Mass. *pop* 31,635 **2** town *cen* Tenn. S of Nashville *pop* 62,487 **3** city SE Wis., a SSW suburb of Milwaukee *pop* 35,451 **4** former district Canada in N Northwest Territories including Arctic islands & Boothia & Melville peninsulas; area now divided bet. Nunavut & Northwest Territories
Franklin D. Roosevelt Lake reservoir 151 *mi* (243 *km*) long NE Wash. formed in Columbia River by Grand Coulee Dam
Franks Peak \ˈfraŋks\ mountain 13,140 *ft* (4005 *m*) NW Wyo.; highest in Absaroka Range
Franz Jo·sef Land \ˌfrants-ˈjō-zəf-ˌland, -səf-; ˌfränts-ˈyō-zəf-ˌlänt\ archipelago Russia in Arctic Ocean N of Novaya Zemlya
Fras·ca·ti \frä-ˈskä-tē\ commune *cen* Italy in Lazio SE of Rome *pop* 20,758
Fra·ser \ˈfrā-zər, -zhər\ river 850 *mi* (1368 *km*) Canada in S *cen* B.C. flowing into Strait of Georgia
Frau·en·feld \ˈfrau̇(-ə)n-ˌfelt\ commune NE Switzerland ✻ of Thurgau canton *pop* 19,538
Fred·er·ick \ˈfre-drik, ˈfre-də-rik\ city N Md. *pop* 65,239
Fred·er·icks·burg \ˈfre-driks-ˌbərg, ˈfre-də-riks-\ city NE Va. SW of Alexandria *pop* 24,286
Fred·er·ic·ton \ˈfre-drik-tən, ˈfre-də-rik-\ city Canada ✻ of N.B. on St. John River *pop* 56,224
Fred·er·iks·berg \ˈfre-driks-ˌbərg, ˈfre-də-riks-\ city Denmark on Sjælland Is., W suburb of Copenhagen *pop* 91,435
Free·port \ˈfrē-ˌpȯrt\ **1** city N Ill. W of Rockford *pop* 25,638 **2** village SE N.Y. on Long Is. *pop* 42,860 **3** city NW Bahamas on *cen* Grand Bahama Is. *pop* 26,574
Free State *or* **Vry·staat** \ˈfrā-ˌstät, ˈfrī-\ *or formerly* **Or·ange Free State** \ˈȯr-inj, ˈär-, -ənj\ province E *cen* Republic of South Africa bet. Orange & Vaal rivers *area* 49,992 *sq mi* (129,480 *sq km*), *pop* 2,767,000
Free·town \ˈfrē-ˌtau̇n\ city & port ✻ of Sierra Leone on the Atlantic *pop* 178,600
Frei·burg \ˈfrī-ˌbu̇rg, -ˌbərg, -ˌbu̇rk\ *or* **Freiburg im Breis·gau** \im-ˈbrīs-ˌgau̇\ city SW Germany at W foot of Black Forest *pop* 193,775
Fréjus — see CENIS (Mont) 2
Fré·jus, Mas·sif du \mä-ˌsēf-dᵫ-frā-ˈzhᵫs\ mountain on border bet. France & Italy at SW end of Graian Alps
Fre·man·tle \ˈfrē-ˌman-t^{ə}l\ city Australia in SW Western Australia at mouth of Swan River; port for Perth *pop* 23,834
Fre·mont \ˈfrē-ˌmänt\ **1** city W Calif. SE of Oakland *pop* 214,089 **2** city E Nebr. on Platte River *pop* 26,397
French Broad \ˈbrȯd\ river 210 *mi* (338 *km*) flowing from W N.C. to E Tenn.
French Community former federation comprising France, its overseas departments & territories, & the former French territories in Africa that chose to maintain their ties with France
French Equatorial Africa *or earlier* **French Congo** former country W *cen* Africa N of Congo River comprising a federation of Chad, Gabon, Middle Congo, & Ubangi-Shari territories ✻ Brazzaville
French Guiana country N S. America; an overseas department of France ✻ Cayenne *area* 35,126 *sq mi* (90,976 *sq km*), *pop* 207,500
French Guinea — see GUINEA 2
French India former French possessions in India including Chandernagore (ceded to India 1950) & Puducherry, Karikal, Yanam, & Mahé (ceded to India 1954) ✻ Puducherry
French Indochina — see INDOCHINA 2
French Morocco — see MOROCCO 1
French Polynesia *or formerly* **French Oceania** islands in S. Pacific belonging to France & including Society, Marquesas, Tuamotu, Gambier, & Austral groups ✻ Papeete (on Tahiti) *pop* 259,596
French Somaliland — see DJIBOUTI 1
French Sudan — see MALI 2
French Territory of the Afars and the Issas — see DJIBOUTI 1
French Union former federation (1946–58) comprising metropolitan France & its overseas departments, territories, & associated states — see FRENCH COMMUNITY
French West Africa former federation of French dependencies W Africa consisting of Dahomey, French Guinea, French Sudan, Ivory Coast, Mauritania, Niger, Senegal, & Upper Volta
French West Indies islands of the W. Indies belonging to France & including Guadeloupe, Martinique, Désirade, Les Saintes, Marie Galante, St. Barthélemy, & part of St. Martin
Fres·no \ˈfrez-(ˌ)nō\ city S *cen* Calif. SE of San Francisco *pop* 494,665
Fria, Cape \ˈfrē-ə\ cape NW Namibia on the Atlantic
Fri·bourg \frē-ˈbu̇r\ **1** canton W *cen* Switzerland *area* 645 *sq mi* (1670 *sq km*), *pop* 239,100 **2** commune, its ✻, SW of Bern *pop* 32,096
Frid·ley \ˈfrid-lē\ city SE Minn. N of St. Paul *pop* 27,208
Friends·wood \ˈfren(d)z-ˌwu̇d\ city SE Tex. SE of Houston *pop* 35,805
Fries·land \ˈfrēs-ˌland, ˈfrēz-, -lənd; ˈfrēs-ˌlänt\ **1** old region N Europe bordering on North Sea **2** province N Netherlands ✻ Leeuwarden *area* 1464 *sq mi* (3792 *sq km*), *pop* 636,184
Frio, Cape \ˈfrē-(ˌ)ō\ cape SE Brazil E of Rio de Janeiro
Frisches Haff — see VISLINSKI ZALIV
Fris·co \ˈfris-kō\ city N Texas N of Dallas *pop* 116,989
Fri·sian Islands \ˈfri-zhən, ˈfrē-\ islands NW Europe in North Sea including **West Frisian Islands** (off N Netherlands), **East Frisian Islands** (off NW Germany), & **North Frisian Islands** (off NW Germany & Denmark, including Helgoland & Sylt)
Fri·u·li \frē-ˈü-lē\ district N Italy in Friuli-Venezia Giulia on Slovenia border — **Fri·u·li·an** \frē-ˈü-lē-ən\ *adj or n*
Friuli–Ve·ne·zia Giu·lia \-ve-ˈnet-sē-ə-ˈjül-yä\ region N Italy E of Veneto ✻ Trieste *area* 3028 *sq mi* (7842 *sq km*), *pop* 1,188,594
Fro·bi·sher Bay \ˈfrō-bi-shər\ inlet of the Atlantic N Canada in E Nunavut on SE coast of Baffin Is.
Front Range \ˈfrənt\ range of the Rockies extending from *cen* Colo. N into SE Wyo. — see GRAYS PEAK
Frost·belt \ˈfrȯst-ˌbelt\ the N & NE states of the U.S.
Fro·ward, Cape \ˈfrō-(w)ərd\ headland S Chile N of Strait of Magellan; southernmost point of mainland of S. America at *ab* 53°54′S
Frunze — see BISHKEK
Frý·dek–Mís·tek \ˈfrē-dek-ˈmēs-tek\ city E Czech Republic just S of Ostrava *pop* 61,400
Fu–chou — see FUZHOU
Fuen·la·bra·da \ˌfwān-lä-ˈbrä-t͟hä\ commune *cen* Spain, SSW of Madrid *pop* 182,705
Fujairah *or* **Fujayrah, Al** — see AL FUJAYRAH
Fu·ji, Mount \ˈfü-jē\ *or* **Fu·ji·ya·ma** \ˌfü-jē-ˈyä-mä\ *or* **Fu·ji–san** \-ˈsän\ mountain 12,388 *ft* (3776 *m*) Japan in S *cen* Honshu; highest in Japan
Fu·jian \ˈfü-ˈjyen\ *or* **Fu·kien** \ˈfü-ˈkyen, -ˈjyen\ province SE China bordering on Taiwan Strait ✻ Fuzhou *area* 47,529 *sq mi* (123,575 *sq km*), *pop* 30,048,224
Fu·ji·sa·wa \ˌfü-jē-ˈsä-wä\ city Japan in SE Honshu *pop* 379,185
Fu·ku·o·ka \ˌfü-kü-ˈō-kä\ city & port Japan in N Kyushu on inlet of Tsushima Strait *pop* 1,341,470
Fu·ku·ya·ma \ˌfü-kə-ˈyä-mä\ city Japan in SW Honshu *pop* 378,789
Ful·da \ˈfu̇l-də\ city *cen* Germany *pop* 57,180
Ful·ham \ˈfu̇-ləm\ former metropolitan borough SW London, England, now part of Hammersmith
Ful·ler·ton \ˈfu̇-lər-tən\ city SW Calif. NE of Long Beach *pop* 135,161
Fu·na·ba·shi \ˌfü-nä-ˈbä-shē\ city Japan in SE Honshu, a suburb of Tokyo *pop* 550,074
Fu·na·fu·ti \ˌfü-nä-ˈfü-tē\ island (atoll) *cen* Tuvalu Islands in W Pacific; contains ✻ of the group *pop* 1328
Fun·chal \fün-ˈshäl, ˌfən-\ city & port Portugal ✻ of Madeira Islands *pop* 103,961
Fun·dy, Bay of \ˈfən-dē\ inlet of the Atlantic SE Canada bet. N.B. & N.S.
Fundy National Park scenic & recreational reservation SE Canada in N.B. on upper Bay of Fundy
Fur·neaux \ˈfər-(ˌ)nō\ islands Australia off NE Tasmania
Fur·ness \ˈfər-nəs\ district N England comprising peninsula in Irish Sea in SW Cumbria
Fürth \ˈfu̇rt, ˈfᵫrt\ city S *cen* Germany NW of Nuremberg *pop* 105,297
Fu·shun \ˈfü-ˈshu̇n\ city NE China in NE Liaoning E of Shenyang *pop* 1,202,388
Fu·tu·na \fü-ˈtü-nä\ **1** island SW Pacific in Futuna Islands **2** island SW Pacific in SE Vanuatu
Futuna Islands *or F* **Iles de Hoorn** \ˌēl-də-ˈōrn\ islands SW Pacific NE of Fiji; formerly a French protectorate, since 1959 part of Wallis & Futuna Islands territory *pop* 4732
Fu·xin *or* **Fu·sin** \ˈfü-ˈshin\ city NE China in *cen* Liaoning *pop* 688,000
Fu·zhou \ˈfü-ˈjō\ *or* **Foo·chow** *or* **Fu–chou** \ˈfü-ˈjō, -ˈchau̇\ *or formerly* **Min·how** \ˈmin-ˈhō\ city & port SE China ✻ of Fujian on Min River *pop* 874,809
Fyn \ˈfin\ island Denmark in the Baltic bet. Sjælland & Jutland; chief city Odense *area* 1149 *sq mi* (2987 *sq km*), *pop* 441,795
Ga·bès \ˈgä-ˌbes\ city & port SE Tunisia on **Gulf of Gabès** *or anc* **Syrtis Minor** \ˈsər-təs\ (arm of the Mediterranean) *pop* 83,610
Ga·bon \gä-ˈbō^{n}\ **1** estuary NW Gabon flowing into the Atlantic **2** country W Africa on the Atlantic; formerly a territory of French Equatorial Africa, since 1958 a republic ✻ Libreville *area* 102,317 *sq mi* (265,001 *sq km*), *pop* 1,500,000 — **Gab·o·nese** \ˌga-bə-ˈnēz, -ˈnēs\ *adj or n*
Ga·bo·rone \ˌgä-bō-ˈrō-(ˌ)nā, ˌk̲ä-\ *or formerly* **Ga·be·ro·nes** \-ˈrō-nəs\ town SE Botswana, its ✻ *pop* 133,468
Gad·a·ra \ˈga-də-rə\ town of ancient Palestine SE of Sea of Galilee — **Gad·a·rene** \ˈga-də-ˌrēn, ˌga-də-ˈ\ *adj or n*
Gades *or* **Gadir** — see CÁDIZ — **Gad·i·tan** \ˈga-də-tən\ *adj or n*
Gads·den \ˈgadz-dən\ city NE Ala. on the Coosa *pop* 36,856
Gadsden Purchase tract of land S of Gila River in present Ariz. & N.Mex. purchased 1853 by the U.S. from Mexico *area* 29,640 *sq mi* (77,064 *sq km*)
Gaeseong — see KAESONG
Ga·e·ta \gä-ˈā-tä\ city & port *cen* Italy in Lazio on **Gulf of Gaeta** (inlet of Tyrrhenian Sea N of Bay of Naples) *pop* 22,515
Gaf·sa \ˈgaf-sə\ *or anc* **Cap·sa** \ˈkap-sə\ oasis W *cen* Tunisia
Ga·han·na \gə-ˈha-nə\ city *cen* Ohio NE of Columbus *pop* 33,248
Gaines·ville \ˈgānz-ˌvil, -vəl\ **1** city N *cen* Fla. *pop* 124,354 **2** city N Ga. NE of Atlanta *pop* 33,804
Gaird·ner, Lake \ˈgerd-nər\ salt lake Australia in S. Australia W of Lake Torrens *area* 1840 *sq mi* (4784 *sq km*)
Gai·thers·burg \ˈgā-thərz-ˌbərg\ city W Md. NW of Washington, D.C. *pop* 59,933
Ga·lá·pa·gos Islands \gə-ˈlä-pə-gəs, -ˈla-, -ˌgōs\ *or* **Ar·chi·pié·la·go de Co·lón** \ˌär-chē-ˈpyā-lä-gō-t͟hā-kō-ˈlōn\ island group Ecuador in the

Pacific W of mainland ✻ on San Cristóbal Is. *area* 3093 *sq mi* (8010 *sq km*), *pop* 9785 — see ISABELA ISLAND

Gal·a·ta \'ga-lə-tə\ port & commercial section of Istanbul, Turkey

Ga·la·ți \gä-'läts, -'lät-sē\ city E Romania on the Danube *pop* 298,584

Ga·la·tia \gə-'lā-sh(ē-)ə\ ancient country & Roman province *cen* Asia Minor in region centered on modern Ankara, Turkey — **Ga·la·tian** \-shən\ *adj or n*

Gald·hø·pig·gen \'gäl-ˌhœ-ˌpē-gən\ mountain 8100 *ft* (2469 *m*) S *cen* Norway in Jotunheim Mountains

Gales·burg \'gālz-ˌbərg\ city NW Ill. WNW of Peoria *pop* 32,195

Ga·li·cia \gə-'li-sh(ē-)ə\ **1** region E *cen* Europe including N slopes of the Carpathians & valleys of the upper Vistula, Dniester, Bug, & Seret rivers; former Austrian crown land; belonged to Poland bet. the two world wars; now divided bet. Poland & Ukraine **2** region & ancient kingdom NW Spain bordering on the Atlantic — **Ga·li·cian** \-'li-shən\ *adj or n*

Gal·i·lee \'ga-lə-ˌlē\ hill region N Israel N of Plain of Esdraelon — **Gal·i·le·an** \ˌga-lə-'lē-ən\ *adj or n*

Galilee, Sea of *or mod* **Lake Ti·be·ri·as** \tī-'bir-ē-əs\ *or bib* **Lake of Gen·nes·a·ret** \gə-'ne-sə-ˌret, -rət\ *or* **Sea of Tiberias** *or* **Sea of Chin·ne·reth** \'ki-nə-ˌreth\ *or Heb* **Yam Kin·ne·ret** \'yäm-'ki-nə-ˌret\ lake 13 *mi* (21 *km*) long & 7 *mi* (11 *km*) wide N Israel on Syrian border traversed by Jordan River; *ab* 700 *ft* (212 *m*) below sea level

Gal·la·tin \'ga-lə-tən\ **1** river 125 *mi* (201 *km*) SW Mont. — see THREE FORKS **2** city N Tenn. NE of Nashville *pop* 30,278

Gallatin Range mountain range S Mont. — see ELECTRIC PEAK

Gal·li·nas, Point \gä-'yē-näs\ cape N Colombia; northernmost point of S. America, at 12°15′ N

Gal·lip·o·li \gə-'li-pə-lē\ *or Turk* **Ge·li·bo·lu** \ge-'lē-bò-ˌlü\ peninsula Turkey in Europe bet. the Dardanelles & Saros Gulf — see CHERSONESE

Gal·lo·way \'ga-lə-ˌwā\ former district SW Scotland comprising area formerly in counties of Wigtown & Kirkcudbright — see DUMFRIES AND GALLOWAY — **Gal·we·gian** \gal-'wē-j(ē-)ən\ *adj or n*

Gal·lup \'ga-ləp\ city NW N.Mex. near American Indian reservations *pop* 21,678

Galt \'gölt\ former city Ont., Canada — see CAMBRIDGE 2

Gal·ves·ton \'gal-vəs-tən\ city SE Tex. on **Galveston Island** (30 *mi or* 48 *km* long) at entrance to **Galveston Bay** (inlet of Gulf of Mexico) *pop* 47,743 — **Gal·ves·to·nian** \ˌgal-və-'stō-nē-ən, -nyən\ *n*

Gal·way \'gȯl-ˌwā\ **1** county W Ireland in Connacht bordering on the Atlantic *area* 2293 *sq mi* (5962 *sq km*), *pop* 209,077 **2** municipal borough & port, its ✻, on **Galway Bay** (inlet) *pop* 65,832

Gam·bia \'gam-bē-ə, 'gäm-\ **1** river 700 *mi* (1126 *km*) W Africa flowing from Fouta Djallon in W Guinea W through Senegal into the Atlantic in Gambia **2** *or* **the Gambia** country W Africa; a republic in the Commonwealth of Nations ✻ Banjul *area* 4003 *sq mi* (10,368 *sq km*), *pop* 1,400,000 — **Gam·bi·an** \-bē-ən\ *adj or n*

Gam·bier Islands \'gam-ˌbir\ islands S. Pacific SE of Tuamotu Archipelago belonging to France *pop* 620 — see MANGAREVA

Gan *or* **Kan** \'gän\ river over 500 *mi* (800 *km*) SE China in Jiangxi

Gana — see GHANA 1

Gan·ca \gän-'jä\ *or* **Gyan·dzha** \gyän-'jä\ *or 1935–90* **Ki·ro·va·bad** \ˌkē-rə-və-'bät\ *or earlier* **Eli·sa·vet·pol** *or* **Ye·li·za·vet·pol** \yi-li-zə-'vyet-ˌpȯl\ city W Azerbaijan *pop* 282,200

Gand — see GHENT

Gan·dhi·na·gar \'gən-də-ˌnə-gər\ town W India ✻ of Gujarat *pop* 121,746

Gan·ges \'gan-ˌjēz\ river 1550 *mi* (2494 *km*) N India flowing from the Himalayas SE & E to unite with the Brahmaputra & empty into Bay of Bengal through the vast **Ganges Delta** — see HUGLI — **Gan·get·ic** \gan-'je-tik\ *adj*

Gangetic Plain low-lying plains region India & Bangladesh formed by Ganges River & its tributaries

Gang·tok \'gaŋ-'täk, 'gəŋ-\ town NE India ✻ of Sikkim *pop* 29,162

Gan·nett Peak \'ga-nət\ mountain 13,804 *ft* (4208 *m*) *cen* Wyo.; highest in Wind River Range & in the state

Gan·su *or* **Kan·su** \'gän-'sü\ province N *cen* China ✻ Lanzhou *area* 137,104 *sq mi* (356,470 *sq km*), *pop* 22,371,141

Gao·xiong \'gaů-'shyůŋ\ *or* **Kao–hsiung** \'kaů-'shyůŋ, 'gaů-\ city & port SW Taiwan *pop* 1,509,100

Gar \'gär\ *or* **Ka·erh** \'kä-'ər\ town China in W Tibet

Gar·da, Lake \'gär-dä\ lake *ab* 35 *mi* (56 *km*) long N Italy bet. Lombardy & Veneto draining through the Mincio into the Po

Gar·de·na \gär-'dē-nə\ city SW Calif. S of Los Angeles *pop* 58,829

Garden City **1** city W Kans. on Arkansas River *pop* 26,658 **2** city SE Mich. *pop* 27,692

Garden Grove city SW Calif. SW of Los Angeles *pop* 170,883

Gar·field \'gär-ˌfēld\ city NE N.J. N of Newark *pop* 30,487

Garfield Heights city NE Ohio SSE of Cleveland *pop* 28,849

Garfield Mountain mountain 10,961 *ft* (3341 *m*) SW Mont. near Idaho border; highest in Beaverhead & Bitterroot ranges

Ga·ri·glia·no \ˌgär-ēl-'yä-(ˌ)nō\ river 100 *mi* (161 *km*) *cen* Italy in Lazio flowing SE & SW into Gulf of Gaeta

Gar·land \'gär-lənd\ city NE Tex. NNE of Dallas *pop* 226,876

Gar·misch–Par·ten·kir·chen \'gär-mish-'pär-tᵊn-ˌkir-kən\ city S Germany in Bavaria SW of Munich in foothills of the Alps *pop* 27,094

Ga·ronne \gə-'rän, gä-'rȯn\ river *ab* 355 *mi* (571 *km*) SW France flowing NW to unite with the Dordogne forming Gironde Estuary

Gar·ri·son Dam \'ga-rə-sən\ dam 210 *ft* (64 *m*) high in Missouri River W *cen* N.Dak. — see SAKAKAWEA (Lake)

Gary \'ger-ē\ city NW Ind. on Lake Michigan *pop* 80,294

Gas·co·nade \ˌgas-kə-'nād\ river 265 *mi* (426 *km*) S *cen* Mo. flowing NE into Missouri River

Gas·co·ny \'gas-kə-nē\ *or F* **Gas·cogne** \gä-'skȯnʸ\ region & former province SW France ✻ Auch

Ga·sher·brum \'gə-shər-ˌbrüm, -ˌbrům\ mountain 26,470 *ft* (8068 *m*) N Kashmir in Karakoram Range SE of K2

Gas·pé Peninsula \ga-'spā, 'ga-ˌ\ peninsula Canada in SE Que. bet. mouth of St. Lawrence River & Chaleur Bay — **Gas·pe·sian** \ga-'spē-zhən\ *adj*

Gasteiz — see VITORIA

Gas·ti·neau Channel \'gas-tə-ˌnō\ channel SE Alaska bet. Douglas Is. & mainland on which Juneau is situated

Gas·to·nia \ga-'stō-nē-ə, -nyə\ city SW N.C. W of Charlotte *pop* 71,741

Gates·head \'gāts-ˌhed\ town N England in Tyne and Wear county on the Tyne opposite Newcastle *pop* 196,500

Gates of the Arctic National Park wilderness area N *cen* Alaska in Brooks Range N of the Arctic Circle

Gath \'gath\ city of ancient Philistia ENE of Gaza

Gat·i·neau \ˌga-tə-'nō\ **1** river 240 *mi* (386 *km*) Canada in SW Que. flowing S into Ottawa River at Hull **2** town Canada in SW Que. *pop* 265,349

Ga·tun Lake \gä-'tün\ lake *cen* Panama formed by the **Gatun Dam** in the Chagres; formerly in Canal Zone

Gaul \'gȯl\ *or L* **Gal·lia** \'ga-lē-ə\ ancient country W Europe comprising the region now occupied by France & Belgium & at one time also the Po valley in N Italy — see CISALPINE GAUL, TRANSALPINE GAUL

Gau·teng \'gaů-ˌteŋ\ *or formerly* **Pretoria–Witwatersrand–Vereeniging** province *cen* NE Republic of South Africa *area* 7262 *sq mi* (18,810 *sq km*), *pop* 6,864,000

Ga·var·nie \ˌgä-vär-'nē\ waterfall 1385 *ft* (422 *m*) SW France S of Lourdes in the **Cirque de Gavarnie** \ˌsərk-də-\ (natural amphitheater at head of Gave de Pau) — see PAU 1

Gave de Pau — see PAU 1

Gav·ins Point Dam \'ga-vənz\ dam SE S.Dak. & NE Nebr. in Missouri River — see LEWIS AND CLARK LAKE

Gäv·le \'yev-lə\ city & port E Sweden on Gulf of Bothnia NNW of Stockholm *pop* 91,276

Ga·ya \gə-'yä\ city NE India in *cen* Bihar *pop* 383,197

Ga·za *or Ar* **Ghaz·ze** \'gä-zə, 'ga-\ Palestinian-administered city near the Mediterranean; with surrounding coastal district (**Gaza Strip**, adjoining Sinai Peninsula), administered 1949–67 by Egypt, subsequently by Israel, and since 2005 by the Palestinian Authority *district pop* 1,400,000 — **Ga·zan** \-zən\ *n or adj*

Ga·zi·an·tep \ˌgä-zē-(ˌ)än-'tep\ *or formerly* **Ain·tab** \īn-'täb\ city S Turkey N of Aleppo, Syria *pop* 603,434

Gdańsk \gə-'dän(t)sk, -'dan(t)sk\ *or G* **Dan·zig** \'dan(t)-sig, 'dän(t)-sik\ city & port N Poland on Gulf of Gdańsk *pop* 464,649

Gdańsk, Gulf of *or* **Gulf of Danzig** inlet of S Baltic Sea in N Poland & W Russia

Gdyn·ia \gə-'di-nē-ə\ city & port N Poland on Gulf of Gdańsk NNW of Gdańsk *pop* 250,936

Gebel Katherina — see KATHERINA (Gebel)

Gebel Musa — see MUSA (Gebel)

Ge·diz \gə-'dēz\ *or* **Sa·ra·bat** \ˌsär-ä-'bät\ river 217 *mi* (349 *km*) W Turkey in Asia flowing W into Gulf of Izmir

Gee·long \jə-'lȯŋ\ city & port SE Australia in S Victoria on Port Phillip Bay SW of Melbourne *pop* 13,036

Geelvink Bay — see SARERA BAY

Gel·der·land \'gel-dər-ˌland, 'kel-dər-ˌlänt\ province E Netherlands bordering on IJsselmeer ✻ Arnhem *area* 1981 *sq mi* (5131 *sq km*), *pop* 1,949,233

Gelibolu — see GALLIPOLI

Gel·sen·kir·chen \ˌgel-zᵊn-'kir-kən\ city W Germany in the Ruhr W of Dortmund *pop* 293,839

General San Martín — see SAN MARTÍN

Gen·e·see \ˌje-nə-'sē\ river 144 *mi* (232 *km*) W N.Y. flowing N into Lake Ontario

Ge·ne·va \jə-'nē-və\ *or F* **Ge·nève** \zhə-'nev\ *or G* **Genf** \'genf\ **1** canton SW Switzerland *area* 109 *sq mi* (282 *sq km*), *pop* 414,300 **2** city, its ✻, at SW tip of Lake Geneva on the Rhône *pop* 175,998 — **Gen·e·vese** \ˌje-nə-'vēz, -'vēs\ *adj or n*

Geneva, Lake *or* **Lake Le·man** \'lē-mən, 'le-; lə-'man; lā-'män\ lake 45 *mi* (72 *km*) long on border bet. SW Switzerland & E France; traversed by the Rhône

Genk \'keŋk\ commune NE Belgium *pop* 62,949

Gennesaret, Lake of — see GALILEE (Sea of)

Gen·oa \'je-nō-ə\ *or It* **Ge·no·va** \'je-nō-(ˌ)vä\ *or anc* **Gen·ua** \'jen-yə-wə\ commune & port NW Italy ✻ of Liguria at foot of the Apennines & at head of **Gulf of Genoa** (arm of Ligurian Sea) *pop* 632,366 — **Gen·o·ese** \ˌje-nō-'ēz, -'ēs\ *adj or n* — **Gen·o·vese** \-nə-'vēz, -'vēs\ *adj or n*

Gent — see GHENT

Gen·tof·te \'gen-ˌtȯf-tə\ city Denmark on Sjælland Is., N suburb of Copenhagen *pop* 68,314

George \'jȯrj\ river 345 *mi* (555 *km*) Canada in NE Que. flowing N into Ungava Bay

George, Lake **1** lake 14 *mi* (22 *km*) long NE Fla. in course of St. Johns River WNW of Daytona Beach **2** lake 33 *mi* (53 *km*) long E N.Y. S of Lake Champlain

Georg·es Bank \'jȯr-jəz\ submerged sandbank in the Atlantic E of Mass.

George·town \'jȯrj-ˌtaůn\ **1** section of Washington, D.C., in W part of the city **2** city *cen* Texas N of Austin *pop* 47,400 **3** city & port ✻ of Guyana on the Atlantic *pop* 162,000

George Town \'jȯrj-ˌtaůn\ **1** town ✻ of Cayman Islands on Grand Cayman Is. **2** *or* **Pe·nang** \pə-'naŋ, -'näŋ\ city & port Malaysia ✻ of Penang on Penang Is. *pop* 234,930

George Washington Birthplace National Monument historic site E Va.

George Washington Carver National Monument historic site SW Mo. SE of Joplin

Geor·gia \'jȯr-jə\ **1** state SE U.S. ✻ Atlanta *area* 58,910 *sq mi* (152,577 *sq km*), *pop* 9,687,653 **2** *or* **Republic of Georgia** independent country SW Asia bordering on Black Sea; an ancient & medieval kingdom, later (1936–91) a constituent republic of the U.S.S.R. ✻ Tbilisi *area* 26,911 *sq mi* (69,699 *sq km*), *pop* 4,371,500

Georgia, Strait of channel 150 *mi* (241 *km*) long NW Wash. & SW B.C. bet. S Vancouver Is. & mainland NW of Puget Sound

Georgian Bay inlet of Lake Huron Canada in SE Ont.

Georgian Bay Islands National Park reservation SE Canada in Ont. comprising over 50 small islands in Georgian Bay

\ə\ **a**but \ᵊ\ kitten, F table \ər\ **fur**ther \a\ **a**sh \ā\ **a**ce \ä\ m**o**p, m**a**r
\aů\ **ou**t \ch\ **ch**in \e\ b**e**t \ē\ **ea**sy \g\ **g**o \i\ h**i**t \ī\ **i**ce \j\ **j**ob
\ŋ\ si**ng** \ō\ g**o** \ȯ\ l**aw** \ȯi\ b**oy** \th\ **th**in \t͟h\ **th**e \ü\ l**oo**t \ů\ f**oo**t
\y\ **y**et \zh\ vi**si**on, bei**ge** \k, ⁿ, œ, ue, ʸ\ *see* Guide to Pronunciation

Geor·gi·na \jôr-'jē-nə\ town Canada in SE Ont. *pop* 43,517
Ge·ra \'ger-ə\ city E Germany ESE of Erfurt *pop* 126,521
Ger·la·chov·sky \'ger-lə-ˌkôf-skē\ mountain 8711 *ft* (2655 *m*) N Slovakia in Tatry Mountains; highest in Carpathians
German East Africa former country E Africa comprising Tanganyika & Ruanda-Urundi (now Rwanda & Burundi); a German protectorate 1885–1920
Ger·ma·nia \(ˌ)jər-'mā-nē-ə, -nyə\ 1 region of ancient Europe E of the Rhine & N of the Danube 2 region of Roman Empire just W of the Rhine in what is now NE France & part of Belgium & the Netherlands
German Southwest Africa — see NAMIBIA
Ger·man·town \'jər-mən-ˌtaûn\ 1 city SW Tenn. *pop* 38,844 2 a NW section of Philadelphia, Pa.
Ger·ma·ny \'jər-mə-nē\ or G **Deutsch·land** \'dòich-ˌlänt\ country *cen* Europe bordering on North & Baltic seas, divided 1949–90 into two republics: **Federal Republic of Germany** or **Bun·des·re·pu·blik Deutschland** \ˌbůn-dəs-ˌrā-pü-'blēk\ to the W (❋ Bonn, *area ab* 96,000 *sq mi or* 249,600 *sq km*) & **German Democratic Republic** or **Deutsche De·mo·krat·ische Re·pu·blik** \'dòi-chə-ˌdā-mō-'krä-ti-shə-ˌrā-pü-'blēk\ to the E (❋ East Berlin *area ab* 42,000 *sq mi or* 108,780 *sq km*); ❋ Berlin *area* 137,735 *sq mi* (356,734 *sq km*), *pop* 82,440,300
Ger·mis·ton \'jər-məs-tən\ city NE Republic of South Africa in Gauteng E of Johannesburg *pop* 221,972
Ge·ro·na \hā-'rō-nä\ or **Gi·ro·na** \hē-\ 1 province NE Spain in NE Catalonia *area* 2273 *sq mi* (5887 *sq km*), *pop* 565,304 2 commune, its ❋ *pop* 74,879
Ge·ta·fe \hā-'tä-fā\ commune *cen* Spain, S of Madrid *pop* 151,479
Get·tys·burg \'ge-tēz-ˌbərg\ borough S Pa. WSW of York *pop* 7620
Ge·zi·ra \jə-'zē-rə\ or **Gezira, El** \-el-\ or **Al Ja·zi·rah** \ˌal-jə-'zē-rə\ region E *cen* Sudan bet. the Blue Nile & the White Nile
Gha·da·mes or **Gha·da·mis** or **Ghu·da·mis** \'gə-'də-məs, -'dä-\ oasis & town NW Libya in Tripolitania near Algerian border
Gha·gha·ra \'gä-gə-ˌrä\ river 570 *mi* (1207 *km*) S *cen* Asia flowing S from SW Tibet through Nepal into the Ganges in N India
Gha·na \'gä-nə\ 1 or **Ga·na** ancient empire W Africa in what is now W Mali; flourished 4th–13th centuries 2 country W Africa bordering on Gulf of Guinea; a republic within the Commonwealth of Nations; formerly (as Gold Coast) a Brit. territory comprising Gold Coast Colony, Ashanti, Northern Territories, & Brit. Togoland trust terr. ❋ Accra *area* 92,100 *sq mi* (238,539 *sq km*), *pop* 23,652,000 — **Gha·na·ian** \gä-'nā-ən, ga-, -'nī-ən\ *adj or n* — **Gha·nian** \'gä-nē-ən, 'gä-, -nyən\ *adj or n*
Gharapuri — see ELEPHANTA
Ghar·da·ïa \gär-'dī-ə\ commune N *cen* Algeria *pop* 89,415
Ghats — see EASTERN GHATS, WESTERN GHATS
Ghaz·ni \'gäz-nē\ city E *cen* Afghanistan; once ❋ of a Muslim kingdom extending from the Tigris to the Ganges *pop* 35,900
Ghazze — see GAZA
Ghent \'gent\ or Flem **Gent** \'kent\ or F **Gand** \'gän\ city NW *cen* Belgium ❋ of E. Flanders *pop* 226,220
Giant's Causeway formation of prismatic basaltic columns Northern Ireland on N coast of Moyle
Gib·e·on \'gi-bē-ən\ city of ancient Palestine NW of Jerusalem — **Gib·e·on·ite** \-ə-ˌnīt\ *n*
Gi·bral·tar \jə-'brol-tər\ town & port on Rock of Gibraltar; a Brit. colony *area* 2.5 *sq mi* (6.5 *sq km*), *pop* 28,200 — **Gi·bral·tar·i·an** \jə-ˌbrol-'ter-ē-ən, ji-ˌbrol-\ *n*
Gibraltar, Rock of or anc **Cal·pe** \'kal-(ˌ)pē\ headland on S coast of Spain at E end of Strait of Gibraltar; highest point 1396 *ft* (426 *m*) — see PILLARS OF HERCULES
Gibraltar, Strait of channel bet. Spain & Africa connecting the Atlantic & Mediterranean *ab* 8 *mi* (12.8 *km*) wide at narrowest point
Gies·sen \'gē-s°n\ city W *cen* Germany N of Frankfurt am Main *pop* 73,763
Gi·fu \'gē-(ˌ)fü\ city Japan in *cen* Honshu *pop* 402,751
Gi·jón \hē-'hōn\ city & port NW Spain in Asturias province on Bay of Biscay *pop* 266,419
Gi·la \'hē-lə\ river 630 *mi* (1014 *km*) N.Mex. & Ariz. flowing W into Colorado River
Gila Cliff Dwellings National Monument site SW N.Mex. of cliff-dweller ruins
Gil·bert \'gil-bərt\ town SW *cen* Ariz. SE of Mesa *pop* 208,453
Gilbert and El·lice \'e-lis\ island group W Pacific; until 1976 a Brit. colony; now divided into the independent countries of Kiribati and Tuvalu
Gilbert Islands islands Kiribati in W Pacific — **Gil·bert·ese** \ˌgil-bər-'tēz, -'tēs\ *n or adj*
Gil·boa, Mount \gil-'bō-ə\ mountain 1631 *ft* (497 *m*) N Israel W of Jordan River & S of Plain of Esdraelon
Gil·e·ad \'gi-lē-əd\ mountainous region of ancient Palestine E of Jordan River; now in Jordan — **Gil·e·ad·ite** \-lē-ə-ˌdīt\ *n*
Gil·git \'gil-gət\ 1 region NW Kashmir; under Pakistani control 2 town NW Kashmir on Gilgit River (tributary of the Indus) *pop* 4671
Gil·ling·ham \'ji-liŋ-əm\ town SE England in Kent *pop* 93,300
Gil·roy \'gil-ˌrôi\ city W Calif. SE of San Jose *pop* 48,821
Gin·za \'gin-zə, 'gēn-zä\ shopping street & entertainment district in downtown Tokyo, Japan
Gi·re·sun \ˌgir-ə-'sün\ or **Ke·ra·sun** \ˌker-ə-\ city & port NE Turkey on Black Sea W of Trabzon *pop* 67,536
Girgenti — see AGRIGENTO
Gi·ronde \jə-'ränd, zhə-; zhē-'rōⁿd\ estuary 45 *mi* (72 *km*) W France formed by junction of the Garonne & the Dordogne & flowing NW into Bay of Biscay
Gis·borne \'giz-bərn, -ˌbòrn\ port New Zealand on E North Is. *urban area pop* 31,719
Gi·za \'gē-zə\ or **El Giza** \el-\ or **Al Ji·zah** \äl-'jē-zə\ city N Egypt on W bank of the Nile near Cairo *pop* 2,096,000
Gju·he·zes, Cape \jü-'hə-ˌzəs\ or formerly **Cape Lin·guet·ta** \liŋ-'gwe-tä\ or **Cape Glos·sa** \'glä-sä, 'glò-\ cape SW Albania projecting into Strait of Otranto
Gla·cier Bay \'glā-shər\ also -zhər\ inlet SE Alaska at S end of St. Elias Range in **Glacier Bay National Park**

Glacier National Park 1 — see WATERTON-GLACIER INTERNATIONAL PEACE PARK 2 area of mountains and rainforest W Canada in SE B.C. W of Yoho National Park
Glad·beck \'glät-ˌbek, 'glad-\ city W Germany in the Ruhr *pop* 80,127
Glades \'glādz\ EVERGLADES
Glad·sak·se \'gläth-ˌsäk-sə\ city Denmark, a suburb of Copenhagen *pop* 61,198
Glad·stone \'glad-ˌstōn\ city W Mo. N of Kansas City *pop* 25,410
Gla·mor·gan \glə-'mor-gən\ or **Gla·mor·gan·shire** \-ˌshir, -shər\ former county SE Wales ❋ Cardiff; divided 1974 into Mid Glamorgan, South Glamorgan, and West Glamorgan
Gla·rus \'glär-əs\ or F **Gla·ris** \glä-'rēs\ 1 canton E *cen* Switzerland *area* 264 *sq mi* (684 *sq km*), *pop* 38,300 2 commune, its ❋ *pop* 5634
Glas·gow \'glas-(ˌ)kō, 'glas-(ˌ)gō, 'glaz-(ˌ)gō\ city & port S *cen* Scotland constituting an administrative area on the Clyde *area* 68 *sq mi* (175 *sq km*), *pop* 681,470 — **Glas·we·gian** \gla-'swē-jən, glaz-\ *n or adj*
Glas·ton·bury 1 \'glas-tən-ˌber-ē\ town *cen* Conn. SE of Hartford *pop* 34,427 2 \'glas-tən-b(ə-)rē, 'gläs-\ town SW England in Somerset *pop* 6773
Glen Canyon Dam \'glen\ dam N Ariz. in Glen Canyon of Colorado River forming **Lake Pow·ell** \'paů(-ə)l\ (chiefly in SE Utah)
Glen·coe \glen-'kō\ valley W Scotland SE of Loch Leven
Glen Cove \'glen-'kōv\ city SE N.Y. on NW Long Is. *pop* 26,964
Glen·dale \'glen-ˌdāl\ 1 city *cen* Ariz. NW of Phoenix *pop* 226,721 2 city SW Calif. just N of Los Angeles *pop* 191,719
Glendale Heights village NE Ill. *pop* 34,208
Glen·do·ra \glen-'dôr-ə\ city SW Calif. *pop* 50,073
Glen El·lyn \gle-'ne-lən\ village NE Ill. W of Chicago *pop* 27,450
Glen More \glen-'mòr\ valley *ab* 50 *mi* (80 *km*) long N Scotland running SW to NE & connecting Loche Linnhe & Moray Firth — see CALEDONIAN CANAL
Glen·view \'glen-ˌvyü\ village NE Ill. NNW of Chicago *pop* 44,692
Glit·ter·tind \'gli-tər-ˌtin\ mountain 8110 *ft* (2472 *m*) S *cen* Norway in Jotunheim Mountains; highest in Scandinavia
Gli·wi·ce \gli-'vēt-se\ or G **Glei·witz** \'glī-(ˌ)vits\ city SW Poland in Silesia W of Katowice *pop* 222,084
Glouces·ter \'glos-, 'glòs-\ 1 city NE Mass. on Cape Ann *pop* 28,789 2 former city Canada in SE Ont., now part of Ottawa 3 town SW *cen* England ❋ of Gloucestershire *pop* 91,800
Glouces·ter·shire \'gläs-tər-ˌshir, -shər, 'glòs-\ or **Glouces·ter** \'gläs-tər, 'glòs-\ county SW *cen* England *area* 1055 *sq mi* (2732 *sq km*), *pop* 520,600
Gnossus — see KNOSSOS
Goa or Pg **Gôa** \'gō-ə\ state W India on Malabar Coast; before 1962 belonged to Portugal; with Daman & Diu constituted a union territory 1962–87; ❋ Panaji *area* 1404 *sq mi* (3636 *sq km*), *pop* 1,343,998 — see PORTUGUESE INDIA — **Go·an** \'gō-ən\ *adj or n* — **Goa·nese** \ˌgō-ə-'nēz, -'nēs\ *adj or n*
Go·da·va·ri \gō-'dä-və-rē\ river 900 *mi* (1448 *km*) *cen* India flowing SE across the Deccan into Bay of Bengal
Go·des·berg \'gō-dəs-ˌbərg, -ˌberk\ or **Bad Godesberg** \ˌbät-\ former commune W Germany on the Rhine; became part of Bonn 1969
Godthåb — see NUUK
Godwin Austen — see K2
Go·ge·bic Range \gō-'gē-bik\ iron-bearing region N Wis. & NW Mich.
Goi·â·nia or formerly **Goy·a·nia** \gói-'yä-nə\ city SE *cen* Brazil ❋ of Goiás *pop* 1,093,007
Goi·ás or formerly **Goi·az** or **Goy·az** \gói-'äs\ state SE *cen* Brazil ❋ Goiânia *area* 131,339 *sq mi* (340,168 *sq km*), *pop* 5,003,228
Gök·çe·ada \gœk-jä-'dä\ or formerly **Im·roz** \im-'ròz\ island Turkey in NE Aegean *area* 110 *sq mi* (286 *sq km*)
Go·lan Heights \'gō-ˌlän, -lən\ hilly region NE of Sea of Galilee; annexed by Israel 1981
Gol·con·da \gäl-'kän-də\ ruined city *cen* India in W Andhra Pradesh W of Hyderabad ❋ (1512–1687) of Golconda kingdom
Gold Coast 1 region W Africa on N shore of Gulf of Guinea bet. the Ivory Coast & the Slave Coast 2 former Brit. colony in S Gold Coast region ❋ Accra; now part of Ghana
Golden Chersonese — see CHERSONESE
Golden Gate strait 2 *mi* (3.2 *km*) wide W Calif. connecting San Francisco Bay with Pacific Ocean
Golden Horde region comprising most of what is now Russia in Europe; formed W part of Mongol Empire from mid 13th to end of 14th century
Golden Horn inlet of the Bosporus Turkey; harbor of Istanbul
Golds·boro \'gōl(d)z-ˌbər-ō\ city E *cen* N.C. *pop* 36,437
Golgotha — see CALVARY
Go·ma·ti \'gō-mə-tē\ or formerly **Gum·ti** \'güm-tē\ river *ab* 500 *mi* (805 *km*) N India flowing SE into the Ganges
Gomel — see HOMYEL'
Go·mor·rah \gə-'mòr-ə, -'mär-\ ancient city thought to be in the area now covered by the SW part of the Dead Sea
Go·nâve, Gulf of \gō-'näv\ arm of Caribbean Sea on W coast of Haiti
Gon·der \'gòn-dər\ or **Gon·dar** \-dər, -ˌdär\ city NW Ethiopia N of Lake Tana ❋ of Amhara & former ❋ of Ethiopia *pop* 163,097
Gond·wa·na·land \gän-'dwä-nə-ˌland\ or **Gond·wa·na** \-'dwä-nə\ hypothetical land area believed to have once connected the Indian subcontinent & the landmasses of the southern hemisphere
Gong·ga Shan \gäŋ-gə-'shän\ or **Min·ya Kon·ka** \ˌmi-nyə-'kän-kə\ mountain 24,790 *ft* (7556 *m*) W China in SW *cen* Sichuan; highest in China
Good Hope, Cape of \ˌgůd-'hōp\ cape S Republic of South Africa in SW Western Cape province W of False Bay, at 34°21′ S — see CAPE OF GOOD HOPE 2
Good·win Sands \'gůd-win\ shoals SE England in Strait of Dover off E coast of Kent — see DOWNS 2
Goose Creek city SE S.C. *pop* 35,938
Go·rakh·pur \'gòr-ək-ˌpúr\ city NE India in E Uttar Pradesh N of Varanasi *pop* 624,570
Go·ri·zia \gō-'rēt-syä\ commune NE Italy in Venetia *pop* 37,999
Gorki — see NIZHNIY NOVGOROD
Gör·litz \'gœr-ˌlits, -ləts\ city E Germany on Neisse River *pop* 70,448

Gor·lov·ka \'gȯr-ləf-kə\ *or* **Hor·liv·ka** \'hȯr-\ city E Ukraine in the Donets Basin N of Donetsk *pop* 337,000

Gor·no–Al·tay *or* **Gorno–Al·tai** \'gȯr-nə-ˌäl-'tī\ *or* **Altai** *or* **Altay** \ˌäl-'tī\ *or formerly* **Oy·rot** \'ȯi-rət\ autonomous region S Russia in Asia in SE Altai Territory in Altai Mountains ✹ **Gorno–Al·taysk** \-'tīsk\ *area* 35,753 *sq mi* (92,600 *sq km*), *pop* 197,000

Gor·no–Ba·dakh·shan \'gȯr-(ˌ)nō-ˌbä-ˌdäk-'shän\ autonomous region SE Tajikistan in the Pamirs ✹ Khorog *area* 24,595 *sq mi* (63,701 *sq km*), *pop* 167,100

Gor·zow Wiel·ko·pol·ski \gȯ-zhüf-ˌvyel-kȯ-'pȯl-skē\ city W Poland *pop* 123,350

Go·shen \'gō-shən\ **1** city N Ind. *pop* 31,719 **2** district of ancient Egypt N of the Nile Delta

Gos·port \'gäs-ˌpȯrt\ town S England in Hampshire on Portsmouth harbor *pop* 72,800

Gö·te·borg \ˌyœ-tə-'bȯr-ē\ *or* **Goth·en·burg** \'gä-thən-ˌbərg\ city & port SW Sweden on the Kattegat *pop* 474,921

Go·tha \'gō-tə, 'gō-thə\ city *cen* Germany W of Erfurt *pop* 53,372

Goth·am \'gä-thəm\ NEW YORK CITY — an informal name — **Goth·am·ite** \-thə-ˌmīt\ *n*

Got·land \'gät-ˌland\ island Sweden in the Baltic off SE coast; chief town Visby *area* 1225 *sq mi* (3174 *sq km*), *pop* 57,381

Göt·ting·en \'gœ-tiŋ-ən, 'ge-\ city *cen* Germany *pop* 124,331

Gou·da \'gau̇-də, 'gü-, 'k̲au̇-\ commune SW Netherlands NE of Rotterdam *pop* 71,688

Gov·er·nors Island National Monument \'gə-vər-nərz\ historic fortification New York City in New York Bay

Gow·er \'gau̇-(ə)r\ peninsula S Wales W of Swansea

Go·zo \'gȯd-zō, 'gȯt-sō\ island Malta in Mediterranean Sea NW of Malta Is. *area* 26 *sq mi* (67 *sq km*)

Gra·ham Land \'grā-əm, 'gra(-ə)m\ the N section of the Antarctic Peninsula

Gra·hams·town \'grā-əmz-ˌtau̇n, 'gra(-ə)mz-\ city S Republic of South Africa in Eastern Cape province ENE of Port Elizabeth *pop* 41,302

Grai·an Alps \'grā-ən, 'grī-\ section of W Alps S of Mont Blanc on border bet. France & Italy — see GRAN PARADISO

Grain Coast \'grān\ region W Africa in Liberia on Gulf of Guinea

Gram·pi·an Hills \'gram-pē-ən\ hills *cen* Scotland bet. the Lowlands & the Highlands — see BEN NEVIS

Gra·na·da \grə-'nä-də, grä-'nä-thä\ **1** city SW Nicaragua on NW shore of Lake Nicaragua *pop* 56,232 **2** medieval Moorish kingdom S Spain **3** province S Spain in Andalusia bordering on the Mediterranean *area* 4838 *sq mi* (12,530 *sq km*), *pop* 821,660 **4** city, its ✹, in the Sierra Nevada *pop* 240,661

Gran·by \'gran-bē\ town Canada in S Que. *pop* 63,433

Gran Cha·co \'grän-'chä-(ˌ)kō\ *or* **Chaco** region S *cen* S. America drained by the Paraguay & its chief W tributaries the Pilcomayo & Bermejo; divided bet. Argentina, Bolivia, & Paraguay

Grand **1** river 260 *mi* (418 *km*) SW Mich. flowing N & W into Lake Michigan **2** river 300 *mi* (483 *km*) NW Mo. flowing SE into Missouri River **3** river 200 *mi* (322 *km*) N S.Dak. flowing E into Missouri River **4** the Colorado River from its source to junction with Green River in SE Utah — a former name **5** — see NEOSHO

Grand Atlas — see ATLAS MOUNTAINS

Grand Bahama island Bahamas *area* 530 *sq mi* (1373 *sq km*), *pop* 46,994

Grand Banks shoals in W Atlantic SE of Newfoundland

Grand Canal *or* **Da Yun·he** \'dä-'yün-'hə\ *or* **Ta Yün Ho** \'tä-'yuen-'hō\ canal *ab* 1000 *mi* (1609 *km*) long E China from Hangzhou to Tianjin

Grand Canary *or Sp* **Gran Ca·na·ria** \ˌgrän-kä-'när-yä\ island Spain in the Canaries; chief city Las Palmas *area* 592 *sq mi* (1533 *sq km*)

Grand Canyon gorge of the Colorado NW Ariz. extending from mouth of the Little Colorado W to the Grand Wash Cliffs; over 1 *mi* (1.6 *km*) deep; area largely within **Grand Canyon National Park** — see MARBLE CANYON

Grand Cayman — see CAYMAN ISLANDS

Grand Cou·lee \'kü-lē\ valley E Wash. extending SSW from S wall of canyon of Columbia River where it turns W in forming the Big Bend

Grand Coulee Dam dam NE *cen* Wash. in Columbia River — see FRANKLIN D. ROOSEVELT LAKE

Grande, Rio \ˌrē-ō-'grand, -'gran-dē\ river U.S. & Mexico — see RIO GRANDE **2** \ˌrē-ō-'gran-də, -dē\ river 680 *mi* (1094 *km*) E Brazil in Minas Gerais flowing W to unite with Paranaíba River forming Paraná River

Grande Prai·rie \'grand-'prer-ē, -'prä-rē\ city Canada in W Alta. *pop* 55,032

Grande–Terre \grän-'ter\ island French West Indies constituting the E portion of Guadeloupe *area* 220 *sq mi* (572 *sq km*)

Grand Falls — see CHURCHILL FALLS

Grand Forks city E N.Dak. on Red River *pop* 52,838

Grand Island city SE *cen* Nebr. near Platte River *pop* 48,520

Grand Junction city W Colo. on Colorado River *pop* 58,566

Grand Lac — see TONLE SAP

Grand Ma·nan Island \mə-'nan\ island 20 *mi* (32 *km*) long Canada in N.B. at entrance to Bay of Fundy *pop* 2460

Grand Portage National Monument historic site NE Minn. on Lake Superior

Grand Prairie city NE *cen* Tex. W of Dallas *pop* 175,396

Grand Rapids city SW Mich. *pop* 188,040

Grand Te·ton \'tē-ˌtän, 'tē-'tᵊn\ mountain 13,770 *ft* (4197 *m*) W Wyo. in Grand Teton National Park; highest in Teton Range

Grand Teton National Park main part of Teton Range NW Wyo. including Jackson Lake

Grand Tra·verse Bay \'tra-vərs\ inlet of Lake Michigan in Mich. on NW coast of Lower Peninsula

Grand Turk — see TURKS AND CAICOS

Grand·view \'grand-ˌvyü\ city W Mo. *pop* 24,475

Grange·mouth \'grānj-məth, -ˌmau̇th\ burgh & port *cen* Scotland on Firth of Forth *pop* 21,666

Granicus — see KOCAKAS

Granite City city SW Ill. on Mississippi River *pop* 29,849

Granite Peak mountain 12,799 *ft* (3901 *m*) S Mont. in Beartooth Range (spur of Absaroka Range); highest point in state

Gran Pa·ra·di·so \ˌgrän-ˌpär-ä-'dē-(ˌ)zō\ mountain 13,323 *ft* (4061 *m*) NW Italy in NW Piedmont; highest in Graian Alps

Grants Pass \'gran(t)s\ city SW Oreg. *pop* 34,533

Grape·vine \'grāp-ˌvīn\ city N Tex. NE of Fort Worth *pop* 46,334

Gras·mere \'gras-ˌmir\ lake 1 *mi* (1.6 *km*) long NW England in Cumbria in Lake District

Grasse \'gras, 'gräs\ commune SE France W of Nice *pop* 43,848

Grass·lands National Park \'gras-ˌlandz, -ləndz\ area of prairie & badlands in Canada in SW Sask.

Grau·bün·den \grau̇-'bün-dən, -'bu̇en-\ *or F* **Gri·sons** \grē-'zōⁿ\ canton E Switzerland ✹ Chur *area* 2745 *sq mi* (7110 *sq km*), *pop* 185,700

Graudenz — see GRUDZIADZ

Gravenhage, 's — see HAGUE (The)

Graves·end \ˌgrāvz-'end\ town SE England in Kent *pop* 52,963

Grays Harbor \'grāz\ inlet of the Pacific W Wash.

Grays Peak mountain 14,270 *ft* (4349 *m*) *cen* Colo.; highest in Front Range

Graz \'gräts\ city S Austria on the Mur; chief city of Styria *pop* 226,244

Great Abaco — see ABACO

Great Australian Bight wide bay on S coast of Australia; part of Indian Ocean

Great Barrier Reef coral reef 1250 *mi* (2012 *km*) long Australia in Coral Sea off NE coast of Queensland; most of the area designated a marine park

Great Basin region W U.S. bet. Sierra Nevada & Wasatch Range including most of Nev. & parts of Calif., Idaho, Utah, Wyo., & Oreg. & having no drainage to ocean; contains many isolated mountain ranges (the **Basin Ranges**)

Great Basin National Park area of mountain and desert landscapes E Nev. including Wheeler Peak & Lehman Caves

Great Bear Lake lake Canada in Northwest Territories *area* over 12,000 *sq mi* (31,200 *sq km*)

Great Brit·ain \'bri-tᵊn\ *or* **Britain** **1** island W Europe comprising England, Scotland, & Wales *area* 88,150 *sq mi* (228,300 *sq km*), *pop* 57,103,927 **2** UNITED KINGDOM

Great Crosby — see CROSBY

Great Dismal Swamp — see DISMAL SWAMP

Great Divide — see CONTINENTAL DIVIDE

Great Dividing Range mountain system E Australia extending from Cape York Peninsula to S Victoria &, interrupted by Bass Strait, into Tasmania — see KOSCIUSKO (Mount)

Greater Antilles group of islands in the West Indies including Cuba, Hispaniola, Jamaica, & Puerto Rico

Greater London — see LONDON 2

Greater Manchester metropolitan area NW England comprising Manchester and nearby boroughs *area* 514 *sq mi* (1331 *sq km*), *pop* 2,454,800

Greater Sunda Islands — see SUNDA ISLANDS

Greater Walachia — see MUNTENIA

Great Exuma — see EXUMA

Great Falls **1** waterfall 35 *ft* (11 *m*) in the Potomac N of Washington, D.C. **2** city W *cen* Mont. on Missouri River WSW of the **Great Falls of the Missouri** (waterfall, now in modified form) *pop* 58,505

Great Inagua — see INAGUA

Great Indian Desert — see THAR DESERT

Great Kabylia — see KABYLIA

Great Karoo — see KAROO

Great Lakes chain of five lakes (Superior, Michigan, Huron, Erie, & Ontario) *cen* N. America in the U.S. & Canada draining through St. Lawrence River into the Atlantic **2** group of lakes E *cen* Africa including Lakes Turkana, Albert, Victoria, Tanganyika, & Malawi

Great Namaqualand — see NAMAQUALAND

Great Ouse — see OUSE 1

Great Plains elevated plains region W *cen* U.S. & W Canada E of Rocky Mountains & chiefly W of 100th meridian extending from NE B.C. & NW Alta. SE & S to include the Llano Estacado of N.Mex. & Tex.

Great Rift Valley depression SW Asia & E Africa extending with several breaks from valley of Jordan River S to *cen* Mozambique

Great Saint Ber·nard \ˌsänt-bər-'närd\ mountain pass 8090 *ft* (2468 *m*) through Pennine Alps bet. Switzerland & Italy

Great Salt Lake lake *ab* 80 *mi* (130 *km*) long N Utah having strongly saline waters & no outlet

Great Salt Lake Desert flat barren region NW Utah

Great Sand Dunes National Park area of dunes wilderness S Colo. on W slope of Sangre de Cristo Mountains

Great Slave Lake \'slāv\ lake NW Canada in SE Northwest Territories receiving Slave River on S & draining into Mackenzie River on W *area* *ab* 11,000 *sq mi* (28,400 *sq km*)

Great Smoky Mountains mountains on N.C.-Tenn. boundary partly in **Great Smoky Mountains National Park** — see CLINGMANS DOME

Great Stour — see STOUR 3

Great Yarmouth — see YARMOUTH 2

Greece \'grēs\ *or ModGk* **El·lás** \e-'läs\ *or anc Gk* **Hel·las** \'he-ləs\ country S Europe at S end of Balkan Peninsula; a republic ✹ Athens *area* 50,944 *sq mi* (131,945 *sq km*), *pop* 10,964,020

Gree·ley \'grē-lē\ city N Colo. *pop* 92,889

Green \'grēn\ **1** river 730 *mi* (1175 *km*) W U.S. flowing from Wind River Range in W Wyo. S into Colorado River in SE Utah **2** city NE Ohio S of Akron *pop* 22,817

Green·acres \'grēn-ˌā-kərz\ city SE Fla. S of West Palm Beach *pop* 37,573

Green Bay **1** inlet of NW Lake Michigan 120 *mi* (193 *km*) long in NW Mich. & NE Wis. **2** city NE Wis. on Green Bay *pop* 104,057

Green·belt \'grēn-ˌbelt\ city *cen* Md. *pop* 23,068

Green·field \'grēn-ˌfēld\ city SE Wis. near Milwaukee *pop* 36,720

\ə\ abut \ᵊ\ kitten, F table \ər\ further \a\ ash \ā\ ace \ä\ mop, mar \au̇\ out \ch\ chin \e\ bet \ē\ easy \g\ go \i\ hit \ī\ ice \j\ job \ŋ\ sing \ō\ go \ȯ\ law \ȯi\ boy \th\ thin \t̲h̲\ the \ü\ loot \u̇\ foot \y\ yet \zh\ vision, beige \k̲, ⁿ, œ, ɶ, ᵛ\ see Guide to Pronunciation

Green·land \ˈgrēn-lənd, -ˌland\ *or native* **Ka·laal·lit Nu·naat** \kä-ˈlät-ˌlēt-nü-ˈnät, -ˈlä-\ island in N. Atlantic off NE N. America belonging to Denmark ✱ Nuuk *area* 839,999 *sq mi* (2,175,597 *sq km*), *pop* 57,000 — **Green·land·er** \-lən-dər, -ˌlan-\ *n* — **Green·land·ic** \ˌgrēn-ˈlan-dik\ *adj*

Greenland Sea arm of Arctic Ocean bet. Greenland & Spitsbergen

Green Mountains mountains E N. America in Appalachian system extending from S Que. S through Vt. into W Mass. — see MANSFIELD (Mount)

Gree·nock \ˈgrē-nək\ burgh & port SW Scotland on Firth of Clyde *pop* 57,324

Greens·boro \ˈgrēnz-ˌbər-ō\ city N *cen* N.C. *pop* 269,666

Green·ville \ˈgrēn-ˌvil, -vəl\ **1** city W Miss. on Mississippi River *pop* 34,400 **2** city E N.C. *pop* 84,554 **3** city NW S.C. *pop* 58,409 **4** city NE Tex. NE of Dallas on the Sabine *pop* 25,557

Green·wich **1** \ˈgre-nich, ˈgrēn-ˌwich, ˈgrin-ˌwich\ town SW Conn. on Long Island Sound *pop* 61,171 **2** \ˈgri-nij, ˈgre-, -nich\ borough of E Greater London, England *pop* 200,800

Green·wich Village \ˈgre-nich\ section of New York City in Manhattan on lower W side

Green·wood \ˈgrēn-ˌwu̇d\ city *cen* Ind. *pop* 49,791

Gre·na·da \grə-ˈnā-də\ island Brit. West Indies in S Windward Islands; with S Grenadines, independent member of the Commonwealth of Nations since 1974 ✱ St. George's *area* 133 *sq mi* (346 *sq km*), *pop* 100,895 — **Gre·na·dan** \-ˈnā-dᵊn\ *adj or n* — **Gre·na·di·an** \-ˈnā-dē-ən\ *adj or n*

Gren·a·dines \ˌgre-nə-ˈdēnz, ˈgre-nə-ˌ\ islands Brit. West Indies in *cen* Windward Islands bet. Grenada & St. Vincent; divided administratively bet. Grenada & St. Vincent and the Grenadines

Gre·no·ble \grə-ˈnō-bəl, -ˈnȯblᵊ\ city SE France on the Isère *pop* 153,426

Gresh·am \ˈgre-shəm\ city NW Oreg. E of Portland *pop* 105,594

Grey·lock, Mount \ˈgrā-ˌläk\ mountain 3491 *ft* (1064 *m*) NW Mass.; highest in Berkshire Hills & in state

Grif·fin \ˈgri-fən\ city W *cen* Ga. *pop* 23,643

Grims·by \ˈgrimz-bē\ port E England near mouth of the Humber *pop* 92,147

Grin·del·wald \ˈgrin-dᵊl-ˌwȯld, -ˌvält\ valley & village *cen* Switzerland in Bern canton in the Berner Alpen E of Interlaken

Gri·qua·land West \ˈgri-kwə-ˌland, ˈgrē-\ district NW Republic of South Africa in NE Northern Cape N of Orange River; chief town Kimberley

Gris–Nez, Cape \grē-ˈnā\ headland N France projecting into Strait of Dover

Grisons — see GRAUBÜNDEN

Grod·no \ˈgräd-(ˌ)nō, ˈgrȯd-nə\ *or* **Hrod·na** *or* **Hrod·no** \ˈk̲rȯd-nə\ city W Belarus on the Neman *pop* 284,800

Gro·ning·en \ˈgrō-niŋ-ən, ˈk̲rō-niŋ-ə(n)\ **1** province NE Netherlands *area* 934 *sq mi* (2419 *sq km*), *pop* 570,480 **2** city, its ✱ *pop* 175,569

Gros Morne National Park \grō-ˈmȯrn\ area of varied landscape features in Newfoundland

Gross·glock·ner \ˈgrōs-ˌglȯk-nər\ mountain 12,461 *ft* (3798 *m*) SW Austria; highest in the Hohe Tauern & in Austria

Gros Ventre \ˈgrō-ˌvänt\ river 100 *mi* (161 *km*) W Wyo. flowing W into Snake River

Grot·on \ˈgrä-tᵊn\ town SE Conn. E of New London *pop* 40,115

Grove City \ˈgrōv\ city *cen* Ohio *pop* 35,575

Groz·ny *or* **Groz·nyy** \ˈgrȯz-nē, ˈgräz-\ city S Russia in Europe N of Caucasus Mountains ✱ of Chechnya *pop* 388,000

Gru·dziadz \ˈgrü-ˌjȯnts\ *or G* **Grau·denz** \ˈgrau̇-ˌdents\ city N Poland on the Vistula NE of Bydgoszcz *pop* 100,861

Gua·da·la·ja·ra \ˌgwä-də-lə-ˈhär-ə, ˌgwä-t͟hä-lä-ˈhä-rä\ **1** city W *cen* Mexico ✱ of Jalisco *pop* 1,628,617 **2** province E *cen* Spain in NE New Castile *area* 4707 *sq mi* (12,191 *sq km*), *pop* 174,999 **3** commune, its ✱ *pop* 68,248

Gua·dal·ca·nal \ˌgwä-dᵊl-kə-ˈnal, ˌgwä-də-kə-\ island W Pacific in the SE Solomons *pop* 60,275 — see HONIARA

Gua·dal·qui·vir \ˌgwä-dᵊl-ki-ˈvir, -ˈkwi-vər\ river 408 *mi* (656 *km*) S Spain flowing W & SW into Gulf of Cádiz

Gua·da·lupe \ˈgwä-də-ˌlüp\ river SE Tex. flowing SE into San Antonio River

Gua·da·lupe Hi·dal·go \ˈgwä-də-ˌlüp-hi-ˈdal-(ˌ)gō, ˌgwä-t͟hä-ˈlü-pā-ē-ˈt͟häl-(ˌ)gō\ **1** former city *cen* Mexico N of Mexico City, now part of city of Gustavo A. Madero **2** GUSTAVO A. MADERO (Villa)

Guadalupe Mountains mountains S N.Mex. & W Tex., the S extension of Sacramento Mountains; highest point **Guadalupe Peak,** 8749 *ft* (2667 *m*), in **Guadalupe Mountains National Park** (in Tex.)

Gua·de·loupe \ˈgwä-də-ˌlüp, ˌgwä-də-ˈ\ two islands, Basse-Terre (or Guadeloupe proper) & Grande-Terre, in French West Indies in *cen* Leeward Islands; an overseas department of France ✱ Basse-Terre (in Basse-Terre Is.) *area* 582 *sq mi* (1507 *sq km*), *pop* 422,222 — **Gua·de·lou·pe·an** \ˌgwä-də-ˈlü-pē-ən\ *n*

Gua·di·a·na \ˌgwä-ˈt͟hyä-nä\ river 515 *mi* (829 *km*) Spain & Portugal flowing W & S into Gulf of Cádiz

Guaíra — see SETE QUEDAS

Guam \ˈgwäm\ island W Pacific in S Marianas; unincorporated U.S. territory ✱ Hagåtña *area* 209 *sq mi* (541 *sq km*), *pop* 154,805 — **Gua·ma·ni·an** \gwä-ˈmā-nē-ən\ *adj or n*

Gua·na·ba·coa \ˌgwä-nä-bä-ˈkō-ä\ city W Cuba E of Havana *pop* 100,452

Gua·na·ba·ra Bay \ˌgwä-nä-ˈbär-ə\ inlet of Atlantic Ocean SE Brazil

Gua·na·jua·to \ˌgwä-nä-ˈhwä-(ˌ)tō\ **1** state *cen* Mexico *area* 11,810 *sq mi* (30,588 *sq km*), *pop* 3,982,593 **2** city, its ✱ *pop* 128,171

Guang·dong \ˈgwäŋ-ˈdu̇ŋ\ *or* **Kwang·tung** \ˈgwäŋ-ˈdu̇ŋ, ˈkwäŋ-, -ˈtu̇ŋ\ province SE China bordering on S. China Sea & Gulf of Tonkin ✱ Guangzhou *area* 76,220 *sq mi* (197,410 *sq km*), *pop* 62,829,236

Guang·xi Zhuang·zu \ˈgwäŋ-ˈshē-ˈjwäŋ-ˈdzü\ *or* **Kwang·si Chuang** \ˈgwäŋ-ˈshē-ˈjwäŋ\ region & former province S China W of Guangdong ✱ Nanning *area* 85,096 *sq mi* (221,250 *sq km*), *pop* 42,245,765

Guang·zhou *or* **Kuang–chou** \ˈgwäŋ-ˈjō\ *or* **Can·ton** \ˈkan-ˌtän, kan-ˈ\ city & port SE China ✱ of Guangdong on Zhu River *pop* 2,914,281

Guan·tá·na·mo \gwän-ˈtä-nä-ˌmō\ city SE Cuba NW of **Guantánamo Bay** (inlet of the Caribbean; site of U.S. naval base) *pop* 200,381

Gua·po·ré \ˌgwä-pō-ˈrā\ **1** *or* **Ité·nez** \ē-ˈtā-nes\ river 1087 *mi* (1749 *km*) W Brazil & NE Bolivia flowing NW to the Mamoré **2** — see RONDÔNIA

Guar·da·fui, Cape \ˌg(w)är-dä-ˈfwē, -ˈfü-ē\ cape NE Somalia at entrance to Gulf of Aden

Guá·ri·co \ˈgwär-i-ˌkō\ river W Venezuela flowing SW & S into the Apure

Gua·te·ma·la \ˌgwä-tə-ˈmä-lə, -tā-ˈmä-lä\ **1** country Central America S of Mexico bordering on the Pacific & the Caribbean; a republic *area* 42,042 *sq mi* (109,309 *sq km*), *pop* 11,237,196 **2** *or* **Guatemala City** city, its ✱ *pop* 942,348 — **Gua·te·ma·lan** \-ˈmä-lən\ *adj or n*

Gua·via·re \gwä-ˈvyä-rā\ river 650 *mi* (1046 *km*) Colombia flowing E into the Orinoco

Gua·ya·ma \gwä-ˈyä-mä\ town SE Puerto Rico *pop* 45,362

Gua·ya·nil·la \ˌgwī-ä-ˈnē-yä\ city SW Puerto Rico *pop* 21,581

Gua·ya·quil \ˌgwī-ə-ˈkēl, -ˈkil\ city & port W Ecuador on Guayas River 40 *mi* (64 *km*) from **Gulf of Guayaquil** (inlet of the Pacific) *pop* 1,985,379

Gua·yas \ˈgwī-äs\ river W Ecuador forming delta in Gulf of Guayaquil

Guay·mas \ˈgwī-mäs\ city & port NW Mexico in Sonora on Gulf of California *pop* 134,625

Guay·na·bo \gwī-ˈnä-(ˌ)bō, -(ˌ)vō\ city NE *cen* Puerto Rico *pop* 97,924

Guelph \ˈgwelf\ city Canada in SE Ont. *pop* 121,688

Guern·sey \ˈgərn-zē\ island English Channel in the Channel Islands ✱ St. Peter Port *area* 24 *sq mi* (62 *sq km*), *pop* 55,421

Guer·re·ro \gā-ˈrā-rō\ state S Mexico bordering on the Pacific ✱ Chilpancingo *area* 24,631 *sq mi* (63,794 *sq km*), *pop* 2,620,637

Gui *or* **Kuei** \ˈgwā\ river 200 *mi* (322 *km*) SE China in E Guangxi Zhuangzu flowing S into the Xi

Gui·a·na \gē-ˈa-nə, -ˈä-nə; gī-ˈa-nə\ region N S. America bordering on the Atlantic & bounded on W & S by Orinoco, Negro, & Amazon rivers; includes Guyana, French Guiana, Suriname, & adjoining parts of Brazil & Venezuela — **Gui·a·nan** \-nən\ *adj or n* — **Gui·a·nese** \ˌgī-ə-ˈnēz, ˌgē-ə-, -ˈnēs\ *adj or n*

Gui·enne *or* **Guy·enne** \gwē-ˈyen\ region & former province SW France bordering on Bay of Biscay ✱ Bordeaux — see AQUITAINE

Gui·lin *or* **Kuei–lin** *or* **Kwei·lin** \ˈgwā-ˈlin\ city S China in NE Guangxi Zhuangzu on the Gui *pop* 364,130

Guin·ea \ˈgi-nē\ *or F* **Gui·née** \gē-ˈnā\ **1** region W Africa bordering on the Atlantic from Gambia (on N) to Angola (on S) **2** *or formerly* **French Guinea** republic W Africa bordering on the Atlantic; formerly a territory of French West Africa ✱ Conakry *area* 94,925 *sq mi* (245,856 *sq km*), *pop* 10,058,000 — **Guin·ean** \ˈgi-nē-ən\ *adj or n*

Guinea, Gulf of arm of the Atlantic W *cen* Africa; includes Bights of Benin & Biafra

Guin·ea–Bis·sau \ˌgi-nē-bi-ˈsau̇\ *or formerly* **Portuguese Guinea** republic W Africa S of Senegal; until 1974 a Portuguese colony ✱ Bissau *area* 13,948 *sq mi* (36,265 *sq km*), *pop* 1,548,159

Gui·púz·coa \gē-ˈpüs-kō-ə, -ˈpüth-kō-ä\ province N Spain; in Basque Country ✱ Donostia-San Sebastian *area* 771 *sq mi* (1997 *sq km*), *pop* 673,563

Gui·yang *or* **Kuei–yang** *or* **Kwei·yang** \ˈgwā-ˈyäŋ\ city S China ✱ of Guizhou *pop* 1,018,619

Gui·zhou \ˈgwā-ˈjō\ *or* **Kwei·chow** \ˈgwā-ˈjō\ province S China S of Sichuan ✱ Guiyang *area* 67,181 *sq mi* (174,671 *sq km*), *pop* 32,391,066

Gu·ja·rat *or* **Gu·je·rat** \ˌgü-jə-ˈrät, ˌgu̇-\ **1** region W India where Gujarati is spoken **2** state W India N & E of Gulf of Khambhat ✱ Gandhinagar *area* 72,236 *sq mi* (187,091 *sq km*), *pop* 50,596,992

Guj·ran·wala \ˌgüj-rən-ˈwä-lə, ˌgu̇j-\ city NE Pakistan *pop* 1,132,509

Gulf Islands National Park Reserve protected area SW Canada in Strait of Georgia off SE Vancouver Is., B.C.

Gulf·port \ˈgəlf-ˌpȯrt\ city & port SE Miss. *pop* 67,793

Gulf Stream warm current in N. Atlantic flowing from Gulf of Mexico NE along U.S. coast to Nantucket & thence eastward

Gulja — see YINING

Gumti — see GOMATI

Gun·ni·son \ˈgə-nə-sən\ river 150 *mi* (241 *km*) W *cen* Colo. flowing W & NW into Colorado River — see BLACK CANYON

Gunsan — see KUNSAN

Gun·tur \gu̇n-ˈtu̇r\ city E India in *cen* Andhra Pradesh *pop* 514,707

Gu·ra·bo \gü-ˈrä-bō\ city E *cen* Puerto Rico *pop* 45,369

Gur·nee \ˈgər-nē, gər-ˈnē\ village NE corner of Ill. *pop* 31,295

Gus·ta·vo A. Ma·de·ro, Vil·la \ˈvē-yä-gü-ˈstä-vō-ˌä-mä-ˈt͟hā-rō\ city *cen* Mexico in Distrito Federal N of Mexico City *pop* 1,182,895

Guy·ana \gī-ˈa-nə\ *or formerly* **British Guiana** country N S. America on Atlantic coast; a republic within the Commonwealth of Nations since 1970 ✱ Georgetown *area* 83,000 *sq mi* (215,800 *sq km*), *pop* 751,223 — **Guy·a·nese** \ˌgī-ə-ˈnēz, -ˈnēs\ *adj or n*

Gwa·dar \ˈgwä-dər\ town & port SW Pakistan on Arabian Sea; until 1958 belonged to Sultan of Oman *pop* 17,000

Gwaii Haa·nas National Park Reserve \ˌgwī-ˈhä-nəs\ coastal & Haida heritage site W Canada in Queen Charlotte Islands, W B.C.

Gwa·li·or \ˈgwä-lē-ˌȯr\ **1** former state N *cen* India ✱ Lashkar; part of Madhya Pradesh since 1956 **2** city N *cen* India in NW Madhya Pradesh SSE of Agra *pop* 826,919

Gwangju — see KWANGJU

Gwyn·edd \ˈgwi-ne͟th\ administrative area of NW Wales *area* 984 *sq mi* (2548 *sq km*)

Gyandzha — see GANCA

Gyor \ˈjœr\ city NW Hungary WNW of Budapest *pop* 134,200

Haar·lem \ˈhär-ləm\ city W Netherlands ✱ of N. Holland *pop* 147,831

Haarlemmermeer — see HOOFDDORP

Habana, La — see HAVANA — **Ha·ba·ne·ro** \ˌä-bə-ˈner-ō\ *n*

Ha·chi·o·ji \ˌhä-chē-ˈō-jē\ city Japan on Honshu *pop* 536,046

Hack·en·sack \ˈha-kᵊn-ˌsak\ city NE N.J. *pop* 43,010

Hack·ney \ˈhak-nē\ borough of N Greater London, England *pop* 164,200

Had·ding·ton \ˈha-diŋ-tən\ **1** *or* **Had·ding·ton·shire** \-ˌshir, -shər\ — see EAST LOTHIAN **2** royal burgh Scotland E of Edinburgh *pop* 8117

Ha·dra·mawt *or* **Ha·dhra·maut** \ˌhä-drə-ˈmau̇t\ region S Arabia bordering on Arabian Sea E of Aden, Yemen; chief town Al Mukalla *area* 58,500 *sq mi* (152,100 *sq km*)

Hadrumetum — see SOUSSE

Hae·ju \ˈhī-(ˌ)jü\ city SW N. Korea on inlet of Yellow Sea *pop* 195,000

Ha–erh–pin — see HARBIN

Ha·gåt·ña \hə-ˈgät-nyə\ *or formerly* **Aga·na** \ä-ˈgä-nyä\ town ✳ of Guam on W coast *pop* 1122

Ha·gen \ˈhä-gᵊn\ *or* **Hagen in West·fa·len** \in-ˌvest-ˈfä-lən\ city W Germany ENE of Düsseldorf *pop* 214,085

Ha·ger·man Fossil Beds National Monument \ˈhä-gər-mən\ site S Idaho along the Snake River

Ha·gers·town \ˈhä-gərz-ˌtaun\ city N Md. *pop* 39,662

Hague, Cap de la — see CAP DE LA HAGUE

Hague, The \thə-ˈhäg\ *or D* **'s Gra·ven·ha·ge** \ˈskrä-vᵊn-ˌhä-kə\ city SW Netherlands near coast of North Sea; ✳ of S. Holland & seat of government of the Netherlands *pop* 457,726

Haidarabad — see HYDERABAD

Hai·fa \ˈhī-fə\ city & port NW Israel at foot of Mt. Carmel *pop* 251,000

Hai·kou \ˈhī-ˈkō\ city & port SE China ✳ of Hainan *pop* 280,153

Hai·nan \ˈhī-ˈnän\ island SE China in S. China Sea; a province ✳ Haikou *area* 13,124 *sq mi* (33,991 *sq km*), *pop* 6,557,482

Hai·naut \ä-ˈnō, hä-\ **1** medieval county in Low Countries SE of Flanders in modern SW Belgium & N France **2** province SW Belgium ✳ Mons *area* 1463 *sq mi* (3789 *sq km*), *pop* 1,281,042

Hai·phong \ˈhī-ˈfôn, -ˈfän\ city & port N Vietnam in Tonkin in delta of Red River *metropolitan area pop* 1,726,900

Hai·ti \ˈhā-tē *also* hä-ˈē-tē\ **1** — see HISPANIOLA **2** country W. Indies on W Hispaniola; a republic ✳ Port-au-Prince *area* 10,714 *sq mi* (27,856 *sq km*), *pop* 7,929,048

Ha·ko·da·te \ˌhä-kō-ˈdä-tā\ city & port Japan in SW Hokkaido on Tsugaru Strait *pop* 287,637

Hal·ber·stadt \ˈhäl-bər-ˌshtät, -ˌstät\ city *cen* Germany SE of Brunswick *pop* 47,713

Hal·di·mand \ˈhôl-də-mənd\ city Canada in S Ont. *pop* 44,876

Ha·le·a·ka·la Crater \ˌhä-lā-ˌä-kä-ˈlä\ crater of dormant volcano 10,023 *ft* (3055 *m*) with crater more than 7500 *ft* (762 *m*) deep & 20 *mi* (32 *km*) in circumference Hawaii on E Maui in **Haleakala National Park**

Hal·i·car·nas·sus \ˌha-lə-kär-ˈna-səs\ ancient city SW Asia Minor in SW Caria on Aegean Sea

Hal·i·fax \ˈha-lə-ˌfaks\ **1** municipality & port Canada ✳ of N.S. *pop* 390,096 **2** town N England in W. Yorkshire *pop* 87,488 — **Hal·i·go·ni·an** \ˌha-lə-ˈgō-nē-ən\ *n*

Hal·lan·dale Beach \ˈha-lən-ˌdāl\ city SE Fla. S of Fort Lauderdale *pop* 37,113

Hal·le \ˈhä-lə\ city E *cen* Germany on the Saale NW of Leipzig *pop* 232,396

Hall·statt \ˈhôl-ˌstat, ˈhäl-ˌshtät\ village W *cen* Austria on shore of **Hall·stät·ter Lake** \ˈhôl-ˌste-tər, ˈhäl-ˌshte-\

Hal·ma·hera \ˌhäl-mə-ˈher-ə, ˌhäl-\ island E Indonesia in the Moluccas; largest in the group *area* 6928 *sq mi* (18,013 *sq km*), *pop* 54,000

Halm·stad \ˈhälm-ˌstäd\ city & port SW Sweden *pop* 86,585

Halq al–Wa·di \ˈhälk-äl-ˈwä-dē\ *or* **La Gou·lette** \ˌlä-gü-ˈlet\ city N Tunisia on Bay of Tunis; port for Tunis *pop* 67,685

Hälsingborg — see HELSINGBORG

Hal·tom City \ˈhôl-təm\ city N Tex. NE of Fort Worth *pop* 42,409

Hal·ton Hills \ˈhôl-tᵊn\ town Canada in S Ont. *pop* 59,008

Halys River — see KIZIL IRMAK

Ha·ma *or* **Ha·mah** \ˈhä-ˌmä\ *or bib* **Ha·math** \ˈhä-ˌmath\ city W Syria on the Orontes *pop* 313,000

Ha·mad, Al \ˌäl-hə-ˈmäd\ the SW portion of Syrian Desert

Ha·ma·dan \ˌhä-mə-ˈdan, ˌhä-mə-ˈdän\ *or anc* **Ec·bat·a·na** \ek-ˈba-tə-nə\ city W Iran WSW of Tehran *pop* 479,640

Ha·ma·ma·tsu \ˌhä-mä-ˈmät-(ˌ)sü\ city Japan in S Honshu SE of Nagoya near Pacific coast *pop* 582,095

Ham·burg \ˈham-ˌbərg; ˈhäm-ˌbůrg, -ˌbůrk\ city & port N Germany on the Elbe 68 *mi* (109 *km*) from its mouth; a state of the Federal Republic of Germany 1948–90 & of reunified Germany since then *area* 288 *sq mi* (749 *sq km*), *pop* 1,668,800 — **Ham·burg·er** \-ˌbər-gər, -ˌbůr-\ *n*

Ham·den \ˈham-dən\ town S Conn. N of New Haven *pop* 60,960

Ha·meln \ˈhä-məln\ *or formerly* **Ham·e·lin** \ˈha-mə-lən\ city N *cen* Germany in Lower Saxony SW of Hannover *pop* 58,906

Ham·hung *or* **Ham·heung** \ˈhäm-ˌhůn\ city E *cen* N. Korea near coast *pop* 701,000

Ham·il·ton \ˈha-məl-tən\ **1** city SW Ohio N of Cincinnati *pop* 62,477 **2** town & port ✳ of Bermuda *pop* 969 **3** — see CHURCHILL 2 **4** city & port Canada in SE Ont. on Lake Ontario *pop* 519,949 **5** city New Zealand on *cen* North Is. *urban area pop* 166,128

Hamilton, Mount mountain 4261 *ft* (1299 *m*) W Calif. E of San Jose

Hamilton Inlet inlet of the Atlantic 150 *mi* (241 *km*) long (with Lake Melville) Canada in SE Labrador

Hamm \ˈhäm, ˈham\ city W Germany on Lippe River *pop* 180,323

Ham·mer·fest \ˈha-mər-ˌfest, ˈhä-\ town & port N Norway on island in Arctic Ocean; northernmost town in Europe, at 70°38′N *pop* 6934

Ham·mer·smith and Ful·ham \ˈha-mər-ˌsmith-ənd-ˈfú-ləm\ borough of SW Greater London, England *pop* 136,500

Ham·mond \ˈha-mənd\ city NW Ind. SE of Chicago *pop* 80,830

Hamp·shire \ˈhamp-ˌshir, -shər\ *or* **Hants** \ˈhants\ county S England on English Channel ✳ Winchester *area* 1509 *sq mi* (3908 *sq km*), *pop* 1,511,900

Hamp·stead \ˈhamp-stəd, -ˌsted\ former metropolitan borough NW London, England, now part of Camden

Hamp·ton \ˈhamp-tən\ city & port SE Va. E of Newport News on Hampton Roads *pop* 137,436

Hampton Roads channel SE Va. through which James & Elizabeth rivers flow into Chesapeake Bay

Ham·tramck \ham-ˈtra-mik\ city SE Mich. surrounded by Detroit *pop* 22,423

Han \ˈhän\ **1** river E *cen* China in Shaanxi & Hubei flowing SE into the Chang **2** river *ab* 300 *mi* (483 *km*) N *cen* S. Korea flowing W & NW into Yellow Sea

HaNegev — see NEGEV

Han·ford \ˈhan-fərd\ city S *cen* Calif. SE of Fresno *pop* 53,967

Hang·zhou \ˈhäŋ-ˈjō\ *or* **Hang·chou** \ˈhäŋ-ˈjō\ *or* **Hang·chow** \ˈhäŋ-ˈchaů, ˈhäŋ-ˈjō\ city E China ✳ of Zhejiang at head of **Hangzhou Bay** (inlet of E. China Sea) *pop* 1,099,660

Han·ko \ˈhaŋ-ˌkō\ *or Sw* **Hangö** \ˈhäŋ-ˌœ\ town & port SW Finland on Hanko (Hangö) Peninsula in the Baltic SE of Turku

Han·kow \ˈhaŋ-ˈkaů, -ˈkō; ˈhän-ˈkō\ former city E *cen* China — see WU·HAN

Han·ni·bal \ˈha-nə-bəl\ city NE Mo. on Mississippi River *pop* 17,916

Han·no·ver *or* **Han·o·ver** \ˈha-nō-vər, -nə-vər, *G* hä-ˈnō-fər\ city N *cen* Germany WNW of Brunswick *pop* 517,476

Ha·noi \ha-ˈnòi, ha-\ city ✳ of Vietnam in Tonkin on Red River; formerly ✳ of French Indochina & of N. Vietnam *metropolitan area pop* 2,931,400

Han·o·ver Park \ˈha-ˌnō-vər, -nə-vər\ village NE Ill. *pop* 37,973

Han·yang \ˈhän-ˈyäŋ\ former city E *cen* China — see WUHAN

Haora — see HOWRAH

Ha·rap·pa \hə-ˈra-pə\ locality E Pakistan in Indus Valley between Multan and Lahore; center of a prehistoric civilization

Ha·ra·re \hə-ˈrä-(ˌ)rā\ *or formerly* **Salisbury** city ✳ of Zimbabwe *pop* 1,444,534

Har·bin \ˈhär-bən, här-ˈbin\ *or* **Ha–erh–pin** \ˈhä-ˈər-ˈbin\ *or formerly* **Pin·kiang** \ˈbin-ˈjyäŋ\ city NE China ✳ of Heilongjiang on Songhua River *pop* 2,443,398

Ha·rer \ˈhär-ər\ city E Ethiopia E of Addis Ababa *pop* 105,000

Har·in·gey \ˈha-riŋ-ˌgā\ borough of N Greater London, England *pop* 187,300

Ha·rī·rūd *or* **Ha·ri Rud** \ˈha-rē-ˈrüd\ *or anc* **Ari·us** \ˈer-ē-əs, ə-ˈrī-əs\ river 700 *mi* (1126 *km*) NW Afghanistan, NE Iran, & S Turkmenistan flowing W & N into Kara Kum Desert

Har·lem \ˈhär-ləm\ **1** river channel SE N.Y. NE of Manhattan Is. connecting (with Spuyten Duyvil Creek) Hudson & East rivers **2** section of New York City in N Manhattan bordering on Harlem & East rivers — **Har·lem·ite** \-lə-ˌmīt\ *n*

Har·lin·gen \ˈhär-lən-jən\ city S Tex. NNW of Brownsville *pop* 64,849

Har·ling·en \ˈhär-liŋ-ən\ town & port N Netherlands in Friesland

Har·ney Lake \ˈhär-nē\ intermittent salt lake SE Oreg. in **Harney Basin** (depression, *area* 2500 *sq mi* or 6500 *sq km*)

Harney Peak mountain 7242 *ft* (2207 *m*) SW S.Dak.; highest in Black Hills & in state

Harris — see LEWIS WITH HARRIS

Har·ris·burg \ˈha-rəs-ˌbərg\ city ✳ of Pa. on Susquehanna River *pop* 49,528

Har·ri·son \ˈha-rə-sən\ village SE N.Y. on Long Island Sound *pop* 27,472

Har·ri·son·burg \ˈha-rə-sən-ˌbərg\ city N Va. *pop* 48,914

Har·ro·gate \ˈha-rə-gət, -ˌgāt\ town N England in N. Yorkshire N of Leeds *pop* 66,475

Har·row \ˈha-(ˌ)rō\ borough of NW Greater London, England *pop* 194,300

Hart·ford \ˈhärt-fərd\ city N *cen* Conn., its ✳ *pop* 124,775 — **Hart·ford·ite** \-fər-ˌdīt\ *n*

Hart·le·pool \ˈhärt-lē-ˌpül\ seaport N England on North Sea *pop* 88,200

Har·vard, Mount \ˈhär-vərd\ mountain 14,420 *ft* (4395 *m*) *cen* Colo. in Sawatch Range SE of Mt. Elbert

Har·vey \ˈhär-vē\ city NE Ill. S of Chicago *pop* 25,282

Har·wich \ˈha-rij, -rich\ seaport SE England in Essex on North Sea *pop* 15,076

Har·ya·na \ˌhə-rē-ˈä-nə\ state NW India in E Punjab formed 1966 from S part of former state of Punjab ✳ Chandigarh *area* 17,010 *sq mi* (44,226 *sq km*), *pop* 21,082,989

Harz \ˈhärts\ mountains *cen* Germany bet. the Elbe & the Leine — see BROCKEN

Hasa *or* **Hasa, Al—** — see AL-HASA

Has·selt \ˈhä-səlt\ commune NE Belgium ✳ of Limburg *pop* 68,771

Has·tings \ˈhās-tiŋz\ **1** city S Nebr. *pop* 24,907 **2** resort town SE England in E. Sussex on Strait of Dover *pop* 78,100

Ha·tay \hä-ˈtī\ district S Turkey E of Gulf of Iskenderun

Ha·til·lo \ä-ˈtē-ō\ city NW Puerto Rico *pop* 41,953

Hat·ter·as, Cape \ˈha-tə-rəs\ cape N.C. on SE Hatteras Is.

Hatteras Island island N.C. bet. Pamlico Sound & Atlantic Ocean; a long barrier island

Hat·ties·burg \ˈha-tēz-ˌbərg\ city SE Miss. *pop* 45,989

Hau·ra·ki Gulf \hau-ˈra-kē, -ˈrä-kē\ inlet of the S. Pacific N New Zealand on N coast of North Is.

Ha·vana \hə-ˈva-nə\ *or Sp* **La Ha·ba·na** \ˌlä-ä-ˈbä-nä\ city & port ✳ of Cuba on Gulf of Mexico *pop* 2,096,054 — **Ha·van·an** \hə-ˈva-nən\ *adj or n*

Hav·ant \ˈha-vənt\ town S England in Hampshire NE of Portsmouth *pop* 117,400

Ha·vel \ˈhä-fᵊl\ river 212 *mi* (341 *km*) NE Germany flowing SW through Berlin into the Elbe

Hav·er·ford·west \ˌha-vər-fərd-ˈwest, ˌhär-fərd-\ port SW Wales *pop* 9936

Ha·ver·hill \ˈhāv-rəl, ˈhā-və-rəl\ city NE Mass. *pop* 60,879

Ha·ver·ing \ˈhāv-riŋ, ˈhā-və-riŋ\ borough of NE Greater London, England *pop* 224,400

Ha·ví·rov \ˈhä-vē-ˌzhòf\ city E Czech Republic *pop* 85,855

Havre — see LE HAVRE

Ha·waii \hə-ˈwä-yē, -ˈwä-ē *also* -ˈvä- *or* -ˈwò-; *sometimes* -yə\ **1** *or* **Ha·wai·ian Islands** \-yən\ *or formerly* **Sand·wich Islands** \ˈsand-ˌwich\ group of islands *cen* Pacific belonging to U.S. **2** island SE Hawaii, largest of the group; chief city Hilo *area* 4021 *sq mi* (10,455 *sq km*), *pop* 185,079 **3** state of the U.S. comprising Hawaiian Islands except Midway Islands; annexed 1898, a territory 1900–59 ✳ Honolulu *area* 6471 *sq mi* (16,760 *sq km*), *pop* 1,360,301

Hawaii Volcanoes National Park reservation Hawaii including Mauna Loa & Kilauea volcanoes on Hawaii (island)

Hawke Bay \ˈhòk\ inlet of the S. Pacific N New Zealand on SE coast of North Is.

Haw·thorne \ˈhò-ˌthòrn\ city SW Calif. SW of Los Angeles *pop* 84,293

Hay \ˈhā\ river 530 *mi* (853 *km*) Canada in N Alta. & S Northwest Territories flowing NE into Great Slave Lake

---

\ə\ abut \ᵊ\ kitten, F table \ər\ further \a\ ash \ā\ ace \ä\ mop, mar
\au\ out \ch\ chin \e\ bet \ē\ easy \g\ go \i\ hit \ī\ ice \j\ job
\ŋ\ sing \ō\ go \ò\ law \òi\ boy \th\ thin \th̲\ the \ü\ loot \ů\ foot
\y\ yet \zh\ vision, beige \k̲, ⁿ, œ, ᴜɛ, ᵞ\ see Guide to Pronunciation

Hayes \'hāz\ **1** river 300 *mi* (483 *km*) Canada in E Man. flowing NE into Hudson Bay **2** *or* **Hayes and Har·ling·ton** \'här-liŋ-tən\ former urban district SE England in Middlesex, now part of Hillingdon

Hay·ward \'hā-wərd\ city W Calif. SE of Oakland *pop* 144,186

Ha·zel·wood \'hā-zəl-₁wud\ city E Mo. WNW of St. Louis *pop* 25,703

Ha·zle·ton \'hā-zəl-tən\ city E Pa. S of Wilkes-Barre *pop* 25,340

Heard \'hərd\ island S Indian Ocean SE of Kerguelen at 53°10'S, 74°10'E; administered by Australia

He·bei \'hə-'bā\ *or* **Ho·peh** *or* **Ho·pei** \'hō-'bā\ *or formerly* **Chih·li** \'chē-'lē, 'jir-'lē\ province NE China ✻ Shijiazhuang *area* 77,079 *sq mi* (199,635 *sq km*) *pop* 61,082,439

Heb·ri·des \'he-brə-₁dēz\ islands W Scotland in the Atlantic, divided by Little Minch into **Inner Hebrides** (near the mainland) & **Outer Hebrides** (to NW) *area* 2900 *sq mi* (7540 *sq km*), *pop* 30,660 — see LEWIS WITH HARRIS, WESTERN ISLES — **Heb·ri·de·an** \,he-brə-'dē-ən\ *adj or n*

He·bron \'hē-brən\ *or anc* **Kir·jath–ar·ba** \,kər-yəth-'är-bə, ,kir-\ city West Bank SW of Jerusalem; governed by Palestinian Authority since 1997 *pop* 79,087

Hec·ate Strait \'he-kət\ strait Canada in W B.C.; inlet of the Pacific bet. Queen Charlotte Islands & the coast

Heer·len \'her-lən\ commune SE Netherlands in Limburg NE of Maastricht *pop* 95,004

He·fei *or* **Ho·fei** \'hə-'fā\ *or formerly* **Lu·chow** \'lü-'jō\ city E China ✻ of Anhui W of Nanjing *pop* 733,278

Hei·del·berg \'hī-d³l-₁bərg, -₁berk\ city SW Germany on the Neckar SE of Mannheim *pop* 139,392

Heil·bronn \'hīl-₁brän, hīl-'brón\ city SW Germany on the Neckar N of Stuttgart *pop* 117,427

Heilong, Hei–lung — see AMUR

Hei·long·jiang *or* **Hei–lung·kiang** \'hā-'lúŋ-'jyäŋ\ province NE China in N Manchuria bordering on the Amur ✻ Harbin *area* 178,996 *sq mi* (465,390 *sq km*) *pop* 35,214,873

He·jaz \he-'jaz, hi-\ *or* **Al Hi·jāz** \,äl-hi-'jaz\ region W Saudi Arabia on Red Sea; a viceroyalty ✻ Mecca *area* 134,600 *sq mi* (348,614 *sq km*), *pop* 1,400,000

Hek·la *or* **Hec·la** \'he-klä\ volcano 4747 *ft* (1447 *m*) SW Iceland

Hel·e·na \'he-lə-nə\ city W *cen* Mont., its ✻ *pop* 28,190

Hel·go·land \'hel-gō-₁land, -₁länt\ *or* **Hel·i·go·land** \'he-lə-gō-\ island NW Germany in North Sea, in N. Frisian Islands

Hel·i·con \'he-lə-₁kän, -li-kən\ *or ModGk* **Eli·kón** \,e-lē-'kón\ mountain 5735 *ft* (1748 *m*) E *cen* Greece in SW Boeotia near Gulf of Corinth

He·li·op·o·lis \,hē-lē-'ä-pə-lis\ **1** — see BAALBEK **2** ancient ruined city N Egypt NE of modern Cairo

Hellas — see GREECE

Hel·les, Cape \'he-(,)lēz\ headland Turkey in Europe at S tip of Gallipoli Peninsula

Hellespont, Hellespontus — see DARDANELLES

Hell Gate a narrow part of East River in New York City bet. Long Is. & Manhattan Is.

Hells Canyon \'helz\ canyon of Snake River on Idaho-Oreg. border; deepest in the U.S.

Hel·mand *or* **Hel·mund** \'hel-mənd\ river SW Afghanistan flowing SW & W into swamps on Iran border

Hel·mond \'hel-₁mónt\ commune S Netherlands *pop* 82,853

Helm·stedt \'helm-₁shtet, -₁shtāt\ city *cen* Germany E of Brunswick near former E. Germany–W. Germany border *pop* 27,072

Hel·sing·borg *or* **Häl·sing·borg** \'hel-siŋ-₁bòrg, -₁bòr-ē\ city & port SW Sweden on Øresund opposite Helsingør, Denmark *pop* 117,737

Hel·sing·ør \,hel-siŋ-'ér\ city & port Denmark on N Sjælland Is. *pop* 56,754

Hel·sin·ki \'hel-₁siŋ-kē, hel-'\ *or Sw* **Hel·sing·fors** \'hel-siŋ-₁fòrs\ city & port ✻ of Finland on Gulf of Finland *pop* 559,718

Hel·vel·lyn \hel-'ve-lən\ mountain 3118 *ft* (950 *m*) NW England in Cumbria SW of Ullswater

Helvetia — see SWITZERLAND — **Hel·ve·tian** \hel-'vē-shən\ *adj or n*

Hem·et \'he-mət\ city SE Calif. SE of San Bernardino *pop* 58,812

Hemp·stead \'hem(p)-₁sted, -₁stəd\ village SE N.Y. on Long Is. *pop* 53,891

He·nan \'hə-'nän\ *or* **Ho·nan** \'hō-'nan\ province E *cen* China ✻ Zhengzhou *area* 64,479 *sq mi* (167,645 *sq km*) *pop* 85,509,535

Hen·der·son \'hen-dər-sən\ **1** city NW Ky. *pop* 28,757 **2** city S Nev. *pop* 257,729

Hen·der·son·ville \'hen-dər-sən-₁vil, -vəl\ city N Tenn. NE of Nashville *pop* 51,372

Hen·don \'hen-dən\ urban district SE England in Middlesex; part of Barnet

Heng·yang \'həŋ-'yäŋ\ city SE *cen* China in SE Hunan on the Xiang *pop* 487,148

Hen·ley \'hen-lē\ *or* **Henley on Thames** town SE *cen* England in Oxfordshire W of London *pop* 31,744

Hen·lo·pen, Cape \hen-'lō-pən\ headland SE Del. at entrance to Delaware Bay

Hen·ry, Cape \'hen-rē\ headland SE Va. S of entrance to Chesapeake Bay

He·rat \he-'rät, hə-\ *or anc* **Aria** \'er-ē-ə, ə-'rī-ə\ city NW Afghanistan on the Harīrūd *pop* 177,300

Her·cu·la·ne·um \,hər-kyə-'lā-nē-əm\ ancient city S Italy in Campania on Tyrrhenian Sea; destroyed A.D. 79 by eruption of Mt. Vesuvius

Her·e·ford \'her-ə-fərd, *US also* 'hər-fərd\ **1** *or* **Her·e·ford·shire** \-₁shir, -shər\ county W England on Welsh border **2** town W England in Herefordshire *pop* 49,800

Her·ford \'her-fórt\ city W *cen* Germany in N. Rhine-Westphalia NE of Bielefeld *pop* 64,732

He·ri·sau \'her-ə-₁zaú\ commune NE Switzerland ✻ of Appenzell Outer Rhodes *pop* 15,560

Her·mon, Mount \'hər-mən\ mountain 9232 *ft* (2814 *m*) on border bet. Syria & Lebanon; highest in Anti-Lebanon Mountains

Her·mo·sil·lo \,her-mō-'sē-(₁)yō\ city NW Mexico ✻ of Sonora on Sonora River *pop* 559,154

Hermoúpolis — see ERMOÚPOLIS

Her·ne \'her-nə\ city W Germany in the Ruhr *pop* 179,137

Her·ning \'her-niŋ\ city Denmark in *cen* Jutland *pop* 56,376

Her·ten \'her-t³n\ city W Germany in N. Rhine-Westphalia N of Essen *pop* 69,374

Hert·ford \'här-fərd, 'härt-, *US also* 'hərt-\ town SE England ✻ of Hertfordshire *pop* 21,412

Hert·ford·shire \'här-fərd-₁shir, 'härt-, -shər, *US also* 'hərt-\ *or* **Hertford** \'härt-, *US also* 'hərt-\ county SE England *area* 654 *sq mi* (1699 *sq km*), *pop* 951,500

Hertogenbosch, 's — see 'S HERTOGENBOSCH

Her·ze·go·vi·na \,hert-sə-gō-'vē-nə, ,hərt-, -'gō-və-nə\ *or Serb* **Her·ce·go·vi·na** \'kert-sə-gō-vē-nə\ region S Europe S of Bosnia & NW of Montenegro; part of Bosnia and Herzegovina — **Her·ze·go·vi·nian** \,hert-sə-gō-'vē-nē-ən, ,hərt-, -nyən\ *n*

Hes·pe·ria \he-'spir-ē-ə\ city SE Calif. N of San Bernardino *pop* 90,173

Hesse \'hes, 'he-sē\ *or G* **Hes·sen** \'he-s³n\ **1** region W *cen* Germany N of Baden-Württemberg, divided into **Hesse–Darmstadt** (in the S) & **Hesse–Cas·sel** \-'ka-s³l, -'kä-\ (in the N), the latter being united with Prussia in 1866 as part of the province of **Hesse–Nassau** along with the duchy of Nassau & the city of Frankfurt am Main **2** state of the Weimar Republic, equivalent to Hesse-Darmstadt **3** state of Germany & *formerly* of W. Germany including larger part of Hesse-Darmstadt & part of Hesse-Nassau ✻ Wiesbaden *area* 8151 *sq mi* (21,111 *sq km*), *pop* 5,763,300

Hes·ton and Isle·worth \'hes-tən-ənd-'ī-zəl-(₁)wərth, 'he-s³n-\ former municipal borough SE England in Middlesex, now part of Hounslow

Hi·a·le·ah \,hī-ə-'lē-ə\ city SE Fla. N of Miami *pop* 224,669

Hibernia — see IRELAND 1

Hick·o·ry \'hi-kə-rē\ city W cen N.C. *pop* 40,010

Hi·dal·go \hi-'dal-(₁)gō, ē-'thäl-(₁)gō\ state *cen* Mexico ✻ Pachuca *area* 8103 *sq mi* (20,987 *sq km*), *pop* 1,888,366

Hierosolyma — see JERUSALEM

Hier·ro \'yer-(₁)ō\ *or* **Fer·ro** \'fer-(₁)ō\ island Spain; westernmost of the Canary Islands *area* 107 *sq mi* (278 *sq km*)

Hi·ga·shi·ōsa·ka \hi-₁gä-shē-'ō-sä-kä\ city Japan in S Honshu, suburb of Osaka *pop* 515,094

High Atlas — see ATLAS MOUNTAINS

High·land \'hī-lənd\ **1** city SE Calif. E of San Bernardino *pop* 53,104 **2** town NW Ind. S of Hammond *pop* 23,727 **3** administrative area N Scotland *area* 9806 *sq mi* (25,398 *sq km*)

Highland Park city NE Ill. N of Chicago *pop* 29,763

High·lands \'hī-ləndz\ the chiefly mountainous N part of Scotland N of a line connecting Firth of Clyde & Firth of Tay

Highlands of Navesink — see NAVESINK (Highlands of)

Highlands of the Hudson hilly region SE N.Y. on both sides of Hudson River; includes Storm King (W of the Hudson) 1355 *ft* (413 *m*)

High Plains the Great Plains esp. from Nebr. southward

High Point \'hī-₁póint\ city N *cen* N.C. SW of Greensboro *pop* 104,371

High Sierra the Sierra Nevada (in Calif.)

High Wyc·ombe \'wi-kəm\ town SE *cen* England in Buckinghamshire WNW of London *pop* 60,516

Hii·u·maa \'hē-ə-₁mä\ island Estonia in Baltic Sea N of Sarema Is. *area* 373 *sq mi* (966 *sq km*)

Hijāz, Al — see HEJAZ

Hil·des·heim \'hil-dəs-₁hīm\ city N Germany SSE of Hannover *pop* 105,674

Hil·liard \'hil-yərd\ city *cen* Ohio, a suburb of Columbus *pop* 28,435

Hil·ling·don \'hi-liŋ-dən\ borough of W Greater London, England *pop* 225,800

Hills·boro \'hilz-₁bər-ō\ city NW Oreg. W of Portland *pop* 91,611

Hi·lo \'hē-(₁)lō\ city & port Hawaii in E Hawaii (island) *pop* 43,263

Hil·ton Head Island \'hil-t³n-'hed\ island comprising a town off S.C. coast *pop* 33,862

Hil·ver·sum \'hil-vər-səm\ city *cen* Netherlands in N. Holland SE of Amsterdam *pop* 83,096

Hi·ma·chal Pra·desh \hi-₁mä-chəl-prə-'desh, -'dāsh\ state NW India NW of Uttar Pradesh ✻ Shimla *area* 21,490 *sq mi* (55,659 *sq km*), *pop* 6,077,248

Hi·ma·la·yas \,hi-mə-'lā-əz; hə-'mäl-yəz, -'mäl-ē-əz\ *or the* **Hi·ma·la·ya** \-ə\ mountains S Asia on border bet. India & Tibet & in Kashmir, Nepal, & Bhutan — see EVEREST (Mount)

Hi·me·ji \hē-'mä-jē\ city Japan in W Honshu *pop* 478,309

Hindenburg — see ZABRZE

Hin·du Kush \,hin-(₁)dü-'kúsh, -'kòsh\ *or anc* **Cau·ca·sus In·di·cus** \'kò-kə-səs-'in-di-kəs\ mountain range *cen* Asia SW of the Pamirs on border of Kashmir & in Afghanistan — see TIRICH MIR

Hin·du·stan \,hin-(₁)dü-'stan, -də-, -'stän\ **1** region N India N of the Deccan including the plain drained by the Indus, the Ganges, & the Brahmaputra **2** the subcontinent of India **3** the Republic of India

Hines·ville \'hīnz-₁vil, -vəl\ city SE Ga. *pop* 33,437

Hip·po \'hi-(₁)pō\ *or* **Hippo Re·gi·us** \'rē-jəs, -jē-əs\ ancient city N Africa SW of modern Annaba, Algeria; chief town of Numidia

Hi·ra·ka·ta \,hir-ə-'kä-tä\ city Japan in S Honshu *pop* 402,563

Hi·ro·shi·ma \,hir-ə-'shē-mə, hə-'rō-shə-mə\ city & port Japan in SW Honshu on Inland Sea *pop* 1,126,239

His·pa·nia \hi-'spä-nē-ə, -'spā-nyə, -'spa-\ — see IBERIAN PENINSULA

His·pan·io·la \,his-pə-'nyō-lə\ *or Sp* **Es·pa·ño·la** \,es-₁pä-'nyō-lä\ *or formerly* **Hai·ti** \'hā-tē\ *or* **San·to Do·min·go** \,san-tə-də-'miŋ-(₁)gō\ island West Indies in the Greater Antilles; divided bet. Haiti (on W) & Dominican Republic (on E) *area* 29,371 *sq mi* (76,071 *sq km*)

His·sar·lik \,hi-sər-'lik\ site of ancient Troy NW Turkey in Asia 4 *mi* (6.4 *km*) SE of mouth of the Dardanelles

Hi·was·see \hī-'wä-sē\ river 150 *mi* (241 *km*) E U.S. flowing from NE Ga. WNW through W N.C. into Tennessee River in Tenn.

Ho·bart \'hō-₁bärt, -bərt\ **1** city NW Ind. *pop* 29,059 **2** \-₁bärt\ city & port Australia ✻ of Tasmania *pop* 47,106

Hobbs \'häbz\ city SE corner of N.Mex. *pop* 34,122

Ho·bo·ken \'hō-₁bō-kən\ city NE N.J. N of Jersey City *pop* 50,005

Ho Chi Minh City \'hō-₁chē-'min\ *or formerly* **Sai·gon** \sī-'gän, 'sī-₁\ city & port S Vietnam; formerly (as Saigon) ✻ of S. Vietnam *pop* 5,479,000

Hodeida — see AL HUDAYDAH

Hof \'hōf, 'hóf\ city Germany in Bavaria on the Saale near former E. Germany–W. Germany border *pop* 52,859

Hofei — see HEFEI

Hoff·man Estates \'häf-mən, 'hóf-\ village NE Ill. *pop* 51,895

Hofuf — see AL HUFUF

Hoggar Mountains — see AHAGGAR MOUNTAINS

Ho·hen·zol·lern \'hō-ən-ˌzä-lərn, -ˌtsò-lərn\ region SW Germany; formerly a province of Prussia — see WÜRTTEMBERG

Ho·he Tau·ern \ˌhō-ə-'taú(-ə)rn\ range of the E Alps W Austria bet. Carinthia & Tirol — see GROSSGLOCKNER

Hoh·hot \'hō-'hōt\ *or* **Hu·he·hot** \'hü-hə-'hōt\ *or* **Hu–ho–hao–t'e** \'hü-'hō-'haú-'tə\ city N China ✳ of Inner Mongolia *pop* 652,534

Ho·ho·kam Pi·ma National Monument \'hō-'hō-kəm-'pē-mə\ site S Ariz. containing archaeological remains; not open to the public

Hok·kai·do \hò-'kī-(ˌ)dō\ *or formerly* **Ye·zo** \'ye-(ˌ)zō\ island N Japan N of Honshu *area with adjacent small islands* 30,313 *sq mi* (78,511 *sq km*), *pop* 5,683,062

Hol·guín \(h)òl-'gēn\ city E Cuba in plateau region *pop* 228,052

Hol·land \'hä-lənd\ **1** city W Mich. on Lake Michigan *pop* 33,051 **2** medieval county of Holy Roman Empire bordering on North Sea, now forming N. & S. Holland provinces of the Netherlands **3** — see NETHERLANDS — **Hol·land·er** \-lən-dər\ *n*

Holland, Parts of district & former administrative county E England in SE Lincolnshire ✳ Boston *area* 418 *sq mi* (1083 *sq km*)

Hollandia — see JAYAPURA

Hol·lis·ter \'hä-lə-stər\ city W Calif. E of Monterey Bay *pop* 34,928

Hol·ly·wood \'hä-lē-ˌwùd\ **1** section of Los Angeles, Calif. NW of the downtown district **2** city SE Fla. N of Miami *pop* 140,768

Hol·stein \'hōl-ˌstīn, -ˌstēn; 'hòl-ˌshtīn\ region N Germany S of Jutland Peninsula adjoining Schleswig; once a duchy of Denmark, became a part of Prussia 1866 — see SCHLESWIG-HOLSTEIN

Hol·ston \'hōl-stən\ river 140 *mi* (225 *km*) E Tenn. flowing SW to unite with French Broad River forming the Tennessee River

Holy Cross, Mount of the mountain 14,005 *ft* (4269 *m*) NW *cen* Colo. in Sawatch Range

Holy·head \'hä-lē-ˌhed\ seaport NW Wales on Holy Is.

Ho·ly Island \'hō-lē\ **1** *or* **Lin·dis·farne** \'lin-dəs-ˌfärn\ peninsula which becomes an island at high tide N England off NE coast of Northumberland *pop* 190 **2** *or* **Holyhead Island** island NW Wales in St. George's Channel off W coast of Anglesey

Holy Land the lands comprising ancient Palestine & including the holy land of the Jewish, Christian, & Islamic religions

Holy Loch inlet of Firth of Clyde W Scotland on NW shore of the firth opposite mouth of the Clyde

Hol·yoke \'hō(l)-ˌyōk\ city SW Mass. N of Springfield *pop* 39,880

Holy Roman Empire realm of varying extent in *cen* Europe in medieval & modern periods with Germany as chief component

Home·stead \'hōm-ˌsted\ city SE Fla. SW of Miami *pop* 60,512

Homestead National Monument of America site SE Nebr. of first homestead entered under General Homestead Act of 1862

Home·wood \'hōm-ˌwùd\ city *cen* Ala. *pop* 25,167

Homs \'hòmz, 'hùms\ *or anc* **Em·e·sa** \'e-mə-sə\ city W Syria on the Orontes *pop* 354,508

Ho·myel' \ˌkō-'myel\ *or* **Go·mel** \gò-'mel, -'myel\ *or* **Ho·mel** \hò-\ city SE Belarus *pop* 503,300

Honan — see HENAN

Hon·du·ras \hän-'dùr-əs, -'dyùr-; òn-'dü-räs\ country Central America bordering on the Caribbean & the Pacific; a republic ✳ Tegucigalpa *area* 43,277 *sq mi* (112,087 *sq km*), *pop* 6,535,344 — **Hon·du·ran** \-ən\ *adj or n*

Honduras, Gulf of inlet of the Caribbean bet. S Belize, E Guatemala, & N Honduras

Hon·fleur \ōⁿ-'flœr\ town & port N France on Seine estuary *pop* 8346

Hong — see RED 4

Hong Kong \'häŋ-ˌkäŋ, -ˈkäŋ; 'hòŋ-ˌkòŋ, -ˈkòŋ\ *or* **Chin Xiang·gang** *or* **Hsiang Kang** \'shyäŋ-ˌgäŋ\ **1** special administrative region China on SE coast E of mouth of Zhu River including Hong Kong Is., Jiulong Peninsula & New Territories; & nearby islands; formerly a Brit. crown colony with Victoria as ✳ *area* 424 *sq mi* (1098 *sq km*), *pop* 6,708,389 **2** — see VICTORIA 5 — **Hong Kong·er** *n*

Hong·shui *or* **Hung·shui** \'hùŋ-'shwē\ river S China flowing from E Yunnan E to S Guangxi Zhuangzu

Hong·ze *or* **Hung·tse** \'hùŋ-'dzə\ lake 65 *mi* (105 *km*) long E China in W Jiangsu; traversed by the Huang

Ho·ni·a·ra \ˌhō-nē-'är-ə\ town W Pacific ✳ of Solomon Islands on Guadalcanal Is. *pop* 49,107

Ho·no·lu·lu \ˌhä-nə-'lü-(ˌ)lü, ˌhō-nə-\ city & port ✳ of Hawaii on Oahu *area pop* 953,207 — **Ho·no·lu·lan** \-'lü-lən\ *n*

Hon·shu \'hän-(ˌ)shü, 'hòn-\ *or* **Hon·do** \-(ˌ)dō\ island Japan; chief island of the group *area* 86,246 *sq mi* (223,377 *sq km*), *pop* 100,254,208

Hood, Mount \'hùd\ mountain 11,235 *ft* (3424 *m*) NW Oreg. in Cascade Range; highest point in state

Hood Canal inlet of Puget Sound 80 *mi* (129 *km*) long W Wash. along E shore of Olympic Peninsula

Hoofd·dorp \'hōft-ˌdòrp\ *or* **Haar·lem·mer·meer** \ˌhär-lə-mər-'mār\ commune W Netherlands *pop* 118,553

Hooghly — see HUGLI

Hook of Holland \'hùk\ headland SW Netherlands in S. Holland on coast SW of The Hague

Hoorn, Iles de — see FUTUNA ISLANDS

Hoo·sac Mountains \'hü-sæk\ mountain range NW Mass. & SW Vt., a southern extension of Green Mountains

Hoo·ver \'hü-vər\ city *cen* Ala. *pop* 81,619

Hoover Dam *or formerly* **Boul·der Dam** \'bōl-dər\ dam 726 *ft* (221 *m*) high in Colorado River bet. Nev. & Ariz. — see MEAD (Lake)

Ho·pat·cong, Lake \hə-'pat-ˌkän, -ˌkäŋ\ lake 8 *mi* (13 *km*) long N N.J.

Hopeh *or* **Hopei** — see HEBEI

Hope·well \'hōp-ˌwel, -wəl\ city SE Va. *pop* 22,591

Hop·kins·ville \'häp-kənz-ˌvil\ city SW Ky. *pop* 31,577

Ho·reb, Mount \'hòr-ˌeb\ *or* **Mount Si·nai** \'sī-ˌnī *also* -nē-ˌī\ mountain where according to the Bible the Law was given to Moses; thought to be in the Gebel Musa on Sinai Peninsula

Horlivka — see GORLOVKA

Hor·moz \'hòr-ˌmòz\ *or* **Hor·muz** *same or* hòr-'müz\ island SE Iran in Strait of Hormuz

Hor·muz *or* **Or·muz** \'(h)òr-ˌməz, (h)òr-'müz\ ancient town S Iran on **Strait of Hormuz** (strait connecting Persian Gulf & Gulf of Oman)

Horn \'hòrn\ *or* **North Cape** cape NW Iceland

Horn, Cape headland S Chile on **Horn Island** in Tierra del Fuego; southernmost point of S. America, at 55°59′S

Horn·church \'hòrn-ˌchərch\ former urban district SE England in Essex, now part of Havering

Horn of Africa the easternmost projection of Africa — variously used to refer to the region including Somalia, SE or all of Ethiopia, often Djibouti, and sometimes Eritrea, Sudan, & Kenya

Hor·sens \'hòr-sᵊnz, -sᵊn(t)s\ city & port Denmark *pop* 54,940

Hos·pi·ta·let \ˌ(h)äs-ˌpi-tə-'let, ˌòs-pē-tä-'let\ city NE Spain in Barcelona province, SW suburb of Barcelona *pop* 239,019

Ho·tan \'hō-ˌtän\ *or* **Ho–t'ien** \'hō-tyen\ *or* **Kho·tan** \'kō-ˌtän\ town & oasis W China in SW Xinjiang Uygur on S edge of the Taklimakan

Hot Springs city W *cen* Ark. adjoining **Hot Springs National Park** (reservation containing hot mineral springs) *pop* 35,193

Hou·ma \'hō-mə, 'hü-\ city SE La. *pop* 33,727

Houns·low \'haúnz-(ˌ)lō\ borough of SW Greater London, England *pop* 193,400

Hou·sa·ton·ic \ˌhü-sə-'tä-nik, ˌhü-zə-\ river 148 *mi* (238 *km*) W Mass. & W Conn. flowing from Berkshire Hills S into Long Island Sound

Hous·ton \'hyüs-tən, 'yüs-\ city & port SE Tex. connected with Galveston Bay by **Houston Ship Channel** (50 *mi* or 80 *km* long) *pop* 2,099,451 — **Hous·to·nian** \hyü-'stō-nē-ən, yü-, -nyən\ *n* — **Houston·ite** \'hyüs-tə-ˌnīt, 'yüs-\ *n*

Hove \'hōv\ town S England in E. Sussex *pop* 82,500

Ho·ven·weep National Monument \'hō-vən-ˌwēp\ site SE Utah & SW Colo. of prehistoric pueblos & cliff dwellings

How·rah *or* **Hao·ra** \'haú-rə\ city E India in W. Bengal on the Hugli opposite Calcutta *pop* 1,008,704

Hrodna *or* **Hrodno** — see GRODNO

Hsi — see XI

Hsia–men — see XIAMEN

Hsi–an — see XI'AN

Hsiang — see XIANG

Hsiang–t'an — see XIANGTAN

Hsin–chu — see XINZHU

Hsin–hsiang — see XINXIANG

Hsi–ning — see XINING

Hsinkao — see YÜ SHAN

Hsi–tsang — see TIBET

Hsüan–hua — see XUANHUA

Hsü–chou — see XUZHOU

Huai \'hü-ˌī, 'hwī\ river *over* 600 *mi* (966 *km*) E China flowing from S Henan E into Hongze Lake

Huai–nan \ˌhü-ˌī-'nän, ˌhwī-\ city E China in N *cen* Anhui SW of Bengbu *pop* 703,934

Hual·la·ga \wä-'yä-gä, ˌkwä-\ river 700 *mi* (1126 *km*) N *cen* Peru flowing N into the Marañón

Huam·bo \'wäm-(ˌ)bō, 'hwäm-\ *or formerly* **No·va Lis·boa** \ˌnò-və-ˌlēzh-'bō-ə\ city Angola in W *cen* highlands *pop* 49,823

Huang *or* **Hwang** \'hwäŋ\ *or* **Yellow** river 3396 *mi* (5464 *km*) N China flowing from Kunlun Mountains in Qinghai E into Bo Hai

Huang–pu *or* **Whang–poo** \'hwäŋ-'pü\ river 70 *mi* (113 *km*) E China flowing E & N past Shanghai into the Chang

Huas·ca·rán \ˌwäs-kä-'rän\ mountain 22,205 *ft* (6768 *m*) W Peru; highest in the country

Hu·bei *or* **Hu·peh** *or* **Hu·pei** \'hü-'bā\ province E *cen* China ✳ Wuhan *area* 72,394 *sq mi* (188,224 *sq km*), *pop* 53,969,210

Hu·ber Heights \'hyü-bər, 'yü-\ city W Ohio *pop* 38,101

Hu·bli–Dhar·wad \ˌhü-blē-ˌdär-'wäd\ *or* **Hu·bli–Dhar·war** \-'wär\ city SW India in W Karnataka *pop* 786,018

Hudaydah, Al — see AL HUDAYDAH

Hud·ders·field \'hə-dərz-ˌfēld\ town N England in W. Yorkshire NE of Manchester *pop* 123,888

Hud·dinge \'hü-diŋ-ə\ city E Sweden, just S of Stockholm *pop* 86,457

Hud·son \'həd-sən\ **1** river 306 *mi* (492 *km*) E N.Y. flowing from Adirondack Mountains S into New York Bay **2** town S N.H. *pop* 24,467 — **Hud·so·ni·an** \ˌhəd-'sō-nē-ən\ *adj*

Hudson Bay inlet of the Atlantic in N Canada; an inland sea 850 *mi* (1368 *km*) long

Hudson Strait strait 450 *mi* (724 *km*) long NE Canada bet. S Baffin Is. & N Que. connecting Hudson Bay with the Atlantic

Hue *or* **F Hué** \'hwā, 'wä, hü-'ā, hyü-'ā\ city & port *cen* Vietnam in Annam; formerly ✳ of Annam *pop* 211,718

Huel·va \'wel-vä, 'hwel-\ **1** province SW Spain in Andalusia on Gulf of Cádiz *area* 3894 *sq mi* (10,085 *sq km*), *pop* 462,579 **2** city, its ✳ *pop* 142,284

Hues·ca \'wes-kä, 'hwes-\ **1** province NE Spain in Aragon *area* 6051 *sq mi* (15,672 *sq km*), *pop* 206,502 **2** commune, its ✳ *pop* 46,243

Hufuf, Al — see AL HUFUF

Hu·gli *or* **Hoo·ghly** \'hü-glē\ river 120 *mi* (193 *km*) E India flowing S into Bay of Bengal; most westerly channel of the Ganges in its delta

Huhehot — see HOHHOT

Hui·la \'wē-(ˌ)lä, 'hwē-\ volcano 18,865 *ft* (5750 *m*) SW *cen* Colombia

Hull \'həl\ **1** former town Canada in SW Que. on Ottawa River, now part of Gatineau **2** *or in full* **Kings·ton upon Hull** \'kiŋ-stən\ city & port E England on the Humber *pop* 242,200

Hu·ma·cao \ˌü-mə-'kaú\ town E Puerto Rico *pop* 58,466

Hum·ber \'həm-bər\ estuary 40 *mi* (64 *km*) E England formed by Ouse & Trent rivers & flowing E & SE into North Sea

Hum·boldt \'həm-ˌbōlt\ river 290 *mi* (467 *km*) N Nev. flowing W & SW into Rye Patch reservoir & formerly into Humboldt Lake

Humboldt Bay bay NW Calif. on which Eureka is situated

Humboldt Glacier glacier NW Greenland

Humboldt Lake lake W Nev. formerly receiving Humboldt River; has no outlet but has an intermittent S extension **Humboldt Sink**

Hum·phreys Peak \'həm(p)-frēz\ mountain peak 12,633 *ft* (3851 *m*) N *cen* Ariz. — see SAN FRANCISCO PEAKS

\ə\ **abut** \ᵊ\ **kitten, F table** \ər\ **further** \a\ **ash** \ā\ **ace** \ä\ **mop, mar**
\aú\ **out** \ch\ **chin** \e\ **bet** \ē\ **easy** \g\ **go** \i\ **hit** \ī\ **ice** \j\ **job**
\ŋ\ **sing** \ō\ **go** \ò\ **law** \òi\ **boy** \th\ **thin** \t̷h\ **the** \ü\ **loot** \ù\ **foot**
\y\ **yet** \zh\ **vision, beige** \ḵ, ⁿ, œ, ᴜ, ᵞ\ *see* Guide to Pronunciation

Hu·nan \ˈhü-ˈnän\ province SE *cen* China ✻ Changsha *area* 81,274 *sq mi* (211,312 *sq km*), *pop* 60,659,754
Hun·ga·ry \ˈhəŋ-gə-rē\ *or Hung* **Ma·gyar·or·szág** \ˌmȯ-ˌjȯr-ˈȯr-ˌsäg\ country *cen* Europe; formerly a kingdom, since 1946 a republic ✻ Budapest *area* 35,919 *sq mi* (93,030 *sq km*), *pop* 10,197,119
Hungshui — see HONGSHUI
Hungtse — see HONGZE
Hun·ter \ˈhən-tər\ river 287 *mi* (462 *km*) SE Australia in E New South Wales flowing E into the Pacific
Hunt·ers·ville \ˈhən-tərz-ˌvil\ town N.C. N of Charlotte *pop* 46,773
Hun·ting·don \ˈhən-tiŋ-dən\ **1** *or* **Hun·ting·don·shire** \-ˌshir, -shər\ *or* **Huntingdon and Pe·ter·bor·ough** \ˈpē-tər-ˌbər-ō\ *or* **Hunts** \ˈhənts\ former county E *cen* England ✻ Huntingdon; since 1974 part of Cambridgeshire **2** town E *cen* England in Cambridgeshire *pop* 2859
Hun·ting·ton \ˈhən-tiŋ-tən\ city W W.Va. on Ohio River *pop* 49,138
Huntington Beach city SW Calif. SE of Los Angeles *pop* 189,992
Huntington Park city SW Calif. S of Los Angeles *pop* 58,114
Hunts·ville \ˈhənts-ˌvil, -vəl\ **1** city N Ala. *pop* 180,105 **2** city E Tex. N of Houston *pop* 38,548
Hu·on Gulf \ˈhyü-ˌän\ inlet of Solomon Sea on SE coast of North-East New Guinea S of Huon Peninsula
Hu·ron, Lake \ˈhyu̇r-ˌän, ˈyu̇r-\ lake E *cen* N. America bet. the U.S. & Canada; one of the Great Lakes *area* 23,010 *sq mi* (59,826 *sq km*)
Hurst \ˈhərst\ city NE Tex. NE of Fort Worth *pop* 37,337
Hutch·in·son \ˈhə-chən-sən\ city *cen* Kans. *pop* 42,080
Huy \ˈwē, ˈhwē\ commune E Belgium SW of Liège *pop* 19,297
Huy·ton with Ro·by \ˈhī-t^{ə}n-wit͟h-ˈrō-bē, -with-\ town NW England in Lancashire E of Liverpool *pop* 57,671
Hwaining — see ANQING
Hy·bla \ˈhī-blə\ ancient town in Sicily on S slope of Mt. Etna
Hydaspes — see JHELUM
Hy·der·a·bad \ˈhī-d(ə-)rə-ˌbad, -ˌbäd\ **1** former state S *cen* India in the Deccan ✻ Hyderabad **2** *or* **Hai·dar·a·bad** city S *cen* India ✻ of Andhra Pradesh *pop* 3,449,878 **3** city S Pakistan in Sind on the Indus *pop* 1,166,894
Hy·dra \ˈhī-drə\ *or ModGk* **Ídhra** \ˈē-t͟h-rä\ island Greece in S Aegean Sea off E coast of Peloponnese *area* 20 *sq mi* (52 *sq km*), *pop* 2794 — **Hy·dri·ot** \ˈhī-drē-ət, -drē-ˌät\ *or* **Hy·dri·ote** \-ˌōt, -ət\ *n*
Hydraotes — see RAVI
Hy·ères \ē-ˈer, ˈyer\ commune SE France on Côte d'Azur E of Toulon *pop* 51,412
Hyères Islands *or F* **Îles d'Hyères** \ˌēl-dē-ˈer, ēl-ˈdyer\ islands SE France in the Mediterranean
Hy·met·tus \hī-ˈme-təs\ mountain ridge *ab* 3370 *ft* (1027 *m*) *cen* Greece E & SE of Athens — **Hy·met·ti·an** \-ˈme-tē-ən\ *adj*
Hyr·ca·nia \(ˌ)hər-ˈkā-nē-ə\ province of ancient Persia on SE coast of Caspian NE of Media & NW of Parthia — **Hyr·ca·ni·an** \-nē-ən\ *adj*
Ia·si \ˈyäsh, ˈyä-shē\ *or* **Jas·sy** \ˈyä-sē\ city NE Romania *pop* 321,580
Iba·dan \i-ˈbä-d^{ə}n, -ˈba-\ city SW Nigeria NNE of Lagos *pop* 2,600,000
Ibe·ria \ī-ˈbir-ē-ə\ **1** ancient Spain **2** IBERIAN PENINSULA **3** ancient region S of the Caucasus W of Colchis in modern Republic of Georgia
Ibe·ri·an Peninsula \-ē-ən\ peninsula SW Europe bet. the Mediterranean & the Atlantic occupied by Spain & Portugal
Ibi·cuí \ˌē-bi-ˈkwē\ river S Brazil in Rio Grande do Sul flowing W into Uruguay River
Ibi·za \ē-ˈvē-thä, -ˈbē-, -sə, -zə\ island Spain in the Balearics SW of Majorca *area ab* 220 *sq mi* (570 *sq km*)
Içá — see PUTUMAYO
Icaria — see IKARIA — **Icar·i·an** \ī-ˈker-ē-ən, i-\ *adj or n*
Ice·land \ˈīs-lənd, ˈīs-ˌland\ *or Dan* **Is·land** \ˈēs-ˌlän\ *or Icelandic* **Ís·land** \ˈēs-ˌlänt\ island bet. the Arctic & the Atlantic SE of Greenland; a republic, formerly (1380–1918) belonging to Denmark, later (1918–44) an independent kingdom in personal union with Denmark ✻ Reykjavik *area* 39,702 *sq mi* (102,828 *sq km*), *pop* 313,400 — **Ice·land·er** \ˈīs-ˌlan-dər, ˈīs-lən-\ *n*
I–ch'ang — see YICHANG
Ichi·ka·wa \ē-ˈchē-ˌkä-wə\ city Japan in SE Honshu E of Tokyo *pop* 448,642
Iconium — see KONYA
Ida, Mount — see KAZ DAGI
Ida·ho \ˈī-də-ˌhō\ state NW U.S. ✻ Boise *area* 83,557 *sq mi* (217,248 *sq km*), *pop* 1,567,582 — **Ida·ho·an** \ˌī-də-ˈhō-ən\ *adj or n*
Idaho Falls city SE Idaho on Snake River *pop* 56,813
Id·fu \ˈid-(ˌ)fü\ city S Egypt on the Nile *pop* 34,858
Idhi \ˈē-t͟hē\ *or* **Ida** \ˈī-də\ mountain 8058 *ft* (2456 *m*) Greece in *cen* Crete; highest on island
Idumaea *or* **Idumea** — see EDOM — **Id·u·mae·an** *or* **Id·u·me·an** \ˌi-dyü-ˈmē-ən\ *adj or n*
Ie·per \ˈyā-pər\ *or F* **Ypres** \ˈēpr^{ə}\ commune NW Belgium in W. Flanders *pop* 35,081
Ife \ˈē-(ˌ)fā\ city SW Nigeria NE of Ibadan *pop* 209,100
If·ni \ˈif-nē\ former territory NW coast of Africa administered by Spain 1934–69 ✻ Sidi Ifni; ceded to Morocco 1969
Igua·çú *or* **Igua·zú** \ˌē-gwə-ˈsü\ river S Brazil in Paraná state flowing W into Alto Paraná River; contains **Iguaçú Falls** *or* **Iguazú Falls** (waterfall over 2 *mi or* 3.2 *km* wide composed of numerous cataracts averaging 200 *ft or* 61 *m* in height)
IJs·sel \ˈī-səl, ˈā-\ river 70 *mi* (113 *km*) E Netherlands flowing out of the Rhine N into IJsselmeer
IJs·sel·meer \ˈī-səl-ˌmer, ˈā-\ *or* **Lake Ijs·sel** \ˈī-səl, ˈā-\ freshwater lake N Netherlands separated from North Sea by a dike & bordered by reclaimed lands; part of former Zuider Zee (inlet of North Sea)
Ika·ria \ˌē-kä-ˈrē-ä\ *or* **Ni·ka·ria** \ˌnē-\ *or anc* **Icar·ia** \ī-ˈka-rē-ə, i-\ island Greece in Southern Sporades WSW of Samos *area* 99 *sq mi* (257 *sq km*)
Île–de–France \ˌēl-də-ˈfräⁿs\ region & former province N *cen* France bounded on N by Picardy, on E by Champagne, on S by Orléanais, & on W by Normandy ✻ Paris
Ile des Pins \ˌēl-dā-ˈpaⁿ\ *or* **Isle of Pines** \ˈpīnz\ island SW Pacific; part of overseas dept. of New Caledonia *area* 58 *sq mi* (151 *sq km*)
Île du Diable — see DEVIL'S ISLAND
Îles de la Société — see SOCIETY ISLANDS
Îles du Vent — see WINDWARD ISLANDS 3
Îles sous le Vent — see LEEWARD ISLANDS 2
Il·ford \ˈil-fərd\ former municipal borough SE England in Essex, now part of Redbridge
Il·fra·combe \ˈil-frə-ˌküm\ town SW England in Devon on Bristol Channel *pop* 10,133
Ili \ē-ˈlē\ river 800 *mi* (1287 *km*) *cen* Asia flowing from W Xinjiang Uygur, China, W & NW into Lake Balkhash in Kazakhstan
Ilía — see ELIS
Il·i·am·na \ˌi-lē-ˈam-nə\ volcano 10,016 *ft* (3053 *m*) NE of Iliamna Lake
Iliamna Lake lake 80 *mi* (129 *km*) long SW Alaska NE of Bristol Bay
Ilium — see TROY 3 — **Il·i·an** \ˈi-lē-ən\ *adj or n*
Ill \ˈēl\ river 129 *mi* (208 *km*) NE France flowing into the Rhine
Il·lam·pu \ē-ˈyäm-(ˌ)pü\ **1** *or* **So·ra·ta** \sə-ˈrä-tə\ massif in the Andes W Bolivia E of Lake Titicaca — see ANCOHUMA **2** peak 20,867 *ft* (6360 *m*) in the Illampu Massif
Il·li·ma·ni \ˌē-yē-ˈmä-nē\ mountain 21,201 *ft* (6462 *m*) Bolivia E of La Paz
Il·li·nois \ˌi-lə-ˈnȯi *also* -ˈnȯiz\ **1** river 273 *mi* (439 *km*) Ill. flowing SW into Mississippi River **2** state *cen* U.S. ✻ Springfield *area* 56,400 *sq mi* (146,640 *sq km*), *pop* 12,830,632 — **Il·li·nois·an** \ˌi-lə-ˈnȯi-ən *also* -ˈnȯi-z^{ə}n\ *adj or n*
Il·lyr·ia \i-ˈlir-ē-ə\ ancient region S Europe in Balkan Peninsula bordering on the Adriatic — **Il·lyr·ic** \-ˈlir-ik\ *adj*
Il·lyr·i·cum \i-ˈlir-i-kəm\ province of Roman Empire in Illyria
Il'·men' \ˈil-mən\ lake W Russia in Europe S of Lake Ladoga
Ilo·ilo \ˌē-lō-ˈē-(ˌ)lō\ city Philippines on Panay Is. *pop* 311,000
Im·pe·ria \im-ˈpir-ē-ə, -ˈper-\ commune & port NW Italy in Liguria SW of Genoa *pop* 40,252
Im·pe·ri·al Beach \im-ˈpir-ē-əl\ city SW Calif. S of San Diego *pop* 26,324
Imperial Valley valley U.S. & Mexico in SE Calif. & NE Baja California in Colorado Desert; most of area below sea level
Imp·hal \ˈimp-ˌhəl\ city NE India ✻ of Manipur *pop* 217,275
Imroz — see GÖKÇEADA
Ina·gua \i-ˈnä-gwə\ two islands in SE Bahamas: **Great Inagua** (50 *mi or* 80 *km* long) & **Little Inagua** (8 *mi or* 13 *km* long)
In·chon *or* **In·cheon** \ˈin-ˌchən\ *or formerly* **Che·mul·po** \jə-ˈmu̇l-(ˌ)pō\ city & port NW S. Korea W of Seoul *pop* 2,466,338
In·de·pen·dence \ˌin-də-ˈpen-dən(t)s\ city W Mo. E of Kansas City *pop* 116,830
In·dia \ˈin-dē-ə\ **1** peninsula region (often called a subcontinent) S Asia S of the Himalayas bet. Bay of Bengal & Arabian Sea occupied by India, Pakistan, & Bangladesh & formerly often considered to include Burma (but not Ceylon) **2** those parts of India until 1947 under Brit. rule or protection together with Baluchistan & the Andaman & Nicobar islands &, prior to 1937, Burma **3** country comprising major portion of peninsula; a republic within the Commonwealth of Nations; until 1947 a part of the Brit. Empire ✻ New Delhi *area* 1,195,063 *sq mi* (3,095,472 *sq km*), *pop* 1,200,000,000
In·di·ana \ˌin-dē-ˈa-nə\ state E *cen* U.S. ✻ Indianapolis *area* 36,291 *sq mi* (94,357 *sq km*), *pop* 6,483,802 — **In·di·an·an** \-ˈa-nən\ *adj or n* — **In·di·an·i·an** \-ˈa-nē-ən\ *adj or n*
Indiana Harbor harbor district in E. Chicago, Ind., on Lake Michigan
In·di·a·nap·o·lis \ˌin-dē-ə-ˈna-pə-lis\ city *cen* Ind., its ✻ *pop* 820,445
In·di·an Ocean \ˈin-dē-ən\ ocean E of Africa, S of Asia, W of Australia, & N of Antarctica *area ab* 28,350,500 *sq mi* (73,427,795 *sq km*)
Indian River lagoon 165 *mi* (266 *km*) long E Fla. bet. mainland & coastal islands
Indian States former semi-independent states of the Indian Empire ruled by native princes subject to varying degrees of Brit. authority — see BRITISH INDIA
Indian Territory former territory S U.S. in present state of Okla.
In·dies \ˈin-(ˌ)dēz\ **1** EAST INDIES **2** WEST INDIES
In·di·gir·ka \ˌin-də-ˈgir-kə\ river *over* 1000 *mi* (1609 *km*) E *cen* Russia in Asia in NE Sakha Republic flowing N into E. Siberian Sea
In·dio \ˈin-dē-ˌō\ city SE Calif. SE of San Bernardino *pop* 76,036
In·do·chi·na \ˌin-(ˌ)dō-ˈchī-nə\ **1** peninsula SE Asia; includes Myanmar, Cambodia, Laos, Malay Peninsula, Thailand, & Vietnam **2** *or* **French Indochina** former country SE Asia comprising Annam, Cochin China, & Tonkin (all now part of Vietnam), Cambodia, & Laos ✻ Hanoi
In·do·ne·sia \ˌin-də-ˈnē-zhə, -shə\ **1** country SE Asia in Malay Archipelago comprising Sumatra, Java, S & E Borneo, Sulawesi, W Timor, W New Guinea, the Moluccas, & many adjacent smaller islands; formerly (as **Netherlands Indies**) an overseas territory of the Netherlands ✻ Jakarta *area* 739,773 *sq mi* (1,916,103 *sq km*), *pop* 232,500,000 **2** MALAY ARCHIPELAGO
In·dore \in-ˈdȯr\ **1** former state *cen* India in Narmada valley ✻ Indore; area now in Madhya Pradesh **2** city NW *cen* India in W Madhya Pradesh *pop* 1,597,441
In·dus \ˈin-dəs\ river 1800 *mi* (2897 *km*) S Asia flowing from Tibet NW & SSW through Pakistan into Arabian Sea
In·gle·wood \ˈiŋ-gəl-ˌwu̇d\ city SW Calif. SW of Los Angeles *pop* 109,673
In·gol·stadt \ˈiŋ-gəl-ˌshtät, -ˌstät\ city S Germany in *cen* Bavaria *pop* 107,375
In·gu·she·tia \ˌiŋ-gü-ˈshē-shə\ *or* **In·gu·she·ti·ya** \-ˈshe-tē-yə\ *or* **Ingush Republic** \in-ˈgüsh, iŋ-\ autonomous republic S Russia in Europe N of Caucasus Mountains ✻ Nazran' *area* 1242 *sq mi* (3217 *sq km*), *pop* 1,234,000
Ink·ster \ˈiŋk-stər\ city SE Mich. W of Detroit *pop* 25,369
In·land Empire \ˈin-ˌland, -lənd\ region NW U.S. bet. Cascade Range & Rocky Mountains in E Wash., N Idaho, NW Mont., & NE Oreg.
Inland Sea inlet of the Pacific 240 *mi* (386 *km*) long SW Japan bet. Honshu on E & N, Kyushu on W, & Shikoku on S
Inn \ˈin\ river 320 *mi* (515 *km*) flowing from SE Switzerland NE through Austria into the Danube in SE Germany — see ENGADINE
Inner Hebrides — see HEBRIDES
Inner Mon·go·lia \män-ˈgōl-yə, mäŋ-, -ˈgō-lē-ə\ *or* **Nei Mong·gol** \ˈnā-ˈmän-ˌgōl, -ˈmäŋ-\ *or* **Nei–meng–ku** \ˈnā-ˈməŋ-ˈkü\ region N China in SE Mongolia & W Manchuria ✻ Hohhot *area* 454,633 *sq mi* (1,182,046 *sq km*), *pop* 21,456,798
In·nis·fil \ˈi-nəs-ˌfil, -fəl\ town Canada in SE Ont. *pop* 33,079
Inniskilling — see ENNISKILLEN
Inns·bruck \ˈinz-ˌbru̇k, ˈin(t)s-\ city W Austria *pop* 113,392

Inside Passage protected shipping route from Puget Sound, Wash., to Skagway, Alaska, following channels bet. mainland & coastal islands
In·ter·la·ken \ˈin-tər-ˌlä-kən\ commune W *cen* Switzerland in Bern canton on the Aare bet. Lake of Thun & Lake of Brienz *pop* 5500
International Zone — see MOROCCO 1
In·ver·car·gill \ˌin-vər-ˈkär-gil\ city New Zealand on S coast of South Is. *urban area pop* 46,305 — see BLUFF
In·ver·clyde \ˌin-vər-ˈklīd\ administrative area of W Scotland *area* 62 *sq mi* (162 *sq km*)
In·ver Grove Heights \ˈin-vər\ city SE Minn. *pop* 33,880
In·ver·ness \ˌin-vər-ˈnes\ **1** *or* **In·ver·ness–shire** \-ˈnesh-ˌshir, -shər\ former county NW Scotland **2** burgh NW Scotland, formerly ✻ of Highland region *pop* 63,090
Io·an·ni·na \yō-ˈä-nē-(ˌ)nä\ city NW Greece in N Epirus *pop* 56,496
Io·na \ī-ˈō-nə\ island Scotland in S Inner Hebrides off SW tip of Mull Is. *area* 6 *sq mi* (16 *sq km*), *pop* 120
Io·nia \ī-ˈō-nē-ə\ ancient region W Asia Minor bordering on the Aegean W of Lydia & Caria — **Io·ni·an** \-nē-ən\ *adj or n*
Ionian Islands islands W Greece in Ionian Sea *pop* 191,003
Ionian Sea arm of the Mediterranean Sea bet. SE Italy & W Greece
Io·wa \ˈī-ə-wə\ **1** river 291 *mi* (468 *km*) Iowa flowing SE into Mississippi River **2** state *cen* U.S. ✻ Des Moines *area* 56,275 *sq mi* (145,752 *sq km*), *pop* 3,046,355 — **Io·wan** \-wən\ *adj or n*
Iowa City city E Iowa S of Cedar Rapids *pop* 67,862
I–pin — see YIBIN
Ipoh \ˈē-(ˌ)pō\ city Malaysia ✻ of Perak *pop* 125,766
Ips·wich \ˈip-(ˌ)swich\ **1** city E Australia in SE Queensland *pop* 73,299 **2** town SE England ✻ of Suffolk *pop* 115,500
Iqa·lu·it \ē-ˈka-lü-ət\ city Canada ✻ of Nunavut on Baffin Is. *pop* 6699
Iqui·que \ē-ˈkē-kā\ city & port N Chile on the Pacific *pop* 216,419
Iqui·tos \ē-ˈkē-(ˌ)tōs\ city NE Peru on the Amazon *pop* 269,500
Irák·li·on \i-ˈra-klē-ən, ē-ˈrä-klē-ˌȯn\ *or* **Can·dia** \ˈkan-dē-ə\ city & port Greece ✻ of Crete *pop* 117,167
Iran \i-ˈrän, -ˈran; ī-ˈran\ *or esp formerly by outsiders* **Per·sia** \ˈpər-zhə, *esp Brit* -shə\ country SW Asia bordering in N on Caspian Sea & in S on Persian Gulf & Gulf of Oman; an Islamic republic since 1979, formerly an empire ✻ Tehran *area* 635,932 *sq mi* (1,647,064 *sq km*), *pop* 69,500,000 — **Irani** \-ˈrä-nē, -ˈra-\ *adj or n*
Ira·pua·to \ˌē-rä-ˈpwä-tō\ city *cen* Mexico in Guanajuato *pop* 412,639
Iraq \i-ˈräk, -ˈrak\ country SW Asia in Mesopotamia; a republic since 1958, formerly a kingdom ✻ Baghdad *area* 168,927 *sq mi* (437,521 *sq km*), *pop* 31,500,000 — **Iraqi** \-ˈrä-kē, -ˈra-\ *adj or n*
Irbīl — see ARBĪL
Ire·land \ˈī(-ə)r-lənd\ **1** *or L* **Hi·ber·nia** \hī-ˈbər-nē-ə\ island W Europe in the Atlantic, one of the British Isles *area* 32,052 *sq mi* (83,015 *sq km*); divided bet. Ireland (republic) & Northern Ireland **2** *or* **Ei·re** \ˈer-ə\ country occupying major portion of the island; a republic since 1949; a division of the United Kingdom of Great Britain and Ireland 1801–1921 & (as **Irish Free State**) a dominion of the Commonwealth of Nations 1922–37 ✻ Dublin *area* 26,602 *sq mi* (69,165 *sq km*), *pop* 4,239,848 **3** — see NORTHERN IRELAND
Irish Sea arm of the Atlantic bet. Great Britain & Ireland
Ir·kutsk \ir-ˈkütsk, ˌər-\ city S Russia in Asia on the Angara near Lake Baikal *pop* 639,000
Iron Gate \ˈī(-ə)rn\ gorge 2 *mi* (3.2 *km*) long in the Danube where it cuts around Transylvanian Alps on border bet. Romania & Serbia
Ir·ra·wad·dy \ˌir-ə-ˈwä-dē\ river 1300 *mi* (2092 *km*) Myanmar flowing S into Bay of Bengal through several mouths
Ir·tysh \ir-ˈtish, ˌər-\ *or Chin* **Er·tix** \ˈər-ˈjis—*sic*\ river *over* 2600 *mi* (4180 *km*) *cen* Asia flowing from Altai Mountains in China NW & N through Kazakhstan & into the Ob' in W Russia in Asia
Irún \ē-ˈrün\ commune N Spain in Guipúzcoa *pop* 56,601
Ir·vine \ˈər-ˌvīn\ city SW Calif. SE of Santa Ana *pop* 212,375
Ir·ving \ˈər-viŋ\ city NE Tex. W of Dallas *pop* 216,290
Isa·be·la \ˌē-sä-ˈbā-lä\ city NW Puerto Rico *pop* 45,631
Is·a·bela Island \ˌi-zə-ˈbe-lə, ˌē-sä-ˈbā-lä\ island Ecuador; largest of the Galápagos *area* 1650 *sq mi* (4290 *sq km*), *pop* 336
Isar \ˈē-ˌzär\ river 163 *mi* (262 *km*) W Europe flowing from Tirol, Austria, through Bavaria, Germany, into the Danube
Isau·ria \ī-ˈsȯr-ē-ə\ ancient district in E Pisidia S Asia Minor on N slope of W Taurus Mountains — **Isau·ri·an** \-ē-ən\ *adj or n*
Is·chia \ˈis-kē-ə\ island Italy in Tyrrhenian Sea WSW of Naples *area* 18 *sq mi* (47 *sq km*)
Ise Bay \ˈē-ˌsā\ inlet of the Pacific S Japan on S coast of Honshu
Iseo, Lake \ē-ˈzā-(ˌ)ō\ lake 14 *mi* (22 *km*) long N Italy in Lombardy
Isère \ē-ˈzer\ river 150 *mi* (241 *km*) SE France flowing from Graian Alps WSW into the Rhône
Iser·lohn \ˌē-zər-ˈlōn, ˈē-zər-ˌ\ city W Germany *pop* 96,976
Isfahan — see ESFAHĀN
Ishim \i-ˈshim\ river 1330 *mi* (2140 *km*) flowing from N Kazakhstan N into the Irtysh in W Russia in Asia
Isis \ˈī-səs\ upper course of Thames River, England; a local name
Is·ken·de·run \(ˌ)is-ˌken-də-ˈrün\ *or formerly* **Al·ex·an·dret·ta** \ˌa-lig-(ˌ)zan-ˈdre-tə, ˌe-\ city & port S Turkey on **Gulf of Iskenderun** (inlet of the Mediterranean) *pop* 154,807
Is·lam·a·bad \is-ˈlä-mə-ˌbäd, iz-, -ˈla-mə-ˌbad\ city ✻ of Pakistan in NE part of the country NE of Rawalpindi *pop* 529,180
Island *or* **Ísland** — see ICELAND
Is·lay \ˈī-(ˌ)lā, -lə\ island Scotland in S Inner Hebrides *area* 234 *sq mi* (608 *sq km*), *pop* 3855
Isle au Haut \ˌī-lə-ˈhō(t), ˌē-lə-ˈhō\ island Maine at entrance to Penobscot Bay — see ACADIA NATIONAL PARK
Isle of Anglesey administrative area of Wales comprising Anglesey Is. & Holy Is. ✻ Llangefni *area* 276 *sq mi* (715 *sq km*)
Isle of Av·a·lon \ˈa-və-ˌlän\ Druidic site in Glastonbury, England
Isle of Ely — see ELY (Isle of)
Isle of Man — see MAN (Isle of)
Isle of Pines — see YOUTH (Isle of)
Isle of Wight — see WIGHT (Isle of)
Isle Roy·ale \ˈī(-ə)l-ˈrȯi(-ə)l\ island Mich. in NW Lake Superior in **Isle Royale National Park**
Is·ling·ton \ˈiz-liŋ-tən\ borough of N Greater London, England *pop* 155,200
Is·ma·i·lia \ˌiz-mā-ə-ˈlē-ə, ˌis-\ city NE Egypt on the Suez Canal *pop* 293,184
Isole Eolie — see LIPARI ISLANDS
Ison·zo \ē-ˈzȯn(t)-(ˌ)sō\ *or in Slovenia* **So·ča** \ˈsȯ-chä\ river *ab* 80 *mi* (130 *km*) W Slovenia & NE Italy flowing S into Gulf of Trieste
Ispahan — see ESFAHĀN
Is·par·ta \ˌis-(ˌ)pär-ˈtä\ city SW Turkey N of Antalya *pop* 112,117
Is·ra·el \ˈiz-rē(-ə)l, -(ˌ)rā(-ə)l *also* ˈis- *or* ˈiz-rəl\ **1** kingdom in ancient Palestine comprising the lands occupied by the Hebrew people; established *ab* 1025 B.C.; divided *ab* 933 B.C. into a S kingdom (Judah) & a N kingdom (Israel) **2** *or* **Northern Kingdom** *or* **Ephra·im** \ˈē-frē-əm\ the N portion of the Hebrew kingdom after the division ✻ Samaria **3** country SW Asia bordering on the Mediterranean; a republic established 1948 ✻ Jerusalem *area* 7993 *sq mi* (20,782 *sq km*), *pop* 7,300,000 — see PALESTINE
Is·sus \ˈi-səs\ ancient town S Asia Minor N of modern Iskenderun
Is·syk Kul *or* **Ys·yk–Köl** \ˌi-sik-ˈkəl, -ˈkœl\ lake 115 *mi* (185 *km*) long in NE Kyrgyzstan *area* 2355 *sq mi* (6099 *sq km*)
Is·tan·bul \ˌis-tən-ˈbül, -ˌtan-, -ˌtän-, -ˈbu̇l, ˈis-tən-ˌ, *or with* m *for* n\ *or formerly* **Con·stan·ti·no·ple** \ˌkän-ˌstan-tə-ˈnō-pəl\ *or anc* **By·zan·ti·um** \bə-ˈzan-tē-əm, -ˈzan-sh(ē-)əm\ city NW Turkey on the Bosporus & Sea of Marmara; ✻ of preindependence Turkey & earlier ✻ of Ottoman Empire *pop* 6,620,241
Ister — see DANUBE
Is·tria \ˈis-trē-ə\ *or* **Is·tra** \-trə\ *or* **Is·tri·an Peninsula** \-trē-ən\ peninsula in Croatia & Slovenia projecting into the N Adriatic — **Istrian** *adj or n*
Itai·pu \ē-ˈtī-pü\ dam in Paraná River bet. Brazil & Paraguay
Italian East Africa former territory E Africa comprising Eritrea, Ethiopia, & Italian Somaliland
Italian Somaliland former Italian colony E Africa bordering on Indian Ocean ✻ Mogadishu; since 1960 part of Somalia
It·a·ly \ˈi-tə-lē\ *or It* **Ita·lia** \ē-ˈtäl-yä\ *or L* **Ita·lia** \ə-ˈtal-yə, i-\ **1** peninsula 760 *mi* (1223 *km*) long S Europe projecting into the Mediterranean bet. Adriatic & Tyrrhenian seas **2** country comprising the peninsula of Italy, Sicily, Sardinia, & numerous other islands; a republic since 1946, formerly a kingdom ✻ Rome *area* 116,313 *sq mi* (302,251 *sq km*), *pop* 57,844,017
Ita·na·gar \ˌē-tə-ˈnə-gər\ town NE India ✻ of Arunachal Pradesh *pop* 34,970
Itas·ca, Lake \ī-ˈtas-kə\ lake NW *cen* Minn.; generally considered as source of Mississippi River
Iténez — see GUAPORÉ
Ith·a·ca \ˈi-thi-kə\ **1** city S *cen* N.Y. on Cayuga Lake *pop* 30,014 **2** *or ModGk* **Ithá·ki** \ē-ˈthä-kē\ island W Greece in the Ionian Islands NE of Cephalonia *area* 37 *sq mi* (96 *sq km*) — **Ith·a·can** \ˈi-thi-kən\ *adj or n*
Itsu·ku·shi·ma \ˌēt-ˌsü-kə-ˈshē-mä\ island *ab* 5 *mi* (8 *km*) long Japan in Inland Sea SW of Hiroshima
It·u·raea *or* **It·u·rea** \ˌi-tyü-ˈrē-ə\ country of ancient Palestine S of Damascus — **It·u·rae·an** *or* **It·u·re·an** \-ˈrē-ən\ *adj or n*
Iva·no–Fran·kivs'k \i-ˈvä-nə-frän-ˈkifsk\ *or formerly* **Sta·ni·slav** \ˌstä-nə-ˈsläf, -ˈsläv\ city SW Ukraine *pop* 226,000
Iva·no·vo \ē-ˈvä-nə-və\ *or formerly* **Ivanovo Voz·ne·sensk** \ˌvəz-nə-ˈsen(t)sk\ city *cen* Russia in Europe WNW of Nizhniy Novgorod *pop* 480,000
Ivory Coast *or* **Côte d'Ivoire** \ˌkōt-dē-ˈvwär\ **1** region W Africa bordering on the Atlantic W of the Gold Coast **2** country W Africa including the Ivory Coast & its hinterland; a republic; formerly a territory of French West Africa; official ✻ Yamoussoukro, seat of government Abidjan *area* 124,503 *sq mi* (322,463 *sq km*), *pop* 21,100,000 — **Ivor·i·an** \(ˌ)ī-ˈvȯr-ē-ən\ *adj or n* — **Ivory Coast·er** \ˈkō-stər\ *n*
Iv·va·vik National Park \ˈi-və-ˌvik\ reservation NW Canada in extreme NW Yukon Territory
Iwa·ki \ē-ˈwä-kē\ city Japan on E coast of Honshu *pop* 360,138
Iwo \ˈē-(ˌ)wō\ city SW Nigeria NE of Ibadan *pop* 319,500
Iwo Ji·ma \ˌē-(ˌ)wō-ˈjē-mə\ *or* **Iwo To** \-ˈtō\ island Japan in W Pacific in the Volcano Islands *area* 8 *sq mi* (21 *sq km*)
Ix·elles \ēk-ˈsel\ *or Flem* **El·se·ne** \ˈel-sə-nə\ commune *cen* Belgium in Brabant, suburb of Brussels *pop* 74,377
Ix·ta·ci·huatl *or* **Iz·tac·ci·huatl** \ˌēs-(ˌ)tä-ˈsē-ˌwä-tᵊl\ extinct volcano 17,343 *ft* (5286 *m*) S Mexico N of Popocatepetl
Iza·bal, Lake \ˌē-zə-ˈbäl, -sä-ˈväl\ lake 25 *mi* (40 *km*) long E Guatemala
Izal·co \i-ˈzal-(ˌ)kō, ē-ˈsäl-\ volcano 7828 *ft* (2386 *m*) W El Salvador
Izhevsk \i-ˈzhefsk\ *or 1985–87* **Usti·nov** \ˈüs-ti-ˌnȯf, -ˌnȯv\ city E Russia in Europe ✻ of Udmurtia *pop* 651,000
Iz·may·il \ˌē-smä-ˈēl, ˈiz-mē-əl\ *or Russ* **Iz·ma·il** \ˈiz-mē-əl, ˌis-mə-ˈēl\ *or Romanian* **Is·ma·il** \ˌiz-mä-ˈēl, ˌis-\ city SW Ukraine on delta of the Danube *pop* 95,000
Iz·mir \iz-ˈmir\ *or formerly* **Smyr·na** \ˈsmər-nə\ city & port W Turkey in Asia on **Gulf of Izmir** (inlet of the Aegean) *pop* 1,757,414
Iz·mit *or* **Is·mid** \iz-ˈmit\ *or anc* **As·ta·cus** \ˈas-tə-kəs\ *or* **Nic·o·me·dia** \ˌni-kə-ˈmē-dē-ə\ city & port NW Turkey in Asia on **Gulf of Izmit** (E arm of Sea of Marmara) *pop* 256,882
Iz·nik \iz-ˈnik\ lake 14 *mi* (22 *km*) long NW Turkey in Asia
Jabal Katrinah — see KATHERINA (Gebel)
Ja·bal·pur \ˈjə-bəl-ˌpu̇r\ city *cen* India in *cen* Madhya Pradesh *pop* 951,469
Jack·son \ˈjak-sən\ **1** city S Mich. *pop* 33,534 **2** city ✻ of Miss. on Pearl River *pop* 173,514 **3** city W Tenn. *pop* 65,211
Jackson Hole valley NW Wyo. E of Teton Range containing **Jackson Lake** (reservoir); partly in Grand Teton National Park
Jack·son·ville \ˈjak-sən-ˌvil\ **1** city *cen* Ark. NE of Little Rock *pop* 28,364 **2** city NE Fla. near mouth of St. Johns River *pop* 821,784 **3** city E N.C. *pop* 70,145
Jadotville — see LIKASI
Ja·én \hä-ˈān\ **1** province S Spain in N Andalusia *area* 5212 *sq mi* (13,499 *sq km*), *pop* 643,820 **2** commune, its ✻ *pop* 112,590

\ə\ **ab**ut \ᵊ\ kitt**e**n, F table \ər\ **fur**ther \a\ **a**sh \ā\ **a**ce \ä\ m**o**p, m**ar**
\au̇\ **ou**t \ch\ **ch**in \e\ b**e**t \ē\ **ea**sy \g\ **g**o \i\ h**i**t \ī\ **i**ce \j\ **j**ob
\ŋ\ si**ng** \ō\ g**o** \ȯ\ l**aw** \ȯi\ b**oy** \th\ **th**in \t͟h\ **th**e \ü\ l**oo**t \u̇\ f**oo**t
\y\ **y**et \zh\ vi**si**on, bei**ge** \k, ⁿ, œ, ue, ʸ\ *see* Guide to Pronunciation

Jaf•fa \ˈja-fə, ˈya-, ˈyä-\ *or* **Ya•fo** \yä-ˈfō\ *or anc* **Jop•pa** \ˈjä-pə\ former city W Israel, since 1950 a S section of Tel Aviv
Jaff•na \ˈjäf-nə\ city N Sri Lanka on Jaffna Peninsula *pop* 129,000
Jaffna Peninsula peninsula N extremity of Sri Lanka extending into Palk Strait
Jain•tia Hills \ˈjīn-tē-ə\ hills E India in N *cen* Assam E of Khasi Hills
Jai•pur \ˈjī-ˌpu̇r\ **1** former state NW India, now part of Rajasthan **2** city, its ✻, now ✻ of Rajasthan *pop* 2,324,319
Ja•kar•ta *or* **Dja•kar•ta** \jə-ˈkär-tə\ *or formerly* **Ba•ta•via** \bə-ˈtā-vē-ə\ city & port ✻ of Indonesia in NW Java *pop* 6,503,449
Ja•lan•dhar \ˈjə-lən-dər\ city NW India in Punjab *pop* 701,223
Jalapa — see XALAPA
Ja•lis•co \hə-ˈlis-(ˌ)kō\ state W *cen* Mexico ✻ Guadalajara *area* 30,941 *sq mi* (80,137 *sq km*), *pop* 5,302,689
Jal•u•it \ˈja-lu̇-wət, ˈjal-yu̇-wət\ island (atoll) W Pacific, in Ralik chain of the Marshall Islands
Ja•mai•ca \jə-ˈmā-kə\ island West Indies in the Greater Antilles; a dominion of the Commonwealth of Nations since 1962; formerly a Brit. colony ✻ Kingston *area* 4471 *sq mi* (11,580 *sq km*), *pop* 2,607,632 — **Ja•mai•can** \-kən\ *adj or n*
Jamaica Bay inlet of Atlantic SE N.Y. in SW Long Is.
Jam•bi \ˈjäm-bē\ city & port Indonesia in SE *cen* Sumatra *pop* 340,066
James \ˈjāmz\ **1** *or officially* **Da•ko•ta** \də-ˈkō-tə\ river 710 *mi* (1143 *km*) N.Dak. & S.Dak. flowing S to Missouri River **2** river 340 *mi* (547 *km*) Va. flowing E into Chesapeake Bay at Hampton Roads
James Bay the S extension of Hudson Bay 280 *mi* (448 *km*) long & 150 *mi* (240 *km*) wide Canada bet. NE Ont. & W Que.
James•town \ˈjāmz-ˌtau̇n\ **1** city SW N.Y. *pop* 31,146 **2** ruined village E Va. SW of Williamsburg on James River; first permanent English settlement in America (1607)
Jam•mu \ˈjə-(ˌ)mü\ city S of Srinagar, winter ✻ of Jammu & Kashmir *pop* 378,431
Jammu and Kash•mir \ˈkash-ˌmir, ˈkazh-, kash-ˈ, kazh-ˈ\ *or* **Kashmir** disputed territory N India (subcontinent); claimed as a constituent state (summer ✻ Srinagar, winter ✻ Jammu *area* 53,665 *sq mi*—138,992 *sq km*—*pop* 10,069,917) and partly administered by India, but also claimed and partly controlled by Pakistan
Jam•na•gar \jäm-ˈnə-gər\ city W India in W Gujarat on Gulf of Kachchh *pop* 447,734
Jam•shed•pur \ˈjäm-ˌshed-ˌpu̇r\ city E India in Jharkhand *pop* 570,349
Ja•mu•na \ˈjə-mu̇-nə\ the lower Brahmaputra
Janes•ville \ˈjānz-ˌvil\ city S Wis. SE of Madison *pop* 63,575
Ja•nic•u•lum \jə-ˈni-kyə-ləm\ hill in Rome, Italy, on right bank of the Tiber opposite the seven hills on which the ancient city was built — see AVENTINE
Jan Ma•yen Island \yän-ˈmī-ən\ island in Arctic Ocean E of Greenland & NNE of Iceland belonging to Norway *area* 147 *sq mi* (382 *sq km*)
Ja•pan \jə-ˈpan, ja-\ *or Jp* **Nip•pon** \ni-ˈpän, nē-ˈpȯⁿ\ *or* **Ni•hon** \nē-ˈhȯn\ country E Asia comprising Honshu, Hokkaido, Kyushu, Shikoku, & other islands in the W Pacific; a constitutional monarchy ✻ Tokyo *area* 143,619 *sq mi* (371,973 *sq km*), *pop* 127,756,815
Japan, Sea of *also* **East Sea** arm of the W North Pacific W of Japan
Ja•pu•rá \ˌzhä-pü-ˈrä\ river 1750 *mi* (2816 *km*) S Colombia & NW Brazil flowing SE into the Amazon
Ja•ra•bu•lus \ja-ˈrä-bü-ˌlüs\ *or* **Je•ra•blus** \je-ˈrä-ˌblüs\ town N Syria on the Euphrates near Turkish border
Jar•vis \ˈjär-vis\ island *cen* Pacific in the Line Islands; claimed by U.S.
Jas•per National Park \ˈjas-pər\ reservation W Canada in W Alta. on E slopes of the Rockies NW of Banff National Park
Jassy — see IASI
Ja•strze•bie–Zdroj \yäs-ˈjä-bēz-ˈdrȯi\ city S Poland *pop* 102,661
Ja•va \ˈjä-və, ˈja-\ *or Indonesian* **Dja•wa** \ˈjä-və\ island Indonesia SE of Sumatra; chief city Jakarta *area* 51,007 *sq mi* (132,618 *sq km*), *pop* 107,581,306
Java Head cape Indonesia at W end of Java on Sunda Strait
Ja•va•ri \ˌzhä-vä-ˈrē\ *or Sp* **Ya•va•rí** \ˌyä-vä-ˈrē\ *or formerly* **Ya•ca•ra•na** \ˌyä-kä-ˈrä-nä\ river *ab* 600 *mi* (965 *km*) NW S. America flowing NE on Peru-Brazil boundary into the Amazon
Java Sea arm of the Pacific bounded on S by Java, on W by Sumatra, on N by Borneo, & on E by Sulawesi
Jaxartes — see SYR DAR'YA
Jaya, Puncak — see PUNCAK JAYA
Ja•ya•pu•ra \ˌjä-yä-ˈpü-rä\ *or formerly* **Hol•lan•dia** \hȯ-ˈlän-dē-ə\ *or* **Ko•ta•ba•ru** \ˌkō-tä-ˈbä-rü\ *or* **Su•kar•na•pu•ra** \sü-ˈkär-nä-ˌpü-rä\ city & port Indonesia ✻ of West Papua
Jazirah, Al — see GEZIRA
Jebel, Bahr el — see BAHR AL-GHAZAL
Je•bel ed Druz \ˈje-bəl-ed-ˈdrüz\ *or* **Jebel Druz** region S Syria E of Sea of Galilee on border of Jordan
Jebel Musa — see MUSA (Jebel)
Jebel Toubkal — see TOUBKAL (Jebel)
Jebus — see JERUSALEM
Jed•burgh \ˈjed-b(ə-)rə\ royal burgh SE Scotland SE of Edinburgh
Jef•fer•son \ˈje-fər-sən\ river over 200 *mi* (321 *km*) SW Mont. — see THREE FORKS
Jefferson, Mount mountain 10,495 *ft* (3199 *m*) NW Oreg. in Cascades
Jefferson City city ✻ of Mo. on Missouri River *pop* 43,079
Jef•fer•son•town \ˈje-fər-sən-ˌtau̇n\ city N Ky. E of Louisville *pop* 26,595
Jef•fer•son•ville \ˈje-fər-sən-ˌvil\ city S Ind. *pop* 44,953
Jehol — see CHENGDE
Jeju — see CHEJU
Je•mappes \zhə-ˈmäp\ commune SW Belgium W of Mons
Je•na \ˈyā-nə\ city E *cen* Germany E of Erfurt *pop* 100,967
Jeonju — see CHONJU
Je•qui•ti•nho•nha \zhe-ˌkē-tē-ˈnyō-nyə, -ˈnō-nyə\ river 500 *mi* (805 *km*) E Brazil flowing NE into the Atlantic
Jer•ba *or* **Djer•ba** \ˈjər-bə, ˈjer-\ *or* **Jar•bah** \ˈjer-bə\ island SE Tunisia in the Mediterranean at entrance to Gulf of Gabès *area* 197 *sq mi* (510 *sq km*)
Je•rez \hə-ˈrās, hā-ˈreth, -ˈres\ *or* **Je•rez de la Fron•te•ra** \ˌthā-lä-frōn-ˈtā-rä\ *or formerly* **Xe•res** \ˈsher-ēz\ city SW Spain NE of Cádiz *pop* 183,273
Jer•i•cho \ˈjer-i-ˌkō\ **1** *or Ar* **Ari•ha** \ä-ˈrē-hä\ town West Bank 5 *mi* (8 *km*) NW of Dead Sea **2** city of ancient Palestine near site of modern Jericho
Jer•sey \ˈjər-zē\ **1** island English Channel in the Channel Islands ✻ St. Helier *area* 45 *sq mi* (117 *sq km*) **2** NEW JERSEY — **Jer•sey•an** \-ən\ *n* — **Jer•sey•ite** \-ˌīt\ *n*
Jersey City city & port NE N.J. *pop* 247,597
Je•ru•sa•lem \jə-ˈrü-s(ə-)ləm, -ˈrü-z(ə-)ləm\ *or anc* **Hi•ero•sol•y•ma** \ˌhī-(ə-)rō-ˈsä-lə-mə\ *or bib* **Je•bus** \ˈjē-bəs\ city SW Asia NW of Dead Sea; divided 1948–67 bet. Jordan (old city) & Israel (new city); ✻ of Israel since 1950 & formerly ✻ of ancient kingdoms of Israel & Judah; old city under Israeli control since 1967 *pop* 657,500 — **Je•ru•sa•lem•ite** \-lə-ˌmīt\ *n*
Jer•vis Bay \ˈjär-vis\ inlet of the Pacific SE Australia on SE coast of New South Wales on which is situated district (*area* 28 *sq mi or* 73 *sq km*) that is part of Australian Capital Territory
Jesselton — see KOTA KINABALU
Jewel Cave National Monument limestone cave SW S.Dak.
Jewish Autonomous Oblast *or* **Ye•vrey•ska•ya** \yi-ˈvrā-skə-yə\ autonomous oblast E Russia in Asia, bordering on the Amur ✻ Birobidzhan *area* 13,900 *sq mi* (36,001 *sq km*)
Jez•re•el \ˈjez-rē-ˌel, -ˌrēl\ town of ancient Palestine in Samaria NW of Mt. Gilboa in Valley of Jezreel; now in N Israel
Jezreel, Valley of the E end of the Plain of Esdraelon
Jhan•si \ˈjän(t)-sē\ city N India in S Uttar Pradesh *pop* 383,248
Jhar•khand \ˈjär-kənd\ state NE India ✻ Ranchi *area* 28,832 *sq mi* (74,675 *sq km*), *pop* 26,909,428
Jhe•lum \ˈjā-ləm\ *or anc* **Hy•das•pes** \hī-ˈdas-(ˌ)pēz\ river 450 *mi* (724 *km*) NW India (subcontinent) flowing from Kashmir S & SW into the Chenab
Jia•mu•si *or* **Chia–mu–ssu** *or* **Kia•mu•sze** \ˈjyä-ˈmü-ˈsə\ city NE China in E Heilongjiang *pop* 493,409
Jiang•su *or* **Kiang•su** \ˈjyäŋ-ˈsü\ province E China bordering on Yellow Sea ✻ Nanjing *area* 40,927 *sq mi* (106,001 *sq km*), *pop* 67,056,519
Jiang•xi *or* **Kiang•si** \ˈjyäŋ-shē\ province SE China ✻ Nanchang *area* 63,629 *sq mi* (165,435 *sq km*), *pop* 37,710,281
Jiao•zhou *or* **Kiao•chow** \ˈjyau̇-ˈjō\ bay of Yellow Sea E China in E Shandong *area* 200 *sq mi* (520 *sq km*)
Jid•da *or* **Jid•dah** \ˈji-də\ *or* **Jed•da** *or* **Jed•dah** \ˈje-də\ city W Saudi Arabia in Hejaz on Red Sea; port for Mecca *pop* 561,104
Jih–k'a–tse — see XIGAZÊ
Ji•lin \ˈjē-ˈlin\ *or* **Ki•rin** \ˈkē-ˈrin\ **1** province NE China in E Manchuria ✻ Changchun *area* 72,201 *sq mi* (187,723 *sq km*), *pop* 24,658,721 **2** *or formerly* **Yung•ki** \ˈyüŋ-ˈjē\ city NE China in E *cen* Jilin *pop* 1,036,858
Ji•long *or* **Chi–lung** \ˈjē-ˈlu̇ŋ\ *or* **Kee•lung** \ˈkē-ˈlu̇ŋ\ city & port N Taiwan *pop* 391,950
Ji•nan *or* **Chi•nan** *or* **Tsi•nan** \ˈjē-ˈnän\ city E China ✻ of Shandong *pop* 1,500,000
Jin•ja \ˈjin-jä\ city & port SE Uganda on Lake Victoria *pop* 60,979
Jinmen — see QUEMOY
Jin•zhou *or* **Chin•chow** *or* **Chin–chou** \ˈjin-ˈjō\ city NE China in SW Liaoning *pop* 400,000
Jiu•long \ˈjü-ˈlȯŋ\ *or* **Kow•loon** \ˈkau̇-ˈlün\ **1** peninsula SE China in Hong Kong opposite Hong Kong Is. **2** city on Jiulong Peninsula
Jizah, Al — see GIZA
João Pes•soa \ˌzhwau̇ⁿ-pe-ˈsō-ə\ *or formerly* **Pa•ra•í•ba** \ˌpär-ä-ˈē-bə\ city NE Brazil ✻ of Paraíba *pop* 597,934
Jodh•pur \ˈjäd-pər, -ˌpu̇r\ **1** *or* **Mar•war** \ˈmär-ˌwär\ former state NW India bordering on Thar Desert & Rann of Kachchh, since 1949 part of Rajasthan state **2** city, its ✻ *pop* 846,408
Jod•rell Bank \ˈjä-drəl\ locality NW England in NE Cheshire
Jogjakarta — see YOGYAKARTA
Jo•han•nes•burg \jō-ˈhä-nəs-ˌbərg, -ˈha-\ city NE Republic of South Africa in Gauteng *pop* 654,232
John Day \ˈjän-ˈdā\ river 281 *mi* (452 *km*) N Oreg. flowing W & N into Columbia River
John Day Fossil Beds National Monument park N *cen* Oreg.
John o' Groat's \ˌjän-ō-ˈgrōts\ *or* **John o' Groat's House** locality N Scotland; popularly considered the northernmost point of mainland of Scotland & Great Britain — see DUNNET HEAD
John•son City \ˈjän(t)-sən\ city NE Tenn. S of Va. border *pop* 63,152
John•ston \ˈjän(t)-stən\ **1** island (atoll) *cen* Pacific SW of Oahu; belongs to the U.S. **2** town N R.I. SW of Providence *pop* 28,769
Johns•town \ˈjänz-ˌtau̇n\ city SW *cen* Pa. *pop* 20,978
Jo•hor \jə-ˈhȯr\ state Malaysia in Peninsular Malaysia at S end of Malay Peninsula ✻ Johor Baharu *area* 7360 *sq mi* (19,062 *sq km*), *pop* 2,074,297
Johor Ba•ha•ru \ˈbä-hə-ˌrü\ city S Malaysia (federation) ✻ of Johor on an inlet opposite Singapore Is. *pop* 135,936
Join•vi•le *or formerly* **Join•vil•le** \zhāⁿ-ˈvē-lē\ city S Brazil NNW of Florianópolis *pop* 429,604
Jo•li•et \ˌjō-lē-ˈet, *chiefly by outsiders* ˌjä-\ city NE Ill. *pop* 147,433
Jo•lo \hō-ˈlō\ island S Philippines; chief island of Sulu Archipelago *area* 345 *sq mi* (897 *sq km*)
Jones•boro \ˈjōnz-ˌbər-ō\ city NE Ark. *pop* 67,263
Jön•kö•ping \ˈyœn-ˌshœ-piŋ\ city S Sweden at S end of Vättern Lake *pop* 118,581
Jon•quière \ˌzhōⁿ-ˈkyer\ former town Canada in S *cen* Que., now part of Saguenay
Jop•lin \ˈjä-plin\ city SW Mo. *pop* 50,150
Joppa — see JAFFA
Jor•dan \ˈjȯr-dᵊn\ **1** river *cen* Utah flowing from Utah Lake N into Great Salt Lake **2** river 200 *mi* (322 *km*) SW Asia flowing from Anti-Lebanon Mountains S through Sea of Galilee into Dead Sea **3** *or formerly* **Trans•jor•dan** \(ˌ)tran(t)s-, (ˌ)tranz-\ country SW Asia ✻ Amman *area* 34,575 *sq mi* (89,549 *sq km*), *pop* 5,100,981 — **Jor•da•ni•an** \jȯr-ˈdā-nē-ən\ *adj or n*
Josh•ua Tree National Park \ˈjä-shə-wə\ area containing unusual desert flora S Calif. N of Salton Sea
Jo•tun•heim \ˈyō-tᵊn-ˌhām\ *or Norw* **Jo•tun•hei•men** \-ˌhā-mən\ mountains S *cen* Norway — see GLITTERTIND
Juana Dí•az \ˌwä-nə-ˈdē-ˌäs, ˌhwä-nä-ˈthē-äs\ municipality S Puerto Rico *pop* 50,531
Juan de Fu•ca, Strait of \ˌwän-də-ˈfyü-kə, ˌhwän-\ strait 100 *mi* (161 *km*) long bet. Vancouver Is., B.C., & Olympic Peninsula, Wash.

Juan Fer·nán·dez \ˌwän-fər-ˈnan-dəs, ˌhwän-fer-ˈnän-dās\ three islands SE Pacific W of Chile belonging to Chile *area* 70 *sq mi* (182 *sq km*)

Juan–les–Pins \ˌzhwäⁿ-lā-ˈpaⁿ\ town SE France on Cap d'Antibes

Juárez — see CIUDAD JUÁREZ

Jub·a \ˈjü-bə, -ˌbä\ town ✳ of South Sudan *pop* 244,000

Jub·ba *or* **Ju·ba** \ˈjü-bə\ river 1000 *mi* (1609 *km*) E Africa flowing from S Ethiopia S through Somalia into Indian Ocean

Ju·by, Cape \ˈjü-bē, ˈyü-\ cape NW Africa on NW coast of Western Sahara

Jú·car \ˈhü-ˌkär\ river over 300 *mi* (480 *km*) E Spain flowing S & E into the Mediterranean S of Valencia

Ju·daea *or* **Ju·dea** \jü-ˈdē-ə, -ˈdä-\ the S division of ancient Palestine under Persian, Greek, & Roman rule succeeding the kingdom of Judah; bounded on N by Samaria, on E by Jordan River & Dead Sea, on SW by Sinai Peninsula, & on W by the Mediterranean — **Ju·dae·an** *or* **Ju·de·an** \-ən\ *adj or n*

Ju·dah \ˈjü-də\ kingdom S ancient Palestine ✳ Jerusalem — see ISRAEL

Jugoslavia — see YUGOSLAVIA — **Ju·go·slav** \ˌyü-gō-ˈsläv, -ˈslav\ *or* **Ju·go·sla·vi·an** \-ˈslä-vē-ən\ *adj or n*

Juiz de Fo·ra \ˌzhwēzh-də-ˈfȯr-ə\ city E Brazil in S Minas Gerais *pop* 456,796

Ju·juy \hü-ˈhwē\ city NW Argentina W of Tucumán *pop* 44,188

Ju·lian Alps \ˈjül-yən\ section of E Alps W Slovenia N of Istrian Peninsula; highest peak Triglav 9395 *ft* (2864 *m*)

Julian Venetia — see VENEZIA GIULIA

Jun·cos \ˈhün-kōs\ city E Puerto Rico *pop* 40,290

Ju·neau \ˈjü-(ˌ)nō, jü-ˈ\ city & port ✳ of Alaska in SE coastal strip *pop* 31,275

Jung·frau \ˈyu̇ŋ-ˌfrau̇\ mountain 13,642 *ft* (4158 *m*) SW *cen* Switzerland in Berner Alpen bet. Bern & Valais cantons

Jung·gar Pen·di \ˈju̇ŋ-ˈgär-ˈpən-ˈdē\ *or* **Chun·go·erh P'en·ti** \ˈchün-ˈgō-ˈər-ˈpən-ˈtē\ *or* **Dzun·gar·ian Basin** \jən-ˈger-ē-ən, ju̇n-\ region W China in N Xinjiang Uygur N of the Tian Shan

Ju·ni·a·ta \ˌjü-nē-ˈa-tə\ river 150 *mi* (241 *km*) S *cen* Pa. flowing E into the Susquehanna

Ju·nín \hü-ˈnēn\ 1 city E Argentina W of Buenos Aires *pop* 62,080 2 town *cen* Peru at S end of **Lake Junín** (25 *mi* or 40 *km* long)

Ju·pi·ter \ˈjü-pə-tər\ town SE Fla. *pop* 55,156

Jupiter Island island SE Fla. in the Atlantic

Ju·ra \ˈju̇r-ə\ 1 canton W Switzerland *area* 322 *sq mi* (834 *sq km*), *pop* 69,100 2 mountains France & Switzerland extending *ab* 145 *mi* (233 *km*) along the boundary; highest peak Mount Neige (in France) 5652 *ft* (1723 *m*) 3 island 24 *mi* (39 *km*) long W Scotland in the Inner Hebrides S of Mull

Juramento — see SALADO 1

Ju·ruá \ˌzhu̇r-(ə-)ˈwä\ river NW *cen* S. America flowing from E *cen* Peru NE into the Solimões in NW Brazil

Ju·rue·na \ˌzhu̇r-ˈwä-nə\ river 600 *mi* (966 *km*) W *cen* Brazil flowing N to unite with the Teles Pires forming the Tapajoz

Jut·land \ˈjət-lənd\ *or Dan* **Jyl·land** \ˈyu̇e-ˌlän\ 1 peninsula N Europe projecting into North Sea & comprising mainland of Denmark & N portion of Schleswig-Holstein, Germany 2 the mainland of Denmark

Jy·vas·ky·la \ˈjü-vas-ˌkue-la\ city S *cen* Finland *pop* 81,110

Kaapland — see CAPE OF GOOD HOPE

Kabalega Falls — see MURCHISON FALLS

Kab·ar·di·no–Bal·kar·ia *or* **Kab·ar·di·no–Bal·ka·ri·ya** \ˌka-bər-ˈdē-nō-ˌbȯl-ˈka-rē-ə, -ˌbal-\ autonomous republic S Russia in Europe on N slopes of the Caucasus ✳ Nal'chik *area* 4826 *sq mi* (12,499 *sq km*), *pop* 784,000

Kabarega Falls — see MURCHISON FALLS

Ka·bul \ˈkä-bəl, -ˌbül; kə-ˈbül\ 1 river 435 *mi* (700 *km*) Afghanistan & N Pakistan flowing E into the Indus 2 city ✳ of Afghanistan on Kabul River *pop* 1,424,400 — **Ka·buli** \kä-bə-(ˌ)lē, kə-ˈbü-lē\ *adj or n*

Ka·bwe \ˈkä-(ˌ)bwā\ *or formerly* **Bro·ken Hill** \ˈbrō-kən\ city *cen* Zambia *pop* 166,519

Ka·by·lia \kə-ˈbī-lē-ə, -ˈbi-\ mountainous region N Algeria on coast E of Algiers; comprises: **Great Kabylia** (to W) & **Little Kabylia** (to E)

Kachchh, Gulf of \ˈkȯch\ *or* **Gulf of Kutch** \ˈkȯch\ inlet of Arabian Sea W India N of Kathiawar

Kachchh, Rann of *or* **Rann of Kutch** salt marsh in S Pakistan & W India stretching in an arc from the mouths of the Indus to the head of Gulf of Kachchh

Ka·desh–bar·nea \ˌkä-(ˌ)desh-ˈbär-nē-ə, -bär-ˈnē-ə\ town of ancient Palestine S of Dead Sea; exact location uncertain

Ka·di·koy \ˈkä-ˈdi-kȯi\ *or anc* **Chal·ce·don** \ˈkal-sə-ˌdän, kal-ˈsē-dⁿn\ former city of Asia on the Bosporus, now a district of Istanbul

Kadiyevka — see STAKHANOV

Kaerh — see GAR

Kae·song *or* **Gae·seong** \ˈgā-ˌsȯŋ\ city SW N. Korea SE of Pyongyang *pop* 331,000

Kaf·fe·klub·ben \ˈkä-fə-ˌklü-bən, -ˌklə\ island in Arctic Ocean off N coast of Greenland; northernmost point of land in the world, at 83°40′N

Kaf·frar·ia \kə-ˈfrer-ē-ə, ka-\ region Republic of South Africa in Eastern Cape province S of Lesotho bordering on Indian Ocean

Kafiristan — see NURISTAN

Ka·fue \kä-ˈfü-ā\ river 600 *mi* (965 *km*) Zambia flowing into the Zambezi

Ka·ge·ra \kä-ˈgä-rä\ river 430 *mi* (692 *km*) Burundi, Rwanda, & NW Tanzania flowing N & E into Lake Victoria on Uganda border

Ka·go·shi·ma \kä-gō-ˈshē-mä, kä-ˈgō-shē-\ city & port S Japan in S Kyushu on **Kagoshima Bay** (inlet of the Pacific) *pop* 552,098

Ka·hoo·la·we \ˌkä-hō-ō-ˈlä-(ˌ)vā, -(ˌ)wä\ island Hawaii SW of Maui *area* 45 *sq mi* (117 *sq km*)

Kai·bab Plateau \ˈkī-ˌbab\ plateau N Ariz. & SW Utah N of Grand Canyon

Kai·e·teur Falls \ˌkī-ə-ˈtu̇r, ˌkī-ˈchu̇r\ waterfall 741 *ft* (226 *m*) high & 350 *ft* (107 *m*) wide *cen* Guyana

Kai·feng \ˈkī-ˈfəŋ\ city E *cen* China in NE Henan *pop* 318,000

Kai·lua \kī-ˈlü-ä\ city Hawaii in NE Oahu *pop* 38,635

Kair·ouan \ker-ˈwän\ city NE Tunisia *pop* 117,903

Kai·sers·lau·tern \ˌkī-zərz-ˈlau̇-tərn\ city SW Germany W of Ludwigshafen *pop* 100,541

Kaiser–Wilhelmsland — see NORTH-EAST NEW GUINEA

Ka·ki·na·da \ˌkä-kə-ˈnä-də\ city & port E India in NE Andhra Pradesh on Bay of Bengal *pop* 289,920

Kalaallit Nunaat — see GREENLAND

Ka Lae \kä-ˈlä-ā\ *or* **South Cape** headland Hawaii; southernmost point of Hawaii (island)

Kalaeloa Point — see BARBERS POINT

Kal·a·ha·ri Desert \ˌkä-lə-ˈhär-ē, ˌkä-\ desert region S Africa N of Orange River & S of Lake Ngami in Botswana & NW Republic of South Africa

Kal·a·ma·zoo \ˌka-lə-mə-ˈzü\ city SW Mich. *pop* 74,262

Ka·lat *or* **Khe·lat** \kə-ˈlät\ region NW Pakistan including S & *cen* Baluchistan; a former princely state ✳ Kalat

Ka·le·mie \kä-ˈlā-mē\ *or formerly* **Al·bert·ville** \ˈal-bər-ˌvēl, ˈal-bərt-ˌvil\ city & port E Democratic Republic of the Congo on Lake Tanganyika *pop* 96,212

Kalgan — see ZHANGJIAKOU

Kal·goor·lie–Boul·der \kal-ˈgu̇r-lē-ˈbōl-dər\ town Australia in S *cen* W. Australia *pop* 25,016

Ka·li·man·tan \ˌka-lə-ˈman-ˌtan, ˌkä-lē-ˈmän-ˌtän\ 1 — see BORNEO 2 the S & E part of Borneo belonging to Indonesia; formerly (as **Dutch Borneo**) part of Netherlands Indies

Kalinin — see TVER

Ka·li·nin·grad \kə-ˈlē-nən-ˌgrad, -nyən-, -ˌgrät\ *or G* **Kö·nigs·berg** \ˈkā-nigz-ˌbȯrg, *Ger* ˈkœ-niks-ˌberk\ city & port W Russia in Europe near Vislinski Zaliv; formerly ✳ of E. Prussia *pop* 411,000

Ka·lisz \ˈkä-lēsh\ commune *cen* Poland W of Lodz *pop* 106,087

Kal·mar \ˈkäl-ˌmär, ˈkal-\ city & port SE Sweden *pop* 60,066

Kal·myk·ia *or* **Kal·myk·i·ya** \(ˌ)kal-ˈmi-kē-ə\ autonomous republic S Russia in Europe on NW shore of Caspian Sea W of the Volga ✳ Elista *area* 29,305 *sq mi* (75,900 *sq km*), *pop* 322,000

Ka·lu·ga \kə-ˈlü-gə\ city W *cen* Russia in Europe on Oka River WNW of Tula *pop* 347,000

Ka·ma \ˈkä-mə\ river E Russia in Europe flowing SW into the Volga S of Kazan'

Ka·ma·ku·ra \kä-ˈmä-kə-ˌrä, ˌkä-mä-ˈku̇r-ä\ city Japan in SE Honshu on Sagami Sea S of Yokohama *pop* 167,583

Kam·chat·ka \kam-ˈchat-kə, -ˈchät-\ peninsula 750 *mi* (1207 *km*) long E Russia in Asia bet. Sea of Okhotsk & Bering Sea

Ka·met \ˈkə-ˌmät, kə-ˈmät\ mountain 25,447 *ft* (7756 *m*) N India in Uttarakhand in NW part of the Himalayas

Kam·loops \ˈkam-ˌlüps\ city Canada in S B.C. *pop* 85,678

Kam·pa·la \käm-ˈpä-lä, kam-\ city ✳ of Uganda N of Lake Victoria *pop* 1,200,000

Kampuchea — see CAMBODIA — **Kam·pu·che·an** \ˌkam-pə-ˈchē-ən\ *adj*

Kan — see GAN

Ka·nan·ga \kä-ˈnäŋ-gä\ *or formerly* **Lu·lua·bourg** \ˌlü-lwä-ˈbu̇r\ city S *cen* Democratic Republic of the Congo *pop* 720,000

Kananur — see CANNANORE

Ka·na·wha \kə-ˈnȯ-(w)ə\ river 97 *mi* (156 *km*) W W.Va. flowing NW into Ohio River

Ka·na·za·wa \kä-ˈnä-zä-wä, ˌkä-nä-ˈzä-wä\ city & port Japan in W *cen* Honshu near Sea of Japan *pop* 456,438

Kan·chen·jun·ga \ˌkən-chən-ˈjəŋ-gə, -ˈju̇ŋ-\ *or* **Kang·chen·jun·ga** \ˌkəŋ-\ mountain 28,209 *ft* (8598 *m*) Nepal & Sikkim, India, in the Himalayas; 3d highest in the world

Kan·chi·pu·ram \kän-ˈchē-pə-rəm\ city SE India in N Tamil Nadu SW of Madras *pop* 152,984

Kan·da·har *or* **Qan·da·har** \ˈkən-də-ˌhär\ city SE Afghanistan *pop* 130,212

Kan·dy \ˈkan-dē\ city W *cen* Sri Lanka ENE of Colombo *pop* 104,000 — **Kan·dy·an** \-dē-ən\ *adj*

Kane Basin \ˈkān\ section of the channel bet. NW Greenland & Ellesmere Is. N of Baffin Bay

Ka·ne·o·he \ˌkä-nē-ˈō-ä, -ˈō-(ˌ)hā\ city Hawaii on Kaneohe Bay, Oahu *pop* 34,597

Kaneohe Bay inlet Hawaii on E Oahu

Kan·ka·kee \ˌkaŋ-kə-ˈkē\ 1 river 135 *mi* (217 *km*) Ind. & Ill. flowing SW & W to unite with Des Plaines River forming Illinois River 2 city NE Ill. on Kankakee River *pop* 27,537

Kan·nap·o·lis \kə-ˈna-pə-lis\ town *cen* N.C. *pop* 42,625

Ka·no \ˈkä-(ˌ)nō\ city N Nigeria *pop* 3,000,000

Kan·pur \ˈkän-ˌpu̇r\ city N India in S Uttar Pradesh on the Ganges *pop* 2,532,138

Kan·sas \ˈkan-zəs\ 1 *or* **Kaw** \ˈkȯ\ river 169 *mi* (272 *km*) E Kans. flowing E into Missouri River — see SMOKY HILL 2 state *cen* U.S. ✳ Topeka *area* 82,277 *sq mi* (213,097 *sq km*), *pop* 2,853,118 — **Kan·san** \ˈkan-zən\ *adj or n*

Kansas City 1 city NE Kans. adjacent to Kansas City, Mo. *pop* 145,786 2 city W Mo. on Missouri River *pop* 459,787

Kansu — see GANSU

Kan·ton Island \ˈkan-tⁿn\ island (atoll) *cen* Pacific in Phoenix Islands

Kan·to Plain \ˈkän-(ˌ)tō\ region Japan in E *cen* Honshu in which Tokyo is situated

Kao–hsiung — see GAOXIONG

Ka·pi·da·gi \kä-pi-ˈdau̇\ *or anc* **Cyz·i·cus** \ˈsi-zi-kəs\ peninsula NW Turkey in Asia projecting into Sea of Marmara

Ka·ra·chay–Cher·kes·sia \ˌkär-ə-ˌchī-chir-ˈke-syə\ *or* **Ka·ra·cha·ye·vo–Cher·kes·i·ya** \ˌkär-ə-ˌchī-ə-ˌvō-chir-ˈke-sē-ə\ autonomous region SE Russia in Europe in N Caucasus *area* 5444 *sq mi* (14,100 *sq km*), *pop* 431,000 ✳ Cherkessk

Ka·ra·chi \kə-ˈrä-chē\ city & port S Pakistan ✳ of Sind *pop* 12,100,000

Karafuto — see SAKHALIN

Ka·ra·gan·da \ˌkär-ə-ˈgän-də\ *or* **Qa·ra·ghan·dy** \-dē\ city *cen* Kazakhstan *pop* 446,000

Ka·raj \kä-ˈräj\ city N Iran NW of Tehran *pop* 1,400,000

Ka·ra·kal·pak·stan \ˌka-rə-ˌkäl-'päk-ˌstän\ autonomous republic NW Uzbekistan SE of Aral Sea ✻ Nukus *area* 63,938 *sq mi* (165,599 *sq km*), *pop* 1,273,800

Kar·a·ko·ram Pass \ˌkär-ə-'kòr-əm\ mountain pass 18,290 *ft* (5575 *m*) NE Kashmir through Karakoram Range

Karakoram Range mountain system S *cen* Asia in N Kashmir & NW Tibet on Xinjiang Uygur border connecting the Himalayas with the Pamirs; westernmost system of the Himalayan complex — see K2

Kar·a·ko·rum \ˌka-rə-'kòr-əm\ ruined city Mongolia on the upper Orhon ✻ of Mongol Empire

Ka·ra–Kum \ˌka-rə-'küm, ˌkär-ə-\ desert Turkmenistan S of Aral Sea bet. the Caspian Sea & the Amu Dar'ya *area* 115,830 *sq mi* (300,000 *sq km*)

Ka·ra Sea \'kär-ə\ arm of Arctic Ocean off coast of Russia E of Novaya Zemlya

Ka·ra Su \ˌka-rə-'sü, ˌkär-ə-\ the Euphrates above its junction with the Murat in E *cen* Turkey

Kar·ba·lā' \ˌkär-bə-'lä, 'kär-bə-lə\ city *cen* Iraq SSW of Baghdad *pop* 83,301

Ka·re·lia or **Ka·re·li·ya** \kə-'rē-lē-ə, -'rēl-yə\ autonomous republic NW Russia in Europe; formerly (1940–56), as the **Ka·re·lo–Finn·ish Republic** \kə-'rē-(ˌ)lō-'fi-nish\, constituent republic of the U.S.S.R. ✻ Petrozadovsk *area* 66,564 *sq mi* (172,401 *sq km*), *pop* 800,000

Ka·re·lian Isthmus \kə-'rē-lē-ən, -'rēl-yən\ isthmus Russia in Europe bet. Gulf of Finland & Lake Ladoga

Ka·ri·ba, Lake \kä-'rē-bä\ lake 175 *mi* (282 *km*) long SE Zambia & N Zimbabwe formed in the Zambezi by **Kariba Dam**

Ka·ri·kal \ˌkär-ə-'käl\ **1** territory of former French India S of Puducherry; incorporated 1954 in India *area* 52 *sq mi* (135 *sq km*) **2** or **Ka·rai·kal** \ˌkä-ri-'käl\ city & port, its ✻, on Bay of Bengal *pop* 22,252

Kar·kheh or **Ker·kheh** \'kär-'kä\ or *anc* **Cho·as·pes** \kō-'as-(ˌ)pēz\ river flowing from W Iran S & W into marshlands E of the Tigris in SE Iraq

Karl–Marx–Stadt — see CHEMNITZ

Karls·kro·na \kär(-ə)lz-'krü-nə\ city & port SE Sweden on Baltic Sea *area pop* 60,676

Karls·ru·he \'kär(-ə)lz-ˌrü-ə\ city SW Germany in Baden-Württemberg on the Rhine 278,579 — **Karls·ru·her** \-ˌrü-ər\ *n*

Karl·stad \'kär(-ə)l-ˌstä(d)\ city SW Sweden *pop* 80,934

Kar·nak \'kär-ˌnak\ town S Egypt on the Nile N of Luxor on N part of site of ancient Thebes

Kar·na·ta·ka \kər-'nä-tə-kə\ or *formerly* **My·sore** \mī-'sòr\ state SW India ✻ Bangalore *area* 74,037 *sq mi* (191,756 *sq km*), *pop* 52,733,958

Ka·roo or **Kar·roo** \kə-'rü\ plateau region W Republic of South Africa W of Drakensberg Mountains divided into **Little Karoo** or **Southern Karoo** (in *cen* Western Cape province), **Great Karoo** or **Central Karoo** (in Western Cape & Eastern Cape provinces), & **Northern Karoo** or **Upper Karoo** (in Northern Cape, Free State, & North West provinces)

Kár·pa·thos \'kär-pä-ˌthòs\ island Greece in the S Dodecanese *area* 118 *sq mi* (307 *sq km*), *pop* 8129

Kars \'kärz, 'kärs\ city NE Turkey *pop* 79,496

Karst \'kärst\ or **Kras** \'kräs\ or *It* **Car·so** \'kär-(ˌ)sō\ limestone plateau NE of Istrian Peninsula in W Slovenia extending into E Italy

Ka·run \kä-'rün\ river over 500 *mi* (800 *km*) W Iran flowing into Shatt al Arab

Kar·vi·ná \'kär-vē-ˌnä\ city E Czech Republic just E of Ostrava *pop* 65,141

Ka·sai \kə-'sī\ **1** river 1338 *mi* (2153 *km*) N Angola & W Democratic Republic of the Congo flowing N & W into Congo River **2** region S *cen* Democratic Republic of the Congo

Kashi or **K'a–shih** \'kä-shē, 'kä-\ or **Kash·gar** \'kash-ˌgär, 'kash-\ or *Uighur* **Kax·gar** \'käsh-ˌgär\ city W China in SW Xinjiang Uygur *pop* 174,570

Ka·shi·wa \'kä-shē-(ˌ)wä\ city Japan in E Honshu *pop* 327,851

Kash·mir \'kash-ˌmir, 'kazh-, kash-', kazh-'\ **1** or *formerly* **Cashmere** mountainous region N India (subcontinent) W of Tibet & SW of Xinjiang Uygur; includes valley (**Vale of Kashmir**) watered by the Jhelum **2** — see JAMMU AND KASHMIR

Kas·kas·kia \ka-'kas-kē-ə\ river 320 *mi* (515 *km*) SW Ill. flowing SW into Mississippi River

Kas·sa·la \'ka-sə-lä\ city NE Sudan *pop* 99,000

Kas·sel \'ka-səl, 'kä-\ city *cen* Germany WNW of Erfurt *pop* 196,828

Kas·ser·ine Pass \'ka-sə-ˌrēn\ mountain pass *cen* Tunisia

Ka·stel·lór·i·zon \ˌkäs-te-'lòr-ə-ˌzòn\ or **Ca·stel·lo·ri·zo** \ˌkäs-tə-'lòr-ə-ˌzō\ or *It* **Cas·tel·ros·so** \ˌkäs-ˌtel-'rō-(ˌ)sō\ island Greece in the E Dodecanese off SW coast of Turkey *area* 9 *sq mi* (23 *sq km*)

Ká·stron \'käs-ˌtròn\ town Greece on Lemnos

Ka·tah·din, Mount \kə-'tä-dⁿn\ mountain 5268 *ft* (1606 *m*) N *cen* Maine; highest point in state

Katanga — see SHABA — **Ka·tan·gese** \kə-ˌtän-'gēz, -taŋ-, -'gēs\ *adj*

Ka·te·ri·ni \ˌkä-te-'rē-nē\ town N Greece *pop* 46,304

Kath·er·i·na, Ge·bel \'je-bəl-ˌka-thə-'rē-nə\ or **Ja·bal Kat·ri·nah** \ˌjä-bəl-kä-'trē-nə\ or **Mount Cath·er·ine** \-ka-th(ə-)rən\ mountain 8652 *ft* (2637 *m*) NE Egypt on Sinai Peninsula; highest in the Gebel Musa

Ka·thi·a·war \ˌkä-tē-ə-'wär\ peninsula W India in Gujarat bet. Gulf of Kachchh & Gulf of Khambhat

Kath·man·du or **Kat·man·du** \ˌkat-ˌman-'dü, ˌkät-ˌmän-\ city ✻ of Nepal *pop* 671,846

Kat·mai, Mount \'kat-ˌmī\ volcano 6715 *ft* (2047 *m*) S Alaska in Aleutian Range at NE end of Alaska Peninsula

Katmai National Park volcanic landscape S Alaska including Mt. Katmai & Valley of Ten Thousand Smokes

Ka·to·wi·ce \ˌkä-tò-'vēt-se\ or *G* **Kat·to·witz** \'kä-tə-ˌvits\ city S Poland in Silesia *pop* 367,041

Kat·rine, Loch \'ka-trən\ lake 9 *mi* (14 *km*) long *cen* Scotland E of Loch Lomond

Ka·tsi·na \'kät-sē-nä\ city N Nigeria ✻ of old Hausa kingdom of Katsina *pop* 182,400

Kat·te·gat \'ka-ti-ˌgat\ arm of North Sea bet. Sweden & Jutland Peninsula of Denmark

Kau·ai \kä-'wä-ē\ island Hawaii WNW of Oahu *area* 555 *sq mi* (1437 *sq km*), *pop* 67,091

Kau·nas \'kaù-nəs, -ˌnäs\ or *Russ* **Kov·no** \'kòv-(ˌ)nō, -nə\ city *cen* Lithuania on the Neman; a former (1918–40) ✻ of Lithuania *pop* 378,943

Ka·vá·la or **Ka·vál·la** \kä-'vä-lä\ city & port NE Greece in Macedonia *pop* 58,576

Ka·va·rat·ti \ˌkə-və-'rə-tē\ town S India ✻ of Lakshadweep union territory *pop* 10,113

Kāveri — see CAUVERY

Kāveri Falls — see CAUVERY FALLS

Kaw — see KANSAS 1

Ka·wa·goe \kä-'wä-gō-wä\ city Japan in SE *cen* Honshu *pop* 330,766

Ka·wa·gu·chi \ˌkä-wä-'gü-chē, kä-'wä-gü-(ˌ)chē\ city Japan in E Honshu N of Tokyo *pop* 460,027

Ka·war·tha Lakes \kə-'wòr-thə\ **1** group of lakes Canada in SE Ont. E of Lake Simcoe; traversed by Trent Canal system **2** city Canada in SE Ont. NE of Toronto *pop* 73,214

Ka·wa·sa·ki \ˌkä-wä-'sä-kē\ city Japan in E Honshu on Tokyo Bay, S suburb of Tokyo *pop* 1,249,905

Kaxgar — see KASHI

Kay·se·ri \ˌkī-zə-'rē\ or *anc* **Cae·sa·rea** \ˌsē-zə-'rē-ə, ˌse-zə-, ˌse-sə-\ or **Maz·a·ca** \'ma-zə-kə\ or **Caesarea Mazaca** city *cen* Turkey in Asia at foot of Erciyas Mt.; chief city of ancient Cappadocia *pop* 421,362

Ka·zakh·stan *also* **Ka·zak·stan** \ˌka-(ˌ)zak-'stan; ˌkä(ˌ)zäk-'stän or kə-\ country NW *cen* Asia extending from Caspian Sea to Altai Mountains; a constituent republic of the U.S.S.R. 1936–91 ✻ Astana *area* 1,048,300 *sq mi* (2,715,097 *sq km*), *pop* 15,685,000

Ka·zan \kə-'zan\ river 455 *mi* (732 *km*) Canada flowing through a series of lakes into Baker Lake

Ka·zan' \kə-'zan, -'zän, -'zä-nyə\ city E *cen* Russia in Europe ✻ of Tatarstan *pop* 1,098,000

Kazan Retto — see VOLCANO ISLANDS

Kaz·bek \käz-'bek\ mountain 16,558 *ft* (5047 *m*) bet. Georgia & Russia in Europe in the Caucasus Mountains

Kaz Da·gi \ˌkäz-'dī\ or **Mount Ida** \'ī-də\ mountain 5797 *ft* (1767 *m*) NW Turkey in Asia SE of ancient Troy

Kea \'kä-ä\ or *anc* **Ce·os** \'sē-ˌäs\ island Greece in NW Cyclades; chief town Kea *area* 67 *sq mi* (174 *sq km*)

Ke·a·la·ke·kua Bay \kä-ˌä-lä-kä-'kü-ä\ inlet of the Pacific Hawaii in W Hawaii (island) on Kona coast W of Mauna Loa

Kear·ney \'kär-nē\ city S *cen* Nebr. on Platte River *pop* 30,787

Kear·ny \'kär-nē\ town NE N.J. N of Newark *pop* 40,684

Kecs·ke·met \'kech-ke-ˌmät\ city *cen* Hungary *pop* 108,000

Ked·ah \'ke-də\ state Malaysia in N Peninsular Malaysia on Strait of Malacca ✻ Alor Setar *area* 3660 *sq mi* (9516 *sq km*), *pop* 1,304,800

Keeling Islands — see COCOS ISLANDS

Keelung — see JILONG

Keene \'kēn\ city SW N.H. *pop* 23,409

Kee·wa·tin \kē-'wä-tⁿn, -'wät\ former district Canada in E Northwest Territories N of Man. & Ont. & including the islands in Hudson Bay, area now part of Nunavut

Kefallinía — see CEPHALONIA

Kef·la·vík \'kye-blä-ˌvēk, 'ke-flə-\ town SW Iceland WSW of Reykjavík *pop* 7520

Keigh·ley \'kēth-lē—*sic*\ town N England in W. Yorkshire, NW of Leeds *pop* 57,451

Kei·zer \'kī-zər\ city NW Oreg. N of Salem *pop* 36,478

Kej·im·ku·jik National Park \ˌke-jə-mə-'kü-jik, ˌkej-mə-\ area of lakes and streams Canada in SW N.S.

Ke·lan·tan \kə-'lan-ˌtan\ state Malaysia in N Peninsular Malaysia on S. China Sea ✻ Kota Baharu *area* 5780 *sq mi* (14,970 *sq km*), *pop* 1,181,680

Kel·ler \'ke-lər\ city N Texas N of Fort Worth *pop* 39,627

Ke·low·na \ki-'lō-nə\ city Canada in S B.C. *pop* 117,312

Keltsy — see KIELCE

Ke·me·ro·vo \'kye-mə-rə-və; 'ke-mə-ˌrō-və, -rə-, vō\ city Russia in Asia in Kuznetsk Basin on Tom' River *pop* 521,000

Ke·nai Peninsula \'kē-ˌnī\ peninsula S Alaska E of Cook Inlet; site of **Kenai Fjords National Park** (ice field)

Ken·dal \'ken-dⁿl\ town NW England in Cumbria *pop* 23,411

Ken·il·worth \'ke-nⁿl-ˌwərth\ town *cen* England in Warwickshire *pop* 19,315

Ke·ni·tra \kə-'nē-trə\ or *formerly* **Port Lyau·tey** \ˌpòr-lyō-'tā\ city N Morocco NE of Rabat *pop* 359,142

Ken·ne·bec \'ke-ni-ˌbek, ˌke-ni-'\ river 150 *mi* (240 *km*) S Maine flowing S from Moosehead Lake into the Atlantic

Kennedy, Cape — see CANAVERAL (Cape)

Ken·ne·dy, Mount \'ke-nə-dē\ mountain 13,905 *ft* (4238 *m*) NW Canada in Yukon Territory in St. Elias Range near Alaska border

Ken·ner \'ke-nər\ city SE La. W of New Orleans *pop* 66,702

Ken·ne·saw Mountain \'ke-nə-ˌsò\ mountain 1809 *ft* (551 *m*) NW Ga. NW of Atlanta

Ken·ne·wick \'ke-nə-ˌwik\ city SE Wash. *pop* 73,917

Ke·no·sha \kə-'nō-shə\ city SE Wis. S of Racine *pop* 99,218

Ken·sing·ton and Chel·sea \'ken-ziŋ-tən-ənd-'chel-sē, 'ken(t)-siŋ-\ royal borough of W Greater London, England *pop* 127,600; includes former boroughs of Kensington & Chelsea

Kent \'kent\ **1** city NE Ohio SE of Cleveland *pop* 28,904 **2** city W Wash. S of Seattle *pop* 92,411 **3** county SE England bordering on Strait of Dover; one of kingdoms in Anglo-Saxon heptarchy ✻ Maidstone *area* 1493 *sq mi* (3867 *sq km*), *pop* 1,485,100 — **Kent·ish** \'ken-tish\ *adj*

Kent Island island Md. in Chesapeake Bay 15 *mi* (25 *km*) long; largest island in the bay

Ken·tucky \kən-'tə-kē\ **1** river 259 *mi* (417 *km*) N *cen* Ky. flowing NW into Ohio River **2** state E *cen* U.S. ✻ Frankfort *area* 40,395 *sq mi* (105,027 *sq km*), *pop* 4,339,367 — **Ken·tuck·i·an** \-kē-ən\ *adj* or *n*

Kent·wood \'kent-ˌwüd\ city SW Mich. *pop* 48,707

Ken·ya \'ke-nyə, 'kē-\ or *formerly* **British East Africa** republic E Africa S of Ethiopia bordering on Indian Ocean; member of the Commonwealth of Nations; formerly a Brit. crown colony & protectorate ✻ Nairobi *area* 224,960 *sq mi* (584,896 *sq km*), *pop* 38,600,000 — **Ken·yan** \-nyən\ *adj* or *n*

Kenya, Mount extinct volcano 17,058 *ft* (5199 *m*) *cen* Kenya near the equator

Ker·a·la \\'ker-ə-lə\\ state SW India bordering on Arabian Sea ✳ Thiruvananthapuram *area* 15,007 *sq mi* (38,868 *sq km*), *pop* 31,838,619

Kerasun — see GIRESUN

Kerch \\'kerch\\ **1** peninsula S Ukraine projecting E from Crimea **2** city & port Ukraine in E Crimea on Kerch Strait *pop* 178,000

Kerch Strait *or anc* **Cim·me·ri·an Bosporus** \\sə-'mir-ē-ən\\ strait bet. Kerch & Taman' peninsulas connecting Sea of Azov & Black Sea

Ker·gue·len Islands \\'kər-gə-lən, ˌkər-gə-'len\\ archipelago S Indian Ocean belonging to France *area* 2394 *sq mi* (6200 *sq km*)

Ke·rin·ci *or* **Ke·rin·tji** \\kə-'rin-chē\\ volcano 12,484 *ft* (3805 *m*) Indonesia in W *cen* Sumatra; highest peak on the island

Kerkheh — see KARKHEH

Kerk·ra·de \\'kerk-ˌrä-də\\ commune SE Netherlands

Kérkyra — see CORFU

Ker·mad·ec Islands \\(ˌ)kər-'ma-dək\\ islands SW Pacific NE of New Zealand, belonging to New Zealand *area* 13 *sq mi* (34 *sq km*), *pop* 9

Ker·man \\kər-'män, ker-\\ **1** *or anc* **Car·ma·nia** \\kär-'mä-nē-ə, -nyə\\ region SE Iran bordering on Gulf of Oman & Persian Gulf S of ancient Parthia **2** *or anc* **Car·ma·na** \\'kär-'mä-nə, -'ma-, -'mä-\\ city SE *cen* Iran in NW Kerman region *pop* 257,284

Kermanshah — see BĀKHTARĀN

Kern \\'kərn\\ river 150 *mi* (241 *km*) S *cen* Calif. flowing SW into a reservoir

Ker·ry \\'ker-ē\\ county SW Ireland in Munster ✳ Tralee *area* 1815 *sq mi* (4719 *sq km*), *pop* 132,527

Ker·u·len \\'ker-ə-ˌlen\\ river E Mongolia flowing S & E into the Argun in Manchuria

Kes·te·ven, Parts of \\ke-'stē-vən, 'kes-ti-vən\\ district & former administrative county E England in SW Lincolnshire ✳ Sleaford *area* 734 *sq mi* (1901 *sq km*)

Kes·wick \\'ke-zik\\ town NW England in Cumbria in Lake District

Ket·ter·ing \\'ke-tə-riŋ\\ city SW Ohio S of Dayton *pop* 56,163

Keu·ka Lake \\'kyü-kə, kā-'yü-\\ lake 18 *mi* (29 *km*) long W *cen* N.Y.; one of the Finger Lakes

Kew \\'kyü\\ **1** city SE Australia in S Victoria, NE suburb of Melbourne *pop* 27,291 **2** parish S England in Surrey; now in the Greater London borough of Richmond upon Thames

Ke·wee·naw Peninsula \\'kē-wə-ˌnò\\ peninsula NW Mich. projecting from Upper Peninsula into Lake Superior W of **Keweenaw Bay**

Key Lar·go \\'lär-(ˌ)gō\\ island S Fla. in the Florida Keys

Key West \\'west\\ city SW Fla. on Key West (island) at W end of Florida Keys *pop* 24,649 — **Key West·er** \\'wes-tər\\ *n*

Kha·ba·rovsk \\kə-'bär-əfsk, kə-\\ **1** territory E Russia in Asia bordering on Sea of Okhotsk *area* 318,378 *sq mi* (824,599 *sq km*), *pop* 1,855,000 **2** city, its ✳ on the Amur *pop* 615,000

Kha·kas·sia *or* **Kha·ka·si·ya** \\kə-'käs-yə, kə-; kə-'ka-zhə\\ autonomous region S Russia in Asia in SW Krasnoyarsk Territory N of the Sayan Mountains ✳ Abakan *area ab* 24,000 *sq mi* (62,400 *sq km*), *pop* 581,000

Khalkidikí — see CHALCIDICE

Khal·kís \\käl-'kēs, käl-\\ *or* **Chal·cis** \\'kal-səs, -kəs\\ city *cen* Greece ✳ of Euboea on Evripos Strait *pop* 51,482

Kham·bhat \\'kəm-bət\\ *or* **Cam·bay** \\kam-'bā\\ city W India in Gujarat W of Vadodara *pop* 80,439

Khambhat, Gulf of *or* **Gulf of Cambay** inlet of Arabian Sea in India N of Bombay

Khan·ka \\'kaŋ-kə\\ lake E Asia bet. Maritime Territory, Russia & Heilongjiang, China *area* 1700 *sq mi* (4420 *sq km*)

Khan–Ten·gri \\ˌkän-'teŋ-grē\\ mountain 22,949 *ft* (6995 *m*) on border bet. Kyrgyzstan & Xinjiang Uygur (China) in Tian Shan

Khar·kiv \\'kär-kəf, 'kär-\\ *or* **Khar·kov** \\'kär-ˌkóf, 'kär-, -ˌkòv, -kəf\\ city NE Ukraine, its ✳ 1921–34, on edge of Donets Basin *pop* 1,623,000

Khar·toum \\kär-'tüm\\ city ✳ of Sudan at junction of White Nile & Blue Nile *pop* 1,950,000

Khartoum North city *cen* Sudan *pop* 700,887

Kha·si Hills \\'kä-sē\\ hills E India in NW *cen* Assam

Kha·tan·ga \\kə-'täŋ-gə\\ river 800 *mi* (1287 *km*) N Russia in Asia, in NE Krasnoyarsk Territory flowing N into Laptev Sea

Khelat — see KALAT

Kher·son \\ker-'sòn\\ city & port S Ukraine on the Dnieper near its mouth *pop* 365,000

Khíos — see CHIOS

Khir·bat Qum·ran *or* **Khir·bet Qum·ran** \\kir-'bat-küm-'rän\\ locality West Bank on Wadi Qumran near NW shore of Dead Sea; site of an Essene community (*ab* 100 B.C.–A.D. 68) near a series of caves in which the Dead Sea Scrolls were found

Khi·va \\'kē-və\\ **1** *or* **Kho·rezm** \\kə-'re-zəm\\ oasis Uzbekistan on the lower Amu Dar'ya **2** *or* **Khwa·razm** \\kwə-'ra-zəm, kwä-\\ former khanate *cen* Asia including Khiva oasis **3** town in the oasis, ✳ of the khanate *pop* 41,300

Khmer Republic — see CAMBODIA

Khor·a·san \\ˌkór-ə-'sän, ˌkór-\\ *or* **Khu·ra·san** \\ˌkúr-ə-'sän, ˌkúr-\\ region NE Iran; chief city Mashhad

Khor·ra·ma·bad \\kò-'ra-mə-ˌbäd, -ˌbad\\ *or* **Khur·ra·ma·bad** \\kú-'rä-\\ city W Iran *pop* 208,592

Khor·ram·shahr \\ˌkór-əm-'shä(-hə)r, ˌkór-\\ city & port W Iran in Khuzistan on Shatt al Arab NNW of Abadan

Khotan — see HOTAN

Khums, Al — see AL KHUMS

Khu·zi·stan \\ˌkü-zi-'stän, -'stan\\ region SW Iran bordering on Persian Gulf; chief city Khorramshahr

Khy·ber Pass \\'kī-bər\\ mountain pass 33 *mi* (53 *km*) long on border bet. Afghanistan & Pakistan in Safed Koh Range WNW of Peshawar

Kiamusze — see JIAMUSI

Kiangsi — see JIANGXI

Kiangsu — see JIANGSU

Kiaochow — see JIAOZHOU

Ki·bo \\'kē-(ˌ)bò\\ mountain peak 19,340 *ft* (5895 *m*) NE Tanzania; highest peak of Kilimanjaro & highest point in Africa

Kid·der·min·ster \\'ki-dər-ˌmin(t)-stər\\ town W England SW of Birmingham *pop* 51,261

Kid·ron \\'ki-drən, 'kī-\\ valley Israel bet. Jerusalem & Mount of Olives; source of stream (Kidron) flowing E to Dead Sea

Kiel \\'kēl\\ **1** city & port N Germany ✳ of Schleswig-Holstein on SE coast of Jutland Peninsula *pop* 247,107 **2** *or* **Nord–Ost·see** \\'nórt-ˌòst-'zā\\ ship canal 61 *mi* (98 *km*) N Germany across base of Jutland Peninsula connecting Baltic Sea & North Sea

Kiel·ce \\'kēl-(ˌ)tsä, 'kyelt-\\ *or Russ* **Kelt·sy** \\'kelt-sē\\ city S Poland S of Warsaw *pop* 212,901

Ki·ev \\'kē-ˌef, -ˌev, -if\\ *or Ukrainian* **Ky·iv** *or* **Ky·yiv** \\'kyē-ü\\ city ✳ of Ukraine on the Dnieper *pop* 2,587,000 — **Ki·ev·an** \\'kē-ˌe-fən, -vən\\ *adj or n*

Ki·ga·li \\kē-'gä-lē\\ city *cen* Rwanda, its ✳ *pop* 232,733

Kikládhes — see CYCLADES

Ki·lau·ea \\ˌkē-ˌlä-'wä-ä\\ volcano 4190 *ft* (1277 *m*) with crater 2 *mi* (3.2 *km*) wide Hawaii in SE Hawaii (island) in Hawaii Volcanoes National Park

Kil·dare \\kil-'der\\ county E Ireland in Leinster ✳ Naas *area* 654 *sq mi* (1700 *sq km*), *pop* 163,944

Kil·i·man·ja·ro \\ˌki-lə-mən-'jär-(ˌ)ō, -'ja-(ˌ)rō\\ mountain Tanzania on NE mainland near Kenya border — see KIBO

Kil·ken·ny \\kil-'ke-nē\\ **1** county SE Ireland in Leinster *area* 796 *sq mi* (2070 *sq km*), *pop* 80,339 **2** town, its ✳ *pop* 8513

Kil·lar·ney, Lakes of \\ki-'lär-nē\\ three lakes SW Ireland in County Kerry

Kill Dev·il \\'kil-ˌde-vəl\\ hill E N.C. near village of **Kit·ty Hawk** \\'ki-tē-ˌhòk\\ on sand barrier opposite Albemarle Sound

Kil·leen \\ki-'lēn\\ city *cen* Tex. N of Austin *pop* 127,921

Kil·lie·cran·kie \\ˌki-lē-'kraŋ-kē\\ mountain pass *cen* Scotland in the SE Grampians

Kill Van Kull \\ˌkil-(ˌ)van-'kəl, -vən-\\ channel bet. N.J. & Staten Is., N.Y., connecting Newark Bay & Upper New York Bay

Kil·mar·nock \\kil-'mär-nək\\ burgh SW Scotland SW of Glasgow *pop* 52,080

Kim·ber·ley \\'kim-bər-lē\\ city Republic of South Africa in E Northern Cape WNW of Bloemfontein *pop* 105,258

Kimberley Plateau *or* **The Kimberley** plateau region N Western Australia N of 19°30′S

Kin·a·ba·lu \\ˌkē-nä-'bä-lü\\ mountain 13,455 *ft* (4101 *m*) Malaysia in N *cen* Sabah; highest in Borneo Is.

Kin·car·dine \\kin-'kär-dən\\ *or* **Kin·car·dine·shire** \\-ˌshir, -shər\\ *or* **The Mearns** \\'mərnz, 'mernz\\ former county E Scotland ✳ Stonehaven

Ki·nesh·ma \\'kē-nish-mə\\ city *cen* Russia in Europe NE of Moscow *pop* 104,000

King·man \\'kiŋ-mən\\ reef *cen* Pacific at N end of Line Islands

King's — see OFFALY

Kings Canyon National Park \\'kiŋz\\ area of diverse landscapes SE *cen* Calif. in the Sierra Nevada N of Sequoia National Park

King's Lynn \\'kiŋz-'lin\\ *or* **Lynn** *or* **Lynn Re·gis** \\'rē-jəs\\ town E England in Norfolk near The Wash *pop* 33,340

Kings Mountain ridge N.C. & S.C. SW of Gastonia, N.C.

Kings Peak mountain 13,528 *ft* (4123 *m*) NE Utah in Uinta Mountains; highest point in state

Kings·port \\'kiŋz-ˌpòrt\\ city NE Tenn. on the Holston *pop* 48,205

Kings·ton \\'kiŋ-stən\\ **1** city SE N.Y. on the Hudson *pop* 23,893 **2** city Canada in SE Ont. on Lake Ontario near head of St. Lawrence River; ✳ of Canada 1841–44 *pop* 123,363 **3** *or in full* **Kingston upon Thames** royal borough of SW Greater London, England ✳ of Surrey *pop* 130,600 **4** city & port ✳ of Jamaica on **Kingston Harbor** (inlet of the Caribbean) *pop* 103,771

Kingston upon Hull — see HULL 2

Kings·town \\'kiŋz-ˌtaún\\ **1** town & port ✳ of St. Vincent and the Grenadines on St. Vincent Is. *pop* 15,670 **2** — see DUN LAOGHAIRE

Kings·ville \\'kiŋz-ˌvil, -vəl\\ city S Tex. *pop* 26,213

Kinmen — see QUEMOY

Kinneret, Yam — see GALILEE (Sea of)

Kin·ross \\kin-'ròs\\ *or* **Kin·ross–shire** \\-'ròsh-ˌshir, -shər\\ former county E *cen* Scotland ✳ Kinross

Kin·sha·sa \\kin-'shä-sə\\ *or formerly* **Lé·o·pold·ville** \\'lē-ə-ˌpōld-ˌvil, 'lā-\\ city ✳ of Democratic Republic of the Congo on Congo River at outlet of Pool Malebo *pop* 3,804,000

Kin·ston \\'kin-stən\\ city E N.C. *pop* 21,677

Kin·tyre \\kin-'tī(-ə)r\\ peninsula 40 *mi* (64 *km*) long SW Scotland bet. the Atlantic & Firth of Clyde terminating in **Mull of Kintyre** \\'məl\\ (cape in N. Channel)

Kioga — see KYOGA

Kirghiz Republic *or* **Kirgiz Republic** — see KYRGYZSTAN

Ki·ri·bati \\'kir-ə-ˌbas—*sic*\\ island nation W Pacific SSE of the Marshalls comprising the Gilbert, Line, & Phoenix groups and Banaba ✳ on Tarawa *area* 277 *sq mi* (717 *sq km*) *pop* 92,533

Ki·rik·ka·le \\kə-'ri-kə-ˌlä\\ city *cen* Turkey E of Ankara *pop* 185,431

Kirin — see JILIN

Ki·ri·ti·mati \\kə-'ris-məs—*sic*\\ *or* **Christ·mas** \\'kris-məs\\ island (atoll) in the Line Islands; largest atoll in the Pacific *area* 234 *sq mi* (608 *sq km*), *pop* 674

Kirjath–arba — see HEBRON

Kirk·caldy \\(ˌ)kər-'kò-dē, -'kòl-, -'kä-\\ royal burgh & port E Scotland on Firth of Forth N of Edinburgh *pop* 46,314

Kirk·cud·bright \\(ˌ)kər-'kü-brē\\ *or* **Kirk·cud·bright·shire** \\-ˌshir, -shər\\ former county S Scotland ✳ Kirkcudbright

Kirk·land \\'kərk-lənd\\ city W Wash. NE of Seattle *pop* 48,787

Kirk·pat·rick, Mount \\ˌkərk-'pa-trik\\ mountain 14,856 *ft* (4528 *m*) E Antarctica in Queen Alexandra Range S of Ross Sea

Kir·kuk \\'kúr-ˌkük\\ city NE Iraq SE of Mosul *pop* 175,303

Kirk·wall \\'kərk-ˌwòl\\ burgh & port N Scotland ✳ of Orkney Islands on Mainland Is. *pop* 5947

Kirk·wood \\'kərk-ˌwúd\\ city E Mo. W of St. Louis *pop* 27,540

Ki·rov \\'kē-ˌròf, -ˌròv, -rəf\\ *or* **Vyat·ka** \\vē-'at-kə, -'ät-kə\\ city E *cen* Russia in Europe *pop* 493,000

Kirovabad — see GANCA

Ki·ro·vo·grad \ki-'rō-və-ˌgrad, -ˌgrät\ *or* **Ki·ro·vo·hrad** \-ˌkrät\ *or formerly* **Zi·nov·ievsk** \zə-'nóv-ˌyefsk\ *or* **Eli·sa·vet·grad** \i-ˌli-zə-'vet-ˌgrad, -ˌgrät\ city S *cen* Ukraine *pop* 278,000

Ki·ru·na \'kē-rü-ˌnä\ city N Sweden in Lapland *pop* 23,555

Ki·san·ga·ni \ˌkē-sän-'gä-nē\ *or formerly* **Stan·ley·ville** \'stan-lē-ˌvil\ city NE Democratic Republic of the Congo on Congo River *pop* 373,397

Kish \'kish\ ancient city of Sumer & Akkad E of site of Babylon

Kishinev — see CHIŞINĂU

Kis·ka \'kis-kə\ island SW Alaska; largest & westernmost of Rat Islands in the Aleutians

Kis·maa·yo \kēs-'mä-yō\ *or* **Kis·ma·yu** \kis-'mī-(ˌ)ü\ city & port S Somalia *pop* 30,115

Kis·sim·mee \ki-'si-mē\ **1** river 140 *mi* (225 *km*) S *cen* Fla. flowing SSE from Tohopekaliga Lake through **Lake Kissimmee** (12 *mi* or 19 *km* long) into Lake Okeechobee **2** city Fla. on Tohopekaliga Lake *pop* 59,682

Kistna — see KRISHNA

Ki·su·mu \kē-'sü-(ˌ)mü\ city W Kenya on Lake Victoria *pop* 336,632

Ki·ta·kyu·shu \kē-ˌtä-'kyü-(ˌ)shü\ city & port Japan in N Kyushu formed 1963 by amalgamation of former cities of Kokura, Moji, Tobata, Wakamatsu, & Yawata *pop* 1,011,471

Kitch·e·ner \'kich-nər, 'ki-chə-\ city Canada in SE Ont. *pop* 219,153

Kithairon — see CITHAERON

Kí·thi·ra *or* **Ky·the·ra** *or* **Ký·thi·ra** \'kē-thē-(ˌ)rä\ island W Greece; southernmost of Ionian Islands **✻** Kíthira *area* 110 *sq mi* (286 *sq km*)

Kit·ta·tin·ny Mountain \ˌki-tə-'ti-nē\ ridge E U.S. in the Appalachians extending from SE N.Y. through NW N.J. into E Pa.

Kit·tery Point \'ki-tə-rē\ cape Maine at S tip

Kitty Hawk — see KILL DEVIL

Kitz·bü·hel \'kits-ˌbyü(-ə)l, -ˌbú(-ə)l\ resort town W Austria in the Tirol *pop* 8119

Ki·vu, Lake \'kē-(ˌ)vü\ lake 60 *mi* (96 *km*) long & 30 *mi* (48 *km*) wide E Democratic Republic of the Congo in Great Rift Valley N of Lake Tanganyika *area* 1042 *sq mi* (2699 *sq km*)

Kı·zıl Ir·mak \kə-ˌzil-ir-'mäk\ *or anc* **Ha·lys River** \'hā-ləs\ river 715 *mi* (1150 *km*) N *cen* Turkey flowing W & NE into Black Sea

Kjö·len Mountains \'chœ-lən\ mountains on border bet. NE Norway & NW Sweden; highest Kebnekaise (in Sweden) 6965 *ft* (2123 *m*)

Kla·gen·furt \'klä-gən-ˌfúrt\ city S Austria **✻** of Carinthia WSW of Graz *pop* 90,141

Klai·pe·da \'klī-pə-də\ *or* **Me·mel** \'mā-məl\ city & port W Lithuania on the Baltic *pop* 192,954

Klam·ath \'kla-məth\ river 250 *mi* (402 *km*) S Oreg. & NW Calif. flowing from Upper Klamath Lake SW into the Pacific

Klamath Mountains mountains S Oreg. & NW Calif. in the Coast Ranges; highest Mt. Eddy (in Calif.) 9038 *ft* (2755 *m*)

Kle·ve \'klā-və\ city W Germany WSW of Münster *pop* 46,450

Klon·dike \'klän-ˌdīk\ **1** river 90 *mi* (145 *km*) Canada in *cen* Yukon Territory flowing W into the Yukon **2** the Klondike River valley

Klu·ane National Park \klü-'ò-nē, -'ä-\ area of mountains and glaciers in Canada in SW Yukon Territory including Mt. Logan

Kly·az'·ma \klē-'az-mə\ river *ab* 390 *mi* (630 *km*) *cen* Russia in Europe flowing E to join the Oka W of Nizhniy Novgorod

Knos·sos *or* **Cnos·sus** *or* **Gnos·sus** \'nä-səs\ ruined city **✻** of ancient Crete near N coast SE of modern Iráklion

Knox·ville \'näks-ˌvil, -vil\ city E Tenn. on Tennessee River *pop* 178,874

Knud Ras·mus·sen Land \'(k)nüd-'ras-mə-sən, -'räs-ˌmú-sⁿn\ region N & NW Greenland bet of Baffin Bay

Ko·ba·rid \'kō-bə-ˌrēd\ *or It* **Ca·po·ret·to** \ˌka-pə-'re-(ˌ)tō, ˌkä-pō-\ village W Slovenia on the Isonzo NE of Udine, Italy

Ko·be \'kō-bē, -ˌbā\ city & port Japan in S Honshu on Osaka Bay *pop* 1,493,398

København — see COPENHAGEN

Ko·blenz *or* **Co·blenz** \'kō-ˌblents\ city W Germany SSE of Cologne at confluence of the Rhine & the Moselle *pop* 109,046

Ko·buk Valley National Park \kō-'búk\ site W Alaska N of the Arctic Circle along **Kobuk River** containing archaeological remains and unusual landscapes

Ko·ca \kō-'jä\ river *ab* 75 *mi* (121 *km*) S Turkey flowing SW & S into the Mediterranean

Ko·ca·bas \ˌkō-jə-'bäsh\ *or anc* **Gra·ni·cus** \grə-'nī-kəs\ river NW Turkey in Asia flowing NE to Sea of Marmara

Ko·chi \'kō-chē\ city & port Japan in S Shikoku *pop* 330,654

Ko·di·ak \'kō-dē-ˌak\ island S Alaska in Gulf of Alaska E of Alaska Peninsula

Ko·dok \'kō-ˌdäk\ *or formerly* **Fa·sho·da** \fə-'shō-də\ town NE South Sudan on White Nile River

Ko·ha·la Mountains \kō-'hä-lä\ mountains Hawaii in N Hawaii (island); highest *ab* 5500 *ft* (1676 *m*)

Ko·hi·ma \kō-'hē-mə, 'kō-hē-\ town NE India **✻** of Nagaland *pop* 78,584

Koil — see ALIGARH

Ko·kand \kō-'kand\ *or* **Qü·qon** \kú-'kòn\ **1** region & former khanate E Uzbekistan **2** city in Kokand region SE of Tashkent *pop* 175,000

Ko·ko·mo \'kō-kə-ˌmō\ city N *cen* Ind. *pop* 45,468

Koko Nor — see QINGHAI

Kok·so·ak \'käk-sō-ˌak\ river 85 *mi* (136 *km*) Canada N Que. formed by confluence of the Caniapiscau and the Larch and flowing into Ungava Bay

Ko·la Peninsula \'kō-lə\ peninsula 250 *mi* (402 *km*) long & 150 *mi* (241 *km*) wide NW Russia in Europe bet. Barents & White seas

Ko·lar Gold Fields \'kō-ˌlär\ city S India in SE Karnataka *pop* 156,398

Kold·ing \'kō-leŋ\ city & port Denmark *pop* 57,128

Kol·ha·pur \'kō-lə-ˌpúr\ city W India in SW Maharashtra SSE of Bombay *pop* 485,183

Kolkata — see CALCUTTA

Kolmar — see COLMAR

Köln — see COLOGNE

Ko·ly·ma *or* **Ko·li·ma** \kə-'lē-mə, ˌkä-li-'mä\ river 1110 *mi* (1786 *km*) NE Russia in Asia flowing from Kolyma Mountains NE into E. Siberian Sea

Kolyma Mountains *or* **Kolima Mountains** mountain range Russia in Asia in NE Khabarovsk Territory parallel to coast of Penzhinskaya Bay

Ko·man·dor·ski Islands \ˌkä-mən-'dòr-skē\ *or* **Com·mand·er Islands** \kə-'man-dər\ islands E Russia in Asia in Bering Sea E of Kamchatka Peninsula *area* 850 *sq mi* (2210 *sq km*)

Ko·ma·ti \kō-'mä-tē\ river 500 *mi* (805 *km*) S Africa flowing from N Drakensberg Mountains in NE Republic of South Africa E & N into Delagoa Bay in S Mozambique

Ko·mi Republic \'kō-mē\ autonomous republic NE Russia in Europe W of N Ural Mountains **✻** Syktyvkar *area* 160,579 *sq mi* (415,900 *sq km*), *pop* 1,255,000

Ko·mo·do \kə-'mō-(ˌ)dō\ island Indonesia in the Lesser Sundas E of Sumbawa Is. & W of Flores Is. *area* 185 *sq mi* (481 *sq km*)

Kom·so·mol'sk–na–Amure \ˌkäm-sə-'mòlsk-ˌnä-ä-'mú-rē\ city E Russia in Asia in S Khabarovsk Territory on the Amur

Ko·na \'kō-nä\ coast region Hawaii in W Hawaii (island)

Königsberg — see KALININGRAD

Kö·niz \'kä-nəts, 'kə(r)-, 'kœ-\ commune W *cen* Switzerland SW of Bern *pop* 36,101

Kon·kan \'kän-kən\ region W India in W Maharashtra bordering on Arabian Sea & extending from Bombay S to Goa

Konstanz — see CONSTANCE

Kon·ya \kō-'nyä\ *or anc* **Ico·ni·um** \ī-'kō-nē-əm\ city SW *cen* Turkey on edge of *cen* plateau *pop* 513,346

Koo·o·lau Range \ˌkō-ō-'lä-(ˌ)ü\ mountains Hawaii in E Oahu

Koo·te·nai *or in Canada* **Koo·te·nay** \'kü-tə-ˌnä, -tə-nē\ river 407 *mi* (655 *km*) SW Canada & NW U.S. in B.C., Mont., & Idaho flowing through **Kootenay Lake** (65 *mi* or 104 *km* long, in B.C.) into Columbia River

Kootenay National Park area of diverse landscapes in Canada in SE B.C. including section of the upper Kootenay River

Ko·per \'kō-ˌper\ *or* **Ko·par** \-ˌpär\ *or It* **Ca·po·dis·tria** \ˌka-pə-'dis-trē-ə, ˌkä-pō-'dēs-\ town & port SW Slovenia at N end of Istrian Peninsula SSW of Trieste *pop* 25,272

Ko·peysk \kə-'pyäsk\ city SW Russia in Asia SE of Chelyabinsk *pop* 78,300

Kor·do·fan \ˌkòr-də-'fan\ region *cen* Sudan W & N of White Nile River; chief city El Obeid

Ko·rea \kə-'rē-ə, *esp South* (ˌ)kō-\ **1** peninsula 600 *mi* (966 *km*) long & 135 *mi* (217 *km*) wide E Asia bet. Yellow Sea & East Sea (Sea of Japan) **2** *or Jp* **Cho·sen** \'chō-'sen\ country coextensive with the peninsula; once a kingdom & (1910–45) a Japanese dependency **✻** Seoul; divided 1948 at 38th parallel into republics of **North Korea** (**✻** Pyongyang *area* 46,609 *sq mi* or 120,717 *sq km, pop* 24,051,200) & **South Korea** (**✻** Seoul *area* 38,022 *sq mi* or 98,477 *sq km, pop* 50,200,000)

Korea Bay arm of Yellow Sea bet. Liaodong Peninsula & N. Korea

Korea Strait channel 120 *mi* (193 *km*) wide bet. S S. Korea & SW Japan connecting Sea of Japan & Yellow Sea

Kórinthos — see CORINTH

Ko·ri·ya·ma \ˌkō-rē-'yä-mä\ city Japan in N *cen* Honshu *pop* 334,824

Kort·rijk \'kòrt-ˌrīk\ *or* **Cour·trai** \kúr-'trā\ commune NW Belgium in W. Flanders on the Leie NNE of Lille *pop* 74,558

Kos *or* **Cos** \'käs, 'kós\ **1** island Greece in the Dodecanese *area* 111 *sq mi* (289 *sq km*) **2** chief town on the island

Kos·ci·us·ko, Mount \ˌkä-zē-'əs-(ˌ)kō, ˌkä-sē-\ mountain 7310 *ft* (2228 *m*) SE Australia in SE New South Wales; highest in Great Dividing Range & in Australia

Ko·shi·ga·ya \kō-'shē-gä-yä; ˌkō-shi-'gī-ə\ city Japan in Honshu N of Tokyo *pop* 308,307

Ko·si·ce \'kō-shēt-ˌsä\ city E Slovakia *pop* 236,093

Ko·so·vo \'kò-sò-ˌvō, 'kä-\ country S Europe in Balkan Peninsula; an autonomous province of Serbia 1946–2008; **✻** Pristina *area* 4203 *sq mi* (10,886 *sq km*), *pop* 2,100,000 — **Ko·so·var** \'kò-sò-ˌvär, 'kä-\ *n or adj*

Kos·rae \'kòs-ˌrī\ islands E Carolines; part of Federated States of Micronesia — **Kos·rae·an** \ˌkòs-'rī-ən\ *n*

Ko·stro·ma \ˌkäs-trə-'mä\ city *cen* Russia in Europe on the Volga *pop* 282,000

Ko·sza·lin \kō-'shä-ˌlēn\ city NW Poland *pop* 107,580

Ko·ta Ba·ha·ru \ˌkō-tə-bä-hä-'rü\ city Malaysia in N Peninsular Malaysia **✻** of Kelantan *pop* 281,161

Kotabaru — see JAYAPURA

Ko·ta Kin·a·ba·lu \'kō-tə-ˌki-nə-bə-'lü\ *or formerly* **Jes·sel·ton** \'je-səl-tən\ city & port Malaysia **✻** of Sabah *pop* 112,758

Ko·tor \'kō-ˌtòr\ *or It* **Cat·ta·ro** \'kä-tä-ˌrò\ town & port SW Montenegro on an inlet of the Adriatic *pop* 22,496

Kottbus — see COTTBUS

Kot·te \'kō-(ˌ)tä\ town W Sri Lanka, a suburb ESE of Colombo *pop* 109,000

Kot·ze·bue Sound \'kät-si-ˌbyü\ arm of Chukchi Sea NW Alaska NE of Bering Strait

Kou·chi·bou·guac National Park \kü-ˌshē-bü-'gwäk\ area of wetland landscapes SE Canada in E N.B.

Kou·dou·gou \kü-'dü-(ˌ)gü\ town *cen* Burkina Faso *pop* 88,184

Kovno — see KAUNAS

Kowloon — see JIULONG

Koy·u·kuk \'kī-ə-ˌkək\ river *ab* 500 *mi* (800 *km*) N *cen* Alaska flowing from Brooks Range SW into Yukon River

Kozhikode — see CALICUT

Kra, Isthmus of \'krä\ isthmus S Thailand in N *cen* Malay Peninsula; 40 *mi* (64 *km*) wide at narrowest part

Krak·a·tau \ˌkra-kə-'taú\ *or* **Krak·a·toa** \-'tō-ə\ island & volcano Indonesia bet. Sumatra & Java

Kra·ków *or* **Cra·cow** \'krä-ˌkaú, 'kra-, 'krä-, -(ˌ)kō, *Pol* 'krä-ˌküf\ *or G* **Kra·kau** \'krä-ˌkaú\ city S Poland on the Vistula *pop* 748,356

Kras — see KARST

Kras·no·dar \ˌkräs-nə-'där\ **1** territory S Russia in Europe in N Caucasus region *area* 32,278 *sq mi* (83,600 *sq km*), *pop* 5,004,000 **2** *or formerly* **Eka·te·ri·no·dar** \i-ˌkä-tə-'rē-nə-ˌdär\ city, its **✻**, on the Kuban' *pop* 635,000

Kras·no·yarsk \ˌkräs-nə-'yärsk\ **1** territory W *cen* Russia in Asia extending along valley of the Yenisey from Arctic Ocean to Sayan Mountains *area* 927,258 *sq mi* (2,401,598 *sq km*), *pop* 3,122,000 **2** city, its **✻**, on the upper Yenisey *pop* 925,000

Kre·feld \'krä-ˌfelt\ *or formerly* **Krefeld–Uer·ding·en** \-'úr-diŋ-ən, -'úer-\ city W Germany on the Rhine WSW of Essen *pop* 245,772

Krish·na \'krish-nə\ *or formerly* **Kist·na** \'kist-nə\ river 800 *mi* (1287 *km*) S India flowing from Western Ghats E into Bay of Bengal

Kristiania — see OSLO

Kris·tian·sand \'kris-chən-ˌsand, 'kris-tē-ən-ˌsän\ city & port SW Norway on the Skagerrak SW of Oslo *pop* 62,546

Kris·tian·sund \'kris-chən-ˌsənd, 'kris-tē-ən-ˌsùn\ city & port W Norway *pop* 16,789

Kríti — see CRETE

Kron·shtadt \'krōn-ˌshtät\ city W Russia in Europe on island in E Gulf of Finland W of St. Petersburg *pop* 45,300

Kru·ger National Park \'krü-gər\ game reserve NE Republic of South Africa in E parts of Limpopo & Mpumalanga provinces on Mozambique border

Kru·gers·dorp \'krü-gərz-ˌdòrp\ city NE Republic of South Africa in Gauteng W of Johannesburg *pop* 92,725

Krung Thep — see BANGKOK

Kryv·yy Rih \kri-'vē-'rik\ *or* **Kri·voy Rog** \ˌkri-ˌvòi-'rōg, -'ròk\ city SE *cen* Ukraine NE of Odessa *pop* 724,000

K2 \ˌkā-'tü\ *or* **God·win Aus·ten** \ˌgä-dwən-'ós-tən, ˌgò-, -'äs-\ mountain 28,250 *ft* (8611 *m*) N Kashmir in Karakoram Range; 2d highest in the world

Kua·la Lum·pur \ˌkwä-lə-'lùm-ˌpùr, -'ləm-, -ˌlùm-'\ city ✱ of Malaysia in Peninsular Malaysia *pop* 1,145,075

Kuang–chou — see GUANGZHOU

Ku·ban' \kü-'banʸ, -'bän\ river *over* 550 *mi* (885 *km*) S Russia in Europe flowing from the Caucasus N & W into Sea of Azov

Ku·ching \'kü-chiŋ\ city & port Malaysia ✱ of Sarawak *pop* 231,490

Ku·dus \'kü-ˌdüs\ city Indonesia in *cen* Java NE of Semarang

Kuei — see GUI

Kuei–lin — see GUILIN

Kuei–yang — see GUIYANG

Kufra — see AL KUFRAH

Ku·iu Island \'kü-(ˌ)yü\ island SE Alaska in *cen* Alexander Archipelago

Ku·la Gulf \'kü-lə\ body of water 17 *mi* (27 *km*) long in the Solomons bet. New Georgia & adjacent islands

Kuldja — see YINING

Kum \'kùm\ river 247 *mi* (398 *km*) *cen* S. Korea flowing into Yellow Sea

Ku·ma·mo·to \ˌkü-mä-'mō-(ˌ)tō\ city Japan in W Kyushu *pop* 662,012

Ku·ma·si \kü-'mä-sē, -'ma-\ city S *cen* Ghana NW of Accra *pop* 385,192

Kumgang — see DIAMOND

Kumilla — see COMILLA

Kunene — see CUNENE

Kun·lun \'kün-'lün\ mountains W China extending from the Pamirs & Karakoram Range E to SE Qinghai — see MUZTAG

Kun·ming \'kùn-'miŋ\ *or formerly* **Yun·nan** \'yü-'nän\ *or* **Yun·nan·fu** \-'fü\ city S China ✱ of Yunnan *pop* 1,127,411

Kun·san *or* **Gun·san** \'gùn-ˌsän\ city & port W S. Korea on Yellow Sea at mouth of the Kum *pop* 218,216

Kuo·pio \'kwò-pē-ˌò\ city S *cen* Finland *pop* 87,347

Ku·pre·a·nof \ˌkü-prē-'a-ˌnòf\ island SE Alaska in E Alexander Archipelago

Ku·ra \kə-'rä, 'kùr-ə\ river 941 *mi* (1514 *km*) W Asia flowing from NE Turkey ESE through Georgia & Azerbaijan into Caspian Sea

Ku·ra·shi·ki \kü-'rä-shē-kē, ˌkùr-ä-'shē-kē\ city Japan in SW Honshu *pop* 430,291

Kur·di·stan \ˌkùr-də-'stan, ˌkər-, -'stän; 'kər-də-ˌ\ region SW Asia chiefly in E Turkey, NW Iran, & N Iraq

Ku·re Atoll \'kùr-ē, 'kyùr-; 'kü-(ˌ)rä\ *or* **Ocean Island** island *cen* Pacific in Hawaii; westernmost of the Leewards

Kurg — see COORG

Kur·gan \kùr-'gan, -'gän\ city SW Russia in Asia *pop* 365,000

Ku·ria Mu·ria Islands \ˌkùr-ē-ə-'mùr-ē-ə, ˌkyùr-, -'myùr-\ islands Oman in Arabian Sea off SW coast area 28 *sq mi* (73 *sq km*), *pop* 85

Ku·ril Islands *or* **Ku·rile Islands** \'kyùr-ˌēl, 'kùr-; kyù-'rēl, kù-\ islands Russia in the Pacific bet. S Kamchatka & NE Hokkaido, Japan; belonged 1875–1945 to Japan *area* 6023 *sq mi* (15,600 *sq km*)

Kurisches Haff — see COURLAND LAGOON

Kursk \'kùrsk\ city SW Russia in Europe on the Seym *pop* 435,000

Kush — see CUSH

Kus·ko·kwim \'kəs-kə-ˌkwim\ river *ab* 600 *mi* (965 *km*) SW Alaska flowing SW into **Kuskokwim Bay** (inlet of Bering Sea)

Kut, Al — see AL KUT

Ku·tah·ya *or* **Ku·ta·iah** \kü-'tä-yə\ city W *cen* Turkey *pop* 130,944

Kutch \'kəch\ former principality & state W India N of Gulf of Kachchh ✱ Bhuj, now part of Gujarat

Kutch, Gulf of — see KACHCHH (Gulf of)

Kutch, Rann of — see KACHCHH (Rann of)

Ku·wait \kü-'wāt\ **1** country W Asia in Arabia at head of Persian Gulf; a sheikhdom, before 1961 under Brit. protection *area* 6880 *sq mi* (17,819 *sq km*), *pop* 3,524,000 **2** city & port, its ✱ *pop* 28,859 — **Ku·waiti** \-'wä-tē\ *adj or n*

Kuybyshev — see SAMARA

Kuz·netsk \küz-'netsk\ city SE *cen* Russia in Europe *pop* 101,000

Kuznetsk Basin basin of the Tom' S Russia in Asia extending from Novokuznetsk to Tomsk

Kwa·ja·lein \'kwä-jə-lən, -ˌlän\ island (atoll) 78 *mi* (126 *km*) long W Pacific in Ralik chain of the Marshalls

Kwan·do \'kwän-(ˌ)dō\ river *ab* 500 *mi* (804 *km*) S Africa flowing from *cen* Angola SE & E into the Zambezi just above Victoria Falls

Kwang·cho·wan \'gwäŋ-'jō-'wän, 'kwäŋ-\ former territory SE China in Kwangtung on Leizhou Peninsula; leased 1898–1946 to France ✱ Fort Bayard *area* 325 *sq mi* (845 *sq km*)

Kwang·ju *or* **Gwang·ju** \'gwäŋ-(ˌ)jü\ city SW S. Korea *pop* 1,350,948

Kwangsi Chuang — see GUANGXI ZHUANGZU

Kwangtung — see GUANGDONG

Kwan·tung \'gwän-'dùŋ, 'kwän-'tùŋ\ former territory NE China in S Manchuria at tip of Liaodong Peninsula; leased to Russia 1898–1905, to Japan 1905–45, & to Russia again 1945–55; included cities of Port Arthur & Dairen

Kwanza — see CUANZA

Kwathlamba — see DRAKENSBERG

Kwa·Zu·lu \kwä-'zü-(ˌ)lü\ former group of noncontiguous black enclaves in E Republic of South Africa; incorporated into KwaZulu-Natal 1994

KwaZulu–Natal province E Republic of South Africa bet. Drakensberg Mountains & Indian Ocean *area* 35,591 *sq mi* (92,180 *sq km*), *pop* 8,553,000

Kweichow — see GUIZHOU

Kweilin — see GUILIN

Kyiv *or* **Kyyiv** — see KIEV

Kyo·ga *or* **Kio·ga** \kē-'ō-gə\ lake *cen* Uganda N of Lake Victoria traversed by the Victoria Nile

Kyo·to \'kyō-(ˌ)tō\ city Japan in W *cen* Honshu NNE of Osaka; formerly (794–1869) ✱ of Japan *pop* 1,467,785

Kyr·gyz·stan \ˌkir-gi-'stan, -'stän; 'kir-gi-ˌ\ independent country W *cen* Asia; a constituent republic (**Kir·giz Republic** *or* **Kir·ghiz Republic** \(ˌ)kir-'gēz\) of the U.S.S.R. 1936–91; ✱ Bishkek *area* 76,641 *sq mi* (198,500 *sq km*), *pop* 5,500,000

Kythera *or* **Kýthira** — see KÍTHIRA

Kyu·shu \'kyü-(ˌ)shü\ island S Japan S of W end of Honshu *area* over 16,200 *sq mi* (41,958 *sq km*), *pop* 13,445,561

Ky·zyl \ki-'zil\ town S Russia in Asia ✱ of Tuva Republic *pop* 88,000

Laa·youne \lä-'yün\ *or* **El Aai·ún** \ˌel-ī-'ün\ town NW Africa ✱ of Western Sahara *pop* 179,000

Labe — see ELBE

Lab·ra·dor \'la-brə-ˌdòr\ **1** peninsula E Canada bet. Hudson Bay & the Atlantic; divided bet. Que. & Nfld. & Lab. *area* 625,000 *sq mi* (1,618,750 *sq km*) **2** the section of the peninsula belonging to Nfld. & Lab. 102,485 *sq mi* (265,436 *sq km*) — **Lab·ra·dor·ean** *or* **Lab·ra·dor·ian** \ˌla-brə-'dòr-ē-ən\ *adj or n*

Labrador Sea arm of the Atlantic bet. Labrador & Greenland

La·bu·an \lä-'bü-än\ island Malaysia off W coast of Sabah *pop* 14,904

Lac·ca·dive Islands \'la-kə-ˌdēv, -ˌdīv, -div\ *or* **Can·na·nore Islands** \'ka-nə-ˌnòr\ islands India in Arabian Sea N of the Maldives

Lacedaemon — see SPARTA — **Lac·e·dae·mo·nian** \ˌla-sə-di-'mō-nē-ən, -nyən\ *adj or n*

La·cey \'lā-sē\ city W Wash. E of Olympia *pop* 42,393

La Chaux–de–Fonds \lä-ˌshō-də-'fòⁿ\ commune W Switzerland in Neuchâtel canton in Jura Mountains WNW of Bern *pop* 36,107

La·chine \lə-'shēn\ former town Canada in S Que. above the **Lachine Rapids** on St. Lawrence River, now part of Montreal (city)

La·chish \'lā-kish\ city of ancient Palestine W of Hebron

Lach·lan \'lä-klən\ river 800 *mi* (1287 *km*) SE Australia in *cen* New South Wales flowing W into the Murrumbidgee

Lac Mai–Ndombe — see MAI-NDOMBE (Lac)

La·co·nia \lə-'kō-nē-ə, -nyə\ ancient country S Greece in SE Peloponnese bordering on the Aegean & the Mediterranean ✱ Sparta — **La·co·ni·an** \-nē-ən, -nyən\ *adj or n*

Laconia, Gulf of inlet of the Mediterranean on S coast of Greece in Peloponnese bet. Capes Taínaron & Malea

La Coruña — see A CORUÑA

La Crosse \lə-'krós\ city W Wis. *pop* 51,320

La·dakh \lə-'däk\ district India in E Kashmir on border of Tibet ✱ Leh *area* 45,762 *sq mi* (118,981 *sq km*) — **La·dakhi** \-'dä-kē\ *adj or n*

Lad·o·ga, Lake \'la-də-gə, 'lä-\ lake W Russia in Europe near St. Petersburg *area* 6835 *sq mi* (17,703 *sq km*); largest in Europe

Ladrone Islands — see MARIANA ISLANDS

La·dy·smith \'lā-dē-ˌsmith\ city E Republic of South Africa in W KwaZulu-Natal *pop* 28,920

Lae \'lä-ˌā\ city Papua New Guinea on Huon Gulf *pop* 78,692

La·fay·ette \ˌla-fē-'et, ˌlä-\ **1** city W Calif. E of Berkeley *pop* 23,893 **2** city N *cen* Colo. NNW of Denver *pop* 24,453 **3** city W *cen* Ind. *pop* 67,140 **4** city S La. *pop* 120,623

La Flo·ri·da \lä-flò-'rē-thä\ city *cen* Chile; formerly a district of SE Santiago *pop* 365,674

La·gash \'lā-ˌgash\ ancient city of Sumer bet. the Euphrates & the Tigris at modern village of Telloh \te-'lò\ in S Iraq

Lagoa dos Patos — see PATOS (Lagoa dos)

La·gos \'lä-ˌgäs, -ˌgòs\ city & port SW Nigeria partly on an island in Bight of Benin; former ✱ of Nigeria *pop* 1,340,000

La Goulette — see HALQ AL-WADI

LaGrange \lə-'grānj\ city W Ga. *pop* 25,998

La Granja — see SAN ILDEFONSO

La Guai·ra \lə-'gwī-rə\ city N Venezuela on the Caribbean; port for Caracas *pop* 20,344

La·gu·na Beach \lə-ˌgü-nə\ city SW Calif. SE of Long Beach *pop* 22,723

Laguna Hills city S Calif. SE of Santa Ana *pop* 30,344

Laguna Madre — see MADRE (Laguna)

La·gu·na Ni·guel \lə-ˌgü-nə-nē-'gel\ city S Calif. *pop* 62,979

La Habana — see HAVANA

La Ha·bra \lə-'hä-brə\ city SW Calif. SE of Los Angeles *pop* 60,239

La Hogue \lə-'hòg\ roadstead NW France in English Channel off E coast of Cotentin Peninsula

La·hore \lə-'hòr\ city Pakistan in E Punjab province *pop* 5,143,495

Lah·ti \'lä-tē\ city S Finland NNE of Helsinki *pop* 97,543

La·jas \'lä-häs\ city SW Puerto Rico *pop* 25,753

La Jol·la \lə-'hói-ə\ a NW section of San Diego, Calif.

Lake Charles \'chär-(ə)lz\ city SW La. *pop* 71,993

Lake Clark National Park \'klärk\ reservation S *cen* Alaska WSW of Anchorage containing scenic wilderness, abundant wildlife

Lake District area NW England in S Cumbria & NW Lancashire containing many lakes & peaks

Lake El·si·no·re \'el-sə-ˌnòr\ city S Calif. SE of Santa Ana *pop* 51,821

Lake Forest city S Calif. SE of Santa Ana *pop* 58,707

Lake Hav·a·su City \'ha-və-ˌsü\ city W Ariz. *pop* 52,527

Lake in the Hills village NE Ill. WNW of Chicago *pop* 28,965

Lake Jack·son \'jak-sən\ city SE Tex. S of Houston *pop* 26,849

Lake·land \'lāk-lənd\ city *cen* Fla. E of Tampa *pop* 97,422
Lake Os·we·go \ä-'swē-(,)gō\ city NW Oreg. S of Portland *pop* 36,619
Lake·shore \'lāk-,shōr\ town Canada in SE Ont. on Lake Saint Clair *pop* 34,546
Lake·ville \'lāk-,vil\ village SE Minn. SE of Minneapolis *pop* 55,954
Lake·wood \'lāk-,wu̇d\ **1** city SW Calif. NE of Long Beach *pop* 80,048 **2** city N *cen* Colo. W of Denver *pop* 142,980 **3** city NE Ohio on Lake Erie *pop* 52,131 **4** city W *cen* Wash., a suburb of Tacoma *pop* 58,163
Lake Worth \'wərth\ city SE Fla. on Lake Worth (lagoon) *pop* 34,910
Lak·shad·weep \lək-'shä-,dwēp\ *or formerly* **Lac·ca·dive, Min·i·coy, and Amin·di·vi Islands** \'la-kə-,dēv, -,dīv; 'mi-ni-,kȯi; ,ə-mən-'dē-vē\ union territory India comprising the Laccadive group ✻ Kavaratti *area* 11 *sq mi* (29 *sq km*), *pop* 60,595
La Lí·nea \lä-'lē-nā-ä\ commune SW Spain on Bay of Algeciras *pop* 59,437
La Lou·vière \,lä-lü-'vyer\ commune SW Belgium *pop* 76,535
La Man·cha \lä-'män-chä, lə-'man-chə\ region S *cen* Spain in S New Castile — **Man·che·gan** \man-'chē-gən, män-'chā-\ *adj or n*
La Mau·ri·cie National Park \lä-,mȯr-ē-'sē\ wilderness and recreational area SE Canada in S Que.
Lam·ba·ré·né \,läm-bä-rā-'nā\ city W Gabon *pop* 17,770
Lam·beth \'lam-bəth, -,beth\ borough of S Greater London, England *pop* 220,100
La Me·sa \lə-'mā-sə\ city SW Calif. NE of San Diego *pop* 57,065
La·mia \lä-'mē-ä\ city E *cen* Greece NW of Thermopylae *pop* 43,898
La Mi·ra·da \,lä-mə-'rä-də\ city SW Calif. SE of Los Angeles *pop* 48,527
Lam·mer·muir \'la-mər-,myu̇r\ *or* **Lam·mer·moor** \-,mu̇r\ hills SE Scotland ESE of Edinburgh
La Mosquitia — see MOSQUITO COAST
Lam·pe·du·sa \,lam-pə-'dü-sə, ,läm-pe-'dü-zə\ island Italy in the Pelagie Islands
La·nai \lə-'nī, lä-\ island Hawaii W of Maui *area* 141 *sq mi* (367 *sq km*)
Lan·ark \'la-nərk\ **1** *or* **Lan·ark·shire** \-,shir, -shər\ former county S *cen* Scotland; chief city Glasgow **2** burgh *cen* Scotland SE of Glasgow *pop* 9778
Lan·ca·shire \'laŋ-kə-,shir, -shər\ *or* **Lan·cas·ter** \'laŋ-kəs-tər\ county NW England bordering on Irish Sea ✻ Preston *area* 1217 *sq mi* (3152 *sq km*), *pop* 1,365,100
Lan·cas·ter \'laŋ-kəs-tər (*usu for 3, 5*), 'lan-,kas-tər (*usu for 1, 2*), 'laŋ-,kas-tər (*usu for 4*)\ **1** city SW Calif. NE of Los Angeles *pop* 156,633 **2** city S *cen* Ohio SE of Columbus *pop* 38,780 **3** city SE Pa. *pop* 59,322 **4** city NE Tex. S of Dallas *pop* 36,361 **5** city NW England in Lancashire *pop* 125,600 — **Lan·cas·tri·an** \laŋ-'kas-trē-ən, lan-\ *adj or n*
Landes \'länᵈ\ coastal region SW France on Bay of Biscay bet. Gironde Estuary & the Adour
Land's End \'landz-'end\ cape SW England at SW tip of Cornwall; extreme W point of England, at 5°41′W
Lang·dale Pikes \'laŋ-,dāl\ two mountain peaks NW England in Cumbria in Lake District
Lang·ford \'laŋ-fərd\ city Canada in B.C. on SE Vancouver Is. *pop* 29,228
Lan·gue·doc \,laŋ-gə-'däk, ,läⁿg-'dȯk\ region & former province S France extending from Auvergne to the Mediterranean
Lan·sing \'lan-siŋ\ **1** village NE Ill. SSE of Chicago *pop* 28,331 **2** city S Mich., its ✻ *pop* 114,297
Lan Tau \'län-'dau̇\ island Hong Kong, China, W of Hong Kong Is. *area* 58 *sq mi* (151 *sq km*)
La·nús \lä-'nüs\ city E Argentina S of Buenos Aires *pop* 466,755
Lan·zhou *or* **Lan–chou** \'län-'jō\ city N *cen* China ✻ of Gansu *pop* 1,194,640
La·od·i·cea \(,)lā-,ä-də-'sē-ə, ,lā-ə-\ **1** ancient city W *cen* Asia Minor in Phrygia **2** — see LATAKIA 2 — **La·od·i·ce·an** \-'sē-ən\ *adj or n*
Laoighis \'lāsh, 'lēsh\ *or* **Leix** \'lāsh, 'lēsh\ *or formerly* **Queen's** county *cen* Ireland in Leinster ✻ Portlaoighise *area* 664 *sq mi* (1726 *sq km*), *pop* 58,744
Laon \läⁿ\ commune N France NE of Paris *pop* 26,241
Laos \'lau̇s, 'lä-(,)ōs, 'lā-,äs\ country SE Asia; a republic, until 1975 a kingdom; formerly a state of French Indochina; ✻ Vientiane *area* 91,428 *sq mi* (236,799 *sq km*), *pop* 5,600,000
La Pal·ma \lä-'päl-mä\ island Spain in Canary Islands; chief town Santa Cruz de la Palma *area* 280 *sq mi* (728 *sq km*)
La Paz \lä-'päz, -'päs\ **1** city, administrative ✻ of Bolivia E of Lake Titicaca at altitude of 12,001 *ft* (3658 *m*), *metropolitan area pop* 711,036 **2** town W Mexico ✻ of Baja California Sur on **La Paz Bay** (inlet of Gulf of California) *pop* 182,418
Lap·land \'lap-,land, -lənd\ region N Europe above the Arctic Circle in N Norway, N Sweden, N Finland, & Kola Peninsula of Russia — **Lap·land·er** \-,lan-dər, -lən-\ *n*
La Pla·ta \lä-'plä-tä\ city E Argentina SE of Buenos Aires *pop* 542,567
La Plata Peak \lə-'pla-tə, -'plä-\ mountain 14,336 *ft* (4370 *m*) *cen* Colo. in Sawatch Mountains
La Porte \lə-'pōrt\ city SE Tex. on Galveston Bay *pop* 33,800
Lap·tev Sea \'lap-,tef, -,tev\ *or formerly* **Nor·den·skjöld Sea** \'nōr-dᵊn-,shəld, -,shəld, -,shēld\ arm of Arctic Ocean Russia bet. Taymyr Peninsula & New Siberian Islands
La Puen·te \lä-'pwen-tā\ city SW Calif. ESE of Los Angeles *pop* 39,816
L'Aqui·la \'lä-kwē-lä\ commune *cen* Italy NE of Rome ✻ of Abruzzi *pop* 70,005
La Quin·ta \lə-'kēn-tə\ city S Calif. SE of Palm Springs *pop* 37,467
Lar·a·mie \'la-rə-mē\ **1** river 216 *mi* (348 *km*) N Colo. & SE Wyo. flowing N & NE into N. Platte River **2** city SE Wyo. *pop* 30,816
Larch \'lärch\ river 270 *mi* (434 *km*) Canada in W Que. flowing NE to unite with the Caniapiskau forming Koksoak River
La·re·do \lə-'rā-(,)dō\ city S Tex. on Rio Grande *pop* 236,091
La·res \'lä-rās\ city W *cen* Puerto Rico *pop* 30,753
Lar·go \'lär-(,)gō\ town W Fla. S of Clearwater *pop* 77,648
La Rio·ja \,lä-rē-'ō-hä\ province N Spain along the upper Ebro ✻ Logroño *area* 1944 *sq mi* (5035 *sq km*), *pop* 276,702
La·ris·sa \lə-'ri-sə\ city N *cen* Greece in E Thessaly *pop* 113,426
Lar·i·stan \,la-rə-'stan\ region S Iran bordering on Persian Gulf
Larne \'lärn\ district NE Northern Ireland, established 1974 *area* 131 *sq mi* (341 *sq km*), *pop* 29,181
La Ro·chelle \,lä-rō-'shel\ city & port W France on Bay of Biscay *pop* 76,711
Lar·vik \'lär-vik\ town & port SE Norway *pop* 38,019
La·Salle \lə-'sal\ **1** town Canada in SE Ont. on Detroit River *pop* 28,643 **2** former town Canada in S Que. now part of Montreal (city)
Las·caux \lä-'skō\ cave SW *cen* France near town of Montignac
Las Cru·ces \läs-'krü-sās\ city S N.Mex. *pop* 97,618
La Se·re·na \,lä-sā-'rā-nä\ city N *cen* Chile *pop* 160,148
Las Pal·mas \läs-'päl-mäs\ **1** province Spain comprising the E Canary Islands *area* 1569 *sq mi* (4064 *sq km*), *pop* 887,676 **2** city & port, its ✻, in NE Grand Canary Is. *pop* 354,863
La Spe·zia \lä-'spet-sē-ä\ city & port NW Italy in Liguria *pop* 95,091
Las Pie·dras \,läs-'pyā-thräs\ city E Puerto Rico *pop* 38,675
Las·sen Peak \'la-sᵊn\ volcano 10,457 *ft* (3187 *m*) N Calif. at S end of Cascade Range; central feature of **Lassen Volcanic National Park**
Las Ve·gas \läs-'vā-gəs\ city SE corner of Nev. *pop* 583,756
Lat·a·kia \,la-tə-'kē-ə\ **1** region NW Syria bordering on the Mediterranean **2** *or anc* **La·od·i·cea** \(,)lā-,ä-də-'sē-ə, ,lā-ə-\ city & port on the Mediterranean; chief town of the region *pop* 284,000
La·ti·na \lä-'tē-nä\ commune *cen* Italy *pop* 115,019
Latin America **1** Spanish America & Brazil **2** all of the Americas S of the U.S. — **Latin American** *adj or n*
Latin Quarter section of Paris, France, S of the Seine frequented by students & artists
Lat·via \'lat-vē-ə\ independent country N *cen* Europe bordering on the Baltic; an independent republic 1918–40, a constituent republic (**Lat·vi·an Republic** \'lat-vē-ən\ ) of the U.S.S.R. 1940–91; ✻ Riga *area* 24,595 *sq mi* (63,701 *sq km*), *pop* 2,400,000
Lau·der·dale Lakes \'lȯ-dər-,dāl\ city SE Fla. *pop* 32,593
Lau·der·hill \'lȯ-dər-,hil\ city SE Fla. *pop* 66,887
Laun·ces·ton \'lȯn(t)-səs-tən, 'län(t)-\ city & port Australia in N Tasmania *pop* 62,504
Lau·ra·sia \lȯ-'rā-zhə, -shə\ hypothetical land area believed to have once connected the landmasses of the northern hemisphere except for the Indian subcontinent
Lau·ren·tian Mountains \lȯ-'ren(t)-shən\ range Canada in S Que. N of the St. Lawrence on S edge of Canadian Shield
Laurentian Plateau — see CANADIAN SHIELD
Lau·ri·um \'lȯr-ē-əm, 'lär-\ mountain SE Greece at SE tip of Attica
Lau·sanne \lō-'zän, -'zan\ commune W Switzerland ✻ of Vaud canton on Lake Geneva *pop* 115,638
Lausitz — see LUSATIA
Lava Beds National Monument area of volcanic features N Calif. SE of Lower Klamath Lake
La·val \lə-'val\ town Canada in S Que. NW of Montreal *pop* 401,553
La Vendée — see VENDÉE
La Verne \lə-'vərn\ city SW Calif. E of Los Angeles *pop* 31,063
Lawn·dale \'lȯn-,dāl, 'län-\ city SW Calif. SSW of Los Angeles *pop* 32,769
Law·rence \'lȯr-ən(t)s, 'lär-\ **1** town *cen* Ind. NE of Indianapolis *pop* 46,001 **2** city NE Kans. WSW of Kansas City *pop* 87,643 **3** city NE corner of Mass. *pop* 76,377
Law·ton \'lȯ-tᵊn\ city SW Okla. *pop* 96,867
Lay·san \'lī-,sän\ island Hawaii in the Leewards NW of Niihau
Lay·ton \'lā-tᵊn\ city N Utah N of Salt Lake City *pop* 67,311
La·zio \'lät-sē-,ō\ *or* **La·tium** \'lā-sh(ē-)əm\ region *cen* Italy bordering on Tyrrhenian Sea & traversed by the Tiber ✻ Rome *pop* 5,302,302
League City \'lēg\ city SE Tex. NW of Galveston *pop* 83,560
League of Nations political organization established by the Allied powers at end of World War I; replaced by United Nations 1946
Leam·ing·ton \'le-miŋ-tən\ **1** municipality Canada in SE Ont. SE of Windsor *pop* 28,403 **2** *or* **Royal Leamington Spa** town S *cen* England in Warwickshire *pop* 44,989
Leav·en·worth \'le-vən-,wərth\ city NE Kans. on Missouri River NW of Kansas City *pop* 35,251
Lea·wood \'lē-,wu̇d\ city E Kans. S of Kansas City *pop* 31,867
Leb·a·non **1** \'le-bə-nən\ city SE *cen* Pa. E of Harrisburg *pop* 25,477 **2** \-nən, -,nän\ country SW Asia bordering on the Mediterranean; a republic since 1944, formerly (1920–44) a French mandate ✻ Beirut *area* 4016 *sq mi* (10,401 *sq km*), *pop* 4,100,000 — **Leb·a·nese** \,le-bə-'nēz, -'nēs\ *adj or n*
Lebanon Mountains *or anc* **Lib·a·nus** \'li-bə-nəs\ mountains Lebanon running parallel to coast W of Bekaa Valley
Le Bour·get \lə-,bu̇r-'zhā\ commune N France, NE suburb of Paris *pop* 12,134
Lec·ce \'lā-chā, 'le-\ commune SE Italy in Puglia *pop* 97,458
Lec·co \'lā-(,)kō, 'le-\ commune N Italy in Lombardy on SE arm (**Lake Lecco**) of Lake Como
Lech \'lek, 'lek\ river Austria & Germany flowing from Vorarlberg N into the Danube
Leeds \'lēdz\ city N England in W. Yorkshire *pop* 674,400
Lees·burg \'lēz-,bərg\ town N Va. near Maryland border *pop* 42,616
Lee's Summit \'lēz\ city W Mo. SE of Kansas City *pop* 91,364
Leeu·war·den \'lā-ü-,vär-də(n)\ commune N Netherlands ✻ of Friesland *pop* 90,516
Lee·ward Islands \'lē-wərd, 'lü-ərd\ **1** island chain *cen* Pacific extending 1250 *mi* (2012 *km*) WNW from main islands of the Hawaiian group; includes Nihoa, Necker, Laysan, Midway, & Kure islands **2** *or F* **Îles sous le Vent** \,ēl-sü-lə-'väⁿ\ islands S. Pacific, W group of the Society Islands *pop* 22,232 **3** islands West Indies in the N Lesser Antilles extending from Virgin Islands (on N) to Dominica (on S) **4** former colony Brit. West Indies in the Leewards including Antigua, St. Kitts and Nevis, & Montserrat
Le·ga·nés \,lā-gä-'nās\ commune *cen* Spain S of Madrid *pop* 173,584
Leg·horn \'leg-,hȯrn\ *or It* **Li·vor·no** \lē-'vȯr-(,)nō\ commune & port *cen* Italy in Tuscany on Tyrrhenian Sea *pop* 171,346
Leg·ni·ca \leg-'nēt-sä\ city SW Poland *pop* 104,196
Leh \'lā\ town India in E Kashmir on the Indus ✻ of Ladakh
Le Ha·vre \lə-'hävrᵊ, -'häv\ *or* **Havre** *or formerly* **Le Havre–de–Grâce** \-də-'gräs\ city & port N France on English Channel on N side of Seine estuary *pop* 190,924
Le·high \'lē-,hī\ river 100 *mi* (161 *km*) E Pa. flowing SW & SE into Delaware River
Leh·man Caves \'lē-mən\ limestone caverns E Nev. on E slope of Wheeler Peak in Great Basin National Park

Leices·ter \'les-tər\ city *cen* England ✳ of Leicestershire *pop* 270,600

Leices·ter·shire \'les-tər-,shir, -shər\ *or* **Leices·ter** \'les-tər\ county *cen* England ✳ Leicester *area* 1021 *sq mi* (2644 *sq km*), *pop* 860,500

Lei·den *or* **Ley·den** \'lī-d°n, *D usu* 'lā-də, -yə\ city W Netherlands in S. Holland on a branch of the lower Rhine *pop* 117,170

Leie — see LYS

Lei·ne \'lī-nə\ river 119 *mi* (192 *km*) *cen* Germany

Lein·ster \'len(t)-stər\ province E Ireland *area* 7581 *sq mi* (19,635 *sq km*), *pop* 2,105,579

Leip·zig \'līp-sig, -sik\ city E Germany in Saxony *pop* 503,191

Leith \'lēth\ port section of Edinburgh, Scotland, on Firth of Forth

Lei·tha \'lī-(,)tä\ river 112 *mi* (180 *km*) E Austria & NW Hungary flowing SE into the Raba

Lei·trim \'lē-trəm\ county NW Ireland in Connacht ✳ Carrick on Shannon *area* 589 *sq mi* (1531 *sq km*), *pop* 25,799

Leix — see LAOIGHIS

Lei·xões \lā-'shói°sh\ town NW Portugal on the Atlantic; port for Porto

Lei·zhou *or* **Lei–chou** \'lā-'jō\ *or* **Lui·chow** \'lwē-'jō, -'chaú\ peninsula SE China in Guangdong bet. S. China Sea & Gulf of Tonkin

Lek \'lek\ river 40 *mi* (64 *km*) Netherlands flowing W into the Atlantic; the N branch of the lower Rhine

Lely·stad \'lā-lē-,stät\ commune *cen* Netherlands ✳ of Flevoland *pop* 66,460

Le Maine — see MAINE 2

Leman, Lake — see GENEVA (Lake)

Le Mans \lə-'mäⁿ\ city NW France on the Sarthe *pop* 146,064

Lemberg — see L'VIV

Lem·nos \'lem-,näs, -nəs\ *or ModGk* **Lím·nos** \'lēm-,nòs\ island Greece in the Aegean ESE of Chalcidice Peninsula; chief town Kástron *area* 177 *sq mi* (458 *sq km*)

Lemon Grove city S Calif. E of San Diego *pop* 25,320

Le·na \'lē-nə, 'lā-; 'lye-nə\ river *ab* 2700 *mi* (4345 *km*) E Russia in Asia flowing from mountains W of Lake Baikal NE & N into Laptev Sea through wide delta

Le·nexa \lə-'nek-sə\ city E Kans. SW of Kansas City *pop* 48,190

Leningrad — see SAINT PETERSBURG 2 — **Len·in·grad·er** \'le-nən-,gra-dər, -,grä-\ *n*

Le·nin Peak \'le-nən, 'lyä-nēn\ mountain 23,405 *ft* (7134 *m*) on border bet. Kyrgyzstan & Tajikistan; highest in Trans Alai Range

Lens \'läⁿs\ city N France SW of Lille *pop* 36,192

Leom·in·ster \'le-mən-stər\ city *cen* Mass. N of Worcester *pop* 40,759

Le·ón \lā-'ōn\ **1** *or* **León de los Al·da·mas** \dä-,lós-äl-'dä-mäs, thä-\ city *cen* Mexico in Guanajuato *pop* 872,453 **2** city W Nicaragua *pop* 90,897 **3** region & ancient kingdom NW Spain W of Old Castile **4** province NW Spain in N León region *area* 5972 *sq mi* (15,467 *sq km*), *pop* 488,751 **5** city, its ✳ *pop* 130,916

Le·o·ne, Mon·te \,môn-tā-lā-'ō-nä\ mountain 11,657 *ft* (3553 *m*) on border bet. Switzerland & Italy SW of Simplon Pass; highest in Lepontine Alps

Leopold II, Lake — see MAI-NDOMBE (Lac)

Léopoldville — see KINSHASA

Le·pon·tine Alps \li-'pän-,tīn, 'le-pən-\ range of *cen* Alps on border bet. Switzerland & Italy — see LEONE (Monte)

Lep·tis Mag·na \,lep-təs-'mag-nə\ ancient seaport N Africa near present-day Al Khums

Lé·ri·da \'ler-i-də, 'lā-rē-thä\ **1** province NE Spain in NW Catalonia *area* 4644 *sq mi* (12,028 *sq km*), *pop* 362,206 **2** — see LLEIDA

Ler·wick \'lər-(,)wik, 'ler-\ burgh & port N Scotland on Mainland Is. in the Shetlands *pop* 7223

Les·bos \'lez-,bäs, -bəs, -,vòs\ *or* **Myt·i·le·ne** \,mi-tə-'lē-nē, ,mē-tē-'lē-\ island Greece in the Aegean off NW Turkey *area* 630 *sq mi* (1632 *sq km*), *pop* 103,700

Les Ey·zies \,lā-zā-'zē\ commune SW *cen* France SE of Périgueux *pop* 909

Le·so·tho \lə-'sō-(,)tō, -'sü-(,)tü\ *or formerly* **Ba·su·to·land** \bə-'sü-tō-,land\ country S Africa surrounded by Republic of South Africa; a constitutional monarchy within the Commonwealth of Nations ✳ Maseru *area* 11,716 *sq mi* (30,462 *sq km*), *pop* 2,157,550

Lesser Antilles islands in the W. Indies including the Virgin, Leeward, & Windward Islands, Trinidad, Barbados, Tobago, & islands in the S Caribbean N of Venezuela

Lesser Armenia — see LITTLE ARMENIA

Lesser Slave Lake \'släv\ lake Canada in *cen* Alta. draining through the **Lesser Slave River** to Athabasca River *area* 461 *sq mi* (1199 *sq km*)

Lesser Sunda Islands — see SUNDA ISLANDS

Leth·bridge \'leth-(,)brij\ city Canada in S Alta. *pop* 83,517

Le·ti·cia \le-'tē-sē-ä\ town SE Colombia on the Amazon *pop* 32,700

Leuc·tra \'lük-trə\ ancient village Greece in Boeotia SW of Thebes

Leu·ven \'lə(r)-və(n), 'lœ-\ *or Fr* **Lou·vain** \lü-'vaⁿ\ city *cen* Belgium in Brabant E of Brussels *pop* 89,152

Le·val·lois–Per·ret \lə-,väl-'wä-pə-'rā\ commune N France on the Seine, NW suburb of Paris *pop* 54,750

Le·vant \lə-'vant\ the countries bordering on the E Mediterranean — **Le·van·tine** \'le-vən-,tīn, -,tēn, lə-'van-\ *adj or n*

Levant States — see SYRIA 2

Le·ven, Loch \'lē-vən\ **1** inlet of Loch Linnhe W Scotland **2** lake 4 *mi* (6.4 *km*) long E Scotland SSE of Perth

Le·ver·ku·sen \'lā-vər-,kü-z°n\ city W Germany on the Rhine SE of Düsseldorf *pop* 161,147

Lé·vis \'lā-vəs, lā-'vē\ city Canada in S Que. *pop* 138,769

Lev·kás \lef-'käs\ island Greece in the Ionians at entrance to Ambracian Gulf *area* 111 *sq mi* (288 *sq km*)

Lew·es \'lü-əs\ **1** the upper Yukon River S of its junction with the Pelly **2** town S England ✳ of E. Sussex on Ouse River S of London

Lewis and Clark Caverns \'lü-əs-ənd-'klärk\ *or formerly* **Mor·ri·son Cave** \'mòr-ə-sən, 'mär-\ caverns *cen* Mont. WNW of Bozeman

Lewis and Clark Lake 30 *mi* (48 *km*) long SE S.Dak. & NE Nebr. formed by Gavins Point Dam

Lew·i·sham \'lü-ə-shəm\ borough of SE Greater London, England *pop* 215,300

Lew·is·ton \'lü-ə-stən\ **1** city NW Idaho on Wash. border *pop* 31,894 **2** city SW Maine on the Androscoggin opposite Auburn *pop* 36,592

Lew·is·ville \'lü-əs-,vil, -vəl\ city N Tex. *pop* 95,290

Lewis with Har·ris \'lü-əs-with-'ha-rəs, -with-\ island NW Scotland in the Outer Hebrides, divided administratively into **Lewis** (in the N; chief town & port Stornoway) & **Harris** (in the S); largest of the Hebrides *area* 770 *sq mi* (2002 *sq km*)

Lex·ing·ton \'lek-siŋ-tən\ **1** city N *cen* Ky. ESE of Frankfort *pop* 295,803 **2** town NE Mass. NW of Boston *pop* 31,394

Leyden — see LEIDEN

Ley·te \'lā-tē\ island Philippines in the Visayan Islands W of **Leyte Gulf** (inlet of the Pacific); chief town Tacloban *area* 2785 *sq mi* (7241 *sq km*)

Ley·ton \'lā-t°n\ former municipal borough SE England in Essex, now part of Waltham Forest

Lha·sa \'lä-sə, 'la-\ city SW China ✳ of Tibet *pop* 106,885

Lho·tse \'lōt-'sä, 'hlōt-\ mountain 27,923 *ft* (8511 *m*) on border bet. Nepal & Tibet in Mt. Everest Massif S of Mt. Everest; 4th highest in the world

Lian·yun·gang \'lyän-'yün-'gäŋ\ *or* **Lien·yün–kang** \le-'ən-'yün-'gäŋ\ *or formerly* **Tung·hai** \'düŋ-'hī\ city E China in N Jiangsu *pop* 354,139

Liao \'lyaú\ river 700 *mi* (1126 *km*) NE China flowing into Gulf of Liaodong

Liao·dong *or* **Liao·tung** \'lyaú-'dúŋ\ peninsula NE China in S Liaoning bet. Korea Bay & **Gulf of Liaodong** (arm of Bo Hai)

Liao·ning \'lyaú-'niŋ\ *or formerly* **Feng·tien** \'fəŋ-'tyen\ province NE China in S Manchuria ✳ Shenyang *area* 58,301 *sq mi* (151,583 *sq km*), *pop* 39,459,697

Liao·si \'lyaú-'shē\ former province (1948–54) NE China in S Manchuria bordering on Gulf of Liaodong ✳ Chin-chou (Jinzhou)

Liao·yang \'lyaú-'yäŋ\ city NE China in *cen* Liaoning NE of Anshan *pop* 492,559

Liaoyuan — see SHUANGLIAO

Li·ard \'lē-ərd\ river 755 *mi* (1215 *km*) W Canada flowing from Stikine Ranges in Yukon Territory E & N into Mackenzie River

Libanus — see LEBANON MOUNTAINS

Li·be·ria \lī-'bir-ē-ə\ country W Africa; a republic ✳ Monrovia *area* 43,000 *sq mi* (111,800 *sq km*), *pop* 3,065,600 — **Li·be·ri·an** \-ē-ən\ *adj or n*

Lib·er·ty \'li-bər-tē\ city NW Mo. NNE of Kansas City *pop* 29,149

Liberty Island *or formerly* **Bed·loe's Island** \'bed-,lōz\ island SE N.Y. in Upper New York Bay; comprises **Statue of Liberty National Monument**

Li·bre·ville \'lē-brə-,vil, -,vēl\ city & port ✳ of Gabon at mouth of Gabon River *pop* 419,596

Lib·ya \'li-bē-ə\ **1** the part of Africa N of the Sahara bet. Egypt & Syrtis Major (Gulf of Sidra) — an ancient name **2** N Africa W of Egypt — an ancient name **3** country N Africa bordering on the Mediterranean; a colony of Italy 1912–43, an independent kingdom 1951–69, a republic since 1969 ✳ Tripoli *area* 679,358 *sq mi* (1,766,331 *sq km*), *pop* 5,678,500

Lib·y·an Desert \'li-bē-ən\ desert N Africa W of the Nile in Libya, Egypt, & Sudan

Lich·field \'lich-,fēld\ city W *cen* England in Staffordshire *pop* 90,700

Lick·ing \'li-kiŋ\ river 320 *mi* (515 *km*) NE Ky. flowing NW into Ohio River

Li·di·ce \'li-də-sē, 'lē-dyēt-,sä\ village W *cen* Czech Republic in W *cen* Bohemia

Li·do \'lē-(,)dō\ island Italy in the Adriatic separating Lagoon of Venice & Gulf of Venice

Liech·ten·stein \'lik-tən-,stīn, 'lik-tən-,shtīn\ country W Europe bet. Switzerland & Austria bordering on the Rhine; a principality ✳ Vaduz *area* 62 *sq mi* (161 *sq km*), *pop* 33,525 — **Liech·ten·stein·er** \-,stī-nər, -,shtī-\ *n*

Li·ège \lē-'ezh, -'äzh\ *or Flem* **Luik** \'līk, 'lœik\ **1** province E Belgium *area* 1497 *sq mi* (3877 *sq km*), *pop* 1,024,130 **2** city, its ✳ *pop* 185,131

Lie·pa·ja \lē-'e-pə-yə, 'lye-pä-yä\ *or G* **Li·bau** \'lē-,baú\ city & port W Latvia on the Baltic *pop* 87,505

Lif·fey \'li-fē\ river 50 *mi* (80 *km*) E Ireland flowing into Dublin Bay

Lif·ford \'li-fərd\ town NW Ireland (republic) in Ulster ✳ of County Donegal *pop* 1478

Li·gu·ria \lə-'gyúr-ē-ə\ region NW Italy bordering on Ligurian Sea ✳ Genoa *pop* 1,621,016 — **Li·gu·ri·an** \-ē-ən\ *adj or n*

Ligurian Sea arm of the Mediterranean N of Corsica

Li·ka·si \lē-'kä-sē\ *or formerly* **Ja·dot·ville** \,zha-dō-'vēl, zha-'dō-,vil\ city SE Democratic Republic of the Congo in SE Shaba *pop* 279,839

Lille \'lēl\ *or formerly* **Lisle** \'lēl, 'līl\ city N France; medieval ✳ of Flanders *pop* 184,647

Li·long·we \li-'lòŋ-(,)gwā\ city ✳ of Malawi *pop* 498,185

Li·ma 1 \'lī-mə\ city NW Ohio *pop* 38,771 **2** \'lē-mə\ city ✳ of Peru on the Rímac *pop* 5,825,900

Li·ma·vady \,li-mə-'va-dē\ district N Northern Ireland, established 1974 *area* 226 *sq mi* (588 *sq km*), *pop* 29,201

Li·may \lē-'mī\ river 250 *mi* (402 *km*) W Argentina flowing out of Lake Nahuel Huapí & joining the Neuquén forming Negro River

Lim·burg \'lim-,bərg\ **1** region W Europe E of the Meuse including parts of present Limburg province, Netherlands, & Limburg province, Belgium **2** province NE Belgium ✳ Hasselt *area* 935 *sq mi* (2422 *sq km*), *pop* 798,583 **3** province SE Netherlands ✳ Maastricht *area* 853 *sq mi* (2209 *sq km*), *pop* 1,143,296

Lime·house \'līm-,haús\ district E London, England, in Tower Hamlets on N bank of Thames River

Lim·er·ick \'li-mə-rik, 'lim-rik\ **1** county SW Ireland in Munster *area* 1037 *sq mi* (2696 *sq km*), *pop* 175,304 **2** city & port, its ✳, on the Shannon *pop* 54,023

Límnos — see LEMNOS

Li·moges \lē-'mōzh, li-\ city SW *cen* France *pop* 133,924

Li·món \lē-'mōn\ *or* **Puer·to Limón** \'pwer-tō\ city & port E Costa Rica on the Caribbean *pop* 64,783

\ə\ abut \ᵊ\ kitten, F table \ər\ further \a\ ash \ā\ ace \ä\ mop, mar \aú\ out \ch\ chin \e\ bet \ē\ easy \g\ go \i\ hit \ī\ ice \j\ job \ŋ\ sing \ō\ go \ò\ law \òi\ boy \th\ thin \th̲\ the \ü\ loot \ú\ foot \y\ yet \zh\ vision, beige \k̲, ⁿ, œ, ᴜe, ᵫ\ *see* Guide to Pronunciation

Li·mou·sin \ˌlē-mü-ˈzaⁿ\ region & former province S cen France W of Auvergne ✻ Limoges

Lim·po·po \lim-ˈpō-(ˌ)pō\ **1** or **Croc·o·dile** \ˈkrä-kə-ˌdīl\ river 1000 mi (1609 km) S Africa flowing from Limpopo province, Republic of South Africa, into Indian Ocean in Mozambique **2** or formerly **North·ern** or **Noord** \ˈnȯrd, ˈnȯrt\ or earlier **Northern Transvaal** province NE Republic of South Africa area 47,598 sq mi (123,280 sq km), pop 5,013,000

Lin·coln \ˈliŋ-kən\ **1** city SE Nebr., its ✻ pop 258,379 **2** city E England ✻ of Lincolnshire pop 81,900

Lincoln Park city SE Mich. SW of Detroit pop 38,144

Lin·coln·shire \ˈliŋ-kən-ˌshir, -shər\ or **Lincoln** county E England ✻ Lincoln area 2354 sq mi (6097 sq km), pop 573,900

Lin·den \ˈlin-dən\ city NE N.J. SSW of Elizabeth pop 40,499

Lin·den·hurst \ˈlin-dən-ˌhərst\ village SE N.Y. in cen Long Is. pop 27,253

Lin·des·nes \ˈlin-dəs-ˌnās\ cape Norway at S tip on North Sea

Lindisfarne — see HOLY ISLAND 1

Lind·sey, Parts of \ˈlin-zē\ district & former administrative county E England in N Lincolnshire ✻ Lincoln area 1520 sq mi (3952 sq km)

Line Islands \ˈlīn\ islands Kiribati in W Pacific S of Hawaii; formerly divided bet. the U.S. (Kingman Reef & Palmyra) & Great Britain (Teraina, Tabuaeran, & Kiritimati) pop 4782

Lin·ga·yen Gulf \ˌliŋ-gä-ˈyen\ inlet of S. China Sea Philippines in NW Luzon

Linguetta, Cape — see GJUHEZES (Cape)

Lin·kö·ping \ˈlin-ˌshȯ(r)-piŋ, -ˌshœ-\ city SE Sweden pop 135,066

Lin·lith·gow \lin-ˈlith-(ˌ)gō\ **1** or **Lin·lith·gow·shire** \-ˌshir, -shər\ — see WEST LOTHIAN 2 **2** burgh SE Scotland W of Edinburgh pop 9524

Linn·he, Loch \ˈlin-ē\ inlet of the Atlantic on W coast of Scotland extending NE from head of Firth of Lorn

Linz \ˈlints, ˈlinz\ city N Austria on the Danube pop 183,504

Li·on, Gulf of \ˈlī-ən\ or F **Golfe du Lion** \ˌgȯlf-dœ-ˈlyōⁿ\ arm of the Mediterranean on S coast of France

Lip·a·ri \ˈli-pə-rē\ or anc **Lip·a·ra** \ˈli-pə-rə\ island, chief of the Lipari Islands

Lipari Islands or It **Iso·le Eo·lie** \ˈē-zò-ˌlā-ā-ˈò-lē-ˌā\ islands Italy in SE Tyrrhenian Sea off NE Sicily area ab 45 sq mi (117 sq km) — see STROMBOLI

Li·petsk \ˈlē-ˌpetsk, -ˌpitsk\ city SW cen Russia in Europe N of Voronezh pop 464,000

Lip·pe \ˈli-pə\ **1** river ab 150 mi (241 km) W Germany flowing from Teutoburg Forest W into the Rhine **2** former principality & state W Germany bet. Teutoburg Forest & the Weser ✻ Detmold

Li·ri \ˈlir-ē\ river 100 mi (161 km) cen Italy flowing into Gulf of Gaeta

Lis·bon \ˈliz-bən\ or Pg **Lis·boa** \lēzh-ˈvō-ə\ city & port ✻ of Portugal on Tagus estuary pop 564,657 — **Lis·bo·an** \liz-ˈbō-ən\ n

Lis·burn \ˈliz-(ˌ)bərn\ district E Northern Ireland, established 1974 area 171 sq mi (445 sq km), pop 99,162

Lis·burne, Cape \ˈliz-(ˌ)bərn\ cape NW Alaska projecting into Arctic Ocean near W end of Brooks Range

Li·sieux \lēz-ˈyə(r), -ˈyœ\ city NW France E of Caen pop 23,171

Li·ta·ni \li-ˈtä-nē\ river 90 mi (144 km) S Lebanon flowing into Mediterranean

Lith·u·a·nia \ˌli-thə-ˈwā-nē-ə, ˌli-thyə-, -nyə\ or Lith **Lie·tu·va** \lye-ˈtü-vä\ country N cen Europe bordering on the Baltic; remnant of a medieval principality extending from Baltic Sea to Black Sea; a republic 1918–40, a constituent republic (**Lithuanian Republic**) of the U.S.S.R. 1940–91; ✻ Vilnius area 25,174 sq mi (65,201 sq km), pop 3,483,972

Little Abaco — see ABACO

Little Armenia or **Lesser Armenia** region S Turkey corresponding to ancient Cilicia

Little Bighorn river 80 mi (129 km) N Wyo. & S Mont. flowing N into Bighorn River

Little Bighorn Battlefield National Monument site SE Mont. on the Little Bighorn River of battle fought 1876

Little Colorado river ab 300 mi (483 km) NE Ariz. flowing NW into Colorado River

Little Diomede — see DIOMEDE ISLANDS

Little Inagua — see INAGUA

Little Kabylia — see KABYLIA

Little Karoo — see KAROO

Little Minch — see MINCH

Little Missouri river 560 mi (901 km) W U.S. flowing from NE Wyo. N into Missouri River in W N.Dak.

Little Namaqualand — see NAMAQUALAND

Lit·tle Rock \ˈli-tᵊl-ˌräk\ city ✻ of Ark. on Arkansas River pop 193,524

Little Saint Ber·nard \ˌsänt-bər-ˈnärd\ mountain pass 7178 ft (2188 m) over Savoy Alps bet. France & Italy S of Mont Blanc

Lit·tle·ton \ˈli-tᵊl-tən\ town N cen Colo. S of Denver pop 41,737

Little Walachia — see OLTENIA

Litzmannstadt — see LODZ

Liv·er·more \ˈli-vər-ˌmȯr\ city W Calif. SE of Oakland pop 80,968

Liv·er·pool \ˈli-vər-ˌpül\ city & port NW England in Merseyside on Mersey estuary pop 448,300 — **Liv·er·pud·li·an** \ˌli-vər-ˈpəd-lē-ən\ adj or n

Liv·ing·stone \ˈli-viŋ-stən\ city S Zambia on the Zambezi pop 82,218

Livingstone Falls rapids in lower Congo River W equatorial Africa below Pool Malebo; a series of cascades dropping nearly 900 ft (273 m) in 220 mi (352 km)

Li·vo·nia \lə-ˈvō-nē-ə, -nyə\ **1** region cen Europe bordering on the Baltic in Latvia & Estonia **2** city SE Mich. W of Detroit pop 96,942 — **Li·vo·ni·an** \-nē-ən, -nyən\ adj or n

Livorno — see LEGHORN

Lizard Point headland SW England in S Cornwall at S tip of **The Lizard** (peninsula projecting into English Channel); extreme S point of Great Britain, at 49°57′30″N, 5°12′W

Lju·blja·na \lē-ˌü-blē-ˈä-nə\ city cen Slovenia, its ✻ pop 323,291

Llan·ber·is \lan-ˈber-əs, hlan-\ village NW Wales near Snowdon at entrance to **Pass of Llanberis** (1169 ft or 354 m)

Llan·drin·dod Wells \lan-ˈdrin-ˌdȯd, hlan-\ town E Wales; formerly ✻ of Powys

Llan·dud·no \lan-ˈdid-(ˌ)nō, hlan-, -ˈdəd-\ town NW Wales pop 18,991

Lla·nel·li or **Lla·nel·ly** \hla-ˈne-hlē, la-ˈne-lē\ town & port S Wales WNW of Swansea pop 73,500

Llan·gef·ni \lan-ˈgev-nē, hlan-\ town NW Wales on Anglesey Is. pop 4265

Lla·no Es·ta·ca·do \ˈla-(ˌ)nō-ˌes-tə-ˈkä-(ˌ)dō, ˈlä-, ˈyä-\ or **Staked Plain** \ˈstāk(t)-\ plateau region E & SE N.Mex. & W Tex.

Llei·da \ˈyä-thä\ or **Lérida** commune ✻ of Lérida province, Spain pop 112,199

Llu·llai·lla·co \ˌyü-ˌyī-ˈyä-(ˌ)kō\ volcano 22,057 ft (6723 m) N Chile in Andes on Argentina border SE of Antofagasta

Lo·an·ge \lō-ˈaŋ-gə\ or Pg **Lu·an·ge** \lü-ˈaŋ-gə\ river 425 mi (684 km) NE Angola & SW Republic of the Congo flowing N into Kasai River

Lo·bam·ba \lō-ˈbäm-bə\ town, legislative ✻ of Swaziland

Lo·bi·to \lō-ˈbē-(ˌ)tō\ city & port W Angola pop 59,528

Lo·bos, Point \ˈlō-(ˌ)bōs\ **1** promontory Calif. in San Francisco on S side of entrance to the Golden Gate **2** promontory Calif. on the Pacific SW of Monterey

Lo·car·no \lō-ˈkär-(ˌ)nō\ commune SE cen Switzerland pop 14,430

Loch·gilp·head \läk-ˈgilp-ˌhed, läk-\ burgh W Scotland at head of arm of Firth of Clyde

Lo·cris \ˈlō-krəs, ˈlä-\ region of ancient Greece N of Gulf of Corinth — **Lo·cri·an** \-krē-ən\ adj or n

Lod \ˈlōd\ city cen Israel pop 45,500

Lo·di 1 \ˈlō-ˌdī\ city cen Calif. SSE of Sacramento pop 62,134 **2** \ˈlō-ˌdī\ borough NE N.J. SE of Paterson pop 24,136 **3** \ˈlò-(ˌ)dē\ commune N Italy in Lombardy SE of Milan pop 41,319

Lodz \ˈlüj, ˈlädz\ or G **Litz·mann·stadt** \ˈlits-män-ˌshtät\ city cen Poland WSW of Warsaw pop 851,690

Lo·fo·ten \ˈlō-ˌfò-tᵊn\ island group Norway off NW coast SW of Vesterålen area 475 sq mi (1235 sq km)

Lo·gan \ˈlō-gən\ city N Utah pop 48,174

Logan, Mount mountain 19,551 ft (5959 m) Canada in SW corner of Yukon; highest in St. Elias & Coast ranges & in Canada & 2d highest in N. America

Lo·gro·ño \lō-ˈgrō-(ˌ)nyō\ commune ✻ of La Rioja province, Spain, on the Ebro pop 133,058

Loire \lə-ˈwär, ˈlwär\ river 634 mi (1020 km) cen France flowing from the Massif Central NW & W into Bay of Biscay

Lo·í·za \lō-ˈē-sä\ city Puerto Rico pop 30,060

Lol·land \ˈlä-lənd\ island Denmark in the Baltic S of Sjælland area 477 sq mi (1240 sq km), pop 69,796

Lo·ma·mi \lō-ˈmä-mē\ river ab 800 mi (1285 km) cen Democratic Republic of the Congo flowing N into Congo River

Lo·mas \ˈlō-ˌmäs\ or **Lo·mas de Za·mo·ra** \dā-zä-ˈmȯr-ä, thä-sä-ˈmō-rä\ city E Argentina SW of Buenos Aires pop 572,769

Lom·bard \ˈläm-ˌbärd\ village NE Ill. W of Chicago pop 43,165

Lom·bar·dy \-ˌbär-dē, -bər- also ˈləm-\ or It **Lom·bar·dia** \ˌläm-bər-ˈdē-ə, ˌlōm-\ region N Italy chiefly N of the Po ✻ Milan pop 9,121,714

Lom·blen \läm-ˈblen\ island Indonesia in the Lesser Sundas E of Flores area 468 sq mi (1217 sq km)

Lom·bok \ˈläm-ˌbäk\ island Indonesia in the Lesser Sundas E of Bali; chief town Mataram area 1825 sq mi (4745 sq km), pop 1,300,234

Lo·mé \lō-ˈmā\ city & port ✻ of Togo pop 920,000

Lo·mond, Ben \ben-ˈlō-mənd\ mountain 3192 ft (973 m) S cen Scotland on E side of Loch Lomond

Lomond, Loch lake 24 mi (39 km) long S cen Scotland; largest in Scotland

Lom·poc \ˈläm-ˌpōk\ city SW Calif. W of Santa Barbara pop 42,434

Lon·don \ˈlən-dən\ **1** city Canada in SE Ont. on Thames River pop 366,151 **2** city & port SE England ✻ of United Kingdom formerly constituting an administrative county; comprises **City of London** or **The City** (approximately coextensive with anc **Lon·din·i·um** \län-ˈdi-nē-əm, ˌlon-\; pop 4000) & 32 other boroughs, which together are referred to as the metropolitan county of **Greater London** (area 632 sq mi or 1637 sq km, pop 6,377,900) — **Lon·don·er** \-də-nər\ n

Lon·don·der·ry 1 \ˈlən-dən-ˌder-ē\ town SE N.H. NE of Nashua pop 23,236 **2** — see DERRY **3** \ˈlən-dən-ˈder-ē, ˈlən-dən-ˌ\ traditional county N Northern Ireland

Long Beach 1 city & port SW Calif. SE of Los Angeles pop 462,257 **2** city SE N.Y. on island S of Long Is. pop 33,275

Long Branch city E cen N.J. on the Atlantic pop 30,719

Long·ford \ˈlȯŋ-fərd\ **1** county E cen Ireland in Leinster area 403 sq mi (1048 sq km), pop 31,068 **2** town, its ✻ pop 6393

Long Island island 118 mi (190 km) long SE N.Y. S of Conn. area 1723 sq mi (4462 sq km) — **Long Islander** n

Long Island City section of New York City in NW Queens

Long Island Sound inlet of the Atlantic bet. Conn. & Long Is.

Long·mont \ˈlȯŋ-ˌmänt\ city N Colo. N of Denver pop 86,270

Longs Peak \ˈlȯŋz\ mountain 14,255 ft (4345 m) N cen Colo. in Front Range in Rocky Mountain National Park

Lon·gueuil \lȯŋ-ˈgāl, -ˈgœ-ē-\ city Canada in S Que. pop 231,409

Long·view \ˈlȯŋ-ˌvyü\ **1** city NE Tex. pop 80,455 **2** city SW Wash. on Columbia River pop 36,648

Long Xuy·en \laúŋ-ˈswē-ən\ city S Vietnam in SW Cochin China on S side of Mekong Delta pop 128,817

Lookout, Cape cape E N.C. on the Atlantic SW of Cape Hatteras

Lookout Mountain ridge 2126 ft (648 m) SE Tenn., NW Ga., & NE Ala.

Lo·rain \lə-ˈrān, lō-\ city N Ohio on Lake Erie pop 64,097

Lord Howe Island \lȯrd-ˈhaú\ island Australia in Tasman Sea ENE of Sydney belonging to New South Wales area 5 sq mi (13 sq km)

Lo·re·to \lə-ˈrä-(ˌ)tō, -ˈre-\ commune cen Italy in Marche pop 11,372

Lo·ri·ent \ˌlȯr-ē-ˈäⁿ\ commune & port NW France in Brittany on Bay of Biscay pop 59,224

Lor·raine \lə-ˈrän, lȯ-\ or G **Lo·thring·en** \ˈlō-triŋ-ən\ region & former duchy NE France around the upper Moselle & the Meuse; remnant (Upper Lorraine) of medieval kingdom of **Lo·tha·rin·gia** \ˌlō-thə-ˈrin-j(ē-)ə\ including also territory to N (Lower Lorraine) bet. the Rhine & the Schelde — see ALSACE-LORRAINE

Los Al·tos \lòs-ˈal-(ˌ)tōs\ city W Calif. SSE of Palo Alto pop 28,976

Los An·ge·les \lòs-'an-jə-ləs *also* -ˌlēz, *sometimes* -'aŋ-gə-ˌlēz\ city & port SW Calif. on the Pacific *pop* 3,792,621 — **Los An·ge·le·no** \-ˌan-jə-'lē-(ˌ)nō *also* -ˌaŋ-gə-'lē-\ *n*

Los Ba·nos \lòs-'ba-nəs\ city W *cen* Calif. *pop* 35,972

Los Gat·os \lòs-'ga-təs\ town W Calif. S of San José *pop* 29,413

Lot \'lät, 'lòt\ river 300 *mi* (483 *km*) S France flowing W into the Garonne

Louang·phra·bang \'lwäŋ-prä-'bäŋ\ *or* **Luang Pra·bang** \'lwäŋ-prä-\ city NW Laos on the Mekong NNW of Vientiane

Lough·bor·ough \'ləf-ˌbər-ə, -ˌbə-rə, -b(ə-)rə\ town *cen* England in Leicestershire S of Nottingham *pop* 47,647

Lou·ise, Lake \lù-'ēz\ lake W Canada in SW Alta. in Banff National Park

Lou·i·si·ade Archipelago \lù-ˌē-zē-'äd, -'ad\ island group in Solomon Sea SE of New Guinea; belongs to Papua New Guinea *area ab* 600 *sq mi* (1555 *sq km*), *pop* 14,599

Lou·i·si·ana \lù-ˌē-zē-'a-nə, ˌlü-ə-zē-, ˌlü-zē-\ state S U.S. ✱ Baton Rouge *area* 48,523 *sq mi* (126,160 *sq km*), *pop* 4,533,372 — **Lou·i·si·an·an** \-'a-nən\ *adj or n* — **Lou·i·si·an·i·an** \-'a-nē-ən, -'a-nyən\ *adj or n*

Louisiana Purchase region W U.S. bet. Mississippi River & the Rockies purchased 1803 from France *area* 885,000 *sq mi* (2,301,000 *sq km*)

Lou·is·ville \'lü-i-ˌvil, -vəl\ city N Ky. on Ohio River *pop* 597,337

Loup \'lüp\ river 290 *mi* (467 *km*) E *cen* Nebr. flowing E into Platte River

Lourdes \'lùrd, 'lùrdz\ commune SW France on the Gave de Pau SSW of Tarbes *pop* 15,242

Lourenço Marques — see MAPUTO

Louth \'laùth\ county E Ireland in Leinster bordering on Irish Sea ✱ Dundalk *area* 317 *sq mi* (824 *sq km*), *pop* 101,821

Louvain — see LEUVEN

Love·land \'ləv-lənd\ city N Colo. N of Denver *pop* 66,859

Loveland Pass mountain pass N *cen* Colo. in Front Range of Rocky Mountains

Low Countries region W Europe bordering on North Sea & comprising modern Belgium, Luxembourg, & the Netherlands

Low·ell \'lō-əl\ city N Mass. NW of Boston *pop* 106,519

Lower Canada the province of Canada 1791–1841 corresponding to modern Que. — see UPPER CANADA

Lower 48 the continental states of the U.S. excluding Alaska

Lower Klamath Lake lake N Calif. on Oreg. border SSE of Upper Klamath Lake (in Oreg.)

Lower Peninsula S part of Mich., S of Straits of Mackinac

Lower Saxony *or G* **Nie·der·sach·sen** \ˌnē-dər-ˌzäk-sən\ state of Germany & formerly of W. Germany bordering on North Sea ✱ Hannover *area* 18,305 *sq mi* (47,410 *sq km*), *pop* 7,387,200 — see SAXONY

Lowes·toft \'lō-stəf(t), -ˌstòft\ port E England in E. Suffolk on North Sea *pop* 55,231

Low·lands \'lō-ləndz, -ˌlandz\ the *cen* & E part of Scotland lying bet. the Highlands & the Southern Uplands

Loyalty Islands islands SW Pacific E of New Caledonia; a dependency of New Caledonia *area ab* 755 *sq mi* (1955 *sq km*), *pop* 17,912

Lu·a·la·ba \ˌlü-ä-'lä-bä\ river 400 *mi* (640 *km*) SE Democratic Republic of the Congo flowing N to join the **Lu·a·pu·la** \-'pü-lä\ (outlet of Lake Bangweulu) forming Congo River

Lu·an·da \lü-'än-də\ city & port ✱ of Angola *pop* 2,600,000

Luangue — see LOANGE

Lub·bock \'lə-bək\ city NW Tex. *pop* 229,573

Lü·beck \'lü-ˌbek, 'lue-\ city & port N Germany NE of Hamburg *pop* 215,999

Lu·blin \'lü-blən, -blēn\ city E Poland SE of Warsaw *pop* 349,672

Lu·bum·ba·shi \ˌlü-büm-'bä-shē\ *or formerly* **Elis·a·beth·ville** \i-'li-zə-bəth-ˌvil\ city SE Democratic Republic of the Congo in SE Shaba *pop* 739,082

Lucania — see BASILICATA

Lu·ca·nia, Mount \lü-'kä-nē-ə, -nyə\ mountain 17,147 *ft* (5226 *m*) Canada in SW Yukon in St. Elias Range N of Mt. Logan

Luc·ca \'lü-kə\ commune *cen* Italy in Tuscany NW of Florence *pop* 85,487

Lu·cerne \lü-'sərn\ *or G* **Lu·zern** \lüt-'sern\ **1** canton *cen* Switzerland *area* 577 *sq mi* (1494 *sq km*), *pop* 350,600 **2** commune, its ✱, on Lake of Lucerne *pop* 57,374

Lucerne, Lake of *or G* **Vier·wald·stät·ter See** \fir-'vält-ˌshte-tər-ˌzā\ lake 24 *mi* (39 *km*) long *cen* Switzerland *area* 44 *sq mi* (114 *sq km*)

Luchow — see HEFEI

Luck·now \'lək-ˌnaù\ city N India ESE of Delhi ✱ of Uttar Pradesh *pop* 2,207,340

Lüda — see DALIAN

Lü·de·ritz \'lü-də-rits, 'lue-\ town & port SW Namibia *pop* 6000

Lu·dhi·a·na \ˌlü-dē-'ä-nə\ city NW India in Punjab SE of Amritsar *pop* 1,395,053

Lud·wigs·burg \'lüd-vigz-ˌbùrg, 'lüt-viks-ˌbùrk\ city SW Germany in Baden-Württemberg N of Stuttgart *pop* 83,913

Lud·wigs·ha·fen am Rhein \ˌlüd-vigz-'hä-fə-näm-'rīn, ˌlüt-viks-\ city SW Germany on the Rhine opposite Mannheim *pop* 165,368

Luf·kin \'ləf-kən\ city E Tex. NNE of Houston *pop* 35,067

Lu·ga·no \lü-'gä-(ˌ)nō\ commune S Switzerland in Ticino canton on Lake Lugano *pop* 26,530

Lugano, Lake lake on border bet. Switzerland & Italy E of Lake Maggiore *area* 19 *sq mi* (49 *sq km*)

Lu·go \'lü-(ˌ)gō\ **1** province NW Spain in NE Galicia on Bay of Biscay *area* 3785 *sq mi* (9803 *sq km*), *pop* 357,648 **2** commune, its ✱ *pop* 88,414

Lu·hans'k \lü-'hän(t)sk\ *or* **Lu·gansk** \-'gän(t)sk\ *or 1935–58 & 1970–89* **Vo·ro·shi·lov·grad** \ˌvòr-ə-'shē-ləf-ˌgrad, ˌvär-, -ləv-, -ˌgräd\ city E Ukraine in Donets Basin *pop* 504,000

Luichow — see LEIZHOU

Luik — see LIÈGE

Lu·leå \'lü-lä-ˌö\ city & port N Sweden near head of Gulf of Bothnia *pop* 72,139

Lu·le·bur·gaz \ˌlü-lə-bùr-'gäz, ˌlue-\ city *cen* Turkey in Europe

Luluabourg — see KANANGA

Lund \'lünd, 'lənd\ city SW Sweden NE of Malmö *pop* 100,402

Lun·dy Island \'lən-dē\ island SW England at mouth of Bristol Channel off coast of Devon *area* 2 *sq mi* (5.2 *sq km*)

Lü·ne·burg \'lü-nə-ˌbùrg, 'lue-nə-ˌbùrk\ city N Germany SE of Hamburg & NE of **Lüneburg Heath** *or G* **Lü·ne·bur·ger Hei·de** \-ˌbùr-gər-ˌhī-də\ (tract of moorland *ab* 55 *mi* or 88 *km* long) *pop* 62,944

Lü·nen \'lü-nən, 'lue-\ city W Germany S of Münster *pop* 88,443

Lu·nen·burg \'lü-nən-ˌbərg\ municipal district Canada in S N.S. *pop* 25,118

Lu·né·ville \'lü-nə-ˌvil, lue-nä-'vēl\ city NE France on the Meurthe SE of Nancy *pop* 20,188

Lungki — see ZHANGZHOU

Luo·yang \lü-'wō-'yäŋ\ *or* **Lo·yang** \'lō-'yäŋ\ city E China in N Henan in the Huang basin *pop* 759,752

Lu·ray Caverns \'lü-ˌrā, lü-'\ caverns N Va. in Blue Ridge Mountains

Lu·sa·ka \lü-'sä-kä\ city ✱ of Zambia *pop* 982,362

Lu·sa·tia \lü-'sä-sh(ē-)ə\ *or G* **Lau·sitz** \'laù-(ˌ)zits\ region E Germany NW of Silesia E of the Elbe

Lü·shun \'lü-'shün\ *or* **Port Ar·thur** \'är-thər\ port NE China in S Liaoning at tip of Liaodong Peninsula; part of greater Dalian

Lusitania — see PORTUGAL — **Lu·si·ta·ni·an** \ˌlü-sə-'tā-nē-ən, -nyən\ *adj or n*

Lu·ta — see DALIAN

Lutetia — see PARIS 2

Lu·ton \'lü-tⁿn\ town SE *cen* England in SE Bedfordshire *pop* 167,300

Lüt·zen \'lüt-sən, 'luet-\ town E Germany in Saxony SW of Leipzig

Lux·em·bourg *or G* **Lux·em·burg** \'lək-səm-ˌbərg, 'lùk-səm-ˌbùrk\ **1** province SE Belgium ✱ Arlon *area* 1706 *sq mi* (4418 *sq km*), *pop* 250,406 **2** country W Europe bet. Belgium, France, & Germany; a grand duchy *area* 999 *sq mi* (2597 *sq km*), *pop* 506,000 **3** city, its ✱ *pop* 75,377 — **Lux·em·bourg·er** \-ˌbər-gər, -ˌbùr-\ *n* — **Lux·em·bourg·i·an** *or* **Lux·em·burg·i·an** \ˌlək-səm-'bər-gē-ən, ˌlùk-səm-'bùr-\ *adj*

Lux·or \'lək-ˌsòr, 'lùk-\ city S Egypt on the Nile on S part of site of ancient Thebes *pop* 142,000

Lu·zon \lü-'zän\ island N Philippines chief island of the group *area* 41,765 *sq mi* (108,171 *sq km*), *pop* 42,784,360

L'viv \lə-'vē-ü, -'vēf\ *or* **L'vov** \lə-'vòf, -'vòv\ *or Pol* **Lwów** \lə-'vüf, -'vüv\ *or G* **Lem·berg** \-ˌberg, -ˌberk\ city W Ukraine *pop* 802,000

Lyallpur — see FAISALABAD

Ly·ca·bet·tus *or Gk* **Ly·ka·bet·tos** \ˌli-kə-'be-təs, ˌlī-\ mountain 909 *ft* (277 *m*) in NE part of Athens, Greece

Ly·ca·o·nia \ˌli-kā-'ō-nē-ə, ˌlī-, -nyə\ ancient region & Roman province SE *cen* Asia Minor N of Cilicia

Ly·cia \'li-sh(ē-)ə\ ancient region & Roman province SW Asia Minor on coast SE of Caria

Lyd·ia \'li-dē-ə\ ancient country W Asia Minor bordering on the Aegean ✱ Sardis

Lynch·burg \'linch-ˌbərg\ city S *cen* Va. on James River *pop* 75,568

Lynn \'lin\ **1** city N Mass. NE of Boston *pop* 90,329 **2** *or* **Lynn Re·gis** — see KING'S LYNN

Lynn Canal narrow inlet of the Pacific 80 *mi* (129 *km*) long SE Alaska extending N from Juneau

Lynn·wood \'lin-ˌwùd\ city N Wash. N of Seattle *pop* 35,836

Lyn·wood \'lin-ˌwùd\ city SW Calif. S of Los Angeles *pop* 69,772

Lyon \'lyōⁿ\ *or* **Ly·ons** \lē-'òⁿ, 'lī-ənz\ *or anc* **Lug·du·num** \ləg-'dü-nəm, ˌlüg-\ city SE France at confluence of the Saône & the Rhône *pop* 445,274

Ly·on·nais *or* **Ly·o·nais** \ˌlē-ò-'nä\ former province SE France NE of Auvergne & W of the Saône & the Rhône ✱ Lyon

Lys \'lēs\ *or in Belgium* **Leie** \'lā-ə, 'lī-ə\ river 120 *mi* (193 *km*) France & Belgium flowing NE into the Schelde

Lyt·tel·ton \'li-tⁿl-tən\ borough New Zealand on South Is.; port for Christchurch on **Port Lyttelton** (inlet) *pop* 3190

Maarianhamina — see MARIEHAMN

Maas — see MEUSE

Maas·tricht *or* **Maes·tricht** \mä-ˌstrikt, -ˌstrik̇t; mä-'\ commune SE Netherlands on the Meuse ✱ of Limburg *pop* 122,005

Ma·cao *or* **Ma·cau** \mə-'kaù\ *or Chin* **Ao·men** \'aù-'mən\ **1** peninsula SE China in Guangdong in Xi delta W of Hong Kong **2** special administrative region SE China comprising Macao Peninsula & two small adjacent islands; formerly a Port. overseas territory with Macao (city) as ✱ *area* 9.1 *sq mi* (23.6 *sq km*), *pop* 488,000 **3** city & port Macao (special administrative region) *pop* 161,252 — **Mac·a·nese** \ˌma-kə-'nēz, -'nēs\ *n*

Ma·ca·pá \ˌmä-kə-'pä\ city & port N Brazil ✱ of Amapá *pop* 283,308

Macassar — see MAKASSAR 1 — **Ma·cas·sar·ese** \mə-ˌka-sə-'rēz, -'rēs\ *n*

Mac·cles·field \'ma-kəlz-ˌfēld\ town W England in E Cheshire SSE of Manchester *pop* 147,000

Mac·don·nell Ranges \mək-'dä-nⁿl\ series of mountain ridges *cen* Australia in S Northern Territory; highest point Mt. Ziel 5023 *ft* (1531 *m*)

Mac·e·do·nia \ˌma-sə-'dō-nē-ə, -nyə\ **1** region S Europe in Balkan Peninsula in NE Greece, the former Yugoslav section of Macedonia, & SW Bulgaria including territory of ancient kingdom of Macedonia (*or* **Mac·e·don** \'ma-sə-dən, -ˌdän\ ✱ Pella) **2** country S *cen* Balkan Peninsula; a federated republic of Yugoslavia 1946–92 ✱ Skopje *area* 9928 *sq mi* (25,714 *sq km*), *pop* 2,016,060

Ma·ceió \ˌma-sä-'ō\ city NE Brazil ✱ of Alagoas *pop* 797,759

Mac·gil·li·cud·dy's Reeks \mə-ˌgi-lə-ˌkə-dēz-'rēks\ mountain range SW Ireland in County Kerry — see CARRANTUOHILL

Ma·chi·da \mä-'chē-dä, 'mä-chē-ˌdä\ city Japan on Honshu *pop* 377,494

Ma·chi·li·pat·nam \ˌmä-chə-lē-'pət-nəm\ *or* **Ban·dar** \'bən-dər\ city & port SE India in E Andhra Pradesh SW of Kakinada *pop* 183,370

Ma·chu Pic·chu \ˌmä-(ˌ)chü-'pē-(ˌ)chü, -'pēk-\ site SE Peru of ancient Inca city on a mountain NW of Cuzco

Macías Nguema Biyogo — see BIOKO

Mac·ken·zie \mə-ˈken-zē\ **1** river 1120 *mi* (1802 *km*) NW Canada in Northwest Territories flowing from Great Slave Lake NW into Beaufort Sea — sometimes considered to include the Finlay, Peace, & Slave rivers (total length 2635 *mi or* 4216 *km*) **2** former district Canada in W Northwest Territories in basin of Mackenzie River; area now split bet. Northwest Territories & the W part of Nunavut

Mackenzie Mountains mountain range NW Canada in the Rockies in Yukon Territory & W Northwest Territories

Mack·i·nac \ˈma-kə-ˌnȯ, -ˌnak\ *or formerly* **Mich·i·li·mack·i·nac** \ˌmi-shə-lē-\ island N Mich. in Straits of Mackinac

Mackinac, Straits of channel N Mich. connecting Lake Huron & Lake Michigan; 4 *mi* (6.4 *km*) wide at narrowest point

Ma·con \ˈmā-kən\ city *cen* Ga. on the Ocmulgee *pop* 91,351

Mâ·con \mä-ˈkō^{n}\ city E *cen* France *pop* 34,472

Mac·quar·ie \mə-ˈkwär-ē\ river 590 *mi* (949 *km*) SE Australia in E *cen* New South Wales flowing NNW to Darling River

Mac·tan \mäk-ˈtän\ island S *cen* Philippines off E coast of Cebu

Mad·a·gas·car \ˌma-də-ˈgas-kər, -kär\ island W Indian Ocean off SE Africa; formerly a French territory; became (1958) a republic of the French Community as the **Mal·a·gasy Republic** \ˌma-lə-ˈga-sē\ *or F* **Ré·pu·blique Mal·gache** \rā-pœ-ˈblēk-mäl-ˈgäsh\; name changed to Madagascar 1975 ✱ Antananarivo *area* 226,657 *sq mi* (589,308 *sq km*), *pop* 19,600,000 — **Mad·a·gas·can** \ˌma-də-ˈgas-kən\ *adj or n*

Ma·dei·ra \mə-ˈdir-ə, -ˈder-ə\ **1** river 2013 *mi* (3239 *km*) W Brazil formed at Bolivian border by confluence of the Mamoré & the Beni & flowing NE to the Amazon **2** islands in N. Atlantic N of the Canaries belonging to Portugal ✱ Funchal *area* 308 *sq mi* (798 *sq km*), *pop* 245,011 **3** island, chief of group *area* 285 *sq mi* (741 *sq km*) — **Ma·dei·ran** \-ˈdir-ən, -ˈder-\ *adj or n*

Ma·de·ra \mə-ˈder-ə\ city S *cen* Calif. NW of Fresno *pop* 61,416

Ma·dhya Bha·rat \ˌmä-dyə-ˈbär-ət\ former state *cen* India; a union of 20 states formed 1948; became part of Madhya Pradesh 1956

Madhya Pra·desh \prə-ˈdesh, -ˈdāsh\ state *cen* India ✱ Bhopal *area* 114,710 *sq mi* (297,099 *sq km*), *pop* 60,385,118 — see CENTRAL PROVINCES AND BERAR, MADHYA BHARAT

Ma·di·nat ash Sha'b \mə-ˈdē-ˌnə-tash-ˈshab\ city S Yemen; formerly a ✱ of People's Democratic Republic of Yemen & (as **Al It·ti·had** \al-ˌi-tə-ˈhad\) ✱ of Federation of South Arabia

Mad·i·son \ˈma-də-sən\ **1** river 180 *mi* (290 *km*) SW Mont. — see THREE FORKS **2** city N Ala. W of Huntsville *pop* 42,938 **3** city S Wis., its ✱ *pop* 233,209

Madison Heights city SE Mich. N of Detroit *pop* 29,694

Ma·dras \mə-ˈdras, -ˈdräs\ **1** — see TAMIL NADU **2** *or* **Chen·nai** \ˈche-ˌnī\ city & port S India ✱ of Tamil Nadu *pop* 4,216,268 — **Ma·drasi** \-ˈdra-sē, -ˈdrä-\ *n*

Ma·dre, La·gu·na \lə-ˌgü-nə-ˈmä-drā\ inlet of Gulf of Mexico S Tex. bet. Padre Is. & mainland

Ma·dre de Dios \ˈmä-drā-(ˌ)dā-dē-ˈōs\ river *ab* 700 *mi* (1126 *km*) rising in SE Peru & flowing E into the Beni in Brazil

Ma·drid \mə-ˈdrid\ **1** province *cen* Spain in NW New Castile *area* 3087 *sq mi* (7995 *sq km*), *pop* 5,423,384 **2** city, its ✱ & ✱ of Spain *pop* 2,938,723 — **Mad·ri·le·nian** \ˌma-drə-ˈlē-nē-ən, -dri-, -nyən\ *adj or n* — **Ma·dri·le·ño** \ˌmä-drə-ˈlā-(ˌ)nyō, -drē-\ *n*

Ma·du·ra *or D* **Ma·doe·ra** \mə-ˈdu̇r-ə\ island Indonesia off coast of NE Java *area* (with adjacent islands) 2113 *sq mi* (5494 *sq km*), *pop* 1,858,183 — **Mad·u·rese** \ˌma-də-ˈrēz, ˌma-jə-, -ˈrēs\ *adj or n*

Ma·du·rai \ˌmä-də-ˈrī\ city S India in S Tamil Nadu *pop* 922,913

Maeander — see MENDERES 1

Ma·fia \ˈmä-fē-ə, ˈma-\ island Tanzania in Indian Ocean S of Zanzibar *area* 170 *sq mi* (442 *sq km*), *pop* 16,748

Maf·i·keng \ˈma-fə-kiŋ\ town N Republic of South Africa in North West province *pop* 6515

Ma·ga·dan \ˌmä-gə-ˈdan, -ˈdän\ city & port E Russia in Asia on N shore of Sea of Okhotsk *pop* 152,000

Ma·ga·dha \ˈmə-gə-də, ˈmä-\ ancient kingdom India including Bihar S of the Ganges

Magallanes — see PUNTA ARENAS

Mag·da·la \ˈmag-də-lə\ city of N ancient Palestine on W shore of Sea of Galilee N of Tiberias

Mag·da·le·na \ˌmag-də-ˈlā-nə, -ˈlē-\ river 956 *mi* (1538 *km*) Colombia flowing N into the Caribbean

Mag·da·len Islands \ˈmag-də-lən\ *or F* **Îles de la Ma·de·leine** \ˌēl-də-lä-mäd-ˈlen, -mä-də-ˈlen\ islands Canada in Que. in Gulf of St. Lawrence bet. Newfoundland & P.E.I. *area* 102 *sq mi* (265 *sq km*)

Mag·de·burg \ˈmäg-də-ˌbu̇rk, ˈmag-də-ˌbərg\ city *cen* Germany on the Elbe ✱ of Saxony-Anhalt *pop* 275,238

Ma·gel·lan, Strait of \mə-ˈje-lən, *chiefly Brit* -ˈge-\ strait 350 *mi* (563 *km*) long at S end of S. America bet. mainland & Tierra del Fuego (Archipelago)

Ma·ger·öy \ˌmä-gə-ˈroi\ island Norway in Arctic Ocean off N coast *area* 111 *sq mi* (288 *sq km*)

Mag·gio·re, Lake \mä-ˈjȯr-ā\ lake 40 *mi* (64 *km*) long N Italy & S Switzerland traversed by Ticino River

Magh·er·a·felt \ˈmär-ə-ˌfelt, ˈma-kə-rə-ˌfelt\ district *cen* Northern Ireland, established 1974 *area* 221 *sq mi* (575 *sq km*), *pop* 35,874

Ma·ghreb *or* **Ma·ghrib** \ˈmä-grəb\ NW Africa &, at time of the Moorish occupation, Spain — now considered to include Morocco, Algeria, Tunisia, & sometimes Libya — **Ma·ghre·bi** *or* **Ma·ghri·bi** \ˈmä-grə-bē\ *adj or n* — **Ma·ghreb·i·an** \mə-ˈgre-bē-ən\ *or* **Ma·ghrib·i·an** \-ˈgri-\ *adj or n*

Mag·na Grae·cia \ˌmag-nə-ˈgrē-shə\ the ancient Greek colonies in S Italian Peninsula including Tarentum, Sybaris, Crotona, Heraclea, & Neapolis

Magnesia — see MANISA

Mag·ni·to·gorsk \mag-ˈnē-tə-ˌgȯrsk\ city W Russia in Asia on Ural River *pop* 441,000

Magyarorszag — see HUNGARY

Ma·ha·jan·ga \ˌmə-hə-ˈjəŋ-gə\ city & port NW Madagascar *pop* 144,023

Mahalla El Kubra, El — see EL MAHALLA EL KUBRA

Ma·ha·na·di \mə-ˈhä-nə-dē\ river *ab* 560 *mi* (900 *km*) E India flowing into Bay of Bengal in Orissa through several mouths

Ma·ha·rash·tra \ˌmä-hə-ˈräsh-trə\ **1** region W *cen* India S of the Narmada; the original home of the Marathas **2** state W India bordering on Arabian Sea, formed 1960 from SE part of former Bombay state ✱ Bombay *area* 118,637 *sq mi* (307,270 *sq km*), *pop* 96,752,247

Ma·hé \mä-ˈhā\ **1** island in Indian Ocean, chief of the Seychelles group *pop* 61,183 **2** *or formerly* **May·ya·li** \mī-ˈyä-lē\ town SW India in N Kerala; a settlement of French India until 1954

Ma·hil·yow *or* **Mo·gi·lev** \mə-gil-ˈyȯf\ city E Belarus on the Dnieper *pop* 363,000

Ma·hón \mə-ˈhōn, mä-ˈōn\ *or* **Port Ma·hon** \mə-ˈhōn\ city & port Spain on Minorca Is. *pop* 23,315

Ma·hone Bay \mə-ˈhōn\ inlet of the Atlantic E Canada in S N.S.

Maid·en·head \ˈmā-d^{ə}n-ˌhed\ town S England in Berkshire on Thames River W of London *pop* 49,038

Maid·stone \ˈmād-stən, -ˌstōn\ town SE England ✱ of Kent on the Medway ESE of London *pop* 133,200

Main \ˈmīn, ˈmān\ river 325 *mi* (523 *km*) S *cen* Germany rising in N Bavaria in the Fichtelgebirge & flowing W into the Rhine

Mai–Ndom·be, Lac \ˌlak-ˌmīn-ˈdȯm-bā\ *or formerly* **Lake Leo·pold II** \ˈlē-ə-ˌpōld\ lake W Democratic Republic of the Congo

Maine \ˈmān\ **1** state NE U.S. ✱ Augusta *area* 33,265 *sq mi* (86,156 *sq km*), *pop* 1,328,361 **2** *or* **Le Maine** \lə-ˈmān, -ˈmen\ region & former province NW France S of Normandy ✱ Le Mans **3** — see MAYENNE — **Main·er** \ˈmā-nər\ *n*

Main·land \ˈmān-ˌland, -lənd\ **1** HONSHU **2** island N Scotland; largest of the Orkneys **3** island N Scotland; largest of the Shetlands

Mainz \ˈmīnts\ *or F* **Ma·yence** \mä-ˈyä^{n}s\ city SW *cen* Germany on the Rhine ✱ of Rhineland-Palatinate *pop* 182,867

Mai·pú \mī-ˈpü\ city *cen* Chile, a SW suburb of Santiago *pop* 468,390

Mait·land \ˈmāt-lənd\ city SE Australia in E New South Wales *pop* 46,909

Ma·jor·ca \mä-ˈjȯr-kə, mə-, -ˈyȯr-\ *or Sp* **Ma·llor·ca** \mä-ˈyȯr-kä\ island Spain; largest of the Balearic Islands; chief city Palma *area* 1405 *sq mi* (3653 *sq km*) — **Ma·jor·can** \-ˈjȯr-kən, -ˈyȯr-\ *adj or n*

Ma·ju·ro \mə-ˈju̇r-(ˌ)ō\ island (atoll) W Pacific in SE Marshall Islands; contains ✱ of the group *pop* 23,700

Ma·ka·lu \ˈmə-kə-ˌlü\ mountain 27,824 *ft* (8481 *m*) in the Himalayas in NE Nepal SE of Mt. Everest; 5th highest in the world

Ma·kas·sar \mə-ˈka-sər\ **1** *or* **Ma·cas·sar** strait Indonesia bet. E Borneo & W Sulawesi **2** — see UJUNG PANDANG — **Ma·kas·sar·ese** \mə-ˌka-sə-ˈrēz, -ˈrēs\ *n*

Ma·kga·di·kga·di Pans \mä-ˌkä-dē-ˈkä-dē\ large salt basin NE Botswana

Ma·khach·ka·la \mə-ˌkäch-kə-ˈlä\ *or formerly* **Pe·trovsk** \pə-ˈtrȯfsk\ city SE Russia in Europe on the Caspian ✱ of Dagestan *pop* 339,000

Ma·ki·yiv·ka *or* **Ma·ke·yev·ka** \mə-ˈkā-yəf-kə\ city E Ukraine in Donets Basin NE of Donetsk *pop* 424,000

Makkah — see MECCA

Mal·a·bar Coast \ˈma-lə-ˌbär\ region SW India on Arabian Sea in Karnataka & Kerala states

Ma·la·bo \mä-ˈlä-(ˌ)bō\ *or formerly* **San·ta Is·a·bel** \ˌsan-tə-ˈi-zə-ˌbel\ city ✱ of Equatorial Guinea on Bioko Is. *pop* 134,400

Malacca — see MELAKA — **Ma·lac·can** \mə-ˈla-kən, -ˈlä-\ *adj*

Ma·lac·ca, Strait of \mə-ˈla-kə, -ˈlä-\ channel 500 *mi* (805 *km*) long bet. S Malay Peninsula & island of Sumatra

Má·la·ga \ˈma-lə-gə, ˈmä-lä-gä\ **1** province S Spain in Andalusia area 2809 *sq mi* (7275 *sq km*), *pop* 1,287,017 **2** city & port, its ✱, NE of Gibraltar *pop* 524,414

Malagasy Republic — see MADAGASCAR

Ma·lai·ta \mə-ˈlā-tə\ island SW Pacific in the SE Solomons NE of Guadalcanal

Ma·lang \mə-ˈläŋ\ city Indonesia in E Java S of Surabaya *pop* 695,618

Mä·lar·en \ˈmā-ˌlär-ən\ lake SE Sweden extending from Baltic Sea 70 *mi* (113 *km*) inland

Ma·la·tya \ˌmä-ˈlä-ˌtyä\ *or anc* **Mel·i·te·ne** \ˌme-lə-ˈtē-nē\ city E Turkey NE of Gaziantep *pop* 281,776

Ma·la·wi \mə-ˈlä-wē\ *or formerly* **Ny·asa·land** \nī-ˈa-sə-ˌland, nē-\ country SE Africa bordering on Lake Malawi; formerly a Brit. protectorate; independent member of the Commonwealth of Nations since 1964; a republic since 1966 ✱ Lilongwe *area* 45,747 *sq mi* (118,485 *sq km*), *pop* 13,100,000 — **Ma·la·wi·an** \-ən\ *adj or n*

Malawi, Lake *or* **Lake Ny·asa** \nī-ˈa-sə, nē-\ lake SE Africa in Great Rift Valley in Malawi, Mozambique, & Tanzania

Ma·laya \mə-ˈlā-ə, mā-\ **1** MALAY PENINSULA **2** BRITISH MALAYA **3** *or* **Federation of Malaya** former country SE Asia; a Brit. dominion 1957–63, since 1963 a territory (now called **Peninsular Malaysia**) of Malaysia ✱ Kuala Lumpur *area* 50,690 *sq mi* (131,794 *sq km*)

Ma·lay Archipelago \mə-ˈlā, ˈmā-(ˌ)lā\ archipelago SE Asia including Sumatra, Java, Borneo, Sulawesi, Moluccas, & Timor — usu. considered to include also the Philippines & sometimes New Guinea

Malay Peninsula peninsula 700 *mi* (1126 *km*) long SE Asia divided bet. Thailand & Malaysia

Malay Sea sea SE Asia surrounding the Malay Archipelago

Ma·lay·sia \mə-ˈlā-zh(ē-)ə, -sh(ē-)ə\ **1** MALAY ARCHIPELAGO **2** country SE Asia, a union of Malaya, Sabah (N. Borneo), Sarawak, & (until 1965) Singapore; a federal constitutional monarchy in the Commonwealth of Nations ✱ Kuala Lumpur *area* 128,727 *sq mi* (333,403 *sq km*), *pop* 27,500,000 — **Ma·lay·sian** \mə-ˈlā-zhən, -shən\ *adj or n*

Mal·den \ˈmȯl-dən\ **1** city E Mass. N of Boston *pop* 59,450 **2** island W Pacific, one of the Line Islands

Mal·dives \ˈmȯl-ˌdēvz, -ˌdīvz *also* ˈmal-, -divz\ islands in Indian Ocean S of the Laccadives; a sultanate under Brit. protection until 1965; now an independent member of the Commonwealth of Nations ✱ Male *area* 115 *sq mi* (299 *sq km*), *pop* 298,968 — **Mal·div·i·an** \mȯl-ˈdi-vē-ən, mal-\ *adj or n*

Ma·le \ˈmä-lē\ island (atoll), chief of the Maldives *pop* 103,693; contains the nation's ✱

Ma·lea, Cape \mä-ˈlē-ä\ cape S Greece at extremity of E peninsula of the Peloponnese

Ma·le·bo, Pool *or* **Malebo Pool** \mä-ˈlā-ˌbō\ *or* **Stanley Pool** expansion of Congo River *ab* 20 *mi* (32 *km*) long 300 *mi* (483 *km*) above its mouth bet. Republic of the Congo & Democratic Republic of the Congo

Mal·e·ku·la *or* **Mal·a·ku·la** \ˌma-lə-ˈkü-lə\ island SW Pacific in Vanuatu *area* 781 *sq mi* (2023 *sq km*), *pop* 19,289

Malgache, République — see MADAGASCAR

Mal·heur Lake \mal-'hûr\ lake SE Oreg. in Harney Basin

Ma·li \'mä-lē, 'ma-\ **1** federation 1959–60 of Senegal & Sudanese Republic **2** or formerly **Sudanese Republic** country W Africa in W Sahara & Sudan regions; a republic; before 1958 constituted **French Sudan** (a territory of France); ✻ Bamako area 478,652 sq mi (1,239,709 sq km), pop 11,995,000 — **Ma·li·an** \-lē-ən\ adj or n

Ma·li·a·kós, Gulf of \mäl-yä-'kòs\ inlet of Aegean Sea on E coast of Greece

Malines — see MECHLIN

Mal·in Head \'ma-lən\ cape Ireland (republic) in County Donegal; northernmost tip of Ireland (island)

Mal·mé·dy \mal-mə-'dē\ commune E Belgium SE of Liège; formerly in Germany, transferred (with Eupen) to Belgium 1919 pop 11,394

Malmö \'mal-,mœ, -(,)mō\ city & port SW Sweden on Øresund opposite Copenhagen, Denmark pop 265,481

Mal·ta \'mòl-tə\ or anc **Mel·i·ta** \'me-lə-tə, mə-'lē-tə\ **1** or **Mal·tese Islands** \mòl-'tēz, -'tēs\ group of islands in the Mediterranean S of Sicily; a republic of the Commonwealth of Nations ✻ Valletta area 122 sq mi (317 sq km), pop 404,000 **2** island, chief of the group area 95 sq mi (247 sq km)

Maluku — see MOLUCCAS

Mal·vern Hills \'mò(l)-vərn\ hills W England SW of Worcester

Malvinas, Islas — see FALKLAND ISLANDS

Mam·be·ra·mo \,mam-bə-'rä-(,)mō\ river 500 mi (805 km) W New Guinea flowing NW into the Pacific

Mam·moth Cave \'ma-məth\ limestone caverns SW cen Kentucky in **Mammoth Cave National Park**

Ma·mo·ré \,mä-mō-'rā\ river 1200 mi (1931 km) Bolivia flowing N to unite with the Beni on Brazilian border forming Madeira River

Man, Isle of \'man\ or anc **Mo·na·pia** \mə-'nā-pē-ə\ or **Mo·na** \'mō-nə\ island British Isles in Irish Sea; a possession of the Brit. Crown; has own legislature & laws ✻ Douglas area 221 sq mi (575 sq km), pop 76,300 — **Manx·man** \'maŋks-mən\ n

Ma·na·do \mä-'nä-(,)dō\ city & port Indonesia on NE Sulawesi Is. on Celebes Sea pop 318,796

Ma·na·gua \mä-'nä-gwä\ city ✻ of Nicaragua on **Lake Managua** (38 mi or 61 km long draining S to Lake Nicaragua) pop 864,201

Ma·na·ma \mə-'na-mə\ city ✻ of Bahrain pop 143,035

Ma·nas·sas \mə-'na-səs\ city NE Va. pop 37,821

Ma·na·tí \,mä-nä-'tē\ city N Puerto Rico pop 44,113

Ma·naus \mə-'naús\ city W Brazil ✻ of Amazonas on Negro River 12 mi (19 km) from its junction with the Amazon pop 1,405,835

Mancha, La — see LA MANCHA

Manche, La — see ENGLISH CHANNEL

Man·ches·ter \'man-,ches-tər, -chəs-tər\ **1** town cen Conn. E of Hartford pop 58,241 **2** city S N.H. on the Merrimack pop 109,565 **3** city NW England ENE of Liverpool pop 406,900 — see GREATER MANCHESTER — **Man·cu·ni·an** \man-'kyü-nē-ən, -nyən\ adj or n applies to sense 3

Man·chu·kuo \,man-'chü-kwō, man-'chü-\ former country (1931–45) E Asia in Manchuria & E Inner Mongolia ✻ Changchun

Man·chu·ria \man-'chùr-ē-ə\ region NE China S of the Amur including Heilongjiang, Jilin, & Liaoning provinces & part of Inner Mongolia — **Man·chu·ri·an** \-ē-ən\ adj or n

Man·da·lay \,man-də-'lā\ city cen Myanmar pop 1,208,100

Man·ga·ia \mäŋ-'gī-ə\ island S. Pacific in SE Cook Islands; completely encircled by reef area 20 sq mi (52 sq km)

Man·ga·lore \'maŋ-gə-,lōr\ city S India in Karnataka on Malabar Coast W of Bangalore pop 398,745

Man·ga·re·va \,mäŋ-gä-'rā-vä, ,mäŋ-ä-\ island S. Pacific, chief of the Gambier Islands area 7 sq mi (18 sq km)

Mang·a·ung \mäŋ-'ā\ municipality cen Republic of South Africa including the city of Bloemfontein

Man·hat·tan \man-'ha-tᵊn, mən-\ **1** city NE cen Kans. on Kansas River pop 52,281 **2** island 13 mi (21 km) long SE N.Y. on New York Bay **3** borough of New York City comprising Manhattan Is., several small adjacent islands, & a small area (Marble Hill) on mainland pop 1,585,873 — **Man·hat·tan·ite** \-,īt\ n

Manhattan Beach city SW Calif. SW of Los Angeles pop 35,135

Ma·ni·hi·ki \,mä-nē-'hē-kē\ island, chief of the Northern Cook Islands; an atoll pop 408

Manihiki Islands — see NORTHERN COOK ISLANDS

Ma·nila \mə-'ni-lə\ city & port ✻ of the Philippines on W coast of Luzon on **Manila Bay** (inlet of S. China Sea) pop 1,587,000

Man·i·pur \,ma-nə-'pûr, -mə-\ **1** river 210 mi (338 km) NE India & W Myanmar flowing into the Chindwin **2** state NE India bet. Assam & Myanmar ✻ Imphal area 8628 sq mi (22,433 sq km), pop 2,388,634

Ma·ni·sa or **Ma·nis·sa** \,mä-nē-'sä\ or anc **Mag·ne·sia** \mag-'nē-shə, -zhə\ city W Turkey NE of Izmir pop 158,928

Man·i·to·ba \,ma-nə-'tō-bə\ province S cen Canada ✻ Winnipeg area 211,468 sq mi (547,703 sq km), pop 1,208,268 — **Man·i·to·ban** \-bən\ adj or n

Manitoba, Lake lake over 120 mi (193 km) long Canada in S Man. area 1817 sq mi (4724 sq km)

Man·i·tou·lin Island \,ma-nə-'tü-lən\ island 80 mi (129 km) long Canada in S Ont. in Lake Huron area 1068 sq mi (2777 sq km)

Man·i·to·woc \'ma-nə-tə-,wäk\ city E Wis. pop 33,736

Ma·ni·za·les \,mä-nə-'zä-ləs, ,mä-nē-'sä-läs\ city W Colombia in Cauca valley pop 327,100

Man·ka·to \man-'kä-(,)tō\ city S Minn. pop 39,309

Man·nar, Gulf of \mə-'när\ inlet of Indian Ocean bet. Sri Lanka & S tip of India S of Palk Strait

Mann·heim \'man-,hīm, 'män-\ city SW Germany at confluence of the Rhine & the Neckar pop 314,685

Mans·field \'manz-,fēld, 'man(t)s-\ **1** city N cen Ohio pop 47,821 **2** city N Texas S of Fort Worth pop 56,368 **3** town N cen England in Nottinghamshire N of Nottingham pop 98,800

Mansfield, Mount mountain 4393 ft (1339 m) N Vt.; highest in Green Mountains & in state

Mansûra, El or **Mansurah, Al** — see EL MANSÛRA

Man·te·ca \man-'tē-kə\ city cen Calif. S of Stockton pop 67,096

Man·tua \'man-chə-wə, 'manch-wə, 'män-tü-ä\ or **Man·to·va** \'män-tō-vä\ commune N Italy in Lombardy WSW of Venice pop 47,969 — **Man·tu·an** \'man-chə-wən, 'manch-wən, 'man-tə-wən\ adj or n

Ma·nua Islands \mä-'nü-ä\ islands SW Pacific in American Samoa E of Tutuila area 22 sq mi (57 sq km)

Ma·nus \'mä-nəs\ island SW Pacific in Admiralty Islands; largest of group area 600 sq mi (1560 sq km)

Man·za·la, Lake \man-'zä-lə\ or anc **Ta·nis** \'tā-nəs\ lagoon N Egypt in Nile Delta W of N entrance of Suez Canal

Man·za·nil·lo \,man-zə-'ni-lō, ,män-sä-'nē-yō\ city & port E Cuba on the Caribbean pop 107,650

Mao·ke Mountains \'maú-kä\ or formerly **Snow Mountains** \'snō\ mountains West Papua, Indonesia — see PUNCAK JAYA

Maple Grove city SE cen Minn. pop 61,567

Maple Heights city NE Ohio SE of Cleveland pop 23,138

Maple Ridge municipality Canada in SW B.C. E of Vancouver pop 76,052

Ma·ple·wood \'mā-pəl-,wùd\ village SE Minn. pop 38,018

Ma·pu·to \mə-'pü-(,)tō, -(,)tü\ or formerly **Lou·ren·ço Mar·ques** \lō-'räⁿ-sü-'mär-kish\ city & port ✻ of Mozambique on Delagoa Bay pop 1,099,102

Ma·quo·ke·ta \mə-'kō-kə-tə\ river 150 mi (241 km) E Iowa flowing SE into Mississippi River

Mar·a·cai·bo \,ma-rə-'kī-(,)bō, ,mär-ä-\ city NW Venezuela on channel bet. Lake Maracaibo & Gulf of Venezuela pop 1,207,513

Maracaibo, Lake S extension of Gulf of Venezuela in NW Venezuela area over 5000 sq mi (12,950 sq km)

Maracanda — see SAMARQAND

Ma·ra·cay \,mär-ä-'kī\ city N Venezuela WSW of Caracas pop 354,428

Marais des Cygnes \,mer-də-'zēn, -'sēn\ river 150 mi (241 km) E Kans. & W Mo. flowing into the Osage

Ma·ra·nhão \,mär-ə-'nyaú⁰\ state NE Brazil bordering on the Atlantic ✻ São Luis area 127,242 sq mi (329,557 sq km), pop 5,651,475

Ma·ra·ñón \,mär-ə-'nyōn\ river N Peru flowing from the Andes NNW & E to join the Ucayali forming the Amazon

Mar·a·thon \'mar-ə-,thän\ **1** plain E Greece in Attica NE of Athens on the Aegean **2** ancient town on the plain

Marble Canyon canyon of Colorado River N Ariz. just above the Grand Canyon — sometimes considered its upper portion

Mar·ble·head \'mär-bəl-,hed, ,mär-bəl-'\ town E Mass. pop 19,808

Mar·burg \'mär-,bûrk, -,bûrg\ city W cen Germany in Hesse N of Frankfurt am Main pop 75,331

Marche \'märsh\ **1** region & former province cen France NW of Auvergne **2** region cen Italy on the Adriatic NW of Abruzzi ✻ Ancona pop 1,469,195

Mar·cus Island \'mär-kəs\ island W Pacific E of the Bonin Islands, belonging to Japan; occupied 1945–68 by U.S. area 1 sq mi (2.6 sq km)

Mar·cy, Mount \'mär-sē\ mountain 5344 ft (1629 m) NE N.Y.; highest in Adirondack Mountains & in state

Mar del Pla·ta \,mär-del-'plä-tä\ city & port E Argentina SSE of Buenos Aires pop 407,024

Mare Island \'mer\ island W Calif. in San Pablo Bay

Ma·rem·ma \mä-'re-mä\ low-lying district W Italy on Tyrrhenian coast in SW Tuscany; formerly swampland

Ma·ren·go \mä-'reŋ-(,)gō\ village NW Italy in SE Piedmont

Mar·e·o·tis \,ma-rē-'ō-təs\ or Ar **Mar·yût** \mər-'yüt\ lake N Egypt in Nile Delta; Alexandria is situated bet. it & the Mediterranean

Ma·reth \'mär-əth, 'ma-rəth\ town SE Tunisia SSE of Gabès

Mar·ga·ri·ta \,mär-gä-'rē-tä\ island N Venezuela in the Caribbean, chief of the **Nue·va Es·par·ta** \'nwä-vä-e-'spär-tä\ group; chief town & port Porlamar 414 sq mi (1072 sq km)

Mar·gate \'mär-,gāt\ **1** city SE Fla. pop 53,284 **2** \-,gāt, -gət\ borough SE England in Kent on coast of Isle of Thanet pop 53,280

Mar·i·ana Islands \,mer-ē-'a-nə\ or formerly **La·drone Islands** \lə-'drōn\ islands W Pacific S of Bonin Islands; comprise commonwealth of Northern Mariana Islands & Guam

Ma·ri·a·nao \,mär-ē-ä-'naú\ city W Cuba, W suburb of Havana pop 133,671

Ma·ri·án·ské Láz·ně \'mär-ē-,än(t)-ske-'läz-ne\ or G **Ma·ri·en·bad** \mə-'rē-ən-,bad, -,bät; 'mer-ē-ən-,\ town W Czech Republic in NW Bohemia NE of Plzeň pop 14,741

Ma·ri·as \mə-'rī-əs, -əz\ river 210 mi (338 km) NW Mont. flowing SE to Missouri River

Marias Pass mountain pass 5215 ft (1590 m) NW Mont. in Lewis Range of the Rocky Mountains at SE corner of Glacier National Park

Ma·ri·bor \'mär-ē-,bòr\ city NE Slovenia pop 153,053

Ma·rie Byrd Land \mə-,rē-'bərd\ region W Antarctica E of Ross Ice Shelf & Ross Sea

Ma·rie Ga·lante \,mä-,rē-gä-'länt\ island E W. Indies in the Leewards; a dependency of Guadeloupe area 60 sq mi (156 sq km), pop 13,463

Ma·rie·hamn \mə-'rē-ə-,hämn\ or **Maa·rian·ha·mi·na** \'mär-yän-,hä-mə-,nä\ seaport SW Finland ✻ of Åland pop 10,067

Ma·ri El or **Ma·riy El** \'mä-rē-'el\ autonomous republic E cen Russia in Europe ✻ Yoshkar-Ola area 8958 sq mi (23,201 sq km), pop 762,000

Mar·i·et·ta \,mer-ē-'e-tə\ city NW Ga. NW of Atlanta pop 56,579

Ma·ri·na \mə-'rē-nə\ city W Calif. on Monterey Bay pop 19,718

Ma·rin·du·que \,ma-rən-'dü-(,)kā, ,mär-ēn-\ island Philippines in Sibuyan Sea S of Luzon; chief town Boac area 355 sq mi (923 sq km), pop 173,715

Mar·i·on \'mer-ē-ən\ **1** city N cen Ind. pop 29,948 **2** city E Iowa NE of Cedar Rapids pop 34,768 **3** city SE cen Ohio pop 36,837

Maritime Alps section of the W Alps SE France & NW Italy extending to the Mediterranean; highest point Punta Argentera 10,817 ft (3297 m)

Maritime Provinces or the **Maritimes** the Canadian provinces of N.B., N.S., & P.E.I. — formerly considered by some to include also Nfld.&Lab. — see ATLANTIC PROVINCES

Maritime Territory or Russ **Pri·mor·skiy Kray** or **Pri·mor·ski Krai** \prē-'mòr-skē-'krī\ territory E Russia in Asia bordering on Sea of Japan ✻ Vladivostok area 64,054 sq mi (165,900 sq km), pop 2,309,000

\ə\ abut \ᵊ\ kitten, F table \ər\ further \a\ ash \ā\ ace \ä\ mop, mar
\aú\ out \ch\ chin \e\ bet \ē\ easy \g\ go \i\ hit \ī\ ice \j\ job
\ŋ\ sing \ō\ go \ò\ law \òi\ boy \th\ thin \th\ the \ü\ loot \ù\ foot
\y\ yet \zh\ vision, beige \k̲, ⁿ, œ, ᵫ, ᵞ\ see Guide to Pronunciation

Ma·ri·tsa \mə-'rēt-sə\ *or Gk* **Év·ros** \'ev-,rós\ *or Turk* **Me·riç** \me-'rēch\ river *ab* 300 *mi* (480 *km*) S Europe flowing from W Rhodope Mountains in S Bulgaria E & S through Thrace into the Aegean

Ma·ri·u·pol \,ma-rē-'ü-,pól, -pəl\ *or 1949–89* **Zhda·nov** \zhə-'dä-nəf\ city E Ukraine *pop* 417,000

Mark·ham \'mär-kəm\ **1** town Canada in SE Ont. NE of Toronto *pop* 301,709 **2** river 200 *mi* (322 *km*) Papua New Guinea flowing S & SE into Solomon Sea

Markham, Mount mountain 14,275 *ft* (4351 *m*) Antarctica W of Ross Ice Shelf

Marl \'märl\ city W Germany in the Ruhr *pop* 91,864

Marl·bor·ough \'märl-,bər-ō, 'mól-\ city E Mass. E of Worcester *pop* 38,499

Mar·ma·ra, Sea of \'mär-mə-rə\ *or anc* **Pro·pon·tis** \prə-'pän-təs\ sea NW Turkey connected with Black Sea by the Bosporus & with Aegean Sea by the Dardanelles *area* 4429 *sq mi* (11,471 *sq km*)

Mar·mo·la·da \,mär-mō-'lä-dä\ mountain 10,965 *ft* (3342 *m*) NE Italy; highest in the Dolomites

Marne \'märn\ river 325 *mi* (523 *km*) NE France flowing W into the Seine

Ma·ro·ni \mä-'rō-nē\ *or D* **Ma·ro·wij·ne** \'mär-ō-,vī-nə\ river 450 *mi* (720 *km*) on border bet. Suriname & French Guiana flowing N into the Atlantic

Maros — see MURES

Mar·que·sas Islands \mär-'kā-zəz, -zəs, -səz, -səs\ *or F* **Îles Mar·quises** \,ēl-mär-'kēz\ islands S. Pacific N of Tuamotu Archipelago in French Polynesia ✳ Taiohae (on Nuku Hiva) *area* 480 *sq mi* (1248 *sq km*), *pop* 7358

Mar·ra·kech *or* **Mar·ra·kesh** \,ma-rə-'kesh, 'ma-rə-, mə-'rä-kish\ *or formerly* **Mo·roc·co** \mə-'rä-(,)kō\ city *cen* Morocco in foothills of the Grand Atlas *pop* 823,154

Mar·sa·la \mär-'sä-lä\ city & port Italy on W coast of Sicily S of Trapani *pop* 80,818

Marsa Matruh — see MATRUH

Mar·seille \mär-'sā\ *or* **Mar·seilles** \mär-'sā, -'sālz\ *or anc* **Mas·sil·ia** \mə-'si-lē-ə\ city & port SE France on Gulf of Lion *pop* 797,491 — **Mar·seil·lais** \,mär-sə-'yä, -'yäz; -sə-'lä, -'läz\ *n*

Mar·shall \'mär-shəl\ city NE Tex. *pop* 23,523

Marshall Islands islands W Pacific ✳ Majuro; part of former Trust Territory of the Pacific Islands; internally self-governing since 1980 *pop* 50,840 — **Mar·shall·ese** \,mär-shə-'lēz, -'lēs\ *adj or n*

Mar·shall·town \'mär-shəl-,taun\ city *cen* Iowa *pop* 27,552

Marsh·field \'märsh-,fēld\ town E Mass. N of Plymouth *pop* 25,132

Mar·ston Moor \'mär-stən\ locality N England in N. Yorkshire W of York

Mar·ta·ban, Gulf of \,mär-tə-'ban, -'bän\ arm of Andaman Sea S Myanmar

Mar·tha's Vineyard \'mär-thəz\ island 20 *mi* (32 *km*) long SE Mass. in the Atlantic off SW coast of Cape Cod WNW of Nantucket — **Vine·yard·er** \'vin-yər-dər\ *n*

Mar·ti·nez \mär-'tē-nəs\ city W Calif. NE of Oakland *pop* 35,824

Mar·ti·nique \,mär-tə-'nēk\ island W. Indies in the Windwards; department of France ✳ Fort-de-France *area* 425 *sq mi* (1101 *sq km*), *pop* 402,000 — **Mar·ti·ni·can** \-'nē-kən\ *adj or n* — **Mar·ti·ni·quais** \-,tē-ni-'kā\ *adj or n*

Marwar — see JODHPUR

Maryborough — see PORTLAOIGHISE

Mary·land \'mer-ə-lənd, *locally also* 'mer-lən(d)\ state E U.S. ✳ Annapolis *area* 10,460 *sq mi* (27,091 *sq km*), *pop* 5,773,552 — **Mary·land·er** \-lən-dər, -,lan-\ *n*

Maryland Heights city E Mo. W of St. Louis *pop* 27,472

Mar·ys·ville \'mer-ēz-,vil\ city NW *cen* Wash. on Puget Sound *pop* 60,020

Maryūt — see MAREOTIS

Mary·ville \'mer-ē-,vil, 'mä-rē-, -vəl\ city E Tenn. *pop* 27,465

Ma·sa·da \mə-'sä-də\ fortress town of ancient Palestine; site in SE Israel W of Dead Sea

Ma·san \'mä-,sän\ *or formerly* **Ma·sam·po** \'mä-,säm-(,)pō\ city & port SE S. Korea on an inlet of Korea Strait W of Pusan *pop* 448,746

Mas·ba·te \mäz-'bä-tē, mäs-\ island *cen* Philippines in the Visayan Islands NE of Panay *area* 1571 *sq mi* (4085 *sq km*)

Mas·ca·rene Islands \,mas-kə-'rēn\ islands W Indian Ocean E of Madagascar including Mauritius, Réunion, and Rodrigues

Mas·couche \ma-'sküsh\ town Canada in S Que. N of Montreal *pop* 42,491

Mas·e·ru \'ma-sə-,rü, -zə-\ city ✳ of Lesotho *pop* 227,880

Mash·had \mə-'shad\ city NE Iran *pop* 2,427,316

Ma·son City \'mä-s°n\ city N Iowa *pop* 28,079

Mason–Dix·on Line \-'dik-sən\ the boundary line from the SW corner of Del. N to Pa. & W to approximately the SW corner of Pa.; often considered the boundary bet. the N & S states

Mas·qat \'məs-,kät\ *or* **Mus·cat** \-,kät, -,kat, -kət\ town & port ✳ of Oman on Gulf of Oman *pop* 24,893

Mas·sa·chu·setts \,ma-sə-'chü-səts, -zəts, -'tü-\ state NE U.S. ✳ Boston *area* 8265 *sq mi* (21,456 *sq km*), *pop* 6,547,629

Massachusetts Bay inlet of the Atlantic E Mass.

Mas·sa·nut·ten Mountain \,ma-sə-'nə-t°n\ ridge N Va. in Blue Ridge Mountains

Mas·sa·wa \mə-'sä-wə, -'saú-ə\ *or* **Mits·'i·wa** \mit-'sē-wə\ city & port Eritrea on an inlet of the Red Sea *pop* 23,100

Mas·sif Cen·tral \ma-'sēf-(,)sen-träl, -(,)sän-\ plateau *cen* France rising sharply just W of the Rhône-Saône valley & sloping N to the Paris basin & W to the basin of Aquitaine

Mas·sil·lon \'ma-sə-,län\ city NE Ohio *pop* 32,149

Mas·sive, Mount \'ma-siv\ mountain 14,421 *ft* (4396 *m*) *cen* Colo. in Sawatch Range N of Mt. Elbert

Ma·su·ria \mə-'zúr-ē-ə, -'sur-\ *or G* **Ma·su·ren** \mə-'zur-ən\ region NE Poland SE of Gulf of Gdansk; formerly in E. Prussia, Germany — **Ma·su·ri·an** \-'zur-ē-ən, -'sur-\ *adj*

Mat·a·be·le·land \,ma-tə-'bē-lē-,land, ,mä-tä-'bä-lä-\ region SW Zimbabwe bet. the Limpopo & the Zambezi; chief town Bulawayo

Ma·ta·di \mä-'tä-dē\ town & port W Democratic Republic of the Congo *pop* 245,900

Mat·a·gor·da Bay \,ma-tə-'gór-də\ inlet of Gulf of Mexico 30 *mi* (48 *km*) long SE Tex.

Ma·ta·mo·ros \,mä-tä-'mór-ōs\ city NE Mexico in Tamaulipas on Rio Grande opposite Brownsville, Tex. *pop* 363,487

Mat·a·nus·ka \,ma-tə-'nüs-kə\ river 90 *mi* (145 *km*) S Alaska flowing SW to head of Cook Inlet

Ma·tan·zas \mə-'tan-zəs, mä-'tän-säs\ city & port W Cuba on Straits of Florida E of Havana *pop* 113,724

Matapan — see TAÍNARON

Ma·thu·ra \'mə-tə-rə\ *or* **Mut·tra** \'mə-trə\ city N India in W Uttar Pradesh NW of Agra *pop* 298,827

Mat·lock \'mat-,läk\ town N England ✳ of Derbyshire *pop* 20,610

Ma·to Gros·so *or formerly* **Mat·to Gros·so** \,mä-tə-'grō-(,)sō, -(,)sü\ **1** state SW Brazil ✳ Cuiabá *area* 352,400 *sq mi* (912,716 *sq km*), *pop* 2,504,353 **2** plateau region in E *cen* Mato Grosso state

Ma·to Gros·so do Sul \-dō-'sül, -dú-\ state SW Brazil ✳ Campo Grande *area* 140,219 *sq mi* (350,548 *sq km*), *pop* 2,078,001

Mato Tepee — see DEVILS TOWER

Ma·truh \mə-'trü\ *or* **Mar·sa Matruh** \'mer-sə\ town NW Egypt

Matsu — see MAZU

Ma·tsu·do \mät-'sü-(,)dō\ city Japan on Honshu, a suburb of Tokyo *pop* 464,841

Ma·tsu·shi·ma \,mät-sü-'shē-mə, mät-'sü-shē-mə\ group of over 200 islets Japan of N Honshu NE of Sendai

Ma·tsu·ya·ma \,mät-sə-'yä-mä\ city Japan in W Shikoku *pop* 473,379

Mat·tag·a·mi \mə-'ta-gə-mē\ river 275 *mi* (442 *km*) Canada in E Ont.

Mat·ta·po·ni \,ma-tə-pə-'nī\ river 125 *mi* (201 *km*) E Va.

Mat·ter·horn \'ma-tər-,hórn, 'mä-\ *or F* **Mont Cer·vin** \mōⁿ-ser-'vaⁿ\ mountain 14,691 *ft* (4478 *m*) in Pennine Alps on border bet. Switzerland & Italy

Ma·tu·rín \,mä-tü-'rēn\ city NE Venezuela *pop* 207,382

Maui \'maú-ē\ island Hawaii NW of Hawaii (island) *area* 728 *sq mi* (1893 *sq km*)

Mau·mee \,mó-'mē\ river 175 *mi* (282 *km*) NE Ind. & NW Ohio flowing NE into Lake Erie at Toledo

Mau·na Kea \,maú-nä-'kä-ä, ,mó-\ extinct volcano 13,796 *ft* (4205 *m*) Hawaii in N *cen* Hawaii (island)

Mauna Loa \-'lō-ə\ volcano 13,680 *ft* (4170 *m*) Hawaii in S *cen* Hawaii (island) in Hawaii Volcanoes National Park

Maures, Monts des \,mōⁿ-dä-'mór\ mountains SE France at W end of the Riviera

Mau·re·ta·nia *or* **Mau·ri·ta·nia** \,mór-ə-'tā-nē-ə, ,mär-, -nyə\ ancient country N Africa W of Numidia in modern Morocco & W Algeria — **Mau·re·ta·ni·an** *or* **Mau·ri·ta·ni·an** \-nē-ən, -nyən\ *adj or n*

Mauritania *or F* **Mau·ri·ta·nie** \mó-rē-tä-'nē\ country NW Africa bordering on the Atlantic N of Senegal River; a republic within the French Community, formerly a territory ✳ Nouakchott *area* 397,955 *sq mi* (1,030,807 *sq km*), *pop* 3,200,000 — **Mau·ri·ta·ni·an** \,mór-ə-'tā-nē-ən, ,mär-, -nyən\ *adj or n*

Mau·ri·ti·us \mó-'ri-sh(ē-)əs\ island in Indian Ocean in *cen* Mascarenes; constitutes with Rodrigues & other dependencies a dominion of the Commonwealth of Nations ✳ Port Louis *area* 720 *sq mi* (1872 *sq km*), *pop* 1,210,196 — **Mau·ri·tian** \-'ri-shən\ *adj or n*

Mawlamyine — see MOULMEIN

May, Cape \'mā\ cape S N.J. at entrance to Delaware Bay

May·a·gua·na \,mä-ə-'gwä-nə\ island in SE Bahamas NNE of Great Inagua Is. *area* 110 *sq mi* (285 *sq km*)

Ma·ya·güez \,mī-ä-'gwez, -'gwes\ city & port W Puerto Rico *pop* 89,080

Ma·ya·pán \,mī-ä-'pän\ ruined city ✳ of the Mayas SE Mexico in Yucatán SSE of Mérida

Mayence — see MAINZ

Ma·yenne \mä-'yen\ river 125 *mi* (201 *km*) NW France uniting with the Sarthe to form the **Maine** \'mān, 'men\ (8 *mi* or 13 *km* long, flowing into the Loire)

May·fair \'mā-,fer\ district of W London, England, in Westminster borough

May·kop \mī-'kóp\ city S Russia in Europe ✳ of Adygeya *pop* 163,000

May·nooth \mā-'nüth\ town E Ireland in County Kildare *pop* 4768

Mayo **1** \'mī-(,)ō\ river 250 *mi* (402 *km*) NW Mexico in Sonora flowing SW into Gulf of California **2** \'mā-(,)ō\ county NW Ireland in Connacht ✳ Castlebar *area* 2084 *sq mi* (5418 *sq km*), *pop* 117,446

Ma·yon \mä-'yōn\ volcano 8077 *ft* (2462 *m*) Philippines in SE Luzon

Ma·yotte \mä-'yät, -'yót\ island of the Comoros; a French dependency *area* 144 *sq mi* (374 *sq km*), *pop* 186,452 — see COMOROS

May·wood \'mā-,wúd\ **1** city SW Calif. SE of downtown Los Angeles *pop* 27,395 **2** village NE Ill. W of Chicago *pop* 24,090

Mayyali — see MAHÉ 2

Mazaca — see KAYSERI

Ma·za·tlán \,mä-zət-'län, -sät-\ city & port W Mexico in Sinaloa on the Pacific *pop* 357,619

Ma·zu *or* **Ma·tsu** \'mät-'sü, 'mat-, -(,)sü\ island off SE China in Taiwan Strait; administered by Taiwan *pop* 11,002

Mba·ba·ne \əm-bä-'bä-nä\ town ✳ of Swaziland *pop* 57,992

Mban·da·ka \əm-bän-'dä-kä\ *or formerly* **Co·quil·hat·ville** \kō-kē-'at-,vil\ city W Democratic Republic of the Congo on Congo River *pop* 263,000

Mbi·ni \əm-'bē-nē\ *or formerly* **Río Mu·ni** \,rē-ō-'mü-nē\ mainland portion of Equatorial Guinea bordering on Gulf of Guinea ✳ Bata *area* 10,040 *sq mi* (26,104 *sq km*) *pop* 749,529

Mbomou — see BOMU

Mbu·ji–Ma·yi \əm-,bü-jē-'mī-,yē\ *or formerly* **Ba·kwan·ga** \bä-'kwäⁿ-gä\ city S Democratic Republic of the Congo *pop* 613,027

Mc·Al·len \mə-'ka-lən\ city S Tex. WNW of Brownsville *pop* 129,877

Mc·Kees·port \mə-'kēz-,pórt\ city SW Pa. S of Pittsburgh *pop* 19,731

Mc·Kin·ley, Mount \mə-'kin-lē\ *or* **De·na·li** \də-'nä-lē\ mountain 20,320 *ft* (6194 *m*) *cen* Alaska in Alaska Range; highest in U.S. & N. America; in **Denali National Park**

Mc·Kin·ney \mə-'ki-nē\ city NE Tex. N of Dallas *pop* 131,117

M'·Clure Strait \mə-'klúr\ channel N Canada bet. Banks Is. & Melville Is. opening on the W into Arctic Ocean

Mc·Minn·ville \mək-'min-,vil, -vəl\ city NW Oreg. NW of Salem *pop* 32,187

Mc·Mur·do Sound \mək-'mər-dō\ inlet of W Ross Sea Antarctica bet. Ross Is. & coast of Victoria Land

Mead, Lake \'mēd\ reservoir NW Ariz. & SE Nev. formed by Hoover Dam in Colorado River

Mearns, The — see KINCARDINE

Meath \'mēth, *by outsiders also* 'mēth\ county E Ireland in NE Leinster ✳ Trim *area* 903 *sq mi* (2348 *sq km*), *pop* 134,005

Meaux \'mō\ commune N France ENE of Paris *pop* 49,348

Mec·ca \'me-kə\ *or Ar* **Mak·kah** \'mä-kə\ city Saudi Arabia ✳ of Hejaz *pop* 1,294,106 — **Mec·can** \-kən\ *adj or n*

Mech·lin \'me-klən\ *or Flem* **Me·che·len** \'mā-kə-lə(n)\ *or F* **Ma·lines** \mä-'lēn\ commune N Belgium *pop* 75,946

Meck·len·burg \'me-klən-ˌbərg, -ˌburk\ region NE Germany SE of Jutland Peninsula & E of the Elbe; in 18th & 19th centuries divided into duchies of **Mecklenburg–Schwe·rin** \-shvä-'rēn\ & **Mecklenburg–Stre·litz** \-'shträ-ləts, -'strä-\, which became grand duchies 1815 & states of Weimar Republic 1919

Mecklenburg–West Pomerania state of Germany bordering on Baltic Sea ✳ Schwerin *area* 9096 *sq mi* (23,559 *sq km*), *pop* 1,924,000

Me·dan \mā-'dän\ city Indonesia in NE Sumatra *pop* 1,730,752

Me·del·lín \ˌme-də-'lēn, ˌmā-thā-'yēn\ city NW Colombia NW of Bogotá *pop* 1,581,400

Med·ford \'med-fərd\ **1** city E Mass. N of Boston *pop* 56,173 **2** city SW Oreg. *pop* 74,907

Me·dia \'mē-dē-ə\ ancient country & province of Persian Empire SW Asia in NW modern Iran — **Me·di·an** \-dē-ən\ *adj or n*

Media Atropatene — see AZERBAIJAN 1

Med·i·cine Bow \ˌme-də-sən-ˌbō\ river 120 *mi* (193 *km*) S Wyo. flowing into N. Platte River

Medicine Bow Mountains mountains N Colo. & S Wyo. in the Rockies; highest **Medicine Bow Peak** (in Wyo.) 12,013 *ft* (3662 *m*)

Medicine Hat city Canada in SE Alta. *pop* 60,005

Me·di·na \mə-'dē-nə\ **1** city N Ohio WNW of Akron 26,678 **2** \mä-'dē-nə\ city W Saudi Arabia *pop* 918,889

Mediolanum — see MILAN

Med·i·ter·ra·nean Sea \ˌme-də-tə-'rā-nē-ən, -nyən\ sea 2300 *mi* (3700 *km*) long bet. Europe & Africa connecting with the Atlantic through Strait of Gibraltar & with Red Sea through Suez Canal

Mé·doc \mā-'däk, -'dȯk\ district SW France N of Bordeaux

Med·way \'med-ˌwā\ river 70 *mi* (113 *km*) SE England in Kent flowing NE into Thames River

Mee·rut \'mā-rət, 'mir-ət\ city N India in NW Uttar Pradesh NE of Delhi *pop* 1,074,229

Meg·a·ra \'me-gə-rə\ city & port Greece on Saronic Gulf W of Athens *pop* 17,294; chief town of ancient **Meg·a·ris** \'me-gə-rəs\ (district bet. Saronic Gulf & Gulf of Corinth) — **Me·gar·i·an** \mə-'ger-ē-ən, me-\ *adj or n*

Me·gha·la·ya \ˌmā-gə-'lā-ə\ state NE India ✳ Shillong *area* 8665 *sq mi* (22,442 *sq km*), *pop* 2,306,069

Megh·na \'meg-nə\ river Bangladesh, the lower course of the Surma

Me·gid·do \mi-'gi-(ˌ)dō\ city of ancient Palestine N of Samaria

Meis·sen \'mī-sᵊn\ city E Germany NW of Dresden *pop* 33,997

Méjico — see MEXICO

Mek·nes \mek-'nes\ city N Morocco WSW of Fez; former ✳ of Morocco *area pop* 229,000

Me·kong \'mā-ˌkȯŋ, -ˈkäŋ; 'mā-ˌ\ river 2600 *mi* (4184 *km*) SE Asia flowing from Qinghai (China) S & SE into S. China Sea in N Vietnam

Me·la·ka *or* **Ma·lac·ca** \mə-'la-kə, -'lä-\ **1** state Malaysia on W coast of Peninsular Malaysia *area* 640 *sq mi* (1648 *sq km*), *pop* 504,502 **2** city, its ✳ *pop* 250,635

Mel·a·ne·sia \ˌme-lə-'nē-zhə, -shə\ the islands in the Pacific NE of Australia & S of Micronesia including Bismarck Archipelago, the Solomons, Vanuatu, New Caledonia, & the Fijis

Mel·bourne \'mel-bərn\ **1** city E Fla. SSW of Cape Canaveral *pop* 76,068 **2** city & port SE Australia ✳ of Victoria on Port Phillip Bay *metropolitan area pop* 2,761,995 — **Mel·bur·ni·an** \mel-'bər-nē-ən\ *n*

Me·lil·la \mə-'lē-yə\ city & port NE Morocco on coast NE of Fez; a Spanish presidio *pop* 66,411

Melita — see MALTA

Melitene — see MALATYA

Me·li·to·pol \ˌme-lə-'tȯ-pəl\ city S Ukraine near Sea of Azov *pop* 177,000

Melos — see MÍLOS

Mel·rose \'mel-ˌrōz\ city E Mass. N of Boston *pop* 26,983

Melrose Park village NE Ill. W of Chicago *pop* 25,411

Mel·ville, Lake \'mel-ˌvil\ lake Canada in Nfld.&Lab. in SE Labrador; the inner basin of Hamilton Inlet *area* 1133 *sq mi* (2946 *sq km*)

Melville Island island N Canada in Parry Islands *area over* 16,250 *sq mi* (42,085 *sq km*)

Melville Peninsula peninsula Canada in Nunavut bet. Foxe Basin & an arm of Gulf of Boothia

Memel — see KLAIPEDA

Mem·phis \'mem(p)-fəs\ **1** city SW Tenn. on Mississippi River *pop* 646,889 **2** ancient city N Egypt on the Nile S of modern Cairo; once ✳ of Egypt — **Mem·phi·an** \-fē-ən\ *adj or n* — **Mem·phite** \'mem-ˌfīt\ *adj or n applies to sense 2*

Mem·phre·ma·gog, Lake \ˌmem(p)-fri-'mā-ˌgäg\ lake 30 *mi* (48 *km*) long on border bet. Canada & the U.S. in Que. & Vt.

Menado — see MANADO

Men·ai Strait \'me-ˌnī\ strait 14 *mi* (22 *km*) long N Wales bet. Anglesey Is. & mainland

Me Nam — see CHAO PHRAYA

Men·den·hall \'men-dən-ˌhȯl\ glacier SE Alaska N of Juneau

Men·de·res \ˌmen-də-'res\ **1** *or anc* **Mae·an·der** \mē-'an-dər\ river 240 *mi* (386 *km*) W Turkey in Asia flowing SW & W into the Aegean **2** *or anc* **Sca·man·der** \skə-'man-dər\ river 60 *mi* (96 *km*) NW Turkey in Asia flowing from Kaz Dagi W & NW across the plain of ancient Troy into the Dardanelles

Men·dip \'men-ˌdip, -dəp\ hills SW England in NE Somerset; highest Blackdown 1068 *ft* (326 *m*)

Men·do·ci·no, Cape \ˌmen-də-'sē-(ˌ)nō\ headland NW Calif. SSW of Eureka; extreme W point of Calif., at 124°8'W

Men·do·ta, Lake \men-'dō-tə\ lake 6 *mi* (9.6 *km*) long S Wis. NW of Madison

Men·do·za \men-'dō-zə, -sä\ city W Argentina *pop* 121,696

Men·lo Park \'men-(ˌ)lō\ city W Calif. SE of San Francisco *pop* 32,026

Me·nom·i·nee \mə-'nä-mə-nē\ river 125 *mi* (201 *km*) NE Wis. flowing SE on Mich.-Wis. border into Green Bay

Menominee Range iron-rich mountain range NE Wis. & NW Mich. in Upper Peninsula

Me·nom·o·nee Falls \mə-'nä-mə-nē\ village SE Wis. *pop* 35,626

Menorca — see MINORCA

Men·ton \män⁻'tō⁻\ *or It* **Men·to·ne** \men-'tō-nā\ city SE France on the Mediterranean ENE of Nice *pop* 28,792

Men·tor \'men-tər\ city NE Ohio NE of Cleveland *pop* 47,159

Men·zel Bour·gui·ba \men-'zel-bür-'gē-bə\ *or formerly* **Fer·ry·ville** \'fer-ē-ˌvil\ city N Tunisia on Lake Bizerte *pop* 42,111

Me·ra·no \mā-'rä-(ˌ)nō\ commune N Italy in Trentino-Alto Adige NW of Bolzano *pop* 34,236

Mer·ced \mər-'sed\ **1** river 150 *mi* (241 *km*) cen Calif. flowing W through Yosemite Valley into the San Joaquin **2** city cen Calif. in San Joaquin valley *pop* 78,958

Mer·cia \'mər-sh(ē-)ə\ ancient Anglian kingdom cen England; one of kingdoms in Anglo-Saxon heptarchy

Mer·gent·heim \'mer-gənt-ˌhīm\ *or* **Bad Mergentheim** \ˌbät-\ town S Germany in Baden-Württemberg NNE of Stuttgart

Meriç — see MARITSA

Mé·ri·da \'mer-ə-də, 'mā-rē-thä\ **1** city SE Mexico ✳ of Yucatán *pop* 557,340 **2** city N Venezuela S of Lake Maracaibo *pop* 167,992

Mer·i·den \'mer-ə-dən\ city S cen Conn. S of Hartford *pop* 60,868

Me·rid·i·an \mə-'ri-dē-ən\ **1** city SW Idaho W of Boise *pop* 75,092 **2** city E cen Miss. *pop* 41,148

Merín — see MIRIM (Lake)

Mer·i·on·eth \ˌmer-ē-'ä-nəth\ *or* **Mer·i·on·eth·shire** \-ˌshir, -shər\ former county NW Wales ✳ Dolgellau

Mer·oë \'mer-ō-(ˌ)ē\ ancient city NE Africa on the Nile; site in N cen Sudan — **Mero·ite** \'mer-ō-ˌīt\ *n* — **Mero·it·ic** \ˌmer-ō-'i-tik\ *adj*

Meroë, Isle of ancient region E Sudan bet. the Nile & Blue Nile rivers & the Atbara

Mer·rill·ville \'mer-əl-ˌvil, -vəl\ town NW Ind. *pop* 35,246

Mer·ri·mack \'mer-ə-ˌmak\ **1** river 110 *mi* (177 *km*) S N.H. & NE Mass. flowing S & NE into the Atlantic **2** town S N.H. *pop* 25,494

Mer·ritt Island \'mer-ət\ island 40 *mi* (64 *km*) long E Fla. W of Canaveral Peninsula bet. Indian River & Banana River

Mer·sey \'mər-zē\ river 70 *mi* (113 *km*) NW England flowing NW & W into Irish Sea through a large estuary

Mer·sey·side \'mər-zē-ˌsīd\ metropolitan county NW England ✳ Liverpool *area* 261 *sq mi* (676 *sq km*), *pop* 1,376,800

Mer·sin \mer-'sēn\ city & port S Turkey on the Mediterranean WSW of Adana *pop* 422,357

Mer·thyr Tyd·fil \ˌmər-thər-'tid-ˌvil\ **1** administrative area of S Wales *area* 43 *sq mi* (111 *sq km*) **2** town S Wales NNW of Cardiff *pop* 59,300

Mer·ton \'mər-tᵊn\ borough of SW Greater London, England *pop* 161,800

Me·ru, Mount \'mā-(ˌ)rü\ mountain 14,979 *ft* (4566 *m*) NE Tanzania

Me·sa \'mā-sə\ city SW cen Ariz. E of Phoenix *pop* 439,041

Me·sa·bi Range \mə-'sä-bē\ range of hills NE Minn. NW of Duluth containing large deposits of iron

Me·sa Verde National Park \'mā-sə-'vərd, -'vər-dē\ reservation SW Colo. containing prehistoric cliff dwellings

Me·se·ta \me-'sä-tə\ the central plateau of Spain

Me·so·amer·i·ca \ˌme-zō-ə-'mer-i-kə, ˌmē-, -sō-\ region of S N. America that was occupied during pre-Columbian times by peoples (as the Olmecs, Mayans, and Aztecs) with shared cultural features — **Me·so·amer·i·can** \-kən\ *adj*

Mes·o·po·ta·mia \ˌme-s(ə-)pə-'tā-mē-ə, -myə\ **1** region SW Asia bet. the Tigris & the Euphrates extending from the mountains of E Asia Minor to the Persian Gulf **2** the entire Tigris-Euphrates valley — **Mes·o·po·ta·mian** \-mē-ən, -myən\ *adj or n*

Mes·quite \mə-'skēt, me-\ city N Tex. E of Dallas *pop* 139,824

Mes·se·ne *or ModGk* **Mes·sí·ni** \me-'sē-nē\ town S Greece in SW Peloponnese; ancient ✳ of Messenia

Mes·se·nia \mə-'sē-nē-ə, -nyə\ region S Greece in SW Peloponnese bordering on Ionian Sea

Messenia, Gulf of inlet of the Mediterranean S Greece on S coast of Peloponnese

Mes·si·na \me-'sē-nä\ *or anc* **Mes·sa·na** \mə-'sä-nə\ *or* **Zan·cle** \'zaŋ-(ˌ)klē\ city & port Italy in NE Sicily *pop* 257,302

Messina, Strait of channel bet. S mainland part of Italy & NE Sicily

Mes·ta \me-'stä\ *or Gk* **Nés·tos** \'nes-ˌtȯs\ river 150 *mi* (240 *km*) SW Bulgaria & NE Greece flowing from W end of Rhodope Mountains SE into the Aegean

Me·ta \'mā-tä\ river over 620 *mi* (995 *km*) NE Colombia flowing into the Orinoco on Venezuela-Colombia boundary

Met·air·ie \'me-tə-rē\ population center SE La. *pop* 138,481

Me·tau·ro \mā-'tau̇-(ˌ)rō\ *or anc* **Me·tau·rus** \-'tȯr-əs\ river 70 *mi* (113 *km*) cen Italy flowing E into the Adriatic

Me·thu·en \mə-'thü-ən, -'thyü-\ city NE Mass. *pop* 47,255

Me·to·hi·ja \me-'tō-hē-yä\ district SW Kosovo

Metz \'mets, F 'mes\ city NE France on the Moselle *pop* 123,704

Meurthe \'mərt, 'mœrt\ river *ab* 100 *mi* (161 *km*) NE France flowing NW from Vosges Mountains to the Moselle

Meuse \'myüz, 'mə(r)z, 'mœz\ *or D* **Maas** \'mäs\ river *ab* 580 *mi* (933 *km*) W Europe flowing from NE France through S Belgium into North Sea in the Netherlands

Mewar — see UDAIPUR

Mex·i·cali \ˌmek-si-'ka-lē, -sē-'kä-\ city NW Mexico ✳ of Baja California (state) on Mexico-Calif. border *pop* 696,034

Mex·i·co \'mek-si-ˌkō\ *or Sp* **Mé·ji·co** \'me-hē-(ˌ)kō\ *or MexSp* **Mé·xi·co** \'me-hē-(ˌ)kō\ **1** country S N. America S of the U.S.; a republic ✳ Mexico *area* 759,530 *sq mi* (1,972,544 *sq km*), *pop* 112,337,000 **2** state

\ə\ abut \ᵊ\ kitten, F table \ər\ further \a\ ash \ā\ ace \ä\ mop, mar \au̇\ out \ch\ chin \e\ bet \ē\ easy \g\ go \i\ hit \ī\ ice \j\ job \ŋ\ sing \ō\ go \ȯ\ law \ȯi\ boy \th\ thin \t̲h\ the \ü\ loot \u̇\ foot \y\ yet \zh\ vision, beige \k, ⁿ, œ, ᵫ, ᵊ\ see Guide to Pronunciation

S *cen* Mexico ✻ Toluca *area* 8286 *sq mi* (21,461 *sq km*), *pop* 9,815,795 **3** *or* **Mexico City** city ✻ of Mexico (republic) in Federal District (area surrounded on three sides by state of Mexico) — see TENOCHTITLÁN
Mexico, Gulf of inlet of the Atlantic on SE coast of N. America
Mé·zenc, Mount \mā-ˈzeŋk\ volcanic mountain 5755 *ft* (1754 *m*) S France; highest in the Cévennes
Mez·zo·gior·no \ˌmet-sō-ˈjȯr-(ˌ)nō, ˌmed-zō-\ the Italian peninsula S of *ab* the latitude of Rome
Mi·ami \mī-ˈa-mē\ city & port SE Fla. on Biscayne Bay *pop* 399,457 — **Mi·ami·an** \-mē-ən\ *n*
Miami Beach city SE Fla. *pop* 87,779
Mich·i·gan \ˈmi-shi-gən\ state N U.S. in Great Lakes region including an upper (NW) & a lower (SE) peninsula ✻ Lansing *area* 58,527 *sq mi* (151,585 *sq km*), *pop* 9,883,640 — **Mich·i·gan·der** \ˌmi-shi-ˈgan-dər\ *n* — **Mich·i·ga·ni·an** \ˌmi-shə-ˈgā-nē-ən, -ˈga-\ *n* — **Mich·i·gan·ite** \ˈmi-shi-gə-ˌnīt\ *n*
Michigan, Lake lake N *cen* U.S.; one of the Great Lakes *area* 22,400 *sq mi* (58,240 *sq km*)
Michigan City city N Ind. on Lake Michigan *pop* 31,479
Michilimackinac — see MACKINAC
Mi·cho·a·cán \ˌmē-chō-ä-ˈkän\ state SW Mexico bordering on the Pacific ✻ Morelia *area* 23,114 *sq mi* (59,865 *sq km*), *pop* 3,548,199
Mi·cro·ne·sia \ˌmī-krə-ˈnē-zhə, -shə\ the islands of the W Pacific E of the Philippines & N of Melanesia including the Caroline, Kiribati, Mariana, & Marshall groups
Micronesia, Federated States of islands W Pacific in the Carolines comprising Kosrae, Pohnpei, Chuuk, & Yap; part of former Trust Territory of the Pacific Islands; internally self-governing since 1986
Mid·del·burg \ˈmi-dᵊl-ˌbərg\ city SW Netherlands ✻ of Zeeland
Middle Congo former French territory W *cen* Africa — see CONGO 3, FRENCH EQUATORIAL AFRICA
Middle East *or* **Mid·east** \ˌmid-ˈēst\ the countries of SW Asia & N Africa — usu. considered to include the countries extending from Libya on the W to Afghanistan on the E — **Middle Eastern** *or* **Mid·east·ern** \ˌmid-ˈē-stərn\ *adj* — **Middle Easterner** *n*
Mid·dles·brough \ˈmi-dᵊlz-brə\ town N England on Tees River *pop* 141,100
Mid·dle·sex \ˈmi-dᵊl-ˌseks\ former county SE England, now absorbed in Greater London
Mid·dle·town \ˈmi-dᵊl-ˌtau̇n\ **1** city *cen* Conn. S of Hartford *pop* 47,648 **2** city SE N.Y. *pop* 28,086 **3** city SW Ohio SW of Dayton *pop* 48,694 **4** town S R.I. N of Newport *pop* 16,150
Mi·di \mē-ˈdē\ the south of France
Mid·i·an \ˈmi-dē-ən\ ancient region NW Arabia E of Gulf of Aqaba
Mid·land \ˈmid-lənd\ **1** city *cen* Mich. NW of Saginaw *pop* 41,863 **2** city W Tex. NE of Odessa *pop* 111,147
Mid·lands \ˈmid-ləndz\ the central counties of England — usu. considered to comprise Bedfordshire, Buckinghamshire, Cambridgeshire, Derbyshire, Leicestershire, Lincolnshire, Northamptonshire, Nottinghamshire, Oxfordshire, Staffordshire, Warwickshire, W. Midlands, & part of the former county of Hereford and Worcester
Mid·lo·thi·an \mid-ˈlō-t͟hē-ən\ administrative area of SE Scotland *area* 137 *sq mi* (356 *sq km*)
Mid·vale \ˈmid-ˌvāl\ city N *cen* Utah S of Salt Lake City *pop* 27,964
Mid·way \ˈmid-ˌwā\ islands (atoll) *cen* Pacific 1300 *mi* (2092 *km*) WNW of Honolulu, Hawaii, belonging to the U.S., in Hawaiian group but not incorporated in state of Hawaii *area* 2 *sq mi* (5.2 *sq km*)
Mid·west \ˌmid-ˈwest\ *or* **Middle West** region N *cen* U.S. including area around Great Lakes & in upper Mississippi River valley from Ohio — sometimes considered to include Ky. on the E to N.Dak., S.Dak., Nebr., & Kans. on the W — **Mid·west·ern** \ˌmid-ˈwes-tərn\ *or* **Middle Western** *adj* — **Mid·west·ern·er** \ˌmid-ˈwes-tə(r)-nər\ *or* **Middle Westerner** *n*
Midwest City city *cen* Okla. E of Oklahoma City *pop* 54,371
Míkonos — see MYKONOS
Mi·lan \mə-ˈlan, -ˈlän\ *or It* **Mi·la·no** \mē-ˈlä-(ˌ)nō\ *or anc* **Me·dio·la·num** \ˌme-dē-ō-ˈlä-nəm\ commune N Italy ✻ of Lombardy *pop* 1,449,403 — **Mil·a·nese** \ˌmi-lə-ˈnēz, -ˈnēs\ *adj or n*
Mi·laz·zo \mē-ˈlät-(ˌ)sō\ *or anc* **My·lae** \ˈmī-(ˌ)lē\ city & port Italy in NE Sicily W of Messina *pop* 32,586
Mi·le·tus \mī-ˈlē-təs, mə-\ ancient city on W coast of Asia Minor in Caria near mouth of Maeander River
Mil·ford \ˈmil-fərd\ **1** town S Conn. on Long Island Sound *pop* 51,271 **2** town E Mass. SE of Worcester *pop* 27,999
Milford Haven town & port SW Wales on Milford Haven (inlet of St. George's Channel) *pop* 13,934
Mi·li·la·ni Town \ˌmē-lē-ˈlä-nē\ town Hawaii on *cen* Oahu *pop* 27,629
Milk \ˈmilk\ river 625 *mi* (1006 *km*) Canada & U.S. in Alta. & Mont. flowing SE into Missouri River
Mille Lacs \mi(l)-ˈlak(s)\ lake 20 *mi* (32 *km*) long E *cen* Minn.
Mill·ville \ˈmil-ˌvil\ city S N.J. *pop* 28,400
Mí·los *or* **Me·los** \ˈmē-ˌlȯs\ island Greece in SW Cyclades *area* 57 *sq mi* (148 *sq km*)
Mil·pi·tas \mil-ˈpē-təs\ city W Calif. N of San Jose *pop* 66,790
Mil·ton \ˈmil-tᵊn\ **1** town E Mass. S of Boston *pop* 27,003 **2** town Canada in SE Ont. SW of Toronto *pop* 84,362
Mil·wau·kee \mil-ˈwȯ-kē\ city & port SE Wis. on Lake Michigan *pop* 594,833 — **Mil·wau·kee·an** \-kē-ən\ *n*
Min \ˈmin\ **1** river 350 *mi* (563 *km*) *cen* China in Sichuan flowing SE into the Chang **2** river 250 *mi* (402 *km*) SE China in Fujian flowing SE into E. China Sea
Mi·nas Basin \ˈmī-nəs\ landlocked bay E Canada in *cen* N.S.; the NE extension of Bay of Fundy; connected with it by **Minas Channel**
Mi·nas Ge·rais \ˌmē-nəs-zhə-ˈrīs\ state E Brazil ✻ Belo Horizonte *area* 226,707 *sq mi* (587,171 *sq km*), *pop* 17,891,494
Minch \ˈminch\ channel NW Scotland comprising **North Minch** & **Little Minch** bet. Outer Hebrides & NW coast of Scotland
Min·cio \ˈmēn-(ˌ)chō, ˈmin-chē-ˌō\ *or anc* **Min·cius** \ˈmin(t)-sh(ē-)əs, -sē-əs\ river 115 *mi* (185 *km*) N Italy issuing from Lake Garda & emptying into the Po
Min·da·nao \ˌmin-də-ˈnä-ˌō, -ˈnau̇\ island S Philippines *area* (including adjacent islands) 38,254 *sq mi* (99,078 *sq km*), *pop* 13,966,000
Mindanao Sea — see BOHOL SEA
Min·do·ro \min-ˈdȯr-(ˌ)ō\ island *cen* Philippines SW of Luzon *area* 3759 *sq mi* (9773 *sq km*), *pop* 473,940
Min·gan Archipelago National Park Reserve \ˈmiŋ-gən\ reservation E Canada in Gulf of St. Lawrence, Que.
Minhow — see FUZHOU
Min·i·coy \ˈmi-ni-ˌkȯi\ island India, southernmost of the Laccadives
Min·i·do·ka Internment National Monument \ˌmi-nə-ˈdō-kə\ historic site S *cen* Idaho
Min·ne·ap·o·lis \ˌmi-nē-ˈa-pə-lis\ city SE Minn. on Mississippi River *pop* 382,578 — **Min·ne·a·pol·i·tan** \-nē-ə-ˈpä-lə-tən\ *n*
Min·ne·so·ta \ˌmi-nə-ˈsō-tə\ **1** river 332 *mi* (534 *km*) S Minn. flowing from Big Stone Lake to Mississippi River **2** state N U.S. ✻ St. Paul *area* 84,068 *sq mi* (218,577 *sq km*), *pop* 5,303,925 — **Min·ne·so·tan** \-ˈsō-tᵊn\ *adj or n*
Min·ne·ton·ka \ˌmi-nə-ˈtäŋ-kə\ city SE Minn. E of **Lake Minnetonka** (12 *mi or* 19 *km* long) *pop* 49,734
Minni — see ARMENIA 1
Mi·nor·ca \mə-ˈnȯr-kə\ *or Sp* **Me·nor·ca** \mā-ˈnȯr-kä\ island Spain in the Balearic Islands ENE of Majorca; chief city Mahón — **Mi·nor·can** \mə-ˈnȯr-kən\ *adj or n*
Mi·not \ˈmī-ˌnät, -nət\ city NW *cen* N.Dak. *pop* 40,888
Minsk \ˈmin(t)sk\ city ✻ of Belarus *pop* 1,800,000
Minya, Al *or* **Minya, El** — see EL MINYA
Minya Konka — see GONGGA SHAN
Mi·que·lon \ˈmi-kə-ˌlän, ˌmē-kə-ˈlōⁿ\ island off S Newfoundland, Canada, belonging to France — see SAINT PIERRE AND MIQUELON
Mi·ra·bel \ˌmē-rä-ˈbel\ city Canada in S Que. *pop* 41,957
Mir·a·mar \ˈmir-ə-ˌmär\ city SE Fla. *pop* 122,041
Mi·rim \mə-ˈrim\ *or Sp* **Me·rín** \mā-ˈrēn\ lake 108 *mi* (174 *km*) long on boundary bet. Brazil & Uruguay near Atlantic coast
Mir·za·pur \ˈmir-zə-ˌpu̇r\ city N India in SE Uttar Pradesh on the Ganges SW of Varanasi *pop* 205,264
Mi·se·num \mī-ˈsē-nəm\ ancient port & naval station S Italy at NW corner of Bay of Naples
Mish·a·wa·ka \ˌmi-shə-ˈwȯ-kə, -ˈwä-\ city N Ind. *pop* 48,252
Miskito Coast — see MOSQUITO COAST
Mis·kolc \ˈmish-ˌkōlts\ city NE Hungary NE of Budapest *pop* 207,300
Mişr — see EGYPT
Mis·sion \ˈmi-shən\ **1** city S Tex. near the Rio Grande *pop* 77,058 **2** municipality Canada in SW B.C. *pop* 36,426
Missionary Ridge mountain SE Tenn. & NW Ga. SE of Chattanooga
Mission Vie·jo \vē-ˈā-(ˌ)hō\ city SW Calif. SE of Santa Ana *pop* 93,305
Mis·sis·sau·ga \ˌmi-sə-ˈsȯ-gə\ city Canada in S Ont. *pop* 713,443
Mis·sis·sip·pi \ˌmi-sə-ˈsi-pē\ **1** river 2340 *mi* (3765 *km*) *cen* U.S. flowing from N *cen* Minn. to Gulf of Mexico — see ITASCA (Lake) **2** river 105 *mi* (169 *km*) Canada in SE Ont. flowing NE & N into Ottawa River **3** state S U.S. ✻ Jackson *area* 47,689 *sq mi* (123,514 *sq km*), *pop* 2,967,297
Mississippi Sound inlet of Gulf of Mexico E of Lake Pontchartrain
Mis·sou·la \mə-ˈzü-lə\ city W Mont. *pop* 66,788
Mis·sou·ri \mə-ˈzu̇r-ē, *by some residents* mə-ˈzu̇r-ə\ **1** river 2466 *mi* (3968 *km*) W U.S. flowing from SW Mont. into Mississippi River in E Mo. — see THREE FORKS **2** state *cen* U.S. ✻ Jefferson City *area* 69,697 *sq mi* (180,515 *sq km*), *pop* 5,988,927 — **Mis·sou·ri·an** \-ˈzu̇r-ē-ən\ *adj or n*
Missouri City city SE Tex. SW of Houston *pop* 67,358
Mis·tas·si·ni \ˌmis-tə-ˈsē-nē\ **1** lake Canada in S *cen* Que. draining W to James Bay *area* 840 *sq mi* (2184 *sq km*) **2** river 185 *mi* (298 *km*) Canada in S Que. flowing S into Lake Saint-Jean
Mis·ti, El \el-ˈmēs-tē, -ˈmis-\ dormant volcano 19,101 *ft* (5822 *m*) S Peru
Mitch·am \ˈmi-chəm\ former municipal borough S England in Surrey, now part of Merton
Mitch·ell, Mount \ˈmi-chəl\ mountain 6684 *ft* (2037 *m*) W N.C. in Black Mountains of the Blue Ridge; highest point in U.S. E of Mississippi River
Mits'iwa — see MASSAWA
Mix·co \ˈmēs-(ˌ)kō\ city S *cen* Guatemala, a suburb of Guatemala City *pop* 384,428
Mi·ya·za·ki \mē-ˌyä-ˈzä-kē, mē-ˈyä-zä-(ˌ)kē\ city & port Japan in Kyushu on SE coast *pop* 305,755
Mi·zo·ram \mi-ˈzȯr-əm\ state NE India ✻ Aizawl *area* 8142 *sq mi* (21,169 *sq km*), *pop* 689,756
Mma·ba·tho \mä-ˈbä-(ˌ)tō\ town N Republic of South Africa near Botswana border; formerly ✻ of Bophuthatswana
Mo·ab \ˈmō-ˌab\ region Jordan E of Dead Sea; in biblical times a kingdom bet. Edom & the country of the Amorites
Mo·bile \mō-ˈbēl, ˈmō-ˌbēl\ **1** river 38 *mi* (61 *km*) long SW Ala. formed by Alabama & Tombigbee rivers & flowing S into **Mobile Bay** (inlet of Gulf of Mexico) **2** city & port SW Ala. *pop* 195,111
Mo·ca \ˈmō-kä\ city NW Puerto Rico *pop* 40,109
Moçambique — see MOZAMBIQUE
Moçâmedes — see NAMIBE
Mo·cha \ˈmō-kə\ *or Ar* **Al Mu·khā** \ˌäl-mu̇-ˈk͟hä\ town & port SW Yemen on the Red Sea *pop* 10,428
Mod·der \ˈmä-dər\ river 180 *mi* (290 *km*) Republic of South Africa in Free State; a tributary of the Vaal
Mo·de·na \ˈmō-də-nə, ˈmȯ-dā-nä\ *or anc* **Mu·ti·na** \ˈmyü-tə-nə\ commune N Italy in Emilia SW of Venice *pop* 176,965 — **Mod·e·nese** \ˌmō-də-ˈnēz, ˌmȯ-, -ˈnēs\ *n*
Mo·des·to \mə-ˈdes-(ˌ)tō\ city *cen* Calif. on the Tuolumne *pop* 201,165
Moe·sia \ˈmē-sh(ē-)ə\ ancient country & Roman province SE Europe in modern Serbia & Bulgaria S of the Danube from the Drina to the Black Sea
Mog·a·di·shu \ˌmä-gə-ˈdi-(ˌ)shü, ˌmō-, -ˈdē-\ *or* **Mog·a·di·scio** \-(ˌ)shō\ city & port ✻ of Somalia on Indian Ocean *pop* 349,245
Mogador — see ESSAOUIRA
Mogilev — see MAHILYOW
Mo·gol·lon Mountains \ˌmə-gə-ˈyōn, ˌmō-\ mountains SW N.Mex.; highest peak Whitewater Baldy 10,895 *ft* (3320 *m*)
Mo·hacs \ˈmō-ˌhach, -ˌhäch\ town S Hungary *pop* 20,700
Mo·hawk \ˈmō-ˌhȯk\ river 148 *mi* (238 *km*) E *cen* N.Y. flowing E into Hudson River
Mo·hen·jo Da·ro \mō-ˈhen-(ˌ)jō-ˈdär-(ˌ)ō\ prehistoric city Pakistan in Indus valley NE of modern Karachi

Mo·ja·ve Desert *or* **Mo·ha·ve Desert** \mə-'hä-vē, mō-\ desert S Calif. SE of S end of the Sierra Nevada

Mo·ji \'mō-(ͺ)jē\ former city Japan in N Kyushu — see KITAKYUSHU

Mok·po \'mäk-(ͺ)pō\ city & port SW S. Korea on Yellow Sea SW of Kwangju *pop* 236,085

Mold \'mōld\ town NE Wales SSW of Liverpool, England

Mol·da·via \mäl-'dā-vē-ə, -vyə\ **1** region Europe in NE Romania & Moldova bet. the Carpathians & Transylvanian Alps on the W & the Dniester on the E **2** — see MOLDOVA — **Mol·da·vian** \-vē-ən, -vyən\ *adj or n*

Mol·do·va \mäl-'dō-və, mȯl-\ country in E Moldavia region; formerly (as **Moldavian Republic** *or* **Moldavia**) a constituent republic of the U.S.S.R.; ✳ Chişinău *area* 13,012 *sq mi* (33,701 *sq km*), *pop* 4,362,000 — **Mol·do·van** \-vən\ *n or adj*

Mo·len·beek \'mō-lən-ͺbäk\ *or* **Molenbeek–Saint–Jean** \-saⁿ-'zhäⁿ\ commune cen Belgium in Brabant W of Brussels *pop* 74,662

Mo·line \mō-'lēn\ city NW Ill. on Mississippi River *pop* 43,483

Mo·li·se \mō-'lē-zā\ region cen Italy bet. the Apennines & the Adriatic S of Abruzzi ✳ Campobasso *pop* 327,177 — see ABRUZZI

Mo·lo·kai \ͺmä-lə-'kī, ͺmō-lō-'kä-ē\ island cen Hawaii *area* 259 *sq mi* (673 *sq km*)

Mo·lo·po \mō-'lō-(ͺ)pō\ river 600 *mi* (966 *km*) S Africa flowing W along border bet. Botswana & Republic of South Africa & thence S into Orange River; now usu. dry

Molotov — see PERM

Mo·luc·cas \mə-'lə-kəz\ *or Indonesian* **Ma·lu·ku** \mə-'lü-(ͺ)kü\ islands Indonesia in Malay Archipelago bet. Sulawesi & New Guinea *area* 32,307 *sq mi* (83,675 *sq km*), *pop* 2,300,000 — see HALMAHERA — **Mo·luc·ca** \mə-'lə-kə\ *or* **Mo·luc·can** \-kən\ *adj*

Mom·ba·sa \mäm-'bä-sə\ **1** island Kenya on coast N of Pemba **2** city & port on Mombasa Is. & adjacent mainland *pop* 900,000

Mona 1 — see ANGLESEY **2** *or* **Monapia** — see MAN (Isle of)

Mo·na·co \'mä-nə-ͺkō *also* mə-'nä-(ͺ)kō\ **1** country S Europe on the Mediterranean coast of France; a principality *area* 480 *acres* (194 *hectares*), *pop* 35,000 **2** commune, its ✳ — **Mo·na·can** \'mä-nə-kən, mə-'nä-kən\ *adj or n* — **Mon·e·gasque** \ͺmä-ni-'gask\ *adj or n*

Mo·nad·nock, Mount \mə-'nad-ͺnäk\ mountain 3165 *ft* (965 *m*) SW N.H.

Mon·a·ghan \'mä-nə-hən, -ͺhan\ **1** county N Ireland (republic) in Ulster *area* 498 *sq mi* (1290 *sq km*), *pop* 52,593 **2** town, its ✳ *pop* 5754

Mo·na Passage \'mō-nə\ strait West Indies bet. Hispaniola & Puerto Rico connecting the Caribbean & the Atlantic

Monastir — see BITOLA

Mön·chen·glad·bach \ͺmœn-kən-'glät-ͺbäk, ͺmœn-kən-'glät-ͺbäk\ *or formerly* **Mün·chen–Glad·bach** \ͺm(y)ün-kən-, ͺmȯen-kən-\ city W Germany W of Düsseldorf *pop* 262,581

Monc·ton \'məŋk-tən\ city Canada in E N.B. *pop* 69,074

Mon·go·lia \män-'gōl-yə, mäŋ-, -'gō-lē-ə\ **1** region E Asia E of Altai Mountains; includes Gobi Desert **2** *or* **Outer Mongolia** country cen Asia comprising major portion of region of Mongolia; a republic ✳ Ulaanbaatar *area* 604,247 *sq mi* (1,565,000 *sq km*), *pop* 2,800,000 **3** INNER MONGOLIA

Mon·he·gan \män-'hē-gən\ island Maine E of Portland

Mon·mouth \'män-məth, 'mən-\ *or* **Mon·mouth·shire** \-ͺshir, -shər\ administrative area of SE Wales, often regarded as part of England *area* 328 *sq mi* (850 *sq km*)

Mo·noc·a·cy \mə-'nä-kə-sē\ river 60 *mi* (96 *km*) S Pa. & N Md. flowing S into the Potomac

Mo·no Lake \'mō-(ͺ)nō\ saline lake 14 *mi* (22 *km*) long E Calif.

Mo·non·ga·he·la \mə-ͺnän-gə-'hē-lə, -ͺnäŋ-gə-, 'hā-lə\ river 128 *mi* (206 *km*) N W.Va. & SW Pa. flowing N to unite with Allegheny River at Pittsburgh forming Ohio River

Mon·roe \mən-'rō\ **1** city N La. *pop* 48,815 **2** city N.C. SE of Charlotte *pop* 32,797

Mon·roe·ville \(ͺ)mən-'rō-ͺvil\ municipality SW Pa. E of Pittsburgh *pop* 28,386

Mon·ro·via \(ͺ)mən-'rō-vē-ə\ **1** city SW Calif. E of Pasadena *pop* 36,590 **2** city & port ✳ of Liberia on the Atlantic *pop* 243,243

Mons \'mōⁿs\ *or Flem* **Ber·gen** \'ber-kə(n)\ commune SW Belgium ✳ of Hainaut *pop* 90,955

Mon·ta·na \män-'ta-nə\ state NW U.S. ✳ Helena *area* 147,138 *sq mi* (381,087 *sq km*), *pop* 989,415 — **Mon·tan·an** \-nən\ *adj or n*

Mont·au·ban \män-tō-'bän, mōⁿ-tō-'bäⁿ\ city SW France on the Tarn N of Toulouse *pop* 51,889

Mon·tauk Point \'män-ͺtȯk\ headland SE N.Y. at E tip of Long Is.

Mont Blanc \mōⁿ-'bläⁿ\ mountain peak 15,771 *ft* (4807 *m*) on border of France, Italy, and Switzerland in Savoy Alps; highest of the Alps

Mont Blanc Tunnel tunnel 7½ *mi* (12 *km*) long France & Italy under Mont Blanc

Mont·clair \mänt-'kler\ city SW Calif. E of Los Angeles *pop* 36,664

Mon·te Al·bán \ͺmän-tē-äl-'bän, ͺmōn-tä-äl-'vän\ ruined city of the Zapotecs S Mexico in Oaxaca (state) SW of Oaxaca

Mon·te·bel·lo \ͺmän-tə-'be-(ͺ)lō\ city SW Calif. *pop* 62,500

Mon·te Car·lo \ͺmän-tē-'kär-(ͺ)lō, ͺmȯn-tä-\ commune Monaco *pop* 15,507

Mon·te·go Bay \män-ͺtē-(ͺ)gō\ city & port NW Jamaica on Montego Bay (inlet of the Caribbean) *pop* 83,446

Mon·te·ne·gro \ͺmän-tə-'nē-(ͺ)grō, -'nā-, -'ne-\ country S Europe on Balkan Peninsula; a constituent republic of Serbia and Montenegro 1992–2006 and of Yugoslavia 1946–92; earlier a kingdom (✳ Cetinje) ✳ Podgorica *area* 5333 *sq mi* (13,812 *sq km*), *pop* 620,145 — **Mon·te·ne·grin** \-grən\ *adj or n*

Mon·te·rey \ͺmän-tə-'rā\ city W Calif. on peninsula at S end of **Monterey Bay** (inlet of the Pacific) *pop* 27,810

Monterey Park city SW Calif. E of Los Angeles *pop* 60,269

Mon·ter·rey \ͺmän-tə-'rā\ city NE Mexico ✳ of Nuevo León *pop* 1,064,197

Mon·te·vi·deo \ͺmän-tə-və-'dā-(ͺ)ō, -'vid-ē-ͺō; ͺmȯn-tä-\ city & port of Uruguay on N shore of Río de la Plata *pop* 1,260,753

Mon·te·zu·ma Castle National Monument \ͺmän-tə-'zü-mə\ reservation cen Ariz. containing prehistoric cliff dwellings

Mont·gom·ery \(ͺ)mən(t)-'gə-mə-rē, män(t)-, -'gä-; -'gəm-rē, -'gäm-\ **1** city ✳ of Ala. on Alabama River *pop* 205,764 **2** *or* **Mont·gom·ery·shire** \-ͺshir, -shər\ former county E Wales ✳ Welshpool

Mont·mar·tre \mōⁿ-'märtrᵊ\ section of Paris, France, on a hill in N cen part of the city

Mont·mo·ren·cy \ͺmänt-mə-'ren(t)-sē, mōⁿ-mȯ-rä-ⁿ-'sē\ commune N France, N suburb of Paris *pop* 20,576

Mont·mo·ren·cy Falls \ͺmänt-mə-'ren(t)-sē\ waterfall *over* 270 *ft* (82 *m*) Canada in S Que. NE of Quebec (city) in **Montmorency River** (60 *mi or* 96 *km* flowing S into St. Lawrence River)

Mont·par·nasse \ͺmōⁿ-(ͺ)pär-'näs, -'nas\ section of Paris, France, in S cen part of the city — **Mont·par·nas·sian** \-'na-shən, -'na-sē-ən\ *adj*

Mont·pe·lier \mänt-'pēl-yər, -'pil-\ city N cen Vt., its ✳ *pop* 7855

Mont·pel·lier \mōⁿ-pel-'yā\ city S France WNW of Marseille *pop* 225,511

Mon·tre·al \ͺmän-trē-'ȯl, ͺmən-\ *or* **Mont·ré·al** \ͺmōⁿ-rā-'äl\ city & port Canada in S Que. on **Montreal Island** (32 *mi or* 51 *km* long, in St. Lawrence River) *pop* 1,649,519 — **Mon·tre·al·er** \ͺmän-trē-'ȯ-lər, ͺmən-\ *n*

Montreal North *or* **Montréal–Nord** \-'nȯr\ former town Canada in S Que. on Montreal Is., now part of Montreal (city)

Mon·treuil \mōⁿ-'trœ-ē\ *or* **Montreuil–sous–Bois** \-ͺsü-'bwä\ commune N France, E suburb of Paris *pop* 90,735

Mont–Roy·al \ͺmōⁿ-rwä-'yäl\ *or* **Mount Roy·al** \maȯnt-'rȯi(-ə)l\ height 769 *ft* (234 *m*) in Montreal, Que.

Mont–Saint–Mi·chel \ͺmōⁿ-saⁿ-mē-'shel\ small island NW France in Gulf of St.-Malo

Mont·ser·rat \ͺmän(t)-sə-'rat\ island Brit. West Indies in the Leewards SW of Antigua ✳ Plymouth *area* 40 *sq mi* (104 *sq km*), *pop* 4482 — **Mont·ser·ra·tian** \ͺmän(t)-sə-'rä-shən\ *n*

Monument Valley region NE Ariz. & SE Utah containing red sandstone buttes, mesas, & arches

Mon·za \'mōnt-sä, 'män-zə\ commune N Italy in Lombardy SE of Milan *pop* 120,900

Moore \'mȯr\ city cen Okla. S of Oklahoma City *pop* 55,081

Mo·oréa \ͺmō-ō-'rā-ə, mō-'rā-\ island S. Pacific in Society Islands NW of Tahiti *area over* 50 *sq mi* (130 *sq km*)

Moor·head \'mȯr-ͺhed, 'mur-\ city W Minn. on Red River opposite Fargo, N.Dak. *pop* 38,065

Moor·park \'mȯr-ͺpärk\ city SW Calif. W of Los Angeles *pop* 34,421

Moose \'müs\ river 50 *mi* (80 *km*) Canada in NE Ont. flowing NE into James Bay; estuary of Abitibi, Mattagami, & other rivers

Moose·head Lake \'müs-ͺhed\ lake 35 *mi* (56 *km*) long NW cen Maine

Moose Jaw city Canada in S Sask. W of Regina *pop* 33,274

Mo·rad·a·bad \mə-'rä-də-ͺbäd, -'ra-də-ͺbad\ city N India in NW Uttar Pradesh ENE of Delhi *pop* 641,240

Mo·ra·tu·wa \mə-'rə-tə-wə, 'mȯr-ə-ͺtü-wä\ city W Sri Lanka on Indian Ocean S of Colombo *pop* 170,000

Mo·ra·va \'mȯr-ä-vä\ **1** river *ab* 220 *mi* (354 *km*) cen Europe flowing S from E Czech Republic & forming part of the borders bet. the Czech Republic & Slovakia and Austria & Slovakia before entering the Danube **2** river 134 *mi* (216 *km*) Serbia flowing N into the Danube

Mo·ra·via \mə-'rā-vē-ə\ *or* **Mo·ra·va** \'mȯr-ä-vä\ region E Czech Republic S of Silesia traversed by Morava River; once an independent kingdom, later under shifting jurisdictions; chief city Brno

Mo·ra·vi·an Gate \mə-'rä-vē-ən\ mountain pass cen Europe bet. Sudety & Carpathian mountains

Moravska Ostrava — see OSTRAVA

Mor·ay \'mər-ē\ **1** administrative area of NE Scotland bordering on North Sea *area* 864 *sq mi* (2238 *sq km*) **2** *or* **Mor·ay·shire** \-ͺshir, -shər\ *or* **Elgin** \'el-gən\ *or* **El·gin·shire** \-ͺshir, -shər\ former county NE Scotland bordering on North Sea ✳ Elgin

Moray Firth inlet of North Sea N Scotland

Mord·vin·ia \mȯrd-'vi-nē-ə\ *or* **Mor·do·via** \(ͺ)mȯr-'dō-vē-ə\ *or* **Mordo·vi·an Republic** \-vē-ən\ autonomous republic cen Russia in Europe S & W of the middle Volga ✳ Saransk *area* 10,116 *sq mi* (26,200 *sq km*), *pop* 964,000 — **Mordvinian** *n*

Mo·reau \'mȯr-(ͺ)ō\ river 290 *mi* (467 *km*) NW S.Dak. flowing E into Missouri River

More·cambe and Hey·sham \'mȯr-kəm-ənd-'hē-shəm\ town NW England in N Lancashire on **Morecambe Bay** (inlet of Irish Sea) *pop* 41,187

Mo·re·lia \mə-'rāl-yə, mō-'räl-yä\ city SW Mexico ✳ of Michoacán *pop* 489,756

Mo·re·los \mə-'rā-ləs, mō-'rä-lōs\ state S cen Mexico ✳ Cuernavaca *area* 1908 *sq mi* (4942 *sq km*), *pop* 1,195,059

Mo·re·no Valley \mə-'rē-(ͺ)nō\ city S Calif. E of Riverside *pop* 193,365

More·ton Bay \'mȯr-tᵊn\ inlet of the Pacific Australia in SE Queensland at mouth of Brisbane River

Mor·gan Hill \'mȯr-gən\ city W Calif. SE of San Jose *pop* 37,882

Mor·gan·town \'mȯr-gən-ͺtaȯn\ city N W.Va. *pop* 29,660

Mo·ri·ah \mə-'rī-ə\ hill in E part of Jerusalem

Mo·roc·co \mə-'rä-(ͺ)kō\ **1** country NW Africa bordering on the Atlantic & the Mediterranean; a kingdom ✳ Rabat, summer ✳ Tangier *area* 172,413 *sq mi* (446,550 *sq km*), *pop* 29,631,000; formerly (1911–56) divided into **French Morocco** (protectorate ✳ Rabat), **Spanish Morocco** (protectorate ✳ Tetuán), & the **International Zone** of Tangier **2** — see MARRAKECH — **Mo·roc·can** \-kən\ *adj or n*

Mo·ro Gulf \'mȯr-(ͺ)ō\ arm of Celebes Sea S Philippines off SW coast of Mindanao

Mo·ro·ni \mȯ-'rō-nē\ city ✳ of Comoros *pop* 41,500

Mo·ro·vis \mō-'rō-vēs\ city cen Puerto Rico *pop* 32,610

Mor·ris Jes·up, Cape \'mȯr-əs-'je-səp, 'mär-\ headland N Greenland in Peary Land on Arctic Ocean; world's northernmost dry land

Morrison, Mount — see YÜ SHAN

Morrison Cave — see LEWIS AND CLARK CAVERN

Mor·ris·town \'mȯr-əs-ͺtaȯn, 'mär-\ city E Tenn. ENE of Knoxville *pop* 29,137

Mos·cow \'mäs-(ͺ)kō, -ͺkaȯ\ *or Russ* **Mos·kva** \mäsk-'vä\ **1** river 315 *mi* (507 *km*) W cen Russia in Europe flowing E into Oka River **2** city

* of Russia & formerly of U.S.S.R. & of Soviet Russia on Moscow River *pop* 8,769,000 — see MUSCOVY
Mo·selle \mō-ˈzel\ *or G* **Mo·sel** \ˈmō-zəl\ river *ab* 340 *mi* (545 *km*) E France & W Germany flowing from Vosges Mountains into the Rhine at Koblenz
Mosquito Coast *or* **Mi·ski·to Coast** \mis-ˈkē-(ˌ)tō\ *or* **La Mo·squi·tia** \lä-ˌmō-skē-ˈtē-ä\ region Central America bordering on the Caribbean in E Honduras & E Nicaragua
Mos·sel Bay \ˈmō-səl\ city & port S Republic of South Africa in S Western Cape on Mossel Bay (inlet of Indian Ocean) *pop* 17,574
Mos·tag·a·nem \mə-ˈsta-gə-ˌnem\ city & port NW Algeria *pop* 114,534
Mós·to·les \ˈmōs-tō-ˌlās\ commune *cen* Spain, SW of Madrid *pop* 196,524
Mo·sul \mō-ˈsül, ˈmō-səl\ city N Iraq on the Tigris *pop* 264,146
Moul·mein \mül-ˈmān, mōl-, -ˈmīn\ *or* **Maw·la·myine** \ˌmō-lə-ˈmyīn\ city S Myanmar on Gulf of Martaban at mouth of the Salween *pop* 171,977
Mountain View city W Calif. NW of San Jose *pop* 74,066
Mount De·sert Island \də-ˈzərt, ˈde-zərt\ island S Maine in the Atlantic *area* 100 *sq mi* (260 *sq km*) — see ACADIA NATIONAL PARK
Mount Pleasant 1 city *cen* Mich. NW of Saginaw *pop* 26,016 2 town SE S.C. on the coast *pop* 67,843 3 village SE Wis. *pop* 26,197
Mount Pros·pect \ˈprä-ˌspekt\ village NE Ill. *pop* 54,167
Mount Rainier National Park — see RAINIER (Mount)
Mount Rev·el·stoke National Park \ˈre-vəl-ˌstōk\ area of varied landscapes in Canada in SE B.C. including Mt. Revelstoke
Mount Royal — see MONT-ROYAL
Mount Ver·non \ˈvər-nən\ 1 city SE N.Y. N of the Bronx *pop* 67,292 2 city NW Wash. *pop* 31,743
Mourne Mountains \ˈmōrn\ mountains SE Northern Ireland
Moyle \ˈmȯi(-ə)l\ district N Northern Ireland, established 1974 *area* 191 *sq mi* (497 *sq km*), *pop* 14,617
Mo·zam·bique \ˌmō-zəm-ˈbēk\ *or Pg* **Mo·çam·bi·que** \ˌmü-säm-ˈbē-kə\ 1 channel 950 *mi* (1529 *km*) long SE Africa bet. Madagascar & Mozambique 2 *or formerly* **Portuguese East Africa** country SE Africa bordering on Mozambique Channel; a republic, until 1975 a dependency of Portugal * Maputo *area* 297,846 *sq mi* (771,421 *sq km*), *pop* 20,530,714 — **Mo·zam·bi·can** \ˌmō-zəm-ˈbē-kən\ *adj or n*
Mpu·ma·lan·ga \əm-ˌpü-mä-ˈläŋ-gä\ *or formerly* **Eastern Transvaal** province NE Republic of South Africa *area* 30,259 *sq mi* (78,370 *sq km*), *pop* 2,911,000
Mtwa·ra \əm-ˈtwär-ä\ city & port Tanzania in SE mainland
Mu·dan·jiang *or* **Mu–tan–chiang** *or* **Mu·tan·kiang** \ˈmü-ˈdän-ˈjyäŋ\ city NE China in S Heilongjiang on the **Mudan River** (310 *mi or* 496 *km* flowing NE into Songhua River) *pop* 571,705
Mu·gu, Point \mə-ˈgü\ cape SW Calif. W of Los Angeles
Muir Woods National Monument \ˈmyu̇r\ redwood grove N Calif. NW of San Francisco
Mui·zen·berg \ˈmī-zᵊn-ˌbərg\ town Republic of South Africa on False Bay, SSE suburb of Cape Town
Mukalla — see AL MUKALLA
Mukden — see SHENYANG
Mukhā, Al — see MOCHA
Mül·heim \ˈmül-ˌhīm, ˈmyül-, ˈmuel-\ *or* **Mülheim an der Ruhr** \än-də(r)-ˈru̇r\ city W Germany on Ruhr River *pop* 177,042
Mul·house \mə-ˈlüz\ commune NE France in Alsace *pop* 110,141
Mull \ˈməl\ island W Scotland in the Inner Hebrides *area* 351 *sq mi* (913 *sq km*), *pop* 1499
Mul·lin·gar \ˌmə-lən-ˈgär\ town N *cen* Ireland * of Westmeath *pop* 8077
Mul·tan \mu̇l-ˈtän\ city NE Pakistan SW of Lahore *pop* 1,197,384
Mult·no·mah Falls \ˌməlt-ˈnō-mə\ waterfall 620 *ft* (189 *m*) NW Oreg. E of Portland in a tributary of Columbia River
Mumbai — see BOMBAY 2
München–Gladbach — see MÖNCHENGLADBACH
Mun·cie \ˈmən(t)-sē\ city E *cen* Ind. *pop* 70,085
Mun·de·lein \ˈmən-də-ˌlīn\ village NE Ill. NW of Chicago *pop* 31,064
Mu·nich \ˈmyü-nik\ *or G* **Mün·chen** \ˈmuen-kən\ city S Germany * of Bavaria on the Isar *pop* 1,229,052
Mun·ster \ˈmən(t)-stər\ province S Ireland *area* 9316 *sq mi* (24,168 *sq km*), *pop* 1,100,614
Mün·ster \ˈmən(t)-stər, ˈmu̇n(t)-, ˈmuen-\ city W Germany; formerly * of Westphalia *pop* 264,181
Mun·te·nia \ˌmən-ˈtē-nē-ə, mün-ˈte-nē-ə\ *or* **Greater Walachia** region SE Romania in E part of Walachia
Mur \ˈmu̇r\ *or* **Mu·ra** \ˈmu̇r-ə\ river 279 *mi* (449 *km*) Austria, NE Slovenia, & N tip of Croatia flowing into the Drava
Mu·rat \mü-ˈrät\ *or anc* **Ar·sa·ni·as** \är-ˈsā-nē-əs\ river 380 *mi* (612 *km*) E Turkey flowing WSW into the Euphrates
Mur·chi·son \ˈmər-chə-sən\ river 440 *mi* (708 *km*) Australia in W Western Australia flowing W into Indian Ocean
Murchison Falls *or* **Ka·ba·le·ga Falls** \kä-bä-ˈlē-gä, -ˈlā-\ *or* **Ka·ba·re·ga Falls** \-ˈrā-\ waterfall 130 *ft* (40 *m*) W Uganda in the Victoria Nile
Mur·cia \ˈmər-sh(ē-)ə\ 1 region & ancient kingdom SE Spain bordering on the Mediterranean 2 province SE Spain bordering on the Mediterranean *area* 4369 *sq mi* (11,316 *sq km*), *pop* 1,197,646 3 commune, its * & * of ancient kingdom of Murcia *pop* 370,745
Mu·res \ˈmü-ˌresh\ *or Hung* **Ma·ros** \ˈmȯr-ˌōsh\ river 450 *mi* (725 *km*) *cen* Romania & E Hungary flowing W into the Tisza
Mur·frees·boro \ˈmər-f(r)ēz-ˌbər-ō\ city *cen* Tenn. *pop* 108,755
Mur·mansk \mu̇r-ˈman(t)sk, -ˈmän(t)sk\ city & port NW Russia in Europe on an inlet of Barents Sea *pop* 468,000
Mur·ray \ˈmər-ē, ˈmə-rē\ 1 city N Utah S of Salt Lake City *pop* 46,746 2 river *over* 1560 *mi* (2510 *km*) SE Australia flowing from near Mt. Kosciusko in E Victoria W into Indian Ocean in SE S. Australia
Mur·ri·eta \ˌmər-ē-ˈe-tə\ city S Calif. *pop* 103,466
Mur·rum·bidg·ee \ˌmər-əm-ˈbi-jē, ˌmə-rəm-\ river *almost* 1000 *mi* (1610 *km*) SE Australia in New South Wales flowing W into Murray River
Murviedro — see SAGUNTO
Mu·sa, Ge·bel \ˈje-bəl-ˈmü-sə\ mountain group NE Egypt in S Sinai Peninsula — see HOREB (Mount), KATHERINA (Gebel)
Mu·sa, Je·bel \ˈje-bəl-ˈmü-sə\ *or anc* **Ab·i·la** *or* **Ab·y·la** \ˈa-bə-lə\ mountain 2775 *ft* (846 *m*) N Morocco opposite Rock of Gibraltar — see PILLARS OF HERCULES
Muscat — see MASQAT
Muscat and Oman — see OMAN
Mus·ca·tine \ˌməs-kə-ˈtēn\ city E Iowa on the Mississippi *pop* 22,886
Mus·co·vy \ˈməs-kə-vē\ 1 the principality of Moscow (founded 1295) which in 15th century came to dominate Russia 2 — see RUSSIA 1
Mus·ke·gon \mə-ˈskē-gən\ 1 river 200 *mi* (322 *km*) W *cen* Mich. flowing SW into Lake Michigan 2 city & port SW Mich. *pop* 38,401
Mus·kin·gum \mə-ˈskiŋ-əm, -gəm\ river 120 *mi* (193 *km*) E Ohio flowing SSE into Ohio River
Mus·ko·gee \(ˌ)mə-ˈskō-gē\ city E Okla. *pop* 39,223
Mus·ko·ka, Lake \mə-ˈskō-kə\ lake Canada in SE Ont. E of Georgian Bay & N of Lake Simcoe *area* 54 *sq mi* (140 *sq km*)
Mus·sel·shell \ˈmə-səl-ˌshel\ river 300 *mi* (483 *km*) *cen* Mont. flowing E & N into Missouri River
Mutina — see MODENA
Mu·tsu Bay \ˈmüt-(ˌ)sü\ inlet N Japan in NE Honshu on Tsugaru Strait
Muttra — see MATHURA
Muz·tag \müs-ˈtäg, məz-\ *or* **Mu–tzu–t'a–ko** \ˈmü-ˈdzü-ˈtä-ˈkō\ mountain 25,340 *ft* (7724 *m*) W China in S Xinjiang Uygur; highest in Kunlun Mountains
Mwe·ru \ˈmwā-rü\ lake 76 *mi* (122 *km*) long on border bet. Democratic Republic of the Congo & Zambia SW of Lake Tanganyika
Myan·mar \ˈmyän-ˌmär\ *or unofficially* **Bur·ma** \ˈbər-mə\ country SE Asia on Bay of Bengal; administrative * Naypyidaw, historic * Yangon *area* 261,789 *sq mi* (680,651 *sq km*), *pop* 52,200,000
Myc·a·le \ˈmi-kə-(ˌ)lē\ promontory W Turkey opposite Samos Is.
My·ce·nae \mī-ˈsē-(ˌ)nē\ ancient city S Greece in NE Peloponnese
My·ko·la·yiv \ˌmē-kə-ˈlä-yif\ *or* **Ni·ko·la·yev** \ˌnē-\ city & port S Ukraine *pop* 514,136
Myk·o·nos \ˈmi-kə-ˌnōs\ *or ModGk* **Mí·ko·nos** \ˈmē-kō-ˌnȯs\ island Greece in the Aegean in NE Cyclades *area* 35 *sq mi* (91 *sq km*)
Mylae — see MILAZZO
My·men·singh \ˌmī-mən-ˈsiŋ\ city N Bangladesh *pop* 198,662
My·ra \ˈmī-rə\ ancient city S Asia Minor on coast of Lycia
Myr·tle Beach \ˈmər-tᵊl\ city E S.C. on the Atlantic *pop* 27,109
My·sia \ˈmi-sh(ē-)ə\ ancient country NW Asia Minor bordering on the Propontis — **My·sian** \-sh(ē-)ən\ *adj or n*
My·sore \mī-ˈsȯr\ 1 — see KARNATAKA 2 city S India in S Karnataka *pop* 742,261
Mys·tic \ˈmis-tik\ river E Mass. flowing SE into Boston harbor
Mytilene — see LESBOS
Naas \ˈnās\ town E Ireland in Leinster * of Kildare *pop* 11,140
Nab·a·taea *or* **Nab·a·tea** \ˌna-bə-ˈtē-ə\ ancient Arab kingdom SE of Palestine — **Nab·a·tae·an** *or* **Nab·a·te·an** \-ˈtē-ən\ *adj or n*
Na·be·rezh·nye Chel·ny \ˌnä-bə-ˈrezh-nə-ˈchel-nē, nə-bir-ˈyezh-ni-yə-chil-ˈnē\ city E Russia in Europe in Tatarstan *pop* 514,000
Nab·lus \ˈna-bləs, ˈnä-\ *or* **Nā·bu·lus** \ˈnä-bu̇-ˈlu̇s\ *or anc* **She·chem** \ˈshe-kəm, -ˌkem\ *or* **Ne·ap·o·lis** \nē-ˈa-pə-lis\ city of ancient Palestine in Samaria; now in N *cen* West Bank *pop* 106,944
Nac·og·do·ches \ˌna-kə-ˈdō-chəz, -chəs\ city E Tex. *pop* 32,996
Nafud *or* **Nafūd, An** — see AN NAFŪD
Na·ga Hills \ˈnä-gə\ hills E India & N Myanmar SE of the Brahmaputra; highest Saramati 12,553 *ft* (3826 *m*)
Na·ga·land \ˈnä-gə-ˌland\ state E India N of Manipur in Naga Hills * Kohima *area* 6366 *sq mi* (16,488 *sq km*), *pop* 1,988,636
Na·ga·no \nä-ˈgä-(ˌ)nō, ˈnä-gə-\ city Japan in *cen* Honshu *pop* 360,112
Na·ga·sa·ki \ˌnä-gä-ˈsä-kē, ˌna-gə-ˈsa-kē\ city & port Japan in W Kyushu on E. China Sea *pop* 423,167
Na·gor·no–Ka·ra·bakh \nə-ˌgȯr-(ˌ)nō-ˈkär-ə-ˌbäk\ region SW Azerbaijan *area* 1700 *sq mi* (4420 *sq km*), *pop* 193,300
Na·goya \nə-ˈgȯi-ə, ˈnä-gō-(ˌ)yä\ city Japan in S *cen* Honshu *pop* 2,171,557
Nag·pur \ˈnäg-ˌpu̇r\ city *cen* India in NE Maharashtra *pop* 2,051,320
Na·gua·bo \nä-ˈgwä-bō\ city E Puerto Rico *pop* 26,720
Na·ha \ˈnä-(ˌ)hä\ city Ryukyu Islands * of Okinawa *pop* 301,032
Na·han·ni National Park Reserve \nä-ˈhä-nē\ wilderness area W Canada in SW Northwest Territories
Na·huel Hua·pí \nä-ˈwel-wä-ˈpē\ lake SW Argentina in the Andes in **Nahuel Huapí National Park**
Nairn \ˈnern\ 1 *or* **Nairn·shire** \-ˌshir, -shər\ former county NE Scotland 2 burgh, its *, on Moray Firth *pop* 10,420
Nai·ro·bi \nī-ˈrō-bē\ city S *cen* Kenya, its * *pop* 2,083,509
Najd — see NEJD — **Naj·di** \ˈnaj-dē, ˈnazh-\ *adj or n*
Nal'·chik \ˈnäl-chik\ town S Russia in Europe * of Kabardino-Balkaria *pop* 242,000
Na·lu·baa·le Dam \ˌnä-lü-ˈbä-lā\ *or formerly* **Owen Falls Dam** dam in Victoria Nile in Uganda — see OWEN FALLS
Na·ma·qua·land \nä-ˈmä-kwä-ˌland\ *or* **Na·ma·land** \ˈnä-mə-\ region SW Africa; divided by Orange River into **Great Namaqualand** (in Namibia) & **Little Namaqualand** (in Northern Cape province, Republic of South Africa)
Na·mib \ˈnä-mib\ desert along entire length of coast of Namibia *ab* 800 *mi* (1287 *km*) long by 30–100 *mi* (48–161 *km*) wide
Na·mi·be \nä-ˈmē-bā\ *or formerly* **Mo·çâ·me·des** \mə-ˈsä-mə-dish\ town & port SW Angola
Na·mib·ia \nə-ˈmi-bē-ə\ *or formerly* **South–West Africa** *or 1884–1919* **German Southwest Africa** country SW Africa on the Atlantic; until 1990 a territory administered by South Africa which captured it from Germany in World War I * Windhoek *area* 318,321 *sq mi* (824,451 *sq km*), *pop* 1,830,330 — **Na·mib·ian** \-bē-ən, -byən\ *adj or n*
Nam·pa \ˈnam-pə\ city SW Idaho W of Boise *pop* 81,557
Nam·po \ˈnam-(ˌ)pō, ˈnäm-\ *or formerly* **Chin·nam·po** \ˈchē(n)-ˌnäm-(ˌ)pō\ city & port SW N. Korea SW of Pyongyang *pop* 130,000
Na·mur \nə-ˈmu̇r, -ˈmyu̇r\ 1 province S Belgium *area* 1413 *sq mi* (3674 *sq km*), *pop* 447,775 2 commune, its * *pop* 105,393
Nan \ˈnän\ river 390 *mi* (628 *km*) N Thailand flowing S to join the Ping forming the Chao Phraya
Na·nai·mo \nə-ˈnī-(ˌ)mō\ city Canada in B.C. on SE Vancouver Is. *pop* 83,810
Nan·chang \ˈnän-ˈchäŋ\ city SE China * of Jiangxi on the Gan SW of Poyang Lake *pop* 1,086,124
Nan·cy \ˈnan(t)-sē, näⁿ-ˈsē\ city NE France on the Meurthe *pop* 103,552

Nan·da De·vi \ˌnən-də-ˈdā-vē\ mountain 25,645 *ft* (7816 *m*) N India in the Himalayas in Uttarakhand

Nan·ga Par·bat \ˌnəŋ-gə-ˈpər-bət\ mountain 26,660 *ft* (8126 *m*) in W Himalayas in region of Jammu and Kashmir under Pakistani control

Nan·jing \ˈnän-ˈjiŋ\ *or* **Nan·king** \ˈnan-ˈkiŋ, ˈnän-\ city E China on the Chang ✻ of Jiangsu & (1928–37 & 1946–49) ✻ of China *pop* 2,090,204

Nan Ling \ˈnän-ˈliŋ\ mountain system SE China roughly separating Guangdong & Guangxi Zhuangzu from Hunan & Guizhou

Nan·ning \ˈnän-ˈniŋ\ *or formerly* **Yung·ning** \ˈyu̇ŋ-ˈniŋ\ city S China ✻ of Guangxi Zhuangzu *pop* 721,877

Nan·terre \nä^{n}-ˈter\ commune N France W of Paris *pop* 84,270

Nantes \ˈnan(t)s, ˈnä^{n}t\ city NW France on the Loire *pop* 270,343

Nan·tong \ˈnän-ˈtu̇ŋ\ *or* **Nan·tung** \-ˈtu̇ŋ\ city & port E China in SE Jiangsu on Chang estuary NW of Shanghai *pop* 343,341

Nan·tuck·et \nan-ˈtə-kət\ island Mass. S of Cape Cod on **Nantucket Sound** (inlet of the Atlantic) *pop* 7446 — **Nan·tuck·et·er** \-kə-tər\ *n*

Napa \ˈna-pə\ city W Calif. N of Vallejo *pop* 76,915

Na·per·ville \ˈnā-pər-ˌvil\ city NE Ill. W of Chicago *pop* 141,853

Na·pi·er \ˈnā-pē-ər\ city New Zealand in E North Is. on Hawke Bay *urban area pop* 113,673

Na·ples \ˈnā-pəlz\ *or It* **Na·po·li** \ˈnä-pō-lē\ *or anc* **Ne·ap·o·lis** \nē-ˈa-pə-ləs\ city & port S Italy on **Bay of Naples** (inlet of Tyrrhenian Sea) ✻ of Campania *pop* 1,000,470

Na·po \ˈnä-(ˌ)pō\ river 550 *mi* (885 *km*) NW S. America rising near Mt. Cotopaxi in *cen* Ecuador & flowing E & SE into the Amazon

Na·ra \ˈnär-ä\ city Japan in W *cen* Honshu E of Osaka; an early ✻ of Japan *pop* 366,185

Na·ran·ji·to \ˌnär-ˌäŋ-ˈhē-tō\ city *cen* Puerto Rico *pop* 30,402

Nar·bonne \när-ˈbän, -ˈbən\ city S France *pop* 46,506

Na·rew \ˈnär-ˌef, -ˌev\ *or Russ* **Na·rev** \ˈnär-if\ river NE Poland flowing W & SW into Bug River

Nar·ma·da \nər-ˈmə-də\ river 800 *mi* (1287 *km*) *cen* India flowing W bet. Vindhya Mountains & Satpura Range into Gulf of Khambhat

Nar·ra·gan·sett Bay \ˌna-rə-ˈgan(t)-sət\ inlet of the Atlantic SE R.I.

Nar·vik \ˈnär-vik\ town & port N Norway *pop* 18,736

Na·shik \ˈnä-shik\ *or* **Na·sik** \ˈnä-sik\ town W India in Maharashtra *pop* 1,076,967

Nash·ua \ˈna-shə-wə *also* -ˌwä\ city S N.H. *pop* 86,494

Nash·ville \ˈnash-ˌvil, -vəl\ city N *cen* Tenn., its ✻ *pop* 601,222 — **Nash·vil·lian** \nash-ˈvil-yən\ *n*

Nas·sau **1** \ˈna-ˌsȯ\ city & port ✻ of Bahamas on New Providence Is. *pop* 248,900 **2** \ˈna-ˌsȯ, *G* ˈnä-ˌsau̇\ region Germany N & E of the Rhine; chief city Wiesbaden

Nassau Range — see SUDIRMAN RANGE

Nasser, Lake — see ASWÂN

Na·tal \nə-ˈtal, -ˈtäl\ **1** city & port NE Brazil ✻ of Rio Grande do Norte *pop* 712,317 **2** former province E Republic of South Africa bet. Drakensberg Mountains & Indian Ocean; now part of KwaZulu-Natal

Natch·ez \ˈna-chəz\ city SW Miss. on Mississippi River *pop* 15,792

Natchez Trace pioneer road bet. Nashville, Tenn., & Natchez, Miss.; constructed in the early 19th century

Na·tick \ˈnā-tik\ town E Mass. W of Boston *pop* 33,006

National City city SW Calif. S of San Diego *pop* 58,582

Natural Bridges National Monument park SE Utah

Nau·cra·tis \ˈnȯ-krə-təs\ ancient Greek city N Egypt in Nile Delta

Nau·ga·tuck \ˈnȯ-gə-ˌtək\ town SW *cen* Conn. *pop* 31,862

Nau·plia \ˈnȯ-plē-ə\ *or* **Nau·pli·on** \-plē-ən\ *or ModGk* **Náv·pli·on** \ˈnäf-plē-ˌȯn\ town & port S Greece in E Peloponnese near head of Gulf of Argolis *pop* 11,453

Na·u·ru \nä-ˈü-(ˌ)rü\ *or formerly* **Pleas·ant Island** \ˈple-zᵊnt\ island (atoll) W Pacific 26 *mi* (42 *km*) S of the equator; formerly a joint Brit., New Zealand, & Australian trust territory; since 1968 an independent republic *area* 8 *sq mi* (21 *sq km*), *pop* 10,065 — **Na·u·ru·an** \-ˈü-rə-wən\ *adj or n*

Na·va·jo National Monument \ˈna-və-ˌhō-, ˈnä-\ area containing cliff dwelling ruins N Ariz. near Utah boundary

Na·varre \nə-ˈvär\ *or Sp* **Na·var·ra** \nä-ˈvär-ä\ **1** region & former kingdom N Spain & SW France in W Pyrenees **2** province N Spain ✻ Pamplona *area* 4024 *sq mi* (10,422 *sq km*), *pop* 555,829

Nav·e·sink, Highlands of *or* **Navesink Highlands** \ˈna-və-ˌsiŋk, ˈne-və(r)-\ range of hills E N.J. from near Sandy Hook to Raritan Bay

Navigators Islands — see SAMOA 1

Náv·pak·tos \ˈnäf-ˌpäk-tȯs\ town & port Greece on N shore of strait connecting Gulf of Corinth & Gulf of Patras

Nax·ci·van \ˌnək-chi-ˈvän\ *or* **Na·khi·che·van** \ˌna-ki-chə-ˈvän\ **1** exclave of Azerbaijan separated from the rest of the country by Armenia *area* 2124 *sq mi* (5501 *sq km*), *pop* 373,000 **2** city, its ✻, on the Aras *pop* 70,000

Nax·os \ˈnak-səs, -ˌsäs\ **1** *or ModGk* **Ná·xos** \ˈnäk-ˌsȯs\ island Greece, largest of the Cyclades *area* 165 *sq mi* (427 *sq km*) **2** oldest Greek colony in Sicily; ruins SW of Taormina

Na·ya·rit \ˌnä-yä-ˈrēt\ state W Mexico bordering on the Pacific ✻ Tepic *area* 10,664 *sq mi* (27,620 *sq km*), *pop* 824,543

Nay·pyi·daw *or* **Nay Pyi Taw** \ˈne-pyē-ˌdȯ\ site S *cen* Myanmar to which national ✻ was moved 2006

Naz·a·reth \ˈna-zə-rəth\ city N Israel in Galilee SE of Haifa *pop* 49,800

Naze, The \ˈnāz\ headland SE England on E coast of Essex

Na·zil·li \ˌnä-zē-ˈlē\ city SW Turkey SE of Izmir *pop* 105,665

Naz·ran' \ˈnäz-rən^{y}\ town S Russia in Europe ✻ of Ingushetia

N'Dja·me·na \ən-jä-ˈmā-nä, -ˈmē-\ *or formerly* **Fort–La·my** \ˌfȯr-lə-ˈmē\ city on the Chari ✻ of Chad *pop* 687,800

Neagh, Lough \ˈnā\ lake *cen* Northern Ireland *area* 153 *sq mi* (398 *sq km*); largest in British Isles

Neapolis **1** — see NABLUS **2** — see NAPLES

Near East the countries of SW Asia & NE Africa — sometimes used interchangeably with *Middle East,* which has become the more common term — **Near Eastern** *adj*

Near Islands \ˈnir\ islands SW Alaska at W end of the Aleutians — see ATTU

Neath and Port Talbot \ˈnēth . . . ˈtȯl-bət, -ˈtal-\ administrative area of S Wales *area* 170 *sq mi* (440 *sq km*)

Nebo, Mount peak Jordan E of N end of Dead Sea 2630 *ft* (802 *m*)

Ne·bras·ka \nə-ˈbras-kə\ state *cen* U.S. ✻ Lincoln *area* 77,355 *sq mi* (200,349 *sq km*), *pop* 1,826,341 — **Ne·bras·kan** \-kən\ *adj or n*

Ne·chako \ni-ˈcha-(ˌ)kō\ river 287 *mi* (462 *km*) Canada in *cen* B.C. flowing N & E into the Fraser

Ne·ches \ˈnā-chəz\ river E Tex. flowing S & SE into Sabine Lake

Neck·ar \ˈne-kər, -ˌkär\ river 228 *mi* (367 *km*) SW Germany rising in the Black Forest & flowing N & W into the Rhine

Neck·er \ˈne-kər\ island Hawaii in Leewards NW of Niihau Is.

Need·ham \ˈnē-dəm\ town E Mass. WSW of Boston *pop* 28,886

Nee·nah \ˈnē-nə\ city E Wis. on Lake Winnebago *pop* 25,501

Ne·ge·ri Sem·bi·lan \ˈne-grē-səm-ˈbē-lən\ state Malaysia in Peninsular Malaysia on Strait of Malacca ✻ Seremban *area* 2590 *sq mi* (6708 *sq km*), *pop* 691,200

Neg·ev \ˈne-ˌgev\ *or* **Neg·eb** \-ˌgeb\ region S Israel; a triangular wedge of desert touching Gulf of Aqaba in S

Ne·gro \ˈnā-(ˌ)grō, ˈne-\ **1** river 400 *mi* (640 *km*) S *cen* Argentina flowing E into the Atlantic **2** river 1400 *mi* (2253 *km*) E Colombia & N Brazil flowing into the Amazon **3** river 434 *mi* (698 *km*) *cen* Uruguay flowing SW into Uruguay River

Ne·gros \ˈnā-(ˌ)grōs, ˈne-\ island S *cen* Philippines in the Visayan Islands SE of Panay Is. *area* 4905 *sq mi* (12,753 *sq km*)

Neige, Mount — see JURA 2

Nei·jiang *or* **Nei–chiang** \ˈnā-ˈjyäŋ\ city *cen* China in S *cen* Sichuan SE of Chengdu *pop* 256,012

Nei Monggol *or* **Nei–meng–ku** — see INNER MONGOLIA

Neis·se \ˈnī-sə\ **1** river 159 *mi* (256 *km*) W Europe flowing from N Czech Republic N into the Oder **2** — see NYSA

Nejd \ˈnejd, ˈnezhd\ *or* **Najd** \ˈnajd, ˈnazhd\ region *cen* & E Saudi Arabia; *area* 447,000 *sq mi* (1,162,200 *sq km*), *pop* 1,200,000 — **Nej·di** \ˈnej-dē, ˈnezh-\ *adj or n*

Nel·son \ˈnel-sən\ **1** river 400 *mi* (644 *km*) Canada in Man. flowing from N end of Lake Winnipeg to Hudson Bay **2** city & port New Zealand on N coast of South Is. *pop* 37,943

Nelson Mandela Bay municipality S Republic of South Africa including the city of Port Elizabeth *pop* 1,005,800

Ne·man \ˈne-mən\ river 582 *mi* (936 *km*) *cen* Europe flowing from *cen* Belarus N & W through Lithuania & along border with exclave of Russia into Courland Lagoon

Ne·mea \ˈnē-mē-ə\ valley & town Greece in NE Peloponnese W of Corinth — **Ne·me·an** \ˈnē-mē-ən, ni-ˈmē-\ *adj*

Ne·nagh \ˈnē-nä, ˈnē-nək\ town S Ireland ✻ of County Tipperary North *pop* 6121

Ne·o·sho \nē-ˈō-(ˌ)shō, -shə\ *or in Okla* **Grand** river 460 *mi* (740 *km*) SE Kans. & NE Okla. flowing SE & S into Arkansas River; now largely submerged in dam-created lakes and reservoirs in its lower course

Ne·pal \nə-ˈpȯl, nā-, -ˈpäl *also* nə-ˈpal\ country Asia on NE border of India in the Himalayas; ✻ Kathmandu *area* 54,362 *sq mi* (140,798 *sq km*), *pop* 23,151,423 — **Nep·a·lese** \ˌne-pə-ˈlēz, -ˈlēs\ *adj or n*

Ne·pe·an \ˈnē-pē-ən\ former city Canada in SE Ont.; now part of Ottawa

Ness, Loch \ˈnes\ lake 23 *mi* (37 *km*) long NW Scotland in NW Highlands

Néstos — see MESTA

Neth·er·lands \ˈne-t͟hər-ləndz\ **1** LOW COUNTRIES — a historical usage **2** *or* **the Netherlands** *or* **Hol·land** \ˈhä-lənd\ *or D* **Ne·der·land** \ˈnā-dər-ˌlänt\ country NW Europe on North Sea; a kingdom, official ✻ Amsterdam, seat of government The Hague *area* 16,033 *sq mi* (41,525 *sq km*), *pop* 16,500,000 — **Neth·er·land** \ˈne-t͟hər-lənd\ *adj* — **Neth·er·land·er** \-ˌlan-dər, -lən-\ *n* — **Neth·er·land·ic** \-ˌlan-dik\ *adj* — **Neth·er·land·ish** \-ˌlan-dish, -lən-\ *adj*

Netherlands Antilles former Dutch overseas territory W. Indies comprising Bonaire, Curaçao, Saba, St. Eustatius, & S part of St. Martin ✻ Willemstad (on Curaçao) *area* over 370 *sq mi* (958 *sq km*)

Netherlands Guiana — see SURINAME 1

Netherlands Indies — see INDONESIA 1

Netherlands New Guinea former name of W half of New Guinea when it was under Dutch control

Netherlands Timor — see TIMOR 1

Néthou, Pic de — see ANETO (Pico de)

Net·tu·no \ne-ˈtü-(ˌ)nō\ commune Italy on Tyrrhenian Sea SSE of Rome adjoining Anzio *pop* 39,290

Neu·châ·tel \ˌnü-shä-ˈtel, ˌnyü-, ˌnə(r)-, ˌnœ-\ **1** canton W Switzerland in Jura Mountains *area* 308 *sq mi* (798 *sq km*), *pop* 166,500 **2** commune, its ✻, on **Lake of Neuchâtel** (*area* 84 *sq mi or* 218 *sq km*), *pop* 31,739

Neuil·ly–sur–Seine \ˌnə(r)-ˌyē-ˌsu̇r-ˈsän, ˌnœ-ˈyē-sœr-ˈsen\ commune N France NW of Paris near the Bois de Boulogne *pop* 59,874

Neu·mün·ster \nȯi-ˈmuen-stər\ city N Germany SSW of Kiel *pop* 81,175

Neu·quén \nyü-ˈkān, nā-u̇-\ river 320 *mi* (515 *km*) W Argentina flowing from the Andes E to join the Limay forming Negro River

Neuse \ˈnüs, ˈnyüs\ river E *cen* N.C. flowing SE into Pamlico Sound

Neuss \ˈnȯis\ city W Germany W of Düsseldorf *pop* 147,663

Neus·tria \ˈnü-strē-ə, ˈnyü-\ **1** the W part of the dominions of the Franks after the conquest by Clovis in 6th century, comprising the NW part of modern France bet. the Meuse, the Loire, & the Atlantic **2** NORMANDY — so called *ab* 11th century — **Neus·tri·an** \-ən\ *adj or n*

Ne·va \ˈnē-və, ˈnā-, nye-ˈvä\ river 40 *mi* (64 *km*) W Russia in Europe flowing from Lake Ladoga to Gulf of Finland at St. Petersburg

Ne·va·da \nə-ˈva-də, *chiefly by outsiders* -ˈvä-\ state W U.S. ✻ Carson City *area* 110,567 *sq mi* (286,368 *sq km*), *pop* 2,700,551 — **Ne·va·dan** \-ˈva-dᵊn, -ˈvä-\ *or* **Ne·va·di·an** \-ˈva-dē-ən, -ˈvä-\ *adj or n*

Ne·vers \nə-ˈver\ city *cen* France SE of Orléans *pop* 40,934

Ne·vis \ˈnē-vəs\ island E West Indies, part of St. Kitts and Nevis in the Leewards; chief town Charlestown *area* 36 *sq mi* (93 *sq km*), *pop* 11,181 — **Ne·vis·ian** \nə-ˈvi-zh(ē-)ən\ *adj or n*

New Albany city S Ind. on Ohio River *pop* 36,372

New Amsterdam town founded *ab* 1625 on Manhattan Is. by the Dutch; renamed New York 1664 by the British

\ə\ **abut** \ᵊ\ kitten, F table \ər\ **further** \a\ ash \ā\ ace \ä\ mop, mar \au̇\ **out** \ch\ **chin** \e\ bet \ē\ **easy** \g\ go \i\ **hit** \ī\ ice \j\ **job** \ŋ\ sing \ō\ **go** \ȯ\ **law** \ȯi\ **boy** \th\ **thin** \t͟h\ **the** \ü\ **loot** \u̇\ **foot** \y\ yet \zh\ vision, beige \k̲, ^{n}, œ, ue, ^{y}\ *see* Guide to Pronunciation

New·ark \ˈnü-ərk, ˈnyü-; *esp 2 & 4* ˈnü-ˌärk, ˈnyü-\ 1 city W Calif. SE of San Francisco *pop* 42,573 2 city NE Del. W of Wilmington *pop* 31,454 3 city & port NE N.J. on **Newark Bay** (W extension of Upper New York Bay) *pop* 277,140 4 city *cen* Ohio *pop* 47,573
New Bedford city & port SE Mass. on W side of Buzzards Bay *pop* 95,072
New Ber·lin \ˈbər-lən\ city SE Wis. W of Milwaukee *pop* 39,584
New Bern \ˈn(y)ü-ˌbərn, -ˈbərn\ city E N.C. *pop* 29,524
New Braun·fels \ˈbrau̇n-fəlz\ city SE *cen* Tex. *pop* 57,740
New Britain 1 city *cen* Conn. *pop* 73,206 2 island Bismarck Archipelago; largest of group *area* 14,160 *sq mi* (36,674 *sq km*), *pop* 263,500
New Brunswick 1 city N *cen* N.J. *pop* 55,181 2 province SE Canada bordering on Gulf of Saint Lawrence & Bay of Fundy ✻ Fredericton *area* 27,633 *sq mi* (71,569 *sq km*), *pop* 751,171
New·burgh \ˈnü-ˌbərg, ˈnyü-\ city SE N.Y. on Hudson River S of Poughkeepsie *pop* 28,866
New Caledonia island SW Pacific SW of Vanuatu; with nearby islands, constitutes an overseas department of France ✻ Nouméa *area* 7367 *sq mi* (19,081 *sq km*), *pop* 230,789
New Castile — see CASTILE
New·cas·tle \ˈnü-ˌka-səl, ˈnyü-, *3 is locally* nü-ˈ, nyü-ˈ\ 1 city & port SE Australia in E New South Wales at mouth of Hunter River *metropolitan area pop* 262,331 2 *or in full* **Newcastle upon Tyne** \ˈtīn\ city & port N England ✻ of Tyne and Wear *pop* 263,000 3 *or in full* **Newcastle–under–Lyme** \-ˈlīm\ town W *cen* England in Staffordshire *pop* 117,400
New Cas·tle \ˈnü-ˌka-səl, ˈnyü-\ city W Pa. ESE of Youngstown, Ohio *pop* 23,273
New Delhi city ✻ of India in Delhi Territory S of city of (old) Delhi *pop* 294,783
New England 1 the NE U.S. comprising the states of Maine, N.H., Vt., Mass., R.I., & Conn. 2 region SE Australia in NE New South Wales; in area of **New England Range** (part of Great Dividing Range) — **New En·gland·er** \ˈiŋ-glən-dər *also* ˈiŋ-lən-\ *n* — **New En·glandy** \-dē\ *adj*
New Forest forested area S England in Hampshire bet. the Avon & Southampton Water; once a royal hunting ground
New·found·land \ˈnü-fən(d)-lənd, ˈnyü-, -ˌland; ˌnü-fən(d)-ˈland, ˌnyü-\ island Canada in the Atlantic E of Gulf of St. Lawrence *area* 43,359 *sq mi* (112,300 *sq km*) — **New·found·land·er** \-lən-dər, -ˌlan-; -ˈlan-dər\ *n*
Newfoundland and Labrador *or 1949–2001* **Newfoundland** province E Canada comprising Newfoundland & part of Labrador ✻ St. John's *area* 143,488 *sq mi* (371,634 *sq km*), *pop* 514,536
New France the possessions of France in N. America before 1763
New Georgia 1 island group W Pacific in *cen* Solomon Islands 2 island 50 *mi* (80 *km*) long; chief island of the group
New Gra·na·da \grə-ˈnä-də\ Spanish viceroyalty in NW S. America 1717–1819 comprising area included in modern Panama, Colombia, Venezuela, & Ecuador
New Guinea 1 *or* **Papua** island in Malay Archipelago N of E Australia divided bet. Indonesia on W & Papua New Guinea on E *area* over 305,000 *sq mi* (789,950 *sq km*) 2 the NE portion of the island of New Guinea; formerly a territory; now part of Papua New Guinea — see NORTH-EAST NEW GUINEA — **New Guin·ean** \ˈgi-nē-ən\ *adj or n*
New·ham \ˈnü-əm, ˈnyü-\ borough of E Greater London, England *pop* 200,200
New Hamp·shire \ˈhamp-shər, -ˌshir\ state NE U.S. ✻ Concord *area* 9279 *sq mi* (24,033 *sq km*), *pop* 1,316,470 — **New Hamp·shire·man** \-mən\ *n* — **New Hamp·shir·ite** \-ˌīt\ *n*
New Ha·ven \ˈhā-vən\ city & port S Conn. *pop* 129,779 — **New Ha·ven·er** \ˈhā-və-nər\ *n*
New Hebrides — see VANUATU
New Iberia city S La. SE of Lafayette *pop* 30,617
New·ing·ton \ˈnü-iŋ-tən, ˈnyü-\ town *cen* Conn. SW of Hartford *pop* 30,562
New Ireland island W Pacific in Bismarck Archipelago N of New Britain *area* 3340 *sq mi* (8684 *sq km*), *pop* (with adjacent islands) 48,774
New Jersey state E U.S. ✻ Trenton *area* 7787 *sq mi* (20,168 *sq km*), *pop* 8,791,894 — **New Jer·sey·an** \-ən\ *n* — **New Jer·sey·ite** \-ˌīt\ *n*
New London city & port SE Conn. on Long Island Sound at mouth of Thames River *pop* 27,620
New·mar·ket \ˈnü-ˌmär-kət, ˈnyü-\ 1 town Canada in SE Ont. N of Toronto *pop* 79,978 2 town E England in Suffolk *pop* 16,129
New Mex·i·co \ˈmek-si-ˌkō\ state SW U.S. ✻ Santa Fe *area* 121,593 *sq mi* (314,926 *sq km*), *pop* 2,059,179 — **New Mex·i·can** \-si-kən\ *adj or n*
New Milford city W Conn. *pop* 28,142
New Neth·er·land \ˈne-t͟hər-lənd\ Dutch colony in N. America 1613–64 occupying lands bordering on Hudson River & later also on lower Delaware River ✻ New Amsterdam
New Or·leans \ˈȯr-lē-ənz, ˈȯr-lənz, ˈȯrl-yənz, (ˌ)ȯr-ˈlēnz\ city & port SE La. bet. Lake Pontchartrain & Mississippi River *pop* 343,829 — **New Or·lea·nian** \(ˌ)ȯr-ˈlē-nyən, -nē-ən\ *n*
New·port \ˈnü-ˌpȯrt, ˈnyü-, -ˌpȯrt\ 1 city & port SE R.I. on Narragansett Bay *pop* 24,672 2 town S England ✻ of Isle of Wight *pop* 23,570 3 administrative area of SE Wales *area* 73 *sq mi* (189 *sq km*) 4 city SE Wales WNW of Bristol *pop* 129,900 — **New·port·er** \-ˌpȯr-tər\ *n*
Newport Beach city SW Calif. SE of Long Beach *pop* 85,186
New·port News \ˈnü-ˌpȯrt-ˈnüz, ˈnyü-ˌpȯrt-ˈnyüz, -pərt-\ city & port SE Va. on James River & Hampton Roads *pop* 180,719
New Providence island in NW *cen* Bahamas E of Andros *area* 80 *sq mi* (207 *sq km*), *pop* 210,832; site of Nassau
New Quebec region Canada in N Que. N of the Eastmain bet. Hudson Bay & Labrador — see UNGAVA
New Quebec Crater *or formerly* **Chubb Crater** \ˈchəb\ lake-filled meteoric crater Canada in N Que., in N Ungava Peninsula
New Ro·chelle \rə-ˈshel\ city SE N.Y. on Long Island Sound E of Mount Vernon *pop* 77,062
New·ry and Mourne \ˈnü-rē, ˈnyü- . . . ˈmȯrn\ district S Northern Ireland *area* 345 *sq mi* (894 *sq km*), *pop* 82,288
New Siberian Islands islands NE Russia in Asia in Arctic Ocean bet. Laptev & E. Siberian seas *area* 11,000 *sq mi* (28,600 *sq km*)
New South Wales state SE Australia bordering on the Pacific ✻ Sydney *area* 309,433 *sq mi* (801,431 *sq km*), *pop* 5,732,032
New Spain Spanish viceroyalty 1535–1821 including territory now in SW U.S., Mexico, Central America N of Panama, much of the West Indies, & the Philippines ✻ Mexico City
New Sweden Swedish colony in N. America 1638–55 mostly on W side of Delaware River from modern Trenton, N.J., to its mouth
New Te·cum·seth \tə-ˈkəm(p)-seth\ town Canada in SE Ont. *pop* 30,234
New Territories Hong Kong exclusive of Hong Kong Is. & Jiulong Peninsula comprising that part of Hong Kong leased to Great Britain by China 1898–1997
New·ton \ˈnü-tᵊn, ˈnyü-\ city E Mass. W of Boston *pop* 85,146
New·town \ˈnü-ˌtau̇n, ˈnyü-\ town SW Conn. E of Danbury *pop* 27,560
New·town·ab·bey \ˌnü-tᵊn-ˈa-bē, ˌnyü-\ district E Northern Ireland, established 1974 *area* 58 *sq mi* (150 *sq km*), *pop* 73,832
New·town Saint Bos·wells \ˈnü-ˌtau̇n-sənt-ˈbäz-wəlz, ˈnyü-, -sānt-\ village S Scotland SE of Edinburgh
New West·min·ster \wes(t)-ˈmin(t)-stər\ city Canada in SW B.C. on the Fraser ESE of Vancouver *pop* 65,976
New Windsor — see WINDSOR
New York 1 state NE U.S. ✻ Albany *area* 49,576 *sq mi* (121,898 *sq km*), *pop* 19,378,102 2 *or* **New York City** city & port SE N.Y. at mouth of Hudson River; includes boroughs of Bronx, Brooklyn, Manhattan, Queens, & Staten Is. *pop* 8,175,133 3 the borough of Manhattan in New York City *pop* 1,585,873 — **New York·er** \ˈyȯr-kər\ *n*
New York Bay inlet of the Atlantic SE N.Y. & NE N.J. at mouth of Hudson River forming harbor of metropolitan New York & consisting of **Upper New York Bay** & **Lower New York Bay** connected by the **Narrows** (strait separating Staten Is. & Long Is.)
New York State Barge Canal — see ERIE CANAL
New Zea·land \ˈzē-lənd\ country SW Pacific ESE of Australia comprising chiefly North Is. & South Is.; a dominion of the Commonwealth of Nations ✻ Wellington *area* 103,736 *sq mi* (269,714 *sq km*), *pop* 4,028,000 — **New Zea·land·er** \-lən-dər\ *n*
Ngaliema, Mount — see STANLEY (Mount)
Nga·mi, Lake \əŋ-ˈgä-mē\ marshy depression NW Botswana N of Kalahari Desert; formerly a large lake
Ngau·ru·hoe \əŋ-ˌgau̇-rə-ˈhō-ē\ volcano 7515 *ft* (2291 *m*) New Zealand in *cen* North Is. in Tongariro National Park
Ni·ag·a·ra Falls \(ˌ)nī-ˈa-g(ə-)rə\ 1 waterfalls on border bet. N.Y. & Ont. in the **Niagara River** (36 *mi or* 58 *km* flowing from Lake Erie N into Lake Ontario); divided by Goat Is. into Horseshoe, or Canadian, Falls (158 *ft or* 48 *m* high) & American Falls (167 *ft or* 51 *m* high) 2 city W N.Y. at the falls *pop* 50,193 3 city Canada in SE Ont. *pop* 82,997
Nia·mey \nē-ˈä-(ˌ)mā, nyä-ˈmā\ city ✻ of Niger *pop* 707,951
Ni·as \ˈnē-ˌäs\ island Indonesia in Indian Ocean off W coast of Sumatra *area* 1569 *sq mi* (4064 *sq km*), *pop* 314,829 — **Ni·as·san** \ˈnē-ə-sən\ *n*
Ni·caea \nī-ˈsē-ə\ *or* **Nice** \ˈnīs\ ancient city of Byzantine Empire; site at modern village of Iznik in NW Turkey in Asia at E end of Iznik Lake — **Ni·cae·an** \nī-ˈsē-ən\ *adj*
Nic·a·ra·gua \ˌni-kə-ˈrä-gwə, ˌnē-kä-ˈrä-gwä\ 1 lake *ab* 100 *mi* (160 *km*) long S Nicaragua 2 country Central America bordering on the Pacific & the Caribbean; a republic ✻ Managua *area* 49,579 *sq mi* (128,410 *sq km*), *pop* 5,142,098 — **Nic·a·ra·guan** \-ˈrä-gwən\ *adj or n*
Nice \ˈnēs\ *or anc* **Ni·caea** \nī-ˈsē-ə\ city & port SE France on the Mediterranean *pop* 343,123
Nic·o·bar Islands \ˈni-kə-ˌbär\ islands India in Indian Ocean S of Andaman Islands *area* 740 *sq mi* (1917 *sq km*), *pop* 14,563 — see ANDAMAN AND NICOBAR
Nicomedia — see IZMIT
Ni·cop·o·lis \nə-ˈkä-pə-lis, nī-\ ancient city NW Greece in Epirus
Nic·o·sia \ˌni-kə-ˈsē-ə\ city *cen* Cyprus, its ✻ *pop* 206,200
Nidwald, Nidwalden — see UNTERWALDEN
Niedersachsen — see LOWER SAXONY
Nieuw·poort *or* **Nieu·port** \ˈnü-ˌpȯrt, ˈnyü-, *F* nyœ-ˈpȯr\ commune NW Belgium in W. Flanders on the Yser *pop* 10,468
Ni·ger \ˈnī-jər, nē-ˈzher\ 1 river 2600 *mi* (4184 *km*) W Africa flowing from Fouta Djallon NE, SE, & S into Gulf of Guinea 2 country W Africa; a republic, until 1958 a territory of French West Africa ✻ Niamey *area* 459,073 *sq mi* (1,188,999 *sq km*), *pop* 15,000,000 — **Ni·ger·ien** \ˌnī-jir-ē-ˈen, nē-ˈzher-ē-ən\ *adj or n* — **Ni·ger·ois** \ˌnē-zhər-ˈwä, -zher-\ *n*
Ni·ge·ria \nī-ˈjir-ē-ə\ country W Africa bordering on Gulf of Guinea; a republic within the Commonwealth of Nations, formerly a colony & protectorate ✻ Abuja *area* 356,669 *sq mi* (927,339 *sq km*), *pop* 167,000,000 — **Ni·ge·ri·an** \-ē-ən\ *adj or n*
Nii·ga·ta \nē-ˈgä-tä, ˈnē-gä-ˌtä\ city & port Japan in N Honshu on Sea of Japan *pop* 501,431
Nii·hau \ˈnē-ˌhau̇\ island Hawaii WSW of Kauai *area* 72 *sq mi* (187 *sq km*)
Nij·me·gen \ˈnī-ˌmā-gən, ˈnā-, -k͟ə(n)\ commune E Netherlands in Gelderland on the Waal S of Arnhem *pop* 154,616
Nikaria — see IKARIA
Nikolayev — see MYKOLAYIV
Ni·ko·pol \ˈnē-kə-ˌpȯl, ˈnyē-, -pəl\ city E *cen* Ukraine on the Dnieper *pop* 159,000
Nile \ˈnī(-ə)l\ river 4160 *mi* (6693 *km*) E Africa flowing from Lake Victoria in Uganda N into the Mediterranean in Egypt; in various sections called specifically: **Vic·to·ria Nile** \vik-ˈtȯr-ē-ə\ *or* **Som·er·set Nile** \ˈsə-mər-sət, -ˌset\ bet. Lake Victoria & Lake Albert; **Al·bert Nile** \ˈal-bərt\ bet. Lake Albert & Lake No; & **White Nile** from Lake No to Khartoum — see BLUE NILE
Niles \ˈnī(-ə)lz\ village NE Ill. NW of Chicago *pop* 29,803
Nil·gi·ri Hills \ˈnil-gə-rē\ hills S India in W Tamil Nadu; highest point Mt. Dodabetta 8640 *ft* (2633 *m*)
Nîmes \ˈnēm\ city S France NE of Montpellier *pop* 133,406
Nimrud — see CALAH
Nin·e·veh \ˈni-nə-və\ *or L* **Ni·nus** \ˈnī-nəs\ ancient city ✻ of Assyria; ruins in Iraq on the Tigris opposite Mosul
Ning·bo *or* **Ning–po** \ˈniŋ-ˈbō\ *or formerly* **Ning·hsien** \ˈniŋ-ˈshyen\ city E China in N Zhejiang ESE of Hangzhou *pop* 552,540
Ninghsia, Ningsia — see YINCHUAN
Ning·xia Hui·zu \ˈniŋ-ˈshyä-ˈhwē-ˈdzü\ *or* **Ning·sia Hui** \ˈniŋ-ˈshyä-ˈhwē\ region N China; formerly a province ✻ Yinchuan *area* 30,039 *sq mi* (78,101 *sq km*), *pop* 4,655,451

Ni·o·brara \nī-ə-'brer-ə\ river 431 *mi* (694 *km*) E Wyo. & N Nebr. flowing E into Missouri River

Niort \nē-'òr\ city W France ENE of La Rochelle *pop* 56,661

Nip·i·gon, Lake \'ni-pə-ˌgän\ lake Canada in W Ont. N of Lake Superior *area* 1870 *sq mi* (4862 *sq km*)

Nip·is·sing, Lake \'ni-pə-sin\ lake Canada in SE Ont. NE of Georgian Bay *area* over 320 *sq mi* (829 *sq km*)

Nippon — see JAPAN

Nip·pur \ni-'pùr\ ancient city of Sumer SSE of Babylon

Nis *or* **Nish** \'nish, 'nēsh\ city E Serbia *pop* 173,724

Ni·shi·no·mi·ya \ˌni-shē-'nō-mē-ˌyä\ city Japan in W Honshu on Osaka Bay E of Kobe *pop* 438,105

Ni·te·rói *or formerly* **Nic·the·roy** \nē-te-'ròi\ city SE Brazil on Guanabara Bay opposite Rio de Janeiro *pop* 459,451

Ni·tra \'ni-trə, 'nyē-trä\ city W Slovakia *pop* 87,285

Nit·ta·ny \'ni-tə-nē\ valley *cen* Pa.

Ni·u·a·fo·'ou \nē-'ü-ä-ˌfō-ō\ island SW *cen* Pacific in the N Tongas *pop* 763

Ni·ue \nē-'ü-(ˌ)ā\ island S *cen* Pacific; a self-governing territory of New Zealand *area* 100 *sq mi* (260 *sq km*), *pop* 1625 — **Ni·ue·an** \nyü-'wā-ən, 'nyü-ˌwä-\ n

Ni·velles \nē-'vel\ commune *cen* Belgium *pop* 23,944

Ni·ver·nais \ˌnē-vər-'nā\ region & former province *cen* France E of the upper Loire ✳ Nevers

Nizh·niy Nov·go·rod *or* **Nizh·ni Novgorod** \'nizh-nē-'näv-gə-ˌräd, -'nòv-gə-rət\ *or 1932–89* **Gor·ki** \'gòr-kē\ city *cen* Russia in Europe at confluence of Oka & Volga rivers *pop* 1,433,000

Nizhniy Ta·gil *or* **Nizhni Tagil** \tə-'gil\ city W Russia in Asia on E slope of the Urals *pop* 437,000

No, Lake \'nō\ lake S *cen* Sudan where Bahr el Jebel & Bahr el Ghazal join to form the White Nile *area* 40 *sq mi* (104 *sq km*)

No·bles·ville \'nō-bəlz-ˌvil\ city *cen* Ind. N of Indianapolis *pop* 51,969

No·gal·es \nō-'ga-ləs, -'gä-lās\ city NW Mexico in Sonora *pop* 133,491

Nome, Cape \'nōm\ cape W Alaska on S side of Seward Peninsula

Noord — see LIMPOPO 2

Noordwes — see NORTH WEST

Noot·ka Sound \'nùt-kə, 'nüt-\ inlet of the Pacific Canada in SW B.C. on W coast of Vancouver Is.

Nor·co \'nòr-(ˌ)kō\ city SE Calif. W of Palm Springs *pop* 27,063

Nordenskjöld Sea — see LAPTEV SEA

Nord·kyn \'nòr-kən, 'nür-ˌkᵊn\ headland NE Norway on Barents Sea; northernmost point of European mainland, at 71°8′N

Nord–Ostsee — see KIEL 2

Nor·folk \'nòr-fək, *US also* -ˌfòk, -ˌfòrk\ **1** city NE Nebr. *pop* 24,210 **2** city & port SE Va. on Elizabeth River S of Hampton Roads *pop* 242,803 **3** county E England bordering on North Sea ✳ Norwich *area* 2152 *sq mi* (5574 *sq km*), *pop* 736,400

Norfolk Broads — see BROADS

Norfolk Island island S. Pacific bet. New Caledonia & New Zealand; administered by Australia *area* 13 *sq mi* (34 *sq km*), *pop* 1912

Norge — see NORWAY

Nor·i·cum \'nòr-i-kəm, 'när-\ ancient country & Roman province W *cen* Europe S of the Danube in modern Austria & S Germany

No·ril'sk \nə-'rēlsk\ city N Russia in Asia, N of arctic circle near mouth of the Yenisey *pop* 165,000

Nor·mal \'nòr-məl\ town *cen* Ill. N of Bloomington *pop* 52,497

Nor·man \'nòr-mən\ city *cen* Okla. on Canadian River *pop* 110,925

Nor·man·dy \'nòr-mən-dē\ *or F* **Nor·man·die** \nòr-mäⁿ-'dē\ region & former province NW France NE of Brittany ✳ Rouen

Nor·ris·town \'nòr-əs-ˌtaùn, 'när-\ borough SE Pa. *pop* 34,324

Norr·kö·ping \'nòr-ˌshœ-pin\ city & port SE Sweden SW of Stockholm at head of an inlet of the Baltic *pop* 123,303

North·al·ler·ton \nòr-'tha-lər-tən\ town N England ✳ of N. Yorkshire *pop* 9556

North America continent of the western hemisphere NW of S. America bounded by Atlantic, Arctic, & Pacific oceans *area* 9,361,791 *sq mi* (24,247,039 *sq km*) — **North American** *adj or n*

North·amp·ton \nòr-'tham(p)-tən, nòrth-'ham(p)-\ **1** city W *cen* Mass. on Connecticut River N of Holyoke *pop* 28,549 **2** town *cen* England N of Northamptonshire *pop* 145,421

North·amp·ton·shire \-ˌshir, -shər\ *or* **Northampton** *or* **North·ants** \nòr-'than(t)s\ county *cen* England ✳ Northampton *area* 947 *sq mi* (2453 *sq km*), *pop* 572,900

North Andover town NE Mass. E of Lawrence *pop* 28,352

North Atlantic — see ATLANTIC OCEAN

North At·tle·bor·ough *or* **North At·tle·boro** \'a-tᵊl-ˌbər-ō\ town SE Mass. *pop* 28,712

North Ayrshire administrative area of W Scotland *area* 341 *sq mi* (884 *sq km*)

North Bay \'nòrth-ˌbā\ city Canada in SE Ont. *pop* 53,651

North Borneo — see SABAH

North Brabant *or D* **Noord–Bra·bant** \ˌnōrt-'brä-ˌbänt\ province S Netherlands ✳ 's Hertogenbosch *area* 1971 *sq mi* (5105 *sq km*), *pop* 2,391,123

North·brook \'nòrth-ˌbrùk\ village NE Ill. NW of Chicago *pop* 33,170

North Canadian river *ab* 800 *mi* (1287 *km*) S *cen* U.S. flowing ESE from NE N.Mex. into Canadian River in E Okla. — see BEAVER

North Cape 1 cape New Zealand at N tip of North Is. **2** cape NE Norway on Mageröy Is. at 71°10′20″N **3** — see HORN

North Car·o·li·na \ˌker(-ə)-'lī-nə, ˌka-rə-\ state E U.S. ✳ Raleigh *area* 52,669 *sq mi* (136,413 *sq km*), *pop* 9,535,483 — **North Car·o·lin·ian** \-'li-nē-ən, -'li-nyən\ *adj or n*

North Cas·cades National Park \kas-'kādz, 'kas-\ area of glaciers and mountain lakes N *cen* Wash. on Canadian border

North Channel strait bet. NE Ireland & SW Scotland connecting Irish Sea & the Atlantic

North Charleston city SE S.C. *pop* 97,471

North Chicago city NE Ill. S of Waukegan *pop* 32,574

North Cow·i·chan \'kaù-ə-chən\ municipality Canada in B.C. on E Vancouver Is. *pop* 28,807

North Da·ko·ta \də-'kō-tə\ state NW *cen* U.S. ✳ Bismarck *area* 70,665 *sq mi* (183,729 *sq km*), *pop* 672,591 — **North Da·ko·tan** \-'kō-tᵊn\ *adj or n*

North Down district E Northern Ireland, established 1974 *area* 28 *sq mi* (73 *sq km*), *pop* 70,308

North Downs hills S England chiefly in Kent & Surrey

North East Frontier Agency — see ARUNACHAL PRADESH

North–East New Guinea *or earlier* **Kai·ser–Wil·helms·land** \'kī-zər-'vil-helms-ˌlänt\ the NE part of mainland Papua New Guinea — a historical usage

Northern *or* **Northern Transvaal** — see LIMPOPO 2

Northern Cape province W Republic of South Africa *area* 139,691 *sq mi* (361,800 *sq km*), *pop* 749,000

Northern Cir·cars \(ˌ)sər-'kärz\ the coast region of E India now in E Andhra Pradesh — a historical usage

Northern Cook Islands \'kùk\ *or* **Ma·ni·hi·ki Islands** \ˌmä-nē-'hē-kē\ islands S *cen* Pacific N of Cook Islands; belong to New Zealand

Northern Ireland country NE Ireland; a division of the United Kingdom of Great Britain and Northern Ireland ✳ Belfast *area* 5452 *sq mi* (14,121 *sq km*), *pop* 1,685,267 — see ULSTER

Northern Karoo — see KAROO

Northern Kingdom — see ISRAEL

Northern Mar·i·ana Islands \ˌmer-ē-'a-nə\ islands W Pacific; in Trust Territory of the Pacific Islands 1947–76 & a U.S. commonwealth since 1986; *area* 184 *sq mi* (478 *sq km*), *pop* 69,221

Northern Rhodesia — see ZAMBIA

Northern Sporades — see SPORADES

Northern Territories former Brit. protectorate W Africa; now part of Ghana

Northern Territory territory *cen* & N Australia bordering on Arafura Sea ✳ Darwin *area* 520,280 *sq mi* (1,347,525 *sq km*), *pop* 169,300

North Frisian — see FRISIAN ISLANDS

North·glenn \'nòrth-ˌglen\ city N *cen* Colo. NE of Denver *pop* 35,789

North Ha·ven \'nòrth-ˌhā-vən\ town S Conn. *pop* 24,093

North Holland *or D* **Noord–Hol·land** \ˌnòrt-'hò-ˌlänt\ province NW Netherlands ✳ Haarlem *area* 1124 *sq mi* (2911 *sq km*), *pop* 2,559,477

North Island island N New Zealand *area* 44,297 *sq mi* (114,729 *sq km*), *pop* 2,829,798

North Kings·town \'kiŋz-taùn\ town S R.I. *pop* 26,486

North Korea — see KOREA — **North Korean** *adj or n*

North Lanarkshire administrative area of W Scotland *area* 183 *sq mi* (484 *sq km*)

North Las Vegas city SE Nev. *pop* 216,961

North Lau·der·dale \'lò-dər-ˌdāl\ city SE Fla. *pop* 41,023

North Little Rock city *cen* Ark. *pop* 62,304

North Miami city SE Fla. *pop* 58,786

North Miami Beach city SE Fla. *pop* 41,523

North Minch — see MINCH

North Olm·sted \'ō(l)m-ˌsted, 'əm-\ city NE Ohio *pop* 32,718

North Ossetia — see ALANIA

North Pacific — see PACIFIC OCEAN

North Platte 1 river 680 *mi* (1094 *km*) W U.S. flowing from N Colo. N & E through Wyo. into Nebr. to unite with the S. Platte forming Platte River **2** city SW *cen* Nebr. *pop* 24,733

North Port city SW Fla. *pop* 57,357

North Providence town NE R.I. *pop* 32,078

North Rhine–Westphalia *or G* **Nord·rhein–West·fa·len** \'nòrt-ˌrīn-ˌvest-'fä-lən\ state of Germany & formerly of W. Germany formed 1946 by union of former Westphalia province, Lippe state, & N Rhine Province ✳ Düsseldorf *area* 13,142 *sq mi* (34,038 *sq km*), *pop* 17,349,700

North Rich·land Hills \'rich-lənd\ town N Tex. *pop* 63,343

North Riding — see YORK

North River estuary of Hudson River bet. SE N.Y. & NE N.J.

North Roy·al·ton \'ròi-(ə)l-tən\ city N Ohio *pop* 30,444

North Saskatchewan — see SASKATCHEWAN

North Sea arm of the Atlantic 600 *mi* (966 *km*) long & 350 *mi* (563 *km*) wide E of Great Britain

North Slope region N Alaska bet. Brooks Range & Arctic Ocean

North Thompson — see THOMPSON

North Ton·a·wan·da \ˌtä-nə-'wän-də\ city W N.Y. N of Buffalo *pop* 31,568

North Truchas Peak — see TRUCHAS PEAK

North·um·ber·land \nòr-'thəm-bər-lənd\ county N England ✳ Newcastle upon Tyne *area* 2013 *sq mi* (5214 *sq km*), *pop* 300,600

Northumberland Strait strait 180 *mi* (290 *km*) long Canada in Gulf of St. Lawrence bet. P.E.I. & the mainland

North·um·bria \nòr-'thəm-brē-ə\ ancient country Great Britain bet. the Humber & Firth of Forth; one of kingdoms in Anglo-Saxon heptarchy

North Vancouver city Canada in SW B.C. *pop* 48,196

North Vietnam — see VIETNAM

North West *or* **Noord·wes** \ˌnòrd-'wes, ˌnòrt-\ province N Republic of South Africa *area* 44,861 *sq mi* (116,190 *sq km*), *pop* 3,349,000

Northwest Angle area of land N Minn. N of Lake of the Woods & bordering on SE Man., Canada *area* 130 *sq mi* (340 *sq km*)

North–West Frontier Province province of Pakistan & formerly of Brit. India on Afghanistan border ✳ Peshawar *pop* 11,658,000

Northwest Passage a passage by sea bet. the Atlantic & the Pacific along the N coast of N. America

Northwest Territories territory NW Canada comprising that area of the mainland N of 60°N bet. Yukon to the W & Nunavut to the E ✳ Yellowknife *area* 456,790 *sq mi* (1,183,085 *sq km*), *pop* 41,462

North York former city Canada in SE Ont., now part of Toronto

North Yorkshire county N England ✳ Northallerton *area* 3327 *sq mi* (8617 *sq km*), *pop* 698,700

Nor·ton Shores \'nòr-tᵊn\ city W Mich. S of Muskegon *pop* 23,994

Norton Sound arm of Bering Sea W Alaska bet. Seward Peninsula & the mouths of Yukon River

Nor·walk \'nòr-ˌwòk\ **1** city SW Calif. SE of Los Angeles *pop* 105,549 **2** city SW Conn. on Long Island Sound *pop* 85,603

Nor·way \ˈnȯr-ˌwā\ *or Norw* **Nor·ge** \ˈnȯr-gə\ country N Europe in Scandinavia bordering on Atlantic & Arctic oceans; a kingdom ✻ Oslo *area* 154,790 *sq mi* (400,906 *sq km*), *pop* 4,900,000
Nor·we·gian Sea \nȯr-ˈwē-jən\ open sea bet. Greenland & Iceland on the W and Spitsbergen & Norway on the E
Nor·wich 1 \ˈnȯr-(ˌ)wich; ˈnȯr-ich, ˈnär-\ city SE Conn. *pop* 40,493 2 \ˈnär-ij, -ich\ city E England ✻ of Norfolk *pop* 120,700
Nor·wood \ˈnȯr-ˌwu̇d\ town E Mass. SW of Boston *pop* 28,602
Not·ta·way \ˈnä-tə-ˌwā\ river 400 *mi* (644 *km*) Canada in SW Que. flowing NW into James Bay
Not·ting·ham \ˈnä-tiŋ-əm, *US also* -ˌham\ city N *cen* England ✻ of Nottinghamshire *pop* 261,500
Not·ting·ham·shire \ˈnä-tiŋ-əm-ˌshir, -shər, *US also* -ˌham-\ *or* **Nottingham** *or* **Notts** \ˈnäts\ county N *cen* England ✻ Nottingham *area* 866 *sq mi* (2243 *sq km*), *pop* 980,600
Nouak·chott \nu̇-ˈäk-ˌshät\ city SW Mauritania, its ✻ *pop* 558,195
Nou·méa \nü-ˈmā-ə\ city & port ✻ of New Caledonia *pop* 76,293
No·va Igua·çu \ˌnȯ-və-ˌē-gwə-ˈsü\ city SE Brazil in Rio de Janeiro state NW of Rio de Janeiro *pop* 920,599
Nova Lisboa — see HUAMBO
No·va·ra \nō-ˈvär-ä\ commune NW Italy in Piedmont *pop* 102,243
No·va Sco·tia \ˌnō-və-ˈskō-shə\ province SE Canada comprising a peninsula (375 *mi or* 600 *km* long) & Cape Breton Is. ✻ Halifax *area* 20,402 *sq mi* (52,840 *sq km*), *pop* 921,727 — see ACADIA — **No·va Sco·tian** \-shən\ *adj or n*
No·va·to \nō-ˈvä-(ˌ)tō\ city W Calif. N of San Francisco *pop* 51,904
No·va·ya Zem·lya \ˈnō-və-yə-ˌzem-lē-ˈä\ two islands NE Russia in Europe in Arctic Ocean bet. Barents Sea & Kara Sea *area* 31,382 *sq mi* (81,279 *sq km*), *pop* 400
Nov·go·rod \ˈnäv-gə-ˌräd, ˈnȯv-gə-rət\ 1 medieval principality E Europe extending from Lake Peipus & Lithuania to the Urals 2 city W Russia in Europe *pop* 235,000
No·vi \ˈnō-ˌvī\ city SE Mich. NW of Detroit *pop* 55,224
No·vi Sad \ˌnō-vē-ˈsäd\ city N Serbia on the Danube; chief city of Vojvodina *pop* 191,405
No·vo·kuz·netsk \ˌnō-(ˌ)vō-ku̇z-ˈnetsk, ˌnȯ-və-küz-ˈnyetsk\ *or formerly* **Sta·linsk** \ˈstä-lin(t)sk, ˈsta-; ˈstäl-yin(t)sk\ city S Russia in Asia at S end of Kuznetsk Basin *pop* 600,000
No·vo·si·birsk \ˌnō-(ˌ)vō-sə-ˈbirsk, ˌnō-və-\ *or formerly* **No·vo·ni·ko·la·evsk** \-ˌni-kə-ˈlī-əfsk\ city S Russia in Asia on the Ob' *pop* 1,442,000
Nu·bia \ˈnü-bē-ə, ˈnyü-\ region & ancient kingdom NE Africa along the Nile in S Egypt & N Sudan
Nu·bi·an Desert \ˈnü-bē-ən, ˈnyü-\ desert NE Sudan E of the Nile
Nu·e·ces \nu̇-ˈā-səs, nyu̇-\ river over 300 *mi* (483 *km*) S Tex. flowing S & SE into **Nueces Bay** at head of Corpus Christi Bay
Nueva Esparta — see MARGARITA
Nue·vo La·re·do \ˈnwā-(ˌ)vō-lä-ˈrā-(ˌ)dō, -t͟hō\ city N Mexico in Tamaulipas on Rio Grande opposite Laredo, Tex. *pop* 275,060
Nuevo Le·ón \lā-ˈōn\ state N Mexico in the Sierra Madre Oriental ✻ Monterrey *area* 24,925 *sq mi* (64,556 *sq km*), *pop* 3,098,736
Nu·ku·'a·lo·fa \ˌnü-kü-ä-ˈlō-fä\ town ✻ of Tonga on Tongatapu Is. *pop* 22,400
Nu·ku Hi·va \ˌnü-kü-ˈhē-vä\ island S. Pacific in the Marquesas; largest in group *area* 60 *sq mi* (155 *sq km*), *pop* 2650; chief town Taiohae
Null·ar·bor Plain \ˈnə-lə-ˌbȯr\ treeless plain SW Australia in Western Australia & S. Australia bordering on Great Australian Bight
Num·foor \ˈnüm-ˌfȯr\ island West Papua, Indonesia in W Schouten Islands *area* 28 *sq mi* (73 *sq km*)
Nu·mid·ia \nu̇-ˈmi-dē-ə, nyu̇-\ ancient country N Africa E of Mauretania in modern Algeria; chief city Hippo — **Nu·mid·i·an** \-dē-ən\ *adj or n*
Nu·na·vut \ˈnü-nə-ˌvüt\ semiautonomous territory NE Canada, created 1999 from E two-thirds of Northwest Territories ✻ Iqaluit *area* 747,534 *sq mi* (1,936,113 *sq km*), *pop* 31,906
Nun·ea·ton \ˌnə-ˈnē-tᵊn\ town *cen* England in Warwickshire E of Birmingham *pop* 71,530
Nu·ni·vak \ˈnü-nə-ˌvak\ island 50 *mi* (80 *km*) long W Alaska in Bering Sea
Nu·rem·berg \ˈnu̇r-əm-ˌbərg, ˈnyu̇r-\ *or G* **Nürn·berg** \ˈnu̇ern-ˌberk\ city S Germany in N *cen* Bavaria *pop* 497,496
Nu·ri·stan \ˌnu̇r-i-ˈstan, -ˈstän\ *or formerly* **Kaf·iri·stan** \ˌka-fə-ri-ˈstan, -ˈstän\ mountainous area E Afghanistan S of the Hindu Kush
Nuuk \ˈnük\ *or* **Godt·håb** \ˈgȯt-ˌhȯp\ town ✻ of Greenland on SW coast *pop* 15,000
Nyasa, Lake — see MALAWI (Lake)
Nyasaland — see MALAWI
Nyir·a·gon·go \nē-ˌir-ə-ˈgȯŋ-(ˌ)gō, -ˈgäŋ-, ˌnyir-\ volcano *ab* 11,400 *ft* (3475 *m*) E Democratic Republic of the Congo in Virunga Mountains NE of Lake Kivu
Nyí·regy·há·za \ˈnē-ˌrej-ˌhä-zȯ\ city NE Hungary *pop* 120,600
Nysa \ˈni-sə\ *or G* **Neis·se** \ˈnī-sə\ river 120 *mi* (193 *km*) SW Poland flowing NE into the Oder
Oa·he Reservoir \ō-ˈä-(ˌ)hē\ reservoir *ab* 225 *mi* (362 *km*) long N S.Dak. & S N.Dak. formed in Missouri River by **Oahe Dam**
Oa·hu \ō-ˈä-(ˌ)hü\ island Hawaii; site of Honolulu *area* 589 *sq mi* (1531 *sq km*), *pop* 953,207
Oak Creek city SE Wis. *pop* 34,451
Oak·dale \ˈōk-ˌdāl\ city E Minn. ENE of St. Paul *pop* 27,378
Oak Forest city NE Ill. S of Chicago *pop* 27,962
Oak·ham \ˈō-kəm\ town E *cen* England in E Leicestershire; ✻ of former county of Rutlandshire *pop* 7996
Oak·land \ˈō-klənd\ city & port W Calif. on San Francisco Bay opposite San Francisco *pop* 390,724
Oakland Park city SE Fla. N of Fort Lauderdale *pop* 41,363
Oak Lawn village NE Ill. SW of Chicago *pop* 56,690
Oak·ley \ˈō-klē\ city Calif. NE of Oakland *pop* 35,432
Oak Park 1 village NE Ill. W of Chicago *pop* 51,878 2 city SE Mich. N of Detroit *pop* 29,319
Oak Ridge city E Tenn. W of Knoxville *pop* 29,330
Oak·ville \ˈōk-ˌvil\ town Canada in SE Ont. SW of Toronto *pop* 182,520
Oa·xa·ca \wä-ˈhä-kä\ 1 state SE Mexico bordering on the Pacific *area* 36,820 *sq mi* (95,364 *sq km*), *pop* 3,019,560 2 city, its ✻ *pop* 212,943 — **Oa·xa·can** \-kən\ *adj*
Ob' \ˈäb, ˈōb\ river *over* 2250 *mi* (3620 *km*) W Russia in Asia flowing NW & N into **Gulf of Ob'** (inlet of Arctic Ocean 500 *mi or* 800 *km* long)
Ober·am·mer·gau \ˌō-bər-ˈä-mər-ˌgau̇\ town S Germany in Bavaria SSW of Munich *pop* 4906
Ober·hau·sen \ˈō-bər-ˌhau̇-zᵊn\ city W Germany in the Ruhr WNW of Essen *pop* 224,559
Oberland — see BERNER ALPEN
Obwald *or* **Obwalden** — see UNTERWALDEN
Ocala \ō-ˈka-lə\ city N *cen* Fla. S of Gainesville *pop* 56,315
Oce·a·nia \ˌō-shē-ˈa-nē-ə, -ˈā-\ the lands of the *cen* & S Pacific including Micronesia, Melanesia, Polynesia (including New Zealand), often Australia, & sometimes the Malay Archipelago — **Oce·a·ni·an** \-nē-ən\ *adj or n*
Ocean Island 1 — see BANABA 2 — see KURE ATOLL
Ocean·side \ˈō-shən-ˌsīd\ city SW Calif. NNW of San Diego *pop* 167,086
Oc·mul·gee \ōk-ˈməl-gē\ river 255 *mi* (410 *km*) *cen* Ga. flowing SE to join the **Oco·nee** \ō-ˈkō-nē\ (250 *mi or* 402 *km*) forming the Altamaha
Ocmulgee National Monument reservation *cen* Ga. at Macon containing American Indian mounds & other remains
Oco·ee \ō-ˈkō-ē\ city *cen* Fla. W of Orlando *pop* 35,579
Ocra·coke Island \ˈō-krə-ˌkōk\ island off *cen* N.C. coast bet. Pamlico Sound & the Atlantic — see CROATAN
Oden·se \ˈō-dᵊn-sə, ˈu̇-ən-zə\ city Denmark in N Fyn Is. *pop* 184,308
Oder \ˈō-dər\ *or* **Odra** \ˈȯ-drə\ river *ab* 565 *mi* (909 *km*) *cen* Europe rising in the mountains of Silesia, Czech Republic & flowing N to join Neisse River & thence N into the Baltic Sea
Odes·sa \ō-ˈde-sə\ 1 city W Tex. *pop* 99,940 2 *or Ukrainian* **Odesa** city & port S Ukraine on Black Sea *pop* 1,101,000
Odisha — see ORISSA
Oea — see TRIPOLI 2
Oe·ta \ˈē-tə\ mountains *cen* Greece, E spur of Pindus Mountains; highest point 7060 *ft* (2152 *m*)
O'·Fal·lon \ō-ˈfa-lən\ city E Mo. WNW of St. Louis *pop* 79,329
Of·fa·ly \ˈȯ-fə-lē, ˈä-\ *or formerly* **King's** county *cen* Ireland in Leinster ✻ Tullamore *area* 771 *sq mi* (2005 *sq km*), *pop* 63,663
Of·fen·bach \ˈȯ-fən-ˌbäk, -ˌbäk\ city SW *cen* Germany on Main River E of Frankfurt am Main *pop* 115,790
Oga·den \ō-ˈgä-ˌdān\ plateau region SE Ethiopia
Ogasawara Islands — see BONIN ISLANDS
Og·bo·mo·sho \ˌōg-bō-ˈmō-(ˌ)shō\ city W Nigeria *pop* 644,200
Og·den \ˈȯg-dən, ˈäg-\ city N Utah *pop* 82,825
Ogee·chee \ō-ˈgē-chē\ river 250 *mi* (402 *km*) E Ga. flowing SE into the Atlantic
Ohio \ō-ˈhī-(ˌ)ō, ə-, -ə\ 1 river *ab* 975 *mi* (1569 *km*) E U.S. flowing from junction of Allegheny & Monongahela rivers in W Pa. into Mississippi River 2 state NE *cen* U.S. ✻ Columbus *area* 41,222 *sq mi* (106,765 *sq km*), *pop* 11,536,504 — **Ohio·an** \-ˈhī-ō-ən\ *n*
Ohře — see EGER
Oise \ˈwäz\ river 188 *mi* (302 *km*) N France flowing SW into the Seine
Oi·ta \ˈȯi-ˌtä, ō-ˈē-tä\ city & port Japan in NE Kyushu *pop* 436,470
Ojos del Sa·la·do \ˈō-(ˌ)hōs-ˌdel-sä-ˈlä-(ˌ)dō, -ˌt͟hel-, -t͟hō\ mountain 22,664 *ft* (6908 *m*) NW Argentina in the Andes W of Tucumán
Oka \ō-ˈkä\ 1 river 530 *mi* (853 *km*) S *cen* Russia in Asia flowing N from the Sayan Mountains into the Angara 2 river 919 *mi* (1479 *km*) *cen* Russia in Europe flowing into the Volga
Oka·nog·an *or in Canada* **Oka·na·gan** \ˌō-kə-ˈnä-gən\ river 300 *mi* (483 *km*) U.S. & Canada flowing from **Okanagan Lake** (in SE B.C.) into Columbia River in NE Wash.
Oka·van·go \ˌō-kä-ˈväŋ-(ˌ)gō\ *or Pg* **Cu·ban·go** \kü-ˈbäŋ-(ˌ)gü\ river 1000 *mi* (1609 *km*) SW *cen* Africa rising in *cen* Angola & flowing S & E to empty into **Okavango Swamps** *or* **Okavango Delta** (great marsh area N of Lake Ngami in NW Botswana)
Oka·ya·ma \ˌō-kä-ˈyä-mä\ city & port Japan in W Honshu on Inland Sea *pop* 626,642
Oka·za·ki \ˌō-kä-ˈzä-kē, ō-ˈkä-zä-kē\ city Japan in S *cen* Honshu SE of Nagoya *pop* 336,583
Okee·cho·bee, Lake \ˌō-kə-ˈchō-bē\ lake 37 *mi* (60 *km*) long S *cen* Fla.
Oke·fe·no·kee \ˌō-kə-fə-ˈnō-kē, ˌō-kē- *also* ˈōk-fə-ˌnōk\ swamp over 600 *sq mi* (1554 *sq km*) SE Ga. & NE Fla.
Okhotsk, Sea of \ō-ˈkätsk, ə-ˈkȯtsk\ inlet of the Pacific E Russia in Asia W of Kamchatka Peninsula & Kuril Islands
Oki Archipelago \ˈō-(ˌ)kē\ archipelago Japan in Sea of Japan off SW Honshu
Oki·na·wa \ˌō-kə-ˈnä-wə, -ˈnau̇-ə\ 1 island group Japan in *cen* Ryukyu Islands; largest city Naha; occupied by the U.S. 1945–1972 2 island in the group; largest in the Ryukyus *area* 454 *sq mi* (1176 *sq km*) — **Oki·na·wan** \-ˈnä-wən, -ˈnau̇-ən\ *adj or n*
Okla·ho·ma \ˌō-klə-ˈhō-mə\ state S *cen* U.S. ✻ Oklahoma City *area* 69,956 *sq mi* (181,186 *sq km*), *pop* 3,751,351 — **Okla·ho·man** \-mən\ *adj or n*
Oklahoma City city ✻ of Okla. on the N. Canadian *pop* 579,999
Öland \ˈə(r)-ˌländ, ˈœ-\ island Sweden in Baltic Sea off SE coast; chief town Borgholm *area* 519 *sq mi* (1349 *sq km*), *pop* 25,382
Ola·the \ō-ˈlā-thə\ city NE Kans. SW of Kansas City *pop* 125,872
Old Castile — see CASTILE
Ol·den·burg \ˈōl-dən-ˌbərg, -ˌbu̇rk\ 1 former state NW Germany bordering on North Sea 2 city NW Germany W of Bremen *pop* 145,161
Old Faithful geyser Yellowstone National Park NW Wyo.
Old·ham \ˈōl-dəm\ city NW England in Greater Manchester *pop* 211,400
Old Point Comfort cape SE Va. on N shore of Hampton Roads
Old Sar·um \ˈser-əm\ *or anc* **Sor·bi·o·du·num** \ˌsȯr-bē-ə-ˈdü-nəm, -ˈdyü-\ ancient city S England in Wiltshire N of Salisbury
Ol·du·vai Gorge \ˈōl-də-ˌvī\ canyon Tanzania in N mainland SE of Serengeti Plain; contains fossil beds
Olek·ma \ō-ˈlek-mə\ river 794 *mi* (1278 *km*) *cen* Russia in Asia rising in Yablonovy Mountains & flowing N into the Lena
Ole·nek \ˌä-lə-ˈnyȯk\ river N Russia in Asia flowing NE into Laptev Sea W of the Lena
Ol·i·fants \ˈä-lə-fən(t)s\ river 350 *mi* (563 *km*) S Africa in Republic of South Africa & Mozambique flowing into the Limpopo
Olives, Mount of *or* **Ol·i·vet** \ˈä-lə-ˌvet, ˌä-lə-ˈ\ mountain ridge 2680 *ft* (817 *m*) West Bank running N & S on E side of Jerusalem

Olo·mouc \ˈȯ-lə-ˌmōts\ *or G* **Ol·mütz** \ˈȯl-ˌmüts, -ˌmyüts, -ˌmuets\ city E Czech Republic in *cen* Moravia *pop* 102,607

Olsz·tyn \ˈȯl-shtən\ *or G* **Al·len·stein** \ˈä-lən-ˌshtīn\ city N Poland NNW of Warsaw *pop* 161,238

Olt \ˈȯlt\ river 308 *mi* (496 *km*) S Romania flowing S through the Transylvanian Alps into the Danube

Ol·te·nia \äl-ˈte-nē-ə\ *or* **Little Walachia** region S Romania W of the Olt; the W division of Walachia

Olym·pia \ə-ˈlim-pē-ə, ō-\ **1** city ✳ of Wash. on Puget Sound *pop* 46,478 **2** plain S Greece in NW Peloponnese along the Alpheus — **Olym·pi·an** \-pē-ən\ *adj or n* — **Olym·pic** \-pik\ *adj*

Olympic Mountains mountains NW Wash. in *cen* Olympic Peninsula — see OLYMPUS (Mount)

Olympic National Park area of varied landscapes NW Wash. including part of Olympic Mountains & land along Pacific coast

Olympic Peninsula peninsula NW Wash. W of Puget Sound

Olym·pus, Mount \ə-ˈlim-pəs, ō-\ **1** mountain 7965 *ft* (2428 *m*) NW Wash.; highest in Olympic Mountains **2** *or* **Olympus** massif NE Greece in Thessaly near west coast of Gulf of Salonika; highest point 9570 *ft* (2917 *m*) **3** — see ULU DAG

Olyn·thus \ō-ˈlin(t)-thəs\ ancient city NE Greece in Macedonia on Chalcidice Peninsula

Om' \ˈȯm\ river 450 *mi* (724 *km*) SW Russia in Asia flowing into the Irtysh

Omagh \ˈō-mə, -ˌmä\ **1** district W Northern Ireland, established 1974 *area* 436 *sq mi* (1134 *sq km*), *pop* 45,343 **2** town W Northern Ireland in *cen* Omagh district *pop* 17,280

Oma·ha \ˈō-mə-ˌhȯ, -ˌhä\ city E Nebr. on Missouri River *pop* 408,958

Omaha Beach W *cen* part of Normandy beaches NW France NW of Bayeux; in World War II landing place of American army during invasion of France June 6, 1944

Oman \ō-ˈmän, -ˈman\ *or formerly* **Muscat and Oman** country SW Asia in SE Arabia bordering on Arabian Sea; a sultanate ✳ Masqat *area* 82,000 *sq mi* (213,200 *sq km*), *pop* 2,968,000 — **Omani** \ō-ˈmä-nē, -ˈma-\ *adj or n*

Oman, Gulf of arm of Arabian Sea bet. Oman & SE Iran

Om·dur·man \ˌäm-dər-ˈman, -ˈmän\ city *cen* Sudan on the Nile opposite Khartoum & Khartoum North *pop* 2,200,000

Omi·ya \ˈō-mē-ˌyä, ō-ˈmē-ä\ city Japan on Honshu, a suburb of Tokyo *pop* 456,271

Omo·lon \ˌä-mə-ˈlȯn\ river 715 *mi* (1150 *km*) E Russia in Asia flowing from the Kolyma Range N into Kolyma River

Omsk \ˈȯm(p)sk, ˈäm(p)sk\ city SW Russia in Asia at confluence of the Irtysh & the Om *pop* 1,169,000

Omu·ra \ō-ˈmü-rä, ō-ˈmü-rä\ city & port Japan in NW Kyushu on **Ōmura Bay** (inlet of E. China Sea) NNE of Nagasaki

One·ga, Lake \ō-ˈne-gə\ lake NW Russia in Europe in S Karelia *area* over 3700 *sq mi* (9583 *sq km*)

Onei·da Lake \ō-ˈnī-də\ lake *ab* 22 *mi* (35 *km*) long *cen* N.Y. NE of Syracuse

On·tar·io \än-ˈter-ē-ˌō\ **1** city SW Calif. NW of Riverside *pop* 163,924 **2** province E Canada bet. Great Lakes & Hudson Bay ✳ Toronto *area* 415,596 *sq mi* (1,076,395 *sq km*), *pop* 12,851,821 — **On·tar·i·an** \-ē-ən\ *adj or n*

Ontario, Lake lake U.S. & Canada in N.Y. & Ont.; easternmost of the Great Lakes *area ab* 7600 *sq mi* (19,684 *sq km*)

Oos Kaap — see EASTERN CAPE

Ope·li·ka \ˌō-pə-ˈlī-kə\ city E Alabama *pop* 26,477

Ope·lou·sas \ˌä-pə-ˈlü-səs\ city S *cen* La. N of Lafayette *pop* 16,634

Opo·le \ō-ˈpȯ-le\ *or G* **Op·peln** \ˈȯ-pəln\ city SW Poland on the Oder *pop* 127,653

Oporto — see PORTO

Oquirrh Mountains \ˈō-kər\ mountain range N *cen* Utah S of Great Salt Lake; highest point *ab* 11,000 *ft* (3353 *m*)

Ora·dea \ȯ-ˈrä-dē-ə\ city NW Romania in Transylvania near Hungarian border *pop* 206,527

Oral \ȯ-ˈräl\ *or* **Uralsk** \ü-ˈrälsk, yü-ˈralsk\ city W Kazakhstan on Ural River *pop* 214,000

Oran \ō-ˈrän\ city & port NW Algeria *pop* 628,558

Or·ange \ˈär-inj, ˈär-(ə)nj, ˈȯr-inj, ˈȯr-(ə)nj\ **1** city SW Calif. N of Santa Ana *pop* 136,416 **2** river 1300 *mi* (2092 *km*) S Africa flowing from the Drakensberg in Lesotho W into the Atlantic

Orange \ȯ-ˈräⁿzh\ city SE France N of Avignon *pop* 27,999

Orange Free State — see FREE STATE

Or·ange·ville \ˈȯr-inj-ˌvil, ˈär-, -ənj-\ town Canada in Ont. NW of Toronto *pop* 27,975

Ordzhonikidze — see VLADIKAVKAZ

Ore·bro \œr-ə-ˈbrü\ city S *cen* Sweden *pop* 125,520

Or·e·gon \ˈȯr-i-gən, ˈär-, *chiefly by outsiders* -ˌgän\ **1** the Columbia River — an early name used esp. prior to discovery of mouth & renaming of river (1792) by Capt. Robert Gray **2** state NW U.S. ✳ Salem *area* 97,073 *sq mi* (251,419 *sq km*), *pop* 3,831,074 — **Or·e·go·nian** \ˌȯr-i-ˈgō-nē-ən, ˌär-, -ˈnyən\ *adj or n*

Oregon Caves limestone caverns SW Oreg. SW of Medford in **Oregon Caves National Monument**

Oregon City city NW Oreg. S of Portland *pop* 31,859

Oregon Country region W N. America bet. Pacific coast & the Rockies and bet. N Calif. & Alaska — so called *ab* 1818–46

Oregon Trail pioneer route to the Pacific Northwest *ab* 2000 *mi* (3219 *km*) long from vicinity of Independence, Mo., to the Willamette-Columbia river region; used esp. 1842–60

Orel \ȯ-ˈrel, ȯr-ˈyȯl\ *or* **Or·yol** \ȯr-ˈyȯl\ city S Russia in Europe SSW of Moscow

Orem \ˈȯr-əm\ city N Utah N of Provo *pop* 88,328

Oren·burg \ˈȯr-ən-ˌbərg, -ˌbùrg\ *or formerly* **Chka·lov** \chə-ˈkä-ləf\ city SE Russia in Europe on Ural River *pop* 557,000

Oren·se \ȯ-ˈren-(ˌ)sā\ *or* **Ou·ren·se** \ō-ü-ˈren-\ **1** province NW Spain *area* 2810 *sq mi* (7278 *sq km*), *pop* 338,446 **2** city, its ✳ *pop* 107,510

Øre·sund \ˈœr-ə-ˌsun\ strait bet. Sjælland Is., Denmark, & S Sweden connecting Kattegat with Baltic Sea

Organ Pipe Cactus National Monument park S Ariz. on Mexican border containing flora not found elsewhere in U.S.

Or·hon \ˈȯr-ˌhȯn, -ˌkȯn\ *or* **Or·khon** \ˈȯr-ˌkȯn, -ˌkȯn\ river N Mongolia flowing NE from N edge of the Gobi into the Selenga

Oril·lia \ȯ-ˈril-yə\ city Canada in SE Ont. on Lake Simcoe *pop* 30,586

Ori·no·co \ˌȯr-ē-ˈnō-(ˌ)kō\ river 1336 *mi* (2150 *km*) Venezuela flowing from Brazilian border to Colombia border & thence into the Atlantic through wide delta

Oris·sa *or* **Odisha** \ō-ˈri-sə\ state E India bordering on Bay of Bengal ✳ Bhubaneswar *area* 60,178 *sq mi* (155,861 *sq km*), *pop* 36,706,920

Ori·za·ba \ˌȯr-ə-ˈzä-bə, ˌȯr-ē-ˈsä-vä\ **1** — see CITLALTÉPETL **2** city E Mexico in Veracruz state *pop* 113,516

Ork·ney Islands \ˈȯrk-nē\ islands N Scotland constituting an administrative area ✳ Kirkwall (on Mainland Is.) *area* 376 *sq mi* (978 *sq km*), *pop* 19,570 — **Ork·ney·an** \ˈȯrk-nē-ən, ȯrk-ˈ\ *adj or n*

Or·lan·do \ȯr-ˈlan-(ˌ)dō\ city E *cen* Fla. NE of Tampa *pop* 238,300

Or·land Park \ˈȯr-lənd\ village NE Ill. SW of Chicago *pop* 56,767

Or·lé·ans \ˌȯr-lā-ˈäⁿ\ commune N *cen* France on the Loire SSW of Paris is ✳ of region & former province of **Or·lé·a·nais** \ˌȯr-lā-ə-ˈnä\ *pop* 113,089

Or·ly \ȯr-ˈlē, ˈȯr-lē\ commune France, SSE suburb of Paris *pop* 20,497

Or·moc Bay \ȯr-ˈmäk\ inlet of Camotes Sea Philippines in NW Leyte Is.

Or·mond Beach \ˈȯr-mənd\ city E Fla. upcoast from Daytona Beach *pop* 38,137

Ormuz — see HORMUZ

Orne \ˈȯrn\ river 95 *mi* (153 *km*) NW France flowing N into Bay of the Seine

Oro·co·vis \ˌȯr-ō-ˈkō-vēs\ city *cen* Puerto Rico *pop* 23,423

Oron·tes \ȯ-ˈrän-(ˌ)tēz\ river 246 *mi* (396 *km*) Syria & Turkey rising in Lebanon in the Bekaa & flowing into the Mediterranean

Oro Valley \ˈȯr-ō\ town S Ariz. N of Tucson *pop* 41,011

Or·ping·ton \ˈȯr-piŋ-tən\ former urban district SE England in Kent, now part of Bromley

Or·re·fors \ˌȯr-ə-ˈfȯrz, -ˈfȯrsh\ town SE Sweden NW of Kalmar

Orsk \ˈȯrsk\ city SE Russia in Europe on Ural River *pop* 273,000

Or·te·gal, Cape \ˈȯr-ti-ˌgäl\ cape NW Spain

Ort·les \ˈȯrt-ˌläs\ *or G* **Ort·ler** \-lər\ mountain range of E Alps N Italy bet. Venezia Tridentina & Lombardy; highest peak 12,792 *ft* (3899 *m*)

Orū·mī·yeh \ˌùr-ü-ˈmē-yə\ *or formerly* **Re·zā·ī·yeh** \ˌre-zä-ˈē-yə\ **1** shallow saline lake NW Iran *area* 1815 *sq mi* (4701 *sq km*) **2** city NW Iran *pop* 583,255

Oru·ro \ō-ˈri-rō\ city W Bolivia *pop* 201,230

Or·vie·to \ˌȯr-ˈvyä-(ˌ)tō, -ˈvye-\ commune *cen* Italy *pop* 20,684

Oryol — see OREL

Osage \ō-ˈsāj, ˈō-ˌ\ river E Kans. & Mo. flowing E into Missouri River; now partly submerged in Lake of the Ozarks

Osa·ka \ō-ˈsä-kä, ˈō-sä-ˌkä\ city & port Japan in S Honshu on **Osaka Bay** (inlet of the Pacific) *pop* 2,598,744

Osh·a·wa \ˈä-shə-wə, -ˌwä, -ˌwȯ\ city Canada in SE Ont. on Lake Ontario ENE of Toronto *pop* 149,607

Osh·kosh \ˈäsh-ˌkäsh\ city E Wis. on Lake Winnebago *pop* 66,083

Osi·jek \ˈō-sē-ˌyek\ city E Croatia in Slavonia *pop* 90,411

Os·lo \ˈäz-(ˌ)lō, ˈäs-\ *or formerly* **Chris·ti·a·nia** *or* **Kris·ti·a·nia** \ˌkris-chē-ˈa-nē-ə, ˌkrish-chē-, ˌkris-tē-, -ˈä-\ city ✳ of Norway at N end of **Oslo Fjord** (inlet of the Skagerrak) *pop* 507,831

Os·na·brück \ˈäz-nə-ˌbrük, ˌȯs-nə-ˈbruek\ city NW Germany in Lower Saxony *pop* 165,143

Osor·no \ō-ˈsȯr-(ˌ)nō\ volcano 8727 *ft* (2644 *m*) S *cen* Chile in lake district

Os·sa, Mount \ˈä-sə\ mountain 6490 *ft* (1967 *m*) NE Greece in E Thessaly

Os·se·tia \ä-ˈsē-sh(ē-)ə\ region SE Russia in Europe in *cen* Caucasus — see ALANIA, SOUTH OSSETIA

Os·si·ning \ˈä-sə-niŋ\ village SE N.Y. on Hudson River *pop* 25,060

Ost·end \ä-ˈstend, ˈä-ˌ\ *or Flem* **Oost·en·de** \ō-ˈsten-də\ *or F* **Os·tende** \ȯ-ˈstäⁿd\ city & port NW Belgium *pop* 67,574

Österreich — see AUSTRIA

Os·tia \ˈäs-tē-ə\ town *cen* Italy at mouth of the Tiber E of site of ancient town of the same name which was the port for Rome

Ostrasia — see AUSTRASIA

Ostra·va \ˈȯs-trə-və\ *or formerly* **Mo·rav·ska Ostrava** \ˈmȯr-əf-skə\ city *cen* E Czech Republic in Moravia *pop* 316,744

Osu·mi Islands \ˈō-sü-(ˌ)mē, ō-ˈsü-mē\ island group Japan in N Ryukyu Islands

Os·we·go \ä-ˈswē-(ˌ)gō\ city N N.Y. on Lake Ontario *pop* 18,142

Oś·wie·cim \ȯsh-ˈfyen-chēm\ *or G* **Ausch·witz** \ˈaùsh-ˌvits\ commune S Poland W of Kraków; site of Nazi concentration camp during World War II *pop* 45,282

Ota·go Harbour \ō-ˈtä-gō\ inlet of the Pacific S New Zealand on E coast of South Is.; Dunedin is situated on it

Otran·to \ō-ˈtran-(ˌ)tō, ō-ˈträn-ˌtō\ commune & port S Italy on coast at SE tip of Puglia *pop* 5341

Otranto, Strait of strait bet. SE Italy & W Albania connecting Adriatic Sea & Ionian Sea

Ot·ta·wa \ˈä-tə-wə, -ˌwä, -ˌwȯ\ **1** river 696 *mi* (1120 *km*) E Canada in SE Ont. & S Que. flowing E into St. Lawrence River **2** city ✳ of Canada in SE Ont. *pop* 883,391

Ot·to·man Empire \ˈä-tə-mən\ former Turkish sultanate in SE Europe, W Asia, & N Africa including at greatest extent Turkey, Syria, Mesopotamia, Palestine, Arabia, Egypt, Barbary States, Balkans, & parts of Russia & Hungary

Ot·tum·wa \ə-ˈtəm-wə, ō-ˈtəm-\ city SE Iowa *pop* 25,023

Oua·chi·ta \ˈwä-shə-ˌtȯ\ river 605 *mi* (974 *km*) SW Ark. & E La. flowing into Black River

Ouachita Mountains mountains W Ark. & SE Okla. S of Arkansas River

Oua·ga·dou·gou \ˌwä-gä-ˈdü-(ˌ)gü\ city *cen* Burkina Faso, its ✳ *pop* 1,475,223

Ouar·gla \ˈwȯr-glə, ˈwär-, -ˌglä\ town & oasis Algeria in the Sahara *pop* 81,721

\ə\ abut \ᵊ\ kitten, F table \ər\ further \a\ ash \ā\ ace \ä\ mop, mar \aù\ out \ch\ chin \e\ bet \ē\ easy \g\ go \i\ hit \ī\ ice \j\ job \ŋ\ sing \ō\ go \ȯ\ law \ȯi\ boy \th\ thin \t͟h\ the \ü\ loot \ù\ foot \y\ yet \zh\ vision, beige \k, ⁿ, œ, ᴔ, ᵞ\ *see* Guide to Pronunciation

Oubangui — see UBANGI
Oubangui–Chari — see UBANGI-SHARI
Ou·den·aar·de \ˌau̇-də-ˈnär-də, ˌō-\ *or F* **Au·de·narde** \ˌō-də-ˈnärd\ commune Belgium in E Flanders on the Schelde *pop* 28,089
Oudh \ˈau̇d\ region N India in E *cen* Uttar Pradesh; formerly a province of British India
Oudts·hoorn \ˈōts-ˌhȯrn\ city S Republic of South Africa in Western Cape province E of Cape Town *pop* 34,124
Oues·sant, Île d' \ˌēl-dwe-ˈsäⁿ\ *or* **Ush·ant** \ˈə-shənt\ island NW France off tip of Brittany
Ouj·da *or* **Oudj·da** \üzh-ˈdä\ city NE Morocco near Algerian border *area pop* 480,000
Ou·lu \ˈau̇-(ˌ)lü, ˈō-\ *or Sw* **Uleå·borg** \ˈü-lä-ō-ˌbȯr-ē\ city N *cen* Finland on Gulf of Bothnia *pop* 123,274
Ourense — see ORENSE
Ou·ro Prê·to \ˌō-(ˌ)rü-ˈprā-(ˌ)tü\ city E Brazil in Minas Gerais *pop* 66,277
Ouse \ˈüz\ **1** *or* **Great Ouse** river 160 *mi* (257 *km*) *cen* & E England flowing into The Wash **2** river 60 *mi* (96 *km*) NE England flowing SE to unite with Trent River forming the Humber
Outer Banks chain of sand islands & peninsulas along N.C. coast
Outer Hebrides — see HEBRIDES
Outer Mongolia — see MONGOLIA 2 — **Outer Mongolian** *adj or n*
Out Islands islands of the Bahamas group excepting New Providence
Ov·am·bo·land \ō-ˈvam-bō-ˌland\ region N Namibia
Over·ijs·sel \ˌō-və-ˈrī-səl\ province E Netherlands ✻ Zwolle *area* 1518 *sq mi* (3932 *sq km*), *pop* 1,094,032
Over·land Park \ˈō-vər-lənd\ city NE Kans. S of Kansas City *pop* 173,372
Ovie·do \ˌō-vē-ˈā-(ˌ)dō, ˌō-ˈvyā-t͟hō\ **1** — see ASTURIAS 2 **2** city NW Spain ✻ of Asturias province *pop* 201,154
Ovie·do \ō-ˈvē-dō\ city E *cen* Fla. NE of Orlando *pop* 33,342
Owas·co Lake \ō-ˈwäs-(ˌ)kō\ lake 11 *mi* (18 *km*) long *cen* N.Y.; one of the Finger Lakes
Ow·en Falls \ˈō-ən\ former waterfall E Africa in Uganda in the Nile N of Lake Victoria; now submerged in water behind Nalubaale Dam
Ow·ens \ˈō-ənz\ river E Calif. formerly flowing into **Owens Lake** (now dry), now supplying water to city of Los Angeles by way of Los Angeles Aqueduct
Ow·ens·boro \ˈō-ənz-ˌbər-ō\ city NW Ky. *pop* 57,265
Owen Stan·ley Range \ˈstan-lē\ mountain range E New Guinea; highest peak Mt. Victoria 13,363 *ft* (4073 *m*)
Owy·hee \ō-ˈwī-(ˌ)(h)ē\ river 250 *mi* (402 *km*) SW Idaho & SE Oreg. flowing N into Snake River
Ox·ford \ˈäks-fərd\ *or ML* **Ox·o·nia** \äk-ˈsō-nē-ə\ city S *cen* England ✻ of Oxfordshire *pop* 109,000 — **Ox·ford·ian** \äks-ˈfȯr-dē-ən\ *adj or n*
Ox·ford·shire \ˈäks-fərd-ˌshir, -shər\ *or* **Oxford** county S *cen* England ✻ Oxford *area* 1044 *sq mi* (2704 *sq km*), *pop* 553,800
Ox·nard \ˈäks-ˌnärd\ city S Calif. SE of Santa Barbara *pop* 197,899
Oxus — see AMU DAR'YA
Oxy·rhyn·chus \ˌäk-si-ˈriŋ-kəs\ *or Ar* **El Bah·na·sa** \el-ˈbä-nə-ˌsä\ archaeological site Egypt N of El Minyâ & S of El Faiyûm
Oyrot — see GORNO-ALTAY
Ozark Plateau \ˈō-ˌzärk\ *or* **Ozark Mountains** eroded tableland region 1500–2500 *ft* (457–762 *m*) high *cen* U.S. N of Arkansas River in N Ark., S Mo., & NE Okla. with E extension in S Ill. — **Ozark·er** \ˈō-ˌzär-kər\ *n* — **Ozark·ian** \ō-ˈzär-kē-ən\ *adj or n*
Ozarks, Lake of the \ˈō-ˌzärks\ reservoir 125 *mi* (200 *km*) long *cen* Mo. formed in Osage River by Bagnell Dam
Pa·ca·rai·ma Mountains \ˌpä-kä-ˈrī-mä\ mountain range N S. America in SE Venezuela, N Brazil, & W Guyana — see RORAIMA
Pa·chu·ca \pä-ˈchü-kä\ city *cen* Mexico ✻ of Hidalgo *pop* 179,440
Pa·cif·i·ca \pə-ˈsi-fi-kə\ city W Calif. S of San Francisco on the Pacific *pop* 37,234
Pa·cif·ic Islands, Trust Territory of the \pə-ˈsi-fik\ former U.S. trust territory comprising the Northern Mariana Islands (until 1978), the Federated States of Micronesia (until 1991), the Marshall Islands (until 1991), and Palau (until 1994)
Pacific Northwest region NW U.S. — usu. considered to include Wash. & Ore. and sometimes Idaho and all or part of Mont.
Pacific Ocean ocean extending from the arctic circle to the antarctic regions & from W N. America & W S. America to E Asia & Australia *area* 69,375,000 *sq mi* (180,375,000 *sq km*); often divided into **North Pacific Ocean** & **South Pacific Ocean**
Pacific Rim the countries bordering on or located in the Pacific Ocean — used esp. of Asian countries on the Pacific
Pacific Rim National Park Reserve scenic coastal area SW Canada in Vancouver Island
Pac·to·lus \pak-ˈtō-ləs\ river Asia Minor in ancient Lydia flowing into the Hermus (modern Gediz) near Sardis
Pa·dang \ˈpä-ˌdäŋ\ city & port Indonesia in W Sumatra *pop* 631,543
Pad·ding·ton \ˈpa-diŋ-tən\ former metropolitan borough NW London, England, now part of Westminster
Pa·dre Island \ˈpä-drē, -drā\ island 113 *mi* (182 *km*) long S Tex. bet. Laguna Madre & Gulf of Mexico
Pad·ua \ˈpa-jə-wə, ˈpa-dyü-wə\ *or It* **Pa·do·va** \ˈpä-dō-ˌvä\ commune NE Italy W of Venice *pop* 209,641 — **Pad·u·an** \ˈpa-jə-wən, ˈpa-dyü-\ *adj or n*
Pa·du·cah \pə-ˈdü-kə, -ˈdyü-\ city W Ky. on Ohio River *pop* 25,024
Padus — see PO
Paes·tum \ˈpes-təm, ˈpēs-\ *or earlier* **Po·sei·do·nia** \ˌpä-ˌsī-ˈdō-nē-ə, ˌpō-\ ancient city S Italy in W Lucania on Gulf of Salerno (ancient **Bay of Paestum**)
Pa·go Pa·go \ˌpä-(ˌ)gō-ˈpä-(ˌ)gō, ˌpäŋ-(ˌ)ō-ˈpäŋ-(ˌ)ō\ town & port ✻ of American Samoa on Tutuila Is.
Pa·hang \pə-ˈhaŋ\ state W Malaysia (federation) bordering on S. China Sea ✻ Kuantan *area* 13,920 *sq mi* (36,053 *sq km*), *pop* 1,036,724
Painted Desert region NE Ariz. E of the Little Colorado
Pais·ley \ˈpāz-lē\ burgh SW Scotland W of Glasgow *pop* 84,789
Pakanbaru — see PEKANBARU
Pa·ki·stan \ˈpa-ki-ˌstan, ˌpä-ki-ˈstän\ country S Asia orig. comprising an E division & a W division; a dominion 1947–56, an Islamic republic since 1956, & a member of the Commonwealth of Nations 1956–72; formed from parts of former Brit. India; ✻ Islamabad *area* 307,373 *sq mi* (796,096 *sq km*), *pop* 153,047,500 — see EAST PAKISTAN, WEST PAKISTAN — **Pa·ki·stani** \ˌpa-ki-ˈsta-nē, ˌpä-ki-ˈstä-\ *adj or n*
Pa·lat·i·nate \pə-ˈla-tə-nət\ *or G* **Pfalz** \ˈ(p)fälts\ either of two districts SW Germany once ruled by counts palatine of the Holy Roman Empire: **Rhenish Palatinate** (on the Rhine E of Saarland) & **Upper Palatinate** (on the Danube around Regensburg) — see RHINELAND-PALATINATE
Pal·a·tine \ˈpa-lə-ˌtīn\ **1** hill in Rome, Italy, one of seven on which the ancient city was built — see AVENTINE **2** village NE Ill. NW of Chicago *pop* 68,557
Pa·lau \pə-ˈlau̇\ *or* **Be·lau** \bə-\ island group W Pacific comprising a republic; usu. considered part of the Carolines *pop* 19,907 — **Pa·lau·an** \pə-ˈlau̇-ən\ *n*
Pa·la·wan \pə-ˈlä-wən, -ˌwän\ island 278 *mi* (445 *km*) long W Philippines W of the Visayan Islands *area* 4550 *sq mi* (11,830 *sq km*), *pop* (with adjacent islands) 528,287
Pa·lem·bang \ˌpä-ləm-ˈbäŋ\ city & port Indonesia in SE Sumatra *pop* 1,141,036
Pa·len·cia \pä-ˈlen-syä, -thyä\ **1** province N Spain *area* 3100 *sq mi* (8029 *sq km*), *pop* 174,143 **2** city, its ✻, NNE of Valladolid *pop* 79,797
Pa·len·que \pä-ˈleŋ-(ˌ)kā\ ruined Mayan city S Mexico in N Chiapas
Pa·ler·mo \pə-ˈlər-(ˌ)mō, pä-ˈler-\ *or anc* **Pan·or·mus** \pa-ˈnȯr-məs\ *or* **Pan·hor·mus** \pan-ˈhȯr-\ city & port Italy ✻ of Sicily *pop* 679,290 — **Pa·ler·mi·tan** \pə-ˈlər-mə-tən, -ˈler-\ *adj or n*
Pal·es·tine \ˈpa-lə-ˌstīn\ *or L* **Pal·aes·ti·na** \ˌpa-lə-ˈstē-nə, -ˈstī-\ **1** ancient region SW Asia bordering on E coast of the Mediterranean & extending E of Jordan River **2** region bordering on the Mediterranean on W & Dead Sea on E; a part of the Ottoman Empire 1516–1917, a Brit. mandate 1923–48; now approx. coextensive with Israel and the West Bank — **Pal·es·tin·ian** \ˌpa-lə-ˈsti-nē-ən, -nyən\ *adj or n*
Pal·i·sades \ˌpa-lə-ˈsādz\ line of cliffs 15 *mi* (24 *km*) long SE N.Y. & NE N.J. on W bank of Hudson River
Palk Strait \ˈpȯ(l)k\ strait 40 *mi* (64 *km*) wide bet. N Sri Lanka & SE India connecting Gulf of Mannar & Bay of Bengal
Pal·ma \ˈpäl-mä\ *or* **Palma de Mal·lor·ca** \dā-mä-ˈyȯr-kä, t͟hā-\ commune & port Spain ✻ of Baleares province on Majorca *pop* 333,801
Pal·mas \ˈpäl-mäs\ city *cen* Brazil ✻ of Tocantins *pop* 137,355
Pal·mas, Cape \ˈpäl-məs\ cape Liberia on extreme SE coast
Palm Bay city E Fla. on Indian River *pop* 103,190
Palm Beach Gardens city SE Fla. *pop* 48,452
Palm Coast city NE Fla. *pop* 75,180
Palm·dale \ˈpäm-ˌdāl, ˈpälm-\ city SW Calif. NE of Los Angeles *pop* 152,750
Palm Desert city SW Calif ESE of Riverside *pop* 48,445
Palm·er Archipelago \ˈpä-mər, ˈpäl-\ *or formerly* **Antarctic Archipelago** islands W of N end of Antarctic Peninsula in British Antarctic Territory
Palmer Land the S section of Antarctic Peninsula
Palmer Peninsula — see ANTARCTIC PENINSULA
Palm·er·ston \ˈpä-mər-stən, ˈpäl-mər-\ island (atoll) *cen* Pacific NW of Rarotonga Is.; belongs to New Zealand *area* 1 *sq mi* (2.6 *sq km*)
Palmerston North city New Zealand on S North Is. NE of Wellington *urban area pop* 72,681
Palm Springs city S Calif. E of Los Angeles *pop* 44,552
Pal·my·ra \pal-ˈmī-rə\ *or bib* **Tad·mor** \ˈtad-ˌmȯr\ ancient city Syria on N edge of Syrian Desert NE of Damascus — **Pal·my·rene** \ˌpal-mə-ˈrēn, -mī-\ *adj or n*
Palmyra Atoll island *cen* Pacific in Line Islands *area* 1 *sq mi* (2.6 *sq km*)
Palo Al·to \ˌpa-lō-ˈal-(ˌ)tō\ city W Calif. SE of San Francisco on San Francisco Bay *pop* 64,403
Pal·o·mar Mountain *or* **Mount Palomar** \ˈpa-lə-ˌmär\ mountain 6138 *ft* (1871 *m*) S Calif. NNE of San Diego
Pa·los \ˈpä-ˌlōs\ *or* **Pa·los de la Fron·te·ra** \t͟hā-lä-frȯn-ˈtā-rä\ town & former port SW Spain SE of Huelva *pop* 7314
Pa·louse \pə-ˈlüs\ **1** river *ab* 140 *mi* (225 *km*) NW Idaho & SE Wash. flowing W & S into Snake River **2** *or* **the Palouse** *or* **Palouse Hills** fertile hilly region E Wash. & NW Idaho N of Snake & Clearwater rivers
Pa·mirs \pə-ˈmirz\ *or* **Pa·mir** \-ˈmir\ mountain region *cen* Asia in Tajikistan & on borders of Xinjiang Uygur, Kashmir, & Afghanistan from which radiate Tian Shan to N, Kunlun & Karakoram to E, & Hindu Kush to W; has many peaks over 20,000 *ft* (6095 *m*)
Pam·li·co \ˈpam-li-ˌkō\ river E N.C., estuary of Tar River, flowing E into **Pamlico Sound** (inlet of the Atlantic bet. the mainland & offshore islands)
Pam·phyl·ia \pam-ˈfi-lē-ə\ ancient district & Roman province S Asia Minor on coast S of Pisidia — **Pam·phyl·i·an** \-lē-ən\ *adj or n*
Pam·plo·na \pam-ˈplō-nə, päm-ˈplō-nä\ *or formerly* **Pam·pe·lu·na** \ˌpam-pə-ˈlü-nə\ city N Spain ✻ of Navarra province & once ✻ of Navarre kingdom *pop* 183,964
Pan·a·ji \ˈpə-nə-jē\ town & port W India ✻ of Goa & formerly ✻ of Portuguese India *pop* 58,785
Pan·a·ma *or Sp* **Pa·na·má** \ˈpa-nə-ˌmä, -ˌmȯ, ˌpa-nə-ˈ; ˌpä-nä-ˈmä\ **1** country S Central America; a republic; before 1903 part of Colombia *area* (including Canal Zone) 30,765 *sq mi* (79,681 *sq km*), *pop* 3,300,000 **2** *or* **Panama City** city & port, its ✻, on Gulf of Panama *pop* 411,549 **3** ship canal 51 *mi* (82 *km*) *cen* Panama connecting the Atlantic (Caribbean Sea) & the Pacific (Gulf of Panama) — **Pan·a·ma·ni·an** \ˌpa-nə-ˈmā-nē-ən\ *adj or n*
Panama, Gulf of inlet of the Pacific on S coast of Panama
Panama, Isthmus of *or formerly* **Isthmus of Dar·i·en** \ˌder-ē-ˈen, ˌdär-\ isthmus Central America connecting N. America & S. America & forming Panama (republic)
Panama Canal Zone — see CANAL ZONE
Panama City **1** city & port NW Fla. on Gulf of Mexico *pop* 36,484 **2** — see PANAMA
Pan·a·mint Mountains \ˈpa-nə-ˌmint, -mənt\ mountains E Calif. W of Death Valley — see TELESCOPE PEAK
Pa·nay \pə-ˈnī\ island Philippines in the Visayan Islands; chief town Iloilo *area* 4446 *sq mi* (11,560 *sq km*)
Pan·gaea \pan-ˈjē-ə\ hypothetical land area believed to have once connected nearly all of the earth's landmasses together — see GONDWANALAND, LAURASIA
Pang–pu — see BENGBU

Pa·ni·pat \'pä-ni-ˌpət\ city NW India in SE Haryana state *pop* 261,665

Panjab — see PUNJAB

Panj·nad \ˌpənj-'näd\ river 50 *mi* (80 *km*) Pakistan formed from the combined stream of the Chenab & the Sutlej & flowing SW into the Indus

Pan·kow \'pän-(ˌ)kō\ NE suburb of Berlin, Germany; formerly seat of E. German government

Pan·mun·jom *or* **Pan·mun·jeom** \ˌpän-ˌmùn-'jəm\ village on N. Korea—S. Korea border SE of Kaesong

Pan·no·nia \pə-'nō-nē-ə\ Roman province SE Europe including territory W of the Danube now in Hungary & adjacent parts of Croatia & Vojvodina

Pantar — see ALOR

Pan·tel·le·ria \ˌpan-ˌte-lə-'rē-ə\ island Italy in the Mediterranean bet. Sicily & Tunisia

Pá·nu·co \'pä-nü-ˌkō\ river *cen* Mexico flowing from Hidalgo state NE into Gulf of Mexico

Pao-chi — see BAOJI

Pão de Açú·car \ˌpaùn-dē-ə-'sü-kər\ *or* **Sugarloaf Mountain** peak 1296 *ft* (395 *m*) SE Brazil in city of Rio de Janeiro on W side of entrance to Guanabara Bay

Paoking — see SHAOYANG

Pao·ting — see BAODING

Pao·t'ou — see BAOTOU

Papal States temporal domain of the popes in *cen* Italy 755–1870

Pa·pee·te \pä-pē-'ā-tē; pə-'pā-tē, -'pē-\ commune & port Society Islands on Tahiti ✱ of French Polynesia *pop* 23,555

Paph·la·go·nia \ˌpa-flə-'gō-nē-ə, -nyə\ ancient country & Roman province N Asia Minor bordering on Black Sea — **Paph·la·go·nian** \-nē-ən, -nyən\ *adj or n*

Pa·phos \'pā-ˌfäs, 'pä-ˌfòs\ town SW Cyprus on coast 10 *mi* (16 *km*) WNW of site of ancient city of Paphos *pop* 27,800

Pa·pua \'pa-pyü-wə, 'pä-pü-wə\ **1** — see NEW GUINEA 1 **2** the SE portion of the island of New Guinea; formerly a territory; now part of Papua New Guinea

Papua, Gulf of arm of Coral Sea SE New Guinea

Papua New Guinea country comprising the E part of the island of New Guinea, Bougainville Is., & the Bismarck Archipelago; before 1975 a U.N. trust territory administered by Australia ✱ Port Moresby *area* 178,260 *sq mi* (461,693 *sq km*), *pop* 5,190,736 — **Papua New Guinean** *adj or n*

Pa·rá \pə-'rä\ **1** river 200 *mi* (322 *km*) N Brazil, the E mouth of the Amazon **2** state N Brazil S of the Amazon — Belém *area* 481,869 *sq mi* (1,248,041 *sq km*), *pop* 6,192,307 **3** — see BELÉM

Par·a·dise \'pa-rə-ˌdīs, -ˌdīz\ **1** town N Calif. N of Sacramento *pop* 26,218 **2** population center Nev. *pop* 223,167

Par·a·guay \'pa-rə-ˌgwī, -ˌgwä; ˌpä-rä-'gwī\ **1** river 1584 *mi* (2549 *km*) *cen* S. America flowing from Mato Grosso plateau in Brazil S into Paraná River in Paraguay **2** country *cen* S. America traversed by Paraguay river; a republic ✱ Asunción *area* 157,043 *sq mi* (406,741 *sq km*), *pop* 4,643,000 — **Par·a·guay·an** \ˌpa-rə-'gwī-ən, -'gwä-\ *adj or n*

Pa·ra·í·ba \ˌpa-rə-'ē-bə\ **1** *or* **Paraíba do Nor·te** \dü-'nòr-tē\ river *ab* 180 *mi* (290 *km*) NE Brazil flowing E into the Atlantic **2** *or* **Paraíba do Sul** \dü-'sül\ river *ab* 600 *mi* (965 *km*) SE Brazil flowing NE into the Atlantic **3** state NE Brazil bordering on the Atlantic ✱ João Pessoa *area* 20,833 *sq mi* (53,957 *sq km*), *pop* 3,443,825

Par·a·mar·i·bo \ˌpa-rə-'ma-rə-ˌbō, -ˌbō\ city & port ✱ of Suriname on Suriname River *pop* 200,000

Par·a·mount \'pa-rə-ˌmaùnt\ city SW Calif. N of Long Beach *pop* 54,098

Pa·ram·us \pə-'ra-məs\ borough NE N.J. *pop* 26,342

Pa·ra·ná \ˌpär-ä-'nä\ **1** *or in upper course* **Al·to Paraná** \'al-(ˌ)tō, 'äl-\ river *ab* 2500 *mi* (4022 *km*) *cen* S. America flowing from junction of Rio Grande & Paranaíba River in Brazil SSW into the Río de la Plata in Argentina **2** state S Brazil E of Paraná River ✱ Curitiba *area* 76,959 *sq mi* (199,324 *sq km*), *pop* 9,563,458 **3** city NE Argentina on Paraná River *pop* 277,338

Pa·ra·na·í·ba *or formerly* **Pa·ra·na·hi·ba** \ˌpä-rə-nə-'ē-bə, ˌpär-ä-nä-\ river S Brazil flowing SW to unite with the Rio Grande forming Paraná River

Par·a·shant National Monument \'pa-rə-shänt\ reservation NW Ariz. containing open space

Par·du·bi·ce \'pär-dü-ˌbit-se\ city *cen* Czech Republic in Bohemia on the Elbe E of Prague *pop* 90,668

Paria, Gulf of inlet of the Atlantic bet. Trinidad & Venezuela

Pa·ria Peninsula \'pär-ē-ä\ peninsula NE Venezuela

Pa·ri·cu·tín \pä-ˌrē-kü-'tēn\ volcano *ab* 9100 *ft* (2775 *m*) SW Mexico in NW Michoacán; first eruption 1943

Parida, La — see BOLÍVAR (Cerro)

Par·is \'pa-rəs, *Fr* pä-'rē\ **1** city NE Tex. *pop* 25,171 **2** *or anc* **Lu·te·tia** \lü-'tē-sh(ē-)ə\ city ✱ of France on the Seine *pop* 2,125,851 — **Pa·ri·sian** \pə-'ri-zhən, -'rē-\ *adj or n*

Par·ker \'pär-kər\ town E *cen* Colo. SSE of Denver *pop* 45,297

Par·kers·burg \'pär-kərz-ˌbərg\ city NW W.Va. *pop* 31,492

Park Forest village NE Ill. S of Chicago *pop* 21,975

Park Ridge city NE Ill. NW of Chicago *pop* 37,480

Par·ma \'pär-mə\ **1** city NE Ohio S of Cleveland *pop* 81,601 **2** commune N Italy in Emilia-Romagna *pop* 170,031

Par·na·í·ba *or formerly* **Par·na·hy·ba** \ˌpär-nə-'ē-bə\ river NE Brazil flowing NE into the Atlantic

Par·nas·sus \pär-'na-səs\ *or* *ModGk* **Par·nas·sós** \ˌpär-nä-'sòs\ mountain 8061 *ft* (2457 *m*) *cen* Greece N of Gulf of Corinth

Pá·ros \'pär-ˌòs\ island Greece in *cen* Cyclades W of Naxos *area* 75 *sq mi* (194 *sq km*)

Par·ra·mat·ta \ˌpa-rə-'ma-tə\ city SE Australia, W suburb of Sydney, on Parramatta River (estuary W arm of Port Jackson) *pop* 132,798

Par·ris Island \'pa-rəs\ island S S.C. in Port Royal Sound

Parry Islands \'pa-rē\ islands Canada in Arctic Archipelago in Arctic Ocean N of Victoria Is.

Parsnip — see FINLAY

Par·thia \'pär-thē-ə\ ancient country SW Asia in NE modern Iran

Pas·a·de·na \ˌpa-sə-'dē-nə\ **1** city SW Calif. just NE of Los Angeles *pop* 137,122 **2** city SE Tex. E of Houston *pop* 149,043 — **Pas·a·de·nan** \-nən\ *n*

Pa·sar·ga·dae \pə-'sär-gə-ˌdē\ city of ancient Persia built by Cyrus the Great; ruins NE of site of later Persepolis

Pa·say \'pä-ˌsī\ municipality Philippines in Luzon on Manila Bay S of Manila *pop* 354,000

Pas·ca·gou·la \ˌpas-kə-'gü-lə\ city & port SE Miss. *pop* 22,392

Pas·co \'pas-(ˌ)kō\ city SE Wash. *pop* 59,781

Pasco, Cerro de — see CERRO DE PASCO

Pascua, Isla de — see EASTER ISLAND

Pas de Calais — see DOVER (Strait of)

Pa·sig \'pä-sig\ river 14 *mi* (23 *km*) Philippines in Luzon flowing from the Laguna de Bay in *cen* part of the island through Manila into Manila Bay

Paso Ro·bles \'pa-sō-'rō-bəlz\ *or in full* **El Paso de Robles** city W Calif. *pop* 29,793

Pas·sa·ic \pə-'sā-ik\ **1** river 80 *mi* (130 *km*) NE N.J. flowing into Newark Bay **2** city NE N.J. SSE of Paterson *pop* 69,781

Pas·sa·ma·quod·dy Bay \ˌpa-sə-mə-'kwä-dē\ inlet of Bay of Fundy bet. E Maine & SW N.B. at mouth of St. Croix River

Pas·se·ro, Cape \'pä-sə-ˌrō, 'pa-\ headland Italy at SE tip of Sicily

Pas·ta·za \pä-'stä-zə, -sä\ river 400 *mi* (644 *km*) Ecuador & Peru flowing S into the Marañón

Pat·a·go·nia \ˌpa-tə-'gō-nyə, -nē-ə\ region S. America in S Argentina & S Chile bet. the Andes & the Atlantic S of *ab* 40°S lat. — sometimes considered to include Tierra del Fuego — **Pat·a·go·nian** \-nyən, -nē-ən\ *adj or n*

Pa·tan \'pä-ˌtən\ city E *cen* Nepal adjoining Kathmandu *pop* 96,109

Pa·tap·sco \pə-'tap-(ˌ)skō, -si-ˌkō\ river 80 *mi* (129 *km*) N *cen* Md. flowing SE into Chesapeake Bay

Pat·er·son \'pa-tər-sən\ city NE N.J. N of Newark *pop* 146,199

Pa·ti·a·la \pə-tē-ä-lä\ **1** former state NW India, now part of Punjab state **2** city, its ✱, SW of Shimla *pop* 302,870

Pat·mos \'pat-məs, 'pät-ˌmòs\ island Greece in the NW Dodecanese

Pat·na \'pət-nə\ city NE India on the Ganges, ✱ of Bihar *pop* 1,376,950

Pa·tos, La·goa dos \ˌlä-gò-ə-dòs-'pä-ˌtòs, -düs-'pä-(ˌ)tüs\ lagoon 124 *mi* (200 *km*) long S Brazil in Rio Grande do Sul

Pa·tras \pə-'tras, pə-'träs\ *or Gk* **Pa·trai** \'pä-tre\ *or anc* **Pa·trae** \'pā-(ˌ)trē\ city & port W Greece in N Peloponnese on Gulf of Patras *pop* 155,180

Patras, Gulf of *or Gk* **Pa·tra·i·kós Kól·pos** \ˌpä-trä-ē-'kòs-'kòl-(ˌ)pòs\ inlet of Ionian Sea W Greece W of Gulf of Corinth

Patrimony of St. Peter — see ROME (Duchy of)

Pa·tux·ent \pə-'tək-sənt\ river 100 *mi* (161 *km*) *cen* Md. flowing S & SE into Chesapeake Bay

Pau \'pō\ **1** *or F* **Gave de Pau** \ˌgäv-də-'pō\ river 100 *mi* (161 *km*) SW France rising in the Pyrenees SW of Pau & flowing to the Adour — see GAVARNIE **2** commune SW France on Pau River *pop* 78,800

Pa·via \pä-'vē-ä\ commune N Italy S of Milan *pop* 73,893

Pav·lof \'pav-ˌlòf\ volcano 8261 *ft* (2518 *m*) SW Alaska on SW Alaska Peninsula in Aleutian Range

Paw·tuck·et \pə-'tə-kət, pò-\ city NE R.I. *pop* 71,148

Pay·san·dú \ˌpī-ˌsän-'dü\ city NW Uruguay *pop* 62,412

Pea·body \'pē-bə-dē, -ˌbä-dē\ city NE Mass. N of Lynn *pop* 51,251

Peace \'pēs\ river 1195 *mi* (1923 *km*) W Canada flowing E & NE in N B.C. & N Alta. into Slave River — see FINLAY

Peach·tree City \'pēch-ˌtrē\ city NW *cen* Ga. SSW of Atlanta *pop* 34,364

Pearl \'pər(-ə)l\ **1** river *ab* 410 *mi* (660 *km*) S Miss. flowing S into Gulf of Mexico **2** — see ZHU

Pear·land \'per-ˌland, -lənd\ city E Texas S of Houston *pop* 91,252

Pearl City unincorporated population center Hawaii in S Oahu *pop* 47,698

Pearl Harbor inlet Hawaii on S coast of Oahu W of Honolulu; site of U.S. Navy base

Pea·ry Land \'pir-ē\ region N Greenland on Arctic Ocean

Pe·chen·ga \'pe-chən-gə, pe-'chen-gä\ *or Finn* **Pet·sa·mo** \'pet-sä-ˌmō\ town & port NW Russia in Europe on inlet of Barents Sea in district that belonged to Finland 1920–44 *pop* 3500

Pe·cho·ra \pi-'chòr-ə\ river over 1100 *mi* (1770 *km*) NE Russia in Europe flowing N into Barents Sea

Pe·cos \'pā-kəs\ river E N.Mex. & W Tex. flowing SE into the Rio Grande

Pecos National Monument archaeological site N *cen* N.Mex. SE of Santa Fe containing Indian villages & a Spanish mission

Pecs \'pāch\ city S Hungary W of the Danube *pop* 179,000

Ped·er·nal·es \ˌpər-də-'na-ləs\ river *cen* Tex. flowing E into Colorado River

Pee·bles \'pē-bəlz\ **1** *or* **Pee·bles·shire** \'pē-bəl-ˌshir, -ˌshər\ former county SE Scotland including upper course of the Tweed **2** burgh SE Scotland on the Tweed — **Tweed·dale** \'twēd-ˌdāl\

Pee Dee \'pē-ˌdē\ river 233 *mi* (375 *km*) N.C. & S.C. flowing SE into Winyah Bay — see YADKIN

Peel \'pēl\ river 425 *mi* (684 *km*) NW Canada rising in W Yukon Territory & flowing E & N into the Mackenzie

Pee·ne \'pā-nə\ river 70 *mi* (113 *km*) NE Germany flowing E through Pomerania and forming **Peene Estuary** which flows N–S

Pee·ne·mün·de \ˌpā-nə-'mün-də, -'myün-, -'mʉen-\ village NE Germany on island at mouth of Peene Estuary

Pei·pus \'pī-pəs\ *or Estonian* **Peip·si** \'pāp-sē\ *or Russ* **Chud·skoe** \chüt-'skò-yə, -'skòi-(y)ə\ lake Europe bet. Estonia & Russia *area* 1390 *sq mi* (3600 *sq km*)

Pe·kan·ba·ru \ˌpā-kən-bär-ü\ *or* **Pa·kan·ba·ru** \ˌpä-\ city Indonesia in *cen* Sumatra *pop* 398,694

Pe·kin \'pē-kən, -ˌkin\ city N *cen* Ill. SSW of Peoria *pop* 33,857

Peking — see BEIJING

Pe·la·gie Islands \pe-'lä-je\ islands Italy in the Mediterranean S of Sicily bet. Malta & Tunisia

Pe·lée, Mount \pə-'lā\ volcano French West Indies in N Martinique; erupted 1902

Pelee, Point — see POINT PELEE NATIONAL PARK

Pe·lee Island \'pē-lē\ island SE Canada in W Lake Erie SW of Point Pelee, Ont. *area* 18 *sq mi* (47 *sq km*), *pop* 287

Pel·e·liu \,pe-lə-'lē-(,)ü, ,pe-lel-,yü\ island W Pacific at S end of Palau Islands *pop* 702

Pe·li·on \'pē-lē-ən\ *or ModGk* **Pí·lion** \'pēl-,yón\ mountain 5089 *ft* (1551 *m*) NE Greece in E Thessaly SE of Mt. Ossa

Pel·la \'pe-lə\ ancient city NE Greece, ancient ✶ of Macedonia

Pel·ly \'pe-lē\ river 330 *mi* (531 *km*) NW Canada in Yukon Territory flowing W into Yukon River

Pel·o·pon·nese \'pe-lə-pə-,nēz, -,nēs, ,pe-lə-pə-'\ *or* **Pel·o·pon·ne·sus** \,pe-lə-pə-'nē-səs\ *or* **Pel·o·pon·ni·sos** \,pe-lə-'pò-nē-,sòs\ peninsula forming S part of mainland of Greece — **Pel·o·pon·ne·sian** \,pe-lə-pə-'nē-zhən, -shən\ *adj or n*

Pem·ba \'pem-bə\ island Tanzania in Indian Ocean N of island of Zanzibar *pop* 265,039

Pem·broke \'pem-,brúk, *US also* -,brōk\ *or* **Pem·broke·shire** \-,shir, -shər\ administrative area of SW Wales *area* 614 *sq mi* (1590 *sq km*)

Pem·broke Pines \'pem-,brōk\ city SE Fla. *pop* 154,750

Pe·nang \pə-'nan\ **1** island SE Asia at N end of Strait of Malacca *area* 108 *sq mi* (281 *sq km*) **2** state Malaysia (federation) comprising Penang Island & mainland opposite, ✶ George Town *area* 400 *sq mi* (1036 *sq km*) *pop* 1,065,075; until 1948 one of the Straits Settlements **3** — see GEORGE TOWN

Pen–ch'i — see BENXI

Pen·del·i·kón \,pen-de-lē-'kòn\ mountain 3638 *ft* (1109 *m*) E Greece in Attica NE of Athens

Pend Oreille \pän-də-'rā\ river 100 *mi* (161 *km*) N Idaho & NE Wash. flowing from **Pend Oreille Lake** (35 *mi* or 56 *km* long, in Idaho) W & N into Columbia River in B.C.

Penedos de São Pedro e São Paulo — see SAINT PETER AND SAINT PAUL ROCKS

Pe·ne·us \pə-'nē-əs\ *or ModGk* **Pi·niós** \pē-'nyòs\ *or formerly* **Sa·lam·bria** \sə-'lam-brē-ə\ river 125 *mi* (201 *km*) N Greece in Thessaly flowing E into Gulf of Salonika

Penghu \'pəŋ-'hü\ *or* **Pes·ca·do·res** \,pes-kə-'dòr-ēz, -əs\ islands E China in Taiwan Strait, attached to Taiwan; chief town Makung (on Penghu, chief island) *area* 49 *sq mi* (127 *sq km*)

Peng–pu — see BENGBU

Pen–hsi — see BENXI

Peninsular Malaysia — see MALAYA 3

Pen·nine Alps \'pe-,nīn\ section of Alps on border bet. Switzerland & Italy NE of Graian Alps — see ROSA (Monte)

Pennine Chain mountains N England extending from Scotland border to Derbyshire & Staffordshire; highest Cross Fell 2930 *ft* (893 *m*)

Penn·syl·va·nia \,pen(t)-səl-'vā-nyə, -nē-ə\ state NE U.S. ✶ Harrisburg *area* 45,333 *sq mi* (117,866 *sq km*), *pop* 12,702,379

Pe·nob·scot \pə-'näb-,skät, -skət\ river 101 *mi* (162 *km*) *cen* Maine flowing S into **Penobscot Bay** (inlet of the Atlantic)

Pen·rhyn \pen-'rin, 'pen-,\ *or* **Ton·ga·re·va** \,täŋ-(g)ä-'rä-vä\ island S *cen* Pacific in the Northern Cook Islands

Pen·sa·co·la \,pen(t)-sə-'kō-lə\ city & port NW Fla. on **Pensacola Bay** (inlet of Gulf of Mexico) *pop* 51,923

Pen·tap·o·lis \pen-'ta-pə-lis\ any of several groups of five ancient cities in Italy, Asia Minor, & Cyrenaica

Pen·te·cost \'pen-ti-,kóst, -'käst\ island SW Pacific in Vanuatu *pop* 31,500

Pen·tic·ton \pen-'tik-tən\ city Canada in S B.C. *pop* 32,877

Pent·land Firth \'pent-lənd\ channel bet. Orkneys & mainland of Scotland

Pentland Hills hills S Scotland; highest peak Scald Law 1898 *ft* (578 *m*)

Pe·ñue·las \pā-nyü-'ā-läs\ city S Puerto Rico *pop* 24,282

Pen·za \'pen-zə\ city S *cen* Russia in Europe W of Samara *pop* 552,000

Pen·zance \pen-'zan(t)s, pən-\ seaside resort SW England in Cornwall on English Channel *pop* 19,521

Pen·zhin·ska·ya \,pen-zhin(t)-skə-yə, 'pen-,zhin(t)-\ *or* **Pen·zhi·na** \'pen-zhə-nə\ bay E Russia in Asia bet. Kamchatka Peninsula & mainland; an arm of Sea of Okhotsk

People's Democratic Republic of Yemen — see YEMEN

People's Republic of China — see CHINA (People's Republic of)

Pe·o·ria \pē-'òr-ē-ə\ **1** town SW *cen* Ariz. *pop* 154,065 **2** city N *cen* Ill. on Illinois River *pop* 115,007

Pep·in, Lake \'pe-pən\ expansion of upper Mississippi River 34 *mi* (55 *km*) long bet. SE Minn. & W Wis.

Pera — see BEYOGLU

Pe·raea *or* **Pe·rea** \pə-'rē-ə\ region of ancient Palestine E of Jordan River

Pe·rak \'per-ə, 'pir-ə, 'per-,ak\ state Malaysia in W Peninsular Malaysia on Strait of Malacca ✶ Ipoh *area* 8030 *sq mi* (20,798 *sq km*), *pop* 1,880,016

Per·di·do \pər-'dē-(,)dō\ river 60 *mi* (96 *km*) rising in SE Ala. & flowing S into Gulf of Mexico forming part of Ala.-Fla. boundary

Per·ga \'pər-gə\ ancient city S Asia Minor in Pamphylia

Per·ga·mum \'pər-gə-məm\ *or* **Per·ga·mus** \-məs\ *or* **Per·ga·mos** \-məs, -,mäs\ **1** ancient Greek kingdom covering most of Asia Minor; at its height 263–133 B.C. **2** *or modern* **Ber·ga·ma** \bər-'gä-mə\ city W Turkey NNE of Izmir ✶ of ancient Pergamum

Pé·ri·gord \,per-ə-'gòr\ old division of N Guienne in SW France ✶ Périgueux

Pé·ri·gueux \,per-ə-'gə(r), pā-rē-'gœ\ commune SW France NE of Bordeaux *pop* 30,152

Pe·rim \pə-'rim, -'rēm\ island in Bab el Mandeb Strait at entrance to Red Sea; belongs to Yemen

Per·lis \'per-ləs\ state Malaysia bordering on Thailand & Andaman Sea ✶ Kangar *area* 310 *sq mi* (803 *sq km*), *pop* 184,070

Perm' \'pərm, 'perm\ *or formerly* **Mo·lo·tov** \'mä-lə-,tòf, 'mò-, 'mō-, -,tòv\ city E Russia in Europe *pop* 1,099,000

Per·nam·bu·co \,pər-nəm-'bü-(,)kō, -'byü-; ,per-nəm-'bü-(,)kü\ **1** state NE Brazil ✶ Recife *area* 39,005 *sq mi* (101,023 *sq km*), *pop* 7,918,344 **2** — see RECIFE

Per·nik \'per-nik\ city W Bulgaria S of Sofia *pop* 81,000

Per·pi·gnan \,per-pē-'nyäⁿ\ city S France SE of Toulouse near Mediterranean coast *pop* 105,096

Per·ris \'per-əs\ city SE Calif. W of Palm Springs *pop* 68,386

Per·sep·o·lis \pər-'se-pə-lis\ city of ancient Persia; site in SW Iran NE of Shiraz

Persia — see IRAN

Persian Gulf arm of Arabian Sea bet. SW Iran & Arabia

Persian Gulf States Kuwait, Bahrain, Qatar, & United Arab Emirates

Per·sis \'pər-sis\ ancient region SW Iran

Perth \'pərth\ **1** city ✶ of Western Australia on Swan River *pop* 80,517 — see FREMANTLE **2** *or* **Perth·shire** \-,shir, -shər\ former county *cen* Scotland **3** burgh *cen* Scotland *pop* 41,998

Perth Am·boy \,pərth-'am-,bói\ city & port NE N.J. on Raritan Bay at mouth of Raritan River *pop* 50,814

Perth and Kinross administrative area of E *cen* Scotland *area* 2051 *sq mi* (5311 *sq km*)

Pe·ru \pə-'rü, pā-\ country W S. America; a republic ✶ Lima *area* 496,222 *sq mi* (1,285,215 *sq km*), *pop* 27,000,000 — **Pe·ru·vi·an** \-'rü-vē-ən\ *adj or n*

Pe·ru·gia \pə-'rü-j(ē-)ə, pā-\ commune *cen* Italy bet. Lake Trasimeno & the Tiber ✶ of Umbria *pop* 158,282

Pe·sa·ro \'pā-zə-,rō\ commune & port *cen* Italy on the Adriatic NW of Ancona *pop* 89,408

Pes·ca·ra \pe-'skär-ä\ commune & port *cen* Italy on the Adriatic *pop* 115,448

Pe·sha·war \pə-'shä-wər, -'shaù(-ə)r\ city N Pakistan ESE of Khyber Pass *pop* 982,816

Pe·tach Tik·va *or* **Pe·tah Tiq·wa** \'pe-tə(k)-'tik-(,)vä, ,pā-\ city W Israel *pop* 148,900

Pet·a·lu·ma \,pe-tə-'lü-mə\ city W Calif. N of San Francisco *pop* 57,941

Pe·ta·re \pe-'tär-(,)ā\ city N Venezuela, a SE suburb of Caracas *pop* 531,866

Pe·ter·bor·ough \'pē-tər-,bər-ō\ **1** city Canada in SE Ont. *pop* 78,698 **2** city E *cen* England *pop* 88,346

Peterborough, Soke of \'sòk\ former administrative county E *cen* England in Northamptonshire; later part of Huntingdonshire & since 1974 in Cambridgeshire

Pe·ters·burg \'pē-tərz-,bərg\ **1** city SE Va. S of Richmond *pop* 32,420 **2** SAINT PETERSBURG

Pet·it·co·di·ac \,pe-tē-'kō-dē-,ak\ river 60 *mi* (96 *km*) SE Canada in SE N.B. flowing to head of Bay of Fundy

Pe·tra \'pē-trə, 'pe-\ ancient city of NW Arabia on slope of Mt. Hor, site now in SW Jordan; ✶ of the Edomites & Nabataeans

Petrified Forest National Park reservation E Ariz. in Painted Desert containing natural exhibit of petrified wood

Pe·tro·dvo·rets \,pi-trə-dvär-'yets\ *or formerly* **Pe·ter·hof** \'pē-tər-,hòf, -,häf\ town W Russia in Europe W of St. Petersburg

Petroglyph National Monument reservation Albuquerque, N.Mex., containing rock carvings

Petrograd — see SAINT PETERSBURG 2

Pet·ro·pav·lovsk \,pe-trə-'pav-,lòfsk, ,pi-trə-'päv-ləfsk\ city N Kazakhstan *pop* 248,300

Petropavlovsk–Kam·chat·skiy \-kam-'chat-skē, -'chät-\ city & port E Russia in Asia on Kamchatka Peninsula *pop* 273,000

Pe·tró·po·lis \pə-'trò-pü-lēs\ city SE Brazil in Rio de Janeiro state *pop* 286,537

Petrovsk — see MAKHACHKALA

Pet·ro·za·vodsk \,pi-trə-zə-'vòtsk\ city NW Russia in Europe ✶ of Karelia on Lake Onega *pop* 280,000

Petsamo — see PECHENGA

Pfalz — see PALATINATE

Pforz·heim \'(p)fòrts-,hīm\ city SW Germany SE of Karlsruhe *pop* 115,547

Phar·os \'fer-,äs\ peninsula N Egypt in city of Alexandria; formerly an island

Pharr \'fär\ city S Tex. E of McAllen *pop* 70,400

Phar·sa·lus \fär-'sä-ləs\ *or* **Phar·sa·la** \'fär-sə-lə\ *or ModGk* **Fár·sa·la** \'fär-sä-lä\ town E *cen* Greece in E Thessaly in ancient district of **Phar·sa·lia** \fär-'säl-yə, -'sä-lē-ə\

Phe·nix City \'fē-niks\ city E Ala. *pop* 32,822

Phe·rae \'fir-ē\ ancient town SE Thessaly

Phil·a·del·phia \,fi-lə-'del-fyə, -fē-ə\ **1** city & port SE Pa. on Delaware River *pop* 1,526,006 **2** — see ALASEHIR **3** — see AMMAN — **Phil·a·del·phian** \-fyən, -fē-ən\ *adj or n*

Phi·lae \'fī-(,)lē\ former island S Egypt in the Nile above Aswân; now submerged

Philippeville — see SKIKDA

Phi·lip·pi \'fi-lə-,pī, fə-'li-,pī\ ancient town NE Greece in N *cen* Macedonia — **Phi·lip·pi·an** \fə-'li-pē-ən\ *adj or n*

Phil·ip·pine Islands \,fi-lə-'pēn, 'fi-lə-,\ islands of the Malay Archipelago NE of Borneo — see PHILIPPINES

Phil·ip·pines \'fi-lə-,pēnz, -,pēnz\ *or Sp* **Fi·li·pi·nas** \,fē-lē-'pē-(,)näs\ *or* **Pilipino** **Pi·li·pi·nas** \,pē-lē-'pē-(,)näs\ country E Asia comprising the Philippine Islands; a republic; once a Spanish possession & (1898–1946) a U.S. possession ✶ Manila *land area* 115,651 *sq mi* (299,536 *sq km*), *pop* 93,600,000 — **Philippine** *adj or n*

Philippine Sea sea comprising the waters of the W Pacific E of & adjacent to the Philippine Islands

Philippopolis — see PLOVDIV

Phi·lis·tia \fə-'lis-tē-ə\ country SW ancient Palestine on the coast; the land of the Philistines

Phnom Penh \(pə-)'näm-'pen, (pə-)'nòm-\ city ✶ of Cambodia on the Mekong *pop* 1,200,000

Pho·caea \fō-'sē-ə\ ancient city of Asia Minor on Aegean Sea in N Ionia — **Pho·cae·an** \-ən\ *adj or n*

Pho·cis \'fō-səs\ region *cen* Greece N of Gulf of Corinth — **Pho·cian** \'fō-sē-ən, -shən\ *adj or n*

Phoe·ni·cia \fi-'ni-sh(ē-)ə, -'nē-\ ancient country SW Asia at E end of the Mediterranean in modern Syria & Lebanon

Phoe·nix \'fē-niks\ city ✶ of Ariz. on Salt River *pop* 1,445,632 — **Phoe·ni·cian** \fē-'ni-shən\ *n*

Phoenix Islands islands W Pacific belonging to Kiribati

Phra Nakhon Si Ayutthaya — see AYUTTHAYA

Phry·gia \'fri-j(ē-)ə\ ancient country W *cen* Asia Minor divided *ab* 400 B.C. into **Greater Phrygia** (the inland region) & **Lesser Phrygia** (region along the Dardanelles)

Pia·cen·za \pyä-'chen-sä\ *or anc* **Pla·cen·tia** \plə-'sen(t)-sh(ē-)ə\ commune N Italy on the Po SE of Milan *pop* 98,407

Pi·auí *or formerly* **Pi·au·hy** \pyaü-'ē, pē-,aü-\ state NE Brazil bordering on the Atlantic E of Parnaíba River ＊ Teresina *area* 97,017 *sq mi* (251,274 *sq km*), *pop* 2,843,278

Pia·ve \'pyä-(,)vä, pē-'ä-\ river 137 *mi* (220 *km*) NE Italy flowing S & SE into the Adriatic

Pic·ar·dy \'pi-kər-dē\ *or F* **Pi·car·die** \pē-kär-'dē\ region & former province N France bordering on English Channel N of Normandy; chief town Amiens — **Pi·card** \'pi-,kärd, -kərd; pi-'kärd\ *adj or n*

Pi·ce·num \pī-'sē-nəm\ district of ancient Italy on the Adriatic SE of Umbria

Pick·er·ing \'pi-k(ə-)riŋ\ city Canada in SE Ont. *pop* 88,721

Pi·co Ri·ve·ra \pē-(,)kō-rə-'vir-ə\ city SW Calif. *pop* 62,942

Pied·mont \'pēd-,mänt\ **1** upland region E U.S. lying E of the Appalachian Mountains bet. SE N.Y. & *cen* Ala. **2** *or It* **Pie·mon·te** \pyä-'mōn-(,)tā\ region NW Italy bordering on France & Switzerland W of Lombardy ＊ Turin *pop* 4,357,559 — **Pied·mon·tese** \,pēd-mən-'tēz, -(,)män-, -'tēs\ *adj or n*

Pie·dras Ne·gras \pē-'ä-drəs-'ne-grəs, 'pyä-thräs-'nä-gräs\ city N Mexico in Coahuila on the Rio Grande *pop* 116,148

Pi·er·ia \pī-'ir-ē-ə, -'er-\ ancient region NE Greece in Macedonia N of Thessaly

Pierre \'pir\ city ＊ of S.Dak. on Missouri River *pop* 13,646

Pierre·fonds \pē-er-'fōⁿ, ,pyer-\ former town Canada in S Que., now part of Montreal (city)

Pie·ter·mar·itz·burg \,pē-tər-'ma-rəts-,bərg\ city E Republic of South Africa in S *cen* KwaZulu-Natal *pop* 128,598

Pigs, Bay of \'pigz\ *or* **Ba·hía de Co·chi·nos** \bä-'ē-ä-thä-kō-'chē-nōs\ bay W Cuba on S coast

Pikes Peak \'pīks\ mountain 14,110 *ft* (4301 *m*) E *cen* Colo. at S end of Front Range

Pik Pobedy — see POBEDA PEAK

Pi·la·tus \pē-'lä-tùs\ mountain 6983 *ft* (2128 *m*) *cen* Switzerland in Unterwalden SW of Lucerne

Pil·co·ma·yo \,pēl-kō-'mä-yō\ river 1000 *mi* (1609 *km*) S *cen* S. America rising in Bolivia & flowing SE on Argentina-Paraguay boundary into Paraguay River

Pílion — see PELION

Pillars of Her·cu·les \'hər-kyə-,lēz\ the two promontories at E end of Strait of Gibraltar: Rock of Gibraltar (in Europe) & Jebel Musa (in Africa)

Pí·los \'pē-,lòs\ town & port SW Greece in SW Peloponnese

Pim·li·co \'pim-li-,kō\ district of W London, England, in SW Westminster

Pi·nar del Río \pē-'när-thel-'rē-(,)ō\ city & port W Cuba *pop* 121,774

Pi·na·tu·bo, Mount \,pē-nä-'tü-(,)bō, ,pi-nə-\ volcano N Philippines on Luzon

Pin·dus Mountains \'pin-dəs\ mountains N Greece bet. Epirus & Thessaly

Pine Bluff \'pīn-'bləf, -,bləf\ city SE *cen* Ark. *pop* 49,083

Pi·nel·las Park \pī-'ne-ləs\ city W Fla. NW of St. Petersburg *pop* 49,079

Pinellas Peninsula peninsula W Fla. W of Tampa Bay

Pines, Isle of **1** — see YOUTH (Isle of) **2** — see ILE DES PINS

Ping \'piŋ\ river 360 *mi* (579 *km*) W Thailand flowing SSE to join Nan River forming the Chao Phraya

Piniós — see PENEUS

Pinkiang — see HARBIN

Pinnacles National Monument reservation W *cen* Calif. in Coast Range SSE of Hollister containing unusual rock formations

Pinsk \'pin(t)sk\ city SW Belarus *pop* 123,800

Pio·tr·ków Try·bu·nal·ski \,pyò-tər-,küf-,tri-bù-'näl-skē, pē-'ò-, -,kùv-\ commune *or* Poland SSE of Lodz *pop* 80,529

Pipe Spring National Monument site NW Ariz. on Kaibab Plateau containing old Mormon fort

Pipe·stone National Monument \'pīp-,stōn\ reservation SW Minn. containing quarry once used by American Indians

Pi·rae·us \pī-'rē-əs, pi-'rā-\ *or* **Pi·rai·evs** \,pē-re-'efs\ city E Greece on Saronic Gulf; port of Athens *pop* 169,622

Pirineos — see PYRENEES

Pir·ma·sens \'pir-mə-,zen(t)s\ city SW Germany near French border E of Saarbrücken *pop* 47,801

Pir·na \'pir-nə\ city E Germany SE of Dresden *pop* 48,001

Pi·sa \'pē-zə, *It* -sä\ commune W *cen* Italy in Tuscany on the Arno *pop* 91,977 — **Pi·san** \'pē-zᵊn\ *adj or n*

Pis·cat·a·qua \pi-'ska-tə-,kwò\ river 12 *mi* (19 *km*) Maine & N.H. formed by junction of Cocheco & Salmon Falls rivers & flowing SE into Maine-N.H. boundary into the Atlantic

Pis·gah, Mount \'piz-gə\ ridge Jordan E of N end of Dead Sea

Pi·sid·ia \pə-'si-dē-ə, pī-\ ancient country S Asia Minor N of Pamphylia — **Pi·sid·i·an** \-dē-ən\ *adj*

Pis·to·ia \pē-'stò-yä\ commune *cen* Italy NW of Florence *pop* 87,275

Pit \'pit\ river N Calif. flowing SW into the Sacramento

Pit·cairn Island \'pit-,kern\ island S. Pacific SE of Tuamotu Archipelago; a Brit. colony, with several smaller islands *pop* 62 — **Pit·cairn·er** \'pit-,ker-nər\ *n*

Pi·tes·ti \pē-'tesht, -'tesh-tē\ city S *cen* Romania *pop* 168,756

Pitts·burg \'pits-,bərg\ city W Calif. NE of Oakland on San Joaquin River *pop* 63,264

Pitts·burgh \'pits-,bərg\ city SW Pa. at confluence of the Allegheny & the Monongahela where they form the Ohio *pop* 305,704 — **Pittsburgh·er** \-,bər-gər\ *n*

Pitts·field \'pits-,fēld\ city W Mass. *pop* 44,737

Piz Bernina — see BERNINA

Pla·cen·tia \plə-'sen(t)-shə\ city SW Calif. *pop* 50,533

Placentia Bay inlet of the Atlantic E Canada in SE Newfoundland

Plac·id, Lake \'pla-səd\ lake 5 *mi* (8 *km*) long NE N.Y. in the Adirondacks

Plain·field \'plān-,fēld\ city NE N.J. *pop* 49,808

Plains of Abra·ham \'ā-brə-,ham\ plateau Canada in W part of city of Quebec

Pla·no \'plā-(,)nō\ city NE Tex. N of Dallas *pop* 259,841

Plantation city SE Fla. W of Fort Lauderdale *pop* 84,955

Plant City \'plant\ city W *cen* Fla. E of Tampa *pop* 34,721

Plas·sey \'pla-sē\ village NE India in W. Bengal N of Calcutta

Pla·ta, Río de la \,rē-ō-,thä-lä-'plä-tä\ *or* **River Plate** \'plāt\ estuary of Paraná & Uruguay rivers S. America bet. Uruguay & Argentina

Pla·taea \plə-'tē-ə\ *or* **Pla·tae·ae** \-'tē-,ē\ ancient city Greece in SE Boeotia S of Thebes — **Pla·tae·an** \-'tē-ən\ *adj or n*

Platte \'plat\ **1** river 310 *mi* (499 *km*) *cen* Nebr. formed by junction of the N. Platte & S. Platte & flowing E into the Missouri **2** river 300 *mi* (483 *km*) SW Iowa & NW Mo. flowing into the Missouri

Plattensee — see BALATON (Lake)

Platts·burgh \'plats-,bərg\ city NE N.Y. on Lake Champlain *pop* 19,989

Plau·en \'plaù-ən\ *or* **Plauen im Vogt·land** \im-'fōkt-,länt\ city E Germany in Saxony *pop* 70,856

Pleasant — see NAURU

Pleasant Grove city N *cen* Utah NNW of Provo *pop* 33,509

Pleasant Hill city W Calif. ENE of Oakland *pop* 33,152

Pleas·an·ton \'ple-zᵊn-tən\ city W Calif. SE of Oakland *pop* 70,285

Plenty, Bay of inlet of the S. Pacific N New Zealand on NE coast of North Is.

Ple·ven \'ple-ven\ city NW Bulgaria *pop* 138,323

Plock \'plótsk\ commune NE *cen* Poland *pop* 121,996

Plo·iesti *or* **Plo·esti** \plò-'yesht, -'yesh-tē\ city SE *cen* Romania *pop* 232,452

Plov·div \'plòv-,dif, -,div\ *or Gk* **Phil·ip·pop·o·lis** \,fē-lē-'pò-pō-,lēs\ city S Bulgaria on the Maritsa N of the Rhodope Mountains *pop* 379,083

Plum \'pləm\ borough SW Pa., a suburb of Pittsburgh *pop* 27,126

Plym·outh \'pli-məth\ **1** town SE Mass.: location of **Plymouth Rock** (spot traditionally considered to be where the Pilgrims first landed) *pop* 56,468 **2** city SE Minn. NW of Minneapolis *pop* 70,576 **3** city & port SW England in Devon *pop* 238,800

Pl·zeň \'pəl-,zen\ city W Czech Republic in Bohemia WSW of Prague *pop* 165,259

Po \'pō\ *or anc* **Pa·dus** \'pä-dəs\ river 405 *mi* (652 *km*) N Italy flowing from slopes of Mt. Viso E into the Adriatic through several mouths

Po·be·da Peak \pō-'be-də, pə-, -'bye-\ *or Russ* **Pik Po·be·dy** \,pēk-pə-'bye-dē, -'be-dē\ mountain 24,406 *ft* (7439 *m*) E Kyrgyzstan; highest in Tian Shan

Po·ca·tel·lo \,pō-kə-'te-(,)lō, -lə\ city SE Idaho *pop* 54,255

Po·co·no Mountains \'pō-kə-,nō\ mountains E Pa. NW of Kittatinny Mountain; highest point *ab* 1600 *ft* (488 *m*)

Pod·go·ri·ca \'pòd-,gòr-ēt-sä\ *or 1946–92* **Ti·to·grad** \'tē-(,)tō-,grad, -,gräd\ city ＊ of Montenegro *pop* 152,242

Po·do·lia \pə-'dō-lē-ə, -'dōl-yə\ *or Russ* **Po·dolsk** \pə-'dólsk\ region W Ukraine N of middle Dniester River

Po·dol'sk \pə-'dólsk\ city W *cen* Russia in Europe S of Moscow *pop* 208,000

Po Hai — see BO HAI

Pohn·pei \'pōn-,pā\ *or* **Po·na·pe** \'pō-nə-,pā\ island E Carolines; part of Federated States of Micronesia

Pointe–à–Pi·tre \,pwant-ə-'pētrᵊ\ city & port French West Indies in Guadeloupe on Grande-Terre *pop* 26,083

Pointe–Claire \,pòint-'kler, pwant-\ town Canada in S Que. on St. Lawrence River SW of Montreal *pop* 30,790

Pointe–Noire \,pwant-'nwär\ city & port SW Republic of the Congo on the Atlantic *pop* 576,206; formerly ＊ of Middle Congo

Point Pe·lee National Park \'pòint-'pē-lē\ reservation Canada in SE Ont. on Point Pelee (cape projecting into Lake Erie)

Poi·tiers *or formerly* **Poic·tiers** \pwä-'tyā, 'pwä-tē-,ā\ city W *cen* France SW of Tours *pop* 83,507

Poi·tou \pwä-'tü\ region & former province W France SE of Brittany ＊ Poitiers

Po·land \'pō-lənd\ *or Pol* **Pol·ska** \'pòl-skä\ country E *cen* Europe bordering on Baltic Sea; in medieval period a kingdom, at one time extending to the lower Dnieper; partitioned 1772, 1793, 1795 among Russia, Prussia, & Austria; again a kingdom 1815–30; lost autonomy 1830–1918; since 1918 a republic ＊ Warsaw *area* 120,756 *sq mi* (312,758 *sq km*), *pop* 38,038,400

Polesye — see PRIPET

Polish Corridor strip of land N Europe in Poland that bet. World War I & World War II separated E. Prussia from main part of Germany; area was before 1919 part of Germany

Pol·ta·va \pəl-'tä-və\ city *cen* Ukraine on Vorskla River WSW of Kharkiv *pop* 320,000

Poltoratsk — see ASHGABAT

Poly·ne·sia \,pä-lə-'nē-zhə, -shə\ the islands of the *cen* & S Pacific including Hawaii, the Line, Phoenix, Tonga, Cook, & Samoa islands, Tuvalu, Easter Is., French Polynesia, & often New Zealand

Pom·er·a·nia \,pä-mə-'rā-nē-ə, -nyə\ *or G* **Pom·mern** \'pò-mərn\ *or Pol* **Po·mo·rze** \pò-'mò-zhe\ **1** region N Europe on Baltic Sea; formerly in Germany, now mostly in Poland **2** former province of Prussia

Pom·er·e·lia \,pä-mə-'rē-lē-ə, -'rēl-yə\ *or G* **Pom·me·rel·len** \,pò-mə-'re-lən\ region N Europe on the Baltic W of the Vistula & E of Pomerania; orig. part of Pomerania

Po·mo·na \pə-'mō-nə\ city SW Calif. E of Los Angeles *pop* 149,058

Pom·pa·no Beach \'päm-pə-,nō, 'pəm-\ city SE Fla. on the Atlantic N of Fort Lauderdale *pop* 99,845

Pom·pe·ii \päm-'pā, -'pā-,ē\ ancient city S Italy SE of Naples destroyed A.D. 79 by eruption of Mt. Vesuvius — **Pom·pe·ian** *or* **Pom·pei·ian** \-'pā-ən\ *adj or n*

Pon·ca City \'päŋ-kə\ city N Okla. on Arkansas River *pop* 25,387

Pon·ce \'pòn(t)-(,)sā\ city & port S Puerto Rico *pop* 166,327

\ə\ abut \ᵊ\ kitten, F table \ər\ further \a\ ash \ā\ ace \ä\ mop, mar \aù\ out \ch\ chin \e\ bet \ē\ easy \g\ go \i\ hit \ī\ ice \j\ job \ŋ\ sing \ō\ go \ò\ law \òi\ boy \th\ thin \th̷\ the \ü\ loot \ù\ foot \y\ yet \zh\ vision, beige \k, ⁿ, œ, ʊ, ᵞ\ *see* Guide to Pronunciation

Pondicherry — see PUDUCHERRY
Pon·ta Del·ga·da \pȯn-tə-del-'gä-də\ city & port Azores on São Miguel Is. *pop* 65,854
Pont·char·train, Lake \'pänt-shər-,trān, ,pänt-shər-'-\ lake SE La. E of the Mississippi & N of New Orleans *area ab* 630 *sq mi* (1632 *sq km*)
Pon·te·fract \'pän-ti-,frakt, *formerly also* 'pəm(p)-frət, 'päm(p)-\ town N England in W. Yorkshire, SE of Leeds *pop* 31,971
Pon·te·ve·dra \,pȯn-tā-'vä-drä\ **1** province NW Spain in SW Galicia on the Atlantic *area* 1729 *sq mi* (4478 *sq km*), *pop* 903,759 **2** commune & port, its *, W of Vigo *pop* 74,942
Pon·ti·ac \'pän-tē-,ak\ city SE Mich. NW of Detroit *pop* 59,515
Pon·ti·a·nak \,pän-tē-'ä-,näk\ city Indonesia on SW coast of Borneo *pop* 398,357
Pon·tine Islands \'pän-,tīn, -,tēn\ islands Italy in Tyrrhenian Sea W of Naples; chief islands **Pon·za** \'pȯnt-sä\ & **Pon·ti·ne** \'pän-,tīn, -,tēn; pȯn-'tē-nä\
Pontine Marshes district *cen* Italy in SW Lazio, separated from sea by low sand hills that prevent natural drainage; now reclaimed
Pon·tus \'pän-təs\ **1** ancient country NE Asia Minor; a kingdom 4th century B.C. to 66 B.C., later a Roman province **2** *or* **Pontus Euxinus** — see BLACK SEA
Pon·ty·pool \,pän-tə-'pül\ town SE Wales NW of Bristol, England *pop* 36,761
Pon·ty·pridd \,pän-tə-'prēth\ town SE Wales NW of Cardiff *pop* 32,992
Poole \'pül\ town S England in Dorset on English Channel *pop* 130,900
Pool Malebo — see MALEBO (Pool)
Poona — see PUNE
Po·o·pó, Lake \pō-ō-'pō, (,)pō-'pō\ lake 60 *mi* (96 *km*) long W *cen* Bolivia S of Lake Titicaca at altitude of 12,000 *ft* (3658 *m*)
Pop·lar \'pä-plər\ former metropolitan borough E London, England, on N bank of the Thames, now part of Tower Hamlets
Po·po·ca·te·petl \pō-pə-'ka-tə-,pe-t'l, -,ka-tə-'; ,pō-pō-kä-'tä-,pe-t'l\ volcano 17,887 *ft* (5452 *m*) SE *cen* Mexico in Puebla
Porcupine river 448 *mi* (721 *km*) in N Yukon Territory & NE Alaska flowing N & W into the Yukon
Pork·ka·la Peninsula \'pȯr-kä-,lä\ peninsula S Finland W of Helsinki
Por·la·mar \,pȯr-lä-'mär\ city & port NE Venezuela on Margarita Is.
Port Adelaide city SE S. Australia on Gulf of St. Vincent at mouth of Torrens River; port for Adelaide *pop* 38,205
Por·tage \'pȯr-tij\ **1** city NW Ind. E of Gary *pop* 36,828 **2** city SW Mich. S of Kalamazoo *pop* 46,292
Port Ar·thur \'är-thər\ **1** city & port SE Tex. on Sabine Lake *pop* 53,818 **2** — see THUNDER BAY **3** — see LÜ-SHUN
Port–au–Prince \,pȯrt-ō-'prin(t)s, ,pȯr-(t)ō-'prans\ city & port * of Haiti on the SE shore of Gulf of Gonâve *pop* 752,600
Port Blair \'bler\ town & port India on S. Andaman Is. * of Andaman and Nicobar union territory *pop* 100,186
Port Ches·ter \'pȯrt-,ches-tər\ village SE N.Y. NE of New Rochelle on Long Island Sound *pop* 28,967
Port Co·quit·lam \kō-'kwit-ləm\ city Canada in SW B.C. *pop* 56,342
Port Eliz·a·beth \i-'li-zə-bəth\ city & port in the municipality of Nelson Mandela Bay S Republic of South Africa in S Eastern Cape province on Algoa Bay *pop* 237,503
Por·ter·ville \'pȯr-tər-,vil\ city S *cen* Calif. *pop* 54,165
Port Ev·er·glades \'e-vər-,glädz\ seaport SE Fla. on the Atlantic at SE point of Fort Lauderdale
Port Hed·land \'hed-lənd\ port Western Australia
Port Hu·ron \'hyúr-,än, 'yúr-, -ən\ city E Mich. on Lake Huron & St. Clair River *pop* 30,184
Port Jack·son \'jak-sən\ inlet of S. Pacific SE Australia in New South Wales; the harbor of Sydney
Port·land \'pȯrt-lənd\ **1** city & port SW Maine on Casco Bay *pop* 66,194 **2** city & port NW Oreg. at confluence of Columbia & Willamette rivers *pop* 583,776 — **Port·land·er** \'pȯrt-lən-dər\ *n*
Portland Canal inlet of the Pacific *ab* 80 *mi* (130 *km*) long Canada & U.S. bet. B.C. & SE tip of Alaska
Port·laoigh·ise \pȯrt-'lē-shə, -'lē-ə-\ *or* **Port Laoi·se** \'lē-shə\ *or* **Mary·bor·ough** \'ma-rē-,bər-ō\ town *cen* Ireland * of County Laoighis *pop* 3773
Port Lou·is \'lü-əs, 'lü-ē\ city & port * of Mauritius *pop* 146,876
Port Lyautey — see KENITRA
Port Mahon — see MAHÓN
Port Moo·dy \'mü-dē\ city Canada in SW B.C. E of Vancouver *pop* 32,975
Port Mores·by \'mȯrz-bē\ city & port SE New Guinea in Papua * of Papua New Guinea *pop* 254,158
Por·to \'pȯr-(,)tü\ *or* **Opor·to** \ō-'pȯr-(,)tü\ city & port NW Portugal on the Douro *pop* 263,131 — see LEIXÕES
Por·to Ale·gre \'pȯr-(,)tü-ä-'lä-grē\ city & port S Brazil * of Rio Grande do Sul state at N end of Lagoa dos Patos *pop* 1,360,590
Por·to·be·lo \,pȯr-tō-'be-(,)lō\ town & port Panama on Caribbean coast; center of S. American trade in 17th & 18th centuries
Port of Spain city & port * of Trinidad and Tobago, on NW Trinidad Is. *pop* 49,031
Por·to–No·vo \,pȯr-tō-'nō-(,)vō\ city & port * of Benin *pop* 192,000
Port Or·ange \'är-inj, 'är-(,)nj, 'ȯr-inj, 'ȯr(-ə)nj\ city E Fla. *pop* 56,048
Porto Rico — see PUERTO RICO
Pȯr·to Vel·ho \,pȯr-tü-'vel-yü\ city W Brazil * of Rondônia *pop* 334,661
Port Phil·lip Bay \'fi-ləp\ inlet of Bass Strait SE Australia in Victoria; the harbor of Melbourne
Port Roy·al \'rȯi(-ə)l\ town Jamaica at entrance to Kingston Harbor; early * of Jamaica, destroyed by earthquakes 1692 & 1907 & partly engulfed by the sea
Port Royal Sound inlet of the Atlantic S S.C.
Port Said \sä-'ēd, 'sīd\ city & port NE Egypt on the Mediterranean at N end of Suez Canal *pop* 262,760
Port Saint Lu·cie \,sānt-'lü-sē\ city E Fla. *pop* 164,603
Ports·mouth \'pȯrts-məth\ **1** city & port SE N.H. on the Atlantic *pop* 20,779 **2** city & port SE Va. on Elizabeth River opposite Norfolk *pop* 95,535 **3** city S England in Hampshire on **Port·sea** \'pȯrt-sē, 'pȯrt-\ (island in English Channel) *pop* 174,700
Port Stanley — see STANLEY
Port Sudan city & port NE Sudan on Red Sea *pop* 100,700

Por·tu·gal \'pȯr-chi-gəl, ,pür-tü-'gäl\ *or anc* **Lu·si·ta·nia** \,lü-sə-'tā-nē-ə, -nyə\ country SW Europe in W Iberian Peninsula bordering on the Atlantic; a kingdom before 1910; now a republic * Lisbon *area* (not including Azores & Madeira) 35,383 *sq mi* (91,642 *sq km*), *pop* 10,356,117
Portuguese East Africa — see MOZAMBIQUE 2
Portuguese Guinea — see GUINEA-BISSAU
Portuguese India former Portuguese possessions on W coast of India peninsula, annexed 1961 by India; comprised territory of Goa & districts of Daman & Diu
Portuguese Timor — see TIMOR 1
Portuguese West Africa — see ANGOLA
Port–Vi·la \,pȯrt-'vē-lə\ *or* **Vila** town & port * of Vanuatu in SW Efate Is. *pop* 44,000
Porz am Rhein \,pȯrts-äm-'rīn\ city W Germany ESE suburb of Cologne *pop* 76,762
Poseidonia — see PAESTUM
Potch·ef·stroom \'pȯ-chəf-,strōm\ city NE Republic of South Africa in E North West province SW of Johannesburg *pop* 51,800
Po·to·mac \pə-'tō-mək, -mik\ river 287 *mi* (462 *km*) E U.S. flowing from W.Va. into Chesapeake Bay & forming S boundary of Md.
Po·to·sí \,pō-tō-'sē\ city S Bolivia *pop* 132,966
Pots·dam \'päts-,dam\ city NE Germany * of Brandenburg *pop* 139,025
Pough·keep·sie \pə-'kip-sē, pō-\ city SE N.Y. *pop* 32,736
Poverty Point National Monument site NE La. featuring prehistoric earthworks
Po·way \'paú-(,)wā\ city S Calif., a suburb of San Diego *pop* 47,811
Pow·der \'paú-dər\ **1** river 150 *mi* (241 *km*) E Oreg. flowing into the Snake **2** river 375 *mi* (604 *km*) N Wyo. & SE Mont. flowing N into the Yellowstone
Powell, Lake — see GLEN CANYON DAM
Pow·ys \'pō-əs\ administrative area of E *cen* Wales *area* 2006 *sq mi* (5196 *sq km*)
Po·yang \'pō-'yäŋ\ lake 90 *mi* (145 *km*) long E China in N Jiangxi
Poz·nan \'pȯz-,nan, 'pȯz-,nän\ *or G* **Po·sen** \'pō-z'n\ city W *cen* Poland on the Warta *pop* 588,715
Poz·zuo·li \pȯt-'swō-lē\ *or anc* **Pu·te·o·li** \pyü-'tē-ə-,lī, pü-\ commune & port S Italy in Campania W of Naples *pop* 82,152
Prague \'präg\ *or Czech* **Pra·ha** \'prä-(,)hä\ city * of Czech Republic & formerly of Czechoslovakia in Bohemia on Vltava River *pop* 1,169,106
Praia \'prī-ə\ town * of Cape Verde on São Tiago Is. *pop* 132,000
Prairie Provinces the Canadian provinces of Man., Sask., & Alta.
Pra·to \'prä-tō\ commune *cen* Italy in Tuscany *pop* 174,513
Pratt·ville \'prat-,vil, -vəl\ city *cen* Ala. NW of Montgomery *pop* 33,960
Pres·cott \'pres-kət, -,kät\ city *cen* Ariz. *pop* 39,843
Prescott Valley town *cen* Ariz. NNW of Phoenix *pop* 38,822
Pre·šov \'pre-,shaü\ city *cen* E Slovakia *pop* 161,782
Presque Isle \presk-'ī(-ə)l\ peninsula NW Pa. in Lake Erie forming **Presque Isle Bay** (harbor of Erie, Pa.)
Pressburg — see BRATISLAVA
Pres·ton \'pres-tən\ **1** former town Ont., Canada — see CAMBRIDGE **2** city NW England NNE of Liverpool * of Lancashire *pop* 126,200
Prest·wich \'prest-(,)wich\ borough NW England in Greater Manchester NNW of Manchester *pop* 31,198
Prest·wick \'prest-(,)wik\ burgh SW Scotland N of Ayr *pop* 13,532
Pre·to·ria \pri-'tȯr-ē-ə\ city, administrative * of Republic of South Africa & formerly * of Transvaal in the municipality of Tshwane *pop* 303,684
Pretoria–Witwatersrand–Vereeniging — see GAUTENG
Prib·i·lof Islands \'pri-bə-,lȯf\ islands Alaska in Bering Sea
Prich·ard \'pri-chərd\ city N Mobile *pop* 22,659
Primorski Krai *or* **Primorskiy Kray** — see MARITIME TERRITORY
Prince Al·bert \'al-bərt\ city Canada in *cen* Sask. *pop* 35,129
Prince Albert National Park reservation Canada in *cen* Sask. in watershed area
Prince Ed·ward Island \'ed-wərd\ island SE Canada in Gulf of Saint Lawrence off E N.B. & N N.S.; a province * Charlottetown *area* 2185 *sq mi* (5660 *sq km*), *pop* 140,204
Prince Edward Island National Park reservation Canada on N coast of P.E.I.
Prince George \'jȯrj\ city Canada in E *cen* B.C. *pop* 71,974
Prince of Wales, Cape \'wālz\ cape Alaska at W tip of Seward Peninsula; most westerly point of mainland of N. America, at 168°W
Prince of Wales Island **1** island SE Alaska; largest in Alexander Archipelago **2** island N Canada bet. Victoria Is. & Somerset Is. *area* 12,830 *sq mi* (33,358 *sq km*)
Prince Ru·pert's Land \'rü-pərts\ historical region N & W Canada comprising drainage basin of Hudson Bay granted 1670 by King Charles II to Hudson's Bay Company; purchased 1869 by Canada
Prince Wil·liam Sound \'wil-yəm\ inlet of Gulf of Alaska S Alaska E of Kenai Peninsula
Prín·ci·pe Island \'prin(t)-si-pē\ island W Africa in Gulf of Guinea N of São Tomé — see SÃO TOMÉ
Prip·et \'pri-,pet, -pət\ *or Russ* **Pri·pyat'** \'pri-pyət\ *or Belarusian* **Pry·pyats'** \'pri-pyäts\ *or Ukrainian* **Pry·p'yat'** \'pri-pyät\ river 500 *mi* (805 *km*) E *cen* Europe in NW Ukraine & S Belarus flowing E through the marshlands called **Po·les·ye** \pə-'les-ye\ *or* **Pripet Marshes** to the Dnieper
Pris·ti·na \'prēsh-tē-,nä\ *or Alb* **Prish·ti·në** \'prēsh-tē-nä\ town * of Kosovo *pop* 155,499
Pro·gre·so \prə-'grā\,sō\ city SE Mexico on Yucatán Peninsula; port for Mérida *pop* 37,806
Pro·ko·pyevsk \prə-'kȯ-pyəfsk\ city S Russia in Asia at S end of Kuznetsk Basin NW of Novokuznetsk *pop* 272,000
Propontis — see MARMARA (Sea of)
Pro·vence \prə-'väⁿ(t)s, prō-'väⁿs\ region & former province SE France bordering on the Mediterranean * Aix-en-Provence
Prov·i·dence \'prä-və-dən(t)s, -,den(t)s\ city & port N R.I., its * *pop* 178,042
Pro·vo \'prō-(,)vō\ city N *cen* Utah on Utah Lake *pop* 112,488
Prud·hoe Bay \'prü-(,)dō, 'prə-; 'prüd-(,)hō, 'prəd-\ inlet of Beaufort Sea N Alaska
Prus·sia \'prə-shə\ *or G* **Preus·sen** \'prȯi-s'n\ **1** historical region N

Germany bordering on Baltic Sea **2** former kingdom & state of Germany ✻ Berlin — see EAST PRUSSIA, WEST PRUSSIA — **Prus·sian** \'prə-shən\ *adj or n*

Prut \'prüt\ river 565 *mi* (909 *km*) E Europe flowing from the Carpathians SSE into the Danube; forming the Romanian boundary with Moldova & Ukraine

Pskov \pə-'skóf, -'skòv\ city W Russia in Europe near **Lake Pskov** (S arm of Peipus Lake) *pop* 209,000

Ptol·e·ma·is \ˌtä-lə-'mā-əs\ **1** ancient town in upper Egypt on left bank of the Nile NW of Thebes **2** ancient town in Cyrenaica NW of Barka; site at modern village of Tolmeta **3** — see ACRE

Pu·chon or **Bu·cheon** \'bü-ˌchən\ city NW S. Korea *pop* 456,292

Pu·du·cher·ry \ˌpü-dü-ˌcher-ē\ or formerly **Pon·di·cher·ry** \ˌpän-də-'cher-ē, -'sher-\ **1** union territory SE India surrounded by Tamil Nadu; a settlement of French India before 1954, area 183 *sq mi* (474 *sq km*), *pop* 973,829 **2** city & port, its ✻ *pop* 220,749

Pueb·la \'pwe-blä\ **1** state SE cen Mexico area 13,096 *sq mi* (33,919 *sq km*), *pop* 4,126,101 **2** or **Puebla de Za·ra·go·za** \dä-ˌza-rə-'gō-zə, thä-ˌsär-ä-'gō-sä\ city, its ✻, SE of Mexico (City) *pop* 1,054,921

Pueb·lo \'pwe-ˌblò\ city SE cen Colo. on the Arkansas *pop* 106,595

Puen·te Al·to \'pwen-tā-'al-tò\ city cen Chile, just S of Santiago *pop* 492,915

Puer·to Bar·rios \'pwer-tō-'bär-ē-ˌōs\ city & port E Guatemala on Gulf of Honduras *pop* 39,088

Puerto La Cruz \lä-'krüz, -'krüs\ city NE Venezuela *pop* 60,546

Puerto Limón — see LIMÓN

Puer·to Ri·co \ˌpór-tə-'rē-(ˌ)kō, ˌpwer-tō-\ or formerly **Por·to Rico** \ˌpór-tə, ˌpór-tō\ island W. Indies E of Hispaniola; a self-governing commonwealth in union with the U.S. ✻ San Juan area 3435 *sq mi* (8931 *sq km*), *pop* 3,725,789 — **Puerto Ri·can** \'rē-kən\ *adj or n*

Pu·get Sound \'pyü-jət\ arm of the Pacific extending 80 *mi* (129 *km*) S into W Wash. from E end of Strait of Juan de Fuca

Pu·glia \'pül-yä\ or **Apu·lia** \ä-'pül-yä\ or **Le Pu·glie** \lə-'pül-yä\ region SE Italy on the Adriatic & Gulf of Taranto ✻ Bari *pop* 4,086,608

Pu·ka·pu·ka \ˌpü-kä-'pü-kä\ or **Dan·ger Islands** \'dān-jər\ group of coral islands cen Pacific N of Cook Islands; administered with Cook Islands by New Zealand

Pu·kas·kwa National Park \pə-'kas-kwə\ wilderness reservation Canada in Ont. bordering on Lake Superior

Pu·la \'pü-lä\ city & port W Croatia at tip of Istria *pop* 62,690

Pul·ko·vo \'pül-kə-və, -ˌvō\ village W Russia in Europe S of St. Petersburg

Pull·man \'pùl-mən\ city SE Wash. S of Spokane *pop* 29,799

Pu·log, Mount \'pü-ˌlóg\ mountain 9606 *ft* (2928 *m*) Philippines in N Luzon at S end of Cordillera Central; highest in Luzon

Pu·na de Ata·ca·ma \'pü-nä-ˌä-tä-'kä-mä\ high plateau region NW Argentina NW of San Miguel de Tucumán

Pun·cak Jaya \'pün-ˌchäk-'jä-yə\ or formerly **Mount Car·stensz** \'kär-stənz\ mountain 16,535 *ft* (5040 *m*) in Sudirman Range, West Papua, Indonesia; highest in New Guinea (island)

Pu·ne \'pü-nə\ or **Poo·na** \'pü-nə\ city W India in Maharashtra ESE of Bombay *pop* 2,540,069

Pun·jab or **Pan·jab** \ˌpən-'jäb, -'jab, ˌpən-ˌ\ **1** region NW Indian subcontinent in Pakistan & NW India occupying valleys of the Indus & its five tributaries; formerly a province of Brit. India ✻ Lahore **2** or **East Punjab** former state NW India in E Punjab divided 1966 into two states of Punjabi Suba & Haryana **3** or formerly **West Punjab** province NE Pakistan ✻ Lahore **4** or **Pun·jabi Su·ba** \ˌpən-'jä-bē-'sü-bə, -'ja-\ state NW India formed from N part of former state of Punjab ✻ Chandigarh area 19,448 *sq mi* (50,370 *sq km*), *pop* 24,289,296

Punt \'pùnt\ a part of Africa not certainly identified but probably Somaliland — an ancient Egyptian name

Pun·ta Are·nas \ˌpün-tä-ə-'rā-näs\ or formerly **Ma·gal·la·nes** \ˌmä-gä-'yä-näs\ city & port S Chile on Strait of Magellan *pop* 119,496

Punta del Es·te \thel-'es-tā\ town S Uruguay *pop* 5272

Pu·ra·cé \ˌpü-rä-'sā\ volcano 15,604 *ft* (4756 *m*) SW cen Colombia

Pur·beck, Isle of \'pər-ˌbek\ peninsula region S England in Dorset extending E into English Channel

Pur·ga·toire \'pər-gə-ˌtwär, 'pi-kə-ˌtwī(-ə)r\ river 190 *mi* (306 *km*) SE Colo. flowing into the Arkansas

Pu·ri \'pùr-ē\ city E India in SE Orissa on Bay of Bengal *pop* 157,610

Pu·rus \pü-'rüs\ river 2000 *mi* (3219 *km*) NW cen S. America rising in the Andes in SE Peru & flowing NE into the Amazon in Brazil

Pu·san \'pü-ˌsän, 'bü-\ or **Bu·san** \'bü-\ city & port SE S. Korea on Korea Strait *pop* 3,655,437

Push·kin \'pùsh-kən\ or formerly **Tsar·skoye Se·lo** \'t)sär-skə-yə-sə-'lò\ or **Det·skoe Selo** \'dyet-skə-yə\ city W Russia in Europe S of St. Petersburg *pop* 95,300

Puteoli — see POZZUOLI

Put–in–Bay \'pùt-ˌin-'bā\ inlet of Lake Erie in Ohio on S. Bass Is.; site of Oliver Hazard Perry's victory over the British fleet 1813

Pu·tra·ja·ya \ˌpü-trə-'jī-ə\ site SW Peninsular Malaysia of planned national ✻

Pu·tu·ma·yo \ˌpü-tü-'mī-(ˌ)ò\ or (in Brazil) **Içá** \ē-'sä\ river 980 *mi* (1577 *km*) NW S. America flowing from SW Colombia into the Amazon in NW Brazil

Puy·al·lup \pyü-'a-ləp\ city W cen Wash. ESE of Tacoma *pop* 37,022

Puy de Dôme — see DÔME (Puy de)

Puy de Sancy — see SANCY (Puy de)

Pya·ti·gorsk \pi-tē-'górsk\ city S Russia in Europe in N Caucasus WNW of Grozny, Chechnya *pop* 132,000

Pyd·na \'pid-nə\ ancient town Macedonia on Gulf of Salonika

Pyong·yang or **Pyeong·yang** \'pyòn-ˌyan, 'pyən-, -'yän\ city ✻ of N. Korea on the Taedong *pop* 2,355,000

Pyramid Lake lake 30 *mi* (48 *km*) long NW Nev. NE of Reno

Pyr·e·nees \'pir-ə-ˌnēz\ or F **Py·ré·nées** \pē-rā-'nā\ or Sp **Pi·ri·ne·os** \pē-rē-'nā-(ˌ)ōs\ mountains along French-Spanish border from Bay of Biscay to Gulf of Lion — see ANETO (Pico de) — **Pyr·e·ne·an** \ˌpir-ə-'nē-ən\ *adj or n*

Qaanaaq — see THULE

Qandahar — see KANDAHAR

Qaraghandy — see KARAGANDA

Qa·tar \'kä-tər, 'gä-, 'gə-; kə-'tär\ country E Arabia on peninsula projecting into Persian Gulf; an independent emirate ✻ Doha area 4400 *sq mi* (11,395 *sq km*), *pop* 1,697,000 — **Qa·tari** \kə-'tär-ē, gə-\ *adj or n*

Qat·ta·ra Depression \kə-'tär-ə\ region NW Egypt, a low area 40 *mi* (64 *km*) from coast; lowest point 440 *ft* (134 *m*) below sea level

Qaz·vin or **Kaz·vin** \kaz-'vēn\ city NW Iran S of Elburz Mountains & NW of Tehran *pop* 248,591

Qe·na \'ke-nə, 'kā-\ city S Egypt N of Luxor *pop* 137,000

Qe·qer·tar·su·aq \ˌke-ker-'tär-ˌsü-äk\ or **Dis·ko** \'dis-kō\ island W Greenland in Davis Strait

Qeshm \'ke-shəm\ island S Iran in Strait of Hormuz *pop* 15,000

Qing·dao \'chin-'daú\ or **Tsing·tao** \'chin-'daú, '(t)sin-'daú\ city & port E China in E Shandong on Jiaozhou Bay *pop* 1,459,195

Qing·hai \'chin-'hī\ or **Ko·ko Nor** \ˌkō-(ˌ)kō-'nòr\ or **Ch'ing–hai** \'chin-'hī\ low saline lake W cen China in NE Qinghai province at altitude of 10,515 *ft* (3205 *m*) **2** or **Tsing·hai** \'chin-'hī\ province W China ✻ Xining area 278,378 *sq mi* (723,783 *sq km*), *pop* 4,456,946

Qin·huang·dao or **Ch'in–huang–tao** or **Chin·wang·tao** \'chin-'hwän-'daú, -'wän-\ city & port NE China in NE Hebei *pop* 210,000

Qi·qi·har \'chē-'chē-'här\ or **Ch'i–ch'i–ha–erh** \'chē-'chē-'hä-'ər\ or **Tsi·tsi·har** \'(t)sēt-sē-ˌhär, 'chē-chē-\ city NE China in W Heilongjiang *pop* 1,500,000

Qi·shon \kē-ˌshòn, kē-\ river 45 *mi* (72 *km*) N Israel flowing NW through Plain of Esdraelon to the Mediterranean

Qom \'küm\ city NW cen Iran *pop* 543,139

Quad Cities the cities of Davenport, Iowa, East Moline, Moline, & Rock Island, Ill. — sometimes considered to include Bettendorf, Iowa, instead of East Moline

Quan·zhou or **Ch'üan–chou** or **Chuan·chow** \'chwän-'jō\ city SE China in SE Fujian on Taiwan Strait *pop* 110,000

Qu'Ap·pelle \kwə-'pel\ river 270 *mi* (434 *km*) Canada in S Sask. flowing E into the Assiniboine

Que·bec \kwi-'bek, ki-\ or **Qué·bec** \kā-'bek\ **1** province E Canada extending from Hudson Bay to Gaspé Peninsula area 595,388 *sq mi* (1,542,056 *sq km*), *pop* 7,903,001 **2** city & port, its ✻, on the St. Lawrence *pop* 516,622 — **Que·bec·er** or **Que·beck·er** \kwi-'be-kər, ki-\ *n*

Que·bra·dil·las \ˌkā-brä-'thē-yäs\ city NW Puerto Rico *pop* 25,919

Queen Char·lotte Islands \'shär-lət\ islands Canada in W B.C. in Pacific Ocean area ab 4000 *sq mi* (10,360 *sq km*)

Queen Charlotte Sound sound S of Queen Charlotte Islands

Queen Eliz·a·beth Islands \i-'li-zə-bəth\ islands N Canada in N Northwest Territories & N Nunavut; include Parry, Sverdrup, Devon, & Ellesmere islands

Queen Maud Land \'mód\ section of Antarctica on the Atlantic

Queens \'kwēnz\ borough of New York City on Long Is. *pop* 2,230,722

Queen's — see LAOIGHIS

Queens·land \'kwēnz-ˌland, -lənd\ state NE Australia ✻ Brisbane area 667,000 *sq mi* (1,727,530 *sq km*), *pop* 3,116,200 — **Queens·land·er** \-ˌlan-dər, -lən-\ *n*

Queenstown — see COBH

Quelpart — see CHEJU

Que·moy \ki-'mói, kwi-; 'kwē-, \ or **Chin Jin·men** \'jin-'mən\ or **Kin·men** \'kin-\ island SE China in Taiwan Strait 15 *mi* (24 *km*) E of Xiamen; garrisoned by Taiwan since 1950 *pop* 60,544

Que·ré·ta·ro \kā-'rā-tä-ˌrō\ **1** state cen Mexico area 4544 *sq mi* (11,769 *sq km*), *pop* 1,051,235 **2** city, its ✻ *pop* 454,049

Quet·ta \'kwe-tə\ city Pakistan in N Baluchistan *pop* 565,137

Que·zal·te·nan·go \ke(t)-ˌsäl-tā-'nän-(ˌ)gō\ city SW Guatemala *pop* 72,745

Que·zon City \'kā-ˌsòn\ city Philippines in Luzon NE of Manila; former (1948–76) official ✻ of the Philippines *pop* 1,632,000

Quil·mes \'kēl-ˌmäs, -ˌmes\ city E Argentina SE of Buenos Aires *pop* 509,445

Quim·per \kaⁿ-'per\ commune NW France W of Rennes *pop* 63,274

Qui·nault \kwi-'nòlt\ river 65 *mi* (105 *km*) W Wash. flowing to the Pacific

Quin·cy **1** \'kwin(t)-sē\ city W Ill. on the Mississippi *pop* 40,633 **2** \'kwin-zē\ city E Mass. SE of Boston *pop* 92,271

Quin·ta·na Roo \kēn-ˌtä-nä-'rò\ state SE Mexico in E Yucatán ✻ Chetumal area 16,228 *sq mi* (42,030 *sq km*), *pop* 493,277

Quin·te, Bay of \'kwin-tē\ inlet of Lake Ontario in Canada in SE Ont.; connected with Georgian Bay by Trent Canal

Quinte West city Canada in SE Ont. *pop* 43,086

Quir·i·nal \'kwir-ə-nªl\ hill in Rome, Italy, one of seven on which the ancient city was built — see AVENTINE

Qui·to \'kē-(ˌ)tò\ city ✻ of Ecuador *pop* 1,100,847

Qul·lai Is·mail So·mo·ni \kü-'lī-ēs-ˌmói(-ə)l-sō-mō-'nē\ or formerly **Communism Peak** mountain 24,590 *ft* (7495 *m*) NE Tajikistan in Pamirs; highest in Tajikistan & the former U.S.S.R.

Qumran, Khirbat — see KHIRBAT QUMRAN

Qüqon — see KOKAND

Qut·ti·nir·paaq National Park \kə-'ti-nir-ˌpäk\ reservation N Canada in NE Ellesmere Is. containing remote wilderness

Ra·ba \'rä-bə\ river 160 *mi* (257 *km*) SE Austria & W Hungary flowing E & NE into the Danube

Ra·bat \rə-'bät\ city ✻ of Morocco on Atlantic coast *pop* 668,000

Ra·baul \rə-'baúl\ city Bismarck Archipelago at E end of New Britain; formerly ✻ of Territory of New Guinea *pop* 17,022

Rabbah Ammon, Rabbath Ammon — see AMMAN

Race, Cape \'räs\ headland, SE point of Newfoundland, Canada

Ra·ci·bórz \rä-'chē-ˌbùsh\ or G **Ra·ti·bor** \'rä-tə-ˌbòr\ city SW Poland in Silesia on the Oder *pop* 62,833

Ra·cine \rə-'sēn, rā-\ city SE Wis. S of Milwaukee *pop* 78,860

Rad·nor \'rad-nər, -ˌnòr\ or **Rad·nor·shire** \-ˌshir, -shər\ former county E Wales; became part of Powys 1974

Ra·dom \'rä-ˌdóm\ commune Poland NE of Kielce *pop* 226,317

Raetia — see RHAETIA — **Rae·tian** \'rē-shən\ *adj or n*

Ragae *or* **Rages** — see RHAGAE
Ra·gu·sa \rə-ˈgü-zə\ commune Italy in SE Sicily *pop* 69,735
Rah·way \ˈrȯ-ˌwā\ city NE N.J. SW of Elizabeth *pop* 27,346
Rainbow Bridge National Monument reservation S Utah near Ariz. boundary containing **Rainbow Bridge** (large natural bridge)
Rai·nier, Mount \rə-ˈnir, rā-\ *or formerly* **Mount Ta·co·ma** \tə-ˈkō-mə\ mountain 14,410 *ft* (4392 *m*) W *cen* Wash.; highest in the Cascade Range & in Wash.; in **Mount Rainier National Park**
Rainy \ˈrā-nē\ river 80 *mi* (129 *km*) on Canada-U.S. boundary bet. Ont. & Minn. flowing from Rainy Lake into Lake of the Woods
Rainy Lake lake Canada & U.S. bet. Ont. & Minn. *area* 360 *sq mi* (932 *sq km*)
Rai·pur \ˈrī-ˌpu̇r\ city E India, ✱ of Chhattisgarh *pop* 605,131
Rai·sin \ˈrā-zᵊn\ river *ab* 115 *mi* (185 *km*) SE Mich. flowing into Lake Erie
Ra·jah·mun·dry \ˌrä-jə-ˈmu̇n-drē\ city E India in E Andhra Pradesh on Godavari River W of Kakinada *pop* 313,347
Ra·jas·than \ˈrä-jə-ˌstän\ state NW India bordering on Pakistan ✱ Jaipur *area* 132,149 *sq mi* (342,266 *sq km*), *pop* 56,473,122
Raj·kot \ˈräj-ˌkōt\ **1** former state W India in N *cen* Kathiawar Peninsula; now part of Gujarat **2** city, its ✱, *pop* 966,642
Raj·pu·ta·na \ˌräj-pə-ˈtä-nə\ *or* **Rajasthan** region NW India bordering on Pakistan & including part of Thar Desert
Ra·leigh \ˈrȯ-lē, ˈrä-lē\ city E *cen* N.C., its ✱ *pop* 403,892
Ra·lik \ˈrä-lik\ the W chain of the Marshall Islands
Ram·a·po Mountains \ˈra-mə-ˌpō\ mountains of the Appalachians N N.J. & S N.Y.; highest point 1164 *ft* (355 *m*)
Ra·mat Gan \rə-ˌmät-ˈgän, ˌrä-mät-\ city W Israel E of Tel Aviv *pop* 122,700
Ram·bouil·let \räⁿ-bü-ˈyā\ town N France SW of Paris *pop* 24,789
Ram·gan·ga \räm-ˈgəŋ-gə\ river *ab* 350 *mi* (563 *km*) N India in Uttar Pradesh flowing S into the Ganges
Ram·pur \ˈräm-ˌpu̇r\ **1** former state N India NW of Bareilly, now in Uttar Pradesh **2** city, its ✱, ENE of Delhi *pop* 281,549
Rams·gate \ˈramz-ˌgāt, -gət\ town SE England in Kent on North Sea N of Dover *pop* 39,642
Ran·ca·gua \rän-ˈkä-gwä, räŋ-\ city *cen* Chile *pop* 214,344
Ran·chi \ˈrän-chē\ city E India, ✱ of Jharkhand *pop* 846,454
Ran·cho Cu·ca·mon·ga \ˈran-(ˌ)chō-ˌkü-kə-ˈməŋ-gə, ˈrän-, -ˈmäŋ-\ city SW Calif. NW of Riverside *pop* 165,269
Rancho Pal·os Ver·des \ˌpa-ləs-ˈvər-dēz\ city SW Calif. on coast S of Torrance *pop* 41,643
Rancho San·ta Mar·ga·ri·ta \ˌsan-tə-ˌmär-gə-ˈrē-tə\ city S Calif. *pop* 47,853
Rand \ˈrand, ˈränd\ WITWATERSRAND
Ran·ders \ˈrä-nərs\ city & port NE Denmark *pop* 61,137
Ran·dolph \ˈran-ˌdälf\ town E Mass. S of Boston *pop* 32,112
Range·ley Lakes \ˈrānj-lē\ chain of lakes W Maine & N N.H.
Ran·goon \ran-ˈgün, raŋ-\ **1** *or* **Yan·gon** \ˌyäŋ-ˈgōn\ river 25 *mi* (40 *km*) S Myanmar, the E outlet of the Irrawaddy **2** — see YANGON 2
Ran·noch, Loch \ˈra-nək, -nək\ lake 9 *mi* (14 *km*) long *cen* Scotland
Rann of Kachchh — see KACHCHH (Rann of)
Ra·pa \ˈrä-pə\ island S. Pacific in SE Tubuai group *area* 15 *sq mi* (39 *sq km*), *pop* 516
Ra·pal·lo \rə-ˈpä-(ˌ)lō\ commune NW Italy in Liguria ESE of Genoa on **Gulf of Rapallo** (inlet of Ligurian Sea) *pop* 29,357
Rapa Nui — see EASTER ISLAND
Rap·i·dan \ˌra-pə-ˈdan\ river 70 *mi* (113 *km*) N Va. rising in Blue Ridge Mountains & flowing E into the Rappahannock
Rap·id City \ˈra-pəd\ city W S.Dak. in Black Hills *pop* 67,956
Rap·pa·han·nock \ˌra-pə-ˈha-nək\ river 212 *mi* (341 *km*) NE Va. flowing into Chesapeake Bay
Rap·ti \ˈräp-tē\ river 400 *mi* (644 *km*) Nepal & N India flowing SE into the Ghaghara
Rar·i·tan \ˈra-rə-tən\ river 75 *mi* (121 *km*) N *cen* N.J. flowing E into **Raritan Bay** (inlet of the Atlantic S of Staten Is., N.Y.)
Rar·o·ton·ga \ˌra-rə-ˈtäŋ-gə, -ˈtäŋ-ə\ island S. Pacific in SW part of Cook Islands *pop* 14,000; site of Avarua (✱ of Cook Islands)
Ra's al Khay·mah *or* **Ras al–Khai·mah** \ˌräs-al-ˈkī-mə, -ˈkī-\ sheikhdom, member of United Arab Emirates
Ra's at Tīb — see BON (Cape)
Ras Da·shen \ˌräs-də-ˈshen\ mountain 15,158 *ft* (4260 *m*) N Ethiopia NE of Lake Tana; highest in Ethiopia
Rashid — see ROSETTA
Rasht \ˈrasht\ city NW Iran near the Caspian *pop* 557,366
Ra·tak \ˈrä-ˌtäk\ the E chain of the Marshall Islands
Rat Islands \ˈrat\ islands SW Alaska in W Aleutians — see AMCHITKA, KISKA
Ra·ton \ra-ˈtōn, rə-, -ˈtün; *usu* -ˈtün *in N Mex*, -ˈtün *in Colo*\ pass 7834 *ft* (2388 *m*) SE Colo. just N of Colo.-N.Mex. border in **Raton Range** (E spur of Sangre de Cristo Mountains)
Ra·ven·na \rä-ˈve-nä\ commune N Italy NE of Florence *pop* 139,771
Ra·vi \ˈrä-vē\ *or anc* **Hy·dra·o·tes** \ˌhī-drə-ˈō-(ˌ)tēz\ river 450 *mi* (724 *km*) N India (subcontinent) flowing SW to the Chenab & forming part of boundary bet. E. Punjab (India) & W. Punjab (Pakistan)
Ra·wal·pin·di \ˌrä-wəl-ˈpin-dē, ˌrau̇l-ˈ, rōl-ˈ\ city NE Pakistan NNW of Lahore *pop* 1,409,768
Ray·town \ˈrā-ˌtau̇n\ city W Mo. SE of Kansas City *pop* 29,526
Read·ing \ˈre-diŋ\ **1** town E Mass. N of Boston *pop* 24,747 **2** city SE Pa. on the Schuylkill *pop* 88,082 **3** town S England ✱ of Berkshire *pop* 122,600
Re·bild \ˈrā-ˌbil\ village N Denmark in N Jutland S of Ålborg in **Rebild Hills** (site of **Rebild National Park**)
Re·ci·fe \ri-ˈsē-fē\ *or formerly* **Per·nam·bu·co** \ˌpər-nəm-ˈbü-(ˌ)kō, -ˈbyü-; ˌper-nəm-ˈbü-(ˌ)kü\ city & port NE Brazil ✱ of Pernambuco state *municipal area pop* 1,422,905
Reck·ling·hau·sen \ˌre-kliŋ-ˈhau-zᵊn\ city W Germany SW of Münster *pop* 125,966
Red \ˈred\ **1** river 1018 *mi* (1638 *km*) flowing E on Okla.-Tex. boundary & into the Atchafalaya & Mississippi in La. **2** river N *cen* U.S. & S *cen* Canada flowing N on Minn.-N.Dak. boundary & into Lake Winnipeg in Man. **3** — see ARCTIC RED **4** *or* **Hong** \ˈhȯŋ\ *or (in China)* **Yuan** \yu̇-ˈän, -ˈan\ river 500 *mi* (805 *km*) SE Asia rising in *cen* Yunnan, China, & flowing SE across N Vietnam into Gulf of Tonkin
Red·bridge \ˈred-(ˌ)brij\ borough of NE Greater London, England *pop* 220,600
Red Deer **1** river 385 *mi* (620 *km*) Canada in S Alta. flowing E & SE into the S. Saskatchewan **2** city Canada in S *cen* Alta. S of Edmonton *pop* 90,564
Red·ding \ˈre-diŋ\ city N Calif. *pop* 89,861
Red Lake lake 38 *mi* (61 *km*) long N Minn. divided into **Upper Red Lake** & **Lower Red Lake**; drained by **Red Lake River** (196 *mi or* 315 *km* flowing W into Red River)
Red·lands \ˈred-lən(d)z\ city S Calif. SE of San Bernardino *pop* 68,747
Red·mond \ˈred-mənd\ city W *cen* Wash. NE of Seattle *pop* 54,144
Re·don·do Beach \ri-ˈdän-dō\ city SW Calif. *pop* 66,748
Red Sea sea 1450 *mi* (2334 *km*) long bet. Arabia & NE Africa
Red Volta river 200 *mi* (322 *km*) S Burkina Faso & N Ghana flowing into Lake Volta
Red·wood City \ˈred-ˌwu̇d\ city W Calif. SE of San Francisco *pop* 76,815
Redwood National Park reservation NW Calif. containing groves of redwoods
Reel·foot \ˈrēl-ˌfu̇t\ lake NW Tenn. near the Mississippi
Re·gens·burg \ˈrā-gənz-ˌbərg, -gəns-ˌbu̇rk\ city SE Germany in Bavaria on the Danube NNE of Munich *pop* 123,002
Reg·gane \re-ˈgän, -ˈgan\ oasis *cen* Algeria in Tanezrouft SSE of Béchar
Reg·gio \ˈre-(ˌ)jō, -jē-(ˌ)ō\ **1** *or* **Reggio di Ca·la·bria** \dē-kä-ˈlä-brē-ä\ *or* **Reggio Calabria** *or anc* **Rhe·gi·um** \ˈrē-jē-əm\ commune & port S Italy on Strait of Messina *pop* 179,509 **2** *or* **Reggio nel·l'Emi·lia** \ˌne-le-ˈmēl-yä\ *or* **Reggio Emilia** commune N Italy in Emilia-Romagna NW of Bologna *pop* 146,092
Re·gi·na \ri-ˈjī-nə\ city Canada ✱ of Sask. *pop* 193,100
Reims *or* **Rheims** \ˈrēmz, *F* ˈraⁿs\ city NE France ENE of Paris *pop* 187,181
Reindeer Lake lake Canada on Man.-Sask. border *area ab* 2500 *sq mi* (6475 *sq km*)
Re·ma·gen \ˈrā-ˌmä-gən\ town W Germany on W bank of the Rhine NW of Koblenz *pop* 15,460
Rem·scheid \ˈrem-ˌshīt\ city W Germany in N. Rhine-Westphalia ESE of Düsseldorf *pop* 123,618
Ren·do·va \ren-ˈdō-və\ island W Pacific in *cen* Solomon Islands off SW *cen* coast of New Georgia Is.
Ren·frew \ˈren-ˌfrü\ *or* **Ren·frew·shire** \-ˌshir, -shər\ former county SW Scotland ✱ Paisley
Renfrewshire administrative area of W Scotland *area* 101 *sq mi* (261 *sq km*)
Rennes \ˈren\ city NW France N of Nantes *pop* 206,194
Re·no \ˈrē-(ˌ)nō\ city W Nev. NNE of Lake Tahoe *pop* 225,221
Ren·ton \ˈren-tᵊn\ city W Wash. SE of Seattle *pop* 90,927
Re·pen·ti·gny \rə-ˌpäⁿ-tē-ˈnyē\ town Canada in S Que. N of Montreal *pop* 82,000
Republican river 445 *mi* (716 *km*) Nebr. & Kans. rising in E Colo. & flowing E to unite with the Smoky Hill forming Kansas River
Re·thondes \rə-ˈtōⁿd\ village N France E of Compiègne *pop* 668
Ré·union \rē-ˈyü-nyən, ˌrā-ue-ˈnyōⁿ\ island W Indian Ocean in the W Mascarene Islands ✱ St.-Denis; an overseas department of France *area* 970 *sq mi* (2522 *sq km*), *pop* 834,000
Reut·ling·en \ˈrȯit-liŋ-ən\ city S Germany in Baden-Württemberg S of Stuttgart *pop* 105,835
Revel — see TALLINN
Re·vere \ri-ˈvir\ city E Mass. NE of Boston *pop* 51,755
Re·vil·la·gi·ge·do \rā-ˈvē-yä-hē-ˈhā-(ˌ)thō\ islands Mexico in the Pacific SW of S end of Baja California
Re·vil·la·gi·ge·do Island \ri-ˌvi-lə-gə-ˈgē-(ˌ)dō, -ˈge-\ island SE Alaska in SE Alexander Archipelago E of Prince of Wales Is.
Reyes, Point \ˈrāz\ cape W Calif. at S extremity of peninsula extending into the Pacific NW of Golden Gate
Reyk·ja·vík \ˈrā-kyə-ˌvik, -ˌvēk\ city & port ✱ of Iceland *pop* 112,490
Reyn·olds·burg \ˈre-nᵊl(d)z-ˌbərg\ city *cen* Ohio *pop* 35,893
Rey·no·sa \rā-ˈnō-sə\ city NE Mexico in Tamaulipas on the Rio Grande *pop* 337,053
Rezāīyeh — see ORŪMĪYEH
Rhae·tia *or* **Rae·tia** \ˈrē-sh(ē-)ə\ ancient Roman province *cen* Europe S of the Danube including most of modern Tirol & Vorarlberg regions of Austria & Graubünden canton of E Switzerland — **Rhae·tian** \-shən\ *adj or n*
Rhaetian Alps section of Alps E Switzerland in E Graubünden — see BERNINA
Rha·gae *or* **Ra·gae** \-(ˌ)jē, -ˌjī\ *or bib* **Ra·ges** \ˈrā-jəz\ city of ancient Media; ruins at modern village of **Rey** \ˈrī\ S of Tehran, Iran
Rhenish Palatinate — see PALATINATE
Rheydt \ˈrīt\ city W Germany S of Mönchengladbach *pop* 100,300
Rhine \ˈrīn\ *or G* **Rhein** \ˈrīn\ *or F* **Rhin** \ˈraⁿ\ *or D* **Rijn** \ˈrīn\ river 820 *mi* (1320 *km*) W Europe flowing from SE Switzerland to North Sea in Netherlands; forms W boundary of Liechtenstein & Austria & SW boundary of Germany — **Rhe·nish** \ˈre-nish, ˈrē-\ *adj*
Rhine·land \ˈrīn-ˌland, -lənd\ *or G* **Rhein·land** \ˈrīn-ˌlänt\ **1** the part of Germany W of the Rhine **2** RHINE PROVINCE — **Rhine·land·er** \ˈrīn-ˌlan-dər, -lən-\ *n*
Rhineland–Palatinate *or G* **Rheinland–Pfalz** \ˈ(p)fälts\ state of Germany & formerly of W. Germany chiefly W of the Rhine ✱ Mainz *area* 7654 *sq mi* (19,900 *sq km*), *pop* 3,642,482
Rhine Province former province of Prussia, Germany, bordering on Belgium ✱ Koblenz
Rhode Is·land \rōd-ˈī-lənd\ **1** *or officially* **Rhode Island and Providence Plantations** state NE U.S. ✱ Providence *area* 1212 *sq mi* (3139 *sq km*), *pop* 1,052,567 **2** — see AQUIDNECK — **Rhode Islander** *n*
Rhodes \ˈrōdz\ *or ModGk* **Ró·dhos** \ˈrȯ-ˌthȯs\ **1** island Greece in the SE Aegean, chief island of the Dodecanese *area* 540 *sq mi* (1399 *sq km*), *pop* 103,295 **2** city, its ✱ *pop* 43,619 — **Rho·di·an** \ˈrō-dē-ən\ *adj or n*
Rho·de·sia \rō-ˈdē-zh(ē-)ə\ **1** region *cen* S Africa comprising Zambia & Zimbabwe; contains rich archaeological findings **2** — see ZIMBABWE 2 — **Rho·de·sian** \-zh(ē-)ən\ *adj or n*
Rhodesia and Nyasaland, Federation of former country S Africa comprising S. Rhodesia, N. Rhodesia, & Nyasaland; a federal state within the Commonwealth; dissolved 1963

Rhod·o·pe \'rä-də-(,)pē, rō-'dō-pē\ mountains S Bulgaria & NE Greece; highest Musala 9596 *ft* (2925 *m*)

Rhon·dda \'rän-də, '(h)rän-thə\ town SE Wales NW of Cardiff *pop* 76,300

Rhondda Cy·non Taff \'kə-nən-'taf\ administrative area of S Wales *area* 164 sq mi (424 sq km)

Rhône \'rōn\ river 505 *mi* (813 *km*) Switzerland & France rising in the Alps and flowing through Lake Geneva into Gulf of Lion

Rhyl \'ril\ town & port NE Wales on Irish Sea *pop* 22,714

Ri·al·to \rē-'al-(,)tō\ 1 city SW Calif. W of San Bernardino *pop* 99,171 2 island & district of Venice, Italy

Ri·au *or* **Du Ri·ouw** \'rē-,au\ archipelago Indonesia S of Singapore *area* 2279 *sq mi* (5925 *sq km*), *pop* 278,966; chief island Bintan

Ri·bei·rão Prê·to \,rē-bə-'raúⁿ-'prä-(,)tü\ city SE Brazil in N *cen* São Paulo state *pop* 504,923

Rich·ard·son \'ri-chərd-sən\ city NE Tex. N of Dallas *pop* 99,223

Rich·e·lieu \'ri-shə-,lü, rē-shəl-'yœ\ river 210 *mi* (338 *km*) Canada in S Que. flowing N from Lake Champlain to head of Lake St. Peter in the St. Lawrence

Rich·field \'rich-,fēld\ city SE Minn.; a S suburb of Minneapolis *pop* 35,228

Rich·land \'rich-lənd\ city SE Wash. at confluence of Yakima & Columbia rivers *pop* 48,058

Rich·mond \'rich-mənd\ 1 city W Calif. NNW of Oakland on San Francisco Bay *pop* 103,701 2 city E Ind. *pop* 36,812 3 city *cen* Ky. *pop* 31,364 4 borough of New York City — see STATEN ISLAND 5 city ✸ of Va. on the James *pop* 204,214 6 city Canada in SW B.C. S of Vancouver *pop* 190,473 7 *or in full* Richmond upon Thames borough of SW Greater London, England *pop* 154,600 — **Rich·mond·er** \-mən-dər\ *n*

Richmond Hill town Canada in SE Ont. N of Toronto *pop* 185,541

Ri·deau Canal \ri-'dō\ canal system Canada 124 *mi* (200 *km*) long in SE Ont. connecting Lake Ontario & Ottawa River & including **Rideau Lake** (20 *mi* or 32 *km* long) & **Rideau River** (flowing into the Ottawa)

Ridge·crest \'rij-,krest\ city S Calif. NE of Bakersfield *pop* 27,616

Ridge·field \'rij-,fēld\ town S Conn. NW of Norwalk *pop* 24,638

Ridge·wood \'rij-,wúd\ village NE N.J. NNE of Paterson *pop* 24,958

Rid·ing Mountain National Park \'rī-diŋ\ wilderness area in Canada in SW Man. surrounded by agricultural land

Rif — see ER RIF

Rift Valley GREAT RIFT VALLEY

Ri·ga \'rē-gə\ city & port ✸ of Latvia at S extremity of the Gulf of Riga *pop* 747,157

Riga, Gulf of inlet of Baltic Sea bordering on Estonia & Latvia

Ri·je·ka *or* **Ri·e·ka** \rē-'ye-kə\ *or It* **Fiu·me** \'fyü-(,)mā, fē-'ü-\ city & port W Croatia *pop* 167,964

Rijs·wijk \'rīs-,vīk\ commune SW Netherlands

Rí·mac \'rē-,mäk\ river 80 *mi* (129 *km*) W Peru flowing SW through Lima into the Pacific

Ri·mi·ni \'ri-mi-(,)nē, 'rē-\ *or anc* **Arim·i·num** \ə-'ri-mə-nəm\ commune & port N Italy on the Adriatic ESE of Ravenna *pop* 131,705

Ri·mou·ski \ri-'müs-kē\ town Canada in S Que. on Gaspé Peninsula *pop* 46,860

Ring of Fire belt of volcanoes & frequent seismic activity nearly encircling the Pacific

Rio \'rē-(,)ō\ RIO DE JANEIRO

Rio Bran·co \,rē-(,)ō-'braŋ-(,)kō, ,rē-(,)ü-'bräŋ-(,)kü\ 1 — see BRANCO 2 city W Brazil, ✸ of Acre *municipal area pop* 253,059

Rio de Ja·nei·ro \,rē-(,)ō-də-zhə-'ner-(,)ō, -dē-; 'rē-ü-dē-zhə-'nä-rü\ 1 state SE Brazil *area* 17,092 *sq mi* (44,268 *sq km*), *pop* 14,391,282 2 city, its ✸ & port on Guanabara Bay; former ✸ of Brazil *pop* 5,857,904

Río de la Plata — see PLATA (Río de la)

Río de Oro \,rē-(,)ō-dē-'ôr-(,)ō\ territory NW Africa comprising the S zone of Western Sahara

Rio Grande 1 \,rē-(,)ō-'grand, -'gran-dē *also* ,rī-ō-'grand\ *or MexSp* **Río Bra·vo** \,rē-(,)ō-'brä-(,)vō\ river 1885 *mi* (3034 *km*) SW U.S. forming part of Mexico-U.S. boundary & flowing from San Juan Mountains in SW Colo. to Gulf of Mexico 2 *or* **Rio Gran·de do Sul** \,rē-ü-'grän-dē-dü-'sül\ city S Brazil in Rio Grande do Sul state W of entrance to Lagoa dos Patos *pop* 186,544 3 \,rē-(,)ō-'grän-dā, -dē\ municipality NE Puerto Rico *pop* 52,362 4 — see GRANDE (Rio)

Rio Grande de Cagayan — see CAGAYAN

Rio Gran·de do Nor·te \,rē-(,)ü-'grän-dē-dü-'nòr-tē\ state NE Brazil ✸ Natal *area* 20,528 *sq mi* (53,168 *sq km*), *pop* 2,776,782

Rio Grande do Sul \-'sül\ state SE Brazil bordering on Uruguay ✸ Pôrto Alegre *area* 108,951 *sq mi* (282,183 *sq km*), *pop* 10,187,798

Rioja, the — see LA RIOJA

Río Muni — see MBINI

Río Pie·dras \'rē-(,)ō-'pyä-drəs, -thräs\ former city, since 1951 part of San Juan, Puerto Rico

Rio Ran·cho \,rē-(,)ō-'ran-(,)chō, -'rän-\ city *cen* N.Mex., a N suburb of Albuquerque *pop* 87,521

Rip·on Falls \'ri-pən, -,pän\ former waterfall in the Victoria Nile N of Lake Victoria; submerged by Nalubaale Dam

Riv·er·side \'ri-vər-,sīd\ 1 city S Calif. *pop* 303,871 2 city SW Ohio E of Dayton *pop* 25,201

Riv·er·ton \'ri-vər-tən\ city N *cen* Utah S of Salt Lake City *pop* 38,753

Riv·i·era \,ri-vē-'er-ə\ coast region SE France & NW Italy bordering on the Mediterranean — see CÔTE D'AZUR

Riviera Beach city SE Fla. N of W. Palm Beach *pop* 32,488

Ri·yadh \rē-'yäd\ city ✸ of the Nejd & of Saudi Arabia *pop* 4,700,000

Rju·kan \'rē-'ü-,kän\ town S Norway W of Oslo near **Rjukan Falls** (waterfall 780 *ft* or 238 *m*)

Ro·a·noke \'rō-(ə-),nōk\ 1 river 380 *mi* (612 *km*) S Va. & NE N.C. flowing E & SE into Albemarle Sound 2 city W *cen* Va. *pop* 97,032

Roanoke Island island N.C. S of entrance to Albemarle Sound

Rob·erts, Point \'rä-bərts\ cape NW Wash. at the tip of a peninsula extending S into Strait of Georgia from B.C. & separated from U.S. mainland by Boundary Bay

Rob·son, Mount \'räb-sən\ mountain 12,972 *ft* (3954 *m*) W Canada in E B.C.; highest in Canadian Rockies

Ro·ca, Cape \'rō-kə\ *or Pg* **Ca·bo da Ro·ca** \'kä-bü-də-'rò-kə\ cape Portugal; westernmost point of continental Europe, at 9°30'W

Roch·dale \'räch-,dāl\ town NW England in Greater Manchester NNE of Manchester *pop* 92,704

Roche·fort \'ròsh-,fòr, 'rōsh-fərt\ *or* **Rochefort–sur–Mer** \-,sīer-'mer\ city W France SSE of La Rochelle *pop* 25,775

Roch·es·ter \'rä-chəs-tər, -,ches-tər\ 1 city SE Minn. *pop* 106,769 2 city SE N.H. *pop* 29,752 3 city W N.Y. on the Genesee *pop* 210,565 4 city SE England in Kent *pop* 52,505

Rock \'räk\ river 300 *mi* (483 *km*) S Wis. & N Ill. flowing S & SW into the Mississippi at Rock Island

Rock·all \'rä-,kòl\ islet N Atlantic NW of Ireland

Rock·ford \'räk-fərd\ city N Ill. NW of Chicago *pop* 152,871

Rock·hamp·ton \räk-'ham(p)-tən, rä-'kam(p)-\ city & port E Australia in E Queensland on Fitzroy River *pop* 61,631

Rock Hill city N S.C. SSW of Charlotte, N.C. *pop* 66,154

Rock Island city NW Ill. on the Mississippi *pop* 39,018

Rock·lin \'räk-lin, -klən\ city E Calif. NE of Sacramento *pop* 56,974

Rock·ville \'räk-,vil, -vəl\ city SW Md. *pop* 61,209

Rockville Centre village SE N.Y. in W *cen* Long Is. *pop* 24,023

Rocky Mount \'rä-kē\ city NE *cen* N.C. *pop* 57,477

Rocky Mountain National Park scenic wilderness N Colo.

Rocky Mountains *or* the **Rock·ies** \'rä-kēz\ mountains W N. America extending from N Alaska SE to N.Mex. — see ELBERT (Mount), ROBSON (Mount)

Ródhos — see RHODES

Ro·dri·gues \rò-'drē-gəs\ island Indian Ocean in the Mascarenes *area* 40 *sq mi* (104 *sq km*), *pop* 36,175; a dependency of Mauritius

Rog·ers \'rä-jərz\ city NW Ark. *pop* 55,964

Rogers Pass mountain pass Canada in SE B.C. in Selkirk Mountains

Rogue \'rōg\ river *ab* 200 *mi* (320 *km*) SW Oreg. rising in Crater Lake National Park & flowing W & SW into the Pacific

Ro·hil·khand \'rō-,hil-,kənd\ *or* **Ba·reil·ly** \bə-'rā-lē\ region N India in Uttar Pradesh; chief city Bareilly

Rohn·ert Park \'rō-nərt\ city W Calif. S of Santa Rosa *pop* 40,971

Rolling Meadows city NE Ill. NW of Chicago *pop* 24,099

Ro·ma·gna \rō-'mä-nyä\ district N Italy on the Adriatic comprising the E part of Emilia-Romagna region

Roman Campagna — see CAMPAGNA DI ROMA

Ro·ma·nia \rú-'mā-nē-ə, rō-, -nyə\ *or* **Ru·ma·nia** \rú-\ country SE Europe bordering on Black Sea ✸ Bucharest *area* 91,699 *sq mi* (237,500 *sq km*), *pop* 21,698,181

Rom·blon \räm-'blōn\ 1 islands Philippines in N Visayan Islands in Sibuyan Sea *area* 524 *sq mi* (1357 *sq km*) 2 island in the group

Rome \'rōm\ 1 city NW Ga. NW of Atlanta *pop* 36,303 2 city E *cen* N.Y. NW of Utica *pop* 33,725 3 *or It* **Ro·ma** \'rō-mä\ *or anc* **Ro·ma** \'rō-ma\ city ✸ of Italy on the Tiber *pop* 2,655,970 4 the Roman Empire

Rome, Duchy of division of Byzantine Empire 6th to 8th century *cen* Italy comprising most of modern Lazio; later a province of the Papal States called **Patrimony of Saint Pe·ter** \'pē-tər\

Rom·ford \'räm(p)-fərd, 'rəm(p)-\ former municipal borough SE England in Essex, now part of Havering

Rom·u·lus \'rä-myə-ləs\ city SE Mich. *pop* 23,989

Ron·ces·va·lles \,rón(t)-səs-'vä-əs\ *or F* **Ron·ce·vaux** \rōⁿs-'vō, rōⁿ-sə-\ commune N Spain 5 *mi* (8 *km*) from French boundary in the Pyrenees near **Pass of Roncesvalles** *pop* 28

Ron·dô·nia \rōⁿ-'dō-nyə\ *or formerly* **Gua·po·ré** \,gwä-pò-'rā\ state W Brazil ✸ Pôrto Velho *area* 93,839 *sq mi* (243,043 *sq km*), *pop* 1,130,400

Rong·er·ik \'rän-ə-,rik, 'ròŋ-\ island W *cen* Pacific in the Marshalls in Ratak chain E of Bikini

Ron·ne Ice Shelf \'rō-nə, 'rə-nə\ area of shelf ice Antarctica in Weddell Sea

Roo·de·poort \'rō-də-,pòrt, 'rō-i-,pòrt\ city Republic of South Africa in Gauteng W of Johannesburg *metropolitan pop* 141,764

Roo·se·velt \'rō-zə-,velt, -vəlt *also* 'rü-\ river *ab* 400 *mi* (644 *km*) W *cen* Brazil flowing from W Mato Grosso state N into the Aripuanã

Ro·rai·ma \rò-'rī-mä\ 1 mountain 9094 *ft* (2772 *m*) N S. America in Pacaraima Mountains on boundary bet. Venezuela, Guyana, & Brazil; has flat top 2 state N Brazil ✸ Boa Vista *area* 88,843 *sq mi* (230,181 *sq km*), *pop* 324,397

Ror·schach \'rór-,shäk, -,shäk\ commune NE Switzerland on S shore of Lake Constance *pop* 9878

Ro·sa, Mon·te \'mòn-tä-'rō-zä\ mountain 15,203 *ft* (4634 *m*) on Swiss-Italian boundary; highest in Pennine Alps

Ro·sa·rio \rō-'zär-ē-,ō, -'sär-\ city E *cen* Argentina on the Paraná *pop* 591,428

Ros·com·mon \räs-'kä-mən\ 1 county *cen* Ireland in Connacht *area* 951 *sq mi* (2473 *sq km*), *pop* 53,774 2 town, its ✸ *pop* 1363

Rose, Mount \'rōz\ mountain 10,778 *ft* (3285 *m*) W Nev. SW of Reno

Ro·seau \rō-'zō\ seaport ✸ of Dominica *pop* 14,847

Ro·selle \rō-'zel\ village NE Ill. *pop* 22,763

Rose·mead \'rōz-,mēd\ city SW Calif. E of Los Angeles *pop* 53,764

Ro·sen·berg \'rō-zⁿn-,bərg\ city SE Tex. *pop* 30,618

Ro·set·ta \rō-'ze-tə\ *or Ar* **Ra·shīd** \rä-'shēd\ *or anc* **Bol·bi·ti·ne** \,bäl-bə-'tī-nē\ 1 river 146 *mi* (235 *km*) N Egypt forming W branch of the Nile in its delta 2 city N Egypt on the Rosetta *pop* 36,711

Rose·ville \'rōz-,vil\ 1 city N *cen* Calif. NE of Sacramento *pop* 118,788 2 city SE Mich. NE of Detroit *pop* 47,299 3 village SE Minn. N of St. Paul *pop* 33,660

Ross and Crom·ar·ty \'ròs-ənd-'krä-mər-tē\ former county N Scotland ✸ Dingwall

Ross Dependency section of Antarctica lying bet. 160°E and 150°W long.; claimed by New Zealand

Ross Ice Shelf area of shelf ice Antarctica in S Ross Sea

Ross Sea arm of S. Pacific extending into Antarctica E of Victoria Land

Ros·tock \'räs-ˌtäk, 'rós-ˌtók\ city & port NE Germany on Warnow River near the Baltic coast *pop* 234,475

Ros·tov–on–Don \rə-'stóf-ˌän-'dän, -'stóv, -ˌón-\ *or Russ* **Ros·tov-na–Do·nu** \rə-'stóf-nä-'dó-nü, -'stóv-\ city S Russia in Europe on the Don *pop* 1,027,000

Ros·well \'räz-ˌwel, -wəl\ **1** city NW *cen* Ga. N of Atlanta *pop* 88,346 **2** city SE N.Mex. *pop* 48,366

Ro·ta \'rō-tə\ **1** island W Pacific at S end of the Marianas *area* 35 *sq mi* (91 *sq km*) **2** town & port SW Spain on the Atlantic *pop* 25,053

Roth·er·ham \'rä-thə-rəm\ town N England in S. Yorkshire NE of Sheffield *area pop* 247,100

Rothe·say \'räth-sē\ royal burgh SW Scotland on island of Bute *pop* 5408

Ro·to·rua \ˌrō-tō-'rü-ə\ city New Zealand in N *cen* North Is. *urban area pop* 52,608

Rot·ter·dam \'rä-tər-ˌdam, -ˌdäm\ city & port SW Netherlands on the Nieuwe Maas (one of the mouths of the Meuse) *pop* 598,660 — **Rot·ter·dam·er** \-ˌda-mər, -ˌdä-\ *n*

Ro·tu·ma \rō-'tü-mə\ island SW Pacific N of Fiji Islands *area* 14 *sq mi* (36 *sq km*); belongs to Fiji

Rou·baix \rü-'bä\ city N France NE of Lille *pop* 96,959

Rou·en \rü-'äⁿ\ city & port N France on the Seine *pop* 106,560

Round Lake Beach village NE Ill. *pop* 28,175

Round Rock town *cen* Tex. N of Austin *pop* 99,887

Rous·sil·lon \ˌrü-sē-'yōⁿ\ region & former province S France bordering on the Pyrenees & the Mediterranean ✷ *Perpignan*

Rou·yn–No·ran·da \'rü-ən-nə-'ran-də, rü-'äⁿ-\ town Canada in SW Que. *pop* 41,012

Row·lett \raú-lət\ city NE Tex., a suburb of Dallas *pop* 56,199

Rox·burgh \'räks-ˌbər-ə, -ˌbə-rə, -b(ə-)rə\ *or* **Rox·burgh·shire** \-ˌshir, -shər\ former county SE Scotland ✷ *Jedburgh*

Roy \'rói\ city NE Utah SW of Ogden *pop* 36,884

Royal Gorge section of the canyon of Arkansas River S *cen* Colo.

Royal Leamington Spa — see LEAMINGTON 2

Royal Oak city SE Mich. N of Detroit *pop* 57,236

Royal Tun·bridge Wells *or* **Tunbridge Wells** \'tən-brij\ town SE England in Kent *pop* 44,506

Ru·an·da–Urun·di \rü-ˌän-də-ü-'rün-dē\ *or* **Belgian East Africa** former trust territory E *cen* Africa bordering on Lake Tanganyika & comprising two districts, **Ruanda** (✷ Kigali) & **Urundi** (✷ Usumbura), administered by Belgium under League of Nations mandate 1919–45 & under U.N. trusteeship 1946–62 ✷ Usumbura — see BURUNDI, RWANDA

Ru·a·pe·hu, Mount \ˌrü-ə-'pā-(ˌ)hü\ volcano 9175 *ft* (2796 *m*) New Zealand in Tongariro National Park; highest peak in North Is.

Rubʻ al–Kha·li \ˌrüb-al-'kä-lē, *Ar* -äl-'kä-\ *or* **Empty Quarter** desert region S Arabia extending from Nejd S to Hadramawt *area ab* 250,000 *sq mi* (647,500 *sq km*)

Ru·bi·con \'rü-bi-ˌkän\ river 15 *mi* (24 *km*) N *cen* Italy flowing E into the Adriatic

Ru·da Slas·ka \ˌrü-də-'shlóⁿ-skə\ commune S Poland *pop* 169,789

Rudolf, Lake — see TURKANA (Lake)

Ru·fisque \rü-'fēsk\ city & port W Senegal *pop* 152,000

Rug·by \'rəg-bē\ town *cen* England in Warwickshire on the Avon *pop* 83,400

Rü·gen \'rü-gən, 'rœ-\ island NE Germany in Baltic Sea off coast of Pomerania *area* 358 *sq mi* (927 *sq km*); chief town Bergen

Ruhr \'rúr\ **1** river 146 *mi* (235 *km*) W Germany flowing NW & W to the Rhine **2** industrial district in valley of the Ruhr

Ruis·lip North·wood \'rīs-ləp-'nórth-ˌwúd\ former urban district S England in Middlesex, now part of Hillingdon

Ru·me·lia \rü-'mēl-yə, -'mē-lē-ə\ a division of the old Ottoman Empire including Albania, Macedonia, & Thrace

Run·ny·mede \'rə-nē-ˌmēd\ meadow S England in Surrey on S bank of the Thames

Ru·pert \'rü-pərt\ river 380 *mi* (612 *km*) Canada in W Que. flowing W into James Bay

Rupert's Land PRINCE RUPERT'S LAND

Ru·se \'rü-(ˌ)sä\ *or Turk* **Rus·chuk** \rús-'chük\ city NE Bulgaria on the Danube S of Bucharest *pop* 158,000

Rush·more, Mount \'rəsh-ˌmór\ mountain 5600 *ft* (1707 *m*) W S.Dak. in Black Hills on which are carved faces of presidents Washington, Jefferson, Lincoln, & Theodore Roosevelt; a national memorial

Rus·sell Cave National Monument \'rə-səl\ reservation NE Ala. including cavern where remains of early pre-Columbian humans have been found

Rus·sell·ville \'rə-səl-ˌvil\ city NW *cen* Ark. *pop* 27,920

Rus·sia \'rə-shə\ *or Russ* **Ros·si·ya** \rä-'sē-yə\ **1** *or formerly* **Mus·co·vy** \'məs-kə-vē\ former empire E Europe & N Asia coextensive (except for Finland & Kars, a mountainous region now in NE Turkey) with the U.S.S.R. ✷ St. Petersburg **2** the U.S.S.R. — a popular usage despite the fact that the U.S.S.R. included other republics besides Russia **3** *or officially* **Russian Federation** independent country in E Europe & N Asia bordering on Arctic & Pacific oceans & on Baltic & Black seas; a constituent republic (**Russian Republic** *or* **Soviet Russia**) of the U.S.S.R. 1922–91 ✷ Moscow *area* 6,592,812 *sq mi* (17,075,383 *sq km*), *pop* 148,000,000

Russian Turkestan region formerly comprising the republics of Soviet Central Asia

Ruthenia — see ZAKARPATS'KA — **Ru·thene** \rü-'thēn\ *n* — **Ru·the·nian** \-'thē-nyən, -nē-ən\ *adj or n*

Rut·land \'rət-lənd\ *or* **Rut·land·shire** \-lənd-ˌshir, -shər\ former county E *cen* England ✷ Oakham

Ru·vu·ma *or Pg* **Ro·vu·ma** \rü-'vü-mə\ river *ab* 450 *mi* (724 *km*) SE Africa rising in S Tanzania & flowing E into Indian Ocean

Ru·wen·zo·ri \ˌrü-ən-'zór-ē\ mountain group E *cen* Africa bet. Lake Albert & Lake Edward, on boundary bet. Uganda & Democratic Republic of the Congo — see STANLEY (Mount)

Rwan·da \rü-'än-də\ *or chiefly formerly* **Ru·an·da** country E *cen* Africa; a republic ✷ Kigali *area* 10,169 *sq mi* (26,338 *sq km*), *pop* 8,128,553 — see RUANDA-URUNDI — **Rwan·dan** \-dən\ *adj or n* — **Rwan·dese** \rü-ˌän-'dēz, -'dēs\ *adj or n*

Rya·zan' \ˌrē-ə-'zan, -'zän\ city *cen* Russia in Europe on Oka River SE of Moscow *pop* 529,000

Ry·binsk \'ri-bən(t)sk\ *or 1946–57* **Shcher·ba·kov** \ˌsh(ch)er-bə-'kóf, -'kóv\ *or 1984–89* **An·dro·pov** \an-'drō-ˌpóf, -ˌpóv\ city W *cen* Russia in Europe *pop* 252,000

Ryb·nik \'rib-nik\ commune S Poland *pop* 142,588

Rye \'rī\ town SE England in E. Sussex *pop* 4293

Ryu·kyu Islands \rē-'yü-(ˌ)kyü, -(ˌ)kü\ islands W Pacific extending bet. Kyushu, Japan, & Taiwan; belonged to Japan 1895–1945; occupied by U.S. 1945; returned to Japan in 1953 (N islands) and 1972 (S islands) *area ab* 850 *sq mi* (2202 *sq km*), *pop* 1,222,458 — see AMAMI, OKINAWA, OSUMI ISLANDS, SAKISHIMA ISLANDS, TOKARA ISLANDS — **Ryu·kyu·an** \-ˌkyü-ən, -ˌkü-\ *adj or n*

Rze·szow \'zhe-ˌshúf\ commune SE Poland *pop* 150,754

Saa·le \'zä-lə, 'sä-\ river 265 *mi* (426 *km*) E *cen* Germany rising in NE Bavaria in the Fichtelgebirge & flowing N into the Elbe

Saan·ich \'sa-nich\ municipality Canada in B.C. on SE Vancouver Is. N of Victoria *pop* 109,752

Saar \'sär, 'zär\ **1** *or F* **Sarre** \'sär\ river *ab* 150 *mi* (241 *km*) Europe flowing from Vosges Mountains in France N to the Moselle in W Germany **2** *or* **Saar·land** \'sär-ˌland, 'zär-\ region W Europe in basin of Saar River bet. France & Germany; once part of Lorraine, became part of Germany in 19th century; administered by League of Nations 1919–35; became a state of Germany 1935; came under control of France after World War II; to W. Germany by a plebiscite Jan. 1, 1957, as a state (**Saarland**) ✷ Saarbrücken *area* 991 *sq mi* (2567 *sq km*), *pop* 1,073,000

Saar·brück·en \zär-'brü-kən, sär-, -'brœ-\ city SW Germany ✷ of Saarland *pop* 192,030

Saaremaa — see SAREMA

Sa·ba \'sä-bə, 'sä-bə\ internally self-governing Dutch island W. Indies in Leeward Islands; chief settlement The Bottom *area* 5 *sq mi* (13 *sq km*), *pop* 1700 **2** — see SHEBA

Sa·ba·dell \ˌsa-bə-'del, sä-\ commune NE Spain NW of Barcelona *pop* 183,788

Sa·bah \'sä-bə\ *or formerly* **North Borneo** state Malaysia in NE Borneo, formerly a Brit. colony ✷ Kota Kinabalu *area* 29,507 *sq mi* (76,423 *sq km*), *pop* 1,736,902

Sa·ba·na Gran·de \sä-'bä-nä-'grän-dā\ city SW Puerto Rico *pop* 25,265

Sa·bar·ma·ti \ˌsä-bər-'mə-tē\ river *ab* 250 *mi* (402 *km*) W India flowing S into head of Gulf of Khambhat

Sa·bi \'sä-bē\ *or in Mozambique* **Sa·ve** \'sä-və\ river 400 *mi* (644 *km*) SE Africa rising in *cen* Zimbabwe & flowing E across S Mozambique to Indian Ocean

Sa·bine \sə-'bēn\ river E Tex. & W La. flowing SE through **Sabine Lake** (15 *mi* or 24 *km* long) & **Sabine Pass** (channel) into Gulf of Mexico

Sa·ble, Cape \'sā-bəl\ **1** cape at SW tip of Fla.; southernmost point of U.S. mainland, at *ab* 25°7′N **2** headland E Canada on an islet S of **Cape Sable Island** (7 *mi* or 11 *km* long, at S end of N.S.)

Sable Island island Canada 20 *mi* (32 *km*) long in the Atlantic SE of Cape Canso; belongs to N.S.

Sab·ra·tha \'sä-brə-thə\ *or anc* **Sab·ra·ta** \-tə\ town Libya on the coast WNW of Tripoli *pop* 30,836

Sachsen — see SAXONY

Sa·co \'só-(ˌ)kō\ river 104 *mi* (167 *km*) E N.H. & SW Maine flowing SE into the Atlantic

Sac·ra·men·to \ˌsa-krə-'men-(ˌ)tō\ **1** river 382 *mi* (615 *km*) N Calif. flowing S into Suisun Bay **2** city ✷ of Calif. on Sacramento River NE of San Francisco *pop* 466,488

Sacramento Mountains mountains S N.Mex. — see GUADALUPE MOUNTAINS, SIERRA BLANCA PEAK

Sa·fed Koh \sə-ˌfed-'kō\ mountain range E Afghanistan on Pakistan border; a S extension of the Hindu Kush

Sa·fi \'sa-fē\ city & port W Morocco SW of Casablanca *pop* 284,750

Sa·ga·mi·ha·ra \sä-ˌgä-mē-'här-ä\ city Japan on Honshu *pop* 605,561

Sa·ga·mi Sea \sä-'gä-mē\ inlet of the Pacific Japan in SE Honshu SW of Tokyo Bay

Saghalien — see SAKHALIN

Sag·i·naw \'sa-gə-ˌnó\ city E *cen* Mich. NNW of Flint *pop* 51,508

Saginaw Bay inlet of Lake Huron in E Mich.

Sa·gres \'sä-grish\ village SW Portugal E of Cape Saint Vincent

Sa·gua·ro National Park \sə-'gwär-ō, -'wär-\ reservation SE Ariz. E of Tucson containing giant saguaro cacti

Sag·ue·nay \'sa-gə-ˌnä, ˌsa-gə-'\ **1** river 105 *mi* (169 *km*) Canada in S Que. flowing from Lake Saint Jean E into the St. Lawrence **2** city Canada in S *cen* Que. on the Saguenay *pop* 144,746

Sa·guia el Ham·ra \'sa-gyə-el-'ham-rə\ territory NW Africa, the N zone of Western Sahara

Sa·gun·to \sä-'gün-(ˌ)tō\ *or formerly* **Mur·vie·dro** \ˌmúr-vē-'ä-(ˌ)drō, ˌmür-'vyä-thrō\ commune E Spain NNE of Valencia *pop* 56,471

Sa·ha·ra \sə-'her-ə, -'här-\ desert region N Africa N of the Sudan region extending from the Atlantic coast to Red Sea — **Sa·ha·ran** \-ən\ *adj*

Sa·ha·ran·pur \sə-'här-ən-ˌpúr\ city N India in NW Uttar Pradesh NNE of Delhi *pop* 452,925

Sa·hel \'sä-hil, sə-'hil\ the semidesert S fringe of the Sahara that stretches from Mauritania to Chad — **Sa·hel·ian** \sə-'hil-yən\ *adj*

Saida — see SIDON

Saigon — see HO CHI MINH CITY — **Sai·gon·ese** \ˌsī-gə-'nēz, -'nēs\ *adj or n*

Sai·maa \'sī-ˌmä\ group of lakes SE Finland of which **Lake Saimaa** is the largest

Saint Al·bans \'ól-bənz\ town SE England in Hertfordshire *pop* 122,400

Saint Al·bert *usu* **St. Albert** \'al-bərt\ city Canada in *cen* Alta. *pop* 61,466

Saint An·drews \'an-ˌdrüz\ burgh E Scotland on **Saint Andrews Bay** (inlet of North Sea) SE of Dundee

Saint Bar·thé·le·my \ˌsaⁿ-bär-tä-lə-'mē\ island French West Indies in department of Guadeloupe; chief town Gustavia *pop* 8000

Saint Bernard — see GREAT SAINT BERNARD, LITTLE SAINT BERNARD

Saint Cath·a·rines *usu* **St. Catharines** \'ka-th(ə-)rənz\ city Canada in SE Ont. NW of Niagara Falls on Welland Canal *pop* 131,400

Saint Charles \'chär(-ə)lz\ **1** city NE Ill. W of Chicago *pop* 32,974 **2** city E Mo. on the Missouri River *pop* 65,794

Saint Clair, Lake \'klér\ lake SE Mich. & SE Ont. area 460 sq mi (1196 sq km), connected by **Saint Clair River** (40 mi or 64 km) with Lake Huron & draining through Detroit River into Lake Erie

Saint Clair Shores city SE Mich. NE of Detroit pop 59,715

Saint–Cloud \sänt-'klaüd, sönt-; saⁿ-'klü\ commune France, WSW suburb of Paris pop 28,164

Saint Cloud \'klaüd\ city cen Minn. on the Mississippi pop 65,842

Saint Croix \sänt-'kròi, sönt-\ 1 river 129 mi (208 km) Canada & U.S. bet. N.B. & Maine 2 river 164 mi (264 km) NW Wis. & E Minn. flowing into the Mississippi 3 or **San·ta Cruz** \san-tə-'krüz\ island W. Indies, largest of the Virgin Islands of the U.S. area 80 sq mi (208 sq km), pop 53,234; chief town Christiansted

Saint Croix Island International Historic Site reservation E Maine on Canada border on island in St. Croix River

Saint–Cyr–l'Ecole \saⁿ-'sir-lā-'kòl\ commune N France W of Versailles pop 14,585

Saint–De·nis \saⁿ(t)-də-'nē\ 1 commune N France NNE of Paris pop 85,994 2 commune ✻ of Réunion Is. pop 109,072

Sainte–Foy \sänt-'fòi, sönt-; saⁿt-'fwä, saⁿ-tə-\ former town Canada in SE Que., now part of Quebec (city)

Sainte–Ju·lie \saⁿt-zhü-'lē\ town Canada in S Que. E of Montreal pop 30,104

Saint Eli·as, Mount \i-'lī-əs\ mountain 18,008 ft (5489 m) on Alaska-Canada boundary in St. Elias Mountains

Saint Elias Mountains mountain range of the Coast Ranges SW Yukon Territory & E Alaska — see LOGAN (Mount)

Saint–Étienne \saⁿ-tā-'tyen\ city SE cen France pop 180,438

Saint–Eus·tache \saⁿ-tyü-'stash\ town Canada in S Que. pop 44,154

Saint Eu·sta·ti·us \sänt-yü-'stā-sh(ē-)əs\ or informally **Sta·tia** \'stā-shə\ internally self-governing Dutch island W. Indies NW of St. Kitts area 7 sq mi (18 sq km), pop 2292

Saint Fran·cis \sänt-'fran(t)-səs, sönt-\ 1 river 425 mi (684 km) SE Mo. & E Ark. flowing S into the Mississippi 2 or **Saint–Fran·çois** \saⁿ-fräⁿ-'swä\ river 165 mi (266 km) Canada in S Que. flowing NW into the St. Lawrence

Saint Francis, Lake expansion of St. Lawrence River Canada above Valleyfield, Que.

Saint Gall \sänt-'gòl, sönt-; saⁿ-'gäl\ or G **Sankt Gal·len** \zänkt-'gä-lən\ 1 canton NE Switzerland area 778 sq mi (2015 sq km), pop 452,600 2 commune, its ✻ pop 69,909

Saint George \'jòrj\ city SW corner of Utah pop 72,897

Saint–Georges \saⁿ-'zhòrzh\ town Canada in S Que. pop 31,173

Saint George's \'jòr-jəz\ town ✻ of Grenada pop 4000

Saint George's Channel strait British Isles bet. SW Wales & Ireland

Saint–Ger·main \saⁿ-zhər-'maⁿ\ or **Saint–Ger·main–en–Laye** \-,maⁿ-,äⁿ-'lā\ commune N France WNW of Paris pop 38,124

Saint Gott·hard \sänt-'gät-hərd, sönt-, 'gät-hərd; saⁿ-gò-'tär\ 1 mountains Switzerland in Lepontine Alps bet. Uri & Ticino cantons 2 mountain pass 6916 ft (2108 m) in St. Gotthard Range

Saint He·le·na \sänt-ə-'lē-nə, ,sänt-hə-'lē-\ island S. Atlantic; a Brit. colony ✻ Jamestown area 47 sq mi (122 sq km), pop 4000

Saint Hel·ens \'sänt-'he-lənz, sönt-\ town NW England in Merseyside ENE of Liverpool pop 98,769

Saint Helens, Mount volcanic peak 8366 ft (2550 m) SW Wash. in Cascades

Saint Hel·ier \'hel-yər\ town Channel Islands ✻ of Jersey pop 28,123

Saint–Hu·bert \sänt-'hyü-bərt, sönt-\ or saⁿ-yü-'ber\ former town Canada in S Que. E of Montreal, now part of Longueuil

Saint–Hy·a·cinthe \sänt-'hī-ə-(,)sin(t)th, sönt-; ,sant-yə-'sant\ town Canada in S Que. E of Montreal pop 53,236

Saint–Jean, Lake or **Lac Saint–Jean** \läk-saⁿ-'zhäⁿ\ lake Canada in S Que. draining through the Saguenay to the St. Lawrence area 414 sq mi (1072 sq km)

Saint–Jean–de–Luz \saⁿ-,zhäⁿ-də-'lüz, -'luez\ town SW France on Bay of Biscay SW of Biarritz pop 13,241

Saint–Jean–sur–Ri·che·lieu \saⁿ-'zhäⁿ-sür-'ri-shə-,lü, -,rē-shəl-'yœ\ town Canada in S Que. SE of Montreal pop 92,394

Saint–Jé·rôme \saⁿ-zhā-'rōm, ,sänt-jə-'rōm\ town Canada in S Que. NW of Montreal pop 68,456

Saint John \sänt-'jän, sönt-\ 1 river 418 mi (673 km) NE U.S. & SE Canada flowing from N Maine into Bay of Fundy in N.B. 2 city & port Canada in S N.B. at mouth of the St. John pop 70,063

Saint John Island island W. Indies, one of the Virgin Islands of the U.S. area 20 sq mi (52 sq km), pop 3504

Saint Johns \'sänz, sönt-\ river 285 mi (459 km) NE Fla. flowing N & E into the Atlantic

Saint John's \sänt-'jänz, sönt-\ 1 city Brit. West Indies ✻ of Antigua and Barbuda on Antigua Is. pop 23,000 2 usu **St. John's** city & port Canada ✻ of Nfld.&Lab. pop 106,172

Saint Jo·seph \-zəf also -səf\ city NW Mo. pop 76,780

Saint Kil·da \'kil-də\ island NW Scotland in the Atlantic; westernmost of the Outer Hebrides

Saint Kitts \'kits\ or **Saint Chris·to·pher** \'kris-tə-fər\ island Brit. West Indies in the Leewards; chief town Basseterre area 68 sq mi (177 sq km); with Nevis, forms independent state of **Saint Kitts and Nevis** (✻ Basseterre area 104 sq mi or 269 sq km, pop 46,111) — **Kit·ti·tian** \kə-'ti-shən\ n or adj

Saint–Lau·rent \saⁿ-lò-'räⁿ, ,sänt-lò-'rent\ former town Canada in S Que. on Montreal Is., now part of Montreal (city)

Saint Law·rence \sänt-'lòr-ən(t)s, sönt-, -'lär-\ river 760 mi (1223 km) E Canada in Ont. & Que. bordering on the U.S. in N.Y., flowing from Lake Ontario NE into the Atlantic, & forming at its mouth a wide bay (the **Gulf of Saint Lawrence**)

Saint Lawrence, Lake expansion of St. Lawrence River Canada & U.S. WSW of Cornwall, Ont.

Saint Lawrence Island island 95 mi (153 km) long W Alaska in N Bering Sea

Saint Lawrence Islands National Park reservation SE Canada in SE Ont.

Saint Lawrence Seaway waterway Canada & U.S. in & along the St. Lawrence River bet. Lake Ontario & Montreal

Saint–Lé·o·nard \saⁿ-,lā-ə-när; sänt-'le-nərd, sönt-\ former town Canada in S Que., now part of Montreal (city)

Saint–Lô \sänt-'lō, sönt-; saⁿ-'lō\ commune NW France pop 20,081

Saint–Lou·is \saⁿ-lü-'ē\ 1 city & port Senegal on island at mouth of Senegal River; formerly ✻ of Senegal pop 180,000 2 city & port Réunion pop 50,500

Saint Lou·is \sänt-'lü-əs, sönt-\ 1 river 160 mi (257 km) NE Minn. flowing to W tip of Lake Superior 2 city E Mo. on the Mississippi pop 319,294 — **Saint Lou·i·san** \'lü-ə-sən\ n — **Saint Lou·i·sian** \'lü-ə-zhən, -shən\ n

Saint Lou·is, Lake \sänt-'lü-ē, sönt-\ expansion of St. Lawrence River Canada above Lachine Rapids

Saint Lou·is Park \sänt-'lü-əs\ city SE Minn. pop 45,250

Saint Lu·cia \sänt-'lü-shə, sönt-\ island Brit. West Indies in the Windwards S of Martinique; an independent member of the Commonwealth of Nations since 1979 ✻ Castries area 238 sq mi (616 sq km), pop 154,750 — **Saint Lu·cian** \-shən\ adj or n

Saint–Ma·lo \saⁿ-'mä-lō\ city & port NW France in Brittany on island in Gulf of Saint-Malo pop 50,697

Saint–Malo, Gulf of arm of English Channel NW France bet. Cotentin Peninsula & Brittany

Saint Mar·tin \sänt-'mär-tᵃn, sönt-\ or D **Sint Maar·ten** \sint-\ island W. Indies in the N Leewards; divided bet. France & Netherlands area 33 sq mi (86 sq km)

Saint Mar·ys \'mer-ēz, 'mä-rēz\ 1 river 175 mi (282 km) on Fla.-Ga. border flowing from Okefenokee Swamp to the Atlantic 2 river ab 70 mi (115 km) bet. Canada & U.S. in Ont. & Upper Peninsula of Mich. flowing from Lake Superior into Lake Huron; descends 20 ft (6.1 m) in a mile at **Saint Marys Falls** — see SAULT SAINTE MARIE CANALS

Saint–Maur–des–Fos·sés \saⁿ-,mòr-dā-fò-'sā\ commune N France SE of Paris on the Marne pop 73,071

Saint Mau·rice \sänt-'mòr-əs, sönt-, -'mär-; ,saⁿ-mə-'rēs\ river 325 mi (523 km) Canada in S Que. flowing S into the St. Lawrence

Saint–Mi·hiel \saⁿ-mē-'yel\ town NE France on the Meuse pop 5251

Saint Mo·ritz \sänt-mə-'rits, ,saⁿ-mə-'rē; G **Sankt Mo·ritz** \zänkt-mə-'rits\ town E Switzerland in Graubunden canton SSE of Chur pop 5900

Saint–Na·zaire \,saⁿ-na-'zer\ commune & port NW France at mouth of the Loire pop 65,868

Saint–Nicolas — see SINT-NIKLAAS

Sain·tonge \saⁿ-'tōⁿzh\ region & former province of France on Bay of Biscay N of the Gironde ✻ Saintes

Saint–Ouen \saⁿ-'twaⁿ\ commune France, N suburb of Paris pop 39,719

Saint Pan·cras \sänt-'paŋ-krəs, sönt-\ former metropolitan borough NW London, England, now part of Camden

Saint Paul \'pòl\ city E Minn., its ✻ pop 285,068 — **Saint Paul·ite** \'pò-,līt\ n

Saint Pe·ter, Lake \sänt-'pē-tər, sönt-\ expansion of St. Lawrence River Canada bet. Sorel-Tracy & Trois-Rivières, Que.

Saint Peter and Saint Paul Rocks or Pg **Pe·ne·dos de São Pe·dro e São Pau·lo** \pə-'nä-düs-dē-,saüⁿ-'päd-rü-ē-,saüⁿ-'paü-lü\ rocky islets in the Atlantic 600 mi (966 km) NE of Natal, Brazil; belong to Brazil

Saint Peter Port town Channel Islands ✻ of Guernsey pop 16,648

Saint Pe·ters \'pē-tərz\ city E Mo. WNW of St. Louis pop 52,575

Saint Pe·ters·burg \'pē-tərz-,bərg\ 1 city W Fla. on Pinellas Peninsula SW of Tampa pop 244,769 2 or 1914–24 **Pet·ro·grad** \'pe-trə-,grad, -,grät\ or 1924–91 **Le·nin·grad** \'le-nən-,grad, -,grät\ city W Russia in Europe, at E end of Gulf of Finland; ✻ of Russian Empire 1712–1917 pop 4,952,000

Saint–Pierre and Mi·que·lon \saⁿ-'pyer-ən(d)-,mē-kə-'lōⁿ\ French islands in the Atlantic off S Newfoundland ✻ St.-Pierre, area 93 sq mi (242 sq km), pop 6125

Saint–Quen·tin \sänt-'kwen-tᵃn, sönt-, F saⁿ-kän-'taⁿ\ commune N France on the Somme NW of Laon pop 59,049

Saint Si·mons Island \sänt-'sī-mənz, sönt-\ island SE Ga. in the Atlantic

Saint Thom·as \'tä-məs\ 1 island W. Indies, one of the Virgin Islands of the U.S. area 32 sq mi (83 sq km), pop 51,181 2 — see CHARLOTTE AMALIE 3 usu **St. Thomas** city Canada in SE Ont. S of London pop 37,905

Saint–Tro·pez \saⁿ-trò-'pä\ commune SE France on the Mediterranean SW of Cannes pop 5480

Saint Vin·cent \sänt-'vin(t)-sənt, sönt-\ island Brit. West Indies in cen Windwards; with N Grenadines became independent 1979 as **Saint Vincent and the Grenadines** (✻ Kingstown area 150 sq mi or 390 sq km, pop 109,000)

Saint Vincent, Cape or Pg **Ca·bo de São Vi·cen·te** \'kä-bü-dē-,saüⁿ-vē-'sä-ntē\ cape SW Portugal

Saint Vincent, Gulf inlet of Indian Ocean Australia in S. Australia E of Yorke Peninsula

Sai·pan \sī-'pan, -'pän, 'sī-,\ island W Pacific in S cen Marianas area 47 sq mi (122 sq km), pop 62,392 — **Sai·pa·nese** \,sī-pə-'nēz, -'nēs\ adj or n

Sa·is \'sā-is\ ancient city Egypt in Nile Delta

Sa·ja·ma \sä-'hä-mä\ mountain 21,391 ft (6520 m) W Bolivia near Chilean boundary

Sa·kai \(,)sä-'kī\ city Japan in S Honshu on Osaka Bay pop 792,018

Sak·a·ka·wea, Lake \,sa-kə-kə-'wē-ə\ reservoir ab 200 mi (322 km) long W N.Dak. formed in the Missouri by the Garrison Dam

Sa·kar·ya \sə-'kär-yə\ river ab 500 mi (804 km) NW Turkey in Asia flowing into the Black Sea E of the Bosporus

Sa·kha \'sä-kə\ or unofficially **Ya·ku·tia** \yä-'kü-sh(ē-)ə\ autonomous republic E cen Russia in Asia ✻ Yakutsk area 1,198,146 sq mi (3,103,198 sq km), pop 1,093,000

Sa·kha·lin \'sa-kə-,lēn, -lən; ,sä-kä-'lēn\ or formerly **Sa·gha·lien** \'sa-gə-,lēn, ,sa-gə-'\ or Jp **Ka·ra·fu·to** \kä-'rä-fə-,tò\ island SE Russia in Asia in Sea of Okhotsk N of Hokkaido; formerly (1905–45) divided bet. Russia & Japan area more than 28,500 sq mi (73,800 sq km)

Sa·ki·shi·ma Islands \ˌsä-kē-ˈshē-mä, sä-ˈkē-shē-mä\ island group Japan in S Ryukyus off E coast of N Taiwan; occupied 1945–72 by the U.S. *area* 343 *sq mi* (888 *sq km*)

Sakkara — see SAQQÂRA

Sa·kon·net River \sə-ˈkə-nət\ inlet of the Atlantic SE R.I., E of Aquidneck Is.

Sal·a·ber·ry–de–Val·ley·field \ˈsa-lə-ˌber-ē-də-ˈva-lē-ˌfēld\ *or* **Valleyfield** town Canada in S Que. SW of Montreal *pop* 40,077

Sa·la·do \sə-ˈlä-(ˌ)dō, sä-ˈlä-t͟hō\ **1** *or in upper course* **Ju·ra·men·to** \ˌhü-rä-ˈmen-(ˌ)tō\ river 1120 *mi* (1802 *km*) N Argentina flowing from the Andes SE into the Paraná **2** *or in upper course* **Des·agua·de·ro** \ˌt͟hä-ˌsä-gwä-ˈt͟her-(ˌ)ō\ river 850 *mi* (1368 *km*) W *cen* Argentina flowing S into the Colorado

Sal·a·man·ca \ˌsa-lə-ˈmaŋ-kə, ˌsä-lä-ˈmäŋ-kä\ **1** province W Spain *area* 4763 *sq mi* (12,336 *sq km*), *pop* 345,609 **2** commune, its ✻, WNW of Madrid *pop* 156,368

Sal·a·maua \ˌsä-lä-ˈmau̇-ä\ town Papua New Guinea on Huon Gulf

Salambria — see PENEUS

Sal·a·mis \ˈsa-lə-məs\ **1** ancient city Cyprus on E coast **2** island Greece in Saronic Gulf off Attica

Sal·da·nha Bay \sal-ˈda-nyə\ inlet of the Atlantic on W coast of Western Cape province, Republic of South Africa

Sa·lé \sa-ˈlā\ *or chiefly formerly* **Sal·lee** \ˈsa-lē\ city & port NW Morocco, N suburb of Rabat *area pop* 849,000

Sa·lem \ˈsā-ləm\ **1** city & port NE Mass. NE of Lynn *pop* 41,340 **2** town SE N.H. E of Nashua *pop* 28,776 **3** city ✻ of Oreg. on Willamette River *pop* 154,637 **4** town W *cen* Va. WNW of Roanoke *pop* 24,802 **5** city S India in N *cen* Tamil Nadu SW of Madras *pop* 693,236

Sa·ler·no \sə-ˈlər-(ˌ)nō, sä-ˈler-\ commune & port S Italy on **Gulf of Salerno** (inlet of Tyrrhenian Sea) ESE of Naples *pop* 141,724 — **Sa·ler·ni·tan** \-ˈlər-nə-tən, -ˈler-\ *adj or n*

Sal·ford \ˈsȯl-fərd\ urban area NW England in Greater Manchester *pop* 98,024

Sa·li·na \sə-ˈlī-nə\ city *cen* Kans. on Smoky Hill River *pop* 47,707

Sa·li·nas \sə-ˈlē-nəs\ **1** river 150 *mi* (241 *km*) W Calif. flowing NW into Monterey Bay **2** city W Calif. near Monterey Bay *pop* 150,441 **3** city S Puerto Rico *pop* 31,078

Salinas Pueblo Missions National Monument area containing archaeological ruins *cen* N.Mex.

Salis·bury \ˈsȯlz-ˌber-ē, -b(ə-)rē, *US also* ˈsalz-\ **1** city SE Md. *pop* 30,343 **2** city W *cen* N.C. SSW of Winston-Salem *pop* 33,662 **3** — see HARARE **4** city S England in Wiltshire on the Avon *pop* 35,355

Salisbury Plain plateau S England in Wiltshire NW of Salisbury

Salm·on \ˈsa-mən\ river 420 *mi* (676 *km*) *cen* Idaho flowing into Snake River

Salmon River Mountains mountains *cen* Idaho; many peaks over 9000 *ft* (2743 *m*)

Salonika — see THESSALONÍKI

Sa·lon·i·ka, Gulf of \sə-ˈlä-ni-kə\ *or Gk* **Ther·ma·ï·kós Kól·pos** \ther-ˌmä-ē-ˈkȯs-ˈkȯl-ˌpȯs\ arm of Aegean Sea N Greece W of Chalcidice

Salop — see SHROPSHIRE — **Sa·lo·pi·an** \sə-ˈlō-pē-ən\ *adj or n*

Salt \ˈsȯlt\ **1** river 200 *mi* (322 *km*) Ariz. flowing W into the Gila **2** river 100 *mi* (161 *km*) N *cen* Ky. flowing into Ohio River **3** river 200 *mi* (322 *km*) NE Mo. flowing SE into Mississippi River

Sal·ta \ˈsäl-tä\ city NW Argentina *pop* 373,857

Sal·til·lo \säl-ˈtē-(ˌ)yō, sal-\ city NE Mexico ✻ of Coahuila *pop* 440,845

Salt Lake City city N Utah, its ✻ *pop* 186,440

Sal·to \ˈsäl-(ˌ)tō\ city & port NW Uruguay on Uruguay River *pop* 74,881

Sal·ton Sea \ˈsȯl-tᵊn\ saline lake *ab* 235 *ft* (72 *m*) below sea level SE Calif. at N end of Imperial Valley formed by diversion of water from Colorado River into depression called **Salton Sink**

Salt Sea — see DEAD SEA

Sa·lu·da \sə-ˈlü-də\ river 200 *mi* (322 *km*) W *cen* S.C. flowing SE to unite with Broad River forming the Congaree

Sal·va·dor \ˈsal-və-ˌdȯr, ˌsal-və-ˈ\ **1** EL SALVADOR **2** *or formerly* **São Salvador** \sau̇ⁿ-\ *or* **Ba·hia** \bä-ˈē-ə\ port NE Brazil ✻ of Bahia *pop* 2,443,107 — **Sal·va·dor·an** \ˌsal-və-ˈdȯr-ən\ *adj or n* — **Sal·va·dor·ean** *or* **Sal·va·dor·ian** \-ē-ən\ *adj or n*

Sal·ween \ˈsal-ˌwēn\ river *ab* 1500 *mi* (2415 *km*) SE Asia flowing from Tibet S into Gulf of Martaban in Myanmar

Salz·burg \ˈsȯlz-ˌbərg, ˈsalz-, ˈsalz-, ˈsȯlts-, *G* ˈzälts-ˌbu̇rk\ city W Austria ESE of Munich, Germany *pop* 142,662

Salz·git·ter \ˈzälts-ˌgi-tər\ *or formerly* **Wa·ten·stedt–Salzgitter** \ˈvä-tᵊn-ˌshtet-, -ˌstet-\ city N *cen* Germany SW of Brunswick *pop* 115,381

Salz·kam·mer·gut \ˈzälts-ˌkä-mər-ˌgüt\ district N Austria E of Salzburg; chief town Bad Ischl

Samanala Kanda — see ADAM'S PEAK

Sa·mar \ˈsä-ˌmär\ island E *cen* Philippines in the Visayan Islands N of Leyte *area* 5050 *sq mi* (13,130 *sq km*)

Sa·ma·ra \sə-ˈmär-ə\ *or 1935–91* **Kuy·by·shev** \ˈkwē-bə-ˌshef, ˈkü-ē-bə-, -ˌshev\ city E Russia in Europe in valley of the Volga *pop* 1,239,000

Sa·mar·ia \sə-ˈmer-ē-ə\ **1** district of ancient Palestine W of the Jordan bet. Galilee & Judaea **2** city, its ✻ & ✻ of the Northern Kingdom (Israel); rebuilt by Herod the Great & renamed **Se·bas·te** \sə-ˈbas-tē\; site in West Bank at modern village of Sebastīyah

Sam·a·rin·da \ˌsa-mə-ˈrin-də\ city Indonesia in E Borneo *pop* 407,339

Sam·ar·qand *or* **Sam·ar·kand** \ˈsa-mər-ˌkand\ *or anc* **Mar·a·can·da** \ˌma-rə-ˈkan-də\ city E Uzbekistan *pop* 370,500

Sam·mam·ish \sə-ˈma-mish\ city W *cen* Wash. *pop* 45,780

Sam·ni·um \ˈsam-nē-əm\ ancient country S *cen* Italy

Sa·moa \sə-ˈmō-ə\ **1** *or formerly* **Navigators Islands** islands SW *cen* Pacific N of Tonga Islands; divided at long. 171°W into American, or Eastern, Samoa & independent Samoa *area* 1209 *sq mi* (3143 *sq km*) — see AMERICAN SAMOA **2** *or formerly* **Western Samoa** islands SW *cen* Pacific W of American Samoa; formerly administered by New Zealand; an independent member of the Commonwealth of Nations since 1962 ✻ Apia (on Upolu Is.) *area* 1100 *sq mi* (2850 *sq km*), *pop* 179,186

Sa·mos \ˈsā-ˌmäs, ˈsä-ˌmȯs\ island Greece in the Aegean off coast of Turkey N of the Dodecanese *area* 184 *sq mi* (477 *sq km*), *pop* 41,850 — **Sa·mi·an** \ˈsā-mē-ən\ *adj or n*

Sam·o·thrace \ˈsa-mə-ˌthrās\ *or ModGk* **Sa·mo·thrá·ki** \ˌsä-mȯ-ˈthrä-kē\ island Greece in the NE Aegean — **Sam·o·thra·cian** \ˌsa-mə-ˈthrā-shən\ *adj or n*

Sam·sun \säm-ˈsün\ city & port N Turkey on Black Sea NW of Ankara *pop* 303,979

San·aa *or* **Sana** \sa-ˈnä, ˈsa-ˌnä\ city S Arabia ✻ of Yemen & formerly ✻ of Yemen Arab Republic *pop* 1,700,000

Sa·nan·daj \ˌsä-nən-ˈdäj\ city NW Iran *pop* 204,537

San An·dre·as Fault \ˌsan-an-ˈdrā-əs\ zone of faults Calif. extending from N coast toward head of Gulf of California

San An·ge·lo \san-ˈan-jə-ˌlō\ city W *cen* Tex. *pop* 93,200

San An·to·nio \ˌsan-ən-ˈtō-nē-ˌō\ **1** river *ab* 200 *mi* (322 *km*) S Tex. flowing SE into Gulf of Mexico **2** city S Tex. on San Antonio River *pop* 1,327,407 — **San An·to·ni·an** \-nē-ən\ *n*

San Be·ni·to \ˌsan-bə-ˈnē-(ˌ)tō\ city S Tex. NW of Brownsville *pop* 24,250

San Ber·nar·di·no \ˌsan-ˌbər-nə(r)-ˈdē-(ˌ)nō\ city SW Calif. E of Los Angeles *pop* 209,924

San Bernardino Mountains mountains S Calif. S of Mojave Desert; highest **San Gor·go·nio Mountain** \ˌsan-gȯr-ˈgō-nē-(ˌ)ō\ 11,502 *ft* (3506 *m*)

San Bru·no \san-ˈbrü-(ˌ)nō\ city W Calif. S of San Francisco *pop* 41,114

San Buenaventura — see VENTURA

San Car·los \san-ˈkär-lōs\ city W Calif. SE of San Francisco *pop* 28,406

San Carlos de Bariloche — see BARILOCHE

San Cle·men·te \ˌsan-klə-ˈmen-tē\ city SW Calif. NW of San Diego *pop* 63,522

San Clemente Island island S Calif., southernmost of Channel Islands

San Cris·to·bal \ˌsan-kri-ˈstō-bəl\ island W Pacific in SE Solomons

San Cris·tó·bal \ˌsan-kri-ˈstō-bəl\ **1** *or* **Chatham Island** island Ecuador in the Galápagos *pop* 1404 **2** city W Venezuela SSW of Lake Maracaibo *pop* 220,697

Sanc·ti Spí·ri·tus \ˌsäŋk-tē-ˈspē-rē-ˌtüs\ city W *cen* Cuba SE of Santa Clara *pop* 85,499

San·cy, Puy de \ˌpwē-də-ˌsäⁿ-ˈsē\ mountain 6188 *ft* (1886 *m*) S *cen* France; highest in the Monts Dore & Auvergne Mountains

San·da·kan \san-ˈdä-kən\ city & port Malaysia in Sabah on Sulu Sea; former ✻ of N. Borneo *pop* 118,417

Sand·hurst \ˈsand-ˌhərst\ village S England in E Berkshire SE of Reading *pop* 6445

San·dia Mountains \san-ˈdē-ə\ mountains N *cen* N.Mex. E of Albuquerque; highest **Sandia Crest** 10,678 *ft* (3255 *m*)

San Di·e·go \ˌsan-dē-ˈā-(ˌ)gō\ city & port SW Calif. on **San Diego Bay** (inlet of the Pacific) *pop* 1,307,402 — **San Di·e·gan** \-gən\ *adj or n*

San Di·mas \san-ˈdē-məs\ city SW Calif. NW of Pomona *pop* 33,371

San Domingo — see DOMINICAN REPUBLIC

San·dring·ham \ˈsan-driŋ-əm\ village E England in NW Norfolk

San·dus·ky \sən-ˈdəs-kē, san-\ **1** river 150 *mi* (241 *km*) N Ohio flowing N into Lake Erie **2** city N Ohio at entrance to **Sandusky Bay** (inlet of Lake Erie) *pop* 25,793

Sand·wich \ˈsan(d)-(ˌ)wich\ town SE England in Kent on Stour River *pop* 4227

Sandwich Islands — see HAWAII 1

Sandy \ˈsan-dē\ city N Utah S of Salt Lake City *pop* 87,461

Sandy Hook peninsula E N.J. extending N toward New York Bay

San Fer·nan·do \ˌsan-fər-ˈnan-(ˌ)dō\ **1** valley S Calif. NW of Los Angeles; partly within Los Angeles city limits **2** city SW Calif. in San Fernando Valley *pop* 23,645

San·ford \ˈsan-fərd\ **1** city E *cen* Fla. NNE of Orlando *pop* 53,570 **2** city *cen* N.C. SW of Raleigh *pop* 28,094

Sanford, Mount mountain 16,237 *ft* (4949 *m*) S Alaska at W end of Wrangell Mountains

San Fran·cis·co \ˌsan-frən-ˈsis-(ˌ)kō\ city & port W Calif. on **San Francisco Bay** & the Pacific *pop* 805,235 — **San Fran·cis·can** \-kən\ *adj or n*

San Francisco Peaks mountain N *cen* Ariz. N of Flagstaff; includes three peaks: Mt. Humphreys 12,633 *ft* (3851 *m*), highest point in the state; Mt. Agassiz 12,340 *ft* (3761 *m*); & Mt. Fremont 11,940 *ft* (3639 *m*)

San Ga·bri·el \san-ˈgā-brē-əl\ city SW Calif. S of Pasadena *pop* 39,718

San Gabriel Mountains mountains S Calif. SW of Mojave Desert & NE of Los Angeles; highest San Antonio Peak 10,080 *ft* (3072 *m*)

San·ga·mon \ˈsaŋ-gə-mən\ river *ab* 250 *mi* (400 *km*) *cen* Ill. flowing SW & W into Illinois River

San·gay \säŋ-ˈgī\ volcano 17,159 *ft* (5230 *m*) SE *cen* Ecuador

San Ger·mán \ˌsäŋ-her-ˈmän\ city SW Puerto Rico *pop* 35,527

San·gi·he Islands \ˌsäŋ-gē-ˈā\ *or* **San·gi Islands** \ˈsäŋ-gē\ islands Indonesia NE of Sulawesi *pop* 194,253; largest of the group **Sangihe** *or* **Sangi**

San Gi·mi·gna·no \ˌsän-ˌjē-mē-ˈnyä-(ˌ)nō\ commune *cen* Italy NW of Siena *pop* 7021

San·gre de Cris·to Mountains \ˌsaŋ-grē-də-ˈkris-(ˌ)tō\ mountains S Colo. & N N.Mex. in Rocky Mountains — see BLANCA PEAK

San·i·bel Island \ˈsa-nə-bəl, -ˌbel\ island SW Fla. SW of Fort Myers

San Il·de·fon·so \ˌsan-ˌil-də-ˈfän(t)-(ˌ)sō, ˌsän-ˌēl-dā-ˈfōn-sō\ *or* **La Gran·ja** \lä-ˈgräŋ-(ˌ)hä\ commune *cen* Spain SE of Segovia *pop* 5093

San Isi·dro \ˌsan-ə-ˈsē-(ˌ)drō\ city E Argentina *pop* 299,022

San Ja·cin·to \ˌsan-jə-ˈsin-tō\ **1** river SE Tex. flowing S into Galveston Bay **2** city S Calif. SE of San Bernardino *pop* 44,199

San Joa·quin \ˌsan-wä-ˈkēn, -wȯ-\ river 350 *mi* (563 *km*) *cen* Calif. flowing from the Sierra Nevada SW & then NW into Sacramento River

San Jo·se \ˌsan-(h)ō-ˈzā\ city W Calif. SSE of San Francisco *pop* 945,942

San Jo·sé \ˌsäŋ-hō-ˈsā, ˌsan-(h)ō-ˈzā\ city *cen* Costa Rica, its ✻ *pop* 330,529

San Juan \san-ˈwän, ˌsän-ˈhwän\ **1** river 360 *mi* (579 *km*) SW Colo., NW N.Mex., & SE Utah flowing W into Colorado River **2** city & port NE Puerto Rico, its ✻ *pop* 395,326 **3** city S Texas near the Mexican border *pop* 33,856 **4** city W Argentina N of Mendoza *pop* 106,564 — **San Jua·ne·ro** \ˌsan-wä-ˈner-(ˌ)ō, -ˈhwä-\ *n*

San Juan Capistrano — see CAPISTRANO

San Juan Hill hill E Cuba near Santiago de Cuba

San Juan Islands islands NW Wash. bet. Vancouver Is. & the mainland

San Juan Mountains mountains SW Colo. in the Rocky Mountains — see UNCOMPAHGRE PEAK

Sankt An·ton am Arl·berg \zäŋkt-ˈän-ˌtōn-ˌäm-ˈär(-ə)l-ˌbərg, -ˌberk\ village W Austria in Tirol W of Innsbruck

Sankt Gallen — see SAINT GALL

Sankt Moritz — see SAINT MORITZ

San Le·an·dro \san-lē-ˈan-(ˌ)drō\ city W Calif. SE of Oakland pop 84,950

Şan·lı·ur·fa \ˌshän-lə-ˈür-fä\ or **Ur·fa** \ˈür-fä\ or anc **Edes·sa** \i-ˈde-sə\ city SE Turkey pop 276,528

San Lo·ren·zo \ˌsän-lō-ˈren-(ˌ)zō\ 1 city E Puerto Rico pop 41,058 2 city S Paraguay E of Asunción

San Lucas, Cape — see CABO SAN LUCAS

San Lu·is \san-ˈlü-əs\ valley S Colo. & N N.Mex. along the upper Rio Grande bet. the San Juan & Sangre de Cristo mountains

San Lu·is Obis·po \san-ˌlü-əs-ə-ˈbis-(ˌ)pō\ city W Calif. NW of Santa Barbara pop 45,119

San Lu·is Po·to·sí \ˌsän-lü-ˌēs-ˌpō-tə-ˈsē\ 1 state cen Mexico area 24,266 sq mi (62,849 sq km), pop 2,003,187 2 city, its ✳, NE of León pop 525,819

San Mar·cos \san-ˈmär-kəs, -kōs\ 1 city SW Calif. NNW of San Diego pop 83,781 2 city S Tex. NE of San Antonio pop 44,894

San Ma·ri·no \ˌsan-mə-ˈrē-(ˌ)nō\ 1 country S Europe on Italian Peninsula SSW of Rimini; a republic area 24 sq mi (62 sq km), pop 26,850 2 town, its ✳ — **Sam·ma·ri·nese** \ˌsa(m)-ˌma-rə-ˈnēz, -ˈnēs\ n — **San Mar·i·nese** \ˌsan-ˌma-\ adj or n

San Mar·tín \ˌsan-mär-ˈtēn\ or **Ge·ne·ral San Martín** \hä-nä-ˈräl\ city E Argentina, NW suburb of Buenos Aires pop 407,506

San Ma·teo \ˌsan-mə-ˈtā-(ˌ)ō\ city W Calif. SSE of San Francisco pop 97,207

San Mi·guel de Tu·cu·mán \ˌsän-mē-ˈgel-dä-ˌtü-kü-män\ or **Tucumán** city NW Argentina at foot of E ranges of the Andes pop 473,014

San Pab·lo \san-ˈpa-(ˌ)blō\ city W Calif. N of Oakland on **San Pablo Bay** (N extension of San Francisco Bay) pop 29,139

San Pe·dro Channel \san-ˈpē-(ˌ)drō, -ˈpā-\ channel SW Calif. bet. Santa Catalina Is. & the mainland

San Pe·dro Su·la \ˌsän-ˈpā-(ˌ)thrō-ˈsü-lä\ city NW Honduras pop 300,400

San Ra·fael \ˌsan-rə-ˈfel\ city W Calif. on San Pablo Bay pop 57,713

San Ra·mon \ˌsan-rə-ˈmōn\ city W Calif. E of Oakland pop 72,148

San Re·mo \san-ˈrä-(ˌ)mō, san-ˈrē-\ city & port NW Italy in Liguria near French border pop 55,786

San Sal·va·dor \san-ˈsal-və-ˌdór, ˌsän-ˈsäl-vä-ˌthór\ 1 island cen Bahamas area 60 sq mi (156 sq km) 2 city W cen El Salvador, its ✳ pop 415,346

San Se·bas·tián \ˌsän-sā-ˌbäs-ˈtyän\ city NW Puerto Rico pop 42,430

San Stefano — see YESILKOY

San·ta Ana \ˌsan-tə-ˈa-nə, ˌsän-tä-ˈä-nä\ 1 city SW Calif. ESE of Long Beach pop 324,528 2 city NW El Salvador pop 168,047

Santa Bar·ba·ra \ˈbär-b(ə-)rə\ city S Calif. pop 88,410

Santa Barbara Channel channel SW Calif. bet. the N Channel Islands & mainland

Santa Barbara Islands — see CHANNEL ISLANDS 1

Santa Catalina — see CATALINA

San·ta Ca·ta·ri·na \ˌsan-tə-ˌka-tə-ˈrē-nə\ state S Brazil bordering on the Atlantic ✳ Florianópolis area 37,060 sq mi (95,985 sq km), pop 4,536,433

Santa Clara \ˈkler-ə\ 1 city W Calif. NW of San Jose pop 116,468 2 city W cen Cuba pop 194,354

San·ta Cla·ri·ta \klə-ˈrē-tə\ city Calif. pop 176,320

Santa Cruz \ˈkrüz\ 1 island SW Calif. in NW Channel Islands 2 city W Calif. S of San Jose on Monterey Bay pop 59,946 3 — see SAINT CROIX 4 river 250 mi (402 km) S Argentina flowing E into the Atlantic 5 city E Bolivia pop 694,616

San·ta Cruz de Te·ne·ri·fe \ˌsän-tä-ˈkrüs-dä-ˌte-nə-ˈrē-(ˌ)fä, -ˈrēf, -ˈrif\ 1 province Spain comprising W Canary Islands area 1239 sq mi (3209 sq km), pop 806,801 2 city & port, its ✳, on NE Tenerife Is. pop 188,477

Santa Cruz Islands islands SW Pacific in SE Solomons N of Vanuatu; until 1978 administratively attached to Brit. Solomon Islands area 362 sq mi (938 sq km)

San·ta Fe \ˌsan-tə-ˈfä\ 1 city N cen N.Mex., its ✳ pop 67,947 2 city cen Argentina on Salado River pop 442,214 — **Santa Fe·an** \ˈfä-ən\ n

Santa Fe Trail pioneer route to the Southwest used esp. 1821–80 from vicinity of Kansas City, Mo., to Santa Fe, N.Mex.

San·ta Is·a·bel \ˌsan-tə-ˈi-zə-ˌbel\ 1 island W Pacific in the E cen Solomons NE of Guadalcanal area ab 1500 sq mi (3900 sq km) 2 — see MALABO

Santa Ma·ría \mə-ˈrē-ə\ city W Calif. NW of Santa Barbara pop 99,553

San·ta Ma·ría \ˌsän-tä-mə-ˈrē-ə\ volcano ab 12,400 ft (3780 m) W Guatemala

Santa Mar·ta \ˈmär-tə\ city & port N Colombia on the Caribbean E of Barranquilla pop 286,500

San·ta Mon·i·ca \ˌsan-tə-ˈmä-ni-kə\ city SW Calif. adjacent to Los Angeles on **Santa Monica Bay** (inlet of the Pacific) pop 89,736

San·tan·der \ˌsän-ˌtän-ˈder, ˌsan-ˌtan-\ 1 — see CANTABRIA 2 city & port N Spain on Bay of Biscay ✳ of Cantabria province pop 180,717

San·ta Pau·la \ˌsan-tə-ˈpó-lə\ city SW Calif. NW of Los Angeles pop 29,321

San·ta·rém \ˌsan-tə-ˈrem\ city N Brazil in W Pará at confluence of the Tapajoz & the Amazon pop 262,538

San·ta Ro·sa \ˌsan-tə-ˈrō-zə\ city W Calif. N of San Francisco pop 167,815

Santa Rosa Island island SW Calif. in NW Channel Islands

San·tee \(ˌ)san-ˈtē, ˈsan-\ 1 river 143 mi (230 km) S.C. flowing SE into the Atlantic — see CONGAREE 2 city S Calif., a suburb of San Diego pop 53,413

San·ti·a·go \ˌsan-tē-ˈä-(ˌ)gō\ 1 city cen Chile, its ✳ metropolitan area pop 4,668,500 2 or **Santiago de los Ca·bal·le·ros** \thä-lōs-ˌkä-vä-ˈyer-(ˌ)ōs\ city N cen Dominican Republic pop 580,745 3 or **Santiago de Com·pos·te·la** \də-ˌkäm-pə-ˈste-lə, -ˌkōm-\ commune NW Spain pop 90,188 — **San·ti·a·gan** \ˌsan-tē-ˈä-gən, ˌsän-\ n

Santiago de Cu·ba \də-ˈkyü-bə, thä-ˈkü-vä\ city & port SE Cuba pop 405,354

Santiago del Es·te·ro \(ˌ)del-ə-ˈster-(ˌ)ō, (ˌ)thel-ä-ˈstā-rō\ city N Argentina SE of San Miguel de Tucumán pop 201,709

San·to An·dré \ˈsän-tü-än-ˈdre\ city SE Brazil pop 649,331

San·to Do·min·go \ˌsan-tə-də-ˈmiŋ-(ˌ)gō\ 1 or formerly **Tru·jil·lo** \trü-ˈhē-(ˌ)yō\ or **Ci·u·dad Trujillo** \syü-ˈthä(th), ˌsē-ü-ˈdad\ city & port ✳ of Dominican Republic on Caribbean Sea pop 1,971,050 2 — see HISPANIOLA 3 — see DOMINICAN REPUBLIC — **San·to Do·min·gan** \ˌsan-tə-də-ˈmiŋ-gən\ adj or n

Santorini — see THIRA

San·tos \ˈsan-tüs\ city & port SE Brazil in SE São Paulo state SSE of São Paulo on an island in a tidal inlet pop 417,983

San·tur·ce \sän-ˈtür-(ˌ)sä\ a NE section of San Juan, Puerto Rico

São Fran·cis·co \ˌsaúⁿ-frən-ˈsēs-(ˌ)kü\ river 1800 mi (2897 km) E Brazil flowing from S cen Minas Gerais NE & E into the Atlantic

São Luís \ˌsaúⁿ-lü-ˈēs\ city & port NE Brazil ✳ of Maranhão state on Maranhão Is. pop 870,028

São Manuel — see TELES PIRES

São Mi·guel \ˌsaúⁿ-mē-ˈgel\ island Portugal in E Azores; chief town Ponta Delgada area 288 sq mi (746 sq km)

Saône \ˈsōn\ river 298 mi (479 km) E France flowing SSW into the Rhône

São Pau·lo \saúⁿ-ˈpaú-(ˌ)lü, -(ˌ)lō\ 1 state SE Brazil area 95,852 sq mi (248,257 sq km), pop 37,032,403 2 city, its ✳ pop 10,434,252

São Ro·que, Cape \saúⁿ-ˈró-kə\ headland NE Brazil N of Natal

São Salvador — see SALVADOR 2

São Tia·go \saúⁿ-tē-ˈä-(ˌ)gü, -(ˌ)gō\ island Cape Verde Islands, largest of the group; chief town Praia area 383 sq mi (992 sq km)

São To·mé \ˌsaúⁿ-tə-ˈmā\ island W Africa in Gulf of Guinea; with Príncipe Is., forms the republic (until 1975 a Portuguese territory) of **São Tomé and Príncipe** (✳ São Tomé area 372 sq mi or 963 sq km, pop 137,599)

São Vicente, Cabo de — see SAINT VINCENT (Cape)

Sap·po·ro \ˈsä-pō-ˌrō; sä-ˈpór-(ˌ)ō\ city Japan on W Hokkaido pop 1,822,368

Saq·qâ·ra or **Saq·qâ·rah** or **Sak·ka·ra** \sə-ˈkär-ə\ village N Egypt SW of ruins of Memphis

Sarabat — see GEDIZ

Sar·a·gos·sa \ˌsa-rə-ˈgä-sə\ or Span **Za·ra·go·za** \ˌthä-rä-ˈgō-thä, ˌsä-rä-ˈgō-sä\ city, ✳ of Zaragoza province, Spain pop 614,905

Sa·ra·je·vo \ˌsa-rə-ˈyä-(ˌ)vō, ˌsär-ə-; ˈsär-ə-ye-ˌvó\ city SE cen Bosnia and Herzegovina, its ✳ — **Sa·ra·je·van** \-vən\ n

Sar·a·nac \ˌsa-rə-ˌnak\ river 100 mi (161 km) NE N.Y. flowing NE from **Saranac Lakes** (three lakes in the Adirondacks: Upper Saranac, Middle Saranac, & Lower Saranac) into Lake Champlain

Sa·ransk \sə-ˈrän(t)sk, -ˈran(t)sk\ city cen Russia in Europe ✳ of Mordvinia pop 322,000

Sar·a·so·ta \ˌsa-rə-ˈsō-tə\ city W Fla. S of Tampa pop 51,917

Sar·a·to·ga \ˌsa-rə-ˈtō-gə\ city W Calif. SW of San Jose pop 29,926

Saratoga Lake lake 7 mi (11 km) long E N.Y. S of Lake George

Saratoga Springs city N N.Y. pop 26,586

Sa·ra·tov \sə-ˈrä-təf\ city cen Russia in Europe on a reservoir of the Volga pop 909,000

Sa·ra·wak \sə-ˈrä-(ˌ)wä(k), -ˌwak\ state Malaysia in N Borneo, formerly a Brit. colony ✳ Kuching area 48,342 sq mi (125,206 sq km), pop 1,648,217

Sardica — see SOFIA

Sar·din·ia \sär-ˈdi-nē-ə, -ˈdi-nyə\ or It **Sar·de·gna** \sär-ˈdā-nyä\ island Italy S of Corsica; with surrounding smaller islands, constitutes a region of Italy ✳ Cagliari area ab 9300 sq mi (24,087 sq km), pop 1,637,639

Sar·dis \ˈsär-dəs\ or **Sar·des** \ˈsär-(ˌ)dēz\ ancient city W Asia Minor ✳ of Lydia; site E of Izmir — **Sar·di·an** \ˈsär-dē-ən\ adj or n

Sa·re·ma or Estonian **Saa·re·maa** \ˈsär-ə-ˌmä\ island Estonia at mouth of Gulf of Riga area ab 1050 sq mi (2720 sq km)

Sa·re·ra Bay \sə-ˈrer-ə\ or formerly **Geel·vink Bay** \ˈgāl-(ˌ)viŋk, ˈkäl-\ inlet Indonesia in N West Papua

Sar·gas·so Sea \sär-ˈga-(ˌ)sō\ tract of comparatively still water N. Atlantic lying chiefly bet. 25° & 35°N & 40° & 70°W and containing thick seaweed growth

Sar·go·dha \sər-ˈgō-də\ city N cen Pakistan WNW of Lahore pop 458,440

Sark \ˈsärk\ island in the English Channel, one of the Channel Islands; a dependency of Guernsey area 2 sq mi (5.2 sq km) — **Sark·ese** \ˌsär-ˈkēz, -ˈkēs\ n

Sar·ma·tia \sär-ˈmä-sh(ē-)ə\ ancient region E Europe in modern Poland & Russia bet. the Vistula & the Volga — **Sar·ma·tian** \-shən\ adj or n

Sar·nia \ˈsär-nē-ə\ city Canada in SE Ont. on St. Clair River opposite Port Huron, Mich. pop 72,366

Sa·ron·ic Gulf \sə-ˈrä-nik\ inlet of the Aegean SE Greece bet. Attica & the Peloponnese

Sa·ros Gulf \ˈser-ˌäs\ inlet of the Aegean SW Turkey in Europe N of Gallipoli Peninsula

Sarre — see SAAR

Sarthe \ˈsärt\ river 175 mi (282 km) NW France flowing S to unite with the Mayenne forming Maine River

Sarum OLD SARUM

Sa·se·bo \ˈsä-se-ˌbó\ city & port Japan in NW Kyushu on an inlet of E. China Sea pop 240,838

Sas·katch·e·wan \sa-ˈska-chə-wən, sa-, -ˌwän\ 1 river 340 mi (547 km) S cen Canada formed by confluence in cen Sask. of two branches rising in the Rockies in Alta., the **North Saskatchewan** (760 mi or 1216 km) & the **South Saskatchewan** (865 mi or 1384 km), & flowing E into Lake Winnipeg 2 province SW Canada ✳ Regina area 220,121 sq mi (570,113 sq km), pop 1,033,381 — **Sas·katch·e·wan·ian** \-ˌska-chə-ˈwä-nē-ən\ adj or n

---

\ə\ abut \ᵊ\ kitten, F table \ər\ further \a\ ash \ā\ ace \ä\ mop, mar

\aú\ out \ch\ chin \e\ bet \ē\ easy \g\ go \i\ hit \ī\ ice \j\ job

\ŋ\ sing \ō\ go \ó\ law \ói\ boy \th\ thin \t͟h\ the \ü\ loot \ú\ foot

\y\ yet \zh\ vision, beige \ḵ, ⁿ, œ, ɶ, ᵜ\ see Guide to Pronunciation

Sas·ka·toon \ˌsas-kə-ˈtün\ city Canada in *cen* Sask. on S. Saskatchewan River *pop* 222,189
Sas·sa·ri \ˈsä-sä-(ˌ)rē\ commune Italy in NW Sardinia *pop* 120,874
Sa·til·la \sə-ˈti-lə\ river 220 *mi* (354 *km*) SE Ga. flowing E into the Atlantic
Sat·pu·ra Range \ˈsät-pə-rə\ range of hills W *cen* India bet. the Narmada & the Tapi
Sa·tu–Ma·re \ˌsä-(ˌ)tü-ˈmär-(ˌ)ā\ city NW Romania in Transylvania on the Somes *pop* 115,630
Sau·di Arabia \ˈsau̇-dē, ˈsȯ-dē, sä-ˈü-dē\ country SW Asia occupying most of Arabia; a kingdom, comprising former kingdoms of Nejd & Hejaz & principality of Asir ✻ Riyadh *area* 865,000 *sq mi* (2,240,350 *sq km*), *pop* 20,800,000 — **Saudi** *adj or n* — **Saudi Arabian** *adj or n*
Sau·gus \ˈsȯ-gəs\ town NE Mass. W of Lynn *pop* 26,628
Sault Sainte Ma·rie *usu* **Sault Ste. Marie** \ˈsü-(ˌ)sānt-mə-ˈrē\ city Canada in Ont. across the St. Marys River from Michigan *pop* 75,141
Sault Sainte Marie Canals *or* **Soo Canals** \ˈsü\ three ship canals (two in the U.S. & one in Canada) at rapids in St. Marys River connecting Lake Superior & Lake Huron
Sau·mur \sō-ˈmu̇r, -ˈmyu̇r, -ˈmœr\ commune NW France on the Loire SE of Angers *pop* 29,916
Sau·rash·tra \sau̇-ˈräsh-trə\ former state (1948–56) W India on Kathiawar Peninsula; in Bombay state 1956–60 & since 1960 in Gujarat
Sa·va \ˈsä-və\ river 584 *mi* (940 *km*) flowing from Italian border E through Slovenia, into Croatia, along Croatia-Bosnia and Herzegovina border, & into Serbia where it flows into the Danube at Belgrade
Sa·vaii \sə-ˈvī-ˌē\ island Samoa (nation) SW Pacific, largest in Samoa islands
Sa·van·nah \sə-ˈva-nə\ **1** river 314 *mi* (505 *km*) E Ga. flowing SE to the Atlantic & forming Ga.-S.C. boundary **2** city & port E Ga. at mouth of Savannah River *pop* 136,286
Save — see SABI
Sa·vo \ˈsä-(ˌ)vō\ island W Pacific in SE Solomons N of W Guadalcanal
Sa·vo·na \sä-ˈvō-nä\ commune & port NW Italy SW of Genoa *pop* 61,911
Sa·voy \sə-ˈvȯi\ *or F* **Sa·voie** \sä-ˈvwä\ *or It* **Sa·vo·ia** \sä-ˈvȯ-yä\ region SE France in Savoy Alps SW of Switzerland & bordering on Italy; duchy 1416–1720, part of kingdom of Sardinia 1720–1860; became part of France 1860 — **Sa·voy·ard** \sə-ˈvȯi-ˌärd, ˌsa-ˌvȯi-ˈärd, ˌsa-ˌvwä-ˈyär(d)\ *adj or n*
Savoy Alps section of W Alps SE France — see MONT BLANC
Sa·watch Range \sə-ˈwäch\ mountain range *cen* Colo. in Rocky Mountains — see ELBERT (Mount)
Saxe \ˈsaks\ SAXONY — its French name; used in English chiefly in names of former duchies in Thuringia: **Saxe–Al·ten·burg** \-ˈäl-tᵊn-ˌbu̇rg\, **Saxe–Co·burg** \-ˈkō-ˌbərg\, **Saxe–Go·tha** \-ˈgō-tə, -thə\, **Saxe–Mei·ning·en** \-ˈmī-niŋ-ən\, & **Saxe–Wei·mar–Ei·se·nach** \-ˈvī-ˌmär-ˈī-zə-ˌnäk, -ˌnäk\
Sax·o·ny \ˈsak-s(ə-)nē\ *or G* **Sach·sen** \ˈzäk-sən\ **1** region & former duchy NW Germany S of Jutland Peninsula bet. the Elbe & the Rhine — see LOWER SAXONY **2** region & state of reunified Germany N of the Erzgebirge ✻ Dresden *area* 7081 *sq mi* (18,340 *sq km*), *pop* 4,764,300 — see SAXE
Saxony–An·halt \-ˈän-ˌhält\ state of *cen* Germany ✻ Magdeburg *area* 7956 *sq mi* (20,606 *sq km*), *pop* 2,874,000
Sa·yan Mountains \sə-ˈyän\ mountains S Russia in Asia on border of Tuva N of Altai Mountains
Sayre·ville \ˈser-ˌvil\ borough E *cen* N.J. *pop* 42,704
Sa·zan \ˈsä-ˌzän\ *or It* **Sa·se·no** \sə-ˈzā-(ˌ)nō, sä-\ island Albania in N Strait of Otranto
Sca Fell \ˌskȯ-ˈfel\ mountain 3162 *ft* (964 *m*) NW England in Cumbrians SW of Keswick; second highest peak in England
Sca·fell Pike \ˌskȯ-ˈfel\ mountain 3210 *ft* (978 *m*) NW England in Cumbria NE of Sca Fell; highest in the Cumbrians & in England
Scamander — see MENDERES 2
Scan·di·na·via \ˌskan-də-ˈnā-vē-ə, -vyə\ **1** peninsula N Europe occupied by Norway & Sweden **2** Denmark, Norway, Sweden — sometimes also considered to include Iceland, the Faeroe Islands, & Finland
Scapa Flow \ˌska-pə-ˈflō\ sea basin N Scotland in the Orkneys
Scar·bor·ough \ˈskär-ˌbər-ō\ **1** former city Canada in SE Ont., now part of Toronto **2** town & port NE England in N. Yorkshire *pop* 107,800
Schaer·beek *or Flem* **Schaar·beek** \ˈskär-ˌbāk, ˈskär-\ commune *cen* Belgium, NE suburb of Brussels *pop* 107,736
Schaff·hau·sen \shäf-ˈhau̇-zᵊn\ **1** canton N Switzerland bordering on SW Germany *area* 115 *sq mi* (298 *sq km*), *pop* 73,400 **2** commune, its ✻ *pop* 33,436
Schaum·burg \ˈshäm-(ˌ)bərg\ village NE Ill. NW of Chicago *pop* 74,227
Schaum·burg–Lip·pe \ˈshau̇m-ˌbu̇rk-ˈli-pə\ state of Germany 1918–33 in NW bet. Westphalia & Hannover
Schel·de \ˈskel-də\ *or* **Scheldt** \ˈskelt\ *or F* **Es·caut** \e-ˈskō\ river 270 *mi* (434 *km*) W Europe flowing from N France through Belgium into North Sea in Netherlands
Sche·nec·ta·dy \skə-ˈnek-tə-dē\ city E N.Y. *pop* 66,135
Scher·er·ville \ˈshir-ər-ˌvil\ town NW Ind. *pop* 29,243
Sche·ve·ning·en \ˈskā-və-ˌniŋ-ə(n), ˈskā-\ seaside resort SW Netherlands on North Sea; part of The Hague
Schie·dam \skē-ˈdäm, skē-\ commune SW Netherlands *pop* 76,576
Schles·wig \ˈshles-(ˌ)wig, -(ˌ)vik\ **1** *or Dan* **Sles·vig** \ˈslis-vē\ region N Germany & S Denmark in S Jutland Peninsula **2** city N Germany *pop ab* 26,938
Schleswig–Hol·stein \-ˈhōl-ˌstīn, -ˌshtīn\ state of Germany & formerly of W. Germany consisting of Holstein & part of Schleswig ✻ Kiel *area* 6046 *sq mi* (15,659 *sq km*), *pop* 2,626,100
Schou·ten Islands \ˈskau̇-tᵊn\ islands Indonesia in N West Papua at mouth of Sarera Bay *area* 1230 *sq mi* (3198 *sq km*)
Schuyl·kill \ˈskü-kᵊl, ˈskül-ˌkil\ river 131 *mi* (211 *km*) SE Pa. flowing SE into Delaware River at Philadelphia
Schwaben — see SWABIA
Schwarzwald — see BLACK FOREST
Schwein·furt \ˈshvīn-ˌfu̇rt\ city S *cen* Germany on Main River *pop* 54,520
Schweiz — see SWITZERLAND
Schwe·rin \shvā-ˈrēn\ city N Germany ✻ of Mecklenburg-West Pomerania *pop* 125,959
Schwyz \ˈshvēts\ **1** canton E *cen* Switzerland *area* 351 *sq mi* (909 *sq km*), *pop* 131,400 **2** town, its ✻, E of Lucerne *pop* 13,934
Scil·ly, Isles of \ˈsi-lē\ island group SW England off Land's End comprising 140 islands ✻ Hugh Town *area* 6 *sq mi* (16 *sq km*), *pop* 2900 — see CORNWALL 2 — **Scil·lo·ni·an** \si-ˈlō-nē-ən\ *adj or n*
Sci·o·to \sī-ˈō-tə\ river 237 *mi* (381 *km*) Ohio flowing S into Ohio River
Scone \ˈskün\ locality E Scotland NE of Perth *pop* 3713
Sco·pus, Mount \ˈskō-pəs\ mountain Israel NE of Jerusalem
Scores·by Sound \ˈskȯrz-bē\ inlet of Norwegian Sea E Greenland N of 70°N
Sco·tia Sea \ˈskō-shə\ part of the S. Atlantic SE of Falkland Islands, W of S. Sandwich Islands, & N of S. Orkney Islands
Scot·land \ˈskät-lənd\ *or L* **Cal·e·do·nia** \ˌka-lə-ˈdō-nyə, -nē-ə\ *or ML* **Sco·tia** \ˈskō-shə\ country N Great Britain; a division of United Kingdom of Great Britain and Northern Ireland ✻ Edinburgh *area* 29,797 *sq mi* (77,174 *sq km*), *pop* 5,062,011
Scottish Bor·ders \-ˈbȯr-dərz\ administrative area of S Scotland *area* 1828 *sq mi* (4734 *sq km*)
Scotts Bluff National Monument \ˈskäts\ reservation W Nebr. on N. Platte River including **Scotts Bluff** (high butte that was a landmark on the Oregon Trail)
Scotts·dale \ˈskäts-ˌdāl\ city SW *cen* Ariz. E of Phoenix *pop* 217,385
Scran·ton \ˈskran-tᵊn\ city NE Pa. *pop* 76,089
Scun·thorpe \ˈskən-ˌthȯrp\ town E England in Lincolnshire WSW of Hull *pop* 60,500
Scu·ta·ri, Lake \ˈskü-tä-rē\ lake NW Albania & S Montenegro *area* 143 *sq mi* (370 *sq km*)
Scyth·ia \ˈsi-thē-ə, -thē-\ the country of the ancient Scythians comprising parts of Europe & Asia N & NE of Black Sea & E of Aral Sea
Sea Islands islands SE U.S. in the Atlantic off coast of S.C., Ga., & Fla. bet. mouths of Santee & St. Johns rivers
Seal Beach city SW Calif. SE of Los Angeles *pop* 24,168
Sea·side \ˈsē-ˌsīd\ city W Calif. on Monterey Bay *pop* 33,025
Sea Tac \ˈsē-ˌtak\ city W *cen* Wash. between Seattle & Tacoma *pop* 26,909
Se·at·tle \sē-ˈa-tᵊl\ city & port W Wash. bet. Puget Sound & Lake Washington *pop* 608,660 — **Se·at·tle·ite** \-tᵊl-ˌīt\ *n*
Se·ba·go Lake \sə-ˈbā-(ˌ)gō\ lake 13 *mi* (21 *km*) long SW Maine
Sebaste — see SAMARIA 2
Sebastea *or* **Sebastia** — see SIVAS
Se·cun·der·a·bad \si-ˈkən-də-rə-ˌbad, -ˌbäd\ city S *cen* India in Andhra Pradesh, NE suburb of Hyderabad *pop* 204,182
Se·dan \si-ˈdan, *F* sə-ˈdäⁿ\ city NE France on the Meuse NE of Reims *pop* 20,547
Sedge·moor \ˈsej-ˌmu̇r, -ˌmȯr\ moorland SW England in *cen* Somerset
Se·go·via \sā-ˈgō-vyə, sə-, -vē-ə\ **1** — see COCO **2** province N *cen* Spain in Old Castile *area* 2683 *sq mi* (6949 *sq km*), *pop* 147,694 **3** commune, its ✻, NW of Madrid *pop* 54,368
Sei·kan Tunnel \ˈsā-ˌkän\ rail tunnel Japan under Tsugaru Strait bet. Honshu & Hokkaido 33.4 *mi* (53.7 *km*) long
Seim — see SEYM
Seine \ˈsān, ˈsen\ river 480 *mi* (772 *km*) N France flowing NW into **Bay of the Seine** (inlet of English Channel)
Se·lang·or \sə-ˈläŋ-ər, -ˈlaŋ-ˌgȯr\ state *cen* Malaysia (federation) on Strait of Malacca *area* 3074 *sq mi* (7962 *sq km*), *pop* 2,289,236
Sel·en·ga \ˌse-lən-ˈgä\ river N *cen* Asia rising in W Mongolia & flowing to Lake Baikal
Se·leu·cia \sə-ˈlü-sh(ē-)ə\ **1** *or* **Seleucia Tra·che·o·tis** \ˌtrā-kē-ˈō-təs\ ancient city SE Asia Minor in Cilicia SW of Tarsus **2** ancient city, chief city of the Seleucid Empire; ruins now in Iraq on the Tigris SSE of Baghdad **3** *or* **Seleucia Pi·er·ia** \pī-ˈir-ē-ə, -ˈer-\ ancient city Asia Minor N of mouth of the Orontes; port for Antioch
Sel·kirk \ˈsel-ˌkərk\ **1** *or* **Sel·kirk·shire** \-ˌshir, -shər\ former county SE Scotland **2** burgh SE of Edinburgh *pop* 5417
Selkirk Mountains mountains SW Canada in SE B.C. W of the Rockies; highest Mt. Sir Sandford 11,555 *ft* (3522 *m*)
Sel·ma \ˈsel-mə\ city *cen* Ala. W of Montgomery *pop* 20,756
Se·ma·rang \sə-ˈmär-ˌäŋ\ city & port Indonesia in *cen* Java on N coast *pop* 1,250,971
Se·mey \ˈse-mā\ *or* **Sem·i·pa·la·tinsk** \ˌse-mi-pə-ˈlä-ˌtin(t)sk\ city NE Kazakhstan on the Irtysh *pop* 344,700
Sem·i·nole, Lake \ˈse-mə-ˌnōl\ reservoir SW Ga. & NW Fla. formed by confluence of Chattahoochee & Flint rivers & emptying by the Apalachicola
Sen·dai \(ˌ)sen-ˈdī\ city Japan in NE Honshu *pop* 1,008,130
Sen·e·ca Lake \ˈse-ni-kə\ lake 35 *mi* (56 *km*) long W *cen* N.Y.; one of the Finger Lakes
Sen·e·gal \ˌse-ni-ˈgȯl, -ˈgäl, ˈse-ni-ˌ\ **1** river 1015 *mi* (1633 *km*) W Africa flowing from Fouta Djallon NW & W into the Atlantic **2** country W Africa on the Atlantic; a republic of the French Community, formerly a territory of French West Africa ✻ Dakar *area* 76,124 *sq mi* (197,161 *sq km*), *pop* 7,899,000 — **Sen·e·ga·lese** \ˌse-ni-gə-ˈlēz, -ˈlēs\ *adj or n*
Sen·e·gam·bia \ˌse-nə-ˈgam-bē-ə\ **1** region W Africa around Senegal & Gambia rivers **2** confederation of Senegal & Gambia 1982–89 — **Sen·e·gam·bi·an** \-ən\ *adj or n*
Sen·lac \ˈsen-ˌlak\ hill SE England in Sussex NW of Hastings
Sen·lis \säⁿ-ˈlēs\ commune N France NNE of Paris *pop* 16,314
Sen·nar *or* **Sen·naar** \sə-ˈnär\ region E Sudan chiefly bet. White Nile & Blue Nile rivers; an ancient kingdom
Sens \ˈsäⁿs\ city NE *cen* France WSW of Troyes *pop* 26,906
Seongnam — see SONGNAM
Seoul \ˈsōl\ city NW S. Korea on Han River *pop* 9,853,972; formerly ✻ of Korea, since 1948 ✻ of S. Korea
Se·pik \ˈsā-pik\ river 600 *mi* (966 *km*) N Papua New Guinea
Se·quoia National Park \si-ˈkwȯi-ə\ reservation SE *cen* Calif. including Mt. Whitney
Se·raing \sə-ˈreⁿ\ commune E Belgium *pop* 60,407
Seram — see CERAM
Ser·bia \ˈsər-bē-ə\ *or formerly* **Ser·via** \-vē-ə\ country S Europe; a constituent republic of Serbia and Montenegro 2003–06 and of Yugoslavia before that (1946–2003) including Kosovo & Vojvodina ✻ Belgrade *area* 34,115 *sq mi* (88,358 *sq km*), *pop* 9,823,000

Serbia and Montenegro *or 1992–2003* **Yugoslavia** former country S Europe on Balkan Peninsula ✳ Belgrade *area* 39,449 *sq mi* (102,173 *sq km*)

Serbs, Croats, and Slovenes, Kingdom of the — see YUGOSLAVIA

Serdica — see SOFIA

Se·re·kun·da \se-re-'kün-də\ city W Gambia *pop* 68,824

Serendib — see CEYLON 1

Ser·en·ge·ti Plain \ser-ən-'ge-tē\ area N Tanzania including **Serengeti National Park** (wild game reserve)

Ser·gi·pe \sər-'zhē-pə\ state NE Brazil ✳ Aracajú *area* 8441 *sq mi* (21,862 *sq km*), *pop* 1,492,400

Se·rin·ga·pa·tam \sə-,riŋ-gə-pə-'tam\ town S India N of city of Mysore

Se·ro·we \sə-'rō-ä\ city E Botswana *pop* 30,264

Ser·ra da Es·tre·la \'ser-ə-(,)dä-ish-'tre-lä\ mountain range Portugal; highest point Malhão da Estrela (highest in Portugal) 6532 *ft* (1991 *m*)

Serra do Mar \dü-'mär\ mountain range S Brazil along coast

Ser·rai \'ser-(,)e, -,ä\ city N Greece *pop* 50,875

Ser·ra Pa·ri·ma \,ser-ə-pə-'rē-mə\ mountain range N S. America on Venezuela-Brazil border; source of the Orinoco

Ses·tos \'ses-təs\ ruined town Turkey in Europe on the Dardanelles

Ses·to San Gio·van·ni \'ses-tō-,sän-jō-'vä-nē\ commune N Italy *pop* 81,687

Sète \'set\ *or formerly* **Cette** \'set\ commune & port S France SSW of Montpellier *pop* 39,579

Se·te Que·das \,se-tē-'kā-dəsh\ *or formerly* **Guaí·ra** \'gwī-(,)rä\ former cataract in Alto Paraná River on Brazil-Paraguay boundary; now submerged in reservoir formed by Itaipu Dam

Sé·tif \sā-'tēf\ commune NE Algeria *pop* 144,200

Se·tú·bal \sə-'tü-bəl, -,bäl\ city & port SW Portugal on **Bay of Setúbal** (inlet of the Atlantic) *pop* 113,934

Se·van \sə-'vän\ lake N Armenia *area* 480 *sq mi* (1243 *sq km*)

Se·vas·to·pol \sə-'vas-tə-,pōl, -,pōl, -pəl; ,se-və-'stō-pəl, -'stō-\ *or formerly* **Se·bas·to·pol** \-'bas-; ,se-bə-\ city & port SW Crimea *pop* 366,000

Se·ver·na·ya Zem·lya \'se-vər-nə-yə-,zem-lē-ä, 'sye-vir-nə-yə-zim-'lyä\ islands N Russia in Asia N of Taymyr Peninsula in Arctic Ocean bet. Kara & Laptev seas *area* 14,300 *sq mi* (37,180 *sq km*)

Sev·ern River \'se-vərn\ **1** inlet of Chesapeake Bay, in Md., on which Annapolis is situated **2** river 610 *mi* (982 *km*) Canada in NW Ont. flowing NE into Hudson Bay **3** river 210 *mi* (338 *km*) Great Britain flowing from E cen Wales into Bristol Channel in England

Se·vier \sə-'vir\ river 280 *mi* (451 *km*) SW cen Utah flowing into **Sevier Lake** (25 *mi* or 40 *km* long; saline)

Se·ville \sə-'vil\ *or Sp* **Se·vil·la** \sā-'vē-(,)yä\ **1** province SW Spain *area* 5406 *sq mi* (14,002 *sq km*), *pop* 1,727,603 **2** city, its ✳, on the Guadalquiver *pop* 684,633

Sè·vres \'sevr'\ commune N France SW of Paris *pop* 22,555

Sew·ard Peninsula \'sü-ərd\ peninsula 180 *mi* (290 *km*) long & 130 *mi* (209 *km*) wide W Alaska projecting into Bering Sea bet. Kotzebue & Norton sounds — see PRINCE OF WALES (Cape)

Sey·chelles \sā-'shel(z)\ island group W Indian Ocean NE of Madagascar ✳ Victoria (on Mahé Is.) *area* 107 *sq mi* (277 *sq km*), *pop* 81,177; formerly a Brit. colony, a republic in the Commonwealth of Nations since 1976 — **Sey·chel·lois** \sā-shəl-'wä, -,shel-\

Sey·han \sā-'hän\ *or* **Sei·hun** \-'hün\ river Turkey flowing SSW into the Mediterranean **2** — see ADANA

Seym *or* **Seim** \'säm\ river 460 *mi* (740 *km*) N Ukraine & Russia in Europe flowing W into the Desna

Sfax \'sfaks\ city & port Tunisia on Gulf of Gabès *pop* 221,770

's Gravenhage — see HAGUE (The)

Shaan·xi \'shän-'shē\ *or* **Shen·si** \'shen-'sē, 'shən-'shē\ province N cen China bordering on the Huang ✳ Xi'an *area* 75,598 *sq mi* (195,799 *sq km*), *pop* 32,882,403

Sha·ba \'shä-bə\ *or formerly* **Ka·tan·ga** \kə-'täŋ-gə, -'taŋ-\ region SE Democratic Republic of the Congo; chief city Lubumbashi

Shak·er Heights \'shä-kər\ city NE Ohio E of Cleveland *pop* 28,448

Shakh·ty \'shäk-tē, 'shäk-\ *or formerly* **Ale·ksan·drovsk-Gru·shev·ski** \,a-lik-'sän-drəfsk-grü-shef-skē\ city S Russia in Europe NE of Rostov-on-Don *pop* 228,000

Shan·dong \'shän-'dȯŋ\ *or* **Shan–tung** \'shan-'təŋ, 'shän-'dùŋ\ **1** peninsula E China projecting ENE bet. Yellow Sea & Bo Hai **2** province E China including Shandong Peninsula ✳ Jinan *area* 59,189 *sq mi* (153,300 *sq km*), *pop* 84,392,827

Shang·hai \shaŋ-'hī\ city & port E China on the Huangpu near the Chang estuary *pop* 12,693,000

Shang·qiu *or* **Shang–ch'iu** \'shäŋ-'chyü\ city E China in E Henan *pop* 164,880

Shan·non \'sha-nən\ river 230 *mi* (370 *km*) W Ireland flowing S & W into the Atlantic

Shan States \'shän, 'shan\ mountainous region SE Asia ruled by the Shan people 12th-16th centuries; now in E Myanmar

Shan·tou \'shän-'tō\ *or* **Swa·tow** \'swä-'taù\ city & port SE China in E Guangdong on S. China Sea *pop* 578,630

Shan·xi \'shän-'shē\ *or* **Shan·si** \-'sē, -'shē\ province N China bordering on the Huang ✳ Taiyuan *area* 60,656 *sq mi* (157,099 *sq km*), *pop* 28,759,014

Shao·xing *or* **Shao–hsing** \'shaù-'shiŋ\ city E China in N Zhejiang SE of Hangzhou *pop* 179,818

Shao·yang \'shaù-'yäŋ\ *or formerly* **Pao·king** \'baù-'chiŋ\ city SE China in cen Hunan W of Hengyang *pop* 247,227

Shari — see CHARI

Sharjah — see ASH SHARIQAH

Shark Bay inlet of Indian Ocean 150 *mi* (241 *km*) long W Western Australia, at *ab* 25°S

Shar·on, Plain of \'sher-ən\ region N Israel on coast bet. Mt. Carmel & Jaffa

Sha·shi \'shä-'shē\ *or* **Sha–shih** \-'shir, -'shē\ city E cen China in S Hubei on the Chang *pop* 281,352

Shas·ta, Mount \'shas-tə\ mountain 14,162 *ft* (4316 *m*) N Calif. in Cascade Range; an isolated volcanic cone

Shatt al Ar·ab \,shat-al-'a-rəb\ river 120 *mi* (193 *km*) SE Iraq formed by the Tigris & the Euphrates & flowing SE into Persian Gulf

Shaw·an·gunk Mountains \'shäŋ-gəm, shə-'wän-(,)gəŋk\ mountain ridge SE N.Y.; part of Kittatinny Mountain

Sha·win·i·gan \shə-'wi-ni-gən\ city Canada in S Que. on the St. Maurice *pop* 50,060

Shaw·nee \shȯ-'nē, 'shȯ-,; shä-'nē, 'shä-,\ **1** city NE Kans. S of Kansas City *pop* 62,209 **2** city cen Okla. *pop* 29,857

Shcherbakov — see RYBINSK

She·ba \'shē-bə\ *or* **Sa·ba** \'sā-bə\ ancient country S Arabia probably including Yemen

She·boy·gan \shi-'bȯi-gən\ city & port E Wis. *pop* 49,288

Shechem — see NABLUS

Shef·field \'she-,fēld\ city N England in S. Yorkshire *pop* 499,700

Shel·i·kof \'she-li-,kȯf\ strait S Alaska bet. Alaska Peninsula & islands of Kodiak & Afognak

Shel·ton \'shel-t°n\ city SW Conn. *pop* 39,559

Shen·an·do·ah \,she-nən-'dō-ə, ,sha-nə-'dō-ə\ river 55 *mi* (88 *km*) N Va. flowing NE bet. Allegheny & Blue Ridge Mountains across NE tip of W.Va. & into the Potomac; forms **Shenandoah Valley**

Shenandoah National Park wilderness area N Va. in Blue Ridge Mountains

Shensi — see SHAANXI

Shen·yang \'shən-'yäŋ\ *or* **Muk·den** \'mük-dən, 'mək-; mük-'den\ *or formerly* **Feng·tien** \'fəŋ-'tyen\ city NE China ✳ of Liaoning; chief city of Manchuria *pop* 3,603,712

Shen·zhen *or* **Shen–chen** \'shən-'jen\ city SE China in S Guangdong just N of Hong Kong *pop* 1,120,400

Sher·brooke \'shər-,bruk\ city E Canada in S Que. *pop* 154,601

Sher·man \'shər-mən\ city NE Tex. N of Dallas *pop* 38,521

's Her·to·gen·bosch \ser-,tō-gən-'bȯs, -,kən-\ city S Netherlands ✳ of N. Brabant *pop* 131,697

Sher·wood Forest \'shər-,wùd- *also* -'sher-\ ancient royal forest cen England chiefly in Nottinghamshire

Shet·land \'shet-lənd\ *or* **Zet·land** \'zet-\ islands N Scotland NE of the Orkneys; constitute an administrative area ✳ Lerwick (on Mainland Is.) *area* 550 *sq mi* (1430 *sq km*), *pop* 21,960 — **Shet·land·er** \'shet-lən-dər\ *n*

Shey·enne \shī-'an, -'en\ river 325 *mi* (523 *km*) SE cen N.Dak. flowing into Red River

Shi·bin al–Kawm *or* **Shi·bîn el Kôm** \shi-,bēn-el-'kōm\ city N Egypt *pop* 153,000

Shigatse — see XIGAZÊ

Shi·jia·zhuang *or* **Shih–chia–chuang** \'shir-'jyä-'jwäŋ, 'shē-\ city NE China ✳ of Hebei *pop* 1,068,439

Shi·kar·pur \shi-'kär-,pùr\ city S cen Pakistan in Sind *pop* 88,000

Shi·ko·ku \shē-'kō-(,)kü\ island S Japan E of Kyushu *area* 7245 *sq mi* (18,765 *sq km*), *pop* 4,154,039

Shil·ka \'shil-kə\ river 345 *mi* (555 *km*) SE Russia in Asia flowing NE to unite with the Argun forming the Amur

Shil·long \shi-'lȯŋ\ city NE India ✳ of Meghalaya *pop* 132,876

Shi·loh \'shī-(,)lō\ **1** locality SW Tenn.; site of American Civil War battle **2** village ancient Palestine on slope of Mt. Ephraim

Shi·mi·zu \shē-'mē-(,)zü, 'shē-mē-,zü\ city & port Japan in cen Honshu on Suruga Bay; port for Shizuoka *pop* 236,818

Shim·la \'shim-lə\ *or* **Sim·la** \'sim-\ city N India N of Delhi ✳ of Himachal Pradesh & former summer ✳ of India *pop* 142,161

Shi·mo·da \shē-'mō-də, -,dä\ city & port Japan in S Honshu SW of Yokohama on Sagami Sea *pop* 27,798

Shi·mo·no·se·ki \,shē-mō-nō-'se-kē\ *or formerly* **Ba·kan** \'bä-,kän\ city & port Japan in SW Honshu on Shimonoseki Strait *pop* 252,389

Shimonoseki Strait strait Japan bet. Honshu & Kyushu connecting Inland Sea & Korea Strait

Shi·nar \'shī-nər, -,när\ a country known to the early Hebrews as a plain in Babylonia; prob. Sumer

Shi·raz \shi-'räz, -'raz\ city S cen Iran *pop* 848,289

Shi·re \shē-(,)rā, 'shir-ē\ river 250 *mi* (400 *km*) S Malawi & cen Mozambique flowing from Lake Malawi S into the Zambezi

Shi·shal·din \shi-'shal-dən\ volcano 9372 *ft* (2856 *m*) SW Alaska on Unimak Is.; highest in Aleutian Range

Shi·zu·o·ka \shē-zü-'wō-kä\ city Japan in cen Honshu near Suruga Bay SW of Shimizu *pop* 469,695

Shko·dër \'shkō-dər\ city NW Albania *pop* 185,395

Sho·la·pur \'shō-lə-,pùr\ *or* **So·la·pur** \'sō-\ city W India in SE Maharashtra SE of Bombay *pop* 873,037

Shore·ditch \'shȯr-,dich\ former metropolitan borough N cen London, England, now part of Hackney

Shore·line \'shȯr-,līn\ city W cen Wash. N of Seattle *pop* 53,007

Shore·view \'shȯr-,vyü\ city E Minn. *pop* 25,043

Short·land Islands \'shȯrt-lənd\ islands W Pacific in the Solomons off S end of Bougainville

Sho·sho·ne \shə-'shō-nē, shə-'shōn\ river 120 *mi* (193 *km*) NW Wyo. flowing NE into Bighorn River

Shoshone Falls waterfall 210 *ft* (64 *m*) S Idaho in Snake River

Shreve·port \'shrēv-,pȯrt\ city NW La. on Red River *pop* 199,311

Shrews·bury \'sh(r)üz-,ber-ē, -b(ə-)rē\ town E Mass. *pop* 35,608 **2** \Brit often 'shrōz-\ town W England ✳ of Shropshire *pop* 59,826

Shrop·shire \'shräp-shər, -,shir\ *or* **Sal·op** \'sa-ləp, -,läp\ county W England bordering on Wales ✳ Shrewsbury *area* 1396 *sq mi* (3616 *sq km*), *pop* 401,600

Shuang·liao \'shwäŋ-'lyaù\ *or formerly* **Liao·yuan** \'lyaù-'ywen\ city NE China in W Jilin S of Changchun on the Liao

Shu·ma·gin \'shü-mə-gən\ islands SW Alaska S of Alaska Peninsula

Shushan — see SUSA

Shym·kent \shim-'kent\ *or* **Chim·kent** \chim-\ city S Kazakhstan N of Tashkent *pop* 438,800

Si — see XI

Si·al·kot \sē-'äl-,kōt\ city NE Pakistan NNE of Lahore *pop* 421,502

Siam — see THAILAND

Siam, Gulf of — see THAILAND (Gulf of)

\ə\ abut \'ə\ kitten, F table \ər\ further \a\ ash \ā\ ace \ä\ mop, mar
\aù\ out \ch\ chin \e\ bet \ē\ easy \g\ go \i\ hit \ī\ ice \j\ job
\ŋ\ sing \ō\ go \ȯ\ law \ȯi\ boy \th\ thin \t͟h\ the \ü\ loot \ù\ foot
\y\ yet \zh\ vision, beige \k̲, ⁿ, œ, ᴜ, ᵸ\ *see* Guide to Pronunciation

Siangtan — see XIANGTAN
Si·be·ria \sī-ˈbir-ē-ə\ region N Asia in Russia extending from the Urals to the Pacific; roughly coextensive with Russia in Asia — **Si·be·ri·an** \-ən\ *adj or n*
Si·biu \sē-ˈbyü\ city W *cen* Romania in Transylvania *pop* 155,045
Si·bu·yan Sea \ˌsē-bü-ˈyän\ body of water *cen* Philippines bounded by Mindoro, S Luzon, & the Visayan Islands
Si·chuan \ˈsēch-ˈwän\ *or* **Sze·chuan** *or* **Sze·chwan** \ˈsech-ˈwän, ˈsesh-\ province SW China ✻ Chengdu *area* 219,691 *sq mi* (571,197 *sq km*), *pop* 107,218,173
Sic·i·ly \ˈsi-s(ə-)lē\ *or It* **Si·ci·lia** \sē-ˈchēl-yä\ *or anc* **Si·cil·ia** \sə-ˈsil-yə\ *or* **Tri·nac·ria** \trə-ˈna-krē-ə, trī-\ island S Italy in the Mediterranean; a region ✻ Palermo *area* 9925 *sq mi* (25,706 *sq km*), *pop* 5,076,700 — **Si·cil·ian** \sə-ˈsil-yən\ *adj or n*
Si·cy·on \ˈsi-shē-ˌän, ˈsi-sē-\ *or Gk* **Sik·y·on** \ˈsē-kē-ˌȯn\ ancient city S Greece in NE Peloponnese NW of Corinth
Si·di Bar·râ·ni \ˈsē-dē-bə-ˈrä-nē\ village NW Egypt on coast
Sidi Bel Ab·bès \ˈsē-dē-ˌbel-ə-ˈbes\ commune NW Algeria *pop* 152,778
Si·don \ˈsī-dᵊn\ *or Ar* **Sai·da** \ˈsī-də\ city & port SW Lebanon; a chief city of ancient Phoenicia — **Si·do·ni·an** \sī-ˈdō-nē-ən\ *adj or n*
Sid·ra, Gulf of \ˈsi-drə\ *or* **Gulf of Sir·te** \ˈsir-tə\ *or anc* **Syr·tis Major** \ˈsər-təs\ inlet of the Mediterranean on coast of Libya
Sie·ben·ge·bir·ge \ˈzē-bən-gə-ˌbir-gə\ hills W Germany on right bank of the Rhine SSE of Bonn — see DRACHENFELS
Si·ena *or* **Si·en·na** \sē-ˈe-nä\ commune *cen* Italy in Tuscany *pop* 54,366 — **Si·en·ese** *or* **Si·en·nese** \ˌsē-ə-ˈnēz, -ˈnēs\ *adj or n*
Si·er·ra Blan·ca Peak \sē-ˌer-ə-ˈblaŋ-kə, ˈsyer-ä-ˈbläŋ-kä\ mountain 12,003 *ft* (3658 *m*) S *cen* N.Mex. in Sierra Blanca Range of the Sacramento Mountains
Sierra de Gre·dos \dā-ˈgrā-(ˌ)dōs, thā-\ mountain range W *cen* Spain; highest peak Plaza de Almanzor *ab* 8500 *ft* (2591 *m*)
Sierra de Gua·dar·ra·ma \dā-ˌgwä-dä-ˈrä-mä\ mountain range *cen* Spain; highest peak Pico de Peñalara 7970 *ft* (2429 *m*)
Sier·ra Le·one \sē-ˌer-ə-lē-ˈōn, ˌsir-ə-, -lē-ˈō-nē\ country W Africa on the Atlantic; a dominion of the Commonwealth of Nations ✻ Freetown *area* 27,699 *sq mi* (71,740 *sq km*), *pop* 4,491,000 — **Sierra Le·on·ean** \-ˈō-nē-ən\ *adj or n*
Si·er·ra Ma·dre del Sur \sē-ˌer-ə-ˈmä-drā-del-ˈsu̇r, ˈsyer-ä-ˈmä-thrā-thel-ˈsür\ mountain range S Mexico along Pacific coast in Guerrero & Oaxaca
Sierra Madre Oc·ci·den·tal \ˌäk-sə-ˌden-ˈtäl, ˌōk-sē-ˌthen-ˈtäl\ mountain range NW Mexico parallel to the Pacific coast
Sierra Madre Ori·en·tal \ˌȯr-ē-ˌen-ˈtäl\ mountain range E Mexico parallel to coast of Gulf of Mexico
Sierra Mo·re·na \mō-ˈrā-nä\ mountain range SW Spain bet. the Guadiana & the Guadalquivir; highest peak Estrella 4339 *ft* (1322 *m*)
Sierra Ne·va·da \nə-ˈva-də, -ˈvä-\ **1** mountain range E Calif. extending into W Nev. — see WHITNEY (Mount) **2** mountain range S Spain; highest peak Mulhacén *ab* 11,410 *ft* (3478 *m*)
Sierra Nevada de Mérida — see CORDILLERA DE MÉRIDA
Sierra Nevada de San·ta Mar·ta \dā-ˌsan-tə-ˈmär-tə, thā-ˌsän-tä-\ mountain range N Colombia on Caribbean coast
Sierra Vis·ta \ˈvis-tə\ city SE Ariz. SE of Tucson *pop* 43,888
Si·kang \ˈshē-ˈkäŋ\ former province S China ✻ Yaan
Si·kho·te–Alin' \ˈsē-kə-ˌtā-ə-ˈlēn\ mountain range SE Russia in Asia in Maritime Territory
Sik·kim \ˈsi-kəm, -ˌkim\ former country SE Asia on S slope of the Himalayas bet. Nepal & Bhutan; since 1975 a state of India ✻ Gangtok *area* 2744 *sq mi* (7107 *sq km*), *pop* 406,457 — **Sik·kim·ese** \ˌsi-kə-ˈmēz, -ˈmēs\ *adj or n*
Si·le·sia \sī-ˈlē-zh(ē-)ə, sə-, -sh(ē-)ə\ region E *cen* Europe in valley of the upper Oder bordering on Sudety Mountains; formerly chiefly in Germany, now chiefly in E Czech Republic & SW Poland — **Si·le·sian** \-zh(ē-)ən, -sh(ē-)ən\ *adj or n*
Silicon Valley region W Calif. bet. San Jose & Palo Alto, a center of high-tech industries
Silk Road *or* **Silk Route** ancient trade route that extended from China to the Mediterranean Sea
Sil·vas·sa \ˌsil-vä-ˈsä\ town W India ✻ of Dadra and Nagar Haveli union territory *pop* 21,890
Sim·birsk \sim-ˈbirsk\ *or 1924–91* **Ul·ya·novsk** \ül-ˈyä-nəfsk\ city SE *cen* Russia in Europe on the Volga *pop* 656,000
Sim·coe, Lake \ˈsim-(ˌ)kō\ lake E Canada in SE Ont. SE of Georgian Bay *area* 280 *sq mi* (728 *sq km*)
Sim·fe·ro·pol \ˌsim(p)-fə-ˈrō-pəl, -ˈrō-\ city S Ukraine *pop* 353,000
Si·mi Valley \sē-ˈmē\ city SW Calif. W of Los Angeles *pop* 124,237
Simla — see SHIMLA
Si·mons·town \ˈsī-mənz-ˌtau̇n\ town & port SW Republic of South Africa in Western Cape province on False Bay S of Cape Town
Sim·plon Pass \ˈsim-ˌplän\ mountain pass 6590 *ft* (2009 *m*) in Lepontine Alps bet. Switzerland & Italy in Valais & Piedmont
Simplon Tunnel tunnel *ab* 12 *mi* (19 *km*) long through Monte Leone (tallest mountain in Lepontine Alps) near Simplon Pass
Sims·bury \ˈsimz-ˌber-ē, -b(ə-)rē\ town N Conn. *pop* 23,511
Si·nai \ˈsī-ˌnī *also* -nē-ˌī\ peninsula extension of continent of Asia NE Egypt bet. Red Sea & the Mediterranean — **Si·na·it·ic** \ˌsī-nē-ˈi-tik\ *adj*
Sinai, Mount — see HOREB (Mount)
Si·na·loa \ˌsē-nä-ˈlō-ä\ state W Mexico bordering on Gulf of California ✻ Culiacán *area* 22,429 *sq mi* (58,091 *sq km*), *pop* 2,204,054
Sind *or* **Sindh** \ˈsind\ province S Pakistan in lower Indus valley ✻ Karachi
Sin·ga·pore \ˈsiŋ-ə-ˌpȯr *also* ˈsiŋ-gə-\ **1** island Malay Archipelago in S. China Sea off S end of Malay Peninsula; formerly a Brit. crown colony, from 1963 to 1965 a state of Malaysia (federation), an independent republic in the Commonwealth of Nations since 1965, *area* 255 *sq mi* (660 *sq km*), *pop* 4,163,700 **2** city & port, its ✻, on Singapore Strait *pop* 206,500 — **Sin·ga·por·ean** \ˌsiŋ-ə-ˈpȯr-ē-ən *also* ˌsiŋ-gə-\ *adj or n*
Singapore Strait channel SE Asia bet. Singapore Is. & Riau Archipelago connecting Strait of Malacca & S. China Sea
Sining — see XINING
Sinkiang Uighur — see XINJIANG UYGUR
Si·nop \sə-ˈnȯp\ *or anc* **Si·no·pe** \-ˈnō-pē\ town & port N Turkey on peninsula in Black Sea NW of Ankara *pop* 25,631
Sinsiang — see XINXIANG
Sint Maarten — see SAINT MARTIN
Sint–Nik·laas \ˈsint-ˈni-kläs\ *or* **Saint–Ni·co·las** \ˌsaⁿ-ˌnē-kȯ-ˈlä\ commune NW *cen* Belgium *pop* 68,473
Sin·tra *or* **Cin·tra** \ˈsēn-trə\ city W Portugal NW of Lisbon *pop* 363,749
Sin·ui·ju \ˈsin-ˈwē-ˈjü\ city W N. Korea on the Yalu opposite Dandong, China *pop* 289,000
Sion **1** \sē-ˈōⁿ\ *or G* **Sit·ten** \ˈzi-tᵊn, ˈsi-\ commune SW *cen* Switzerland ✻ of Valais *pop* 25,350 **2** — see ZION 2
Sioux City \ˈsü\ city NW Iowa on Missouri River *pop* 82,684
Sioux Falls city SE S.Dak. on the Big Sioux *pop* 153,888
Si·ping \ˈsə-ˈpiŋ\ *or* **Ssu–p'ing** \ˈsə-ˈpiŋ\ *or formerly* **Sze·ping·kai** \ˈsə-ˈpiŋ-ˈgī\ city NE China in Jilin SW of Changchun *pop* 317,223
Sip·par \si-ˈpär\ ancient city of Babylonia on the Euphrates SSW of modern Baghdad
Siracusa — see SYRACUSE 2
Si·ret \si-ˈret\ river 280 *mi* (450 *km*) E Romania flowing from the Carpathians SE into the Danube
Sir·mi·lik National Park \ˈsər-mə-lik\ reservation N Canada in N Nunavut on Baffin Is.
Síros — see SYROS
Sis·ki·you Mountains \ˈsis-ki-ˌyü\ mountains N Calif. & SW Oreg., highest Mt. Ashland (in Oreg.) 7533 *ft* (2296 *m*)
Sit·tang \ˈsi-ˌtäŋ\ river 260 *mi* (418 *km*) E *cen* Myanmar flowing S into Gulf of Martaban
Sit·twe \ˈsi-ˌtwā\ *or formerly* **Ak·yab** \a-ˈkyab\ city & port W Myanmar; chief town of Arakan coast *pop* 42,329
Si·vas \si-ˈväs\ *or anc* **Se·bas·tea** *or* **Se·bas·tia** \sə-ˈbas-ch(ē-)ə, -tē-ə\ city E *cen* Turkey on the upper Kizil Irmak *pop* 221,512
Si·wa \ˈsē-wə\ *or anc* **Am·mo·ni·um** \ə-ˈmō-nē-əm\ oasis & town NW Egypt W of Qattara Depression *pop* 4999
Si·wa·lik Range \si-ˈwä-lik\ foothills of the Himalayas N India extending SE from N Punjab into Uttar Pradesh
Sjæl·land \ˈshe-ˌlän\ island, largest of islands of Denmark; site of Copenhagen *area* 2709 *sq mi* (7043 *sq km*), *pop* 2,096,449
Skag·er·rak \ˈska-gə-ˌrak\ arm of the North Sea bet. Norway & Denmark
Skag·it \ˈska-jət\ river 163 *mi* (262 *km*) SW B.C. & NW Wash. flowing S & W into Puget Sound
Skan·e·at·e·les Lake \ˌska-nē-ˈat-ləs, ˌski-nē-\ lake 16 *mi* (26 *km*) long *cen* N.Y. SW of Syracuse; one of the Finger Lakes
Skaw, The \ˈskȯ\ *or* **Ska·gens Od·de** \ˈskä-gənz-ˌȯ-də\ cape Denmark at N extremity of Jutland
Skee·na \ˈskē-nə\ river 360 *mi* (579 *km*) Canada in W B.C. flowing S & W into Hecate Strait
Skid·daw \ˈski-ˌdȯ\ mountain 3053 *ft* (930 *m*) NW England in NW *cen* Cumbria
Skik·da \ˈskik-(ˌ)dä\ *or formerly* **Phi·lippe·ville** \ˈfi-ləp-ˌvil, fi-ˌlēp-ˈvēl\ city & port NE Algeria N of Constantine *pop* 128,747
Skíros — see SKYROS
Sko·kie \ˈskō-kē\ village NE Ill. N of Chicago *pop* 64,784
Skop·je \ˈskȯ-pye, -pyə\ city ✻ of Macedonia on the Vardar *pop* 470,642
Skunk river 264 *mi* (425 *km*) SE Iowa flowing SE into Mississippi River
Skye \ˈskī\ island Scotland, one of the Inner Hebrides *area* 670 *sq mi* (1742 *sq km*)
Sky·ros \ˈskī-rəs, -ˌräs\ *or Gk* **Skí·ros** \ˈskē-ˌrȯs\ island Greece in the Northern Sporades E of Euboea
Slave \ˈslāv\ river 258 *mi* (415 *km*) Canada flowing from W end of Lake Athabasca N into Great Slave Lake
Slave Coast region W Africa bordering on Bight of Benin bet. Benin & Volta rivers
Slav·kov \ˈsläf-ˌkȯf, ˈsläv-ˌkȯv\ *or* **Aus·ter·litz** \ˈȯ-stər-ˌlits, ˈau̇-\ town SE Czech Republic ESE of Brno
Sla·vo·nia \slə-ˈvō-nē-ə, -nyə\ region E Croatia bet. the Sava, the Drava, & the Danube — **Sla·vo·ni·an** \-nē-ən, -nyən\ *adj or n*
Slea·ford \ˈslē-fərd\ town E England in SW Lincolnshire SSE of Lincoln
Slesvig — see SCHLESWIG 1
Sli·dell \slī-ˈdel\ city SE La. NE of New Orleans *pop* 27,068
Slide Mountain \ˈslīd\ mountain 4204 *ft* (1281 *m*) SE N.Y. W of Kingston; highest in the Catskills
Sli·go \ˈslī-(ˌ)gō\ **1** county N Ireland (republic) in N Connacht *area* 693 *sq mi* (1795 *sq km*), *pop* 58,200 **2** town & port, its ✻, on **Sligo Bay** (inlet of the Atlantic) *pop* 17,297
Slough \ˈslau̇\ town SE *cen* England in Berkshire *pop* 98,600
Slo·va·kia \slō-ˈvä-kē-ə, -ˈva-\ *or* **Slo·ven·sko** \ˈslȯ-ven-ˌskȯ\ country *cen* Europe; a constituent republic of Czechoslovakia 1918–92 ✻ Bratislava *area* 18,923 *sq mi* (49,011 *sq km*), *pop* 5,379,455
Slo·ve·nia \slō-ˈvē-nē-ə, -nyə\ country S Europe N & W of Croatia; a federated republic of Yugoslavia 1946–91 ✻ Ljubljana *area* 7819 *sq mi* (20,251 *sq km*), *pop* 1,975,164
Smoky Hill river 540 *mi* (869 *km*) *cen* Kans. flowing E to unite with Republican River forming the Kansas River
Smo·lensk \smō-ˈlen(t)sk\ city W Russia in Europe on the upper Dnieper WSW of Moscow *pop* 352,000
Smyr·na \ˈsmər-nə\ **1** town NW Ga. NW of Atlanta *pop* 51,271 **2** town *cen* Tenn. SE of Nashville *pop* 39,974 **3** — see IZMIR
Snake \ˈsnāk\ river 1038 *mi* (1670 *km*) NW U.S. flowing from NW Wyo. across S Idaho & into Columbia River in Wash.
Snake Range mountain range E Nevada
Sno·qual·mie Falls \snō-ˈkwäl-mē\ waterfall 270 *ft* (80 *m*) W *cen* Wash. in **Snoqualmie River** 70 *mi* (118 *km*)
Snow — see MAOKE
Snow·don \ˈsnō-dᵊn\ massif 3560 *ft* (1085 *m*) NW Wales in Gwynedd; highest point in Wales
Snow·do·nia \snō-ˈdō-nē-ə, -nyə\ mountain region NW Wales centering around Snowdon
Snowy river 278 *mi* (447 *km*) SE Australia flowing from Snowy Mountains to the Pacific in SE Victoria
Snowy Mountains mountains SE Australia in SE New South Wales
So·bat \ˈsō-ˌbat\ river 460 *mi* (740 *km*) W Ethiopia & SE Sudan flowing W into White Nile River
Soča — see ISONZO

So·chi \'sō-chē\ city & port S Russia in Europe on NE coast of Black Sea *pop* 344,000

So·ci·e·ty Islands \sə-'sī-ə-tē\ *or F* Îles de la So·ci·é·té \,ēl-də-la-sò-syā-'tā\ islands S. Pacific belonging to France ✱ Papeete (on Tahiti) *area* 621 *sq mi* (1608 *sq km*), *pop* 162,573

So·cor·ro \sə-'kôr-(,)ō\ city Tex., a S suburb of El Paso *pop* 32,013

So·co·tra \sə-'kō-trə\ island Indian Ocean E of Gulf of Aden in Yemen; chief town Tamridah *area* 1400 *sq mi* (3640 *sq km*), *pop* 8000

Sö·der·täl·je \,sə(r)-dər-'tel-yə, ,sœ-\ town SE Sweden, a suburb of Stockholm *pop* 79,613

Sod·om \'sä-dəm\ ancient city thought to be in the area now covered by the SW part of the Dead Sea

So·fia \'sō-fē-ə, 'sò-, ,sō-\ *or* Bulg **So·fi·ya** \'sò-fē-ə\ *or anc* **Ser·di·ca** \'sər-di-kə\ *or* **Sar·di·ca** \'sär-\ city W Bulgaria, its ✱ *pop* 1,141,142

Sog·di·a·na \,säg-dē-'a-nə, -'ä-nə, -'ä-nə\ province of ancient Persian Empire bet. the Jaxartes (Syr Dar'ya) & Oxus (Amu Dar'ya) ✱ Maracanda (Samarqand)

Sog·ne Fjord \'sòn-nə\ inlet of Norwegian Sea SW Norway; longest fjord in Norway

So·hâg \sō-'häj\ city *cen* Egypt on the Nile SE of Asyût *pop* 190,132

So·ho \'sō-,hō\ district of *cen* London, England, in Westminster

Sois·sons \swä-'sō\ commune N France NW of Paris *pop* 29,439

Solapur — see SHOLAPUR

So·lent, The \'sō-lənt\ channel S England bet. Isle of Wight & the mainland

So·li·hull \,sō-li-'həl\ town *cen* England in W. Midlands SE of Birmingham *pop* 194,100

So·li·mões \,sü-lē-'móiⁿsh\ the upper Amazon, Brazil, from Peruvian border to the mouth of Negro River

So·ling·en \'zō-liŋ-ən, 'sō-\ city W Germany in the Ruhr ESE of Düsseldorf *pop* 165,924

Sol·o·mon Islands \'sä-lə-mən\ islands W Pacific E of New Guinea divided bet. Papua New Guinea & the independent country (formerly a Brit. protectorate of the Solomon Islands (✱ Honiara) *area* 11,500 *sq mi* (29,785 *sq km*), *pop* 536,000

Solomon Sea arm of Coral Sea W of Solomon Islands

So·lo·thurn \'zō-lə-,tùrn, 'sō-\ 1 canton NW Switzerland *area* 305 *sq mi* (790 *sq km*), *pop* 245,500 2 commune, its ✱, on the Aare *pop* 15,130

Sol·way Firth \'säl-,wä\ inlet of Irish Sea in Great Britain on boundary bet. England & Scotland

So·ma·lia \sō-'mä-lē-ə, sə-, -'mäl-yə\ country E Africa bordering on Gulf of Aden & Indian Ocean; formed 1960 by union of Brit. Somaliland & Italian Somaliland ✱ Mogadishu *area* 246,154 *sq mi* (637,539 *sq km*), *pop* 9,400,000 — **So·ma·lian** \-'mä-lē-ən, -'mäl-yən\ *adj or n*

So·ma·li·land \sō-'mä-lē-,land, sə-\ region E Africa comprising Somalia, Djibouti, & the Ogaden region of E Ethiopia

Som·er·set \'sə-mər-,set, -sət\ *or* **Som·er·set·shire** \-,shir, -shər\ county SW England ✱ Taunton *area* 1383 *sq mi* (3582 *sq km*), *pop* 459,100

Somerset Island island N Canada in Nunavut N of Boothia Peninsula *area* 9370 *sq mi* (24,362 *sq km*)

Somerset Nile — see NILE

Som·er·ville \'sə-mər-,vil\ city E Mass. N of Cambridge *pop* 75,754

So·mes \sō-'mesh\ *or Hung* Sza·mos \'sò-,mōsh\ river NE Hungary & NW Romania flowing NW into the Tisza

Somme \'säm, 'sòm\ river *ab* 150 *mi* (241 *km*) N France flowing NW into the English Channel

Song·hua \'sòŋ-'hwä\ *or* Sun·ga·ri \'sùŋ-gə-rē\ river *over* 1000 *mi* (1609 *km*) NE China in E Manchuria flowing from N. Korea border NW & NE into the Amur; dammed in upper part to form Songhua Reservoir

Song·nam *or* Seong·nam \'səŋ-'näm\ city NW S. Korea *pop* 447,692

So·no·ra \sə-'nòr-ə\ 1 river 250 *mi* (400 *km*) NW Mexico flowing SW into upper Gulf of California 2 state NW Mexico bordering on U.S. & Gulf of California ✱ Hermosillo *area* 71,403 *sq mi* (184,934 *sq km*), *pop* 1,823,606 — **So·no·ran** \-ən\ *adj or n*

Sonoran Desert desert SW U.S. & NW Mexico in S Ariz., SE Calif., & N Sonora

Soo Canals — see SAULT SAINTE MARIE CANALS

Soochow — see SUZHOU

Sop·ron \'shō-,prōn\ city W Hungary *pop* 57,500

Sorata — see ILLAMPU

Sorbiodunum — see OLD SARUM

So·rel–Tra·cy \sò-'rel-tra-'sē\ city Canada in S Que. *pop* 34,600

So·ria \'sòr-ē-ə\ 1 province N *cen* Spain *area* 3972 *sq mi* (10,287 *sq km*), *pop* 90,717 2 commune, its ✱, W of Saragossa *pop* 35,151

So·ro·ca·ba \,sòr-ə-'ka-bə, -'kä-\ city SE Brazil in SE São Paulo state *pop* 493,468

Sor·ren·to \sə-'ren-(,)tō\ *or anc* **Sur·ren·tum** \,sə-ren-təm\ commune & port S Italy on S side of Bay of Naples *pop* 17,429

Sos·no·wiec \sä-'snō-,vyets\ city SW Poland NE of Katowice *pop* 259,269

Sou·fri·ère \,sü-frē-'er\ 1 volcano 4813 *ft* (1467 *m*) French West Indies in S Basse-Terre, Guadeloupe 2 volcano 4048 *ft* (1234 *m*) Brit. West Indies on St. Vincent Is.

Sou·ris \'sùr-əs\ river 450 *mi* (724 *km*) Canada & U.S. flowing from SE Sask. SE into N N.Dak. & N into the Assiniboine in SW Man.

Sousse \'süs\ *or anc* **Had·ru·me·tum** \,ha-drə-'mē-təm\ city & port NE Tunisia *pop* 69,530

South Africa, Republic of country S Africa S of the Limpopo, Molopo, & Orange rivers bordering on Atlantic & Indian oceans; a republic, until 1961 (as **Union of South Africa**) a Brit. dominion; administrative ✱ Pretoria, legislative ✱ Cape Town, judicial ✱ Bloemfontein *area* 471,445 *sq mi* (1,221,043 *sq km*), *pop* 44,819,778

South African Republic — see TRANSVAAL

Sou·thall \'sau-,thòl\ former municipal borough S England in Middlesex, now part of Ealing

South America continent of the western hemisphere lying bet. the Atlantic & Pacific oceans SE of N. America & chiefly S of the equator *area* 6,880,706 *sq mi* (17,821,029 *sq km*) — **South American** *adj or n*

South·amp·ton \sau-'tham(p)-tən, saùth-'ham(p)-\ city & port S England in Hampshire on Southampton Water (estuary) *pop* 194,400

Southampton Island island N Canada in Nunavut, bet. Hudson Bay & Foxe Channel *area* 15,700 *sq mi* (40,820 *sq km*)

South Arabia, Federation of former Brit. protectorate comprising crown colony of Aden & numerous semi-independent Arab sultanates & emirates; made part of People's Democratic Republic of Yemen 1967

South Atlantic — see ATLANTIC OCEAN

South Australia state S Australia ✱ Adelaide *area* 380,070 *sq mi* (988,182 *sq km*), *pop* 1,462,900

South·aven \'saù-,thā-vən\ city N Miss. near Tenn. border *pop* 48,982

South Ayrshire administrative area of W Scotland *area* 464 *sq mi* (1202 *sq mi*)

South Bend \'bend\ city N Ind. NW of Fort Wayne *pop* 101,168

South Canadian — see CANADIAN

South Cape — see KA LAE

South Car·o·li·na \,ker-(ə)-'lī-nə, ,ka-rə-\ state SE U.S. ✱ Columbia *area* 31,113 *sq mi* (80,583 *sq km*), *pop* 4,625,364 — **South Car·o·lin·ian** \-'li-nē-ən, -'li-nyən\ *adj or n*

South China Sea part of W Pacific enclosed by SE China, Taiwan, Philippines, Indochina, Malaya, & Borneo

South Da·ko·ta \də-'kō-tə\ state NW *cen* U.S. ✱ Pierre *area* 77,116 *sq mi* (199,730 *sq km*), *pop* 814,180 — **South Da·ko·tan** \-'kō-tªn\ *adj or n*

South Downs hills S England chiefly in Sussex

South·end–on–Sea \,saù-,thend-,òn-'sē, -,än-\ seaside resort SE England in Essex at mouth of Thames estuary *pop* 153,700

Southern Alps mountain range New Zealand in W South Is. extending almost the length of the island — see COOK (Mount)

Southern Karoo — see KAROO

Southern Ocean *or* **Antarctic Ocean** the ocean surrounding Antarctica including the southern parts of the S. Atlantic, S. Pacific, & Indian oceans esp. S of *ab* 60°S

Southern Rhodesia — see ZIMBABWE 2

Southern Up·lands \'əp-lən(d)z, -,lan(d)z\ elevated moorland region S Scotland

Southern Yemen — see YEMEN

South Euclid city NE Ohio E of Cleveland *pop* 22,295

South·field \'saùth-,fēld\ city SE Mich. NW of Detroit *pop* 71,739

South·gate \'saùth-,gāt\ city SE Mich. S of Detroit *pop* 30,047

South Gate \,gāt\ city SW Calif. SE of Los Angeles *pop* 94,396

South Georgia island S. Atlantic E of Tierra del Fuego *area* 1450 *sq mi* (3770 *sq km*); administered by Britain

South Holland *or D* **Zuid–Hol·land** \zīt-'hò-,länt\ province SW Netherlands ✱ The Hague *area* 1259 *sq mi* (3261 *sq km*), *pop* 3,423,780

South·ing·ton \'sə-thiŋ-tən\ town W *cen* Conn. *pop* 43,069

South Island island S New Zealand *area* 59,439 *sq mi* (153,947 *sq km*), *pop* 906,756

South Jordan city N *cen* Utah S of Salt Lake City *pop* 50,418

South Kings·town \'kiŋ-stən, -,staùn\ town S R.I. *pop* 30,639

South Korea — see KOREA 2

South Lake Tahoe city E Calif. on Lake Tahoe *pop* 21,403

South Lanarkshire administrative area of W Scotland *area* 684 *sq mi* (1771 *sq km*)

South Mountain ridge S Pa. & W Md. at N end of Blue Ridge

South Na·han·ni \nə-'ha-nē\ river 350 *mi* (563 *km*) Canada in SW Northwest Territories flowing SE into the Liard

South Orkney Islands islands S. Atlantic SE of the Falklands in British Antarctic Territory *area* 240 *sq mi* (622 *sq km*)

South Os·se·tia \ä-'sē-shə\ autonomous region N Republic of Georgia ✱ Tskhinvali *area ab* 1500 *sq mi* (3900 *sq km*), *pop* 99,000

South Pacific — see PACIFIC OCEAN

South Pasadena city SW Calif. *pop* 25,619

South Pass broad valley SW *cen* Wyo. crossing Continental Divide

South Platte river 424 *mi* (682 *km*) Colo. & Nebr. flowing E to join N. Platte River forming the Platte River

South·port \'saùth-,pòrt\ town NW England in Merseyside on coast N of Liverpool *pop* 89,745

South Portland city SW Maine *pop* 25,002

South Sandwich Islands islands S. Atlantic SE of S. Georgia Is. *area* 120 *sq mi* (312 *sq km*); administered by Britain

South San Francisco city W Calif. *pop* 63,632

South Saskatchewan — see SASKATCHEWAN

South Seas the areas of the Atlantic, Indian, & Pacific oceans in the southern hemisphere — used esp. of the S. Pacific

South Shetland Islands British islands S. Atlantic SE of Cape Horn off tip of Antarctic Peninsula

South Shields \'shēldz\ seaport N England in Tyne and Wear at mouth of the Tyne E of Newcastle *pop* 87,203

South Sudan country E Africa ✱ Juba *area* 239,284 *sq mi* (619,746 *sq km*), *pop* 8,260,500

South Thompson — see THOMPSON

South Tirol — see ALTO ADIGE

South Vietnam — see VIETNAM

South·wark \'sə-thərk, 'saùth-wərk\ borough of S London, England *pop* 196,500

South–West Africa — see NAMIBIA

South Windsor town N Conn. NE of Hartford *pop* 25,709

South Yemen — see YEMEN — **South Ye·me·ni** \'ye-mə-nē\ *adj*

South Yorkshire metropolitan county N England ✱ Barnsley *area* 624 *sq mi* (1616 *sq km*), *pop* 1,248,500

So·vetsk \sə-'vyetsk\ *or G* Til·sit \'til-sət, -zit\ city W Russia in Europe on the Neman *pop* 42,300

So·vet·ska·ya Ga·van' \sə-'vyet-skə-yə-'gä-vən, -'gä-və-nyə\ city & port SE Russia in Asia on Tatar Strait *pop* 30,600

Soviet Central Asia the portion of *cen* Asia formerly belonging to the U.S.S.R. & comprising the Kyrgyzstan, Tajikistan, Turkmenistan, & Uzbekistan republics & sometimes Kazakhstan

Soviet Russia 1 — see RUSSIA 2 the U.S.S.R.

Soviet Union — see UNION OF SOVIET SOCIALIST REPUBLICS

So·we·to \sō-'wä-tō, -'we-, -tü\ township NE Republic of South Africa in Gauteng adjoining SW Johannesburg — **So·we·tan** \-t²n\ n
Spa \'spä\ town E Belgium SE of Liège pop 10,394
Spain \'spän\ or Sp **Es·pa·ña** \ä-'spä-nyä\ country SW Europe in the Iberian Peninsula; a kingdom ✻ Madrid area 194,881 sq mi (504,742 sq km), pop 39,141,000
Span·dau \'shpän-,daů, 'spän-\ a W section of Berlin, Germany
Spanish America 1 the Spanish-speaking countries of the Americas 2 the parts of America settled & formerly governed by the Spanish
Spanish Guinea former Spanish colony W Africa bordering on Gulf of Guinea including Río Muni (Mbini), Fernando Póo (Bioko) & other islands — see EQUATORIAL GUINEA
Spanish Main \'män\ 1 the mainland of Spanish America esp. along N coast of S. America 2 the Caribbean Sea & adjacent waters esp. at the time when region was infested with pirates
Spanish Morocco — see MOROCCO 1
Spanish Peaks two mountains (**East Spanish Peak** 12,683 ft or 3866 m & **West Spanish Peak** 13,623 ft or 4152 m) S Colo.
Spanish Sahara former Spanish possessions Río de Oro & Saguia el Hamra — see WESTERN SAHARA
Spanish Town town SE Jamaica; former ✻ of Jamaica pop 131,056
Sparks \'spärks\ city W Nev. E of Reno pop 90,264
Spar·ta \'spär-tə\ or **Lac·e·dae·mon** \,la-sə-'dē-mən\ ancient city S Greece in Peloponnese ✻ of Laconia
Spar·tan·burg \'spär-t²n-,bərg\ city NW S.C. pop 37,013
Spen·cer Gulf \'spen(t)-sər\ inlet of Indian Ocean SE S. Australia
Spey \'spā\ river 110 mi (177 km) NE Scotland flowing into Moray Firth
Spey·er \'shpī(-ə)r, 'spī(-ə)r\ or **Spires** \'spī(-ə)rz\ city SW Germany on W bank of the Rhine SW of Heidelberg pop 47,456
Spezia, La — see LA SPEZIA
Spits·ber·gen \'spits-,bər-gən\ group of islands in Arctic Ocean N of Norway; belongs to Norway area 23,641 sq mi (61,230 sq km) — see SVALBARD
Split \'split\ city & port S Croatia on Dalmatian coast pop 200,459
Spo·kane \spō-'kan\ 1 river 120 mi (193 km) N Idaho & E Wash. flowing from Coeur d'Alene Lake W into Columbia River 2 city E Wash. at **Spokane Falls** in Spokane River pop 208,916
Spo·le·to \spō-'lä-(,)tō, -'lē-\ commune cen Italy SE of Perugia pop 37,802
Spor·a·des \'spȯr-ə-,dēz, 'spär-\ two island groups Greece in the Aegean: the **Northern Sporades** (chief island Skyros, N of Euboea & E of Thessaly) & the **Southern Sporades** (chiefly Samos, Ikaria, & the Dodecanese, off SW Turkey)
Sprat·ly Islands \'sprat-lē\ islands cen S. China Sea SE of Cam Ranh Bay; claimed by several countries
Spree \'shprā, 'sprā\ river 247 mi (397 km) E Germany flowing N into the Havel
Spree·wald \-,vält\ marshy district E Germany in Spree River valley
Spring·dale \'sprin̄-,dāl\ city NW Ark. pop 69,797
Spring·field \'sprin̄-,fēld\ 1 city ✻ of Ill. on the Sangamon pop 116,250 2 city SW Mass. on Connecticut River pop 153,060 3 city SW Mo. pop 159,498 4 city W cen Ohio NE of Dayton pop 60,608 5 city W Oreg. on the Willamette E of Eugene pop 59,403
Spring Mountains range SE Nevada W of Las Vegas
Springs \'sprin̄z\ city NE Republic of South Africa in Gauteng pop 142,812
Spring Valley village SE N.Y. N of New York City pop 31,347
Spuy·ten Duy·vil Creek \,spī-t²n-'dī-vəl\ channel New York City N of Manhattan Is. connecting Hudson & Harlem rivers
Sri Ja·ya·war·de·ne·pu·ra Kot·te \,srē-jä-yä-wär-,dä-nä-'pü-rə-'kȯ-tä\ legislative ✻ of Sri Lanka, a suburb of Colombo
Sri Lan·ka \(,)srē-'län̄-kə, (,)shrē-, -'lan̄-\ or formerly **Cey·lon** \si-'län, sā-\ country coextensive with island of Ceylon; an independent republic in the Commonwealth of Nations ✻ Colombo area 25,332 sq mi (65,863 sq km), pop 17,829,500 — **Sri Lan·kan** \-'län-kən, -'lan̄-\ adj or n
Sri·na·gar \srē-'nə-gər\ city India, summer ✻ of Jammu and Kashmir, in W Kashmir on the Jhelum NNE of Lahore pop 894,940
Srp·ska, Re·pu·bli·ka \'sərp-skä, re-'pü-blē-kä\ autonomous region of Bosnia and Herzegovina in N, E, & SE area 9686 sq mi (25,087 sq km), pop 1,392,000
Ssu·p'ing — see SIPING
Staf·fa \'sta-fə\ islet W Scotland in the Inner Hebrides W of Mull — see FINGAL'S CAVE
Staf·ford \'sta-fərd\ town W cen England ✻ of Staffordshire pop 117,000
Staf·ford·shire \'sta-fərd-,shir, -shər\ or **Stafford** county W cen England ✻ Stafford area 1086 sq mi (2813 sq km), pop 1,020,300
Staked Plain — see LLANO ESTACADO
Sta·kha·nov \stə-'kä-nəf, -'kä-\ or formerly **Ka·di·yev·ka** \kə-'dē-yəf-kə\ city E Ukraine pop 113,000
Stalin 1 — see BRASOV 2 — see DONETSK 3 — see VARNA
Stalinabad — see DUSHANBE
Stalingrad — see VOLGOGRAD
Stalino — see DONETSK
Stalinsk — see NOVOKUZNETSK
Stam·ford \'stam-fərd\ city SW Conn. pop 122,643
Stanislav — see IVANO-FRANKIVS'K
Stan·ley \'stan-lē\ or **Port Stanley** town ✻ of the Falklands
Stanley, Mount or in Democratic Republic of the Congo **Mount Nga·lie·ma** \ən-gäl-'yä-mä\ mountain with two peaks (higher 16,763 ft or 5109 m) E cen Africa; highest of Ruwenzori
Stanley Falls — see BOYOMA FALLS
Stanley Pool — see MALEBO (Pool)
Stanleyville — see KISANGANI
Stan·o·voy \,sta-nə-'vȯi\ mountain range SE Russia in Asia N of the Amur
Stan·ton \'stan-t²n\ city SW Calif. SE of Los Angeles pop 38,186
Sta·ra Za·go·ra \,stär-ə-zə-'gȯr-ə\ city cen Bulgaria pop 164,553
State College borough cen Pa. NE of Altoona pop 42,034
Stat·en Island \'sta-t²n\ 1 island SE N.Y. SW of mouth of Hudson River 2 or formerly **Rich·mond** \'rich-mənd\ borough of New York City including Staten Is. pop 468,730

States·boro \'stāts-,bər-ō\ city E Ga. NW of Savannah pop 28,422
States·ville \'stāts-,vil, -vəl\ city W cen N.C. N of Charlotte pop 24,532
Statia — see SAINT EUSTATIUS
Statue of Liberty National Monument — see LIBERTY ISLAND
Staun·ton \'stan-t²n\ city NW cen Va. pop 23,746
Sta·van·ger \stə-'vän̄-ər, -'van-\ city & port SW Norway pop 107,866
Stav·ro·pol' \sta-'vrō-pəl, -'vrō-, 'stä-vrə-pəl\ 1 territory S Russia in Europe N of the Caucasus area 31,120 sq mi (80,600 sq km), pop 2,536,000 2 city, its ✻ pop 332,000 3 — see TOL'YATTI
Ste·bark \'stem-,bärk\ or G **Tan·nen·berg** \'ta-nən-,bərg, 'tä-nən-,berk\ village NE Poland SW of Olsztyn
Steens Mountain \'stēnz\ mountain mass SE Oreg.; highest point ab 9700 ft (2955 m)
Stel·len·bosch \'ste-lən-,bäs, -,bäsh, Afrik ,ste-ləm-'bȯs\ city SW Republic of South Africa in SW Western Cape province pop 29,955
Step·ney \'step-nē\ former metropolitan borough E London, England, on N bank of Thames River, now part of Tower Hamlets
Ster·ling Heights \'stər-lin̄\ city SE Mich. N of Detroit pop 129,699
Stettin — see SZCZECIN
Ste·vens Point \'stē-vənz\ city cen Wis. pop 26,717
Stew·art \'stü-ərt, 'styü-\ river 331 mi (532 km) Canada in cen Yukon flowing W into Yukon River
Stewart Island island New Zealand S of South Is. area 675 sq mi (1748 sq km)
Sti·kine \sti-'kēn\ river 335 mi (539 km) Canada & Alaska flowing from **Stikine Ranges** (in B.C. & Yukon) into the Pacific
Still·wa·ter \'stil-,wȯ-tər, -,wä-\ city N cen Okla. pop 45,688
Stir·ling \'stər-lin̄\ 1 or **Stir·ling·shire** \-,shir, -shər\ administrative area of cen Scotland area 848 sq mi (2196 sq km) 2 city cen Scotland on the Forth pop 38,638
Stock·holm \'stäk-,hō(l)m\ city & port ✻ of Sweden on Mälaren Lake pop 758,148 — **Stock·holm·er** \-,hō(l)-mər\ n
Stock·port \'stäk-,pȯrt\ town NW England in Greater Manchester S of Manchester pop 276,800
Stock·ton \'stäk-tən\ city cen Calif. on the San Joaquin pop 291,707
Stoke New·ing·ton \,stōk-'nü-in-tən, -'nyü-\ former metropolitan borough N London, England, now part of Hackney
Stoke—on—Trent \'stōk-,än-'trent, -,ȯn-\ city W cen England in Staffordshire pop 244,800
Stone·ha·ven \stōn-'hä-vən, stän-'hiv\ burgh & port E Scotland SSW of Aberdeen pop 7885
Stone·henge \'stōn-,henj, (,)stōn-'\ assemblage of chief megaliths S England in Wiltshire on Salisbury Plain erected by prehistoric peoples
Stone Mountain mountain 1686 ft (514 m) NW cen Ga. E of Atlanta
Stones \'stōnz\ river 60 mi (96 km) cen Tenn. flowing NW into Cumberland River
Stor·mont \'stȯr-mənt\ E suburb of Belfast, Northern Ireland; site of Parliament House
Stor·no·way \'stȯr-nə-,wā\ burgh NW Scotland in Lewis, chief town of Lewis with Harris pop 8660
Stough·ton \'stȯ-t²n\ town E Mass. NW of Brockton pop 26,962
Stour 1 \'stůr\ river 47 mi (76 km) SE England flowing E bet. Essex & Suffolk into the North Sea 2 \'staůr, 'stůr\ river 55 mi (88 km) S England in Dorset & Hampshire flowing SE into Avon River 3 or **Great Stour** \'stůr also 'staů(-ə)r\ river 40 mi (64 km) SE England in Kent flowing NE into the North Sea 4 \'staů(-ə)r, 'stůr\ river 20 mi (32 km) cen England in Oxfordshire & Warwickshire flowing NW into Avon River 5 (same as 4) river 20 mi (32 km) W cen England flowing S into Severn River
Stour·bridge \'staů(-ə)r-,brij, 'stȯr-\ town W cen England in W. Midlands W of Birmingham pop 54,661
Stow \'stō\ city NE Ohio NE of Akron pop 34,837
Stra·bane \strə-'ban\ district W Northern Ireland, established 1974 area 336 sq mi (874 sq km), pop 35,668
Straits Settlements former country SE Asia on Strait of Malacca comprising Singapore Is., Penang, & Melaka area 1242 sq mi (3229 sq km); now divided bet. Singapore (republic) & Malaysia (federation)
Stral·sund \'shtrál-,zúnt, 'strál-, -,súnt\ city & port NE Germany on the Baltic opposite Rügen Is. pop 71,618
Stras·bourg \'sträs-,bůrg, 'sträz-, -,bərg\ or G **Strass·burg** \'shträs-,bůrk\ city NE France on Ill River pop 263,941
Strat·ford \'strat-fərd\ 1 town SW Conn. pop 51,384 2 city Canada in SE Ont. W of Kitchener pop 30,886
Stratford—upon—Avon \-'ā-vən, -'a-\ town cen England in Warwickshire SSE of Birmingham pop 20,858
Strath·clyde \strath-'klīd\ Celtic kingdom of 6th to 11th centuries S Scotland & NW England ✻ Dumbarton; its S part called **Cum·bria** \'kəm-brē-ə\
Strath·more \strath-'mȯr\ great valley of E cen Scotland S of the Grampians
Stream·wood \'strēm-,wůd\ village NE Ill. E of Elgin pop 39,858
Stre·sa \'strā-zə\ town NW Italy on Lake Maggiore
Stret·ford \'stret-fərd\ town NW England in Greater Manchester SW of Manchester pop 47,600
Stri·món, Gulf of \strē-'mȯn\ or **Stri·mon·i·kós Kól·pos** \strē-,mȯ-nē-'kȯs-'kȯl-pȯs\ or **Stry·mon·ic Gulf** \strī-'mä-nik\ inlet of the Aegean NE Greece NE of Chalcidice Peninsula
Strom·bo·li \'sträm-bō-(,)lē\ or anc **Stron·gy·le** \'strän-jə-,lē\ 1 island Italy in Lipari Islands 2 volcano 3038 ft (926 m) on the island
Strom·lo, Mount \'sträm-(,)lō\ hill 2500 ft (758 m) SE Australia in Australian Capital Territory W of Canberra
Strongs·ville \'strȯnz-,vil\ city NE Ohio SW of Cleveland pop 44,750
Stry·mon \'strī-,män\ or Bulg **Stru·ma** \'strü-mə\ river W Bulgaria & NE Greece flowing SE into Gulf of Strimón
Stutt·gart \'shtút-,gärt, 'stút-, 'stət-\ city SW Germany ✻ of Baden-Württemberg on the Neckar pop 591,946
Styr \'stir\ river 271 mi (436 km) NW Ukraine flowing N into the Pripet in the Pripet Marshes
Styr·ia \'stir-ē-ə\ or Ger **Stei·er·mark** \'shtī(-ə)r-,märk, 'stī(-ə)r-\ region cen & SE Austria; chief city Graz — **Styr·i·an** \'stir-ē-ən\ adj or n
Sua·kin \'swä-kən\ town & port NE Sudan on Red Sea
Su·bic \'sü-bik\ town Philippines in W Luzon at head of **Subic Bay** (inlet of S. China Sea NW of Bataan Peninsula) pop 30,340
Su·bo·ti·ca \'sü-bȯ-,tēt-sä\ city N Serbia in N Vojvodina pop 150,666

Süchow 1 — see XUZHOU 2 — see YIBIN
Su·cre \ˈsü-(ˌ)krā\ city, constitutional ✽ of Bolivia, SE of La Paz *pop* 193,876
Su·dan \sü-ˈdan, -ˈdän\ 1 region N Africa bet. the Atlantic & the upper Nile S of the Sahara including basins of Lake Chad & Niger River & the upper Nile 2 former country NE Africa; until 1956 a territory (**Anglo–Egyptian Sudan**) under joint Brit. & Egyptian rule; later a republic ✽ Khartoum; split 2011 into Sudan (sense 3) and South Sudan 3 country NE Africa N of South Sudan ✽ Khartoum *area* 728,216 *sq mi* (1,886,079 *sq km*), *pop* 31,118,500 — **Su·da·nese** \ˌsü-də-ˈnēz, -ˈnēs\ *adj or n*
Sudanese Republic — see MALI 2
Sud·bury \ˈsəd-ˌber-ē, -b(ə-)rē\ city Canada in SE Ont. N of Georgian Bay *greater Sudbury pop* 160,274
Sudd \ˈsəd\ swamp region S. Sudan drained by White Nile River
Su·de·ten·land \sü-ˈdā-tᵊn-ˌland, -ˌlänt\ region N Czech Republic in Sudety Mountains
Su·de·ty *Czech* ˈsu̇-de-tē, *Polish* su̇-ˈde-tē\ *or* **Su·de·ten** \sü-ˈdā-tᵊn\ mountains *cen* Europe W of the Carpathians bet. Czech Republic & Poland — **Sudeten** *adj or n*
Su·dir·man Range \sü-ˈdir-mən\ *or formerly* **Nas·sau Range** \ˈna-ˌsȯ\ mountain range *cen* West Papua, Indonesia — see PUNCAK JAYA
Su·ez \sü-ˈez, ˈsü-ˌez, *chiefly Brit* ˈsü-iz\ city & port NE Egypt at S end of Suez Canal on **Gulf of Suez** (arm of Red Sea) *pop* 506,000
Suez, Isthmus of isthmus NE Egypt bet. Mediterranean & Red seas connecting Africa & Asia
Suez Canal canal over 100 *mi* (161 *km*) long NE Egypt traversing Isthmus of Suez
Suf·folk \ˈsə-fək, *US also* -ˌfȯk\ 1 city SE Va. *pop* 84,585 2 county E England bordering on North Sea ✽ Ipswich *area* 1520 *mi* (3937 *km*), *pop* 629,900; formerly divided into administrative counties of **East Suffolk** (✽ Ipswich) & **West Suffolk** (✽ Bury St. Edmunds)
Suffolk Broads — see BROADS
Sugar Land city SE Tex. SW of Houston *pop* 78,817
Sugarloaf Mountain — see PÃO DE AÇÚCAR
Suisse — see SWITZERLAND
Sui·sun Bay \sə-ˈsün\ the E extension of San Pablo Bay *cen* Calif.
Suisun City city *cen* Calif. SW of Sacramento *pop* 28,111
Su·i·ta \ˈsü-ē-ˌtä\ city Japan on Honshu *pop* 347,929
Sukarnapura — see JAYAPURA
Su·khu·mi \ˈsu̇-kə-mē, su̇-ˈku̇-mē\ city & port NW Georgia ✽ of Abkhazia on Black Sea *pop* 39,000
Su·la·we·si \ˌsü-lä-ˈwā-sē\ *or* **Ce·le·bes** \ˈse-lə-ˌbēz, sə-ˈlē-bēz\ island Indonesia E of Borneo ✽ Ujung Pandang *area* 72,775 *sq mi* (188,487 *sq km*), *pop* 12,520,711
Sul·grave \ˈsəl-ˌgrāv\ village England in S Northamptonshire
Su·lu Archipelago \ˈsü-(ˌ)lü\ archipelago SW Philippines SW of Mindanao
Sulu Sea sea W Philippines N of Celebes Sea
Su·ma·tra \su̇-ˈmä-trə\ island W Indonesia S of Malay Peninsula *area* 182,542 *sq mi* (472,784 *sq km*) — **Su·ma·tran** \-trən\ *adj or n*
Sum·ba \ˈsüm-bə\ island Indonesia in the Lesser Sundas *area* 4306 *sq mi* (11,196 *sq km*), *pop* 251,126
Sum·ba·wa \süm-ˈbä-wə\ island Indonesia in the Lesser Sundas *area* 5693 *sq mi* (14,745 *sq km*), *pop* 195,554
Su·mer \ˈsü-mər\ the S division of ancient Babylonia — see AKKAD, SHINAR
Sum·mer·ville \ˈsə-mər-ˌvil\ town SE S.C. *pop* 43,392
Sum·qay·it \su̇m-ˈkī-it\ *or* **Sum·ga·it** \-ˈgī-\ city & port Azerbaijan on the Caspian NW of Baku *pop* 236,200
Sum·ter \ˈsəm-tər\ city E *cen* S.C. E of Columbia *pop* 40,524
Sun·belt \ˈsən-ˌbelt\ region S & SW U.S.
Sun·da Islands \ˈsün-də, ˈsən-\ islands Malay Archipelago comprising the **Greater Sunda Islands** (Sumatra, Java, Borneo, Sulawesi, & adjacent islands) & the **Lesser Sunda Islands** (from Bali E to Timor); with exception of N Borneo & East Timor, belongs to Indonesia
Sunda Strait strait bet. Java & Sumatra
Sun·der·land \ˈsən-dər-lənd\ seaport N England in Tyne and Wear on North Sea *pop* 286,800
Sunds·vall \ˈsən(t)s-ˌväl, ˈsu̇ndz-\ city & port E Sweden on Gulf of Bothnia *pop* 93,252
Sungari — see SONGHUA
Sun·ny·vale \ˈsə-nē-ˌvāl\ city W Calif. WNW of San Jose *pop* 140,081
Sun·rise \ˈsən-ˌrīz\ city SE Fla. W of Fort Lauderdale *pop* 84,439
Sunset Crater volcanic crater N *cen* Ariz. in **Sunset Crater Volcano National Monument**
Suomi — see FINLAND
Su·pe·ri·or \su̇-ˈpir-ē-ər\ city & port NW Wis. on Lake Superior *pop* 27,244
Superior, Lake lake U.S. & Canada; largest, northernmost, & westernmost of the Great Lakes *area* 31,800 *sq mi* (82,362 *sq km*)
Superstition Mountains range S *cen* Ariz. E of Phoenix
Sur — see TYRE
Sur, Point \ˈsər\ promontory Calif. on the Pacific SSW of Monterey — see BIG SUR
Su·ra·ba·ya \ˌsu̇r-ə-ˈbī-ə\ city & port Indonesia in NE Java on **Surabaya Strait** (bet. Java & W end of Madura) *pop* 2,483,871
Su·ra·kar·ta \ˌsu̇r-ə-ˈkär-tə\ city Indonesia in *cen* Java *pop* 504,176
Su·rat \ˈsu̇r-ət, sə-ˈrat\ city W India in SE Gujarat *pop* 2,433,787
Sur·bi·ton \ˈsər-bə-tən\ former municipal borough S England in Surrey WSW of London, now part of Kingston upon Thames
Su·ri·ba·chi, Mount \ˌsu̇r-ē-ˈbä-chē\ volcano 548 *ft* (167 *m*) in the Volcano Islands at S end of Iwo Jima
Su·ri·na·me \ˌsu̇r-ə-ˈnä-mə\ 1 *or formerly* **Dutch Guiana** *or* **Netherlands Guiana** country N S. America bet. Guyana & French Guiana; a republic, until 1975 territory of the Netherlands ✽ Paramaribo *area* 63,251 *sq mi* (163,820 *sq km*), *pop* 492,829 2 river N Suriname flowing N into the Atlantic — **Su·ri·nam·er** \ˈsu̇r-ə-ˌnä-mər, ˌsu̇r-ə-ˈnä-\ *n* — **Su·ri·nam·ese** \ˌsu̇r-ə-nə-ˈmēz, -ˈmēs\ *adj or n*
Sur·ma \ˈsu̇r-mə\ river 560 *mi* (901 *km*) NE India (subcontinent) in Manipur & Bangladesh — see MEGHNA
Sur·prise \sər-ˈprīz\ city S *cen* Ariz. W of Phoenix *pop* 117,517
Surrentum — see SORRENTO
Sur·rey \ˈsər-ē, ˈsə-rē\ 1 county SE England S of London ✽ Kingston upon Thames *area* 662 *sq mi* (1714 *sq km*), *pop* 998,000 2 city Canada in SW B.C. SE of Vancouver *pop* 468,251
Surts·ey \ˈsərt-ˌsā, ˈsu̇rt-\ island Iceland off S coast *area* 1 *sq mi* (2.6 *sq km*); formed 1963 by volcanic eruption
Su·ru·ga Bay \ˈsu̇r-ə-gə, sü-ˈrü-gä\ inlet of the Pacific Japan on coast of SE Honshu W of Sagami Sea
Su·sa \ˈsü-zə\ *or bib* **Shu·shan** \ˈshü-shən, -ˌshan\ ancient city ✽ of Elam; ruins in SW Iran
Susiana — see ELAM
Sus·que·han·na \ˌsəs-kwə-ˈha-nə\ river 444 *mi* (714 *km*) E U.S. flowing from *cen* N.Y. S through Pa. & into Chesapeake Bay in N Md.
Sus·sex \ˈsə-siks, *US also* -ˌseks\ former county SE England bordering on English Channel; one of kingdoms in Anglo-Saxon heptarchy — see EAST SUSSEX, WEST SUSSEX
Suth·er·land \ˈsə-t͟hər-lənd\ *or* **Suth·er·land·shire** \-lən(d)-ˌshir, -shər\ former county N Scotland ✽ Dornoch
Sutherland Falls waterfall 1904 *ft* (580 *m*) New Zealand in SW South Is.
Sut·lej \ˈsət-ˌlej\ river *ab* 900 *mi* (1448 *km*) N India (subcontinent) flowing from Tibet W & SW through the Punjab to join the Chenab
Sut·ton \ˈsə-tᵊn\ borough of S Greater London, England *pop* 164,300
Sutton Cold·field \ˈkōl(d)-ˌfēld\ town *cen* England in W. Midlands NE of Birmingham *pop* 86,494
Sutton–in–Ash·field \-ˈash-ˌfēld\ town N *cen* England in Nottinghamshire N of Nottingham *pop* 41,270
Su·va \ˈsü-və\ city & port ✽ of Fiji on Viti Levu Is. *pop* 86,178
Su·wał·ki \su̇-ˈvau̇-kē\ 1 district NE Poland 2 city in the district *pop* 69,000
Su·wan·nee \sə-ˈwä-nē, ˈswä-\ river 250 *mi* (400 *km*) SE Ga. & N Fla. flowing SW into Gulf of Mexico
Su·won \ˈsü-ˌwän\ city NW S. Korea S of Seoul *pop* 430,752
Su·zhou \ˈsü-ˈjō\ *or* **Soo·chow** \-ˈjō, -ˈchau̇\ *or formerly* **Wu·hsien** \ˈwü-ˈshyen\ city E China in SE Jiangsu W of Shanghai *pop* 706,459
Sval·bard \ˈsväl-ˌbär\ island group in the Arctic Ocean including Spitsbergen, Bear Is., & other small islands *area* 23,958 *sq mi* (62,052 *sq km*); under Norwegian administration
Sverdlovsk — see YEKATERINBURG
Sver·drup Islands \ˈsver-drəp\ islands N Canada W of Ellesmere Is. including Axel Heiberg, Ellef Ringnes, & Amund Ringnes islands
Swa·bia \ˈswā-bē-ə\ *or G* **Schwa·ben** \ˈshvä-bən\ region and medieval county SW Germany chiefly in area comprising modern Baden-Württemberg & W Bavaria — **Swa·bi·an** \ˈswā-bē-ən\ *adj or n*
Swan \ˈswän\ *or in its upper course* **Av·on** \ˈa-vən\ river *ab* 240 *mi* (386 *km*) SW Western Australia flowing W into Indian Ocean
Swan Islands two islands in the Caribbean NE of Honduras
Swan·sea \ˈswän-zē *also* -ˌsē\ 1 administrative area of S Wales *area* 146 *sq mi* (378 *sq km*) 2 city & port S Wales *pop* 182,100
Swat \ˈswät\ river 400 *mi* (644 *km*) Pakistan flowing into Kabul River
Swatow — see SHANTOU
Swa·zi·land \ˈswä-zē-ˌland\ country SE Africa bet. Republic of South Africa & Mozambique; a former Brit. protectorate; an independent kingdom since 1968 administrative ✽ Mbabane, legislative ✽ Lobamba *area* 6705 *sq mi* (17,433 *sq km*), *pop* 1,000,000
Swe·den \ˈswē-dᵊn\ *or Sw* **Sve·ri·ge** \ˈsve-rē-yə\ country N Europe on Scandinavian peninsula W of Baltic Sea; a kingdom ✽ Stockholm *area* 173,665 *sq mi* (449,792 *sq km*), *pop* 9,400,000
Swin·don \ˈswin-dən\ town S England in NE Wiltshire *pop* 91,136
Świ·no·ujś·cie \ˌshfē-nō-ˈü-ēsh-ˌche\ city & port NW Poland on N coast of Uznam (Usedom) Is. NNW of Szczecin *pop* 42,886
Swin·ton and Pen·dle·bury \ˈswin-tᵊn-ənd-ˈpen-dᵊl-ˌber-ē, -b(ə-)rē\ town NW England in Greater Manchester *pop* 39,621
Swit·zer·land \ˈswit-sər-lənd\ *or F* **Suisse** \ˈswʸēs\ *or G* **Schweiz** \ˈshvīts\ *or It* **Sviz·ze·ra** \ˈzvēt-tsā-rä\ *or L* **Hel·ve·tia** \hel-ˈvē-sh(ē-)ə\ country W Europe in the Alps; a federal republic ✽ Bern *area* 15,940 *sq mi* (41,285 *sq km*), *pop* 7,800,000
Syb·a·ris \ˈsi-bə-rəs\ ancient Greek city S Italy on Gulf of Tarentum; destroyed 510 B.C.
Syd·ney \ˈsid-nē\ city & port SE Australia on Port Jackson ✽ of New South Wales *metropolitan area pop* 3,097,956 — **Syd·ney·ite** \-ˌīt\ *n* — **Syd·ney·sid·er** \-ˌsī-dər\ *n*
Syene — see ASWĀN
Syk·tyv·kar \ˌsik-tif-ˈkär\ town NE Russia in Europe ✽ of Komi Republic *pop* 226,000
Sylt \ˈzilt, ˈsilt\ island NW Germany, chief of the N. Frisian Islands *area* 36 *sq mi* (94 *sq km*)
Syr·a·cuse \ˈsir-ə-ˌkyüs, -ˌkyüz\ 1 city *cen* N.Y. near Oneida Lake *pop* 145,170 2 *or It* **Si·ra·cu·sa** \ˌsē-rä-ˈkü-zä\ *or anc* **Syr·a·cu·sae** \ˌsir-ə-ˈkyü-(ˌ)sē, -(ˌ)zē\ city & port Italy in SE Sicily *pop* 125,673 — **Syr·a·cu·san** \ˌsir-ə-ˈkyü-sᵊn, -zᵊn\ *adj or n*
Syr Dar'·ya \sir-ˈdär-yə\ *or anc* **Jax·ar·tes** \jak-ˈsär-(ˌ)tēz\ river *ab* 1370 *mi* (2204 *km*) Tajikistan & S Kazakhstan flowing from Tian Shan W & NW into Aral Sea
Syr·ia \ˈsir-ē-ə\ 1 ancient region SW Asia bordering on the Mediterranean & covering modern Syria, Lebanon, Israel, & Jordan 2 former French mandate (1920–44) comprising the **Le·vant States** \lə-ˈvant\ (Syria, Lebanon, Latakia, & Jebel ed Druz), administrative ✽ Beirut, legislative ✽ Damascus 3 country SW Asia bordering on the Mediterranean; a republic 1944–58 & since 1961; a province of United Arab Republic 1958–61 ✽ Damascus *area* 71,498 *sq mi* (185,180 *sq km*), *pop* 21,000,000 — **Syr·i·an** \ˈsir-ē-ən\ *adj or n*
Syrian Desert desert W Asia bet. Mediterranean coast & the Euphrates covering N Saudi Arabia, NE Jordan, SE Syria, & W Iraq
Syros *or Gk* **Síros** \ˈsē-ˌrȯs\ 1 island Greece in the Cyclades S of Andros 2 — see ERMOÚPOLIS
Syrtis Major — see SIDRA (Gulf of)
Syrtis Minor — see GABÈS (Gulf of)

\ə\ **abut** \ᵊ\ **kitten, F table** \ər\ **further** \a\ **ash** \ā\ **ace** \ä\ **mop, mar** \au̇\ **out** \ch\ **chin** \e\ **bet** \ē\ **easy** \g\ **go** \i\ **hit** \ī\ **ice** \j\ **job** \ŋ\ **sing** \ō\ **go** \ȯ\ **law** \ȯi\ **boy** \th\ **thin** \t͟h\ **the** \ü\ **loot** \u̇\ **foot** \y\ **yet** \zh\ **vision, beige** \k̲, ⁿ, œ, ue, ʸ\ *see* **Guide to Pronunciation**

Szamos — see SOMES
Szcze·cin \'shche-ˌchēn\ *or G* **Stet·tin** \shte-'tēn\ city & port NW Poland *pop* 412,058
Szechuan, Szechwan — see SICHUAN
Sze·ged \'se-ˌged\ city S Hungary *pop* 184,000
Sze·kes·fe·her·var \'sā-ˌkesh-ˌfe-hār-ˌvär\ city W *cen* Hungary *pop* 111,200
Szepingkai — see SIPING
Szol·nok \'sōl-ˌnōk\ city E *cen* Hungary *pop* 82,900
Szom·bat·hely \'sōm-ˌbȯt-ˌhā\ city W Hungary *pop* 87,700
Ta·bas·co \tə-'bas-(ˌ)kō\ state SE Mexico on the Caribbean SW of Yucatán Peninsula ✻ Villahermosa *area* 9522 *sq mi* (24,662 *sq km*), *pop* 1,501,744
Ta·blas \'tä-bläs\ island *cen* Philippines in Romblon group
Table Bay harbor of Cape Town, Republic of South Africa
Table Mountain mountain 3563 *ft* (1086 *m*) Republic of South Africa S of Cape Town
Ta·bor, Mount \'tā-bər, -ˌbȯr\ mountain 1929 *ft* (588 *m*) N Israel E of Nazareth
Ta·bo·ra \tä-'bȯr-ä\ city W *cen* Tanzania *pop* 67,392
Ta·briz \tə-'brēz\ city NW Iran in Azerbaijan *pop* 971,482
Ta·bu·a·er·an \tə-ˌbü-ə-'er-ən\ *or formerly* **Fan·ning** \'fa-niŋ\ island W Pacific in the Line Islands *area* 15 *sq mi* (39 *sq km*), *pop* 376
Tac·na \'täk-nä\ city S Peru near Chilean border *pop* 150,200; in region (**Tacna–Ari·ca** \-ä-'rē-kä\) occupied 1884–1930 by Chile & now divided bet. Chile & Peru
Ta·co·ma \tə-'kō-mə\ city & port W Wash. on Puget Sound S of Seattle *pop* 198,397
Tacoma, Mount — see RAINIER (Mount)
Ta·con·ic Range \tə-'kä-nik\ mountains along N part of Conn.-N.Y. boundary & entire Mass.-N.Y. boundary & in SW Vt.; highest peak Mt. Equinox (in Vt.) 3816 *ft* (1163 *m*)
Ta·djou·ra, Gulf of \tə-'jür-ə\ inlet of Gulf of Aden in E Djibouti
Tadmor — see PALMYRA
Tae·dong \ta-'dúŋ, tī-\ river *cen* N. Korea flowing SW into Korea Bay
Tae·gu \'tā-gü, 'dā-\ *or* **Dae·gu** \'dā-\ city SE S. Korea NNW of Pusan *pop* 2,473,990
Tae·jon \'tā-'jən, 'dā-\ *or* **Dae·jeon** \'dā-\ city *cen* S. Korea NW of Taegu *pop* 1,365,961
Ta·gan·rog \'ta-gən-ˌräg\ city S Russia in Europe on **Gulf of Taganrog** (NE arm of Sea of Azov) *pop* 293,000
Ta·gus \'tā-gəs\ *or Sp* **Ta·jo** \'tä-(ˌ)hō\ *or Pg* **Te·jo** \'tā-(ˌ)zhü\ river 626 *mi* (1007 *km*) Spain & Portugal flowing W into the Atlantic
Ta·hi·ti \tə-'hē-tē\ island S. Pacific in Windward group of the Society Islands; chief town Papeete *area* 402 *sq mi* (1045 *sq km*), *pop* 131,309
Ta·hoe, Lake \'tä-ˌhō\ lake 22 *mi* (35 *km*) long on Calif.-Nev. boundary
Tai·bei \'tī-'bā\ *or* **Tai·pei** \'tī-'pā, -'bā\ city ✻ of (Nationalist) Republic of China, on Taiwan *pop* 2,632,600
Tai Hu \'tī-'hü\ lake *ab* 45 *mi* (72 *km*) long E China in Jiangsu
T'ai–nan \'tī-'nän\ city SW Taiwan *pop* 702,237
Taí·na·ron \'tā-nä-ˌrȯn\ *or* **Mat·a·pan** \ˌma-tə-'pan\ cape S Greece at S tip of Peloponnese bet. Gulfs of Laconia & Messenia
Tai·o·hae \ˌtī-ō-'hē\ town Nuku Hiva Is. ✻ of the Marquesas
Tai Shan \'tī-'shän\ mountain 5000 *ft* (1524 *m*) E China in W Shandong
Tai·wan \'tī-'wän\ *or* **For·mo·sa** \fȯr-'mō-sə, fər-, -zə\ island China off SE coast E of Fujian; belonged to Japan 1895–1945; since 1949 seat of (Nationalist) Republic of China (✻ Taibei) *area* 13,807 *sq mi* (35,760 *sq km*), *pop* 22,300,929 — **Tai·wan·ese** \ˌtī-wə-'nēz, -'nēs\ *adj or n*
Taiwan Strait *or* **Formosa Strait** strait bet. Taiwan & Fujian, China connecting E. China & S. China seas
Tai·yu·an \'tī-'ywen, -'ywän\ *or formerly* **Yang·ku** \'yäŋ-'kü\ city N China ✻ of Shanxi *pop* 1,533,884
Tai·zhong \'tī-'júŋ\ *or* **Tai·chung** \'tī-'chúŋ\ city W Taiwan *pop* 1,004,400
Tai·zhou *or* **T'ai–chou** \'tī-'jō\ city E China in *cen* Jiangsu
Ta·jik·i·stan \tä-ˌji-ki-'stan, tə-, -ˌjē-, -'stän; -'ji-ki-ˌ, -'jē-\ country W *cen* Asia bordering on China & Afghanistan; a constituent republic (**Tadzhik Republic** \tä-'jik, tə-, -'jēk\ *or* **Ta·dzhik·i·stan** *same as* TAJIKISTAN\ ) of the U.S.S.R. 1929–91 ✻ Dushanbe *area* 55,251 *sq mi* (143,100 *sq km*), *pop* 6,127,000
Ta·ju·mul·co \ˌtä-hü-'mül-(ˌ)kō\ mountain 13,845 *ft* (4220 *m*) W Guatemala; highest in Central America
Ta·ka·ma·tsu \ˌtä-kä-'mät-(ˌ)sü, tä-'kä-mät-ˌsü\ city & port Japan in NE Shikoku on Inland Sea *pop* 332,865
Ta·ka·tsu·ki \tä-'kät-sü-(ˌ)kē\ city Japan in S Honshu *pop* 357,438
Tak·ka·kaw \'ta-kə-ˌkȯ\ waterfall 1650 *ft* (503 *m*) Canada in SE B.C. in Yoho National Park; highest in Canada
Ta·kli·ma·kan *or* **Ta·kla Ma·kan** \ˌtä-klə-mə-'kän\ desert W China in *cen* Xinjiang Uygur bet. Tian Shan & Kunlun Mountains
Ta·la·ud Islands \'tä-ˌlä-ˌüd\ *or* **Ta·laur Islands** \-ˌlä-ˌúr\ islands Indonesia NE of Sulawesi *area* 494 *sq mi* (1284 *sq km*), *pop* 194,253
Tal·ca \'täl-kä\ city *cen* Chile S of Santiago *pop* 201,797
Tal·ca·hua·no \ˌtäl-kä-'wä-(ˌ)nō, -'hwä-\ city & port S *cen* Chile NW of Concepción *pop* 250,348
Ta–lien — see DALIAN
Tal·la·has·see \ˌta-lə-'ha-sē\ city N Fla., its ✻ *pop* 181,376
Tal·la·hatch·ie \ˌta-lə-'ha-chē\ river 230 *mi* (370 *km*) N Miss. flowing SW
Tal·la·poo·sa \ˌta-lə-'pü-sə\ river 268 *mi* (431 *km*) NW Ga. & E Ala. flowing SW to join the Coosa forming Alabama River
Tal·linn \'ta-lən, 'tä-\ *or formerly* **Re·vel** \'rā-vəl\ city & port ✻ of Estonia *pop* 398,434
Ta·ma·le \tä-'mä-lā\ town N Ghana *pop* 135,952
Tam·al·pais, Mount \ˌta-məl-'pī-əs\ mountain 2572 *ft* (784 *m*) W Calif. NW of San Francisco
Ta·man' \tə-'män\ peninsula S Russia in Europe in Ciscaucasia bet. Sea of Azov & Black Sea
Tam·an·ras·set \ˌta-mən-'ra-sət\ wadi & oasis SE Algeria
Ta·mar \'tā-mər\ **1** river 40 *mi* (64 *km*) Australia in N Tasmania flowing N to Bass Strait **2** river 60 *mi* (96 *km*) SW England flowing SE from NW Devon into English Channel
Tam·a·rac \'ta-mə-ˌrak\ city SE Fla. *pop* 60,427
Tamatave — see TOAMASINA
Ta·mau·li·pas \ˌtä-ˌmaú-'lē-päs, tə-\ state NE Mexico bordering on Gulf of Mexico ✻ Ciudad Victoria *area* 30,822 *sq mi* (79,829 *sq km*), *pop* 2,249,581
Tam·bo·ra \täm-'bȯr-ə\ volcano 9350 *ft* (2850 *m*) Indonesia on Sumbawa Is.
Tam·bov \täm-'bȯf, -'bȯv\ city S *cen* Russia in Europe SE of Moscow *pop* 311,000
Tam·il Na·du \ˌta-məl-'nä-(ˌ)dü, ˌtä-\ *or formerly* **Madras** state SE India bordering on Bay of Bengal ✻ Madras *area* 50,180 *sq mi* (129,966 *sq km*), *pop* 55,858,946
Tam·pa \'tam-pə\ city W Fla. on **Tampa Bay** (inlet of Gulf of Mexico) *pop* 335,709 — **Tam·pan** \-pən\ *adj or n*
Tam·pe·re \'tam-pe-ˌrā, 'täm-\ city SW Finland *pop* 197,774
Tam·pi·co \tam-'pē-(ˌ)kō\ city & port E Mexico in S Tamaulipas on the Pánuco 7 *mi* (11 *km*) from its mouth *pop* 271,636
Ta·na \'tä-nä\ river 440 *mi* (708 *km*) E Africa in Kenya flowing into the Indian Ocean
Ta·na, Lake \'tä-nə\ lake NW Ethiopia; source of the Blue Nile *area* 1418 *sq mi* (3687 *sq km*)
Ta·na·gra \'ta-nə-grə, tə-'na-grə\ village E *cen* Greece E of Thebes; an important town of ancient Boeotia
Tan·a·na \'ta-nə-ˌnȯ\ river 550 *mi* (885 *km*) E & *cen* Alaska flowing NW into Yukon River
Tananarive, Tananarivo — see ANTANANARIVO
Tan·ez·rouft \ˌta-nəz-'rüft\ extremely arid region of W Sahara in SW Algeria & N Mali
Tan·ga \'taŋ-gə\ city & port Tanzania on NE mainland *pop* 187,634
Tan·gan·yi·ka \ˌtan-gə-'nyē-kə, ˌtaŋ-gə-, -'nē-\ former country E Africa bet. Lake Tanganyika & Indian Ocean; administered by Britain 1920–61; became an independent member of the Commonwealth of Nations 1961 ✻ Dar es Salaam; since 1964 united with Zanzibar as Tanzania — see GERMAN EAST AFRICA — **Tan·gan·yi·kan** \-kən\ *adj or n*
Tanganyika, Lake lake E Africa in Great Rift Valley bet. Democratic Republic of the Congo & Tanzania *area* 12,700 *sq mi* (33,020 *sq km*)
Tan·gier \tan-'jir\ **1** city & port N Morocco on Strait of Gibraltar; summer ✻ of Morocco *pop* 187,894 **2** the International Zone of Tangier — see MOROCCO — **Tan·ger·ine** \ˌtan-jə-'rēn\ *adj or n*
Tang·shan \'däŋ-'shän, 'täŋ-\ city NE China in E Hebei *pop* 1,044,194
Ta·nim·bar Islands \tə-'nim-ˌbär, tä-\ islands Indonesia in SE Moluccas ENE of Timor *pop* 50,000
Ta·nis \'tā-nəs\ *or bib* **Zo·an** \'zō-ˌan\ ancient city N Egypt in E Nile Delta near Lake Tanis
Tanis, Lake — see MANZALA (Lake)
Tan·jung·ka·rang \ˌtän-jüŋ-'kä-räŋ\ *or* **Ban·dar Lam·pung** \'bən-dər-'läm-púŋ\ city & port Indonesia in S Sumatra *pop* 636,706
Tan·jung·pri·ok \ˌtän-ˌjüŋ-prē-'ȯk\ port of Jakarta, Indonesia
Tan·na \'tä-nə\ island SW Pacific in Vanuatu *pop* 19,825
Tannenberg — see STĘBARK
Tan·ta \'tän-tə\ city N Egypt in *cen* Nile Delta *pop* 372,000
Tan–tung — see DANDONG
Tan·za·nia \ˌtan-zə-'nē-ə, ˌtän-\ republic E Africa formed 1964 by union of Tanganyika & Zanzibar; legislative ✻ Dodoma, historic ✻ Dar es Salaam *area* 364,900 *sq mi* (945,091 *sq km*), *pop* 34,443,603 — **Tan·za·ni·an** \-'nē-ən\ *adj or n*
Taor·mi·na \taúr-'mē-nä\ *or anc* **Tau·ro·me·ni·um** \ˌtȯr-ə-'mē-nē-əm\ commune Italy in NE Sicily *pop* 10,697
Ta·pa·jos *or* **Ta·pa·joz** \ˌta-pə-'zhȯs, ˌtä-\ river N Brazil flowing NE into the Amazon — see JURUENA
Ta·pi \'tä-pē\ river 436 *mi* (702 *km*) W India S of Satpura Range flowing W into Gulf of Khambhat
Tap·pan Zee \ˌta-pən-'zē\ expansion of Hudson River SE N.Y.
Taprobane — see CEYLON
Ta·qua·ri \ˌta-kwə-'rē, ˌtä-\ river 350 *mi* (565 *km*) S *cen* Brazil rising in S *cen* Mato Grosso & flowing WSW into Paraguay River
Tar \'tär\ river 215 *mi* (346 *km*) NE N.C. — see PAMLICO
Tara \'ta-rə\ village Ireland in County Meath NW of Dublin near **Hill of Tara** (seat of ancient Irish kings)
Tarābulus **1** — see TRIPOLI 1 **2** — see TRIPOLI 2
Taranaki — see EGMONT (Mount)
Ta·ran·to \'tär-än-ˌtō, tə-'ran-(ˌ)tō\ *or anc* **Ta·ren·tum** \tə-'ren-təm\ city & port SE Italy on **Gulf of Taranto** (inlet of Ionian Sea) *pop* 207,199
Ta·ra·wa \tə-'rä-wə, 'ta-rə-ˌwä\ island W Pacific containing ✻ of Kiribati *area* 8 *sq mi* (21 *sq km*), *pop* 41,194
Tarbes \'tärb\ city SW France ESE of Pau *pop* 46,433
Tar·gu–Mu·res *or* **Tir·gu–Mu·res** \'tər-gü-'múr-esh\ city NE *cen* Romania *pop* 149,577
Ta·ri·fa, Cape \tä-'rē-fə, tə-\ cape S Spain; southernmost point of continental Europe, at 36°01′N
Ta·rim \'dä-'rēm, 'tä-\ river 1250 *mi* (2012 *km*) W China in Xinjiang Uygur in the Taklimakan flowing E & SE into a marshy depression
Tar·lac \'tär-ˌläk\ city Philippines in *cen* Luzon *pop* 72,000
Tarn \'tärn\ river 233 *mi* (375 *km*) S France flowing W into the Garonne
Tar·nów \'tär-ˌnüf\ city S Poland E of Kraków *pop* 120,385
Tar·qui·nia \tär-'kwē-nyə, -'kwi-, -nē-ə\ *or formerly* **Cor·ne·to** \kȯr-'nā-(ˌ)tō\ *or anc* **Tar·quin·ii** \tär-'kwi-nē-ˌī\ town *cen* Italy in N Lazio
Tar·ra·go·na \ˌtar-ə-'gō-nə, ˌtär-ä-'gō-nä\ **1** province NE Spain on the Mediterranean *area* 2426 *sq mi* (6283 *sq km*), *pop* 609,673 **2** commune & port, its ✻, SW of Barcelona *pop* 113,129
Tarrasa — see TERRASSA
Tar·shish \'tär-(ˌ)shish\ ancient maritime country referred to in the Bible, located by some in S Spain & identified with Tartessus
Tar·sus \'tär-səs\ city S Turkey near the Cilician Gates ✻ of ancient Cilicia *pop* 187,508
Tar·ta·ry \'tär-tə-rē\ *or* **Ta·ta·ry** \'tä-\ a vast historical region in Asia & E Europe roughly extending from the Sea of Japan to the Dnieper
Tar·tes·sus *or* **Tar·tes·sos** \tär-'te-səs\ ancient kingdom on SW coast of Spanish peninsula — see TARSHISH
Tar·tu \'tär-(ˌ)tü\ *or G* **Dor·pat** \'dȯr-ˌpät\ city E Estonia W of Lake Peipus *pop* 101,140
Tash·kent \tash-'kent, täsh-\ city ✻ of Uzbekistan E of the Syr Dar'ya *pop* 2,073,000
Tas·man, Mount \'taz-mən\ mountain 11,475 *ft* (3498 *m*) New Zealand in South Is. in Southern Alps NE of Mt. Cook

Tas•ma•nia \taz-ˈmā-nē-ə, -nyə\ *or formerly* **Van Die•men's Land** \van-ˈdē-mənz\ island SE Australia S of Victoria; a state ✻ Hobart *area* 26,383 *sq mi* (68,332 *sq km*), *pop* 471,400 — **Tas•ma•ni•an** \taz-ˈmā-nē-ən, -nyən\ *adj or n*
Tasman Sea the S. Pacific bet. SE Australia & W New Zealand
Ta•ta•ban•ya \ˈtò-tò-ˌbä-(ˌ)nyò\ city NW Hungary *pop* 75,300
Ta•tar•stan \ˌta-tər-ˈstan, ˌtä-tər-ˈstän\ autonomous republic E *cen* Russia in Europe ✻ Kazan' *area* 26,255 *sq mi* (68,000 *sq km*), *pop* 3,696,000
Ta•tar Strait \ˈtä-ˌtär, tə-ˈtär\ strait bet. Sakhalin Is. & mainland of Asia
Ta•try \ˈtä-trē\ *or* **Ta•tra** \ˈtä-trə\ mountain group N Slovakia & S Poland in *cen* Carpathian Mountains — see GERLACHOVSKY
Tatung — see DATONG
Tau•ghan•nock Falls \tə-ˈga-nək\ waterfall 215 *ft* (66 *m*) S *cen* N.Y. NW of Ithaca
Taun•ton \ˈtȯn-t^{ə}n, ˈtän-\ city SE Mass. *pop* 55,874
Tau•nus \ˈtau̇-nəs\ mountain range SW *cen* Germany E of the Rhine & N of lower Main River; highest peak Grosser Feldberg 2886 *ft* (880 *m*)
Tauric Chersonese — see CHERSONESE
Tau•rus \ˈtȯr-əs\ *or Turk* **To•ros** \tò-ˈròs\ mountains S Turkey parallel to Mediterranean coast
Tax•co \ˈtäs-(ˌ)kō\ *or* **Taxco de Alar•cón** \t͟hā-ˌä-ˌlär-ˈkòn\ city S Mexico in Guerrero SSW of Mexico City *pop* 86,811
Tay \ˈtā\ river 120 *mi* (193 *km*) E *cen* Scotland flowing into North Sea through **Loch Tay** and **Firth of Tay**
Tay•lor \ˈtā-lər\ city SE Mich. SW of Detroit *pop* 63,131
Tay•lors•ville \ˈtā-lərz-ˌvil\ city N *cen* Utah *pop* 58,652
Tay•myr Peninsula \tī-ˈmir\ peninsula N Russia in Asia bet. the Yenisey & the Khatanga — see CHELYUSKIN (Cape)
Ta Yün Ho — see GRAND CANAL
Tbi•li•si \tə-ˈbē-lə-sē, tə-bə-ˈlē-sē\ *or* **Tif•lis** \ˈti-fləs, tə-ˈflēs\ city ✻ of Republic of Georgia on the Kura *pop* 1,260,000
Tchad — see CHAD
Teche, Bayou \ˈtesh\ stream 175 *mi* (282 *km*) S La. flowing SE into the Atchafalaya
Tees \ˈtēz\ river 70 *mi* (113 *km*) N England flowing E into North Sea
Tees•side \ˈtē(z)-ˌsīd\ urban area N England on the Tees
Te•gu•ci•gal•pa \tə-ˌgü-sə-ˈgal-pə, tā-ˌgü-sē-ˈgäl-pä\ city ✻ of Honduras *pop* 879,000
Te•hach•a•pi Mountains \ti-ˈha-chə-pē\ mountains SE Calif. N of Mojave Desert running E–W bet. S end of Sierra Nevada & the Coast Ranges; highest peak Double Mountain 7988 *ft* (2435 *m*); at E end is **Tehachapi Pass** 3793 *ft* (1156 *m*)
Teh•ran \ˌtā-(ə-)ˈran, te-ˈran, -ˈrän\ city ✻ of Iran at foot of S slope of Elburz Mountains *pop* 7,797,520
Teh•ri \ˈtā-rē\ *or* **Tehri Garh•wal** \(ˌ)gər-ˈwäl\ former state N India in NW Uttar Pradesh on Tibet border; chief town Tehri
Te•huan•te•pec, Isthmus of \tə-ˈwän-tə-ˌpek\ the narrowest section of Mexico, bet. **Gulf of Tehuantepec** (on Pacific side) & Bay of Campeche; 137 *mi* (220 *km*) wide at narrowest point
Tejo — see TAGUS
Tel Aviv \ˌtel-ə-ˈvēv\ city W Israel on the Mediterranean *pop* 353,200 — see JAFFA — **Tel Avi•vi•an** \-ˈvē-vē-ən\ *n*
Tel el Amar•na \ˈtel-ˌel-ə-ˈmär-nə\ locality *cen* Egypt on E bank of the Nile NW of Asyût; site of ruins
Tel•e•mark \ˈte-lə-ˌmärk\ mountain region SW Norway
Telescope Peak mountain 11,049 *ft* (3368 *m*) E Calif., highest in Panamint Mountains
Te•les Pi•res \ˈtā-lēs-ˈpē-rēs\ *or formerly* **São Ma•nuel** \ˌsau̇^{n}-mä-ˈnwel\ river 600 *mi* (966 *km*) E Brazil flowing NW to join the Juruena forming the Tapajos
Te•ma \ˈtā-mä\ city & port Ghana E of Accra *pop* 100,052
Te•mec•u•la \tə-ˈme-kyü-lə\ city S Calif. bet. San Bernardino & San Diego *pop* 100,097
Temeš — see TIMIȘ
Tem•pe \tem-ˈpē, *chiefly by outsiders* ˈtem-pē\ city S *cen* Ariz. SE of Phoenix *pop* 161,719
Tem•pe, Vale of \ˈtem-pē\ *or ModGk* **Tém•bi** \ˈtem-bē\ valley in NE Thessaly bet. Mounts Olympus & Ossa
Tem•ple \ˈtem-pəl\ city NE *cen* Tex. SSW of Waco *pop* 66,102
Temple City city SW Calif. SE of Pasadena *pop* 35,558
Te•mu•co \tā-ˈmü-(ˌ)kō\ city S *cen* Chile *pop* 245,347
Tenedos — see BOZCAADA
Te•ne•ri•fe \ˌte-nə-ˈrē-(ˌ)fā, -ˈrēf, -ˈrif\ *or formerly* **Ten•er•iffe** \ˌte-nə-ˈrif, -ˈrēf\ island Spain, largest of the Canary Islands; chief town Santa Cruz de Tenerife *area* 795 *sq mi* (2059 *sq km*)
Ten•nes•see \ˌte-nə-ˈsē, ˈte-nə-ˌ\ **1** river 652 *mi* (1049 *km*) E U.S. in Tenn., Ala., & Ky. flowing into Ohio River **2** state SE *cen* U.S. ✻ Nashville *area* 42,144 *sq mi* (109,153 *sq km*), *pop* 6,346,105 — **Ten•nes•se•an** *or* **Ten•nes•see•an** \ˌte-nə-ˈsē-ən\ *adj or n*
Tennessee–Tom•big•bee Waterway \-täm-ˈbig-bē\ waterway 234 *mi* (374 *km*) long from Tennessee River on Tenn.-Miss. border to Tombigbee River in W *cen* Ala.
Te•noch•ti•tlán \tā-ˌnòch-tēt-ˈlän\ MEXICO CITY — name used when it was capital of the Aztec Empire
Ten•sas \ˈten-ˌsò\ river 250 *mi* (402 *km*) NE La. uniting with Ouachita River to form Black River
Ten•saw \ˈten-ˌsò\ river 40 *mi* (64 *km*) SW Ala. formed by Tombigbee & Alabama rivers & flowing S into Mobile Bay
Te•o•ti•hua•cán \ˌtā-ō-ˌtē-wä-ˈkän\ city S *cen* Mexico in Mexico state NE of Mexico City; once ✻ of the Toltecs *pop* 2238
Te•pic \tā-ˈpēk\ city W Mexico ✻ of Nayarit *pop* 292,780
Te•quen•da•ma Falls \ˌtā-kän-ˈdä-mä\ waterfall *cen* Colombia S of Bogotá
Te•rai•na \te-ˈrī-nə\ *or formerly* **Washington** island W Pacific in the Line Islands *pop* 1155
Ter•cei•ra \tər-ˈser-ə, -ˈsir-\ island *cen* Azores *area* 153 *sq mi* (396 *sq km*)
Te•reng•ga•nu \te-reŋ-ˈgä-nü\ state E Malaysia on S. China Sea ✻ Kuala Terengganu *area* 5000 *sq mi* (12,950 *sq km*), *pop* 770,931
Te•re•si•na \ˌtā-rā-ˈzē-nə\ city NE Brazil ✻ of Piauí *pop* 715,360
Termonde — see DENDERMONDE
Ter•na•te \ter-ˈnä-(ˌ)tā\ **1** island Indonesia in N Moluccas off W Halmahera *pop* 33,964 **2** city & port, chief city on Ternate *pop* 24,287
Ter•ni \ˈter-nē\ commune *cen* Italy NNE of Rome *pop* 110,020
Ter•ra•ci•na \ˌter-ä-ˈchē-nä\ city & port *cen* Italy in Lazio SE of Pontine Marshes *pop* 39,393
Ter•ra No•va National Park \ˌter-ə-ˈnō-və\ area of varied landscapes E Canada in E Newfoundland (island)
Ter•ras•sa \te-ˈrä-sä\ *or* **Tar•ra•sa** \tä-ˈrä-sä\ commune NE Spain NNW of Barcelona *pop* 173,775
Terre•bonne \ˈter-ə-ˌbän, ter-ˈbòn\ city Canada in Que. N of Montreal *pop* 106,322
Ter•re Haute \ˌter-ə-ˈhōt *also* -ˈhət\ city W Ind. *pop* 60,785
Te•ruel \ˌter-ü-ˈwel\ **1** province E Spain in S Aragon *area* 5715 *sq mi* (14,802 *sq km*), *pop* 135,858 **2** commune, its ✻ *pop* 31,158
Teschen — see CIESZYN
Tessin — see TICINO
Te•thys \ˈtē-thəs\ hypothetical sea believed to have extended into E Pangaea & later to have separated Laurasia to the N & Gondwanaland to the S with the Mediterranean being a remnant of it — **Te•thy•an** \-thē-ən\ *adj*
Te•ton Range \ˈtē-ˌtän, ˈtē-t^{ə}n\ mountain range NW Wyo. — see GRAND TETON
Té•touan \tā-ˈtwä^{n}\ *or Sp* **Te•tuán** \te-ˈtwän\ city & port N Morocco on the Mediterranean *pop* 320,539
Teu•to•burg Forest \ˈtü-tə-ˌbərg, ˈtyü-\ *or G* **Teu•to•bur•ger Wald** \ˈtòi-tə-ˌbu̇r-gər-ˌvält\ range of forested hills W Germany in region bet. Ems & Weser rivers; highest point 1530 *ft* (466 *m*)
Tewkes•bury \ˈtüks-ˌber-ē, ˈtyüks-, ˈtu̇ks-, -b(ə-)rē\ town SW *cen* England in Gloucestershire on Avon & Severn rivers *pop* 9554
Tewks•bury \ˈtüks-ˌber-ē, ˈtyüks-, ˈtu̇ks-, -b(ə-)rē\ town NE Mass. *pop* 28,961
Tex•ar•kana \ˌtek-sər-ˈka-nə, -sär-\ **1** city SW Ark. *pop* 29,919 **2** city NE Tex. adjacent to Texarkana, Ark. *pop* 36,411
Tex•as \ˈtek-səs, -siz\ state S U.S. ✻ Austin *area* 266,807 *sq mi* (691,030 *sq km*), *pop* 25,145,561 — **Tex•an** \-sən\ *adj or n*
Texas City city & port SE Tex. on Galveston Bay *pop* 45,099
Tex•co•co \tes-ˈkō-(ˌ)kō\ city *cen* Mexico in Mexico state E of Mexico City *pop* 18,044
Thai•land \ˈtī-ˌland, -lənd\ *or formerly* **Si•am** \sī-ˈam\ country SE Asia on Gulf of Thailand; a kingdom ✻ Bangkok *area* 198,455 *sq mi* (513,998 *sq km*), *pop* 66,000,000 — **Thai•land•er** \-ˌlan-dər, -lən-\ *n*
Thailand, Gulf of *or formerly* **Gulf of Siam** arm of S. China Sea bet. Indochina & Malay Peninsula
Thames **1** \ˈtemz, ˈthāmz, ˈtāmz\ river 15 *mi* (24 *km*) SE Conn., an estuary flowing S into Long Island Sound **2** \ˈtemz\ river 135 *mi* (217 *km*) Canada in SE Ont. flowing S & SW into Lake St. Clair **3** \ˈtemz\ river *over* 200 *mi* (322 *km*) S England flowing from the Cotswolds in Gloucestershire E into the North Sea — see ISIS
Tha•ne \ˈtä-nə\ town W India in Maharashtra NNE of Bombay *pop* 1,261,517
Than•et, Isle of \ˈtha-nət\ tract of land SE England in NE Kent cut off from mainland by arms of Stour River *area* 42 *sq mi* (109 *sq km*)
Thar Desert \ˈtär\ *or* **Great Indian Desert** desert S Asia in Pakistan & India bet. Aravalli Range & the Indus
Thá•sos \ˈthä-ˌsòs\ island Greece in the N Aegean E of Chalcidice Peninsula *area* 146 *sq mi* (378 *sq km*)
The•ba•id \ˈthi-ˈbā-əd, ˈthē-bā-ˌid\ ancient district surrounding Thebes in Egypt or in Greece
Thebes \ˈthēbz\ **1** *or anc* **The•bae** \ˈthē-(ˌ)bē\ *or* **Di•os•po•lis** \dī-ˈäs-pə-lis\ ancient city S Egypt on the Nile S of modern Qena — see KARNAK, LUXOR **2** ancient city E Greece in Boeotia NNW of Athens — **The•ban** \ˈthē-bən\ *adj or n*
The Colony city N Tex. *pop* 36,328
The Hague — see HAGUE (The)
The•o•dore Roosevelt National Park \ˈthē-ə-ˌdòr, -dər\ badlands W N.Dak. in three areas on the Little Missouri
Thermaïkós Kólpos — see SALONIKA (Gulf of)
Ther•mop•y•lae \(ˌ)thər-ˈmä-pə-(ˌ)lē\ locality E Greece bet. Mt. Oeta & Gulf of Maliakós; once a narrow pass along the coast, now a rocky plain 6 *mi* (9.6 *km*) from the sea
Thes•sa•lo•ní•ki \ˌthe-sä-lō-ˈnē-kē\ *or formerly* **Sa•lo•ni•ka** \sə-ˈlä-ni-kə\ *or anc* **Thes•sa•lo•ni•ca** \ˌthe-sə-ˈlä-ni-kə, -lə-ˈnē-kə\ city & port N Greece in Macedonia *pop* 402,443
Thes•sa•ly \ˈthe-sə-lē\ *or Gk* **Thes•sa•lía** \ˌthe-sä-ˈlē-ä\ region E Greece bet. Pindus Mountains & the Aegean — **Thes•sa•lian** \the-ˈsā-lē-ən, -ˈsāl-yən\ *adj or n*
Thet•ford Mines \ˈthet-fərd\ town Canada in S Que. *pop* 25,709
Thim•phu \tim-ˈpü\ city W *cen* Bhutan, its ✻ *pop* 79,185
Thí•ra \ˈthē-rä\ *or* **San•to•ri•ni** \ˌsan-tə-ˈrē-nē\ *or anc* **The•ra** \ˈthir-ə\ island Greece in S Cyclades 29 *sq mi* (75 *sq km*)
Thi•ru•van•an•tha•pur•am \ˌtir-ü-və-ˌnən-tə-ˈpu̇r-əm\ *or* **Tri•van•drum** \tri-ˈvan-drəm\ city & port S India NW of Cape Comorin ✻ of Kerala *pop* 744,739
Tho•hoy•an•dou \tō-ˌhòi-an-ˈdü\ town NE Republic of South Africa; formerly ✻ of Venda
Thomp•son \ˈtäm(p)-sən\ river 304 *mi* (489 *km*) Canada in S B.C. flowing S (as the **North Thompson**) & thence W & SW into the Fraser; joined by a branch, the **South Thompson**
Thorn•ton \ˈthòrn-t^{ə}n\ city NE *cen* Colo. N of Denver *pop* 118,772
Thousand Islands island group Canada & U.S. in St. Lawrence River in Ont. & N.Y.
Thousand Oaks city SW Calif. W of Los Angeles *pop* 126,683
Thrace \ˈthrās\ region SE Europe in Balkan Peninsula N of the Aegean; as ancient country (**Thra•ce** \ˈthrā-(ˌ)sē\ *or* **Thra•cia** \ˈthrā-sh(ē-)ə\), extended to the Danube; modern remnant divided bet. Greece (**Western Thrace**) & Turkey (**Eastern Thrace**, constituting Turkey in Europe) — **Thra•cian** \ˈthrā-shən\ *adj or n*
Thracian Chersonese — see CHERSONESE
Three Forks city SW Mont. where Missouri River is formed by confluence of Gallatin, Jefferson, & Madison rivers *pop* 1869

\ə\ **abut** \ᵊ\ **kitten**, F **table** \ər\ **further** \a\ **ash** \ā\ **ace** \ä\ **mop**, **mar**
\au̇\ **out** \ch\ **chin** \e\ **bet** \ē\ **easy** \g\ **go** \i\ **hit** \ī\ **ice** \j\ **job**
\ŋ\ **sing** \ō\ **go** \ȯ\ **law** \ȯi\ **boy** \th\ **thin** \t͟h\ **the** \ü\ **loot** \u̇\ **foot**
\y\ **yet** \zh\ **vision, beige** \k, ^{n}, œ, ue, ^{y}\ *see* Guide to Pronunciation

Three Mile Island island in Susquehanna River SE *cen* Pa.
Thu·le \ˈtü-lē\ *or* **Qaa·naaq** \kä-ˈnäk\ settlement NW Greenland
Thun \ˈtün\ commune E *cen* Switzerland *pop* 37,950
Thun, Lake of \ˈtün\ *or* **Thun·er·see** \ˈtü-nər-ˌzā\ lake 10 *mi* (16 *km*) long *cen* Switzerland; an expansion of Aare River
Thunder Bay city Canada in SW Ont. on Lake Superior, formed 1970 by consolidation of Fort William & Port Arthur *pop* 108,359
Thur·gau \ˈtu̇r-ˌgau̇\ *or F* **Thur·go·vie** \tu̇er-gō-ˈvē\ canton NE Switzerland ✻ Frauenfeld *area* 389 *sq mi* (1008 *sq km*), *pop* 228,200
Thu·rin·gia \thu̇-ˈrin-j(ē-)ə, thyu̇-\ *or G* **Thü·ring·en** \ˈtu̇e-riŋ-ən\ region *cen* Germany including the **Thu·rin·gian Forest** \thu̇-ˈrin-j(ē-)ən, thyu̇-\ *or G* **Thü·ring·er Wald** \ˈtu̇e-riŋ-ər-ˌvält\ (wooded mountain range bet. the upper Werra & the Czech border); included in a state of reunified Germany ✻ Erfurt *area* 6275 *sq mi* (16,252 *sq km*), *pop* 2,611,300
Thur·rock \ˈthər-ək, ˈthə-rək\ former urban district SE England in Essex
Thursday Island island NE Australia off N Queensland in Torres Strait
Thyatira — see AKHISAR
Ti·a·hua·na·co \ˌtē-ä-wä-ˈnä-(ˌ)kō\ locality W Bolivia near SE end of Lake Titicaca; site of prehistoric ruins
Tian·jin \ˈtyän-ˈjin\ *or* **Tien·tsin** \ˈtyen-ˈtsin, ˈtin-\ municipality & port NE China SE of Beijing *pop* 7,764,141
Tian Shan *or* **Tien Shan** \ˈtyen-ˈshän, -ˈshan\ mountain system *cen* Asia extending from the Pamirs NE into Xinjiang Uygur — see POBEDA PEAK
Ti·ber \ˈtī-bər\ *or It* **Te·ve·re** \ˈtā-vā-rā\ river 252 *mi* (405 *km*) *cen* Italy flowing through Rome into Tyrrhenian Sea
Ti·be·ri·as \tī-ˈbir-ē-əs\ city NE Israel in Galilee on W shore of Sea of Galilee *pop* 23,900
Tiberias, Lake *or* **Tiberias, Sea of** — see GALILEE (Sea of)
Ti·bes·ti Mountains \tə-ˈbes-tē\ mountains N *cen* Africa in the Sahara in NW Chad; highest peak Emi Koussi 11,204 *ft* (3415 *m*)
Ti·bet \tə-ˈbet\ *or* **Xi·zang** *or* **Hsi–tsang** \ˈshēd-ˈzäŋ\ region SW China on high plateau (average altitude 16,000 *ft or* 4877 *m*) N of the Himalayas ✻ Lhasa *area* 471,660 *sq mi* (1,226,316 *sq km*), *pop* 2,196,010
Ti·bet·an Plateau \tə-ˈbe-t^{ə}n\ *or* **Plateau of Tibet** tableland rising to 15,000 *ft* (4570 *m*) Tibet extending into surrounding Chinese provinces
Ti·bu·rón \ˌtē-bü-ˈrōn\ island 34 *mi* (55 *km*) long NW Mexico in Gulf of California off coast of Sonora
Ti·ci·no \tē-ˈchē-(ˌ)nō\ **1** river 154 *mi* (248 *km*) Switzerland & Italy flowing from slopes of St. Gotthard Range SE & SW through Lake Maggiore into the Po **2** *or F* **Tes·sin** \te-ˈsa^{n}\ canton S Switzerland bordering on Italy ✻ Bellinzona *area* 1085 *sq mi* (2821 *sq km*), *pop* 311,900 — **Ti·ci·nese** \ˌti-chə-ˈnēz, -ˈnēs\ *adj or n*
Tientsin — see TIANJIN
Tier·ra del Fue·go \tē-ˈer-ə-(ˌ)del-fü-ˈā-(ˌ)gō, ˈtyer-ä-(ˌ)thel-ˈfwā-gō\ **1** archipelago off S S. America S of Strait of Magellan; in Argentina & Chile *area over* 28,400 *sq mi* (73,556 *sq km*) **2** chief island of the archipelago; divided bet. Chile and Argentina *area* 18,530 *sq mi* (48,178 *sq km*)
Tiflis — see TBILISI
Ti·gard \ˈtī-gərd\ city NW Oreg. SSW of Portland *pop* 48,035
Ti·gre **1** \ˈtē-(ˌ)grā\ city E Argentina, NW suburb of Buenos Aires, on islands in Paraná Delta *pop* 256,005 **2** \ti-ˈgrā, ˈti-(ˌ)grā\ region N Ethiopia bordering on Eritrea — **Ti·gre·an** \ti-ˈgrā-ən\ *adj or n*
Ti·gris \ˈtī-grəs\ river 1180 *mi* (1899 *km*) SE Turkey & Iraq flowing SSE & uniting with the Euphrates to form the Shatt al Arab
Ti·jua·na \ˌtē-ə-ˈwä-nə, tē-ˈhwä-nä\ city NW Mexico on U.S. border in Baja California *pop* 991,592
Ti·kal \tē-ˈkäl\ ancient Mayan city N Guatemala
Til·burg \ˈtil-ˌbərg\ commune S Netherlands SE of Rotterdam *pop* 197,358
Til·bury \ˈtil-b(ə-)rē, *US also* -ˌber-ē\ town & port SE England in Essex on Thames River E of London
Til·la·mook Bay \ˈti-lə-ˌmək, -ˌmu̇k\ inlet of the Pacific NW Oreg.
Tilsit — see SOVETSK
Ti·ma·ga·mi, Lake \tə-ˈmä-gə-mē\ lake Canada in Ont. N of Lake Nipissing
Timbuktu — see TOMBOUCTOU
Tim·gad \ˈtim-ˌgad\ ancient Roman city NE Algeria
Ti·miş \ˈtē-mēsh\ *or in Serbia* **Te·meš** \ˈte-mesh\ river *ab* 200 *mi* (322 *km*) Romania & Serbia flowing W & S into the Danube downstream from Belgrade
Ti·mi·soa·ra \ˌtē-mē-ˈshwär-ä\ city W Romania *pop* 317,651
Tim·mins \ˈti-mənz\ city Canada in E Ont. N of Sudbury *pop* 43,165
Ti·mor \ˈtē-ˌmȯr, tē-ˈ\ **1** island SE Asia in Lesser Sunda Islands *area* 13,094 *sq mi* (34,044 *sq km*), *pop* 3,000,000; W part (formerly **Netherlands Timor**) belonged to the Dutch until 1946, and is now part of Indonesia; E part (formerly **Portuguese Timor**) belonged to Portugal until 1975, was annexed by Indonesia 1976, and gained independence 2002 as East Timor **2** sea bet. Timor Is. & Australia — **Ti·mor·ese** \(ˌ)tē-ˌmȯ-ˈrēz, -ˈrēs\ *adj or n*
Timor–Leste — see EAST TIMOR
Tim·pa·no·gos, Mount \ˌtim-pə-ˈnō-gəs\ mountain 12,008 *ft* (3660 *m*) N *cen* Utah N of Provo; highest in Wasatch Range
Timpanogos Cave National Monument series of limestone caverns N *cen* Utah on N slope of Mt. Timpanogos
Ti·ni·an \ˌti-nē-ˈan\ island W Pacific in the S Marianas
Tin·ley Park \ˈtin-lē\ village NE Ill. *pop* 56,703
Tí·nos \ˈtē-ˌnȯs\ island Greece in N Cyclades SE of Andros
Tin·tag·el Head \tin-ˈta-jəl\ headland SW England in NW Cornwall
Tip·pe·ca·noe \ˌti-pē-kə-ˈnü\ river 200 *mi* (322 *km*) N Ind. flowing SW into the Wabash
Tip·per·ary \ˌti-pə-ˈrer-ē\ **1** former county S Ireland in Munster; now divided into **Tipperary South** ✻ Clonmel & **Tipperary North** ✻ Nenagh *area* 1643 *sq mi* (4272 *sq km*), *pop* 140,131 **2** town in SW County Tipperary South *pop* 4783
Ti·ra·në *or* **Ti·ra·na** \ti-ˈrä-nə, tē-\ city *cen* Albania, its ✻ *pop* 519,720
Tirgu–Mures — see TARGU-MURES
Ti·rich Mir \ˌtir-ich-ˈmir\ mountain *ab* 25,260 *ft* (7699 *m*) Pakistan on Afghan border; highest in the Hindu Kush
Ti·rol *or* **Ty·rol** \tə-ˈrōl; ˈtī-ˌrōl, tī-; ˈtir-əl\ *or It* **Ti·ro·lo** \tē-ˈrȯ-(ˌ)lō\ region Europe in E Alps chiefly in Austria; the section S of Brenner Pass has belonged since 1919 to Italy — **Ti·ro·le·an** \tə-ˈrō-lē-ən, tī-; ˌtir-ə-ˈ, ˌtī-rə-ˈ\ *adj or n* — **Ti·ro·lese** \ˌtir-ə-ˈlēz, ˌtī-rə-, -ˈlēs\ *adj or n*
Ti·ruch·chi·rap·pal·li \ˌtir-ə-chə-ˈrä-pə-lē\ city S India in *cen* Tamil Nadu *pop* 746,062
Ti·ryns \ˈtir-ənz, ˈtī-rənz\ city of pre-Homeric Greece; ruins in E Peloponnese SE of Argos
Ti·sza \ˈti-ˌsȯ\ river *ab* 600 *mi* (965 *km*) E Europe flowing from the Carpathians in W Ukraine W & SW into the Danube
Ti·ti·ca·ca, Lake \ˌti-ti-ˈkä-kä, ˌtē-tē-\ lake on Peru-Bolivia boundary at altitude of 12,500 *ft* (3810 *m*), *area* 3200 *sq mi* (8320 *sq km*)
Titograd — see PODGORICA
Ti·tus·ville \ˈtī-təs-ˌvil, -vəl\ city E Fla. E of Orlando *pop* 43,761
Tiv·o·li \ˈti-və-lē, ˈtē-vō-\ *or anc* **Ti·bur** \ˈtī-bər\ commune *cen* Italy in Lazio ENE of Rome *pop* 52,990
Tjilatjap — see CILACAP
Tlax·ca·la \tlä-ˈskä-lä\ **1** state *cen* Mexico *area* 1511 *sq mi* (3913 *sq km*), *pop* 761,277 **2** city, its ✻, E of Mexico City *pop* 50,631
Tlem·cen \tlem-ˈsen\ *or* **Ti·lim·sen** \tə-lim-ˈsen\ city NW Algeria *pop* 126,882
Toa Al·ta \ˌtō-ä-ˈäl-tä\ municipality NE *cen* Puerto Rico *pop* 74,066
Toa Ba·ja \ˈbä-(ˌ)hä\ municipality NE Puerto Rico W of San Juan *pop* 89,609
To·a·ma·si·na \ˌtō-ə-mə-ˈsē-nə\ *or formerly* **Ta·ma·tave** \ˌtə-mə-ˈtäv, ˌtä-\ city & port E coast of Madagascar *pop* 191,041
To·ba·go \tə-ˈbā-(ˌ)gō\ island SE W. Indies, a territory of Trinidad and Tobago; chief town Scarborough *area* 116 *sq mi* (302 *sq km*), *pop* 54,084 — **To·ba·go·ni·an** \ˌtō-bə-ˈgō-nē-ən, -nyən\ *n*
To·bol \tə-ˈbȯl\ river N Kazakhstan & SW Russia in Asia flowing from SE foothills of the Urals NNE into the Irtysh
To·bruk \tō-ˈbru̇k, ˈtō-ˌ\ city & port NE Libya *pop* 34,200
To·can·tins \ˌtō-kən-ˈtēnz, ˌtü-kən-ˈtē^{n}s\ **1** river *ab* 1700 *mi* (2736 *km*) E *cen* & NE Brazil rising in S *cen* Goiás & flowing N into Pará River **2** state NE *cen* Brazil ✻ Palmas *area* 116,573 *sq mi* (301,294 *sq km*), *pop* 1,157,098
To·go \ˈtō-(ˌ)gō\ republic W Africa on Bight of Benin ✻ Lomé *area* 21,853 *sq mi* (56,599 *sq km*), *pop* 6,191,000 — **To·go·lese** \ˌtō-gə-ˈlēz, -ˈlēs\ *adj or n*
To·go·land \ˈtō-(ˌ)gō-ˌland\ region W Africa on Gulf of Guinea bet. Benin & Ghana; until 1919 a German protectorate, then divided into two trust territories: British Togoland (in W; since 1957 part of Ghana) & French Togo (in E; since 1958 Togo) — **To·go·land·er** \ˈtō-(ˌ)gō-ˌlan-dər\ *n*
To·ho·pe·kal·i·ga Lake \tə-ˌhō-pi-ˈka-li-gə\ lake *cen* Fla. S of Orlando
To·ka·ra Islands \tō-ˈkär-ä\ island group Japan in N Ryukyus
To·ke·lau Islands \ˈtō-kə-ˌlau̇\ islands *cen* Pacific N of Samoa belonging to New Zealand *pop* 1466 — **To·ke·lau·an** \ˌtō-kə-ˈlau̇-ən\ *n*
To·ko·ro·za·wa \ˌtō-kō-ˈrō-zä-(ˌ)wä\ city Japan on Honshu, a suburb of Tokyo *pop* 330,100
To·kyo \ˈtō-kē-ˌō, -ˌkyō\ *or formerly* **Edo** \ˈe-(ˌ)dō\ *or* **Ye·do** \ˈye-(ˌ)dō\ city ✻ of Japan in SE Honshu on **Tokyo Bay** (inlet of the Pacific) *pop* 12,064,101 — **To·kyo·ite** \ˈtō-kē-(ˌ)ō-ˌīt\ *n*
To·le·do \tə-ˈlē-(ˌ)dō, -ˈlē-də, *for 2 & 3 also* tō-ˈlā-thō\ **1** city & port NW Ohio on the Maumee River *pop* 287,208 **2** province *cen* Spain in W New Castile *area* 5934 *sq mi* (15,369 *sq km*), *pop* 541,379 **3** commune, its ✻ *pop* 68,382 — **To·le·dan** \-ˈlē-d^{ə}n\ *adj or n* — **To·le·do·an** \-ˈlē-dō-ən\ *adj or n*
To·li·ma \tō-ˈlē-mä\ dormant volcano W *cen* Colombia 17,110 *ft* (5215 *m*)
To·lu·ca \tō-ˈlü-kä\ *or* **Toluca de Ler·do** \thā-ˈler-(ˌ)dō\ city *cen* Mexico ✻ of Mexico state *pop* 487,630
Toluca, Ne·va·do de \nā-ˈvä-thō-thā-\ extinct volcano 15,016 *ft* (4577 *m*) S *cen* Mexico in Mexico state
Tol'·yat·ti *or* **To·gliat·ti** \tȯl-ˈyä-tē\ *or formerly* **Stav·ro·pol'** \stav-ˈrō-pəl, -ˈrō-; ˈstä-vrə-ˌpəl\ city SE *cen* Russia in Europe NW of Samara *pop* 666,000
Tom' \ˈtäm, ˈtȯm\ river 450 *mi* (724 *km*) S Russia in Asia rising in NW Altai Mountains & flowing into the Ob'
Tom·big·bee \täm-ˈbig-bē\ river NE Miss. & W Ala. flowing S to Mobile & Tensaw rivers
Tom·bouc·tou \tō^{n}-bük-ˈtü\ *or* **Tim·buk·tu** \ˌtim-ˌbək-ˈtü, tim-ˈbək-(ˌ)tü\ town W Africa in Mali near Niger River *pop* 31,925
Tomb·stone \ˈtüm-ˌstōn\ city SE corner of Ariz. *pop* 1380; site of gunfight at O.K. Corral in 1881
Tomsk \ˈtäm(p)sk, ˈtȯm(p)sk\ city S *cen* Russia in Asia on Tom' River near its junction with the Ob' *pop* 505,000
Ton·ga \ˈtäŋ-gə, ˈtäŋ-ə, ˈtȯŋ-ä\ islands SW Pacific E of Fiji; a kingdom in the Commonwealth of Nations ✻ Nuku'alofa *area* 270 *sq mi* (702 *sq km*), *pop* 101,134
Tongareva — see PENRHYN
Ton·ga·ri·ro \ˌtäŋ-gə-ˈrir-(ˌ)ō, ˌtäŋ-ə-\ volcano 6516 *ft* (1986 *m*) New Zealand in *cen* North Is. in **Tongariro National Park**
Tong·hua \ˈtu̇ŋ-ˈhwä, ˈtȯŋ-ˈwä\ *or* **T'ung–hua** *or* **Tung·hwa** \ˈtu̇ŋ-\ city NE China in S Jilin *pop* 158,000
Tongue \ˈtəŋ\ river 246 *mi* (396 *km*) N Wyo. & S Mont. flowing N into Yellowstone River
Ton·kin \ˈtäŋ-kən; ˈtän-ˈkin, ˈtäŋ-\ *or* **Tong·king** \ˈtäŋ-ˈkiŋ\ region N Indochina bordering on China, since 1946 forming N part of Vietnam; chief city Hanoi — **Ton·kin·ese** \ˌtäŋ-kə-ˈnēz, ˌtän-, -ˈnēs\ *or* **Tong·king·ese** \ˌtäŋ-kiŋ-ˈēz, -ˈēs\ *adj or n*
Tonkin, Gulf of arm of S. China Sea E of N Vietnam
Ton·le Sap \ˌtän-ˌlā-ˈsap\ *or F* **Grand Lac** \grä^{n}-ˈläk\ lake 87 *mi* (140 *km*) long SW Indochina in W Cambodia
Ton·to National Monument \ˈtän-(ˌ)tō\ area of cliff-dweller ruins S *cen* Ariz. E of Phoenix
Too·ele \tü-ˈe-lə\ city NW *cen* Utah S of Great Salt Lake *pop* 31,605
Too·woom·ba \tə-ˈwu̇m-bə\ city E Australia in SE Queensland *pop* 81,043
To·pe·ka \tə-ˈpē-kə\ city ✻ of Kans. on Kansas River *pop* 127,473
To·po·lo·bam·po \tō-ˌpō-lō-ˈbäm-(ˌ)pō\ town & port NW Mexico in Sinaloa on Gulf of California
Tor·bay \(ˌ)tȯr-ˈbā\ former county borough SW England in Devon on **Tor Bay** (inlet of English Channel)
Tor·cel·lo \tȯr-ˈche-(ˌ)lō\ island Italy in Lagoon of Venice

Tor·de·sil·las \ˌtȯr-dā-ˈsē-yäs, -ˈsēl-yäs\ village NW Spain SW of Valladolid *pop* 8045

Tor·faen \ˈtȯr-ˌvīn\ administrative area of SE Wales *area* 49 *sq mi* (126 *sq km*)

Torino — see TURIN

Tor·ne \ˈtȯr-nə\ *or Finn* **Tor·nio** \ˈtȯr-nē-ˌō\ river 354 *mi* (570 *km*) NE Sweden flowing S, forming part of Finnish-Swedish border, to head of Gulf of Bothnia

Torn·gat Mountains National Park \ˈtȯrn-ˌgat\ wilderness area E Canada in Nfld. & Lab. at N tip of Labrador

To·ron·to \tə-ˈrän-(ˌ)tō, -ˈrän-ə\ city & port Canada ✱ of Ont. on Lake Ontario *pop* 2,615,060 — **To·ron·to·ni·an** \tə-ˌrän-ˈtō-nē-ən; ˌtȯr-ən-, ˌtär-ən-\ *adj or n*

Toros — see TAURUS

Tor·rance \ˈtȯr-ən(t)s, ˈtär-\ city SW Calif. SSW of Los Angeles *pop* 145,438

Tor·re An·nun·zi·a·ta \ˈtȯr-ā-ā-ˌnün(t)-sē-ˈä-tä\ commune S Italy on Bay of Naples SE of Naples *pop* 56,471

Torre de Cerredo — see CERREDO

Tor·re del Gre·co \ˈtȯr-ā-del-ˈgre-(ˌ)kō, -ˈgrä-\ commune S Italy on Bay of Naples *pop* 103,577

Tor·rens, Lake \ˈtȯr-ənz, ˈtär-\ salt lake Australia in E S. Australia N of Spencer Gulf 92 *ft* (28 *m*) above sea level

Tor·re·ón \ˌtȯr-ā-ˈōn\ city N Mexico in Coahuila *pop* 459,809

Tor·res Strait \ˈtȯr-əs\ strait 80 *mi* (129 *km*) wide bet. island of New Guinea & N tip of Cape York Peninsula, Australia

Tor·res Ve·dras \ˌtȯr-iz-ˈve-drəsh\ town W Portugal N of Lisbon *pop* 72,250

Tor·ring·ton \ˈtȯr-iŋ-tən, ˈtär-\ city NW Conn. *pop* 36,383

Tow·son \ˈtau̇-sᵊn\ unincorporated population center N Md. N of Baltimore *pop* 55,197

Tor·to·la \tȯr-ˈtō-lə\ island Brit. West Indies; chief of the Brit. Virgin Islands; site of Road Town *area* 21 *sq mi* (54 *sq km*), *pop* 9730

Tor·tu·ga \tȯr-ˈtü-gə\ island Haiti off N coast; a stronghold of pirates in 17th century *pop* 13,723

To·ruń \ˈtȯr-ˌün, -ˌü-nyə\ city N Poland on the Vistula *pop* 200,822

Toscana — see TUSCANY

Tot·ten·ham \ˈtä-tə-nəm\ former municipal borough SE England in Middlesex, now part of Haringey

Toub·kal, Je·bel \ˈje-bəl-tüb-ˈkäl\ mountain 13,665 *ft* (4165 *m*) W *cen* Morocco; highest in Atlas Mountains

Toug·gourt \tə-ˈgu̇rt\ town & oasis NE Algeria S of Biskra *pop* 70,645

Tou·lon \tü-ˈlōⁿ\ commune & port SE France on the Mediterranean *pop* 160,712

Tou·louse \tü-ˈlüz\ city SW France on the Garonne *pop* 390,301

Tou·raine \tü-ˈrän, -ˈren\ region & former province NW *cen* France ✱ Tours

Tourane — see DA NANG

Tour·coing \tu̇r-ˈkwaⁿ\ city N France NE of Lille *pop* 93,531

Tour·nai *or* **Tour·nay** \tu̇r-ˈnā\ *or Flem* **Door·nik** \ˈdȯr-nik\ commune SW Belgium on the Schelde *pop* 67,232

Tours \ˈtu̇r\ city NW *cen* France *pop* 132,677

Tower Hamlets borough of E Greater London, England *pop* 153,500

Towns·ville \ˈtau̇nz-ˌvil, -vəl\ city & port NE Australia in NE Queensland *pop* 101,398

Tow·son \ˈtau̇-sᵊn\ unincorporated population center N Md. N of Baltimore *pop* 55,197

To·ya·ma \tō-ˈyä-mä\ city Japan in *cen* Honshu near **Toyama Bay** (inlet of Sea of Japan) *pop* 325,700

To·yo·ha·shi \ˌtōi-ō-ˈhä-shē\ city Japan in S Honshu SE of Nagoya *pop* 364,856

To·yo·na·ka \ˌtōi-ō-ˈnä-kə\ city Japan in S Honshu *pop* 391,726

To·yo·ta \ˌtōi-ˈō-tä\ city Japan in S Honshu *pop* 351,101

Trab·zon \trab-ˈzän\ *or* **Treb·i·zond** \ˈtre-bə-ˌzänd\ *or anc* **Trap·e·zus** \ˈtra-pi-zəs\ city & port NE Turkey on Black Sea *pop* 143,941

Tra·cy \ˈtrā-sē\ city *cen* Calif. SSW of Stockton *pop* 82,922

Tra·fal·gar, Cape \trə-ˈfal-gər, ˌtra-fäl-ˈgär\ cape SW Spain SE of Cádiz at W end of Strait of Gibraltar

Tra·lee \trə-ˈlē\ seaport SW Ireland ✱ of County Kerry *pop* 17,109

Trans Alai \ˈträn(t)s-ə-ˈlī, -ˌlī\ mountain range Kyrgyzstan & Tajikistan in NW Pamirs — see LENIN PEAK

Transalpine Gaul the part of Gaul lying chiefly in what is now France & Belgium

Transcaucasia — see CAUCASUS — **Trans·cau·ca·sian** \ˌtran(t)s-kȯ-ˈkā-zhən, -ˈka-\ *adj or n*

Transjordan — see JORDAN 3 — **Trans·jor·da·ni·an** \ˌtran(t)s-jȯr-ˈdā-nē-ən, ˌtranz-\ *adj or n*

Trans·kei \(ˌ)tran(t)s-ˈkī\ former black enclave in the Republic of South Africa ✱ Umtata; granted independence 1976; abolished 1994 — **Trans·kei·an** \-ən\ *adj or n*

Trans·vaal \tran(t)s-ˈväl, tranz-\ former province NE Republic of South Africa bet. the Vaal & the Limpopo; in 19th century a Boer republic (**South African Republic**) ✱ Pretoria *area* 109,621 *sq mi* (283,918 *sq km*)

Tran·syl·va·nia *or Romanian* **Tran·sil·va·nia** \ˌtran(t)-səl-ˈvā-nyə, -nē-ə\ region NW Romania bounded on the N, E, & S by the Carpathians & the Transylvanian Alps; part of Hungary 1867–1918 — **Tran·syl·va·nian** \-nyən, -nē-ən\ *adj or n*

Transylvanian Alps a S extension of the Carpathian Mountains in *cen* Romania

Tra·pa·ni \ˈträ-pä-nē\ commune & port Italy at NW tip of Sicily *pop* 69,221

Tra·si·me·no, Lake \ˌtra-zē-ˈmā-nō\ lake 10 *mi* (16 *km*) wide *cen* Italy W of Perugia

Trav·an·core \ˈtra-vən-ˌkȯr\ region & former state SW India on Malabar Coast extending N from Cape Comorin; included (1949–56) in former **Travancore and Co·chin** \ˈkō-chən\ state (✱ Thiruvananthapuram); became part of Kerala 1956

Trav·erse, Lake \ˈtra-vərs\ lake NE S.Dak. & W Minn.; drained by the Bois de Sioux (headstream of Red River)

Treb·bia \ˈtre-bē-ä\ *or anc* **Tre·bia** \ˈtrē-bē-ə\ river 71 *mi* (114 *km*) NW Italy flowing N into the Po

Treb·i·zond \ˈtre-bə-ˌzänd\ **1** — see TRABZON **2** Greek empire 1204–1461, an offshoot of Byzantine Empire; at greatest extent included Georgia, Crimea, & S coast of Black Sea E of the Sakarya

Treng·ga·nu \treŋ-ˈgä-(ˌ)nü\ state Malaysia in NE Peninsular Malaysia on S. China Sea ✱ Kuala Trengganu *area* 5000 *sq mi* (12,950 *sq km*)

Trent \ˈtrent\ **1** river 150 *mi* (241 *km*) Canada in SE Ont. flowing from Kawartha Lakes through Rice Lake into Lake Ontario (Bay of Quinte) **2** river 170 *mi* (274 *km*) *cen* England flowing NNE & uniting with Ouse River to form the Humber

Trent Canal canal system Canada 224 *mi* (360 *km*) long in SE Ont. connecting Lake Huron (Georgian Bay) with Lake Ontario (Bay of Quinte)

Tren·ti·no–Al·to Adi·ge \tren-ˈtē-nō-ˌäl-tō-ˈä-dē-ˌjä\ region N Italy ✱ Trento *area* 5526 *sq mi* (13,613 *sq km*), *pop* 943,123

Tren·to \ˈtren-(ˌ)tō\ commune N Italy *pop* 105,942

Tren·ton \ˈtren-tᵊn\ city ✱ of N.J. on Delaware River *pop* 84,913

Tre·vi·so \trā-ˈvē-(ˌ)zō\ commune NE Italy NW of Venice *pop* 82,450

Trier \ˈtrir\ city W Germany on the Moselle near Luxembourg border *pop* 98,752

Tri·este \trē-ˈest, -ˈes-tē, -ˈes-tä\ *or Slovene and Croatian* **Trst** \ˈtȯrst\ city & port NE Italy ✱ of Friuli-Venezia Giulia on **Gulf of Trieste** (inlet at head of the Adriatic NW of the Istrian Peninsula) *pop* 215,096; once belonged to Austria; part of Italy 1919–47; in 1947 made with surrounding territory the **Free Territory of Trieste** under administration of the United Nations; city with N part of Free Territory returned to Italy 1953, S part of territory having previously been absorbed into Yugoslavia — **Tri·es·tine** \trē-ˈes-tən, -ˌtēn\ *adj*

Tri·ka·la *or* **Trik·ka·la** \ˈtri-kə-lə, ˈtrē-kä-lä\ city *cen* Greece *pop* 48,810

Trim \ˈtrim\ town E Ireland ✱ of County Meath *pop* 1781

Trinacria — see SICILY — **Tri·nac·ri·an** \trə-ˈna-krē-ən, trī-\ *adj*

Trin·co·ma·lee \ˌtriŋ-kə-mə-ˈlē, triŋ-ˈkə-mə-lē\ city & port NE Sri Lanka on Bay of Bengal *pop* 50,000

Trin·i·dad \ˈtri-nə-ˌdad\ island SE W. Indies off coast of NE Venezuela *pop* 1,208,282; with Tobago, a dominion (**Trinidad and Tobago**) ✱ of the Commonwealth of Nations since 1962; formerly a Brit. colony ✱ Port of Spain *area* 1980 *sq mi* (5128 *sq km*), *pop* 1,262,366 — **Trin·i·da·di·an** \ˌtri-nə-ˈdä-dē-ən, -ˈda-\ *adj or n*

Trin·i·ty \ˈtri-nə-tē\ river N Tex. flowing SE into Galveston Bay

Trip·o·li \ˈtri-pə-lē\ **1** *or Ar* **Ṭa·rā·bu·lus** \tə-ˈrä-bə-ləs\ *or anc* **Trip·o·lis** \ˈtri-pə-ləs\ city & port NW Lebanon NNE of Beirut *pop* 127,611 **2** *or Ar* **Ṭarābulus** *or anc* **Oea** \ˈē-ə\ city & port NW Libya, its ✱ *pop* 591,062 **3** Tripolitania when it was one of the Barbary States — **Trip·o·li·tan** \tri-ˈpä-lə-tən\ *adj or n*

Tri·po·li·ta·nia \ˌtri-ˌpä-lə-ˈtā-nyə, ˌtri-pə-lə-\ *or anc* **Trip·o·lis** \ˈtri-pə-ləs\ region & former province NW Libya bordering on the Mediterranean — **Tri·po·li·ta·nian** \-nyən, -nē-ən\ *adj or n*

Tri·pu·ra \ˈtri-pə-rə\ state E India bet. Bangladesh & Assam ✱ Agartala *area* 4035 *sq mi* (10,451 *sq km*), *pop* 3,191,168

Tris·tan da Cu·nha \ˌtris-tən-də-ˈkü-nə, -nyə\ island S. Atlantic, chief of the Tristan da Cunha Islands attached to Brit. colony of St. Helena *area* 38 *sq mi* (98 *sq km*), *pop* 274; volcanic eruptions 1961

Trivandrum — see THIRUVANANTHAPURAM

Tro·as \ˈtrō-ˌas\ **1** *or* **Tro·ad** \-ˌad\ territory surrounding the ancient city of Troy in NW Mysia, Asia Minor **2** ancient city of Mysia S of site of Troy — **Tro·ad·ic** \trō-ˈa-dik\ *adj*

Tro·bri·and \ˈtrō-brē-ˌänd, -ˌand\ islands SW Pacific in Solomon Sea; attached to Papua New Guinea *area* 170 *sq mi* (442 *sq km*) — **Tro·bri·and·er** \ˌtrō-brē-ˈän-dər, -ˌan-\ *or* **Trobriand Islander** *n*

Trois–Ri·vières \ˌt(r)wä-ri-ˈvyer\ city Canada in S Que. NE of Montreal on N bank of St. Lawrence River *pop* 131,338; includes former town of **Trois–Ri·vières–Ouest** \ˌt(r)wä-ri-ˌvyer-ˈwest\

Trom·sö \ˈträm-ˌsō, -ˌsœ\ city & port N Norway *pop* 50,754

Trond·heim \ˈträn-ˌhām\ city & port *cen* Norway on **Trondheim Fjord** (80 *mi* or 128 *km* long), *pop* 142,891

Tros·sachs \ˈträ-səks, -ˌsaks\ valley *cen* Scotland bet. Loch Katrine & Loch Achray

Trot·wood \ˈträt-ˌwu̇d\ city SW Ohio W of Dayton *pop* 24,431

Trou·ville \trü-ˈvēl\ *or* **Trouville–sur–Mer** \-(ˌ)su̇r-ˈmer\ town & port N France on English Channel S of Le Havre *pop* 5410

Trow·bridge \ˈtrō-(ˌ)brij\ town S England ✱ of Wiltshire *pop* 22,984

Troy \ˈtrȯi\ **1** city SE Mich. N of Detroit *pop* 80,980 **2** city E N.Y. on Hudson River NNE of Albany *pop* 50,129 **3** *or* **Il·i·um** \ˈi-lē-əm\ *or* **Tro·ja** \ˈtrō-jə, -yə\ ancient city NW Asia Minor in Troas SW of the Dardanelles

Troyes \ˈt(r)wä\ city NE France SE of Paris *pop* 60,903

Tru·chas Peak \ˈtrü-chəs\ *or* **North Truchas Peak** mountain 13,110 *ft* (3996 *m*) N N.Mex. in Sangre de Cristo Mountains NE of Santa Fe; highest of three peaks forming **Truchas Peaks**

Trucial Oman, Trucial States — see UNITED ARAB EMIRATES

Truck·ee \ˈtrə-kē\ river 120 *mi* (193 *km*) E Calif. & W Nev. flowing from Lake Tahoe into Pyramid Lake

Tru·ji·llo \trü-ˈhē-(ˌ)yō\ **1** city NW Peru NW of Lima *pop* 193,528 **2** — see SANTO DOMINGO 1

Trujillo Al·to \ˈäl-(ˌ)tō\ municipality NE *cen* Puerto Rico *pop* 74,842

Truk — see CHUUK

Trum·bull \ˈtrəm-bəl\ town SW Conn. N of Bridgeport *pop* 36,018

Tru·ro \ˈtru̇r-(ˌ)ō\ town SW England ✱ of Cornwall and Isles of Scilly *pop* 16,277

Tsang·po \ˈ(t)säŋ-ˈpō\ the upper Brahmaputra in Tibet

Tsaritsyn — see VOLGOGRAD

Tsarskoye Selo — see PUSHKIN

Tshwa·ne \ˈchwä-nä\ municipality Republic of South Africa including the city of Pretoria

Tsinan — see JINAN

Tsinghai — see QINGHAI

Tsingtao — see QINGDAO

Tsitsihar — see QIQIHAR

Tskhin·va·li \ˈ(t)skin-və-lē\ town N Republic of Georgia NW of Tbilisi ✱ of South Ossetia *pop* 42,600

Tsu·ga·ru Strait \'(t)sü-gä-ˌrü\ strait Japan bet. Honshu & Hokkaido
Tsu·shi·ma \(t)sü-'shē-mä\ island Japan in Korea Strait separated from Kyushu and Honshu by **Tsushima Strait** (the SE part of Korea Strait) *area* 271 *sq mi* (705 *sq km*)
Tu·a·la·tin \ˌtü-'ä-lə-tən\ city NW Oreg. SSW of Portland *pop* 26,054
Tu·a·mo·tu Archipelago \ˌtü-ä-'mō-(ˌ)tü\ archipelago S. Pacific E of Society Islands; belongs to France *area* 330 *sq mi* (858 *sq km*), *pop* 14,900
Tü·bing·en \'tü-biŋ-ən, 'tyü-, 'tue-\ city SW Germany on the Neckar S of Stuttgart *pop* 82,483
Tuc·son \'tü-ˌsän, *esp locally* tü-'sän\ city SE Ariz. *pop* 520,116 — **Tuc·son·an** \'tü-ˌsä-nən\ *n*
Tucumán — see SAN MIGUEL DE TUCUMÁN
Tu·ge·la \tü-'gā-lä\ river 312 *mi* (502 *km*) E Republic of South Africa in *cen* KwaZulu-Natal flowing E to Indian Ocean; near its source on Mont Aux Sources are the **Tugela Falls** (3110 *ft or* 948 *m*)
Tuk·tut No·gait National Park \'tůk-ˌtət-'näg-ˌgīd, 'twäk-\ Arctic landscape N Canada in N Northwest Territories on Nunavut border
Tu·la \'tü-lä\ **1** *or* **Tula de Al·len·de** \(ˌ)thā-ä-'yen-dā\ city *cen* Mexico in SW Hidalgo N of Mexico City; ancient ✻ of the Toltecs *pop* 71,622 **2** city SW *cen* Russia in Europe S of Moscow *pop* 541,000
Tu·la·gi \tü-'lä-gē\ island S. Pacific in S *cen* Solomons
Tu·lare \tü-'ler(-ē)\ city S *cen* Calif. SE of Fresno *pop* 59,278
Tulare Lake former lake S *cen* Calif. S of Hanford; drained for farmland
Tul·la·more \ˌtə-lə-'mȯr\ town *cen* Ireland ✻ of County Offaly *pop* 8623
Tul·sa \'təl-sə\ city NE Okla. on Arkansas River *pop* 391,906 — **Tul·san** \-sən\ *n*
Tu·men \'tü-'mən\ river 324 *mi* (521 *km*) E Asia on border bet. N. Korea, China, & Russia flowing NE & SE into Sea of Japan
Tu·muc–Hu·mac Mountains \tü-ˌmü-kü-'mäk\ *or Pg* **Ser·ra Tu·mu·cu·ma·que** \'se-rə-tü-ˌmü-kü-'mä-kā, -kē\ range of low mountains NE Brazil on Suriname-French Guiana boundary
Tunbridge Wells — see ROYAL TUNBRIDGE WELLS
T'ung–hua *or* **Tonghua** — see TONGHUA
Tun·gu·ska \tůŋ-'gü-skə, tən-\ any of three rivers in *cen* Russia in Asia, tributaries of the Yenisey: **Lower Tunguska, Stony Tunguska,** & **Upper Tunguska** (lower course of the Angara)
Tu·nis \'tü-nəs, 'tyü-\ **1** city ✻ of Tunisia near site of ancient Carthage *pop* 674,100 **2** TUNISIA — used esp. of the former Barbary State
Tu·ni·sia \tü-'nē-zh(ē-)ə, tyü-, -'ni-\ country N Africa bordering on the Mediterranean; formerly one of the Barbary States; a French protectorate 1881–1956, a monarchy 1956–57, & a republic since 1957 ✻ Tunis *area* 63,378 *sq mi* (164,149 *sq km*), *pop* 10,374,000 — **Tu·ni·sian** \-zh(ē-)ən\ *adj or n*
Tu·ol·um·ne \tů-'ä-lə-mē\ river 155 *mi* (249 *km*) *cen* Calif. flowing W from Yosemite National Park into the San Joaquin
Tu·pe·lo \'tü-pə-ˌlō, 'tyü-\ city NE Miss. *pop* 34,546
Tu·pun·ga·to \ˌtü-püŋ-'gä-(ˌ)tō\ mountain 22,310 *ft* (6800 *m*) in the Andes on Argentina-Chile boundary ENE of Santiago, Chile
Tu·rin \'tůr-ən, 'tyůr-; tů-'rin, tyů-\ *or It* **To·ri·no** \tō-'rē-(ˌ)nō\ commune NW Italy on the Po ✻ of Piedmont *pop* 900,987 — **Tu·rin·ese** \ˌtůr-ə-'nēz, ˌtyůr-, -'nēs\ *adj or n*
Tur·kana, Lake \tər-'ka-nə\ *or* **Lake Ru·dolf** \'rü-ˌdȯlf, -ˌdälf\ lake N Kenya in Great Rift Valley *area* 2473 *sq mi* (6405 *sq km*)
Tur·key \'tər-kē\ country W Asia & SE Europe bet. Mediterranean & Black seas; formerly center of an empire (✻ Constantinople), since 1923 a republic ✻ Ankara *area* 301,380 *sq mi* (780,574 *sq km*), *pop* 73,085,000 — see OTTOMAN EMPIRE
Tur·ki·stan *or* **Tur·ke·stan** \ˌtər-kə-'stan, -'stän; 'tər-kə-ˌ\ region *cen* Asia bet. Iran & Siberia; now divided bet. Turkmenistan, Uzbekistan, Tajikistan, Kyrgyzstan, Kazakhstan, China, & Afghanistan — see CHINESE TURKESTAN, RUSSIAN TURKESTAN
Turk·men·i·stan \(ˌ)tərk-ˌme-nə-'stan, -'stän; (ˌ)tərk-'me-nə-ˌ\ country *cen* Asia bordering on Afghanistan, Iran, & the Caspian Sea; a constituent republic (**Turk·men Republic** \'tərk-mən\ ) of the U.S.S.R. 1925–91✻ Ashgabat *area* 188,455 *sq mi* (488,098 *sq km*), *pop* 5,478,900 — **Turk·men** \-mən\ *adj* — **Turk·me·ni·an** \ˌtərk-'mē-nē-ən\ *adj*
Turks and Cai·cos \'tərks-ənd-'kā-kəs, -ˌkōs\ two groups of islands (Turks Islands & Caicos Islands) Brit. West Indies at SE end of Bahamas; a Brit. colony; seat of government on **Grand Turk** (7 *mi or* 11 *km* long) *area* 166 *sq mi* (432 *sq km*), *pop* 19,886
Tur·ku \'tůr-(ˌ)kü\ city & port SW Finland *pop* 173,686
Tur·lock \'tər-ˌläk\ city *cen* Calif. SE of Modesto *pop* 68,549
Tur·tle Bay \'tər-tᵊl\ section of New York City in E *cen* Manhattan on East River; site of United Nations headquarters
Tus·ca·loo·sa \ˌtəs-kə-'lü-sə\ city W *cen* Ala. on Black Warrior River SW of Birmingham *pop* 90,468
Tus·ca·ny \'təs-kə-nē\ *or It* **To·sca·na** \tō-'skä-nä\ region NW *cen* Italy bordering on Ligurian & Tyrrhenian seas ✻ Florence *area* 8876 *sq mi* (22,989 *sq km*), *pop* 3,547,604
Tus·cu·lum \'təs-kyə-ləm, -kə-\ ancient town Italy in Lazio SE of Rome
Tus·tin \'təs-tən\ city SW Calif. E of Santa Ana *pop* 75,540
Tu·tu·i·la \ˌtü-tü-'wē-lä\ island, chief of American Samoa group *area* 52 *sq mi* (135 *sq km*) — **Tu·tu·i·lan** \-lən\ *adj or n*
Tu·va·lu \tü-'vä-(ˌ)lü, -'vär-(ˌ)ü\ *or formerly* **El·lice Islands** \'e-lis\ islands W Pacific N of Fiji; a Brit. territory 1976–78; became an independent member of the Commonwealth of Nations 1978 ✻ Funafuti *area* 9 *sq mi* (23 *sq km*), *pop* 9561 — see GILBERT AND ELLICE
Tu·va Republic \'tü-və\ autonomous republic S Russia in Asia N of Mongolia ✻ Kyzyl *area* 65,380 *sq mi* (169,334 *sq km*), *pop* 306,000
Tux·tla \'tüst-lə\ *or* **Tuxtla Gu·tiér·rez** \gü-'tyer-es\ city SE Mexico ✻ of Chiapas *pop* 386,135
Tu·zi·goot National Monument \'tü-zi-ˌgüt\ area containing ruins of prehistoric pueblo *cen* Ariz. SW of Flagstaff
Tver' \'tver\ *or 1932–90* **Ka·li·nin** \kä-'lē-nin\ city W *cen* Russia in Europe on the Volga *pop* 456,000
Tweed \'twēd\ river 97 *mi* (156 *km*) SE Scotland & NE England flowing E into North Sea
Tweeddale — see PEEBLES
Twick·en·ham \'twi-kə-nəm, 'twit-nəm\ former municipal borough SE England in Middlesex, now part of Richmond upon Thames
Twin Cities the cities of Minneapolis & St. Paul, Minn.
Twin Falls city S Idaho SW of Twin Falls (waterfall in Snake River) *pop* 44,125
Two Sic·i·lies \'si-s(ə-)lēz\ former kingdom consisting of Sicily & S Italy
Ty·chy \'ti-kē, -ki\ town S Poland *pop* 189,874
Ty·ler \'tī-lər\ city E Tex. ESE of Dallas *pop* 96,900
Tyn·dall, Mount \'tin-dᵊl\ **1** mountain 14,018 *ft* (4273 *m*) S *cen* Calif. in Sierra Nevada NW of Mt. Whitney **2** mountain 8280 *ft* (2524 *m*) New Zealand in *cen* South Is. in Southern Alps
Tyne \'tīn\ river 30 *mi* (48 *km*) N England flowing E into North Sea
Tyne and Wear \'wir\ metropolitan county N England ✻ Newcastle upon Tyne *area* 216 *sq mi* (559 *sq km*), *pop* 1,087,000
Tyne·mouth \'tīn-ˌmau̇th, -məth\ town N England in Tyne and Wear on North Sea at mouth of the Tyne *pop* 60,022
Tyre \'tī(-ə)r\ *or* **Ty·rus** \'tī-rəs\ port & chief city of ancient Phoenicia; site at modern town of Sur on the Mediterranean coast in S Lebanon — **Tyr·i·an** \'tir-ē-ən\ *adj or n*
Ty·ree, Mount \tī-'rē\ mountain 16,290 *ft* (4965 *m*) W Antarctica in Ellsworth Mountains NW of Vinson Massif
Tyrol — see TIROL — **Ty·ro·le·an** \tə-'rō-lē-ən, tī-; ˌtir-ə-', ˌtī-rə-'\ *adj or n* — **Ty·ro·lese** \ˌtir-ə-'lēz, ˌtī-rə-, -'lēs\ *adj or n*
Ty·rone \ti-'rōn\ former county W *cen* Northern Ireland ✻ Omagh
Tyr·rhe·ni·an Sea \tə-'rē-nē-ən\ the part of the Mediterranean W of Italy, N of Sicily, & E of Sardinia & Corsica
Tyu·men' \tyü-'men\ city W Russia in Asia on the **Tu·ra** \tů-'rä\ (a tributary of the Tobol) *pop* 496,000
Tzu–kung — see ZIGONG
Tzu–po — see ZIBO
Uap — see YAP
Uau·pés \wau̇-'pes\ *or Sp* **Vau·pés** \vau̇-\ river Colombia & Brazil flowing ESE into Negro River
Uban·gi \ü-'bäŋ-gē, yü-'baŋ-\ *or F* **Ou·ban·gui** \ü-bäⁿ-'gē\ river 700 *mi* (1126 *km*) W *cen* Africa on NW border of Democratic Republic of the Congo flowing W & S into Congo River — see UELE
Ubangi–Sha·ri \-'shär-ē\ *or F* **Oubangui–Cha·ri** \-shä-'rē\ former French territory N *cen* Africa — see CENTRAL AFRICAN REPUBLIC
Uca·ya·li \ˌü-kä-'yä-lē\ river *ab* 1000 *mi* (1609 *km*) *cen* & N Peru flowing N to unite with the Marañón forming the Amazon
Uc·cle \'üklᵊ, 'uekl\ *or Flem* **Uk·kel** \'ə-kəl, 'œ-\ commune *cen* Belgium *pop* 74,952
Udai·pur \ů-'dī-ˌpůr\ **1** *or* **Me·war** \mā-'wär\ former state NW India, now part of Rajasthan state **2** city, its ✻ *pop* 389,317
Udi·ne \'ü-dē-ˌnā\ commune NE Italy NE of Venice in Friuli-Venezia Giulia region *pop* 95,321
Ud·mur·tia \ůd-'můr-shə, -shē-ə\ *or* **Ud·mur·ti·ya** \-tē-yə\ autonomous republic E Russia in Europe in W foothills of the Urals ✻ Izhevsk *area* 16,255 *sq mi* (42,101 *sq km*), *pop* 1,637,000
Ue·le \'we-lē\ river 700 *mi* (1126 *km*) *cen* Africa flowing W in N Democratic Republic of the Congo to unite with the Bomu forming Ubangi River
Ufa \ü-'fä\ **1** river E Russia in Europe in S Urals flowing NW & SW into the Belaya **2** city E Russia in Europe ✻ of Bashkortostan *pop* 1,097,000
Ugan·da \ü-'gän-də, yü-, -'gan-\ republic E Africa N of Lake Victoria; member of the Commonwealth of Nations ✻ Kampala *area* 91,134 *sq mi* (236,037 *sq km*), *pop* 33,796,000 — **Ugan·dan** \-dən\ *adj or n*
Uga·rit \ü-'gär-it, yü-\ ancient city Syria on Mediterranean coast
Uin·ta Mountains \yü-'in-tə\ mountain range NE Utah — see KINGS PEAK
Uj·jain \'ü-ˌjīn\ city NW *cen* India in W Madhya Pradesh *pop* 429,933
Ujung Pan·dang \ü-ˌjůŋ-(ˌ)pän-'däŋ\ *or formerly* **Ma·kas·sar** \mə-'kasər\ city & port Indonesia in SW Sulawesi *pop* 944,685
Uk·ku·sik·sa·lik National Park \ˌü-kü-'sik-sə-lik\ coastal tundra region N Canada in E mainland portion of Nunavut
Ukraine \yü-'krān, 'yü-ˌ, *also* yü-'krīn\ *or* **Ukra·yi·na** \ˌü-krä-'yē-nä\ *or chiefly formerly* **the Ukraine** country E Europe on N coast of Black Sea; a constituent republic of the U.S.S.R. 1923–91 ✻ Kiev *area* 233,089 *sq mi* (603,701 *sq km*), *pop* 45,858,000
usage In the past Ukraine was frequently referred to as *the Ukraine;* however, since Ukraine declared independence in 1991, most newspapers and magazines have adopted the style of referring to Ukraine without the *the,* and this has become the more common styling.
Ulaan·baa·tar *or* **Ulan Ba·tor** \ˌü-ˌlän-'bä-ˌtȯr\ *or formerly* **Ur·ga** \'ůr-gə\ city N *cen* Mongolia (republic), its ✻ *pop* 760,077
Ulan–Ude \ˌü-ˌlän-ů-'dā\ *or formerly* **Verkh·ne·u·dinsk** \ˌverk-nə-'ü-ˌdin(t)sk\ city S Russia in Asia ✻ of Buryatia on the Selenga *pop* 366,000
Uleåborg — see OULU
Ulls·wa·ter \'əlz-ˌwȯ-tər, -ˌwä-\ lake 7 *mi* (11 *km*) long NW England in Cumbria
Ulm \'ůlm\ city S Germany in E Baden-Württemberg *pop* 112,173
Ul·san \'ül-'sän\ city SE S. Korea *pop* 1,012,110
Ul·ster \'əl-stər\ **1** region N Ireland (island) comprising Northern Ireland & N Ireland (republic); ancient kingdom, later a province comprising nine counties, three of which in 1921 joined Irish Free State (now Ireland) while the rest remained with United Kingdom **2** province N Ireland (republic) comprising counties Cavan, Donegal, & Monaghan *area* 3093 *sq mi* (8042 *sq km*), *pop* 246,714 **3** NORTHERN IRELAND — used unofficially — **Ul·ster·ite** \-stə-ˌrīt\ *n* — **Ul·ster·man** \-stər-mən\ *n*
Ulu Dag \ˌü-lə-'dä(g)\ *or anc* **Mount Olym·pus** \ə-'lim-pəs, ō-\ mountain 8343 *ft* (2543 *m*) NW Turkey in Asia SE of Bursa
Ulu·ru \ü-'lü-rü\ *or* **Ayers Rock** \'erz\ outcrop *cen* Australia in SW Northern Territory; 1143 *ft* (348 *m*) high
Ulyanovsk — see SIMBIRSK
Uma·til·la \ˌyü-mə-'ti-lə\ river 80 *mi* (129 *km*) NE Oreg. flowing W & N into Columbia River
Um·bria \'əm-brē-ə\ region *cen* Italy in the Apennines ✻ Perugia *pop* 840,482
Umeå \'ü-mā-(ˌ)ō\ city & port N Sweden on Gulf of Bothnia *pop* 106,525
Umm al Qay·wayn *or* **Umm al–Qai·wain** \'ům-äl-kī-'wīn\ sheikhdom, member of United Arab Emirates
Um·nak \'üm-ˌnak\ island SW Alaska in Fox Islands

Ump·qua \ˈəm(p)-ˌkwȯ\ river 200 *mi* (322 *km*) SW Oreg. flowing into the Pacific

Um·ta·ta \u̇m-ˈtä-tə\ city Republic of South Africa; formerly ✻ of Transkei

Un·alas·ka \ˌə-nə-ˈlas-kə\ island SW Alaska in Fox Islands

Unalaska Bay inlet SW Alaska on N coast of Unalaska Is.

Un·com·pah·gre Peak \ˌən-kəm-ˈpä-grē\ mountain 14,309 *ft* (4361 *m*) SW Colo.; highest in San Juan Mountains

Uncompahgre Plateau tableland W Colo. SW of the Gunnison

Un·gava \ˌən-ˈga-və\ region Canada N of the Eastmain & W of Labrador including Ungava Peninsula, divided bet. Que. & Nfld.&Lab. — see NEW QUEBEC

Ungava Bay inlet of Hudson Strait Canada in N Que.

Ungava Peninsula peninsula Canada in N Que. bet. Hudson Bay & Ungava Bay

Uni·mak \ˈyü-nə-ˌmak\ island SW Alaska in Fox Islands

Union City 1 city W Calif. S of Oakland *pop* 69,516 2 city NE N.J. N of Jersey City *pop* 66,455

Union of South Africa — see SOUTH AFRICA (Republic of)

Union of Soviet Socialist Republics *or* **Soviet Union** country 1922–91 E Europe & N Asia bordering on the Arctic & Pacific oceans & Baltic & Black seas; a union of 15 constituent republics ✻ Moscow *area* 8,649,512 *sq mi* (22,402,236 *sq km*)

United Arab Emirates *or formerly* **Tru·cial States** \ˈtrü-shəl\ *or* **Tru·cial Oman** \ō-ˈmän, -ˈman\ country NE Arabia on Persian Gulf bet. Qatar & Oman; a republic composed of seven sheikhdoms (Abu Dhabi, ʿAjman, Al Fujayrah, Ash Shariqah, Dubayy, Ra's al Khaymah, & Umm al Qaywayn) formerly under Brit. protection ✻ Abu Dhabi *area* 30,000 *sq mi* (77,700 *sq km*), *pop* 4,104,695

United Arab Republic 1 former union of Egypt & Syria (1958–61) 2 EGYPT — a former name (1961–71)

United Kingdom 1 *or* **United Kingdom of Great Britain and Northern Ireland** country W Europe in British Isles comprising Great Britain & Northern Ireland ✻ London *area* 94,251 *sq mi* (244,110 *sq km*), *pop* 58,789,194 2 *or* **United Kingdom of Great Britain and Ireland** country 1801–1921 comprising Great Britain & Ireland

United Nations political organization established 1945; headquarters in New York City in E *cen* Manhattan overlooking East River — see TURTLE BAY

United Provinces *or* **United Provinces of Agra and Oudh** former province N India formed 1902 ✻ Allahabad; as Uttar Pradesh, became a state of India (republic) 1950

United States of America *or* **United States** \yu̇-ˈnī-təd-ˈstāts, *esp Southern* ˈyü-ˌ\ country N. America bordering on Atlantic, Pacific, & Arctic oceans; a federal republic ✻ Washington *area* 3,619,969 *sq mi* (9,375,720 *sq km*), *pop* 308,745,538

University City city E Mo. WNW of St. Louis *pop* 35,371

University Park city NE Tex. within city of Dallas *pop* 23,068

University Place city W *cen* Wash. near Tacoma *pop* 31,144

Un·ter·wal·den \ˈu̇n-tər-ˌväl-dən\ former canton *cen* Switzerland, now divided into two cantons (formerly half cantons): **Nid·wal·den** \ˈnēt-ˌväl-dən\ *or F* **Nid·wald** \nēd-ˈväld\ (✻ Stans *area* 106 *sq mi or* 276 *sq km, pop* 38,600) & **Ob·wal·den** \ˈȯp-ˌväl-dən\ *or F* **Ob·wald** \ȯb-ˈväld\ (✻ Sarnen *area* 189 *sq mi or* 490 *sq km, pop* 32,700)

Up·land \ˈəp-lənd\ city SW Calif. W of San Bernardino *pop* 73,732

Upo·lu \ü-ˈpō-(ˌ)lü\ island S. Pacific in independent Samoa

Upper Adige — see ALTO ADIGE

Upper Arlington city *cen* Ohio W of Columbus *pop* 33,771

Upper Canada the Canadian province 1791–1841 corresponding to the S part of modern Ont. — see LOWER CANADA

Upper Karoo — see KAROO

Upper Klamath Lake lake 30 *mi* (48 *km*) long S Oreg. SSE of Crater Lake drained by Klamath River — see LOWER KLAMATH LAKE

Upper Palatinate — see PALATINATE

Upper Peninsula the N part of Mich. bet. Lake Superior to the N & Lakes Michigan & Huron to the S

Upper Volta — see BURKINA FASO — **Upper Vol·tan** \ˈväl-tᵊn, ˈvōl-, ˈvȯl-\ *adj or n*

Upp·sa·la \ˈüp-ˌsä-lə, ˈəp-, -lä\ city E Sweden NNW of Stockholm *pop* 179,673

Ur \ˈər, ˈu̇r\ city of ancient Sumer; site in S Iraq NW of Basra

Ural \ˈyu̇r-əl\ river *over* 1500 *mi* (2414 *km*) Russia & Kazakhstan rising at S end of Ural Mountains & flowing S into the Caspian

Ural Mountains mountain system Russia & Kazakhstan extending from Kara Sea to steppes N of Aral Sea; usu. considered the dividing line bet. Asia & Europe; highest peak Narodnaya 6214 *ft* (1894 *m*)

Uralsk — see ORAL

Ura·ri·coe·ra \ˌü-ˌrär-i-ˈkwer-ə\ river *ab* 300 *mi* (483 *km*) N Brazil, a headstream of the Rio Branco

Ura·wa \ü-ˈrä-wä\ city Japan in Honshu N of Tokyo *pop* 484,845

Ur·bana \ˌər-ˈba-nə\ city E *cen* Ill. *pop* 41,250

Ur·ban·dale \ˈər-bən-ˌdāl\ city S *cen* Iowa *pop* 39,463

Ur·bi·no \u̇r-ˈbē-(ˌ)nō\ commune *cen* Italy *pop* 15,240

Urfa — see ŞANLIURFA

Urga — see ULAANBAATAR

Uri \ˈu̇r-ē\ canton *cen* Switzerland S of Lake of Lucerne ✻ Altdorf *area* 415 *sq mi* (1079 *sq km*), *pop* 35,000

Uru·bam·ba \ˌü-rü-ˈbäm-bä\ river 450 *mi* (724 *km*) *cen* Peru flowing NNW to unite with the Apurímac forming the Ucayali

Uru·guay \ˈu̇r-ə-ˌgwī, ˈyu̇r-; ˈyu̇r-ə-ˌgwā; ˌü-rü-ˈgwī\ 1 river *ab* 1000 *mi* (1609 *km*) SE S. America rising in Brazil & flowing into the Río de la Plata 2 *or* **Re·pú·bli·ca Ori·en·tal del Uru·guay** \rā-ˈpü-blē-(ˌ)kä-ˌȯr-ē-ˌen-ˈtäl-thel-\ *or formerly* **Ban·da Ori·en·tal** \ˈbän-də-ˌȯr-ē-ˌen-ˈtäl\ country SE S. America bet. the lower Uruguay & the Atlantic; a republic ✻ Montevideo *area* 68,039 *sq mi* (176,221 *sq km*), *pop* 3,241,003 — **Uru·guay·an** \ˌu̇r-ə-ˈgwī-ən, ˌyu̇r-; ˌyu̇r-ə-ˈgwā-\ *adj or n*

Ürüm·qi \ˈue-ˈrue̅m-ˈchē\ *or* **Urum·chi** \u̇-ˈru̇m-chē, ˌu̇r-əm-ˈ\ *or* **Wu·lu–mu–ch'i** \ˈwü-ˈlü-ˈmü-ˈchē\ city NW China ✻ of Xinjiang Uygur on N side of Tian Shan *pop* 1,046,898

Urundi — see BURUNDI

Ushant — see OUESSANT, ÎLE D'

Us·hua·ia \ü-ˈswī-ä\ town S Argentina on S coast of Tierra del Fuego Is.; southernmost city in the world, at 54°48'S *pop* 45,430

Usk \ˈəsk\ river 60 *mi* (96 *km*) S Wales & W England flowing E & S into Severn estuary

Üs·kü·dar \ˌu̇s-kue-ˈdär\ suburb of Istanbul, Turkey, on Asian side of the Bosporus

Us·pal·la·ta Pass \ˌüs-pä-ˈyä-tä, -ˈzhä-\ *or* **La Cum·bre** \lä-ˈküm-(ˌ)brā\ mountain pass (12,572 *ft or* 3832 *m*) & tunnel S S. America in the Andes bet. Mendoza, Argentina & Santiago, Chile

Us·su·ri \u̇-ˈsu̇r-ē\ river 365 *mi* (587 *km*) E Asia on border bet. Russia & China flowing N into the Amur

Usti nad La·bem \ˈüs-tē-ˈnäd-lä-ˌbem\ city NW Czech Republic in N Bohemia on the Elbe *pop* 95,436

Ustinov — see IZHEVSK

Usumbura — see BUJUMBURA

Utah \ˈyü-ˌtȯ, -ˌtä\ state W U.S. ✻ Salt Lake City *area* 84,899 *sq mi* (219,888 *sq km*), *pop* 2,763,885 — **Utah·an** \-ˌtȯ(-ə)n, -ˌtä(-ə)n\ *adj or n* — **Utahn** \-ˌtȯ(-ə)n, -ˌtä(-ə)n\ *n*

Utah Lake lake 23 *mi* (37 *km*) long N *cen* Utah drained by Jordan River

Uti·ca \ˈyü-ti-kə\ 1 city E *cen* N.Y. on Mohawk River *pop* 62,235 2 ancient city N Africa on Mediterranean coast NW of Carthage

Utrecht \ˈyü-ˌtrekt, ˈue-ˌtrekt\ 1 province *cen* Netherlands S of the IJsselmeer *area* 538 *sq mi* (1393 *sq km*), *pop* 1,139,925 2 city, its ✻ *pop* 260,625

Utsu·no·mi·ya \ˌüt-sə-ˈnō-mē-ˌyä\ city Japan in *cen* Honshu N of Tokyo *pop* 443,808

Ut·ta·ra·khand \ˈü-tä-rä-ˌkänd\ *or formerly* **Ut·ta·ran·chal** \ˈu̇-tə-ˌrän-chəl\ state N India ✻ Dehra Dun *area* 24,385 *sq mi* (63,157 *sq km*), *pop* 8,479,562

Ut·tar Pra·desh \ˌu̇-tər-prə-ˈdesh, -ˈdāsh\ state N India bordering on Tibet & Nepal ✻ Lucknow *area* 89,270 *sq mi* (231,209 *sq km*), *pop* 166,052,859 — see UNITED PROVINCES

Utua·do \ü-ˈtwä-thō\ city W *cen* Puerto Rico *pop* 33,149

Ux·bridge \ˈəks-(ˌ)brij\ former municipal borough SE England in Middlesex, now part of Hillingdon

Ux·mal \üsh-ˈmäl, üs-\ site of ancient Mayan city SE Mexico in W Yucatán

Uz·bek·i·stan \(ˌ)u̇z-ˌbe-ki-ˈstan, ˌəz-, -ˈstän; -ˈbe-ki-ˌ\ country W *cen* Asia E of the Amu Dar'ya; a constituent republic (**Uz·bek Republic** \ˈu̇z-ˌbek, ˈəz-, u̇z-ˈ\) of the U.S.S.R. 1924–91 ✻ Tashkent *area* 173,591 *sq mi* (449,601 *sq km*), *pop* 25,640,000

Uzh·go·rod \ˈu̇zh-gə-rət\ *or Ukrainian* **Uzh·ho·rod** \ˈüzh-hȯ-ˌrȯd\ city SW Ukraine ✻ of Zakarpats'ka *pop* 123,000

Vaal \ˈväl\ river 720 *mi* (1158 *km*) Republic of South Africa rising in Mpumalanga & flowing W into Orange River in Northern Cape

Vaa·sa *or Sw* **Va·sa** \ˈvä-sə\ city & port W Finland *pop* 57,014

Vac·a·ville \ˈva-kə-ˌvil\ city W Calif. SW of Sacramento *pop* 92,428

Va·do·da·ra \və-ˈdō-də-ˌrä\ *or* **Ba·ro·da** \bə-ˈrō-də\ city W India in SE Gujarat SE of Ahmadabad *pop* 1,306,035

Va·duz \vä-ˈdüts\ commune ✻ of Liechtenstein on the Rhine *pop* 4949

Váh \ˈvä(k)\ *or Hung* **Vág** \ˈväg\ river over 240 *mi* (386 *km*) W Slovakia rising in Tatry Mountains & flowing W & S into the Danube

Va·lais \va-ˈlā\ *or G* **Wal·lis** \ˈvä-lis\ canton SW *cen* Switzerland bordering on France & Italy ✻ Sion *area* 2020 *sq mi* (5232 *sq km*), *pop* 278,200

Val·dai Hills \väl-ˈdī\ hills W Russia in Europe SE of Lake Il'men'; highest point 1053 *ft* (321 *m*)

Val–d'Or \ˈval-ˌdȯr\ town Canada in SW Que. *pop* 31,862

Val·dos·ta \val-ˈdäs-tə\ city S Ga. *pop* 54,518

Va·lence \va-ˈläⁿs\ commune SE France S of Lyon *pop* 64,222

Va·len·cia \və-ˈlen(t)-sh(ē-)ə, -sē-ə\ 1 region & ancient kingdom E Spain bet. Andalusia & Catalonia 2 province E Spain *area* 4156 *sq mi* (10,764 *sq km*), *pop* 2,216,285 3 commune & port on the Mediterranean, its ✻ *pop* 738,441 4 city N Venezuela WSW of Caracas *pop* 1,200,000

Va·len·ci·ennes \və-ˌlen(t)-sē-ˈen(z)\ city N France *pop* 41,251

Va·len·tia \və-ˈlen(t)-sh(ē-)ə\ island SW Ireland in County Kerry in the Atlantic S of entrance to Dingle Bay

Vale of Glamorgan administrative area of S Wales *area* 130 *sq mi* (337 *sq km*)

Val·la·do·lid \ˌva-lə-də-ˈlid, ˌvä-yä-thō-ˈlēth\ 1 province NW *cen* Spain *area* 3166 *sq mi* (8200 *sq km*), *pop* 498,094 2 commune, its ✻, NNW of Madrid *pop* 316,580

Val·lau·ris \ˌvä-lō-ˈrēs\ village SE France NE of Cannes *pop* 25,765

Val·le d'Ao·sta \ˌvä-lā-dä-ˈȯs-tä\ *or* **Val d'Ao·sta** \ˌväl-dä-\ autonomous region NW Italy bordering on France & Switzerland NW of Piedmont ✻ Aosta *area* 1260 *sq mi* (3263 *sq km*), *pop* 120,589

Val·le·jo \və-ˈlā-(ˌ)ō\ city W Calif. on San Pablo Bay *pop* 115,942

Val·let·ta \və-ˈle-tə\ city & port ✻ of Malta *pop* 7200

Valleyfield — see SALABERRY-DE-VALLEYFIELD

Valley of Ten Thousand Smokes volcanic region SW Alaska in Katmai National Park

Valley Stream village SE N.Y. on Long Is. *pop* 37,511

Va·lois \ˈval-ˌwä, väl-ˈwä\ medieval county & duchy N France in NE Île-de-France ✻ Crépy-en-Valois

Valona — see VLORË

Val·pa·rai·so 1 \ˌval-pə-ˈrā-(ˌ)zō\ city NW Ind. SE of Gary *pop* 31,730 2 \-ˈrī-(ˌ)zō, -ˈrā-\ *or Sp* **Val·pa·ra·í·so** \ˌväl-pä-rä-ˈē-sō\ city & port, seat of legislature of Chile WNW of Santiago *pop* 275,982

Van \ˈvan\ salt lake E Turkey in Asia *area* 1419 *sq mi* (3675 *sq km*)

Van·cou·ver \van-ˈkü-vər\ 1 city SW Wash. on Columbia River opposite Portland, Oreg. *pop* 161,791 2 city & port Canada in SW B.C. on Burrard Inlet *pop* 603,502 — **Van·cou·ver·ite** \-və-ˌrīt\ *n*

Vancouver, Mount mountain 15,700 *ft* (4785 *m*) on Alaska-Yukon boundary in St. Elias Range

Vancouver Island island W Canada in B.C. off SW coast; chief city Victoria *area* 12,408 *sq mi* (32,261 *sq km*)

Van Die·men Gulf \van-ˈdē-mən\ inlet of Arafura Sea N Australia in N Northern Territory

Van Diemen's Land — see TASMANIA

\ə\ **abut** \ᵊ\ **kitten**, F **table** \ər\ **further** \a\ **ash** \ā\ **ace** \ä\ **mop, mar**
\au̇\ **out** \ch\ **chin** \e\ **bet** \ē\ **easy** \g\ **go** \i\ **hit** \ī\ **ice** \j\ **job**
\ŋ\ **sing** \ō\ **go** \ȯ\ **law** \ȯi\ **boy** \th\ **thin** \th\ **the** \ü\ **loot** \u̇\ **foot**
\y\ **yet** \zh\ **vision, beige** \k, ⁿ, œ, ue, ʸ\ *see* Guide to Pronunciation

Vä·nern \ˈve-nərn\ lake SW Sweden *area* 2156 *sq mi* (5584 *sq km*)
Van·taa \ˈvän-(ˌ)tä\ town S Finland N of Helsinki *pop* 179,856
Va·nua Le·vu \və-ˌnü-ə-ˈle-(ˌ)vü, ˌvän-wä-ˈlā-\ island S. Pacific in the Fijis NE of Viti Levu *area* 2137 *sq mi* (5535 *sq km*)
Van·u·atu \ˌvan-ˌwä-ˈtü, ˌvän- *also* -ˈwä-(ˌ)tü\ *or formerly* **New Heb·ri·des** \ˈhe-brə-ˌdēz\ islands SW Pacific W of Fiji; formerly under joint Brit. & French administration; a republic since 1980 ✻ Port-Vila (on Efate) *area* 5700 *sq mi* (14,820 *sq km*), *pop* 186,678
Va·ra·na·si \və-ˈrä-nə-sē\ *or* **Ba·na·ras** *or* **Be·na·res** \bə-ˈnär-əs\ city N India in SE Uttar Pradesh *pop* 1,100,748
Var·dar \ˈvär-ˌdär\ river 241 *mi* (388 *km*) Macedonia (country) & N Greece flowing S into Gulf of Salonika
Va·re·se \vä-ˈrā-sā\ commune N Italy NW of Milan *pop* 83,830
Var·na \ˈvär-nə\ *or formerly* **Sta·lin** \ˈstä-lən, ˈsta-, -ˌlēn\ city & port E Bulgaria on Black Sea *pop* 314,913
Väs·ter·ås \ˌves-tə-ˈrōs\ city E Sweden on Mälaren Lake NW of Stockholm *pop* 128,902
Vaté — see EFATE
Vat·i·can City \ˈva-ti-kən\ *or It* **Cit·tà del Va·ti·ca·no** \chēt-ˈtä-del-ˌvä-tē-ˈkä-nō\ independent papal state within commune of Rome, Italy; created Feb. 11, 1929 *area* 109 *acres* (43 *hectares*), *pop* 467
Vät·tern \ˈve-tərn\ lake S Sweden *area* 738 *sq mi* (1911 *sq km*)
Vaud \ˈvō\ *or G* **Waadt** \ˈvät\ canton W Switzerland N of Lake Geneva ✻ Lausanne *area* 1240 *sq mi* (3212 *sq km*), *pop* 626,200
Vau·dreuil–Do·ri·on \vō-ˌdrœ-ē-ˈdȯr-ē-ˌō^{n}\ town Canada in S Que. *pop* 33,305
Vaughan \ˈvȯn, ˈvän\ city Canada in SE Ont. N of Toronto *pop* 288,301
Vaupés — see UAUPÉS
Ve·ga Al·ta \ˈvā-gə-ˈäl-tə\ city N Puerto Rico *pop* 39,951
Ve·ga Ba·ja \ˈvā-gə-ˈbä-(ˌ)hä\ municipality N Puerto Rico *pop* 59,662
Vegas LAS VEGAS
Ve·ii \ˈvē-ˌī, ˈvā-\ ancient city of Etruria in *cen* Italy NNW of Rome
Vej·le \ˈvī-lə\ city & port Denmark *pop* 50,879
Vel·bert \ˈfel-bərt\ city W Germany in N. Rhine-Westphalia in Ruhr valley NE of Düsseldorf *pop* 89,347
Vel·la La·vel·la \ˈve-lə-lə-ˈve-lə\ island SW Pacific in *cen* Solomons
Vel·lore \və-ˈlȯr, ve-\ city SE India in N Tamil Nadu *pop* 177,413
Vel·sen \ˈvel-sən, -zən\ commune W Netherlands; outer port for Amsterdam *pop* 67,407
Vence \ˈvä^{n}s\ commune SE France W of Nice *pop* 16,970
Ven·da \ˈven-də\ former black enclave in the Republic of South Africa ✻ Thohoyandou; granted independence 1979; abolished 1994
Ven·dée \vä^{n}-ˈdā\ *or* **La Vendée** \lä-\ region W France bordering on Bay of Biscay S of Brittany
Ven·dôme \vä^{n}-ˈdōm\ town N *cen* France WSW of Orléans
Ve·ne·tia \və-ˈnē-sh(ē-)ə\ *or It* **Ve·ne·zia** \ve-ˈnet-sē-ä\ **1** area NE Italy, W Slovenia, & W Croatia including territory bet. the lower Po & the Alps **2** VENEZIA EUGANEA — **Ve·ne·tian** \-ˈnē-shən\ *adj*
Ve·ne·to \ˈve-nä-ˌtō, ˈvā-\ region NE Italy comprising most of Venezia Euganea ✻ Venice *area* 7096 *sq mi* (18,379 *sq km*), *pop* 4,540,853
Ve·ne·zia Eu·ga·nea \vā-ˈnet-sē-ä-ˌā-ü-ˈgä-nē-ä\ the S portion of Venetia
Venezia Giu·lia \ˈjül-yä\ the E portion of Venetia including Julian Alps & Istria; now mainly in Slovenia & Croatia
Venezia Tri·den·ti·na \ˌtrē-ˌden-ˈtē-nä\ the NW portion of Venetia N of Lake Garda; included in Trentino-Alto Adige region
Ven·e·zu·e·la \ˌve-nə-ˈzwā-lə, -zə-ˈwā-; ˌbā-nā-ˈswā-lä\ country N S. America; a republic ✻ Caracas *area* 352,143 *sq mi* (912,050 *sq km*), *pop* 29,000,000 — **Ven·e·zu·e·lan** \-lən\ *adj or n*
Venezuela, Gulf of inlet of the Caribbean NW Venezuela N of Lake Maracaibo
Ven·ice \ˈve-nəs\ *or It* **Ve·ne·zia** \ve-ˈnet-sē-ä\ *or L* **Ve·ne·tia** \və-ˈnē-sh(ē-)ə\ city & port NE Italy ✻ of Veneto, on islands in **Lagoon of Venice** (inlet of Gulf of Venice) *pop* 275,368 — **Ve·ne·tian** \və-ˈnē-shən\ *adj or n*
Venice, Gulf of arm of the Adriatic bet. Po Delta & Istria
Ven·lo *or* **Ven·loo** \ˈven-(ˌ)lō\ commune SE Netherlands on Maas (Meuse) River near German border *pop* 91,400
Ven·ta \ˈven-tə\ river 217 *mi* (349 *km*) in Lithuania & Latvia flowing into the Baltic
Ven·ti·mi·glia \ˌven-tē-ˈmēl-yä\ commune NW Italy on Ligurian Sea W of San Remo near Menton, France *pop* 26,725
Vents·pils \ˈvent-ˌspils, -ˌspilz\ *or G* **Win·dau** \ˈvin-ˌdau̇\ city & port Latvia at mouth of the Venta *pop* 44,004
Ven·tu·ra \ven-ˈtu̇r-ə, -ˈtyu̇r-\ *or officially* **San Buen·a·ven·tu·ra** \(ˌ)san-ˌbwe-nə-ˌven-\ city & port SW Calif. on Santa Barbara Channel ESE of Santa Barbara *pop* 106,433
Venue, Ben — see BEN VENUE
Ve·ra·cruz \ˌver-ə-ˈkrüz, -ˈkrüs\ **1** state E Mexico ✻ Jalapa *area* 28,114 *sq mi* (72,815 *sq km*), *pop* 6,228,239 **2** city & port E Mexico in Veracruz state on Gulf of Mexico *pop* 327,522
Ver·cel·li \ver-ˈche-lē, (ˌ)vər-\ commune NW Italy *pop* 48,016
Verde, Cape \ˈvərd\ *or* **Cap Vert** \ˌkäp-ˈver\ promontory W Africa in Senegal; westernmost point in Africa, at 17°30′ W
Ver·di·gris \ˈvər-də-grəs\ river 351 *mi* (565 *km*) SE Kans. & NE Okla. flowing into Arkansas River
Ver·dun \(ˌ)vər-ˈdən, ver-\ **1** former town Canada in S Que. on Montreal Is., now part of Montreal (city) **2** *or* **Verdun–sur–Meuse** \-ˌsu̇r-\ city NE France on the Meuse ESE of Reims *pop* 19,624
Ver·ee·ni·ging \fə-ˈrā-nə-giŋ, -nə-k̲əŋ\ city NE Republic of South Africa in Gauteng on the Vaal S of Johannesburg *pop* 94,500
Verkhneudinsk — see ULAN-UDE
Ver·mont \vər-ˈmänt\ state NE U.S. ✻ Montpelier *area* 9609 *sq mi* (24,983 *sq km*), *pop* 625,741 — **Ver·mont·er** \-ˈmän-tər\ *n*
Ver·non \ˈvər-nən\ **1** town N *cen* Conn. NE of Hartford *pop* 29,179 **2** city Canada in S B.C. *pop* 38,150
Vernyi — see ALMATY
Vé·roia \ˈver-yä\ *or anc* **Be·rea** *or* **Be·roea** \bə-ˈrē-ə\ town NE Greece in Macedonia W of Thessaloníki
Ve·ro·na \ve-ˈrō-nä\ commune NE Italy on the Adige *pop* 257,477 — **Ver·o·nese** \ˌver-ə-ˈnēz, -ˈnēs\ *adj or n*
Ver·sailles \(ˌ)vər-ˈsī, ver-\ city N France, WSW suburb of Paris *pop* 85,761
Ves·ta·via Hills \ve-ˈstā-vē-ə\ city *cen* Ala. S of Birmingham *pop* 34,033
Ves·ter·ål·en \ˈves-tə-ˌrȯ-lən\ island group Norway off NW coast NE of Lofoten island group
Ve·su·vi·us \və-ˈsü-vē-əs\ *or It* **Ve·su·vio** \vā-ˈsü-vyō, -ˈzü-\ volcano 4190 *ft* (1277 *m*) Italy in Campania on Bay of Naples
Vet·lu·ga \vet-ˈlü-gə\ river 528 *mi* (850 *km*) *cen* Russia in Europe flowing S into the Volga
Ve·vey \və-ˈvā\ commune W Switzerland in Vaud *pop* 16,139
Vi·cen·te Ló·pez \vē-ˈsen-tē-ˈlō-ˌpez, -ˌpes\ city E Argentina, N suburb of Buenos Aires, on Río de la Plata *pop* 289,142
Vi·cen·za \vē-ˈchen-sä\ commune NE Italy W of Venice *pop* 110,454
Vi·chu·ga \vi-ˈchü-gə\ city *cen* Russia in Europe *pop* 49,700
Vi·chy \ˈvi-shē, ˈvē-\ commune *cen* France on the Allier *pop* 26,501
Vicks·burg \ˈviks-ˌbərg\ city W Miss. *pop* 23,856
Vic·to·ria \vik-ˈtȯr-ē-ə\ **1** city SE Tex. on Guadalupe River *pop* 62,592 **2** city Canada ✻ of B.C. on SE Vancouver Is. *pop* 80,017 **3** river 350 *mi* (563 *km*) Australia in NW Northern Territory flowing N & NW to Timor Sea **4** state SE Australia ✻ Melbourne *area* 87,884 *sq mi* (228,498 *sq km*), *pop* 4,244,221 **5** *or* **Hong Kong** \ˈhäŋ-ˌkäŋ, -ˈkäŋ; ˈhȯŋ-ˌkȯŋ, -ˈkȯŋ\ city & port Hong Kong special administrative region, China on NW Hong Kong Is.; served as ✻ of Hong Kong colony *pop* 1,035,000 — **Vic·to·ri·an** \vik-ˈtȯr-ē-ən\ *adj or n*
Victoria, Lake lake E Africa in Tanzania, Kenya, & Uganda *area* 26,828 *sq mi* (69,484 *sq km*)
Victoria Falls waterfall 355 *ft* (108 *m*) S Africa in the Zambezi on border bet. Zambia & Zimbabwe
Victoria Island island N Canada SE of Banks Is. *area* 81,930 *sq mi* (213,018 *sq km*)
Victoria Land region E Antarctica S of New Zealand on W shore of Ross Sea & Ross Ice Shelf
Victoria Nile — see NILE
Vic·to·ri·a·ville \vik-ˈtȯr-ē-ə-ˌvil\ town Canada in S Que. *pop* 43,462
Vic·tor·ville \ˈvik-tər-ˌvil\ city SE Calif. N of San Bernardino *pop* 115,903
Vied·ma \ˈvyād-mä\ town S *cen* Argentina *pop* 46,948
Vi·en·na \vē-ˈe-nə, -ˈa-\ *or G* **Wien** \ˈvēn\ city ✻ of Austria on the Danube *pop* 1,550,123 — **Vi·en·nese** \ˌvē-ə-ˈnēz, -ˈnēs\ *adj or n*
Vi·enne \vē-ˈen\ **1** river 217 *mi* (349 *km*) SW *cen* France flowing NW into the Loire **2** city SE France on the Rhône *pop* 29,930
Vien·tiane \(ˌ)vyen-ˈtyän\ city ✻ of Laos, near Thailand border *pop* 200,000
Vie·ques \vē-ˈā-kās\ island W. Indies off E Puerto Rico, belonging to Puerto Rico *pop* 9301; chief town Isabel Segunda
Vierwaldstätter See — see LUCERNE (Lake of)
Viet·nam \vē-ˈet-ˈnäm, vyet-, ˌvē-ət-, vēt-, -ˈnam\ country SE Asia in Indochina; state, including Tonkin & N Annam, set up 1945–46; with S Annam & Cochin China, an associated state of French Union 1950–54; after civil war, divided 1954–75 at 17th parallel into republics of **North Vietnam** (✻ Hanoi) & **South Vietnam** (✻ Saigon); reunited 1975 ✻ Hanoi *area* 127,207 *sq mi* (330,738 *sq km*), *pop* 87,100,000
Vi·go \ˈvē-(ˌ)gō\ city & port NW Spain on **Vigo Bay** (inlet of the Atlantic) *pop* 280,186
Viipuri — see VYBORG
Vi·ja·ya·na·gar \ˌvi-jə-yə-ˈnə-gər\ Hindu kingdom (1336–1565) S India S of the Krishna
Vi·ja·ya·wa·da \ˌvi-jə-yə-ˈwä-də\ *or formerly* **Bez·wa·da** \be-ˈzwä-də\ city SE India in E Andhra Pradesh on the Krishna *pop* 825,436
Vila — see PORT-VILA
Vi·la No·va de Ga·ia \ˈvē-lə-ˈnȯ-və-dē-ˈgī-ə\ city NW Portugal, just S of Porto *pop* 288,749
Villa Cisneros — see DAKHLA
Villa Gustavo A. Madero — see GUSTAVO A. MADERO (Villa)
Vil·la·her·mo·sa \ˌvē-yä-ˌer-ˈmō-sä\ city SE Mexico ✻ of Tabasco state *pop* 158,216
Vil·lal·ba \vē-ˈyäl-bä\ city S *cen* Puerto Rico *pop* 26,073
Ville·franche \ˌvēl-ˈfrä^{n}sh, ˌvē-lə-\ **1** *or* **Villefranche–sur–Mer** \-sœr-ˈmer\ commune & port SE France E of Nice *pop* 6825 **2** *or* **Villefranche–sur–Saône** \-ˈsōn\ commune E *cen* France NNW of Lyon *pop* 30,630
Vil·leur·banne \(ˌ)vē-ˌyœr-ˈban, -ˈbän\ commune E France, E suburb of Lyon *pop* 124,152
Vil·ni·us \ˈvil-nē-əs\ city ✻ of Lithuania *pop* 542,287
Vi·lyui *or* **Vi·lyuy** \vil-ˈyü-ē\ river *over* 1500 *mi* (2410 *km*) *cen* Russia in Asia flowing E into the Lena
Vim·i·nal \ˈvi-mə-n^{ə}l\ hill in Rome, Italy, one of seven upon which the ancient city was built — see AVENTINE
Vi·my Ridge \ˈvē-mē, vi-ˈmē\ ridge near Vimy commune (*pop* 4672) N France N of Arras
Vi·ña del Mar \ˈvē-nyä-(ˌ)t̲h̲el-ˈmär\ city & port *cen* Chile E of Valparaiso *pop* 286,931
Vin·cennes \va^{n}-ˈsen\ commune N France E of Paris *pop* 43,580
Vin·dhya Mountains \ˈvin-dyə, -dē-ə\ mountain range N *cen* India N of & parallel to the Narmada River
Vindhya Pra·desh \prə-ˈdesh, -ˈdāsh\ former state NE *cen* India ✻ Rewa; became (1956) part of Madhya Pradesh
Vine·land \ˈvīn-lənd\ city S N.J. *pop* 60,724
Vineyard, the MARTHA'S VINEYARD
Vin·land \ˈvin-lənd\ a portion of the coast of N. America visited & so called by Norse voyagers *ab* A.D. 1000; thought to be located along the Atlantic in what is now E or NE Canada
Vin·ny·tsya *or* **Vin·ni·tsa** \ˈvi-nət-syə\ city W *cen* Ukraine *pop* 381,000
Vin·son Massif \ˈvin(t)-sən\ mountain 16,066 *ft* (4897 *m*) W Antarctica S of Ellsworth Land in Ellsworth Mountains; highest in Antarctica
Vir·gin \ˈvər-jən\ river 200 *mi* (322 *km*) SW Utah & SE Nev. flowing to Lake Mead
Vir·gin·ia \vər-ˈji-nyə, -ˈji-nē-ə\ state E U.S. ✻ Richmond *area* 40,767 *sq mi* (105,586 *sq km*), *pop* 8,001,024 — **Vir·gin·ian** \-nyən, -nē-ən\ *adj or n*
Virginia Beach city SE Va. on the Atlantic *pop* 437,994
Virginia Capes Cape Charles & Cape Henry in Va. forming entrance to Chesapeake Bay
Virgin Islands group of islands W. Indies E of Puerto Rico — see BRITISH VIRGIN ISLANDS, VIRGIN ISLANDS OF THE UNITED STATES
Virgin Islands Coral Reef National Monument reservation U.S. Virgin Islands in waters surrounding St. John Is.

Virgin Islands National Park scenic and historic area W. Indies in Virgin Islands of the U.S. on and around St. John Is.

Virgin Islands of the United States the W islands of the Virgin Islands group including St. Croix, St. John, & St. Thomas; a territory ✳ Charlotte Amalie (on St. Thomas Is.) *area* 132 *sq mi* (343 *sq km*), *pop* 108,612 — see DANISH WEST INDIES

Vi·run·ga \vē-'rùŋ-gä\ volcanic mountain range E *cen* Africa in E Democratic Republic of the Congo, SW Uganda, & NW Rwanda N of Lake Kivu; highest peak Karisimbi 14,780 *ft* (4505 *m*)

Vi·sa·lia \vī-'sāl-yə\ city S *cen* Calif. SE of Fresno *pop* 124,442

Vi·sa·yan \və-'sī-ən\ islands *cen* Philippines bet. Luzon & Mindanao — see BOHOL, CEBU, LEYTE, MASBATE, NEGROS, PANAY, ROMBLON, SAMAR

Vis·by \'viz-bē\ city & port Sweden on Gotland Is. in the Baltic *pop* 19,319

Vish·a·kha·pat·nam \vi-,shä-kə-'pət-nəm\ *or* **Vis·a·kha·pat·nam** \vi-,sä-\ city & port E India in NE Andhra Pradesh *pop* 969,608

Vis·lin·ski Za·liv \vis-'lin-skē-zä-'lyif\ *or Pol* **Za·lew Wiś·la·ny** \'zä-lef-vēsh-'lä-nē\ *or G* **Fri·sches Haff** \'fri-shəs-,häf\ lagoon N Poland & W Russia in Europe; inlet of Gulf of Gdańsk

Vi·so \'vē-(,)zō\ mountain 12,602 *ft* (3841 *m*) NW Italy in Piedmont SW of Turin near French border; highest in Cottian Alps

Vis·ta \'vis-tə\ city SW Calif. N of San Diego *pop* 93,834

Vis·tu·la \'vis-chə-lə, 'vish-chə-, 'vis-tə-\ *or Pol* **Wis·ła** \'vē-(,)swä\ river *over* 660 *mi* (1062 *km*) Poland flowing N from the Carpathians into Gulf of Gdańsk

Vi·tebsk \'vē-,tepsk, -,tebsk, və-'\ *or* **Vit·syebsk** \'vēt-syipsk\ city NE Belarus on Dvina River *pop* 1,434,200

Vi·ter·bo \vi-'ter-(,)bō\ commune *cen* Italy in Lazio *pop* 60,387

Vi·ti Le·vu \,vē-tē-'le-(,)vü\ island SW Pacific, largest of the Fiji group *area* 4010 *sq mi* (10,386 *sq km*)

Vi·tim \və-'tēm\ river 1133 *mi* (1823 *km*) S Russia in Asia flowing NE & N into the Lena

Vi·to·ria \vi-'tòr-ē-ə\ *or* **Gas·teiz** \'gäsh-,tās\ city N Spain ✳ of Álava province SSE of Bilbao *pop* 216,852

Vi·tó·ria \vi-'tòr-ē-ə\ city & port E Brazil ✳ of Espírito Santo state *pop* 292,304

Vi·try–sur–Seine \vē-,trē-,sur-'sän, -'sen\ commune N France, SSE suburb of Paris *pop* 78,908

Viz·ca·ya \vēs-'kī-ä\ *or* **Bis·ca·ya** \bēs-\ *or* **Bis·cay** \'bis-,kā, -kē\ province N Spain on Bay of Biscay; in Basque Country ✳ Bilbao *area* 853 *sq mi* (2209 *sq km*), *pop* 1,122,637

Vlaanderen — see FLANDERS

Vlaar·ding·en \'vlär-diŋ-ə(n)\ commune & port SW Netherlands W of Rotterdam *pop* 73,935

Vlad·i·kav·kaz \,vla-di-kəf-'kaz, -,käf-'käz, -,kaf-'kaz\ *or 1932–43 & 1955–91* **Or·dzha·ni·kid·ze** \,òr-jä-nə-'kid-zə\ *or 1944–54* **Dzau·dzhi·kau** \(d)zaù-'jē-,kaù\ city S Russia in Europe *pop* 325,000

Vla·di·mir \'vla-də-,mir, vlə-'dē-,mir\ city *cen* Russia in Europe on the Klyaz'ma E of Moscow *pop* 356,000

Vlad·i·vos·tok \,vla-də-və-'stäk, -'väs-,täk\ city & port SE Russia in Asia ✳ of Maritime Territory *pop* 648,000

Vlis·sing·en \'vli-siŋ-ə(n)\ *or* **Flush·ing** \'flə-shiŋ\ city & port SW Netherlands in Zeeland

Vlo·rë \'vlòr-ə\ *or* **Va·lo·na** \və-'lō-nə\ *or formerly* **Av·lo·na** \av-'lō-nə\ city & port S Albania *pop* 147,128

Vlta·va \'vəl-tə-və\ river 270 *mi* (434 *km*) W Czech Republic in Bohemia flowing N into the Elbe

Vogelkop — see DOBERAI

Voiotía — see BOEOTIA

Voj·vo·di·na \'vòi-vò-,dē-nä\ province N Serbia; chief city Novi Sad *area* 8683 *sq mi* (22,576 *sq km*), *pop* 2,012,605

Volcano Islands *or Jp* **Ka·zan Ret·to** \,kä-,zän-'re-(,)tō\ islands W Pacific S of Bonin Islands; belong to Japan; under U.S. control 1945–68 *area* 11 *sq mi* (28 *sq km*) — see IWO JIMA

Vol·ga \'väl-gə, 'vòl-, 'võl-\ river *ab* 2300 *mi* (3700 *km*) Russia in Europe rising in Valdai Hills & flowing into the Caspian

Vol·go·grad \'väl-gə-,grad, 'vòl-, 'võl-, -,grät\ *or formerly* **Sta·lin·grad** \'stä-lən-,grad, 'sta-, -,grät\ *or* **Tsa·ri·tsyn** \(t)sə-'rēt-sən\ city S Russia in Europe on the Volga *pop* 1,006,000

Vo·log·da \'vò-ləg-də\ city *cen* Russia in Europe NNE of Moscow *pop* 290,000

Vó·los \'vò-,lòs\ city & port E Greece on Gulf of Vólos (inlet of the Aegean)

Vol·ta \'väl-tə, 'vòl-, 'võl-\ river W Africa flowing from Lake Volta (reservoir *area* 3275 *sq mi* or 8515 *sq km* receiving the Black Volta & White Volta) in N *cen* Ghana S into Bight of Benin — see RED VOLTA

Vol·ta Re·don·da \'väl-tə-ri-'dän-də, 'vòl-, 'võl-\ city E Brazil on Paraíba River NW of city of Rio de Janeiro *pop* 242,063

Vol·tur·no \väl-'tùr-(,)nō, vòl-, võl-\ river 110 *mi* (177 *km*) S *cen* Italy flowing from the Apennines SE & SW into Gulf of Gaeta

Vor·arl·berg \'fòr-,ärl-,bərg, -,berk\ province W Austria W of Tirol bordering on Switzerland ✳ Bregenz *pop* 333,128

Vo·ro·nezh \və-'rò-nish\ city S *cen* Russia in Europe near Don River *pop* 902,000

Voroshilovgrad — see LUHANS'K

Vor·skla \'vòr-sklə\ river Russia & Ukraine flowing into the Dnieper

Vosges \'vōzh\ mountains NE France on W side of Rhine valley; highest point 4672 *ft* (1424 *m*)

Voy·a·geurs National Park \,vòi-ə-'zhərz\ area of interconnected lakes N Minn. on Canadian border

Vrangelya — see WRANGEL

Vrystaat — see FREE STATE

Vun·tut National Park \'vùn-,tùt\ wilderness area NW Canada in NW Yukon on Alaska border

Vyat·ka \vē-'ät-kə\ **1** river *ab* 800 *mi* (1287 *km*) E *cen* Russia in Europe flowing into the Kama **2** — see KIROV

Vy·borg \'vē-,bòrg\ *or Finn* **Vii·pu·ri** \'vē-pü-rē\ city & port W Russia in Europe on arm of Gulf of Finland; belonged to Finland 1917–40 *pop* 81,100

Vy·cheg·da \'vi-chig-də\ river 700 *mi* (1120 *km*) NE *cen* Russia in Europe flowing W to the Northern Dvina

Waadt — see VAUD

Waal \'väl\ river Netherlands, the S branch of the lower Rhine

Wa·bash \'wò-,bash\ river 475 *mi* (764 *km*) Ind. & Ill. flowing into Ohio River

Wa·co \'wā-(,)kō\ city NE *cen* Tex. on the Brazos *pop* 124,805

Wad·den·zee \,vä-d°n-'zā\ inlet of North Sea N Netherlands bet. W. Frisian Islands & IJsselmeer

Wad·ding·ton, Mount \'wä-diŋ-tən\ mountain 13,176 *ft* (4016 *m*) W Canada in SW B.C. in Coast Mountains; highest in the province

Wadi al–'Arabah, Wadi 'Arabah, Wadi el–'Arabah — see 'ARABAH (Wadi)

Wad Me·da·ni \wäd-'me-də-nē\ city E *cen* Sudan on the Blue Nile *pop* 106,715

Wa·gram \'vä-,gräm\ village Austria NE of Vienna

Wai·a·le·a·le, Mount \wī-,ä-lā-'ä-lä\ mountain 5200 *ft* (1585 *m*) Hawaii in *cen* Kauai

Wai·ka·to \wī-'kä-(,)tō\ river 264 *mi* (425 *km*) New Zealand in NW North Is. flowing NW into Tasman Sea

Wai·ki·ki \,wī-ki-'kē, -,kē-\ resort section of Honolulu, Hawaii NW of Diamond Head on Waikiki Beach

Wai·ma·lu \wī-'mä-lü\ unincorporated population center Hawaii on Pearl Harbor, Oahu *pop* 13,730

Wai·mea Canyon \wī-'mā-ä\ gorge Hawaii on SW coast of Kauai

Wai·pa·hu \wī-'pä-(,)hü\ city Hawaii in SW Oahu *pop* 38,216

Wai·ta·ki \wī-'tä-kē\ river 130 *mi* (209 *km*) New Zealand in SE *cen* South Is. flowing ESE into the Pacific

Wa·ka·ya·ma \,wä-kä-'yä-mä\ city & port Japan in SW Honshu on Inland Sea *pop* 386,551

Wake·field \'wāk-,fēld\ **1** town E Mass. N of Boston *pop* 24,932 **2** city N England ✳ of W. Yorkshire *pop* 60,540

Wake Island \'wāk\ island N. Pacific N of Marshall Islands belonging to the U.S.

Wa·la·chia *or* **Wal·la·chia** \wä-'lā-kē-ə\ region S Romania bet. the Transylvanian Alps & the Danube; includes Muntenia & Oltenia; chief city Bucharest — **Wa·la·chi·an** *or* **Wal·la·chi·an** \-ən\ *adj or n*

Wał·brzych \'vaùb-,zhik, -,zhik\ *or G* **Wal·den·burg** \'wäl-dən-,bərg, 'väl-dən-,bùrk\ city SW Poland *pop* 141,139

Wal·deck \'väl-,dek\ former county, principality, & state of Germany bet. Westphalia & Hesse-Nassau ✳ Arolsen

Wal·den Pond \'wòl-dən\ pond NE Mass. S of Concord

Wales \'wālz\ *or W* **Cym·ru** \'kəm-,rē\ *or ML* **Cam·bria** \'kam-brē-ə\ principality SW Great Britain; a division of the United Kingdom of Great Britain and Northern Ireland ✳ Cardiff *area* 8016 *sq mi* (20,761 *sq km*), *pop* 2,903,085

Wal·la·sey \'wä-lə-sē\ town NW England in Merseyside on coast W of Liverpool *pop* 90,057

Wal·la Wal·la \'wä-lə-,wä-lə, 'wä-lə-,\ city SE Wash. *pop* 31,731

Wal·ling·ford \'wä-liŋ-fərd\ town S Conn. NNE of New Haven *pop* 45,135

Wallis — see VALAIS

Wal·lis Islands \'wä-ləs\ islands SW Pacific NE of Fiji Islands; with Futuna Islands, constitute a French overseas territory (**Wallis and Futuna Islands** *pop* 13,484)

Wal·lo·nia \wä-'lō-nē-ə\ semiautonomous region S Belgium *pop* 3,358,560

Wal·lops Island \'wä-ləps\ island E Va. in the Atlantic SW of Chincoteague Bay

Wal·lowa Mountains \wä-'laù-ə\ mountains NE Oreg. E of Blue Mountains; highest Sacajawea Peak 9838 *ft* (2999 *m*)

Walnut city SW Calif. E of Los Angeles *pop* 29,172

Walnut Canyon National Monument area containing cliff dwellings N *cen* Ariz. ESE of Flagstaff

Walnut Creek city W Calif. E of Berkeley *pop* 64,173

Wal·pole \'wòl-,pōl, 'wäl-\ town E Mass. SW of Boston *pop* 24,070

Wal·sall \'wòl-,sòl, -,säl\ town W *cen* England in W. Midlands NNW of Birmingham *pop* 255,600

Wal·tham \'wòl-,tham, *chiefly by outsiders* -thəm\ city E Mass. W of Boston *pop* 60,632

Waltham Forest \'wòl-thəm\ borough of NE Greater London, England *pop* 203,400

Wal·tham·stow \'wòl-thəm-,stō\ former municipal borough SE England in Essex, now part of Waltham Forest

Wal·vis Bay \'wòl-vəs\ town & port W Namibia on Walvis Bay (inlet of the Atlantic) W of Windhoek; formerly an exclave of Republic of South Africa forming a district *area* (of district) 434 *sq mi* (1124 *sq km*)

Wands·worth \'wän(d)z-(,)wərth\ borough of SW Greater London, England *pop* 237,500

Wang·a·nui \,wäŋ-gə-'nü-ē, ,wäŋ-ə-\ **1** river 180 *mi* (290 *km*) New Zealand in SW *cen* North Is. flowing into Tasman Sea **2** city & port New Zealand in North Is. on Tasman Sea *urban area pop* 39,423

Wan·ne–Eick·el \'vä-nə-'ī-kəl\ city W Germany in the Ruhr N of Bochum *pop* 100,300

Wan·stead and Wood·ford \'wän-stəd-°n-'wùd-fərd\ former municipal borough S England in Essex, now part of Redbridge

Wap·si·pin·i·con \,wäp-si-'pi-ni-kən\ river 225 *mi* (362 *km*) SE Minn. & E Iowa flowing SE into Mississippi River

Wa·pusk National Park \'wä-,pùsk\ wilderness area in Canada in NE Man. bordering Hudson Bay; protects polar bears & waterfowl

Wa·ran·gal \wə-'rəŋ-gəl\ city S *cen* India in N Andhra Pradesh NE of Hyderabad *pop* 528,570

War·bur·ton Creek \'wòr-bər-t°n\ river 275 *mi* (442 *km*) Australia in NE S. Australia flowing SW into Lake Eyre

War·ley \'wòr-lē\ town W *cen* England, a NW suburb of Birmingham *pop* 152,455

War·ner Rob·ins \'wòr-nər-'rä-bənz\ city *cen* Ga. *pop* 66,588

War·ren \'wòr-ən, 'wär-\ **1** city SE Mich. N of Detroit *pop* 134,056 **2** city NE Ohio NW of Youngstown *pop* 41,557

War·ring·ton \'wòr-iŋ-tən, 'wär-\ town NW England in Cheshire on the Mersey E of Liverpool *pop* 57,389

\ə\ **abut** \ᵊ\ **kitten**, F **table** \ər\ **further** \a\ **ash** \ā\ **ace** \ä\ **mop, mar**
\aù\ **out** \ch\ **chin** \e\ **bet** \ē\ **easy** \g\ **go** \i\ **hit** \ī\ **ice** \j\ **job**
\ŋ\ **sing** \ō\ **go** \ò\ **law** \òi\ **boy** \th\ **thin** \tẖ\ **the** \ü\ **loot** \ù\ **foot**
\y\ **yet** \zh\ **vision, beige** \ḵ, ⁿ, œ, ᴜ, ᵞ\ *see* Guide to Pronunciation

War·saw \'wȯr-ˌsȯ\ *or Pol* **War·sza·wa** \vär-'shä-vä\ *or G* **War·schau** \'vär-ˌshau̇\ city ✻ of Poland on the Vistula *pop* 1,655,063

War·ta \'vär-tə\ *or G* **War·the** \'vär-tə\ river 502 *mi* (808 *km*) Poland flowing NW & W into the Oder

War·wick \'wär-ik, *US also* 'wȯr-ik, 'wȯr-(ˌ)wik\ **1** city *cen* R.I. S of Providence on Narragansett Bay *pop* 82,672 **2** town *cen* England ✻ of Warwickshire *pop* 21,936

War·wick·shire \'wär-ik-ˌshir, -shər, *US also* 'wȯr-ik-, 'wȯr-(ˌ)wik-\ *or* **Warwick** county *cen* England ✻ Warwick *area* 792 *sq mi* (2051 *sq km*), *pop* 477,000

Wa·satch Range \'wȯ-ˌsach\ mountain range SE Idaho & N & *cen* Utah — see TIMPANOGOS (Mount)

Wash, The \'wȯsh, 'wäsh\ inlet of North Sea E England bet. Norfolk & Lincolnshire

Wash·ing·ton \'wȯ-shiŋ-tən, 'wä-, *chiefly Midland also* 'wȯr-shiŋ- *or* 'wär-\ **1** state NW U.S. ✻ Olympia *area* 68,192 *sq mi* (177,299 *sq km*), *pop* 6,724,540 **2** city ✻ of the U.S., coextensive with District of Columbia and often collectively referred to as **Washington, D.C.** *pop* 601,723 **3** — see TERAINA — **Wash·ing·to·nian** \ˌwȯ-shiŋ-'tō-nē-ən, ˌwä-, -nyən\ *adj or n*

Washington, Lake lake 20 *mi* (32 *km*) long W Wash. E of Seattle

Washington, Mount mountain 6288 *ft* (1916 *m*) N N.H.; highest in White Mountains

Wash·i·ta \'wä-shə-ˌtȯ, 'wȯ-\ river 500 *mi* (805 *km*) NW Tex. & SW Okla. flowing SE into Red River

Wa·tau·ga \wä-'tȯ-gə\ river 60 *mi* (96 *km*) NW N.C. & NE Tenn. flowing into S fork of the Holston

Watenstedt–Salzgitter — see SALZGITTER

Wa·ter·bury \'wȯ-tə(r)-ˌber-ē, 'wä-\ city W *cen* Conn. NNW of New Haven *pop* 110,366

Wa·ter·ee \'wȯ-tə-ˌrē, 'wä-\ river S.C., lower course of the Catawba — see CONGAREE

Wa·ter·ford \'wȯ-tər-fərd, 'wä-\ **1** county S Ireland in Munster *area* 710 *sq mi* (1846 *sq km*), *pop* 101,546 **2** city & port, its ✻ *pop* 44,594

Wa·ter·loo \ˌwȯ-tər-'lü, ˌwä-; 'wȯ-tər-ˌlü, 'wä-\ **1** city NE *cen* Iowa *pop* 68,406 **2** town *cen* Belgium S of Brussels *pop* 28,898 **3** city Canada in SE Ont. W of Kitchener *pop* 98,780

Wa·ter·ton–Glacier International Peace Park \'wȯ-tər-tən, 'wä-\ area of adjoining national parks on U.S.-Canada border in Rocky Mountains comprising **Glacier National Park** in NW Mont. & **Waterton Lakes National Park** in S Alta.

Wa·ter·town \'wȯ-tər-ˌtau̇n, 'wä-\ **1** city E Mass. W of Boston *pop* 31,915 **2** city N *cen* N.Y. SE of Kingston, Ont. *pop* 27,023

Wat·ford \'wät-fərd\ town SE England in Hertfordshire *pop* 72,100

Wat·son·ville \'wät-sən-ˌvil\ city W Calif. *pop* 51,199

Wat·ten·scheid \'vä-tᵊn-ˌshīt\ city W Germany E of Essen *pop* 80,527

Watts \'wäts\ section of Los Angeles, Calif. S of the downtown district

Wau·ke·gan \wȯ-'kē-gən\ city NE Ill. N of Chicago *pop* 89,078

Wau·ke·sha \'wȯ-kə-ˌshȯ\ city SE Wis. *pop* 70,718

Wau·sau \'wȯ-ˌsȯ, -sə\ city N *cen* Wis. *pop* 39,106

Wau·wa·to·sa \ˌwȯ-wə-'tō-sə\ city SE Wis. *pop* 46,396

Wa·zir·i·stan \wə-ˌzir-i-'stan, -'stän\ region W Pakistan on border of Afghanistan NE of Baluchistan

Weald \'wēld\ region SE England in Kent, Surrey, & Sussex, bet. N. Downs & S. Downs; once heavily forested

Wear \'wir\ river 67 *mi* (108 *km*) N England flowing into North Sea at Sunderland

Web·ster Groves \'web-stər\ city E Mo. *pop* 22,995

Wed·dell Sea \wə-'del, 'we-dᵊl\ arm of the S. Atlantic E of Antarctic Peninsula

Wei \'wā\ river *ab* 535 *mi* (860 *km*) N *cen* China flowing E to join the Huang

Wei·fang \'wā-'fäŋ\ city E China in E *cen* Shandong *pop* 428,522

Wei·hai \'wā-'hī\ city & port E China in NE Shandong on Yellow Sea *pop* 128,888

Wei·mar \'vī-ˌmär, 'wī-\ city E *cen* Germany E of Erfurt *pop* 64,000

Weimar Republic the German republic 1919–33

Wel·land \'we-lənd\ city Canada in SE Ont. SW of Niagara Falls *pop* 50,631

Welland Canal *or* **Welland Ship Canal** canal 27 *mi* (44 *km*) Canada in SE Ont. connecting Lake Erie & Lake Ontario

Welles·ley \'welz-lē\ town E Mass. WSW of Boston *pop* 27,982

Wel·ling·ton \'we-liŋ-tən\ **1** village SE Fla. *pop* 56,508 **2** city & port ✻ of New Zealand in SW North Is. on Port Nicholson (Wellington Harbor) on Cook Strait *pop* 179,466

Wells \'welz\ city SW England in Somerset *pop* 8374

Welsh·pool \'welsh-ˌpül\ town E Wales near English border *pop* 7317

Wel·wyn Garden City \'we-lən\ town SE England in Hertfordshire N of London *pop* 40,369

Wem·bley \'wem-blē\ former municipal borough SE England in Middlesex, now part of Brent

We·natch·ee \wə-'na-chē\ city *cen* Wash. *pop* 31,925

Wen·zhou *or* **Wen·chow** *or* **Wen–chou** \'wən-'jō\ city & port E China in S Zhejiang on E. China Sea *pop* 401,871

Wer·ra \'ver-ə\ river 180 *mi* (290 *km*) *cen* Germany flowing N

We·ser \'vā-zər\ river 273 *mi* (439 *km*) *cen* & NW Germany flowing into North Sea

Wes·la·co \'wes-li-ˌkō\ city S Tex. W of Harlingen *pop* 35,670

Wes·sex \'we-siks\ ancient Anglian kingdom S England ✻ Winchester; one of kingdoms in Anglo-Saxon heptarchy

West Al·lis \'a-ləs\ city SE Wis. *pop* 60,411

West Antarctica — see ANTARCTICA

West Bank area Middle East W of Jordan River; occupied by Israel since 1967 with parts having been transferred to Palestinian administration since 1993 — **West Bank·er** \'baŋ-kər\ *n*

West Bend \'bend\ city SE Wis. NNW of Milwaukee *pop* 31,078

West Bengal state E India comprising the W third of former Bengal province ✻ Calcutta *area* 33,852 *sq mi* (87,677 *sq km*), *pop* 68,077,965

West Beskids — see BESKIDS

West Brom·wich \'brä-mich\ town W *cen* England in W. Midlands NW of Birmingham *pop* 154,930

West Chicago city NE Ill. *pop* 27,086

West Co·vi·na \kō-'vē-nə\ city SW Calif. *pop* 106,098

West Des Moines city S *cen* Iowa *pop* 56,609

West Dunbartonshire administrative area of W Scotland *area* 62 *sq mi* (162 *sq km*)

Wes·ter·ly \'wes-tər-lē\ town SW R.I. *pop* 17,936

Western Australia state W Australia on Indian Ocean ✻ Perth *area* 975,920 *sq mi* (2,537,392 *sq km*), *pop* 1,676,400

Western Cape *or* **Wes–Kaap** \'wes-ˌkäp, 'ves-\ province SW Republic of South Africa *area* 49,950 *sq mi* (129,370 *sq km*), *pop* 3,635,000

Western Ghats \'gäts, 'gȯts, 'gəts\ chain of mountains SW India extending SSE parallel to coast from mouth of the Tapi to Cape Comorin; highest peak 8842 *ft* (2695 *m*) — see EASTERN GHATS

Western Isles **1** *or Scot* **Ei·lean Siar** \'e-lən-'shē(-ə)r\ the Outer Hebrides, constituting an administrative area of W Scotland ✻ Stornoway *area* 1120 *sq mi* (2912 *sq km*), *pop* 29,410 **2** — used unofficially of the entire Hebrides group

Western Reserve tract of land NE Ohio on S shore of Lake Erie; part of W lands of Conn., ceded 1800 *area ab* 5470 *sq mi* (14,222 *sq km*)

Western Sahara *or formerly* **Spanish Sahara** territory NW Africa; formerly a Spanish possession, divided 1975 bet. Mauritania, which gave up its claim in Aug. 1979, & Morocco, which subsequently occupied the entire territory *area* 102,703 *sq mi* (266,001 *sq km*), *pop* 416,500 — **Western Saharan** *adj*

Western Samoa — see SAMOA 2

Western Thrace — see THRACE

Wes·ter·ville \'wes-tər-ˌvil, -vəl\ city *cen* Ohio *pop* 36,120

West·field \'west-ˌfēld\ **1** city SW Mass. WNW of Springfield *pop* 41,094 **2** town NE N.J. WSW of Elizabeth *pop* 30,316

West Flanders province NW Belgium bordering on North Sea ✻ Brugge *area* 1210 *sq mi* (3134 *sq km*), *pop* 1,132,275

West Frisian Islands — see FRISIAN ISLANDS

West Germany the Federal Republic of Germany — see GERMANY

West Ham \'ham\ former county borough SE England in Essex, now part of Newham

West Hartford town *cen* Conn. *pop* 63,268

West Ha·ven \'west-ˌhā-vən\ city S Conn. *pop* 55,564

West Hollywood city SW Calif. *pop* 34,399

West Indies **1** the islands lying bet. SE N. America & N S. America bordering the Caribbean & comprising the Greater Antilles, Lesser Antilles, & Bahamas **2** *or* **West Indies Federation** former country including all of the Brit. West Indies except the Bahamas & the Brit. Virgin Islands; established 1958, dissolved 1961 — **West Indian** *adj or n*

West Jordan city N *cen* Utah *pop* 103,712

West Kelowna municipality Canada in S B.C. *pop* 30,892

West Lafayette city W *cen* Ind. *pop* 29,596

West·lake \'west-ˌlāk\ city N Ohio W of Cleveland *pop* 32,729

West·land \'west-lənd\ city SE Mich. W of Detroit *pop* 84,094

West Lo·thi·an \'lō-t͟hē-ən\ **1** administrative area of S Scotland *area* 164 *sq mi* (425 *sq km*) **2** *or earlier* **Lin·lith·gow** \lin-'lith-(ˌ)gō\ *or* **Lin·lith·gow·shire** \-ˌshir, -shər\ former county SE Scotland bordering on Firth of Forth ✻ Linlithgow

West Malaysia the peninsular part of Malaysia — see MALAYA 3

West·meath \(ˌ)west-'mēt͟h, -'mēth\ county E *cen* Ireland in Leinster ✻ Mullingar *area* 681 *sq mi* (1771 *sq km*), *pop* 71,858

West Memphis city E Ark. on Mississippi River *pop* 26,245

West Midlands metropolitan county W *cen* England ✻ Birmingham *area* 360 *sq mi* (932 *sq km*), *pop* 2,499,300

West·min·ster \'wes(t)-ˌmin(t)-stər\ **1** city SW Calif. E of Long Beach *pop* 89,701 **2** city N *cen* Colo. NW of Denver *pop* 106,114 **3** *or* **City of Westminster** borough of W *cen* Greater London, England *pop* 181,500

West·mont \'west-ˌmänt\ city NE Ill. *pop* 24,685

West·mor·land \'west-mər-lənd, *US also* west-'mȯr-\ former county NW England ✻ Kendal

West New York town NE N.J. on Hudson River *pop* 49,708

Wes·ton \'wes-tən\ city SE Fla. W of Fort Lauderdale *pop* 65,333

Wes·ton–su·per–Mare \-ˌsü-pər-'mer\ seaside resort SW England in Avon on Bristol Channel *pop* 57,980

West Pakistan the former W division of Pakistan, now coextensive with Pakistan

West Palm Beach city SE Fla. on Lake Worth inlet *pop* 99,919

West·pha·lia \west-'fāl-yə, -'fā-lē-ə\ *or G* **West·fa·len** \ˌvest-'fä-lən\ region W Germany bordering on Netherlands E of the Rhine; includes Ruhr valley; a province of Prussia 1816–1945 ✻ Münster — see NORTH RHINE-WESTPHALIA — **West·pha·lian** \west-'fāl-yən, -'fā-lē-ən\ *adj or n*

West Point population center SE New York on W bank of Hudson River N of New York City *pop* 6763; site of U.S. military academy

West·port \'west-ˌpȯrt\ town SW Conn. *pop* 26,391

West Prussia region N Europe bordering on the Baltic bet. Pomerania & E. Prussia; since 1945 in Poland

West Punjab — see PUNJAB 3

West Quod·dy Head \'kwä-dē\ cape NE Maine at entrance to Passamaquoddy Bay

Wes·tra·lia \we-'strāl-yə, -'strā-lē-ə\ WESTERN AUSTRALIA

West Riding — see YORK 3

West Sacramento city N *cen* Calif. *pop* 48,744

West Springfield town SW Mass. on Connecticut River *pop* 28,391

West Suffolk — see SUFFOLK 2

West Sus·sex \'sə-siks, *US also* -ˌseks\ county S England ✻ Chichester *area* 806 *sq mi* (2088 *sq km*), *pop* 692,800

West Valley City city N Utah S of Salt Lake City *pop* 129,480

West Vancouver municipality Canada in SW B.C. *pop* 42,694

West Virginia state E U.S. ✻ Charleston *area* 24,181 *sq mi* (62,871 *sq km*), *pop* 1,852,994 — **West Virginian** *adj or n*

West Warwick town *cen* R.I. *pop* 29,191

West Yorkshire metropolitan county NW England ✻ Wakefield *area* 816 *sq mi* (2113 *sq km*), *pop* 1,984,700

Weth·ers·field \'we-t͟hərz-ˌfēld\ town *cen* Conn. *pop* 26,668

Wex·ford \'weks-fərd\ **1** county SE Ireland in Leinster *area* 908 *sq mi* (2352 *sq km*), *pop* 116,596 **2** town & port, its ✻ *pop* 9537

Wey·mouth \'wā-məth\ city E Mass. SE of Boston *pop* 53,743

Whales, Bay of inlet of Ross Sea Antarctica in Ross Ice Shelf

Whangpoo — see HUANGPU

Whea·ton \'hwē-tᵊn, 'wē-\ city NE Ill. W of Chicago *pop* 52,894

Wheat Ridge city N *cen* Colo. W of Denver *pop* 30,166

Whee·ler Peak \ˈhwē-lər, ˈwē-\ **1** mountain 13,063 *ft* (3982 *m*) E Nev. in Snake Range **2** mountain 13,161 *ft* (4013 *m*) N N.Mex. in Sangre de Cristo Mountains; highest in the state
Whee·ling \ˈhwē-liŋ, ˈwē-\ **1** village NE Ill. NNE of Chicago *pop* 37,648 **2** city N W.Va. on Ohio River *pop* 28,486
Whid·bey Island \ˈhwid-bē, ˈwid-\ island 40 *mi* (64 *km*) long NW Wash. at N end of Puget Sound E of Admiralty Inlet
Whit·by \ˈhwit-bē, ˈwit-\ town Canada in S Ont. *pop* 122,022
Whit·church–Stouff·ville \ˈhwi(t)-ˌchərch-ˈstō-ˌvil, ˈwi(t)-\ town Canada in SE Ont. *pop* 37,628
White **1** river 690 *mi* (1110 *km*) N Ark. & SW Mo. flowing SE into Mississippi River **2** river 250 *mi* (402 *km*) NW Colo. & E Utah flowing W into Green River **3** river 50 *mi* (80 *km*) SW Ind. flowing W into the Wabash **4** river 325 *mi* (523 *km*) S S.Dak. flowing E into Missouri River **5** river 130 *mi* (209 *km*) NW Tex.
White Bear Lake city E Minn. NE of St. Paul *pop* 23,797
White·chap·el \ˈhwīt-ˌcha-pəl, ˈwīt-\ district of E London, England, N of Thames River in Tower Hamlets
White·friars \ˈhwīt-ˌfrī(-ə)rz, ˈwīt-\ district of *cen* London, England, on Thames River
White·horse \ˈhwīt-ˌhȯrs, ˈwīt-\ city NW Canada ✻ of Yukon Territory on upper Yukon River *pop* 23,276
White Mountains **1** mountains E Calif. & SE Nev. **2** mountains N N.H. in the Appalachians — see WASHINGTON (Mount)
White Nile — see NILE
White Pass mountain pass 2890 *ft* (881 *m*) SE Alaska on Canada (B.C.) border
White Plains city SE N.Y. NE of Yonkers *pop* 56,853
White Sands National Monument area of gypsum sand dunes S N.Mex. SW of Alamogordo
White Sea *or Russ* **Be·lo·ye Mo·re** \ˈbye-lə-yə-ˈmȯr-yə, ˈbe-lə-\ inlet of Barents Sea NW Russia in Europe enclosed on the N by Kola Peninsula
White Volta — see VOLTA
Whit·ney, Mount \ˈhwit-nē, ˈwit-\ mountain 14,494 *ft* (4419 *m*) SE *cen* Calif. in Sierra Nevada in Sequoia National Park; highest in the U.S. outside of Alaska
Whit·ti·er \ˈhwi-tē-ər, ˈwi-\ city SW Calif. SE of Los Angeles *pop* 85,331
Wich·i·ta \ˈwi-chə-ˌtȯ\ **1** city S *cen* Kans. on Arkansas River *pop* 382,368 **2** river 250 *mi* (402 *km*) N Tex. flowing ENE into Red River
Wichita Falls city N Tex. on Wichita River *pop* 104,553
Wichita Mountains range SW Okla.; highest 2464 *ft* (751 *m*)
Wick·low \ˈwi-(ˌ)klō\ **1** county E Ireland in Leinster *area* 782 *sq mi* (2033 *sq km*), *pop* 114,676 **2** town & port, its ✻, SSE of Dublin *pop* 5847
Wicklow Mountains range Ireland along E coast; highest point Lugnaquilla 3039 *ft* (926 *m*)
Wien — see VIENNA
Wies·ba·den \ˈvēs-ˌbä-d^{ə}n\ city SW *cen* Germany on the Rhine W of Frankfurt am Main ✻ of Hesse *pop* 264,022
Wig·an \ˈwi-gən\ town NW England in Greater Manchester W of Manchester *metropolitan area pop* 301,900
Wight, Isle of \ˈwīt\ island S England in English Channel ✻ Newport *area* 152 *sq mi* (394 *sq km*), *pop* 126,600
Wig·town \ˈwig-tən, -ˌtau̇n\ *or* **Wig·town·shire** \-ˌshir, -shər\ former county SW Scotland ✻ Wigtown
Wilderness Road trail from SW Va. to *cen* Ky. through Cumberland Gap blazed to site of Boonesborough by Daniel Boone 1775 & later extended to falls of the Ohio at Louisville
Wild·wood \ˈwī(-ə)ld-ˌwu̇d\ city E Mo. *pop* 35,517
Wil·helms·ha·ven \ˌvil-ˌhelmz-ˈhä-fən, ˈvi-ləmz-ˌ\ city & port NW Germany NW of Bremen *pop* 91,149
Wilkes–Barre \ˈwilks-ˌba-rə, -ˌba-rē, -ˌber\ city NE Pa. on the Susquehanna SW of Scranton *pop* 41,498
Wilkes Land \ˈwilks\ coast region E Antarctica extending along Indian Ocean S of Australia
Wil·lam·ette \wə-ˈla-mət\ river 300 *mi* (485 *km*) NW Oreg. flowing N into Columbia River
Wil·la·pa Bay \ˈwi-lə-ˌpȯ, -ˌpä\ inlet of the Pacific SW Wash.
Wil·lem·stad \ˈvi-ləm-ˌstät\ city, Curaçao, formerly ✻ of Netherlands Antilles *pop* 93,600
Willes·den \ˈwilz-dən\ former municipal borough SE England in Middlesex, now part of Brent
Wil·liams·burg \ˈwil-yəmz-ˌbərg\ city SE Va. NNW of Newport News; ✻ of Virginia 1699–1780; site of large-scale restoration *pop* 14,068
Wil·liam·son, Mount \ˈwil-yəm-sən\ mountain 14,375 *ft* (4382 *m*) SE *cen* Calif. in Sierra Nevada NNW of Mt. Whitney
Wil·liams·port \ˈwil-yəmz-ˌpȯrt\ city N *cen* Pa. on W branch of the Susquehanna *pop* 29,381
Wil·lough·by \ˈwi-lə-bē\ city NE Ohio NE of Cleveland *pop* 22,268
Wil·mette \wil-ˈmet\ village NE Ill. N of Chicago *pop* 27,087
Wil·ming·ton \ˈwil-miŋ-tən\ **1** city & port N Del. *pop* 70,851 **2** city & port SE N.C. *pop* 106,476
Wil·son \ˈwil-sən\ city E *cen* N.C. E of Raleigh *pop* 49,167
Wilson, Mount mountain 5710 *ft* (1740 *m*) SW Calif. NE of Pasadena
Wilt·shire \ˈwilt-ˌshir, -shər\ county S England ✻ Trowbridge *area* 1392 *sq mi* (3605 *sq km*), *pop* 553,300
Wim·ble·don \ˈwim-bəl-dən\ former municipal borough SE England in Surrey, now part of Merton
Win·ches·ter \ˈwin-ˌches-tər, -chəs-tər\ **1** city N Va. *pop* 26,203 **2** city S England ✻ of Hampshire *pop* 30,642
Wind \ˈwind\ river W *cen* Wyo., the upper course of Bighorn River
Windau — see VENTSPILS
Wind Cave limestone cavern SW S.Dak. in Black Hills in **Wind Cave National Park**
Win·der·mere \ˈwin-də(r)-ˌmir\ lake 10 *mi* (16 *km*) long NW England in Cumbria; largest in England
Wind·ham \ˈwin-dəm\ town E *cen* Conn. *pop* 25,268
Wind·hoek \ˈvint-ˌhu̇k\ city ✻ of Namibia *pop* 233,529
Wind River Canyon gorge of Bighorn River W *cen* Wyo.
Wind River Range mountain range W *cen* Wyo. — see GANNETT PEAK
Wind·sor \ˈwin-zər\ **1** town Calif. N of San Francisco *pop* 26,801 **2** town N *cen* Conn. N of Hartford *pop* 29,044 **3** city Canada in SE Ont. on Detroit River opposite Detroit, Mich. *pop* 210,891 **4** *or* **New Windsor** town S England in Berkshire on Thames River *pop* 30,065
Wind·ward Islands \ˈwind-wərd\ **1** islands W. Indies in the S Lesser Antilles extending S from Martinique but not including Barbados, Tobago, or Trinidad **2** former colony Brit. West Indies comprising territories of St. Lucia, St. Vincent, & Grenada in the Windward group & Dominica in the Leewards **3** *or F* **Îles du Vent** \ˌēl-due-ˈvä^{n}\ islands S. Pacific, E group of the Society Islands, including Tahiti *pop* 184,224
Windward Passage channel bet. Cuba & Hispaniola
Win·ne·ba·go, Lake \ˌwi-nə-ˈbā-(ˌ)gō\ lake 30 *mi* (48 *km*) long E Wis.
Win·ni·peg \ˈwi-nə-ˌpeg\ **1** river *ab* 500 *mi* (804 *km*) Canada in W Ont. & SE Man. flowing from Lake of the Woods to Lake Winnipeg **2** city Canada ✻ of Man. *pop* 663,617 — **Win·ni·peg·ger** \-ˌpe-gər\ *n*
Winnipeg, Lake lake *ab* 260 *mi* (418 *km*) long Canada in S *cen* Man. drained by Nelson River
Win·ni·pe·go·sis, Lake \ˌwi-nə-pə-ˈgō-səs\ lake Canada in W Man. W of Lake Winnipeg *area* 2075 *sq mi* (5374 *sq km*)
Win·ni·pe·sau·kee, Lake \ˌwi-nə-pə-ˈsȯ-kē\ lake *cen* N.H. *area* 71 *sq mi* (185 *sq km*)
Wi·no·na \wə-ˈnō-nə\ city SE Minn. *pop* 27,592
Wi·noo·ski \wə-ˈnüs-kē\ river 100 *mi* (161 *km*) N *cen* Vt. flowing into Lake Champlain
Win·ston–Sa·lem \ˌwin(t)-stən-ˈsā-ləm\ city N N.C. *pop* 229,617
Winter Haven city *cen* Fla. E of Lakeland *pop* 33,874
Winter Park city E Fla. N of Orlando *pop* 27,852
Winter Springs city E *cen* Fla. N of Orlando *pop* 33,282
Win·ter·thur \ˈvin-tər-ˌtu̇r\ commune N Switzerland in Zurich canton NE of Zurich *pop* 89,612
Win·yah Bay \ˈwin-ˌyȯ\ inlet of the Atlantic E S.C.
Wis·con·sin \wi-ˈskän(t)-sən\ **1** river 430 *mi* (692 *km*) *cen* Wis. flowing S & W into Mississippi River **2** state N *cen* U.S. ✻ Madison *area* 56,154 *sq mi* (145,439 *sq km*), *pop* 5,686,986 — **Wis·con·sin·ite** \-sə-ˌnīt\ *n*
Wisconsin Dells \ˈdelz\ gorge of Wisconsin River in S *cen* Wis.
Wisła — see VISTULA
Wis·mar \ˈvis-ˌmär, ˈwiz-ˌmär\ city & port N Germany *pop* 54,471
Wis·sa·hick·on Creek \ˌwi-sə-ˈhi-kən\ stream SE Pa. flowing into the Schuylkill at Philadelphia
With·la·coo·chee \ˌwith-lə-ˈkü-chē\ **1** river 110 *mi* (177 *km*) S Ga. & NW Fla. flowing SE into the Suwannee **2** river 120 *mi* (193 *km*) NW *cen* Fla. flowing NW into Gulf of Mexico
Wit·ten \ˈvi-t^{ə}n\ city W Germany SW of Dortmund *pop* 105,242
Wit·ten·berg \ˈwi-t^{ə}n-ˌbərg, ˈvi-t^{ə}n-ˌberk\ city E *cen* Germany E of Dessau *pop* 48,718
Wit·wa·ters·rand \ˈwit-ˌwȯ-tərz-ˌrand, -ˌwä-, -ˌränd, -ˌränt\ ridge of gold-bearing rock 62 *mi* (100 *km*) long & 23 *mi* (37 *km*) wide NE Republic of South Africa in Gauteng and North West provinces
Wło·cła·wek \vwȯt-ˈswä-ˌvek\ commune N *cen* Poland on the Vistula *pop* 120,823
Wo·burn \ˈwü-bərn, ˈwō-\ city E Mass. NW of Boston *pop* 38,120
Wo·dzi·sław Śl ą·ski \vȯ-ˈjē-swäf-ˈshlȯn-skē\ town S Poland *pop* 111,329
Wolds, The \ˈwōldz\ chalk hills NE England stretching from N. Yorkshire to N Lincolnshire
Wolfs·burg \ˈwu̇lfs-ˌbərg, ˈvȯlfs-ˌbu̇rk\ city N *cen* Germany *pop* 128,995
Wol·lon·gong \ˈwu̇-lən-ˌgäŋ, -ˌgȯŋ\ city SE Australia in E New South Wales S of Sydney *pop* 211,417
Wol·ver·hamp·ton \ˌwu̇l-vər-ˈham(p)-tən\ city W *cen* England in W. Midlands NW of Birmingham *pop* 236,582
Won·san \ˈwən-ˌsän\ city & port N. Korea on E coast *pop* 274,000
Wood Buffalo National Park wilderness area W Canada in N Alta. & SE Northwest Territories featuring buffalo
Wood·bury \ˈwu̇d-ˌber-ē, -bə-rē\ city E Minn., a suburb of St. Paul *pop* 61,961
Wood Green former municipal borough SE England in Middlesex, now part of Haringey
Wood·land \ˈwu̇d-lənd\ city W Calif. NW of Sacramento *pop* 55,468
Wood·lark \ˈwu̇d-ˌlärk\ island W Pacific in Solomon Sea off SE New Guinea; attached to Papua New Guinea *area* 400 *sq mi* (1040 *sq km*)
Wood·ridge \ˈwu̇d-(ˌ)rij\ village NE Ill. *pop* 32,971
Woods, Lake of the lake S Canada & N U.S. in Ont., Man., & Minn. SE of Lake Winnipeg *area* 1679 *sq mi* (4349 *sq km*)
Wood·stock \ˈwu̇d-ˌstäk\ city Canada in SE Ont. *pop* 37,754
Wool·wich \ˈwu̇-lij, -lich\ former metropolitan borough E London, England, now part of Greenwich
Woom·era \ˈwu̇-mə-rə\ town S. Australia W of Lake Torrens
Woon·sock·et \wün-ˈsä-kət, ˈwün-ˌ\ city N R.I. *pop* 41,186
Woos·ter \ˈwu̇s-tər\ city N *cen* Ohio SW of Akron *pop* 26,119
Worces·ter \ˈwu̇s-tər\ **1** city E *cen* Mass. W of Boston *pop* 181,045 **2** *or* **Worces·ter·shire** \-tə(r)-ˌshir, -shər\ county W *cen* England ✻ Worcester *area* 704 *sq mi* (1823 *sq km*), *pop* 538,200 **3** city, ✻ of Worcestershire & formerly of Hereford and Worcester *pop* 81,000
World War II Valor in the Pacific National Monument park comprising nine sites in Hawaii, Calif., & Alaska
Worms \ˈwərmz, ˈvȯrm(p)s\ city SW Germany on the Rhine NNW of Mannheim *pop* 77,429
Worth, Lake \ˈwərth\ inlet (lagoon) of the Atlantic SE Fla.
Wor·thing \ˈwər-thiŋ\ town S England in W. Sussex on English Channel *pop* 94,100
Wound·ed Knee \ˌwün-dəd-ˈnē\ locality SW S.Dak.; site of 1890 massacre of American Indians by U.S. troops *pop* 382
Wran·gel \ˈraŋ-gəl\ *or Russ* **Vran·ge·lya** \ˈvrän-gəl-yə\ island in Arctic Ocean off NE coast of Russia in Asia
Wran·gell \ˈraŋ-gəl\ island SE Alaska NE of Prince of Wales Is.
Wrangell, Cape cape SW Alaska on Attu Is. in Aleutians
Wrangell, Mount active volcano 14,163 *ft* (4317 *m*) S Alaska in Wrangell Mountains NW of Mt. Blackburn
Wrangell Mountains mountain range S Alaska NW of St. Elias Range — see BLACKBURN (Mount)

\ə\ **abut** \$^{ə}$\ **kitten**, F **table** \ər\ **further** \a\ **ash** \ā\ **ace** \ä\ **mop, mar** \au̇\ **out** \ch\ **chin** \e\ **bet** \ē\ **easy** \g\ **go** \i\ **hit** \ī\ **ice** \j\ **job** \ŋ\ **sing** \ō\ **go** \ȯ\ **law** \ȯi\ **boy** \th\ **thin** \th\ **the** \ü\ **loot** \u̇\ **foot** \y\ **yet** \zh\ **vision, beige** \k, ^{n}, œ, ue, ^{y}\ *see* Guide to Pronunciation

Wrangell–Saint Eli·as National Park \-sänt-i-'lī-əs\ wilderness area S *cen* Alaska; world's largest park 8,331,604 *acres* (3,374,300 *hectares*)

Wrath, Cape \'rath, *Sc* 'röth *or* 'räth\ extreme NW point of Scotland, at 58°35'N

Wrex·ham \'rek-səm\ **1** administrative area of NE Wales *area* 192 *sq mi* (497 *sq km*) **2** borough NE Wales near English border *pop* 40,272

Wro·claw \'vrot-,swäf, -,släv\ *or G* **Bres·lau** \'bres-,laů, 'brez-\ city SW Poland, chief city of Silesia *pop* 642,334

Wu \'wü\ river 700 *mi* (1126 *km*) *cen* China rising in W Guizhou & flowing through Sichuan into the Chang

Wu·chang \'wü-'chäŋ\ former city E *cen* China — see WUHAN

Wu·han \'wü-'hän\ city E *cen* China * of Hubei at junction of Han & Chang rivers; formed from the former separate cities of Hankow, Hanyang, & Wuchang *pop* 3,284,229

Wuhsien — see SUZHOU

Wu·hu \'wü-'hü\ city E China in E Anhui *pop* 425,740

Wu–lu–mu–ch'i — see ÜRÜMQI

Wu·pat·ki National Monument \wü-'pat-kē\ area containing prehistoric Indian dwellings N Ariz. NNE of Flagstaff

Wup·per·tal \'vů-pər-,täl\ city W Germany in Ruhr valley ENE of Düsseldorf *pop* 385,463

Würt·tem·berg \'wərt-əm-,bərg, 'wůrt-; 'vůer-təm-,berk\ region SW Germany bet. Baden & Bavaria; chief city Stuttgart; once a duchy, kingdom (1813–1918), state (1918–45); divided 1945–51, S part being joined to Hohenzollern forming **Württemberg–Hohenzollern** state & N part to N Baden forming **Württomberg Baden** state; since 1951 part of Baden-Württemberg state

Würz·burg \'wərts-,bərg, 'wůrts-; 'vůerts-,bůrk\ city S *cen* Germany on Main River in N Bavaria NW of Nuremberg *pop* 128,512

Wutsin — see CHANGZHOU

Wu·xi *or* **Wu–hsi** \'wü-'shē\ city E China in S Jiangsu NW of Suzhou

Wu·zhou *or* **Wu–chou** *or* **Wu·chow** \'wü-'jō\ city S China in E Guangxi Zhuangzu at junction of the Gui & the Xi *pop* 210,452

Wy·an·dotte \'wī-ən-,dät *also* 'wīn-\ city SE Mich. *pop* 25,883

Wye \'wī\ river 130 *mi* (209 *km*) E Wales & W England flowing into Severn River

Wy·o·ming \wī-'ō-miŋ\ **1** state NW U.S. * Cheyenne *area* 97,914 *sq mi* (254,576 *sq km*), *pop* 563,626 **2** valley NE Pa. along the Susquehanna **3** city SW Mich. *pop* 72,125 — **Wy·o·ming·ite** \-miŋ-,īt\ *n*

Xa·la·pa *or* **Ja·la·pa** \hə-'lä-pə\ city E Mexico * of Veracruz *pop* 279,451

Xan·thus \'zan(t)-thəs\ city of ancient Lycia; site near mouth of Koca River in SW Turkey

Xe·nia \'zē-nyə, -nē-ə\ city SW *cen* Ohio *pop* 25,719

Xeres — see JEREZ

Xi *or* **Hsi** *or* **Si** \'shē\ river 300 *mi* (483 *km*) SE China in Guangxi Zhuangzu & Guangdong flowing E into S. China Sea

Xia·men *or* **Hsia–men** \'shyä-'mən\ *or* **Amoy** \ä-'mòi, a-, ə-\ city & port SE China in S Fujian on two islands *pop* 308,000

Xi'·an *or* **Hsi–an** \'shē-'än\ *or formerly* **Chang·an** \'chäŋ-'än\ city E *cen* China * of Shaanxi on the Wei *pop* 1,959,044

Xiang *or* **Hsiang** \'shyäŋ\ river 350 *mi* (560 *km*) SE *cen* China flowing from N Guangxi Zhuangzu N into Hunan

Xianggang — see HONG KONG

Xiang·tan *or* **Hsiang–t'an** *or* **Siang·tan** \'shyäŋ-'tän, -'tan\ city SE China in E Hunan on the Xiang S of Changsha *pop* 441,968

Xi·ga·zê \'shē-'gä-'dzə\ *or* **Shi·ga·tse** \shi-'gä-'dzə\ *or* **Jih–k'a–tse** \'zhir-'kä-'dzə\ town W China in SE Tibet on the Tsangbo W of Lhasa

Xin·gu \shēŋ-'gü\ river 1230 *mi* (1979 *km*) *cen* & N Brazil rising on Mato Grosso plateau & flowing N into the Amazon near its mouth

Xi·ning *or* **Si·ning** *or* **Hsi–ning** \'shē-'niŋ\ city NW China * of Qinghai *pop* 551,776

Xin·jiang Uy·gur *or* **Sin·kiang Ui·ghur** \'shin-'jyäŋ-'wē-gər\ *often shortened to* **Xinjiang** *or* **Sinkiang** region W China bet. the Kunlun & Altai mountains; formerly a province * Ürümqi *area* 635,829 *sq mi* (1,653,154 *sq km*), *pop* 15,155,778

Xin·xiang *or* **Hsin–hsiang** *or* **Sin·siang** \'shin-'shyäŋ\ city E China in N Henan N of Zhengzhou *pop* 473,762

Xin·zhu \'shin-'jü\ *or* **Hsin–chu** \'shin-'chü\ city & port China in NW Taiwan on coast SW of Taibei *pop* 332,524

Xizang — see TIBET

Xo·chi·mil·co \,sō-chē-'mēl(,)-kō, ,sō-shi-, -'mil-\ city S *cen* Mexico, SE suburb of Mexico City *pop* 271,020

Xuan·hua *or* **Hsüan–hua** \'shwän-'hwä, 'shwan-, -'wä\ city NE China in NW Hebei NW of Beijing *pop* 114,000

Xu·zhou \'shü-'jō\ *or* **Hsü–chou** *or* **Sü·chow** \'shü-'jō, 'sü-; 'sü-'chaů\ city E China in NW Jiangsu *pop* 805,695

Ya·blo·no·vy Mountains *or* **Ya·blo·no·vyy Mountains** \,yä-blə-nə-'vē\ mountain range S Russia in Asia

Ya·bu·coa \,yä-bü-'kō-ä\ city SE Puerto Rico *pop* 37,941

Yacarana — see JAVARI

Yad·kin \'yad-kən\ river 202 *mi* (325 *km*) *cen* N.C., the upper course of the Pee Dee

Yafo — see JAFFA

Yak·i·ma \'ya-kə-,mò\ **1** river 200 *mi* (322 *km*) S Wash. flowing SE into Columbia River **2** city S *cen* Wash. *pop* 91,067

Yak·u·tat Bay \'ya-kə-,tat\ inlet of the Pacific SE Alaska

Yakutia — see SAKHA

Ya·kutsk \yə-'kütsk\ city E *cen* Russia in Asia *pop* 198,000

Ya·long *or* **Ya·lung** \'yä-'lůŋ\ river SW China in W Sichuan flowing S into the Chang

Yal·ta \'yòl-tə\ city & port Ukraine on S coast of Crimea *pop* 89,000

Ya·lu \'yä-(,)lü\ river *ab* 500 *mi* (804 *km*) SE Manchuria & NW N. Korea flowing N, W, & SW into Korea Bay

Ya·mal \yä-'mäl\ peninsula NW Russia in Asia at N end of Ural Mountains bet. Gulf of Ob' & Kara Sea

Ya·mous·sou·kro \,yä-mə-'sü-krō\ town *cen* Ivory Coast; its official * *pop* 106,786

Yam·pa \'yam-pə\ river 250 *mi* (400 *km*) NW Colo. flowing W into Green River in Dinosaur National Monument

Ya·mu·na \'yə-mə-nə\ river 860 *mi* (1384 *km*) N India in Uttar Pradesh flowing from the Himalayas S & SE into the Ganges

Ya·na \'yä-nə\ river N Russia in Asia flowing N into Laptev Sea

Ya·nam \yə-'näm\ town SE India in Puducherry terr.; a settlement of French India until 1954 *pop* 20,297

Yan'·an *or* **Yen·an** \'ye-'nän\ city NE *cen* China in *cen* Shaanxi *pop* 113,277

Yangku — see TAIYUAN

Yan·gon \,yän-'gòn\ **1** — see RANGOON 1 **2** *or formerly and now unofficially* **Rangoon** city & port historic * of Myanmar on Rangoon River 21 *mi* (34 *km*) from its mouth *pop* 4,477,600

Yang·quan *or* **Yang·chüan** \'yäŋ-'chwän, -'chwen\ city N China in E Shanxi E of Taiyuan *pop* 362,268

Yangtze — see CHANG

Yang·zhou *or* **Yang–chou** \'yäŋ-'jō\ city E China in SW Jiangsu NE of Nanjing *pop* 312,892

Yan·tai \'yän-'tī\ *or* **Yen–t'ai** \'yən-\ *or* **Che·foo** \'jə-'fü\ city & port E China in NE Shandong on Shandong Peninsula on Bo Hai *pop* 452,127

Yaoun·dé \yaůn-'dä\ city S *cen* Cameroon, its * *pop* 1,800,000

Yap \'yap, 'yäp\ *or* **Uap** \'wäp\ islands W Carolines, part of Federated States of Micronesia — **Yap·ese** \ya-'pēz, yä-, -'pēs\ *adj*

Ya·quí \yä-'kē\ river 420 *mi* (676 *km*) NW Mexico in Sonora flowing SW into Gulf of California

Yar·kand \yär-'känd\ *or* **Yar·kant** \-'känt\ river Kashmir & China flowing from Karakoram Range N & W to join the Hotan in Xinjiang Uygur forming the Tarim

Yar·mouth \'yär-məth\ **1** city SE Mass. on Cape Cod E of Barnstable *pop* 23,793 **2** *or* **Great Yarmouth** port E England in Norfolk on North Sea *pop* 50,152

Ya·ro·slavl' \,yär-ə-'slä-vᵊl\ city *cen* Russia in Europe on the Volga NE of Moscow *pop* 637,000

Yau·co \'yaů-,kō\ municipality SW Puerto Rico *pop* 42,043

Yavarí — see JAVARI

Ya·wa·ta \yä-'wä-tä\ former city Japan in N Kyushu — see KITAKYUSHU

Yazd \'yazd\ *or* **Yezd** \'yezd\ city *cen* Iran *pop* 432,194

Yaz·oo \ya-'zü, 'ya-(,)zü\ river 189 *mi* (304 *km*) Miss. flowing SW into Mississippi River

Yedo — see TOKYO

Ye·gor'·yevsk \yə-'gòr-yəfsk, -əfsk\ city W Russia in Europe SE of Moscow *pop* 74,200

Ye·ka·te·rin·burg \yi-'ka-tə-rən-,bərg, yi-,kä-ti-rēm-'bůrk\ *or* 1924–91 **Sverd·lovsk** \sverd-'lòfsk\ city W Russia in Asia in *cen* Ural Mountains *pop* 1,371,000

Yelizavetpol — see GANCA

Yellow — see HUANG

Yel·low·knife \'ye-lō-,nīf\ city Canada * of Northwest Territories on Great Slave Lake *pop* 19,234

Yellow Sea inlet of E. China Sea bet. N China, N. Korea, & S. Korea

Yel·low·stone \'ye-lō-,stōn\ river 671 *mi* (1080 *km*) NW Wyo. & S & E Mont. flowing N through **Yellowstone Lake** (*area* 140 *sq mi or* 364 *sq km*) & **Grand Canyon of the Yellowstone** in Yellowstone National Park & NE into Missouri River in NW N.Dak. near Mont. border

Yellowstone Falls two waterfalls NW Wyo. in Yellowstone River at head of Grand Canyon of the Yellowstone; upper fall 109 *ft* (33 *m*), lower fall 308 *ft* (94 *m*)

Yellowstone National Park area NW Wyo., E Idaho, & S Mont. including numerous geysers & hot springs

Ye·men \'ye-mən\ country S Arabia bordering on Red Sea & Gulf of Aden; a republic formed 1990 by merger of **Yemen Arab Republic** (* Sanaa) with **People's Democratic Republic of Yemen** *or* **Southern Yemen** (* Aden) * Sanaa *area* 203,849 *sq mi* (527,969 *sq km*), *pop* 19,700,000 — **Ye·me·ni** \'ye-mə-nē\ *adj or n* — **Ye·men·ite** \-mə-,nīt\ *n or adj*

Yen·i·sey \,yi-ni-'sä\ river *over* 2500 *mi* (4022 *km*) Russia in Asia flowing N into Arctic Ocean

Yen–t'ai — see YANTAI

Yeosu — see YOSU

Ye·re·van \,yer-ə-'vän\ city * of Armenia *pop* 1,100,000

Ye·sil Ir·mak \ya-'shēl-ir-'mäk\ river N Turkey in Asia flowing N into Black Sea

Ye·sil·koy \'yā-,shēl-'kòi\ *or formerly* **San Ste·fa·no** \san-'ste-fə-,nō\ town Turkey in Europe on Sea of Marmara W of Istanbul

Yevreyskaya — see JEWISH AUTONOMOUS OBLAST

Yezo — see HOKKAIDO

Yi·bin \'yē-'bēn\ *or* **I–pin** \'ē-'bēn, -'pin\ *or formerly* **Sü·chow** \'shu-'jō, 'sü-; 'sü-'chaů\ city *cen* China in S Sichuan on the Chang *pop* 805,695

Yi·chang \'yē-'chäŋ\ *or* **I–ch'ang** \'ē-'chäŋ\ city *cen* China in W Hubei *pop* 371,601

Yin·chuan \'yin-'chwän, -'chwen\ *or formerly* **Ning·sia** *or* **Ning·hsia** \'niŋ-'shyä\ city N China * of Ningxia Huizu on the Huang *pop* 356,652

Ying·kou \'yiŋ-'kō\ *or* **Ying·kow** \'yin-'kaů, -'kō\ city & port NE China in *cen* Liaoning on Gulf of Liaodong *pop* 421,589

Yi·ning \'yē-'niŋ\ *or* **Gul·ja** \'gůl-(,)jä\ *or* **Kul·dja** \'kůl-(,)jä\ city W China in NW Xinjiang Uygur *pop* 177,193

Yog·ya·kar·ta \,yō-gyə-'kär-tə\ *or* **Jog·ja·kar·ta** \,jōg-yə-\ city Indonesia in S Java *pop* 412,392

Yo·ho National Park \'yō-(,)hō\ area W Canada in SE B.C. on W slopes of Rocky Mountains

Yo·ko·ha·ma \,yō-kō-'hä-mä\ city & port Japan in SE Honshu on Tokyo Bay S of Tokyo *pop* 3,426,651

Yo·ko·su·ka \'yō-'kò-s(ə-)kä\ city & port Japan in Honshu W of entrance to Tokyo Bay *pop* 428,645

Yon·kers \'yäŋ-kərz\ city SE N.Y. N of New York City *pop* 195,976

Yonne \'yən, 'yòn\ river 182 *mi* (293 *km*) NE France flowing NNW into the Seine

Yor·ba Lin·da \,yòr-bə-'lin-də\ city SW Calif. *pop* 64,234

York \'yòrk\ **1** city SE Pa. S of Harrisburg *pop* 43,718 **2** municipality Canada in SE Ont. *pop* 1,032,524 **3** *or* **York·shire** \,shir, -shər\ former county N England bordering on North Sea comprising city of York & (former) administrative counties of **East Rid·ing** \'rī-diŋ\ (* Beverley), **North Riding** (* Northallerton), & **West Riding** (* Wakefield) — see NORTH YORKSHIRE, SOUTH YORKSHIRE, WEST YORKSHIRE **4** *or anc* **Ebo·ra·cum** \i-'bòr-ə-kəm, -'bär-\ city N England in N. Yorkshire on Ouse River *pop* 100,600

York, Cape — see CAPE YORK PENINSULA

Yorke Peninsula \'yòrk\ peninsula Australia in SE S. Australia bet. Spencer Gulf and Gulf St. Vincent

York River estuary 40 *mi* (64 *km*) E Va. flowing SE into Chesapeake Bay

Yo·sem·i·te Falls \yō-'se-mə-tē\ waterfall E *cen* Calif. descending from rim of Yosemite Valley in two falls (upper fall 1430 *ft* or 436 *m*, lower fall 320 *ft* or 98 *m*) connected by cascades

Yosemite Valley glaciated valley of Merced River E *cen* Calif. on W slope of Sierra Nevada in **Yosemite National Park**

Yosh·kar-Ola \yəsh-'kär-ə-'lä\ town E Russia in Europe ✳ of Mari El *pop* 249,000

Yo·su \'yō-(,)sü\ *or* **Yeo·su** \'yə-(,)sü\ city & port S S. Korea on Korea Strait *pop* 171,933

Yough·io·ghe·ny \,yä-kə-'gā-nē, ,yò-hə-, -'ge-nē\ river 135 *mi* (217 *km*) NE W.Va., NW Md., & SW Pa. flowing N & NW into the Monongahela

Youngs·town \'yəŋz-,taùn\ city NE Ohio E of Akron *pop* 66,982

Youth, Isle of *or formerly* **Isle of Pines** island W Cuba in the Caribbean *area* 1180 *sq mi* (3068 *sq km*)

Ypres — see IEPER

Yser \ē-'zer\ river 48 *mi* (77 *km*) France & Belgium flowing into North Sea

Ysyk–Köl — see ISSYK KUL

Yu·an \'ywen, 'ywän\ **1** river 500 *mi* (805 *km*) SE *cen* China flowing from Guizhou NE to NE Hunan **2** — see RED 4

Yu·ba City \'yü-bə\ city N Calif. N of Sacramento *pop* 64,925

Yu·cai·pa \yü-'kī-pə\ city S Calif. E of Riverside *pop* 51,367

Yu·ca·tán \,yü-kə-'tan, -kä-'tän\ **1** peninsula SE Mexico & N Central America including Belize & part of Guatemala **2** state SE Mexico at N end of Yucatán Peninsula ✳ Mérida *area* 16,749 *sq mi* (43,380 *sq km*), *pop* 1,362,940 — **Yu·ca·te·can** \-'te-kən\ *adj*

Yucatán Channel channel bet. Yucatán & W end of Cuba

Yuc·ca House National Monument \'yə-kə\ reservation SW Colo.; contains prehistoric ruins

Yu·go·sla·via *also* **Ju·go·sla·via** \,yü-gō-'slä-vē-ə, ,yü-gə-\ **1** former country S Europe on Balkan Peninsula consisting of Serbia, Montenegro, Slovenia, Croatia, Bosnia and Herzegovina, & Macedonia; established 1918 as a kingdom (**Kingdom of the Serbs, Croats, and Slovenes**), became a federal republic 1945 ✳ Belgrade **2** — see SERBIA AND MONTENEGRO — **Yu·go·slav** \,yü-gō-'släv, -'slav; 'yü-gō-\ *or* **Yu·go·sla·vi·an** \,yü-gō-'slä-vē-ən, -gə-\ *adj or n*

Yu·kon \'yü-,kän\ **1** river 1979 *mi* (3185 *km*) Yukon (territory) & Alaska flowing NW & SW into Bering Sea — see LEWES **2** *or formerly* **Yukon Territory** territory NW Canada bet. Alaska & B.C. bordering on Arctic Ocean ✳ Whitehorse *area* 205,345 *sq mi* (531,843 *sq km*), *pop* 33,897 — **Yu·kon·er** \-,kä-nər\ *n*

Yu·ma \'yü-mə\ city SW Ariz. on Colorado River *pop* 93,064

Yungki — see JILIN

Yungning — see NANNING

Yun·nan \'yü-'nän\ **1** province SW China bordering on Indochina & Myanmar ✳ Kunming *area* 168,417 *sq mi* (437,884 *sq km*), *pop* 36,972,610 **2** *or* **Yunnanfu** *or* **Yun·nan·ese** \,yü-nan-'nēz, -'nēs\ *adj or n*

Yun·que, El \'el-'yüŋ-(,)kā\ mountain 3496 *ft* (1066 *m*) E Puerto Rico

Yü Shan \'yue-'shän, 'yü-\ *or* **Hsin·kao** \'shin-'kaù\ *or* **Mount Mor·ri·son** \'mòr-ə-sən, 'mär-\ mountain 13,113 *ft* (3997 *m*) *cen* Taiwan; highest on island

Yver·don \ē-ver-'dōⁿ\ commune W Switzerland N of Lausanne *pop* 20,802

Zaan·stad \'zän-,stät\ commune N Netherlands *pop* 137,669

Za·brze \'zäb-(,)zhä\ *or G* **Hin·den·burg** \'hin-dən-bərg, -,bùrk\ city SW Poland in Silesia *pop* 195,293

Za·ca·te·cas \,zä-kə-'tä-kəs, ,sä-kä-'tä-käs\ **1** state N Mexico *area* 28,973 *sq mi* (75,040 *sq km*), *pop* 1,276,323 **2** city, its ✳ *pop* 226,265

Za·dar \'zä-,där\ *or It* **Za·ra** \'zär-ä\ city & port Croatia; held by Italy 1920–47 *pop* 80,355

Zag·a·zig \'za-gə-,zig\ *or* **Az–Za·qā·zīq** \,az-zə-,kä-'zēk\ city N Egypt NNE of Cairo *pop* 302,840

Za·greb \'zä-,greb\ city ✳ of Croatia *pop* 779,145

Zag·ros Mountains \'za-grəs, -,grōs\ mountains W & S Iran bordering on Turkey, Iraq, & Persian Gulf; highest over 14,000 *ft* (4267 *m*)

Za·he·dan \,zä-hi-'dän\ city E Iran *pop* 567,449

Za·ire \zä-'ir\ **1** river in Africa — see CONGO 1 **2** — see CONGO 2 — **Za·ir·ean** *or* **Za·ir·ian** \zä-'ir-ē-ən\ *adj or n*

Za·kar·pat·s'ka \,zä-kär-'pät-skə\ *or formerly* **Car·pa·thi·an Ru·the·nia** \kär-'pä-thē-ən-rü-'thē-nyə, -nē-ə\ *or* **Ruthenia** region W Ukraine S of the Carpathian Mountains; part of Hungary before 1918 & 1939–45; a province of Czechoslovakia 1918–38 ✳ Uzhgorod *area* 4942 *sq mi* (12,800 *sq km*), *pop* 1,258,264

Zá·kin·thos \'zä-kēn-,thòs\ **1** island W Greece, one of the Ionian Islands, SSE of Cephalonia *area* 157 *sq mi* (407 *sq km*), *pop* 32,746 **2** its chief town *pop* 11,200

Zalew Wiślany — see VISLINSKI ZALIV

Za·ma \'zä-mə, 'zä-\ ancient town N Africa SW of Carthage

Zam·be·zi *or* **Zam·be·si** \zam-'bē-zē, zäm-'bä-zē\ river *ab* 1700 *mi* (2735 *km*) SE Africa flowing from NW Zambia into Mozambique Channel

Zam·bia \'zam-bē-ə\ *or formerly* **Northern Rhodesia** country S Africa; formerly a Brit. protectorate; independent republic within the Commonwealth of Nations since 1964 ✳ Lusaka *area* 290,585 *sq mi* (752,615 *sq km*), *pop* 13,200,000 — **Zam·bi·an** \'zam-bē-ən\ *adj or n*

Zam·bo·an·ga \,zam-bō-'äŋ-gə\ city & port Philippines on SW coast of Mindanao *pop* 442,000

Za·mo·ra \zə-'mòr-ə\ **1** province NW Spain in *cen* León *area* 4077 *sq mi* (10,559 *sq km*), *pop* 199,090 **2** city, its ✳ *pop* 64,845

Zancle — see MESSINA

Zanes·ville \'zānz-,vil\ city E *cen* Ohio *pop* 25,487

Zan·jan \zan-'jän\ city NW Iran *pop* 349,713

Zan·zi·bar \'zan-zə-,bär\ **1** island E Africa off NE Tanzania mainland *area* 600 *sq mi* (1554 *sq km*), *pop* 700,000; formerly a sultanate, with Pemba & adjacent islands forming a Brit. protectorate; became independent 1963; united 1964 with Tanganyika to form Tanzania **2** city & port ✳ of the island & formerly of protectorate *pop* 205,807 — **Zan·zi·bari** \,zan-zə-'bär-ē\ *n or adj*

Za·po·rizh·zhya \zä-pə-'rēzh-zhyə\ *or Russ* **Za·po·rozh'·ye** \zä-pə-'rò-zhə\ *or formerly* **Ale·ksan·drovsk** \,a-lik-'san-drəfsk\ city SE Ukraine *pop* 815,256

Za·ra·go·za \,za-rə-'gō-zə\ *or* **Sar·a·gos·sa** \,sa-rə-'gä-sə\ **1** province NE Spain in W Aragon *area* 6639 *sq mi* (17,195 *sq km*), *pop* 861,855 **2** — see SARAGOSSA

Zee·brug·ge \'zā-,brə-gə, -,brü-\ town NW Belgium; port for Brugge

Zee·land \'zē-lənd, 'zā-; 'zā-,länt\ province SW Netherlands ✳ Middelburg *area* 1043 *sq mi* (2701 *sq km*), *pop* 377,235

Zem·po·al·te·pec \zem-pō-'äl-tə-,pek\ *or* **Zem·po·al·te·petl** \-,äl-'tä-,pe-tᵊl, -,äl-tə-\ mountain 11,138 *ft* (3395 *m*) SE Mexico in Oaxaca

Zer·matt \(t)ser-'mät\ village SW *cen* Switzerland in Valais in Pennine Alps NE of the Matterhorn

Zetland — see SHETLAND 2

Zhang·jia·kou *or* **Chang–chia–k'ou** \'jän-'jyä-'kō\ *or* **Kal·gan** \'kal-'gan\ city NE China in NW Hebei NW of Beijing *pop* 529,136

Zhang·zhou *or* **Chang–chou** \'jän-'jō\ *or formerly* **Lung·ki** \'lùŋ-kē\ city SE China in S Fujian

Zhdanov — see MARIUPOL'

Zhe·jiang *or* **Che·kiang** \'jə-'jyäŋ\ province E China bordering on E. China Sea ✳ Hangzhou *area* 39,305 *sq mi* (102,193 *sq km*), *pop* 41,445,930

Zheng·zhou *or* **Cheng–chou** *or* **Cheng·chow** \'jəŋ-'jō\ city NE *cen* China ✳ of Henan on the Huang *pop* 1,159,679

Zhen·jiang *or* **Chen–chiang** \'jən-'jyäŋ\ city & port E China in NW *cen* Jiangsu *pop* 368,316

Zhou·shan *or* **Chou–shan** \'jō-'shän\ archipelago E China in E. China Sea at entrance to Hangzhou Bay

Zhu \'jü\ *or* **Chu** \'jü, 'chü\ *or* **Pearl** river SE China flowing from Guangzhou in Guangdong Province to S. China Sea

Zhu·zhou *or* **Chu–chou** *or* **Chu·chow** \'jü-'jō\ city SE China in E Hunan *pop* 409,924

Zhy·to·myr *or* **Zhi·to·mir** \zhi-'tò-,mir\ city W Ukraine *pop* 284,236

Zi·bo *or* **Tzu–po** \'(d)zə-'bō\ city E China in *cen* Shandong *pop* 1,138,074

Zie·lo·na Go·ra \zhe-'lò-nä-'gùr-ä\ city W *cen* Poland *pop* 118,300

Zi·gong *or* **Tzu–kung** \'(d)zə-'gùŋ\ city S *cen* China in S *cen* Sichuan *pop* 393,184

Zim·ba·bwe \zim-'bä-bwē, -,(,)bwä\ **1** archaeological site NE Zimbabwe (country) **2** *or formerly* **Southern Rhodesia** *or* 1970–79 **Rhodesia** country S Africa S of the Zambezi; a self-governing Brit. colony that declared itself a republic 1970; adopted majority rule 1979 ✳ Harare *area* 150,820 *sq mi* (390,624 *sq km*), *pop* 11,634,663 — **Zim·ba·bwe·an** \-ən\ *adj or n*

Zinovievsk — see KIROVOGRAD

Zi·on \'zī-ən\ **1** city NE Ill. N of Waukegan *pop* 24,413 **2** *or* **Mount Zion** *or* **Sion** \'sī-ən, 'zī-\ *or* **Mount Sion** hill E Jerusalem, Israel; orig. the stronghold of Jerusalem conquered by David; occupied in ancient times by the Jewish Temple

Zi·on National Park \'zī-ən\ reservation SW Utah centering around **Zion Canyon** of Virgin River

Zi·pan·gu \zə-'paŋ-(,)gü\ JAPAN — the name used by Marco Polo

Zi·pa·qui·rá \,sē-pä-kē-'rä\ town *cen* Colombia N of Bogotá

Zla·to·ust \,zlä-tə-'üst\ city W Russia in Asia in the S Urals *pop* 208,000

Zoan — see TANIS

Zoe·ter·meer \,zü-tər-'mer\ commune W Netherlands *pop* 110,500

Zom·ba \'zòm-\ city SE Malawi S of Lake Malawi *pop* 87,366

Zon·gul·dak \,zòŋ-gəl-'däk\ city & port NW Turkey *pop* 116,725

Zug \'(t)sük, 'züg\ *or F* **Zoug** \'züg\ **1** canton N *cen* Switzerland *area* 92 *sq mi* (238 *sq km*), *pop* 100,900 **2** commune, its ✳, on Lake of Zug *pop* 23,000

Zug, Lake of lake N *cen* Switzerland in Zug & Schwyz cantons N of Lake of Lucerne *area* 15 *sq mi* (39 *sq km*)

Zug·spit·ze \'(t)sük-,shpit-sə, 'züg-, -,spit-\ mountain 9721 *ft* (2963 *m*) S Germany; highest in Bavarian Alps & in Germany

Zui·der Zee \,zī-dər-'zā, -'zē\ former inlet of North Sea N Netherlands — see IJSSELMEER

Zuid–Holland — see SOUTH HOLLAND

Zu·lu·land \'zü-(,)lü-,land\ territory E Republic of South Africa in NE KwaZulu-Natal bordering on Indian Ocean N of the Tugela *area* 10,362 *sq mi* (26,838 *sq km*)

Zu·rich \'zùr-ik\ *or G* **Zü·rich** \'tsʏ-rik\ **1** canton N Switzerland *area* 668 *sq mi* (1730 *sq km*), *pop* 1,228,600 **2** city, its ✳, at NW end of Lake of Zurich *pop* 363,300 — **Zü·rich·er** \-i-kər, -ri-kər\ *n*

Zurich, Lake of lake 25 *mi* (40 *km*) long N *cen* Switzerland

Zut·phen \'zət-fən\ commune E Netherlands on the IJssel

Zwick·au \'tsfi-,kaù, 'zwi-\ city E Germany S of Leipzig *pop* 112,565

Zwol·le \'zvò-lə, 'zwò-\ city E Netherlands ✳ of Overijssel *pop* 109,000

\ə\ **abut** \ᵊ\ kitten, F table \ər\ **further** \a\ **ash** \ā\ **ace** \ä\ **mop, mar**
\aù\ **out** \ch\ **chin** \e\ bet \ē\ **easy** \g\ **go** \i\ **hit** \ī\ **ice** \j\ **job**
\ŋ\ **sing** \ō\ **go** \ò\ **law** \òi\ **boy** \th\ **thin** \t̲h̲\ **the** \ü\ **loot** \ù\ **foot**
\y\ **yet** \zh\ **vision, beige** \ḵ, ⁿ, œ, ᵫ, ᵛ\ see Guide to Pronunciation

Signs and Symbols

Astronomy

SUN, GREATER PLANETS, ETC.

⊙ the sun; Sunday
○ *or* ☽ the moon; Monday
● new moon
☽, ◖, *or*) first quarter
○ full moon
☾, ◗, *or* (last quarter
☿ Mercury; Wednesday
♀ Venus; Friday
⊕ *or* ♁ Earth
♂ Mars; Tuesday
♃ Jupiter; Thursday
♄ *or* ♄ Saturn; Saturday

♅, ♅, *or* ♅ Uranus
♆, ♆, *or* ♃ Neptune
♇ Pluto
☄ comet
✳ *or* ✶ fixed star

ASPECTS AND NODES

☌ conjunction
□ quadrature
△ trine
☍ opposition
☊ ascending node
☋ descending node
(for astrological symbols see ZODIAC table)

Biology

○ an individual, specif., a female—used chiefly in inheritance charts
□ an individual, specif., a male—used chiefly in inheritance charts
♀ female
♂ *or* ♁ male
× crossed with; hybrid

+ wild type
P_1 parental generation usu. consisting of two or more different pure strains
F_1 first filial generation, offspring of a mating between different P_1 strains
F_2 second filial generation, offspring of an $F_1 \times F_1$ mating

Business and Finance

a/c account ⟨in a/c with⟩
@ at; each ⟨4 apples @ 5¢ = 20¢⟩
P principal; present value
i, r rate of interest
n number of periods (as of interest) and esp. years
/ *or* ℔ per
c/o care of
number if it precedes a numeral ⟨track #3⟩; pounds if it follows ⟨a 5 # sack of sugar⟩

℔ pound; pounds
% percent
‰ per thousand
© copyrighted
® registered trademark
$ dollars
¢ cents
£ pounds
/ shillings
(for other currency symbols see MONEY table)

Chemistry

+ signifies "plus," "and," "together with"—used between the symbols of substances brought together for, or produced by, a reaction; placed to the right of a symbol above the line, it signifies a unit charge of positive electricity: Ca^{++} *or* Ca^{2+} denotes the ion of calcium, which carries two positive charges; also used to indicate a dextrorotatory compound [as (+)-tartaric acid]

− signifies a unit charge of negative electricity when placed to the right of a symbol above the line: Cl^- denotes a chlorine ion carrying a negative charge; also used to indicate a levorotatory compound [as (−)-quinine]; also used to indicate the removal of a part from a compound (as − CO_2)

− signifies a single bond—used between the symbols of elements or groups which unite to form a compound: (as H−O−H for H_2O)

· —used to separate parts of a compound regarded as loosely joined (as $CuSO_4 \cdot 5H_2O$); the centered dot is also used to denote the presence of a single unpaired electron (as H·)

= indicates a double bond; placed to the right of a symbol above the line, it signifies two unit charges of negative electricity (as $SO_4^=$, the negative ion of sulfuric acid, carrying two negative charges)

≡ signifies a triple bond or a triple negative charge

: —used to indicate an unshared pair of electrons (as $:NH_3$); also sometimes used to indicate a double bond (as in $CH_2:CH_2$)

( ) marks groups within a compound [as in $C_6H_4(CH_3)_2$, the formula for xylene which contains two methyl groups (CH_3)]

⌐ *or* ⌐ joins attached atoms or groups in structural formulas for cyclic compounds, as that for glucose

$$\overline{}O\overline{}$$
$$CH_2OHCH(CHOH)_3CHOH$$

⬡ *or* ⬡ denotes the benzene ring
= gives or forms
→ gives, leads to, or is converted to
⇄ forms and is formed from, is in equilibrium with
↓ indicates precipitation of the substance

↑	indicates that the substance passes off as a gas
↔	indicates a reversible reaction or resonance structures
Δ	indicates that heat is required or produced
≡	is equivalent—used in statements to show how much of one substance will react with a given quantity of another so as to leave no excess of either
m, n, x	—used to indicate a variable or unknown number of atoms or groups esp. in polymers [as in $(C_5H_8)_n$]
1, 2, etc.	—used to indicate various quantities (as mass number $\langle ^{12}C\rangle$, atomic number $\langle _6C\rangle$, number of atoms or groups $\langle (C_6H_5)_2\rangle$, or quantity of electric charge $\langle Ca^{2+}\rangle$); also used in names to indicate the positions of substituting groups, attached to the first, etc., of the numbered atoms of the parent compound (as glucose-6-phosphate)
I, II, III, etc.	—used to indicate oxidation state $\langle Fe^{III}\rangle$
H	enthalpy
^{2}H *also* H^2	deuterium
^{3}H *also* H^3	tritium
M	metal
R	organic group, alkyl or aryl group
S	entropy
X	halogen atom
Z	atomic number
′	—used to distinguish between different substituents of the same kind (as R′, R″, R‴ to indicate different organic groups) (for element symbols see ELEMENT table)

Computers

?	wildcard used esp. to represent any single character in a keyword search (as in a search for "f?n" to find *fan*, *fin*, and *fun*)
*	wildcard used esp. to represent zero or more characters in a keyword search (as in a search for "key*" to find *key*, *keys*, *keyed*, *keying*, etc.)
@	at sign—used to introduce the domain name in an e-mail address
:-) *and* :-(etc.	emoticons (e.g., smile, frown, etc.)
/ *or* \	—used to introduce or separate parts of a computer address
.	dot—used to separate parts of a computer address or file name
⟨ ⟩	—used to enclose tags in a markup language (as ⟨title⟩Dictionary⟨/title⟩)

Home Electronics

◯	on
│	off
⏻ *or* ⏼ *or* ⏽	power switch
⇋	USB port
☼	brightness
▶	play
▶▶	fast forward
◀	rewind
◀◀	fast rewind
+	increase
-	decrease
◀ *or* 🔇	mute
🎧	headphone jack
◑	contrast
‖	pause
■	stop
●	record
▲	eject

Mathematics

+	plus; positive $\langle a + b = c\rangle$—also used to indicate omitted figures or an approximation
–	minus; negative
±	plus or minus; positive or negative ⟨the square root of $4a^2$ is $\pm 2a$⟩ ⟨an age of 120,000 years $\pm 12,000$⟩ ⟨a tolerance of ± 5 percent⟩
×	multiplied by; times $\langle 6 \times 4 = 24\rangle$—also indicated by placing a dot between the factors $\langle 6{\cdot}4 = 24\rangle$ or by writing the factors one after the other, often enclosed in parentheses, without explicitly indicating multiplication $\langle (4)(5)(3) = 60\rangle$ $\langle -4abc\rangle$
÷ *or* :	divided by $\langle 24 \div 6 = 4\rangle$—also indicated by writing the divisor under the dividend with a line between $\langle \frac{24}{6} = 4\rangle$ or by writing the divisor after the dividend with a slash between $\langle 3/8\rangle$
E	times 10 raised to an indicated exponent ⟨4.52E5 $= 4.52 \times 10^5$⟩—used esp. in electronic displays
=	equals $\langle 6 + 2 = 8\rangle$
≠ *or* ＋	is not equal to
>	is greater than $\langle 6 > 5\rangle$
<	is less than $\langle 3 < 4\rangle$
≧ *or* ≥	is greater than or equal to
≦ *or* ≤	is less than or equal to
≯	is not greater than
≮	is not less than
≈	is approximately equal to
≡	is identical to
~	is similar to; the negation of; the negative of
≅	is congruent to
∝	varies directly as; is proportional to
:	is to; the ratio of
∴	therefore
∞	infinity
∠	angle; the angle ⟨∠ ABC⟩
∟	right angle ⟨∟ ABC⟩
⊥	the perpendicular; is perpendicular to ⟨AB ⊥ CD⟩
‖	parallel; is parallel to ⟨AB ‖ CD⟩
⊙ *or* ○	circle
⌒	arc of a circle
△	triangle
□	square
▭	rectangle
√ *or* √	root—used without an index to indicate a square root (as in $\sqrt{4} = 2$) or with an index above the sign to indicate a higher degree (as in $\sqrt[3]{3}$, $\sqrt[3]{7}$); also denoted by a fractional index at the right of a number whose denominator expresses the degree of the root $\langle 3^{1/3} = \sqrt[3]{3}\rangle$
( )	parentheses ⎫
[ ]	brackets ⎬ —used to indicate associated quantities and the order of operations
{ }	braces ⎭
—	(when placed above quantities) vinculum

Δ the operation of finding the difference between two nearby values of a variable (as y) or of a function (as f) for two values of its independent variable (as x) differing by a small nonzero amount (as h) $\langle \Delta y = y_2 - y_1 \rangle$ $\langle \Delta f(x) = f(x) + h) - f(x) \rangle$

$\int$ integral; integral of $\langle \int 2x\,dx = x^2 + C \rangle$

$\int_b^a$ the integral taken from the value b to the value a of the variable

$\dfrac{df(x)}{dx}$ the derivative of the function $f(x)$ with respect to x

$\dfrac{\partial f(x,y)}{\partial x}$ the partial derivative of the function $f(x,y)$ with respect to x

δ_j^i Kronecker delta

s standard deviation of a sample taken from a population

σ standard deviation of a population

s^2 variance of a sample from a population

σ^2 variance

Σ sum; summation $\langle \sum_{i=1}^n x_i = x_1 + x_2 + \ldots + x_n \rangle$

$\bar{x}$ arithmetic mean of a sample of a variable x

μ (1) micrometer (2) arithmetic mean of a population

χ^2 chi-square

P the probability of obtaining a result as great as or greater than the observed result in a statistical test if the null hypothesis is true

r correlation coefficient

$E(x)$ expected value of the random variable x

π pi; the number 3.14159265+; the ratio of the circumference of a circle to its diameter

Π product $\langle \prod_{i=1}^n x_i = (x_1)(x_2) \ldots (x_n) \rangle$

$!$ factorial $\langle n! = n(n-1)(n-2) \ldots 1 \rangle$

e or ϵ (1) the number 2.7182818+; the base of the natural system of logarithms (2) the eccentricity of a conic section

i the positive square root of minus one $\sqrt{-1}$

n an unspecified number (as an exponent) esp. when integral

$\circ$ degree $\langle 60° \rangle$

$'$ minute; foot $\langle 30' \rangle$—also used to distinguish between different values of the same variable or between different variables (as a', a'', a''', usually read a prime, a double prime, a triple prime) or between the first and higher derivatives of a func-

tion (as f', f'' or $f'(x)$, $f''(x)$ for the first and second derivatives of f or $f(x)$)

$''$ second; inch $\langle 30'' \rangle$

$0, 1, 2, 3$, etc. —used as exponents placed above and at the right of an expression to indicate that it is raised to a power whose degree is indicated by the figure $\langle a^0$ equals $1 \rangle$ $\langle a^1$ equals $a \rangle$ $\langle a^2$ is the square of $a \rangle$

$-1, -2, -3$, etc. —used as exponents placed above and at the right of an expression to indicate that the reciprocal of the expression is raised to the power whose degree is indicated by the figure $\langle a^{-1}$ equals $1/a \rangle$ $\langle a^{-2}$ equals $1/a^2 \rangle$

θ angle or measure of an angle esp. in radians

$\sin^{-1}x$ arcsine of x

$\cos^{-1}x$ arccosine of x

$\tan^{-1}x$ arctangent of x

f function

f^{-1} the inverse of the function f

$|z|$ the absolute value of z

$[a_{ij}]$ matrix with element a_{ij} in the ith row and jth column

$|a_{ij}|$ determinant of a square matrix with elements a_{ij}

$\|A\|$ or $\|\mathbf{x}\|$ norm of the matrix A or the vector $\mathbf{x}$

A^{-1} inverse of the matrix A

A^T transpose of the matrix A

$\oplus$ an operation in a mathematical system (as a group or ring) with $A \oplus B$ indicating the sum of the two elements A and B

$\otimes$ an operation in a mathematical system (as a group or ring) with $A \otimes B$ indicating the product of the two elements A and B

$[x]$ the greatest integer not greater than x

(a,b) the open interval $a < x < b$

$[a,b]$ the closed interval $a \le x \le b$

$\aleph_0$ aleph-null

ω the ordinal number of the positive integers

$\ni$ or : such that $\langle$ choose a and $b \ni a + b = 6 \rangle$

$\exists$ there exists $\langle \exists\, a \ni a + 2 = 4 \rangle$

$\forall$ for every, for all $\langle \forall\, a \ni a$ is a real number, $a^2 \ge 0 \rangle$

$\cup$ union of two sets

$\cap$ intersection of two sets

$\subset$ is included in, is a subset of

$\supset$ contains as a subset

$\in$ or ϵ is an element of

$\notin$ is not an element of

Λ or 0 or $\emptyset$ or $\{\,\}$ empty set, null set

Miscellaneous

$\&$ and

$\&c$ et cetera, and so forth

$"$ or $"$ ditto marks

$/$ slash (or diagonal or slant or solidus or virgule)—used to mean "or" (as in and/or), "and/or" (as in dead/wounded), "per" (as in feet/second); used to indicate end of a line of verse; used to separate the figures of a date (4/4/73)

☞ index or fist

$<$ derived from

$>$ whence derived

$+$ and

} used in linguistics

$*$ hypothetical; ungrammatical

$\dagger$ died—used esp. in genealogies

$+$ cross (for variations see CROSS illustration)

✶ monogram from Greek XP signifying Christ

Ⓤ or Ⓚ kosher certification

✡ Magen David

☥ ankh

℣ versicle

℟ response

✳ —used in Roman Catholic and Anglican service books to divide each verse of a psalm, indicating where the response begins

✠ or + —used in some service books to indicate where the sign of the cross is to be made; also used by certain Roman Catholic and Anglican prelates as a sign of the cross preceding their signatures

LXX Septuagint

卐 swastika

$f/$ or f: relative aperture of a photographic lens

℞ take—used on prescriptions; prescription; treatment

☠ poison

☣ biohazard, biohazardous materials

☢ or ☢ radiation, radioactive materials

🜨 civil defense

☢ fallout shelter

☮ peace

x or $\times$ by $\langle 3 \times 5$ cards $\rangle$

☯ yin and yang

♲ recycle, recyclable

Physics

α	alpha particle
β	beta particle, beta ray
γ	gamma, photon; surface tension
ϵ	permittivity
η	efficiency; viscosity
λ	wavelength
μ	micro-; micron; muon; permeability
ν	frequency; neutrino
ρ	density; resistivity
σ	conductivity; cross section; surface tension
ϕ	luminous flux; magnetic flux
Ω	ohm
Å	angstrom
B	magnetic induction; magnetic field
c	speed of light
e	electron; electronic charge
E	electric field; energy; illumination; modulus of elasticity; potential difference
h	Planck's constant
$\hbar$	a constant equal to $h/2\pi$

H	magnetic field strength
J	angular momentum
L	inductance, self-inductance
n	refractive index; neutron
p	momentum of a particle; proton
q	charge; quark
S	entropy
T	absolute temperature; period
V	electrical potential
W	work
X	power of magnification; reactance
Y	admittance
Z	impedance

CIRCUIT ELEMENTS

$\dashv\vdash$ *or* $\dashv\vdash$	DC power, battery
$-\!\!\bigcirc\!\!-$	AC power, generator
$\dashv\vdash$	capacitor
$-\!\!\text{vvv}\!\!-$	resistor
$-\!\!\text{mmm}\!\!-$	inductor
$-\!\!/\!\!\circ\!\!-$	switch
m *or* $\perp$	grounded connection

Reference Marks

*	asterisk *or* star
†	dagger
‡	double dagger
§	section *or* numbered clause

‖	parallels
¶ *or* ⁋	paragraph
	(for editing marks see PROOFREADERS' MARKS table)

Stamps and Stamp Collecting

★ *or* *	unused
★★ *or* **	unused with original gum intact and never mounted with a stamp hinge

⊙ *or* ○ *or* 0	used
⊞	block of four
⊠	entire cover or card

Weather

	Barometer, changes of:
$\diagup$	Rising, then falling
$\diagup$	Rising, then steady; or rising, then rising more slowly
$/$	Rising steadily, or unsteadily
$\diagdown$	Falling or steady, then rising; or rising, then rising more quickly
—	Steady, same as 3 hours ago
$\diagdown$	Falling, then rising, same or lower than 3 hours ago
$\diagdown$	Falling, then steady; or falling, then falling more slowly
$\backslash$	Falling steadily, or unsteadily
$\diagdown$	Steady or rising, then falling; or falling, then falling more quickly
◎	calm
○	clear
◑	cloudy (partly)
●	cloudy (completely overcast)
⊹	drifting or blowing snow
⸴	drizzle
≡	fog

∞	freezing rain
▲▲▲▲	front, cold
▬▬▬	warm
▬▲▬▲	occluded
▼▲▼	stationary
⫴	funnel clouds
∞	haze
●	hurricane
◯	tropical storm
↔	ice needles
●	rain
⸱*	rain and snow
⋺⋹	rime
↭	sandstorm or dust storm
▽	shower(s)
▽̇	shower of rain
▽̇	shower of hail
△	sleet
✳	snow
⌐̌	thunderstorm
⌐	visibility reduced by smoke

A Handbook of Style

Punctuation

Punctuation marks are used in written English to separate groups of words for meaning and emphasis; to convey an idea of the variations of pitch, volume, pauses, and intonation of the spoken language; and to help avoid ambiguity. The uses of the standard punctuation marks are discussed and illustrated in the following pages. For an explanation of the punctuation marks used in the entries in this dictionary, see the Explanatory Notes in the front of the book.

Apostrophe '

1. Indicates the possessive of nouns and indefinite pronouns. The possessive of singular nouns and some plural nouns is formed by adding -'s. The possessive of plural nouns ending in an s or z sound is usually formed by adding only an apostrophe; the possessive of irregular plurals is formed by adding -'s.

the boy's mother	birds' migrations
Douglas's crimes	the Stevenses' house
anyone's guess	people's opinions
Degas's drawings	children's laughter

2. Marks the omission of letters in contracted words.

didn't   they're   she'd

3. Marks the omission of digits in numerals.

class of '03   in the '90s

4. Often forms plurals of letters, figures, abbreviations, symbols, and words referred to as words.

dot your *i*'s and cross your *t*'s

three 8's *or* three 8s

these Ph.D.'s *or* these Ph.D.s

used &'s instead of *and*'s

Brackets [ ]

1. Enclose editorial comments or clarifications inserted into quoted material.

His embarrassment had peaked [sic] her curiosity.

2. Enclose insertions that supply missing letters or that alter the form of the original word.

His letter continues, "If D[eutsch] won't take the manuscript, perhaps someone at Faber will."

He dryly observed that they bought the stock because "they want[ed] to see themselves getting richer."

3. Function as parentheses within parentheses.

Posner's recent essays (like his earlier *Law and Literature* [1988]) bear this out

Colon :

1. Introduces an amplifying word, phrase, or clause that acts as an appositive.

That year Handley's old obsession was replaced with a new one: jazz.

The issue comes down to this: Will we offer a reduced curriculum, or will we simply cancel the program?

2. Introduces a list or series.

Three abstained: Britain, France, and Belgium.

3. Introduces a clause or phrase that explains, illustrates, amplifies, or restates what has gone before.

Dawn was breaking: the distant peaks were already glowing with the sun's first rays.

4. Introduces lengthy quoted material set off from the rest of the text by indentation but not by quotation marks. It may also be used before a quotation enclosed by quotation marks in running text.

The *Rumpole* series has been well described as follows:

Rumpled, disreputable, curmudgeonly barrister Horace Rumpole often wins cases despite the disdain of his more aristocratic colleagues. Fond of cheap wine ("Château Thames Embankment") and. . . .

The inscription reads: "Here lies one whose name was writ in water."

5. Separates elements in bibliographic publication data and page references, in biblical citations, and in formulas used to express time and ratios.

Boston: Houghton Mifflin, 1997

Scientific American 240 (Jan.):122-33

John 4:10   8:30 a.m.   a ratio of 3:5

6. Separates titles and subtitles.

Southwest Stories: Tales from the Desert

7. Follows the salutation in formal correspondence.

Dear Judge Wright: Ladies and Gentlemen:

8. Follows headings in memorandums and business letters.

TO: Reference:

9. Is placed outside quotation marks and parentheses when it punctuates the larger sentence.

The problem becomes most acute in "Black Rose and Destroying Angel": plot simply ceases to exist.

, Comma

1. Separates main clauses joined by a coordinating conjunction (such as *and, but, or, nor, so*), and occasionally short parallel clauses not joined by conjunctions.

She knew very little about the new system, and he volunteered nothing.

The trial lasted for nine months, but the jury took only four hours to reach its verdict.

She came, she saw, she conquered.

2. Sets off adverbial clauses and phrases that begin or interrupt a sentence. If the sentence can be easily read without a comma, the comma may be omitted.

Having agreed to disagree, they turned to other matters.

The report, after being read aloud, was put up for consideration.

In January the roof fell in.

As cars age they depreciate.

3. Sets off transitional words and phrases (such as *indeed, however*) and words that introduce examples (such as *namely, for example*).

Indeed, no one seemed to have heard of him.

They concluded, however, that it was meaningless.

Three have complied, namely, Togo, Benin, and Ghana.

4. Sets off contrasting expressions within a sentence.

This project will take six months, not six weeks.

5. Separates words, phrases, or clauses in a series. Many writers omit the comma before the last item in a series whenever this would not result in ambiguity.

Men, women[,] and children crowded aboard the train.

Her job required her to pack quickly, to travel often[,] and to have no personal life.

He came down the steps as reporters shouted questions, flashbulbs popped[,] and the crowd pushed closer.

6. Separates two or more adjectives that modify a noun. It is not used between two adjectives when the first modifies the combination of the second plus the noun it modifies.

in a calm, reflective manner

the harsh, damp, piercing wind

a good used car   the lone bald eagle

7. Sets off a nonrestrictive (nonessential) word, phrase, or clause that is in apposition to a preceding or following noun.

We visited Verdun, site of the famous battle.

A cherished landmark, the Hotel Sandburg was spared.

Its author, Maria Olevsky, was an expert diver.

8. Separates a direct quotation from a phrase identifying its source or speaker. The comma is omitted when the quotation ends with a question mark or exclamation point, and usually omitted when the quoted phrase itself is the subject or object of the larger sentence.

She answered, "I'm leaving."

"I suspect," Bob observed, "we'll be hearing more."

"How about another round?" Elaine piped up.

"The network is down" was the reply she feared.

9. Sets off words in direct address and mild interjections.

The facts, my fellow Americans, are very different.

This is our final notice, Mr. Sutton.

Ah, the mosaics in Ravenna are matchless.

10. Precedes a tag question.

That's obvious, isn't it?

11. Indicates the omission of a word or phrase used in a parallel construction earlier in the sentence. In short sentences, the comma may be omitted.

Eight councillors cast their votes for O'Reilly; six, for Mendez.

Seven voted in favor, three against.

12. Is used to avoid ambiguity that might arise from adjacent words.

Under Mr. James, Madison High School flourished.

13. Groups numerals into units of three to separate thousands, millions, and so on. It is not used in street addresses, page numbers, and four-digit years.

2,000 case histories   12537 Wilshire Blvd.

a fee of $12,500   page 1415

numbering 3,450,000   in 3000 B.C.

14. Separates a surname from a following title or degree, and often from the abbreviations *Jr.* and *Sr.*

Sandra H. Cobb, Vice President

Lee Herman Melville, M.D.

Douglas Fairbanks, Jr.   *or*   Douglas Fairbanks Jr.

15. Sets off elements of an address (except for zip codes) and full dates. When only the month and year are given, the comma is usually omitted.

> Write to Bureau of the Census, Washington, DC 20233.
>
> In Reno, Nevada, their luck ran out.
>
> On July 26, 2000, the court issued its opinion.
>
> October 1929 brought an end to all that.

16. Follows the salutation in informal correspondence and follows the complimentary close in a letter.

> Dear Aunt Sarah,   Sincerely yours,

Dash   —

1. Marks an abrupt change or break in the structure of a sentence.

> The students seemed happy enough with the new plan, but the alumni—there was the problem

2. Is used in place of commas or parentheses to emphasize parenthetical or amplifying material. In general, no punctuation immediately precedes an opening dash or immediately follows a closing dash.

> It will prevent corporations—large and small—from buying influence with campaign contributions.

3. Introduces defining phrases and lists.

> The motion was then tabled—that is, removed indefinitely from consideration.
>
> Davis was a leading innovator in at least three styles—bebop, cool jazz, and jazz-rock fusion.

4. Often precedes the attribution of a quotation, either immediately after the quotation or on the next line.

> Only the sign is for sale.—Søren Kierkegaard
>
> *or*
>
> Only the sign is for sale.
>   —Søren Kierkegaard

5. Sets off an interrupting clause or phrase. An exclamation point or question mark may immediately precede a dash.

> If we don't succeed—and the critics say we won't—then the whole project is in jeopardy.
>
> His hobby was getting on people's nerves—especially mine!—and he was very good at it.

Ellipsis . . . .

1. Indicates the omission of one or more words within a quoted sentence. Omission of a word or phrase is indicated by three ellipsis points. If an entire sentence or more is omitted, the end punctuation of the preceding sentence (including a period) is followed by three ellipsis points. Punctuation used in the original that falls on either side of the ellipsis is often omitted; however, it may be retained, especially if this helps clarify the sentence structure. (The second and third examples below are shortened versions of the first.)

> Is it so bad, then, to be misunderstood? Pythagoras was misunderstood, and Socrates, and Jesus, and

Luther, and Copernicus, and Galileo, and Newton, and every pure and wise spirit that ever took flesh. To be great is to be misunderstood.—Emerson

> Is it so bad, then, to be misunderstood? Pythagoras was misunderstood, and Socrates, and Jesus, . . . and every pure and wise spirit that ever took flesh.
>
> Is it so bad, then, to be misunderstood? . . . To be great is to be misunderstood.

2. Indicates that one or more lines have been omitted from a poem. The row of ellipsis points usually matches the length of the line above.

> When I heard the learned astronomer,
> . . . .
> How soon unaccountable I became tired and sick,
> Til rising and gliding out I wandered off by myself,

3. Indicates faltering speech or an unfinished sentence in dialogue.

> "I mean . . . " he stammered, "like . . . How?"

Exclamation Point   !

1. Ends an emphatic phrase, sentence, or interjection.

> Without a trace!
>
> There is no alternative!
>
> Encore!

2. Is placed within brackets, dashes, parentheses, and quotation marks when it punctuates only the enclosed material. It is placed outside them when it punctuates the entire sentence. If it falls where a comma could also go, the comma is dropped.

> All of this proves—at long last!—that we were right from the start.
>
> Somehow the dog got the gate open (for the third time!) and ran into the street.
>
> He sprang to his feet and shouted "Point of order!"
>
> At this rate, the national anthem will soon be replaced by "You Are My Sunshine"!
>
> "Absolutely not!" he snapped.
>
> They wouldn't dare! she told herself over and over.

Hyphen   -

1. Is often used to link elements in compound words. Consult the dictionary in doubtful cases.

> secretary-treasurer   spin-off
>
> cost-effective   light-year
>
> middle-of-the-road   president-elect

2. Is used to separate a prefix, suffix, or combining form from an existing word if the base word is capitalized, and often when the base word is more than two syllables long, or when identical letters would otherwise be adjacent to each other. Consult the dictionary in doubtful cases.

> pre-Victorian   wall-like
>
> industry-wide   co-opted
>
> recession-proof   anti-inflationary

3. Is used in compound nouns containing a particle (usually a preposition or adverb).

on-ramp	falling-out
runner-up	right-of-way

4. Is used in most compound modifiers when placed before the noun.

the fresh-cut grass	a made-up excuse
her gray-green eyes	the well-worded statement

5. Is used with the first of two prefixes or modifiers forming a compound with the same base word.

pre- and postoperative care

anti- or pro-Revolutionary sympathies

early- and mid-20th-century painters

6. Is used with written-out numbers, both cardinal and ordinal, between 21 and 99.

forty-one years old	his forty-first birthday
one hundred forty-one	

7. Is used in a written-out fraction employed as a modifier. A fraction used as a noun is often left open.

a one-half share

three fifths of the vote   *or*   three-fifths of the vote

one one-hundredth of an inch

8. Is used between numbers and dates with the meaning "(up) to and including." In typeset material the hyphen is replaced by the longer en dash.

pages 128–34

the years 1995–99

9. Is used as the equivalent of *to, and,* or *versus* to indicate linkage or opposition. In typeset material the longer en dash is used.

the New York–Paris flight

the Lincoln–Douglas debates

a final score of 7–2.

10. Marks an end-of-line division of a word.

In 1975 smallpox, formerly a great scourge, was declared eradicated.

( ) Parentheses

1. Enclose phrases and clauses that provide examples, explanations, or supplementary facts.

Nominations for principal officers (president, vice president, treasurer, and secretary) were approved.

Four computers (all outdated models) were replaced.

Although we liked Mille Fiori (their risotto was the best), we hadn't been there in several months.

2. Enclose numerals that confirm a spelled-out number in a business or legal context.

Delivery will be made in thirty (30) days.

The fee is four thousand dollars ($4,000.00).

3. Enclose numbers or letters indicating individual items in a series within a sentence.

Sentences can be classified as (1) simple, (2) multiple or compound, and (3) complex.

4. Enclose abbreviations that follow their spelled-out forms, or spelled-out forms that follow their abbreviations.

the Food and Drug Administration (FDA)

the ABA (American Booksellers Association)

5. Indicate alternative terms.

Please sign and return the enclosed form(s).

6. Often enclose cross-references and bibliographic references, as well as publishing data in bibliographic citations.

Specialized services are also available (see list below).

The diagram (Fig. 3) illustrates the action of the pump.

Subsequent studies (Braxton 1998; Roh and Weinglass 2002) have confirmed these findings.

3. See Stendhal, *Love* (New York: Penguin, 1975), 342.

7. Are used with other punctuation marks as follows: If an independent sentence is enclosed in parentheses, its first word is capitalized and a period is placed inside the parentheses. If the parenthetical expression occurs within a sentence, it is uncapitalized unless it is a quotation, and does not end with a period but may end with an exclamation point, a question mark, or quotation marks. No punctuation immediately precedes an opening parenthesis within a sentence; if punctuation is required, it follows the closing parenthesis.

The discussion was held in the boardroom. (The results are still confidential.)

This short section (musicians would call it the *bridge*) has the song's most distinctive harmonies.

The background music is always Bach (does the chairman have such good taste?).

He was distraught ("It's my whole career!") and refused to see anyone.

I'll get back to you tomorrow (Friday), when I have more details.

. Period

1. Ends a sentence or a sentence fragment that is neither a question nor an exclamation. Only one period ends a sentence.

She asked if we were swing dancers.

Give it your best.

Unlikely. In fact, inconceivable.

She liked best the sentence that read "Leda Rubin has made the impossible possible."

2. Follows most abbreviations and some contractions.

Calif.	e.g.	Dr.
Sept.	p.m.	Jr.
etc.	dept.	Assn.
Ph.D. *or* PhD		C.E.O. *or* CEO

3. Is used with a person's initials.

    F. Scott Fitzgerald   J. B. S. Haldane

4. Follows numerals and letters when used without parentheses in outlines and vertical lists.

    I. Objectives
     A. Economy
       1. Low initial cost
       2. Low maintenance cost
     B. Ease of operation

Question Mark   ?

1. Ends a direct question.

    "When do they arrive?" she asked.

    Was anyone seen in the area after 10 p.m.?

2. Ends a question that forms part of a sentence, but does not follow an indirect question.

    What was her motive? you may be asking.

    I naturally wondered, Will it really work?

    He asked when the club normally closed.

3. Indicates uncertainty about a fact.

    Geoffrey Chaucer, English poet (1342?–1400)

4. Is used with other punctuation marks exactly like the exclamation point (see p. 1606).

Quotation   "   "
Marks, Double

1. Enclose direct quotations but not indirect quotations.

    "I'm leaving," she whispered. "This could last forever."

    She whispered that she was leaving.

    He asked, "What went wrong?"

    The question is, What went wrong?

2. Enclose words or phrases borrowed from others, and words of obvious informality.

    They required a "biodata summary"—that is, a résumé.

    He called himself "emperor," but he was really just a dictator.

    They were afraid the patient had "stroked out"—had had a cerebrovascular accident.

3. Enclose titles of poems, short stories, essays, articles in periodicals, chapters of books, and episodes of radio and television programs.

    the article "After the Genocide" in the *New Yorker*

    "The Death of the Hired Man" by Robert Frost

    Poe's "The Murders in the Rue Morgue"

    John Barth's essay "The Literature of Exhaustion"

    The Jungle Book's ninth chapter, "Rikki-tikki-tavi"

    *M*A*S*H*'s finale, "Goodbye, Farewell and Amen"

4. Enclose lines of poetry run in with the text.

    When Gilbert advised, "Stick close to your desks and never go to sea, / And you all may be rulers of the Queen's Navee!" this latest appointee was obviously paying attention.

5. Are used with other punctuation marks as follows: A period or comma is placed within the quotation marks. A colon or semicolon is placed outside them. A dash, question mark, or exclamation point is placed inside the quotation marks when it punctuates the quoted matter only, but outside when it punctuates the whole sentence.

    He smiled and said, "I'm happy for you."

    "Too easy," she shot back.

    There was only one real "issue": noise.

    She spoke of her "little cottage in the country"; she might better have called it a mansion.

    "I can't see how—" he started to say.

    Saturdays there were dances—"sock hops"—in the gym.

    He asked, "When did she leave?"

    What is the meaning of "the open door"?

    She collapsed in her seat with a stunned "Good grief!"

    Save us from his "mercy"!

Quotation Marks,
Single   '   '

1. Enclose quoted material within quoted material.

    "I distinctly heard him say, 'Don't be late,' and then I heard the door close."

    This analysis is indebted to Del Banco's "Elizabeth Bishop's 'Insomnia': An Inverted View."

2. In British usage, may enclose quoted material, in which case a quotation within a quotation is set off by double quotation marks.

    'I distinctly heard him say, "Don't be late," and then I heard the door close.'

Semicolon   ;

1. Separates related independent clauses joined without a coordinating conjunction.

    Cream the butter and sugar; add the eggs and beat well.

    The river overflowed its banks; roads vanished; freshly plowed fields turned into lakes.

2. Joins two clauses when the second includes a conjunctive adverb (such as *however, indeed, thus*) or a phrase that acts like one (such as *in that case, as a result, on the other hand*).

    It won't be easy to sort out the facts; a decision must be made, however.

    The case could take years; as a result, many plaintiffs will accept settlements.

3. Is often used before introductory expressions such as *for example, that is,* and *namely*.

> We were fairly successful; that is, we made our deadlines and met our budget.

4. Separates phrases or items in a series when they contain commas.

> The assets include $22 million in land, buildings, and equipment; $34 million in cash and investments; and $8 million in inventory.

> The Pissarro exhibition will travel to Washington, D.C.; Manchester, N.H.; Portland, Ore.; and Oakland, Cal.

> The votes against were: Precinct 1, 418; Precinct 2, 332; Precinct 3, 256.

5. Is placed outside quotation marks and parentheses.

> They again demanded "complete autonomy"; the demand was again rejected.

> She found him urbane and entertaining (if somewhat overbearing); he found her charmingly ingenuous.

/   Slash

1. Separates alternatives, usually representing the words *or* or *and/or*.

> alumni/ae   his/her

2. Replaces the word *to* or *and* in some compound terms and ranges.

> 1998/99   *or*   1998–99

> the May/June issue   *or*   the May–June issue

3. Separates lines of poetry that are run in with the text. A space usually precedes and follows the slash.

> In Pope's words: "'Tis with our judgments as our watches, none / Go just alike, yet each believes his own."

4. Separates the elements in a numerical date, and numerators and denominators in fractions.

> on 9/11/01   a 7/8-mile course

5. Represents the word *per* or *to* when used between units of measure or the terms of a ratio.

> 400,000 tons/year   price/earnings ratio

> 29 mi/gal   20/20 vision

6. Punctuates some abbreviations.

> w/o [*for* without]   I/O [*for* input/output]

> c/o [*for* care of]   P/E [*for* price/earnings]

7. Punctuates Internet addresses.

> http://unabridged.Merriam-Webster.com/

Foreign Marks

1. Guillemets « » often enclose quotations in French and other European languages.

> Marie Antoinette est censée dire «qu'ils mangent de la brioche».

2. Spanish exclamation points ¡ ! are used in pairs to enclose an exclamatory sentence in Spanish writing.

> ¡Qué buen día!

3. Spanish question marks ¿ ? are used in pairs to enclose an interrogatory sentence in Spanish writing.

> ¿Qué es esto?

Capitals and Italics

Words and phrases are capitalized or italicized to indicate that they have a special significance in particular contexts. The following rules and examples describe the most common uses of capitals and italics.

Beginnings

1. The first word of a sentence or sentence fragment is capitalized.

> The play lasted nearly three hours.

> So many people, so many opinions.

> Bravo!

2. The first word of a sentence contained within parentheses is capitalized. However, a parenthetical sentence within another sentence is not capitalized unless it is a complete quoted sentence.

> No one answered the telephone. (They were probably on vacation.)

> Having waited in line for an hour (why do we do these things?), we finally left.

> After some initial defensiveness ("Was it my fault?"), he gradually got over it.

3. The first word of a direct quotation is capitalized. However, if the quotation is interrupted in mid-sentence, the second part does not begin with a capital. When a quotation is syntactically dependent on the sentence in which it occurs, it usually does not begin with a capital.

> Hart repeated, "We have no budget for new computers."

> "We have no budget for new computers," repeated Hart, "but we may next year."

> Hart made it clear that "we have no budget for new computers."

4. The first word of a sentence within a sentence that is not a direct quotation is usually capitalized. Examples include mottoes and rules, unspoken or imaginary dialogue, and direct questions.

> You know the saying "Fools rush in where angels fear to tread."

> The first rule is, When in doubt, spell it out.

> My first thought was, How can I avoid this assignment?

> The question is, When can we go?

5. The first word following a colon is usually lowercased, even when it begins a complete sentence. However, when the sentence introduced is lengthy and distinctly separate from the preceding clause, it is often capitalized.

> The advantage of this system is clear: it's inexpensive.

> The situation is critical: This company cannot hope to recoup the fourth-quarter losses that were sustained in five operating divisions.

6. The first word of a line of poetry is traditionally capitalized. However, in modern poetry the line beginnings are often lowercased. The poem's original capitalization should always be retained.

> The best lack all conviction, while the worst
> Are full of passionate intensity.
> —W. B. Yeats

> If tributes cannot
> be implicit
> give me diatribes and the fragrance of iodine,
> the cork oak acorn grown in Spain . . .
> —Marianne Moore

7. The first words of items in vertical lists are usually capitalized. However, numbered phrases within a sentence are lowercased.

> The English peerage consists of five ranks:
> 1. Duke (Duchess)
> 2. Marquess (Marchioness)
> 3. Earl (Countess)
> 4. Viscount (Viscountess)
> 5. Baron (Baroness)

> Among the fastest animals are (1) the cheetah, clocked at 70 mph; (2) the pronghorn, at 61 mph; (3) the lion, at 50 mph; (4) the quarter horse, at 47 mph; and (5) the elk, at 45 mph.

8. The first word in an outline heading is capitalized.

> I. Prose texts
>   A. Typeface
>   1. Alphabets
>   2. Characteristics
>   B. Type page and trim size

9. The first word and courtesy titles of the salutation of a letter and the first word of a complimentary close are capitalized.

> Dear Sir or Madam: Sincerely yours,

> To whom it may concern: Love,

Proper Nouns and Adjectives

Awards and Prizes

1. Names of awards and prizes are capitalized. Words and phrases that are not actually part of the award's name are lowercased.

> Academy Award   Rhodes Scholarship
> Nobel Prize in medicine   Rhodes scholar

Derivatives of Proper Nouns

2. Derivatives of proper nouns are capitalized when used in their primary sense. If the derived term has taken on a specialized meaning, it is often lowercased. Consult the dictionary when in doubt.

Roman sculpture	chinaware
Edwardian era	french fries
Hodgkin's disease	quixotic

Geographical References

3. Terms that identify divisions of the earth's surface and distinct regions, places, or districts are capitalized, as are derivative nouns and adjectives.

Tropic of Cancer	the Highlands
Asia Minor	Highland attitudes
the Great Lakes	Burgundy
Arnhem Land	Burgundians

4. Popular names of localities are capitalized.

the Left Bank	the Sunbelt
Little Italy	the Loop

5. Words designating global, national, regional, or local political divisions are capitalized when they are essential elements of specific names. They are usually lowercased when they precede a proper noun or are not part of a specific name.

the Roman Empire	New York City
the fall of the empire	the city of New York

6. Generic geographical terms (such as *lake, mountain*) are capitalized if they are part of a proper noun.

Lake Tanganyika	Atlas Mountains
Yosemite Valley	Mount Everest

7. Generic geographical terms preceding two or more names are usually capitalized.

Lakes Huron and Erie

Mounts McKinley, Whitney, and Shasta

8. Generic terms that are not used as part of a single proper noun are not capitalized. These include plural terms that follow two or more proper nouns, and terms that are used descriptively or alone.

Maine and Oak streets

the Oder and Nysa rivers

the Pacific coast of Mexico

the river delta

9. Compass points are capitalized when they refer to a geographical region or form part of a place-name or street name. They are lowercased when they refer to a simple direction.

the Southwest	East Coast
North Pole	north of the Rio Grande
West 12th Street	went west on 12th Street

10. Nouns and adjectives that are derived from compass points and that designate or refer to a specific geographical region are usually capitalized.

Easterners	Southern hospitality
Northern Europeans	Southwestern recipes

11. Names of streets, monuments, parks, landmarks, and other public places are capitalized. Generic terms (such as *street, park, bridge*) are lowercased when used alone.

State Street	the Plaza Hotel
Golden Gate Bridge	back to the hotel

Governmental and Judicial Bodies

12. Full names of legislative, executive, and administrative bodies are capitalized, as are easily recognizable short forms of these names. However, nonspecific noun and adjective references to them are usually lowercased.

United States Congress

Congress

congressional hearings

Federal Trade Commission

a federal agency

13. Full names of high courts are capitalized. Short forms of such names are usually lowercased, as are names of city and county courts. However, both the full and short names of the U.S. Supreme Court are capitalized.

International Court of Justice

the state supreme court

Springfield municipal court

small-claims court

the Supreme Court of the United States

the Court

Historical Periods and Events

14. Names of some historical and cultural periods and movements are capitalized. When in doubt, consult a dictionary or encyclopedia.

Bronze Age	Third Reich
the Renaissance	Victorian era
Fifth Republic	Age of Pericles
Prohibition	the atomic age

15. Names of conferences, councils, and specific historical, cultural, and sporting events are capitalized.

Yalta Conference	San Francisco Earthquake
Council of Trent	Cannes Film Festival
Boston Tea Party	World Cup

16. Full names of specific treaties, laws, and acts are capitalized.

Treaty of Versailles	First Amendment rights
the Bill of Rights	Clean Air Act of 1990

Legal Cases

17. Names of the plaintiff and defendant in legal case titles are italicized, as are short forms of case titles. The *v.* (for *versus*) may be roman or italic. When the party involved rather than the case itself is being discussed, the reference is not italicized.

Smith et. al. v. [or v.] Jones

a quick decision in the *Jones* case

She covered the Lemuel Jones trial for the newspaper.

Military Units

18. Full titles of branches and units of the U.S. armed forces are capitalized, as are standard short forms. However, the plurals of *army, navy, air force,* and *coast guard* are lowercased.

U.S. Marine Corps	the Third Army
the Marines	allied armies

Organizations

19. Names of organizations, corporations, and institutions are capitalized, as are derivative terms to designate their members. However, common nouns occurring after the names of two or more organizations are lowercased.

the Rotary Club	AT&T Corporation
all Rotarians	League of Women Voters
University of Wisconsin	
Yale and Harvard universities	

20. Words such as *agency, department, division, group,* or *office* that designate corporate and organizational units are capitalized only as part of a specific proper noun.

manager of the Sales Division of K2 Outfitters

a memo to the sales divisions of both companies

People

21. Names and initials of persons are capitalized. If a name is hyphenated, both elements are capitalized. Particles forming the initial elements of surnames (such as *de, della, du, la, ten, ter, van,* and *von*) may or may not be capitalized, depending on the practice of the individual. The prefixes *Mac, Mc,* and *O'* are always capitalized.

Cecil Day-Lewis	Martin Van Buren
Cecil B. DeMille	Wernher von Braun
Agnes de Mille	Archibald MacLeish
W. E. B. DuBois	Sean O'Casey

22. Titles preceding the name of a person and epithets or nicknames used instead of a name are capitalized. However, titles used alone or as part of a phrase following a name are usually lowercased.

President Lincoln

Honest Abe

King Henry VIII

Henry VIII, king of England

Logex Corp.'s president

23. Words of family relationship preceding or used in place of a person's name are capitalized; otherwise they are lowercased.

Uncle Fred	Mother's birthday
Cousin Julia	my mother's birthday

24. Words designating languages, nationalities, peoples, races, religious groups, and tribes are capitalized. Designations based on skin color are usually lowercased.

Spanish	Iroquois
Spaniards	Asians
Muslims	blacks and whites

Personifications

25. Abstract concepts or qualities are capitalized when they are personified.

as Autumn paints each leaf in fiery colors

the statue of Justice with her scales

Religious Terms

26. Words designating the supreme being are capitalized. Plural references to deities are lowercased.

Allah	the Almighty
Brahma	in the eyes of God
Jehovah	the angry gods

27. Personal pronouns referring to the supreme being are often capitalized in religious writing.

God made His presence known

28. Traditional designations of apostles, prophets, and saints are capitalized.

the Madonna	the Twelve
the Prophet	St. John of the Cross
Moses the Lawgiver	John the Baptist

29. Names of religions, denominations, creeds and confessions, and religious orders are capitalized, as are derivatives of these names.

Judaism	Apostles' Creed
Islam	a Buddhist
Eastern Orthodox	Society of Jesus
Church of England	Jesuit teachers

30. Full names of specific places of worship are capitalized, but terms such as *church, synagogue,* and *mosque* are lowercased when used alone.

Hunt Memorial Church	the Blue Mosque
Beth Israel Synagogue	the mosque's minaret

31. Names of the Bible and other sacred works, their books and parts, and versions or editions of them are capitalized but not italicized. Adjectives derived from such names are capitalized except for the words *biblical* and *scriptural.*

Bible	Talmud
the Scriptures	Bhagavad Gita
Old Testament	Revised Standard Version
Koran *also* Quran *or* Qur'an	
Koranic *also* Quranic *or* Qur'anic	

Scientific Terms

32. Names of planets and their satellites, stars, constellations, and other specific celestial objects are capitalized. However, the words *sun, earth,* and *moon* are usually lowercased unless they occur with other astronomical names.

Jupiter	Halley's comet
Ganymede	Mars, Venus, and Earth
the North Star	life on earth
Ursa Major	the new moon

33. New Latin genus names in zoology and botany are capitalized and italicized. The second term in binomial scientific names, identifying the species, is lowercased and italicized, as are the names of races, varieties, or subspecies.

the California condor (*Gymnogyps californianus*)

a common buttercup (*Ranunculus acris*)

the Florida panther (*Felis concolor coryi*)

34. In zoology and botany, New Latin names of all groups above genus (such as class or family) are capitalized but not italicized. Their derivative nouns and adjectives are lowercased.

the class Gastropoda	the order Diptera
gastropod	dipteran flies
the family Ascaridae	Bryophyta
ascarid	bryophytic

35. Names of geological time divisions are capitalized. The generic terms that follow them are lowercased.

Mesozoic era	Paleocene epoch
Quaternary period	the Upper Cretaceous

Time Periods and Dates

36. Names of days of the week, months, and holidays and holy days are capitalized. Names of the seasons are lowercased.

Tuesday	Veterans Day	Easter
January	Yom Kippur	winter

Titles of Works

37. Words in titles of books, magazines, newspapers, plays, movies, long poems, and works of art such as paintings and sculpture are capitalized except for internal articles, coordinating conjunctions, prepositions, and the *to* of infinitives. Prepositions of four or more letters are often capitalized. The entire title is italicized. (Titles of articles in periodicals, short poems, short stories, essays, lectures, chapters of books, and episodes of radio and television programs are similarly capitalized but enclosed in quotation marks rather than italicized; see examples at "Quotation Marks, Double" on p. 1608.)

Of Mice and Men	*Lawrence of Arabia*
Publishers Weekly	Eliot's *The Waste Land*
USA Today	Monet's *Water-Lily Pool*
Miller's *The Crucible*	Rodin's *Thinker*

38. Titles of long musical compositions are usually capitalized and italicized; the titles of songs and short compositions are capitalized and enclosed in quotation marks, as are the popular names of longer works. The titles of compositions identified by their musical forms (such as *quartet, sonata, concerto*) are capitalized only, as are movements.

Mozart's *The Magic Flute*

Loesser's *Guys and Dolls*

"My Funny Valentine"

Beethoven's "Für Elise"

the "Moonlight" Sonata

his Violin Concerto in D

Quartet in D, Op. 64, No. 5

the Adagietto movement

39. Common titles of book sections (such as *chapter, preface, index*) are usually capitalized only when they refer to a section of the same book in which the reference appears.

See the Appendix for further information.

In a long introduction, the author explained her goals.

40. Nouns used with numbers or letters to designate major reference headings in books or periodicals are usually capitalized. Nouns designating minor elements are usually lowercased.

in Volume 5	see page 101
of Chapter 2	at paragraph 6.1
in Table 3	in line 8

Trademarks

41. Registered trademarks, service marks, and brand names are capitalized.

Coke	Kleenex	Xerox
Walkman	Band-Aid	Prozac
Levi's	Jacuzzi	Express Mail

Transportation

42. Names of ships, airplanes, and space vehicles are capitalized and italicized. The designations *USS, SS,* and *HMS* are not italicized.

HMS *Bounty*	*Challenger*
Spirit of St. Louis	*Apollo 13*

43. Names of train lines, types of aircraft, and space programs are capitalized but not italicized.

Metroliner	Concorde
Boeing 727	Pathfinder Program

Other Styling Conventions

44. Italics are used to emphasize or draw attention to words in a sentence.

Students must notify the dean's office *in writing* of any added or dropped courses.

She was not *the* star, merely *a* star.

45. Italics are often used for letters referred to as letters, words referred to as words, and numerals referred to as numerals.

The *g* in *align* is silent.

Purists still insist that *data* is a plural noun.

The first *2* and the last *0* are barely legible.

46. Unfamiliar words or words having a specialized meaning are italicized when first introduced and defined in a text, but not subsequently.

In the *direct-to-consumer* transaction, the publisher markets directly to the individual by mail.

Vitiligo is a condition in which skin pigment cells stop making pigment. Treatment for vitiligo includes . . .

47. Foreign words and phrases that have not been fully adopted into English are italicized. In general, any word that appears in the main A-Z vocabulary of this dictionary does not need to be italicized.

At the club such behavior was distinctly *mal vu*.

The prix fixe lunch was $25.

Documentation of Sources

Writers are often required to specify the source of a quotation or piece of information borrowed from another work. Though formal documentation is omitted from popular writing, where quotations or information sources are acknowledged only casually (e.g., "As Stephen Hawking observed in his *Brief History of Time*, . . . "), the systematic use of notes, references, and bibliographies is required in most serious nonfiction and all scholarly writing, in which such documentation is an important indicator of the quality of the writer's research.

Footnotes, which are placed at the bottom of a page, and *endnotes,* which are placed at the end of an article, chapter, or book, have been the preferred form of documentation in serious works intended for a wide general readership and traditionally also in scholarly works in the humanities. Numbers within the text refer the reader to the footnotes or endnotes, which contain full bibliographical information on the works cited.

In scholarly works in the social and natural sciences, and increasingly in the humanities as well, *parenthetical references*—very brief references enclosed in parentheses within the actual text—refer the reader to a list of sources at the end. In works that employ parenthetical references, footnotes or endnotes may be used to provide ancillary information.

Regardless of which system is used, most carefully documented works include a *bibliography* or *list of sources* at the end.

The following paragraphs discuss and illustrate standard styles for references, notes, and bibliographic entries in scholarly fields. Fuller treatment can be found in *Merriam-Webster's Manual for Writers and Editors, The Chicago Manual of Style,* Kate Turabian's *Manual for Writers of Term Papers, Theses, and Dissertations,* the *MLA Handbook for Writers of Research Papers* (for the humanities), the *Publication Manual of the American Psychological Association* (for the social sciences), and *Scientific Style and Format* (for the natural sciences). However, the most efficient way to master the standard documentation style employed in any given discipline may be simply to study the citations in one of its leading journals.

Footnotes and Endnotes

Footnotes and endnotes are indicated by superscript numerals, usually placed immediately after the borrowed text. In an article, the numbering is consecutive throughout; in a book, it starts over with each new chapter. The notes themselves begin with numbers (either superscript, or now more commonly, full size with a period) that correspond to the superscript reference numbers in the text. Word-processing programs have greatly simplified the placement and numbering of footnotes and endnotes.

The first thirteen examples below (each of which is keyed to an item in the "Bibliographies" section at the end) illustrate the style to be used for the first reference to a book (nos. 1–9) or article (nos. 10–13). For journals, the abbreviations *vol.* and *no.* are now usually omitted. The reference normally ends with a page reference, though the abbreviations *p.* and *pp.* are usually omitted. In typescript, underlining may be used in place of italics. Any element of the reference that appears in the text itself (e.g., the author's name) can be omitted from the note. Note that citations of online sources (nos. 14–15) replace any physical place of publication with an Internet address, and end with the date on which the user consulted the source. An example of a substantive note (a note providing information other than straight bibliographical data) is also included (no. 16). Subsequent references to a book or article (nos. 17–18) generally consist of only the author's name and the new page reference; a shortened version of the work's title may be added to distinguish two or more cited works by the same author.

One author	1. Elizabeth Bishop, *The Complete Poems: 1927–79* (New York: Farrar, Straus & Giroux, 1983), 46.
Two or more authors	2. John S. Kenyon and Thomas A. Knott, *A Pronouncing Dictionary of American English* (Springfield, Mass.: Merriam-Webster, 1953), xv.
	3. Randolph Quirk et al., *A Comprehensive Grammar of the English Language* (London: Longman, 1985), 135.
Edition and/or translation	4. Arthur S. Banks and Thomas C. Muller, eds., *Political Handbook of the World: 2000–2002* (Binghamton, N.Y.: CSA Publications, 2003), 719–22.
	5. Simone de Beauvoir, *The Second Sex,* trans. and ed. H. M. Parshley (New York: Knopf, 1953; Vintage, 1989), 446.
Second or later edition	6. Albert Hourani and Malise Ruthven, *A History of the Arab Peoples,* 2d ed. (Belknap–Harvard Univ. Press, 2003), 66.

Article in a collection	7. Chester Himes, "Headwaiter," in *Calling the Wind,* ed. Clarence Major (New York: HarperCollins, 1993), 83.
Work in two or more volumes	8. Frederic G. Cassidy and Joan Houston Hall, eds., *Dictionary of American Regional English* (Belknap–Harvard Univ. Press, 1985–), 3:447.
Corporate author	9. *Who's Who in America: 2003* (New Providence, N.J.: Marquis Who's Who, 2002), 1:995.
Monthly magazine	10. Vannevar Bush, "As We May Think," *Atlantic Monthly,* July 1945, 101–8.
Weekly magazine	11. Christopher Hitchens, review of *C. L. R. James* by Farrukh Dhondy, *Times Literary Supplement,* 18 Jan. 2002, 34.
Journal paginated consecutively throughout annual volume	12. Lawrence M. Davis, Charles L. Houck, and Clive Upton, "'Sett Out Verry Eairly Wensdy': The Spelling and Grammar in the Lewis and Clark Journals," *American Speech* 75 (Summer 2000): 138.
Newspaper	13. Carol Kaesuk Yoon, "Scientists Say Orangutans Can Exhibit 'Culture,'" *New York Times,* 3 Jan. 2003, A14.
Electronic source	14. Jim Marchand, "Translating Crescentia," 27 Dec. 2002, Medieval Texts Discussion List ⟨http://listserv.uiuc.edu/wa.cgi?A2=ind0212&L=medtextl&P=20109⟩ (10 Jan. 2003).
	15. John Rothgeb, "The Tristan Chord: Identity and Origin," *Music Theory Online,* 1.1 (Jan. 1995), ⟨http://www.societymusictheory.org/mto/issues/mto.95.1.1/ mto.95.1.1.rothgeb.art⟩ (12 June 1999).
Substantive note	16. Both "globalization" and "global village" date at least from the 1960s, with Zbigniew Brzezinski and Marshall McLuhan emphasizing respectively the universal status of the North American model of modernity and the technological convergence of the world. See Mattelart, 115.
Subsequent reference	17. Quirk et al., 106.
	18. Beauvoir, *Second Sex,* 251.

Parenthetical References

Parenthetical references, though not used in works intended for a wide audience, are standard in scholarly works in the social sciences and natural sciences, and are increasingly being used in the humanities as well. These highly abbreviated references are embedded within the text itself and direct the reader to the more complete source information given in a bibliography at the end.

In the natural sciences, parenthetical references include only the author's last name and the year of publication ("author-date style," or "name-year style"). In the social sciences, writers use either the author-date style or an alternative style that also includes a page reference ("author-date-page style"). In the humanities, a page reference normally takes the place of the year of publication ("author-page style"). To distinguish two works published in the same year, the date may be followed by a lowercase letter—"(Chavis 1999a)," "(Chavis 1999b)." To distinguish among cited works by the same author, a shortened form of the work's title may be added—"(Faulkner, *Absalom* 220)," "(Faulkner, *Intruder* 151)."

The examples below illustrate the use of parenthetical references in, respectively, the natural sciences, the social sciences, and the humanities.

A historical assessment of many small, isolated populations found that every group with fewer than 50 individuals became extinct within 50 years (Berger 1990).

The land in West Africa was quite difficult to settle, and the mortality rate during the passage was "shockingly high" (Schick 1980, 27).

García Lorca critics have pointed out that, although Pepe sets the action of *La casa de Bernarda Alba* in motion, he never appears onstage (Gabriele 388; Urrea 51).

As with footnotes and endnotes, any information evident from the textual context—name, date, or title—is omitted from the reference. As a result, many references in the social sciences and humanities consist simply of page numbers.

References to electronic sources, which usually lack page references, may instead use paragraph numbers, if provided—"(Mather ¶ 16)"—or the number of the paragraph under a given heading within the article—"(Ortiz & Lane, Conclusions, para. 4)."

Other Systems

A newer style of citation, now often used in the natural sciences, is the *citation-sequence system.* Every source is given a number corresponding to the order of its first appearance in the article, and every later citation of that source employs the same number. The numbers themselves are either set in the main text as superscripts or are shown full-size in parentheses or brackets. There is usually no bibliography. The excerpt below (in which the source with the lower number had first appeared earlier in the article) is followed by the corresponding entries in the article's list of sources, in a style employing minimal punctuation and italicization.

> The relation between bone mass and breast cancer may also involve endogenous androgens, which are determinants of bone mass[100] and which have also been associated with the risk of breast cancer.[21]
>
> **21.** Zhang Y, Kiel DP, Kreger BE, et al. Bone mass and the risk of breast cancer among postmenopausal women. N Engl J Med 1997;336:611–7.
>
> **100.** Buchanan JR, Myers C, Lloyd T, Leuenberger P, Demers LM. Determinants of peak trabecular bone density in women: the role of androgens, estrogen, and exercise. J Bone Miner Res 1988;3:673–80.

Another newer system, sometimes used when the intended audience includes both general readers and scholars, is the *white-copy system,* which provides endnotes but omits any reference to them at all on the text pages. The general reader can thus completely ignore the documentation, while the scholar can check sources at will. The excerpt is followed by its corresponding endnotes.

> Aiken was on his way out of the flat when Ezra asked him if there was nobody genuinely *modern* he could recommend? Maybe someone at Harvard, 'something DIFFERENT'? Aiken thought for a moment, and answered: 'Oh well, there is Eliot.' Ezra asked who Eliot was, and was told: 'A guy at Harvard doing funny stuff.' Actually, added Aiken, Eliot was in England at the moment, so Ezra could meet him if he wanted to. Ezra told Aiken to arrange it.
>
> 257 'something DIFFERENT', PH 21 Dec '56. 'Oh well', Doob 128. 'A guy', Lyndall Gordon, *Eliot's Early Years,* Oxford University Press, 1977, 66.

The style of white-copy endnotes continues to vary widely from publication to publication. Here the abbreviations "PH" (indicating an unpublished collection of letters) and "Doob" (indicating a book) are explained in the book's bibliographic appendix; the third item, not being one of the book's important sources, is omitted from the appendix and instead given its full citation here.

Bibliographies

A bibliography is usually provided at the end of any properly documented work (except those using the citation-sequence style). In works that rely on parenthetical references, a bibliography is essential, since the full citations are given nowhere else. In works that rely on footnotes or endnotes, the bibliography generally simply provides a convenient listing, alphabetized by the author's last name, of the bibliographic information that first appeared in the notes. Bibliography entries differ from notes chiefly in their punctuation. They include all the information in a full footnote or endnote except specific page references; however, when a journal article or a piece in a collection is being cited, the entry provides the range of pages for the entire article or piece.

The following bibliographies illustrate standard styles employed in, respectively, the humanities and the social and natural sciences. These differ principally in four respects: in the sciences, (1) the author's first and middle names are abbreviated, often without periods, (2) the date directly follows the author's name, (3) all words in book and article titles are lowercased except the first word, the first word of any subtitle, and proper nouns and adjectives, and (4) article titles are not enclosed in quotation marks. Also, in many scientific publications today, book and journal titles are not italicized. In journal citations, the abbreviations *vol.* and *no.* are generally omitted; the issue number either appears in parentheses or is omitted altogether, since pagination alone is sufficient to identify the issue when pagination is continuous throughout the volume. The titles of scientific journals are usually given in standard abbreviated forms.

HUMANITIES

Banks, A. S., and Thomas C. Muller, eds. *Political Handbook of the World: 2000–2002.* Binghamton, N.Y.: CSA Publications, 2003.

Beauvoir, Simone de. *The Second Sex.* Trans. and ed. H. M. Parshley. New York: Alfred A. Knopf, 1953. Reprint: New York: Vintage, 1989.

Bishop, Elizabeth. *The Complete Poems: 1927–79.* New York: Farrar, Straus & Giroux, 1983.

Bush, Vannevar. "As We May Think." *Atlantic Monthly.* July 1945: 101–8.

Cassidy, Frederic G., and Joan Houston Hall, eds. *Dictionary of American Regional English.* 4 vols. to date. Cambridge, Mass.: Belknap–Harvard Univ. Press, 1985–.

Davis, Lawrence M., Charles L. Houck, and Clive Upton. "'Sett Out Verry Eairly Wensdy': The Spelling and Grammar in the Lewis and Clark Journals." *American Speech* 75 (Summer 2000): 137–148.

Himes, Chester. "Headwaiter." In Clarence Major, ed., *Calling the Wind.* New York: HarperCollins, 1993: 79–93.

Hitchens, Christopher. Review of *C. L. R. James,* by Farrukh Dhondy. *Times Literary Supplement.* 18 Jan. 2002: 34.

Hourani, Albert, and Malise Ruthven. *A History of the Arab Peoples.* 2d ed. Cambridge, Mass.: Belknap–Harvard Univ. Press, 2003.

Kenyon, John S., and Thomas A. Knott. *A Pronouncing Dictionary of American English.* Springfield, Mass.: Merriam-Webster, 1953.

Marchand, Jim. "Translating Crescentia." Medieval Texts Discussion List. 27 Dec. 2002. ⟨http://listserv.uiuc.edu/wa.cgi?A2=ind0212&L=medtextl&P=20109⟩ (10 Jan. 2003).

Quirk, Randolph, et al. *A Comprehensive Grammar of the English Language.* London: Longman, 1985.

Rothgeb, John. "The Tristan Chord: Identity and Origin." *Music Theory Online* 1.1 (Jan. 1995). ⟨http://societymusictheory.org/mto/issues/mto.95.1.1/mto.95.1.1.rothgeb.art⟩ (12 June 1999).

Who's Who in America: 2003. 3 vols. New Providence, N.J.: Marquis Who's Who, 2002.

Yoon, Carol Kaesuk. "Scientists Say Orangutans Can Exhibit 'Culture.'" *New York Times.* 3 Jan. 2003: A14.

SCIENCES

American Ornithologists' Union. 1998. *The A.O.U. checklist of North American birds.* 7th ed. Washington, D.C.: American Ornithologists' Union.

Borio, L., et al. 2001. Death Due to bioterrorism-related inhalational anthrax. *JAMA* 286:2554–59.

Charney, R., and A. Lytchak. 2001. Metric characterizations of spherical and Euclidean buildings. *Geom. and Topol.* 5, paper 17: 521–550. ⟨http://www.maths.warwick.ac.uk/gt/GTVol5/paper17.abs.html⟩ (8 Aug. 2002).

Gould, S.J., and N. Eldredge. 1977. Punctuated equilibria: The tempo and mode of evolution reconsidered. *Paleobiology* 3: 115–151.

Hölldobler, B., and E.O. Wilson. 1990. *The ants.* Cambridge, Mass.: Belknap–Harvard Univ. Press.

Mayr, E. 1982. Processes of speciation in animals. In: C. Barigozzi, ed. *Mechanisms of speciation.* New York: Alan R. Liss. 1–19.

McGraw-Hill yearbook of science and technology: 2003. 2003. New York: McGraw-Hill.

Nowak, R.M. 1999. *Walker's mammals of the world.* 6th ed. 2 vols. Baltimore: Johns Hopkins Univ. Press.

Forms of Address

The relationship between individual correspondents defines the form of address used in letters, so no guidelines apply for all occasions. The following examples provide generally accepted options, with the most formal usage listed first. Both male and female names are shown, usually alternating; for any given entry the form of address for the opposite sex can be easily determined. The female equivalent of "Sir" standing alone is "Madam" ("Madame" for foreign addressees); the male equivalent of "Madam" standing alone is "Sir." The female equivalent of "Mr." is "Ms." (or "Mrs. " or "Miss" if either is preferred by the addressee) when it immediately precedes a name, and "Madam" when it immediately precedes a title. The male equivalent of "Ms." is "Mr."

Religious

ROMAN CATHOLIC

Pope   His Holiness the Pope *or* His Holiness John Paul II
SALUTATION: Your Holiness:
or
Most Holy Father:

Cardinal   His Eminence Anthony Cardinal Benelli (*add, if appropriate:* , Archbishop of ——)
SALUTATION: Your Eminence:
or
Dear Cardinal Benelli:

Apostolic Delegate   His Excellency The Most Reverend Peter Rouleau, Archbishop of ——, The Apostolic Delegate
SALUTATION: Dear Archbishop:

Archbishop   His Excellency The Most Reverend Anthony Benelli, Archbishop of ——
SALUTATION: Dear Archbishop:
or
Most Reverend Sir:
or
Your Excellency:

Bishop   The Most Reverend Peter Rouleau, Bishop of ——
SALUTATION: Most Reverend Sir:
or
Your Excellency:
or
Dear Bishop Rouleau:

Abbot   The Right Reverend (*or* Rt. Rev.) Anthony Benelli, O.S.B. (*or other order initials*), Abbot of ——
SALUTATION: Right Reverend Abbot:
or
Dear Father Abbot:

Prior   The Very Reverend Peter Rouleau, O.P. (*or other order initials*), Prior of ——
SALUTATION: Dear Father Prior:

Monsignor   The Very Reverend Monsignor (*or* Very Rev. Msgr.) Anthony Benelli (*papal chamberlain*); The Reverend Monsignor (*or* Rev. Msgr.) Anthony Benelli (*domestic prelate*)
SALUTATION: Very Reverend and Dear Monsignor Benelli: (*papal chamberlain*)
or
Reverend and Dear Monsignor Benelli: (*domestic prelate*)

Superior, Mother Superior, Father Superior   The Reverend Mother Superior, Convent of —— *or* Reverend Mother Mary Angelica, S.M. (*or other order initials*),

Convent of —— / The Very Reverend Anthony Benelli, C.P. (*or other order initials*), Superior of —— (*religious community*)
SALUTATION: Reverend Mother: *or* Dear Reverend Mother: / Dear Father Superior:

Priest   The Reverend Father Benelli *or* The Reverend Anthony Benelli *or* The Reverend Anthony Benelli, S.T.D. (*or other earned doctorate*)
SALUTATION: Reverend Father:
or
Dear Father Benelli:
or
Dear Father:

Monk, Nun   Brother James, O.S.F. (*or other order initials*) / Sister Mary Angelica, S.C. (*or other order initials*)
SALUTATION: Dear Brother James: / Dear Sister Mary Angelica:

Deacon   The Reverend Mr. Peter Rouleau (*permanent deacon*); Mr. Peter Rouleau (*transitional deacon*)
SALUTATION: Dear Deacon:

PROTESTANT (except Episcopal)

Bishop   Bishop Michael R. Taylor
SALUTATION: Dear Bishop Taylor:

Minister   The Reverend Diane L. Clark *or* The Reverend Diane L. Clark, Ph.D. (*or other earned doctorate*) *or* The Reverend Doctor (*or* Rev. Dr.) Diane L. Clark (*if individual uses title*)
SALUTATION: Dear Ms. Clark:
or
Dear Dr. Clark: (*if individual uses title*)
or
Dear Pastor Clark: (*chiefly Lutheran*)

EPISCOPAL

Bishop   The Right Reverend (*or* Rt. Rev.) Michael R. Taylor, Bishop of —— (*diocesan bishop*); The Most Reverend Michael R. Taylor, Presiding Bishop (*presiding bishop*)
SALUTATION: Right Reverend Sir: *or* Dear Bishop Taylor: (*diocesan bishop*); Most Reverend Sir: *or* Dear Bishop: *or* Dear Bishop Taylor: (*presiding bishop*)

Archdeacon   The Venerable (*or* Ven.) Diane L. Clark, Archdeacon of ——
SALUTATION: Venerable Madam:
or
Dear Archdeacon Clark:

Dean   The Very Reverend Michael R. Taylor, —— Ca-

thedral (*or* —— Seminary) *or* Dean Michael R. Taylor, —— Cathedral (*or* —— Seminary)
SALUTATION: Very Reverend Sir:
or
Dear Dean Taylor:

Prior The Very Reverend Michael R. Taylor, O.H.R. (*or other order initials*)
SALUTATION: Dear Father Prior:

Canon The Reverend Diane L. Clark, Canon of —— Cathedral
SALUTATION: Dear Canon Clark:

Priest The Reverend Michael R. Taylor / The Reverend Diane L. Clark, (*add position title, as:* Rector of ——, Vicar of ——)
SALUTATION: Dear Father Taylor: / Dear Ms. Clark:
(*individual may prefer* Mrs. *or* Mother)

Deacon The Reverend Ms. Diane L. Clark (*permanent deacon*); Mr. Michael R. Taylor (*transitional deacon*)
SALUTATION: Dear Deacon:

EASTERN ORTHODOX

Patriarch His All Holiness Ecumenical Patriarch Bartholomew; His All Holiness Patriarch George (*Greek Orthodox*); His Holiness Alexy II, Patriarch of Moscow and All Russia (*Russian Orthodox*); His Beatitude Ignatius IV the Patriarch of —— (*other Orthodox; usage varies*)
SALUTATION: Your All Holiness: (*Greek Orthodox*); Your Holiness: *or* Your Beatitude: (*other Orthodox; usage varies*)

Primate His Beatitude the Most Blessed Theodosius, Archbishop of ——, Metropolitan of —— *or* His Beatitude the Most Reverend George, Patriarchal Vicar of —— *or* His Holiness Metropolitan George, Primate of —— (*usage varies*)
SALUTATION: Your Beatitude:

Archbishop His Eminence Archbishop George, (*add position title, as:* Metropolitan of ——)
SALUTATION: Your Eminence:

Bishop, Mitered Archpriest His Grace Bishop George, (*add position title*) *or* The Right Reverend (*or* Rt. Rev.) George, (*add position title*) (*Greek Orthodox*); His Excellency Bishop Alexander, (*add position title*) *or* The Right Reverend (*or* Rt. Rev.) Alexander, (*add position title*) (*Russian Orthodox*)
SALUTATION: Your Grace: (*Greek Orthodox*)
or
Your Excellency: (*Russian Orthodox*)

Archpriest, Archimandrite The Very Reverend Father (*or* V. Rev. Fr.) George Costas (*Greek Orthodox*); The Very Reverend Alexander Ivanov (*Russian Orthodox*)
SALUTATION: Dear Father Costas:

Priest The Reverend Father (*or* Rev. Fr.) George Costas
SALUTATION: Dear Father Costas:

Deacon The Reverend Deacon George Costas (*Greek Orthodox*); The Reverend Alexander Ivanov (*Russian Orthodox*)
SALUTATION: Dear Deacon Costas:

JEWISH

Rabbi Rabbi Rebecca K. Meyer *or* Rabbi Rebecca K. Meyer, D.H.L. (*or other earned doctorate*)
SALUTATION: Dear Rabbi Meyer:
or
Dear Dr. Meyer: (*if individual uses title*)

Cantor Cantor David R. Cohen
SALUTATION: Dear Cantor Cohen:

ISLAMIC

For all: *First line in letter:* "In the Name of Allah The Most Gracious, The Most Merciful" (*from a Muslim*), *or* "In the Name of God (*or* Allah) The Most Gracious, The Most Merciful" (*from a non-Muslim*)

Grand Mufti His Eminence Ahmad Kabbani Al-Dhahiri, The Grand Mufti of ——
SALUTATION: Your Eminence:

Imam The Honored Sheikh Abdul Al-Rashid, Imam of —— Mosque (*or* Masjid al- ——)
SALUTATION: Brother Sheikh Al-Rashid: *or* Hujjat al-Islam Sheikh Al-Rashid: (*from a Muslim*)
or
Dear Sheikh Al-Rashid: (*from a non-Muslim*)

BUDDHIST

Dalai Lama His Holiness The Dalai Lama (*Tibetan Buddhism*)
SALUTATION: Your Holiness:

Monk The Venerable (*or* Ven.) Ajahn Thera, —— Monastery (*or other community*); The Venerable Doctor (*or* Ven. Dr.) Ajahn Thera (*if individual uses title*), —— Monastery (*or other community*) (*Theravada Buddhist tradition, Southeast Asia; for Mahayana tradition, usage varies*)
SALUTATION: Venerable Sir: (*Theravada tradition*)

Governmental

FOREIGN LEADERS

Premier, President, Prime Minister Her Excellency Joan K. Evans, Prime Minister of ——
SALUTATION: Excellency:
or
Dear Madame Prime Minister:

DIPLOMATS

U.N. Secretary-General His Excellency Kofi Annan, Secretary-General of the United Nations
SALUTATION: Excellency:
or
Dear Mr. Secretary-General:

Foreign Ambassador Her Excellency Joan K. Evans, Ambassador of ——
SALUTATION: Excellency:
or
Dear Madame Ambassador:

American Ambassador The Honorable James T. Snyder, American Ambassador *or* (*if in Canada or Latin America*) The Ambassador of the United States of America
SALUTATION: Sir:
or
Dear Mr. Ambassador:

Foreign Chargé d'Affaires Joan K. Evans, Esq., Chargé d'Affaires of ——
SALUTATION: Madame:
or
Dear Ms. Evans:

American Chargé d'Affaires   James T. Snyder, Esq., American Chargé d'Affaires *or* (*if in Canada or Latin America*) James T. Snyder, Esq., The United States Chargé d'Affaires
SALUTATION: Sir:
or
        Dear Mr. Snyder:

Foreign Consul   The Consul of ―― *or* The Honorable Joan K. Evans, ―― Consul *or* The Honorable Joan K. Evans, Consul of ――
SALUTATION: Madame:
or
        Dear Ms. Evans:

American Consul   The American Consul *or* (*if in Canada or Latin America*) The Consul of the United States of America *or* James T. Snyder, Esq., American Consul *or* (*if in Canada or Latin America*) James T. Snyder, Esq., Consul of the United States of America
SALUTATION: Sir:
or
        Dear Sir:
or
        Dear Mr. Snyder:

FEDERAL OFFICIALS

President   The President, The White House
SALUTATION: Mr. President:
or
        Dear Mr. President:

Vice President   The Vice President of the United States, United States Senate *or* The Honorable James T. Snyder, Vice President of the United States
SALUTATION: Sir:
or
        Dear Mr. Vice President:

Speaker of the House   The Honorable Speaker of the House of Representatives *or* The Honorable Joan K. Evans, Speaker of the House of Representatives
SALUTATION: Madam:
or
        Dear Madam Speaker:
or
        Dear Ms. Evans:

Chief Justice   The Chief Justice of the United States, The Supreme Court of the United States *or* The Chief Justice, The Supreme Court
SALUTATION: Sir:
or
        Dear Mr. Chief Justice:

Associate Justice   Madam Justice Evans, The Supreme Court of the United States
SALUTATION: Madam:
or
        Dear Madam Justice:
or
        Dear Justice Evans:

Cabinet member (*other than Attorney General*)   The Secretary of ―― *or* The Honorable James T. Snyder, Secretary of ――
SALUTATION: Sir:
or
        Dear Mr. Secretary:
or
        Dear Mr. Snyder:

Attorney General   The Honorable Joan K. Evans, Attorney General
SALUTATION: Madam:
or
        Dear Madam Attorney General:

Commissioner   The Honorable James T. Snyder, Commissioner
SALUTATION: Dear Mr. Commissioner:
or
        Dear Commissioner Snyder:

Director of an agency   The Honorable Joan K. Evans, Director
SALUTATION: Dear Ms. Evans:

Federal judge   The Honorable James T. Snyder, Judge of the U.S. District Court of the ―― District of ――
SALUTATION: Sir:
or
        Dear Judge Snyder:

U.S. Senator   The Honorable Joan K. Evans, U.S. Senate
SALUTATION: Dear Senator Evans:

U.S. Representative   The Honorable James T. Snyder, U.S. House of Representatives *or* (*for a local address*) The Honorable James T. Snyder, Representative in Congress
SALUTATION: Sir:
or
        Dear Representative Snyder:
or
        Dear Mr. Snyder:

STATE AND LOCAL OFFICIALS

Governor   The Honorable Joan K. Evans, Governor of ―― *or* Her Excellency, the Governor of ――
SALUTATION: Madam:
or
        Dear Governor Evans:

Lieutenant Governor   The Honorable Lieutenant Governor of ―― *or* The Honorable James T. Snyder, Lieutenant Governor of ――
SALUTATION: Sir:
or
        Dear Mr. Snyder:

President of State Senate   The Honorable Joan K. Evans, President of the Senate of the State of ――
SALUTATION: Madam:
or
        Dear Senator Evans:
or
        Dear Ms. Evans:

Speaker, State Assembly (House of Delegates, House of Representatives)   The Honorable James T. Snyder, Speaker of the ――
SALUTATION: Sir:
or
        Dear Mr. Snyder:

Chief Justice of State Supreme Court   The Honorable Joan K. Evans, Chief Justice of the Supreme Court of ――
SALUTATION: Madam:
or
        Dear Madam Chief Justice:

Associate Justice of State Supreme Court   The Honorable James T. Snyder, Associate Justice of the Supreme Court of ――
SALUTATION: Sir:
or
        Dear Justice Snyder:

Attorney General   The Honorable Joan K. Evans, Attorney General of the State of ――
SALUTATION: Madam:
or
        Dear Madam Attorney General:

Secretary of State The Honorable Secretary of State of —— or The Honorable James T. Snyder, Secretary of State of ——
SALUTATION: Sir:
> or
> Dear Mr. Secretary:

Judge The Honorable Joan K. Evans, (*add position title, as:* Judge of the —— Court of ——)
SALUTATION: Dear Judge Evans:

State Senator The Honorable James T. Snyder, The Senate of ——
SALUTATION: Dear Senator Snyder:

State Representative (Assemblyman, Delegate) The Honorable Joan K. Evans, House of Representatives (State Assembly, House of Delegates)
SALUTATION: Madam:
> or
> Dear Ms. Evans:

Mayor The Honorable James T. Snyder, Mayor of ——
SALUTATION: Sir:
> or
> Dear Mr. Mayor:
> or
> Dear Mayor Snyder:

Alderman (Councilman), City Attorney, County Clerk The Honorable Joan K. Evans, (*add position title, as:* Clerk of —— County)
SALUTATION: Dear Ms. Evans:

Military

The appropriate form of address for **all ranks** is: *Full or abbreviated rank + full name + comma + abbreviation for branch of service* (USA, USAF, USMC, USN, USCG).

In practice, salutations will differ according to the relationship between individual correspondents; the most formal will employ the addressee's full title.

ARMY, AIR FORCE, MARINE CORPS

General General Carl R. Berger, USA (*or other branch, as:* USAF, USMC) *or* GEN (*Army*) / Gen (*Air Force, Marine Corps*) Carl R. Berger, USA (USAF, USMC)
SALUTATION: Dear General Berger:

Lieutenant General, Major General, Brigadier General *Similar to* General, *with* LTG, MG, BG (*Army*); Lt-Gen, MajGen, BGen (*Air Force*); LtGen, MajGen, BrigGen (*Marine Corps*)
SALUTATION: Dear —— General Berger: (*give full rank*)

Colonel Colonel Susan B. Miller, USAF (*or* USA, USMC) *or* Col (*Air Force, Marine Corps*) / COL (*Army*) Susan B. Miller, USAF (USA, USMC)
SALUTATION: Dear Colonel Miller:

Lieutenant Colonel *Similar to* Colonel, *with* LTC (*Army*), LtCol (*Air Force, Marine Corps*)
SALUTATION: Dear Colonel Miller:

Major Major Carl R. Berger, USMC (*or* USA, USAF) *or* Maj (*Air Force, Marine Corps*) / MAJ (*Army*) Carl R. Berger, USMC (USA, USAF)
SALUTATION: Dear Major Berger:

Captain Captain Susan B. Miller, USA (*or* USAF, USMC) *or* CPT (*Army*) / Capt (*Air Force, Marine Corps*) Susan B. Miller, USA (USAF, USMC)
SALUTATION: Dear Captain Miller:

First Lieutenant First Lieutenant Carl R. Berger, USAF (*or* USA, USMC) *or* 1stLt (*Air Force, Marine Corps*) / 1LT (*Army*) Carl R. Berger, USAF (USA, USMC)
SALUTATION: Dear Lieutenant Berger:

Second Lieutenant Second Lieutenant Susan B. Miller, USMC (*or* USA, USAF) *or* 2ndLt (*Air Force, Marine Corps*) / 2LT (*Army*) Susan B. Miller, USMC (USA, USAF)
SALUTATION: Dear Lieutenant Miller:

Chief Warrant Officer Chief Warrant Officer Carl R. Berger, USA (*or* USMC) *or* CW5, CW4, CW3, CW2 (*Army*) / CWO5, CWO4, CWO3, CWO2 (*Marine Corps*) Carl R. Berger, USA (USMC)
SALUTATION: Dear Chief Warrant Officer Berger:

Warrant Officer Warrant Officer Susan B. Miller, USMC (*or* USA) *or* WO1 (*Army*) / WO (*Marine Corps*) Susan B. Miller, USMC (USA)
SALUTATION: Dear Warrant Officer Miller:

Sergeant Sergeant Carl R. Berger, USA (*or* USMC) *or* SGT (*Army*) / Sgt (*Marine Corps*) Carl R. Berger, USA (USMC). *Similar pattern for other sergeant ranks:* **Sergeant Major of the Army** *or* SMA; **Chief Master Sergeant of the Air Force** *or* CMSgt; **Sergeant Major of the Marine Corps** *or* SMMC; **Command Sergeant Major** *or* CSM (*Army*); **Sergeant Major** *or* SGM (*Army*) / SgtMaj (*Marine Corps*); **Master Gunnery Sergeant** *or* MGySgt (*Marine Corps*); **First Sergeant** *or* 1SG (*Army*) / 1stSgt (*Marine Corps*); **Master Sergeant** *or* MSG (*Army*) / MSgt (*Air Force, Marine Corps*); **Senior Master Sergeant** *or* SMSgt (*Air Force*); **Sergeant First Class** *or* SFC (*Army*); **Gunnery Sergeant** *or* GySgt (*Marine Corps*); **Staff Sergeant** *or* SSG (*Army*) / SSgt (*Air Force, Marine Corps*); **Technical Sergeant** *or* TSgt (*Air Force*)
SALUTATION: Dear —— Sergeant Berger: (*give full rank*)

Corporal Corporal Susan B. Miller, USA (*or* USMC) *or* CPL (*Army*) / Cpl (*Marine Corps*) Susan B. Miller, USA (USMC). *Similar pattern for* **Lance Corporal** *or* L/Cpl (*Marine Corps*)
SALUTATION: Dear Corporal / Lance Corporal Miller:

Specialist Specialist Carl R. Berger, USA *or* SPC Carl R. Berger, USA
SALUTATION: Dear Specialist Berger:

Private Private Susan B. Miller, USMC (*or* USA) *or* Pvt (*Marine Corps*) / PVT (*Army*) Susan B. Miller, USMC (USA). *Similar pattern for* **Private First Class** *or* PFC (*Army, Marine Corps*)
SALUTATION: Dear Private —— Miller: (*give full rank*)

Airman Airman (*or* Amn) Carl R. Berger, USAF. *Similar pattern for* **Airman Basic** *or* AB, **Airman First Class** *or* A1C, *and* **Senior Airman** *or* SrA
SALUTATION: Dear —— Airman —— Berger: (*give full rank*)

NAVY, COAST GUARD

Admiral Admiral (*or* ADM) Carl R. Berger, USN (*or* USCG). *Similar pattern for* **Fleet Admiral** *or* FADM (*wartime,* USN *only*); **Vice Admiral** *or* VADM; *and* **Rear Admiral** *or* RADM
SALUTATION: Dear —— Admiral Berger: (*give full rank*)

Captain Captain (*or* CAPT) Susan B. Miller, USN (*or* USCG)
SALUTATION: Dear Captain Miller:

Commander Commander (*or* CDR) Carl R. Berger, USN (*or* USCG). *Similar pattern for* **Lieutenant Commander** *or* LCDR
SALUTATION: Dear —— Commander Berger: (*give full rank*)

Lieutenant   Lieutenant (*or* LT) Susan B. Miller, USN (*or* USCG)
SALUTATION: Dear Lieutenant Miller:
or
Dear Ms. Miller:

Lieutenant Junior Grade   Lieutenant (j.g.) Carl R. Berger, USN (*or* USCG) *or* LTJG Carl R. Berger, USN (*or* USCG)
SALUTATION: Dear Lieutenant Berger:
or
Dear Mr. Berger:

Ensign   Ensign (*or* ENS) Susan B. Miller, USN (*or* USCG)
SALUTATION: Dear Ensign Miller:
or
Dear Ms. Miller:

Chief Warrant Officer   Chief Warrant Officer (*or* CWO4, CWO3, CWO2) Carl R. Berger, USN (*or* USCG)
SALUTATION: Dear Chief Warrant Officer Berger:
or
Dear Mr. Berger:

Master Chief Petty Officer   Master Chief Petty Officer (*or* MCPO) Susan B. Miller, USN (*or* USCG). *Similar pattern for other petty officer ranks:* **Senior Chief Petty Officer** *or* SCPO; **Chief Petty Officer** *or* CPO; **Petty Officer First Class** *or* PO1; **Petty Officer Second Class** *or* PO2; **Petty Officer Third Class** *or* PO3
SALUTATION: Dear ——— Petty Officer ——— Miller: (*give full rank*)

Seaman   Seaman Carl R. Berger, USN (*or* USCG). *Similar pattern for* **Seaman Apprentice** *or* SA, and **Seaman Recruit** *or* SR
SALUTATION: Dear Seaman Berger:

Miscellaneous

Attorney   Ms. Helen E. Clark, Attorney-at-Law *or* Helen E. Clark, Esq.
SALUTATION: Dear Ms. Clark:

Certified Public Accountant   Bruce P. Richards, C.P.A.
SALUTATION: Dear Mr. Richards:

Dentist   Helen E. Clark, D.D.S. (*or* D.M.D.) *or* Dr. Helen E. Clark
SALUTATION: Dear Dr. Clark:

Physician   Bruce P. Richards, M.D. *or* Dr. Bruce P. Richards (*medical doctor*); Bruce P. Richards, D.O. *or* Dr. Bruce P. Richards (*osteopathic physician*)
SALUTATION: Dear Dr. Richards:

Professor   Ms. Helen E. Clark, Assistant Professor / Associate Professor / Professor of ——— (*academic field*), Department of ——— *or* Dr. Helen E. Clark (*with doctorate*), Assistant Professor / Associate Professor / Professor of ——— (*academic field*), Department of ———
SALUTATION: Dear Professor Clark:
or
Dear Dr. Clark: (*with doctorate; usage varies by institutional practice and individual preference*)
or
Dear Ms. Clark:

Veterinarian   Bruce P. Richards, D.V.M. (*or* V.M.D.) *or* Dr. Bruce P. Richards
SALUTATION: Dear Dr. Richards:

Index

Merriam-Webster's Language Research Service and award-winning Web sites provide answers to your language questions.

Merriam-Webster's Language Research Service offers owners of *Merriam-Webster's Collegiate® Dictionary* the opportunity to take advantage of the editorial resources of America's foremost dictionary publisher—at no cost. If you have a question specific to language, a particular word or its origin, an inquiry to the Language Research Service will bring an accurate and concise reply from a Merriam-Webster editor.

E-mail queries to **LRS@Merriam-Webster.com** or mail questions to:

Language Research Service, P.O. Box 281, Springfield, MA 01102

Letters from correspondents in the U.S. should include a self-addressed, stamped envelope.

Merriam-Webster Online (Merriam-Webster.com)
Newly redesigned, Merriam-Webster.com delivers a wealth of clear and precise language information and offers free access to *Merriam-Webster's Collegiate® Dictionary* and *Thesaurus*. Additional features include audio pronunciations, a free *Word of the Day* e-mail, crosswords and word games. Trend Watch and Top Ten Lists entertain and educate visitors with facts and stories about language.

Merriam-Webster Unabridged (Merriam-WebsterUnabridged.com)
This premium service provides unlimited access to the complete text of *Webster's Third New International Dictionary, Unabridged*—America's largest and most comprehensive dictionary—in an advertising-free environment. Additional features include a comprehensive reference library, premium word games, and Word.com, a monthly newsletter from Merriam-Webster's editors.

Merriam-Webster's Word Central (WordCentral.com)
Word Central is a lively site for kids, parents, and teachers devoted to fostering a lifelong interest in words and language. Its centerpiece is the fully searchable *Merriam-Webster's Online Student Dictionary*, the only age-specific dictionary available on the Web. Other features include *Merriam-Webster's Online Student Thesaurus*, interactive word games, and Build Your Own Dictionary.

Merriam-Webster's Learner's Dictionary (LearnersDictionary.com)
Designed especially for ESL students and teachers, LearnersDictionary.com features the free, fully searchable *Merriam-Webster's Advanced Learner's English Dictionary*. The site offers a free *Learner's Word of the Day* e-mail, interactive language exercises, audio pronunciations, and an Ask the Editors blog.